W9-BUI-780

NORTHERN EUROPEAN RUSSIA
pp 124-125
SOUTHERN EUROPEAN RUSSIA
pp 126-127

ASIA pp 148 – 163
NORTHEASTERN CHINA, MONGOLIA & KOREA
pp162-163
WESTERN CHINA
pp158-159
AFGHANISTAN & PAKISTAN
EASTERN CHINA
pp160-161
NORTHERN INDIA & THE HIMALAYAN STATES
pp152-153
SOUTHERN INDIA & SRI LANKA
pp154-155

Svalbard
p 92
THE RUSSIAN FEDERATION
pp122-123
KAZAKHSTAN
pp144-145
ASIA
pp 128-173
(also see inset)
TURKEY & THE CAUCASUS
pp136-137
CENTRAL ASIA
pp146-147
THE MEDITERRANEAN
pp 120-121
Cyprus
p 121
THE NEAR EAST
pp138-139
IRAN & THE GULF STATES
pp142-143
THE ARABIAN PENINSULA
pp140-141
SOUTH ASIA
pp150-151
MAINLAND EAST ASIA
pp 156-157
JAPAN
pp 164-165
Izu-shoto, Ogasawara-shoto & Kazan-retto
p 165
Ryukyu Islands
p 165
Sakishima-shoto
p 165
THE PACIFIC OCEAN
pp 192-193
MAINLAND SOUTHEAST ASIA
pp 166-167
Mariana Islands
p 188
Wake Island
p 189
Saipan
p 188
Guam
p 188
MICRONESIA
pp 188-189
Yap
p 188
Chuuk Islands
p 189
Pohnpei
p 189
Marshall Islands
p 189
Babeldaob
p 188
Majuro Atoll
p 189
Palau
p 188
Micronesia
pp 188-189
Kosrae
p 189
Nauru
p 189
Tarawa
p 190
Kiribati
p 191
Maldives
p 151
WESTERN MARITIME SOUTHEAST ASIA
pp 168-169
EASTERN MARITIME SOUTHEAST ASIA
pp 170-171
Tuvalu
p 190
Funafuti Atoll
p 190
AFRICA
pp 66-83
EAST AFRICA
pp 80-81
CENTRAL AFRICA
pp 78-79
Seychelles
p 172
Comoro Islands
p 172
THE INDIAN OCEAN
pp 172-173
MELANESIA
pp 186-187
Madagascar
p 172
Mauritius
p 173
Réunion
p 173
SOUTHERN AFRICA
pp 82-83
AUSTRALASIA & OCEANIA
pp 174-193
AUSTRALIA
pp 180-181
SOUTHEAST AUSTRALIA
pp 182-183
NEW ZEALAND
pp 184-185
ANTARCTICA
pp 194-195

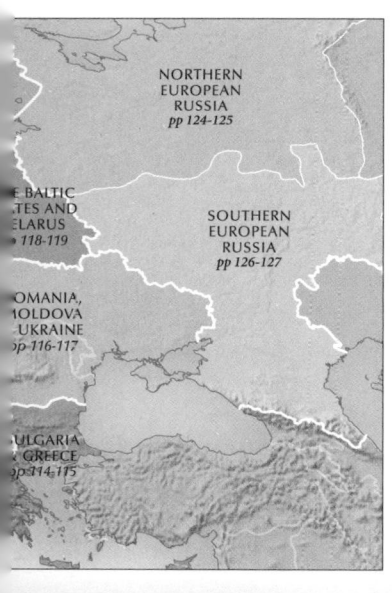

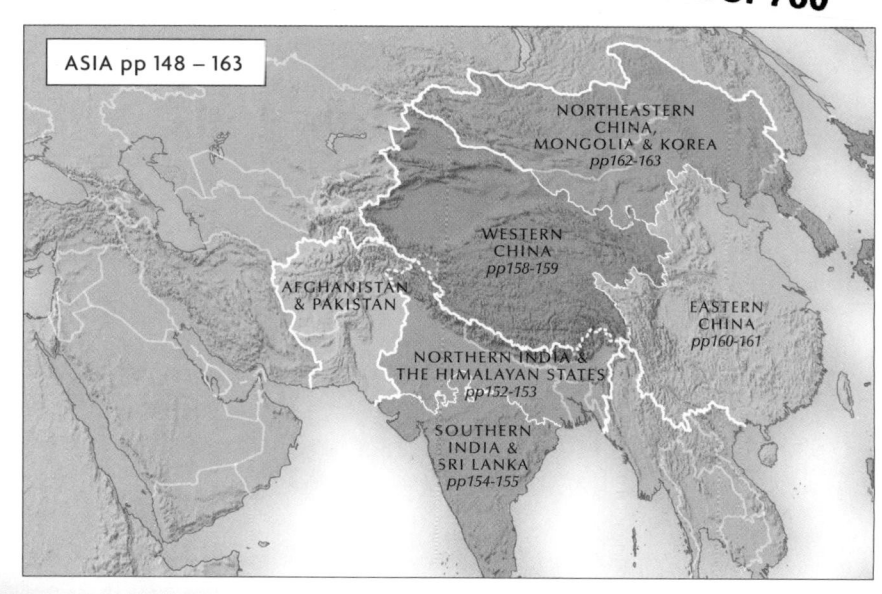

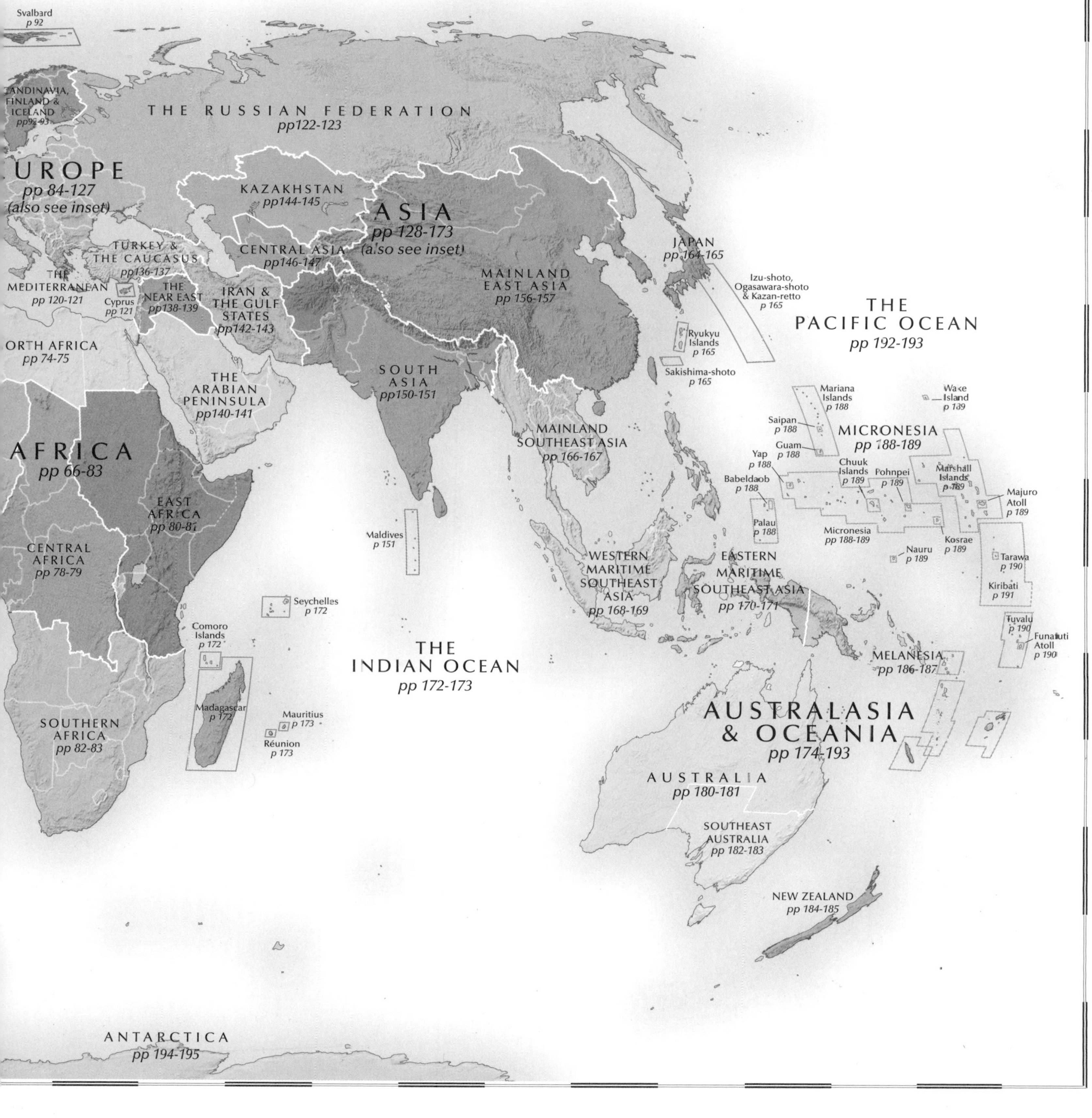

WORLD ATLAS

CONCISE

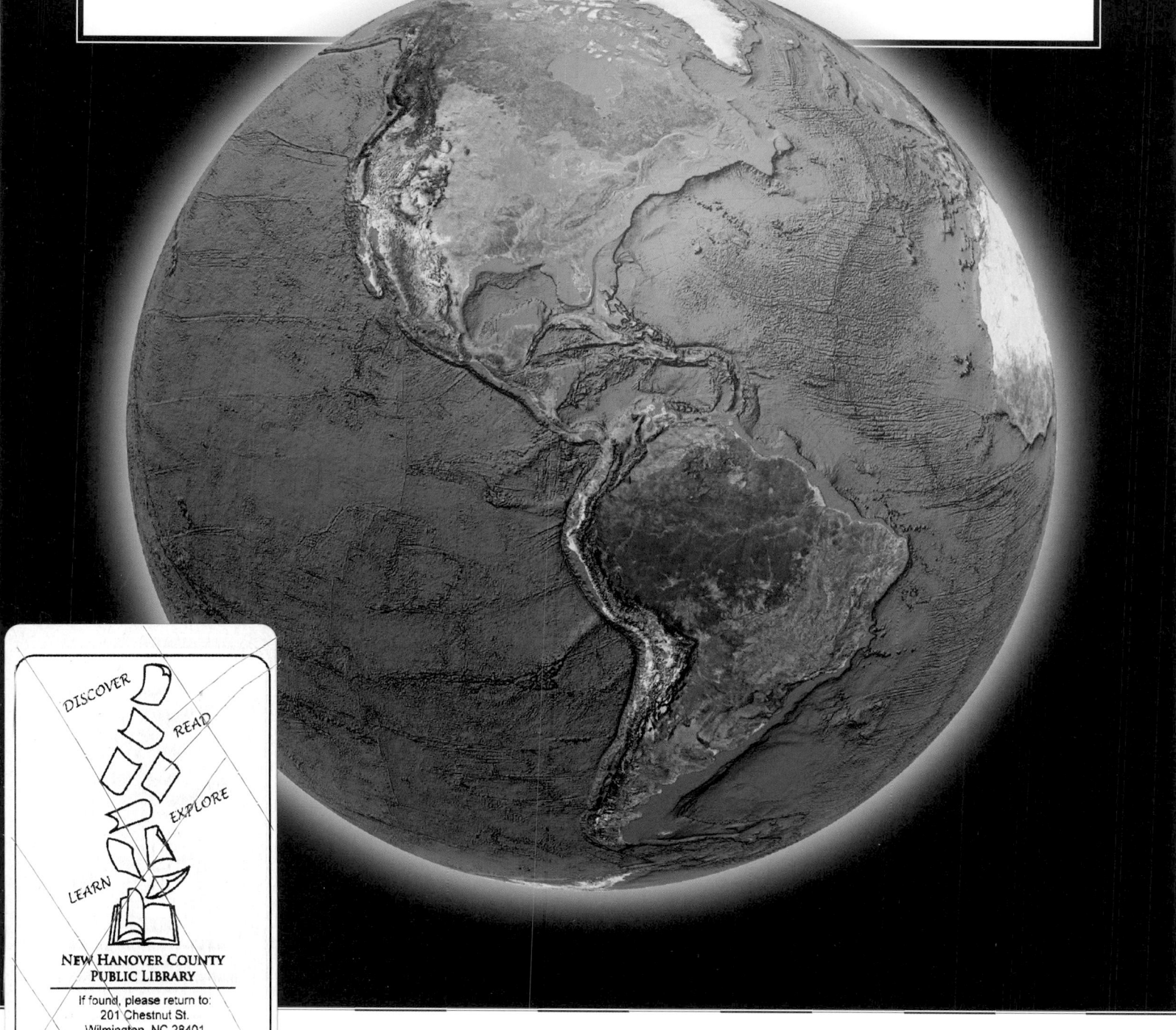

DISCOVER
READ
EXPLORE
LEARN

NEW HANOVER COUNTY
PUBLIC LIBRARY

If found, please return to:
201 Chestnut St.
Wilmington, NC 28401
(910) 798-6300
http://www.nhclibrary.org

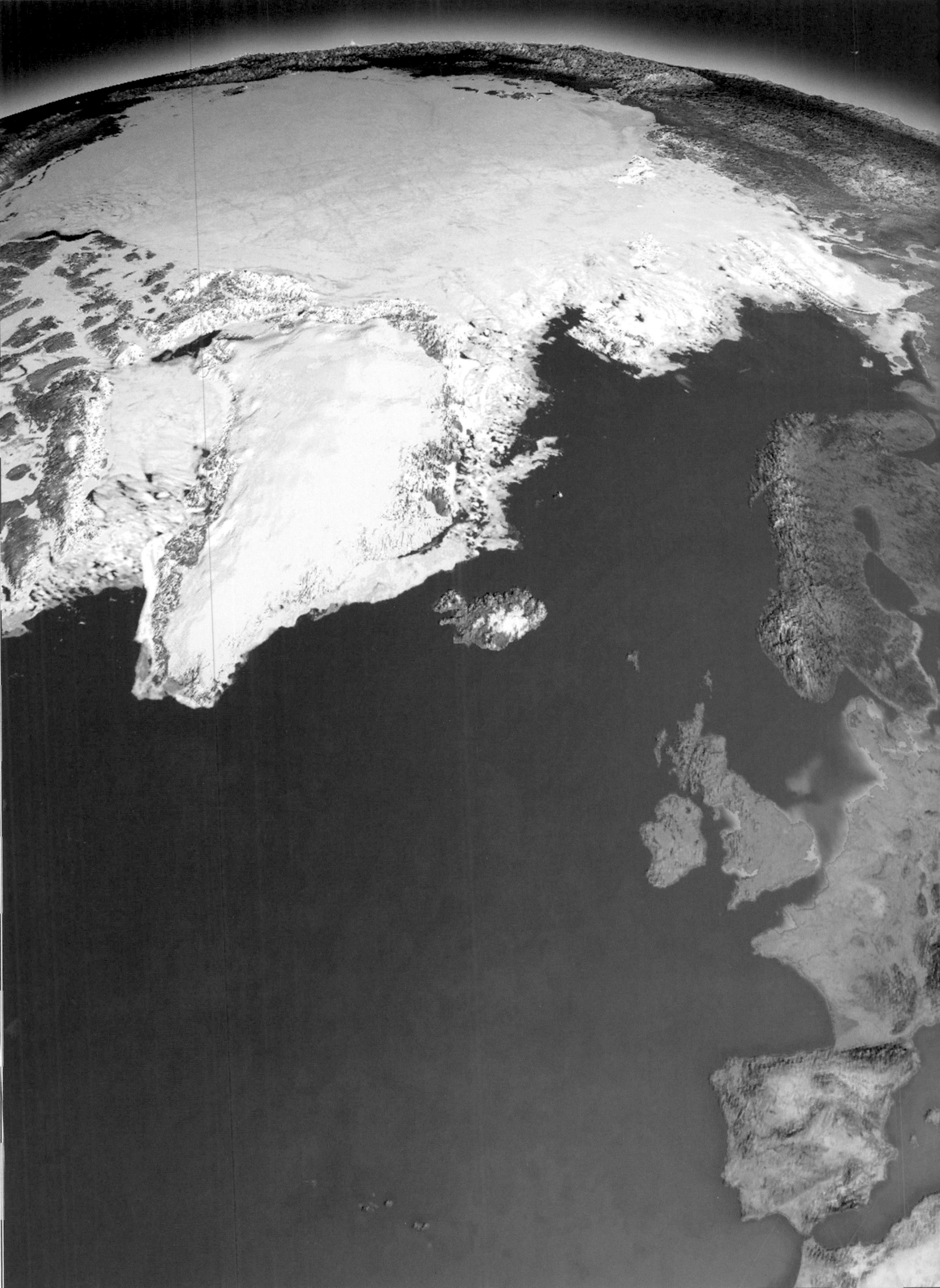

London • New York • Melbourne • Munich • Delhi

WORLD ATLAS

CONCISE

Previously published as *Concise Atlas of the World* and also includes content published in *Reference World Atlas*

**NEW HANOVER COUNTY
PUBLIC LIBRARY
201 CHESTNUT STREET
WILMINGTON, NC 28401**

LONDON, NEW YORK, MELBOURNE, MUNICH, DELHI

FOR THE FIFTH EDITION

Publisher Jonathan Metcalf   **Art Director** Philip Ormerod   **Associate Publisher** Liz Wheeler
Managing Cartographer David Roberts   **Senior Cartographic Editor** Simon Mumford   **Designers** Encompass Graphics Ltd, Brighton, UK • Philip Rowles
Cartographers Paul Eames • Iorwerth Watkins   **Jacket Designer** Philip Ormerod   **Production Controller** Linda Dare   **Production Editor** Joanna Byrne

General Geographical Consultants

Physical Geography Denys Brunsden, Emeritus Professor, Department of Geography, King's College, London
Human Geography Professor J Malcolm Wagstaff, Department of Geography, University of Southampton
Place Names Caroline Burgess, Permanent Committee on Geographical Names, London
Boundaries International Boundaries Research Unit, Mountjoy Research Centre, University of Durham

Digital Mapping Consultants

DK Cartopia developed by George Galfalvi and XMap Ltd, London
Professor Jan-Peter Muller, Department of Photogrammetry and Surveying, University College, London
Cover globes, planets and information on the Solar System provided by Philip Eales and Kevin Tildsley, Planetary Visions Ltd, London

Regional Consultants

North America Dr David Green, Department of Geography, King's College, London • Jim Walsh, Head of Reference, Wessell Library, Tufts University, Medford, Massachussetts
South America Dr David Preston, School of Geography, University of Leeds   **Europe** Dr Edward M Yates, formerly of the Department of Geography, King's College, London
Africa Dr Philip Amis, Development Administration Group, University of Birmingham • Dr Ieuan Ll Griffiths, Department of Geography, University of Sussex
Dr Tony Binns, Department of Geography, University of Sussex
Central Asia Dr David Turnock, Department of Geography, University of Leicester   **South and East Asia** Dr Jonathan Rigg, Department of Geography, University of Durham
Australasia and Oceania Dr Robert Allison, Department of Geography, University of Durham

Acknowledgments

Digital terrain data created by Eros Data Center, Sioux Falls, South Dakota, USA. Processed by GVS Images Inc, California, USA and Planetary Visions Ltd, London, UK
Cambridge International Reference on Current Affairs (CIRCA), Cambridge, UK • Digitization by Robertson Research International, Swanley, UK • Peter Clark
British Isles maps generated from a dataset supplied by Map Marketing Ltd/European Map Graphics Ltd in combination with DK Cartopia copyright data

DORLING KINDERSLEY CARTOGRAPHY

Editor-in-Chief Andrew Heritage   **Managing Cartographer** David Roberts   **Senior Cartographic Editor** Roger Bullen
Editorial Direction Louise Cavanagh   **Database Manager** Simon Lewis   **Art Direction** Chez Picthall

Cartographers

Pamela Alford • James Anderson • Caroline Bowie • Dale Buckton • Tony Chambers • Jan Clark • Bob Croser • Martin Darlison • Damien Demaj • Claire Ellam • Sally Gable
Jeremy Hepworth • Geraldine Horner • Chris Jackson • Christine Johnston • Julia Lunn • Michael Martin • Ed Merritt • James Mills-Hicks • Simon Mumford • John Plumer
John Scott • Ann Stephenson • Gail Townsley • Julie Turner • Sarah Vaughan • Jane Voss • Scott Wallace • Iorwerth Watkins • Bryony Webb • Alan Whitaker • Peter Winfield

Digital Maps Created in DK Cartopia by
Tom Coulson • Thomas Robertshaw
Philip Rowles • Rob Stokes
Managing Editor
Lisa Thomas
Editors
Thomas Heath • Wim Jenkins • Jane Oliver
Siobhan Ryan • Elizabeth Wyse
Editorial Research
Helen Dangerfield • Andrew Rebeiro-Hargrave
Additional Editorial Assistance
Debra Clapson • Robert Damon • Ailsa Heritage
Constance Novis • Jayne Parsons • Chris Whitwell

Placenames Database Team
Natalie Clarkson • Ruth Duxbury • Caroline Falce • John Featherstone • Dan Gardiner
Ciárán Hynes • Margaret Hynes • Helen Rudkin • Margaret Stevenson • Annie Wilson
Senior Managing Art Editor
Philip Lord
Designers
Scott David • Carol Ann Davis • David Douglas • Rhonda Fisher
Karen Gregory • Nicola Liddiard • Paul Williams
Illustrations
Ciárán Hughes • Advanced Illustration, Congleton, UK
Picture Research
Melissa Albany • James Clarke • Anna Lord
Christine Rista • Sarah Moule • Louise Thomas

First American edition, 2001. This revised edition, 2011.

Published in the United States by DK Publishing, 375 Hudson Street, New York, New York 10014

11 12 13 14 15   10 9 8 7 6 5 4 3 2 1

179963 — January 2011

Copyright © 2001, 2003, 2004, 2005, 2008, 2011 Dorling Kindersley Limited. All rights reserved

Without limiting the rights under copyright reserved above, no part of this publication may be reproduced, stored in or introduced into
a retrieval system, or transmitted, in any form, or by any means (electronic, mechanical, photocopying, recording, or otherwise),
without the prior written permission of both the copyright owner and the above publisher of this book.

Published in Great Britain by Dorling Kindersley Ltd. A Penguin company.

DK Publishing books are available at special
discounts when purchased in bulk for sales promotion,
premiums, fundraising, or educational use.
For details, contact:
DK Publishing Special Markets, 375 Hudson Street,
New York, New York 10014 or specialsales@dk.com

A catalog record for this book is avaiable from the Library of Congress

ISBN 978-0-7566-7146-4

Printed and bound in Singapore by Star Standard.

Discover more at **www.dk.com**

Introduction

EVERYTHING YOU NEED TO KNOW ABOUT OUR PLANET TODAY

For many, the outstanding legacy of the twentieth century was the way in which the Earth shrank. In the third millennium, it is increasingly important for us to have a clear vision of the world in which we live. The human population has increased fourfold since 1900. The last scraps of *terra incognita*— the polar regions and ocean depths—have been penetrated and mapped. New regions have been colonized and previously hostile realms claimed for habitation. The growth of air transportation and mass tourism allows many of us to travel further, faster, and more frequently than ever before. In doing so we are given a bird's-eye view of the Earth's surface denied to our forebears.

At the same time, the amount of information about our world has grown enormously. Our multi-media environment hurls uninterrupted streams of data at us, on the printed page, through the airwaves, and across our television, computer, and phone screens; events from all corners of the globe reach us instantaneously and are witnessed as they unfold. Our sense of stability and certainty has been eroded; instead, we are aware that the world is in a constant state of flux and change. Natural disasters, man-made cataclysms, and conflicts between nations remind us daily of the enormity and fragility of our domain. The ongoing threat of international terrorism throws into very stark relief the difficulties that arise when trying to "know" or "understand" our planet and its many cultures.

The current crisis in our "global" culture has made the need greater than ever before for everyone to possess an atlas. DK's **CONCISE** WORLD **ATLAS** has been conceived to meet this need. At its core, like all atlases, it seeks to define where places are located, to describe their main characteristics, and to map them in relation to other places. Every attempt has been made to produce information and maps that are as clear, accurate, and accessible as possible using the latest digital cartographic techniques. In addition, each page of the atlas provides a wealth of further information, bringing the maps to life. Using photographs, diagrams, at-a-glance maps, introductory texts, and captions, the atlas builds up a detailed portrait of those features—cultural, political, economic, and geomorphological—that make each region unique, and which are also the main agents of change.

This fifth edition of the **CONCISE** WORLD **ATLAS** incorporates hundreds of revisions and updates affecting every map and every page, distilling the burgeoning mass of information available through modern technology into an extraordinarily detailed and reliable view of our world.

CONTENTS

THE WORLD

ATLAS OF THE WORLD

North America

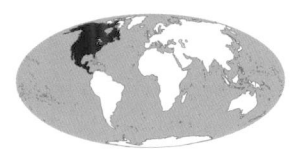

South America

Africa

Europe

Asia

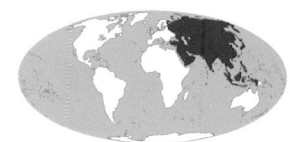

Australasia & Oceania

INDEX–GAZETTEER

Key to maps

Regional

Physical features

elevation

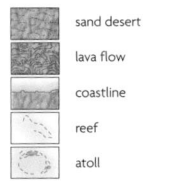

6000m / 19,686ft
4000m / 13,124ft
3000m / 9843ft
2000m / 6562ft
1000m / 3281ft
500m / 1640ft
250m / 820ft
100m / 328ft
sea level
below sea level

▲ elevation above sea level (mountain height)
▲ volcano
✕ pass
▼ elevation below sea level (depression depth)

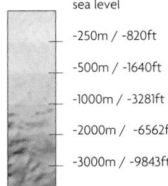

sand desert
lava flow
coastline
reef
atoll

sea depth

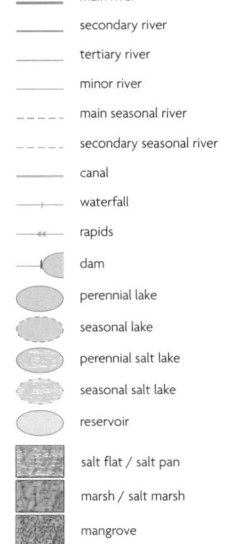

sea level
-250m / -820ft
-500m / -1640ft
-1000m / -3281ft
-2000m / -6562ft
-3000m / -9843ft

▲ seamount / guyot symbol
▼ undersea spot depth

Drainage features

main river
secondary river
tertiary river
minor river
main seasonal river
secondary seasonal river
canal
waterfall
rapids
dam
perennial lake
seasonal lake
perennial salt lake
seasonal salt lake
reservoir

salt flat / salt pan
marsh / salt marsh
mangrove
wadi
spring / well / waterhole / oasis

Ice features

ice cap / sheet
ice shelf
glacier / snowfield
• • • summer pack ice limit
◦ ◦ ◦ winter pack ice limit

Communications

——— motorway / highway
- - - - motorway / highway (under construction)
——— major road
——— minor road
→···· tunnel (road)
——— main railroad
——— minor railroad
→···· tunnel (railroad)
✈ international airport

Borders

━━━ full international border
▪ ▪ ▪ undefined international border
━ ▪ ━ disputed de facto border
━ ▪ ━ disputed territorial claim border
━ ━ ━ indication of country extent (Pacific only)
━ ━ ━ indication of dependent territory extent (Pacific only)
• • • • demarcation / cease fire line
——— autonomous / federal region border
——— 2nd order internal administrative border
——— 3rd order internal administrative border

Settlements

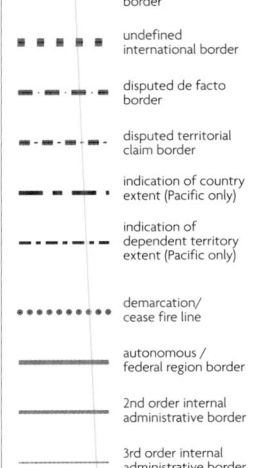

built up area

settlement population symbols

▪ more than 5 million
▣ 1 million to 5 million
◉ 500,000 to 1 million
◎ 100,000 to 500,000
⊕ 50,000 to 100,000
○ 10,000 to 50,000
○ fewer than 10,000

■ ● ● country / dependent territory capital city
■ ● ● autonomous / federal region / 2nd order internal administrative center
■ ● ● 3rd order internal administrative center

Miscellaneous features

▫▫▫▫▫ ancient wall
◇ site of interest
● scientific station

Graticule features

——— lines of latitude / longitude / Equator
- - - Tropics / Polar circles
45° degrees of longitude / latitude

Typographic key

Physical features

landscape features ... *Namib Desert*
Massif Central
ANDES

headland .... *Nordkapp*

elevation / volcano / pass .... Mount Meru
4556 m

drainage features .... *Lake Geneva*

rivers / canals
spring / well /
waterhole / oasis /
waterfall /
rapids / dam .... *Mekong*

ice features .... *Vatnajökull*

sea features .... *Golfe de Lion*
Andaman Sea
INDIAN OCEAN

undersea features ... *Barracuda Fracture Zone*

Regions

country .... **ARMENIA**

dependent territory
with parent state .... **NIUE** (to NZ)

region outside
feature area .... ANGOLA

autonomous /
federal region .... MINAS GERAIS

2nd order internal
administrative
region .... MINSKAYA
VOBLASTS'

3rd order internal
administrative
region .... Vaucluse

cultural region .... New England

Settlements

capital city .... **BEIJING**

dependent territory
capital city .... FORT-DE-FRANCE

other settlements ··· **Chicago**
Adana
Tizi Ozou
Yonezawa
Farnham

Miscellaneous

sites of interest /
miscellaneous .... Valley of the Kings

Tropics /
Polar circles .... *Antarctic Circle*

How to use this Atlas

The atlas is organized by continent, moving eastward from the International Date Line. The opening section describes the world's structure, systems, and its main features. The Atlas of the World which follows, is a continent-by-continent guide to today's world, starting with a comprehensive insight into the physical, political, and economic structure of each continent, followed by integrated mapping and descriptions of each region or country.

The world

The introductory section of the Atlas deals with every aspect of the planet, from physical structure to human geography, providing an overall picture of the world we live in. Complex topics such as the landscape of the Earth, climate, oceans, population, and economic patterns are clearly explained with the aid of maps and diagrams drawn from the latest information.

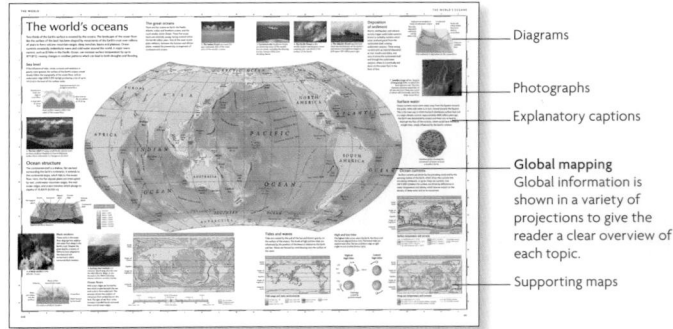

Diagrams
Photographs
Explanatory captions

Global mapping
Global information is shown in a variety of projections to give the reader a clear overview of each topic.

Supporting maps

The political continent

The political portrait of the continent is a vital reference point for every continental section, showing the position of countries relative to one another, and the relationship between human settlement and geographic location. The complex mosaic of languages spoken in each continent is mapped, as is the effect of communications networks on the pattern of settlement.

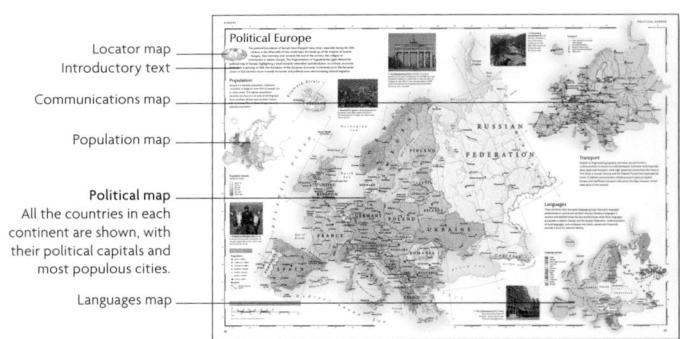

Locator map
Introductory text
Communications map
Population map

Political map
All the countries in each continent are shown, with their political capitals and most populous cities.

Languages map

Continental resources

The Earth's rich natural resources, including oil, gas, minerals, and fertile land, have played a key role in the development of society. These pages show the location of minerals and agricultural resources on each continent, and how they have been instrumental in dictating industrial growth and the varieties of economic activity across the continent.

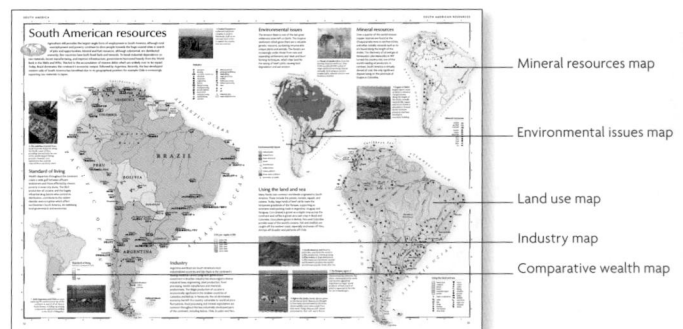

Mineral resources map
Environmental issues map
Land use map
Industry map
Comparative wealth map

The physical continent

The astonishing variety of landforms, and the dramatic forces that created and continue to shape the landscape, are explained in the continental physical spread. Cross-sections, illustrations, and terrain maps highlight the different parts of the continent, showing how nature's forces have produced the landscapes we see today.

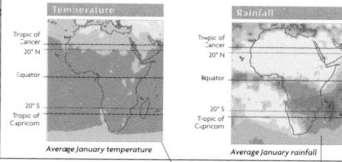

Climate charts
Rainfall and temperature charts clearly show the continental patterns of rainfall and temperature.

Climate map
Climatic regions vary across each continent. The map displays the differing climatic regions, as well as daily hours of sunshine at selected weather stations.

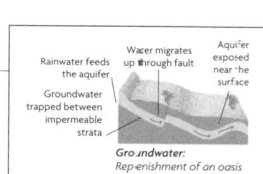

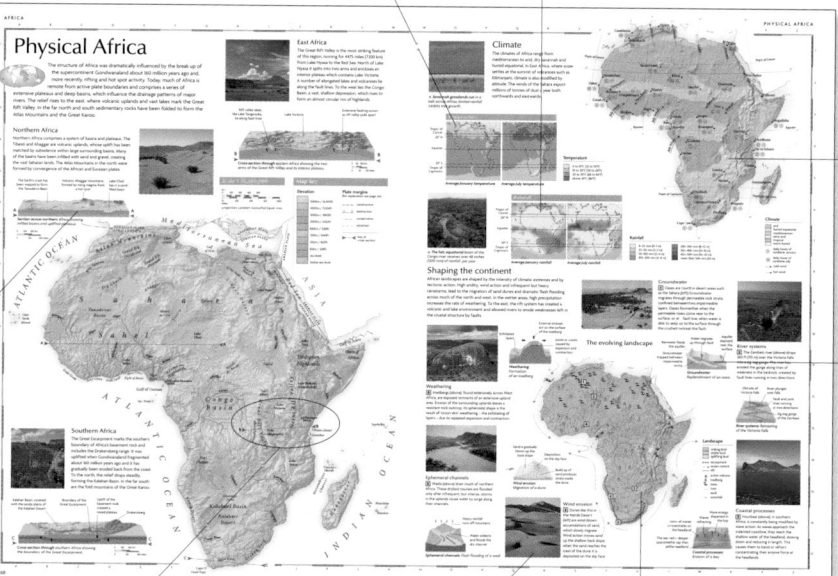

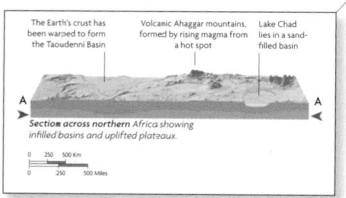

The Earth's crust has been warped to form the Taoudenni Basin

Volcanic Ahaggar mountains, formed by rising magma from a hot spot

Lake Chad lies in a sand-filled basin

Section across northern Africa showing infilled basins and uplifted plateaus.

Cross-sections
Detailed cross-sections through selected parts of the continent show the underlying geomorphic structure.

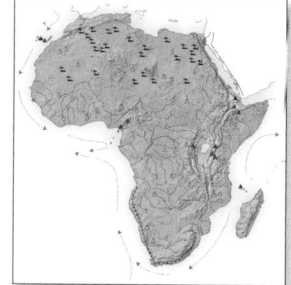

Rainwater feeds the aquifer

Water migrates up through fault

Aquifer exposed near the surface

Groundwater trapped between impermeable strata

Groundwater: Replenishment of an oasis

Landform diagrams
The complex formation of many typical landforms is summarized in these easy-to-understand illustrations.

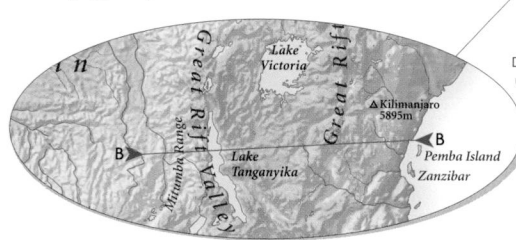

Main physical map
Detailed satellite data has been used to create an accurate and visually striking picture of the surface of the continent.

Photographs
A wide range of beautiful photographs bring the world's regions to life.

Landscape evolution map
The physical shape of each continent is affected by a variety of forces which continually sculpt and modify the landscape. This map shows the major processes which affect different parts of the continent.

Regional mapping

The main body of the Atlas is a unique regional map set, with detailed information on the terrain, the human geography of the region, and its infrastructure. Around the edge of the map, additional "at-a-glance" maps, give an instant picture of regional industry, land use, and agriculture. The detailed terrain map (shown in perspective), focuses on the main physical features of the region, and is enhanced by annotated illustrations, and photographs of the physical structure.

Key to transportation symbols
❶ Extent of national paved road network.
❷ Extent of motorways, freeways, or major national highways.
❸ Extent of commercial railroad network.
❹ Extent of inland waterways navigable by commercial craft.

Transportation network
❶ 340,090 miles (544,344km)		❷ 4813 miles (7700 km)
❸ 12,872 miles (20,592 km)		❹ 2108 miles (3389 km)

New York's commercial success is tied historically to its transportation connections. The Erie Canal, completed in 1825, opened up the Great Lakes and the interior to New York's markets and carried a stream of immigrants into the Midwest.

Transportation network
The differing extent of the transportation network for each region is shown here, along with key facts about the transportation system.

Regional Locator
This small map shows the location of each country in relation to its continent.

Key to main map
A key to the population symbols and land heights accompanies the main map.

World locator
This locates the continent in which the region is found on a small world map.

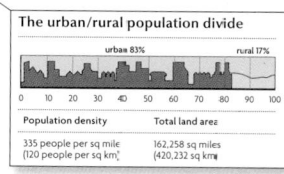

Land use map
This shows the different types of land use which characterize the region, as well as indicating the principal agricultural activities.

Map keys
Each supporting map has its own key.

Grid reference
The framing grid provides a location reference for each place listed in the Index.

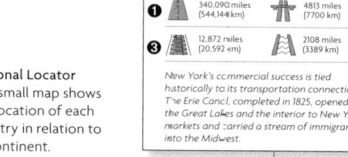

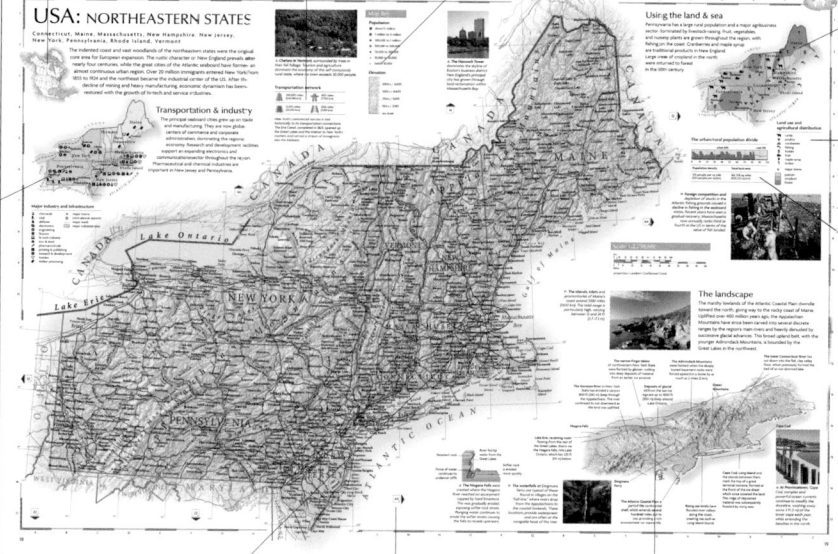

The urban/rural population divide

urban 83% · rural 17%

Population density	Total land area
335 people per sq mile (120 people per sq km)	162,258 sq miles (420,232 sq km)

Urban/rural population divide
The proportion of people in the region who live in urban and rural areas, as well as the overall population density and land area are clearly shown in these simple graphics.

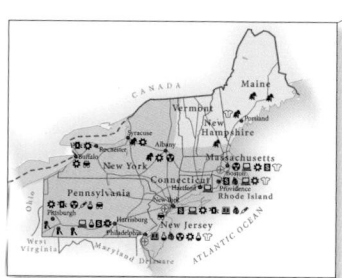

Transportation and industry map
The main industrial areas are mapped, and the most important industrial and economic activities of the region are shown.

Continuation symbols
These symbols indicate where adjacent maps can be found.

Landscape map
The computer-generated terrain model accurately portrays an oblique view of the landscape. Annotations highlight the most important geographic features of the region.

Main regional map
A wealth of information is displayed on the main map, building up a rich portrait of the interaction between the physical landscape and the human and political geography of each region. The key to the regional maps can be found on page viii.

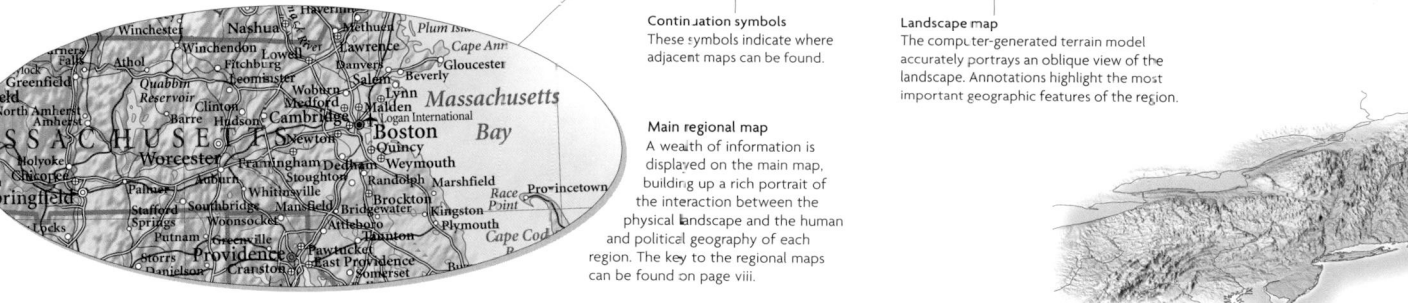

The Solar System

Nine major planets, their satellites, and countless minor planets (asteroids) orbit the Sun to form the Solar System. The Sun, our nearest star, creates energy from nuclear reactions deep within its interior, providing all the light and heat which make life on Earth possible. The Earth is unique in the Solar System in that it supports life: its size, gravitational pull and distance from the Sun have all created the optimum conditions for the evolution of life. The planetary images seen here are composites derived from actual spacecraft images (not shown to scale).

Orbits

All the Solar System's planets and dwarf planets orbit the Sun in the same direction and (apart from Pluto) roughly in the same plane. All the orbits have the shapes of ellipses (stretched circles). However, in most cases, these ellipses are close to being circular: only Pluto and Eris have very elliptical orbits. Orbital period (the time it takes an object to orbit the Sun) increases with distance from the Sun. The more remote objects not only have further to travel with each orbit, they also move more slowly.

Mercury Venus Earth Mars

Ceres
(dwarf planet)

Jupiter

The Sun

- ⊖ *Diameter: 854,948 miles (1,392,000 km)*
- ● *Mass: 1990 million million million million tons*

The Sun was formed when a swirling cloud of dust and gas contracted, pulling matter into its center. When the temperature at the center rose to 1,000,000°C, nuclear fusion – the fusing of hydrogen into helium, creating energy – occurred, releasing a constant stream of heat and light.

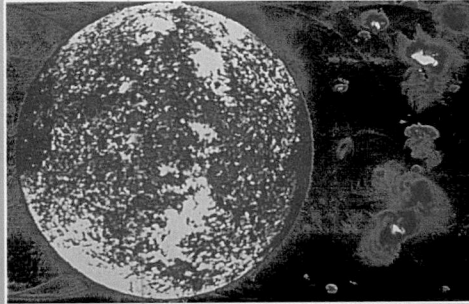

▲ **Solar flares are** *sudden bursts of energy from the Sun's surface. They can be 125,000 miles (200,000 km) long.*

The formation of the Solar System

The cloud of dust and gas thrown out by the Sun during its formation cooled to form the Solar System. The smaller planets nearest the Sun are formed of minerals and metals. The outer planets were formed at lower temperatures, and consist of swirling clouds of gases.

Solar eclipse

A solar eclipse occurs when the Moon passes between Earth and the Sun, casting its shadow on Earth's surface. During a total eclipse *(below)*, viewers along a strip of Earth's surface, called the area of totality, see the Sun totally blotted out for a short time, as the umbra (Moon's full shadow) sweeps over them. Outside this area is a larger one, where the Sun appears only partly obscured, as the penumbra (partial shadow) passes over.

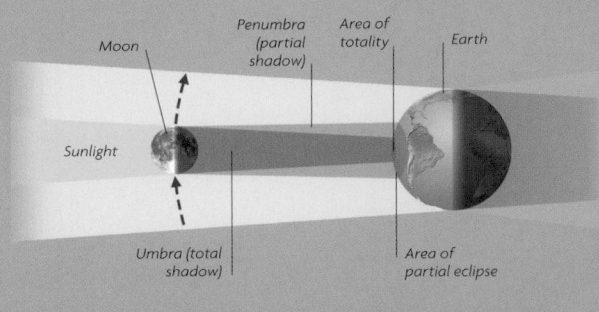

Penumbra *(partial shadow)*

Area of totality

Earth

Moon

Sunlight

Umbra *(total shadow)*

Area of partial eclipse

PLANETS

DWARF PLANETS

	MERCURY	VENUS	EARTH	MARS	JUPITER	SATURN	URANUS	NEPTUNE	CERES	PLUTO	ERIS
DIAMETER	3029 miles (4875 km)	7521 miles (12,104 km)	7928 miles (12,756 km)	4213 miles (6780 km)	88,846 miles (142,984 km)	74,898 miles (120,536 km)	31,763 miles (51,118 km)	30,775 miles (49,528 km)	590 miles (950 km)	1432 miles (2304 km)	1429-1553 miles (2300-2500 km)
AVERAGE DISTANCE FROM THE SUN	36 mill. miles (57.9 mill. km)	67.2 mill. miles (108.2 mill. km)	93 mill. miles (149.6 mill. km)	141.6 mill. miles (227.9 mill. km)	483.6 mill. miles (778.3 mill. km)	889.8 mill. miles (1431 mill. km)	1788 mill. miles (2877 mill. km)	2795 mill. miles (4498 mill. km)	257 mill. miles (414 mill. km)	3675 mill. miles (5915 mill. km)	6344 mill. miles (10,210 mill. km)
ROTATION PERIOD	58.6 days	243 days	23.93 hours	24.62 hours	9.93 hours	10.65 hours	17.24 hours	16.11 hours	9.1 hours	6.38 days	not known
ORBITAL PERIOD	88 days	224.7 days	365.26 days	687 days	11.86 years	29.37 years	84.1 years	164.9 years	4.6 years	248.6 years	557 years
SURFACE TEMPERATURE	-180°C to 430°C (-292°F to 806°F)	480°C (896°F)	-70°C to 55°C (-94°F to 131°F)	-120°C to 25°C (-184°F to 77°F)	-110°C (-160°F)	-140°C (-220°F)	-200°C (-320°F)	-200°C (-320°F)	-107°C (-161°F)	-230°C (-380°F)	-243°C (-405°F)

AVERAGE DISTANCE FROM THE SUN

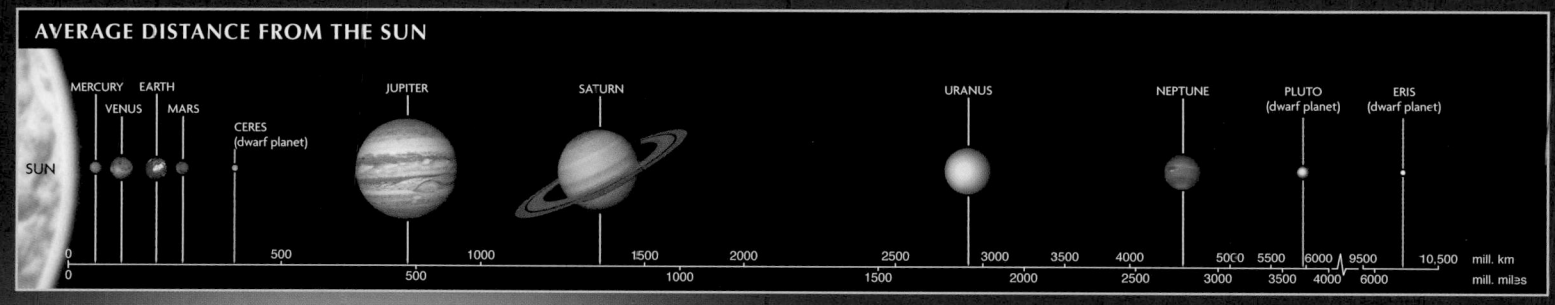

SUN · MERCURY · VENUS · EARTH · MARS · CERES (dwarf planet) · JUPITER · SATURN · URANUS · NEPTUNE · PLUTO (dwarf planet) · ERIS (dwarf planet)

0 500 1000 1500 2000 2500 3000 3500 4000 5000 5500 6000 9500 10,500 mill. km
0 500 1000 1500 2000 2500 3000 3500 4000 6000 mill. miles

Saturn

Uranus

Neptune

Pluto (dwarf planet)

Eris (dwarf planet)

Space Debris

Millions of objects, remnants of planetary formation, circle the Sun in a zone lying between Mars and Jupiter: the asteroid belt. Fragments of asteroids break off to form meteoroids, which can reach the Earth's surface. Comets, composed of ice and dust, originated outside our Solar System. Their elliptical orbit brings them close to the Sun and into the inner Solar System.

▲ *Meteor Crater in Arizona is 4200 ft (1300 m) wide and 660 ft (200 m) deep. It was formed over 10,000 years ago.*

Possible and actual meteorite craters

Map key
◯ Possible impact craters
◯ Meteorite impact craters

The Earth's Atmosphere

During the early stages of the Earth's formation, ash, lava, carbon dioxide, and water vapor were discharged onto the surface of the planet by constant volcanic eruptions. The water formed the oceans, while carbon dioxide entered the atmosphere or was dissolved in the oceans. Clouds, formed of water droplets, reflected some of the Sun's radiation back into space. The Earth's temperature stabilized and early life forms began to emerge, converting carbon dioxide into life-giving oxygen.

▲ *It is thought that the gases that make up the Earth's atmosphere originated deep within the interior, and were released many millions of years ago during intense volcanic activity, similar to this eruption at Mount St. Helens.*

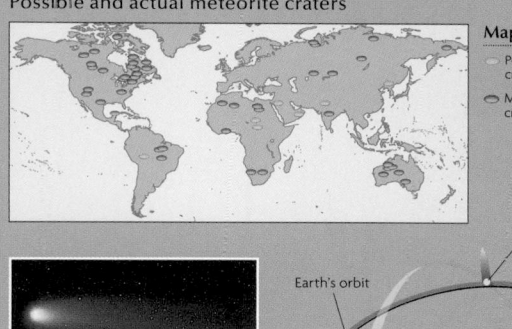

▲ *The orbit of Halley's Comet brings it close to the Earth every 76 years. It last visited in 1986.*

Halley's Comet

Earth's orbit

Halley's orbit

Orbit of Halley's Comet around the Sun

The physical world

The Earth's surface is constantly being transformed: it is uplifted, folded, and faulted by tectonic forces; weathered and eroded by wind, water, and ice. Sometimes change is dramatic, the spectacular results of earthquakes or floods. More often it is a slow process lasting millions of years. A physical map of the world represents a snapshot of the ever-evolving architecture of the Earth. This terrain map shows the whole surface of the Earth, both above and below the sea.

The world in section

These cross-sections around the Earth, one in the northern hemisphere; one straddling the Equator, reveal the limited areas of land above sea level in comparison with the extent of the sea floor. The greater erosive effects of weathering by wind and water limit the upward elevation of land above sea level, while the deep oceans retain their dramatic mountain and trench profiles.

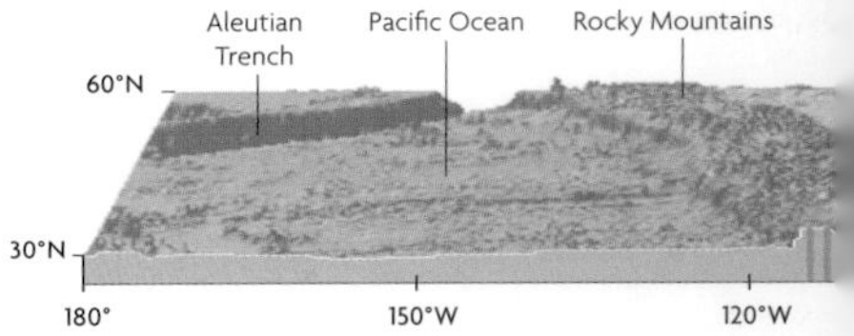

Cross-section: Northern hemisphere

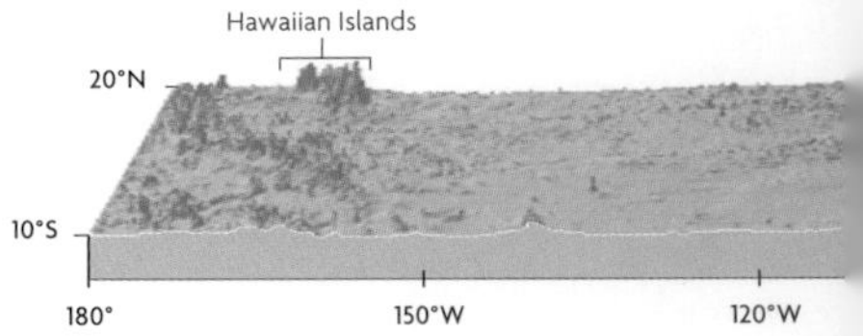

Cross-section: Southern hemisphere

Map key

Geographical regions

- ice
- tundra
- needleleaf forest
- broadleaf forest
- cultivated land
- hot desert
- cold desert
- tropical grassland
- tropical rain forest
- mountain
- submarine regions

Scale 1:73,000,000

Km 0 250 500 1000 1500 2000

Miles 0 250 500 1000 1500 2000

projection: Wagner VII

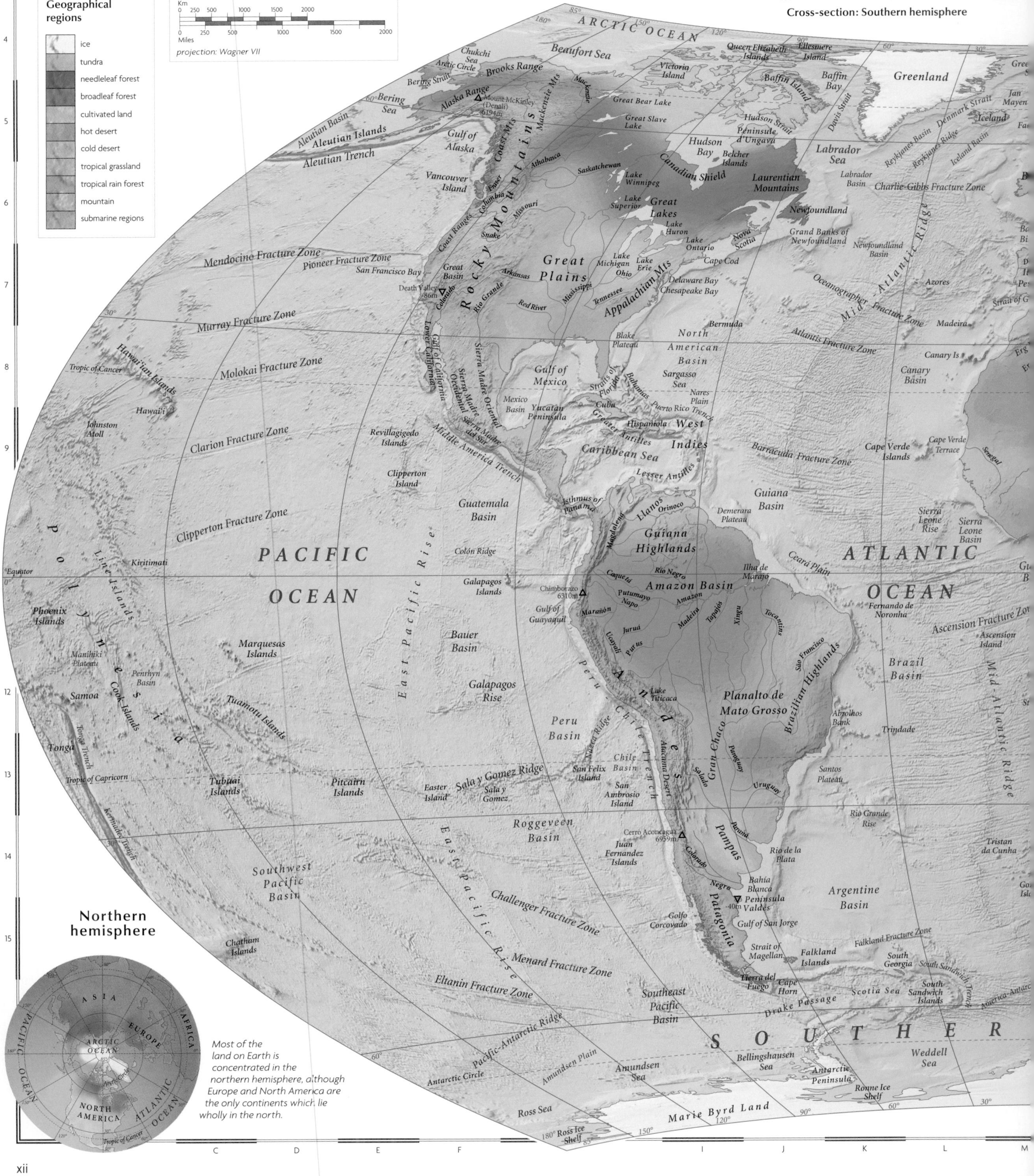

Northern hemisphere

Most of the land on Earth is concentrated in the northern hemisphere, although Europe and North America are the only continents which lie wholly in the north.

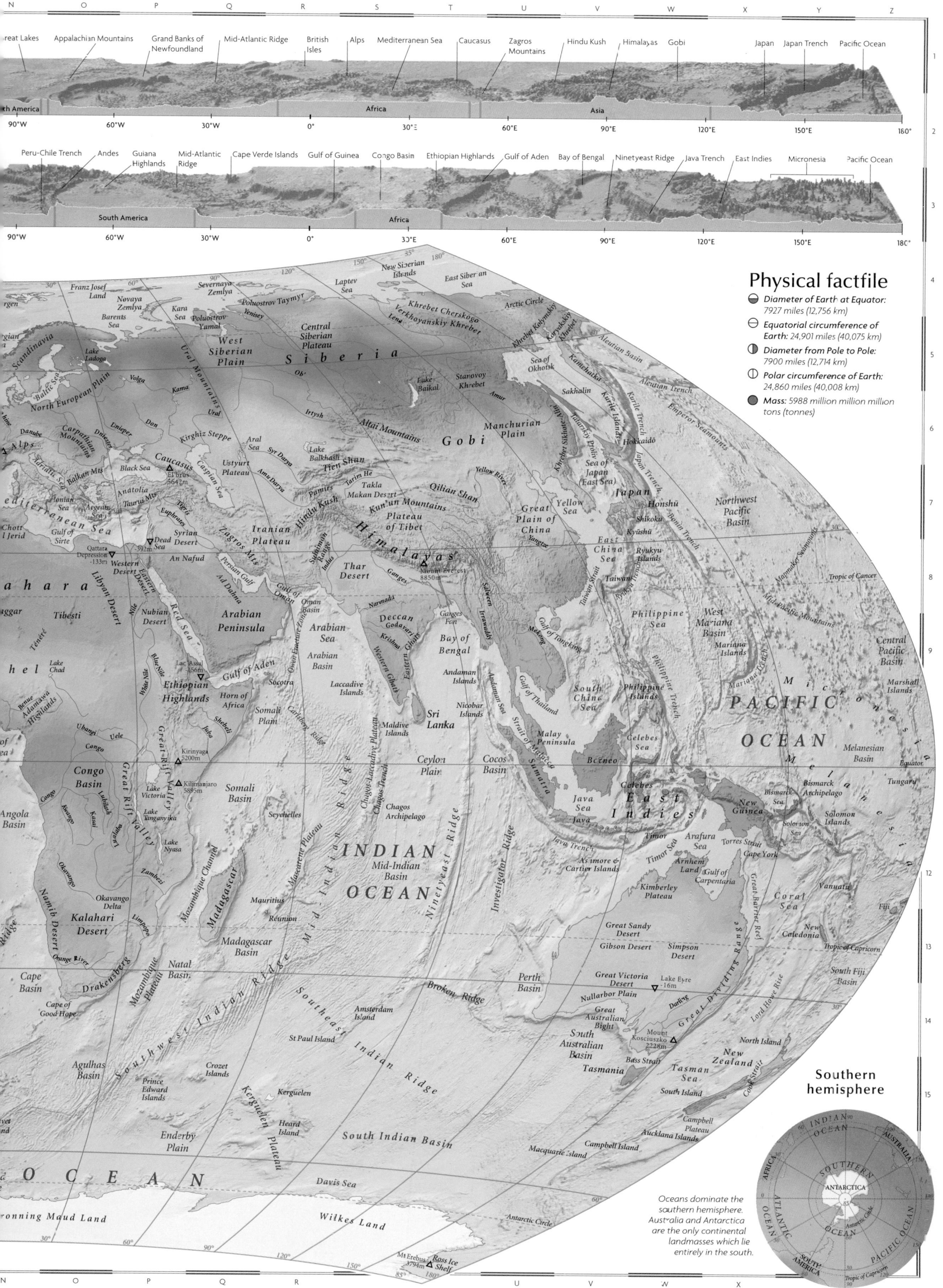

Physical factfile

- **Diameter of Earth at Equator:** 7927 miles (12,756 km)
- **Equatorial circumference of Earth:** 24,901 miles (40,075 km)
- **Diameter from Pole to Pole:** 7900 miles (12,714 km)
- **Polar circumference of Earth:** 24,860 miles (40,008 km)
- **Mass:** 5988 million million million tons (tonnes)

Southern hemisphere

Oceans dominate the southern hemisphere. Australia and Antarctica are the only continental landmasses which lie entirely in the south.

Structure of the Earth

The Earth as it is today is just the latest phase in a constant process of evolution which has occurred over the past 4.5 billion years. The Earth's continents are neither fixed nor stable; over the course of the Earth's history, propelled by currents rising from the intense heat at its center, the great plates on which they lie have moved, collided, joined together, and separated. These processes continue to mold and transform the surface of the Earth, causing earthquakes and volcanic eruptions and creating oceans, mountain ranges, deep ocean trenches, and island chains.

Inside the Earth

The Earth's hot inner core is made up of solid iron, while the outer core is composed of liquid iron and nickel. The mantle nearest the core is viscous, whereas the rocky upper mantle is fairly rigid. The crust is the rocky outer shell of the Earth. Together, the upper mantle and the crust form the lithosphere.

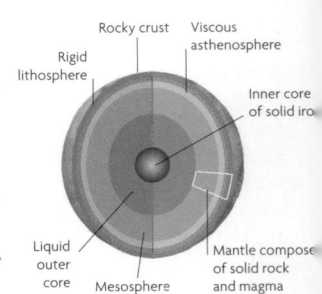

Rocky crust
Rigid lithosphere
Viscous asthenosphere
Inner core of solid iron
Liquid outer core
Mesosphere
Mantle composed of solid rock and magma

The dynamic Earth

The Earth's crust is made up of eight major (and several minor) rigid continental and oceanic tectonic plates, which fit closely together. The positions of the plates are not static. They are constantly moving relative to one another. The type of movement between plates affects the way in which they alter the structure of the Earth. The oldest parts of the plates, known as shields, are the most stable parts of the Earth and little tectonic activity occurs here.

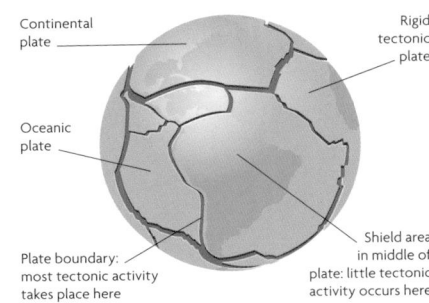

Continental plate
Rigid tectonic plate
Oceanic plate
Plate boundary: most tectonic activity takes place here
Shield area in middle of plate: little tectonic activity occurs here

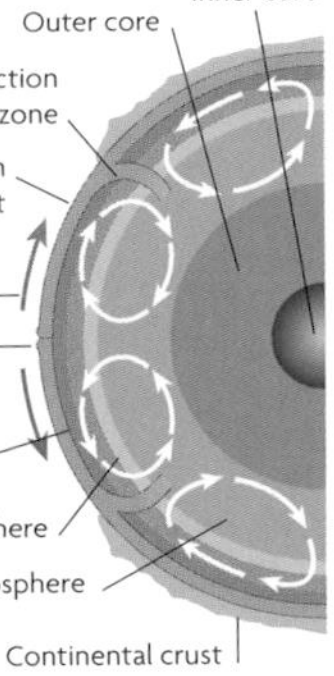

Convection currents

Deep within the Earth, at its inner core, temperatures may exceed 8,100°F (4,500°C). This heat warms rocks in the mesosphere which rise through the partially molten mantle, displacing cooler rocks just below the solid crust, which sink, and are warmed again by the heat of the mantle. This process is continuous, creating convection currents which form the moving force beneath the Earth's crust.

Inner core
Outer core
Subduction zone
Ocean crust
Movement of plate
Mid-ocean ridge
Lithosphere
Asthenosphere
Mesosphere
Continental crust

Plate boundaries

The boundaries between the plates are the areas where most tectonic activity takes place. Three types of movement occur at plate boundaries: the plates can either move toward each other, move apart, or slide past each other. The effect this has on the Earth's structure depends on whether the margin is between two continental plates, two oceanic plates, or an oceanic and continental plate.

Mid-ocean ridges

—— Mid-ocean ridges are formed when two adjacent oceanic plates pull apart, allowing magma to force its way up to the surface, which then cools to form solid rock. Vast amounts of volcanic material are discharged at these mid-ocean ridges which can reach heights of 10,000 ft (3000 m).

▲ *The Mid-Atlantic Ridge* rises above sea level in Iceland, producing geysers and volcanoes.

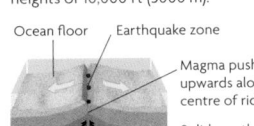

Ocean floor
Earthquake zone
Magma pushed upwards along centre of ridge
Solid mantle

Formation of a mid-ocean ridge

▲ *Mount Pinatubo is an* active volcano, lying on the Pacific "Ring of Fire."

Ocean plates meeting

△△ Oceanic crust is denser and thinner than continental crust; on average it is 3 miles (5 km) thick, while continental crust averages 18–24 miles (30–40 km). When oceanic plates of similar density meet, the crust is contorted as one plate overrides the other, forming deep sea trenches and volcanic island arcs above sea level.

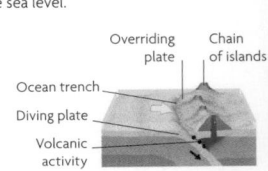

Overriding plate
Chain of islands
Ocean trench
Diving plate
Volcanic activity

Ocean plates meeting to form an island arc

Tectonic activity

- – – – – uncertain plate boundary
- ▲ volcanic zone
- ● earthquake zone
- ● hot spot
- ＶＶＶＶＶ rift valley

[World map with plate boundaries, showing: JUAN DE FUCA PLATE, NORTH AMERICAN PLATE, EURASIAN PLATE, ANATOLIAN PLATE, IRANIAN PLATE, ARABIAN PLATE, CARIBBEAN PLATE, COCOS PLATE, PACIFIC PLATE, AFRICAN PLATE, SOUTH AMERICAN PLATE, NAZCA PLATE, PHILIPPINE PLATE, CAROLINE PLATE, BISMARCK PLATE, SOLOMON PLATE, FIJI PLATE, INDO-AUSTRALIAN PLATE, SCOTIA PLATE, ANTARCTIC PLATE. Map lines include Arctic Circle, Tropic of Cancer, Equator, Tropic of Capricorn, Antarctic Circle.]

Diving plates

△△ When an oceanic and a continental plate meet, the denser oceanic plate is driven underneath the continental plate, which is crumpled by the collision to form mountain ranges. As the ocean plate plunges downward, it heats up, and molten rock (magma) is forced up to the surface.

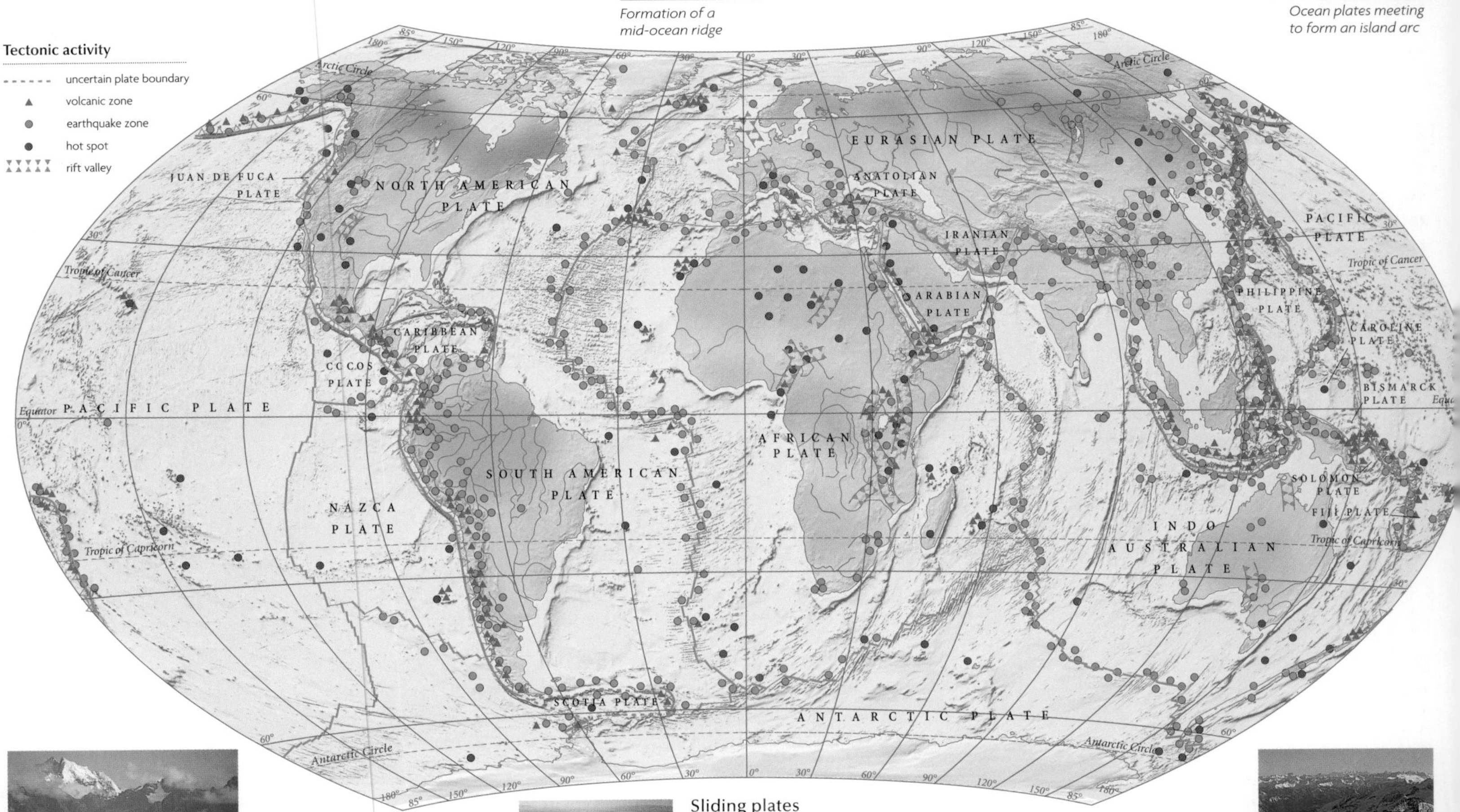

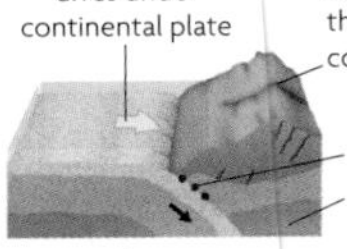

◄ *The Andean mountain* chain is the typical result of the impact of a diving plate.

Oceanic plate dives under continental plate
Mountains thrust up by collision
Earthquake zone
Continental plate

Diving plate

▲ *The deep fracture* caused by the sliding plates of the San Andreas Fault can be clearly seen in parts of California.

Sliding plates

—— When two plates slide past each other, friction is caused along the fault line which divides them. The plates do not move smoothly, and the uneven movement causes earthquakes.

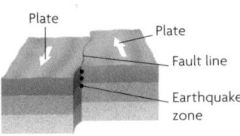

Plate
Plate
Fault line
Earthquake zone

Sliding plates

▶ *The Alps were* formed when the African Plate collided with the Eurasian Plate, about 65 million years ago.

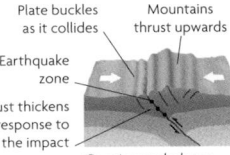

Plate buckles as it collides
Mountains thrust upwards
Earthquake zone
Crust thickens in response to the impact

Continental plates colliding to form a mountain range

Colliding plates

▲▲▲ When two continental plates collide, great mountain chains are thrust upward as the crust buckles and folds under the force of the impact.

Continental drift

Although the plates which make up the Earth's crust move only a few inches in a year, over the millions of years of the Earth's history, its continents have moved many thousands of miles, to create new continents, oceans, and mountain chains

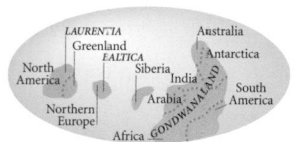

1: Cambrian period
570–510 million years ago. Most continents are in tropical latitudes. The supercontinent of Gondwana reaches the South Pole.

2: Devonian period
408–362 million years ago. The continents of Gondwanaland and Laurentia are drifting northward.

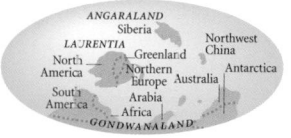

3: Carboniferous period
362–290 million years ago. The Earth is dominated by three continents; Laurentia, Angaraland, and Gondwanaland.

4: Triassic period
245–208 million years ago. All three major continents have joined to form the super-continent of Pangea.

5: Jurassic period
208–145 million years ago. The super-continent of Pangea begins to break up, causing an overall rise in sea levels.

6: Cretaceous period
145–65 million years ago. Warm, shallow seas cover much of the land: sea levels are about 80 ft (25 m) above present levels.

7: Tertiary period
65–2 million years ago. Although the world's geography is becoming more recognizable, major events such as the creation of the Himalayan mountain chain, are still to occur during this period.

Continental shields

The centers of the Earth's continents, known as shields, were established between 2500 and 500 million years ago; some contain rocks over three billion years old. They were formed by a series of turbulent events: plate movements, earthquakes, and volcanic eruptions. Since the Pre-Cambrian period, over 570 million years ago, they have experienced little tectonic activity, and today, these flat, low-lying slabs of solidified molten rock form the stable centers of the continents. They are bounded or covered by successive belts of younger sedimentary rock.

The Hawai'ian island chain

A hot spot lying deep beneath the Pacific Ocean pushes a plume of magma from the Earth's mantle up through the Pacific Plate to form volcanic islands. While the hot spot remains stationary, the plate on which the islands sit is moving slowly. A long chain of islands has been created as the plate passes over the hot spot.

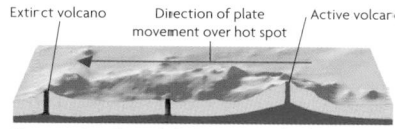

Extinct volcano   Direction of plate movement over hot spot   Active volcano

Cross-section through the Hawai'ian Islands

Evolution of the Hawai'ian Islands

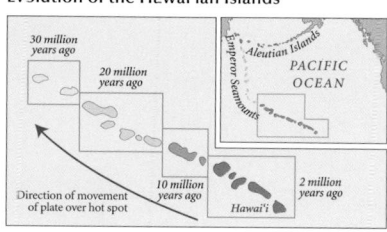

30 million years ago
20 million years ago
10 million years ago
2 million years ago
Aleutian Islands
Emperor Seamounts
PACIFIC OCEAN
Direction of movement of plate over hot spot
Hawai'i

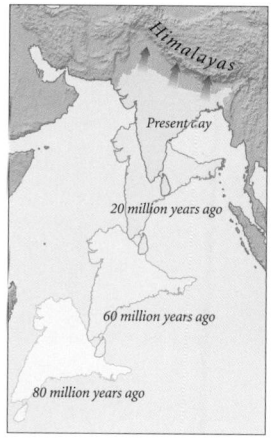

Creation of the Himalayas

Between 10 and 20 million years ago, the Indian subcontinent, part of the ancient continent of Gondwanaland, collided with the continent of Asia. The Indo-Australian Plate continued to move northward, displacing continental crust and uplifting the Himalayas, the world's highest mountain chain.

Movements of India

Himalayas
Present day
20 million years ago
60 million years ago
80 million years ago

Force of collision pushes up mountains

Cross-section through the Himalayas

▲ The Himalayas were uplifted when the Indian subcontinent collided with Asia.

The Earth's geology

The Earth's rocks are created in a continual cycle. Exposed rocks are weathered and eroded by wind, water, and chemicals and deposited as sediments. If they pass into the Earth's crust they will be transformed by high temperatures and pressures into metamorphic rocks or they will melt and solidify as igneous rocks.

Sandstone

[8] Sandstones are sedimentary rocks formed mainly in deserts, beaches, and deltas. Desert sandstones are formed of grains of quartz which have been well rounded by wind erosion.

▲ Rock stacks of desert sandstone, at Bryce Canyon National Park, Utah, US.

◄ Extrusive igneous rocks are formed during volcanic eruptions, as here in Hawai'i.

Andesite

[7] Andesite is an extrusive igneous rock formed from magma which has solidified on the Earth's crust after a volcanic eruption.

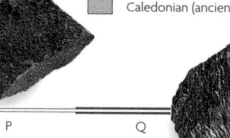

Gneiss

[1] Gneiss is a metamorphic rock made at great depth during the formation of mountain chains, when intense heat and pressure transform sedimentary or igneous rocks.

▲ Gneiss formations in Norway's Jotunheimen Mountains.

Basalt

[2] Basalt is an igneous rock, formed when small quantities of magma lying close to the Earth's surface cool rapidly.

◄ Basalt columns at Giant's Causeway, Northern Ireland, UK.

Limestone

[3] Limestone is a sedimentary rock, which is formed mainly from the calcite skeletons of marine animals which have been compressed into rock.

▲ Limestone hills, Guilin, China.

Coral

[4] Coral reefs are formed from the skeletons of millions of individual corals.

▲ Great Barrier Reef, Australia.

Geological regions
- continental shield
- sedimentary cover
- coral formation
- igneous rock types

Mountain ranges
- Alpine (new)
- Hercynian (old)
- Caledonian (ancient)

Schist

[1] Schist is a metamorphic rock formed during mountain building, when temperature and pressure are comparatively high. Both mudstones and shales reform into schist under these conditions

▶ Schist formations in the Atlas Mountains, northwestern Africa

Granite

[5] Granite is an intrusive igneous rock formed from magma which has solidified deep within the Earth's crust. The magma cools slowly, producing a coarse-grained rock.

▶ Namibia's Namaqualand Plateau is formed of granite.

Shaping the landscape

The basic material of the Earth's surface is solid rock: valleys, deserts, soil, and sand are all evidence of the powerful agents of weathering, erosion, and deposition which constantly shape and transform the Earth's landscapes. Water, either flowing continually in rivers or seas, or frozen and compacted into solid sheets of ice, has the most clearly visible impact on the Earth's surface. But wind can transport fragments of rock over huge distances and strip away protective layers of vegetation, exposing rock surfaces to the impact of extreme heat and cold.

Coastal water

The world's coastlines are constantly changing; every day, tides deposit, sift and sort sand, and gravel on the shoreline. Over longer periods, powerful wave action erodes cliffs and headlands and carves out bays.

▶ *A low, wide* sandy beach on South Africa's Cape Peninsula is continually re-shaped by the action of the Atlantic waves.

▲ *The sheer chalk* cliffs at Seven Sisters in southern England are constantly under attack from waves.

Water

Less than 2% of the world's water is on the land, but it is the most powerful agent of landscape change. Water, as rainfall, groundwater, and rivers, can transform landscapes through both erosion and deposition. Eroded material carried by rivers forms the world's most fertile soils.

▲ *Waterfalls such as* the Iguaçu Falls on the border between Argentina and southern Brazil, erode the underlying rock, causing the falls to retreat.

Groundwater

In regions where there are porous rocks such as chalk, water is stored underground in large quantities; these reservoirs of water are known as aquifers. Rain percolates through topsoil into the underlying bedrock, creating an underground store of water. The limit of the saturated zone is called the water table.

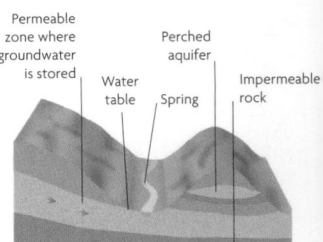
Permeable zone where groundwater is stored · Perched aquifer · Water table · Spring · Impermeable rock
Storage of groundwater in an aquifer

World river systems

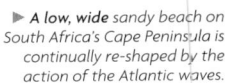
drainage basin

World river systems:
Sediment deposited annually per drainage basin

tons per sq mile per year 9120 · 6080 · 1520 · 760 · 400 · 200 and less · 2400 · 1600
tonnes per sq km per year

ARCTIC OCEAN
Arctic Circle · Yukon · Mackenzie · Nelson · Columbia · St. Lawrence · Colorado · Mississippi/Missouri · Rio Grande · Orinoco · Amazon · São Francisco · Paraná · Rhine · Danube · Tigris/Euphrates · Niger · Nile · Congo · Zambezi · Orange · Yenisey · Lena · Volga · Ob' · Amur · Yellow River · Indus · Ganges/Brahmaputra · Yangtze · Mekong · Murray/Darling

PACIFIC OCEAN · ATLANTIC OCEAN · INDIAN OCEAN · PACIFIC OCEAN
Tropic of Cancer · Equator · Tropic of Capricorn · Antarctic Circle

Rivers

Rivers erode the land by grinding and dissolving rocks and stones. Most erosion occurs in the river's upper course as it flows through highland areas. Rock fragments are moved along the river bed by fast-flowing water and deposited in areas where the river slows down, such as flat plains, or where the river enters seas or lakes.

River valleys

Over long periods of time rivers erode uplands to form characteristic V-shaped valleys with smooth sides.

Resistant rock · River · Chemical erosion cuts valley in softer rock
River valley erosion

Deltas

When a river deposits its load of silt and sediment (alluvium) on entering the sea, it may form a delta. As this material accumulates, it chokes the mouth of the river, forcing it to create new channels to reach the sea.

▶ *The Nile forms* a broad delta as it flows into the Mediterranean.

Drainage basins

The drainage basin is the area of land drained by a major trunk river and its smaller branch rivers or tributaries. Drainage basins are separated from one another by natural boundaries known as watersheds.

Watershed · Major trunk river · Alps · Dolomites · Apennines · Tributary river · Delta · River mouth · Po Valley
The drainage basin of the Po river, northern Italy.

Meanders

In their lower courses, rivers flow slowly. As they flow across the lowlands, they form looping bends called meanders.

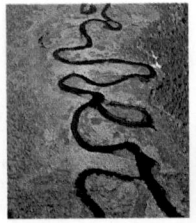
▲ *The Mississippi River* forms meanders as it flows across the southern US.

▲ *The meanders of* Utah's San Juan River have become deeply incised.

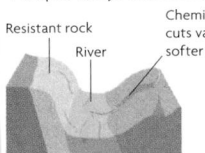
◀ *Mud is deposited* by China's Yellow River in its lower course.

Deposition

When rivers have deposited large quantities of fertile alluvium, they are forced to find new channels through the alluvium deposits, creating braided river systems.

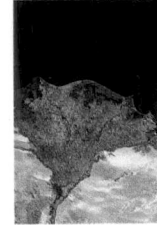

Landslides

Heavy rain and associated flooding on slopes can loosen underlying rocks, which crumble, causing the top layers of rock and soil to slip.

▶ *A huge landslide in* the Swiss Alps has left massive piles of rocks and pebbles called scree.

Gullies

In areas where soil is thin, rainwater is not effectively absorbed, and may flow overland. The water courses downhill in channels, or gullies, and may lead to rapid erosion of soil.

▲ *A deep gully* in the French Alps caused by the scouring of upper layers of turf.

Ice

During its long history, the Earth has experienced a number of glacial episodes when temperatures were considerably lower than today. During the last Ice Age, 18,000 years ago, ice covered an area three times larger than it does today. Over these periods, the ice has left a remarkable legacy of transformed landscapes.

Glaciers

Glaciers are formed by the compaction of snow into "rivers" of ice. As they move over the landscape, glaciers pick up and carry a load of rocks and boulders which erode the landscape they pass over, and are eventually deposited at the end of the glacier.

▲ *A massive glacier advancing down a valley in southern Argentina.*

Post-glacial features

When a glacial episode ends, the retreating ice leaves many features. These include depositional ridges called moraines, which may be eroded into low hills known as drumlins; sinuous ridges called eskers; kames, which are rounded hummocks; depressions known as kettle holes and windblown loess deposits.

Glacial valleys

Glaciers can erode much more powerfully than rivers. They form steep-sided, flat-bottomed valleys with a typical U-shaped profile. Valleys created by tributary glaciers, whose floors have not been eroded to the same depth as the main glacial valley floor, are called hanging valleys

▲ *The U-shaped profile and piles of morainic debris are characteristic of a valley once filled by a glacier.*

▲ *A series of hanging valleys high up in the Chilean Andes.*

▲ *The profile of the Matterhorn has been formed by three cirques lying "back-to-back."*

Cirques

Cirques are basin-shaped hollows which mark the head of a glaciated valley. Where neighboring cirques meet, they are divided by sharp rock ridges called arêtes. It is these arêtes which give the Matterhorn its characteristic profile.

Fjords

Fjords are ancient glacial valleys flooded by the sea following the end of a period of glaciation. Beneath the water, the valley floor can be 4000 ft (1300 m) deep.

▲ *A fjord fills a former glacial valley in southern New Zealand.*

Periglaciation

Periglacial areas occur near to the edge of ice sheets. A layer of frozen ground lying just beneath the surface of the land is known as permafrost. When the surface melts in the summer, the water is unable to drain into the frozen ground, and so "creeps" downhill, a process known as solifluction.

Past and present world ice-cover and glacial features

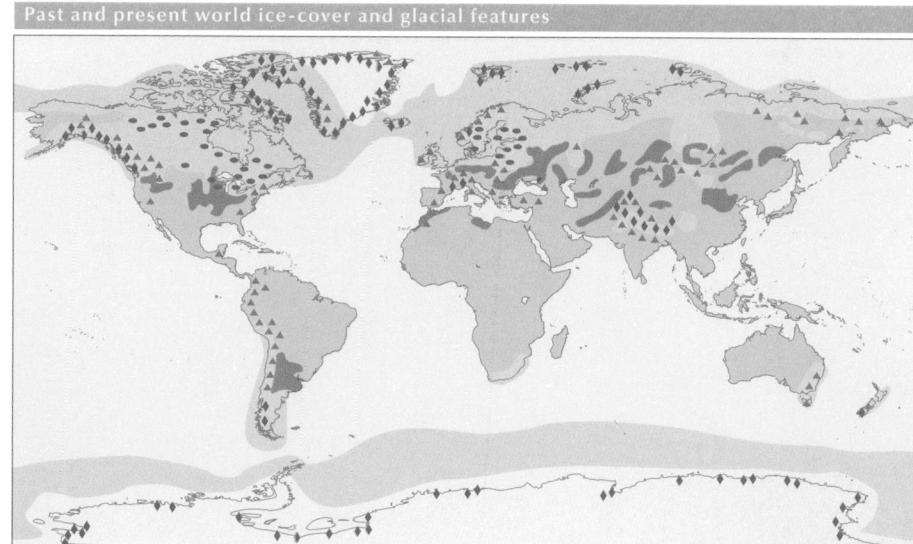

Past and present world ice cover and glacial features

- extent of last Ice Age
- loess deposits
- post-glacial feature
- glacial feature
- present day ice cover
- glacial field

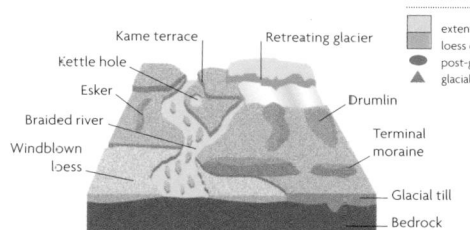

Kame terrace — Retreating glacier — Kettle hole — Esker — Braided river — Windblown loess — Drumlin — Terminal moraine — Glacial till — Bedrock

Post-glacial landscape features

Ice shattering

Water drips into fissures in rocks and freezes, expanding as it does so. The pressure weakens the rock, causing it to crack, and eventually to shatter into polygonal patterns.

▲ *Irregular polygons show through the sedge-grass tundra in the Yukon, Canada.*

Wind

Strong winds can transport rock fragments great distances, especially where there is little vegetation to protect the rock. In desert areas, wind picks up loose, unprotected sand particles, carrying them over great distances. This powerfully abrasive debris is blasted at the surface by the wind, eroding the landscape into dramatic shapes.

Prevailing winds and dust trajectories

Prevailing winds

- northeast trade
- southeast trade
- westerly
- westerly
- polar easterly
- polar easterly

Dust trajectories

- trajectory of aeolian dust

Hot and cold deserts

Main desert types

- hot arid
- semi-arid
- cold polar

Temperature

Most of the world's deserts are in the tropics. The cold deserts which occur elsewhere are arid because they are a long way from the rain-giving sea. Rock in deserts is exposed because of lack of vegetation and is susceptible to changes in temperature; extremes of heat and cold can cause both cracks and fissures to appear in the rock.

Deposition

The rocky, stony floors of the world's deserts are swept and scoured by strong winds. The smaller, finer particles of sand are shaped into surface ripples, dunes, or sand mountains, which rise to a height of 650 ft (200 m). Dunes usually form single lines, running perpendicular to the direction of the prevailing wind. These long, straight ridges can extend for over 100 miles (160 km).

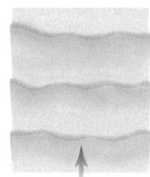

▲ *Barchan dunes in the Arabian Desert.*

▲ *Complex dune system in the Sahara.*

Heat

Fierce sun can heat the surface of rock, causing it to expand more rapidly than the cooler, underlying layers. This creates tensions which force the rock to crack or break up. In arid regions, the evaporation of water from rock surfaces dissolves certain minerals within the water, causing salt crystals to form in small openings in the rock. The hard crystals force the openings to widen into cracks and fissures.

Desert abrasion

Abrasion creates a wide range of desert landforms from faceted pebbles and wind ripples in the sand, to large-scale features such as yardangs (low, streamlined ridges), and scoured desert pavements.

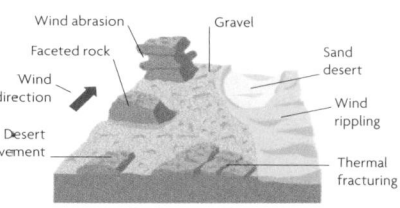

Wind abrasion — Gravel — Faceted rock — Wind direction — Sand desert — Wind rippling — Desert pavement — Thermal fracturing

Features of a desert surface

▲ *The cracked and parched floor of Death Valley, California. This is one of the hottest deserts on Earth.*

◄ *This dry valley at Ellesmere Island in the Canadian Arctic is an example of a cold desert. The cracked floor and scoured slopes are features also found in hot deserts.*

Dunes

Dunes are shaped by wind direction and sand supply. Where sand supply is limited, crescent-shaped barchan dunes are formed.

Wind direction

Types of dune

Transverse dune

Barchan dune

Linear dune

Star dune

The world's oceans

Two-thirds of the Earth's surface is covered by the oceans. The landscape of the ocean floor, like the surface of the land, has been shaped by movements of the Earth's crust over millions of years to form volcanic mountain ranges, deep trenches, basins, and plateaus. Ocean currents constantly redistribute warm and cold water around the world. A major warm current, such as El Niño in the Pacific Ocean, can increase surface temperature by up to 10°F (8°C), causing changes in weather patterns which can lead to both droughts and flooding.

The great oceans

There are five oceans on Earth: the Pacific, Atlantic, Indian, and Southern oceans, and the much smaller Arctic Ocean. These five ocean basins are relatively young, having evolved within the last 80 million years. One of the most recent plate collisions, between the Eurasian and African plates, created the present-day arrangement of continents and oceans.

▲ *The Indian Ocean* accounts for approximately 20% of the total area of the world's oceans.

Sea level

If the influence of tides, winds, currents, and variations in gravity were ignored, the surface of the Earth's oceans would closely follow the topography of the ocean floor, with an underwater ridge 3000 ft (915 m) high producing a rise of up to 3 ft (1 m) in the level of the surface water.

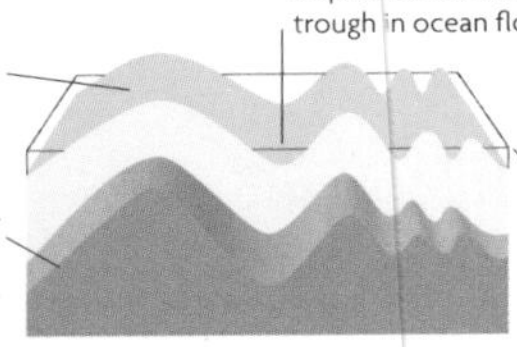

How surface waters reflect the relief of the ocean floor

- Elevated sea level over ridge in ocean floor
- Actual relief of ocean floor
- Depressed sea level over trough in ocean floor
- Base level of the sea surface at 0 ft (0 m)

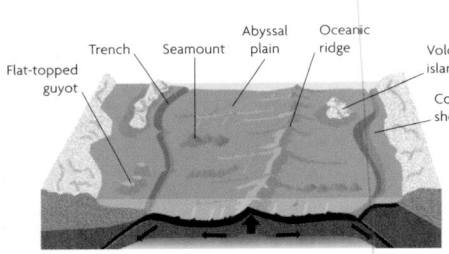

▲ *The low relief* of many small Pacific islands such as these atolls at Huahine in French Polynesia makes them vulnerable to changes in sea level.

Ocean structure

The continental shelf is a shallow, flat seabed surrounding the Earth's continents. It extends to the continental slope, which falls to the ocean floor. Here, the flat abyssal plains are interrupted by vast, underwater mountain ranges, the mid-ocean ridges, and ocean trenches which plunge to depths of 35,828 ft (10,920 m).

Flat-topped guyot · Trench · Seamount · Abyssal plain · Oceanic ridge · Volcanic island · Continental shelf

Typical sea-floor features

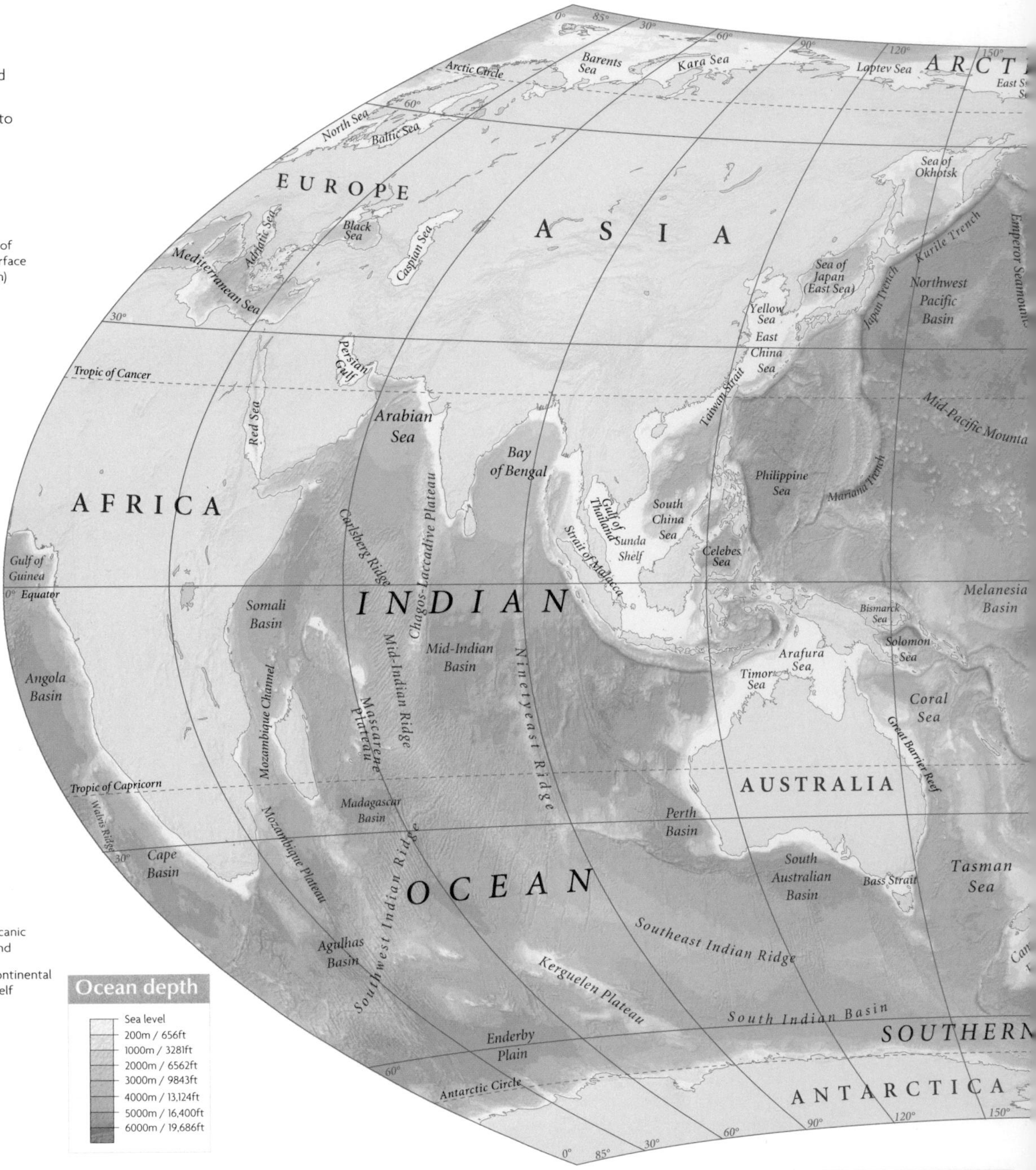

Ocean depth

	Sea level
	200m / 656ft
	1000m / 3281ft
	2000m / 6562ft
	3000m / 9843ft
	4000m / 13,124ft
	5000m / 16,400ft
	6000m / 19,686ft

Black smokers

These vents in the ocean floor disgorge hot, sulfur-rich water from deep in the Earth's crust. Despite the great depths, a variety of lifeforms have adapted to the chemical-rich environment which surrounds black smokers.

▲ *A black smoker* in the Atlantic Ocean.

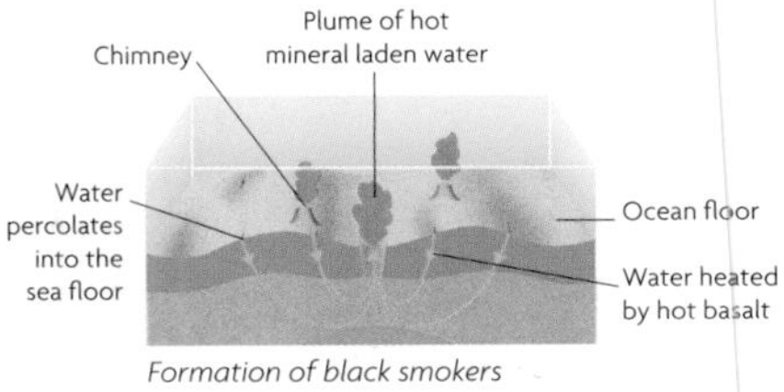

Plume of hot mineral laden water · Chimney · Water percolates into the sea floor · Ocean floor · Water heated by hot basalt

Formation of black smokers

▲ *Surtsey, near Iceland,* is a volcanic island lying directly over the Mid-Atlantic Ridge. It was formed in the 1960s following intense volcanic activity nearby.

Ocean floors

Mid-ocean ridges are formed by lava which erupts beneath the sea and cools to form solid rock. This process mirrors the creation of volcanoes from cooled lava on the land. The ages of sea floor rocks increase in parallel bands outward from central ocean ridges.

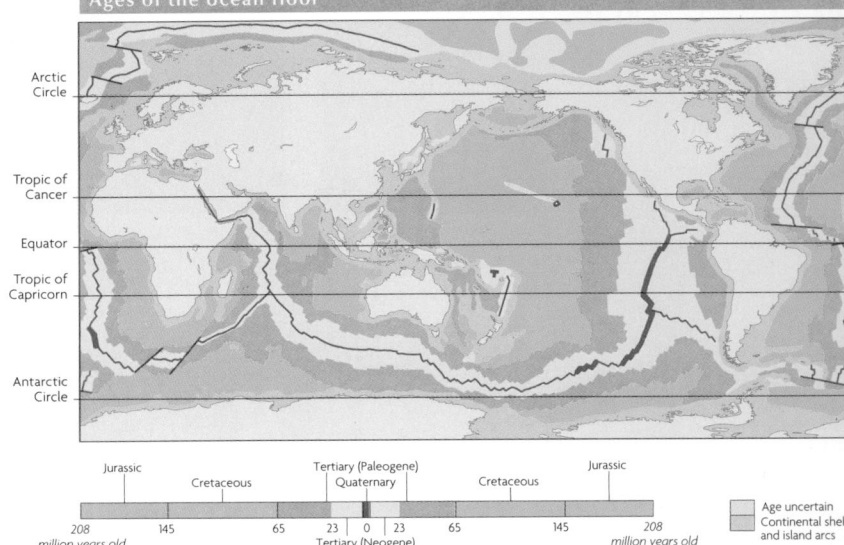

Ages of the ocean floor

Arctic Circle · Tropic of Cancer · Equator · Tropic of Capricorn · Antarctic Circle

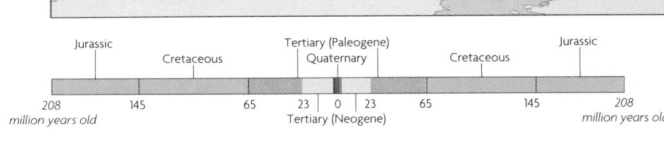

Jurassic · Cretaceous · Tertiary (Paleogene) · Quaternary · Cretaceous · Jurassic

208 *million years old* · 145 · 65 · 23 · 0 · 23 · 65 · 145 · 208 *million years old*
Tertiary (Neogene)

Age uncertain · Continental shelf and island arcs

Map labels: Arctic Circle · Barents Sea · Kara Sea · Laptev Sea · ARCTIC · East S... · North Sea · Baltic Sea · EUROPE · Black Sea · Caspian Sea · ASIA · Sea of Okhotsk · Mediterranean Sea · Adriatic Sea · Aegean Sea · Sea of Japan (East Sea) · Kurile Trench · Emperor Seamount · Japan Trench · Northwest Pacific Basin · Yellow Sea · East China Sea · Taiwan Strait · Tropic of Cancer · Persian Gulf · Red Sea · Arabian Sea · Gulf of Guinea · Equator · AFRICA · Carlsberg Ridge · Chagos-Laccadive Plateau · Bay of Bengal · Gulf of Thailand · Sunda Shelf · Strait of Malacca · South China Sea · Philippine Sea · Mariana Trench · Mid-Pacific Mounta... · Celebes Sea · Somali Basin · INDIAN · Mid-Indian Basin · Mid-Indian Ridge · Ninetyeast Ridge · Bismarck Sea · Melanesia Basin · Solomon Sea · Arafura Sea · Timor Sea · Coral Sea · Great Barrier Reef · Angola Basin · Mozambique Channel · Mascarene Plateau · AUSTRALIA · Tropic of Capricorn · Walvis Ridge · Madagascar Basin · Perth Basin · Tasman Sea · Mozambique Plateau · Cape Basin · OCEAN · South Australian Basin · Bass Strait · Agulhas Basin · Southwest Indian Ridge · Southeast Indian Ridge · Kerguelen Plateau · South Indian Basin · SOUTHERN · Enderby Plain · Antarctic Circle · ANTARCTICA

▲ **Currents in the** Southern Ocean are driven by some of the world's fiercest winds, including the Roaring Forties, Furious Fifties, and Shrieking Sixties.

▲ **The Pacific Ocean is** the world's largest and deepest ocean, covering over one-third of the surface of the Earth.

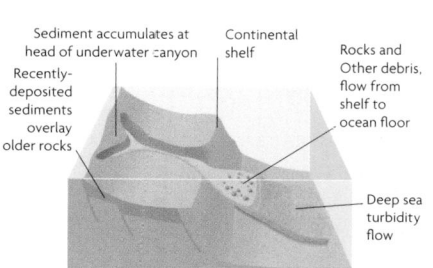

▲ **The Atlantic Ocean** was formed when the landmasses of the eastern and western hemispheres began to drift apart 180 million years ago.

Deposition of sediment

Storms, earthquakes, and volcanic activity trigger underwater currents known as turbidity currents which scour sand and gravel from the continental shelf, creating underwater canyons. These strong currents pick up material deposited at river mouths and deltas, and carry it across the continental shelf and through the underwater canyons, where it is eventually laid down on the ocean floor in the form of fans.

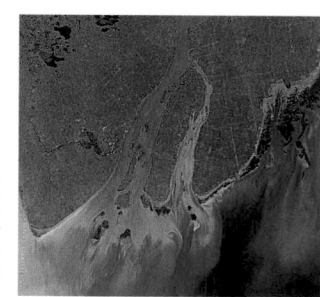

How sediment is deposited on the ocean floor

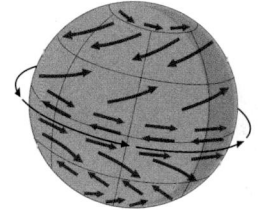

▶ **Satellite image of** the Yangtze (Chang Jiang) Delta, in which the land appears red. The river deposits immense quantities of silt into the East China Sea, much of which will eventually reach the deep ocean floor.

Surface water

Ocean currents move warm water away from the Equator toward the poles, while cold water is, in turn, moved towards the Equator. This is the main way in which the Earth distributes surface heat and is a major climatic control. Approximately 4000 million years ago, the Earth was dominated by oceans and there was no land to interrupt the flow of the currents, which would have flowed as straight lines, simply influenced by the Earth's rotation.

Idealized globe showing the movement of water around a landless Earth.

Ocean currents

Surface currents are driven by the prevailing winds and by the spinning motion of the Earth, which drives the currents into circulating whirlpools,or gyres. Deep sea currents, over 330 ft (100 m) below the surface, are driven by differences in water temperature and salinity, which have an impact on the density of deep water and on its movement.

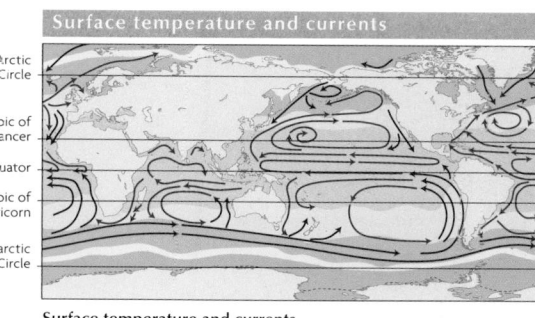

Surface temperature and currents

- ..... Ice-shelf (below 0°C / 32°F)
- Sea-ice* (average) below -2°C / 28°F
- Sea-water -2–0°C / 28–32°F
- * Sea-water freezes at -1.9°C / 28.4°F
- 0–10°C / 32–50°F
- 10–20°C / 50–68°F
- 20–30°C / 68–86°F
- → warm current
- → cold current

Tides and waves

Tides are created by the pull of the Sun and Moon's gravity on the surface of the oceans. The levels of high and low tides are influenced by the position of the Moon in relation to the Earth and Sun. Waves are formed by wind blowing over the surface of the water.

High and low tides

The highest tides occur when the Earth, the Moon and the Sun are aligned (below left). The lowest tides are experienced when the Sun and Moon align at right angles to one another (below right).

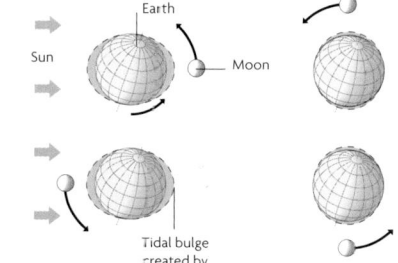

Tidal range and wave environments

- less than 2m / 7ft
- 2–4m / 7–13ft
- greater than 4m / 13ft
- east coast swell
- west coast swell
- tropical cyclone
- storm wave
- ice-shelf

Highest high tides

Earth

Sun

Moon

Lowest high tides

Tidal bulge created by gravitational pull

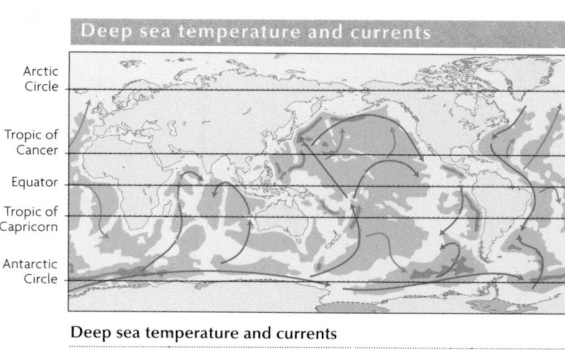

Deep sea temperature and currents

- Ice-shelf (below 0°C / 32°F)
- Sea-water -2–0°C / 28–32°F (below 5000m / 16,400ft)
- Sea-water 0–5°C / 32–41°F (below 4000m / 13,12Oft)
- → Primary currents
- → Secondary currents

The global climate

The Earth's climatic types consist of stable patterns of weather conditions averaged out over a long period of time. Different climates are categorized according to particular combinations of temperature and humidity. By contrast, weather consists of short-term fluctuations in wind, temperature, and humidity conditions. Different climates are determined by latitude, altitude, the prevailing wind, and circulation of ocean currents. Longer-term changes in climate, such as global warming or the onset of ice ages, are punctuated by shorter-term events which comprise the day-to-day weather of a region, such as frontal depressions, hurricanes, and blizzards.

The atmosphere, wind and weather

The Earth's atmosphere has been compared to a giant ocean of air which surrounds the planet. Its circulation patterns are similar to the currents in the oceans and are influenced by three factors; the Earth's orbit around the Sun and rotation about its axis, and variations in the amount of heat radiation received from the Sun. If both heat and moisture were not redistributed between the Equator and the poles, large areas of the Earth would be uninhabitable.

◀ *Heavy fogs, as* here in southern England, form as moisture-laden air passes over cold ground.

Temperature

The world can be divided into three major climatic zones, stretching like large belts across the latitudes: the tropics which are warm; the cold polar regions and the temperate zones which lie between them. Temperatures across the Earth range from above 86°F (30°C) in the deserts to as low as -70°F (-55°C) at the poles. Temperature is also controlled by altitude; because air becomes cooler and less dense the higher it gets, mountainous regions are typically colder than those areas which are at, or close to, sea level.

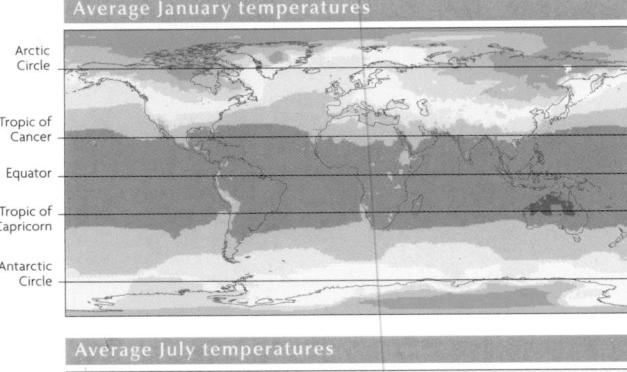

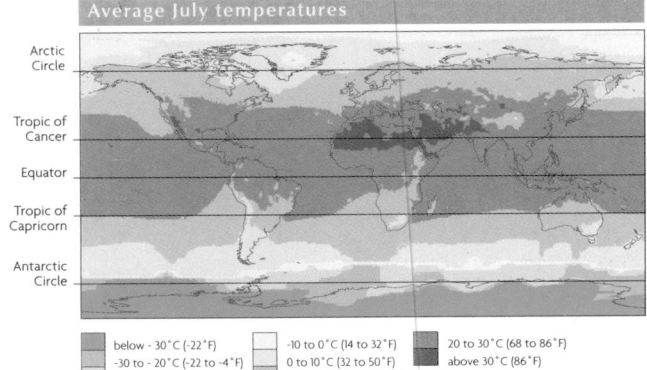

below - 30°C (-22°F)	-10 to 0°C (14 to 32°F)	20 to 30°C (68 to 86°F)
-30 to 20°C (-22 to -4°F)	0 to 10°C (32 to 50°F)	above 30°C (86°F)
-20 to -10°C (-4 to 14°F)	10 to 20°C (50 to 68°F)	

Global air circulation

Air does not simply flow from the Equator to the poles, it circulates in giant cells known as Hadley and Ferrel cells. As air warms it expands, becoming less dense and rising; this creates areas of low pressure. As the air rises it cools and condenses, causing heavy rainfall over the tropics and slight snowfall over the poles. This cool air then sinks, forming high pressure belts. At surface level in the tropics these sinking currents are deflected poleward as the westerlies and toward the equator as the trade winds. At the poles they become the polar easterlies.

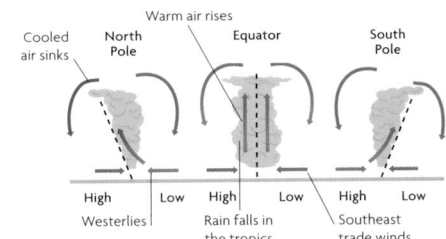

▲ *The Antarctic pack* ice expands its area by almost seven times during the winter as temperatures drop and surrounding seas freeze.

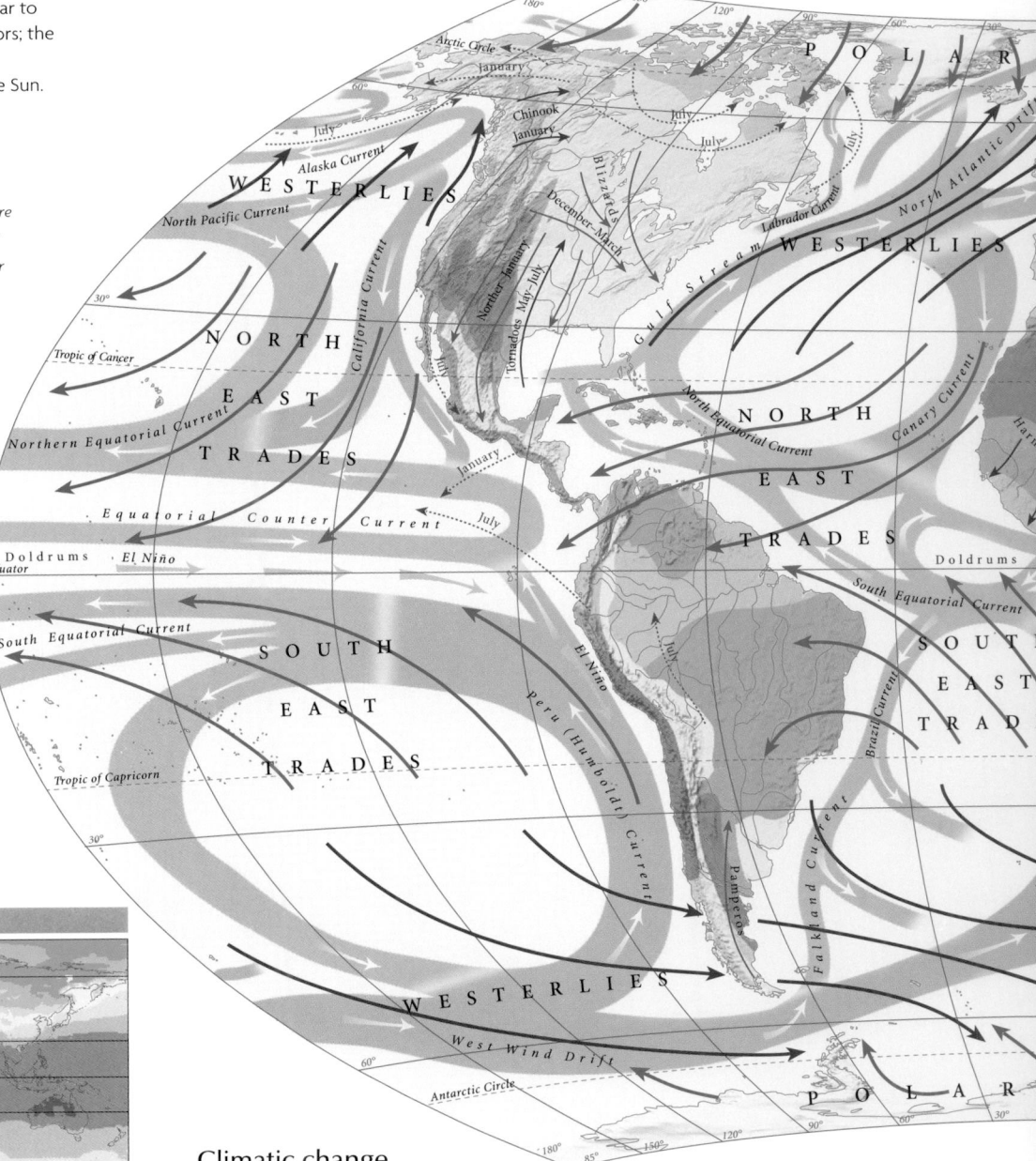

Climatic change

The Earth is currently in a warm phase between ice ages. Warmer temperatures result in higher sea levels as more of the polar ice caps melt. Most of the world's population lives near coasts, so any changes which might cause sea levels to rise, could have a potentially disastrous impact.

▲ *This ice fair, painted by Pieter Brueghel the Younger in the 17th century, shows the Little Ice Age which peaked around 300 years ago.*

The greenhouse effect

Gases such as carbon dioxide are known as "greenhouse gases" because they allow shortwave solar radiation to enter the Earth's atmosphere, but help to stop longwave radiation from escaping. This traps heat, raising the Earth's temperature. An excess of these gases, such as that which results from the burning of fossil fuels, helps trap more heat and can lead to global warming.

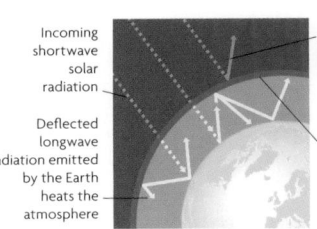

◄ *The islands of the Caribbean, Mexico's Gulf coast and the southeastern US are often hit by hurricanes formed far out in the Atlantic.*

Oceanic water circulation

In general, ocean currents parallel the movement of winds across the Earth's surface. Incoming solar energy is greatest at the Equator and least at the poles. So, water in the oceans heats up most at the Equator and flows poleward, cooling as it moves north or south toward the Arctic or Antarctic. The flow is eventually reversed and cold water currents move back toward the Equator. These ocean currents act as a vast system for moving heat from the Equator toward the poles and are a major influence on the distribution of the Earth's climates.

▲ *In marginal climatic zones years of drought can completely dry out the land and transform grassland to desert.*

Map key

Climate zones
- ice cap
- subarctic
- tundra
- continental
- temperate
- warm temperate
- mediterranean
- semi-arid
- arid
- hot humid
- humid equatorial
- tropical

Ocean currents
→ warm
→ cold

Prevailing winds
→ warm
→ cold

Local winds
→ warm
→ cold
June → seasonal*
*(seasonal winds which can either be warm or cold)

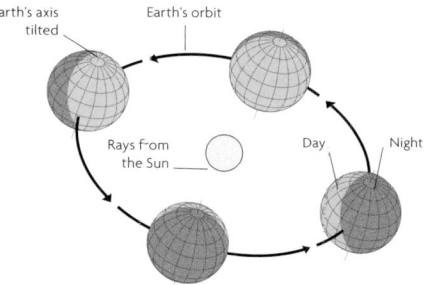

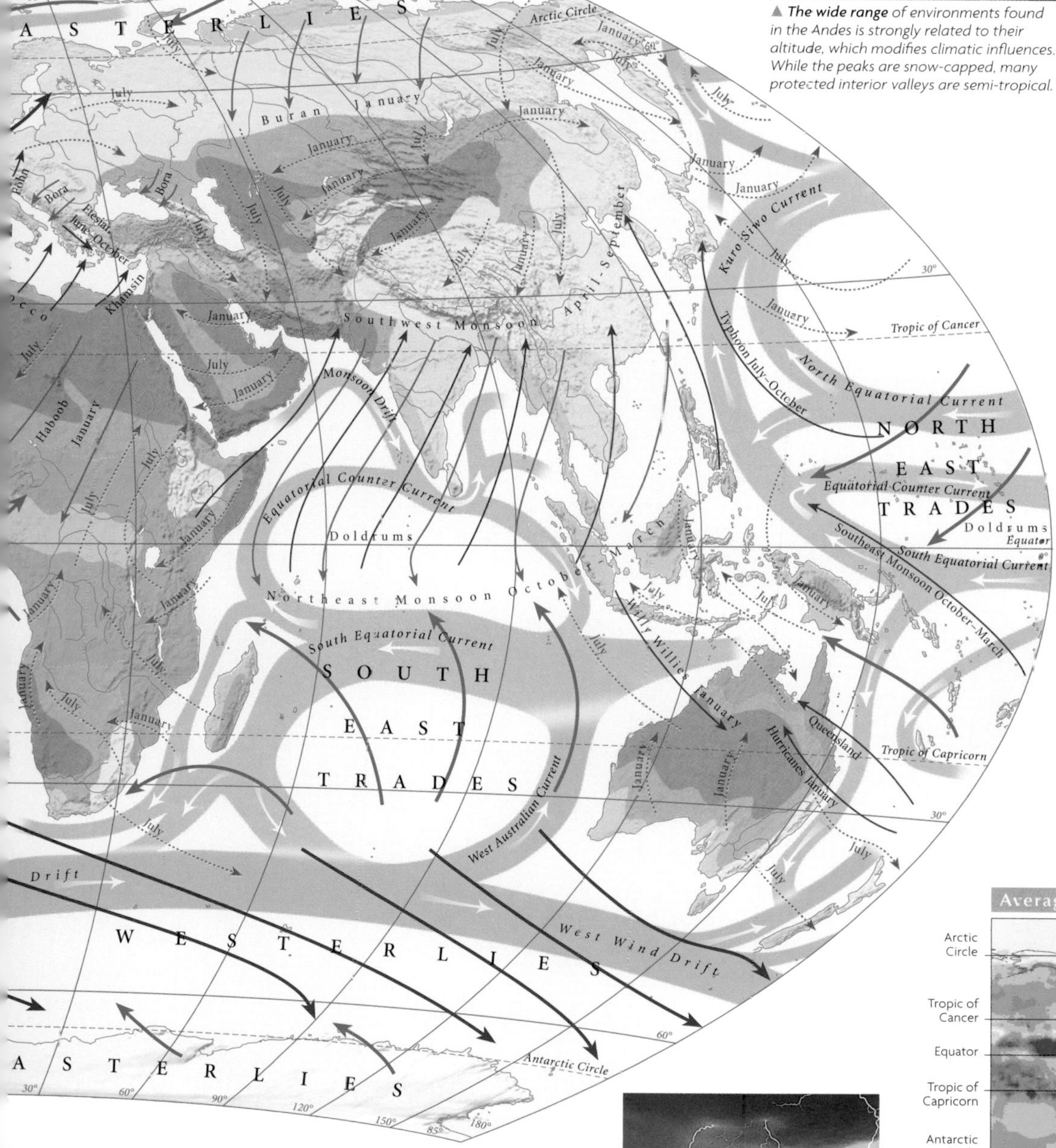

▲ *The wide range of environments found in the Andes is strongly related to their altitude, which modifies climatic influences. While the peaks are snow-capped, many protected interior valleys are semi-tropical.*

Tilt and rotation

The tilt and rotation of the Earth during its annual orbit largely control the distribution of heat and moisture across its surface, which correspondingly controls its large-scale weather patterns. As the Earth annually rotates around the Sun, half its surface is receiving maximum radiation, creating summer and winter seasons. The angle of the Earth means that on average the tropics receive two and a half times as much heat from the Sun each day as the poles.

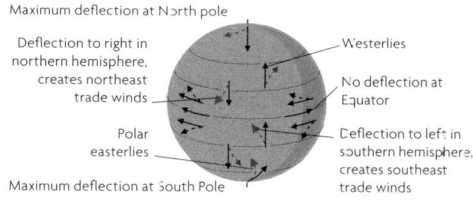

Earth's axis tilted — Earth's orbit
Rays from the Sun — Day — Night

The Coriolis effect

The rotation of the Earth influences atmospheric circulation by deflecting winds and ocean currents. Winds blowing in the northern hemisphere are deflected to the right and those in the southern hemisphere are deflected to the left, creating large-scale patterns of wind circulation, such as the northeast and southeast trade winds and the westerlies. This effect is greatest at the poles and least at the Equator.

Maximum deflection at North pole
Deflection to right in northern hemisphere, creates northeast trade winds
Westerlies
No deflection at Equator
Polar easterlies
Deflection to left in southern hemisphere, creates southeast trade winds
Maximum deflection at South Pole

Precipitation

When warm air expands, it rises and cools, and the water vapor it carries condenses to form clouds. Heavy, regular rainfall is characteristic of the equatorial region, while the poles are cold and receive only slight snowfall. Tropical regions have marked dry and rainy seasons, while in the temperate regions rainfall is relatively unpredictable.

▲ *Monsoon rains, which affect southern Asia from May to September, are caused by sea winds blowing across the warm land.*

▲ *Heavy tropical rainstorms occur frequently in Papua New Guinea, often causing soil erosion and landslides in cultivated areas.*

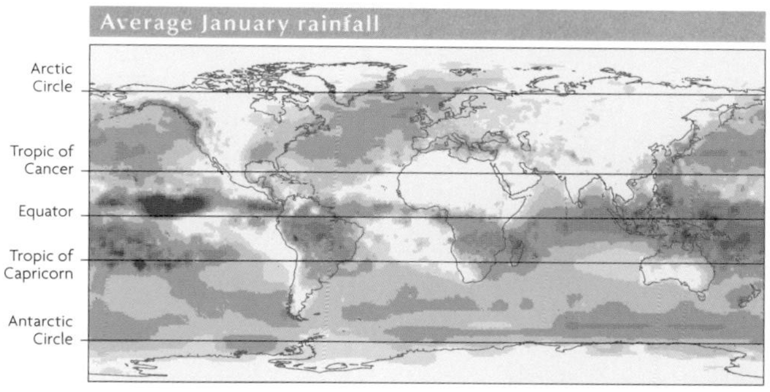

Average January rainfall
Arctic Circle
Tropic of Cancer
Equator
Tropic of Capricorn
Antarctic Circle

Average July rainfall
Arctic Circle
Tropic of Cancer
Equator
Tropic of Capricorn
Antarctic Circle

☐ 0–25 mm (0–1 in)
☐ 25–50 mm (1–2 in)
☐ 50–100 mm (2–4 in)
☐ 100–200 mm (4–8 in)
☐ 200–300 mm (8–12 in)
☐ 300–400 mm (12–16 in)
☐ 400–500 mm (16–20 in)
☐ above 500 mm (20 in)

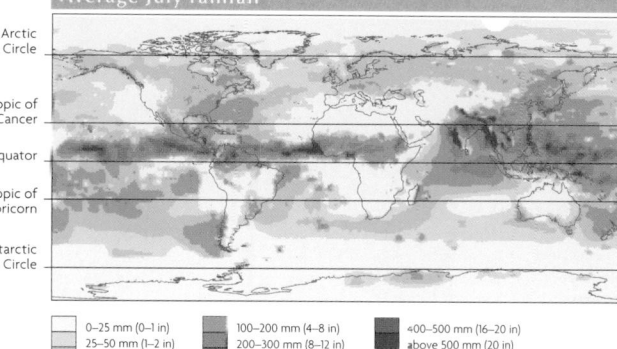

▲ *Violent thunderstorms occur along advancing cold fronts, when cold, dry air masses meet warm, moist air, which rises rapidly, its moisture condensing into thunderclouds. Rain and hail become electrically charged, causing lightning.*

◄ *The intensity of some blizzards in Canada and the northern US can give rise to snowdrifts as high as 10 ft (3 m).*

◄ *The Atacama Desert in Chile is one of the driest places on Earth, with an average rainfall of less than 2 inches (50 mm) per year.*

The rainshadow effect

When moist air is forced to rise by mountains, it cools and the water vapor falls as precipitation, either as rain or snow. Only the dry, cold air continues over the mountains, leaving inland areas with little or no rain. This is called the rainshadow effect and is one reason for the existence of the Mojave Desert in California, which lies east of the Coast Ranges.

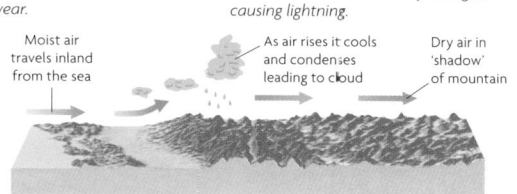

Moist air travels inland from the sea
As air rises it cools and condenses leading to cloud
Dry air in 'shadow' of mountain

The rainshadow effect

(Map labels: ASTERLIES, Buran, January, July, Arctic Circle, Bora, Bise, Bora, June–October, Mistral, Khamsin, Southwest Monsoon, April–September, Monsoon Drift, Sirocco, Haboob, Equatorial Counter Current, Doldrums, Kuro-Siwo Current, North Equatorial Current, NORTH EAST TRADES, Tropic of Cancer, Typhoon July–October, Equatorial Counter Current, Doldrums, Equator, South Equatorial Current, Southeast Monsoon October–March, Northeast Monsoon October, SOUTH EAST TRADES, South Equatorial Current, Willy Willies January, Queensland, Hurricanes January, West Australian Current, Tropic of Capricorn, West Wind Drift, WESTERLIES, Drift, ASTERLIES, Antarctic Circle)

Life on Earth

A unique combination of an oxygen-rich atmosphere and plentiful water is the key to life on Earth. Apart from the polar ice caps, there are few areas which have not been colonized by animals or plants over the course of the Earth's history. Plants process sunlight to provide them with their energy, and ultimately all the Earth's animals rely on plants for survival. Because of this reliance, plants are known as primary producers, and the availability of nutrients and temperature of an area is defined as its primary productivity, which affects the quantity and type of animals which are able to live there. This index is affected by climatic factors – cold and aridity restrict the quantity of life, whereas warmth and regular rainfall allow a greater diversity of species.

Biogeographical regions

The Earth can be divided into a series of biogeographical regions, or biomes, ecological communities where certain species of plant and animal coexist within particular climatic conditions. Within these broad classifications, other factors including soil richness, altitude, and human activities such as urbanization, intensive agriculture, and deforestation, affect the local distribution of living species within each biome.

Polar regions
☐ A layer of permanent ice at the Earth's poles covers both seas and land. Very little plant and animal life can exist in these harsh regions.

Tundra
☐ A desolate region, with long, dark freezing winters and short, cold summers. With virtually no soil and large areas of permanently frozen ground known as permafrost, the tundra is largely treeless, though it is briefly clothed by small flowering plants in the summer months.

Needleleaf forests
☐ With milder summers than the tundra and less wind, these areas are able to support large forests of coniferous trees.

Broadleaf forests
☐ Much of the northern hemisphere was once covered by deciduous forests, which occurred in areas with marked seasonal variations. Most deciduous forests have been cleared for human settlement.

Temperate rain forests
☐ In warmer wetter areas, such as southern China, temperate deciduous forests are replaced by evergreen forest.

Deserts
☑ Deserts are areas with negligible rainfall. Most hot deserts lie within the tropics; cold deserts are dry because of their distance from the moisture-providing sea.

Mediterranean
☐ Hot, dry summers and short winters typify these areas, which were once covered by evergreen shrubs and woodland, but have now been cleared by humans for agriculture.

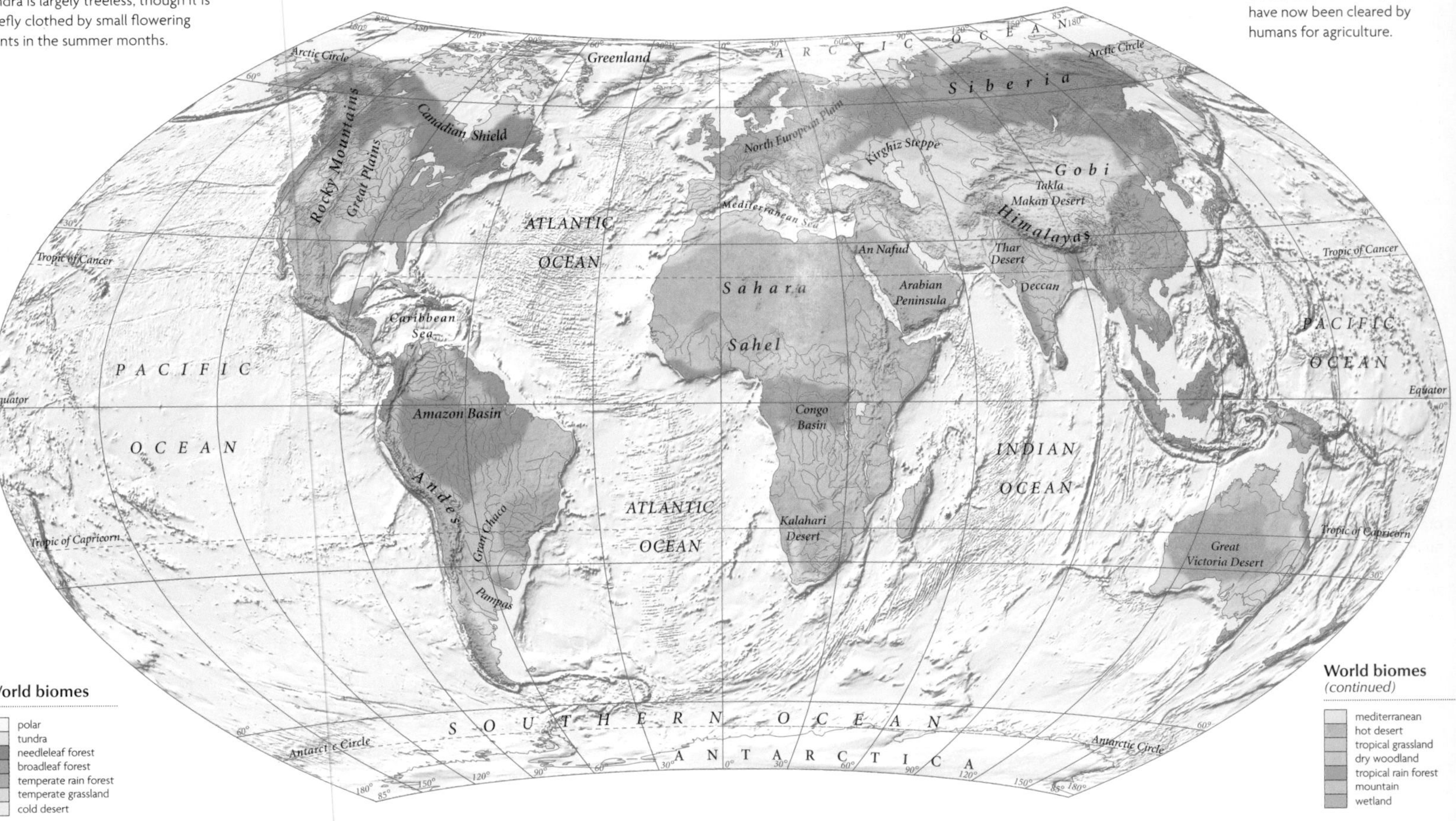

World biomes
☐ polar
☐ tundra
☐ needleleaf forest
☐ broadleaf forest
☐ temperate rain forest
☐ temperate grassland
☐ cold desert

World biomes (continued)
☐ mediterranean
☐ hot desert
☐ tropical grassland
☐ dry woodland
☐ tropical rain forest
☐ mountain
☐ wetland

[World map with labels: Arctic Circle, Greenland, ARCTIC OCEAN, Siberia, Rocky Mountains, Canadian Shield, Great Plains, North European Plain, Kirghiz Steppe, Gobi, Takla Makan Desert, Himalayas, ATLANTIC OCEAN, Mediterranean Sea, An Nafud, Thar Desert, Tropic of Cancer, Sahara, Arabian Peninsula, Deccan, PACIFIC OCEAN, Caribbean Sea, Sahel, Amazon Basin, Congo Basin, INDIAN OCEAN, Equator, OCEAN, Andes, Gran Chaco, ATLANTIC OCEAN, Kalahari Desert, Great Victoria Desert, Tropic of Capricorn, Pampas, SOUTHERN OCEAN, Antarctic Circle, ANTARCTICA]

Tropical and temperate grasslands
☑ The major grassland areas are found in the centers of the larger continental landmasses. In Africa's tropical savannah regions, seasonal rainfall alternates with drought. Temperate grasslands, also known as steppes and prairies are found in the northern hemisphere, and in South America, where they are known as the pampas.

Dry woodlands
☐ Trees and shrubs, adapted to dry conditions, grow widely spaced from one another, interspersed by savannah grasslands.

Tropical rain forests
☐ Characterized by year-round warmth and high rainfall, tropical rain forests contain the highest diversity of plant and animal species on Earth.

Mountains
☐ Though the lower slopes of mountains may be thickly forested, only ground-hugging shrubs and other vegetation will grow above the tree line which varies according to both altitude and latitude.

Wetlands
☐ Rarely lying above sea level, wetlands are marshes, swamps, and tidal flats. Some, with their moist, fertile soils, are rich feeding grounds for fish and breeding grounds for birds. Others have little soil structure and are too acidic to support much plant and animal life.

Biodiversity

The number of plant and animal species, and the range of genetic diversity within the populations of each species, make up the Earth's biodiversity. The plants and animals which are endemic to a region – that is, those which are found nowhere else in the world – are also important in determining levels of biodiversity. Human settlement and intervention have encroached on many areas of the world once rich in endemic plant and animal species. Increasing international efforts are being made to monitor and conserve the biodiversity of the Earth's remaining wild places.

Animal adaptation

The degree of an animal's adaptability to different climates and conditions is extremely important in ensuring its success as a species. Many animals, particularly the largest mammals, are becoming restricted to ever-smaller regions as human development and modern agricultural practices reduce their natural habitats. In contrast, humans have been responsible – both deliberately and accidentally – for the spread of some of the world's most successful species. Many of these introduced species are now more numerous than the indigenous animal populations.

Polar animals

The frozen wastes of the polar regions are able to support only a small range of species which derive their nutritional requirements from the sea. Animals such as the walrus *(left)* have developed insulating fat, stocky limbs, and double-layered coats to enable them to survive in the freezing conditions.

Desert animals

Many animals which live in the extreme heat and aridity of the deserts are able to survive for days and even months with very little food or water. Their bodies are adapted to lose heat quickly and to store fat and water. The Gila monster *(above)* stores fat in its tail.

Amazon rain forest

The vast Amazon Basin is home to the world's greatest variety of animal species. Animals are adapted to live at many different levels from the treetops to the tangled undergrowth which lies beneath the canopy. The sloth *(below)* hangs upside down in the branches. Its fur grows from its stomach to its back to enable water to run off quickly.

Diversity of animal species

Number of animal species per country
- more than 2000
- 1000–1999
- 700–999
- 400–699
- 200–399
- 100–199
- 0–99
- data not available

Marine biodiversity

The oceans support a huge variety of different species, from the world's largest mammals like whales and dolphins down to the tiniest plankton. The greatest diversities occur in the warmer seas of continental shelves, where plants are easily able to photosynthesize, and around coral reefs, where complex ecosystems are found. On the ocean floor, nematodes can exist at a depth of more than 10,000 ft (3000 m) below sea level.

High altitudes

Few animals exist in the rarefied atmosphere of the highest mountains. However, birds of prey such as eagles and vultures *(above)*, with their superb eyesight can soar as high as 23,000 ft (7000 m) to scan for prey below.

Urban animals

The growth of cities has reduced the amount of habitat available to many species. A number of animals are now moving closer into urban areas to scavenge from the detritus of the modern city *(left)* Rodents, particularly rats and mice, have existed in cities for thousands of years, and many insects, especially moths, quickly develop new coloring to provide them with camouflage

Endemic species

Isolated areas such as Australia and the island of Madagascar, have the greatest range of endemic species. In Australia, these include marsupials such as the kangaroo *(below)*, which carry their young in pouches on their bodies. Destruction of habitat, pollution, hunting, and predators introduced by humans, are threatening this unique biodiversity.

Plant adaptation

Environmental conditions, particularly climate, soil type, and the extent of competition with other organisms, influence the development of plants into a number of distinctive forms. Similar conditions in quite different parts of the world create similar adaptations in the plants, which may then be modified by other, local, factors specific to the region.

Cold conditions

In areas where temperatures rarely rise above freezing, plants such as lichens *(left)* and mosses grow densely, close to the ground.

Rain forests

Most of the world's largest and oldest plants are found in rain forests; warmth and heavy rainfall provide ideal conditions for vast plants like the world's largest flower, the rafflesia *(left)*.

Hot, dry conditions

Arid conditions lead to the development of plants whose surface area has been reduced to a minimum to reduce water loss. In cacti *(above)*, which can survive without water for months leaves are minimal or not present at all.

Ancient plants

Some of the world's most primitive plants still exist today, including algae, cycads, and many ferns *(above)*, reflecting the success with which they have adapted to changing conditions.

Resisting predators

A great variety of plants have developed devices including spines *(above)*, poisons, stinging hairs, and an unpleasant taste or smell to deter animal predators.

Diversity of plant species

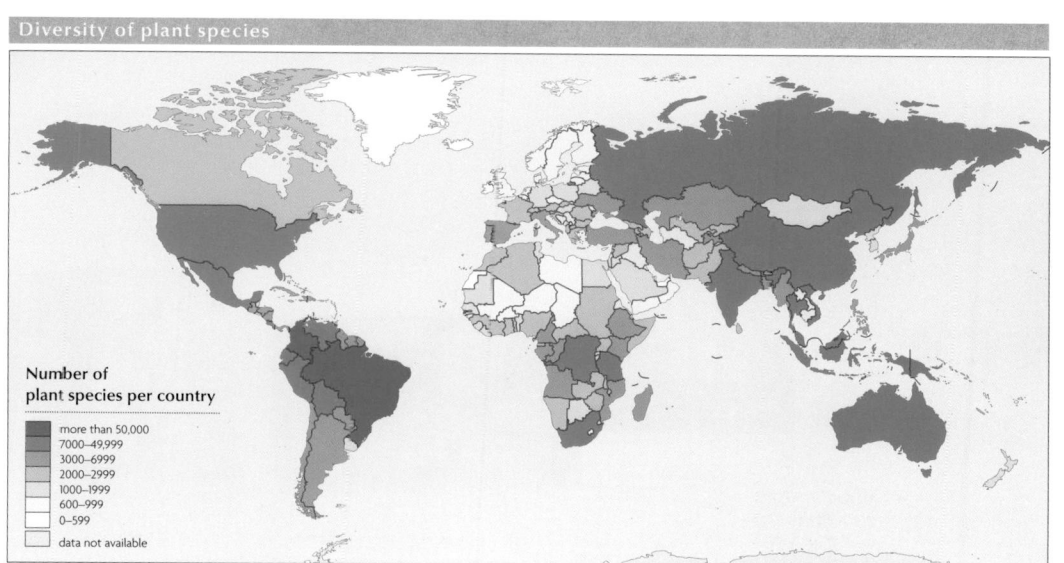

Number of plant species per country
- more than 50,000
- 7000–49,999
- 3000–6999
- 2000–2999
- 1000–1999
- 600–999
- 0–599
- data not available

Weeds

Weeds such as bindweed *(above)* are fast-growing, easily dispersed, and tolerant of a number of different environments, enabling them to quickly colonize suitable habitats. They are among the most adaptable of all plants.

Population and settlement

The Earth's population is projected to rise from its current level of about 6.5 billion to reach some 10 billion by 2025. The global distribution of this rapidly growing population is very uneven, and is dictated by climate, terrain, and natural and economic resources. The great majority of the Earth's people live in coastal zones, and along river valleys. Deserts cover over 20% of the Earth's surface, but support less than 5% of the world's population. It is estimated that over half of the world's population live in cities – most of them in Asia – as a result of mass migration from rural areas in search of jobs. Many of these people live in the so-called "megacities," some with populations as great as 40 million.

Patterns of settlement

The past 200 years have seen the most radical shift in world population patterns in recorded history.

Nomadic life

All the world's peoples were hunter-gatherers 10,000 years ago. Today nomads, who live by following available food resources, account for less than 0.0001% of the world's population. They are mainly pastoral herders, moving their livestock from place to place in search of grazing land.

Nomadic population

Nomadic population area

The growth of cities

In 1900 there were only 14 cities in the world with populations of more than a million, mostly in the northern hemisphere. Today, as more and more people in the developing world migrate to towns and cities, there are over 30 cities whose population exceeds 5 million, and around 440 "million-cities."

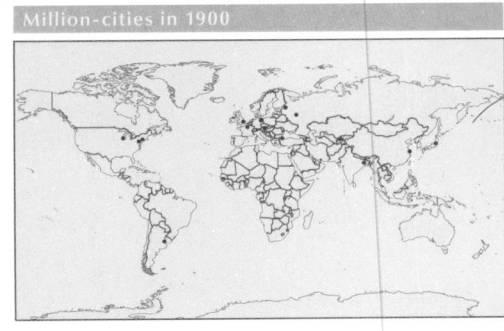

Million-cities in 1900

● Cities over 1 million population

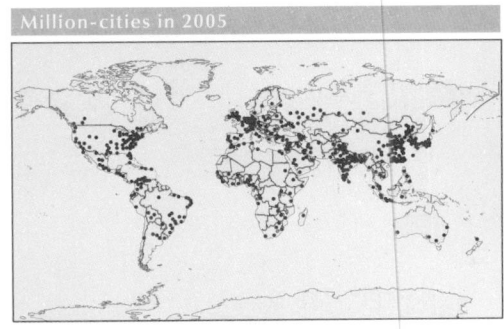

Million-cities in 2005

● Cities over 1 million population

North America

The eastern and western seaboards of the US, with huge expanses of interconnected cities, towns, and suburbs, are vast, densely-populated megalopolises. Central America and the Caribbean also have high population densities. Yet, away from the coasts and in the wildernesses of northern Canada the land is very sparsely settled.

▼ **Vancouver on Canada's** west coast, grew up as a port city. In recent years it has attracted many Asian immigrants, particularly from the Pacific Rim.

▲ **North America's central** plains, the continent's agricultural heartland, are thinly populated and highly productive.

Europe

With its temperate climate, and rich mineral and natural resources, Europe is generally very densely settled. The continent acts as a magnet for economic migrants from the developing world, and immigration is now widely restricted. Birthrates in Europe are generally low, and in some countries, such as Germany, the populations have stabilized at zero growth, with a fast-growing elderly population.

▲ **Many European cities,** like Siena, once reflected the "ideal" size for human settlements. Modern technological advances have enabled them to grow far beyond the original walls.

▲ **Within the densely-populated** Netherlands the reclamation of coastal wetlands is vital to provide much-needed land for agriculture and settlement.

Population density
(inhabitants per sq mile)

- 520–2600
- 260–520
- 130–260
- 52–130
- 26–52
- 13–26
- 3–13
- Fewer than 3

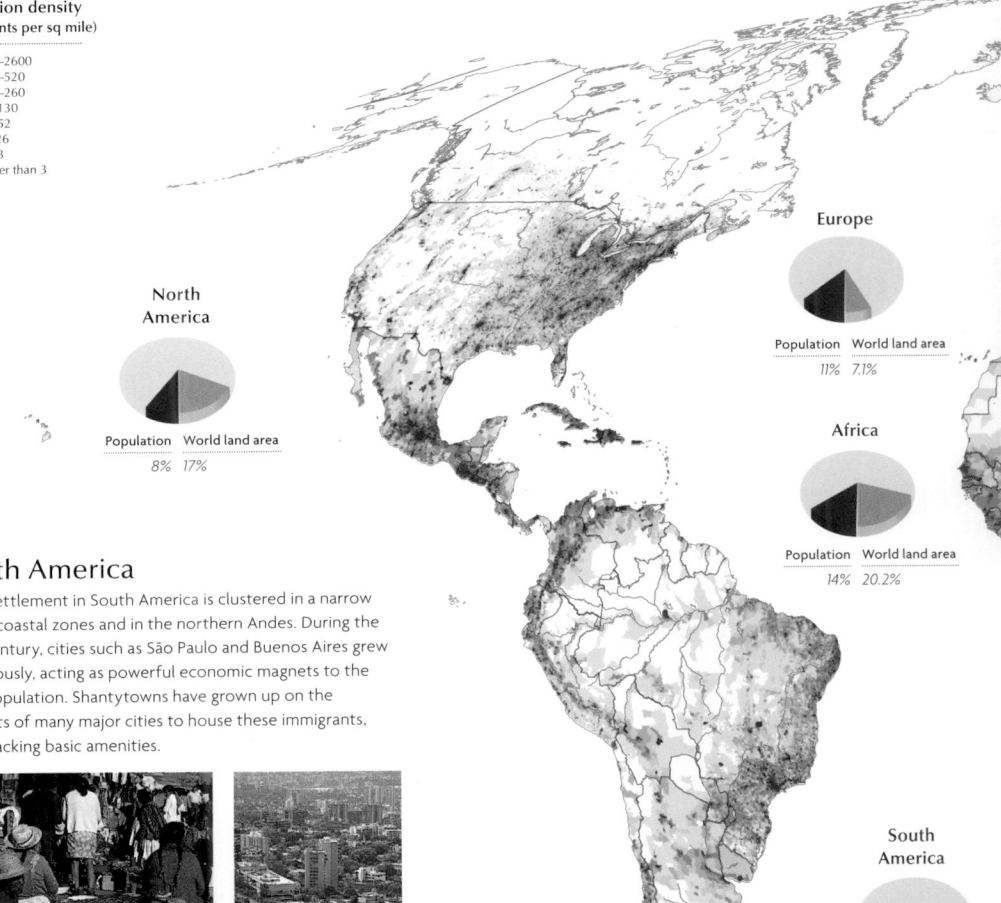

North America

Population 8% World land area 17%

Europe

Population 11% World land area 7.1%

Africa

Population 14% World land area 20.2%

South America

Population 6% World land area 11.8%

South America

Most settlement in South America is clustered in a narrow belt in coastal zones and in the northern Andes. During the 20th century, cities such as São Paulo and Buenos Aires grew enormously, acting as powerful economic magnets to the rural population. Shantytowns have grown up on the outskirts of many major cities to house these immigrants, often lacking basic amenities.

▲ **Many people in** western South America live at high altitudes in the Andes, both in cities and in villages such as this one in Bolivia.

▲ **Venezuela is one** of the most highly urbanized countries in South America, with nearly 90% of the population living in cities such as Caracas.

Africa

The arid climate of much of Africa means that settlement of the continent is sparse, focusing in coastal areas and fertile regions such as the Nile Valley. Africa still has a high proportion of nomadic agriculturalists, although many are now becoming settled, and the population is predominantly rural.

▲ **Cities such as** Nairobi (above), Cairo, and Johannesburg have grown rapidly in recent years, although only Cairo has a significant population on a global scale.

▼ **Traditional lifestyles and** homes persist across much of Africa, which has a higher proportion of rural or village-based population than any other continent.

Asia

Most Asian settlement originally centered around the great river valleys such as the Indus, the Ganges, and the Yangtze. Today, almost 60% of the world's population lives in Asia, many in burgeoning cities – particularly in the economically-buoyant Pacific Rim countries. Even rural population densities are high in many countries; practices such as terracing in Southeast Asia making the most of the available land.

▲ **Many of China's** cities are now vast urban areas with populations of more than 5 million people.

▲ **This stilt village** in Bangladesh is built to resist the regular flooding. Pressure on land, even in rural areas, forces many people to live in marginal areas.

Population structures

Population pyramids are an effective means of showing the age structures of different countries, and highlighting changing trends in population growth and decline. The typical pyramid for a country with a growing, youthful population, is broad-based *(left)*, reflecting a high birthrate and a far larger number of young rather than elderly people. In contrast, countries with populations whose numbers are stabilizing have a more balanced distribution of people in each age band, and may even have lower numbers of people in the youngest age ranges, indicating both a high life expectancy, and that the population is now barely replacing itself *(right)*. The Russian Federation *(center)* is suffering from a declining population, forcing the government to consider a number of measures, including tax incentives and immigration, in an effort to stabilize the population.

Youthful population
(India)

Males / Females
80+, 70–79, 60–69, 50–59, 40–49, 30–39, 20–29, 10–19, 0–9
100 80 60 40 20 0 20 40 60 80 100
Population in millions

Declining population
(Russian Federation)

Males / Females
80+, 70–79, 60–69, 50–59, 40–49, 30–39, 20–29, 10–19, 0–9
12 10 8 6 4 2 0 2 4 6 8 10 12
Population in millions

Ageing population
(United States of America)

Males / Females
80+, 70–79, 60–69, 50–59, 40–49, 30–39, 20–29, 10–19, 0–9
20 16 12 8 4 0 4 8 12 16 20
Population in millions

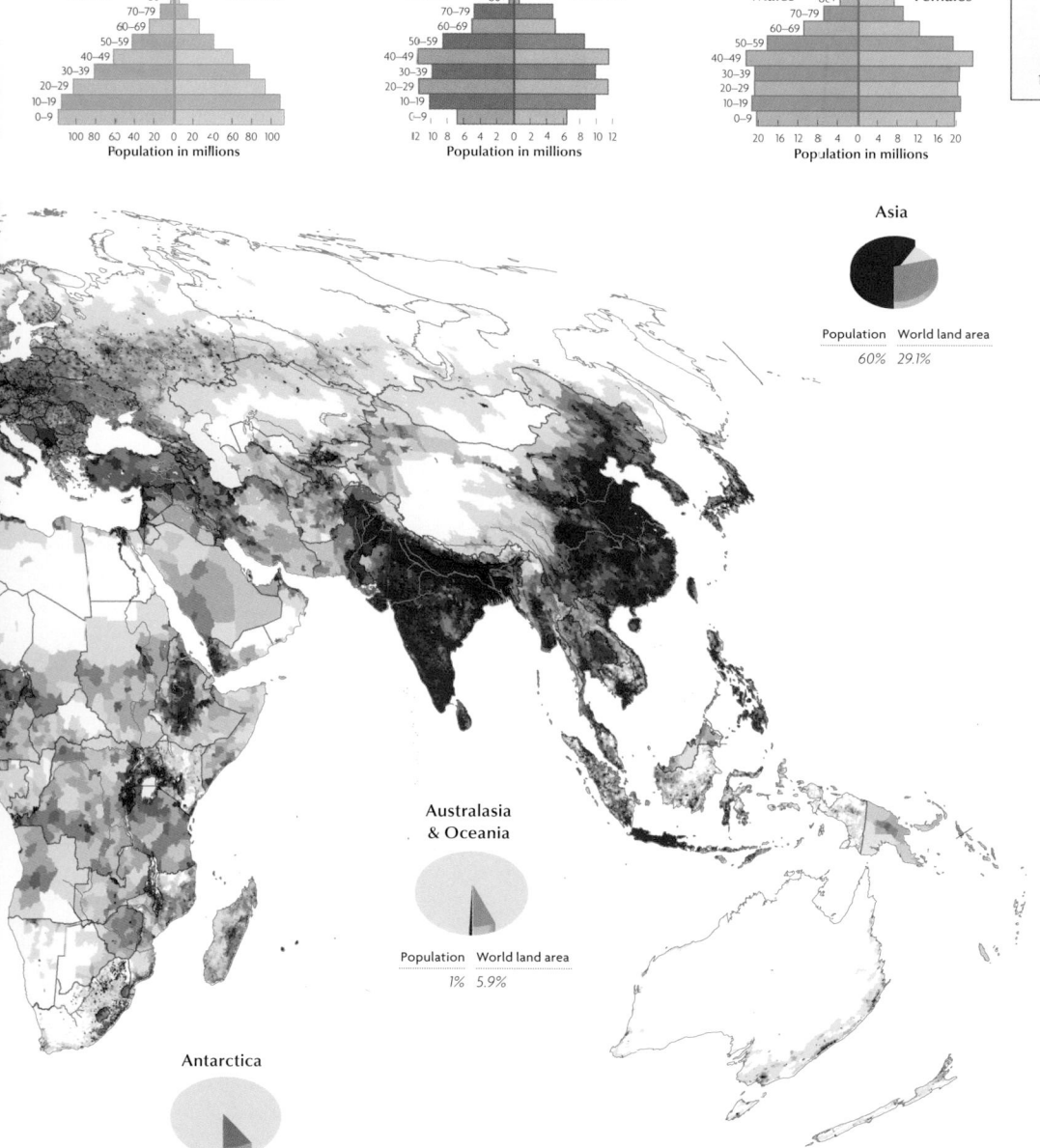

Asia

Population 60% / World land area 29.1%

Australasia & Oceania

Population 1% / World land area 5.9%

Antarctica

Population 0% / World land area 8.9%

Population growth

Improvements in food supply and advances in medicine have both played a major role in the remarkable growth in global population, which has increased five-fold over the last 150 years. Food supplies have risen with the mechanization of agriculture and improvements in crop yields. Better nutrition, together with higher standards of public health and sanitation, have led to increased longevity and higher birthrates.

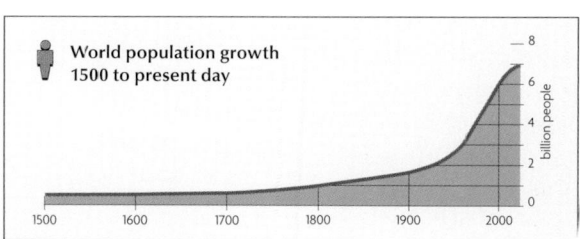

World population growth 1500 to present day

1500 1600 1700 1800 1900 2000
billion people: 8 6 4 2 0

World nutrition

Two-thirds of the world's food supply is consumed by the industrialized nations, many of which have a daily calorific intake far higher than is necessary for their populations to maintain a healthy body weight. In contrast, in the developing world, about 800 million people do not have enough food to meet their basic nutritional needs.

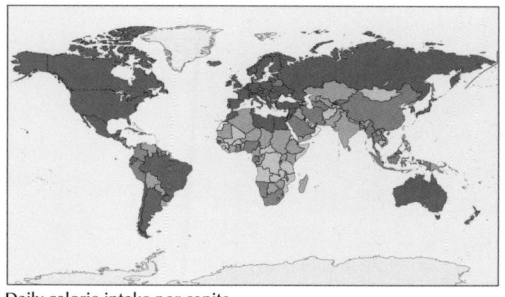

Daily calorie intake per capita

above 3000 / 2500–2999 / 2000–2499 / below 2000 / data not available

World life expectancy

Improved public health and living standards have greatly increased life expectancy in the developed world, where people can now expect to live twice as long as they did 100 years ago. In many of the world's poorest nations, inadequate nutrition and disease, means that the average life expectancy still does not exceed 45 years.

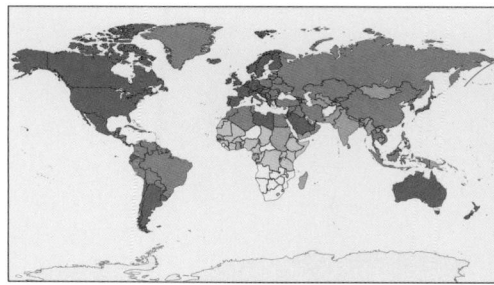

Life expectancy at birth

above 75 years / 65–74 years / 55–64 years / 45–54 years / below 44 years / data not available

Australasia and Oceania

This is the world's most sparsely settled region. The peoples of Australia and New Zealand live mainly in the coastal cities, with only scattered settlements in the arid interior. The Pacific islands can only support limited populations because of their remoteness and lack of resources.

▶ *Brisbane, on Australia's Gold Coast is the most rapidly expanding city in the country. The great majority of Australia's population lives in cities near the coasts.*

◀ *The remote highlands of Papua New Guinea are home to a wide variety of peoples, many of whom still subsist by traditional hunting and gathering.*

Average world birth rates

Birthrates are much higher in Africa, Asia, and South America than in Europe and North America. Increased affluence and easy access to contraception are both factors which can lead to a significant decline in a country's birthrate.

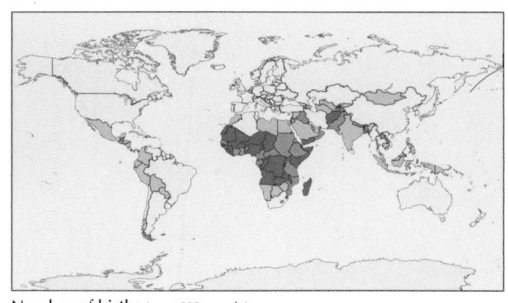

Number of births (per 1000 people)

above 40 / 30–39 / 20–29 / below 20 / data not available

World infant mortality

In parts of the developing world infant mortality rates are still high; access to medical services such as immunization, adequate nutrition, and the promotion of breast-feeding have been important in combating infant mortality.

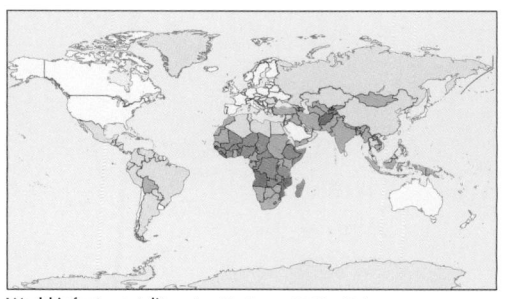

World infant mortality rates (deaths per 1000 live births)

above 125 / 75–124 / 35–74 / 15–34 / below 15 / data not available

The economic system

The wealthy countries of the developed world, with their aggressive, market-led economies and their access to productive new technologies and international markets, dominate the world economic system. At the other extreme, many of the countries of the developing world are locked in a cycle of national debt, rising populations, and unemployment. The state-managed economies of the former communist bloc began to be dismantled during the 1990s, and China is emerging as a major economic power following decades of isolation.

Trade blocs

Trade blocs

EU	NAFTA	ASEAN	LAIA
CACM	SADC	ECOWAS	CEEAC

Trade blocs

International trade blocs are formed when groups of countries, often already enjoying close military and political ties, join together to offer mutually preferential terms of trade for both imports and exports. Increasingly, global trade is dominated by three main blocs: the EU, NAFTA, and ASEAN. They are supplanting older trade blocs such as the Commonwealth, a legacy of colonialism.

International trade flows

World trade acts as a stimulus to national economies, encouraging growth. Over the last three decades, as heavy industries have declined, services – banking, insurance, tourism, airlines, and shipping – have taken an increasingly large share of world trade. Manufactured articles now account for nearly two-thirds of world trade; raw materials and food make up less than a quarter of the total.

Shipping
Ships carry 80% of international cargo, and extensive container ports, where cargo is stored, are vital links in the international transportation network.

Multinationals
Multinational companies are increasingly penetrating inaccessible markets. The reach of many American commodities is now global.

Primary products
Many countries, particularly in the Caribbean and Africa, are still reliant on primary products such as rubber and coffee, which makes them vulnerable to fluctuating prices.

Service industries
Service industries such as banking, tourism and insurance were the fastest-growing industrial sector in the last half of the 20th century. Lloyds of London is the center of the world insurance market.

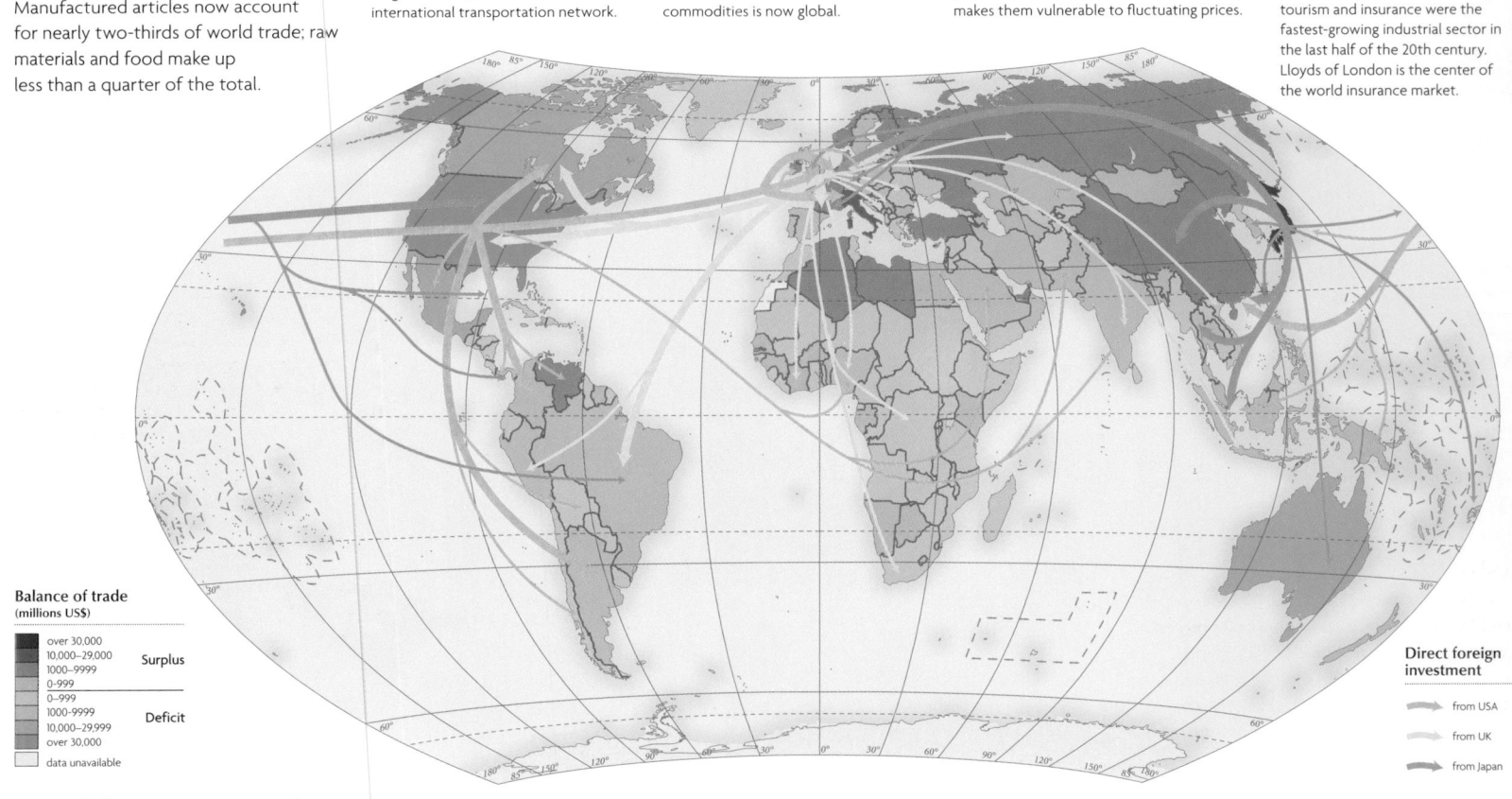

Balance of trade
(millions US$)

over 30,000	
10,000–29,000	
1000–9999	Surplus
0–999	
0–999	
1000–9999	
10,000–29,999	Deficit
over 30,000	
data unavailable	

Direct foreign investment

- from USA
- from UK
- from Japan

World money markets

The financial world has traditionally been dominated by three major centers – Tokyo, New York, and London, which house the headquarters of stock exchanges, multinational corporations and international banks. Their geographic location means that, at any one time in a 24-hour day, one major market is open for trading in shares, currencies, and commodities. Since the late 1980s, technological advances have enabled transactions between financial centers to occur at ever-greater speed, and new markets have sprung up throughout the world.

New stock markets
New stock markets are now opening in many parts of the world, where economies have recently emerged from state controls. In Moscow and Beijing, and several countries in eastern Europe, newly-opened stock exchanges reflect the transition to market-driven economies.

The developing world
International trade in capital and currency is dominated by the rich nations of the northern hemisphere. In parts of Africa and Asia, where exports of any sort are extremely limited, home-produced commodities are simply sold in local markets.

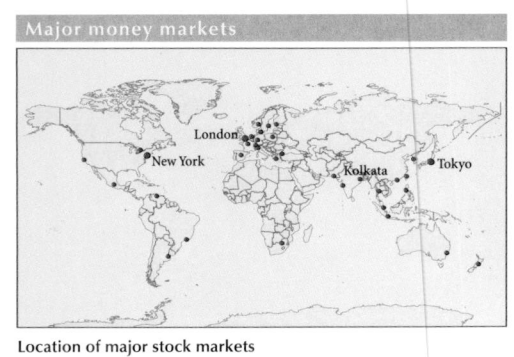

Major money markets

Location of major stock markets

- Major stock markets

▲ *The Tokyo Stock Market* crashed in 1990, leading to a slow-down in the growth of the world's most powerful economy, and a refocusing on economic policy away from export-led growth and toward the domestic market.

▲ *Dealers at the* Kolkata Stock Market. The Indian economy has been opened up to foreign investment and many multinationals now have bases there.

▲ *Markets have thrived* in communist Vietnam since the introduction of a liberal economic policy.

World wealth disparity

A global assessment of Gross Domestic Product (GDP) by nation reveals great disparities. The developed world, with only a quarter of the world's population, has 80% of the world's manufacturing income. Civil war, conflict, and political instability further undermine the economic self-sufficiency of many of the world's poorest nations.

Urban sprawl

Cities are expanding all over the developing world, attracting economic migrants in search of work and opportunities. In cities such as Rio de Janeiro, housing has not kept pace with the population explosion, and squalid shanty towns (favelas) rub shoulders with middle-class housing.

▲ **The favelas of** Rio de Janeiro sprawl over the hills surrounding the city.

Agricultural economies

In parts of the developing world, people survive by subsistence farming – only growing enough food for themselves and their families. With no surplus product, they are unable to exchange goods for currency, the only means of escaping the poverty trap. In other countries, farmers have been encouraged to concentrate on growing a single crop for the export market. This reliance on cash crops leaves farmers vulnerable to crop failure and to changes in the market price of the crop.

▲ **The Ugandan uplands** are fertile, but poor infrastructure hampers the export of cash crops.

Urban decay

Although the US still dominates the global economy, it faces deficits in both the federal budget and the balance of trade. Vast discrepancies in personal wealth, high levels of unemployment, and the dismantling of welfare provisions throughout the 1980s have led to severe deprivation in several of the inner cities of North America's industrial heartland.

▲ **Cities such as** Detroit have been badly hit by the decline in heavy industry.

Booming cities

Since the 1980s the Chinese government has set up special industrial zones, such as Shanghai, where foreign investment is encouraged through tax incentives. Migrants from rural China pour into these regions in search of work, creating "boomtown" economies.

◄ **Foreign investment has** encouraged new infrastructure development in cities like Shanghai.

Economic "tigers"

The economic "tigers" of the Pacific Rim – China, Singapore, and South Korea – have grown faster than Europe and the US over the last decade. Their export- and service-led economies have benefited from stable government, low labor costs, and foreign investment.

▲ **Hong Kong, with** its fine natural harbour, is one of the most important ports in Asia.

The affluent West

The capital cities of many countries in the developed world are showcases for consumer goods, reflecting the increasing importance of the service sector, and particularly the retail sector, in the world economy. The idea of shopping as a leisure activity is unique to the western world. Luxury goods and services attract visitors, who in turn generate tourist revenue.

Comparative world wealth

World economies - average GDP per capita (US$)

- above 20,000
- 5000–20,000
- 2000–5000
- below 2000
- data unavailable

▲ **A shopping arcade** in Paris displays a great profusion of luxury goods.

◄ **In rural Southeast Asia,** babies are given medical checks by UNICEF as part of a global aid program sponsored by the UN.

Tourism

In 2004, there were over 700 million tourists worldwide. Tourism is now the world's biggest single industry, employing over 130 million people, though frequently in low-paid unskilled jobs. While tourists are increasingly exploring inaccessible and less-developed regions of the world, the benefits of the industry are not always felt at a local level. There are also worries about the environmental impact of tourism, as the world's last wildernesses increasingly become tourist attractions.

▲ **Botswana's Okavango Delta** is an area rich in wildlife. Tourists go on safaris to the region, but the impact of tourism is controlled.

Money flows

Foreign investment in the developing world during the 1970s led to a global financial crisis in the 1980s, when many countries were unable to meet their debt repayments. The International Monetary Fund (IMF) was forced to reschedule the debts and, in some cases, write them off completely. Within the developing world, austerity programs have been initiated to cope with the debt, leading in turn to high unemployment and galloping inflation. In many parts of Africa, stricken economies are now dependent on international aid.

Tourist arrivals

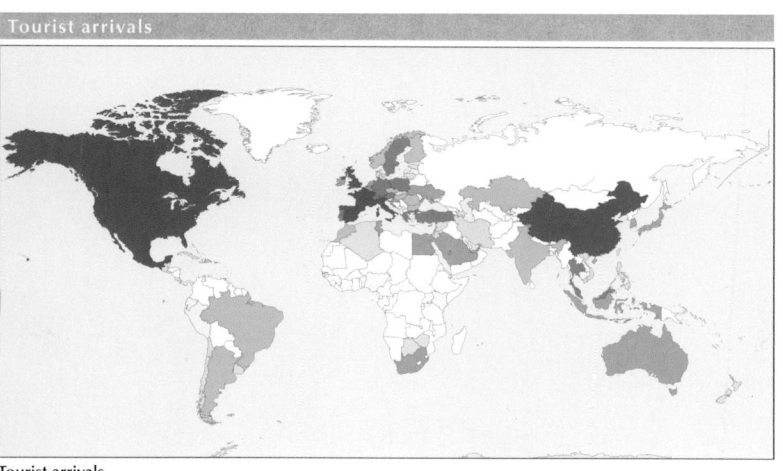

Tourist arrivals

- over 20 million
- 10–20 million
- 5–10 million
- 2.5–5 million
- 1–2.5 million
- 700,000–999,000
- under 700,000
- data unavailable

International debt

International debt (as percentage of GNI)

- over 100%
- 70–99%
- 50–69%
- 30–49%
- 10–29%
- below 10%
- data unavailable

The political world

There are 195 independent countries in the world today. With the exception of Antarctica, where territorial claims have been deferred by international treaty, every land area of the Earth's surface either belongs to, or is claimed by, one country or another. The largest country in the world is the Russian Federation, the smallest is Vatican City. Some 60 overseas dependent territories remain, administered variously by France, Australia, Denmark, New Zealand, Norway, Portugal, the UK, the US, and the Netherlands.

International borders

The map shows three main types of boundary between states. Full borders represent internationally agreed and recognized territorial boundaries. Undefined borders exist where no fixed boundary between states has been demarcated; the boundaries indicated in this way show approximate areas of sovereignty. A disputed border is indicated where a *de facto* territorial boundary exists, which is not agreed or is subject to arbitration.

Most densely populated country
Monaco: 43,561 people per sq mile
(16,754 people per sq km)

Smallest country
Vatican City: 0.17 sq miles (0.44 sq km)

Longest land borders
Russian Federation:
12,427 miles (20,000 km)

Longest single land border
Canada/USA: 5526 miles
(8893 km)

Largest country
Russian Federation:
6,592,735 sq miles
(17,075,200 sq km)

Most populous City
Tokyo: 34,200,000
people

Most sparsely populated country
Mongolia:
4 people per sq mile
(2 people per sq km)

Most populous country
China: 1,331,400,000 people

Largest island country
Australia: 2,967,893 sq miles
(7,686,850 sq km)

Smallest island country
Nauru: 8.2 sq miles
(21.2 sq km)

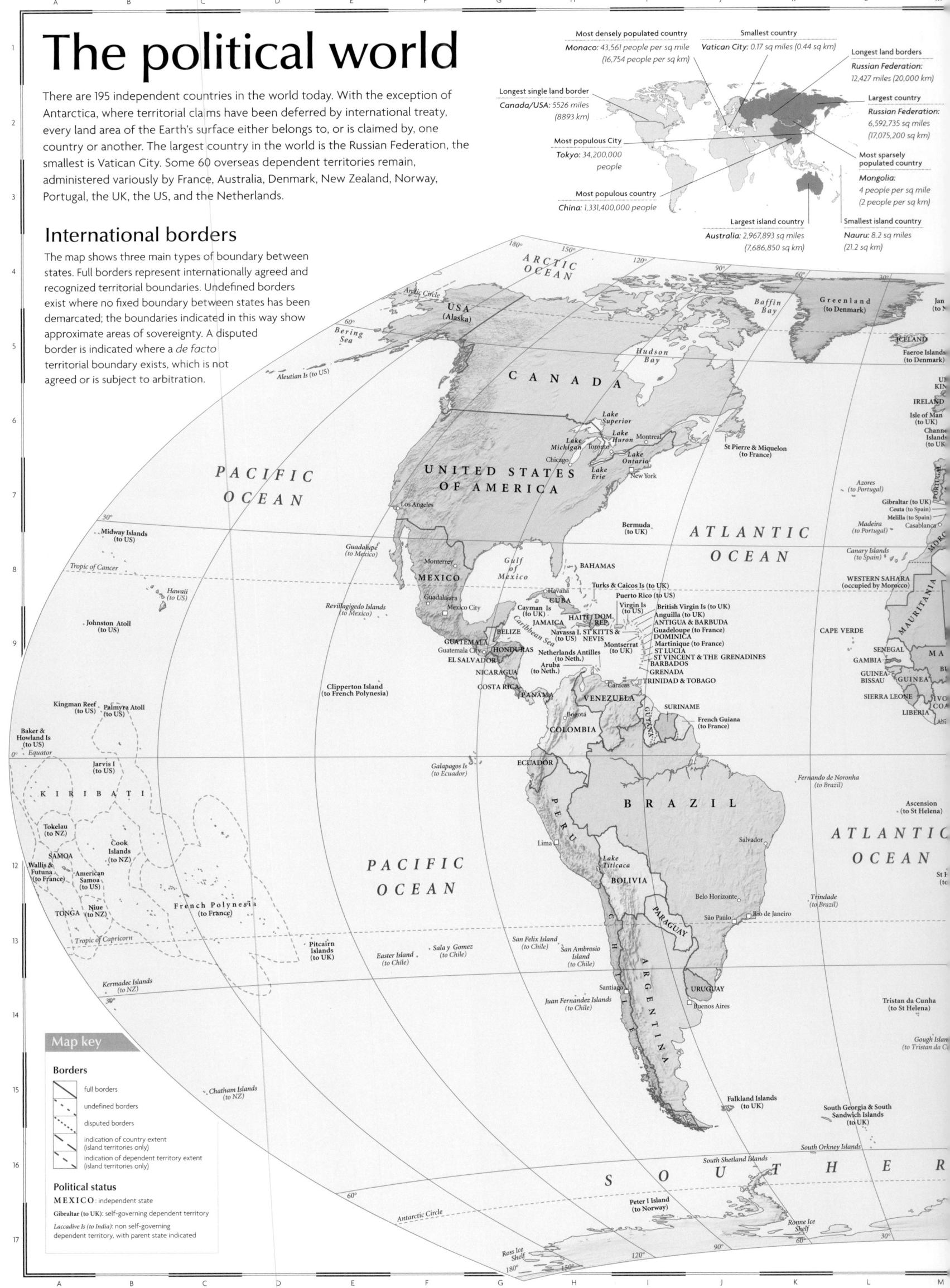

Map key

Borders

full borders

undefined borders

disputed borders

indication of country extent
(island territories only)

indication of dependent territory extent
(island territories only)

Political status

MEXICO: independent state

Gibraltar (to UK): self-governing dependent territory

Laccadive Is (to India): non self-governing
dependent territory, with parent state indicated

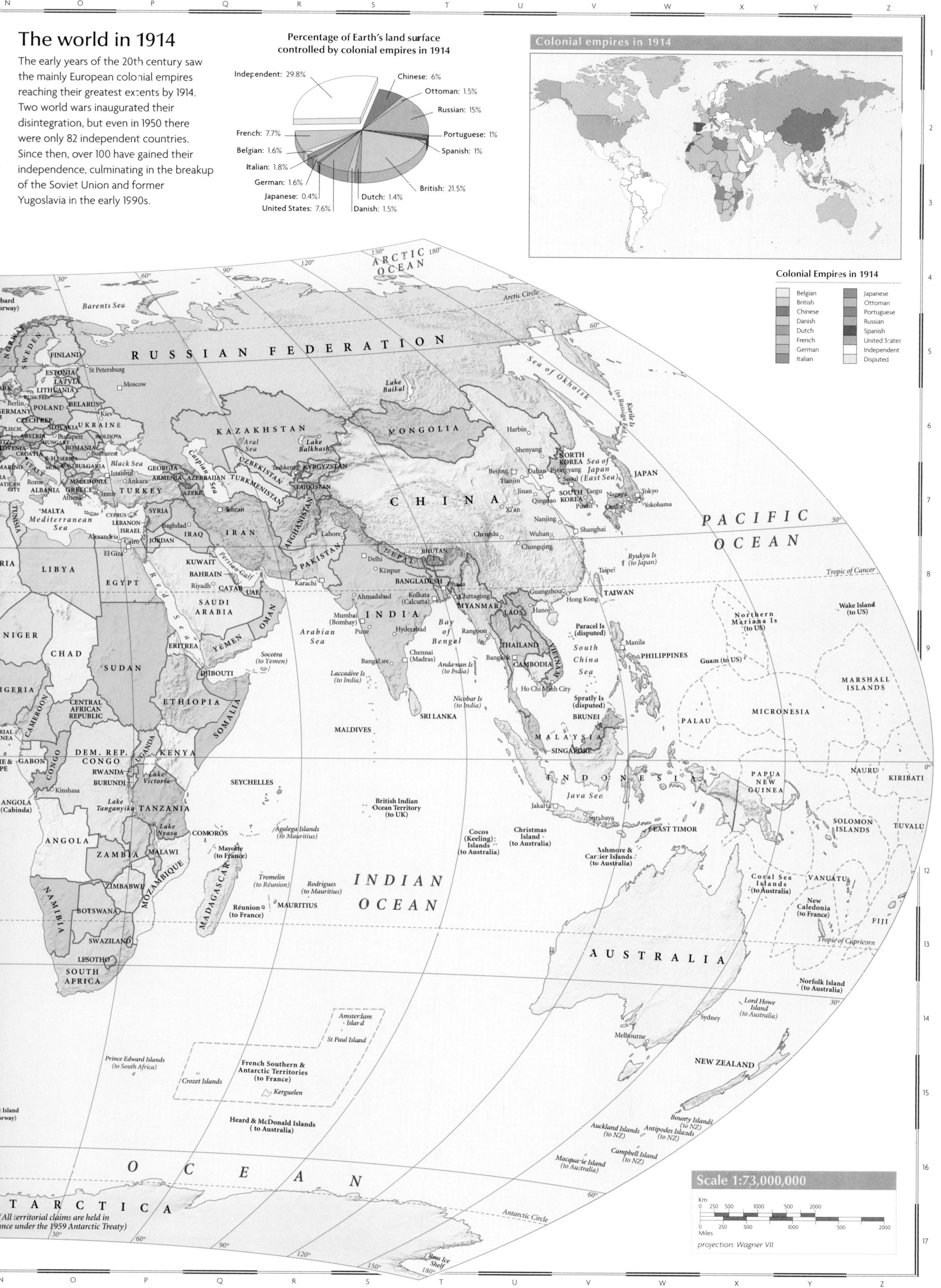

The world in 1914

The early years of the 20th century saw the mainly European colonial empires reaching their greatest extents by 1914. Two world wars inaugurated their disintegration, but even in 1950 there were only 82 independent countries. Since then, over 100 have gained their independence, culminating in the breakup of the Soviet Union and former Yugoslavia in the early 1990s.

Percentage of Earth's land surface controlled by colonial empires in 1914

- Independent: 29.8%
- Chinese: 6%
- Ottoman: 1.5%
- Russian: 15%
- Portuguese: 1%
- Spanish: 1%
- British: 21.5%
- French: 7.7%
- Belgian: 1.6%
- Italian: 1.8%
- German: 1.6%
- Japanese: 0.4%
- Dutch: 1.4%
- United States: 7.6%
- Danish: 1.5%

Colonial empires in 1914

Colonial Empires in 1914
- Belgian
- British
- Chinese
- Danish
- Dutch
- French
- German
- Italian
- Japanese
- Ottoman
- Portuguese
- Russian
- Spanish
- United States
- Independent
- Disputed

Scale 1:73,000,000

projection: Wagner VII

States and boundaries

There are over 190 sovereign states in the world today; in 1950 there were only 82. Over the last half-century national self-determination has been a driving force for many states with a history of colonialism and oppression. As more borders have been added to the world map, the number of international border disputes has increased.

In many cases, where the impetus toward independence has been religious or ethnic, disputes with minority groups have also caused violent internal conflict. While many newly-formed states have moved peacefully toward independence, successfully establishing government by multiparty democracy, dictatorship by military regime or individual despot is often the result of the internal power-struggles which characterize the early stages in the lives of new nations.

The nature of politics

Democracy is a broad term: it can range from the ideal of multiparty elections and fair representation to, in countries such as Singapore, a thin disguise for single-party rule. In despotic regimes, on the other hand, a single, often personal authority has total power; institutions such as parliament and the military are mere instruments of the dictator.

◀ **The stars and** stripes of the US flag are a potent symbol of the country's status as a federal democracy.

Types of government

- Multiparty democracy for more than 10 yrs
- Multiparty democracy within last 10 yrs
- Single-party government
- Military regime
- Theocracy
- Monarchy
- Non-party system
- Transitional regime
- ♟ Current civil unrest

The changing world map

Decolonization

In 1950, large areas of the world remained under the control of a handful of European countries *(page xxxiii)*. The process of decolonization had begun in Asia, where, following the Second World War, much of southern and southeastern Asia sought and achieved self-determination. In the 1960s, a host of African states achieved independence, so that by 1965, most of the larger tracts of the European overseas empires had been substantially eroded. The final major stage in decolonization came with the breakup of the Soviet Union and the Eastern bloc after 1990. The process continues today as the last toeholds of European colonialism, often tiny island nations, press increasingly for independence.

New nations 1945–1965

New nations 1965–present

▲ **Icons of communism,** including statues of former leaders such as Lenin and Stalin, were destroyed when the Soviet bloc was dismantled in 1989, creating several new nations.

▲ **Iran has been** one of the modern world's few true theocracies; Islam has an impact on every aspect of political life.

▲ **North Korea is** an independent communist republic. Power is concentrated in the hands of Kim Jong Il.

Administration at the time of independence

Australia	Malaysia
Aust/NZ/UK	Netherlands
Belgium	New Zealand
China	Pakistan
Czechoslovakia	Portugal
Egypt/UK	South Africa
Ethiopia	Spain
France	UK
France/UK	Unified country
Indonesia	USA
Italy	USSR
Japan	Yugoslavia

◀ **Saddam Hussein former** autocratic leader of Iraq, promoted an extreme personality cult for over 20 years. He was ousted by a US-led coalition in 2003.

◀ **South Africa became** a democracy in 1994, when elections ended over a century of white minority rule.

▲ **In Brunei the** Sultan has ruled by decree since 1962; power is closely tied to the royal family. The Sultan's brothers are responsible for finance and foreign affairs.

Lines on the map

The determination of international boundaries can use a variety of criteria. Many of the borders between older states follow physical boundaries; some mirror religious and ethnic differences; others are the legacy of complex histories of conflict and colonialism, while others have been imposed by international agreements or arbitration.

Post-colonial borders

When the European colonial empires in Africa were dismantled during the second half of the 20th century, the outlines of the new African states mirrored colonial boundaries. These boundaries had been drawn up by colonial administrators, often based on inadequate geographical knowledge. Such arbitrary boundaries were imposed on people of different languages, racial groups, religions, and customs. This confused legacy often led to civil and international war.

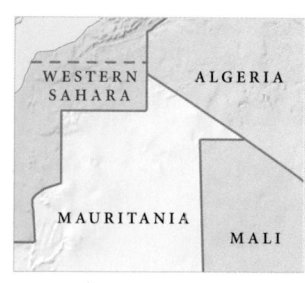

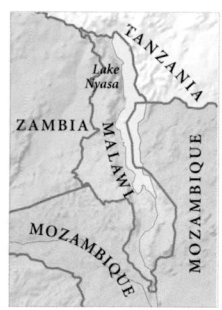

▲ *The conflict that* has plagued many African countries since independence has caused millions of people to become refugees.

Physical borders

Many of the world's countries are divided by physical borders: lakes, rivers, mountains. The demarcation of such boundaries can, however, lead to disputes. Control of waterways, water supplies, and fisheries are frequent causes of international friction.

Enclaves

The shifting political map over the course of history has frequently led to anomalous situations. Parts of national territories may become isolated by territorial agreement, forming an enclave. The West German part of the city of Berlin, which until 1989 lay a hundred miles (160km) within East German territory, was a famous example

▲ *Since the independence* of Lithuania and Belarus, the peoples of the Russian enclave of Kaliningrad have become physically isolated.

Antarctica

When Antarctic exploration began a century ago, seven nations, Australia, Argentina, Britain, Chile, France, New Zealand, and Norway, laid claim to the new territory. In 1961 the Antarctic Treaty, now signed by 45 nations, agreed to hold all territorial claims in abeyance.

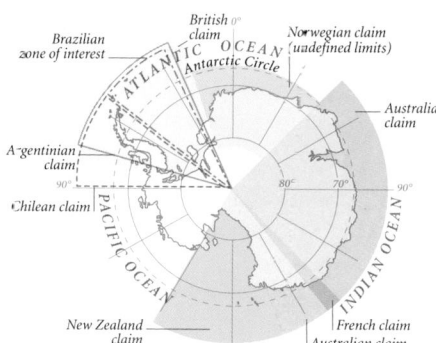

Geometric borders

Straight lines and lines of longitude and latitude have occasionally been used to determine international boundaries; and indeed the world's second longest continuous international boundary, between Canada and the USA follows the 49th Parallel for over one-third of its course. Many Canadian, American, and Australian internal administrative boundaries are similarly determined using a geometric solution.

▲ *Different farming techniques* in Canada and the US clearly mark the course of the international boundary in this satellite map.

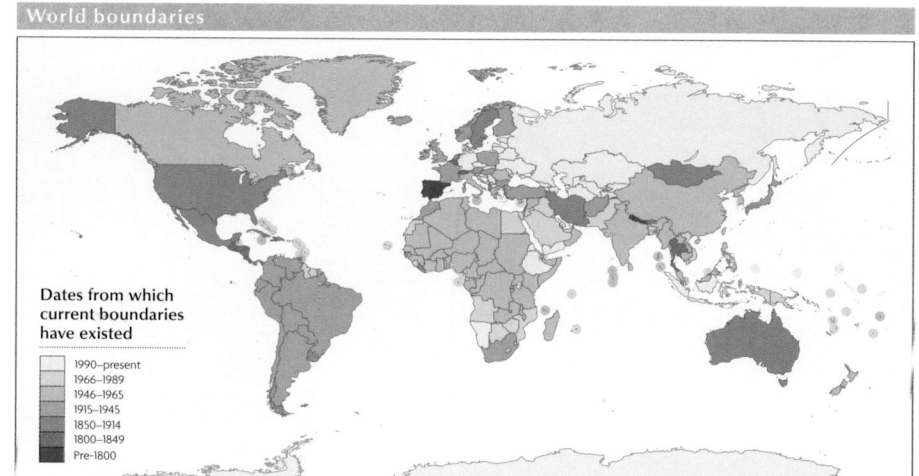

World boundaries

Dates from which current boundaries have existed

- 1990–present
- 1966–1989
- 1946–1965
- 1915–1945
- 1850–1914
- 1800–1849
- Pre-1800

Lake borders

Countries which lie next to lakes usually fix their borders in the middle of the lake. Unusually the Lake Nyasa border between Malawi and Tanzania runs along Tanzania's shore.

▲ *Complicated agreements between* colonial powers led to the awkward division of Lake Nyasa.

River borders

Rivers alone account for one-sixth of the world's borders. Many great rivers form boundaries between a number of countries. Changes in a river's course and interruptions of its natural flow can lead to disputes, particularly in areas where water is scarce. The center of the river's course is the nominal boundary line.

▲ *The Danube forms* all or part of the border between nine European nations.

Mountain borders

Mountain ranges form natural barriers and are the basis for many major borders, particularly in Europe and Asia. The watershed is the conventional boundary demarcation line, but its accurate determination is often problematic.

▲ *The Pyrenees form* a natural mountain border between France and Spain.

Shifting boundaries – Poland

Borders between countries can change dramatically over time. The nations of eastern Europe have been particularly affected by changing boundaries. Poland is an example of a country whose boundaries have changed so significantly that it has literally moved around Europe. At the start of the 16th century, Poland was the largest nation in Europe. Between 1772 and 1795, it was absorbed into Prussia, Austria, and Russia, and it effectively ceased to exist. After the First World War, Poland became an independent country once more, but its borders changed again after the Second World War following invasions by both Soviet Russia and Nazi Germany.

▲ *In 1634, Poland was* the largest nation in Europe. Its eastern boundary reaching toward Moscow.

▲ *From 1772–1795, Poland was* gradually partitioned between Austria, Russia, and Prussia. Its eastern boundary receded by over 100 miles (160 km).

▲ *Following the First World War,* Poland was reinstated as an independent state, but it was less than half the size it had been in 1634.

▲ *After the Second World War,* the Baltic Sea border was extended westward, but much of the eastern territory was annexed by Russia.

International disputes

There are more than 60 disputed borders or territories in the world today. Although many of these disputes can be settled by peaceful negotiation, some areas have become a focus for international conflict. Ethnic tensions have been a major source of territorial disagreement throughout history, as has the ownership of, and access to, valuable natural resources. The turmoil of the postcolonial era in many parts of Africa is partly a result of the 19th century "carve-up" of the continent, which created potential for conflict by drawing often arbitrary lines through linguistic and cultural areas.

Jammu and Kashmir

Disputes over Jammu and Kashmir have caused three serious wars between India and Pakistan since 1947. Pakistan wishes to annex the largely Muslim territory, while India refuses to cede any territory or to hold a referendum, and also lays claim to the entire territory. Most international maps show the "line of control" agreed in 1972 as the *de facto* border. In addition, India has territorial disputes with neighboring China. The situation is further complicated by a Kashmiri independence movement, active since the late 1980s.

▲ **Indian army troops** maintain their positions in the mountainous terrain of northern Kashmir.

North and South Korea

Since 1953, the *de facto* border between North and South Korea has been a cease-fire line which straddles the 38th Parallel and is designated as a demilitarized zone. Both countries have heavy fortifications and troop concentrations behind this zone.

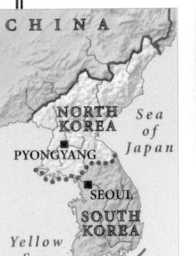

▲ **Heavy fortifications on** the border between North and South Korea.

Cyprus

Cyprus was partitioned in 1974, following an invasion by Turkish troops. The south is now the Greek Cypriot Republic of Cyprus, while the self-proclaimed Turkish Republic of Northern Cyprus is recognized only by Turkey.

▲ **The so-called** "green line" divides Cyprus into Greek and Turkish sectors.

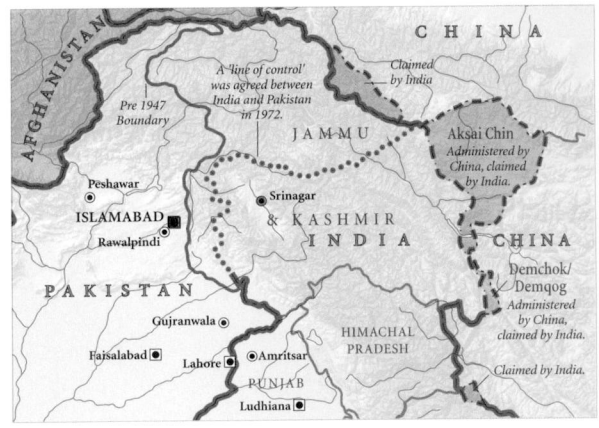

The Falkland Islands

The British dependent territory of the Falkland Islands was invaded by Argentina in 1982, sparking a full-scale war with the UK. In 1995, the UK and Argentina reached an agreement on the exploitation of oil reserves around the islands.

◀ **British warships in** Falkland Sound during the 1982 war with Argentina.

Israel

Israel was created in 1948 following the 1947 UN Resolution (147) on Palestine. Until 1979 Israel had no borders, only cease-fire lines from a series of wars in 1948, 1967, and 1973. Treaties with Egypt in 1979 and Jordan in 1994 led to these borders being defined and agreed. Negotiations over Israeli settlements and Palestinian self-government seen little effective progress since 2000.

▲ **Barbed-wire fences** surround a settlement in the Golan Heights.

Former Yugoslavia

Following the disintegration in 1991 of the communist state of Yugoslavia, the breakaway states of Croatia and Bosnia and Herzegovina came into conflict with the "parent" state (consisting of Serbia and Montenegro). Warfare focused on ethnic and territorial ambitions in Bosnia. The tenuous Dayton Accord of 1995 sought to recognize the post-1990 borders, whilst providing for ethnic partition and required international peace-keeping troops to maintain the terms of the peace.

▲ **Most claimant states** have small military garrisons on the Spratly Islands.

The Spratly Islands

The site of potential oil and natural gas reserves, the Spratly Islands in the South China Sea have been claimed by China, Vietnam, Taiwan, Malaysia, and the Philippines since the Japanese gave up a wartime claim in 1951.

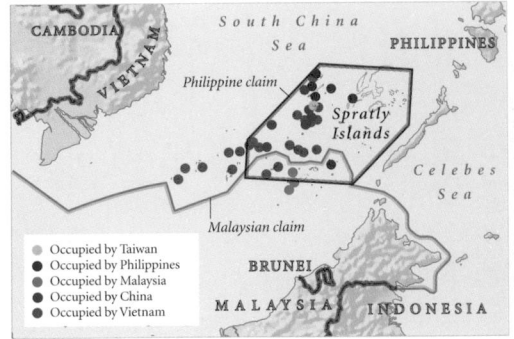

Conflicts and international disputes

- Countries contributing troops to coalition force in Iraq (as of 2008)
- Major active territorial or border disputes
- Countries involved in internal conflict
- Active territorial or border disputes and internal conflict

ATLAS
OF THE WORLD

THE MAPS IN THIS ATLAS ARE ARRANGED CONTINENT BY CONTINENT, STARTING FROM THE INTERNATIONAL DATE LINE, AND MOVING EASTWARD. THE MAPS PROVIDE A UNIQUE VIEW OF TODAY'S WORLD, COMBINING TRADITIONAL CARTOGRAPHIC TECHNIQUES WITH THE LATEST REMOTE-SENSED AND DIGITAL TECHNOLOGY.

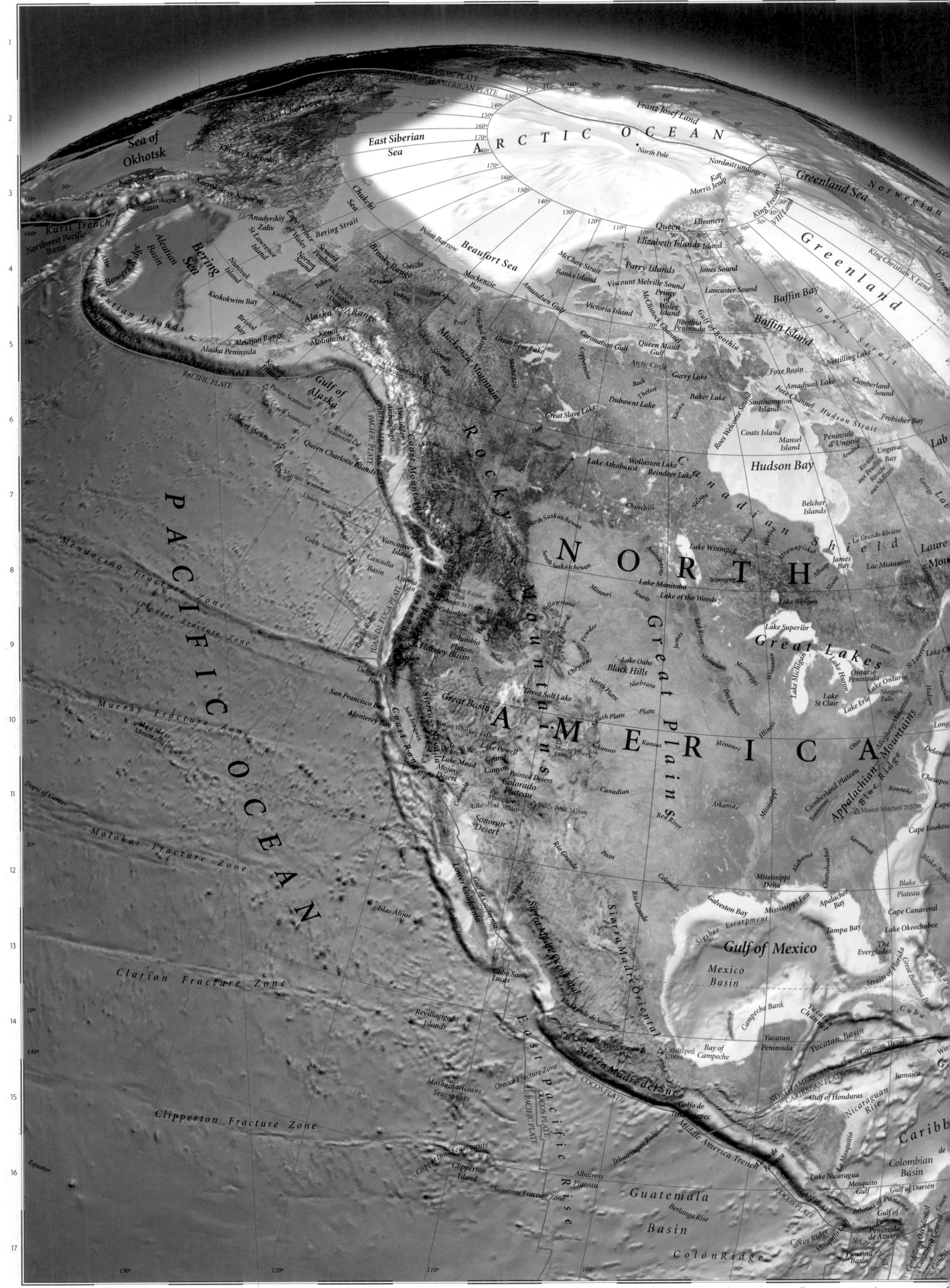

ARCTIC OCEAN

North Pole

Franz Josef Land

Greenland Sea

Norwegian

Greenland

Kap
Morris Jesup

King Frederik
VIII Land

Nordostrundingen

King Christian X Land

Ice

Queen
Elizabeth Islands

Ellesmere
Island

Davis Strait

Parry Islands

Jones Sound

McClure Strait

Banks Island

Baffin Bay

Viscount Melville Sound

Lancaster Sound

Prince
of
Wales
Island

M'Clintock Channel

Gulf
of Boothia

Baffin Island

Victoria Island

Boothia
Peninsula

Coronation Gulf

Queen Maud
Gulf

Foxe Basin

Netilling Lake

Cumberland
Sound

Sea of
Okhotsk

Ratmol Churkchov

Khrebet Kolymskiy

East Siberian
Sea

Chukchi
Sea

Anadyrskiy
Zaliv

Cape Prince
of Wales

Seward
Peninsula

Bering Strait

Point Barrow

Beaufort Sea

Mackenzie
Bay

Amundsen Gulf

Kamchatka

Koryakskoye Nagor'ye

Kaukhandorskaya
Basin

St Lawrence
Island

Nunivak
Island

Norton
Sound

Brooks Range

Yukon

Colville

Peel

Porcupine

Coppermine

Back

Thelon

Dubawnt Lake

Garry Lake

Baker Lake

Arctic Circle

Great Bear Lake

Kazan

Southampton
Island

Foxe Channel

Kurit Trench

Northwest Pacific
Basin

Aleutian
Basin

Bering
Sea

Kuskokwim Bay

Kuskokwim

Bristol
Bay

Kenai
Mountains

Alaska
Range

Mount McKinley
6194m

Yukon

Tanana

Mackenzie
Mountains

Liard

Great Slave Lake

Hay

Wollaston Lake

Athabasca

Lake Athabasca

Reindeer Lake

Roes Welcome Sound

Coats Island

Hudson Strait

Frobisher Bay

Péninsule
d'Ungava

Rivière
aux Feuilles
Rivière aux Mélèzes

Ungava
Bay

Baie
aux Feuilles

George

Lab

Bowers Ridge

Attu

Aleutian Islands

Kodiak
Island

Gulf of
Alaska

Alaska Peninsula

Alaska Peninsula

Aleutian Range

NORTH AMERICAN PLATE

PACIFIC PLATE

Patton Seamount

Cowie Seamount

Dickins
Seamount

Gilbert Seamounts

Queen Charlotte Islands

Merton Seamount

Union Seamount

Cobb Seamount

Vancouver
Island

Coast Mountains

Cascadia
Basin

Rocky

Mansel
Island

Hudson Bay

Belcher
Islands

Churchill

Nelson

La Grande Rivière

James
Bay

Lac Mistassini

Laure

Mou

Canadian Shield

NORTH

Lake Winnipeg

Attawapiskat

Severn

Winisk

Albany

Ottawa

St Lawrence

Lake

PACIFIC PLATE

Mendocino Fracture Zone

Pioneer Fracture Zone

Murray Fracture Zone

Moonless
Mountains

Molokai Fracture Zone

PACIFIC OCEAN

Tropic of Cancer

Clarion Fracture Zone

JUAN DE FUCA PLATE

Gorda Ridge

Astoria
Fan

Delgada Fan

San Francisco Bay

Monterey Bay

San Joaquin

Coast Ranges

Sierra Nevada

Mount Rainier
4392m

Mount St Helens

Columbia

Mount Hood

Columbia
Plateau

Harney Basin

Snake

Yellowstone

Powder

Great Basin

Mount Whitney 4418m

Death
Valley

Lake
Mead

Mojave
Desert

Lake Powell

Grand
Canyon

Painted Desert

Colorado
Plateau

Baldy Peak 3476m

Gila

Gila Peak 3505m

Sonoran
Desert

Colorado

Columbia

Owyhee

Rocky Mountains

Great Salt Lake

Black Hills

Lake Oahe

North Platte

Niobrara

Cheyenne

South Platte

Platte

Arkansas

Kansas

Mount Elbert
4399m

Great Plains

AMERICA

Missouri

Souris

Lake Manitoba

Lake of the Woods

Red River

Assiniboine

South Saskatchewan

North Saskatchewan

Des Moines

Missouri

Illinois

Wisconsin

Mississippi

Minnesota

Lake Nipigon

Lake Superior

Great Lakes

Lake Michigan

Lake Huron

Ontario
Peninsula

Lake
St Clair

Lake Erie

Niagara
Falls

Lake Ontario

Seaway

Allegheny Mountains

Appalachian Mountains

Blue Ridge

Mount Mitchell 2037m

Cumberland Plateau

Tennessee

Ohio

Arkansas

Mississippi

Roanoke

Delaware

Chesa

Long

Cape

Cape Lookout

Islas Alijos

Gulf of California

Baja California

Sierra Madre Occidental

Red River

Canadian

Pecos

Rio Grande

Colorado

Mississippi
Delta

Galveston Bay

Sigsbee Escarpment

Mississippi Fan

Alabama

Chattahoochee

Apalachee
Bay

Tampa Bay

Blake
Plateau

Cape Canaveral

Lake Okeechobee

The
Everglades

Gulf of Mexico

Mexico
Basin

Straits of Florida

Great Bahama Bank

Cabo San
Lucas

Revillagigedo
Islands

Río de Santiago

Lago de Chapala

Popocatépetl 5452m

Citlaltépetl
5700m

Sierra Madre del Sur

East Pacific Rise

COCOS PLATE

Campeche Bank

Campeche

Yucatán
Channel

Yucatán
Peninsula

Bay of
Campeche

Yucatan Basin

Cuba

Cayman Trench

Jamaica

G

Caribb

Mathematicians
Seamounts

Orozco Fracture Zone

Clipperton Fracture Zone

Clipperton Seamounts

Clipperton
Island

Siqueiros Fracture Zone

Equator

Albatross
Plateau

Berlanga Rise

Sierra Madre de Sur

PACIFIC PLATE

COCOS
PLATE

Golfo de
Tehuantepec

Tehuantepec Ridge

Middle America Trench

NORTH AMERICAN PLATE

CARIBBEAN PLATE

Gulf of Honduras

Nicaraguan
Rise

Lake Nicaragua

Guatemala
Basin

Mosquito
Gulf

Lake Managua

Mosquito
Coast

Gulf of Darién

Colombian
Basin

Cordillera Oriental

Colón Ridge

Cocos Ridge

Panama
Basin

Gulf of
Panama

Peninsula
de Azuero

Isthmus of Panama

NAZCA
PLATE

North America

North America is the world's third largest continent with a total area of 9,358,340 sq miles

(24,238,000 sq km) including Greenland and the Caribbean islands.

It lies wholly within the Northern Hemisphere.

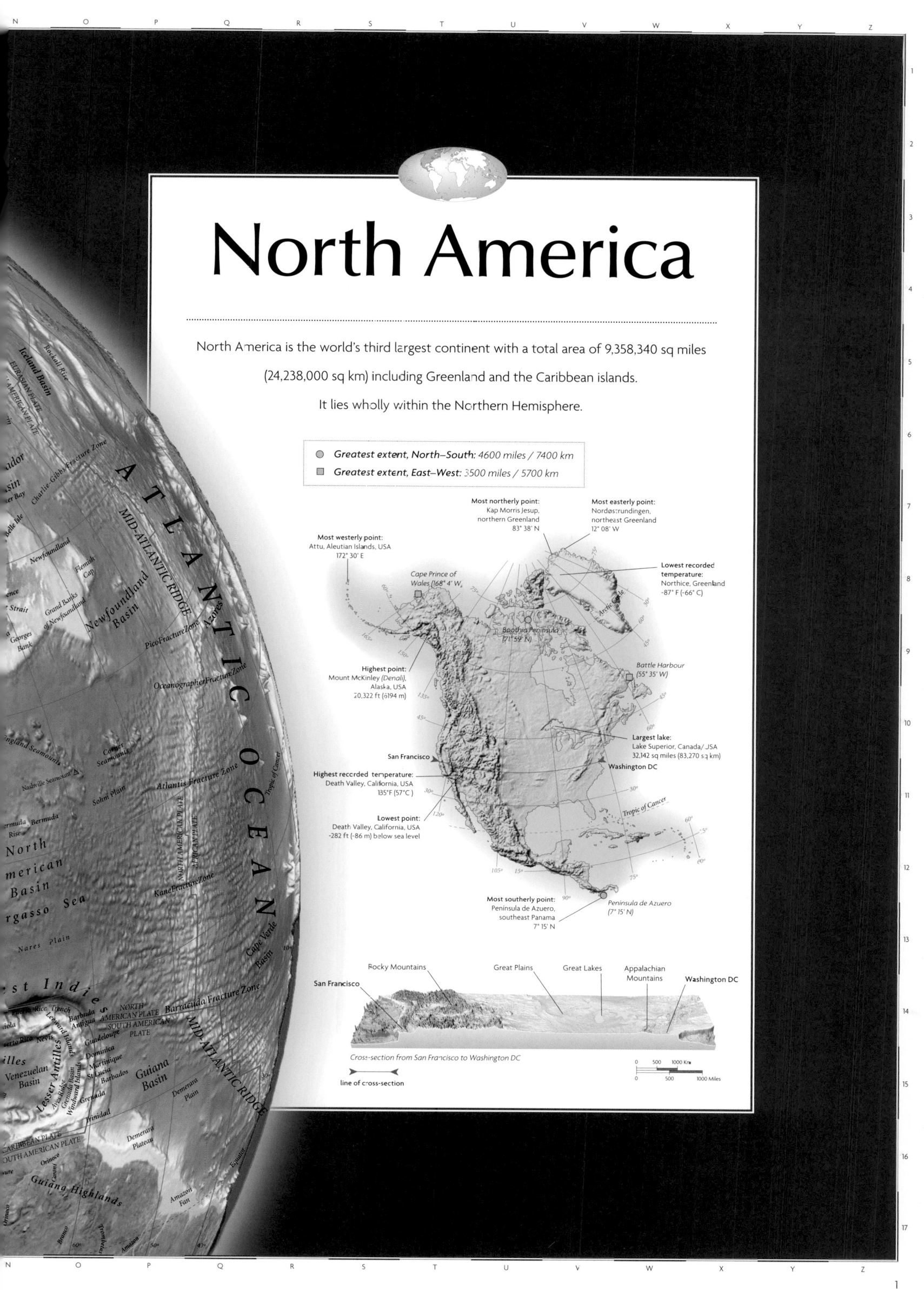

● **Greatest extent, North–South:** 4600 miles / 7400 km

■ **Greatest extent, East–West:** 3500 miles / 5700 km

Most northerly point:
Kap Morris Jesup,
northern Greenland
83° 38' N

Most easterly point:
Nordøstrundingen,
northeast Greenland
12° 08' W

Most westerly point:
Attu, Aleutian Islands, USA
172° 30' E

Cape Prince of
Wales (168° 4' W)

**Lowest recorded
temperature:**
Northice, Greenland
-87° F (-66° C)

Boothia Peninsula
(71° 59' N)

Highest point:
Mount McKinley (Denali),
Alaska, USA
20,322 ft (6194 m)

Battle Harbour
(55° 35' W)

Largest lake:
Lake Superior, Canada/USA
32,142 sq miles (83,270 sq km)

San Francisco

Washington DC

Highest recorded temperature:
Death Valley, California, USA
135°F (57°C)

Tropic of Cancer

Lowest point:
Death Valley, California, USA
-282 ft (-86 m) below sea level

Most southerly point:
Peninsula de Azuero,
southeast Panama
7° 15' N

Peninsula de Azuero
(7° 15' N)

Rocky Mountains   Great Plains   Great Lakes   Appalachian Mountains   **Washington DC**

San Francisco

Cross-section from San Francisco to Washington DC

line of cross-section

0   500   1000 Km
0   500   1000 Miles

ATLANTIC OCEAN
MID-ATLANTIC RIDGE

Iceland Basin
EURASIAN PLATE
NORTH AMERICAN PLATE
Rockall Rise
Charlie-Gibbs Fracture Zone
Newfoundland
Flemish Cap
Newfoundland Basin
Grand Banks of Newfoundland
Georges Bank
Pico Fracture Zone
Azores
Oceanographer Fracture Zone
New England Seamounts
Corner Seamounts
Nashville Seamount
Sohm Plain
Atlantis Fracture Zone
Tropic of Cancer
NORTH AMERICAN PLATE
AFRICAN PLATE
Bermuda Rise
Bermuda
North American Basin
Kane Fracture Zone
Sargasso Sea
Nares Plain
Cape Verde Basin
West Indies
Puerto Rico Trench
Barbuda
Leeward Islands
Antigua
NORTH AMERICAN PLATE
Barracuda Fracture Zone
SOUTH AMERICAN PLATE
Hispaniola
Puerto Rico
Nevis
Guadeloupe
Dominica
Lesser Antilles
Martinique
St Lucia
Venezuelan Basin
Grenada Basin
Barbados
Windward Islands
Grenada
Aves Ridge
Guiana Basin
MID-ATLANTIC RIDGE
Demerara Plain
Trinidad
CARIBBEAN PLATE
SOUTH AMERICAN PLATE
Demerara Plateau
Orinoco
Guiana Highlands
Equator
Amazon Fan
Amazon

Physical North America

The North American continent can be divided into a number of major structural areas: the Western Cordillera, the Canadian Shield, the Great Plains, and Central Lowlands, and the Appalachians. Other smaller regions include the Gulf Atlantic Coastal Plain which borders the southern coast of North America from the southern Appalachians to the Great Plains. This area includes the expanding Mississippi Delta. A chain of volcanic islands, running in an arc around the margin of the Caribbean Plate, lie to the east of the Gulf of Mexico.

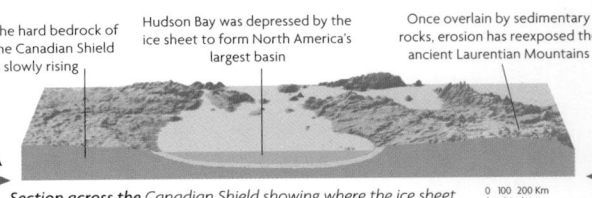

The Canadian Shield

Spanning northern Canada and Greenland, this geologically stable plain forms the heart of the continent, containing rocks more than two billion years old. A long history of weathering and repeated glaciation has scoured the region, leaving flat plains, gentle hummocks, numerous small basins and lakes, and the bays and islands of the Arctic.

The Western Cordillera

About 80 million years ago the Pacific and North American plates collided, uplifting the Western Cordillera. This consists of the Aleutian, Coast, Cascade, and Sierra Nevada mountains, and the inland Rocky Mountains. These run parallel from the Arctic to Mexico.

The weight of the ice sheet, 1.8 miles (3 km) thick, has depressed the land to 0.6 miles (1 km) below sea level

▲ This computer-generated view shows the ice-covered island of Greenland without its ice cap.

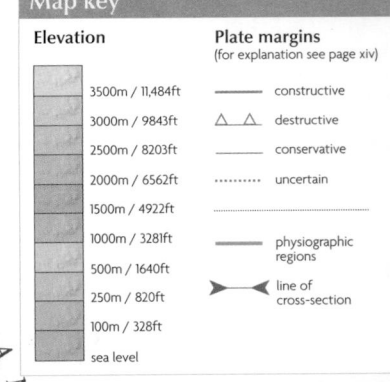

The hard bedrock of the Canadian Shield is slowly rising

Hudson Bay was depressed by the ice sheet to form North America's largest basin

Once overlain by sedimentary rocks, erosion has reexposed the ancient Laurentian Mountains

Section across the Canadian Shield showing where the ice sheet has depressed the underlying rock and formed bays and islands.

Strata have been thrust eastward along fault lines

Volcanic rock

The Rocky Mountain Trench is the longest linear fault on the continent

B   B

Cross-section through the Western Cordillera showing direction of mountain building.

Map key

Elevation

	3500m / 11,484ft
	3000m / 9843ft
	2500m / 8203ft
	2000m / 6562ft
	1500m / 4922ft
	1000m / 3281ft
	500m / 1640ft
	250m / 820ft
	100m / 328ft
	sea level

Plate margins
(for explanation see page xiv)

——	constructive
△ △	destructive
——	conservative
········	uncertain
——	physiographic regions
►◄	line of cross-section

Scale 1:42,000,000

projection: Lambert Azimuthal Equal Area

The Great Plains & Central Lowlands

Deposits left by retreating glaciers and rivers have made this vast flat area very fertile. In the north this is the result of glaciation, with deposits up to one mile (1.7 km) thick, covering the basement rock. To the south and west, the massive Missouri/Mississippi river system has for centuries deposited silt across the plains, creating broad, flat floodplains and deltas.

The Appalachians

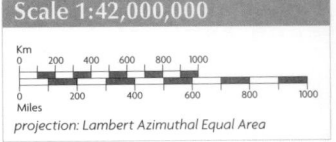

The Appalachian Mountains, uplifted about 400 million years ago, are some of the oldest in the world. They have been lowered and rounded by erosion and now slope gently toward the Atlantic across a broad coastal plain.

Horizontal strata

Sedimentary strata folded and faulted into ridges and valleys

Softer strata has been crumpled against the harder basement rock

Hard basement rock

C   C

Cross-section through the Appalachians showing the numerous folds, which have subsequently been weathered to create a rounded relief.

Sedimentary layers overlay domed basement rock

Upland rivers drain south toward the Mississippi Basin

Confluence of the Missouri and Mississippi Rivers

D   D

Section across the Great Plains and Central Lowlands showing river systems and structure.

Map labels

ASIA
Bering Strait
Beaufort Sea
Brooks Range
Mackenzie Delta
Mount McKinley 6194m
Mackenzie Mountains
Alaska Range
Aleutian Range
Mackenzie
Great Bear Lake
Bering Sea
Aleutian Islands
Gulf of Alaska
NORTH AMERICAN PLATE
PACIFIC PLATE
Coast Mountains
Great Slave Lake
Lake Athabasca
WESTERN CORDILLERA
CANADIAN SHIELD
Reindeer Lake
ROCKY MOUNTAINS
Lake Winnipeg
Lake Manitoba
CENTRAL LOWLANDS
Mount Rainier 4392m
Mount St Helens 2549m
Great Basin
Great Salt Lake
Sierra Nevada
San Joaquin
San Andreas Fault
Death Valley -86m
Mojave Desert
Colorado
Colorado Plateau
Grand Canyon
GREAT PLAINS
Sonoran Desert
Arkansas
Ohio
Missouri
Mississippi
Lake California
Gulf of California
Sierra Madre Occidental
Rio Grande
Sierra Madre Oriental
GULF ATLANTIC COASTAL PLAIN
Mississippi Delta
Gulf of Mexico
Volcán Pico de Orizaba 5700m
Sierra Madre del Sur
Yucatan Peninsula
Lake Nicaragua
Isthmus of Panama
PACIFIC OCEAN
COCOS PLATE
CARIBBEAN PLATE
Caribbean Sea
West Indies
Greater Antilles
Lesser Antilles
SOUTH AMERICAN PLATE
SOUTH AMERICA
Greenland
Baffin Bay
Baffin Island
Davis Strait
Foxe Basin
Hudson Strait
Labrador Sea
Labrador
ATLANTIC OCEAN
Hudson Bay
Laurentian Mountains
Newfoundland
Nova Scotia
Lake Superior
Lake Huron
Lake Ontario
Lake Erie
Lake Michigan
Great Lakes
St Lawrence
APPALACHIAN MOUNTAINS
APPALACHIANS
Cape Cod

Climate

North America's climate includes extremes ranging from freezing Arctic conditions in Alaska and Greenland, to desert in the southwest, and tropical conditions in southeastern Florida, the Caribbean, and Central America. Central and southern regions are prone to severe storms including tornadoes and hurricanes.

▲ *"Tornado alley" in the Mississippi Valley suffers frequent tornadoes.*

▲ *Much of the southwest is semi-desert; receiving less than 12 inches (300 mm) of rainfall a year.*

Climate

- ice cap
- tundra
- subarctic
- cool continental
- warm humid
- semiarid
- arid
- humid equatorial
- tropical

☼ daily hours of sunshine, January
☼ daily hours of sunshine, July
→ direction of hurricanes
🌀 tornado zones

Temperature

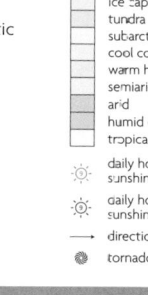
Average January temperature

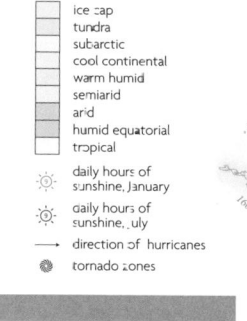
Average July temperature

Temperature
- below -30°C (-22°F)
- -30 to -20°C (-22 to -4°F)
- -20 to -10°C (-4 to 14°F)
- -10 to 0°C (14 to 32°F)
- 0 to 10°C (32 to 50°F)
- 10 to 20°C (50 to 68°F)
- 20 to 30°C (68 to 86°F)
- above 30°C (86°F)

Rainfall

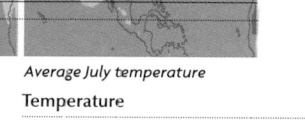
Average January rainfall

Average July rainfall

Rainfall
- 0–25 mm (0–1 in)
- 25–50 mm (1–2 in)
- 50–100 mm (2–4 in)
- 100–200 mm (4–8 in)
- 200–300 mm (8–12 in)
- 300–400 mm (12–16 in)
- 400–500 mm (16–20 in)
- more than 500 mm (20 in)

Cities labelled: Nome, Fairbanks, Aklavik, Kugluktuk, Resolute, Eismitte, Iqaluit, Haines Junction, Juneau, Fort Vermilion, Fort St John, Churchill, Happy Valley - Goose Bay, Torbay, Vancouver, Medicine Hat, Winnipeg, Montréal, Toronto, Boise, Sioux City, New York, Salt Lake City, Denver, San Francisco, Las Vegas, Atlanta, Cape Hatteras, Phoenix, Los Angeles, Little Rock, Houston, Guaymas, Chihuahua, New Orleans, Miami, Nassau, Santo Domingo, Fort-de-France, Mérida, Kingston, Acapulco, San Salvador, San José

◄ *The lush, green mountains of the Lesser Antilles receive annual rainfalls of up to 360 inches (9000 mm).*

Shaping the continent

Glacial processes affect much of northern Canada, Greenland, and the Western Cordillera. Along the western coast of North America, Central America, and the Caribbean, underlying plates moving together lead to earthquakes and volcanic eruptions. The vast river systems, fed by mountain streams, constantly erode and deposit material along their paths.

Volcanic activity

1 Mount St. Helens volcano (right) in the Cascade Range erupted violently in May 1980, killing 57 people and leveling large areas of forest. The lateral blast filled a valley with debris for 15 miles (25 km).

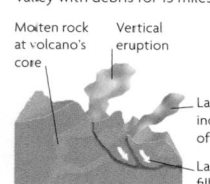

- Molten rock at volcano's core
- Vertical eruption
- Lateral explosion increases extent of damage
- Landslide fills valley

Volcanic activity: Eruption of Mount St Helens

Seismic activity

5 The San Andreas Fault (above) places much of the North America's west coast under constant threat from earthquakes. It is caused by the Pacific Plate grinding past the North American Plate at a faster rate, though in the same direction.

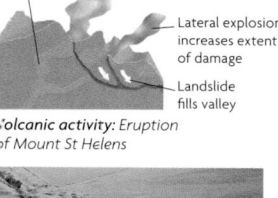

- Pacific Plate
- San Andreas Fault
- Fault is caused by faster movement of Pacific Plate
- North American Plate

Seismic activity: Action of the San Andreas Fault

River erosion

6 The Grand Canyon (above) in the Colorado Plateau was created by the downward erosion of the Colorado River, combined with the gradual uplift of the plateau, over the past 30 million years. The contours of the canyon formed as the softer rock layers eroded into gentle slopes, and the hard rock layers into cliffs. The depth varies from 3855–6560 ft (1175–2000 m).

Periglaciation

2 The ground in the far north is nearly always frozen: the surface thaws only in summer. This freeze-thaw process produces features such as pingos (left); formed by the freezing of groundwater. With each successive winter ice accumulates producing a mound with a core of ice.

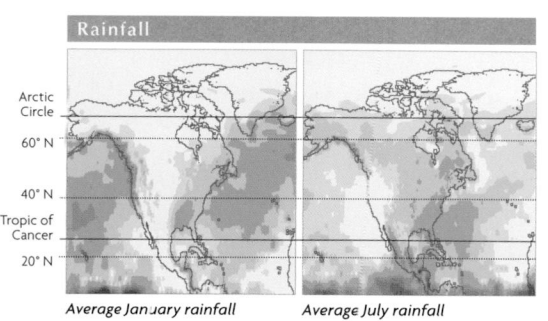

- Ice core pushes up ground to form pingo
- Unfrozen lake
- Groundwater attracted to ice core

Periglaciation: Formation of a pingo in the Mackenzie Delta

The evolving landscape

Landscape
- limestone region
- sinking land
- stable land
- uplifting land

▲ active volcano
⋯ area of tectonic activity
--- limit of permafrost
— maximum limit of glaciation
→ ocean current

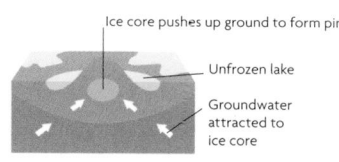

- Soft rock is easily eroded into gentle slopes
- Hard rock resists erosion
- Colorado River cuts down through rock

River Erosion: Formation of the Grand Canyon

Post-glacial lakes

3 A chain of lakes from Great Bear Lake to the Great Lakes (above) was created as the ice retreated northward. Glaciers scoured hollows in the softer lowland rock. Glacial deposits at the lip of the hollows, and ridges of harder rock, trapped water to form lakes.

- Retreating glacier
- Ice-scoured hollow filled with glacial meltwater to form a lake
- Harder rock creates a barrier between lakes
- Softer lowland rock

Post-glacial lakes: Formation of the Great Lakes

Weathering

4 The Yucatan Peninsula is a vast, flat limestone plateau in southern Mexico. Weathering action from both rainwater and underground streams has enlarged fractures in the rock to form caves and hollows, called sinkholes (above).

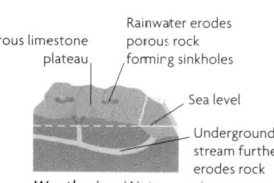

- Rainwater erodes porous rock forming sinkholes
- Porous limestone plateau
- Sea level
- Underground stream further erodes rock

Weathering: Water erosion on the Yucatan Peninsula

Political North America

Democracy is well established in some parts of the continent but is a recent phenomenon in others. The economically dominant nations of Canada and the US have a long democratic tradition but elsewhere, notably in the countries of Central America, political turmoil has been more common. In Nicaragua and Haiti, harsh dictatorships have only recently been superseded by democratically elected governments. North America's largest countries, Canada, Mexico, and the US have federal state systems, sharing political power between national and state governments. The US has intervened militarily on several occasions in Central America and the Caribbean to protect its strategic interests.

Transportation

In the 19th century, railroads opened up the North American continent. Air transportation is now more common for long distance passenger travel, although railroads are still extensively used for bulk freight transportation. Waterways like the Mississippi River are important for the transportation of bulk materials, and the Panama Canal is a vital link between the Pacific and Atlantic Oceans. In the 20th century, road transportation increased massively, with the introduction of cheap, mass-produced motor cars and extensive highway construction.

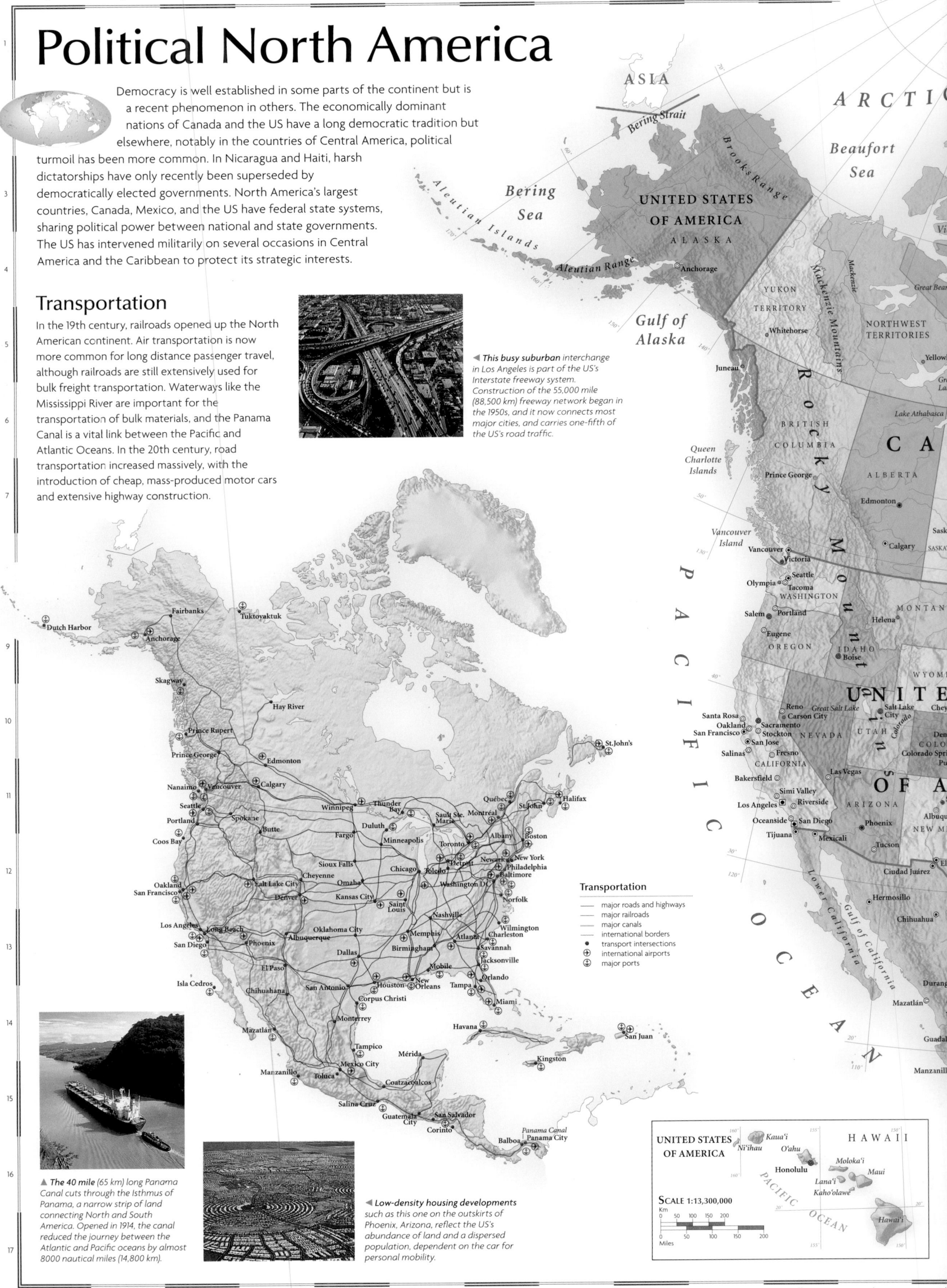

◀ *This busy suburban interchange in Los Angeles is part of the US's Interstate freeway system. Construction of the 55,000 mile (88,500 km) freeway network began in the 1950s, and it now connects most major cities, and carries one-fifth of the US's road traffic.*

Transportation

- ⋯⋯⋯ major roads and highways
- ─── major railroads
- ─── major canals
- ─── international borders
- ● transport intersections
- ⊕ international airports
- ⊕ major ports

UNITED STATES OF AMERICA

SCALE 1:13,300,000

Km 0 50 100 150 200
Miles 0 50 100 150 200

▲ *The 40 mile (65 km) long Panama Canal cuts through the Isthmus of Panama, a narrow strip of land connecting North and South America. Opened in 1914, the canal reduced the journey between the Atlantic and Pacific oceans by almost 8000 nautical miles (14,800 km).*

◀ *Low-density housing developments such as this one on the outskirts of Phoenix, Arizona, reflect the US's abundance of land and a dispersed population, dependent on the car for personal mobility.*

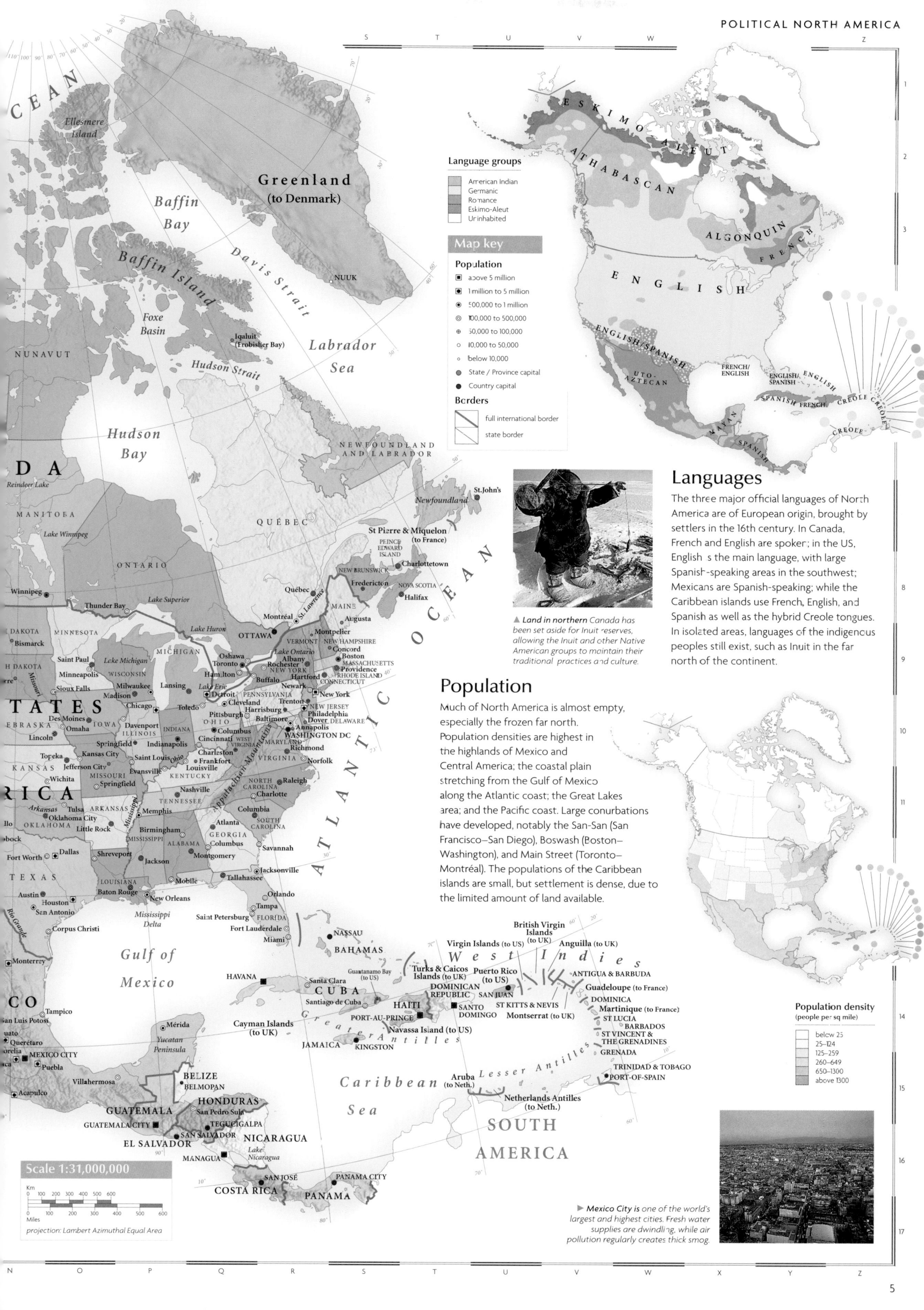

Languages

The three major official languages of North America are of European origin, brought by settlers in the 16th century. In Canada, French and English are spoken; in the US, English is the main language, with large Spanish-speaking areas in the southwest; Mexicans are Spanish-speaking; while the Caribbean islands use French, English, and Spanish as well as the hybrid Creole tongues. In isolated areas, languages of the indigenous peoples still exist, such as Inuit in the far north of the continent.

▲ *Land in northern Canada has been set aside for Inuit reserves, allowing the Inuit and other Native American groups to maintain their traditional practices and culture.*

Population

Much of North America is almost empty, especially the frozen far north. Population densities are highest in the highlands of Mexico and Central America; the coastal plain stretching from the Gulf of Mexico along the Atlantic coast; the Great Lakes area; and the Pacific coast. Large conurbations have developed, notably the San-San (San Francisco–San Diego), Boswash (Boston–Washington), and Main Street (Toronto–Montréal). The populations of the Caribbean islands are small, but settlement is dense, due to the limited amount of land available.

▶ *Mexico City is one of the world's largest and highest cities. Fresh water supplies are dwindling, while air pollution regularly creates thick smog.*

Language groups
- American Indian
- Germanic
- Romance
- Eskimo-Aleut
- Uninhabited

Map key

Population
- above 5 million
- 1 million to 5 million
- 500,000 to 1 million
- 100,000 to 500,000
- 50,000 to 100,000
- 10,000 to 50,000
- below 10,000
- State / Province capital
- Country capital

Borders
- full international border
- state border

Population density
(people per sq mile)
- below 25
- 25–124
- 125–259
- 260–649
- 650–1300
- above 1300

Scale 1:31,000,000

projection: Lambert Azimuthal Equal Area

North American resources

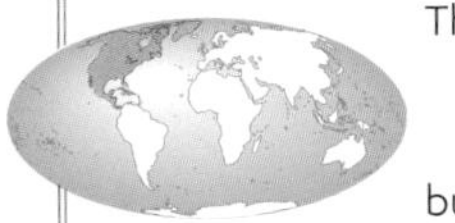

The two northern countries of Canada and the US are richly endowed with natural resources that have helped to fuel economic development. The US is the world's largest economy, although today it is facing stiff competition from the Far East. Mexico has relied on oil revenues but there are hopes that the North American Free Trade Agreement (NAFTA), will encourage trade growth with Canada and the US. The poorer countries of Central America and the Caribbean depend largely on cash crops and tourism.

Standard of living

The US and Canada have one of the highest overall standards of living in the world. However, many people still live in poverty, especially in urban ghettos and some rural areas. Central America and the Caribbean are markedly poorer than their wealthier northern neighbors. Haiti is the poorest country in the western hemisphere.

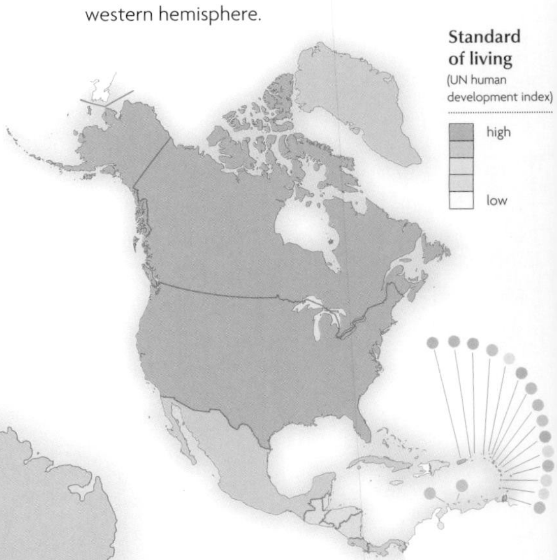

Industry

The modern, industrialized economies of the US and Canada contrast sharply with those of Mexico, Central America, and the Caribbean. Manufacturing is especially important in the US; vehicle production is concentrated around the Great Lakes, while electronic and hi-tech industries are increasingly found in the western and southern states. Mexico depends on oil exports and assembly work, taking advantage of cheap labor. Many Central American and Caribbean countries rely heavily on agricultural exports.

◀ *After its purchase* from Russia in 1867, Alaska's frozen lands were largely ignored by the US. Oil reserves similar in magnitude to those in eastern Texas were discovered in Prudhoe Bay, Alaska in 1968. Freezing temperatures and a fragile environment hamper oil extraction.

Standard of living
(UN human development index)

high

low

▲ *Fish such as* cod, flounder, and plaice are caught in the Grand Banks, off the Newfoundland coast, and processed in many North Atlantic coastal settlements.

▲ *South of San Francisco,* "Silicon Valley" is both a national and international center for hi-tech industries, electronic industries, and research institutions.

▲ *Multinational companies rely* on cheap labor and tax benefits to facilitate the assembly of vehicle parts in Mexican factories.

▲ *The health of* the Wall Street stock market in New York is the standard measure of the state of the world's economy.

Map labels

ARCTIC OCEAN
Beaufort Sea
Bering Strait
RUSS. FED.
Bering Sea
Prudhoe Bay
USA
Gulf of Alaska
Baffin Bay
Greenland (to Denmark)
Labrador Sea
Hudson Strait
Hudson Bay
PACIFIC OCEAN
CANADA
Vancouver
Calgary
Seattle
Winnipeg
Portland
Montréal
Minneapolis
Toronto
Boston
Milwaukee
Buffalo
Albany
Detroit
Cleveland
New York
UNITED STATES
Chicago
Pittsburgh
Baltimore
Philadelphia
OF AMERICA
Dayton
Cincinnati
San Francisco
Denver
Kansas City
Saint Louis
Wichita
Greensboro
Nashville
Charlotte
Los Angeles
Phoenix
Tulsa
Atlanta
San Diego
Birmingham
Tijuana
Dallas
Ciudad Juárez
El Paso
Jacksonville
Houston
New Orleans
Orlando
ATLANTIC OCEAN
Tampa
Miami
Monterrey
Gulf of Mexico
MEXICO
West Indies
Guadalajara
Havana
CUBA
BAHAMAS
Virgin Islands (to US)
British Virgin Islands (to UK)
ANGUILLA (to UK)
ST KITTS & NEVIS
ANTIGUA & BARBUDA
Turks & Caicos Islands (to UK)
Puerto Rico (to US)
MONTSERRAT (to UK)
Guadeloupe (to France)
DOMINICA
Martinique (to France)
ST LUCIA
BARBADOS
ST VINCENT & THE GRENADINES
GRENADA
Port-of-Spain
TRINIDAD & TOBAGO
San Juan
DOMINICAN REPUBLIC
Santo Domingo
HAITI
Port-au-Prince
Cayman Islands (to UK)
JAMAICA
Greater Antilles
Navassa Island (to US)
Lesser Antilles
Aruba (to Neth.)
Netherlands Antilles (to Neth.)
Caribbean Sea
VENEZUELA
Mexico City
BELIZE
GUATEMALA
Guatemala City
HONDURAS
Tegucigalpa
EL SALVADOR
San Salvador
NICARAGUA
Managua
San José
COSTA RICA
Panama City
PANAMA
COLOMBIA

Industry

- ✈ aerospace
- brewing
- car/vehicle manufacture
- chemicals
- defense
- electronics
- engineering
- film industry
- $ finance
- food processing
- hi-tech industry
- iron & steel
- pharmaceuticals
- printing & publishing
- research & development
- shipbuilding
- sugar processing
- textiles
- timber processing
- tobacco processing
- coal
- oil
- gas
- industrial cities
- major industrial areas

GNI per capita (US$)

- below 1999
- 2000–4999
- 5000–9999
- 10,000–19,999
- 20,000–24,999
- above 25,000

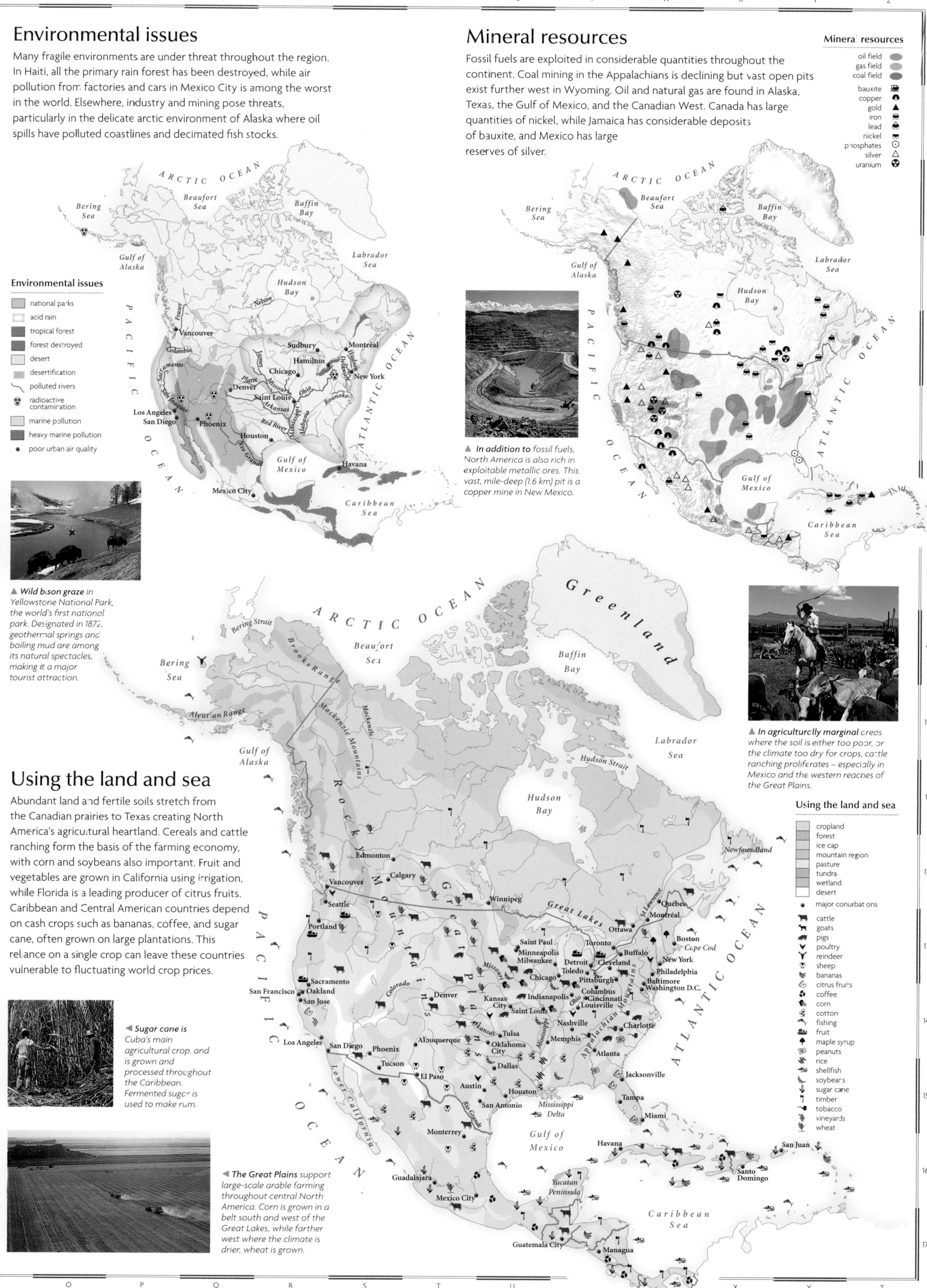

Environmental issues

Many fragile environments are under threat throughout the region. In Haiti, all the primary rain forest has been destroyed, while air pollution from factories and cars in Mexico City is among the worst in the world. Elsewhere, industry and mining pose threats, particularly in the delicate arctic environment of Alaska where oil spills have polluted coastlines and decimated fish stocks.

Environmental issues
- national parks
- acid rain
- tropical forest
- forest destroyed
- desert
- desertification
- polluted rivers
- radioactive contamination
- marine pollution
- heavy marine pollution
- poor urban air quality

▲ **Wild bison graze** in Yellowstone National Park, the world's first national park. Designated in 1872, geothermal springs and boiling mud are among its natural spectacles, making it a major tourist attraction.

Mineral resources

Fossil fuels are exploited in considerable quantities throughout the continent. Coal mining in the Appalachians is declining but vast open pits exist further west in Wyoming. Oil and natural gas are found in Alaska, Texas, the Gulf of Mexico, and the Canadian West. Canada has large quantities of nickel, while Jamaica has considerable deposits of bauxite, and Mexico has large reserves of silver.

Mineral resources
- oil field
- gas field
- coal field
- bauxite
- copper
- gold
- iron
- lead
- nickel
- phosphates
- silver
- uranium

▲ **In addition to** fossil fuels, North America is also rich in exploitable metallic ores. This vast, mile-deep (1.6 km) pit is a copper mine in New Mexico.

▲ **In agriculturally marginal areas** where the soil is either too poor, or the climate too dry for crops, cattle ranching proliferates – especially in Mexico and the western reaches of the Great Plains.

Using the land and sea

Abundant land and fertile soils stretch from the Canadian prairies to Texas creating North America's agricultural heartland. Cereals and cattle ranching form the basis of the farming economy, with corn and soybeans also important. Fruit and vegetables are grown in California using irrigation, while Florida is a leading producer of citrus fruits. Caribbean and Central American countries depend on cash crops such as bananas, coffee, and sugar cane, often grown on large plantations. This reliance on a single crop can leave these countries vulnerable to fluctuating world crop prices.

Using the land and sea
- cropland
- forest
- ice cap
- mountain region
- pasture
- tundra
- wetland
- desert
- major conurbations
- cattle
- goats
- pigs
- poultry
- reindeer
- sheep
- bananas
- citrus fruits
- coffee
- corn
- cotton
- fishing
- fruit
- maple syrup
- peanuts
- rice
- shellfish
- soybeans
- sugar cane
- timber
- tobacco
- vineyards
- wheat

◄ **Sugar cane is** Cuba's main agricultural crop, and is grown and processed throughout the Caribbean. Fermented sugar is used to make rum.

◄ **The Great Plains** support large-scale arable farming throughout central North America. Corn is grown in a belt south and west of the Great Lakes, while farther west where the climate is drier, wheat is grown.

Canada

Canada is the second largest country in the world, and with only about one-tenth of its land area inhabited, it is one of the most sparsely populated. Canada became a confederation in 1867, though Newfoundland did not join until 1949. As a founding member of the UN and of the Commonwealth, Canada has played an important role in international affairs. A constitutional crisis, focusing on the French-speaking Québécois, and Inuit, and Native American land rights, dominated politics in the 1990s. In 1999, part of the Northwest Territories, Nunavut, became a self-governing homeland for the Inuit.

◀ *The Selwyn Mountains* in northwestern Canada form part of the Rocky Mountains. The highest point, Keele Peak, rises to 9750 ft (2972 m).

Transportation and industry

Abundant energy in the form of coal, oil, natural gas, and hydroelectric power underpins Canadian industry. Over 75% of manufacturing is concentrated in the Great Lakes–St. Lawrence region, including prospering aerospace, transportation, and hi-tech industries. Across Canada as a whole, manufacturing has developed around a diversified, high-quality resource base and a wide range of metallic and nonmetallic minerals.

◀ *Canada has one* of the world's highest rates of energy consumption per person. It is endowed with vast hydroelectric potential from which more than 60% of its electricity requirements are generated.

Major industry and infrastructure

- ✈ aerospace
- 🚗 car manufacture
- 🧪 chemicals
- ⚙ engineering
- 🍴 food processing
- 💻 hi-tech industry
- ⚡ hydroelectric power
- 🛢 oil & gas
- ⛏ mining
- 🌲 timber processing
- ● capital cities
- • major towns
- ✈ international airports
- — major roads
- ▨ major industrial areas

Transportation network

🛣	309,019 miles (497,375 km)	🛣	10,500 miles (16,900 km)
🚆	8049 miles (12,995 km)	⚡	1864 miles (3000 km)

In recent years the road network has been expanded, especially links to remote areas. Meanwhile, for long-distance travel, air transportation now supersedes the declining rail network, which focuses mainly on east–west routes.

Using the land and sea

The majority of Canada's agricultural land is found in the prairies, which cover 140 million acres (57 million ha) and support wheat and grain-fed cattle. More specialized crops, such as fruit and vegetables, are grown in pockets of agricultural land in the east and west. Of Canada's many islands, only Prince Edward Island has notable farmland. Further north, boreal forests, exploited for timber, run in an almost unbroken arc, giving way to uncultivable tundra and ice sheets in the far north.

The urban/rural population divide

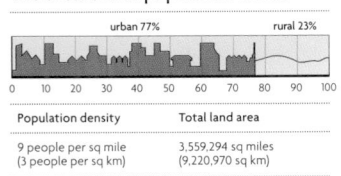

urban 77%   rural 23%

0 10 20 30 40 50 60 70 80 90 100

Population density	Total land area
9 people per sq mile (3 people per sq km)	3,559,294 sq miles (9,220,970 sq km)

Land use and agricultural distribution

- 🐄 cattle
- 🌾 cereals
- 🐟 fishing
- 🍒 fruit
- 🌲 timber
- ■ capital cities
- • major towns

- pasture
- cropland
- forest
- wetland
- mountain region
- barren
- tundra

◀ *The climate and* topography of the prairies makes them ideally suited to farming. Long summer days, moderate temperatures, limited rainfall, and flat plains provide excellent conditions for wheat farming.

Scale 1:14,700,000

Km 0 25 50 75 100 150 200 250 300 350
Miles 0 25 50 100 150 200 250 300

projection: Lambert Azimuthal Equal Area

The landscape

Glaciers on islands in the Arctic Ocean are the last remnants of the ice sheet that once covered and shaped Canada. Hudson Bay is the center of the Canadian Shield, a huge, eroded plateau marked at its southern extremity by a string of lakes running southeastward from Great Bear Lake to the Great Lakes. In contrast to the rolling relief of the Shield and the central lowland region, the Rocky Mountains rise to peaks of over 13,000 ft (4000 m), stretching 500 miles (800 km) along the west coast.

► **Permanently frozen ground** known as permafrost is common in Canada's northern tundra. It thickens farther north, becoming hundreds of yards deep in parts of the Arctic.

Permanently frozen ground

Top layer thaws in the summer

Marginal areas of permafrost thaw in summer

Unfrozen ground where temperature is more moderate

The Mackenzie river, flowing north over the permafrost, forms a wide river channel with many tributaries. Together with the Peel river it has created a long, narrow delta at its mouth. The entire river freezes during the winter.

Fertile prairies stretch from the southern rim of the Canadian Shield, south into the US.

Exposure to three phases of mountain-building and subsequent erosion over millions of years has molded the ancient Canadian Shield into a series of basins and ridges.

▲ **Along the northeastern** coast of Baffin Island the mountains rise to 8000 ft (2440 m). Glaciers move down through the valleys to the sea, eroding wide U-shaped valleys.

Great Bear Lake

The Rocky Mountains were formed some 80 million years ago, when the Pacific plate was driven under the North American plate, forcing up the land.

The Great Lakes lie on the Canada–US border. The basins they now occupy were fashioned by repeated ice advance. At one time, Lakes Superior, Huron, and Michigan formed a single large lake, Lake Nipissing.

The St. Lawrence River is 2350 miles (3782 km) long. It flows from the western shore of Lake Superior through the Great Lakes and on to the Atlantic Ocean. From December to April, the St. Lawrence Seaway freezes between Lake Ontario and Montréal.

► **The Great Lakes** are drained by the St. Lawrence River which flows down through a wide tectonic depression. It forms a broad estuary for much of its course, the width varying from 1.2 miles (1.9 km) in the upper reaches to 90 miles (145 km) at its mouth.

Isolated pillars, known as hoodoos near Red Deer river in the badlands of Alberta are a product of wind and water erosion, especially flash floods. The badlands lie in the rain shadow of the Rocky Mountains, which creates a semiarid climate.

Map key

Population
- ⊙ 1 million to 5 million
- ⊙ 500,000 to 1 million
- ⊙ 100,000 to 500,000
- ⊕ 50,000 to 100,000
- ○ 10,000 to 50,000
- ○ below 10,000

Elevation
- 6000m / 19,686ft
- 4000m / 13,124ft
- 3000m / 9843ft
- 2000m / 6562ft
- 1000m / 3281ft
- 500m / 1640ft
- 250m / 820ft
- 100m / 328ft
- sea level

Canada:
WESTERN PROVINCES

Alberta, British Columbia, Manitoba,
Saskatchewan, Yukon Territory

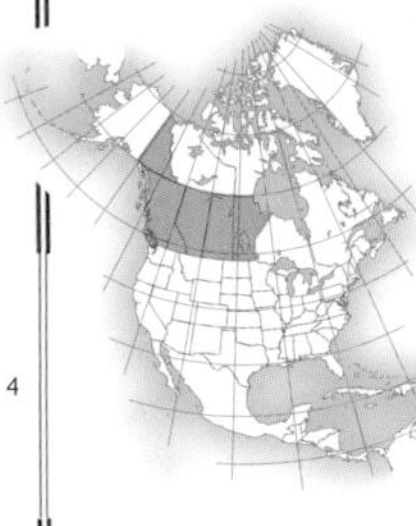

The mountains of the west coast, incorporating British Columbia
and the Yukon Territory, descend into the vast, flat prairies of
Alberta, Saskatchewan, and Manitoba. The empty lands and
fertile soils of the prairie provinces attracted migrants, and
the descendants of early European immigrants still make up
a large proportion of the population. The mechanization
of agriculture has reduced the need for labor, and rural
population densities remain low. The majority of the
people live within 100 miles (160 km) of the southern
Canada–US border, and in British Columbia, one of the leading Canadian
provinces in terms of economic wealth. The Yukon Territory, in the far
north, remains a relatively unspoiled wilderness, containing large,
untapped mineral reserves. This province has a significant population of
Native American people, many of whom maintain a traditional lifestyle.

Using the land and sea

Wheat farming is the economic mainstay of Alberta, Manitoba, and
Saskatchewan, which contain 82% of farmland in Canada. Cattle
are also raised on the prairies. Forestry and fishing are the most
prominent resource-based industries in British Columbia. Despite
the mountainous terrain, fruit and specialized grains can be grown
in the Okanagan and Fraser valleys.

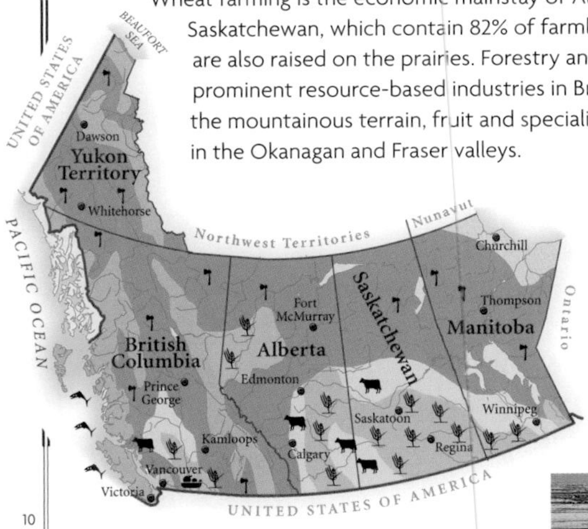

Land use and agricultural distribution

- cattle
- cereals
- fishing
- fruit
- timber
- major towns

- pasture
- cropland
- forest
- wetland
- barren
- tundra

The urban/rural population divide

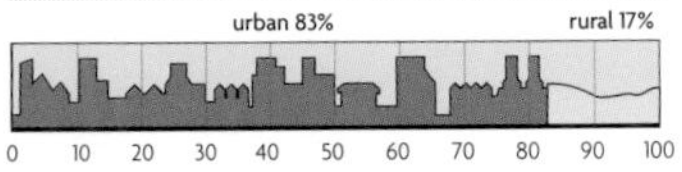

urban 83%   rural 17%

0 10 20 30 40 50 60 70 80 90 100

Population density	Total land area
8 people per sq mile (3 people per sq km)	1,230,547 sq miles (3,187,120 sq km)

▲ Large, highly-mechanized and
often very specialized farms,
requiring huge investment but little
labor, characterize modern
farming in the prairies.

Transportation & industry

The western provinces contain a wealth of mineral resources.
Alberta holds the bulk of Canada's fossil fuels; the other
provinces contain reserves of metallic ores, such as zinc, lead,
and silver. Isolation from markets has slowed the development
of manufacturing, restricting it to the large cities like Vancouver,
Winnipeg, and Calgary. Hydroelectric power is widely exploited,
although there is increasing concern about potential
ecological damage.

Transportation network

82,438 miles (135,145 km)	
6459 miles (10,401 km)	
24,041 miles (38,694 km)	
None	

The transportation network of
the western provinces is
dominated by east–west routes
that weave through mountain
passes and spread across the
plains. Access to some northern
areas is restricted to air travel.

Major industry and infrastructure

- aerospace
- chemicals
- coal
- engineering
- food processing
- hydroelectric power
- mining
- oil & gas
- timber processing

- major towns
- international airports
- major roads
- major industrial areas

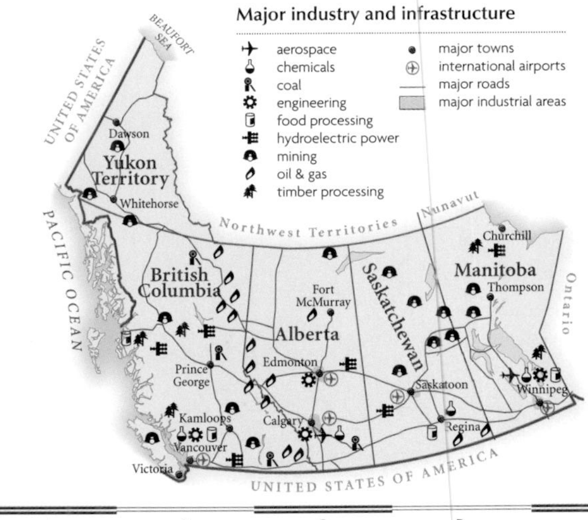

▲ The Fraser River valley is a major
area of settlement in British
Columbia. Railroads cross the
Rocky Mountains via this valley.

▲ Established in 1907,
Jasper National Park lies
in the heart of the Rocky
Mountains. It is noted for
its spectacular alpine
scenery and contains
part of the large
Columbia Icefield.

◀ Much of the Yukon Territory
is uninhabited tundra. Industry
is based on the extraction of
mineral resources, and to a
lesser extent, on the scattered
forests of the south.

The landscape

The massive Rocky Mountains form a continental divide between rivers flowing eastward and westward. The interior plains lie east of the mountains, stretching from the Arctic Circle south into the US. Covered with glacial deposits from the last Ice Age, these are interspersed with hilly regions and long, steep escarpments.

Map key

Population
- 500,000 to 1 million
- 100,000 to 500,000
- 50,000 to 100,000
- 10,000 to 50,000
- below 10,000

Elevation
- 6000m / 19,686ft
- 4000m / 13,124ft
- 3000m / 9843ft
- 2000m / 6562ft
- 1000m / 3281ft
- 500m / 1640ft
- 250m / 820ft
- 100m / 328ft
- sea level

Scale 1:8,250,000

projection: Lambert Conformal Conic

Mount Logan rises 19,551 ft (5959 m). It is the highest peak in Canada.

The Columbia Icefield in the Rocky Mountains is the source of two major rivers, the Athabasca and the North Saskatchewan.

Vegetated island — Bar
River flow is diverted by deposited sediments — Sand flat

▲ Braided rivers are shallow and fast-flowing. The interlaced branches are formed when excess sediments, which can no longer be transported, are deposited. The sediments collect in the river channel forming bars and sand flats. Islands form when the bars are colonized by vegetation.

The badlands of Alberta were created when east-flowing rivers, swollen by meltwater at the end of the last Ice Age, cut deep, wide canyons producing eroded, barren landscapes.

South Saskatchewan River

▲ Across the tundra of northern Manitoba, widespread permafrost inhibits water from permeating the soil. This causes rivers like the Churchill to flow in many channels, which can be frozen for up to six months during the winter.

The Nelson and Churchill rivers drain northward across the Canadian Shield to Hudson Bay. The shield covers three-fifths of Saskatchewan.

Setting Lake

The Rocky Mountain Trench is the longest linear fault in the world. It has formed a straight, flat-bottomed valley between 2–9 miles (4–15 km) wide, and up to 3280 ft (1000 m) deep.

Hundreds of islands dot the fjord-indented coast of British Columbia; the largest is Vancouver Island.

Three major passes cut through the Rocky Mountains: Yellowhead, Kicking Horse, and Crowsnest. They are all used as transportation routes through the mountains.

The Cypress Hills rise to 4806 ft (1465 m) above the surrounding plain. Having escaped the last glaciation they contain unique plant and animal life. The silvery lupine, bunchberry, and lodgepole pine all grow in the cool, moist climate of the hills.

The Alberta and Saskatchewan plains bear strong testament to past glaciations. The Assiniboine, Saskatchewan and Qu'Appelle rivers occupy flat-bottomed, steep-sided valleys eroded during the last Ice Age by glacial meltwater.

▲ Ancient granite outcrops, part of the Canadian Shield, rise above the surface of Setting Lake, which was initially formed by meltwater from the last Ice Age.

The lowlands of Manitoba are a basin that once held the vast post-glacial Lake Agassiz, remnants of which include Lake Winnipeg, Lake Winnipegosis, and Lake Manitoba.

Canada: EASTERN PROVINCES

New Brunswick, Newfoundland & Labrador, Nova Scotia, Ontario, Prince Edward Island, Québec, *St Pierre & Miquelon (to France)*

Colonized by both the English and the French during the 16th century, Canada's eastern provinces are still marked by their dual influences. They contain the last fragment of once-sizeable French territories, the islands of St. Pierre and Miquelon. French remains Canada's second official language and Québec's first language. The population of the eastern provinces is highly concentrated in the south, especially along the border with the US. A recent decline in fishing in the Atlantic provinces has encouraged a steady flow of westerly migration to more prosperous regions. The north, around Hudson Bay, remains snow-covered for most of the year and the indigenous Inuit people make up the bulk of its sparse population.

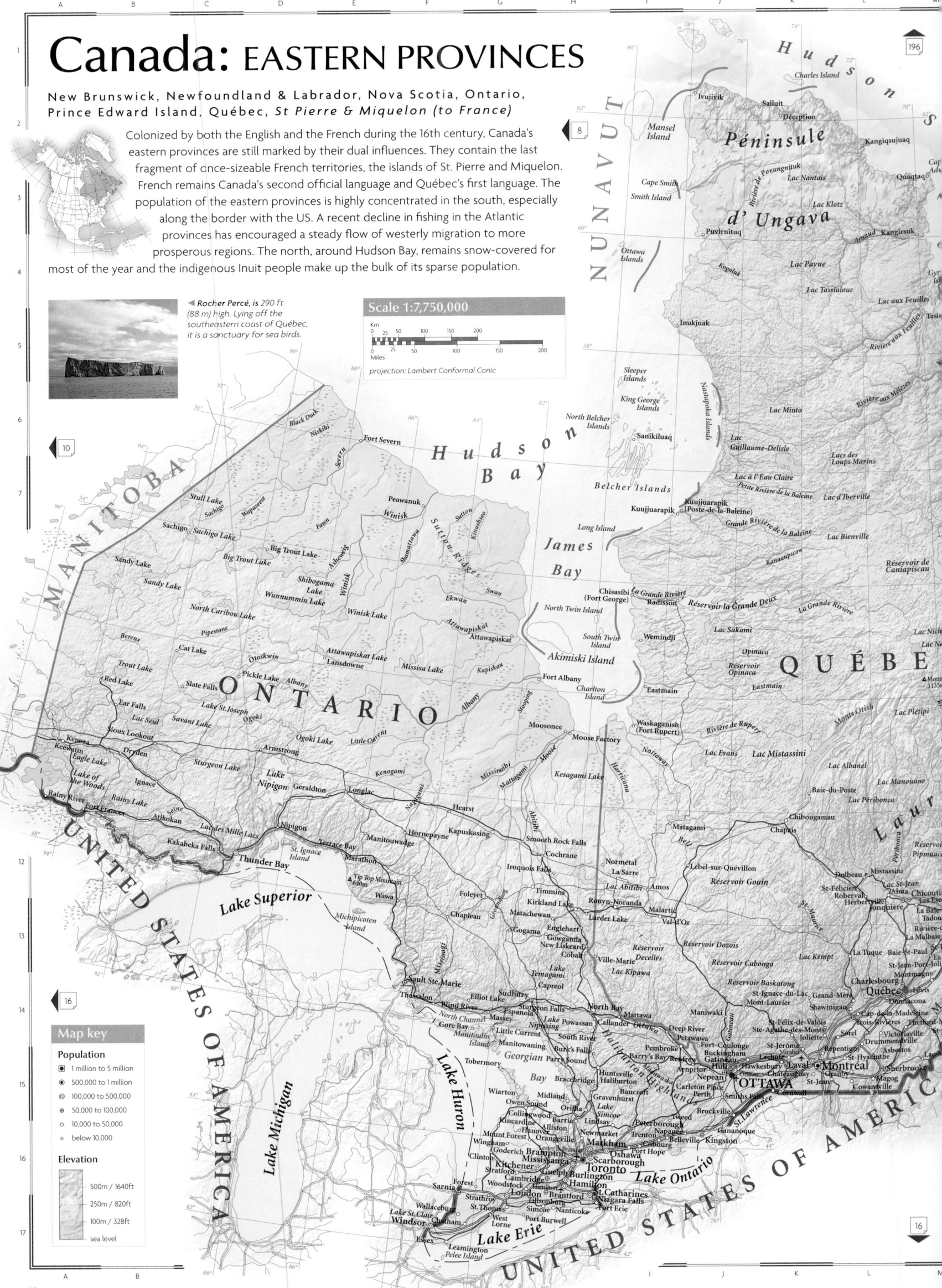

◀ *Rocher Percé, is 290 ft (88 m) high. Lying off the southeastern coast of Québec, it is a sanctuary for sea birds.*

Scale 1:7,750,000

projection: Lambert Conformal Conic

Map key

Population
- ◉ 1 million to 5 million
- ◎ 500,000 to 1 million
- ◉ 100,000 to 500,000
- ◉ 50,000 to 100,000
- ○ 10,000 to 50,000
- ∘ below 10,000

Elevation
- 500m / 1640ft
- 250m / 820ft
- 100m / 328ft
- sea level

The landscape

Much of eastern Canada is part of the Canadian Shield. Glaciers have scoured the land leaving deposits that have dammed and diverted streams, to create a rocky landscape strewn with lakes and swamps. Much of the ground is subject to permafrost, which further impedes drainage. The uplands in the far east are the most northerly extension of the Appalachian mountain chain.

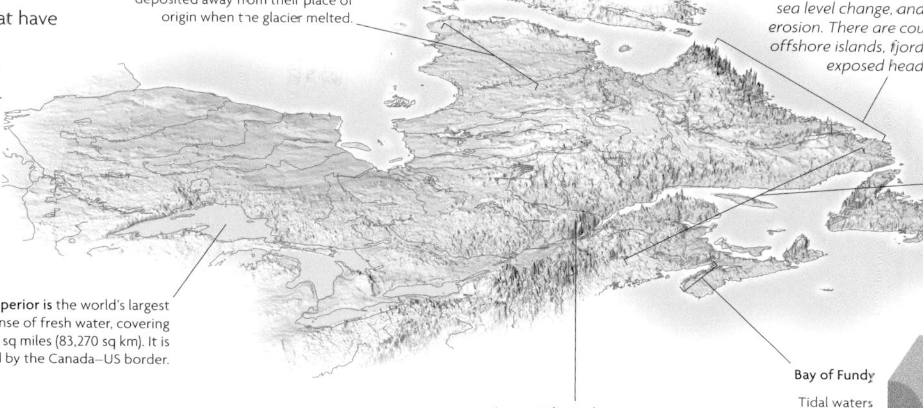

The Péninsule d'Ungava is littered with erratics – isolated rocks which were carried by glaciers and deposited away from their place of origin when the glacier melted.

Lake Superior is the world's largest expanse of fresh water, covering 32,150 sq miles (83,270 sq km). It is crossed by the Canada–US border.

Laurentides Park

Bay of Fundy

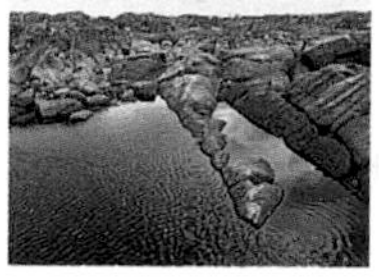

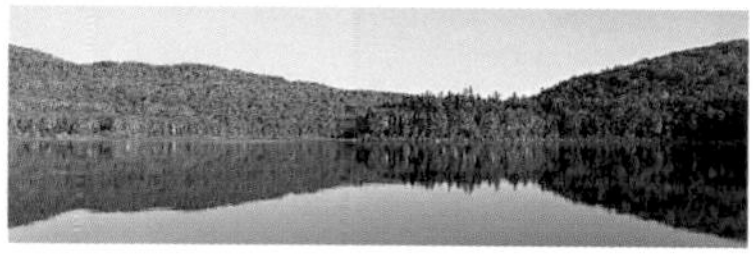

The eroded highlands of New Brunswick, Nova Scotia and Newfoundland are part of the Appalachian mountain chain, formed over 400 million years ago.

▶ *Labrador's indented coast is a product of past glaciations, which caused sea level change, and wave erosion. There are countless offshore islands, fjords, and exposed headlands.*

▶ *The forested Laurentides Park incorporates part of the Laurentian Mountains. Within its boundaries are over 1600 lakes*

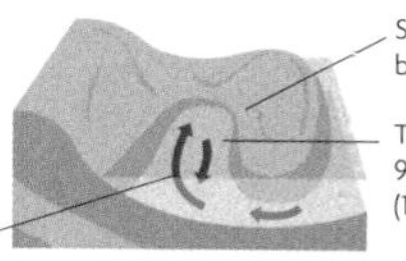

Steep cliffs bound the bay
The bay is 94 miles (151 km) long
Tidal waters are channeled down the bay

▲ *At the Bay of Fundy, incoming waves are funneled down the long, narrow, steep-sided bay. These topographical features cause fast-flowing tides which can rise 70 ft (21 m).*

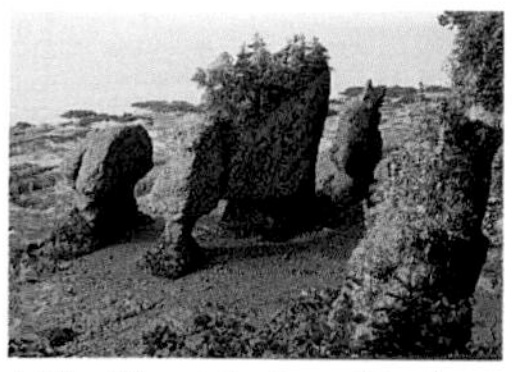

▲ *The tides at the Bay of Fundy are among the highest in the world. At low tide the tree-topped rocks have been likened to flowerpots.*

Transportation & industry

Both Québec and Ontario have a diversified manufacturing sector located in the south. Across the rest of the region, industry is largely based around local resources, which accounts for the large number of fish and timber processing plants and mines. Many of the fast-flowing rivers are also gradually being harnessed for hydroelectric power.

LABRADOR SEA
Hudson Bay
Manitoba
Ontario
Québec
Schefferville
Thunder Bay
Sault Ste. Marie
OTTAWA
Toronto
Montréal
Québec
Newfoundland & Labrador
St. John's
New Brunswick
Prince Edward Island
Nova Scotia
Halifax
ATLANTIC OCEAN
UNITED STATES OF AMERICA

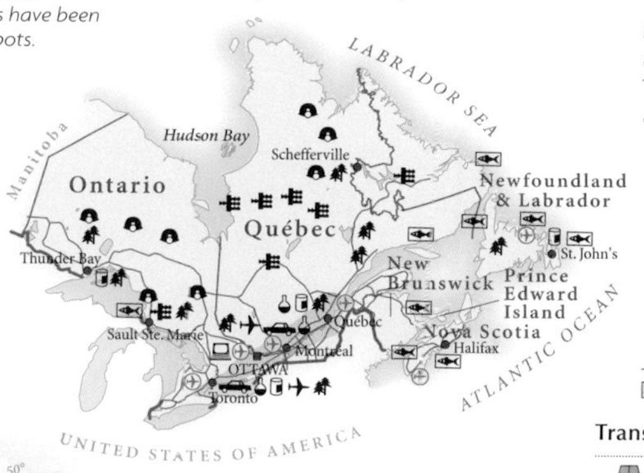

Major industry and infrastructure

- aerospace
- vehicle manufacture
- chemicals
- fish processing
- food processing
- hi-tech industry
- hydroelectric power
- mining
- timber processing
- capital cities
- major towns
- international airports
- major roads
- major industrial areas

Transportation network

- 84,522 miles (136,325 km)
- 1858 miles (2998 km)
- 20,602 miles (33,159 km)
- 376 miles (606 km)

The majority of Canada's large ports lie in the east. Since the 1960s the region's rail network has been steadily reduced; Newfoundland recently lost its last remaining line, the Long-Cross Island line.

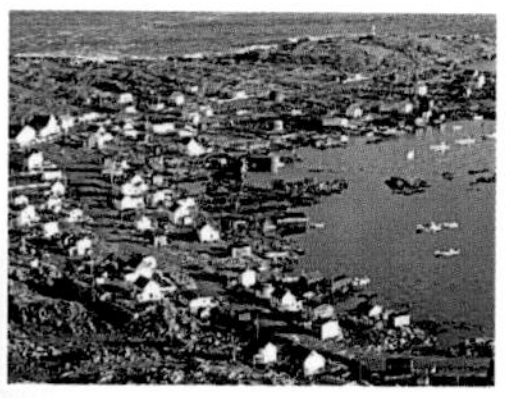

▲ *Fish processing is a major industry in the Atlantic provinces. Fogo Island, off Newfoundland, has barely a thousand inhabitants but it is able to sustain a number of cod canneries.*

Using the land & sea

With thin soils restricting farming to the south, the forests that grow in vast unbroken tracts across eastern Canada provide an important source of revenue. Coastal communities rely heavily on the rich fishing grounds of the Atlantic Ocean, although foreign competition and overfishing have resulted in strict policies to conserve stocks.

LABRADOR SEA
Hudson Bay
Manitoba
Ontario
Québec
Thunder Bay
Sault Ste. Marie
OTTAWA
Toronto
Montréal
Québec
Newfoundland & Labrador
St. John's
New Brunswick
Prince Edward Island
Nova Scotia
Halifax
ATLANTIC OCEAN
UNITED STATES OF AMERICA

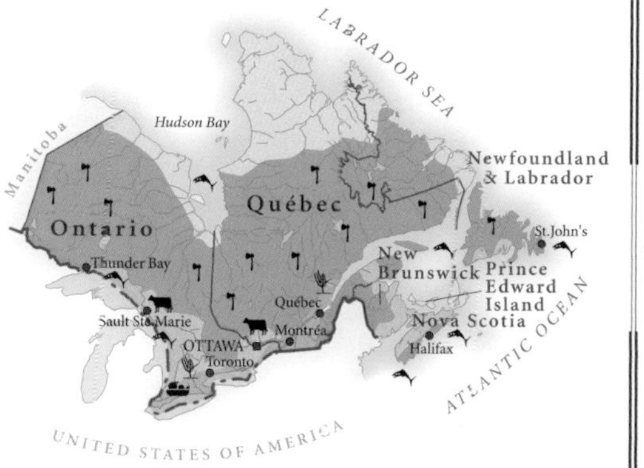

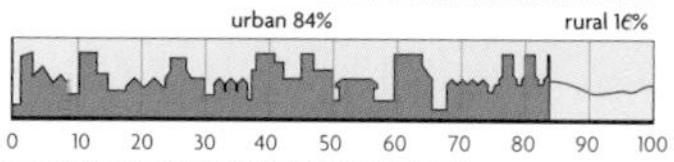

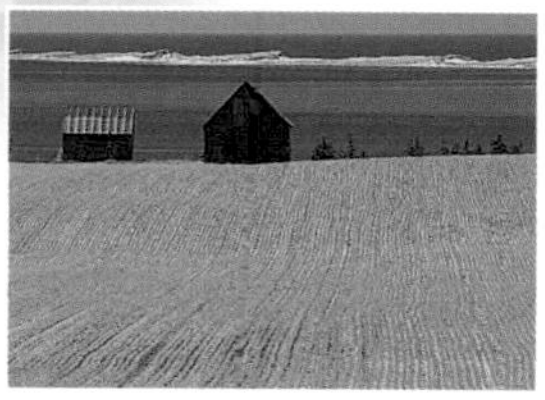

Land use and agricultural distribution

- cattle
- cereals
- fishing
- fruit
- timber
- capital cities
- major towns
- pasture
- cropland
- forest
- tundra

The urban/rural population divide

urban 84%
rural 16%
0
10
20
30
40
50
60
70
80
90
100

Population density	Total land area
21 people per sq mile (8 people per sq km)	1,076,227 sq miles (2,787,431 sq km)

▶ *Prince Edward Island is the only Atlantic province with notable agricultural land. The island is Canada's leading producer of potatoes.*

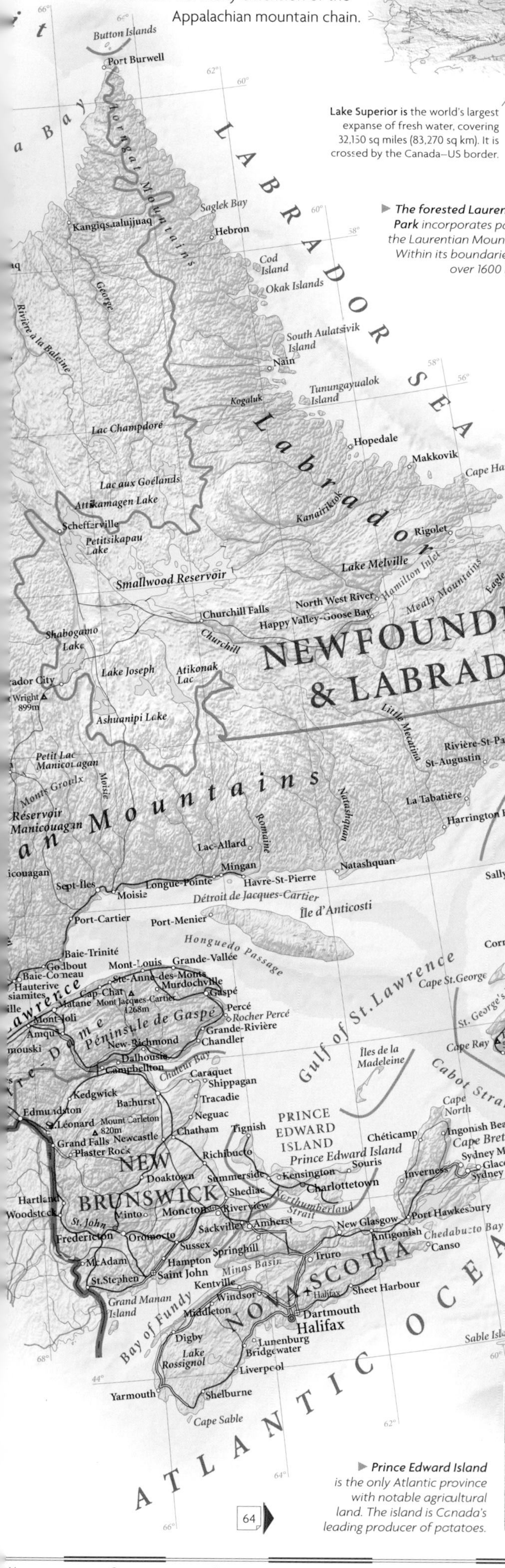

Button Islands
Port Burwell
LABRADOR SEA
Torngat Mountains
Saglek Bay
Kangiqsualujjuaq
Hebron
Cod Island
Okak Islands
George
Rivière à la Baleine
South Aulatsivik Island
Nain
Tunungayualok Island
Kogaluk
Labrador
Lac Champdoré
Hopedale
Makkovik
Cape Harrison
Lac aux Goélands
Attikamagen Lake
Kanairiktok
Schefferville
Petitsikapau Lake
Rigolet
Cartwright
Lake Melville
Smallwood Reservoir
Hamilton Inlet
Mealy Mountains
Eagle
Churchill Falls
North West River
Happy Valley-Goose Bay
Shabogamo Lake
Churchill
NEWFOUNDLAND & LABRADOR
Port Hope Simpson
Lake Joseph
Atikonak Lac
Belle Isle
Wright 899m
Ashuanipi Lake
Little Mecatina
Red Bay
Cape Bauld
Forteau
St. Anthony
Strait of Belle Isle
Rivière-St-Paul
St-Augustin
Petit Lac Manicouagan
Moisie
Natashquan
Roddickton
Grey Islands
Réservoir Manicouagan
Mountains
La Tabatière
Port Saunders
Harrington Harbour
White Bay
Romaine
Long Range Mountains
Baie Verte
Fogo Island
Lac-Allard
Notre Dame Bay
Mingan
Natashquan
Sally's Cove
Gros Morne 808m
Sept-Îles
Longue-Pointe
Havre-St-Pierre
Moisie
Détroit de Jacques-Cartier
Île d'Anticosti
Gander
Bonavista Bay
Bonavista
Deer Lake
Grand Lake
Grand Falls
Port-Cartier
Port-Menier
Buchans
Red Indian Lake
Honguedo Passage
Corner Brook
Newfoundland
Clarenville
Baie-Trinité
Godbout
Mont-Louis
Grande-Vallée
Stephenville
Baie-Comeau
Ste-Anne-des-Monts
Murdochville
Cape St. George
Trinity Bay
Carbonear
St.John's
Hauterive
Cap-Chat
Gaspé
Meelpaeg Lake
Matane
Mont Jacques-Cartier 1268m
Gulf of St. Lawrence
St. George's Bay
Percé
Rocher Percé
Mont-Joli
Péninsule de Gaspé
Grande-Rivière
Burgeo
Placentia
Chandler
Table Mountain 587m
Avalon Peninsula
New Richmond
Cape Ray
Harbour Breton
Placentia Bay
Campbellton
Îles de la Madeleine
Channel-Port aux Basques
Marystown
Cape Race
Dalhousie
Chaleur Bay
Caraquet
Cabot Strait
Grand Bank
Shippagan
Kedgwick
Bathurst
Tracadie
Cape North
ST PIERRE & MIQUELON (to France)
Edmundston
St-Léonard
Mount Carleton 820m
Neguac
PRINCE EDWARD ISLAND
Chéticamp
Ingonish Beach
Grand Falls
Newcastle
Chatham
Tignish
Cape Breton Island
Plaster Rock
Sydney Mines
Glace Bay
Richibucto
Prince Edward Island
Souris
Sydney
NEW BRUNSWICK
Doaktown
Summerside
Kensington
Charlottetown
Inverness
Hartland
Shediac
Woodstock
Minto
Moncton
Riverview
Northumberland Strait
Port Hawkesbury
Sackville
Amherst
New Glasgow
Antigonish
Chedabucto Bay
Fredericton
Oromocto
Sussex
Canso
Hampton
Springhill
Truro
St. John
McAdam
Minas Basin
St.Stephen
Saint John
NOVA SCOTIA
Kentville
Sheet Harbour
Grand Manan Island
Windsor
Bay of Fundy
Middleton
Halifax
Dartmouth
Halifax
Digby
Lunenburg
Bridgewater
Lake Rossignol
Sable Island
Liverpool
Yarmouth
Shelburne
Cape Sable
ATLANTIC OCEAN

64

Southeastern Canada

Southern Ontario, Southern Québec

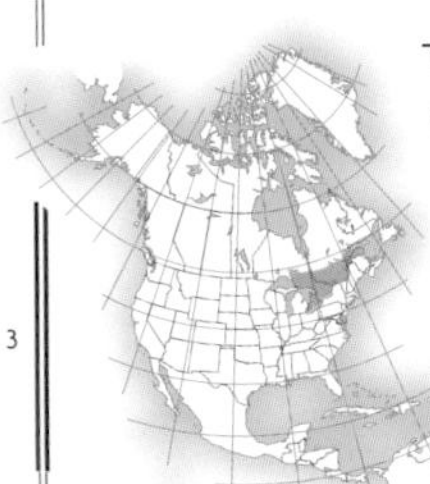

The southern parts of Québec and Ontario form the economic heart of Canada. The two provinces are divided by their language and culture; in Québec, French is the main language, whereas English is spoken in Ontario. Separatist sentiment in Québec has led to a provincial referendum on the question of a sovereignty association with Canada. The region contains Canada's capital, Ottawa and its two largest cities: Toronto, the center of commerce and Montréal, the cultural and administrative heart of French Canada.

▶ *Niagara Falls lies on the border between Canada and the US. It comprises a system of two falls: American Falls, in New York, is separated from Horseshoe Falls, in Ontario, by Goat Island. Horseshoe Falls, seen here, plunges 184 ft (56 m) and is 2500 ft (762 m) wide.*

▲ *The port at Montréal is situated on the St. Lawrence Seaway. A network of 16 locks allows oceangoing vessels access to routes once plied by fur-trappers and early settlers.*

Transportation & industry

The cities of southern Québec and Ontario, and their hinterlands, form the heart of Canadian manufacturing industry. Toronto is Canada's leading financial center, and Ontario's motor and aerospace industries have developed around the city. A major center for nickel mining lies to the north of Toronto. Most of Québec's industry is located in Montréal, the oldest port in North America. Chemicals, paper manufacture, and the construction of transportation equipment are leading industrial activities.

Major industry and infrastructure

- 🚗 car manufacture
- chemicals
- ⚙ engineering
- S finance
- food processing
- hi-tech industry
- mining
- iron & steel
- textiles
- paper industry
- timber processing
- capital cities
- major towns
- ⊕ international airports
- major roads
- major industrial areas

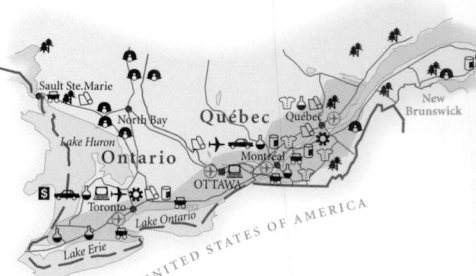

Transportation network

The opening of the St. Lawrence Seaway in 1959 finally allowed oceangoing ships (up to 24,000 tons (tonnes)) access to the interior of Canada, creating a vital trading route.

Map key

Population
- ▣ 1 million to 5 million
- ◉ 500,000 to 1 million
- ◎ 100,000 to 500,000
- ⊕ 50,000 to 100,000
- ○ 10,000 to 50,000
- · below 10,000

Elevation
- 500m / 1640ft
- 250m / 820ft
- 100m / 328ft
- sea level

▶ *Montréal, on the banks of the St. Lawrence River, is Québec's leading metropolitan center and one of Canada's two largest cities – Toronto is the other. Montréal clearly reflects French culture and traditions.*

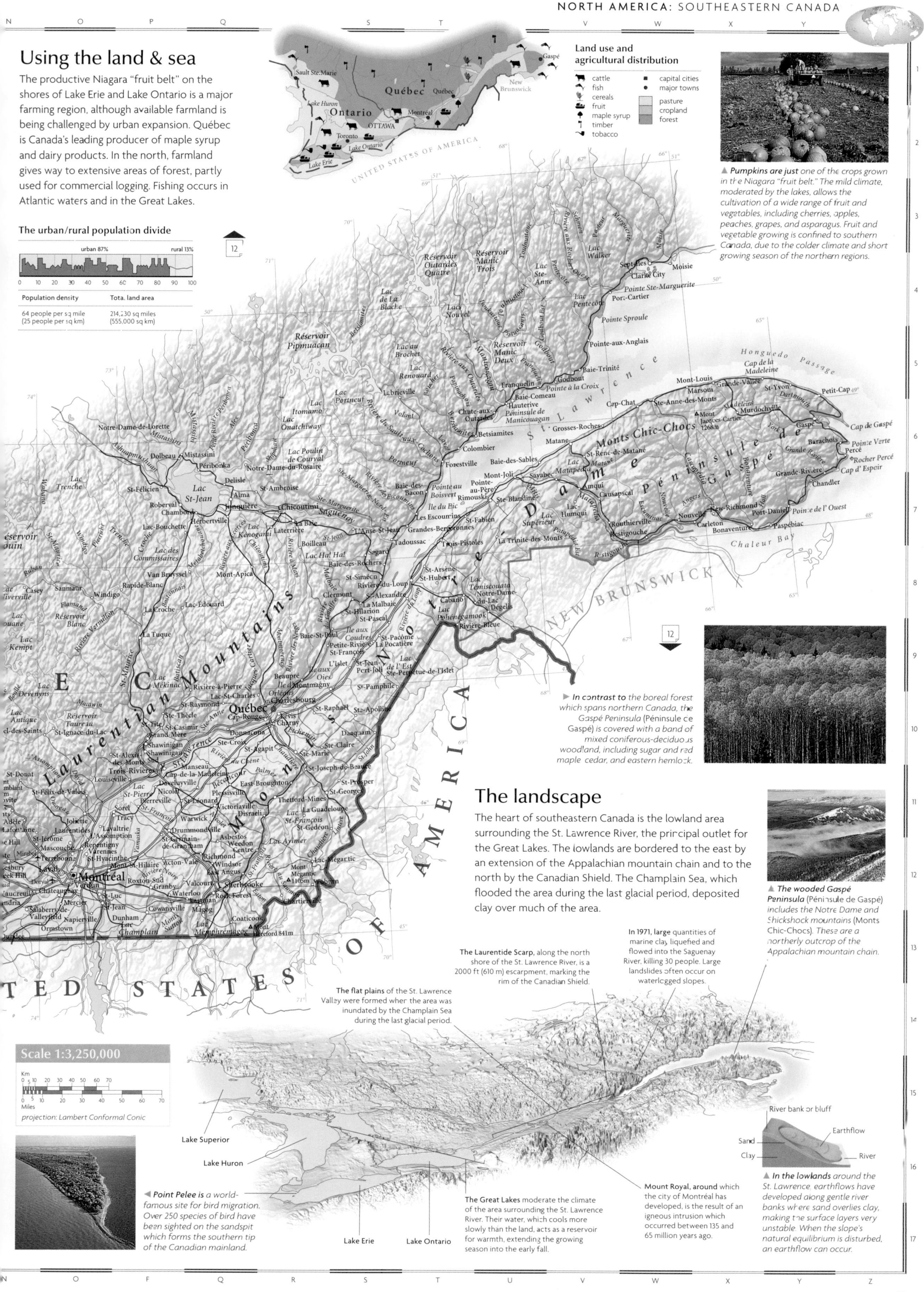

Using the land & sea

The productive Niagara "fruit belt" on the shores of Lake Erie and Lake Ontario is a major farming region, although available farmland is being challenged by urban expansion. Québec is Canada's leading producer of maple syrup and dairy products. In the north, farmland gives way to extensive areas of forest, partly used for commercial logging. Fishing occurs in Atlantic waters and in the Great Lakes.

The urban/rural population divide

urban 87%   rural 13%

0 10 20 30 40 50 60 70 80 90 100

Population density	Total land area
64 people per sq mile (25 people per sq km)	214,730 sq miles (555,000 sq km)

Land use and agricultural distribution

- cattle
- fish
- cereals
- fruit
- maple syrup
- timber
- tobacco
- ■ capital cities
- • major towns
- pasture
- cropland
- forest

▲ **Pumpkins are just** one of the crops grown in the Niagara "fruit belt." The mild climate, moderated by the lakes, allows the cultivation of a wide range of fruit and vegetables, including cherries, apples, peaches, grapes, and asparagus. Fruit and vegetable growing is confined to southern Canada, due to the colder climate and short growing season of the northern regions.

▶ **In contrast to** the boreal forest which spans northern Canada, the Gaspé Peninsula (Péninsule de Gaspé) is covered with a band of mixed coniferous-deciduous woodland, including sugar and red maple, cedar, and eastern hemlock.

The landscape

The heart of southeastern Canada is the lowland area surrounding the St. Lawrence River, the principal outlet for the Great Lakes. The lowlands are bordered to the east by an extension of the Appalachian mountain chain and to the north by the Canadian Shield. The Champlain Sea, which flooded the area during the last glacial period, deposited clay over much of the area.

▲ **The wooded Gaspé Peninsula** (Péninsule de Gaspé) includes the Notre Dame and Shickshock mountains (Monts Chic-Chocs). These are a northerly outcrop of the Appalachian mountain chain.

In 1971, large quantities of marine clay liquefied and flowed into the Saguenay River, killing 30 people. Large landslides often occur on waterlogged slopes.

The Laurentide Scarp, along the north shore of the St. Lawrence River, is a 2000 ft (610 m) escarpment, marking the rim of the Canadian Shield.

The flat plains of the St. Lawrence Valley were formed when the area was inundated by the Champlain Sea during the last glacial period.

Scale 1:3,250,000

Km
0 5 10 20 30 40 50 60 70

Miles
0 5 10 20 30 40 50 60 70

projection: Lambert Conformal Conic

◀ **Point Pelee is** a world-famous site for bird migration. Over 250 species of bird have been sighted on the sandspit which forms the southern tip of the Canadian mainland.

The Great Lakes moderate the climate of the area surrounding the St. Lawrence River. Their water, which cools more slowly than the land, acts as a reservoir for warmth, extending the growing season into the early fall.

Mount Royal, around which the city of Montréal has developed, is the result of an igneous intrusion which occurred between 135 and 65 million years ago.

▲ **In the lowlands** around the St. Lawrence, earthflows have developed along gentle river banks where sand overlies clay, making the surface layers very unstable. When the slope's natural equilibrium is disturbed, an earthflow can occur.

River bank or bluff
Earthflow
Sand
Clay
River

Lake Superior
Lake Huron
Lake Erie
Lake Ontario

15

The United States of America

COTERMINOUS US (FOR ALASKA AND HAWAII SEE PAGES 38-39)

The US's progression from frontier territory to economic and political superpower has taken less than 200 years. The 48 coterminous states, along with the outlying states of Alaska and Hawaii, are part of a federal union, held together by the guiding principles of the US Constitution, which embodies the ideals of democracy and liberty for all. Abundant fertile land and a rich resource base fueled and sustained US economic development. With the spread of agriculture and the growth of trade and industry came the need for a larger workforce, which was supplied by millions of immigrants, many seeking an escape from poverty and political or religious persecution. Immigration continues today, particularly from Central America and Asia.

▲ *Washington DC was established as the si[te] for the nation's capital in 1790. It is home to the seat of national government, on Capitol Hill, as well as the President's official residence, the White House.*

▶ *The clear waters of Niaga[ra] Falls cascade 190 ft (58 m) into th[e] gorge below. It is one of America[']s most famous spectacles and leading tourist attraction. The fa[lls] are slowly receding and the gorg[e] may one day stretch fro[m] Lake Ontario to Lake Er[ie].*

▲ *Mount Rainier is a dormant volcano in the Cascade Range, Washington. This 14,090 ft (4392 m) peak is flanked by the most extensive glacier outside Alaska.*

8
192
40

Transportation & industry

The US has been the industrial powerhouse of the world since the Second World War, pioneering mass-production and the consumer lifestyle. Initially, heavy engineering and manufacturing in the northeast led the economy. Today, heavy industry has declined and the US economy is driven by service and financial industries, with the most important being defense, hi-tech, and electronics.

Transportation network

3,875,040 miles (6,240,000 km)	52,388 miles (84,361 km)
148,308 miles (235,238 km)	25,467 miles (41,009 km)

Transportation in the US is dominated by the car which, with the extensive Interstate Highway system, allows great personal mobility. Today, internal air flights between major cities provide the most rapid cross-country travel.

Major industry and infrastructure

- aerospace
- car manufacture
- chemicals
- coal
- electronics
- engineering
- food processing
- hi-tech industry
- oil & gas
- research & development
- textiles
- tourism
- capital cities
- major towns
- international airports
- major roads
- major industrial areas

The landscape

The high, rugged mountain ranges of the west are about 80 million years old, geologically young compared to the old, eroded, Appalachian mountain chain, which dates from when North America and Europe were joined together as part of the supercontinent Pangaea, 400 million years ago. In contrast, the Great Plains and Mississippi Basin have a low relief and fertile soils.

Mount Rainier • Great Plains • The Great Lakes • Niagara Falls

Death Valley, California, 282 ft (86 m) below sea level, is the lowest point in the western hemisphere, and one of the hottest places on Earth. Temperatures of 135° F (57° C) have been recorded here.

Monument Valley's striking sandstone spires and pillars (buttes) have been formed by the action of wind, water, heat, and cold.

The deep gullies of South Dakota's badlands are created by periodic, torrential rainfall, which erodes the soft soils and rocks. Their form has been greatly affected by changes in land use.

◄ Devils Tower, in Wyoming is a 1280 ft (390 m) intrusion of basalt rock, which cooled to form octagonal pillars. In 1906 it became the first US National Monument.

Most of the US is drained by the great Mississippi River system. At its mouth, where levées are breached, floodwaters are carried to the swamps through a series of channels. This region is known as the bayou.

Barrier beaches, bars and spits are typical of the Atlantic coast. These sand formations around Cape Hatteras stretch along the coast for 200 miles (320 km).

The Great Smoky Mountains, part of the ancient Appalachian mountain chain, formed a natural barrier to early settlers attempting to penetrate the country's interior.

The Everglades are a vast area of sawgrass swamp covering 4000 sq miles (10,300 sq km) of southern Florida.

Missouri River
Ohio River
Mississippi River
Mississippi Delta

▲ The massive drainage basin of the Mississippi covers 1,250,000 sq miles (3,200,000 sq km). It includes all areas drained by the Mississippi and its chief tributaries, the Missouri and Ohio Rivers, and drains the entire region from the Appalachians to the Rockies.

Map key

Population
- ⊡ above 5 million
- ⊡ 1 million to 5 million
- ◉ 500,000 to 1 million
- ◎ 100,000 to 500,000
- ⊕ 50,000 to 100,000
- ○ 10,000 to 50,000
- ∘ below 10,000

Elevation
- 4000m / 13,124ft
- 3000m / 9843ft
- 2000m / 6562ft
- 1000m / 3281ft
- 500m / 1640ft
- 250m / 820ft
- 100m / 328ft
- sea level

Using the land and sea

Over half of the US is used for agriculture, typified by the large cereal grain farms and cattle ranches of the Great Plains and Midwest prairie regions. Although wheat and corn are still primary crops, a diverse range of fruits and vegetables are grown in the fertile areas, particularly near the east and west coasts. Despite the abundance of cultivable land, inadequate soil management has resulted in a third of the topsoil being lost through wind and water erosion.

▶ Fakahatchee Strand is part of the extensive subtropical swamps in the Florida Everglades. The swamps support a wide variety of animal life, including many rare birds, fish, alligators, and crocodiles.

Land use and agricultural distribution

- cattle
- pigs
- poultry
- citrus fruits
- cotton
- fishing
- fruit
- corn
- peanuts
- shellfish
- soybeans
- timber
- tobacco
- wheat

- ■ capital cities
- • major towns

- pasture
- cropland
- forest
- wetland
- desert
- mountain region

The urban/rural population divide

urban 76%   rural 24%

0 10 20 30 40 50 60 70 80 90 100

Population density	Total land area
98 people per sq mile (38 people per sq km)	2,959,045 sq miles (7,663,631 sq km)

◄ Farming on the Great Plains and in the Midwest is characterized by large-scale, mechanized wheat farms.

USA: NORTHEASTERN STATES

Connecticut, Maine, Massachusetts, New Hampshire, New Jersey,
New York, Pennsylvania, Rhode Island, Vermont

The indented coast and vast woodlands of the northeastern states were the original core area for European expansion. The rustic character of New England prevails after nearly four centuries, while the great cities of the Atlantic seaboard have formed an almost continuous urban region. Over 20 million immigrants entered New York from 1855 to 1924 and the northeast became the industrial center of the US. After the decline of mining and heavy manufacturing, economic dynamism has been restored with the growth of hi-tech and service industries.

Transportation & industry

The principal seaboard cities grew up on trade and manufacturing. They are now global centers of commerce and corporate administration, dominating the regional economy. Research and development facilities support an expanding electronics and communications sector throughout the region. Pharmaceutical and chemical industries are important in New Jersey and Pennsylvania.

Major industry and infrastructure

- chemicals
- coal
- defense
- electronics
- engineering
- finance
- hi-tech industry
- iron & steel
- pharmaceuticals
- printing & publishing
- research & development
- textiles
- timber processing
- major towns
- international airports
- major roads
- major industrial area

▲ *Chelsea in Vermont,* surrounded by trees in their fall foliage. Tourism and agriculture dominate the economy of this self-consciously rural state, where no town exceeds 30,000 people.

Transportation network

340,090 miles (544,144 km)	4813 miles (7700 km)
12,872 miles (20,592 km)	2108 miles (3389 km)

New York's commercial success is tied historically to its transportation connections. The Erie Canal, completed in 1825, opened up the Great Lakes and the interior to New York's markets and carried a stream of immigrants into the Midwest.

Map key

Population
- ■ above 5 million
- ■ 1 million to 5 million
- ● 500,000 to 1 million
- ◎ 100,000 to 500,000
- ● 50,000 to 100,000
- ○ 10,000 to 50,000
- ○ below 10,000

Elevation
- 1000m / 3281ft
- 500m / 1640ft
- 250m / 820ft
- 100m / 328ft
- sea level

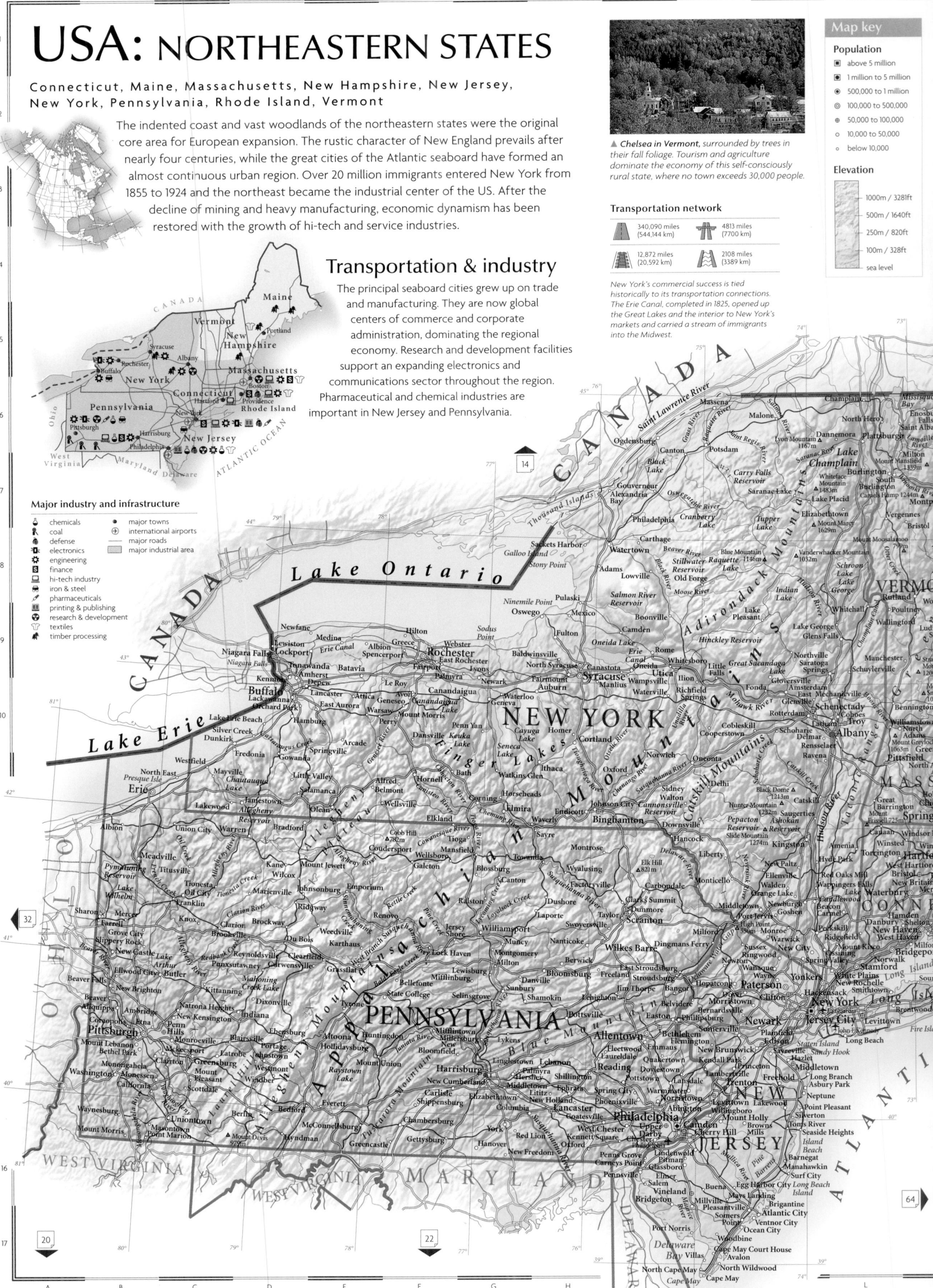

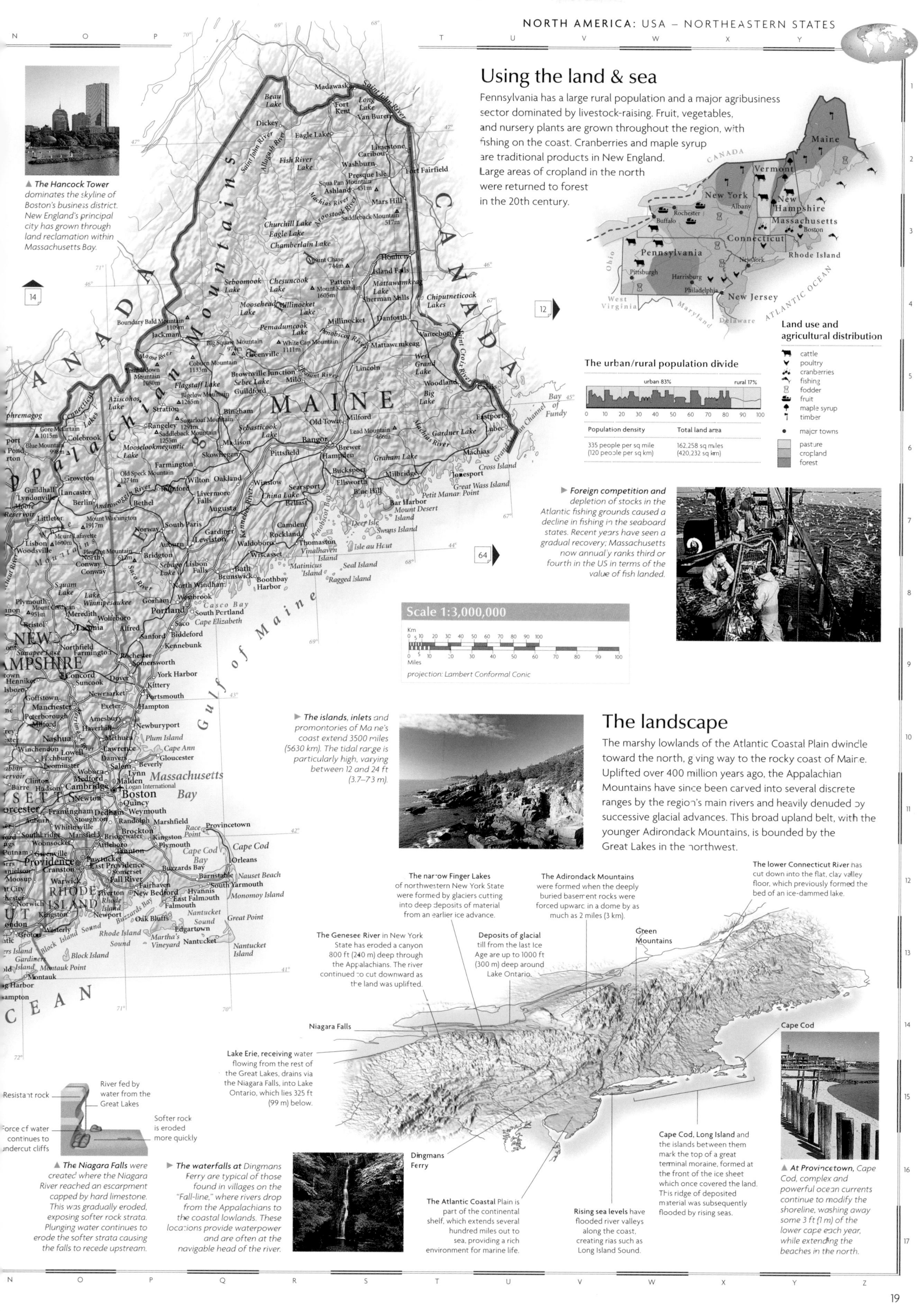

▲ *The Hancock Tower dominates the skyline of Boston's business district. New England's principal city has grown through land reclamation within Massachusetts Bay.*

Using the land & sea

Pennsylvania has a large rural population and a major agribusiness sector dominated by livestock-raising. Fruit, vegetables, and nursery plants are grown throughout the region, with fishing on the coast. Cranberries and maple syrup are traditional products in New England. Large areas of cropland in the north were returned to forest in the 20th century.

Land use and agricultural distribution

- cattle
- poultry
- cranberries
- fishing
- fodder
- fruit
- maple syrup
- timber

↑ major towns

- pasture
- cropland
- forest

The urban/rural population divide

urban 83%   rural 17%

0 10 20 30 40 50 60 70 80 90 100

Population density	Total land area
335 people per sq mile (120 people per sq km)	162,258 sq miles (420,232 sq km)

▶ *Foreign competition and depletion of stocks in the Atlantic fishing grounds caused a decline in fishing in the seaboard states. Recent years have seen a gradual recovery; Massachusetts now annually ranks third or fourth in the US in terms of the value of fish landed.*

Scale 1:3,000,000

Km
0 5 10 20 30 40 50 60 70 80 90 100

Miles
0 5 10 20 30 40 50 60 70 80 90 100

projection: Lambert Conformal Conic

▶ *The islands, inlets and promontories of Maine's coast extend 3500 miles (5630 km). The tidal range is particularly high, varying between 12 and 24 ft (3.7–7.3 m).*

The landscape

The marshy lowlands of the Atlantic Coastal Plain dwindle toward the north, giving way to the rocky coast of Maine. Uplifted over 400 million years ago, the Appalachian Mountains have since been carved into several discrete ranges by the region's main rivers and heavily denuded by successive glacial advances. This broad upland belt, with the younger Adirondack Mountains, is bounded by the Great Lakes in the northwest.

The narrow Finger Lakes of northwestern New York State were formed by glaciers cutting into deep deposits of material from an earlier ice advance.

The Adirondack Mountains were formed when the deeply buried basement rocks were forced upward in a dome by as much as 2 miles (3 km).

The lower Connecticut River has cut down into the flat, clay valley floor, which previously formed the bed of an ice-dammed lake.

The Genesee River in New York State has eroded a canyon 800 ft (240 m) deep through the Appalachians. The river continued to cut downward as the land was uplifted.

Deposits of glacial till from the last Ice Age are up to 1000 ft (300 m) deep around Lake Ontario.

Green Mountains

Niagara Falls

Cape Cod

Lake Erie, receiving water flowing from the rest of the Great Lakes, drains via the Niagara Falls, into Lake Ontario, which lies 325 ft (99 m) below.

Resistant rock

River fed by water from the Great Lakes

Force of water continues to undercut cliffs

Softer rock is eroded more quickly

▲ *The Niagara Falls were created where the Niagara River reached an escarpment capped by hard limestone. This was gradually eroded, exposing softer rock strata. Plunging water continues to erode the softer strata causing the falls to recede upstream.*

▶ *The waterfalls at Dingmans Ferry are typical of those found in villages on the "Fall-line," where rivers drop from the Appalachians to the coastal lowlands. These locations provide waterpower and are often at the navigable head of the river.*

Dingmans Ferry

The Atlantic Coastal Plain is part of the continental shelf, which extends several hundred miles out to sea, providing a rich environment for marine life.

Rising sea levels have flooded river valleys along the coast, creating rias such as Long Island Sound.

Cape Cod, Long Island and the islands between them mark the top of a great terminal moraine, formed at the front of the ice sheet which once covered the land. This ridge of deposited material was subsequently flooded by rising seas.

▲ *At Provincetown, Cape Cod, complex and powerful ocean currents continue to modify the shoreline, washing away some 3 ft (1 m) of the lower cape each year, while extending the beaches in the north.*

19

USA: MID-EASTERN STATES

Delaware, District of Columbia, Kentucky,
Maryland, North Carolina, South Carolina,
Tennessee, Virginia, West Virginia

Key events in American history took place in this diverse region, which
became the front line between the North and the South during the Civil
War of the 1860s. Strong regional contrasts exist between the fertile
coastal plains, the isolated upcountry of the Appalachian Mountains, and
the cotton-growing areas of the Mississippi lowlands to the west. While
coal mining, a traditional industry in the Appalachians, has declined in
recent years leaving much rural poverty, service industries elsewhere
have increased, especially in Washington DC, the nation's capital.

Transportation & industry

In the urbanized northeast, manufacturing remains
important, alongside a burgeoning service sector. North
Carolina is a major center for industrial research and
development. Traditional industries include Tennessee
whiskey and textiles in South Carolina. The decline of
open-pit coal mining in the Appalachians has been
hastened by environmental controls, although
adventure-tourism is a flourishing new industry.

Major industry and infrastructure

- adventure-tourism
- car manufacture
- coal
- electronics
- engineering
- finance
- food processing
- hi-tech industry
- mining
- research & development
- textiles
- capital cities
- major towns
- international airports
- major roads
- major industrial areas

Map key

Population
- 500,000 to 1 million
- 100,000 to 500,000
- 50,000 to 100,000
- 10,000 to 50,000
- below 10,000

Elevation
- 6000m / 19,686ft
- 4000m / 13,124ft
- 3000m / 9843ft
- 2000m / 6562ft
- 1000m / 3281ft
- 500m / 1640ft
- 250m / 820ft
- 100m / 328ft
- sea level

Scale 1:3,250,000

Km 0 5 10 20 30 40 50 60 70 80
Miles 0 5 10 20 30 40 50 60 70 80

projection: Lambert Conformal Conic

▲ The Bluegrass region of Kentucky centers
on the town of Lexington. This exceptionally
fertile rolling plain is well known for its
thoroughbred horse-breeding ranches.

Transportation network

- 452,218 miles (723,548 km)
- 5737 miles (8267 km)
- 18,336 miles (29,503 km)
- 4404 miles (7081 km)

Tennessee's rivers are part of an important inland
bulk transportation network. Memphis connects
with New Orleans in the south, and with cities as
distant as Minneapolis, Sioux City, Chicago, and
Pittsburgh, via the Mississippi and its tributaries.

The landscape

The eastern tributaries of the Mississippi drain the
interior lowlands. The Cumberland Plateau and the
parallel ranges of the Appalachians have been
successively uplifted and eroded over time, with the
eastern side reduced to a series of foothills known as the
Piedmont. The broad coastal plain gradually falls away
into salt marshes, lagoons, and offshore
bars, broken by flooded estuaries along
the shores of the Atlantic.

The Mammoth Cave is part of an
extensive cave system in the limestone
region of southwestern Kentucky.
It stretches for over 300 miles (485 km)
on five different levels and contains
three rivers and three lakes.

The Mississippi River and its
tributary the Ohio River form the
western border of the region.

◄ The Great Smoky Mountains form
the western escarpment of the
Appalachians. The region is heavily
forested, with over 130 species of tree.

The Cumberland Plateau is the
most southwesterly part of the
Appalachians. Big Black
Mountain at 4180 ft (1274 m) is
the highest point in the range.

The Blue Ridge mountains
are a steep ridge, culminating
in Mount Mitchell, the highest
point in the Appalachians,
at 6684 ft (2037 m).

Natural Bridge in eastern
Kentucky is an arch 78 ft
(26 m) long and 65 ft (20 m)
high. It has been shaped from
resistant sandstone by
gradual weathering processes,
which removed the softer
rock lying underneath.

The Allegheny Mountains
form the northwestern
edge of the Appalachian
mountain chain. Continuous
folding has formed rich
seams of bituminous coal.

Appalachian Mountains

◄ Farmland on the eastern
shores of Chesapeake Bay is
sustained by artificial
drainage. The area also
provides refuge for a variety
of waterfowl.

The many inlets of Chesapeake Bay
are the flooded tributaries of the
main river valley, which have been
inundated by rising sea levels.

Salt marshes such as Great Dismal
Swamp, develop where the coast
is sheltered. Vast areas of such
marshland have been reclaimed for
farmland and settlement.

Cape Hatteras is the easternmost
point of an offshore barrier island,
a wave-deposited sand-bar which
has become permanent,
establishing its own vegetation.

Barrier islands

These intertidal
mudflats become
submerged at high tide

Tidal inlet

Barrier island

▲ Barrier islands are common along
the coasts of North and South
Carolina. As sea levels rise, wave action
builds up ridges of sand and pebbles
parallel to the coast, separated by
lagoons or intertidal mud flats, which
are flooded at high tide.

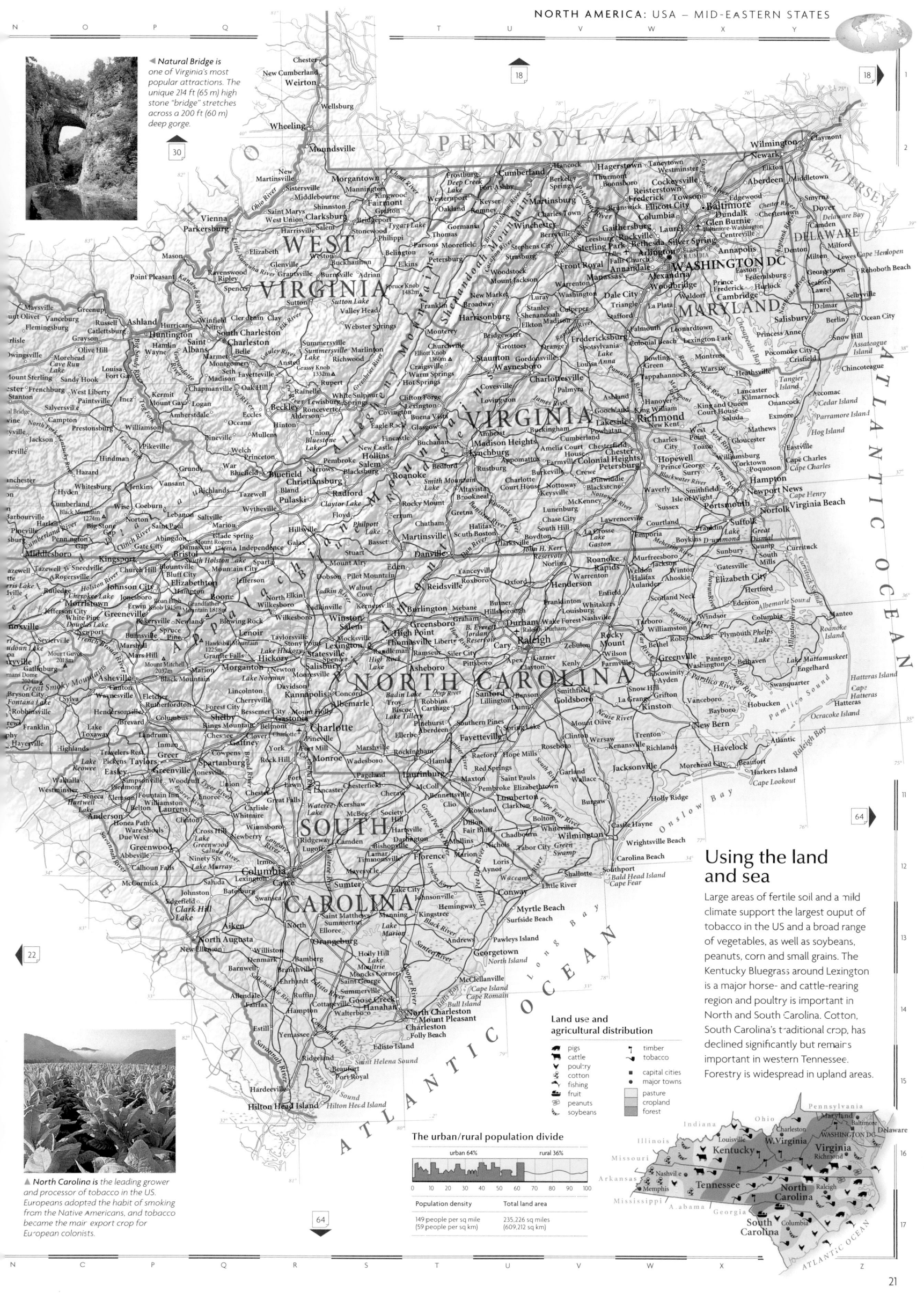

◄ *Natural Bridge* is one of Virginia's most popular attractions. The unique 214 ft (65 m) high stone "bridge" stretches across a 200 ft (60 m) deep gorge.

▲ *North Carolina is* the leading grower and processor of tobacco in the US. Europeans adopted the habit of smoking from the Native Americans, and tobacco became the main export crop for European colonists.

Using the land and sea

Large areas of fertile soil and a mild climate support the largest ouput of tobacco in the US and a broad range of vegetables, as well as soybeans, peanuts, corn and small grains. The Kentucky Bluegrass around Lexington is a major horse- and cattle-rearing region and poultry is important in North and South Carolina. Cotton, South Carolina's traditional crop, has declined significantly but remains important in western Tennessee. Forestry is widespread in upland areas.

Land use and agricultural distribution

- pigs
- cattle
- poultry
- cotton
- fishing
- fruit
- peanuts
- soybeans
- timber
- tobacco
- ■ capital cities
- • major towns
- pasture
- cropland
- forest

The urban/rural population divide

urban 64% rural 36%

0 10 20 30 40 50 60 70 80 90 100

Population density

149 people per sq mile
(59 people per sq km)

Total land area

235,226 sq miles
(609,212 sq km)

21

USA: TEXAS

First explored by Spaniards moving north from Mexico in search of gold, Texas was controlled by Spain and then by Mexico, before becoming an independent republic in 1836, and joining the Union of States in 1845. During the 19th century, many migrants who came to Texas raised cattle on the abundant land; in the 20th century, they were joined by prospectors attracted by the promise of oil riches. Today, although natural resources, especially oil, still form the basis of its wealth, the diversified Texan economy includes thriving hi-tech and financial industries. The major urban centers, home to 80% of the population, lie in the south and east, and include Houston, the "oil-city," and Dallas–Fort Worth. Hispanic influences remain strong, especially in southern and western Texas.

▲ *Dallas was founded* in 1841 as a prairie trading post and its development was stimulated by the arrival of railroads. Cotton and then oil funded the town's early growth. Today, the modern, high rise skyline of Dallas reflects the city's position as a leading center of banking, insurance, and the petroleum industry in the southwest.

Using the land

Cotton production and livestock-raising, particularly cattle, dominate farming, although crop failures and the demands of local markets have led to some diversification. Following the introduction of modern farming techniques, cotton production spread out from the east to the plains of western Texas. Cattle ranches are widespread, while sheep and goats are raised on the dry Edwards Plateau.

Land use and agricultural distribution
- cattle
- goats
- sheep
- cereals
- cotton
- • major towns
- pasture
- cropland
- forest
- barren

The urban/rural population divide
urban 80%   rural 20%
0 10 20 30 40 50 60 70 80 90 100

Population density | Total land area
84 people per sq mile (33 people per sq km) | 261,797 sq miles (678,028 sq km)

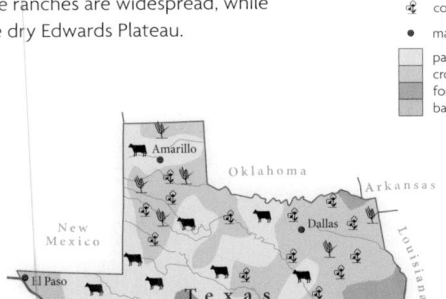
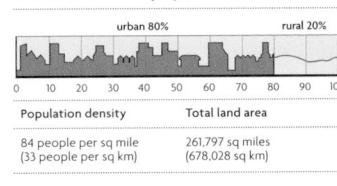
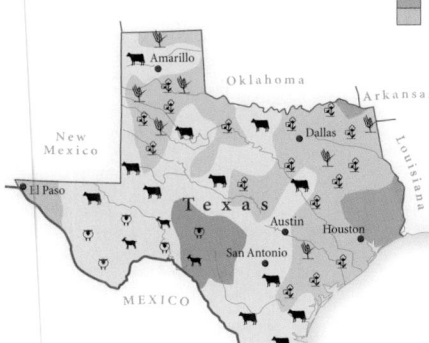

▲ *Cap Rock Escarpment* juts out from the plains, running 200 miles (320 km) from north to south. Its height varies from 300 ft (90 m) rising to sheer cliffs up to 1000 ft (300 m).

▲ *The huge cattle* ranches of Texas developed during the 19th century when land was plentiful and could be acquired cheaply. Today, more cattle and sheep are raised in Texas than in any other state.

The landscape

Texas is made up of a series of massive steps descending from the mountains and high plains of the west and northwest to the coastal lowlands in the southeast. Many of the state's borders are delineated by water. The Rio Grande flows from the Rocky Mountains to the Gulf of Mexico, marking the border with Mexico.

The Llano Estacado or Staked Plain in northern Texas is known for its harsh environment. In the north, freezing winds carrying ice and snow sweep down from the Rocky Mountains. To the south, sandstorms frequently blow up, scouring anything in their paths. Flash floods, in the wide, flat riverbeds that remain dry for most of the year, are another hazard.

The Guadalupe Mountains lie in the southern Rocky Mountains. They incorporate Guadalupe Peak, the highest in Texas, rising 8749 ft (2667 m).

The Red River flows for 1300 miles (2090 km), marking most of the northern border of Texas. A dam and reservoir along its course provide vital irrigation and hydroelectric power to the surrounding area.

The Rio Grande flows from the Rocky Mountains through semi-arid land, supporting sparse vegetation. The river actually shrinks along its course, losing more water through evaporation and seepage than it gains from its tributaries and rainfall.

Big Bend National Park

Edwards Plateau is a limestone outcrop. It is part of the Great Plains, bounded to the southeast by the Balcones Escarpment, which marks the southerly limit of the plains.

Sabine River

Extensive forests of pine and cypress grow in the eastern corner of the coastal lowlands where the average rainfall is 45 inches (1145 mm) a year. This is higher than the rest of the state and over twice the average in the west.

In the coastal lowlands of southeastern Texas the Earth's crust is warping, causing the land to subside and allowing the sea to invade. Around Galveston, the rate of downward tilting is 6 inches (15 cm) per year. Erosion of the coast is also exacerbated by hurricanes.

Oil deposits
Oil accumulates beneath impermeable cap rock
Oil trapped by fault
Impermeable rock strata
Oil deposits migrate through reservoir rocks such as shale
Salt dome

▲ *Oil deposits are* found beneath much of Texas. They collect as oil migrates upward through porous layers of rock until it is trapped, either by a cap of rock above a salt dome, or by a fault line which exposes impermeable rock through which the oil cannot rise.

Laguna Madre in southern Texas has been almost completely cut off from the sea by Padre Island. This sand bank was created by wave action, carrying and depositing material along the coast. The process is known as longshore drift.

◀ *Flowing through* 1500 ft (450 m) high gorges, the shallow, muddy Rio Grande makes a 90° bend. This marks the southern border of Big Bend National Park, and gives it its name. The area is a mixture of forested mountains, deserts, and canyons.

Padre Island

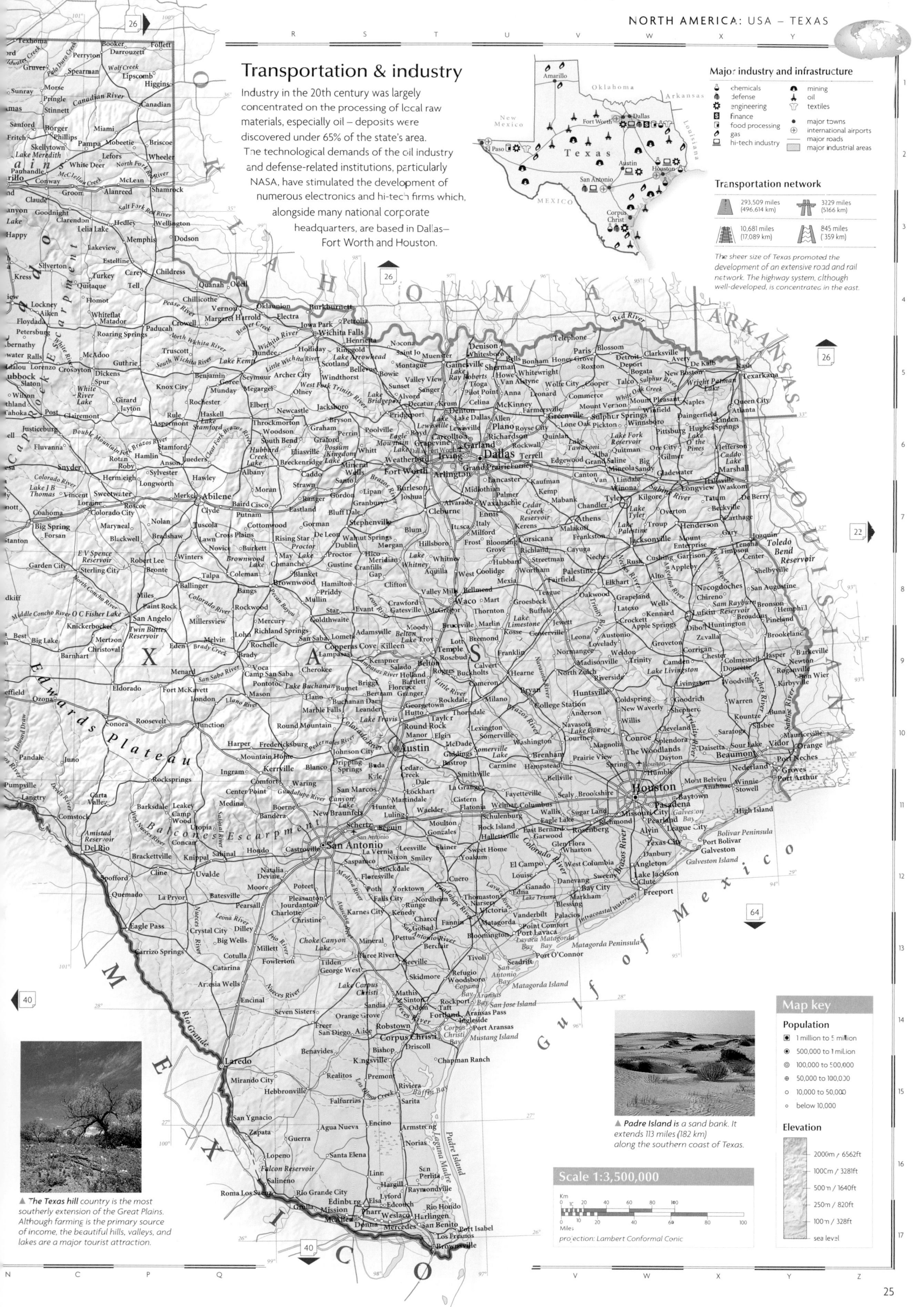

Transportation & industry

Industry in the 20th century was largely concentrated on the processing of local raw materials, especially oil – deposits were discovered under 65% of the state's area. The technological demands of the oil industry and defense-related institutions, particularly NASA, have stimulated the development of numerous electronics and hi-tech firms which, alongside many national corporate headquarters, are based in Dallas–Fort Worth and Houston.

Major industry and infrastructure

- chemicals
- defense
- engineering
- finance
- food processing
- gas
- hi-tech industry
- mining
- oil
- textiles
- major towns
- international airports
- major roads
- major industrial areas

Transportation network

293,509 miles (496,614 km)	3229 miles (5166 km)
10,681 miles (17,089 km)	845 miles (359 km)

The sheer size of Texas promoted the development of an extensive road and rail network. The highway system, although well-developed, is concentrated in the east.

▲ Padre Island is a sand bank. It extends 113 miles (182 km) along the southern coast of Texas.

▲ The Texas hill country is the most southerly extension of the Great Plains. Although farming is the primary source of income, the beautiful hills, valleys, and lakes are a major tourist attraction.

Map key

Population
- 1 million to 5 million
- 500,000 to 1 million
- 100,000 to 500,000
- 50,000 to 100,000
- 10,000 to 50,000
- below 10,000

Elevation
- 2000m / 6562ft
- 1000m / 3281ft
- 500m / 1640ft
- 250m / 820ft
- 100m / 328ft
- sea level

Scale 1:3,500,000

projection: Lambert Conformal Conic

USA: SOUTH MIDWESTERN STATES

Arkansas, Kansas, Missouri, Oklahoma

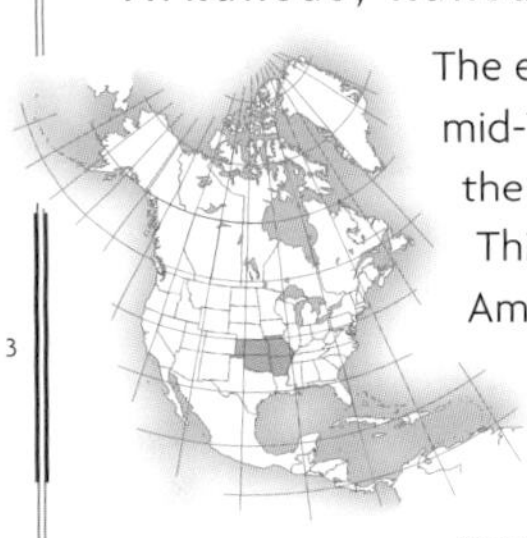

The expansion of the US focused on this region in the mid-19th century. Settlers spread from the confluence of the Missouri and Mississippi rivers up onto the Great Plains. This treeless expanse, which early explorers had called the Great American Desert was turned into one of the world's richest agricultural regions. But periodic droughts, coupled with overintensive farming, led to the "dustbowl" soil erosion crisis of the 1930s, the abandonment of many farms, and a mass exodus to the west coast. The land has since recovered, although the mechanization of agriculture has led to a decline in the rural population. In recent years, suburban residential development has spread rapidly across the wooded Ozark Plateau in the east of the region.

Transportation & industry

The processing of agricultural products, such as brewing and meatpacking, has been traditionally important in these states. In Kansas and Oklahoma, diversified manufacturing now supplements income from fossil fuels; Wichita has become a world center for aeronautical engineering, an industry which also employs many people in neighboring Missouri.

Major industry and infrastructure

- ✈ aerospace
- ✿ engineering
- S finance
- ▣ food processing
- ◊ gas
- ⛏ mining
- ♠ oil
- vehicle manufacture
- • major towns
- ⊕ international airports
- — major roads
- major industrial areas

▶ *Agricultural produce from the plains is moved by barges along the Mississippi. The river now carries a far greater tonnage of freight than any other waterway system in the US.*

Transportation network

- 380,307 miles (608,491 km)
- 4068 miles (6508 km)
- 16,185 miles (25,896 km)
- 1994 miles (3208 km)

The Arkansas River and its tributaries allow access to over half of the US's navigable inland waterways. A system of locks and dams along the river provides Tulsa, in Oklahoma, with a navigable water route to the Gulf of Mexico.

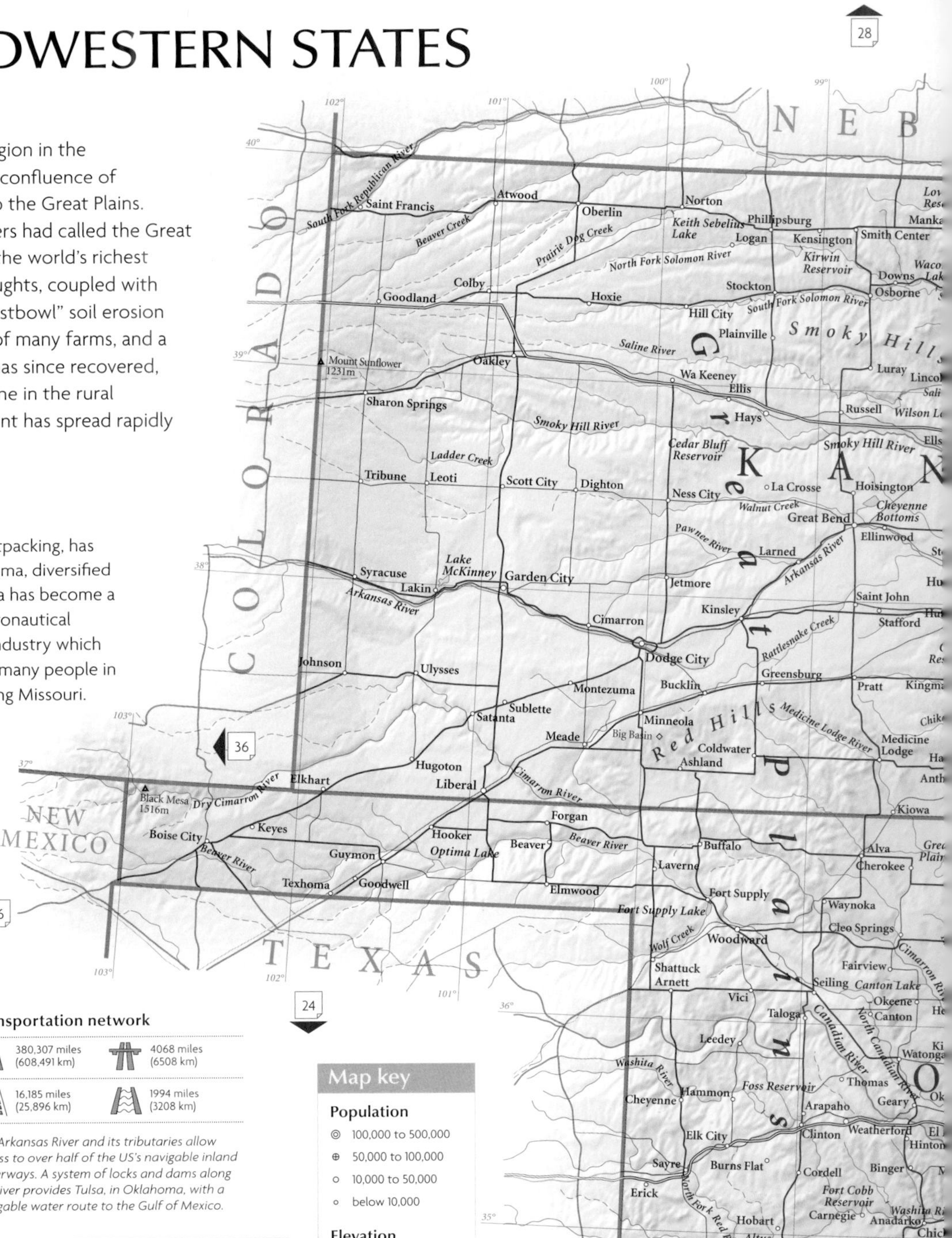

Map key

Population

- ◎ 100,000 to 500,000
- ⊕ 50,000 to 100,000
- ○ 10,000 to 50,000
- ○ below 10,000

Elevation

- 1000m / 3281ft
- 500m / 1640ft
- 250m / 820ft
- 100m / 328ft
- sea level

The landscape

Most of the region consists of high, treeless plains, which gradually descend east from the Rocky Mountains. Drainage follows this slope, with rivers flowing toward the alluvial lowlands of the Mississippi in the southeast. Between the plains and the lowlands lie various ranges of wooded hills, including the deeply incised Ozark Plateau.

▲ *The Mississippi, North America's longest river, is joined by the Missouri, its main tributary, on a flood plain which spreads south to the Gulf of Mexico.*

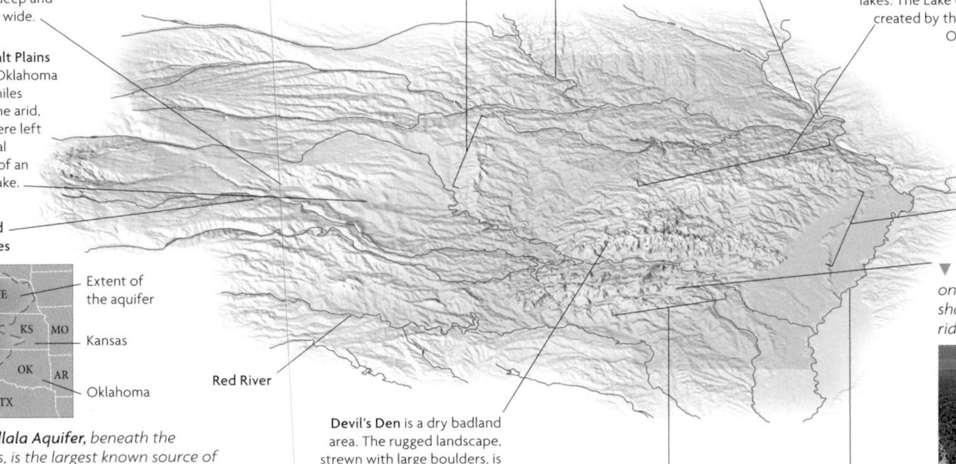

Collapsed limestone caverns led to the formation of Big Basin in Kansas; a depression 100 ft (33 m) deep and 1 mile (1.6 km) wide.

Flint Hills is the region's easternmost major escarpment. Steep, grassy uplands are interspersed with rocky, wooded ravines and outcrops of limestone and chert.

Missouri River

The Ozark Plateau is a wooded, hilly region of rivers and narrow, winding lakes. The Lake of the Ozarks was created by the damming of the Osage River in 1930.

The Great Salt Plains of northern Oklahoma cover 45 sq miles (116 sq km). The arid, white flats were left by the gradual evaporation of an ancient salt lake.

Crowleys Ridge is a long, sandy ridge, rising from the Mississippi floodplain. It was formed over thousands of years by the deposition of sand blown eastward from the Great Plains.

Underground water reserves

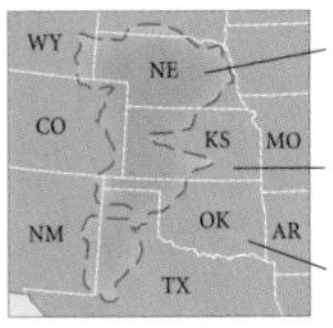

Scale 1:3,250,000

Km 0 5 10 20 30 40 50 60 70
Miles 0 5 10 20 30 40 50 60 70

projection: Lambert Conformal Conic

▼ *Lake Ouachita, in Arkansas is one of a number of irregularly-shaped lakes found among the ridges of the Ouachita Mountains.*

▲ *The Ogallala Aquifer, beneath the Great Plains, is the largest known source of underground water in the world. There is concern about the rapid depletion of this finite water supply by irrigation schemes.*

- Extent of the aquifer
- Kansas
- Oklahoma

Red River

Devil's Den is a dry badland area. The rugged landscape, strewn with large boulders, is the eroded remnant of a spur extending from the Arbuckle Mountains to the west.

Ouachita Mountains

Mississippi River

▲ *The landscape of northeast Kansas is interlaced by rivers which have cut broad wooded valleys through the gentle hills. All the rivers in Kansas form part of the massive Missouri/Mississippi drainage basin.*

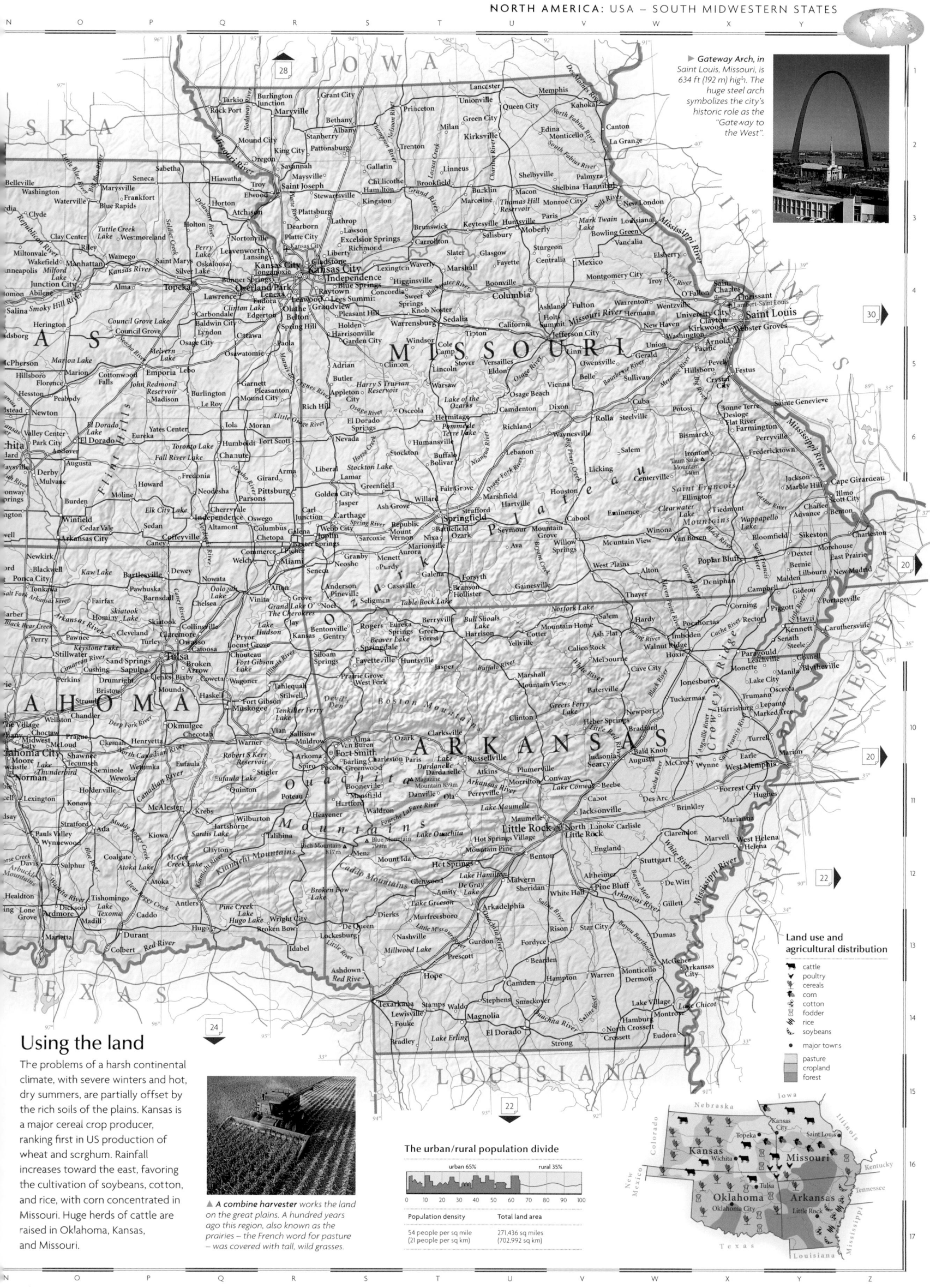

▶ *Gateway Arch, in Saint Louis, Missouri, is 634 ft (192 m) high. The huge steel arch symbolizes the city's historic role as the "Gateway to the West".*

Using the land

The problems of a harsh continental climate, with severe winters and hot, dry summers, are partially offset by the rich soils of the plains. Kansas is a major cereal crop producer, ranking first in US production of wheat and sorghum. Rainfall increases toward the east, favoring the cultivation of soybeans, cotton, and rice, with most concentrated in Missouri. Huge herds of cattle are raised in Oklahoma, Kansas, and Missouri.

▲ *A combine harvester works the land on the great plains. A hundred years ago this region, also known as the prairies – the French word for pasture – was covered with tall, wild grasses.*

The urban/rural population divide

urban 65%   rural 35%

0   10   20   30   40   50   60   70   80   90   100

Population density	Total land area
54 people per sq mile (21 people per sq km)	271,436 sq miles (702,992 sq km)

Land use and agricultural distribution

- 🐄 cattle
- 🦃 poultry
- 🌾 cereals
- 🌽 corn
- 🌱 cotton
- fodder
- rice
- soybeans
- major towns

- pasture
- cropland
- forest

USA: UPPER PLAINS STATES

Iowa, Minnesota, Nebraska, North Dakota, South Dakota

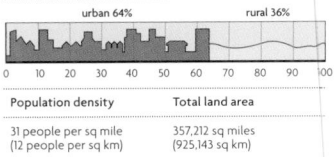

Lying at the very heart of the North American continent, much of this region was acquired from France as part of the Louisiana Purchase in 1803. The area was largely bypassed by the early waves of westward migrants. When Europeans did settle, during the 19th century, they displaced the Native Americans who lived on the plains. The settlers planted arable crops and raised cattle on the immensely fertile prairie land, founding an agrarian tradition which flourishes today. Most of this region remains rural; of the five states, only in Minnesota has there been significant diversification away from agriculture and resource-based industries into the hi-tech and service sectors.

Using the land

The popular image of these states as agricultural is entirely justified; prairies stretch uninterrupted across most of the area. Croplands fall into two regions: the wheat belt of the plains, and the corn belt of the central US. Cash crops, such as soybeans, are grown to supplement incomes. Livestock, particularly pigs and cattle, are raised throughout this region.

▶ *Dark, fertile prairie soils* in the southeast provide Minnesota's most productive farmland. Hot, humid summers create a long growing season for corn cultivation.

Land use and agricultural distribution

- 🐄 cattle
- 🐖 pigs
- 🌽 corn
- soybeans
- wheat
- • major towns
- pasture
- cropland
- forest
- wetland

The urban/rural population divide

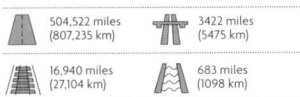

urban 64%   rural 36%

0 10 20 30 40 50 60 70 80 90 100

Population density	Total land area
31 people per sq mile (12 people per sq km)	357,212 sq miles (925,143 sq km)

Transportation & industry

Food processing and the production of farm machinery are supported by the large agricultural sector. Mineral exploitation is also an important activity: gold is mined in the ore-rich Black Hills of South Dakota, and both North Dakota and Nebraska are emerging as major petroleum producers.

▶ *Water erosion along* the Little Missouri River has carried away sedimentary deposits, creating rugged landscapes known as badlands.

Major industry and infrastructure

- coal
- engineering
- electronics
- finance
- food processing
- oil & gas
- mining
- • major towns
- ⊕ international airports
- major roads
- major industrial areas

Transportation network

504,522 miles (807,235 km)		3422 miles (5475 km)	
16,940 miles (27,104 km)		683 miles (1098 km)	

Nebraska's central location has made it an important transportation artery for east–west traffic. Minnesota's road network radiates out from the hub of the twin cities, Minneapolis–Saint Paul.

The landscape

These states straddle the Great Plains and the lowlands of the central US, with Minnesota lying in a transition zone between the eastern forests and the prairies. The region was shaped by repeated ice advances and retreats, leaving a flat relief, broken only by the numerous lakes and broad river networks that drain the prairies.

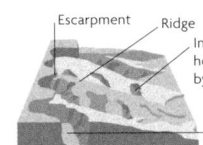

Escarpment   Ridge

In permeable strata hollows are formed by small mudslides

Water flowing into gullies erodes back the escarpment

▲ *Badlands are formed* by stormwater run-off. This flows down the impermeable strata of the escarpment and saturates the permeable strata, leading to mudslides and the formation of gullies.

The Minnesota landscape contains many post-glacial features, including its numerous lakes, boulder-strewn hills, and mineral-rich deposits.

North Dakota Badlands

Although it escaped the last glaciation, the limestone bedrock of southeastern Minnesota has been eroded by surface and subterranean streams, leaving a network of underground caverns and steepsided valleys.

▲ *In the badlands* of North and South Dakota, horizontal layers of sandstone have been eroded by rivers, leaving a landscape of narrow gullies, sharp crests and pinnacles.

South Dakota Badlands

▲ *Chimney Rock is a remnant* of an ancient land surface, eroded by the North Platte River. The tip of its spire stands 500 ft (150 m) above the plain.

Missouri River

Mississippi River

◀ *In northeastern Iowa,* the Mississippi and its tributaries have deeply incised the underlying bedrock creating a hilly terrain, with bluffs standing 300 ft (90 m) above the valley.

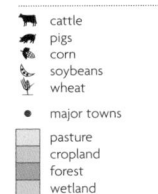
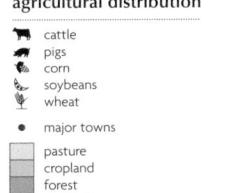
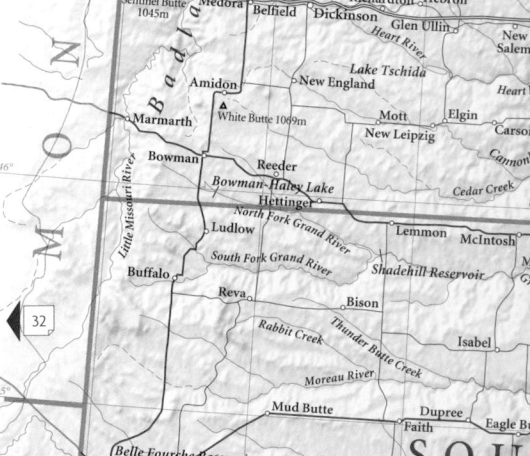

► Along the shores of Lake Superior in Minnesota, the average number of frostfree days can be as few as 90, and frosts may occur in any month of the year.

Map key

Population
◎ 100,000 to 500,000
⊕ 50,000 to 100,000
○ 10,000 to 50,000
∘ below 10,000

Elevation
2000m / 6562ft
1000m / 3281ft
500m / 1640ft
250m / 820ft
100m / 328ft
sea level

Scale 1:3,500,000

Km
0 20 40 60 80 100 120

Miles
0 20 40 60 80 100 120

projection: Lambert Conformal Conic

USA: GREAT LAKES STATES

Illinois, Indiana, Michigan, Ohio, Wisconsin

The states bordering the Great Lakes developed rapidly in the second half of the 19th century as a result of improvements in communications: railroads to the west and waterways to the south and east. Fertile land and good links with growing eastern seaboard cities encouraged the development of agriculture and food processing. Migrants from Europe and other parts of the US flooded into the region and for much of the 20th century the region's economy boomed. However, in recent years heavy industry has declined, earning the region the unwanted label the "Rustbelt."

Transportation & industry

The Great Lakes region is the center of the US car industry. Since the early part of the 20th century, its prosperity has been closely linked to the fortunes of automobile manufacturing. Iron and steel production has expanded to meet demand from this industry. In the 1970s, nationwide recession, cheaper foreign competition in the automobile sector, pollution in and around the Great Lakes, and the collapse of the meatpacking industry, centered on Chicago, forced these states to diversify their industrial base. New industries have emerged, notably electronics, service, and finance industries.

Transportation network

540,682 miles (865,091 km)		6550 miles (10,480 km)	
24,928 miles (39,884 km)		2330 miles (3748 km)	

Few areas of the US have a comparable system. Chicago is a principal transportation terminus with a dense network of roads, railroads, and Interstate freeways that radiates out from the city.

▶ Ever since Ransom Olds and Henry Ford started mass-producing automobiles in Detroit early in the 20th century, the city's name has become synonymous with the American automotive industry.

Major industry and infrastructure

- car manufacture
- coal
- electronics
- engineering
- finance
- food processing
- iron & steel
- oil
- research & development
- textiles
- major towns
- international airports
- major roads
- major industrial areas

The landscape

Much of this region shows the impact of glaciation which lasted until about 10,000 years ago, and extended as far south as Illinois and Ohio. Although the relief of the region slopes toward the Great Lakes, because the ice sheets blocked northerly drainage, most of the rivers today flow southward, forming part of the massive Mississippi/Missouri drainage basin.

The many lakes and marshes of Wisconsin and Michigan are the result of glacial erosion and deposition which occurred during the last Ice Age.

Southwestern Wisconsin is known as a "driftless" area. Unlike most of the region, low hills protected it from erosion by the advancing ice sheet.

Most of the water used in northern Illinois is pumped from underground reservoirs. Due to increased demand, many areas now face a water shortage. Around Joliet, the water table was lowered by more than 700 ft (210 m) over the last century.

◀ The dunes near Sleeping Bear Point rise 400 ft (120 m) from the banks of Lake Michigan. They are constantly being resculpted by wind action.

Lake Michigan

Lake Erie is the shallowest of the five Great Lakes. Its average depth is about 62 ft (19 m). Storms sweeping across from Canada erode its shores and cause the silting of its harbors.

The Appalachian plateau stretches eastward from Ohio. It is dissected by streams flowing west into the Mississippi and Ohio rivers.

Illinois plains

▲ The plains of Illinois are characteristic of drift landscapes, scoured and flattened by glacial erosion and covered with fertile glacial deposits.

Mississippi River

Ohio River

Relic landforms from the last glaciation, such as shallow basins and ridges, cover all but the south of this region. Ridges, known as moraines, up to 300 ft (100 m) high, lie to the south of Lake Michigan.

Unlike the level prairie to the north, southern Indiana is relatively rugged. Limestone in the hills has been dissolved by water, producing features such as sinkholes and underground caves.

Glacial till

Present-day river or stream

Channels caused by outwash from melting glacier

Most recent till deposits

Older till sheet

Bedrock

▲ As a result of successive glacial depositions, the total depth of till along the former southern margin of the Laurentide ice sheet can exceed 1300 ft (400 m).

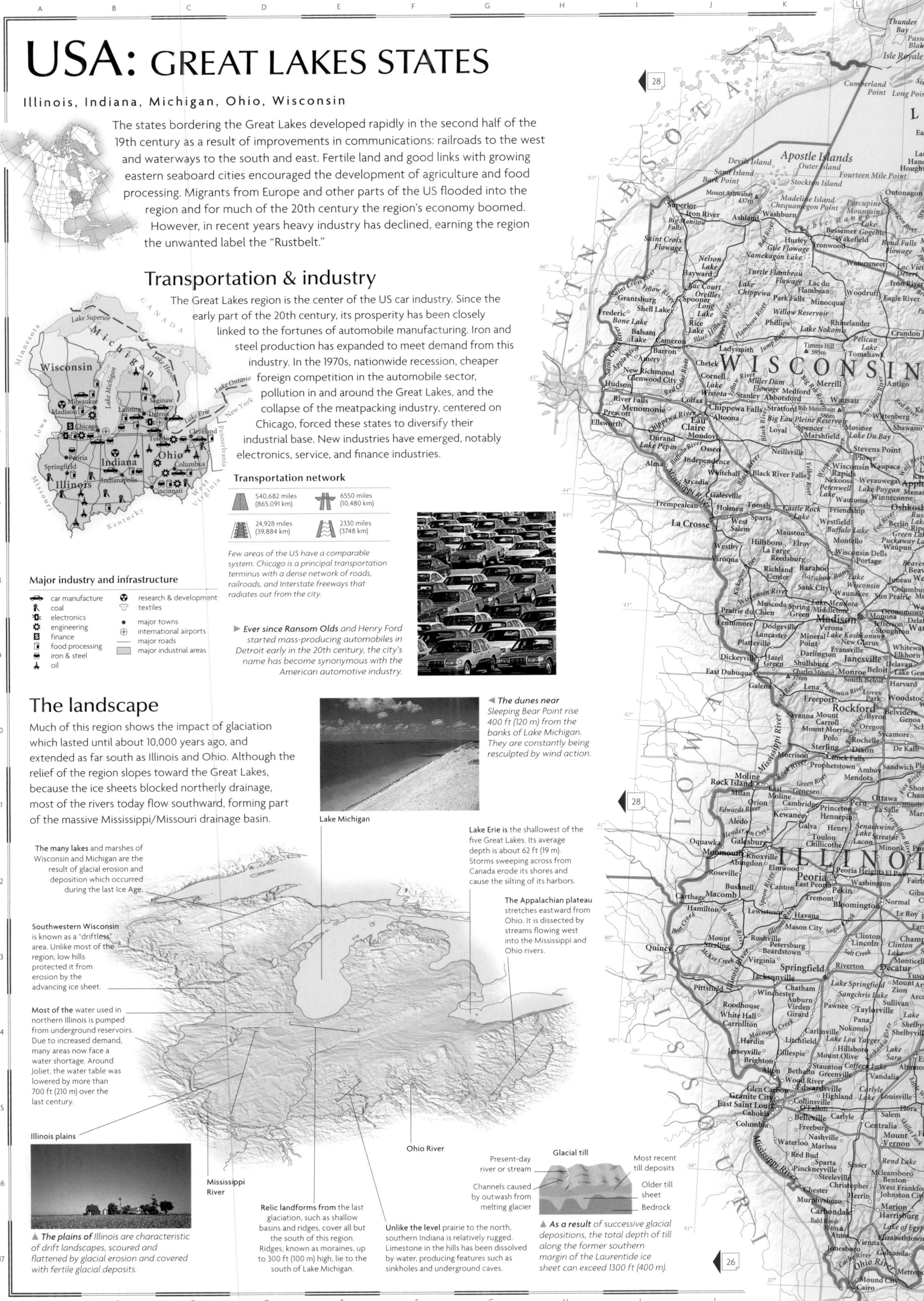

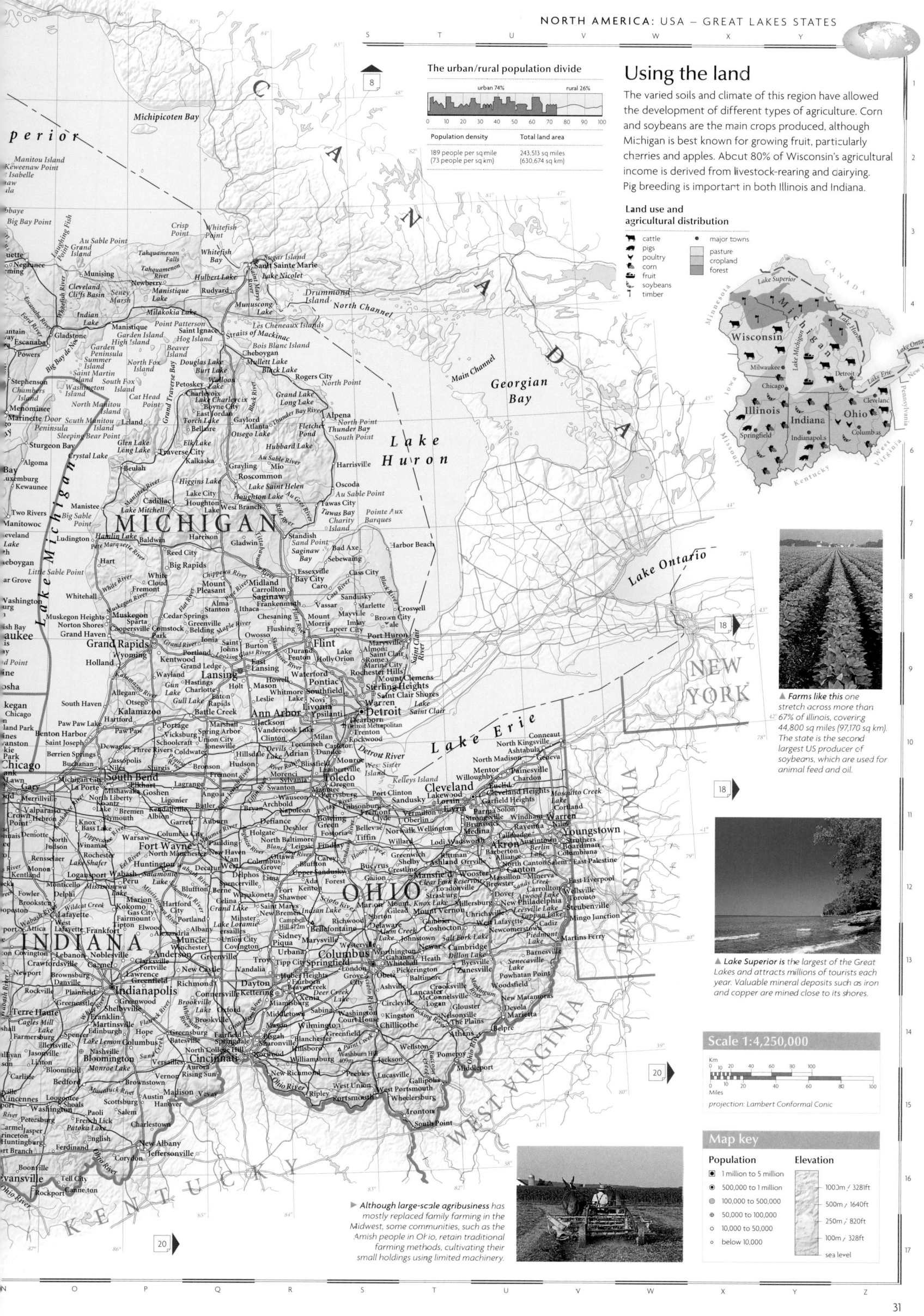

The urban/rural population divide

urban 74%   rural 26%

0 10 20 30 40 50 60 70 80 90 100

Population density	Total land area
189 people per sq mile (73 people per sq km)	243,513 sq miles (630,674 sq km)

Using the land

The varied soils and climate of this region have allowed the development of different types of agriculture. Corn and soybeans are the main crops produced, although Michigan is best known for growing fruit, particularly cherries and apples. About 80% of Wisconsin's agricultural income is derived from livestock-rearing and dairying. Pig breeding is important in both Illinois and Indiana.

Land use and agricultural distribution

- cattle
- pigs
- poultry
- corn
- fruit
- soybeans
- timber
- major towns
- pasture
- cropland
- forest

▲ Farms like this one stretch across more than 67% of Illinois, covering 44,800 sq miles (97,170 sq km). The state is the second largest US producer of soybeans, which are used for animal feed and oil.

▲ Lake Superior is the largest of the Great Lakes and attracts millions of tourists each year. Valuable mineral deposits such as iron and copper are mined close to its shores.

Scale 1:4,250,000

Km
0 10 20   40   60   80   100

Miles
0   20   40   60   80   100

projection: Lambert Conformal Conic

Map key

Population
- ▣ 1 million to 5 million
- ◉ 500,000 to 1 million
- ◎ 100,000 to 500,000
- ⊕ 50,000 to 100,000
- ○ 10,000 to 50,000
- ○ below 10,000

Elevation
- 1000m / 3281ft
- 500m / 1640ft
- 250m / 820ft
- 100m / 328ft
- sea level

▶ Although large-scale agribusiness has mostly replaced family farming in the Midwest, some communities, such as the Amish people in Ohio, retain traditional farming methods, cultivating their small holdings using limited machinery.

USA: NORTH MOUNTAIN STATES

Idaho, Montana, Oregon, Washington, Wyoming

The remoteness of the northwestern states, coupled with the rugged landscape, ensured that this was one of the last areas settled by Europeans in the 19th century. Fur-trappers and gold-prospectors followed the Snake River westward as it wound its way through the Rocky Mountains. The states of the northwest have pioneered many conservationist policies, with the first US National Park opened at Yellowstone in 1872. More recently, the Cascades and Rocky Mountains have become havens for adventure tourism. The mountains still serve to isolate the western seaboard from the rest of the continent. This isolation has encouraged West Coast cities to expand their trade links with countries of the Pacific Rim.

▲ *The Snake River* has cut down into the basalt of the Columbia Basin to form Hells Canyon, the deepest in the US, with cliffs up to 7900 ft (2408 m) high.

Map key

Population
◉ 500,000 to 1 million
◎ 100,000 to 500,000
⊕ 50,000 to 100,000
○ 10,000 to 50,000
∘ below 10,000

Elevation
4000m / 13,124ft
3000m / 9843ft
2000m / 6562ft
1000m / 3281ft
500m / 1640ft
250m / 820ft
100m / 328ft
sea level

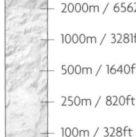

▶ *Fine-textured, volcanic* soils in the hilly Palouse region of eastern Washington are susceptible to erosion.

Using the land

Wheat farming in the east gives way to cattle ranching as rainfall decreases. Irrigated farming in the Snake River valley produces large yields of potatoes and other vegetables. Dairying and fruit-growing take place in the wet western lowlands between the mountain ranges.

The urban/rural population divide
urban 74%   rural 26%

Population density
26 people per sq mile
(10 people per sq km)

Total land area
487,970 sq miles
(1,263,716 sq km)

Scale 1:4,250,000
projection: Lambert Conformal Conic

Land use and agricultural distribution
🐄 cattle
🦃 poultry
🌾 cereals
🍎 fruit
🥔 potatoes
🌲 timber
• major towns
pasture
cropland
forest

Transportation & industry

Minerals and timber are extremely important in this region. Uranium, precious metals, copper, and coal are all mined, the latter in vast open-cast pits in Wyoming; oil and natural gas are extracted further south. Manufacturing, notably related to the aerospace and electronics industries, is important in western cities.

Transportation network
347,857 miles (556,571 km)
4200 miles (6720 km)
12,354 miles (19,766 km)
1108 miles (1782 km)

Major industry and infrastructure
⬙ adventure tourism
✈ aerospace
⚒ coal
🧪 chemicals
electronics
🍴 food processing
⛏ mining
oil & gas
🪵 timber processing
• major towns
✈ international airports
major roads
major industrial areas

The Union Pacific Railroad has been in service across Wyoming since 1867. The route through the Rocky Mountains is now shared with the Interstate 80, a major east–west highway.

◀ *Seattle lies in* one of Puget Sound's many inlets. The city receives oil and other resources from Alaska, and benefits from expanding trade across the Pacific.

◀ *Crater Lake, Oregon,* is 6 miles (10 km) wide and 1800 ft (600 m) deep. It marks the site of a volcanic cone, which collapsed after an eruption within the last 7000 years.

The landscape

The Rocky Mountains are flanked by lower parallel ranges, which spread onto the Great Plains in the east and surmount the broad lava plateau which extends westward. The Cascade Range divides the Columbia Basin from the coastlands, where the low areas around Puget Sound are broken by the steep, volcanic Olympic Mountains and the wooded hills of the Coast Ranges.

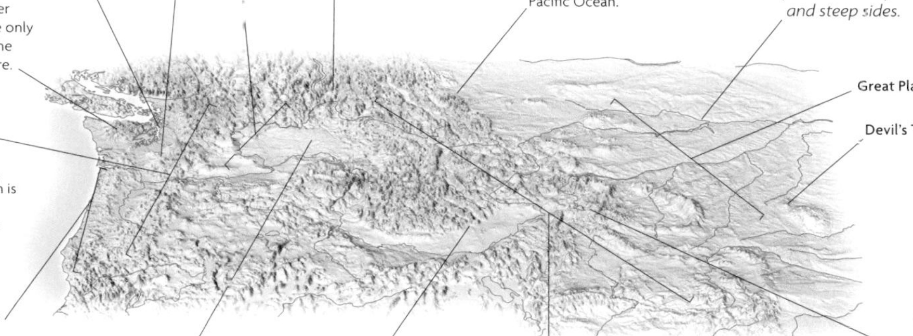

Puget Sound

Glacial valleys on the seaward side of the Olympic Mountains receive about 142 inches (3600 mm) of rain per year, supporting the only true rain forest of the northern hemisphere.

Mount St. Helens erupted in 1980, killing 57 people and devastating a huge area.

Columbia Basin

Grand Coulee and the lesser coulees (ravines) were cut by cataclysmic floods, from the release of an ice-dammed lake, at the end of the last Ice Age.

The Continental Divide, or watershed, crosses the Lewis Range. From here, rivers flow east to Hudson Bay, south to the Gulf of Mexico and west to the Pacific Ocean.

▶ Piney Buttes are the remnants of an older, higher land surface gradually weathered and eroded into isolated outcrops with flat tops and steep sides.

The Cascades are glacially scoured volcanic mountains, the highest of which is Mount Rainier, a dormant volcano at 14,409 ft (4392 m).

Coast Ranges

Great Plains

Devil's Tower

Molten rock pools, forming parallel columns

Surrounding strata eroded away

Molten rock wells up from the Earth's core

▲ Devil's Tower in Wyoming is an igneous intrusion, formed below the Earth's surface. Molten rock intruded through cracks in the overlying strata and cooled. Over time, the softer rock layers have been eroded away, leaving only the tower standing.

The plateaus of the Columbia and Snake rivers represent one of the world's largest accumulations of lava. Over 5 million years ago, successive flows of molten basalt buried the existing land surface by up to 450 ft (150 m).

The contorted rock shapes at "Craters of the Moon" National Monument in Idaho were left 2000 years ago by the sporadic upwelling of viscous lava from fissures in the basalt plateau.

Rocky Mountains

▲ Water from the hot springs in Yellowstone National Park deposits minerals as it cools in rock pools. Long periods of deposition have created these rock terraces.

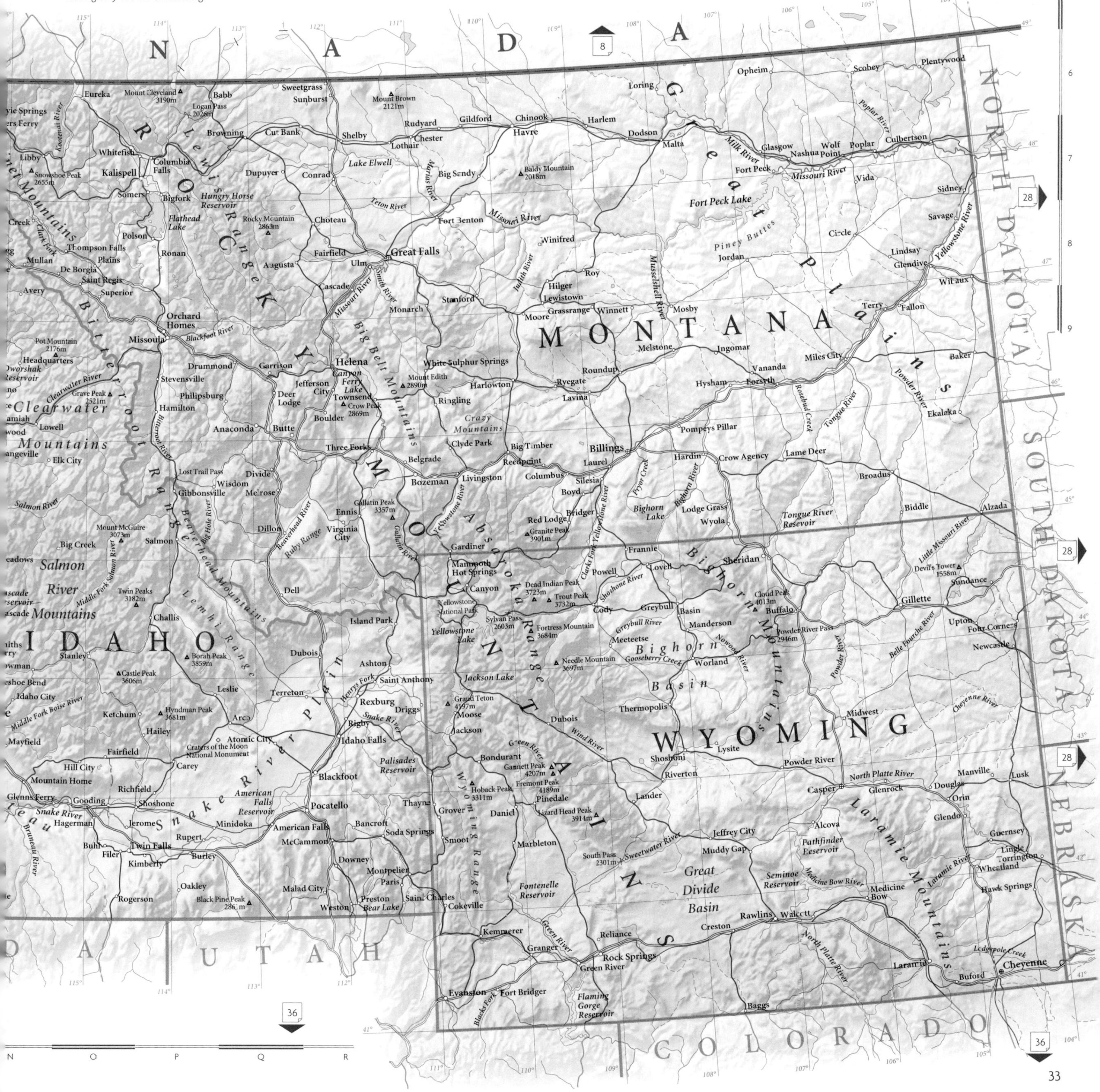

[Map of North Mountain States: Montana, Wyoming, Idaho, with portions of North Dakota, South Dakota, Nebraska, Colorado, Utah, and Canada]

USA: CALIFORNIA & NEVADA

The Gold Rush of 1849 attracted the first major wave of European settlers to the West Coast. The pleasant climate, beautiful scenery, and dynamic economy continue to attract immigrants – despite the ever-present danger of earthquakes – and California has become the US's most populous state. The overwhelmingly urban population is concentrated in the vast conurbations of Los Angeles, San Francisco, and San Diego; new immigrants include people from South Korea, the Philippines, Vietnam, and Mexico. Nevada's arid lands were initially exploited for minerals; in recent years, revenue from mining has been superseded by income from the tourist and gambling centers of Las Vegas and Reno.

Map key

Population
- ◉ 1 million to 5 million
- ◉ 500,000 to 1 million
- ◎ 100,000 to 500,000
- ⊕ 50,000 to 100,000
- ⊙ 10,000 to 50,000
- ∘ below 10,000

Elevation
- 4000m / 13,124ft
- 3000m / 9843ft
- 2000m / 6562ft
- 1000m / 3281ft
- 500m / 1640ft
- 250m / 820ft
- 100m / 328ft
- sea level

Scale 1:3,250,000

projection: Lambert Conformal Conic

Transportation & industry

Nevada's rich mineral reserves ushered in a period of mining wealth which has now been replaced by revenue generated from gambling. California supports a broad set of activities including defense-related industries and research and development facilities. "Silicon Valley," near San Francisco, is a world leading center for micro-electronics, while tourism and the Los Angeles film industry also generate large incomes.

Major industry and infrastructure

- ✈ aerospace
- 🚗 car manufacture
- ⚙ defense
- 🎬 film industry
- S finance
- 🍴 food processing
- 🎰 gambling
- 💻 hi-tech industry
- ⛏ mining
- pharmaceuticals
- research & development
- textiles
- tourism
- ● major towns
- ⊕ international airports
- — major roads
- ▦ major industrial areas

Transportation network

211,459 miles (338,334 km)	2944 miles (4710 km)
7822 miles (12,595 km)	190 miles (360 km)

In California, the motor vehicle is a vital part of daily life, and an extensive freeway system runs throughout the state, cementing its position as the most important mode of transport.

◀ *Gambling was legalized in Nevada in 1931. Las Vegas has since become the center of this multimillion dollar industry.*

The landscape

The broad Central Valley divides California's coastal mountains from the Sierra Nevada. The San Andreas Fault, running beneath much of the state, is the site of frequent earth tremors and sometimes more serious earthquakes. East of the Sierra Nevada, the landscape is characterized by the basin and range topography with stony deserts and many salt lakes.

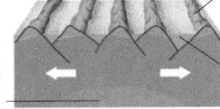

Rising molten rock causes stretching of the Earth's crust

Extensive cracking (faulting) uplifted a series of ridges

As ridges are eroded they fill intervening valleys with sediments

▲ *Molten rock (magma) welling up to form a dome in the Earth's interior, causes the brittle surface rocks to stretch and crack. Some areas were uplifted to form mountains (ranges), while others sunk to form flat valleys (basins).*

◀ *The General Sherman sequoia tree in Sequoia National Park is around 2500 years old and at 275 ft (84 m) is one of the largest living things on earth.*

Most of California's agriculture is confined to the fertile and extensively irrigated Central Valley, running between the Coast Ranges and the Sierra Nevada. It incorporates the San Joaquin and Sacramento valleys.

The dramatic granitic rock formations of Half Dome and El Capitan, and the verdant coniferous forests, attract millions of visitors annually to Yosemite National Park in the Sierra Nevada.

Sierra Nevada

The Great Basin dominates most of Nevada's topography containing large open basins, punctuated by eroded features such as *buttes* and *mesas.* River flow tends to be seasonal, dependent upon spring showers and winter snow melt.

Wheeler Peak is home to some of the world's oldest trees, bristlecone pines, which live for up to 5000 years.

Using the land

California is the leading agricultural producer in the US, although low rainfall makes irrigation essential. The long growing season and abundant sunshine allow many crops to be grown in the fertile Central Valley including grapes, citrus fruits, vegetables, and cotton. Almost 17 million acres (6.8 million hectares) of California's forests are used commercially. Nevada's arid climate and poor soil are largely unsuitable for agriculture; 85% of its land is state owned and large areas are used for underground testing of nuclear weapons.

Land use and agricultural distribution

- 🐄 cattle
- citrus fruits
- 🍎 fruit
- irrigation
- timber
- vineyards
- ● major towns
- pasture
- cropland
- forest
- desert

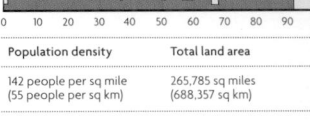

When the Hoover Dam across the Colorado River was completed in 1936, it created Lake Mead, one of the largest artificial lakes in the world, extending for 115 miles (285 km) upstream.

Amargosa Desert

The San Andreas Fault is a transverse fault which extends for 650 miles (1050 km) through California. Major earthquakes occur when the land either side of the fault moves at different rates. San Francisco was devastated by an earthquake in 1906.

Death Valley

▶ *Named by migrating settlers in 1849, Death Valley is the driest, hottest place in North America, as well as being the lowest point on land in the western hemisphere, at 282 ft (86 m) below sea level.*

The sparsely populated Mojave Desert receives less than 8 inches (200 mm) of rainfall a year. It is used extensively for weapons-testing and military purposes.

The Salton Sea was created accidentally between 1905 and 1907 when an irrigation channel from the Colorado River broke out of its banks and formed this salty 300 sq mile (777 sq km), landlocked lake.

▲ *The Sierra Nevada create a "rainshadow," preventing rain from reaching much of Nevada. Pacific air masses, passing over the mountains, are stripped of their moisture.*

▲ *Without considerable irrigation, this fertile valley at Palm Springs would still be part of the Sonoran Desert. California's farmers account for about 80% of the state's total water usage.*

The urban/rural population divide

urban 92%   rural 8%

0 10 20 30 40 50 60 70 80 90 100

Population density	Total land area
142 people per sq mile (55 people per sq km)	265,785 sq miles (688,357 sq km)

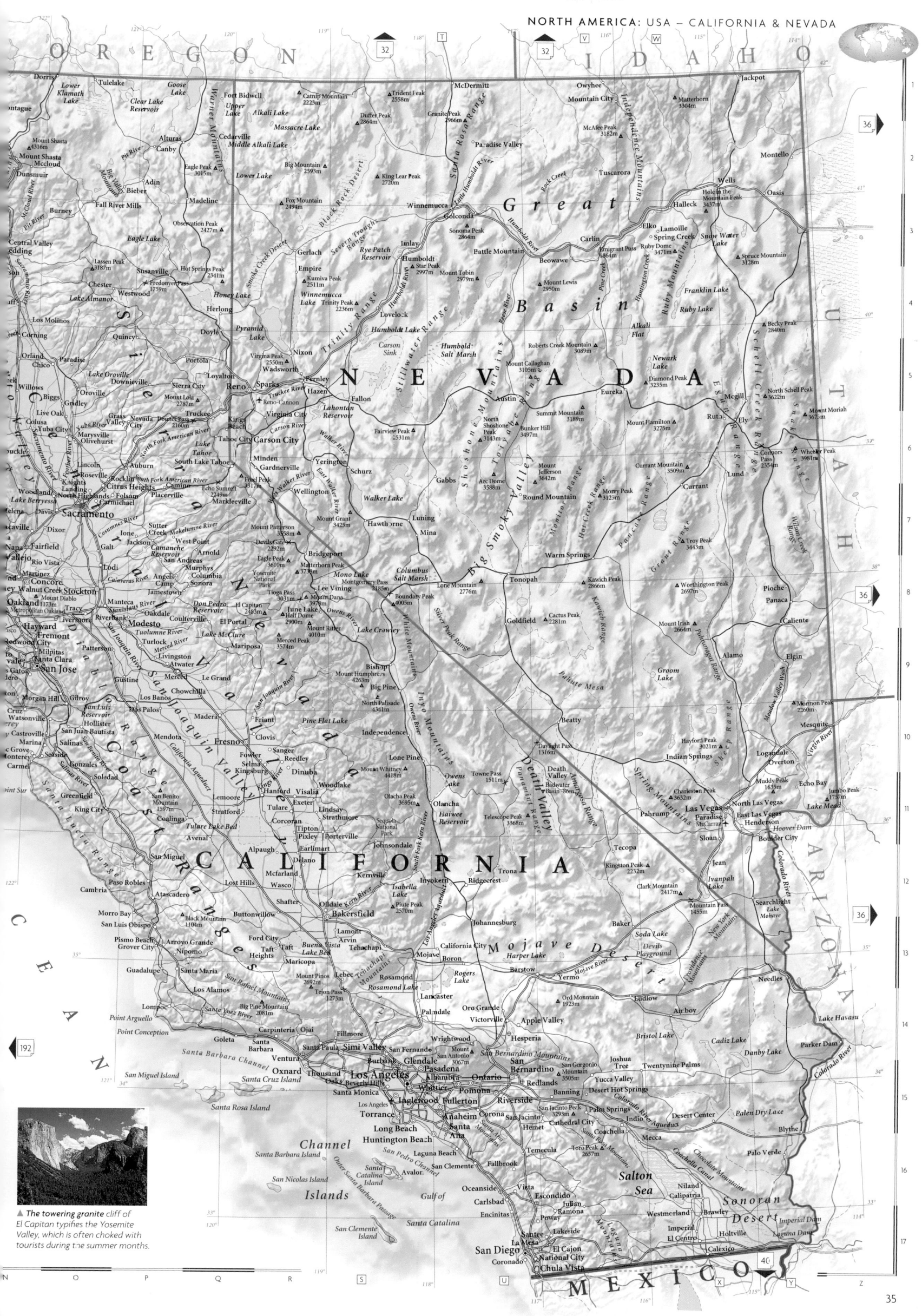

OREGON

IDAHO

Dorris
Lower Klamath Lake
Tulelake
Goose Lake
Jackpot
Montague
Mount Shasta 4316m
Clear Lake Reservoir
Upper Lake
Fort Bidwell
Catnip Mountain 2223m
McDermitt
Owyhee
Mountain City
Matterhorn 3304m
Mount Shasta
Mccloud
Alturas
Canby
Cedarville
Alkali Lake
Trident Peak 2558m
Granite Peak 2966m
Paradise Valley
McAfee Peak 3182m
Montello
Dunsmuir
Middle Alkali Lake
Massacre Lake
Duffer Peak 2864m
Wells
Burney
Bieber
Madeline
Big Mountain 2593m
Fox Mountain 2494m
Winnemucca
Golconda
Great
Halleck
Elko
Lamoille
Hole in the Mountain Peak 3437m
Oasis
Fall River Mills
Adin
Observation Peak 2427m
King Lear Peak 2720m
Sonoma Peak 2864m
Humboldt River
Battle Mountain
Carlin
Emigrant Pass
Ruby Dome 3471m
Snow Water Lake
Spring Creek
Montello

Basin

NEVADA

UTAH

CALIFORNIA

MEXICO

PACIFIC OCEAN

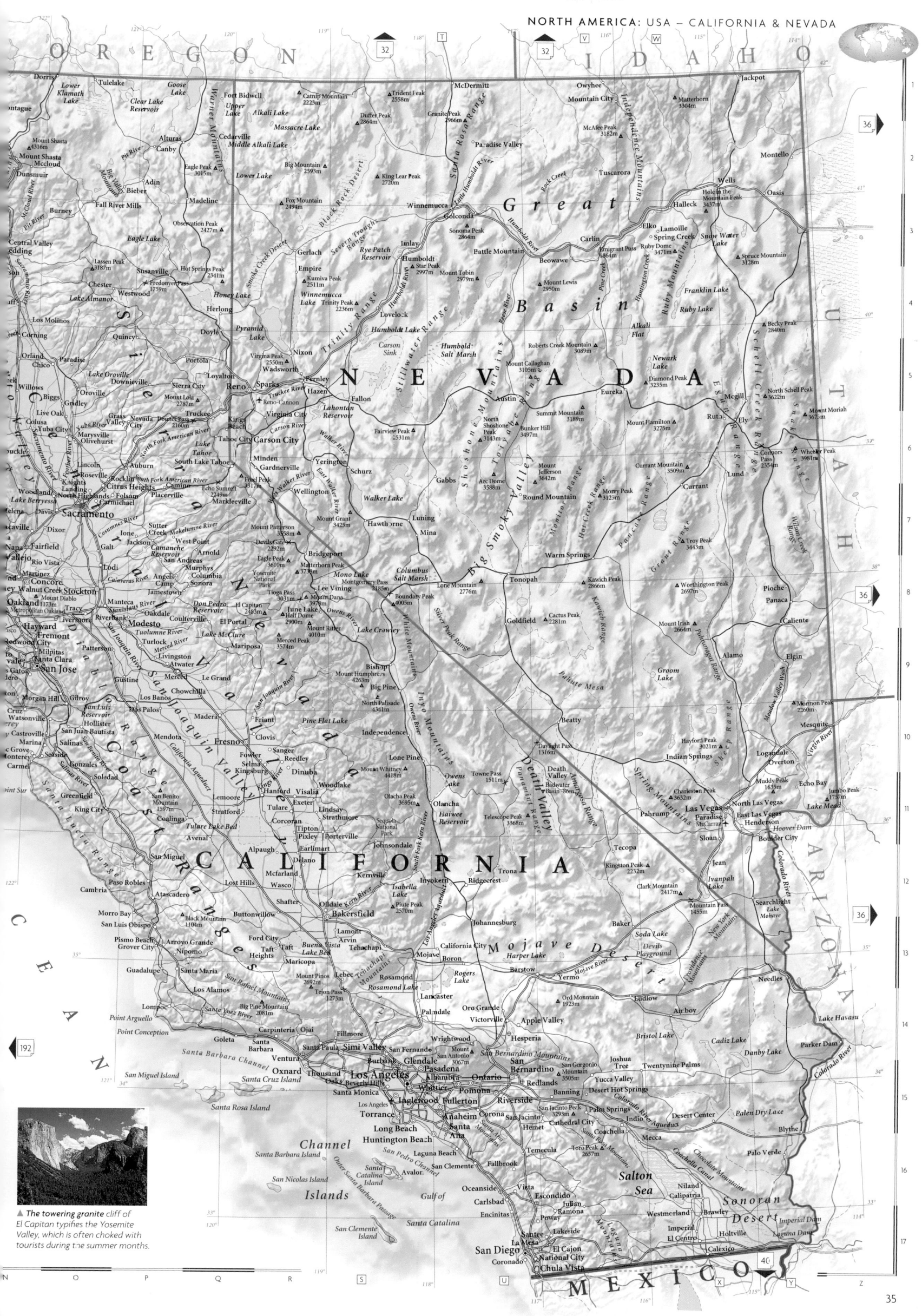
▲ The towering granite cliff of El Capitan typifies the Yosemite Valley, which is often choked with tourists during the summer months.

USA: SOUTH MOUNTAIN STATES

Arizona, Colorado, New Mexico, Utah

This arid region, characterized by expansive plateaus and spectacular canyons is home to several distinct peoples. The ruins of cliff dwellings built a thousand years ago by the Anasazi people still exist today, and native Americans own one-third of the land in Arizona. Spanish and Mexican conquest and settlement left a hispanic presence which is strongest in New Mexico. The Mormons, who came to the Great Salt Lake seeking religious freedom in 1847, were among the earliest Anglo-American settlers and now make up over 70% of Utah's population. The region's mineral wealth drove rapid development in the 20th century, yet the constraints of a fragile environment, including widespread water shortages, may limit prospects for growth.

The landscape

The arid, rocky expanse of the Colorado Plateau is dissected by immense canyons of the Colorado River. Desert lies to the north and south and branches of the Rocky Mountains run east and west. The Great Salt Lake and Desert lie within the Great Basin, a barren region of parallel mountain ranges that extends into Arizona.

When water evaporates it leaves a salt pan

Mudflats

Lake is fed by seasonal snow melt

Water level of lake varies according to quantity of run-off received from snow melt

▲ *The Great Salt Lake is an ephemeral lake; it can remain dry for extended periods, leaving a pan of evaporated mineral salts in its center.*

Over 13 million years of weathering has created thousands of spires and pinnacles from the alternating rock strata of Bryce Canyon.

The parallel basins and ridges, which run north–south along the Great Basin, reflect a major series of block-faults in the underlying bedrock.

Parts of the Grand Canyon, which cuts through the Colorado Plateau, are 16 miles (25 km) wide. The Colorado River has cut down 6262 ft (2000 m), exposing rock strata more than 2 billion years old.

Lake Powell

The Rio Grande has its source in several meltwater streams, which have cut deep valleys into the platform of the San Juan Mountains.

Sand dunes, 600 ft (180 m) high, have been deposited in San Luis Valley, by winds funnelled through the San Juan and Sangre de Cristo mountains in the Rockies.

Rainbow Bridge is the world's largest natural arch. The 309 ft (94 m) span probably began to grow when the sandstone spur of a meandering creek was breached during a flash flood.

The striking color effects seen in the Painted Desert come from minerals such as gypsum and haematite, combined with ambient heat and dust.

Petrified Forest

▶ *In the arid landscape of Petrified Forest National Park in Arizona, the grain of prehistoric trees has been preserved as a fossil imprint in the rocks. The bog-preserved trees were gradually turned to stone by seeping mineral-rich water.*

Shifting gypsum sands produce a constantly changing land surface, overwhelming plants and any other obstacles in Tularosa Valley.

▶ *The intricate stalactites of Carlsbad Caverns have grown with the seepage of calcium-rich water over the last 100,000 years. The huge caves are home to around 100,000 Mexican freetail bats..*

Transportation & industry

New industries have helped reduce the region's dependence on the extraction of minerals and fossil fuels. Precision manufacture has grown rapidly, particularly in Arizona and Colorado. Salt Lake City and Denver are well-established financial centers and New Mexico, the main US producer of uranium, is a prominent region for nuclear research. Colorado is the most important US center for winter sports.

Transportation network

232,434 miles (373,986 km)	4059 miles (6515 km)
8627 miles (13,881 km)	none

The Colorado Rockies are crossed by 32 mountain passes, some as high as 12,183 ft (3713 m). The Eisenhower Tunnel west of Denver carries Interstate Highway 70 straight through the Continental Divide.

Major industry and infrastructure

- chemicals
- coal
- defense
- finance
- food processing
- hi-tech industry
- oil & gas
- mining
- research & development
- winter sports
- major towns
- international airports
- major roads
- major industrial areas

▲ *Glen Canyon Dam on the Colorado river was completed in 1964, it provides hydroelectric power and irrigation water as part of a long-term project to harness the river.*

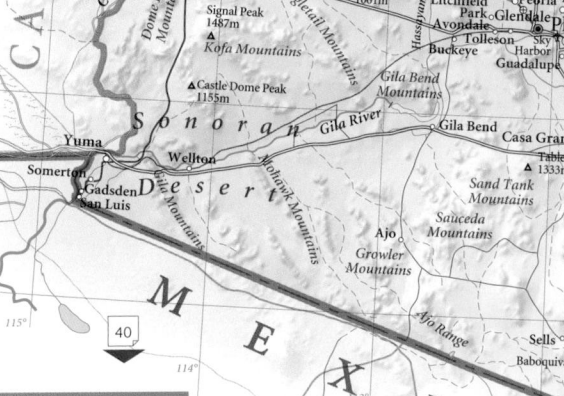

◀ *The flat tablelands (mesas), and the isolated pinnacles (buttes) which rise from the floor of Monument Valley are the resistant remnants of an earlier land surface, gradually cut back by erosion under arid conditions.*

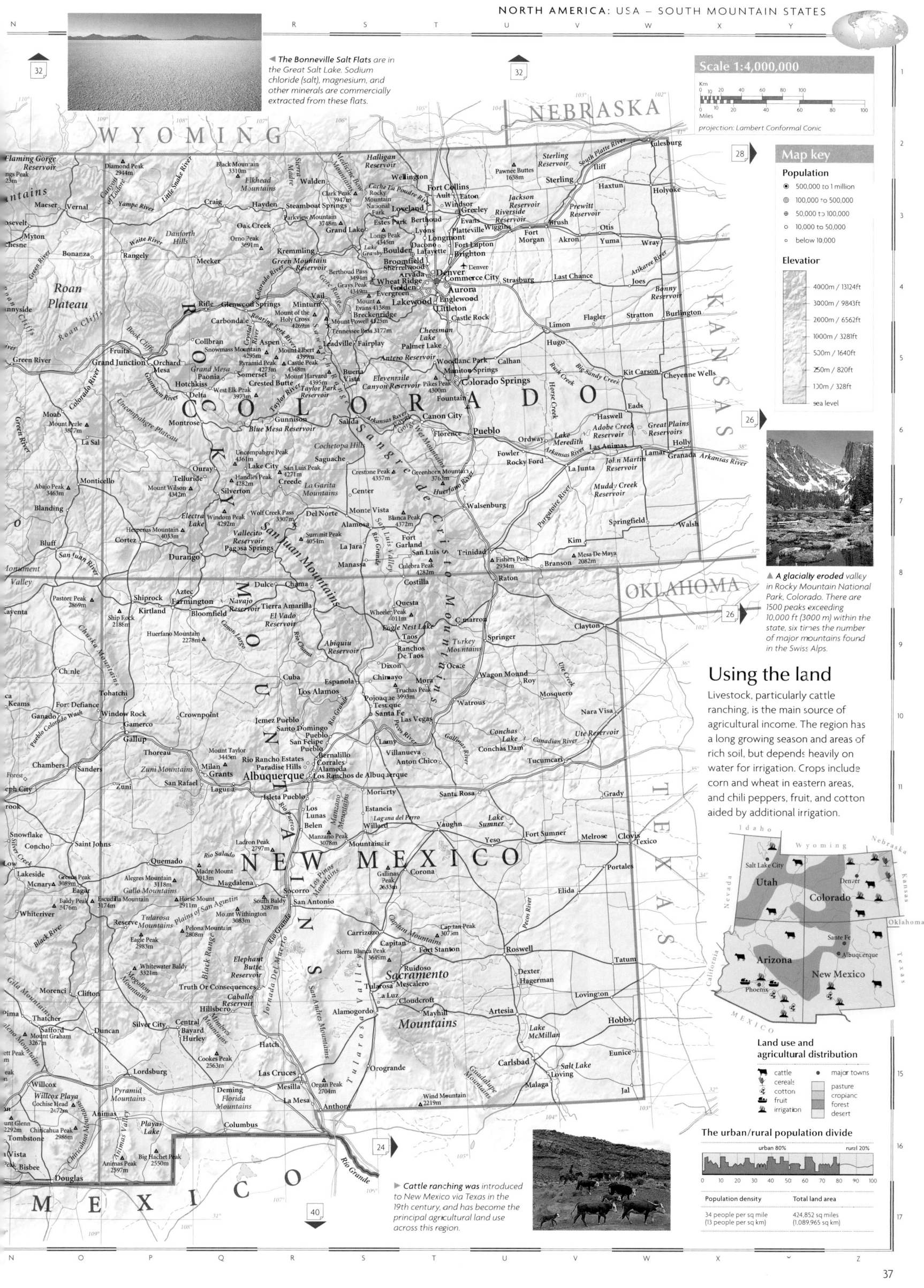

◀ *The Bonneville Salt Flats* are in the Great Salt Lake. Sodium chloride (salt), magnesium, and other minerals are commercially extracted from these flats.

Scale 1:4,000,000

projection: Lambert Conformal Conic

Map key

Population

◉ 500,000 to 1 million
◎ 100,000 to 500,000
⊕ 50,000 to 100,000
⊙ 10,000 to 50,000
∘ below 10,000

Elevation

4000m / 13124ft
3000m / 9843ft
2000m / 6562ft
1000m / 3281ft
500m / 1640ft
250m / 820ft
100m / 328ft
sea level

▲ *A glacially eroded* valley in Rocky Mountain National Park, Colorado. There are 1500 peaks exceeding 10,000 ft (3000 m) within the state, six times the number of major mountains found in the Swiss Alps.

Using the land

Livestock, particularly cattle ranching, is the main source of agricultural income. The region has a long growing season and areas of rich soil, but depends heavily on water for irrigation. Crops include corn and wheat in eastern areas, and chili peppers, fruit, and cotton aided by additional irrigation.

Land use and agricultural distribution

🐄 cattle
🌾 cereals
🌱 cotton
🍎 fruit
💧 irrigation

• major towns
pasture
cropland
forest
desert

The urban/rural population divide

urban 80%   rural 20%

0 10 20 30 40 50 60 70 80 90 100

Population density	Total land area
34 people per sq mile (13 people per sq km)	424,852 sq miles (1,089,965 sq km)

▶ *Cattle ranching was* introduced to New Mexico via Texas in the 19th century, and has become the principal agricultural land use across this region.

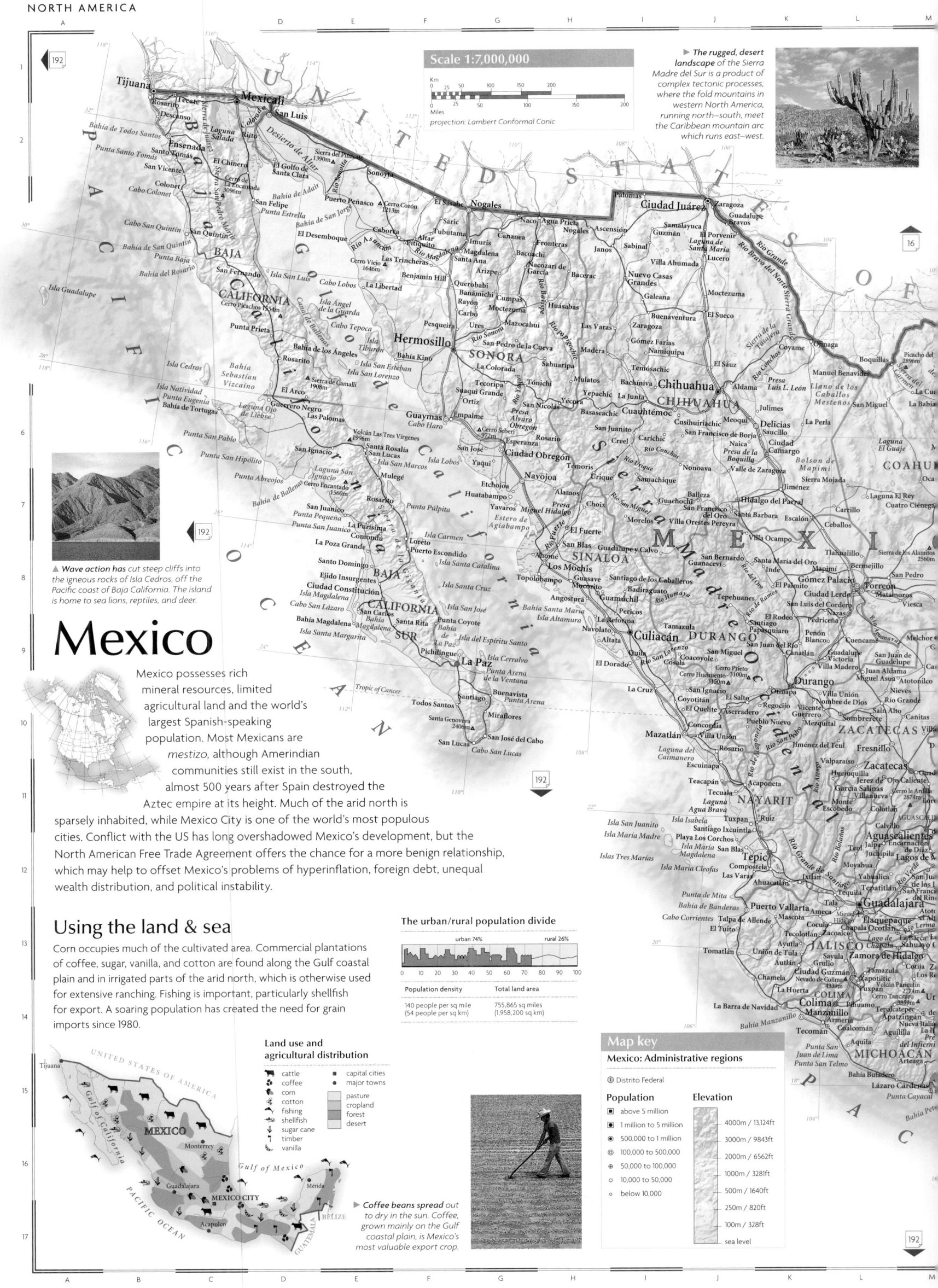

▶ *The rugged, desert landscape* of the Sierra Madre del Sur is a product of complex tectonic processes, where the fold mountains in western North America, running north–south, meet the Caribbean mountain arc which runs east–west.

Scale 1:7,000,000

projection: Lambert Conformal Conic

▲ *Wave action has* cut steep cliffs into the igneous rocks of Isla Cedros, off the Pacific coast of Baja California. The island is home to sea lions, reptiles, and deer.

Mexico

Mexico possesses rich mineral resources, limited agricultural land and the world's largest Spanish-speaking population. Most Mexicans are *mestizo*, although Amerindian communities still exist in the south, almost 500 years after Spain destroyed the Aztec empire at its height. Much of the arid north is sparsely inhabited, while Mexico City is one of the world's most populous cities. Conflict with the US has long overshadowed Mexico's development, but the North American Free Trade Agreement offers the chance for a more benign relationship, which may help to offset Mexico's problems of hyperinflation, foreign debt, unequal wealth distribution, and political instability.

Using the land & sea

Corn occupies much of the cultivated area. Commercial plantations of coffee, sugar, vanilla, and cotton are found along the Gulf coastal plain and in irrigated parts of the arid north, which is otherwise used for extensive ranching. Fishing is important, particularly shellfish for export. A soaring population has created the need for grain imports since 1980.

The urban/rural population divide

urban 74%   rural 26%

0 10 20 30 40 50 60 70 80 90 100

Population density	Total land area
140 people per sq mile (54 people per sq km)	755,865 sq miles (1,958,200 sq km)

Land use and agricultural distribution

- cattle
- coffee
- corn
- cotton
- fishing
- shellfish
- sugar cane
- timber
- vanilla

- capital cities
- major towns

- pasture
- cropland
- forest
- desert

Map key

Mexico: Administrative regions

Ⓓ Distrito Federal

Population
- ▪ above 5 million
- ▪ 1 million to 5 million
- ◉ 500,000 to 1 million
- ◎ 100,000 to 500,000
- ⊙ 50,000 to 100,000
- ○ 10,000 to 50,000
- ○ below 10,000

Elevation
- 4000m / 13,124ft
- 3000m / 9843ft
- 2000m / 6562ft
- 1000m / 3281ft
- 500m / 1640ft
- 250m / 820ft
- 100m / 328ft
- sea level

▶ *Coffee beans spread* out to dry in the sun. Coffee, grown mainly on the Gulf coastal plain, is Mexico's most valuable export crop.

N O P Q R S T U V W X Y

The landscape

The great central plateau rises gently southward from the Rio Grande, isolated from the coastal plains by the Sierra Madre Oriental and Occidental. The two ranges converge from east and west respectively, culminating in high volcanic peaks around Mexico City. Further ranges of the Sierra Madre rise to the south of the Balsas basin, skirted by the low-lying Isthmus of Tehuantepec (*Istmo de Tehuantepec*) and Yucatan Peninsula.

The long, narrow, extremely arid peninsula of Baja (lower) California is an elongated granite block, separated from the mainland by the flooded rift valley of the Gulf of California (*Golfo de California*).

Wave action has constructed sand bars which shelter lagoons along the shore of the Gulf coastal plain.

The dormant cone of Volcán Pico de Orizaba is, at 18,700 ft (5700 m), the highest peak in Mexico. In North America, only Mount McKinley and Mount Logan are taller.

▲ *Tropical rainforest abounds* in the Yucatan Peninsula, a broad, low limestone shelf. Rivers are rare due to the porous nature of limestone, so the forest is mostly fed by streams and underground water.

Sierra Madre Oriental

Rio Grande

The heavily-forested Isthmus of Tehuantepec (*Istmo de Tehuantepec*) is a graben; a low-lying trough created by downward movement of the bedrock between two fault lines.

Formation of the Gulf of California

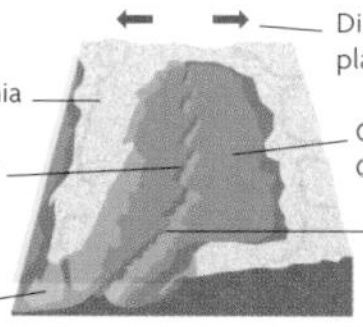

Direction of plate movement
Baja California
Transform fault
Gulf of California
Edge of continental crust
Spreading oceanic ridge

Sierra Madre Occidental

▲ *The Gulf of California* (*Golfo de California*) began to open out about 4 million years ago as a result of rifting and plate displacement along transform faults.

▲ *Popocatépetl is a dormant* volcano, part of the Pacific "Ring of Fire." The crater is over half a mile (1 km) wide.

Río Balsas

Popocatépetl

The unstable, earthquake-prone, upland basin around Mexico City was once a region of shallow lakes. Flood control measures and domestic consumption over the last four centuries have caused the virtual disappearance of this surface water.

The highlands of Chiapas are a series of *horsts*, blocks of land thrust upward between two fault lines. Volcanic cones have developed where lava has flowed out from the faults.

Transportation & industry

Oil and gas on the Gulf coast are Mexico's main sources of export income. Metal mining has declined but the country remains a leading global producer of silver. Manufacturing is heavily concentrated around the metropolitan area of Mexico City, while the duty-free movement of goods in the US border region, under the *Maquiladora* (twin plant) scheme, has created new hi-tech and service growth centers.

Major industry and infrastructure

- brewing
- car manufacture
- chemicals
- electronics
- fish processing
- maquiladoras
- mining
- oil & gas
- textiles
- capital cities
- major towns
- international airports
- major roads
- major industrial areas

Transportation network

67,564 miles (108,746 km)

3994 miles (6429 km)

16,561 miles (26,656 km)

1801 miles (2900 km)

Fast, modern highways or autopistas now link Mexico City with Toluca, Puebla and other satellite cities, yet distant centers like Chihuahua are still served by narrow roads and an outdated railroad network.

▲ *A stone figure reclines by the* Temple of Warriors, within the Mayan city of Chichén-Itzá. The Maya civilization flourished across the Yucatan Peninsula between 200 and 900 AD.

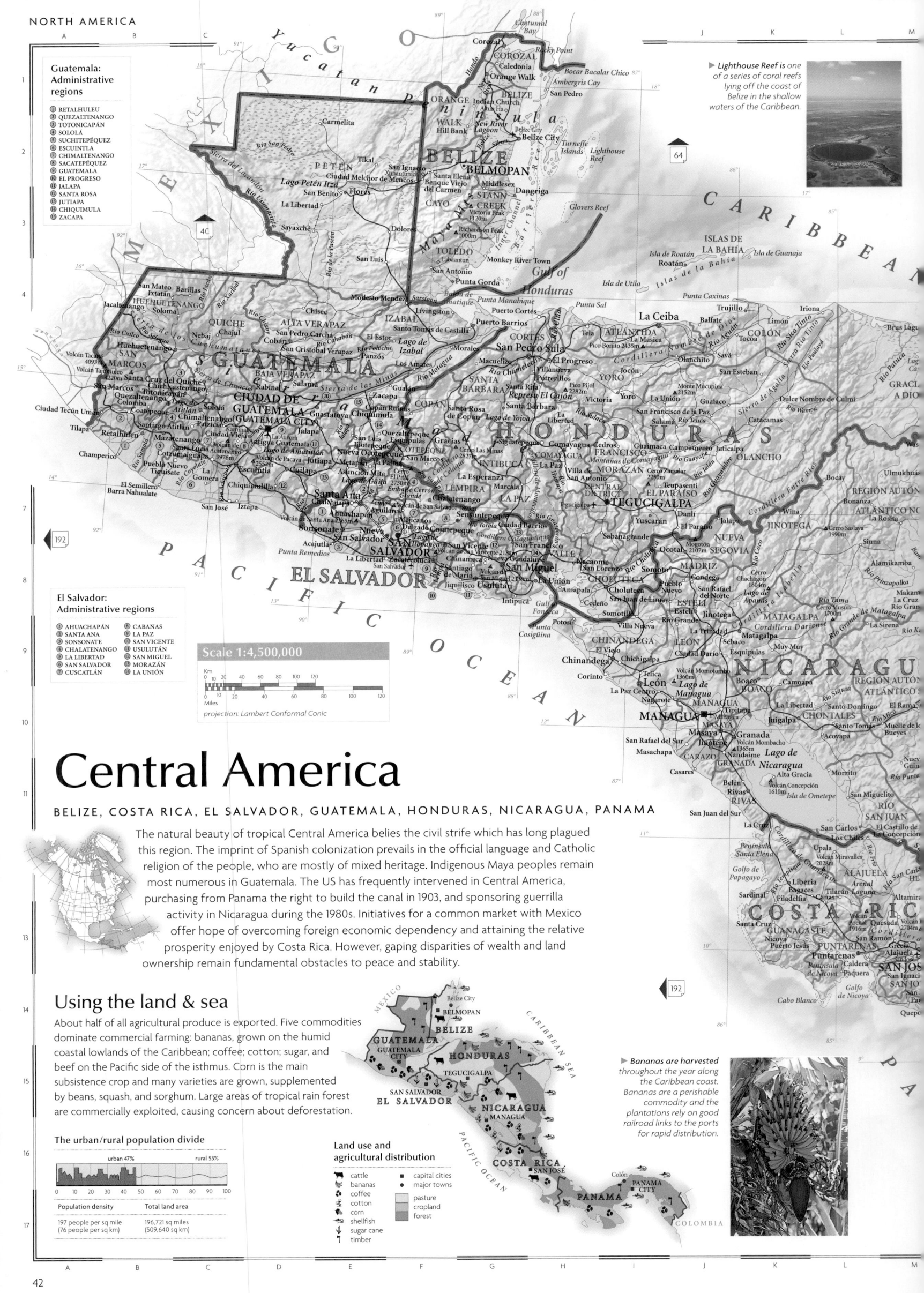

Guatemala: Administrative regions

1. RETALHULEU
2. QUEZALTENANGO
3. TOTONICAPÁN
4. SOLOLÁ
5. SUCHITEPÉQUEZ
6. ESCUINTLA
7. CHIMALTENANGO
8. SACATEPÉQUEZ
9. GUATEMALA
10. EL PROGRESO
11. JALAPA
12. SANTA ROSA
13. JUTIAPA
14. CHIQUIMULA
15. ZACAPA

▶ *Lighthouse Reef is one of a series of coral reefs lying off the coast of Belize in the shallow waters of the Caribbean.*

El Salvador: Administrative regions

1. AHUACHAPÁN
2. SANTA ANA
3. SONSONATE
4. CHALATENANGO
5. LA LIBERTAD
6. SAN SALVADOR
7. CUSCATLÁN
8. CABAÑAS
9. LA PAZ
10. SAN VICENTE
11. USULUTÁN
12. SAN MIGUEL
13. MORAZÁN
14. LA UNIÓN

Scale 1:4,500,000

projection: Lambert Conformal Conic

Central America

BELIZE, COSTA RICA, EL SALVADOR, GUATEMALA, HONDURAS, NICARAGUA, PANAMA

The natural beauty of tropical Central America belies the civil strife which has long plagued this region. The imprint of Spanish colonization prevails in the official language and Catholic religion of the people, who are mostly of mixed heritage. Indigenous Maya peoples remain most numerous in Guatemala. The US has frequently intervened in Central America, purchasing from Panama the right to build the canal in 1903, and sponsoring guerrilla activity in Nicaragua during the 1980s. Initiatives for a common market with Mexico offer hope of overcoming foreign economic dependency and attaining the relative prosperity enjoyed by Costa Rica. However, gaping disparities of wealth and land ownership remain fundamental obstacles to peace and stability.

Using the land & sea

About half of all agricultural produce is exported. Five commodities dominate commercial farming: bananas, grown on the humid coastal lowlands of the Caribbean; coffee; cotton; sugar, and beef on the Pacific side of the isthmus. Corn is the main subsistence crop and many varieties are grown, supplemented by beans, squash, and sorghum. Large areas of tropical rain forest are commercially exploited, causing concern about deforestation.

The urban/rural population divide

urban 47%   rural 53%

0 10 20 30 40 50 60 70 80 90 100

Population density	Total land area
197 people per sq mile (76 people per sq km)	196,721 sq miles (509,640 sq km)

Land use and agricultural distribution

- cattle
- bananas
- coffee
- cotton
- corn
- shellfish
- sugar cane
- timber
- ● capital cities
- ▪ major towns
- pasture
- cropland
- forest

▶ *Bananas are harvested throughout the year along the Caribbean coast. Bananas are a perishable commodity and the plantations rely on good railroad links to the ports for rapid distribution.*

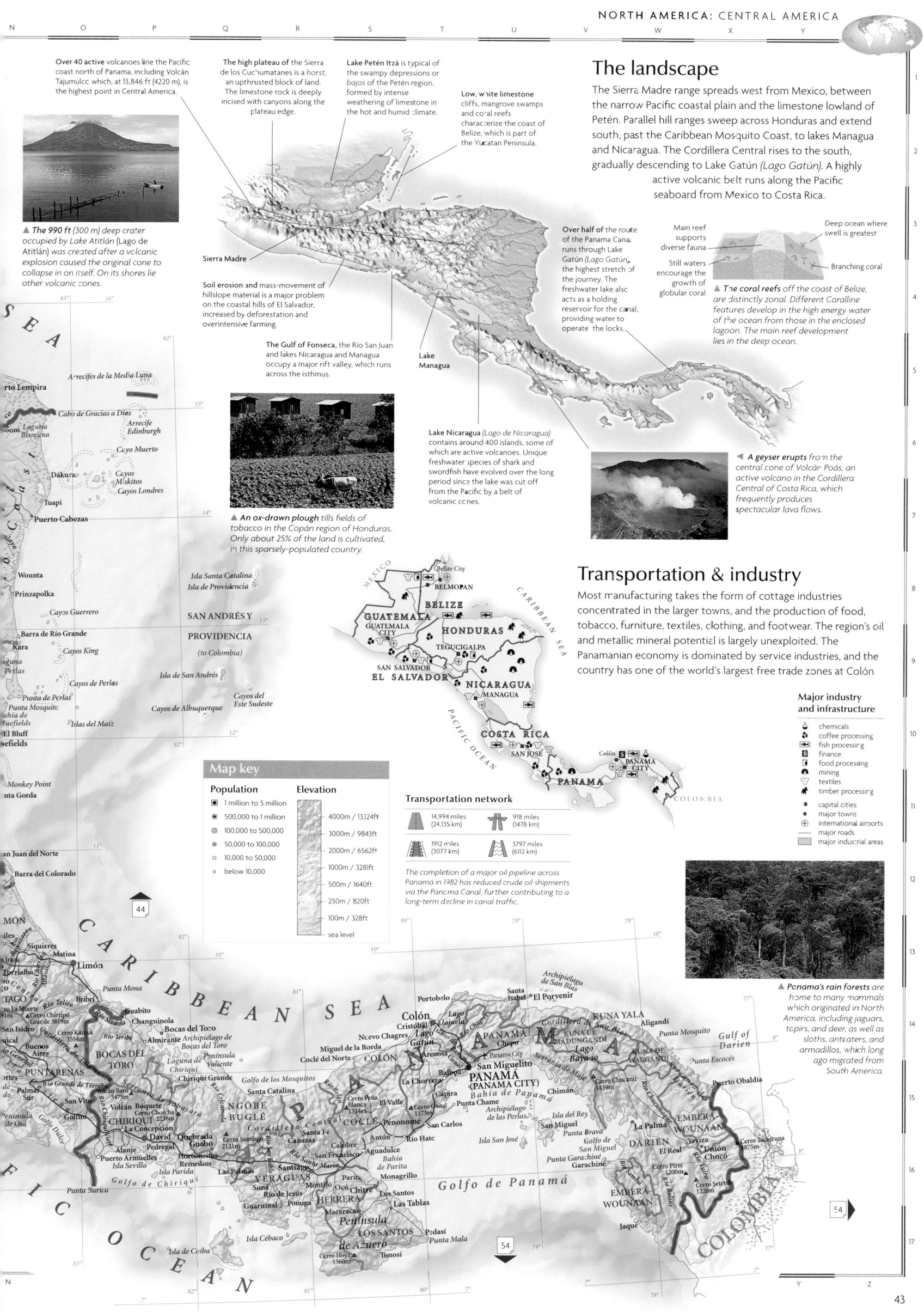

Over 40 active volcanoes line the Pacific coast north of Panama, including Volcán Tajumulco which, at 13,846 ft (4220 m), is the highest point in Central America.

▲ *The 990 ft (300 m) deep crater occupied by Lake Atitlán (Lago de Atitlán) was created after a volcanic explosion caused the original cone to collapse in on itself. On its shores lie other volcanic cones.*

Sierra Madre

Soil erosion and mass-movement of hillslope material is a major problem on the coastal hills of El Salvador, increased by deforestation and overintensive farming.

The high plateau of the Sierra de los Cuchumatanes is a *horst,* an upthrusted block of land. The limestone rock is deeply incised with canyons along the plateau edge.

Lake Petén Itzá is typical of the swampy depressions or *bajos* of the Petén region, formed by intense weathering of limestone in the hot and humid climate.

Low, white limestone cliffs, mangrove swamps and coral reefs characterize the coast of Belize, which is part of the Yucatan Peninsula.

The Gulf of Fonseca, the Río San Juan and lakes Nicaragua and Managua occupy a major rift valley, which runs across the isthmus.

Lake Managua

Over half of the route of the Panama Canal runs through Lake Gatún (*Lago Gatún*), the highest stretch of the journey. The freshwater lake also acts as a holding reservoir for the canal, providing water to operate the locks.

Lake Nicaragua (*Lago de Nicaragua*) contains around 400 islands, some of which are active volcanoes. Unique freshwater species of shark and swordfish have evolved over the long period since the lake was cut off from the Pacific by a belt of volcanic cones.

▲ *An ox-drawn plough* tills fields of tobacco in the Copán region of Honduras. Only about 25% of the land is cultivated, in this sparsely-populated country.

The landscape

The Sierra Madre range spreads west from Mexico, between the narrow Pacific coastal plain and the limestone lowland of Petén. Parallel hill ranges sweep across Honduras and extend south, past the Caribbean Mosquito Coast, to lakes Managua and Nicaragua. The Cordillera Central rises to the south, gradually descending to Lake Gatún (*Lago Gatún*). A highly active volcanic belt runs along the Pacific seaboard from Mexico to Costa Rica.

Main reef supports diverse fauna

Still waters encourage the growth of globular coral

Deep ocean where swell is greatest

Branching coral

▲ *The coral reefs* off the coast of Belize, are distinctly zonal. Different Coralline features develop in the high energy water of the ocean from those in the enclosed lagoon. The main reef development lies in the deep ocean.

▲ *A geyser erupts* from the central cone of Volcán Poás, an active volcano in the Cordillera Central of Costa Rica, which frequently produces spectacular lava flows.

Transportation & industry

Most manufacturing takes the form of cottage industries concentrated in the larger towns, and the production of food, tobacco, furniture, textiles, clothing, and footwear. The region's oil and metallic mineral potential is largely unexploited. The Panamanian economy is dominated by service industries, and the country has one of the world's largest free trade zones at Colón

Major industry and infrastructure

- chemicals
- coffee processing
- fish processing
- finance
- food processing
- mining
- textiles
- timber processing

- capital cities
- major towns
- international airports
- major roads
- major industrial areas

Map key

Population
- 1 million to 5 million
- 500,000 to 1 million
- 100,000 to 500,000
- 50,000 to 100,000
- 10,000 to 50,000
- below 10,000

Elevation
- 4000m / 13,124ft
- 3000m / 9843ft
- 2000m / 6562ft
- 1000m / 3281ft
- 500m / 1640ft
- 250m / 820ft
- 100m / 328ft
- sea level

Transportation network

14,994 miles (24,135 km)   918 miles (1478 km)

1912 miles (3077 km)   3797 miles (6112 km)

The completion of a major oil pipeline across Panama in 1982 has reduced crude oil shipments via the Panama Canal, further contributing to a long-term decline in canal traffic.

▲ *Panama's rain forests are home to many mammals which originated in North America, including jaguars, tapirs, and deer, as well as sloths, anteaters, and armadillos, which long ago migrated from South America.*

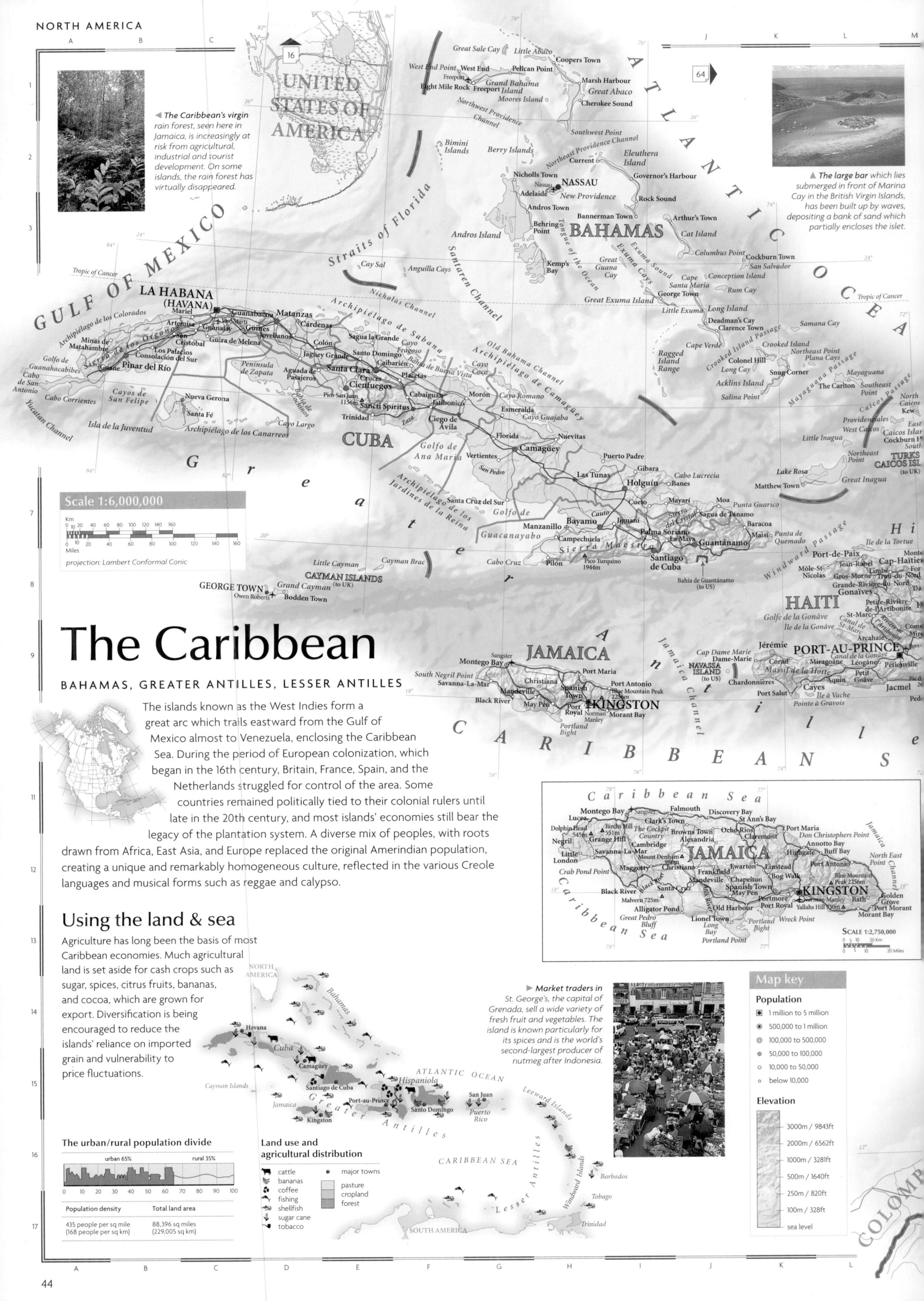

The Caribbean

BAHAMAS, GREATER ANTILLES, LESSER ANTILLES

The islands known as the West Indies form a great arc which trails eastward from the Gulf of Mexico almost to Venezuela, enclosing the Caribbean Sea. During the period of European colonization, which began in the 16th century, Britain, France, Spain, and the Netherlands struggled for control of the area. Some countries remained politically tied to their colonial rulers until late in the 20th century, and most islands' economies still bear the legacy of the plantation system. A diverse mix of peoples, with roots drawn from Africa, East Asia, and Europe replaced the original Amerindian population, creating a unique and remarkably homogeneous culture, reflected in the various Creole languages and musical forms such as reggae and calypso.

Using the land & sea

Agriculture has long been the basis of most Caribbean economies. Much agricultural land is set aside for cash crops such as sugar, spices, citrus fruits, bananas, and cocoa, which are grown for export. Diversification is being encouraged to reduce the islands' reliance on imported grain and vulnerability to price fluctuations.

◄ *The Caribbean's virgin rain forest, seen here in Jamaica, is increasingly at risk from agricultural, industrial and tourist development. On some islands, the rain forest has virtually disappeared.*

▲ *The large bar which lies submerged in front of Marina Cay in the British Virgin Islands, has been built up by waves, depositing a bank of sand which partially encloses the islet.*

▶ *Market traders in St. George's, the capital of Grenada, sell a wide variety of fresh fruit and vegetables. The island is known particularly for its spices and is the world's second-largest producer of nutmeg after Indonesia.*

Scale 1:6,000,000

projection: Lambert Conformal Conic

SCALE 1:2,750,000

The urban/rural population divide

urban 65% rural 35%

Population density	Total land area
435 people per sq mile (168 people per sq km)	88,396 sq miles (229,005 sq km)

Land use and agricultural distribution

- cattle
- bananas
- coffee
- fishing
- shellfish
- sugar cane
- tobacco
- major towns
- pasture
- cropland
- forest

Map key

Population
- 1 million to 5 million
- 500,000 to 1 million
- 100,000 to 500,000
- 50,000 to 100,000
- 10,000 to 50,000
- below 10,000

Elevation
- 3000m / 9843ft
- 2000m / 6562ft
- 1000m / 3281ft
- 500m / 1640ft
- 250m / 820ft
- 100m / 328ft
- sea level

Transportation & industry

Caribbean industry remains, with few exceptions, agricultural, and export-led, or service-based, supporting the flourishing tourist industry. However, several countries including Jamaica, Barbados, Trinidad and Tobago, and Puerto Rico have developed important mineral industries, and Cuba is attempting to diversify its economy by importing capital goods to start up new manufacturing businesses.

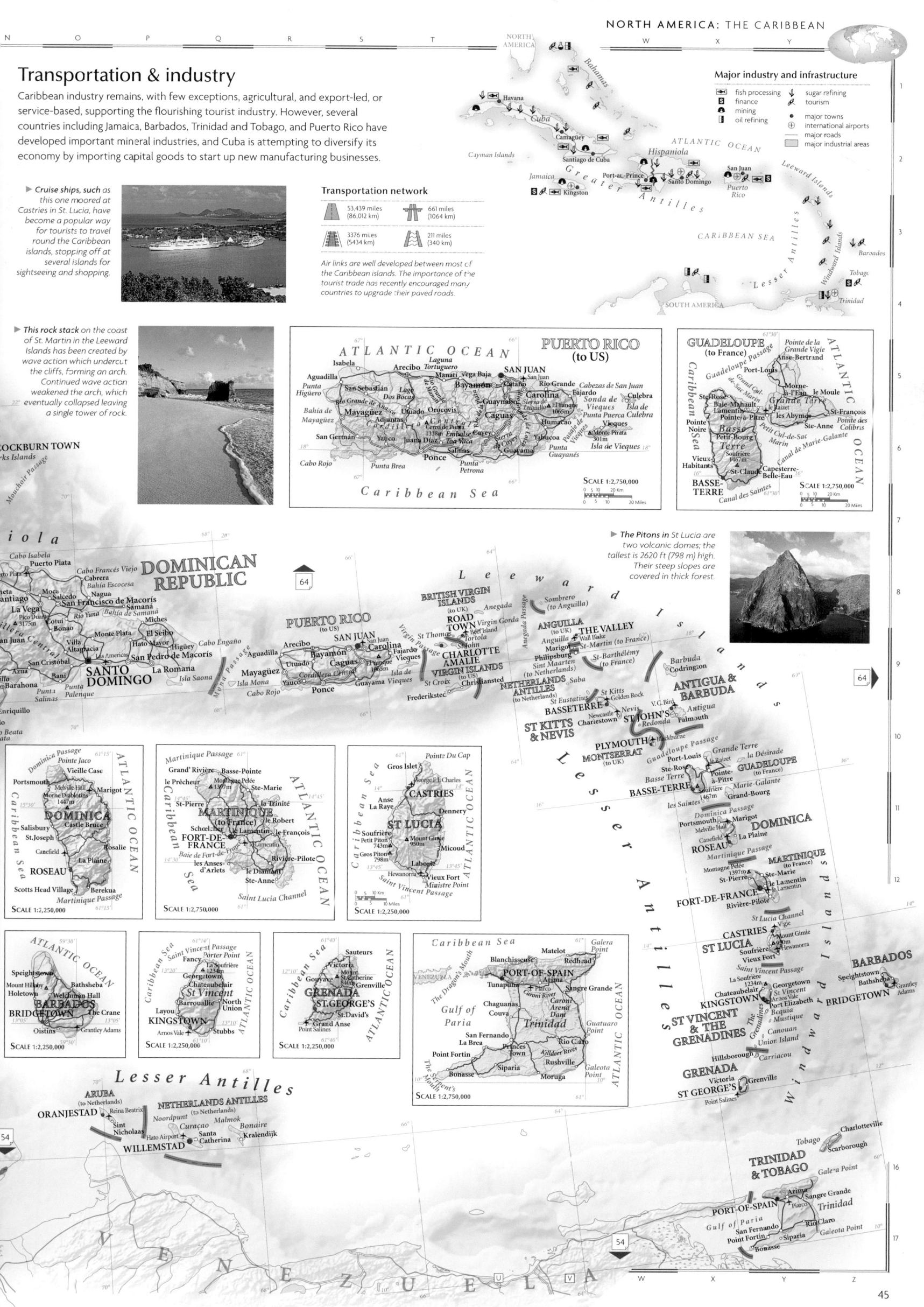

▶ Cruise ships, such as this one moored at Castries in St. Lucia, have become a popular way for tourists to travel round the Caribbean islands, stopping off at several islands for sightseeing and shopping.

Transportation network

53,439 miles (86,012 km)		661 miles (1064 km)	
3376 miles (5434 km)		211 miles (340 km)	

Air links are well developed between most of the Caribbean islands. The importance of the tourist trade has recently encouraged many countries to upgrade their paved roads.

Major industry and infrastructure

- fish processing
- finance
- mining
- oil refining
- sugar refining
- tourism
- major towns
- international airports
- major roads
- major industrial areas

▶ This rock stack on the coast of St. Martin in the Leeward Islands has been created by wave action which undercut the cliffs, forming an arch. Continued wave action weakened the arch, which eventually collapsed leaving a single tower of rock.

▶ The Pitons in St Lucia are two volcanic domes; the tallest is 2620 ft (798 m) high. Their steep slopes are covered in thick forest.

South America

Reaching from the humid tropics down into the cold south Atlantic, South America has an area of 6,886,000 sq miles (17,835,000 sq km). There are 12 separate countries, with the largest, Brazil, covering almost half the continent.

- ● **Greatest extent, North–South:** *4750 miles / 7640 km*
- ■ **Greatest extent, East–West:** *3100 miles / 4990 km*

Most northerly point:
Punta Gallinas, Colombia 12° 28' N

Punta Gallinas, Colombia 12° 28' N

Most westerly point:
Galapagos Islands,
Ecuador 92° W

Equator

Punta Pariñas, Peru
81° 20' W

Cabo Branco /
Ponta do Seixas,
Brazil 34° 50' W

Largest lake: Lake Titicaca,
Bolivia/Peru 3220 sq miles
(8340 sq km)

Highest recorded temperature:
Rivadavia, Argentina
120°F (49°C)

Tropic of Capricorn

Antofagasta

São Paulo

Most easterly point:
Ilhas Martin Vaz, Brazil
28° 51' W

Highest point:
Cerro Aconcagua, Argentina
22,833 ft (6959 m)

Lowest point:
Peninsula Valdés, Argentina
-131 ft (-40 m) below sea level

Lowest recorded temperature:
Sarmiento, Argentina
-27°F (-33°C)

Froward Cape, Chile
53° 54' S

Most southerly point:
Cape Horn, Chile
55° 59' S

Antofagasta,
Chile

Atacama Desert

Andes

Paraguay river

Planalto de Mato Grosso

São Paulo, Brazil

Cross-section from Antofagasta, Chile to São Paulo, Brazil

line of cross-section

0 250 500 750 1000 Km

0 250 500 750 1000 Miles

AMERICA

Mississippi Fan
Apalachee Bay
Apalachicola Escarpment
Cape Canaveral
Lake Okeechobee
Bahamas
Hatteras Plain
Sargasso Sea
Nares Plain

Gulf of Mexico
Straits of Florida
Great Bahama Bank
West Indies
Tropic of Cancer
Cape Verde Basin
Cape Verde Islands

Yucatan Peninsula
Cuba
Great Bahama Bank
Puerto Rico Trench
NORTH AMERICAN PLATE
SOUTH AMERICAN PLATE
Gambia Plain

Cayman Trench
Gulf of Honduras
Yucatan Basin
Greater Antilles
Jamaica
Windward Passage
Hispaniola
Puerto Rico
Leeward Islands
Barbuda
Antigua
Guadeloupe
Nevis

AMERICAN PLATE
Gulf of Fonseca
Mosquito Coast
del Sur
CARIBBEAN PLATE
Nicaraguan Rise
Caribbean Sea
Punta Gallinas
Aruba
Bonaire
Curaçao
Lesser Antilles
Isla de Margarita
Grenada
Tobago
Trinidad
Dominica
Martinique
Saint Lucia
Barbados
AFRICAN PLATE
Doldrums Fracture Zone

Guatemala Trench
Gulf of Honduras
Mosquito Gulf
Gulf of Darien
Peninsula de la Guajira
Gulf of Venezuela
Lake Maracaibo
Cordillera de la Costa
Apure
Orinoco
Demerara Plain
Guiana Basin
Four North Fracture Zone
Saint Paul Fracture Zone
Equator

Colón Ridge
Panama Basin
Gulf of Darien
Colombian Basin
Serrania
CARIBBEAN PLATE
SOUTH AMERICAN PLATE
Cordillera Central
Cordillera Oriental
Meta
Arauca
Llanos
Casanare
Guaviare
Guiana Highlands
Charicoera
Caroni
Essequibo
Courantune
Maroni
Oyapok
Tumuc-Humac Mountains
Amazon Fan
Ceará Plain

Isthmus of Panama
Gulf of Panama
Peninsula de Azuero
Cordillera Occidental
Serra Parima
Orinoco
Branco
Uaupés
Rio Negro
Içá
Japurá
Trombetas
Para de Oeste
Jari
Amazon
Xingu
Paru
Araguari
Ilha de Marajó
Baía de Marajó
Represa de Tucuruí
Baía de São Marcos
AFRICAN PLATE
Cabo de São Roque
Atol das Rocas
Fernando de Noronha

Galápagos
Colombian Basin
Chimborazo 6310m
Cordillera Real
Putumayo
Napo
Caquetá
Ucayali
Rio Negro
Amazon
Purus
Madeira
AMAZON BASIN
SOUTH AMERICA
Curuá
Iriri
Tocantins
Tapajós
Araguaia
Represa de Sobradinho
P.analto da Borborema
Cabo Branco
Fernambuco
Represa de Itaparica

Gulf of Guayaquil
Punta Parinas
Marañón
Jurua
Juruá
Purus
Tapauá
Teffé
Acre
Madre de Dios
Beni
Mamoré
Serra do Cachimbo
Chapada dos Parecis
São Manuel
Serra Formosa
Juruena
Serra do Roncador
Serra Geral de Goiás
Chapada Diamantina
Chapada das Mangabeiras
Represa de Sobradinho
Brazilian Highlands
Serra da Espinhaço
Baía de Todos os Santos
Brazil Basin

Mendaña Fracture Zone
Peru Basin
Cordillera Oriental
Cordillera Occidental
Yungas
Lago Poopó
Lake Titicaca
Altiplano
ANDES
Planalto de Mato Grosso
Pantanal
Paraguay
Itaquai
Taquari
Aporé
Rio Grande
São Francisco
Paraná
Serra do Paranapiacaba
Serra do Mar
Serra da Mantiqueira
Tropic of Capricorn

Chile Basin
Nazca Ridge
Atacama Desert
Salinas Grandes
Gran Chaco
Pilcomayo
Paraná
Uruguay
Represa de Itaipu
Iguaçu
Paraná
Serra do Mar
Ilha de São Sebastião
Santos Plateau
Rio Grande Rise

Easter Island
Sala y Gomez Fracture Zone
Islas de los Desventurados
Salado
Shores de Córdoba
Mar Chiquita
Laguna Mar Chiquita
Aconcagua 6959m
Mesopotamia
Paraná
Embalse de Río Negro
Cuchilla Grande
Mirim Lagoon
Lagoa dos Patos
Rio de la Plata

Roggeveen Basin
Juan Fernandez Islands
ANDES
Neuquén
Pampas
Colorado
Río Negro
Bahía Blanca
Argentine Basin

Limay
Chubut
Golfo San Matías
Argentine Plain

NAZCA PLATE
ANTARCTIC PLATE
Patagonia
Gulf of San Jorge
Falkland Escarpment
Maurice Ewing Bank
South Sandwich Trench
South Georgia Rise

West Pacific Rise
Lago Buenos Aires
Golfo Corcovado
Chico
Deseado
Bahía Grande
Falkland Plateau
Falkland Islands
South Georgia
SOUTH AMERICAN PLATE
SCOTIA PLATE
Sandwich Islands

ANTARCTIC PLATE
PACIFIC PLATE
Archipiélago de los Chonos
Strait of Magellan
Tierra del Fuego
Cape Horn
Scotia Ridge
Scotia Sea
SCOTIA PLATE
ANTARCTIC PLATE
South Orkney Islands
South Shetland Islands

Weddell Sea
ANTARCTICA

MID-ATLANTIC RIDGE
ATLANTIC OCEAN
PACIFIC OCEAN

Physical South America

Three major physiographic regions characterize South America. The oldest, the ancient Brazilian Shield and the smaller Guiana and Patagonian shields, form the stable core of the continent. Stretching along the entire west coast are the younger Andean fold mountains with many summits rising to 20,000 ft (6100 m). These two diverse regions are separated by a number of sedimentary basins carrying South America's large river systems to the sea. These include the massive Amazon Basin and the basin of the Gran Chaco.

The Amazon Basin and Guiana Shield

The Amazon river occupies a large depression in the Earth's crust, formed by the uplift of the Andes. It is covered by thick volcanic deposits and layers of alluvium – these have been laid down by the Amazon's many tributaries. To the north is the smaller Guiana Shield.

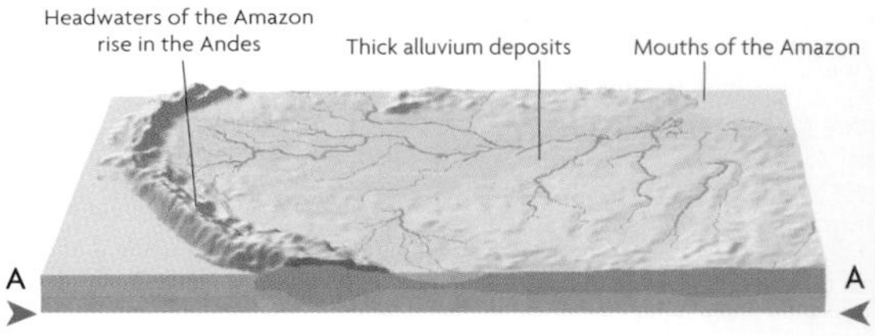

Headwaters of the Amazon rise in the Andes | Thick alluvium deposits | Mouths of the Amazon

Section across northern South America showing Amazon Basin and its drainage pattern.

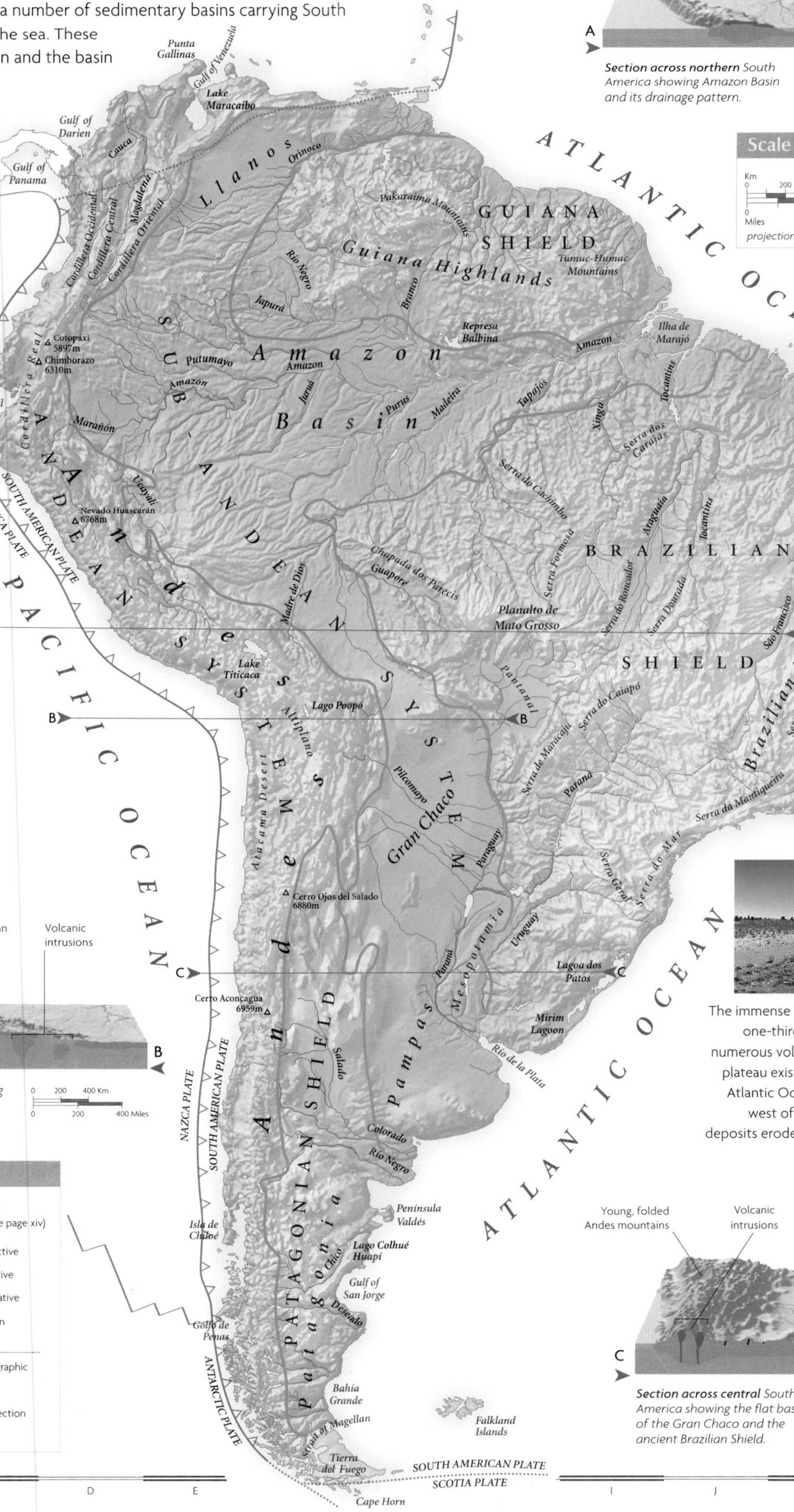

0   500   1000 Km
0   500   1000 Miles

Scale 1:30,500,000

Km
0   200   400   600   800
Miles
0   200   400   600   800

projection: Lambert Azimuthal Equal Area

The Andean Uplands

The Andean Uplands run along the west coast of South America. They are being uplifted as the Nazca Plate is subducted beneath the South American Plate. They contain some of the world's largest volcanoes, such as Cotopaxi, and Lake Titicaca which occupies a dormant site. The far south has many large ice-sheets and a fragmented coastline.

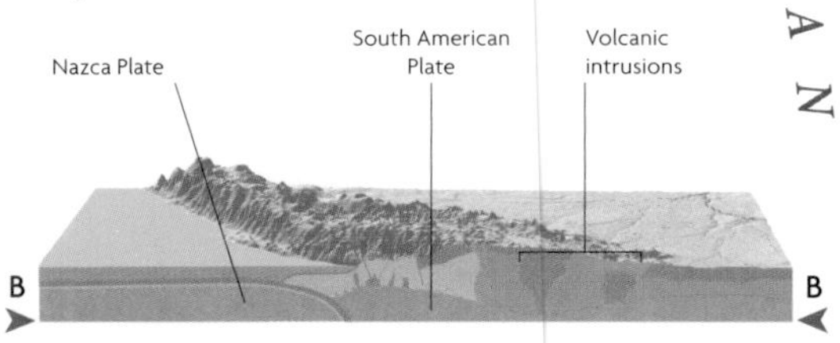

Nazca Plate | South American Plate | Volcanic intrusions

Cross-section through the Andes showing the subduction of the Nazca Plate beneath the South American Plate.

0   200   400 Km
0   200   400 Miles

Map key

Elevation

6000m / 19,686ft
4000m / 13,124ft
3000m / 9843ft
2000m / 6562ft
1000m / 3281ft
500m / 1640ft
250m / 820ft
100m / 328ft
sea level

Plate margins
(for explanation see page xiv)

— constructive
△ △ destructive
— conservative
···· uncertain

— physiographic regions
◄► line of cross-section

The Brazilian Shield and Gran Chaco

The immense Brazilian Shield underlies more than one-third of South America. It is pitted with numerous volcanic intrusions, and a large basaltic plateau exists between the Paraná river and the Atlantic Ocean. The flat Gran Chaco lies to the west of the shield, covered by sedimentary deposits eroded from the Andes, and transported by South America's mighty rivers.

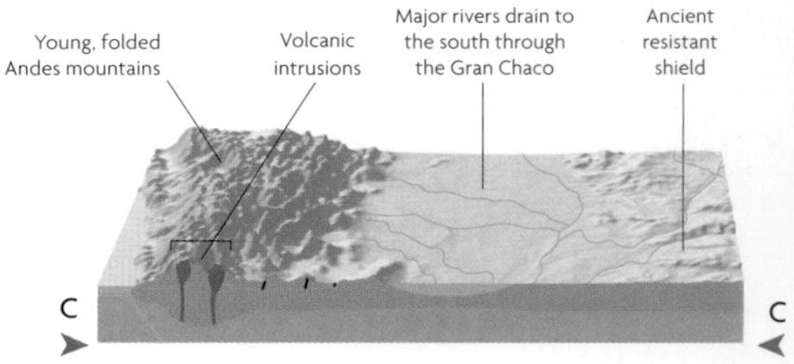

Young, folded Andes mountains | Volcanic intrusions | Major rivers drain to the south through the Gran Chaco | Ancient resistant shield

Section across central South America showing the flat basin of the Gran Chaco and the ancient Brazilian Shield.

0   200   400 Km
0   200   400 Miles

COCOS PLATE
NAZCA PLATE

Punta Gallinas
Gulf of Venezuela
Lake Maracaibo
Gulf of Darien
Gulf of Panama
Cauca
Magdalena
Cordillera Occidental
Cordillera Central
Cordillera Oriental
Llanos
Orinoco
Pakaraima Mountains
GUIANA SHIELD
Guiana Highlands
Tumuc-Humac Mountains
Rio Negro
Branco
Japurá
Putumayo
Cotopaxi 5897m
Chimborazo 6310m
Cordillera Real
Gulf of Guayaquil
Marañón
Amazon
Amazon
Amazon Basin
Represa Balbina
Ilha de Marajó
Tapajós
Xingu
Tocantins
Cabo de São Roque
Punta Negra
Nevado Huascarán 6768m
Ucayali
Juruá
Purus
Madeira
Serra dos Carajás
Serra do Cachimbo
Serra Formosa
Araguaia
Tocantins
Planalto da Borborema
Madre de Dios
Chapada dos Parecis
Guaporé
BRAZILIAN
Represa de Sobradinho
Lake Titicaca
Planalto de Mato Grosso
Serra do Catapó
Serra do Roncador
Serra Dourada
São Francisco
SHIELD
Lago Poopó
Altiplano
Pantanal
Brazilian Highlands
Serra do Espinhaço
Atacama Desert
ANDEAN SYSTEM
Pilcomayo
Serra de Maracaju
Paraná
Serra da Mantiqueira
Gran Chaco
Paraguay
Paraná
Serra Geral
Serra do Mar
Cerro Ojos del Salado 6880m
Paraguay
Uruguay
Mesopotamia
Cerro Aconcagua 6959m
Paraná
Lagoa dos Patos
Pampas
Uruguay
Mirim Lagoon
Rio de la Plata
Salado
Colorado
Rio Negro
PATAGONIAN SHIELD
Península Valdés
Isla de Chiloé
Lago Colhué Huapi
Gulf of San Jorge
Deseado
Patagonia
Golfo de Penas
Bahía Grande
Strait of Magellan
Falkland Islands
Tierra del Fuego
Cape Horn

NAZCA PLATE
SOUTH AMERICAN PLATE
PACIFIC OCEAN
ATLANTIC OCEAN
ANTARCTIC PLATE
SOUTH AMERICAN PLATE
SCOTIA PLATE

Climate

The climate of South America is influenced by three principal factors: the seasonal shift of high pressure air masses over the tropics, cold ocean currents along the western coast, affecting temperature and precipitation, and the mountain barrier produced by by the Andes, which creates a rain shadow over much of the south.

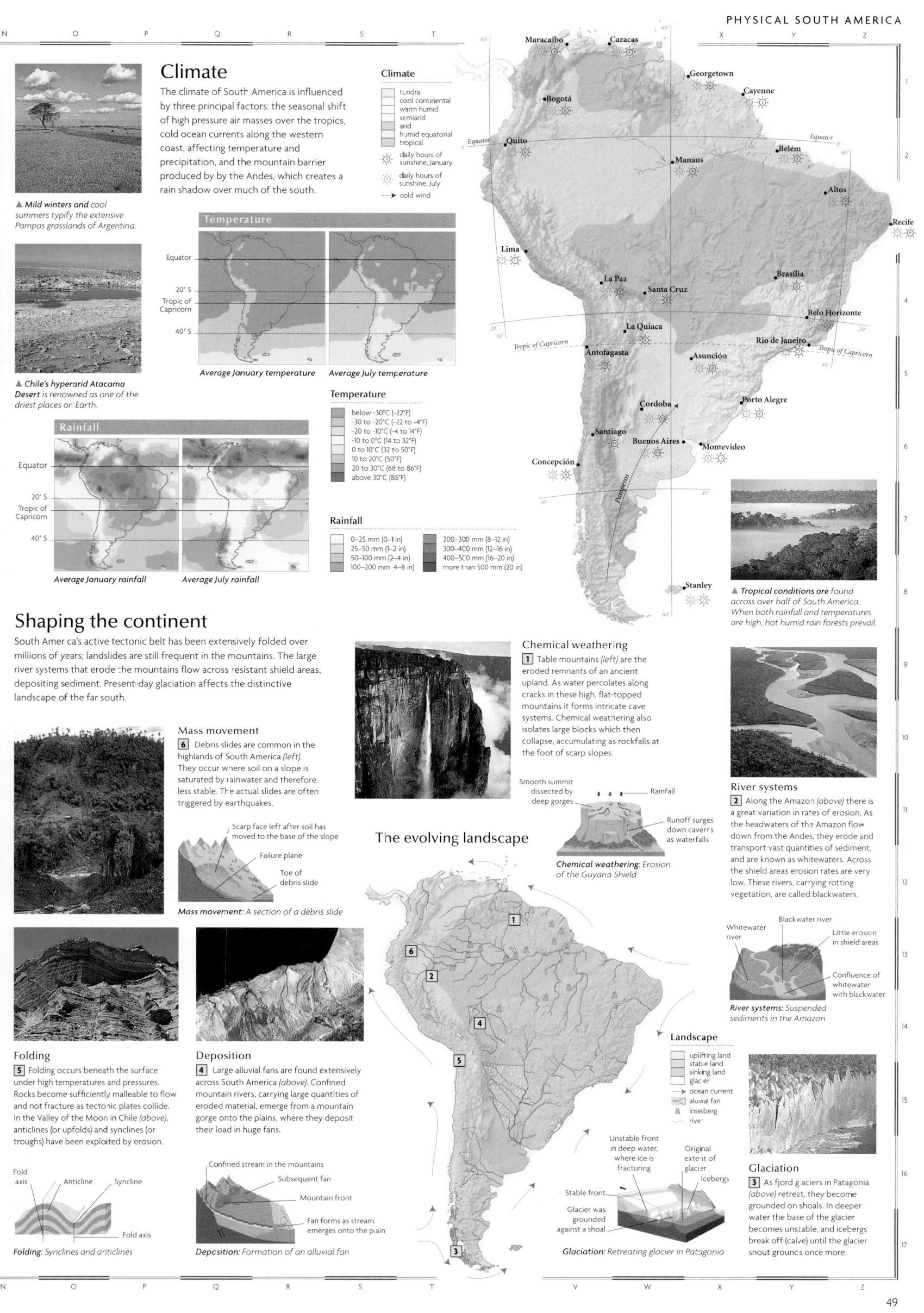

▲ Mild winters and cool summers typify the extensive Pampas grasslands of Argentina.

▲ Chile's hyperarid Atacama Desert is renowned as one of the driest places on Earth.

Climate
- tundra
- cool continental
- warm humid
- semiarid
- arid
- humid equatorial
- tropical
- ☼ daily hours of sunshine, January
- ☼ daily hours of sunshine, July
- → cold wind

Temperature

Average January temperature

Average July temperature

Temperature
- below -30°C (-22°F)
- -30 to -20°C (-22 to -4°F)
- -20 to -10°C (-4 to 14°F)
- -10 to 0°C (14 to 32°F)
- 0 to 10°C (32 to 50°F)
- 10 to 20°C (50°F)
- 20 to 30°C (68 to 86°F)
- above 30°C (86°F)

Rainfall

Average January rainfall

Average July rainfall

Rainfall
- 0–25 mm (0–1 in)
- 25–50 mm (1–2 in)
- 50–100 mm (2–4 in)
- 100–200 mm (4–8 in)
- 200–300 mm (8–12 in)
- 300–400 mm (12–16 in)
- 400–500 mm (16–20 in)
- more than 500 mm (20 in)

Cities labeled on map: Maracaibo, Caracas, Georgetown, Cayenne, Bogotá, Quito, Manaus, Belém, Altos, Recife, Lima, La Paz, Santa Cruz, Brasília, Belo Horizonte, La Quiaca, Rio de Janeiro, Antofagasta, Asunción, Cordoba, Porto Alegre, Santiago, Buenos Aires, Montevideo, Concepción, Stanley. Equator, Tropic of Capricorn, Pampero.

▲ Tropical conditions are found across over half of South America. When both rainfall and temperatures are high, hot humid rain forests prevail.

Shaping the continent

South America's active tectonic belt has been extensively folded over millions of years; landslides are still frequent in the mountains. The large river systems that erode the mountains flow across resistant shield areas, depositing sediment. Present-day glaciation affects the distinctive landscape of the far south.

Mass movement

6 Debris slides are common in the highlands of South America (left). They occur where soil on a slope is saturated by rainwater and therefore less stable. The actual slides are often triggered by earthquakes.

Scarp face left after soil has moved to the base of the slope
Failure plane
Toe of debris slide

Mass movement: A section of a debris slide

Chemical weathering

1 Table mountains (left) are the eroded remnants of an ancient upland. As water percolates along cracks in these high, flat-topped mountains it forms intricate cave systems. Chemical weathering also isolates large blocks which then collapse, accumulating as rockfalls at the foot of scarp slopes.

Smooth summit dissected by deep gorges
Rainfall
Runoff surges down caverns as waterfalls

Chemical weathering: Erosion of the Guyana Shield

The evolving landscape

River systems

2 Along the Amazon (above) there is a great variation in rates of erosion. As the headwaters of the Amazon flow down from the Andes, they erode and transport vast quantities of sediment, and are known as whitewaters. Across the shield areas erosion rates are very low. These rivers, carrying rotting vegetation, are called blackwaters.

Whitewater river
Blackwater river
Little erosion in shield areas
Confluence of whitewater with blackwater

River systems: Suspended sediments in the Amazon

Folding

5 Folding occurs beneath the surface under high temperatures and pressures. Rocks become sufficiently malleable to flow and not fracture as tectonic plates collide. In the Valley of the Moon in Chile (above), anticlines (or upfolds) and synclines (or troughs) have been exploited by erosion.

Fold axis
Anticline
Syncline
Fold axis

Folding: Synclines and anticlines

Deposition

4 Large alluvial fans are found extensively across South America (above). Confined mountain rivers, carrying large quantities of eroded material, emerge from a mountain gorge onto the plains, where they deposit their load in huge fans.

Confined stream in the mountains
Subsequent fan
Mountain front
Fan forms as stream emerges onto the plain

Deposition: Formation of an alluvial fan

Landscape
- uplifting land
- stable land
- sinking land
- glacier
- ocean current
- alluvial fan
- inselberg
- river

Unstable front in deep water, where ice is fracturing
Original extent of glacier
Icebergs
Stable front
Glacier was grounded against a shoal

Glaciation: Retreating glacier in Patagonia

Glaciation

3 As fjord glaciers in Patagonia (above) retreat, they become grounded on shoals. In deeper water the base of the glacier becomes unstable, and icebergs break off (calve) until the glacier snout grounds once more.

Political South America

Modern South America's political boundaries have their origins in the territorial endeavors of explorers during the 16th century, who claimed almost the entire continent for Portugal and Spain. The Portuguese land in the east later evolved into the federal state of Brazil, while the Spanish vice-royalties eventually emerged as separate independent nation-states in the early 19th century. South America's growing population has become increasingly urbanized, with the growth of coastal cities into large conurbations like Rio de Janeiro and Buenos Aires. In Brazil, Argentina, Chile, and Uruguay, a succession of military dictatorships has given way to fragile, but strengthening, democracies.

◀ **Europe retains a** small foothold in South America. Kourou in French Guiana was the site chosen by the European Space Agency to launch the Ariane rocket. As a result of its status as a French overseas department, French Guiana is actually part of the European Union.

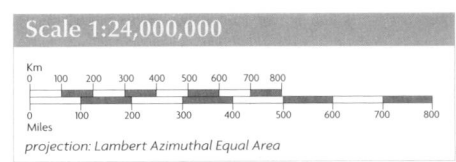

Scale 1:24,000,000

projection: Lambert Azimuthal Equal Area

Transportation

Most major road and rail routes are confined to the coastal regions by the forbidding natural barriers of the Andes mountains and the Amazon Basin. Few major cross-continental routes exist, although Buenos Aires serves as a transportation center for the main rail links to La Paz and Valparaíso, while the construction of the Trans-Amazon and Pan-American Highways have made direct road travel possible from Recife to Lima and from Puerto Montt up the coast into central America. A new waterway project is proposed to transform the River Paraguay into a major shipping route, although it involves considerable wetland destruction.

▶ **South America's most** extensive rail network is centered on the Argentinian capital, Buenos Aires. The construction of new rail lines ouward from this important port, allowed the colonization of the Pampas lands for agriculture.

Languages

Prior to European exploration in the 16th century, a diverse range of indigenous languages were spoken across the continent. With the arrival of Iberian settlers, Spanish became the dominant language, with Portuguese spoken in Brazil, and Native American languages such as Quechua and Guaraní, becoming concentrated in the continental interior. Today this pattern persists, although successive European colonization has led to Dutch being spoken in Suriname, English in Guyana, and French in French Guiana, while in large urban areas, Japanese and Chinese are increasingly common.

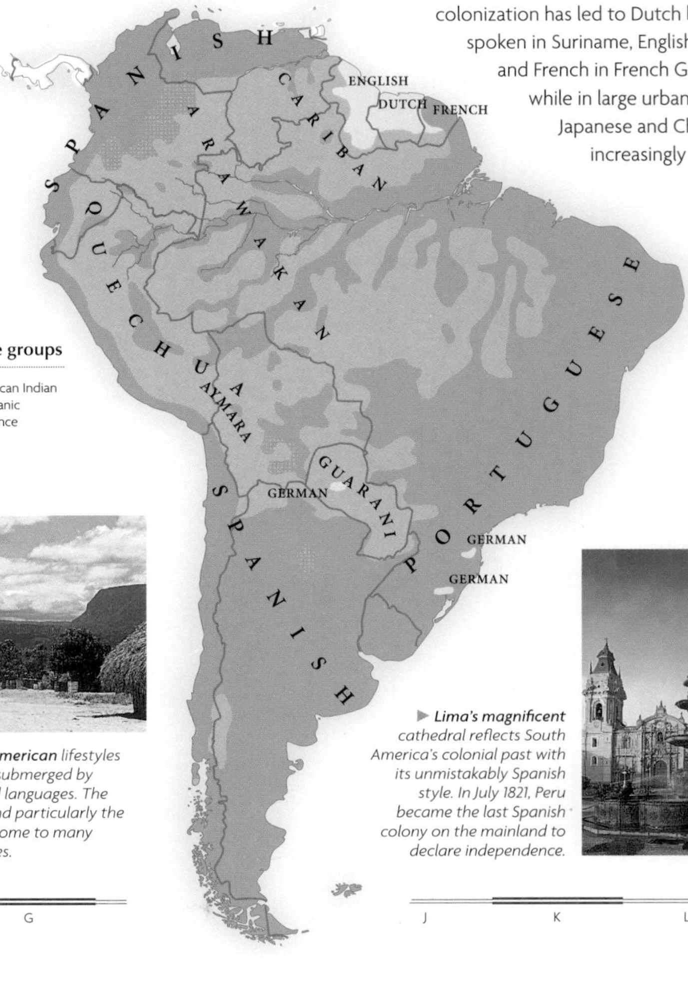

Transportation

- — major roads and highways
- — major railroads
- — international borders
- • transport intersections
- ⊕ international airports
- ⊕ major ports

Language groups

- American Indian
- Germanic
- Romance

▶ **Chile's main port,** Valparaíso, is a vital national shipping center, in addition to playing a key role in the growing trade with Pacific nations. The country's awkward, elongated shape means that sea transportation is frequently used for internal travel and communications in Chile.

▲ **Indigenous South American** lifestyles have not been totally submerged by European cultures and languages. The continental interior, and particularly the Amazon Basin, is still home to many different ethnic peoples.

▶ **Lima's magnificent** cathedral reflects South America's colonial past with its unmistakably Spanish style. In July 1821, Peru became the last Spanish colony on the mainland to declare independence.

Caribbean Sea

PANAMA
Gulf of Panama
Gulf of Darien

Santa Marta
Barranquilla
Cartagena
Maracaibo
Valledupar
Cabimas
Lake Maracaibo
Valencia
CARACAS
Maracay
Barquisimeto
Cumaná
Monteria
Cúcuta
Barinas
San Cristóbal
Bucaramanga
Medellín
Manizales
Pereira
Armenia
Ibagué
BOGOTÁ
Cali
Pasto

VENEZUELA
Orinoco
Ciudad Guayana
Venezuelan territorial claim
GEORGETOWN
Linden
PARAMARIBO
CAYENNE
GUYANA
SURINAME
French Guiana (to France)
Surinamese territorial claims

Llanos
Rio Negro
Guiana Highlands
Boa Vista
RORAIMA

COLOMBIA
Esmeraldas
Equator
QUITO
ECUADOR
Portoviejo
Ambato
Riobamba
Babahoyo
Guayaquil
Cuenca
Machala
Piura
Chiclayo
Trujillo

Caquetá
Japurá
Putumayo
Amazon
Iquitos
Marañón
Amazon

AMAPÁ
Macapá
Represa Balbina
Manaus
Santarém
Belém
São Luís
Fortaleza

AMAZONAS BASIN
PARÁ
MARANHÃO
Teresina
CEARÁ
Natal
RIO GRANDE DO NORTE
PARAÍBA
João Pessoa
Jaboatão
Recife
PERNAMBUCO

PERU
ANDES
Callao
LIMA
Huancayo
Cusco
Arequipa

ACRE
Rio Branco
Porto Velho
RONDÔNIA

BRAZIL

BOLIVIA
La Paz
Lake Titicaca
Cochabamba
Oruro
SUCRE
Santa Cruz
Tacna
Arica
Lago Poopó
Iquique
Tocopilla
Antofagasta

MATO GROSSO
Planalto de Mato Grosso
Cuiabá
BRASÍLIA
DISTRITO FEDERAL
Goiânia
GOIÁS
MINAS GERAIS
Belo Horizonte
Juazeiro
Represa de Sobradinho
BAHIA
Salvador
Aracaju
SERGIPE
Maceió
ALAGOAS
Palmas
TOCANTINS
Brazilian Highlands

Campo Grande
MATO GROSSO DO SUL
Ribeirão Preto
SÃO PAULO
Londrina
Campinas
Osasco
Sorocaba
São Paulo
Santos
Nova Iguaçu
Niterói
Rio de Janeiro
RIO DE JANEIRO
Vitória
ESPÍRITO SANTO
Juiz de Fora

PARAGUAY
Gran Chaco
San Salvador de Jujuy
Salta
Formosa
ASUNCIÓN
Villarrica
Ciudad del Este
PARANÁ
Curitiba
SANTA CATARINA
Florianópolis
Posadas
Corrientes
Resistencia
San Miguel de Tucumán
Santiago del Estero
La Rioja
RIO GRANDE DO SUL
Santa Maria
Porto Alegre

ARGENTINA
CHILE
La Serena
Coquimbo
San Juan
Córdoba
Mendoza
San Luis
Santa Fe
Paraná
Rosario
Tacuarembó
Melo
URUGUAY
MONTEVIDEO
BUENOS AIRES
La Plata
Rio de la Plata
Viña del Mar
Valparaíso
SANTIAGO
Linares
Concepción
Lota
Temuco
Valdivia
Puerto Montt
Santa Rosa
Bahía Blanca
Mar del Plata
Neuquén
Rio Negro
Colorado
Pampas
Patagonia
Rawson
Lago Colhué Huapí
Golfo de San Jorge
Bahía Grande
Rio Gallegos
Falkland Islands (to UK)
STANLEY
Punta Arenas
Ushuaia
Beagle Channel
Cape Horn
Strait of Magellan

PACIFIC OCEAN
ATLANTIC OCEAN

Tropic of Capricorn
Equator

▶ In April 1960, Brazil's government began the move from Rio de Janeiro to Brasília, a futuristic new city built in the sparsely populated interior. Brasília is now the federal capital of Brazil.

▶ Rapid urbanization was a feature of most South American countries in the latter half of the 20th century. In many cases, this unchecked growth has led to the development of sprawling slums, lacking adequate water and sewerage facilities.

▲ Perched high in the Andes like many of the cities in western South America, La Paz, Bolivia is the world's highest capital city at over 11,500 ft (3500 m).

Map key

Population
- ■ above 5 million
- ■ 1 million to 5 million
- ⊡ 500,000 to 1 million
- ⊙ 100,000 to 500,000
- ⊕ 50,000 to 100,000
- ○ 10,000 to 50,000
- ○ below 10,000
- ● Country capital
- ● State capital

Borders
- full international border
- disputed de facto border
- disputed territorial claim border
- state border

Population

Almost half of South America's population lives in Brazil but, due to the large uninhabited expanses of the Amazon Basin, its overall population density is much lower than in other countries. During the 20th century the most important population trend was the movement from rural to urban areas, giving rise to great population concentrations in large cities like São Paulo, Rio de Janeiro, Caracas, Lima, Bogotá, and Buenos Aires.

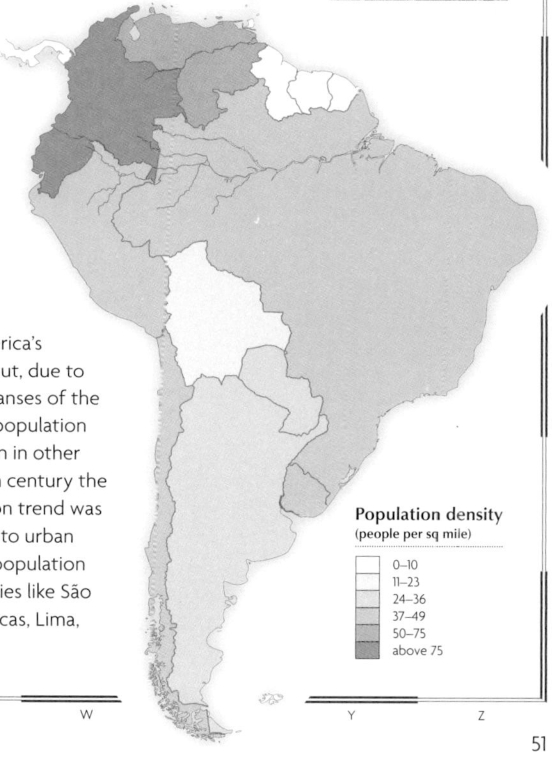

Population density (people per sq mile)
- 0–10
- 11–23
- 24–36
- 37–49
- 50–75
- above 75

TRINIDAD & TOBAGO

51

South American resources

Agriculture still provides the largest single form of employment in South America, although rural unemployment and poverty continue to drive people towards the huge coastal cities in search of jobs and opportunities. Mineral and fuel resources, although substantial, are distributed unevenly; few countries have both fossil fuels and minerals. To break industrial dependence on raw materials, boost manufacturing, and improve infrastructure, governments borrowed heavily from the World Bank in the 1960s and 1970s. This led to the accumulation of massive debts which are unlikely ever to be repaid. Today, Brazil dominates the continent's economic output, followed by Argentina. Recently, the less-developed western side of South America has benefited due to its geographical position; for example Chile is increasingly exporting raw materials to Japan.

◀ *Ciudad Guayana is a planned industrial complex in eastern Venezuela, built as an iron and steel center to exploit the nearby iron ore reserves.*

Industry

✈	aerospace	⚕	pharmaceuticals
	brewing		printing & publishing
	car/vehicle manufacture		shipbuilding
	chemicals		sugar processing
	electronics		textiles
⚙	engineering		timber processing
$	finance		tobacco processing
	fish processing		wine
	food processing	⚓	oil
	hi-tech industry		gas
	iron & steel	•	industrial cities
	meat processing	▨	major industrial areas
△	metal refining		
	narcotics		

Caribbean Sea

Barranquilla
Cartagena
Maracaibo
Barquisimeto
Caracas
Valencia
Ciudad Guayana

VENEZUELA

Medellín
Bogotá
Cali

COLOMBIA

Georgetown
Paramaribo

GUYANA

SURINAME

French Guiana (to France)

PANAMA

Gulf of Panama

Quito
ECUADOR
Guayaquil
Iquitos

Belém

A m a z o n

B a s i n

Manaus

Fortaleza

B R A Z I L

Nata

Recife

Maceió

▲ *The cold Peru Current flows north from the Antarctic along the Pacific coast of Peru, providing rich nutrients for one of the world's largest fishing grounds. However, over exploitation has severely reduced Peru's anchovy catch.*

Chiclayo
Chimbote
PERU
Lima
Cusco
Arequipa

Salvador

Standard of living

Wealth disparities throughout the continent create a wide gulf between affluent landowners and those afflicted by chronic poverty in inner city slums. The illicit production of cocaine, and the hugely influential drug barons who control its distribution, contribute to the violent disorder and corruption which affect northwestern South America, destabilizing local governments and economies.

BOLIVIA
La Paz
Santa Cruz
Sucre
Arica
Iquique
Chuquicamata
Antofagasta

Brasília

Belo Horizonte

PARAGUAY

Asunción
Ciudad del Este

São Paulo
Rio de Janeiro
Curitiba

San Miguel de Tucumán
Corrientes

Porto Alegre

P A C I F I C   O C E A N

Córdoba
Santa Fe
Rosario
Valparaíso
Mendoza
Santiago
Buenos Aires

URUGUAY
Rio Grande
Montevideo

Talca
Concepción

ARGENTINA

Bahía Blanca
Neuquén

Valdivia

Standard of living
(UN human development index)

low

high

▶ *Both Argentina and Chile are now exploring the southernmost tip of the continent in search of oil. Here in Punta Arenas, a drilling rig is being prepared for exploratory drilling in the Strait of Magellan.*

Comodoro Rivadavia
Gulf of San Jorge

Falkland Islands (to UK)

Bahía Grande

Punta Arenas

Cape Horn

GNI per capita (US$)

below 999
1000–1999
2000–2999
3000–3999
4000–4999
above 5000

Industry

Argentina and Brazil are South America's most industrialized countries and São Paulo is the continent's leading industrial center. Long-term government investment in Brazilian industry has encouraged a diverse industrial base; engineering, steel production, food processing, textile manufacture, and chemicals predominate. The illegal production of cocaine is economically significant in the Andean countries of Colombia and Bolivia. In Venezuela, the oil-dominated economy has left the country vulnerable to world oil price fluctuations. Food processing and mineral exploitation are common throughout the less industrially developed parts of the continent, including Bolivia, Chile, Ecuador, and Peru.

Environmental issues

The Amazon Basin is one of the last great wilderness areas left on Earth. The tropical rain forests which grow there are a valuable genetic resource, containing innumerable unique plants and animals. The forests are increasingly under threat from new and expanding settlements and "slash-and-burn" farming techniques, which clear land for the raising of beef cattle, causing land degradation and soil erosion.

▲ **Clouds of smoke** billow from the burning Amazon rainforest. Over 11,500 sq miles (30,000 sq km) of virgin rainforest are being cleared annually, destroying an ancient, irreplaceable, natural resource and biodiverse habitat.

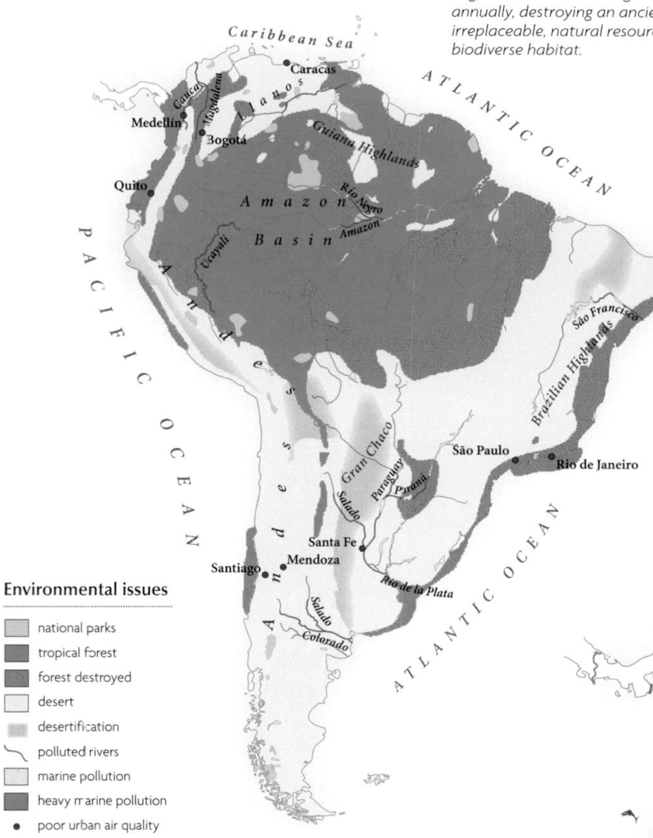

Environmental issues

- national parks
- tropical forest
- forest destroyed
- desert
- desertification
- polluted rivers
- marine pollution
- heavy marine pollution
- poor urban air quality

Mineral resources

Over a quarter of the world's known copper reserves are found at the Chuquicamata mine in northern Chile, and other metallic minerals such as tin are found along the length of the Andes. The discovery of oil and gas at Venezuela's Lake Maracaibo in 1917 turned the country into one of the world's leading oil producers. In contrast, South America is virtually devoid of coal, the only significant deposit being on the peninsula of Guajira in Colombia.

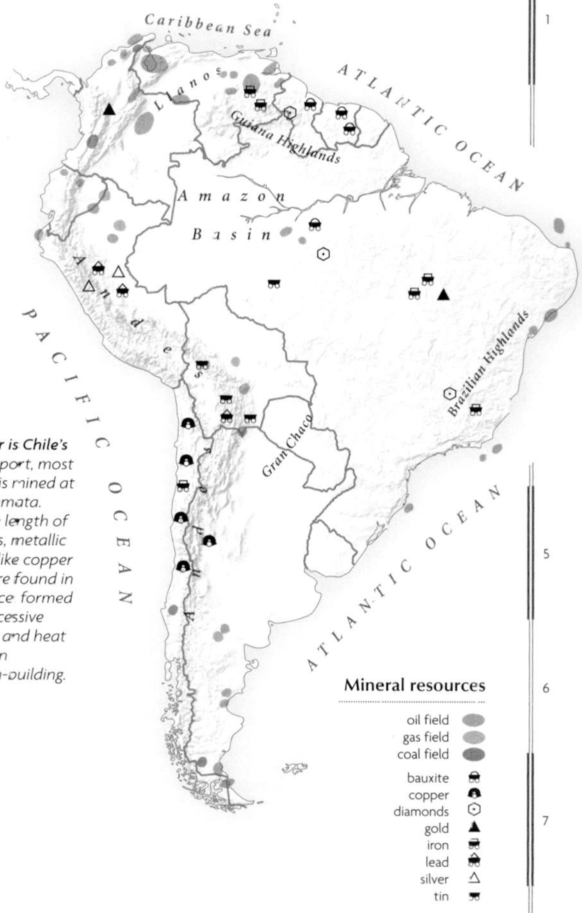

▲ **Copper is Chile's** largest export, most of which is mined at Chuquicamata. Along the length of the Andes, metallic minerals like copper and tin are found in abundance formed by the excessive pressures and heat involved in mountain-building.

Mineral resources

- oil field
- gas field
- coal field
- bauxite
- copper
- diamonds
- gold
- iron
- lead
- silver
- tin

Using the land and sea

Many foods now common worldwide originated in South America. These include the potato, tomato, squash, and cassava. Today, large herds of beef cattle roam the temperate grasslands of the Pampas, supporting an extensive meatpacking trade in Argentina, Uruguay and Paraguay. Corn is grown as a staple crop across the continent and coffee is grown as a cash crop in Brazil and Colombia. Coca plants grown in Bolivia, Peru, and Colombia provide most of the world's cocaine. Fish and shellfish are caught off the western coast, especially anchovies off Peru, shrimps off Ecuador and pilchards off Chile.

◄ **South America, and** Brazil in particular, now leads the world in coffee production, mainly growing Coffea Arabica in large plantations. Coffee beans are harvested, roasted and brewed to produce the world's second most popular drink, after tea.

◄ **The Pampas region** of southeast South America is characterized by extensive, flat plains, and populated by cattle and ranchers (gauchos). Argentina is a major world producer of beef, much of which is exported to the US for use in hamburgers.

◄ **High in the Andes**, hardy alpacas graze on the barren land. Alpacas are thought to have been domesticated by the Incas, whose nobility wore robes made from their wool. Today, they are still reared and prized for their soft, warm fleeces.

Using the land and sea

- barren land
- cropland
- desert
- forest
- mountain region
- pasture
- major conurbations
- cattle
- pigs
- sheep
- bananas
- corn
- citrus fruits
- cocoa
- cotton
- coffee
- fishing
- oil palms
- peanuts
- rubber
- shellfish
- soybeans
- sugar cane
- vineyards
- wheat

53

Northern South America

COLOMBIA, GUYANA, SURINAME, VENEZUELA, French Guiana (to France)

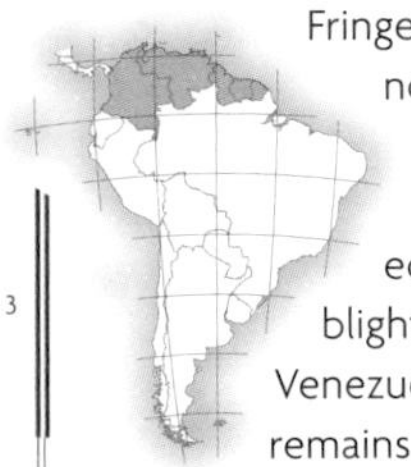

Fringed by the Pacific and Atlantic oceans and the Caribbean Sea, South America's northern region has a rich range of natural resources, some exploited for centuries by colonial powers including the Spanish, French, Dutch, and British, others still to be fully explored. The prospects for further economic development in Colombia, Guyana, and Suriname are blighted by drug-related violence and political instability. Venezuela, despite huge incomes from its oil reserves, remains less developed in other industrial sectors. French Guiana is an overseas *département* of France, now seeking greater autonomy. Most of the major population centers, such as Bogotá, have grown up in the temperate conditions of the high Andes or, like Caracas, at strategic points along the Caribbean coast.

► *Flowers grown in Colombia are exported all over the world, and include fine carnations and roses. Here, workers are cutting roses which have been grown in plastic greenhouses.*

Map key

Population
- ⊞ 1 million to 5 million
- ◉ 500,000 to 1 million
- ◎ 100,000 to 500,000
- ⊕ 50,000 to 100,000
- ○ 10,000 to 50,000
- ○ below 10,000

Elevation
- 4000m / 13,124ft
- 3000m / 9843ft
- 2000m / 6562ft
- 1000m / 3281ft
- 500m / 1640ft
- 250m / 820ft
- 100m / 328ft
- sea level

▲ *Large open squares like the Plaza de Bolívar in Bogotá are characteristic of many cities founded by the Spanish.*

◄ *Scattered farms and villages have grown up on the gentle slopes of this Colombian river valley, utilizing the fertile soils for farming.*

Scale 1:7,250,000

Km 0 25 50 100 150 200
Miles 0 25 50 100 150 200

projection: Lambert Azimuthal Equal Area

▲ *The Orinoco river flows from its source in the southern Guiana Highlands to form a broad delta on Venezuela's Atlantic coast. One of its distributary channels opens into a wide bay called the Serpent's Mouth.*

Transportation & industry

Many mineral resources are mined in Colombia, including fuels, gold, and precious and semiprecious stones. Revenues from coffee and exports of illegal narcotics are crucial to the economy. Venezuela's major economic activity is the oil industry around Lake Maracaibo (Lago de Maracaibo). Sugar and bauxite are exported from Guyana and Suriname.

Transportation network

31,720 miles (51,054 km)	
3411 miles (5490 km)	
2448 miles (3940 km)	
22,429 miles (36,100 km)	

Rivers are an important means of transportation in Colombia; many are extensively navigable. The Pan-American Highway runs through Colombia. In Venezuela, much infrastructure investment is linked to the oil industry.

Major industry and infrastructure

- chemicals
- finance
- food processing
- iron & steel
- narcotics
- mining
- oil
- oil refining
- pharmaceuticals
- textiles
- timber processing
- ■ capital cities
- • major towns
- ⊕ international airports
- — major roads
- major industrial areas

▲ *Vast oil reserves* around Lake Maracaibo (Lago de Maracaibo) form the focus of Venezuelan industry. Incomes from oil are used to invest in other industries and in the development of infrastructure.

Using the land

The Andean basins support cereals and potatoes. Livestock graze at higher altitudes and on the drier tropical grasslands known as the *llanos*; hardy goats are reared in scrubland areas. Grown at higher elevations, coffee is an important cash crop, as is cotton, sugar cane, bananas, citrus fruits, cocoa, and rice, farmed on the Caribbean lowlands. Coca is the most widely grown narcotic plant, with heroin poppies grown in Colombia and marijuana in lowland areas throughout the region.

The urban/rural population divide

urban 80%   rural 20%

0 10 20 30 40 50 60 70 80 90 100

Population density	Total land area
78 people per sq mile (30 people per sq km)	1,111,317 sq miles (2,879,060 sq km)

Land use and agricultural distribution

- cattle
- goats
- bananas
- cereals
- coffee
- cotton
- sugar cane
- ■ capital cities
- • major towns
- pasture
- cropland
- forest
- wetlands
- mountain region

▲ *The Sierra Nevada de Santa Marta* is a granite massif which rises sharply from the Caribbean lowlands to snow-covered peaks, the tallest of which is 18,947 ft (5775 m) high.

Guiana Shield
- Alluvial plains
- Inselbergs
- Table mountains

▲ *The Guiana Shield* is one of the oldest land surfaces in the world – probably formed more than 4 billion years ago. Chemical weathering over millions of years has created flat-topped table mountains and large numbers of inselbergs.

Over 80% of Suriname is covered by tropical rain forest.

Lake Maracaibo (Lago de Maracaibo) is not a true lake but a shallow inlet of the Caribbean Sea. It is the main source of Venezuela's oil.

The drainage basin of the Magdalena River and the Cauca, its main tributary, covers over 20% of Colombia's total surface area.

In the Guiana Highlands, Venezuela's most remote region, the ancient crystalline rocks contain deposits of iron ore, gold and diamonds.

Angel Falls (Salto Angel), at 3212 ft (979 m), is the world's highest waterfall.

Igneous intrusions into the crystalline plateau which forms most of central Guyana have led to the formation of the many rapids that characterize Guyana's rivers.

The landscape

At its northernmost reaches, in western Colombia and Venezuela, the great Andean mountain chain splits into three distinct ranges: the Cordillera Oriental, Cordillera Central, and Cordillera Occidental, intercut by a complex series of lesser ranges and basins. The relief becomes lower toward the coast and the interior plains of the northern Amazon Basin, rising again into the tropical hills of the Guiana Highlands.

Cordillera Occidental
Cordillera Central
Cordillera Oriental

Colombia's eastern lowlands are known locally as llanos, meaning grasslands.

▶ *The Potaru river* descends 741 ft (226 m) over a sandstone ledge at the Kaieteur Falls in Guyana.

Potaru river

Most of the land in French Guiana is low-lying; here, the rocks of the Guiana Highlands have been eroded by rivers flowing toward the sea.

Map labels:

Caribbean Sea, PANAMA, Barranquilla, Maracaibo, Valencia, CARACAS, Cumaná, ATLANTIC OCEAN, GEORGETOWN, PARAMARIBO, Cayenne, Ciudad Guayana, VENEZUELA, GUYANA, SURINAME, FRENCH GUIANA, Medellín, PACIFIC OCEAN, BOGOTÁ, COLOMBIA, Cali, ECUADOR, PERU, BRAZIL

N SEA, Isla Blanquilla, Isla de Margarita, Islas Los Testigos, TRINIDAD & TOBAGO, NUEVA ESPARTA, Juangriego, La Asunción, Pampatar, Punta de Porlamar, Boca de Pozo, Araya, Juan Griego, Cariaco, El Pilar, Irapa, Güiria, Puerto de Hierro, Gulf of Paria, Cumaná, Carúpano, Río Caribe, La Cruz, Barcelona, SUCRE, Casanay, Caripe, Caripito, Maturín, Pedernales, The Serpent's Mouth, Punta Baja, MONAGAS, ANZOÁTEGUI, El Tigre, San José de Guanipa, Barrancas, Tucupita, DELTA AMACURO, Curiapo, Río Orinoco, Guayabones, Waini Point, Waini, ATLANTIC OCEAN

Ciudad Guayana, Soledad, El Pao, Upata, El Palmar, Port Kaituma, Charity, Ciudad Bolívar, Embalse de Guri, Arakaka, Matthews Ridge, Barama River, Spring Garden, Essequibo Islands, GEORGETOWN, Ciudad Piar, Guasipati, Kurucki, Aurora, Parika, Bartica, New Amsterdam, Ross Hall, Corriverton, BOLÍVAR, El Dorado, Cuyuni River, Enachu Landing, Peters Mine, Rockstone, Linden, Nieuw Nickerie, Friendship, Cerro Turagua 1838m, Canaima, Kamarang, Imbaimadai, Issano, Wageningen, Totness, Groningen, SARAMACCA, WANICA COMMEWIJNE, Nieuw Amsterdam, Mana, La Paragua, Auyan Tepuy 2950m, Mount Roraima 2810m, Ayanganna Mountain 2042m, GUYANA, Ituni, Kabalebo River, Ledydorp, PARAMARIBO, Onverwacht, Albina, St-Laurent-du-Maroni, Iles du Salut, Cerro Guaiquinima 2100m, Cerro Venamo 1563m, Uruyén, Kaieteur Falls, Glendor Mountains, Kurupukari, Oreallo, Wasjabo, Donderkamp, Kwakoegron, Berg en Dal, Brownsweg, Brokopondo, Herminadorp, Citron, Apoera, W.J. van Blommesteinmeer, Iracoubo, Sinnamary, Centre Spatial Guyanais, Kourou, Uonán, Santa María de Erebato, Caruana de Montaña, Lethem, Rupununi River, Kanuku Mountains, Sauriwaunawa, Jacobs Ladder Fals, Bergi, Bott-Pasi, Grand-Santi, Pokeeti, FRENCH GUIANA (to France), Tafelberg 1026m, Hendrik Top 957m, Djoemoe, SURINAME, St-Elie, Délices, Caca, Saül, Montagnes Bellevue de l'Inini, Rémire, Matoury, CAYENNE, Cayenne, Pointe Béhague

Santa María de Uairén, Santa Elena de Uairén, Pakaraima Mountains, (Venezuela claims all of Guyana west of Essequibo river), Juliana Top 1230m, Lucie River, Apetina, Tapanahony River, Apikalo, SIPALIWINI, Alimimuni Piek 728m, Massif du Mitaraka 690m, Mont Saint-Marcel 635m, Trois Sauts, Maripasoula, Pedima, Baie de l'Oyapok, St-Georges, Xuyuwini Landing, Johi Village, Acarai Mountains, Tumuc-Humac Mountains, L'Oyapok Fleuve, Camopi, Maroni River, (Claimed by Suriname), Equator, BRAZIL

Western South America

BOLIVIA, ECUADOR, PERU

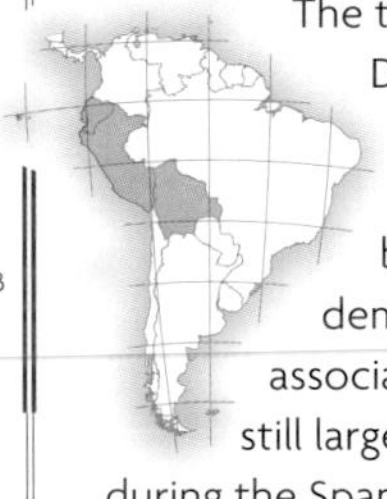

The three states of Western South America share a similar geography and recent history. Dominated by the Inca empire until Spanish conquest in the 16th century, they achieved independence from Spain in the early 19th century. The precipitous terrain of the Andes presents severe difficulties for overland transportation and continues to be a barrier to national unity and stability. Although Ecuador is now a relatively stable democracy, the military is highly influential in Peru and Bolivia, while the drug trade and associated corruption discourages external aid and economic progress. Wealth and power are still largely concentrated in the hands of a small elite of families, who attained their position during the Spanish colonial period. Energy resources and political recognition for the indigenous peoples are becoming increasingly important issues, particularly in Bolivia.

The landscape

Bolivia, Peru, and Ecuador each possess a high Andean mountain region and an eastern region consisting of tropical lowlands and the Andean slope leading down to them. Toward the south of the region, the mountains widen to form the high plateau of the Altiplano. Peru and Ecuador also have fertile, lowland coastal plains. A wide variety of environments include *selva* (tropical rain forest), *montaña* (mountain forest), and grassland.

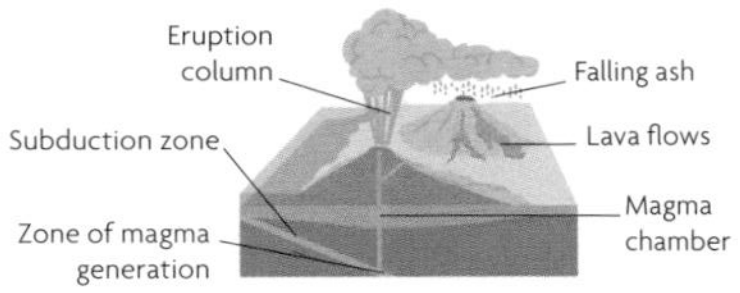

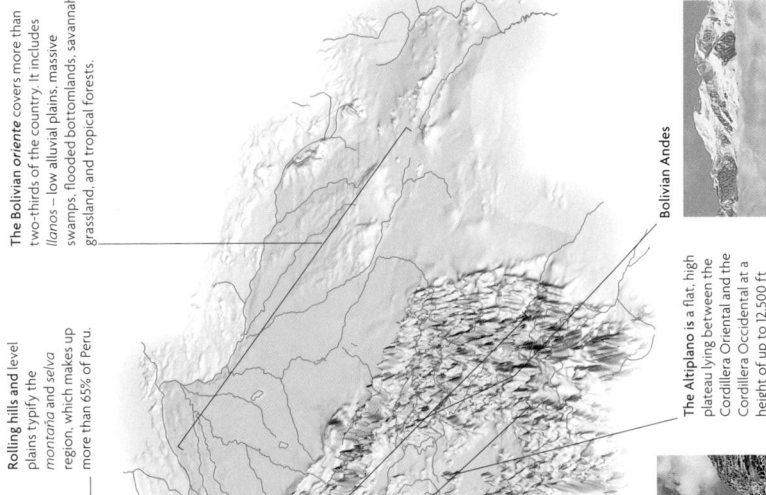

▲ **There are many** large and active volcanoes in the Andes. Magma generated in the heart of the volcano erupts in a huge cloud of ash. Ashfall deposits are common throughout the Andes and the rock produced is known as *andesite*. This is rapidly soaked by heavy rain, causing massive debris flows.

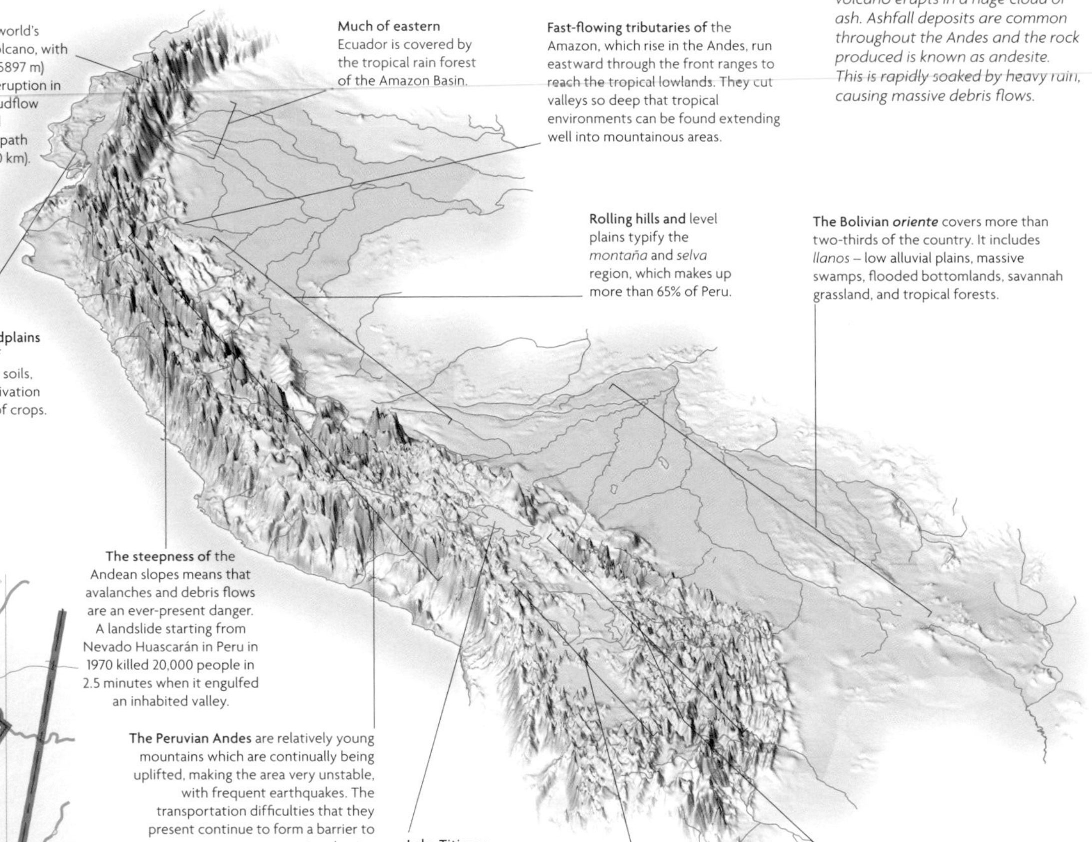

Eruption column
Falling ash
Lava flows
Subduction zone
Magma chamber
Zone of magma generation

Fast-flowing tributaries of the Amazon, which rise in the Andes, run eastward through the front ranges to reach the tropical lowlands. They cut valleys so deep that tropical environments can be found extending well into mountainous areas.

Much of eastern Ecuador is covered by the tropical rain forest of the Amazon Basin.

Cotopaxi is the world's highest active volcano, with a peak 19,347 ft (5897 m) high. A massive eruption in 1877 caused a mudflow which destroyed everything in its path for 150 miles (240 km).

Rolling hills and level plains typify the *montaña* and *selva* region, which makes up more than 65% of Peru.

The coastal floodplains are the source of Ecuador's richest soils, enabling the cultivation of a wide range of crops.

▲ **Ecuador's capital city,** Quito, lies high in the Andes, nestling between snowcapped peaks. At 9350 ft (2850 m), Quito is the second highest capital in the world – La Paz in Bolivia is the highest.

The steepness of the Andean slopes means that avalanches and debris flows are an ever-present danger. A landslide starting from Nevado Huascarán in Peru in 1970 killed 20,000 people in 2.5 minutes when it engulfed an inhabited valley.

The Peruvian Andes are relatively young mountains which are continually being uplifted, making the area very unstable, with frequent earthquakes. The transportation difficulties that they present continue to form a barrier to national unity.

The Bolivian *oriente* covers more than two-thirds of the country. It includes *llanos* – low alluvial plains, massive swamps, flooded bottomlands, savannah grassland, and tropical forests.

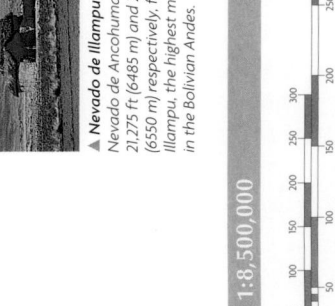

Bolivian Andes

▲ **Nevado de Illampu** and Nevado de Ancohuma, at 21,275 ft (6485 m) and 21,490 ft (6550 m) respectively, form Illampu, the highest mountain in the Bolivian Andes.

The Altiplano is a flat, high plateau lying between the Cordillera Oriental and the Cordillera Occidental at a height of up to 12,500 ft (3800 m). At its margins lie many spurs and alluvial fans.

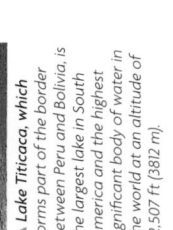

Lake Titicaca

▲ **Lake Titicaca, which** forms part of the border between Peru and Bolivia, is the largest lake in South America and the highest significant body of water in the world at an altitude of 12,507 ft (3812 m).

Scale 1:8,500,000

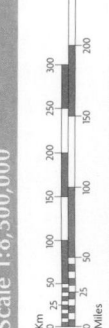

Projection: Lambert Azimuthal Equal Area

Map key

Population
- ■ above 5 million
- ⊡ 1 million to 5 million
- ◉ 500,000 to 1 million
- ◎ 100,000 to 500,000
- ⊙ 50,000 to 100,000
- ○ 10,000 to 50,000
- ∘ below 10,000

Elevation
- 6000m / 19,686ft
- 4000m / 13,124ft
- 3000m / 9843ft
- 2000m / 6562ft
- 1000m / 3281ft
- 500m / 1640ft
- 250m / 820ft
- 100m / 328ft
- sea level

Ecuador: Administrative regions
- ① CARCHI
- ② TUNGURAHUA
- ③ BOLIVAR
- ④ CHIMBORAZO
- ⑤ ZAMORA CHINCHIPE

COLOMBIA

ECUADOR

PERU

BRAZIL

Equator

56

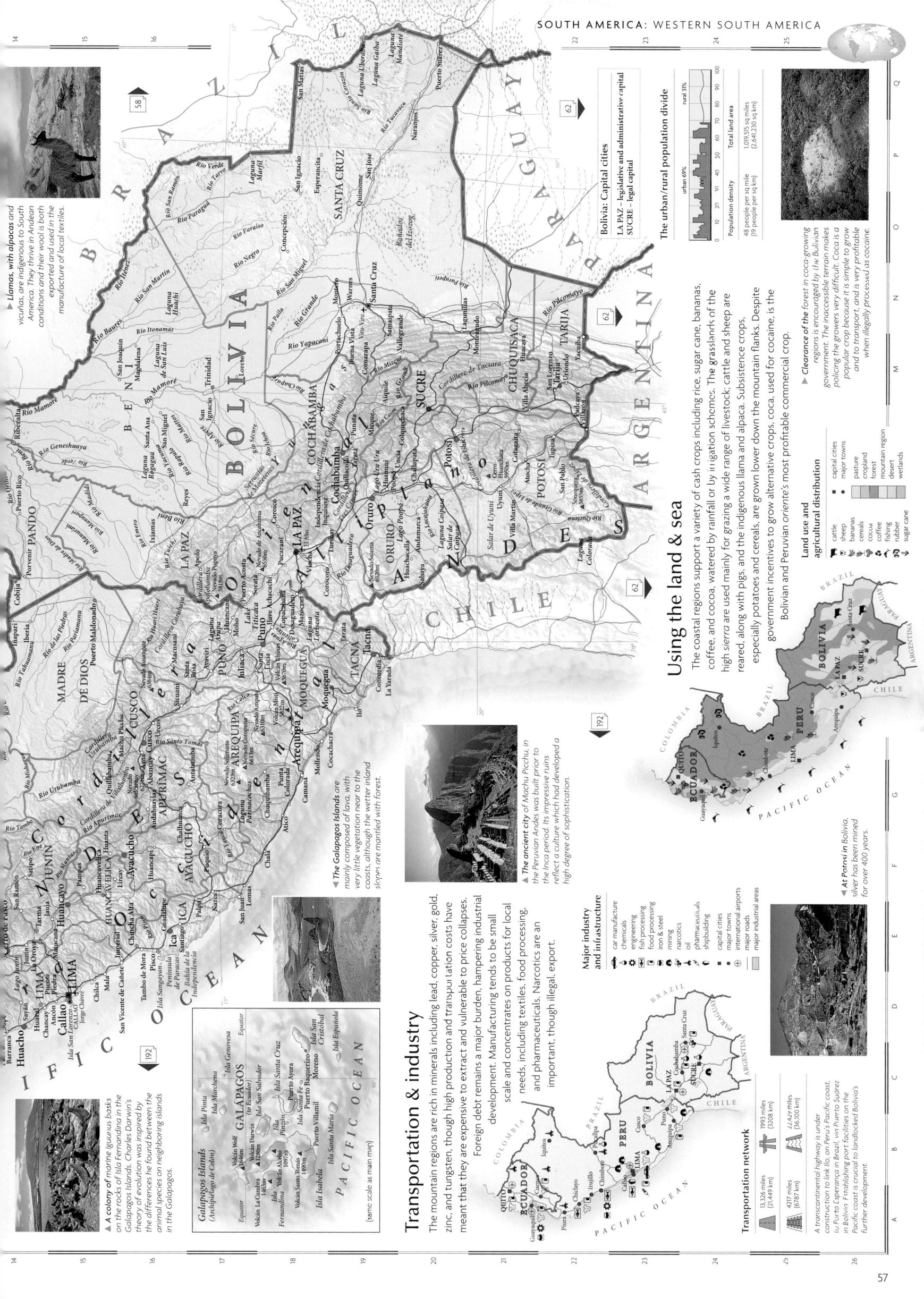

▲ *Llamas, with alpacas and vicuñas, are indigenous to South America. They thrive in Andean conditions and their wool is both exported and used in the manufacture of local textiles.*

Bolivia: Capital cities
LA PAZ – legislative and administrative capital
SUCRE – legal capital

The urban/rural population divide

urban 69%   rural 31%

Population density   Total land area
48 people per sq mile   1,019,515 sq miles
(19 people per sq km)   (2,641,230 sq km)

▲ *Clearance of the forest in coca-growing regions is encouraged by the Bolivian government. The inaccessible terrain makes policing the growers very difficult. Coca is a popular crop because it is simple to grow and to transport, and is very profitable when illegally processed as cocaine.*

Using the land & sea

The coastal regions support a variety of cash crops including rice, sugar cane, bananas, coffee, and cocoa, watered by rainfall or by irrigation schemes. The grasslands of the high *sierra* are used mainly for grazing a wide range of livestock: cattle and sheep are reared, along with pigs, and the indigenous llama and alpaca. Subsistence crops, especially potatoes and cereals, are grown lower down the mountain flanks. Despite government incentives to grow alternative crops, coca, used for cocaine, is the Bolivian and Peruvian *oriente*'s most profitable commercial crop.

Land use and agricultural distribution

- cattle
- sheep
- bananas
- cocoa
- coffee
- fishing
- rubber
- sugar cane
- capital cities
- major towns
- pasture
- cropland
- forest
- mountain region
- desert
- wetlands

▲ *At Potosí in Bolivia, silver has been mined for over 400 years.*

▲ *A colony of marine iguanas basks on the rocks of Isla Fernandina in the Galapagos Islands. Charles Darwin's theory of evolution was inspired by the differences he found between the animal species on neighboring islands in the Galapagos.*

▼ *The Galapagos Islands are mainly composed of lava, with very little vegetation near to the coasts, although the wetter inland slopes are mantled with forest.*

▲ *The ancient city of Machu Picchu, in the Peruvian Andes was built prior to the Inca period. Its impressive ruins reflect a culture which had developed a high degree of sophistication.*

Galapagos Islands
(Archipiélago de Colón)

(same scale as main map)

Transportation & industry

The mountain regions are rich in minerals including lead, copper, silver, gold, zinc, and tungsten, though high production and transportation costs have meant that they are expensive to extract and vulnerable to price collapses. Foreign debt remains a major burden, hampering industrial development. Manufacturing tends to be small scale and concentrates on products for local needs, including textiles, food processing, and pharmaceuticals. Narcotics are an important, though illegal, export.

Major industry and infrastructure

- car manufacture
- chemicals
- engineering
- fish processing
- food processing
- iron & steel
- mining
- narcotics
- oil
- pharmaceuticals
- shipbuilding
- capital cities
- major towns
- international airports
- major roads
- major industrial areas

Transportation network

13,326 miles (21,449 km)	1993 miles (3208 km)
4217 miles (6787 km)	22,429 miles (36,100 km)

A transcontinental highway is under construction to link Ilo, on Peru's Pacific coast, to Porto Esperanza in Brazil, via Puerto Suárez in Bolivia. Establishing port facilities on the Pacific coast is crucial to landlocked Bolivia's further development.

Brazil

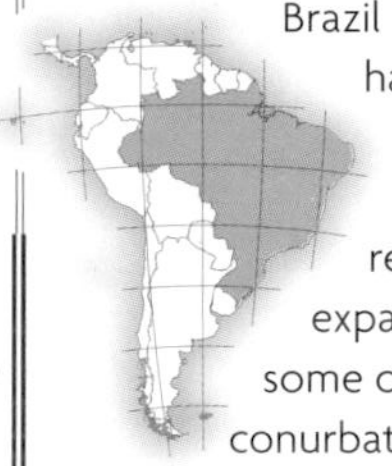

Brazil is the largest country in South America, with a population of 191 million – almost half the combined total of the continent. The 26 states which make up the federal republic of Brazil are administered from the purpose-built capital, Brasília. Tropical rain forest, covering more than one-third of the country, contains rich natural resources, but great tracts are sacrificed to agriculture, industry and urban expansion on a daily basis. Most of Brazil's multiethnic population now live in cities, some of which are vast areas of urban sprawl; São Paulo is one of the world's biggest conurbations, with more than 20 million inhabitants. Although prosperity is a reality for some, many people still live in great poverty, and mounting foreign debts continue to damage Brazil's prospects of economic advancement.

Using the land

Brazil has immense natural resources, including minerals and hardwoods, many of which are found in the fragile rain forest. Brazil is the world's leading coffee grower and a major producer of livestock, sugar, and orange juice concentrate. Soybeans for animal feed, particularly for poultry feed, have become the country's most significant crop.

The urban/rural population divide

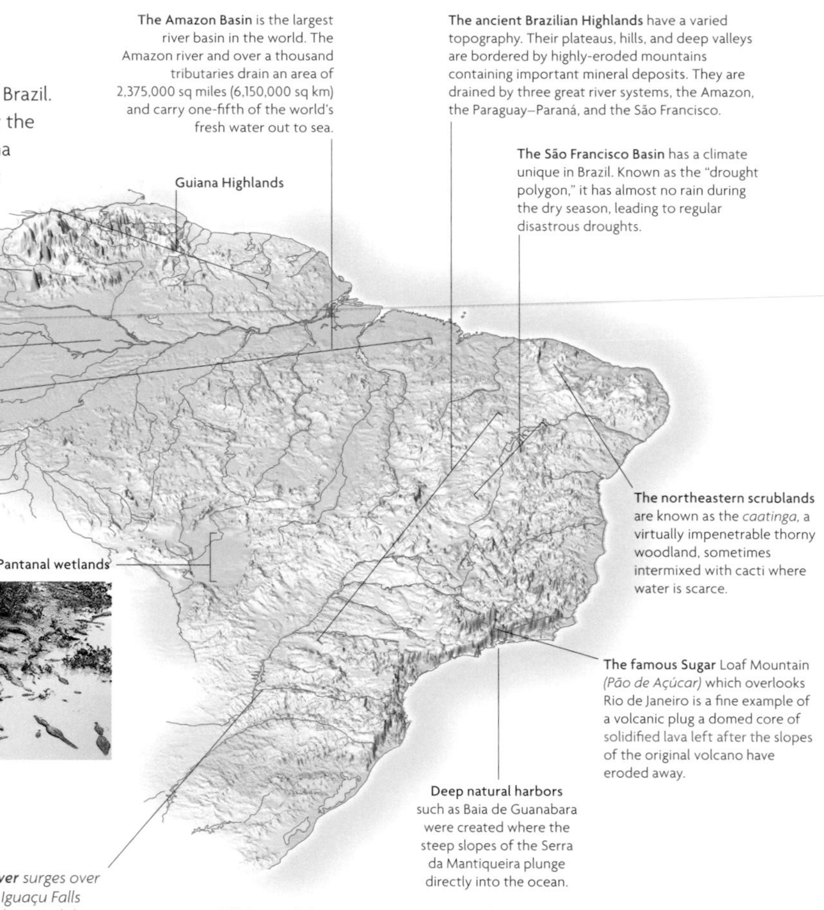

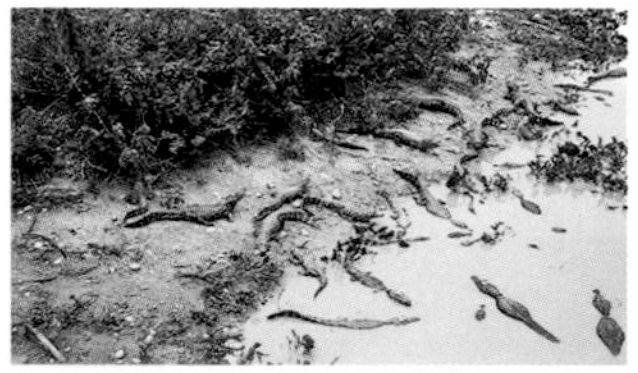

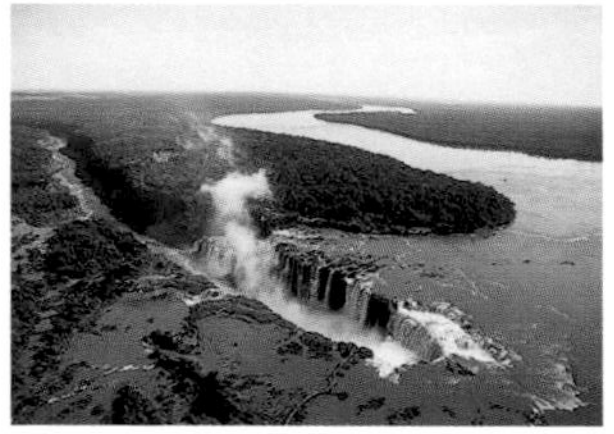

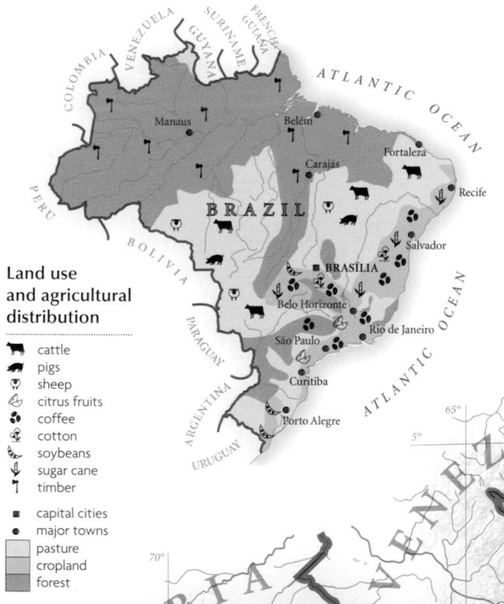

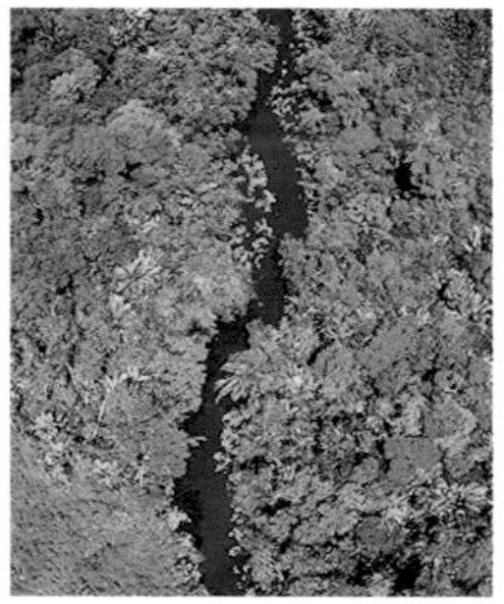

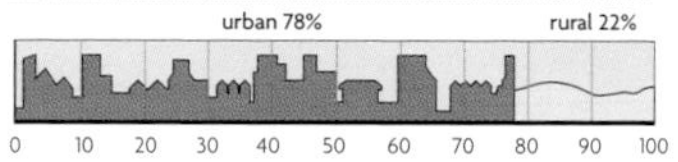

urban 78%
rural 22%
0 10 20 30 40 50 60 70 80 90 100

Population density	Total land area
55 people per sq mile (21 people per sq km)	3,286,472 sq miles (8,511,970 sq km)

BRAZIL
BRASÍLIA
Manaus
Belém
Carajás
Fortaleza
Recife
Salvador
Belo Horizonte
Rio de Janeiro
São Paulo
Curitiba
Porto Alegre
COLOMBIA
VENEZUELA
GUYANA
SURINAME
FRENCH GUIANA
PERU
BOLIVIA
PARAGUAY
ARGENTINA
URUGUAY
ATLANTIC OCEAN
Land use and agricultural distribution
cattle
pigs
sheep
citrus fruits
coffee
cotton
soybeans
sugar cane
timber
capital cities
major towns
pasture
cropland
forest

► *The fecundity of parts of Brazil's rain forest results from exceptionally high levels of rainfall and the quantities of silt deposited by the Amazon river system.*

The landscape

The Amazon Basin, containing the largest area of tropical rain forest on Earth, covers nearly half of Brazil. It is bordered by two shield areas: in the south by the Brazilian Highlands, and in the north by the Guiana Highlands. The east coast is dominated by a great escarpment which runs for 1600 miles (2565 km).

The Amazon Basin is the largest river basin in the world. The Amazon river and over a thousand tributaries drain an area of 2,375,000 sq miles (6,150,000 sq km) and carry one-fifth of the world's fresh water out to sea.
The ancient Brazilian Highlands have a varied topography. Their plateaus, hills, and deep valleys are bordered by highly-eroded mountains containing important mineral deposits. They are drained by three great river systems, the Amazon, the Paraguay–Paraná, and the São Francisco.
The São Francisco Basin has a climate unique in Brazil. Known as the "drought polygon," it has almost no rain during the dry season, leading to regular disastrous droughts.
Guiana Highlands
Brazil's highest mountain is the Pico da Neblina which was only discovered in 1962. It is 9888 ft (3014 m) high.
The floodplains which border the Amazon river are made up of a variety of different features including shallow lakes and swamps, mangrove forests in the tidal delta area, and fertile levées on river banks and point bars.
The northeastern scrublands are known as the *caatinga*, a virtually impenetrable thorny woodland, sometimes intermixed with cacti where water is scarce.
Pantanal wetlands
The famous Sugar Loaf Mountain (*Pão de Açúcar*) which overlooks Rio de Janeiro is a fine example of a volcanic plug a domed core of solidified lava left after the slopes of the original volcano have eroded away.
Deep natural harbors such as Baia de Guanabara were created where the steep slopes of the Serra da Mantiqueira plunge directly into the ocean.

► *The Pantanal region in the south of Brazil is an extension of the Gran Chaco plain. The swamps and marshes of this area are renowned for their beauty, and abundant and unique wildlife, including wildfowl and these caimans, a type of crocodile.*

◄ *The Iguaçu river surges over the spectacular Iguaçu Falls (Saltos do Iguaçu) toward the Paraná river. Falls like these are increasingly under pressure from large-scale hydroelectric projects such as that at Itaipú.*

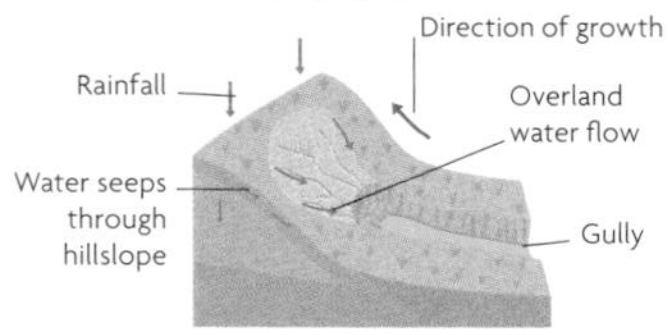

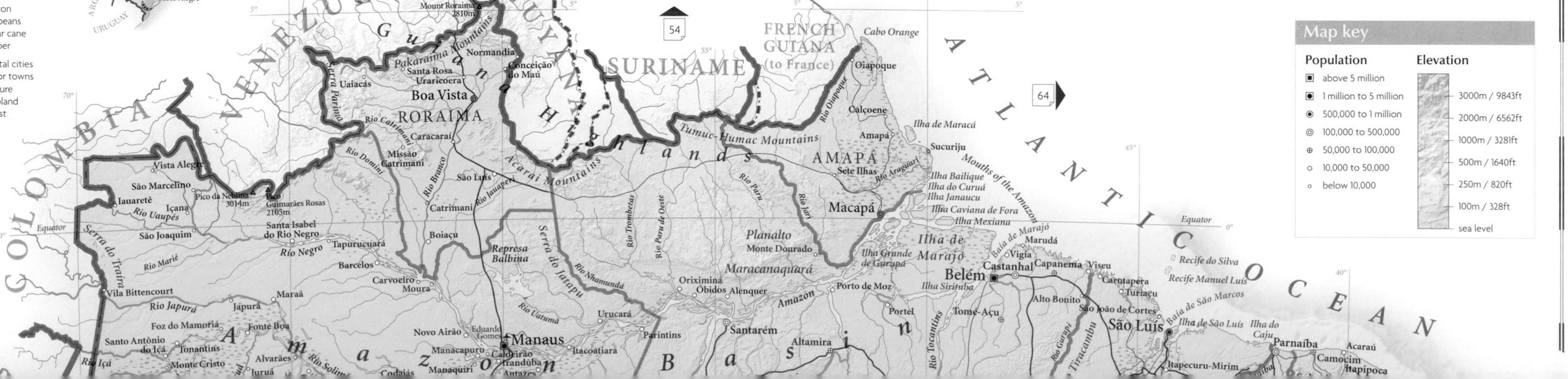

Hillslope gullying

Rainfall
Direction of growth
Overland water flow
Water seeps through hillslope
Gully

◄ *Large-scale gullies are common in Brazil, particularly on hillslopes from which vegetation has been removed. Gullies grow headwards (up the slope), aided by a combination of erosion through water seepage and rainwater runoff.*

54
64
56
VENEZUELA
GUYANA
SURINAME
FRENCH GUIANA (to France)
COLOMBIA
ATLANTIC OCEAN
Guiana Highlands
RORAIMA
AMAPÁ
Boa Vista
Macapá
Belém
Manaus
São Luís
Santarém
Mount Roraima 2810m
Pico da Neblina 3014m
Tumuc-Humac Mountains
Acaraí Mountains
Pakaraima Mountains
Serra Parima
Serra do Tatapu
Planalto Maracanaquará
Ilha de Marajó
Mouths of the Amazon
Cabo Orange
Oiapoque
Equator
Map key
Population
above 5 million
1 million to 5 million
500,000 to 1 million
100,000 to 500,000
50,000 to 100,000
10,000 to 50,000
below 10,000
Elevation
3000m / 9843ft
2000m / 6562ft
1000m / 3281ft
500m / 1640ft
250m / 820ft
100m / 328ft
sea level

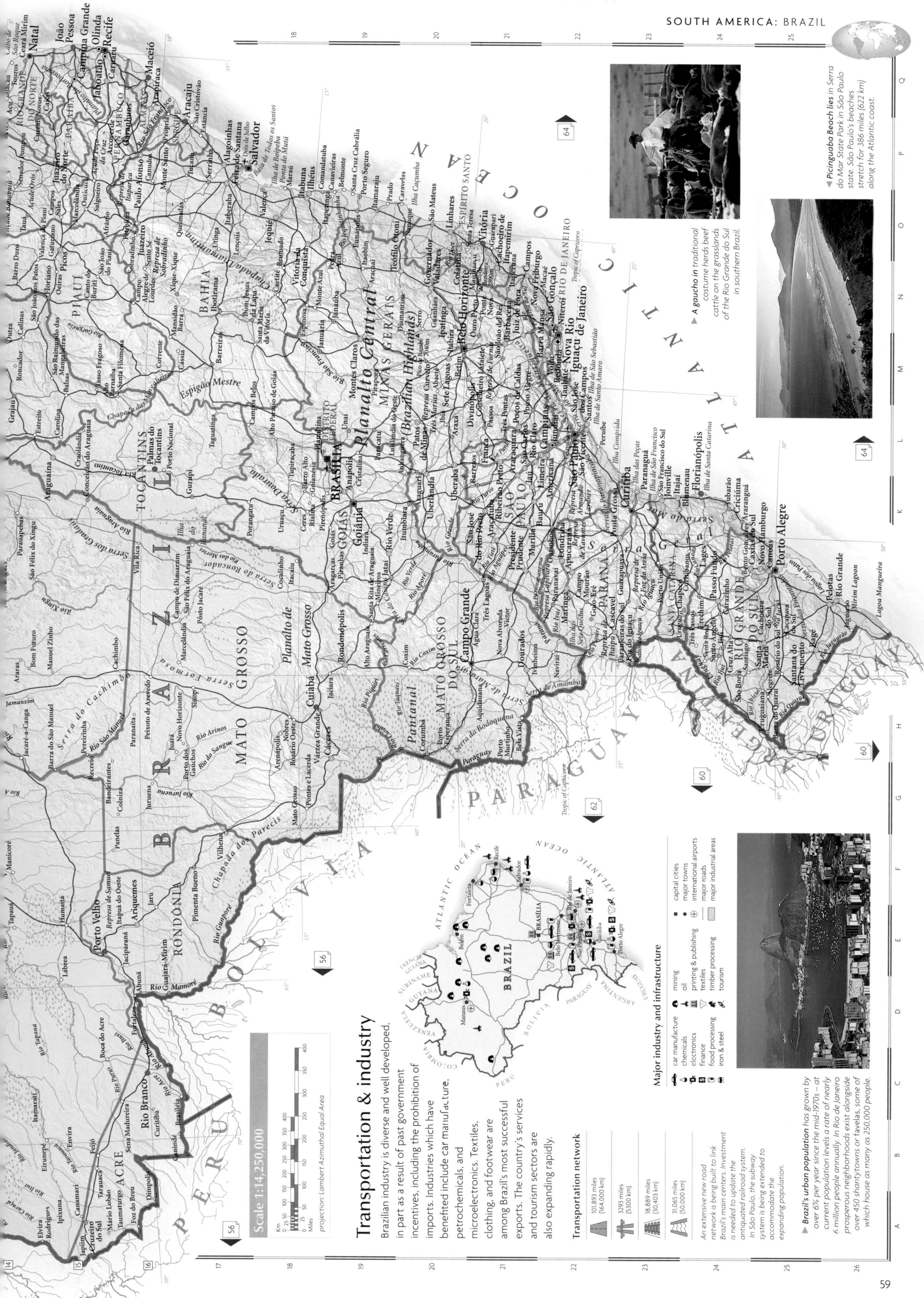

▲ *Picinguaba Beach* lies in Serra do Mar State Park in São Paulo state. São Paulo's beaches stretch for 386 miles (622 km) along the Atlantic coast.

▲ *A gaucho in traditional costume herds beef cattle on the grasslands of the Rio Grande do Sul in southern Brazil.*

Transportation & industry

Brazilian industry is diverse and well developed, in part as a result of past government incentives, including the prohibition of imports. Industries which have benefited include car manufacture, petrochemicals, and microelectronics. Textiles, clothing, and footwear are among Brazil's most successful exports. The country's services and tourism sectors are also expanding rapidly.

Scale 1:14,250,000

Km
0 25 50   100 150 200 250 300 350 400
Miles
0   25 50   100   150   200 250 300 350 400

projection: Lambert Azimuthal Equal Area

Transportation network

101,893 miles (164,000 km)

3293 miles (5300 km)

18,889 miles (30,403 km)

31,065 miles (50,000 km)

An extensive new road network is being built to link Brazil's main centers. Investment is needed to update the antiquated railroad system. In São Paulo, the subway system is being extended to accommodate the expanding population.

▲ *Brazil's urban population* has grown by over 6% per year since the mid-1970s – at current population levels a rate of nearly 6 million people annually. In Rio de Janeiro prosperous neighborhoods exist alongside over 450 shantytowns or favelas, some of which house as many as 250,000 people.

Major industry and infrastructure

- car manufacture
- chemicals
- electronics
- finance
- food processing
- iron & steel
- mining
- oil
- printing & publishing
- textiles
- timber processing
- tourism

- capital cities
- major towns
- international airports
- major roads
- major industrial areas

Eastern South America

URUGUAY, NORTHEAST ARGENTINA, SOUTHEAST BRAZIL

The vast conurbations of Rio de Janeiro, São Paulo, and Buenos Aires form the core of South America's highly-urbanized eastern region. São Paulo state, with over 40 million inhabitants, is among the world's 20 most powerful economies, and São Paulo is the fastest growing city on the continent. Rio de Janeiro and Buenos Aires, transformed in the last hundred years from port cities to great metropolitan areas each with more than 10 million inhabitants, typify the unstructured growth and wealth disparities of South America's great cities. In Uruguay, over two fifths of the population lives in the capital, Montevideo, which faces Buenos Aires across the Plate River (Rio de la Plata). Immigration from the countryside has created severe pressure on the urban infrastructure, particularly on available housing, leading to a profusion of crowded shanty settlements (favelas or barrios).

Using the land

Most of Uruguay and the Pampas of northern Argentina are devoted to the rearing of livestock, especially cattle and sheep, which are central to both countries' economies. Soybeans, first produced in Brazil's Rio Grande do Sul, are now more widely grown for large-scale export, as are cereals, sugar cane, and grapes. Subsistence crops, including potatoes, corn and sugar beets, are grown on the remaining arable land.

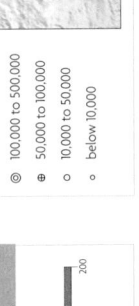

▲ Soybeans are harvested, pressed, and processed into soyacake, which is used as animal feed. The cake is fed mainly to chickens on large-scale factory farms, and the growth in soy production has been an important factor in the expansion of the Brazilian poultry trade.

Land use and agricultural distribution

- cattle
- sheep
- cereals
- coffee
- fruit
- soybeans
- sugar cane
- capital cities
- major towns

- pasture
- cropland
- forest
- wetlands
- barren land

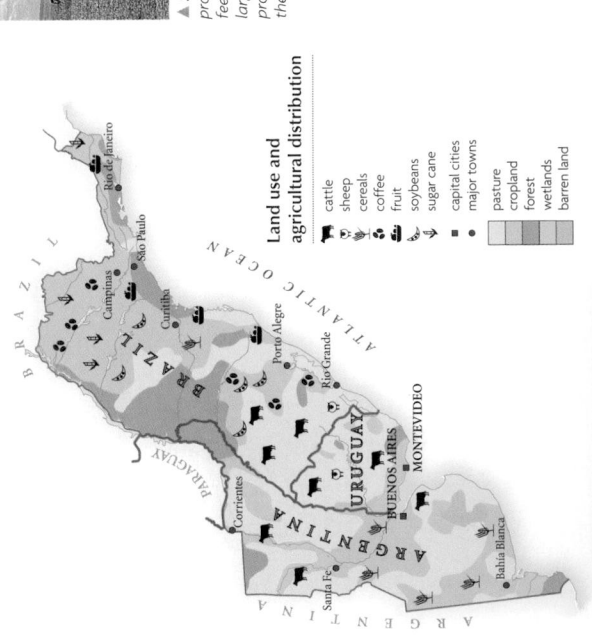

▼ The rolling grasslands of Uruguay are ideally suited to the rearing of cattle, which are concentrated in great herds throughout the region.

Transportation & industry

Southeast Brazil is home to much of the important motor and capital goods industry, largely based around São Paulo; iron and steel production is also concentrated in this region. Uruguay's economy continues to be based mainly on the export of livestock products including meat and leather goods. Buenos Aires is Argentina's chief port, and the region has a varied and sophisticated economic base including service-based industries such as finance and publishing, as well as primary processing.

Major industry and infrastructure

- car manufacture
- chemicals
- engineering
- finance
- food processing
- iron & steel
- meat processing
- printing & publishing
- shipbuilding
- textiles
- timber processing
- capital cities
- major towns
- international airports
- major roads
- major industrial areas

Transportation network

Throughout the region, road networks need to be expanded to cope with urban development. Plans are underway to build a bridge over the Plate River (Rio de la Plata) to link Colonia and Buenos Aires.

▲ The Itaipú dam on the Paraná river is one of the largest hydroelectric projects in the world, jointly financed by Brazil and Paraguay.

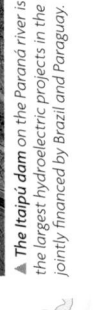

▲ Rio de Janeiro's annual carnival, Mardi Gras, which ushers in the start of Lent, is an extravagant five-day parade through the city, characterized by fantastically decorated floats, exuberant

Scale 1:7,000,000

projection: Lambert Azimuthal Equal Area

Map key

Population
- ■ above 5 million
- ■ 1 million to 5 million
- ■ 500,000 to 1 million
- ⊕ 100,000 to 500,000
- ⊙ 50,000 to 100,000
- ◉ 10,000 to 50,000
- ○ below 10,000

Elevation
- 2000m / 6562ft
- 1000m / 328ft
- 500m / 1640ft
- 250m / 820ft
- 100m / 328ft
- sea level

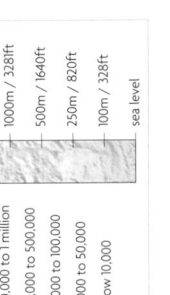

The landscape

The southern reaches of the Brazilian Highlands follow the Atlantic coast to form low, rolling hills in the northeast of Uruguay. Much of South America's mid-eastern region and all of Uruguay has a gentle relief with land rarely rising above 300 ft (100 m). Argentina's northeast comprises two main regions: a long, narrow lowland known as Mesopotamia; and part of the Pampas grasslands.

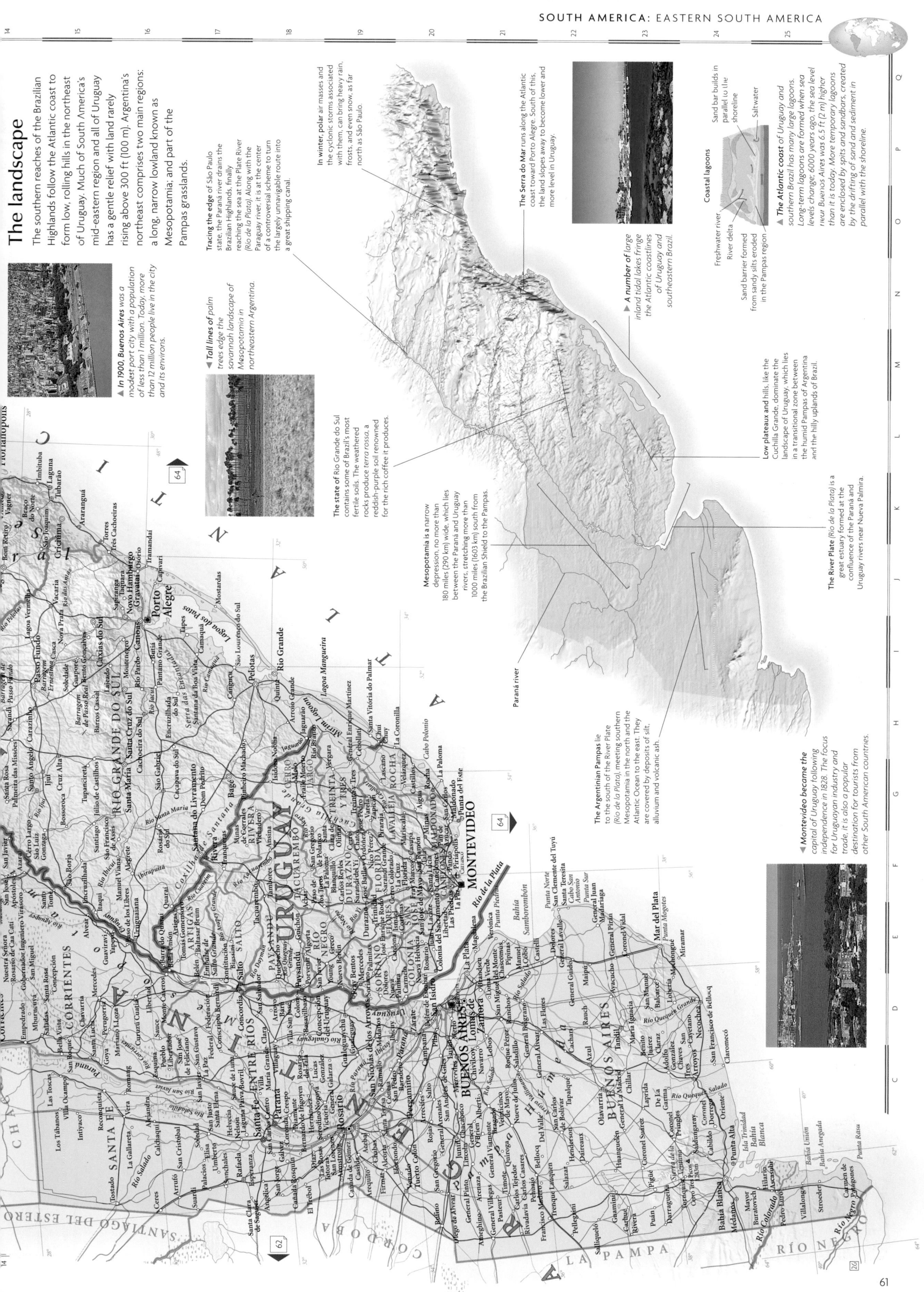

▲ In 1900, Buenos Aires was a modest port city with a population of less than 1 million. Today, more than 12 million people live in the city and its environs.

Tracing the edge of São Paulo state, the Paraná river drains the Brazilian Highlands, finally reaching the sea at the Plate River (Rio de la Plata). Along with the Paraguay river, it is at the center of a controversial scheme to turn the largely unnavigable route into a great shipping canal.

▼ Tall lines of palm trees edge the savannah landscape of Mesopotamia in northeastern Argentina.

In winter, polar air masses and the cyclonic storms associated with them, can bring heavy rain, frosts, and even snow, as far north as São Paulo.

The Serra do Mar runs along the Atlantic coast toward Porto Alegre. South of this, the land slopes away to become lower and more level in Uruguay.

▲ A number of large inland tidal lakes fringe the Atlantic coastlines of Uruguay and southeastern Brazil.

Coastal lagoons

Sand bar builds in parallel to the shoreline

Saltwater

Freshwater river

River delta

Sand barrier formed from sandy silts eroded in the Pampas region.

▲ The Atlantic coast of Uruguay and southern Brazil has many large lagoons. Long-term lagoons are formed when sea levels change; 6000 years ago, the sea level near Buenos Aires was 6.5 ft (2 m) higher than it is today. More temporary lagoons are enclosed by spits and sandbars, created by the drifting of sand and sediment in parallel with the shoreline.

The state of Rio Grande do Sul contains some of Brazil's most fertile soils. The weathered rocks produce terra rossa, a reddish-purple soil renowned for the rich coffee it produces.

Mesopotamia is a narrow depression, no more than 180 miles (290 km) wide, which lies between the Paraná and Uruguay rivers, stretching more than 1000 miles (1603 km) south from the Brazilian Shield to the Pampas.

Low plateaux and hills, like the Cuchilla Grande, dominate the landscape of Uruguay, which lies in a transitional zone between the humid Pampas of Argentina and the hilly uplands of Brazil.

Paraná river

The River Plate (Rio de la Plata) is a great estuary formed at the confluence of the Paraná and Uruguay rivers near Nueva Palmira.

The Argentinian Pampas lie to the south of the River Plate (Rio de la Plata), meeting southern Mesopotamia in the north and the Atlantic Ocean to the east. They are covered by deposits of silt, alluvium and volcanic ash.

▼ Montevideo became the capital of Uruguay following independence in 1828. The focus for Uruguayan industry and trade, it is also a popular destination for tourists from other South American countries.

▲ **Floodwaters cover the** land in the Gran Chaco, partly submerging its vegetation of fan palms and hyacinths.

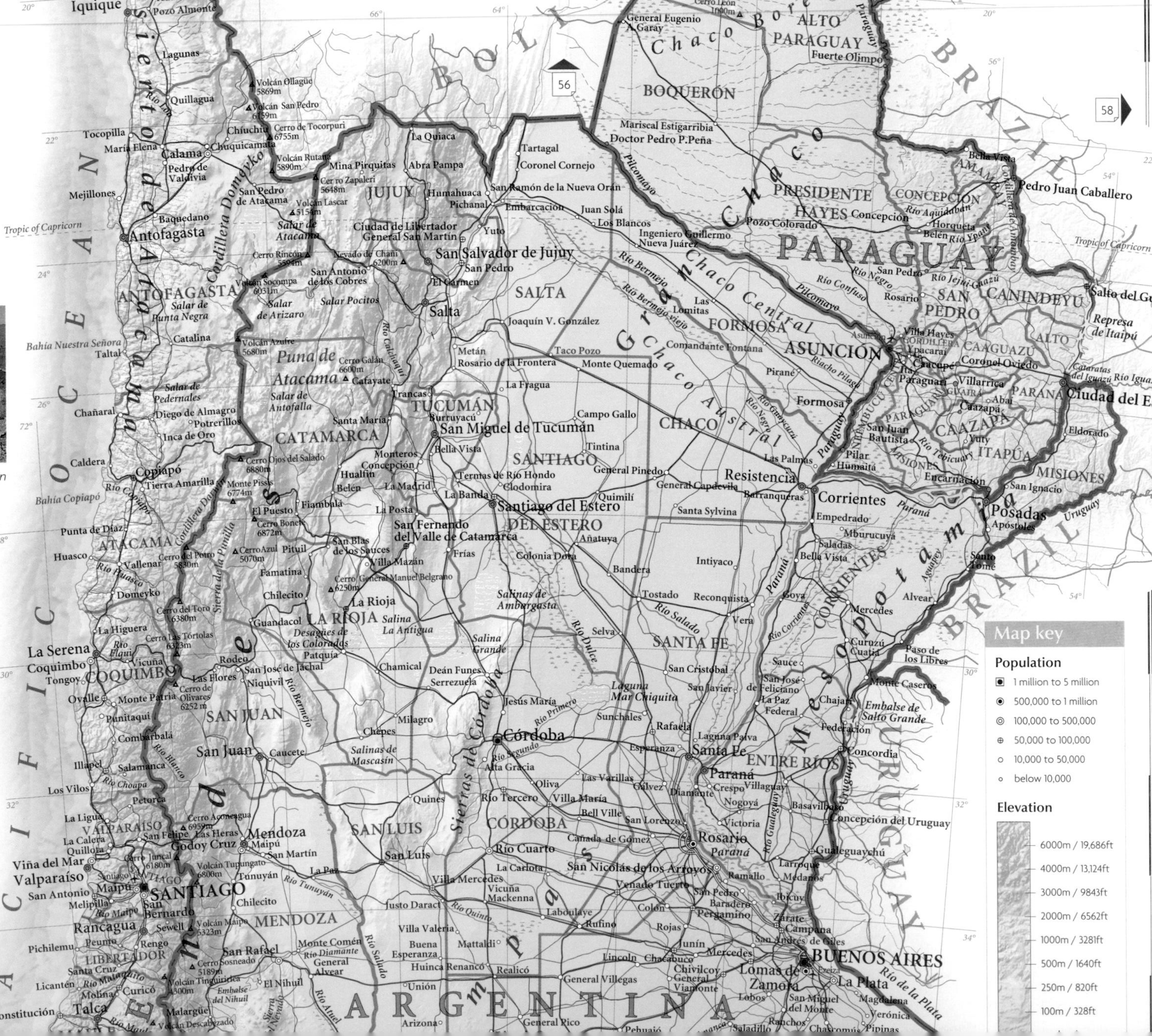

▲ **Boiling water and steam emerge** from a volcanic vent, one of the Tatio geysers which lie at the foot of Cerro de Tocorpuri near Chile's border with Bolivia.

Southern South America

ARGENTINA, CHILE, PARAGUAY

South America's cone-shaped southern region is shared by Argentina and Chile, two overwhelmingly urbanized nations whose populations live mainly in or around the capital cities, Buenos Aires and Santiago. The people are largely *mestizo* or of European origin; in the early 20th century Argentina absorbed waves of new European immigrants, many from Italy and Germany. Paraguay is far less urbanized than its neighbors, with a homogeneous population of mixed Spanish and Guaraní origin, who retain their Indian roots through the Guaraní language. Though most Paraguayans live in the southeast, near Asunción, the indigenous Indians live in the sparsely populated Gran Chaco. The Gran Chaco is also home to some of Argentina's minority indigenous peoples, who otherwise live mainly in Andean regions. Chile's estimated 800,000 Mapauche Indians live almost exclusively in the south.

Transportation & industry

Food processing and agricultural exports remain a fundamental part of Argentina's economy. The growth of manufacturing is regularly hampered by hyper-inflation and massive foreign debts. The world's most important copper producer and one of the top twenty gold producers, Chile also has a thriving wine and grape industry. Most Paraguayan exports involve primary processing, although domestic goods are produced for home markets.

▲ **Chuquicamata copper mine,** lies on a desert plateau near Calama in the Andes of northern Chile. It is the world's largest open-pit copper mine.

Major industry and infrastructure

- chemicals
- engineering
- food processing
- meat processing
- mining
- oil
- textiles
- timber processing
- capital cities
- major towns
- international airports
- major roads
- major industrial areas

Transportation network

55,062 miles (93,453 km)	3038 miles (4889 km)
26,811 miles (43,153 km)	9180 miles (14,775 km)

Argentina's state transportation system is undergoing privatization, though the outmoded rail network requires updating. Paraguay requires foreign investment to upgrade its roads and railroads. Essential internal air routes, especially across the Andes, are well established in all three countries.

Map key

Population

- ● 1 million to 5 million
- ● 500,000 to 1 million
- ● 100,000 to 500,000
- ● 50,000 to 100,000
- ○ 10,000 to 50,000
- ○ below 10,000

Elevation

6000m / 19,686ft	
4000m / 13,124ft	
3000m / 9843ft	
2000m / 6562ft	
1000m / 3281ft	
500m / 1640ft	
250m / 820ft	
100m / 328ft	

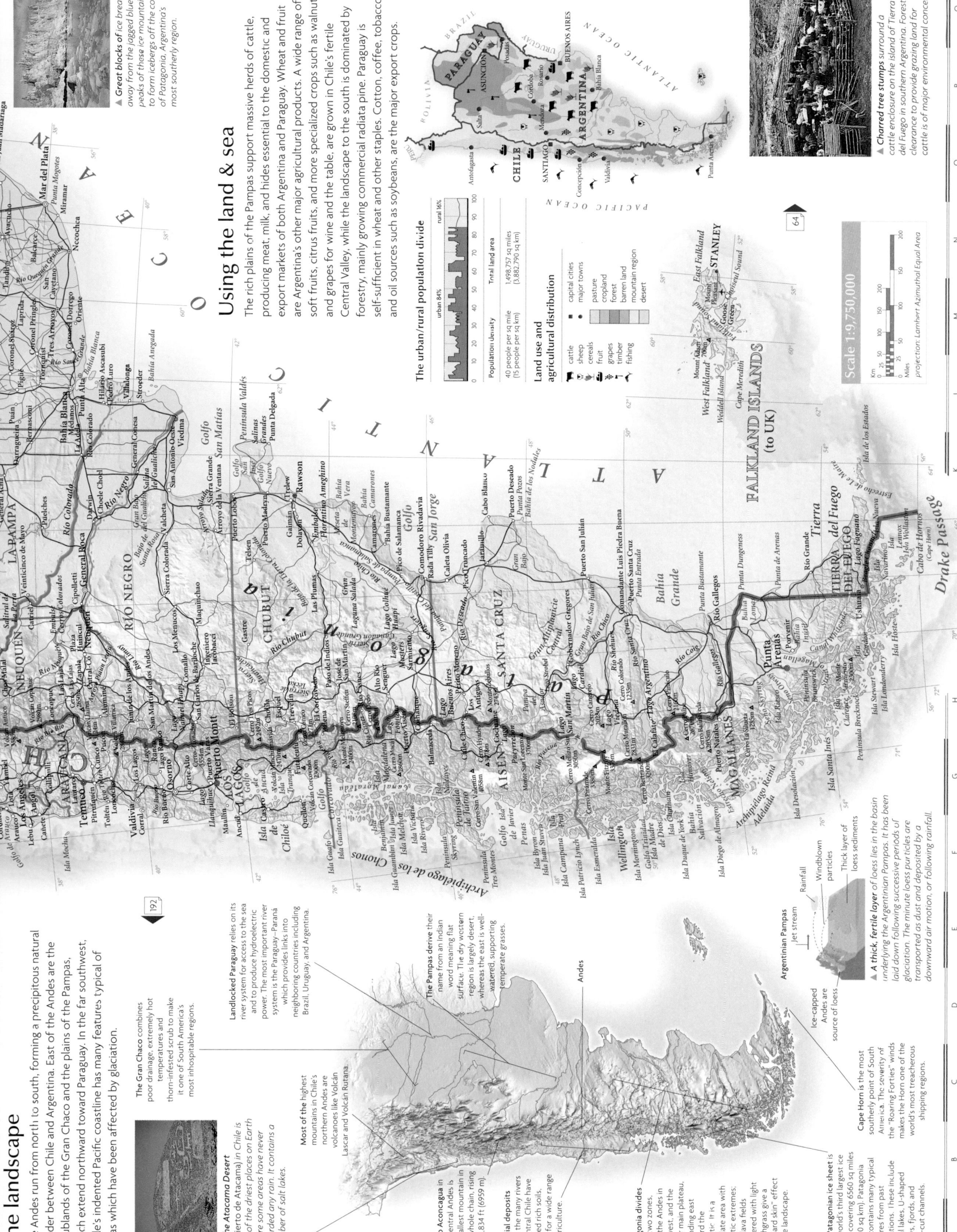

▲ **Great blocks** of ice break away from the jagged blue peaks of these ice mountains to form icebergs off the coast of Patagonia, Argentina's most southerly region.

▲ **Charred tree stumps** surround a cattle enclosure on the island of Tierra del Fuego in southern Argentina. Forest clearance to provide grazing land for cattle is of major environmental concern.

The landscape

The Andes run from north to south, forming a precipitous natural border between Chile and Argentina. East of the Andes are the scrublands of the Gran Chaco and the plains of the Pampas, which extend northward toward Paraguay. In the far southwest, Chile's indented Pacific coastline has many features typical of areas which have been affected by glaciation.

▲ **The Atacama Desert** (Desierto de Atacama) in Chile is one of the driest places on Earth where some areas have never recorded any rain. It contains a number of salt lakes.

The Gran Chaco combines poor drainage, extremely hot temperatures and thorn-infested scrub to make it one of South America's most inhospitable regions.

Landlocked Paraguay relies on its river system for access to the sea and to produce hydroelectric power. The most important river system is the Paraguay–Paraná which provides links into neighboring countries including Brazil, Uruguay, and Argentina.

The Pampas derive their name from an Indian word meaning flat surface. The dry western region is largely desert; whereas the east is well-watered, supporting temperate grasses.

Cerro Aconcagua in the central Andes is the tallest mountain in the whole chain, rising to 22,834 ft (6959 m).

Alluvial deposits from the many rivers in central Chile have created rich soils, ideal for a wide range of agriculture.

Most of the highest mountains in Chile's northern Andes are volcanoes like Volcán Lascar and Volcán Rutana.

Patagonia divides into two zones, with the west, and the lower main plateau, extending east toward the Atlantic. It is a desolate area with climatic extremes; dark lava fields scattered with light bunchgrass give a "leopard skin" effect to the landscape.

Cape Horn is the most southerly point of South America. The severity of the "Roaring Forties" winds makes the Horn one of the world's most treacherous shipping regions.

The Patagonian ice sheet is the world's third largest ice field, covering 6560 sq miles (17,000 sq km). Patagonia also contains many typical features from past glaciations. These include glacial lakes, U-shaped valleys, fjords, and deep-cut channels.

Ice-capped Andes are source of loess

Andes

Argentinian Pampas

Rainfall

Windblown particles

Jet stream

Thick layer of loess sediments

▲ **A thick, fertile layer** of loess lies in the basin underlying the Argentinian Pampas. It has been laid down following successive periods of glaciation. The minute loess particles are transported as dust and deposited by a downward air motion, or following rainfall.

Using the land & sea

The rich plains of the Pampas support massive herds of cattle, producing meat, milk, and hides essential to the domestic and export markets of both Argentina and Paraguay. Wheat and fruit are Argentina's other major agricultural products. A wide range of soft fruits, citrus fruits, and more specialized crops such as walnuts, and grapes for wine and the table, are grown in Chile's fertile Central Valley, while the landscape to the south is dominated by forestry, mainly growing commercial radiata pine. Paraguay is self-sufficient in wheat and other staples. Cotton, coffee, tobacco, and oil sources such as soybeans, are the major export crops.

The urban/rural population divide

urban 84%   rural 16%

Population density

40 people per sq mile
(15 people per sq km)

Total land area

1,498,757 sq miles
(3,882,790 sq km)

Land use and agricultural distribution

- cattle
- sheep
- cereals
- fruit
- grapes
- timber
- fishing

- capital cities
- major towns
- pasture
- cropland
- forest
- barren land
- mountain region
- desert

Scale 1:9,750,000

Km 0 25 50 100 150 200
Miles 0 25 50 100 150 200

projection: Lambert Azimuthal Equal Area

The Atlantic Ocean

The Atlantic is the youngest of the world's oceans, formed about 180 million years ago when the landmasses of the eastern and western hemispheres separated. Its underwater topography is dominated by the Mid-Atlantic Ridge, a huge mountain system running north to south along the center of the ocean. Although most of the ridge's peaks lie below the sea, some emerge as volcanic islands, like Iceland and the Azores. The Atlantic contains a wealth of resources, including substantial oil and gas reserves and rich fishing grounds. Until the 1950s, the north Atlantic was the world's busiest shipping route; cheaper air transportation and alternative routes have shifted patterns of world trade.

Resources

Development of the oil and gas reserves in the Atlantic began in the 1940s around the Gulf of Mexico. Since then other areas have been exploited, including the North Sea, the west coast of Africa and the area east of Newfoundland and Nova Scotia. There is also extensive mining of sand, gravel, and shell deposits by the US and UK. For centuries, the north Atlantic's fishing grounds have been utilized more heavily than other oceans, leading to a serious decline in many fish stocks.

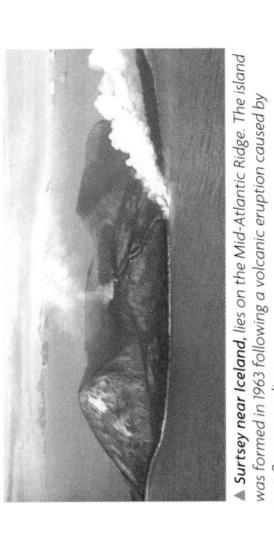

▲ *Surtsey near Iceland*, lies on the Mid-Atlantic Ridge. The island was formed in 1963 following a volcanic eruption caused by sea-floor spreading.

Resources (including wildlife)
- fish
- whales
- aggregates
- oil & gas
- major towns
- major ports

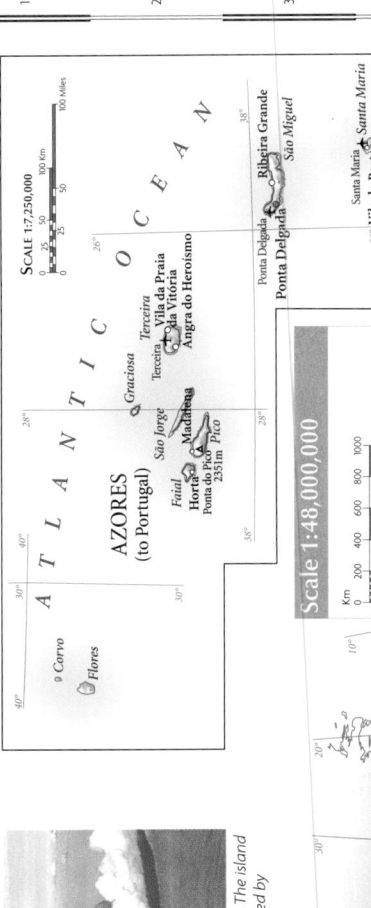

▲ *Fishing in the seas* around northwestern Europe dates back over 1500 years. The high nutrient content of the seas makes them ideal breeding grounds for many species of fish.

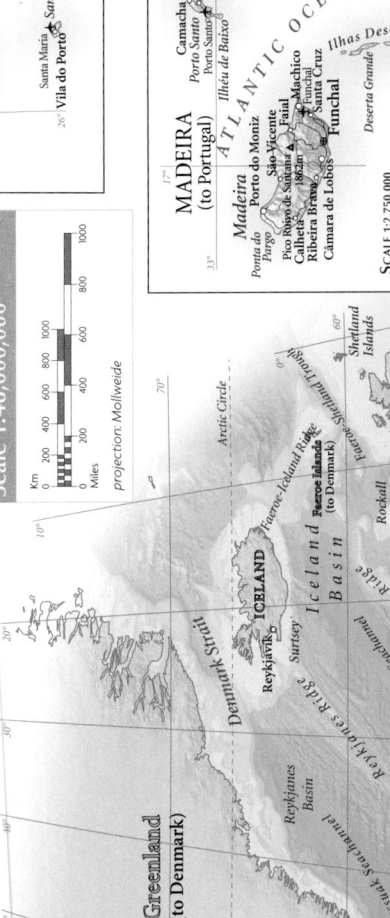

▲ *On January 5 1993*, the oil tanker Braer ran aground in the Shetland Islands, spilling 83,660 tons (85,000 tonnes) of light crude oil into the ocean, devastating the local marine ecosystem.

AZORES (to Portugal)
ATLANTIC OCEAN

Scale 1:7,250,000

Corvo
Flores
Graciosa
São Jorge
Terceira
Faial
Madalena
Horta
Pico
Pico do Pico 2351m
Ponta Delgada
São Miguel
Ponta Delgada
Ribeira Grande
Vila da Praia da Vitória
Angra do Heroísmo
Santa Maria
Vila do Porto
Santa Maria

MADEIRA (to Portugal)
ATLANTIC OCEAN

Scale 1:2,750,000

Porto Santo
Camacha
Porto Santo
Ilhéu de Baixo
São Vicente
Porto do Moniz
Machico
Funchal
Câmara de Lobos
Ponta do Pargo
Pico Ruivo de Santana 1862m
Ribeira Brava
Calheta
Ilhas Desertas
Bugio
Deserta Grande
Ilha Chão

ISLAS CANARIAS (CANARY ISLANDS) (to Spain)

Scale 1:7,250,000

Alegranza
Graciosa
Arrecife
Teguise
Lanzarote
La Oliva
Puerto del Rosario
Fuerteventura
Tinajo
Antigua
Las Palmas
La Palma
Santa Cruz de la Palma
Tenerife
Santa Cruz de Tenerife
Pico de Teide 3718m
La Gran Canaria
Las Palmas de Gran Canaria
Gáldar
San Sebastián
La Orotava
Puerto de la Cruz
Gomera
Valverde
Hierro
Villahermoso
ATLANTIC OCEAN

BERMUDA (to UK)

Scale 1:550,000

St Catherine Point
St George
St George's Island
St David's Island
Tucker's Town
HAMILTON
Somerset
Spanish Point
Great Sound
Ireland Island North
Ireland Island South

Scale 1:48,000,000
projection: Mollweide

ATLANTIC OCEAN

EUROPE
AFRICA
NORTH AMERICA
SOUTH AMERICA

Rotterdam
North Sea
Shetland Islands
UNITED KINGDOM
IRELAND
Irish Sea
Celtic Sea
Celtic Shelf
Milford Haven
Southampton
English Channel
Nantes
FRANCE
Bordeaux
Bay of Biscay
Bilbao
Gijón
SPAIN
PORTUGAL
Lisbon
Gibraltar
Strait of Gibraltar
MOROCCO
Casablanca
Safi
Western Sahara (occupied by Morocco)
ALGERIA
NIGERIA
Lagos
Porto-Novo
BENIN
TOGO
GHANA
IVORY COAST
Abidjan
LIBERIA
SIERRA LEONE
Freetown
GUINEA
Conakry
GUINEA-BISSAU
Bissau
SENEGAL
Dakar
Banjul
GAMBIA
MAURITANIA
Nouakchott
Nouâdhibou

Arctic Circle
Denmark Strait
ICELAND
Reykjavík
Iceland Basin
Iceland-Faroe Ridge
Faroe Islands (to Denmark)
Rockall
Rockall Bank
Rockall Trough
Porcupine Bank
Porcupine Plain
Biscay Plain
Iberian Plain
Tagus Plain
Madeira (to Portugal)
Canary Islands (to Spain)
Cape Verde Terrace
Cape Verde
CAPE VERDE
Gambia Plain
Sierra Leone Basin

GREENLAND (to Denmark)
Baffin Bay
Baffin Basin
Baffin Island
Foxe Basin
Hudson Strait
Davis Strait
Labrador Sea
Labrador Basin
Cumberland Sound
Ungava Bay
CANADA
Newfoundland
Gulf of St Lawrence
Nova Scotia
Halifax
Grand Banks of Newfoundland
Flemish Cap
Newfoundland Basin
Newfoundland Ridge
Northwest Atlantic Mid-Ocean Canyon
Orphan Knoll
Milne Seamounts
New England Seamounts
Sohm Plain
Nashville Seamount

NORTH AMERICA
UNITED STATES OF AMERICA
Boston
New York
Baltimore
Savannah
Jacksonville
Mobile
New Orleans
Gulf of Mexico
Campeche Bank
MEXICO
Tampico
Veracruz
Bay of Campeche
Yucatan
Yucatan Basin
Yucatan Channel
BELIZE
Belize City
HONDURAS
GUATEMALA
NICARAGUA
Bluefields
COSTA RICA
PANAMA
Colón
Cristóbal
Gulf of Panama
Darien Basin
CUBA
BAHAMAS
Great Bahama Bank
Little Bahama Bank
Straits of Florida
HAITI
DOMINICAN REPUBLIC
JAMAICA
Hispaniola
PUERTO RICO (to USA)
Puerto Rico Trench
Turks & Caicos Islands (to UK)
Bermuda (to UK)
Bermuda Rise
Caribbean Sea
Cayman Trough
Colombian Basin
Venezuelan Basin
Muertos Trough
Aves Ridge
Leeward Islands
BARBADOS
TRINIDAD & TOBAGO
Windward Islands
Nares Plain
Hatteras Plain
Blake Plateau
Blake-Bahama Ridge
Corner Seamounts

ATLANTIC OCEAN
Mid-Atlantic Ridge
Reykjanes Ridge
Reykjanes Basin
Charlie-Gibbs Fracture Zone
Oceanographer Fracture Zone
Atlantis Fracture Zone
Kane Fracture Zone
Vema Fracture Zone
Barracuda Fracture Zone
Doldrums Fracture Zone
East Azores Fracture Zone
East Thulean Rise
West Thulean Rise
Kings Trough
Azores (to Portugal)
Great Meteor Tablemount
Cruiser Tablemount
Krylov Seamount
Atlantis Seamount
Barracuda Ridge
Demerara Plain
Demerara Plateau

VENEZUELA
La Guaira
Maracaibo
Gulf of Venezuela
COLOMBIA
GUYANA
Georgetown
SOUTH AMERICA
Rio de Janeiro
Buenos Aires
Cape Town
AFRICA
Reykjavík
Rotterdam
New York
New Orleans
Gibraltar
Lagos
La Guaira
Cristóbal
Sargasso Sea
Scotia Sea
Weddell Sea
ANTARCTICA

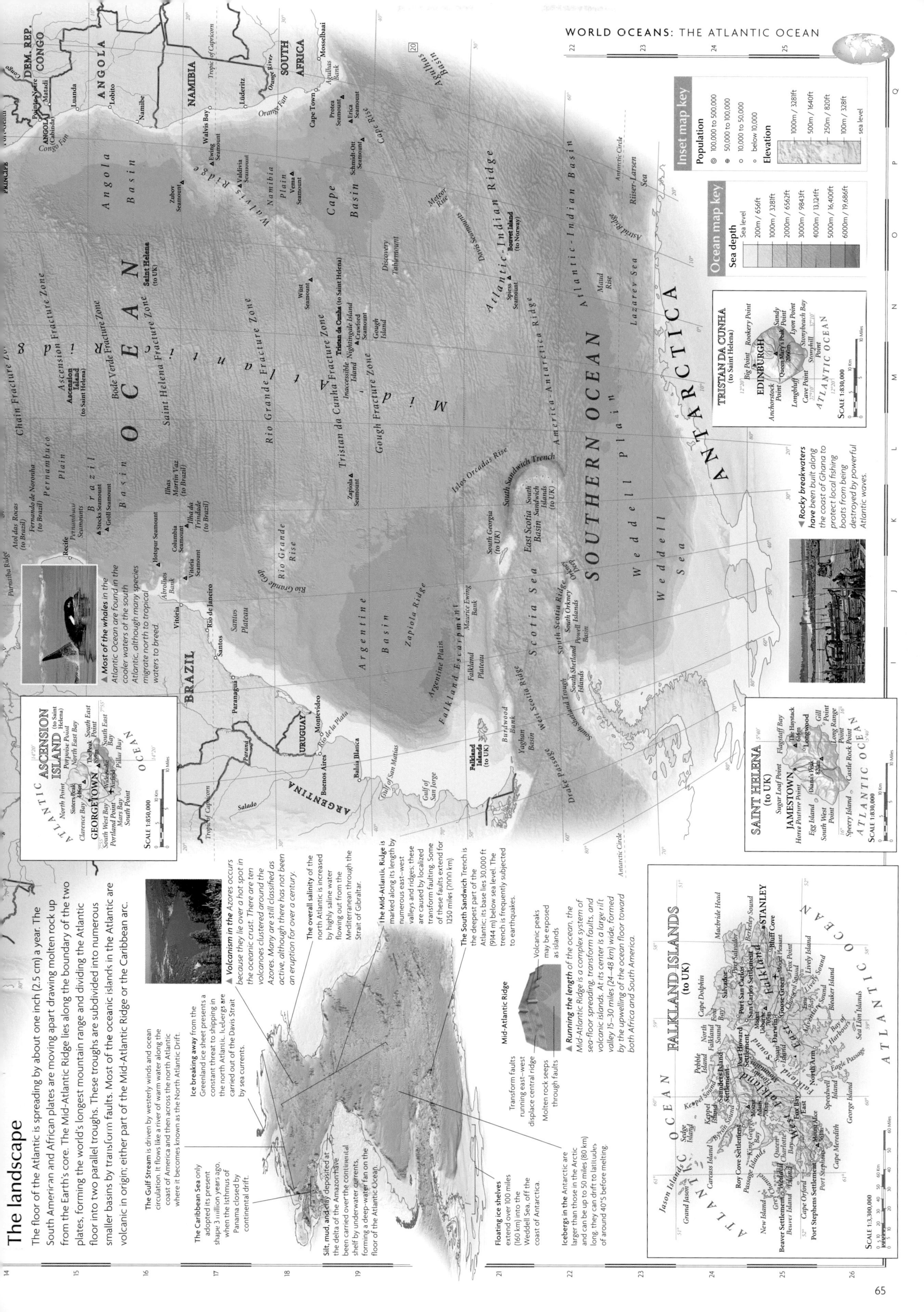

The landscape

The floor of the Atlantic is spreading by about one inch (2.5 cm) a year. The South American and African plates are moving apart drawing molten rock up from the Earth's core. The Mid-Atlantic Ridge lies along the boundary of the two plates, forming the world's longest mountain range and dividing the Atlantic floor into two parallel troughs. These troughs are subdivided into numerous smaller basins by transform faults. Most of the oceanic islands in the Atlantic are volcanic in origin; either part of the Mid-Atlantic Ridge or the Caribbean arc.

The Gulf Stream is driven by westerly winds and ocean circulation. It flows like a river of warm water along the coast of America and then across the north Atlantic where it becomes known as the North Atlantic Drift.

Ice breaking away from the Greenland ice sheet presents a constant threat to shipping in the north Atlantic. Icebergs are carried out of the Davis Strait by sea currents.

The Caribbean Sea only adopted its present shape 3 million years ago, when the Isthmus of Panama closed by continental drift.

Silt, mud, and clay deposited at the delta of the Amazon have been carried over the continental shelf by underwater currents, forming a deep-water fan on the floor of the Atlantic Ocean.

Floating ice shelves extend over 100 miles (160 km) into the Weddell Sea, off the coast of Antarctica.

Icebergs in the Antarctic are larger than those in the Arctic and can be up to 50 miles (80 km) long, they can drift to latitudes of around 40°S before melting.

Transform faults running east–west displace central ridge

Molten rock seeps through faults

Mid-Atlantic Ridge

▲ **Running the length** of the ocean, the Mid-Atlantic Ridge is a complex system of sea-floor spreading, transform faults, and volcanic islands. At its center is a large rift valley 15–30 miles (24–48 km) wide, formed by the upwelling of the ocean floor toward both Africa and South America.

Volcanic peaks may be exposed as islands

▲ **Volcanism in the Azores** occurs because they lie over a hot spot in the oceanic crust. There are ten volcanoes clustered around the Azores. Many are still classified as active, although there has not been an eruption for over a century.

The overall salinity of the north Atlantic is increased by highly saline water flowing out from the Mediterranean through the Strait of Gibraltar.

The Mid-Atlantic Ridge is marked along its length by numerous east–west valleys and ridges; these are caused by localized transform faulting. Some of these faults extend for 1250 miles (2000 km).

The South Sandwich Trench is the deepest part of the Atlantic. Its base lies 30,000 ft (9144 m) below sea level. The trench is frequently subjected to earthquakes.

▲ **Most of the whales** in the Atlantic Ocean are found in the cooler waters of the south Atlantic, although many species migrate north to tropical waters to breed.

▲ **Rocky breakwaters have been built** along the coast of Ghana to protect local fishing boats from being destroyed by powerful Atlantic waves.

ASCENSION ISLAND (to Saint Helena)
SCALE 1:850,000

TRISTAN DA CUNHA (to Saint Helena)
SCALE 1:830,000

SAINT HELENA (to UK)
SCALE 1:830,000

FALKLAND ISLANDS (to UK)
SCALE 1:3,300,000

Inset map key — Population / Elevation

Ocean map key — Sea depth

Africa

The world's second largest continent, Africa covers an area of 11,712,434 sq miles (30,335,000 sq km). It has 53 separate countries, including Madagascar in the Indian Ocean – the highest number of any continent.

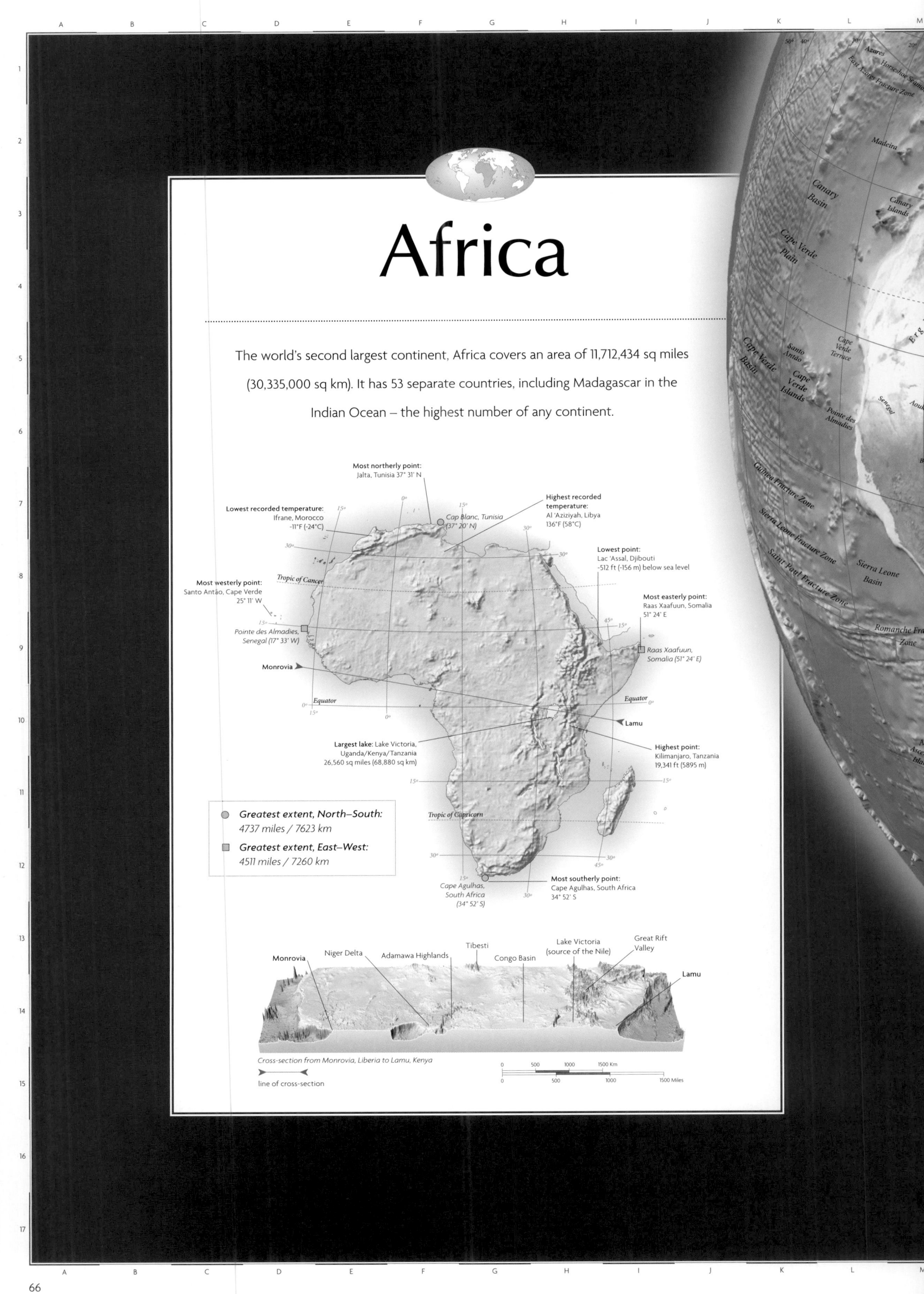

Most northerly point:
Jalta, Tunisia 37° 31' N

Lowest recorded temperature:
Ifrane, Morocco
-11°F (-24°C)

Highest recorded temperature:
Al 'Aziziyah, Libya
136°F (58°C)

Most westerly point:
Santo Antão, Cape Verde
25° 11' W

Lowest point:
Lac 'Assal, Djibouti
-512 ft (-156 m) below sea level

Pointe des Almadies,
Senegal (17° 33' W)

Most easterly point:
Raas Xaafuun, Somalia
51° 24' E

Monrovia

Raas Xaafuun,
Somalia (51° 24' E)

Tropic of Cancer

Equator

Equator

Lamu

Largest lake: Lake Victoria,
Uganda/Kenya/Tanzania
26,560 sq miles (68,880 sq km)

Highest point:
Kilimanjaro, Tanzania
19,341 ft (5895 m)

● **Greatest extent, North–South:**
4737 miles / 7623 km

■ **Greatest extent, East–West:**
4511 miles / 7260 km

Tropic of Capricorn

Most southerly point:
Cape Agulhas, South Africa
34° 52' S

Cape Agulhas,
South Africa
(34° 52' S)

Monrovia · Niger Delta · Adamawa Highlands · Tibesti · Congo Basin · Lake Victoria (source of the Nile) · Great Rift Valley · Lamu

Cross-section from Monrovia, Liberia to Lamu, Kenya

line of cross-section

| 0 | 500 | 1000 | 1500 Km |
| 0 | 500 | 1000 | 1500 Miles |

Canary
Basin

Madeira

Canary
Islands

Cape Verde
Plain

Cape
Verde
Terrace

Cape Verde
Basin

Santo
Antão

Cape
Verde
Islands

Pointe des
Almadies

Senegal

Aouk

Erg &

Guinea Fracture Zone

Sierra Leone Fracture Zone

Saint Paul Fracture Zone

Sierra Leone
Basin

Romanche Fra
Zone

Assa
Islan

Azores

West Thulean Fracture Zone

Horseshoe Seamo

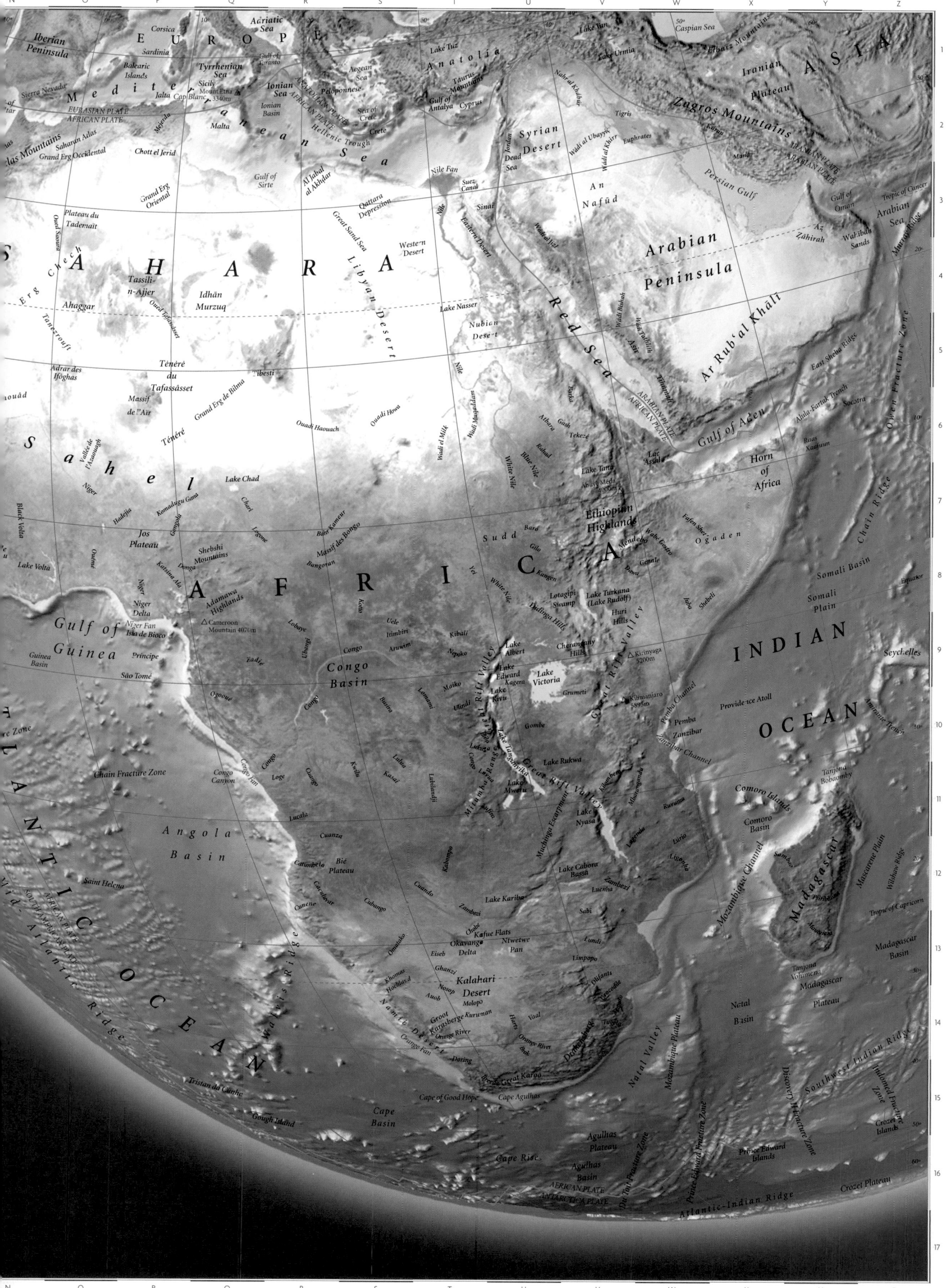

Iberian
Peninsula
EUROPE
Corsica
Adriatic
Sea
Sardinia
Balearic
Islands
Sierra Nevada
Tyrrhenian
Sea
Sicily
Mount Etna
3340m
Ionian
Sea
Gulf of
Taranto
Aegean
Sea
Peloponnese
Ionian
Basin
Malta
Hellenic Trough
Sea of
Crete
Crete
Lake Tuz
Anatolia
Taurus
Mountains
Gulf of
Antalya
Cyprus
Lake Van
Lake Urmia
Elbars Mountains
Iranian
Plateau
ASIA
Zagros Mountains
Caspian Sea

Jalta
Cap Blanc
Chott el Jerid
EURASIAN PLATE
AFRICAN PLATE
Merdja
Mediterranean
Sea
Gulf of
Sirte
Al Jabal
al Akhdar
Nahr al Khabur
Tigris
Euphrates
Syrian
Desert
Dead
Sea
Wadi al Ubayyiḍ
Manḏi
Karun
Persian Gulf
Gulf of
Oman
Arabian
Sea
Murray Ridge

las Mountains
Grand Erg Occidental
Saharan Atlas
Grand Erg
Oriental
Plateau du
Tademaït
Oued Saoura
 Erg Chech
Tanezrouft
Ahaggar
Adrar des
Ifoghas
Tassili-
n-Ajjer
Idhān
Murzuq
Oued Tafassasset
Massif
de l'Aïr
Ténéré
du
Tafassâsset
Tibesti
Grand Erg de Bilma
Ténéré
SAHARA
Libyan Desert
Great Sand Sea
Qattara
Depression
Western
Desert
Nile Fan
Suez
Canal
Sinai
Nile
Lake Nasser
Nubian
Desert
Eastern Desert
Red Sea
An
Nafūd
Wadi Bishah
Arabian
Peninsula
Az
Zāhirah
Wabi al
Batin
Sands
Ar Rub' al Khāli
Tropic of Cancer

Erg
Tademaït
Wadi ad Dawāsir
'Asīr
Wadi al Milk
Wadi
Mejerda
ARABIAN PLATE
AFRICAN PLATE
East Sheba Ridge
Alula-Fartak Trench
Socotra
Owen Fracture Zone

Adrar des
Ifoghas
Sahel
Black Volta
Niger
Hadejia
Komadugu Gana
Lake Chad
Chari
Logone
Bahr Kameur
Wadi Howar
Ouadi Howa
Ouadi Haouach
White Nile
Blue Nile
Atbara
Gash
Tekezé
Abbay
Nile
Setit
Tomi
Lac
Assal
Gulf of Aden
Raas
Xaafuun
Horn
of
Africa

Lake Volta
eu
Onetone
Jos
Plateau
Katsina Ala
Donga
Shebshi
Mountains
Bangoran
Massif des Bongo
Yei
Sudd
Baro
Gilo
Lake Tana
Abuye Meda
2000m
Ethiopian
Highlands
Mendebo
Babi Gwani
Genale
Fafen
Shet
Ogaden
Dawa
Shebeli
Somali Basin
Chain Ridge
Somali
Plain
Equator

Niger
Adamawa
Highlands
AFRICA
Kotto
Uele
Kangen
Lotagipi
Swamp
Dudinga Hills
Lake Turkana
(Lake Rudolf)
Huri
Hills
Jubo
Shebeli
Somali
Plain

Niger
Delta
Gulf of
Guinea
Niger Fan
Isla de Bioco
Príncipe
Guinea
Basin
São Tomé
△ Cameroon
Mountain 4070m
Lobaye
Ubangi
Zadié
Congo
Congo
Basin
Itimbiri
Aruwimi
Ngoko
Kibali
Maiko
Lomami
Lualaba
Lake
Albert
Lake
Edward
Lake
Kivu
Cherangany
Hills
Kagera
Lake
Victoria
Grumeti
△ Kirinyaga
5200m
INDIAN
Seychelles

tre Zone
Ogooué
Atlantic Ocean
Chain Fracture Zone
Congo
Congo
Loge
Congo Fan
Congo
Canyon
Kwilu
Kasai
Busira
Ulindi
Gombe
Eastern Rift Valley
Western Rift Valley
Kalungwishi
Luapula
Lake
Tanganyika
Great Rift Valley
Kilombero
Lake
Mweru
△ Kilimanjaro
5895m
Pemba Channel
Pemba
Zanzibar
Zanzibar Channel
Providence Atoll
OCEAN
Tanjona
Bobaomby

Lucala
Angola
Basin
Saint Helena
Cuanza
Catumbela
Bié
Plateau
Cubango
Cuando
Zambezi
Muchinga Escarpment
Lake
Nyasa
Kilombero
Luwegu
Lake Rukwa
Ruvuma
Comoro Islands
Comoro
Basin
Madagascar
Mascarene Plain
Wilhelm Ridge

Walvis Ridge
Cunene
Okavango
Delta
Kwando
Kafue Flats
Lake Kariba
Luangwa
Lake Cabora
Bassa
Luenha
Sabi
Lundi
Limpopo
Lurio
Mozambique Channel
Mozambique Plateau
Madagascar
Basin
Tropic of Capricorn

SOUTH AMERICAN PLATE
AFRICAN PLATE
Khomas
Hochland
Ghanzi
Nosop
Molopo
Kalahari
Desert
Omaruru
Eiseb
Ntwetwe
Pan
Chobe
Olifants
Changane
Tanjona
Vohimena
Madagascar
Plateau
Madagascar

Mid-Atlantic Ridge
Namib Desert
Auob
Groot
Karrasberge
Kuruman
Vaal
Hari
Crocodile
Save
Incomati
Natal
Basin

ATLANTIC OCEAN
Orange
Khomas
Orange River
Darling
Great Karoo
Cape of Good Hope
Cape Agulhas
Natal Valley
Southwest Indian Ridge
Discovery II Fracture Zone
Indomed Fracture Zone

Tristan da Cunha
Cape
Basin
Gough Island
Agulhas
Plateau
Cape Rise
Agulhas
Basin
AFRICAN PLATE
ANTARCTICA PLATE
Atlantic-Indian Ridge
Prince Edward
Fracture Zone
Prince Edward
Islands
Crozet
Islands
Crozet Plateau

Physical Africa

The structure of Africa was dramatically influenced by the break up of the supercontinent Gondwanaland about 160 million years ago and, more recently, rifting and hot spot activity. Today, much of Africa is remote from active plate boundaries and comprises a series of extensive plateaus and deep basins, which influence the drainage patterns of major rivers. The relief rises to the east, where volcanic uplands and vast lakes mark the Great Rift Valley. In the far north and south sedimentary rocks have been folded to form the Atlas Mountains and the Great Karoo.

East Africa

The Great Rift Valley is the most striking feature of this region, running for 4475 miles (7200 km) from Lake Nyasa to the Red Sea. North of Lake Nyasa it splits into two arms and encloses an interior plateau which contains Lake Victoria. A number of elongated lakes and volcanoes lie along the fault lines. To the west lies the Congo Basin, a vast, shallow depression, which rises to form an almost circular rim of highlands.

Rift valley lakes, like Lake Tanganyika, lie along fault lines

Lake Victoria

Extensive faulting occurs as rift valley pulls apart

Cross-section through eastern Africa showing the two arms of the Great Rift Valley and its interior plateau.

Northern Africa

Northern Africa comprises a system of basins and plateaus. The Tibesti and Ahaggar are volcanic uplands, whose uplift has been matched by subsidence within large surrounding basins. Many of the basins have been infilled with sand and gravel, creating the vast Saharan lands. The Atlas Mountains in the north were formed by convergence of the African and Eurasian plates.

The Earth's crust has been warped to form the Taoudenni Basin

Volcanic Ahaggar mountains, formed by rising magma from a hot spot

Lake Chad lies in a sand-filled basin

Section across northern Africa showing infilled basins and uplifted plateaus.

Scale 1:40,000,000

projection: Lambert Azimuthal Equal Area

Map key

Elevation

5000m / 16,405ft
4000m / 13,124ft
3000m / 9843ft
2000m / 6562ft
1000m / 3281ft
500m / 1640ft
250m / 820ft
100m / 328ft
sea level
below sea level

Plate margins
(for explanation see page xiv)

constructive
destructive
conservative
uncertain
line of cross-section

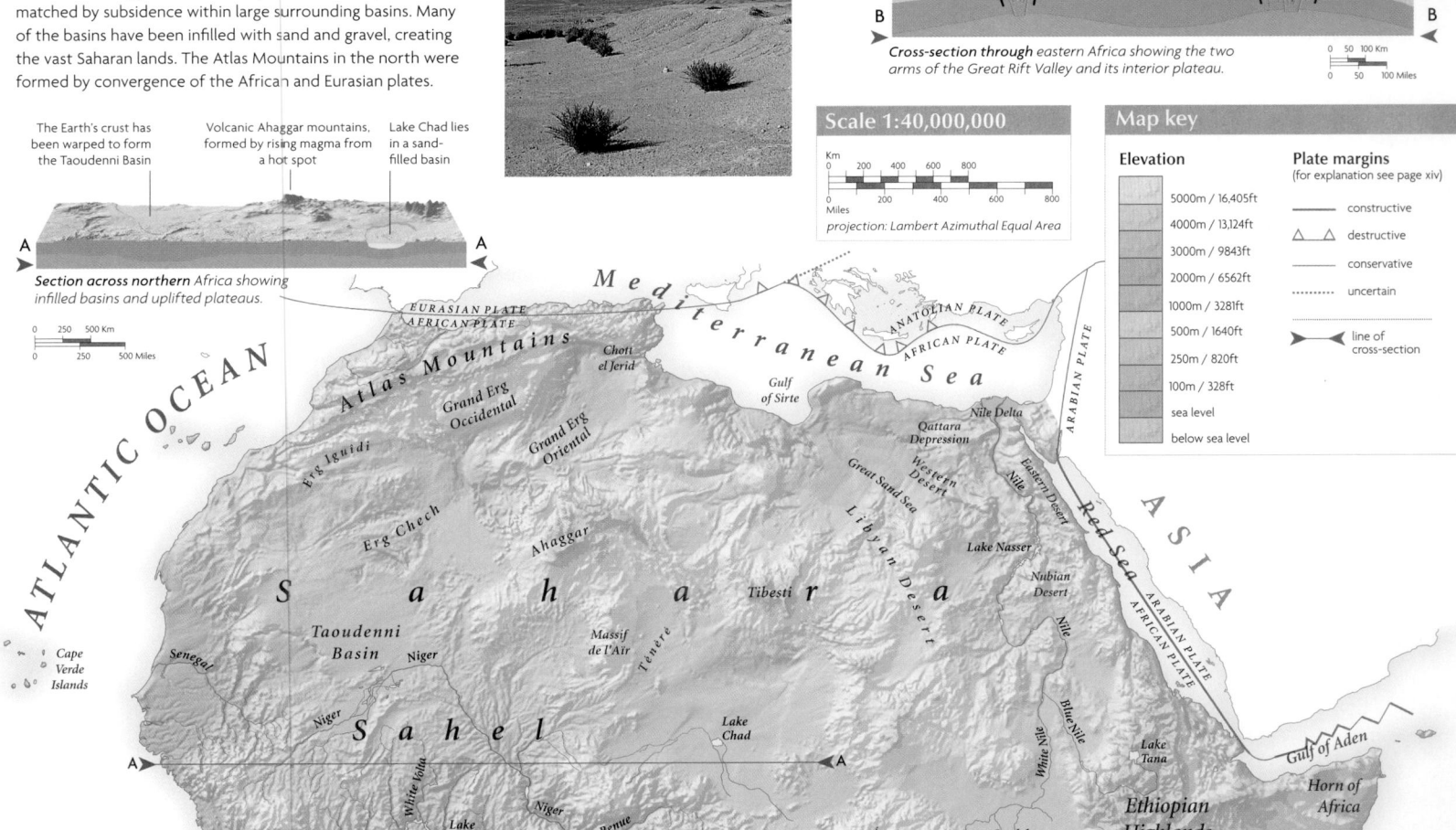

EURASIAN PLATE
AFRICAN PLATE
ANATOLIAN PLATE
AFRICAN PLATE
ARABIAN PLATE

Mediterranean Sea

ATLANTIC OCEAN

Atlas Mountains
Chott el Jerid
Grand Erg Occidental
Grand Erg Oriental
Gulf of Sirte
Nile Delta
Qattara Depression
Western Desert
Great Sand Sea
Libyan Desert
Erg Iguidi
Erg Chech
Ahaggar
Tibesti
Ténéré
Massif de l'Air
Lake Nasser
Nubian Desert
Nile

S a h a r a

ASIA
Red Sea
ARABIAN PLATE
AFRICAN PLATE

Taoudenni Basin
Senegal
Niger
Cape Verde Islands

Sahel
Niger
Lake Chad
Blue Nile
White Nile
Lake Tana
Gulf of Aden
Horn of Africa

White Volta
Lake Volta
Niger
Benue
Adamawa Highlands
Cameroon Mountain 4070m
Niger Delta
Slave Coast
Grain Coast
Ivory Coast
Gold Coast
Bight of Benin
Gulf of Guinea
São Tomé

Ethiopian Highlands
Shebeli
Lake Turkana (Lake Rudolf)
Juba

Ubangi
Massif des Bongo
Sudd
Congo

Congo Basin
Lake Albert
Lake Victoria
Mitumba Range
Great Rift Valley
Kilimanjaro 5895m
Lake Tanganyika
Pemba Island
Zanzibar
Seychelles

ATLANTIC OCEAN

Congo

Bié Plateau
Lake Nyasa
Comoro Islands
Zambezi
Madagascar
Mauritius
Réunion

INDIAN OCEAN

Namib Desert
Okavango Delta
Kalahari Basin
Kalahari Desert
Zambezi
Limpopo
Mozambique Channel

Orange River
Drakensberg
Great Karoo
Cape of Good Hope

Southern Africa

The Great Escarpment marks the southern boundary of Africa's basement rock and includes the Drakensberg range. It was uplifted when Gondwanaland fragmented about 160 million years ago and it has gradually been eroded back from the coast. To the north, the relief drops steadily, forming the Kalahari Basin. In the far south are the fold mountains of the Great Karoo.

Kalahari Basin, covered with the sandy plains of the Kalahari Desert

Boundary of the Great Escarpment

Uplift of the basement rock created a raised plateau

Drakensberg

Cross-section through southern Africa showing the boundary of the Great Escarpment.

Climate

The climates of Africa range from mediterranean to arid, dry savannah, and humid equatorial. In East Africa, where snow settles at the summit of volcanoes such as Kilimanjaro, climate is also modified by altitude. The winds of the Sahara export millions of tonnes of dust a year both northward and eastward.

▲ *Savannah grasslands run* in a belt across Africa; limited rainfall inhibits tree growth.

Temperature

Average January temperature

Average July temperature

Temperature
- 0 to 10°C (32 to 50°F)
- 10 to 20°C (50 to 68°F)
- 20 to 30°C (68 to 86°F)
- above 30°C (86°F)

▲ *The hot, equatorial* basin of the Congo river receives over 48 inches (1200 mm) of rainfall per year.

Rainfall

Average January rainfall

Average July rainfall

Rainfall
- 0–25 mm (0–1 in)
- 25–50 mm (1–2 in)
- 50–100 mm (2–4 in)
- 100–200 mm (4–8 in)
- 200–300 mm (8–12 in)
- 300–400 mm (12–16 in)
- 400–500 mm (16–20 in)
- more than 500 mm (20 in)

Climate
- arid
- humid equatorial
- mediterranean
- sem-arid
- tropical
- warm humid
- daily hours of sunshine, January
- daily hours of sunshine, July
- cold wind
- hot wind

Shaping the continent

African landscapes are shaped by the intensity of climatic extremes and by tectonic action. High aridity, wind action, and infrequent but heavy rainstorms, lead to the migration of sand dunes and dramatic flash flooding across much of the north and west. In the wetter areas, high precipitation increases the rate of weathering. To the east, the rift system has created a volcanic and lake environment and allowed rivers to erode weaknesses left in the crustal structure by faults.

Groundwater

1 Oases are found in desert areas such as the Sahara (left). Groundwater migrates through permeable rock strata, confined between two impermeable layers. Oases form either when the permeable rocks come near to the surface, or at a fault line, when water is able to seep up to the surface through the crushed rocks at the fault.

Weathering: Formation of an inselberg

External stresses act on the surface of the inselberg

Exfoliated layers

Joints or cracks caused by expansion and contraction

The evolving landscape

Rainwater feeds the aquifer

Water migrates up through fault

Aquifer exposed near the surface

Groundwater trapped between impermeable strata

Groundwater: Replenishment of an oasis

River systems

2 The Zambezi river (above) drops 360 ft (110 m) over the Victoria Falls into a zigzag gorge. The river has eroded the gorge along lines of weakness in the bedrock, created by fault lines running in two directions.

Old site of Victoria Falls

River plunges over falls

River plunges over falls

Fault and joint lines running in two directions

Zigzag gorge of the Zambezi

River systems: Retreating of the Victoria Falls

Weathering

6 Inselbergs (above), found extensively across West Africa, are exposed remnants of an extensive upland area. Erosion of the surrounding uplands leaves a resistant rock outcrop. Its spheroidal shape is the result of "onion-skin" weathering – the exfoliating of layers – due to repeated expansion and contraction.

Landscape
- sinking land
- stable land
- uplifting land
- escarpment
- ocean current
- rift
- active volcano
- inselberg
- oasis
- river
- wadi
- waterfall

Ephemeral channels

5 Wadis (above) drain much of northern Africa. These dry bed courses are flooded only after infrequent, but intense, storms in the uplands cause water to surge along their channels.

Heavy rainfall runs off mountains

Water collects and floods the dry channel

Ephemeral channels: Flash flooding of a wadi

Sand is gradually blown up the back slope

Deposition on the slip face

Build up of sand produces strata inside the dune

Wind erosion: Migration of a dune

Wind erosion

4 Dunes like this in the Namib Desert (left) are wind-blown accumulations of sand, which slowly migrate. Wind action moves sand up the shallow back slope; when the sand reaches the crest of the dune it is deposited on the slip face.

Wave energy dispersed in the bay

Waves refracting

Force of waves concentrates on the headland

The sea bed is deeper opposite the bay than at the headland

Coastal processes: Erosion of a bay

Coastal processes

3 Houtbaai (above), in southern Africa, is constantly being modified by wave action. As waves approach the indented coastline, they reach the shallow water of the headland, slowing down and reducing in length. This causes them to bend or refract, concentrating their erosive force at the headlands.

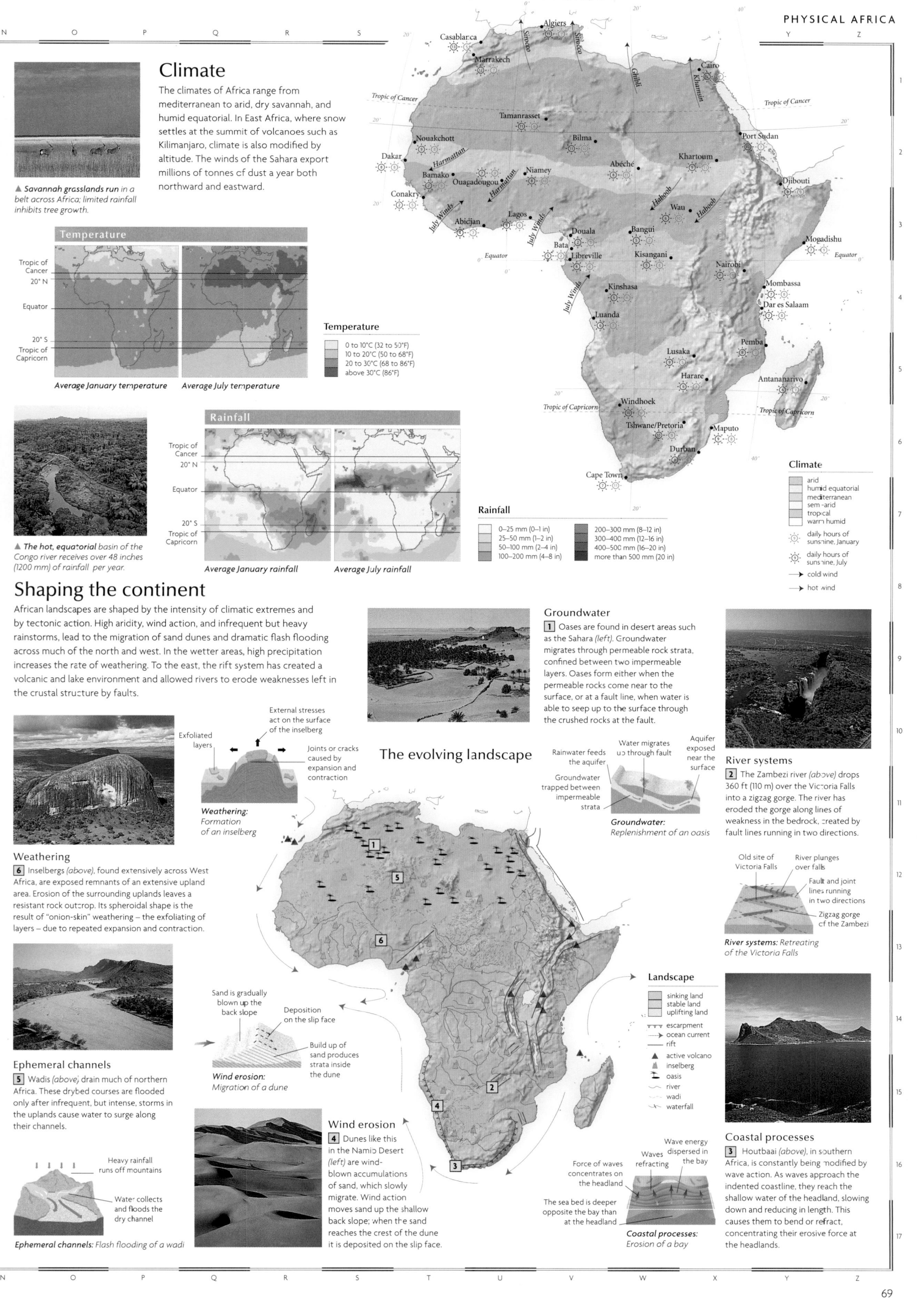

69

African resources

The economies of most African countries are dominated by subsistence and cash crop agriculture, with limited industrialization. Manufacturing is largely confined to South Africa. Many countries depend on a single resource, such as copper or gold, or a cash crop, such as coffee, for export income, which can leave them vulnerable to fluctuations in world commodity prices. In order to diversify their economies and develop a wider industrial base, investment from overseas is being actively sought by many African governments.

Industry

Many African industries concentrate on the extraction and processing of raw materials. These include the oil industry, food processing, mining, and textile production. South Africa accounts for over half of the continent's industrial output with much of the remainder coming from the countries along the northern coast. Over 60% of Africa's workforce is employed in agriculture.

◀ The unspoiled natural splendor of wildlife reserves, like the Serengeti National Park in Tanzania, attract tourists to Africa from around the globe. The tourist industry in Kenya and Tanzania is particularly well developed, where it accounts for almost 10% of GNI.

Standard of living

Since the 1960s most countries in Africa have seen significant improvements in life expectancy, healthcare, and education. However, 28 of the 30 most deprived countries in the world are African, and the continent as a whole lies well behind the rest of the world in terms of meeting many basic human needs.

Standard of living
(UN human development index)

- high
- low

GNI per capita (US $)

- below 499
- 500–999
- 1000–1999
- 2000–2999
- 3000–3999
- above 4000

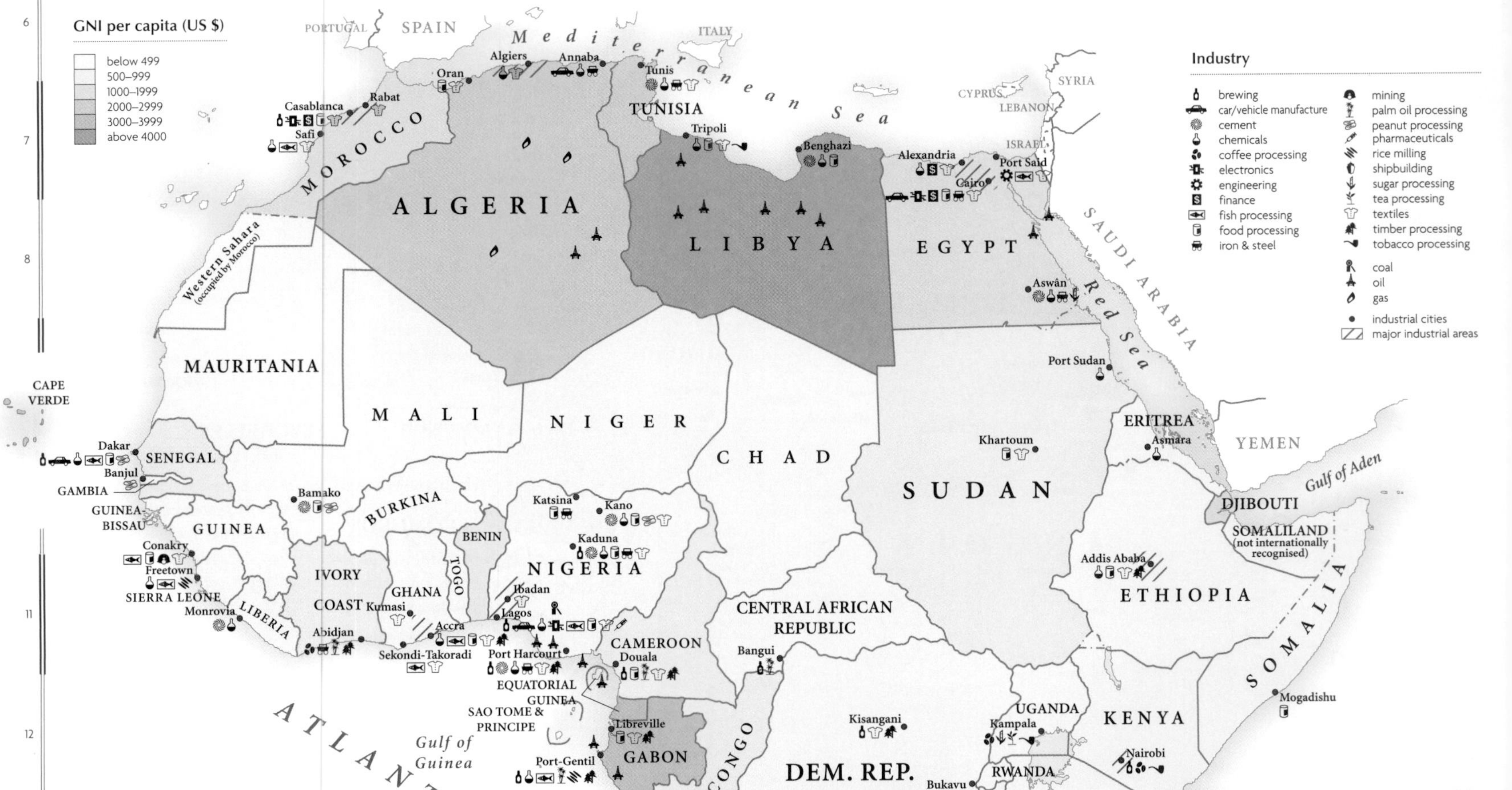

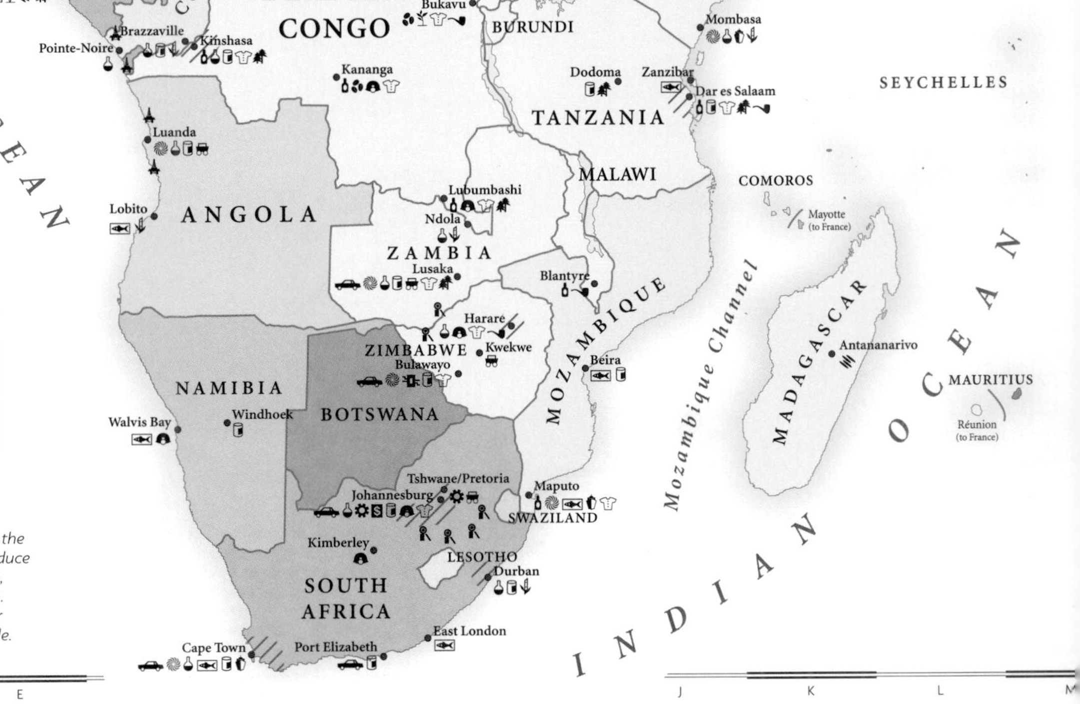

Industry

- brewing
- car/vehicle manufacture
- cement
- chemicals
- coffee processing
- electronics
- engineering
- finance
- fish processing
- food processing
- iron & steel
- mining
- palm oil processing
- peanut processing
- pharmaceuticals
- rice milling
- shipbuilding
- sugar processing
- tea processing
- textiles
- timber processing
- tobacco processing
- coal
- oil
- gas
- industrial cities
- major industrial areas

◀ The discovery of oil in the swampy Niger Delta during the 1960s made Nigeria one of Africa's richer nations. As world oil prices fell in the 1980s, the Nigerian economy faltered.

▶ Exotic rugs and brightly colored textiles are sold in a street market along the banks of the river Nile in Luxor, Egypt.

◀ The Rössing uranium mines in Namibia are one of the largest in the world. Canada and Australia produce over half the world's uranium ore, used to fuel nuclear power plants. Elsewhere, South Africa and Niger also mine uranium on a large scale.

PORTUGAL · SPAIN · ITALY · Mediterranean Sea · CYPRUS · LEBANON · SYRIA · ISRAEL

MOROCCO · Western Sahara (occupied by Morocco) · ALGERIA · TUNISIA · LIBYA · EGYPT · SAUDI ARABIA

Oran · Algiers · Annaba · Tunis · Tripoli · Benghazi · Alexandria · Port Said · Cairo · Aswân · Red Sea

Casablanca · Rabat · Safi

MAURITANIA · MALI · NIGER · CHAD · SUDAN · ERITREA · YEMEN

CAPE VERDE

Dakar · SENEGAL · Banjul · GAMBIA · GUINEA BISSAU · GUINEA · Conakry · Freetown · SIERRA LEONE · Monrovia · LIBERIA · IVORY COAST · GHANA · Kumasi · Abidjan · Sekondi-Takoradi · Accra · TOGO · BENIN · Bamako · BURKINA · Katsina · Kano · Kaduna · NIGERIA · Ibadan · Lagos · Port Harcourt · Douala · CAMEROON · Port Sudan · Khartoum · Asmara · DJIBOUTI · SOMALILAND (not internationally recognised) · Addis Ababa · ETHIOPIA · SOMALIA · Mogadishu

CENTRAL AFRICAN REPUBLIC · Bangui

EQUATORIAL GUINEA · SAO TOME & PRINCIPE · Libreville · GABON · Port-Gentil · CONGO · Brazzaville · Pointe-Noire · Kinshasa · DEM. REP. CONGO · Kisangani · Bukavu · UGANDA · Kampala · RWANDA · BURUNDI · KENYA · Nairobi · Mombasa

ATLANTIC OCEAN · Gulf of Guinea

Luanda · Kananga · Dodoma · Zanzibar · Dar es Salaam · TANZANIA · SEYCHELLES

Lobito · ANGOLA · Lubumbashi · Ndola · ZAMBIA · Lusaka · MALAWI · Blantyre · Beira · COMOROS · Mayotte (to France) · MOZAMBIQUE · Mozambique Channel · MADAGASCAR · Antananarivo

Harare · ZIMBABWE · Kwekwe · Bulawayo

NAMIBIA · Windhoek · BOTSWANA · Walvis Bay

Tshwane/Pretoria · Johannesburg · Maputo · SWAZILAND · Kimberley · LESOTHO · Durban · SOUTH AFRICA · East London · Cape Town · Port Elizabeth

INDIAN OCEAN · MAURITIUS · Réunion (to France)

Gulf of Aden

Environmental issues

One of Africa's most serious environmental problems occurs in marginal areas such as the Sahel where scrub and forest clearance, often for cooking fuel, combined with overgrazing, are causing desertification. Game reserves in southern and eastern Africa have helped to preserve many endangered animals, although the needs of growing populations have led to conflict over land use, and poaching is a serious problem.

Environmental issues
- national parks
- tropical forest
- forest destroyed
- desert
- desertification
- polluted rivers
- radioactive contamination
- marine pollution
- heavy marine pollution
- poor urban air quality

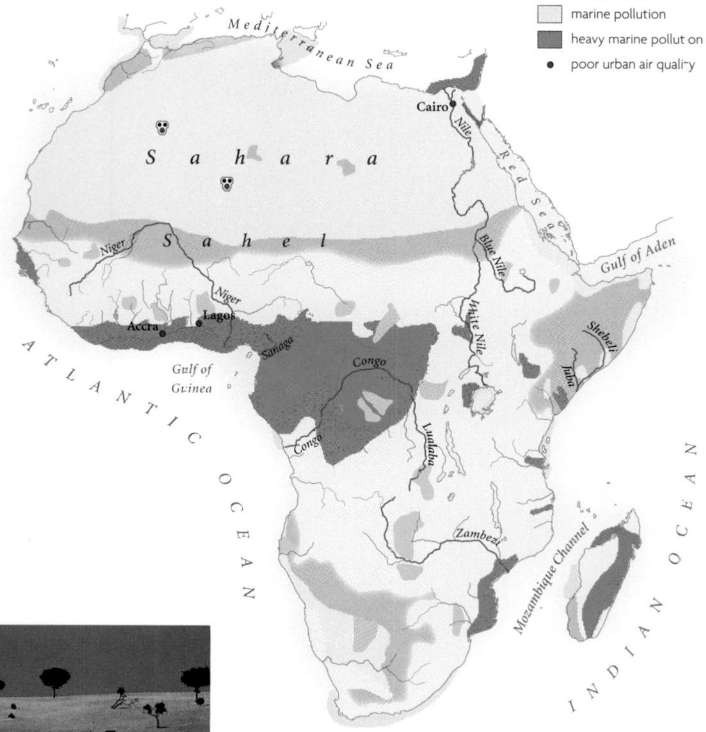

▲ The Sahel's delicate natural equilibrium is easily destroyed by the clearing of vegetation, drought, and overgrazing. This causes the Sahara to advance south, engulfing the savannah grasslands.

Mineral resources

Africa's ancient plateaus contain some of the world's most substantial reserves of precious stones and metals. About 15% of the world's gold is mined in South Africa; Zambia has great copper deposits; and diamonds are mined in Botswana, Dem. Rep. Congo, and South Africa. Oil has brought great economic benefits to Algeria, Libya, and Nigeria.

Mineral resources
- oil field
- gas field
- coal field
- bauxite
- copper
- diamonds
- gold
- iron
- phosphates
- tin
- uranium

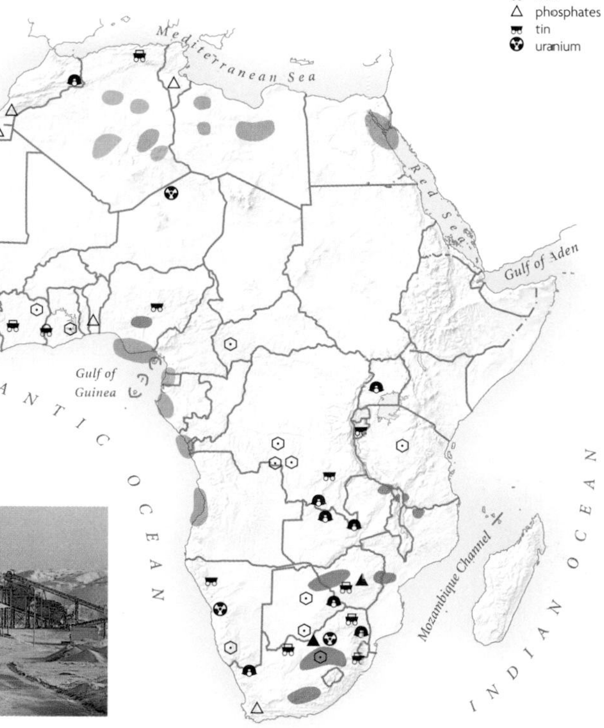

▲ North and West Africa have large deposits of white phosphate minerals which are used in making fertilizers. Morocco, Senegal, and Tunisia are among the continent's leading producers.

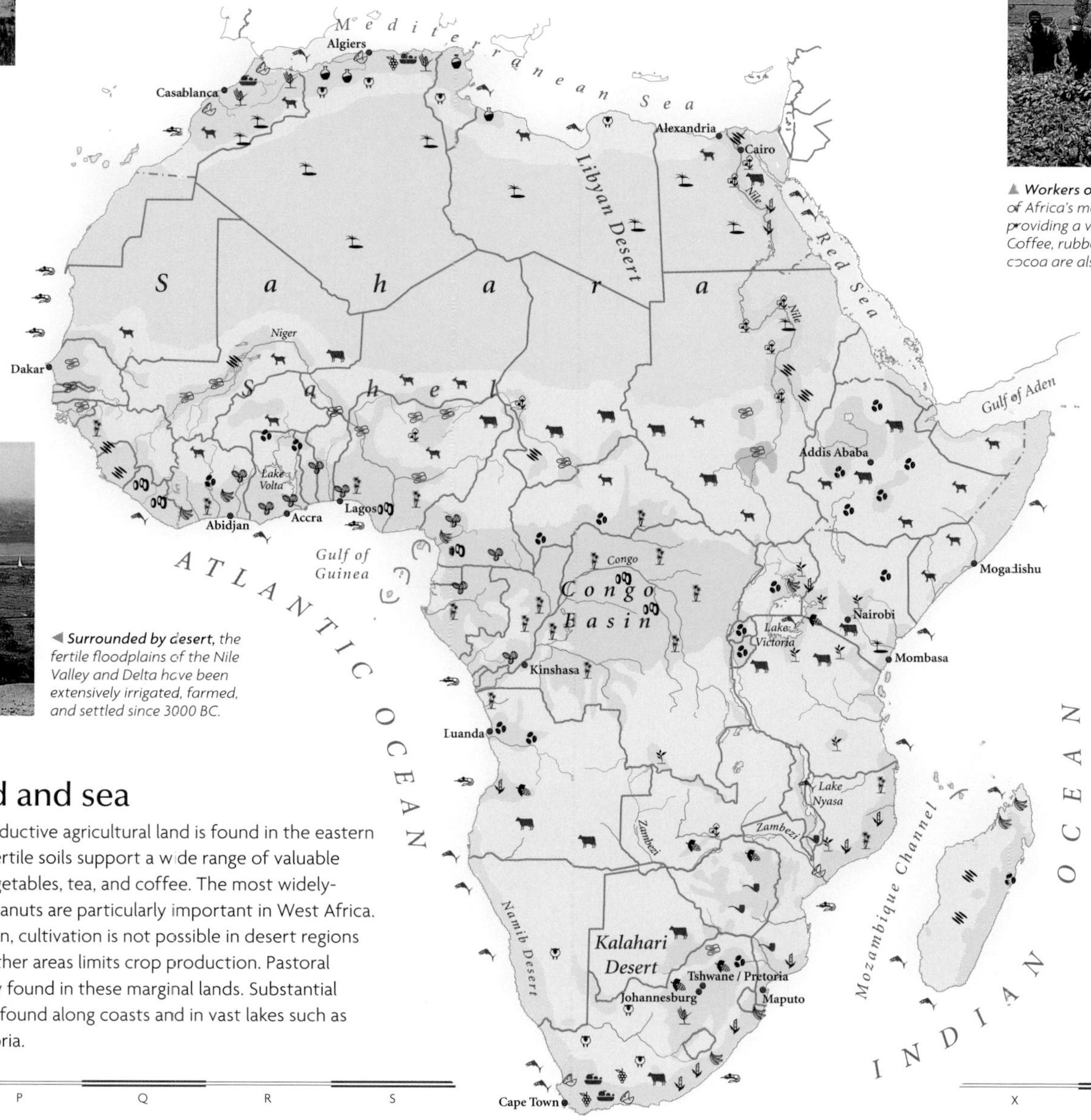

▲ Workers on a tea plantation gather one of Africa's most important cash crops, providing a valuable source of income. Coffee, rubber, bananas, cotton, and cocoa are also widely grown as cash crops.

◄ Surrounded by desert, the fertile floodplains of the Nile Valley and Delta have been extensively irrigated, farmed, and settled since 3000 BC.

Using the land and sea

Some of Africa's most productive agricultural land is found in the eastern volcanic uplands, where fertile soils support a wide range of valuable export crops including vegetables, tea, and coffee. The most widely-grown grain is corn and peanuts are particularly important in West Africa. Without intensive irrigation, cultivation is not possible in desert regions and unreliable rainfall in other areas limits crop production. Pastoral herding is most commonly found in these marginal lands. Substantial local fishing industries are found along coasts and in vast lakes such as Lake Nyasa and Lake Victoria.

Using the land and sea
- cropland
- desert
- forest
- pasture
- wetland
- major conurbations
- cattle
- goats
- cereals
- sheep
- bananas
- corn
- citrus fruits
- cocoa
- cotton
- coffee
- dates
- fishing
- fruit
- oil palms
- olives
- peanuts
- rice
- rubber
- shellfish
- sugar cane
- tea
- tobacco
- vineyards
- wheat

North Africa

ALGERIA, EGYPT, LIBYA, MOROCCO, TUNISIA, WESTERN SAHARA

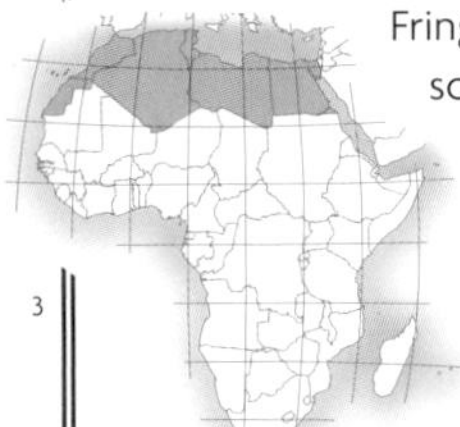

Fringed by the Mediterranean along the northern coast and by the arid Sahara in the south, North Africa reflects the influence of many invaders, both European and, most importantly, Arab, giving the region an almost universal Islamic flavor and a common Arabic language. The countries lying to the west of Egypt are often referred to as the Maghreb, an Arabic term for "west." Today, Morocco and Tunisia exploit their culture and landscape for tourism, while rich oil and gas deposits aid development in Libya and Algeria, despite political turmoil. Egypt, with its fertile, Nile-watered agricultural land and varied industrial base, is the most populous nation.

▲ These rock piles in Algeria's Ahaggar mountains are the result of weathering caused by extremes of temperature. Great cracks or joints appear in the rocks, which are then worn and smoothed by the wind.

The landscape

The Atlas Mountains, which extend across much of Morocco, northern Algeria, and Tunisia, are part of the fold mountain system which also runs through much of southern Europe. They recede to the south and east, becoming a steppe landscape before meeting the Sahara desert which covers more than 90% of the region. The sediments of the Sahara overlie an ancient plateau of crystalline rock, some of which is more than four billion years old.

Map key

Population
- ■ above 5 million
- ■ 1 million to 5 million
- ◉ 500,000 to 1 million
- ◎ 100,000 to 500,000
- ⊕ 50,000 to 100,000
- ⊙ 10,000 to 50,000
- ○ below 10,000

Elevation
- 4000m / 13,124ft
- 3000m / 9843ft
- 2000m / 6562ft
- 1000m / 3281ft
- 500m / 1640ft
- 250m / 820ft
- 100m / 328ft
- sea level

Scale 1:12,250,000

projection: Lambert Azimuthal Equal Area

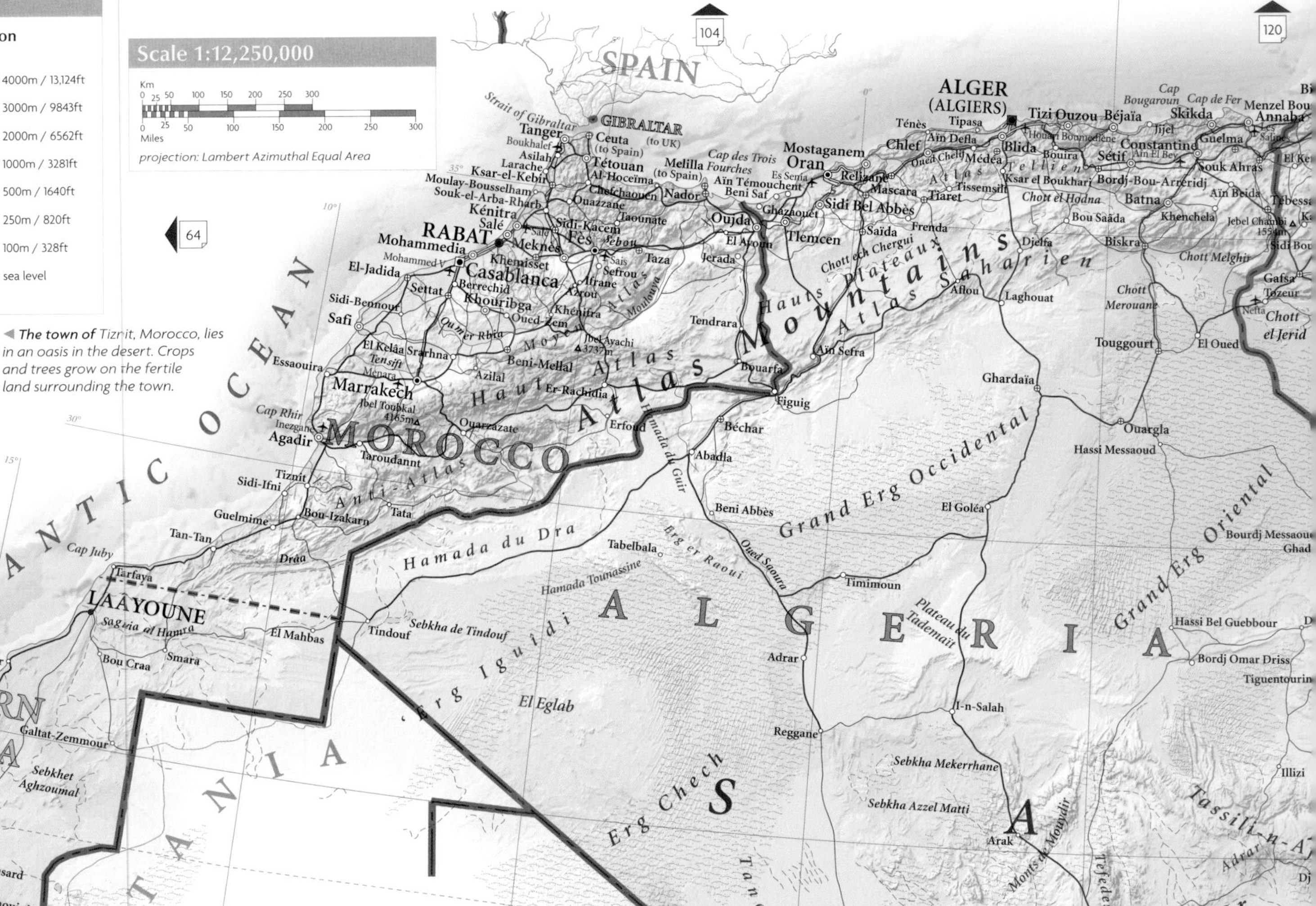

◀ The town of Tiznit, Morocco, lies in an oasis in the desert. Crops and trees grow on the fertile land surrounding the town.

▶ The Grand Erg Occidental is one of Algeria's great Saharan sand seas. Wind force and direction determines the nature of landforms such as the linear or seif dunes in the foreground.

Using the land & sea

Sheltered valleys in the Atlas Mountains, the Nile Valley and Delta, and the Mediterranean coast are the main sources of good farming land. A wide variety of valuable crops including cereals, rice, and cotton, and woods such as cedar and cork, are grown. Typical Mediterranean crops such as olives, figs, dates, and citrus fruits also thrive in these areas. The Nile Valley is particularly fertile, and most of Egypt's population lives close to the river. Elsewhere, irrigation is essential to improve crop yields on the desert margins.

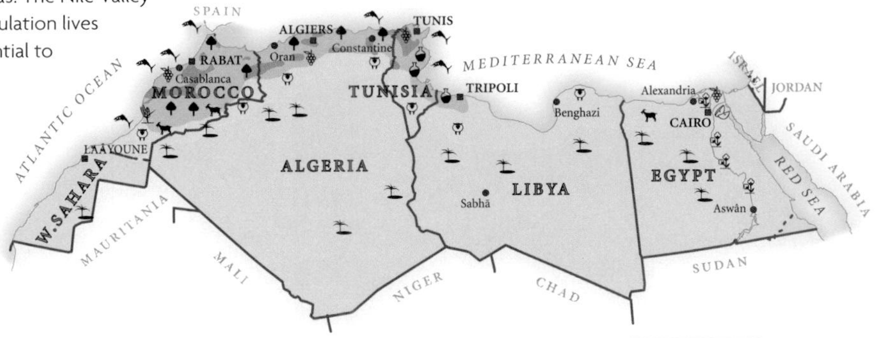

The urban/rural population divide

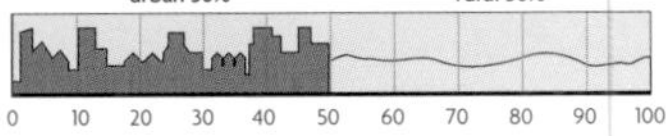

urban 50% | rural 50%

0 10 20 30 40 50 60 70 80 90 100

Population density	Total land area
65 people per sq mile (25 people per sq km)	2,215,020 sq miles (5,738,394 sq km)

Land use and agricultural distribution
- goats
- sheep
- cereals
- citrus fruits
- cork
- cotton
- dates
- fishing
- olives
- vineyards
- ■ capital cities
- ■ major towns
- pasture
- cropland
- forest
- desert

▲ Many North African nomads, such as the Bedouin, maintain a traditional pastoral lifestyle on the desert fringes, moving their herds of sheep, goats, and camels from place to place – crossing country borders in order to find sufficient grazing land.

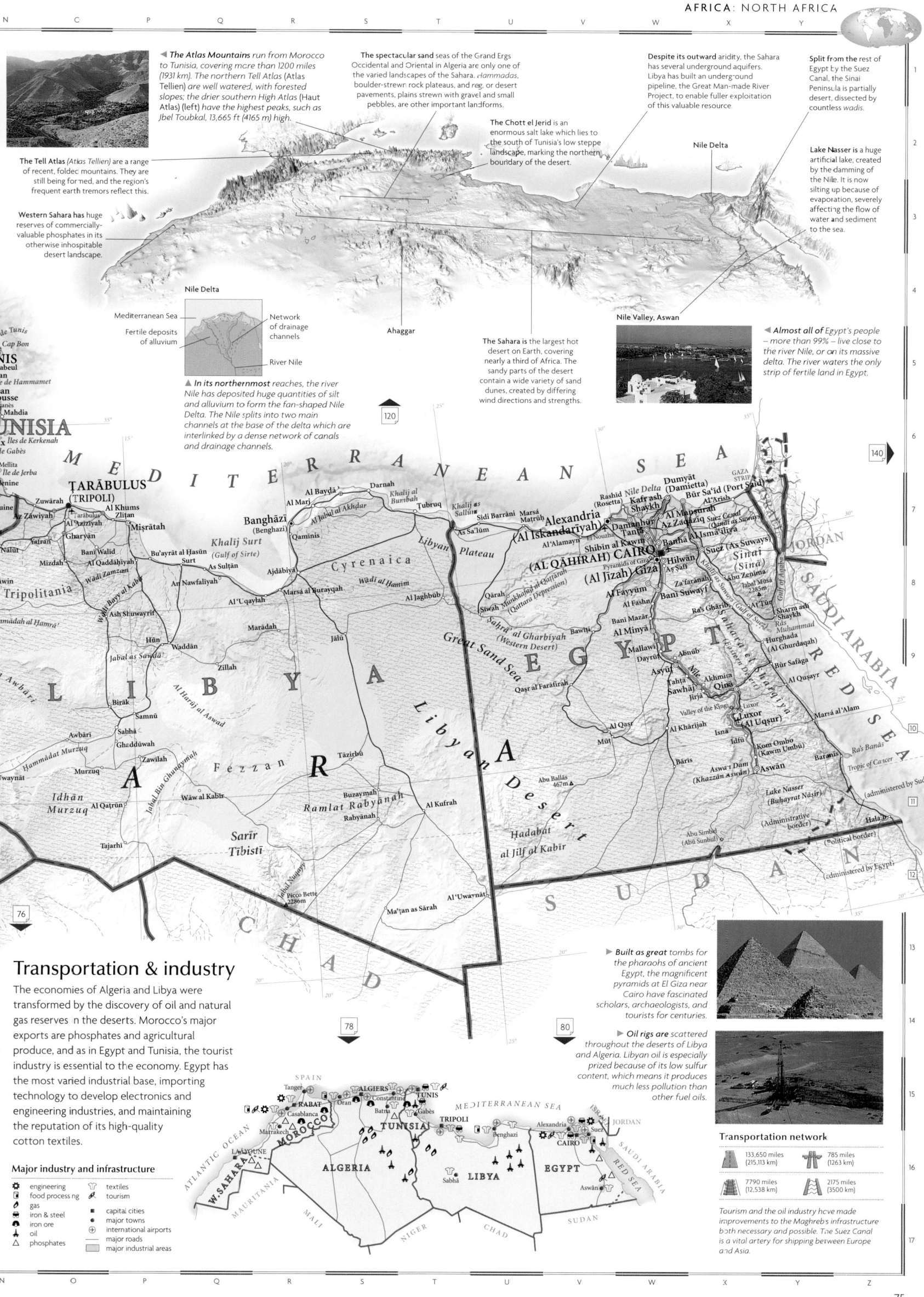

The Atlas Mountains run from Morocco to Tunisia, covering more than 1200 miles (1931 km). The northern Tell Atlas (Atlas Tellien) are well watered, with forested slopes; the drier southern High Atlas (Haut Atlas) (left) have the highest peaks, such as Jbel Toubkal, 13,665 ft (4165 m) high.

The spectacular sand seas of the Grand Ergs Occidental and Oriental in Algeria are only one of the varied landscapes of the Sahara. *Hammadas*, boulder-strewn rock plateaus, and *reg*, or desert pavements, plains strewn with gravel and small pebbles, are other important landforms.

Despite its outward aridity, the Sahara has several underground aquifers. Libya has built an underground pipeline, the Great Man-made River Project, to enable fuller exploitation of this valuable resource.

Split from the rest of Egypt by the Suez Canal, the Sinai Peninsula is partially desert, dissected by countless *wadis*.

The Tell Atlas (Atlas Tellien) are a range of recent, folded mountains. They are still being formed, and the region's frequent earth tremors reflect this.

The Chott el Jerid is an enormous salt lake which lies to the south of Tunisia's low steppe landscape, marking the northern boundary of the desert.

Nile Delta

Lake Nasser is a huge artificial lake, created by the damming of the Nile. It is now silting up because of evaporation, severely affecting the flow of water and sediment to the sea.

Western Sahara has huge reserves of commercially-valuable phosphates in its otherwise inhospitable desert landscape.

Nile Delta

Mediterranean Sea
Fertile deposits of alluvium
Network of drainage channels
River Nile

Ahaggar

Nile Valley, Aswan

In its northernmost reaches, the river Nile has deposited huge quantities of silt and alluvium to form the fan-shaped Nile Delta. The Nile splits into two main channels at the base of the delta which are interlinked by a dense network of canals and drainage channels.

The Sahara is the largest hot desert on Earth, covering nearly a third of Africa. The sandy parts of the desert contain a wide variety of sand dunes, created by differing wind directions and strengths.

Almost all of Egypt's people – more than 99% – live close to the river Nile, or on its massive delta. The river waters the only strip of fertile land in Egypt.

Transportation & industry

The economies of Algeria and Libya were transformed by the discovery of oil and natural gas reserves in the deserts. Morocco's major exports are phosphates and agricultural produce, and as in Egypt and Tunisia, the tourist industry is essential to the economy. Egypt has the most varied industrial base, importing technology to develop electronics and engineering industries, and maintaining the reputation of its high-quality cotton textiles.

Major industry and infrastructure

- ⚙ engineering
- 🏭 food processing
- 🛢 gas
- iron & steel
- iron ore
- oil
- ▲ phosphates
- ⊺ textiles
- tourism
- ■ capital cities
- ● major towns
- ⊕ international airports
- — major roads
- ▨ major industrial areas

Built as great tombs for the pharaohs of ancient Egypt, the magnificent pyramids at El Giza near Cairo have fascinated scholars, archaeologists, and tourists for centuries.

Oil rigs are scattered throughout the deserts of Libya and Algeria. Libyan oil is especially prized because of its low sulfur content, which means it produces much less pollution than other fuel oils.

Transportation network

- 133,650 miles (215,113 km)
- 785 miles (1263 km)
- 7790 miles (12,538 km)
- 2175 miles (3500 km)

Tourism and the oil industry have made improvements to the Maghreb's infrastructure both necessary and possible. The Suez Canal is a vital artery for shipping between Europe and Asia.

West Africa

BENIN, BURKINA, CAPE VERDE, GAMBIA, GHANA, GUINEA, GUINEA-BISSAU, IVORY COAST, LIBERIA, MALI, MAURITANIA, NIGER, NIGERIA, SENEGAL, SIERRA LEONE, TOGO

West Africa is an immensely diverse region, encompassing the desert landscapes and mainly Muslim populations of the southern Saharan countries, and the tropical rain forests of the more humid south, with a great variety of local languages and cultures. The rich natural resources and accessibility of the area were quickly exploited by Europeans; most of the Africans taken by slave traders came from this region, causing serious depopulation. The very different influences of West Africa's leading colonial powers, Britain and France, remain today, reflected in the languages and institutions of the countries they once governed.

▶ *The dry scrub of the Sahel is only suitable for grazing herd animals like these cattle in Mali.*

Transportation & industry

Abundant natural resources including oil and metallic minerals are found in much of West Africa, although investment is required for their further exploitation. Nigeria experienced an oil boom during the 1970s but subsequent growth has been sporadic. Most industry in other countries has a primary basis, including mining, logging, and food processing.

Transportation network

62,154 miles (100,038 km)		1037 miles (1669 km)	
6752 miles (10,867 km)		10,192 miles (16,405 km)	

The road and rail systems are most developed near the coasts. Some of the landlocked countries remain disadvantaged by the difficulty of access to ports, and their poor road networks.

Scale 1:10,000,000

Km 0 25 50 100 150 200 250
Miles 0 25 50 100 150 200 250
projection: Lambert Azimuthal Equal Area

Major industry and infrastructure

- chemicals
- cotton spinning
- food processing
- mining
- oil
- palm oil processing
- peanut processing
- textiles
- vehicle manufacture

- ■ capital cities
- • major towns
- ✈ international airports
- — major roads
- major industrial areas

Map key

Population
- ▣ 1 million to 5 million
- ◉ 500,000 to 1 million
- ◎ 100,000 to 500,000
- ⊕ 50,000 to 100,000
- ○ 10,000 to 50,000
- ∘ below 10,000

Elevation
- 2000m / 6562ft
- 1000m / 3281ft
- 500m / 1640ft
- 250m / 820ft
- 100m / 328ft
- sea level

CAPE VERDE

Santo Antão, Pombas, Ilhas de Barlavento, Mindelo, Ribeira Brava, Pedra Lume, São Vicente, Amílcar Cabral, Sal, São Nicolau, Boa Vista, João Barrosa, ATLANTIC OCEAN, Tarrafal, Maio, Fogo, São Filipe, Santiago, Maio, PRAIA, Ilhas de Sotavento

(same scale as main map)

◀ *The southern regions of West Africa still contain great swathes of tropical rainforest, including some of the world's most prized hardwood trees, such as mahogany and iroko.*

Using the land & sea

The humid southern regions are most suitable for cultivation; in these areas, cash crops such as coffee, cotton, cocoa, and rubber are grown in large quantities. Peanuts are grown throughout West Africa. In the north, advancing desertification has made the Sahel increasingly uncultivable, and pastoral farming is more common. Great herds of sheep, cattle, and goats are grazed on the savannah grasses. Fishing is important in coastal and delta areas.

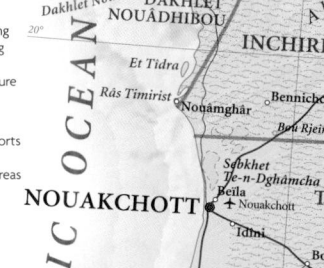

▲ *The Gambia, mainland Africa's smallest country, produces great quantities of peanuts. Winnowing is used to separate the nuts from their stalks.*

Land use and agricultural distribution

- goats
- sheep
- cocoa
- coffee
- cotton
- oil palms
- peanuts
- rubber
- shellfish
- ■ capital cities
- • major towns
- pasture
- cropland
- forest
- desert

The urban/rural population divide

urban 36%   rural 64%

0 10 20 30 40 50 60 70 80 90 100

Population density	Total land area
104 people per sq mile (40 people per sq km)	2,337,137 sq miles (6,054,760 sq km)

[Main map labels:]

WESTERN SAHARA (occupied by Morocco), TIRIS ZEMMOUR, Yetti, Aïn Ben Tili, Bir Mogrein, 'Ayoûn 'Abd el Mâlek, Kâghet, El Mreiti, Zouérat, El Hammâmi, Fdérik, Touâjil, Tourine, Chār, El Mrâyer, Choûm, Ouadâne, ADRAR, Atâr, Chinguetti, Ouârâne, Erg, Râs Nouâdhibou, Nouâdhibou, Dakhlet Nouâdhibou, DAKHLET NOUÂDHIBOU, INCHIRI, Akjoujt, Râs Timiris, Nouâmghâr, El Mreyyé, Et Tidra, Bennichâb, Ouffeft, MAURITANIA, TAGANT, HODH, ECH CHARGUI, Sebkhet Te-n-Dghâmcha, Beîla, Nouâkchott, Rachid, Tidjikja, Tichît, Oualâta, NOUAKCHOTT, TRARZA, Idini, Moudjéria, Boumdeïd, Tâmchekket, HODH EL GHARBI, Boutilimit, Magta' Lahjar, Tiguent, Mederdra, Rkiz, ALEG, Guérou, Kiffa, Ayoûn el 'Atroûs, Néma, Rosso, BRAKNA, Bogué, Kaédi, Kankossa, Timbedgha, Amourj, Richard Toll, Dagana, Podor, Bababé, Monguel, ASSABA, Kobenni, Bassikounou, Saint Louis, Lac de Guier, Matam, GORGOL, Mbagne, GUIDIMAKA, Oudî Yénjé, Adel Bagro, Louga, Mékhé, Kébémer, Dara, Linguère, Ranérou, Sélibabi, Yélimané, Nioro, Ballé, Nara, Tivaouane, Thiès, Touba, Mbaké, Vélingara, Baké, Ambidédi, Sandaré, Diéma, Mourdiah, DAKAR, Diourbel, Bambey, SENEGAL, Kayes, Kayes, Maréna, Mbour, Joal-Fadiout, Fatick, Saloum, Kaolack, Koungheul, Goudiri, Diamou, Sadiola, Bafoulabé, KAYES, Kokani, Didiéni, Banamba, Sokone, Nioro du Rip, Kaffrine, Tambacounda, Dialakoto, Kéniéba, Kita, Toukoto, Sébékoro, Kolokani, Koulikoro, BANJUL, Gambia, Bisse Santa, Georgetown, KOULIKORO, GAMBIA, Brikama, Mansa Konko, Koussanar, Saraya, Manantali, Lac de Manantali, Kangaba, Kolda, Vélingara, Médina Gounas, Niagassola, Bamako, BAMAKO, Dioulouloum, Bignona, Sédhiou, Mali, Kédougou, Satadougou, Kokofata, Ziguinchor, Farim, Kolda, Gambia, Saraya, 1538m, Maléa, Doko, Ouéllébougou, GUINEA-BISSAU, Cacheu, Bissorã, Gabú, Koundâra, Fouta, Tangue, Kangaba, Dioïla, Quinhámel, Mansôa, Bafatá, Dinguiraye, Tikinso, Siguiri, Yanfolila, SIKASSO, BISSAU, Bolama, Fulacunda, Gaoual, Djallon, Labé, Tougué, Kouroussa, Mandiana, Manankoro, Arquipélago dos Bijagós, Buba, Catió, Boké, Pita, Dalaba, Dabola, Manankoro, Kamsar, Télimélé, Kavendou, 1421m, Mamou, Kankan, Sanguilla, Kouto, Fria, Boffa, Konkouré, Kindia, Faranah, Madinani, Odienné, Cap Verga, Dubréka, GUINEA, Kérouané, Pic de Tibé, Bako, Conakry, Coyah, Forécariah, Tokounou, Kissidougou, 1504m, Boron, CONAKRY, Kambia, Pendembu, Dabola, Kailahun, Port Loko, Makeni, Bintimani, 1945m, Koidu, Guéckédou, Macenta, Beyla, Lungi, Pepel, Lunsar, Magburaka, Voinjama, FREETOWN, Moyamba, Shenge, Bo, Kenema, Yomou, Nzérékoré, Lola, SIERRA LEONE, Bonthe, Matru, Pujehun, Zorzor, Nzérékoré, Yekepa, Biankouma, Man, Sherbro Island, Sulima, Gbanga, Ganta, Tapeta, Touba, Séguéla, Robertsport, Tubmanburg, Kakata, Duékoué, Daloa, MONROVIA, Monrovia, Harbel, Saint John, Guiglo, Marshall, Zwedru, Toupoue, Buchanan, Taï, IVORY, Buyo, Lac de Buyo, River Cess, Greenville, Sassandra, LIBERIA, ATLANTIC OCEAN, Plibo, Grand Cess, Harper, Grand-Be, Cape Palmas, Tabou

[Inset map country labels:] MOROCCO, W. SAHARA, ALGERIA, LIBYA, MAURITANIA, NOUAKCHOTT, MALI, NIGER, CHAD, DAKAR, SENEGAL, BANJUL, GAMBIA, BISSAU, GUINEA-BISSAU, CONAKRY, GUINEA, FREETOWN, SIERRA LEONE, MONROVIA, LIBERIA, ATLANTIC OCEAN, BAMAKO, BURKINA, OUAGADOUGOU, NIAMEY, NIGERIA, ABUJA, BENIN, TOGO, GHANA, IVORY COAST, ACCRA, LOMÉ, PORTO-NOVO, Lagos, CAMEROON, YAMOUSSOUKRO

The dry grasslands of the Sahel border the southern reaches of the Sahara. Overgrazing, drought, and the cutting down of trees for firewood, means that much of the Sahel is turning irrevocably to desert.

▶ The Niger river flows for 2600 miles (4181 km) from Fouta Djallon, on the plateau of Guinea, via southern Mali, where it supports rich fish stocks, on through the desert, and finally through Nigeria to the Gulf of Guinea.

▲ Inselbergs, found across the Sahel, are isolated hills, or outcrops, formed where the surrounding plain has eroded away, leaving only the more resistant remnants of the original plateau.

The landscape

There are two major topographical areas in West Africa: the northern deserts are part of the Saharan region which stretches across the whole continent; the grasslands of the Sahel and the southern Guinea coast are part of Africa's central plateau. The landscape is generally low, rarely rising above 1500 ft (457 m) and consists mainly of plains, broken by an occasional high plateau or mountain range.

Two types of coastline characterize West Africa. Swampy, muddy coasts, colonized by mangroves occur on river deltas and where ocean currents are weak, like the coast of Senegal. Sandy beaches, with barrier ridges and lagoons, form where currents are stronger.

Virgin rain forest which once covered much of the West African coast, has been drastically reduced by logging and agricultural land clearance.

As it nears the Gulf of Guinea, the Niger forks into many strands. When the river floods, alluvium is deposited over a wide area. This creates fertile soils, able to support both crops and livestock.

Lake Volta is an artificial lake, created by the damming of the Volta river. It links the drier northern areas with the coast and is intended to provide fresh water for drinking, fisheries, and irrigation.

Barrier beaches

Fluvial deposits — Lagoon
River dammed by — Barrier beach
barrier beach
— Estuarine deposits

▲ Along much of the West African coast, barrier beaches have built up and dammed river mouths, forming fluvial and estuarine plains.

Central Africa

CAMEROON, CENTRAL AFRICAN REPUBLIC, CHAD, CONGO, DEM. REP. CONGO, EQUATORIAL GUINEA, GABON, SAO TOME & PRINCIPE

The great rain forest basin of the Congo river embraces most of remote Central Africa. The interior was largely unknown to Europeans until late in the 19th century, when its tribal kingdoms were split – principally between France and Belgium – with Sao Tome and Principe the lone Portuguese territory, and Equatorial Guinea controlled by Spain. Open democracy and regional economic integration are important goals for these nations – several of which have only recently emerged from restrictive regimes – and investment is needed to improve transportation infrastructures. Many of the small, but fast-growing and increasingly urban population, speak French, the regional *lingua franca*, along with several hundred Pygmy, Bantu, and Sudanic dialects.

The landscape

Lake Chad lies in a desert basin bounded by the volcanic Tibesti mountains in the north, plateaus in the east and, in the south, the broad watershed of the Congo basin. The vast circular depression of the Congo is isolated from the coastal plain by the granite Massif du Chaillu. To the northwest, the volcanoes and fold mountains of the Cameroon Ridge (*Dorsale Camerounaise*) extend as islands into the Gulf of Guinea. The high fold mountains fringing the east of the Congo Basin fall steeply to the lakes of the Great Rift Valley.

Transportation & industry

Large reserves of valuable minerals are found in Central Africa: copper, cobalt, zinc, and diamonds are mined in Dem. Rep. Congo and manganese in Gabon. Congo, Cameroon, Gabon, and Equatorial Guinea have oil deposits and oil has also been recently discovered in Chad. Goods such as palm oil and rubber are processed for export.

The Tibesti mountains are the highest in the Sahara. They were pushed up by the movement of the African Plate over a hot spot, which first formed the northern Ahaggar mountains and is now thought to lie under the Great Rift Valley.

The Congo river is second only to the Amazon in the volume of water it carries, and in the size of its drainage basin.

Lake Tanganyika, the world's second deepest lake, is the largest of a series of linear "ribbon" lakes occupying a trench within the Great Rift Valley.

Rich mineral deposits in the "Copper Belt" of Dem. Rep. Congo were formed under intense heat and pressure when the ancient African Shield was uplifted to form the region's mountains.

▼ *Virgin tropical rain forest* covers the Ruwenzori range on the borders of Dem. Rep. Congo and Uganda.

The lakelike expansion of the Congo river at Stanley Pool is the lowest point of the interior basin, although the river still descends more than 1000 ft (300 m) to reach the sea.

▲ *The Congo river flows* sluggishly through the rain forest of the interior basin. Toward the coast, the river drops steeply in a series of waterfalls and cataracts. At this point, the erosional power of the river becomes so great that it has formed a deep submarine canyon offshore.

Waterfalls and cataracts

Submarine canyon

Broad, shallow basin

Lake Chad is the remnant of an inland sea, which once occupied much of the surrounding basin. A series of droughts since the 1970s has reduced the area of this shallow freshwater lake to about 1000 sq miles (2599 sq km).

▲ *A plug of resistant lava*, at the southwestern end of the Cameroon Ridge (Dorsale Camerounaise), is all that remains of an eroded volcano.

The volcanic massif of Cameroon Mountain occupies an area which remains volcanically active.

Massif du Chaillu

Gulf of Guinea

▲ *The ancient rocks* of Dem. Rep. Congo hold immense and varied mineral reserves. This open pit copper mine is at Kolwezi in the far south.

▲ *The vast sandflats* surrounding Lake Chad were once covered by water. Changing climatic patterns caused the lake to shrink, and desert now covers much of its previous area.

Map key

Population
- ⊡ 1 million to 5 million
- ◉ 500,000 to 1 million
- ⊕ 100,000 to 500,000
- ⊙ 50,000 to 100,000
- ○ 10,000 to 50,000
- ○ below 10,000

Elevation
- 4000m / 13124ft
- 3000m / 9843ft
- 2000m / 6561ft
- 1000m / 3281ft
- 500m / 1640ft
- 250m / 820ft
- 100m / 328ft
- sea level

Scale 1:10,500,000

Km 0 25 50 100 150 200 250
Miles 0 25 50 100 150 200 250

projection: Lambert Azimuthal Equal Area

Major industry and infrastructure

- ♨ brewing
- ⚗ chemicals
- ⬡ cobalt
- ⊙ copper
- ◈ diamonds
- ⊕ food processing
- ◬ manganese
- △ oil
- ⋔ palm oil processing
- ⊞ textiles
- ⊕ tin
- ■ capital cities
- ▪ major towns
- ✈ international airports
- ⊕ major roads
- ▦ major industrial areas

Transportation network

102,747 miles (165,774 km)	37 miles (60 km)
3985 miles (6414 km)	14,110 miles (22,710 km)

The Trans-Gabon railroad, which began operating in 1987, has opened up new sources of timber and manganese. Elsewhere, much investment is needed to update and improve road, rail, and water transportation.

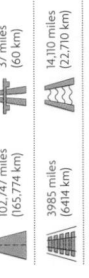

74

76

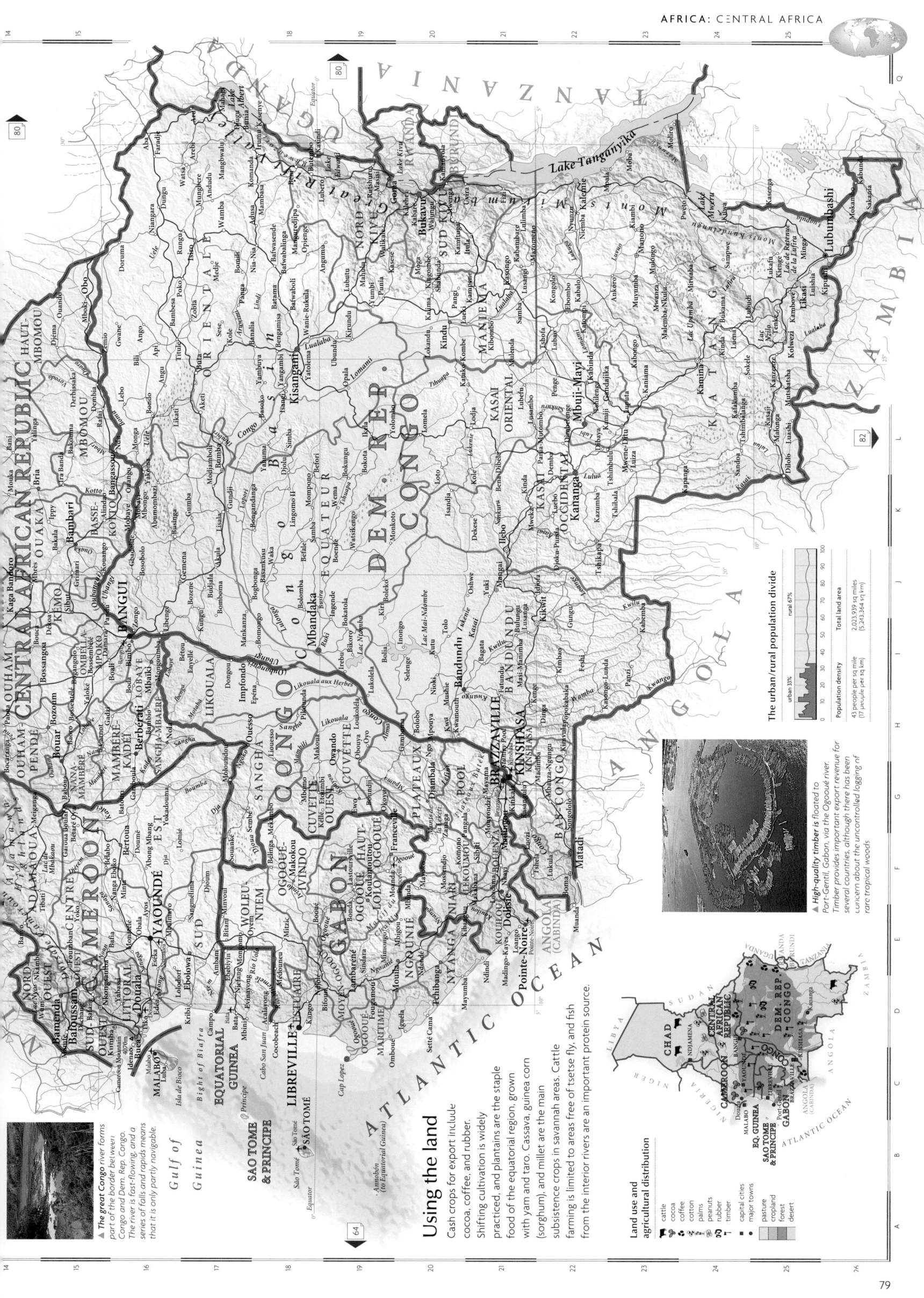

Using the land

Cash crops for export include cocoa, coffee, and rubber. Shifting cultivation is widely practiced, and plantains are the staple food of the equatorial region, grown with yam and taro. Cassava, guinea corn (sorghum), and millet are the main subsistence crops in savannah areas. Cattle farming is limited to areas free of tsetse fly, and fish from the interior rivers are an important protein source.

Land use and agricultural distribution

▲ *The great Congo river forms part of the border between Congo and Dem. Rep. Congo. The river is fast-flowing, and a series of falls and rapids means that it is only partly navigable.*

▲ *High-quality timber is floated to Port-Gentil, Gabon, via the Ogooué river. Timber provides important export revenue for several countries, although there has been concern about the uncontrolled logging of rare tropical woods*

The urban/rural population divide

East Africa

BURUNDI, DJIBOUTI, ERITREA, ETHIOPIA, KENYA, RWANDA, SOMALIA, SUDAN, TANZANIA, UGANDA

The countries of East Africa divide into two distinct cultural regions. Sudan and the "Horn" nations have been influenced by the Middle East; Ethiopia was the home of one of the earliest Christian civilizations, and Sudan reflects both Muslim and Christian influences. The southern countries share a closer cultural affinity with other sub-Saharan nations. Some of Africa's most densely populated countries lie in this region, and the needs of a growing number of people have put pressure on marginal lands and fragile environments. Although most East African economies remain strongly agricultural, Kenya has developed a varied industrial base.

The landscape

East Africa's most significant landscape feature is the Great Rift Valley, which formed during the most recent phase of continental movement when the rigid basement rocks cracked and buckled. Great blocks of land were raised and lowered, creating huge flat-bottomed valleys and steep escarpments, sometimes covered by volcanic extrusions in highland areas.

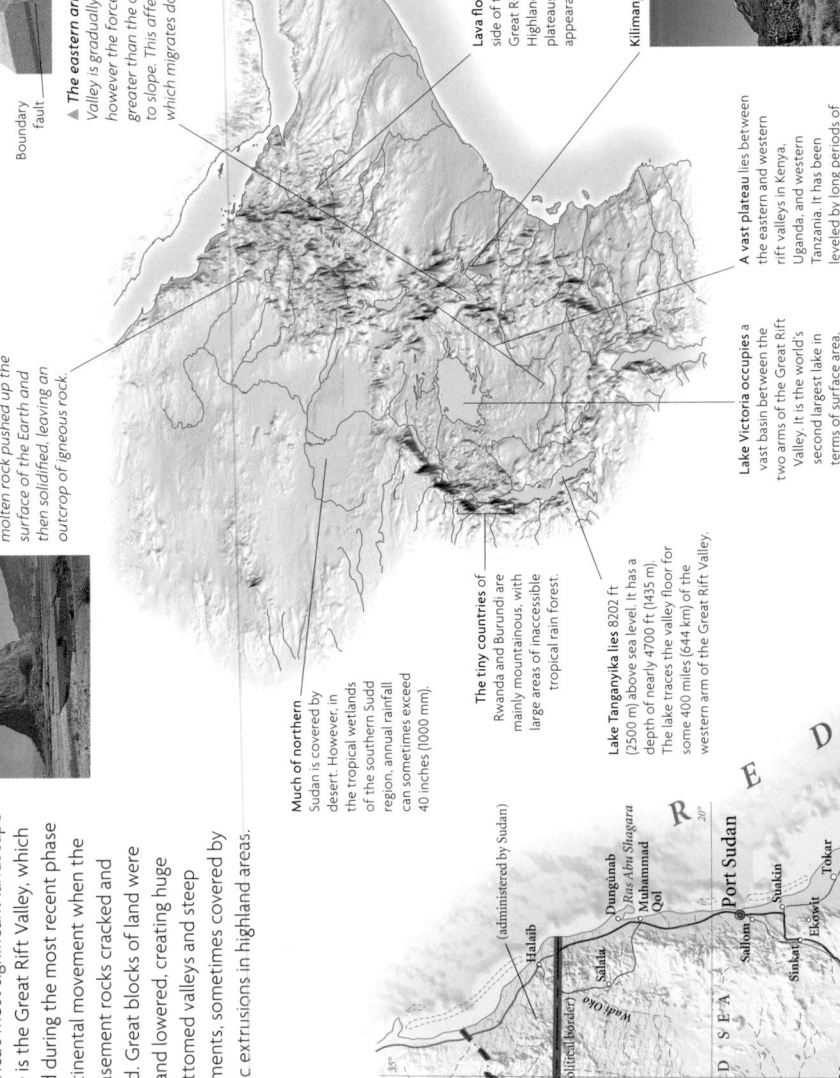

Ephemeral lake forms at far edge of slope

Central block slopes towards main fault

Boundary fault

▲ **The eastern arm** of the Great Rift Valley is gradually being pulled apart; however the forces on one side are greater than the other causing the land to slope. This affects regional drainage which migrates down the slope.

▼ **This dome at** Gonder, in Ethiopia, is a volcanic intrusion, formed when molten rock pushed up the surface of the Earth and then solidified, leaving an outcrop of igneous rock.

Much of northern Sudan is covered by desert. However, in the tropical wetlands of the southern Sudd region, annual rainfall can sometimes exceed 40 inches (1000 mm).

The tiny countries of Rwanda and Burundi are mainly mountainous, with large areas of inaccessible tropical rain forest.

Lake Tanganyika lies 8202 ft (2500 m) above sea level. It has a depth of nearly 4700 ft (1435 m). The lake traces the valley floor for some 400 miles (644 km) of the western arm of the Great Rift Valley.

Lake Victoria occupies a vast basin between the two arms of the Great Rift Valley. It is the world's second largest lake in terms of surface area, extending 26,560 sq miles (68,880 sq km). The lake contains numerous islands and coral reefs.

A vast plateau lies between the eastern and western rift valleys in Kenya, Uganda, and western Tanzania. It has been leveled by long periods of erosion to form a peneplain, but is dotted with inselbergs – outcrops of more resistant rocks.

Lava flows on uplifted areas either side of the eastern branch of the Great Rift Valley gave the Ethiopian Highlands – a series of high, wide plateaus – their distinctive rounded appearance and fertile soils.

Kilimanjaro

▲ **An extinct volcano.** Kilimanjaro is Africa's highest mountain, rising 19,340 ft (5895 m). Once famed for its snow-capped peak, this has almost competely melted due to changing climatic conditions.

▲ **The Kassala region** in eastern Sudan is watered by the Atbara River, an important tributary of the Nile. Most of the population is engaged in agriculture, growing cotton and cereals.

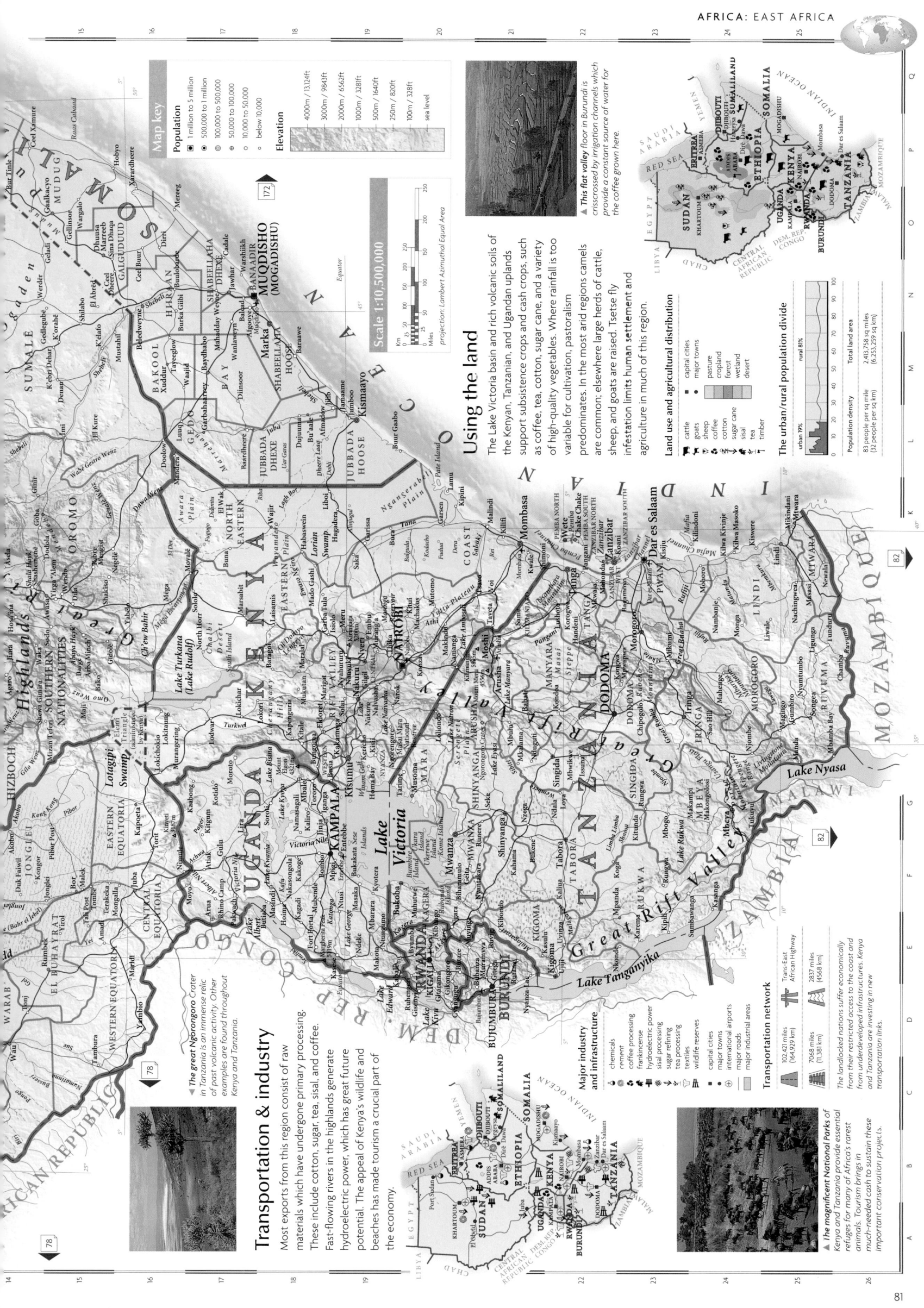

Using the land

The Lake Victoria basin and rich volcanic soils of the Kenyan, Tanzanian, and Ugandan uplands support subsistence crops and cash crops, such as coffee, tea, cotton, sugar cane, and a variety of high-quality vegetables. Where rainfall is too variable for cultivation, pastoralism predominates. In the most arid regions camels are common; elsewhere large herds of cattle, sheep, and goats are raised. Tsetse fly infestation limits human settlement and agriculture in much of this region.

Land use and agricultural distribution

- cattle
- goats
- sheep
- coffee
- cotton
- sugar cane
- sisal
- tea
- timber

- capital cities
- major towns
- pasture
- cropland
- forest
- wetland
- desert

The urban/rural population divide

urban 19%   rural 81%

Population density
83 people per sq mile
(32 people per sq km)

Total area
2,413,758 sq miles
(6,253,259 sq km)

Transportation & industry

Most exports from this region consist of raw materials which have undergone primary processing. These include cotton, sugar, tea, sisal, and coffee. Fast-flowing rivers in the highlands generate hydroelectric power, which has great future potential. The appeal of Kenya's wildlife and beaches has made tourism a crucial part of the economy.

Major industry and infrastructure

- chemicals
- cement
- coffee processing
- frankincense
- hydroelectric power
- sisal processing
- sugar refining
- tea processing
- textiles
- wildlife reserves
- capital cities
- major towns
- international airports
- major roads
- major industrial areas

Transportation network

Trans-East African Highway

102,421 miles (164,929 km)
7068 miles (11,381 km)
2837 miles (4568 km)

The landlocked nations suffer economically from their restricted access to the coast and from underdeveloped infrastructures. Kenya and Tanzania are investing in new transportation links.

▼ *The great Ngorongoro Crater in Tanzania is an immense relic of past volcanic activity. Other examples are found throughout Kenya and Tanzania.*

▲ *This flat valley floor in Burundi is crisscrossed by irrigation channels which provide a constant source of water for the coffee grown here.*

▲ *The magnificent National Parks of Kenya and Tanzania provide essential refuges for many of Africa's rarest animals. Tourism brings in much-needed cash to sustain these important conservation projects.*

Map key

Population

- 1 million to 5 million
- 500,000 to 1 million
- 100,000 to 500,000
- 50,000 to 100,000
- 10,000 to 50,000
- below 10,000

Elevation

- 4000m / 13,124ft
- 3000m / 9843ft
- 2000m / 6562ft
- 1000m / 3281ft
- 500m / 1640ft
- 250m / 820ft
- 100m / 328ft
- sea level

Scale 1:10,500,000

projection: Lambert Azimuthal Equal Area

Southern Africa

ANGOLA, BOTSWANA, LESOTHO, MALAWI, MOZAMBIQUE, NAMIBIA, SOUTH AFRICA, SWAZILAND, ZAMBIA, ZIMBABWE

Africa's vast southern plateau has been a contested homeland for disparate peoples for many centuries. The European incursion began with the slave trade and quickened in the 19th century, when the discovery of enormous mineral wealth secured South Africa's regional economic dominance. The struggle against white minority rule led to strife in Namibia, Zimbabwe, and the former Portuguese territories of Angola and Mozambique. South Africa's notorious apartheid laws, which denied basic human rights to more than 75% of the people, led to the state being internationally ostracized until 1994, when the first fully democratic elections inaugurated a new era of racial justice.

Transportation & industry

South Africa, the world's largest exporter of gold, has a varied economy which generates about 75% of the region's income and draws migrant labor from neighboring states. Angola exports petroleum; Botswana and Namibia rely on diamond mining; and Zambia is seeking to diversify its economy to compensate for declining copper reserves.

▲ Almost all new mining ventures in Zimbabwe are now subject to government control. This mine at Bindura in northeastern Zimbabwe produces nickel, one of the country's top three minerals in terms of economic value

The landscape

Most of southern Africa rests on a concave plateau comprising the Kalahari basin and a mountainous fringe, skirted by a coastal plain which widens out in Mozambique. The plateau extends north, toward the Planalto de Bié in Angola, the Congo Basin and the lake-filled troughs of the Great Rift Valley. The eastern region is drained by the Zambezi and Limpopo rivers, and the Orange is the major western river.

At Victoria Falls, the Zambezi river has cut a spectacular gorge taking advantage of large joints in the basalt, which were first formed as the lava cooled and contracted.

▲ The fast-flowing Zambezi river cuts a deep, wide channel as it flows along the Zimbabwe/Zambia border.

Lake Nyasa occupies one of the deep troughs of the Great Rift Valley, where the land has been displaced downward by as much as 3000 ft (920 m).

Great Rift Valley

Limpopo river

Bushveld intrusion

Volcanic lava, over 250 million years old, caps the peaks of the Drakensberg range, which lie on the mountainous rim of southern Africa's interior plateau.

Broad, flat-topped mountains characterize the Great Karoo. These have been cut from level rock strata under extremely arid conditions.

The Okavango/Cubango River flows from the Planalto de Bié to the swamplands of the Okavango Delta, one of the world's largest inland deltas, where it divides into countless distributary channels, feeding out into the desert.

Planalto de Bié

Thousands of years of evaporating water have produced the Etosha Pan, one of the largest salt flats in the world. Lake and river sediments in the area indicate that the region was once less arid.

▲ Finger Rock, near Khorixas, Namibia is a remnant of a former land surface, which has been denuded by erosion over the last 5 million years. These occasional stacks of partially weathered rocks interrupt the plains of the dry southern interior.

Khorixas, Namibia

The Kalahari desert is the largest continuous sand surface in the world. Iron oxide gives a distinctive red color to the windblown sand, which, in eastern areas covers the bedrock by over 200 ft (60 m).

Namib Desert

The Orange River, one of the longest rivers in Africa, rises in Lesotho and is the only major river in the south which flows westward, rather than to the east coast.

The mountains of the Little Karoo are composed of sedimentary rocks which have been substantially folded and faulted.

Transportation network

| | | 746 miles (1202 km) | | 3815 miles (6144 km) |

| | 84,213 miles (135,609 km) | | 23,208 miles (37,372 km) |

Southern Africa's Cape-gouge rail network is by far the largest in the continent. About two-thirds of the 20,000 mile (32,000 km) system lies within South Africa. Lines such as the Harare–Bulawayo route have become corridors for industrial growth.

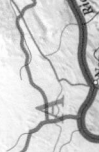

▲ Following a series of droughts, this baobab tree in Zimbabwe now stands alone in a field once filled by sugar cane. The thick trunk and small leaves of the baobab help it to conserve water, enabling it to survive even in drought conditions.

Major industry and infrastructure

- car manufacture
- coal
- copper
- diamonds
- gold
- oil
- textiles
- uranium
- food processing

- capital cities
- major towns
- international airports
- major roads
- wildlife reserves
- major industrial areas

Map key

Population
- ⊛ 1 million to 5 million
- ◉ 500,000 to 1 million
- ⊜ 100,000 to 500,000
- ⊕ 50,000 to 100,000
- ⊙ 10,000 to 50,000
- ∘ below 10,000

Elevation
- 3000m / 9843ft
- 2000m / 6562ft
- 1000m / 3281ft
- 500m / 1640ft
- 250m / 820ft
- 100m / 328ft
- sea level

South Africa: Capital cities
TSHWANE / PRETORIA – administrative capital
CAPE TOWN – legislative capital
BLOEMFONTEIN – judicial capital

The Bushveld intrusion lies on South Africa's high "veld." Molten magma intruded into the Earth's crust creating a saucer-shaped feature, more than 180 miles (300 km) across, containing regular layers of precious minerals, overlain by a dome of granite.

Granite
Chromite
Bushveld intrusion
Gabbro and peridotite
Magnetite
Platinum minerals

Scale 1:10,500,000

Km 0 25 50 100 150 200 250 300
Miles 0 25 50 100 150 200 250 300
projection: Lambert Azimuthal Equal Area

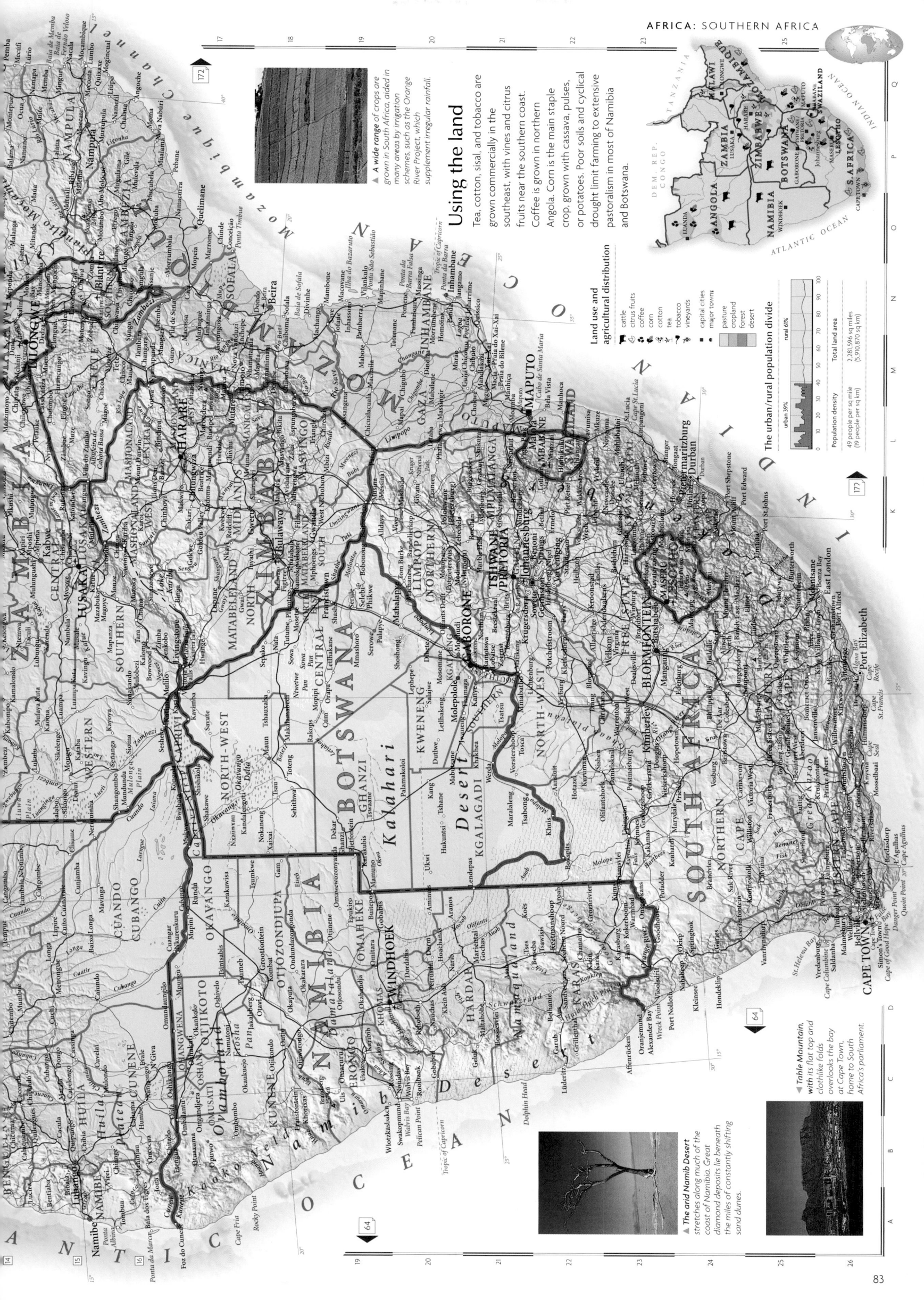

▲ *A wide range* of crops are grown in South Africa, aided in many areas by irrigation schemes, such as the Orange River Project, which supplement irregular rainfall.

Using the land

Tea, cotton, sisal, and tobacco are grown commercially in the southeast, with vines and citrus fruits near the southern coast. Coffee is grown in northern Angola. Corn is the main staple crop, grown with cassava, pulses, or potatoes. Poor soils and cyclical drought limit farming to extensive pastoralism in most of Namibia and Botswana.

Land use and agricultural distribution

- cattle
- citrus fruits
- coffee
- corn
- cotton
- tea
- tobacco
- vineyards
- capital cities
- major towns

- pasture
- cropland
- forest
- desert

The urban/rural population divide

urban 39%   rural 61%

Total land area: 2,281,596 sq miles (5,910,870 sq km)

Population density: 49 people per sq mile (19 people per sq km)

▲ *The arid Namib Desert* stretches along much of the coast of Namibia. Great diamond deposits lie beneath the miles of constantly shifting sand dunes.

▲ *Table Mountain,* with its flat top and clothlike folds overlooks the bay at Cape Town, home to South Africa's parliament.

ARCTIC OCEAN
North Pole

Ellesmere Island

Greenland

King Frederik
VIII Land

King Christian X Land

Laptev Sea

Severnaya
Zemlya

Poluostrov Taymyr

Kara Sea

Mys
Flissingskiy

Franz Josef Land

NORTH AMERICAN PLATE
EURASIAN PLATE

Spitsbergen

Greenland
Sea

Novaya Zemlya

Barents
Sea

Bjørnøya

Baydaratskaya Guba

Poluostrov Yamal

Gulf of Ob

Yenisey

West Siberian
Plain

A S

Jan Mayen Fracture Zone
Jan Mayen

Barents
Trough

North Cape Nordkinn

Murmansk Rise

Ob'

Irtysh

Kolbeinsey Ridge

Iceland
Plateau

Norwegian Sea

Norwegian
Basin

Tromsøflaket
Fugløya Bank

Vesterålen

Inarijärvi

Ostrov
Kolguyev
Kanin

Pechora

Timanskiy Kryazh

Gora Narodnaya

Tobol

Arctic Circle

Denmark Strait

Iceland
Plateau

Jan Mayen Ridge

Voring Plateau

Lofoten

Kebnekaise
2117m

Kola Peninsula
Ozero
Imandra

White Sea

Mezen'

Northern Dvina

Vychegda

Bjargtangar

Iceland
Vatnajökull

Faeroe-Iceland Ridge

Traena
Bank

Kaitra

Tornälven

Onega Bay

Lake
Ladoga

Ozero
Vygozero

Volga

Reykjanes Ridge

Iceland
Basin

Faeroe Islands

Galdhøpiggen
2469m

Scandinavia

Luleälven

Kemijoki

Oulujoki

Lake
Onega

Onega

Ozero
Beloye

Sukhona

Yug

Kama

Chusovaya

Irtysh

Hatton Ridge

Bill Baileys
Bank

Faeroe-Shetland Trough

Shetland
Islands

Lhangan

Glama

Ljusnan

Åland

Gulf of Finland

Lake
Peipus

Msta

Rybinsk
Reservoir

Gor'kiy
Reservoir

Urzhuka

Vyatka

Izhevsk

Votkinsk
Reservoir

Ural

Rockall
Rise

Feni Ridge

Rockall Trough

Viking Bank

Outer Hebrides

Orkney Islands

Norwegian Trench

Vänern

Vättern

Gotland

Gulf of
Riga

Lake Pskov

Lake Ilmen

Lake
Beloye

Moskva

Oka

Klyaz'ma

Volga Upland

Kuybyshev
Reservoir

Samara

Ben Nevis
1343m

Grampian
Mountains

North Channel

Pennines

Jutland
Bank

Skagerrak

Kattegat

Baltic Sea

Neman

Western Dvina

Dnieper Lowlands

Don

Khoper

Ural

North
Sea

Great
Fisher
Bank

Jylland

Sjælland

Bug

Vistula

Byeraznia

Dnieper

Seym

Desna

Don

Donets

Manych

Yergeni

British
Isles

Ireland

Irish Sea

Snowdon
1083m

Trent

Britain

Severn

Dogger
Bank

Frisian Islands

Elbe
Oder

Warta

Harz

EUROPE

Pripet
Marshes

Kiev
Reservoir

Kremenchuk
Reservoir

Dniester Podil's'ka Vysochina

Pivdennyy Buh

Tsimlyansk
Reservoir

Kirghiz

Shannon

Celtic Sea

St. George's
Channel

Celtic
Shelf

Bristol Channel

Thames

Strait of Dover

Land's End

English Channel

Channel Islands

Ardennes

Rhine

Moselle

Seine

Marne

Meuse

Danube

Vosges

Black
Forest

Lake Constance

Morava

Carpathian
Mountains

Tisza

Bakony

Lake Balaton

Great
Hungarian
Plain

Sava

Drava

Transylvanian Alps

Danube

Siret

Prut

Black Sea Lowland

Sea of
Azov

Crimea

Kerch Strait

Kuban'

Bosporus

porcupine
Plain

Azores-Biscay Rise

Charcot Seamounts

Bay of
Biscay

Biscay
Plain

Biscay

Loire

Vienne

Cher

Saone

Lake Geneva

Mont
Blanc

Lake Garda

Po

Adige

Adriatic Sea

Dinaric Alps

Drin

Balkan Mountains

Rhodope Mountains

Maritsa

Black Sea

EURASIAN PLATE
ANATOLIAN PLATE

Theta Gap

Galicia
Bank

Garonne

Dordogne

Massif
Central

Cévennes

Lot

Ligurian
Sea

Tiber

Corno Grande
2912m

Adriatic
Basin

Strait of Otranto

Lake Scutari

Lake
Ohrid

Lake
Prespa

Sea of
Marmara

Anatolia

Iberian
Plain

Cordillera Cantábrica

Iberian

Mino

Douro

Aragon

Duero

Ebro

Sistema Ibérico

Gulf of Lion

Corsica

Strait of Bonifacio

Sardinia

Tyrrhenian
Sea

Tyrrhenian
Basin

Gulf of
Taranto

Ionian Sea

Peloponnese

Aegean Sea

Lake Eğirdir

Lake Tuz

Tagus Plain

Peninsula

Tagus

Gorringe
Ridge

Cape
Saint Vincent

Guadiana

Sierra Morena

Guadalquivir

Júcar

Gulf of
Valencia

Balearic Islands

Algerian Basin

Sistemas Béticos

Sierra Nevada

Segura

Mediterranean Sea

Mount Etna
3340m

Sicily

Ionian Basin

Malta

Mirtoun
Sea

Sea of Crete

Rhodes

Cyprus

Cyprus
Basin

Horseshoe Seamounts

Ampère Seamount

Seine Plain

Seine Seamount

Madeira

Cabo
da Roca

Punta de
Tarifa

Strait of
Gibraltar

Alboran Sea

Rif

Tell Atlas

EURASIAN PLATE
AFRICAN PLATE

Gávdos

Mediterranean Ridge

Levantine Basin

Nile Fan

Dacia Seamount

Canary Islands

Agadir Canyon

Oued Chelif

Sebou

Rbia

Middle Atlas

High Atlas

Atlas Mountains

Saharan Atlas

Chott el Jerid

Gulf of
Sirte

Qattara Depression
-133m

Western Desert

Suez Canal

Nile

'Erg Iguidi

Erg Chech

Grand Erg Occidental

Grand Erg Oriental

Libyan Desert

SAHARA

AFRICA

Europe

Europe is the world's second smallest continent, covering 4,053,309 sq miles (10,498,000 sq km). It comprises 46 separate countries, including Turkey and the Russian Federation, although the greater parts of these nations lie in Asia.

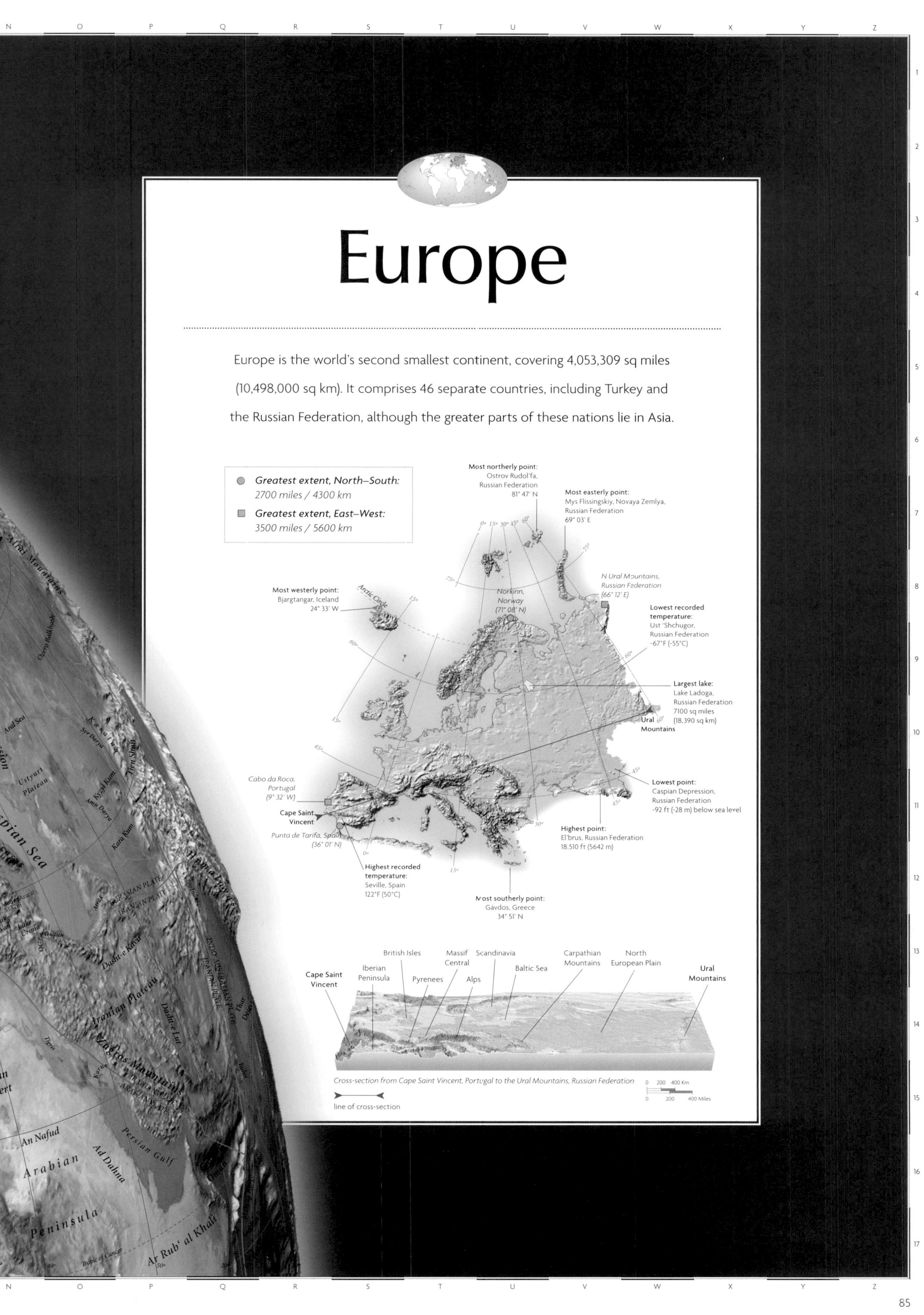

● *Greatest extent, North–South:*
2700 miles / 4300 km

■ *Greatest extent, East–West:*
3500 miles / 5600 km

Most northerly point:
Ostrov Rudol'fa,
Russian Federation
81° 47' N

Most easterly point:
Mys Flissingskiy, Novaya Zemlya,
Russian Federation
69° 03' E

Most westerly point:
Bjargtangar, Iceland
24° 33' W

*N Ural Mountains,
Russian Federation
(66° 12' E)*

*Nordkinn,
Norway
(71° 08' N)*

Lowest recorded
temperature:
Ust 'Shchugor,
Russian Federation
-67°F (-55°C)

Arctic Circle

Largest lake:
Lake Ladoga,
Russian Federation
7100 sq miles
(18,390 sq km)

Ural
Mountains

*Cabo da Roca,
Portugal
(9° 32' W)*

Cape Saint
Vincent

*Punta de Tarifa, Spain
(36° 01' N)*

Lowest point:
Caspian Depression,
Russian Federation
-92 ft (-28 m) below sea level

Highest point:
El'brus, Russian Federation
18,510 ft (5642 m)

Highest recorded
temperature:
Seville, Spain
122°F (50°C)

Most southerly point:
Gávdos, Greece
34° 51' N

Cape Saint
Vincent

Iberian
Peninsula

British Isles

Pyrenees

Massif
Central

Alps

Scandinavia

Baltic Sea

Carpathian
Mountains

North
European Plain

Ural
Mountains

Cross-section from Cape Saint Vincent, Portugal to the Ural Mountains, Russian Federation

line of cross-section

0   200   400 Km

0   200   400 Miles

Altai Mountains

Ozero Balkhash

Aral Sea

Ka ra Kum

Syr Darya

Tien Shan

Kyzyl Kum

Amu Darya

Ustyurt
Plateau

Kara Kum

Caspian Sea

EURASIAN PLATE

IRANIAN PLATE

Lake
Urmia

Dasht-e Kavir

Iranian Plateau

Dasht-e Lut

Tigris

Zagros Mountains

ARABIAN PLATE

An Nafud

Arabian

Ad Dahna

Persian Gulf

Peninsula

Ar Rub' al Khali

Tropic of Cancer

Political Europe

The political boundaries of Europe have changed many times, especially during the 20th century in the aftermath of two world wars, the breakup of the empires of Austria-Hungary, Nazi Germany and, toward the end of the century, the collapse of communism in eastern Europe. The fragmentation of Yugoslavia has again altered the political map of Europe, highlighting a trend toward nationalism and devolution. In contrast, economic federalism is growing. In 1958, the formation of the European Economic Community (now the European Union or EU) started a move toward economic and political union and increasing internal migration.

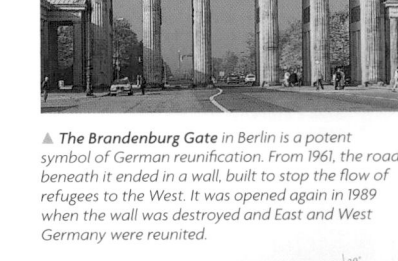

▲ *The Brandenburg Gate* in Berlin is a potent symbol of German reunification. From 1961, the road beneath it ended in a wall, built to stop the flow of refugees to the West. It was opened again in 1989 when the wall was destroyed and East and West Germany were reunited.

Population

Europe is a densely populated, urbanized continent; in Belgium over 90% of people live in urban areas. The highest population densities are found in an area stretching east from southern Britain and northern France, into Germany. The northern fringes are only sparsely populated.

▲ *Demand for space* in densely populated European cities like London has led to the development of high-rise offices and urban sprawl.

Population density
(people per sq mile)

	below 130
	130–259
	260–379
	380–519
	520–780
	above 780

▲ *Traditional lifestyles still* persist in many remote and rural parts of Europe, especially in the south, east, and in the far north.

Map key

Population

- ▪ above 5 million
- ▣ 1 million to 5 million
- ◉ 500,000 to 1 million
- ◎ 100,000 to 500,000
- ⊕ 50,000 to 100,000
- ○ 10,000 to 50,000
- ● Country capital

Borders

full international border

Scale 1:17,250,000

Km 0 100 200 300 400 500 600 700

Miles 0 100 200 300 400 500 600 700

projection: Lambert Azimuthal Equal Area

Denmark Strait

REYKJAVÍK
ICELAND
Arctic Circle

Denmark Strait

ATLANTIC OCEAN

Norwegian Sea

Faeroe Islands (to Denmark)

Shetland Islands

Outer Hebrides
Orkney Islands

North Sea

NORWAY
Trondheim
Bergen
Stavanger
Kristiansand
OSLO

SWEDEN
Uppsala
Örebro
STOCKHOLM
Vänern
Vättern
Gothenburg
Jönköping
Gotland

FINLAND
Tampere
Turku
HELSINKI
Åland
St Peter

Murman

Gulf of Bothnia

ESTONIA
TALLINN

LATVIA
RIGA
Ventspils
Liepāja
Western Dvina

LITHUANIA
Kaunas
VILNIUS
Vitsyebsk

MINSK

BELARUS
Babruysk
Brest

SCOTLAND
Aberdeen
Glasgow
Dundee
Edinburgh
NORTHERN IRELAND
Belfast
Newcastle upon Tyne

IRELAND
DUBLIN
Isle of Man (to UK)
Liverpool
Leeds
Manchester
Sheffield

UNITED KINGDOM
WALES
Birmingham
ENGLAND
Cardiff
Southampton
LONDON
Thames

Channel Islands (to UK)
English Channel
le Havre

DENMARK
Aalborg
COPENHAGEN
Odense
Helsingborg
Malmö
Baltic Sea

Groningen
AMSTERDAM NETH.
THE HAGUE
Rotterdam
Nijmegen
Antwerp
BELGIUM
BRUSSELS
Liège
Bonn
Düsseldorf

Hamburg
Bremen
Hannover
BERLIN
Leipzig
Dresden
GERMANY
Frankfurt am Main
Nuremberg
Stuttgart
Munich
Elbe
Oder
Rhine

RUSS. FED. (Kaliningrad)
Gdańsk
Bydgoszcz
Poznań
Łódź
Wrocław
WARSAW
POLAND
Kraków
Vistula

PRAGUE
CZECH REPUBLIC

Chernivtsi
UK
L'viv
Drв

MOL
Chişinău

Rennes
PARIS
Orléans
Strasbourg
FRANCE
Nantes
St-Nazaire
Loire
Seine
Limoges
Bordeaux
Lyon
Toulouse
Marseille
Nice
Rhône

Bay of Biscay

BERN
Geneva
Zürich
SWITZERLAND
LIECHTENSTEIN
Innsbruck
Milan
Turin
Verona
Salzburg
Danube
AUSTRIA
VIENNA
BRATISLAVA
SLOVAKIA
Győr
Miskolc
BUDAPEST
HUNGARY
LJUBLJANA
SLOVENIA
ZAGREB
CROATIA
Venice
Trieste
Genoa
Bologna
Florence
Po

A Coruña
Porto
Bilbao
Valladolid
Duero
Ebro
PORTUGAL
Tagus
LISBON
Setúbal
MADRID
SPAIN
Zaragoza
ANDORRA LA VELLA
ANDORRA
Pyrenees
Barcelona
Valencia
Seville
Córdoba
Murcia
Cádiz
Málaga
Gibraltar (to UK)
Ceuta (to Spain)
Melilla (to Spain)

Corsica
MONACO
Pisa
VATICAN CITY
ROME
SAN MARINO
ITALY
Naples
Sardinia
Cagliari
Palermo
Sicily
Catania
Messina
Cosenza

Ibiza
Mallorca
Palma
Menorca
Balearic Islands

Mediterranean Sea

Adriatic Sea
BOS. & HERZ.
SARAJEVO
Mostar
MONTENEGRO
PODGORICA
BELGRADE
SERBIA
KOSOVO (disputed)
PRISTINA
SKOPJE
MACEDONIA
TIRANA
ALBANIA
Bari

ROMANIA
Cluj-Napoca
Braşov
BUCHAREST
Danube
Ruse
Constanţ

BULGARIA
SOFIA
Stara Zagora

Tyrrhenian Sea

Ionian Sea

GREECE
Larisa
Aegean Sea
Piraeus
ATHENS
Salonica
Istan

MALTA
VALLETTA

Crete
Irákleio

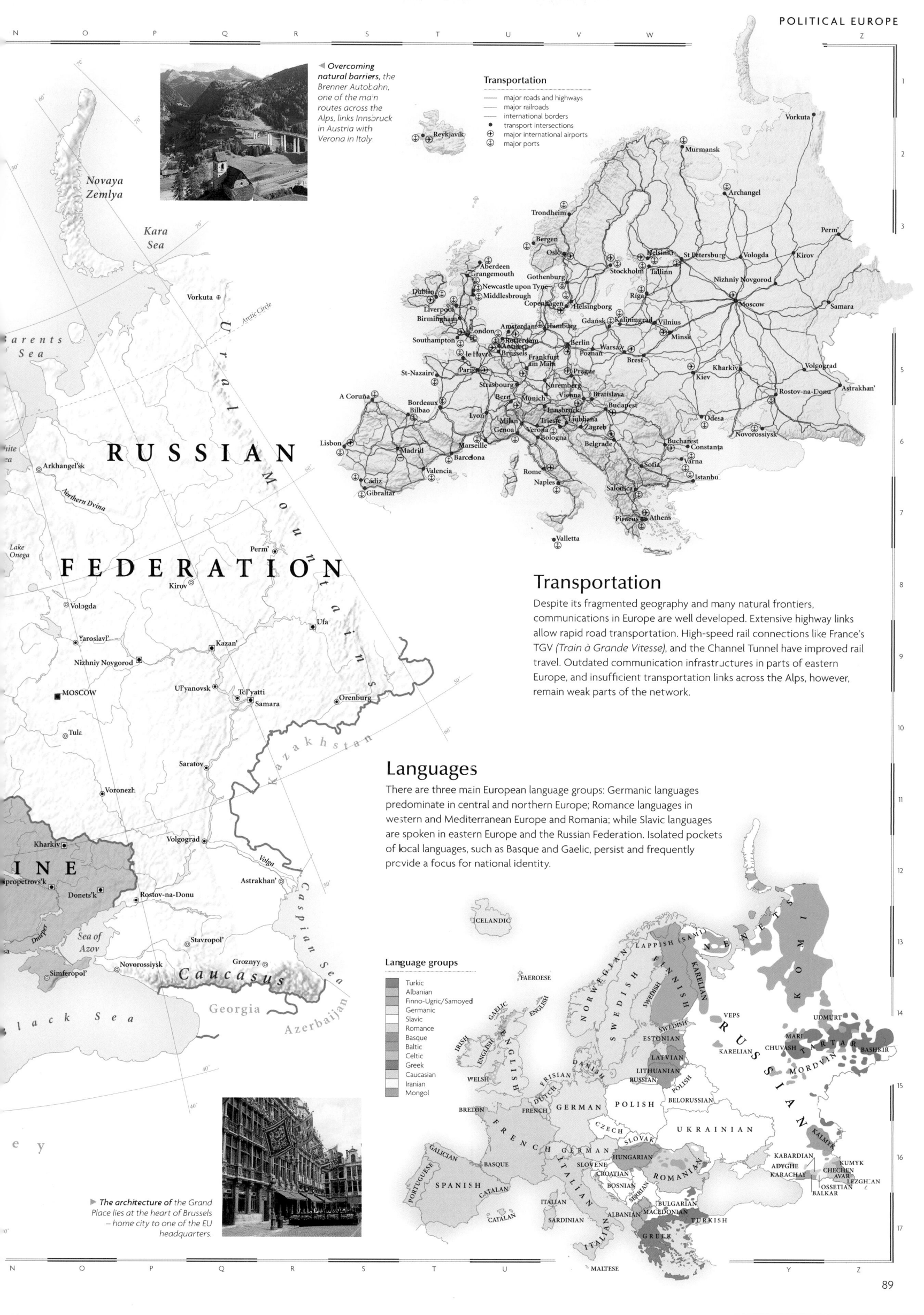

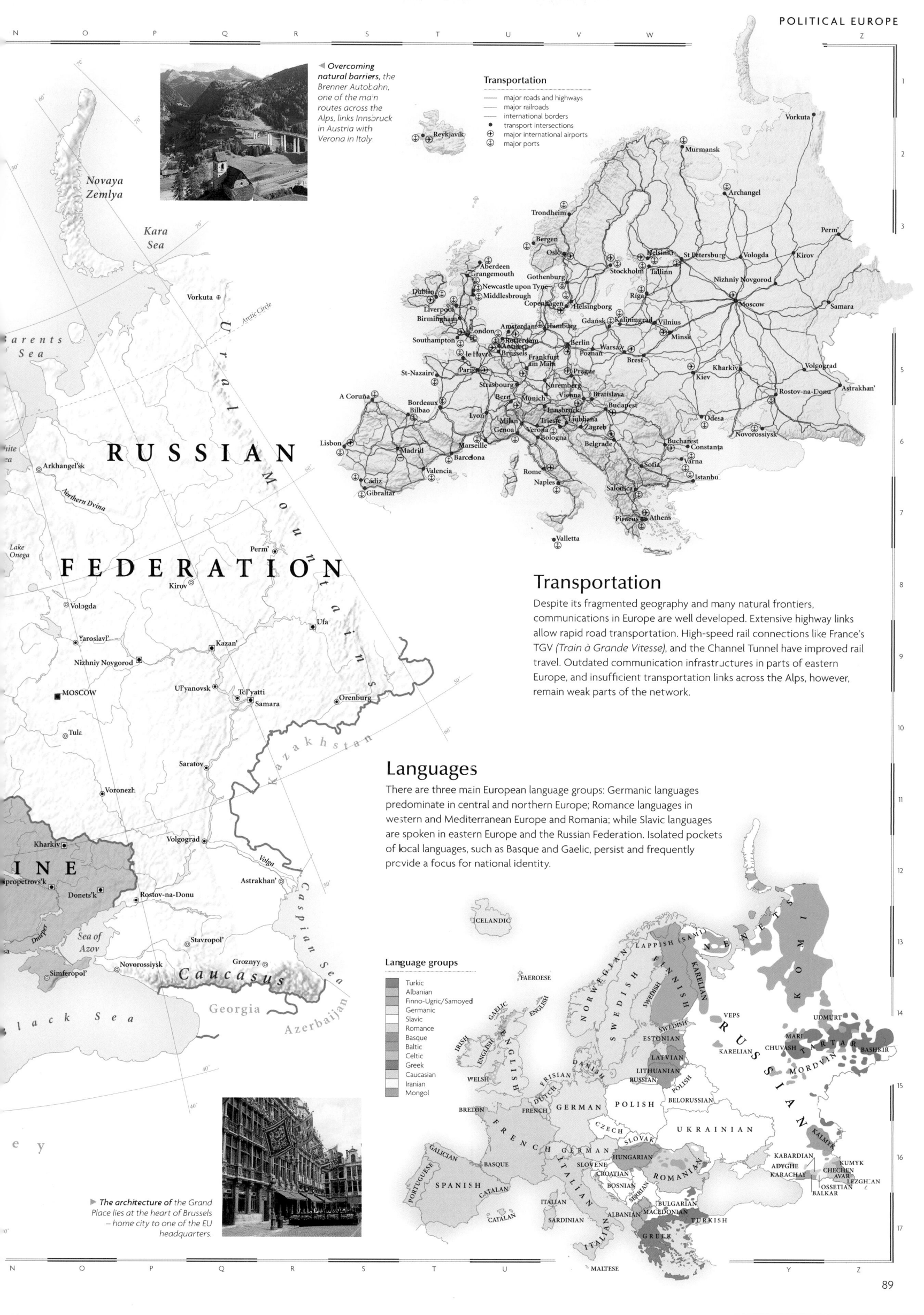
◄ *Overcoming natural barriers, the Brenner Autobahn, one of the main routes across the Alps, links Innsbruck in Austria with Verona in Italy*

Transportation
— major roads and highways
— major railroads
— international borders
• transport intersections
⊕ major international airports
⊕ major ports

Novaya Zemlya

Kara Sea

Barents Sea

White Sea

RUSSIAN

FEDERATION

Ural Mountains

Lake Onega

Arkhangel'sk

Northern Dvina

Vologda

Kirov

Perm'

Yaroslavl'

Ufa

Nizhniy Novgorod

Kazan'

■ MOSCOW

Ul'yanovsk

Tel'yatti

Samara

Orenburg

Tula

Saratov

Voronezh

Kazakhstan

Kharkiv

Volgograd

Volga

Astrakhan'

Caspian Sea

NE

Dnipropetrovs'k

Donets'k

Rostov-na-Donu

Dnieper

Sea of Azov

Simferopol'

Novorossiysk

Stavropol'

Groznyy

Caucasus

Georgia

Azerbaijan

Black Sea

Turkey

Reykjavik

Vorkuta ⊕

Murmansk

Archangel

Vorkuta

Perm'

Trondheim

Bergen

Oslo

Helsinki

St Petersburg

Vologda

Kirov

Nizhniy Novgorod

Aberdeen

Grangemouth

Newcastle upon Tyne

Middlesbrough

Gothenburg

Stockholm

Tallinn

Moscow

Samara

Dublin

Liverpool

Birmingham

Copenhagen

Helsingborg

Riga

London

Southampton

Amsterdam

Rotterdam

Antwerp

Brussels

le Havre

Hamburg

Gdańsk

Kaliningrad

Vilnius

Minsk

Volgograd

Berlin

Warsaw

Poznań

Brest

Kharkiv

Rostov-na-Donu

Astrakhan'

St-Nazaire

Paris

Strasbourg

Frankfurt am Main

Nuremberg

Prague

Kiev

Odesa

A Coruña

Bordeaux

Bilbao

Lyon

Bern

Munich

Vienna

Innsbruck

Bratislava

Budapest

Milan

Trieste

Ljubljana

Zagreb

Bucharest

Constanţa

Lisbon

Madrid

Genoa

Verona

Bologna

Belgrade

Varna

Marseille

Barcelona

Valencia

Rome

Sofia

Istanbul

Cádiz

Gibraltar

Naples

Salonica

Novorossiysk

Piraeus

Athens

Valletta

Transportation

Despite its fragmented geography and many natural frontiers, communications in Europe are well developed. Extensive highway links allow rapid road transportation. High-speed rail connections like France's TGV *(Train à Grande Vitesse)*, and the Channel Tunnel have improved rail travel. Outdated communication infrastructures in parts of eastern Europe, and insufficient transportation links across the Alps, however, remain weak parts of the network.

Languages

There are three main European language groups: Germanic languages predominate in central and northern Europe; Romance languages in western and Mediterranean Europe and Romania; while Slavic languages are spoken in eastern Europe and the Russian Federation. Isolated pockets of local languages, such as Basque and Gaelic, persist and frequently provide a focus for national identity.

Language groups
- Turkic
- Albanian
- Finno-Ugric/Samoyed
- Germanic
- Slavic
- Romance
- Basque
- Baltic
- Celtic
- Greek
- Caucasian
- Iranian
- Mongol

ICELANDIC

FAEROESE

NORWEGIAN

LAPPISH (SAMI)

NENETS

KOMI

SWEDISH

FINNISH

KARELIAN

SWEDISH

SWEDISH

VEPS

UDMURT

GAELIC

ENGLISH

ESTONIAN

KARELIAN

MARI

CHUVASH

TATAR

BASHKIR

IRISH

ENGLISH

ENGLISH

LATVIAN

RUSSIAN

MORDVIN

WELSH

FRISIAN

DANISH

LITHUANIAN

RUSSIAN

KALMYK

BRETON

DUTCH

FRENCH

GERMAN

POLISH

BELORUSSIAN

FRENCH

GERMAN

CZECH

UKRAINIAN

GALICIAN

SLOVAK

KABARDIAN

KUMYK

PORTUGUESE

BASQUE

ITALIAN

SLOVENE

HUNGARIAN

ADYGHE

CHECHEN

AVAR

KARACHAY

LEZGHIAN

SPANISH

CATALAN

CROATIAN

ROMANIAN

OSSETIAN

BALKAR

ITALIAN

BOSNIAN

SERBIAN

BULGARIAN

CATALAN

ALBANIAN

MACEDONIAN

SARDINIAN

GREEK

TURKISH

ITALIAN

MALTESE

► *The architecture of the Grand Place lies at the heart of Brussels – home city to one of the EU headquarters.*

Scandinavia, Finland & Iceland

DENMARK, NORWAY, SWEDEN, FINLAND, ICELAND

Jutting into the Arctic Circle, this northern swath of Europe has some of the continent's harshest environments, but benefits from great reserves of oil, gas, and natural evergreen forests. While most early settlers came from the south, migrants to Finland came from the east, giving it a distinct language and culture. Since the late 19th century, the Scandinavian states have developed strong egalitarian traditions. Today, their welfare benefits systems are among the most extensive in the world, and standards of living are high. The Lapps, or Sami, maintain their traditional lifestyle in the northern regions of Norway, Sweden, and Finland.

The landscape

Glaciers up to 10,000 ft (3000 m) deep covered most of Scandinavia and Finland during the last Ice Age. The effects of glaciation mark the entire landscape, from the mountains to the lowlands, across the tundra landscape of Lapland, and the lake districts of Sweden and Finland.

Lapland, north of the Arctic Circle, is an area of undulating fells and plains known as tundra. The subsoil is permanently frozen and therefore impermeable. There are many peat bogs. Pools reappear in the summer when the surface thaws.

Using the land & sea

The cold climate, short growing season, poorly developed soil, steep slopes, and exposure to high winds across northern regions means that most agriculture is concentrated, with the population, in the south. Most of Finland and much of Norway and Sweden are covered by dense forests of pine, spruce, and birch, which supply the timber industries.

Land use and agricultural distribution

- fishing
- pigs
- reindeer
- sheep
- timber
- capital cities
- major towns
- pasture
- cropland
- forest
- mountain region
- tundra

cereals

Population density Total land area
51 people per sq mile 473,970 sq miles

The urban/rural population divide
urban 77%   rural 23%

Scale 1:9,000,000
projection: Lambert Conformal Conic
Km 0 20 40 60 80 100
Miles 0 20 40 60 80 100

Scale 1:5,500,000
Km 0 10 20 40 60 80 100 120 140 160
Miles 0 10 20 40 60 80 100 120 140 160
projection: Lambert Conformal Conic

(same scale as main map)

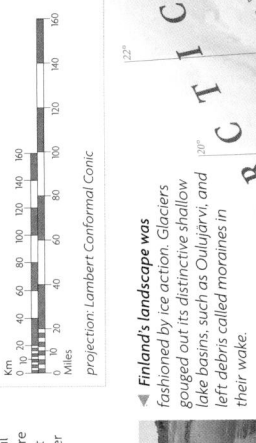

▼ Finland's landscape was fashioned by ice action. Glaciers gouged out its distinctive shallow lake basins, such as Oulujärvi, and left debris called moraines in their wake.

Oulujärvi

▲ Scandinavia is still recovering from the last Ice Age, when ice depressed the land by 2000 ft (600 m). This gradual uplift is known as isostatic rebound.

Area of maximum yearly uplift 0.3 in/yr (9 mm/yr)

Slower rates of uplift 0.1 in/yr (3 mm/yr)

Halti Mountain is Finland's highest point, at 4356 ft (1328 m).

The Lofoten Islands were one of the first areas exposed as the ice sheet melted.

Geysers are a by-product of Iceland's volcanic activity. Geysir, Iceland's largest spring, gives them their name.

Sjælland coast

▲ On the coast of Sjælland, these cliffs have been eroded by the sea, exposing layers of chalk and limestone.

Fjords

▲ The fjords on the western coast of Norway were once gentle river valleys. Their deep floors and steep sides were carved out by glaciers during the last Ice Age, and they were later flooded by the sea.

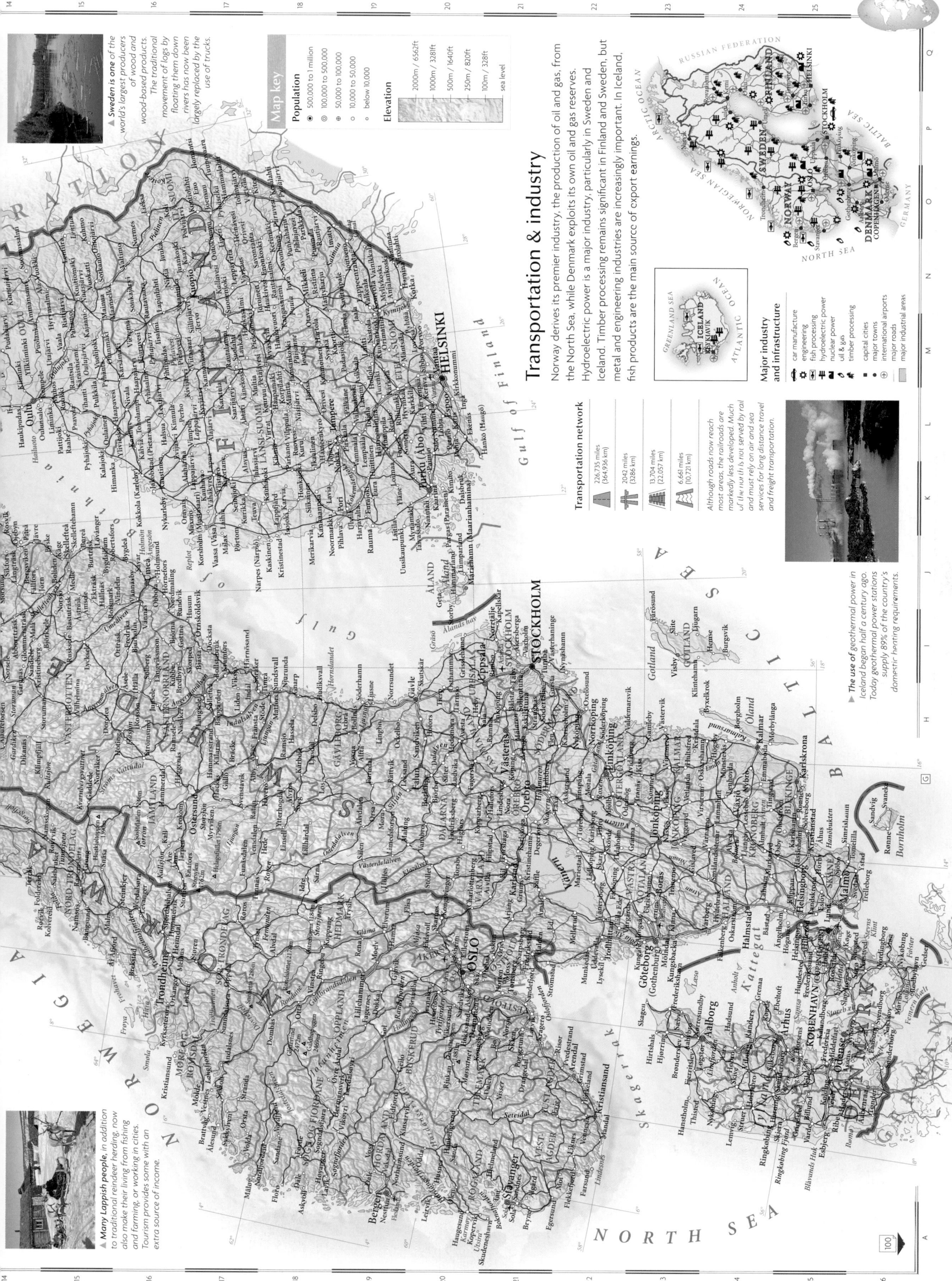

▲ *Sweden is one of the world's largest producers of wood and wood-based products. The traditional movement of logs by floating them down rivers has now been largely replaced by the use of trucks.*

Map key

Population
- ◉ 500,000 to 1 million
- ⊚ 100,000 to 500,000
- ⊕ 50,000 to 100,000
- ○ 10,000 to 50,000
- ∘ below 10,000

Elevation
- 2000m / 6562ft
- 1000m / 3281ft
- 500m / 1640ft
- 250m / 820ft
- 100m / 328ft
- sea level

Transportation & industry

Norway derives its premier industry, the production of oil and gas, from the North Sea, while Denmark exploits its own oil and gas reserves. Hydroelectric power is a major industry, particularly in Sweden and Iceland. Timber processing remains significant in Finland and Sweden, but metal and engineering industries are increasingly important. In Iceland, fish products are the main source of export earnings.

Transportation network

- 226,735 miles (364,936 km)
- 2042 miles (3386 km)
- 13,704 miles (22,057 km)
- 6,661 miles (10,721 km)

Although roads now reach most areas, the railroads are markedly less developed. Much of the north is not served by rail services for long distance travel and must rely on air and sea transportation.

Major industry and infrastructure

- car manufacture
- engineering
- fish processing
- hydroelectric power
- nuclear power
- oil & gas
- timber processing
- capital cities
- major towns
- international airports
- major roads
- major industrial areas

▲ *The use of geothermal power in Iceland began half a century ago. Today geothermal power stations supply 89% of the country's domestic heating requirements.*

▲ *Many Lappish people, in addition to traditional reindeer herding, now also make their living from fishing and farming, or working in cities. Tourism provides some with an extra source of income.*

Southern Scandinavia

SOUTHERN NORWAY, SOUTHERN SWEDEN, DENMARK

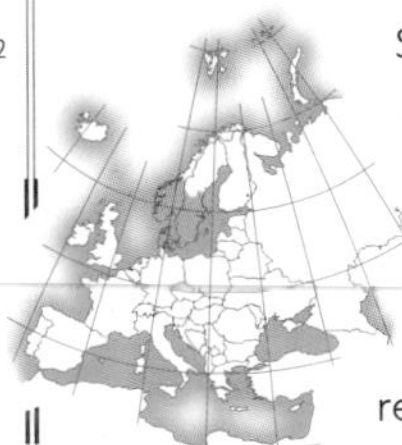

Scandinavia's economic and political hub is the more habitable and accessible southern region. Many of the area's major cities are on the southern coasts, including Oslo and Stockholm, the capitals of Norway and Sweden. In Denmark, most of the population and the capital, Copenhagen, are located on its many islands. A cultural unity links the three Scandinavian countries. Their main languages, Danish, Swedish, and Norwegian, are mutually intelligible, and they all retain their monarchies, although the parliaments have legislative control.

Using the land

Agriculture in southern Scandinavia is highly mechanized although farms are small. Denmark is the most intensively farmed country and its western pastureland is used mainly for pig farming. Cereal crops including wheat, barley, and oats, predominate in eastern Denmark and in the far south of Sweden. Southern Norway, and Sweden have large tracts of forest which are exploited for logging.

Land use and agricultural distribution

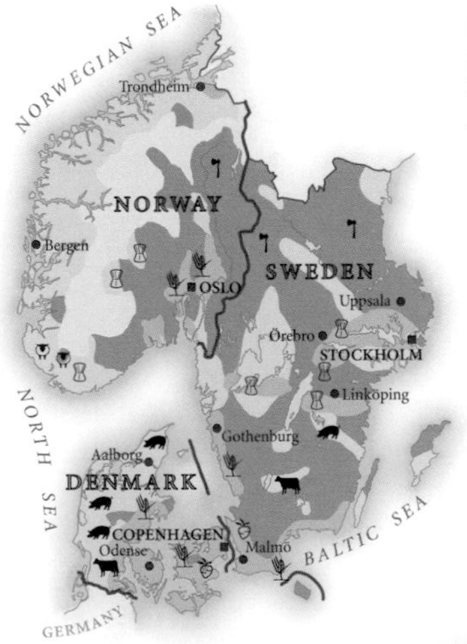

- cattle
- pigs
- sheep
- cereals
- fodder
- root crops
- timber

capital cities
major towns
pasture
cropland
forest
mountain region

The urban/rural population divide

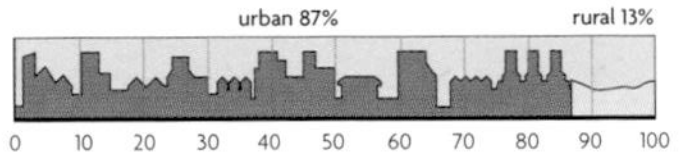

urban 87% rural 13%

Total land area
173,487 sq miles
(456,564 sq km)

Population density
112 people per sq mile
(43 people per sq km)

The landscape

Southern Scandinavia, with the exception of Norway, has a flatter terrain than the rest of the region. Denmark and southern Sweden are both extensions of the North European Plain. In this area, because of glacial deposition rather than erosion, the soils are deeper and more fertile.

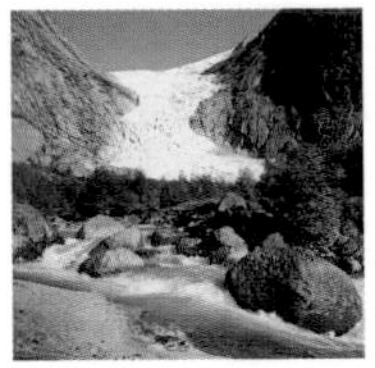

Acid rain, caused by industrial pollution, carried north from elsewhere in Europe, harms plant and animal life in Scandinavian forests and lakes. The region's surface rocks lack lime to neutralize the acid, so making the problem more serious.

Distinctive low ridges, called eskers, are found across southern Sweden. They are formed from sand and gravel deposits left by retreating glaciers.

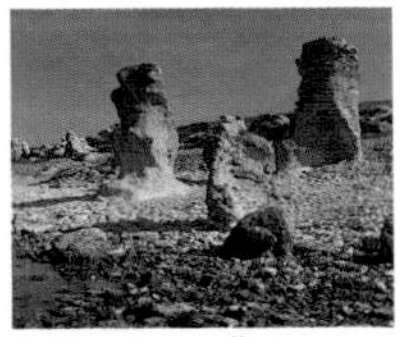

▲ Limestone pillars eroded by the sea dot the coast of Gotland and surrounding islands.

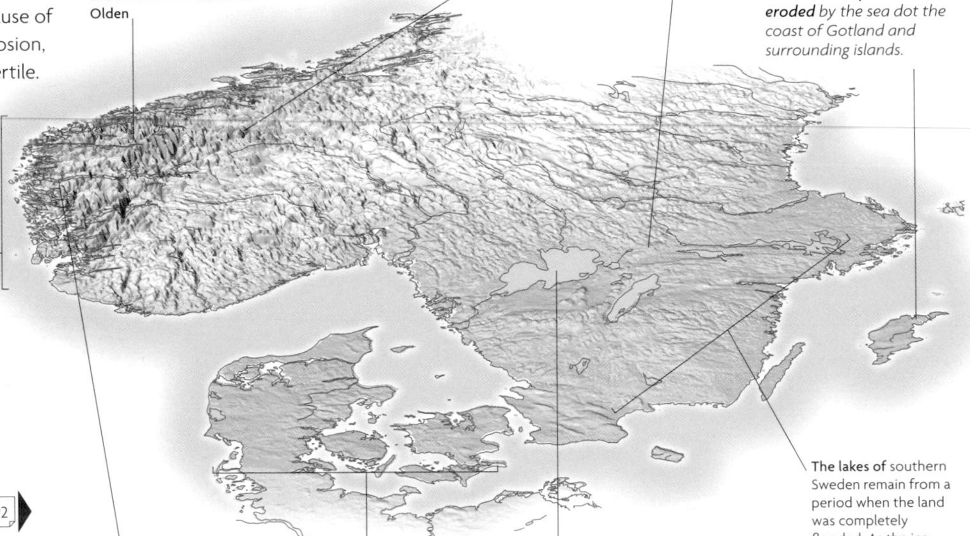

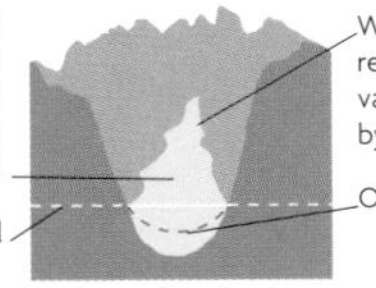

The lakes of southern Sweden remain from a period when the land was completely flooded. As the ice which covered the area melted, the land rose, leaving lakes in shallow, ice-scoured depressions. Sweden has over 90,000 lakes.

Vänern in Sweden is the largest lake in Scandinavia. It covers an area of 2080 sq miles (5390 sq km).

The peak of Glittertind in the Jotunheimen mountains is 8110 ft (2472 m) high.

▼ In the past, glaciers such as this one in Olden, Norway, were much larger. Today, many are retreating to yield the spectacular glacial scenery.

Denmark's flat and fertile soils are formed on glacial deposits between 100–160 ft (30–50 m) deep.

When the ice retreated the valley was flooded by the sea
Old valley floor
Sea level
Erosion by glaciers deepened existing river valleys

Sognefjorden

▲ Sognefjorden is the deepest of Norway's many fjords. It drops to 4291 ft (1308 m) below sea level.

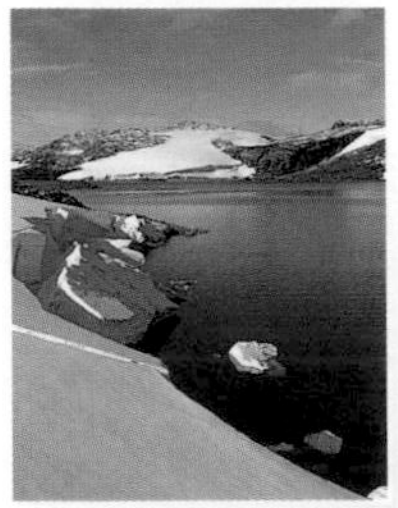

Map key

Population
- ◉ 500,000 to 1 million
- ◎ 100,000 to 500,000
- ⊕ 50,000 to 100,000
- ○ 10,000 to 50,000
- ○ below 10,000

Elevation
2000m / 6562ft
1000m / 3281ft
500m / 1640ft
250m / 820ft
100m / 328ft
sea level

Scale 1:3,250,000

projection: Lambert Conformal Conic

▲ In Norway winters are longer and colder inland than in coastal areas, where the warm current of the North Atlantic Drift moderates the climate.

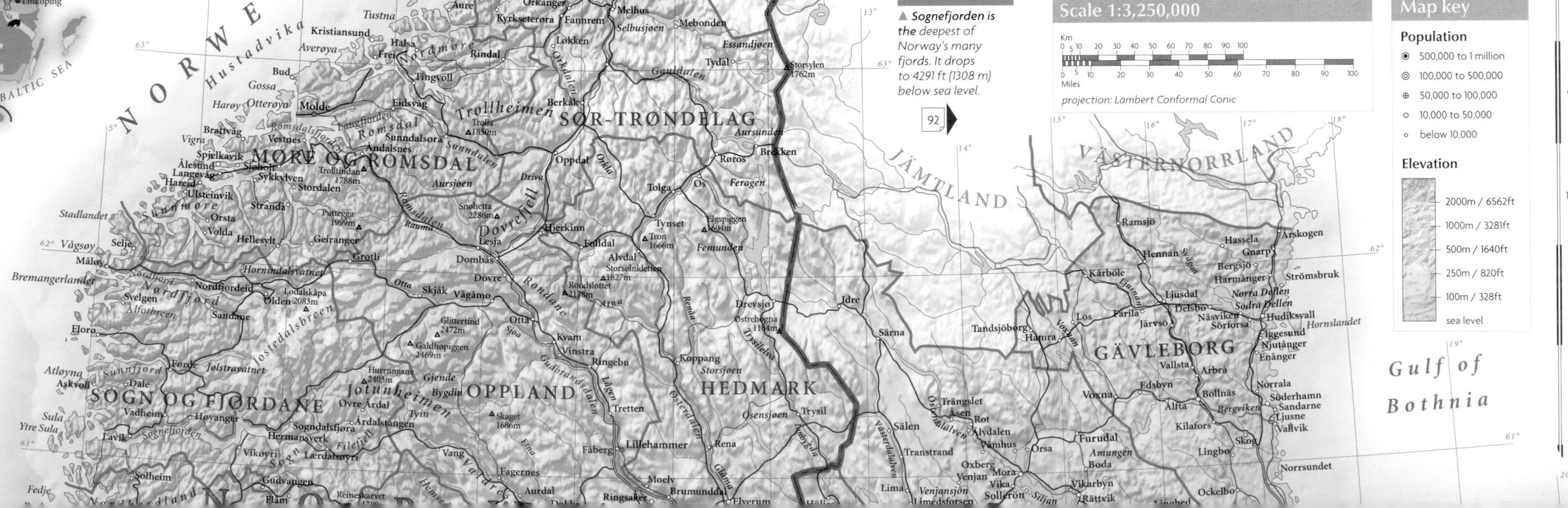

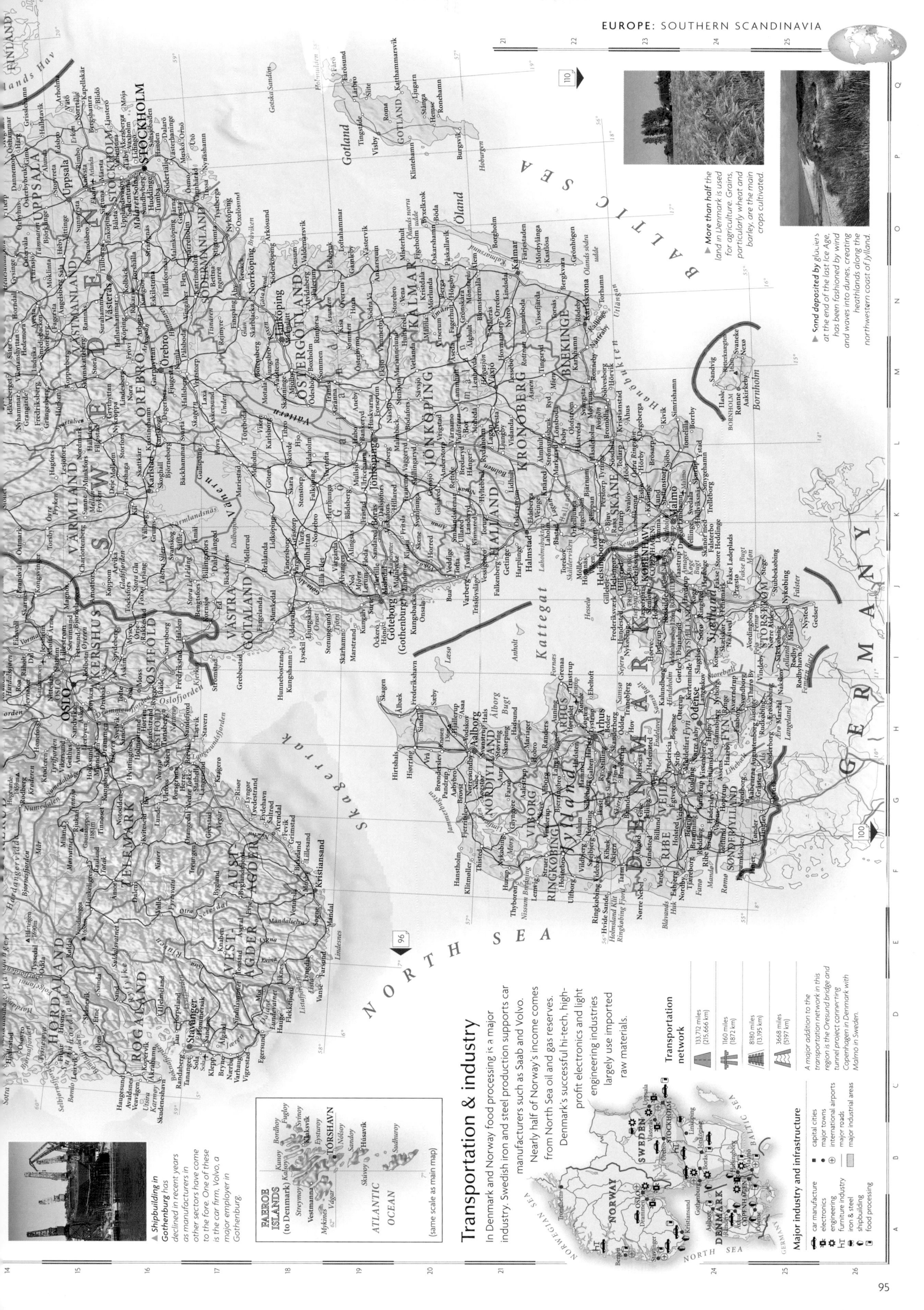

▲ *More than half the land in Denmark is used for agriculture. Grains, particularly wheat and barley, are the main crops cultivated.*

▲ *Sand deposited by glaciers at the end of the last Ice Age, has been fashioned by wind and waves into dunes, creating heathlands along the northwestern coast of Jylland.*

Transportation & industry

In Denmark and Norway food processing is a major industry. Swedish iron and steel production supports car manufacturers such as Saab and Volvo. Nearly half of Norway's income comes from North Sea oil and gas reserves. Denmark's successful hi-tech, high-profit electronics and light engineering industries largely use imported raw materials.

Transportation network

🚗	133,712 miles (215,666 km)	
🚂	1160 miles (1872 km)	
🚢	8180 miles (13,195 km)	
✈	3668 miles (5197 km)	

A major addition to the transportation network in this region is the Øresund bridge and tunnel project connecting Copenhagen in Denmark with Malmö in Sweden.

Major industry and infrastructure

- car manufacture
- electronics
- engineering
- furniture industry
- iron & steel
- shipbuilding
- food processing
- ■ capital cities
- ▪ major towns
- ⊕ international airports
- major roads
- major industrial areas

▲ *Shipbuilding in Gothenburg has declined in recent years as manufacturers in other sectors have come to the fore. One of these is the car firm, Volvo, a major employer in Gothenburg.*

FAEROE ISLANDS
(to Denmark)

(same scale as main map)

TÓRSHAVN

ATLANTIC OCEAN

The British Isles

UNITED KINGDOM, IRELAND

The British Isles have for centuries played a central role in European and world history. England, Wales, Scotland, and Northern Ireland together form the United Kingdom (UK), while the southern portion of Ireland is an independent country, self-governing since 1921. Although England has tended to be the politically and economically dominant partner in the UK, the Scots, Welsh, and Irish maintain independent cultures, distinct national identities and languages. Southeastern England is the most densely populated part of this crowded region, with over eight million people living in and around the London area.

The landscape

Rugged uplands dominate the landscape of Scotland, Wales, and northern England. All the peaks in the British Isles over 4000 ft (1219 m) lie in highland Scotland. Lowland England rises into several ranges of rolling hills, including the older Mendips, and the Cotswolds and the Chilterns, which were formed at the same time as the Alps in southern Europe.

▲ *The valley of Glen Coe in the Scottish Highlands is a U-shaped valley, typical of the north and west of the British Isles, where glaciers shaped much of the landscape.*

The Pennines, sometimes called "the backbone of England," are formed of limestones and grits.

Ben Nevis at 4409 ft (1343 m) is the highest peak in the UK.

▲ *Ullswater in the Lake District fills a deep valley formed by glacial erosion.*

The Fens are a low-lying area reclaimed from the sea.

The Cotswold Hills are characterized by a series of limestone ridges overlooking clay vales.

Chiltern Hills

Durdle Door

▲ *Coastal erosion around the British Isles forms striking features such as this limestone arch, Durdle Door in Dorset.*

Over 600 islands, mostly uninhabited, lie west and north of the Scottish mainland.

Snowdon is the highest mountain in England and Wales reaching 3556 ft (1085 m).

The lowlands of Scotland, drained by the Tay, Forth, and Clyde rivers, are centered on a rift valley. The region contains valuable coal reserves.

Thousands of hexagonal basalt columns form Giant's Causeway on the north coast of Antrim. These were created by volcanic activity.

Lake District

Peat bogs dot the poorly-drained Irish lowlands.

The British Isles have no large-scale river systems. The Shannon is the longest, at 230 miles (370 km).

▲ *Dartmoor, studded with tors, is an exposed part of a vast granite dome, formed when molten rock intruded into the Earth's crust.*

Black Ven, Lyme Regis

Cracks
Sandstone
Clay
Limestone
Water
Mudslide
Sea

▲ *Much of the south coast is subject to landslides. Following rain, porous sandstones feed water into the underlying, less permeable clays which then crumble and slide into the sea.*

Map key

Population

■	above 5 million
◉	1 million to 5 million
⊙	500,000 to 1 million
⊚	100,000 to 500,000
○	50,000 to 100,000
○	10,000 to 50,000
∘	below 10,000

Elevation

1000m / 328ft
500m / 1640ft
250m / 820ft
100m / 328ft
sea level

Transportation & industry

The British Isles' industrial base was founded primarily on coal, iron, and textiles, based largely in the north. Today, the most productive sectors include hi-tech industries clustered mainly in the southeastern England, chemicals, finance, and the service sector, particularly tourism.

Major industry and infrastructure

- 🚗 car manufacture
- ⚙ chemicals
- 🔧 engineering
- 💻 hi-tech industry
- 🏭 iron & steel
- 🏖 tourism

- ■ capital cities
- ● major cities
- ● major towns
- ⊕ international airports
- ▨ major roads
- ▬ major industrial areas

Transportation network

| ▲ | 285,947 miles (460,240 km) | | 2023 miles (3578 km) |
| 🏭 | 11,825 miles (19,032km) | | 3976 miles (6400 km) |

The UK's congested roads have become a major focus of environmental concern in recent years. No longer an island, the UK was finally linked to continental Europe by the Channel Tunnel in 1994.

▼ *Clew Bay in western Ireland, is characteristic of the heavily indented west coast, where deep wide-mouthed bays separate the mountains of Mayo, Donegal, and Kerry as they thrust out into the Atlantic Ocean.*

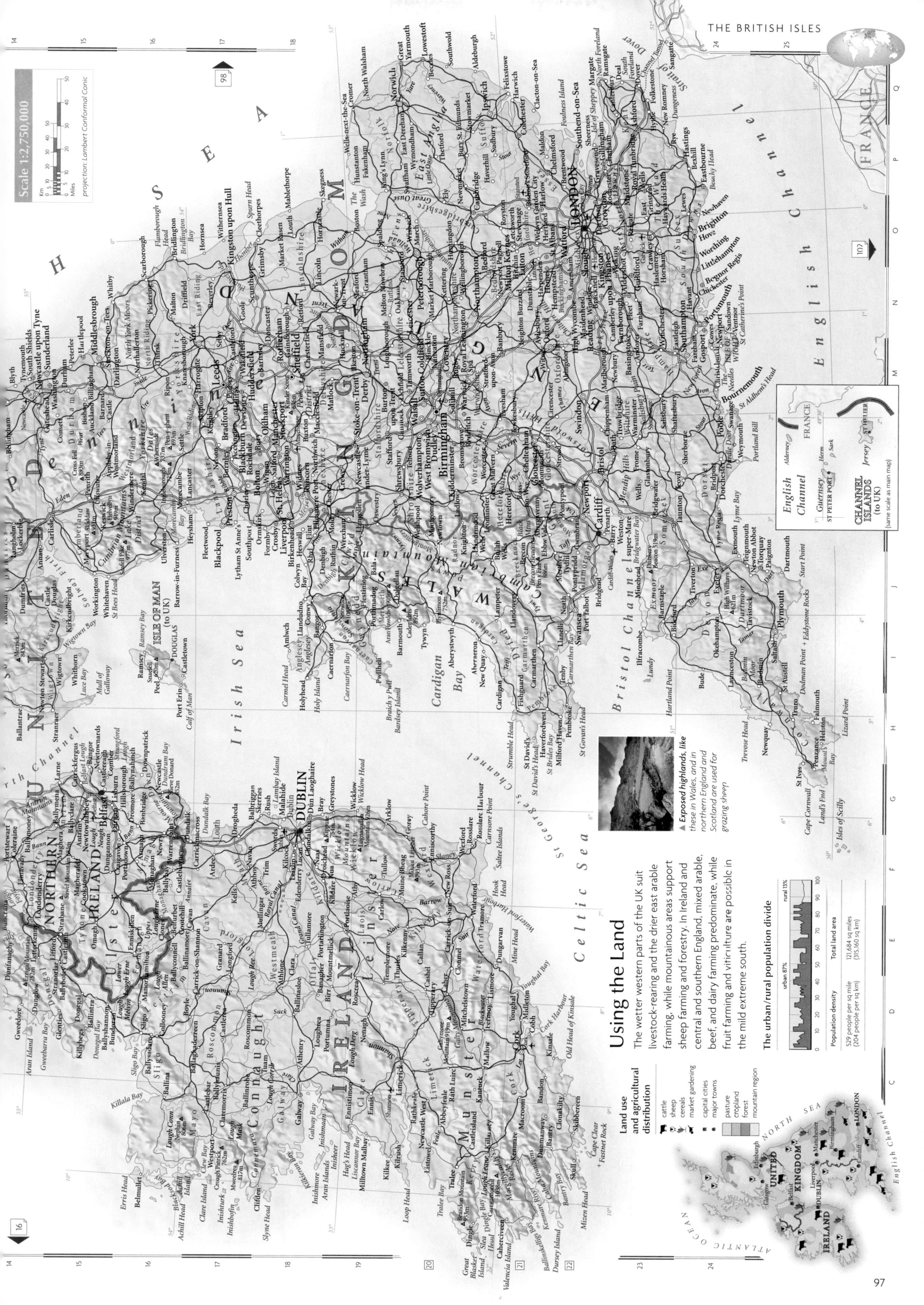

Using the Land

The wetter western parts of the UK suit livestock-rearing and the drier east arable farming, while mountainous areas support sheep farming and forestry. In Ireland and central and southern England, mixed arable, beef, and dairy farming predominate, while fruit farming and viticulture are possible in the mild extreme south.

The urban/rural population divide

urban 87% rural 13%

Population density	Total land area
529 people per sq mile (204 people per sq km)	121,684 sq miles (315,160 sq km)

Land use and agricultural distribution

- cattle
- sheep
- cereals
- market gardening
- capital cities
- major towns
- pasture
- cropland
- forest
- mountain region

▲ *Exposed highlands, like these in Wales, and in northern England and Scotland are used for grazing sheep*

Scale 1:2,750,000
projection: Lambert Conformal Conic

The Low Countries

BELGIUM, LUXEMBOURG, NETHERLANDS

One of northwestern Europe's strategic crossroads, the Low Countries are united by a common history in which they have often been a battleground in European wars. For over a thousand years they were ruled by foreign powers. Even after they achieved independence, the three countries maintained close links, later forming the world's first totally free labor and goods market, the Benelux Economic Union, which became the core of the European Community (now the European Union or EU). These states have remained at the forefront of wider European cooperation; Brussels, The Hague, and Luxembourg are hosts to major institutions of the EU.

The landscape

The main geographical regions of the Netherlands are the northern glacial heathlands, the low-lying lands of the Rhine and Maas/Meuse, the reclaimed polders, and the dune coast and islands. Belgium includes part of the Ardennes, together with the coalfields on its northern flanks, and the fertile Flanders plain.

▲ Extensive sand dune systems along the coast have prevented flooding of the land. Behind the dunes, marshy land is drained to form polders, usable land suitable for agriculture.

Since the Middle Ages the people of the Netherlands have used ditches and drainage dikes to reclaim land from the sea. These reclaimed areas are known as polders.

The loess soils of the Flanders Plain in western Belgium provide excellent conditions for arable farming.

▲ Uplifted and folded 220 million years ago, the Ardennes have since been reduced to relatively level plateaus, then sharply incised by rivers such as the Maas/Meuse.

Sea
Polder
Drainage ditch
Dune system
Sand dunes
Schoorl

▼ Heathlands, like these at Schoorl, are found along the coast of the Netherlands. Much of the coast was breached by the sea in the 5th century, creating its distinctive inlets and islands.

▲ One-third of the Netherlands lies below sea level and flooding is a constant threat. Barrages have been built across the mouths of many rivers to contain floodwaters.

The parallel valleys of the Maas/Meuse and Rhine rivers were created when the Rhine was deflected from its previous course by the ice sheet which formed during the last Ice Age.

Silts and sands eroded by the Rhine throughout its course are deposited to form a delta on the west coast of the Netherlands.

Hautes Fagnes is the highest part of Belgium. The bogs and streams in this upland region result from high rainfall and low temperatures.

Ardennes

Transportation & industry

In the western Netherlands, a massive, sprawling industrialized zone encompasses many new hi-tech and service industries. Belgium's central region has emerged as the country's light manufacturing and services center. Luxembourg city is home to more than 160 banks and the European headquarters of many international companies.

The Low Countries hold a key position on the North Sea, containing Europe's two largest ports, Rotterdam and Antwerp, which are connected to a comprehensive system of inland waterways.

Transportation network

🛫	140,588 miles (226,281 km)	🚂	2565 miles (4129 km)
	4099 miles (6598 km)	🚢	4134 miles (6653 km)

Major industry and infrastructure

- ✈ aerospace
- Ⓢ finance
- ⚙ engineering
- ⚒ hi-tech industry
- ⚗ pharmaceuticals
- 🧵 textiles
- ■ capital cities
- ● major cities
- • major towns
- ⊕ international airports
- — major roads
- ▨ major industrial areas

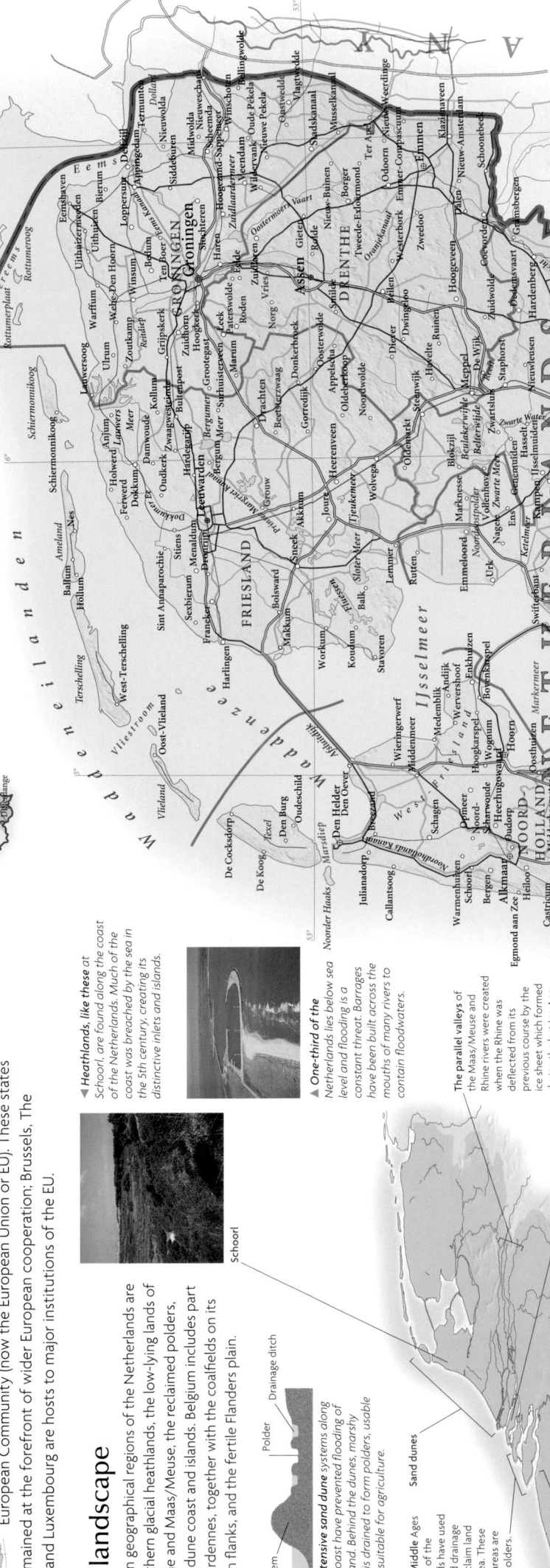

NETHERLANDS

GRONINGEN

FRIESLAND

DRENTHE

OVERIJSSEL

IJsselmeer

NOORD-HOLLAND

FLEVOLAND

GELDERLAND

AMSTERDAM

UTRECHT

Haarlem
Leiden

'S-GRAVENHAGE
(THE HAGUE)

ZUID-HOLLAND

Rotterdam

GERMANY

NORTH SEA

GERMANY

LUXEMBOURG
LUXEMBOURG

NETHERLANDS
AMSTERDAM
THE HAGUE
BELGIUM
BRUSSELS

FRANCE

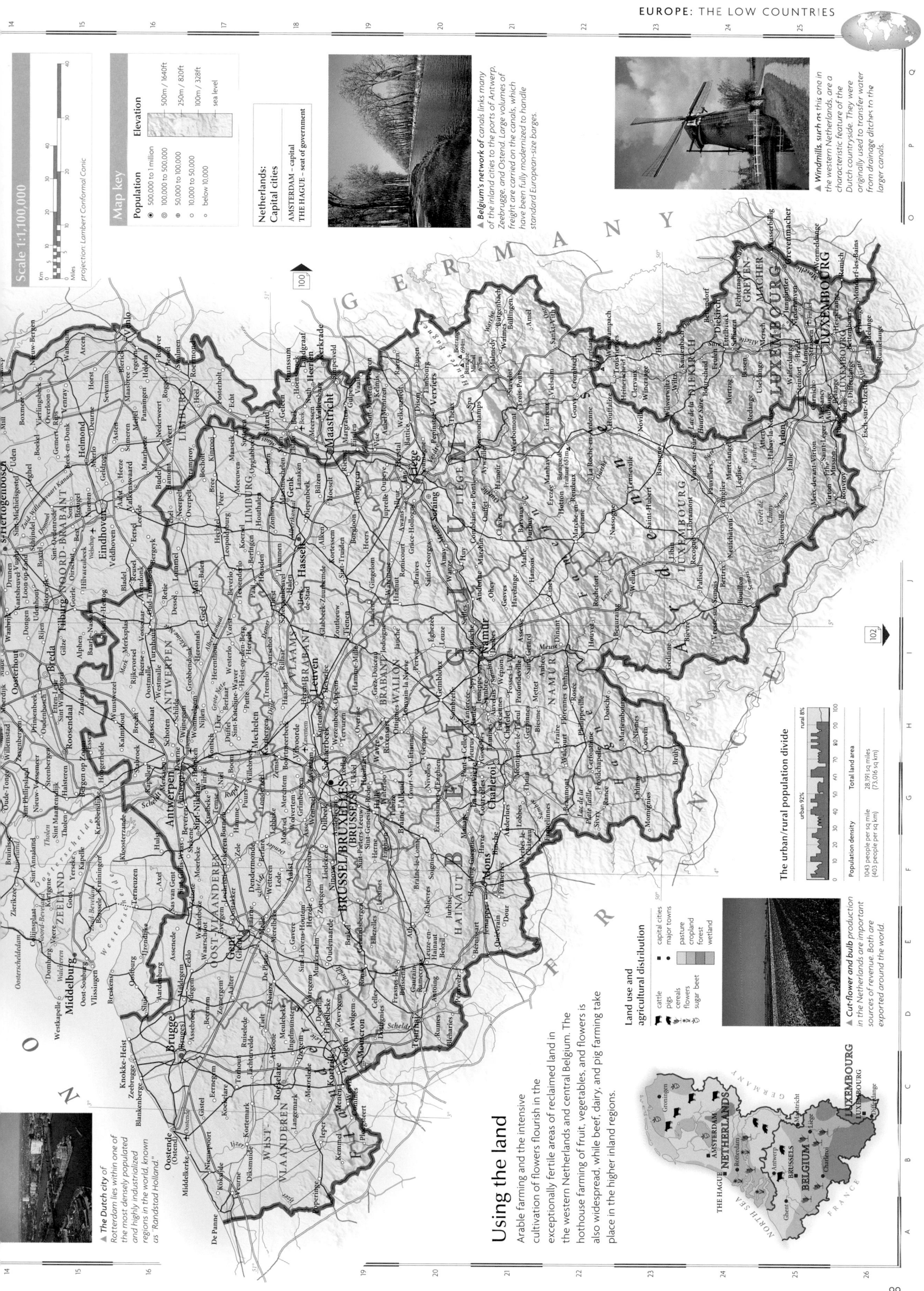

Scale 1:1,100,000

projection: Lambert Conformal Conic

Map key

Population
- ◉ 500,000 to 1 million
- ⊕ 100,000 to 500,000
- ⊙ 50,000 to 100,000
- ○ 10,000 to 50,000
- ○ below 10,000

Elevation
- 500m / 1640ft
- 250m / 820ft
- 100m / 328ft
- sea level

Netherlands:
Capital cities

AMSTERDAM – capital
THE HAGUE – seat of government

▲ *Belgium's network of canals links many of the inland cities to the ports of Antwerp, Zeebrugge, and Ostend. Large volumes of freight are carried on the canals, which have been fully modernized to handle standard European-size barges.*

▲ *Windmills, such as this one in the western Netherlands, are a characteristic feature of the Dutch countryside. They were originally used to transfer water from drainage ditches to the larger canals.*

▲ *The Dutch city of Rotterdam lies within one of the most densely populated and highly industrialized regions in the world, known as 'Randstad Holland.'*

Using the land

Arable farming and the intensive cultivation of flowers flourish in the exceptionally fertile areas of reclaimed land in the western Netherlands and central Belgium. The hothouse farming of fruit, vegetables, and flowers is also widespread, while beef, dairy, and pig farming take place in the higher inland regions.

Land use and agricultural distribution
- cattle
- pigs
- cereals
- flowers
- sugar beet
- ▪ capital cities
- ▫ major towns
- pasture
- cropland
- forest
- wetland

▲ *Cut-flower and bulb production in the Netherlands are important sources of revenue. Both are exported around the world.*

The urban/rural population divide

Population density: 1043 people per sq mile (403 people per sq km)

Total land area: 28,191 sq miles (73,016 sq km)

urban 92% | rural 8%

Germany

Despite the devastation of its industry and infrastructure during the Second World War and its separation from eastern Germany during the Cold War, West Germany made a rapid recovery in the following generation to become Europe's most formidable economic power. When the Berlin Wall was dismantled in 1989, the two halves of Germany were politically united for the first time in 40 years. Complete social and economic unity remain a longer term goal, as East German industry and society adapt to a free market. Germany has been a key player in the creation of the European Union (EU) and in moves toward a single European currency.

The landscape

The plains of northern Germany, the volcanic plateaus and mountains of the central uplands, and the Bavarian Alps are the three principal geographic regions in Germany. North to south the land rises steadily from barely 300 ft (90 m) in the plains to 6500 ft (2000 m) in the Bavarian Alps, which are a small but distinct region in the far south.

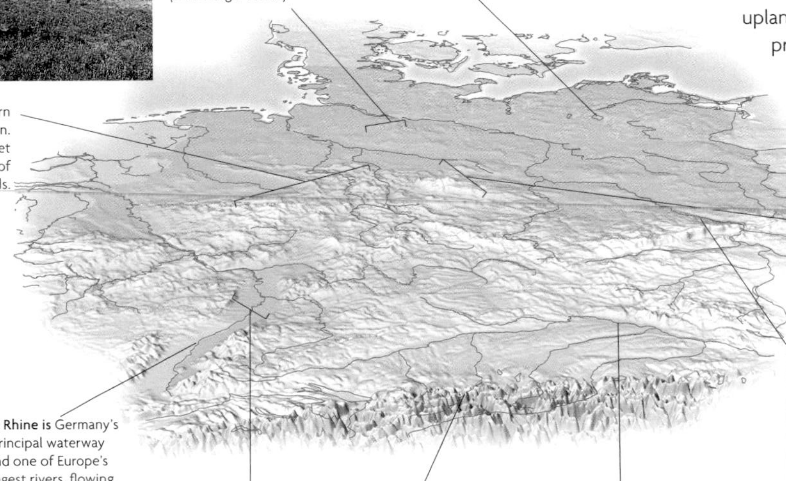

Müritz lake covers 45 sq miles (117 sq km), but is only 108 ft (33 m) deep. It lies in a shallow valley formed by meltwater flowing out from a retreating ice sheet. These valleys are known as *Urstromtäler*.

The Harz Mountains were formed 300 million years ago. They are block-faulted mountains, formed when a section of the Earth's crust was thrust up between two faults.

The Danube rises in the Black Forest (*Schwarzwald*) and flows east, across a wide valley, on its course to the Black Sea.

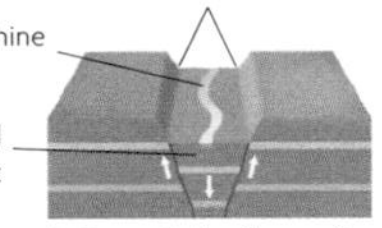

Zugspitze, the highest peak in Germany at 9719 ft (2962 m), was formed during the Alpine mountain-building period, 30 million years ago.

The Rhine is Germany's principal waterway and one of Europe's longest rivers, flowing 820 miles (1320 km).

Rhine Rift Valley

▲ **Part of the** floor of the Rhine Rift Valley was let down between two parallel faults in the Earth's crust.

Fault lines
Rhine
Downfaulted block

Much of the landscape of northern Germany has been shaped by glaciation. During the last Ice Age, the ice sheet advanced as far the northern slopes of the central uplands.

▲ **The heathlands of** northern Germany are covered by glacial deposits of sandy outwash soil which makes them largely infertile. They support only sheep and solitary trees.

Lüneburg Heath (Lüneburger Heide)

▲ *The Elbe flows in wide meanders across the north German plain to the North Sea. At its mouth it is 10 miles (16 km) wide.*

Elbe river

92
96
98
110

Scale 1:2,500,000

projection: Lambert Conformal Conic

Using the land

Germany has a large, efficient agricultural sector, and produces more than three-quarters of its own food. The major crops grown are cereals and sugar beet on the more fertile soils, and root crops, rye, oats, and fodder on the poorer soils of the northern plains and central uplands. Southern Germany is also a principal producer of high quality wines. Vineyards cover the slopes surrounding the Rhine and its tributaries.

Land use and agricultural distribution

cattle
pigs
cereals
sugar beet
vineyards

● capital cities
● major towns

pasture
cropland
forest

The urban/rural population divide

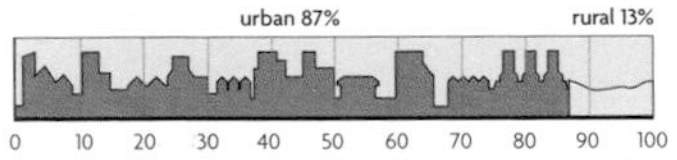

urban 87% rural 13%

Population density	
612 people per sq mile (236 people per sq km)	

Total land area	
13,804 sq miles (356,910 sq km)	

▲ *The Moselle river flows through the Rhine State Uplands (Rheinisches Schiefergebirge). During a period of uplift, preexisting river meanders were deeply incised, to form its present dramatic contours.*

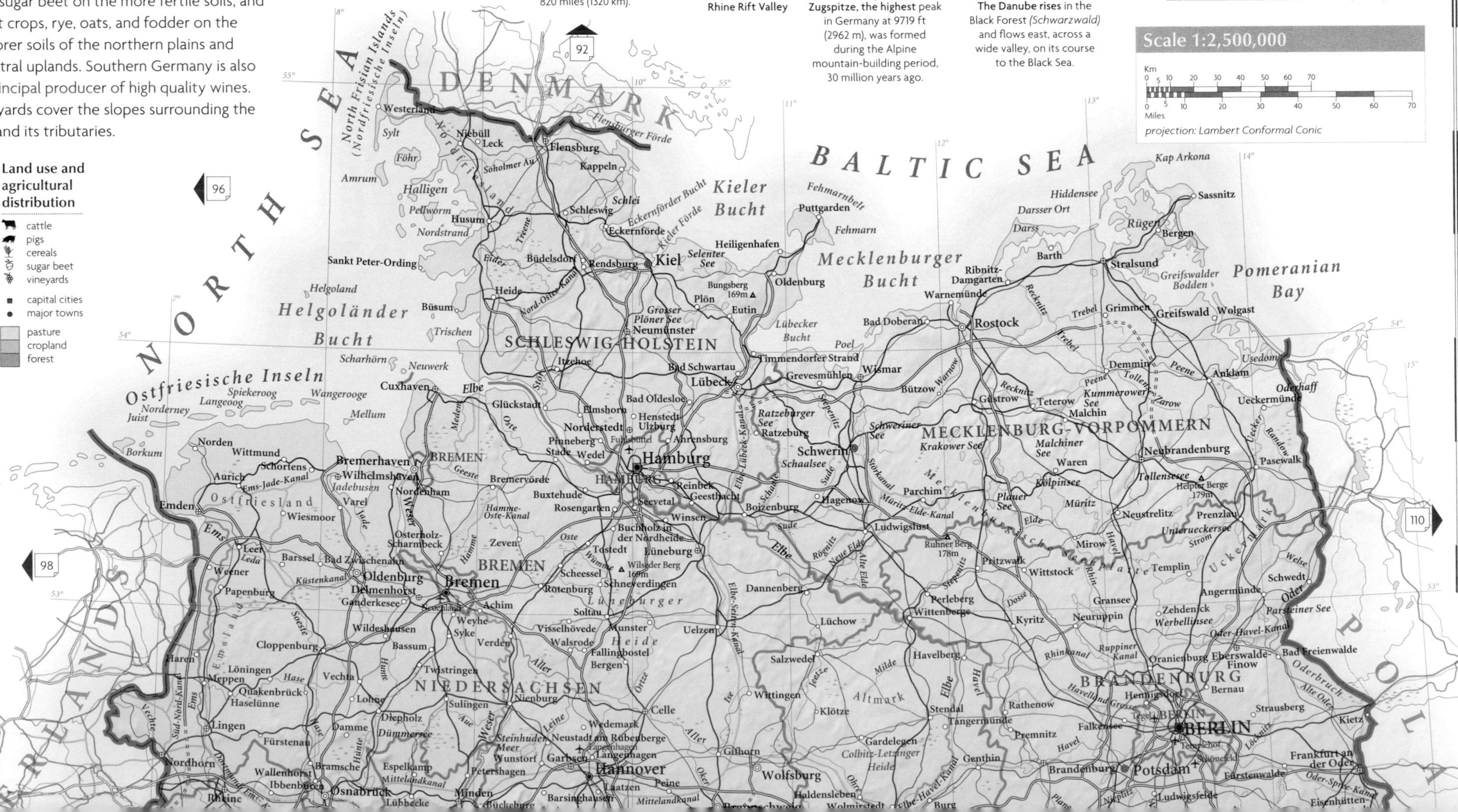

Map place names

POLAND
BALTIC SEA
DENMARK
CZECH REPUBLIC
AUSTRIA
SWITZ.
FRANCE
BELG.
LUX.
NETHERLANDS
NORTH SEA

BERLIN
Hamburg
Bremen
Leipzig
Dresden
Dortmund
Essen
Düsseldorf
Cologne
Frankfurt am Main
Nürnberg
Stuttgart
Saarbrücken
Munich

BALTIC SEA
NORTH SEA
Pomeranian Bay
POLAND

MECKLENBURG-VORPOMMERN
SCHLESWIG-HOLSTEIN
NIEDERSACHSEN
BRANDENBURG
BREMEN
BERLIN

DENMARK

North Frisian Islands (*Nordfriesische Inseln*)
Ostfriesische Inseln
Helgoländer Bucht
Kieler Bucht
Mecklenburger Bucht

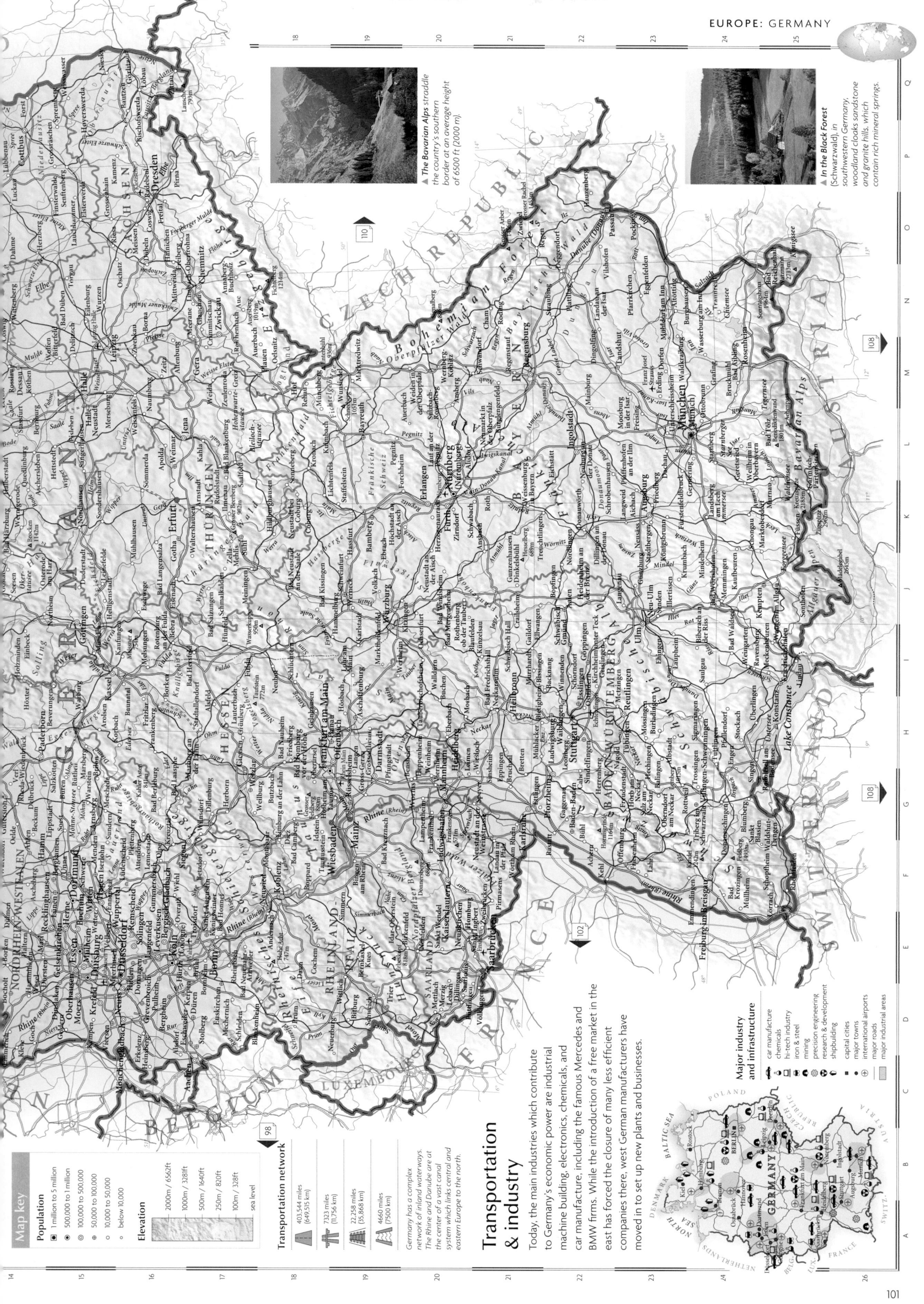

▲ The Bavarian Alps straddle the country's southern border at an average height of 6500 ft (2000 m).

▲ In the Black Forest (Schwarzwald), in southwestern Germany, woodland clocks sandstone and granite hills, which contain rich mineral springs.

Transportation & industry

Today, the main industries which contribute to Germany's economic power are industrial machine building, electronics, chemicals, and car manufacture, including the famous Mercedes and BMW firms. While the introduction of a free market in the east has forced the closure of many less efficient companies there, west German manufacturers have moved in to set up new plants and businesses.

Germany has a complex network of inland waterways. The Rhine and Danube are at the center of a vast canal system which links central and eastern Europe to the north.

Transportation network

403,544 miles (649,515 km)

7333 miles (11,756 km)

22,258 miles (35,868 km)

4660 miles (7500 km)

Map key

Population

- 1 million to 5 million
- 500,000 to 1 million
- 100,000 to 500,000
- 50,000 to 100,000
- 10,000 to 50,000
- below 10,000

Elevation

- 2000m / 6562ft
- 1000m / 3281ft
- 500m / 1640ft
- 250m / 820ft
- 100m / 328ft
- sea level

Major industry and infrastructure

- car manufacture
- chemicals
- hi-tech industry
- iron & steel
- mining
- precision engineering
- research & development
- shipbuilding
- capital cities
- major cities
- major towns
- international airports
- major roads
- major industrial areas

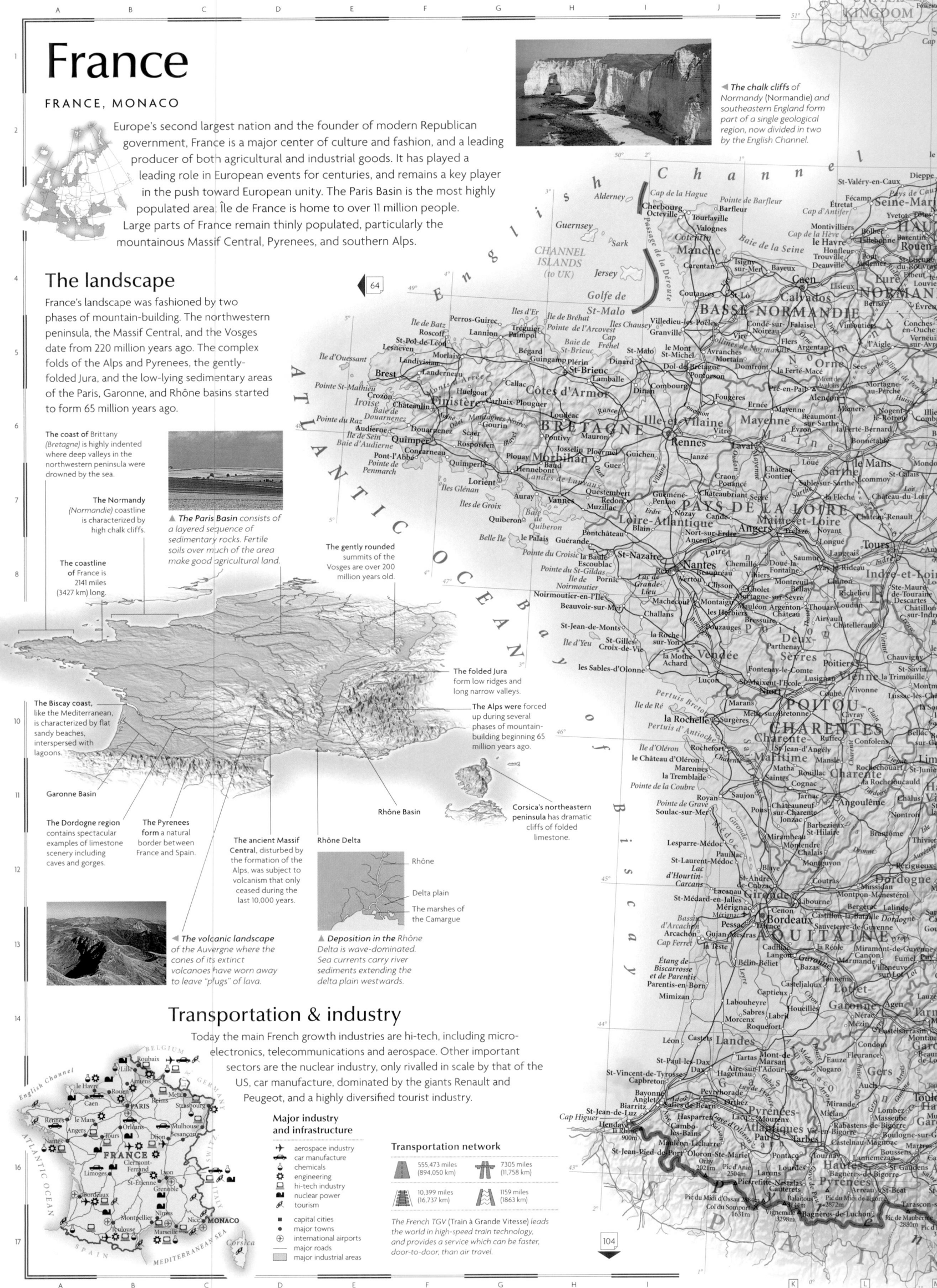

France

FRANCE, MONACO

Europe's second largest nation and the founder of modern Republican government, France is a major center of culture and fashion, and a leading producer of both agricultural and industrial goods. It has played a leading role in European events for centuries, and remains a key player in the push toward European unity. The Paris Basin is the most highly populated area. Île de France is home to over 11 million people. Large parts of France remain thinly populated, particularly the mountainous Massif Central, Pyrenees, and southern Alps.

◄ *The chalk cliffs* of Normandy (Normandie) and southeastern England form part of a single geological region, now divided in two by the English Channel.

The landscape

France's landscape was fashioned by two phases of mountain-building. The northwestern peninsula, the Massif Central, and the Vosges date from 220 million years ago. The complex folds of the Alps and Pyrenees, the gently-folded Jura, and the low-lying sedimentary areas of the Paris, Garonne, and Rhône basins started to form 65 million years ago.

The coast of Brittany (Bretagne) is highly indented where deep valleys in the northwestern peninsula were drowned by the sea.

The Normandy (Normandie) coastline is characterized by high chalk cliffs.

The coastline of France is 2141 miles (3427 km) long.

▲ *The Paris Basin* consists of a layered sequence of sedimentary rocks. Fertile soils over much of the area make good agricultural land.

The gently rounded summits of the Vosges are over 200 million years old.

The folded Jura form low ridges and long narrow valleys.

The Alps were forced up during several phases of mountain-building beginning 65 million years ago.

Corsica's northeastern peninsula has dramatic cliffs of folded limestone.

The Biscay coast, like the Mediterranean, is characterized by flat sandy beaches, interspersed with lagoons.

Garonne Basin

The Dordogne region contains spectacular examples of limestone scenery including caves and gorges.

The Pyrenees form a natural border between France and Spain.

The ancient Massif Central, disturbed by the formation of the Alps, was subject to volcanism that only ceased during the last 10,000 years.

Rhône Basin

Rhône Delta

Rhône
Delta plain
The marshes of the Camargue

◄ *The volcanic landscape* of the Auvergne where the cones of its extinct volcanoes have worn away to leave "plugs" of lava.

▲ *Deposition in the* Rhône Delta is wave-dominated. Sea currents carry river sediments extending the delta plain westwards.

Transportation & industry

Today the main French growth industries are hi-tech, including micro-electronics, telecommunications and aerospace. Other important sectors are the nuclear industry, only rivalled in scale by that of the US, car manufacture, dominated by the giants Renault and Peugeot, and a highly diversified tourist industry.

Major industry and infrastructure

✈ aerospace industry
🚗 car manufacture
⚗ chemicals
⚙ engineering
💻 hi-tech industry
⚛ nuclear power
🌴 tourism

■ capital cities
• major towns
⊕ international airports
— major roads
▨ major industrial areas

Transportation network

555,473 miles (894,050 km)	7305 miles (11,758 km)
10,399 miles (16,737 km)	1159 miles (1863 km)

The French TGV (Train à Grande Vitesse) leads the world in high-speed train technology, and provides a service which can be faster, door-to-door, than air travel.

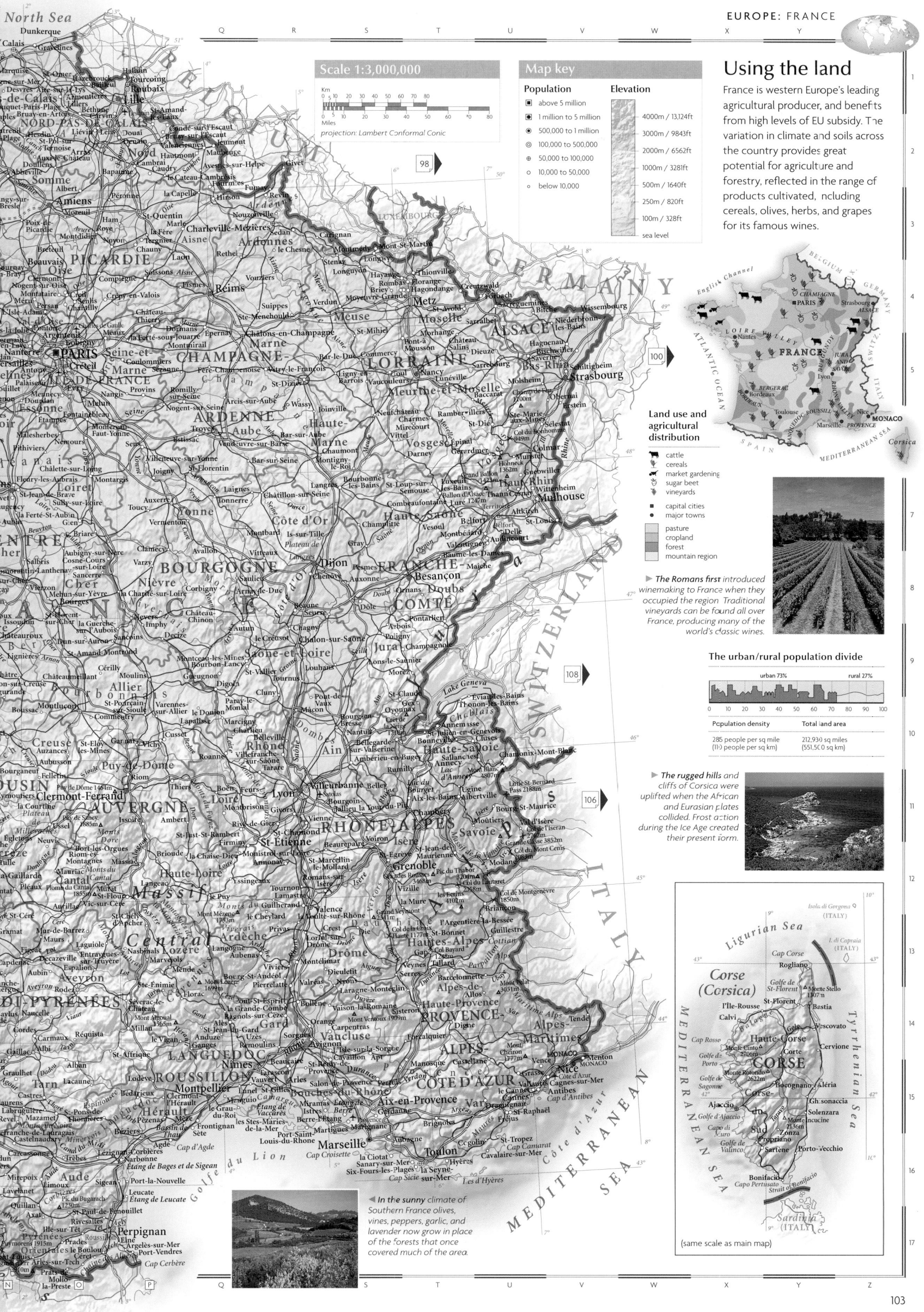

Using the land

France is western Europe's leading agricultural producer, and benefits from high levels of EU subsidy. The variation in climate and soils across the country provides great potential for agriculture and forestry, reflected in the range of products cultivated, including cereals, olives, herbs, and grapes for its famous wines.

Land use and agricultural distribution

- cattle
- cereals
- market gardening
- sugar beet
- vineyards
- ■ capital cities
- ● major towns
- pasture
- cropland
- forest
- mountain region

► *The Romans first* introduced winemaking to France when they occupied the region. Traditional vineyards can be found all over France, producing many of the world's classic wines.

The urban/rural population divide

urban 73%	rural 27%

Population density	Total land area
285 people per sq mile (110 people per sq km)	212,930 sq miles (551,500 sq km)

► *The rugged hills* and cliffs of Corsica were uplifted when the African and Eurasian plates collided. Frost action during the Ice Age created their present form.

◄ *In the sunny* climate of Southern France olives, vines, peppers, garlic, and lavender now grow in place of the forests that once covered much of the area.

Scale 1:3,000,000

projection: Lambert Conformal Conic

Map key

Population

- ■ above 5 million
- ■ 1 million to 5 million
- ◉ 500,000 to 1 million
- ◎ 100,000 to 500,000
- ⊕ 50,000 to 100,000
- ○ 10,000 to 50,000
- • below 10,000

Elevation

- 4000m / 13,124ft
- 3000m / 9843ft
- 2000m / 6562ft
- 1000m / 3281ft
- 500m / 1640ft
- 250m / 820ft
- 100m / 328ft
- sea level

(same scale as main map)

The Iberian peninsula

ANDORRA, GIBRALTAR, PORTUGAL,
SPAIN (Azores, Canary Islands, Madeira on p.64)

The Iberian peninsula is separated from the rest of
Europe by the Pyrenees, and at its most southerly
point is only 5 miles (8 km) from North Africa.
The location of Iberia has been central to its
diverse history. The Greeks, Carthaginians, Romans,
Visigoths, and most recently the Moors, invaded
Iberia at various times. For much of the 20th century,
both Spain and Portugal were governed by right-wing
dictators. Since the establishment of democratic governments in the
mid-1970s, modernization has been rapid and both countries are now
among the most popular of European holiday destinations.

Using the land

The principal crops grown in Iberia are
cereals, especially wheat and barley. Both
countries are major wine producers, most
notably of Rioja, sherry, and port. Sheep
are kept throughout the region, and citrus
fruits thrive on the Mediterranean coast.
The successful forest industry in Iberia
produces 84% of the world's cork.

▲ *The steep, terraced slopes of the
Douro Valley in northern Portugal,
are used to cultivate vines. The
grapes harvested produce
Portugal's famous port wine.*

Land use and agricultural distribution

- sheep
- cereals
- citrus fruit
- olives
- vineyards
- cork
- capital cities
- major towns

pasture
cropland
forest
mountain region

The urban/rural population divide

urban 68%   rural 32%

0 10 20 30 40 50 60 70 80 90 100

Population density	Total land area
215 people per sq mile (83 people per sq km)	230,569 sq miles (597,170 sq km)

Transportation & industry

Since the 1970s, the economies of Spain and Portugal
have expanded and diversified. In both countries,
tourism has outstripped agriculture in economic
importance. Spain's resource base is varied, including
coal, iron, and the world's largest reserves of mercury.
Portugal is a leading producer of tungsten ore.

Major industry and infrastructure

- car manufacture
- chemicals
- engineering
- fish processing
- mining
- textiles
- tourism
- capital cities
- major towns
- international airports
- major roads
- major industrial areas

Transportation network

241,720 miles (388,990 km)	1552 miles (2529 km)
11,793 miles (18,979 km)	1159 miles (1865 km)

*Radiating from Madrid, the road network in
Spain dates from the 18th century, but now
includes many highways. Portugal's road
system has been completely modernized in
recent years.*

◄ *The eroded cliffs of the
Algarve in southern Portugal
were carved by Atlantic waves.
The numerous rocky bays and
beaches, and the region's
pleasant climate, have made it
a popular tourist destination.*

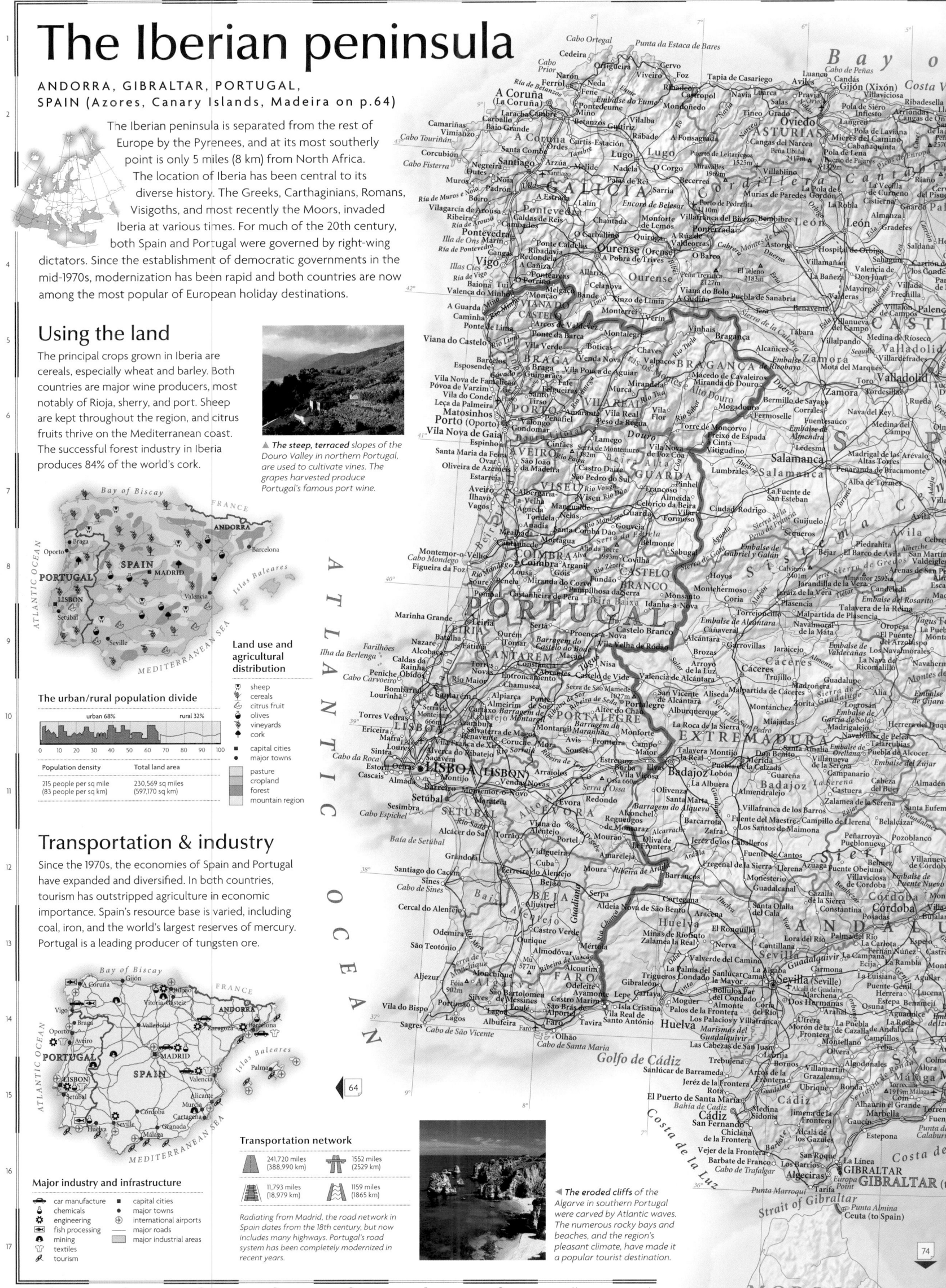

▶ **The climate in** northwestern Spain is milder in both summer and winter than in the rest of the country, creating a verdant environment, more commonly associated with northwestern Europe.

Map key

Population

- ▣ 1 million to 5 million
- ◉ 500,000 to 1 million
- ◎ 100,000 to 500,000
- ⊕ 50,000 to 100,000
- ○ 10,000 to 50,000
- ∘ below 10,000

Elevation

3000m / 9843ft
2000m / 6562ft
1000m / 3281ft
500m / 1640ft
250m / 820ft
100m / 328ft
sea level

Scale 1:3,000,000

Km 0 10 20 30 40 50 60 70 80

Miles 0 10 20 30 40 50 60 70 80

projection: Lambert Conformal Conic

The landscape

A vast plateau, the Meseta dominates the centre of the peninsula, enclosed by the Cordillera Cantábrica to the north and the Sierra Morena to the south. It is drained by three major rivers, the Douro/Duero, the Tagus, and the Guadalquivir. The peninsula experiences great variations in climate and rainfall, both regionally and locally.

▲ **The Pyrenees form** Iberia's northeastern boundary, running for 270 miles (440 km), dividing the peninsula from the rest of Europe.

The Ebro river has formed the peninsula's largest delta. Recently, sediment flows have been seriously disturbed by nearby reservoirs.

On the northeastern coast sea level changes are evident from wave-cut beaches which rise up to 200 ft (60 m) above the present sea level.

Cordillera Cantábrica

Douro/Duero river

The Meseta plateau averages 1970 ft (600 m) in height and is now largely dry and treeless.

Tagus River

Mountain front

Weathered material

Pediment

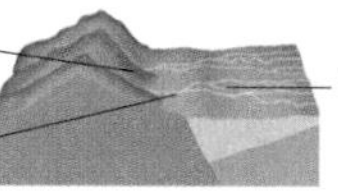

▲ **Pediments are characteristic** of semiarid lands across Iberia. A pediment is a flat, low-lying, eroded platform, cut into the bedrock. Weathered material is transported by streams and deposited in broad fan shapes on the pediment.

The Guadalquivir river brings vital irrigation water to the plains, and like many of Iberia's rivers, is prone to flooding.

Sierra Morena

The Sierra Nevada in southern Spain contain Iberia's highest peak, Mulhacén, which rises 11,418 ft (3481 m).

The Balearic Islands (Islas Baleares) are characterized by jagged limestones and plains.

▶ **In the Sierra de los Filabres** deforestation and overgrazing, which cause soil erosion, have created semidesert badlands.

105

The Italian peninsula

ITALY, SAN MARINO, VATICAN CITY

The Italian peninsula is a land of great contrasts. Until unification in 1861, Italy was a collection of independent states, whose competitiveness during the Renaissance resulted in the architectural and artistic magnificence of cities such as Rome, Florence, and Venice. The majority of Italy's population and economic activity is concentrated in the north, centered on the sophisticated industrial city of Milan. Southern Italy, the *Mezzogiorno*, has a harsh terrain, and remains far less developed than the north. Attempts to attract industry and investment in the south are frequently deterred by the entrenched network of organized crime and corruption.

The landscape

The mainly mountainous and hilly Italian peninsula took its present form following a collision between the African and Eurasian tectonic plates. The Alps in the northwest rise to a high point of 15,772 ft (4807 m) at Mont Blanc (*Monte Bianco*) on the French border, while the Apennines (*Appennino*) form a rugged backbone, running along the entire length of the country.

Mont Blanc
(*Monte Bianco*)

▲ *The island of Sardinia is an ancient land mass; an uplifted section of very old igneous rocks. Its rugged mountainous regions provide pasture for sheep and goats, while its valleys support some agriculture.*

Costa Smeralda

▲ *The Dolomites* (Alpi Dolomitiche) *are formed of thick limestones, overlying weaker marine strata. They have distinctive serrated peaks and many massive landslides occur.*

The distinctive square shape of the Gulf of Taranto (Golfo di Taranto) was defined by numerous block faults. Earthquakes are common in this region.

The Strait of Messina (Stretto di Messina) *is between 2 and 12 miles (3–19 km) wide, and is a rich fishing ground.*

Vesuvius (*Vesuvio*)

The Pontine Marshes (Agro Pontino) *are bounded by low sand hills which prevent natural drainage.*

The Apennines (Appennino) *are the source of most of Italy's rivers. They run 823 miles (1324 km) down the length of the peninsula.*

Sicily is the largest island in the Mediterranean at 9926 sq miles (25,708 sq km).

The southwestern tip of Sicily lies 95 miles (152 km) from the north African mainland and is part of the same geological region.

The Po Valley once formed part of the Adriatic Sea. Sediments of gravel, sand, and clay washed down from the Alps gradually filling the bay and forming a broad, cultivable plain.

Sardinia is the second largest island in the Mediterranean Sea. The highest point is Punta La Marmora at 6607 ft (1834 m).

Present-day crater has developed within the old crater of Monte Somma

▲ *There have been four volcanoes on the site of Vesuvius since volcanic activity began here more than 10,000 years ago.*

Vesuvius (*Vesuvio*)

Monte Somma

Old crater

Using the land

Italy produces 95% of its own food. The best farming land is in the Po Valley in northern Italy, where soft wheat and rice are grown. Irrigation is essential to agriculture in much of the south. Italy is a major producer and exporter of citrus fruits, olives, tomatoes, and wine.

The urban/rural population divide

urban 67%   rural 33%

Population density
506 people per sq mile
(195 people per sq km)

Total land area
116,320 sq miles
(301,270 sq km)

Land use and agricultural distribution

- cattle
- cereals
- citrus fruits
- olive oil
- rice

- capital cities
- major towns
- pasture
- cropland
- forest

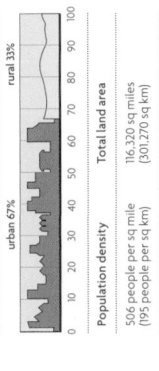
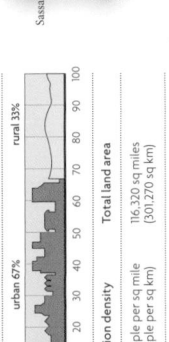

Scale 1:2,750,000

Projection: Lambert Conformal Conic

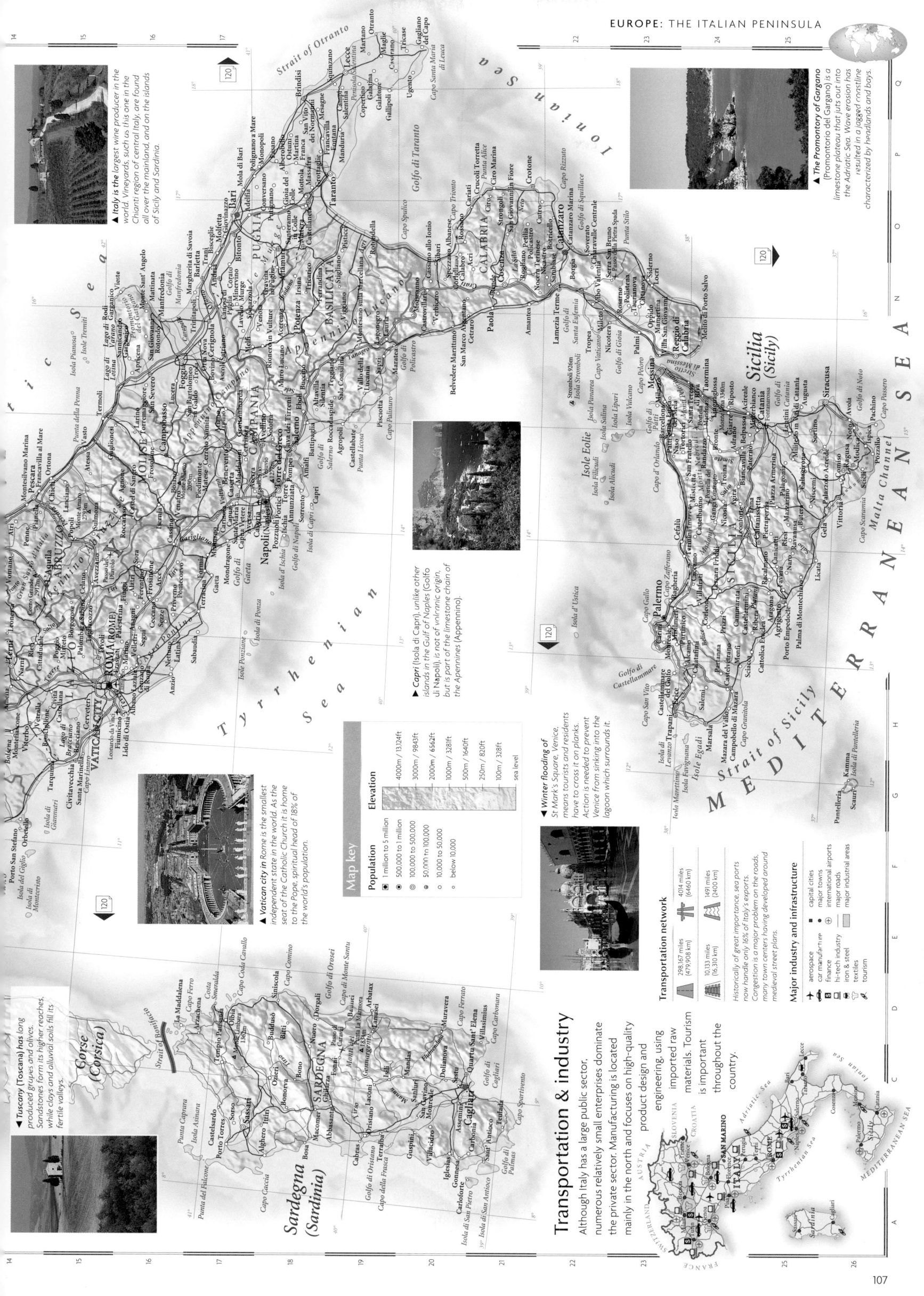

▲ **Italy is the** largest wine producer in the world. Vineyards, such as this one in the Chianti region of central Italy, are found all over the mainland, and on the islands of Sicily and Sardinia.

▲ **The Promontory of Gargano** (Promontorio del Gargano) is a limestone plateau that juts out into the Adriatic Sea. Wave erosion has resulted in a jagged coastline characterized by headlands and bays.

▲ **Capri** (Isola di Capri), unlike other islands in the Gulf of Naples (Golfo di Napoli), is not of volcanic origin, but is part of the limestone chain of the Apennines (Appennino).

▲ **Vatican city** in Rome is the smallest independent state in the world. As the seat of the Catholic Church it is home to the Pope, spiritual head of 18% of the world's population.

▼ **Winter flooding of** St Mark's Square, Venice, means tourists and residents have to cross it on planks. Action is needed to prevent Venice from sinking into the lagoon which surrounds it.

▼ **Tuscany (Toscana) has** long produced grapes and olives. Sandstones form its higher reaches, while clays and alluvial soils fill its fertile valleys.

Map key

Population

- ◉ 1 million to 5 million
- ◎ 500,000 to 1 million
- ⊙ 100,000 to 500,000
- ⊚ 50,000 to 100,000
- ○ 10,000 to 50,000
- ○ below 10,000

Elevation

- 4000m / 13124ft
- 3000m / 9843ft
- 2000m / 6562ft
- 1000m / 3281ft
- 500m / 1640ft
- 250m / 820ft
- 100m / 328ft
- sea level

Transportation & industry

Although Italy has a large public sector, numerous relatively small enterprises dominate the private sector. Manufacturing is located mainly in the north and focuses on high-quality product design and engineering, using imported raw materials. Tourism is important throughout the country.

Transportation network

- 298,167 miles (479,908 km)
- 4014 miles (6460 km)
- 10,133 miles (16,310 km)
- 1491 miles (2400 km)

Historically of great importance, sea ports now handle only 16% of Italy's exports. Congestion is a major problem on the roads, many town centers having developed around medieval street plans.

Major industry and infrastructure

- capital cities
- major towns
- international airports
- major roads
- major industrial areas

- aerospace
- car manufacture
- finance
- hi-tech industry
- iron & steel
- textiles
- tourism

The Alpine states

AUSTRIA, LIECHTENSTEIN, SLOVENIA, SWITZERLAND

The Alpine countries of Austria, Switzerland, Liechtenstein, and Slovenia form a narrow strip across western Europe's geographical core, lying on the main north–south trading routes across the Alps. Switzerland, politically neutral since 1815, is an important international meeting place and houses one of the headquarters of the United Nations, it only became a member in 2002. Austria, once at the heart of the great Habsburg Empire has been a fully independent nation since 1955, and maintains a deserved reputation as an international center of culture. Slovenia declared independence from the former Yugoslavia in 1991 and despite initial economic hardship, is now starting to achieve the prosperity enjoyed by its Alpine neighbors.

Using the land

The Alpine region's mountainous terrain discourages cultivation over much of the land area. The primary agricultural activity is the raising of dairy and beef cattle on the pasture land of the lower mountain slopes. Austria is self-supporting in grains, and crops such as wheat, barley, and grapes are grown on the east Austrian lowlands. Woodlands are more prevalent in the eastern Alps; both Austria and Slovenia have large tracts of forest.

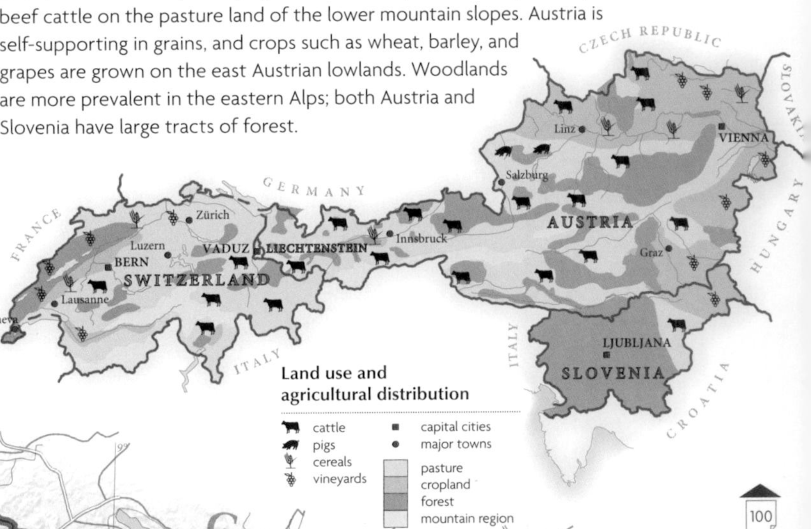

Land use and agricultural distribution

- cattle
- pigs
- cereals
- vineyards
- capital cities
- major towns
- pasture
- cropland
- forest
- mountain region

◀ **The Matterhorn**, on the Swiss-Italian border, is one of the highest mountains in the Alps, at 14,692 ft (4478 m). The term "horn" refers to its distinctive peak, formed by three glaciers eroding hollows, known as cirques, in each of its sides.

The landscape

The Alps occupy three-fifths of Switzerland, most of southern Austria and the northwest of Slovenia. They were formed by the collision of the African and Eurasian tectonic plates, which began 65 million years ago. Their complex geology is reflected in the differing heights and rock types of the various ranges. The Rhine flows along Liechtenstein's border with Switzerland, creating a broad floodplain in the north and west of Liechtenstein. In the far northeast and east are a number of lowland regions, including the Vienna Basin, Burgenland, and the plain of the Danube. Slovenia's major rivers largely flow across the lower eastern regions; in the west, the rivers flow underground through the limestone Karst region.

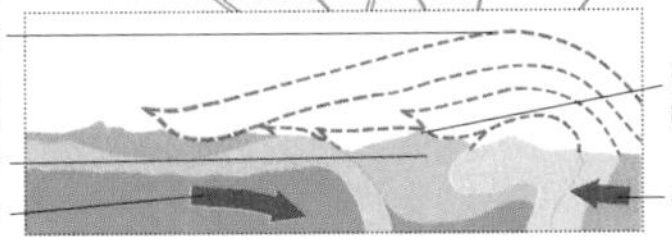

Original height after uplift and folding

Folded strata are overturned creating a nappe

Eurasian Plate

Present-day height of Alps

African Plate

▲ **The convergence of** the African and Eurasian plates compressed and folded huge masses of rock strata. As the plates continued to move together, the folded strata were overturned, creating complex nappes. Much of the rock strata has since been eroded, resulting in the current topography of the Alps.

▲ **Constricted as it** cuts through ridges in the Alps, the Danube meanders across the lowlands, where uplift combined with river erosion has deepened meanders.

The **Vienna Basin** lies mainly below 390 ft (120 m). It gradually subsided and filled with sediment as the Alps were uplifted.

Neusiedler See straddles the border of Austria and Hungary; the area around it provides some of the best wine-growing land in Austria.

The **Austrian Alps** comprise three distinct mountain ranges, separated by deep trenches. The northern and southern ranges are rugged limestones, while the Tauern range is formed of crystalline rocks.

The **Tauern range** in the central Austrian Alps contains the highest mountain in Austria, the towering Grossglockner, rising 12,461 ft (3798 m).

The **limestone cave** system at Postojna extends for more than 10 miles (16 km) and includes caverns reaching 125 ft (40 m) in height and width.

▶ **The deep, blue** lakes of the Karst region are part of a drainage network which runs largely underground through this limestone area.

The first road through the Brenner Pass was built in 1772, although it has been used as a mountain route since Roman times. It is the lowest of the main Alpine passes at 4298 ft (1374 m).

The Rhine, like other major Alpine rivers, follows a broad, flat trough between the mountains. Along part of its course, the Rhine forms the boundary between Switzerland and Liechtenstein.

The Bernese Alps (Berner Alpen) contain the Aletsch, which at 15 miles (24 km) is the longest Alpine glacier.

Tectonic activity has resulted in dramatic changes in land height over very short distances. Lake Geneva, lying at 1221 ft (372 m) is only 43 miles (70 km) away from the 15,772 ft (4807 m) peak of Mont Blanc, on the France–Italy border.

The mountains of the Jura form a natural border between Switzerland and France. Their marine limestones date from over 200 million years ago. When the Alps were formed the Jura were folded into a series of parallel ridges and troughs.

Karst region

The urban/rural population divide

urban 66%   rural 34%

Population density	Total land area	
314 people per sq mile (121 people per sq km)	56,135 sq miles (145,390 sq km)	

◀ *In this mountainous region, the flatter, more accessible areas are often used for both cattle grazing and recreation.*

◀ *These converging glaciers are marked by dark lines of moraine. This eroded material is carried by glaciers, and deposited as the ice melts.*

Scale 1:2,000,000

projection: Lambert Conformal Conic

Transportation & industry

All four nations concentrate on high-quality manufacturing and services. Austrian iron and steel production is complemented by construction industries; and Slovenia, traditionally the industrial powerhouse of the western Balkans has increasingly diversified industries. Liechtenstein and Switzerland, lacking raw materials, produce pharmaceuticals and precision instruments, such as watches, and act as international banking centers. The spectacular scenery of the region encourages tourism all year round.

Transportation network

181,107 miles (291,497 km)	2116 miles (3405 km)
6368 miles (10,249 km)	993 miles (1598 km)

Tunnels and passes through the Alps are an important feature of this region. The NEAT project, providing two new high-speed rail links between Basel and Milan, was given approval in 1992.

▶ *The Austrian Tirol contains some of the most spectacular Alpine scenery. Snow cover is a permanent feature in the highest reaches.*

Map key

Population

◉	1 million to 5 million
◉	500,000 to 1 million
◎	100,000 to 500,000
⊕	50,000 to 100,000
⊙	10,000 to 50,000
∘	below 10,000

Elevation

4000m / 13,124ft	
3000m / 9843ft	
2000m / 6562ft	
1000m / 3281ft	
500m / 1640ft	
250m / 820ft	
100m / 328ft	
sea level	

Major industry and infrastructure

🚗	car manufacture
⚗	chemicals
⚙	engineering
S	finance
	food processing
	iron & steel
	pharmaceuticals
	textiles
	tourism
	watch making
	winter sports
■	capital cities
■	major towns
✈	international airports
—	major roads
	major industrial areas

▲ *The Schönbrunn Palace in Vienna was the summer residence of the Habsburg monarchy. Today, it is a major tourist attraction.*

Central Europe

CZECH REPUBLIC, HUNGARY, POLAND, SLOVAKIA

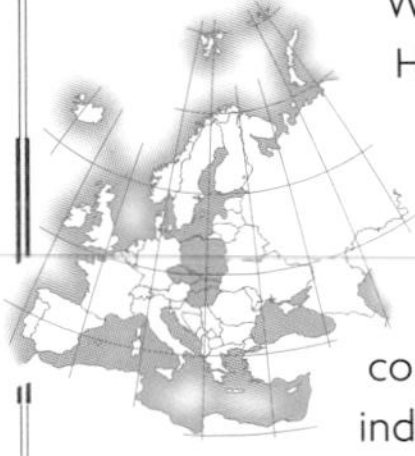

When Slovakia and the Czech Republic became separate countries in 1993, they joined Hungary and Poland in a new role as independent nation states, following centuries of shifting boundaries and imperial strife. This turbulent history bequeathed the region a rich cultural heritage, shared through the works of its many great writers and composers, and celebrated in the vibrant historic capitals of Prague, Budapest, and Warsaw. Having shaken off years of Soviet domination in 1989, these states are confronting the challenge of winning commercial investment to modernize outmoded industries as they integrate their economies with those of the European Union.

Transportation & industry

Heavy industry has dominated postwar life in Central Europe. Poland has large coal reserves, having inherited the Silesian coalfield from Germany after the Second World War, allowing the export of large quantities of coal, along with other minerals. Hungary specializes in consumer goods and services, while Slovakia's industrial base is still relatively small. The Czech Republic's traditional glassworks and breweries bring some stability to its precarious Soviet-built manufacturing sector.

Major industry and infrastructure

- car manufacture
- chemicals
- engineering
- food processing
- mining
- shipbuilding
- tourism

- ■ capital cities
- ● major towns
- ⊕ international airports
- — major roads
- major industrial areas

Transportation network

213,997 miles (344,600 km)	
817 miles (315 km)	
27,479 miles (44,249 km)	
3784 miles (6094 km)	

The huge growth of tourism and business has prompted major investment in the transportation infrastructure, with new roadbuilding schemes within and between the main cities of the region.

▲ Budapest, the capital of Hungary, straddles the Danube. It comprises the historic towns of Buda, on the west bank, and Pest, which contains the Parliament Building, seen here on the far bank.

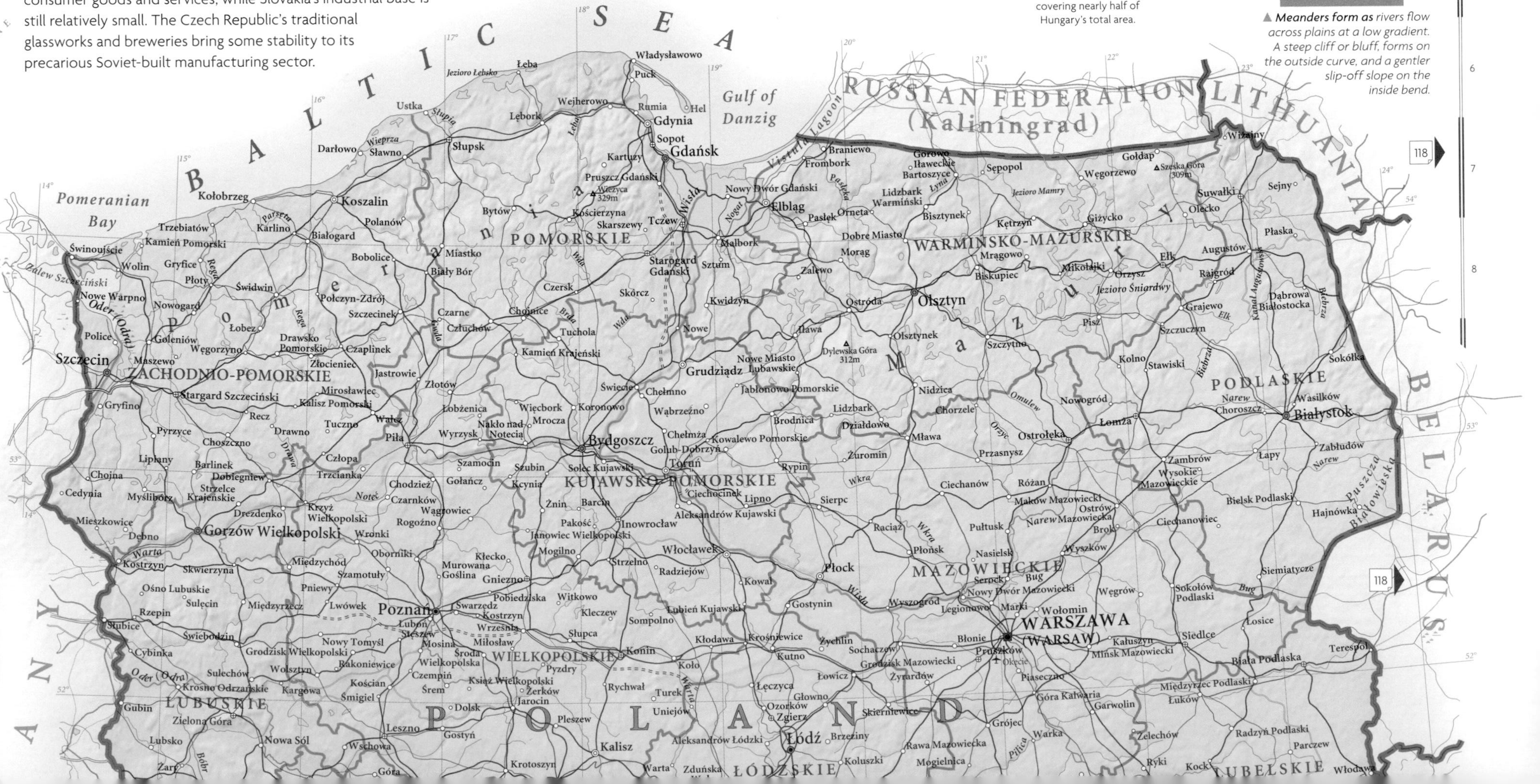

The landscape

The forested Carpathian Mountains, uplifted with the Alps, lie southeast of the older Bohemian Massif, which contains the Sudeten and Krusné Hory (Erzgebirge) ranges. They divide the fertile plains of the Danube to the south and the Vistula (Wisła), which flows north across vast expanses of glacial deposits into the Baltic Sea.

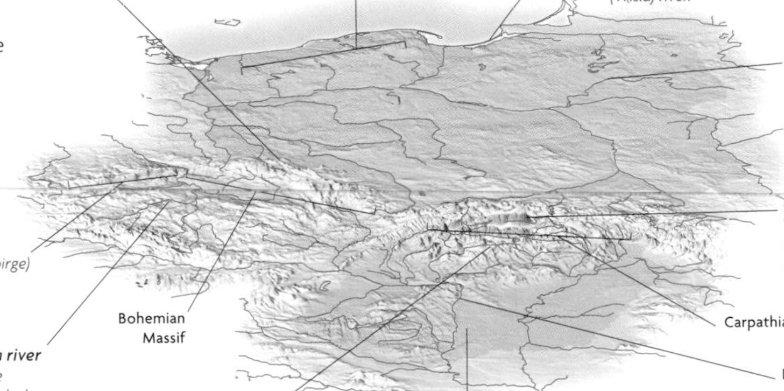

▲ The Biebrza river has left meanders and oxbow lakes as it flows across low-lying ground.

Longshore currents moving east along the Baltic coast have built a 40 mile (65 km) spit composed of material from the Vistula (Wisła) river.

Hot mineral springs occur where geothermally heated water wells up through faults and fractures in the rocks of the Sudeten Mountains.

Pomerania is a sandy coastal region of glacially-formed lakes stretching west from the Vistula (Wisła).

Gerlachovský Štít, in the Tatra Mountains, is Slovakia's highest mountain, at 8711ft (2655 m).

Carpathian Mountains

Danube river

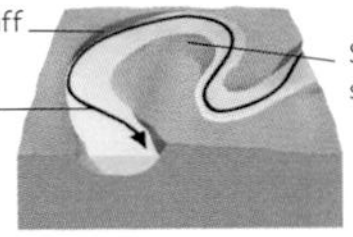

▲ Meanders form as rivers flow across plains at a low gradient. A steep cliff or bluff, forms on the outside curve, and a gentler slip-off slope on the inside bend.

Slip-off slope

Bluff

Direction of flow

The Great Hungarian Plain formed by the floodplain of the Danube is a mixture of steppe and cultivated land, covering nearly half of Hungary's total area.

The Slovak Ore Mountains (Slovenské Rudohorie) are noted for their mineral resources, including high-grade iron ore.

Bohemian Massif

Krusne Hory (Erzgebirge)

▲ The Berounka river cuts through the precipitous wooded landscape of the Bohemian Massif, banked by a broad floodplain.

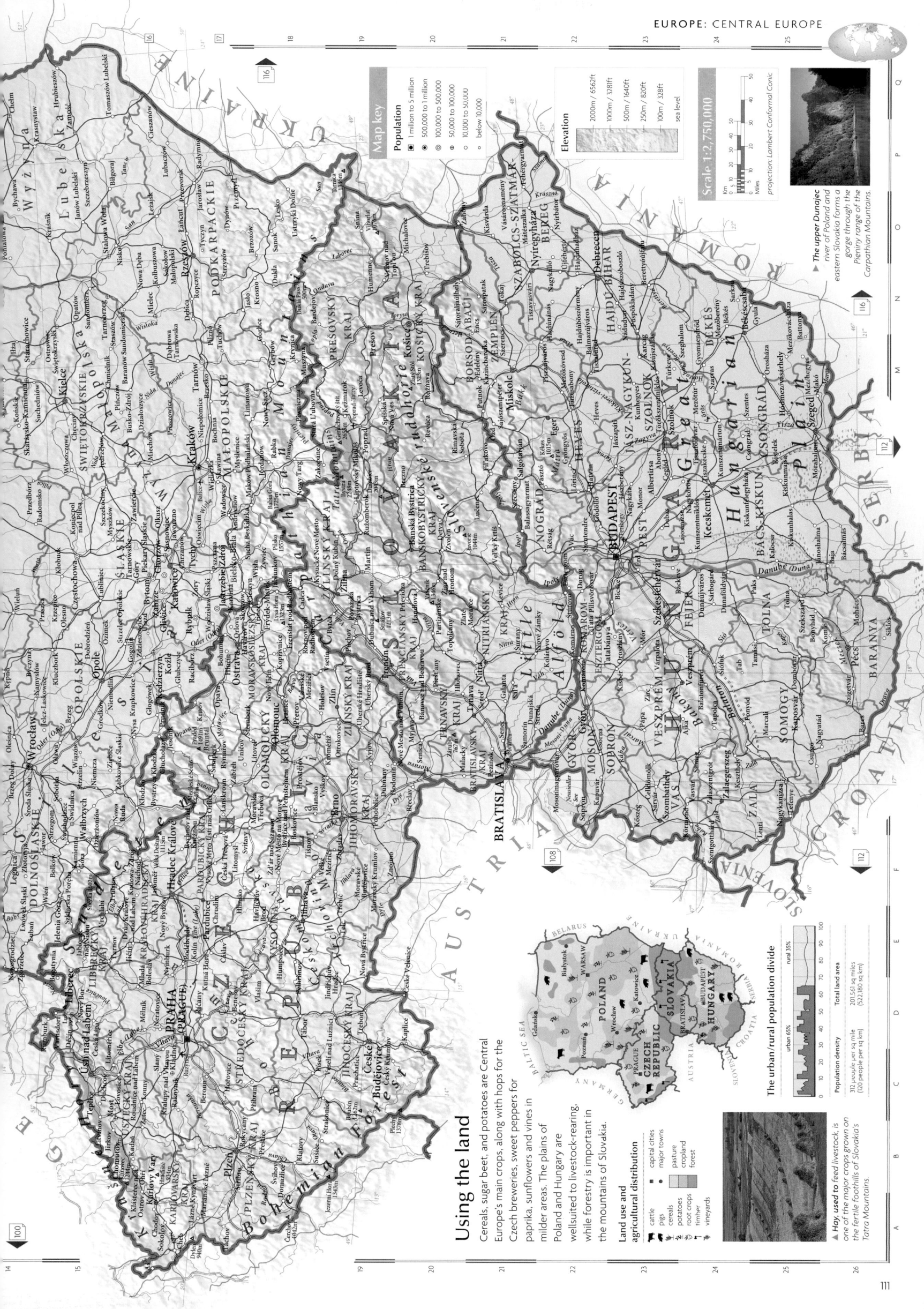

▲ The upper Dunajec river of Poland and eastern Slovakia forms a gorge through the Pieniny range of the Carpathian Mountains.

Map key

Population

◉	1 million to 5 million
◎	500,000 to 1 million
◉	100,000 to 500,000
⊕	50,000 to 100,000
⊙	10,000 to 50,000
○	below 10,000

Elevation

	2000m / 6562ft
	1000m / 3281ft
	500m / 1640ft
	250m / 820ft
	100m / 328ft
	sea level

Scale 1:2,750,000

projection: Lambert Conformal Conic

Using the land

Cereals, sugar beet, and potatoes are Central Europe's main crops, along with hops for the Czech breweries, sweet peppers for paprika, sunflowers and vines in milder areas. The plains of Poland and Hungary are wellsuited to livestock-rearing, while forestry is important in the mountains of Slovakia.

Land use and agricultural distribution

🐄	cattle	● capital cities
🐖	pigs	∘ major towns
🌾	cereals	pasture
🥔	potatoes	cropland
	root crops	forest
	timber	
	vineyards	

▲ Hay, used to feed livestock, is one of the major crops grown on the fertile foothills of Slovakia's Tatra Mountains.

The urban/rural population divide

urban 65%   rural 35%

Population density	Total land area
312 people per sq mile (120 people per sq km)	201,561 sq miles (522,180 sq km)

111

Southeast Europe

ALBANIA, BOSNIA & HERZEGOVINA, CROATIA, KOSOVO, MACEDONIA, MONTENEGRO, SERBIA

For 46 years the federation of Yugoslavia held together the most diverse ethnic region in Europe, along the picturesque mountain hinterland of the Dalmatian coast. Economic collapse resulted in internal tensions. In the early 1990s, civil war broke out in both Croatia and Bosnia as the ethnic populations struggled to establish their own exclusive territories. Peace was only restored by the UN after NATO launched air strikes in 1995. Montenegro voted to split from Serbia in 2006. More recently, Kosovo controversially declared independence from Serbia in 2008, although this may take some time to be fully recognized. Neighboring Albania is slowly improving its fragile economy but remains one of Europe's poorest nations.

The landscape

The Tisza, Sava, and Drava Rivers drain the broad northern lowland, meeting the Danube after it crosses the Hungarian border. In the west, the Dinaric Alps divide the Adriatic Sea from the interior. Mainland valleys and elongated islands run parallel to the steep Dalmatian (Dalmacija) coastline, following alternating bands of resistant limestone.

Scale 1:2,750,000

projection: Lambert Conformal Conic

▲ **Hot, dry summers** and mild winters offer excellent conditions for viticulture in Montenegro. The precipitous Dinaric Alps have kept this region relatively isolated for centuries.

Dalmatian (Dalmacija) coast

▲ **Limestone cliffs along the** Dalmatian (Dalmacija) shoreline are heavily eroded, as salt water dissolves the rock along existing horizontal cracks, or joints. This tends to form a platform of rock at the foot of the cliff.

The elongated islands, promontories and straits of the Dalmatian (Dalmacija) coast were formed as the Adriatic Sea rose to flood valleys running parallel to the shore.

Sava river

A series of river valleys breaking through the Dinaric Alps from the lowlands of western Albania, give access to the interior.

Drava river

At least 70% of the fresh water in the western Balkans drains eastward into the Black Sea, mostly via the Danube (Dunav).

The river floodplains of the Pannonian Basin are flanked by terraces of gravel and wind-blown glacial deposits known as loess.

Tisza river

At Iron Gate (Derdap), on the border with Romania, the Danube narrows and cuts through foothills of the Balkan and Carpathian mountains, forming the deepest gorge in Europe.

▲ **Rain and underground** water dissolve limestone along massive vertical joints (cracks). This creates poljes: depressions several miles across with steep walls and broad, flat floors.

Polje in the Kosovo region

Sheer limestone walls enclose all sides

Flat polje floor

Underground drainage along joints in the rock

Spring at foot of cliff

A major earthquake at Skopje, Macedonia, in 1963 killed 1000 people. The whole region lies on an active crustal plate margin.

Lake Ohrid

▲ **Lake Ohrid borders** Albania and Macedonia. Ohrid is the deepest lake in the western Balkans, reaching depths of 938 ft (286 m).

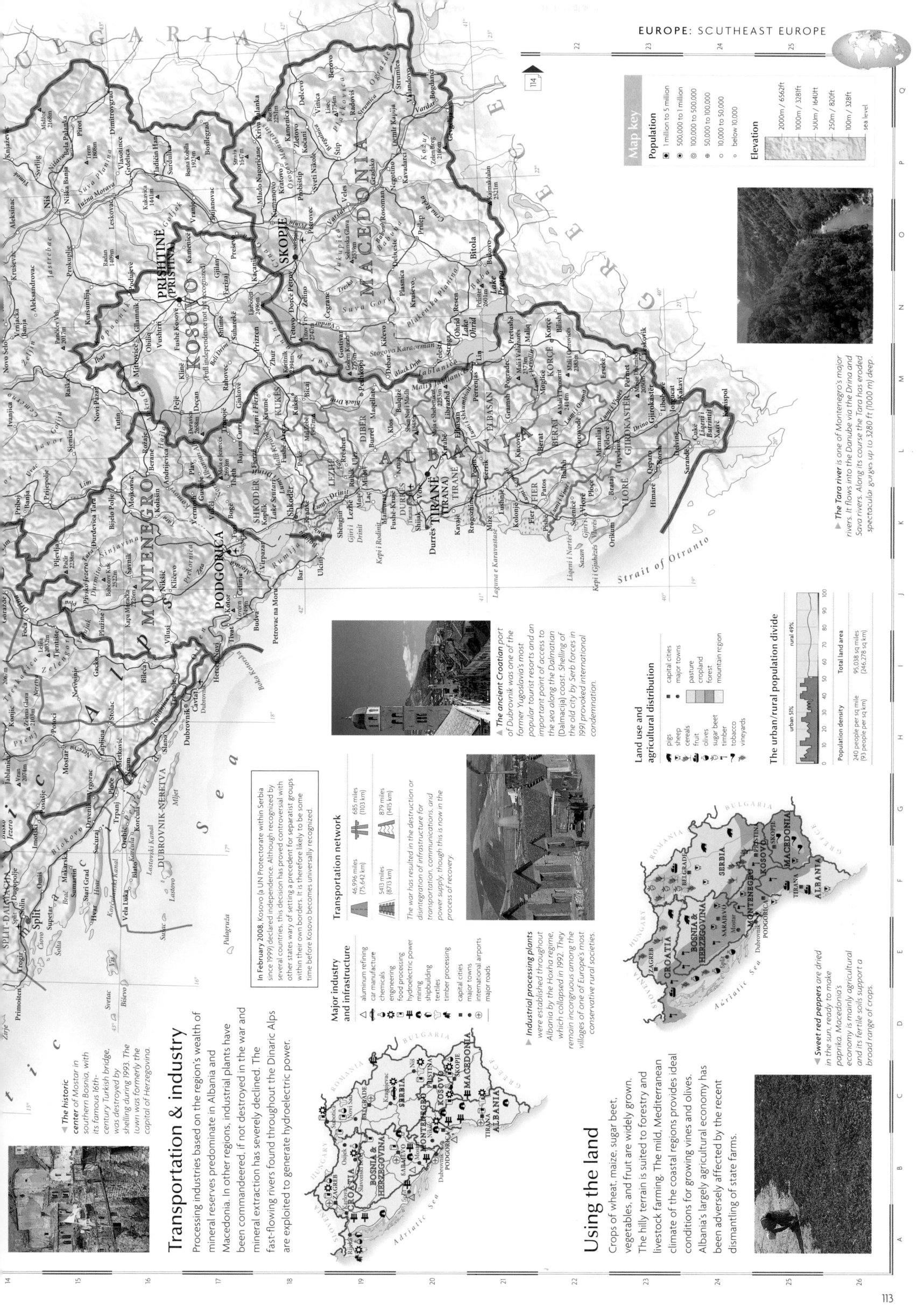

Map key

Population
- ● 1 million to 5 million
- ◉ 500,000 to 1 million
- ◎ 100,000 to 500,000
- ⊕ 50,000 to 100,000
- ○ 10,000 to 50,000
- ∘ below 10,000

Elevation
- 2000m / 6562ft
- 1000m / 3281ft
- 500m / 1640ft
- 250m / 820ft
- 100m / 328ft
- sea level

▲ *The Tara river is one of Montenegro's major rivers. It flows into the Danube via the Drina and Sava rivers. Along its course the Tara has eroded spectacular gorges up to 3280 ft (1000 m) deep.*

▲ *The ancient Croatian port of Dubrovnik was one of the former Yugoslavia's most popular tourist resorts and an important point of access to the sea along the Dalmatian (Dalmacija) coast. Shelling of the old city by Serb forces in 1991 provoked international condemnation.*

In February 2008, Kosovo (a UN Protectorate within Serbia since 1999) declared independence. Although recognized by several countries, this decision has proved controversial with other states wary of setting a precedent for separatist groups within their own borders. It is therefore likely to be some time before Kosovo becomes universally recognized.

Transportation network

46,996 miles (75,642 km)	685 miles (1103 km)
5413 miles (8713 km)	879 miles (1415 km)

The war has resulted in the destruction or disintegration of infrastructure for transportation, communications, and power supply, though this is now in the process of recovery.

Major industry and infrastructure

- aluminum refining
- car manufacture
- chemicals
- engineering
- food processing
- hydroelectric power
- mining
- shipbuilding
- textiles
- timber processing
- capital cities
- major towns
- international airports
- major roads

▲ *Industrial processing plants were established throughout Albania by the Hoxha regime, which collapsed in 1992. They remain incongruous among the villages of one of Europe's most conservative rural societies.*

Transportation & industry

Processing industries based on the region's wealth of mineral reserves predominate in Albania and Macedonia. In other regions, industrial plants have been commandeered, if not destroyed in the war and mineral extraction has severely declined. The fast-flowing rivers found throughout the Dinaric Alps are exploited to generate hydroelectric power.

▲ *The historic center of Mostar in southern Bosnia, with its famous 16th-century Turkish bridge, was destroyed by shelling during 1993. The town was formerly the capital of Herzegovina.*

Land use and agricultural distribution

- pigs
- sheep
- cereals
- fruit
- olives
- sugar beet
- tobacco
- vineyards
- capital cities
- major towns
- pasture
- cropland
- forest
- mountain region

The urban/rural population divide

urban 51% / rural 49%

Population density	Total land area
240 people per sq mile (93 people per sq km)	95,038 sq miles (246,278 sq km)

▼ *Sweet red peppers are dried in the sun, ready to make paprika. Macedonia's economy is mainly agricultural and its fertile soils support a broad range of crops.*

Using the land

Crops of wheat, maize, sugar beet, vegetables, and fruit are widely grown. The hilly terrain is suited to forestry and livestock farming. The mild, Mediterranean climate of the coastal regions provides ideal conditions for growing vines and olives. Albania's largely agricultural economy has been adversely affected by the recent dismantling of state farms.

Bulgaria & Greece

Including EUROPEAN TURKEY

Greece is renowned as the original hearth of western civilization. The rugged terrain and numerous islands have profoundly affected its development, creating a strong agricultural and maritime tradition.

In the past 50 years, this formerly rural society has rapidly urbanized, with one third of the population now living in the capital, Athens, and in the northern city of Salonica. Bulgaria, dominated for centuries by the Ottoman Turks, became part of the eastern bloc after the Second World War, only slowly emerging from Soviet influence in 1989. Moves toward democracy led to some instability in Bulgaria and Greece, now outweighed by the challenge of integration with the European Union.

Transportation & industry

Soviet investment introduced heavy industry into Bulgaria, and the processing of agricultural produce, such as tobacco, is important throughout the country. Both countries have substantial shipyards and Greece has one of the world's largest merchant fleets. Many small craft workshops, producing textiles and processed foods, are clustered around Greek cities. The service and construction sectors have profited from the successful tourist industry.

Major industry and infrastructure

- chemicals
- engineering
- food processing
- shipbuilding
- textiles
- tourism
- capital cities
- major towns
- international airports
- major roads
- major industrial areas

Transportation network

103,930 miles (167,630 km)	
345 miles (557 km)	
4346 miles (6995 km)	
294 miles (474 km)	

Bulgaria's railroads require investment to revive an outdated infrastructure. In Greece, despite a developing road network, ferry-boats remain the most effective form of transportation in many areas.

The landscape

Bulgaria's Balkan mountains divide the Danubian Plain (*Dunavska Ravnina*) and Maritsa Basin, meeting the Black Sea in the east along sandy beaches. The steep Rhodope Mountains form a natural barrier with Greece, while the younger Pindus form a rugged central spine which descends into the Aegean Sea to give a vast archipelago of over 2000 islands, the largest of which is Crete.

Ancient metamorphic rock, formed miles below the surface

Mount Olympus

Limestone rocks exposed by erosion of metamorphic rocks

Younger limestones created in shallow seas

▲ **Mount Olympus is a composite** of rocks formed by two major tectonic events. First the older metamorphic rocks were thrust over the limestones, then two million years ago regional warping and subsequent erosion, reexposed the limestone.

Mount Olympus is the mythical home of the Greek Gods and, at 9570 ft (2917 m), is the highest mountain in Greece.

The Peloponnese consist of several mountainous peninsulas, linked to the mainland by the isthmus of Corinth. The Corinth Canal (*Dioryga Korinthou*), built in 1893, cuts through the isthmus, linking the Aegean and Ionian Seas.

The Danube, Europe's second longest river, forms most of Bulgaria's northern border. The Danubian plain (*Dunavska Ravnina*), extending from the southern bank, is extremely fertile.

Balkan Mountains

Maritsa Basin

Pindus Mountains

▲ **The Arda river cuts through** the Rhodope Mountains in rugged, rocky gorges.

The islands of Crete, Kythira, Karpathos, and Rhodes are part of an arc which bends southeastward from the Peloponnese, forming the southern boundary of the Aegean.

▲ **Layers of black** volcanic ash still cover the island of Santorini. This volcano last erupted 3500 years ago, but still shows signs of volcanic activity.

Rhodes

Karpathos

Crete

Kythira

Rhodope Mountains

Corinth Canal (*Dioryga Korinthou*)

Scale 1:2,750,000

projection: Lambert Conformal Conic

▲ **A towering pinnacle** at Metéora in central Greece is home to the monastery of Roussánou. The 24 rock towers which dominate the plain of Thessaly (Thessalía) are remnants of an old plateau. Long-term weathering along fissures in the rock has worn away the rest of the plateau.

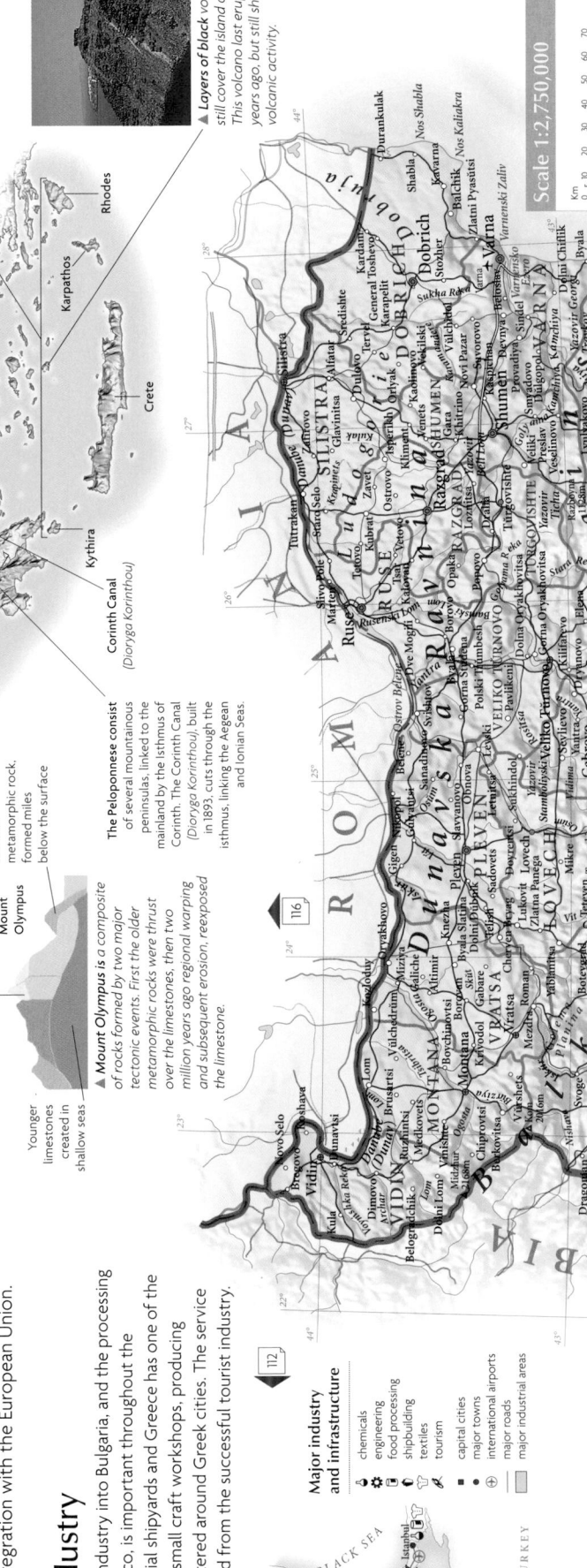

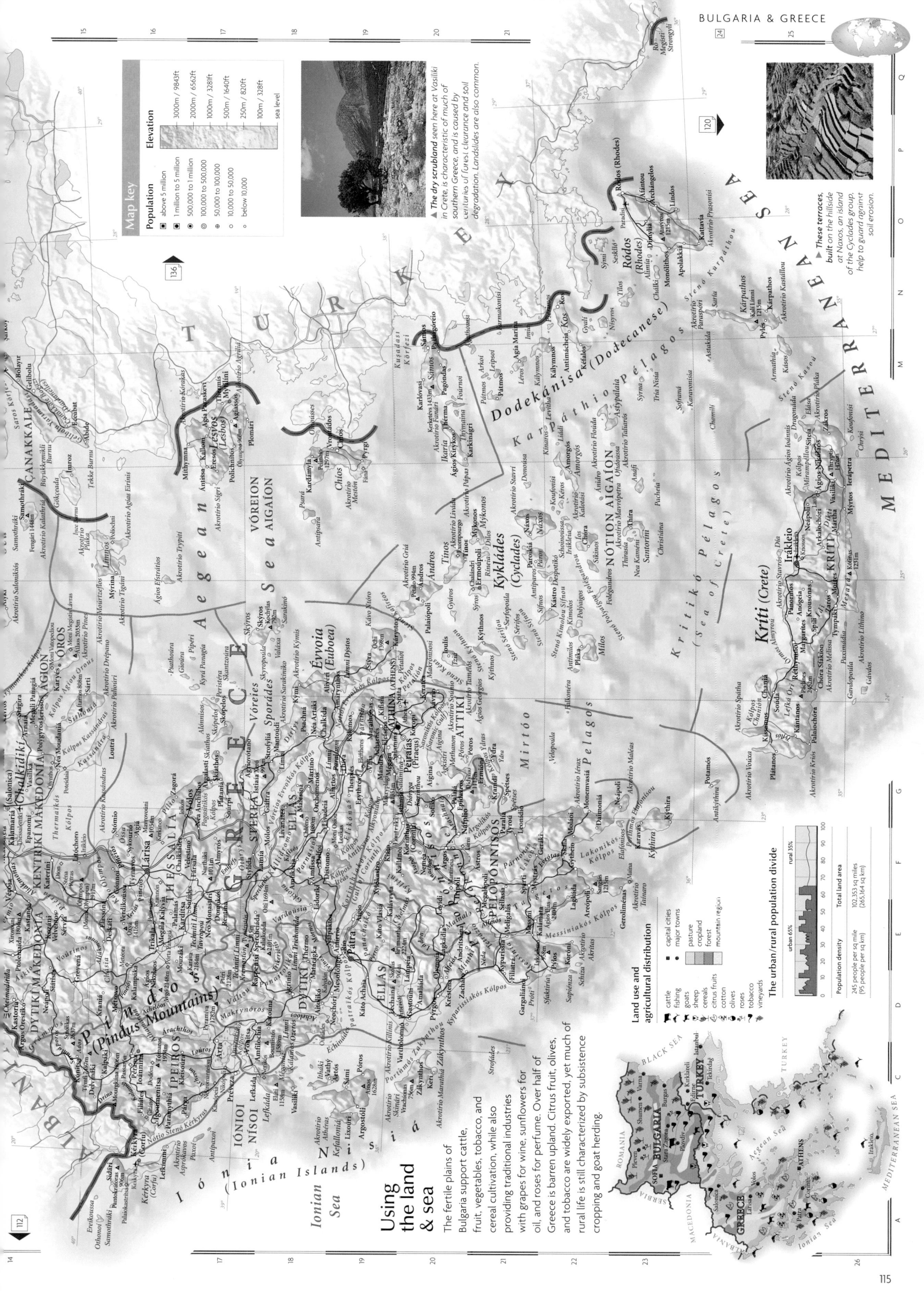

Using the land & sea

The fertile plains of Bulgaria support cattle, fruit, vegetables, tobacco, and cereal cultivation, while also providing traditional industries with grapes for wine, sunflowers for oil, and roses for perfume. Over half of Greece is barren upland. Citrus fruit, olives, and tobacco are widely exported, yet much of rural life is still characterized by subsistence cropping and goat herding.

▲ The dry scrubland seen here at Vasiliki in Crete, is characteristic of much of southern Greece, and is caused by centuries of forest clearance and soil degradation. Landslides are also common.

▲ These terraces, built on the hillside at Naxos, an island of the Cyclades group, help to guard against soil erosion.

Map key

Population
- ■ above 5 million
- ◻ 1 million to 5 million
- ◉ 500,000 to 1 million
- ◎ 100,000 to 500,000
- ⊙ 50,000 to 100,000
- ○ 10,000 to 50,000
- ∘ below 10,000

Elevation
- 3000m / 9843ft
- 2000m / 6562ft
- 1000m / 3280ft
- 500m / 1640ft
- 250m / 820ft
- 100m / 328ft
- sea level

Land use and agricultural distribution
- cattle
- fishing
- goats
- sheep
- cereals
- citrus fruits
- cotton
- olives
- roses
- tobacco
- vineyards

- ● capital cities
- • major towns
- pasture
- cropland
- forest
- mountain region

The urban/rural population divide

urban 65%   rural 35%

Population density	Total land area
245 people per sq mile (95 people per sq km)	102,353 sq miles (265,164 sq km)

Romania, Moldova & Ukraine

The industrial, social, and cultural make-up of Romania and the former Soviet states of Moldova and Ukraine still bear the imprint of their communist past. As part of the USSR, Ukraine was a leading agricultural, industrial, and energy producer. These industries, like those in Moldova and Romania, are now being reoriented more firmly toward western markets. As a result of shifting borders, and Soviet policy actively encouraging Russian immigration into other Soviet states like Ukraine and Moldova, all three countries now contain large numbers of foreign nationals. Moldovans and Romanians are still close in terms of language and culture, although Moldova is striving to remain an independent nation.

Using the land

The fertile black soils of Ukraine, often called "the breadbasket of Europe," have enabled the cultivation of a variety of cereals and vegetables, which are widely exported. Romania and Moldova also grow cereals, sunflowers, and vegetables, and are noted for the quality of their wines.

◀ *The fertile lands and tolerant climate of Moldova are ideally suited to growing grapes for wine.*

Land use and agricultural distribution

- cattle
- pigs
- poultry
- sheep
- cereals
- cotton
- sugar beet
- sunflowers
- vineyards

- ■ capital cities
- ● major towns
- pasture
- cropland
- forest
- wetland

The urban/rural population divide

urban 65%   rural 35%

0 10 20 30 40 50 60 70 80 90 100

Population density	Total land area
222 people per sq mile (86 people per sq km)	334,947 sq miles (867,740 sq km)

◀ *Glacial lakes are found throughout the Transylvanian Alps (Carpatii Meridionali), although the mountains no longer have any permanent snow cover.*

Transportation & industry

Heavy industry using local raw materials characterizes much of this region. The industrial heartland of Ukraine, specializing in metal and machine-building industries, is based around its vast mineral reserves in the Donbass region. In Moldova, food processing draws on produce from its agricultural sector. Romanian industry relies both on local raw materials and imported iron, steel, and oil.

Major industry and infrastructure

- car manufacture
- chemicals
- coal
- engineering
- food processing
- mining
- oil & gas
- textiles
- tourism

- ■ capital cities
- ● major towns
- ✈ international airports
- major roads
- major industrial areas

Transportation network

170,707 miles (274,757 km)		1170 miles (1883 km)	
21,474 miles (34,563 km)		4130 miles (6647 km)	

Increased industrialization has necessitated the upgrading of road and rail networks in all three countries. Modernization has tended to focus only on major cities and industrial areas.

▶ *During the 1960s and 1970s, many industries, like this carbon factory, developed using the mineral resources on the flanks of the Transylvanian Alps (Carpatii Meridionali).*

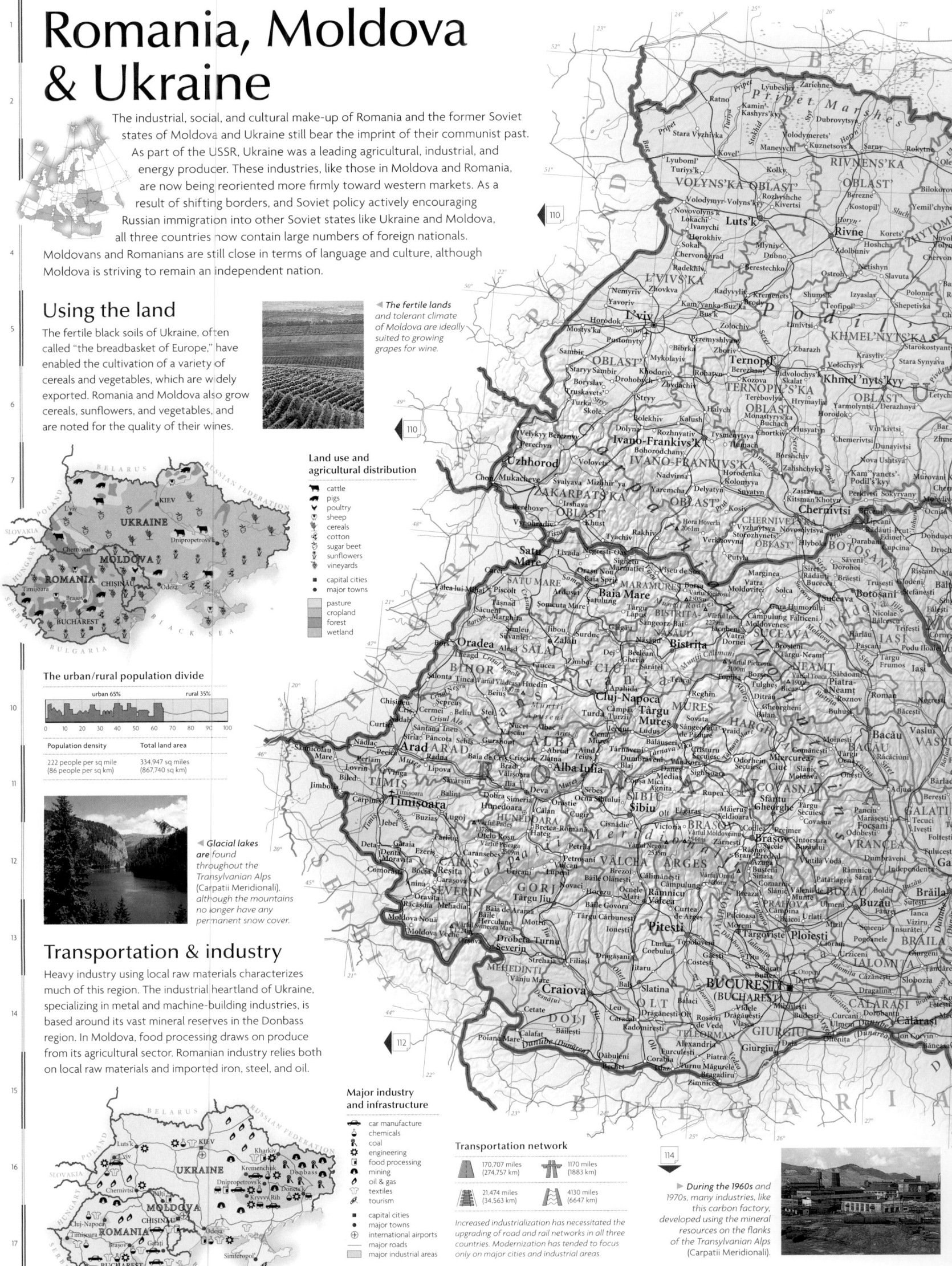

Scale 1:3,500,000

Km
0 10 20 30 40 50 60 70 80 90 100

Miles
0 10 20 30 40 50 60 70 80 90 100

projection: Lambert Conformal Conic

Map key

Population
- 1 million to 5 million
- 500,000 to 1 million
- 100,000 to 500,000
- 50,000 to 100,000
- 10,000 to 50,000
- below 10,000

Elevation
- 2000m / 6562ft
- 1000m / 3281ft
- 500m / 1640ft
- 250m / 820ft
- 100m / 328ft
- sea level

▲ The Swallow's Nest castle at Yalta is one of many tourist resorts on the Crimean (Krym) coast, dubbed the "Russian Riviera."

The landscape

Vast flat lowlands and gently rolling hills cover most of southeastern Europe. In the southwest, the Carpathian Mountains form a gentle arc. To the south of the Carpathian Mountains lies the Danube Plain, across which the Danube river flows to the Black Sea. To the north and east, the hills of Moldova level out into low plains, running east to the steppes of Ukraine.

▶ Divided into crystalline massifs, the southern arm of the Carpathian Mountains, the Transylvanian Alps (Carpatii Meridionali), extend 170 miles (274 km) across southwestern Romania.

The Codrii Hills dominate the landscape of central Moldova; they are intersected by deep, flat valleys and ravines.

Steppe landscape covers two-thirds of Ukraine. These flat, treeless grasslands extend from central Europe to central Asia.

Most of the major rivers in southeastern Europe, like the Danube, the Dniester, and Dnieper flow south and east to the Black Sea.

Uplifted and folded at the same time as the Alps, some 250 miles (400 km) of the eastern Carpathian Mountains contain ancient volcanic cones and craters.

The Apuseni Mountains (Muntii Apuseni) are rich in mineral deposits, including gold and iron ore.

Transylvanian Alps (Carpatii Meridionali)

The Danube forms a natural border between Romania and Bulgaria.

The three branches of the Danube Delta (Delta Dunării) form a triangle of wetlands covering some 1950 sq miles (5050 sq km).

At Kryms'ki Hory, three flat-topped, parallel limestone ridges run 80 miles (128 km) along the southern coast of the Crimean (Krym) Peninsula.

Old glaciated valley

Water has eroded a new post-glacial valley

▲ Balkas are common throughout Ukraine. They are large U-shaped valleys, formed during the last ice Age, which contain narrower deep valleys. These were incised by a sudden flow of water, following an icemelt.

Counterclockwise currents have created the sandspits which fringe the Sea of Azov.

The Baltic states & Belarus

BELARUS, ESTONIA, LATVIA, LITHUANIA, Kaliningrad

Occupying Europe's main corridor to Russia, the four distinct cultures of Estonia, Latvia, Lithuania, and Belarus share a history of struggle for nationhood against the interests of more powerful neighbors. As the first republics to declare their independence from the Soviet Union in 1990–91, the Baltic states of Estonia, Latvia, and Lithuania sought an economic role in the EU, while reaffirming their European cultural roots through the church and a strong musical tradition. Meanwhile, Belarus has shown economic and political allegiance to Russia by joining the Commonwealth of Independent States.

▲ *The seaport of Riga is Latvia's capital and the center of economic and cultural life. With a 32% Russian minority in Latvia, language and the right to national citizenship are key issues.*

Using the land

Across the four nations cattle and pig farming are widespread, together with diverse arable crops, including flax for making linen, potatoes used to produce vodka, cereals, and other vegetables. Almost a third of the land is forested; demand for timber has increased the importance of forest management.

Land use and agricultural distribution

- cattle
- pigs
- cereals
- flax
- potatoes
- timber
- capital cities
- major towns
- pasture
- cropland
- forest
- wetland

The urban/rural population divide

urban 69%   rural 31%

Population density: 122 people per sq mile (47 people per sq km)

Total land area: 145,006 sq miles (375,656 sq km)

▲ *A pine forest in northern Belarus. Conifers in the north give way to hardwood forest farther south. Timber mills are supplied with logs floated along the country's many navigable waterways.*

▲ *The Western Dvina river provides hydroelectric power and, during the summer months, access to the Baltic Sea. The lower course of the river freezes from December to April.*

Map key

Population
- ◉ 1 million to 5 million
- ◎ 500,000 to 1 million
- ⊕ 100,000 to 500,000
- ⊙ 50,000 to 100,000
- ○ 10,000 to 50,000
- ∘ below 10,000

Elevation
- 250m / 820ft
- 100m / 328ft
- sea level

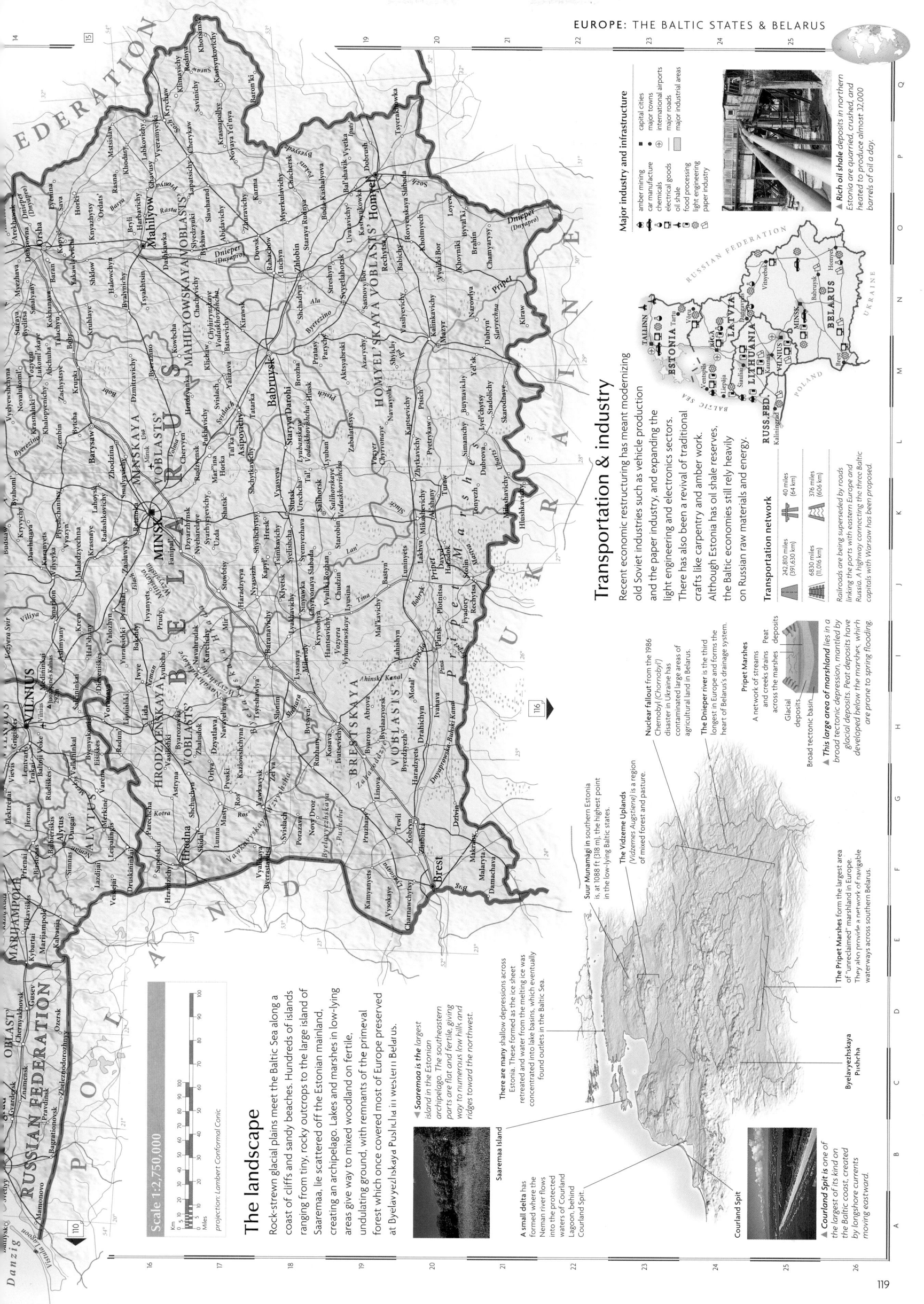

The landscape

Rock-strewn glacial plains meet the Baltic Sea along a coast of cliffs and sandy beaches. Hundreds of islands ranging from tiny, rocky outcrops to the large island of Saaremaa, lie scattered off the Estonian mainland, creating an archipelago. Lakes and marshes in low-lying areas give way to mixed woodland on fertile, undulating ground, with remnants of the primeval forest which once covered most of Europe preserved at Byelavyezhskaya Pushcha in western Belarus.

▲ *Saaremaa is the largest island in the Estonian archipelago. The southeastern parts are flat and fertile, giving way to numerous low hills and ridges toward the northwest.*

Saaremaa Island

A small delta has formed where the Neman river flows into the protected waters of Courland Lagoon, behind Courland Spit.

There are many shallow depressions across Estonia. These formed as the ice sheet retreated and water from the melting ice was concentrated into lake basins, which eventually found outlets in the Baltic Sea.

Courland Spit

▲ *Courland Spit is one of the largest of its kind on the Baltic coast, created by longshore currents moving eastward.*

Transportation & industry

Recent economic restructuring has meant modernizing old Soviet industries such as vehicle production and the paper industry, and expanding the light engineering and electronics sectors. There has also been a revival of traditional crafts like carpentry and amber work. Although Estonia has oil shale reserves, the Baltic economies still rely heavily on Russian raw materials and energy.

Transportation network

Railroads are being superseded by roads linking the ports with eastern Europe and Russia. A highway connecting the three Baltic capitals with Warsaw has been proposed.

Major industry and infrastructure

▲ *Rich oil shale deposits in northern Estonia are quarried, crushed, and heated to produce almost 32,000 barrels of oil a day.*

The Videme Uplands (Vidzemes Augstiene) is a region of mixed forest and pasture.

Suur Munamägi in southern Estonia is, at 1088 ft (318 m), the highest point in the low-lying Baltic states.

Nuclear fallout from the 1986 Chernobyl (Chornobyl') disaster in Ukraine has contaminated large areas of agricultural land in Belarus.

The Dnieper river is the third longest in Europe and forms the heart of Belarus's drainage system.

Pripet Marshes

A network of streams and creeks drains across the marshes.

▲ *This large area of marshland lies in a broad tectonic depression, mantled by glacial deposits. Peat deposits have developed below the marshes, which are prone to spring flooding.*

The Pripet Marshes form the largest area of "unreclaimed" marshland in Europe. They also provide a network of navigable waterways across southern Belarus.

Scale 1:2,750,000

The Mediterranean

The Mediterranean Sea stretches over 2500 miles (4000 km) east to west, separating Europe from Africa. At its westernmost point it is connected to the Atlantic Ocean through the Strait of Gibraltar. In the east, the Suez canal, opened in 1869, gives passage to the Indian Ocean. In the northeast, linked by the Sea of Marmara, lies the Black Sea. The Mediterranean is bordered by almost 30 states and territories, and more than 100 million people live on its shores and islands. Throughout history, the Mediterranean has been a focal area for many great empires and civilizations, reflected in the variety of cultures found on its shores. Since the 1960s, development along the southern coast of Europe has expanded rapidly to accommodate increasing numbers of tourists and to enable the exploitation of oil and gas reserves. This has resulted in rising levels of pollution, threatening the future of the sea.

▲ *Monte Carlo is* just one of the luxurious resorts scattered along the Riviera, which stretches along the coast from Cannes in France to La Spezia in Italy. The region's mild winters and hot summers have attracted wealthy tourists since the early 19th century.

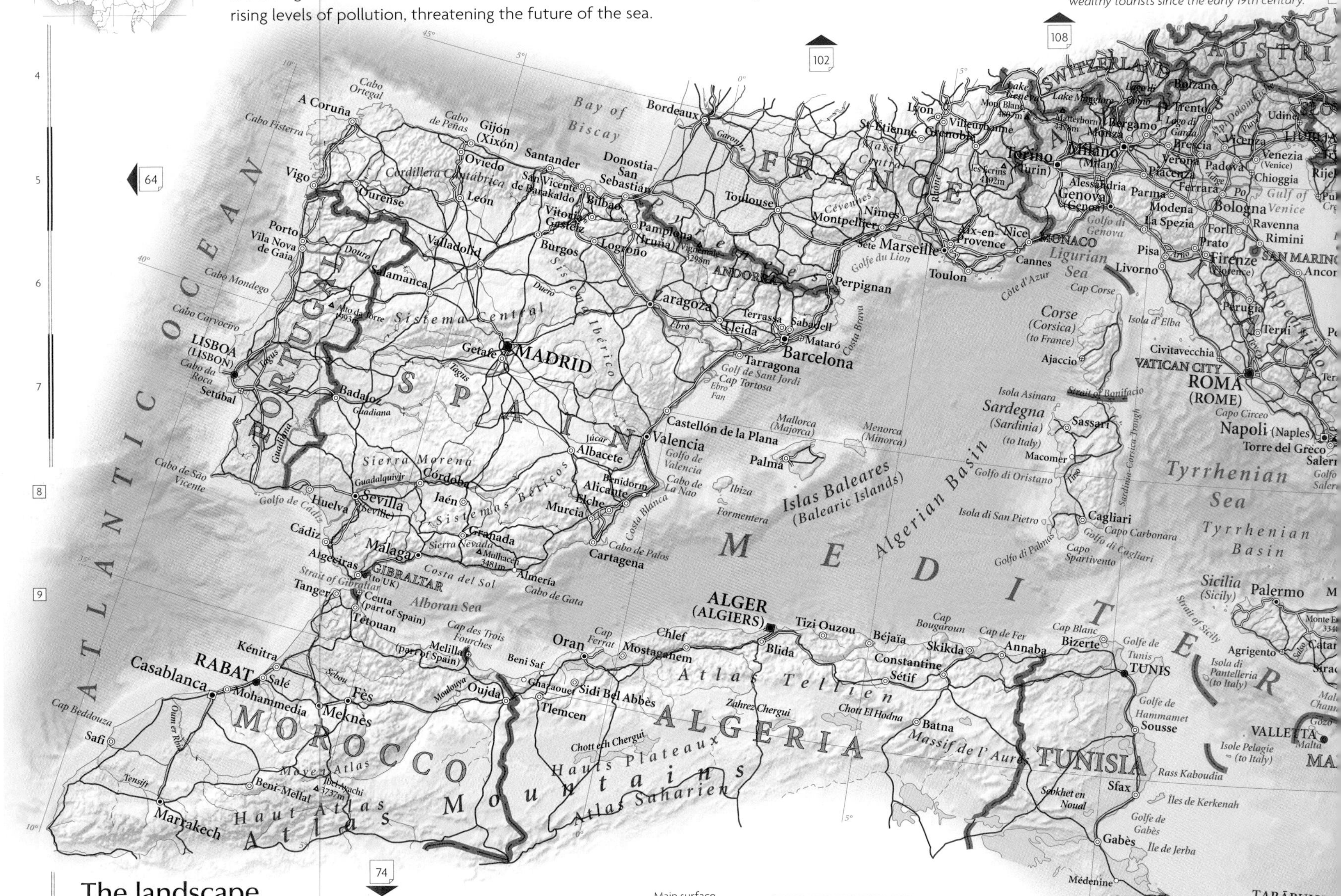

The landscape

The Mediterranean Sea is almost totally landlocked, joined to the Atlantic Ocean through the Strait of Gibraltar, which is only 8 miles (13 km) wide. Lying on an active plate margin, sea floor movements have formed a variety of basins, troughs, and ridges. A submarine ridge running from Tunisia to the island of Sicily divides the Mediterranean into two distinct basins. The western basin is characterized by broad, smooth abyssal (or ocean) plains. In contrast, the eastern basin is dominated by a large ridge system, running east to west.

The narrow Strait of Gibraltar inhibits water exchange between the Mediterranean Sea and the Atlantic Ocean, producing a high degree of salinity and a low tidal range within the Mediterranean. The lack of tides has encouraged the build-up of pollutants in many semienclosed bays.

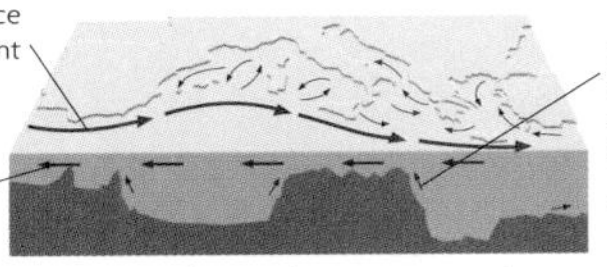

Main surface current

Dense currents sink below surface

Denser, more saline currents flow back to Atlantic

▲ *Because the Mediterranean* is almost enclosed by land, its circulation is quite different to the oceans. There is one major current which flows in from the Atlantic and moves east. Currents flowing back to the Atlantic are denser and flow below the main current.

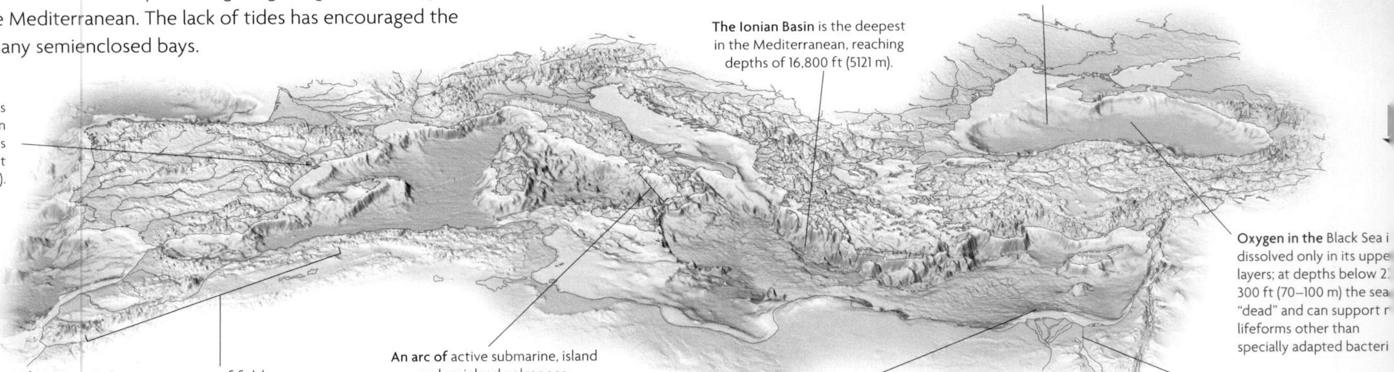

Industrial pollution flowing from the Dnieper and Danube rivers has destroyed a large proportion of the fish population that used to inhabit the upper layers of the Black Sea.

The Ionian Basin is the deepest in the Mediterranean, reaching depths of 16,800 ft (5121 m).

The edge of the Eurasian Plate is edged by a continental shelf. In the Mediterranean Sea this is widest at the Ebro Fan where it extends 60 miles (96 km).

Oxygen in the Black Sea is dissolved only in its upper layers; at depths below 2,300 ft (70–100 m) the sea is "dead" and can support no lifeforms other than specially adapted bacteria.

◀ *The Atlas Mountains* are a range of fold mountains that lie in Morocco and Algeria. They run parallel to the Mediterranean, forming a topographical and climatic divide between the Mediterranean coast and the western Sahara.

An arc of active submarine, island and mainland volcanoes, including Etna and Vesuvius, lie in and around southern Italy. The area is also susceptible to earthquakes and landslides.

Nutrient flows into the eastern Mediterranean, and sediment flows to the Nile Delta have been severely lowered by the building of the Aswan Dam across the Nile in Eygpt. This is causing the delta to shrink.

The Suez Canal, opened in 1869, extends 100 miles (160 km) from Port Said to the Gulf of Suez.

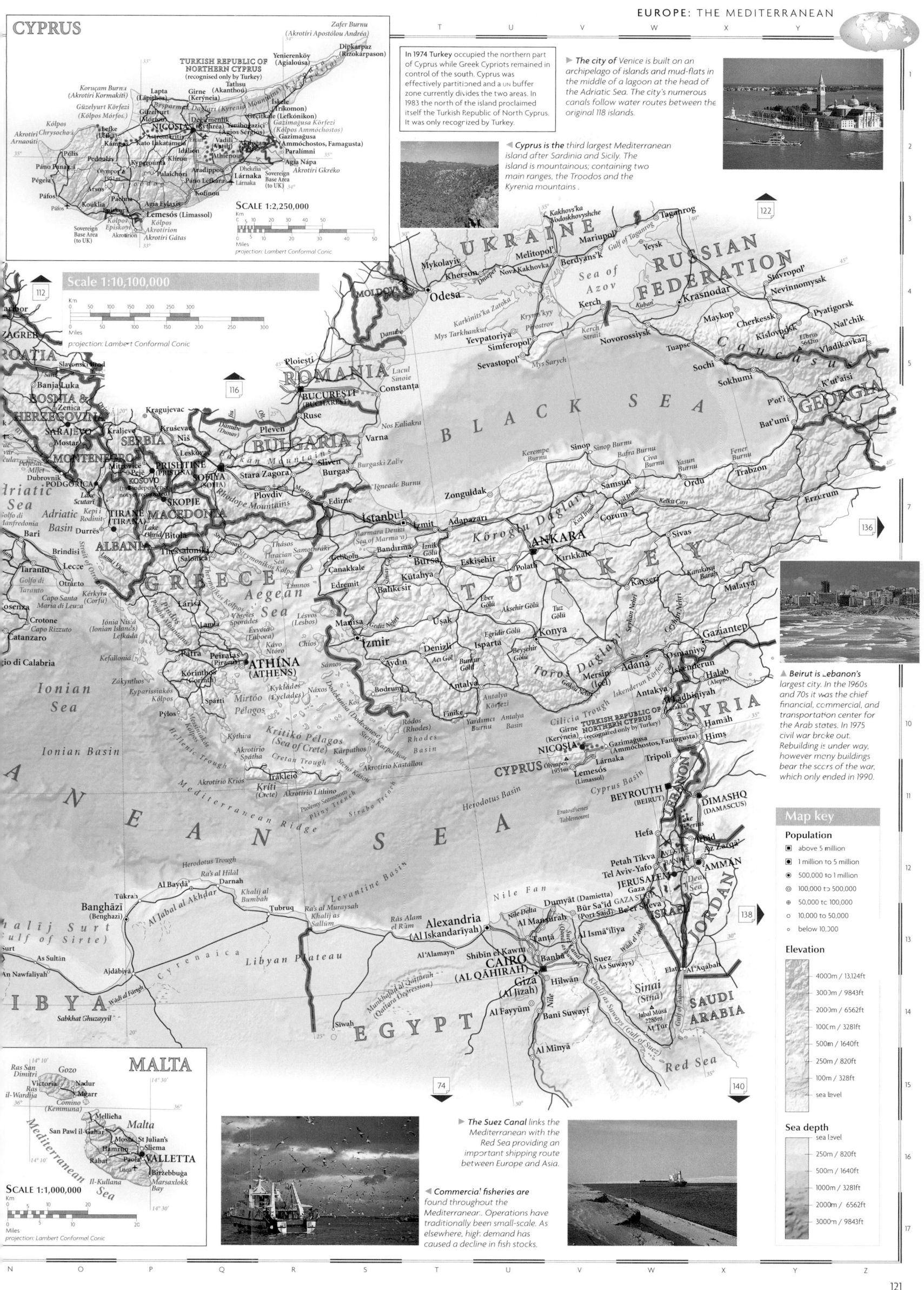

CYPRUS

TURKISH REPUBLIC OF NORTHERN CYPRUS
(recognised only by Turkey)

SCALE 1:2,250,000
projection: Lambert Conformal Conic

Scale 1:10,100,000
projection: Lambert Conformal Conic

In 1974 Turkey occupied the northern part of Cyprus while Greek Cypriots remained in control of the south. Cyprus was effectively partitioned and a UN buffer zone currently divides the two areas. In 1983 the north of the island proclaimed itself the Turkish Republic of North Cyprus. It was only recognized by Turkey.

► The city of Venice is built on an archipelago of islands and mud-flats in the middle of a lagoon at the head of the Adriatic Sea. The city's numerous canals follow water routes between the original 118 islands.

◄ Cyprus is the third largest Mediterranean island after Sardinia and Sicily. The island is mountainous; containing two main ranges, the Troodos and the Kyrenia mountains.

▲ Beirut is Lebanon's largest city. In the 1960s and 70s it was the chief financial, commercial, and transportation center for the Arab states. In 1975 civil war broke out. Rebuilding is under way, however many buildings bear the scars of the war, which only ended in 1990.

Map key

Population
- above 5 million
- 1 million to 5 million
- 500,000 to 1 million
- 100,000 to 500,000
- 50,000 to 100,000
- 10,000 to 50,000
- below 10,000

Elevation
- 4000m / 13,124ft
- 3000m / 9843ft
- 2000m / 6562ft
- 1000m / 3281ft
- 500m / 1640ft
- 250m / 820ft
- 100m / 328ft
- sea level

Sea depth
- sea level
- 250m / 820ft
- 500m / 1640ft
- 1000m / 3281ft
- 2000m / 6562ft
- 3000m / 9843ft

MALTA

SCALE 1:1,000,000
projection: Lambert Conformal Conic

► The Suez Canal links the Mediterranean with the Red Sea providing an important shipping route between Europe and Asia.

◄ Commercial fisheries are found throughout the Mediterranean. Operations have traditionally been small-scale. As elsewhere, high demand has caused a decline in fish stocks.

The Russian Federation

The Cold War era of global relations was concluded in 1991 with the formal dissolution of the Soviet Union. The Russian Federation declared its separate sovereignty from the foundering communist empire following independence declarations from a number of former Soviet republics. As the leading member of the Commonwealth of Independent States, the Russian Federation has a central role in the development of post-Soviet Eurasia. Crossing 11 time zones, the Russian Federation is almost twice the size of the US, and with more than 150 ethnic minorities and 21 autonomous republics, regionalist dissent within its own territory remains a danger.

THE RUSSIAN FEDERATION: ADMINISTRATIVE REGIONS

The administrative area names in European Russia have been omitted west of the Ural Mountains. Please refer to pages 124–125 and 126–127 where these areas are shown at a larger scale.

124-125
126-127

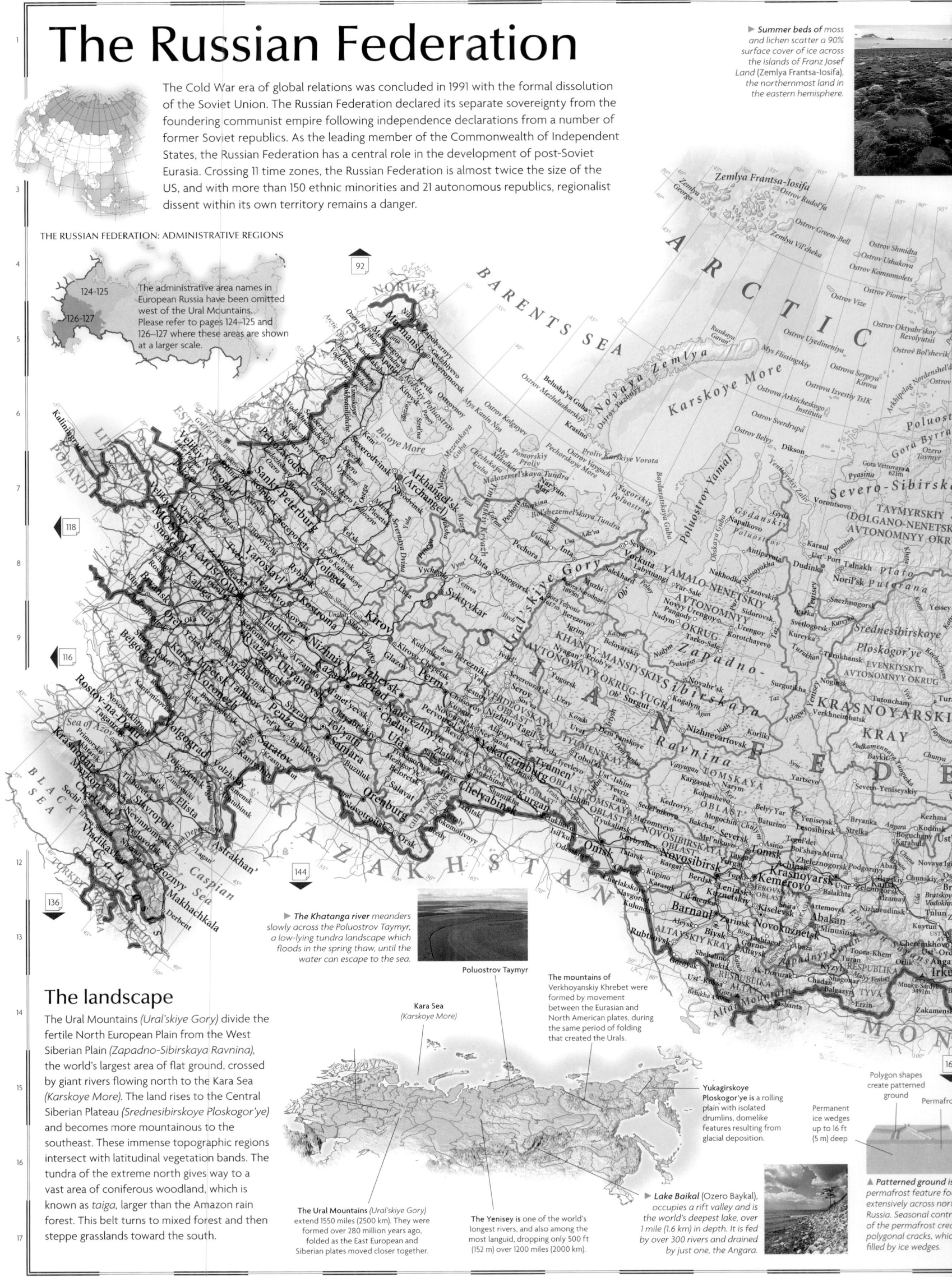

▶ *Summer beds of* moss and lichen scatter a 90% surface cover of ice across the islands of Franz Josef Land (Zemlya Frantsa-Iosifa), the northernmost land in the eastern hemisphere.

▶ *The Khatanga river* meanders slowly across the Poluostrov Taymyr, a low-lying tundra landscape which floods in the spring thaw, until the water can escape to the sea.

Poluostrov Taymyr

Kara Sea
(Karskoye More)

The mountains of Verkhoyanskiy Khrebet were formed by movement between the Eurasian and North American plates, during the same period of folding that created the Urals.

Yukagirskoye Ploskogor'ye is a rolling plain with isolated drumlins, domelike features resulting from glacial deposition.

Permanent ice wedges up to 16 ft (5 m) deep

Polygon shapes create patterned ground

Permafros

▲ *Patterned ground is* permafrost feature fou extensively across nort Russia. Seasonal contra of the permafrost crea polygonal cracks, whic filled by ice wedges.

The landscape

The Ural Mountains (Ural'skiye Gory) divide the fertile North European Plain from the West Siberian Plain (Zapadno-Sibirskaya Ravnina), the world's largest area of flat ground, crossed by giant rivers flowing north to the Kara Sea (Karskoye More). The land rises to the Central Siberian Plateau (Srednesibirskoye Ploskogor'ye) and becomes more mountainous to the southeast. These immense topographic regions intersect with latitudinal vegetation bands. The tundra of the extreme north gives way to a vast area of coniferous woodland, which is known as *taiga*, larger than the Amazon rain forest. This belt turns to mixed forest and then steppe grasslands toward the south.

The Ural Mountains (Ural'skiye Gory) extend 1550 miles (2500 km). They were formed over 280 million years ago, folded as the East European and Siberian plates moved closer together.

The Yenisey is one of the world's longest rivers, and also among the most languid, dropping only 500 ft (152 m) over 1200 miles (2000 km).

▶ *Lake Baikal* (Ozero Baykal), occupies a rift valley and is the world's deepest lake, over 1 mile (1.6 km) in depth. It is fed by over 300 rivers and drained by just one, the Angara.

Transportation & industry

Raw materials, particularly fossil fuels, ores, and precious metals are abundant, yet often found at sites far from habitation. This inherent "friction of distance" problem was met starting in the 1930s by Soviet commitment to heavy industry and the strategic location of plants east of the Urals. It has left a pattern of isolated and often vast industrial complexes, in remote areas from Vladivostok to Murmansk, in the far north and across European Russia, with lighter manufacturing concentrated in urban areas.

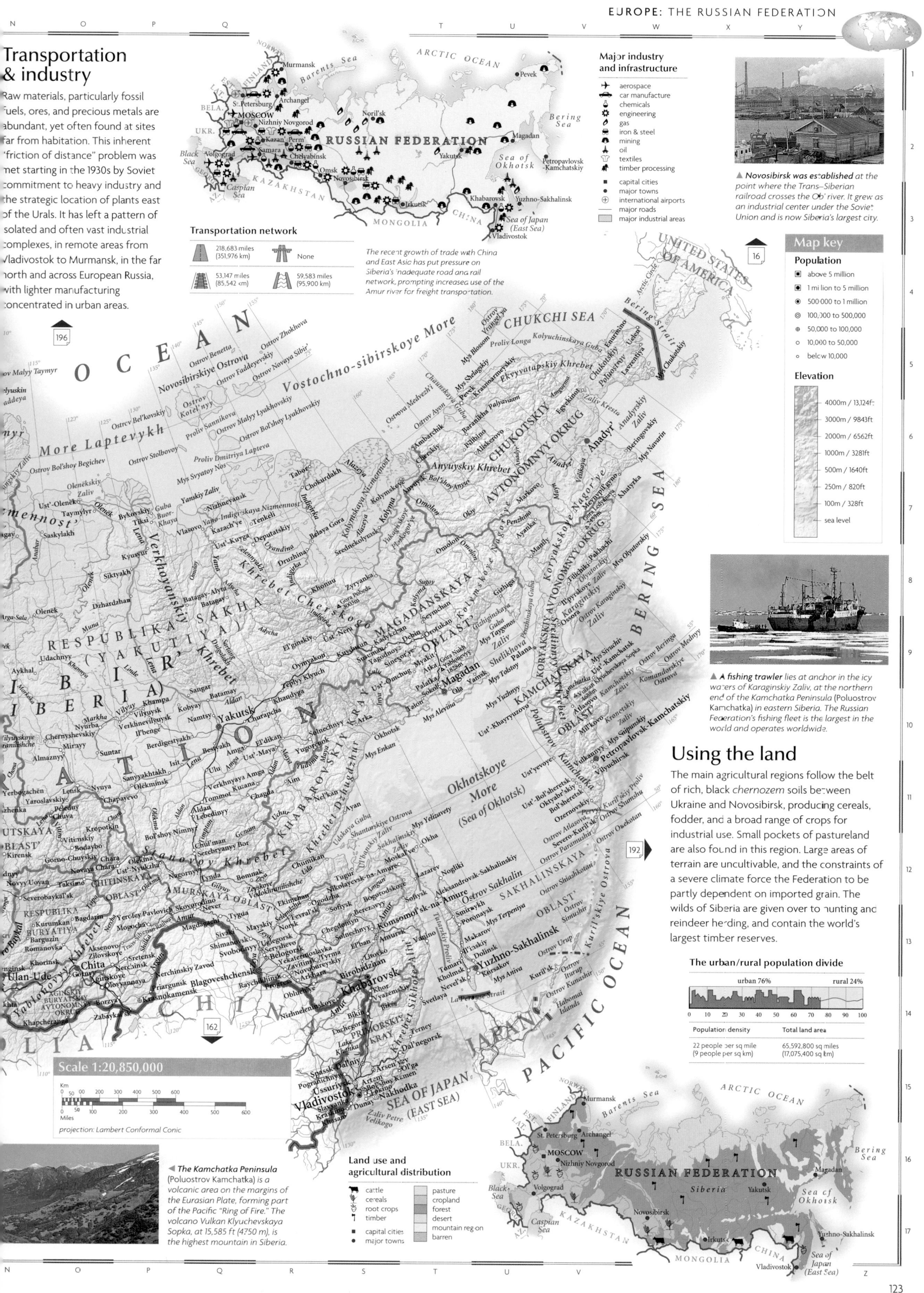

Major industry and infrastructure

- aerospace
- car manufacture
- chemicals
- engineering
- gas
- iron & steel
- mining
- oil
- textiles
- timber processing
- capital cities
- major towns
- international airports
- major roads
- major industrial areas

Transportation network

218,683 miles (351,976 km)

53,147 miles (85,542 km)

59,583 miles (95,900 km)

None

The recent growth of trade with China and East Asia has put pressure on Siberia's inadequate road and rail network, prompting increased use of the Amur river for freight transportation.

▲ *Novosibirsk was established* at the point where the Trans–Siberian railroad crosses the Ob' river. It grew as an industrial center under the Soviet Union and is now Siberia's largest city.

Map key

Population

- above 5 million
- 1 million to 5 million
- 500,000 to 1 million
- 100,000 to 500,000
- 50,000 to 100,000
- 10,000 to 50,000
- below 10,000

Elevation

- 4000m / 13,124ft
- 3000m / 9843ft
- 2000m / 6562ft
- 1000m / 3281ft
- 500m / 1640ft
- 250m / 820ft
- 100m / 328ft
- sea level

▲ *A fishing trawler* lies at anchor in the icy waters of Karaginskiy Zaliv, at the northern end of the Kamchatka Peninsula (Poluostrov Kamchatka) in eastern Siberia. The Russian Federation's fishing fleet is the largest in the world and operates worldwide.

Using the land

The main agricultural regions follow the belt of rich, black *chernozem* soils between Ukraine and Novosibirsk, producing cereals, fodder, and a broad range of crops for industrial use. Small pockets of pastureland are also found in this region. Large areas of terrain are uncultivable, and the constraints of a severe climate force the Federation to be partly dependent on imported grain. The wilds of Siberia are given over to hunting and reindeer herding, and contain the world's largest timber reserves.

The urban/rural population divide

urban 76%   rural 24%

0 10 20 30 40 50 60 70 80 90 100

Population density

22 people per sq mile (9 people per sq km)

Total land area

65,592,800 sq miles (17,075,400 sq km)

Scale 1:20,850,000

Km
0 100 200 300 400 500 600

Miles
0 100 200 300 400 500 600

projection: Lambert Conformal Conic

◄ *The Kamchatka Peninsula* (Poluostrov Kamchatka) is a volcanic area on the margins of the Eurasian Plate, forming part of the Pacific "Ring of Fire." The volcano Vulkan Klyuchevskaya Sopka, at 15,585 ft (4750 m), is the highest mountain in Siberia.

Land use and agricultural distribution

- cattle
- cereals
- root crops
- timber
- capital cities
- major towns
- pasture
- cropland
- forest
- desert
- mountain region
- barren

Northern European Russia

Reaching into the Arctic Circle, this region of lakeland, forest and tundra is historically bound to Europe by St Petersburg, the old imperial capital of Tsarist Russia and home to a third of the region's population. Communist rule from Moscow left the north politically marginalized, contributing to the present problems of outmoded industry, poor infrastructure and serious environmental neglect. However, with borders embracing Finland, Norway, the Baltic and the northern sea route to the Atlantic, the region's success in foreign trade is now of prime importance to the Russian economy.

The landscape

The ancient bedrock of the Scandinavian Shield lies exposed across the glacially scoured Khibiny Mountains of the Kola Peninsula (Kol'skiy Poluostrov), becoming mantled with till toward the North European Plain. The Valdai Hills (Valdayskaya Vozvyshennost') form an important watershed for the plain's rivers, while thick forest veils a complicated topography of moraines, lakes, and ground disturbed by frost action. The Ural Mountains (Ural'skiye Gory) form a border with Asia in the east.

◄ *The Kola Peninsula* (Kol'skiy Poluostrov) *is part of the Scandinavian Shield, an area of ancient bedrock underlying Scandinavia. Rocks in excess of 2500 million years old are exposed across the peninsula.*

▲ *The Khibiny mountains were formed by volcanic intrusions into the Scandinavian Shield, over 570 million years ago.*

Kola Peninsula (Kol'skiy Poluostrov)

Karst features, including sinkholes, lakes, and caverns, are found in limestone outcrops across the plain of the Severnaya Dvina and Mezen' rivers.

The low-lying plains of the Pechora, Mezen', and Severnaya Dvina rivers were flooded by the sea while the land was still isostatically depressed following the last Ice Age, a process which has hidden the landforms created by glacial deposition.

Retreating glacier — Meltwater channels

Terminal moraine

▲ *Terminal moraines are* crescent-shaped ridges of glacial deposits, widely found in central Russia. Detritus is carried by the glacier and deposited at its terminus (snout) as it melts, marking the limit of the ice advance.

Ural Mountains (Ural'skiye Gory)

Two of Europe's biggest rivers, the Volga and Western Dvina, rise in the swampy uplands of the Valdai Hills (Valdayskaya Vozvyshennost.)

◄ *Lake Onega* (Onezhskoye Ozero) *is the remnant of a body of water which, 12,000 years ago, connected the White Sea* (Beloye More) *with the Gulf of Finland and the Baltic Sea.*

Using the land & sea

The cold climate confines agriculture mainly to southern and western provinces, where dairy farming predominates and arable land is given over to fodder crops as well as flax, potatoes, oats, and rye. Areas beyond the northern margins of cultivation are used for forestry, hunting, herding, and fishing, with some vegetables grown in hothouses around urban areas.

Land use and agricultural distribution

- cattle
- fishing
- reindeer
- timber
- fodder
- • major towns
- pasture
- cropland
- forest
- mountain region
- wetland
- tundra
- barren
- ice

RUSSIAN FEDERATION

The urban/rural population divide

urban 80%   rural 20%

0 10 20 30 40 50 60 70 80 90 100

Population density	Total land area
26 people per sq mile (10 people per sq km)	829,398 sq miles (2,148,700 sq km)

◄ *Many rapids are found along the 175 mile (280 km) course of the Suna river.*

▶ *St. Peter and Paul Fortress is the oldest building in St Petersburg, founded by Peter the Great in 1703 as a modern, European capital for Russia.*

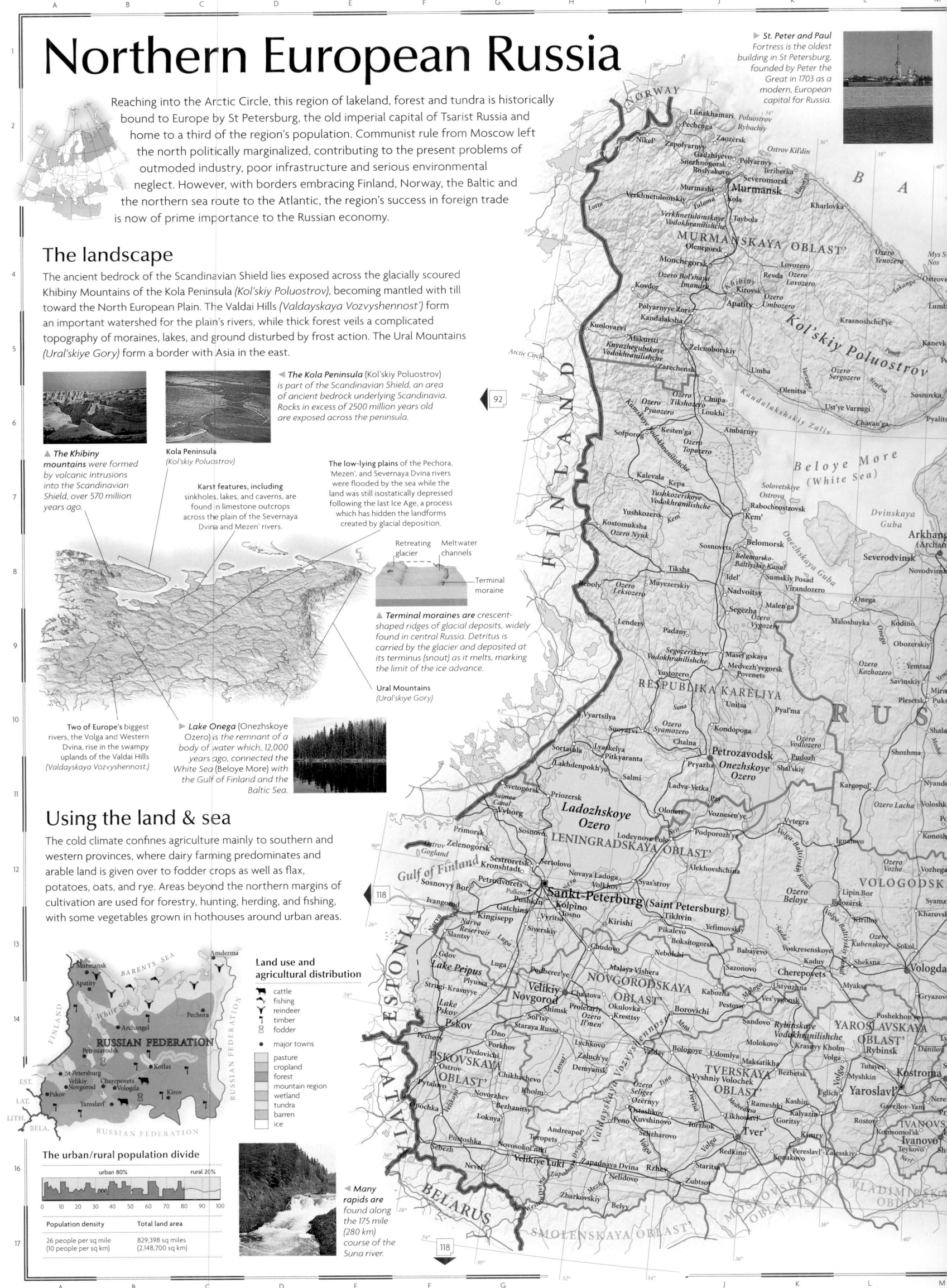

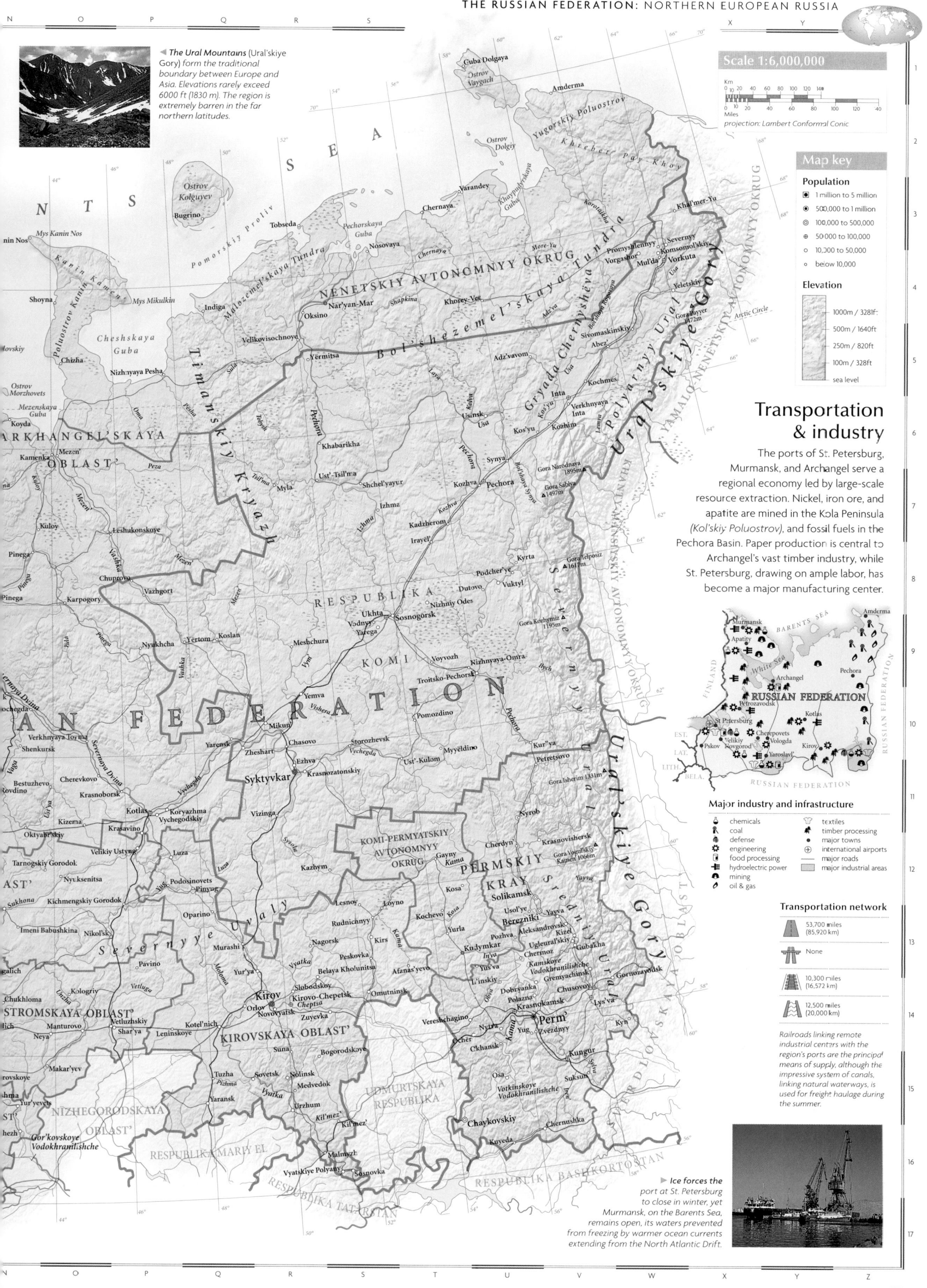

◄ *The Ural Mountains* (Ural'skiye Gory) form the traditional boundary between Europe and Asia. Elevations rarely exceed 6000 ft (1830 m). The region is extremely barren in the far northern latitudes.

Scale 1:6,000,000

projection: Lambert Conformal Conic

Map key

Population
- ◉ 1 million to 5 million
- ◎ 500,000 to 1 million
- ⊙ 100,000 to 500,000
- ⊕ 50,000 to 100,000
- ○ 10,000 to 50,000
- ○ below 10,000

Elevation
- 1000m / 3281ft
- 500m / 1640ft
- 250m / 820ft
- 100m / 328ft
- sea level

Transportation & industry

The ports of St. Petersburg, Murmansk, and Archangel serve a regional economy led by large-scale resource extraction. Nickel, iron ore, and apatite are mined in the Kola Peninsula (Kol'skiy Poluostrov), and fossil fuels in the Pechora Basin. Paper production is central to Archangel's vast timber industry, while St. Petersburg, drawing on ample labor, has become a major manufacturing center.

Major industry and infrastructure

- chemicals
- coal
- defense
- engineering
- food processing
- hydroelectric power
- mining
- oil & gas
- textiles
- timber processing
- major towns
- international airports
- major roads
- major industrial areas

Transportation network

- 53,700 miles (85,920 km)
- None
- 10,300 miles (16,572 km)
- 12,500 miles (20,000 km)

Railroads linking remote industrial centers with the region's ports are the principal means of supply, although the impressive system of canals, linking natural waterways, is used for freight haulage during the summer.

► *Ice forces the port at St. Petersburg to close in winter, yet Murmansk, on the Barents Sea, remains open, its waters prevented from freezing by warmer ocean currents extending from the North Atlantic Drift.*

125

▶ *Kaliningrad has been a Russian enclave since 1945. The port is an important center for the Russian Federation's Baltic fishing fleet.*

◀ *St Basil's Cathedral, completed in 1561, stands in Moscow's Red Square next to the Kremlin; the original fortified stronghold of the city.*

Southern European Russia

This region, divided from Asia by desert, seas, and mountains, has exerted a powerful influence both east and west since the 13th century. Over 70 years of Communist rule produced a highly urbanized, industrial society dominated by Moscow, which was the capital of the Soviet Union until 1991. Almost two-thirds of the Russian Federation's population live in this core area, with a relatively high per capita share of its wealth. However, the rapid growth of a market economy has caused great social upheaval, with rising crime and political instability.

The landscape

Ancient folds in the deep sedimentary strata of the North European Plain have created a sequence of high and low regions. The Central Russian Upland *(Srednerusskaya Vozvyshennost')* in the west is deeply incised by rivers draining into the lowland of the Oka and Don rivers. In the east the Volga, Europe's longest river, flows south to the Caspian Sea, dividing the Volga Uplands *(Privolzhskaya Vozvyshennost')* from the foothills of the Ural Mountains *(Ural'skiye Gory)*. The Caucasus mountains and the Black Sea form a natural border to the southwest.

▲ *A plantation of Scots pine helps consolidate the loose sandy soils of the Meshchera Lowland (Meshcherskaya Nizmennost'), which lies on the bed of an old glacial lake.*

The Smolensk-Moscow Upland *(Smolensko-Moskovskaya Vozvyshennost')* is a series of terminal moraine ridges marking the southern extent of the last glaciation.

Glacial till covers the bedrock to the north of the North European Plain, giving a gentle surface relief.

The lowland of the Oka and Don rivers lies over a broad trough, between the upfolds of the Volga Uplands *(Privolzhskaya Vozvyshennost')* to the east, and the Central Russian Upland *(Srednerusskaya Vozvyshennost')* to the west.

The southern Ural mountains *(Ural'skiye Gory)* consist of several parallel ranges of ancient fold mountains running from north to south.

Central Russian Upland *(Srednerusskaya Vozvyshennost').*

The floodplain of the Volga forms a long oasis of verdant vegetation, contrasting with the aridity of the surrounding Caspian hinterland.

The marshlands of the Volga Delta are visited by over 260 species of bird each year, migrating between South Africa and Arctic Siberia.

The Caspian Depression is a large downfold (or syncline) which became flooded, forming the Caspian Sea. The shoreline is 98 ft (30 m) below sea level.

◀ *The Caucasus mountains run from the Black Sea to the Caspian Sea. They include El'brus which, at 18,511 ft (5642 m), is the highest point in Europe. It is still uplifting at a rate of 0.4 inches (10 mm) per year.*

Drifting sand occupies large areas of the south, forming dunes up to 50 ft (15 m) high.

Salt dome

Salt dome is forced up and through the rock strata

Sedimentary strata

Salts are forced upwards by denser overlying strata

▲ *Salt domes, rounded hills up to 500 ft (150 m) high, are produced as less dense rock salts are displaced under the extreme pressure of denser, overlying strata and forced up toward the surface creating domes. They are widespread in the Caspian Depression.*

Scale 1:6,000,000

projection: Lambert Conformal Conic

Map key

Population

- above 5 million
- 1 million to 5 million
- 500,000 to 1 million
- 100,000 to 500,000
- 50,000 to 100,000
- 10,000 to 50,000
- below 10,000

Elevation

- 4000m / 13,124ft
- 3000m / 9843ft
- 2000m / 6562ft
- 1000m / 3281ft
- 500m / 1640ft
- 250m / 820ft
- 100m / 328ft
- sea level

Using the land

In the cold, humid north and in the southern Urals (Ural'skiye Gory), small grains, potatoes, and flax are commonly rotated with legumes which support livestock farming. The rich chernozem (or black earth) areas support diverse crops such as sugar beet, hemp, sunflowers, millet, and vegetables. Further south, aridity restricts husbandry to extensive grazing, with intensive fruit and rice cultivation along the oasis of the Volga.

The urban/rural population divide

urban 71%   rural 29%

0 10 20 30 40 50 60 70 80 90 100

Population density

115 people per sq mile
(45 people per sq km)

Total land area

705,916 sq miles
(1,828,800 sq km)

Land use and agricultural distribution

- sheep
- flax
- potatoes
- rice
- sunflowers
- sugar beet
- timber
- capital cities
- major towns
- pasture
- cropland
- forest
- wetland
- mountain region
- tundra

Transportation & industry

Manufacturing is largely based around Moscow and the Volga region, which became a major industrial area during the Second World War. Both Moscow and Nizhniy Novgorod are centers of skilled labor for light manufacturing and engineering. Most of Russia's main chemical plants are located along the Volga, and one of the world's largest car factories was recently opened in Tol'yatti. Processing and machine construction plants use oil, gas, and hydroelectric power from the Volga Basin and metallic minerals from the Urals (Ural'skiye Gory) and Kursk.

◀ Industrial plants are massed along the Volga. Environmental stress from decades of unbridled industrial development has prompted widespread concern about pollution levels.

Transportation network

250,000 miles (402,000 km)   None

28,000 miles (44,800 km)   16,300 miles (26,080 km)

Seventy private and national flag airlines have been created from the reorganization of the state airline Aeroflot, which maintained the world's largest fleet of aircraft during the Soviet era.

Major industry and infrastructure

- aerospace
- car manufacture
- chemicals
- defense
- electronics
- engineering
- gas
- mining
- oil
- textiles
- capital cities
- major towns
- international airports
- major roads
- major industrial areas

Asia

Asia, the world's largest continent, covers 16,838,365 sq miles (43,608,000 sq km).
It comprises 49 separate countries, including 97% of Turkey and 72% of the
Russian Federation. Almost 60% of the world's population lives in Asia.

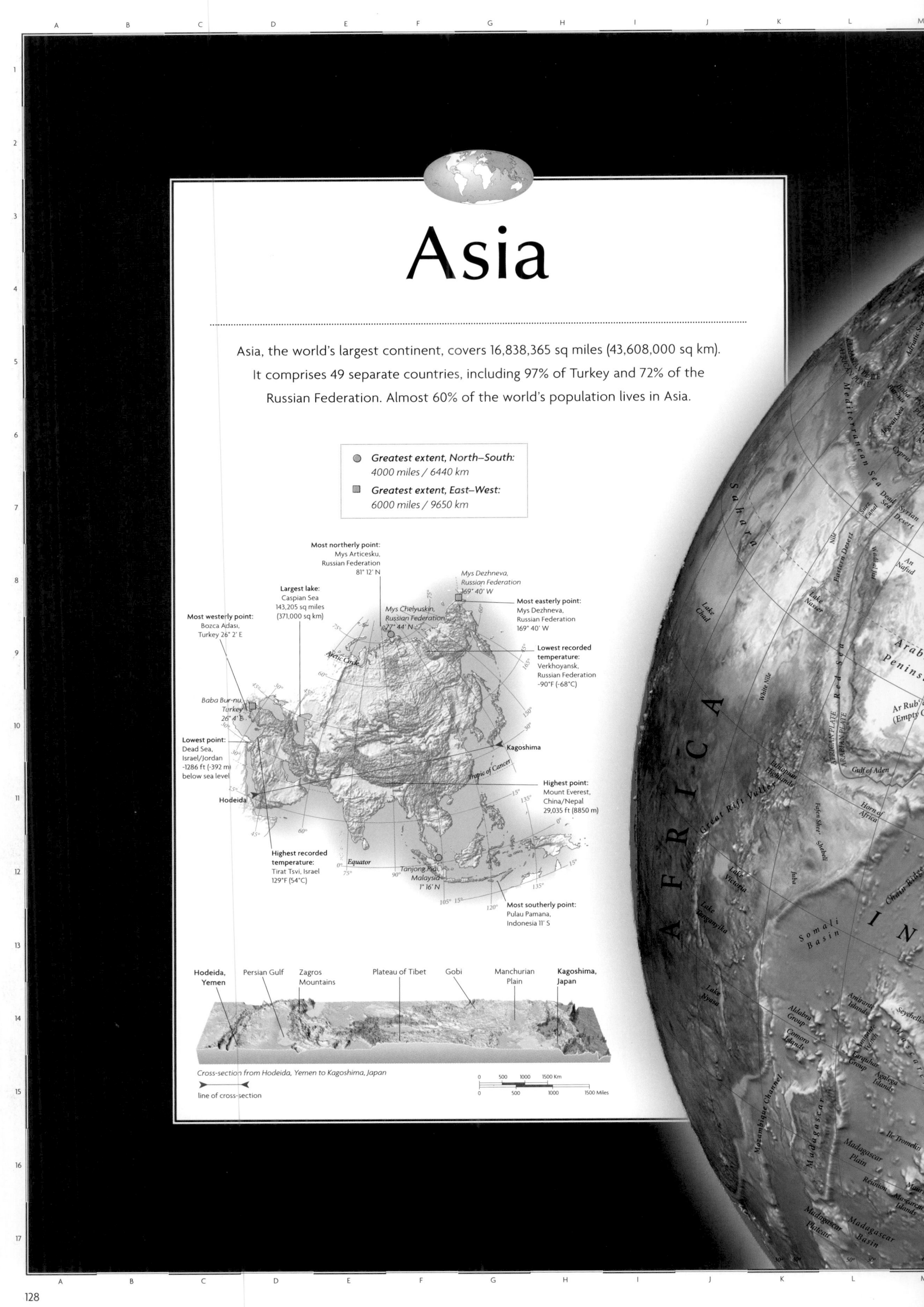

- **Greatest extent, North–South:**
  4000 miles / 6440 km
- **Greatest extent, East–West:**
  6000 miles / 9650 km

Most northerly point:
Mys Articesku,
Russian Federation
81° 12' N

Largest lake:
Caspian Sea
143,205 sq miles
(371,000 sq km)

Mys Dezhneva,
Russian Federation
169° 40' W

Mys Chelyuskin,
Russian Federation
77° 44' N

Most easterly point:
Mys Dezhneva,
Russian Federation
169° 40' W

Most westerly point:
Bozca Adası,
Turkey 26° 2' E

Lowest recorded
temperature:
Verkhoyansk,
Russian Federation
-90°F (-68°C)

Baba Bur-nu,
Turkey
26° 4' E

Lowest point:
Dead Sea,
Israel/Jordan
-1286 ft (-392 m)
below sea level

Kagoshima

Highest point:
Mount Everest,
China/Nepal
29,035 ft (8850 m)

Hodeida

Highest recorded
temperature:
Tirat Tsvi, Israel
129°F (54°C)

Equator

Tanjong Piai,
Malaysia
1° 16' N

Most southerly point:
Pulau Pamana,
Indonesia 11' S

Hodeida,   Persian Gulf   Zagros   Plateau of Tibet   Gobi   Manchurian   Kagoshima,
Yemen   Mountains   Plain   Japan

Cross-section from Hodeida, Yemen to Kagoshima, Japan

line of cross-section

0   500   1000   1500 Km

0   500   1000   1500 Miles

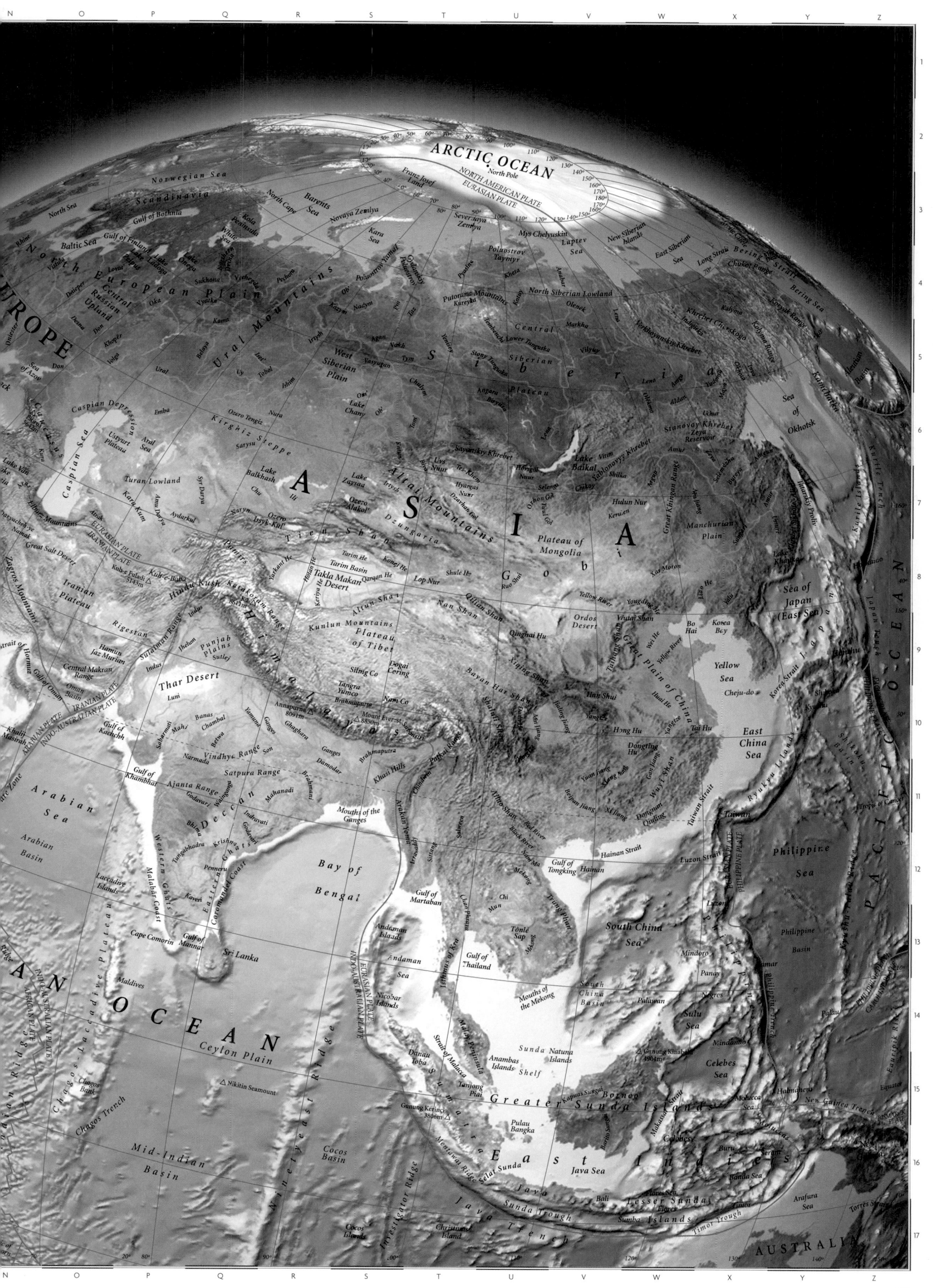

ARCTIC OCEAN
North Pole
NORTH AMERICAN PLATE
EURASIAN PLATE

Norwegian Sea

Scandinavia

North Sea

Baltic Sea

Barents Sea

North Cape

Novaya Zemlya

Kara Sea

Gulf of Bothnia

Gulf of Finland

White Sea

Kola Peninsula

Franz Josef Land

Severnaya Zemlya

Mys Chelyuskin

Laptev Sea

New Siberian Islands

East Siberian Sea

Long Strait

Bering Strait

Bering Sea

Chukot Range

Koryak Range

EUROPE

North European Plain

Central Russian Upland

Ural Mountains

West Siberian Plain

S i b e r i a

Central Siberian Plateau

North Siberian Lowland

Putorana Mountains

Khrebet Cherskogo

Kolyma Range

Sea of Okhotsk

Kuril Trench

Caspian Depression

Kirghiz Steppe

A S I A

Altai Mountains

Plateau of Mongolia

G o b i

Manchurian Plain

Lake Baikal

Stanovoy Khrebet

Zeya Reservoir

Amur

Aral Sea

Turan Lowland

Lake Balkhash

Tien Shan

Dzungaria

Hulun Nur

Sea of Japan (East Sea)

Caspian Sea

Caucasus

Iranian Plateau

Zagros Mountains

Hindu Kush

Takla Makan Desert

Tarim Basin

Lop Nur

Altun Shan

Nan Shan

Qilian Shan

Ordos Desert

Yellow River

Wu Tai Shan

Great Plain of China

Bo Hai

Korea Bay

Yellow Sea

Cheju-do

Kyushu

East China Sea

Ryukyu Islands

Taiwan

Kunlun Mountains

Plateau of Tibet

H i m a l a y a s

Mount Everest 8850m

Thar Desert

Iranian Plateau

Arabian Sea

Arabian Basin

Deccan

Western Ghats

Eastern Ghats

Bay of Bengal

Mouths of the Ganges

Arakan Yoma

Gulf of Martaban

Andaman Islands

Andaman Sea

Gulf of Thailand

Tônlé Sap

South China Sea

Mindoro

Palawan

Philippine Sea

Philippine Basin

Luzon

PHILIPPINE PLATE

PACIFIC OCEAN

Japan Trench

Ceylon Plain

Laccadive Islands

Maldives

Cape Comorin

Gulf of Mannar

Sri Lanka

Isthmus of Kra

Nicobar Islands

Mouths of the Mekong

South China Basin

Sulu Sea

Celebes Sea

Chagos-Laccadive Plateau

Chagos Bank

Nikitin Seamount

INDO-AUSTRALIAN PLATE EURASIAN PLATE

Malay Peninsula

Sunda Shelf

Natuna Islands

Anambas Islands

Borneo

Gunung Kinabalu 4101m

Greater Sunda Islands

Halmahera

Celebes

Buru

Ceram

New Guinea Trench

Chagos Trench

Mid-Indian Basin

I N D I A N O C E A N

Ninetyeast Ridge

Cocos Basin

Sumatra

Danau Toba

Strait of Malacca

Tanjong Piai

Gunung Kerinci 3806m

Pulau Bangka

Selat Sunda

Java Sea

E a s t I n d i e s

Java

Bali

Lesser Sundas

Sumba Islands

Timor

Banda Sea

Arafura Sea

Torres Strait

Cocos Islands

Christmas Island

Java Trench

Sunda Trough

Timor Trough

AUSTRALIA

Physical Asia

The structure of Asia can be divided into two distinct regions. The landscape of
northern Asia consists of old mountain chains, shields, plateaus, and basins, like the
Ural Mountains in the west and the Central Siberian Plateau to the east. To the
south of this region, are a series of plateaus and basins, including the vast Plateau of
Tibet and the Tarim Basin. In contrast, the landscapes of southern Asia are much younger, formed by
tectonic activity beginning about 65 million years ago, leading to an almost continuous mountain
chain running from Europe, across much of Asia, and culminating in the mighty Himalayan mountain
belt, formed when the Indo-Australian Plate collided with the Eurasian Plate. They are still being
uplifted today. North of the mountains lies a belt of deserts, including the Gobi and the Takla Makan.
In the far south, tectonic activity has formed narrow island arcs, extending over 4000 miles (7000 km).
To the west lies the Arabian Shield, once part of the African Plate. As it was rifted apart from Africa,
the Arabian Plate collided with the Eurasian Plate, uplifting the Zagros Mountains.

Coastal Lowlands and Island Arcs

The coastal plains that fringe Southeast Asia contain
many large delta systems, caused by high levels of
rainfall and erosion of the Himalayas, the Plateau of
Tibet, and relict loess deposits. To the south is an
extensive island archipelago, lying on the drowned
Sunda Shelf. Most of these islands are volcanic in origin,
caused by the subduction of the Indo-Australian Plate
beneath the Eurasian Plate.

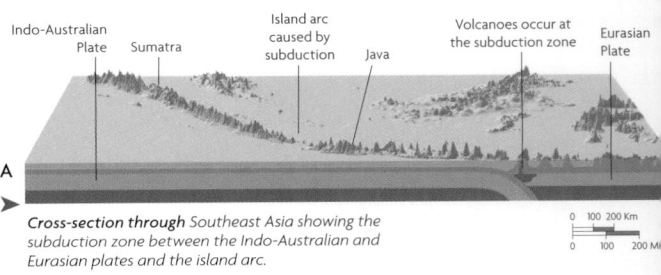

Cross-section through Southeast Asia showing the
subduction zone between the Indo-Australian and
Eurasian plates and the island arc.

The Indian Shield and Himalayan System

The large shield area beneath the Indian
subcontinent is between 2.5 and 3.5 billion
years old. As the floor of the southern
Indian Ocean spread, it pushed the Indian
Shield north. This was eventually driven
beneath the Plateau of Tibet. This process
closed up the ancient Tethys Sea and
uplifted the world's highest mountain
chain, the Himalayas. Much of the uplifted
rock strata was from the seabed of the
Tethys Sea, partly accounting for the
weakness of the rocks and the high levels
of erosion found in the Himalayas.

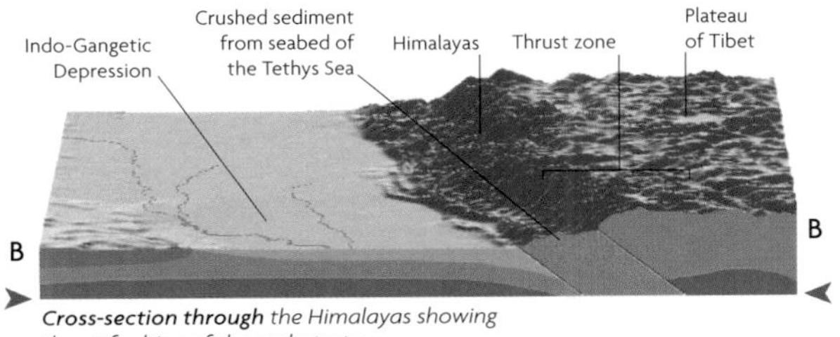

Cross-section through the Himalayas showing
thrust faulting of the rock strata.

East Asian Plains and Uplands

Several, small, isolated shield areas, such as the
Shandong Peninsula, are found in east Asia. Between
these stable shield areas, large river systems like
the Yangtze and the Yellow River have deposited
thick layers of sediment, forming extensive
alluvial plains. The largest of these is the
Great Plain of China, the relief of which
does not rise above 300 ft (100 m).

Map key

Elevation

	6000m / 19,686ft
	4000m / 13,124ft
	3000m / 9843ft
	2000m / 6562ft
	1000m / 3281ft
	500m / 1640ft
	250m / 820ft
	100m / 328ft
	sea level

Plate margins
(for explanation see page xiv)

	constructive
	destructive
	conservative
	uncertain
	physiographic regions
	line of cross-section

Scale 1:63,000,000

projection: Lambert Azimuthal Equal Area

The Arabian Shield and Iranian Plateau

Approximately five million years ago, rifting of
the continental crust split the Arabian Plate from
the African Plate and flooded the Red Sea. As this
rift spread, the Arabian Plate collided with the
Eurasian Plate, transforming part of the Tethys
seabed into the Zagros Mountains which run
northwest-southeast across western Iran.

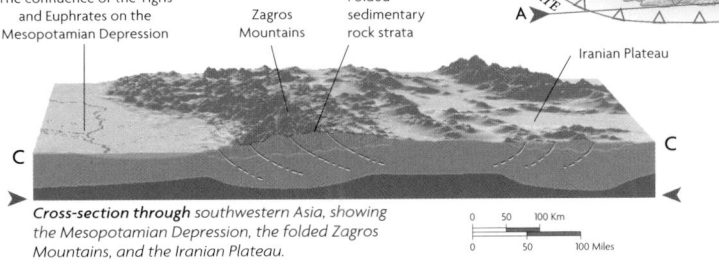

Cross-section through southwestern Asia, showing
the Mesopotamian Depression, the folded Zagros
Mountains, and the Iranian Plateau.

Climate

he climate of Asia exhibits marked differences from region to region, with
eezing polar conditions in the north, hot and cold deserts in central regions
d subtropical conditions throughout the south. Much of this variation can
e attributed to enormous mountain barriers and internal depressions found
ross the continent. Monsoon winds, which reverse semiannually, cause
ternate wet and dry seasons across southern Asia. These air
asses moving north from the ocean are stripped of their
oisture over the Himalayas causing arid
nditions across the Plateau of
bet. Both the south and east
e susceptible to tropical
clones or typhoons.

▲ *Tropical cyclones occur principally
during late summer and early fall. The
intense winds and heavy rainfall can
devastate entire villages.*

Temperature

Average January temperature

Average July temperature

Temperature

below -30°C (-22°F)	0 to 10°C (32 to 50°F)
-30 to -20°C (-22 to -4°F)	10 to 20°C (50°F)
-20 to -10°C (-4 to 14°F)	20 to 30°C (68 to 86°F)
-10 to 0°C (14 to 32°F)	above 30°C (86°F)

Climate

tundra	☼ daily hours of sunshine, January
subarctic	
cool continental	☼ daily hours of sunshine, July
warm humid	
mediterranean	→ cyclone
semi-arid	→ typhoon
arid	→ cold/dry monsoon
humid equatorial	→ warm/wet monsoon
tropical	→ cold wind

▶ *The Gobi Desert experiences major
extremes in climate, with winter temperatures
sometimes falling below -40°C (-40°F) and
summer temperatures exceeding 45°C (113°F).*

Rainfall

Average January rainfall

Average July rainfall

Rainfall

0 – 25 mm (0–1 in)
25–50 mm (1–2 in)
50–100 mm (2–4 in)
100–200 mm (4–8 in)
200–300 mm (8–12 in)
300–400 mm (12–16 in)
400–500 mm (16–20 in)
more than 500 mm (20 in)

◀ *Through India, the southwest
monsoon, which brings heavy rainfall
from May to September, accounts for
80% of annual precipitation.*

haping the landscape

the north, melting of extensive permafrost leads to typical
riglacial features such as thermokarst. In the arid areas wind action
ansports sand creating extensive dune systems. An active tectonic
argin in the south causes continued uplift, and volcanic and seismic
tivity, but also high rates of weathering and erosion. Across the
ntinent, huge rivers erode and transport vast quantities of
diment depositing it on the plains or forming large deltas.

River systems

1 Vast river systems flow across Asia,
many originating in the Himalayas and
the Plateau of Tibet. Seasonal melting of
snow and monsoon rains swell the river
flow leading to flooding and erosion.
The Yellow River *(right)* gets its color
from the high level of eroded material
from the loess plateau.

*River systems: erosion of
the loess plateau by the
yellow river*

Chemical weathering

2 Tower karsts are widespread
across south China *(left)* and
Vietnam. It is thought the karstic
towers were formed under a soil
cover, where small depressions in
the limestone bedrock began to
be weathered by soil water acids,
eventually creating larger hollows.
This process continued over
millions of years, deepening the
hollows and leaving steep-sided
limestone hills.

*Chemical weathering:
formation of tower karst*

Sedimentation

4 The Ganges/Brahmaputra is a tide-
dominated delta *(below)*. The two rivers
transport huge quantities of mountain
sediment, which is deposited on the delta plain.
This debris is then redistributed by tidal
currents, to form extensions to the bars, beach
ridges, and deltaic deposits.

*Sedimentation: the
destruction of a delta*

lcanic activity

Volcanic eruptions
ur frequently across
theast Asia's island
s *(below)*. Low-level
otions occur when
undwater, superheated
underlying magma,
omes pressurized,
ing hot fluid and rocks
through cracks in the
canic cone. This is known
phreatic eruption.

*Volcanic activity: a
phreatic eruption*

Landscape

▨ limestone region	••• area of tectonic activity
sinking land	
stable land	--- limit of permafrost
uplifting land	
▲ active volcano	→ ocean current

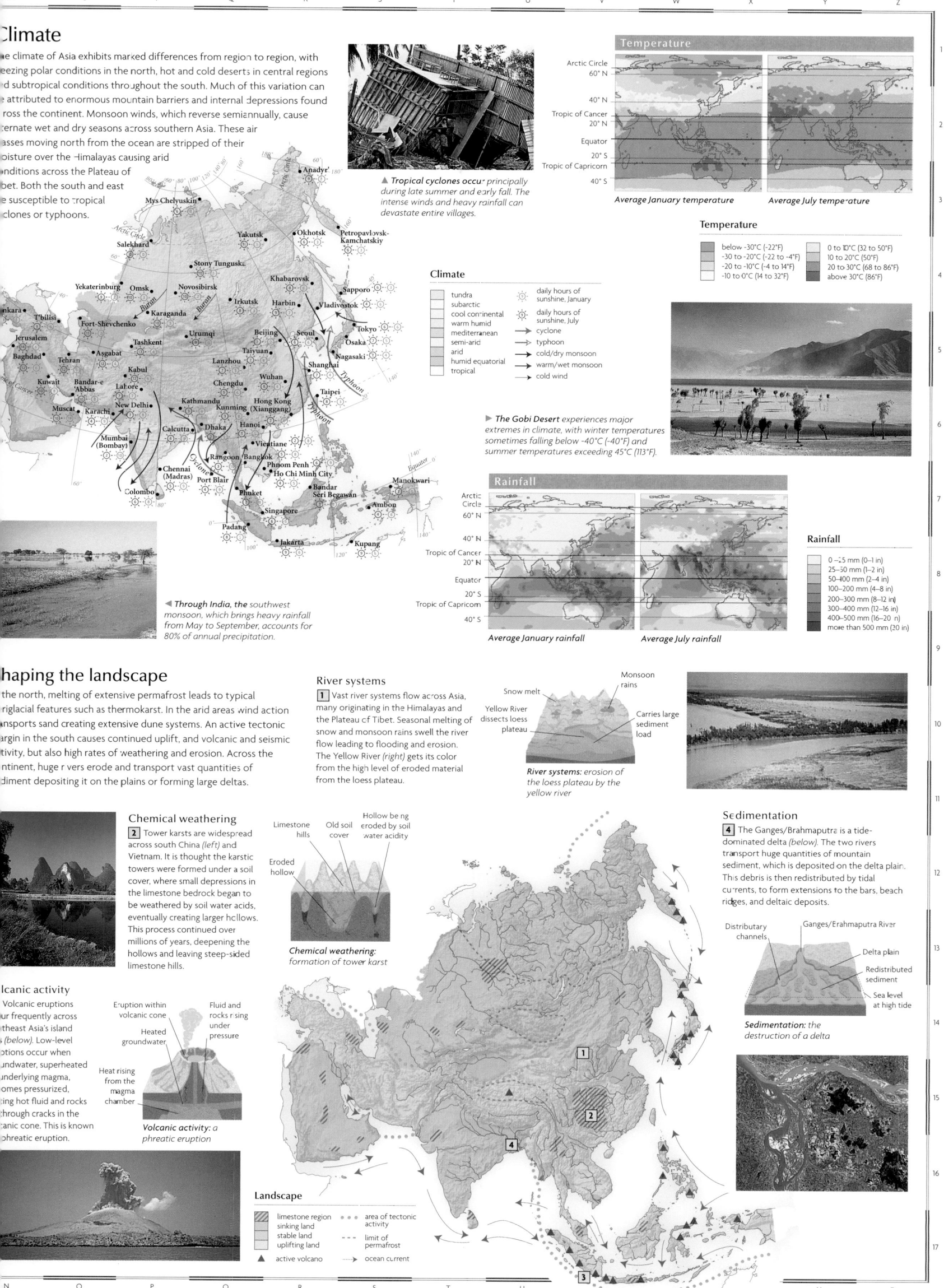

Political Asia

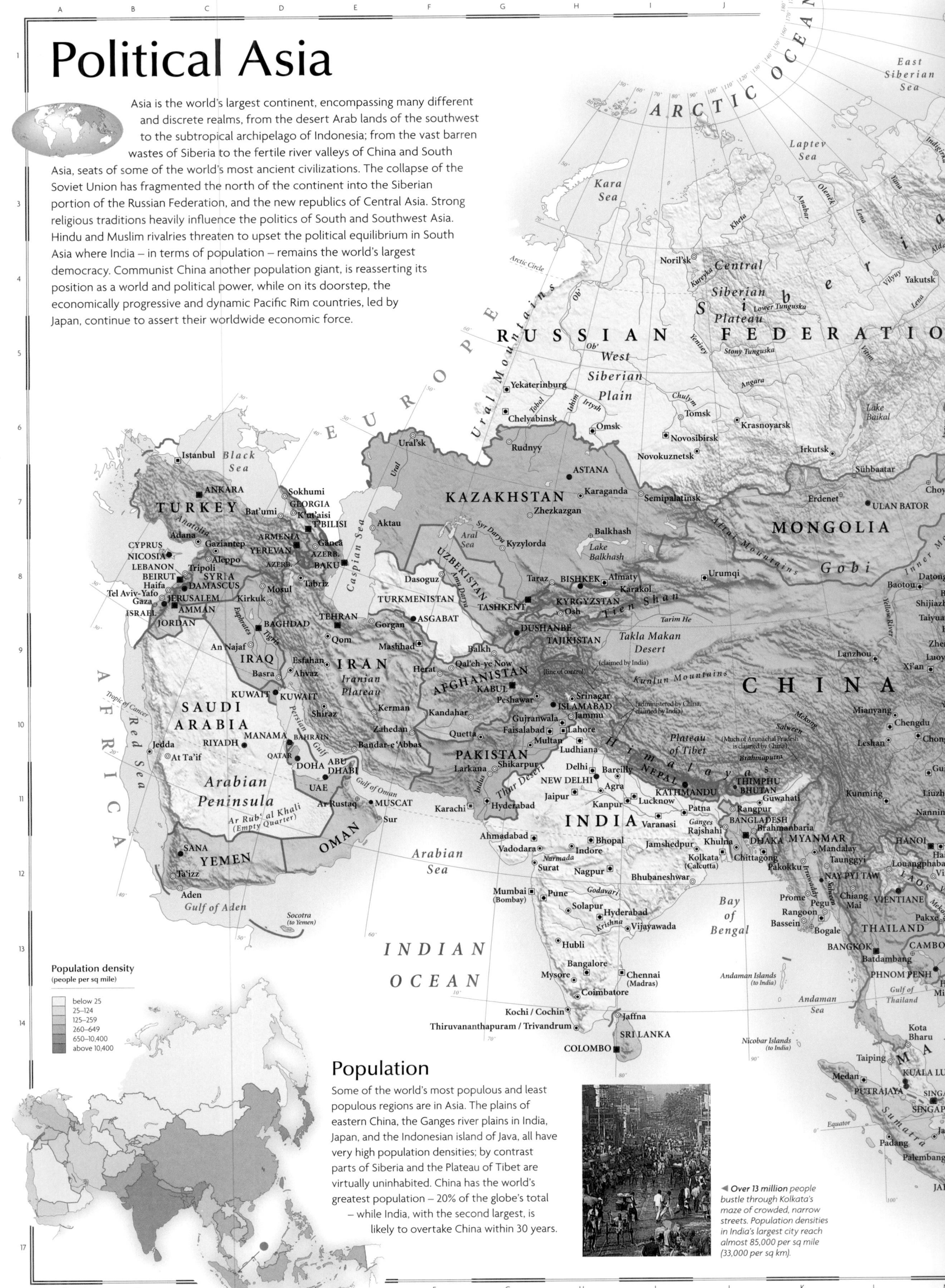

Asia is the world's largest continent, encompassing many different and discrete realms, from the desert Arab lands of the southwest to the subtropical archipelago of Indonesia; from the vast barren wastes of Siberia to the fertile river valleys of China and South Asia, seats of some of the world's most ancient civilizations. The collapse of the Soviet Union has fragmented the north of the continent into the Siberian portion of the Russian Federation, and the new republics of Central Asia. Strong religious traditions heavily influence the politics of South and Southwest Asia. Hindu and Muslim rivalries threaten to upset the political equilibrium in South Asia where India – in terms of population – remains the world's largest democracy. Communist China another population giant, is reasserting its position as a world and political power, while on its doorstep, the economically progressive and dynamic Pacific Rim countries, led by Japan, continue to assert their worldwide economic force.

Population density
(people per sq mile)

- below 25
- 25–124
- 125–259
- 260–649
- 650–10,400
- above 10,400

Population

Some of the world's most populous and least populous regions are in Asia. The plains of eastern China, the Ganges river plains in India, Japan, and the Indonesian island of Java, all have very high population densities; by contrast parts of Siberia and the Plateau of Tibet are virtually uninhabited. China has the world's greatest population – 20% of the globe's total – while India, with the second largest, is likely to overtake China within 30 years.

◄ *Over 13 million people bustle through Kolkata's maze of crowded, narrow streets. Population densities in India's largest city reach almost 85,000 per sq mile (33,000 per sq km).*

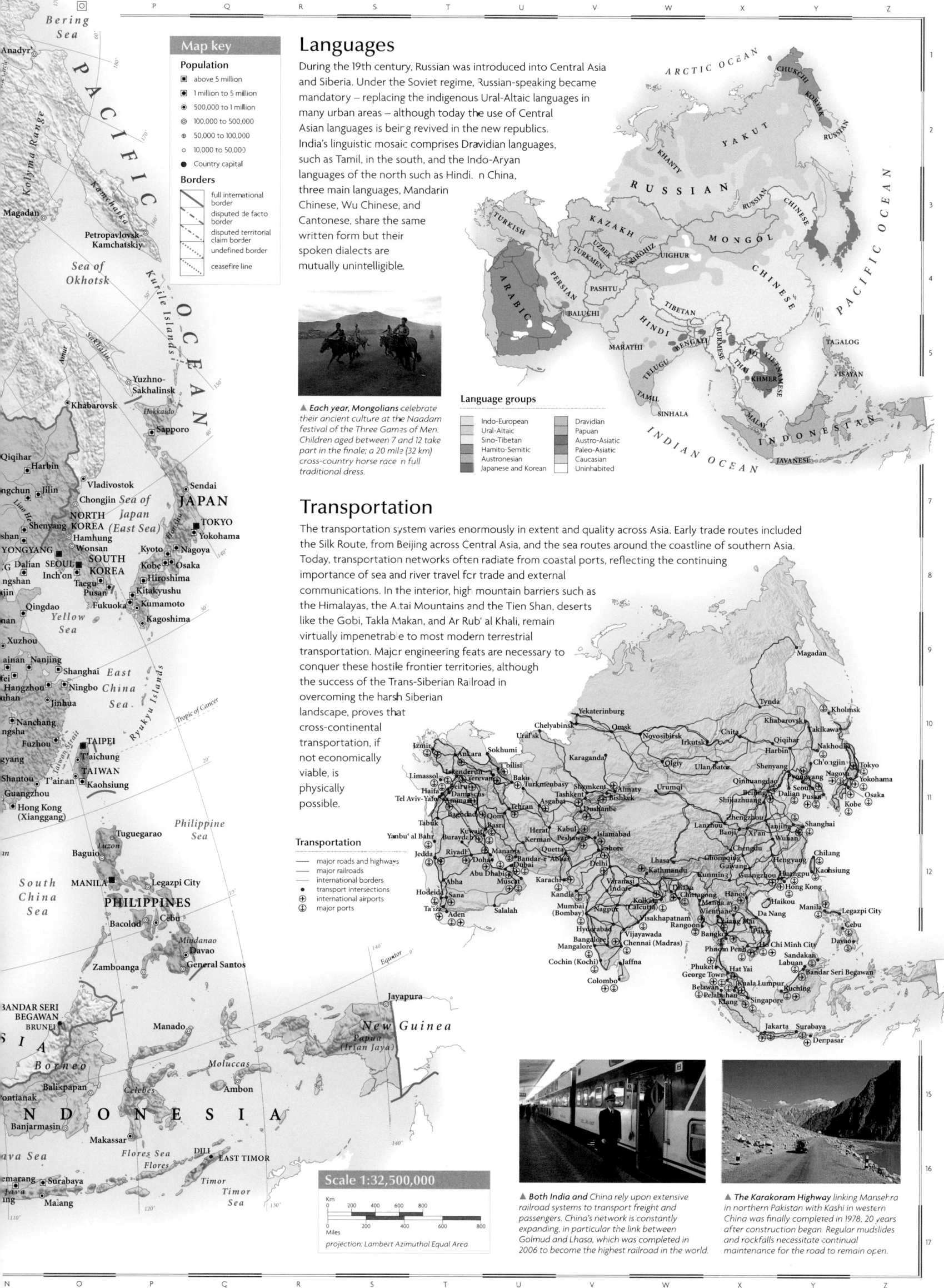

Map key

Population
- ■ above 5 million
- ◨ 1 million to 5 million
- ◉ 500,000 to 1 million
- ◎ 100,000 to 500,000
- ⊕ 50,000 to 100,000
- ○ 10,000 to 50,000
- ■ Country capital

Borders
- full international border
- disputed de facto border
- disputed territorial claim border
- undefined border
- ceasefire line

Languages

During the 19th century, Russian was introduced into Central Asia and Siberia. Under the Soviet regime, Russian-speaking became mandatory – replacing the indigenous Ural-Altaic languages in many urban areas – although today the use of Central Asian languages is being revived in the new republics. India's linguistic mosaic comprises Dravidian languages, such as Tamil, in the south, and the Indo-Aryan languages of the north such as Hindi. In China, three main languages, Mandarin Chinese, Wu Chinese, and Cantonese, share the same written form but their spoken dialects are mutually unintelligible.

▲ Each year, Mongolians celebrate their ancient culture at the Naadam festival of the Three Games of Men. Children aged between 7 and 12 take part in the finale; a 20 mile (32 km) cross-country horse race in full traditional dress.

Language groups
- Indo-European
- Ural-Altaic
- Sino-Tibetan
- Hamito-Semitic
- Austronesian
- Japanese and Korean
- Dravidian
- Papuan
- Austro-Asiatic
- Paleo-Asiatic
- Caucasian
- Uninhabited

Transportation

The transportation system varies enormously in extent and quality across Asia. Early trade routes included the Silk Route, from Beijing across Central Asia, and the sea routes around the coastline of southern Asia. Today, transportation networks often radiate from coastal ports, reflecting the continuing importance of sea and river travel for trade and external communications. In the interior, high mountain barriers such as the Himalayas, the Altai Mountains and the Tien Shan, deserts like the Gobi, Takla Makan, and Ar Rub' al Khali, remain virtually impenetrable to most modern terrestrial transportation. Major engineering feats are necessary to conquer these hostile frontier territories, although the success of the Trans-Siberian Railroad in overcoming the harsh Siberian landscape, proves that cross-continental transportation, if not economically viable, is physically possible.

Transportation
- major roads and highways
- major railroads
- international borders
- • transport intersections
- ⊕ international airports
- ⊕ major ports

Scale 1:32,500,000

Km
0 200 400 600 800

Miles
0 200 400 600 800

projection: Lambert Azimuthal Equal Area

▲ Both India and China rely upon extensive railroad systems to transport freight and passengers. China's network is constantly expanding, in particular the link between Golmud and Lhasa, which was completed in 2006 to become the highest railroad in the world.

▲ The Karakoram Highway linking Mansehra in northern Pakistan with Kashi in western China was finally completed in 1978, 20 years after construction began. Regular mudslides and rockfalls necessitate continual maintenance for the road to remain open.

Asian resources

Although agriculture remains the economic mainstay of most Asian countries, the number of people employed in agriculture has steadily declined, as new industries have been developed during the past 30 years. China, Indonesia, Malaysia, Thailand, and Turkey have all experienced far-reaching structural change in their economies, while the breakup of the Soviet Union has created a new economic challenge in the Central Asian republics. The countries of The Persian Gulf illustrate the rapid transformation from rural nomadism to modern, urban society which oil wealth has brought to parts of the continent. Asia's most economically dynamic countries, Japan, Singapore, South Korea, and Taiwan, fringe the Pacific Ocean and are known as the Pacific Rim. In contrast, other Southeast Asian countries like Laos and Cambodia remain both economically and industrially underdeveloped.

Industry

East Asian industry leads the continent in both productivity and efficiency; electronics, hi-tech industries, car manufacture, and shipbuilding are important. The so-called economic "tigers" of the Pacific Rim are Japan, South Korea, and Taiwan and in recent years China has rediscovered its potential as an economic superpower. Heavy industries such as engineering, chemicals, and steel typify the industrial complexes along the corridor created by the Trans-Siberian Railroad, the Fergana Valley in Central Asia, and also much of the huge industrial plain of east China. The discovery of oil in the Persian Gulf has brought immense wealth to countries that previously relied on subsistence agriculture on marginal desert land.

Standard of living

Despite Japan's high standards of living, and Southwest Asia's oil-derived wealth, immense disparities exist across the continent. Afghanistan remains one of the world's most underdeveloped nations, as do the mountain states of Nepal and Bhutan. Further rapid population growth is exacerbating poverty and overcrowding in many parts of India and Bangladesh.

Standard of living
(UN human development index)

low

high

▲ *On a small island* at the southern tip of the Malay Peninsula lies Singapore, one of the Pacific Rim's most vibrant economic centers. Multinational banking and finance form the core of the city's wealth.

GNI per capita (US$)

- below 1999
- 2000–4999
- 5000–9999
- 10,000–19,999
- 20,000–24,999
- above 25,000

Industry

- ✈ aerospace
- brewing
- 🚗 car/vehicle manufacture
- cement
- chemicals
- electronics
- engineering
- 💲 finance
- fish processing
- food processing
- hi-tech industry
- iron & steel
- pharmaceuticals
- printing & publishing
- shipbuilding
- sugar processing
- tea processing
- textiles
- timber processing
- tobacco processing
- coal
- oil
- gas
- • industrial cities
- ▨ major industrial areas

▲ *Iron and steel,* engineering, and shipbuilding typify the heavy industry found in eastern China's industrial cities, especially the nation's leading manufacturing center, Shanghai.

◄ *Traditional industries are* still crucial to many rural economies across Asia. Here, on the Vietnamese coast, salt has been extracted from seawater by evaporation and is being loaded into a van to take to market.

Environmental issues

The transformation of Uzbekistan by the former Soviet Union into the world's fifth largest producer of cotton led to the diversion of several major rivers for irrigation. Starved of this water, the Aral Sea diminished in volume by over 75% since 1960, irreversibly altering the ecology of the area. Heavy industries in eastern China have polluted coastal waters, rivers, and urban air, while in Myanmar, Malaysia, and Indonesia, ancient hardwood rainforests are felled faster than they can regenerate.

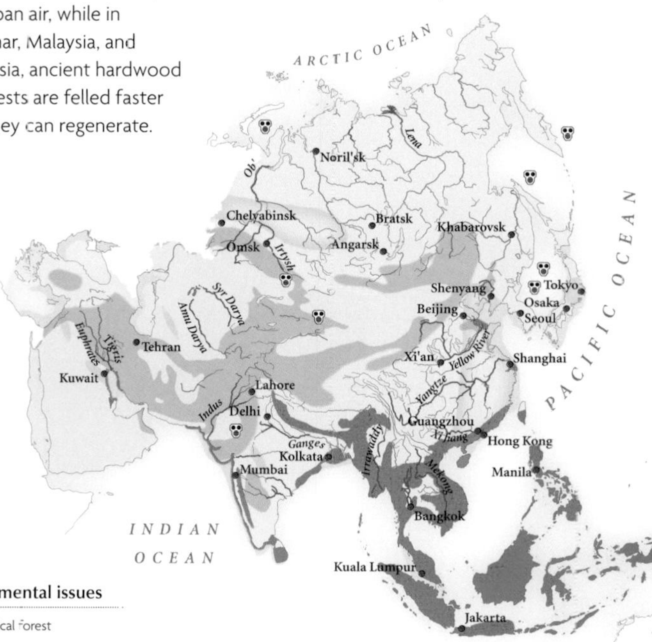

Environmental issues

- tropical forest
- forest destroyed
- desert
- desertification
- acid rain
- polluted rivers
- marine pollution
- heavy marine pollution
- radioactive contamination
- poor urban air quality

▲ Although Siberia remains a quintessentially frozen, inhospitable wasteland, vast untapped mineral reserves – especially the oil and gas of the West Siberian Plain – have lured industrial development to the area since the 1950s and 1960s.

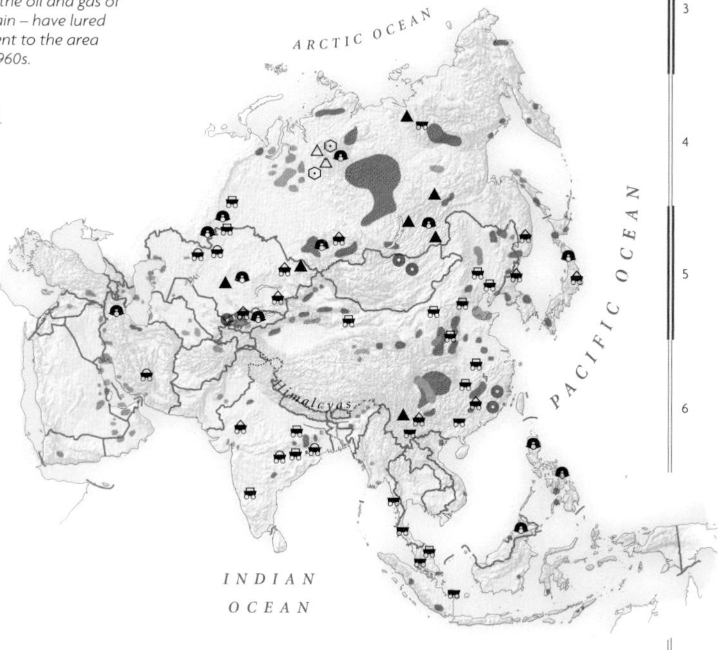

◀ The long-term environmental impact of the Gulf War (1991) is still uncertain. As Iraqi troops left Kuwait, equipment was abandoned to rust and thousands of oil wells were set alight, pouring crude oil into the Persian Gulf.

Mineral resources

At least 60% of the world's known oil and gas deposits are found in Asia; notably the vast oil fields of the Persian Gulf, and the less-exploited oil and gas fields of the Ob' basin in west Siberia. Immense coal reserves in Siberia and China have been utilized to support large steel industries. Southeast Asia has some of the world's largest deposits of tin, found in a belt running down the Malay Peninsula to Indonesia.

Mineral resources

- oil field
- gas field
- coal field
- chromite
- copper
- gold
- iron
- lead
- nickel
- platinum
- tin
- wolfram

Using the land and sea

Vast areas of Asia remain uncultivated as a result of unsuitable climatic and soil conditions. In favourable areas such as river deltas, farming is intensive. Rice is the staple crop of most Asian countries, grown in paddy fields on waterlogged alluvial plains and terraced hillsides, and often irrigated for higher yields. Across the black earth region of the Eurasian steppe in southern Siberia and Kazakhstan, wheat farming is the dominant activity. Cash crops, like tea in Sri Lanka and dates in the Arabian Peninsula, are grown for export, and provide valuable income. The sovereignty of the rich fishing grounds in the South China Sea is disputed by China, Malaysia, Taiwan, the Philippines, and Vietnam because of potential oil reserves.

▲ Date palms have been cultivated in oases throughout the Arabian Peninsula since antiquity. In addition to the fruit, palms are used for timber, fuel, rope, and for making vinegar, syrup and a liquor known as arrack.

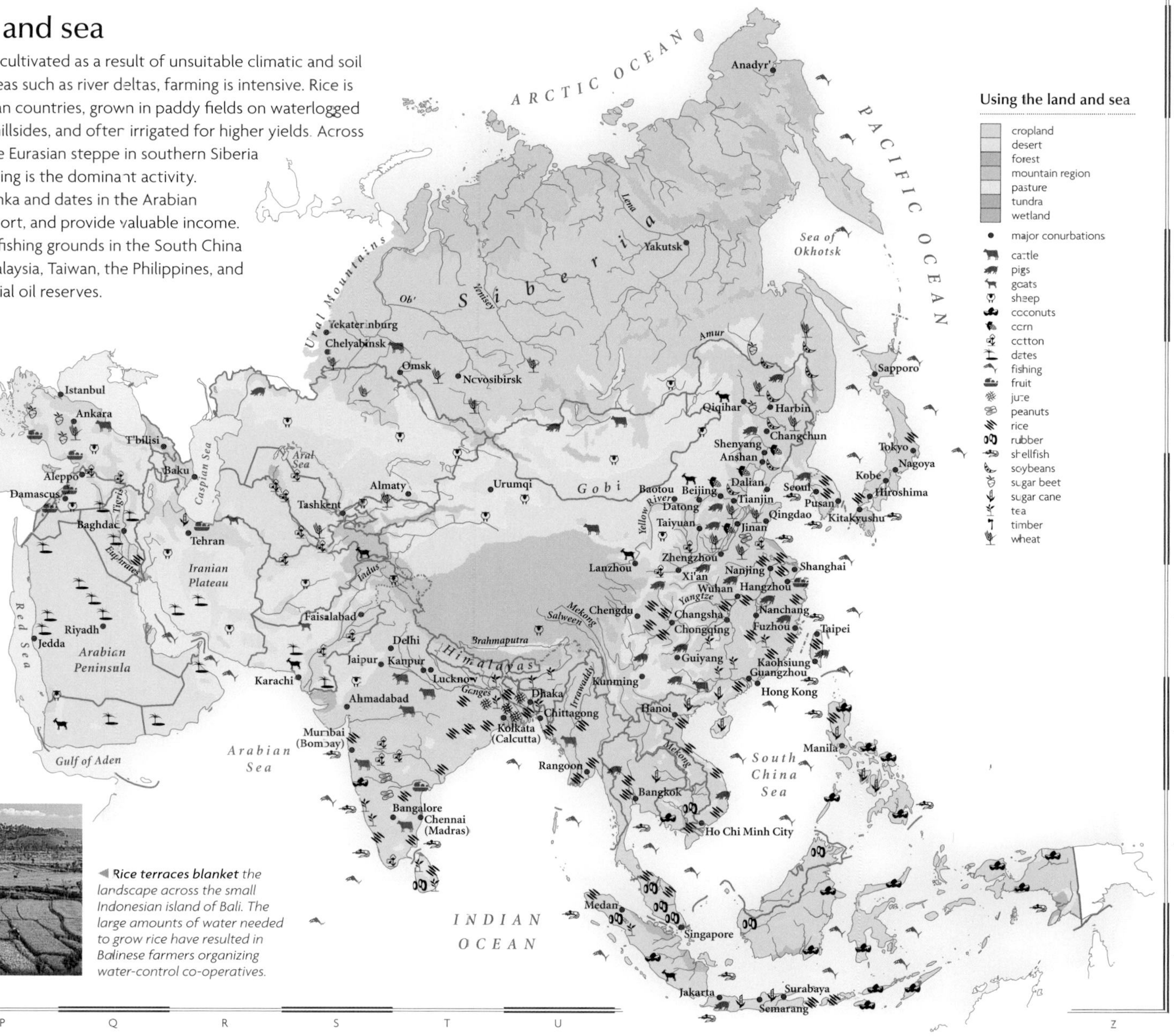

Using the land and sea

- cropland
- desert
- forest
- mountain region
- pasture
- tundra
- wetland
- major conurbations
- cattle
- pigs
- goats
- sheep
- coconuts
- corn
- cotton
- dates
- fishing
- fruit
- jute
- peanuts
- rice
- rubber
- shellfish
- soybeans
- sugar beet
- sugar cane
- tea
- timber
- wheat

◀ Rice terraces blanket the landscape across the small Indonesian island of Bali. The large amounts of water needed to grow rice have resulted in Balinese farmers organizing water-control co-operatives.

135

Turkey & the Caucasus

ARMENIA, AZERBAIJAN, GEORGIA, TURKEY

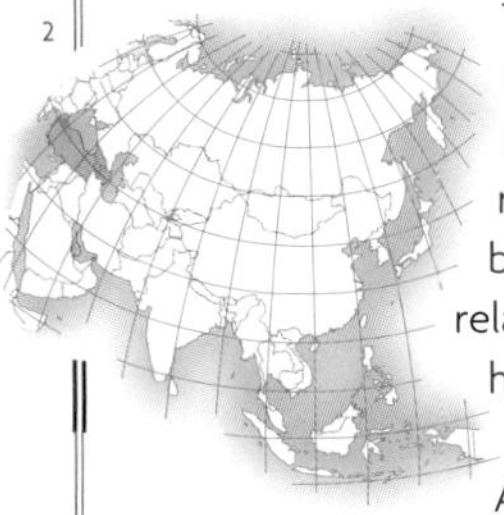

This region occupies the fragmented junction between Europe, Asia, and the Russian Federation. Sunni Islam provides a common identity for the secular state of Turkey, which the revered leader Kemal Atatürk established from the remnants of the Ottoman Empire after the First World War. Turkey has a broad resource base and expanding trade links with Europe, but the east is relatively undeveloped and strife between the state and a large Kurdish minority has yet to be resolved. Georgia is similarly challenged by ethnic separatism, while the Christian state of Armenia and the mainly Muslim and oil-rich Azerbaijan are locked in conflict over the territory of Nagorno-Karabakh.

Using the land & sea

Turkey is largely self-sufficient in food. The irrigated Black Sea coastlands have the world's highest yields of hazelnuts. Tobacco, cotton, sultanas, tea, and figs are the region's main cash crops and a great range of fruit and vegetables are grown. Wine grapes are among the labor-intensive crops which allow full use of limited agricultural land in the Caucasus. Sturgeon fishing is particularly important in Azerbaijan.

Transportation & industry

Turkey leads the region's well diversified economy. Petrochemicals, textiles, engineering, and food processing are the main industries. Azerbaijan is able to export oil, while the other states rely heavily on hydroelectric power and imported fuel. Georgia produces precision machinery. War and earthquake damage have devastated Armenia's infrastructure.

▲ **Azerbaijan has substantial** oil reserves, located in and around the Caspian Sea. They were some of the earliest oilfields in the world to be exploited.

Land use and agricultural distribution

- cattle
- goats
- cotton
- fishing
- fruit
- hazelnuts
- olives
- sugar beet
- tobacco
- vineyards

- capital cities
- major towns

- pasture
- cropland
- forest

The urban/rural population divide

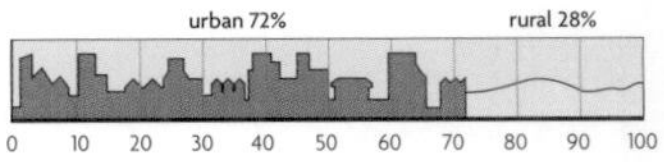

urban 72%   rural 28%

0 10 20 30 40 50 60 70 80 90 100

Population density	Total land area
238 people per sq mile (92 people per sq km)	368,912 sq miles (955,730 sq km)

Major industry and infrastructure

- carpet weaving
- cement
- chemicals
- coal
- engineering
- food processing
- oil
- textiles
- tourism
- vehicle manufacture

- capital cities
- major towns
- international airports
- major roads
- major industrial areas

Transportation network

114,867 miles (184,882 km)

5778 miles (9300 km)

8120 miles (13,069 km)

745 miles (1200 km)

Physical and political barriers have severely limited communications between Armenia, Georgia and Azerbaijan. Turkey has a relatively well-developed transportation network.

▲ **For many centuries,** Istanbul has held tremendous strategic importance as a crucial gateway between Europe and Asia. Founded by the Greeks as Byzantium, the city became the center of the East Roman Empire and was known as Constantinople to the Romans. From the 15th century onward the city became the center of the great Ottoman Empire.

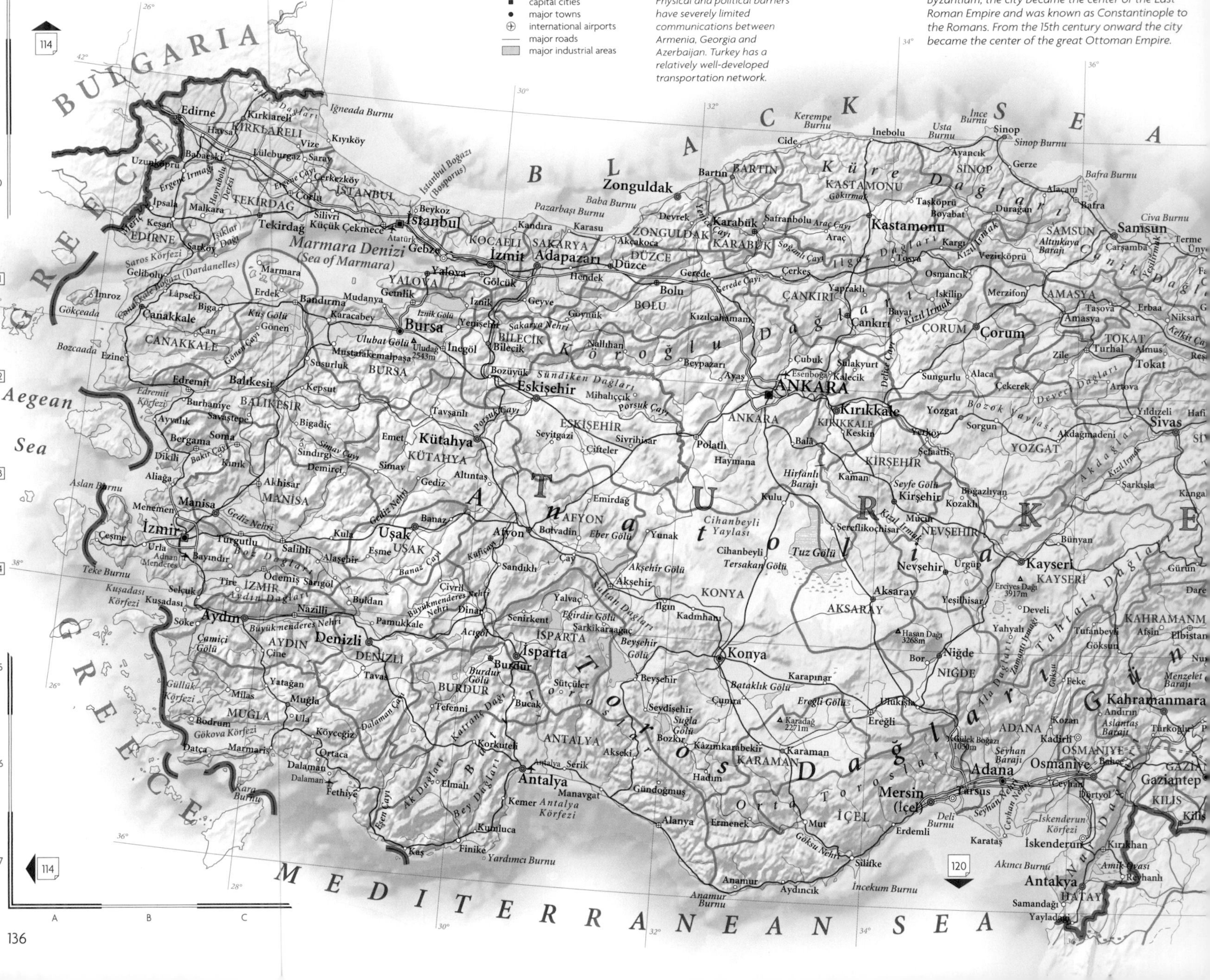

The landscape

The deeply eroded hills and salty basins of the Anatolian Plateau are bordered by several mountain ranges along the Black Sea coast, and the limestone Taurus Mountains (Toros Daglari) in the south. A lowland trough divides the Caucasus and the Lesser Caucasus, which form a formidable barrier of peaks in the north.

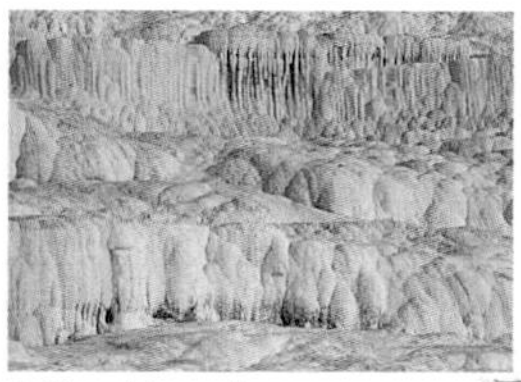

Limestone weathering in the Anatolian Plateau

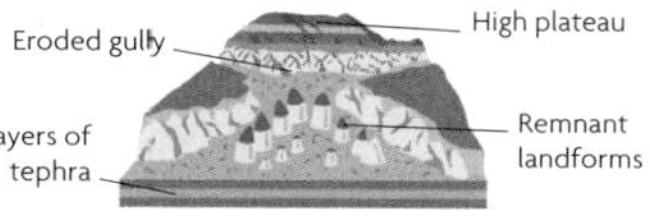

Eroded gully — High plateau
Layers of tephra — Remnant landforms

▲ In central Turkey, rainwater has chemically weathered away numerous layers of limestone, leaving isolated outcrops and pinnacles and deep eroded gullies.

▶ The Caucasus are fold mountains, which formed around the same time as the Taurus Mountains (Toros Daglari) around 65 million years ago and have since been modified by volcanic erruptions.

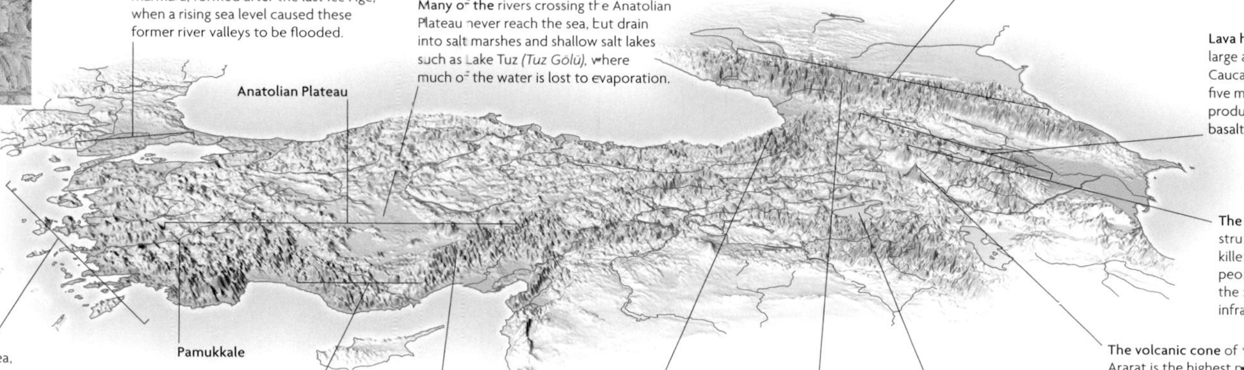

▲ The white rock terraces at Pamukkale in western Turkey were formed when underground water, heated by volcanic activity, dissolved minerals in the rocks. When the water reached the surface and evaporated the minerals were left behind in these extraordinary formations.

The straits of the Bosporus and the Dardanelles, respectively linking the Black and Mediterranean seas with the Sea of Marmara, formed after the last Ice Age, when a rising sea level caused these former river valleys to be flooded.

Many of the rivers crossing the Anatolian Plateau never reach the sea, but drain into salt marshes and shallow salt lakes such as Lake Tuz (Tuz Golu), where much of the water is lost to evaporation.

Lava has flowed over large areas of the Lesser Caucasus within the last five million years, producing extensive basalt plateaus.

The earthquake that struck Armenia in 1988 killed over 55,000 people and devastated the country's infrastructure.

Long, parallel mountain ranges run from east to west into the Aegean Sea, which has risen since the last Ice Age to form a drowned coastline of numerous islands and extended inlets.

The folded peaks of the Taurus Mountains (Toros Daglari) were formed 60–65 million years ago, at the same time as the Alps. The rock is mainly limestone, with deep caves, gorges, and underground rivers.

The Cilician Gates (Gulek Bogaz), a major pass through the Taurus Mountains (Toros Daglari), is the point where streams flow from the interior plateau onto the lowland of Adana.

Thick, temperate forest veils the seaward slopes of the Kaçkar Daglari. The southern slopes, which lie in a rainshadow, are dry and barren.

The granite massif near Surami divides the lowlands of Georgia from the oil-rich basin of Azerbaijan's Kura river, which has built a large delta into the Caspian Sea.

The shallow, saline Lake Van (Van Golu) is the largest lake in Turkey. Dry terraces mark a previous shoreline 181 ft (55 m) above the present water level.

The volcanic cone of Mount Ararat is the highest peak in Turkey, with an altitude of 16,853 ft (5137 m).

▶ Since the 6th century BC, the pinnacles and caves of east-central Anatolia have been utilized as dwellings. Many are still inhabited today.

Map key

Population
- above 5 million
- 1 million to 5 million
- 500,000 to 1 million
- 100,000 to 500,000
- 50,000 to 100,000
- 10,000 to 50,000
- below 10,000

Elevation
- 4000m / 13,124ft
- 3000m / 9843ft
- 2000m / 6562ft
- 1000m / 3281ft
- 500m / 1640ft
- 250m / 820ft
- 100m / 328ft
- sea level

Scale 1:4,500,000

projection: Lambert Conformal Conic

▲ The fisheries of Azerbaijan are noted for their hauls of sturgeon, and the Caspian Sea accounts for 80% of the world's total catch. However, stocks are now under serious threat due to overfishing.

▲ Traditional steam baths are found throughout the region, and are used for socializing as well as for bathing.

The Near East

IRAQ, ISRAEL, JORDAN, LEBANON, SYRIA

Some of the world's oldest civilizations developed in this region – the Fertile Crescent – which is venerated by Jews, Muslims, and Christians, but torn by competing religious, ethnic, and national claims to the land. Turkish Ottoman rule ended with the First World War and the region was divided into areas administered by Britain and France. The UN endorsed calls for a Jewish homeland in what was then Palestine and in 1948 the state of Israel was declared. Hostility towards the Jewish state led to a series of wars with its Arab neighbors. After 2000, attempts to broker peaceful resolutions with both the Palestinian population and with adjacent Arab states were hampered by a revival of Islamic militarism and conflicting international interests in the oil-rich region. This led to an Israeli retrenchment and culminated in a US-led invasion of Iraq in 2003, which toppled the Ba'athist regime of Saddam Hussein in the name of a "war on terror".

Using the land & sea

Water scarcity limits cropland to the north and to areas watered principally by the Tigris, Euphrates, and Jordan rivers. In Israel, new irrigation techniques are allowing cultivation in the arid Negev. Wheat is the chief grain and large areas of scrub support livestock herding. Commercial produce includes dates, tobacco, citrus fruits, olives, grapes, and cotton, which is Syria's main export crop. Fishing is still important in the Mediterranean.

The urban/rural population divide

urban 70%   rural 30%

Population density	Total land area
217 people per sq mile (84 people per sq km)	325,460 sq miles (843,160 sq km)

Land use and agricultural distribution

- sheep
- cereals
- citrus fruits
- cotton
- dates
- fishing
- rice
- tobacco

- capital cities
- major towns

- pasture
- cropland
- wetland
- desert

Transportation & industry

The petrochemical industry is well established, and central to the economies of Syria and Iraq, which was the world's second largest oil exporter before the war with Iran which began in 1980. Lebanon has traditionally been a center for commerce, while Israel has a well-diversified economy with an expanding tourist industry, despite few natural resources.

Transportation network

	49,859 miles (80,249 km)	
	1365 miles (2197 km)	
	3826 miles (6158 km)	
	1171 miles (1885 km)	

Jordan's seaport of Al 'Aqabah is connected to Damascus in Syria by road and rail. This route to the Red Sea provides for large exports of phosphate and trade with states in the Persian Gulf.

Major industry and infrastructure

- car manufacture
- cement
- chemicals
- electronics
- finance
- food processing
- iron & steel
- oil
- oil refining
- textiles

- capital cities
- major towns
- international airports
- major roads
- major industrial areas

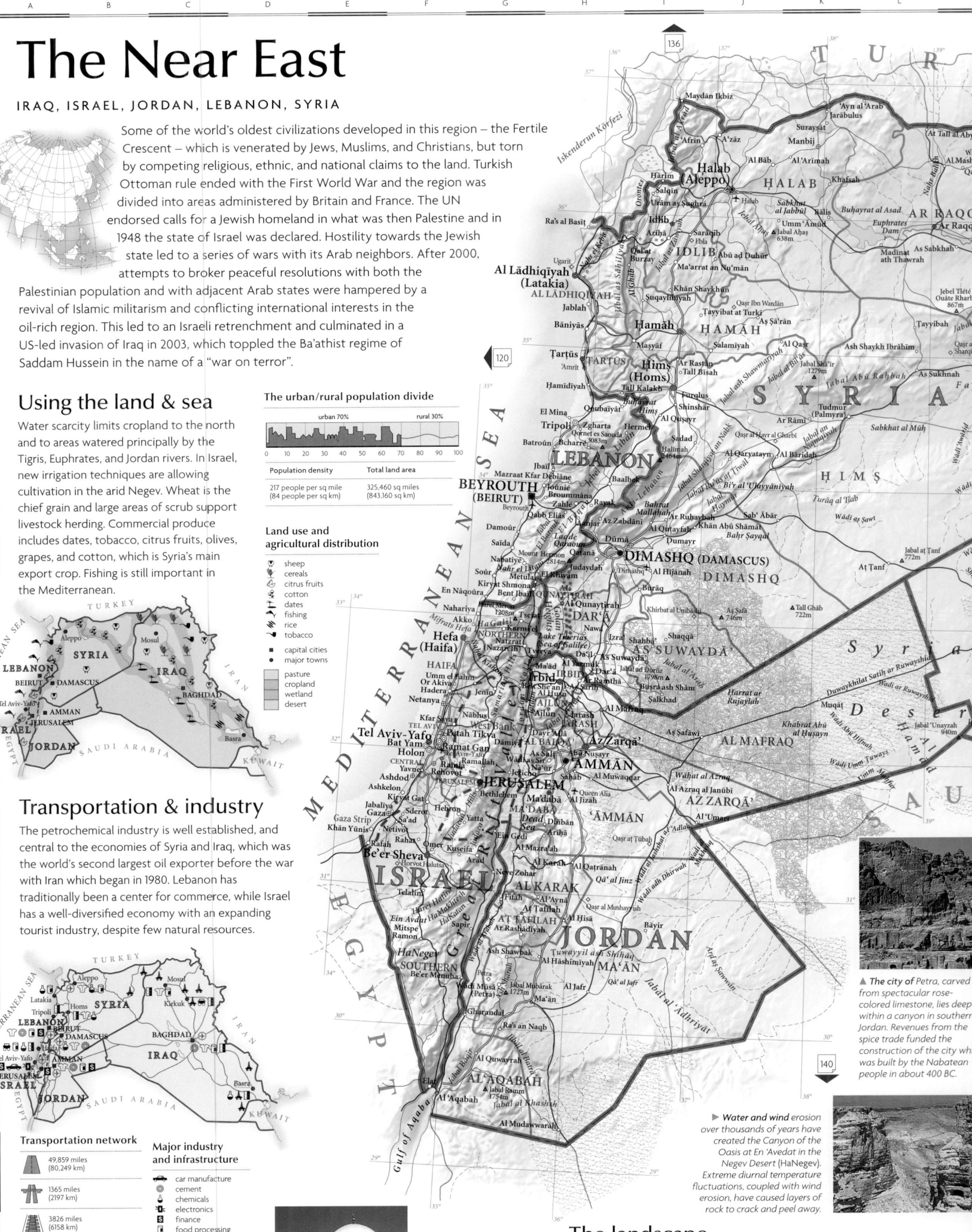

▲ *The city of Petra, carved from spectacular rose-colored limestone, lies deep within a canyon in southern Jordan. Revenues from the spice trade funded the construction of the city which was built by the Nabatean people in about 400 BC.*

▶ *Water and wind erosion over thousands of years have created the Canyon of the Oasis at En 'Avedat in the Negev Desert (HaNegev). Extreme diurnal temperature fluctuations, coupled with wind erosion, have caused layers of rock to crack and peel away.*

◄ *The Dome of the Rock in Jerusalem is a magnificent mosque, revered by Muslims. Close by is the Wailing Wall, the city's most sacred Jewish landmark and the Church of the Holy Sepulchre, a famous Christian place of worship.*

The landscape

The Al Jazirah plateau divides the Euphrates and Tigris rivers, which cross the Mesopotamian plain to reach their confluence in the southeast. The rocky Syrian Desert extends west to the northern extremity of the Great Rift Valley, which runs from the mountains of Lebanon to the Gulf of Aqaba. The Jordan river flows south along this trough into the Dead Sea, divided from the Mediterranean coastal plain by a steep-sided plateau.

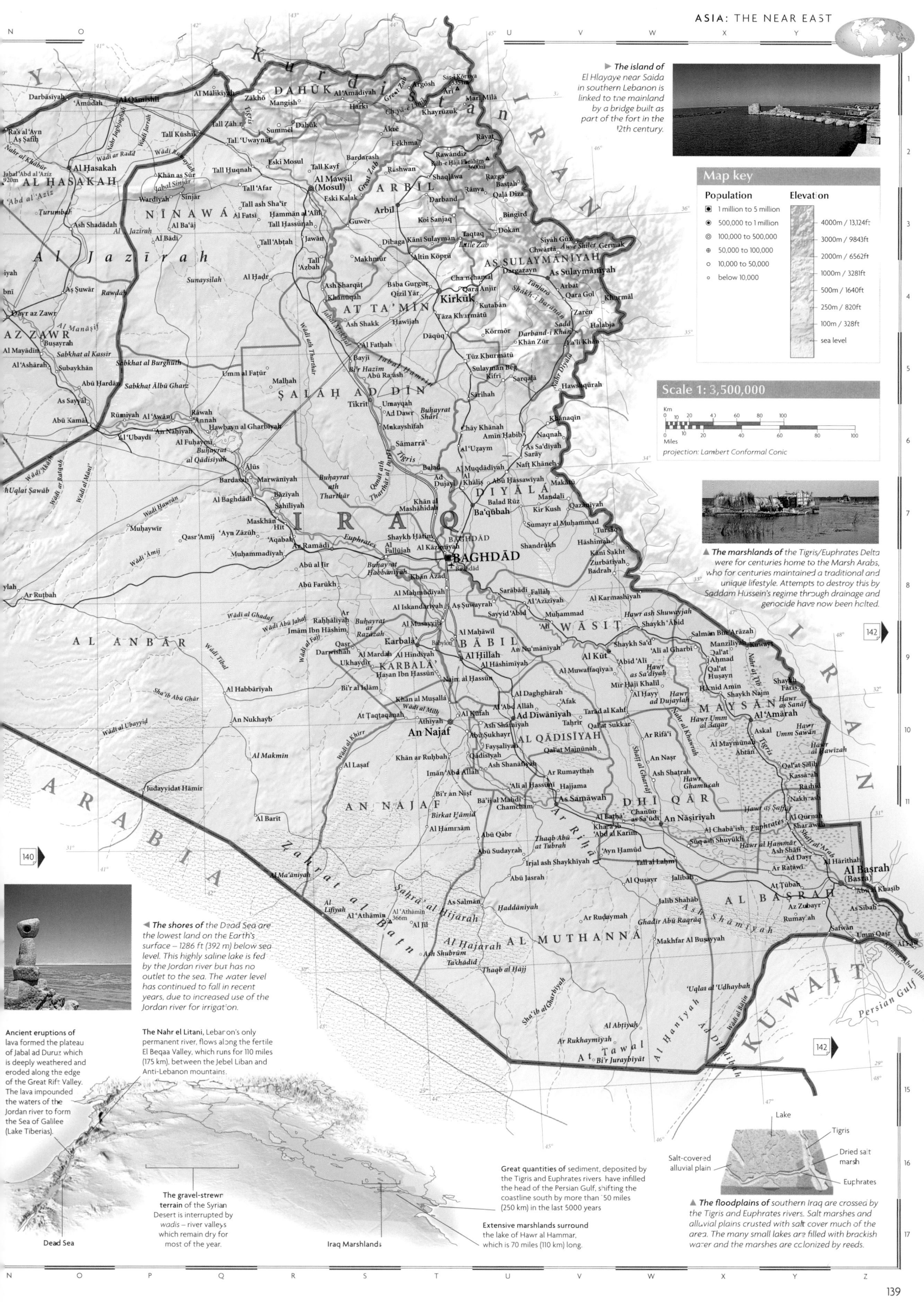

▶ The island of El Hlayaye near Saida in southern Lebanon is linked to the mainland by a bridge built as part of the fort in the 12th century.

Map key

Population

- ◙ 1 million to 5 million
- ◉ 500,000 to 1 million
- ⊚ 100,000 to 500,000
- ⊕ 50,000 to 100,000
- ○ 10,000 to 50,000
- ○ below 10,000

Elevation

- 4000m / 13,124ft
- 3000m / 9843ft
- 2000m / 6562ft
- 1000m / 3281ft
- 500m / 1640ft
- 250m / 820ft
- 100m / 328ft
- sea level

Scale 1: 3,500,000

Km
0 10 20 40 60 80 100

Miles
0 10 20 40 60 80 100

projection: Lambert Conformal Conic

▲ The marshlands of the Tigris/Euphrates Delta were for centuries home to the Marsh Arabs, who for centuries maintained a traditional and unique lifestyle. Attempts to destroy this by Saddam Hussein's regime through drainage and genocide have now been halted.

◀ The shores of the Dead Sea are the lowest land on the Earth's surface – 1286 ft (392 m) below sea level. This highly saline lake is fed by the Jordan river but has no outlet to the sea. The water level has continued to fall in recent years, due to increased use of the Jordan river for irrigation.

Ancient eruptions of lava formed the plateau of Jabal ad Duruz which is deeply weathered and eroded along the edge of the Great Rift Valley. The lava impounded the waters of the Jordan river to form the Sea of Galilee (Lake Tiberias).

The Nahr el Litani, Lebanon's only permanent river, flows along the fertile El Beqaa Valley, which runs for 110 miles (175 km), between the Jebel Liban and Anti-Lebanon mountains.

Dead Sea

The gravel-strewn terrain of the Syrian Desert is interrupted by wadis – river valleys which remain dry for most of the year.

Iraq Marshlands

Great quantities of sediment, deposited by the Tigris and Euphrates rivers have infilled the head of the Persian Gulf, shifting the coastline south by more than 150 miles (250 km) in the last 5000 years.

Extensive marshlands surround the lake of Hawr al Hammar, which is 70 miles (110 km) long.

Lake
Tigris
Salt-covered alluvial plain
Dried salt marsh
Euphrates

▲ The floodplains of southern Iraq are crossed by the Tigris and Euphrates rivers. Salt marshes and alluvial plains crusted with salt cover much of the area. The many small lakes are filled with brackish water and the marshes are colonized by reeds.

The Arabian Peninsula

BAHRAIN, KUWAIT, OMAN, QATAR, SAUDI ARABIA, UNITED ARAB EMIRATES (UAE), YEMEN

Huge expanses of desert cover much of the Arabian Peninsula, limiting settlement to oases, the mountains along the Red Sea, and coastal belts. The most populous area is the fertile highlands of Yemen. The Islamic faith and Arabic language give the region a cultural and religious unity, and the Saudi city of Mecca *(Makkah)* is Islam's most holy place, visited by over two million pilgrims each year. More than half the world's oil reserves are contained in this region, and the exploitation of oil and gas has brought great wealth, particularly to Saudi Arabia. Yemen and Oman are the least developed of the Arabian states, with large rural populations. Within Saudi Arabia over 86% of the people live in urban areas.

Using the land

Most of the Arabian Peninsula is unsuited to settled agriculture, making irrigation and land reclamation projects essential. The narrow coastal plain and isolated oases, commonly amounting to less than 1% of the land area, are used to cultivate grains, coffee, and exotic fruits. Goats, sheep, and camels are widespread throughout the region.

The urban/rural population divide

urban 64%   rural 36%

0 10 20 30 40 50 60 70 80 90 100

Population density	Total land area
50 people per sq mile (19 people per sq km)	1,147,856 sq miles (2,973,720 sq km)

Land use and agricultural distribution

- goats
- sheep
- cereals
- coffee
- dates
- fruit
- capital cities
- major towns
- pasture
- cropland
- desert

◄ **The fertile soils** of Yemen have encouraged settlement of almost all of the land from sea level up to the mountains at 10,000 ft (3050 m). In the higher reaches elaborate terraces have been constructed to facilitate crop cultivation.

The landscape

A plateau more than 2500 ft (760 m) high extends across much of the Arabian Peninsula. The plateau slopes eastward from the massive, rifted escarpment along the coast of the Red Sea, to the shallow waters of the Persian Gulf. The interior is characterized by *cuestas* and valleys, drained by a system of *wadis*. A crescent of sand and gravel deserts lies to the east.

The An Nafud Desert is covered with *barchan* dunes varying between 30–100 ft (10–30 m) high. The "horns" of the crescent-shaped dunes reflect the direction in which they are being moved by the wind.

Inselbergs are dotted over a wide area of the Najd Plateau. These resistant remnants of the ancient basement rock are left standing when the softer weathered rock has been worn away.

Evaporation / Crusted layer left behind / Storm surge flooding / Normal level of tidal range / Salt wedge penetrates inland water

▲ **A sabkha is** a flat, salt-encrusted plain which occurs near the coast just above the high water mark. Flooding by sea water leads to saturation of the land with saline-rich groundwater. As this evaporates, a cracked layer of sand, cemented together with salt, gypsum, and calcium carbonate is left behind.

Few areas in the Arabian Peninsula have rivers flowing through them. Most are drained by ephemeral watercourses called *wadis*.

The Hejaz (Al Hijaz) and Asir mountains form part of the same geological region as the highlands of Sudan and Eritrea, to which they were once joined. They were separated when faulting opened the Red Sea, over 50 million years ago.

Across the Najd Plateau the flat relief is broken by *mesas*; steep-sided rock plateaus and *cuestas*; ridges with one steep and one gentle slope.

▲ **Ar Rub' al Khali,** also known as the Empty Quarter, is the most arid part of the Arabian Peninsula. It is the largest uninterrupted sand desert in the world. Ridges of sand up to 25 miles (40 km) long, run northeast–southwest, giving characteristic linear dunes.

The Jabal an Nabi Shu'ayb in Yemen is the highest point on the peninsula, rising to 12,336 ft (3760 m).

The Arabian Shield underpins the west of the peninsula. It is a fragment of the ancient continent, Gondwanaland, which was separated by rifting millions of years ago.

▲ **Every Muslim must** make at least one pilgrimage or hajj to Mecca (Makkah), in Saudi Arabia, during their lifetime. The cloth-covered shrine is called the Ka'bah, and is regarded by Muslims as the most sacred place on Earth.

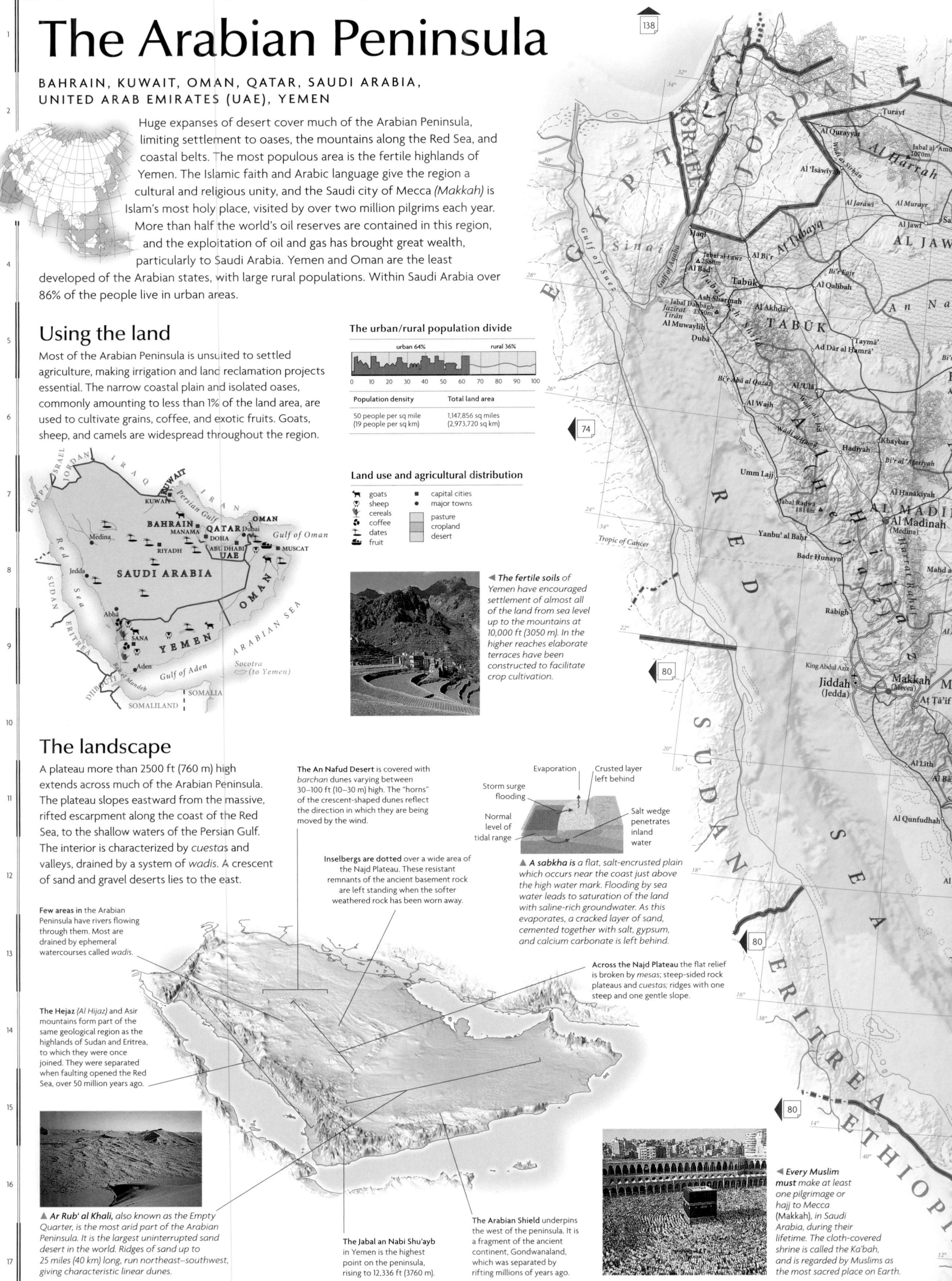

Transportation & industry

The extraction and refining of oil and gas are the major industrial activities in the Arabian Peninsula. The region also has an active construction sector, with many Arab cities reflecting the wealth generated by the oil industry. The service sector is dominated by financial and technical institutions, which, like the construction sector, mainly serve the oil industry. Traditional handicrafts such as carpet-weaving are found in rural areas.

◀ *Saudi Arabia contains the world's largest oil reserves, lying mainly along the Persian Gulf coast. Each day the region produces around 10 million barrels of oil. Here, in the desert, excess oil is being burnt off.*

Transportation network

🛣	44,832 miles (72,159 km)	🚉	673 miles (1083 km)
🚂	670 miles (1078 km)		none

Internal surface transportation is poorly developed across the peninsula. Along the coast, commercial routes have developed, but connections between bordering states rely on major airports.

Major industry and infrastructure

- cement
- chemicals
- iron & steel
- oil
- oil refining
- food processing
- capital cities
- major towns
- international airports
- major roads
- major industrial areas

▶ *Seasonal watercourses or wadis drain much of the interior of the Arabian Peninsula. Although they remain dry for much of the year, they are prone to flash floods after heavy rains.*

Map key

Population
- 1 million to 5 million
- 500,000 to 1 million
- 100,000 to 500,000
- 50,000 to 100,000
- 10,000 to 50,000
- below 10,000

Elevation
- 3000m / 9843ft
- 2000m / 6562ft
- 1000m / 3281ft
- 500m / 640ft
- 250m / 820ft
- 100m / 328ft
- sea level

Scale 1:8,250,000

projection: Lambert Conformal Conic

Iran & the Gulf states

BAHRAIN, IRAN, KUWAIT, QATAR, UNITED ARAB EMIRATES (UAE)

The discovery of oil in the Persian Gulf in the 1930s brought great wealth to the surrounding states. The revenue was largely used to modernize industry and infrastructure, initiating great social change in these formerly agrarian countries. Today, over 90% of the people in the Gulf states live in urban areas, and foreign nationals make up a sizeable proportion of the population in Kuwait, Qatar, and the United Arab Emirates. The importance of control of the oil reserves has led to a number of territorial disputes, including most recently the Iran–Iraq War (1980-88) and the First Gulf War (1991). Islam is practiced almost exclusively throughout the region and two distinct strands are found; Sunni Muslims in Qatar, Kuwait, and UAE, and Shi'a Muslims in Iran and Bahrain. In 1979 Iran became the world's largest theocracy.

The landscape

The land rises steeply from the fragmented coastal lowlands bordering the Persian Gulf, to reach Iran's interior plateau, bounded by heavily eroded mountain chains. An unstable plate boundary runs northwest to southeast across Iran causing frequent earthquakes. On the sandy west coast of the Persian Gulf, the relief is generally flat, with patches of salt marsh. Bahrain consists of two groups of islands, which are mostly small and rocky.

Pyroclastic layers | Lava flow

Lava flow layers

▲ *Qolleh-ye Damavand in the Elburz Mountains is a composite volcano. It comprises layers of lava and pyroclasts fragmentary rocks which accumulate on the slopes of the volcano after being ejected into the air.*

▲ *Marine sediments from deep beneath the ancient Tethys Sea have been uplifted to form the Elburz Mountains, which stretch along the shores of the Caspian Sea, northern Iran.*

Lava and ash from previous volcanic activity covers a 200 mile (320 km) stretch from the border with Azerbaijan to the Caspian Sea.

Iran's two mountain chains, the Zagros and Elburz, were uplifted at the same time as the Alps in Europe, when the African Plate collided with the Eurasian Plate.

Caspian Sea

Qolleh-ye Damavand

Dominated by a vast, semi-arid interior plateau, most of Iran lies above 1640 ft (500 m). The region is poorly drained with many of its basins remaining dry for months at a time.

The fierce Shamal wind affects much of this region. Every summer it blows dust south from the flood plains of the Tigris and Euphrates, reducing visibility to such an extent that Kuwait International Airport is frequently forced to close.

Prolific springs tapping artesian water make cultivation possible across the north of Bahrain's main island. This provides a sharp contrast to the sandy plains in the south and west.

The oilfields of the Persian Gulf are formed from marine shale deposits lying in sedimentary basins at the margins of the Zagros Mountains.

Autumn winds blowing across the Persian Gulf can reach speeds of up to 95 mph (150 kmph) causing severe storms, squalls, and waterspouts.

Numerous islands lie along the southern coast of the Persian Gulf. Some of these are salt domes, created when less dense salts were displaced and forced up to the surface by denser, overlying strata.

The Dasht-e Lut

◀ *The Dasht-e Lut covers a large portion of eastern Iran with its dry, wind-eroded plain of scattered sandstone pillars and salty depressions. During the summer, temperatures soar, making it one of the world's hottest, driest places.*

Using the land & sea

Along the coast of the Caspian Sea, desalinated water allows fruits and vegetables to be produced, although water shortages and desert soils still limit farming. Sheep are the most important livestock raised in Iran and commercial forests cover the northwest of the country. Shrimp stocks were decimated by pollution during the Gulf War, but fishing remains important for domestic and export markets.

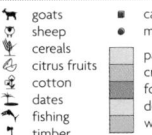

◀ *All of the Gulf states have commercial fishing fleets. Before the discovery of oil, fishing was the region's leading industry.*

◀ *The Kuwait Towers in the center of Kuwait are symbols of the vast wealth oil has brought to the country. Before 1960, the city had only one main street and was surrounded by a mud wall.*

Land use and agricultural distribution

- goats
- sheep
- cereals
- citrus fruits
- cotton
- dates
- fishing
- timber
- capital cities
- major towns
- pasture
- cropland
- forest
- desert
- wetland

The urban/rural population divide

urban 65% | rural 35%

0 10 20 30 40 50 60 70 80 90 100

Population density	Total land area
112 people per sq mile (43 people per sq km)	642,883 sq miles (1,665,500 sq km)

Map labels

TURKEY, ARMENIA, AZERBAIJAN, Máku, Aras, Siāh Chashmeh, Khvoy, Zonūz, Marand, Ahar, Kūhhā-ye Sabalān 4811m, Ardabīl, Salmās, Sūfīān, Tabrīz, Bostānābād, Qūshchī, Orūmīyeh, AZARBĀYJĀN-E SHARQĪ, Bonāb, Hashtrūd, Mīāneh, Khalkhāl, Rasht, Fowman, Marāgheh, Kūh-e Ḩāji Ebrāhīm 3600m, Naqadeh, Mīāndowāb, Piranshahr, Mahābād, AZARBĀYJĀN-E GHARBĪ, Bukān, Soltānīyeh, ZANJĀN, Zanjān, Qazvīn, Bāneh, Saqqez, Qezel Owzan, Qeydār, Abhar, Dīvāndarreh, KORDESTĀN, Bījār, Āb Garm, Marīvān, Rūdkhāneh, Razan, Avaj, Sanandaj, Qorveh, Kabūd Rahang, Nowshan, Paveh, Songor, HAMADĀN, Hamadān, Qaṣr-e Shīrīn, Kermānshāh (Bākhtarān), Kangavar, Tuyserkān, Āshtiā, Sar-e Pol-e Zahāb, KERMĀNSHĀH, Nahāvand, Malāyer, Arāk, Eslāmābād, Borūjerd, Tareh, MARK, Eyvān, Īlām, Do Rūd, Aligū, Golp, LORESTĀN, Khorramābād, ĪLĀM, Darreh Shahr, Daryācheh-ye Sadd-e Dez, Dehlorān, Amīrābād, Mehrān, Andīmeshk, Dezfūl, Shūsh, Shūshtar, Masjed Soleymān, Izeh, KHŪZESTĀN, Sūsangerd, Ahvāz, Rāmh, Kārūn, Omīdīyeh, Āg, Khorramshahr, Behbah, Ābādān, Bandar-e Māhshahr, Al Qash'ānīyah, Ar Rawḍatayn, Jazīrat Būbiyān, KUWAIT, Waḏī al Bāṭin, Al Jahrā, Ḩūn al Kuwayt, Faylakah, As Sālimī, AL KUWAYT (KUWAIT), Al Aḥmadī, Al Fuḩayḩil, Aṣ Ṣubayḩīyah, Al Wafrah, Al Khīrān, SAUDI ARABIA, Persi, AL MANĀ (MANAM)

Inset map (bottom left)

TURKEY, ARMENIA, AZERBAIJAN, Caspian Sea, TURKMENISTAN, Tabriz, Mashhad, TEHRAN, IRAN, AFGHANISTAN, IRAQ, Esfahan, Kerman, Abadan, Shiraz, PAKISTAN, KUWAIT, KUWAIT, Bandar-e Abbas, Persian Gulf, BAHRAIN, MANAMA, SAUDI ARABIA, QATAR, DOHA, ABU DHABI, U.A.E., Gulf of Oman, OMAN

◄ Many volcanoes lie in Iran's 1200 mile (1930 km) volcanic belt, including the country's highest peak, the now-extinct Qolleh-ye Damavand at 18,600 ft (5671 m).

► Extensive oil and gas exploitation in the Gulf region has allowed the economic transformation of the Gulf states. Consequently, many of these states have a hugely improved per capita income compared to the 1960's.

Transportation & industry

Both onshore and offshore oil reserves are exploited throughout the region. Kuwait not only extracts but also refines 80% of its oil. Bahrain has diversified its economy to become the main commercial and financial center in the Persian Gulf. Iran produces a wide range of products: textile mills are widespread and carpet weaving is an important export industry.

Major industry and infrastructure

- carpet manufacture
- chemicals
- finance
- food processing
- oil
- oil refining
- textiles
- capital city
- major towns
- international airports
- major roads
- major industrial areas

Transportation network

63,543 miles (102,274 km)	884 miles (1423 km)
3822 miles (6151 km)	562 miles (904 km)

Major towns and neighboring countries are linked by adequate road networks, although rural areas are less well served. Bahrain is linked to the mainland by a 15 mile (25 km) long causeway.

Map key

Population

- above 5 million
- 1 million to 5 million
- 500,000 to 1 million
- 100,000 to 500,000
- 50,000 to 100,000
- 10,000 to 50,000
- below 10,000

Elevation

- 4000m / 13,124ft
- 3000m / 9843ft
- 2000m / 6562ft
- 1000m / 3281ft
- 500m / 1640ft
- 250m / 820ft
- 100m / 328ft
- sea level

Scale 1:6,000,000

Km
0 10 20 40 60 80 100 120 140 160 180 200

Miles
0 10 20 40 60 80 100 120 140 160 180 200

projection: Lambert Conformal Conic

A B C D E F G H I J K L M

Kazakhstan

Abundant natural resources lie in the immense steppe grasslands, deserts, and central plateau of the former Soviet republic of Kazakhstan. An intensive program of industrial and agricultural development to exploit these resources during the Soviet era resulted in catastrophic industrial pollution, including fallout from nuclear testing and the shrinkage of the Aral Sea. Since independence, the government has encouraged foreign investment and liberalized the economy to promote growth. The adoption of Kazakh as the national language is intended to encourage a new sense of national identity in a state where living conditions for the majority remain harsh, both in cramped urban centers and impoverished rural areas.

Transportation & industry

The single most important industry in Kazakhstan is mining, based around extensive oil deposits near the Caspian Sea, the world's largest chromium mine, and vast reserves of iron ore. Recent foreign investment has helped to develop industries including food processing and steel manufacture, and to expand the exploitation of mineral resources. The Russian space program is still based at Baykonyr, near Kyzylorda in central Kazakhstan.

Major industry and infrastructure

- ⚗ chemicals
- ⚙ engineering
- 🐟 fish processing
- 🍴 food processing
- 🏭 iron & steel
- △ metallurgy
- ⛏ mining
- ⚓ oil

- ■ capital cities
- ● major towns
- ✈ international airports
- — major roads
- major industrial areas

Transportation network

- 48,263 miles (77,680 km)
- none
- 8483 miles (13,660 km)
- 3900 miles (2423 km)

Industrial areas in the north and east are well-connected to Russia. Air and rail links with Germany and China have been established through foreign investment. Better access to Baltic ports is being sought.

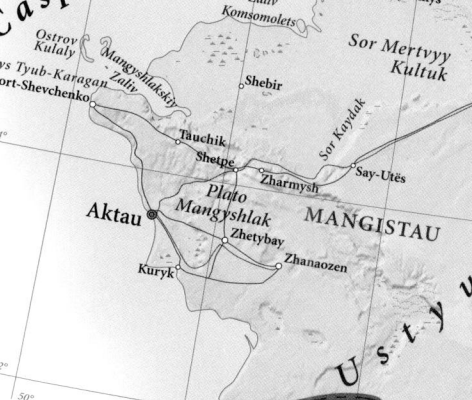

An open-pit coal mine in Kazakhstan. Foreign investment is being actively sought by the Kazakh government in order to fully exploit the potential of the country's rich mineral reserves.

Map key

Population

- ▣ 1 million to 5 million
- ◉ 500,000 to 1 million
- ◎ 100,000 to 500,000
- ⊕ 50,000 to 100,000
- ⊙ 10,000 to 50,000
- ○ below 10,000

Elevation

- 4000m / 13,124ft
- 3000m / 9843ft
- 2000m / 6562ft
- 1000m / 3281ft
- 500m / 1640ft
- 250m / 820ft
- 100m / 328ft
- sea level

Using the land & sea

The rearing of large herds of sheep and goats on the steppe grasslands forms the core of Kazakh agriculture. Arable cultivation and cotton-growing in pasture and desert areas was encouraged during the Soviet era, but relative yields are low. The heavy use of fertilizers and the diversion of natural water sources for irrigation has degraded much of the land.

Land use and agricultural distribution

- 🐄 cattle
- 🐐 goats
- 🐑 sheep
- cotton
- 🐟 fishing
- 🌾 wheat

- ■ capital cities
- ● major towns

- pasture
- cropland
- forest
- mountain region
- desert

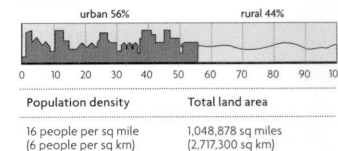

The urban/rural population divide

urban 56%	rural 44%

0 10 20 30 40 50 60 70 80 90 100

Population density	Total land area
16 people per sq mile (6 people per sq km)	1,048,878 sq miles (2,717,300 sq km)

▲ **The nomadic peoples** who moved their herds around the steppe grasslands are now largely settled, although echoes of their traditional lifestyle, in particular their superb riding skills, remain.

122

Scale 1:7,000,000

Km
0 25 50 100 150 200 250

Miles
0 25 50 100 150 200 250

projection: Lambert Conformal Conic

The landscape

Stretching more than 1250 miles (2000 km) from the Caspian Sea in the west to China in the east, more than 40% of Kazakhstan is covered by steppe grasslands which give way to barren desert in the south. The land rises eastward towards the mineral-rich central plateau, to form the Altai Mountains.

▲ *Since 1960, the* Aral Sea has shrunk by 75%, become extremely saline, and lost all but five of its once-abundant fish species. Factors in this ecological disaster include the excessive use of fertilizers, defoliants and the diversion of its main source rivers for the irrigation of desert lands.

The Caspian Sea is the largest body of inland water in the world.

The desert of Peski Bol'shiye Barsuki is mainly sandy displaying a number of classic dune formations. Groundwater supports a small amount of vegetation.

A large number of salt lakes fill depressions in the rolling uplands of central Kazakhstan.

▶ *The Altai Mountains* lie on Kazakhstan's eastern borders with China and the Russian Federation. Cold and largely barren, they are the source of many of the rivers which flow across the steppe.

Its waters taken for industry and irrigation, the Syr Darya, one of Kazakhstan's major rivers, now barely reaches the Aral Sea which it used to fill. Like many Kazakh rivers it has been heavily polluted with chemicals and its flow has been restricted by up to 60%.

The waters of Lake Balkhash (Ozero Balkhash), unlike those of the Aral Sea, are still able to support a fishing industry.

The central Kazakh Uplands (Kazakhskiy Melkosopochnik) contain much of the country's mineral riches. The landscape is largely flat with occasional rocky outcrops and hillocks.

▶ *Immense stretches* of steppe grasslands characterize much of the Kazakh landscape. These lowland areas have been used for arable cultivation in recent years, although problems with irrigation have meant that much of the land is being allowed to revert to its natural vegetation and pastoral usage.

▲ *Rows of pine* trees edge this valley near Almaty. The snow-covered slopes in the background are used for skiing.

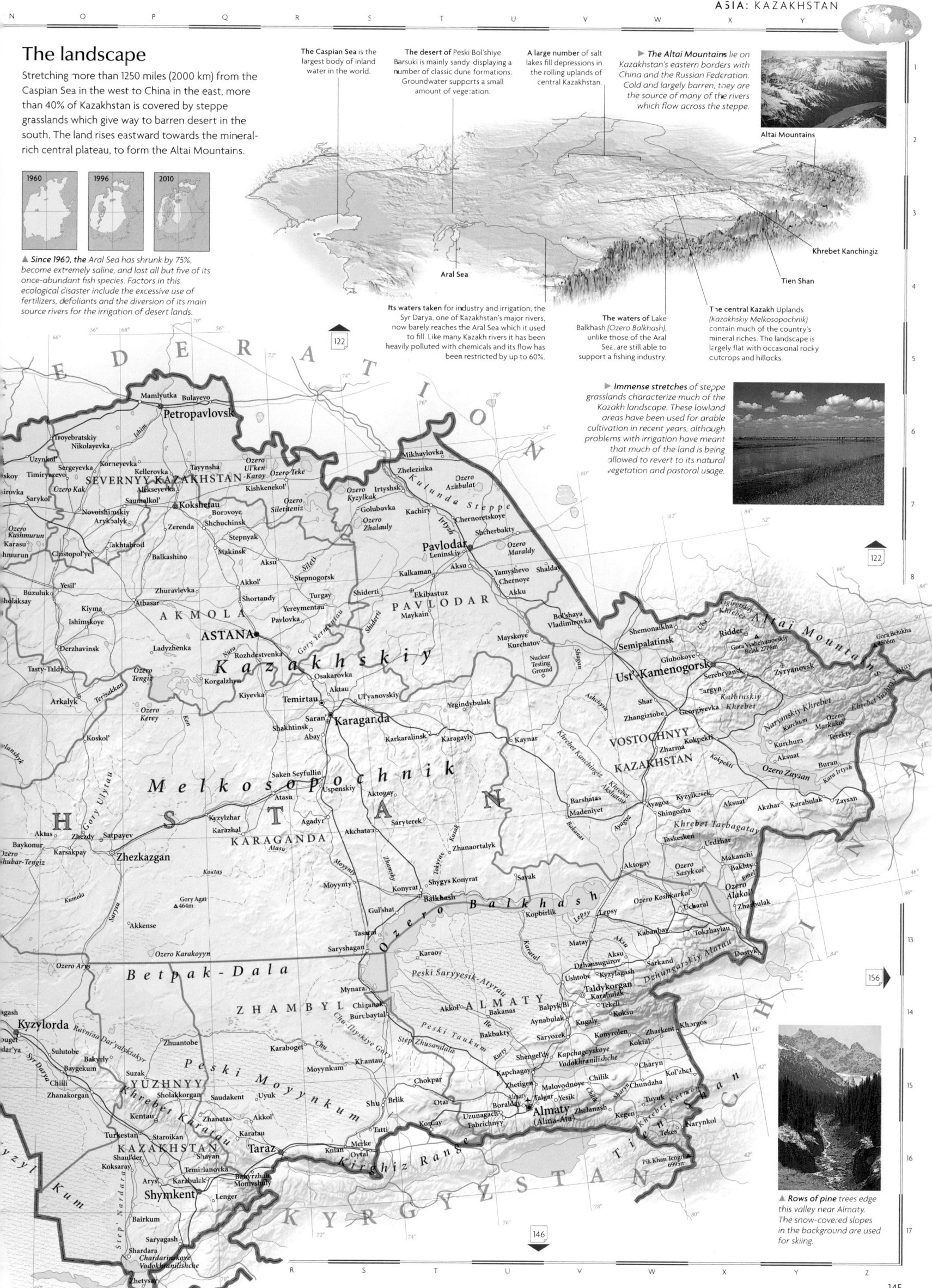

Central Asia

KYRGYZSTAN, TAJIKISTAN, TURKMENISTAN, UZBEKISTAN

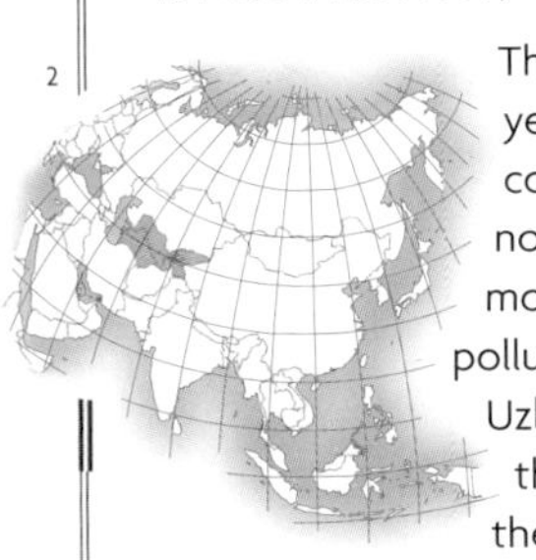

The four republics that declared independence in 1991 were created in the early years of the Soviet Union, promoting ethnic divisions in a region whose common focus, since the 8th century, has been Islam. Traditional rural, nomadic ways of life have survived the Soviet era, while the benefits of modern industry and grand irrigation schemes have resulted in severe pollution in the delicate, arid environment of the steppe, particularly in Uzbekistan. Many ethnic minority groups are scattered among the four republics, with isolated communities in the mountains of Kyrgzstan.

The current Islamic revival has brought hope of greater regional unity, in spite of religious factionalism which, in 1992, plunged Tajikistan into civil war.

▲ *The southern shoreline* of the Aral Sea has retreated over 30 miles (48 km) since 1960. A major cause is the diversion of water from the Amu Darya river for irrigation via the Kara Kum Canal (Garagum Kanaly).

◄ *The desert of the Kara Kum* (Garagum) occupies over 70% of Turkmenistan; its wind-scoured surface of dune ridges and depressions severely limits human settlement.

Map key

Population

- ◉ 1 million to 5 million
- ◉ 500,000 to 1 million
- ⊚ 100,000 to 500,000
- ⊕ 50,000 to 100,000
- ○ 10,000 to 50,000
- ∘ below 10,000

Elevation

6000m / 19,686ft
4000m / 13,124ft
3000m / 9843ft
2000m / 6562ft
1000m / 3281ft
500m / 1640ft
250m / 820ft
100m / 328ft
sea level

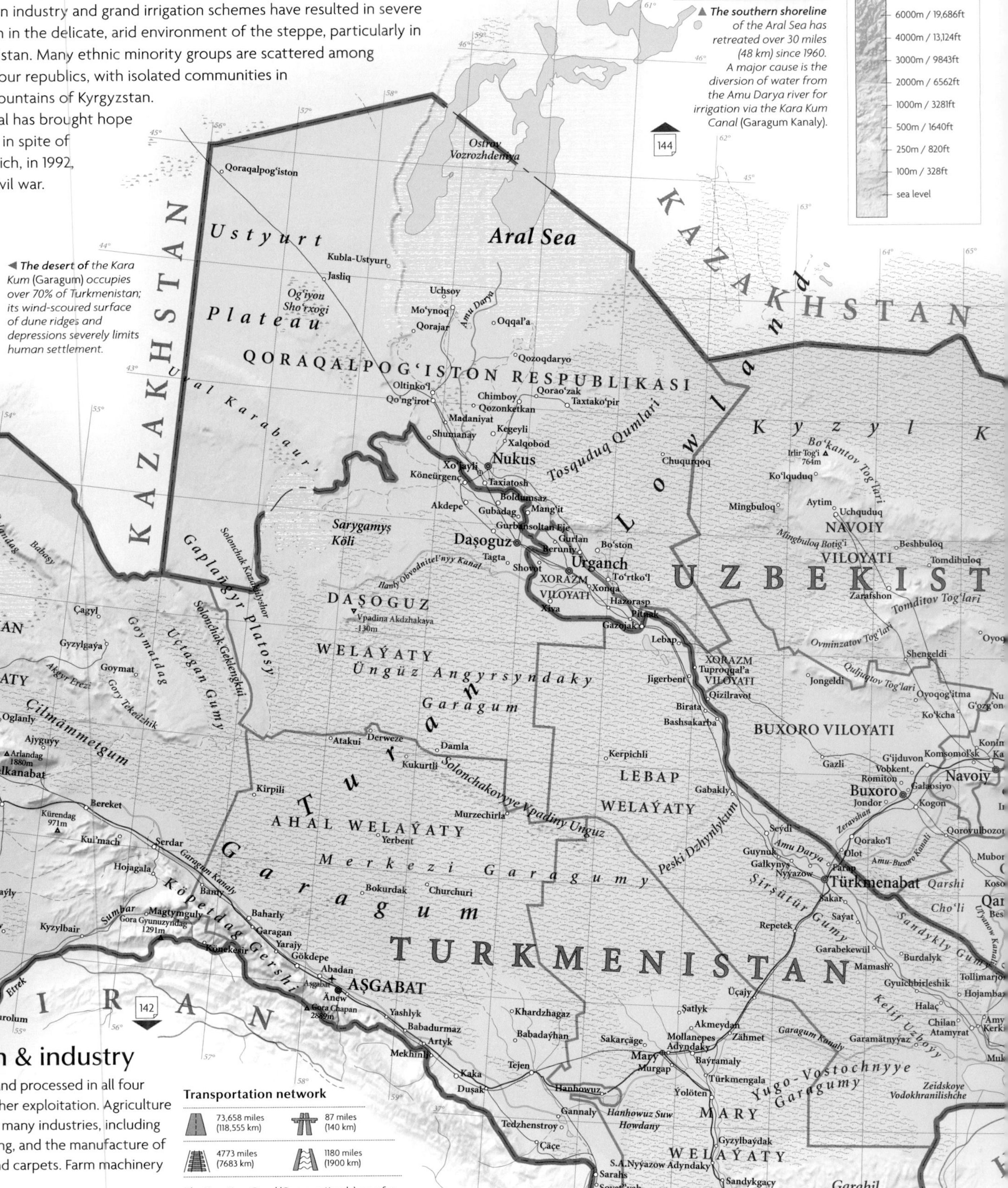

Transportation & industry

Fossil fuels are extracted and processed in all four states, with scope for further exploitation. Agriculture provides raw materials for many industries, including food and textiles processing, and the manufacture of leather goods, clothing, and carpets. Farm machinery is also produced.

Transportation network

73,658 miles (118,555 km)	87 miles (140 km)
4773 miles (7683 km)	1180 miles (1900 km)

The Kara Kum Canal (Garagum Kanaly) runs for 870 miles (1400 km) from the Amu Darya river to the Caspian Sea. The canal is principally used for irrigation but is navigable for 280 miles (450 km).

Major industry and infrastructure

- carpet weaving
- chemicals
- engineering
- food processing
- oil & gas
- textiles
- ■ capital cities
- • major towns
- ⊕ international airports
- major roads
- major industrial areas

The landscape

The great Tien Shan and Pamir ranges meet in a succession of high mountain chains. These mountains encircle the fertile Fergana Valley and reach west into the desert of the Kyzyl Kum, dividing the Syr Darya and Amu Darya rivers. Sandy steppeland extends to the shores of the Caspian Sea, with the desert of the Kara Kum (Garagum) in the south. The Amu Darya drains into the Aral Sea in the north.

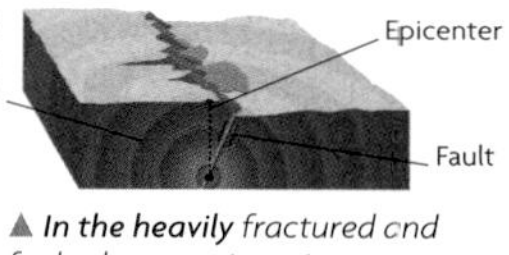

Salt marshes fill many of the depressions in the Ustyurt Plateau, a barren, rocky tableland about 650 ft (200 m) above sea level.

Some of the world's largest deposits of marine salts are found in Garabogaz Aylagy. This shallow, saline gulf has an average depth of only 33 ft (10 m), and a very high evaporation rate, producing the salty deposits.

The Kara Kum (Garagum) is one of the world's largest expanses of sand. Wind action has created a terrain of shifting, crescent-shaped sand dunes known as barchans.

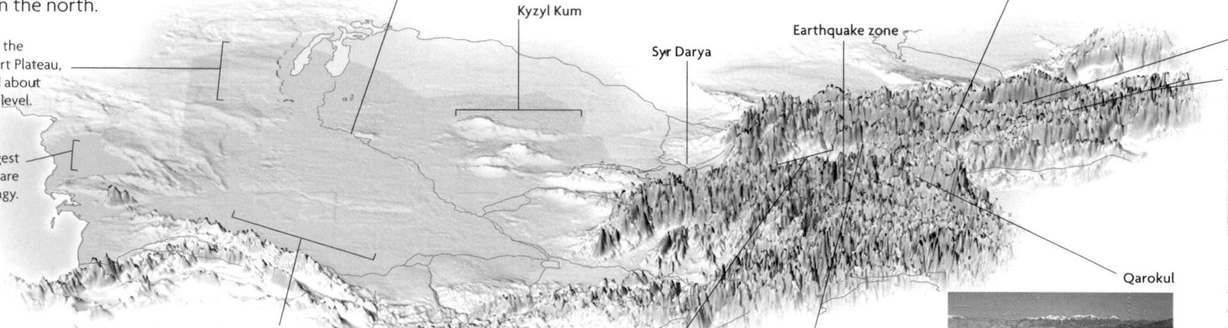

The Amu Darya is the only river in Central Asia with a sufficient volume of water to cross the desert of the Kara Kum (Garagum) from the Pamirs to the Aral Sea, where it forms a delta largely vegetated by scrub grasses.

Kyzyl Kum

Syr Darya

Earthquake zone

Shock waves travel through ground

Epicenter

Fault

▲ *In the heavily* fractured and faulted mountain region, earthquakes are common, caused by the sudden release of tension along active fault lines.

A series of major rock faults has created the Fergana Valley, a deep depression surrounded by high mountains. Water from the Syr Darya river and from underground sources supports intensive agriculture, despite minimal rainfall.

Qullai Ismoili Somoni, was formerly known as Mount Communism, so named because it was the highest point in the the former Soviet Union, rising to 24,590 ft (7495 m).

Qarokul

Naryn river

◄ *Bare mountains provide a* stark background to the croplands along the Naryn river in Kyrgyzstan. Irrigation is essential for cultivation in this dry region.

Ozero Issyk-Kul' lies at an altitude of 5193 ft (1584 m). The lake remains ice-free throughout the year, due to the slight salinity of the water.

Tien Shan

▲ *The Tien Shan* extend from China in the east, reaching heights over 24,400 ft (7439 m) and branching into many parallel ranges in the west.

◄ *Nestling high in* the Pamir range, and fed by glacial meltwater, Qarokul is the largest of the lakes in this region.

Scale 1:4,750,000

projection: Lambert Conformal Conic

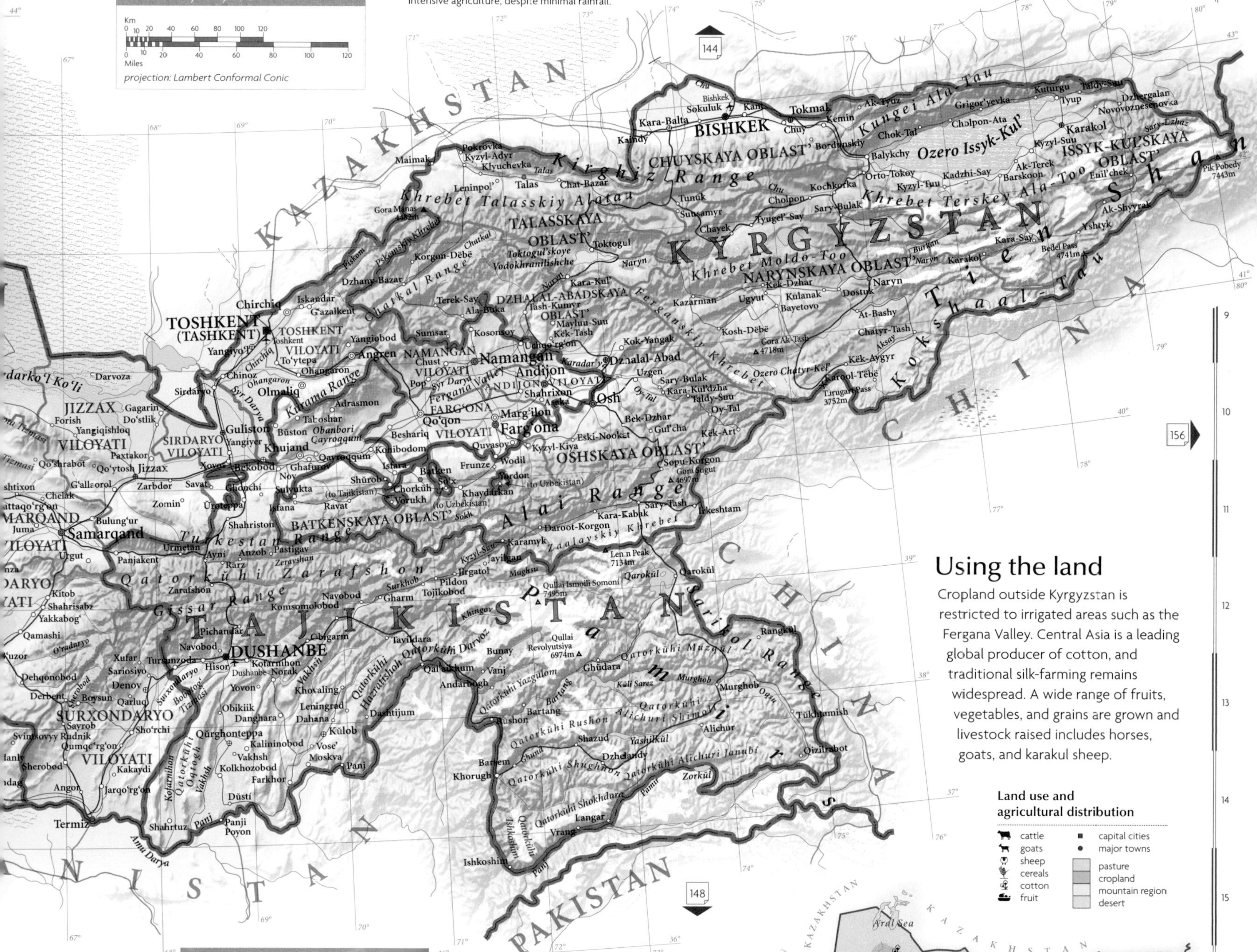

Using the land

Cropland outside Kyrgyzstan is restricted to irrigated areas such as the Fergana Valley. Central Asia is a leading global producer of cotton, and traditional silk-farming remains widespread. A wide range of fruits, vegetables, and grains are grown and livestock raised includes horses, goats, and karakul sheep.

Land use and agricultural distribution

- cattle
- goats
- sheep
- cereals
- cotton
- fruit
- capital cities
- major towns
- pasture
- cropland
- mountain region
- desert

▶ *Plentiful sunshine*, rich soils and massive irrigation schemes have made Uzbekistan the world's fifth largest cotton producer, although water shortages now prevent any further expansion of irrigated land.

The urban/rural population divide

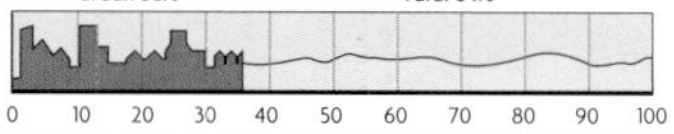

urban 36%   rural 64%

Population density	Total land area
88 people per sq mile (34 people per sq km)	492,961 sq miles (1 277,100 sq km)

147

Afghanistan & Pakistan

Pakistan was created by the partition of British India in 1947, becoming the western arm of a new Islamic state for Indian Muslims; the eastern sector, in Bengal, seceded to become the separate country of Bangladesh in 1971. Over half of Pakistan's 158 million people live in the Punjab, at the fertile head of the great Indus Basin. The river sustains a national economy based on irrigated agriculture, including cotton for the vital textiles industry. Afghanistan, a mountainous, landlocked country, with an ancient and independent culture, has been wracked by war since 1979. Factional strife escalated into an international conflict in late 2001, as US-led troops ousted the militant and fundamentally Islamist *taliban* regime as part of their "war on terror."

◀ *The town of* Bamian lies high in the Hindu Kush west of Kabul. Between the 2nd and 5th centuries two huge statues of Buddha were carved into the nearby rock, the largest of which stood 125 ft (38 m) high. The statues were destroyed by the taliban regime in March 2001.

Transportation & industry

Pakistan is highly dependent on the cotton textiles industry, although diversified manufacture is expanding around cities such as Karachi and Lahore. Afghanistan's limited industry is based mainly on the processing of agricultural raw materials and includes traditional crafts such as carpet weaving.

Major industry and infrastructure

- carpet weaving
- chemicals
- engineering
- finance
- food processing
- iron & steel
- oil & gas
- textiles
- capital cities
- major towns
- international airports
- major roads
- major industrial areas

Transportation network

- 96,154 miles (154,763 km)
- 211 miles (340 km)
- 4852 miles (7814 km)
- 745 miles (1200 km)

The Karakoram Highway was completed after 20 years of construction in 1978. It breaches the Himalayan mountain barrier providing a commercial motor route linking lowland Pakistan and China.

▶ *The Karakoram Highway* is one of the highest major roads in the world. It took over 24,000 workers almost 20 years to complete.

The landscape

Afghanistan's topography is dominated by the mountains of the Hindu Kush, which spread south and west into numerous mountain spurs. The dry plateau of southwestern Afghanistan extends into Pakistan and the hills which overlook the great Indus Basin. In northern Pakistan the Hindu Kush, Himalayan, and Karakoram ranges meet to form one of the world's highest mountain regions.

◀ *The Hunza river* rises in the northern Karakoram Range, running for 120 miles (193 km) before joining the Gilgit river.

Hunza river

The plains and foothills which extend from the northern slopes of the Hindu Kush are part of the great grassy steppe lands of Central Asia.

▶ *The arid Hindu Kush* makes much of Afghanistan uninhabitable, with over 50% of the land lying above 6500 ft (2000 m).

Hindu Kush

K2 (Mount Godwin Austen), in the Karakoram Range, is the second highest mountain in the world, at an altitude of 28,251 ft (8611 m).

Some of the largest glaciers outside the polar regions are found in the Karakoram Range, including Siachen Glacier (Siachen Muztagh), which is 40 miles (72 km) long.

Frequent earthquakes mean that mountain-building processes are continuing in this region, as the Indo-Australian Plate drifts northward, colliding with the Eurasian Plate.

Himalayas

The soils of the Punjab plain are nourished by enormous quantities of sediment, carried from the Himalayas by the five tributaries of the Indus river.

Mountain chains running southwest from the Hindu Kush into Pakistan form a barrier to the humid winds which blow from the Indian Ocean, creating arid conditions across southern Afghanistan.

The Indus Basin is part of the Indus-Ganges lowland, a vast depression which has been filled with layers of sediment over the last 50 million years. These deposits are estimated to be over 16,400 ft (5000 m) deep.

The Indus Delta is prone to heavy flooding and high levels of salinity. It remains a largely uncultivated wilderness area.

Glacis covered by coarse-grained sediment

Sediments washed down from mountains accumulate on glacis slopes

Fine sediments deposited on salt flats are removed by wind erosion.

Bedrock

▲ *Glacis are gentle,* debris-covered slopes which lead into saltflats or deserts. They typically occur at the base of mountains in arid regions such as Afghanistan.

Scale 1:5,000,000

Km
0 10 20   40   60   80   100   120   140   160

Miles
0 10 20   40   60   80   100   120   140   160

projection: Lambert Conformal Conic

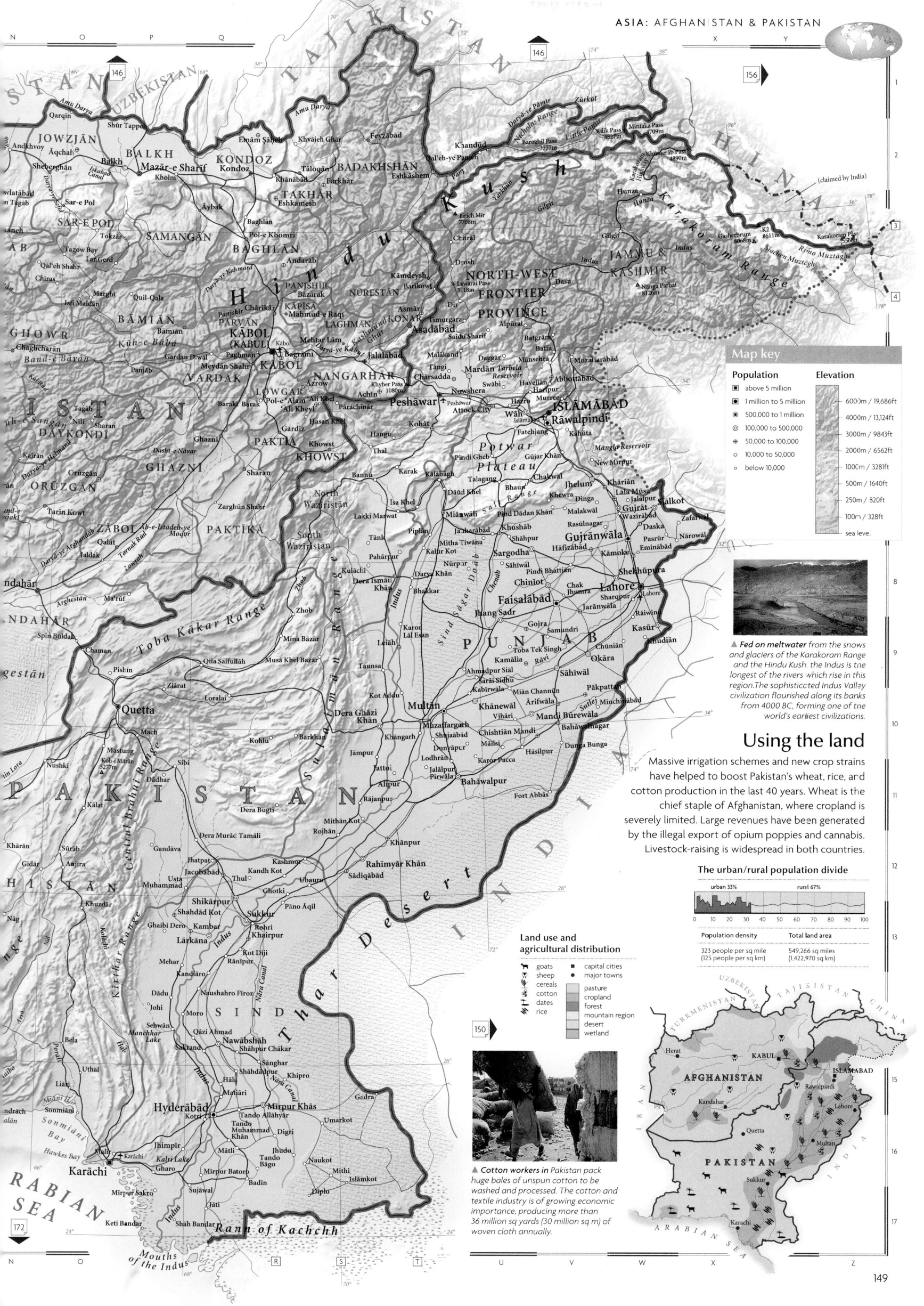

Map key

Population
- ■ above 5 million
- ■ 1 million to 5 million
- ◉ 500,000 to 1 million
- ◎ 100,000 to 500,000
- ⊕ 50,000 to 100,000
- ○ 10,000 to 50,000
- ○ below 10,000

Elevation
- 6000m / 19,686ft
- 4000m / 13,124ft
- 3000m / 9843ft
- 2000m / 6562ft
- 1000m / 3281ft
- 500m / 1640ft
- 250m / 320ft
- 100m / 328ft
- sea level

▲ *Fed on meltwater* from the snows and glaciers of the Karakoram Range and the Hindu Kush, the Indus is the longest of the rivers which rise in this region. The sophisticated Indus Valley civilization flourished along its banks from 4000 BC, forming one of the world's earliest civilizations.

Using the land

Massive irrigation schemes and new crop strains have helped to boost Pakistan's wheat, rice, and cotton production in the last 40 years. Wheat is the chief staple of Afghanistan, where cropland is severely limited. Large revenues have been generated by the illegal export of opium poppies and cannabis. Livestock-raising is widespread in both countries.

The urban/rural population divide

urban 33%   rural 67%

0 10 20 30 40 50 60 70 80 90 100

Population density	Total land area
323 people per sq mile (125 people per sq km)	549,266 sq miles (1,422,970 sq km)

Land use and agricultural distribution

- goats
- sheep
- cereals
- cotton
- dates
- rice

- ● capital cities
- ● major towns

- pasture
- cropland
- forest
- mountain region
- desert
- wetland

▲ *Cotton workers in* Pakistan pack huge bales of unspun cotton to be washed and processed. The cotton and textile industry is of growing economic importance, producing more than 36 million sq yards (30 million sq m) of woven cloth annually.

South Asia

BANGLADESH, BHUTAN, INDIA, MALDIVES, NEPAL, PAKISTAN, SRI LANKA

The landscape

South Asia is effectively isolated from the rest of Asia by desert along the western flank of Pakistan, and a continuous wall of mountains, dominated by the Himalayas, to the north and east. The great basins of the Indus and Ganges separate this mountain fringe from the rolling plateau of the Indian peninsula, which is bordered by a line of coastal hills, the Eastern and Western Ghats.

More than one-fifth of the world's population lives in the south Asian subcontinent. Great cultural diversity has come from a long succession of foreign invaders, including Hindu Aryans, Islamic Moguls, and the British, whose empire incorporated the princely states of the Maharajas and extended to the borders of Nepal and Bhutan in the Himalayas.

Independent since 1947, India is the world's largest democracy, and at the current rate of growth, may overtake China as the world's most populous country during the 21st century. There are points of tension in the region over claims for independence by the Sikhs in the Indian Punjab and the Tamil separatists in Sri Lanka, and the long-standing dispute with Pakistan over Jammu and Kashmir in the north.

▼ *The towering Karakoram and Hindu Kush ranges, formed at the same time as the Himalayas, dominate Pakistan's northern borders. K2 on the border of northern Pakistan is the second highest mountain on Earth, at 28,251 ft (8611 m).*

▼ *The Indus valley near Skardu in northern Pakistan has been partially infilled by great quantities of eroded sediment. Most of this is carried from the region's bare slopes by swollen rivers during the spring thaw and mass movement activity.*

The Himalayas are the highest and most extensive mountain system in the world. They were formed when the Indo-Australian Plate collided with the Eurasian Plate about 40 million years ago, thrusting up huge masses of land and creating a "ripple" effect, which formed lesser mountain ranges in Tibet and Southeast Asia. Mount Everest is the world's tallest mountain at 29,035 ft (8850 m).

Almost all of Bangladesh lies in the immense delta formed by the Ganges and the Brahmaputra which merge and flow out into the Bay of Bengal.

Ganges delta

Deccan plateau

▲ *The Deccan plateau covers an area of more than 123,553 sq miles (320,000 sq km). It is formed of deep layers of volcanic basalt, reaching thicknesses of more than 9800 ft (3000 m) toward the coast. Distinctive stepped valleys cut in the basalt plateau by rivers are known as "traps."*

Layers of volcanic basalt

Stepped valleys or 'traps'

Eastern Ghats

Bharatpur

▲ *Rivers flowing from the Himalayas into a broad depression in northern India have formed marshes around Bharatpur. They are now a sanctuary for numerous bird species.*

Coastal deposition has formed many typical features along the western coast of Sri Lanka. These include spits and bars, sometimes enclosing lagoons.

Trivandrum in southern India normally receives the first of the monsoon rains, which are essential to south Asian agriculture and moderate the extreme summer heat. The monsoon then moves northward over a period of about two months.

The Western Ghats are formed by a fault scarp which runs unbroken for more than 930 miles (1500 km). They reach their highest point at the southern Cardamom Hills.

The Indus river flows more than 1970 miles (3180 km) from southwestern Tibet to its mouth on the Arabian Sea. It has an estimated catchment area of 450,000 sq miles (1,165,500 sq km).

The coast of western Pakistan is a staircase of folded rock strata caused by successive periods of rapid uplift.

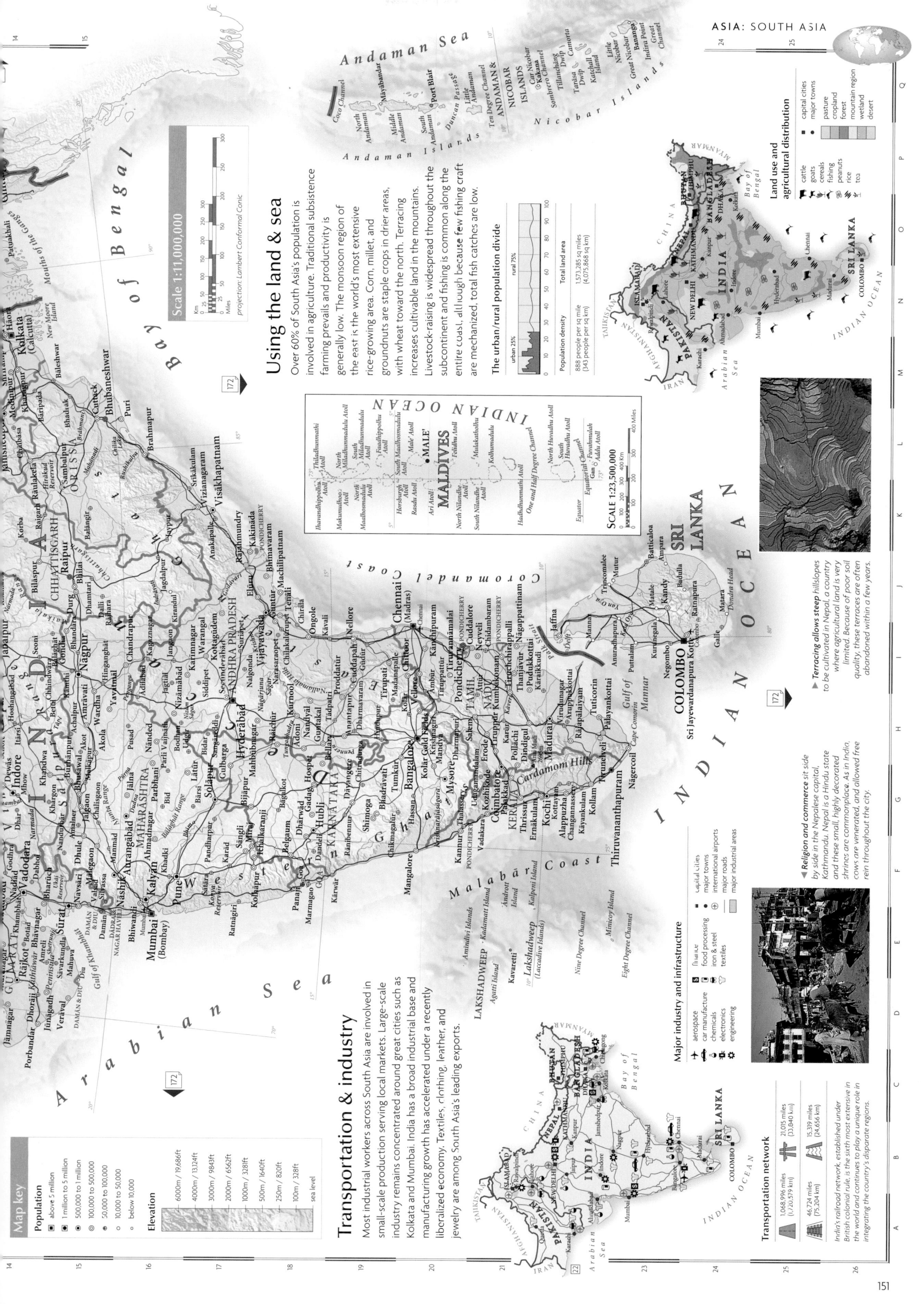

Using the land & sea

Over 60% of South Asia's population is involved in agriculture. Traditional subsistence farming prevails and productivity is generally low. The monsoon region of the east is the world's most extensive rice-growing area. Corn, millet, and groundnuts are staple crops in drier areas, with wheat toward the north. Terracing increases cultivable land in the mountains. Livestock-raising is widespread throughout the subcontinent and fishing is common along the entire coast, although because few fishing craft are mechanized, total fish catches are low.

The urban/rural population divide

urban 25%   rural 75%

Population density   Total land area
888 people per sq mile   1,573,285 sq miles
(343 people per sq km)   (4,075,868 sq km)

Land use and agricultural distribution

capital cities
major towns
pasture
cropland
forest
mountain region
wetland
desert

cattle
goats
cereals
peanuts
tea

fishing
rice
tea

▲ Terracing allows steep hillslopes to be cultivated in Nepal, a country where agricultural land is very limited. Because of poor soil quality, these terraces are often abandoned within a few years.

Transportation & industry

Most industrial workers across South Asia are involved in small-scale production serving local markets. Large-scale industry remains concentrated around great cities such as Kolkata and Mumbai. India has a broad industrial base and manufacturing growth has accelerated under a recently liberalized economy. Textiles, clothing, leather, and jewelry are among South Asia's leading exports.

Major industry and infrastructure

aerospace
car manufacture
chemicals
electronics
engineering
finance
food processing
iron & steel
textiles

capital cities
major towns
international airports
major roads
major industrial areas

Transportation network

21,015 miles (33,040 km)
46,724 miles (75,204 km)
1,068,996 miles (1/20,579 km)
15,339 miles (24,656 km)

India's railroad network, established under British colonial rule, is the sixth most extensive in the world and continues to play a unique role in integrating the country's disparate regions.

▲ Religion and commerce sit side by side in the Nepalese capital, Kathmandu. Nepal is a Hindu state and these small, highly decorated shrines are commonplace. As in India, cows are venerated, and allowed free rein throughout the city.

Map key

Population
■ above 5 million
■ 1 million to 5 million
● 500,000 to 1 million
● 100,000 to 500,000
● 50,000 to 100,000
○ 10,000 to 50,000
○ below 10,000

Elevation
6000m / 19,686ft
4000m / 13,124ft
3000m / 9843ft
2000m / 6562ft
1000m / 3281ft
500m / 1640ft
250m / 820ft
100m / 328ft
sea level

Scale 1:11,000,000
projection: Lambert Conformal Conic

SCALE 1:23,500,000

MALDIVES
MALE'

Northern India & the Himalayan states

BANGLADESH, BHUTAN, NEPAL, Arunachal Pradesh, Assam, Bihar, Chandigarh, Delhi, Haryana, Himachal Pradesh, Jammu & Kashmir, Jharkhand, Manipur, Meghalaya, Mizoram, Nagaland, Punjab, Rajasthan, Sikkim, Tripura, Uttarakhand, Uttar Pradesh, West Bengal

The Ganges and Brahmaputra river basins and the massive mountain barrier of the Himalayas define this region's landscape and have served to reinforce potent cultural and religious differences among its people. Hinduism pervades most aspects of national life and is a growing political force within India, a secular country which also encompasses the center of Sikhism at Amritsar and the world's largest Muslim minority. Nepal is a crowded mountain state, which faces severe ecological problems from deforestation, while the tiny Himalayan Buddhist kingdom of Bhutan is emerging from long-term isolation, to welcome selected visitors. The Muslim state of Bangladesh, formerly East Pakistan, is one of the world's most densely populated countries and one of the poorest, with more than 145 million people living largely on the massive Ganges/Brahmaputra delta. Many Bangladeshis live under threat of repeated, catastrophic floods.

◀ *The Golden Temple in Amritsar, the most sacred shrine of the Sikh religion, was the scene of violent clashes between Sikh separatists and government forces in 1984.*

Map key

Population
- ▣ 1 million to 5 million
- ◉ 500,000 to 1 million
- ◎ 100,000 to 500,000
- ⊕ 50,000 to 100,000
- ○ 10,000 to 50,000
- ○ below 10,000

Elevation
- 6000m / 19,686ft
- 4000m / 13,124ft
- 3000m / 9843ft
- 2000m / 6562ft
- 1000m / 3281ft
- 500m / 1640ft
- 250m / 820ft
- 100m / 328ft
- sea level

Transportation & industry

Textiles, engineering, chemicals, and electronics are leading industries in north India. The plateau of Chota Nagpur provides ore for iron and steel production in the major industrial region northeast of Kolkata. Bangladesh processes jute and Nepal has a small manufacturing sector based on agricultural produce, while Bhutan's limited industry is concentrated in the southern lowland area.

Scale 1:6,500,000

projection: Lambert Conformal Conic

Major industry and infrastructure
- ⌂ adventure tourism
- 🚗 car manufacture
- ⚗ chemicals
- coal
- ⚙ electronics
- engineering
- $ finance
- food processing
- iron & steel
- jute processing
- ↟ oil
- tea processing
- textiles
- ■ capital cities
- • major towns
- ✈ international airports
- major roads
- major industrial areas

Transportation network
Over 60% of Bangladesh's internal trade is carried by boat. The country has a very disjointed land transportation network, with no bridges over the Brahmaputra and few road crossings on the Ganges river.

The landscape

Most of the region is drained by the Ganges river, which meets the Brahmaputra in Bangladesh to form an immense delta before flowing into the Bay of Bengal. The Himalayas extend eastward over 1500 miles (2400 km), from the parallel ranges running through Jammu and Kashmir. The Thar Desert occupies the southwest.

The Indian Punjab lies mainly to the west of the Ganges watershed and its rivers flow into the Indus. Control of this water resource has been a source of great friction with neighboring Pakistan.

The border between India and Pakistan runs through the Thar Desert, an area of sandy seif dunes 50–100 ft (15–30 m) in height. Fossils found in the desert indicate that the dunes, stabilized by vegetation, have been in their current position for about 3000 years.

Sambhar Salt Lake in Rajasthan is India's largest lake. Unlike most of the Himalayan lakes which are glacial in origin – formed in ice-scoured basins or as the result of depositional damming – it is an ephemeral salt lake filled periodically by flash flooding.

▶ **The Pir Panjal** Range in southwestern Kashmir rises to elevations of 12,500 ft (3810 m). Despite the freezing conditions, settlements and extensive pastures are found above the tree line.

The Ganges river, sacred to the Hindu people, drains a vast lowland area at the base of the Himalayas. The northern plains are covered by sandy deposits, broken by mud banks formed when the river floods.

The rapid deforestation of Himalayan valleys has led to acute soil erosion and increased rates of rainwater runoff, both cited as possible causes of the worsening floods downstream in the Ganges/Brahmaputra delta, although natural rates are high and may be the real cause.

The northern ranges of the Himalayas contain the highest mountains in the world, with average heights of more than 23,000 ft (7000 m) and many peaks higher than 26,000 ft (8000 m).

In the last 40 million years, the course of the Brahmaputra has been diverted hundreds of miles to the east by the rising landmass of the Himalayas.

The Khasi Hills are an example of a *horst*, a fractured block of bedrock which has been thrust upward.

Over half of the great Ganges/Brahmaputra delta floods each year during the monsoon as rivers, swollen by meltwater from the Himalayas and by excess rainwater, break their banks and fertilize the land with nutrient-rich sediment

▲ **The summit of** Machhapuchhre rises to 22,942 ft (6993 m). It is also known as the "Fish's Tail" because of its distinctive peak.

Debris slides in the middle Himalayas

Debris fans at base of slope
Soil blocks
Slide plain

▲ **Soil loss in** the middle Himalayas has largely been attributed to debris slides, where large blocks of soil are mobilized by saturation along a slide plane. Once mobile, the soil slides down the slope, gaining speed and thinning to form a fan at the base of the slope.

Using the land

Grain production dominates land use. Rice is most widely grown in the east. Irrigation and new crop strains have dramatically increased yields in the Punjab, a major wheat-producing area. River floodplains are intensively farmed and livestock herding is widespread, particularly in Bhutan. Regional crops include jute in Bangladesh, tea in Assam, cardamom in Sikkim, and saffron in Kashmir.

The urban/rural population divide

urban 23%   rural 77%

0 10 20 30 40 50 60 70 80 90 100

Population density	Total land area
993 people per sq mile (384 people per sq km)	665,104 sq miles (1,723,068 sq km)

Land use and agricultural distribution

- cattle
- goats
- sheep
- cereals
- jute
- rice
- tea
- ■ capital cities
- • major towns
- pasture
- cropland
- forest
- mountain region
- wetland
- desert

▲ **An adverse climate**, steep slopes, and poor soils limit crop cultivation in Bhutan, which is a largely agrarian economy. Rice, corn, and wheat are the main staples although orchards are being established as the soil and climate suit this type of farming.

▲ **Flooded streets** in Dhaka, Bangladesh are a testament to the region's vulnerability to flooding. In 1988 alone, 75% of the country was flooded, leaving thousands of people dead and over 25 million homeless.

Southern India & Sri Lanka

SRI LANKA, Andhra Pradesh, Chhattisgarh, Dadra & Nagar Haveli, Daman & Diu, Goa, Gujarat, Karnataka, Kerala, Lakshadweep, Madhya Pradesh, Maharashtra, Orissa, Pondicherry, Tamil Nadu

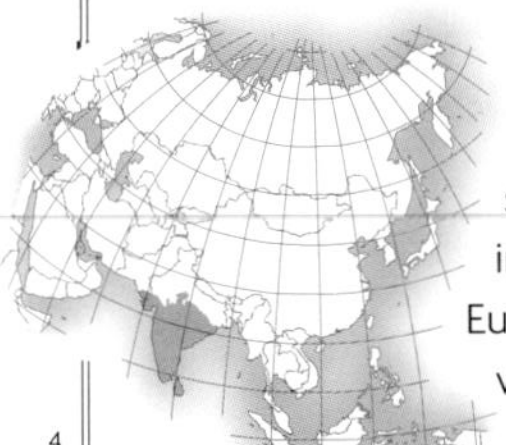

The unique and highly independent southern states reflect the diverse and decentralized nature of India, which has fourteen official languages. The southern half of the peninsula lay beyond the reach of early invaders from the north and retained the distinct and ancient culture of Dravidian peoples such as the Tamils, whose language is spoken in preference to Hindi throughout southern India. The interior plateau of southern India is less densely populated than the coastal lowlands, where the European colonial imprint is strongest. Urban and industrial growth is accelerating, but southern India's vast population remains predominantly rural. The island of Sri Lanka has two distinct cultural groups; the mainly Buddhist Sinhalese majority, and the Tamil minority whose struggle for a homeland in the northeast has led to prolonged civil war.

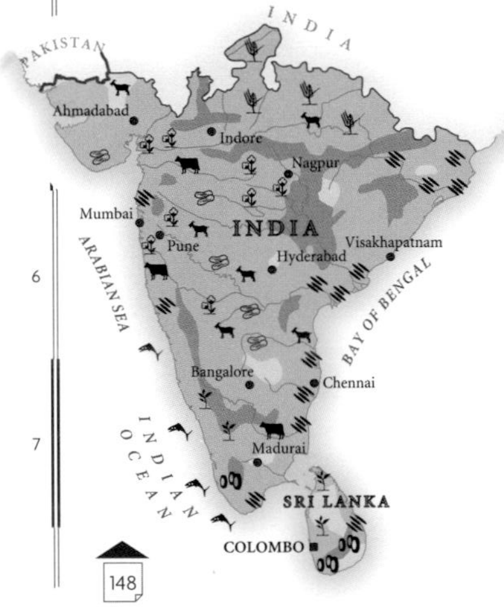

Using the land and sea

Rice is the main staple in the east, in Sri Lanka and along the humid Malabar Coast. Peanuts are grown on the Deccan plateau, with wheat, corn, and chickpeas, toward the north. Sri Lanka is a leading exporter of tea, coconuts and rubber. Cotton plantations supply local mills around Nagpur and Mumbai. Fishing supports many communities in Kerala and the Laccadive Islands.

Land use and agricultural distribution

cattle — pasture
goats — cropland
cereals — forest
cotton — wetland
fishing
peanuts
rice
rubber
tea

■ capital cities
• major towns

The urban/rural population divide

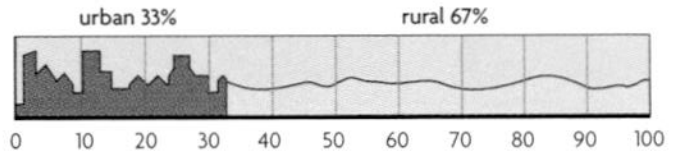

urban 33%   rural 67%

Population density
730 people per sq mile
(282 people per sq km)

Total land area
698,295 sq miles
(1,809,054 sq km)

The landscape

The undulating Deccan plateau underlies most of southern India; it slopes gently down toward the east and is largely enclosed by the Ghats coastal hill ranges. The Western Ghats run continuously along the Arabian Sea coast, while the Eastern Ghats are interrupted by rivers which follow the slope of the plateau and flow across broad lowlands into the Bay of Bengal. The plateaus and basins of Sri Lanka's central highlands are surrounded by a broad plain.

Along the northern boundary of the Deccan plateau, old basement rocks are interspersed with younger sedimentary strata. This creates spectacular scarplands, cut by numerous waterfalls along the softer sedimentary strata.

The interior uplands of southern India are broadly known as the Deccan plateau. River erosion of the plateau's volcanic rock has created distinctive stepped valleys called traps.

Deep layers of river sediment have created a broad lowland plain along the eastern coast, with rivers such as the Krishna forming extensive deltas.

The island of Sri Lanka is essentially an extension of the Deccan plateau. It lies on the Indian continental shelf and is composed of the same hard, crystalline rocks.

Ocean currents cause sediment build up

Sri Lanka

Adam's Bridge

Relict of ancient tombolo

Adam's Bridge

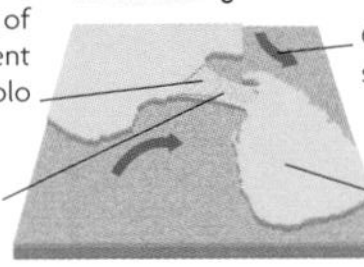

▲ Adam's Bridge (Rama's Bridge) is a chain of sandy shoals lying about 4 ft (1.2 m) under the sea between India and Sri Lanka. They once formed the world's longest tombolo, or land bridge, before the sea level began to rise several thousand years ago.

The Rann of Kachchh tidal marshes encircle the low-lying Kachchh peninsula. For several months during the rainy season the water level of the marshes rises and Kachchh becomes an island.

▼ The Western Ghats run north-south marking the western boundary of the Deccan plateau. Their height rises to the south where their summits reach altitudes of 8000 ft (2500m).

The Konkan coast, which runs between Daman and Goa, is characterized by rocky headlands, and bays with crescent-shaped beaches. Flooded river valleys known as rias extend inland.

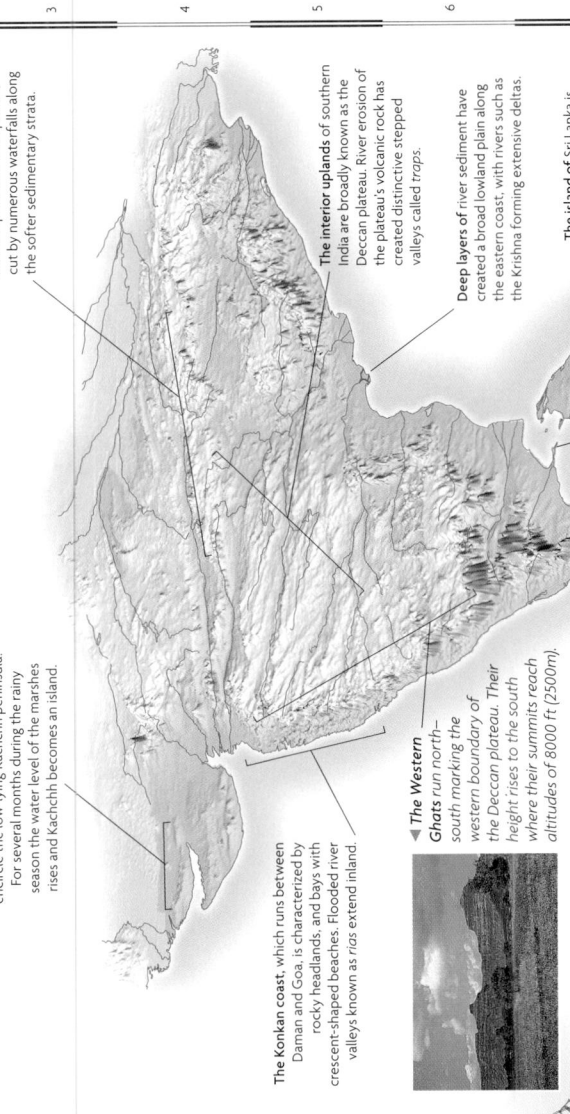

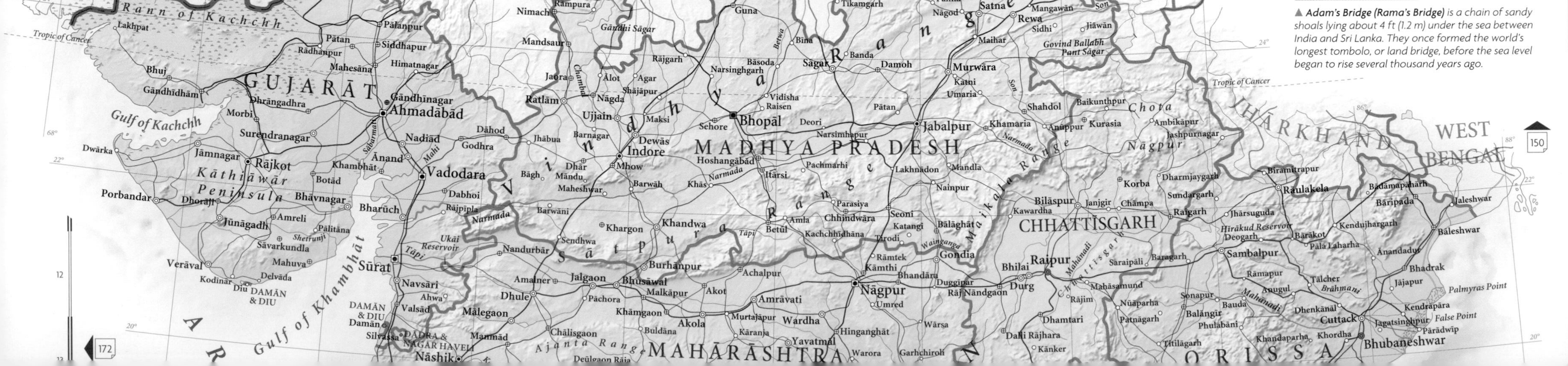

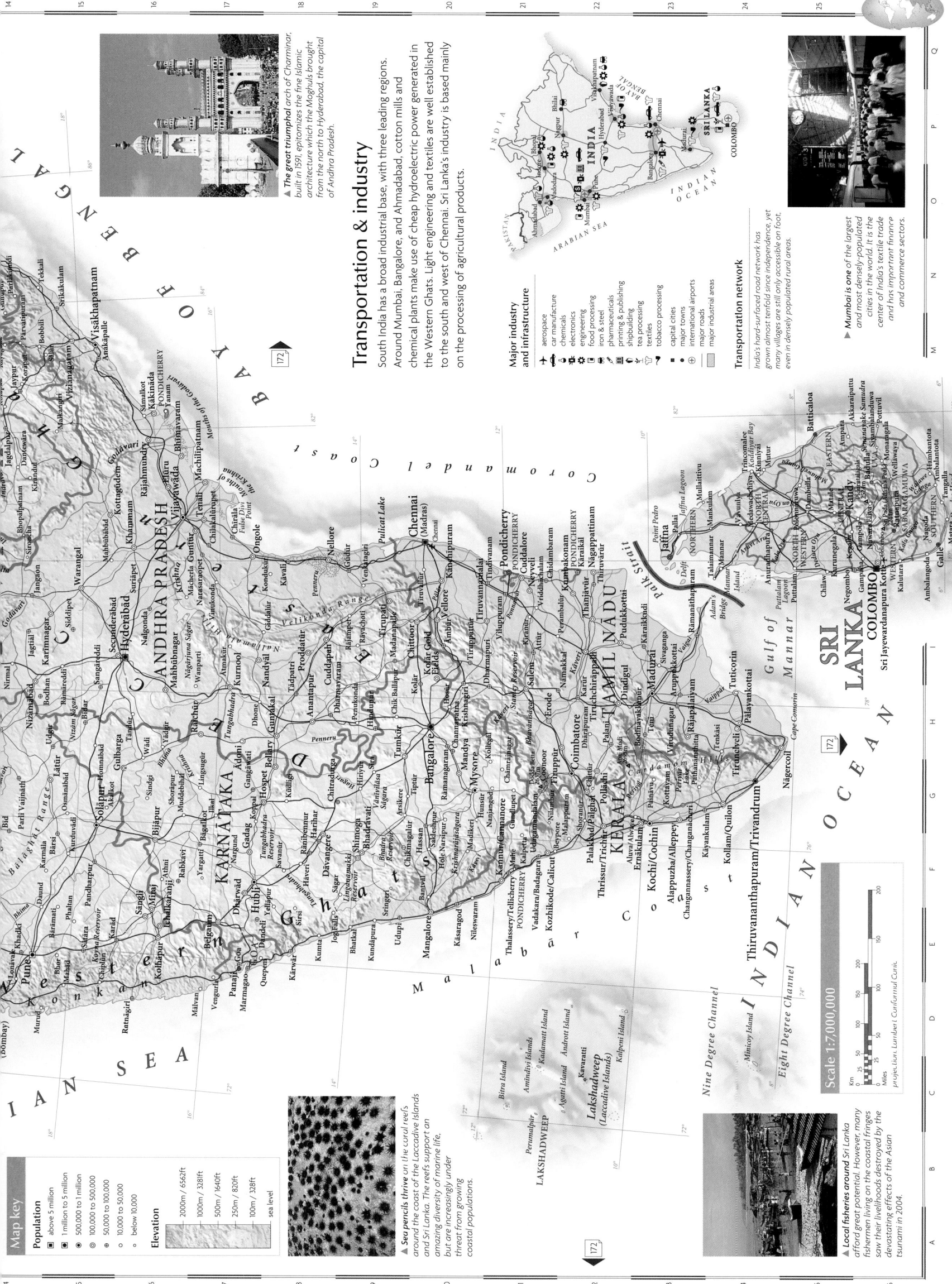

▲ The great triumphal arch of Charminar, built in 1591, epitomizes the fine Islamic architecture which the Moghuls brought from the north to Hyderabad, the capital of Andhra Pradesh.

Transportation & industry

South India has a broad industrial base, with three leading regions. Around Mumbai, Bangalore, and Ahmadabad, cotton mills and chemical plants make use of cheap hydroelectric power generated in the Western Ghats. Light engineering and textiles are well established to the south and west of Chennai. Sri Lanka's industry is based mainly on the processing of agricultural products.

Major industry and infrastructure

- aerospace
- car manufacture
- chemicals
- electronics
- engineering
- food processing
- iron & steel
- pharmaceuticals
- printing & publishing
- shipbuilding
- tea processing
- textiles
- tobacco processing
- capital cities
- major cities
- major towns
- international airports
- major roads
- major industrial areas

Transportation network

India's hard-surfaced road network has grown almost tenfold since independence, yet many villages are still only accessible on foot, even in densely populated rural areas.

▲ Mumbai is one of the largest and most densely-populated cities in the world. It is the center of India's textile trade and has important finance and commerce sectors.

Map key

Population

- above 5 million
- 1 million to 5 million
- 500,000 to 1 million
- 100,000 to 500,000
- 50,000 to 100,000
- 10,000 to 50,000
- below 10,000

Elevation

- 2000m / 6562ft
- 1000m / 3281ft
- 500m / 1640ft
- 250m / 820ft
- 100m / 328ft
- sea level

▲ Sea pencils thrive on the coral reefs around the coast of the Laccadive Islands and Sri Lanka. The reefs support an amazing diversity of marine life, but are increasingly under threat from growing coastal populations.

▲ Local fisheries around Sri Lanka afford great potential. However, many fishermen living on the coastal fringes saw their livelihoods destroyed by the devastating effects of the Asian tsunami in 2004.

Scale 1:7,000,000

projection: Lambert Conformal Conic.

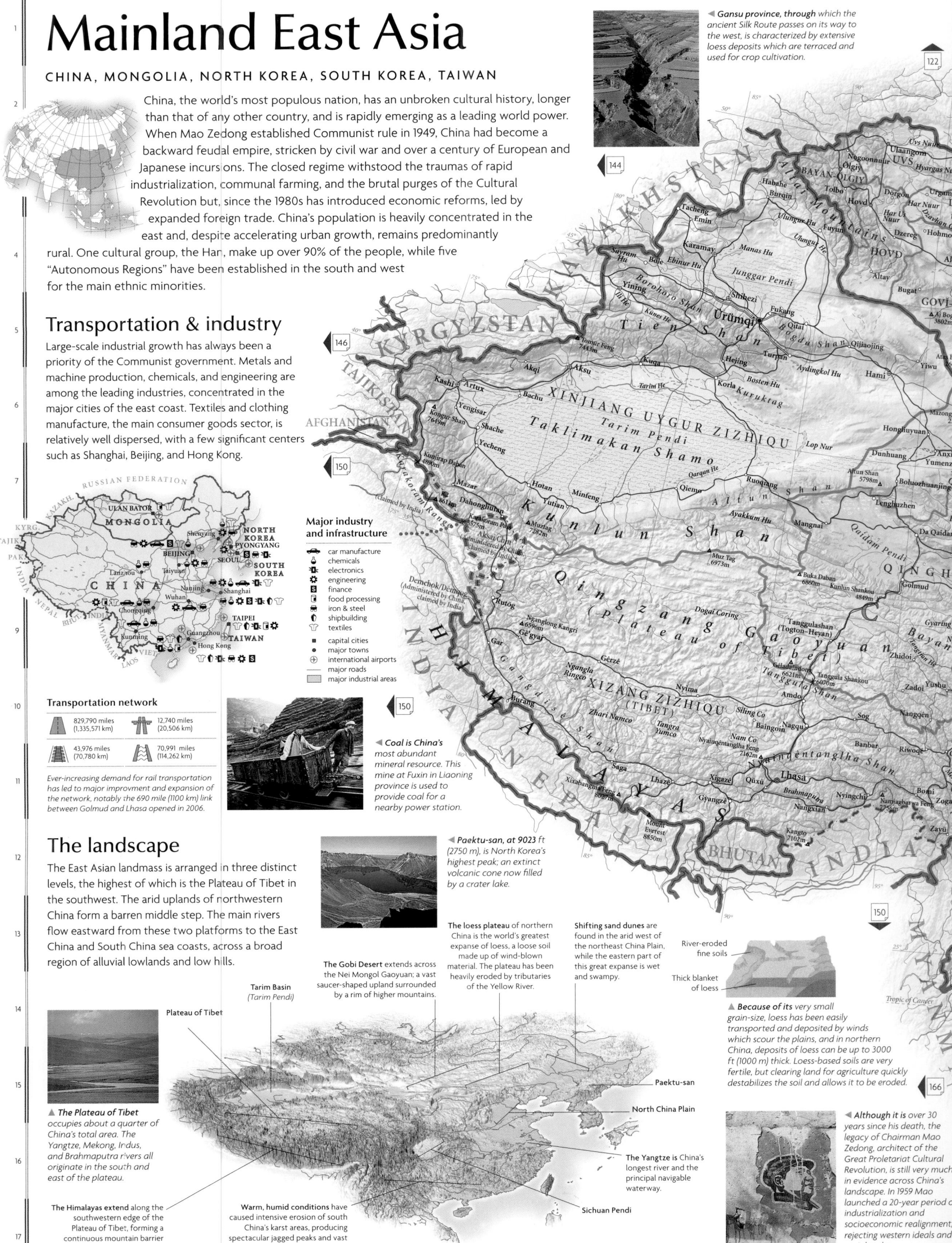

Mainland East Asia

CHINA, MONGOLIA, NORTH KOREA, SOUTH KOREA, TAIWAN

China, the world's most populous nation, has an unbroken cultural history, longer than that of any other country, and is rapidly emerging as a leading world power. When Mao Zedong established Communist rule in 1949, China had become a backward feudal empire, stricken by civil war and over a century of European and Japanese incursions. The closed regime withstood the traumas of rapid industrialization, communal farming, and the brutal purges of the Cultural Revolution but, since the 1980s has introduced economic reforms, led by expanded foreign trade. China's population is heavily concentrated in the east and, despite accelerating urban growth, remains predominantly rural. One cultural group, the Han, make up over 90% of the people, while five "Autonomous Regions" have been established in the south and west for the main ethnic minorities.

Transportation & industry

Large-scale industrial growth has always been a priority of the Communist government. Metals and machine production, chemicals, and engineering are among the leading industries, concentrated in the major cities of the east coast. Textiles and clothing manufacture, the main consumer goods sector, is relatively well dispersed, with a few significant centers such as Shanghai, Beijing, and Hong Kong.

Major industry and infrastructure

- car manufacture
- chemicals
- electronics
- engineering
- finance
- food processing
- iron & steel
- shipbuilding
- textiles

- capital cities
- major towns
- international airports
- major roads
- major industrial areas

Transportation network

829,790 miles (1,335,571 km)	12,740 miles (20,506 km)
43,976 miles (70,780 km)	70,991 miles (114,262 km)

Ever-increasing demand for rail transportation has led to major improvment and expansion of the network, notably the 690 mile (1100 km) link between Golmud and Lhasa opened in 2006.

◄ *Coal is China's most abundant mineral resource. This mine at Fuxin in Liaoning province is used to provide coal for a nearby power station.*

The landscape

The East Asian landmass is arranged in three distinct levels, the highest of which is the Plateau of Tibet in the southwest. The arid uplands of northwestern China form a barren middle step. The main rivers flow eastward from these two platforms to the East China and South China sea coasts, across a broad region of alluvial lowlands and low hills.

◄ *Gansu province, through which the ancient Silk Route passes on its way to the west, is characterized by extensive loess deposits which are terraced and used for crop cultivation.*

◄ *Paektu-san, at 9023 ft (2750 m), is North Korea's highest peak; an extinct volcanic cone now filled by a crater lake.*

The Gobi Desert extends across the Nei Mongol Gaoyuan; a vast saucer-shaped upland surrounded by a rim of higher mountains.

The loess plateau of northern China is the world's greatest expanse of loess, a loose soil made up of wind-blown material. The plateau has been heavily eroded by tributaries of the Yellow River.

Shifting sand dunes are found in the arid west of the northeast China Plain, while the eastern part of this great expanse is wet and swampy.

River-eroded fine soils

Thick blanket of loess

▲ *Because of its very small grain-size, loess has been easily transported and deposited by winds which scour the plains, and in northern China, deposits of loess can be up to 3000 ft (1000 m) thick. Loess-based soils are very fertile, but clearing land for agriculture quickly destabilizes the soil and allows it to be eroded.*

Tarim Basin (Tarim Pendi)

Plateau of Tibet

Paektu-san

North China Plain

The Yangtze is China's longest river and the principal navigable waterway.

Sichuan Pendi

▲ *The Plateau of Tibet occupies about a quarter of China's total area. The Yangtze, Mekong, Indus, and Brahmaputra rivers all originate in the south and east of the plateau.*

The Himalayas extend along the southwestern edge of the Plateau of Tibet, forming a continuous mountain barrier over 1500 miles (2500 km) long.

Warm, humid conditions have caused intensive erosion of south China's karst areas, producing spectacular jagged peaks and vast caves in the limestone.

◄ *Although it is over 30 years since his death, the legacy of Chairman Mao Zedong, architect of the Great Proletariat Cultural Revolution, is still very much in evidence across China's landscape. In 1959 Mao launched a 20-year period of industrialization and socioeconomic realignment, rejecting western ideals and social codes.*

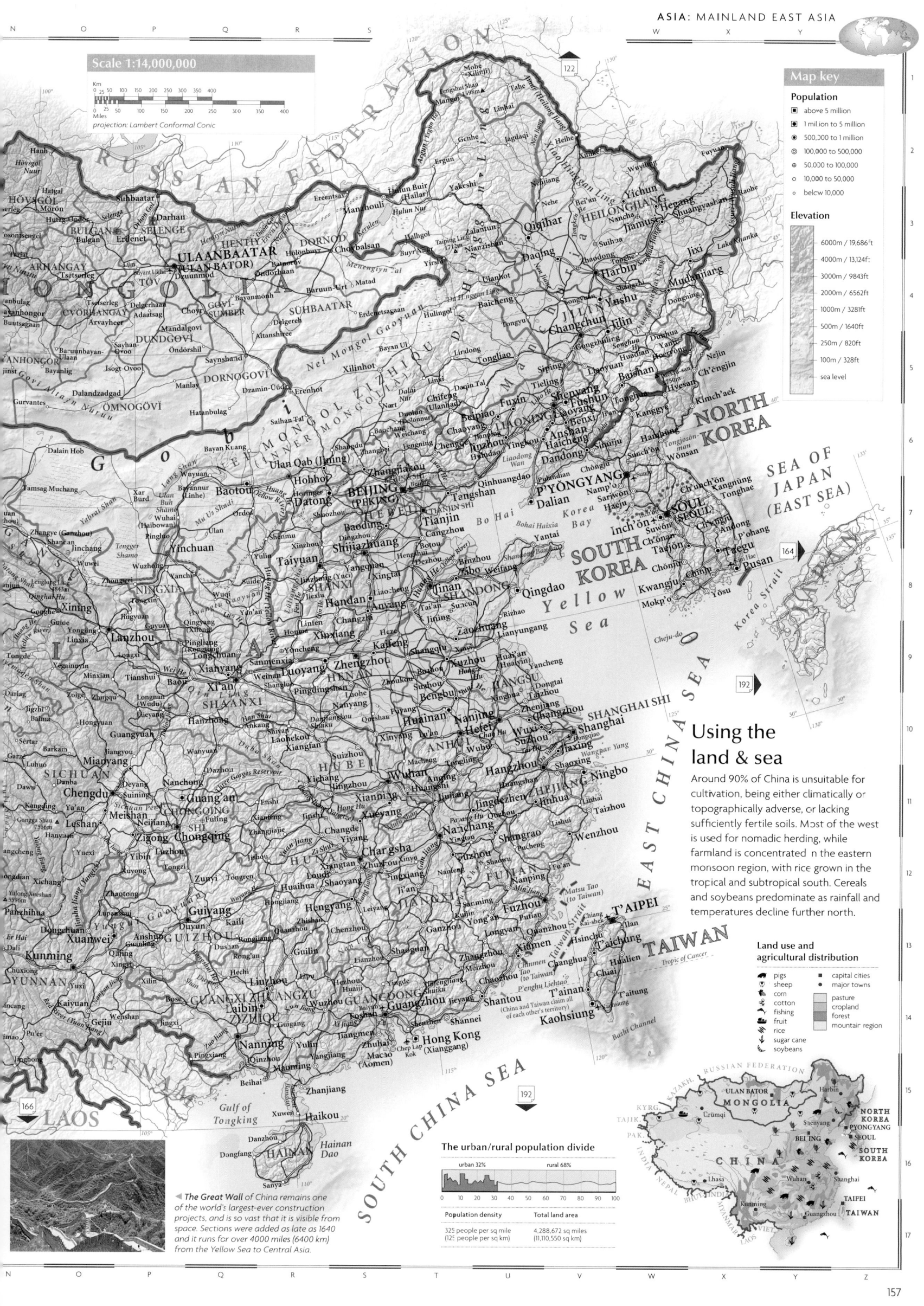

Using the land & sea

Around 90% of China is unsuitable for cultivation, being either climatically or topographically adverse, or lacking sufficiently fertile soils. Most of the west is used for nomadic herding, while farmland is concentrated in the eastern monsoon region, with rice grown in the tropical and subtropical south. Cereals and soybeans predominate as rainfall and temperatures decline further north.

The Great Wall of China remains one of the world's largest-ever construction projects, and is so vast that it is visible from space. Sections were added as late as 1640 and it runs for over 4000 miles (6400 km) from the Yellow Sea to Central Asia.

157

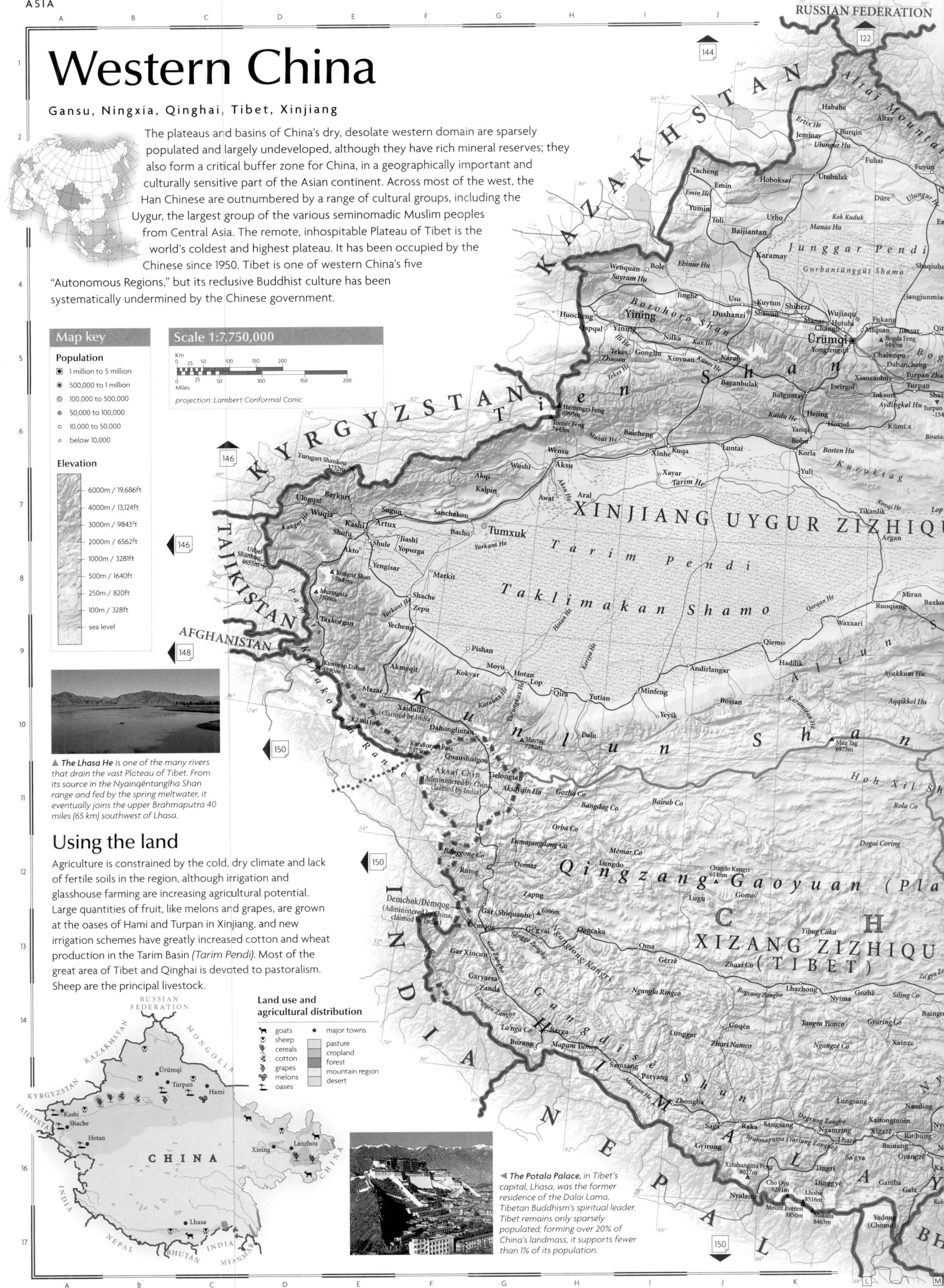

RUSSIAN FEDERATION

Western China

Gansu, Ningxia, Qinghai, Tibet, Xinjiang

The plateaus and basins of China's dry, desolate western domain are sparsely populated and largely undeveloped, although they have rich mineral reserves; they also form a critical buffer zone for China, in a geographically important and culturally sensitive part of the Asian continent. Across most of the west, the Han Chinese are outnumbered by a range of cultural groups, including the Uygur, the largest group of the various seminomadic Muslim peoples from Central Asia. The remote, inhospitable Plateau of Tibet is the world's coldest and highest plateau. It has been occupied by the Chinese since 1950. Tibet is one of western China's five "Autonomous Regions," but its reclusive Buddhist culture has been systematically undermined by the Chinese government.

Map key

Population
- ▣ 1 million to 5 million
- ◉ 500,000 to 1 million
- ◎ 100,000 to 500,000
- ⊕ 50,000 to 100,000
- ⊙ 10,000 to 50,000
- ○ below 10,000

Elevation
- 6000m / 19,686ft
- 4000m / 13,124ft
- 3000m / 9843ft
- 2000m / 6562ft
- 1000m / 3281ft
- 500m / 1640ft
- 250m / 820ft
- 100m / 328ft
- sea level

Scale 1:7,750,000

projection: Lambert Conformal Conic

▲ **The Lhasa He** is one of the many rivers that drain the vast Plateau of Tibet. From its source in the Nyainqêntanglha Shan range and fed by the spring meltwater, it eventually joins the upper Brahmaputra 40 miles (65 km) southwest of Lhasa.

Using the land

Agriculture is constrained by the cold, dry climate and lack of fertile soils in the region, although irrigation and glasshouse farming are increasing agricultural potential. Large quantities of fruit, like melons and grapes, are grown at the oases of Hami and Turpan in Xinjiang, and new irrigation schemes have greatly increased cotton and wheat production in the Tarim Basin (Tarim Pendi). Most of the great area of Tibet and Qinghai is devoted to pastoralism. Sheep are the principal livestock.

Land use and agricultural distribution
- 🐐 goats
- 🐑 sheep
- 🌾 cereals
- cotton
- 🍇 grapes
- melons
- oases
- • major towns
- pasture
- cropland
- forest
- mountain region
- desert

◀ **The Potala Palace,** in Tibet's capital, Lhasa, was the former residence of the Dalai Lama, Tibetan Buddhism's spiritual leader. Tibet remains only sparsely populated; forming over 20% of China's landmass, it supports fewer than 1% of its population.

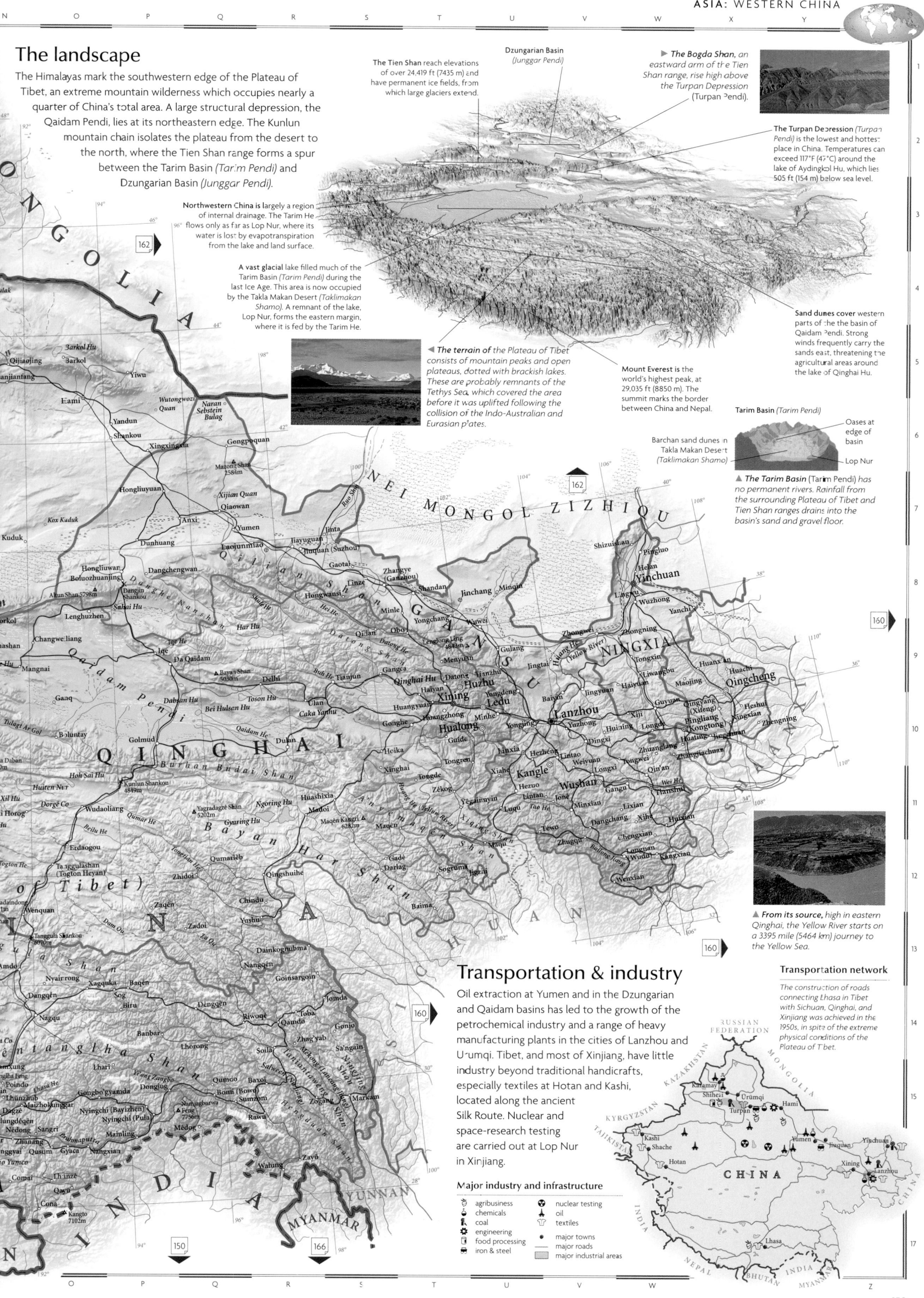

The landscape

The Himalayas mark the southwestern edge of the Plateau of Tibet, an extreme mountain wilderness which occupies nearly a quarter of China's total area. A large structural depression, the Qaidam Pendi, lies at its northeastern edge. The Kunlun mountain chain isolates the plateau from the desert to the north, where the Tien Shan range forms a spur between the Tarim Basin (Tarim Pendi) and Dzungarian Basin (Junggar Pendi).

Dzungarian Basin (Junggar Pendi)

The Tien Shan reach elevations of over 24,419 ft (7435 m) and have permanent ice fields, from which large glaciers extend.

▶ The Bogda Shan, an eastward arm of the Tien Shan range, rise high above the Turpan Depression (Turpan Pendi).

The Turpan Depression (Turpan Pendi) is the lowest and hottest place in China. Temperatures can exceed 117°F (47°C) around the lake of Aydingkol Hu, which lies 505 ft (154 m) below sea level.

Northwestern China is largely a region of internal drainage. The Tarim He flows only as far as Lop Nur, where its water is lost by evapotranspiration from the lake and land surface.

A vast glacial lake filled much of the Tarim Basin (Tarim Pendi) during the last Ice Age. This area is now occupied by the Takla Makan Desert (Taklimakan Shamo). A remnant of the lake, Lop Nur, forms the eastern margin, where it is fed by the Tarim He.

◀ The terrain of the Plateau of Tibet consists of mountain peaks and open plateaus, dotted with brackish lakes. These are probably remnants of the Tethys Sea, which covered the area before it was uplifted following the collision of the Indo-Australian and Eurasian plates.

Mount Everest is the world's highest peak, at 29,035 ft (8850 m). The summit marks the border between China and Nepal.

Sand dunes cover western parts of the the basin of Qaidam Pendi. Strong winds frequently carry the sands east, threatening the agricultural areas around the lake of Qinghai Hu.

Tarim Basin (Tarim Pendi)

Oases at edge of basin

Barchan sand dunes in Takla Makan Desert (Taklimakan Shamo)

Lop Nur

▲ The Tarim Basin (Tarim Pendi) has no permanent rivers. Rainfall from the surrounding Plateau of Tibet and Tien Shan ranges drains into the basin's sand and gravel floor.

▲ From its source, high in eastern Qinghai, the Yellow River starts on a 3395 mile (5464 km) journey to the Yellow Sea.

Transportation & industry

Oil extraction at Yumen and in the Dzungarian and Qaidam basins has led to the growth of the petrochemical industry and a range of heavy manufacturing plants in the cities of Lanzhou and Urumqi. Tibet, and most of Xinjiang, have little industry beyond traditional handicrafts, especially textiles at Hotan and Kashi, located along the ancient Silk Route. Nuclear and space-research testing are carried out at Lop Nur in Xinjiang.

Transportation network

The construction of roads connecting Lhasa in Tibet with Sichuan, Qinghai, and Xinjiang was achieved in the 1950s, in spite of the extreme physical conditions of the Plateau of Tibet.

Major industry and infrastructure

- agribusiness
- chemicals
- coal
- engineering
- food processing
- iron & steel
- nuclear testing
- oil
- textiles
- major towns
- major roads
- major industrial areas

159

Eastern China

TAIWAN, Anhui, Beijing, Chongqing, Fujian, Guangdong, Guangxi, Guizhou, Hainan, Hebei, Henan, Hubei, Hunan, Jiangsu, Jiangxi, Shaanxi, Shandong, Shanghai, Shanxi, Sichuan, Tianjin, Yunnan, Zhejiang

The east is China's heartland. Massive industrial development since 1949 has transformed much of the densely populated rural landscape, in a region still prone to flooding and drought. Over 30 cities have populations of over a million, including the giant metropolis of Shanghai and the capital Beijing, which has been China's cultural and political center since the 13th century. The ethnically diverse southwest and the oil-rich interior provinces of Sichuan and Shaanxi have largely missed out on the remarkable economic growth occurring in designated free-trade areas along the coasts of the South and East China seas. The republic of Taiwan was established in 1949 by Chinese nationalists ousted from the mainland by the victorious Communist forces. Taiwan now has one of the strongest economies in the world but its sovereignty is not recognized by China. Hong Kong provides a major international trade link for China; a 99-year "lease" period of British control was concluded in 1997.

▲ *North of the* Qin Ling range in Shaanxi province, is an agriculturally fertile region covered with fine, wind-blown deposits and known as the loess plateau. The loose sediments are vulnerable to water erosion.

Using the land & sea

This is a region of intensive cultivation. Wheat, millet, sorghum, and cotton are the main crops of the Yellow River basin. South from Sichuan, rice becomes the principal crop, grown with wheat, corn, and cotton along the Yangtze river. Tea is produced in the hills and sugar cane along the coast of the southeast, where flat land is limited. Pigs and poultry are raised in great numbers.

Land use and agricultural distribution

- 🐂 cattle
- 🐖 pigs
- 🌾 cereals
- 🌽 corn
- 🌿 cotton
- 🐟 fishing
- 🥜 peanuts
- 🌾 rice
- 🎋 sugar cane
- 🍃 tea

- ■ capital cities
- • major towns

- pasture
- cropland
- forest
- mountain region

▲ *On the hills* above the North China Plain, slopes are terraced to utilize the rich loess soils of the Taihang Shan range.

Map key

Population
- ▣ above 5 million
- ▦ 1 million to 5 million
- ◉ 500,000 to 1 million
- ⊙ 100,000 to 500,000
- ⊚ 50,000 to 100,000
- ○ 10,000 to 50,000
- ∘ below 10,000

Elevation
- 6000m / 19,686ft
- 4000m / 13,124ft
- 3000m / 9843ft
- 2000m / 6562ft
- 1000m / 3281ft
- 500m / 1640ft
- 250m / 820ft
- 100m / 328ft
- sea level

Scale 1:8,500,000

Km 0 25 50 100 150 200 250 300
Miles 0 25 50 100 150 200 250 300

projection: Lambert Conformal Conic

◄ *The former* *Portuguese* territory of Macao, with its colonial architecture, bars and casinos, reverted to Chinese rule in 1999.

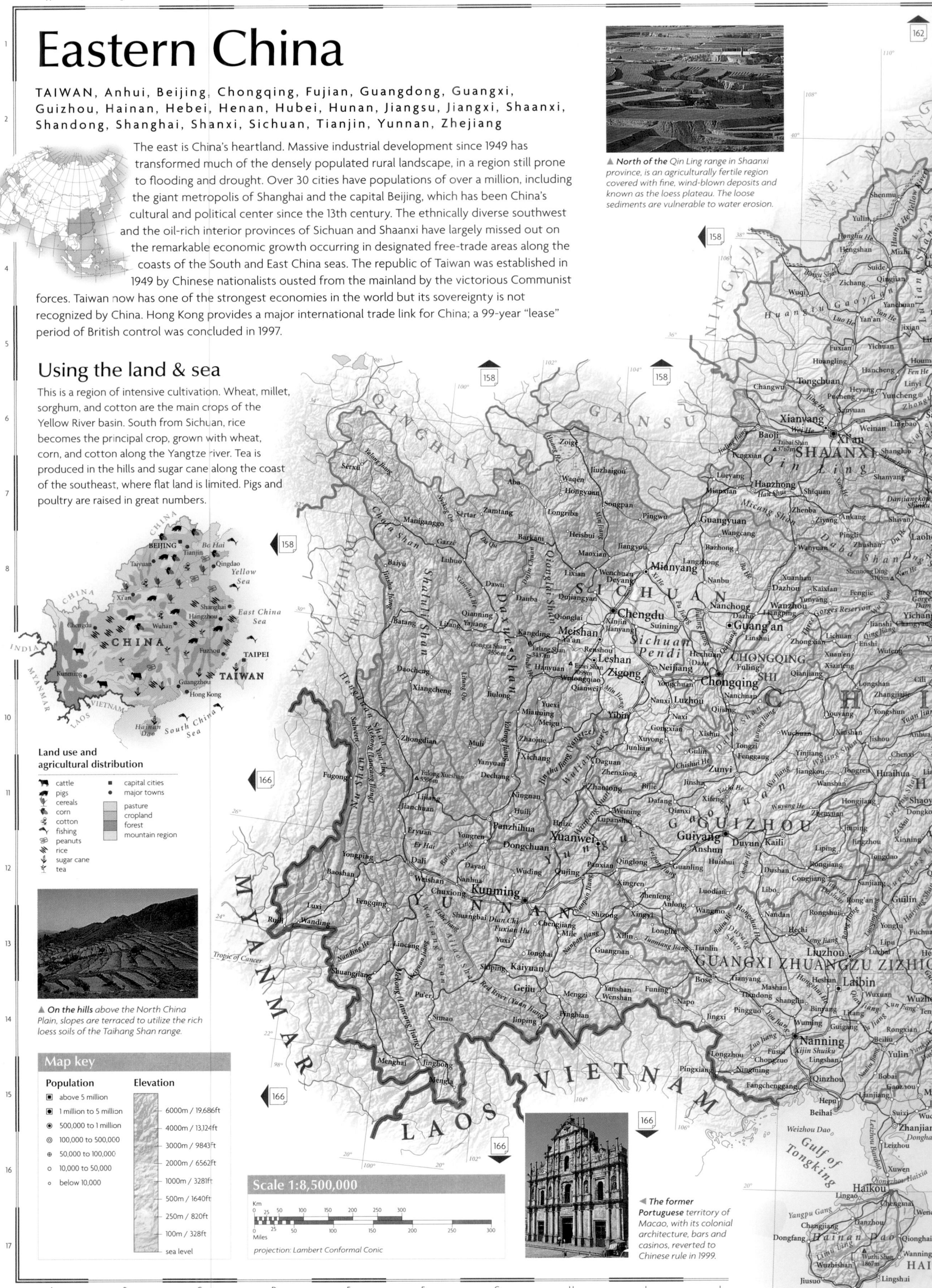

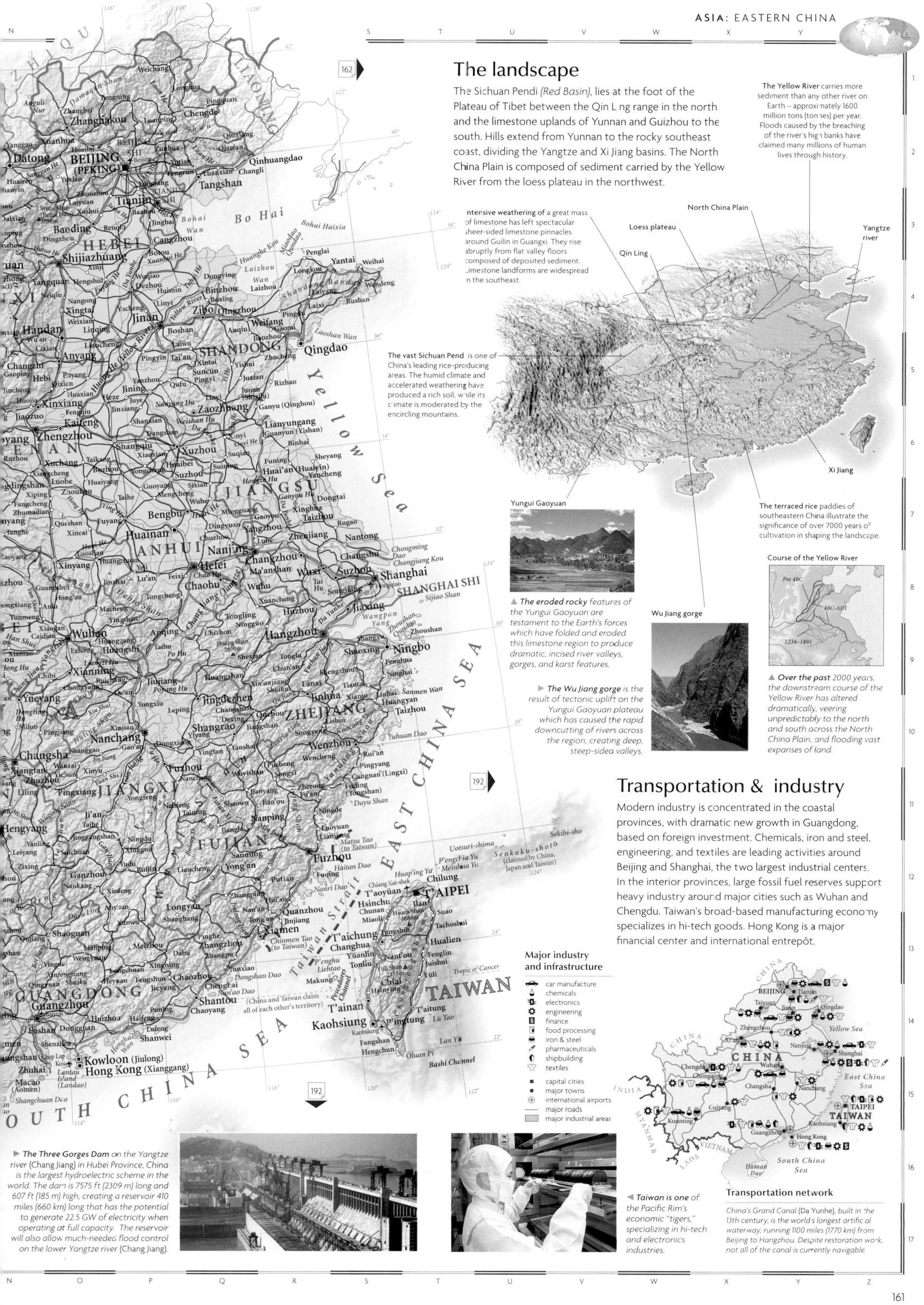

The landscape

The Sichuan Pendi (Red Basin), lies at the foot of the Plateau of Tibet between the Qin Ling range in the north and the limestone uplands of Yunnan and Guizhou to the south. Hills extend from Yunnan to the rocky southeast coast, dividing the Yangtze and Xi Jiang basins. The North China Plain is composed of sediment carried by the Yellow River from the loess plateau in the northwest.

The Yellow River carries more sediment than any other river on Earth – approximately 1600 million tons (tonnes) per year. Floods caused by the breaching of the river's high banks have claimed many millions of human lives through history.

Intensive weathering of a great mass of limestone has left spectacular sheer-sided limestone pinnacles around Guilin in Guangxi. They rise abruptly from flat valley floors composed of deposited sediment. Limestone landforms are widespread in the southeast.

North China Plain

Loess plateau

Qin Ling

Yangtze river

Xi Jiang

The vast Sichuan Pend is one of China's leading rice-producing areas. The humid climate and accelerated weathering have produced a rich soil, while its climate is moderated by the encircling mountains.

Yungui Gaoyuan

▲ The eroded rocky features of the Yungui Gaoyuan are testament to the Earth's forces which have folded and eroded this limestone region to produce dramatic, incised river valleys, gorges, and karst features.

Wu Jiang gorge

▶ The Wu Jiang gorge is the result of tectonic uplift on the Yungui Gaoyuan plateau which has caused the rapid downcutting of rivers across the region, creating deep, steep-sided valleys.

The terraced rice paddies of southeastern China illustrate the significance of over 7000 years of cultivation in shaping the landscape.

Course of the Yellow River

Pre 4BC

4BC–AD1

1234–1891

▲ Over the past 2000 years, the downstream course of the Yellow River has altered dramatically, veering unpredictably to the north and south across the North China Plain, and flooding vast expanses of land.

Transportation & industry

Modern industry is concentrated in the coastal provinces, with dramatic new growth in Guangdong, based on foreign investment. Chemicals, iron and steel, engineering, and textiles are leading activities around Beijing and Shanghai, the two largest industrial centers. In the interior provinces, large fossil fuel reserves support heavy industry around major cities such as Wuhan and Chengdu. Taiwan's broad-based manufacturing economy specializes in hi-tech goods. Hong Kong is a major financial center and international entrepôt.

Major industry and infrastructure

- car manufacture
- chemicals
- electronics
- engineering
- finance
- food processing
- iron & steel
- pharmaceuticals
- shipbuilding
- textiles

- ■ capital cities
- ■ major towns
- ⊕ international airports
- — major roads
- ▨ major industrial areas

▶ The Three Gorges Dam on the Yangtze river (Chang Jiang) in Hubei Province, China is the largest hydroelectric scheme in the world. The dam is 7575 ft (2309 m) long and 607 ft (185 m) high, creating a reservoir 410 miles (660 km) long that has the potential to generate 22.5 GW of electricity when operating at full capacity. The reservoir will also allow much-needed flood control on the lower Yangtze river (Chang Jiang).

◀ Taiwan is one of the Pacific Rim's economic "tigers," specializing in hi-tech and electronics industries.

Transportation network

China's Grand Canal (Da Yunhe), built in the 13th century, is the world's longest artificial waterway, running 1100 miles (1770 km) from Beijing to Hangzhou. Despite restoration work, not all of the canal is currently navigable.

Northeastern China, Mongolia & Korea

MONGOLIA, NORTH KOREA, SOUTH KOREA, Heilongjiang, Inner Mongolia, Jilin, Liaoning

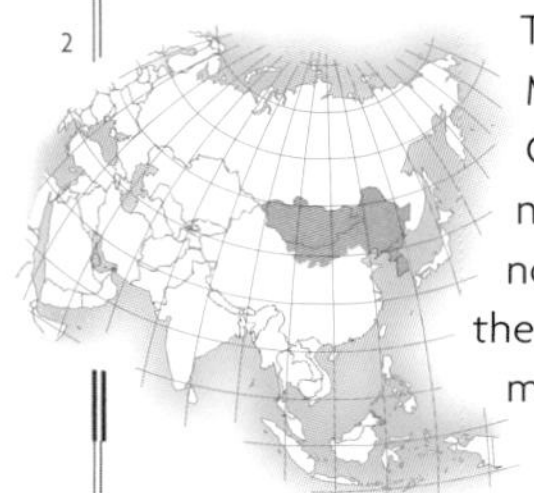

This northerly region has been a domain of shifting borders and competing colonial powers for centuries. Mongolia was the heartland of Chinghiz Khan's vast Mongol empire in the 13th century, while northeastern China was home to the Manchus, China's last ruling dynasty (1644–1911). The mineral and forest wealth of the northeast helped make this China's principal region of heavy industry, although the outdated state factories now face decline. South Korea's state-led market economy has grown dramatically and Seoul is now one of the world's largest cities. The austere communist regime of North Korea has isolated itself from the expanding markets of the Pacific Rim and faces continuing economic stagnation.

▲ *The Eurasian steppe* stretches from the mouth of the Danube in Europe, to Mongolia. In Mongolia, nomadic people have lived in felt huts called yurts or gers, for thousands of years.

Map key

Population
- ▣ above 5 million
- ◼ 1 million to 5 million
- ◉ 500,000 to 1 million
- ◎ 100,000 to 500,000
- ⊕ 50,000 to 100,000
- ○ 10,000 to 50,000
- ○ below 10,000

Elevation
- 4000m / 13,124ft
- 3000m / 9843ft
- 2000m / 6562ft
- 1000m / 3281ft
- 500m / 1640ft
- 250m / 820ft
- 100m / 328ft
- sea level

Scale 1:7,750,000

projection: Lambert Conformal Conic

The landscape

The great North China Plain is largely enclosed by mountain ranges including the Great and Lesser Khingan Ranges (*Da Hinggan Ling* and *Xiao Hinggan Ling*) in the north, and the Changbai Shan, which extend south into the rugged peninsula of Korea. The broad steppeland plateau of Nei Mongol Gaoyuan borders the southeastern edge of the great cold desert of the Gobi which extends west across the southern reaches of Mongolia. In northwest Mongolia the Altai Mountains and various lesser ranges are interspersed with lakeland basins.

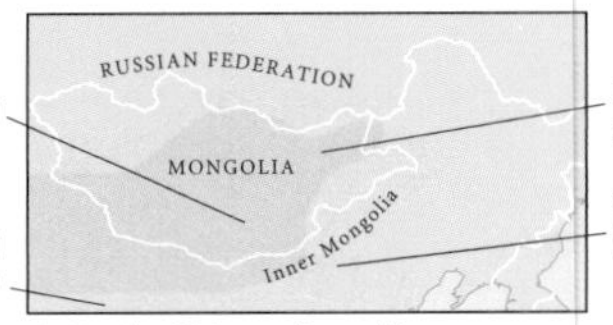

▲ *Much of Mongolia* and Inner Mongolia is a vast desert area. To the south and east, a semiarid region extends into China proper.

▲ *The Gobi desert* stretches from Central Asia, through Mongolia and into China. Bare rock surfaces, rather than sand dunes, typify the cold desert landscape of the Gobi.

Tributaries of the Amur river follow U-shaped valleys through the Great Khingan Range (*Da Hinggan Ling*). These were cut by ice-age glaciers between 3 and 10 million years ago.

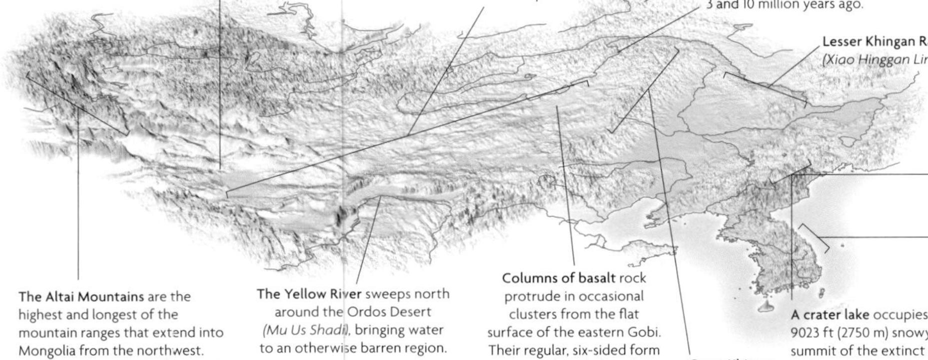

Lesser Khingan Range (*Xiao Hinggan Ling*)

Changbai Shan

T'aebaek-sanmaek

The Altai Mountains are the highest and longest of the mountain ranges that extend into Mongolia from the northwest. These mountains provide one of the last refuges for the endangered snow leopard.

The Yellow River sweeps north around the Ordos Desert (*Mu Us Shadi*), bringing water to an otherwise barren region.

Columns of basalt rock protrude in occasional clusters from the flat surface of the eastern Gobi. Their regular, six-sided form was produced when the rock cooled and contracted from its molten state.

Great Khingan Range (*Da Hinggan Ling*)

A crater lake occupies the 9023 ft (2750 m) snowy summit of the extinct volcano Paektu-san, the highest peak in the mountains of the Changbai Shan.

◀ *The wooded mountain* range of T'aebaek-sanmaek forms the backbone of the Korean peninsula, running north–south along the eastern coastline.

Transportation & industry

North Korea's centrally-planned economy is strongly oriented toward heavy industry, while South Korea has a broad manufacturing base which includes textiles, steel, electronics, and one of the world's largest shipbuilding industries. Mongolia and Inner Mongolia's great mineral resource potential is largely undeveloped. The heavy industrial region around Shenyang produces iron, steel, chemicals, and cement on a massive scale.

Major industry and infrastructure

- car manufacture
- chemicals
- coal
- electronics
- engineering
- finance
- food processing
- iron & steel
- pharmaceuticals
- shipbuilding
- textiles
- ■ capital cities
- ● major towns
- ✈ international airports
- — major roads
- major industrial areas

Transportation network

Liaoning has China's most comprehensive railroad network, the legacy of the Japanese occupation of Manchuria in the 20th century. The railroads are used primarily for freight transportation.

▲ *Ulan Bator, the Mongolian capital bears many of the hallmarks of Soviet-style central planning, the result of economic and industrial assistance from the Soviet Union following Mongolian independence in 1921.*

▶ *While North Korea has remained politically and economically isolated from the rest of the world, South Korea has enjoyed immense economic growth. It has benefited considerably from US economic aid in the aftermath of the Korean war of 1950–1953.*

Using the land & sea

Mongolia and Inner Mongolia rely heavily on livestock farming, with only about 1% of the land area cultivated. Northeastern China produces wheat, corn, soybeans, and sugar beet. The cool climate limits the range of crops and large upland areas of the northeast remain forested. Rice is the staple food of North and South Korea. The latter has become a leading ocean-fishing nation.

Land use and agricultural distribution

- goats
- pigs
- sheep
- corn
- fishing
- rice
- soybeans
- sugar beet
- wheat
- ■ capital cities
- ● major towns
- pasture
- cropland
- forest
- mountain region
- desert

Japan

In the years since the end of the Second World War, Japan has become the world's most dynamic industrial nation. The country comprises a string of over 4000 islands which lie in a great northeast to southwest arc in the northwest Pacific. Four major islands: Hokkaido, Honshu, Shikoku, and Kyushu are home to the great majority of Japan's population of 128 million people, although the mountainous terrain of the central region means that most cities are situated on the coast. A densely populated industrial belt stretches along much of Honshu's southern coast, including Japan's crowded capital, Tokyo. Alongside its spectacular economic growth and the increasing westernization of its cities, Japan still maintains a highly individual culture, reflected in its traditional food, formal behavioral codes, unique Shinto religion, and a deep reverence for the emperor.

Using the land & sea

Although only about 11% of Japan is suitable for cultivation, substantial government support, a favorable climate and intensive farming methods enable the country to be virtually self-sufficient in rice production. Northern Hokkaido, the largest and most productive farming region, has an open terrain and climate similar to that of the American Midwest, and produces over half of Japan's cereal requirements. Farmers are being encouraged to diversify by growing fruit, vegetables, and wheat, as well as raising livestock.

Land use and agricultural distribution

- cattle
- pigs
- fishing
- cereals
- citrus fruits
- fruit
- herbs
- rice
- root crops
- tobacco
- ■ capital cities
- ● major towns
- pasture
- cropland
- forest

The urban/rural population divide

urban 78%   rural 22%

0 10 20 30 40 50 60 70 80 90 100

Population density	Total land area
885 people per sq mile (342 people per sq km)	145,869 sq miles (377,800 sq km)

The landscape

The islands of Japan lie on the Pacific "Ring of Fire," and form a series of clearly defined arcs. The largely mountainous landscape was formed very recently in geological terms. Volcanic eruptions and earthquakes continue to reshape the terrain and shake the country's complex infrastructure. There is no single continuous mountain range; the mountains divide into many small land blocks separated by lowlands and dissected by numerous river valleys.

▶ *Cutting terraces maximizes the limited agricultural land, enabling Japan to produce large quantities of rice.*

Sea of Japan (East Sea)
Active volcanic island
Japan Trench (subduction zone)

▲ *Japan is part of an arc of volcanic islands, formed by the Pacific Plate diving under the Eurasian Plate. This process generates intense stress which is periodically released as earthquakes.*

◀ *Mount Fuji is Japan's highest mountain, rising 12,388 ft (3776 m) above the Kanto Plain in the central region of Honshu. The flat land below is suitable for growing crops such as tea. Like many Japanese mountains, it is revered as a sacred site.*

Mount Fuji

A number of rivers which emerge from the volcanic parts of northwestern Honshu are so highly acidic that their water is unsuitable for irrigation and consumption.

▶ *Trees cling to the sheer slopes of the waterfalls on the northern island of Hokkaido. The island's climate is similar to that in northern Europe, with long, cold winters and short, warm summers.*

In much of Kyushu the coast is subsiding, giving a highly indented coastline. In some places, former hilltops are barely visible above the current sea level.

There are over 60 active volcanoes – like Asahi-dake, Hokkaido's highest peak – throughout Japan. This accounts for more than 10% of the world's total.

The Inland Sea (Seto-naikai) has resulted from the depression of faulted blocks which has allowed sea water to invade the region between northern Shikoku and western Honshu.

Strong southeasterly winds blowing onshore during the winter create sand dunes which extend for miles along the eastern coasts.

Biwa-ko is the largest lake in Japan, covering 260 sq miles (673 sq km) in central Honshu. The depression in which it lies was created by recent faulting of the underlying rocks.

Rising land on the Pacific coast of Honshu leads to typical features such as raised beaches, some lying over 1000 ft (300 m) above sea level.

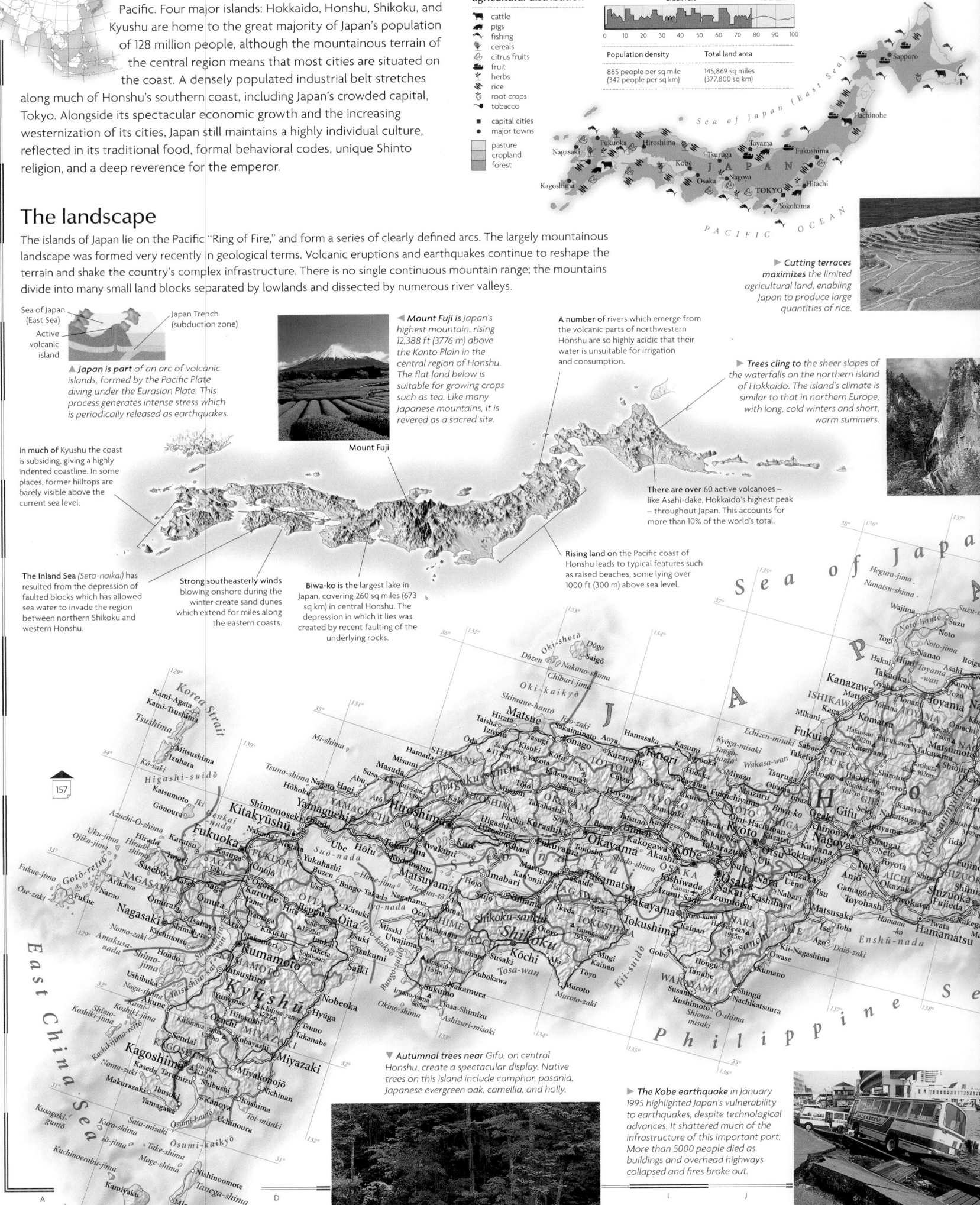

▼ *Autumnal trees near Gifu, on central Honshu, create a spectacular display. Native trees on this island include camphor, pasania, Japanese evergreen oak, camellia, and holly.*

▶ *The Kobe earthquake in January 1995 highlighted Japan's vulnerability to earthquakes, despite technological advances. It shattered much of the infrastructure of this important port. More than 5000 people died as buildings and overhead highways collapsed and fires broke out.*

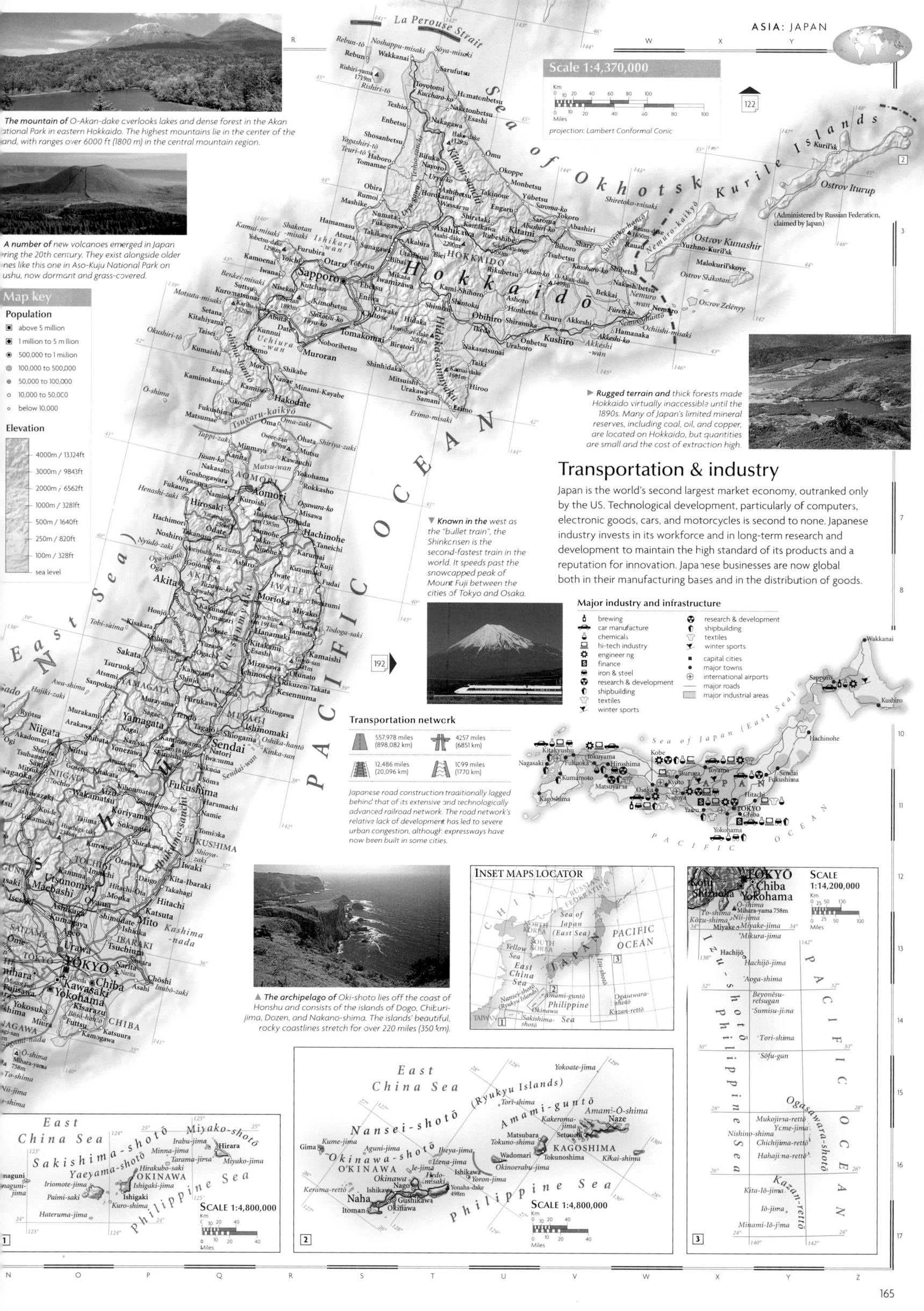

The mountain of O-Akan-dake overlooks lakes and dense forest in the Akan National Park in eastern Hokkaido. The highest mountains lie in the center of the island, with ranges over 6000 ft (1800 m) in the central mountain region.

A number of new volcanoes emerged in Japan during the 20th century. They exist alongside older ones like this one in Aso-Kuju National Park on Kyushu, now dormant and grass-covered.

Map key

Population

- ■ above 5 million
- ■ 1 million to 5 million
- ◉ 500,000 to 1 million
- ◎ 100,000 to 500,000
- ⊕ 50,000 to 100,000
- ○ 10,000 to 50,000
- ○ below 10,000

Elevation

- 4000m / 13,124ft
- 3000m / 9843ft
- 2000m / 6562ft
- 1000m / 3281ft
- 500m / 1640ft
- 250m / 820ft
- 100m / 328ft
- sea level

Scale 1:4,370,000

projection: Lambert Conformal Conic

▶ *Rugged terrain and* thick forests made Hokkaido virtually inaccessible until the 1890s. Many of Japan's limited mineral reserves, including coal, oil, and copper, are located on Hokkaido, but quantities are small and the cost of extraction high.

Transportation & industry

Japan is the world's second largest market economy, outranked only by the US. Technological development, particularly of computers, electronic goods, cars, and motorcycles is second to none. Japanese industry invests in its workforce and in long-term research and development to maintain the high standard of its products and a reputation for innovation. Japanese businesses are now global both in their manufacturing bases and in the distribution of goods.

▼ *Known in the* west as the "bullet train", the Shinkansen is the second-fastest train in the world. It speeds past the snowcapped peak of Mount Fuji between the cities of Tokyo and Osaka.

Major industry and infrastructure

- brewing
- car manufacture
- chemicals
- hi-tech industry
- engineering
- finance
- iron & steel
- research & development
- shipbuilding
- textiles
- winter sports
- research & development
- shipbuilding
- textiles
- winter sports
- ■ capital cities
- ● major towns
- ⊕ international airports
- — major roads
- major industrial areas

Transportation network

557,978 miles (898,082 km)	4257 miles (6851 km)
12,486 miles (20,096 km)	1099 miles (1770 km)

Japanese road construction traditionally lagged behind that of its extensive and technologically advanced railroad network. The road network's relative lack of development has led to severe urban congestion, although expressways have now been built in some cities.

▲ *The archipelago of* Oki-shoto lies off the coast of Honshu and consists of the islands of Dogo, Chiburi-jima, Dozen, and Nakano-shima. The islands' beautiful, rocky coastlines stretch for over 220 miles (350 km).

INSET MAPS LOCATOR

TOKYO SCALE 1:14,200,000

East China Sea

SCALE 1:4,800,000

SCALE 1:4,800,000

Mainland Southeast Asia

CAMBODIA, LAOS, MYANMAR, THAILAND, VIETNAM

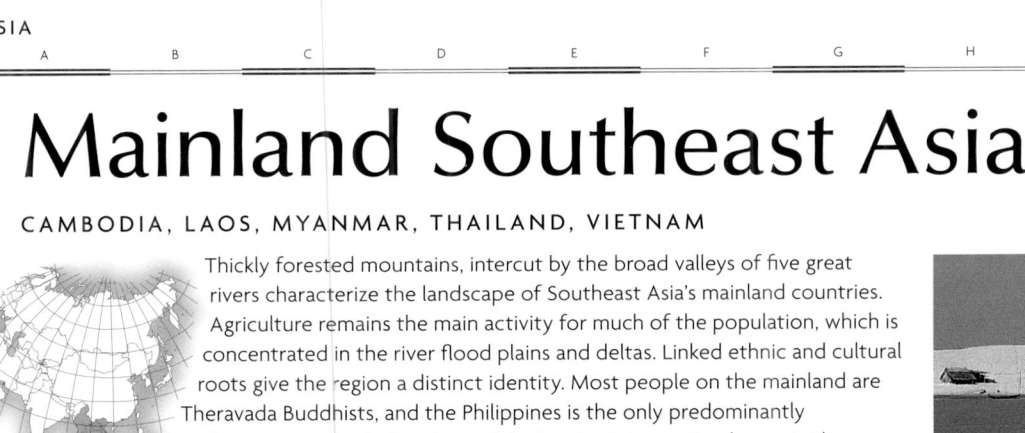

Thickly forested mountains, intercut by the broad valleys of five great rivers characterize the landscape of Southeast Asia's mainland countries. Agriculture remains the main activity for much of the population, which is concentrated in the river flood plains and deltas. Linked ethnic and cultural roots give the region a distinct identity. Most people on the mainland are Theravada Buddhists, and the Philippines is the only predominantly Christian country in Southeast Asia. Foreign intervention began in the 16th century with the opening of the spice trade; Cambodia, Laos and Vietnam were French colonies until the end of the Second World War, Myanmar was under British control. Only Thailand was never colonized. Today, Thailand is poised to play a leading role in the economic development of the Pacific Rim, and Laos and Vietnam have begun to mend the devastation of the Vietnam War, and to develop their economies. With continuing political instability and a shattered infrastructure, Cambodia faces an uncertain future, while Myanmar is seeking investment and the ending of its long isolation from the world community.

▲ The Irrawaddy river is Myanmar's vital central artery, watering the ricefields and providing a rich source of fish, as well as an important transport link, particularly for local traffic.

The landscape

A series of mountain ranges runs north–south through the mainland, formed as the result of the collision between the Eurasian Plate and the Indian subcontinent, which created the Himalayas. They are interspersed by the valleys of a number of great rivers. On their passage to the sea these rivers have deposited sediment, forming huge, fertile flood plains and deltas.

The coastline of the Isthmus of Kra

Longshore drift
Eroded coastline
Spit
Lagoon
Wave attack

◄ The east and west coasts of the Isthmus of Kra differ greatly. The tectonically uplifting west coast is exposed to the harsh south-westerly monsoon and is heavily eroded. On the east coast, longshore currents produce depositional features such as spits and lagoons.

Hkakabo Razi is the highest point in mainland Southeast Asia. It rises 19,300 ft (5885 m) at the border between China and Myanmar.

Mountains dominate the Laotian landscape with more than 90% of the land lying more than 600 ft (180 m) above sea level. The mountains of the Chaîne Annamitique form the country's eastern border.

The Red River delta in northern Vietnam is fringed to the north by steep-sided, round-topped limestone hills, typical of karst scenery.

The Irrawaddy river runs virtually north–south, draining the plains of northern Myanmar. The Irrawaddy delta is the country's main rice-growing area.

Salween River

▲ The coast of the Isthmus of Kra, in southeast Thailand has many small, precipitous islands like these, formed by chemical erosion on limestone, which is weathered along vertical cracks. The humidity of the climate in Southeast Asia increases the rate of weathering.

Isthmus of Kra

Malay Peninsula

Tonle Sap, a freshwater lake, drains into the Mekong delta via the Mekong river. It is the largest lake in Southeast Asia.

The Mekong river flows through southern China and Myanmar, then for much of its length forms the border between Laos and Thailand, flowing through Cambodia before terminating in a vast delta on the southern Vietnamese coast.

◄ The fast-flowing waters of the Mekong river cascade over this waterfall in Champasak province in Laos. The force of the water erodes rocks at the base of the fall.

Using the land and sea

The fertile flood plains of rivers such as the Mekong and Salween, and the humid climate, enable the production of rice throughout the region. Cambodia, Laos, and Myanmar still have substantial forests, producing hardwoods such as teak and rosewood. Cash crops include tropical fruits such as coconuts, bananas and pineapples, rubber, oil palm, sugar cane and the jute substitute, kenaf. Pigs and cattle are the main livestock raised. Large quantities of marine and freshwater fish are caught throughout the region.

▲ Commercial logging – still widespread in Myanmar – has now been stopped in Thailand because of over-exploitation of the tropical rainforest.

The urban/rural population divide

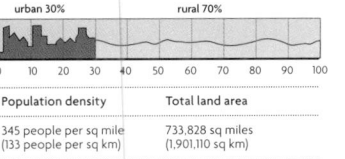

urban 30%   rural 70%

0 10 20 30 40 50 60 70 80 90 100

Population density	Total land area
345 people per sq mile (133 people per sq km)	733,828 sq miles (1,901,110 sq km)

Land use and agricultural distribution

- cattle
- pigs
- bananas
- coconuts
- fishing
- oil palms
- rice
- rubber
- sugar cane
- timber
- ■ capital cities
- • major towns
- pasture
- cropland
- forest
- wetland

Transportation & industry

Industrial manufacturing has become increasingly important in Thailand and Vietnam in recent years. The assembling of component-based electrical and electronic goods is becoming more common throughout this region, with foreign companies benefiting from low labour costs and the upgrading of technology. The economies of Myanmar and Cambodia are still based on agricultural produce and the processing of raw materials. Tin is the region's most important metal, and nickel, copper and chromite are also mined, although the quantities produced are not significant on a global scale. Thailand's successful tourist industry is the country's highest earner of foreign exchange.

Transportation network

🛣	82,958 miles (133,524 km)	🛤	267 miles (430 km)
🚆	7500 miles (12,071 km)	✈	28,585 miles (46,008 km)

Transportation development has concentrated on the building of road networks. Water and sea transport remain important, although air links have improved, particularly in Thailand and the Philippines.

Major industry and infrastructure

- chemicals
- electronics
- engineering
- finance
- food processing
- iron & steel
- oil & gas
- mining
- shipbuilding
- textiles
- timber processing
- capital cities
- major towns
- international airports
- major roads
- major industrial areas

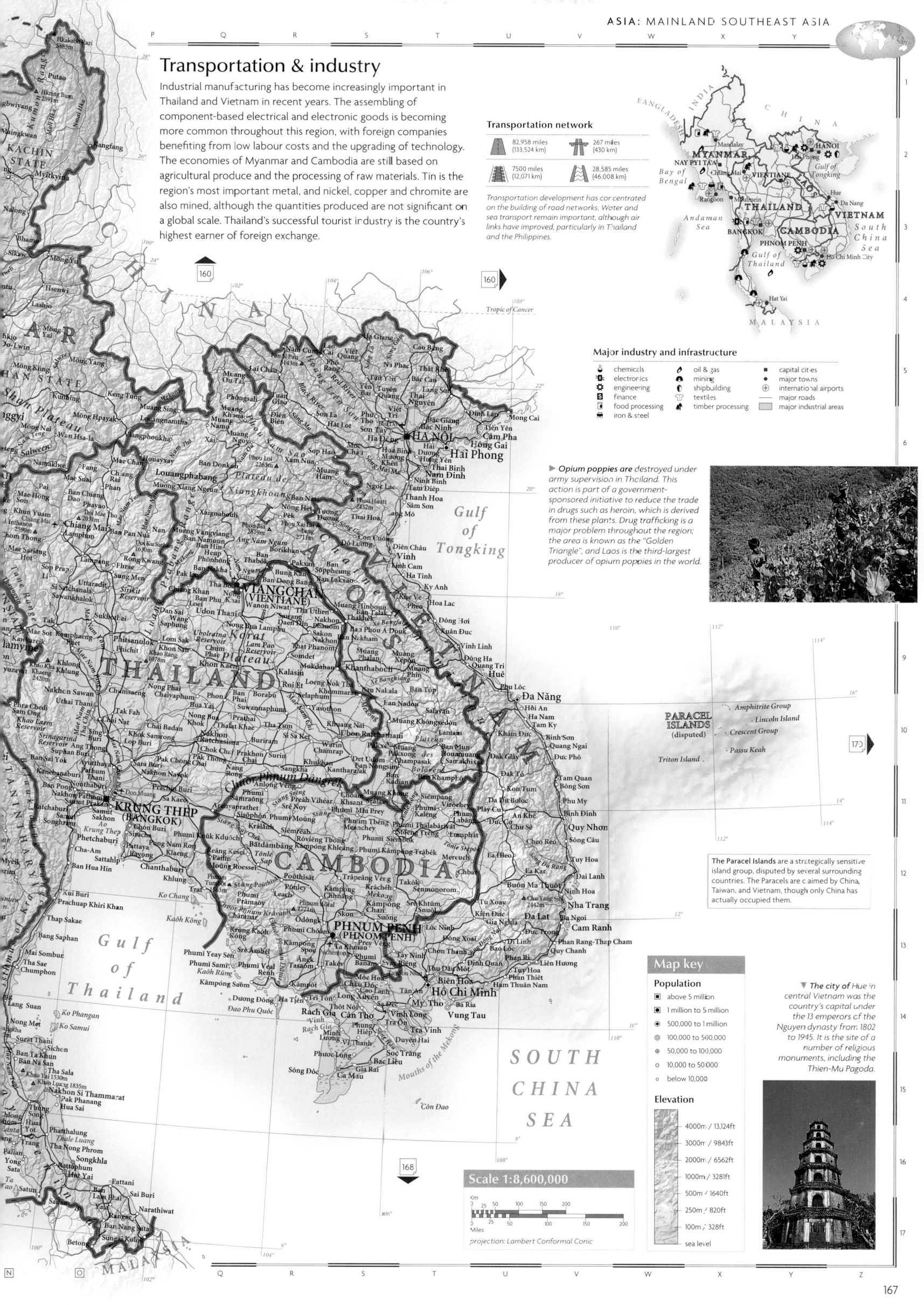

▶ *Opium poppies are destroyed under army supervision in Thailand. This action is part of a government-sponsored initiative to reduce the trade in drugs such as heroin, which is derived from these plants. Drug trafficking is a major problem throughout the region; the area is known as the "Golden Triangle", and Laos is the third-largest producer of opium poppies in the world.*

The Paracel Islands are a strategically sensitive island group, disputed by several surrounding countries. The Paracels are claimed by China, Taiwan, and Vietnam, though only China has actually occupied them.

Map key

Population
- ■ above 5 million
- ▣ 1 million to 5 million
- ◉ 500,000 to 1 million
- ◎ 100,000 to 500,000
- ◌ 50,000 to 100,000
- ○ 10,000 to 50,000
- · below 10,000

Elevation
- 4000m / 13,124ft
- 3000m / 9843ft
- 2000m / 6562ft
- 1000m / 3281ft
- 500m / 1640ft
- 250m / 820ft
- 100m / 328ft
- sea level

▼ *The city of Hue in central Vietnam was the country's capital under the 13 emperors of the Nguyen dynasty from 1802 to 1945. It is the site of a number of religious monuments, including the Thien-Mu Pagoda.*

Scale 1:8,600,000

projection: Lambert Conformal Conic

Western Maritime Southeast Asia

BRUNEI, INDONESIA, MALAYSIA, SINGAPORE

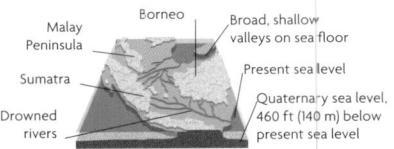

The world's largest archipelago, Indonesia's myriad islands stretch 3100 miles (5000 km) eastward across the Pacific, from the Malay Peninsula to western New Guinea. Only about 1500 of the 13,677 islands are inhabited and the huge, predominently Muslim population is unevenly distributed, with some two-thirds crowded onto the western islands of Java, Madura, and Bali. The national government is trying to resettle large numbers of people from these islands to other parts of the country to reduce population pressure there. Malaysia, split between the mainland and the east Malaysian states of Sabah and Sarawak on Borneo, has a diverse population, as well as a fast-growing economy, although the pace of its development is still far outstripped by that of Singapore. This small island nation is the financial and commercial capital of Southeast Asia. The Sultanate of Brunei in northern Borneo, one of the world's last princely states, has an extremely high standard of living, based on its oil revenues.

The landscape

Indonesia's western islands are characterized by rugged volcanic mountains cloaked with dense tropical forest, which slope down to coastal plains covered by thick alluvial swamps. The Sunda Shelf, an extension of the Eurasian Plate, lies between Java, Bali, Sumatra, and Borneo. These islands' mountains rise from a base below the sea, and they were once joined together by dry land, which has since been submerged by rising sea levels.

▲ **The Sunda Shelf** underlies this whole region. It is one of the largest submarine shelves in the world, covering an area of 714,285 sq miles (1,850,000 sq km). During the early Quaternary period, when sea levels were lower, the shelf was exposed.

◄ **Danau (lake) Toba** in Sumatra fills an enormous caldera 18 miles (30 km) wide and 62 miles (100 km) long – the largest in the world. It was formed through a combination of volcanic action and tectonic activity.

Malay Peninsula has a rugged east coast, but the west coast, fronting the Strait of Malacca, has many sheltered beaches and bays. The two coasts are divided by the Banjaran Titiwangsa, which run the length of the peninsula.

Gunung Kinabalu is the highest peak in Malaysia, rising 13,455 ft (4101 m).

◄ **The river of** Sungai Mahakam cuts through the central highlands of Borneo, the third largest island in the world, with a total area of 290,000 sq miles (757,050 sq km). Although mountainous, Borneo is one of the most stable of the Indonesian islands, with little volcanic activity.

The island of Krakatau (Pulau Rakata), lying between Sumatra and Java, was all but destroyed in 1883, when the volcano erupted. The release of gas and dust into the atmosphere disrupted cloud cover and global weather patterns for several years.

Gunung Semeru

Indonesia has more than 220 volcanoes, most of which are still active. They are strung out along the island arc from Sumatra through the Lesser Sunda Islands, into the Moluccas and Celebes.

Transportation & industry

Singapore has a thriving economy based on international trade and finance. Annual trade through the port is among the highest of any in the world. Indonesia's western islands still depend on natural resources, particularly petroleum, gas, and wood, although the economy is rapidly diversifying with manufactured exports including garments, consumer electronics, and footwear. A high-profile aircraft industry has developed in Bandung on Java. Malaysia has a fast-growing and varied manufacturing sector, although oil, gas, and timber remain important resource-based industries.

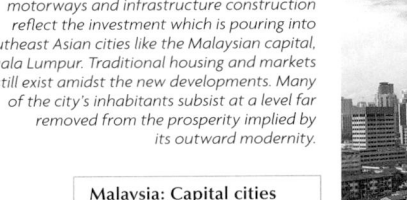

▶ **Ranks of gleaming** skyscrapers, new motorways and infrastructure construction reflect the investment which is pouring into Southeast Asian cities like the Malaysian capital, Kuala Lumpur. Traditional housing and markets still exist amidst the new developments. Many of the city's inhabitants subsist at a level far removed from the prosperity implied by its outward modernity.

Malaysia: Capital cities
KUALA LUMPUR – capital
PUTRAJAYA – administrative capital

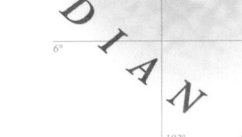

Using the land and sea

Rice is the most important arable crop in Indonesia and Malaysia, and both countries manage to meet almost all of their domestic demand. Malaysian rubber accounts for 25% of world production and is the main cash crop, grown on plantations and small farms, along with oil palms and copra. Timber is exported from both Malaysia and Indonesia. Modern agricultural techniques enable Singapore to produce fruits and vegetables despite a shortage of suitable land.

▶ Spiral cuts in the bark of this rubber palm show where it has been tapped. Sophisticated 'cloning' techniques mean that trees which produce consistently high quantities of rubber can be easily reproduced.

Transportation network

165,272 miles
(266,010 km)

958 miles
(1,542 km)

5,061 miles
(8,146 km)

18,070 miles
(29,084 km)

Singapore's metro system, completed in 1991, is among the most efficient in the world. Malaysia has several fast, modern highways and most roads are paved. Indonesia's many islands make improvement of the shipping infrastructure a priority.

Major industry and infrastructure

- aerospace
- copra processing
- chemicals
- electronics
- engineering
- finance
- food processing
- iron & steel
- oil
- ship building
- timber processing
- textiles

■ capital cities
● major towns
⊕ international airports
— major roads
▨ major industrial areas

Land use and agricultural distribution

- coconuts
- fishing
- oil palms
- rice
- rubber
- shellfish
- sugar cane
- timber

■ capital cities
● major towns

pasture
cropland
forest
wet and

The urban/rural population divide

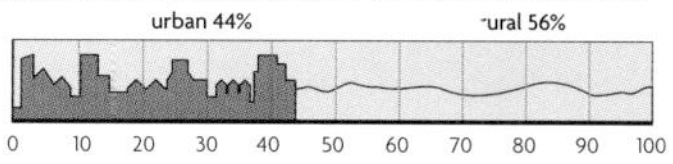

urban 44%   rural 56%

0 10 20 30 40 50 60 70 80 90 100

Population density	Total land area
297 people per sq mile (115 people per sq km)	828,356 sq miles (2,146,000 sq km)

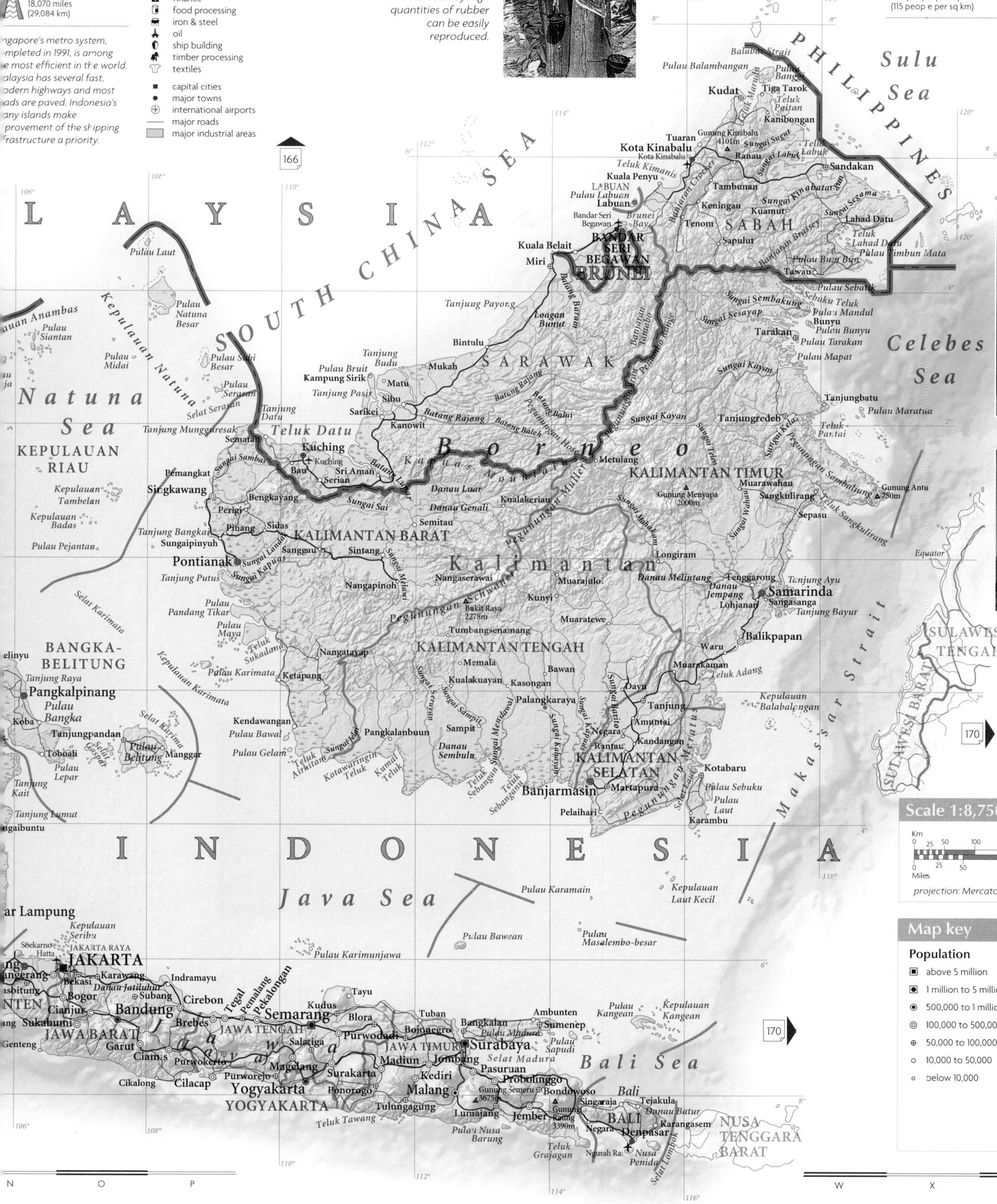

▼ This tiny island near Kota Kinabalu, in Sabah, eastern Malaysia, is a part of a designated national park. Thickly forested, it is surrounded by broad, sandy beaches and shallow inland seas.

▲ The volcano of Gunung Semeru in eastern Java lies on the Pacific "Ring of Fire". It is part of the ancient Tennegger volcano and remains highly active.

Scale 1:8,750,000

Km
0 25 50 100 150 200

Miles
0 25 50 100 150 200

projection: Mercator

Map key

Population

- ▣ above 5 million
- ◧ 1 million to 5 million
- ◉ 500,000 to 1 million
- ◎ 100,000 to 500,000
- ⊕ 50,000 to 100,000
- ⊙ 10,000 to 50,000
- ○ below 10,000

Elevation

4000m / 13,124ft
3000m / 9843ft
2000m / 6562ft
1000m / 3281ft
500m / 1640ft
250m / 820ft
100m / 328ft
sea level

A B C D E F G H I J K L M

Eastern Maritime Southeast Asia

EAST TIMOR, INDONESIA, PHILIPPINES

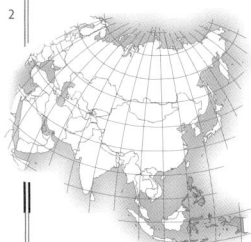

The Philippines takes its name from Philip II of Spain who was king when the islands were colonized during the 16th century. Almost 400 years of Spanish, and later US, rule have left their mark on the country's culture; English is widely spoken and over 90% of the population is Christian. The Philippines' economy is agriculturally based – inadequate infrastructure and electrical power shortages have so far hampered faster industrial growth. Indonesia's eastern islands are less economically developed than the rest of the country. Papua (Irian Jaya), which constitutes the western portion of New Guinea, is one of the world's last great wildernesses. East Timor is the newest independent state in the world, gaining full autonomy in 2002.

▲ *The traditional boat-shaped* houses of the Toraja people in Sulawesi. Although now Christian, the Toraja still practice the animist traditions and rituals of their ancestors. They are famous for their elaborate funeral ceremonies and burial sites in cliffside caves.

The landscape

Located on the Pacific "Ring of Fire" the Philippines' 7100 islands are subject to frequent earthquakes and volcanic activity. Their terrain is largely mountainous, with narrow coastal plains and interior valleys and plains. Luzon and Mindanao are by far the largest islands and comprise roughly 66% of the country's area. Indonesia's eastern islands are mountainous and dotted with volcanoes, both active and dormant.

▶ *Lake Taal on* the Philippines island of Luzon lies within the crater of an immense volcano that erupted twice in the 20th century, first in 1911 and again in 1965, causing the deaths of more than 3200 people.

The Spratly Islands are a strategically sensitive island group, disputed by several surrounding countries. The Spratlys are claimed by China, Taiwan, Vietnam, Malaysia, and the Philippines and are particularly important as they lie on oil and gas deposits.

Mindanao has five mountain ranges many of which have large numbers of active volcanoes. Lying just west of the Philippines Trench, which forms the boundary between the colliding Philippine and Eurasian plates, the entire island chain is subject to earthquakes and volcanic activity.

The 1000 islands of the Moluccas are the fabled Spice Islands of history, whose produce attracted traders from around the globe. Most of the northern and central Moluccas have dense vegetation and rugged mountainous interiors where elevations often exceed 3000 feet (9144 m).

▲ *Bohol in the* southern Philippines is famous for its so-called "chocolate hills". There are more than 1000 of these regular mounds on the island. The hills are limestone in origin, the smoothed remains of an earlier cycle of erosion. Their brown appearance in the dry season gives them their name.

The four-pronged island of Celebes is the product of complex tectonic activity which ruptured and then reattached small fragments of the Earth's crust to form the island's many peninsulas.

Coral islands such as Timor in eastern Indonesia show evidence of very recent and dramatic movements of the Earth's plates. Reefs in Timor have risen by as much as 4000 ft (1300 m) in the last million years.

The Pegunungan Jayawijaya range in central Papua (Irian Jaya) contains the world's highest range of limestone mountains, some with peaks more than 16,400 ft (5000 m) high. Heavy rainfall and high temperatures, which promote rapid weathering, have led to the creation of large underground caves and river systems such as the river of Sungai Baliem.

Using the land and sea

Indonesia's eastern islands are less intensively cultivated than those in the west. Coconuts, coffee and spices such as cloves and nutmeg are the major commercial crops while rice, corn and soybeans are grown for local consumption. The Philippines' rich, fertile soils support year-round production of a wide range of crops. The country is one of the world's largest producers of coconuts and a major exporter of coconut products, including one-third of the world's copra. Although much of the arable land is given over to rice and corn, the main staple food crops, tropical fruits such as bananas, pineapples and mangos, and sugar cane are also grown for export.

Land use and agricultural distribution

- coconuts
- fishing
- rice
- rubber
- shellfish
- sugar cane
- ■ capital cities
- ● major towns
- pasture
- cropland
- forest
- wetland

The urban/rural population divide

urban 45%   rural 55%

0 10 20 30 40 50 60 70 80 90 100

Population density	Total land area
258 people per sq mile (160 people per sq km)	654,771 sq miles (1,053,755 sq km)

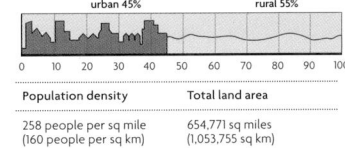

▲ *More than two-thirds* of Papua's (Irian Jaya) land area is heavily forested and the population of around 1.5 million live mainly in isolated tribal groups using more than 80 distinct languages.

◀ *The terracing of* land to restrict soil erosion and create flat surfaces for agriculture is a common practice throughout Southeast Asia, particularly where land is scarce. These terraces are on Luzon in the Philippines.

Map labels:
SOUTH CHINA SEA
SPRATLY ISLANDS (disputed)
Palawan
Quez
Brooke's Point
Balabac Island
Balabac Strait
MALAYSI
KALIMANTA TIMUR
KALIMANTAN SELATAN
Equator
Java Sea
NUSA TENGG
Mataram
Bayan
Sumbawabesar
Gunung Tambor
Lombok
Kuta
Gunung Tambor 140m

Luzon Strait
Luzon
Baguio
MANILA
Philippine Sea
South China Sea
PHILIPPINES
Cebu
Butuan
Sulu Sea
Mindanao
Zamboanga
Davao
MALAYSIA
Celebes Sea
Manado
Halmahera
PACIFIC OCEAN
Celebes
Maluku (Moluccas)
Ceram
Ambon
Jayapura
Banda Sea
Makassar
New Guinea
PAPUA NEW GUINEA
INDONESIA
Arafura Sea
Lombok
Sumbawa
Flores
Sumba
DILI
EAST TIMOR
Timor
Kupang
Timor Sea
INDIAN OCEAN

168

Transportation & industry

The Philippines' economy is primarily a mixture of agriculture and light industry. The manufacturing sector is still developing; many factories are licensees of foreign companies producing finished goods for export. Mining is also important – the country's chromite, nickel, and copper deposits are among the largest in the world. Agriculture is the main activity in eastern Indonesia. Most industry has a primary basis, including logging, food-processing, and mining. Nickel, the most important metal, is produced on Sulawesi, in Papua (Irian Jaya), and in the Moluccas.

Major industry and infrastructure

- copra processing
- chemicals
- finance
- food processing
- mining
- oil
- timber processing
- textiles
- capital cities
- major towns
- international airports
- major roads
- major industrial areas

Transportation network

- 16,652 miles (26,800 km)
- None
- 500 miles (805 km)
- 8704 miles (14,008 km)

Sulawesi has some good roads, but on Papua (Irian Jaya) and the Moluccas there are few road interconnections between major settled areas. Water and sea transportation remain important although air links have improved in the Philippines.

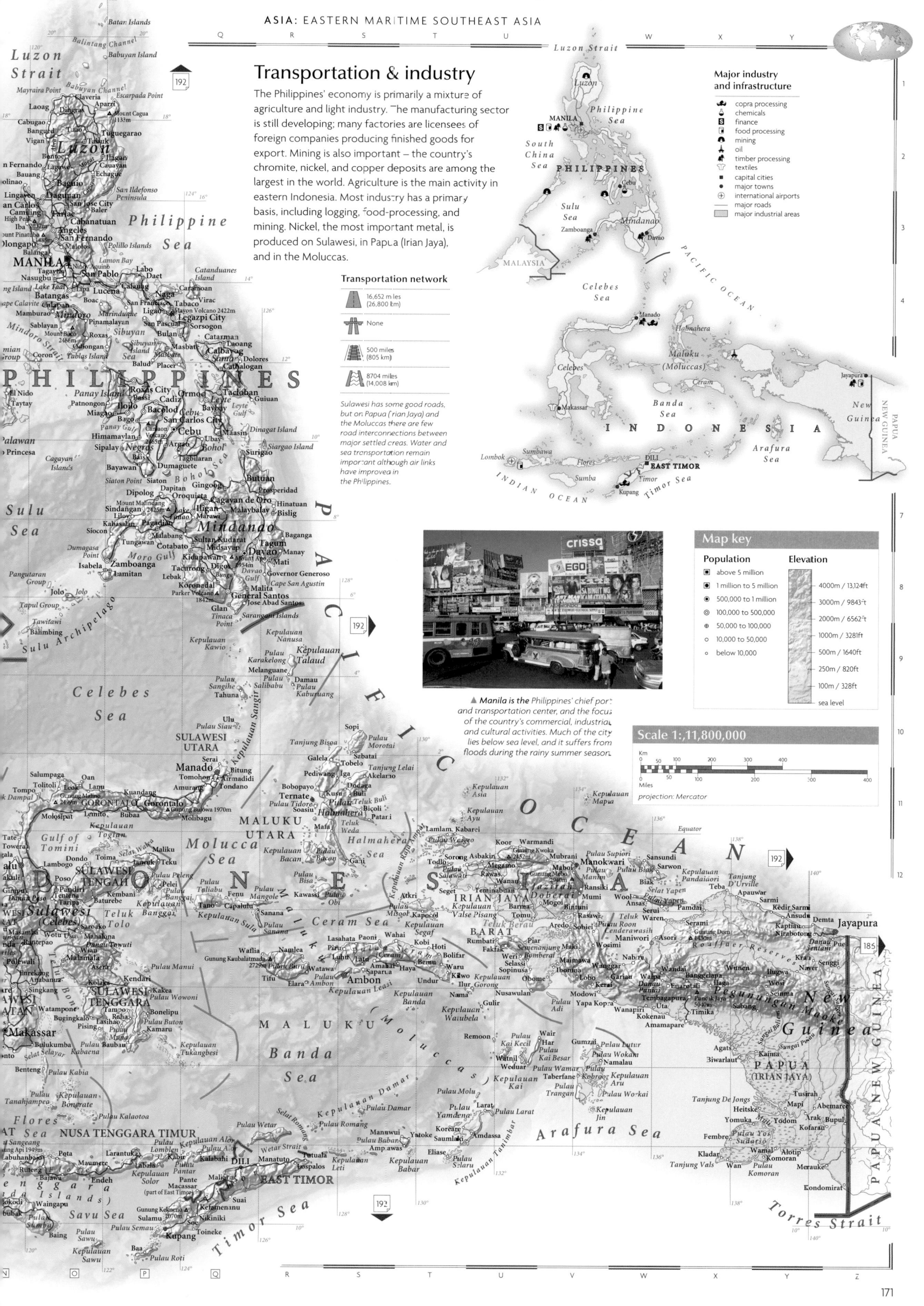

▲ **Manila is the** Philippines' chief port and transportation center, and the focus of the country's commercial, industrial, and cultural activities. Much of the city lies below sea level, and it suffers from floods during the rainy summer season.

Map key

Population
- above 5 million
- 1 million to 5 million
- 500,000 to 1 million
- 100,000 to 500,000
- 50,000 to 100,000
- 10,000 to 50,000
- below 10,000

Elevation
- 4000m / 13,124ft
- 3000m / 9843ft
- 2000m / 6562ft
- 1000m / 3281ft
- 500m / 1640ft
- 250m / 820ft
- 100m / 328ft
- sea level

Scale 1:11,800,000

projection: Mercator

The Indian Ocean

Despite being the smallest of the three major oceans, the evolution of the Indian Ocean was the most complex. The ocean basin was formed during the breakup of the supercontinent Gondwanaland, when the Indian subcontinent moved northeast, Africa moved west, and Australia separated from Antarctica. Like the Pacific Ocean, the warm waters of the Indian Ocean are punctuated by coral atolls and islands. About one-fifth of the world's population – over a billion people – live on its shores. In 2004, over 290,000 died and millions more were left homeless after a tsunami devastated large stretches of the ocean's coastline.

The landscape

The Indian Ocean began forming about 150 million years ago, but in its present form it is relatively young, only about 36 million years old. Along the three subterranean mountain chains of its mid-ocean ridge the seafloor is still spreading. The Indian Ocean has fewer trenches than other oceans and only a narrow continental shelf around most of its surrounding land.

Sediments come from Ganges/Brahmaputra river system

Submarine canyons transport sediment to fan – some of these are more than 1500 miles (2500 km) long

Sri Lanka

▲ *The Ganges Fan is one of the world's largest submarine accumulations of sediment, extending far beyond Sri Lanka. It is fed by the Ganges/Brahmaputra river system, whose sediment is carried through a network of underwater canyons at the edge of the continental shelf.*

The mid-oceanic ridge runs from the Arabian Sea. It diverges east of Madagascar. One arm runs southwest to join the Mid-Atlantic Ridge, the other branches southeast, joining the Pacific-Antarctic Ridge, southeast of Tasmania.

The Ninetyeast Ridge takes its name from the line of longitude it follows. It is the world's longest and straightest under-sea ridge.

Two of the world's largest rivers flow into the Indian Ocean: the Indus and the Ganges/Brahmaputra. Both have deposited enormous fans of sediment.

Indus River

▶ *A large proportion of the coast of Thailand, on the Isthmus of Kra, is stabilized by mangrove thickets. They act as an important breeding ground for wildlife.*

The Java Trench is the world's longest, it runs 1600 miles (2570 km) from the southwest of Java, but is only 50 miles (80 km) wide.

The relief of Madagascar rises from a low-lying coastal strip in the east, to the central plateau. The plateau is also a major watershed separating Madagascar's three main river basins.

▶ *The central group of the Seychelles are mountainous, granite islands. They have a narrow coastal belt and lush, tropical vegetation cloaks the highlands.*

The Kerguelen Islands in the Southern Ocean were created by a hot spot in the Earth's crust. The islands were formed in succession as the Antarctic Plate moved slowly over the hot spot.

The circulation in the northern Indian Ocean is controlled by the monsoon winds. Biannually these winds reverse their pattern, causing a reversal in the surface currents and alternative high and low pressure conditions over Asia and Australia.

Resources

Many of the small islands in the Indian Ocean rely exclusively on tuna-fishing and tourism to maintain their economies. Most fisheries are artisanal, although large-scale tuna-fishing does take place in the Seychelles, Mauritius and the western Indian Ocean. Other resources include oil in the Persian Gulf, pearls in the Red Sea, and tin from deposits off the shores of Myanmar, Thailand, and Indonesia.

Resources (including wildlife)

fish		△	tin deposits
penguins		⚓	tourism
shellfish		•	major towns
whales		⊕	major ports
oil & gas			

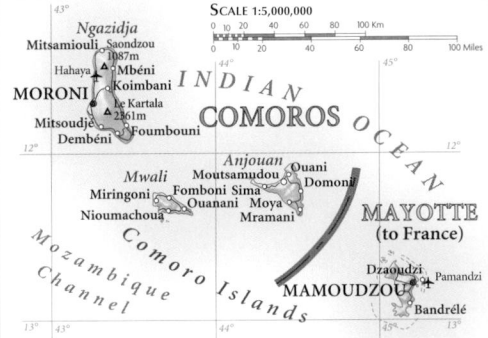

▶ *The recent use of large dragnets for tuna-fishing has not only threatened the livelihoods of many small-scale fisheries, but also caused widespread environmental concern about the potential impact on other marine species.*

▲ *Coral reefs support an enormous diversity of animal and plant life. Many species of tropical fish, like these squirrel fish, live and feed around the profusion of reefs and atolls in the Indian Ocean.*

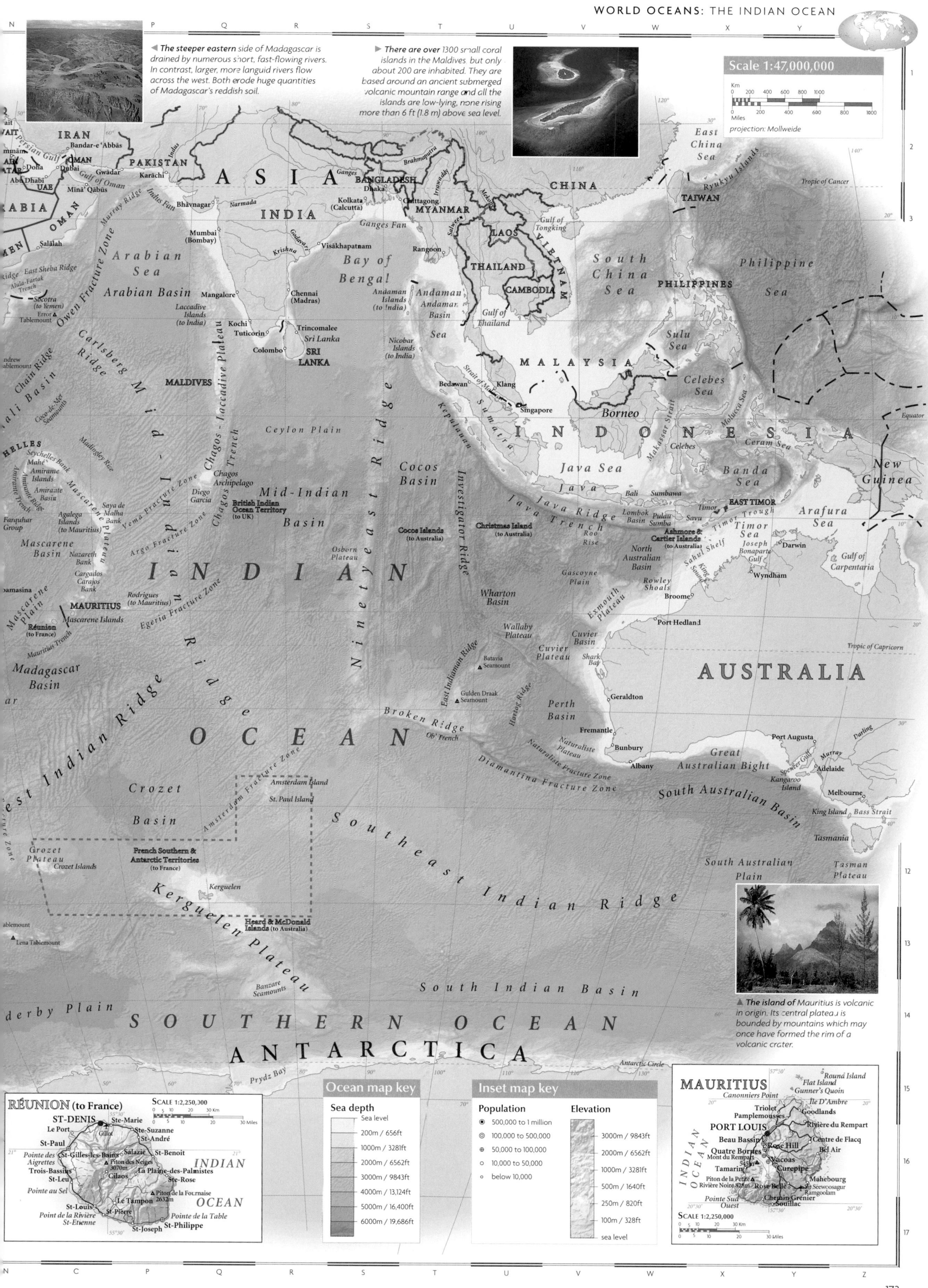

► The steeper eastern side of Madagascar is drained by numerous short, fast-flowing rivers. In contrast, larger, more languid rivers flow across the west. Both erode huge quantities of Madagascar's reddish soil.

► There are over 1300 small coral islands in the Maldives, but only about 200 are inhabited. They are based around an ancient submerged volcanic mountain range and all the islands are low-lying, none rising more than 6 ft (1.8 m) above sea level.

Scale 1:47,000,000

projection: Mollweide

▲ The island of Mauritius is volcanic in origin. Its central plateau is bounded by mountains which may once have formed the rim of a volcanic crater.

Ocean map key

Sea depth

	Sea level
	200m / 656ft
	1000m / 3281ft
	2000m / 6562ft
	3000m / 9843ft
	4000m / 13,124ft
	5000m / 16,400ft
	6000m / 19,686ft

Inset map key

Population

◉	500,000 to 1 million
◎	100,000 to 500,000
⊕	50,000 to 100,000
⊙	10,000 to 50,000
○	below 10,000

Elevation

	3000m / 9843ft
	2000m / 6562ft
	1000m / 3281ft
	500m / 1640ft
	250m / 820ft
	100m / 328ft
	sea level

RÉUNION (to France)

SCALE 1:2,250,000

ST-DENIS
Ste-Marie
Le Port
Ste-Suzanne
St-Paul
St-André
Pointe des Aigrettes
St-Gilles-les-Bains
Salazie
St-Benoit
Trois-Bassins
Cilaos
Piton des Neiges 3070m
La Plaine-des-Palmistes
St-Leu
Ste-Rose
Pointe au Sel
Le Tampon 2632m
Piton de la Fournaise
St-Louis
St-Pierre
Pointe de la Rivière
Pointe de la Table
St-Etienne
St-Joseph
St-Philippe

INDIAN OCEAN

MAURITIUS

Round Island
Flat Island
Gunner's Quoin
Canonniers Point
Île D'Ambre
Triolet
Goodlands
Pamplemousses
Rivière du Rempart
PORT LOUIS
Beau Bassin
Centre de Flacq
Quatre Bornes
Rose Hill
Bel Air
Mont du Rempart
Vacoas
Tamarin
Curepipe
Piton de la Petite
Rivière Noire 828m
Rose Belle
Mahebourg
Pointe Sud Ouest
Chemin Grenier
Seewoosagur Ramgoolam
Souillac

SCALE 1:2,250,000

INDIAN OCEAN

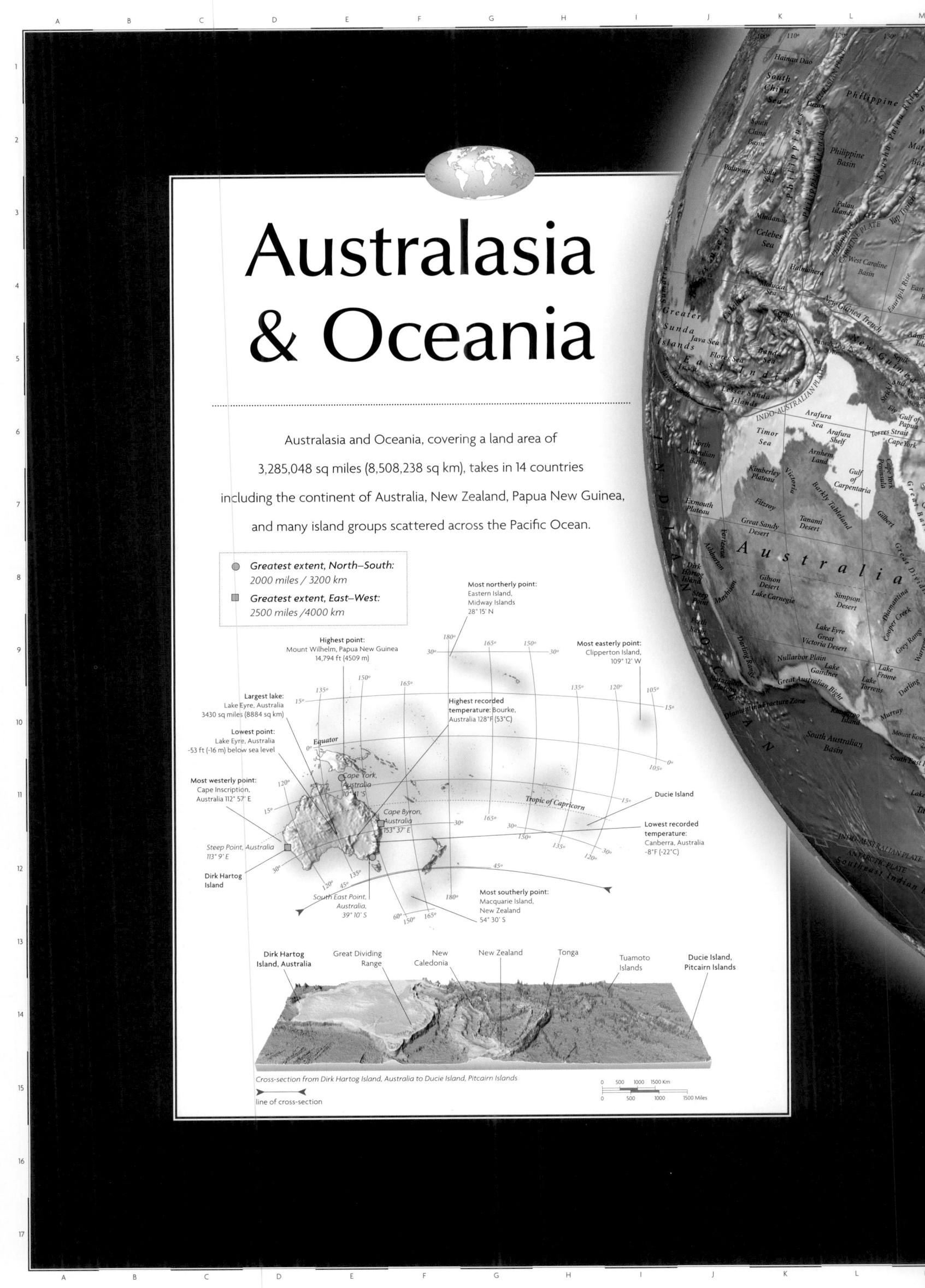

Australasia & Oceania

Australasia and Oceania, covering a land area of
3,285,048 sq miles (8,508,238 sq km), takes in 14 countries
including the continent of Australia, New Zealand, Papua New Guinea,
and many island groups scattered across the Pacific Ocean.

● **Greatest extent, North–South:**
2000 miles / 3200 km

■ **Greatest extent, East–West:**
2500 miles /4000 km

Most northerly point:
Eastern Island,
Midway Islands
28° 15' N

Highest point:
Mount Wilhelm, Papua New Guinea
14,794 ft (4509 m)

Most easterly point:
Clipperton Island,
109° 12' W

Largest lake:
Lake Eyre, Australia
3430 sq miles (8884 sq km)

**Highest recorded
temperature:** Bourke,
Australia 128°F (53°C)

Lowest point:
Lake Eyre, Australia
-53 ft (-16 m) below sea level

Most westerly point:
Cape Inscription,
Australia 112° 57' E

Cape York,
Australia
10° 41' S

Ducie Island

Cape Byron,
Australia
153° 37' E

**Lowest recorded
temperature:**
Canberra, Australia
-8°F (-22°C)

Steep Point, Australia
113° 9' E

**Dirk Hartog
Island**

*South East Point,
Australia,
39° 10' S*

Most southerly point:
Macquarie Island,
New Zealand
54° 30' S

**Dirk Hartog
Island, Australia**

**Great Dividing
Range**

**New
Caledonia**

New Zealand

Tonga

**Tuamoto
Islands**

**Ducie Island,
Pitcairn Islands**

Cross-section from Dirk Hartog Island, Australia to Ducie Island, Pitcairn Islands

line of cross-section

| 0 | 500 | 1000 | 1500 Km |
| 0 | 500 | 1000 | 1500 Miles |

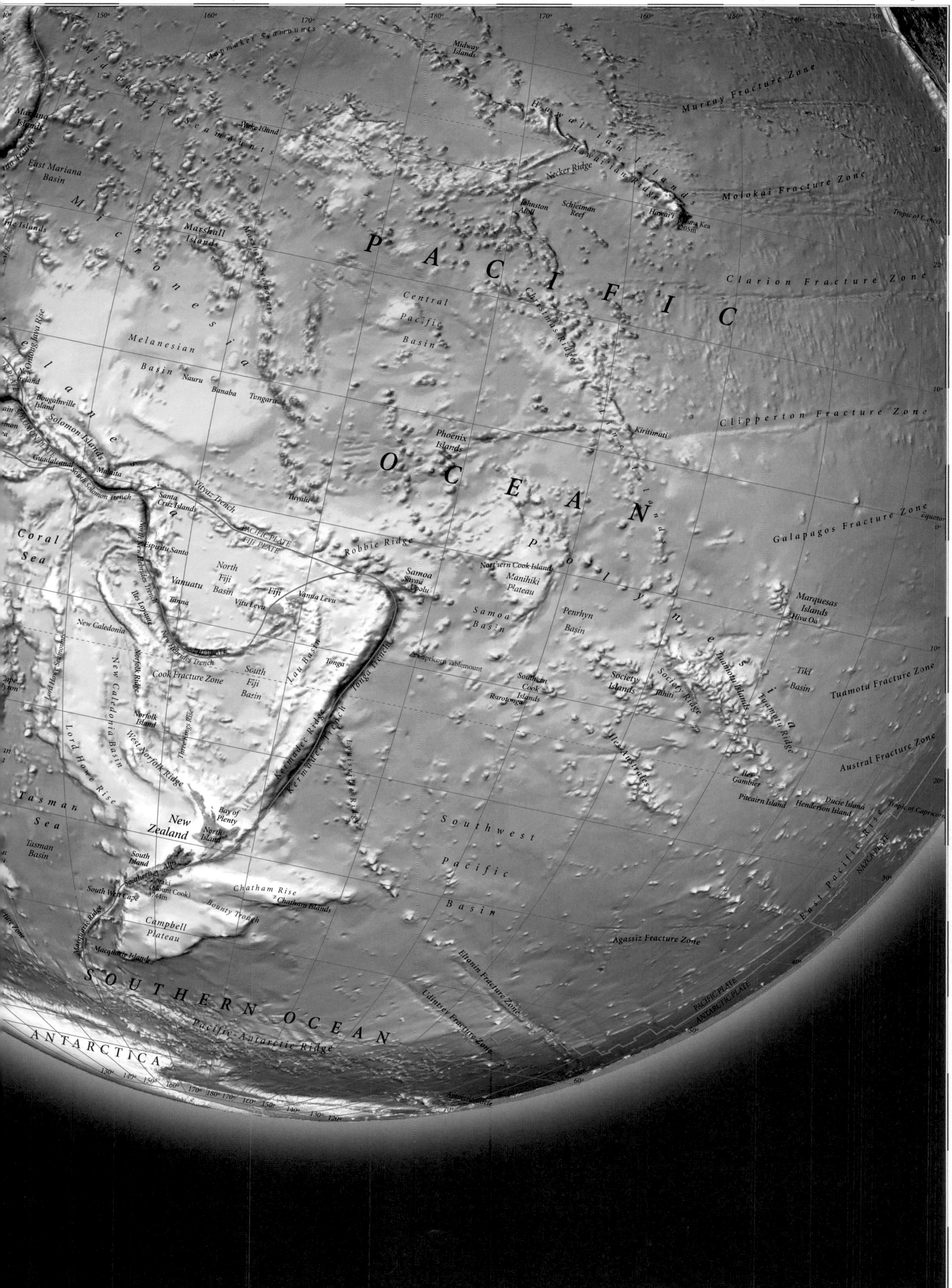

Mid-Pacific Seamounts

Mapmaker Seamounts

Midway Islands

Murray Fracture Zone

Mariana Islands

Wake Island

Hawaiian Islands

Necker Ridge

Johnston Atoll

Schietman Reef

Hawai'i

Mauna Kea 205m

Molokai Fracture Zone

Tropic of Cancer

East Mariana Basin

M i c r o n e s i a

Marshall Islands

Mid-Pacific Seamounts

P A C I F I C

Clarion Fracture Zone

Ifa Islands

Central Pacific Basin

Christmas Ridge

Melanesian Basin

Nauru

Banaba

Tungaru

Clipperton Fracture Zone

Ontong Java Rise

New Ireland

Phoenix Islands

Kiritimati

O C E A N

Bougainville Island

Solomon Islands

Guadalcanal

Malaita

North Solomon Trench

Vityaz Trench

Santa Cruz Islands

Tuvalu

Robbie Ridge

Galapagos Fracture Zone

equator

Coral Sea

Espíritu Santo

PACIFIC PLATE

FIJI PLATE

North Fiji Basin

Samoa

Savai'i

Upolu

Northern Cook Islands

Manihiki Plateau

Penrhyn Basin

Marquesas Islands

Hiva Oa

Vanuatu

Tanna

Fiji

Vitu Levu

Vanua Levu

Samoa Basin

P o l y n e s i a

Ile Loyaute

New Caledonia

Norfolk Ridge

Cook Fracture Zone

South Fiji Basin

Lau Basin

Tonga

Capricorn Tablemount

Southern Cook Islands

Rarotonga

Society Islands

Society Ridge

Tahiti

Tuamotu Islands

Tuamotu Ridge

Tiki Basin

Tuamotu Fracture Zone

New Hebrides Trench

North Norfolk Ridge

Norfolk Island

Three Kings Rise

Kermadec Ridge

Louisville Ridge

Australes

Iles Gambier

Austral Fracture Zone

Tasman Sea

Lord Howe Rise

New Caledonia Basin

West Norfolk Ridge

Kermadec Trench

Tonga Trench

Pitcairn Island

Henderson Island

Ducie Island

Tropic of Capricorn

Lord Howe Seamounts

Bay of Plenty

North Island

Southwest

Cape Byron

New Zealand

Tasman Basin

South Island

Southern Alps

Aoraki (Mount Cook) 3244m

Chatham Rise

Chatham Islands

Pacific

East Pacific Rise

NAZCA PLATE

South West Cape

Bounty Trough

Basin

Macquarie Ridge

Campbell Plateau

Agassiz Fracture Zone

Macquarie Island

Eltanin Fracture Zone

PACIFIC PLATE

ANTARCTIC PLATE

SOUTHERN OCEAN

Udintsev Fracture Zone

ANTARCTICA

Pacific-Antarctic Ridge

Antarctic Circle

Political Australasia & Oceania

Vast expanses of ocean separate this geographically fragmented realm, characterized more by each country's isolation than by any political unity. Australia's and New Zealand's traditional ties with the United Kingdom, as members of the Commonwealth, are now being called into question as Australasian and Oceanian nations are increasingly looking to forge new relationships with neighboring Asian countries like Japan. External influences have featured strongly in the politics of the Pacific Islands; the various territories of Micronesia were largely under US control until the late 1980s, and France, New Zealand, the US, and the UK still have territories under colonial rule in Polynesia. Nuclear weapons-testing by Western superpowers was widespread during the Cold War period, but has now been discontinued.

Population

Density of settlement in the region is generally low. Australia is one of the least densely populated countries on Earth with over 80% of its population living within 25 miles (40 km) of the coast – mostly in the southeast of the country. New Zealand, and the island groups of Melanesia, Micronesia, and Polynesia, are much more densely populated, although many of the smaller islands remain uninhabited.

◀ *Western Australia's mineral* wealth has transformed its state capital, Perth, into one of Australia's major cities. Perth is one of the world's most isolated cities – over 2500 miles (4000 km) from the population centers of the eastern seaboard.

Scale 1:35,500,000

projection: Lambert Azimuthal Equal Area

Population density
(people per sq mile)

- below 10
- 10-62
- 63-130
- 131-259
- 260-519
- 520-780
- above 780

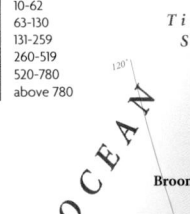

▲ *The myriad of* small coral islands that are scattered across the Pacific Ocean are often uninhabited, as they offer little shelter from the weather, often no fresh water, and only limited food supplies.

◀ *The planes of* the Australian Royal Flying Doctor Service are able to cover large expanses of barren land quickly, bringing medical treatment to the most inaccessible and far-flung places.

Map labels:

Philippine Sea, Northern Mariana Islands (to US), Saipan, Mariana Islands, Micronesia, Guam (to US), HAGÅTNA, Bikini Atoll, Yap, Caroline Islands, Chuuk, Pohnpei, PALIKIR, Kosrae, MELEKEOK, Babeldaob, MICRONESIA, PALAU, Melanesia, NAURU, PAPUA NEW GUINEA, Bismarck Sea, New Ireland, Wewak, New Britain, Rabaul, Solomon Islands, New Guinea, Madang, Ubai, Arawa, Bougainville Island, SOLOMON ISLANDS, Mount Hagen, Lae, Solomon Sea, New Georgia Islands, HONIARA, Guadalcanal, Santa Cruz Islands, Tapini, PORT MORESBY, VANU..., Espíritu Santo, Malekula, Arafura Sea, Torres Strait, Coral Sea, New Caledonia (to France), PORT..., Coral Sea Islands (to Australia), NOUMÉA, Cape York Peninsula, Great Barrier Reef, Timor Sea, Darwin, Arnhem Land, Gulf of Carpentaria, Cairns, Joseph Bonaparte Gulf, Katherine, Normanton, Wyndham, Townsville, Great Dividing Range, Kimberley Plateau, NORTHERN TERRITORY, Hughenden, Mackay, Derby, Tennant Creek, Tanami Desert, Mount Isa, QUEENSLAND, Rockhampton, Broome, Barcaldine, Great Sandy Desert, Charleville, Miles, Brisbane, Port Hedland, Alice Springs, Simpson Desert, Toowoomba, Norfolk Island (to A...), AUSTRALIA, Cunnamulla, Grafton, Lord Howe Island (to Australia), Hamersley Range, Gibson Desert, Lake Eyre North, Bourke, Grey Range, Barwon, Darling, Wilcannia, NEW SOUTH WALES, Dubbo, Newcastle, Great Victoria Desert, Lake Torrens, SOUTH AUSTRALIA, Flinders Ranges, Carnavon, Lake Everard, Lake Gairdner, Port Augusta, Murray, Campbelltown, Sydney, Wollongong, Mount Magnet, Whyalla, Wagga Wagga, CANBERRA, AUSTRALIAN CAPITAL TERRITORY, Ceduna, Adelaide, Kalgoorlie, Bendigo, Horsham, VICTORIA, Tasman Sea, Geraldton, Great Australian Bight, Kangaroo Island, Ballarat, Melbourne, Geelong, Mount Gambier, Bass Strait, Launceston, TASMANIA, Perth, Esperance, Tasmania, Hobart, Albany, INDIAN OCEAN, Tropic of Capricorn

Languages

English is spoken throughout Australia and New Zealand. In Australia, English has been superimposed on a mosaic of Aboriginal languages. In New Zealand, the indigenous language, Maori, is the official language besides English. In Papua New Guinea, Melanesian Pidgin has become a lingua franca alongside several hundred indigenous languages. Across the region, the indigenous languages can be grouped into (1) the Aboriginal languages of Australia, (2) the Papuan languages spoken mostly inland in Papua New Guinea, and (3) the widely dispersed Austronesian, which includes coastal languages of Papua New Guinea, New Zealand Maori, and languages of Oceania.

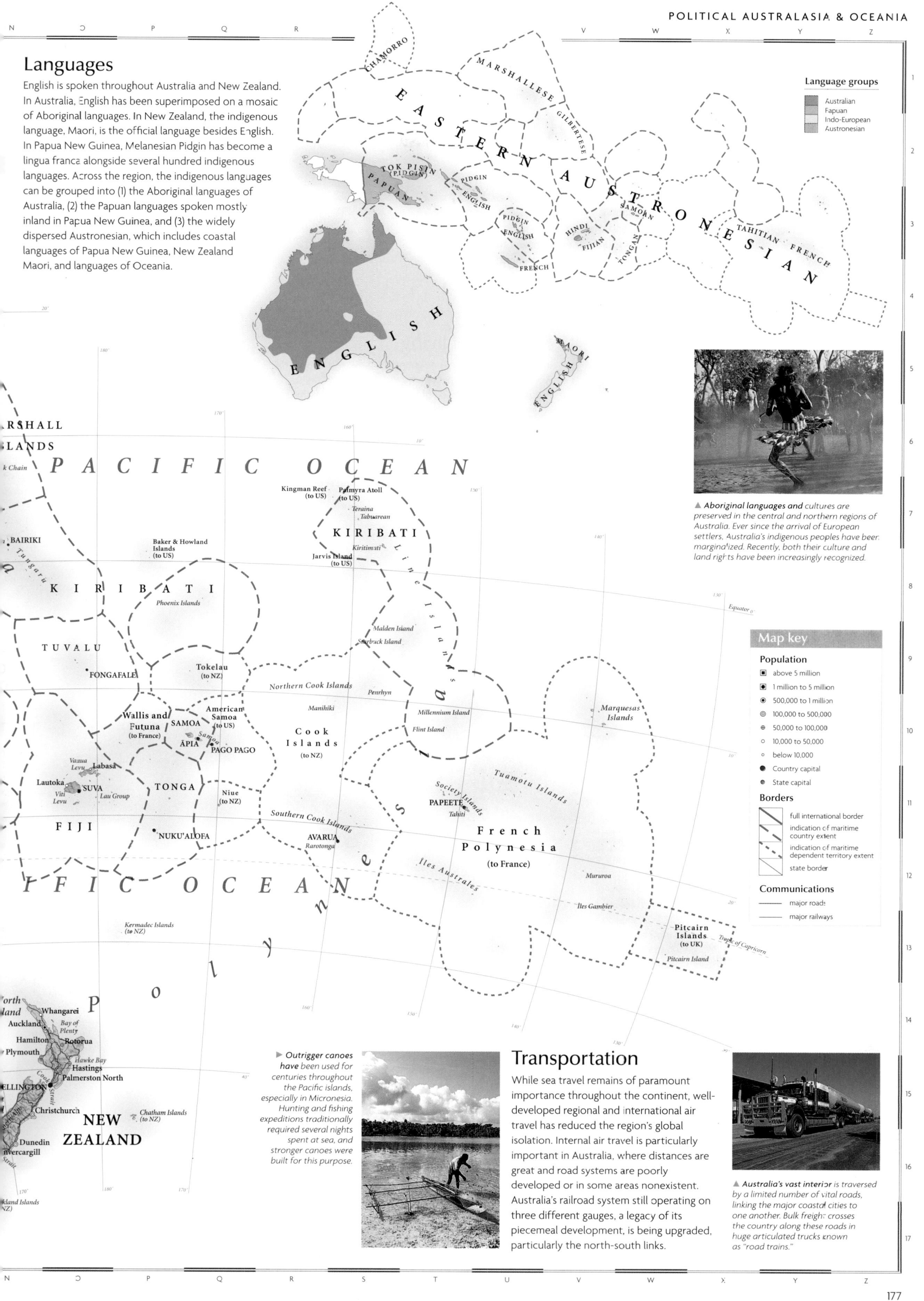

Language groups

- Australian
- Papuan
- Indo-European
- Austronesian

▲ *Aboriginal languages and* cultures are preserved in the central and northern regions of Australia. Ever since the arrival of European settlers, Australia's indigenous peoples have been marginalized. Recently, both their culture and land rights have been increasingly recognized.

Map key

Population

- ▪ above 5 million
- ▫ 1 million to 5 million
- ◉ 500,000 to 1 million
- ◎ 100,000 to 500,000
- ⊕ 50,000 to 100,000
- ⊙ 10,000 to 50,000
- ∘ below 10,000
- ● Country capital
- ◉ State capital

Borders

- full international border
- indication of maritime country extent
- indication of maritime dependent territory extent
- state border

Communications

- major roads
- major railways

▶ *Outrigger canoes have* been used for centuries throughout the Pacific islands, especially in Micronesia. Hunting and fishing expeditions traditionally required several nights spent at sea, and stronger canoes were built for this purpose.

Transportation

While sea travel remains of paramount importance throughout the continent, well-developed regional and international air travel has reduced the region's global isolation. Internal air travel is particularly important in Australia, where distances are great and road systems are poorly developed or in some areas nonexistent. Australia's railroad system still operating on three different gauges, a legacy of its piecemeal development, is being upgraded, particularly the north-south links.

▲ *Australia's vast interior is traversed by a limited number of vital roads, linking the major coastal cities to one another. Bulk freight crosses the country along these roads in huge articulated trucks known as "road trains."*

Australia

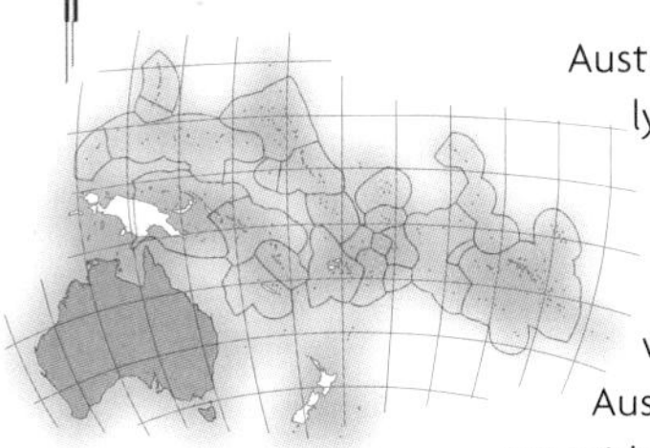

Australia is the world's smallest continent, a stable landmass lying between the Indian and Pacific oceans. Previously home to its aboriginal peoples only, since the end of the 18th century immigration has transformed the face of the country. Initially settlers came mainly from western Europe, particularly the UK, and for years Australia remained wedded to its British colonial past. More recent immigrants have come from eastern Europe, and from Asian countries such as Japan, South Korea, and Indonesia. Australia is now forging strong trading links with these "Pacific Rim" countries and its economic future seems to lie with Asia and the Americas, rather than Europe, its traditional partner.

Using the land

Over 104 million sheep are dispersed in vast herds around the country, contributing to a major export industry. Cattle-ranching is important, particularly in the west. Wheat, and grapes for Australia's wine industry, are grown mainly in the south. Much of the country is desert, unsuitable for agriculture unless irrigation is used.

The urban/rural population divide

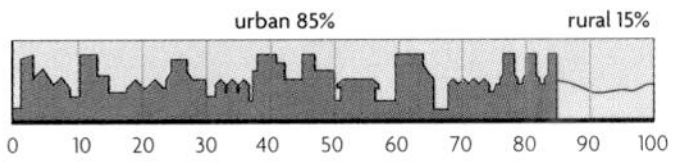

urban 85% rural 15%

Population density	Total land area
6 people per sq mile (2 people per sq km)	2,967,893 sq miles (7,686,850 sq km)

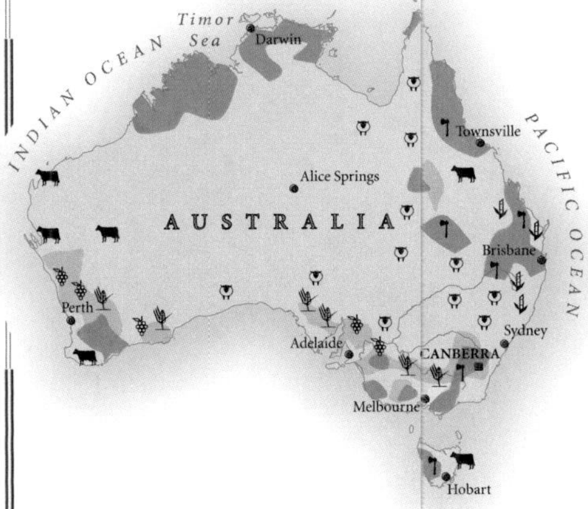

Land use and agricultural distribution

- cattle
- sheep
- cereals
- sugar cane
- timber
- vineyards
- capital cities
- major towns
- pasture
- cropland
- forest
- desert
- mountain region

▲ Lines of ripening vines stretch for miles in Barossa Valley, a major wine-growing region near Adelaide.

The landscape

Australia consists of many eroded plateaus, lying firmly in the middle of the Indo-Australian Plate. It is the world's flattest continent, and the driest, after Antarctica. The coasts tend to be more hilly and fertile, especially in the east. The mountains of the Great Dividing Range form a natural barrier between the eastern coastal areas and the flat, dry plains and desert regions of the Australian "outback."

▲ The Great Barrier Reef is the world's largest area of coral islands and reefs. It runs for about 1240 miles (2000 km) along the Queensland coast.

▲ The Pinnacles are a series of rugged sandstone pillars. Their strange shapes have been formed by water and wind erosion.

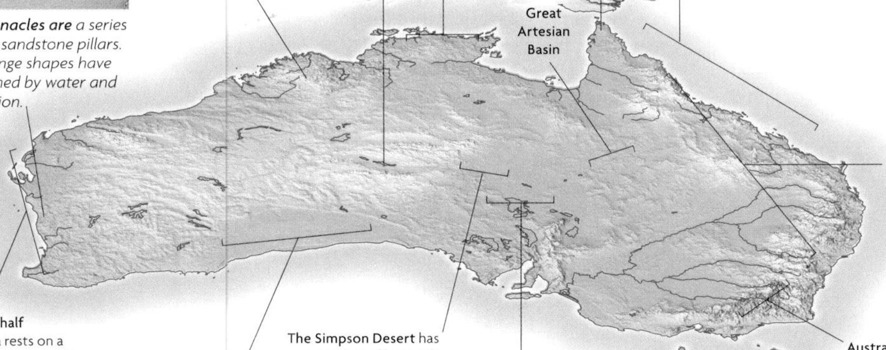

The ancient Kimberley Plateau is the source of some of Australia's richest mineral deposits, including diamonds.

Uluru (Ayers Rock)

Arnhem Land

The tropical rain forest of the Cape York Peninsula contains more than 600 different varieties of tree.

Great Artesian Basin

More than half of Australia rests on a uniform shield over 600 million years old. It is one of the Earth's original geological plates.

The Nullarbor Plain is a low-lying limestone plateau which is so flat that the Trans-Australian Railway runs through it in a straight line for more than 300 miles (483 km).

The Simpson Desert has a number of large salt pans, created by the evaporation of past rivers and now sourced by seasonal rains. Some are crusted with gypsum, but most are covered with common salt crystals.

The Lake Eyre basin, lying 51 ft (16 m) below sea level, is one of the largest inland drainage systems in the world, covering an area of more than 500,000 sq miles (1,300,000 sq km).

The Great Dividing Range forms a watershed between east- and west-flowing rivers. Erosion has created deep valleys, gorges, and waterfalls where rivers tumble over escarpments on their way to the sea.

Australian Alps

Tasmania has the same geological structure as the Australian Alps. During the last period of glaciation, 18,000 years ago, sea levels were some 300 ft (100 m) lower and it was joined to the mainland.

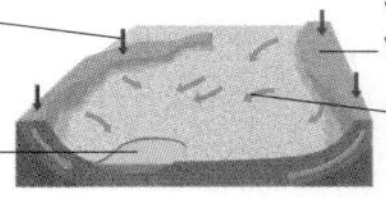

◄ Uluru (Ayers Rock), the world's largest free-standing rock, is a massive outcrop of red sandstone in Australia's desert center. Wind and sandstorms have ground the rock into the smooth curves seen here. Uluru is revered as a sacred site by many aboriginal peoples.

Scale 1:11,500,000

projection: Lambert Conformal Conic

Map key

Population
- 1 million to 5 million
- 500,000 to 1 million
- 100,000 to 500,000
- 50,000 to 100,000
- 10,000 to 50,000
- below 10,000

Elevation
- 2000m / 6562ft
- 1000m / 3281ft
- 500m / 1640ft
- 250m / 820ft
- 100m / 328ft
- sea level

Great Artesian Basin

Rainwater replenishes aquifer

Lake Eyre

Aquifers from which artesian water is obtained

Underground water movements

▲ The Great Artesian Basin underlies nearly 20% of the total area of Australia, providing a valuable store of underground water, essential to Australian agriculture. The ephemeral rivers which drain the northern part of the basin have highly braided courses and, in consequence, the area is known as "channel country."

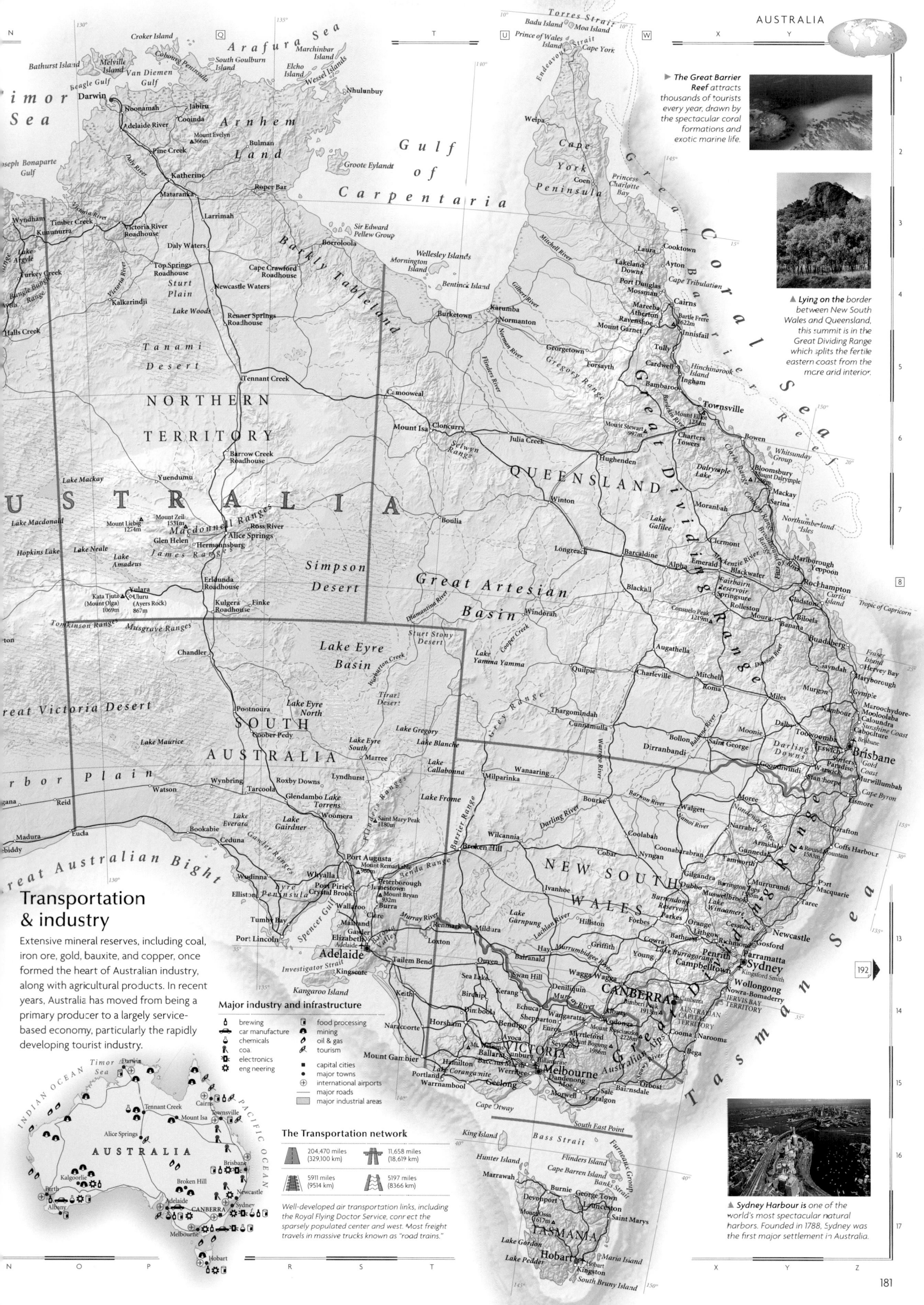

► **The Great Barrier Reef** attracts thousands of tourists every year, drawn by the spectacular coral formations and exotic marine life.

▲ **Lying on the** border between New South Wales and Queensland, this summit is in the Great Dividing Range which splits the fertile eastern coast from the more arid interior.

Transportation & industry

Extensive mineral reserves, including coal, iron ore, gold, bauxite, and copper, once formed the heart of Australian industry, along with agricultural products. In recent years, Australia has moved from being a primary producer to a largely service-based economy, particularly the rapidly developing tourist industry.

Major industry and infrastructure

- brewing
- car manufacture
- chemicals
- coal
- electronics
- engineering
- food processing
- mining
- oil & gas
- tourism
- ■ capital cities
- ⊕ major towns
- ⊕ international airports
- — major roads
- major industrial areas

The Transportation network

204,470 miles (329,100 km)	11,658 miles (18,619 km)
5911 miles (9514 km)	5197 miles (8366 km)

Well-developed air transportation links, including the Royal Flying Doctor Service, connect the sparsely populated center and west. Most freight travels in massive trucks known as "road trains."

▲ **Sydney Harbour is** one of the world's most spectacular natural harbors. Founded in 1788, Sydney was the first major settlement in Australia.

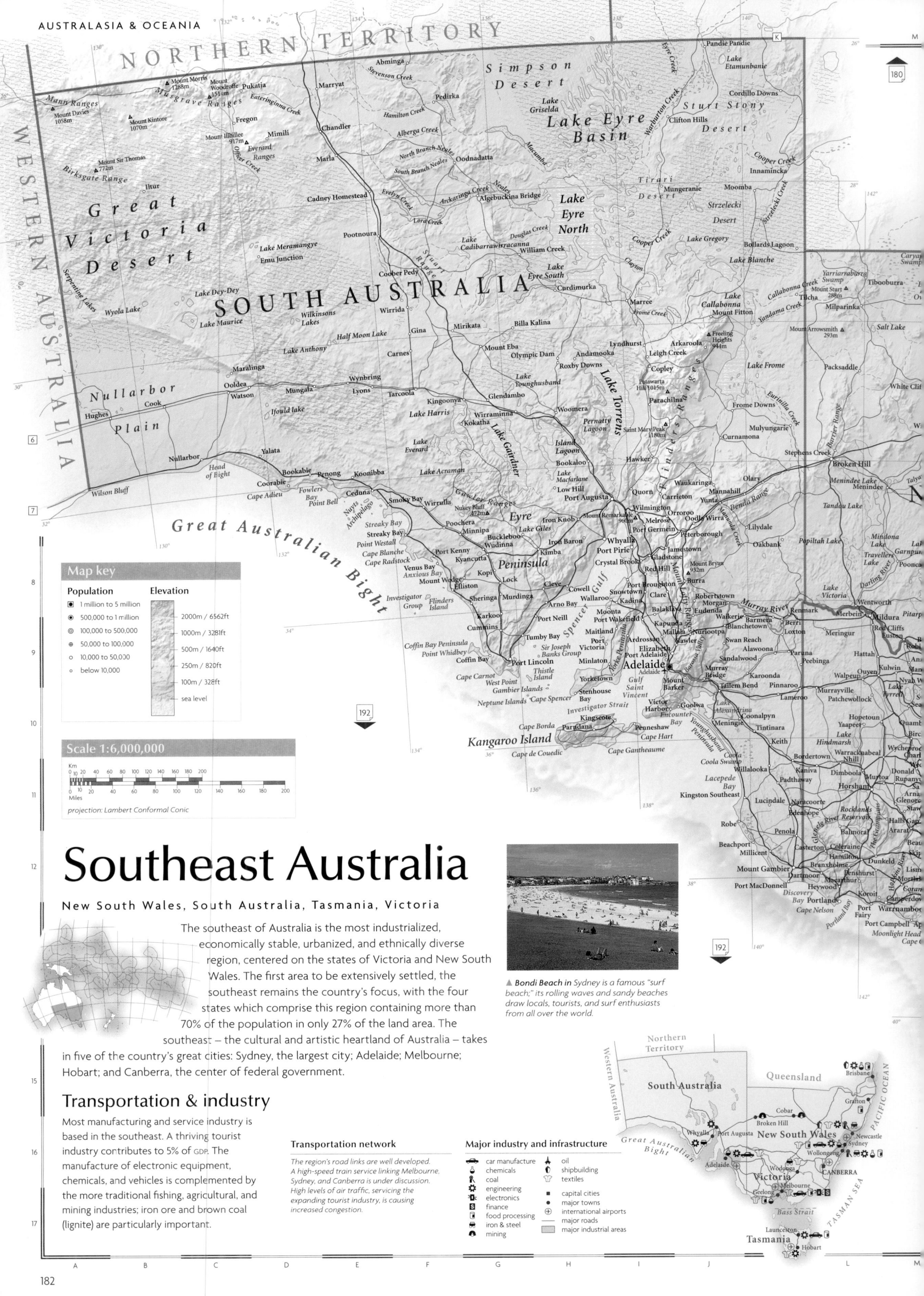

Map key

Population

- 1 million to 5 million
- 500,000 to 1 million
- 100,000 to 500,000
- 50,000 to 100,000
- 10,000 to 50,000
- below 10,000

Elevation

- 2000m / 6562ft
- 1000m / 3281ft
- 500m / 1640ft
- 250m / 820ft
- 100m / 328ft
- sea level

Scale 1:6,000,000

Km 0 10 20 40 60 80 100 120 140 160 180 200

Miles 0 10 20 40 60 80 100 120 140 160 180 200

projection: Lambert Conformal Conic

Southeast Australia

New South Wales, South Australia, Tasmania, Victoria

The southeast of Australia is the most industrialized, economically stable, urbanized, and ethnically diverse region, centered on the states of Victoria and New South Wales. The first area to be extensively settled, the southeast remains the country's focus, with the four states which comprise this region containing more than 70% of the population in only 27% of the land area. The southeast – the cultural and artistic heartland of Australia – takes in five of the country's great cities: Sydney, the largest city; Adelaide; Melbourne; Hobart; and Canberra, the center of federal government.

Transportation & industry

Most manufacturing and service industry is based in the southeast. A thriving tourist industry contributes to 5% of GDP. The manufacture of electronic equipment, chemicals, and vehicles is complemented by the more traditional fishing, agricultural, and mining industries; iron ore and brown coal (lignite) are particularly important.

▲ **Bondi Beach in** Sydney is a famous "surf beach;" its rolling waves and sandy beaches draw locals, tourists, and surf enthusiasts from all over the world.

Transportation network

The region's road links are well developed. A high-speed train service linking Melbourne, Sydney, and Canberra is under discussion. High levels of air traffic, servicing the expanding tourist industry, is causing increased congestion.

Major industry and infrastructure

- car manufacture
- chemicals
- coal
- engineering
- electronics
- finance
- food processing
- iron & steel
- mining
- oil
- shipbuilding
- textiles
- capital cities
- major towns
- international airports
- major roads
- major industrial areas

Using the land & sea

The western flanks of the Great Dividing Range and the northern deserts of South Australia support massive herds of sheep and cattle, while more intensive stockrearing occurs near the cities. Sugar cane is the most important industrial crop, and cereal grains including wheat, corn, barley, and sorghum are also grown. Grapes, citrus, and orchard fruits are among the wide range of fruit and vegetables cultivated in this region. Tasmania's forestry and fishing contributes to over one-third of the state's exports.

▲ The fertile Darling Downs, known as the "breadbasket of Australia," support a wide range of crops including cereals, sugar cane, and fruit.

▶ The Murray River has its source in the eastern uplands of the Great Dividing Range. Fed by melting snow, it runs for 1609 miles (2589 km) and has sufficient volume to reach the ocean southeast of Adelaide despite a minimal gradient for most of its lower reaches.

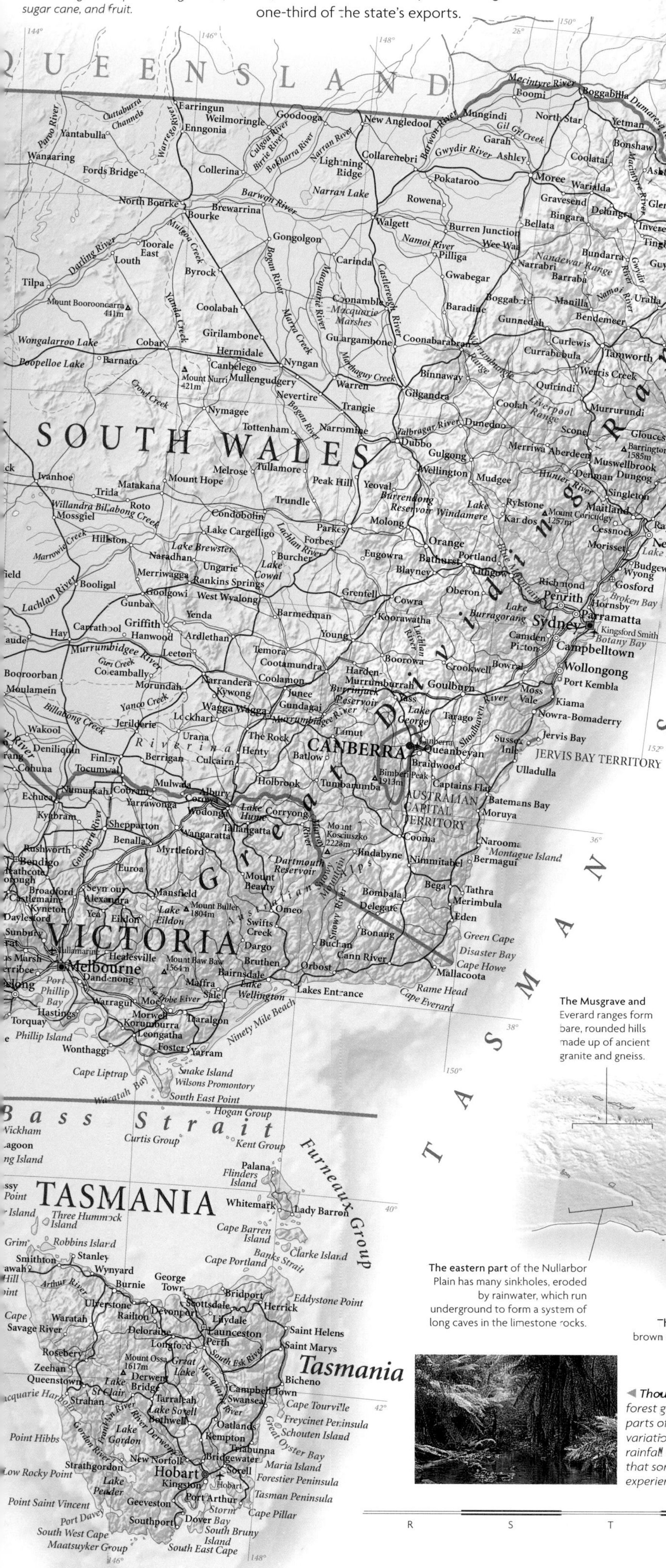

The urban/rural population divide

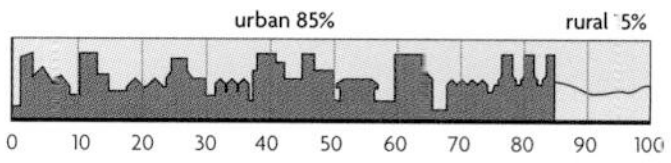

urban 85%   rural 15%

0   10   20   30   40   50   60   70   80   90   100

Population density	Total land area
18 people per sq mile (7 people per sq km)	778,022 sq miles (2,015,600 sq km)

Land use and agricultural distribution

- cattle
- sheep
- bananas
- fishing
- fruit
- sugar cane
- vineyards
- wheat
- capital cities
- major towns
- pasture
- cropland
- forest
- desert
- mountain region

The landscape

The southern half of the Great Dividing Range runs parallel to the eastern coast of Victoria and New South Wales as far as Tasmania, which, though divided from the mainland is part of the same mountain chain. South Australia comprises the Australian shield and half of the dry, flat Nullarbor Plain. The Murray/Darling river basin is the only major river system.

◀ The heavily folded Flinders Ranges is part of an arc of sedimentary rocks reaching northward from Kangaroo Island.

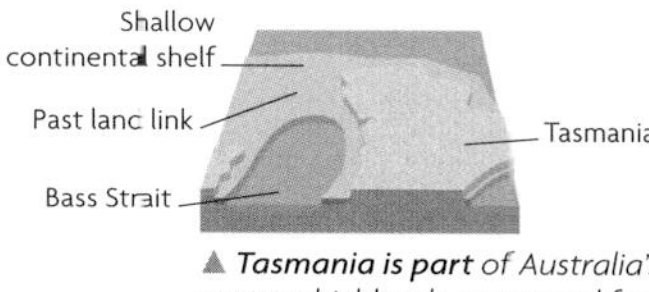

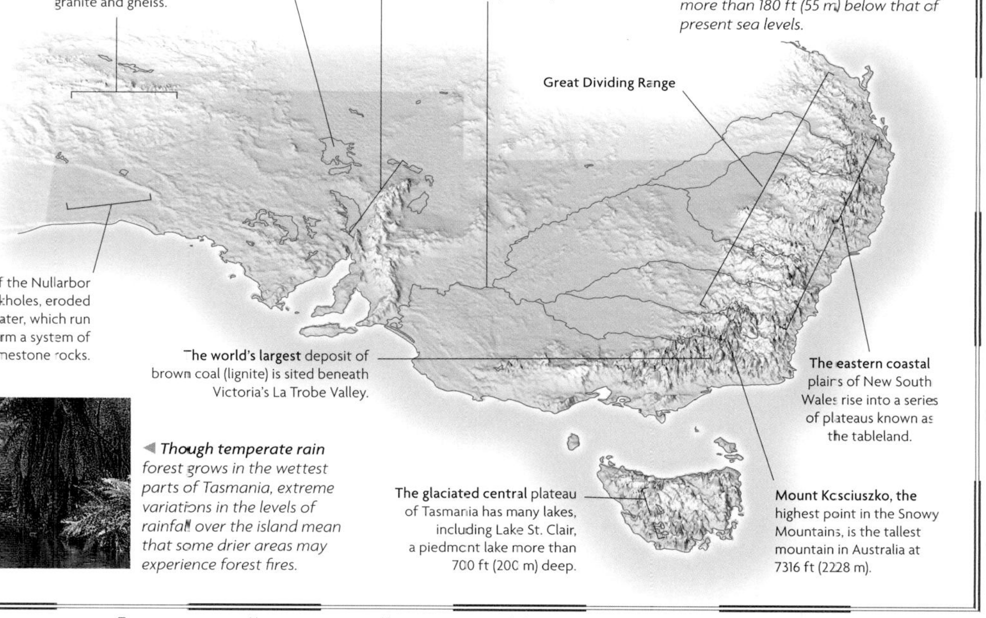

Lake Eyre is the largest of southern Australia's dry lakes. Lying -51 ft (-16 m) below sea level, it has flooded only three times in the last century.

The Musgrave and Everard ranges form bare, rounded hills made up of ancient granite and gneiss.

The Murray/Darling is Australia's longest river at 1703 miles (2739 km).

Shallow continental shelf
Past land link
Bass Strait
Tasmania

▲ Tasmania is part of Australia's eastern highlands, separated from the mainland by 155 miles (250 km) of the Bass Strait. In the recent geological past, dry land links between Tasmania and Victoria would have been possible during periods of world-wide glaciation, when the sea level was more than 180 ft (55 m) below that of present sea levels.

Great Dividing Range

The eastern part of the Nullarbor Plain has many sinkholes, eroded by rainwater, which run underground to form a system of long caves in the limestone rocks.

The world's largest deposit of brown coal (lignite) is sited beneath Victoria's La Trobe Valley.

The eastern coastal plains of New South Wales rise into a series of plateaus known as the tableland.

◀ Though temperate rain forest grows in the wettest parts of Tasmania, extreme variations in the levels of rainfall over the island mean that some drier areas may experience forest fires.

The glaciated central plateau of Tasmania has many lakes, including Lake St. Clair, a piedmont lake more than 700 ft (200 m) deep.

Mount Kosciuszko, the highest point in the Snowy Mountains, is the tallest mountain in Australia at 7316 ft (2228 m).

New Zealand

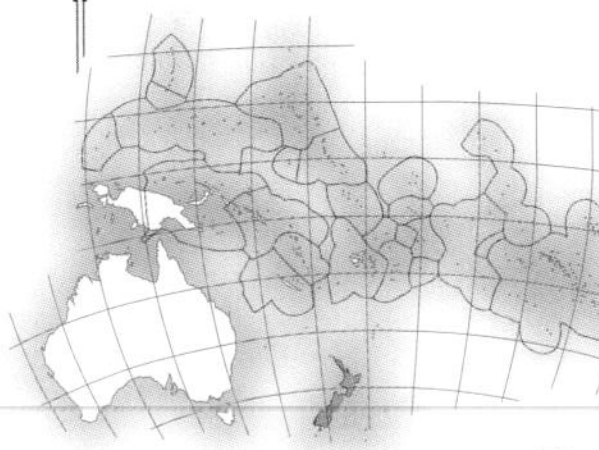

Lying 1500 miles east-southeast of Australia, New Zealand was originally settled by the Maori people of Polynesia. It was visited by Europeans for the first time only as recently as the 1770s. The islands' rugged topography means that most settlement has concentrated in coastal areas. People of European origin make up about 70% of the population of 4 million, following immigration which began in the 1920s. Many recent settlers have come from Asia, including India and China, and a number of the Pacific islands.

The Maori now make up a minority of less than half a million. Their ancient claims to at least half of national territory, however, are gaining increasing legal credence.

The landscape

New Zealand comprises two large islands and many scattered smaller islands. On South Island the Alpine Fault marks the boundary between the Pacific and Indo-Australian plates. Tectonic activity has strongly influenced the formation of the Southern Alps, snowcapped mountains with several peaks over 9800 ft (3000 m). North Island has a lower and less extensive mountain region, containing forested hills, a central volcanic plateau, and downlands.

Mountain-building in the Southern Alps

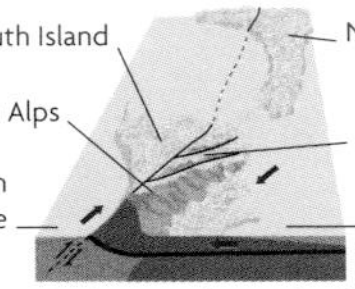

North Island
Alpine Fault
Pacific Plate
South Island
Southern Alps
Indo-Australian Plate

▲ **The Southern Alps** have been formed by "slip" faulting. The Indo-Australian and Pacific plates run in opposite directions along the Alpine Fault. Although they slide past each other, they are also being thrust over one another, causing the continental crust of the Pacific Plate to be uplifted to form the Alps.

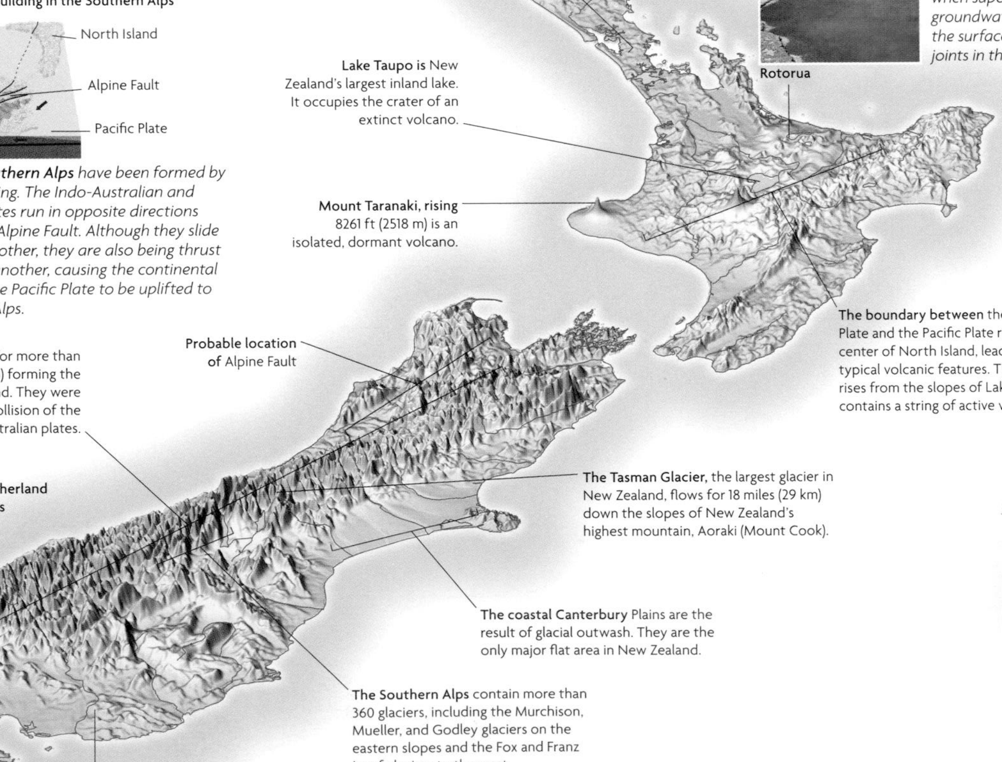

Fiordland, in the far south west, contains a large number of flooded glacial valleys.

The Southern Alps run for more than 300 miles, (483 km) forming the backbone of South Island. They were uplifted following the collision of the Pacific and Indo-Australian plates.

Sutherland Falls

High levels of rainfall and a steep topography has made New Zealand's rivers swift-running. In the southern reaches of both islands, rivers such as the Mokoreta form broad, braided streams.

Probable location of Alpine Fault

Mount Taranaki, rising 8261 ft (2518 m) is an isolated, dormant volcano.

Lake Taupo is New Zealand's largest inland lake. It occupies the crater of an extinct volcano.

The Southern Alps contain more than 360 glaciers, including the Murchison, Mueller, and Godley glaciers on the eastern slopes and the Fox and Franz Josei glaciers to the west.

The coastal Canterbury Plains are the result of glacial outwash. They are the only major flat area in New Zealand.

The Tasman Glacier, the largest glacier in New Zealand, flows for 18 miles (29 km) down the slopes of New Zealand's highest mountain, Aoraki (Mount Cook).

The boundary between the Indo-Australian Plate and the Pacific Plate runs through the center of North Island, leading to many typical volcanic features. The plateau which rises from the slopes of Lake Taupo contains a string of active volcanoes.

▲ **Clouds of steam** rise from White Island, an active, offshore volcano lying in the Bay of Plenty, off the northern coast of North Island.

▶ **The Northland region** is characterized by many coastal inlets. These are lined by mangrove swamps, signaling the change to a subtropical climate in the far north of the island.

Northland

▼ **The Rotorua and Taupo** valleys have some of the largest and most spectacular thermal springs in New Zealand. These occur when superheated groundwater rises to the surface through joints in the rocks.

Rotorua

Scale 1:3,000,000
projection: Lambert Conformal Conic

PACIFIC OCEAN

TASMAN SEA

NEW ZEALAND

NORTH ISLAND

SOUTH ISLAND

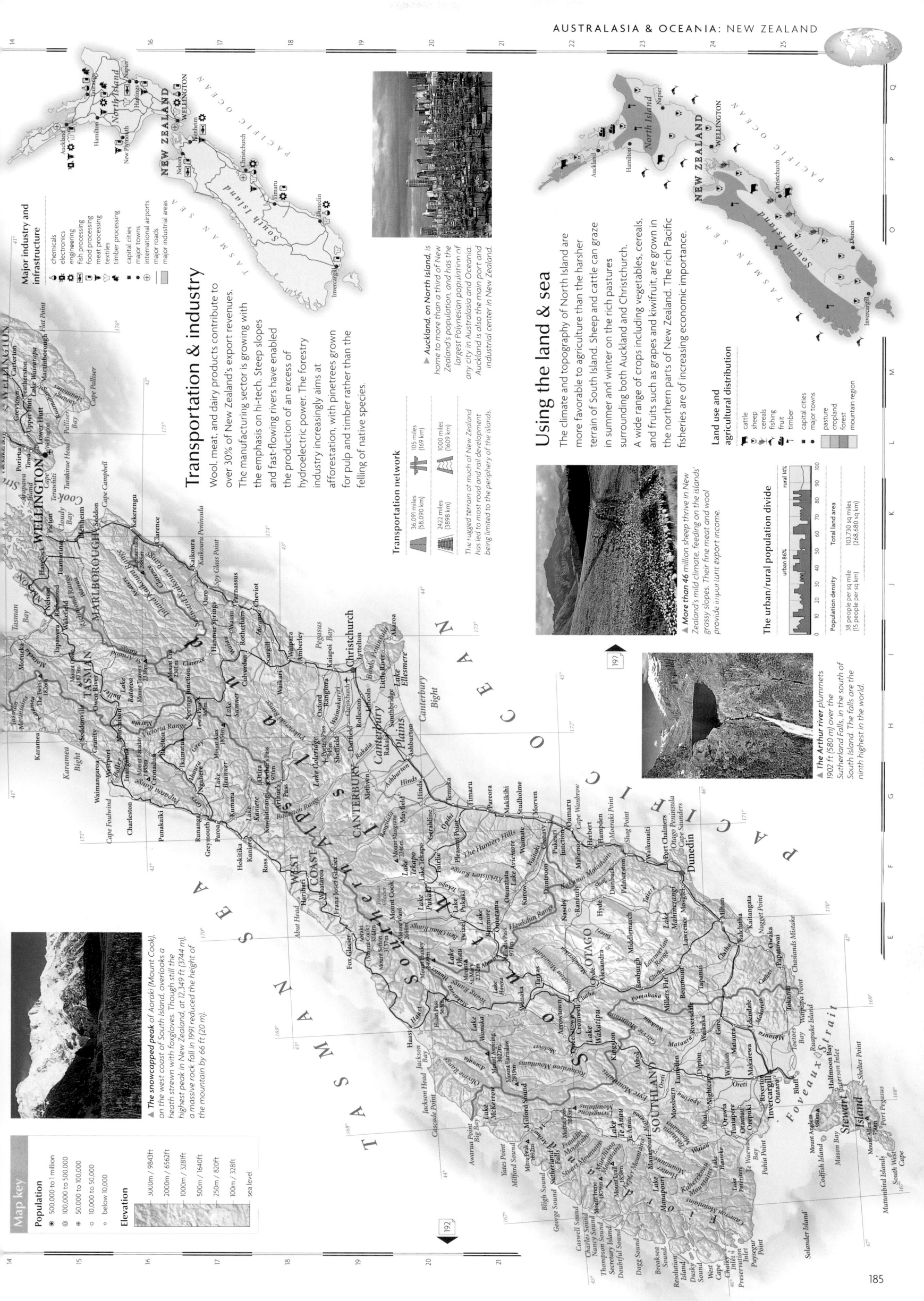

Map key

Population

- ⊙ 500,000 to 1 million
- ⊛ 100,000 to 500,000
- ⊕ 50,000 to 100,000
- ○ 10,000 to 50,000
- ○ below 10,000

Elevation

- 3000m / 9843ft
- 2000m / 6562ft
- 1000m / 3281ft
- 500m / 1640ft
- 250m / 820ft
- 100m / 328ft
- sea level

▲ *The snowcapped peak of Aoraki (Mount Cook), on the west coast of South Island, overlooks a heath strewn with foxgloves. Though still the highest peak in New Zealand, at 12,349 ft (3744 m), a massive rock fall in 1991 reduced the height of the mountain by 66 ft (20 m).*

Major industry and infrastructure

- ☼ chemicals
- ⚙ electronics
- ⚙ engineering
- ◷ food processing
- ⚓ fish processing
- 🗡 meat processing
- ◉ textiles
- 🌲 timber processing
- ● capital cities
- ● major towns
- ✈ international airports
- ▨ major industrial areas

Transportation & industry

Wool, meat, and dairy products contribute to over 30% of New Zealand's export revenues. The manufacturing sector is growing with the emphasis on hi-tech. Steep slopes and fast-flowing rivers have enabled the production of an excess of hydroelectric power. The forestry industry increasingly aims at afforestation, with pinetrees grown for pulp and timber rather than the felling of native species.

Transportation network

🛫	36,091 miles (58,090 km)
⛟	105 miles (169 km)
🚆	2442 miles (3898 km)
🚗	1000 miles (1609 km)

The rugged terrain of much of New Zealand has led to most road and rail development being limited to the periphery of the islands.

▲ *Auckland, on North Island, is home to more than a third of New Zealand's population, and has the largest Polynesian population of any city in Australasia and Oceania. Auckland is also the main port and industrial center in New Zealand.*

Using the land & sea

The climate and topography of North Island are more favorable to agriculture than the harsher terrain of South Island. Sheep and cattle can graze in summer and winter on the rich pastures surrounding both Auckland and Christchurch. A wide range of crops including vegetables, cereals, and fruits such as grapes and kiwifruit, are grown in the northern parts of New Zealand. The Pacific fisheries are of increasing economic importance.

Land use and agricultural distribution

- 🐄 cattle
- 🐑 sheep
- 🌾 cereals
- 🐟 fishing
- 🍎 fruit
- 🌲 timber
- ● capital cities
- ● major towns
- pasture
- cropland
- forest
- mountain region

▲ *More than 46 million sheep thrive in New Zealand's mild climate, feeding on the islands' grassy slopes. Their fine meat and wool provide important export income.*

▲ *The Arthur river plummets 1902 ft (580 m) over the Sutherland Falls, in the south of South Island. The falls are the ninth highest in the world.*

The urban/rural population divide

rural 14%
urban 86%

Population density	Total land area
38 people per sq mile (15 people per sq km)	103,730 sq miles (268,680 sq km)

Melanesia

FIJI, New Caledonia (to France), PAPUA NEW GUINEA, SOLOMON ISLANDS, VANUATU

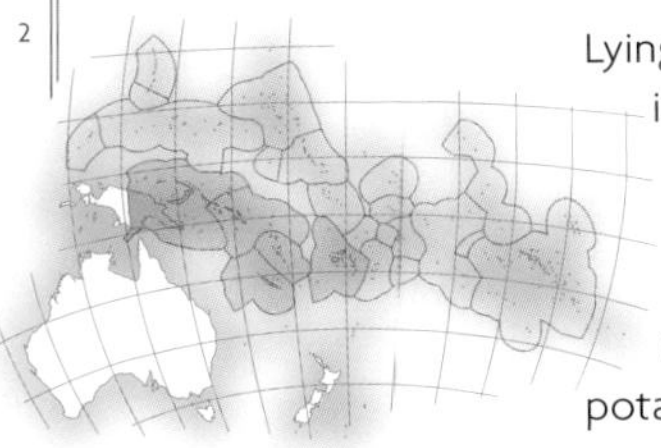

Lying in the southwest Pacific Ocean, northeast of Australia and south of the Equator, the islands of Melanesia form one of the three geographic divisions (along with Polynesia and Micronesia) of Oceania. Melanesia's name derives from the Greek melas, "black," and nesoi, "islands." Most of the larger islands are volcanic in origin. The smaller islands tend to be coral atolls and are mainly uninhabited. Rugged mountains, covered by dense rain forest, take up most of the land area. Melanesian's cultivate yams, taro, and sweet potatoes for local consumption and live in small, usually dispersed, homesteads.

▲ Huli tribesmen from Southern Highlands Province in Papua New Guinea parade in ceremonial dress, their powdered wigs decorated with exotic plumage and their faces and bodies painted with colored pigments.

Map key

Population
- ⊚ 100,000 to 500,000
- ⊕ 50,000 to 100,000
- ○ 10,000 to 50,000
- ○ below 10,000

Elevation
- 4000m / 13,124ft
- 3000m / 9843ft
- 2000m / 6562ft
- 1000m / 3281ft
- 500m / 1640ft
- 250m / 820ft
- 100m / 328ft
- sea level

Transportation & Industry

The processing of natural resources generates significant export revenue for the countries of Melanesia. The region relies mainly on copra, tuna, and timber exports, with some production of cocoa and palm oil. The islands have substantial mineral resources including the world's largest copper reserves on Bougainville Island; gold, and potential oil and natural gas. Tourism has become the fastest growing sector in most of the countries' economies.

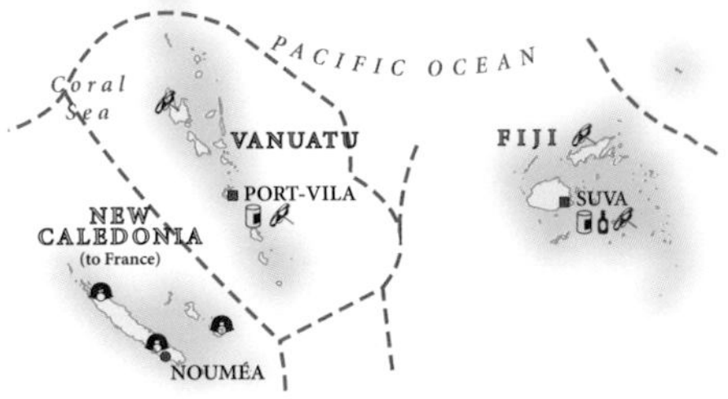

◄ On New Caledonia's main island, relatively high interior plateaus descend to coastal plains. Nickel is the most important mineral resource, but the hills also harbor metallic deposits including chrome, cobalt, iron, gold, silver, and copper.

◄ Lying close to the banks of the Sepik river in northern Papua New Guinea, this building is known as the Spirit House. It is constructed from leaves and twigs, ornately woven and trimmed into geometric patterns. The house is decorated with a mask and topped by a carved statue.

▲ On one of Vanuatu's many islands, beach houses stand at the water's edge, surrounded by coconut palms and other tropical vegetation. The unspoilt beaches and tranquillity of its islands are drawing ever-larger numbers of tourists to Vanuatu.

Transportation network

1236 miles (1990 km)		None
370 miles (595 km)		6924 miles (11,143 km)

As most of the islands of Melanesia lie off the major sea and air routes, services to and from the rest of the world are infrequent. Transportation by road on rugged terrain is difficult and expensive.

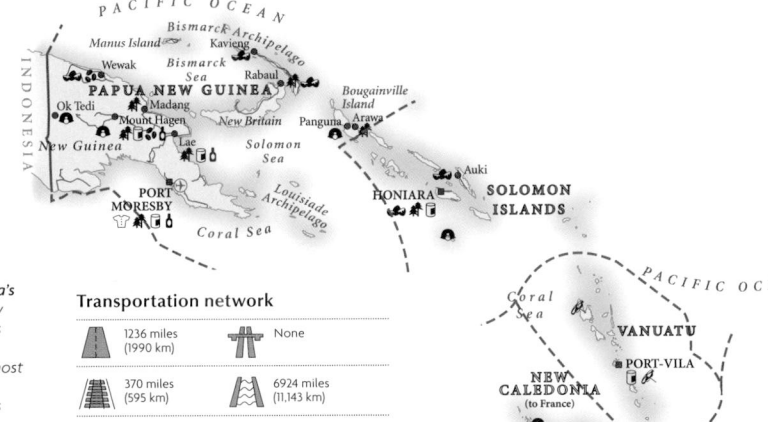

Major industry and infrastructure

- beverages
- coffee processing
- copra processing
- food processing
- mining
- textiles
- timber processing
- tourism
- ■ capital cities
- ● major towns
- ⊕ international airports
- major roads

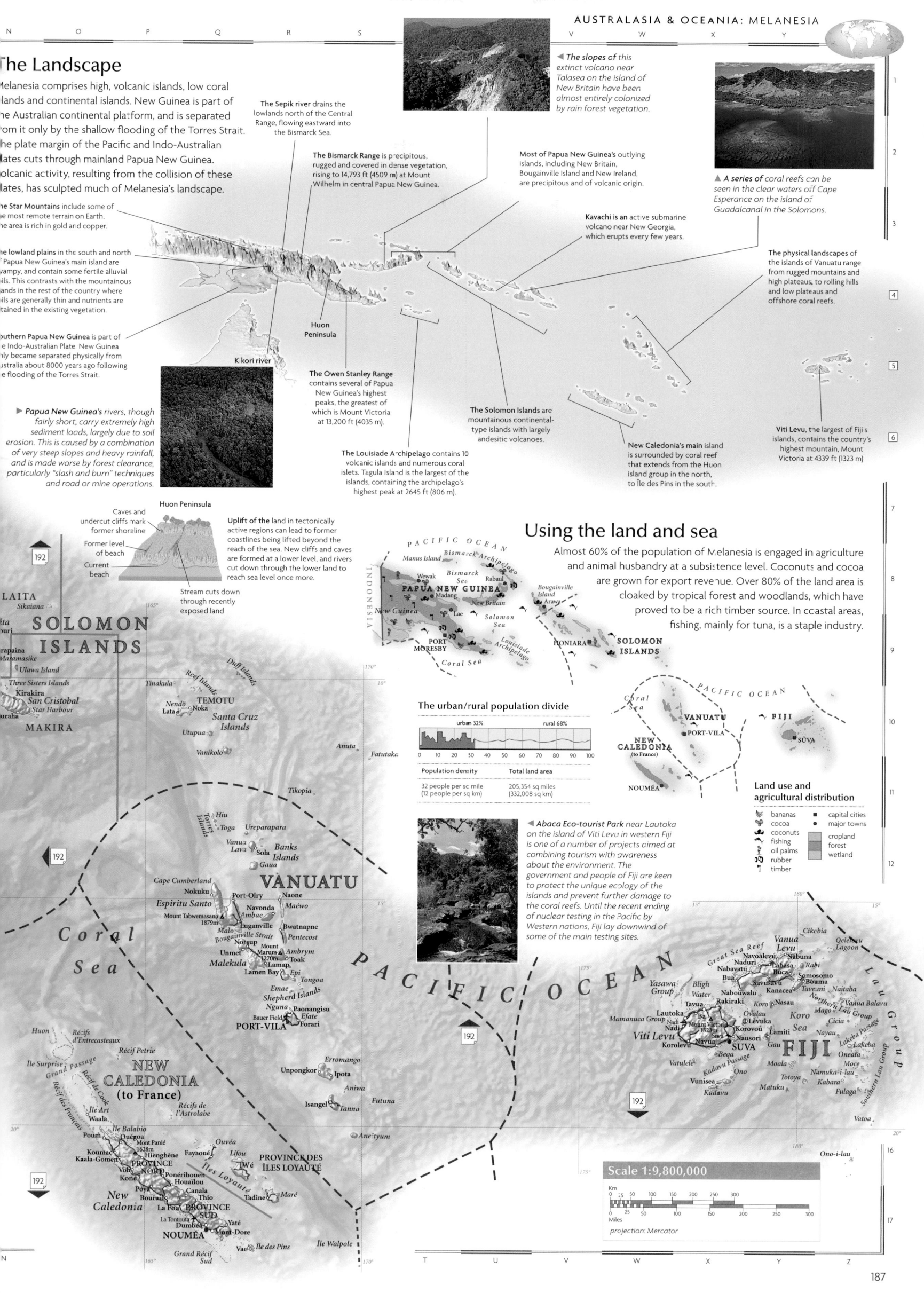

The Landscape

Melanesia comprises high, volcanic islands, low coral islands and continental islands. New Guinea is part of the Australian continental platform, and is separated from it only by the shallow flooding of the Torres Strait. The plate margin of the Pacific and Indo-Australian plates cuts through mainland Papua New Guinea. Volcanic activity, resulting from the collision of these plates, has sculpted much of Melanesia's landscape.

The Star Mountains include some of the most remote terrain on Earth. The area is rich in gold and copper.

The lowland plains in the south and north of Papua New Guinea's main island are swampy, and contain some fertile alluvial soils. This contrasts with the mountainous lands in the rest of the country where soils are generally thin and nutrients are retained in the existing vegetation.

Southern Papua New Guinea is part of the Indo-Australian Plate. New Guinea only became separated physically from Australia about 8000 years ago following the flooding of the Torres Strait.

► Papua New Guinea's rivers, though fairly short, carry extremely high sediment loads, largely due to soil erosion. This is caused by a combination of very steep slopes and heavy rainfall, and is made worse by forest clearance, particularly "slash and burn" techniques and road or mine operations.

◄ The slopes of this extinct volcano near Talasea on the island of New Britain have been almost entirely colonized by rain forest vegetation.

▲ A series of coral reefs can be seen in the clear waters off Cape Esperance on the island of Guadalcanal in the Solomons.

The Sepik river drains the lowlands north of the Central Range, flowing eastward into the Bismarck Sea.

The Bismarck Range is precipitous, rugged and covered in dense vegetation, rising to 14,793 ft (4509 m) at Mount Wilhelm in central Papua New Guinea.

Most of Papua New Guinea's outlying islands, including New Britain, Bougainville Island and New Ireland, are precipitous and of volcanic origin.

Kavachi is an active submarine volcano near New Georgia, which erupts every few years.

The physical landscapes of the islands of Vanuatu range from rugged mountains and high plateaus, to rolling hills and low plateaus and offshore coral reefs.

Huon Peninsula

Kikori river

The Owen Stanley Range contains several of Papua New Guinea's highest peaks, the greatest of which is Mount Victoria at 13,200 ft (4035 m).

The Solomon Islands are mountainous continental-type islands with largely andesitic volcanoes.

New Caledonia's main island is surrounded by coral reef that extends from the Huon island group in the north, to Île des Pins in the south.

Viti Levu, the largest of Fiji's islands, contains the country's highest mountain, Mount Victoria at 4339 ft (1323 m)

The Louisiade Archipelago contains 10 volcanic islands and numerous coral islets. Tagula Island is the largest of the islands, containing the archipelago's highest peak at 2645 ft (806 m).

Huon Peninsula

Caves and undercut cliffs mark former shoreline

Former level of beach

Current beach

Stream cuts down through recently exposed land

Uplift of the land in tectonically active regions can lead to former coastlines being lifted beyond the reach of the sea. New cliffs and caves are formed at a lower level, and rivers cut down through the lower land to reach sea level once more.

Using the land and sea

Almost 60% of the population of Melanesia is engaged in agriculture and animal husbandry at a subsistence level. Coconuts and cocoa are grown for export revenue. Over 80% of the land area is cloaked by tropical forest and woodlands, which have proved to be a rich timber source. In coastal areas, fishing, mainly for tuna, is a staple industry.

The urban/rural population divide

urban 32%   rural 68%

0 10 20 30 40 50 60 70 80 90 100

Population density	Total land area
32 people per sq mile (12 people per sq km)	205,354 sq miles (332,008 sq km)

◄ Abaca Eco-tourist Park near Lautoka on the island of Viti Levu in western Fiji is one of a number of projects aimed at combining tourism with awareness about the environment. The government and people of Fiji are keen to protect the unique ecology of the islands and prevent further damage to the coral reefs. Until the recent ending of nuclear testing in the Pacific by Western nations, Fiji lay downwind of some of the main testing sites.

Land use and agricultural distribution

- bananas
- cocoa
- coconuts
- fishing
- oil palms
- rubber
- timber
- capital cities
- major towns
- cropland
- forest
- wetland

PACIFIC OCEAN
Manus Island
Bismarck Archipelago
Wewak
Bismarck Sea
Rabaul
INDONESIA
PAPUA NEW GUINEA
Madang
New Britain
Bougainville Island
Arawa
New Guinea
Lae
Solomon Sea
Louisiade Archipelago
HONIARA
SOLOMON ISLANDS
PORT MORESBY
Coral Sea

PACIFIC OCEAN
Coral Sea
VANUATU
PORT-VILA
FIJI
SUVA
NEW CALEDONIA (to France)
NOUMÉA

Map labels (main map):

SOLOMON ISLANDS
LAITA
Sikaiana
Tita
Buri
Arapaina
Maramasike
Ulawa Island
MAKIRA
Kirakira
San Cristobal
Star Harbour
uraha
Three Sisters Islands

Reef Islands
Duff Islands
Tinakula
Nendö
Noka
Lata
TEMOTU
Santa Cruz Islands
Utupua
Vanikolo
Anuta
Fatutaka

Tikopia

Hiu
Toga
Ureparapara
Torres Islands
Vanua Lava
Sola
Banks Islands
Gaua

VANUATU
Cape Cumberland
Nokuku
Port-Olry
Naone
Navonda
Maéwo
Espiritu Santo
Ambae
Mount Tabwemasana 1879m
Luganville
Malo
Pentecost
Bougainville Strait
Bwatnapne
Norsup
Mount Marum 1270m
Ambrym
Unmet
Toak
Malekula
Laman
Lamen Bay
Epi
Tongoa
Emae
Shepherd Islands
Nguna
Paonangisu
Bauer Field
Efate
Forari
PORT-VILA

Coral Sea
Huon
Récifs d'Entrecasteaux
Récif Petrie
Île Surprise
Grand Passage
NEW CALEDONIA (to France)
Récifs de l'Astrolabe
Erromango
Unpongkor
Ipota
Aniwa
Isangel
Tanna
Futuna
Aneityum

Île Art
Waala
Poum
Ouégoa
Mont Panié 1628m
Île Balabio
Koumac
Hienghène
Fayaoué
Ouvéa
Lifou
Kaala-Gomen
PROVINCE NORD
Voh
Ponérihouen
Koné
Houailou
Poya
Canala
Bourail
Thio
La Foa
PROVINCE SUD
Tadine
Maré
La Tontouta
Dumbéa
Yaté
NOUMÉA
Mont-Dore
Vao
Île des Pins
Grand Récif Sud
Îles Loyauté
PROVINCE DES ÎLES LOYAUTÉ
Wé
New Caledonia

PACIFIC OCEAN

FIJI
Cikobia
Qelelevu Lagoon
Vanua Levu
Great Sea Reef
Navoalevu
Nabuna
Naduri
Labasa
Rabi
Nabavatu
Buca
Somosomo
Bua
Savusavu
Bouma
Yasawa Group
Bligh Water
Nabouwalu
Kanacea
Taveuni
Naitaba
Tavua
Koro
Nasau
Mago
Vanua Balavu
Lautoka
Ba
Ovalau
Cicia
Nadi
Levuka
Lamiti
Nausori
Mamanuca Group
Mount Victoria 1323m
Korovou
Nayau
Viti Levu
Navua
SUVA
Gau
Lakeba
Korolevu
Beqa
Koro Sea
Northern Lau Group
Vatulele
Moala
Totoya
Oneata
Moce
Vunisea
Ono
Matuku
Kabara
Kadavu
Kadavu Passage
Fulaga
Vatoa
Ono-i-lau
Lau Group
Southern Lau Group

Scale 1:9,800,000

Km
0 25 50 100 150 200 250 300
Miles
0 25 50 100 150 200 250 300

projection: Mercator

Micronesia

MARSHALL ISLANDS, MICRONESIA, NAURU, PALAU,
Guam, Northern Mariana Islands, Wake Island

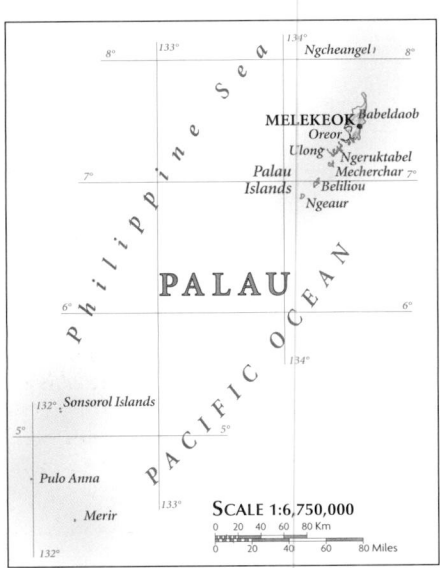

The Micronesian islands lie in the western reaches of the Pacific Ocean and are all part of the same volcanic zone. The Federated States of Micronesia is the largest group, with more than 600 atolls and forested volcanic islands in an area of more than 1120 sq miles (2900 sq km). Micronesia is a mixture of former colonies, overseas territories, and dependencies. Most of the region still relies on aid and subsidies to sustain economies limited by resources, isolation, and an emigrating population, drawn to New Zealand and Australia by the attractions of a western lifestyle.

Palau

Palau is an archipelago of over 200 islands, only eight of which are inhabited. It was the last remaining UN trust territory in the Pacific, controlled by the US until 1994, when it became independent. The economy operates on a subsistence level, with coconuts and cassava the principal crops. Fishing licenses and tourism provide foreign currency.

SCALE 1:825,000

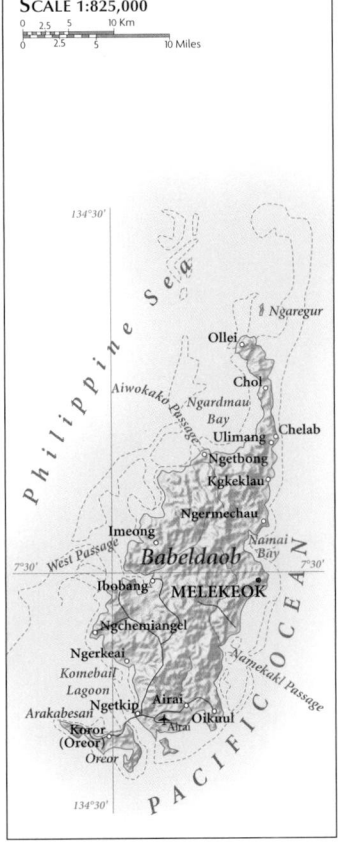

SCALE 1:6,750,000

Guam (to US)

Lying at the southern end of the Mariana Islands, Guam is an important US military base and tourist destination. Social and political life is dominated by the indigenous Chamorro, who make up just under half the population, although the increasing prevalence of western culture threatens Guam's traditional social stability.

◄ The tranquility of these coastal lagoons, at Inarajan in southern Guam, belies the fact that the island lies in a region where typhoons are common.

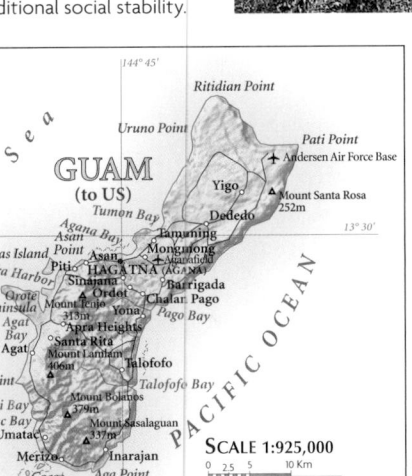

SCALE 1:925,000

Northern Mariana Islands (to US)

A US Commonwealth territory, the Northern Marianas comprise the whole of the Mariana archipelago except for Guam. The islands retain their close links with the US and continue to receive American aid. Tourism, though bringing in much-needed revenue, has speeded the decline of the traditional subsistence economy. Most of the population lives on Saipan.

SCALE 1:550,000

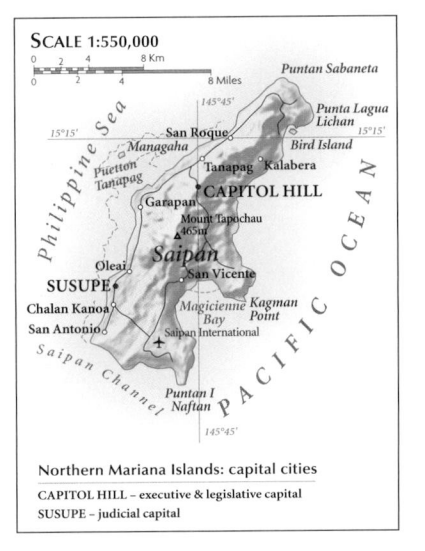

Northern Mariana Islands: capital cities

CAPITOL HILL – executive & legislative capital
SUSUPE – judicial capital

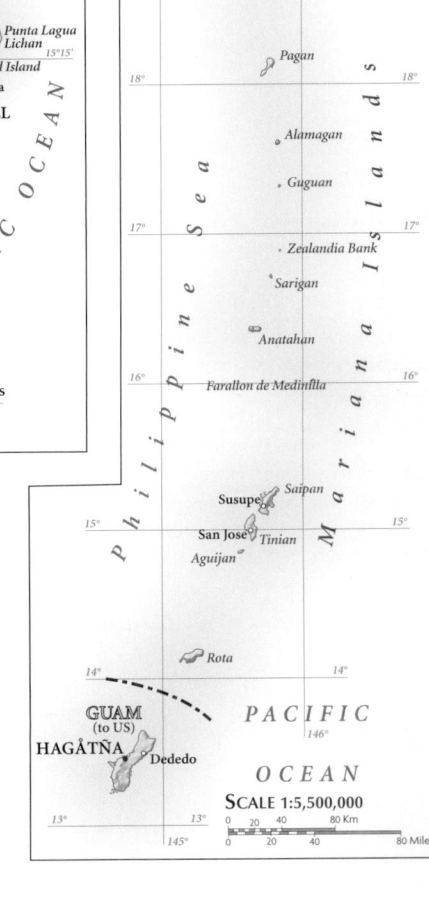

SCALE 1:5,500,000

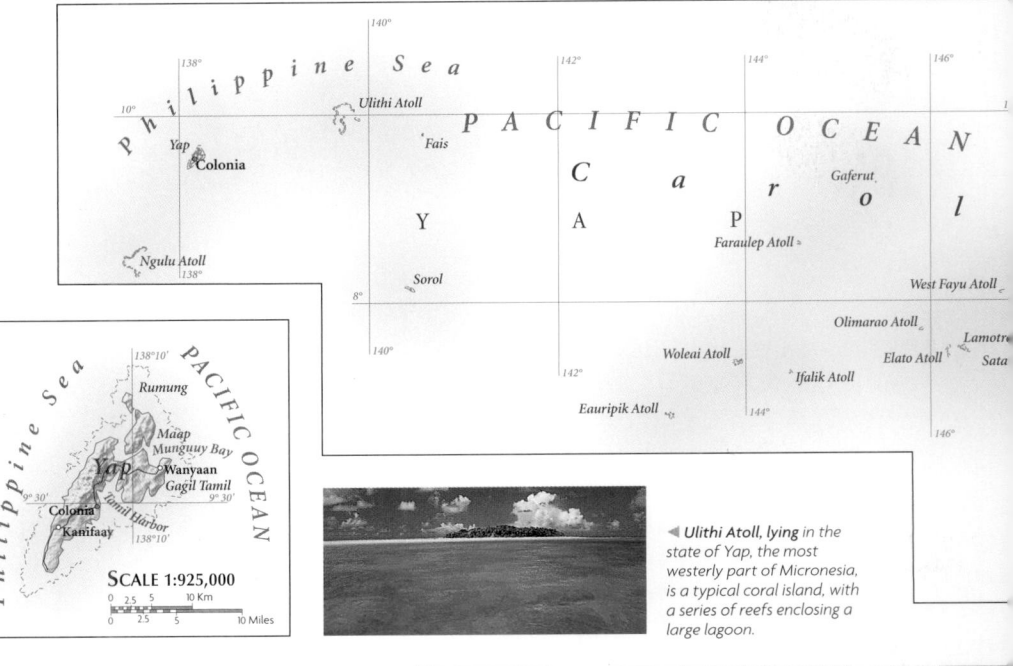

▲ The Palau Islands have numerous hidden lakes and lagoons. These sustain their own ecosystems which have developed in isolation. This has produced adaptations in the animals and plants that are often unique to each lake.

Micronesia

A mixture of high volcanic islands and low-lying coral atolls, the Federated States of Micronesia include all the Caroline Islands except Palau. Pohnpei, Kosrae, Chuuk, and Yap are the four main island cluster states, each of which has its own language, with English remaining the official language. Nearly half the population is concentrated on Pohnpei, the largest island. Independent since 1986, the islands continue to receive considerable aid from the US which supplements an economy based primarily on fishing and copra processing.

◄ Ulithi Atoll, lying in the state of Yap, the most westerly part of Micronesia, is a typical coral island, with a series of reefs enclosing a large lagoon.

Marshall Islands

A group of 34 widely-scattered atolls in the central Pacific Ocean, the Marshall Islands include some of the largest atolls in the world, formed from low coral islands with sandy beaches and enclosing vast lagoons. Formerly under US protection as part of the UN Trust Territory of the Pacific Islands, and including the former US nuclear testing sites of Bikini atoll and Enewetak Atoll, the Marshall Islands became self-governing in 1979. The economy is reliant on US aid and on the rent paid by the US for its missile base on Kwajalein atoll.

SCALE 1:1,100,000

Majuro Atoll

PACIFIC OCEAN

MARSHALL ISLANDS

Ratak Chain

Ralik Chain

▲ *Majuro Atoll is* the Marshall Islands' capital and commercial center. Almost half the population live on the narrow islands, often in overcrowded conditions.

SCALE 1:7,250,000

Nauru

A former British colony, the tiny island of Nauru, with an area of only 8.2 sq miles (21.2 sq km), has been exploited for its substantial phosphate deposits by the UK, Australia, and New Zealand. Since independence in 1968, the phosphate industry has made its citizens some of the wealthiest in the world, and scars from the vast mining operation pit the island's landscape. Phosphate reserves are now virtually exhausted and investment overseas will in future form the bulk of Nauru's income.

NAURU

PACIFIC OCEAN

SCALE 1:250,000

◀ *A series of* coral pinnacles stand exposed in the shallow water off the coast of Nauru. Much of the island has an extraordinary "lunar" landscape, created by years of phosphate extraction.

Wake Island *(to US)*

An unincorporated territory of the US with a tiny population, Wake Island remains strategically important to US forces, and has been used as a base in several conflicts. Formed by the rim of an extinct underwater volcano, it is now used as an emergency airstrip for trans-Pacific flights, and as a stopover for cargo planes.

SCALE 1:725,000

PACIFIC OCEAN

PALIKIR

Pohnpei

▲ *Canoes, built following* tradition, are still important in Micronesia, and are used for transportation and for fishing. This large canoe, on Satawal, in the state of Yap, needs nearly 20 people to return it to the boathouse.

Chuuk Islands

PACIFIC OCEAN

SCALE 1:1,750,000

WAKE ISLAND
(to US)

Wake Lagoon

PACIFIC OCEAN

SCALE 1:275,000

PACIFIC OCEAN

Kosrae

SCALE 1:550,000

CHUUK

MICRONESIA

PALIKIR *Pohnpei*

POHNPEI

PACIFIC OCEAN

KOSRAE

SCALE 1:9,000,000

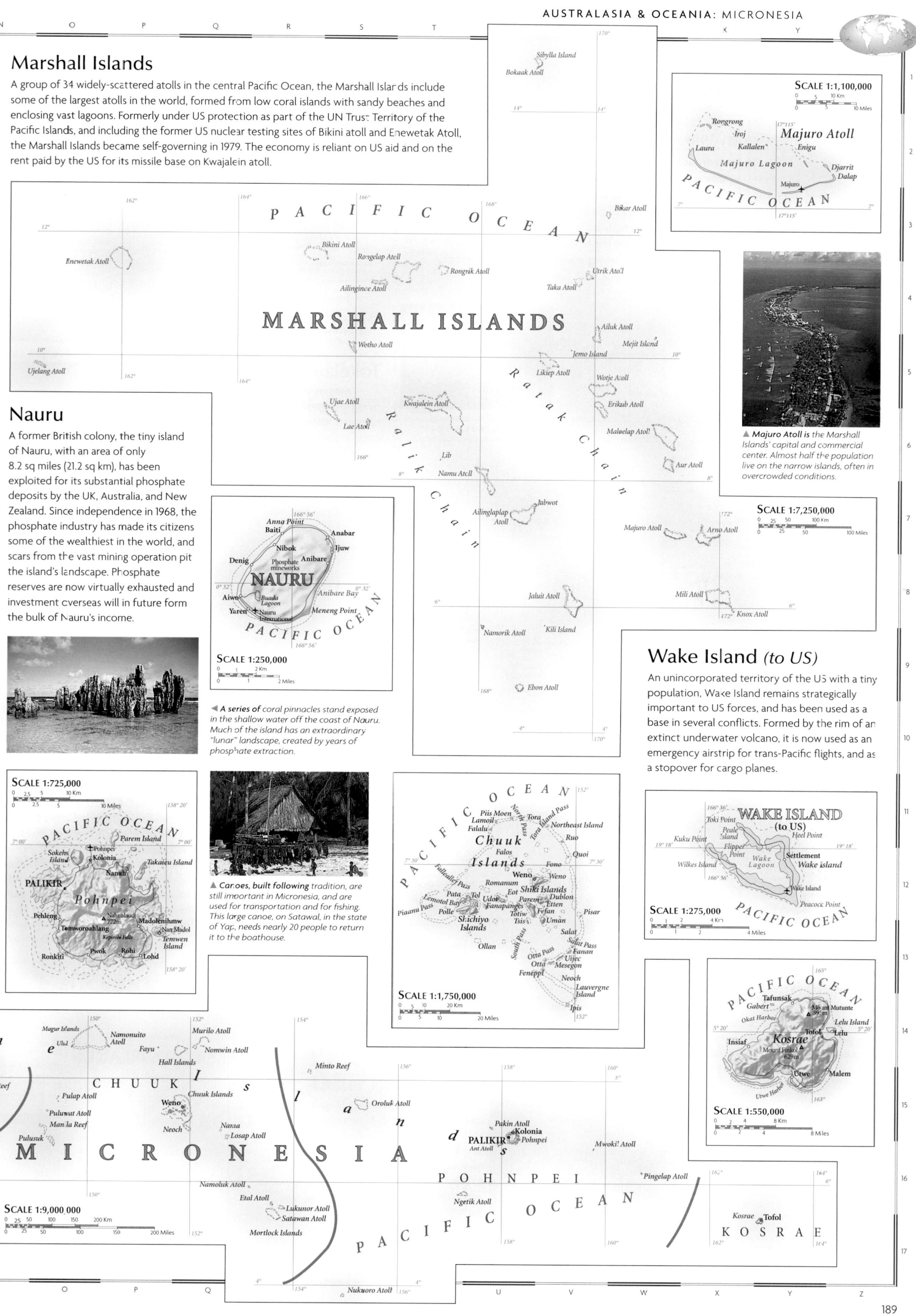

The Pacific Ocean

The Pacific is the world's largest and deepest ocean. It is nearly twice the area of the Atlantic and contains almost three times as much water. The ocean is dotted with islands and surrounded by some of the world's most populous states; over half the world's population lives on its shores. The Pacific is bordered by active plate margins known as the "Ring of Fire," causing earthquakes and tsunamis, and creating volcanic islands and subterranean mountain chains. The largest underwater mountains break the surface as island arcs. The fisheries of the Pacific are some of the most productive in the world and provide a vital resource for many of the Pacific islands. Since the Second World War there has been a shift in trading patterns, with a considerable growth in trade between the US and the countries of the Pacific Rim.

The Ring of Fire

The active plate margins surrounding the Pacific have created numerous land and island volcanoes along its border. The actual basin of the Pacific is made up of a number of separate tectonic plates which move away from each other, colliding with other plates. When they collide, the oceanic plates, being thinner, are forced beneath the thicker continental plates, forming deep ocean trenches and high ridges. These collision zones are known as subduction zones and are characterized by intense seismic and volcanic activity.

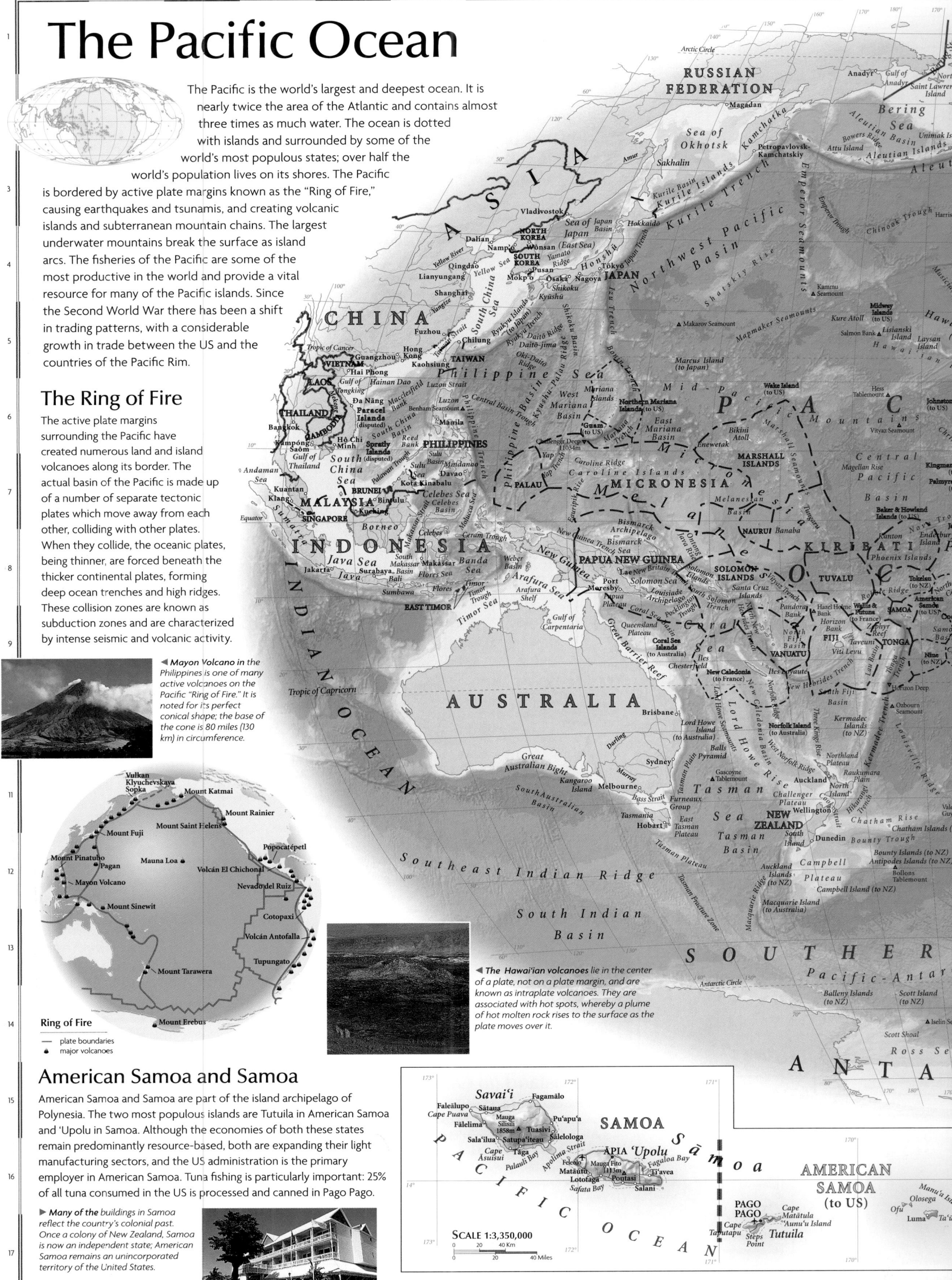

◀ **Mayon Volcano** in the Philippines is one of many active volcanoes on the Pacific "Ring of Fire." It is noted for its perfect conical shape; the base of the cone is 80 miles (130 km) in circumference.

Ring of Fire

— plate boundaries
● major volcanoes

◀ **The Hawai'ian volcanoes** lie in the center of a plate, not on a plate margin, and are known as intraplate volcanoes. They are associated with hot spots, whereby a plume of hot molten rock rises to the surface as the plate moves over it.

American Samoa and Samoa

American Samoa and Samoa are part of the island archipelago of Polynesia. The two most populous islands are Tutuila in American Samoa and 'Upolu in Samoa. Although the economies of both these states remain predominantly resource-based, both are expanding their light manufacturing sectors, and the US administration is the primary employer in American Samoa. Tuna fishing is particularly important: 25% of all tuna consumed in the US is processed and canned in Pago Pago.

▶ **Many of the** buildings in Samoa reflect the country's colonial past. Once a colony of New Zealand, Samoa is now an independent state; American Samoa remains an unincorporated territory of the United States.

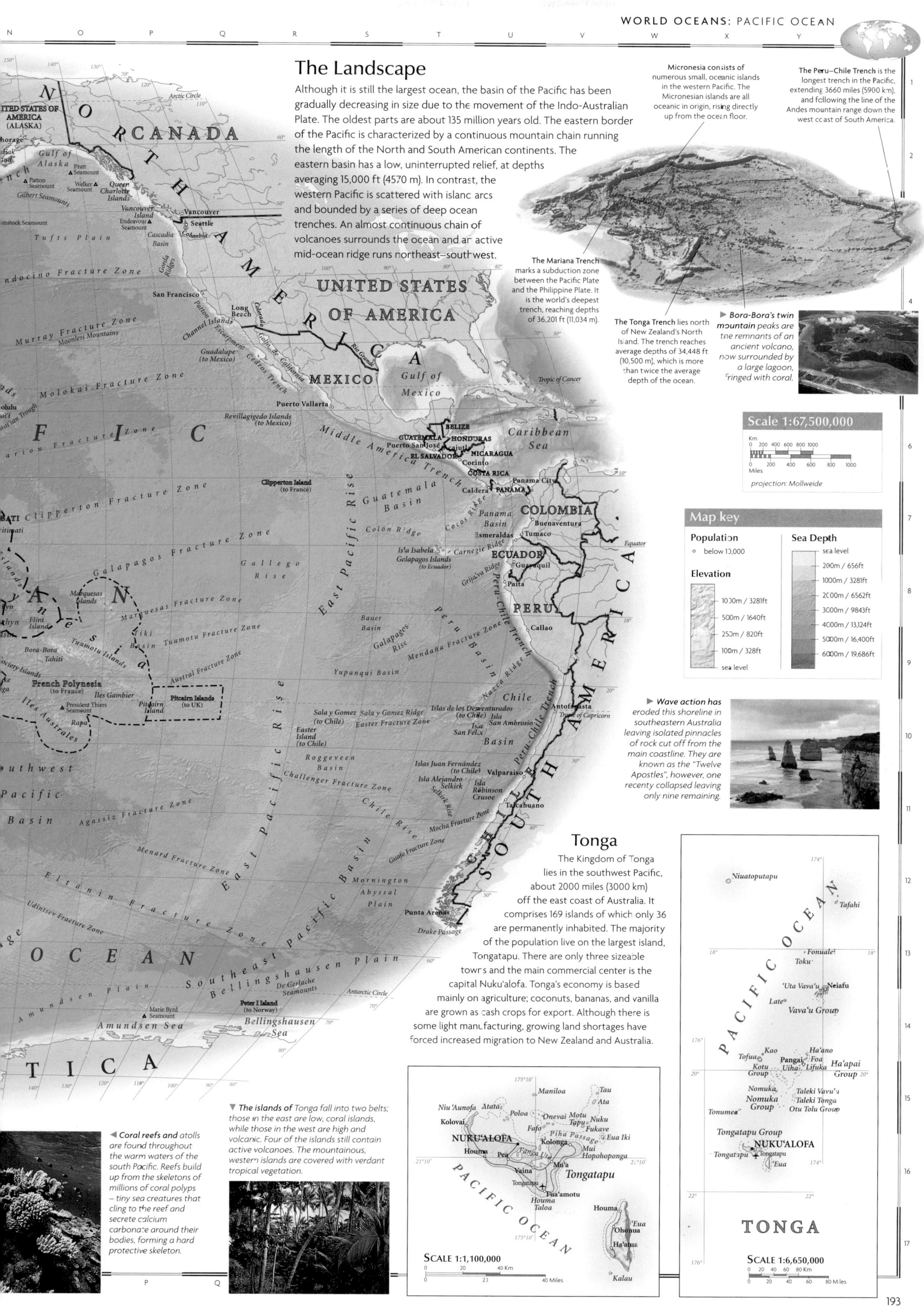

The Landscape

Although it is still the largest ocean, the basin of the Pacific has been gradually decreasing in size due to the movement of the Indo-Australian Plate. The oldest parts are about 135 million years old. The eastern border of the Pacific is characterized by a continuous mountain chain running the length of the North and South American continents. The eastern basin has a low, uninterrupted relief, at depths averaging 15,000 ft (4570 m). In contrast, the western Pacific is scattered with island arcs and bounded by a series of deep ocean trenches. An almost continuous chain of volcanoes surrounds the ocean and an active mid-ocean ridge runs northeast–southwest.

Micronesia consists of numerous small, oceanic islands in the western Pacific. The Micronesian islands are all oceanic in origin, rising directly up from the ocean floor.

The Peru–Chile Trench is the longest trench in the Pacific, extending 3660 miles (5900 km), and following the line of the Andes mountain range down the west coast of South America.

The Mariana Trench marks a subduction zone between the Pacific Plate and the Philippine Plate. It is the world's deepest trench, reaching depths of 36,201 ft (11,034 m).

The Tonga Trench lies north of New Zealand's North Island. The trench reaches average depths of 34,448 ft (10,500 m), which is more than twice the average depth of the ocean.

▶ **Bora-Bora's twin mountain** peaks are the remnants of an ancient volcano, now surrounded by a large lagoon, fringed with coral.

Scale 1:67,500,000

Km
0 200 400 600 800 1000

0   200   400   600   800   1000
Miles

projection: Mollweide

Map key

Population
○ below 10,000

Elevation
1000m / 3281ft
500m / 1640ft
250m / 820ft
100m / 328ft
sea level

Sea Depth
sea level
200m / 656ft
1000m / 3281ft
2000m / 6562ft
3000m / 9843ft
4000m / 13,124ft
5000m / 16,400ft
6000m / 19,686ft

▶ **Wave action has** eroded this shoreline in southeastern Australia leaving isolated pinnacles of rock cut off from the main coastline. They are known as the "Twelve Apostles", however, one recently collapsed leaving only nine remaining.

Tonga

The Kingdom of Tonga lies in the southwest Pacific, about 2000 miles (3000 km) off the east coast of Australia. It comprises 169 islands of which only 36 are permanently inhabited. The majority of the population live on the largest island, Tongatapu. There are only three sizeable towns and the main commercial center is the capital Nuku'alofa. Tonga's economy is based mainly on agriculture; coconuts, bananas, and vanilla are grown as cash crops for export. Although there is some light manufacturing, growing land shortages have forced increased migration to New Zealand and Australia.

◀ **Coral reefs and** atolls are found throughout the warm waters of the south Pacific. Reefs build up from the skeletons of millions of coral polyps – tiny sea creatures that cling to the reef and secrete calcium carbonate around their bodies, forming a hard protective skeleton.

▼ **The islands of** Tonga fall into two belts; those in the east are low, coral islands, while those in the west are high and volcanic. Four of the islands still contain active volcanoes. The mountainous, western islands are covered with verdant tropical vegetation.

SCALE 1:1,100,000

0   20   40 Km

0   20   40 Miles

SCALE 1:6,650,000

0 20 40 60 80 Km

0   20   40   60   80 Miles

TONGA

Antarctica

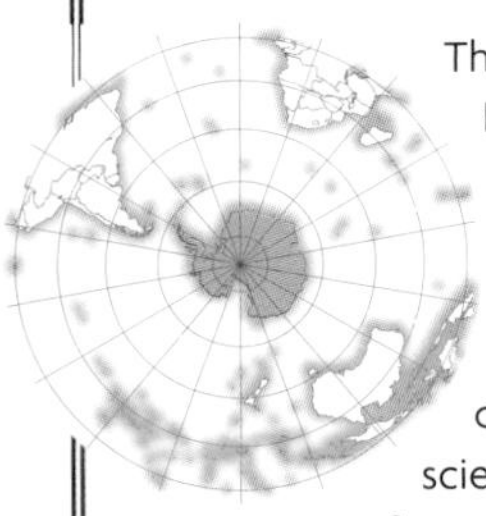

The ice-covered continent of Antarctica, which is the Earth's most southerly region, has drawn explorers and entrepreneurs seeking challenge and riches in its wintry lands for over 200 years. The extreme climate has deterred any large-scale settlement of the continent, and though commercial hunters built outposts in the past, habitation is now limited to scientific bases. The Antarctic Treaty, which came into force in 1961, provides for international governance and scientific cooperation in place of potential territorial conflict.

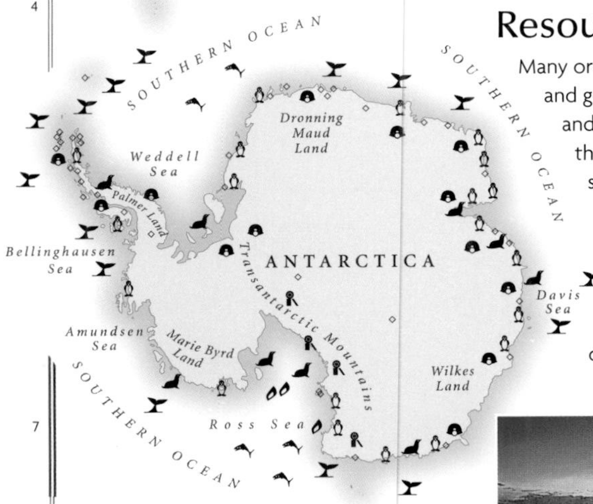

192

Resources

Many ore minerals, including iron and gold, are found in the Antarctic, and there are also coal reserves in the Transantarctic Mountains. The severe conditions and environmental importance of the region mean that exploitation of potential mineral resources is both uneconomic and undesirable. The unique wildlife and landscape draw a small number of tourists annually.

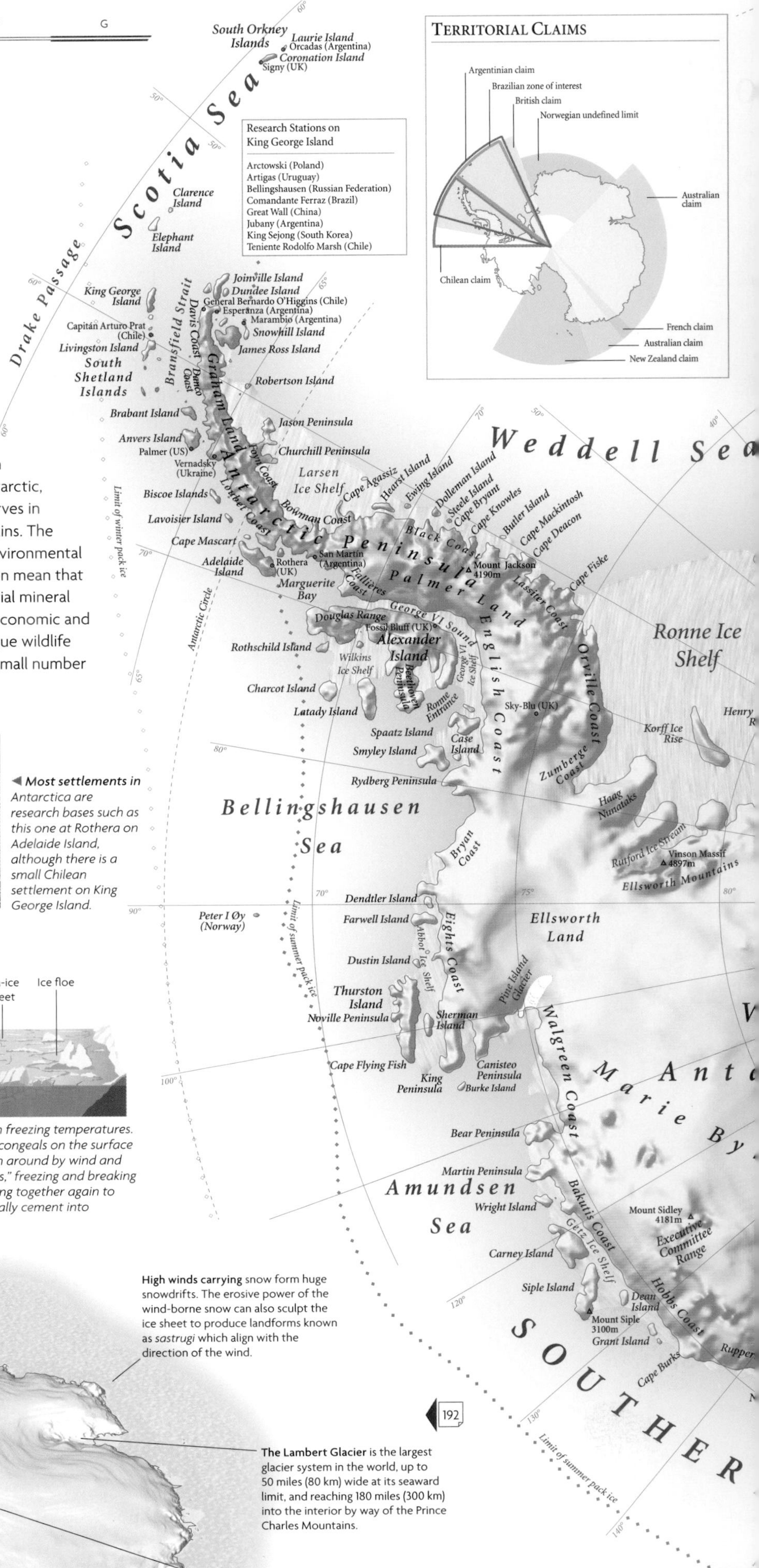

TERRITORIAL CLAIMS

Argentinian claim
Brazilian zone of interest
British claim
Norwegian undefined limit
Australian claim
Chilean claim
French claim
Australian claim
New Zealand claim

Research Stations on King George Island

Arctowski (Poland)
Artigas (Uruguay)
Bellingshausen (Russian Federation)
Comandante Ferraz (Brazil)
Great Wall (China)
Jubany (Argentina)
King Sejong (South Korea)
Teniente Rodolfo Marsh (Chile)

◄ *Most settlements in Antarctica are research bases such as this one at Rothera on Adelaide Island, although there is a small Chilean settlement on King George Island.*

The landscape

There are two distinct parts to Antarctica: West Antarctica, a series of ice-covered, mountainous islands, joined together by the ice, and the high plateau of East Antarctica. The Ross Sea and the Weddell Sea are outliers of the Southern Ocean – deep bays partially covered by thick ice shelves.

Grease ice · Pancake ice · Sea-ice sheet · Ice floe

◄ *On Elephant Island, the coast is edged by glaciers, although the land is not permanently covered by ice.*

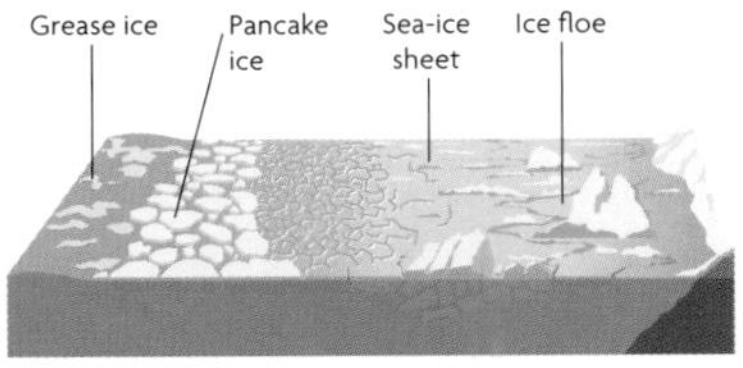

▲ *Pack ice forms out at sea in freezing temperatures. At the outer limits, grease ice congeals on the surface of the ocean. This is then spun around by wind and waves into irregular "pancakes," freezing and breaking up several times before bonding together again to form sea-ice sheets, which finally cement into enormous ice floes.*

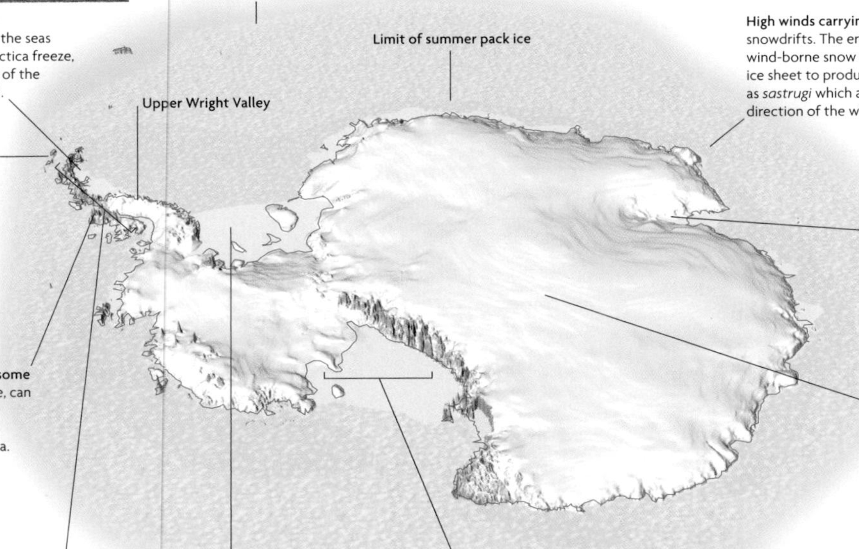

Limit of winter pack ice
Limit of summer pack ice
Upper Wright Valley
Elephant Island

During the winter the seas surrounding Antarctica freeze, increasing the size of the continent by 100%.

High winds carrying snow form huge snowdrifts. The erosive power of the wind-borne snow can also sculpt the ice sheet to produce landforms known as *sastrugi* which align with the direction of the wind.

Many volcanoes, some of them still active, can be found in the mountains of the Antarctic Peninsula.

The Lambert Glacier is the largest glacier system in the world, up to 50 miles (80 km) wide at its seaward limit, and reaching 180 miles (300 km) into the interior by way of the Prince Charles Mountains.

Antarctica is the highest continent on Earth, because of the great thickness of ice which overlays the land. In places the ice alone can each up to 15,700 ft (4800 m) thick. Much of the basement rock of west Antarctica lies below sea level, pushed down by the weight of the ice.

The mountainous Antarctic Peninsula is formed of rocks 65–225 million years old, overlain by more recent rocks and glacial deposits. It is connected to the Andes in South America by a submarine ridge.

Nearly half – 44% – of the Antarctic coastline is bounded by ice shelves, like the Ronne Ice Shelf, which float on the Ocean. These are joined to the inland ice sheet by dome-shaped ice "rises."

More than 30% of Antarctic ice is contained in the Ross Ice Shelf.

◄ *The barren, flat-bottomed Upper Wright Valley was once filled by a glacier, but is now dry, strewn with boulders and pebbles. In some dry valleys, there has been no rain for over 2 million years.*

▲ *Large colonies of seabirds live in the extremely harsh Antarctic climate. The Emperor penguins seen here, the smaller Adélie penguin, the Antarctic petrel, and the South Polar skua are the only birds that breed exclusively on the continent.*

Resources (including wildlife)
- coal
- fish
- minerals
- oil & gas
- penguins
- seals
- whales
- polar research base

◀ The sun sets over the Antarctic Peninsula for more than six months during the winter. However, there are more hours of sunshine during the brief Antarctic summer than most equatorial countries experience in a whole year.

▲ Immense, flat-topped icebergs are formed when blocks of ice break away from the main ice sheet. Though the exposed area is enormous, the volume of ice concealed beneath the water may be many times greater.

Scale 1:16,500,000

projection: Lambert Azimuthal Equal Area

A   B   C   D   E   F   G   H   I   J   K   L   M

The Arctic

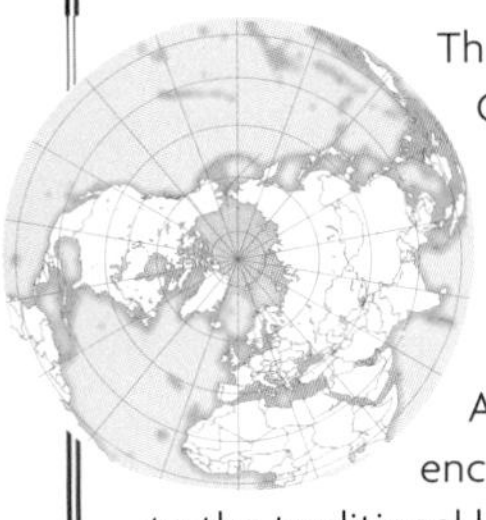

Three continents, Asia, North America, and Europe, reach into the Arctic Circle at their northernmost limits, almost entirely encircling the Arctic Ocean. Despite the region's extraordinarily harsh climate, it has been inhabited for thousands of years by peoples such as the European Lapps, the Russian Nenet, and the North American Inuit, who draw a living from fishing, herding, and hunting. More recently, particularly in the Russian Arctic, opportunities to exploit oil and other mineral reserves have encouraged immigration. Pollution of the Arctic's unique ecology and damage to the traditional lifestyles of many native peoples have been the unfortunate results of this activity, and international cooperation is needed to safeguard the future of the region.

Map key

Population
- ◼ above 5 million
- ◾ 1 million to 5 million
- ◉ 500,000 to 1 million
- ◎ 100,000 to 500,000
- ⊕ 50,000 to 100,000
- ○ 10,000 to 50,000
- ∘ below 10,000

Sea depth

	Sea level
	200m / 656ft
	1000m / 3281ft
	2000m / 6562ft
	3000m / 9843ft
	4000m / 13,124ft
	5000m / 16,400ft
	6000m / 19,686ft

Scale 1:23,500,000

Km 0 100 200 300 400 500 600
Miles 0 100 200 300 400 500 600

projection: Lambert Azimuthal Equal Area

▲ *Windblown snow etches deep patterns in the ice sheet known as sastrugi. They align with the direction of the wind*

Resources

Large quantities of coal, oil, and natural gas are to be found in the basins of the Arctic Ocean, and in northern Canada, Alaska, and the Russian Federation. The cost and difficulty of extraction and, more recently, awareness of damage to the environment, have limited exploitation to coastal regions. The unfrozen waters have stocks of fish including cod, flounder, and haddock. Quotas have now been put in place to restrict the number of fish caught annually. Reindeer are herded in large numbers by many of the native Arctic peoples. Most grain and vegetables are imported from elsewhere.

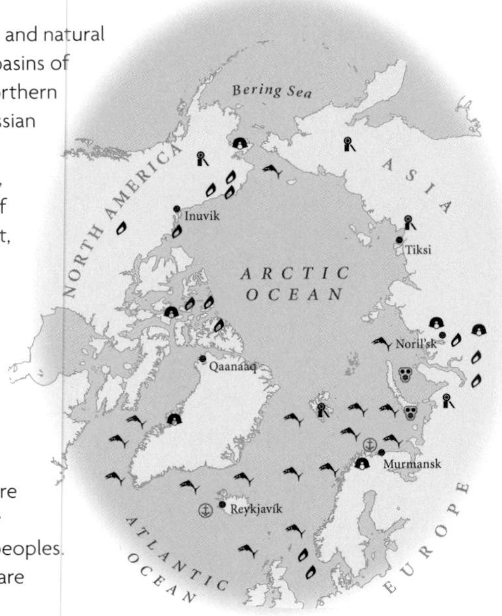

Bering Sea

NORTH AMERICA

ASIA

Inuvik

Tiksi

ARCTIC OCEAN

Noril'sk

Qaanaaq

Murmansk

Reykjavík

ATLANTIC OCEAN

EUROPE

▲ *Icebreakers are ships with specially strengthened hulls, designed to break a path through the ice. They are used to keep important routes open during the winter, when falling temperatures cause much of the Arctic Ocean to freeze over.*

Resources

- 🟥 coal
- fish
- mining
- 🔵 oil & gas
- ☢ radioactive contamination
- • major towns
- ⊕ major ports

The landscape

The Arctic Ocean comprises two large ocean basins divided by three submarine ridges, the greatest of which, the Lomonosov Ridge, is a huge underwater mountain range which has an average height of more than 10,000 ft (3000 m). The lands which encircle the Arctic Ocean are underlain by great shield areas of ancient rocks, which were heavily glaciated during the last Ice Age.

◀ *Icebergs are constantly broken up and reshaped by wind and the oceans. This flat-topped iceberg has been undercut, leaving a craggy ice cliff.*

The Canadian Shield underlies almost all of the Canadian Arctic. It is a very stable plateau of ancient rock, now covered by glacial lakes and sediment, which supports tundra vegetation.

The Arctic Ocean is the world's smallest ocean with a total area of 5,440,000 sq miles (15,100,000 sq km).

At a latitude of more than 75° N, the Arctic Ocean is almost permanently covered by pack ice, though high winds and the movement of the seas may cause the ice to crack and break up.

In the more southerly reaches of the Arctic, like Siberia, much of the land is covered by permafrost. In the summer, higher temperatures warm the frozen ground, causing a number of typical phenomena. These include solifluction, the fast downhill movement of top soil layers; freeze/thaw activity, which patterns the ground into regular polygonal shapes, and the formation of large domes with a frozen ice core, known as pingos.

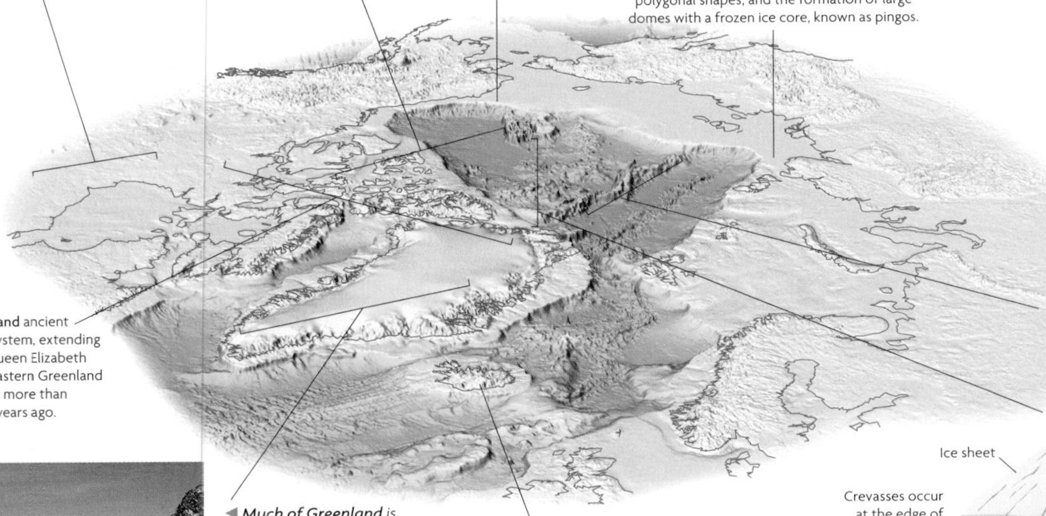

A complex and ancient mountain system, extending from the Queen Elizabeth Islands to eastern Greenland was formed more than 245 million years ago.

◀ *Much of Greenland is covered by a massive ice sheet more than 650,000 sq miles (1,683,400 sq km) in extent. The weight of the ice has depressed the central land area to form a basin lying more than 1000 ft (300 m) below sea level. Only at the edges of the island is bare rock visible.*

Iceland has five major glaciers, sustained by heavy snowfall. Parts of the ice cap cover active volcanoes, such as Bárdharbunga, which periodically erupt causing the melted ice to form a great lake at the glacier margins.

Lomonosov Ridge

Arctic ice shelf

Ice sheet

Crevasses occur at the edge of the ice sheet

Iceberg

Sea water melts the edge of the ice sheet

▲ *At the boundary of the Arctic ice shelves, sea water flows under the ice causing melting and forming crevasses on the surface. This eventually weakens blocks of ice which break away as icebergs. This process is known as calving.*

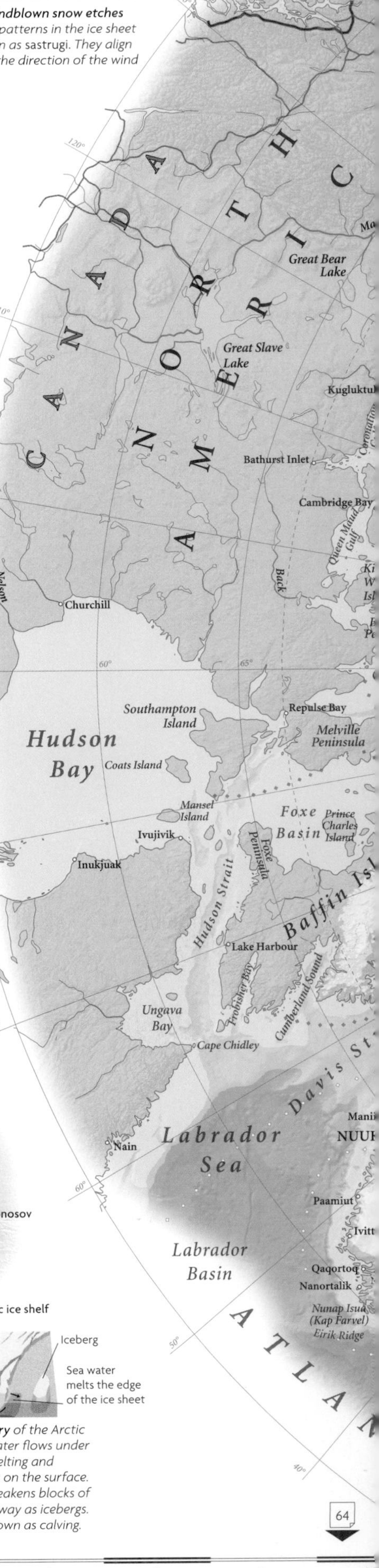

Map place names (right side)

NORTH AMERICA

CANADA

Great Bear Lake

Great Slave Lake

Kugluktuk

Bathurst Inlet

Cambridge Bay

Nelson

Buck

Churchill

Repulse Bay

Southampton Island

Melville Peninsula

Hudson Bay

Coats Island

Mansel Island

Foxe Basin

Prince Charles Island

Ivujivik

Inukjuak

Hudson Strait

Baffin Is

Lake Harbour

Cumberland Sound

Ungava Bay

Cape Chidley

Davis St

Nain

Labrador Sea

Manii

NUU

Paamiut

Labrador Basin

Ivitt

Qaqortoq

Nanortalik

Numap Isua (Kap Farvel)

Eirik Ridge

ATLAN

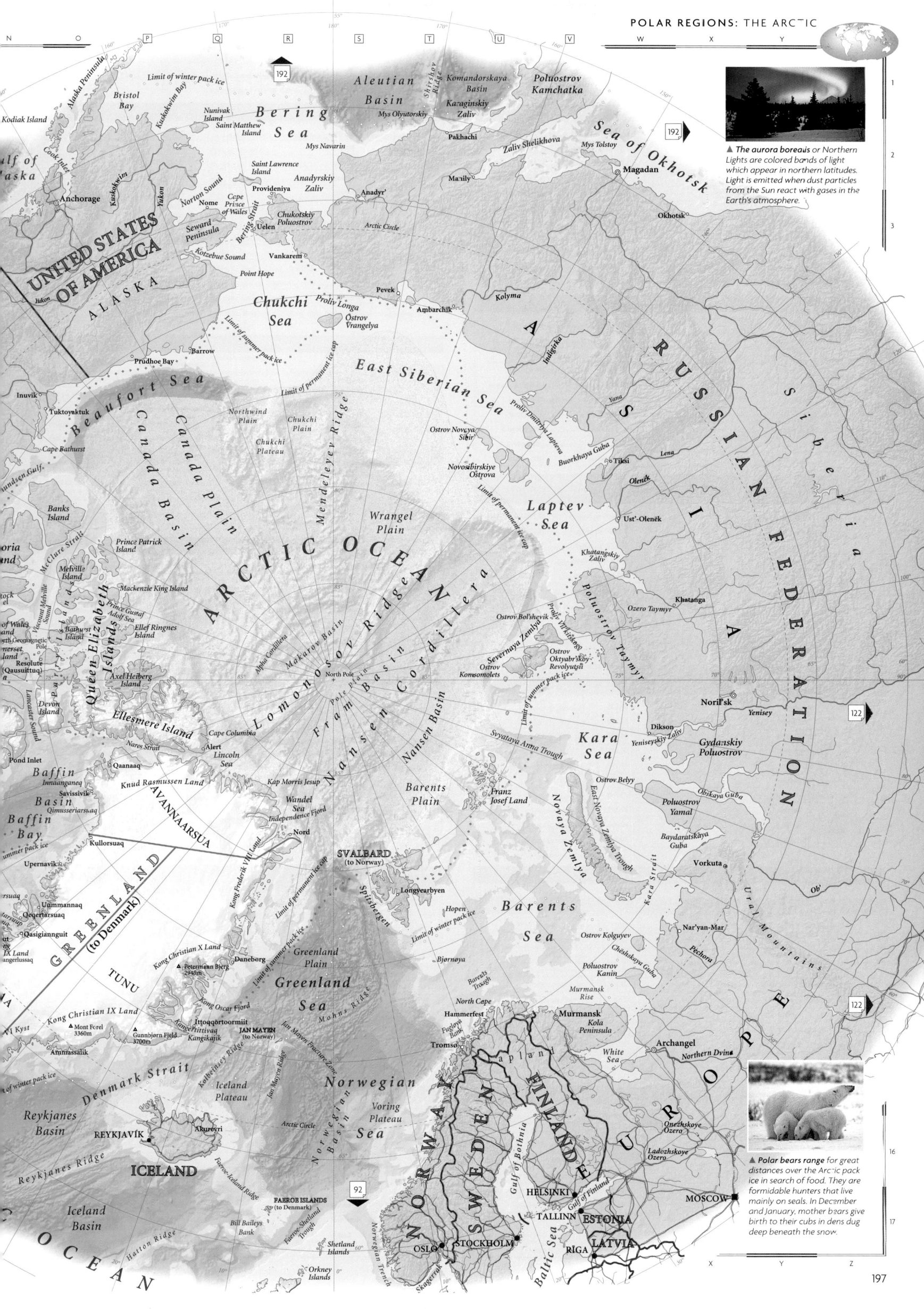

▲ **The aurora borealis** or Northern Lights are colored bands of light which appear in northern latitudes. Light is emitted when dust particles from the Sun react with gases in the Earth's atmosphere.

▲ **Polar bears range** for great distances over the Arctic pack ice in search of food. They are formidable hunters that live mainly on seals. In December and January, mother bears give birth to their cubs in dens dug deep beneath the snow.

The time zones

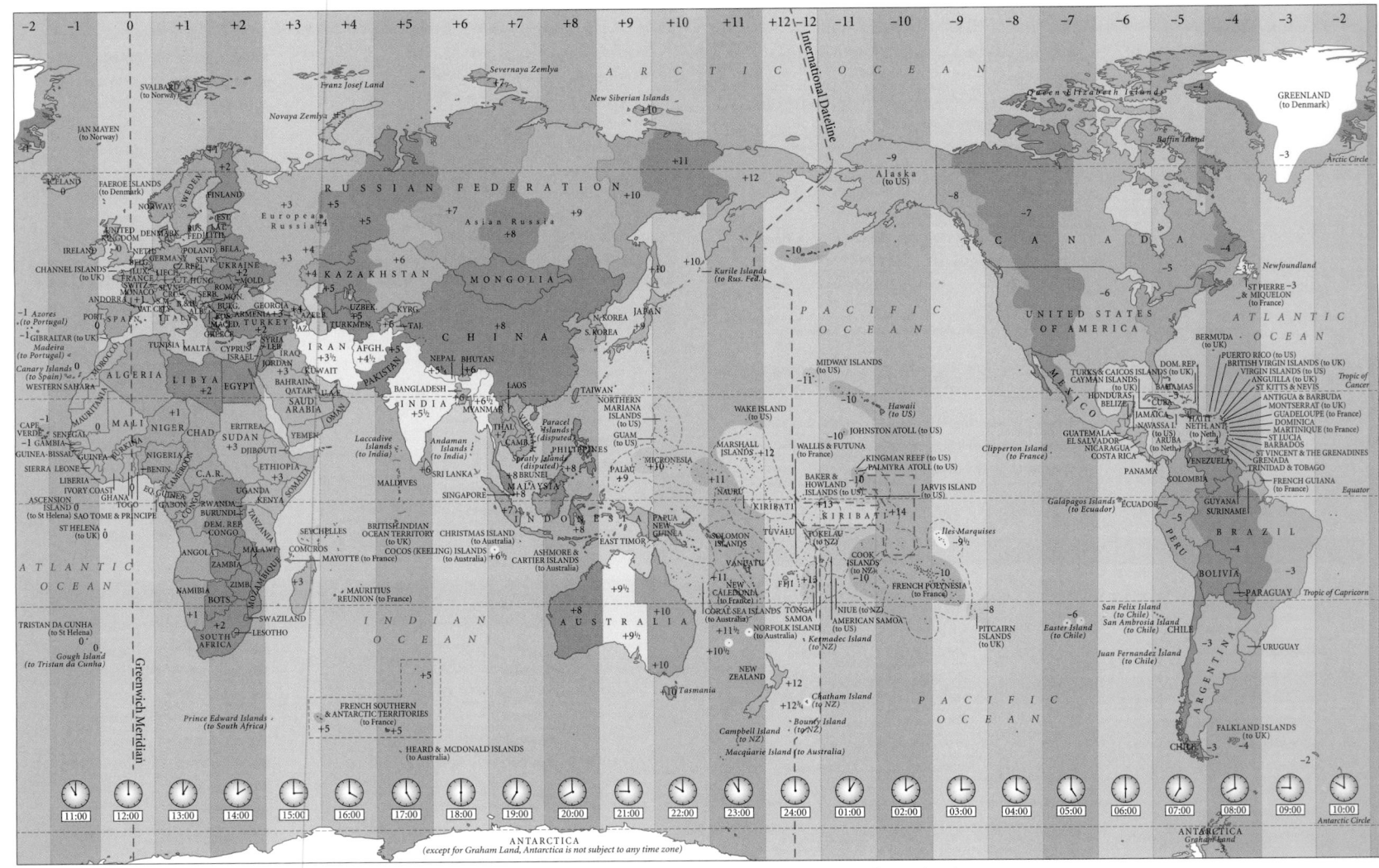

The numbers at the top of the map indicate the number of hours each time zone is ahead or behind Coordinated Universal Time (UTC).
The clocks and 24-hour times given at the bottom of the map show the time in each time zone when it is 12:00 hours noon (UTC)

Time Zones

Because Earth is a rotating sphere, the Sun shines on only half of its surface at any one time. Thus, it is simultaneously morning, evening and night time in different parts of the world *(see diagram below).* Because of these disparities, each country or part of a country adheres to a local time.

A region of Earth's surface within which a single local time is used is called a time zone. There are 24 one hour time zones around the world, arranged roughly in longitudinal bands.

Standard Time

Standard time is the official local time in a particular country or part of a country. It is defined by the

Day and night around the world

time zone or zones associated with that country or region. Although time zones are arranged roughly in longitudinal bands, in many places the borders of a zone do not fall exactly on longitudinal meridians, as can be seen on the map *(above),* but are determined by geographical factors or by borders between countries or parts of countries. Most countries have just one time zone and one standard time, but some large countries (such as the US, Canada, and Russia) are split between several time zones, so standard time varies across those countries. For example, the coterminous United States straddles four time zones and so has four standard times, called the Eastern, Central, Mountain, and Pacific standard times. China is unusual in that just one standard time is used for the whole country, even though it extends across 60° of longitude from west to east.

Coordinated Universal Time (UTC)

Coordinated Universal Time (UTC) is a reference by which the local time in each time zone is set. For example, Australian Western Standard Time (the local time in Western Australia) is set 8 hours ahead of UTC (it is

UTC+8) whereas Eastern Standard Time in the United States is set 5 hours behind UTC (it is UTC-5). UTC is a successor to, and closely approximates, Greenwich Mean Time (GMT). However, UTC is based on an atomic clock, whereas GMT is determined by the Sun's position in the sky relative to the 0° longitudinal meridian, which runs through Greenwich, UK.

The International Dateline

The International Dateline is an imaginary line from pole to pole that roughly corresponds to the 180° longitudinal meridian. It is an arbitrary marker between calendar days. The dateline is needed because of the use of local times around the world rather than a single universal time. When moving from west to east across the dateline, travelers have to set their watches back one day. Those traveling in the opposite direction, from east to west, must add a day.

Daylight Saving Time

Daylight saving is a summertime adjustment to the local time in a country or region, designed to cause a higher proportion of its citizens' waking hours to pass during daylight. To follow the system, timepieces are advanced by an hour on a pre-decided date in spring and reverted back in the fall. About half of the world's nations use daylight saving.

Countries of the World

There are currently 195 independent countries in the world – more than at any previous time – and 59 dependencies. Antarctica is the only land area on Earth that is not officially part of, and does not belong to, any single country.

In 1950, the world comprised 82 countries. In the decades following, many more states came into being as they achieved independence from their former colonial rulers. Most recent additions were caused by the breakup of the former Soviet Union in 1991, and the former Yugoslavia in 1992, which swelled the ranks of independent states. In February 2008, Kosovo became the latest country to be formed by controversially declaring independence from Serbia.

Country factfile key

Formation Date of independence / date current borders were established

Population Total population / population density – based on total *land* area / percentage of urban-based population

Languages An asterisk (*) denotes the official language(s)

Calorie consumption Average number of calories consumed daily per person

AFGHANISTAN
Central Asia

Official name The Islamic Republic of Afghanistan
Formation 1919 / 1919
Capital Kabul
Population 32.3 million / 128 people per sq mile (50 people per sq km) / 24%
Total area 250,000 sq. miles (647,500 sq. km)
Languages Pashtu*, Tajik, Dari*, Farsi, Uzbek, Turkmen
Religions Sunni Muslim 84%, Shi'a Muslim 15%, Other 1%
Ethnic mix Pashtun 38%, Tajik 25%, Hazara 19%, Uzbek and Turkmen 15%, Other 3%
Government Presidential system
Currency Afghani = 100 puls
Literacy rate 28%
Calorie consumption 1539 calories

ALBANIA
Southeast Europe

Official name Republic of Albania
Formation 1912 / 1921
Capital Tirana
Population 3.2 million / 302 people per sq mile (117 people per sq km) / 44%
Total area 11,100 sq. miles (28,748 sq. km)
Languages Albanian*, Greek
Religions Sunni Muslim 70%, Orthodox Christian 20%, Roman Catholic 10%
Ethnic mix Albanian 93%, Greek 5%, Other 2%
Government Parliamentary system
Currency Lek = 100 qindarka (qintars)
Literacy rate 99%
Calorie consumption 2848 calories

ALGERIA
North Africa

Official name People's Democratic Republic of Algeria
Formation 1962 / 1962
Capital Algiers
Population 33.9 million / 37 people per sq mile (14 people per sq km) / 59%
Total area 919,590 sq. miles (2,381,740 sq. km)
Languages Arabic*, Tamazight (Kabyle, Shawia, Tamashek), French
Religions Sunni Muslim 99%, Christian and Jewish 1%
Ethnic mix Arab 75%, Berber 24%, European and Jewish 1%
Government Presidential system
Currency Algerian dinar = 100 centimes
Literacy rate 70%
Calorie consumption 3022 calories

ANDORRA
Southwest Europe

Official name Principality of Andorra
Formation 1278 / 1278
Capital Andorra la Vella
Population 71,822 / 399 people per sq mile (154 people per sq km) / 91%
Total area 181 sq. miles (468 sq. km)
Languages Spanish, Catalan*, French, Portuguese
Religions Roman Catholic 94%, Other 6%
Ethnic mix Spanish 46%, Andorran 28%, Other 18%, French 8%
Government Parliamentary system
Currency Euro = 100 cents
Literacy rate 99%
Calorie consumption Not available

ANGOLA
Southern Africa

Official name Republic of Angola
Formation 1975 / 1975
Capital Luanda
Population 16.9 million / 35 people per sq mile (14 people per sq km) / 36%
Total area 481,351 sq. miles (1,246,700 sq. km)
Languages Portuguese*, Umbundu, Kimbundu, Kikongo
Religions Roman Catholic 50%, Other 30%, Protestant 20%
Ethnic mix Ovimbundu 37%, Other 25%, Kimbundu 25%, Bakongo 13%
Government Presidential system
Currency Readjusted kwanza = 100 lwei
Literacy rate 67%
Calorie consumption 2083 calories

ANTIGUA & BARBUDA
West Indies

Official name Antigua and Barbuda
Formation 1981 / 1981
Capital St. John's
Population 69,481 / 409 people per sq mile (158 people per sq km) / 38%
Total area 170 sq. miles (442 sq. km)
Languages English*, English patois
Religions Anglican 45%, Other Protestant 42%, Roman Catholic 10%, Other 2%, Rastafarian 1%
Ethnic mix Black African 95%, Other 5%
Government Parliamentary system
Currency Eastern Caribbean dollar = 100 cents
Literacy rate 86%
Calorie consumption 2349 calories

ARGENTINA
South America

Official name The Argentine Republic
Formation 1816 / 1816
Capital Buenos Aires
Population 39.5 million / 37 people per sq mile (14 people per sq km) / 90%
Total area 1,058,296 sq. miles (2,766,890 sq. km)
Languages Spanish*, Italian, Amerindian languages
Religions Roman Catholic 90%, Other 6%, Protestant 2%, Jewish 2%
Ethnic mix Indo-European 83%, Mestizo 14%, Jewish 2%, Amerindian 1%
Government Presidential system
Currency new Argentine peso = 100 centavos
Literacy rate 97%
Calorie consumption 2992 calories

ARMENIA
Southwest Asia

Official name Republic of Armenia
Formation 1991 / 1991
Capital Yerevan
Population 3 million / 261 people per sq mile (101 people per sq km) / 64%
Total area 11,506 sq. miles (29,800 sq. km)
Languages Armenian*, Azeri, Russian
Religions Armenian Apostolic Church (Orthodox) 88%, Other 6%, Armenian Catholic Church 6%
Ethnic mix Armenian 98%, Other 1%, Yezidi 1%
Government Parliamentary system
Currency Dram = 100 luma
Literacy rate 99%
Calorie consumption 2268 calories

AUSTRALIA
Australasia & Oceania

Official name Commonwealth of Australia
Formation 1901 / 1901
Capital Canberra
Population 20.9 million / 7 people per sq mile (3 people per sq km) / 92%
Total area 2,967,893 sq. miles (7,686,850 sq. km)
Languages English*, Italian, Cantonese, Greek, Arabic, Vietnamese, Aboriginal languages
Religions Roman Catholic 26%, Anglican 24%, Other 23%, Nonreligious 13%, United Church 8%, Other Protestant 6%
Ethnic mix European 92%, Asian 5%, Aboriginal 2%, Other 1%
Government Parliamentary system
Currency Australian dollar = 100 cents
Literacy rate 99%
Calorie consumption 3054 calories

AUSTRIA
Central Europe

Official name Republic of Austria
Formation 1918 / 1919
Capital Vienna
Population 8.2 million / 257 people per sq mile (99 people per sq km) / 66%
Total area 32,378 sq. miles (83,858 sq. km)
Languages German*, Croatian, Slovenian, Hungarian (Magyar)
Religions Roman Catholic 78%, Nonreligious 9%, Other (including Jewish and Muslim) 8%, Protestant 5%
Ethnic mix Austrian 93%, Croat, Slovene, and Hungarian 6%, Other 1%
Government Parliamentary system
Currency Euro = 100 cents
Literacy rate 99%
Calorie consumption 3673 calories

AZERBAIJAN
Southwest Asia

Official name Republic of Azerbaijan
Formation 1991 / 1991
Capital Baku
Population 8.5 million / 254 people per sq mile (98 people per sq km) / 50%
Total area 33,436 sq. miles (86,600 sq. km)
Languages Azeri*, Russian
Religions Shi'a Muslim 68%, Sunni Muslim 26%, Russian Orthodox 3%, Armenian Apostolic Church (Orthodox) 2%, Other 1%
Ethnic mix Azeri 91%, Other 3%, Lazs 2%, Armenian 2%, Russian 2%
Government Presidential system
Currency New manat = 100 gopik
Literacy rate 99%
Calorie consumption 2575 calories

BAHAMAS
West Indies

Official name Commonwealth of the Bahamas
Formation 1973 / 1973
Capital Nassau
Population 305,655 / 79 people per sq mile (31 people per sq km) / 90%
Total area 5382 sq. miles (13,940 sq. km)
Languages English*, English Creole, French Creole
Religions Baptist 32%, Anglican 20%, Roman Catholic 19%, Other 17%, Methodist 6%, Church of God 6%
Ethnic mix Black African 85%, Other 15%
Government Parliamentary system
Currency Bahamian dollar = 100 cents
Literacy rate 96%
Calorie consumption 2755 calories

BAHRAIN
Southwest Asia

Official name Kingdom of Bahrain
Formation 1971 / 1971
Capital Manama
Population 708,573 / 2596 people per sq mile (1004 people per sq km) / 90%
Total area 239 sq. miles (620 sq. km)
Languages Arabic
Religions Muslim (mainly Shi'a) 99%, Other 1%
Ethnic mix Bahraini 70%, Iranian, Indian, and Pakistani 24%, Other Arab 4%, European 2%
Government Mixed monarchical–parliamentary system
Currency Bahraini dinar = 1000 fils
Literacy rate 87%
Calorie consumption Not available

BANGLADESH
South Asia

Official name People's Republic of Bangladesh
Formation 1971 / 1971
Capital Dhaka
Population 147 million / 2845 people per sq mile (1098 people per sq km) / 25%
Total area 55,598 sq. miles (144,000 sq. km)
Languages Bengali*, Urdu, Chakma, Marma (Magh), Garo, Khasi, Santhali, Tripuri, Mro
Religions Muslim (mainly Sunni) 87%, Hindu 12%, Other 1%
Ethnic mix Bengali 98%, Other 2%
Government Transitional regime
Currency Taka = 100 poisha
Literacy rate 41%
Calorie consumption 2205 calories

BARBADOS
West Indies

Official name Barbados
Formation 1966 / 1966
Capital Bridgetown
Population 280,946 / 1692 people per sq mile (653 people per sq km) / 52%
Total area 166 sq. miles (430 sq. km)
Languages English*, Bajan (Barbadian English)
Religions Anglican 40%, Other 24%, Nonreligious 17%, Pentecostal 8%, Methodist 7%, Roman Catholic 4%
Ethnic mix Black African 92%, White 3%, Other 3%, Mixed race 2%
Government Parliamentary system
Currency Barbados dollar = 100 cents
Literacy rate 99%
Calorie consumption 3091 calories

BELARUS
Eastern Europe

Official name Republic of Belarus
Formation 1991 / 1991
Capital Minsk
Population 9.6 million / 120 people per sq mile (46 people per sq km) / 71%
Total area 80,154 sq. miles (207,600 sq. km)
Languages Belorussian*, Russian*
Religions Orthodox Christian 60%, Other 32%, Roman Catholic 8%
Ethnic mix Belorussian 81%, Russian 11%, Polish 4%, Other 2%, Ukrainian 2%
Government Presidential system
Currency Belorussian rouble = 100 kopeks
Literacy rate 99%
Calorie consumption 3000 calories

BELGIUM
Northwest Europe

Official name Kingdom of Belgium
Formation 1830 / 1919
Capital Brussels
Population 10.5 million / 829 people per sq mile (320 people per sq km) / 97%
Total area 11,780 sq. miles (30,510 sq. km)
Languages Dutch*, French*, German*
Religions Roman Catholic 88%, Other 10%, Muslim 2%
Ethnic mix Fleming 58%, Walloon 33%, Other 6%, Italian 2%, Moroccan 1%
Government Parliamentary system
Currency Euro = 100 cents
Literacy rate 99%
Calorie consumption 3584 calories

BELIZE
Central America

Official name Belize
Formation 1981 / 1981
Capital Belmopan
Population 294,385 / 33 people per sq mile (13 people per sq km) / 48%
Total area 8867 sq. miles (22,966 sq. km)
Languages English*, English Creole, Spanish, Mayan, Garifuna (Carib)
Religions Roman Catholic 62%, Other 13%, Anglican 12%, Methodist 6%, Mennonite 4%, Seventh-day Adventist 3%
Ethnic mix Mestizo 49%, Creole 25%, Maya 11%, Other 6%, Garifuna 6%, Asian Indian 3%
Government Parliamentary system
Currency Belizean dollar = 100 cents
Literacy rate 75%
Calorie consumption 2869 calories

BENIN
West Africa

Official name Republic of Benin
Formation 1960 / 1960
Capital Porto-Novo
Population 9 million / 211 people per sq mile (81 people per sq km) / 45%
Total area 43,483 sq. miles (112,620 sq. km)
Languages French*, Fon, Bariba, Yoruba, Adja, Houeda, Somba
Religions Voodoo 50%, Muslim 30%, Christian 20%
Ethnic mix Fon 41%, Other 21%, Adja 16%, Yoruba 12%, Bariba 10%
Government Presidential system
Currency CFA franc = 100 centimes
Literacy rate 35%
Calorie consumption 2548 calories

BHUTAN
South Asia

Official name Kingdom of Bhutan
Formation 1656 / 1865
Capital Thimphu
Population 2.3 million / 127 people per sq mile (49 people per sq km) / 9%
Total area 18,147 sq. miles (47,000 sq. km)
Languages Dzongkha*, Nepali, Assamese
Religions Mahayana Buddhist 70%, Hindu 24%, Other 6%
Ethnic mix Bhute 50%, Other 25%, Nepalese 25%
Government Mixed monarchical–parliamentary system
Currency Ngultrum = 100 chetrum
Literacy rate 47%
Calorie consumption Not available

BOLIVIA
South America

Official name Republic of Bolivia
Formation 1825 / 1938
Capital La Paz (administrative); Sucre (judicial)
Population 9.5 million / 23 people per sq mile (9 people per sq km) / 64%
Total area 424,162 sq. miles (1,098,580 sq. km)
Languages Aymara*, Quechua*, Spanish*
Religions Roman Catholic 93%, Other 7%
Ethnic mix Quechua 37%, Aymara 32%, Mixed race 13%, European 10%, Other 8%
Government Presidential system
Currency Boliviano = 100 centavos
Literacy rate 87%
Calorie consumption 2235 calories

BOSNIA & HERZEGOVINA
Southeast Europe

Official name Bosnia and Herzegovina
Formation 1992 / 1992
Capital Sarajevo
Population 3.9 million / 198 people per sq mile (76 people per sq km) / 45%
Total area 19,741 sq. miles (51,129 sq. km)
Languages Bosnian*, Croatian*, Serbian*
Religions Muslim (mainly Sunni) 40%, Orthodox Christian 31%, Roman Catholic 15%, Other 10%, Protestant 4%
Ethnic mix Bosniak 44%, Serb 31%, Croat 17%, Other 8%
Government Parliamentary system
Currency Marka = 100 pfeninga
Literacy rate 97%
Calorie consumption 2894 calories

BOTSWANA
Southern Africa

Official name Republic of Botswana
Formation 1966 / 1966
Capital Gaborone
Population 1.8 million / 8 people per sq mile (3 people per sq km) / 52%
Total area 231,803 sq. miles (600,370 sq. km)
Languages English*, Setswana, Shona, San, Khoikhoi, isiNdebele
Religions Traditional beliefs 50%, Christian (mainly Protestant) 30%, Other (including Muslim) 20%
Ethnic mix Tswana 98%, Other 2%
Government Presidential system
Currency Pula = 100 thebe
Literacy rate 81%
Calorie consumption 2151 calories

BRAZIL
South America

Official name Federative Republic of Brazil
Formation 1822 / 1828
Capital Brasília
Population 191 million / 59 people per sq mile (23 people per sq km) / 84%
Total area 3,286,470 sq. miles (8,511,965 sq. km)
Languages Portuguese*, German, Italian, Spanish, Polish, Japanese, Amerindian languages
Religions Roman Catholic 74%, Protestant 15%, Atheist 7%, Other 4%
Ethnic mix White 54%, Mixed race 38%, Black 6%, Other 2%
Government Presidential system
Currency Real = 100 centavos
Literacy rate 89%
Calorie consumption 3049 calories

BRUNEI
Southeast Asia

Official name Brunei Darussalam
Formation 1984 / 1984
Capital Bandar Seri Begawan
Population 374,577 / 184 people per sq mile (71 people per sq km) / 77%
Total area 2228 sq. miles (5770 sq. km)
Languages Malay*, English, Chinese
Religions Muslim (mainly Sunni) 66%, Buddhist 14%, Other 10%, Christian 10%
Ethnic mix Malay 67%, Chinese 16%, Other 11%, Indigenous 6%
Government Monarchy
Currency Brunei dollar = 100 cents
Literacy rate 93%
Calorie consumption 2855 calories

BULGARIA
Southeast Europe

Official name Republic of Bulgaria
Formation 1908 / 1947
Capital Sofia
Population 7.6 million / 178 people per sq mile (69 people per sq km) / 70%
Total area 42,822 sq. miles (110,910 sq. km)
Languages Bulgarian*, Turkish, Romani
Religions Orthodox Christian 83%, Muslim 12%, Other 4%, Roman Catholic 1%
Ethnic mix Bulgarian 84%, Turkish 9%, Roma 5%, Other 2%
Government Parliamentary system
Currency Lev = 100 stotinki
Literacy rate 98%
Calorie consumption 2848 calories

BURKINA
West Africa

Official name Burkina Faso
Formation 1960 / 1960
Capital Ouagadougou
Population 14 million / 132 people per sq mile (51 people per sq km) / 18%
Total area 105,869 sq. miles (274,200 sq. km)
Languages French*, Mossi, Fulani, Tuareg, Dyula, Songhai
Religions Muslim 55%, Traditional beliefs 35%, Roman Catholic 9%, Other Christian 1%
Ethnic mix Mossi 48%, Other 21%, Peul 10%, Lobi 7%, Bobo 7%, Mandé 7%
Government Presidential system
Currency CFA franc = 100 centimes
Literacy rate 22%
Calorie consumption 2462 calories

BURUNDI
Central Africa

Official name Republic of Burundi
Formation 1962 / 1962
Capital Bujumbura
Population 8.1 million / 818 people per sq mile (316 people per sq km) / 10%
Total area 10,745 sq. miles (27,830 sq. km)
Languages Kirundi*, French*, Kiswahili
Religions Christian (mainly Roman Catholic) 60%, Traditional beliefs 39%, Muslim 1%
Ethnic mix Hutu 85%, Tutsi 14%, Twa 1%
Government Presidential system
Currency Burundian franc = 100 centimes
Literacy rate 59%
Calorie consumption 1649 calories

CAMBODIA
Southeast Asia

Official name Kingdom of Cambodia
Formation 1953 / 1953
Capital Phnom Penh
Population 14.6 million / 214 people per sq mile (83 people per sq km) / 19%
Total area 69,900 sq. miles (181,040 sq. km)
Languages Khmer*, French, Chinese, Vietnamese, Cham
Religions Buddhist 93%, Muslim 6%, Christian 1%
Ethnic mix Khmer 90%, Other 5%, Vietnamese 4%, Chinese 1%
Government Parliamentary system
Currency Riel = 100 sen
Literacy rate 74%
Calorie consumption 2046 calories

CAMEROON
Central Africa

Official name Republic of Cameroon
Formation 1960 / 1961
Capital Yaoundé
Population 16.3 million / 94 people per sq mile (36 people per sq km) / 52%
Total area 183,567 sq. miles (475,400 sq. km)
Languages English*, French*, Bamileke, Fang, Fulani
Religions Roman Catholic 35%, Traditional beliefs 25%, Muslim 22%, Protestant 18%
Ethnic mix Cameroon highlanders 31%, Other 21%, Equatorial Bantu 19%, Kirdi 11%, Fulani 10%, Northwestern Bantu 8%
Government Presidential system
Currency CFA franc = 100 centimes
Literacy rate 68%
Calorie consumption 2273 calories

CANADA
North America

Official name Canada
Formation 1867 / 1949
Capital Ottawa
Population 32.9 million / 9 people per sq mile (4 people per sq km) / 81%
Total area 3,854,085 sq. miles (9,984,670 sq. km)
Languages English*, French*, Chinese, Italian, German, Ukrainian, Portuguese, Inuktitut, Cree
Religions Roman Catholic 44%, Protestant 29%, Other and nonreligious 27%
Government Parliamentary system
Currency Canadian dollar = 100 cents
Literacy rate 99%
Calorie consumption 3589 calories

CAPE VERDE
Atlantic Ocean

Official name Republic of Cape Verde
Formation 1975 / 1975
Capital Praia
Population 423,613 / 272 people per sq mile (105 people per sq km) / 57%
Total area 1557 sq. miles (4033 sq. km)
Languages Portuguese*, Portuguese Creole
Religions Roman Catholic 97%, Other 2%, Protestant (Church of the Nazarene) 1%
Ethnic mix Mestiço 60%, African 30%, Other 10%
Government Mixed presidential–parliamentary system
Currency Cape Verde escudo = 100 centavos
Literacy rate 76%
Calorie consumption 3243 calories

CENTRAL AFRICAN REPUBLIC
Central Africa

Official name Central African Republic
Formation 1960 / 1960
Capital Bangui
Population 4.2 million / 17 people per sq mile (7 people per sq km) / 43%
Total area 240,534 sq. miles (622,984 sq. km)
Languages French*, Sango, Banda, Gbaya
Religions Traditional beliefs 60%, Christian (mainly Roman Catholic) 35%, Muslim 5%
Ethnic mix Baya 34%, Banda 27%, Mandjia 21%, Sara 10%, Other 8%
Government Presidential system
Currency CFA franc = 100 centimes
Literacy rate 49%
Calorie consumption 1980 calories

CHAD
Central Africa

Official name Republic of Chad
Formation 1960 / 1960
Capital N'Djamena
Population 10.3 million / 21 people per sq mile (8 people per sq km) / 25%
Total area 495,752 sq. miles (1,284,000 sq. km)
Languages Arabic*, French*, Sara, Maba
Religions Muslim 55%, Traditional beliefs 35%, Christian 10%
Ethnic mix Other 30%, Sara 28%, Mayo-Kebbi 12%, Arab 12%, Ouaddai 9%, Kanem-Bornou 9%
Government Presidential system
Currency CFA franc = 100 centimes
Literacy rate 26%
Calorie consumption 2114 calories

CHILE
South America

Official name Republic of Chile
Formation 1818 / 1883
Capital Santiago
Population 16.6 million / 57 people per sq mile (22 people per sq km) / 87%
Total area 292,258 sq. miles (756,950 sq. km)
Languages Spanish*, Amerindian languages
Religions Roman Catholic 80%, Other and nonreligious 20%
Ethnic mix Mixed race and European 90%, Other Amerindian 9%, Mapuche 1%
Government Presidential system
Currency Chilean peso = 100 centavos
Literacy rate 96%
Calorie consumption 2863 calories

CHINA
East Asia

Official name People's Republic of China
Formation 960 / 1999
Capital Beijing
Population 1.33 billion / 370 people per sq mile (143 people per sq km) / 40%
Total area 3,705,386 sq. miles (9,596,960 sq. km)
Languages Mandarin*, Wu, Cantonese, Hsiang, Min, Hakka, Kan
Religions Nonreligious 59%, Traditional beliefs 20%, Other 13%, Buddhist 6%, Muslim 2%
Ethnic mix Han 92%, Other 4%, Hui 1%, Miao 1%, Manchu 1%, Zhuang 1%
Government One-party state
Currency Renminbi (known as yuan) = 10 jiao = 100 fen
Literacy rate 91%
Calorie consumption 2951 calories

COLOMBIA
South America

Official name Republic of Colombia
Formation 1819 / 1903
Capital Bogotá
Population 47 million / 117 people per sq mile (45 people per sq km) / 77%
Total area 439,733 sq. miles (1,138,910 sq. km)
Languages Spanish*, Wayuu, Páez, and other Amerindian languages
Religions Roman Catholic 95%, Other 5%
Ethnic mix Mestizo 58%, White 20%, European–African 14%, African 4%, African–Amerindian 3%, Amerindian 1%
Government Presidential system
Currency Colombian peso = 100 centavos
Literacy rate 93%
Calorie consumption 2585 calories

COMOROS
Indian Ocean

Official name Union of the Comoros
Formation 1975 / 1975
Capital Moroni
Population 711,417 / 826 people per sq mile (319 people per sq km) / 36%
Total area 838 sq. miles (2170 sq. km)
Languages Arabic*, Comoran*, French*
Religions Muslim (mainly Sunni) 98%, Other 1%, Roman Catholic 1%
Ethnic mix Comoran 97%, Other 3%
Government Presidential system
Currency Comoros franc = 100 centimes
Literacy rate 56%
Calorie consumption 1754 calories

CONGO
Central Africa

Official name Republic of the Congo
Formation 1960 / 1960
Capital Brazzaville
Population 4.2 million / 32 people per sq mile (12 people per sq km) / 54%
Total area 132,046 sq. miles (342,000 sq. km)
Languages French*, Kongo, Teke, Lingala
Religions Traditional beliefs 50%, Roman Catholic 25%, Protestant 23%, Muslim 2%
Ethnic mix Bakongo 51%, Teke 17%, Other 16%, Mbochi 11%, Mbédé 5%
Government Presidential system
Currency CFA franc = 100 centimes
Literacy rate 83%
Calorie consumption 2162 calories

CONGO, DEM. REP.
Central Africa

Official name Democratic Republic of the Congo
Formation 1960 / 1960
Capital Kinshasa
Population 61.2 million / 70 people per sq mile (27 people per sq km) / 33%
Total area 905,563 sq. miles (2,345,410 sq. km)
Languages French*, Kiswahili, Tshiluba, Kikongo, Lingala
Religions Roman Catholic 50%, Protestant 20%, Traditional beliefs and other 10%, Muslim 10%, Kimbanguist 10%
Ethnic mix Other 55%, Mongo, Luba, Kongo, and Mangbetu-Azande 45%
Government Presidential system
Currency Congolese franc = 100 centimes
Literacy rate 67%
Calorie consumption 1599 calories

COSTA RICA
Central America

Official name Republic of Costa Rica
Formation 1838 / 1838
Capital San José
Population 4.5 million / 228 people per sq mile (88 people per sq km) / 61%
Total area 19,730 sq. miles (51,100 sq. km)
Languages Spanish*, English Creole, Bribri, Cabecar
Religions Roman Catholic 76%, Other (including Protestant) 24%
Ethnic mix Mestizo and European 96%, Black 2%, Chinese 1%, Amerindian 1%
Government Presidential system
Currency Costa Rican colón = 100 céntimos
Literacy rate 95%
Calorie consumption 2876 calories

CROATIA
Southeast Europe

Official name Republic of Croatia
Formation 1991 / 1991
Capital Zagreb
Population 4.6 million / 211 people per sq mile (81 people per sq km) / 59%
Total area 21,831 sq. miles (56,542 sq. km)
Languages Croatian*
Religions Roman Catholic 88%, Other 7%, Orthodox Christian 4%, Muslim 1%
Ethnic mix Croat 90%, Other 5%, Serb 5%
Government Parliamentary system
Currency Kuna = 100 lipa
Literacy rate 98%
Calorie consumption 2799 calories

CUBA
West Indies

Official name Republic of Cuba
Formation 1902 / 1902
Capital Havana
Population 11.3 million / 264 people per sq mile (102 people per sq km) / 76%
Total area 42,803 sq. miles (110,860 sq. km)
Languages Spanish
Religions Nonreligious 49%, Roman Catholic 40%, Atheist 6%, Other 4%, Protestant 1%
Ethnic mix White 66%, European–African 22%, Black 12%
Government One-party state
Currency Cuban peso = 100 centavos
Literacy rate 99%
Calorie consumption 3152 calories

CYPRUS
Southeast Europe

Official name Republic of Cyprus
Formation 1960 / 1960
Capital Nicosia
Population 788,457 / 221 people per sq mile (85 people per sq km) / 69%
Total area 3571 sq. miles (9250 sq. km)
Languages Greek*, Turkish*
Religions Orthodox Christian 78%, Muslim 18%, Other 4%
Ethnic mix Greek 81%, Turkish 11%, Other 8%
Government Presidential system
Currency Euro (Turkish lira in TRNC) = 100 cents (euro); 100 kurus (Turkish lira)
Literacy rate 97%
Calorie consumption 3255 calories

CZECH REPUBLIC
Central Europe

Official name Czech Republic
Formation 1993 / 1993
Capital Prague
Population 10.2 million / 335 people per sq mile (129 people per sq km) / 74%
Total area 30,450 sq. miles (78,866 sq. km)
Languages Czech*, Slovak, Hungarian (Magyar)
Religions Roman Catholic 39%, Atheist 38%, Other 18%, Protestant 3%, Hussite 2%
Ethnic mix Czech 90%, Other 4%, Moravian 4%, Slovak 2%
Government Parliamentary system
Currency Czech koruna = 100 haleru
Literacy rate 99%
Calorie consumption 3171 calories

DENMARK
Northern Europe

Official name Kingdom of Denmark
Formation 950 / 1944
Capital Copenhagen
Population 5.5 million / 336 people per sq mile (130 people per sq km) / 85%
Total area 16,639 sq. miles (43,094 sq. km)
Languages Danish
Religions Evangelical Lutheran 89%, Other 10%, Roman Catholic 1%
Ethnic mix Danish 96%, Other (including Scandinavian and Turkish) 3%, Faeroese and Inuit 1%
Government Parliamentary system
Currency Danish krone = 100 øre
Literacy rate 99%
Calorie consumption 3439 calories

DJIBOUTI
East Africa

Official name Republic of Djibouti
Formation 1977 / 1977
Capital Djibouti
Population 496,374 / 55 people per sq mile (21 people per sq km) / 84%
Total area 8494 sq. miles (22,000 sq. km)
Languages Arabic*, French*, Somali, Afar
Religions Muslim (mainly Sunni) 94%, Christian 6%
Ethnic mix Issa 60%, Afar 35%, Other 5%
Government Presidential system
Currency Djibouti franc = 100 centimes
Literacy rate 66%
Calorie consumption 2220 calories

DOMINICA
West Indies

Official name Commonwealth of Dominica
Formation 1978 / 1978
Capital Roseau
Population 72,386 / 250 people per sq mile (97 people per sq km) / 72%
Total area 291 sq. miles (754 sq. km)
Languages English*, French Creole
Religions Roman Catholic 77%, Protestant 15%, Other 8%
Ethnic mix Black 87%, Mixed race 9%, Carib 3%, Other 1%
Government Parliamentary system
Currency Eastern Caribbean dollar = 100 cents
Literacy rate 88%
Calorie consumption 2763 calories

DOMINICAN REPUBLIC
West Indies

Official name Dominican Republic
Formation 1865 / 1865
Capital Santo Domingo
Population 9.1 million / 487 people per sq mile (188 people per sq km) / 60%
Total area 18,679 sq. miles (48,380 sq. km)
Languages Spanish*, French Creole
Religions Roman Catholic 92%, Other and nonreligious 8%
Ethnic mix Mixed race 75%, White 15%, Black 10%
Government Presidential system
Currency Dominican Republic peso = 100 centavos
Literacy rate 87%
Calorie consumption 2347 calories

EAST TIMOR
Southeast Asia

Official name Democratic Republic of Timor-Leste
Formation 2002 / 2002
Capital Dili
Population 1.1 million / 192 people per sq mile (74 people per sq km) / 8%
Total area 5756 sq. miles (14,874 sq. km)
Languages Tetum (Portuguese/Austronesian)*, Bahasa Indonesia, and Portuguese*
Religions Roman Catholic 95%, Other (including Muslim and Protestant) 5%
Government Parliamentary system
Currency US dollar = 100 cents
Literacy rate 59%
Calorie consumption 2806 calories

ECUADOR
South America

Official name Republic of Ecuador
Formation 1830 / 1942
Capital Quito
Population 13.6 million / 127 people per sq mile (49 people per sq km) / 62%
Total area 109,483 sq. miles (283,560 sq. km)
Languages Spanish*, Quechua, other Amerindian languages
Religions Roman Catholic 93%, Protestant, Jewish, and other 7%
Ethnic mix Mestizo 55%, Amerindian 25%, White 10%, Black 10%
Government Presidential system
Currency US dollar = 100 cents
Literacy rate 91%
Calorie consumption 2754 calories

EGYPT
North Africa

Official name Arab Republic of Egypt
Formation 1936 / 1982
Capital Cairo
Population 76.9 million / 200 people per sq mile (77 people per sq km) / 42%
Total area 386,660 sq. miles (1,001,450 sq. km)
Languages Arabic*, French, English, Berber
Religions Muslim (mainly Sunni) 94%, Coptic Christian and other 6%
Ethnic mix Egyptian 99%, Nubian, Armenian, Greek, and Berber 1%
Government Presidential system
Currency Egyptian pound = 100 piastres
Literacy rate 71%
Calorie consumption 3338 calories

EL SALVADOR
Central America

Official name Republic of El Salvador
Formation 1841 / 1841
Capital San Salvador
Population 7.1 million / 888 people per sq mile (343 people per sq km) / 60%
Total area 8124 sq. miles (21,040 sq. km)
Languages Spanish
Religions Roman Catholic 80%, Evangelical 18%, Other 2%
Ethnic mix Mestizo 94%, Amerindian 5%, White 1%
Government Presidential system
Currency Salvadorean colón & US dollar = 100 centavos (colón); 100 cents (US dollar)
Literacy rate 80%
Calorie consumption 2584 calories

EQUATORIAL GUINEA
Central Africa

Official name Republic of Equatorial Guinea
Formation 1968 / 1968
Capital Malabo
Population 551,201 / 51 people per sq mile (20 people per sq km) / 49%
Total area 10,830 sq. miles (28,051 sq. km)
Languages French*, Spanish*, Fang, Bubi
Religions Roman Catholic 90%, Other 10%
Ethnic mix Fang 85%, Other 11%, Bubi 4%
Government Presidential system
Currency CFA franc = 100 centimes
Literacy rate 87%
Calorie consumption Not available

ERITREA
East Africa

Official name State of Eritrea
Formation 1993 / 2002
Capital Asmera
Population 4.7 million / 104 people per sq mile (40 people per sq km) / 20%
Total area 46,842 sq. miles (121,320 sq. km)
Languages Tigrinya*, English*, Tigre, Afar, Arabic*, Bilen, Kunama, Nara, Saho, Hadareb
Religions Christian 45%, Muslim 45%, Other 10%
Ethnic mix Tigray 50%, Tigray and Kunama 40%, Afar 4%, Other 3%, Saho 3%
Government Transitional regime
Currency Nakfa = 100 cents
Literacy rate 57%
Calorie consumption 1513 calories

ESTONIA
Northeast Europe

Official name Republic of Estonia
Formation 1991 / 1991
Capital Tallinn
Population 1.3 million / 75 people per sq mile (29 people per sq km) / 70%
Total area 17,462 sq. miles (45,226 sq. km)
Languages Estonian*, Russian
Religions Evangelical Lutheran 56%, Orthodox Christian 25%, Other 19%
Ethnic mix Estonian 68%, Russian 26%, Other 4%, Ukrainian 2%
Government Parliamentary system
Currency Kroon = 100 senti
Literacy rate 99%
Calorie consumption 3002 calories

ETHIOPIA
East Africa

Official name Federal Democratic Republic of Ethiopia
Formation 1896 / 2002
Capital Addis Ababa
Population 81.2 million / 189 people per sq mile (73 people per sq km) / 16%
Total area 435,184 sq. miles (1,127,127 sq. km)
Languages Amharic*, Tigrinya, Galla, Sidamo, Somali, English, Arabic
Religions Orthodox Christian 40%, Muslim 40%, Traditional beliefs 15%, Other 5%
Ethnic mix Oromo 32%, Amhara 30%, Other 22%, Tigrean 6%, Somali 6%, Guragie 4%
Government Parliamentary system
Currency Ethiopian birr = 100 cents
Literacy rate 42%
Calorie consumption 1857 calories

FIJI
Australasia & Oceania

Official name Republic of the Fiji Islands
Formation 1970 / 1970
Capital Suva
Population 918,675 / 130 people per sq mile (50 people per sq km) / 52%
Total area 7054 sq. miles (18,270 sq. km)
Languages Fijian, English*, Hindi, Urdu, Tamil, Telugu
Religions Hindu 38%, Methodist 37%, Roman Catholic 9%, Other 8%, Muslim 8%
Ethnic mix Melanesian 51%, Indian 44%, Other 5%
Government Transitional regime
Currency Fiji dollar = 100 cents
Literacy rate 93%
Calorie consumption 2894 calories

FINLAND
Northern Europe

Official name Republic of Finland
Formation 1917 / 1947
Capital Helsinki
Population 5.3 million / 45 people per sq mile (17 people per sq km) / 61%
Total area 130,127 sq. miles (337,030 sq. km)
Languages Finnish*, Swedish*, Sámi
Religions Evangelical Lutheran 89%, Other 9%, Orthodox Christian 1%, Roman Catholic 1%
Ethnic mix Finnish 93%, Other (including Sámi) 7%
Government Parliamentary system
Currency Euro = 100 cents
Literacy rate 99%
Calorie consumption 3100 calories

FRANCE
Western Europe

Official name French Republic
Formation 987 / 1919
Capital Paris
Population 60.9 million / 287 people per sq mile (111 people per sq km) / 76%
Total area 211,208 sq. miles (547,030 sq. km)
Languages French*, Provençal, German, Breton, Catalan, Basque
Religions Roman Catholic 88%, Muslim 8%, Protestant 2%, Buddhist 1%, Jewish 1%
Ethnic mix French 90%, North African (mainly Algerian) 6%, German (Alsace) 2%, Breton 1%, Other (including Corsicans) 1%
Government Mixed presidential–parliamentary system
Currency Euro = 100 cents
Literacy rate 99%
Calorie consumption 3654 calories

GABON
Central Africa

Official name Gabonese Republic
Formation 1960 / 1960
Capital Libreville
Population 1.4 million / 14 people per sq mile (5 people per sq km) / 84%
Total area 103,345 sq. miles (267,667 sq. km)
Languages Fang, French*, Punu, Sira, Nzebi, Mpongwe
Religions Christian (mainly Roman Catholic) 55%, Traditional beliefs 40%, Other 4%, Muslim 1%
Ethnic mix Fang 26%, Shira-punu 24%, Other 16%, Foreign residents 15%, Nzabi-duma 11%, Mbédé-Teke 8%
Government Presidential system
Currency CFA franc = 100 centimes
Literacy rate 71%
Calorie consumption 2637 calories

GAMBIA
West Africa

Official name Republic of the Gambia
Formation 1965 / 1965
Capital Banjul
Population 1.6 million / 414 people per sq mile (160 people per sq km) / 26%
Total area 4363 sq. miles (11,300 sq. km)
Languages English*, Mandinka, Fulani, Wolof, Jola, Soninke
Religions Sunni Muslim 90%, Christian 9%, Traditional beliefs 1%
Ethnic mix Mandinka 40%, Fulani 19%, Wolof 15%, Jola 11%, Serahuli 9%, Other 6%
Government Presidential system
Currency Dalasi = 100 butut
Literacy rate 38%
Calorie consumption 2273 calories

GEORGIA
Southwest Asia

Official name Georgia
Formation 1991 / 1991
Capital Tbilisi
Population 4.4 million / 164 people per sq mile (63 people per sq km) / 52%
Total area 26,911 sq. miles (69,700 sq. km)
Languages Georgian*, Russian, Azeri, Armenian, Mingrelian, Ossetian, Abkhazian* *(in Abkhazia)*
Religions Georgian Orthodox 65%, Muslim 11%, Russian Orthodox 10%, Armenian Apostolic Church (Orthodox) 8%, Other 6%
Ethnic mix Georgian 84%, Armenian 6%, Azeri 6%, Russian 2%, Other 1%, Ossetian 1%
Government Presidential system
Currency Lari = 100 tetri
Literacy rate 99%
Calorie consumption 2354 calories

GERMANY
Northern Europe

Official name Federal Republic of Germany
Formation 1871 / 1990
Capital Berlin
Population 82.7 million / 613 people per sq mile (237 people per sq km) / 88%
Total area 137,846 sq. miles (357,021 sq. km)
Languages German*, Turkish
Religions Protestant 34%, Roman Catholic 33%, Other 30%, Muslim 3%
Ethnic mix German 92%, Other European 3%, Other 3%, Turkish 2%
Government Parliamentary system
Currency Euro = 100 cents
Literacy rate 99%
Calorie consumption 3496 calories

GHANA
West Africa

Official name Republic of Ghana
Formation 1957 / 1957
Capital Accra
Population 23 million / 259 people per sq mile (100 people per sq km) / 46%
Total area 92,100 sq. miles (238,540 sq. km)
Languages English*, Twi, Fanti, Ewe, Ga, Adangbe, Gurma, Dagomba (Dagbani)
Religions Christian 69%, Muslim 16%, Traditional beliefs 9%, Other 6%
Ethnic mix Akan 49%, Mole-Dagbani 17%, Ewe 13%, Other 9%, Ga and Ga-Adangbe 8%, Guan 4%
Government Presidential system
Currency Cedi = 100 pesewas
Literacy rate 58%
Calorie consumption 2667 calories

GREECE
Southeast Europe

Official name Hellenic Republic
Formation 1829 / 1947
Capital Athens
Population 11.2 million / 222 people per sq mile (86 people per sq km) / 61%
Total area 50,942 sq. miles (131,940 sq. km)
Languages Greek*, Turkish, Macedonian, Albanian
Religions Orthodox Christian 98%, Other 1%, Muslim 1%
Ethnic mix Greek 98%, Other 2%
Government Parliamentary system
Currency Euro = 100 cents
Literacy rate 96%
Calorie consumption 3721 calories

GRENADA
West Indies

Official name Grenada
Formation 1974 / 1974
Capital St. George's
Population 89,971 / 687 people per sq mile (265 people per sq km) / 41%
Total area 131 sq. miles (340 sq. km)
Languages English*, English Creole
Religions Roman Catholic 68%, Anglican 17%, Other 15%
Ethnic mix Black African 82%, Mulatto (mixed race) 13%, East Indian 3%, Other 2%
Government Parliamentary system
Currency Eastern Caribbean dollar = 100 cents
Literacy rate 96%
Calorie consumption 2932 calories

GUATEMALA
Central America

Official name Republic of Guatemala
Formation 1838 / 1838
Capital Guatemala City
Population 13.2 million / 315 people per sq mile (122 people per sq km) / 47%
Total area 42,042 sq. miles (108,890 sq. km)
Languages Spanish*, Quiché, Mam, Cakchiquel, Kekchi
Religions Roman Catholic 65%, Protestant 33%, Other and nonreligious 2%
Ethnic mix Amerindian 60%, Mestizo 30%, Other 10%
Government Presidential system
Currency Quetzal = 100 centavos
Literacy rate 69%
Calorie consumption 2219 calories

GUINEA
West Africa

Official name Republic of Guinea
Formation 1958 / 1958
Capital Conakry
Population 9.8 million / 103 people per sq mile (40 people per sq km) / 35%
Total area 94,925 sq. miles (245,857 sq. km)
Languages French*, Pulaar, Malinke, Soussou
Religions Muslim 65%, Traditional beliefs 33%, Christian 2%
Ethnic mix Peul 39%, Malinké 23%, Other 16%, Soussou 11%, Kissi 6%, Kpellé 5%
Government Presidential system
Currency Guinea franc = 100 centimes
Literacy rate 30%
Calorie consumption 2409 calories

GUINEA-BISSAU
West Africa

Official name Republic of Guinea-Bissau
Formation 1974 / 1974
Capital Bissau
Population 1.7 million / 157 people per sq mile (60 people per sq km) / 35%
Total area 13,946 sq. miles (36,120 sq. km)
Languages Portuguese*, Portuguese Creole, Balante, Fulani, Malinke
Religions Traditional beliefs 52%, Muslim 40%, Christian 8%
Ethnic mix Balante 30%, Fulani 20%, Other 17%, Mandyako 14%, Mandinka 12%, Papel 7%
Government Presidential system
Currency CFA franc = 100 centimes
Literacy rate 40%
Calorie consumption 2024 calories

GUYANA
South America

Official name The Co-operative Republic of Guyana
Formation 1966 / 1966
Capital Georgetown
Population 769,095 / 10 people per sq mile (4 people per sq km) / 38%
Total area 83,000 sq. miles (214,970 sq. km)
Languages English*, English Creole, Hindi, Tamil, Amerindian languages
Religions Christian 57%, Hindu 33%, Muslim 9%, Other 1%
Ethnic mix East Indian 43%, Black African 30%, Mixed race 17%, Amerindian 9%, Other 1%
Government Presidential system
Currency Guyanese dollar = 100 cents
Literacy rate 97%
Calorie consumption 2692 calories

HAITI
West Indies

Official name Republic of Haiti
Formation 1804 / 1844
Capital Port-au-Prince
Population 8.8 million / 827 people per sq mile (319 people per sq km) / 38%
Total area 10,714 sq. miles (27,750 sq. km)
Languages French*, French Creole*
Religions Roman Catholic 80%, Protestant 16%, Other (including Voodoo) 3%, Nonreligious 1%
Ethnic mix Black African 95%, Mulatto (mixed race) and European 5%
Government Presidential system
Currency Gourde = 100 centimes
Literacy rate 52%
Calorie consumption 2086 calories

HONDURAS
Central America

Official name Republic of Honduras
Formation 1838 / 1838
Capital Tegucigalpa
Population 7.5 million / 174 people per sq mile (67 people per sq km) / 46%
Total area 43,278 sq. miles (112,090 sq. km)
Languages Spanish*, Garifuna (Carib), English Creole
Religions Roman Catholic 97%, Protestant 3%
Ethnic mix Mestizo 90%, Black African 5%, Amerindian 4%, White 1%
Government Presidential system
Currency Lempira = 100 centavos
Literacy rate 80%
Calorie consumption 2356 calories

HUNGARY
Central Europe

Official name Republic of Hungary
Formation 1918 / 1947
Capital Budapest
Population 10 million / 280 people per sq mile (108 people per sq km) / 66%
Total area 35,919 sq. miles (93,030 sq. km)
Languages Hungarian (Magyar)*
Religions Roman Catholic 52%, Calvinist 16%, Other 15%, Nonreligious 14%, Lutheran 3%
Ethnic mix Magyar 94%, Other 5%, Roma 1%
Government Parliamentary system
Currency Forint = 100 fillér
Literacy rate 99%
Calorie consumption 3483 calories

ICELAND
Northwest Europe

Official name Republic of Iceland
Formation 1944 / 1944
Capital Reykjavík
Population 301,931 / 8 people per sq mile (3 people per sq km) / 93%
Total area 39,768 sq. miles (103,000 sq. km)
Languages Icelandic*
Religions Evangelical Lutheran 93%, Nonreligious 6%, Other (mostly Christian) 1%
Ethnic mix Icelandic 94%, Other 5%, Danish 1%
Government Parliamentary system
Currency Icelandic króna = 100 aurar
Literacy rate 99%
Calorie consumption 3249 calories

INDIA
South Asia

Official name Republic of India
Formation 1947 / 1947
Capital New Delhi
Population 1.14 billion / 989 people per sq mile (382 people per sq km) / 29%
Total area 1,269,338 sq. miles (3,287,590 sq. km)
Languages Hindi*, English*, Urdu, Bengali, Marathi, Telugu, Tamil, Bihari, Gujarati, Kanarese
Religions Hindu 81%, Muslim 13%, Christian 2%, Sikh 2%, Other 1%, Buddhist 1%
Ethnic mix Indo-Aryan 72%, Dravidian 25%, Mongoloid and other 3%
Government Parliamentary system
Currency Indian rupee = 100 paise
Literacy rate 61%
Calorie consumption 2459 calories

INDONESIA
Southeast Asia

Official name Republic of Indonesia
Formation 1949 / 1999
Capital Jakarta
Population 228 million / 329 people per sq mile (127 people per sq km) / 47%
Total area 741,096 sq. miles (1,919,440 sq. km)
Languages Bahasa Indonesia*, Javanese, Sundanese, Madurese, Dutch
Religions Sunni Muslim 87%, Protestant 6%, Roman Catholic 3%, Hindu 2%, Other 1%, Buddhist 1%
Ethnic mix Javanese 42%, Sundanese 15%, Coastal Malays 12%, Madurese 3%, Other 28%
Government Presidential system
Currency Rupiah = 100 sen
Literacy rate 90%
Calorie consumption 2904 calories

IRAN
Southwest Asia

Official name Islamic Republic of Iran
Formation 1502 / 1990
Capital Tehran
Population 71.2 million / 113 people per sq mile (44 people per sq km) / 67%
Total area 636,293 sq. miles (1,648,000 sq. km)
Languages Farsi*, Azeri, Luri, Gilaki, Kurdish, Mazanderani, Turkmen, Arabic, Baluchi
Religions Shi'a Muslim 93%, Sunni Muslim 6%, Other 1%
Ethnic mix Persian 50%, Azari 24%, Other 10%, Kurdish 8%, Lur and Bakhtiari 8%
Government Islamic theocracy
Currency Iranian rial = 100 dinars
Literacy rate 77%
Calorie consumption 3085 calories

IRAQ
Southwest Asia

Official name Republic of Iraq
Formation 1932 / 1990
Capital Baghdad
Population 30.3 million / 179 people per sq mile (69 people per sq km) / 67%
Total area 168,753 sq. miles (437,072 sq. km)
Languages Arabic*, Kurdish*, Turkic languages, Armenian, Assyrian
Religions Shi'a Muslim 60%, Sunni Muslim 35%, Other (including Christian) 5%
Ethnic mix Arab 80%, Kurdish 15%, Turkmen 3%, Other 2%
Government Parliamentary system
Currency New Iraqi dinar = 1000 fils
Literacy rate 74%
Calorie consumption 2197 calories

IRELAND
Northwest Europe

Official name Ireland
Formation 1922 / 1922
Capital Dublin
Population 4.3 million / 162 people per sq mile (62 people per sq km) / 60%
Total area 27,135 sq. miles (70,280 sq. km)
Languages English*, Irish Gaelic*
Religions Roman Catholic 88%, Other and nonreligious 9%, Anglican 3%
Ethnic mix Irish 99%, Other 1%
Government Parliamentary system
Currency Euro = 100 cents
Literacy rate 99%
Calorie consumption 3656 calories

ISRAEL
Southwest Asia

Official name State of Israel
Formation 1948 / 1994
Capital Jerusalem (not internationally recognized)
Population 7 million / 892 people per sq mile (344 people per sq km) / 92%
Total area 8019 sq. miles (20,770 sq. km)
Languages Hebrew*, Arabic*, Yiddish, German, Russian, Polish, Romanian, Persian
Religions Jewish 76%, Muslim (mainly Sunni) 16%, Other 4%, Druze 2%, Christian 2%
Ethnic mix Jewish 76%, Other (mostly Arab) 24%
Government Parliamentary system
Currency Shekel = 100 agorot
Literacy rate 97%
Calorie consumption 3666 calories

ITALY
Southern Europe

Official name Italian Republic
Formation 1861 / 1947
Capital Rome
Population 58.2 million / 513 people per sq mile (198 people per sq km) / 67%
Total area 116,305 sq. miles (301,230 sq. km)
Languages Italian*, German, French, Rhaeto-Romanic, Sardinian
Religions Roman Catholic 85%, Other and nonreligious 13%, Muslim 2%
Ethnic mix Italian 94%, Other 4%, Sardinian 2%
Government Parliamentary system
Currency Euro = 100 cents
Literacy rate 98%
Calorie consumption 3671 calories

IVORY COAST
West Africa

Official name Republic of Côte d'Ivoire
Formation 1960 / 1960
Capital Yamoussoukro
Population 18.8 million / 153 people per sq mile (59 people per sq km) / 45%
Total area 124,502 sq. miles (322,460 sq. km)
Languages Akan, French*, Krou, Voltaique
Religions Muslim 38%, Traditional beliefs 25%, Roman Catholic 25%, Other 6%, Protestant 6%
Ethnic mix Akan 42%, Voltaique 18%, Mandé du Nord 17%, Krou 11%, Mandé du Sud 10%, Other 2%
Government Presidential system
Currency CFA franc = 100 centimes
Literacy rate 49%
Calorie consumption 2631 calories

JAMAICA
West Indies

Official name Jamaica
Formation 1962 / 1962
Capital Kingston
Population 2.7 million / 646 people per sq mile (249 people per sq km) / 52%
Total area 4243 sq. miles (10,990 sq. km)
Languages English*, English Creole
Religions Other and nonreligious 45%, Other Protestant 20%, Church of God 18%, Baptist 10%, Anglican 7%
Ethnic mix Black African 92%, Mulatto (mixed race) 6%, East Indian 1%, European and Chinese 1%
Government Parliamentary system
Currency Jamaican dollar = 100 cents
Literacy rate 80%
Calorie consumption 2685 calories

JAPAN
East Asia

Official name Japan
Formation 1590 / 1972
Capital Tokyo
Population 128 million / 883 people per sq mile (341 people per sq km) / 66%
Total area 145,882 sq. miles (377,835 sq. km)
Languages Japanese*, Korean, Chinese
Religions Shinto and Buddhist 76%, Buddhist 16%, Other (including Christian) 8%
Ethnic mix Japanese 99%, Other (mainly Korean) 1%
Government Parliamentary system
Currency Yen = 100 sen
Literacy rate 99%
Calorie consumption 2761 calories

JORDAN
Southwest Asia

Official name Hashemite Kingdom of Jordan
Formation 1946 / 1967
Capital Amman
Population 6 million / 175 people per sq mile (67 people per sq km) / 79%
Total area 35,637 sq. miles (92,300 sq. km)
Languages Arabic*
Religions Muslim (mainly Sunni) 92%, Other (mostly Christian) 8%
Ethnic mix Arab 98%, Circassian 1%, Armenian 1%
Government Monarchy
Currency Jordanian dinar = 1000 fils
Literacy rate 90%
Calorie consumption 2673 calories

KAZAKHSTAN
Central Asia

Official name Republic of Kazakhstan
Formation 1991 / 1991
Capital Astana
Population 14.8 million / 14 people per sq mile (5 people per sq km) / 56%
Total area 1,049,150 sq. miles (2,717,300 sq. km)
Languages Kazakh*, Russian, Ukrainian, German, Uzbek, Tatar, Uighur
Religions Muslim (mainly Sunni) 47%, Orthodox Christian 44%, Other 9%
Ethnic mix Kazakh 57%, Russian 27%, Other 8%, Uzbek 3%, Ukrainian 3%, German 2%
Government Presidential system
Currency Tenge = 100 tiyn
Literacy rate 99%
Calorie consumption 2677 calories

KENYA
East Africa

Official name Republic of Kenya
Formation 1963 / 1963
Capital Nairobi
Population 36 million / 164 people per sq mile (63 people per sq km) / 40%
Total area 224,961 sq. miles (582,650 sq. km)
Languages Kiswahili*, English*, Kikuyu, Luo, Kalenjin, Kamba
Religions Christian 60%, Traditional beliefs 25%, Other 9%, Muslim 6%
Ethnic mix Other 31%, Kikuyu 20%, Luhya 14%, Luo 13%, Kalenjin 11%, Kamba 11%
Government Mixed Presidential–Parliamentary system
Currency Kenya shilling = 100 cents
Literacy rate 74%
Calorie consumption 2090 calories

KIRIBATI
Australasia & Oceania

Official name Republic of Kiribati
Formation 1979 / 1979
Capital Bairiki (Tarawa Atoll)
Population 107,817 / 393 people per sq mile (152 people per sq km) / 49%
Total area 277 sq. miles (717 sq. km)
Languages English*, Kiribati
Religions Roman Catholic 53%, Kiribati Protestant Church 39%, Other 8%
Ethnic mix Micronesian 99%, Other 1%
Government Nonparty system
Currency Australian dollar = 100 cents
Literacy rate 99%
Calorie consumption 2859 calories

KOSOVO (not yet fully recognized)
Southeast Europe

Official name Republic of Kosovo
Formation 2008 / 2008
Capital Pristina
Population 2.1 million / 499 people per sq mile (193 people per sq km) / 40%
Total area 4212 sq miles (10,908 sq km)
Languages Albanian*, Serbian*, Bosniak, Gorani, Roma, Turkish
Religions Muslim 92%, Roman Catholic 4%, Orthodox Christian 4%
Ethnic mix Albanian 92%, Serb 4%, Bosniak and Gorani 2%, Turkish 1%, Roma 1%
Government Parliamentary system
Currency Euro = 100 cents
Literacy rate 92%
Calorie consumption Not available

KUWAIT
Southwest Asia

Official name State of Kuwait
Formation 1961 / 1961
Capital Kuwait City
Population 2.8 million / 407 people per sq mile (157 people per sq km) / 96%
Total area 6880 sq. miles (17,820 sq. km)
Languages Arabic*, English
Religions Sunni Muslim 45%, Shi'a Muslim 40%, Christian, Hindu, and other 15%
Ethnic mix Kuwaiti 45%, Other Arab 35%, South Asian 9%, Other 7%, Iranian 4%
Government Monarchy
Currency Kuwaiti dinar = 1000 fils
Literacy rate 93%
Calorie consumption 3010 calories

KYRGYZSTAN
Central Asia

Official name Kyrgyz Republic
Formation 1991 / 1991
Capital Bishkek
Population 5.4 million / 70 people per sq mile (27 people per sq km) / 34%
Total area 76,641 sq. miles (198,500 sq. km)
Languages Kyrgyz*, Russian*, Uzbek, Tatar, Ukrainian
Religions Muslim (mainly Sunni) 70%, Orthodox Christian 30%
Ethnic mix Kyrgyz 65%, Uzbek 14%, Russian 13%, Other 6%, Dungan 1%Ukrainian 1%
Government Presidential system
Currency Som = 100 tyiyn
Literacy rate 99%
Calorie consumption 2999 calories

LAOS
Southeast Asia

Official name Lao People's Democratic Republic
Formation 1953 / 1953
Capital Vientiane
Population 6.2 million / 70 people per sq mile (27 people per sq km) / 21%
Total area 91,428 sq. miles (236,800 sq. km)
Languages Lao*, Mon-Khmer, Yao, Vietnamese, Chinese, French
Religions Buddhist 85%, Other (including animist) 15%
Ethnic mix Lao Loum 66%, Lao Theung 30%, Other 2%, Lao Soung 2%
Government One-party state
Currency New kip = 100 at
Literacy rate 69%
Calorie consumption 2312 calories

LATVIA
Northeast Europe

Official name Republic of Latvia
Formation 1991 / 1991
Capital Riga
Population 2.3 million / 92 people per sq mile (36 people per sq km) / 66%
Total area 24,938 sq. miles (64,589 sq. km)
Languages Latvian*, Russian
Religions Lutheran 55%, Roman Catholic 24%, Other 12%, Orthodox Christian 9%
Ethnic mix Latvian 59%, Russian 29%, Belarussian 4%, Polish 3%, Ukrainian 3%, Other 2%
Government Parliamentary system
Currency Lats = 100 santimi
Literacy rate 99%
Calorie consumption 2938 calories

LEBANON
Southwest Asia

Official name The Lebanese Republic
Formation 1941 / 1941
Capital Beirut
Population 3.7 million / 937 people per sq mile (362 people per sq km) / 88%
Total area 4015 sq. miles (10,400 sq. km)
Languages Arabic*, French, Armenian, Assyrian
Religions Muslim 70%, Christian 30%
Ethnic mix Arab 94%, Armenian 4%, Other 2%
Government Parliamentary system
Currency Lebanese pound = 100 piastres
Literacy rate 86%
Calorie consumption 3196 calories

LESOTHO
Southern Africa

Official name Kingdom of Lesotho
Formation 1966 / 1966
Capital Maseru
Population 1.8 million / 154 people per sq mile (59 people per sq km) / 18%
Total area 11,720 sq. miles (30,355 sq. km)
Languages English*, Sesotho*, isiZulu
Religions Christian 90%, Traditional beliefs 10%
Ethnic mix Sotho 97%, European and Asian 3%
Government Parliamentary system
Currency Loti = 100 lisente
Literacy rate 82%
Calorie consumption 2638 calories

LIBERIA
West Africa

Official name Republic of Liberia
Formation 1847 / 1847
Capital Monrovia
Population 3.5 million / 94 people per sq mile (36 people per sq km) / 47%
Total area 43,000 sq. miles (111,370 sq. km)
Languages English*, Kpelle, Vai, Bassa, Kru, Grebo, Kissi, Gola, Loma
Religions Christian 68%, Traditional beliefs 18%, Muslim 14%
Ethnic mix Indigenous tribes (16 main groups) 95%, Americo-Liberians 5%
Government Presidential system
Currency Liberian dollar = 100 cents
Literacy rate 58%
Calorie consumption 1900 calories

LIBYA
North Africa

Official name The Great Socialist People's Libyan Arab Jamahiriyah
Formation 1951 / 1951
Capital Tripoli
Population 6.1 million / 9 people per sq mile (3 people per sq km) / 87%
Total area 679,358 sq. miles (1,759,540 sq. km)
Languages Arabic*, Tuareg
Religions Muslim (mainly Sunni) 97%, Other 3%
Ethnic mix Arab and Berber 95%, Other 5%
Government One-party state
Currency Libyan dinar = 1000 dirhams
Literacy rate 82%
Calorie consumption 3320 calories

LIECHTENSTEIN
Central Europe

Official name Principality of Liechtenstein
Formation 1719 / 1719
Capital Vaduz
Population 34,247 / 552 people per sq mile (214 people per sq km) / 22%
Total area 62 sq. miles (160 sq. km)
Languages German*, Alemannish dialect, Italian
Religions Roman Catholic 81%, Other 12%, Protestant 7%
Ethnic mix Liechtensteiner 66%, Other 12%, Swiss 10%, Austrian 6%, German 3%, Italian 3%
Government Parliamentary system
Currency Swiss franc = 100 rappen/centimes
Literacy rate 99%
Calorie consumption Not available

LITHUANIA
Northeast Europe

Official name Republic of Lithuania
Formation 1991 / 1991
Capital Vilnius
Population 3.4 million / 135 people per sq mile (52 people per sq km) / 67%
Total area 25,174 sq. miles (65,200 sq. km)
Languages Lithuanian*, Russian
Religions Roman Catholic 83%, Other 12%, Protestant 5%
Ethnic mix Lithuanian 83%, Polish 7%, Russian 6%, Other 3%, Belorussian 1%
Government Parliamentary system
Currency Litas = 100 centu
Literacy rate 99%
Calorie consumption 3324 calories

LUXEMBOURG
Northwest Europe

Official name Grand Duchy of Luxembourg
Formation 1867 / 1867
Capital Luxembourg-Ville
Population 480,222 / 481 people per sq mile (186 people per sq km) / 92%
Total area 998 sq. miles (2586 sq. km)
Languages French*, German*, Luxembourgish*
Religions Roman Catholic 97%, Protestant, Orthodox Christian, and Jewish 3%
Ethnic mix Luxembourger 62%, Foreign residents 38%
Government Parliamentary system
Currency Euro = 100 cents
Literacy rate 99%
Calorie consumption 3701 calories

MACEDONIA
Southeast Europe

Official name Republic of Macedonia
Formation 1991 / 1991
Capital Skopje
Population 2 million / 201 people per sq mile (78 people per sq km) / 60%
Total area 9781 sq. miles (25,333 sq. km)
Languages Macedonian*, Albanian*, Turkish, Romani, Serbian
Religions Orthodox Christian 59%, Muslim 26%, Other 10%, Roman Catholic 4%, Protestant 1%
Ethnic mix Macedonian 64%, Albanian 25%, Turkish 4%, Roma 3%, Other 2%, Serb 2%
Government Mixed presidential–parliamentary system
Currency Macedonian denar = 100 deni
Literacy rate 96%
Calorie consumption 2655 calories

MADAGASCAR
Indian Ocean

Official name Republic of Madagascar
Formation 1960 / 1960
Capital Antananarivo
Population 19.6 million / 87 people per sq mile (34 people per sq km) / 27%
Total area 226,656 sq. miles (587,040 sq. km)
Languages French*, Malagasy*, English*
Religions Traditional beliefs 52%, Christian (mainly Roman Catholic) 41%, Muslim 7%
Ethnic mix Other Malay 46%, Merina 26%, Betsimisaraka 15%, Betsileo 12%, Other 1%
Government Presidential system
Currency Ariary = 5 iraimbilanja
Literacy rate 71%
Calorie consumption 2005 calories

MALAWI
Southern Africa

Official name Republic of Malawi
Formation 1964 / 1964
Capital Lilongwe
Population 13.5 million / 372 people per sq mile (143 people per sq km) / 17%
Total area 45,745 sq. miles (118,480 sq. km)
Languages English*, Chewa, Lomwe, Yao, Ngoni
Religions Protestant 55%, Roman Catholic 20%, Muslim 20%, Traditional beliefs 5%
Ethnic mix Bantu 99%, Other 1%
Government Presidential system
Currency Malawi kwacha = 100 tambala
Literacy rate 64%
Calorie consumption 2155 calories

MALAYSIA
Southeast Asia

Official name Malaysia
Formation 1963 / 1965
Capital Kuala Lumpur; Putrajaya (administrative)
Population 26.2 million / 207 people per sq mile (80 people per sq km) / 64%
Total area 127,316 sq. miles (329,750 sq. km)
Languages Bahasa Malaysia*, Malay, Chinese, Tamil, English
Religions Muslim (mainly Sunni) 53%, Buddhist 19%, Chinese faiths 12%, Other 7%, Christian 7%, Traditional beliefs 2%
Ethnic mix Malay 50%, Chinese 25%, Indigenous tribes 11%, Other 7%, Indian 7%
Government Parliamentary system
Currency Ringgit = 100 sen
Literacy rate 89%
Calorie consumption 2881 calories

MALDIVES
Indian Ocean

Official name Republic of Maldives
Formation 1965 / 1965
Capital Male'
Population 369,031 / 3181 people per sq mile (1230 people per sq km) / 29%
Total area 116 sq. miles (300 sq. km)
Languages Dhivehi (Maldivian)*, Sinhala, Tamil, Arabic
Religions Sunni Muslim 100%
Ethnic mix Arab–Sinhalese–Malay 100%
Government Presidential system
Currency Rufiyaa = 100 laari
Literacy rate 96%
Calorie consumption 2548 calories

MALI
West Africa

Official name Republic of Mali
Formation 1960 / 1960
Capital Bamako
Population 14.3 million / 30 people per sq mile (12 people per sq km) / 33%
Total area 478,764 sq. miles (1,240,000 sq. km)
Languages French*, Bambara, Fulani, Senufo, Soninke
Religions Muslim (mainly Sunni) 80%, Traditional beliefs 18%, Christian 1%, Other 1%
Ethnic mix Bambara 32%, Other 26%, Fulani 14%, Senufu 12%, Soninka 9%, Tuareg 7%
Government Presidential system
Currency CFA franc = 100 centimes
Literacy rate 19%
Calorie consumption 2174 calories

MALTA
Southern Europe

Official name Republic of Malta
Formation 1964 / 1964
Capital Valletta
Population 401,880 / 3241 people per sq mile (1256 people per sq km) / 92%
Total area 122 sq. miles (316 sq. km)
Languages Maltese*, English*
Religions Roman Catholic 98%, Other and nonreligious 2%
Ethnic mix Maltese 96%, Other 4%
Government Parliamentary system
Currency Euro = 100 cents
Literacy rate 88%
Calorie consumption 3587 calories

MARSHALL ISLANDS
Australasia & Oceania

Official name Republic of the Marshall Islands
Formation 1986 / 1986
Capital Majuro
Population 61,815 / 883 people per sq mile (342 people per sq km) / 67%
Total area 70 sq. miles (181 sq. km)
Languages Marshallese*, English*, Japanese, German
Religions Protestant 90%, Roman Catholic 8%, Other 2%
Ethnic mix Micronesian 97%, Other 3%
Government Presidential system
Currency US dollar = 100 cents
Literacy rate 91%
Calorie consumption Not available

MAURITANIA
West Africa

Official name Islamic Republic of Mauritania
Formation 1960 / 1960
Capital Nouakchott
Population 3.2 million / 8 people per sq mile (3 people per sq km) / 63%
Total area 397,953 sq. miles (1,030,700 sq. km)
Languages Hassaniyah Arabic*, Wolof, French
Religions Sunni Muslim 100%
Ethnic mix Maure 81%, Wolof 7%, Tukolor 5%, Other 4%, Soninka 3%
Government Presidential system
Currency Ouguiya = 5 khoums
Literacy rate 51%
Calorie consumption 2772 calories

MAURITIUS
Indian Ocean

Official name Republic of Mauritius
Formation 1968 / 1968
Capital Port Louis
Population 1.3 million / 1811 people per sq mile (699 people per sq km) / 44%
Total area 718 sq. miles (1860 sq. km)
Languages English*, French Creole, Hindi, Urdu, Tamil, Chinese, French
Religions Hindu 52%, Roman Catholic 26%, Muslim 17%, Other 3%, Protestant 2%
Ethnic mix Indo-Mauritian 68%, Creole 27%, Sino-Mauritian 3%, Franco-Mauritian 2%
Government Parliamentary system
Currency Mauritian rupee = 100 cents
Literacy rate 84%
Calorie consumption 2955 calories

MEXICO
North America

Official name United Mexican States
Formation 1836 / 1848
Capital Mexico City
Population 110 million / 149 people per sq mile (57 people per sq km) / 76%
Total area 761,602 sq. miles (1,972,550 sq. km)
Languages Spanish*, Nahuatl, Mayan, Zapotec, Mixtec, Otomi, Totonac, Tzotzil, Tzeltal
Religions Roman Catholic 88%, Other 7%, Protestant 5%
Ethnic mix Mestizo 60%, Amerindian 30%, European 9%, Other 1%
Government Presidential system
Currency Mexican peso = 100 centavos
Literacy rate 91%
Calorie consumption 3145 calories

MICRONESIA
Australasia & Oceania

Official name Federated States of Micronesia
Formation 1986 / 1986
Capital Palikir (Pohnpei Island)
Population 107,862 / 398 people per sq mile (154 people per sq km) / 30%
Total area 271 sq. miles (702 sq. km)
Languages English*, Trukese, Pohnpeian, Mortlockese, Kosraean
Religions Roman Catholic 50%, Protestant 48%, Other 2%
Ethnic mix Chuukese 49%, Pohnpeian 24%, Other 14%, Kosraean 6%, Yapese 5%, Asian 2%
Government Nonparty system
Currency US dollar = 100 cents
Literacy rate 81%
Calorie consumption Not available

MOLDOVA
Southeast Europe

Official name Republic of Moldova
Formation 1991 / 1991
Capital Chisinau
Population 4.2 million / 323 people per sq mile (125 people per sq km) / 46%
Total area 13,067 sq. miles (33,843 sq. km)
Languages Moldovan*, Ukrainian, Russian
Religions Orthodox Christian 98%, Jewish 2%
Ethnic mix Moldovan 64%, Ukrainian 14%, Russian 13%, Gagauz 4%, Other 3%, Bulgarian 2%
Government Parliamentary system
Currency Moldovan leu = 100 bani
Literacy rate 98%
Calorie consumption 2806 calories

MONACO
Southern Europe

Official name Principality of Monaco
Formation 1861 / 1861
Capital Monaco-Ville
Population 32,671 / 43,561 people per sq mile (16,754 people per sq km) / 100%
Total area 0.75 sq. miles (1.95 sq. km)
Languages French*, Italian, Monégasque, English
Religions Roman Catholic 89%, Protestant 6%, Other 5%
Ethnic mix French 32%, Other 29%, Italian 20%, Monégasque 19%
Government Mixed monarchical–parliamentary system
Currency Euro = 100 cents
Literacy rate 99%
Calorie consumption Not available

MONGOLIA
East Asia

Official name Mongolia
Formation 1924 / 1924
Capital Ulan Bator
Population 2.7 million / 4 people per sq mile (2 people per sq km) / 57%
Total area 604,247 sq. miles (1,565 000 sq. km)
Languages Khalkha Mongolian*, Kazakh, Chinese, Russian
Religions Tibetan Buddhist 96%, Muslim 4%
Ethnic mix Khalkh 82%, Other 9%, Kazakh 4%, Dorvod 3%, Bayad 2%
Government Mixed presidential–parliamentary system
Currency Tugrik (tögrög) = 100 möngö
Literacy rate 98%
Calorie consumption 2249 calories

MONTENEGRO
Southeast Europe

Official name Republic of Montenegro
Formation 2006 / 2006
Capital Podgorica
Population 684,736 / 128 people per sq mile (50 people per sq km) / 62%
Total area 5332 sq. miles (13,812 sq. km)
Languages Montenegrin*, Serbian, Albanian, Bosniak, Croatian
Religions Orthodox Christian 74%, Muslim 18%, Other 4%Roman Catholic 4%
Ethnic mix Montenegrin 43%, Serb 32%, Other 12%, Bosniak 8%, Albanian 5%
Government Parliamentary system
Currency Euro = 100 cents
Literacy rate 98%
Calorie consumption Not available

MOROCCO
North Africa

Official name Kingdom of Morocco
Formation 1956 / 1969
Capital Rabat
Population 32.4 million / 188 people per sq mile (73 people per sq km) / 58%
Total area 172,316 sq. miles (446,300 sq. km)
Languages Arabic*, Tamazight (Berber), French, Spanish
Religions Muslim (mainly Sunni) 99%, Other (mostly Christian) 1%
Ethnic mix Arab 70%, Berber 29%, European 1%
Government Mixed monarchical–parliamentary system
Currency Moroccan dirham = 100 centimes
Literacy rate 52%
Calorie consumption 3052 calories

MOZAMBIQUE
Southern Africa

Official name Republic of Mozambique
Formation 1975 / 1975
Capital Maputo
Population 20.5 million / 68 people per sq mile (26 people per sq km) / 37%
Total area 309,494 sq. miles (801,590 sq. km)
Languages Portuguese*, Makua, Xitsonga, Sena, Lomwe
Religions Traditional beliefs 56%, Christian 30%, Muslim 14%
Ethnic mix Makua Lomwe 47%, Tsonga 23%, Malawi 12%, Shona 11%, Yao 4%, Other 3%
Government Presidential system
Currency New metical = 100 centavos
Literacy rate 46%
Calorie consumption 2079 calories

MYANMAR
Southeast Asia

Official name Union of Myanmar
Formation 1948 / 1948
Capital Nay Pyi Taw
Population 51.5 million / 203 people per sq mile (78 people per sq km) / 30%
Total area 261,969 sq. miles (678,500 sq. km)
Languages Burmese*, Shan, Karen, Rakhine, Chin, Yangbye, Kachin, Mon
Religions Buddhist 87%, Christian 6%, Muslim 4%, Other 2%, Hindu 1%
Ethnic mix Burman (Bamah) 68%, Other 13%, Shan 9%, Karen 6%, Rakhine 4%
Government Military-based regime
Currency Kyat = 100 pyas
Literacy rate 90%
Calorie consumption 2937 calories

NAMIBIA
Southern Africa

Official name Republic of Namibia
Formation 1990 / 1994
Capital Windhoek
Population 2.1 million / 7 people per sq mile (3 people per sq km) / 33%
Total area 318,694 sq. miles (825,418 sq. km)
Languages English*, Ovambo Kavango, Bergdama, German, Afrikaans
Religions Christian 90%, Traditional beliefs 10%
Ethnic mix Ovambo 50%, Other tribes 24%, Kavango 9%, Damara 8%, Herero 8%, Other 1%
Government Presidential system
Currency Namibian dollar = 100 cents
Literacy rate 85%
Calorie consumption 2278 calories

NAURU
Australasia & Oceania

Official name Republic of Nauru
Formation 1968 / 1968
Capital None
Population 13,528 / 1670 people per sq mile (644 people per sq km) /
Total area 8.1 sq. miles (21 sq. km)
Languages Nauruan*, Kiribati, Chinese, Tuvaluan, English
Religions Nauruan Congregational Church 60%, Roman Catholic 35%, Other 5%
Ethnic mix Nauruan 62%, Other Pacific islanders 27%, Asian 8%, European 3%
Government Nonparty system
Currency Australian dollar = 100 cents
Literacy rate 95%
Calorie consumption Not available

NEPAL
South Asia

Official name Nepal
Formation 1769 / 1769
Capital Kathmandu
Population 28.2 million / 534 people per sq mile (206 people per sq km) / 15%
Total area 54,363 sq. miles (140,800 sq. km)
Languages Nepali*, Maithili, Bhojpuri
Religions Hindu 90%, Buddhist 5%, Muslim 3%, Other (including Christian) 2%
Ethnic mix Other 52%, Chhetri 16%, Hill Brahman 13%, Tharu 7%, Magar 7%, Tamang 5%
Government Parliamentary system
Currency Nepalese rupee = 100 paisa
Literacy rate 49%
Calorie consumption 2453 calories

NETHERLANDS
Northwest Europe

Official name Kingdom of the Netherlands
Formation 1648 / 1839
Capital Amsterdam; The Hague (administrative)
Population 16.4 million / 1252 people per sq mile (483 people per sq km) / 66%
Total area 15,033 sq. miles (41,526 sq. km)
Languages Dutch*, Frisian
Religions Roman Catholic 36%, Other 34%, Protestant 27%, Muslim 3%
Ethnic mix Dutch 82%, Other 12%, Surinamese 2%, Turkish 2%, Moroccan 2%
Government Parliamentary system
Currency Euro = 100 cents
Literacy rate 99%
Calorie consumption 3362 calories

NEW ZEALAND
Australasia & Oceania

Official name New Zealand
Formation 1947 / 1947
Capital Wellington
Population 4.1 million / 40 people per sq mile (15 people per sq km) / 86%
Total area 103,737 sq. miles (268,680 sq. km)
Languages English*, Maori*
Religions Anglican 24%, Other 22%, Presbyterian 18%, Nonreligious 16%, Roman Catholic 15%, Methodist 5%
Ethnic mix European 75%, Maori 15%, Other 7%, Samoan 3%
Government Parliamentary system
Currency New Zealand dollar = 100 cents
Literacy rate 99%
Calorie consumption 3219 calories

NICARAGUA
Central America

Official name Republic of Nicaragua
Formation 1838 / 1838
Capital Managua
Population 5.7 million / 124 people per sq mile (48 people per sq km) / 58%
Total area 49,998 sq. miles (129,494 sq. km)
Languages Spanish*, English Creole, Miskito
Religions Roman Catholic 80%, Protestant Evangelical 17%, Other 3%
Ethnic mix Mestizo 69%, White 14%, Black 8%, Amerindian 5%, Zambo 4%
Government Presidential system
Currency Córdoba oro = 100 centavos
Literacy rate 77%
Calorie consumption 2298 calories

NIGER
West Africa

Official name Republic of Niger
Formation 1960 / 1960
Capital Niamey
Population 14.9 million / 30 people per sq mile (12 people per sq km) / 23%
Total area 489,188 sq. miles (1,267,000 sq. km)
Languages French*, Hausa, Djerma, Fulani, Tuareg, Teda
Religions Muslim 85%, Traditional beliefs 14%, Other (including Christian) 1%
Ethnic mix Hausa 55%, Djerma and Songhai 21%, Peul 9%, Tuareg 9%, Other 6%
Government Presidential system
Currency CFA franc = 100 centimes
Literacy rate 29%
Calorie consumption 2130 calories

NIGERIA
West Africa

Official name Federal Republic of Nigeria
Formation 1960 / 1961
Capital Abuja
Population 137 million / 390 people per sq mile (151 people per sq km) / 47%
Total area 356,667 sq. miles (923,768 sq. km)
Languages English*, Hausa, Yoruba, Ibo
Religions Muslim 50%, Christian 40%, Traditional beliefs 10%
Ethnic mix Other 29%, Hausa 21%, Yoruba 21%, Ibo 18%, Fulani 11%
Government Presidential system
Currency Naira = 100 kobo
Literacy rate 67%
Calorie consumption 2726 calories

NORTH KOREA
East Asia

Official name Democratic People's Republic of Korea
Formation 1948 / 1953
Capital Pyongyang
Population 22.7 million / 488 people per sq mile (189 people per sq km) / 61%
Total area 46,540 sq. miles (120,540 sq. km)
Languages Korean*
Religions Atheist 100%
Ethnic mix Korean 100%
Government One-party state
Currency North Korean won = 100 chon
Literacy rate 98%
Calorie consumption 2142 calories

NORWAY
Northern Europe

Official name Kingdom of Norway
Formation 1905 / 1905
Capital Oslo
Population 4.7 million / 40 people per sq mile (15 people per sq km) / 80%
Total area 125,181 sq. miles (324,220 sq. km)
Languages Norwegian* (Bokmål "book language" and Nynorsk "new Norsk"), Sámi
Religions Evangelical Lutheran 89%, Other and nonreligious 10%, Roman Catholic 1%
Ethnic mix Norwegian 93%, Other 6%, Sámi 1%
Government Parliamentary system
Currency Norwegian krone = 100 øre
Literacy rate 99%
Calorie consumption 3484 calories

OMAN
Southwest Asia

Official name Sultanate of Oman
Formation 1951 / 1951
Capital Muscat
Population 2.7 million / 33 people per sq mile (13 people per sq km) / 78%
Total area 82,031 sq. miles (212,460 sq. km)
Languages Arabic*, Baluchi, Farsi, Hindi, Punjabi
Religions Ibadi Muslim 75%, Other Muslim and Hindu 25%
Ethnic mix Arab 88%, Baluchi 4%, Persian 3%, Indian and Pakistani 3%, African 2%
Government Monarchy
Currency Omani rial = 1000 baisa
Literacy rate 81%
Calorie consumption Not available

PAKISTAN
South Asia

Official name Islamic Republic of Pakistan
Formation 1947 / 1971
Capital Islamabad
Population 165 million / 553 people per sq mile (214 people per sq km) / 34%
Total area 310,401 sq. miles (803,940 sq. km)
Languages Urdu*, Punjabi, Sindhi, Pashtu, Baluchi, Brahui
Religions Sunni Muslim 77%, Shi'a Muslim 20%, Hindu 2%, Christian 1%
Ethnic mix Punjabi 56%, Pathan (Pashtun) 15%, Sindhi 14%, Mohajir 7%, Other 4%, Baluchi 4%
Government Presidential system
Currency Pakistani rupee = 100 paisa
Literacy rate 50%
Calorie consumption 2419 calories

PALAU
Australasia & Oceania

Official name Republic of Palau
Formation 1994 / 1994
Capital Melekeok
Population 20,842 / 106 people per sq mile (41 people per sq km) / 68%
Total area 177 sq. miles (458 sq. km)
Languages Palauan*, English*, Japanese, Angaur, Tobi, Sonsorolese
Religions Christian 66%, Modekngei 34%
Ethnic mix Palauan 74%, Filipino 16%, Other 6%, Chinese and other Asian 4%
Government Nonparty system
Currency US dollar = 100 cents
Literacy rate 98%
Calorie consumption Not available

PANAMA
Central America

Official name Republic of Panama
Formation 1903 / 1903
Capital Panama City
Population 3.3 million / 112 people per sq mile (43 people per sq km) / 57%
Total area 30,193 sq. miles (78,200 sq. km)
Languages English Creole, Spanish*, Amerindian languages, Chibchan languages
Religions Roman Catholic 86%, Other 8%, Protestant 6%
Ethnic mix Mestizo 60%, White 14%, Black 12%, Amerindian 8%, Asian 4%, Other 2%
Government Presidential system
Currency Balboa = 100 centésimos
Literacy rate 92%
Calorie consumption 2272 calories

PAPUA NEW GUINEA
Australasia & Oceania

Official name Independent State of Papua New Guinea
Formation 1975 / 1975
Capital Port Moresby
Population 6.1 million / 35 people per sq mile (13 people per sq km) / 13%
Total area 178,703 sq. miles (462,840 sq. km)
Languages English*, Pidgin English, Papuan, Motu, 750 (est.) native languages
Religions Protestant 60%, Roman Catholic 37%, Other 3%
Ethnic mix Melanesian and mixed race 100%
Government Parliamentary system
Currency Kina = 100 toea
Literacy rate 57%
Calorie consumption 2193 calories

PARAGUAY
South America

Official name Republic of Paraguay
Formation 1811 / 1938
Capital Asunción
Population 6.4 million / 42 people per sq mile (16 people per sq km) / 58%
Total area 157,046 sq. miles (406,750 sq. km)
Languages Spanish* Guarani, German
Religions Roman Catholic 96%, Protestant (including Mennonite) 4%
Ethnic mix Mestizo 91%, Other 7%, Amerindian 2%
Government Presidential system
Currency Guaraní = 100 céntimos
Literacy rate 93%
Calorie consumption 2565 calories

PERU
South America

Official name Republic of Peru
Formation 1824 / 1941
Capital Lima
Population 28.8 million / 58 people per sq mile (22 people per sq km) / 74%
Total area 496,223 sq. miles (1,285,200 sq. km)
Languages Spanish*, Quechua*, Aymara
Religions Roman Catholic 95%, Other 5%
Ethnic mix Amerindian 50%, Mestizo 40%, White 7%, Other 3%
Government Presidential system
Currency New sol = 100 céntimos
Literacy rate 88%
Calorie consumption 2571 calories

PHILIPPINES
Southeast Asia

Official name Republic of the Philippines
Formation 1946 / 1946
Capital Manila
Population 85.9 million / 746 people per sq mile (288 people per sq km) / 62%
Total area 115,830 sq. miles (300,000 sq. km)
Languages English*, Filipino*, Tagalog, Cebuano, Ilocano, Hiligaynon, many other local languages
Religions Roman Catholic 83%, Protestant 9%, Muslim 5%, Other (including Buddhist) 3%
Ethnic mix Other 34%, Tagalog 28%, Cebuano 13%, Ilocano 9%, Hiligaynon 8%, Bisaya 8%
Government Presidential system
Currency Philippine peso = 100 centavos
Literacy rate 93%
Calorie consumption 2379 calories

POLAND
Northern Europe

Official name Republic of Poland
Formation 1918 / 1945
Capital Warsaw
Population 38.5 million / 328 people per sq mile (126 people per sq km) / 62%
Total area 120,728 sq. miles (312,685 sq. km)
Languages Polish*
Religions Roman Catholic 93%, Other and nonreligious 5%, Orthodox Christian 2%
Ethnic mix Polish 97%, Other 3%
Government Parliamentary system
Currency Zloty = 100 groszy
Literacy rate 99%
Calorie consumption 3374 calories

PORTUGAL
Southwest Europe

Official name The Portuguese Republic
Formation 1139 / 1640
Capital Lisbon
Population 10.6 million / 299 people per sq mile (115 people per sq km) / 55%
Total area 35,672 sq. miles (92,391 sq. km)
Languages Portuguese*
Religions Roman Catholic 97%, Other 2%, Protestant 1%
Ethnic mix Portuguese 98%, African and other 2%
Government Parliamentary system
Currency Euro = 100 cents
Literacy rate 92%
Calorie consumption 3741 calories

QATAR
Southwest Asia

Official name State of Qatar
Formation 1971 / 1971
Capital Doha
Population 907,229 / 214 people per sq mile (82 people per sq km) / 92%
Total area 4416 sq. miles (11,437 sq. km)
Languages Arabic*
Religions Muslim (mainly Sunni) 95%, Other 5%
Ethnic mix Arab 40%, Indian 18%, Pakistani 18%, Other 14%, Iranian 10%
Government Monarchy
Currency Qatar riyal = 100 dirhams
Literacy rate 89%
Calorie consumption Not available

ROMANIA
Southeast Europe

Official name Romania
Formation 1878 / 1947
Capital Bucharest
Population 21.5 million / 242 people per sq mile (93 people per sq km) / 55%
Total area 91,699 sq. miles (237,500 sq. km)
Languages Romanian*, Hungarian (Magyar), Romani, German
Religions Romanian Orthodox 87%, Roman Catholic 5%, Protestant 4%, Other 2%, Greek Orthodox 1%, Greek Catholic (Uniate) 1%
Ethnic mix Romanian 89%, Magyar 7%, Roma 2%, Other 2%
Government Presidential system
Currency New Romanian leu = 100 bani
Literacy rate 97%
Calorie consumption 3455 calories

RUSSIAN FEDERATION
Europe / Asia

Official name Russian Federation
Formation 1480 / 1991
Capital Moscow
Population 142 million / 22 people per sq mile (8 people per sq km) / 73%
Total area 6,592,735 sq. miles (17,075,200 sq. km)
Languages Russian*, Tatar, Ukrainian, Chavash, various other national languages
Religions Orthodox Christian 75%, Muslim 14%, Other 11%
Ethnic mix Russian 80%, Other 12%, Tatar 4%, Ukrainian 2%, Bashkir 1%, Chavash 1%
Government Mixed Presidential–Parliamentary system
Currency Russian rouble = 100 kopeks
Literacy rate 99%
Calorie consumption 3072 calories

RWANDA
Central Africa

Official name Republic of Rwanda
Formation 1962 / 1962
Capital Kigali
Population 9.4 million / 976 people per sq mile (377 people per sq km) / 20%
Total area 10,169 sq. miles (26,338 sq. km)
Languages Kinyarwanda*, French*, English*, Kiswahili
Religions Roman Catholic 56%, Traditional beliefs 25%, Muslim 10%, Protestant 9%
Ethnic mix Hutu 90%, Tutsi 9%, Other (including Twa) 1%
Government Presidential system
Currency Rwanda franc = 100 centimes
Literacy rate 65%
Calorie consumption 2084 calories

SAINT KITTS & NEVIS
West Indies

Official name Federation of Saint Christopher and Nevis
Formation 1983 / 1983
Capital Basseterre
Population 39,349 / 283 people per sq mile (109 people per sq km) / 32%
Total area 101 sq. miles (261 sq. km)
Languages English*, English Creole
Religions Anglican 33%, Methodist 29%, Other 22%, Moravian 9%, Roman Catholic 7%
Ethnic mix Black 95%, Mixed race 3%, White 1%, Other and Amerindian 1%
Government Parliamentary system
Currency Eastern Caribbean dollar = 100 cents
Literacy rate 98%
Calorie consumption 2609 calories

SAINT LUCIA
West Indies

Official name Saint Lucia
Formation 1979 / 1979
Capital Castries
Population 170,649 / 723 people per sq mile (280 people per sq km) / 31%
Total area 239 sq. miles (620 sq. km)
Languages English*, French Creole
Religions Roman Catholic 90%, Other 10%
Ethnic mix Black 83%, Mulatto (mixed race) 13%, Asian 3%, Other 1%
Government Parliamentary system
Currency Eastern Caribbean dollar = 100 cents
Literacy rate 95%
Calorie consumption 2988 calories

SAINT VINCENT & THE GRENADINES
West Indies

Official name Saint Vincent and the Grenadines
Formation 1979 / 1979
Capital Kingstown
Population 118,149 / 902 people per sq mile (347 people per sq km) / 59%
Total area 150 sq. miles (389 sq. km)
Languages English*, English Creole
Religions Anglican 47%, Methodist 28%, Roman Catholic 13%, Other 12%
Ethnic mix Black 77%, Mulatto (mixed race) 16%, Other 3%, Carib 3%, Asian 1%
Government Parliamentary system
Currency Eastern Caribbean dollar = 100 cents
Literacy rate 88%
Calorie consumption 2599 calories

SAMOA
Australasia & Oceania

Official name Independent State of Samoa
Formation 1962 / 1962
Capital Apia
Population 214,265 / 196 people per sq mile (76 people per sq km) / 22%
Total area 1104 sq. miles (2860 sq. km)
Languages Samoan*, English*
Religions Christian 99%, Other 1%
Ethnic mix Polynesian 90%, Euronesian 9%, Other 1%
Government Parliamentary system
Currency Tala = 100 sene
Literacy rate 99%
Calorie consumption 2945 calories

SAN MARINO
Southern Europe

Official name Republic of San Marino
Formation 1631 / 1631
Capital San Marino
Population 29,615 / 1234 people per sq mile (485 people per sq km) / 89%
Total area 23.6 sq. miles (61 sq. km)
Languages Italian*
Religions Roman Catholic 93%, Other and nonreligious 7%
Ethnic mix Sammarinese 88%, Italian 10%, Other 2%
Government Parliamentary system
Currency Euro = 100 cents
Literacy rate 99%
Calorie consumption Not available

SÃO TOMÉ & PRÍNCIPE
West Africa

Official name The Democratic Republic of Sao Tome and Principe
Formation 1975 / 1975
Capital São Tomé
Population 199,579 / 538 people per sq mile (208 people per sq km) / 38%
Total area 386 sq. miles (1001 sq. km)
Languages Portuguese*, Portuguese Creole
Religions Roman Catholic 84%, Other 16%
Ethnic mix Black 90%, Portuguese and Creole 10%
Government Presidential system
Currency Dobra = 100 céntimos
Literacy rate 83%
Calorie consumption 2460 calories

SAUDI ARABIA
Southwest Asia

Official name Kingdom of Saudi Arabia
Formation 1932 / 1932
Capital Riyadh
Population 25.8 million / 32 people per sq mile (12 people per sq km) / 88%
Total area 756,981 sq. miles (1,960,582 sq. km)
Languages Arabic*
Religions Sunni Muslim 85%, Shi'a Muslim 15%
Ethnic mix Arab 90%, Afro-Asian 10%
Government Monarchy
Currency Saudi riyal = 100 halalat
Literacy rate 79%
Calorie consumption 2844 calories

SENEGAL
West Africa

Official name Republic of Senegal
Formation 1960 / 1960
Capital Dakar
Population 12.2 million / 164 people per sq mile (63 people per sq km) / 50%
Total area 75,749 sq. miles (196,190 sq. km)
Languages French*, Wolof, Pulaar, Serer, Diola, Mandinka, Malinke, Soninke
Religions Sunni Muslim 90%, Christian (mainly Roman Catholic) 5%, Traditional beliefs 5%
Ethnic mix Wolof 43%, Serer 15%, Other 14%, Peul 14%, Toucouleur 9%, Diola 5%
Government Presidential system
Currency CFA franc = 100 centimes
Literacy rate 39%
Calorie consumption 2279 calories

SERBIA
Southeast Europe

Official name Republic of Serbia
Formation 2006 / 2008
Capital Belgrade
Population 8.1 million / 271 people per sq mile (105 people per sq km) / 52%
Total area 29,905 sq miles (77,453 sq km)
Languages Serbian*, Hungarian (Magyar)
Religions Orthodox Christian 85%, Other 6%, Roman Catholic 6%, Muslim 3%
Ethnic mix Serb 83%, Other 10%, Magyar 4%, Bosniak 2%, Roma 1%
Government Parliamentary system
Currency Dinar = 100 para
Literacy rate 96%
Calorie consumption 2678 calories

SEYCHELLES
Indian Ocean

Official name Republic of Seychelles
Formation 1976 / 1976
Capital Victoria
Population 81,895 / 787 people per sq mile (303 people per sq km) / 50%
Total area 176 sq. miles (455 sq. km)
Languages French Creole*, English*, French*
Religions Roman Catholic 90%, Anglican 8%, Other (including Muslim) 2%
Ethnic mix Creole 89%, Indian 5%, Other 4%, Chinese 2%
Government Presidential system
Currency Seychelles rupee = 100 cents
Literacy rate 92%
Calorie consumption 2465 calories

SIERRA LEONE
West Africa

Official name Republic of Sierra Leone
Formation 1961 / 1961
Capital Freetown
Population 5.8 million / 210 people per sq mile (81 people per sq km) / 40%
Total area 27,698 sq. miles (71,740 sq. km)
Languages English*, Mende, Temne, Krio
Religions Muslim 30%, Traditional beliefs 30%, Other 30%, Christian 10%
Ethnic mix Mende 35%, Temne 32%, Other 21%, Limba 8%, Kuranko 4%
Government Presidential system
Currency Leone = 100 cents
Literacy rate 35%
Calorie consumption 1936 calories

SINGAPORE
Southeast Asia

Official name Republic of Singapore
Formation 1965 / 1965
Capital Singapore
Population 4.4 million / 18644 people per sq mile (7213 people per sq km) / 100%
Total area 250 sq. miles (648 sq. km)
Languages Mandarin*, Malay*, Tamil*, English*
Religions Buddhist 55%, Taoist 22%, Muslim 16%, Hindu, Christian, and Sikh 7%
Ethnic mix Chinese 77%, Malay 14%, Indian 8%, Other 1%
Government Parliamentary system
Currency Singapore dollar = 100 cents
Literacy rate 93%
Calorie consumption Not available

SLOVAKIA
Central Europe

Official name Slovak Republic
Formation 1993 / 1993
Capital Bratislava
Population 5.4 million / 285 people per sq mile (110 people per sq km) / 58%
Total area 18,859 sq. miles (48,845 sq. km)
Languages Slovak*, Hungarian (Magyar), Czech
Religions Roman Catholic 60%, Other 18%, Atheist 10%, Protestant 8%, Orthodox Christian 4%
Ethnic mix Slovak 86%, Magyar 10%, Roma 2%, Other 1%, Czech 1%
Government Parliamentary system
Currency Euro = 100 cents
Literacy rate 99%
Calorie consumption 2889 calories

SLOVENIA
Central Europe

Official name Republic of Slovenia
Formation 1991 / 1991
Capital Ljubljana
Population 2 million / 256 people per sq mile (99 people per sq km) / 51%
Total area 7820 sq. miles (20,253 sq. km)
Languages Slovenian*
Religions Roman Catholic 96%, Other 3%, Muslim 1%
Ethnic mix Slovene 83%, Other 12%, Serb 2%, Croat 2%, Bosniak 1%
Government Parliamentary system
Currency Euro = 100 cents
Literacy rate 99%
Calorie consumption 3001 calories

SOLOMON ISLANDS
Australasia & Oceania

Official name Solomon Islands
Formation 1978 / 1978
Capital Honiara
Population 566,842 / 52 people per sq mile (20 people per sq km) / 17%
Total area 10,985 sq. miles (28,450 sq. km)
Languages English*, Pidgin English, Melanesian Pidgin
Religions Church of Melanesia (Anglican) 34%, Roman Catholic 19%, South Seas Evangelical Church 17%, Methodist 11%, Seventh-day Adventist 10%, Other 9%
Ethnic mix Melanesian 94%, Polynesian 4%, Other 2%
Government Parliamentary system
Currency Solomon Islands dollar = 100 cents
Literacy rate 77%
Calorie consumption 2265 calories

SOMALIA
East Africa

Official name The Somali Democratic Republic
Formation 1960 / 1960
Capital Mogadishu
Population 8.8 million / 36 people per sq mile (14 people per sq km) / 35%
Total area 246,199 sq. miles (637,657 sq. km)
Languages Somali*, Arabic*, English, Italian
Religions Sunni Muslim 98%, Christian 2%
Ethnic mix Somali 85%, Other 15%
Government Transitional regime
Currency Somali shilin = 100 senti
Literacy rate 24%
Calorie consumption 1628 calories

SOUTH AFRICA
Southern Africa

Official name Republic of South Africa
Formation 1934 / 1994
Capital Pretoria; Cape Town; Bloemfontein
Population 47.7 million / 101 people per sq mile (39 people per sq km) / 57%
Total area 471,008 sq. miles (1,219,912 sq. km)
Languages English, isiZulu, isiXhosa, Afrikaans, Sepedi, Setswana, Sesotho, Xitsonga, siSwati, Tshivenda, isiNdebele
Religions Christian 68%, Traditional beliefs and animist 29%, Muslim 2%, Hindu 1%
Ethnic mix Black 79%, Colored 10%, White 9%, Asian 2%
Government Presidential system
Currency Rand = 100 cents
Literacy rate 82%
Calorie consumption 2956 calories

SOUTH KOREA
East Asia

Official name Republic of Korea
Formation 1948 / 1953
Capital Seoul
Population 48.1 million / 1262 people per sq mile (487 people per sq km) / 81%
Total area 38,023 sq. miles (98,480 sq. km)
Languages Korean*
Religions Mahayana Buddhist 47%, Protestant 38%, Roman Catholic 11%, Confucianist 3%, Other 1%
Ethnic mix Korean 100%
Government Presidential system
Currency South Korean won = 100 chon
Literacy rate 98%
Calorie consumption 3058 calories

SPAIN
Southwest Europe

Official name Kingdom of Spain
Formation 1492 / 1713
Capital Madrid
Population 43.6 million / 226 people per sq mile (87 people per sq km) / 77%
Total area 194,896 sq. miles (504,782 sq. km)
Languages Spanish*, Catalan*, Galician*, Basque*
Religions Roman Catholic 96%, Other 4%
Ethnic mix Castilian Spanish 72%, Catalan 17%, Galician 6%, Basque 2%, Other 2%, Roma 1%
Government Parliamentary system
Currency Euro = 100 cents
Literacy rate 98%
Calorie consumption 3371 calories

SRI LANKA
South Asia

Official name Democratic Socialist Republic of Sri Lanka
Formation 1948 / 1948
Capital Colombo
Population 21.1 million / 844 people per sq mile (326 people per sq km) / 21%
Total area 25,332 sq. miles (65,610 sq. km)
Languages Sinhala*, Tamil*, Sinhala-Tamil, English
Religions Buddhist 69%, Hindu 15%, Muslim 8%, Christian 8%
Ethnic mix Sinhalese 82%, Tamil 9%, Moor 8%, Other 1%
Government Mixed presidential–parliamentary system
Currency Sri Lanka rupee = 100 cents
Literacy rate 91%
Calorie consumption 2385 calories

SUDAN
East Africa

Official name Republic of the Sudan
Formation 1956 / 1956
Capital Khartoum
Population 37.8 million / 39 people per sq mile (15 people per sq km) / 40%
Total area 967,493 sq. miles (2,505,810 sq. km)
Languages Arabic / Arabic, Dinka, Nuer, Nubian, Beja, Zande, Bari, Fur, Shilluk, Lotuko
Religions Muslim (mainly Sunni) 70%, Traditional beliefs 20%, Christian 9%, Other 1%
Ethnic mix Other Black 52%, Arab 40%, Dinka and Beja 7%, Other 1%
Government Presidential system
Currency new Sudanese pound or dinar = 100 piastres
Literacy rate 61%
Calorie consumption 2228 calories

SURINAME
South America

Official name Republic of Suriname
Formation 1975 / 1975
Capital Paramaribo
Population 470,784 / 8 people per sq mile (3 people per sq km) / 77%
Total area 63,039 sq. miles (163,270 sq. km)
Languages Sranan (Creole), Dutch*, Javanese, Sarnami Hindi, Saramaccan, Chinese, Carib
Religions Hindu 27%, Protestant 25%, Roman Catholic 23%, Muslim 20%, Traditional beliefs 5%
Ethnic mix Creole 34%, South Asian 34%, Javanese 18%, Black 9%, Other 5%
Government Parliamentary system
Currency Surinamese dollar = 100 cents
Literacy rate 90%
Calorie consumption 2652 calories

SWAZILAND
Southern Africa

Official name Kingdom of Swaziland
Formation 1968 / 1968
Capital Mbabane
Population 1 million / 151 people per sq mile (58 people per sq km) / 24%
Total area 6704 sq. miles (17,363 sq. km)
Languages English*, siSwati*, isiZulu, Xitsonga
Religions Christian 60%, Traditional beliefs 40%
Ethnic mix Swazi 97%, Other 3%
Government Monarchy
Currency Lilangeni = 100 cents
Literacy rate 80%
Calorie consumption 2322 calories

SWEDEN
Northern Europe

Official name Kingdom of Sweden
Formation 1523 / 1921
Capital Stockholm
Population 9.1 million / 57 people per sq mile (22 people per sq km) / 83%
Total area 173,731 sq. miles (449,964 sq. km)
Languages Swedish*, Finnish, Sámi
Religions Evangelical Lutheran 82%, Other 13%, Roman Catholic 2%, Muslim 2%, Orthodox Christian 1%
Ethnic mix Swedish 86%, Foreign-born or first-generation immigrant 12%, Finnish and Sámi 2%
Government Parliamentary system
Currency Swedish krona = 100 öre
Literacy rate 99%
Calorie consumption 3185 calories

SWITZERLAND
Central Europe

Official name Swiss Confederation
Formation 1291 / 1857
Capital Bern
Population 7.3 million / 475 people per sq mile (184 people per sq km) / 68%
Total area 15,942 sq. miles (41,290 sq. km)
Languages German*, Swiss-German, French*, Italian*, Romansch
Religions Roman Catholic 42%, Protestant 35%, Other and nonreligious 19%, Muslim 4%
Ethnic mix German 64%, French 20%, Other 9%, Italian 6%, Romansch 1%
Government Parliamentary system
Currency Swiss franc = 100 rappen/centimes
Literacy rate 99%
Calorie consumption 3526 calories

SYRIA
Southwest Asia

Official name Syrian Arab Republic
Formation 1941 / 1967
Capital Damascus
Population 20 million / 281 people per sq mile (109 people per sq km) / 50%
Total area 71,498 sq. miles (184,180 sq. km)
Languages Arabic*, French, Kurdish, Armenian, Circassian, Turkic languages, Assyrian, Aramaic
Religions Sunni Muslim 74%, Other Muslim 16%, Christian 10%
Ethnic mix Arab 89%, Kurdish 6%, Other 3%, Armenian, Turkmen, and Circassian 2%
Government One-party state
Currency Syrian pound = 100 piastres
Literacy rate 80%
Calorie consumption 3038 calories

TAIWAN
East Asia

Official name Republic of China (ROC)
Formation 1949 / 1949
Capital Taipei
Population 22.9 million / 1835 people per sq mile (709 people per sq km) / 80%
Total area 13,892 sq. miles (35,980 sq. km)
Languages Amoy Chinese, Mandarin Chinese*, Hakka Chinese
Religions Buddhist, Confucianist, and Taoist 93%, Christian 5%, Other 2%
Ethnic mix Han (pre-20th-century migration) 84%, Han (20th-century migration) 14%, Aboriginal 2%
Government Presidential system
Currency Taiwan dollar = 100 cents
Literacy rate 97%
Calorie consumption Not available

TAJIKISTAN
Central Asia

Official name Republic of Tajikistan
Formation 1991 / 1991
Capital Dushanbe
Population 6.7 million / 121 people per sq mile (47 people per sq km) / 25%
Total area 55,251 sq. miles (143,100 sq. km)
Languages Tajik*, Uzbek, Russian
Religions Sunni Muslim 80%, Other 15%, Shi'a Muslim 5%
Ethnic mix Tajik 80%, Uzbek 15%, Other 3%, Russian 1%, Kyrgyz 1%
Government Presidential system
Currency Somoni = 100 diram
Literacy rate 99%
Calorie consumption 1828 calories

TANZANIA
East Africa

Official name United Republic of Tanzania
Formation 1964 / 1964
Capital Dodoma
Population 39.7 million / 116 people per sq mile (45 people per sq km) / 36%
Total area 364,898 sq. miles (945,087 sq. km)
Languages Kiswahili*, Sukuma, Chagga, Nyamwezi, Hehe, Makonde, Yao, Sandawe, English*
Religions Muslim 33%, Christian 33%, Traditional beliefs 30%, Other 4%
Ethnic mix Native African (over 120 tribes) 99%, European, Asian, and Arab 1%
Government Presidential system
Currency Tanzanian shilling = 100 cents
Literacy rate 69%
Calorie consumption 1975 calories

THAILAND
Southeast Asia

Official name Kingdom of Thailand
Formation 1238 / 1907
Capital Bangkok
Population 68.3 million / 346 people per sq mile (134 people per sq km) / 32%
Total area 198,455 sq. miles (514,000 sq. km)
Languages Thai*, Chinese, Malay, Khmer, Mon, Karen, Miao
Religions Buddhist 95%, Muslim 4%, Other (including Christian) 1%
Ethnic mix Thai 83%, Chinese 12%, Malay 3%, Khmer and Other 2%
Government Parliamentary system
Currency Baht = 100 satang
Literacy rate 93%
Calorie consumption 2467 calories

TOGO
West Africa

Official name The Togolese Republic
Formation 1960 / 1960
Capital Lomé
Population 6.5 million / 310 people per sq mile (120 people per sq km) / 36%
Total area 21,924 sq. miles (56,785 sq. km)
Languages French*, Ewe, Kabye, Gurma
Religions Traditional beliefs 50%, Christian 35%, Muslim 15%
Ethnic mix Ewe 46%, Other African 41%, Kabye 12%, European 1%
Government Presidential system
Currency CFA franc = 100 centimes
Literacy rate 53%
Calorie consumption 2345 calories

TONGA
Australasia & Oceania

Official name Kingdom of Tonga
Formation 1970 / 1970
Capital Nuku'alofa
Population 116,921 / 421 people per sq mile (162 people per sq km) / 34%
Total area 289 sq. miles (748 sq. km)
Languages English*, Tongan*
Religions Free Wesleyan 41%, Other 17%, Roman Catholic 16%, Church of Jesus Christ of Latter-day Saints 14%, Free Church of Tonga 12%
Ethnic mix Tongan 98%, Other 2%
Government Monarchy
Currency Pa'anga (Tongan dollar) = 100 seniti
Literacy rate 99%
Calorie consumption Not available

TRINIDAD & TOBAGO
West Indies

Official name Republic of Trinidad and Tobago
Formation 1962 / 1962
Capital Port-of-Spain
Population 1.3 million / 656 people per sq mile (253 people per sq km) / 76%
Total area 1980 sq. miles (5128 sq. km)
Languages English Creole, English*, Hindi, French, Spanish
Religions Roman Catholic 32%, Hindu 24%, Protestant 14%, Anglican 14%, Other and nonreligious 9%, Muslim 7%
Ethnic mix East Indian 40%, Black 40%, Mixed race 18%, Other 1%, White and Chinese 1%
Government Parliamentary system
Currency Trinidad and Tobago dollar = 100 cents
Literacy rate 99%
Calorie consumption 2732 calories

TUNISIA
North Africa

Official name The Tunisian Republic
Formation 1956 / 1956
Capital Tunis
Population 10.3 million / 172 people per sq mile (66 people per sq km) / 64%
Total area 63,169 sq. miles (163,610 sq. km)
Languages Arabic*, French
Religions Muslim (mainly Sunni) 98%, Christian 1%, Jewish 1%
Ethnic mix Arab and Berber 98%, Jewish 1%, European 1%
Government Presidential system
Currency Tunisian dinar = 1000 millimes
Literacy rate 74%
Calorie consumption 3238 calories

TURKEY
Asia / Europe

Official name Republic of Turkey
Formation 1923 / 1939
Capital Ankara
Population 75.2 million / 253 people per sq mile (98 people per sq km) / 67%
Total area 301,382 sq. miles (780,580 sq. km)
Languages Turkish*, Kurdish, Arabic, Circassian, Armenian, Greek, Georgian, Ladino
Religions Muslim (mainly Sunni) 99%, Other 1%
Ethnic mix Turkish 70%, Kurdish 20%, Other 8%, Arab 2%
Government Parliamentary system
Currency new Turkish lira = 100 kurus
Literacy rate 98%
Calorie consumption 3357 calories

TURKMENISTAN
Central Asia

Official name Turkmenistan
Formation 1991 / 1991
Capital Ashgabat
Population 5 million / 27 people per sq mile (10 people per sq km) / 46%
Total area 188,455 sq. miles (488,100 sq. km)
Languages Turkmen*, Uzbek, Russian, Kazakh, Tatar
Religions Sunni Muslim 87%, Orthodox Christian 11%, Other 2%
Ethnic mix Turkmen 77%, Uzbek 9%, Russian 7%, Other 4%, Kazakh 2%, Tatar 1%
Government One-party state
Currency Manat = 100 tenge
Literacy rate 99%
Calorie consumption 2742 calories

TUVALU
Australasia & Oceania

Official name Tuvalu
Formation 1978 / 1978
Capital Fongafale, on Funafuti Atoll
Population 11,992 / 1199 people per sq mile (461 people per sq km) / 57%
Total area 10 sq. miles (26 sq. km)
Languages English*, Tuvaluan, Kiribati
Religions Church of Tuvalu 97%, Baha'i 1%, Seventh-day Adventist 1%, Other 1%
Ethnic mix Polynesian 92%, Other 6%, Kiribati 2%
Government Nonparty system
Currency Australian dollar and Tuvaluan dollar = 100 cents
Literacy rate 98%
Calorie consumption Not available

UGANDA
East Africa

Official name Republic of Uganda
Formation 1962 / 1962
Capital Kampala
Population 30.9 million / 401 people per sq mile (155 people per sq km) / 12%
Total area 91,135 sq. miles (236,040 sq. km)
Languages English*, Luganda, Nkole, Chiga, Lango, Acholi, Teso, Lugbara
Religions Roman Catholic 38%, Protestant 33%, Traditional beliefs 13%, Muslim (mainly Sunni) 8%, Other 8%
Ethnic mix Other 50%, Baganda 17%, Banyankole 10%, Basoga 9%, Iteso 7%, Bakiga 7%
Government Presidential system
Currency New Uganda shilling = 100 cents
Literacy rate 67%
Calorie consumption 2410 calories

UKRAINE
Eastern Europe

Official name Ukraine
Formation 1991 / 1991
Capital Kiev
Population 45.5 million / 195 people per sq mile (75 people per sq km) / 67%
Total area 233,089 sq. miles (603,700 sq. km)
Languages Ukrainian*, Russian, Tatar
Religions Christian (mainly Orthodox) 95%, Other 5%
Ethnic mix Ukrainian 78%, Russian 17%, Other 5%
Government Presidential system
Currency Hryvna = 100 kopiykas
Literacy rate 99%
Calorie consumption 3054 calories

UNITED ARAB EMIRATES
Southwest Asia

Official name United Arab Emirates
Formation 1971 / 1972
Capital Abu Dhabi
Population 4.8 million / 149 people per sq mile (57 people per sq km) / 85%
Total area 32,000 sq. miles (82,880 sq. km)
Languages Arabic*, Farsi, Indian and Pakistani languages
Religions Muslim (mainly Sunni) 96%, Christian, Hindu, and other 4%
Ethnic mix Asian 60%, Emirian 25%, Other Arab 12%, European 3%
Government Monarchy
Currency UAE dirham = 100 fils
Literacy rate 77%
Calorie consumption 3225 calories

UNITED KINGDOM
Northwest Europe

Official name United Kingdom of Great Britain and Northern Ireland
Formation 1707 / 1922
Capital London
Population 60 million / 643 people per sq mile (248 people per sq km) / 89%
Total area 94,525 sq. miles (244,820 sq. km)
Languages English*, Welsh* *(in Wales)*, Scottish Gaelic, Irish Gaelic
Religions Anglican 45%, Roman Catholic 9%, Presbyterian 4%, Other 42%
Ethnic mix English 80%, Scottish 9%, West Indian, Asian, and other 5%, Northern Irish 3%, Welsh 3%
Government Parliamentary system
Currency Pound sterling = 100 pence
Literacy rate 99%
Calorie consumption 3412 calories

UNITED STATES
North America

Official name United States of America
Formation 1776 / 1959
Capital Washington D.C.
Population 304 million / 86 people per sq mile (33 people per sq km) / 80%
Total area 3,717,792 sq. miles (9,626,091 sq. km)
Languages English*, Spanish, Chinese, French, German, Tagalog, Vietnamese, Italian, Korean, Russian, Polish
Religions Protestant 52%, Roman Catholic 25%, Muslim 2%, Jewish 2%, Other 19%
Ethnic mix White 62%, Hispanic 13%, Black American/African 13%, Other 7%, Asian 4%, Native American 1%
Government Presidential system
Currency US dollar = 100 cents
Literacy rate 99%
Calorie consumption 3774 calories

URUGUAY
South America

Official name The Oriental Republic of Uruguay
Formation 1828 / 1828
Capital Montevideo
Population 3.5 million / 52 people per sq mile (20 people per sq km) / 93%
Total area 68,039 sq. miles (176,220 sq. km)
Languages Spanish*
Religions Roman Catholic 66%, Other and nonreligious 30%, Jewish 2%, Protestant 2%
Ethnic mix White 90%, Mestizo 6%, Black 4%
Government Presidential system
Currency Uruguayan peso = 100 centésimos
Literacy rate 98%
Calorie consumption 2828 calories

UZBEKISTAN
Central Asia

Official name Republic of Uzbekistan
Formation 1991 / 1991
Capital Tashkent
Population 27.4 million / 159 people per sq mile (61 people per sq km) / 37%
Total area 172,741 sq. miles (447,400 sq. km)
Languages Uzbek*, Russian, Tajik, Kazakh
Religions Sunni Muslim 88%, Orthodox Christian 9%, Other 3%
Ethnic mix Uzbek 80%, Other 6%, Russian 6%, Tajik 5%, Kazakh 3%
Government Presidential system
Currency Som = 100 tiyin
Literacy rate 99%
Calorie consumption 2241 calories

VANUATU
Australasia & Oceania

Official name Republic of Vanuatu
Formation 1980 / 1980
Capital Port Vila
Population 211,971 / 45 people per sq mile (17 people per sq km) / 23%
Total area 4710 sq. miles (12,200 sq. km)
Languages Bislama* (Melanesian pidgin), English*, French*, other indigenous languages
Religions Presbyterian 37%, Other 19%, Anglican 15%, Roman Catholic 15%, Traditional beliefs 8%, Seventh-day Adventist 6%
Ethnic mix Melanesian 98%, Other 1%, European 1%
Government Parliamentary system
Currency Vatu = 100 centimes
Literacy rate 74%
Calorie consumption 2587 calories

VATICAN CITY
Southern Europe

Official name The Vatican City
Formation 1929 / 1929
Capital Vatican City
Population 821 / 4829 people per sq mile (1866 people per sq km) / 100%
Total area 0.17 sq. miles (0.44 sq. km)
Languages Italian*, Latin*
Religions Roman Catholic 100%
Government Papal state
Currency Euro = 100 cents
Literacy rate 99%
Calorie consumption Not available

VENEZUELA
South America

Official name Bolivarian Republic of Venezuela
Formation 1830 / 1830
Capital Caracas
Population 27.7 million / 81 people per sq mile (31 people per sq km) / 88%
Total area 352,143 sq. miles (912,050 sq. km)
Languages Spanish*, Amerindian languages
Religions Roman Catholic 89%, Protestant and other 11%
Ethnic mix Mestizo 69%, White 20%, Black 9%, Amerindian 2%
Government Presidential system
Currency Bolívar = 100 céntimos
Literacy rate 93%
Calorie consumption 2336 calories

VIETNAM
Southeast Asia

Official name Socialist Republic of Vietnam
Formation 1976 / 1976
Capital Hanoi
Population 86.4 million / 688 people per sq mile (266 people per sq km) / 26%
Total area 127,243 sq. miles (329,560 sq. km)
Languages Vietnamese*, Chinese, Thai, Khmer, Muong, Nung, Miao, Yao, Jarai
Religions Nonreligious 81%, Buddhist 9%, Christian 7%, Other 3%
Ethnic mix Vietnamese 86%, Other 10%, Tay 2%, Thai 2%
Government One-party state
Currency Dông = 10 hao = 100 xu
Literacy rate 90%
Calorie consumption 2566 calories

YEMEN
Southwest Asia

Official name Republic of Yemen
Formation 1990 / 1990
Capital Sana
Population 22.3 million / 103 people per sq mile (40 people per sq km) / 26%
Total area 203,849 sq. miles (527,970 sq. km)
Languages Arabic*
Religions Sunni Muslim 55%, Shi'a Muslim 42%, Christian, Hindu, and Jewish 3%
Ethnic mix Arab 99%, Other 1%
Government Presidential system
Currency Yemeni rial = 100 fils
Literacy rate 49%
Calorie consumption 2038 calories

ZAMBIA
Southern Africa

Official name Republic of Zambia
Formation 1964 / 1964
Capital Lusaka
Population 12.1 million / 42 people per sq mile (16 people per sq km) / 36%
Total area 290,584 sq. miles (752,614 sq. km)
Languages English*, Bemba, Tonga, Nyanja, Lozi, Lala-Bisa, Nsenga
Religions Christian 63%, Traditional beliefs 36%, Muslim and Hindu 1%
Ethnic mix Bemba 34%, Other African 26%, Tonga 16%, Nyanja 14%, Lozi 9%, European 1%
Government Presidential system
Currency Zambian kwacha = 100 ngwee
Literacy rate 68%
Calorie consumption 1927 calories

ZIMBABWE
Southern Africa

Official name Republic of Zimbabwe
Formation 1980 / 1980
Capital Harare
Population 13.2 million / 88 people per sq mile (34 people per sq km) / 35%
Total area 150,803 sq. miles (390,580 sq. km)
Languages English*, Shona, isiNdebele
Religions Syncretic (Christian/traditional beliefs) 50%, Christian 25%, Traditional beliefs 24%, Other (including Muslim) 1%
Ethnic mix Shona 71%, Ndebele 16%, Other African 11%, White 1%, Asian 1%
Government Presidential system
Currency Zimbabwe dollar = 100 cents
Literacy rate 90%
Calorie consumption 1943 calories

207

GLOSSARY

This glossary lists all geographical, technical, and foreign language terms which appear in the text, followed by a brief definition of the term. Any acronyms used in the text are also listed in full. Terms in italics are for cross-reference and indicate that the word is separately defined in the glossary.

A

Aboriginal The original (*indigenous*) inhabitants of a country or continent. Especially used with reference to Australia.

Abyssal plain A broad *plain* found in the depths of the ocean, more than 10,000 ft (3,000 m) below sea level.

Acid rain Rain, sleet, snow, or mist which has absorbed waste gases from fossil-fueled power stations and vehicle exhausts, becoming more acid. It causes severe environmental damage.

Adaptation The gradual evolution of plants and animals so that they become better suited to survive and reproduce in their *environment*.

Afforestation The planting of new forest in areas that were once forested but have been cleared.

Agribusiness A term applied to activities such as the growing of crops, rearing of animals, or the manufacture of farm machinery, which eventually leads to the supply of agricultural produce at market.

Air mass A huge, homogeneous mass of air, within which horizontal patterns of temperature and *humidity* are consistent. Air masses are separated by *fronts*.

Alliance An agreement between two or more states, to work together to achieve common purposes.

Alluvial fan A large fan-shaped deposit of fine sediments deposited by a river as it emerges from a narrow, mountain valley onto a broad, open *plain*.

Alluvium Material deposited by rivers. Nowadays usually only applied to finer particles of silt and clay.

Alpine Mountain *environment*, between the *treeline* and the level of permanent snow cover.

Alpine mountains Ranges of mountains formed between 30 and 65 million years ago, by *folding*, in western and central Europe.

Amerindian A term applied to people *indigenous* to North, Central, and South America.

Animal husbandry The business of rearing animals.

Antarctic circle The parallel which lies at *latitude* of 66° 32' S.

Anticline A geological *fold* that forms an arch shape, curving upward in the rock *strata*.

Anticyclone An area of relatively high atmospheric pressure.

Aquaculture Collective term for the farming of produce derived from the sea, including fish-farming, the cultivation of shellfish, and plants such as seaweed.

Aquifer A body of rock that can absorb water. Also applied to any rock strata that have sufficient porosity to yield *groundwater* through wells or springs.

Arable Land which has been plowed and is being used, or is suitable, for growing crops.

Archipelago A group or chain of islands.

Arctic Circle The parallel that lies at a *latitude* of 66° 32' N.

Arête A thin, jagged mountain ridge that divides two adjacent *cirques*, found in regions where *glaciation* has occurred.

Arid Dry. An area of low rainfall, where the rate of *evaporation* may be greater than that of *precipitation*. Often defined as those areas that receive less than one inch (25 mm) of rain a year. In these areas only drought-resistant plants can survive.

Artesian well A naturally occurring source of underground water, stored in an *aquifer*.

Artisanal Small-scale, manual operation, such as fishing, using little or no machinery.

ASEAN Association of Southeast Asian Nations. Established in 1967 to promote economic, social, and cultural cooperation. Its members include Brunei, Indonesia, Malaysia, Philippines, Singapore, and Thailand.

Aseismic A region where *earthquake* activity has ceased.

Asteroid A minor planet circling the Sun, mainly between the orbits of Mars and Jupiter.

Asthenosphere A zone of hot, partially melted rock, which underlies the *lithosphere*, within the Earth's *crust*.

Atmosphere The envelope of odorless, colorless and tasteless gases surrounding the Earth, consisting of *oxygen* (23%), *nitrogen* (75%), argon (1%), *carbon dioxide* (0.03%), as well as tiny proportions of other gases.

Atmospheric pressure The pressure created by the action of gravity on the gases surrounding the Earth.

Atoll A ring-shaped island or *coral reef* often enclosing a *lagoon* of sea water.

Avalanche The rapid movement of a mass of snow and ice down a steep slope. Similar movements of other materials are described as *rock avalanches* or *landslides* and *sand avalanches*.

B

Badlands A landscape that has been heavily eroded and dissected by rainwater, and which has little or no vegetation.

Back slope The gentler windward slope of a sand *dune* or gentler slope of a *cuesta*.

Bajos An *alluvial fan* deposited by a river at the base of mountains and hills that encircle *desert* areas.

Bar, coastal An offshore strip of sand or shingle, either above or below the water. Usually parallel to the shore but sometimes crescent-shaped or at an oblique angle.

Barchan A crescent-shaped sand *dune*, formed where wind direction is very consistent. The horns of the crescent point downwind and where there is enough sand the barchan is mobile.

Barrio A Spanish term for the shantytowns – settlements of shacks – that are clustered around many South and Central American cities (*see also Favela*).

Basalt Dark, fine-grained *igneous rock* that is formed near the Earth's surface from fast-cooling *lava*.

Base level The level below which flowing water cannot erode the land.

Basement rock A mass of ancient rock often of *PreCambrian age*, covered by a layer of more recent *sedimentary rocks*. Commonly associated with *shield* areas.

Beach Lake or sea shore where waves break and there is an accumulation of loose sand, mud, gravel, or pebbles.

Bedrock Solid, consolidated and relatively unweathered rock, found on the surface of the land or just below a layer of soil or *weathered* rock.

Biodiversity The quantity of animal or plant species in a given area.

Biomass The total mass of organic matter – plants and animals – in a given area. It is usually measured in kilogrammes per square meter. Plant biomass is proportionally greater than that of animals, except in cities.

Biosphere The zone just above and below the Earth's surface, where all plants and animals live.

Blizzard A severe windstorm with snow and sleet. Visibility is often severely restricted.

Bluff The steep bank of a *meander*, formed by the erosive action of a river.

Boreal forest Tracts of mainly coniferous forest found in northern *latitudes*.

Breccia A type of rock composed of sharp fragments, cemented by a fine-grained material such as clay.

Butte An isolated, flat-topped hill with steep or vertical sides, buttes are the eroded remnants of a former land surface

C

Caatinga Portuguese (Brazilian) term for thorny woodland growing in areas of pale granitic soils.

CACM Central American Common Market. Established in 1960 to further economic ties between its members, which are Costa Rica, El Salvador, Guatemala, Honduras, and Nicaragua.

Calcite Hexagonal crystals of calcium carbonate.

Caldera A huge volcanic vent, often containing a number of smaller vents, and sometimes a crater lake.

Carbon cycle The transfer of carbon to and from the *atmosphere*. This occurs on land through *photosynthesis*. In the sea, *carbon dioxide* is absorbed, some returning to the air and some taken up into the bodies of sea creatures.

Carbon dioxide A colorless, odorless gas (CO_2) that makes up 0.03% of the *atmosphere*.

Carbonation The process whereby rocks are broken down by carbonic acid. Carbon dioxide in the air dissolves in rainwater, forming carbonic acid. *Limestone* terrain can be rapidly eaten away.

Cash crop A single crop grown specifically for export sale, rather than for local use. Typical examples include coffee, tea, and citrus fruits.

Cassava A type of grain meal, used to produce tapioca. A staple crop in many parts of Africa.

Castle kopje Hill or rock outcrop, especially in southern Africa, where steep sides, and a summit composed of blocks, give a castle-like appearance.

Cataracts A series of stepped waterfalls created as a river flows over a band of hard, resistant rock.

Causeway A raised route through marshland or a body of water.

CEEAC Economic Community of Central African States. Established in 1983 to promote regional cooperation and if possible, establish a common market between 16 Central African nations.

Chemical weathering The chemical reactions leading to the decomposition of rocks. Types of chemical weathering include *carbonation*, *hydrolysis*, and *oxidation*.

Chernozem A fertile soil, also known as "black earth" consisting of a layer of dark topsoil, rich in decaying vegetation, overlying a lighter chalky layer.

Cirque Armchair-shaped basin, found in mountain regions, with a steep back, or rear, wall and a raised rock lip, often containing a lake (or *tarn*). The cirque floor has been eroded by a *glacier*, while the back wall is eroded both by the *glacier* and by *weathering*.

Climate The average weather conditions in a given area over a period of years, sometimes defined as 30 years or more.

Cold War A period of hostile relations between the US and the Soviet Union and their allies after the Second World War.

Composite volcano Also known as a strato-volcano, the volcanic cone is composed of alternating deposits of *lava* and *pyroclastic* material.

Compound A substance made up of *elements* chemically combined in a consistent way.

Condensation The process whereby a gas changes into a liquid. For example, water vapor in the *atmosphere* condenses around tiny airborne particles to form droplets of water.

Confluence The point at which two rivers meet.

Conglomerate Rock composed of large, water-worn or rounded pebbles, held together by a natural cement.

Coniferous forest A forest type containing trees which are generally, but not necessarily, *evergreen* and have slender, needlelike leaves. Coniferous trees reproduce by means of seeds contained in a cone.

Continental drift The theory that the continents of today are fragments of one or more prehistoric *supercontinents* which have moved across the Earth's surface, creating ocean basins. The theory has been superseded by a more sophisticated one – *plate tectonics*.

Continental shelf An area of the continental crust, below sea level, which slopes gently. It is separated from the deep ocean by a much more steeply inclined *continental slope*.

Continental slope A steep slope running from the edge of the *continental shelf* to the ocean floor.

Conurbation A vast metropolitan area created by the expansion of towns and cities into a virtually continuous urban area.

Cool continental A rainy *climate* with warm summers [warmest month below 76°F (22°C)] and often severe winters [coldest month below 32°F (0°C)].

Copra The dried, white kernel of a coconut, from which coconut oil is extracted.

Coral reef An underwater barrier created by colonies of the coral polyp. Polyps secrete a protective skeleton of calcium carbonate, and reefs develop as live polyps build on the skeletons of dead generations.

Core The center of the Earth, consisting of a dense mass of iron and nickel. It is thought that the outer core is molten or liquid, and that the hot inner core is solid due to extremely high pressures.

Coriolis effect A deflecting force caused by the rotation of the Earth. In the northern hemisphere a body, such as an *air mass* or ocean current, is deflected to the right, and in the southern hemisphere to the left. This prevents winds from blowing straight from areas of high to low pressure.

Coulées A US / Canadian term for a ravine formed by river *erosion*.

Craton A large block of the Earth's *crust* which has remained stable for a long period of *geological time*. It is made up of ancient *shield* rocks.

Cretaceous A period of *geological time* beginning about 145 million years ago and lasting until about 65 million years ago.

Crevasse A deep crack in a *glacier*.

Crust The hard, thin outer shell of the Earth. The crust floats on the *mantle*, which is softer and more dense. Under the oceans (oceanic crust) the crust is 3.7–6.8 miles (6–11 km) thick. Continental crust averages 18–24 miles (30–40 km).

Crystalline rock Rocks formed when molten *magma* crystallizes (*igneous rocks*) or when heat or pressure cause re-crystallization (*metamorphic rocks*). Crystalline rocks are distinct from *sedimentary rocks*.

Cuesta A hill which rises into a steep slope on one side but has a gentler gradient on its other slope.

Cyclone An area of low *atmospheric pressure*, occurring where the air is warm and relatively low in density, causing low level winds to spiral. *Hurricanes* and *typhoons* are tropical cyclones.

D

De facto
1 Government or other activity that takes place, or exists in actuality if not by right.
2 A border, which exists in practice, but which is not officially recognized by all the countries it adjoins.

Deciduous forest A forest of trees that shed their leaves annually at a particular time or season. In *temperate* climates the fall of leaves occurs in the autumn. Some *coniferous* trees, such as the larch, are deciduous. Deciduous vegetation contrasts with *evergreen*, which keeps its leaves for more than a year.

Defoliant Chemical spray used to remove foliage (leaves) from trees.

Deforestation The act of cutting down and clearing large areas of forest for human activities, such as agricultural land or urban development.

Delta Low-lying, fan-shaped area at a river mouth, formed by the *deposition* of successive layers of *sediment*. Slowing as it enters the sea, a river deposits sediment and may, as a result, split into numerous smaller channels, known as *distributaries*.

Denudation The combined effect of *weathering*, *erosion*, and *mass movement*, which, over long periods, exposes underlying rocks.

Deposition The laying down of material that has accumulated:
(1) after being *eroded* and then transported by physical forces such as wind, ice, or water;
(2) as organic remains, such as coal and coral;
(3) as the result of *evaporation* and chemical *precipitation*.

Depression
1 In climatic terms it is a large low pressure system.
2 A complex *fold*, producing a large valley, which incorporates both a *syncline* and an *anticline*.

Desert An *arid* region of low rainfall, with little vegetation or animal life, which is adapted to the dry conditions. The term is now applied not only to hot tropical and subtropical regions, but to arid areas of the continental interiors and to the ice deserts of the *Arctic* and *Antarctic*.

Desertification The gradual extension of *desert* conditions in *arid* or *semiarid* regions, as a result of climatic change or human activity, such as over-grazing and *deforestation*.

Despot A ruler with absolute power. Despots are often associated with oppressive regimes.

Detritus Piles of rock deposited by an erosive agent such as a river or *glacier*.

Distributary A minor branch of a river, which does not rejoin the main stream, common at *deltas*.

Diurnal Daily, something that occurs each day. Diurnal temperature refers to the variation in temperature over the course of a full day and night.

Divide A US term describing the area of high ground separating two *drainage basins*.

Donga A steep-sided *gully*, resulting from *erosion* by a river or by floods.

Dormant A term used to describe a *volcano* which is not currently erupting. They differ from extinct volcanoes as dormant volcanoes are still considered likely to erupt in the future.

Drainage basin The area drained by a single river system, its boundary is marked by a *watershed* or *divide*.

Drought A long period of continuously low rainfall.

Drumlin A long, streamlined hillock composed of material deposited by a *glacier*. They often occur in groups known as swarms.

Dune A mound or ridge of sand, shaped, and often moved, by the wind. They are found in hot *deserts* and on low-lying coasts where onshore winds blow across sandy beaches.

Dyke A wall constructed in low-lying areas to contain floodwaters or protect from high tides.

E

Earthflow The rapid movement of soil and other loose surface material down a slope, when saturated by water. Similar to a mudflow but not as fast-flowing, due to a lower percentage of water.

Earthquake Sudden movements of the Earth's *crust*, causing the ground to shake. Frequently occurring at *tectonic plate* margins. The shock, or series of shocks, spreads out from an *epicenter*.

EC The European Community (*see* EU).

Ecosystem A system of living organisms – plants and animals – interacting with their *environment*.

ECOWAS Economic Community of West African States. Established in 1975, it incorporates 16 West African states and aims to promote closer regional and economic cooperation.

Element
1 A constituent of the *climate* – *precipitation*, *humidity*, temperature, *atmospheric pressure*, or wind.
2 A substance that cannot be separated into simpler substances by chemical means.

El Niño A climatic phenomenon, the El Niño effect occurs about 14 times each century and leads to major shifts in global air circulation. It is associated with unusually warm currents off the coasts of Peru, Ecuador and Chile. The anomaly can last for up to two years.

Environment The conditions created by the surroundings (both natural and artificial) within which an organism lives. In human geography the word includes the surrounding economic, cultural, and social conditions.

Eon (aeon) Traditionally a long, but indefinite, period of *geological time*.

Ephemeral A nonpermanent feature, often used in connection with seasonal rivers or lakes in dry areas.

Epicenter The point on the Earth's surface directly above the underground origin – or focus – of an *earthquake*.

Equator The line of *latitude* which lies equidistant between the North and South Poles.

Erg An extensive area of sand *dunes*, particularly in the Sahara Desert.

Erosion The processes which wear away the surface of the land. *Glaciers*, wind, rivers, waves, and currents all carry debris which causes *erosion*. Some definitions also include *mass movement* due to gravity as an agent of erosion.

Escarpment A steep slope at the margin of a level, upland surface. In a landscape created by *folding*, escarpments (or scarps) frequently lie behind a more gentle backward slope.

Esker A narrow, winding ridge of sand and gravel deposited by streams of water flowing beneath or at the edge of a *glacier*.

Erratic A rock transported by a *glacier* and deposited some distance from its place of origin.

Eustacy A world-wide fall or rise in ocean levels.

EU The European Union. Established in 1965, it was formerly known as the EEC (European Economic Community) and then the EC (European Community). Its members are Austria, Belgium, Denmark, Finland, France, Germany, Greece, Ireland, Italy, Luxembourg, Netherlands, Portugal, Spain, Sweden, and UK. It seeks to establish an integrated European common market and eventual federation.

Evaporation The process whereby a liquid or solid is turned into a gas or vapor. Also refers to the diffusion of water vapor into the *atmosphere* from exposed water surfaces such as lakes and seas.

Evapotranspiration The loss of moisture from the Earth's surface through a combination of *evaporation*, and *transpiration* from the leaves of plants.

Evergreen Plants with long-lasting leaves, which are not shed annually or seasonally.

Exfoliation A kind of *weathering* whereby scalelike flakes of rock are peeled or broken off by the development of salt crystals in water within the rocks. *Groundwater*, which contains dissolved salts, seeps to the surface and evaporates, precipitating a film of salt crystals, which expands causing fine cracks. As these grow, flakes of rock break off.

Extrusive rock *Igneous* rock formed when molten material (*magma*) pours forth at the Earth's surface and cools rapidly. It usually has a glassy texture.

F

Factionalism The actions of one or more minority political group acting against the interests of the majority government.

Fault A fracture or crack in rock, where strains (*tectonic* movement) have caused blocks to move, vertically or laterally, relative to each other.

Fauna Collective name for the animals of a particular period of time, or region.

Favela Brazilian term for the shantytowns or temporary huts that have grown up around the edge of many South and Central American cities.

Ferrel cell A component in the global pattern of air circulation, which rises in the colder *latitudes* (60° N and S) and descends in warmer *latitudes* (30° N and S). The Ferrel cell forms part of the world's three-cell air circulation pattern, with the *Hadley* and Polar cells.

Fissure A deep crack in a rock or a *glacier*.

Fjord A deep, narrow inlet, created when the sea inundates the *U-shaped valley* created by a *glacier*.

Flash flood A sudden, short-lived rise in the water level of a river or stream, or surge of water down a dry river channel, or *wadi*, caused by heavy rainfall.

Flax A plant used to make linen.

Floodplain The broad, flat part of a river valley, adjacent to the river itself, formed by *sediment* deposited during flooding.

Flora The collective name for the plants of a particular period of time or region.

Flow The movement of a river within its banks, particularly in terms of the speed and volume of water.

Fold A bend in the rock *strata* of the Earth's *crust*, resulting from compression.

Fossil The remains, or traces,of a dead organism preserved in the Earth's *crust*.

Fossil dune A *dune* formed in a once-*arid* region which is now wetter. *Dunes* normally move with the wind, but in these cases vegetation makes them stable.

Fossil fuel Fuel – coal, natural gas or oil – composed of the fossilized remains of plants and animals.

Front The boundary between two *air masses*, which contrast sharply in temperature and *humidity*.

Frontal depression An area of low pressure caused by rising warm air. They are generally 600–1,200 miles (1,000–2,000 km) in diameter. Within *depressions* there are both warm and cold fronts.

Frost shattering A form of *weathering* where water freezes in cracks, causing expansion. As temperatures fluctuate and the ice melts and refreezes, it eventually causes the rocks to shatter and fragments of rock to break off.

G

Gaucho South American term for a stock herder or cowboy who works on the grassy *plains* of Paraguay, Uruguay, and Argentina.

Geological timescale The chronology of the Earth's history as revealed in its rocks. Geological time is divided into a number of periods: *eon*, era, period, epoch, age, and chron (the shortest). These units are not of uniform length.

Geosyncline A concave fold (*syncline*) or large depression in the Earth's *crust*, extending hundreds of miles. This basin contains a deep layer of sediment, especially at its center, from the land masses around it.

Geothermal energy Heat derived from hot rocks within the Earth's *crust* and resulting in hot springs, steam, or hot rocks at the surface. The energy is generated by rock movements, and from the breakdown of radioactive elements occurring under intense pressure.

GDP Gross Domestic Product. The total value of goods and services produced by a country excluding income from foreign countries.

Geyser A jet of steam and hot water that intermittently erupts from vents in the ground in areas that are, or were, *volcanic*. Some geysers occasionally reach heights of 196 ft (60 m).

Ghetto An area of a city or region occupied by an overwhelming majority of people from one racial or religious group, who may be subject to persecution or containment.

Glaciation The growth of *glaciers* and *ice sheets*, and their impact on the landscape.

Glacier A body of ice moving downslope under the influence of gravity and consisting of compacted and frozen snow. A glacier is distinct from an *ice sheet*, which is wider and less confined by features of the landscape.

Glacio-eustacy A world-wide change in the level of the oceans, caused when the formation of *ice sheets* takes up water or when their melting returns water to the ocean. The formation of ice sheets in the *Pleistocene* epoch, for example, caused sea level to drop by about 320 ft (100-m).

Glaciofluvial To do with glacial *meltwater*, the landforms it creates and its processes; *erosion*, transportation, and *deposition*. Glaciofluvial effects are more powerful and rapid where they occur within or beneath the *glacier*, rather than beyond its edge.

Glacis A gentle slope or *pediment*.

Global warming An increase in the average temperature of the Earth. At present the *greenhouse effect* is thought to contribute to this.

GNP Gross National Product. The total value of goods and services produced by a country.

Gondwanaland The *supercontinent* thought to have existed over 200 million years ago in the southern hemisphere. Gondwanaland is believed to have comprised today's Africa, Madagascar, Australia, parts of South America, *Antarctica*, and the Indian subcontinent.

Graben A block of rock let down between two parallel *faults*. Where the graben occurs within a valley, the structure is known as a *rift valley*.

Grease ice Slicks of ice which form in *Antarctic* seas, when ice crystals are bonded together by wind and wave action.

Greenhouse effect A change in the temperature of the *atmosphere*. Short-wave solar radiation travels through the *atmosphere* unimpeded to the Earth's surface, whereas outgoing, long-wave terrestrial radiation is absorbed by materials that reradiate it back to the Earth. Radiation trapped in this way, by water vapor, carbon dioxide, and other "greenhouse gases," keeps the Earth warm. As more *carbon dioxide* is released into the atmosphere by the burning of *fossil fuels*, the greenhouse effect may cause a global increase in temperature.

Groundwater Water that has seeped into the pores, cavities, and cracks of rocks or into soil and water held in an *aquifer*.

Gully A deep, narrow channel eroded in the landscape by *ephemeral* streams.

Guyot A small, flat-topped submarine mountain, formed as a result of subsidence which occurs during *sea-floor spreading*.

Gypsum A soft mineral *compound* (hydrated calcium sulphate), used as the basis of many forms of plaster, including plaster of Paris.

H

Hadley cell A large-scale component in the global pattern of air circulation. Warm air rises over the *Equator* and blows at high altitude toward the poles, sinking in subtropical regions (30° N and 30° S) and creating high pressure. The air then flows at the surface toward the *Equator* in the form of trade winds. There is one cell in each hemisphere. Named after G. Hadley, who published his theory in 1735.

Hamada An Arabic word for a plateau of bare rock in a *desert*.

Hanging valley A tributary valley that ends suddenly, high above the bed of the main valley. The effect is found where the main valley has been more deeply eroded by a *glacier*, than has the tributary valley. A stream in a hanging valley will descend to the floor of the main valley as a waterfall or *cataract*.

Headwards The action of a river eroding back upstream, as opposed to the normal process of downstream *erosion*. Headwards erosion is often associated with *gullying*.

Hoodos Pinnacles of rock that have been worn away by *weathering* in *semiarid* regions.

Horst A block of the Earth's *crust* which has been left upstanding by the sinking of adjoining blocks along fault lines.

Hot spot A region of the Earth's *crust* where high thermal activity occurs, often leading to volcanic eruptions. Hot spots often occur far from plate boundaries, but their movement is associated with *plate tectonics*.

Humid equatorial Rainy *climate* with no winter, where the coolest month is generally above 64°F (18°C).

Humidity The relative amount of moisture held in the Earth's *atmosphere*.

Hurricane
1 A tropical *cyclone* occurring in the Caribbean and western North Atlantic.
2 A wind of more than 65 knots (75 kmph).

Hydroelectric power Energy produced by harnessing the rapid movement of water down steep mountain slopes to drive turbines to generate electricity.

Hydrolysis The chemical breakdown of rocks in reaction with water, forming new compounds.

I

Ice Age A period in the Earth's history when surface temperatures in the temperate *latitudes* were much lower and *ice sheets* expanded considerably. There have been *ice ages* from *Pre-Cambrian* times onward. The most recent began two million years ago and ended 10,000 years ago.

Ice cap A permanent dome of ice in highland areas. The term ice cap is often seen as distinct from *ice sheet*, which denotes a much wider covering of ice; and is also used refer to the very extensive polar and Greenland ice caps.

Ice floe A large, flat mass of ice floating free on the ocean surface. It is usually formed after the break-up of winter ice by heavy storms.

Ice sheet A continuous, very thick layer of ice and snow. The term is usually used of ice masses which are continental in extent.

Ice shelf A floating mass of ice attached to the edge of a coast. The seaward edge is usually a sheer cliff up to 100 ft (30-m) high.

Ice wedge Massive blocks of ice up to 6.5-ft (2-m) wide at the top and extending 32-ft (10-m) deep. They are found in cracks in *polygonally-patterned* ground in *periglacial* regions.

Iceberg A large mass of ice in a lake or a sea, which has broken off from a floating *ice sheet* (an *ice shelf*) or from a *glacier*.

Igneous rock Rock formed when molten material, *magma*, from the hot, lower layers of the Earth's *crust*, cools, solidifies, and crystallizes, either within the Earth's *crust* (*intrusive*) or on the surface (*extrusive*).

IMF International Monetary Fund. Established in 1944 as a UN agency, it contains 182 members around the world and is concerned with world monetary stability and economic development.

Incised meander A *meander* where the river, following its original course, cuts deeply into *bedrock*. This may occur when a mature, meandering river begins to erode its bed much more vigorously after the surrounding land has been uplifted.

Indigenous People, plants, or animals native to a particular region.

Infrastructure The communications and services – roads, railroads, and telecommunications – necessary for the functioning of a country or region.

Inselberg An isolated, steep-sided hill, rising from a low *plain* in *semiarid* and *savannah* landscapes. Inselbergs are usually composed of a rock, such as granite, which resists *erosion*.

Interglacial A period of global *climate*, between two *ice ages*, when temperatures rise and *ice sheets* and *glaciers* retreat.

Intraplate volcano A *volcano* which lies in the centre of one of the Earth's *tectonic plates*, rather than, as is more common, at its edge. They are thought to have been formed by a *hot spot*.

Intrusion (intrusive igneous rock) Rock formed when molten material, *magma*, penetrates existing rocks below the Earth's surface before cooling and solidifying. These rocks cool more slowly than extrusive rock and therefore tend to have coarser grains.

Irrigation The artificial supply of agricultural water to dry areas, often involving the creation of canals and the diversion of natural watercourses.

Island arc A curved chain of islands. Typically, such an arc fringes an ocean trench, formed at the margin between two *tectonic plates*. As one plate overrides another, *earthquakes* and volcanic activity are common and the islands themselves are often volcanic cones.

Isostasy The state of equilibrium that the Earth's *crust* maintains as its lighter and heavier parts float on the denser underlying mantle.

Isthmus A narrow strip of land connecting two larger landmasses or islands.

J

Jet stream A narrow belt of westerly winds in the *troposphere*, at altitudes above 39,000 ft (12,000 m). Jet streams tend to blow more strongly in winter and include: the subtropical jet stream; the *polar* front jet stream in mid-*latitudes*; the *Arctic* jet stream; and the polar-night jet stream.

Joint A crack in a rock, formed where blocks of rock have not shifted relative to each other, as is the case with a *fault*. Joints are created by *folding*; by shrinkage in *igneous rock* as it cools or *sedimentary rock* as it dries out; and by the release of pressure in a rock mass when overlying materials are removed by *erosion*.

Jute A plant fiber used to make coarse ropes, sacks, and matting.

K

Kame A mound of stratified sand and gravel with steep sides, deposited in a *crevasse* by *meltwater* running over a *glacier*. When the ice retreats, this forms an undulating terrain of hummocks.

Karst A barren *limestone* landscape created by carbonic acid in streams and rainwater, in areas where *limestone* is close to the surface. Typical features include caverns, towerlike hills, *sinkholes*, and flat limestone pavements.

Kettle hole A round hollow formed in a glacial deposit by a detached block of glacial ice, which later melted. They can fill with water to form kettle-lakes.

L

Lagoon A shallow stretch of coastal salt-water behind a partial barrier such as a sandbank or *coral reef*. Lagoon is also used to describe the water encircled by an *atoll*.

LAIA Latin American Integration Association. Established in 1980, its members are Argentina, Bolivia, Brazil, Chile, Colombia, Ecuador, Mexico, Paraguay, Peru, Uruguay, and Venezuala It aims to promote economic cooperation between member states.

Landslide The sudden downslope movement of a mass of rock or earth on a slope, caused either by heavy rain; the impact of waves; an *earthquake* or human activity.

Laterite A hard red deposit left by *chemical weathering* in tropical conditions, and consisting mainly of oxides of iron and aluminium.

Latitude The angular distance from the *Equator*, to a given point on the Earth's surface. Imaginary lines of *latitude* running parallel to the Equator encircle the Earth, and are measured in degrees north or south of the Equator. The Equator is 0°, the poles 90° South and North respectively. Also called parallels.

Laurasia In the theory of *continental drift*, the northern part of the great *supercontinent* of *Pangaea*. Laurasia is said to consist of N America, Greenland and all of Eurasia north of the Indian subcontinent.

Lava The molten rock, *magma*, which erupts onto the Earth's surface through a *volcano* or through a *fault* or crack in the Earth's *crust*. Lava refers to the rock both in its molten and in its later, solidified form.

Leaching The process whereby water dissolves minerals and moves them down through layers of soil or rock.

Levée A raised bank alongside the channel of a river. Levées are either human-made or formed in times of flood when the river overflows its channel, slows and deposits much of its *sediment* load.

Lichen An organism which is the symbiotic product of an algae and a fungus. Lichens form in tight crusts on stones and trees, and are resistant to extreme cold. They are often found in tundra regions.

Lignite Low-grade coal, also known as brown coal. Found in large deposits in eastern Europe.

Limestone A porous *sedimentary* rock formed from carbonate materials.

Lingua franca The language adopted as the common language between speakers whose native languages are different. This is common in former colonial states.

Lithosphere The rigid upper layer of the Earth, comprising the *crust* and the upper part of the *mantle*.

Llanos Vast grassland *plains* of northern South America.

Loess Fine-grained, yellow deposits of unstratified silts and sands. Loess is believed to be wind-carried *sediment* created in the last *Ice Age*. Some deposits may later have been redistributed by rivers. Loess-derived soils are of high quality, fertile, and easy to work.

Longitude A division of the Earth which pinpoints how far east or west a given place is from the Prime Meridian (0°) which runs through the Royal Observatory at Greenwich, England (UK). Imaginary lines of longitude are drawn around the world from pole to pole. The world is divided into 360 degrees.

Longshore drift The movement of sand and silt along the coast, carried by waves hitting the beach at an angle.

M

Magma Underground, molten rock, which is very hot and highly charged with gas. It is generated at great pressure, at depths 10 miles (16 km) or more below the Earth's surface. It can issue as *lava* at the Earth's surface or, more often, solidify below the surface as *intrusive igneous rock*.

Mantle The layer of the Earth between the *crust* and the *core*. It is about 1,800 miles (2,900-km) thick. The uppermost layer of the mantle is the soft, 125-mile (200 km) thick *asthenosphere* on which the more rigid *lithosphere* floats.

Maquiladoras Factories on the Mexico side of the Mexico/US border, that are allowed to import raw materials and components duty-free and use low-cost labor to assemble the goods finally exporting them for sale in the US

Market gardening The intensive growing of fruit and vegetables close to large local markets.

Mass movement Downslope movement of weathered materials such as rock, often helped by rainfall or glacial *meltwater*. Mass movement may be a gradual process or rapid, as in a *landslide* or rockfall.

Massif A single very large mountain or an area of mountains with uniform characteristics and clearly-defined boundaries.

Meander A looplike bend in a river, which is found typically in the lower, mature reaches of a river but can form wherever the valley is wide and the slope gentle.

Mediterranean climate A temperate *climate* of hot, dry summers and warm, damp winters. This is typical of the western fringes of the world's continents in the warm temperate regions between *latitudes* of 30° and 40° (north and south).

Meltwater Water resulting from the melting of a *glacier* or *ice sheet*.

Mesa A broad, flat-topped hill, characteristic of *arid* regions.

Mesosphere A layer of the Earth's *atmosphere*, between the *stratosphere* and the *thermosphere*. Extending from about 25–50 miles (40–80 km) above the surface of the Earth.

Mestizo A person of mixed *Amerindian* and European origin.

Metallurgy The refining and working of metals.

Metamorphic rocks Rocks that have been altered from their original form, in terms of texture, composition, and structure by intense heat, pressure, or by the introduction of new chemical substances – or a combination of more than one of these.

Meteor A body of rock, metal or other material, that travels through space at great speeds. Meteors are visible as they enter the Earth's *atmosphere* as shooting stars and fireballs.

Meteorite The remains of a *meteor* that has fallen to Earth.

Meteoroid A *meteor* that is still traveling in space, outside the Earth's *atmosphere*.

Mezzogiorno A term applied to the southern portion of Italy.

Milankovitch hypothesis A theory suggesting that there are a series of cycles that slightly alter the Earth's position when rotating about the Sun. The cycles identified all affect the amount of *radiation* the Earth receives at different *latitudes*. The theory is seen as a key factor in the cause of *ice ages*.

Millet A grain-crop, forming part of the staple diet in much of Africa.

Mistral A strong, dry, cold northerly or north-westerly wind, which blows from the Massif Central of France to the Mediterranean Sea. It is common in winter and its cold blasts can cause crop damage in the Rhône Delta, in France.

Mohorovicic discontinuity (Moho) The structural divide at the margin between the Earth's *crust* and the *mantle*. On average it is 20 miles (35-km) below the continents and 6-miles (10 km) below the oceans. The different densities of the *crust* and the mantle cause *earthquake* waves to accelerate at this point.

Monarchy A form of government in which the head of state is a single hereditary monarch. The monarch may be a mere figurehead, or may retain significant authority.

Monsoon A wind that changes direction biannually. The change is caused by the reversal of pressure over landmasses and the adjacent oceans. Because the inflowing moist winds bring rain, the term monsoon is also used to refer to the rains themselves. The term is derived from and most commonly refers to the seasonal winds of south and east Asia.

Montaña Mountain areas along the west coast of South America.

Moraine Debris, transported and deposited by a *glacier* or *ice sheet* in unstratified, mixed, piles of rock, boulders, pebbles, and clay.

Mountain-building The formation of *fold* mountains by tectonic activity. Also known as orogeny, mountain-building often occurs on the margin where two *tectonic plates* collide. The periods when most mountain-building occurred are known as orogenic phases and lasted many millions of years.

Mudflow An *avalanche* of mud that occurs when a mass of soil is drenched by rain or melting snow. It is a type of *mass movement*, faster than an *earthflow* because it is lubricated by water.

N

Nappe A mass of rocks which has been overfolded by repeated thrust *faulting*.

NAFTA The North American Free Trade Association. Established in 1994 between Canada, Mexico, and the US to set up a free-trade zone.

NASA The North American Space Agency. It is a government body, established in 1958 to develop manned and unmanned space programs.

NATO The North Atlantic Treaty Organization. Established in 1949 to promote mutual defense and cooperation between its members, which are Belgium, Canada, Czech Republic, Denmark, France, Germany, Greece, Iceland, Italy, Luxembourg, the Netherlands, Norway, Portugal, Poland, Spain, Turkey, UK, and US.

Nitrogen The odorless, colorless gas that makes up 78% of the atmosphere. Within the soil, it is a vital nutrient for plants.

Nomads (nomadic) Wandering communities that move around in search of suitable pasture for their herds of animals.

Nuclear fusion A technique used to create a new nucleus by the merging of two lighter ones, resulting in the release of large quantities of energy.

O

Oasis A fertile area in the midst of a *desert*, usually watered by an underground *aquifer*.

Oceanic ridge A mid-ocean ridge formed, according to the theory of *plate tectonics*, when plates drift apart and hot *magma* pours through to form new oceanic *crust*.

Oligarchy The government of a state by a small, exclusive group of people – such as an elite class or a family group.

Onion-skin weathering The *weathering* away or *exfoliation* of a rock or outcrop by the peeling off of surface layers.

Oriente A flatter region lying to the east of the Andes in South America.

Outwash plain *Glaciofluvial* material (typically clay, sand, and gravel) carried beyond an ice sheet by *meltwater* streams, forming a broad, flat deposit.

Oxbow lake A crescent-shaped lake formed on a river *floodplain* when a river erodes the outside bend of a *meander*, making the neck of the *meander* narrower until the river cuts across the neck. The meander is cut off and is dammed off with sediment, creating an oxbow lake. Also known as a cut-off or mortlake.

Oxidation A form of *chemical weathering* where *oxygen* dissolved in water reacts with minerals in rocks – particularly iron – to form oxides. Oxidation causes brown or yellow staining on rocks, and eventually leads to the break down of the rock.

Oxygen A colorless, odorless gas which is one of the main constituents of the Earth's *atmosphere* and is essential to life on Earth.

Ozone layer A layer of enriched *oxygen* (O_3) within the stratosphere, mostly between 18–50 miles (30–80 km) above the Earth's surface. It is vital to the existence of life on Earth because it absorbs harmful shortwave ultraviolet radiation, while allowing beneficial longer wave ultraviolet radiation to penetrate to the Earth's surface.

P

Pacific Rim The name given to the economically-dynamic countries bordering the Pacific Ocean.

Pack ice Ice masses more than 10 ft (3-m) thick that form on the sea surface and are not attached to a landmass.

Pancake ice Thin discs of ice, up to 8 ft (2.4 m) wide which form when slicks of *grease ice* are tossed together by winds and stormy seas.

Pangaea In the theory of continental drift, Pangaea is the original great land mass which, about 190 million years ago, began to split into Gondwanaland in the south and Laurasia in the north, separated by the Tethys Sea.

Pastoralism Grazing of livestock– usually sheep, goats, or cattle. Pastoralists in many drier areas have traditionally been *nomadic*.

Parallel *see Latitude*.

Peat Ancient, partially-decomposed vegetation found in wet, boggy conditions where there is little *oxygen*. It is the first stage in the development of coal and is often dried for use as fuel. It is also used to improve soil quality.

Pediment A gently-sloping ramp of *bedrock* below a steeper slope, often found at mountain edges in *desert* areas, but also in other climatic zones. Pediments may include depositional elements such as *alluvial fans*.

Peninsula A thin strip of land surrounded on three of its sides by water. Large examples include Florida and Korea.

Per capita Latin term meaning "for each person."

Periglacial Regions on the edges of *ice sheets* or *glaciers* or, more commonly, cold regions experiencing intense frost action, *permafrost* or both. Periglacial climates bring long, freezing winters and short, mild summers.

Permafrost Permanently frozen ground, typical of *Arctic* regions. Although a layer of soil above the permafrost melts in summer, the melted water does not drain through the permafrost.

Permeable rocks Rocks through which water can seep, because they are either porous or cracked.

Pharmaceuticals The manufacture of medicinal drugs.

Phreatic eruption A volcanic eruption which occurs when *lava* combines with *groundwater*, superheating the water and causing a sudden emission of steam at the surface.

Physical weathering (mechanical weathering) The breakdown of rocks by physical, as opposed to chemical, processes. Examples include: changes in pressure or temperature; the effect of windblown sand; the pressure of growing salt crystals in cracks within rock; and the expansion and contraction of water within rock as it freezes and thaws.

Pingo A dome of earth with a core of ice, found in *tundra* regions. Pingos are formed either when *groundwater* freezes and expands, pushing up the land surface, or when trapped, freezing water in a lake expands and pushes up lake *sediments* to form the pingo dome.

Placer A belt of mineral-bearing rock *strata* lying at or close to the Earth's surface, from which minerals can be easily extracted.

Plain A flat, level region of land, often relatively low-lying.

Plateau A highland tract of flat land.

Plate *see Tectonic plates*.

Plate tectonics The study of *tectonic plates*, that helps to explain *continental drift*, mountain formation and volcanic activity. The movement of tectonic plates may be explained by the currents of rock rising and falling from within the Earth's *mantle*, as it heats up and then cools. The boundaries of the plates are known as plate margins and most mountains, *earthquakes*, and *volcanoes* occur at these margins. Constructive margins are moving apart; destructive margins are crunching together and conservative margins are sliding past one another.

Pleistocene A period of *geological time* spanning from about 5.2 million years ago to 1.6 million years ago.

Plutonic rock *Igneous* rocks found deep below the surface. They are coarse-grained because they cooled and solidified slowly.

Polar The zones within the *Arctic* and *Antarctic* circles.

Polje A long, broad *depression* found in *karst* (*limestone*) regions.

Polygonal patterning Typical ground patterning, found in areas where the soil is subject to severe frost action, often in *periglacial* regions.

Porosity A measure of how much water can be held within a rock or a soil. Porosity is measured as the percentage of holes or pores in a material, compared to its total volume. For example, the porosity of slate is less than 1% whereas that of gravel is 25–35%.

Prairies Originally a French word for grassy *plains* with few or no trees.

Pre-Cambrian The earliest period of *geological time* dating from over 570-million years ago.

Precipitation The fall of moisture from the *atmosphere* onto the surface of the Earth, whether as dew, hail, rain, sleet, or snow.

Pyramidal peak A steep, isolated mountain summit, formed when the back walls of three or more *cirques* are cut back and move toward each other. The cliffs around such a horned peak, or horn, are divided by sharp *arêtes*. The Matterhorn in the Swiss Alps is an example.

Pyroclasts Fragments of rock ejected during volcanic eruptions.

Q

Quaternary The current period of *geological time*, which started about 1.6-million years ago.

R

Radiation The emission of energy in the form of particles or waves. Radiation from the sun includes heat, light, ultraviolet rays, gamma rays, and X-rays. Only some of the solar energy radiated into space reaches the Earth.

Rainforest Dense forests in tropical zones with high rainfall, temperature and *humidity*. Strictly, the term applies to the equatorial rain forest in tropical lowlands with constant rainfall and no seasonal change. The Congo and Amazon basins are examples. The term is applied more loosely to lush forest in other climates. Within rain forests organic life is dense and varied: at least 40% of all plant and animal species are found here and there may be as many as 100 tree species per hectare.

Rainshadow An area which experiences low rainfall, because of its position on the leeward side of a mountain range.

Reg A large area of stony *desert*, where tightly-packed gravel lies on top of clayey sand. A reg is formed where the wind blows away the finer sand.

Remote-sensing Method of obtaining information about the *environment* using unmanned equipment, such as a satellite, that relays the information to a point where it is collected and used.

Resistance The capacity of a rock to resist *denudation*, by processes such as *weathering* and *erosion*.

Ria A flooded *V-shaped river valley* or estuary, flooded by a rise in sea level (*eustacy*) or sinking land. It is shorter than a *fjord* and gets deeper as it meets the sea.

Rift valley A long, narrow depression in the Earth's *crust*, formed by the sinking of rocks between two *faults*.

River channel The trough which contains a river and is molded by the flow of water within it.

Roche moutonée A rock found in a glaciated valley. The side facing the flow of the *glacier* has been smoothed and rounded, while the other side has been left more rugged because the *glacier*, as it flows over it, has plucked out frozen fragments and carried them away.

Runoff Water draining from a land surface by flowing across it.

S

Sabkha The floor of an isolated *depression* that occurs in an *arid environment* – usually covered by salt deposits and devoid of vegetation.

SADC Southern African Development Community. Established in 1992 to promote economic integration between its member states, which are Angola, Botswana, Lesotho, Malawi, Mauritius, Mozambique, Namibia, South Africa, Swaziland, Tanzania, Zambia, and Zimbabwe.

Salt plug A rounded hill produced by the upward doming of rock *strata* caused by the movement of salt or other evaporite deposits under intense pressure.

Sastrugi Ice ridges formed by wind action. They lie parallel to the direction of the wind.

Savannah Open grassland found between the zone of *deserts*, and that of tropical *rain forests* in the tropics and subtropics. Scattered trees and shrubs are found in some kinds of savannah. A savannah *climate* usually has wet and dry seasons.

Scarp *see Escarpment*.

Scree Piles of rock fragments beneath a cliff or rock face, caused by mechanical *weathering*, especially *frost shattering*, where the expansion and contraction of freezing and thawing water within the rock, gradually breaks it up.

Sea-floor spreading The process whereby *tectonic plates* move apart, allowing hot *magma* to erupt and solidify. This forms a new sea floor and, ultimately, widens the ocean.

Seamount An isolated, submarine mountain or hill, probably of volcanic origin.

Season A period of time linked to regular changes in the weather, especially the intensity of solar *radiation*.

Sediment Grains of rock transported and deposited by rivers, sea, ice, or wind.

Sedimentary rocks Rocks formed from the debris of preexisting rocks or of organic material. They are found in many *environments* – on the ocean floor, on beaches, rivers, and *deserts*. Organically-formed sedimentary rocks include coal and chalk. Other sedimentary rocks, such as flint, are formed by chemical processes. Most of these rocks contain *fossils*, which can be used to date them.

Seif A sand *dune* which lies parallel to the direction of the prevailing wind. Seifs form steep-sided ridges, sometimes extending for miles.

Seismic activity Movement within the Earth, such as an *earthquake or tremor*.

Selva A region of wet forest found in the Amazon Basin.

Semiarid, semidesert The *climate* and landscape which lies between *savannah* and *desert* or between savannah and a *mediterranean* climate. In semiarid conditions there is a little more moisture than in a true *desert*; and more patches of drought-resistant vegetation can survive.

Shale (marine shale) A compacted *sedimentary rock*, with fine-grained particles. Marine shale is formed on the seabed. Fuel such as oil may be extracted from it.

Sheetwash Water that runs downhill in thin sheets without forming channels. It can cause *sheet erosion*.

Sheet erosion The washing away of soil by a thin film or sheet of water, known as *sheetwash*.

Shield A vast stable block of the Earth's *crust*, which has experienced little or no *mountain-building*.

Sierra The Spanish word for mountains.

Sinkhole A circular *depression* in a *limestone* region. They are formed by the collapse of an underground cave system or the *chemical weathering* of the *limestone*.

Sisal A plant-fiber used to make matting.

Slash and burn A farming technique involving the cutting down and burning of scrub forest, to create agricultural land. After a number of seasons this land is abandoned and the process is repeated. This practice is common in Africa and South America.

Slip face The steep leeward side of a sand *dune* or slope. Opposite side to a *back slope*.

Soil A thin layer of rock particles mixed with the remains of dead plants and animals. This occurs naturally on the surface of the Earth and provides a medium for plants to grow.

Soil creep The very gradual downslope movement of rock debris and soil, under the influence of gravity. This is a type of *mass movement*.

Soil erosion The wearing away of soil more quickly than it is replaced by natural processes. Soil can be carried away by wind as well as by water. Human activities, such as over-grazing and the clearing of land for farming, accelerate the process in many areas.

Solar energy Energy derived from the Sun. Solar energy is converted into other forms of energy. For example, the wind and waves, as well as the creation of plant material in photosynthesis, depend on solar energy.

Solifluction A kind of *soil creep*, where water in the surface layer has saturated the soil and rock debris which slips slowly downhill. It often happens where frozen top-layer deposits thaw, leaving frozen layers below them.

Sorghum A type of grass found in South America, similar to sugar cane. When refined it is used to make molasses.

Spit A thin linear deposit of sand or shingle extending from the sea shore. Spits are formed as angled waves shift sand along the beach, eventually extending a ridge of sand beyond a change in the angle of the coast. Spits are common where the coastline bends, especially at estuaries.

Squash A type of edible gourd.

Stack A tall, isolated pillar of rock near a coastline, created as wave action erodes away the adjacent rock.

Stalactite A tapering cylinder of mineral deposit, hanging from the roof of a cave in a *karst* area. It is formed by calcium carbonate, dissolved in water, which drips through the roof of a *limestone* cavern.

Stalagmite A cone of calcium carbonate, similar to a *stalactite*, rising from the floor of a *limestone* cavern and formed when drops of water fall from the roof of a *limestone* cave. If the water has dripped from a *stalactite* above the stalagmite, the two may join to form a continuous pillar.

Staple crop The main crop on which a country is economically and or physically reliant. For example, the major crop grown for large-scale local consumption in South Asia is rice.

Steppe Large areas of dry grassland in the northern hemisphere – particularly found in southeast Europe and central Asia.

Strata The plural of stratum, a distinct, virtually horizontal layer of deposited material, lying parallel to other layers.

Stratosphere A layer of the *atmosphere*, above the *troposphere*, extending from about 7–30 miles (11–50 km) above the Earth's surface. In the lower part of the stratosphere, the temperature is relatively stable and there is little moisture.

Strike-slip fault Occurs where plates move sideways past each other and blocks of rocks move horizontally in relation to each other, not up or down as in normal *faults*.

Subduction zone A region where two *tectonic plates* collide, forcing one beneath the other. Typically, a dense oceanic plate dips below a lighter continental plate, melting in the heat of the *asthenosphere*. This is why the zone is also called a destructive margins (*see Plate tectonics*). These zones are characterized by *earthquakes*, volcanoes, *mountain–building*, and the development of oceanic trenches and *island arcs*.

Submarine canyon A steep-sided valley, that extends along the *continental shelf* to the ocean floor. Often formed by *turbidity currents*.

Submarine fan Deposits of silt and *alluvium*, carried by large rivers forming great fan-shaped deposits on the ocean floor.

Subsistence agriculture An agricultural practice in which enough food is produced to support the farmer and his dependents, but not providing any surplus to generate an income.

Subtropical A term applied loosely to *climates* which are nearly tropical or tropical for a part of the year – areas north or south of the *tropics* but outside the *temperate zone*.

Supercontinent A large continent that breaks up to form smaller continents or that forms when smaller continents merge. In the theory of *continental drift*, the supercontinents are *Pangaea*, *Gondwanaland*, and *Laurasia*.

Sustainable development An approach to development, especially applied to economies across the world which exploit natural resources without destroying them or the *environment*.

Syncline A basin-shaped downfold in rock *strata*, created when the *strata* are compressed, for example where *tectonic plates* collide.

T

Tableland A highland area with a flat or gently undulating surface.

Taiga The belt of *coniferous* forest found in the north of Asia and North America. The conifers are adapted to survive low temperatures and long periods of snowfall.

Tarn A Scottish term for a small mountain lake, usually found at the head of a *glacier*.

Tectonic plates Plates, or tectonic plates, are the rigid slabs which form the Earth's outer shell, the *lithosphere*. Eight big plates and several smaller ones have been identified.

Temperate A moderate *climate* without extremes of temperature, typical of the mid-*latitudes* between the *tropics* and the *polar* circles.

Theocracy A state governed by religious laws – today Iran is the world's largest theocracy.

Thermokarst Subsidence created by the thawing of ground ice in *periglacial* areas, creating depressions.

Thermosphere A layer of the Earth's *atmosphere* which lies above the *mesophere*, about 60–300 miles (100–500 km) above the Earth

Terraces Steps cut into steep slopes to create flat surfaces for cultivating crops. They also help reduce soil *erosion* on unconsolidated slopes. They are most common in heavily-populated parts of Southeast Asia.

Till Unstratified glacial deposits or drift left by a *glacier* or *ice sheet*. Till includes mixtures of clay, sand, gravel, and boulders.

Topography The typical shape and features of a given area such as land height and terrain.

Tombolo A large sand *spit* which attaches part of the mainland to an island.

Tornado A violent, spiraling windstorm, with a center of very low pressure. Wind speeds reach 200 mph (320 kmph) and there is often thunder and heavy rain.

Transform fault In *plate tectonics*, a *fault* of continental scale, occurring where two plates slide past each other, staying close together for example, the San Andreas Fault, USA. The jerky, uneven movement creates *earthquakes* but does not destroy or add to the Earth's *crust*

Transpiration The loss of water vapor through the pores (or stomata) of plants. The process helps to return moisture to the *atmosphere*.

Trap An area of fine-grained *igneous rock* that has been extruded and cooled on the Earth's surface in stages, forming a series of steps or terraces.

Treeline The line beyond which trees cannot grow, dependent on *latitude* and altitude, as well as local factors such as soil.

Tremor A slight *earthquake*.

Trench (oceanic trench) A long, deep trough in the ocean floor, formed, according to the theory of *plate tectonics*, when two plates collide and one dives under the other, creating a *subduction zone*.

Tropics The zone between the *Tropic of Cancer* and the *Tropic of Capricorn* where the *climate* is hot. Tropical climate is also applied to areas rather further north and south of the *Equator* where the climate is similar to that of the true tropics.

Tropic of Cancer A line of *latitude* or imaginary circle round the Earth, lying at 23° 28' N.

Tropic of Capricorn A line of *latitude* or imaginary circle round the Earth, lying at 23° 28' S.

Troposphere The lowest layer of the Earth's *atmosphere*. From the surface, it reaches a height of between 4–10 miles (7–16 km). It is the most turbulent zone of the atmosphere and accounts for the generation of most of the world's weather. The layer above it is called the *stratosphere*.

Tsunami A huge wave created by shock waves from an *earthquake* under the sea. Reaching speeds of up to 600 mph (960-kmph), the wave may increase to heights of 50 ft (15 m) on entering coastal waters; and it can cause great damage.

Tundra The treeless *plains* of the *Arctic Circle*, found south of the *polar* region of permanent ice and snow, and north of the belt of *coniferous* forests known as *taiga*. In this region of long, very cold winters, vegetation is usually limited to mosses, *lichens*, sedges, and rushes, although flowers and dwarf shrubs blossom in the brief summer.

Turbidity current An oceanic feature. A turbidity current is a mass of *sediment*-laden water thathas substantial erosive power. Turbidity currents are thought to contribute to the formation of *submarine canyons*.

Typhoon A kind of *hurricane* (or tropical cyclone) bringing violent winds and heavy rain, a typhoon can do great damage. They occur in the South China Sea, especially around the Philippines.

U

U-shaped valley A river valley that has been deepened and widened by a *glacier*. They are characteristically flat-bottomed and steep-sided and generally much deeper than river valleys.

UN United Nations. Established in 1945, it contains 188 nations and aims to maintain international peace and security, and promote cooperation over economic, social, cultural, and humanitarian problems.

UNICEF United Nations Children's Fund. A UN organization set up to promote family and child related programs.

Urstromtäler A German word used to describe *meltwater* channels that flowed along the front edge of the advancing *ice sheet* during the last Ice Age, 18,000–20 000 years ago.

V

V-shaped valley A typical valley eroded by a river in its upper course.

Virgin rain forest Tropical *rain-forest* in its original state, untouched by human activity such as logging, clearance for agriculture, settlement, or roadbuilding.

Viticulture The cultivation of grapes for wine.

Volcano An opening or vent in the Earth's *crust* where molten rock, *magma*, erupts. Volcanoes tend to be conical but may also be a crack in the Earth's surface or a hole blasted through a mountain. The magma is accompanied by other materials such as gas, steam, and fragments of rock, or *pyroclasts*. They tend to occur on destructive or constructive tectonicplate margins.

W-Z

Wadi The dry bed left by a torrent of water. Also classified as a *ephemeral* stream, found in *arid* and *semiarid* regions, which are subject to sudden and often severe flash flooding.

Warm humid climate A rainy climate with warm summers and mild winters.

Water cycle The continuous circulation of water between the Earth's surface and the *atmosphere*. The processes include *evaporation* and *transpiration* of moisture into the atmosphere, and its return as *precipitation*, some of which flows into lakes and oceans.

Water table The upper level of *groundwater* saturation in permeable rock *strata*.

Watershed The dividing line between one *drainage basin* – an area where all streams flow into a single river system – and another. In the US, watershed also means the whole drainage basin of a single river system – its catchment area.

Waterspout A rotating column of water in the form of cloud, mist, and spray which form on open water. Often has the appearance of a small *tornado*.

Weathering The decay and breakup of rocks at or near the Earth's surface, caused by water, wind, heat or ice, organic material, or the *atmosphere*. *Physical weathering* includes the effects of frost and temperature changes. Biological weathering includes the effects of plant roots, burrowing animals and the acids produced by animals, especially as they decay after death. *Carbonation* and *hydrolysis* are among many kinds of *chemical weathering*.

Geographical names

The following glossary lists geographical terms occurring on the maps and in main-entry names in the Index-Gazetteer. These terms may precede, follow, or be run together with the proper element of the name; where they precede it the term is reversed for indexing purposes - thus Poluostrov Yamal is indexed as Yamal, Poluostrov..

Key

Geographical term
Language, Term

A

Å *Danish, Norwegian*, River
Āb *Persian*, River
Adrar *Berber*, Mountains
Agía, Ágios *Greek*, Saint
Air *Indonesian*, River
Ákra *Greek*, Cape, point
Alpen *German*, Alps
Alt- *German*, Old
Altiplanicie *Spanish*, Plateau
Älve(en) *Swedish*, River
-ån *Swedish*, River
Anse *French*, Bay
'Aqabat *Arabic*, Pass
Archipiélago *Spanish*, Archipelago
Arcipelago *Italian*, Archipelago
Arquipélago *Portuguese*, Archipelago
Arrecife(s) *Spanish*, Reef(s)
Aru *Tamil*, River
Augstiene *Latvian*, Upland
Aukštuma *Lithuanian*, Upland
Aust- *Norwegian*, Eastern
Avtonomnyy Okrug *Russian*, Autonomous district
Āw *Kurdish*, River
'Ayn *Arabic*, Spring, well
'Ayoûn *Arabic*, Wells

B

Baelt *Danish*, Strait
Bahía *Spanish*, Bay
Baḩr *Arabic*, River
Baía *Portuguese*, Bay
Baie *French*, Bay
Bañado *Spanish*, Marshy land
Bandao *Chinese*, Peninsula
Banjaran *Malay*, Mountain range
Baraji *Turkish*, Dam
Barragem *Portuguese*, Reservoir
Bassin *French*, Basin
Batang *Malay*, Stream
Beinn, Ben *Gaelic*, Mountain
-berg *Afrikaans, Norwegian*, Mountain
Besar *Indonesian, Malay*, Big
Birkat, Birket *Arabic*, Lake, well, cistern
Boğazi *Turkish*, Strait, defile
Boka *Serbo-Croatian*, Bay
Bol'sh-aya, -iye, -oy, -oye *Russian*, Big
Botigh(i) *Uzbek*, Depression basin
-bre(en) *Norwegian*, Glacier
Bredning *Danish*, Bay
Bucht *German*, Bay
Bugt(en) *Danish*, Bay
Buḩayrat *Arabic*, Lake, reservoir
Buḩeiret *Arabic*, Lake
Bukit *Malay*, Mountain
-bukta *Norwegian*, Bay
bukten *Swedish*, Bay
Bulag *Mongolian*, Spring
Bulak *Uighur*, Spring
Burnu *Turkish*, Cape, point
Buuraha *Somali*, Mountains

C

Cabo *Portuguese*, Cape
Caka *Tibetan*, Salt lake
Canal *Spanish*, Channel
Cap *French*, Cape
Capo *Italian*, Cape, headland
Cascada *Portuguese*, Waterfall
Cayo(s) *Spanish*, Islet(s), rock(s)
Cerro *Spanish*, Mountain
Chaîne *French*, Mountain range
Chapada *Portuguese*, Hills, upland
Chau *Cantonese*, Island
Chāy *Turkish*, River
Chhâk *Cambodian*, Bay
Chhu *Tibetan*, River
-chŏsuji *Korean*, Reservoir
Chott *Arabic*, Depression, salt lake
Chŭli *Uzbek*, Grassland, steppe
Ch'ün-tao *Chinese*, Island group
Chuŏr Phnum *Cambodian*, Mountains
Ciudad *Spanish*, City, town
Co *Tibetan*, Lake
Colline(s) *French*, Hill(s)
Cordillera *Spanish*, Mountain range
Costa *Spanish*, Coast
Côte *French*, Coast
Coxilha *Portuguese*, Mountains
Cuchilla *Spanish*, Mountains

D

Daban *Mongolian, Uighur*, Pass
Daği *Azerbaijani, Turkish*, Mountain
Dağlari *Azerbaijani, Turkish*, Mountains
-dake *Japanese*, Peak
-dal(en) *Norwegian*, Valley
Danau *Indonesian*, Lake
Dao *Chinese*, Island
Đao *Vietnamese*, Island
Daryā *Persian*, River
Daryācheh *Persian*, Lake
Dasht *Persian*, Desert, plain
Dawḩat *Arabic*, Bay
Denizi *Turkish*, Sea
Dere *Turkish*, Stream
Desierto *Spanish*, Desert
Dili *Azerbaijani*, Spit
-do *Korean*, Island
Dooxo *Somali*, Valley
Düzü *Azerbaijani*, Steppe
-dwīp *Bengali*, Island

E

-eilanden *Dutch*, Islands
Embalse *Spanish*, Reservoir
Ensenada *Spanish*, Bay
Erg *Arabic*, Dunes
Estany *Catalan*, Lake
Estero *Spanish*, Inlet
Estrecho *Spanish*, Strait
Étang *French*, Lagoon, lake
-ey *Icelandic*, Island
Ezero *Bulgarian, Macedonian*, Lake
Ezers *Latvian*, Lake

F

Feng *Chinese*, Peak
-fjella *Norwegian*, Mountain
Fjord *Danish*, Fjord
-fjord(en) *Danish, Norwegian, Swedish*, fjord
-fjordhur *Faeroese*, Fjord
Fleuve *French*, River
Fliegu *Maltese*, Channel
-fljór *Icelandic*, River
-flói *Icelandic*, Bay
Forêt *French*, Forest

G

-gan *Japanese*, Rock
-gang *Korean*, River
Ganga *Hindi, Nepali, Sinhala*, River
Gaoyuan *Chinese*, Plateau
Garagumy *Turkmen*, Sands
-gawa *Japanese*, River
Gebel *Arabic*, Mountain
-gebirge *German*, Mountain range
Ghadīr *Arabic*, Well
Ghubbat *Arabic*, Bay
Gjiri *Albanian*, Bay
Gol *Mongolian*, River
Golfe *French*, Gulf
Golfo *Italian, Spanish*, Gulf
Göl(ü) *Turkish*, Lake
Golyam, -a *Bulgarian*, Big
Gora *Russian, Serbo-Croatian*, Mountain
Góra *Polish*, mountain
Gory *Russian*, Mountain
Gryada *Russian*, ridge
Guba *Russian*, Bay
-gundo *Korean*, island group
Gunung *Malay*, Mountain

H

Ḩadd *Arabic*, Spit
-haehyŏp *Korean*, Strait
Haff *German*, Lagoon
Hai *Chinese*, Bay, lake, sea
Haixia *Chinese*, Strait
Ḩammādah *Arabic*, Desert
Ḩammādat *Arabic*, Rocky plateau
Hāmūn *Persian*, Lake
-hantō *Japanese*, Peninsula
Har, Haré *Hebrew*, Mountain
Ḩarrat *Arabic*, Lava-field
Hav(et) *Danish, Swedish*, Sea
Hawr *Arabic*, Lake
Hāyk' *Amharic*, Lake
He *Chinese*, River
-hegység *Hungarian*, Mountain range
Heide *German*, Heath, moorland
Helodrano *Malagasy*, Bay
Higashi- *Japanese*, East(ern)
Ḩiṣā' *Arabic*, Well
Hka *Burmese*, River
-ho *Korean*, Lake
Hô *Korean*, Reservoir
Holot *Hebrew*, Dunes
Hora *Belarussian, Czech*, Mountain
Hrada *Belarussian*, Mountain, ridge
Hsi *Chinese*, River
Hu *Chinese*, Lake
Huk *Danish*, Point

I

Île(s) *French*, Island(s)
Ilha(s) *Portuguese*, Island(s)
Ilhéu(s) *Portuguese*, Islet(s)
-isen *Norwegian*, Ice shelf
Imeni *Russian*, In the name of
Inish- *Gaelic*, Island
Insel(n) *German*, Island(s)
Irmağı, Irmak *Turkish*, River
Isla(s) *Spanish*, Island(s)
Isola (Isole) *Italian*, Island(s)

J

Jabal *Arabic*, Mountain
Jāl *Arabic*, Ridge
-järv *Estonian*, Lake
-järvi *Finnish*, Lake
Jazā'ir *Arabic*, Islands
Jazīrat *Arabic*, Island
Jazīreh *Persian*, Island
Jebel *Arabic*, Mountain
Jezero *Serbo-Croatian*, Lake
Jezioro *Polish*, Lake
Jiang *Chinese*, River
-jima *Japanese*, Island
Jižní *Czech*, Southern
-jōgi *Estonian*, River
-joki *Finnish*, River
-jökull *Icelandic*, Glacier
Jūn *Arabic*, Bay
Juzur *Arabic*, Islands

K

Kaikyō *Japanese*, Strait
-kaise *Lappish*, Mountain
Kali *Nepali*, River
Kalnas *Lithuanian*, Mountain
Kalns *Latvian*, Mountain
Kang *Chinese*, Harbour
Kangri *Tibetan*, Mountain(s)
Kaôh *Cambodian*, Island
Kapp *Norwegian*, Cape
Káto *Greek*, Lower
Kavīr *Persian*, Desert
K'edi *Georgian*, Mountain range
Kediet *Arabic*, Mountain
Kepi *Albanian*, Cape, point
Kepulauan *Indonesian, Malay*, Island group
Khalîg, Khalīj *Arabic*, Gulf
Khawr *Arabic*, Inlet
Khola *Nepali*, River
Khrebet *Russian*, Mountain range
Ko *Thai*, Island
-ko *Japanese*, Inlet, lake
Kólpos *Greek*, Bay
-kopf *German*, Peak
Körfäzi *Azerbaijani*, Bay
Körfezi *Turkish*, Bay
Kõrgustik *Estonian*, Upland
Kosa *Russian, Ukrainian*, Spit
Koshi *Nepali*, River
Kou *Chinese*, River-mouth
Kowtal *Persian*, Pass
Kray *Russian*, Region, territory
Kryazh *Russian*, Ridge
Kuduk *Uighur*, Well
Kūh(hā) *Persian*, Mountain(s)
-kul' *Russian*, Lake
Kŭl(i) *Tajik, Uzbek*, Lake
-kundo *Korean*, Island group
-kysten *Norwegian*, Coast
Kyun *Burmese*, Island

L

Laaq *Somali*, Watercourse
Lac *French*, Lake
Lacul *Romanian*, Lake
Lagh *Somali*, Stream
Lago *Italian, Portuguese, Spanish*, Lake
Lagoa *Portuguese*, Lagoon
Laguna *Italian, Spanish*, Lagoon, lake
Laht *Estonian*, Bay
Laut *Indonesian*, Bay
Lembalemba *Malagasy*, Plateau
Lerr *Armenian*, Mountain
Lerrnashght'a *Armenian*, Mountain range
Les *Czech*, Forest
Lich *Armenian*, Lake
Liehtao *Chinese*, Island group
Liqeni *Albanian*, Lake
Límni *Greek*, Lake
Ling *Chinese*, Mountain range
Llano *Spanish*, Plain, prairie
Lumi *Albanian*, River
Lyman *Ukrainian*, Estuary

M

Madīnat *Arabic*, City, town
Mae Nam *Thai*, River
-mägi *Estonian*, Hill
Maja *Albanian*, Mountain
Mal *Albanian*, Mountains
Mal-aya, -oye, -yy, *Russian*, Small
-man *Korean*, Bay
Mar *Spanish*, Lake
Marios *Lithuanian*, Lake
Massif *French*, Mountains
Meer *German*, Lake
-meer *Dutch*, Lake
Melkosopochnik *Russian*, Plain
-meri *Estonian*, Sea
Mifraz *Hebrew*, Bay
Minami- *Japanese*, South(ern)
-misaki *Japanese*, Cape, point
Monkhafad *Arabic*, Depression
Montagne(s) *French*, Mountain(s)
Montañas *Spanish*, Mountains
Mont(s) *French*, Mountain(s)
Monte *Italian, Portuguese*, Mountain
More *Russian*, Sea
Mörön *Mongolian*, River
Mys *Russian*, Cape, point

N

-nada *Japanese*, Open stretch of water
Nadi *Bengali*, River
Nagor'ye *Russian*, Upland
Naḩal *Hebrew*, River
Nahr *Arabic*, River
Nam *Laotian*, River
Namakzār *Persian*, Salt desert
Né-a, -on, -os *Greek*, New
Nedre- *Norwegian*, Lower
-neem *Estonian*, Cape, point
Nehri *Turkish*, River
-nes *Norwegian*, Cape, point
Nevado *Spanish*, Mountain (snow-capped)
Nieder- *German*, Lower
Nishi- *Japanese*, West(ern)
-nísi *Greek*, Island
Nisoi *Greek*, Islands
Nizhn-eye, -iy, -iye, -yaya *Russian*, Lower
Nizmennost' *Russian*, Lowland, plain
Nord *Danish, French, German*, North
Norte *Portuguese, Spanish*, North
Nos *Bulgarian*, Point, spit
Nosy *Malagasy*, Island
Nov-a, -i, *Bulgarian, Serbo-Croatian*, New
Nov-aya, -o, -oye, -yy, -yye *Russian*, New
Now-a, -e, -y *Polish*, New
Nur *Mongolian*, Lake
Nuruu *Mongolian*, Mountains
Nuur *Mongolian*, Lake
Nyzovyna *Ukrainian*, Lowland, plain

O

-ø *Danish*, Island
Ober- *German*, Upper
Oblast' *Russian*, Province
Órmos *Greek*, Bay
Orol(i) *Uzbek*, Island
Øster- *Norwegian*, Eastern
Ostrov(a) *Russian*, Island(s)
Otok *Serbo-Croatian*, Island
Oued *Arabic*, Watercourse
-oy *Faeroese*, Island
-øy(a) *Norwegian*, Island
Oya *Sinhala*, River
Ozero *Russian, Ukrainian*, Lake

P

Passo *Italian*, Pass
Pegunungan *Indonesian, Malay*, Mountain range
Pélagos *Greek*, Sea
Pendi *Chinese*, Basin
Penisola *Italian*, Peninsula
Pertuis *French*, Strait
Peski *Russian*, Sands
Phanom *Thai*, Mountain
Phou *Laotian*, Mountain
Pi *Chinese*, Point
Pic *Catalan, French*, Peak
Pico *Portuguese, Spanish*, Peak
-piggen *Danish*, Peak
Pik *Russian*, Peak
Pivostriv *Ukrainian*, Peninsula
Planalto *Portuguese*, Plateau
Planina, Planini *Bulgarian, Macedonian, Serbo-Croatian*, Mountain range
Plato *Russian*, Plateau
Ploskogor'ye *Russian*, Upland
Poluostrov *Russian*, Peninsula
Ponta *Portuguese*, Point
Porthmós *Greek*, Strait
Pótamos *Greek*, River
Presa *Spanish*, Dam
Prokhod *Bulgarian*, Pass
Proliv *Russian*, Strait
Pulau *Indonesian Malay*, Island
Pulu *Malay*, Island
Punta *Spanish*, Point
Pushcha *Belorussian*, Forest
Puszcza *Polish*, Forest

Q

Qā' *Arabic*, Depression
Qalamat *Arabic*, Well
Qatorkŭh(i) *Tajik*, Mountain
Qiuling *Chinese*, Hills
Qolleh *Persian*, Mountain
Qu *Tibetan*, Stream
Quan *Chinese*, Well
Qulla(i) *Tajik*, Peak
Qundao *Chinese*, Island group

R

Raas *Somali*, Cape
-rags *Latvian*, Cape
Ramlat *Arabic*, Sands
Ra's *Arabic*, Cape, headland, point
Ravnina *Bulgarian, Russian*, Plain
Récif *French*, Reef
Recife *Portuguese*, Reef
Reka *Bulgarian*, River
Represa (Rep.) *Portuguese, Spanish*, Reservoir
Reshteh *Persian*, Mountain range
Respublika *Russian*, Republic, first-order administrative division
Respublika(si) *Uzbek*, Republic, first-order administrative division
-retsugan *Japanese*, Chain of rocks
-rettō *Japanese*, Island chain
Riacho *Spanish*, Stream
Riban' *Malagasy*, Mountains
Rio *Portuguese*, River
Río *Spanish*, River
Riu *Catalan*, River
Rivier *Dutch*, River
Rivière *French*, River
Rowd *Pashtu*, River
Rt *Serbo-Croatian*, Point
Rūd *Persian*, River
Rūdkhāneh *Persian*, River
Rudohorie *Slovak*, Mountains
Ruisseau *French*, Stream

S

-saar *Estonian*, Island
-saari *Finnish*, Island
Sabkhat *Arabic*, Salt marsh
Sāgar(a) *Hindi*, Lake, reservoir
Şaḩrā' *Arabic*, Desert
Saint, Sainte *French*, Saint
Salar *Spanish*, Salt-pan
Salto *Portuguese, Spanish*, Waterfall
Samudra *Sinhala*, Reservoir
-san *Japanese, Korean*, Mountain
-sanchi *Japanese*, Mountains
-sandur *Icelandic*, Beach
Sankt *German, Swedish*, Saint
-sanmaek *Korean*, Mountain range
-sanmyaku *Japanese*, Mountain range
San, Santa, Santo *Italian, Portuguese, Spanish*, Saint
São *Portuguese*, Saint
Sarīr *Arabic*, Desert
Sebkha, Sebkhet *Arabic*, Depression, salt marsh
Sedlo *Czech*, Pass
See *German*, Lake
Selat *Indonesian*, Strait
Selatan *Indonesian*, Southern
-selkä *Finnish*, Lake, ridge
Selseleh *Persian*, Mountain range
Serra *Portuguese*, Mountain
Serranía *Spanish*, Mountain
-seto *Japanese*, Channel, strait
Sever-naya, -noye, -nyy, -o *Russian*, Northern
Sha'ib *Arabic*, Watercourse
Shākh *Kurdish*, Mountain
Shamo *Chinese*, Desert
Shan *Chinese*, Mountain(s)
Shankou *Chinese*, Pass
Shanmo *Chinese*, Mountain range
Shaţţ *Arabic*, Distributary
Shet' *Amharic*, River
Shi *Chinese*, Municipality
-shima *Japanese*, Island
Shiqqat *Arabic*, Depression
-shotō *Japanese*, Group of islands
Shuiku *Chinese*, Reservoir
Shŭrkhog(i) *Uzbek*, Salt marsh
Sierra *Spanish*, Mountains
Sint *Dutch*, Saint
-sjø(en) *Norwegian*, Lake
-sjön *Swedish*, Lake
Solonchak *Russian*, Salt lake
Solonchakovyye Vpadiny *Russian*, Salt basin, wetlands
Son *Vietnamese*, Mountain
Sông *Vietnamese*, River
Sør- *Norwegian*, Southern
-spitze *German*, Peak
Star-á, -é *Czech*, Old
Star-aya, -oye, -yy, -yye *Russian*, Old
Stenó *Greek*, Strait
Step' *Russian*, Steppe
Štít *Slovak*, Peak
Stœng *Cambodian*, River
Stolovaya Strana *Russian*, Plateau
Stredné *Slovak*, Middle
Střední *Czech*, Middle
Stretto *Italian*, Strait
Su Anbari *Azerbaijani*, Reservoir
-suidō *Japanese*, Channel, strait
Sund *Swedish*, Sound, strait
Sungai *Indonesian, Malay*, River
Suu *Turkish*, River

T

Tal *Mongolian*, Plain
Tandavan' *Malagasy*, Mountain range
Tangorombohitr' *Malagasy*, Mountain massif
Tanjung *Indonesian, Malay*, Cape, point
Tao *Chinese*, Island
Ţaraq *Arabic*, Hills
Tassili *Berber*, Mountain, plateau
Tau *Russian*, Mountain(s)
Taungdan *Burmese*, Mountain range
Techníti Límni *Greek*, Reservoir
Tekojärvi *Finnish*, Reservoir
Teluk *Indonesian, Malay*, Bay
Tengah *Indonesian*, Middle
Terara *Amharic*, Mountain
Timur *Indonesian*, Eastern
-tind(an) *Norwegian*, Peak
Tizma(si) *Uzbek*, Mountain range, ridge
-tō *Japanese*, island
Tog *Somali*, Valley
-tōge *Japanese*, pass
Togh(i) *Uzbek*, mountain
Tônlé *Cambodian*, Lake
Top *Dutch*, Peak
-tunturi *Finnish*, Mountain
Ţurāq *Arabic*, hills
Tur'at *Arabic*, Channel

U

Udde(n) *Swedish*, Cape, point
'Uqlat *Arabic*, Well
Utara *Indonesian*, Northern
Uul *Mongolian*, Mountains

V

Väin *Estonian*, Strait
Vallée *French*, Valley
-vatn *Icelandic*, Lake
-vatnet *Norwegian*, Lake
Velayat *Turkmen*, Province
-vesi *Finnish*, Lake
Vestre- *Norwegian*, Western
-vidda *Norwegian*, Plateau
-vík *Icelandic*, Bay
-viken *Swedish*, Bay, inlet
Vinh *Vietnamese*, Bay
Víztárloló *Hungarian*, Reservoir
Vodaskhovishcha *Belarussian*, Reservoir
Vodokhranilishche (Vdkhr.) *Russian*, Reservoir
Vodoskhovyshche (Vdskh.) *Ukrainian*, Reservoir
Volcán *Spanish*, Volcano
Vostochn-o, yy *Russian*, Eastern
Vozvyshennost' *Russian*, Upland, plateau
Vozyera *Belarussian*, Lake
Vpadina *Russian*, Depression
Vrchovina *Czech*, Mountains
Vrha *Macedonian*, Peak
Vychodné *Slovak*, Eastern
Vysochyna *Ukrainian*, Upland
Vysočina *Czech*, Upland

W

Waadi *Somali*, Watercourse
Wādī *Arabic* Watercourse
Wāḩat, Wâhat *Arabic*, Oasis
Wald *German*, Forest
Wan *Chinese*, Bay
Way *Indonesian*, River
Webi *Somali*, River
Wenz *Amharic*, River
Wiloyat(i) *Uzbek*, Province
Wyżyna *Polish*, Upland
Wzgórza *Polish*, Upland
Wzvyshsha *Belarussian*, Upland

X

Xé *Laotian*, River
Xi *Chinese*, Stream

Y

-yama *Japanese*, Mountain
Yanchi *Chinese*, Salt lake
Yang *Chinese*, Bay
Yanhu *Chinese*, Salt lake
Yarımadası *Azerbaijani, Turkish*, Peninsula
Yaylası *Turkish*, Plateau
Yazovir *Bulgarian*, Reservoir
Yoma *Burmese*, Mountains
Ytre- *Norwegian*, Outer
Yü *Chinese*, Island
Yunhe *Chinese*, Canal
Yuzhn-o, -yy *Russian*, Southern

Z

-zaki *Japanese*, Cape, point
Zaliv *Bulgarian, Russian*, Bay
-zan *Japanese*, Mountain
Zangbo *Tibetan*, River
Zapadn-aya, -o, -yy *Russian*, Western
Západné *Slovak*, Western
Západní *Czech*, Western
Zatoka *Polish, Ukrainian*, Bay
-zee *Dutch*, Sea
Zemlya *Russian*, Earth, land
Zizhiqu *Chinese*, Autonomous region

100 Mile House – Abū Sunbul

Index

Glossary of Abbreviations

This glossary provides a comprehensive guide to the abbreviations used in this Atlas, and in the Index.

A
abbrev. abbreviated
AD Anno Domini
Afr. Afrikaans
Alb. Albanian
Amh. Amharic
anc. ancient
approx. approximately
Ar. Arabic
Arm. Armenian
ASEAN Association of South East Asian Nations
ASSR Autonomous Soviet Socialist Republic
Aust. Australian
Az. Azerbaijani
Azerb. Azerbaijan

B
Basq. Basque
BC before Christ
Bel. Belorussian
Ben. Bengali
Ber. Berber
B-H Bosnia-Herzegovina
bn billion (one thousand million)
BP British Petroleum
Bret. Breton
Brit. British
Bul. Bulgarian
Bur. Burmese

C
C central
C. Cape
°C degrees Centigrade
CACM Central America Common Market
Cam. Cambodian
Cant. Cantonese
CAR Central African Republic
Cast. Castilian
Cat. Catalan
CEEAC Central America Common Market
Chin. Chinese
CIS Commonwealth of Independent States
cm centimetre(s)
Cro. Croat
Cz. Czech
Czech Rep. Czech Republic

D
Dan. Danish
Div. Divehi
Dom. Rep. Dominican Republic
Dut. Dutch

E
E east
EC *see* EU
EEC *see* EU
ECOWAS Economic Community of West African States
ECU European Currency Unit
EMS European Monetary System
Eng. English
est estimated
Est. Estonian
EU European Union (previously European Community [EC], European Economic Community [EEC])

F
°F degrees Fahrenheit
Faer. Faeroese
Fij. Fijian
Fin. Finnish
Fr. French
Fris. Frisian
ft foot/feet
FYROM Former Yugoslav Republic of Macedonia

G
g gram(s)
Gael. Gaelic
Gal. Galician
GDP Gross Domestic Product (the total value of goods and services produced by a country excluding income from foreign countries)
Geor. Georgian
Ger. German
Gk Greek
GNP Gross National Product (the total value of goods and services produced by a country)

H
Heb. Hebrew
HEP hydro-electric power
Hind. Hindi
hist. historical
Hung. Hungarian

I
I. Island
Icel. Icelandic
in inch(es)
In. Inuit (Eskimo)
Ind. Indonesian
Intl International
Ir. Irish
Is Islands
It. Italian

J
Jap. Japanese

K
Kaz. Kazakh
kg kilogram(s)
Kir. Kirghiz
km kilometre(s)
km² square kilometre (singular)
Kor. Korean
Kurd. Kurdish

L
L. Lake
LAIA Latin American Integration Association
Lao. Laotian
Lapp. Lappish
Lat. Latin
Latv. Latvian
Liech. Liechtenstein
Lith. Lithuanian
Lus. Lusatian
Lux. Luxembourg

M
m million/metre(s)
Mac. Macedonian
Maced. Macedonia
Mal. Malay
Malg. Malagasy
Malt. Maltese
mi. mile(s)
Mong. Mongolian
Mt. Mountain
Mts Mountains

N
N north
NAFTA North American Free Trade Agreement
Nep. Nepali
Neth. Netherlands
Nic. Nicaraguan
Nor. Norwegian
NZ New Zealand

P
Pash. Pashtu
PNG Papua New Guinea
Pol. Polish
Poly. Polynesian
Port. Portuguese
prev. previously

R
Rep. Republic
Res. Reservoir
Rmsch Romansch
Rom. Romanian
Rus. Russian
Russ. Fed. Russian Federation

S
S south
SADC Southern Africa Development Community
SCr. Serbian, Croatian
Sinh. Sinhala
Slvk Slovak
Slvn. Slovene
Som. Somali
Sp. Spanish
St., St Saint
Strs Straits
Swa. Swahili
Swe. Swedish
Switz. Switzerland

T
Taj. Tajik
Th. Thai
Thai. Thailand
Tib. Tibetan
Turk. Turkish
Turkm. Turkmenistan

U
UAE United Arab Emirates
Uigh. Uighur
UK United Kingdom
Ukr. Ukrainian
UN United Nations
Urd. Urdu
US/USA United States of America
USSR Union of Soviet Socialist Republics
Uzb. Uzbek

V
var. variant
Vdkhr. Vodokhranilishche (Russian for reservoir)
Vdskh. Vodoskhovyshche (Ukrainian for reservoir)
Vtn. Vietnamese

W
W west
Wel. Welsh

This index lists all the placenames and features shown on the regional and continental maps in this Atlas. Placenames are referenced to the largest scale map on which they appear. The policy followed throughout the Atlas is to use the local spelling or local name at regional level; commonly-used English language names may occasionally be added (in parentheses) where this is an aid to identification e.g. Firenze (Florence). English names, where they exist, have been used for all international features e.g. oceans and country names; they are also used on the continental maps and in the introductory World Today section; these are then fully cross-referenced to the local names found on the regional maps. The index also contains commonly-found alternative names and variant spellings, which are also fully cross-referenced.

All main entry names are those of settlements unless otherwise indicated by the use of italicized definitions or representative symbols, which are keyed at the foot of each page.

1

10 *M16* **100 Mile House** *var.* Hundred Mile House. British Columbia, SW Canada *51°39′ °19′W*
25 de Mayo *see* Veinticinco de Mayo
137 *Y13* **26 Bakı Komissarı** *Rus.* Imeni 26 Bakinskikh Komissarov. SE Azerbaijan *39°18′N 49°13′E*
26 Baku Komissarlary Adyndaky *see* Uzboý

A

Aa *see* Gauja
95 *G24* **Aabenraa** *var.* Åbenrå, *Ger.* Apenrade. Sønderjylland, SW Denmark *55°03′N 09°26′E*
95 *G20* **Aabybro** *var.* Åbybro. Nordjylland, N Denmark *57°09′N 09°32′E*
101 *C16* **Aachen** *Dut.* Aken, *Fr.* Aix-la-Chapelle; *anc.* Aquae Grani, Aquisgranum. Nordrhein-Westfalen, W Germany *50°47′N 06°06′E*
Aaiún *see* Laâyoune
95 *M24* **Aakirkeby** *var.* Åkirkeby. Bornholm, E Denmark *55°04′N 14°56′E*
95 *G20* **Aalborg** *var.* Ålborg, Ålborg-Nørresundby; *anc.* Alburgum. Nordjylland, N Denmark *57°03′N 09°56′E*
Aalborg Bugt *see* Ålborg Bugt
101 *J21* **Aalen** Baden-Württemberg, S Germany *48°50′N 10°06′E*
95 *G21* **Aalestrup** *var.* Ålestrup. Viborg, NW Denmark *56°42′N 09°31′E*
98 *I11* **Aalsmeer** Noord-Holland, C Netherlands *52°17′N 04°43′E*
99 *F18* **Aalst** Oost-Vlaanderen, C Belgium *50°57′N 04°03′E*
99 *K18* **Aalst** *Fr.* Alost. Noord-Brabant, S Netherlands *51°23′N 05°29′E*
98 *O12* **Aalten** Gelderland, E Netherlands *51°56′N 06°35′E*
99 *D17* **Aalter** Oost-Vlaanderen, NW Belgium *51°05′N 03°28′E*
Aanaar *see* Inari
Aanaarjävri *see* Inarijärvi
93 *M17* **Äänekoski** Länsi-Suomi, W Finland *62°34′N 25°45′E*
138 *H7* **Aanjar** *var.* 'Anjar. C Lebanon *33°45′N 35°56′E*
83 *G21* **Aansluit** Northern Cape, N South Africa *26°41′S 22°24′E*
Aar *see* Aare
108 *F7* **Aarau** Aargau, N Switzerland *47°22′N 08°00′E*
108 *D8* **Aarberg** Bern, W Switzerland *47°19′N 07°54′E*
99 *D16* **Aardenburg** Zeeland, SW Netherlands *51°16′N 03°27′E*
108 *D8* **Aare** *var.* Aar. ≈ W Switzerland
108 *F7* **Aargau** *Fr.* Argovie. ⬖ *canton* N Switzerland
Aarhus *see* Århus
Aarlen *see* Arlon
95 *G21* **Aars** *var.* Års. Nordjylland, N Denmark *56°49′N 09°32′E*
99 *I17* **Aarschot** Vlaams Brabant, C Belgium *50°59′N 04°50′E*
Aassi, Nahr el *see* Orontes
Aat *see* Ath
160 *G7* **Aba** *prev.* Ngawa. Sichuan, C China *32°51′N 101°46′E*
79 *P16* **Aba** Orientale, NE Dem. Rep. Congo *03°52′N 30°14′E*
77 *V17* **Aba** Abia, S Nigeria *05°06′N 07°22′E*
140 *J6* **Abā al Qazāz, Bi'r** *well* NW Saudi Arabia
Abā as Su'ūd *see* Najrān
59 *G14* **Abacaxis, Rio** ≈ NW Brazil
Abaco Island *see* Great Abaco/Little Abaco
Abaco Island *see* Great Abaco, N Bahamas
142 *K10* **Ābādān** Khūzestān, SW Iran *30°24′N 48°18′E*
146 *F13* **Abadan** *prev.* Bezmein, Büzmeýin, *Rus.* Byuzmeyin. Ahal Welaýaty, C Turkmenistan *38°08′N 57°53′E*
143 *O10* **Ābādeh** Fārs, C Iran *31°06′N 52°40′E*
74 *H8* **Abadla** W Algeria *31°04′N 02°39′W*
59 *M20* **Abaeté** Minas Gerais, SE Brazil *19°10′S 45°24′W*
62 *P7* **Abaí** Caazapá, S Paraguay *25°58′S 55°54′W*
Abai *see* Blue Nile
191 *O2* **Abaiang** *var.* Apia; *prev.* Charlotte Island. *atoll* Tungaru, W Kiribati
Abaj *see* Abay
77 *U15* **Abaji** Federal Capital District, C Nigeria *08°35′N 06°54′E*
37 *O7* **Abajo Peak** ▲ Utah, W USA *37°51′N 109°28′W*
77 *V16* **Abakaliki** Ebonyi, SE Nigeria *06°18′N 08°07′E*
122 *K13* **Abakan** Respublika Khakasiya, S Russian Federation *53°43′N 91°25′E*
77 *S11* **Abala** Tillabéri, SW Niger *14°55′N 03°27′E*
77 *U11* **Abalak** Tahoua, C Niger *15°28′N 06°18′E*
119 *N14* **Abalyanka** *Rus.* Obolyanka. ≈ N Belarus
122 *L12* **Aban** Krasnoyarskiy Kray, S Russian Federation *56°41′N 96°04′E*
143 *P9* **Āb Anbār-e Kān Sorkh** Yazd, C Iran *31°22′N 53°38′E*
57 *G16* **Abancay** Apurímac, SE Peru *13°37′S 72°52′W*
190 *H2* **Abaokoro** *atoll* Tungaru, W Kiribati
Abariringa *see* Kanton
143 *P10* **Abarkūh** Yazd, C Iran *31°07′N 53°17′E*
165 *V3* **Abashiri** *var.* Abasiri. Hokkaidō, NE Japan *44°N 144°15′E*
165 *U3* **Abashiri-ko** ◎ Hokkaidō, NE Japan
Abasiri *see* Abashiri
41 *P10* **Abasolo** Tamaulipas, C Mexico *24°02′N 98°18′W*
186 *F9* **Abau** Central, S Papua New Guinea *10°04′S 148°34′E*
145 *R10* **Abay** *var.* Abaj. Karaganda, C Kazakhstan *49°38′N 72°50′E*
81 *I15* **Ābaya Hāyk'** *Eng.* Lake Margherita, *It.* Abbaia. ◎ SW Ethiopia
Ābay Wenz *see* Blue Nile
122 *K13* **Abaza** Respublika Khakasiya, S Russian Federation *52°40′N 89°58′E*
Abbaia *see* Ābaya Hāyk'
143 *Q13* **Āb Bārīk** Fārs, S Iran
107 *C18* **Abbasanta** Sardegna, Italy, C Mediterranean Sea *40°08′N 08°49′E*
Abbatis Villa *see* Abbeville
30 *M3* **Abbaye, Point** *headland* Michigan, N USA *46°58′N 88°08′W*
Abbazia *see* Opatija
Abbé, Lake *see* Abhe, Lake
103 *N2* **Abbeville** *anc.* Abbatis Villa. Somme, N France *50°06′N 01°50′E*
23 *R7* **Abbeville** Alabama, S USA *31°35′N 85°16′W*
23 *U6* **Abbeville** Georgia, SE USA *31°58′N 83°18′W*
22 *I9* **Abbeville** Louisiana, S USA *29°58′N 92°08′W*
21 *P12* **Abbeville** South Carolina, SE USA *34°10′N 82°23′W*
97 *B20* **Abbeyfeale** *Ir.* Mainistir na Féile. SW Ireland *52°24′N 09°21′W*
106 *D8* **Abbiategrasso** Lombardia, NW Italy *45°24′N 08°55′E*
93 *I14* **Abborrträsk** Norrbotten, N Sweden *65°24′N 19°33′E*
194 *J9* **Abbot Ice Shelf** *ice shelf* Antarctica
10 *M17* **Abbotsford** British Columbia, SW Canada *49°02′N 122°18′W*
30 *K6* **Abbotsford** Wisconsin, N USA *44°57′N 90°19′W*
149 *U5* **Abbottābād** North-West Frontier Province, NW Pakistan *34°12′N 73°15′E*
119 *M14* **Abchuha** *Rus.* Obchuga. Minskaya Voblasts', NW Belarus *54°30′N 29°22′E*
98 *I10* **Abcoude** Utrecht, C Netherlands *52°17′N 04°59′E*
139 *N2* **'Abd al 'Azīz, Jabal** ▲▲ NE Syria
141 *U17* **'Abd al Kūrī** *island* SE Yemen
139 *Z13* **'Abd Allāh, Khawr** *bay* Iraq/Kuwait
127 *U6* **Abdulino** Orenburgskaya Oblast', W Russian Federation *53°37′N 53°39′E*
78 *J10* **Abéché** *var.* Abécher, Abeshr. Ouaddaï, SE Chad *13°49′N 20°49′E*
Abécher *see* Abéché
143 *S8* **Āb-e Garm va Sard** Yazd, E Iran
77 *R8* **Abeïbara** Kidal, NE Mali *19°07′N 01°52′E*
105 *P5* **Abejar** Castilla-León, N Spain *41°48′N 02°47′W*
54 *E9* **Abejorral** Antioquia, W Colombia *05°48′N 75°28′W*
Abela *see* Ávila
Abellinum *see* Avellino
92 *Q2* **Abeløya** *island* Kong Karls Land, E Svalbard
80 *I13* **Ābeltī** Oromīya, C Ethiopia *08°09′N 37°31′E*
191 *O2* **Abemama** *var.* Apamama; *prev.* Roger Simpson Island. *atoll* Tungaru, W Kiribati
171 *Y15* **Abemaree** *var.* Abermarre. Papua, E Indonesia *07°03′S 140°10′E*
77 *O16* **Abengourou** E Ivory Coast *06°42′N 03°27′W*
Åbenrå *see* Aabenraa
101 *L22* **Abens** ≈ SE Germany
77 *S16* **Abeokuta** Ogun, SW Nigeria *07°07′N 03°21′E*
97 *I20* **Aberaeron** SW Wales, United Kingdom *52°15′N 04°15′W*
Aberbrothock *see* Arbroath
Abercorn *see* Mbala
29 *R6* **Abercrombie** North Dakota, N USA *46°25′N 96°42′W*
183 *T7* **Aberdeen** New South Wales, SE Australia *32°09′S 150°55′E*
11 *T15* **Aberdeen** Saskatchewan, S Canada *52°15′N 106°19′W*
83 *H25* **Aberdeen** Eastern Cape, S South Africa *32°30′S 24°00′E*
96 *L9* **Aberdeen** *anc.* Devana. NE Scotland, United Kingdom *57°10′N 02°04′W*
21 *X2* **Aberdeen** Maryland, NE USA *39°28′N 76°09′W*
23 *N3* **Aberdeen** Mississippi, S USA *33°49′N 88°32′W*
21 *T10* **Aberdeen** North Carolina, SE USA *35°07′N 79°25′W*
29 *P8* **Aberdeen** South Dakota, N USA *45°27′N 98°29′W*
32 *F8* **Aberdeen** Washington, NW USA *46°57′N 123°48′W*
96 *K9* **Aberdeen** *cultural region* NE Scotland, United Kingdom
8 *L8* **Aberdeen Lake** ◎ Nunavut, NE Canada
96 *J10* **Aberfeldy** C Scotland, United Kingdom *56°38′N 03°49′W*
97 *K21* **Abergavenny** *anc.* Gobannium. SE Wales, United Kingdom *51°50′N 03°W*
Abergwaun *see* Fishguard
Abermarre *see* Abemaree
25 *N5* **Abernathy** Texas, SW USA *33°49′N 101°50′W*
Abersee *see* Wolfgangsee
Abertawe *see* Swansea
Aberteifi *see* Cardigan
32 *I15* **Abert, Lake** ◎ Oregon, NW USA
97 *I20* **Aberystwyth** W Wales, United Kingdom *52°25′N 04°05′W*
Abeshr *see* Abéché
Ábeskovvu *see* Abisko
106 *F10* **Abetone** Toscana, C Italy *44°09′N 10°42′E*
125 *V5* **Abez'** Respublika Komi, NW Russian Federation *66°32′N 61°41′E*
142 *M5* **Āb Garm** Qazvīn, N Iran
141 *N12* **Abhā** 'Asīr, SW Saudi Arabia *18°16′N 42°32′E*
142 *M5* **Abhar** Zanjān, NW Iran *36°05′N 49°18′E*
Abhé Bad/Ābhē Bid Hāyk' *see* Abhe, Lake
80 *K12* **Abhe, Lake** *var.* Lake Abbé, *Amh.* Ābhē Bid Hāyk', *Som.* Abhé Bad. ◎ Djibouti/Ethiopia
77 *V17* **Abia** ⬖ *state* SE Nigeria
139 *V9* **'Abīd 'Alī** Wāsiṭ, E Iraq *32°20′N 45°58′E*
119 *O17* **Abidavichy** *Rus.* Obidovichi. Mahilyowskaya Voblasts', E Belarus *53°20′N 30°25′E*
115 *L15* **Abide** Çanakkale, NW Turkey *40°04′N 26°13′E*
77 *N17* **Abidjan** S Ivory Coast *05°19′N 04°01′W*
Āb-i-Istāda *see* Īstādeh-ye Moqor, Āb-e-
27 *N4* **Abilene** Kansas, C USA *38°55′N 97°14′W*
25 *Q7* **Abilene** Texas, SW USA *32°27′N 99°44′W*
Abindonia *see* Abingdon
97 *M21* **Abingdon** *anc.* Abindonia. S England, United Kingdom *51°41′N 01°17′W*
30 *K12* **Abingdon** Illinois, N USA *40°48′N 90°24′W*
21 *P8* **Abingdon** Virginia, NE USA *36°42′N 81°59′W*
Abingdon *see* Pinta, Isla
18 *J15* **Abington** Pennsylvania, NE USA *40°06′N 75°05′W*
126 *K14* **Abinsk** Krasnodarskiy Kray, SW Russian Federation *44°51′N 38°12′E*
37 *R9* **Abiquiu Reservoir** ⊠ New Mexico, SW USA
Āb-i-safed *see* Sefīd, Darya-ye
92 *I10* **Abisko** *Lapp.* Ábeskovvu. Norrbotten, N Sweden *68°21′N 18°50′E*
12 *G12* **Abitibi** ≈ Ontario, S Canada
12 *H12* **Abitibi, Lac** ◎ Ontario/Québec, S Canada
80 *J10* **Ābīy Ādī** Tigray, N Ethiopia *13°40′N 38°57′E*
118 *H6* **Abja-Paluoja** Viljandimaa, S Estonia *58°08′N 25°20′E*
Abkhazia *see* Ap'khazet'i
182 *F1* **Abminga** South Australia *26°07′S 134°49′E*
75 *W9* **Abnūb** *var.* Abnûb. C Egypt *27°18′N 31°09′E*
Abnûb *see* Abnūb
Åbo *see* Turku
152 *G9* **Abohar** Punjab, N India *30°11′N 74°14′E*
77 *O17* **Aboisso** SE Ivory Coast *05°26′N 03°13′W*
78 *H5* **Abo, Massif d'** ▲▲ NW Chad
77 *R16* **Abomey** S Benin *07°14′N 02°00′E*
79 *F16* **Abong Mbang** Est, SE Cameroon *03°58′N 13°10′E*
111 *L23* **Abony** Pest, C Hungary *47°10′N 20°00′E*
78 *J11* **Abou-Déïa** Salamat, SE Chad *11°30′N 19°18′E*
Aboudouhour *see* Abū aḍ Ḍuhūr
Abou Kémal *see* Abū Kamāl
Abou Simbel *see* Abū Sunbul
137 *T12* **Abovyan** C Armenia *40°16′N 44°33′E*
141 *P15* **Abrād, Wādī** *seasonal river* W Yemen
Abraham Bay *see* The Carlton
104 *G10* **Abrantes** *var.* Abrántes. Santarém, C Portugal *39°28′N 08°12′W*
62 *J4* **Abra Pampa** Jujuy, N Argentina *22°47′S 65°41′W*
Abrashlare *see* Brezovo
54 *G7* **Abrego** Norte de Santander, N Colombia *08°08′N 73°14′W*
Abrene *see* Pytalovo
40 *C7* **Abreojos, Punta** *headland* NW Mexico *26°43′N 113°36′W*
65 *J16* **Abrolhos Bank** *undersea feature* W Atlantic Ocean *18°30′S 38°45′W*
119 *H19* **Abrova** *Rus.* Obrovo. Brestskaya Voblasts', SW Belarus *52°30′N 25°34′E*
116 *G11* **Abrud** *Ger.* Gross-Schlatten, *Hung.* Abrudbánya. Alba, SW Romania *46°16′N 23°05′E*
Abrudbánya *see* Abrud
118 *E6* **Abruka** *island* SW Estonia
107 *J15* **Abruzzese, Appennino** ▲▲ C Italy
107 *J14* **Abruzzo** ⬖ *region* C Italy
141 *N14* **'Abs** *var.* Sūq 'Abs. W Yemen *16°42′N 42°55′E*
33 *T12* **Absaroka Range** ▲▲ Montana/Wyoming, NW USA
137 *Z11* **Abşeron Yarımadası** *Rus.* Apsheronskiy Poluostrov. *peninsula* E Azerbaijan
143 *N6* **Āb Shīrīn** Eşfahān, C Iran *34°17′N 51°17′E*
139 *X10* **Abtān** Maysān, SE Iraq *31°37′N 47°06′E*
109 *R6* **Abtenau** Salzburg, NW Austria *47°33′N 13°21′E*
152 *E14* **Ābu** Rājasthān, N India *24°41′N 72°50′E*
164 *E12* **Abu** Yamaguchi, Honshū, SW Japan *34°30′N 131°26′E*
138 *I4* **Abū aḍ Ḍuhūr** *Fr.* Aboudouhour. Idlib, NW Syria *35°30′N 37°00′E*
143 *P17* **Abū al Abyaḍ** *island* C United Arab Emirates
138 *K10* **Abū al Ḥuṣayn, Khabrat** ◎ N Jordan
139 *R8* **Abū al Jīr** Al Anbār, C Iraq *33°16′N 42°55′E*
139 *Y12* **Abū al Khaṣīb** *var.* Abul Khasib. Al Başrah, SE Iraq *30°26′N 48°00′E*
139 *U12* **Abū at Tubrah, Thaqb** *well* S Iraq
Abu Balâs *see* Abu Ballās
75 *V11* **Abu Ballās** *var.* Abu Balâs. ▲ SW Egypt *24°28′N 27°36′E*
Abu Dhabi *see* Abū Ẓabī
139 *R8* **Abū Farūkh** Al Anbār, C Iraq *33°06′N 43°18′E*
80 *C12* **Abu Gabra** Southern Darfur, W Sudan *11°02′N 26°50′E*
139 *P10* **Abū Ghār, Sha'īb** *dry watercourse* S Iraq
80 *G7* **Abu Hamed** River Nile, N Sudan *19°32′N 33°20′E*
139 *O5* **Abū Ḥardān** *var.* Hajîne. Dayr az Zawr, E Syria *34°45′N 40°49′E*
139 *T7* **Abū Ḥāssawīyah** Diyālá, E Iraq *33°52′N 44°47′E*
138 *K10* **Abū Ḥifnah, Wādī** *dry watercourse* N Jordan
77 *V15* **Abuja** ● (Nigeria) Federal Capital District, C Nigeria *09°04′N 07°28′E*
139 *R9* **Abū Jahaf, Wādī** *dry watercourse* C Iraq
56 *F12* **Abujao, Río** ≈ E Peru
139 *U12* **Abū Jasrah** Al Muthanná, S Iraq *30°43′N 44°50′E*
139 *O6* **Abū Kamāl** *Fr.* Abou Kémal. Dayr az Zawr, E Syria *34°29′N 40°56′E*
165 *P12* **Abukuma-sanchi** ▲▲ Honshū, C Japan
Abula *see* Ávila
Abul Khasib *see* Abū al Khaṣīb
79 *K16* **Abumombazi** *var.* Abumonbazi. Equateur, N Dem. Rep. Congo *03°43′N 22°06′E*
Abumonbazi *see* Abumombazi
59 *D15* **Abunã** Rondônia, W Brazil *09°41′S 65°20′W*
56 *K13* **Abunã, Rio** *var.* Río Abuná. ≈ Bolivia/Brazil
138 *G10* **Abū Nuşayr** *var.* Abu Nuseir. 'Ammān, W Jordan *32°03′N 35°58′E*
Abu Nuseir *see* Abū Nuşayr
139 *T12* **Abū Qabr** Al Muthanná, S Iraq *31°03′N 44°34′E*
138 *K5* **Abū Raḥbah, Jabal** ▲▲ C Syria
139 *S5* **Abū Rajāsh** Şalāḥ ad Dīn, N Iraq *34°47′N 43°36′E*
139 *W13* **Abū Raqrāq, Ghadīr** *well* S Iraq
152 *E14* **Ābu Road** Rājasthān, N India *24°29′N 72°47′E*
80 *I6* **Abu Shagara, Ras** *headland* NE Sudan *18°04′N 38°31′E*
Abu Simbel *see* Abū Sunbul
139 *U12* **Abū Sudayrah** Al Muthanná, S Iraq *30°55′N 44°58′E*
139 *T10* **Abū Şukhayr** Al Qādisīyah, S Iraq *31°54′N 44°27′E*
Abū Sunbul *see* Abū Sunbul

◆ Country ● Country Capital ◇ Dependent Territory ○ Dependent Territory Capital ⬖ Administrative Regions ✈ International Airport ▲ Mountain ▲▲ Mountain Range ⛰ Volcano ≈ River ◎ Lake ⊠ Reservoir

Abut Head – Aigen im Mülkreis

185 *E18* **Abut Head** *headland* South Island, New Zealand *43°06´S 170°16´E*
80 *E9* **Abu 'Urug** Northern Kordofan, C Sudan *15°52´N 30°25´E*
80 *K12* **Ābuyē Mēda** ▲ C Ethiopia *10°28´N 39°44´E*
80 *D11* **Abu Zabad** Western Kordofan, C Sudan *12°21´N 29°16´E*
143 *P16* **Abū Ẓabī** *var.* **Abū Ẓaby,** *Eng.* Abu Dhabi. ● (United Arab Emirates) Abū Ẓaby, C United Arab Emirates *24°30´N 54°20´E*
Abū Ẓabī *see* Abū Ẓabī
75 *X8* **Abu Zenîma** E Egypt *29°01´N 33°08´E*
95 *N17* **Åby** Östergötland, S Sweden *58°40´N 16°10´E*
Abyaḍ, Al Baḥr al *see* White Nile
Åbybro *see* Aabybro
80 *D13* **Abyei** Western Kordofan, S Sudan *09°35´N 28°28´E*
Abyla *see* Ávila
Abymes *see* les Abymes
Abyssinia *see* Ethiopia
Açâba *see* Assaba
54 *F11* **Acacías** Meta, C Colombia *03°59´N 73°46´W*
58 *L13* **Açailandia** Maranhão, E Brazil *04°51´S 47°26´W*
Acaill *see* Achill Island
42 *E8* **Acajutla** Sonsonate, W El Salvador *13°34´N 89°50´W*
79 *D17* **Acalayong** SW Equatorial Guinea *01°05´N 09°34´E*
41 *N13* **Acámbaro** Guanajuato, C Mexico *20°01´N 100°42´W*
54 *C6* **Acandí** Chocó, NW Colombia *08°32´N 77°20´W*
104 *H4* **A Cañiza** *var.* La Cañiza. Galicia, NW Spain *42°13´N 08°15´W*
40 *J11* **Acaponeta** Nayarit, C Mexico *22°30´N 105°21´W*
40 *J11* **Acaponeta, Río de** ⚡ C Mexico
41 *O16* **Acapulco** *var.* Acapulco de Juárez. Guerrero, S Mexico *16°51´N 99°53´W*
Acapulco de Juárez *see* Acapulco
55 *T13* **Acarai Mountains** *Sp.* Serra Acaraí. ▲▲ Brazil/Guyana
Acaraí, Serra *see* Acarai Mountains
58 *O13* **Acaraú** Ceará, NE Brazil *04°35´S 37°37´W*
54 *J6* **Acarigua** Portuguesa, N Venezuela *09°35´N 69°12´W*
42 *C6* **Acatenango, Volcán de** ▲ S Guatemala *14°30´N 90°52´W*
41 *Q15* **Acatlán** *var.* Acatlán de Osorio. Puebla, S Mexico *18°12´N 98°02´W*
Acatlán de Osorio *see* Acatlán
41 *S15* **Acayucan** *var.* Acayucán. Veracruz-Llave, E Mexico *17°59´N 94°58´W*
Accho *see* Akko
21 *Y5* **Accomac** Virginia, NE USA *37°43´N 75°41´N*
77 *Q17* **Accra** ● (Ghana)SE Ghana *05°33´N 00°15´W*
97 *L17* **Accrington** NW England, United Kingdom *53°46´N 02°21´W*
61 *B19* **Acebal** Santa Fe, C Argentina *33°14´S 60°50´W*
168 *H8* **Aceh** *off.* Daerah Istimewa Aceh, *var.* Acheen, Achin, Atchin, Atjeh. ◆ *autonomous district* NW Indonesia
107 *M18* **Acerenza** Basilicata, S Italy *40°46´N 15°51´E*
107 *K17* **Acerra** *anc.* Acerrae. Campania, S Italy *40°56´N 14°22´E*
Acerrae *see* Acerra
57 *J17* **Achacachi** La Paz, W Bolivia *16°01´S 68°44´W*
54 *K7* **Achaguas** Apure, C Venezuela *07°46´N 68°14´W*
154 *H12* **Achalpur** *prev.* Elichpur, Ellichpur. Mahārāshtra, C India *21°19´N 77°30´E*
61 *F18* **Achar** Tacuarembó, C Uruguay *32°20´S 56°15´W*
137 *R10* **Achara** *var.* Ajaria. ◆ *autonomous republic* SW Georgia
115 *H19* **Acharnés** *var.* Aharnes; *prev.* Akharnaí. Attikí, C Greece *38°09´N 23°58´E*
Ach'asar Lerr *see* Achkasar
Acheen *see* Aceh
99 *K16* **Achel** Limburg, NE Belgium *51°15´N 05°31´E*
115 *D16* **Achelóos** *var.* Akhelóös, Aspropótamos; *anc.* Achelous. ⚡ W Greece
Achelous *see* Achelóos
163 *W8* **Acheng** Heilongjiang, NE China *45°32´N 126°56´E*
109 *N6* **Achenkirch** Tirol, W Austria *47°31´N 11°42´E*
101 *L24* **Achenpass** *pass* Austria/Germany
109 *N7* **Achensee** ◎ W Austria
101 *F22* **Achern** Baden-Württemberg, SW Germany *48°37´N 08°04´E*
115 *C16* **Acherón** ⚡ W Greece
77 *W11* **Achétinamou** ⚡ S Niger
152 *J12* **Achhnera** Uttar Pradesh, N India *27°10´N 77°45´E*
42 *C7* **Achiguate, Río** ⚡ S Guatemala
97 *A16* **Achill Head** *Ir.* Ceann Acla. *headland* W Ireland *53°58´N 10°14´W*
97 *A16* **Achill Island** *Ir.* Acaill. *island* W Ireland
100 *H11* **Achim** Niedersachsen, NW Germany *53°01´N 09°01´E*
149 *S5* **Achīn** Nangarhār, E Afghanistan *34°04´N 70°41´E*
Achin *see* Aceh
122 *K12* **Achinsk** Krasnoyarskiy Kray, S Russian Federation *56°21´N 90°25´E*
162 *E5* **Achit Nuur** ◎ NW Mongolia
137 *T11* **Achkasar** *Arm.* Ach'asar Lerr. ▲ Armenia/Georgia *41°09´N 43°55´E*
126 *K13* **Achuyevo** Krasnodarskiy Kray, SW Russian Federation *46°00´N 38°01´E*
81 *F16* **Achwa** *var.* Aswa. ⚡ N Uganda
136 *E15* **Acıgöl** *salt lake* SW Turkey
107 *L24* **Acireale** Sicilia, Italy, C Mediterranean Sea *37°36´N 15°10´E*
Aciris *see* Agri
25 *N7* **Ackerly** Texas, SW USA *32°31´N 101°43´W*
22 *M4* **Ackerman** Mississippi, S USA *33°18´N 89°10´W*
29 *W13* **Ackley** Iowa, C USA *42°33´N 93°03´W*
44 *J5* **Acklins Island** *island* SE Bahamas
Acla, Ceann *see* Achill Head
62 *H11* **Aconcagua, Cerro** ▲ W Argentina *32°36´S 69°53´W*
Açores/Açores, Arquipélago dos/Açores, Ilhas dos *see* Azores
104 *H2* **A Coruña** *Cast.* La Coruña, *Eng.* Corunna; *anc.* Caronium. Galicia, NW Spain *43°22´N 08°24´W*
104 *G2* **A Coruña** *Cast.* La Coruña. ◆ *province* Galicia, NW Spain
42 *L10* **Acoyapa** Chontales, S Nicaragua *11°58´N 85°10´W*
106 *H13* **Acquapendente** Lazio, C Italy *42°44´N 11°52´E*
106 *J13* **Acquasanta Terme** Marche, C Italy *42°46´N 13°24´E*
106 *I13* **Acquasparta** Lazio, C Italy *42°41´N 12°31´E*
106 *C9* **Acqui Terme** Piemonte, NW Italy *44°41´N 08°28´E*
Acrae *see* Palazzolo Acreide
182 *F7* **Acraman, Lake** *salt lake* South Australia
59 *A15* **Acre** *off.* Estado do Acre. ◆ *state* W Brazil
Acre *see* Akko
59 *C16* **Acre, Rio** ⚡ W Brazil
107 *N20* **Acri** Calabria, SW Italy *39°30´N 16°22´E*
Acte *see* Ágion Óros
191 *Y12* **Actéon, Groupe** *island group* Îles Tuamotu, SE French Polynesia
15 *P12* **Acton-Vale** Québec, SE Canada *45°39´N 72°31´W*
41 *P13* **Actopan** *var.* Actopán. Hidalgo, C Mexico *20°19´N 98°59´W*
59 *P14* **Açu** *var.* Assu. Rio Grande do Norte, E Brazil *05°33´S 36°55´W*
Acunum Acusio *see* Montélimar
77 *Q17* **Ada** SE Ghana *05°47´N 00°42´E*
112 *L8* **Ada** Vojvodina, N Serbia *45°48´N 20°08´E*
29 *R5* **Ada** Minnesota, N USA *47°18´N 96°31´W*
31 *R12* **Ada** Ohio, N USA *40°46´N 83°49´W*
27 *O12* **Ada** Oklahoma, C USA *34°47´N 96°41´W*
162 *L8* **Adaatsag** *var.* Tavin. Dundgovĭ, C Mongolia *46°27´N 105°43´E*
Ada Bazar *see* Adapazarı
40 *D3* **Adair, Bahía de** *bay* NW Mexico
104 *M7* **Adaja** ⚡ N Spain
38 *H17* **Adak Island** *island* Aleutian Islands, Alaska, USA
Adalia *see* Antalya
Adalia, Gulf of *see* Antalya Körfezi
141 *X9* **Adam** N Oman *22°22´N 57°30´E*
Adama *see* Nazrēt
60 *I8* **Adamantina** São Paulo, S Brazil *21°41´S 51°04´W*
79 *E14* **Adamaoua** *Eng.* Adamawa. ◆ *province* N Cameroon
68 *F11* **Adamaoua, Massif d'** *Eng.* Adamawa Highlands. *plateau* NW Cameroon
77 *Y14* **Adamawa** ◆ *state* E Nigeria
Adamawa *see* Adamaoua
Adamawa Highlands *see* Adamaoua, Massif d'
106 *F6* **Adamello** ▲ N Italy *46°09´N 10°33´E*
81 *J14* **Ādamī Tulu** Oromīya, C Ethiopia *07°52´N 38°39´E*
63 *M23* **Adam, Mount** *var.* Monte Independencia. ▲ West Falkland, Falkland Islands *51°36´S 60°00´W*
29 *R16* **Adams** Nebraska, C USA *40°25´N 96°30´W*
18 *H8* **Adams** New York, NE USA *43°48´N 75°57´W*
29 *Q3* **Adams** North Dakota, N USA *48°23´N 98°01´W*
155 *I23* **Adam's Bridge** *chain of shoals* NW Sri Lanka
32 *H10* **Adams, Mount** ▲ Washington, NW USA *46°12´N 121°29´W*
Adam's Peak *see* Sri Pada
191 *R16* **Adam's Rock** *island* Pitcairn Island, Pitcairn Islands
191 *P16* **Adamstown** ○ (Pitcairn Islands)Pitcairn Island, Pitcairn Islands *25°04´S 130°05´W*
20 *G10* **Adamsville** Tennessee, S USA *35°14´N 88°23´W*
25 *S9* **Adamsville** Texas, SW USA *31°15´N 98°09´W*
141 *O17* **'Adan** *Eng.* Aden. SW Yemen *12°51´N 45°05´E*
136 *K16* **Adana** *var.* Seyhan. Adana, S Turkey *37°N 35°19´E*
136 *K16* **Adana** *var.* Seyhan. ◆ *province* S Turkey
Adâncata *see* Horlivka
169 *V12* **Adang, Teluk** *bay* Borneo, C Indonesia
136 *F11* **Adapazarı** *prev.* Ada Bazar. Sakarya, NW Turkey *40°49´N 30°24´E*
80 *H8* **Adarama** River Nile, NE Sudan *17°04´N 34°57´E*
195 *Q16* **Adare, Cape** *cape* Antarctica
Ādavāni *see* Ādoni
106 *E6* **Adda** *anc.* Addua. ⚡ N Italy
80 *A13* **Adda** ⚡ W Sudan
143 *Q17* **Aḍ Ḍab'īyah** Abū Ẓaby, C United Arab Emirates *24°17´N 54°08´E*
143 *O18* **Aḍ Ḍafrah** *desert* S United Arab Emirates
141 *Q6* **Ad Dahnā'** *desert* E Saudi Arabia
74 *A11* **Ad Dakhla** *var.* Dakhla. SW Western Sahara *23°46´N 15°56´W*
Ad Dalanj *see* Dilling
Ad Damar *see* Ed Damer
Ad Damazīn *see* Ed Damazin
Ad Dāmir *see* Ed Damer
173 *N2* **Ad Dammām** *desert* NE Saudi Arabia
141 *R6* **Ad Dammān** *var.* Dammām. Ash Sharqīyah, NE Saudi Arabia *26°23´N 50°05´E*
Ad Dāmūr *see* Damoûr
140 *K5* **Ad Dār al Ḥamrā'** Tabūk, NW Saudi Arabia *27°22´N 37°46´E*
140 *M13* **Ad Darb** Jīzān, SW Saudi Arabia *17°45´N 42°15´E*
141 *O8* **Ad Dawādimī** Ar Riyāḍ, C Saudi Arabia *24°32´N 44°21´E*
143 *N16* **Ad Dawḥah** *Eng.* Doha. ● (Qatar) C Qatar *25°15´N 51°36´E*
143 *N16* **Ad Dawḥah** *Eng.* Doha. ✈ C Qatar *25°11´N 51°37´E*
139 *S6* **Ad Dawr** Ṣalāḥ ad Dīn, N Iraq *34°30´N 43°49´E*
139 *Y12* **Ad Dayr** *var.* Dayr, Shahbān. Al Baṣrah, E Iraq *30°45´N 47°36´E*
Addi Arkay *see* Ādī Ārk'ay
139 *X15* **Ad Dibdibah** *physical region* Iraq/Kuwait
Ad Diffah *see* Libyan Plateau
Addis Ababa *see* Ādīs Ābeba
Addison *see* Webster Springs
139 *U10* **Ad Dīwānīyah** *var.* Diwaniyah. C Iraq *32°00´N 44°57´E*
Addoo Atoll *see* Addu Atoll
Addua *see* Adda
151 *K22* **Addu Atoll** *var.* Addoo Atoll, Seenu Atoll. *atoll* S Maldives
Ad Dujail *see* Ad Dujayl
139 *T7* **Ad Dujayl** *var.* Ad Dujail. Ṣalāḥ ad Dīn, N Iraq *33°49´N 44°16´E*
Ad Duwaym/Ad Duwēm *see* Ed Dueim
99 *D16* **Adegem** Oost-Vlaanderen, NW Belgium *51°12´N 03°31´E*
23 *U7* **Adel** Georgia, SE USA *31°08´N 83°25´W*
29 *U14* **Adel** Iowa, C USA *41°36´N 94°01´W*
182 *I9* **Adelaide** *state capital* South Australia *34°56´S 138°36´E*
44 *H2* **Adelaide** New Providence, N Bahamas *24°59´N 77°30´W*
182 *I9* **Adelaide** ✈ South Australia *34°55´S 138°31´E*
194 *H6* **Adelaide Island** *island* Antarctica
181 *P2* **Adelaide River** Northern Territory, N Australia *13°12´S 131°06´E*
76 *M10* **'Adel Bagrou** Hodh ech Chargui, SE Mauritania *15°33´N 07°04´W*
186 *D6* **Adelbert Range** ▲▲ N Papua New Guinea
180 *K3* **Adele Island** *island* Western Australia
107 *O17* **Adelfia** Puglia, SE Italy *41°01´N 16°52´E*
195 *V16* **Adélie Coast** *physical region* Antarctica
195 *V14* **Adélie, Terre** *physical region* Antarctica
Adelnau *see* Odolanów
Adelsberg *see* Postojna
Aden *see* Khormaksar
Aden *see* 'Adan
141 *Q17* **Aden, Gulf of** *gulf* SW Arabian Sea
77 *V10* **Aderbissinat** Agadez, C Niger *15°30´N 07°57´E*
Adhaim *see* Al 'Uẓaym
143 *R16* **Adh Dhayd** *var.* Al Dhaid. Ash Shāriqah, NE United Arab Emirates *25°19´N 55°51´E*
140 *M4* **'Adhfā'** *spring/well* NW Saudi Arabia *29°15´N 41°24´E*
138 *I13* **'Adhrīyāt, Jabāl al** ▲▲ S Jordan
80 *I10* **Ādī Ārk'ay** *var.* Addi Arkay. Āmara, N Ethiopia *13°18´N 37°56´E*
182 *C7* **Adieu, Cape** *headland* South Australia *32°01´S 132°12´E*
106 *H8* **Adige** *Ger.* Etsch. ⚡ N Italy
80 *J10* **Ādīgrat** Tigray, N Ethiopia *14°17´N 39°27´E*
80 *J10* **'Adi Kh'eyih** C Eritrea *19°58´N 39°06´E*
154 *I13* **Ādilābād** *var.* Ādilābād. Andhra Pradesh, C India *19°40´N 78°31´E*
35 *P2* **Adin** California, W USA *41°10´N 120°57´W*
171 *V14* **Adi, Pulau** *island* E Indonesia
18 *K8* **Adirondack Mountains** ▲▲ New York, NE USA
80 *J13* **Ādīs Ābeba** *Eng.* Addis Ababa. ● (Ethiopia) Ādīs Ābeba, C Ethiopia *8°59´N 38°43´E*
80 *J13* **Ādīs Ābeba** ✈ Ādīs Ābeba, C Ethiopia *08°58´N 38°53´E*
80 *I11* **Ādīs Zemen** Āmara, N Ethiopia *12°00´N 37°43´E*
Adi Ugri *see* Mendefera
137 *N15* **Adıyaman** Adıyaman, SE Turkey *37°46´N 38°15´E*
137 *N15* **Adıyaman** ◆ *province* S Turkey
116 *L11* **Adjud** Vrancea, E Romania *46°07´N 27°10´E*
45 *T6* **Adjuntas** C Puerto Rico *18°10´N 66°42´W*
Adjuntas, Presa de las *see* Vicente Guerrero, Presa
Ādkup *see* Erikub Atoll
126 *L15* **Adler** Krasnodarskiy Kray, SW Russian Federation *43°25´N 39°58´E*
Adler *see* Orlice
108 *G7* **Adliswil** Zürich, NW Switzerland *47°19´N 08°32´E*
32 *G7* **Admiralty Inlet** *inlet* Washington, NW USA
39 *X13* **Admiralty Island** *island* Alexander Archipelago, Alaska, USA
186 *E5* **Admiralty Islands** *island group* N Papua New Guinea
136 *B14* **Adnan Menderes** ✈ (İzmir) İzmir, W Turkey *38°16´N 27°09´E*
37 *V6* **Adobe Creek Reservoir** ⊡ Colorado, C USA
77 *T16* **Ado-Ekiti** Ekiti, SW Nigeria *07°42´N 05°13´E*
Adola *see* Kibre Mengist
61 *C23* **Adolfo González Chaues** Buenos Aires, E Argentina
155 *H17* **Ādoni** *var.* Ādavāni. Andhra Pradesh, C India *15°38´N 77°16´E*
102 *K15* **Adour** *anc.* Aturus. ⚡ SW France
Adowa *see* Ādwa
105 *O15* **Adra** Andalucía, S Spain *36°45´N 03°01´W*
107 *L24* **Adrano** Sicilia, Italy, C Mediterranean Sea *37°39´N 14°49´E*
74 *I9* **Adrar** C Algeria *27°56´N 00°12´W*
76 *K7* **Adrar** ◆ *region* C Mauritania
74 *L11* **Adrar** ▲▲ SE Algeria
74 *A12* **Adrar Souttouf** ▲▲ SW Western Sahara
Adrasman *see* Adrasmon
147 *Q10* **Adrasmon** *Rus.* Adrasman. NW Tajikistan *40°33´N 69°56´E*
78 *K10* **Adré** Ouaddaï, E Chad *13°26´N 22°14´E*
106 *H9* **Adria** *anc.* Atria, Hadria, Hatria. Veneto, NE Italy *45°03´N 12°04´E*
31 *R10* **Adrian** Michigan, N USA *41°54´N 84°02´W*
29 *S11* **Adrian** Minnesota, N USA *43°38´N 95°55´W*
27 *R5* **Adrian** Missouri, C USA *38°24´N 94°21´W*
24 *M2* **Adrian** Texas, SW USA *35°16´N 102°39´W*
21 *S4* **Adrian** West Virginia, NE USA *38°53´N 80°14´W*
Adrianople/Adrianopolis *see* Edirne
121 *P7* **Adriatic Basin** *undersea feature* Adriatic Sea, N Mediterranean Sea *42°00´N 17°30´E*
Adriatico, Mare *see* Adriatic Sea
106 *L13* **Adriatic Sea** *Alb.* Deti Adriatik, *It.* Mare Adriatico, *SCr.* Jadransko More, *Slvn.* Jadransko Morje. *sea* N Mediterranean Sea
Adriatik, Deti *see* Adriatic Sea
Adua *see* Ādwa
Aduana del Sásabe *see* El Sásabe
79 *O17* **Adusa** Orientale, NE Dem. Rep. Congo *01°25´N 28°05´E*
118 *J13* **Adutiškis** Vilnius, E Lithuania *55°09´N 26°34´E*
27 *Y7* **Advance** Missouri, C USA *37°06´N 89°54´W*
65 *D25* **Adventure Sound** *bay* East Falkland, Falkland Islands
80 *J10* **Ādwa** *var.* Adowa, *It.* Adua. Tigray, N Ethiopia *14°08´N 38°51´E*
123 *Q8* **Adycha** ⚡ NE Russian Federation
126 *L14* **Adygeya, Respublika** ◆ *autonomous republic* SW Russian Federation
Adzhikui *see* Ajyguýy
77 *N17* **Adzopé** SE Ivory Coast *06°07´N 03°49´W*
125 *U4* **Adz'va** ⚡ NW Russian Federation
125 *U5* **Adz'vavom** Respublika Komi, NW Russian Federation *66°35´N 59°13´E*
Ædua *see* Autun
115 *K19* **Aegean Islands** *island group* Greece/Turkey
Aegean North *see* Vóreion Aigaíon
115 *I17* **Aegean Sea** *Gk.* Aigaíon Pelagos, Aigaío Pélagos, *Turk.* Ege Denizi. *sea* NE Mediterranean Sea
Aegean South *see* Nótion Aigaíon
118 *H3* **Aegviidu** *Ger.* Charlottenhof. Harjumaa, NW Estonia *59°17´N 25°37´E*
Aegyptus *see* Egypt
Aelana *see* Al 'Aqabah
Aelok *see* Ailuk Atoll
Aelōninae *see* Ailinginae Atoll
Aelōnlaplap *see* Ailinglaplap Atoll
Æmilia *see* Emilia-Romagna
Æmilianum *see* Millau
Aemona *see* Ljubljana
Aenaria *see* Ischia
Aeolian Islands *see* Eolie, Isole
191 *Z3* **Aeon Point** *headland* Kiritimati, NE Kiribati *01°46´N 157°11´W*
Æsernia *see* Isernia
104 *G3* **A Estrada** Galicia, NW Spain *42°41´N 08°29´W*
115 *C18* **Aetós** Itháki, Iónia Nísoi, Greece, C Mediterranean Sea *38°21´N 20°40´E*
191 *Q8* **Afaahiti** Tahiti, W French Polynesia *17°43´S 149°18´W*
139 *U10* **'Afak** Al Qādisīyah, C Iraq *32°04´N 45°17´E*
Afanasjevo *see* Afanas'yevo
125 *T14* **Afanas'yevo** *var.* Afanasjevo. Kirovskaya Oblast', NW Russian Federation *58°55´N 53°13´E*
Afándou *see* Afántou
115 *O23* **Afántou** *var.* Afándou. Ródos, Dodekánisa, Greece, Aegean Sea *36°17´N 28°10´E*
80 *K11* **Āfar** ◆ *region* NE Ethiopia
Afar Depression *see* Danakil Desert
191 *O7* **Afareaitu** Moorea, W French Polynesia *17°33´S 149°47´W*
140 *L7* **'Afarīyah, Bi'r al** *well* NW Saudi Arabia
Afars et des Issas, Territoire Français des *see* Djibouti
83 *D22* **Affenrücken** Karas, SW Namibia *28°05´S 15°49´E*
Afghānestān, Dowlat-e Eslāmī-ye *see* Afghanistan
148 *M6* **Afghanistan** *off.* Islamic Republic of Afghanistan, *Per.* Dowlat-e Eslāmī-ye Afghānestān; *prev.* Republic of Afghanistan. ◆ *islamic state* C Asia
Afgoi *see* Afgooye
81 *N17* **Afgooye** *It.* Afgoi. Shabeellaha Hoose, S Somalia *02°09´N 45°07´E*
141 *N8* **'Afīf** Ar Riyāḍ, C Saudi Arabia *23°57´N 42°57´E*
77 *V17* **Afikpo** Ebonyi, S Nigeria *05°52´N 07°58´E*
Afiun Karahissar *see* Afyon
Åfjord *see* Ål Åfjord
109 *V6* **Aflenz Kurort** Steiermark, E Austria *47°33´N 15°14´E*
74 *J6* **Aflou** N Algeria *34°09´N 02°06´E*
81 *L18* **Afmadow** Jubbada Hoose, S Somalia *0°24´N 42°04´E*
39 *Q14* **Afognak Island** *island* Alaska, USA
104 *J2* **A Fonsagrada** Galicia, NW Spain *43°09´N 07°03´W*
186 *E9* **Afore** Northern, S Papua New Guinea *09°10´S 148°30´E*
59 *O15* **Afrânio** Pernambuco, E Brazil *08°32´S 40°54´W*
66-67 **Africa** *continent*
68 *L11* **Africa, Horn of** *physical region* Ethiopia/Somalia
172 *K11* **Africana Seamount** *undersea feature* SW Indian Ocean *37°10´S 29°10´E*
86 *A14* **African Plate** *tectonic plate*
138 *I2* **'Afrīn** Ḥalab, N Syria *36°31´N 36°51´E*
136 *M15* **Afşin** Kahramanmaraş, C Turkey *38°14´N 36°54´E*
98 *J7* **Afsluitdijk** *dam* N Netherlands
29 *U15* **Afton** Iowa, C USA *41°01´N 94°12´W*
29 *W9* **Afton** Minnesota, N USA *44°54´N 92°46´W*
27 *R8* **Afton** Oklahoma, C USA *36°41´N 94°57´W*
136 *F14* **Afyon** *prev.* Afyonkarahisar. Afyon, W Turkey *38°46´N 30°32´E*
136 *F14* **Afyon** *var.* Afiun Karahissar, Afyonkarahisar. ◆ *province* W Turkey
Afyonkarahisar *see* Afyon
Agadès *see* Agadez
77 *V10* **Agadez** *prev.* Agadès. Agadez, C Niger *16°57´N 07°56´E*
77 *W8* **Agadez** ◆ *department* N Niger
74 *E8* **Agadir** SW Morocco *30°30´N 09°37´W*
64 *M9* **Agadir Canyon** *undersea feature* SE Atlantic Ocean *32°30´N 12°50´W*
145 *R12* **Agadyr'** Karaganda, C Kazakhstan *48°15´N 72°55´E*
173 *O7* **Agalega Islands** *island group* N Mauritius
42 *K6* **Agalta, Sierra de** ▲▲ E Honduras
122 *I10* **Agan** ⚡ C Russian Federation
Agana/Agaña *see* Hagåtña
188 *B15* **Agana Bay** *bay* NW Guam
188 *C15* **Aganafield Bay** NW Guam
171 *Kk13* **Agano-gawa** ⚡ Honshū, C Japan
188 *B17* **Aga Point** *headland* S Guam
154 *G9* **Agar** Madhya Pradesh, C India *23°44´N 76°01´E*
81 *I14* **Āgaro** Oromīya, C Ethiopia *07°52´N 36°36´E*
153 *V15* **Agartala** *state capital* Tripura, NE India *23°49´N 91°15´E*
194 *I5* **Agassiz, Cape** *headland* Antarctica *68°29´S 62°59´W*
175 *V13* **Agassiz Fracture Zone** *tectonic feature* S Pacific Ocean
9 *N2* **Agassiz Ice Cap** *Ice feature* Nunavut, N Canada
188 *B16* **Agat** W Guam *13°20´N 144°38´E*
188 *B16* **Agat Bay** *bay* W Guam
145 *P13* **Agat, Gory** *hill* C Kazakhstan
Agatha *see* Agde
115 *M20* **Agathónisi** *island* Dodekánisa, Greece, Aegean Sea
171 *X14* **Agats** Papua, E Indonesia *05°33´S 138°07´E*
155 *C21* **Agatti Island** *island* Lakshadweep, India, N Indian Ocean
38 *D16* **Agattu Island** *island* Aleutian Islands, Alaska, USA
38 *D16* **Agattu Strait** *strait* Aleutian Islands, Alaska, USA
14 *B8* **Agawa** ⚡ Ontario, S Canada
14 *B8* **Agawa Bay** *lake bay* Ontario, S Canada
77 *N17* **Agboville** SE Ivory Coast *05°55´N 04°15´W*
137 *V12* **Ağdam** *Rus.* Agdam. SW Azerbaijan *40°04´N 46°00´E*
Agdam *see* Ağdam
103 *P16* **Agde** *anc.* Agatha. Hérault, S France *43°19´N 03°29´E*
103 *P16* **Agde, Cap d'** *headland* S France *43°17´N 03°30´E*
Agedabia *see* Ajdābiyā
102 *L14* **Agen** *anc.* Aginnum. Lot-et-Garonne, SW France *44°12´N 00°37´E*
Agendicum *see* Sens
165 *O13* **Ageo** Saitama, Honshū, S Japan *35°58´N 139°36´E*
109 *R5* **Ager** ⚡ N Austria
Agere Hiywet *see* Hāgere Hiywet
108 *G8* **Ägerisee** ◎ W Switzerland
142 *M10* **Āghā Jārī** Khūzestān, SW Iran *30°48´N 49°45´E*
39 *P15* **Aghiyuk Island** *island* Alaska, USA
74 *B12* **Aghouinit** SE Western Sahara *22°14´N 13°10´W*
Aghri Dagh *see* Büyükağrı Dağı
74 *B10* **Aghzoumal, Sebkhet** *var.* Sebjet Agsumal. *salt lake* E Western Sahara
115 *F15* **Agiá** *var.* Ayiá. Thessalía, C Greece *39°43´N 22°45´E*
40 *G7* **Agiabampo, Estero de** *estuary* NW Mexico
121 *P3* **Agía Fýlaxis** *var.* Ayia Phyla. S Cyprus *34°43´N 33°02´E*
Agialoúsa *see* Yenierenköy
115 *M21* **Agía Marína** Léros, Dodekánisa, Greece, Aegean Sea *37°09´N 26°51´E*
121 *Q2* **Agía Nápa** *var.* Ayia Napa. E Cyprus *34°59´N 34°00´E*
115 *L16* **Agía Paraskeví** Lésvos, E Greece *39°13´N 26°19´E*
115 *J15* **Agías Eirínis, Akrotírio** *headland* Límnos, E Greece *39°47´N 25°21´E*
Agiasós *see* Agiassós
115 *L17* **Agiassós** *var.* Agiasós, Ayiásos, Ayiássos. Lésvos, E Greece *39°05´N 26°23´E*
127 *T3* **Agidel'** Respublika Bashkortostan, W Russian Federation *55°54´N 53°57´E*
Aginnum *see* Agen
123 *O14* **Aginskiy Buryatskiy Avtonomnyy Okrug** ◆ *autonomous district* S Russian Federation
123 *O14* **Aginskoye** Aginskiy Buryatskiy Avtonomnyy Okrug, S Russian Federation *51°10´N 114°32´E*
115 *I14* **Ágion Óros** *Eng.* Mount Athos. ◆ *monastic republic* NE Greece
115 *H14* **Ágion Óros** *var.* Akte, Aktí; *anc.* Acte. *peninsula* NE Greece
114 *D13* **Ágios Achílleios** *religious building* Dytikí Makedonía, N Greece
115 *J16* **Ágios Efstrátios** *var.* Áyios Evstratios, Hagios Evstrátios. *island* E Greece *39°30´N 25°00´E*
115 *H20* **Ágios Geórgios** *island* Kykládes, Greece, Aegean Sea
Ágios Geórgios *see* Ro
115 *E21* **Ágios Ilías** ▲ S Greece *36°57´N 22°19´E*
115 *K25* **Ágios Ioánnis, Akrotírio** *headland* Kríti, Greece, E Mediterranean Sea *35°19´N 25°46´E*
115 *L20* **Ágios Kírykos** *var.* Áyios Kírikos. Ikaría, Dodekánisa, Greece, Aegean Sea *37°34´N 26°15´E*
115 *K25* **Ágios Nikólaos** *var.* Áyios Nikólaos. Kríti, Greece, E Mediterranean Sea *35°12´N 25°43´E*
115 *D16* **Ágios Nikolaos** Thessalía, C Greece *39°33´N 21°21´E*
115 *H14* **Agíou Órous, Kólpos** *gulf* N Greece
107 *K24* **Agira** *anc.* Agyrium. Sicilia, Italy, C Mediterranean Sea *37°39´N 14°32´E*
115 *G20* **Agkístri** *island* S Greece
114 *G12* **Agkístro** *var.* Angistro. ▲ NE Greece *41°21´N 23°29´E*
103 *O17* **Agly** ⚡ S France
Agnetheln *see* Agnita
14 *E10* **Agnew Lake** ◎ Ontario, S Canada
77 *O16* **Agnibilékrou** E Ivory Coast *07°10´N 03°11´W*
116 *I11* **Agnita** *Ger.* Agnetheln, *Hung.* Szentágota. Sibiu, SW Romania *45°59´N 24°40´E*
107 *K15* **Agnone** Molise, C Italy *41°49´N 14°21´E*
164 *K14* **Ago** Mie, Honshū, SW Japan *34°18´N 136°50´E*
106 *C8* **Agogna** ⚡ N Italy
Agoitz *see* Agoiz
105 *R3* **Agoiz** *var.* Agoitz, Aoiz. Navarra, N Spain *42°47´N 01°23´W*
77 *P17* **Agona Swedru** *var.* Swedru. SE Ghana *05°31´N 00°42´W*
Agordat *see* Ak'ordat
Agosta *see* Augusta
103 *N15* **Agout** ⚡ S France
152 *J12* **Āgra** Uttar Pradesh, N India *27°09´N 78°E*
Agra and Oudh, United Provinces of *see* Uttar Pradesh
Agram *see* Zagreb
105 *U5* **Agramunt** Cataluña, NE Spain *41°48´N 01°07´E*
105 *Q5* **Agreda** Castilla-León, N Spain *41°51´N 01°55´W*
137 *S13* **Ağrı** *var.* Karaköse; *prev.* Karakılısse. Ağrı, NE Turkey *39°44´N 43°04´E*
137 *S13* **Ağrı** ◆ *province* NE Turkey
107 *N19* **Agri** *anc.* Aciris. ⚡ S Italy
Agri Dagi *see* Büyükağrı Dağı
107 *J24* **Agrigento** *Gk.* Akragas; *prev.* Girgenti. Sicilia, Italy, C Mediterranean Sea *37°19´N 13°33´E*
188 *K4* **Agrihan** *island* N Northern Mariana Islands
115 *L17* **Agriliá, Akrotírio** *prev.* Ákra Maléas. *cape* Lésvos, E Greece
115 *D18* **Agrínio** *prev.* Agrinion. Dytikí Ellás, W Greece *38°38´N 21°25´E*
Agrinion *see* Agrínio
115 *G17* **Agriovótano** Évvoia, C Greece *39°00´N 23°18´E*
107 *L18* **Agropoli** Campania, S Italy *40°22´N 14°59´E*
127 *T3* **Agryz** Udmurtskaya Respublika, NW Russian Federation *56°27´N 52°58´E*
137 *U11* **Ağstafa** *Rus.* Akstafa. NW Azerbaijan *41°06´N 45°28´E*
137 *X11* **Ağsu** *Rus.* Akhsu. C Azerbaijan
Agsumal, Sebjet *see* Aghzoumal, Sebkhet
40 *J11* **Agua Brava, Laguna** *lagoon* W Mexico
54 *F7* **Aguachica** Cesar, N Colombia *08°16´N 73°35´W*
59 *J20* **Água Clara** Mato Grosso do Sul, SW Brazil *20°21´S 52°58´W*
44 *D5* **Aguada de Pasajeros** Cienfuegos, C Cuba *22°23´N 80°51´W*
54 *J5* **Aguada Grande** Lara, N Venezuela *10°38´N 69°29´W*
45 *S5* **Aguadilla** W Puerto Rico *18°27´N 67°08´W*
43 *S16* **Aguadulce** Coclé, S Panama *08°16´N 80°31´W*
104 *L14* **Aguadulce** Andalucía, S Spain *37°15´N 04°59´W*
41 *O8* **Agualeguas** Nuevo León, NE Mexico *26°17´N 99°30´W*
40 *L9* **Aguanaval, Río** ⚡ C Mexico
42 *J5* **Aguán, Río** ⚡ N Honduras
25 *R16* **Agua Nueva** Texas, SW USA *26°57´N 98°34´W*
60 *J8* **Aguapeí, Rio** ⚡ S Brazil
61 *E14* **Aguapey, Río** ⚡ NE Argentina
40 *G3* **Agua Prieta** Sonora, NW Mexico *31°16´N 109°33´W*
104 *G5* **A Guarda** *var.* A Guardia, Laguardia, La Guardia. Galicia, NW Spain *41°54´N 08°53´W*
A Guardia *see* A Guarda
56 *E6* **Aguarico, Río** ⚡ Ecuador/Peru
55 *O6* **Aguasay** Monagas, NE Venezuela *09°25´N 63°44´W*
40 *M12* **Aguascalientes** Aguascalientes, C Mexico *21°54´N 102°17´W*
40 *L12* **Aguascalientes** ◆ *state* C Mexico
57 *I18* **Aguas Calientes, Río** ⚡ S Peru
105 *R7* **Aguasvivas** ⚡ NE Spain
60 *J7* **Água Vermelha, Represa de** ⊡ S Brazil
56 *E12* **Aguaytía** Ucayali, C Peru *09°02´S 75°30´W*
104 *I5* **A Gudiña** *var.* La Gudiña. Galicia, NW Spain *42°04´N 07°08´W*
104 *G7* **Águeda** Aveiro, N Portugal *40°34´N 08°28´W*
104 *J8* **Águeda** ⚡ Portugal/Spain
77 *Q8* **Aguelhok** Kidal, NE Mali *19°18´N 00°50´E*
77 *V12* **Aguié** Maradi, S Niger *13°28´N 07°43´E*
188 *K8* **Aguijan** *island* S Northern Mariana Islands
104 *M14* **Aguilar** *var.* Aguilar de la Frontera. Andalucía, S Spain *37°31´N 04°40´W*
104 *M3* **Aguilar de Campóo** Castilla-León, N Spain *42°47´N 04°15´W*
Aguilar de la Frontera *see* Aguilar
42 *F7* **Aguilares** San Salvador, C El Salvador *13°56´N 89°05´W*
105 *Q14* **Aguilas** Murcia, SE Spain *37°24´N 01°36´W*
40 *L15* **Aguililla** Michoacán, SW Mexico *18°43´N 102°45´W*
Agulhas *see* L'Agulhas
172 *J11* **Agulhas Bank** *undersea feature* SW Indian Ocean *35°30´S 21°00´E*
172 *K11* **Agulhas Basin** *undersea feature* SW Indian Ocean *47°00´S 27°00´E*
83 *F26* **Agulhas, Cape** *Afr.* Kaap Agulhas. *headland* SW South Africa *34°51´S 19°59´E*
Agulhas, Kaap *see* Agulhas, Cape
60 *O9* **Agulhas Negras, Pico das** ▲ SE Brazil *22°21´S 44°39´W*
172 *K11* **Agulhas Plateau** *undersea feature* SW Indian Ocean *40°00´S 26°00´E*
165 *S16* **Aguni-jima** *island* Nansei-shotō, SW Japan
Agurain *see* Salvatierra
54 *G5* **Agustín Codazzi** *var.* Codazzi. Cesar, N Colombia *10°02´N 73°15´W*
Agyrium *see* Agira
74 *L12* **Ahaggar** *high plateau region* SE Algeria
146 *E12* **Ahal Welaýaty** *Rus.* Akhalskiy Velayat. ◆ *province* C Turkmenistan
142 *K2* **Ahar** Āzarbāyjān-e Sharqī, NW Iran *38°25´N 47°07´E*
Aharnes *see* Acharnés
138 *I3* **Aḥaṣ, Jabal** ▲ NW Syria
138 *I3* **Aḥaṣ, Jebal** ▲ W Syria
185 *G16* **Ahaura** ⚡ South Island, New Zealand
100 *E13* **Ahaus** Nordrhein-Westfalen, NW Germany *52°04´N 07°01´E*
191 *U9* **Ahe** *atoll* Îles Tuamotu, C French Polynesia
184 *N10* **Ahimanawa Range** ▲▲ North Island, New Zealand
119 *I19* **Ahinski Kanal** *Rus.* Oginskiy Kanal. *canal* SW Belarus
186 *G10* **Ahioma** SE Papua New Guinea *10°20´S 150°35´E*
184 *I2* **Ahipara** Northland, North Island, New Zealand *35°11´S 173°07´E*
184 *I2* **Ahipara Bay** *bay* SE Tasman Sea
Áhkká *see* Akka
39 *N13* **Ahklun Mountains** ▲▲ Alaska, USA
137 *R14* **Ahlat** Bitlis, E Turkey *38°45´N 42°28´E*
101 *F14* **Ahlen** Nordrhein-Westfalen, W Germany *51°46´N 07°53´E*
154 *D10* **Ahmadābād** *var.* Ahmedabad. Gujarāt, W India *23°03´N 72°40´E*
143 *R10* **Aḥmadābād** Kermān, C Iran *35°51´N 59°36´E*
Ahmadi *see* Al Aḥmadī
Ahmad Khel *see* Ḥasan Khēl
155 *F14* **Ahmadnagar** *var.* Ahmednagar. Mahārāshtra, W India *19°08´N 74°48´E*
149 *T9* **Ahmadpur Siāl** Punjab, E Pakistan *30°40´N 71°52´E*
77 *N5* **Aḥmar, 'Erg el** *desert* N Mali
80 *K13* **Ahmar Mountains** ▲▲ C Ethiopia
Ahmedabad *see* Ahmadābād
Ahmednagar *see* Ahmadnagar
114 *N12* **Ahmetbey** Kırklareli, NW Turkey *41°26´N 27°35´E*
14 *H12* **Ahmic Lake** ◎ Ontario, S Canada
190 *G12* **Ahoa** Île Uvea, E Wallis and Futuna *13°17´S 176°12´W*
40 *G8* **Ahomé** Sinaloa, C Mexico *25°55´N 109°10´W*
21 *X8* **Ahoskie** North Carolina, SE USA *36°17´N 76°59´W*
101 *D17* **Ahr** ⚡ W Germany
143 *N12* **Ahram** *var.* Ahrom. Būshehr, S Iran *28°52´N 51°18´E*
100 *J9* **Ahrensburg** Schleswig-Holstein, N Germany *53°41´N 10°14´E*
Ahrom *see* Ahram
93 *L17* **Ähtäri** Länsi-Suomi, W Finland *62°34´N 24°08´E*
40 *K12* **Ahuacatlán** Nayarit, C Mexico *21°02´N 104°30´W*
42 *E7* **Ahuachapán** Ahuachapán, W El Salvador *13°55´N 89°51´W*
42 *A9* **Ahuachapán** ◆ *department* W El Salvador
191 *V16* **Ahu Akivi** *var.* Siete Moai. *ancient monument* Easter Island, Chile, E Pacific Ocean
191 *W11* **Ahunui** *atoll* Îles Tuamotu, C French Polynesia
185 *E20* **Ahuriri** ⚡ South Island, New Zealand
95 *L22* **Åhus** Skåne, S Sweden *55°55´N 14°18´E*
Ahu Tahira *see* Ahu Vinapu
191 *V16* **Ahu Tepeu** *ancient monument* Easter Island, Chile, E Pacific Ocean
191 *V17* **Ahu Vinapu** *var.* Ahu Tahira. *ancient monument* Easter Island, Chile, E Pacific Ocean
142 *L9* **Ahvāz** *var.* Ahwāz; *prev.* Nāsiri. Khūzestān, SW Iran *31°20´N 48°38´E*
Ahvenanmaa *see* Åland
154 *E12* **Ahwa** Gujarāt, W India *20°44´N 73°41´E*
141 *Q16* **Aḥwar** SW Yemen *13°34´N 46°41´E*
Ahwāz *see* Ahvāz
94 *H7* **Åi Åfjord** *var.* Åfjord, Årnes. Sør-Trøndelag, C Norway *63°57´N 10°12´E*
Aibak *see* Āybak
101 *K22* **Aichach** Bayern, SE Germany *48°26´N 11°06´E*
164 *L14* **Aichi** *off.* Aichi-ken, *var.* Aiti. ◆ *prefecture* Honshū, SW Japan
Aidin *see* Aydın
Aidussina *see* Ajdovščina
Aifir, Clochán an *see* Giant's Causeway
Aigaíon Pelagos/Aigaío Pélagos *see* Aegean Sea
109 *S3* **Aigen im Mülkreis** Oberösterreich, N Austria *48°39´N 13°57´E*

◆ Country
● Country Capital
◇ Dependent Territory
○ Dependent Territory Capital
◆ Administrative Regions
✈ International Airport
▲ Mountain
▲▲ Mountain Range
Volcano
⚡ River
◎ Lake
⊡ Reservoir

Column 1

115 G20 **Aígina** var. Aíyina, Egina. Aígina, C Greece 37°45′N 23°26′E

115 G20 **Aígina** island S Greece

115 E18 **Aígio** var. Egio; prev. Aíyion. Dytikí Ellás, S Greece 38°15′N 22°05′E

108 C10 **Aigle** Vaud, SW Switzerland 46°20′N 06°58′E

103 P14 **Aigoual, Mont ▲** S France 44°09′N 03°34′E

173 O16 **Aigrettes, Pointe des** headland W Réunion 21°02′S 55°14′E

61 G19 **Aiguá** var. Aigua. Maldonado, S Uruguay 34°13′S 54°46′W

103 S13 **Aigues ₤** SE France

103 N10 **Aigurande** Indre, C France 46°26′N 01°49′E

Ai-hun see Heihe

163 N10 **Aikawa** Niigata, Sado, C Japan 38°04′N 138°15′E

21 Q13 **Aiken** South Carolina, SE USA 33°34′N 81°44′W

25 N4 **Aiken** Texas, SW USA 34°06′N 101°31′W

160 F13 **Ailao Shan ▲** SW China

189 R4 **Ailinginae Atoll** var. Aelõninae. atoll Ralik Chain, SW Marshall Islands

189 T7 **Ailinglaplap Atoll** var. Aelõnlaplap. atoll Ralik Chain, S Marshall Islands

Aillionn, Loch see Allen, Lough

96 H13 **Ailsa Craig** island SW Scotland, United Kingdom

189 V5 **Ailuk Atoll** var. Aelok. atoll Ratak Chain, NE Marshall Islands

123 R11 **Aim** Khabarovskiy Kray, E Russian Federation 58°45′N 134°08′E

103 R11 **Ain ♦** department E France

103 S10 **Ain ₤** E France

118 G7 **Ainaži** Est. Heinaste, Ger. Hainasch. Limbaži, N Latvia 57°51′N 24°24′E

74 L6 **Aïn Beïda** NE Algeria 35°52′N 07°25′E

76 K4 **'Aïn Ben Tili** Tiris Zemmour, N Mauritania 25°58′N 09°30′W

74 J5 **Aïn Defla** var. Aïn Eddefla. N Algeria 36°16′N 01°58′E

Aïn Eddefla see Aïn Defla

74 L5 **Aïn El Bey ✈** (Constantine) NE Algeria 36°15′N 06°35′E

115 C19 **Aínos ▲** Kefalloniá, Ióniá Nísoi, Greece, C Mediterranean Sea 38°08′N 20°39′E

105 T4 **Ainsa** Aragón, NE Spain 42°25′N 00°08′E

74 I7 **Aïn Sefra** NW Algeria 32°45′N 00°32′W

29 N13 **Ainsworth** Nebraska, C USA 42°33′N 99°51′W

Aintab see Gaziantep

74 H5 **Aïn Témouchent** N Algeria 35°18′N 01°09′W

186 C6 **Aiome** Madang, N Papua New Guinea 05°08′S 144°45′E

Aïoun el Atrous/Aïoun el Atroûss see 'Ayoûn 'el 'Atroûs

54 E11 **Aipe** Huila, C Colombia 03°15′N 75°17′W

56 D9 **Aipena, Río ₤** N Peru

57 L19 **Aiquile** Cochabamba, C Bolivia 18°10′S 65°10′W

Air, Massif de l' see Aïr, Massif de l'

188 E10 **Airai** Babeldaob, C Palau

188 E10 **Airai ✈** (Oreor) Babeldaob, N Palau 07°22′N 134°34′E

168 I11 **Airbangis** Sumatera, NW Indonesia 0°12′N 99°22′E

11 Q16 **Airdrie** Alberta, SW Canada 51°20′N 114°00′W

96 I12 **Airdrie** S Scotland, United Kingdom 55°52′N 03°55′W

Aïr du Azbine see Aïr, Massif de l'

97 M17 **Aire ₤** N England, United Kingdom

102 K15 **Aire-sur-l'Adour** Landes, SW France 43°43′N 00°16′W

103 O1 **Aire-sur-la-Lys** Pas-de-Calais, N France 50°39′N 02°24′E

9 Q6 **Air Force Island** island Baffin Island, Nunavut, NE Canada

169 Q11 **Airhitam, Teluk** bay Borneo, C Indonesia

171 Q11 **Airmadidi** Sulawesi, N Indonesia 01°25′N 124°59′E

77 V8 **Aïr, Massif de l'** var. Aïr, Aïr du Azbine, Asben. ▲ NC Niger

108 G10 **Airolo** Ticino, S Switzerland 46°32′N 08°38′E

102 K9 **Airvault** Deux-Sèvres, W France 46°51′N 00°07′W

115 K19 **Aisch ₤** S Germany

63 G20 **Aisén** off. Región Aisén del General Carlos Ibáñez del Campo, var. Aysen. ♦ region S Chile

10 H7 **Aishihik Lake** ◎ Yukon Territory, W Canada

103 P3 **Aisne ♦** department N France

103 R4 **Aisne ₤** N France

109 T4 **Aist ₤** N Austria

114 K13 **Aisými** Anatolikí Makedonía kai Thráki, NE Greece 41°00′N 25°55′E

105 S11 **Aitana ▲** E Spain

186 B5 **Aitape** var. Eitape. Sandaun, NW Papua New Guinea 03°10′S 142°17′E

31 N4 **Aitkin** Minnesota, N USA 46°31′N 93°42′W

115 D18 **Aitolikó** var. Etoliko; prev. Aitolikón. Dytikí Ellás, C Greece 38°26′N 21°21′E

Aitolikón see Aitolikó

190 L15 **Aitutaki** island S Cook Islands

116 H11 **Aiud** Ger. Strassburg, Hung. Nagyenyed; prev. Engeten. Alba, SW Romania 46°19′N 23°43′E

118 I9 **Aivieskte ₤** C Latvia

189 Q8 **Aiwo** Aiwo Nauru 0°32′S 166°54′E

188 E8 **Aiwokako Passage** passage Babeldaob, N Palau

103 S15 **Aix-en-Provence** var. Aix; anc. Aquae Sextiae. Bouches-du-Rhône, SE France 43°31′N 05°27′E

Aix-la-Chapelle see Aachen

103 T11 **Aix-les-Bains** Savoie, E France 45°40′N 05°55′E

Column 2

186 A6 **Aiyang, Mount ▲** NW Papua New Guinea 05°08′S 141°15′E

Aíyina see Aígina

Aíyion see Aígio

153 W15 **Aizawl** state capital Mizoram, NE India 23°41′N 92°45′E

118 H9 **Aizkraukle** Aizkraukle, S Latvia 56°39′N 25°07′E

118 C9 **Aizpute** Liepāja, W Latvia 56°43′N 21°32′E

165 O11 **Aizu-Wakamatsu** var. Aizuwakamatu, Fukushima, Honshū, C Japan 37°30′N 139°58′E

Aizuwakamatu see Aizu-Wakamatsu

103 X15 **Ajaccio** Corse, France, C Mediterranean Sea 41°54′N 08°43′E

103 X15 **Ajaccio, Golfe d'** gulf Corse, France, C Mediterranean Sea

41 Q15 **Ajalpán** Puebla, S Mexico 18°26′N 97°20′W

154 F13 **Ajanta Range ▲** C India

Ajaria see Achara

Ajastan see Armenia

191 X11 **Akiaki** atoll Îles Tuamotu, E French Polynesia

93 G14 **Ajaureforsen** Västerbotten, N Sweden 65°31′N 15°44′E

185 H17 **Ajax, Mount ▲** South Island, New Zealand 42°34′S 172°06′E

162 F9 **Aj Bogd Uul ▲** SW Mongolia 44°49′N 95°01′E

75 R8 **Ajdābiyā** var. Agedabia, Ajdābiyah. NE Libya 30°46′N 20°14′E

Ajdābiyah see Ajdābiyā

109 S12 **Ajdovščina** Ger. Haidenschaft, It. Aidussina. W Slovenia 45°52′N 13°55′E

165 Q7 **Ajigasawa** Aomori, Honshū, C Japan 40°45′N 140°11′E

111 H23 **Ajka** Veszprém, W Hungary 47°14′N 17°32′E

138 G9 **'Ajlūn** Irbid, N Jordan 32°20′N 35°45′E

138 H9 **'Ajlūn, Jabal ▲** W Jordan

143 R15 **'Ajmān** var. Ajman, 'Ujmān. 'Ajmān, NE United Arab Emirates 25°24′N 55°42′E

152 G12 **Ajmer** var. Ajmere. Rājasthān, N India 26°29′N 74°40′E

36 J15 **Ajo** Arizona, SW USA 32°22′N 112°51′W

105 N2 **Ajo, Cabo de** headland N Spain 43°31′N 03°36′W

36 J16 **Ajo Range ▲** Arizona, SW USA

146 C14 **Ajuguýy** Rus. Adzhikui. Balkan Welaýaty, W Turkmenistan 39°46′N 53°57′E

165 T3 **Akabira** Hokkaidō, NE Japan 43°30′N 142°04′E

165 N10 **Akadomari** Niigata, Sado, C Japan 37°54′N 138°24′E

81 E20 **Akagera ₤** Rwanda/Tanzania see also Kagera

191 W16 **Akahanga, Punta** headland Easter Island, Chile, E Pacific Ocean

80 J13 **Ãk'ak'ï** Oromīya, SW Ethiopia 08°50′N 38°46′E

155 G15 **Akalkot** Mahārāshtra, W India 17°36′N 76°10′E

Akamagaseki see Shimonoseki

165 V3 **Akan** Hokkaidō, NE Japan 44°06′N 144°03′E

165 U4 **Akan** Hokkaidō, NE Japan 43°30′N 144°08′E

165 U4 **Akan-ko ◎** Hokkaidō, NE Japan

Akanthoú see Tatlısu

185 I19 **Akaroa** Canterbury, South Island, New Zealand 43°48′S 172°58′E

80 E9 **Akasha** Northern, N Sudan 21°03′N 30°46′E

164 I13 **Akashi** var. Akasi. Hyōgo, Honshū, SW Japan 34°39′N 135°00′E

Akasi see Akashi

92 K11 **Äkäsjokisuu** Lappi, N Finland 28°28′N 23°44′E

137 S11 **Akbaba Dağı ▲** Armenia/Turkey 41°04′N 43°28′E

Akbük Limanı see Güllük Körfezi

127 O11 **Akbulak** Orenburgskaya Oblast', W Russian Federation 51°01′N 55°35′E

137 O11 **Akçadağ** Malatya, C Turkey 38°21′N 37°59′E

136 H11 **Akçakoca** Düzce, NW Turkey 41°05′N 31°08′E

76 H7 **Akchâr** desert W Mauritania

145 S12 **Akchatau** Kaz. Aqshatau. Karagandā, C Kazakhstan 47°59′N 74°02′E

136 L13 **Akdağ ▲** C Turkey

136 E17 **Ak Dağları ▲** SW Turkey

136 K13 **Akdağmadeni** Yozgat, C Turkey 39°40′N 35°52′E

146 G8 **Akdepe** prev. Ak-Tepe, Leninsk, Turkm. Lenin. Dașoguz Welaýat, N Turkmenistan 42°04′N 59°17′E

121 P2 **Ak-Dere** see Byala

121 P2 **Ak-Dovurak** Respublika Tyva, S Russian Federation 51°09′N 90°36′E

146 F9 **Akdzhakaya, Vpadina** var. Vpadina Akchakaya. depression N Turkmenistan

139 S2 **Akēchā** Ar. 'Aqrah. Dahūk, N Iraq 36°46′N 43°52′E

95 C16 **Åkrehamn** Rogaland, S Norway 59°15′N 05°13′E

77 V9 **Akérrèb** Agadez, C Niger 17°45′N 09°07′E

154 H12 **Akot** Mahārāshtra, C India 20°44′N 77°00′E

81 J9 **Akordat** var. Ak'ordat, Agordat. Akurdet. C Eritrea 15°33′N 38°01′E

77 N16 **Akosombo Dam** dam SE Ghana

154 H12 **Akot** Mahārāshtra, C India 20°44′N 77°00′E

8 K7 **Akpatok Island** island Nunavut, E Canada

31 U12 **Akron** Ohio, N USA 41°05′N 81°31′W

37 V3 **Akron** Colorado, C USA 40°09′N 103°12′W

92 H3 **Akranes** Vesturland, W Iceland 64°19′N 22°01′W

Column 3

Akheloós see Acheloós

39 Q15 **Akhiok** Kodiak Island, Alaska, USA 56°57′N 154°12′W

136 C13 **Akhisar** Manisa, W Turkey 38°54′N 27°50′E

75 X10 **Akhmîm** var. Akhmîm; anc. Panopolis. C Egypt 26°35′N 31°48′E

152 H6 **Akhnûr** Jammu and Kashmir, NW India 32°53′N 74°46′E

114 N10 **Akhtopol** Burgas, E Bulgaria 42°06′N 27°57′E

127 P11 **Akhtuba ₤** SW Russian Federation

127 P11 **Akhtubinsk** Astrakhanskaya Oblast', SW Russian Federation 48°17′N 46°14′E

164 H14 **Aki** Kōchi, Shikoku, SW Japan 33°30′N 133°53′E

39 N12 **Akiachak** Alaska, USA 60°54′N 161°25′W

39 N12 **Akiak** Alaska, USA 60°54′N 161°12′W

191 X11 **Akiaki** atoll Îles Tuamotu, E French Polynesia

12 M9 **Akimiski Island** island Nunavut, C Canada

136 M17 **Akıncı Burnu** headland S Turkey 36°21′N 35°47′E

136 F11 **Akıncılar** see Selçuk

147 U10 **Akinovka** Zaporiz'ka Oblast', S Ukraine 35°44′N 34°09′E

165 P8 **Akita** Akita, Honshū, C Japan 39°44′N 140°06′E

165 Q8 **Akita** off. Akita-ken. ♦ prefecture Honshū, C Japan

76 H8 **Akjoujt** prev. Fort-Repoux. Inchiri, W Mauritania 19°42′N 14°28′W

92 H11 **Akka** Lapp. Áhkká. ▲ N Sweden 67°33′N 17°27′E

92 H11 **Akkajaure ◎** N Sweden

155 L23 **Akkaraipattu** Eastern Province, E Sri Lanka 07°13′N 81°51′E

145 P13 **Akkense** Kaz. Aqkense. Karagandā, C Kazakhstan 46°39′N 68°06′E

145 X11 **Aksuat** Vostochnyy Kazakhstan, E Kazakhstan 47°48′N 82°51′E

145 Y11 **Aksuat** Vostochnyy Kazakhstan, E Kazakhstan 48°03′N 83°39′E

127 S4 **Aksubayevo** Respublika Tatarstan, W Russian Federation 54°52′N 50°50′E

158 M1 **Aksu He ₤** China/Kyrgyzstan see also Sary-Dzhaz

80 J10 **Āksum** Tigray, N Ethiopia 14°06′N 38°42′E

124 I5 **Aktarriti** Murmanskaya Oblast', NW Russian Federation 66°50′N 30°27′E

145 O12 **Aktas** Kaz. Aqtas. Karagandā, C Kazakhstan 48°03′N 66°21′E

147 V9 **Ak-Tash, Gora ▲** C Kyrgyzstan 40°53′N 74°39′E

145 R10 **Aktau** Kaz. Aqtaū. Karagandā, C Kazakhstan 50°13′N 73°06′E

144 E11 **Aktau** Kaz. Aqtaū; prev. Shevchenko. Mangistau, W Kazakhstan 43°25′N 51°14′E

80 J11 **Ālamat'a** Tigray, N Ethiopia 12°22′N 39°32′E

78 R11 **Aktuau** see Ágion Óros

145 X7 **Ak-Terek** Issyk-Kul'skaya Oblast', E Kyrgyzstan 42°14′N 77°46′E

Aktí see Ágion Óros

147 Q9 **Aktjubinsk/Aktyubinsk** see Aktobe

144 I10 **Akto** Xinjiang Uygur Zizhiqu, NW China 39°07′N 75°43′E

144 I10 **Aktobe** prev. Aktjubinsk. headland W Latvia 56°49′N 21°03′E

158 M9 **Akmeqit** Xinjiang Uygur Zizhiqu, NW China 37°10′N 76°59′E

146 J14 **Akmeydan** Mary Welaýaty, C Turkmenistan 37°50′N 62°05′E

145 P9 **Akmola** off. Akmolinskaya Oblast', Kaz. Aqmola Oblysy; prev. Tselinogradskaya Oblast'. ♦ province C Kazakhstan

Akmola see Astana

Akmolinsk see Astana

Akmolinskaya Oblast' see Akmola

118 I11 **Akniste** Jēkabpils, S Latvia 56°09′N 25°43′E

81 F18 **Akobo** Jonglei, SE Sudan 07°50′N 33°05′E

81 F18 **Akobo** var. Ākobowenz. ₤ Ethiopia/Sudan

Ākobowenz see Akobo

154 H12 **Akola** Mahārāshtra, C India 20°44′N 77°00′E

81 G18 **Akordat** var. Ak'ordat, Agordat. Akurdet. C Eritrea 15°33′N 38°01′E

77 N16 **Akosombo Dam** dam SE Ghana

154 H12 **Akot** Mahārāshtra, C India 20°44′N 77°00′E

77 N16 **Akoupé** SE Ivory Coast 06°19′N 03°54′W

12 M3 **Akpatok Island** island Nunavut, E Canada

158 G7 **Akqi** Xinjiang Uygur Zizhiqu, NW China 40°47′N 78°20′E

23 U7 **Akron** Colorado, C USA

84 A4 **Akron** see Acre

94 H3 **Akranes** Vesturland, W Iceland 64°19′N 22°01′W

Column 4

121 P3 **Akrotírion, Kólpos** var. Akrotiri Bay. bay S Cyprus

121 O3 **Akrotiri Sovereign Base Area** UK military installation S Cyprus

158 F11 **Aksai Chin** Chin. Aksayqin. disputed region China/India

136 I15 **Aksaray** Aksaray, C Turkey 38°23′N 33°59′E

136 I15 **Aksaray ♦** province C Turkey

144 G8 **Aksay** var. Aksaj. Kaz. Aqsay. Zapadnyy Kazakhstan, NW Kazakhstan 51°11′N 53°00′E

127 O10 **Aksay** Volgogradskaya Oblast', SW Russian Federation 47°59′N 43°54′E

147 W10 **Ak-say ₤** China/Kyrgyzstan

Aksay/Aksu see Aksu

147 W10 **Aksay Kaz.** Aqsū. ₤ SE Kazakhstan

158 G15 **Aksayqin Hu ◎** NW China

136 C14 **Akșehir** Konya, W Turkey 38°22′N 31°24′E

136 C14 **Akșehir Gölü ◎** C Turkey

136 G16 **Akseki** Antalya, SW Turkey 37°04′N 31°48′E

123 P13 **Aksenovo-Zilovskoye** Chitinskaya Oblast', S Russian Federation 53°01′N 117°26′E

145 Y11 **Aksu** Almaty, SE Kazakhstan 46°39′N 80°20′E

145 X11 **Aksu Kaz.** Aqsū. Akmola, N Kazakhstan 52°31′N 72°09′E

145 W13 **Aksu Kaz.** Aqsū. Almaty, SE Kazakhstan 45°31′N 79°28′E

145 T11 **Aksu** var. Jermak, Kaz. Ermak; prev. Yermak. Pavlodar, NE Kazakhstan 52°03′N 76°55′E

145 X11 **Aksu Kaz.** Aqsū. ₤ SE Kazakhstan

147 V11 **Akshatau, Khrebet** ▲ E Kazakhstan

147 X9 **Ak-Shyyrak** Issyk-Kul'skaya Oblast', E Kyrgyzstan 41°46′N 78°34′E

158 H7 **Aksu Xinjiang Uygur Zizhiqu, NW China 41°17′N 80°15′E**

145 R8 **Aksu Kaz.** Aqsū. Akmola, N Kazakhstan 52°31′N 72°09′E

137 T11 **Alaverdi** N Armenia 41°06′N 44°37′E

145 X11 **Aksu Kaz.** Aqsū. ₤ SE Kazakhstan

93 L16 **Alajärvi** Länsi-Suomi, W Finland 63°00′N 23°50′E

118 K6 **Alajõe** Ida-Virumaa, NE Estonia 59°00′N 27°26′E

42 M13 **Alajuela** Alajuela, C Costa Rica 10°00′N 84°12′W

42 L13 **Alajuela** off. Provincia de Alajuela. ♦ province N Costa Rica

43 T14 **Alajuela, Lago** ◎ C Panama

38 M11 **Alakanuk** Alaska, USA 62°41′N 164°37′W

145 X13 **Alakol', Ozero Kaz.** Alaköl. ◎ SE Kazakhstan

145 X13 **Alaköl** see Alakol', Ozero

92 M11 **Alakurtti** Murmanskaya Oblast', NW Russian Federation 66°57′N 30°27′E

124 J5 **Alakurtti** Murmanskaya Oblast', NW Russian Federation 66°57′N 30°27′E

75 U8 **Al 'Alamayn** var. El 'Alamein. N Egypt 30°50′N 28°57′E

139 R1 **Al 'Amādīyah** Dahūk, N Iraq 37°09′N 43°27′E

188 E5 **Alamagan** island C Northern Mariana Islands

139 X10 **Al 'Amārah** var. Amara. Maysān, E Iraq 31°51′N 47°10′E

80 J1 **Ālamat'a** Tigray, N Ethiopia 12°22′N 39°32′E

121 T13 **'Alam el Rûm, Râs** headland N Egypt 31°21′N 27°23′E

106 B9 **Alamicamba** var. Alamikamb. Región Autónoma Atlántico Norte, NE Nicaragua 13°34′N 84°09′W

Alamikamb see Alamicamba

42 M8 **Alamitos, Sierra de los ▲** NE Mexico 26°15′N 102°14′W

41 O8 **Álamo** Veracruz-Llave, C Mexico 20°55′N 97°41′W

35 X9 **Alamo** Nevada, W USA 37°21′N 115°08′W

20 F9 **Alamo** Tennessee, S USA 35°47′N 89°09′W

37 S14 **Alamogordo** New Mexico, SW USA 32°52′N 105°57′W

40 H7 **Alamos** Sonora, NW Mexico 26°59′N 108°53′W

37 S7 **Alamosa** Colorado, C USA 37°25′N 105°51′W

93 J20 **Åland** var. Åland Islands, Fin. Ahvenanmaa. ♦ province SW Finland

93 J20 **Åland** var. Åland Islands, Fin. Ahvenanmaa. island group SW Finland

Åland Islands see Åland

95 Q14 **Åland Sea** var. Ålands Hav. strait Baltic Sea/Gulf of Bothnia

43 P16 **Alanje** Chiriquí, SW Panama 08°26′N 82°33′W

25 O2 **Alanreed** Texas, SW USA 35°12′N 100°45′W

136 G17 **Alanya** Antalya, S Turkey 36°32′N 32°02′E

23 V17 **Alapaha River ₤** Florida/Georgia, SE USA

122 G11 **Alapayevsk** Sverdlovskaya Oblast', C Russian Federation 57°48′N 61°50′E

138 G10 **Al Balqā' ♦** governorate NW Jordan

14 F11 **Alban** Ontario, S Canada 46°00′N 80°37′W

103 O15 **Alban** Tarn, S France 43°52′N 02°30′E

12 K11 **Albanel, Lac ◎** Québec, SE Canada

113 L20 **Albania off.** Republic of Albania, Alb. Republika e Shqipërisë, Shqipëria; prev. People's Socialist Republic of Albania. ♦ republic SE Europe

23 O6 **Albania** see Aubagne

107 H15 **Albano Laziale** Lazio, C Italy 41°45′N 12°40′E

180 J7 **Albany** Western Australia 35°03′S 117°54′E

23 S7 **Albany** Georgia, SE USA 31°35′N 84°09′W

31 P13 **Albany** Indiana, N USA 40°18′N 85°14′W

Column 5

147 S9 **Ala-Buka** Dzhalal-Abadskaya Oblast', W Kyrgyzstan 41°22′N 71°22′E

136 J12 **Alaca** Çorum, N Turkey 40°10′N 34°52′E

136 K10 **Alaçam** Samsun, N Turkey 41°36′N 35°35′E

23 V9 **Alachua** Florida, SE USA 29°48′N 82°29′W

137 S13 **Aladağlar ▲** W Turkey

136 L15 **Aladağ ▲** C Turkey

162 I5 **Alag-Erdene ₤** Manhan. Hövsgöl, N Mongolia 50°05′N 100°01′E

127 O16 **Alagir** Respublika Severnaya Osetiya, SW Russian Federation 43°01′N 44°10′E

126 B6 **Alagna Valsesia** Valle d'Aosta, NW Italy 45°51′N 07°50′E

102 P9 **Alagnon ₤** C France

59 P16 **Alagoas off.** Estado de Alagoas. ♦ state E Brazil

59 P17 **Alagoinhas** Bahia, E Brazil 12°09′S 38°21′W

105 R5 **Alagón** Aragón, NE Spain 41°46′N 01°07′W

104 J9 **Alagón ₤** W Spain

93 K16 **Alahärmä** Länsi-Suomi, W Finland 63°15′N 22°50′E

al Ahdar see Al Akhdar

93 K16 **Alahärmä** see Altaelva

142 K12 **Al Ahmadī** var. Ahmadi. E Kuwait 29°02′N 48°01′E

147 V11 **Ai Ain** see Al 'Ayn

145 Z8 **Alaior** prev. Alayor. Menorca, Spain, W Mediterranean Sea 39°57′N 04°08′E

147 T11 **Alai Range Rus.** Alayskiy Khrebet. ▲ Kyrgyzstan/Tajikistan

Alais see Alès

145 N8 **Al 'Aja'iz** E Oman 19°53′N 57°12′E

145 N8 **Al 'Aja'iz** SE Oman

137 T11 **Alaverdi** N Armenia 41°06′N 44°37′E

93 N14 **Ala-Vuokki** Oulu, E Finland 64°46′N 29°29′E

93 K17 **Alavus Swe.** Alavo. Länsi-Suomi, W Finland 62°33′N 23°38′E

42 L13 **Alajuela off.** Provincia de Alajuela. ♦ province N Costa Rica

139 P6 **Al 'Awānī** Al Anbār, W Iraq 34°28′N 41°43′E

75 U12 **Al Awaynāt** SE Libya 21°46′N 24°51′E

182 K9 **Alawoona** South Australia 34°45′S 140°28′E

Alaykel'/Alay-Kuu see Kök-Art

143 R17 **Al 'Ayn** var. Al Ain. Abū Ȥaby, E United Arab Emirates 24°13′N 55°44′E

143 R17 **Al 'Ayn** var. Al Ain. ✈ Abū Ȥaby, E United Arab Emirates 24°16′N 55°31′E

138 G12 **Al 'Aynā** Al Karak, W Jordan 30°59′N 35°43′E

Alayor see Alaior

Alayskiy Khrebet see Alai Range

123 S6 **Alazeya ₤** NE Russian Federation

139 U8 **Al 'Azīzīyah** var. Aziziya. Wāsiṭ, E Iraq 32°54′N 45°05′E

120 M12 **Al 'Azīzīyah** NW Libya 32°32′N 13°01′E

138 I10 **Al Azraq al Janūbī** Az Zarqā', N Jordan 31°49′N 36°48′E

25 V6 **Alba** Texas, SW USA 32°47′N 95°37′W

116 G11 **Alba ♦** county W Romania

139 P3 **Al Ba'āj** Nīnawā, N Iraq 36°02′N 41°43′E

138 J2 **Al Bāb** Ḩalab, N Syria 36°24′N 37°32′E

105 P11 **Albacete** Castilla-La Mancha, C Spain 39°N 01°52′W

105 P11 **Albacete ♦** province Castilla-La Mancha, C Spain

140 I4 **Al Bad'** Tabūk, NW Saudi Arabia 28°20′N 35°00′E

104 L7 **Alba de Tormes** Castilla-León, N Spain 40°50′N 05°30′W

139 P3 **Al Bādī** Nīnawā, N Iraq 35°57′N 41°31′E

141 N8 **Al Badī'a** var. (Abū Ȥaby) Abū Ȥaby, C United Arab Emirates 24°27′N 54°39′E

143 P17 **Al Badī'ah** var. Al Bedei'ah. spring/well C United Arab Emirates 23°44′N 53°50′E

140 J4 **Al Bāḩah** var. Al Bāha. Al Bāḩah, SW Saudi Arabia 20°01′N 41°29′E

140 M11 **Al Bāḩah** var. Al Bāha. ♦ province W Saudi Arabia

Al Bahrayn see Bahrain

105 S11 **Albaida** País Valenciano, E Spain 38°51′N 00°31′W

116 H11 **Alba Iulia Ger.** Weissenburg, Hung. Gyulafehérvár; prev. Bálgrad, Karlsburg, Károly-Fehérvár. Alba, W Romania 46°04′N 23°33′E

Albak see Akēchā

139 G10 **Al Balqā' ♦** governorate NW Jordan

14 F11 **Alban** Ontario, S Canada 46°00′N 80°37′W

143 O5 **Albania off.** Republic of Albania 113 L20

113 L20 **Albania** see Aubagne

105 Q14 **Albanchez** Andalucía, S Spain 37°21′N 02°29′W

101 H23 **Albstadt** Baden-Württemberg, S Germany

23 Q6 **Albany** Georgia, SE USA 31°35′N 84°09′W

37 Q11 **Albuquerque** New Mexico, SW USA 35°05′N 106°38′W

43 Q7 **Albuquerque, Cayos de ◊** NW Colombia, Caribbean Sea

Column 6

136 D14 **Alașehir** Manisa, W Turkey 38°19′N 28°30′E

139 N5 **Al 'Ashārah** var. Ashara. Dayr az Zawr, E Syria 34°51′N 40°36′E

141 Z9 **Al Ashkharah** var. Al Ashkhara. NE Oman 21°47′N 59°30′E

Al 'Aşimah see 'Ammān

39 P8 **Alaska** off. State of Alaska, also known as Land of the Midnight Sun, The Last Frontier, Seward's Folly; prev. Russian America. ♦ state NW USA

39 P13 **Alaska, Gulf of** var. Golfo de Alasca. gulf Canada/USA

39 O15 **Alaska Peninsula** peninsula Alaska, USA

39 Q11 **Alaska Range ▲** Alaska, USA

Al-Asnam see Chlef

106 B10 **Alassio** Liguria, NW Italy 44°01′N 08°12′E

137 Y12 **Älät Rus.** Alyaty-Pristan'. SE Azerbaijan 39°57′N 49°24′E

Alat see Olot

139 S13 **Al 'Athāmīn** An Najaf, S Iraq 30°27′N 43°41′E

39 P7 **Alatna River ₤** Alaska, USA

107 J15 **Alatri** Lazio, C Italy 41°43′N 13°21′E

127 P5 **Alatyr'** Chuvashskaya Respublika, W Russian Federation 54°50′N 46°28′E

56 C7 **Alausí** Chimborazo, C Ecuador 02°11′S 78°52′W

105 O3 **Álava Basq.** Araba. ♦ province País Vasco, N Spain

21 S10 **Albemarle** North Carolina, SE USA 35°21′N 80°12′W

21 N8 **Albemarle Sound** inlet W Atlantic Ocean

106 B10 **Albenga** Liguria, NW Italy 44°03′N 08°13′E

104 L8 **Alberche ₤** C Spain

103 O17 **Albères, Chaîne des** var. les Albères, Montes Albères. ▲ France/Spain

182 F2 **Alberga Creek** seasonal river South Australia

104 G7 **Albergaria-a-Velha** Aveiro, N Portugal 40°42′N 08°28′W

105 S10 **Alberic** País Valenciano, E Spain 39°07′N 00°31′W

107 L18 **Alberobello** Puglia, SE Italy 40°47′N 17°14′E

108 J7 **Alberschwende** Vorarlberg, W Austria 47°28′N 09°50′E

103 O3 **Albert** Somme, N France 50°N 02°38′E

11 O12 **Alberta ♦** province SW Canada

Albert Edward Nyanza see Edward, Lake

61 C20 **Alberti** Buenos Aires, E Argentina 35°03′S 60°15′W

111 K23 **Albertirsa** Pest, C Hungary 47°15′N 19°36′E

99 I16 **Albertkanaal** canal N Belgium

81 F16 **Albert Lea** Minnesota, N USA 43°39′N 93°22′W

81 F16 **Albert Nile ₤** NW Uganda

81 F16 **Albert Nyanza** see Albert, Lake

103 T11 **Albertville** Savoie, E France 45°41′N 06°24′E

23 Q2 **Albertville** Alabama, S USA 34°16′N 86°12′W

Albertville see Kalemie

103 N15 **Albi anc.** Albiga. Tarn, S France 43°55′N 02°09′E

29 W15 **Albia** Iowa, C USA 41°01′N 92°48′W

55 X9 **Albina** Marowijne, NE Suriname 05°29′N 54°08′W

83 A15 **Albina, Ponta** headland SW Angola 15°52′S 11°45′E

30 M16 **Albion** Illinois, N USA 38°20′N 88°03′W

31 P11 **Albion** Indiana, N USA 41°23′N 85°26′W

29 P14 **Albion** Nebraska, C USA 41°41′N 98°00′W

18 E9 **Albion** New York, NE USA 43°13′N 78°09′W

18 B12 **Albion** Pennsylvania, NE USA 41°50′N 80°18′W

140 J4 **Al Bi'r** var. Bi'r Ibn Hirmās. Tabūk, NW Saudi Arabia 28°52′N 36°16′E

141 Q9 **Al Biyāḏ** desert C Saudi Arabia

98 H13 **Alblasserdam** Zuid-Holland, SW Netherlands 51°52′N 04°40′E

105 T8 **Albocàsser** var. Albocasser. País Valenciano, E Spain 40°21′N 00°01′E

105 O17 **Alborán, Isla de** island S Spain

Alborán, Mar de see Alboran Sea

105 N17 **Alboran Sea Sp.** Mar de Alborán, sea SW Mediterranean Sea

95 H21 **Ålborg var.** Aalborg, Ålborg-Nørresundby; anc. Alburgum. Nordjylland, N Denmark 57°03′N 10°52′E

95 H21 **Ålborg Bugt var.** Aalborg Bugt. bay N Denmark

Ålborg-Nørresundby see Ålborg

143 O5 **Alborz, Reshteh-ye Kūhhā-ye,** Eng. Elburz Mountains. ▲ N Iran

105 Q14 **Albox** Andalucía, S Spain 37°22′N 02°08′W

101 H23 **Albstadt** Baden-Württemberg, S Germany 48°12′N 09°01′E

104 G14 **Albufeira** Beja, S Portugal 37°05′N 08°15′W

139 P5 **Ālbū Ghar, Sabkhat** ◎ NW Iraq

105 O15 **Albuñol** Andalucía, S Spain 36°47′N 03°11′W

Column 7

29 U7 **Albany** Minnesota, N USA 45°39′N 94°33′W

27 R2 **Albany** Missouri, C USA 40°15′N 94°15′W

18 L10 **Albany** state capital New York, NE USA 42°39′N 73°45′W

32 G12 **Albany** Oregon, NW USA 44°38′N 123°06′W

25 Q6 **Albany** Texas, SW USA 32°44′N 99°18′W

12 F10 **Albany ₤** Ontario, S Canada

Alba Pompeia see Alba

Alba Regia see Székesfehérvár

138 J6 **Al Bāridah** var. Bāridah. Ḩimṣ, C Syria 34°15′N 37°39′E

139 Q11 **Al Bārit** Al Anbār, S Iraq 31°16′N 42°28′E

105 R8 **Albarracín** Aragón, NE Spain 40°24′N 01°25′E

139 Y13 **Al Başrah Eng.** Basra, also Busra, Bussora. ♦ governorate SE Iraq

139 Y12 **Al Başrah Eng.** Basra, also Busra, Bussora. Al Başrah, SE Iraq 30°30′N 47°50′E

139 V11 **Al Baṭḥā'** Dhī Qār, SE Iraq 31°06′N 46°09′E

141 X8 **Al Bāṭinah** var. Batinah. coastal region N Oman

0 H16 **Albatross Plateau** undersea feature E Pacific Ocean

121 Q12 **Al Baydā'** var. Beida. NE Libya 32°46′N 21°43′E

141 P16 **Al Bayḍā'** var. Al Beida. Al Bedei'ah var. Al Badī'ah. SW Yemen 13°58′N 45°38′E

21 S10 **Albemarle** North Carolina, SE USA 35°21′N 80°12′W

21 N8 **Albemarle Island** see Isabela, Isla

21 N8 **Albemarle Sound** inlet W Atlantic Ocean

106 B10 **Albenga** Liguria, NW Italy 44°03′N 08°13′E

104 L8 **Alberche ₤** C Spain

Alberga Creek seasonal river

138 J6 **Al Bāridah** var. Bāridah

139 Q11 **Al Bārit**

105 R8 **Albarracín**

139 Y13 **Al Başrah**

29 U7 **Albany** Minnesota, N USA

27 R2 **Albany** Missouri, C USA

18 L10 **Albany** state capital New York

32 G12 **Albany** Oregon, NW USA

25 Q6 **Albany** Texas, SW USA

12 F10 **Albany ₤** Ontario, S Canada

138 J6 **Al Bāridah**

105 R8 **Albarracín**

37 Q11 **Albuquerque** New Mexico, SW USA

43 Q7 **Albuquerque, Cayos de ◊** NW Colombia, Caribbean Sea

Column 8

29 U7 **Albany** Minnesota, N USA 45°39′N 94°33′W

27 R2 **Albany** Missouri, C USA 40°15′N 94°15′W

18 L10 **Albany** state capital New York, NE USA 42°39′N 73°45′W

32 G12 **Albany** Oregon, NW USA 44°38′N 123°06′W

25 Q6 **Albany** Texas, SW USA 32°44′N 99°18′W

12 F10 **Albany ₤** Ontario, S Canada

Alba Pompeia see Alba

Alba Regia see Székesfehérvár

138 J6 **Al Bāridah** var. Bāridah. Ḩimṣ, C Syria 34°15′N 37°39′E

139 Q11 **Al Bārit** Al Anbār, S Iraq 31°16′N 42°28′E

105 R8 **Albarracín** Aragón, NE Spain 40°24′N 01°25′E

139 Y13 **Al Başrah Eng.** Basra, also Busra, Bussora. ♦ governorate SE Iraq

139 Y12 **Al Başrah** Al Başrah, SE Iraq 30°30′N 47°50′E

139 V11 **Al Baṭḥā'** Dhī Qār, SE Iraq

141 X8 **Al Bāṭinah** var. Batinah

0 H16 **Albatross Plateau** undersea feature E Pacific Ocean

121 Q12 **Al Baydā'** var. Beida

141 P16 **Al Bayḍā'** var. Al Beida

37 Q11 **Albuquerque** New Mexico, SW USA 35°05′N 106°38′W

43 Q7 **Albuquerque, Cayos de ◊** NW Colombia, Caribbean Sea

◆ Country ◇ Dependent Territory ◆ Administrative Regions ▲ Mountain ⛰ Volcano ◎ Lake
● Country Capital ○ Dependent Territory Capital ✈ International Airport ▲ Mountain Range ₤ River ▨ Reservoir

Al Buraymī – Alme

143 *R17* **Al Buraymī** *var.* Buraimi. *spring/well* Oman/United Arab Emirates *24°27′N 55°33′E*
Al Burayqah *see* Marsá al Burayqah
Alburgum *see* Aalborg
104 *I10* **Alburquerque** Extremadura, W Spain *39°12′N 07°00′W*
181 *V14* **Albury** New South Wales, SE Australia *36°03′S 146°53′E*
141 *T14* **Al Buzūn** SE Yemen *15°40′N 50°53′E*
93 *G17* **Alby** Västernorrland, C Sweden *62°30′N 15°25′E*
Albyn, Glen *see* Mor, Glen
104 *G12* **Alcácer do Sal** Setúbal, W Portugal *38°22′N 08°29′W*
Alcalá de Chisvert/Alcalá de Chivert *see* Alcalá de Xivert
104 *K14* **Alcalá de Guadaira** Andalucía, S Spain *37°20′N 05°50′W*
105 *O8* **Alcalá de Henares** *Ar.* Alkal'a; *anc.* Complutum. Madrid, C Spain *40°28′N 03°22′W*
104 *K16* **Alcalá de los Gazules** Andalucía, S Spain *36°29′N 05°43′W*
105 *T8* **Alcalá de Xivert** *var.* Alcalá de Chisvert, *Cast.* Alcalá de Chivert. País Valenciano, E Spain *40°19′N 00°13′E*
105 *N14* **Alcalá La Real** Andalucía, S Spain *37°28′N 03°55′W*
107 *I23* **Alcamo** Sicilia, Italy, C Mediterranean Sea *37°58′N 12°58′E*
105 *T4* **Alcanadre** ≈ NE Spain
105 *T8* **Alcanar** Cataluña, NE Spain *40°33′N 00°28′E*
104 *J5* **Alcañices** Castilla-León, N Spain *41°41′N 06°21′W*
105 *T7* **Alcañiz** Aragón, NE Spain *41°03′N 00°09′W*
104 *I9* **Alcántara** Extremadura, W Spain *39°42′N 06°54′W*
104 *J9* **Alcántara, Embalse de** ⊠ W Spain
105 *R13* **Alcantarilla** Murcia, SE Spain *37°59′N 01°12′W*
105 *P11* **Alcaraz** Castilla-La Mancha, C Spain *38°40′N 02°29′W*
105 *P12* **Alcaraz, Sierra de** ▲▲ C Spain
104 *I12* **Alcarrache** ≈ SW Spain
105 *T6* **Alcarràs** Cataluña, NE Spain *41°34′N 00°31′E*
105 *N14* **Alcaudete** Andalucía, S Spain *37°35′N 04°05′W*
Alcázar *see* Ksar-el-Kebir
105 *O10* **Alcázar de San Juan** *anc.* Alce. Castilla-La Mancha, C Spain *39°24′N 03°12′W*
Alcazarquivir *see* Ksar-el-Kebir
Alce *see* Alcázar de San Juan
57 *B17* **Alcebo, Volcán** ⛰ Galapagos Islands, Ecuador, E Pacific Ocean *0°25′S 91°06′W*
139 *X12* **Al Chabā'ish** *var.* Al Kaba'ish. Dhī Qār, SE Iraq *30°58′N 47°02′E*
117 *Y7* **Alchevs'k** *prev.* Kommunarsk, Voroshilovsk. Luhans'ka Oblast', E Ukraine *48°29′N 38°52′E*
Alcira *see* Alzira
21 *N9* **Alcoa** Tennessee, S USA *35°47′N 83°58′W*
104 *F9* **Alcobaça** Leiria, C Portugal *39°32′N 08°59′W*
105 *N8* **Alcobendas** Madrid, C Spain *40°32′N 03°38′W*
Alcoi *see* Alcoy
105 *P7* **Alcolea del Pinar** Castilla-La Mancha, C Spain *41°02′N 02°28′W*
104 *I11* **Alconchel** Extremadura, W Spain *38°31′N 07°04′W*
Alcora *see* L'Alcora
105 *N8* **Alcorcón** Madrid, C Spain *40°20′N 03°52′W*
105 *S7* **Alcorisa** Aragón, NE Spain *40°53′N 00°23′W*
61 *B19* **Alcorta** Santa Fe, C Argentina *33°32′S 61°07′W*
104 *H14* **Alcoutim** Faro, S Portugal *37°28′N 07°29′W*
33 *W15* **Alcova** Wyoming, C USA *42°33′N 106°40′W*
105 *S11* **Alcoy** *Cat.* Alcoi. País Valenciano, E Spain *38°42′N 00°29′W*
105 *Y9* **Alcúdia** Mallorca, Spain, W Mediterranean Sea *39°51′N 03°06′E*
105 *Y9* **Alcúdia, Badia d'** *bay* Mallorca, Spain, W Mediterranean Sea
172 *M7* **Aldabra Group** *island group* SW Seychelles
139 *U10* **Al Daghghārah** Bābil, C Iraq *32°10′N 44°57′E*
40 *J5* **Aldama** Chihuahua, N Mexico *28°50′N 105°52′W*
41 *P11* **Aldama** Tamaulipas, C Mexico *22°54′N 98°05′W*
123 *Q11* **Aldan** Respublika Sakha (Yakutiya), NE Russian Federation *58°31′N 125°15′E*
123 *Q10* **Aldan** ≈ NE Russian Federation
Aldar *see* Aldarhaan
al Dar al Baida *see* Rabat
162 *G7* **Aldarhaan** *var.* Aldar. Dzavhan, W Mongolia *47°43′N 96°36′E*
97 *Q20* **Aldeburgh** E England, United Kingdom *52°12′N 01°36′E*
105 *P5* **Aldehuela de Calatañazor** Castilla-León, N Spain *41°42′N 02°46′W*
Aldeia Nova *see* Aldeia Nova de São Bento
104 *H13* **Aldeia Nova de São Bento** *var.* Aldeia Nova. Beja, S Portugal *37°55′N 07°24′W*
29 *V11* **Alden** Minnesota, N USA *43°40′N 93°34′W*
184 *N6* **Aldermen Islands, The** *island group* N New Zealand
97 *L25* **Alderney** *island* Channel Islands
97 *N22* **Aldershot** S England, United Kingdom *51°15′N 00°47′W*
21 *R6* **Alderson** West Virginia, NE USA *37°43′N 80°38′W*
Al Dhaid *see* Adh Dhayd
30 *J11* **Aledo** Illinois, N USA *41°12′N 90°45′W*
76 *H9* **Aleg** Brakna, SW Mauritania *17°03′N 13°53′W*
64 *Q10* **Alegranza** *island* Islas Canarias, Spain, NE Atlantic Ocean
37 *P12* **Alegres Mountain** ▲ New Mexico, SW USA *34°09′N 108°11′W*
61 *F15* **Alegrete** Rio Grande do Sul, S Brazil *29°46′S 55°46′W*
61 *C16* **Alejandra** Santa Fe, C Argentina *29°54′S 59°50′W*
193 *T11* **Alejandro Selkirk, Isla** *island* Islas Juan Fernández, Chile, E Pacific Ocean
124 *I12* **Alekhovshchina** Leningradskaya Oblast', NW Russian Federation *60°22′N 33°57′E*
39 *O13* **Aleknagik** Alaska, USA *59°16′N 158°37′W*
Aleksandriya *see* Oleksandriya
Aleksandropol' *see* Gyumri
126 *L3* **Aleksandrov** Vladimirskaya Oblast', W Russian Federation *56°24′N 38°42′E*
113 *N14* **Aleksandrovac** Serbia, C Serbia *43°28′N 21°05′E*
127 *R9* **Aleksandrov Gay** Saratovskaya Oblast', W Russian Federation *50°08′N 48°34′E*
127 *U6* **Aleksandrovka** Orenburgskaya Oblast', W Russian Federation *52°47′N 54°14′E*
Aleksandrovka *see* Oleksandrivka
125 *V13* **Aleksandrovsk** Permskaya Oblast', NW Russian Federation *59°12′N 57°27′E*
Aleksandrovsk *see* Zaporizhzhya
127 *N14* **Aleksandrovskoye** Stavropol'skiy Kray, SW Russian Federation *44°43′N 42°56′E*
123 *T12* **Aleksandrovsk-Sakhalinskiy** Ostrov Sakhalin, Sakhalinskaya Oblast', SE Russian Federation *50°55′N 142°12′E*
110 *J10* **Aleksandrów Kujawski** Kujawskio-pormorskie, C Poland *52°52′N 18°40′E*
110 *K12* **Aleksandrów Łódzki** Łódzkie, C Poland *51°49′N 19°19′E*
Alekseevka *see* Akkol', Akmola, Kazakhstan
Alekseevka *see* Terekty
145 *P7* **Alekseyevka** *Kaz.* Alekseevka. Akmola, N Kazakhstan *53°32′N 69°30′E*
126 *L9* **Alekseyevka** Belgorodskaya, W Russian Federation *50°35′N 38°41′E*
127 *S7* **Alekseyevka** Samarskaya Oblast', W Russian Federation *52°37′N 51°20′E*
Alekseyevka *see* Akkol', Akmola, Kazakhstan
Alekseyevka *see* Terekty, Vostochnyy Kazakhstan, Kazakhstan
127 *R4* **Alekseyevskoye** Respublika Tatarstan, W Russian Federation *55°18′N 50°11′E*
126 *K5* **Aleksin** Tul'skaya Oblast', W Russian Federation *54°30′N 37°08′E*
113 *O14* **Aleksinac** Serbia, SE Serbia *43°33′N 21°43′E*
190 *G11* **Alele** Île Uvea, E Wallis and Futuna *13°14′S 176°09′W*
95 *N20* **Ålem** Kalmar, S Sweden *56°57′N 16°25′E*
102 *L6* **Alençon** Orne, N France *48°26′N 00°04′E*
58 *I12* **Alenquer** Pará, NE Brazil *01°58′S 54°45′W*
38 *G10* **'Alenuihaha Channel** *var.* Alenuihaha Channel. *channel* Hawai'i, USA, C Pacific Ocean
Alep/Aleppo *see* Ḥalab
103 *Y15* **Aléria** Corse, France, C Mediterranean Sea *42°06′N 09°29′E*
197 *Q11* **Alert** Ellesmere Island, Nunavut, N Canada *82°28′N 62°13′W*
103 *Q14* **Alès** *prev.* Alais. Gard, S France *44°08′N 04°05′E*
116 *G9* **Aleşd** *Hung.* Élesd. Bihor, SW Romania *47°03′N 22°22′E*
106 *C9* **Alessandria** *Fr.* Alexandrie. Piemonte, N Italy *44°54′N 08°37′E*
Ålestrup *see* Aalestrup
94 *D9* **Ålesund** Møre og Romsdal, S Norway *62°28′N 06°11′E*
108 *E10* **Aletschhorn** ▲ SW Switzerland *46°33′N 08°01′E*
197 *S1* **Aleutian Basin** *undersea feature* Bering Sea *57°00′N 177°00′E*
38 *H17* **Aleutian Islands** *island group* Alaska, USA
39 *P14* **Aleutian Range** ▲▲ Alaska, USA
0 *B5* **Aleutian Trench** *undersea feature* S Bering Sea *57°00′N 177°00′W*
123 *T10* **Alevina, Mys** *cape* E Russian Federation
15 *Q6* **Alex** ≈ Québec, SE Canada
28 *J3* **Alexander** North Dakota, N USA *47°48′N 103°38′W*
39 *W14* **Alexander Archipelago** *island group* Alaska, USA
Alexanderbaai *see* Alexander Bay
83 *D23* **Alexander Bay** *Afr.* Alexanderbaai. Northern Cape, W South Africa *28°40′S 16°30′E*
23 *Q5* **Alexander City** Alabama, S USA *32°56′N 85°57′W*
194 *J6* **Alexander Island** *island* Antarctica
Alexander Range *see* Kirghiz Range
183 *O12* **Alexandra** Victoria, SE Australia *37°12′S 145°43′E*
185 *D22* **Alexandra** Otago, South Island, New Zealand *45°15′S 169°25′E*
115 *F14* **Alexándreia** *var.* Alexándria. Kentrikí Makedonía, N Greece *40°38′N 22°27′E*
Alexandretta *see* İskenderun
Alexandretta, Gulf of *see* İskenderun Körfezi
15 *N13* **Alexandria** Ontario, SE Canada *45°19′N 74°37′W*
121 *U13* **Alexandria** *Ar.* Al Iskandarīyah. N Egypt *31°07′N 29°51′E*
44 *J12* **Alexandria** C Jamaica *18°18′N 77°21′W*
116 *J15* **Alexandria** Teleorman, S Romania *43°58′N 25°18′E*
31 *P13* **Alexandria** Indiana, N USA *40°15′N 85°40′W*
20 *M4* **Alexandria** Kentucky, S USA *38°59′N 84°22′W*
22 *H7* **Alexandria** Louisiana, S USA *31°19′N 92°27′W*
29 *T7* **Alexandria** Minnesota, N USA *45°54′N 95°22′W*
29 *Q11* **Alexandria** South Dakota, N USA *43°39′N 97°46′W*
21 *W4* **Alexandria** Virginia, NE USA *38°49′N 77°06′W*
Alexándria *see* Alexándreia
18 *I7* **Alexandria Bay** New York, NE USA *44°20′N 75°54′W*
Alexandrie *see* Alessandria
182 *J10* **Alexandrina, Lake** ◎ South Australia
114 *K13* **Alexandroúpoli** *var.* Alexandroúpolis, *Turk.* Dedeagaç, Dedeagach. Anatolikí Makedonía kai Thráki, NE Greece *40°52′N 25°53′E*
Alexandroúpolis *see* Alexandroúpoli
10 *L15* **Alexis Creek** British Columbia, SW Canada *52°06′N 123°25′W*
122 *I13* **Aleysk** Altayskiy Kray, S Russian Federation *52°32′N 82°46′E*
139 *S8* **Al Fallūjah** *var.* Falluja. Al Anbār, C Iraq *33°21′N 43°46′E*
105 *R8* **Alfambra** ≈ E Spain
Al Faqa *see* Faq'
141 *R15* **Al Farḍah** C Yemen *14°51′N 48°33′E*
105 *Q4* **Alfaro** La Rioja, N Spain *42°13′N 01°45′W*
105 *U5* **Alfarràs** Cataluña, NE Spain *41°50′N 00°34′E*
Al Fāshir *see* El Fasher
75 *W8* **Al Fashn** *var.* El Fashn. C Egypt *28°49′N 30°54′E*
114 *M7* **Alfatar** Silistra, NE Bulgaria *43°56′N 27°17′E*
139 *S5* **Al Fatḥah** Şalāḥ ad Dīn, C Iraq *35°06′N 43°34′E*
139 *Q3* **Al Fatsī** Nīnawá, N Iraq *36°04′N 42°39′E*
139 *Z13* **Al Fāw** *var.* Fao. Al Başrah, SE Iraq *29°55′N 48°26′E*
75 *W8* **Al Fayyūm** *var.* El Faiyûm. N Egypt *29°19′N 30°50′E*
El Faiyûm *see* Al Fayyūm
115 *D20* **Alfeiós** *prev.* Alfiós; *anc.* Alpheius, Alpheus. ≈ S Greece
100 *I13* **Alfeld** Niedersachsen, C Germany *51°58′N 09°49′E*
Alfiós *see* Alfeiós
Alföld *see* Great Hungarian Plain
94 *C11* **Ålfotbreen** *glacier* S Norway
19 *P9* **Alfred** Maine, NE USA *43°29′N 70°44′W*
18 *F11* **Alfred** New York, NE USA *42°15′N 77°47′W*
61 *K14* **Alfredo Vagner** Santa Catarina, S Brazil *27°40′S 49°22′W*
94 *M12* **Alfta** Gävleborg, C Sweden *61°20′N 16°05′E*
140 *K12* **Al Fuḥayḥīl** *var.* Fahaheel. SE Kuwait *29°01′N 48°05′E*
139 *Q6* **Al Fuḥaymī** Al Anbār, C Iraq *34°18′N 42°09′E*
143 *S16* **Al Fujayrah** *Eng.* Fujairah. Al Fujayrah, NE United Arab Emirates *25°09′N 56°18′E*
143 *S16* **Al Fujayrah** *Eng.* Fujairah. ✈ Al Fujayrah, NE United Arab Emirates *25°04′N 56°12′E*
Al-Furāt *see* Euphrates
144 *I10* **Alga** *Kaz.* Algha. Aktyubinsk, NW Kazakhstan *49°56′N 57°19′E*
144 *G9* **Algabas** *Kaz.* Alghabas. Zapadnyy Kazakhstan, NW Kazakhstan *50°43′N 52°09′E*
95 *C17* **Ålgård** Rogaland, S Norway *58°45′N 05°52′E*
104 *G14* **Algarve** *cultural region* S Portugal
182 *G3* **Algebuckina Bridge** South Australia *28°03′S 135°48′E*
104 *K16* **Algeciras** Andalucía, SW Spain *36°08′N 05°27′W*
105 *S10* **Algemesí** País Valenciano, E Spain *39°11′N 00°27′W*
Al-Genain *see* El Geneina
120 *F9* **Alger** *var.* Algiers, El Djazaïr, Al Jazair. ● (Algeria) N Algeria *36°47′N 02°58′E*
74 *H9* **Algeria** *off.* Democratic and Popular Republic of Algeria. ◆ *republic* N Africa
Algeria, Democratic and Popular Republic of *see* Algeria
120 *J8* **Algerian Basin** *var.* Balearic Plain. *undersea feature* W Mediterranean Sea
Algha *see* Alga
138 *I4* **Al Ghāb** *Valley* NW Syria
141 *X10* **Al Ghābah** *var.* Ghaba. C Oman *21°22′N 57°14′E*
Alghabas *see* Algabas
141 *U14* **Al Ghayḍah** E Yemen *16°15′N 52°13′E*
140 *M6* **Al Ghazālah** Ḥā'il, NW Saudi Arabia *26°55′N 41°23′E*
107 *B17* **Alghero** Sardegna, Italy, C Mediterranean Sea *40°34′N 08°19′E*
95 *M20* **Älghult** Kronoberg, S Sweden *57°00′N 15°34′E*
Al Ghurdaqah *see* Hurghada
Algiers *see* Alger
105 *S10* **Alginet** País Valenciano, E Spain *39°16′N 00°28′W*
83 *I26* **Algoa Bay** *bay* S South Africa
104 *L15* **Algodonales** Andalucía, S Spain *36°54′N 05°24′W*
105 *N9* **Algodor** ≈ C Spain
Al Golea *see* El Goléa
31 *N6* **Algoma** Wisconsin, N USA *44°41′N 87°24′W*
29 *U12* **Algona** Iowa, C USA *43°04′N 94°13′W*
20 *L8* **Algood** Tennessee, S USA *36°12′N 85°27′W*
105 *O2* **Algorta** País Vasco, N Spain *43°20′N 03°00′W*
61 *E18* **Algorta** Río Negro, W Uruguay *32°26′S 57°18′W*
Al Haba *see* Haba
139 *Q10* **Al Habbārīyah** Al Anbār, S Iraq *32°16′N 42°12′E*
Al Hadhar *see* Al Ḥaḍr
139 *Q4* **Al Ḥaḍr** *var.* Al Hadhar; *anc.* Hatra. Nīnawýa, NW Iraq *35°34′N 42°44′E*
139 *T13* **Al Ḥajarah** *desert* S Iraq
141 *W8* **Al Ḥajar al Gharbī** ▲▲ N Oman
141 *Y8* **Al Hajar ash Sharqī** ▲▲ NE Oman
141 *R15* **Al Ḥajarayn** C Yemen *15°29′N 48°24′E*
138 *L10* **Al Ḥamād** *desert* Jordan/Saudi Arabia
Al Hamad *see* Syrian Desert
75 *N9* **Al Ḥamādah al Ḥamrā'** *var.* Al Ḥamrā'. *desert* NW Libya
105 *N15* **Alhama de Granada** Andalucía, S Spain *37°00′N 03°59′W*
105 *R13* **Alhama de Murcia** Murcia, SE Spain *37°51′N 01°25′W*
35 *T15* **Alhambra** California, W USA *34°08′N 118°06′W*
139 *T12* **Al Ḥammām** An Najaf, S Iraq *31°09′N 44°04′E*
141 *X8* **Al Ḥamrā'** NE Oman *23°07′N 57°23′E*
Al Ḥamrā' *see* Al Ḥamādah al Ḥamrā'
141 *O6* **Al Ḥamūdīyah** *spring/well* N Saudi Arabia *27°05′N 44°24′E*
140 *M7* **Al Ḥanākīyah** Al Madīnah, W Saudi Arabia *24°55′N 40°31′E*
139 *W14* **Al Ḥanīyah** *escarpment* Iraq/Saudi Arabia
139 *Y12* **Al Ḥārithah** Al Başrah, SE Iraq *30°43′N 47°44′E*
140 *L3* **Al Ḥarrah** *desert* NW Saudi Arabia
75 *Q10* **Al Harūj al Aswad** *desert* C Libya
Al Hasaifin *see* Al Ḥusayfīn
139 *N2* **Al Hasakah** *var.* Al Hasijah, El Haseke, *Fr.* Hassetché. Al Ḥasakah, NE Syria *36°22′N 40°44′E*
139 *O2* **Al Hasakah** *off.* Muḥāfaẓat al Ḥasakah, *var.* Al Hasakah, Āl Hasakah, Hasakah, Hassakeh. ◈ *governorate* NE Syria
Al Hasakah *see* 'Āmūdah
Al Hasakah *see* Al Ḥasakah
139 *T9* **Al Hāshimīyah** Bābil, C Iraq *32°24′N 44°39′E*
138 *G13* **Al Hāshimīyah** Ma'ān, S Jordan *30°31′N 35°46′E*
Al Hasijah *see* Al Ḥasakah
104 *M15* **Alhaurín el Grande** Andalucía, S Spain *36°39′N 04°41′W*
141 *Q16* **Al Ḥawrā** S Yemen *13°54′N 47°36′E*
139 *V10* **Al Ḥayy** *var.* Kut al Hai, Kūt al Ḥayy. Wāsiț, E Iraq *32°11′N 46°03′E*
141 *U11* **Al Hibāk** *desert* E Saudi Arabia
138 *H8* **Al Hījānah** *var.* Hejanah, Hijanah. Dimashq, W Syria *33°23′N 36°34′E*
140 *K7* **Al Ḥijāz** *Eng.* Hejaz. *physical region* NW Saudi Arabia
Al Hilbeh *see* 'Ulayyānīyah, Bi'r al
139 *T9* **Al Ḥillah** *var.* Hilla. Bābil, C Iraq *32°28′N 44°29′E*
139 *T9* **Al Hindīyah** *var.* Hindiya. Bābil, C Iraq *32°32′N 44°14′E*
138 *G12* **Al Ḥisā** Aț Ţafīlah, W Jordan *30°49′N 35°58′E*
74 *G5* **Al-Hoceïma** *var.* al Hoceima, Al-Hoceima, Alhucemas; *prev.* Villa Sanjurjo. N Morocco *35°14′N 03°56′W*
Alhucemas *see* Al-Hoceïma
105 *N17* **Alhucemas, Peñon de** *island group* S Spain
141 *N15* **Al Ḥudaydah** *Eng.* Hodeida. W Yemen *15°N 42°50′E*
141 *N15* **Al Ḥudaydah** *var.* Hodeida. ✈ W Yemen *14°45′N 43°01′E*
140 *M4* **Al Ḥudūd ash Shamālīyah** *var.* Minţaqat al Ḥudūd ash Shamālīyah, *Eng.* Northern Border Region. ◈ *province* N Saudi Arabia
141 *S7* **Al Hufūf** *var.* Hofuf. Ash Sharqīyah, NE Saudi Arabia *25°21′N 49°34′E*
al-Hurma *see* Al Khurmah
141 *X7* **Al Ḥusayfīn** *var.* Al Hasaifin. N Oman *24°33′N 56°33′E*
138 *G9* **Al Ḥuşn** *var.* Husn. Irbid, N Jordan *32°29′N 35°53′E*
139 *U9* **'Alī** Wāsiţ, E Iraq *32°43′N 45°21′E*
104 *L10* **Alia** Extremadura, W Spain *39°25′N 05°12′W*
143 *P9* **'Alīābād** Yazd, C Iran *36°55′N 54°33′E*
'Alīābad *see* Qā'emshahr
105 *S7* **Aliaga** Aragón, NE Spain *40°40′N 00°42′W*
136 *B13* **Aliağa** İzmir, W Turkey *38°49′N 26°59′E*
Aliákmon *see* Aliákmonas
115 *F14* **Aliákmonas** *prev.* Aliákmon; *anc.* Haliacmon. ≈ N Greece
139 *W9* **'Alī al Gharbī** Maysān, E Iraq *32°28′N 46°42′E*
139 *U11* **'Alī al Ḥassūnī** Al Qādisīyah, S Iraq *31°25′N 44°50′E*
115 *G18* **Alíartos** Stereá Ellás, C Greece *38°23′N 23°06′E*
137 *Y12* **Äli-Bayramlı** *Rus.* Ali-Bayramly. SE Azerbaijan *39°57′N 48°54′E*
Ali-Bayramly *see* Äli-Bayramlı
114 *P12* **Alibey Barajī** ⊠ NW Turkey
77 *S13* **Alibori** ≈ N Benin
112 *M10* **Alibunar** Vojvodina, NE Serbia *45°06′N 20°59′E*
105 *S12* **Alicante** *Cat.* Alacant, *Lat.* Lucentum. País Valenciano, SE Spain *38°21′N 00°29′W*
105 *S12* **Alicante** ◈ *province* País Valenciano, SE Spain
105 *S12* **Alicante** ✈ Murcia, E Spain *38°21′N 00°29′W*
83 *I25* **Alice** Eastern Cape, S South Africa *32°47′S 26°50′E*
25 *S14* **Alice** Texas, SW USA *27°45′N 98°06′W*
83 *I25* **Alicedale** Eastern Cape, S South Africa *33°19′S 26°05′E*
65 *B25* **Alice, Mount** *hill* West Falkland, Falkland Islands
107 *P20* **Alice, Punta** *headland* S Italy *39°24′N 17°09′E*
181 *Q7* **Alice Springs** Northern Territory, C Australia *23°42′S 133°52′E*
23 *N4* **Aliceville** Alabama, S USA *33°07′N 88°09′W*
147 *U13* **Alichur** SE Tajikistan *37°49′N 73°45′E*
147 *U14* **Alichuri Janubí, Qatorkŭhi** *Rus.* Yuzhno-Alichurskiy Khrebet. ▲▲ SE Tajikistan
147 *U13* **Alichuri Shimolí, Qatorkŭhi** *Rus.* Severo-Alichurskiy Khrebet. ▲▲ SE Tajikistan
107 *K22* **Alicudi, Isola** *island* Isole Eolie, S Italy
Alifu Atoll *see* Ari Atoll
43 *W14* **Aligandí** Kuna Yala, NE Panama *09°15′N 78°05′W*
152 *J11* **Alīgarh** Uttar Pradesh, N India *27°54′N 78°04′E*
142 *M7* **Alīgūdarz** Lorestān, W Iran *33°24′N 49°19′E*
163 *U5* **Alihe** *var.* Oroqen Zizhiqi. Nei Mongol Zizhiqu, N China *50°34′N 123°40′E*
0 *F12* **Alijos, Islas** *islets* California, SW USA
149 *R6* **'Alī Kbel** *Pash.* 'Alī Khēl. Paktīkā, E Afghanistan *33°55′N 69°49′E*
Ali Khel *see* 'Alī Kheyl, Paktīā, Afghanistan
'Alī Khēl *see* 'Alī Kbel, Paktīkā, Afghanistan
149 *R6* **'Alī Kheyl** *var.* Ali Khel, Jajı. Paktīā, SE Afghanistan *33°55′N 69°46′E*
141 *V17* **Al Ikhwān** *island group* SE Yemen
Aliki *see* Alykí
79 *H19* **Alima** ≈ C Congo
Al Imārāt al 'Arabīyahal Muttaḥidah *see* United Arab Emirates
115 *N23* **Alimía** *island* Dodekánisa, Greece, Aegean Sea
55 *V12* **Alimimuni Piek** ▲ S Suriname *02°26′N 55°46′W*
79 *K15* **Alindao** Basse-Kotto, S Central African Republic *04°58′N 21°16′E*
95 *J18* **Alingsås** Västra Götaland, S Sweden *57°55′N 12°30′E*
81 *K18* **Alinjugul** *spring/well* E Kenya *0°03′S 40°31′E*
153 *S16* **Ālīpur** West Bengal, NE India *22°32′N 88°20′E*
149 *S11* **Alīpur** Punjab, E Pakistan *29°22′N 70°59′E*
153 *T12* **Alīpur Duār** West Bengal, NE India *26°28′N 89°25′E*
18 *B14* **Aliquippa** Pennsylvania, NE USA *40°36′N 80°15′W*
80 *L12* **'Ali Sabieh** *var.* 'Alī Sabīḥ. S Djibouti *11°07′N 42°44′E*
'Alī Sabīḥ *see* 'Ali Sabieh
140 *K3* **Al 'Īsāwīyah** Al Jawf, NW Saudi Arabia *30°41′N 37°58′E*
104 *J10* **Aliseda** Extremadura, W Spain *39°25′N 06°42′W*
139 *T8* **Al Iskandarīyah** Bābil, C Iraq *32°53′N 44°22′E*
Al Iskandarīyah *see* Alexandria
123 *T6* **Aliskerovo** Chukotskiy Avtonomnyy Okrug, NE Russian Federation *67°40′N 167°37′E*
75 *W7* **Al Ismā'īlīya** *var.* Ismailia, Ismâ'ilîya. N Egypt *30°32′N 32°13′E*
114 *H13* **Alistráti** Kentrikí Makedonía, NE Greece *41°03′N 23°58′E*
39 *P15* **Alitak Bay** *bay* Kodiak Island, Alaska, USA
Al Ittiḥād *see* Madīnat ash Sha'b
115 *H18* **Alivéri** *var.* Alivérion. Évvoia, C Greece *38°24′N 24°02′E*
Alivérion *see* Alivéri
Aliwal-Noord *see* Aliwal North
83 *I24* **Aliwal North** *Afr.* Aliwal-Noord. Eastern Cape, SE South Africa *30°42′S 26°43′E*
121 *Q13* **Al Jabal al Akhḍar** ▲▲ NE Libya
138 *H13* **Al Jafr** Ma'ān, S Jordan *30°18′N 36°13′E*
75 *T8* **Al Jaghbūb** NE Libya *29°45′N 24°31′E*
142 *K11* **Al Jahrā'** *var.* Al Jahrah, Jahra. C Kuwait *29°18′N 47°36′E*
Al Jahrah *see* Al Jahrā'
Al Jamāhīrīyah al 'Arabīyah al Lībīyah ash Sha'bīyah al Ishtirākīy *see* Libya
140 *K3* **Al Jarāwī** *spring/well* NW Saudi Arabia *30°12′N 38°48′E*
141 *X11* **Al Jawārah** *oasis* SE Oman
140 *L3* **Al Jawf** *off.* Jauf. Al Jawf, NW Saudi Arabia *29°51′N 39°49′E*
140 *L4* **Al Jawf** *var.* Minţaqat al Jawf. ◈ *province* N Saudi Arabia
Al Jawlān *see* Golan Heights
Al Jazair *see* Alger
139 *N4* **Al Jazīrah** *physical region* Iraq/Syria
104 *F14* **Aljezur** Faro, S Portugal *37°18′N 08°49′W*
139 *S13* **Al Jīl** An Najaf, S Iraq *30°28′N 43°57′E*
138 *G11* **Al Jīzah** *var.* Jiza. 'Ammān, N Jordan *31°42′N 35°57′E*
Al Jīzah *see* Gîza
Al Jubail *see* Al Jubayl
141 *S6* **Al Jubayl** *var.* Al Jubail. Ash Sharqīyah, NE Saudi Arabia *27°N 49°36′E*
141 *T10* **Āl Juḥaysh, Qalamat** *well* SE Saudi Arabia
143 *N15* **Al Jumaylīyah** N Qatar *25°37′N 51°05′E*
Al Junaynah *see* El Geneina
104 *G13* **Aljustrel** Beja, S Portugal *37°52′N 08°10′W*
Al Kaba'ish *see* Al Chabā'ish
Al-Kadhimain *see* Al Kāẓimīyah
Al Kāf *see* El Kef
Alkal'a *see* Alcalá de Henares
35 *W4* **Alkali Flat** *salt flat* Nevada, W USA
35 *Q1* **Alkali Lake** ◎ Nevada, W USA
141 *Z9* **Al Kāmil** NE Oman *22°14′N 58°15′E*
138 *G11* **Al Karak** *var.* El Kerak, Karak, Kerak; *anc.* Kir Moab, Kir of Moab. Al Karak, W Jordan *31°11′N 35°42′E*
138 *G12* **Al Karak** *off.* Muḥāfaẓat al Karak. ◈ *governorate* W Jordan
139 *W8* **Al Karmashīyah** Wāsiţ, E Iraq *32°57′N 46°10′E*
Al-Kashaniya *see* Al Qash'ānīyah
Al-Kasr al-Kebir *see* Ksar-el-Kebir
139 *T8* **Al Kāẓimīyah** *var.* Al-Kadhimain, Kadhimain. Baghdād, C Iraq *33°22′N 44°20′E*
99 *J18* **Alken** Limburg, NE Belgium *50°52′N 05°19′E*
141 *X8* **Al Khābūrah** *var.* Khabura. N Oman *23°57′N 57°06′E*
Al Khalīl *see* Hebron
139 *T7* **Al Khāliş** Diyālá, C Iraq *33°51′N 44°33′E*
Al Khaluf *see* Khalūf
75 *W10* **Al Khārijah** *var.* El Khârga. C Egypt *25°31′N 30°36′E*
141 *Q8* **Al Kharj** Ar Riyāḍ, C Saudi Arabia *24°12′N 47°12′E*
141 *W6* **Al Khaşab** *var.* Khasab. N Oman *26°11′N 56°18′E*
Al Khaur *see* Al Khawr
143 *N15* **Al Khawr** *var.* Al Khaur, Al Khor. N Qatar *25°40′N 51°33′E*
142 *K12* **Al Khīrān** *var.* Al Khiran. SE Kuwait *28°34′N 48°21′E*
141 *W9* **Al Khīrān** *spring/well* NW Oman *22°31′N 55°42′E*
Al Khiyām *see* El Khiyam
Al-Khobar *see* Al Khubar
Al Khor *see* Al Khawr
141 *S6* **Al Khubar** *var.* Al-Khobar. Ash Sharqīyah, NE Saudi Arabia *26°00′N 50°00′E*
120 *M12* **Al Khums** *var.* Homs, Khoms, Khums. NW Libya *32°39′N 14°16′E*
141 *R15* **Al Khuraybah** C Yemen *15°05′N 48°17′E*
140 *M9* **Al Khurmah** *var.* al-Hurma. Makkah, W Saudi Arabia *21°59′N 42°00′E*
141 *V9* **Al Kidan** *desert* NE Saudi Arabia
127 *V4* **Alkino-2** Respublika Bashkortostan, W Russian Federation *54°30′N 55°40′E*
98 *H9* **Alkmaar** Noord-Holland, NW Netherlands *52°37′N 04°45′E*
139 *T10* **Al Kūfah** *var.* Kufa. An Najaf, S Iraq *32°02′N 44°25′E*
75 *T11* **Al Kufrah** SE Libya *24°11′N 23°19′E*
141 *T10* **Al Kursū'** *desert* E Saudi Arabia
139 *V9* **Al Kūt** *var.* Kūt al 'Amārah, Kut al Imara. Wāsiţ, E Iraq *32°30′N 45°51′E*
Al-Kuwait *see* Al Kuwayt
Al Kuwayr *see* Guwēr
142 *K11* **Al Kuwayt** *var.* Al-Kuwait, *Eng.* Kuwait, Kuwait City; *prev.* Qurein. ● (Kuwait) E Kuwait *29°23′N 48°00′E*
142 *K11* **Al Kuwayt** ✈ C Kuwait *29°13′N 47°57′E*
115 *G19* **Alkyonidón, Kólpos** *gulf* C Greece
141 *N4* **Al Labbah** *physical region* N Saudi Arabia
138 *G4* **Al Lādhiqīyah** *Eng.* Latakia, *Fr.* Lattaquié; *anc.* Laodicea, Laodicea ad Mare. Al Lādhiqīyah, W Syria *35°31′N 35°47′E*
138 *H4* **Al Lādhiqīyah** *off.* Muḥāfaẓat al Lādhiqīyah, *var.* Al Lathqiyah, Latakia, Lattakia. ◈ *governorate* W Syria
19 *R2* **Allagash River** ≈ Maine, NE USA
152 *M13* **Allahābād** Uttar Pradesh, N India *25°27′N 81°50′E*
143 *S3* **Allāh Dāgh, Reshteh-ye** ▲▲ NE Iran
39 *Q8* **Allakaket** Alaska, USA *66°34′N 152°39′W*
141 *X12* **Al Lakbī** S Oman *18°27′N 56°37′E*
11 *T15* **Allan** Saskatchewan, S Canada *51°50′N 105°59′W*
Allanmyo *see* Aunglan
83 *I22* **Allanridge** Free State, C South Africa *27°45′S 26°40′E*
104 *H4* **Allariz** Galicia, NW Spain *42°11′N 07°48′W*
139 *R11* **Al Laşaf** *var.* Al Lussuf. An Najaf, S Iraq *31°38′N 43°16′E*
Al Lathqiyah *see* Al Lādhiqīyah
23 *S2* **Allatoona Lake** ⊠ Georgia, SE USA
83 *J19* **Alldays** Limpopo, NE South Africa *22°39′S 29°04′E*
Alle *see* Łyna
31 *P10* **Allegan** Michigan, N USA *42°31′N 85°51′W*
18 *E14* **Allegheny Mountains** ▲▲ NE USA
18 *E12* **Allegheny Plateau** ▲▲ New York/Pennsylvania, NE USA
18 *D11* **Allegheny Reservoir** ⊠ New York/Pennsylvania, NE USA
18 *E12* **Allegheny River** ≈ New York/Pennsylvania, NE USA
22 *K9* **Allemands, Lac des** ◎ Louisiana, S USA
25 *U6* **Allen** Texas, SW USA *33°06′N 96°40′W*
21 *R14* **Allendale** South Carolina, SE USA *33°01′N 81°19′W*
41 *N6* **Allende** Coahuila, NE Mexico *28°22′N 100°50′W*
41 *O9* **Allende** Nuevo León, NE Mexico *25°20′N 100°01′W*
97 *D16* **Allen, Lough** *Ir.* Loch Aillionn. ◎ NW Ireland
185 *B26* **Allen, Mount** ▲ Stewart Island, Southland, SW New Zealand *47°05′S 167°49′E*
109 *V2* **Allensteig** Niederösterreich, N Austria *48°40′N 15°24′E*
Allenstein *see* Olsztyn
18 *I14* **Allentown** Pennsylvania, NE USA *40°37′N 75°30′W*
155 *G23* **Alleppey** *var.* Alappuzha. Kerala, SW India *09°30′N 76°22′E* *see also* Alappuzha
100 *J12* **Aller** ≈ NW Germany
29 *V16* **Allerton** Iowa, C USA *40°42′N 93°22′W*
99 *K19* **Alleur** Liège, E Belgium *50°40′N 05°33′E*
101 *J25* **Allgäuer Alpen** ▲▲ Austria/Germany
28 *J13* **Alliance** Nebraska, C USA *42°08′N 102°54′W*
31 *U12* **Alliance** Ohio, N USA *40°55′N 81°06′W*
103 *O10* **Allier** ◈ *department* N France
139 *R13* **Al Līfīyah** *well* An Najaf, S Iraq
44 *J13* **Alligator Pond** C Jamaica *17°52′N 77°34′W*
21 *Y9* **Alligator River** ≈ North Carolina, SE USA
29 *W12* **Allison** Iowa, C USA *42°45′N 92°48′W*
14 *G14* **Alliston** Ontario, S Canada *44°09′N 79°51′W*
140 *L11* **Al Līth** Makkah, SW Saudi Arabia *21°N 41°E*
Al Liwā' *see* Līwā
96 *J12* **Alloa** C Scotland, United Kingdom *56°07′N 03°49′W*
103 *U14* **Allos** Alpes-de-Haute-Provence, SE France *44°16′N 06°37′E*
108 *D6* **Allschwil** Basel-Land, NW Switzerland *47°34′N 07°32′E*
Al Lubnān *see* Lebanon
141 *N14* **Al Luḥayyah** W Yemen *15°44′N 42°45′E*
14 *K12* **Allumettes, Île des** *island* Québec, SE Canada
Al Lussuf *see* Al Laşaf
109 *S5* **Alm** ≈ N Austria
15 *Q7* **Alma** Québec, SE Canada *48°32′N 71°41′W*
27 *S10* **Alma** Arkansas, C USA *35°28′N 94°13′W*
23 *V7* **Alma** Georgia, SE USA *31°32′N 82°27′W*
27 *P4* **Alma** Kansas, C USA *39°01′N 96°17′W*
31 *Q8* **Alma** Michigan, N USA *43°22′N 84°39′W*
29 *O17* **Alma** Nebraska, C USA *40°06′N 99°21′W*
30 *I7* **Alma** Wisconsin, N USA *44°21′N 91°54′W*
139 *R12* **Al Ma'ānīyah** *well* An Najaf, S Iraq
Alma-Ata *see* Almaty
Alma-Atinskaya Oblast' *see* Almaty
Almacellas *see* Almacelles
105 *T5* **Almacelles** *var.* Almacellas. Cataluña, NE Spain *41°44′N 00°26′E*
104 *F11* **Almada** Setúbal, W Portugal *38°40′N 09°09′W*
104 *L11* **Almadén** Castilla-La Mancha, C Spain *38°47′N 04°50′W*
66 *L6* **Almadies, Pointe des** *headland* W Senegal *14°44′N 17°31′W*
140 *L7* **Al Madīnah** *Eng.* Medina. Al Madīnah, W Saudi Arabia *24°25′N 39°29′E*
140 *L7* **Al Madīnah** *off.* Minţaqat al Madīnah. ◈ *province* W Saudi Arabia
138 *H9* **Al Mafraq** *var.* Mafraq. Al Mafraq, N Jordan *32°20′N 36°12′E*
138 *J10* **Al Mafraq** *off.* Muḥāfaẓat al Mafraq. ◈ *governorate* NW Jordan
141 *R15* **Al Maghārīm** C Yemen *15°00′N 47°49′E*
105 *N11* **Almagro** Castilla-La Mancha, C Spain *38°54′N 03°43′W*
Al Maḥallah al Kubrá *see* El Maḥalla el Kubra
139 *T9* **Al Maḥāwīl** *var.* Khān al Maḥāwīl. Bābil, C Iraq *32°39′N 44°28′E*
Al Mahdīyah *see* Mahdia
139 *T8* **Al Maḥmūdīyah** *var.* Mahmudiya. Baghdād, C Iraq *33°04′N 44°22′E*
141 *T14* **Al Mahrah** ▲▲ E Yemen
141 *P7* **Al Majma'ah** Ar Riyāḍ, C Saudi Arabia *25°55′N 45°19′E*
139 *Q11* **Al Makmīn** *well* S Iraq
139 *Q1* **Al Mālikīyah** *var.* Malkiye. Al Ḥasakah, N Syria *37°12′N 42°13′E*
Almalyk *see* Olmaliq
Al Mamlakah *see* Morocco
Al Mamlaka al Urdunīya al Hashemīyah *see* Jordan
143 *Q18* **Al Manādir** *var.* Al Manadir. *desert* Oman/United Arab Emirates
142 *L15* **Al Manāmah** *Eng.* Manama. ● (Bahrain) N Bahrain *26°13′N 50°33′E*
139 *O5* **Al Manāşif** ▲▲ E Syria
35 *O4* **Almanor, Lake** ⊠ California, W USA
105 *R11* **Almansa** Castilla-La Mancha, C Spain *38°52′N 01°06′W*
75 *W7* **Al Manşūrah** *var.* Manşûra, El Manşûra. N Egypt *31°03′N 31°23′E*
104 *L3* **Almanza** Castilla-León, N Spain *42°40′N 05°01′W*
104 *L8* **Almanzor** ▲ W Spain *40°13′N 05°18′W*
105 *P14* **Almanzora** ≈ SE Spain
139 *S9* **Al Mardah** Karbalā', C Iraq *32°35′N 43°30′E*
Al-Mariyya *see* Almería
75 *R7* **Al Marj** *var.* Barka, *It.* Barce. NE Libya *32°30′N 20°54′E*
138 *L2* **Al Mashrafah** Ar Raqqah, N Syria *36°25′N 39°07′E*
141 *X8* **Al Maşna'ah** *var.* Al Muşana'a. NE Oman *23°45′N 57°38′E*
Almassora *see* Almazora
Almatinskaya Oblast' *see* Almaty
145 *U15* **Almaty** *var.* Alma-Ata. Almaty, SE Kazakhstan *43°19′N 76°55′E*
145 *S14* **Almaty** *off.* Almatinskaya Oblast', *Kaz.* Almaty Oblysy; *prev.* Alma-Atinskaya Oblast'. ◈ *province* SE Kazakhstan
145 *U15* **Almaty** ✈ Almaty, SE Kazakhstan *43°15′N 76°57′E*
Almaty Oblysy *see* Almaty
al-Mawailih *see* Al Muwayliḥ
139 *R3* **Al Mawşil** *Eng.* Mosul. Nīnawá, N Iraq *36°21′N 43°08′E*
139 *N5* **Al Mayādīn** *var.* Mayadin, *Fr.* Meyadine. Dayr az Zawr, E Syria *35°00′N 40°31′E*
139 *X10* **Al Maymūnah** *var.* Maimuna. Maysān, SE Iraq *31°43′N 46°55′E*
141 *N5* **Al Mayyāh** Ḥā'il, N Saudi Arabia *27°57′N 42°53′E*
Al Ma'zam *see* Al Ma'zim
105 *P6* **Almazán** Castilla-León, N Spain *41°29′N 02°31′W*
141 *W8* **Al Ma'zim** *var.* Al Ma'zam. NW Oman *23°22′N 56°16′E*
123 *N11* **Almaznyy** Respublika Sakha (Yakutiya), NE Russian Federation *62°19′N 114°14′E*
105 *T9* **Almazora** *Cat.* Almassora. País Valenciano, E Spain *39°55′N 00°02′W*
Al Mazra' *see* Al Mazra'ah
138 *G11* **Al Mazra'ah** *var.* Al Mazra', Mazra'a. Al Karak, W Jordan *31°18′N 35°32′E*
101 *G15* **Alme** ≈ W Germany

◆ Country ● Country Capital ◇ Dependent Territory ○ Dependent Territory Capital ◈ Administrative Regions ✈ International Airport ▲ Mountain ▲▲ Mountain Range ⛰ Volcano ≈ River ◎ Lake ⊠ Reservoir

ALMEIDA – ÄMMÄNSAARI

104 I7 Almeida Guarda, N Portugal 40°43′N 06°53′W
104 G10 Almeirim Santarém, C Portugal 39°12′N 08°37′W
98 O10 Almelo Overijssel, E Netherlands 52°22′N 06°42′E
105 S9 Almenara País Valenciano, E Spain 39°46′N 00°14′W
105 P12 Almenaras ▲ S Spain 38°31′N 02°27′W
105 P5 Almenar de Soria Castilla-León, N Spain 41°41′N 02°12′W
104 J6 Almendra, Embalse de ▣ Castilla-León, NW Spain
104 J11 Almendralejo Extremadura, W Spain 38°41′N 06°25′W
98 J10 Almere var. Almere-stad. Flevoland, C Netherlands 52°22′N 05°12′E
98 J10 Almere-Buiten Flevoland, C Netherlands 52°24′N 05°15′E
98 J10 Almere-Haven Flevoland, C Netherlands 52°20′N 05°13′E
Almere-stad see Almere
105 P15 Almería Ar. Al-Mariyya; anc. Unci, Lat. Portus Magnus. Andalucía, S Spain 36°50′N 02°26′W
105 P14 Almería ◆ province Andalucía, S Spain
105 P15 Almería, Golfo de gulf S Spain
127 S5 Al'met'yevsk Respublika Tatarstan, W Russian Federation 54°53′N 52°20′E
95 L21 Älmhult Kronoberg, S Sweden 56°32′N 14°10′E
141 U9 Al Miḥrāḍ desert NE Saudi Arabia
Al Mīnā' see El Mina
104 L17 Almina, Punta headland Ceuta, Spain, N Africa 35°54′N 05°16′W
75 W9 Al Minyā var. El Minya, Minya. C Egypt 28°06′N 30°40′E
Al Miqdādīyah see Al Muqdādīyah
43 P14 Almirante Bocas del Toro, NW Panama 09°20′N 82°22′W
Almirós see Almyrós
140 M9 Al Mislaḥ spring/well W Saudi Arabia 22°46′N 40°47′E
Almissa see Omiš
104 G13 Almodôvar var. Almodóvar. Beja, S Portugal 37°31′N 08°03′W
104 M11 Almodóvar del Campo Castilla-La Mancha, C Spain 38°43′N 04°10′W
105 Q9 Almodóvar del Pinar Castilla-La Mancha, C Spain 39°44′N 01°55′W
31 S9 Almont Michigan, N USA 42°53′N 83°02′W
14 L13 Almonte Ontario, SE Canada 45°13′N 76°12′W
104 J14 Almonte Andalucía, S Spain 37°16′N 06°31′W
104 K9 Almonte ≈ W Spain
152 K9 Almora Uttarakhand, N India 29°36′N 79°40′E
104 M8 Almorox Castilla-La Mancha, C Spain 40°13′N 04°22′W
141 S7 Al Mubarraz Ash Sharqīyah, E Saudi Arabia 25°28′N 49°34′E
Al Muḍaibī see Al Muḍaybī
138 G15 Al Mudawwarah Ma'ān, SW Jordan 29°20′N 36°E
141 Y9 Al Muḍaybī var. Al Muḍaibī. NE Oman 22°35′N 58°08′E
Almudébar see Almudévar
105 S5 Almudévar var. Almudébar. Aragón, NE Spain 42°03′N 00°34′W
141 S15 Al Mukallā var. Mukalla. SE Yemen 14°36′N 49°07′E
141 N16 Al Mukhā Eng. Mocha. SW Yemen 13°18′N 43°17′E
105 N15 Almuñécar Andalucía, S Spain 36°44′N 03°41′W
139 U7 Al Muqdādīyah var. Al Miqdādīyah. Diyālá, C Iraq 33°58′N 44°58′E
140 L3 Al Murayr spring/well NW Saudi Arabia 30°06′N 39°54′E
136 M12 Almus Tokat, N Turkey 40°22′N 36°54′E
Al Muşana'a see Al Maşna'ah
139 T9 Al Musayyib var. Musaiyib. Bābil, C Iraq 32°47′N 44°20′E
139 W14 Al Muthannā ◆ governorate S Iraq
139 V9 Al Muwaffaqīyah Wāsiţ, S Iraq 32°19′N 45°22′E
138 H10 Al Muwaqqar var. El Muwaqqar. 'Ammān, W Jordan 31°49′N 36°06′E
140 J5 Al Muwayliḥ var. al-Mawailih. Tabūk, NW Saudi Arabia 27°39′N 35°33′E
115 F17 Almyrós var. Almirós. Thessalía, C Greece 39°11′N 22°45′E
115 I24 Almyroú, Órmos bay Kríti, Greece, E Mediterranean Sea
Al Nūwfalīyah see An Nawfalīyah
96 L13 Alnwick N England, United Kingdom 55°27′N 01°44′W
Al Obayyid see El Obeid
Al Odaid see Al 'Udayd
190 B16 Alofi ○ (Niue) W Niue 19°01′S 169°55′E
190 A16 Alofi Bay bay W Niue, C Pacific Ocean
190 E13 Alofi, Île island S Wallis and Futuna
190 E13 Alofitai Île Alofi, W Wallis and Futuna 14°21′S 178°03′W
Aloha State see Hawai'i
118 G7 Aloja Limbaži, N Latvia 57°47′N 24°53′E
153 X10 Along Arunāchal Pradesh, NE India 28°15′N 94°56′E
115 H16 Alónnisos island Vóreies Sporádes, Greece, Aegean Sea
104 M15 Álora Andalucía, S Spain 36°50′N 04°43′W
171 Q16 Alor, Kepulauan island group E Indonesia
171 Q16 Alor, Pulau prev. Ombai. island Kepulauan Alor, E Indonesia
171 O16 Alor, Selat strait Flores Sea/Savu Sea
168 I7 Alor Setar var. Alor Star, Alur Setar. Kedah, Peninsular Malaysia 06°06′N 100°23′E
Alor Star see Alor Setar
Alost see Aalst
154 F9 Ālot Madhya Pradesh, C India 23°56′N 75°40′E
186 G10 Alotau Milne Bay, SE Papua New Guinea 10°20′S 150°23′E
171 Y16 Alotip Papua, E Indonesia 08°07′S 140°06′E
Al Oued see El Oued
35 R12 Alpaugh California, W USA 35°52′N 119°29′W
Alpen see Alps
31 R6 Alpena Michigan, N USA 45°04′N 83°27′W
Alpes see Alps
103 S14 Alpes-de-Haute-Provence ◆ department SE France
103 U14 Alpes-Maritimes ◆ department SE France
181 W8 Alpha Queensland, E Australia 23°40′S 146°38′E
197 R9 Alpha Cordillera var. Alpha Ridge. undersea feature Arctic Ocean 85°30′N 125°00′W
Alpha Ridge see Alpha Cordillera
Alpheius see Alfeiós
99 I15 Alphen Noord-Brabant, S Netherlands 51°29′N 04°57′E
Alphen see Alphen aan den Rijn
98 H11 Alphen aan den Rijn var. Alphen. Zuid-Holland, C Netherlands 52°08′N 04°40′E
Alpheus see Alfeiós
Alpi see Alps
104 G10 Alpiarça Santarém, C Portugal 39°15′N 08°35′W
24 K10 Alpine Texas, SW USA 30°22′N 103°40′W
108 F8 Alpnach Unterwalden, W Switzerland 46°56′N 08°17′E
108 D11 Alps Fr. Alpes, Ger. Alpen, It. Alpi. ▲▲ C Europe
149 U5 Alpurai var. Alpuri. North-West Frontier Province, N Pakistan 34°54′N 72°39′E
Alpuri see Alpurai
141 W8 Al Qābil var. Qabil. N Oman 23°55′N 55°50′E
Al Qadārif see Gedaref
75 P8 Al Qaddāḥiyah N Libya 31°21′N 15°16′E
139 V10 Al Qādisīyah ◆ governorate S Iraq
Al Qāhirah see Cairo
140 K4 Al Qalībah Tabūk, NW Saudi Arabia 28°29′N 37°40′E
139 O1 Al Qāmishlī var. Kamishli, Qamishly. Al Ḥasakah, NE Syria 37°N 41°E
138 I6 Al Qaryatayn var. Qaryatayn, Fr. Qariateïne. Ḥimş, C Syria 34°13′N 37°13′E
142 K11 Al Qash'ānīyah var. Al-Kashaniya. NE Kuwait 29°59′N 47°42′E
141 N7 Al Qaşīm var. Minţaqat Qaşīm, Qassim. ◆ province C Saudi Arabia
75 V10 Al Qaşr var. El Qaşr. C Egypt 25°43′N 28°54′E
138 J5 Al Qaşr Ḥimş, C Syria 35°06′N 37°39′E
Al Qaşr see Al Qaşr
Al Qaşrayn see Kasserine
141 S6 Al Qaţīf Ash Sharqīyah, NE Saudi Arabia 26°27′N 50°01′E
138 G11 Al Qaţrānah var. El Qatrani, Qatrana. Al Karak, W Jordan 31°14′N 36°03′E
75 P11 Al Qaţrūn SW Libya 24°57′N 14°40′E
Al Qayrawān see Kairouan
Al-Qsar al-Kbir see Ksar-el-Kebir
Al Qubayyāt see Qoubaïyât
Al Quds/Al Quds ash Sharīf see Jerusalem
104 H12 Alqueva, Barragem do ▣ Portugal/Spain
138 G8 Al Qunayţirah var. El Kuneitra, El Quneitra, Kuneitra, Qunaytra. Al Qunayţirah, SW Syria 33°08′N 35°49′E
138 G8 Al Qunayţirah off. Muḩāfaẓat al Qunayţirah, var. El Q'unayţirah, Qunaytirah, Fr. Kuneitra. ◆ governorate SW Syria
140 M11 Al Qunfudhah Makkah, SW Saudi Arabia 19°19′N 41°03′E
140 K2 Al Qurayyāt Al Jawf, NW Saudi Arabia 31°25′N 37°26′E
139 Y11 Al Qurnah var. Kurna. Al Başrah, SE Iraq 31°01′N 47°27′E
75 Y10 Al Quşayr var. Al Quşayr var. Qusair, Quseir. E Egypt 26°05′N 34°16′E
139 V12 Al Quşayr Al Muthannā, S Iraq 30°36′N 45°52′E
138 I6 Al Quşayr var. El Quseir, Quşayr, Fr. Kousseir. Ḥimş, W Syria 34°36′N 36°36′E
Al Quşayr see Al Quşayr
138 H7 Al Quţayfah var. Quţayfah, Quţayfe, Quteife, Fr. Kouteifé. Dimashq, W Syria 33°44′N 36°33′E
141 P8 Al Quwayʿīyah Ar Riyāḑ, C Saudi Arabia 24°06′N 45°18′E
Al Quwayr see Guwêr
138 F14 Al Quwayrah var. El Quweira. Al 'Aqabah, SW Jordan 29°47′N 35°18′E
Al Rayyan see Ar Rayyān
Al Ruweis see Ar Ruways
95 G24 Als Ger. Alsen. island SW Denmark
103 U5 Alsace Ger. Elsass; anc. Alsatia. ◆ region NE France
11 R16 Alsask Saskatchewan, S Canada 51°24′N 109°55′W
Alsasua see Altsasu
Alsatia see Alsace
101 C16 Alsdorf Nordrhein-Westfalen, W Germany 50°52′N 06°09′E
10 G8 Alsek ≈ Canada/USA
Alsen see Als
101 F19 Alsenz ≈ W Germany
101 H17 Alsfeld Hessen, C Germany 50°45′N 09°14′E
119 K20 Al'shany Rus. Ol'shany. Brestskaya Voblasts', SW Belarus 52°05′N 27°21′E
Alsókubin see Dolný Kubín
118 C9 Alsunga Kuldīga, W Latvia 56°59′N 21°31′E
Alt see Olt
92 K9 Alta Fin. Alattio. Finnmark, N Norway 69°58′N 23°17′E
29 T12 Alta Iowa, C USA 42°40′N 95°17′W
108 I7 Altach Vorarlberg, W Austria 47°22′N 09°39′E
92 K9 Altaelva Lapp. Álaheaieatnu. ≈ N Norway
92 J8 Altafjorden fjord NE Norwegian Sea
62 K10 Alta Gracia Córdoba, C Argentina 31°42′S 64°25′W
42 K11 Alta Gracia Rivas, SW Nicaragua 11°35′N 85°38′W
54 H4 Altagracia Zulia, NW Venezuela 10°44′N 71°30′W
54 M5 Altagracia de Orituco Guárico, N Venezuela 09°54′N 66°24′W
Altai see Altai Mountains
129 T7 Altai Mountains var. Altai, Chin. Altay Shan, Rus. Altay. ▲▲ Asia/Europe
23 V6 Altamaha River ≈ Georgia, SE USA
58 J13 Altamira Pará, NE Brazil 03°13′S 52°15′W
54 D12 Altamira Huila, S Colombia 02°04′N 75°47′W
42 M13 Altamira Alajuela, N Costa Rica 10°25′N 84°21′W
41 Q11 Altamira Tamaulipas, C Mexico 22°25′N 97°55′W
30 L15 Altamont Illinois, N USA 39°03′N 88°45′W
27 Q7 Altamont Kansas, C USA 37°11′N 95°18′W
32 H16 Altamont Oregon, NW USA 42°12′N 121°44′W
20 K10 Altamont Tennessee, S USA 35°28′N 85°42′W
23 X11 Altamonte Springs Florida, SE USA 28°39′N 81°22′W
107 O17 Altamura anc. Lupatia. Puglia, SE Italy 40°50′N 16°33′E
40 H9 Altamura, Isla island C Mexico
Altan see Erdenehayrhan
Altanbulag see Bayanhayrhan
163 Q7 Altan Emel var. Xin Barag Youqi. Nei Mongol Zizhiqu, N China 48°37′N 116°40′E
Altan-Ovoo see Tsenher
163 N9 Altanshiree var. Chamdmanī. Dornigovĭ, SE Mongolia 45°36′N 110°30′E
Altanteel see Dzereg
162 D5 Altantsögts var. Tsagaantüngi. Bayan-Ölgiy, NW Mongolia 49°06′N 90°26′E
40 F3 Altar Sonora, NW Mexico 30°41′N 111°53′W
40 D2 Altar, Desierto de var. Sonoran Desert. desert Mexico/USA see also Sonoran Desert
Altar, Desierto de see Sonoran Desert
105 Q8 Altas, Sierra ▲ N Spain 40°29′N 01°36′W
40 H9 Altata Sinaloa, C Mexico 24°40′N 107°54′W
42 D4 Alta Verapaz off. Departamento de Alta Verapaz. ◆ department C Guatemala
Alta Verapaz, Departamento de see Alta Verapaz
107 L18 Altavilla Silentia Campania, S Italy 40°32′N 15°06′E
21 T7 Altavista Virginia, NE USA 37°06′N 79°17′W
158 L2 Altay Xinjiang Uygur Zizhiqu, NW China 47°51′N 88°06′E
162 D6 Altay var. Chihertey. Bayan-Ölgiy, W Mongolia 48°10′N 89°35′E
162 G8 Altay prev. Yösönbulag. Govĭ-Altay, W Mongolia 46°23′N 96°17′E
162 E8 Altay var. Bor-Üdzüür. Hovd, W Mongolia 45°46′N 92°13′E
Altay see Altai Mountains, Asia/Europe
Altay see Bayantes, Mongolia
122 J14 Altay, Respublika var. Gornyy Altay; prev. Gorno-Altayskaya Respublika. ◆ autonomous republic S Russian Federation
Altay Shan see Altai Mountains
123 I13 Altayskiy Kray ◆ territory S Russian Federation
Altbetsche see Bečej
101 L20 Altdorf Bayern, SE Germany 49°23′N 11°22′E
108 G8 Altdorf var. Altorf. Uri, C Switzerland 46°53′N 08°38′E
105 T11 Altea País Valenciano, E Spain 38°37′N 00°03′W
100 L10 Alte Elde ≈ N Germany
101 M16 Altenburg Thüringen, E Germany 50°59′N 12°27′E
Altenburg see București, Romania
Altenburg see Baia de Criș, Romania
100 P12 Alte Oder ≈ NE Germany
104 H10 Alter do Chão Portalegre, C Portugal 39°12′N 07°40′W
92 I10 Altevatnet Lapp. Álttesjávri. ⊗ N Norway
27 V12 Altheimer Arkansas, C USA 34°19′N 91°51′W
109 T9 Althofen Kärnten, S Austria 46°52′N 14°27′E
114 H7 Altimir Vratsa, NW Bulgaria 43°33′N 23°48′E
136 K11 Altınkaya Barajı ▣ N Turkey
139 S3 Altin Köprü var. Altun Kupri. At Ta'mīm, N Iraq 35°50′N 44°10′E
136 E13 Altıntaş Kütahya, W Turkey 39°05′N 30°07′E
57 K18 Altiplano physical region W South America
Altkanischa see Kanjiža
103 U7 Altkirch Haut-Rhin, NE France 47°37′N 07°14′E
Altlublau see Stará L'ubovňa
100 L12 Altmark cultural region N Germany
Altmoldowa see Moldova Veche
25 W8 Alto Texas, SW USA 31°39′N 95°04′W
104 H11 Alto Alentejo physical region S Portugal
59 I19 Alto Araguaia Mato Grosso, C Brazil 17°19′S 53°10′W
58 L12 Alto Bonito Pará, NE Brazil 01°48′S 46°18′W
83 O15 Alto Molócuè Zambézia, NE Mozambique 15°38′S 37°42′E
30 K15 Alton Illinois, N USA 38°53′N 90°10′W
27 W8 Alton Missouri, C USA 36°41′N 91°25′W
11 X17 Altona Manitoba, S Canada 49°06′N 97°33′W
18 E14 Altoona Pennsylvania, NE USA 40°32′N 78°23′W
30 J6 Altoona Wisconsin, N USA 44°49′N 91°22′W
62 N3 Alto Paraguay off. Departamento del Alto Paraguay. ◆ department N Paraguay
Alto Paraguay, Departamento del see Alto Paraguay
59 L17 Alto Paraíso de Goiás Goiás, S Brazil 14°04′S 47°15′W
62 P6 Alto Paraná off. Departamento del Alto Paraná. ◆ department E Paraguay
Alto Paraná see Paraná
Alto Paraná, Departamento del see Alto Paraná
59 L15 Alto Parnaíba Maranhão, E Brazil 09°08′S 45°56′W
56 H13 Alto Purús, Río ≈ E Peru
Altorf see Altdorf
63 H19 Alto Río Senguer var. Alto Río Senguerr. Chubut, S Argentina 45°01′S 70°55′W
Alto Río Senguerr see Alto Río Senguer
41 Q13 Altotonga Veracruz-Llave, E Mexico 19°46′N 97°14′W
101 N23 Altötting Bayern, SE Germany 48°12′N 12°37′E
Altpasua see Stara Pazova
Altraga see Bayandzürh
105 P3 Altsasu Cast. Alsasua. Navarra, N Spain 42°54′N 02°10′W
Alt-Schwanenburg see Gulbene
Altsohl see Zvolen
108 I7 Altstätten Sankt Gallen, NE Switzerland 47°22′N 09°33′E
Álttesjávri see Altevatnet
42 G1 Altun Ha ruins Belize, N Belize
Altun Kupri see Altin Köprü
158 D8 Altun Shan ▲ C China 39°19′N 93°37′E
158 L9 Altun Shan var. Altyn Tagh. ▲▲ NW China
35 P2 Alturas California, W USA 41°28′N 120°32′W
26 K12 Altus Oklahoma, C USA 34°39′N 99°21′W
26 K11 Altus Lake ▣ Oklahoma, C USA
Altvater see Praděd
Altyn Tagh see Altun Shan
Alu see Shortland Island
al-'Ubaila see Al 'Ubaylah
139 O6 Al 'Ubaydī Al Anbār, W Iraq 34°22′N 41°15′E
141 T9 Al 'Ubaylah var. al-'Ubaila. Ash Sharqīyah, E Saudi Arabia 22°02′N 50°57′E
141 T9 Al 'Ubaylah spring/well E Saudi Arabia 22°02′N 50°56′E
Al Ubayyiḍ see El Obeid
141 T7 Al 'Udayd var. Al Odaid. Abū Ẓaby, W United Arab Emirates 24°34′N 51°27′E
118 J8 Alūksne Ger. Marienburg. Alūksne, NE Latvia 57°26′N 27°02′E
140 K6 Al 'Ulā Al Madīnah, NW Saudi Arabia 26°39′N 37°55′E
173 N4 Alula-Fartak Trench var. Illaue Fartak Trench. undersea feature W Indian Ocean 14°04′N 51°47′E
138 I11 Al 'Umarī 'Ammān, E Jordan 37°30′N 31°30′E
31 S13 Alum Creek Lake ▣ Ohio, N USA
63 H15 Aluminé Neuquén, C Argentina 39°15′S 71°00′W
95 O14 Alunda Uppsala, C Sweden 60°04′N 18°04′E
117 T14 Alupka Respublika Krym, S Ukraine 44°24′N 34°01′E
75 P8 Al 'Uqaylah N Libya 30°13′N 19°12′E
Al Uqşur see Luxor
Al Urdunn see Jordan
168 J9 Alur Panal bay Sumatera, W Indonesia
Alur Setar see Alor Setar
141 V10 Al 'Urūq al Mu'tariḍah salt lake SE Saudi Arabia
139 Q7 Ālūs Al Anbār, C Iraq 34°05′N 42°27′E
117 T13 Alushta Respublika Krym, S Ukraine 44°41′N 34°24′E
151 G22 Aluva var. Alwaye. Kerala, SW India 10°06′N 76°23′E see also Alwaye
75 N11 Al 'Uwaynāt var. Al Awaynāt. SW Libya 25°47′N 10°34′E
139 T6 Al 'Uẓaym var. Adhaim. Diyālá, E Iraq 34°12′N 44°31′E
26 L8 Alva Oklahoma, C USA 36°48′N 98°40′W
104 H8 Alva ≈ N Portugal
95 J18 Älvängen Västra Götaland, S Sweden 57°56′N 12°09′E
14 F14 Alvanley Ontario, S Canada 44°33′N 81°05′W
41 S14 Alvarado Veracruz-Llave, E Mexico 18°47′N 95°45′W
25 T7 Alvarado Texas, SW USA 32°24′N 97°12′W
58 D13 Alvarães Amazonas, NW Brazil 03°13′S 64°53′W
40 G6 Álvaro Obregón, Presa ▣ W Mexico
94 H10 Alvdal Hedmark, S Norway 62°07′N 10°39′E
94 K12 Älvdalen Dalarna, C Sweden 61°13′N 14°04′E
61 E15 Alvear Corrientes, NE Argentina 29°05′S 56°35′W
104 F10 Alverca do Ribatejo Lisboa, C Portugal 38°56′N 09°01′W
95 L20 Alvesta Kronoberg, S Sweden 56°52′N 14°34′E
25 W12 Alvin Texas, SW USA 29°25′N 95°14′W
94 O13 Älvkarleby Uppsala, C Sweden 60°34′N 17°30′E
25 S5 Alvord Texas, SW USA 33°22′N 97°39′W
93 G18 Älvros Jämtland, C Sweden 62°04′N 14°30′E
92 J13 Älvsbyn Norrbotten, N Sweden 65°41′N 21°00′E
142 K12 Al Wafrā' SE Kuwait 28°38′N 47°57′E
140 J6 Al Wajh Tabūk, NW Saudi Arabia 26°16′N 36°30′E
143 N16 Al Wakrah var. Wakra. C Qatar 25°09′N 51°36′E
138 M8 al Walaj, Sha'īb dry watercourse W Iraq
152 I11 Alwar Rājasthān, N India 27°32′N 76°35′E
141 Q5 Al Wari'ah Ash Sharqīyah, N Saudi Arabia 27°54′N 47°23′E
155 G22 Alwaye var. Aluva. Kerala, SW India 10°06′N 76°23′E see also Aluva
Alxa Zuoqi see Bayan Hot
Alx Youqi see Ehen Hudag
Al Yaman see Yemen
138 G9 Al Yarmūk Irbid, N Jordan 32°41′N 35°55′E
Alyat/Alyaty-Pristan' see Älät
115 I14 Alykí var. Aliki. Thásos, N Greece 40°36′N 24°45′E
119 F14 Alytus Pol. Olita. Alytus, S Lithuania 54°24′N 24°02′E
119 F15 Alytus ◆ province S Lithuania
101 N23 Alz ≈ SE Germany
33 Y11 Alzada Montana, NW USA 45°00′N 104°24′W
122 L12 Alzamay Irkutskaya Oblast', S Russian Federation 55°33′N 98°36′E
99 M25 Alzette ≈ S Luxembourg
105 S10 Alzira var. Alcira; anc. Saetabicula, Suero. País Valenciano, E Spain 39°10′N 00°27′W
Al Zubair see Az Zubayr
181 O8 Amadeus, Lake seasonal lake Northern Territory, C Australia
81 E15 Amadi Western Equatoria, SW Sudan 05°32′N 30°20′E
9 R7 Amadjuak Lake ⊗ Baffin Island, Nunavut, N Canada
95 J23 Amager island E Denmark
165 N14 Amagi-san ▲ Honshū, S Japan 34°51′N 138°57′E
171 S13 Amahai var. Masohi. Pulau Seram, E Indonesia 03°19′S 128°56′E
38 M16 Amak Island island Alaska, USA
164 B14 Amakusa-nada gulf SW Japan
95 J16 Åmål Västra Götaland, S Sweden 59°04′N 12°41′E
54 E8 Amalfi Antioquia, N Colombia 06°54′N 75°04′W
107 L18 Amalfi Campania, S Italy 40°37′N 14°35′E
115 D19 Amaliáda var. Amaliás. Dytikí Elláda, S Greece 37°48′N 21°21′E
Amaliás see Amaliáda
154 F12 Amalner Mahārāshtra, C India 21°03′N 75°04′E
171 W14 Amamapare Papua, E Indonesia 04°51′S 136°44′E
59 H21 Amambaí, Serra de var. Cordillera de Amambay, Serra de Amambay. ▲ Brazil/Paraguay see also Amambay, Cordillera de
62 P4 Amambay off. Departamento del Amambay. ◆ department E Paraguay
62 P5 Amambay, Cordillera de var. Serra de Amambaí, Serra de Amambay. ▲ Brazil/Paraguay see also Amambaí, Serra de
Amambay, Departamento del see Amambay
Amambay, Serra de see Amambaí, Serra de/Amambay, Cordillera de
165 U16 Amami-guntō island group SW Japan
165 V15 Amami-Ō-shima island S Japan
186 A5 Amanab Sandaun, NW Papua New Guinea 03°38′S 141°16′E
106 J13 Amandola Marche, C Italy 42°58′N 13°22′E
107 N21 Amantea Calabria, SW Italy 39°06′N 16°05′E
191 W10 Amanu island Îles Tuamotu, C French Polynesia
58 J10 Amapá Amapá, NE Brazil 02°00′N 50°50′W
58 J11 Amapá off. Estado de Amapá; prev. Território de Amapá. ◆ state NE Brazil
Amapá, Estado de see Amapá
42 H8 Amapala Valle, S Honduras 13°16′N 87°39′W
Amapá, Território de see Amapá
80 J12 Āmara ◆ federal region N Ethiopia
Amara see Al 'Amārah
104 H6 Amarante Porto, N Portugal 41°16′N 08°05′W
166 M5 Amarapura Mandalay, C Myanmar (Burma) 21°54′N 96°01′E
Amardalay see Delgertsogt
104 I12 Amareleja Beja, S Portugal 38°12′N 07°13′W
35 V11 Amargosa Range ▲ California, W USA
25 N2 Amarillo Texas, SW USA 35°13′N 101°50′W
Amarinthos see Amárynthos
107 K15 Amaro, Monte ▲ C Italy 42°03′N 14°06′E
115 H18 Amárynthos var. Amarinthos. Évvoia, C Greece 38°24′N 23°53′E
Amasia see Amasya
136 K12 Amasya anc. Amasia. Amasya, N Turkey 40°37′N 35°50′E
136 K11 Amasya ◆ province N Turkey
42 F4 Amatique, Bahía de bay Gulf of Honduras, W Caribbean Sea
42 D6 Amatitlán, Lago de ⊗ S Guatemala
107 J14 Amatrice Lazio, C Italy 42°38′N 13°19′E
190 C8 Amatuku atoll C Tuvalu
99 J20 Amay Liège, E Belgium 50°33′N 05°19′E
48 F7 Amazon Sp. Amazonas. ≈ Brazil/Peru
59 C14 Amazonas off. Estado do Amazonas. ◆ state N Brazil
54 G15 Amazonas off. Comisaria del Amazonas. ◆ province SE Colombia
56 C10 Amazonas off. Departamento de Amazonas. ◆ department N Peru
54 M12 Amazonas off. Territorio Amazonas. ◆ federal territory S Venezuela
Amazonas see Amazon
Amazonas, Comisaria del see Amazonas
Amazonas, Departamento de see Amazonas
Amazonas, Estado do see Amazonas
Amazonas, Territorio see Amazonas
48 F7 Amazon Basin basin N South America
47 V5 Amazon Fan undersea feature W Atlantic Ocean 05°00′N 47°30′W
58 K11 Amazon, Mouths of the delta NE Brazil
187 R13 Ambae var. Aoba, Omba. island C Vanuatu
152 I9 Ambāla Haryāna, NW India 30°19′N 76°49′E
155 J26 Ambalangoda Southern Province, SW Sri Lanka 06°14′N 80°03′E
155 K26 Ambalantota Southern Province, S Sri Lanka 06°07′N 81°01′E
172 I6 Ambalavao Fianarantsoa, C Madagascar 21°50′S 46°56′E
54 E10 Ambalema Tolima, C Colombia 04°49′N 74°48′W
79 E17 Ambam Sud, S Cameroon 02°23′N 11°17′E
172 J2 Ambanja Antsiranana, N Madagascar 13°40′S 48°27′E
123 T6 Ambarchik Respublika Sakha (Yakutiya), NE Russian Federation 69°33′N 162°08′E
62 K9 Ambargasta, Salinas de salt lake C Argentina
124 J6 Ambarnyy Respublika Kareliya, NW Russian Federation 65°53′N 33°44′E
56 C7 Ambato Tungurahua, C Ecuador 01°18′S 78°39′W
172 I6 Ambatofinandrahana Fianarantsoa, SE Madagascar
172 I5 Ambatolampy Antananarivo, C Madagascar 19°21′S 47°27′E
172 H4 Ambatomainty Mahajanga, W Madagascar 17°40′S 45°39′E
172 J4 Ambatondrazaka Toamasina, C Madagascar 17°49′S 48°28′E
101 L20 Amberg var. Amberg in der Oberpfalz. Bayern, SE Germany 49°26′N 11°52′E
Amberg in der Oberpfalz see Amberg
42 H1 Ambergris Cay island NE Belize
103 S11 Ambérieu-en-Bugey Ain, E France 45°57′N 05°21′E
185 I18 Amberley Canterbury, South Island, New Zealand 43°09′S 172°43′E
103 P11 Ambert Puy-de-Dôme, C France 45°33′N 03°45′E
Ambianum see Amiens
76 J11 Ambidédi Kayes, SW Mali 14°37′N 11°49′W
154 M10 Ambikāpur Chhattīsgarh, C India 23°09′N 83°12′E
172 J2 Ambilobe Antsiranana, N Madagascar 13°10′S 49°03′E
39 O7 Ambler Alaska, USA 67°05′N 157°51′W
Amblève see Amel
Ambo see Hägere Hiywet
172 I8 Amboasary Toliara, S Madagascar 25°01′S 46°23′E
172 J4 Ambodifotatra var. Ambodifototra. Toamasina, E Madagascar 16°59′S 49°51′E
Amboenten see Ambunten
172 I5 Ambohidratrimo Antananarivo, C Madagascar 18°48′S 47°26′E
172 I6 Ambohimahasoa Fianarantsoa, SE Madagascar 21°07′S 47°13′E
172 K3 Ambohitralanana Antsiranana, NE Madagascar 15°13′S 50°28′E
Amboina see Ambon
102 M8 Amboise Indre-et-Loire, C France 47°25′N 01°00′E
171 S13 Ambon prev. Amboina, Amboyna. Pulau Ambon, E Indonesia 03°41′S 128°10′E
171 S13 Ambon, Pulau island E Indonesia
81 I20 Amboseli, Lake ⊗ Kenya/Tanzania
172 I6 Ambositra Fianarantsoa, SE Madagascar 20°31′S 47°15′E
172 I8 Ambovombe Toliara, S Madagascar 25°10′S 46°06′E
35 W14 Amboy California, W USA 34°33′N 115°44′W
30 L11 Amboy Illinois, N USA 41°42′N 89°19′W
Amboyna see Ambon
Ambracia see Árta
Ambre, Cap d' see Bobaomby, Tanjona
18 B14 Ambridge Pennsylvania, NE USA 40°33′N 80°11′W
Ambrim see Ambrym
82 A11 Ambriz Bengo, NW Angola 07°55′S 13°11′E
Ambrizete see N'Zeto
187 R13 Ambrym var. Ambrim. island C Vanuatu
169 T16 Ambunten prev. Amboenten. Pulau Madura, E Indonesia 06°55′S 113°45′E
186 B6 Ambunti East Sepik, NW Papua New Guinea 04°12′S 142°49′E
155 I20 Āmbūr Tamil Nādu, SE India 12°48′N 78°44′E
38 E17 Amchitka Island island Aleutian Islands, Alaska, USA
38 F17 Amchitka Pass strait Aleutian Islands, Alaska, USA
141 R15 'Amd C Yemen 15°10′N 47°58′E
78 J10 Am Dam Ouaddaï, E Chad 12°46′N 20°29′E
171 U16 Amdassa Pulau Yamdena, E Indonesia 07°40′S 131°24′E
125 U1 Amderma Nenetskiy Avtonomnyy Okrug, NW Russian Federation 69°45′N 61°36′E
159 N14 Amdo Xizang Zizhiqu, W China 32°15′N 91°43′E
40 K13 Ameca Jalisco, SW Mexico 20°34′N 104°03′W
41 P14 Amecameca var. Amecameca de Juárez. México, C Mexico 19°08′N 98°48′W
Amecameca de Juárez see Amecameca
61 A20 Ameghino Buenos Aires, E Argentina 34°51′S 62°28′W
99 M21 Amel Fr. Amblève. Liège, E Belgium 50°20′N 06°13′E
98 K4 Ameland Fris. It Amelân. island Waddeneilanden, N Netherlands
Amelân, It see Ameland
107 H14 Amelia Umbria, C Italy 42°33′N 12°26′E
21 V6 Amelia Court House Virginia, NE USA 37°20′N 77°59′W
23 W8 Amelia Island island Florida, SE USA
18 L12 Amenia New York, NE USA 41°51′N 73°31′W
America see United States of America
65 M21 America-Antarctica Ridge undersea feature S Atlantic Ocean
America in Miniature see Maryland
60 L9 Americana São Paulo, S Brazil 22°44′S 47°19′W
33 Q15 American Falls Idaho, NW USA 42°47′N 112°51′W
33 Q15 American Falls Reservoir ▣ Idaho, NW USA
36 L3 American Fork Utah, W USA 40°24′N 111°47′W
192 K16 American Samoa ◇ US unincorporated territory W Polynesia
23 S6 Americus Georgia, SE USA 32°04′N 84°13′W
98 K12 Amerongen Utrecht, C Netherlands 52°00′N 05°30′E
98 K11 Amersfoort Utrecht, C Netherlands 52°09′N 05°23′E
97 N21 Amersham SE England, United Kingdom 51°40′N 00°37′W
30 I5 Amery Wisconsin, N USA 45°18′N 92°20′W
195 W6 Amery Ice Shelf ice shelf Antarctica
29 V13 Ames Iowa, C USA 42°01′N 93°37′W
19 P10 Amesbury Massachusetts, NE USA 42°51′N 70°55′W
Amestratus see Mistretta
115 F18 Amfíkleia var. Amfiklia. Stereá Elláda, C Greece 38°38′N 22°35′E
Amfíklia see Amfíkleia
115 D17 Amfilochía var. Amfilokhía. Dytikí Elláda, C Greece 38°52′N 21°09′E
Amfilokhía see Amfilochía
114 H13 Amfípoli anc. Amphipolis. site of ancient city Kentrikí Makedonía, NE Greece
115 F18 Ámfissa Stereá Elláda, C Greece 38°32′N 22°22′E
123 Q10 Amga Respublika Sakha (Yakutiya), NE Russian Federation 60°55′N 131°45′E
123 Q11 Amga ≈ NE Russian Federation
163 R7 Amgalang var. Xin Barag Zuoqi. Nei Mongol Zizhiqu, N China 48°12′N 118°15′E
123 V5 Amguema ≈ NE Russian Federation
123 S12 Amgun' ≈ SE Russian Federation
13 P15 Amherst Nova Scotia, SE Canada 45°50′N 64°14′W
18 M11 Amherst Massachusetts, NE USA 42°22′N 72°31′W
18 D10 Amherst New York, NE USA 42°57′N 78°47′W
24 M4 Amherst Texas, SW USA 33°59′N 102°24′W
21 U6 Amherst Virginia, NE USA 37°35′N 79°04′W
Amherst see Kyaikkami
14 C18 Amherstburg Ontario, S Canada 42°05′N 83°06′W
21 Q6 Amherstdale West Virginia, NE USA 37°46′N 81°46′W
14 K15 Amherst Island island Ontario, SE Canada
Amida see Diyarbakır
28 J6 Amidon North Dakota, N USA 46°29′N 103°19′W
103 O3 Amiens anc. Ambianum, Samarobriva. Somme, N France 49°54′N 02°18′E
139 P8 'Āmij, Wādī var. Wadi 'Amīj. dry watercourse W Iraq
136 L17 Amik Ovası ⊗ S Turkey
76 E9 Amilcar Cabral ✈ Sal, NE Cape Verde
Amilhayt, Wādī see Umm al Ḥayt, Wādī
Amíndaion/Amindeo see Amýntaio
155 C21 Amīndīvi Islands island group Lakshadweep, India, N Indian Ocean
139 U6 Āmin Ḥabīb Diyālá, E Iraq 34°17′N 45°10′E
83 E20 Aminuis Omaheke, E Namibia 23°43′S 19°21′E
'Amīq, Wadi see 'Āmij, Wādī
142 J7 Amīrābād Īlām, NW Iran 33°20′N 46°16′E
Amirante Bank see Amirante Ridge
173 N6 Amirante Basin undersea feature W Indian Ocean 07°00′S 54°00′E
173 N6 Amirante Islands var. Amirantes Group. island group C Seychelles
173 N7 Amirante Ridge var. Amirante Bank. undersea feature W Indian Ocean 06°00′S 53°10′E
Amirantes Group see Amirante Islands
173 N7 Amirante Trench undersea feature W Indian Ocean 08°00′S 52°30′E
11 U13 Amisk Lake ⊗ Saskatchewan, C Canada
Amistad, Presa de la see Amistad Reservoir
25 O12 Amistad Reservoir var. Presa de la Amistad. ▣ Mexico/USA
Amisus see Samsun
22 K8 Amite var. Amite City. Louisiana, S USA 30°40′N 90°30′W
Amite City see Amite
27 T12 Amity Arkansas, C USA 34°15′N 93°27′W
154 H11 Amla prev. Amulla. Madhya Pradesh, C India 21°53′N 78°10′E
38 I17 Amlia Island island Aleutian Islands, Alaska, USA
97 I18 Amlwch NW Wales, United Kingdom 53°25′N 04°23′W
Ammaia see Portalegre
138 H10 'Ammān var. Amman; anc. Philadelphia, Bibl. Rabbah Ammon, Rabbath Ammon. ● (Jordan) 'Ammān, NW Jordan 31°57′N 35°56′E
138 H10 'Ammān off. Muḩāfaẓat 'Ammān; prev. Al 'Āşimah. ◆ governorate NW Jordan
'Ammān, Muḩāfaẓat see 'Ammān
93 N14 Ämmänsaari Oulu, E Finland 64°51′N 28°58′E

◆ Country
● Country Capital
◇ Dependent Territory
○ Dependent Territory Capital
◆ Administrative Regions
✈ International Airport
▲ Mountain
▲▲ Mountain Range
Volcano
≈ River
⊗ Lake
▣ Reservoir

Ammarnäs – Anthony

92 H13 Ammarnäs Västerbotten, N Sweden 65°58′N 16°10′E
197 O15 Ammassalik var. Angmagssalik. Tunu, S Greenland 65°51′N 37°30′W
101 K24 Ammer ≈ SE Germany
101 K24 Ammersee ⊚ SE Germany
98 J13 Ammerzoden Gelderland, C Netherlands 51°46′N 05°07′E
Ammóchostos see Gazimağusa
Ammóchostos, Kólpos see Gazimağusa Körfezi
Amnok-kang see Yalu
Amoea see Portalegre
Amoentai see Amuntai
Amoerang see Amurang
143 O4 Āmol var. Amul. Māzandarān, N Iran 36°31′N 52°24′E
115 K21 Amorgós Amorgós, Kykládes, Greece, Aegean Sea 36°49′N 25°54′E
115 K22 Amorgós island Kykládes, Greece, Aegean Sea
23 N3 Amory Mississippi, S USA 33°58′N 88°29′W
12 I13 Amos Québec, SE Canada 48°34′N 78°08′W
95 G15 Åmot Buskerud, S Norway 59°52′N 09°55′E
95 E15 Åmot Telemark, S Norway 59°34′N 07°59′E
95 J15 Åmotfors Värmland, C Sweden 59°46′N 12°24′E
76 L10 Amourj Hodh ech Chargui, SE Mauritania 16°04′N 07°12′W
Amoy see Xiamen
172 H7 Ampanihy Toliara, SW Madagascar 24°40′S 44°45′E
155 L25 Ampara var. Amparai. Eastern Province, E Sri Lanka 07°17′N 81°41′E
172 J4 Amparafaravola Toamasina, E Madagascar 17°33′S 48°13′E
Amparai see Ampara
60 M9 Amparo São Paulo, S Brazil 22°40′S 46°49′W
172 J5 Ampasimanolotra Toamasina, E Madagascar 18°49′S 49°04′E
57 H17 Ampato, Nevado ▲ S Peru 15°52′S 71°51′W
101 L23 Amper ≈ SE Germany
64 M9 Ampère Seamount undersea feature E Atlantic Ocean 35°05′N 13°00′W
Amphipolis see Amfípoli
167 X10 Amphitrite Group island group N Paracel Islands
171 T16 Amplawas var. Emplawas. Pulau Babar, E Indonesia 08°01′S 129°42′E
105 U7 Amposta Cataluña, NE Spain 40°43′N 00°34′E
15 V7 Amqui Québec, SE Canada 48°28′N 67°27′W
141 O14 ʿAmrān W Yemen 15°39′N 43°59′E
Amraoti see Amrāvati
154 H12 Amrāvati prev. Amraoti. Mahārāshtra, C India 20°56′N 77°45′E
154 C11 Amreli Gujarāt, W India 21°36′N 71°20′E
108 H6 Amriswil Thurgau, NE Switzerland 47°33′N 09°18′E
138 H5 ʿAmrīt ruins Tarṭūs, W Syria
152 H7 Amritsar Punjab, N India 31°38′N 74°55′E
152 J10 Amroha Uttar Pradesh, N India 28°54′N 78°29′E
100 G7 Amrum island NW Germany
93 J15 Åmsele Västerbotten, N Sweden 64°31′N 19°24′E
98 I10 Amstelveen Noord-Holland, C Netherlands 52°18′N 04°50′E
98 I10 Amsterdam ● (Netherlands) Noord-Holland, C Netherlands 52°22′N 04°54′E
18 K10 Amsterdam New York, NE USA 42°56′N 74°11′W
173 Q11 Amsterdam Fracture Zone tectonic feature S Indian Ocean
173 R11 Amsterdam Island island NE French Southern and Antarctic Territories
109 U4 Amstetten Niederösterreich, N Austria 48°08′N 14°52′E
78 J11 Am Timan Salamat, SE Chad 11°02′N 20°17′E
146 L12 Amu-Buxoro Kanali var. Aral-Bukhorskiy Kanal. canal C Uzbekistan
139 O1 ʿĀmūdah var. Amude. Al Ḥasakah, N Syria 37°06′N 40°56′E
147 O15 Amu Darya Rus. Amudar'ya, Taj. Dar"yoi Amu, Turkm. Amyderya, Uzb. Amudaryo; anc. Oxus. ≈ C Asia
Amu-Dar'ya see Amyderýa
Amudar'ya/Amudaryo/Amu, Dar"yoi see Amu Darya
Amude see ʿĀmūdah
140 L3 ʿAmūd, Jabal al ▲ NW Saudi Arabia 30°59′N 39°17′E
38 J17 Amukta Island island Aleutian Islands, Alaska, USA
38 I17 Amukta Pass strait Aleutian Islands, Alaska, USA
Amul see Āmol
Amulla see Amla
Amundsen Basin see Fram Basin
195 X3 Amundsen Bay bay Antarctica
195 P10 Amundsen Coast physical region Antarctica
193 O14 Amundsen Plain undersea feature S Pacific Ocean
195 Q9 Amundsen-Scott US research station Antarctica 89°59′S 10°00′E
194 J11 Amundsen Sea sea S Pacific Ocean
94 M12 Amungen ⊚ C Sweden
169 U13 Amuntai prev. Amoentai. Borneo, C Indonesia 02°24′S 115°14′E
129 W6 Amur Chin. Heilong Jiang. ≈ China/Russian Federation
171 Q11 Amurang prev. Amoerang. Sulawesi, C Indonesia 01°12′N 124°37′E
105 O3 Amurrio País Vasco, N Spain 43°03′N 03°00′W
123 S13 Amursk Khabarovskiy Kray, SE Russian Federation 50°13′N 136°34′E
123 Q12 Amurskaya Oblast' ⬖ province SE Russian Federation
80 G7 ʿAmur, Wadi ≈ NE Sudan
115 C17 Amvrakikós Kólpos gulf W Greece
Amvrosiyevka see Amvrosiyivka
117 X8 Amvrosiyivka Rus. Amvrosiyevka. Donets'ka Oblast', SE Ukraine 47°46′N 38°30′E
146 M14 Amyderýa Rus. Amu-Dar'ya. Lebap Welaýaty, NE Turkmenistan 37°58′N 65°14′E
Amyderya see Amu Darya
114 E13 Amýntaio var. Amindeo; prev. Amíndaion. Dytikí Makedonía, N Greece 40°42′N 21°42′E
14 B6 Amyot Ontario, S Canada 48°28′N 84°58′W
191 U10 Anaa atoll Îles Tuamotu, C French Polynesia
Anabanoea see Anabanua
171 N14 Anabanua prev. Anabanoea. Sulawesi, C Indonesia 03°58′S 120°07′E
189 R8 Anabar NE Nauru 0°30′S 166°56′E
123 N8 Anabar ≈ NE Russian Federation
An Abhainn Mhór see Blackwater
55 O6 Anaco Anzoátegui, NE Venezuela 09°30′N 64°28′W
33 Q10 Anaconda Montana, NW USA 46°09′N 112°56′W
32 H7 Anacortes Washington, NW USA 48°30′N 122°36′W
26 M11 Anadarko Oklahoma, C USA 35°04′N 98°16′W
114 N12 Ana Dere ≈ NW Turkey
104 G8 Anadia Aveiro, N Portugal 40°26′N 08°27′W
Anadolu Dağları see Doğu Karadeniz Dağları
123 V6 Anadyr' Chukotskiy Avtonomnyy Okrug, NE Russian Federation 64°41′N 177°22′E
123 V6 Anadyr' ≈ NE Russian Federation
Anadyr, Gulf of see Anadyrskiy Zaliv
129 X4 Anadyrskiy Khrebet var. Chukot Range. ▲▲ NE Russian Federation
123 W6 Anadyrskiy Zaliv Eng. Gulf of Anadyr. gulf NE Russian Federation
115 K22 Anáfi anc. Anaphe. island Kykládes, Greece, Aegean Sea
107 J15 Anagni Lazio, C Italy 41°43′N 13°12′E
ʿAnah see ʿAnnah
35 T15 Anaheim California, W USA 33°50′N 117°54′W
10 L15 Anahim Lake British Columbia, SW Canada 52°26′N 125°13′W
38 B8 Anahola Kauaʿi, Hawaiʿi, USA, C Pacific Ocean 22°09′N 159°19′W
41 O7 Anáhuac Nuevo León, NE Mexico 27°13′N 100°09′W
25 X11 Anahuac Texas, SW USA 29°44′N 94°41′W
155 G22 Anai Mudi ▲ S India 10°16′N 77°08′E
Anaiza see ʿUnayzah
155 M15 Anakāpalle Andhra Pradesh, E India 17°42′N 83°06′E
191 W15 Anakena, Playa de beach Easter Island, Chile, E Pacific Ocean
39 Q7 Anaktuvuk Pass Alaska, USA 68°08′N 151°44′W
39 Q6 Anaktuvuk River ≈ Alaska, USA
172 J3 Analalava Mahajanga, NW Madagascar 14°38′S 47°46′E
44 F6 Ana Maria, Golfo de gulf N Caribbean Sea
Anambas Islands see Anambas, Kepulauan
169 N8 Anambas, Kepulauan var. Anambas Islands. island group W Indonesia
77 U17 Anambra ⬖ state SE Nigeria
29 N4 Anamoose North Dakota, N USA 47°50′N 100°14′W
29 Y13 Anamosa Iowa, C USA 42°06′N 91°17′W
136 H17 Anamur İçel, S Turkey 36°06′N 32°49′E
136 H17 Anamur Burnu headland S Turkey 36°03′N 32°49′E
154 D11 Ānand Gujarāt, India 22°34′N 73°01′E
154 O12 Ānandadur Orissa, E India 21°14′N 86°10′E
155 H18 Anantapur Andhra Pradesh, S India 14°41′N 77°36′E
152 H5 Anantnāg var. Islamabad. Jammu and Kashmir, NW India 33°44′N 75°11′E
Ananyev see Anan'yiv
117 O9 Anan'yiv Rus. Ananyev. Odes'ka Oblast', SW Ukraine 47°43′N 29°51′E
126 J14 Anapa Krasnodarskiy Kray, SW Russian Federation 44°55′N 37°20′E
Anaphe see Anáfi
59 K18 Anápolis Goiás, C Brazil 16°19′S 48°58′W
143 R10 Anār Kermān, C Iran 30°49′N 55°18′E
Anár see Inari
143 P7 Anārak Eşfahān, C Iran 33°21′N 53°43′E
Anar Dara see Anār Darreh
148 J7 Anār Darreh var. Anar Dara. Farāh, W Afghanistan 32°45′N 61°38′E
Anárjohka see Inarijoki
23 X9 Anastasia Island island Florida, SE USA
188 K7 Anatahan island C Northern Mariana Islands
128 M6 Anatolia plateau C Turkey
86 F14 Anatolian Plate tectonic feature Asia/Europe
114 H13 Anatolikí Makedonía kai Thráki Eng. Macedonia East and Thrace. ⬖ region NE Greece
Anatom see Aneityum
62 L8 Añatuya Santiago del Estero, N Argentina 28°28′S 62°52′W
An Baile Meánach see Ballymena
An Bhearú see Barrow
An Bhóinn see Boyne
An Blascaod Mór see Great Blasket Island
An Cabhán see Cavan
An Caisleán Nua see Newcastle
An Caisleán Riabhach see Castlerea, Ireland
An Caisleán Riabhach see Castlereagh
56 C13 Ancash off. Departamento de Ancash. ⬖ department W Peru
Ancash, Departamento de see Ancash
An Cathair see Caher
102 J8 Ancenis Loire-Atlantique, NW France 47°23′N 01°10′W
An Chanáil Ríoga see Royal Canal
An Cheacha see Caha Mountains
39 R11 Anchorage Alaska, USA 61°13′N 149°52′W
39 R12 Anchorage ✕ Alaska, USA 61°08′N 150°00′W
39 Q13 Anchor Point Alaska, USA 59°46′N 151°49′W
An Chorr Chríochach see Cookstown
65 M24 Anchorstock Point headland W Tristan da Cunha 37°07′S 12°21′W
An Clár see Clare
An Clochán see Clifden
An Clochán Liath see Dunglow
23 U12 Anclote Keys island group Florida, SE USA
An Cóbh see Cobh
57 J17 Ancohuma, Nevado de ▲ W Bolivia 15°51′S 68°33′W
An Comar see Comber
57 D14 Ancón Lima, W Peru 11°45′S 77°08′W
106 J12 Ancona Marche, C Italy 43°38′N 13°30′E
Ancuabe see Ancuabi
82 Q13 Ancuabi var. Ancuabe. Cabo Delgado, NE Mozambique 13°00′S 39°50′E
63 F17 Ancud prev. San Carlos de Ancud. Los Lagos, S Chile 41°53′S 73°50′W
63 G17 Ancud, Golfo de gulf S Chile
Ancyra see Ankara
163 V8 Anda Heilongjiang, NE China 46°25′N 125°20′E
57 G16 Andahuaylas Apurímac, S Peru 13°39′S 73°24′W
An Daingean see Dingle
153 R15 Āndāl West Bengal, NE India 23°35′N 87°14′E
94 E9 Åndalsnes Møre og Romsdal, S Norway 62°33′N 07°42′E
104 K13 Andalucía Eng. Andalusia. ⬖ autonomous community S Spain
23 P7 Andalusia Alabama, S USA 31°18′N 86°29′W
Andalusia see Andalucía
151 Q21 Andaman and Nicobar Islands var. Andamans and Nicobars. ⬖ union territory India, NE Indian Ocean
173 T4 Andaman Basin undersea feature NE Indian Ocean 10°00′N 94°00′E
151 P19 Andaman Islands island group India, NE Indian Ocean
Andamans and Nicobars see Andaman and Nicobar Islands
173 T4 Andaman Sea sea NE Indian Ocean
57 K19 Andamarca Oruro, C Bolivia 18°46′S 67°31′W
182 H5 Andamooka South Australia 30°26′S 137°12′E
141 Y9 ʿAndām, Wādī seasonal river NE Oman
172 J3 Andapa Antsirañana, NE Madagascar 14°39′S 49°40′E
149 R4 Andarāb var. Banow. Baghlān, NE Afghanistan 35°36′N 69°18′E
Andarbag see Andarbogh
147 S13 Andarbogh Rus. Andarbag, Anderbak. S Tajikistan 37°51′N 71°45′E
109 Z5 Andau Burgenland, E Austria 47°47′N 17°02′E
108 I10 Andeer Graubünden, S Switzerland 46°36′N 09°24′E
92 H9 Andenes Nordland, C Norway 69°18′N 16°10′E
99 J20 Andenne Namur, SE Belgium 50°29′N 05°06′E
77 S11 Andéramboukane Gao, E Mali 15°24′N 03°03′E
Anderbak see Andarbogh
99 G18 Anderlecht Brussels, C Belgium 50°50′N 04°18′E
99 G21 Anderlues Hainaut, S Belgium 50°24′N 04°16′E
108 G9 Andermatt Uri, C Switzerland 46°39′N 08°36′E
101 E17 Andernach anc. Antunnacum. Rheinland-Pfalz, SW Germany 50°26′N 07°24′E
188 D15 Andersen Air Force Base air base NE Guam 13°34′N 144°55′E
39 R9 Anderson Alaska, USA 64°20′N 149°11′W
35 N4 Anderson California, W USA 40°26′N 122°21′W
31 P13 Anderson Indiana, N USA 40°06′N 85°40′W
27 R8 Anderson Missouri, C USA 36°39′N 94°26′W
21 P11 Anderson South Carolina, SE USA 34°30′N 82°39′W
25 V10 Anderson Texas, SW USA 30°29′N 96°00′W
95 K20 Anderstorp Jönköping, S Sweden 57°17′N 13°38′E
54 D9 Andes Antioquia, W Colombia 05°40′N 75°56′W
47 P7 Andes ▲▲ W South America
29 P12 Andes, Lake ⊚ South Dakota, N USA
92 H9 Andfjorden fjord E Norwegian Sea
155 H16 Andhra Pradesh ⬖ state E India
98 J8 Andijk Noord-Holland, NW Netherlands 52°38′N 05°00′E
147 S10 Andijon Rus. Andizhan. Andijon Viloyati, E Uzbekistan 40°46′N 72°19′E
147 S10 Andijon Viloyati Rus. Andizhanskaya Oblast'. ⬖ province E Uzbekistan
Andikíthira see Antikýthira
172 J4 Andilamena Toamasina, C Madagascar 17°00′S 48°35′E
142 L8 Andīmeshk var. Andimishk; prev. Salehābād. Khūzestān, SW Iran 32°30′N 48°26′E
Andimishk see Andīmeshk
Andipáros see Antíparos
Andípaxi see Antípaxoi
Andípsara see Antípsara
136 L16 Andırın Kahramanmaraş, S Turkey 37°33′N 36°18′E
158 J8 Andirlangar Xinjiang Uygur Zizhiqu, NW China 37°38′N 83°40′E
Andírrion see Antírrio
Ándissa see Ántissa
Andizhan see Andijon
Andizhanskaya Oblast' see Andijon Viloyati
149 N2 Andkhvoy Fāryāb, N Afghanistan 36°56′N 65°08′E
105 Q2 Andoain País Vasco, N Spain 43°13′N 02°02′W
163 Y15 Andong Jap. Antō. E South Korea 36°34′N 128°44′E
109 R4 Andorf Oberösterreich, N Austria 48°22′N 13°33′E
105 S7 Andorra Aragón, NE Spain 40°59′N 00°27′W
105 V4 Andorra off. Principality of Andorra, Cat. Valls d'Andorra, Fr. Vallée d'Andorre. ◆ monarchy SW Europe
Andorra see Andorra la Vella
105 V4 Andorra la Vella var. Andorra, Fr. Andorre la Vielle, Sp. Andorra la Vieja. ● (Andorra) C Andorra 42°30′N 01°30′E
Andorra la Vieja see Andorra la Vella
Andorra, Principality of see Andorra
Andorra, Valls d'/Andorra, Vallée d' see Andorra
Andorre la Vielle see Andorra la Vella
97 M22 Andover S England, United Kingdom 51°13′N 01°28′W
27 N6 Andover Kansas, C USA 37°42′N 97°08′W
92 G10 Andøya island C Norway
60 I8 Andradina São Paulo, S Brazil 20°54′S 51°19′W
105 X9 Andratx Mallorca, Spain, W Mediterranean Sea 39°35′N 02°25′E
39 N10 Andreafsky River ≈ Alaska, USA
38 H17 Andreanof Islands island group Aleutian Islands, Alaska, USA
124 H16 Andreapol' Tverskaya Oblast', W Russian Federation 56°38′N 32°17′E
Andreas, Cape see Zafer Burnu
Andreevka see Kabanbay
21 N10 Andrews North Carolina, SE USA 35°19′N 84°01′W
21 T13 Andrews South Carolina, SE USA 33°27′N 79°33′W
24 M7 Andrews Texas, SW USA 32°19′N 102°34′W
173 N5 Andrew Tablemount var. Gora Andryu. undersea feature W Indian Ocean 06°45′N 50°30′E
Andreyevka see Kabanbay
107 N17 Andria Puglia, SE Italy 41°13′N 16°17′E
113 K16 Andrijevica E Montenegro 42°45′N 19°45′E
115 E20 Andrítsaina Pelopónnisos, S Greece 37°29′N 21°52′E
An Droichead Nua see Newbridge
Andropov see Rybinsk
115 J19 Ándros Ándros, Kykládes, Greece, Aegean Sea 37°49′N 24°54′E
115 J20 Ándros island Kykládes, Greece, Aegean Sea
19 O7 Androscoggin River ≈ Maine/New Hampshire, NE USA
44 F3 Andros Island island NW Bahamas
127 R7 Androsovka Samarskaya Oblast', W Russian Federation 52°41′N 49°34′E
44 G3 Andros Town Andros Island, NW Bahamas 24°40′N 77°47′W
155 D21 Āndrott Island island Lakshadweep, India, N Indian Ocean
117 N5 Andrushivka Zhytomyrs'ka Oblast', N Ukraine 50°01′N 29°02′E
111 K17 Andrychów Małopolskie, S Poland 49°51′N 19°18′E
Andryu, Gora see Andrew Tablemount
92 I10 Andselv Troms, N Norway 69°05′N 18°30′E
79 O17 Andudu Orientale, NE Dem. Rep. Congo 02°26′N 28°39′E
105 N13 Andújar anc. Illiturgis. Andalucía, SW Spain 38°02′N 04°03′W
82 C12 Andulo Bié, W Angola 11°29′S 16°43′E
103 Q14 Anduze Gard, S France 44°03′N 03°59′E
An Earagail see Errigal Mountain
95 L19 Aneby Jönköping, S Sweden 57°50′N 14°45′E
Anécho see Aného
77 Q9 Anéfis Kidal, NE Mali 18°05′N 00°38′E
45 U8 Anegada island NE British Virgin Islands
61 B25 Anegada, Bahía bay E Argentina
45 U9 Anegada Passage passage Anguilla/British Virgin Islands
77 R17 Aného var. Anécho; prev. Petit-Popo. S Togo 06°14′N 01°36′E
197 D17 Aneityum var. Anatom; prev. Kéamu. island S Vanuatu
117 N10 Anenii Noi Rus. Novyye Aneny. C Moldova 46°52′N 29°10′E
186 F7 Anepmete New Britain, E Papua New Guinea 05°47′S 148°37′E
105 U4 Aneto ▲ NE Spain 42°36′N 00°37′E
146 F13 Änew Rus. Annau. Ahal Welaýaty, C Turkmenistan 37°51′N 58°22′E
Änewetak see Enewetak Atoll
77 Y8 Aney Agadez, NE Niger 19°22′N 13°00′E
An Fheoir see Nore
122 L12 Angara ≈ C Russian Federation
122 M13 Angarsk Irkutskaya Oblast', S Russian Federation 52°31′N 103°55′E
Angaur see Ngeaur
93 G17 Ånge Västernorrland, C Sweden 62°31′N 15°40′E
Angel see Úhlava
40 D4 Ángel de la Guarda, Isla island NW Mexico
171 O3 Angeles off. Angeles City. Luzon, N Philippines 15°16′N 120°37′E
Angeles City see Angeles
Angel Falls see Ángel, Salto
95 J22 Ängelholm Skåne, S Sweden 56°14′N 12°52′E
61 A17 Angélica Santa Fe, C Argentina 31°33′S 61°33′W
25 W8 Angelina River ≈ Texas, SW USA
55 Q9 Ángel, Salto Eng. Angel Falls. waterfall E Venezuela
95 M15 Ängelsberg Västmanland, C Sweden 59°57′N 16°01′E
35 P8 Angels Camp California, W USA 38°03′N 120°31′W
109 W7 Anger Steiermark, SE Austria 47°16′N 15°41′E
Angerapp see Ozersk
Angerburg see Węgorzewo
93 H15 Ångermanälven ≈ N Sweden
100 P11 Angermünde Brandenburg, NE Germany 53°02′N 13°59′E
102 K7 Angers anc. Juliomagus. Maine-et-Loire, NW France 47°30′N 00°33′W
15 W7 Angers ≈ Québec, SE Canada
93 J16 Ängesön island N Sweden
Angistro see Ágkistro
114 H13 Angítis ≈ NE Greece
167 R13 Ângk Tasaôm prev. Angtassom. Takêv, S Cambodia
185 C25 Anglem, Mount ▲ Stewart Island, Southland, SW New Zealand 46°44′S 167°56′E
97 I18 Anglesey cultural region NW Wales, United Kingdom
97 I18 Anglesey island NW Wales, United Kingdom
102 I15 Anglet Pyrénées-Atlantiques, SW France 43°29′N 01°30′W
25 W12 Angleton Texas, SW USA 29°10′N 95°27′W
Anglia see England
14 H9 Angliers Québec, SE Canada 47°33′N 79°17′W
Anglo-Egyptian Sudan see Sudan
Angmagssalik see Ammassalik
167 Q7 Ang Nam Ngum ⊚ C Laos
79 N16 Ango Orientale, N Dem. Rep. Congo 04°01′N 25°52′E
83 Q15 Angoche Nampula, E Mozambique 16°10′S 39°58′E
63 G14 Angol Araucanía, C Chile 37°47′S 72°45′W
31 Q11 Angola Indiana, N USA 41°37′N 85°00′W
82 A9 Angola off. Republic of Angola; prev. People's Republic of Angola, Portuguese West Africa. ◆ republic SW Africa
65 P15 Angola Basin undersea feature E Atlantic Ocean 15°00′S 03°00′E
Angola, People's Republic of see Angola
Angola, Republic of see Angola
39 X13 Angoon Admiralty Island, Alaska, USA 57°33′N 134°30′W
147 O14 Angor Surkhondaryo Viloyati, S Uzbekistan 37°30′N 67°06′E
Angora see Ankara
186 C6 Angoram East Sepik, NW Papua New Guinea 04°04′S 144°04′E
40 H8 Angostura Sinaloa, C Mexico 25°18′N 108°10′W
Angostura see Ciudad Bolívar
41 U17 Angostura, Presa de la ⊠ SE Mexico
28 J11 Angostura Reservoir ⊠ South Dakota, N USA
102 L11 Angoulême anc. Iculisma. Charente, W France 45°39′N 00°10′E
102 K11 Angoumois cultural region W France
64 O2 Angra do Heroísmo Terceira, Azores, Portugal, NE Atlantic Ocean 38°40′N 27°14′W
60 O10 Angra dos Reis Rio de Janeiro, SE Brazil 22°59′S 44°17′W
Angra Pequena see Lüderitz
147 Q10 Angren Toshkent Viloyati, E Uzbekistan 41°05′N 70°18′E
Angtassom see Ângk Tasaôm
167 O10 Ang Thong var. Angthong. Ang Thong, C Thailand 14°35′N 100°25′E
Angthong see Ang Thong
79 M16 Angu Orientale, N Dem. Rep. Congo 03°38′N 24°14′E
105 S5 Angües Aragón, NE Spain 42°07′N 00°10′W
45 U9 Anguilla ◇ UK dependent territory E West Indies
45 V9 Anguilla island E West Indies
44 F4 Anguilla Cays islets SW Bahamas
Angul see Anugul
161 N1 Anguli Nur ⊚ E China
79 O18 Angumu Orientale, E Dem. Rep. Congo 0°10′S 27°42′E
14 G14 Angus Ontario, S Canada 44°19′N 79°52′W
96 J10 Angus cultural region E Scotland, United Kingdom
59 K19 Anhanguera Goiás, S Brazil 18°12′S 48°19′W
99 I21 Anhée Namur, S Belgium 50°18′N 04°52′E
95 I21 Anholt island C Denmark
160 M11 Anhua var. Dongping. Hunan, S China 28°25′N 111°10′E
161 P8 Anhui var. Anhui Sheng, Anhwei, Wan. ⬖ province E China
AnhuiSheng/Anhwei Wan see Anhui
39 O11 Aniak Alaska, USA 61°34′N 159°31′W
39 O12 Aniak River ≈ Alaska, USA
An Iarmhí see Westmeath
189 R8 Anibare E Nauru 0°31′S 166°56′E
189 R8 Anibare Bay bay E Nauru, W Pacific Ocean
Anicium see le Puy
115 K22 Ánidro island Kykládes, Greece, Aegean Sea
77 R15 Anié C Togo 07°48′N 01°12′E
77 Q15 Anié ≈ C Togo
102 J16 Anie, Pic d' ▲ SW France 42°56′N 00°44′W
127 Y7 Anikhovka Orenburgskaya Oblast', W Russian Federation 51°27′N 60°17′E
14 G9 Anima Nipissing Lake ⊚ Ontario, S Canada
37 O16 Animas New Mexico, SW USA 31°55′N 108°49′W
37 P16 Animas Peak ▲ New Mexico, SW USA 31°34′N 108°46′W
37 P16 Animas Valley valley New Mexico, SW USA
116 F13 Anina Ger. Steierdorf, Hung. Stájerlakanina; prev. Ştaierdorf-Anina, Steierdorf-Anina, Steyerlak-Anina. Caraş-Severin, SW Romania 45°05′N 21°51′E
153 Y9 Anini Arunāchal Pradesh, NE India 28°48′N 95°54′E
29 U14 Anita Iowa, C USA 41°27′N 94°45′W
123 U14 Aniva, Mys headland Ostrov Sakhalin, SE Russian Federation 46°02′N 143°25′E
187 S15 Aniwa island S Vanuatu
93 M19 Anjalankoski Etelä-Suomi, S Finland 60°39′N 26°54′E
ʿAnjar see Aanjar
Anjiangying see Luanping
14 B8 Anjigami Lake ⊚ Ontario, S Canada
149 N13 Anjīra Balūchistān, SW Pakistan 28°19′N 66°19′E
164 K14 Anjō var. Anzyô. Aichi, Honshū, SW Japan 34°56′N 137°05′E
102 J8 Anjou cultural region NW France
172 I13 Anjouan var. Ndzouani, Nzwani. island SE Comoros
172 J4 Anjozorobe Antananarivo, C Madagascar 18°22′S 47°52′E
163 W13 Anju W North Korea 39°36′N 125°44′E
98 M5 Anjum Fris. Eanjum. Friesland, N Netherlands 53°22′N 06°09′E
172 G6 Ankaboa, Tanjona Fr. Cap Saint-Vincent. headland W Madagascar 21°57′S 43°16′E
160 L7 Ankang prev. Xing'an. Shaanxi, C China 32°45′N 109°00′E
136 I12 Ankara prev. Angora; anc. Ancyra. ● (Turkey) Ankara, C Turkey 39°55′N 32°50′E
136 H12 Ankara ⬖ province C Turkey
95 N19 Ankarsrum Kalmar, S Sweden 57°40′N 16°19′E
172 H6 Ankazoabo Toliara, SW Madagascar 22°18′S 44°30′E
172 I4 Ankazobe Antananarivo, C Madagascar 18°20′S 47°07′E
29 V14 Ankeny Iowa, C USA 41°43′N 93°37′W
167 V11 An Khê Gia Lai, C Vietnam 13°57′N 108°39′E
100 O9 Anklam Mecklenburg-Vorpommern, NE Germany 53°51′N 13°42′E
80 K13 Ānkober Āmara, N Ethiopia 09°36′N 39°44′E
77 O17 Ankobra ≈ S Ghana
79 N22 Ankoro Katanga, SE Dem. Rep. Congo 06°45′S 26°58′E
99 L24 Anlier, Forêt d' forest SE Belgium
160 I13 Anlong var. Xin'an. Guizhou, S China 25°05′N 105°29′E
An Longfort see Longford
167 R11 Ânlong Vêng Siĕmréab, NW Cambodia 14°16′N 104°08′E
An Lorgain see Lurgan
161 N8 Anlu Hubei, C China 31°15′N 113°41′E
An Mhí see Meath
An Mhuir Cheilteach see Celtic Sea
An Muileann gCearr see Mullingar
93 F16 Ånn Jämtland, C Sweden 63°19′N 12°34′E
126 M8 Anna Voronezhskaya Oblast', W Russian Federation 51°31′N 40°23′E
30 L17 Anna Illinois, N USA 37°27′N 89°15′W
25 U5 Anna Texas, SW USA 33°21′N 96°33′W
74 L5 Annaba prev. Bône. NE Algeria 36°55′N 07°47′E
An Nabatīyah at Taḥtā see Nabatîyé
101 N17 Annaberg-Buchholz Sachsen, E Germany 50°35′N 13°01′E
109 T9 Annabichl ✕ (Klagenfurt) Kärnten, S Austria 46°39′N 14°21′E
140 M5 An Nafūd desert NW Saudi Arabia
139 P6 ʿAnnah var. ʿĀnah. Al Anbār, NW Iraq 34°50′N 42°00′E
139 P6 An Nāḥiyah Al Anbār, W Iraq 34°24′N 41°33′E
139 S11 An Najaf ⬖ governorate S Iraq
139 T10 An Najaf var. Najaf. An Najaf, S Iraq 31°59′N 44°19′E
21 V5 Anna, Lake ⊠ Virginia, NE USA
97 F16 Annalee ≈ N Ireland
167 S9 Annamitique, Chaîne ▲▲ C Laos
97 J14 Annan S Scotland, United Kingdom 55°N 03°20′W
29 U8 Annandale Minnesota, N USA 45°15′N 94°07′W
21 W4 Annandale Virginia, NE USA 38°48′N 77°10′W
189 Q7 Anna Point headland N Nauru 0°30′S 166°56′E
21 X3 Annapolis state capital Maryland, NE USA 38°59′N 76°30′W
188 A10 Anna, Pulo island S Palau
153 O10 Annapurna ▲ C Nepal 28°30′N 83°50′E
An Nāqūrah see En Nâqoûra
31 R10 Ann Arbor Michigan, N USA 42°17′N 83°45′W
An Nás see Naas
139 W12 An Nāṣirīyah var. Nasiriya. Dhī Qār, SE Iraq 31°04′N 46°17′E
139 W11 An Naṣr Dhī Qār, E Iraq 31°34′N 46°08′E
Annau see Änew
121 O13 An Nawfalīyah var. Al Nūwfalīyah. N Libya 30°46′N 17°48′E
19 P10 Ann, Cape headland Massachusetts, NE USA 42°39′N 70°35′W
180 I10 Annean, Lake ⊚ Western Australia
Anneciacum see Annecy
103 T11 Annecy anc. Anneciacum. Haute-Savoie, E France 45°53′N 06°09′E
103 T11 Annecy, Lac d' ⊚ E France
103 T10 Annemasse Haute-Savoie, E France 46°10′N 06°13′E
39 Z14 Annette Island island Alexander Archipelago, Alaska, USA
An Nhon see Binh Đinh
An Nīl al Abyaḍ see White Nile
An Nīl al Azraq see Blue Nile
23 Q3 Anniston Alabama, S USA 33°39′N 85°49′W
79 A19 Annobón island W Equatorial Guinea
103 R12 Annonay Ardèche, E France 45°15′N 04°40′E
44 K12 Annotto Bay C Jamaica 18°16′N 76°47′W
141 R5 An Nuʿayrīyah var. Nariya. Ash Sharqīyah, NE Saudi Arabia 27°30′N 48°30′E
182 M9 Annuello Victoria, SE Australia 34°54′S 142°50′E
139 Q10 An Nukhayb Al Anbār, S Iraq 32°02′N 42°15′E
139 U9 An Nuʿmānīyah Wāsiṭ, E Iraq 32°34′N 45°23′E
Áno Arkhánai see Archánes
115 J25 Anógeia var. Anogia, Anóyia. Kríti, Greece, E Mediterranean Sea 35°17′N 24°53′E
Anogia see Anógeia
29 V8 Anoka Minnesota, N USA 45°15′N 93°26′W
An Ómaigh see Omagh
172 I1 Anorontany, Tanjona Fr. Cap Saint-Sébastien. headland N Madagascar
172 J5 Anosibe An'Ala Toamasina, E Madagascar 19°24′S 48°11′E
Anóyia see Anógeia
An Pointe see Warrenpoint
161 P9 Anqing Anhui, E China 30°32′N 116°59′E
161 Q5 Anqiu Shandong, E China 36°25′N 119°10′E
An Ráth see Ráth Luirc
An Ribhéar see Kenmare River
An Ros see Rush
99 K19 Ans Liège, E Belgium 50°39′N 05°32′E
Anṣāb see Niṣāb
171 W12 Ansas Papua, E Indonesia 01°44′S 135°52′E
101 J20 Ansbach Bayern, SE Germany 49°18′N 10°36′E
An Sciobairín see Skibbereen
An Scoil see Skull
An Seancheann see Old Head of Kinsale
45 Y5 Anse-Bertrand Grande Terre, N Guadeloupe 16°28′N 61°31′W
172 H17 Anse Boileau Mahé, NE Seychelles 04°43′S 55°29′E
45 S11 Anse La Raye NW Saint Lucia 13°57′N 61°01′W
54 D9 Anserma Caldas, W Colombia 05°15′N 75°47′W
109 T4 Ansfelden Oberösterreich, N Austria 48°12′N 14°17′E
163 U12 Anshan Liaoning, NE China 41°06′N 122°55′E
160 J12 Anshun Guizhou, S China 26°15′N 105°58′E
61 F17 Ansina Tacuarembó, C Uruguay 31°58′S 55°28′W
29 O15 Ansley Nebraska, C USA 41°16′N 99°22′W
25 P6 Anson Texas, SW USA 32°45′N 99°55′W
77 Q10 Ansongo Gao, E Mali 15°39′N 00°33′E
An Srath Bán see Strabane
21 R5 Ansted West Virginia, NE USA 38°08′N 81°06′W
171 Y13 Ansudu Papua, E Indonesia 02°09′S 139°19′E
57 G15 Anta Cusco, S Peru 13°30′S 72°08′W
57 G16 Antabamba Apurímac, C Peru 14°23′S 72°54′W
Antafalva see Kovačica
136 L17 Antakya anc. Antioch, Antiochia. Hatay, S Turkey 36°12′N 36°10′E
172 K3 Antalaha Antsirañana, NE Madagascar 14°53′S 50°16′E
136 F17 Antalya prev. Adalia; anc. Attaleia, Bibl. Attalia. Antalya, SW Turkey 36°53′N 30°42′E
136 F17 Antalya ⬖ province SW Turkey
136 F16 Antalya ✕ Antalya, SW Turkey 36°53′N 30°45′E
121 U10 Antalya Basin undersea feature E Mediterranean Sea
Antalya, Gulf of see Antalya Körfezi
136 F16 Antalya Körfezi var. Gulf of Adalia, Eng. Gulf of Antalya. gulf SW Turkey
172 J5 Antanambao Manampotsy Toamasina, E Madagascar 19°30′S 48°36′E
172 I5 Antananarivo prev. Tananarive. ● (Madagascar) Antananarivo, C Madagascar 18°52′S 47°30′E
172 I4 Antananarivo ⬖ province C Madagascar
172 J5 Antananarivo ✕ Antananarivo, C Madagascar 18°52′S 47°30′E
An tAonach see Nenagh
194-195 Antarctica continent
194 I5 Antarctic Peninsula peninsula Antarctica
174 L13 Antarctic Plate tectonic feature Africa/Antarctica/Australia/South America Atlantic Ocean/Indian Ocean/Pacific Ocean
61 J15 Antas, Rio das ≈ S Brazil
189 U16 Ant Atoll atoll Caroline Islands, E Micronesia
An Teampall Mór see Templemore
Antep see Gaziantep
104 M15 Antequera anc. Anticaria, Antiquaria. Andalucía, S Spain 37°01′N 04°34′W
Antequera see Oaxaca
37 S5 Antero Reservoir ⊠ Colorado, C USA
26 M7 Anthony Kansas, C USA 37°10′N 98°02′W
37 R16 Anthony New Mexico, SW USA 32°00′N 106°36′W

◆ Country
● Country Capital
◇ Dependent Territory
○ Dependent Territory Capital
⬖ Administrative Regions
✕ International Airport
▲ Mountain
▲▲ Mountain Range
Volcano
≈ River
⊚ Lake
⊠ Reservoir

ANTHONY, LAKE – ARÉVALO

182 D5 **Anthony, Lake** salt lake South Australia
74 E8 **Anti-Atlas** ▲▲ SW Morocco
103 U15 **Antibes** anc. Antipolis. Alpes-Maritimes, SE France 43°35′N 07°07′E
103 U15 **Antibes, Cap d'** headland SE France 43°33′N 07°08′E
Anticaria see Antequera
13 Q11 **Anticosti, Île d'** Eng. Anticosti Island. island Québec, E Canada
Anticosti Island see Anticosti, Île d'
102 K3 **Antifer, Cap d'** headland N France 49°43′N 00°10′E
30 L6 **Antigo** Wisconsin, N USA 45°10′N 89°10′W
13 Q15 **Antigonish** Nova Scotia, SE Canada 45°39′N 62°00′W
64 P11 **Antigua** Fuerteventura, Islas Canarias, NE Atlantic Ocean
45 X10 **Antigua** island S Antigua and Barbuda, Leeward Islands
Antigua see Antigua Guatemala
45 W9 **Antigua and Barbuda** ◆ commonwealth republic E West Indies
42 C6 **Antigua Guatemala** var. Antigua. Sacatepéquez, SW Guatemala 14°33′N 90°42′W
41 P11 **Antiguo Morelos** var. Antiguo-Morelos. Tamaulipas, C Mexico 22°35′N 99°08′W
115 F19 **Antíkyras, Kólpos** gulf C Greece
115 G24 **Antikýthira** var. Andikíthira. island S Greece
138 I7 **Anti-Lebanon** var. Jebel esh Sharqi, Ar. Al Jabal ash Sharqī, Fr. Anti-Liban. ▲▲ Lebanon/Syria
Anti-Liban see Anti-Lebanon
115 M22 **Antimácheia** Kos, Dodekánisa, Greece 47°19′N 07°54′E
115 I22 **Antímilos** island Kykládes, Greece, Aegean Sea
36 L6 **Antimony** Utah, W USA 38°07′N 112°00′W
An tInbhear Mór see Arklow
30 M10 **Antioch** Illinois, N USA 42°28′N 88°06′W
Antioch see Antakya
102 I10 **Antioche, Pertuis d'** inlet W France
Antiochia see Antakya
54 D8 **Antioquia** Antioquia, C Colombia 06°36′N 75°53′W
54 E8 **Antioquia** off. Departamento de Antioquia. ◈ province C Colombia
Antioquia, Departamento de see Antioquia
115 J21 **Antíparos** var. Andipáros. island Kykládes, Greece, Aegean Sea
115 B17 **Antípaxoi** var. Andipaxi. island Iónia Nísiá, Greece, C Mediterranean Sea
122 J8 **Antipayuta** Yamalo-Nenetskiy Avtonomnyy Okrug, N Russian Federation 69°08′N 76°43′E
192 L12 **Antipodes Islands** island group S New Zealand
Antipolis see Antibes
115 J18 **Antípsara** var. Andípsara. island E Greece
Antiquaria see Antequera
15 N10 **Antique, Lac** ◎ Québec, SE Canada
115 E18 **Antírrio** var. Andírrion. Dytikí Ellás, C Greece 38°20′N 21°46′E
115 K16 **Ántissa** var. Ándissa. Lésvos, E Greece 39°15′N 26°00′E
An tIúr see Newry
Antivari see Bar
56 C6 **Antizana** ▲ N Ecuador 0°29′S 78°08′W
27 Q13 **Antlers** Oklahoma, C USA 34°15′N 95°38′W
93 J14 **Antnäs** Norrbotten, N Sweden 65°32′N 21°53′E
Antō see Andong
62 G5 **Antofagasta** Antofagasta, N Chile 23°40′S 70°23′W
62 G6 **Antofagasta** off. Región de Antofagasta. ◈ region N Chile
Antofagasta, Región de see Antofagasta
62 I7 **Antofalla, Salar de** salt lake NW Argentina
99 D20 **Antoing** Hainaut, SW Belgium 50°34′N 03°26′E
43 S16 **Antón** Coclé, C Panama 08°23′N 80°15′W
24 M5 **Anton** Texas, SW USA 33°48′N 102°09′W
37 T11 **Anton Chico** New Mexico, SW USA 35°12′N 105°09′W
60 K12 **Antonina** Paraná, S Brazil 25°28′S 48°43′W
188 C16 **Antonio B. Won Pat International** ✈ (Agana) C Guam 13°28′N 144°48′E
103 O5 **Antony** Hauts-de-Seine, N France 48°45′N 02°17′E
Antratsit see Antratsyt
117 Y8 **Antratsyt** Rus. Antratsit. Luhans'ka Oblast', E Ukraine 48°07′N 39°05′E
97 G15 **Antrim** Ir. Aontroim. NE Northern Ireland, United Kingdom 54°43′N 06°13′W
97 G14 **Antrim** Ir. Aontroim. cultural region NE Northern Ireland, United Kingdom
97 G14 **Antrim Mountains** ▲▲ NE Northern Ireland, United Kingdom
172 H5 **Antsalova** Mahajanga, W Madagascar 18°40′S 44°37′E
Antserana see Antsirañana
An tSionainn see Shannon
172 J2 **Antsirañana** var. Antserana; prev. Antsirane, Diégo-Suarez. Antsirañana, N Madagascar 12°19′S 49°17′E
172 J2 **Antsirañana** ◈ province N Madagascar
Antsirane see Antsirañana
An tSiúir see Suir
118 I7 **Antsla** Ger. Anzen. Võrumaa, SE Estonia 57°52′N 26°33′E
An tSláine see Slaney
172 J3 **Antsohihy** Mahajanga, NW Madagascar 14°50′S 47°58′E
63 G14 **Antuco, Volcán** ⛰ C Chile 37°29′S 71°25′W
169 W10 **Antu, Gunung** ▲ Borneo, N Indonesia 0°57′N 118°51′E
An Tullach see Tullow
An-tung see Dandong
Antunnacum see Andernach
Antwerp see Antwerpen
99 G16 **Antwerpen** Eng. Antwerp, Fr. Anvers. Antwerpen, N Belgium 51°13′N 04°25′E
99 H16 **Antwerpen** Eng. Antwerp. ◈ province N Belgium
An Uaimh see Navan
154 N12 **Anugul** var. Angul. Orissa, E India 20°51′N 84°59′E
152 F9 **Anūpgarh** Rājasthān, NW India 29°10′N 73°14′E
154 K10 **Anūppur** Madhya Pradesh, C India 23°05′N 81°45′E
155 K24 **Anuradhapura** North Central Province, C Sri Lanka 08°20′N 80°25′E
Anvers see Antwerpen
194 G4 **Anvers Island** island Antarctica
39 N11 **Anvik** Alaska, USA 62°39′N 160°12′W
39 N10 **Anvik River** ≈ Alaska, USA
38 F17 **Anvil Peak** ▲ Semisopochnoi Island, Alaska, USA 51°59′N 179°36′E
159 P7 **Anxi** var. Yuanquan. Gansu, N China 40°32′N 95°50′E
182 F8 **Anxious Bay** bay South Australia
161 O5 **Anyang** Henan, C China 36°11′N 114°18′E
159 S11 **A'nyêmaqên Shan** ▲▲ C China
118 H12 **Anykščiai** Utena, E Lithuania 55°30′N 25°34′E
161 P13 **Anyuan** var. Xinshan. Jiangxi, S China 25°10′N 115°25′E
123 T7 **Anyuysk** Chukotskiy Avtonomnyy Okrug, NE Russian Federation 68°22′N 161°33′E
123 T7 **Anyuyskiy Khrebet** ▲▲ NE Russian Federation
54 D8 **Anza** Antioquia, C Colombia 06°18′N 75°54′W
Anzen see Antsla
107 I16 **Anzio** Lazio, C Italy 41°28′N 12°38′E
55 O6 **Anzoátegui** off. Estado Anzoátegui. ◈ state NE Venezuela
Anzoátegui, Estado see Anzoátegui
147 P12 **Anzob** W Tajikistan 39°24′N 68°55′E
Anzyô see Anjō
Aoba see Ambae
165 X13 **Aoga-shima** island Izu-shotō, SE Japan
Aohan Qi see Xinhui
Aoiz see Agoiz
167 O11 **Ao Krung Thep** var. Krung Thep Mahanakhon, Eng. Bangkok. ● (Thailand) Bangkok, C Thailand 13°44′N 100°30′E
186 M9 **Aola** var. Tenaghau. Guadalcanal, C Solomon Islands 09°32′S 160°28′E
166 M15 **Ao Luk Nua** Krabi, SW Thailand 08°21′N 98°43′E
Aomen see Macao
172 N8 **Aomori** Aomori, Honshū, C Japan 40°50′N 140°43′E
172 N8 **Aomori** off. Aomori-ken. ◈ prefecture Honshū, C Japan
Aomori-ken see Aomori
Aontroim see Antrim
115 C15 **Aóos** var. Vijosa, Vijosë, Alb. Lumi i Vjosës. ≈ Albania/Greece see also Vjosës, Lumi i
Aóos see Vjosës, Lumi i
191 Q7 **Aorai, Mont** ⛰ Tahiti, W French Polynesia 17°36′S 149°29′W
185 E19 **Aoraki** prev. Aorangi, Mount Cook. ▲ South Island, New Zealand 43°38′S 170°05′E
167 R13 **Aôral, Phnum** prev. Phnom Aural. ▲ W Cambodia 12°01′N 104°10′E
Aorangi see Aoraki
185 L15 **Aorangi Mountains** ▲▲ North Island, New Zealand
184 H13 **Aorere** ≈ South Island, New Zealand
106 A7 **Aosta** anc. Augusta Praetoria. Valle d'Aosta, NW Italy 45°43′N 07°20′E
77 O11 **Aougoundou, Lac** ◎ S Mali
76 K9 **Aoukâr** var. Aouker. plateau C Mauritania
78 J13 **Aouk, Bahr** ≈ Central African Republic/Chad
Aouker see Aoukâr
74 B11 **Aousard** SE Western Sahara 22°42′N 14°22′W
164 H12 **Aoya** Tottori, Honshū, SW Japan 35°31′N 134°01′E
Aoyang see Shanggao
78 H5 **Aozou** Borkou-Ennedi-Tibesti, N Chad 22°01′N 17°11′E
26 M11 **Apache** Oklahoma, C USA 34°57′N 98°21′W
36 L14 **Apache Junction** Arizona, SW USA 33°25′N 111°33′W
24 J9 **Apache Mountains** ▲▲ Texas, SW USA
36 M16 **Apache Peak** ▲ Arizona, SW USA 31°50′N 110°25′W
116 H10 **Apahida** Cluj, NW Romania 46°49′N 23°45′E
23 T9 **Apalachee Bay** bay Florida, SE USA
23 T3 **Apalachee River** ≈ Georgia, SE USA
23 S10 **Apalachicola** Florida, SE USA 29°43′N 84°58′W
23 S10 **Apalachicola Bay** bay Florida, SE USA
23 R9 **Apalachicola River** ≈ Florida, SE USA
Apam see Apan
Apamama see Abemama
41 P14 **Apan** var. Apam. Hidalgo, C Mexico 19°48′N 98°25′W
42 J8 **Apanás, Lago de** ◎ NW Nicaragua
54 H14 **Apaporis, Río** ≈ Brazil/Colombia
185 C23 **Aparima** ≈ South Island, New Zealand
171 O1 **Aparri** Luzon, N Philippines 18°16′N 121°42′E
112 J9 **Apatin** Vojvodina, NW Serbia 45°40′N 19°01′E
124 J4 **Apatity** Murmanskaya Oblast', NW Russian Federation 67°34′N 33°26′E
55 X9 **Apatou** NW French Guiana 05°10′N 54°22′W
40 M14 **Apatzingán** var. Apatzingán de la Constitución. Michoacán, SW Mexico 19°05′N 102°20′W
Apatzingán de la Constitución see Apatzingán
171 X12 **Apauwar** Papua, E Indonesia 01°36′S 138°10′E
Apaxtla see Apaxtla de Castrejón
41 O15 **Apaxtla de Castrejón** var. Apaxtla. Guerrero, S Mexico 18°06′N 99°55′W
118 J7 **Ape** Alūksne, NE Latvia 57°32′N 26°42′E
98 L11 **Apeldoorn** Gelderland, E Netherlands 52°13′N 05°57′E
Apennines see Appennino
Apenrade see Aabenraa
57 L17 **Apere, Río** ≈ C Bolivia
55 W11 **Apetina** Sipaliwini, SE Suriname 03°30′N 55°03′W
21 U9 **Apex** North Carolina, SE USA 35°43′N 78°51′W
79 M16 **Api** Orientale, N Dem. Rep. Congo 03°40′N 25°26′E
152 M9 **Api** ▲ NW Nepal 30°07′N 80°57′E
192 H16 **Āpia** ● (Samoa) Upolu, SE Samoa 13°50′S 171°47′W
Apia see Abaiang
60 K11 **Apiaí** São Paulo, S Brazil 24°29′S 48°51′W
170 M16 **Api, Gunung** ▲ Pulau Sangeang, S Indonesia 08°09′S 119°03′E
187 N9 **Apio** Maramasike Island, N Solomon Islands 09°36′S 161°25′E
41 O15 **Apipilulco** Guerrero, S Mexico 18°11′N 99°40′W
41 P14 **Apizaco** Tlaxcala, S Mexico 19°26′N 98°09′W
137 Q8 **Ap'khazet'i** var. Abkhazia. ◈ autonomous republic NW Georgia
104 I4 **A Pobla de Trives** Cast. Puebla de Trives. Galicia, NW Spain 42°21′N 07°16′W
55 U9 **Apoera** Sipaliwini, NW Suriname 05°12′N 57°13′W
115 O23 **Apolakkiá** Ródos, Dodekánisa, Greece, Aegean Sea 36°02′N 27°48′E
101 L16 **Apolda** Thüringen, C Germany 51°02′N 11°31′E
192 H16 **Apolima Strait** strait C Pacific Ocean
182 M13 **Apollo Bay** Victoria, SE Australia 38°40′S 143°44′E
Apollonia see Sozopol
57 J16 **Apolo** La Paz, W Bolivia 14°48′S 68°31′W
57 J16 **Apolobamba, Cordillera** ▲▲ Bolivia/Peru
171 Q8 **Apo, Mount** ⛰ Mindanao, S Philippines 06°54′N 125°16′E
23 W11 **Apopka** Florida, SE USA 28°40′N 81°30′W
23 W11 **Apopka, Lake** ◎ Florida, SE USA
59 J19 **Aporé, Rio** ≈ SW Brazil
30 K2 **Apostle Islands** island group Wisconsin, N USA
Apostolas Andreas, Cape see Zafer Burnu
61 F14 **Apóstoles** Misiones, NE Argentina 27°54′S 55°45′W
Apostólou Andréa, Akrotíri see Zafer Burnu
117 S9 **Apostolove** Rus. Apostolovo. Dnipropetrovs'ka Oblast', E Ukraine 47°40′N 33°45′E
Apostolovo see Apostolove
17 S10 **Appalachian Mountains** ▲▲ E USA
95 K14 **Äppelbo** Dalarna, C Sweden 60°30′N 14°00′E
98 N7 **Appelscha** Fris. Appelskea. Friesland, N Netherlands 52°57′N 06°19′E
Appelskea see Appelscha
106 G11 **Appennino** Eng. Apennines. ▲▲ Italy/San Marino
107 L17 **Appennino Campano** ▲▲ C Italy
108 I7 **Appenzell** Appenzell, NW Switzerland 47°20′N 09°25′E
108 H7 **Appenzell** ◈ canton NE Switzerland
55 V12 **Appikalo** Sipaliwini, S Suriname 02°07′N 56°16′W
98 O5 **Appingedam** Groningen, NE Netherlands 53°18′N 06°52′E
25 X8 **Appleby** Texas, SW USA 31°43′N 94°36′W
97 L15 **Appleby-in-Westmorland** Cumbria, NW England, United Kingdom 54°35′N 02°26′W
30 K10 **Apple River** ≈ Illinois, N USA
30 I5 **Apple River** ≈ Wisconsin, N USA
25 W9 **Apple Springs** Texas, SW USA 31°13′N 94°57′W
29 S8 **Appleton** Minnesota, N USA 45°12′N 96°01′W
30 M7 **Appleton** Wisconsin, N USA 44°17′N 88°24′W
27 S5 **Appleton City** Missouri, C USA 38°11′N 94°01′W
35 U14 **Apple Valley** California, W USA 34°30′N 117°11′W
29 V9 **Apple Valley** Minnesota, N USA 44°43′N 93°13′W
21 U6 **Appomattox** Virginia, NE USA 37°21′N 78°51′W
188 B16 **Apra Harbor** harbor W Guam
188 B16 **Apra Heights** W Guam
106 F6 **Aprica, Passo dell'** pass N Italy
107 M15 **Apricena** anc. Hadria Picena. Puglia, SE Italy 41°47′N 15°27′E
114 I9 **Apriltsi** Lovech, N Bulgaria 42°50′N 24°54′E
126 L14 **Apsheronsk** Krasnodarskiy Kray, SW Russian Federation 44°27′N 39°45′E
Apsheronskiy Poluostrov see Abşeron Yarımadası
103 S15 **Apt** anc. Apta Julia. Vaucluse, SE France 43°54′N 05°24′E
Apta Julia see Apt
38 H12 **'Apua Point** var. Apua Point. headland Hawai'i, USA, C Pacific Ocean 19°15′N 155°13′W
60 I10 **Apucarana** Paraná, S Brazil 23°34′S 51°28′W
Apulia see Puglia
54 K8 **Apure** off. Estado Apure. ◈ state C Venezuela
Apure, Estado see Apure
54 J7 **Apure, Río** ≈ W Venezuela
57 F16 **Apurímac** off. Departamento de Apurímac. ◈ department C Peru
Apurímac, Departamento de see Apurímac
57 F15 **Apurímac, Río** ≈ S Peru
116 G10 **Apuseni, Munții** ▲▲ W Romania
Aqaba/'Aqaba see Al 'Aqabah
138 F15 **Aqaba, Gulf of** var. Gulf of Elat, Ar. Khalīj al 'Aqabah; anc. Sinus Aelaniticus. gulf NE Red Sea
139 R7 **'Aqabah** Al Anbār, C Iraq 33°33′N 42°55′E
'Aqabah, Khalīj al see Aqaba, Gulf of
149 O2 **Āqchah** var. Āqcheh. Jowzjān, N Afghanistan 37°N 66°07′E
Āqcheh see Āqchah
Aqkengse see Akkense
Aqköl see Akkol'
Aqmola see Astana
Aqmola Oblysy see Akmola
158 L10 **Aqqikkol Hu** ◎ NW China
Aqqū see Akku
Aqqystaū see Akkystau
'Aqrah see Ākrē
Aqsay see Aksay
Aqshataū see Akchatau
Aqsū see Aksu
Aqsūat see Aksuat
Aqtas see Aktas
Aqtaū see Aktau
Aqtöbe see Aktobe
Aqtöbe Oblysy see Aktyubinsk
Aqtoghay see Aktogay
Aquae Augustae see Dax
Aquae Calidae see Bath
Aquae Flaviae see Chaves
Aquae Grani see Aachen
Aquae Panoniae see Baden
Aquae Sextiae see Aix-en-Provence
Aquae Solis see Bath
Aquae Tarbelicae see Dax
36 J11 **Aquarius Mountains** ▲▲ Arizona, SW USA
62 O5 **Aquidabán, Río** ≈ E Paraguay
59 H20 **Aquidauana** Mato Grosso do Sul, S Brazil 20°27′S 55°45′W
40 L15 **Aquila** Michoacán, S Mexico 18°36′N 103°32′W
Aquila/Aquila degli Abruzzi see L'Aquila
25 T8 **Aquilla** Texas, SW USA 31°51′N 97°13′W
44 L9 **Aquin** S Haiti 18°16′N 73°24′W
Aquisgranum see Aachen
102 J13 **Aquitaine** ◈ region SW France
Aqzhar see Akzhar
153 P13 **Āra** prev. Arrah. Bihār, N India 25°34′N 84°40′E
105 S4 **Ara** ≈ NE Spain
23 P2 **Arab** Alabama, S USA 34°19′N 86°30′W
Araba see Álava
138 G12 **'Arabah, Wādī al** Heb. Ha'Arava. dry watercourse Israel/Jordan
117 U12 **Arabats'ka Strilka, Kosa** spit S Ukraine
117 U12 **Arabats'ka Zatoka** gulf S Ukraine
'Arab, Baḩr al see Arab, Bahr el
80 C12 **Arab, Bahr el** var. Baḩr al 'Arab. ≈ S Sudan
56 E7 **Arabela, Río** ≈ N Peru
173 O4 **Arabian Basin** undersea feature N Arabian Sea 11°30′N 65°00′E
Arabian Desert see Sahara el Sharqîya
141 N9 **Arabian Peninsula** peninsula SW Asia
85 P15 **Arabian Plate** tectonic feature Africa/Asia/Europe
141 W14 **Arabian Sea** sea NW Indian Ocean
Arabicus, Sinus see Red Sea
'Arabī, Khalīj al see Gulf, The
Arabistan see Khūzestān
'Arabīyah as Su'ūdīyah, Al Mamlakah al see Saudi Arabia
'Arabīyah Jumhūrīyah, Miṣr al see Egypt
138 I9 **'Arab, Jabal al** ▲▲ S Syria
Arab Republic of Egypt see Egypt
139 Y12 **'Arab, Shaṭṭ al** Eng. Shatt al Arab, Per. Arvand Rūd. ≈ Iran/Iraq
136 I11 **Araç** Kastamonu, N Turkey 41°14′N 33°20′E
59 P16 **Aracaju** state capital Sergipe, E Brazil 10°45′S 37°07′W
54 F5 **Aracataca** Magdalena, N Colombia 10°38′N 74°09′W
58 P13 **Aracati** Ceará, E Brazil 04°32′S 37°45′W
60 J8 **Araçatuba** São Paulo, S Brazil 21°12′S 50°24′W
136 I11 **Araç Çayı** ≈ N Turkey
104 J13 **Aracena** Andalucía, S Spain 37°54′N 06°33′W
115 F20 **Arachnaío** ▲▲ S Greece
115 D16 **Árachthos** var. Arta, prev. Árakhthos; anc. Arachthus. ≈ W Greece
Arachthus see Árachthos
59 N19 **Araçuai** Minas Gerais, SE Brazil 16°52′S 42°03′W
138 F11 **Arad** Southern, S Israel 31°16′N 35°09′E
116 F11 **Arad** Arad, W Romania 46°12′N 21°20′E
116 F11 **Arad** ◈ county W Romania
78 J9 **Arada** Biltine, NE Chad 15°00′N 20°38′E
143 P18 **'Arādah** Abū Ẓaby, S United Arab Emirates 22°57′N 53°24′E
Aradhippou see Aradíppou
121 Q3 **Aradíppou** var. Aradhippou. SE Cyprus 34°57′N 33°37′E
174 K6 **Arafura Sea** Ind. Laut Arafuru. sea W Pacific Ocean
174 L6 **Arafura Shelf** undersea feature C Arafura Sea
Arafuru, Laut see Arafura Sea
59 J18 **Aragarças** Goiás, C Brazil 15°55′S 52°12′W
Aragats, Gora see Aragats Lerr
137 T12 **Aragats Lerr** Rus. Gora Aragats. ▲ W Armenia 40°31′N 44°06′E
32 E14 **Arago, Cape** headland Oregon, NW USA 43°17′N 124°25′W
105 R6 **Aragón** autonomous community E Spain
105 Q4 **Aragón** ≈ NE Spain
107 I24 **Aragona** Sicilia, Italy, C Mediterranean Sea 37°25′N 13°37′E
105 Q7 **Aragoncillo** ▲ C Spain 40°59′N 02°01′W
54 L5 **Aragua** off. Estado Aragua. ◈ state N Venezuela
55 N6 **Aragua de Barcelona** Anzoátegui, NE Venezuela 09°30′N 64°51′W
55 O5 **Aragua de Maturín** Monagas, NE Venezuela 09°58′N 63°30′W
Aragua, Estado see Aragua
59 K15 **Araguaia, Río** var. Araguaya. ≈ C Brazil
59 K19 **Araguari** Minas Gerais, SE Brazil 18°38′S 48°13′W
58 J11 **Araguari, Rio** ≈ SW Brazil
Araguaya see Araguaia, Río
104 K14 **Arahal** Andalucía, S Spain 37°15′N 05°33′W
165 N11 **Arai** Niigata, Honshū, C Japan 37°02′N 138°17′E
Árainn see Inishmore
Árainn Mhór see Aran Island
Ara Jovis see Aranjuez
74 J11 **Arak** C Algeria 25°17′N 03°45′E
171 Y15 **Arak** Papua, E Indonesia 07°14′S 139°40′E
142 M7 **Arāk** prev. Sultānābād. Markazī, W Iran 34°07′N 49°39′E
188 D10 **Arakabesan** island Palau Islands, N Palau
55 S7 **Arakaka** NW Guyana 07°37′N 59°58′W
166 K6 **Arakan State** var. Rakhine State. ◈ state W Myanmar (Burma)
166 K5 **Arakan Yoma** ▲▲ W Myanmar (Burma)
165 O10 **Arakawa** Niigata, Honshū, C Japan 38°06′N 139°25′E
Árakhthos see Árachthos
Araks/Arak's see Aras
158 H7 **Aral** Xinjiang Uygur Zizhiqu, NW China 40°40′N 81°19′E
Aral see Aralsk, Kazakhstan
Aral see Vose', Tajikistan
Aral-Bukhorskiy Kanal see Amu-Buxoro Kanali
137 T12 **Aralik** İgdır, E Turkey 39°54′N 44°28′E
146 H5 **Aral Sea** Kaz. Aral Tengizi, Rus. Aral'skoye More, Uzb. Orol Dengizi. inland sea Kazakhstan/Uzbekistan
144 L13 **Aral'sk** Kaz. Aral. Kzylorda, SW Kazakhstan 46°48′N 61°40′E
Aral'skoye More/Aral Tengizi see Aral Sea
41 O10 **Aramberri** Nuevo León, NE Mexico 24°05′N 99°52′W
186 B8 **Aramia** ≈ SW Papua New Guinea
143 N6 **Ārān** var. Golārā. Eşfahān, C Iran 34°03′N 51°30′E
105 N5 **Aranda de Duero** Castilla-León, N Spain 41°40′N 03°41′W
112 M12 **Aranđelovac** prev. Arandjelovac. Serbia, C Serbia 44°18′N 20°32′E
Arandjelovac see Aranđelovac
97 J19 **Aran Fawddwy** ▲ NW Wales, United Kingdom 52°48′N 03°42′W
97 C14 **Aran Island** Ir. Árainn Mhór. island NW Ireland
97 A18 **Aran Islands** island group W Ireland
105 N9 **Aranjuez** anc. Ara Jovis. Madrid, C Spain 40°02′N 03°37′W
83 E20 **Aranos** Hardap, SE Namibia 24°10′S 19°08′E
25 U14 **Aransas Bay** inlet Texas, SW USA
25 T14 **Aransas Pass** Texas, SW USA 27°54′N 97°09′W
191 O3 **Aranuka** prev. Nanouki. atoll Tungaru, W Kiribati
167 Q11 **Aranyaprathet** Prachin Buri, S Thailand 13°42′N 102°32′E
Aranyosasztal see Zlatý Stôl
Aranyosgyéres see Câmpia Turzii
Aranyosmarót see Zlaté Moravce
164 C14 **Arao** Kumamoto, Kyūshū, SW Japan 32°58′N 130°26′E
77 O8 **Araouane** Tombouctou, N Mali 18°53′N 03°31′W
26 L10 **Arapaho** Oklahoma, C USA 35°34′N 98°57′W
29 N16 **Arapahoe** Nebraska, C USA 40°18′N 99°54′W
57 I16 **Arapa, Laguna** ◎ SE Peru
185 K14 **Arapawa Island** island C New Zealand
61 E17 **Arapey Grande, Río** ≈ N Uruguay
59 P16 **Arapiraca** Alagoas, E Brazil 09°45′S 36°40′W
140 M3 **'Ar'ar** Al Ḩudūd ash Shamālīyah, NW Saudi Arabia 31°N 41°E
54 G15 **Araracuara** Caquetá, S Colombia 0°36′S 72°24′W
61 K15 **Araranguá** Santa Catarina, S Brazil 28°56′S 49°30′W
60 L8 **Araraquara** São Paulo, S Brazil 21°46′S 48°08′W
59 O13 **Araras** Ceará, E Brazil 04°08′S 40°30′W
58 I14 **Araras** Pará, N Brazil 06°04′S 54°34′W
60 L9 **Araras** São Paulo, S Brazil 22°21′S 47°21′W
60 H11 **Araras, Serra das** ▲▲ S Brazil
137 U12 **Ararat** S Armenia 39°49′N 44°45′E
182 M12 **Ararat** Victoria, SE Australia 37°20′S 143°00′E
Ararat, Mount see Büyükağrı Dağı
140 M3 **'Ar'ar, Wādī** dry watercourse Iraq/Saudi Arabia
129 N7 **Aras** Arm. Arak's, Az. Araz Nehri, Per. Rūd-e Aras, Rus. Araks; prev. Araxes. ≈ SW Asia
Aras de Alpuente see Aras de los Olmos
105 R9 **Aras de los Olmos** prev. Aras de Alpuente. País Valenciano, E Spain 39°55′N 01°09′W
137 S13 **Aras Güneyi Dağları** ▲▲ NE Turkey
Aras, Rūd-e see Aras
191 U9 **Aratika** atoll Îles Tuamotu, C French Polynesia
Aratürük see Yiwu
54 I8 **Arauca** Arauca, NE Colombia 07°03′N 70°47′W
54 I8 **Arauca** off. Intendencia de Arauca. ◈ province NE Colombia
Arauca, Intendencia de see Arauca
63 G15 **Araucanía** off. Regíon de la Araucanía. ◈ region C Chile
Araucanía, Regíon de la see Araucanía
54 L7 **Arauca, Río** ≈ Colombia/Venezuela
63 F14 **Arauco** Bío Bío, C Chile 37°15′S 73°22′W
63 F14 **Arauco, Golfo de** gulf S Chile
54 H8 **Arauquita** Arauca, C Colombia 06°57′N 71°19′W
Arausio see Orange
152 F13 **Arāvali Range** ▲▲ N India
186 J7 **Arawa** Bougainville Island, NE Papua New Guinea 06°15′S 155°35′E
185 C20 **Arawata** ≈ South Island, New Zealand
186 F7 **Arawe Islands** island group E Papua New Guinea
59 L20 **Araxá** Minas Gerais, SE Brazil 19°37′S 46°50′W
Araxes see Aras
55 O5 **Araya** Sucre, N Venezuela 10°34′N 64°15′W
Araz Nehri see Aras
105 R4 **Arba** ≈ N Spain
81 I15 **Ārba Minch'** Southern Nationalities, S Ethiopia 06°02′N 37°34′E
139 U4 **Arbat** As Sulaymānīyah, NE Iraq 35°26′N 45°34′E
107 D19 **Arbatax** Sardegna, Italy, C Mediterranean Sea 39°57′N 09°42′E
Arbe see Rab
Arbela see Arbīl
139 S3 **Arbīl** ◈ governorate N Iraq
139 S3 **Arbīl** var. Erbil, Irbīl, Kurd. Hawlēr; anc. Arbela. Arbīl, N Iraq 36°12′N 44°01′E
95 M16 **Arboga** Västmanland, C Sweden 59°24′N 15°50′E
95 M16 **Arbogaån** ≈ C Sweden
103 S9 **Arbois** Jura, E France 46°54′N 05°45′E
54 D6 **Arboletes** Antioquia, NW Colombia 08°52′N 76°25′W
11 X15 **Arborg** Manitoba, S Canada 50°52′N 97°20′W
94 N12 **Arbrå** Gävleborg, C Sweden 61°27′N 16°21′E
96 K10 **Arbroath** anc. Aberbrothock. E Scotland, United Kingdom 56°34′N 02°35′W
35 N6 **Arbuckle** California, W USA 39°00′N 122°05′W
27 N12 **Arbuckle Mountains** ▲▲ Oklahoma, C USA
162 I5 **Arbulag** var. Mandal. Hövsgöl, N Mongolia 49°55′N 99°21′E
Arbuzinka see Arbuzynka
117 Q8 **Arbuzynka** Rus. Arbuzinka. Mykolayivs'ka Oblast', S Ukraine 47°54′N 31°19′E
103 U12 **Arc** ≈ E France
102 J13 **Arcachon** Gironde, SW France 44°40′N 01°11′W
102 J13 **Arcachon, Bassin d'** inlet SW France
18 E10 **Arcade** New York, NE USA 42°32′N 78°19′W
23 W14 **Arcadia** Florida, SE USA 27°13′N 81°51′W
22 H5 **Arcadia** Louisiana, S USA 32°33′N 92°55′W
30 J7 **Arcadia** Wisconsin, N USA 44°15′N 91°30′W
Arcae Remorum see Châlons-en-Champagne
44 L9 **Arcahaie** C Haiti 18°46′N 72°32′W
34 K3 **Arcata** California, W USA 40°51′N 124°06′W
35 U6 **Arc Dome** ▲ Nevada, W USA 38°52′N 117°20′W
107 J16 **Arce** Lazio, C Italy 41°35′N 13°34′E
41 O15 **Arcelia** Guerrero, S Mexico 18°20′N 100°16′W
99 M15 **Arcen** Limburg, SE Netherlands 51°28′N 06°10′E
115 J25 **Archánes** var. Áno Arkhánai, Epáno Archánes; prev. Epáno Arkhánai. Kríti, Greece, E Mediterranean Sea 35°12′N 25°10′E
Archangel see Arkhangel'sk
Archangel Bay see Chëshskaya Guba
115 O23 **Archángelos** var. Arhangelos, Arkhángelos. Ródos, Dodekánisa, Greece, Aegean Sea 36°13′N 28°07′E
114 F7 **Archar** ≈ NW Bulgaria
31 R11 **Archbold** Ohio, N USA 41°31′N 84°18′W
105 R12 **Archena** Murcia, SE Spain 38°07′N 01°17′W
25 R5 **Archer City** Texas, SW USA 33°36′N 98°37′W
104 M14 **Archidona** Andalucía, S Spain 37°06′N 04°23′W
106 G13 **Arcidosso** Toscana, C Italy 42°52′N 11°30′E
103 Q5 **Arcis-sur-Aube** Aube, N France 48°32′N 04°09′E
182 F3 **Arckaringa Creek** seasonal river South Australia
106 G7 **Arco** Trentino-Alto Adige, N Italy 45°53′N 10°52′E
33 Q14 **Arco** Idaho, NW USA 43°38′N 113°18′W
30 M14 **Arcola** Illinois, N USA 39°39′N 88°19′W
105 P6 **Arcos de Jalón** Castilla-León, N Spain 41°12′N 02°13′W
104 K15 **Arcos de la Frontera** Andalucía, S Spain 36°45′N 05°49′W
104 G5 **Arcos de Valdevez** Viana do Castelo, N Portugal 41°51′N 08°25′W
59 P15 **Arcoverde** Pernambuco, E Brazil 08°23′S 37°W
102 H5 **Arcovest, Pointe de l'** headland NW France 48°49′N 02°58′W
Arctic Mid Oceanic Ridge see Nansen Cordillera
197 R8 **Arctic Ocean** ocean
8 G7 **Arctic Red River** ≈ Northwest Territories/Yukon Territory, NW Canada
Arctic Red River see Tsiigehtchic
39 S6 **Arctic Village** Alaska, USA 68°07′N 145°32′W
194 H1 **Arctowski** Polish research station South Shetland Islands, Antarctica 61°57′S 58°23′W
114 I12 **Arda** var. Ardhas, Gk. Ardas. ≈ Bulgaria/Greece see also Ardas
142 L2 **Ardabīl** var. Ardebil. Ardabīl, NW Iran 38°15′N 48°18′E
142 L2 **Ardabīl** off. Ostān-e Ardabīl. ◈ province NW Iran
Ardabīl, Ostān-e see Ardabīl
137 R11 **Ardahan** Ardahan, NE Turkey 41°08′N 42°41′E
137 S11 **Ardahan** ◈ province Ardahan, Turkey
143 O10 **Ardakān** Fārs, SE Iran 30°16′N 52°01′E
143 P8 **Ardakān** Yazd, C Iran 32°20′N 53°59′E
94 E12 **Årdalstangen** Sogn Og Fjordane, S Norway 61°14′N 07°45′E
137 R11 **Ardanuç** Artvin, NE Turkey 41°07′N 42°04′E
114 L12 **Ardas** var. Ardhas, Bul. Arda. ≈ Bulgaria/Greece see also Arda
138 I13 **Arḑ aş Şawwān** var. Ardh es Suwwān. plain S Jordan
127 N4 **Ardatov** Nizhegorodskaya Oblast', W Russian Federation 55°14′N 43°06′E
127 P5 **Ardatov** Respublika Mordoviya, W Russian Federation 54°49′N 46°13′E
14 G12 **Ardbeg** Ontario, S Canada 45°38′N 80°05′W
Ardeal see Transylvania
Ardebil see Ardabīl
103 Q13 **Ardèche** ◈ department E France
103 Q13 **Ardèche** ≈ C France
97 F17 **Ardee** Ir. Baile Átha Fhirdhia. Louth, NE Ireland 53°52′N 06°33′W
103 Q3 **Ardennes** ◈ department NE France
99 J23 **Ardennes** physical region Belgium/France
137 Q11 **Ardeşen** Rize, NE Turkey 41°14′N 41°00′E
143 O7 **Ardestān** var. Ardistan. Eşfahān, C Iran 33°29′N 52°17′E
108 J9 **Ardez** Graubünden, SE Switzerland 46°47′N 10°09′E
Ardhas see Arda/Ardas
Ardh es Suwwān see Arḑ aş Şawwān
Ardila see Ardila, Ribeira de
104 I12 **Ardila, Ribeira de** Sp. Ardilla. ≈ Portugal/Spain see also Ardilla
Ardila, Ribeira de see Ardilla
11 T17 **Ardill** Saskatchewan, S Canada 49°56′N 105°49′W
104 I12 **Ardilla** Port. Ribeira de Ardila. ≈ Portugal/Spain see also Ardila, Ribeira de
40 M11 **Ardilla, Cerro la** ▲ C Mexico 22°15′N 102°33′W
114 J12 **Ardino** Kŭrdzhali, S Bulgaria 41°38′N 25°22′E
Ardistan see Ardestān
183 P9 **Ardlethan** New South Wales, SE Australia 34°24′S 146°52′E
Ard Mhacha see Armagh
23 P1 **Ardmore** Alabama, S USA 34°59′N 86°51′W
27 N13 **Ardmore** Oklahoma, C USA 34°11′N 97°08′W
20 J10 **Ardmore** Tennessee, S USA 35°00′N 86°48′W
96 G10 **Ardnamurchan, Point of** headland N Scotland, United Kingdom 56°42′N 06°15′W
Árdni see Arnøya
99 C17 **Ardooie** West-Vlaanderen, W Belgium 50°59′N 03°10′E
182 I9 **Ardrossan** South Australia 34°27′S 137°54′E
116 H9 **Ardusat** Hung. Erdőszáda. Maramureş, N Romania 47°36′N 23°25′E
93 F16 **Åre** Jämtland, C Sweden 63°25′N 13°04′E
79 P16 **Arebi** Orientale, NE Dem. Rep. Congo 02°47′N 29°35′E
45 T5 **Arecibo** C Puerto Rico 18°29′N 66°44′W′N
171 V13 **Aredo** Papua, E Indonesia 02°27′S 133°59′E
59 P14 **Areia Branca** Rio Grande do Norte, E Brazil 04°53′S 37°03′W
119 O14 **Arekhawsk** Rus. Orekhovsk. Vitsyebskaya Voblasts', N Belarus 54°42′N 30°30′E
Arel see Arlon
Arelas/Arelate see Arles
Arenal, Embalse de see Arenal Laguna
42 L12 **Arenal Laguna** var. Embalse de Arenal. ◎ NW Costa Rica
42 L13 **Arenal, Volcán** ⛰ NW Costa Rica 10°21′N 84°42′W
34 K6 **Arena, Point** headland California, W USA 38°57′N 123°44′W
59 H17 **Arenápolis** Mato Grosso, W Brazil 14°25′S 56°52′W
40 G10 **Arena, Punta** headland NW Mexico 23°28′N 109°24′W
104 L8 **Arenas de San Pedro** Castilla-León, N Spain 40°12′N 05°05′W
63 I24 **Arenas, Punta de** headland S Argentina 53°10′S 68°15′W
61 B20 **Arenaza** Buenos Aires, E Argentina 34°55′S 61°45′W
95 F17 **Arendal** Aust-Agder, S Norway 58°27′N 08°45′E
99 J16 **Arendonk** Antwerpen, N Belgium 51°18′N 05°06′E
43 T15 **Arenosa** Panamá, N Panama 09°02′N 79°57′W
Arensburg see Kuressaare
105 W5 **Arenys de Mar** Cataluña, NE Spain 41°35′N 02°33′E
106 C9 **Arenzano** Liguria, NW Italy 44°25′N 08°43′E
115 F22 **Areópoli** prev. Areópolis. Pelopónnisos, S Greece 36°40′N 22°24′E
Areópolis see Areópoli
57 H18 **Arequipa** Arequipa, SE Peru 16°24′S 71°33′W
57 G17 **Arequipa** off. Departamento de Arequipa. ◈ department Arequia SW Peru
Arequipa, Departamento de see Arequipa
61 B19 **Arequito** Santa Fe, C Argentina 33°09′S 61°28′W
104 M7 **Arévalo** Castilla-León, N Spain 41°04′N 04°44′W

◆ Country
● Country Capital
◇ Dependent Territory
○ Dependent Territory Capital
◈ Administrative Regions
✈ International Airport
▲ Mountain
▲▲ Mountain Range
⛰ Volcano
≈ River
◎ Lake
⊠ Reservoir

Arezzo – Asino

106 H12 Arezzo anc. Arretium. Toscana, C Italy 43°28′N 11°50′E
105 Q4 Arga N Spain
Argaeus see Erciyes Dağı
115 G17 Argalastí Thessalía, C Greece 39°13′N 23°13′E
105 O10 Argamasilla de Alba Castilla-La Mancha, C Spain 39°08′N 03°05′W
158 L8 Argan Xinjiang Uygur Zizhiqu, NW China 40°09′N 88°16′E
105 O8 Arganda Madrid, C Spain 40°19′N 03°26′W
104 H8 Arganil Coimbra, N Portugal 40°13′N 08°03′W
171 P6 Argao Cebu, C Philippines 09°52′N 123°33′E
153 V15 Argartala Tripura, NE India
123 N9 Arga-Sala Respublika Sakha (Yakutiya), NE Russian Federation
103 P17 Argelès-sur-Mer Pyrénées-Orientales, S France 42°33′N 03°01′E
103 T15 Argens SE France
106 H9 Argenta Emilia-Romagna, N Italy 44°37′N 11°49′E
102 K5 Argentan Orne, N France 48°45′N 00°01′W
103 N12 Argentat Corrèze, C France 45°06′N 01°57′E
106 A9 Argentera Piemonte, NE Italy 44°25′N 06°57′E
103 N5 Argenteuil Val-d'Oise, N France 48°57′N 02°13′E
62 K13 Argentina off. Argentine Republic. ◆ republic S South America
Argentina Basin see Argentine Basin
Argentine Abyssal Plain see Argentine Plain
65 I19 Argentine Basin var. Argentina Basin. undersea feature SW Atlantic Ocean 45°00′S 45°00′W
65 I20 Argentine Plain var. Argentine Abyssal Plain. undersea feature SW Atlantic Ocean 47°31′S 50°00′W
Argentine Republic see Argentina
Argentine Rise see Falkland Plateau
63 H22 Argentino, Lago ◎ S Argentina
102 K8 Argenton-Château Deux-Sèvres, W France 46°59′N 00°22′W
102 M9 Argenton-sur-Creuse Indre, C France 46°34′N 01°32′E
Argentoratum see Strasbourg
116 I12 Argeş ◆ county S Romania
116 K14 Argeş S Romania
149 O8 Arghandāb, Daryā-ye SE Afghanistan
Arghastān see Arghestān
149 O8 Arghestān Pash. Arghastān. SE Afghanistan
Argirocastro see Gjirokastër
80 E7 Argo Northern, N Sudan 19°31′N 30°25′E
173 P7 Argo Fracture Zone tectonic feature C Indian Ocean
115 F20 Argolikós Kólpos gulf S Greece
103 R4 Argonne physical region NE France
115 F20 Árgos Pelopónnisos, S Greece 37°38′N 22°43′E
139 S1 Argōsh Dahūk, N Iraq 37°07′N 44°13′E
115 D14 Árgos Orestikó Dytikí Makedonía, N Greece 40°27′N 21°15′E
115 B19 Argostóli var. Argostólion. Kefallonía, Iónia Nisiá, Greece, C Mediterranean Sea 38°13′N 20°29′E
Argostólion see Argostóli
Argovie see Aargau
35 O14 Arguello, Point headland California, W USA 34°34′N 120°39′W
127 P16 Argun Chechenskaya Respublika, SW Russian Federation 43°16′N 45°53′E
157 T2 Argun Chin. Ergun He, Rus. Argun'. China/Russian Federation
77 T12 Argungu Kebbi, NW Nigeria 12°45′N 04°24′E
Argut see Guchin-Us
181 N3 Argyle, Lake salt lake Western Australia
96 G12 Argyll cultural region W Scotland, United Kingdom
Argyrokastron see Gjirokastër
162 I7 Arhangay ◆ province C Mongolia
Arhangelos see Archángelos
95 P14 Arholma Stockholm, C Sweden 59°51′N 19°01′E
95 G22 Århus var. Aarhus. Århus, C Denmark 56°09′N 10°11′E
95 G22 Århus ◆ county C Denmark
139 T1 Ārī Arbīl, E Iraq 37°07′N 44°34′E
Aria see Herāt
83 F22 Ariamsvlei Karas, SE Namibia 28°08′S 19°50′E
107 L17 Ariano Irpino Campania, S Italy 41°08′N 15°00′E
54 F11 Ariari, Río C Colombia
151 K19 Ari Atoll var. Alifu Atoll. atoll C Maldives
77 P11 Aribinda N Burkina 14°12′N 00°50′W
62 G2 Arica hist. San Marcos de Arica. Tarapacá, N Chile 18°31′S 70°18′W
54 H16 Arica Amazonas, S Colombia 02°09′S 71°48′W
62 G2 Arica ✈ Tarapacá, N Chile 18°30′S 70°20′W
114 E13 Aridaía var. Aridea, Aridhaía. Dytikí Makedonía, N Greece 40°59′N 22°04′E
Aridea see Aridaía
172 I15 Aride, Île island Inner Islands, NE Seychelles
Aridhaía see Aridaía
103 N17 Ariège ◆ department S France
102 M16 Ariège var. la Riege. Andorra/France
116 H11 Arieş W Romania
149 U10 Ārifwāla Punjab, E Pakistan 30°15′N 73°08′E
Ariguanì see El Difícil
138 G11 Arīḥā Al Karak, W Jordan 31°25′N 35°47′E
138 I3 Arīḥā var. Arīhā. Idlib, W Syria 35°50′N 36°36′E
Arīhā see Arīḥā
Arīḥā see Jericho
37 W4 Arikaree River Colorado/Nebraska, C USA
112 L13 Arilje Serbia, W Serbia 43°45′N 20°06′E
45 U14 Arima Trinidad, Trinidad and Tobago 10°38′N 61°17′W
Arime see Al 'Arīmah
Ariminum see Rimini
59 H16 Arinos, Rio W Brazil
40 M14 Ario de Rosales var. Ario de Rosáles. Michoacán, SW Mexico 19°12′N 101°42′W
Ario de Rosáles see Ario de Rosales
118 F12 Ariogala Kaunas, C Lithuania 55°16′N 23°30′E
47 T7 Aripuanã W Brazil
59 E15 Ariquemes Rondônia, W Brazil 09°55′S 63°06′W
121 W13 'Arish, Wâdi el NE Egypt
54 K6 Arismendi Barinas, C Venezuela 08°29′N 68°22′W
10 J14 Aristazabal Island island SW Canada
60 F13 Aristóbulo del Valle Misiones, NE Argentina 27°09′S 54°54′W
172 I5 Arivonimamo ✈ (Antananarivo) Antananarivo, C Madagascar 19°00′S 47°11′E
Arixang see Wenquan
105 Q6 Ariza Aragón, NE Spain 41°19′N 02°03′W
62 I6 Arizaro, Salar de salt lake NW Argentina
105 O2 Arizgoiti var. Basauri. País Vasco, N Spain 43°13′N 02°54′W
62 K13 Arizona San Luis, C Argentina 35°44′S 65°16′W
36 J12 Arizona off. State of Arizona, also known as Copper State, Grand Canyon State. ◆ state SW USA
40 G4 Arizpe Sonora, NW Mexico 30°20′N 110°11′W
95 J16 Årjäng Värmland, C Sweden 59°24′N 12°09′E
143 P8 Arjenān Yazd, C Iran 32°19′N 53°48′E
92 I13 Arjeplog Norrbotten, N Sweden 66°04′N 18°E
54 E5 Arjona Bolívar, N Colombia 10°14′N 75°22′W
105 N13 Arjona Andalucía, S Spain 37°56′N 04°04′W
123 S10 Arka Khabarovskiy Kray, E Russian Federation 60°04′N 142°17′E
22 L2 Arkabutla Lake Mississippi, S USA
127 O7 Arkadak Saratovskaya Oblast', W Russian Federation 51°55′N 43°29′E
27 T13 Arkadelphia Arkansas, C USA 34°07′N 93°06′W
115 J25 Arkalochóri; prev. Arkalokhórion. Kríti, Greece, E Mediterranean Sea 35°09′N 25°15′E
Arkalohori/Arkalokhórion see Arkalochóri
145 O10 Arkalyk Kaz. Arqalyq. Kostanay, N Kazakhstan 50°17′N 66°51′E
27 U10 Arkansas off. State of Arkansas, also known as The Land of Opportunity. ◆ state S USA
27 W14 Arkansas City Arkansas, C USA 33°36′N 91°12′W
27 O7 Arkansas City Kansas, C USA 37°03′N 97°02′W
16 K11 Arkansas River C USA
182 J5 Arkaroola South Australia 30°21′S 139°20′E
Arkhángelos see Archángelos
124 L8 Arkhangel'sk Eng. Archangel. Arkhangel'skaya Oblast', NW Russian Federation 64°32′N 40°40′E
124 L9 Arkhangel'skaya Oblast' ◆ province NW Russian Federation
127 O14 Arkhangel'skoye Stavropol'skiy Kray, SW Russian Federation 44°37′N 44°03′E
123 R14 Arkhara Amurskaya Oblast', S Russian Federation 49°20′N 130°04′E
97 G19 Arklow Ir. An tInbhear Mór. SE Ireland 52°48′N 06°09′W
115 M20 Arkoí island Dodekánisa, Greece, Aegean Sea
27 R11 Arkoma Oklahoma, C USA 35°19′N 94°27′W
100 O7 Arkona, Kap headland NE Germany 54°40′N 13°24′E
95 N17 Arkösund Östergötland, S Sweden 58°28′N 16°55′E
122 J6 Arkticheskogo Instituta, Ostrova island N Russian Federation
95 O15 Arlanda ✈ (Stockholm) Stockholm, C Sweden 59°40′N 17°58′E
146 C11 Arlandag Rus. Gora Arlan. ▲ W Turkmenistan 39°39′N 54°28′E
Arlan, Gora see Arlandag
105 O5 Arlanza N Spain
105 N5 Arlanzón N Spain
103 R15 Arles var. Arles-sur-Rhône; anc. Arelas, Arelate. Bouches-du-Rhône, SE France 43°41′N 04°38′E
Arles-sur-Rhône see Arles
103 O17 Arles-sur-Tech Pyrénées-Orientales, S France 42°27′N 02°37′E
29 U9 Arlington Minnesota, N USA 44°36′N 94°04′W
29 R15 Arlington Nebraska, C USA 41°27′N 96°21′W
32 J11 Arlington Oregon, NW USA 45°43′N 120°10′W
29 R10 Arlington South Dakota, N USA 44°21′N 97°07′W
20 E10 Arlington Tennessee, S USA 35°17′N 89°40′W
25 T6 Arlington Texas, SW USA 32°44′N 97°05′W
21 W4 Arlington Virginia, NE USA 38°54′N 77°09′W
32 H7 Arlington Washington, NW USA 48°12′N 122°07′W
30 M10 Arlington Heights Illinois, N USA 42°08′N 88°03′W
77 U8 Arlit Agadez, C Niger 18°54′N 07°25′E
99 L24 Arlon Dut. Aarlen, Ger. Arel, Lat. Orolaunum. Luxembourg, SE Belgium 49°41′N 05°49′E
27 R7 Arma Kansas, C USA 37°32′N 94°42′W
97 F16 Armagh Ir. Ard Mhacha. S Northern Ireland, United Kingdom 54°15′N 06°33′W
97 F16 Armagh cultural region S Northern Ireland, United Kingdom
102 K15 Armagnac cultural region S France
103 Q7 Armançon C France
60 K10 Armando Laydner, Represa S Brazil
115 M24 Armathía island SE Greece
137 T12 Armavir prev. Hoktemberyan, Rus. Oktemberyan. SW Armenia 40°09′N 43°58′E
126 M14 Armavir Krasnodarskiy Kray, SW Russian Federation 44°59′N 41°07′E
54 E10 Armenia Quindío, W Colombia 04°32′N 75°40′W
137 T12 Armenia off. Republic of Armenia, var. Ajastan, Arm. Hayastani Hanrapetut'yun; prev. Armenian Soviet Socialist Republic. ◆ republic SW Asia
Armenian Soviet Socialist Republic see Armenia
Armenia, Republic of see Armenia
Armenierstadt see Gherla
103 O1 Armentières Nord, N France 50°41′N 02°53′E
40 K14 Armería Colima, SW Mexico 18°55′N 103°59′W
183 T5 Armidale New South Wales, SE Australia 30°32′S 151°40′E
29 P11 Armour South Dakota, N USA 43°19′N 98°21′W
61 B18 Armstrong Santa Fe, C Argentina 32°46′S 61°39′W
11 N16 Armstrong British Columbia, SW Canada 50°27′N 119°14′W
12 D11 Armstrong Ontario, S Canada 50°20′N 89°02′W
29 U11 Armstrong Iowa, C USA 43°24′N 94°28′W
25 S16 Armstrong Texas, SW USA 26°55′N 97°47′W
117 S11 Armyans'k Rus. Armyansk. Respublika Krym, S Ukraine 46°05′N 33°43′E
115 H14 Arnaía Cont. Arnea. Kentrikí Makedonía, N Greece 40°30′N 23°36′E
121 N2 Arnaoúti, Akrotíri var. Arnaoúti, Cape Arnaouti. headland W Cyprus 35°06′N 32°16′E
Arnaouti, Cape/Arnaoútis see Arnaoúti, Akrotíri
12 L4 Arnaud Québec, E Canada
103 Q8 Arnay-le-Duc Côte d'Or, C France 47°08′N 04°27′E
Arnea see Arnaía
105 Q4 Arnedo La Rioja, N Spain 42°14′N 02°05′W
95 I14 Årnes Akershus, S Norway 60°07′N 11°28′E
Årnes see Åi Åfjord
26 K9 Arnett Oklahoma, C USA 36°08′N 99°46′W
98 L12 Arnhem Gelderland, SE Netherlands 51°59′N 05°54′E
181 Q2 Arnhem Land physical region Northern Territory, N Australia
106 F11 Arno C Italy
Arno see Arno Atoll
189 W7 Arno Atoll var. Arno. atoll Ratak Chain, NE Marshall Islands
182 H8 Arno Bay South Australia 33°55′S 136°31′E
35 Q8 Arnold California, W USA 38°15′N 120°19′W
27 X5 Arnold Missouri, C USA 38°25′N 90°22′W
29 N15 Arnold Nebraska, C USA 41°25′N 100°11′W
109 R10 Arnoldstein Slvn. Pod Klošter. Kärnten, S Austria 46°34′N 13°43′E
103 N9 Arnon C France
45 P14 Arnos Vale ✈ (Kingstown) Saint Vincent, SE Saint Vincent and the Grenadines 13°08′N 61°13′W
92 I8 Arnøya Lapp. Árdni. island N Norway
14 L12 Arnprior Ontario, SE Canada 45°31′N 76°11′W
101 G15 Arnsberg Nordrhein-Westfalen, W Germany 51°24′N 08°04′E
101 K16 Arnstadt Thüringen, C Germany 50°50′N 10°57′E
Arnswalde see Choszczno
54 K5 Aroa Yaracuy, N Venezuela 10°26′N 68°54′W
83 E21 Aroab Karas, SE Namibia 26°47′S 19°40′E
Ároania see Chelmós
191 O6 Aroa, Pointe headland Moorea, W French Polynesia 17°27′S 149°45′W
Aroe Islands see Aru, Kepulauan
101 H15 Arolsen Niedersachsen, C Germany 51°23′N 09°00′E
106 C7 Arona Piemonte, NE Italy 45°45′N 08°33′E
19 R3 Aroostook River Canada/USA
Arop Island see Long Island
38 M12 Aropuk Lake ◎ Alaska, USA
191 P4 Arorae atoll Tungaru, W Kiribati
190 G16 Arorangi Rarotonga, S Cook Islands 21°13′S 159°49′W
108 I9 Arosa Graubünden, S Switzerland 46°48′N 09°42′E
104 F4 Arousa, Ría de estuary E Atlantic Ocean
184 P8 Arowhana ▲ North Island, New Zealand 38°07′S 177°52′E
137 V12 Arp'a Az. Arpaçay. Armenia/Azerbaijan
137 S11 Arpaçay Kars, NE Turkey 40°51′N 43°20′E
Arpaçay see Arp'a
Arqalyq see Arkalyk
149 N14 Arra SW Pakistan
Arrabona see Győr
Arrah see Āra
Ar Rahad see Er Rahad
139 R9 Ar Raḥḥālīyah Al Anbār, C Iraq 32°53′N 43°21′E
60 Q10 Arraial do Cabo Rio de Janeiro, SE Brazil 22°57′S 42°00′W
104 H11 Arraiolos Évora, S Portugal 38°44′N 07°59′W
139 R8 Ar Ramādī var. Ramadi, Rumadiya. Al Anbār, SW Iraq 33°27′N 43°19′E
138 J6 Ar Rāmī Ḥimṣ, C Syria 34°32′N 37°54′E
Ar Rams see Rams
138 H9 Ar Ramthā var. Ramtha. Irbid, N Jordan 32°34′N 36°00′E
96 H13 Arran, Isle of island SW Scotland, United Kingdom
138 L3 Ar Raqqah var. Rakka; anc. Nicephorium. Ar Raqqah, N Syria 35°57′N 39°03′E
138 L3 Ar Raqqah off. Muḥāfaẓat al Raqqah, var. Raqqah, Fr. Rakka. ◆ governorate N Syria
103 O2 Arras anc. Nemetocenna. Pas-de-Calais, N France 50°17′N 02°46′E
105 P3 Arrasate Cast. Mondragón. País Vasco, N Spain 43°04′N 02°30′W
138 G12 Ar Rashādīyah Aṭ Ṭafīlah, W Jordan 30°42′N 35°38′E
138 I5 Ar Rastān var. Rastâne. Ḥimṣ, W Syria 34°57′N 36°43′E
139 X12 Ar Raṭāwī Al Baṣrah, E Iraq 30°37′N 47°12′E
102 L15 Arrats S France
141 N10 Ar Rawḍah Makkah, S Saudi Arabia 21°19′N 42°48′E
141 Q15 Ar Rawḍah S Yemen 14°26′N 47°14′E
142 K11 Ar Rawḍatayn var. Raudhatain. N Kuwait 29°80′N 47°50′E
143 N16 Ar Rayyān var. Al Rayyan. C Qatar 25°18′N 51°29′E
102 L17 Arreau Hautes-Pyrénées, S France 42°55′N 00°21′E
64 Q11 Arrecife var. Arrecife de Lanzarote, Puerto Arrecife. Lanzarote, Islas Canarias, NE Atlantic Ocean 28°57′N 13°33′W
Arrecife de Lanzarote see Arrecife
43 P6 Arrecife Edinburgh reef NE Nicaragua
61 C19 Arrecifes Buenos Aires, E Argentina 34°06′S 60°09′W
102 F6 Arrée, Monts d' ▲ NW France
Ar Refā'ī see Ar Rifā'ī
Arretium see Arezzo
Arriaca see Guadalajara
109 S9 Arriach Kärnten, S Austria 46°43′N 13°52′E
41 T16 Arriaga Chiapas, SE Mexico 16°14′N 93°54′W
41 N12 Arriaga San Luis Potosí, C Mexico 21°55′N 101°23′W
139 W10 Ar Rifā'ī var. Ar Refā'ī. Dhī Qār, SE Iraq 31°47′N 46°07′E
139 V12 Ar Riḥāb salt flat S Iraq
104 L2 Arriondas Asturias, N Spain 43°23′N 05°11′W
141 Q7 Ar Riyāḍ Eng. Riyadh. ● (Saudi Arabia) Ar Riyāḍ, C Saudi Arabia 24°50′N 46°50′E
141 O8 Ar Riyāḍ off. Minṭaqat ar Riyāḍ. ◆ province C Saudi Arabia
141 S15 Ar Riyān S Yemen 14°43′N 49°18′E
Arrö see Ærø
61 H18 Arroio Grande Rio Grande do Sul, S Brazil 32°15′S 53°02′W
102 K15 Arros S France
103 Q9 Arroux C France
25 R5 Arrowhead, Lake Texas, SW USA
182 L5 Arrowsmith, Mount hill New South Wales, SE Australia
185 D21 Arrowtown Otago, South Island, New Zealand 44°57′S 168°51′E
61 D17 Arroyo Barú Entre Ríos, E Argentina 31°52′S 58°26′W
104 J10 Arroyo de la Luz Extremadura, W Spain 39°28′N 06°36′W
63 J16 Arroyo de la Ventana Río Negro, SE Argentina 41°41′S 66°03′W
35 P13 Arroyo Grande California, W USA 35°07′N 120°35′W
Ar Ru'ays see Ar Ruways
141 R11 Ar Rub 'al Khālī Eng. Empty Quarter, Great Sandy Desert. desert SW Asia
139 V13 Ar Ruḍaymah Al Muthanná, S Iraq 30°20′N 45°26′E
61 A16 Arrufó Santa Fe, C Argentina 30°15′S 61°45′W
138 I7 Ar Ruḥaybah var. Ruhaybeh, Fr. Rouhaïbé. Dimashq, W Syria 33°45′N 36°40′E
139 V15 Ar Rukhaymīyah well S Iraq
139 U11 Ar Rumaythah var. Rumaitha. Al Muthanná, S Iraq 31°31′N 45°15′E
141 X8 Ar Rustāq var. Rostak, Rustaq. N Oman 23°34′N 57°25′E
139 N8 Ar Ruṭbah var. Rutba. Al Anbār, SW Iraq 33°03′N 40°16′E
140 M3 Ar Rūthīyah spring/well NW Saudi Arabia 31°18′N 41°23′E
ar-Ruwaida see Ar Ruwayḍah
141 O8 Ar Ruwayḍah var. ar-Ruwaida. Jīzān, C Saudi Arabia 23°48′N 44°44′E
143 N15 Ar Ruways var. Al Ruweis, Ar Ru'ays, Ruwais. N Qatar 26°08′N 51°13′E
143 O17 Ar Ruways var. Ar Ru'ays. Abū Ẓaby, W United Arab Emirates 24°09′N 52°57′E
Ārs see Aars
Arsanias see Murat Nehri
123 S15 Arsen'yev Primorskiy Kray, SE Russian Federation 44°09′N 133°28′E
155 G19 Arsikere Karnātaka, W India 13°20′N 76°13′E
127 R3 Arsk Respublika Tatarstan, W Russian Federation 56°07′N 49°54′E
94 N10 Årskogen Gävleborg, C Sweden 62°07′N 17°19′E
121 O3 Ársos C Cyprus 34°51′N 32°46′E
94 N13 Årsunda Gävleborg, C Sweden 60°31′N 16°45′E
115 C17 Árta anc. Ambracia. Ípeiros, W Greece 39°08′N 20°59′E
105 Y9 Artà Mallorca, Spain, W Mediterranean Sea 39°42′N 03°20′E
Arta see Árachthos
137 T12 Artashat S Armenia 39°57′N 44°34′E
40 M15 Arteaga Michoacán, SW Mexico 18°22′N 102°18′W
123 S15 Artem Primorskiy Kray, SE Russian Federation 43°24′N 132°20′E
44 C4 Artemisa La Habana, W Cuba 22°49′N 82°47′W
117 W7 Artemivs'k Donets'ka Oblast', E Ukraine 48°35′N 37°58′E
122 K13 Artemovsk Krasnoyarskiy Kray, S Russian Federation 54°22′N 93°24′E
105 U5 Artesa de Segre Cataluña, NE Spain 41°54′N 01°03′E
37 U14 Artesia New Mexico, SW USA 32°50′N 104°24′W
25 Q14 Artesia Wells Texas, SW USA 28°13′N 99°18′W
108 G8 Arth Schwyz, C Switzerland 47°05′N 08°39′E
14 F15 Arthur Ontario, S Canada 43°49′N 80°31′W
30 M14 Arthur Illinois, N USA 39°42′N 88°28′W
28 L14 Arthur Nebraska, C USA 41°35′N 101°42′W
29 Q5 Arthur North Dakota, N USA 47°03′N 97°12′W
185 B21 Arthur South Island, New Zealand
18 B13 Arthur, Lake Pennsylvania, NE USA
183 N15 Arthur River Tasmania, SE Australia
185 G18 Arthur's Pass Canterbury, South Island, New Zealand 42°59′S 171°33′E
185 G17 Arthur's Pass pass South Island, New Zealand
44 I3 Arthur's Town Cat Island, C Bahamas 24°34′N 75°39′W
44 M9 Artibonite, Rivière de l' C Haiti
61 E16 Artigas prev. San Eugenio, San Eugenio del Cuareim. Artigas, N Uruguay 30°25′S 56°28′W
61 E16 Artigas ◆ department N Uruguay
194 H1 Artigas Uruguayan research station Antarctica 61°57′S 58°23′W
137 T11 Art'ik W Armenia 40°38′N 43°58′E
187 O16 Art, Île island Îles Belep, W New Caledonia
103 O2 Artois cultural region N France
136 L12 Artova Tokat, N Turkey 40°04′N 36°17′E
105 Y9 Artrutx, Cap d' var. Cabo Dartuch. cape Menorca, Spain, W Mediterranean Sea
Artsiz see Artsyz
117 N11 Artsyz Rus. Artsiz. Odes'ka Oblast', SW Ukraine 45°59′N 29°26′E
158 E7 Artux Xinjiang Uygur Zizhiqu, NW China 39°40′N 76°10′E
137 R11 Artvin Artvin, NE Turkey 41°12′N 41°48′E
137 R11 Artvin ◆ province NE Turkey
146 G14 Artyk Ahal Welaýaty, C Turkmenistan 37°32′N 59°16′E
79 Q16 Aru Orientale, NE Dem. Rep. Congo 02°53′N 30°50′E
81 E17 Arua NW Uganda 03°02′N 30°56′E
104 I4 A Rúa de Valdeorras var. La Rúa. Galicia, NW Spain 42°22′N 07°12′W
Aruângua see Luangwa
45 O15 Aruba var. Oruba. ◇ Dutch autonomous region S West Indies
47 Q4 Aruba island Aruba, Lesser Antilles
Aru Islands see Aru, Kepulauan
171 W15 Aru, Kepulauan Eng. Aru Islands; prev. Aroe Islands. island group E Indonesia
153 W10 Arunāchal Pradesh prev. North East Frontier Agency, North East Frontier Agency of Assam. ◆ state NE India
Arun Qi see Naji
155 H23 Aruppukkottai Tamil Nādu, SE India 09°31′N 78°03′E
81 I20 Arusha Arusha, N Tanzania 03°23′S 36°40′E
81 I21 Arusha ◆ region E Tanzania
81 I20 Arusha ✈ Arusha, N Tanzania 03°26′S 37°07′E
54 C9 Arusí, Punta headland NW Colombia 05°36′N 77°30′W
155 J23 Aruvi Aru NW Sri Lanka
79 M17 Aruwimi var. Ituri (upper course). NE Dem. Rep. Congo
Árva see Orava
37 T4 Arvada Colorado, C USA 39°48′N 105°06′W
Arvand Rūd see 'Arab, Shaṭṭ al
162 J8 Arvayheer Övörhangay, C Mongolia 46°13′N 102°47′E
9 O10 Arviat prev. Eskimo Point. Nunavut, C Canada 61°10′N 94°15′W
93 I14 Arvidsjaur Norrbotten, N Sweden 65°34′N 19°12′E
95 J15 Arvika Värmland, C Sweden 59°41′N 12°38′E
92 J8 Årviksand Troms, N Norway 70°10′N 20°30′E
35 S13 Arvin California, W USA 35°12′N 118°52′W
163 S8 Arxan Nei Mongol Zizhiqu, N China 47.11N 119.58′E
145 P7 Arykbalyk Kaz. Aryqbalyq. Severnyy Kazakhstan, N Kazakhstan 53°00′N 68°11′E
Aryqbalyq see Arykbalyk
145 P17 Arys' Kaz. Arys. Yuzhnyy Kazakhstan, S Kazakhstan 42°26′N 68°49′E
Arys see Arys'
Arys see Orzysz
Arys Köli see Arys, Ozero
145 O14 Arys, Ozero Kaz. Arys Köli. ◎ C Kazakhstan
107 D16 Arzachena Sardegna, Italy, C Mediterranean Sea 41°05′N 09°21′E
127 O4 Arzamas Nizhegorodskaya Oblast', W Russian Federation 55°25′N 43°51′E
141 V13 Arzāt S Oman 17°00′N 54°18′E
104 H3 Arzúa Galicia, NW Spain 42°55′N 08°10′W
111 A16 Aš Ger. Asch. Karlovarský Kraj, W Czech Republic 50°18′N 12°12′E
95 H15 Ås Akershus, S Norway 59°40′N 10°50′E
Åsa see Asaa
95 H20 Asaa var. Åsa. Nordjylland, N Denmark 57°07′N 10°24′E
83 E21 Asab Karas, S Namibia 25°29′S 17°59′E
77 U16 Asaba Delta, S Nigeria 06°10′N 06°44′E
76 J10 Assaba var. Açâba. ◆ region S Mauritania
149 S4 Asadābād var. Asadābād; prev. Chaghasarāy. Konar, E Afghanistan 34°52′N 71°09′E
Asadābād see Asadābād
138 K3 Asad, Buḥayrat al Eng. Lake Assad. ◎ N Syria
63 H20 Asador, Pampa del plain S Argentina
165 P14 Asahi Chiba, Honshū, S Japan 35°43′N 140°38′E
164 M11 Asahi Toyama, Honshū, SW Japan 36°56′N 137°34′E
165 T13 Asahi-dake ▲ Hokkaidō, N Japan 43°42′N 142°50′E
165 T3 Asahikawa Hokkaidō, N Japan 43°46′N 142°23′E
147 S10 Asaka Rus. Assake; prev. Leninsk. Andijon Viloyati, E Uzbekistan 40°39′N 72°16′E
77 P17 Asamankese SE Ghana 05°47′N 00°41′W
188 B15 Asan W Guam 13°28′N 144°43′E
188 B15 Asan Point headland W Guam
153 R15 Āsānsol West Bengal, NE India 23°40′N 86°59′E
80 K12 Āsayita Āfar, NE Ethiopia 11°35′S 41°23′E
171 T12 Asbakin Papua, E Indonesia 0°45′S 131°40′E
Asben see Aïr, Massif de l'
15 Q12 Asbestos Québec, SE Canada 45°46′N 71°56′W
29 Y13 Asbury Iowa, C USA 42°30′N 90°45′W
18 K15 Asbury Park New Jersey, NE USA 40°13′N 74°00′W
41 Z12 Ascención, Bahiá de la bay NW Caribbean Sea
40 I3 Ascensión Chihuahua, N Mexico 31°07′N 107°59′W
65 M14 Ascension Fracture Zone tectonic feature C Atlantic Ocean
65 G14 Ascension Island ◇ dependency of St.Helena C Atlantic Ocean
65 N16 Ascension Island island C Atlantic Ocean
Asch see Aš
109 S3 Aschach an der Donau Oberösterreich, N Austria 48°22′N 14°00′E
101 H18 Aschaffenburg Bayern, SW Germany 49°58′N 09°10′E
101 F14 Ascheberg Nordrhein-Westfalen, W Germany 51°46′N 07°36′E
101 L14 Aschersleben Sachsen-Anhalt, C Germany 51°46′N 11°28′E
106 G12 Asciano Toscana, C Italy 43°15′N 11°32′E
106 J13 Ascoli Piceno anc. Asculum Picenum. Marche, C Italy 42°51′N 13°34′E
107 M17 Ascoli Satriano anc. Asculub, Ausculum Apulum. Puglia, SE Italy 41°13′N 15°32′E
108 G11 Ascona Ticino, S Switzerland 46°10′N 08°45′E
Asculub see Ascoli Satriano
Asculum Picenum see Ascoli Piceno
80 L11 'Aseb var. Assab, Amh. Āseb. SE Eritrea 13°04′N 42°36′E
95 M20 Åseda Kronoberg, S Sweden 57°10′N 15°20′E
127 T6 Asekeyevo Orenburgskaya Oblast', W Russian Federation 53°36′N 52°53′E
81 J14 Āsela var. Asella, Aselle, Asselle. Oromīya, C Ethiopia 07°55′N 39°08′E
93 H15 Åsele Västerbotten, N Sweden 64°10′N 17°20′E
Asella/Aselle see Āsela
98 N7 Assen Drenthe, NE Netherlands 53°N 06°34′E
94 K12 Äsen Dalarna, C Sweden 61°18′N 13°49′E
114 J11 Asenovgrad prev. Stanimaka. Plovdiv, C Bulgaria 42°00′N 24°53′E
171 O13 Asera Sulawesi, C Indonesia 03°24′S 121°42′E
95 F17 Åseral Vest-Agder, S Norway 58°37′N 07°27′E
118 J3 Aseri var. Asserien, Ger. Asserin. Ida-Virumaa, NE Estonia 59°29′N 26°51′E
40 J10 Aserradero Durango, W Mexico
146 F13 Aşgabat prev. Ashgabat, Ashkhabad, Poltoratsk. ● (Turkmenistan) Ahal Welaýaty, C Turkmenistan 37°58′N 58°22′E
146 F13 Aşgabat ✈ Ahal Welaýaty, C Turkmenistan 38°06′N 58°10′E
95 H16 Åsgårdstrand Vestfold, S Norway 59°22′N 10°27′E
Ashara see Al 'Ashārah
23 T6 Ashburn Georgia, SE USA 31°42′N 83°39′W
185 G19 Ashburton Canterbury, South Island, New Zealand 43°55′S 171°47′E
185 G19 Ashburton South Island, New Zealand
180 H8 Ashburton River Western Australia
145 V10 Ashchysu E Kazakhstan
10 M16 Ashcroft British Columbia, SW Canada 50°41′N 121°17′W
138 E10 Ashdod anc. Azotos, Lat. Azotus. Central, W Israel 31°48′N 34°38′E
27 S14 Ashdown Arkansas, C USA 33°40′N 94°09′W
21 T9 Asheboro North Carolina, SE USA 35°42′N 79°50′W
11 X15 Ashern Manitoba, S Canada 51°10′N 98°22′W
21 P10 Asheville North Carolina, SE USA 35°36′N 82°33′W
12 E8 Asheweig Ontario, C Canada
27 V9 Ash Flat Arkansas, C USA 36°13′N 91°36′W
183 T4 Ashford New South Wales, SE Australia 29°18′S 151°09′E
97 P22 Ashford SE England, United Kingdom 51°09′N 00°52′E
36 K11 Ash Fork Arizona, SW USA 35°12′N 112°31′W
Ashgabat see Aşgabat
27 T7 Ash Grove Missouri, C USA 37°19′N 93°35′W
165 O12 Ashikaga var. Asikaga. Tochigi, Honshū, S Japan 36°21′N 139°26′E
165 Q8 Ashiro Iwate, Honshū, C Japan 40°04′N 141°00′E
164 F15 Ashizuri-misaki Shikoku, SW Japan
138 E10 Ashkelon prev. Ashqelon. Southern, C Israel 31°40′N 34°35′E
143 P9 Ashkezar Yazd, C Iran 31°56′N 54°16′E
Ashkhabad see Aşgabat
23 Q4 Ashland Alabama, S USA 33°16′N 85°50′W
26 K7 Ashland Kansas, C USA 37°12′N 99°47′W
21 P5 Ashland Kentucky, S USA 38°28′N 82°40′W
19 S2 Ashland Maine, NE USA 46°36′N 68°24′W
22 M1 Ashland Mississippi, S USA 34°51′N 89°10′W
27 U4 Ashland Missouri, C USA 38°46′N 92°15′W
29 S15 Ashland Nebraska, C USA 41°01′N 96°21′W
31 T12 Ashland Ohio, N USA 40°52′N 82°19′W
32 G15 Ashland Oregon, NW USA 42°11′N 122°42′W
21 W6 Ashland Virginia, NE USA 37°45′N 77°28′W
30 K3 Ashland Wisconsin, N USA 46°34′N 90°54′W
20 I8 Ashland City Tennessee, S USA 36°16′N 87°05′W
183 S4 Ashley New South Wales, SE Australia 29°21′S 149°49′E
29 O7 Ashley North Dakota, N USA 46°00′N 99°22′W
173 W7 Ashmore and Cartier Islands ◇ Australian external territory E Indian Ocean
119 I14 Ashmyany Rus. Oshmyany. Hrodzyenskaya Voblasts', W Belarus 54°24′N 25°57′E
18 K12 Ashokan Reservoir New York, NE USA
165 U4 Ashoro Hokkaidō, NE Japan 43°16′N 143°33′E
Ashqelon see Ashkelon
Ashraf see Behshahr
139 O3 Ash Shadādah var. Ash Shaddādah, Jisr ash Shadadi, Shaddādī, Shedadi, Tell Shedadi. Al Ḥasakah, NE Syria 36°00′N 40°42′E
Ash Shaddādah see Ash Shadādah
139 Y12 Ash Shāfī Al Baṣrah, E Iraq 30°49′N 47°30′E
139 R4 Ash Shakk var. Shaykh. Ṣalāḥ ad Dīn, C Iraq 35°15′N 43°27′E
Ash Sham/Ash Shām see Dimashq
139 T10 Ash Shāmīyah var. Shamiya. Al Qādisīyah, C Iraq 31°56′N 44°37′E
139 Y13 Ash Shāmīyah var. Al Bādiyah al Janūbīyah. desert S Iraq
139 T11 Ash Shanāfīyah var. Ash Shināfīyah. Al Qādisīyah, S Iraq 31°35′N 44°38′E
138 G13 Ash Sharāh var. Esh Sharā. ▲ W Jordan
143 R16 Ash Shāriqah Eng. Sharjah. Ash Shāriqah, NE United Arab Emirates 25°22′N 55°28′E
143 R16 Ash Shāriqah var. Sharjah. ✈ Ash Shāriqah, NE United Arab Emirates 25°19′N 55°37′E
140 I4 Ash Sharmah var. Šarma. Tabūk, NW Saudi Arabia 28°02′N 35°16′E
139 R4 Ash Sharqāṭ Nīnawýa, NW Iraq 35°31′N 43°15′E
141 S10 Ash Sharqīyah off. Al Minṭaqah ash Sharqīyah, Eng. Eastern Region. ◆ province E Saudi Arabia
Ash Sharqīyah see Al 'Ubaylah
139 W11 Ash Shaṭrah var. Shatra. Dhī Qār, SE Iraq 31°26′N 46°10′E
138 G13 Ash Shawbak Ma'ān, W Jordan 30°32′N 35°34′E
138 L5 Ash Shaykh Ibrāhīm Ḥimṣ, C Syria 35°03′N 38°50′E
141 O17 Ash Shaykh 'Uthmān SW Yemen 12°53′N 45°00′E
141 S15 Ash Shiḥr SE Yemen 14°45′N 49°24′E
Ash Shināfīyah see Ash Shanāfīyah
141 V12 Ash Shiṣar var. Shisur. SW Oman 18°13′N 53°35′E
139 S13 Ash Shubrūm well S Iraq
141 R10 Ash Shuqqān desert E Saudi Arabia
75 O9 Ash Shuwayrif var. Ash Shwayrif. N Libya 29°54′N 14°16′E
Ash Shwayrif see Ash Shuwayrif
31 U10 Ashtabula Ohio, N USA 41°54′N 80°46′W
29 Q5 Ashtabula, Lake North Dakota, N USA
137 T12 Ashtarak W Armenia 40°18′N 44°22′E
142 M6 Āshtīān var. Āshtiyān. Markazī, W Iran 34°23′N 49°55′E
Āshtiyān see Āshtīān
33 R13 Ashton Idaho, NW USA 44°04′N 111°27′W
13 O10 Ashuanipi Lake ◎ Newfoundland and Labrador, E Canada
15 P6 Ashuapmushuan Québec, SE Canada
23 Q3 Ashville Alabama, S USA 33°50′N 86°15′W
31 S14 Ashville Ohio, N USA 39°43′N 82°57′W
30 K3 Ashwabay, Mount hill Wisconsin, N USA
128-129 Asia continent
171 T11 Asia, Kepulauan island group E Indonesia
154 N13 Āsika Orissa, E India 19°38′N 84°41′E
Asikaga see Ashikaga
93 M18 Asikkala var. Vääksy. Etelä-Suomi, S Finland 61°09′N 25°36′E
74 G5 Asilah N Morocco 35°32′N 06°04′W
'Aṣī, Nahr al see Orontes
107 B16 Asinara, Isola island W Italy
122 J12 Asino Tomskaya Oblast', C Russian Federation 56°56′N 86°02′E

◆ Country
● Country Capital
◇ Dependent Territory
○ Dependent Territory Capital
◆ Administrative Regions
✈ International Airport
▲ Mountain
▲ Mountain Range
Volcano
River
◎ Lake
Reservoir

ASINTORF – AVARUA HARBOUR

119 O14 **Asintorf** *Rus.* Osintorf. Vitsyebskaya Voblasts', N Belarus 54°43′N 30°35′E
119 L17 **Asipovichy** *Rus.* Osipovichi. Mahilyowskaya Voblasts', C Belarus 53°18′N 28°40′E
141 N12 **'Asīr** *off.* Minṭaqat 'Asīr. ◈ *province* SW Saudi Arabia
140 M11 **'Asīr** *Eng.* Asir. ▲▲ SW Saudi Arabia
'Asīr, Minṭaqat *see* 'Asīr
139 X10 **Askal** Maysān, E Iraq 31°45′N 47°07′E
137 P13 **Aşkale** Erzurum, NE Turkey 39°56′N 40°39′E
117 T11 **Askaniya-Nova** Khersons'ka Oblast', S Ukraine 46°27′N 33°54′E
95 H15 **Asker** Akershus, S Norway 59°52′N 10°26′E
95 L17 **Askersund** Örebro, C Sweden 58°55′N 14°55′E
Askī Kalak *see* Eski Kaļak
95 I15 **Askim** Østfold, S Norway 59°15′N 11°10′E
127 V3 **Askino** Respublika Bashkortostan, W Russian Federation 56°07′N 56°39′E
115 D14 **Áskio** ▲▲ N Greece
152 L9 **Askot** Uttarakhand, N India 29°44′N 80°20′E
94 C12 **Askvoll** Sogn Og Fjordane, S Norway 61°21′N 05°04′E
136 A13 **Aslan Burnu** *headland* W Turkey 38°44′N 26°43′E
136 L16 **Aslantaş Barajı** ⊠ S Turkey
149 S4 **Asmār** *var.* Bar Kunar. Kunar, E Afghanistan 34°59′N 71°29′E
Asmara *see* Asmera
80 I9 **Asmera** *var.* Asmara. ● (Eritrea) C Eritrea 15°15′N 38°58′E
95 L21 **Åsnen** ◎ S Sweden
115 F19 **Asopós** ≈ S Greece
171 W13 **Asori** Papua, E Indonesia 02°37′S 136°06′E
80 G12 **Āsosa** Bīnishangul Gumuz, W Ethiopia 10°06′N 34°27′E
32 M10 **Asotin** Washington, NW USA 46°18′N 117°03′W
Aspadana *see* Eşfahān
Aspang *see* Aspang Markt
109 X6 **Aspang Markt** *var.* Aspang. Niederösterreich, E Austria 47°34′N 16°06′E
105 S12 **Aspe** País Valenciano, E Spain 38°21′N 00°43′W
37 R5 **Aspen** Colorado, C USA 39°12′N 106°49′W
25 P6 **Aspermont** Texas, SW USA 33°08′N 100°14′W
Asphaltites, Lacus *see* Dead Sea
Aspinwall *see* Colón
185 C20 **Aspiring, Mount** ▲ South Island, New Zealand 44°21′S 168°47′E
115 B16 **Asprókavos, Akrotírio** *headland* Kérkyra, Iónia Nísiá, Greece, C Mediterranean Sea 39°22′N 20°07′E
Aspropótamos *see* Achelóos
Assab *see* 'Aseb
138 L4 **As Sabkhah** *var.* Sabkha. Ar Raqqah, NE Syria 35°30′N 35°54′E
139 U6 **As Sa'dīyah** Diyālá, E Iraq 34°11′N 45°09′E
Assad, Lake *see* Asad, Buḩayrat al
138 I8 **Aş Şafā** ▲ S Syria 33°03′N 37°07′E
138 I10 **Aş Şafāwī** Al Mafraq, N Jordan 37°12′N 32°30′E
75 W8 **Aş Şaff** *var.* El Şaff. N Egypt 29°34′N 31°16′E
139 N2 **Aş Şafīḩ** Al Ḩasakah, N Syria 36°42′N 40°12′E
Aş Şaḩrā' ash Sharqīyah *see* Sahara el Sharqîya
Assake *see* Asaka
As Salamīyah *see* Salamīyah
141 Q4 **As Sālimī** *var.* Salemy. SW Kuwait 29°07′N 46°41′E
67 W7 **'Assal, Lac** ◎ C Djibouti
139 T13 **As Salmān** Al Muthanná, S Iraq 30°29′N 44°34′E
138 G10 **As Salṭ** *var.* Salt. Al Balqā', NW Jordan 32°03′N 35°44′E
75 T7 **As Sallūm** *var.* Salûm. NW Egypt 31°31′N 25°09′E
142 M16 **As Salwā** *var.* Salwa, Salwah. S Qatar 24°44′N 50°52′E
153 V12 **Assam** ◈ *state* NE India
Assamaka *see* Assamakka
77 T8 **Assamakka** *var.* Assamaka. Agadez, NW Niger 19°24′N 05°53′E
139 U11 **As Samāwah** *var.* Samawa. Al Muthanná, S Iraq 31°17′N 45°06′E
As Saqia al Hamra *see* Saguia al Hamra
138 J4 **Aş Şā'rān** Ḩamāh, C Syria 35°15′N 37°28′E
138 G9 **Aş Şarīḩ** Irbid, N Jordan 32°31′N 35°54′E
21 Z5 **Assateague Island** *island* Maryland, NE USA
139 O6 **As Sayyāl** *var.* Sayyāl. Dayr az Zawr, E Syria 34°37′N 40°52′E
99 G18 **Asse** Vlaams Brabant, C Belgium 50°55′N 04°12′E
99 D16 **Assebroek** West-Vlaanderen, NW Belgium 51°12′N 03°16′E
Asselle *see* Āsela
107 C20 **Assemini** Sardegna, Italy, C Mediterranean Sea 39°16′N 08°58′E
99 E16 **Assenede** Oost-Vlaanderen, NW Belgium 51°15′N 03°43′E
95 G24 **Assens** Fyn, C Denmark 55°16′N 09°54′N
Asserien/Asserin *see* Aseri
99 I21 **Assesse** Namur, SE Belgium 50°22′N 05°01′E
141 Y8 **As Sīb** *var.* Seeb. NE Oman 23°40′N 58°03′E
139 Z13 **As Sībah** *var.* Sibah. Al Başrah, SE Iraq 30°13′N 47°24′E
11 T17 **Assiniboia** Saskatchewan, S Canada 49°39′N 105°59′W
11 V15 **Assiniboine** ≈ Manitoba, S Canada
11 P16 **Assiniboine, Mount** ▲ Alberta/British Columbia, SW Canada 50°54′N 115°43′W
Assiout *see* Asyūţ
60 J9 **Assis** São Paulo, S Brazil 22°37′S 50°25′W
106 I13 **Assisi** Umbria, C Italy 43°04′N 12°36′E
Assiut *see* Asyūţ
Assling *see* Jesenice
Assouan *see* Aswān
Assu *see* Açu
Assuan *see* Aswān
142 K12 **Aş Şubayḩīyah** *var.* Subiyah. S Kuwait 28°55′N 47°57′E
141 R16 **As Sufāl** S Yemen 14°06′N 48°42′E
138 L5 **As Sukhnah** *var.* Sukhne, *Fr.* Soukhné. Ḩimş, C Syria 34°56′N 38°52′E
139 U4 **As Sulaymānīyah** *off.* Muḩāfaẓat as Sulaymānīyah. ◈ *governorate* NE Iraq
139 U4 **As Sulaymānīyah** *var.* Sulaimaniya, *Kurd.* Slēmānī. As Sulaymānīyah, NE Iraq 35°32′N 45°27′E
141 P11 **As Sulayyil** Ar Riyāḑ, S Saudi Arabia 20°29′N 45°33′E
121 O13 **As Sulṭān** N Libya 31°01′N 17°21′E
141 Q5 **Aş Şummān** *desert* N Saudi Arabia
141 Q16 **Aş Şurrah** SW Yemen 13°56′N 46°23′E
139 N4 **Aş Şuwār** *var.* Şuwār. Dayr az Zawr, E Syria 35°31′N 40°37′E
138 H9 **As Suwaydā'** *var.* El Suweida, Es Suweida, Suweida, *Fr.* Soueida. As Suwaydā', SW Syria 32°43′N 36°33′E
138 H9 **As Suwaydā'** *off.* Muḩāfaẓat as Suwaydā', *var.* As Suwaydā, Suwaydá, Suweida. ◈ *governorate* S Syria
141 Z9 **As Suwayḩ** NE Oman 22°07′N 59°42′E
141 X8 **As Suwayq** *var.* Suwaik. N Oman 23°49′N 57°30′E
139 T8 **Aş Şuwayrah** *var.* Suwaira. Wāsiţ, E Iraq 32°57′N 44°47′E
As Suways *see* Suez
Asta Colonia *see* Asti
Astacus *see* İzmit
115 M23 **Astakída** *island* SE Greece
145 Q9 **Astana** *prev.* Akmola, Akmolinsk, Tselinograd, Aqmola. ● (Kazakhstan) Akmola, N Kazakhstan 51°13′N 71°25′E
142 M3 **Āstāneh** Gīlān, NW Iran 37°17′N 49°58′E
Asta Pompeia *see* Asti
137 Y14 **Astara** S Azerbaijan 38°28′N 48°51′E
Astarabad *see* Gorgān
99 L15 **Asten** Noord-Brabant, SE Netherlands 51°24′N 05°45′E
Asterābād *see* Gorgān
106 C8 **Asti** *anc.* Asta Colonia, Asta Pompeia, Hasta Colonia, Hasta Pompeia. Piemonte, NW Italy 44°54′N 08°11′E
Astigi *see* Ecija
Astipálaia *see* Astypálaia
148 L16 **Astola Island** *island* SW Pakistan
152 H4 **Astor** Jammu and Kashmir, NW India 35°21′N 74°52′E
104 K4 **Astorga** *anc.* Asturica Augusta. Castilla-León, N Spain 42°27′N 06°04′W
32 F10 **Astoria** Oregon, NW USA 46°12′N 123°50′W
0 F8 **Astoria Fan** *undersea feature* E Pacific Ocean 45°15′N 126°15′W
95 J22 **Åstorp** Skåne, S Sweden 56°09′N 12°57′E
Astrabad *see* Gorgān
127 Q13 **Astrakhan'** Astrakhanskaya Oblast', SW Russian Federation 46°20′N 48°01′E
Astrakhan-Bazar *see* Cälilabad
127 Q11 **Astrakhanskaya Oblast'** ◈ *province* SW Russian Federation
93 J15 **Åsträsk** Västerbotten, N Sweden 64°38′N 20°00′E
Astrida *see* Butare
65 O22 **Astrid Ridge** *undersea feature* S Atlantic Ocean
187 P15 **Astrolabe, Récifs de l'** *reef* C New Caledonia
121 P2 **Astromerítis** N Cyprus 35°09′N 33°02′E
115 F20 **Ástros** Pelopónnisos, S Greece 37°24′N 22°43′E
119 G16 **Astryna** *Rus.* Ostryna. Hrodzyenskaya Voblasts', W Belarus 53°44′N 24°33′E
104 J2 **Asturias** ◈ *autonomous community* NW Spain
Asturias *see* Oviedo
Asturica Augusta *see* Astorga
115 L22 **Astypálaia** *var.* Astipálaia, *It.* Stampalia. *island* Kykládes, Greece, Aegean Sea
192 G16 **Āsuisui, Cape** *headland* Savai'i, W Samoa 13°44′S 172°29′W
195 S2 **Asuka** *Japanese research station* Antarctica 71°49′S 23°52′E
62 O6 **Asunción** ● (Paraguay) Central, S Paraguay 25°17′S 57°36′W
62 O6 **Asunción** ✈ Central, S Paraguay 25°15′S 57°40′W
188 K3 **Asuncion Island** *island* N Northern Mariana Islands
42 E6 **Asunción Mita** Jutiapa, SE Guatemala 14°20′N 89°42′W
Asunción Nochixtlán *see* Nochixtlán
40 E3 **Asunción, Río** ≈ NW Mexico
95 M18 **Åsunden** ◎ S Sweden
118 K11 **Asvyeya** *Rus.* Osveya. Vitsyebskaya Voblasts', N Belarus 56°00′N 28°05′E
Aswa *see* Achwa
75 X11 **Aswān** *var.* Assouan, Assuan, Aswân; *anc.* Syene. SE Egypt 24°03′N 32°59′E
Aswân *see* Aswān
Aswân Dam *see* Khazzān Aswān
75 W9 **Asyūţ** *var.* Assiout, Assiut, Asyût, Siut; *anc.* Lycopolis. C Egypt 27°06′N 31°11′E
Asyût *see* Asyūţ
193 W15 **Ata** *island* Tongatapu Group, SW Tonga
62 G8 **Atacama** *off.* Región de Atacama. ◈ *region* C Chile
Atacama Desert *see* Atacama, Desierto de
62 H4 **Atacama, Desierto de** *Eng.* Atacama Desert. *desert* N Chile
62 I6 **Atacama, Puna de** ▲▲ NW Argentina
Atacama, Región de *see* Atacama
62 I5 **Atacama, Salar de** *salt lake* N Chile
54 E11 **Ataco** Tolima, C Colombia 03°36′N 75°23′W
190 H8 **Atafu Atoll** *island* NW Tokelau
190 H8 **Atafu Village** Atafu Atoll, NW Tokelau 08°40′S 172°40′W
74 K12 **Atakor** ▲▲ SE Algeria
77 R14 **Atakora, Chaîne de l'** *var.* Atakora Mountains. ▲▲ N Benin
Atakora Mountains *see* Atakora, Chaîne de l'
77 R16 **Atakpamé** C Togo 07°32′N 01°08′E
146 F11 **Atakui** Ahal Welaýaty, C Turkmenistan 40°04′N 58°03′E
58 B13 **Atalaia do Norte** Amazonas, N Brazil 04°22′S 70°10′W
146 M14 **Atamyrat** *prev.* Kerki. Lebap Welaýaty, E Turkmenistan 37°52′N 65°06′E
76 I7 **Aţâr** Adrar, W Mauritania 20°30′N 13°03′W
162 G10 **Atas Bogd** ▲ SW Mongolia 43°17′N 96°47′E
35 P12 **Atascadero** California, W USA 35°28′N 120°40′W
25 S13 **Atascosa River** ≈ Texas, SW USA
145 R11 **Atasu** Karaganda, C Kazakhstan 48°42′N 71°38′E
145 R12 **Atasu** ≈ Karaganda, C Kazakhstan
193 V15 **Atata** *island* Tongatapu Group, S Tonga
136 H10 **Atatürk** ✈ (İstanbul) İstanbul, NW Turkey 40°58′N 28°50′E
137 N16 **Atatürk Barajī** ⊠ S Turkey
115 O23 **Atavýros** *prev.* Attavyros. Ródos, Dodekánisa, Aegean Sea 36°10′N 27°50′E
115 O23 **Atavýros** *prev.* Attávyros. ▲ Ródos, Dodekánisa, Greece, Aegean Sea 36°10′N 27°50′E
Atax *see* Aude
80 G8 **Atbara** *var.* 'Aţbārah. River Nile, NE Sudan 17°42′N 34°E
80 H8 **Atbara** *var.* Nahr 'Aţbarah. ≈ Eritrea/Sudan
'Aţbārah/'Aţbarah, Nahr *see* Atbara
145 P9 **Atbasar** Akmola, N Kazakhstan 51°49′N 68°18′E
At-Bashi *see* At-Bashy
147 W9 **At-Bashy** *var.* At-Bashi. Narynskaya Oblast', C Kyrgyzstan 41°07′N 75°48′E
22 I10 **Atchafalaya Bay** *bay* Louisiana, S USA
22 I8 **Atchafalaya River** ≈ Louisiana, S USA
Atchin *see* Aceh
27 Q3 **Atchison** Kansas, C USA 39°31′N 95°07′W
77 P16 **Atebubu** C Ghana 07°47′N 01°00′W
105 Q6 **Ateca** Aragón, NE Spain 41°20′N 01°49′W
40 K11 **Atengo, Río** ≈ C Mexico
Aternum *see* Pescara
107 K15 **Atessa** Abruzzo, C Italy 42°03′N 14°25′E
Ateste *see* Este
99 E19 **Ath** *var.* Aat. Hainaut, SW Belgium 50°38′N 03°47′E
11 Q13 **Athabasca** Alberta, SW Canada 54°44′N 113°15′W
11 Q12 **Athabasca** *var.* Athabaska. ≈ Alberta, SW Canada
11 R10 **Athabasca, Lake** ◎ Alberta/Saskatchewan, SW Canada
Athabaska *see* Athabasca
115 C16 **Athamánon** ▲▲ C Greece
97 F17 **Athboy** *Ir.* Baile Átha Buí. E Ireland 53°38′N 06°55′W
Athenae *see* Athína
97 C18 **Athenry** *Ir.* Baile Átha an Rí. W Ireland 53°19′N 08°49′W
23 P2 **Athens** Alabama, S USA 34°48′N 86°58′W
23 T3 **Athens** Georgia, SE USA 33°57′N 83°24′W
31 T14 **Athens** Ohio, N USA 39°20′N 82°06′W
20 M10 **Athens** Tennessee, S USA 35°27′N 84°38′W
25 V7 **Athens** Texas, SW USA 32°12′N 95°51′W
Athens *see* Athína
115 B18 **Athéras, Akrotírio** *headland* Kefalloniá, Iónia Nísiá, Greece, C Mediterranean Sea 38°20′N 20°24′E
181 W4 **Atherton** Queensland, NE Australia 17°18′S 145°29′E
81 I19 **Athi** ≈ S Kenya
121 Q2 **Athiénou** SE Cyprus 35°01′N 33°31′E
115 H19 **Athína** *Eng.* Athens, *prev.* Athínai; *anc.* Athenae. ● (Greece) Attikí, C Greece 37°59′N 23°44′E
Athínai *see* Athína
139 S10 **Athīyah** An Najaf, C Iraq 32°01′N 44°04′E
97 D18 **Athlone** *Ir.* Baile Átha Luain. C Ireland 53°25′N 07°56′W
155 F16 **Athni** Karnātaka, W India 16°43′N 75°04′E
185 C23 **Athol** Southland, South Island, New Zealand 45°30′S 168°35′E
19 N11 **Athol** Massachusetts, NE USA 42°35′N 72°11′W
115 I15 **Áthos** ▲ NE Greece 40°10′N 24°21′E
Athos, Mount *see* Ágion Óros
Ath Thawrah *see* Madīnat ath Thawrah
141 P5 **Ath Thumāmī** *spring/well* N Saudi Arabia 27°56′N 45°06′E
99 L25 **Athus** Luxembourg, SE Belgium 49°34′N 05°50′E
97 E19 **Athy** *Ir.* Baile Átha Í. C Ireland 52°59′N 06°59′W
78 I10 **Ati** Batha, C Chad 13°11′N 18°20′E
81 F16 **Atiak** NW Uganda 03°14′N 32°05′E
57 G17 **Atico** Arequipa, SW Peru 16°13′S 73°13′W
105 O6 **Atienza** Castilla-La Mancha, C Spain 41°12′N 02°52′W
39 Q6 **Atigun Pass** *pass* Alaska, USA
12 B12 **Atikokan** Ontario, S Canada 48°45′N 91°38′W
13 O9 **Atikonak Lac** ◎ Newfoundland and Labrador, E Canada
42 C6 **Atitlán, Lago de** ◎ W Guatemala
190 L16 **Atiu** *island* S Cook Islands
Atjeh *see* Aceh
123 T9 **Atka** Magadanskaya Oblast', E Russian Federation 60°45′N 151°35′E
38 H17 **Atka** Atka Island, Alaska, USA 52°12′N 174°14′W
38 H17 **Atka Island** *island* Aleutian Islands, Alaska, USA
127 O7 **Atkarsk** Saratovskaya Oblast', W Russian Federation 52°15′N 43°48′E
27 U11 **Atkins** Arkansas, C USA 35°15′N 92°56′W
29 O13 **Atkinson** Nebraska, C USA 42°31′N 98°57′W
171 T12 **Atkri** Papua, E Indonesia 01°45′S 130°04′E
41 O13 **Atlacomulco** *var.* Atlacomulco de Fabela. México, C Mexico 19°49′N 99°54′W
Atlacomulco de Fabela *see* Atlacomulco
23 S3 **Atlanta** *state capital* Georgia, SE USA 33°45′N 84°23′W
31 R6 **Atlanta** Michigan, N USA 45°01′N 84°07′W
25 X6 **Atlanta** Texas, SW USA 33°06′N 94°09′W
29 T15 **Atlantic** Iowa, C USA 41°24′N 95°00′W
21 Y10 **Atlantic** North Carolina, SE USA 34°52′N 76°20′W
23 W8 **Atlantic Beach** Florida, SE USA 30°19′N 81°24′W
18 J17 **Atlantic City** New Jersey, NE USA 39°23′N 74°27′W
172 L14 **Atlantic-Indian Basin** *undersea feature* SW Indian Ocean 60°00′S 15°00′E
172 K13 **Atlantic-Indian Ridge** *undersea feature* SW Indian Ocean 53°00′S 15°00′E
54 E4 **Atlántico** *off.* Departamento del Atlántico. ◈ *province* NW Colombia
64-65 **Atlantic Ocean** *ocean*
Atlántico, Departamento del *see* Atlántico
42 K7 **Atlántico Norte, Región Autónoma** *prev.* Zelaya Norte. ◈ *autonomous region* NE Nicaragua
42 L10 **Atlántico Sur, Región Autónoma** *prev.* Zelaya Sur. ◈ *autonomous region* SE Nicaragua
42 I5 **Atlántida** ◈ *department* N Honduras
77 Y15 **Atlantika Mountains** ▲▲ E Nigeria
64 J10 **Atlantis Fracture Zone** *tectonic feature* NW Atlantic Ocean
74 H7 **Atlas Mountains** ▲▲ NW Africa
123 V11 **Atlasova, Ostrov** *island* SE Russian Federation
123 V10 **Atlasovo** Kamchatskaya Oblast', E Russian Federation 55°42′N 159°35′E
120 G11 **Atlas Saharien** *var.* Saharan Atlas. ▲▲ Algeria/Morocco
Atlas, Tell *see* Atlas Tellien
120 H10 **Atlas Tellien** *Eng.* Tell Atlas. ▲▲ N Algeria
10 I9 **Atlin** British Columbia, W Canada 59°31′N 133°41′W
10 I9 **Atlin Lake** ◎ British Columbia, W Canada
41 P14 **Atlixco** Puebla, S Mexico 18°55′N 98°26′W
94 B11 **Atløyna** *island* S Norway
155 I17 **Ātmakūr** Andhra Pradesh, C India 15°52′N 78°42′E
23 O8 **Atmore** Alabama, S USA 31°01′N 87°29′W
101 J20 **Atmühl** ≈ S Germany
94 H11 **Atna** ≈ S Norway
164 E13 **Atō** Yamaguchi, Honshū, SW Japan 34°24′N 131°42′E
57 L21 **Atocha** Potosí, S Bolivia 20°55′S 66°14′W
27 P12 **Atoka** Oklahoma, C USA 34°22′N 96°08′W
27 O12 **Atoka Lake** *var.* Atoka Reservoir. ⊠ Oklahoma, C USA
Atoka Reservoir *see* Atoka Lake
33 Q14 **Atomic City** Idaho, NW USA 43°26′N 112°48′W
40 L10 **Atotonilco** Zacatecas, C Mexico 24°12′N 102°46′W
Atotonilco *see* Atotonilco el Alto
40 M13 **Atotonilco el Alto** *var.* Atotonilco. Jalisco, SW Mexico 20°35′N 102°30′W
77 N7 **Atouila, 'Erg** *desert* N Mali
41 N16 **Atoyac** *var.* Atoyac de Alvarez. Guerrero, S Mexico 17°12′N 100°28′W
Atoyac de Alvarez *see* Atoyac
41 P15 **Atoyac, Río** ≈ S Mexico
39 O5 **Atqasuk** Alaska, USA 70°28′N 157°24′W
Atrak/Atrak, Rūd-e *see* Etrek
95 J20 **Ätran** ≈ S Sweden
54 C7 **Atrato, Río** ≈ NW Colombia
Atrek *see* Etrek
107 K14 **Atri** Abruzzo, C Italy 42°35′N 13°59′E
Atria *see* Adria
165 P9 **Atsumi** Yamagata, Honshū, C Japan 38°38′N 139°36′E
165 S3 **Atsuta** Hokkaidō, NE Japan 43°28′N 141°24′E
143 Q17 **Aţ Ţaff** *desert* C United Arab Emirates
138 G12 **Aţ Ţafīlah** *var.* Et Tafila, Tafila. Aţ Ţafīlah, W Jordan 30°52′N 35°36′E
138 G12 **Aţ Ţafīlah** *off.* Muḩāfaẓat aţ Ţafīlah. ◈ *governorate* W Jordan
140 L10 **Aţ Ţā'if** Makkah, W Saudi Arabia 21°50′N 40°50′E
Attaleia/Attalia *see* Antalya
23 Q3 **Attalla** Alabama, S USA 34°01′N 86°05′W
138 L2 **At Tall al Abyaḑ** *var.* Tall al Abyaḑ, Tell Abyad, *Fr.* Tell Abiad. Ar Raqqah, N Syria 36°36′N 34°00′E
139 S5 **At Ta'mīn** *off.* Muḩāfaẓat at Ta'mīm. ◈ *governorate* N Iraq
138 L7 **Aţ Ţanf** Ḩimş, S Syria 33°29′N 38°39′E
163 N9 **Attanshiree** Dornogovĭ, SE Mongolia 45°36′N 110°30′E
Attapu *see* Samakhixai
139 S10 **At Ţaqţaqānah** An Najaf, C Iraq 32°03′N 43°54′E
Attávyros *see* Atavýros
139 V15 **At Tawal** *desert* Iraq/Saudi Arabia
12 G9 **Attawapiskat** Ontario, C Canada 52°55′N 82°26′W
12 F9 **Attawapiskat** ≈ Ontario, S Canada
12 D9 **Attawapiskat Lake** ◎ Ontario, C Canada
At Taybé *see* Ţayyibah
101 F16 **Attendorn** Nordrhein-Westfalen, W Germany 51°07′N 07°54′E
109 R5 **Attersee** Salzburg, NW Austria 47°55′N 13°31′E
109 R5 **Attersee** ◎ N Austria
99 L24 **Attert** Luxembourg, SE Belgium 49°45′N 05°47′E
138 M4 **At Tibnī** *var.* Tibnī. Dayr az Zawr, NE Syria 35°30′N 39°48′E
31 N13 **Attica** Indiana, N USA 40°17′N 87°15′W
18 E10 **Attica** New York, NE USA 42°51′N 78°13′W
Attica *see* Attikí
13 N7 **Attikamagen Lake** ◎ Newfoundland and Labrador, E Canada
115 H20 **Attikí** *Eng.* Attica. ◈ *region* C Greece
19 O12 **Attleboro** Massachusetts, NE USA 41°55′N 71°15′W
109 R5 **Attnang** Oberösterreich, N Austria 48°02′N 13°44′E
149 U6 **Attock City** Punjab, E Pakistan 33°52′N 72°20′E
Attopeu *see* Samakhixai
25 X8 **Attoyac River** ≈ Texas, SW USA
38 D16 **Attu** Attu Island, Alaska, USA 52°53′N 173°18′E
139 Y12 **Aţ Ţūbah** Al Başrah, E Iraq 30°29′N 47°28′E
140 K4 **Aţ Ţubayq** *plain* Jordan/Saudi Arabia
38 C16 **Attu Island** *island* Aleutian Islands, Alaska, USA
75 X8 **Aţ Ţūr** *var.* El Ţûr. NE Egypt 28°14′N 33°36′E
155 I21 **Āttūr** Tamil Nādu, SE India 11°34′N 78°39′E
141 N17 **At Turbah** SW Yemen 12°42′N 43°31′E
62 I12 **Atuel, Río** ≈ C Argentina
191 X7 **Atuona** Hiva Oa, NE French Polynesia 09°47′S 139°03′W
Aturus *see* Adour
95 M18 **Åtvidaberg** Östergötland, S Sweden 58°12′N 16°00′E
35 P9 **Atwater** California, W USA 37°19′N 120°33′W
29 T8 **Atwater** Minnesota, N USA 45°08′N 94°48′W
26 I2 **Atwood** Kansas, C USA 39°48′N 101°03′W
31 U12 **Atwood Lake** ⊠ Ohio, N USA
127 P5 **Atyashevo** Respublika Mordoviya, W Russian Federation 54°36′N 46°04′E
144 F12 **Atyrau** *prev.* Gur'yev. Atyrau, W Kazakhstan 47°07′N 51°56′E
144 E11 **Atyrau** *off.* Atyrauskaya Oblast', *var.Kaz.* Atyraū Oblysy; *prev.* Gur'yevskaya Oblast'. ◈ *province* W Kazakhstan
Atyraū Oblysy/ Atyrauskaya Oblast' *see* Atyrau
Atyrauskaya Oblast' *see* Atyrau
108 J7 **Au** Vorarlberg, NW Austria 47°19′N 10°01′E
186 B4 **Aua Island** *island* NW Papua New Guinea
103 S16 **Aubagne** *anc.* Albania. Bouches-du-Rhône, SE France 43°17′N 05°35′E
99 L25 **Aubange** Luxembourg, SE Belgium 49°35′N 05°49′E
103 Q6 **Aube** ◈ *department* N France
103 R6 **Aube** ≈ N France
99 L19 **Aubel** Liège, E Belgium 50°45′N 05°49′E
103 Q13 **Aubenas** Ardèche, E France 44°37′N 04°24′E
103 O8 **Aubigny-sur-Nère** Cher, C France 47°30′N 02°27′E
103 O13 **Aubin** Aveyron, S France 44°30′N 02°18′E
103 O13 **Aubrac, Monts d'** ▲▲ S France
36 J10 **Aubrey Cliffs** *cliff* Arizona, SW USA
23 R5 **Auburn** Alabama, S USA 32°37′N 85°30′W
35 P6 **Auburn** California, W USA 38°53′N 121°03′W
30 K14 **Auburn** Illinois, N USA 39°35′N 89°45′W
31 Q11 **Auburn** Indiana, N USA 41°22′N 85°03′W
20 J7 **Auburn** Kentucky, S USA 36°52′N 86°42′W
19 P8 **Auburn** Maine, NE USA 44°05′N 70°15′W
19 N11 **Auburn** Massachusetts, NE USA 42°11′N 71°47′W
29 S16 **Auburn** Nebraska, C USA 40°23′N 95°50′W
18 H10 **Auburn** New York, NE USA 42°55′N 76°31′W
32 H8 **Auburn** Washington, NW USA 47°18′N 122°13′W
103 N11 **Aubusson** Creuse, C France 45°58′N 02°10′E
118 E10 **Auce** *Ger.* Autz. Dobele, SW Latvia 56°28′N 22°54′E
102 L15 **Auch** *Lat.* Augusta Auscorum, Elimberrum. Gers, S France 43°40′N 00°37′E
77 U16 **Auchi** Edo, S Nigeria 07°01′N 06°17′E
23 T9 **Aucilla River** ≈ Florida/Georgia, SE USA
184 L6 **Auckland** Auckland, North Island, New Zealand 36°53′S 174°46′E
184 K5 **Auckland** *off.* Auckland Region. ◈ *region* North Island, New Zealand
184 L6 **Auckland** ✈ Auckland, North Island, New Zealand 37°01′S 174°49′E
192 J12 **Auckland Islands** *island group* S New Zealand
Auckland Region *see* Auckland
103 O16 **Aude** ◈ *department* S France
103 N16 **Aude** *anc.* Atax. ≈ S France
Audenarde *see* Oudenaarde
Audern *see* Audru
102 E6 **Audierne** Finistère, NW France 48°01′N 04°30′W
102 E6 **Audierne, Baie d'** *bay* NW France
103 U7 **Audincourt** Doubs, E France 47°29′N 06°50′E
118 G5 **Audru** *Ger.* Audern. Pärnumaa, SW Estonia 58°24′N 24°22′E
29 T14 **Audubon** Iowa, C USA 41°44′N 94°56′W
101 N17 **Aue** Sachsen, E Germany 50°35′N 12°42′E
100 H12 **Aue** ≈ NW Germany
100 L9 **Auerbach** Bayern, SE Germany 49°41′N 11°41′E
101 M17 **Auerbach** Sachsen, E Germany 50°30′N 12°24′E
108 I10 **Auererrhein** ≈ SW Switzerland
101 N17 **Auersberg** ▲ E Germany 50°30′N 12°42′E
181 W9 **Augathella** Queensland, E Australia 25°54′S 146°38′E
31 Q12 **Auglaize River** ≈ Ohio, N USA
83 F22 **Augrabies Falls** *waterfall* W South Africa
31 R7 **Au Gres River** ≈ Michigan, N USA
Augsbourg *see* Augsburg
101 K22 **Augsburg** *Fr.* Augsbourg; *anc.* Augusta Vindelicorum. Bayern, S Germany 48°22′N 10°54′E
180 I14 **Augusta** Western Australia 34°18′S 115°10′E
107 L25 **Augusta** *It.* Agosta. Sicilia, Italy, C Mediterranean Sea 37°14′N 15°14′E
27 W11 **Augusta** Arkansas, C USA 35°16′N 91°21′W
23 V3 **Augusta** Georgia, SE USA 33°29′N 81°58′W
27 O6 **Augusta** Kansas, C USA 37°40′N 96°59′W
19 Q7 **Augusta** *state capital* Maine, NE USA 44°20′N 69°44′W
33 Q8 **Augusta** Montana, NW USA 47°28′N 112°23′W
Augusta *see* London
Augusta Auscorum *see* Auch
Augusta Emerita *see* Mérida
Augusta Praetoria *see* Aosta
Augusta Suessionum *see* Soissons
Augusta Trajana *see* Stara Zagora
Augusta Treverorum *see* Trier
Augusta Vangionum *see* Worms
Augusta Vindelicorum *see* Augsburg
95 G24 **Augustenborg** *Ger.* Augustenburg. Sønderjylland, SW Denmark 54°57′N 09°53′E
Augustenburg *see* Augustenborg
39 Q13 **Augustine Island** *island* Alaska, USA
14 L9 **Augustines, Lac des** ◎ Québec, SE Canada
Augustobona Tricassium *see* Troyes
Augustodunum *see* Autun
Augustodurum *see* Bayeux
Augustoritum Lemovicensium *see* Limoges
110 O8 **Augustów** *Rus.* Avgustov. Podlaskie, NE Poland 53°52′N 22°58′E
Augustow Canal *see* Augustowski, Kanał
110 O8 **Augustowski, Kanał** *Eng.* Augustow Canal, *Rus.* Avgustovskiy Kanal. *canal* NE Poland
180 I9 **Augustus, Mount** ▲ Western Australia 24°42′S 117°42′E
186 M9 **Auki** Malaita, N Solomon Islands 08°48′S 160°45′E
21 W8 **Aulander** North Carolina, SE USA 36°15′N 77°16′W
180 L7 **Auld, Lake** *salt lake* C Western Australia
Aulie Ata/Auliye-Ata *see* Taraz
Äūlīeköl *see* Auliyekol'
144 M8 **Auliyekol'** *Kaz.* Äūlīeköl; *prev.* Semiozernoye. Kostanay, N Kazakhstan 52°22′N 64°06′E
106 E10 **Aulla** Toscana, C Italy 44°15′N 10°00′E
102 F6 **Aulne** ≈ NW France
Aulong *see* Ulong
37 T3 **Ault** Colorado, C USA 40°34′N 104°43′W
95 F22 **Aulum** *var.* avlum. Ringkøbing, C Denmark 56°16′N 08°48′E
103 N3 **Aumale** Seine-Maritime, N France 49°45′N 01°43′E
Auminzatau, Gory *see* Ovminzatovo Tog'lari
77 T14 **Auna** Niger, W Nigeria 10°13′N 04°43′E
166 L6 **Aunglan** *var.* Allanmyo, Myaydo. Magway, C Myanmar (Burma) 19°25′N 95°13′E
95 H21 **Auning** Århus, C Denmark 56°26′N 10°23′E
192 K17 **'Aunu'u Island** *island* W American Samoa
83 E20 **Auob** *var.* Oup. ≈ Namibia/South Africa
93 K19 **Aura** Länsi-Suomi, SW Finland 60°37′N 22°35′E
109 R5 **Aurach** ≈ N Austria
Aural, Phnom *see* Aôral, Phnum
153 O14 **Aurangābād** Bihār, N India 24°46′N 84°23′E
154 F13 **Aurangābād** Mahārāshtra, C India 19°52′N 75°22′E
189 V7 **Aur Atoll** *atoll* E Marshall Islands
102 G7 **Auray** Morbihan, NW France 47°40′N 02°59′W
94 G13 **Aurdal** Oppland, S Norway 60°51′N 09°25′E
94 F8 **Aure** Møre og Romsdal, S Norway 63°16′N 08°31′E
29 T12 **Aurelia** Iowa, C USA 42°42′N 95°26′W
Aurelia Aquensis *see* Baden-Baden
Aurelianum *see* Orléans
120 J10 **Aurès, Massif de l'** ▲▲ NE Algeria
100 F10 **Aurich** Niedersachsen, NW Germany 53°28′N 07°28′E
103 O13 **Aurillac** Cantal, C France 44°56′N 02°26′E
Aurine, Alpi *see* Zillertaler Alpen
Aurium *see* Ourense
14 H15 **Aurora** Ontario, S Canada 44°00′N 79°26′W
55 S8 **Aurora** NW Guyana 06°46′N 59°45′W
37 T4 **Aurora** Colorado, C USA 39°42′N 104°51′W
30 M11 **Aurora** Illinois, N USA 41°46′N 88°19′W
31 Q15 **Aurora** Indiana, N USA 39°01′N 84°55′W
29 W4 **Aurora** Minnesota, N USA 47°31′N 92°14′W
27 S8 **Aurora** Missouri, C USA 36°58′N 93°43′W
29 P16 **Aurora** Nebraska, C USA 40°52′N 98°00′W
36 J5 **Aurora** Utah, W USA 38°55′N 111°55′W
Aurora *see* San Francisco, Philippines
Aurora *see* Maéwo, Vanuatu
94 F10 **Aursjøen** ◎ S Norway
94 I9 **Aursunden** ◎ S Norway
83 D21 **Aus** Karas, SW Namibia 26°38′S 16°19′E
Ausa *see* Vic
14 E16 **Ausable** ≈ Ontario, S Canada
31 S7 **Au Sable Point** *headland* Michigan, N USA 44°19′N 83°20′W
31 O3 **Au Sable Point** *headland* Michigan, N USA 46°40′N 86°08′W
31 R6 **Au Sable River** ≈ Michigan, N USA
57 H16 **Ausangate, Nevado** ▲ C Peru 13°47′S 71°13′W
Auschwitz *see* Oświęcim
Ausculum Apulum *see* Ascoli Satriano
105 Q4 **Ausejo** La Rioja, N Spain 42°21′N 02°10′W
Aussig *see* Ústí nad Labem
95 F17 **Aust-Agder** ◈ *county* S Norway
92 P2 **Austfonna** *glacier* NE Svalbard
31 P15 **Austin** Indiana, N USA 38°45′N 85°48′W
29 W11 **Austin** Minnesota, N USA 43°40′N 92°58′W
35 U5 **Austin** Nevada, W USA 39°30′N 117°05′W
25 S10 **Austin** *state capital* Texas, SW USA 30°16′N 97°45′W
180 J10 **Austin, Lake** *salt lake* Western Australia
31 V11 **Austintown** Ohio, N USA 41°06′N 80°45′W
25 V9 **Austonio** Texas, SW USA 31°09′N 95°39′W
Australes, Archipel des *see* Australes, Îles
Australes et Antarctiques Françaises, Terres *see* French Southern and Antarctic Territories
191 T14 **Australes, Îles** *var.* Archipel des Australes, Îles Tubuai, Tubuai Islands, *Eng.* Austral Islands. *island group* SW French Polynesia
175 Y11 **Austral Fracture Zone** *tectonic feature* S Pacific Ocean
174 M8 **Australia** *continent*
181 O7 **Australia** *off.* Commonwealth of Australia. ◆ *commonwealth republic*
Australia, Commonwealth of *see* Australia
183 Q12 **Australian Alps** ▲▲ SE Australia
183 R11 **Australian Capital Territory** *prev.* Federal Capital Territory. ◈ *territory* SE Australia
Australie, Bassin Nord de l' *see* North Australian Basin
Austral Islands *see* Australes, Îles
Austrava *see* Ostrov
109 T6 **Austria** *off.* Republic of Austria, *Ger.* Österreich. ◆ *republic* C Europe
Austria, Republic of *see* Austria
92 K3 **Austurland** ◈ *region* SE Iceland
92 G10 **Austvågøya** *island* C Norway
Ausuitoq *see* Grise Fiord
58 G13 **Autazes** Amazonas, N Brazil 03°37′S 59°08′W
102 M16 **Auterive** Haute-Garonne, S France 43°22′N 01°28′E
Autesiodorum *see* Auxerre
103 N2 **Authie** ≈ N France
Autissiodorum *see* Auxerre
40 K14 **Autlán** *var.* Autlán de Navarro. Jalisco, SW Mexico 19°48′N 104°20′W
Autlán de Navarro *see* Autlán
Autricum *see* Chartres
103 Q9 **Autun** *anc.* Ædua, Augustodunum. Saône-et-Loire, C France 46°58′N 04°18′E
Autz *see* Auce
99 H20 **Auvelais** Namur, S Belgium 50°27′N 04°38′E
103 P11 **Auvergne** ◈ *region* C France
102 M12 **Auvézère** ≈ W France
103 P7 **Auxerre** *anc.* Autesiodorum, Autissiodorum. Yonne, C France 47°48′N 03°35′E
103 N2 **Auxi-le-Château** Pas-de-Calais, N France 50°14′N 02°06′E
103 S8 **Auxonne** Côte d'Or, C France 47°12′N 05°22′E
55 P9 **Auyan Tebuy** ▲ SE Venezuela 05°48′N 62°27′W
103 O10 **Auzances** Creuse, C France 46°01′N 02°29′E
27 U8 **Ava** Missouri, C USA 36°57′N 92°39′W
142 M5 **Āvaj** Qazvin, N Iran
95 C15 **Avaldsnes** Rogaland, S Norway 59°21′N 05°16′E
103 Q8 **Avallon** Yonne, C France 47°30′N 03°54′E
102 K6 **Avaloirs, Mont des** ▲ NW France 48°27′N 00°11′W
35 S16 **Avalon** Santa Catalina Island, California, W USA 33°20′N 118°19′W
18 J17 **Avalon** New Jersey, NE USA 39°04′N 74°42′W
13 V13 **Avalon Peninsula** *peninsula* Newfoundland and Labrador, E Canada
197 Q11 **Avannaarsua** ◈ *province* N Greenland
60 K10 **Avaré** São Paulo, S Brazil 23°06′S 48°57′W
Avaricum *see* Bourges
190 H16 **Avarua** ○ (Cook Islands) Rarotonga, S Cook Islands 21°12′S 159°46′E
190 H16 **Avarua Harbour** *harbor* Rarotonga, S Cook Islands

◆ Country
● Country Capital
◇ Dependent Territory
○ Dependent Territory Capital
◈ Administrative Regions
✈ International Airport
▲ Mountain
▲▲ Mountain Range
Volcano
≈ River
◎ Lake
⊠ Reservoir

AVASFELSŐFALU – BAGNI DI LUCCA

Avasfelsőfalu *see* Negreşti-Oaş
38 *L17* **Avatanak Island** *island* Aleutian Islands, Alaska, USA
190 *B16* **Avatele** S Niue *19°06′S 169°55′E*
190 *H15* **Avatiu Harbour** *harbor* Rarotonga, S Cook Islands
Avdeyevka *see* Avdiyivka
114 *J13* **Ávdira** Anatolikí Makedonía kai Thráki, NE Greece *40°58′N 24°58′E*
117 *X8* **Avdiyivka** *Rus.* Avdeyevka. Donets'ka Oblast', SE Ukraine *48°06′N 37°46′E*
Avdzaga *see* Gurvanbulag
104 *G6* **Ave** ⇝ N Portugal
104 *G7* **Aveiro** *anc.* Talabriga. Aveiro, W Portugal *40°38′N 08°40′W*
104 *G7* **Aveiro** ◈ *district* N Portugal
Avela *see* Ávila
99 *D18* **Avelgem** West-Vlaanderen, W Belgium *50°46′N 03°25′E*
61 *D20* **Avellaneda** Buenos Aires, E Argentina *34°43′S 58°23′W*
107 *L17* **Avellino** *anc.* Abellinum. Campania, S Italy *40°54′N 14°46′E*
35 *Q12* **Avenal** California, W USA *36°00′N 120°07′W*
Avenio *see* Avignon
94 *E8* **Averøya** *island* S Norway
107 *K17* **Aversa** Campania, S Italy *40°58′N 14°13′E*
33 *N9* **Avery** Idaho, NW USA *47°14′N 115°48′W*
25 *W5* **Avery** Texas, SW USA *33°33′N 94°46′W*
Aves, Islas de *see* Las Aves, Islas
Avesnes *see* Avesnes-sur-Helpe
103 *Q2* **Avesnes-sur-Helpe** *var.* Avesnes. Nord, N France *50°08′N 03°57′E*
64 *G12* **Aves Ridge** *undersea feature* SE Caribbean Sea *14°00′N 63°30′W*
95 *M14* **Avesta** Dalarna, C Sweden *60°09′N 16°10′E*
103 *O14* **Aveyron** ◈ *department* S France
103 *N14* **Aveyron** ⇝ S France
107 *J15* **Avezzano** Abruzzo, C Italy *42°02′N 13°26′E*
115 *D16* **Avgó** ▲ C Greece *39°31′N 21°24′E*
Avgustov *see* Augustów
Avgustovskiy Kanal *see* Augustowski, Kanał
96 *J9* **Aviemore** N Scotland, United Kingdom *57°06′N 04°01′W*
185 *F21* **Aviemore, Lake** ◎ South Island, New Zealand
103 *R15* **Avignon** *anc.* Avenio. Vaucluse, SE France *43°57′N 04°49′E*
104 *M7* **Ávila** *var.* Avila; *anc.* Abela, Abula, Abyla, Avela. Castilla-León, C Spain *40°39′N 04°42′W*
104 *L8* **Ávila** ◈ *province* Castilla-León, C Spain
104 *K2* **Avilés** Asturias, NW Spain *43°33′N 05°55′W*
118 *J4* **Avinurme** *Ger.* Awwinorm. Ida-Virumaa, NE Estonia *58°58′N 26°53′E*
104 *H10* **Avis** Portalegre, C Portugal *39°03′N 07°53′W*
Avlum *see* Aulum
182 *M11* **Avoca** Victoria, SE Australia *37°09′S 143°34′E*
29 *T14* **Avoca** Iowa, C USA *41°27′N 95°20′W*
182 *M11* **Avoca River** ⇝ Victoria, SE Australia
107 *L25* **Avola** Sicilia, Italy, C Mediterranean Sea *36°54′N 15°08′E*
18 *F10* **Avon** New York, NE USA *42°53′N 77°41′W*
29 *P12* **Avon** South Dakota, N USA *43°00′N 98°03′W*
97 *M23* **Avon** ⇝ S England, United Kingdom
97 *L20* **Avon** ⇝ C England, United Kingdom
36 *K13* **Avondale** Arizona, SW USA *33°25′N 112°20′W*
23 *X13* **Avon Park** Florida, SE USA *27°36′N 81°30′W*
102 *J5* **Avranches** Manche, N France *48°42′N 01°21′W*
Avveel *see* Ivalojoki, Finland
186 *M6* **Avuavu** *var.* Kolotambu. Guadalcanal, C Solomon Islands *09°52′S 160°25′E*
103 *O3* **Avure** ⇝ N France
Avveel *see* Ivalo, Finland
Avvil *see* Ivalo
77 *O17* **Awaaso** *var.* Awaso. SW Ghana *06°10′N 02°18′W*
141 *X8* **Awābī** *var.* Al 'Awābī. NE Oman *23°20′N 57°35′E*
184 *L9* **Awakino** Waikato, North Island, New Zealand *38°40′S 174°37′E*
142 *M15* **'Awālī** C Bahrain *26°07′N 50°33′E*
99 *K19* **Awans** Liège, E Belgium *50°39′N 05°30′E*
184 *I2* **Awanui** Northland, North Island, New Zealand *35°01′S 173°15′E*
148 *M14* **Awārān** Baluchistān, SW Pakistan *26°31′N 65°10′E*
81 *K16* **Awara Plain** *plain* NE Kenya
80 *M13* **Āwarē** Sumalē, E Ethiopia *08°12′N 44°09′E*
138 *M6* **'Awāriḑ, Wādī** *dry watercourse* E Syria
185 *B20* **Awarua Point** *headland* South Island, New Zealand *44°15′S 168°03′E*
81 *J14* **Āwasa** Southern Nationalities, S Ethiopia *06°54′N 38°26′E*
80 *K13* **Āwash** Āfar, NE Ethiopia *08°59′N 40°16′E*
80 *K12* **Āwash** *var.* Hawash. ⇝ C Ethiopia
Awaso *see* Awaaso
158 *H7* **Awat** Xinjiang Uygur Zizhiqu, NW China *40°36′N 80°22′E*
185 *J15* **Awatere** ⇝ South Island, New Zealand
75 *O10* **Awbārī** SW Libya *26°35′N 12°46′E*
75 *N9* **Awbārī, Idhān** *var.* Edeyen d'Oubari. *desert* Algeria/Libya
80 *M12* **Awdal** *off.* Gobolka Awdal. ◈ N Somalia
80 *C13* **Aweil** Northern Bahr el Ghazal, SW Sudan *08°42′N 27°20′E*
96 *H11* **Awe, Loch** ◎ W Scotland, United Kingdom
77 *U16* **Awka** Anambra, SW Nigeria *06°12′N 07°04′E*
39 *O6* **Awuna River** ⇝ Alaska, USA
Awwinorm *see* Avinurme
Ax *see* Dax
Axarfjördhur *see* Öxarfjördhur
103 *N17* **Axat** Aude, S France *42°47′N 02°14′E*
99 *F16* **Axel** Zeeland, SW Netherlands *51°16′N 03°55′E*
197 *P9* **Axel Heiberg Island** *var.* Axel Heiburg. *island* Nunavut, N Canada
Axel Heiburg *see* Axel Heiberg Island
77 *O17* **Axim** S Ghana *04°53′N 02°14′W*
114 *F13* **Axiós** *var.* Vardar. ⇝ Greece/FYR Macedonia *see also* Vardar
Axiós *see* Vardar
103 *N17* **Ax-les-Thermes** Ariège, S France *42°43′N 01°49′E*
120 *D11* **Ayachi, Jbel** ▲ C Morocco *32°30′N 05°00′W*
61 *D22* **Ayacucho** Buenos Aires, E Argentina *37°09′S 58°30′W*
57 *F15* **Ayacucho** Ayacucho, S Peru *13°10′S 74°15′W*
57 *E16* **Ayacucho** *off.* Departamento de Ayacucho. ◈ *department* SW Peru
Ayacucho, Departamento de *see* Ayacucho
145 *W11* **Ayagoz** *var.* Ayaguz, *Kaz.* Ayaköz; *prev.* Sergiopol. Vostochnyy Kazakhstan, E Kazakhstan *47°54′N 80°25′E*
145 *V12* **Ayagoz** *var.* Ayaguz, *Kaz.* Ayakoz. ⇝ E Kazakhstan
Ayaguz *see* Ayagoz
Ayakagytma *see* Oyoqog'itma
Ayakkuduk *see* Oyoqquduq
158 *L10* **Ayakkum Hu** ◎ NW China
Ayaköz *see* Ayagoz
104 *H14* **Ayamonte** Andalucía, S Spain *37°13′N 07°24′W*
123 *S11* **Ayan** Khabarovskiy Kray, E Russian Federation *56°27′N 138°09′E*
136 *J10* **Ayancık** Sinop, N Turkey *41°56′N 34°35′E*
55 *S9* **Ayanganna Mountain** ▲ C Guyana *05°21′N 59°54′W*
77 *U16* **Ayangba** Kogi, C Nigeria *07°36′N 07°10′E*
123 *U7* **Ayanka** Koryakskiy Avtonomnyy Okrug, E Russian Federation *63°42′N 167°31′E*
54 *E7* **Ayapel** Córdoba, NW Colombia *08°16′N 75°10′W*
136 *H12* **Ayaş** Ankara, N Turkey *40°02′N 32°21′E*
57 *I16* **Ayaviri** Puno, S Peru *14°53′S 70°35′W*
149 *P3* **Āybak** *var.* Aibak, Haibak; *prev.* Samangān. Samangān, NE Afghanistan *36°16′N 68°04′E*
147 *N10* **Aydarko'l Ko'li** *Rus.* Ozero Aydarkul'. ◎ C Uzbekistan
Aydarkul', Ozero *see* Aydarko'l Ko'li
21 *W10* **Ayden** North Carolina, SE USA *35°28′N 77°25′W*
136 *C15* **Aydın** *var.* Aïdin; *anc.* Tralles Aydin. Aydın, SW Turkey *37°51′N 27°51′E*
136 *C15* **Aydın** *var.* Aïdin. ◈ *province* SW Turkey
136 *I17* **Aydıncık** İçel, S Turkey *36°08′N 33°17′E*
136 *C15* **Aydın Dağları** ▲ W Turkey
158 *L6* **Aydingkol Hu** ◎ NW China
127 *X7* **Aydyrlinskiy** Orenburgskaya Oblast', W Russian Federation *52°03′N 59°54′E*
105 *S4* **Ayerbe** Aragón, NE Spain *42°16′N 00°41′W*
Ayers Rock *see* Uluru
Ayeyarwady *see* Irrawaddy
Ayiá *see* Agiá
Ayia Napa *see* Agía Nápa
Ayia Phyla *see* Agía Fýlaxis
Ayiásos/Ayiassos *see* Agiasos
Áyios Evstrátios *see* Ágios Efstrátios
Áyios Kírikos *see* Ágios Kírykos
Áyios Nikólaos *see* Ágios Nikólaos
80 *I11* **Āykel** Āmara, N Ethiopia *12°33′N 37°01′E*
123 *N9* **Aykhal** Respublika Sakha (Yakutiya), NE Russian Federation *66°07′N 110°25′E*
14 *J12* **Aylen Lake** ◎ Ontario, SE Canada
97 *N21* **Aylesbury** SE England, United Kingdom *51°50′N 00°50′W*
105 *O6* **Ayllón** Castilla-León, N Spain *41°25′N 03°23′W*
14 *F17* **Aylmer** Ontario, S Canada *42°46′N 80°57′W*
14 *L12* **Aylmer** Québec, SE Canada *45°23′N 75°51′W*
15 *R12* **Aylmer, Lac** ◎ Québec, SE Canada
8 *L9* **Aylmer Lake** ◎ Northwest Territories, NW Canada
145 *V14* **Aynabulak** *Kaz.* Aynabulaq. Almaty, SE Kazakhstan *44°37′N 77°59′E*
Aynabulaq *see* Aynabulak
138 *K2* **'Ayn al 'Arab** Ḩalab, N Syria *36°55′N 38°21′E*
Aynayn *see* 'Aynīn
139 *V12* **'Ayn Ḩamūd** Dhī Qār, S Iraq *30°51′N 45°37′E*
147 *P12* **Ayni** *prev.* Varzimanor Ayni. W Tajikistan *39°24′N 68°30′E*
140 *M10* **'Aynīn** *var.* Aynayn. *spring/well* SW Saudi Arabia *20°52′N 41°41′E*
21 *U12* **Aynor** South Carolina, SE USA *33°59′N 79°11′W*
139 *Q7* **'Ayn Zāzūh** Al Anbār, C Iraq *33°29′N 42°34′E*
153 *N12* **Ayodhya** Uttar Pradesh, N India *26°47′N 82°12′E*
123 *S6* **Ayon, Ostrov** *island* NE Russian Federation
105 *R11* **Ayora** País Valenciano, E Spain *39°04′N 01°04′W*
77 *Q11* **Ayorou** Tillabéri, W Niger *14°45′N 00°54′E*
79 *E16* **Ayos** Centre, S Cameroon *03°53′N 12°31′E*
76 *L5* **'Ayoûn 'Abd el Mâlek** *well* N Mauritania
76 *K10* **'Ayoûn el 'Atroûs** *var.* Aïoun el Atrous, Aïoun el Atroûss. Hodh el Gharbi, SE Mauritania *16°38′N 09°36′W*
96 *I13* **Ayr** W Scotland, United Kingdom *55°28′N 04°38′W*
96 *I13* **Ayr** ⇝ W Scotland, United Kingdom
96 *I13* **Ayrshire** *cultural region* SW Scotland, United Kingdom
Aysen *see* Aisén
80 *L12* **Āysha** Sumalē, E Ethiopia *10°36′N 42°31′E*
144 *L14* **Ayteke Bi** *Kaz.* Zhangaqazaly; *prev.* Novokazalinsk. Kzylorda, SW Kazakhstan *45°53′N 62°10′E*
146 *K8* **Aytim** Navoiy Viloyati, N Uzbekistan *42°15′N 63°25′E*
181 *W4* **Ayton** Queensland, NE Australia *15°54′S 145°19′E*
114 *M9* **Aytos** Burgas, E Bulgaria *42°43′N 27°14′E*
171 *T11* **Ayu, Kepulauan** *island group* E Indonesia
A Yun Pa *see* Cheo Reo
169 *V11* **Ayu, Tanjung** *headland* Borneo, N Indonesia *0°25′N 117°34′E*
41 *P16* **Ayutlá** *var.* Ayutla de los Libres. Guerrero, S Mexico *16°51′N 99°16′W*
40 *K13* **Ayutla** Jalisco, C Mexico *20°07′N 104°18′W*
Ayutla de los Libres *see* Ayutlá
167 *O11* **Ayutthaya** *var.* Phra Nakhon Si Ayutthaya. Phra Nakhon Si Ayutthaya, C Thailand *14°20′N 100°35′E*
136 *B13* **Ayvalık** Balıkesir, W Turkey *39°18′N 26°42′E*
99 *L20* **Aywaille** Liège, E Belgium *50°28′N 05°40′E*
141 *R13* **'Aywat aş Şay'ar, Wādī** *seasonal river* N Yemen
Azaffal *see* Azeffâl
105 *T9* **Azahar, Costa del** *coastal region* E Spain
105 *S6* **Azaila** Aragón, NE Spain *41°17′N 00°20′W*
104 *F10* **Azambuja** Lisboa, C Portugal *39°04′N 08°52′W*
153 *N13* **Āzamgarh** Uttar Pradesh, N India *26°03′N 83°10′E*
77 *O9* **Azaouâd** *desert* C Mali
77 *S10* **Azaouagh, Vallée de l'** *var.* Azaouak. ⇝ W Niger
Azaouak *see* Azaouagh, Vallée de l'
61 *F14* **Azara** Misiones, NE Argentina *28°03′S 55°42′W*
Azaran *see* Hashtrūd
Azärbaycan/Azärbaycan Respublikası *see* Azerbaijan
Āzarbāyjān-e Bākhtarī *see* Āzarbāyjān-e Gharbī
142 *I4* **Āzarbāyjān-e Gharbī** *off.* Ostān-e Āzarbāyjān-e Gharbī, *Eng.* West Azerbaijan; *prev.* Āzarbāyjān-e Bākhtarī. ◈ *province* NW Iran
Āzarbāyjān-e Gharbī, Ostān-e *see* Āzarbāyjān-e Gharbī
Āzarbāyjān-e Khāvarī *see* Āzarbāyjān-e Sharqī
142 *J3* **Āzarbāyjān-e Sharqī** *off.* Ostān-e Āzarbāyjān-e Sharqī, *Eng.* East Azerbaijan; *prev.* Āzarbāyjān-e Khāvarī. ◈ *province* NW Iran
Āzarbāyjān-e Sharqī, Ostān-e *see* Āzarbāyjān-e Sharqī
77 *W13* **Azare** Bauchi, N Nigeria *11°41′N 10°09′E*
119 *M19* **Azarychy** *Rus.* Ozarichi. Homyel'skaya Voblasts', SE Belarus *51°31′N 29°19′E*
102 *L8* **Azay-le-Rideau** Indre-et-Loire, C France *47°16′N 00°25′E*
138 *I2* **A'zāz** Ḩalab, NW Syria *36°35′N 37°03′E*
76 *H7* **Azeffâl** *var.* Azaffal. *desert* Mauritania/Western Sahara
137 *V12* **Azerbaijan** *off.* Azerbaijani Republic, *Az.* Azärbaycan, Azärbaycan Respublikası; *prev.* Azerbaijan SSR. ◆ *republic* SE Asia
Azerbaijani Republic *see* Azerbaijan
Azerbaijan SSR *see* Azerbaijan
145 *T7* **Azhbulat, Ozero** ◎ NE Kazakhstan
74 *F7* **Azilal** C Morocco *31°58′N 06°53′W*
Azimabad *see* Patna
19 *O6* **Aziscohos Lake** ⊠ Maine, NE USA
Azizbekov *see* Vayk'
Azizie *see* Telish
Aziziya *see* Al 'Azīzīyah
127 *T4* **Aznakayevo** Respublika Tatarstan, W Russian Federation *54°55′N 53°15′E*
56 *C8* **Azogues** Cañar, S Ecuador *02°44′S 78°48′W*
64 *N2* **Azores** *var.* Açores, Ilhas dos Açores, *Port.* Arquipélago dos Açores. *island group* Portugal, NE Atlantic Ocean
64 *L8* **Azores-Biscay Rise** *undersea feature* E Atlantic Ocean *19°00′W 42°40′N*
Azotos/Azotus *see* Ashdod
78 *K11* **Azoum, Bahr** *seasonal river* SE Chad
126 *L12* **Azov** Rostovskaya Oblast', SW Russian Federation *47°07′N 39°26′E*
126 *J13* **Azov, Sea of** *Rus.* Azovskoye More, *Ukr.* Azovs'ke More. *sea* NE Black Sea
Azovs'ke More/Azovskoye More *see* Azov, Sea of
138 *I10* **Azraq, Wāḩat al** *oasis* N Jordan
Āzro *see* Āzrow
74 *G6* **Azrou** C Morocco *33°30′N 05°12′W*
149 *R5* **Āzrow** *var.* Āzro. Lowgar, E Afghanistan *34°11′N 69°39′E*
37 *P8* **Aztec** New Mexico, SW USA *36°49′N 107°59′W*
36 *M13* **Aztec Peak** ▲ Arizona, SW USA *33°48′N 110°54′W*
45 *N9* **Azua** *var.* Azua de Compostela. S Dominican Republic *18°29′N 70°44′W*
Azua de Compostela *see* Azua
104 *K12* **Azuaga** Extremadura, W Spain *38°16′N 05°40′W*
56 *B8* **Azuay** ◈ *province* W Ecuador
164 *C13* **Azuchi-Ō-shima** *island* SW Japan
105 *O11* **Azuer** ⇝ C Spain
43 *S17* **Azuero, Península de** *peninsula* S Panama
62 *I6* **Azufre, Volcán** *var.* Volcán Lastarria. ✱ N Chile *25°16′S 68°35′W*
116 *J12* **Azuga** Prahova, SE Romania *45°27′N 25°34′E*
61 *C22* **Azul** Buenos Aires, E Argentina *36°46′S 59°50′W*
62 *I8* **Azul, Cerro** ▲ NW Argentina *28°28′S 68°43′W*
56 *E12* **Azul, Cordillera** ▲ C Peru
165 *P11* **Azuma-san** ▲ Honshū, C Japan *37°44′N 140°05′E*
103 *V15* **Azur, Côte d'** *coastal region* SE France
191 *Z3* **Azur Lagoon** ◎ Kiritimati, E Kiribati
'Azza *see* Gaza
Az Zāb al Kabīr *see* Great Zab
138 *H7* **Az Zabdānī** *var.* Zabadani. Dimashq, W Syria *33°45′N 36°07′E*
141 *W8* **Az Zāhirah** *desert* NW Oman
141 *S6* **Az Zahrān** *Eng.* Dhahran. Ash Sharqīyah, NE Saudi Arabia *26°18′N 50°02′E*
141 *R6* **Az Zahrān al Khubar** *var.* Dhahran Al Khobar. ✈ Ash Sharqīyah, NE Saudi Arabia *26°28′N 49°42′E*
75 *W7* **Az Zaqāzīq** *var.* Az Zaqāzīq *var.* Zagazig. N Egypt *30°36′N 31°32′E*
Az Zaqāzīq *see* Az Zaqāzīq
138 *H10* **Az Zarqā'** *var.* Zarqa. Az Zarqā', NW Jordan *32°04′N 36°06′E*
138 *I11* **Az Zarqā'** *off.* Muḩāfazat az Zarqā', *var.* Zarqa. ◈ *governorate* N Jordan
75 *O7* **Az Zāwiyah** *var.* Zawia. NW Libya *32°45′N 12°44′E*
141 *N15* **Az Zaydīyah** W Yemen *15°20′N 43°03′E*
74 *I11* **Azzel Matti, Sebkha** *var.* Sebkra Azz el Matti. *salt flat* C Algeria
141 *P6* **Az Zilfī** Ar Riyāḑ, N Saudi Arabia *26°17′N 44°48′E*
139 *Y13* **Az Zubayr** *var.* Al Zubair. Al Başrah, SE Iraq *30°24′N 47°45′E*
Az Zuqur *see* Jabal Zuqar, Jazīrat

B

187 *X15* **Ba** *prev.* Mba. Viti Levu, W Fiji *17°35′S 177°40′E*
Ba *see* Da Rằng, Sông
171 *P17* **Baa** Pulau Rote, C Indonesia *10°44′S 123°06′E*
138 *H7* **Baalbek** *var.* Ba'labakk; *anc.* Heliopolis. E Lebanon *34°00′N 36°15′E*
108 *G8* **Baar** Zug, N Switzerland *47°12′N 08°32′E*
81 *L17* **Baardheere** *var.* Bardere, *It.* Bardera. Gedo, SW Somalia *02°13′N 42°19′E*
80 *Q12* **Baargaal** Bari, NE Somalia *11°12′N 51°04′E*
99 *I15* **Baarle-Hertog** Antwerpen, N Belgium *51°26′N 04°56′E*
99 *I15* **Baarle-Nassau** Noord-Brabant, S Netherlands *51°27′N 04°56′E*
98 *J11* **Baarn** Utrecht, C Netherlands *52°13′N 05°16′E*
162 *H9* **Baatsagaan** *var.* Bayansayr. Bayanhongor, C Mongolia *45°36′N 99°27′E*
114 *D13* **Baba** *var.* Buševa, *Gk.* Varnoús. ▲ FYR Macedonia/Greece
76 *H10* **Bababé** Brakna, W Mauritania *16°22′N 13°57′W*
135 *G10* **Baba Burnu** *headland* NW Turkey *41°18′N 31°24′E*
117 *N13* **Babadag** Tulcea, SE Romania *44°53′N 28°47′E*
137 *X10* **Babadağ Dağı** ▲ NE Azerbaijan *41°02′N 48°04′E*
146 *H14* **Babadayhan** *Rus.* Babadaykhan; *prev.* Kirovsk. Ahal Welaýaty, C Turkmenistan *37°39′N 60°17′E*
Babadaykhan *see* Babadayhan
146 *G14* **Babadurmaz** Ahal Welaýaty, C Turkmenistan *37°39′N 59°03′E*
114 *M12* **Babaeski** Kırklareli, NW Turkey *41°26′N 27°06′E*
139 *T4* **Bāba Gurgur** At Ta'mīn, N Iraq *35°34′N 44°18′E*
56 *B7* **Babahoyo** *prev.* Bodegas. Los Ríos, C Ecuador *01°53′S 79°31′W*
149 *P5* **Bābā, Kūh-e** ▲ C Afghanistan
171 *N12* **Babana** Sulawesi, C Indonesia *02°03′S 119°13′E*
Babao *see* Qilian
171 *Q12* **Babar, Kepulauan** *island group* E Indonesia
171 *T12* **Babar, Pulau** *island* Kepulauan Babar, E Indonesia
152 *G4* **Bābāsar Pass** *pass* India/Pakistan
Babashy, Gory *see* Babaşy
146 *C9* **Babaşy** *Rus.* Gory Babashy. ▲ W Turkmenistan
168 *M13* **Babat** Sumatera, W Indonesia *02°45′S 104°01′E*
Babatag, Khrebet *see* Bototog', Tizmasi
81 *H21* **Babati** Manyara, NE Tanzania *04°12′S 35°45′E*
124 *J13* **Babayevo** Vologodskaya Oblast', NW Russian Federation *59°23′N 35°52′E*
127 *Q15* **Babayurt** Respublika Dagestan, SW Russian Federation *43°38′N 46°49′E*
33 *P6* **Babb** Montana, NW USA *48°51′N 113°26′W*
29 *X4* **Babbitt** Minnesota, N USA *47°42′N 91°56′W*
188 *E9* **Babeldaob** *var.* Babeldaop, Babelthuap. *island* N Palau
Babeldaop *see* Babeldaob
141 *N17* **Bab el Mandeb** *strait* Gulf of Aden/Red Sea
Babelthuap *see* Babeldaob
111 *K17* **Babia Góra** *var.* Babia Hora. ▲ Poland/Slovakia *49°33′N 19°32′E*
Babia Hora *see* Babia Góra
Babian Jiang *see* Black River
Babichi *see* Babichy
119 *N19* **Babichy** *Rus.* Babichi. Homyel'skaya Voblasts', SE Belarus *52°17′N 30°00′E*
139 *U9* **Bābil** ◈ *governorate* S Iraq
112 *I10* **Babina Greda** Vukovar-Srijem, E Croatia *45°09′N 18°33′E*
10 *K13* **Babine Lake** ◎ British Columbia, SW Canada
143 *O4* **Bābol** *var.* Babul, Balfrush, Barfrush; *prev.* Barfurush. Māzandarān, N Iran *36°34′N 52°39′E*
143 *O4* **Bābolsar** *var.* Babulsar; *prev.* Meshed-i-Sar. Māzandarān, N Iran *36°41′N 52°39′E*
36 *L16* **Baboquivari Peak** ▲ Arizona, SW USA *31°46′N 111°36′W*
79 *G15* **Baboua** Nana-Mambéré, W Central African Republic *05°46′N 14°47′E*
119 *M17* **Babruysk** *Rus.* Bobruysk. Mahilyowskaya Voblasts', E Belarus *53°07′N 29°13′E*
Babu *see* Hezhou
Babul *see* Bābol
Babulsar *see* Bābolsar
113 *O19* **Babuna** ▲ C FYR Macedonia
113 *O19* **Babuna** ⇝ C FYR Macedonia
148 *K7* **Bābūs, Dasht-e** *Pash.* Bebas, Dasht-i. ▲ W Afghanistan
171 *O1* **Babuyan Channel** *channel* N Philippines
171 *O1* **Babuyan Islands** *island* N Philippines
139 *T9* **Babylon** *site of ancient city* C Iraq
112 *J9* **Bač** *Ger.* Batsch. Vojvodina, NW Serbia *45°24′N 19°17′E*
58 *M13* **Bacabal** Maranhão, E Brazil *04°15′S 44°45′W*
41 *Y14* **Bacalar** Quintana Roo, SE Mexico *18°38′N 88°17′W*
41 *Y14* **Bacalar Chico, Boca** *strait* SE Mexico
171 *Q12* **Bacan, Kepulauan** *island group* E Indonesia
171 *S12* **Bacan, Pulau** *prev.* Batjan. *island* Maluku, E Indonesia
116 *L10* **Bacău** *Hung.* Bákó. Bacău, NE Romania *46°36′N 26°56′E*
116 *K11* **Bacău** ◈ *county* E Romania
Bắc Bộ, Vịnh *see* Tongking, Gulf of
167 *T5* **Bắc Can** *var.* Bach Thong. Bắc Thai, N Vietnam *22°07′N 105°50′E*
103 *T5* **Baccarat** Meurthe-et-Moselle, NE France *48°27′N 06°46′E*
183 *N12* **Bacchus Marsh** Victoria, SE Australia *37°41′S 144°30′E*
40 *H4* **Bacerac** Sonora, NW Mexico *30°27′N 108°55′W*
116 *L11* **Băcești** Vaslui, E Romania *46°50′N 27°14′E*
167 *T6* **Bắc Giang** Ha Bắc, N Vietnam *21°17′N 106°12′E*
54 *I5* **Bachaquero** Zulia, NW Venezuela *09°57′N 71°09′W*
Bacher *see* Pohorje
118 *M13* **Bacheykava** *Rus.* Bocheykovo. Vitsyebskaya Voblasts', N Belarus *55°01′N 29°09′E*
40 *I5* **Bachíniva** Chihuahua, N Mexico *28°41′N 107°13′W*
Bach Thong *see* Bắc Can
158 *G8* **Bachu** Xinjiang Uygur Zizhiqu, NW China *39°46′N 78°30′E*
9 *N8* **Back** ⇝ Nunavut, N Canada
112 *K10* **Bačka Palanka** *prev.* Palanka. Serbia, NW Serbia *44°22′N 20°57′E*
112 *K8* **Bačka Topola** *Hung.* Topolya; *prev. Hung.* Bácstopolya. Vojvodina, N Serbia *45°48′N 19°39′E*
95 *J17* **Bäckefors** Västra Götaland, S Sweden *58°49′N 12°07′E*
Bäckermühle Schulzenmühle *see* Żywiec
95 *L16* **Bäckhammar** Värmland, C Sweden *59°09′N 14°13′E*
112 *K9* **Bački Petrovac** *Hung.* Petrőcz; *prev.* Petrovac, Petrovácz. Vojvodina, NW Serbia *45°22′N 19°34′E*
101 *I21* **Backnang** Baden-Württemberg, SW Germany *48°57′N 09°26′E*
167 *S15* **Bac Liêu** *var.* Vinh Loi. Minh Hai, S Vietnam *09°17′N 105°44′E*
167 *T6* **Bắc Ninh** Ha Bắc, N Vietnam *21°10′N 106°04′E*
40 *G4* **Bacoachi** Sonora, NW Mexico *30°36′N 110°00′W*
171 *P6* **Bacolod** *off.* Bacolod City. Negros, C Philippines *10°43′N 122°58′E*
Bacolod City *see* Bacolod
171 *O4* **Baco, Mount** ▲ Mindoro, N Philippines *12°50′N 121°08′E*
111 *K25* **Bácsalmás** Bács-Kiskun, S Hungary *46°07′N 19°20′E*
Bácsjózseffalva *see* Žednik
111 *J24* **Bács-Kiskun** *off.* Bács-Kiskun Megye. ◈ *county* S Hungary
Bács-Kiskun Megye *see* Bács-Kiskun
Bácsszenttamás *see* Srbobran
Bácstopolya *see* Bačka Topola
Bactra *see* Balkh
Bada *see* Xilin
155 *F21* **Badagara** *var.* Vadakara. Kerala, SW India *11°36′N 75°34′E* *see also* Vadakara
101 *M24* **Bad Aibling** Bayern, SE Germany *47°52′N 12°00′E*
162 *I13* **Badain Jaran Shamo** *desert* N China
104 *I11* **Badajoz** *anc.* Pax Augusta. Extremadura, W Spain *38°53′N 06°58′W*
104 *J11* **Badajoz** ◈ *province* Extremadura, W Spain
149 *S2* **Badakhshān** ◈ *province* NE Afghanistan
105 *W6* **Badalona** *anc.* Baetulo. Cataluña, E Spain *41°27′N 02°15′E*
154 *O11* **Bādāmapāhārh** Orissa, E India *22°04′N 86°06′E*
152 *K8* **Badarīnāth** ▲ N India *30°44′N 79°29′E*
169 *O10* **Badas, Kepulauan** *island group* W Indonesia
109 *S6* **Bad Aussee** Salzburg, E Austria *47°35′N 13°44′E*
31 *S8* **Bad Axe** Michigan, N USA *43°48′N 83°00′W*
101 *G16* **Bad Berleburg** Nordrhein-Westfalen, W Germany *51°03′N 08°24′E*
101 *L17* **Bad Blankenburg** Thüringen, C Germany *50°43′N 11°19′E*
Bad Borseck *see* Borsec
101 *G18* **Bad Camberg** Hessen, W Germany *50°18′N 08°15′E*
100 *L8* **Bad Doberan** Mecklenburg-Vorpommern, N Germany *54°06′N 11°55′E*
101 *N14* **Bad Düben** Sachsen, E Germany *51°35′N 12°34′E*
109 *X4* **Baden** *var.* Baden bei Wien; *anc.* Aquae Panoniae, Thermae Pannonicae. Niederösterreich, NE Austria *48°01′N 16°14′E*
108 *F9* **Baden** Aargau, N Switzerland *47°28′N 08°19′E*
101 *G21* **Baden-Baden** *anc.* Aurelia Aquensis. Baden-Württemberg, SW Germany *48°46′N 08°14′E*
Baden bei Wien *see* Baden
101 *G22* **Baden-Württemberg** *Fr.* Bade-Wurtemberg. ◈ *state* SW Germany
112 *A10* **Baderna** Istra, NW Croatia *45°12′N 13°45′E*
Bade-Wurtemberg *see* Baden-Württemberg
101 *H20* **Bad Fredrichshall** Baden-Württemberg, S Germany *49°13′N 09°15′E*
100 *P11* **Bad Freienwalde** Brandenburg, NE Germany *52°47′N 14°04′E*
109 *Q8* **Badgastein** *var.* Gastein. Salzburg, NW Austria *47°07′N 13°09′E*
Badger State *see* Wisconsin
148 *L4* **Bādghīs** ◈ *province* NW Afghanistan
109 *T5* **Bad Hall** Oberösterreich, N Austria *48°03′N 14°13′E*
101 *J14* **Bad Harzburg** Niedersachsen, C Germany *51°52′N 10°34′E*
101 *I16* **Bad Hersfeld** Hessen, C Germany *50°52′N 09°42′E*
98 *I10* **Badhoevedorp** Noord-Holland, C Netherlands *52°21′N 04°46′E*
109 *Q8* **Bad Hofgastein** Salzburg, NW Austria *47°11′N 13°07′E*
Bad Homburg *see* Bad Homburg vor der Höhe
101 *G18* **Bad Homburg vor der Höhe** *var.* Bad Homburg. Hessen, W Germany *50°14′N 08°37′E*
101 *E17* **Bad Honnef** Nordrhein-Westfalen, W Germany *50°39′N 07°13′E*
149 *Q17* **Badīn** Sind, SE Pakistan *24°38′N 68°53′E*
21 *S10* **Badin Lake** ⊠ North Carolina, SE USA
40 *I8* **Badiraguato** Sinaloa, C Mexico *25°21′N 107°31′W*
109 *R6* **Bad Ischl** Oberösterreich, N Austria *47°43′N 13°36′E*
Badjawa *see* Bajawa
Badje-Sohppar *see* Övre Soppero
101 *J18* **Bad Kissingen** Bayern, SE Germany *50°12′N 10°04′E*
Bad Königswart *see* Lázně Kynžvart
101 *F19* **Bad Kreuznach** Rheinland-Pfalz, SW Germany *49°51′N 07°52′E*
101 *F24* **Bad Krozingen** Baden-Württemberg, SW Germany *47°55′N 07°43′E*
101 *G16* **Bad Laasphe** Nordrhein-Westfalen, W Germany *50°57′N 08°24′E*
28 *J6* **Badlands** *physical region* North Dakota/South Dakota, N USA
101 *K16* **Bad Langensalza** Thüringen, C Germany *51°05′N 10°40′E*
109 *T3* **Bad Leonfelden** Oberösterreich, N Austria *48°31′N 14°17′E*
101 *I20* **Bad Mergentheim** Baden-Württemberg, SW Germany *49°30′N 09°46′E*
101 *H17* **Bad Nauheim** Hessen, W Germany *50°22′N 08°45′E*
101 *E17* **Bad Neuenahr-Arhweiler** Rheinland-Pfalz, W Germany *50°33′N 07°07′E*
Bad Neustadt *see* Bad Neustadt an der Saale
101 *J18* **Bad Neustadt an der Saale** *var.* Bad Neustadt. Berlin, C Germany *50°21′N 10°13′E*
Badnur *see* Betūl
100 *H13* **Bad Oeynhausen** Nordrhein-Westfalen, NW Germany *52°12′N 08°48′E*
100 *J9* **Bad Oldesloe** Schleswig-Holstein, N Germany *53°49′N 10°22′E*
77 *Q16* **Badou** C Togo *07°37′N 00°37′E*
Bad Polzin *see* Połczyn-Zdrój
100 *H13* **Bad Pyrmont** Niedersachsen, C Germany *51°58′N 09°16′E*
109 *X9* **Bad Radkersburg** Steiermark, SE Austria *46°40′N 16°02′E*
139 *V8* **Badrah** Wāsiţ, E Iraq *33°06′N 45°58′E*
Badrah *see* Tarialan
101 *N24* **Bad Reichenhall** Bayern, SE Germany *47°43′N 12°52′E*
140 *K8* **Badr Ḩunayn** Al Madīnah, W Saudi Arabia *23°46′N 38°45′E*
28 *M10* **Bad River** ⇝ South Dakota, N USA
30 *K4* **Bad River** ⇝ Wisconsin, N USA
100 *H13* **Bad Salzuflen** Nordrhein-Westfalen, NW Germany *52°06′N 08°45′E*
101 *J16* **Bad Salzungen** Thüringen, C Germany *50°48′N 10°15′E*
109 *V8* **Bad Sankt Leonhard im Lavanttal** Kärnten, S Austria *46°55′N 14°51′E*
100 *K9* **Bad Schwartau** Schleswig-Holstein, N Germany *53°55′N 10°42′E*
101 *L24* **Bad Tölz** Bayern, SE Germany *47°44′N 11°34′E*
181 *U1* **Badu Island** *island* Queensland, NE Australia
155 *K25* **Badulla** Uva Province, C Sri Lanka *06°59′N 81°03′E*
109 *X5* **Bad Vöslau** Niederösterreich, NE Austria *47°58′N 16°13′E*
101 *I24* **Bad Waldsee** Baden-Württemberg, S Germany *47°54′N 09°44′E*
35 *U11* **Badwater Basin** *depression* California, W USA
101 *J20* **Bad Windsheim** Bayern, C Germany *49°30′N 10°25′E*
101 *J23* **Bad Wörishofen** Bayern, S Germany *48°00′N 10°36′E*
100 *G10* **Bad Zwischenahn** Niedersachsen, NW Germany *53°10′N 08°01′E*
104 *M13* **Baena** Andalucía, S Spain *37°37′N 04°20′W*
Baeterrae/Baeterrae Septimanorum *see* Béziers
Baetic Cordillera/Baetic Mountains *see* Béticos, Sistemas
Baetulo *see* Badalona
57 *K18* **Baeza** Napo, NE Ecuador *0°30′S 77°52′W*
105 *N13* **Baeza** Andalucía, S Spain *38°00′N 03°28′W*
79 *D15* **Bafang** Ouest, W Cameroon *05°10′N 10°11′E*
76 *H12* **Bafatá** C Guinea-Bissau *12°09′N 14°38′W*
149 *U5* **Baffa** North-West Frontier Province, NW Pakistan *34°30′N 73°18′E*
197 *O11* **Baffin Basin** *undersea feature* N Labrador Sea
197 *N12* **Baffin Bay** *bay* Canada/Greenland
25 *T15* **Baffin Bay** *inlet* Texas, SW USA
196 *M12* **Baffin Island** *island* Nunavut, NE Canada
79 *E15* **Bafia** Centre, C Cameroon *04°49′N 11°14′E*
77 *R14* **Bafilo** NE Togo *09°23′N 01°20′E*
76 *J12* **Bafing** ⇝ W Africa
76 *J12* **Bafoulabé** Kayes, W Mali *13°43′N 10°49′W*
79 *D15* **Bafoussam** Ouest, W Cameroon *05°31′N 10°25′E*
143 *R9* **Bāfq** Yazd, C Iran *31°35′N 55°21′E*
136 *L10* **Bafra** Samsun, N Turkey *41°34′N 35°56′E*
136 *L10* **Bafra Burnu** *headland* N Turkey *41°42′N 36°02′E*
143 *S12* **Bāft** Kermān, S Iran *29°12′N 56°36′E*
79 *N18* **Bafwabalinga** Orientale, NE Dem. Rep. Congo *0°52′N 26°55′E*
79 *N18* **Bafwaboli** Orientale, NE Dem. Rep. Congo *0°36′N 26°08′E*
79 *N17* **Bafwasende** Orientale, NE Dem. Rep. Congo *01°00′N 27°09′E*
42 *K13* **Bagaces** Guanacaste, NW Costa Rica *10°31′N 85°18′W*
153 *O12* **Bagaha** Bihār, N India *27°08′N 84°04′E*
155 *F16* **Bāgalkot** Karnātaka, W India *16°11′N 75°42′E*
81 *J22* **Bagamoyo** Pwani, E Tanzania *06°26′S 38°55′E*
Bagan Datok *see* Bagan Datuk
168 *J8* **Bagan Datuk** *var.* Bagan Datok. Perak, Peninsular Malaysia *03°58′N 100°47′E*
171 *R7* **Baganga** Mindanao, S Philippines *07°31′N 126°34′E*
168 *J9* **Bagansiapiapi** *var.* Pasirpangarayan. Sumatera, W Indonesia *02°06′N 100°52′E*
162 *M8* **Baganuur** *var.* Nüürst. Töv, C Mongolia *47°44′N 108°22′E*
Bagaria *see* Bagheria
77 *T11* **Bagaroua** Tahoua, W Niger *14°34′N 04°24′E*
79 *I20* **Bagata** Bandundu, W Dem. Rep. Congo *03°47′S 17°57′E*
Bagdad *see* Baghdād
123 *O13* **Bagdarin** Respublika Buryatiya, S Russian Federation *54°27′N 113°34′E*
61 *G17* **Bagé** Rio Grande do Sul, S Brazil *31°22′S 54°06′W*
Bagenalstown *see* Muine Bheag
153 *T16* **Bagerhat** *var.* Bagherhat. Khulna, S Bangladesh *22°40′N 89°48′E*
103 *P16* **Bages et de Sigean, Étang de** ◎ S France
152 *K10* **Bāgeshwar** Uttarakhand, N India *29°50′N 79°46′E*
33 *W17* **Baggs** Wyoming, C USA *41°02′N 107°39′W*
154 *F11* **Bāgh** Madhya Pradesh, C India *22°22′N 74°49′E*
139 *T8* **Baghdād** *off.* Muḩāfaẓat Baghdād. ◈ *governorate* C Iraq
139 *T8* **Baghdād** *var.* Bagdad, *Eng.* Baghdad. ● Baghdād, C Iraq *33°20′N 44°26′E*
139 *T8* **Baghdād** ✈ (Baghdād) Baghdād, C Iraq *33°20′N 44°26′E*
Baghdad *see* Baghdād
Baghdād, Muḩāfaẓat *see* Baghdād
Bagherhat *see* Bagerhat
107 *J23* **Bagheria** *var.* Bagaria. Sicilia, Italy, C Mediterranean Sea *38°05′N 13°31′E*
143 *S10* **Bāghīn** Kermān, C Iran *30°50′N 57°00′E*
149 *Q3* **Baghlān** Baghlān, NE Afghanistan *36°11′N 68°44′E*
149 *Q3* **Baghlān** *var.* Bāghlān. ◈ *province* NE Afghanistan
Bāghlān *see* Baghlān
148 *M7* **Bāghrān** Helmand, S Afghanistan *32°55′N 64°57′E*
29 *T4* **Bagley** Minnesota, N USA *47°31′N 95°24′W*
106 *H10* **Bagnacavallo** Emilia-Romagna, C Italy *44°00′N 12°59′E*
102 *K16* **Bagnères-de-Bigorre** Hautes-Pyrénées, S France *43°04′N 00°09′E*
102 *L17* **Bagnères-de-Luchon** Hautes-Pyrénées, S France *42°46′N 00°34′E*
106 *F11* **Bagni di Lucca** Toscana, C Italy *44°01′N 10°38′E*

◆ Country ● Country Capital ◇ Dependent Territory ○ Dependent Territory Capital ◈ Administrative Regions ✈ International Airport ▲ Mountain ▲ Mountain Range ✱ Volcano ⇝ River ◎ Lake ⊠ Reservoir

BAGNO DI ROMAGNA – BANDAR-E DAYYER

106 H11 **Bagno di Romagna** Emilia-Romagna, C Italy 43°51′N 11°57′E
103 R14 **Bagnols-sur-Cèze** Gard, S France 44°10′N 04°37′E
162 M14 **Bag Nur** ◎ N China
166 L8 **Bago** *var.* Pegu. Bago, SW Myanmar (Burma) 17°18′N 96°31′E
171 P6 **Bago** *off.* Bago City. Negros, C Philippines 10°30′N 122°49′E
166 L7 **Bago** *var.* Pegu. ◆ *division* S Myanmar (Burma)
Bago City *see* Bago
76 M13 **Bagoé** ~ Ivory Coast/Mali
Bagrāmē *see* Bagrāmī
149 R5 **Bagrāmī** *var.* Bagrāmē. Kābōl, E Afghanistan 34°29′N 69°16′E
119 B14 **Bagrationovsk** *Ger.* Preussisch Eylau. Kaliningradskaya Oblast', W Russian Federation 54°24′N 20°39′E
Bagrax *see* Bohu
Bagrax Hu *see* Bosten Hu
56 C10 **Bagua** Amazonas, NE Peru 05°37′S 78°36′W
171 O2 **Baguio** *off.* Baguio City. Luzon, N Philippines 16°25′N 120°36′E
Baguio City *see* Baguio
77 V9 **Bagzane, Monts** ▲ N Niger 17°48′N 08°43′E
Bāḩah, Minṭaqat al *see* Al Bāḩah
Bahama Islands *see* Bahamas
44 H3 **Bahamas** *off.* Commonwealth of the Bahamas. ◆ *commonwealth republic* N West Indies
0 L13 **Bahamas** *var.* Bahama Islands. *island group* N West Indies
Bahamas, Commonwealth of the *see* Bahamas
153 S15 **Baharampur** *prev.* Berhampore. West Bengal, NE India 24°06′N 88°19′E
146 E12 **Baharly** *var.* Bäherden, *Rus.* Bakharden; *prev.* Bakherden. Ahal Welaýaty, C Turkmenistan 38°30′N 57°18′E
149 U10 **Bahāwalnagar** Punjab, E Pakistan 30°00′N 73°03′E
149 T11 **Bahāwalpur** Punjab, E Pakistan 29°25′N 71°40′E
136 L16 **Bahçe** Osmaniye, S Turkey 37°14′N 36°34′E
160 J8 **Ba He** ~ C China
Bäherden *see* Baharly
59 N16 **Bahia** *off.* Estado da Bahia. ◆ *state* E Brazil
61 B24 **Bahía Blanca** Buenos Aires, E Argentina 38°43′S 62°19′W
40 L15 **Bahía Bufadero** Michoacán, SW Mexico
63 J19 **Bahía Bustamante** Chubut, SE Argentina 45°06′S 66°30′W
40 D5 **Bahía de los Ángeles** Baja California Norte, NW Mexico
40 C6 **Bahía de Tortugas** Baja California Sur, NW Mexico 27°42′N 114°54′W
Bahia, Estado da *see* Bahia
42 J4 **Bahía, Islas de la** *Eng.* Bay Islands. *island group* N Honduras
40 E5 **Bahía Kino** Sonora, NW Mexico 28°48′N 111°55′W
40 E9 **Bahía Magdalena** *var.* Puerto Magdalena. Baja California Sur, NW Mexico 24°34′N 112°07′W
54 C8 **Bahía Solano** *var.* Ciudad Mutis, Solano. Chocó, W Colombia 06°13′N 77°27′W
80 I11 **Bahir Dar** *var.* Bahr Dar, Bahrdar Giyorgis. Āmara, N Ethiopia 11°34′N 37°23′E
141 X8 **Bahlā'** *var.* Bahlah, Bahlat. NW Oman 22°58′N 57°16′E
Bāhla *see* Bālān
Bahlah/Bahlat *see* Bahlā'
152 M11 **Bahraich** Uttar Pradesh, N India 27°35′N 81°36′E
143 M14 **Bahrain** *off.* State of Bahrain, Dawlat al Bahrayn, *Ar.* Al Baḩrayn, *prev.* Bahrein; *anc.* Tylos, Tyros. ◆ *monarchy* SW Asia
142 M14 **Bahrain** ✈ C Bahrain 26°15′N 50°39′E
142 M15 **Bahrain, Gulf of** *gulf* Persian Gulf, NW Arabian Sea
Bahrain, State of *see* Bahrain
138 I7 **Baḩrat Mallāḩah** ◎ W Syria
Bahrayn, Dawlat al *see* Bahrain
Bahr Dar/Bahrdar Giyorgis *see* Bahir Dar
Bahrein *see* Bahrain
Bahr el, Azraq *see* Blue Nile
Bahr el Gebel *see* Central Equatoria
Bahr el Jebel *see* Central Equatoria
80 E13 **Bahr ez Zaref** ~ C Sudan
67 R8 **Bahr Kameur** ~ N Central African Republic
Bahr Tabariya, Sea of *see* Tiberias, Lake
143 W15 **Bāhū Kalāt** Sīstān va Balūchestān, SE Iran 25°42′N 61°28′E
118 N13 **Bahushewsk** *Rus.* Bogushëvsk. Vitsyebskaya Voblasts', NE Belarus 54°51′N 30°13′E
Bai *see* Tagow Bāy
116 G13 **Baia de Aramă** Mehedinți, SW Romania 45°00′N 22°43′E
116 G11 **Baia de Criș** *Ger.* Altenburg, *Hung.* Körösbánya. Hunedoara, SW Romania 46°10′N 22°41′E
83 A16 **Baia dos Tigres** Namibe, SW Angola 16°36′S 11°44′E
82 A13 **Baia Farta** Benguela, W Angola 12°38′S 13°12′E
116 H9 **Baia Mare** *Ger.* Frauenbach, *Hung.* Nagybánya; *prev.* Neustadt. Maramureș, NW Romania 47°40′N 23°35′E
116 H8 **Baia Sprie** *Ger.* Mittelstadt, *Hung.* Felsőbánya. Maramureș, NW Romania 47°40′N 23°42′E
78 G13 **Baïbokoum** Logone-Oriental, SW Chad 07°46′N 15°43′E
160 F12 **Baicao Ling** ▲ SW China
163 U9 **Baicheng** *var.* Pai-ch'eng; *prev.* T'aon-an. Jilin, NE China 45°32′N 122°51′E
158 I6 **Baicheng** *var.* Bay. Xinjiang Uygur Zizhiqu, NW China 41°49′N 81°45′E
116 J13 **Băicoi** Prahova, SE Romania 45°02′N 25°51′E
Baidoa *see* Baydhabo
15 U6 **Baie-Comeau** Québec, SE Canada 49°12′N 68°10′W
15 U6 **Baie-des-Sables** Québec, SE Canada 48°41′N 67°55′W
15 T7 **Baie-des-Bacon** Québec, SE Canada 48°31′N 69°17′W
15 S8 **Baie-des-Rochers** Québec, SE Canada 47°57′N 69°50′W
12 K11 **Baie-du-Poste** Québec, SE Canada 50°20′N 73°50′W
172 H17 **Baie Lazare** Mahé, NE Seychelles 04°45′S 55°29′E
45 Y5 **Baie-Mahault** Basse Terre, C Guadeloupe 16°16′N 61°35′W
15 R9 **Baie-St-Paul** Québec, SE Canada 47°27′N 70°30′W
15 V5 **Baie-Trinité** Québec, SE Canada 49°25′N 67°20′W
13 T11 **Baie Verte** Newfoundland and Labrador, SE Canada 49°55′N 56°12′W
Baiguan *see* Shangyu
Baihe *see* Erdaobaihe
139 U11 **Bā'ij al Mahdī** Al Muthannā, S Iraq 31°21′N 44°57′E
Baiji *see* Bayjī
158 K4 **Baijiantan** *var.* Uxin Qi. Xinjiang Uygur Zizhiqu, NW China 45°38′N 85°11′E
Baikal, Lake *see* Baykal, Ozero
154 L11 **Baikunthpur** Chhattīsgarh, SW India 23°18′N 82°32′E
Bailādila *see* Kirandul
Baile an Chaistil *see* Ballycastle
Baile an Róba *see* Ballinrobe
Baile an tSratha *see* Ballintra
Baile Átha an Rí *see* Athenry
Baile Átha Buí *see* Athboy
Baile Átha Cliath *see* Dublin
Baile Átha Fhirdhia *see* Ardee
Baile Átha Í *see* Athy
Baile Átha Luain *see* Athlone
Baile Átha Troim *see* Trim
Baile Brigín *see* Balbriggan
Baile Easa Dara *see* Ballysadare
116 I13 **Băile Govora** Vâlcea, SW Romania 45°00′N 24°08′E
116 F13 **Băile Herculane** *Ger.* Herkulesbad, *Hung.* Herkulesfürdő. Caraș-Severin, SW Romania 44°51′N 22°24′E
Baile Locha Riach *see* Loughrea
Baile Mhistéala *see* Mitchelstown
Baile Monaidh *see* Ballymoney
105 N12 **Bailén** Andalucía, S Spain 38°06′N 03°46′W
Baile na hInse *see* Ballynahinch
Baile na Lorgan *see* Castleblayney
Baile na Mainistreach *see* Newtownabbey
Baile Nua na hArda *see* Newtownards
116 I12 **Băile Olănești** Vâlcea, SW Romania 45°14′N 24°18′E
116 H14 **Băilești** Dolj, SW Romania 44°01′N 23°20′E
163 N12 **Bailingmiao** *var.* Darhan Muminggan Lianheqi. Nei Mongol Zizhiqu, N China 41°41′N 110°25′E
58 K11 **Bailique, Ilha** *island* NE Brazil
103 O1 **Bailleul** Nord, N France 50°43′N 02°43′E
78 H12 **Ba Illi** Chari-Baguirmi, SW Chad 10°31′N 16°29′E
159 V12 **Bailong Jiang** ~ C China
82 C13 **Bailundo** *Port.* Vila Teixeira da Silva. Huambo, C Angola 12°12′S 15°52′E
159 T13 **Baima** *var.* Sêraitang. Qinghai, C China 32°55′N 100°44′E
Baima *see* Baxoi
186 C8 **Baimuru** Gulf, S Papua New Guinea 07°34′S 144°49′E
158 M16 **Bainang** Xizang Zizhiqu, W China 28°57′N 89°31′E
23 S8 **Bainbridge** Georgia, SE USA 30°54′N 84°33′W
171 O17 **Baing** Pulau Sumba, SE Indonesia 10°09′S 120°34′E
158 M14 **Baingoin** *var.* Pubao. Xizang Zizhiqu, W China 31°22′N 90°00′E
104 G2 **Baio Grande** Galicia, NW Spain 43°08′N 08°58′W
104 G4 **Baiona** Galicia, NW Spain 42°06′N 08°49′W
163 V7 **Baiquan** Heilongjiang, NE China 47°37′N 126°04′E
Bā'ir *see* Bāyir
158 I11 **Bairab Co** ◎ W China
25 Q7 **Baird** Texas, SW USA 32°23′N 99°24′W
39 N7 **Baird Mountains** ▲ Alaska, USA
Baireuth *see* Bayreuth
190 H3 **Bairiki** ● (Kiribati) Tarawa, NW Kiribati 01°20′N 173°01′E
Bairin Youqi *see* Daban
Bairin Zuoqi *see* Lindong
145 P17 **Bairkum** *Kaz.* Bayyrqum. Yuzhnyy Kazakhstan, S Kazakhstan 41°57′N 68°05′E
183 P12 **Bairnsdale** Victoria, SE Australia 37°51′S 147°38′E
171 P6 **Bais** Negros, S Philippines 09°36′N 123°07′E
102 L15 **Baïse** *var.* Baise. ~ S France
Baise *see* Baïse
163 W11 **Baishan** *prev.* Hunjiang. Jilin, NE China 41°57′N 126°31′E
Baishan *see* Mashan
118 F12 **Baisogala** Šiauliai, C Lithuania 55°38′N 23°44′E
189 Q7 **Baiti** N Nauru 0°30′S 166°55′E
Baitou Shan *see* Paektu-san
104 G13 **Baixo Alentejo** *physical region* S Portugal
64 P5 **Baixo, Ilhéu de** *island* Madeira, Portugal, NE Atlantic Ocean
83 E15 **Baixo Longa** Cuando Cubango, SE Angola 15°39′S 18°39′E
159 V10 **Baiyin** Gansu, C China 36°33′N 104°11′E
160 E8 **Baiyü** *var.* Jianshe. Sichuan, C China 30°37′N 97°15′E
161 N14 **Baiyun** ✈ (Guangzhou) Guangdong, S China 23°12′N 113°19′E
160 K4 **Baiyu Shan** ▲ C China
111 J25 **Baja** Bács-Kiskun, S Hungary 46°13′N 18°56′E
40 C4 **Baja California** *Eng.* Lower California. *peninsula* NW Mexico
40 C4 **Baja California Norte** ◆ *state* NW Mexico
40 E9 **Baja California Sur** ◆ *state* NW Mexico
Bājah *see* Béja
Bajan *see* Bayan
191 V16 **Baja, Punta** *headland* Easter Island, Chile, E Pacific Ocean 27°10′S 109°21′W
40 B4 **Baja, Punta** *headland* NW Mexico 29°57′N 115°48′W
55 R5 **Baja, Punta** *headland* NE Venezuela
42 D5 **Baja Verapaz** *off.* Departamento de Baja Verapaz. ◆ *department* C Guatemala
Baja Verapaz, Departamento de *see* Baja Verapaz
171 N16 **Bajawa** *prev.* Badjawa. Flores, S Indonesia 08°46′S 120°59′E
153 S16 **Baj Baj** *prev.* Budge-Budge. West Bengal, E India 22°29′N 88°11′E
141 N15 **Bājil** W Yemen 15°05′N 43°16′E
183 U4 **Bajimba, Mount** ▲ New South Wales, SE Australia 29°19′S 152°04′E
112 K13 **Bajina Bašta** Serbia, W Serbia 43°58′N 19°33′E
153 U14 **Bajitpur** Dhaka, E Bangladesh 24°12′N 90°57′E
112 K8 **Bajmok** Vojvodina, NW Serbia 45°59′N 19°25′E
Bajo Boquete *see* Boquete
113 L17 **Bajram Curri** Kukës, N Albania 42°23′N 20°06′E
79 J14 **Bakala** Ouaka, C Central African Republic 06°03′N 20°31′E
127 T4 **Bakaly** Respublika Bashkortostan, W Russian Federation 55°10′N 53°46′E
Bakan *see* Shimonoseki
145 U14 **Bakanas** *Kaz.* Baqanas. Almaty, SE Kazakhstan 44°50′N 76°13′E
145 V12 **Bakanas** *Kaz.* Baqanas. ~ E Kazakhstan
149 R4 **Bākārak** Panjshīr, NE Afghanistan 35°16′N 69°28′E
145 U14 **Bakbakty** *Kaz.* Baqbaqty. Almaty, SE Kazakhstan 44°36′N 76°41′E
122 J12 **Bakchar** Tomskaya Oblast', C Russian Federation 56°58′N 81°59′E
76 I11 **Bakel** E Senegal 14°54′N 12°26′W
35 W13 **Baker** California, W USA 35°15′N 116°04′W
22 J8 **Baker** Louisiana, S USA 30°35′N 91°10′W
33 Y9 **Baker** Montana, NW USA 46°22′N 104°16′W
32 L12 **Baker** Oregon, NW USA 44°46′N 117°50′W
192 L7 **Baker and Howland Islands** ◇ *US unincorporated territory* W Polynesia
36 L12 **Baker Butte** ▲ Arizona, SW USA 34°24′N 111°22′W
39 X15 **Baker Island** *island* Alexander Archipelago, Alaska, USA
9 N9 **Baker Lake** Nunavut, N Canada 64°20′N 96°10′W
9 N9 **Baker Lake** ◎ Nunavut, N Canada
32 H6 **Baker, Mount** ▲ Washington, NW USA 48°46′N 121°48′W
35 R13 **Bakersfield** California, W USA 35°22′N 119°01′W
24 M9 **Bakersfield** Texas, SW USA 30°54′N 102°21′W
21 P9 **Bakersville** North Carolina, SE USA 36°01′N 82°09′W
Bākhābī *see* Bū Khābī
Bakharden *see* Baharly
Bakhardok *see* Bokurdak
143 U5 **Bākharz, Kuhhā-ye** ▲ NE Iran
152 D13 **Bākhāsar** Rājasthān, NW India 24°42′N 71°11′E
Bakhchisaray *see* Bakhchysaray
117 T13 **Bakhchysaray** *Rus.* Bakhchisaray. Respublika Krym, S Ukraine 44°44′N 33°53′E
Bakherden *see* Baharly
117 R3 **Bakhmach** Chernihivs'ka Oblast', N Ukraine 51°10′N 32°48′E
Bākhtarān *see* Kermānshāh
143 Q11 **Bakhtegān, Daryācheh-ye** ◎ C Iran
145 X12 **Bakhty** Vostochnyy Kazakhstan, E Kazakhstan 46°41′N 82°45′E
137 Z11 **Bakı** *Eng.* Baku. ● (Azerbaijan) E Azerbaijan 40°24′N 49°51′E
80 M12 **Baki** Awdal, N Somalia 10°10′N 43°45′E
137 Z11 **Bakı** ✈ E Azerbaijan 40°26′N 49°55′E
136 C13 **Bakır Çayı** ~ W Turkey
92 L1 **Bakkafjördhur** Austurland, NE Iceland 66°01′N 14°49′W
92 L1 **Bakkaflói** *sea area* W Norwegian Sea
81 I15 **Bako** Southern Nationalities, S Ethiopia 05°45′N 36°39′E
76 L15 **Bako** NW Ivory Coast 09°08′N 07°40′W
Bákó *see* Bacău
111 H23 **Bakony** *Eng.* Bakony Mountains, *Ger.* Bakonywald. ▲ W Hungary
Bakony Mountains/Bakonywald *see* Bakony
81 M16 **Bakool** *off.* Gobolka Bakool. ◆ *region* W Somalia
Bakool, Gobolka *see* Bakool
79 L15 **Bakouma** Mbomou, SE Central African Republic 05°42′N 22°43′E
127 N15 **Baksan** Kabardino-Balkarskaya Respublika, SW Russian Federation 43°43′N 43°31′E
119 I16 **Bakshty** Hrodzyenskaya Voblasts', W Belarus 53°56′N 26°11′E
Baku *see* Bakı
194 K12 **Bakutis Coast** *physical region* Antarctica
Bakwanga *see* Mbuji-Mayi
145 O15 **Bakyrly** Yuzhnyy Kazakhstan, S Kazakhstan 44°30′N 67°41′E
14 H13 **Bala** Ontario, S Canada 45°01′N 79°37′W
136 I13 **Balā** Ankara, C Turkey 39°34′N 33°07′E
97 J19 **Bala** NW Wales, United Kingdom 52°54′N 03°31′W
170 L7 **Balabac Island** *island* W Philippines
Balabac, Selat *see* Balabac Strait
169 V5 **Balabac Strait** *var.* Selat Balabac. *strait* Malaysia/Philippines
Ba'labakk *see* Baalbek
187 P16 **Balabio, Île** *island* Province Nord, W New Caledonia
116 I14 **Balaci** Teleorman, S Romania 44°21′N 24°55′E
139 S7 **Balad** Ṣalāḩ ad Dīn, N Iraq 34°00′N 44°07′E
139 U7 **Balad Rūz** Diyālá, E Iraq 33°42′N 45°04′E
154 J11 **Bālāghāt** Madhya Pradesh, C India 21°48′N 80°11′E
155 F14 **Bālāghāt Range** ▲ W India
103 X14 **Balagne** *physical region* Corse, France, C Mediterranean Sea
105 U5 **Balaguer** Cataluña, NE Spain 41°48′N 00°48′E
105 S3 **Balaïtous** *var.* Pic de Balaitous. ▲ France/Spain 42°51′N 00°17′W
Balaitous, Pic de *see* Balaïtous
Bálák *see* Ballangen
127 O3 **Balakhna** Nizhegorodskaya Oblast', W Russian Federation 56°26′N 43°43′E
122 L12 **Balakhta** Krasnoyarskiy Kray, S Russian Federation 55°22′N 91°24′E
182 I9 **Balaklava** South Australia 34°10′S 138°22′E
Balakleya *see* Balakliya
117 V6 **Balakliya** *Rus.* Balakleya. Kharkivs'ka Oblast', E Ukraine 49°27′N 36°53′E
127 Q7 **Balakovo** Saratovskaya Oblast', W Russian Federation 52°03′N 47°47′E
83 P14 **Balama** Cabo Delgado, N Mozambique 13°18′S 38°39′E
169 U6 **Balambangan, Pulau** *island* East Malaysia
148 L3 **Bālā Morghāb** Laghmān, NW Afghanistan 35°38′N 63°21′E
152 E11 **Bālān** *prev.* Bāhla. Rājasthān, NW India 27°45′N 71°32′E
116 J10 **Bălan** *Hung.* Balánbánya. Harghita, C Romania 46°39′N 25°47′E
Balánbánya *see* Bălan
171 O3 **Balanga** Luzon, N Philippines 14°40′N 120°32′E
154 M12 **Balāngīr** *prev.* Bolangir. Orissa, E India 20°41′N 83°30′E
127 N8 **Balashov** Saratovskaya Oblast', W Russian Federation 51°32′N 43°14′E
Balasore *see* Bāleshwar
111 K21 **Balassagyarmat** Nógrád, N Hungary 48°06′N 19°17′E
29 S10 **Balaton** Minnesota, N USA 44°13′N 95°52′W
111 H24 **Balaton** *var.* Lake Balaton, *Ger.* Plattensee. ◎ W Hungary
111 I23 **Balatonfüred** *var.* Füred. Veszprém, W Hungary 46°59′N 17°53′E
Balaton, Lake *see* Balaton
116 I11 **Bălăușeri** *Ger.* Bladenmarkt, *Hung.* Balavásár. Mureș, C Romania 46°24′N 24°41′E
Balavásár *see* Bălăușeri
105 Q11 **Balazote** Castilla-La Mancha, C Spain 38°54′N 02°09′W
Balázsfalva *see* Blaj
119 F14 **Balbieriškis** Kaunas, S Lithuania 54°29′N 23°52′E
186 J7 **Balbi, Mount** ▲ Bougainville Island, NE Papua New Guinea 05°51′S 154°58′E
58 F11 **Balbina, Represa** ☒ NW Brazil
43 T15 **Balboa** Panamá, C Panama 08°55′N 79°36′W
97 G17 **Balbriggan** *Ir.* Baile Brigín. E Ireland 53°37′N 06°11′W
Balbunar *see* Kubrat
81 N17 **Balcad** Shabeellaha Dhexe, C Somalia 02°19′N 45°19′E
61 D23 **Balcarce** Buenos Aires, E Argentina 37°51′S 58°16′W
11 U16 **Balcarres** Saskatchewan, S Canada 50°49′N 103°31′W
114 O8 **Balchik** Dobrich, NE Bulgaria 43°25′N 28°11′E
185 E24 **Balclutha** Otago, South Island, New Zealand 46°15′S 169°45′E
25 Q12 **Balcones Escarpment** *escarpment* Texas, SW USA
18 F14 **Bald Eagle Creek** ~ Pennsylvania, NE USA
Baldenburg *see* Biały Bór
21 V12 **Bald Head Island** *island* North Carolina, SE USA
27 W10 **Bald Knob** Arkansas, C USA 35°18′N 91°34′W
30 K17 **Bald Knob** *hill* Illinois, N USA
Baldohn *see* Baldone
118 G9 **Baldone** *Ger.* Baldohn. Rīga, W Latvia 56°46′N 24°18′E
22 I9 **Baldwin** Louisiana, S USA 29°50′N 91°32′W
31 P7 **Baldwin** Michigan, N USA 43°54′N 85°50′W
27 Q4 **Baldwin City** Kansas, C USA 38°43′N 95°12′W
39 N8 **Baldwin Peninsula** *headland* Alaska, USA 66°45′N 162°19′W
18 H9 **Baldwinsville** New York, NE USA 43°09′N 76°19′W
23 N2 **Baldwyn** Mississippi, S USA 34°30′N 88°38′W
11 W15 **Baldy Mountain** ▲ Manitoba, S Canada 51°29′N 100°46′W
33 T7 **Baldy Mountain** ▲ Montana, NW USA 48°09′N 109°39′W
37 O13 **Baldy Peak** ▲ Arizona, SW USA 33°56′N 109°37′W
Bâle *see* Basel
Balearic Plain *see* Algerian Basin
Baleares *see* Illes Baleares
105 X11 **Baleares, Islas** *Eng.* Balearic Islands. *island group* Spain, W Mediterranean Sea
Baleares Major *see* Mallorca
Balearic Islands *see* Baleares, Islas
Balearis Minor *see* Menorca
169 S9 **Baleh, Batang** ~ East Malaysia
12 J8 **Baleine, Grande Rivière de la** ~ Québec, E Canada
12 K7 **Baleine, Petite Rivière de la** ~ Québec, NE Canada
12 K7 **Baleine, Petite Rivière de la** ~ Québec, SE Canada
13 N6 **Baleine, Rivière à la** ~ Québec, E Canada
99 J16 **Balen** Antwerpen, N Belgium 51°12′N 05°12′E
171 O3 **Baler** Luzon, N Philippines 15°47′N 121°30′E
154 P11 **Bāleshwar** *prev.* Balasore. Orissa, E India 21°31′N 86°59′E
77 S12 **Baléyara** Tillabéri, W Niger 13°48′N 02°57′E
127 T1 **Balezino** Udmurtskaya Respublika, NW Russian Federation 57°57′N 53°03′E
42 J4 **Balfate** Colón, N Honduras 15°47′N 86°24′W
11 O17 **Balfour** British Columbia, SW Canada 49°39′N 116°57′W
29 N3 **Balfour** North Dakota, N USA 47°55′N 100°34′W
Balfrush *see* Bābol
122 L14 **Balgazyn** Respublika Tyva, S Russian Federation 50°53′N 95°12′E
11 U16 **Balgonie** Saskatchewan, S Canada 50°30′N 104°12′W
Bălgrad *see* Alba Iulia
81 J19 **Balguda** *spring/well* S Kenya 01°28′S 39°50′E
158 K6 **Balguntay** Xinjiang Uygur Zizhiqu, NW China 42°45′N 86°18′E
141 R16 **Balḩāf** S Yemen 14°02′N 48°16′E
152 F13 **Bāli** Rājasthān, N India 25°10′N 73°20′E
169 U17 **Bali** ◆ *province* S Indonesia
169 T17 **Bali** *island* C Indonesia
111 K16 **Balice** ✈ (Kraków) Małopolskie, S Poland 49°57′N 19°49′E
171 Y14 **Baliem, Sungai** ~ Papua, E Indonesia
136 C12 **Balıkesir** Balıkesir, W Turkey 39°38′N 27°52′E
136 C12 **Balıkesir** ◆ *province* NW Turkey
138 L3 **Balīkh, Nahr** ~ N Syria
169 V12 **Balikpapan** Borneo, C Indonesia 01°15′S 116°50′E
Bali Laut *see* Bali Sea
171 N9 **Balimbing** Tawitawi, SW Philippines 05°10′N 120°00′E
186 B8 **Balimo** Western, SW Papua New Guinea 08°00′S 143°00′E
Bálinc *see* Balinț
101 H23 **Balingen** Baden-Württemberg, SW Germany 48°16′N 08°51′E
116 F11 **Balinț** *Hung.* Bálinc. Timiș, W Romania 45°48′N 21°54′E
171 O1 **Balintang Channel** *channel* N Philippines
138 K3 **Bālis** Ḩalab, N Syria 36°01′N 38°03′E
169 T16 **Bali Sea** *Ind.* Bali Laut. *sea* C Indonesia
98 K7 **Balk** Friesland, N Netherlands 52°54′N 05°34′E
146 B11 **Balkanabat** *Rus.* Nebitdag. Balkan Welaýaty, W Turkmenistan 39°33′N 54°19′E
121 R6 **Balkan Mountains** *Bul./SCr.* Stara Planina. ▲ Bulgaria/Serbia
Balkanskiy Welayat *see* Balkan Welaýaty
146 B9 **Balkan Welaýaty** *Rus.* Balkanskiy Velayat. ◆ *province* W Turkmenistan
145 P8 **Balkashino** Akmola, N Kazakhstan 52°36′N 68°46′E
149 O2 **Balkh** *anc.* Bactra. Balkh, N Afghanistan 36°46′N 66°54′E
149 P2 **Balkh** ◆ *province* N Afghanistan
145 T13 **Balkhash** *Kaz.* Balqash. Karaganda, SE Kazakhstan 46°52′N 74°55′E
Balkhash, Lake *see* Balkhash, Ozero
145 T13 **Balkhash, Ozero** *Eng.* Lake Balkhash, *Kaz.* Balqash. ◎ SE Kazakhstan
Balla Balla *see* Mbalabala
96 H10 **Ballachulish** N Scotland, United Kingdom 56°40′N 05°10′W
180 M12 **Balladonia** Western Australia 32°21′S 123°32′E
97 C16 **Ballaghaderreen** *Ir.* Bealach an Doirín. C Ireland 53°51′N 08°29′W
92 H10 **Ballangen** *Lapp.* Bálák. Nordland, NW Norway 68°18′N 16°48′E
97 H14 **Ballantrae** W Scotland, United Kingdom 55°05′N 05°W
183 N12 **Ballarat** Victoria, SE Australia 37°36′S 143°51′E
180 K11 **Ballard, Lake** *salt lake* Western Australia
Ballari *see* Bellary
76 L11 **Ballé** Koulikoro, W Mali 15°18′N 08°31′W
40 D7 **Ballenas, Bahía de** *bay* NW Mexico
40 D5 **Ballenas, Canal de** *channel* NW Mexico
195 R17 **Balleny Islands** *island group* Antarctica
40 J7 **Balleza** *var.* San Pablo Balleza. Chihuahua, N Mexico 26°55′N 106°21′W
114 M13 **Ballı** Tekirdağ, NW Turkey 40°48′N 27°03′E
153 O13 **Ballia** Uttar Pradesh, N India 25°45′N 84°09′E
183 V4 **Ballina** New South Wales, SE Australia 28°50′S 153°37′E
97 C16 **Ballina** *Ir.* Béal an Átha. W Ireland 54°07′N 09°09′W
97 D16 **Ballinamore** *Ir.* Béal an Átha Móir. NW Ireland 54°03′N 07°47′W
97 D18 **Ballinasloe** *Ir.* Béal Átha na Sluaighe. W Ireland 53°20′N 08°13′W
25 P8 **Ballinger** Texas, SW USA 31°44′N 99°57′W
97 C17 **Ballinrobe** *Ir.* Baile an Róba. W Ireland 53°37′N 09°14′W
97 A21 **Ballinskelligs Bay** *Ir.* Bá na Scealg. *inlet* SW Ireland
97 D15 **Ballintra** *Ir.* Baile an tSratha. NW Ireland 54°35′N 08°07′W
103 T7 **Ballon d'Alsace** ▲ NE France 47°50′N 06°54′E
Ballon de Guebwiller *see* Grand Ballon
113 K21 **Ballsh** *var.* Ballshi. Fier, SW Albania 40°35′N 19°45′E
Ballshi *see* Ballsh
98 K4 **Ballum** Friesland, N Netherlands 53°27′N 05°40′E
97 F16 **Ballybay** *Ir.* Béal Átha Beithe. N Ireland 54°08′N 06°54′W
97 E14 **Ballybofey** *Ir.* Bealach Féich. NW Ireland 54°49′N 07°47′W
97 G14 **Ballycastle** *Ir.* Baile an Chaistil. N Northern Ireland, United Kingdom 55°12′N 06°14′W
97 G15 **Ballyclare** *Ir.* Bealach Cláir. E Northern Ireland, United Kingdom 54°45′N 06°W
97 E16 **Ballyconnell** *Ir.* Béal Átha Conaill. N Ireland 54°07′N 07°35′W
97 C17 **Ballyhaunis** *Ir.* Beál Átha hAmhnais. W Ireland 53°45′N 08°45′W
97 G14 **Ballymena** *Ir.* An Baile Meánach. NE Northern Ireland, United Kingdom 54°52′N 06°17′W
97 F14 **Ballymoney** *Ir.* Baile Monaidh. NE Northern Ireland, United Kingdom 55°10′N 06°30′W
97 G15 **Ballynahinch** *Ir.* Baile na hInse. SE Northern Ireland, United Kingdom 54°24′N 05°54′W
97 D16 **Ballysadare** *Ir.* Baile Easa Dara. NW Ireland 54°13′N 08°30′W
97 D15 **Ballyshannon** *Ir.* Béal Átha Seanaidh. NW Ireland 54°30′N 08°11′W
63 H19 **Balmaceda** Aisén, S Chile 45°52′S 72°43′W
63 G23 **Balmaceda, Cerro** ▲ S Chile 51°27′S 73°26′W
111 N22 **Balmazújváros** Hajdú-Bihar, E Hungary 47°36′N 21°18′E
108 E10 **Balmhorn** ▲ SW Switzerland 46°27′N 07°41′E
182 L12 **Balmoral** Victoria, SE Australia 37°16′S 141°38′E
24 K9 **Balmorhea** Texas, SW USA 30°58′N 103°44′W
Balneario Claromecó *see* Claromecó
Balochistān *see* Baluchistān
82 B13 **Balombo** *Port.* Norton de Matos, Vila Norton de Matos. Benguela, W Angola 12°21′S 14°46′E
82 B13 **Balombo** ~ W Angola
181 X10 **Balonne River** ~ Queensland, E Australia
152 E13 **Bālotra** Rājasthān, N India 25°50′N 72°21′E
145 V14 **Balpyk Bi** *prev.* Kirovskiy, *Kaz.* Kīrov. Almaty, SE Kazakhstan 44°54′N 78°13′E
Balqā'/Balqā', Muḩāfaẓat al *see* Al Balqā'
Balqash *see* Balkhash/Balkhash, Ozero
152 M12 **Balrāmpur** Uttar Pradesh, N India 27°25′N 82°10′E
182 M9 **Balranald** New South Wales, SE Australia 34°39′S 143°33′E
116 H14 **Balș** Olt, S Romania 44°20′N 24°06′E
14 H11 **Balsam Creek** Ontario, S Canada 46°26′N 79°10′W
30 I5 **Balsam Lake** Wisconsin, N USA 45°27′N 92°28′W
14 I14 **Balsam Lake** ◎ Ontario, SE Canada
59 M14 **Balsas** Maranhão, E Brazil 07°30′S 46°W
40 M15 **Balsas, Río** *var.* Río Mexcala. ~ S Mexico
43 W16 **Balsas, Río** ~ SE Panama
119 O18 **Bal'shavik** *Rus.* Bol'shevik. Homyel'skaya Voblasts', SE Belarus 52°34′N 30°53′E
95 O15 **Bålsta** Uppsala, C Sweden 59°31′N 17°32′E
108 E7 **Balsthal** Solothurn, NW Switzerland 47°18′N 07°42′E
117 O8 **Balta** Odes'ka Oblast', SW Ukraine 47°58′N 29°39′E
105 N5 **Baltanás** Castilla-León, N Spain 41°56′N 04°12′W
61 E16 **Baltasar Brum** Artigas, N Uruguay 30°44′S 57°19′W
116 M9 **Bălți** *Rus.* Bel'tsy. N Moldova 47°45′N 27°57′E
Baltic Port *see* Paldiski
118 B10 **Baltic Sea** *Ger.* Ostee, *Rus.* Baltiskoye More. *sea* N Europe
21 X3 **Baltimore** Maryland, NE USA 39°17′N 76°37′W
31 T13 **Baltimore** Ohio, N USA 39°48′N 82°33′W
21 X3 **Baltimore-Washington** ✈ Maryland, E USA 39°10′N 76°40′W
Baltischport/Baltiski *see* Paldiski
Baltiskoye More *see* Baltic Sea
119 A14 **Baltiysk** *Ger.* Pillau. Kaliningradskaya Oblast', W Russian Federation 54°39′N 19°54′E
Baltkrievija *see* Belarus
119 H14 **Baltoji Voke** Vilnius, SE Lithuania 54°35′N 25°13′E
Balūchestān va Sīstān *see* Sīstān va Balūchestān
148 M12 **Baluchistān** *var.* Balochistān, Beluchistan. ◆ *province* SW Pakistan
171 P5 **Balud** Masbate, N Philippines 12°03′N 123°12′E
169 T9 **Balui, Batang** ~ East Malaysia
153 S13 **Bālurghat** West Bengal, NE India 25°12′N 88°50′E
118 J8 **Balvi** Balvi, NE Latvia 57°07′N 27°14′E
147 W7 **Balykchy** *Kir.* Ysyk-Köl; *prev.* Issyk-Kul', Rybach'ye. Issyk-Kul'skaya Oblast', NE Kyrgyzstan 42°29′N 76°08′E
56 B7 **Balzar** Guayas, W Ecuador 01°25′S 79°54′W
108 I8 **Balzers** S Liechtenstein 47°04′N 09°32′E
143 T12 **Bam** Kermān, SE Iran 29°08′N 58°27′E
77 Y13 **Bama** Borno, NE Nigeria 11°28′N 13°46′E
76 L12 **Bamako** ● (Mali) Capital District, SW Mali 12°39′N 08°02′W
77 P10 **Bamba** Gao, C Mali 17°03′N 01°19′W
42 M8 **Bambana, Río** ~ NE Nicaragua
79 J15 **Bambari** Ouaka, C Central African Republic 05°45′N 20°37′E
181 W5 **Bambaroo** Queensland, NE Australia 19°00′S 146°16′E
101 K19 **Bamberg** Bayern, SE Germany 49°54′N 10°53′E
21 R14 **Bamberg** South Carolina, SE USA 33°16′N 81°02′W
79 M16 **Bambesa** Orientale, N Dem. Rep. Congo 03°25′N 25°43′E
76 G11 **Bambey** W Senegal 14°43′N 16°26′W
79 H16 **Bambio** Sangha-Mbaéré, SW Central African Republic 03°57′N 16°54′E
83 I24 **Bamboesberge** ▲ S South Africa 31°24′S 26°10′E
79 D14 **Bamenda** Nord-Ouest, W Cameroon 05°55′N 10°09′E
10 K17 **Bamfield** Vancouver Island, British Columbia, SW Canada 48°48′N 125°05′W
Bami *see* Bamy
149 P4 **Bāmīān** *var.* Bāmiān. Bāmīān, NE Afghanistan 34°50′N 67°50′E
149 O4 **Bāmīān** ◆ *province* C Afghanistan
79 J14 **Bamingui** Bamingui-Bangoran, C Central African Republic 07°38′N 20°06′E
78 J13 **Bamingui** ~ N Central African Republic
78 J13 **Bamingui-Bangoran** ◆ *prefecture* N Central African Republic
143 V13 **Bampūr** Sīstān va Balūchestān, SE Iran 27°13′N 60°28′E
186 C8 **Bamu** ~ SW Papua New Guinea
146 E12 **Bamy** *Rus.* Bami. Ahal Welaýaty, C Turkmenistan 38°42′N 56°47′E
Bán *see* Bánovce nad Bebravou
81 N17 **Banaadir** *off.* Gobolka Banaadir. ◆ *region* S Somalia
Banaadir, Gobolka *see* Banaadir
191 N3 **Banaba** *var.* Ocean Island. *island* Tungaru, W Kiribati
59 O14 **Banabuiú, Açude** ☒ NE Brazil
57 O19 **Bañados del Izozog** *salt lake* SE Bolivia
97 D18 **Banagher** *Ir.* Beannchar. C Ireland 53°12′N 07°56′W
79 M17 **Banalia** Orientale, N Dem. Rep. Congo 01°33′N 25°23′E
76 L12 **Banamba** Koulikoro, W Mali 13°29′N 07°22′W
40 G4 **Banámichi** Sonora, NW Mexico 30°00′N 110°14′W
181 Y9 **Banana** Queensland, E Australia 24°33′S 150°07′E
191 Z2 **Banana** *prev.* Main Camp. Kiritimati, E Kiribati 02°00′N 157°25′W
59 K16 **Bananal, Ilha do** *island* C Brazil
23 Y12 **Banana River** *lagoon* Florida, SE USA
151 Q22 **Bananga** Andaman and Nicobar Islands, India, NE Indian Ocean 06°57′N 93°54′E
Banaras *see* Vārānasi
114 N13 **Banarlı** Tekirdağ, NW Turkey 41°04′N 27°21′E
152 H12 **Banās** ~ N India
75 Z11 **Banâs, Râs** *headland* E Egypt 23°55′N 35°47′E
112 N10 **Banatski Karlovac** Vojvodina, NE Serbia 45°03′N 21°02′E
141 P16 **Banā, Wādī** *dry watercourse* SW Yemen
136 E14 **Banaz** Uşak, W Turkey 38°47′N 29°46′E
136 E14 **Banaz Çayı** ~ W Turkey
159 P14 **Banbar** *var.* Coka. Xizang Zizhiqu, W China 31°01′N 94°43′E
97 G15 **Banbridge** *Ir.* Droichead na Banna. SE Northern Ireland, United Kingdom 54°21′N 06°16′W
Ban Bua Yai *see* Bua Yai
97 M21 **Banbury** S England, United Kingdom 52°04′N 01°20′W
167 O7 **Ban Chiang Dao** Chiang Mai, NW Thailand 19°22′N 98°59′E
96 K9 **Banchory** NE Scotland, United Kingdom 58°05′N 00°35′W
14 J13 **Bancroft** Ontario, SE Canada 45°03′N 77°52′W
33 R15 **Bancroft** Idaho, NW USA 42°43′N 111°54′W
29 U11 **Bancroft** Iowa, C USA 43°17′N 94°13′W
154 I9 **Bānda** Madhya Pradesh, C India 24°01′N 78°59′E
152 L13 **Bānda** Uttar Pradesh, N India 25°28′N 80°20′E
168 F7 **Bandaaceh** *var.* Banda Atjeh; *prev.* Koetaradja, Kutaradja, Kutaraja. Sumatera, W Indonesia 05°30′N 95°20′E
Banda Atjeh *see* Bandaaceh
171 S14 **Banda, Kepulauan** *island group* E Indonesia
Banda, Laut *see* Banda Sea
77 N17 **Bandama** *var.* Bandama Fleuve. ~ S Ivory Coast
77 N15 **Bandama Blanc** ~ C Ivory Coast
Bandama Fleuve *see* Bandama
Bandar 'Abbās *see* Bandar-e 'Abbās
153 W16 **Bandarban** Chittagong, SE Bangladesh 22°13′N 92°13′E
80 Q13 **Bandarbeyla** *var.* Bender Beila, Bender Beyla. Bari, NE Somalia 09°28′N 50°48′E
143 R14 **Bandar-e 'Abbās** *var.* Bandar 'Abbās; *prev.* Gombroon. Hormozgān, S Iran 27°11′N 56°11′E
142 M3 **Bandar-e Anzalī** Gīlān, NW Iran 37°26′N 49°29′E
143 N12 **Bandar-e Būshehr** *var.* Būshehr, *Eng.* Bushire. Būshehr, S Iran 28°59′N 50°50′E
143 O13 **Bandar-e Dayyer** *var.* Deyyer. Būshehr, SE Iran 27°50′N 51°55′E

◆ Country ● Country Capital ◇ Dependent Territory ○ Dependent Territory Capital ◆ Administrative Regions ✈ International Airport ▲ Mountain ▲ Mountain Range ~ Volcano ~ River ◎ Lake ☒ Reservoir

Bandar-e Gonāveh – Bartang

142 M11 **Bandar-e Gonāveh** *var.* Ganāveh; *prev.* Gonāveh. Būshehr, SW Iran *29°33′N 50°39′E*
143 T15 **Bandar-e Jāsk** *var.* Jāsk. Hormozgān, SE Iran *25°35′N 58°06′E*
143 O13 **Bandar-e Kangān** *var.* Kangān. Būshehr, S Iran *25°50′N 57°30′E*
143 R14 **Bandar-e Khamīr** Hormozgān, S Iran *27°00′N 55°50′E*
Bandar-e Langeh *see* Bandar-e Lengeh
143 Q14 **Bandar-e Lengeh** *var.* Bandar-e Langeh, Lingeh. Hormozgān, S Iran *26°34′N 54°52′E*
142 L10 **Bandar-e Māhshahr** *var.* Māh-Shahr; *prev.* Bandar-e Ma'shūr. Khūzestān, SW Iran *30°34′N 49°10′E*
Bandar-e Ma'shūr *see* Bandar-e Māhshahr
143 O14 **Bandar-e Nakhīlū** Hormozgān, S Iran
Bandar-e Shāh *see* Bandar-e Torkaman
143 P4 **Bandar-e Torkaman** *var.* Bandar-e Torkeman, Bandar-e Torkman; *prev.* Bandar-e Shāh. Golestán, N Iran *36°55′N 54°05′E*
Bandar-e Torkeman/ Bandar-e Torkman *see* Bandar-e Torkaman
Bandar Kassim *see* Boosaaso
168 M15 **Bandar Lampung** *var.* Bandarlampung, Tanjungkarang-Telukbetung; *prev.* Tandjoengkarang, Tanjungkarang, Teloekbetoeng, Telukbetung. Sumatera, W Indonesia *05°28′S 105°16′E*
Bandarlampung *see* Bandar Lampung
Bandar Maharani *see* Muar
Bandar Masulipatnam *see* Machilīpatnam
Bandar Penggaram *see* Batu Pahat
169 T7 **Bandar Seri Begawan** *prev.* Brunei Town. ● (Brunei) N Brunei *04°56′N 114°58′E*
169 T7 **Bandar Seri Begawan** ✈ N Brunei *04°56′N 114°58′E*
171 R15 **Banda Sea** *var.* Laut Banda. *sea* E Indonesia
104 H5 **Bande** Galicia, NW Spain *42°01′N 07°58′W*
59 G15 **Bandeirantes** Mato Grosso, W Brazil *09°04′S 57°53′W*
59 N20 **Bandeira, Pico da** ▲ SE Brazil *20°25′S 41°45′W*
83 K19 **Bandelierkop** Limpopo, NE South Africa *23°21′S 29°46′E*
62 L8 **Bandera** Santiago del Estero, N Argentina *28°53′S 62°15′W*
25 Q11 **Bandera** Texas, SW USA *29°44′N 99°06′W*
40 J13 **Banderas, Bahía de** *bay* W Mexico
77 O11 **Bandiagara** Mopti, C Mali *14°20′N 03°37′W*
152 I12 **Bāndīkūi** Rājasthān, N India *27°01′N 76°33′E*
136 C11 **Bandırma** *var.* Penderma. Balıkesir, NW Turkey *40°21′N 27°58′E*
Bandjarmasin *see* Banjarmasin
Bandoeng *see* Bandung
97 C21 **Bandon** *Ir.* Droicheadna Bandan. SW Ireland *51°44′N 08°44′W*
32 E14 **Bandon** Oregon, NW USA *43°07′N 124°24′W*
167 R8 **Ban Dong Bang** Nong Khai, E Thailand *18°00′N 104°08′E*
167 Q6 **Ban Donkon** Oudômxai, N Laos *20°20′N 101°37′E*
172 J14 **Bandrélé** SE Mayotte
79 H20 **Bandundu** *prev.* Banningville. Bandundu, W Dem. Rep. Congo *03°19′S 17°24′E*
79 I21 **Bandundu** *off.* Région de Bandundu. ◈ *region* W Dem. Rep. Congo
Bandundu, Région de *see* Bandundu
169 O16 **Bandung** *prev.* Bandoeng. Jawa, C Indonesia *06°47′S 107°28′E*
116 L15 **Băneasa** Constanța, SW Romania *45°56′N 27°55′E*
142 J4 **Bāneh** Kordestān, N Iran *35°58′N 45°54′E*
44 I7 **Banes** Holguín, E Cuba *20°58′N 75°43′W*
11 P16 **Banff** Alberta, SW Canada *51°10′N 115°34′W*
96 K8 **Banff** NE Scotland, United Kingdom *57°39′N 02°33′W*
96 K8 **Banff** *cultural region* NE Scotland, United Kingdom
Bánffyhunyad *see* Huedin
77 N14 **Banfora** SW Burkina *10°36′N 04°45′W*
155 H19 **Bangalore** *var.* Bengalooru. *state capital* Karnātaka, S India *12°58′N 77°35′E*
153 S16 **Bangaon** West Bengal, NE India *23°01′N 88°50′E*
79 L15 **Bangassou** Mbomou, SE Central African Republic *04°51′N 22°55′E*
186 D7 **Bangeta, Mount** ▲ C Papua New Guinea *06°11′S 147°02′E*
171 P12 **Banggai, Kepulauan** *island group* C Indonesia
171 Q12 **Banggai, Pulau** *island* Kepulauan Banggai, N Indonesia
171 X13 **Banggelapa** Papua, E Indonesia *03°47′S 136°53′E*
Banggi *see* Banggi, Pulau
169 V6 **Banggi, Pulau** *var.* Banggi. *island* East Malaysia
152 K5 **Banggong Co** *var.* Pangong Tso. ◎ China/India *see also* Pangong Tso
121 P13 **Banghāzī** *Eng.* Bengazi, Benghazi, *It.* Bengasi. NE Libya *32°07′N 20°04′E*
Bang Hieng *see* Xé Banghiang
169 O13 **Bangka-Belitung** *off.* Propinsi Bangka-Belitung. ◈ *province* W Indonesia
169 P11 **Bangkai, Tanjung** *var.* Bankai. *headland* Borneo, N Indonesia *0°21′N 108°53′E*
169 S16 **Bangkalan** Pulau Madura, C Indonesia *07°05′S 112°44′E*
169 N12 **Bangka, Pulau** *island* W Indonesia
169 N13 **Bangka, Selat** *strait* Sumatera, W Indonesia
169 N13 **Bangka, Selat** *var.* Selat Likupang. *strait* Sulawesi, N Indonesia
168 J11 **Bangkinang** Sumatera, W Indonesia *0°21′N 100°52′E*
168 K12 **Bangko** Sumatera, W Indonesia *02°05′S 102°20′E*
Bangkok *see* Ao Krung Thep
Bangkok, Bight of *see* Krung Thep, Ao
153 T14 **Bangladesh** *off.* People's Republic of Bangladesh; *prev.* East Pakistan. ◆ *republic* S Asia
Bangladesh, People's Republic of *see* Bangladesh
167 V13 **Ba Ngoi** Khanh Hoa, S Vietnam *11°56′N 109°07′E*
Bangong Co *see* Pangong Tso
97 I18 **Bangor** NW Wales, United Kingdom *53°13′N 04°08′W*
97 G15 **Bangor** *Ir.* Beannchar. E Northern Ireland, United Kingdom *54°40′N 05°40′W*
19 R6 **Bangor** Maine, NE USA *44°48′N 68°47′W*
18 I14 **Bangor** Pennsylvania, NE USA *40°52′N 75°12′W*
67 R8 **Bangoran** ≈ S Central African Republic
Bang Phra *see* Trat
Bang Pla Soi *see* Chon Buri
25 Q8 **Bangs** Texas, SW USA *31°43′N 99°07′W*
167 N13 **Bang Saphan** *var.* Bang Saphan Yai. Prachuap Khiri Khan, SW Thailand *11°10′N 99°33′E*
Bang Saphan Yai *see* Bang Saphan
36 I8 **Bangs, Mount** ▲ Arizona, SW USA *36°47′N 113°51′W*
93 E15 **Bangsund** Nord-Trøndelag, C Norway *64°22′N 11°22′E*
171 O2 **Bangued** Luzon, N Philippines *17°36′N 120°40′E*
79 I15 **Bangui** ● (Central African Republic) Ombella-Mpoko, SW Central African Republic *04°21′N 18°32′E*
79 I15 **Bangui** ✈ Ombella-Mpoko, SW Central African Republic *04°19′N 18°34′E*
83 N16 **Bangula** Southern, S Malawi *16°38′S 35°04′E*
Bangwaketse *see* Southern
82 K12 **Bangweulu, Lake** *var.* Lake Bengweulu. ◎ N Zambia
121 V13 **Banhā** *var.* Benha. N Egypt *30°28′N 31°11′E*
Ban Hat Yai *see* Hat Yai
167 Q7 **Ban Hin Heup** Viangchan, C Laos *18°37′N 102°19′E*
Ban Houayxay/Ban Houei Sai *see* Houayxay
167 O12 **Ban Hua Hin** *var.* Hua Hin. Prachuap Khiri Khan, SW Thailand *12°34′N 99°58′E*
79 L14 **Bani** Haute-Kotto, E Central African Republic *07°06′N 22°51′E*
45 O9 **Baní** S Dominican Republic *18°19′N 70°21′W*
77 N12 **Bani** ≈ S Mali
Banias *see* Bāniyās
77 S11 **Bani Bangou** Tillabéri, SW Niger *15°04′N 02°40′E*
76 M12 **Banifing** *var.* Ngorolaka. ≈ Burkina/Mali
Banijska Palanka *see* Glina
77 R13 **Banikoara** N Benin *11°18′N 02°26′E*
75 W9 **Banī Mazār** *var.* Beni Mazâr. C Egypt *28°29′N 30°48′E*
114 K8 **Baniski Lom** ≈ N Bulgaria
21 U7 **Banister River** ≈ Virginia, NE USA
121 V14 **Banī Suwayf** *var.* Beni Suef. N Egypt *29°09′N 31°04′E*
75 O8 **Banī Walīd** NW Libya *31°46′N 13°59′E*
138 H5 **Bāniyās** *var.* Banias, Baniyas, Paneas. Tarṭūs, W Syria *35°12′N 35°57′E*
113 K14 **Banja** Serbia, W Serbia *43°33′N 19°35′E*
Banjak, Kepulauan *see* Banyak, Kepulauan
112 J12 **Banja Koviljača** Serbia, W Serbia *44°31′N 19°11′E*
112 G11 **Banja Luka** ◈ Republika Srpska, NW Bosnia and Herzegovina
169 T13 **Banjarmasin** *prev.* Bandjarmasin. Borneo, C Indonesia *03°22′S 114°33′E*
76 F11 **Banjul** *prev.* Bathurst. ● (Gambia) W Gambia *13°26′N 16°43′W*
76 F11 **Banjul** ✈ W Gambia *13°18′N 16°39′W*
Bank *see* Bankä
137 Y13 **Bankä** *Rus.* Bank. SE Azerbaijan *39°25′N 49°13′E*
167 S11 **Ban Kadian** *var.* Ban Kadiene. Champasak, S Laos *14°25′N 105°42′E*
Ban Kadiene *see* Ban Kadian
Bankai *see* Bangkai, Tanjung
166 M14 **Ban Kam Phuam** Phangnga, SW Thailand *09°16′N 98°24′E*
Ban Kantang *see* Kantang
77 O11 **Bankass** Mopti, S Mali *14°05′N 03°30′W*
95 L19 **Bankeryd** Jönköping, S Sweden *57°51′N 14°07′E*
83 K16 **Banket** Mashonaland West, N Zimbabwe *17°23′S 30°24′E*
167 T11 **Ban Khamphô** Attapu, S Laos *14°35′N 106°18′E*
23 O4 **Bankhead Lake** ⊠ Alabama, S USA
77 Q11 **Bankilaré** Tillabéri, SW Niger *14°34′N 00°41′E*
Banks, Îles *see* Banks Islands
10 I14 **Banks Island** *island* British Columbia, SW Canada
187 R12 **Banks Islands** *Fr.* Îles Banks. *island group* N Vanuatu
23 U8 **Banks Lake** ◎ Georgia, SE USA
32 K8 **Banks Lake** ⊠ Washington, NW USA
185 I19 **Banks Peninsula** *peninsula* South Island, New Zealand
183 Q15 **Banks Strait** *strait* SW Tasman Sea
Ban Kui Nua *see* Kui Buri
153 R16 **Bānkura** West Bengal, NE India *23°14′N 87°05′E*
167 S8 **Ban Lakxao** *var.* Lak Sao. Bolikhamxai, C Laos *18°10′N 104°58′E*
167 O16 **Ban Lam Phai** Songkhla, SW Thailand *06°43′N 100°57′E*
Ban Mae Sot *see* Mae Sot
Ban Mae Suai *see* Mae Suai
Ban Mak Khaeng *see* Udon Thani
166 M3 **Banmauk** Sagaing, N Myanmar (Burma) *24°26′N 95°54′E*
Banmo *see* Bhamo
167 T10 **Ban Mun-Houamuang** S Laos *15°11′N 106°44′E*
97 F14 **Bann** *var.* Lower Bann, Upper Bann. ≈ N Northern Ireland, United Kingdom
167 S10 **Ban Nadou** Salavan, S Laos *15°51′N 105°38′E*
167 S9 **Ban Nakala** Savannakhét, S Laos *16°14′N 105°09′E*
167 Q8 **Ban Nakha** Viangchan, C Laos *18°13′N 102°29′E*
167 S9 **Ban Nakham** Khammouan, S Laos *17°10′N 105°25′E*
167 P7 **Ban Namoun** Xaignabouli, N Laos *18°40′N 101°34′E*
167 O17 **Ban Nang Sata** Yala, SW Thailand *06°15′N 101°13′E*
167 N15 **Ban Na San** Surat Thani, SW Thailand *08°53′N 99°17′E*
167 R7 **Ban Nasi** Xiangkhoang, N Laos *19°37′N 103°33′E*
44 I3 **Bannerman Town** Eleuthera Island, C Bahamas *24°38′N 76°09′W*
35 V15 **Banning** California, W USA *33°55′N 116°52′W*
Banningville *see* Bandundu
167 S11 **Ban Nongsim** Champasak, S Laos *14°45′N 106°00′E*
149 S7 **Bannu** *prev.* Edwardesabad. North-West Frontier Province, NW Pakistan *33°00′N 70°36′E*
Bañolas *see* Banyoles
56 C7 **Baños** Tungurahua, C Ecuador *01°26′S 78°24′W*
Bánovce *see* Bánovce nad Bebravou
111 I19 **Bánovce nad Bebravou** *var.* Bánovce, *Hung.* Bán. Trenčiansky Kraj, W Slovakia *48°43′N 18°15′E*
112 I12 **Banovići** ◈ Federacija Bosna I Hercegovina, E Bosnia and Herzegovina
Banow *see* Andarāb
Ban Pak Phanang *see* Pak Phanang
167 O7 **Ban Pan Nua** Lampang, NW Thailand *18°51′N 99°57′E*
167 Q9 **Ban Phai** Khon Kaen, E Thailand *16°00′N 102°42′E*
167 T9 **Ban Phou A Douk** Khammouan, C Laos *17°12′N 106°07′E*
167 Q8 **Ban Phu** Uthai Thani, W Thailand
167 O11 **Ban Pong** Ratchaburi, W Thailand *13°49′N 99°53′E*
190 I3 **Banraeaba** Tarawa, W Kiribati *01°20′N 173°02′E*
167 N10 **Ban Sai Yok** Kanchanaburi, W Thailand *14°24′N 98°54′E*
Ban Sattahip/Ban Sattahipp *see* Sattahip
Ban Sichon *see* Sichon
Ban Si Racha *see* Siracha
111 J19 **Banská Bystrica** *Ger.* Neusohl, *Hung.* Besztercebánya. Banskobystricky Kraj, C Slovakia *48°46′N 19°08′E*
111 K20 **Banskobystrický Kraj** ◈ *region* C Slovakia
167 R8 **Ban Sôppheung** Bolikhamxai, C Laos *18°33′N 104°18′E*
Ban Sop Prap *see* Sop Prap
152 G15 **Bānswāra** Rājasthān, N India *23°32′N 74°28′E*
167 N15 **Ban Ta Khun** Surat Thani, SW Thailand *08°53′N 98°52′E*
Ban Takua Pa *see* Takua Pa
167 S8 **Ban Talak** Khammouan, C Laos *17°33′N 105°40′E*
77 R15 **Bantè** W Benin *08°25′N 01°58′E*
167 N16 **Banten** *off.* Propinsi Banten. ◈ *province* W Indonesia
Propinsi Banten *see* Banten
167 Q8 **Ban Thabôk** Bolikhamxai, C Laos *18°21′N 103°12′E*
167 T9 **Ban Tôp** Savannakhét, S Laos *16°07′N 106°07′E*
97 B21 **Bantry** *Ir.* Beanntraí. Cork, SW Ireland *51°41′N 09°27′W*
97 A21 **Bantry Bay** *Ir.* Bá Bheanntraí. *bay* SW Ireland
155 F19 **Bantvāl** *var.* Bantwāl. Karnātaka, E India *12°57′N 75°04′E*
Bantwāl *see* Bantvāl
114 N9 **Banya** Burgas, E Bulgaria *42°46′N 27°49′E*
168 G10 **Banyak, Kepulauan** *prev.* Kepulauan Banjak. *island group* NW Indonesia
105 U8 **Banya, La** *headland* E Spain *40°34′N 00°37′E*
79 E14 **Banyo** Adamaoua, NW Cameroon *06°47′N 11°50′E*
105 X4 **Banyoles** *var.* Bañolas. Cataluña, NE Spain *42°07′N 02°46′E*
167 N16 **Ban Yong Sata** Trang, SW Thailand *07°09′N 99°42′E*
195 X14 **Banzare Coast** *physical region* Antarctica
173 Q14 **Banzare Seamounts** *undersea feature* S Indian Ocean
Banzart *see* Bizerte
163 Q12 **Baochang** *var.* Taibus Qi. Nei Mongol Zizhiqu, N China *41°55′N 115°22′E*
161 O3 **Baoding** *var.* Pao-ting; *prev.* Tsingyuan. Hebei, E China *38°47′N 115°30′E*
Baoebaoe *see* Baubau
Baoi, Oileán *see* Dursey Island
160 J6 **Baoji** *var.* Pao-chi, Paoki. Shaanxi, C China *34°23′N 107°16′E*
163 U9 **Baokang** *var.* Hoqin Zuoyi Zhongji. Nei Mongol Zizhiqu, N China *44°08′N 123°18′E*
186 L8 **Baolo** Santa Isabel, N Solomon Islands *07°41′S 158°47′E*
167 U13 **Bao Lôc** Lâm Đông, S Vietnam *11°33′N 107°48′E*
163 Z7 **Baoqing** Heilongjiang, NE China *46°15′N 132°12′E*
Baoqing *see* Shaoyang
79 H15 **Baoro** Nana-Mambéré, W Central African Republic *05°40′N 16°00′E*
160 E12 **Baoshan** *var.* Pao-shan. Yunnan, SW China *25°05′N 99°07′E*
163 N13 **Baotou** *var.* Pao-t'ou, Paotow. Nei Mongol Zizhiqu, N China *40°38′N 109°59′E*
76 L14 **Baoulé** ≈ S Mali
76 K12 **Baoulé** ≈ W Mali
Bao Yèn *see* Phô Rang
103 O2 **Bapaume** Pas-de-Calais, N France *50°06′N 02°50′E*
14 J13 **Baptiste Lake** ◎ Ontario, SE Canada
Bapu *see* Meigu
Baqanas *see* Bakanas
Baqbaqty *see* Bakbakty
159 P14 **Baqên** *var.* Dartang. Xizang Zizhiqu, W China *31°50′N 94°08′E*
138 F14 **Bāqir, Jabal** ▲▲ S Jordan
139 T7 **Ba'qūbah** *var.* Qubba. Diyālá, C Iraq *33°45′N 44°40′E*
62 H5 **Baquedano** Antofagasta, N Chile *23°20′S 69°50′W*
Baquerizo Moreno *see* Puerto Baquerizo Moreno
113 J18 **Bar** *It.* Antivari. S Montenegro *42°02′N 19°09′E*
116 M6 **Bar** Vinnyts'ka Oblast', C Ukraine *49°05′N 27°40′E*
80 E10 **Bara** Northern Kordofan, C Sudan *13°42′N 30°21′E*
81 M18 **Baraawe** *It.* Brava. Shabeellaha Hoose, S Somalia *01°10′N 43°59′E*
152 M12 **Bāra Banki** Uttar Pradesh, N India *26°56′N 81°11′E*
30 L8 **Baraboo** Wisconsin, N USA *43°27′N 89°45′W*
30 K8 **Baraboo Range** *hill range* Wisconsin, N USA
Baracaldo *see* San Vicente de Barakaldo
15 Y6 **Barachois** Québec, SE Canada *48°37′N 64°14′W*
44 J7 **Baracoa** Guantánamo, E Cuba *20°23′N 74°31′W*
61 C19 **Baradero** Buenos Aires, E Argentina *33°50′S 59°30′W*
183 R6 **Baradine** New South Wales, SE Australia *30°55′S 149°03′E*
Baraf Daja Islands *see* Damar, Kepulauan
154 M12 **Baragarh** *var.* Bargarh. Orissa, E India *21°25′N 83°35′E*
81 I17 **Baragoi** Rift Valley, W Kenya *01°39′N 36°46′E*
45 N9 **Barahona** SW Dominican Republic *18°13′N 71°07′W*
153 W13 **Barail Range** ▲▲ NE India
Baraka *see* Barka
80 G10 **Barakat** Gezira, C Sudan *14°18′N 33°32′E*
Barakī *see* Barakī Barak
149 Q6 **Barakī Barak** *var.* Barakī, Baraki Rajan. Lowgar, E Afghanistan *33°58′N 68°58′E*
Baraki Rajan *see* Barakī Barak
154 N11 **Bārākot** Orissa, E India *21°35′N 85°00′E*
55 S7 **Barama River** ≈ N Guyana
155 E14 **Bārāmati** Mahārāshtra, W India *18°12′N 74°39′E*
152 H5 **Bārāmūla** Jammu and Kashmir, NW India *34°15′N 74°24′E*
119 N14 **Baran'** Vitsyebskaya Voblasts', NE Belarus *54°29′N 30°18′E*
152 I14 **Bārān** Rājasthān, N India *25°08′N 76°32′E*
139 U4 **Barānān, Shākh-i** ▲▲ E Iraq
119 I17 **Baranavichy** *Pol.* Baranowicze, *Rus.* Baranovichi. Brestskaya Voblasts', SW Belarus *53°08′N 26°02′E*
75 Y11 **Baranīce** *var.* Berenice, Mînâ Baranîs. SE Egypt *23°58′N 35°29′E*
123 T6 **Baranikha** Chukotskiy Avtonomnyy Okrug, NE Russian Federation *68°29′N 168°13′E*
116 M4 **Baranivka** Zhytomyrs'ka Oblast', N Ukraine *50°16′N 27°40′E*
39 W14 **Baranof Island** *island* Alexander Archipelago, Alaska, USA
Baranovichi/Baranowicze *see* Baranavichy
111 N15 **Baranów Sandomierski** Podkarpackie, SE Poland *50°28′N 21°31′E*
111 I26 **Baranya** *off.* Baranya Megye. ◈ *county* S Hungary
Baranya Megye *see* Baranya
153 R13 **Barāri** Bihār, NE India *25°31′N 87°23′E*
22 L10 **Barataria Bay** *bay* Louisiana, S USA
Barat Daya, Kepulauan *see* Damar, Kepulauan
118 L12 **Baravukha** *Rus.* Borovukha. Vitsyebskaya Voblasts', N Belarus *55°34′N 28°36′E*
54 E11 **Baraya** Huila, C Colombia *03°11′N 75°04′W*
59 M21 **Barbacena** Minas Gerais, SE Brazil *21°13′S 43°47′W*
54 B13 **Barbacoas** Nariño, SW Colombia *01°38′N 78°08′W*
54 L6 **Barbacoas** Aragua, N Venezuela *09°29′N 66°58′W*
45 Z13 **Barbados** ◆ *commonwealth republic* SE West Indies
47 S3 **Barbados** *island* Barbados
105 U11 **Barbaria, Cap de** *var.* Cabo de Berberia. *headland* Formentera, E Spain *38°39′N 01°24′E*
114 N13 **Barbaros** Tekirdağ, NW Turkey *40°55′N 27°28′E*
74 A11 **Barbas, Cap** *headland* S Western Sahara *22°14′N 16°45′W*
105 T5 **Barbastro** Aragón, NE Spain *42°02′N 00°07′E*
104 K16 **Barbate** ≈ SW Spain
104 K16 **Barbate de Franco** Andalucía, S Spain *36°11′N 05°55′W*
83 K21 **Barberton** Mpumalanga, NE South Africa *25°48′S 31°03′E*
31 U12 **Barberton** Ohio, N USA *41°02′N 81°37′W*
102 K12 **Barbezieux-St-Hilaire** Charente, W France *45°28′N 00°09′W*
54 G9 **Barbosa** Boyaca, C Colombia *05°57′N 73°37′W*
21 N7 **Barbourville** Kentucky, S USA *36°52′N 83°54′W*
45 W9 **Barbuda** *island* N Antigua and Barbuda
181 W8 **Barcaldine** Queensland, E Australia *23°33′S 145°21′E*
Barcarozsnyó *see* Râşnov
104 I11 **Barcarrota** Extremadura, W Spain *38°31′N 06°51′W*
Barcău *see* Berettyó
Barce *see* Al Marj
107 L23 **Barcellona** *var.* Barcellona Pozzo di Gotto. Sicilia, Italy, C Mediterranean Sea *38°10′N 15°15′E*
Barcellona Pozzo di Gotto *see* Barcellona
105 W6 **Barcelona** *anc.* Barcino, Barcinona. Cataluña, E Spain *41°25′N 02°10′E*
55 N5 **Barcelona** Anzoátegui, NE Venezuela *10°08′N 64°43′W*
105 S5 **Barcelona** ◈ *province* Cataluña, NE Spain
105 W6 **Barcelona** ✈ Cataluña, E Spain *41°25′N 02°10′E*
103 U14 **Barcelonnette** Alpes-de-Haute-Provence, SE France *44°24′N 06°37′E*
58 E12 **Barcelos** Amazonas, N Brazil *0°59′S 62°58′W*
104 G5 **Barcelos** Braga, N Portugal *41°32′N 08°37′W*
110 I10 **Barcin** *Ger.* Bartschin. Kujawski-pomorskie, C Poland *52°51′N 17°55′E*
Barcino/Barcinona *see* Barcelona
Barcoo *see* Cooper Creek
111 H26 **Barcs** Somogy, SW Hungary *45°58′N 17°26′E*
137 W11 **Bärdä** *Rus.* Barda. C Azerbaijan *40°25′N 47°07′E*
Barda *see* Bärdä
78 H5 **Bardaï** Borkou-Ennedi-Tibesti, N Chad *21°21′N 16°56′E*
139 R2 **Bardaṛash** Dahūk, N Iraq *36°32′N 43°36′E*
139 Q7 **Bardasah** Al Anbār, SW Iraq *34°02′N 42°28′E*
153 S16 **Barddhamān** West Bengal, NE India *23°10′N 88°03′E*
111 N18 **Bardejov** *Ger.* Bartfeld, *Hung.* Bártfa. Presovský Kraj, E Slovakia *49°17′N 21°18′E*
105 R4 **Bárdenas Reales** *physical region* N Spain
Bardera/Bardere *see* Baardheere
Bardesīr *see* Bardsīr
92 K3 **Bárdharbunga** ▲ C Iceland *64°39′N 17°30′W*
Bardhë, Drini i *see* Beli Drim
106 E9 **Bardi** Emilia-Romagna, C Italy *44°39′N 09°44′E*
106 A8 **Bardonecchia** Piemonte, W Italy *45°04′N 06°40′E*
97 H19 **Bardsey Island** *island* NW Wales, United Kingdom
143 S11 **Bardsīr** *var.* Bardesīr, Mashīz. Kermān, C Iran *29°58′N 56°29′E*
20 L6 **Bardstown** Kentucky, S USA *37°49′N 85°29′W*
Barduli *see* Barletta
20 G7 **Bardwell** Kentucky, S USA *36°52′N 89°01′W*
152 K11 **Bareilly** *var.* Bareli. Uttar Pradesh, N India *28°20′N 79°24′E*
Bareli *see* Bareilly
Baren *see* Jiashi
98 H13 **Barendrecht** Zuid-Holland, SW Netherlands *51°52′N 04°31′E*
102 M3 **Barentin** Seine-Maritime, N France *49°33′N 00°57′E*
92 N3 **Barentsburg** Spitsbergen, W Svalbard *78°01′N 14°19′E*
Barentsevo More/Barents Havet *see* Barents Sea
92 O3 **Barentsøya** *island* E Svalbard
197 T11 **Barents Plain** *undersea feature* N Barents Sea
125 P3 **Barents Sea** *Nor.* Barents Havet, *Rus.* Barentsevo More. *sea* Arctic Ocean
197 U14 **Barents Trough** *undersea feature* SW Barents Sea *75°00′N 29°00′E*
80 I9 **Barentu** W Eritrea *15°08′N 37°35′E*
102 J3 **Barfleur** Manche, N France *49°41′N 01°18′W*
102 J3 **Barfleur, Pointe de** *headland* N France *49°46′N 01°09′W*
Barfrush/Barfurush *see* Bābol
158 H14 **Barga** Xizang Zizhiqu, W China *30°51′N 81°20′E*
Bargarh *see* Baragarh
105 N9 **Bargas** Castilla-La Mancha, C Spain *39°56′N 04°00′W*
81 I15 **Bargē** Southern Nationalities, S Ethiopia *06°11′N 37°04′E*
106 A9 **Barge** Piemonte, NE Italy *44°49′N 07°21′E*
153 U16 **Barguna** Barisal, S Bangladesh *22°09′N 90°07′E*
Bärguşad *see* Vorotan
123 N13 **Barguzin** Respublika Buryatiya, S Russian Federation *53°37′N 109°47′E*
153 O13 **Barhaj** Uttar Pradesh, N India *26°16′N 83°44′E*
183 N10 **Barham** New South Wales, SE Australia *35°39′S 144°09′E*
152 J12 **Barhan** Uttar Pradesh, N India *27°21′N 78°11′E*
19 S7 **Bar Harbor** Mount Desert Island, Maine, NE USA *44°23′N 68°14′W*
153 R14 **Barharwa** Jhārkhand, NE India *24°52′N 87°47′E*
153 P15 **Barhi** Jhārkhand, N India *24°19′N 85°25′E*
107 O17 **Bari** *var.* Bari delle Puglie; *anc.* Barium. Puglia, SE Italy *41°06′N 16°52′E*
80 P12 **Bari** *Off.* Gobolka Bari. ◈ *region* NE Somalia
167 T14 **Ba Ria** *var.* Châu Thanh. Ba Ria-Vung Tau, S Vietnam *10°30′N 107°10′E*
Bāridah *see* Al Bāridah
Bari delle Puglie *see* Bari
Bari, Gobolka *see* Bari
Barikot *see* Barīkowṭ
149 T4 **Barīkowṭ** *var.* Barikot. Konar, NE Afghanistan *35°18′N 71°36′E*
42 C4 **Barillas** *var.* Santa Cruz Barillas. Huehuetenango, NW Guatemala *15°50′N 91°20′W*
54 J6 **Barinas** Barinas, W Venezuela *08°36′N 70°15′W*
54 I7 **Barinas** *off.* Estado Barinas; *prev.* Zamora. ◈ *state* C Venezuela
Barinas, Estado *see* Barinas
54 I6 **Barinitas** Barinas, NW Venezuela *08°45′N 70°26′W*
154 P11 **Bāripada** Orissa, E India *21°56′N 86°43′E*
60 K9 **Bariri** São Paulo, S Brazil *22°04′S 48°46′W*
75 W11 **Bārīs** *var.* Bârîs. S Egypt *24°28′N 30°39′E*
152 G14 **Bari Sādri** Rājasthān, N India *24°25′N 74°28′E*
153 U16 **Barisal** Barisal, S Bangladesh *22°41′N 90°20′E*
153 U16 **Barisal** ◈ *division* S Bangladesh
168 I10 **Barisan, Pegunungan** ▲▲ Sumatera, W Indonesia
169 T12 **Barito, Sungai** ≈ Borneo, C Indonesia
Barium *see* Bari
Bårjås *see* Porjus
80 I9 **Barka** *var.* Baraka, *Ar.* Khawr Barakah. *seasonal river* Eritrea/Sudan
Barka *see* Al Marj
160 H8 **Barkam** Sichuan, C China *31°56′N 102°22′E*
118 J9 **Barkava** Madona, C Latvia *56°43′N 26°34′E*
10 M15 **Barkerville** British Columbia, SW Canada *53°06′N 121°35′W*
149 R11 **Bārkhān** Baluchistān, SW Pakistan *29°54′N 69°31′E*
14 J12 **Bark Lake** ◎ Ontario, SE Canada
20 H7 **Barkley, Lake** ⊠ Kentucky/Tennessee, S USA
10 K17 **Barkley Sound** *inlet* British Columbia, W Canada
83 J24 **Barkly East** *Afr.* Barkly-Oos. Eastern Cape, SE South Africa *30°58′S 27°35′E*
Barkly-Oos *see* Barkly East
181 S4 **Barkly Tableland** *plateau* Northern Territory/Queensland, N Australia
Barkly-Wes *see* Barkly West
83 H22 **Barkly West** *Afr.* Barkly-Wes. Northern Cape, N South Africa *28°32′S 24°32′E*
159 O5 **Barkol** *var.* Barkol Kazak Zizhixian. Xinjiang Uygur Zizhiqu, NW China *43°37′N 93°01′E*
159 O5 **Barkol Hu** ◎ NW China
Barkol Kazak Zizhixian *see* Barkol
30 J3 **Bark Point** *headland* Wisconsin, N USA *46°53′N 91°11′W*
25 P11 **Barksdale** Texas, SW USA *29°43′N 100°03′W*
Bar Kunar *see* Asmār
116 L11 **Bârlad** *prev.* Bîrlad. Vaslui, E Romania *46°12′N 27°39′E*
116 M11 **Bârlad** *prev.* Bîrlad. ≈ E Romania
76 D9 **Barlavento, Ilhas de** *var.* Windward Islands. *island group* N Cape Verde
103 R5 **Bar-le-Duc** *var.* Bar-sur-Ornain. Meuse, NE France *48°46′N 05°10′E*
180 K11 **Barlee, Lake** ◎ Western Australia
180 H8 **Barlee Range** ▲▲ Western Australia
107 N16 **Barletta** *anc.* Barduli. Puglia, SE Italy *41°20′N 16°17′E*
110 E10 **Barlinek** *Ger.* Berlinchen. Zachodnio-pomorskie, NW Poland *53°N 15°11′E*
27 S11 **Barling** Arkansas, C USA *35°19′N 94°18′W*
171 U12 **Barma** Papua, E Indonesia *01°55′S 132°57′E*
183 Q9 **Barmedman** New South Wales, SE Australia *34°09′S 147°21′E*
Barmen-Elberfeld *see* Wuppertal
152 D12 **Bārmer** Rājasthān, NW India *25°43′N 71°25′E*
182 K9 **Barmera** South Australia *34°14′S 140°26′E*
97 I19 **Barmouth** NW Wales, United Kingdom *52°44′N 04°04′W*
154 F10 **Barnagar** Madhya Pradesh, C India *23°01′N 75°28′E*
152 H9 **Barnāla** Punjab, NW India *30°26′N 75°33′E*
97 L15 **Barnard Castle** N England, United Kingdom *54°35′N 01°55′W*
183 O6 **Barnato** New South Wales, SE Australia *31°39′S 145°01′E*
112 I13 **Barnaul** Altayskiy Kray, C Russian Federation *53°21′N 83°45′E*
109 V8 **Bärnbach** Steiermark, SE Austria *47°05′N 15°07′E*
18 K16 **Barnegat** New Jersey, NE USA *39°43′N 74°12′W*
23 S4 **Barnesville** Georgia, SE USA *33°03′N 84°09′W*
29 R6 **Barnesville** Minnesota, N USA *46°39′N 96°25′W*
31 U13 **Barnesville** Ohio, N USA *39°59′N 81°10′W*
98 K11 **Barneveld** *var.* Barnveld. Gelderland, C Netherlands *52°08′N 05°34′E*
25 O9 **Barnhart** Texas, SW USA *31°07′N 101°09′W*
27 P8 **Barnsdall** Oklahoma, C USA *36°33′N 96°09′W*
97 M17 **Barnsley** N England, United Kingdom *53°34′N 01°28′W*
19 Q12 **Barnstable** Massachusetts, NE USA *41°42′N 70°17′W*
97 I23 **Barnstaple** SW England, United Kingdom *51°05′N 04°04′W*
Barnveld *see* Barneveld
21 Q14 **Barnwell** South Carolina, SE USA *33°14′N 81°21′W*
77 U15 **Baro** Niger, C Nigeria *08°35′N 06°28′E*
67 U8 **Baro** *var.* Baro Wenz. ≈ Ethiopia/Sudan
Baro *see* Baro Wenz
Baroda *see* Vadodara
149 U2 **Baroghil Pass** *var.* Kowtal-e Barowghīl. *pass* Afghanistan/Pakistan
119 Q17 **Baron'ki** *Rus.* Boron'ki. Mahilyowskaya Voblasts', E Belarus *53°09′N 32°08′E*
182 J9 **Barossa Valley** *valley* South Australia
Baroui *see* Salisbury
81 H14 **Baro Wenz** *var.* Baro, Nahr Barū. ≈ Ethiopia/Sudan
Baro Wenz *see* Baro
Barowghīl, Kowtal-e *see* Baroghil Pass
153 U12 **Barpeta** Assam, NE India *26°19′N 91°05′E*
31 S7 **Barques, Pointe Aux** *headland* Michigan, N USA *44°04′N 82°57′W*
54 I5 **Barquisimeto** Lara, NW Venezuela *10°03′N 69°18′W*
59 N16 **Barra** Bahia, E Brazil *11°06′S 43°15′W*
96 E9 **Barra** *island* NW Scotland, United Kingdom
183 T5 **Barraba** New South Wales, SE Australia *30°24′S 150°37′E*
60 L9 **Barra Bonita** São Paulo, S Brazil *22°30′S 48°35′W*
64 J12 **Barracuda Fracture Zone** *var.* Fifteen Twenty Fracture Zone. *tectonic feature* SW Atlantic Ocean
64 G11 **Barracuda Ridge** *undersea feature* N Atlantic Ocean
43 N12 **Barra del Colorado** Limón, NE Costa Rica *10°44′N 83°35′W*
43 N9 **Barra de Río Grande** Región Autónoma Atlántico Sur, E Nicaragua *12°56′N 83°30′W*
82 A11 **Barra do Cuanza** Luanda, NW Angola *09°12′S 13°08′E*
60 O9 **Barra do Piraí** Rio de Janeiro, SE Brazil *22°30′S 43°47′W*
61 D16 **Barra do Quaraí** Rio Grande do Sul, SE Brazil *31°03′S 58°10′W*
59 G14 **Barra do São Manuel** Pará, N Brazil *07°12′S 58°03′W*
83 N19 **Barra Falsa, Ponta da** *headland* S Mozambique *22°57′S 35°36′E*
96 E10 **Barra Head** *headland* NW Scotland, United Kingdom *56°46′N 07°37′W*
60 O9 **Barra Mansa** Rio de Janeiro, SE Brazil *22°25′S 44°03′W*
57 D14 **Barranca** Lima, W Peru *10°46′S 77°46′W*
54 F8 **Barrancabermeja** Santander, N Colombia *07°01′N 73°51′W*
54 H4 **Barrancas** La Guajira, N Colombia *10°59′N 72°46′W*
54 J6 **Barrancas** Barinas, NW Venezuela *08°47′N 70°07′W*
55 Q6 **Barrancas** Monagas, NE Venezuela *08°45′N 62°12′W*
54 F6 **Barranco de Loba** Bolívar, N Colombia *08°56′N 74°07′W*
104 I12 **Barrancos** Beja, S Portugal *38°08′N 06°59′W*
62 N7 **Barranqueras** Chaco, N Argentina *27°29′S 58°54′W*
54 E4 **Barranquilla** Atlántico, N Colombia *10°59′N 74°48′W*
83 N20 **Barra, Ponta da** *headland* S Mozambique *23°46′S 35°33′E*
105 P11 **Barrax** Castilla-La Mancha, C Spain *39°04′N 02°12′W*
19 N11 **Barre** Massachusetts, NE USA *42°24′N 72°06′W*
18 M7 **Barre** Vermont, NE USA *44°09′N 72°25′W*
59 M17 **Barreiras** Bahia, E Brazil *12°09′S 44°58′W*
104 F11 **Barreiro** Setúbal, W Portugal *38°40′N 09°05′W*
20 K7 **Barren River Lake** ⊠ Kentucky, S USA
60 L7 **Barretos** São Paulo, S Brazil *20°33′S 48°33′W*
11 P14 **Barrhead** Alberta, SW Canada *54°10′N 114°22′W*
14 G14 **Barrie** Ontario, S Canada *44°22′N 79°42′W*
11 N16 **Barrière** British Columbia, SW Canada *51°10′N 120°06′W*
14 H8 **Barrière, Lac** ◎ Québec, SE Canada
182 L6 **Barrier Range** *hill range* New South Wales, SE Australia
42 G3 **Barrier Reef** *reef* E Belize
188 C16 **Barrigada** C Guam *13°27′N 144°48′E*
Barrington Island *see* Santa Fe, Isla
183 T7 **Barrington Tops** ▲ New South Wales, SE Australia *32°06′S 151°18′E*
183 O4 **Barringun** New South Wales, SE Australia *29°02′S 145°45′E*
59 K18 **Barro Alto** Goiás, S Brazil *15°07′S 48°56′W*
59 N14 **Barro Duro** Piauí, NE Brazil *05°49′S 42°30′W*
30 I5 **Barron** Wisconsin, N USA *45°24′N 91°50′W*
14 J12 **Barron** ≈ Ontario, SE Canada
61 H15 **Barros Cassal** Rio Grande do Sul, S Brazil *29°12′S 52°33′W*
45 P14 **Barrouallie** Saint Vincent , W Saint Vincent and the Grenadines *13°14′N 61°17′W*
39 O4 **Barrow** Alaska, USA *71°17′N 156°47′W*
97 E20 **Barrow** *Ir.* An Bhearú. ≈ SE Ireland
181 Q6 **Barrow Creek Roadhouse** Northern Territory, N Australia *21°30′S 133°52′E*
97 J16 **Barrow-in-Furness** NW England, United Kingdom *54°07′N 03°14′W*
180 G7 **Barrow Island** *island* Western Australia
39 O4 **Barrow, Point** *headland* Alaska, USA *71°23′N 156°28′W*
11 V14 **Barrows** Manitoba, S Canada *52°49′N 101°36′W*
97 J22 **Barry** S Wales, United Kingdom *51°24′N 03°18′W*
14 J12 **Barry's Bay** Ontario, SE Canada *45°30′N 77°41′W*
144 K14 **Barsakel'mes, Ostrov** *island* SW Kazakhstan
Baršć Łužyca *see* Forst
147 S14 **Barsem** S Tajikistan *37°36′N 71°43′E*
145 V11 **Barshatas** Vostochnyy Kazakhstan, E Kazakhstan *48°13′N 78°33′E*
155 F14 **Bārsi** Mahārāshtra, W India *18°14′N 75°42′E*
100 I13 **Barsinghausen** Niedersachsen, C Germany *53°19′N 09°30′E*
147 X8 **Barskoon** Issyk-Kul'skaya Oblast', E Kyrgyzstan *42°07′N 77°34′E*
100 F10 **Barssel** Niedersachsen, NW Germany *53°10′N 07°46′E*
35 U14 **Barstow** California, W USA *34°52′N 117°00′W*
24 L8 **Barstow** Texas, SW USA *31°27′N 103°23′W*
103 R6 **Bar-sur-Aube** Aube, NE France *48°13′N 04°43′E*
Bar-sur-Ornain *see* Bar-le-Duc
103 Q6 **Bar-sur-Seine** Aube, N France *48°06′N 04°22′E*
147 S13 **Bartang** S Tajikistan *38°06′N 71°48′E*
147 T13 **Bartang** ≈ SE Tajikistan

◆ Country
● Country Capital
◇ Dependent Territory
○ Dependent Territory Capital
◈ Administrative Regions
✈ International Airport
▲ Mountain
▲▲ Mountain Range
⛰ Volcano
≈ River
◎ Lake
⊠ Reservoir

BARTENSTEIN – BEČEJ

Bartenstein *see* Bartoszyce
Bártfa/Bartfeld *see* Bardejov
100 *N7* **Barth** Mecklenburg-Vorpommern, NE Germany *54°21′N 12°43′E*
27 *W13* **Bartholomew, Bayou** ≈ Arkansas/Louisiana, S USA
55 *T8* **Bartica** N Guyana *06°24′N 58°36′W*
136 *H10* **Bartın** Bartın, NW Turkey *41°37′N 32°20′E*
136 *H10* **Bartın** ⬖ *province* NW Turkey
181 *W4* **Bartle Frere** ▲ Queensland, E Australia *17°15′S 145°43′E*
27 *P8* **Bartlesville** Oklahoma, C USA *36°44′N 95°59′W*
29 *P14* **Bartlett** Nebraska, C USA *41°51′N 98°32′W*
20 *E10* **Bartlett** Tennessee, S USA *35°12′N 89°52′W*
25 *T9* **Bartlett** Texas, SW USA *30°47′N 97°25′W*
36 *L13* **Bartlett Reservoir** ⊠ Arizona, SW USA
19 *N6* **Barton** Vermont, NE USA *44°44′N 72°09′W*
110 *L7* **Bartoszyce** *Ger.* Bartenstein. Warmińsko-mazurskie, NE Poland *54°16′N 20°49′E*
23 *W12* **Bartow** Florida, SE USA *27°54′N 81°50′W*
Bartschin *see* Barcin
168 *J10* **Barumun, Sungai** ≈ Sumatera, W Indonesia
Barū, Nahr *see* Baro Wenz
169 *S17* **Barung, Nusa** *island* S Indonesia
168 *H9* **Barus** Sumatera, NW Indonesia *02°02′N 98°20′E*
162 *I9* **Baruunbayan-Ulaan** *var.* Höövör. Övörhangay, C Mongolia *45°10′N 101°19′E*
Baruunsuu *see* Tsogttsetsiy
163 *P8* **Baruun-Urt** Sühbaatar, E Mongolia *46°40′N 113°17′E*
43 *P15* **Barú, Volcán** *var.* Volcán de Chiriquí. ⛰ W Panama *08°49′N 82°32′W*
99 *K21* **Barvaux** Luxembourg, SE Belgium *50°21′N 05°30′E*
42 *M13* **Barva, Volcán** ⛰ NW Costa Rica *10°07′N 84°08′W*
117 *W6* **Barvinkove** Kharkivs'ka Oblast', E Ukraine *48°54′N 37°03′E*
154 *G11* **Barwāh** Madhya Pradesh, C India *22°17′N 76°01′E*
Bärwalde Neumark *see* Mieszkowice
154 *F11* **Barwāni** Madhya Pradesh, C India *22°02′N 74°56′E*
183 *P5* **Barwon River** ≈ New South Wales, SE Australia
119 *L15* **Barysaw** *Rus.* Borisov. Minskaya Voblasts', NE Belarus *54°14′N 28°30′E*
127 *Q6* **Barysh** Ul'yanovskaya Oblast', W Russian Federation *53°32′N 47°06′E*
117 *Q4* **Baryshivka** Kyyivs'ka Oblast', N Ukraine *50°21′N 31°21′E*
79 *J17* **Basankusu** Equateur, NW Dem. Rep. Congo *01°12′N 19°50′E*
117 *N11* **Basarabeasca** *Rus.* Bessarabka. SE Moldova *46°22′N 28°56′E*
116 *M14* **Basarabi** Constanța, SW Romania *44°10′N 28°26′E*
40 *H6* **Basaseachic** Chihuahua, NW Mexico *28°18′N 108°13′W*
Basauri *see* Arizgoiti
61 *D18* **Basavilbaso** Entre Ríos, E Argentina *32°23′S 58°55′W*
79 *F21* **Bas-Congo** *off.* Région du Bas-Congo; *prev.* Bas-Zaïre. ⬖ *region* SW Dem. Rep. Congo
108 *E6* **Basel** *Eng.* Basle, *Fr.* Bâle. Basel-Stadt, NW Switzerland *47°33′N 07°36′E*
108 *E7* **Basel** *Eng.* Basle, *Fr.* Bâle. ⬖ *canton* NW Switzerland
143 *T14* **Bashākerd, Kūhhā-ye** ▲▲ SE Iran
11 *Q15* **Bashaw** Alberta, SW Canada *52°40′N 112°53′W*
146 *K16* **Bashbedeng** Mary Welaýaty, S Turkmenistan *35°44′N 63°07′E*
161 *T15* **Bashi Channel** *Chin.* Pa-shih Hai-hsia. *channel* Philippines/Taiwan
Bashkiria *see* Bashkortostan, Respublika
122 *F11* **Bashkortostan, Respublika** *prev.* Bashkiria. ⬖ *autonomous republic* W Russian Federation
127 *N6* **Bashmakovo** Penzenskaya Oblast', W Russian Federation *53°13′N 43°00′E*
146 *J10* **Bashsakarba** Lebap Welaýaty, NE Turkmenistan *40°25′N 62°16′E*
117 *R9* **Bashtanka** Mykolayivs'ka Oblast', S Ukraine *47°24′N 32°27′E*
22 *H8* **Basile** Louisiana, S USA *30°29′N 92°36′W*
107 *M18* **Basilicata** ⬖ *region* S Italy
33 *V13* **Basin** Wyoming, C USA *44°22′N 108°02′W*
97 *N22* **Basingstoke** S England, United Kingdom *51°16′N 01°08′W*
143 *U8* **Başīrān** Khorāsān-e Janūbī, E Iran *31°57′N 59°07′E*
112 *B10* **Baška** *It.* Bescanuova. Primorje-Gorski Kotar, NW Croatia *44°58′N 14°46′E*
137 *T15* **Başkale** Van, SE Turkey *38°03′N 43°59′E*
14 *L10* **Baskatong, Réservoir** ⊠ Québec, SE Canada
137 *O14* **Baskil** Elazığ, E Turkey *38°38′N 38°47′E*
Basle *see* Basel
154 *H9* **Bāsoda** Madhya Pradesh, C India *23°54′N 77°58′E*
79 *L17* **Basoko** Orientale, N Dem. Rep. Congo *01°14′N 23°26′E*
Basque Country, The *see* País Vasco
Basra *see* Al Başrah
103 *U5* **Bas-Rhin** ⬖ *department* NE France
Bassam *see* Grand-Bassam
11 *Q16* **Bassano** Alberta, SW Canada *50°48′N 112°28′W*
106 *H7* **Bassano del Grappa** Veneto, NE Italy *45°45′N 11°45′E*
77 *Q15* **Bassar** *var.* Bassari. NW Togo *09°15′N 00°47′E*
Bassari *see* Bassar
172 *L9* **Bassas da India** *island group* W Madagascar
108 *D7* **Bassecourt** Jura, W Switzerland *47°20′N 07°16′E*
Bassein *see* Pathein
79 *J15* **Basse-Kotto** ⬖ *prefecture* S Central African Republic
105 *V5* **Bassella** Cataluña, NE Spain *42°01′N 01°17′E*
102 *J5* **Basse-Normandie** *Eng.* Lower Normandy. ⬖ *region* N France
45 *Q11* **Basse-Pointe** N Martinique *14°52′N 61°07′W*
76 *H12* **Basse Santa Su** E Gambia *13°18′N 14°10′W*
Basse-Saxe *see* Niedersachsen
45 *X6* **Basse-Terre** ○ (Guadeloupe) Basse Terre, SW Guadeloupe *16°08′N 61°40′W*
45 *V10* **Basseterre** ● (Saint Kitts and Nevis) Saint Kitts, Saint Kitts and Nevis *17°16′N 62°45′W*
45 *X6* **Basse Terre** *island* W Guadeloupe
29 *O13* **Bassett** Nebraska, C USA *42°34′N 99°32′W*
21 *S7* **Bassett** Virginia, NE USA *36°45′N 79°59′W*
37 *N15* **Bassett Peak** ▲ Arizona, SW USA *32°30′N 110°16′W*
76 *M10* **Bassikounou** Hodh ech Chargui, SE Mauritania *15°55′N 05°59′W*
77 *R15* **Bassila** W Benin *08°25′N 01°58′E*
Bass, Îlots de *see* Marotiri
31 *O11* **Bass Lake** Indiana, N USA *41°12′N 86°35′W*
183 *O14* **Bass Strait** *strait* SE Australia
100 *H11* **Bassum** Niedersachsen, NW Germany *52°52′N 08°44′E*
29 *X3* **Basswood Lake** ◎ Canada/USA
95 *J21* **Båstad** Skåne, S Sweden *56°25′N 12°50′E*
139 *U2* **Bastah** As Sulaymānīyah, E Iraq *36°20′N 45°14′E*
143 *Q14* **Bastak** Fārs, SW Iran *27°14′N 54°27′E*
153 *N12* **Basti** Uttar Pradesh, N India *26°48′N 82°44′E*
103 *X14* **Bastia** Corse, France, C Mediterranean Sea *42°42′N 09°27′E*
99 *L23* **Bastogne** Luxembourg, SE Belgium *50°N 05°43′E*
22 *I5* **Bastrop** Louisiana, S USA *32°46′N 91°54′W*
25 *T11* **Bastrop** Texas, SW USA *30°07′N 97°21′W*
93 *J15* **Bastuträsk** Västerbotten, N Sweden *64°47′N 20°05′E*
119 *J19* **Bastyn'** *Rus.* Bostyn'. Brestskaya Voblasts', SW Belarus *52°23′N 26°45′E*
Basuo *see* Dongfang
Basutoland *see* Lesotho
119 *O15* **Basya** ≈ E Belarus
117 *V8* **Basyl'kivka** Dnipropetrovs'ka Oblast', E Ukraine *48°12′N 36°00′E*
Bas-Zaïre *see* Bas-Congo
79 *D17* **Bata** NW Equatorial Guinea *01°51′N 09°48′E*
79 *D17* **Bata** ✈ S Equatorial Guinea *01°55′N 09°48′E*
Batae Coritanorum *see* Leicester
123 *Q8* **Batagay** Respublika Sakha (Yakutiya), NE Russian Federation *67°36′N 134°44′E*
123 *P8* **Batagay-Alyta** Respublika Sakha (Yakutiya), NE Russian Federation *67°48′N 130°15′E*
112 *L10* **Batajnica** Vojvodina, N Serbia *44°55′N 20°17′E*
136 *H15* **Bataklık Gölü** ◎ S Turkey
114 *H11* **Batak, Yazovir** ⊠ SW Bulgaria
152 *H7* **Batāla** Punjab, N India *31°48′N 75°12′E*
104 *F9* **Batalha** Leiria, C Portugal *39°40′N 08°50′W*
79 *N17* **Batama** Orientale, NE Dem. Rep. Congo *0°54′N 26°25′E*
123 *Q10* **Batamay** Respublika Sakha (Yakutiya), NE Russian Federation *63°28′N 129°33′E*
160 *F9* **Batang** *var.* Bazhong. Sichuan, C China *30°04′N 99°10′E*
79 *I14* **Batangafo** Ouham, NW Central African Republic *07°19′N 18°22′E*
171 *P8* **Batangas** *off.* Batangas City. Luzon, N Philippines *13°47′N 121°03′E*
Batangas City *see* Batangas
Bătania *see* Battonya
171 *Q10* **Batan Islands** *island group* N Philippines
60 *L8* **Batatais** São Paulo, S Brazil *20°54′S 47°37′W*
18 *E10* **Batavia** New York, NE USA *43°00′N 78°11′W*
Batavia *see* Jakarta
173 *T9* **Batavia Seamount** *undersea feature* E Indian Ocean *27°42′S 100°36′E*
126 *L12* **Bataysk** Rostovskaya Oblast', SW Russian Federation *47°10′N 39°46′E*
14 *B9* **Batchawana** ≈ Ontario, S Canada
14 *B9* **Batchawana Bay** Ontario, S Canada *46°55′N 84°36′W*
167 *Q12* **Bătdâmbâng** *prev.* Battambang. Bătdâmbâng, NW Cambodia *13°06′N 103°13′E*
79 *G20* **Batéké, Plateaux** *plateau* S Congo
183 *S11* **Batemans Bay** New South Wales, SE Australia *35°45′S 150°09′E*
21 *Q13* **Batesburg** South Carolina, SE USA *33°54′N 81°33′W*
28 *K12* **Batesland** South Dakota, N USA *43°05′N 102°07′W*
27 *V10* **Batesville** Arkansas, C USA *35°45′N 91°39′W*
31 *Q14* **Batesville** Indiana, N USA *39°18′N 85°13′W*
22 *L2* **Batesville** Mississippi, S USA *34°18′N 89°56′W*
25 *Q13* **Batesville** Texas, SW USA *28°56′N 99°38′W*
149 *V5* **Batgrām** North-West Frontier Province, N Pakistan *34°40′N 73°03′E*
44 *L13* **Bath** E Jamaica *17°57′N 76°22′W*
97 *L22* **Bath** *hist.* Akermanceaster; *anc.* Aquae Calidae, Aquae Solis. SW England, United Kingdom *51°23′N 02°22′W*
19 *Q8* **Bath** Maine, NE USA *43°54′N 69°49′W*
18 *F11* **Bath** New York, NE USA *42°20′N 77°16′W*
Bath *see* Berkeley Springs
78 *I10* **Batha** *off.* Préfecture du Batha. ⬖ *prefecture* C Chad
78 *I10* **Batha** *seasonal river* C Chad
Batha, Préfecture du *see* Batha
141 *Y8* **Baṭḥā', Wādī al** *dry watercourse* NE Oman
152 *H9* **Bathinda** Punjab, NW India *30°14′N 74°54′E*
98 *M11* **Bathmen** Overijssel, E Netherlands *52°15′N 06°16′E*
45 *Z14* **Bathsheba** E Barbados *13°13′N 59°31′W*
183 *R8* **Bathurst** New South Wales, SE Australia *33°32′S 149°35′E*
13 *O13* **Bathurst** New Brunswick, SE Canada *47°37′N 65°40′W*
Bathurst *see* Banjul
8 *H6* **Bathurst, Cape** *headland* Northwest Territories, NW Canada *70°33′N 128°00′W*
196 *L8* **Bathurst Inlet** Nunavut, N Canada *66°23′N 107°00′W*
196 *L8* **Bathurst Inlet** *inlet* Nunavut, N Canada
181 *N1* **Bathurst Island** *island* Northern Territory, N Australia
197 *O9* **Bathurst Island** *island* Parry Islands, Nunavut, N Canada
77 *O14* **Batié** SW Burkina *09°53′N 02°53′W*
Batinah *see* Al Bāţinah
141 *Y9* **Bāţin, Wādī al** *dry watercourse* SW Asia
15 *P9* **Batiscan** ≈ Québec, SE Canada
136 *F16* **BatıToroslar** ▲▲ SW Turkey
Batjan *see* Bacan, Pulau
147 *R11* **Batken** Batenskaya Oblast', SW Kyrgyzstan *40°03′N 70°50′E*
Batken Oblasty *see* Batkenskaya Oblast'
147 *Q11* **Batkenskaya Oblast'** *Kir.* Batken Oblasty. ⬖ *province* SW Kyrgyzstan
Batlle y Ordóñez *see* José Batlle y Ordóñez
183 *Q10* **Batlow** New South Wales, SE Australia *35°32′S 148°09′E*
137 *Q15* **Batman** *var.* İluh. Batman, SE Turkey *37°52′N 41°06′E*
137 *Q15* **Batman** ⬖ *province* SE Turkey
74 *L6* **Batna** NE Algeria *35°34′N 06°10′E*
163 *O7* **Batnorov** *var.* Dundbürd. Hentiy, E Mongolia *47°55′N 111°37′E*
Batoe *see* Batu, Kepulauan
162 *K7* **Bat-Öldziy** *var.* Övt. Övörhangay, C Mongolia *46°50′N 102°15′E*
Bat-Öldziyt *see* Dzaamar
22 *J8* **Baton Rouge** *state capital* Louisiana, S USA *30°28′N 91°09′W*
79 *G15* **Batouri** Est, E Cameroon *04°26′N 14°27′E*
138 *G14* **Batrā', Jibāl al** ▲▲ S Jordan
138 *G6* **Batroûn** *var.* Al Batrūn. N Lebanon *34°15′N 35°42′E*
Batsch *see* Bač
Batsevichi *see* Batsevichy
119 *M17* **Batsevichy** *Rus.* Batsevichi. Mahilyowskaya Voblasts', E Belarus *53°24′N 29°14′E*
92 *M7* **Båtsfjord** Finnmark, N Norway *70°37′N 29°42′E*
Batshireet *see* Hentiy
162 *L7* **Batsümber** *var.* Mandal. Töv, C Mongolia *48°24′N 106°47′E*
Battambang *see* tBătdâmbâng
195 *X3* **Batterbee, Cape** *headland* Antarctica
155 *L24* **Batticaloa** Eastern Province, E Sri Lanka *07°44′N 81°43′E*
99 *L19* **Battice** Liège, E Belgium *50°39′N 05°50′E*
107 *L18* **Battipaglia** Campania, S Italy *40°36′N 14°59′E*
11 *R15* **Battle** ≈ Alberta/Saskatchewan, SW Canada
Battle Born State *see* Nevada
31 *Q10* **Battle Creek** Michigan, N USA *42°20′N 85°10′W*
27 *T7* **Battlefield** Missouri, C USA *37°07′N 93°22′W*
11 *S15* **Battleford** Saskatchewan, S Canada *52°45′N 108°20′W*
29 *S6* **Battle Lake** Minnesota, N USA *46°16′N 95°42′W*
35 *U3* **Battle Mountain** Nevada, W USA *40°37′N 116°55′W*
111 *M25* **Battonya** *Rom.* Bătania. Békés, SE Hungary *46°16′N 21°00′E*
162 *J7* **Battsengel** *var.* Jargalant. Arhangay, C Mongolia *47°46′N 101°56′E*
168 *D11* **Batu, Kepulauan** *prev.* Batoe. *island group* W Indonesia
137 *Q10* **Bat'umi** W Georgia *41°39′N 41°38′E*
168 *K10* **Batu Pahat** *prev.* Bandar Penggaram. Johor, Peninsular Malaysia *01°51′N 102°56′E*
171 *O12* **Baturebe** Sulawesi, N Indonesia *01°43′S 121°43′E*
122 *J12* **Baturino** Tomskaya Oblast', C Russian Federation *57°46′N 85°08′E*
117 *R3* **Baturyn** Chernihivs'ka Oblast', N Ukraine *51°20′N 32°54′E*
138 *F10* **Bat Yam** Tel Aviv, C Israel *32°01′N 34°45′E*
127 *Q4* **Batyrevo** Chuvashskaya Respublika, W Russian Federation *55°04′N 47°34′E*
Batys Qazaqstan Oblysy *see* Zapadnyy Kazakhstan
102 *F5* **Batz, Île de** *island* NW France
169 *Q10* **Bau** Sarawak, East Malaysia *01°25′N 110°10′E*
171 *N2* **Bauang** Luzon, N Philippines *16°33′N 120°19′E*
171 *P14* **Baubau** *var.* Baoebaoe. Pulau Buton, C Indonesia *05°30′S 122°37′E*
77 *W14* **Bauchi** Bauchi, NE Nigeria *10°18′N 09°46′E*
77 *W14* **Bauchi** ⬖ *state* C Nigeria
102 *H7* **Baud** Morbihan, NW France *47°52′N 02°59′W*
154 *N13* **Bauda** *var.* Baudh. Orissa, SW India *20°50′N 84°19′E*
29 *T2* **Baudette** Minnesota, N USA *48°42′N 94°36′W*
Baudh *see* Bauda
193 *S9* **Bauer Basin** *undersea feature* E Pacific Ocean *10°00′S 101°45′W*
187 *R14* **Bauer Field** *var.* Port Vila. ✈ (Port-Vila) Éfaté, C Vanuatu *17°42′S 168°21′E*
13 *T9* **Bauld, Cape** *headland* Newfoundland and Labrador, E Canada *51°35′N 55°22′W*
103 *T8* **Baume-les-Dames** Doubs, E France *47°22′N 06°20′E*
101 *I15* **Baunatal** Hessen, C Germany *51°15′N 09°25′E*
107 *D18* **Baunei** Sardegna, Italy, C Mediterranean Sea *40°04′N 09°36′E*
57 *M15* **Baures, Río** ≈ N Bolivia
60 *K9* **Bauru** São Paulo, S Brazil *22°19′S 49°07′W*
Baushar *see* Bawshar
118 *G10* **Bauska** *Ger.* Bauske. Bauska, S Latvia *56°25′N 24°11′E*
Bauske *see* Bauska
101 *Q15* **Bautzen** *Lus.* Budyšin. Sachsen, E Germany *51°11′N 14°29′E*
145 *Q16* **Bauyrzhan Momyshuly** *Kaz.* Baūyrzhan Momyshuly; *prev.* Burnoye. Zhambyl, S Kazakhstan *42°36′N 70°46′E*
Bauzanum *see* Bolzano
Bavaria *see* Bayern
109 *N7* **Bavarian Alps** *Ger.* Bayrische Alpen. ▲▲ Austria/Germany
Bavière *see* Bayern
40 *H4* **Bavispe, Río** ≈ NW Mexico
127 *T5* **Bavly** Respublika Tatarstan, W Russian Federation *54°20′N 53°21′E*
169 *P13* **Bawal, Pulau** *island* N Indonesia
169 *T12* **Bawan** Borneo, C Indonesia *01°36′S 113°55′E*
183 *O12* **Baw Baw, Mount** ▲ Victoria, SE Australia *37°49′S 146°16′E*
169 *S15* **Bawean, Pulau** *island* S Indonesia
75 *V9* **Bawīţī** *var.* Bawîţi. N Egypt *28°19′N 28°53′E*
Bawîţi *see* Bawīţī
77 *Q13* **Bawku** N Ghana *11°00′N 00°12′W*
167 *N7* **Bawlakè** Kayah State, C Myanmar (Burma) *19°10′N 97°19′E*
169 *H11* **Bawo Ofuloa** Pulau Tanahmasa, W Indonesia *0°10′S 98°24′E*
141 *Y8* **Bawshar** *var.* Baushar. NE Oman *23°32′N 58°24′E*
Baxian *see* Bazhou
Ba Xian *see* Bazhou
158 *M8* **Baxkorgan** Xinjiang Uygur Zizhiqu, W China *39°05′N 90°00′E*
23 *V6* **Baxley** Georgia, SE USA *31°46′N 82°21′W*
159 *R15* **Baxoi** *var.* Baima. Xizang Zizhiqu, W China *30°01′N 96°53′E*
29 *W14* **Baxter** Iowa, C USA *41°49′N 93°09′W*
29 *U6* **Baxter** Minnesota, N USA *46°21′N 94°18′W*
27 *R8* **Baxter Springs** Kansas, C USA *37°01′N 94°45′W*
81 *M17* **Bay** *off.* Gobolka Bay. ⬖ *region* SW Somalia
Bay *see* Baicheng
44 *H7* **Bayamo** Granma, E Cuba *20°21′N 76°38′W*
45 *U5* **Bayamón** E Puerto Rico *18°24′N 66°09′W*
163 *W8* **Bayan** Heilongjiang, NE China *46°05′N 127°24′E*
170 *L16* **Bayan** *prev.* Bajan. Pulau Lombok, C Indonesia *08°16′S 116°28′E*
162 *M8* **Bayan** *var.* Maanĭt. Töv, C Mongolia *47°14′N 107°34′E*
Bayan *see* Hölönbuyr, Dornod, Mongolia
Bayan *see* Ihhet, Dornogovĭ, Mongolia
Bayan *see* Bayan-Uul, Govĭ-Altay, Mongolia
Bayan *see* Bayanhutag, Hentiy, Mongolia
Bayan *see* Bürentogtoh, Hövsgol, Mongolia
152 *I12* **Bayāna** Rājasthān, N India *26°55′N 77°18′E*
149 *N5* **Bāyān, Band-e** ▲▲ C Afghanistan
162 *H8* **Bayanbulag** Bayanhongor, C Mongolia *46°46′N 98°07′E*
Bayanbulag *see* Ömnödelger
158 *J5* **Bayanbulak** Xinjiang Uygur Zizhiqu, W China *43°05′N 84°05′E*
162 *L7* **Bayanchandmanĭ** *var.* Ihsüüj. Töv, C Mongolia *48°12′N 106°23′E*
162 *J11* **Bayandalay** *var.* Dalay. Ömnögovĭ, S Mongolia *43°27′N 103°30′E*
163 *O9* **Bayandelger** *var.* Shireet. Sühbaatar, SE Mongolia *45°33′N 112°19′E*
162 *I5* **Bayandzürh** *var.* Altraga. Hövsgöl, N Mongolia *50°08′N 98°54′E*
Bayan Gol *see* Dengkou, China
Bayangol *see* Bugat, Mongolia
162 *I9* **Bayangovĭ** *var.* Örgön. Bayanhongor, C Mongolia *44°43′N 100°23′E*
159 *R12* **Bayan Har Shan** *var.* Bayan Khar. ▲▲ C China
162 *G6* **Bayanhayrhan** *var.* Altanbulag. Dzavhan, N Mongolia *49°16′N 96°22′E*
162 *I8* **Bayanhongor** Bayanhongor, C Mongolia *46°08′N 100°42′E*
162 *H9* **Bayanhongor** ⬖ *province* C Mongolia
162 *K14* **Bayan Hot** *var.* Alxa Zuoqi. Nei Mongol Zizhiqu, N China *38°49′N 105°40′E*
163 *O8* **Bayanhutag** *var.* Bayan. Hentiy, C Mongolia *47°13′N 110°57′E*
163 *T9* **Bayan Huxu** *var.* Horqin Zuoyi Zhongqi. Nei Mongol Zizhiqu, N China *45°02′N 121°28′E*
Bayan Khar *see* Bayan Har Shan
163 *N12* **Bayan Kuang** *prev.* Bayan Obo. Nei Mongol Zizhiqu, N China *41°45′N 109°58′E*
168 *J7* **Bayan Lepas** ✈ (George Town) Pinang, Peninsular Malaysia *05°18′N 100°15′E*
162 *I10* **Bayanlig** *var.* Hatansuudal. Bayanhongor, C Mongolia *44°34′N 100°41′E*
162 *K13* **Bayan Mod** Nei Mongol Zizhiqu, N China *40°45′N 104°29′E*
163 *N8* **Bayanmönh** *var.* Ulaan-Ereg. Hentiy, E Mongolia *46°50′N 109°39′E*
162 *L12* **Bayannur** *var.* Linhe. Nei Mongol Zizhiqu, N China *40°46′N 107°27′E*
Bayan Nuru *see* Xar Burd
162 *E5* **Bayannuur** *var.* Tsul-Ulaan. Bayan-Ölgiy, W Mongolia *48°51′N 91°13′E*
Bayan Obo *see* Bayan Kuang
43 *V15* **Bayano, Lago** ◎ E Panama
162 *C5* **Bayan-Ölgiy** ⬖ *province* NW Mongolia
162 *H9* **Bayan-Öndör** *var.* Bulgan. Bayanhongor, C Mongolia *44°48′N 98°39′E*
162 *K8* **Bayan-Öndör** *var.* Bumbat. Övörhangay, C Mongolia *46°30′N 104°08′E*
162 *L8* **Bayan-Önjüül** *var.* Ihhayrhan. Töv, C Mongolia *46°57′N 105°51′E*
163 *O7* **Bayan-Ovoo** *var.* Javhlant. Hentiy, E Mongolia *47°46′N 112°06′E*
162 *L11* **Bayan-Ovoo** *var.* Erdenetsogt. Ömnögovĭ, S Mongolia *42°54′N 106°16′E*
Bayansayr *see* Baatsagaan
159 *Q9* **Bayan Shan** ▲ C China *37°36′N 96°23′E*
162 *J9* **Bayanteeg** Övörhangay, C Mongolia *45°39′N 101°30′E*
162 *G5* **Bayantes** *var.* Altay. Dzavhan, N Mongolia *49°40′N 96°21′E*
Bayantöhöm *see* Büren
162 *M8* **Bayantsagaan** *var.* Dzogsool. Töv, C Mongolia *46°46′N 107°18′E*
163 *P7* **Bayantümen** *var.* Tsagaanders. Dornod, NE Mongolia *48°03′N 114°16′E*
Bayan-Uhaa *see* Ih-Uul
163 *R10* **Bayan Ul** *var.* Xi Ujimqin Qi. Nei Mongol Zizhiqu, N China *44°31′N 117°36′E*
Bayan-Ulaan *see* Dzüünbayan-Ulaan
163 *O7* **Bayan-Uul** *var.* Javarthushuu. Dornod, NE Mongolia *49°05′N 112°40′E*
162 *F7* **Bayan-Uul** *var.* Bayan. Govĭ-Altay, W Mongolia *47°05′N 95°13′E*
162 *M8* **Bayanuur** *var.* Tsul-Ulaan. Töv, C Mongolia *47°44′N 108°22′E*
28 *J14* **Bayard** Nebraska, C USA *41°45′N 103°19′W*
37 *P15* **Bayard** New Mexico, SW USA *32°45′N 108°07′W*
103 *T13* **Bayard, Col** *pass* SE France
Bayasgalant *see* Mönhhaan
136 *J12* **Bayat** Çorum, N Turkey *40°34′N 34°07′E*
171 *P6* **Bayawan** Negros, C Philippines *09°22′N 122°50′E*
143 *R10* **Bayāẓ** Kermān, C Iran *30°41′N 55°29′E*
171 *Q6* **Baybay** Leyte, C Philippines *10°41′N 124°49′E*
21 *X10* **Bayboro** North Carolina, SE USA *35°08′N 76°49′W*
137 *P12* **Bayburt** Bayburt, NE Turkey *40°15′N 40°16′E*
137 *P12* **Bayburt** ⬖ *province* NE Turkey
31 *R8* **Bay City** Michigan, N USA *43°35′N 83°52′W*
25 *V12* **Bay City** Texas, SW USA *28°59′N 96°00′W*
Baydarata Bay *see* Baydaratskaya Guba
122 *J7* **Baydaratskaya Guba** *var.* Baydarata Bay. *bay* N Russian Federation
81 *M16* **Baydhabo** *var.* Baydhowa, Isha Baydhabo, *It.* Baidoa. Bay, SW Somalia *03°08′N 43°39′E*
Baydhowa *see* Baydhabo
77 *U17* **Bayelsa** ⬖ *state* S Nigeria
101 *N21* **Bayerischer Wald** ▲▲ SE Germany
101 *K21* **Bayern** *Eng.* Bavaria, *Fr.* Bavière. ⬖ *state* SE Germany
147 *V9* **Bayetovo** Narynskaya Oblast', C Kyrgyzstan *41°14′N 74°55′E*
102 *K4* **Bayeux** *anc.* Augustodurum. Calvados, N France *49°16′N 00°42′W*
14 *E15* **Bayfield** ≈ Ontario, S Canada
145 *O15* **Baygekum** *Kaz.* Bäygequm. Kzylorda, S Kazakhstan *44°15′N 66°34′E*
Bäygequm *see* Baygekum
136 *C14* **Bayındır** Izmır, SW Turkey *38°12′N 27°40′E*
138 *H12* **Bāyir** *var.* Bā'ir. Ma'ān, S Jordan *30°46′N 36°40′E*
Bay Islands *see* Bahía, Islas de la
Bayizhen *see* Nyingchi
139 *R5* **Bayjī** *var.* Baiji. Şalāḩ ad Dīn, N Iraq *34°56′N 43°29′E*
Baykadam *see* Saudakent
123 *N13* **Baykal, Ozero** *Eng.* Lake Baikal. ◎ S Russian Federation
123 *M14* **Baykal'sk** Irkutskaya Oblast', S Russian Federation *51°30′N 104°03′E*
137 *R15* **Baykan** Siirt, SE Turkey *38°08′N 41°43′E*
123 *L11* **Baykit** Evenkiyskiy Avtonomnyy Okrug, C Russian Federation *61°37′N 96°23′E*
145 *N12* **Baykonur** *var.* Baykonyr. Karaganda, C Kazakhstan *47°50′N 75°33′E*
Baykonur *see* Baykonyr
144 *M14* **Baykonyr** *var.* Baykonur, *Kaz.* Bayqongyr; *prev.* Leninsk. Kyzylorda, S Kazakhstan *45°38′N 63°20′E*
Baykonyr *see* Baykonur
158 *E7* **Baykurt** Xinjiang Uygur Zizhiqu, W China *39°56′N 75°33′E*
14 *I9* **Bay, Lac** ◎ Québec, SE Canada
127 *W6* **Baymak** Respublika Bashkortostan, W Russian Federation *52°34′N 58°20′E*
23 *O8* **Bay Minette** Alabama, S USA *30°52′N 87°46′W*
143 *O17* **Baynūnah** *desert* W United Arab Emirates
184 *O8* **Bay of Plenty** *off.* Bay of Plenty Region. ⬖ *region* North Island, New Zealand
Bay of Plenty Region *see* Bay of Plenty
191 *Z3* **Bay of Wrecks** *bay* Kiritimati, E Kiribati
Bayonnaise Rocks *see* Beyonēsu-retsugan
102 *I15* **Bayonne** *anc.* Lapurdum. Pyrénées-Atlantiques, SW France *43°30′N 01°28′W*
22 *H4* **Bayou D'Arbonne Lake** ⊠ Louisiana, S USA
23 *N9* **Bayou La Batre** Alabama, S USA *30°24′N 88°15′W*
Bayou State *see* Mississippi
Bayqadam *see* Saudakent
Bayqongyr *see* Baykonyr
Bayram-Ali *see* Baýramaly
146 *J14* **Baýramaly** *var.* Bayramaly; *prev.* Bayram-Ali. Mary Welaýaty, S Turkmenistan *37°33′N 62°08′E*
101 *L19* **Bayreuth** *var.* Baireuth. Bayern, SE Germany *49°57′N 11°34′E*
Bayrische Alpen *see* Bavarian Alps
Bayrūt *see* Beyrouth
22 *L9* **Bay Saint Louis** Mississippi, S USA *30°18′N 89°19′W*
Baysān *see* Beit She'an
Bayshint *see* Öndörshireet
14 *H13* **Bays, Lake of** ◎ Ontario, S Canada
22 *M6* **Bay Springs** Mississippi, S USA *31°58′N 89°17′W*
Bay State *see* Massachusetts
Baysun *see* Boysun
14 *H13* **Baysville** Ontario, S Canada *45°10′N 79°03′W*
141 *N15* **Bayt al Faqīh** W Yemen *14°30′N 43°20′E*
158 *M4* **Baytik Shan** ▲▲ China/Mongolia
Bayt Laḩm *see* Bethlehem
25 *W11* **Baytown** Texas, SW USA *29°43′N 94°59′W*
169 *V11* **Bayur, Tanjung** *headland* Borneo, N Indonesia *0°43′S 117°32′E*
121 *N14* **Bayy al Kabīr, Wādī** *dry watercourse* NW Libya
Bayyrqum *see* Bairkum
105 *P14* **Baza** Andalucía, S Spain *37°30′N 02°45′W*
137 *X10* **Bazardüzü Dağı** *Rus.* Gora Bazardyuzyu. ▲ N Azerbaijan *41°13′N 47°50′E*
Bazardyuzyu, Gora *see* Bazardüzü Dağı
Bazargic *see* Dobrich
83 *N18* **Bazaruto, Ilha do** *island* SE Mozambique
102 *K14* **Bazas** Gironde, SW France *44°27′N 00°11′W*
105 *O14* **Baza, Sierra de** ▲▲ S Spain
160 *J8* **Bazhong** *var.* Bazhou. Sichuan, C China *31°55′N 106°44′E*
Bazhong *see* Batang
161 *P3* **Bazhou** *prev.* Baxian, Ba Xian. Hebei, E China *39°05′N 116°24′E*
Bazhou *see* Bazhong
14 *M9* **Bazin** ≈ Québec, SE Canada
Bazin *see* Pezinok
139 *Q7* **Bāzīyah** Al Anbār, C Iraq *33°50′N 42°41′E*
138 *H6* **Bcharré** *var.* Bcharreh, Bsharrī, Bsherri. NE Lebanon *34°16′N 36°01′E*
Bcharreh *see* Bcharré
28 *J5* **Beach** North Dakota, N USA *46°55′N 104°00′W*
182 *K12* **Beachport** South Australia *37°29′S 140°03′E*
97 *O23* **Beachy Head** *headland* SE England, United Kingdom *50°44′N 00°16′E*
18 *K13* **Beacon** New York, NE USA *41°30′N 73°54′W*
63 *J25* **Beagle Channel** *channel* Argentina/Chile
181 *O1* **Beagle Gulf** *gulf* Northern Territory, N Australia
Bealach an Doirín *see* Ballaghaderreen
Bealach Cláir *see* Ballyclare
Bealach Féich *see* Ballybofey
172 *J3* **Bealanana** Mahajanga, NE Madagascar *14°33′S 48°44′E*
Béal an Átha *see* Ballina
Béal an Átha Móir *see* Ballinamore
Béal an Mhuirhead *see* Belmullet
Béal Átha Beithe *see* Ballybay
Béal Átha Conaill *see* Ballyconnell
Beál Átha hAmhnais *see* Ballyhaunis
Béal Átha na Sluaighe *see* Ballinasloe
Béal Átha Seanaidh *see* Ballyshannon
Bealdovuopmi *see* Peltovuoma
Béal Feirste *see* Belfast
Béal Tairbirt *see* Belturbet
Beanna Boirche *see* Mourne Mountains
Beannchar *see* Banagher, Ireland
Beannchar *see* Bangor, Northern Ireland, UK
Beanntraí *see* Bantry
Bearalváhki *see* Berlevåg
23 *N2* **Bear Creek** ≈ Alabama/Mississippi, S USA
30 *J13* **Bear Creek** ≈ Illinois, N USA
27 *U13* **Bearden** Arkansas, C USA *33°43′N 92°37′W*
195 *Q10* **Beardmore Glacier** *glacier* Antarctica
30 *K13* **Beardstown** Illinois, N USA *40°01′N 90°25′W*
28 *L14* **Bear Hill** ▲ Nebraska, C USA *41°24′N 101°49′W*
Bear Island *see* Bjørnøya
14 *H12* **Bear Lake** Ontario, S Canada *45°28′N 79°31′W*
36 *M1* **Bear Lake** ◎ Idaho/Utah, NW USA
39 *U11* **Bear, Mount** ▲ Alaska, USA *61°16′N 141°09′W*
102 *J16* **Béarn** *cultural region* SW France
194 *J11* **Bear Peninsula** *peninsula* Antarctica
152 *I7* **Beās** ≈ India/Pakistan
105 *P3* **Beasain** País Vasco, N Spain *43°03′N 02°11′W*
105 *O12* **Beas de Segura** Andalucía, S Spain *38°16′N 02°54′W*
45 *N10* **Beata, Cabo** *headland* SW Dominican Republic *17°34′N 71°25′W*
45 *N10* **Beata, Isla** *island* SW Dominican Republic
64 *F11* **Beata Ridge** *undersea feature* N Caribbean Sea *16°00′N 72°30′W*
29 *R17* **Beatrice** Nebraska, C USA *40°14′N 96°43′W*
83 *L16* **Beatrice** Mashonaland East, NE Zimbabwe *18°15′S 30°55′E*
11 *N11* **Beatton** ≈ British Columbia, W Canada
11 *N11* **Beatton River** British Columbia, W Canada *57°35′N 121°45′W*
35 *V10* **Beatty** Nevada, W USA *36°53′N 116°44′W*
21 *N6* **Beattyville** Kentucky, S USA *37°33′N 83°44′W*
173 *X16* **Beau Bassin** W Mauritius *20°13′S 57°27′E*
103 *R15* **Beaucaire** Gard, S France *43°49′N 04°37′E*
14 *I8* **Beauchastel, Lac** ◎ Québec, SE Canada
14 *I10* **Beauchêne, Lac** ◎ Québec, SE Canada
183 *V3* **Beaudesert** Queensland, E Australia *28°00′S 152°27′E*
182 *M12* **Beaufort** Victoria, SE Australia *37°27′S 143°24′E*
21 *X11* **Beaufort** North Carolina, SE USA *34°44′N 76°41′W*
21 *R15* **Beaufort** South Carolina, SE USA *32°23′N 80°40′W*
38 *M11* **Beaufort Sea** *sea* Arctic Ocean
Beaufort-Wes *see* Beaufort West
83 *G25* **Beaufort West** *Afr.* Beaufort-Wes. Western Cape, SW South Africa *32°21′S 22°35′E*
103 *N7* **Beaugency** Loiret, C France *47°46′N 01°38′E*
19 *R1* **Beau Lake** ⊠ Maine, NE USA
96 *I8* **Beauly** N Scotland, United Kingdom *57°29′N 04°29′W*
99 *G21* **Beaumont** Hainaut, S Belgium *50°12′N 04°13′E*
185 *E23* **Beaumont** Otago, South Island, New Zealand *45°48′S 169°32′E*
22 *M7* **Beaumont** Mississippi, S USA *31°10′N 88°55′W*
25 *X10* **Beaumont** Texas, SW USA *30°05′N 94°06′W*
102 *M15* **Beaumont-de-Lomagne** Tarn-et-Garonne, S France *43°54′N 01°00′E*
102 *L6* **Beaumont-sur-Sarthe** Sarthe, NW France *48°15′N 00°07′E*
103 *R8* **Beaune** Côte d'Or, C France *47°02′N 04°50′E*
15 *R9* **Beaupré** Québec, SE Canada *47°03′N 70°52′W*
102 *J8* **Beaupréau** Maine-et-Loire, NW France *47°13′N 00°57′W*
99 *I22* **Beauraing** Namur, SE Belgium *50°07′N 04°57′E*
103 *R12* **Beaurepaire** Isère, E France *45°20′N 05°03′E*
11 *Y16* **Beausejour** Manitoba, S Canada *50°04′N 96°30′W*
103 *N4* **Beauvais** *anc.* Bellovacum, Caesaromagus. Oise, N France *49°27′N 02°04′E*
11 *S13* **Beauval** Saskatchewan, C Canada *55°10′N 107°37′W*
102 *I9* **Beauvoir-sur-Mer** Vendée, NW France *46°54′N 02°03′W*
39 *R8* **Beaver** Alaska, USA *66°22′N 147°31′W*
26 *J8* **Beaver** Oklahoma, C USA *36°48′N 100°32′W*
18 *B14* **Beaver** Pennsylvania, NE USA *40°39′N 80°19′W*
36 *K6* **Beaver** Utah, W USA *38°16′N 112°38′W*
10 *L9* **Beaver** ≈ British Columbia/Yukon Territory, W Canada
11 *S13* **Beaver** ≈ Saskatchewan, C Canada
29 *N17* **Beaver City** Nebraska, C USA *40°08′N 99°49′W*
10 *G6* **Beaver Creek** Yukon Territory, W Canada *62°20′N 140°45′W*
31 *R14* **Beavercreek** Ohio, N USA *39°42′N 83°58′W*
39 *S8* **Beaver Creek** ≈ Alaska, USA
26 *H3* **Beaver Creek** ≈ Kansas/Nebraska, C USA
28 *J5* **Beaver Creek** ≈ Montana/North Dakota, N USA
29 *Q14* **Beaver Creek** ≈ Nebraska, C USA
25 *Q4* **Beaver Creek** ≈ Texas, SW USA
30 *M8* **Beaver Dam** Wisconsin, N USA *43°28′N 88°49′W*
30 *M8* **Beaver Dam Lake** ◎ Wisconsin, N USA
18 *B14* **Beaver Falls** Pennsylvania, NE USA *40°45′N 80°20′W*
33 *P12* **Beaverhead Mountains** ▲▲ Idaho/Montana, NW USA
33 *Q12* **Beaverhead River** ≈ Montana, NW USA
65 *A25* **Beaver Island** *island* W Falkland Islands
31 *P5* **Beaver Island** *island* Michigan, N USA
27 *S9* **Beaver Lake** ⊠ Arkansas, C USA
11 *N13* **Beaverlodge** Alberta, W Canada *55°11′N 119°29′W*
18 *I8* **Beaver River** ≈ New York, NE USA
26 *J8* **Beaver River** ≈ Oklahoma, C USA
18 *B13* **Beaver River** ≈ Pennsylvania, NE USA
65 *A25* **Beaver Settlement** Beaver Island, W Falkland Islands *51°30′S 61°15′W*
Beaver State *see* Oregon
14 *H14* **Beaverton** Ontario, S Canada *44°24′N 79°07′W*
32 *G11* **Beaverton** Oregon, NW USA *45°29′N 122°49′W*
152 *G12* **Beāwar** Rājasthān, N India *26°08′N 74°22′E*
Bebas, Dasht-i *see* Bābūs, Dasht-e
60 *L8* **Bebedouro** São Paulo, S Brazil *20°58′S 48°28′W*
101 *I16* **Bebra** Hessen, C Germany *50°59′N 09°46′E*
41 *W12* **Becal** Campeche, SE Mexico *19°49′N 90°28′W*
15 *Q11* **Bécancour** ≈ Québec, SE Canada
97 *Q19* **Beccles** E England, United Kingdom *52°27′N 01°32′E*
112 *L9* **Bečej** *Ger.* Altbetsche, *Hung.* Óbecse, Rácz-Becse; *prev.* Magyar-Becse, Stari Bečej. Vojvodina, N Serbia *45°36′N 20°02′E*

◆ Country
● Country Capital
◇ Dependent Territory
○ Dependent Territory Capital
⬖ Administrative Regions
✈ International Airport
▲ Mountain
▲▲ Mountain Range
⛰ Volcano
≈ River
◎ Lake
⊠ Reservoir

BECERRÉA – BERBERIA, CABO DE

104 I3 **Becerréa** Galicia, NW Spain 42°51′N 07°10′W
74 H7 **Béchar** prev. Colomb-Béchar. W Algeria 31°38′N 02°11′W
39 O14 **Becharof Lake** ◎ Alaska, USA
116 H15 **Bechet** var. Bechetu. Dolj, SW Romania 43°45′N 23°57′E
Bechetu see Bechet
21 R6 **Beckley** West Virginia, NE USA 37°46′N 81°12′W
101 G14 **Beckum** Nordrhein-Westfalen, W Germany 51°45′N 08°03′E
25 X7 **Beckville** Texas, SW USA 32°14′N 94°27′W
35 X4 **Becky Peak** ▲ Nevada, W USA 39°59′N 114°33′W
116 I9 **Beclean** Hung. Bethlen; prev. Betlen. Bistriţa-Năsăud, N Romania 47°10′N 24°11′E
Bécs see Wien
111 H18 **Bečva** Ger. Betschau, Pol. Beczwa. ≈ E Czech Republic
Beczwa see Bečva
103 P15 **Bédarieux** Hérault, S France 43°37′N 03°10′E
120 B10 **Beddouza, Cap** headland W Morocco 32°35′N 09°16′W
80 I13 **Bedelē** Oromīya, C Ethiopia 08°25′N 36°21′E
147 Y8 **Bedel Pass** Rus. Pereval Bedel. pass China/Kyrgyzstan
Bedel, Pereval see Bedel Pass
95 H22 **Beder** Århus, C Denmark 56°03′N 10°13′E
97 N20 **Bedford** E England, United Kingdom 52°08′N 00°29′W
31 O15 **Bedford** Indiana, N USA 38°51′N 86°29′W
29 U16 **Bedford** Iowa, C USA 40°40′N 94°43′W
20 L4 **Bedford** Kentucky, S USA 38°36′N 85°18′W
18 D15 **Bedford** Pennsylvania, NE USA 40°00′N 78°29′W
21 T6 **Bedford** Virginia, NE USA 37°20′N 79°31′W
97 N20 **Bedfordshire** cultural region E England, United Kingdom
127 N5 **Bednodem'yanovsk** Penzenskaya Oblast', W Russian Federation 53°55′N 43°14′E
98 N5 **Bedum** Groningen, NE Netherlands 53°18′N 06°36′E
27 V11 **Beebe** Arkansas, C USA 35°04′N 91°52′W
Beechy Group see Chichijima-rettō
45 T9 **Beef Island** ✈ (Road Town) Tortola, E British Virgin Islands 18°25′N 64°31′W
Beehive State see Utah
99 L18 **Beek** Limburg, SE Netherlands 50°56′N 05°47′E
99 L18 **Beek** ✈ (Maastricht) Limburg, SE Netherlands 50°55′N 05°47′E
99 K14 **Beek-en-Donk** Noord-Brabant, S Netherlands 51°31′N 05°37′E
138 F13 **Be'er Menuha** prev. Be'ér Menuha. Southern, S Israel 30°22′N 35°09′E
Be'ér Menuha see Be'er Menuha
99 D16 **Beernem** West-Vlaanderen, NW Belgium 51°09′N 03°18′E
99 I16 **Beerse** Antwerpen, N Belgium 51°20′N 04°52′E
Beersheba see Be'er Sheva
138 E11 **Be'er Sheva** var. Beersheba, Ar. Bir es Saba; prev. Be'ér Sheva'. Southern, S Israel 31°15′N 34°47′E
Be'ér Sheva' see Be'er Sheva
98 J13 **Beesd** Gelderland, C Netherlands 51°52′N 05°12′E
99 M16 **Beesel** Limburg, SE Netherlands 51°16′N 06°02′E
83 J21 **Beestekraal** North-West, N South Africa 25°21′S 27°40′E
194 J7 **Beethoven Peninsula** peninsula Alexander Island, Antarctica
Beetstersweach see Beetsterzwaag
98 M6 **Beetsterzwaag** Fris. Beetstersweach. Friesland, N Netherlands 53°03′N 06°04′E
25 S13 **Beeville** Texas, SW USA 28°25′N 97°47′W
79 J18 **Befale** Equateur, NW Dem. Rep. Congo 0°25′N 20°48′E
Befandriana see Befandriana Avaratra
172 J3 **Befandriana Avaratra** var. Befandriana, Befandriana Nord. Mahajanga, NW Madagascar 15°14′S 48°33′E
Befandriana Nord see Befandriana Avaratra
79 K18 **Befori** Equateur, N Dem. Rep. Congo 0°09′N 22°18′E
172 I7 **Befotaka** Fianarantsoa, S Madagascar 23°49′S 47°00′E
183 R11 **Bega** New South Wales, SE Australia 36°43′S 149°50′E
102 G5 **Bégard** Côtes d'Armor, NW France 48°37′N 03°18′W
112 M9 **Begejski Kanal** canal Vojvodina, NE Serbia
94 G13 **Begna** ≈ S Norway
Begoml' see Byahoml'
Begovat see Bekobod
153 Q13 **Begusarai** Bihār, NE India 25°25′N 86°08′E
143 R9 **Behābād** Yazd, C Iran 32°23′N 59°50′E
Behagle see Laï
55 Z10 **Béhague, Pointe** headland E French Guiana 04°38′N 51°52′W
Behar see Bihār
142 M10 **Behbahān** var. Behbehān. Khūzestān, SW Iran 30°38′N 50°07′E
Behbehān see Behbahān
44 G3 **Behring Point** Andros Island, W Bahamas 24°28′N 77°44′W
143 P4 **Behshahr** prev. Ashraf. Māzandarān, N Iran 36°42′N 53°36′E
163 V6 **Bei'an** Heilongjiang, NE China 48°16′N 126°29′E
Beibunar see Sredishte
Beibu Wan see Tongking, Gulf of
Beida see Al Bayḍā'
80 H13 **Beigi** Oromīya, C Ethiopia 09°13′N 34°48′E
160 L16 **Beihai** Guangxi Zhuangzu Zizhiqu, S China 21°29′N 109°10′E
159 Q10 **Bei Hulsan Hu** ◎ C China
161 N13 **Bei Jiang** ≈ S China
161 O2 **Beijing** var. Pei-ching, Eng. Peking; prev. Pei-p'ing. ● (China) Beijing Shi, E China 39°58′N 116°23′E
161 P2 **Beijing** ✈ Beijing Shi, N China 39°54′N 116°22′E
Beijing see Beijing Shi, China
161 O2 **Beijing Shi** var. Beijing, Jing, Pei-ching, Eng. Peking; prev. Pei-p'ing. ◈ municipality E China
76 G8 **Beïla** Trarza, W Mauritania 18°07′N 15°56′W
98 N7 **Beilen** Drenthe, NE Netherlands 52°52′N 06°27′E
160 L15 **Beiliu** var. Lingcheng. Guangxi Zhuangzu Zizhiqu, S China 22°50′N 110°22′E
159 O12 **Beilu He** ≈ W China
Beilul see Beylul
163 U12 **Beining** prev. Beizhen. Liaoning, NE China 41°34′N 121°51′E
96 H8 **Beinn Dearg** ▲ N Scotland, United Kingdom 57°47′N 04°52′W
Beinn MacDuibh see Ben Macdui
160 I12 **Beipan Jiang** ≈ S China
163 T12 **Beipiao** Liaoning, NE China 41°49′N 120°45′E
83 N17 **Beira** Sofala, C Mozambique 19°45′S 34°56′E
83 N17 **Beira** ✈ Sofala, C Mozambique 19°39′S 35°05′E
104 I7 **Beira Alta** former province N Portugal
104 H9 **Beira Baixa** former province C Portugal
104 G8 **Beira Litoral** former province N Portugal
Beirut see Beyrouth
Beisān see Beit She'an
11 Q16 **Beiseker** Alberta, SW Canada 51°20′N 113°34′W
Beitai Ding see Wutai Shan
83 K19 **Beitbridge** Matabeleland South, S Zimbabwe 22°10′S 30°02′E
Beit Lekhem see Bethlehem
138 G9 **Beit She'an** Ar. Baysān, Beisān; anc. Scythopolis, prev. Bet She'an. Northern, N Israel 32°30′N 35°30′E
116 G10 **Beiuş** Hung. Belényes. Bihor, NW Romania 46°40′N 22°21′E
Beizhen see Beining
104 H12 **Beja** anc. Pax Julia. Beja, SE Portugal 38°01′N 07°52′W
74 M5 **Béja** var. Bājah. N Tunisia 36°45′N 09°04′E
104 G13 **Beja** ◈ district S Portugal
120 I9 **Béjaïa** var. Bejaïa, Fr. Bougie; anc. Saldae. NE Algeria 36°49′N 05°03′E
Bejaïa see Béjaïa
104 K8 **Béjar** Castilla-León, N Spain 40°24′N 05°45′W
Bejraburi see Phetchaburi
Bekaa Valley see El Beqaa
Bekabad see Bekobod
Békás see Bicaz
169 O15 **Bekasi** Jawa, C Indonesia 06°14′S 106°595′E
Bek-Budi see Qarshi
Bekdaş/Bekdash see Garabogaz
147 T10 **Bek-Dzhar** Oshskaya Oblast', SW Kyrgyzstan 40°22′N 73°08′E
111 N24 **Békés** Rom. Bichiş. Békés, SE Hungary 46°45′N 21°09′E
111 M24 **Békés** off. Békés Megye. ◈ county SE Hungary
111 M24 **Békéscsaba** Rom. Bichiş-Ciaba. Békés, SE Hungary 46°40′N 21°05′E
Békés Megye see Békés
139 S2 **Bēkhma** Arbīl, E Iraq 36°40′N 44°15′E
172 H7 **Bekily** Toliara, S Madagascar 24°12′S 45°20′E
165 W4 **Bekkai** var. Betsukai. Hokkaidō, NE Japan 43°23′N 145°07′E
147 Q11 **Bekobod** Rus. Bekabad; prev. Begovat. Toshkent Viloyati, E Uzbekistan 40°17′N 69°11′E
127 O7 **Bekovo** Penzenskaya Oblast', W Russian Federation 52°27′N 43°41′E
Bel see Beliu
152 M13 **Bela** Uttar Pradesh, N India 25°55′N 82°00′E
149 N15 **Bela** Baluchistān, SW Pakistan 26°12′N 66°20′E
79 F15 **Bélabo** Est, C Cameroon 04°54′N 13°10′E
112 N10 **Bela Crkva** Ger. Weisskirchen, Hung. Fehértemplom. Vojvodina, W Serbia 44°55′N 21°28′E
173 Y16 **Bel Air** var. Rivière Sèche. E Mauritius
104 L12 **Belalcázar** Andalucía, S Spain 38°33′N 05°07′W
113 P15 **Bela Palanka** Serbia, SE Serbia 43°13′N 22°19′E
119 H16 **Belarus** off. Republic of Belarus, var. Belorussia, Latv. Baltkrievija; prev. Belorussian SSR, Rus. Belorusskaya SSR. ◆ republic E Europe
Belarus, Republic of see Belarus
Belau see Palau
59 H21 **Bela Vista** Mato Grosso do Sul, SW Brazil 22°04′S 56°25′W
83 L21 **Bela Vista** Maputo, S Mozambique 26°20′S 32°40′E
168 I8 **Belawan** Sumatera, W Indonesia 03°46′N 98°44′E
Běla Woda see Weisswasser
127 U4 **Belaya** ≈ W Russian Federation
123 R7 **Belaya Gora** Respublika Sakha (Yakutiya), NE Russian Federation 68°25′N 146°12′E
126 M11 **Belaya Kalitiva** Rostovskaya Oblast', SW Russian Federation 48°09′N 40°43′E
125 R14 **Belaya Kholunitsa** Kirovskaya Oblast', NW Russian Federation 58°54′N 50°52′E
Belaya Tserkov' see Bila Tserkva
77 V11 **Belbédji** Zinder, S Niger 14°35′N 08°00′E
111 K14 **Bełchatów** var. Belchatow. Łódzski, C Poland 51°23′N 19°20′E
Belchatow see Bełchatów
Belcher, Îles see Belcher Islands
12 H7 **Belcher Islands** Fr. Îles Belcher. island group Nunavut, SE Canada
105 S6 **Belchite** Aragón, NE Spain 41°18′N 00°45′W
29 O2 **Belcourt** North Dakota, N USA 48°50′N 99°44′W
31 P9 **Belding** Michigan, N USA 43°06′N 85°13′W
127 U5 **Belebey** Respublika Bashkortostan, W Russian Federation 54°04′N 54°13′E
81 N16 **Beledweyne** var. Belet Huen, It. Belet Uen. Hiiraan, C Somalia 04°39′N 45°12′E
146 B10 **Belek** Balkan Welaýaty, W Turkmenistan 39°57′N 53°51′E
58 L12 **Belém** var. Pará. state capital Pará, N Brazil 01°27′S 48°29′W
65 I14 **Belém Ridge** undersea feature C Atlantic Ocean
62 I7 **Belén** Catamarca, NW Argentina 27°36′N 67°00′W
54 G9 **Belén** Boyacá, C Colombia 06°01′N 72°55′W
42 J11 **Belén** Rivas, SW Nicaragua 11°30′N 85°55′W
62 O5 **Belén** Concepción, C Paraguay 23°25′S 57°14′W
61 D16 **Belén** Salto, N Uruguay 30°47′S 57°47′W
37 R12 **Belen** New Mexico, SW USA 34°37′N 106°46′W
61 D20 **Belén de Escobar** Buenos Aires, E Argentina 34°21′S 58°47′W
114 J7 **Belene** Pleven, N Bulgaria 43°39′N 25°09′E
114 J7 **Belene, Ostrov** island N Bulgaria
43 R15 **Belén, Río** ≈ C Panama
Belényes see Beiuş
Embalse de Belesar see Belesar, Encoro de
104 H3 **Belesar, Encoro de** Sp. Embalse de Belesar. ⊠ NW Spain
Belet Huen/Belet Uen see Beledweyne
126 J5 **Belëv** Tul'skaya Oblast', W Russian Federation 53°48′N 36°07′E
19 R7 **Belfast** Maine, NE USA 44°25′N 69°02′W
97 G15 **Belfast** Ir. Béal Feirste. ◐ E Northern Ireland, United Kingdom 54°35′N 05°55′W
97 G15 **Belfast Aldergrove** ✈ E Northern Ireland, United Kingdom 54°37′N 06°11′W
97 G15 **Belfast Lough** Ir. Loch Lao. inlet E Northern Ireland, United Kingdom
28 K5 **Belfield** North Dakota, N USA 46°53′N 103°12′W
103 U7 **Belfort** Territoire-de-Belfort, E France 47°38′N 06°52′E
Belgard see Białogard
155 E17 **Belgaum** Karnātaka, W India 15°52′N 74°30′E
Belgian Congo see Congo (Democratic Republic of)
195 T3 **Belgicafjella** var. Mount Victor. ▲ Antarctica 72°49′S 33°01′E
België/Belgique see Belgium
99 F20 **Belgium** off. Kingdom of Belgium, Dut. België, Fr. Belgique. ◆ monarchy NW Europe
Belgium, Kingdom of see Belgium
126 J8 **Belgorod** Belgorodskaya Oblast', W Russian Federation 50°38′N 36°37′E
Belgorod-Dnestrovskiy see Bilhorod-Dnistrovs'kyy
126 J8 **Belgorodskaya Oblast'** ◈ province W Russian Federation
Belgrad see Beograd
29 T8 **Belgrade** Minnesota, N USA 45°27′N 94°59′W
33 S11 **Belgrade** Montana, NW USA 45°46′N 111°10′W
Belgrade see Beograd
Belgrano, Cabo see Meredith, Cape
195 N5 **Belgrano II** Argentinian research station Antarctica 77°50′S 35°25′W
21 X9 **Belhaven** North Carolina, SE USA 35°36′N 76°50′W
107 I23 **Belice** anc. Hypsas. ≈ Sicilia, Italy, C Mediterranean Sea
Belice see Belize/Belize City
113 M16 **Beli Drim** Alb. Drini i Bardhë. ≈ Albania/Serbia
127 R17 **Belidzhi** Respublika Dagestan, SW Russian Federation 41°53′N 48°24′E
Beligrad see Berat
188 C8 **Beliliou** prev. Peleliu. island S Palau
114 L8 **Beli Lom, Yazovir** ⊠ NE Bulgaria
112 I8 **Beli Manastir** Hung. Pélmonostor; prev. Monostor. Osijek-Baranja, NE Croatia 45°46′N 16°38′E
102 J13 **Bélin-Béliet** Gironde, SW France 44°30′N 00°48′W
79 F17 **Bélinga** Ogooué-Ivindo, NE Gabon 01°05′N 13°12′E
21 S4 **Belington** West Virginia, NE USA 39°01′N 79°57′W
127 O6 **Belinskiy** Penzenskaya Oblast', W Russian Federation 52°58′N 43°25′E
169 N12 **Belinyu** Pulau Bangka, W Indonesia 01°37′S 105°45′E
169 O13 **Belitung, Pulau** island W Indonesia
116 F10 **Beliu** Hung. Bel. Arad, W Romania 46°31′N 21°57′E
114 I9 **Beli Vit** ≈ NW Bulgaria
42 G2 **Belize** Sp. Belice; prev. British Honduras, Colony of Belize. ◆ commonwealth republic Central America
42 F2 **Belize** Sp. Belice. ◈ district NE Belize
42 G2 **Belize** ≈ Belize/Guatemala
Belize see Belize City
42 G2 **Belize City** var. Belize, Sp. Belice. Belize, NE Belize 17°29′N 88°10′W
42 G2 **Belize City** ✈ Belize, NE Belize 17°31′N 88°15′W
Belize, Colony of see Belize
Beljak see Villach
39 N16 **Belkofski** Alaska, USA 55°07′N 162°04′W
123 O6 **Bel'kovskiy, Ostrov** island Novosibirskiye Ostrova, NE Russian Federation
14 J8 **Bell** ≈ Québec, SE Canada
10 J15 **Bella Bella** British Columbia, SW Canada 52°04′N 128°07′W
102 M10 **Bellac** Haute-Vienne, C France 46°07′N 01°04′E
10 K15 **Bella Coola** British Columbia, SW Canada 52°23′N 126°46′W
106 D6 **Bellagio** Lombardia, N Italy 45°58′N 09°15′E
31 P6 **Bellaire** Michigan, N USA 44°59′N 85°12′W
106 D6 **Bellano** Lombardia, N Italy 46°06′N 09°21′E
155 G17 **Bellary** var. Ballari. Karnātaka, S India 15°11′N 76°54′E
183 S5 **Bellata** New South Wales, SE Australia 29°58′S 149°49′E
61 D16 **Bella Unión** Artigas, N Uruguay 30°18′S 57°35′W
61 C14 **Bella Vista** Corrientes, NE Argentina 28°30′S 59°03′W
62 J7 **Bella Vista** Tucumán, N Argentina 27°05′S 65°19′W
62 P4 **Bella Vista** Amambay, C Paraguay 22°08′S 56°20′W
56 B10 **Bellavista** Cajamarca, N Peru 05°43′S 78°48′W
56 D11 **Bellavista** San Martín, N Peru 07°04′S 76°35′W
183 U6 **Bellbrook** New South Wales, SE Australia 30°48′S 152°32′E
27 V5 **Belle** Missouri, C USA 38°17′N 91°43′W
21 Q5 **Belle** West Virginia, NE USA 38°13′N 81°32′W
31 R13 **Bellefontaine** Ohio, N USA 40°22′N 83°45′W
18 F14 **Bellefonte** Pennsylvania, NE USA 40°54′N 77°43′W
28 J9 **Belle Fourche** South Dakota, N USA 44°40′N 103°50′W
28 J9 **Belle Fourche Reservoir** ⊠ South Dakota, N USA
28 K9 **Belle Fourche River** ≈ South Dakota/Wyoming, N USA
103 S10 **Bellegarde-sur-Valserine** Ain, E France 46°06′N 05°49′E
23 Y14 **Belle Glade** Florida, SE USA 26°40′N 80°40′W
102 G8 **Belle Île** island NW France
13 T9 **Belle Isle** island Belle Isle, Newfoundland and Labrador, E Canada
13 S10 **Belle Isle, Strait of** strait Newfoundland and Labrador, E Canada
Bellenz see Bellinzona
29 W14 **Belle Plaine** Iowa, C USA 41°54′N 92°16′W
29 V9 **Belle Plaine** Minnesota, N USA 44°39′N 93°47′W
14 I9 **Belleterre** Québec, SE Canada 47°24′N 78°40′W
14 J15 **Belleville** Ontario, SE Canada 44°10′N 77°22′W
103 R10 **Belleville** Rhône, E France 46°09′N 04°42′E
30 K15 **Belleville** Illinois, N USA 38°31′N 89°58′W
27 N3 **Belleville** Kansas, C USA 39°51′N 97°38′W
29 Z13 **Bellevue** Iowa, C USA 42°15′N 90°25′W
29 S15 **Bellevue** Nebraska, C USA 41°08′N 95°53′W
31 S11 **Bellevue** Ohio, N USA 41°16′N 82°50′W
25 S5 **Bellevue** Texas, SW USA 33°38′N 98°00′W
32 H8 **Bellevue** Washington, NW USA 47°36′N 122°12′W
55 Y11 **Bellevue de l'Inini, Montagnes** ▲▲ S French Guiana
103 S11 **Belley** Ain, E France 45°46′N 05°41′E
Bellin see Kangirsuk
183 V6 **Bellingen** New South Wales, SE Australia 30°27′S 152°53′E
97 L14 **Bellingham** N England, United Kingdom 55°09′N 02°16′W
32 H6 **Bellingham** Washington, NW USA 48°46′N 122°29′W
Belling Hausen Mulde see Southeast Pacific Basin
194 H2 **Bellingshausen** Russian research station South Shetland Islands, Antarctica 61°57′S 58°23′W
Bellingshausen see Motu One
Bellingshausen Abyssal Plain see Bellingshausen Plain
196 R14 **Bellingshausen Plain** var. Bellingshausen Abyssal Plain. undersea feature SE Pacific Ocean 64°00′S 90°00′W
194 I8 **Bellingshausen Sea** sea Antarctica
98 P6 **Bellingwolde** Groningen, NE Netherlands 53°07′N 07°10′E
108 H11 **Bellinzona** Ger. Bellenz. Ticino, S Switzerland 46°12′N 09°02′E
25 T8 **Bellmead** Texas, SW USA 31°36′N 97°02′W
54 E8 **Bello** Antioquia, W Colombia 06°19′N 75°34′W
61 B21 **Bellocq** Buenos Aires, E Argentina 35°55′S 61°32′W
Bello Horizonte see Belo Horizonte
186 L10 **Bellona** var. Mungiki. island S Solomon Islands
Bellovacum see Beauvais
182 D7 **Bell, Point** headland South Australia 32°13′S 133°08′E
20 F9 **Bells** Tennessee, S USA 35°42′N 89°05′W
25 U5 **Bells** Texas, SW USA 33°36′N 96°24′W
92 N3 **Bellsund** inlet SW Svalbard
106 H6 **Belluno** Veneto, NE Italy 46°08′N 12°13′E
62 L11 **Bell Ville** Córdoba, C Argentina 32°35′S 62°41′W
83 E26 **Bellville** Western Cape, SW South Africa 33°50′S 18°43′E
25 U11 **Bellville** Texas, SW USA 29°57′N 96°15′W
104 L12 **Belmez** Andalucía, S Spain 38°16′N 05°12′W
29 V12 **Belmond** Iowa, C USA 42°51′N 93°36′W
18 E11 **Belmont** New York, NE USA 42°14′N 78°02′W
21 R10 **Belmont** North Carolina, SE USA 35°13′N 81°01′W
59 O18 **Belmonte** Bahia, E Brazil 15°53′S 38°54′W
104 I8 **Belmonte** Castelo Branco, C Portugal 40°21′N 07°20′W
105 P10 **Belmonte** Castilla-La Mancha, C Spain 39°34′N 02°43′W
42 G2 **Belmopan** ● (Belize) Cayo, C Belize 17°13′N 88°48′W
97 B16 **Belmullet** Ir. Béal an Mhuirhead. Mayo, W Ireland 54°14′N 09°59′W
99 E20 **Belœil** Hainaut, SW Belgium 50°33′N 03°45′E
123 R13 **Belogorsk** Amurskaya Oblast', SE Russian Federation 50°53′N 128°24′E
Belogorsk see Bilohirs'k
114 F7 **Belogradchik** Vidin, NW Bulgaria 43°37′N 22°42′E
172 H8 **Beloha** Toliara, S Madagascar 25°09′S 45°04′E
59 M20 **Belo Horizonte** prev. Bello Horizonte. state capital Minas Gerais, SE Brazil 19°54′S 43°54′W
26 M3 **Beloit** Kansas, C USA 39°27′N 98°06′W
30 L9 **Beloit** Wisconsin, N USA 42°31′N 89°01′W
Belokorovichi see Novi Bilokorovychi
124 J8 **Belomorsk** Respublika Kareliya, NW Russian Federation 64°30′N 34°43′E
124 J8 **Belomorsko-Baltiyskiy Kanal** Eng. White Sea-Baltic Canal, White Sea Canal. canal NW Russian Federation
153 V15 **Belonia** Tripura, NE India 23°15′N 91°25′E
Beloozersk see Byelaazyorsk
Belopol'ye see Bilopillya
105 O4 **Belorado** Castilla-León, N Spain 42°25′N 03°11′W
126 L14 **Belorechensk** Krasnodarskiy Kray, SW Russian Federation 44°46′N 39°53′E
127 W5 **Beloretsk** Respublika Bashkortostan, W Russian Federation 53°56′N 58°26′E
Belorussia/Belorussian SSR see Belarus
Belorusskaya Gryada see Byelaruskaya Hrada
Belorusskaya SSR see Belarus
Beloshchel'ye see Nar'yan-Mar
114 N8 **Beloslav** Varna, E Bulgaria 43°13′N 27°42′E
Belostok see Białystok
Belo-sur-Tsiribihina see Belo Tsiribihina
172 H5 **Belo Tsiribihina** var. Belo-sur-Tsiribihina. Toliara, W Madagascar 19°40′S 44°30′E
Belovár see Bjelovar
Belovezhskaya, Pushcha see Białowieska, Puszcza/Byelavyezhskaya, Pushcha
114 H10 **Belovo** Pazardzhik, C Bulgaria 42°10′N 24°01′E
Belovodsk see Bilovods'k
122 H9 **Beloyarskiy** Khanty-Mansiyskiy Avtonomnyy Okrug-Yugra, N Russian Federation 63°40′N 66°31′E
124 K7 **Beloye More** Eng. White Sea. sea NW Russian Federation
124 K13 **Beloye, Ozero** ◎ NW Russian Federation
114 J10 **Belozem** Plovdiv, C Bulgaria 42°11′N 25°00′E
124 K13 **Belozërsk** Vologodskaya Oblast', NW Russian Federation 59°59′N 37°49′E
108 D8 **Belp** Bern, W Switzerland 46°54′N 07°31′E
108 D8 **Belp** ✈ (Bern) Bern, C Switzerland 46°55′N 07°29′E
107 L24 **Belpasso** Sicilia, Italy, C Mediterranean Sea 37°35′N 14°59′E
31 U14 **Belpre** Ohio, N USA 39°14′N 81°34′W
98 M8 **Belterwijde** ◎ N Netherlands
27 R4 **Belton** Missouri, C USA 38°48′N 94°31′W
21 P11 **Belton** South Carolina, SE USA 34°31′N 82°29′W
25 T9 **Belton** Texas, SW USA 31°04′N 97°30′W
25 S9 **Belton Lake** ⊠ Texas, SW USA
Bel'tsy see Bălţi
97 E16 **Belturbet** Ir. Béal Tairbirt. Cavan, N Ireland 54°06′N 07°26′W
Beluchistan see Baluchistān
145 Z9 **Belukha, Gora** ▲ Kazakhstan/Russian Federation 49°50′N 86°44′E
107 M20 **Belvedere Marittimo** Calabria, SW Italy 39°37′N 15°52′E
30 L10 **Belvidere** Illinois, N USA 42°15′N 88°50′W
18 J14 **Belvidere** New Jersey, NE USA 40°50′N 75°05′W
Bely see Belyy
127 V8 **Belyayevka** Orenburgskaya Oblast', W Russian Federation 51°25′N 56°26′E
Belynichi see Byalynichy
124 H17 **Belyy** var. Bely, Beyj. Tverskaya Oblast', W Russian Federation 55°51′N 32°57′E
126 I6 **Belyye Berega** Bryanskaya Oblast', W Russian Federation 53°11′N 34°42′E
122 J6 **Belyy, Ostrov** island N Russian Federation
122 J11 **Belyy Yar** Tomskaya Oblast', C Russian Federation 58°26′N 84°57′E
100 N13 **Belzig** Brandenburg, NE Germany 52°09′N 12°37′E
22 K4 **Belzoni** Mississippi, S USA 33°10′N 90°29′W
172 H4 **Bemaraha** var. Plateau du Bemaraha. ▲▲ W Madagascar
Bemaraha, Plateau du see Bemaraha
82 B10 **Bembe** Uíge, NW Angola 07°03′S 14°25′E
77 S14 **Bembèrèkè** var. Bimbéréké. N Benin 10°10′N 02°41′E
104 K12 **Bembézar** ≈ SW Spain
104 J3 **Bembibre** Castilla-León, N Spain 42°37′N 06°25′W
29 T4 **Bemidji** Minnesota, N USA 47°27′N 94°53′W
98 L12 **Bemmel** Gelderland, SE Netherlands 51°53′N 05°54′E
171 T13 **Bemu** Pulau Seram, E Indonesia 03°21′S 129°58′E
Benāb see Bonāb
105 T5 **Benabarre** var. Benavarn. Aragón, NE Spain 42°06′N 00°28′E
Benaco see Garda, Lago di
79 L20 **Bena-Dibele** Kasai-Oriental, C Dem. Rep. Congo 04°01′S 22°50′E
105 R9 **Benagéber, Embalse de** E Spain
183 O11 **Benalla** Victoria, SE Australia 36°33′S 146°00′E
104 M14 **Benamejí** Andalucía, S Spain 37°16′N 04°33′W
Benares see Vārānasi
Benavarn see Benabarre
104 F10 **Benavente** Santarém, C Portugal 38°59′N 08°49′W
104 K5 **Benavente** Castilla-León, N Spain 42°N 05°40′W
25 S15 **Benavides** Texas, SW USA 27°36′N 98°24′W
96 F8 **Benbecula** island NW Scotland, United Kingdom
Bencovazzo see Benkovac
32 H13 **Bend** Oregon, NW USA 44°04′N 121°19′W
182 K7 **Benda Range** ▲▲ South Australia
183 T6 **Bendemeer** New South Wales, SE Australia 30°54′S 151°12′E
Bender see Tighina
Bender Beila/Bender Beyla see Bandarbeyla
Bender Cassim/Bender Qaasim see Boosaaso
Bendery see Tighina
183 N11 **Bendigo** Victoria, SE Australia 36°46′S 144°19′E
118 E10 **Bēne** Dobele, SW Latvia 56°30′N 23°04′E
98 K13 **Beneden-Leeuwen** Gelderland, C Netherlands 51°52′N 05°32′E
101 L24 **Benediktenwand** ▲ S Germany 47°39′N 11°28′E
Benemérita de San Cristóbal see San Cristóbal
77 N12 **Bénéna** Ségou, S Mali 13°04′N 04°20′W
172 I7 **Benenitra** Toliara, S Madagascar 23°25′S 45°06′E
Beneschau see Benešov
Beneški Zaliv see Venice, Gulf of
111 D17 **Benešov** Ger. Beneschau. Středočeský Kraj, W Czech Republic 49°48′N 14°41′E
123 Q5 **Benetta, Ostrov** island Novosibirskiye Ostrova, NE Russian Federation
107 L17 **Benevento** anc. Beneventum, Malventum. Campania, S Italy 41°07′N 14°45′E
Beneventum see Benevento
173 S3 **Bengal, Bay of** bay N Indian Ocean
Bengalooru see Bangalore
79 M17 **Bengamisa** Orientale, N Dem. Rep. Congo 0°58′N 25°11′E
Bengasi see Banghāzī
Bengazi see Banghāzī
161 P7 **Bengbu** var. Peng-pu. Anhui, E China 32°57′N 117°17′E
32 L9 **Benge** Washington, NW USA 46°55′N 118°01′W
Benghazi see Banghāzī
168 K10 **Bengkalis** Pulau Bengkalis, W Indonesia 01°27′N 102°10′E
168 K10 **Bengkalis, Pulau** island W Indonesia
169 Q10 **Bengkayang** Borneo, C Indonesia 0°45′N 109°28′E
168 K14 **Bengkulu** prev. Bengkoeloe, Benkoelen, Benkulen. Sumatera, W Indonesia 03°46′S 102°16′E
168 K13 **Bengkulu** off. Propinsi Bengkulu; prev. Bengkoeloe, Benkoelen, Benkulen. ◈ province W Indonesia
Bengkulu, Propinsi see Bengkulu
82 A11 **Bengo** ◈ province W Angola
95 J16 **Bengtsfors** Västra Götaland, S Sweden 59°03′N 12°14′E
82 B13 **Benguela** var. Benguella. Benguela, W Angola 12°35′S 13°30′E
83 A14 **Benguela** ◈ province W Angola
Benguella see Benguela
138 F10 **Ben Gurion** ✈ Tel Aviv, C Israel 32°04′N 34°45′E
Bengweulu, Lake see Bangweulu, Lake
Benha see Banhā
192 F6 **Benham Seamount** undersea feature W Philippine Sea 15°48′N 124°15′E
96 H6 **Ben Hope** ▲ N Scotland, United Kingdom 58°25′N 04°36′W
79 P18 **Beni** Nord-Kivu, NE Dem. Rep. Congo 0°31′N 29°30′E
57 L15 **Beni** var. El Beni. ◈ department N Bolivia
74 H8 **Beni Abbès** W Algeria 30°07′N 02°09′W
105 T8 **Benicarló** País Valenciano, E Spain 40°25′N 00°25′E
105 T9 **Benicàssim** Cat. Benicàssim. País Valenciano, E Spain 40°03′N 00°03′E
Benicàssim see Benicàssim
105 T12 **Benidorm** País Valenciano, SE Spain 38°33′N 00°09′W
Beni Mazâr see Banī Mazār
121 C11 **Beni-Mellal** C Morocco 32°20′N 06°21′W
77 R14 **Benin** off. Republic of Benin; prev. Dahomey. ◆ republic W Africa
77 S17 **Benin, Bight of** gulf W Africa
77 U16 **Benin City** Edo, SW Nigeria 06°23′N 05°40′E
Benin, Republic of see Benin
57 K16 **Beni, Río** ≈ N Bolivia
120 F10 **Beni Saf** var. Beni-Saf. NW Algeria 35°19′N 01°23′W
Beni-Saf see Beni Saf
105 T11 **Benissa** País Valenciano, E Spain 38°43′N 00°03′E
Beni Suef see Banī Suwayf
11 V15 **Benito** Manitoba, S Canada 51°57′N 101°24′W
Benito see Uolo, Río
61 C23 **Benito Juárez** Buenos Aires, E Argentina 37°43′S 59°48′W
41 P14 **Benito Juaréz Internacional** ✈ (México) México, S Mexico 19°24′N 99°02′W
25 P5 **Benjamin** Texas, SW USA 33°35′N 99°49′W
58 B13 **Benjamin Constant** Amazonas, N Brazil 04°22′S 70°02′W
40 F4 **Benjamín Hill** Sonora, NW Mexico 30°13′N 111°08′W
63 F19 **Benjamín, Isla** island Archipiélago de los Chonos, S Chile
164 Q4 **Benkei-misaki** headland Hokkaidō, NE Japan 42°49′N 140°10′E
28 L17 **Benkelman** Nebraska, C USA 40°04′N 101°30′W
96 I7 **Ben Klibreck** ▲ N Scotland, United Kingdom 58°15′N 04°23′W
Benkoelen/Bengkoeloe see Bengkulu
112 D13 **Benkovac** It. Bencovazzo. Zadar, SW Croatia 44°02′N 15°36′E
Benkulen see Bengkulu
96 I11 **Ben Lawers** ▲ C Scotland, United Kingdom 56°33′N 04°13′W
96 J9 **Ben Macdui** var. Beinn MacDuibh. ▲ C Scotland, United Kingdom 57°02′N 03°42′W
96 G11 **Ben More** ▲ W Scotland, United Kingdom 56°26′N 06°00′W
96 I11 **Ben More** ▲ C Scotland, United Kingdom 56°22′N 04°31′W
96 H7 **Ben More Assynt** ▲ N Scotland, United Kingdom 58°09′N 04°51′W
185 E20 **Benmore, Lake** ◎ South Island, New Zealand
98 L12 **Bennekom** Gelderland, SE Netherlands 52°00′N 05°40′E
21 T11 **Bennettsville** South Carolina, SE USA 34°36′N 79°40′W
96 H10 **Ben Nevis** ▲ N Scotland, United Kingdom 56°80′N 05°00′W
184 M9 **Benneydale** Waikato, North Island, New Zealand 38°31′S 175°22′E
Bennichab see Bennichchâb
76 H8 **Bennichchâb** var. Bennichab. Inchiri, W Mauritania 19°26′N 15°21′W
18 L10 **Bennington** Vermont, NE USA 42°51′N 73°09′W
185 E20 **Ben Ohau Range** ▲▲ South Island, New Zealand
83 J21 **Benoni** Gauteng, NE South Africa 26°04′S 28°18′E
172 J2 **Be, Nosy** var. Nossi-Bé. island NW Madagascar
Bénoué see Benue
42 F2 **Benque Viejo del Carmen** Cayo, W Belize 17°04′N 89°08′W
101 G19 **Bensheim** Hessen, W Germany 49°41′N 08°38′E
37 N16 **Benson** Arizona, SW USA 31°55′N 110°16′W
29 S8 **Benson** Minnesota, N USA 45°19′N 95°36′W
21 U10 **Benson** North Carolina, SE USA 35°22′N 78°33′W
171 N15 **Benteng** Pulau Selayar, C Indonesia 06°07′S 120°28′E
83 A14 **Bentiaba** Namibe, SW Angola 14°18′S 12°27′E
181 T4 **Bentinck Island** island Wellesley Islands, Queensland, N Australia
80 E13 **Bentiu** Wahda, S Sudan 09°14′N 29°49′E
138 G8 **Bent Jbaïl** var. Bint Jubayl. S Lebanon 33°07′N 35°26′E
11 Q15 **Bentley** Alberta, SW Canada 52°27′N 114°02′W
61 I15 **Bento Gonçalves** Rio Grande do Sul, S Brazil 29°12′S 51°34′W
27 U12 **Benton** Arkansas, C USA 34°34′N 92°35′W
30 L16 **Benton** Illinois, N USA 38°00′N 88°55′W
20 H7 **Benton** Kentucky, S USA 36°51′N 88°21′W
22 G5 **Benton** Louisiana, S USA 32°41′N 93°44′W
27 Y7 **Benton** Missouri, C USA 37°05′N 89°34′W
20 M10 **Benton** Tennessee, S USA 35°10′N 84°39′W
31 O10 **Benton Harbor** Michigan, N USA 42°07′N 86°27′W
27 S9 **Bentonville** Arkansas, C USA 36°23′N 94°13′W
77 V16 **Benue** ◈ state SE Nigeria
78 F13 **Benue** Fr. Bénoué. ≈ Cameroon/Nigeria
163 V12 **Benxi** prev. Pen-ch'i, Penhsihu, Penki. Liaoning, NE China 41°20′N 123°45′E
Benyakoni see Byenyakoni
112 K10 **Beočin** Vojvodina, N Serbia 45°13′N 19°43′E
Beodericsworth see Bury St Edmunds
112 M11 **Beograd** Eng. Belgrade, Ger. Belgrad; anc. Singidunum. ● (Serbia) Serbia, N Serbia 44°48′N 20°27′E
112 L11 **Beograd** Eng. Belgrade. ✈ Serbia, N Serbia 44°45′N 20°21′E
76 M16 **Béoumi** C Ivory Coast 07°40′N 05°34′W
35 V3 **Beowawe** Nevada, W USA 40°33′N 116°31′W
164 E14 **Beppu** Ōita, Kyūshū, SW Japan 33°18′N 131°30′E
187 X15 **Beqa** prev. Mbengga. island W Fiji
45 Y14 **Bequia** island C Saint Vincent and the Grenadines
113 L16 **Berane** prev. Ivangrad. E Montenegro 42°51′N 19°51′E
113 L21 **Berat** var. Berati, SCr. Beligrad. Berat, C Albania 40°43′N 19°58′E
113 L21 **Berat** ◈ district C Albania
Berătău see Berettyó
Berati see Berat
Beraun see Berounka, Czech Republic
Beraun see Beroun, Czech Republic
171 U13 **Berau, Teluk** var. MacCluer Gulf. bay Papua, E Indonesia
80 G8 **Berber** River Nile, NE Sudan 18°01′N 34°00′E
80 N12 **Berbera** Sahil, NW Somalia 10°24′N 45°02′E
79 H16 **Berbérati** Mambéré-Kadéï, SW Central African Republic 04°14′N 15°50′E
Berberia, Cabo de see Barbaria, Cap de

◆ Country
● Country Capital
◇ Dependent Territory
○ Dependent Territory Capital
◈ Administrative Regions
✈ International Airport
▲ Mountain
▲▲ Mountain Range
Volcano
≈ River
◎ Lake
⊠ Reservoir

BERBICE RIVER – BĪJĀR

55 T9 **Berbice River** ⛆ NE Guyana
Berchid *see* Berrechid
103 N2 **Berck-Plage** Pas-de-Calais, N France *50°24′N 01°35′E*
25 T13 **Berclair** Texas, SW USA *28°33′N 97°32′W*
117 W10 **Berda** ⛆ SE Ukraine
Berdichev *see* Berdychiv
123 P10 **Berdigestyakh** Respublika Sakha (Yakutiya), NE Russian Federation *62°02′N 127°03′E*
122 J12 **Berdsk** Novosibirskaya Oblast', C Russian Federation *54°42′N 82°56′E*
117 W10 **Berdyans'k** *Rus.* Berdyansk; *prev.* Osipenko. Zaporiz'ka Oblast', SE Ukraine *46°46′N 36°49′E*
117 W10 **Berdyans'ka Kosa** *spit* SE Ukraine
117 V10 **Berdyans'ka Zatoka** *gulf* S Ukraine
117 N5 **Berdychiv** *Rus.* Berdichev. Zhytomyrs'ka Oblast', N Ukraine *49°54′N 28°39′E*
20 M6 **Berea** Kentucky, S USA *37°34′N 84°18′W*
Beregovo/Beregszász *see* Berehove
116 G8 **Berehove** *Cz.* Berehovo, *Hung.* Beregszász, *Rus.* Beregovo. Zakarpats'ka Oblast', W Ukraine *48°13′N 22°39′E*
Berehovo *see* Berehove
186 D9 **Bereina** Central, S Papua New Guinea *08°29′S 146°30′E*
146 C11 **Bereket** *prev. Rus.* Gazandzhyk, Kazandzhik, *Turkm.* Gazanjyk. Balkan Welaýaty, W Turkmenistan *39°17′N 55°27′E*
45 O12 **Berekua** S Dominica *15°14′N 61°19′W*
77 O16 **Berekum** W Ghana *07°27′N 02°35′W*
Berenice *see* Baranīs
11 O14 **Berens** ⛆ Manitoba/Ontario, C Canada
11 X14 **Berens River** Manitoba, C Canada *52°22′N 97°00′W*
29 R12 **Beresford** South Dakota, N USA *43°02′N 96°45′W*
116 J4 **Berestechko** Volyns'ka Oblast', NW Ukraine *50°21′N 25°06′E*
116 M11 **Bereşti** Galaţi, E Romania *46°04′N 27°54′E*
117 U6 **Berestova** ⛆ E Ukraine
Beretău *see* Berettyó
111 N23 **Berettyó** *Rom.* Barcău; *prev.* Berătău, Beretău. ⛆ Hungary/Romania
111 N23 **Berettyóújfalu** Hajdú-Bihar, E Hungary *47°15′N 21°33′E*
Berëza/Bereza Kartuska *see* Byaroza
117 Q4 **Berezan'** Kyyivs'ka Oblast', N Ukraine *50°18′N 31°30′E*
117 Q10 **Berezanka** Mykolayivs'ka Oblast', S Ukraine *46°51′N 31°24′E*
116 J6 **Berezhany** *Pol.* Brzeżany. Ternopil's'ka Oblast', W Ukraine *49°29′N 25°00′E*
Berezina *see* Byerezino
Berezino *see* Byerazino
117 P10 **Berezivka** *Rus.* Berezovka. Odes'ka Oblast', SW Ukraine *47°12′N 30°56′E*
117 Q2 **Berezna** Chernihivs'ka Oblast', NE Ukraine *51°35′N 31°50′E*
116 L3 **Berezne** Rivnens'ka Oblast', NW Ukraine *51°00′N 26°46′E*
117 R9 **Bereznehuvate** Mykolayivs'ka Oblast', S Ukraine *47°18′N 32°52′E*
125 N10 **Bereznik** Arkhangel'skaya Oblast', NW Russian Federation *62°50′N 42°40′E*
125 U13 **Berezniki** Permskaya Oblast', NW Russian Federation *59°26′N 56°49′E*
Berëzovka *see* Byarozawka, Belarus
Berezovka *see* Berezivka, Ukraine
122 H9 **Berezovo** Khanty-Mansiyskiy Avtonomnyy Okrug-Yugra, N Russian Federation *63°48′N 64°38′E*
127 O9 **Berezovskaya** Volgogradskaya Oblast', SW Russian Federation *50°17′N 43°58′E*
123 S13 **Berezovyy** Khabarovskiy Kray, E Russian Federation *51°42′N 135°39′E*
83 E25 **Berg** ⛆ W South Africa
Berg *see* Berg bei Rohrbach
105 V4 **Berga** Cataluña, NE Spain *42°06′N 01°41′E*
95 N20 **Berga** Kalmar, S Sweden *57°13′N 16°03′E*
136 B13 **Bergama** İzmir, W Turkey *39°08′N 27°10′E*
106 E7 **Bergamo** *anc.* Bergomum. Lombardia, N Italy *45°42′N 09°40′E*
105 P3 **Bergara** País Vasco, N Spain *43°05′N 02°25′W*
109 S3 **Berg bei Rohrbach** *var.* Berg. Oberösterreich, N Austria *48°34′N 14°02′E*
100 O6 **Bergen** Mecklenburg-Vorpommern, NE Germany *54°25′N 13°25′E*
101 I11 **Bergen** Niedersachsen, NW Germany *52°49′N 09°57′E*
98 H8 **Bergen** Noord-Holland, NW Netherlands *52°40′N 04°42′E*
94 C13 **Bergen** Hordaland, S Norway *60°24′N 05°19′E*
Bergen *see* Mons
55 W9 **Berg en Dal** Brokopondo, C Suriname *05°15′N 55°20′W*
99 G15 **Bergen op Zoom** Noord-Brabant, S Netherlands *51°30′N 04°17′E*
102 L13 **Bergerac** Dordogne, SW France *44°51′N 00°30′E*
99 J16 **Bergeyk** Noord-Brabant, S Netherlands *51°19′N 05°21′E*
101 D16 **Bergheim** Nordrhein-Westfalen, W Germany *50°57′N 06°39′E*
55 X10 **Bergi** Sipaliwini, E Suriname *04°36′N 54°24′W*
101 E16 **Bergisch Gladbach** Nordrhein-Westfalen, W Germany *50°59′N 07°09′E*
101 F14 **Bergkamen** Nordrhein-Westfalen, W Germany *51°32′N 07°41′E*
95 N21 **Bergkvara** Kalmar, S Sweden *56°22′N 16°04′E*
Bergomum *see* Bergamo
98 K13 **Bergse Maas** ⛆ S Netherlands
95 P15 **Bergshamra** Stockholm, C Sweden *59°37′N 18°40′E*
94 N10 **Bergsjö** Gävleborg, C Sweden *62°00′N 17°10′E*
93 J14 **Bergsviken** Norrbotten, N Sweden *65°16′N 21°24′E*
98 L6 **Bergum** *Fris.* Burgum. Friesland, N Netherlands *53°12′N 05°59′E*
98 M6 **Bergumer Meer** ◎ N Netherlands
94 N12 **Bergviken** ◎ C Sweden
168 M11 **Berhala, Selat** *strait* Sumatera, W Indonesia
Berhampore *see* Baharampur
99 J17 **Beringen** Limburg, NE Belgium *51°04′N 05°14′E*
39 T12 **Bering Glacier** *glacier* Alaska, USA
Beringov Proliv *see* Bering Strait
192 L2 **Bering Sea** *sea* N Pacific Ocean
38 L9 **Bering Strait** *Rus.* Beringov Proliv. *strait* Bering Sea/Chukchi Sea
Berislav *see* Beryslav
105 O15 **Berja** Andalucía, S Spain *36°51′N 02°56′W*
94 H9 **Berkåk** Sør-Trøndelag, S Norway *62°50′N 10°01′E*
98 N11 **Berkel** ⛆ Germany/Netherlands
35 N8 **Berkeley** California, W USA *37°52′N 122°16′W*
65 E24 **Berkeley Sound** *sound* NE Falkland Islands
21 V2 **Berkeley Springs** *var.* Bath. West Virginia, NE USA *39°38′N 78°14′W*
195 N6 **Berkner Island** *island* Antarctica
114 G8 **Berkovitsa** Montana, NW Bulgaria *43°15′N 23°05′E*
97 M22 **Berkshire** *former county* S England, United Kingdom
99 H17 **Berlaar** Antwerpen, N Belgium *51°08′N 04°39′E*
Berlanga *see* Berlanga de Duero
105 P6 **Berlanga de Duero** *var.* Berlanga. Castilla-León, N Spain *41°28′N 02°51′W*
0 I16 **Berlanga Rise** *undersea feature* E Pacific Ocean *08°30′N 93°30′W*
99 F17 **Berlare** Oost-Vlaanderen, NW Belgium *51°02′N 04°01′E*
104 E9 **Berlenga, Ilha da** *island* C Portugal
92 M7 **Berlevåg** *Lapp.* Bearalváhki. Finnmark, N Norway *70°51′N 29°04′E*
100 O12 **Berlin** ● (Germany) Berlin, NE Germany *52°31′N 13°26′E*
21 Z4 **Berlin** Maryland, NE USA *38°19′N 75°13′W*
19 O7 **Berlin** New Hampshire, NE USA *44°27′N 71°13′W*
18 D16 **Berlin** Pennsylvania, NE USA *39°54′N 78°57′W*
30 L7 **Berlin** Wisconsin, N USA *43°57′N 88°59′W*
100 O12 **Berlin** ◈ *state* NE Germany
Berlinchen *see* Barlinek
31 U12 **Berlin Lake** ⊠ Ohio, N USA
183 R11 **Bermagui** New South Wales, SE Australia *36°26′S 150°01′E*
40 L8 **Bermejillo** Durango, C Mexico *25°55′N 103°39′W*
62 L5 **Bermejo, Río** ⛆ N Argentina
62 I10 **Bermejo, Río** ⛆ W Argentina
62 M6 **Bermejo viejo, Río** ⛆ N Argentina
105 P2 **Bermeo** País Vasco, N Spain *43°25′N 02°44′W*
104 K6 **Bermillo de Sayago** Castilla-León, N Spain *41°22′N 06°08′W*
106 E6 **Bermina, Pizzo** *Rmsch.* Piz Bernina. ▲ Italy/Switzerland *46°22′N 09°52′E see also* Bermina, Piz
64 A12 **Bermuda** *var.* Bermuda Islands, Bermudas; *prev.* Somers Islands. ◇ *UK crown colony* NW Atlantic Ocean
1 N11 **Bermuda** *var.* Great Bermuda, Long Island, Main Island. *island* Bermuda
Bermuda Islands *see* Bermuda
Bermuda-New England Seamount Arc *see* New England Seamounts
1 N11 **Bermuda Rise** *undersea feature* C Sargasso Sea *32°30′N 65°00′W*
Bermudas *see* Bermuda
108 D8 **Bern** *Fr.* Berne. ● (Switzerland) Bern, W Switzerland *46°57′N 07°26′E*
108 D9 **Bern** *Fr.* Berne. ◈ *canton* W Switzerland
37 R11 **Bernalillo** New Mexico, SW USA *35°18′N 106°33′W*
14 H12 **Bernard Lake** ◎ Ontario, S Canada
61 B18 **Bernardo de Irigoyen** Santa Fe, NE Argentina *32°09′S 61°06′W*
18 J14 **Bernardsville** New Jersey, NE USA *40°43′N 74°34′W*
63 K14 **Bernasconi** La Pampa, C Argentina *37°55′S 63°44′W*
100 O12 **Bernau** Brandenburg, NE Germany *52°41′N 13°36′E*
102 L4 **Bernay** Eure, N France *49°05′N 00°36′E*
101 L14 **Bernburg** Sachsen-Anhalt, C Germany *51°47′N 11°45′E*
109 X5 **Berndorf** Niederösterreich, NE Austria *47°58′N 16°08′E*
31 Q12 **Berne** Indiana, N USA *40°39′N 84°57′W*
Berne *see* Bern
108 D10 **Berner Alpen** *var.* Berner Oberland, *Eng.* Bernese Oberland. ▲▲ SW Switzerland
Berner Oberland/Bernese Oberland *see* Berner Alpen
109 Y2 **Bernhardsthal** Niederösterreich, N Austria *48°40′N 16°51′E*
22 H4 **Bernice** Louisiana, S USA *32°49′N 92°39′W*
27 Y8 **Bernie** Missouri, C USA *36°40′N 89°58′W*
180 G9 **Bernier Island** *island* Western Australia
Bernina Pass *see* Bernina, Passo del
108 J10 **Bernina, Passo del** *Eng.* Bernina Pass. *pass* SE Switzerland
108 J10 **Bernina, Piz** *It.* Pizzo Bernina. ▲ Italy/Switzerland *46°22′N 09°55′E see also* Bernina, Pizzo
Bernina, Piz *see* Bernina, Pizzo
99 E20 **Bernissart** Hainaut, SW Belgium *50°29′N 03°37′E*
101 E18 **Bernkastel-Kues** Rheinland-Pfalz, W Germany *49°55′N 07°04′E*
Beroea *see* Ḩalab
172 H6 **Beroroha** Toliara, SW Madagascar *21°40′S 45°10′E*
Béroubouay *see* Gbéroubouè
111 C17 **Beroun** *Ger.* Beraun. Středočeský Kraj, W Czech Republic *49°58′N 14°05′E*
111 C16 **Berounka** *Ger.* Beraun. ⛆ W Czech Republic
113 Q18 **Berovo** E FYR Macedonia *41°45′N 22°50′E*
74 F6 **Berrechid** *var.* Berchid. W Morocco *33°16′N 07°32′W*
103 R15 **Berre, Étang de** ◎ SE France
103 S15 **Berre-l'Étang** Bouches-du-Rhône, SE France *43°28′N 05°10′E*
182 K9 **Berri** South Australia *34°16′S 140°35′E*
31 O10 **Berrien Springs** Michigan, N USA *41°57′N 86°20′W*
183 O10 **Berrigan** New South Wales, SE Australia *35°41′S 145°50′E*
103 N9 **Berry** *cultural region* C France
35 N7 **Berryessa, Lake** ◎ California, W USA
44 G2 **Berry Islands** *island group* N Bahamas
27 T9 **Berryville** Arkansas, C USA *36°22′N 93°35′W*
21 V3 **Berryville** Virginia, NE USA *39°08′N 77°59′W*
83 D21 **Berseba** Karas, S Namibia *26°00′S 17°46′E*
117 O8 **Bershad'** Vinnyts'ka Oblast', C Ukraine *48°20′N 29°30′E*
28 L3 **Berthold** North Dakota, N USA *48°16′N 101°48′W*
37 T3 **Berthoud** Colorado, C USA *40°18′N 105°04′W*
37 S4 **Berthoud Pass** *pass* Colorado, C USA
79 F15 **Bertoua** Est, E Cameroon *04°34′N 13°42′E*
25 S10 **Bertram** Texas, SW USA *30°44′N 98°03′W*
63 G22 **Bertrand, Cerro** ▲ S Argentina *50°00′S 73°27′W*
99 J23 **Bertrix** Luxembourg, SE Belgium *49°52′N 05°15′E*
191 P3 **Beru** *var.* Peru. *atoll* Tungaru, W Kiribati
Beruni *see* Beruniy
146 I9 **Beruniy** *var.* Biruni, *Rus.* Beruni. Qoraqalpog'iston Respublikasi, W Uzbekistan *41°48′N 60°39′E*
58 F13 **Beruri** Amazonas, NW Brazil *03°44′S 61°13′W*
18 H14 **Berwick** Pennsylvania, NE USA *41°03′N 76°13′W*
96 K12 **Berwick** *cultural region* SE Scotland, United Kingdom
96 L12 **Berwick-upon-Tweed** N England, United Kingdom *55°46′N 02°00′W*
117 S10 **Beryslav** *Rus.* Berislav. Khersons'ka Oblast', S Ukraine *46°51′N 33°26′E*
Berytus *see* Beyrouth
172 H4 **Besalampy** Mahajanga, W Madagascar *16°43′S 44°29′E*
103 T8 **Besançon** *anc.* Besontium, Vesontio. Doubs, E France *47°14′N 06°01′E*
103 P10 **Besbre** ⛆ C France
Bescanuova *see* Baška
Besdan *see* Bezdan
Besed' *see* Byesyedz'
147 R10 **Beshariq** *Rus.* Besharyk; *prev.* Kirovo. Farg'ona Viloyati, E Uzbekistan *40°26′N 70°33′E*
Besharyk *see* Beshariq
146 L9 **Beshbuloq** *Rus.* Beshulak. Navoiy Viloyati, N Uzbekistan *41°55′N 64°13′E*
Beshenkovichi *see* Byeshankovichy
146 M13 **Beshkent** Qashqadaryo Viloyati, S Uzbekistan *38°47′N 65°42′E*
Beshulak *see* Beshbuloq
112 L10 **Beška** Vojvodina, N Serbia *45°09′N 20°04′E*
Beskra *see* Biskra
127 O16 **Beslan** Respublika Severnaya Osetiya, SW Russian Federation *43°12′N 44°33′E*
113 P16 **Besna Kobila** ▲ SE Serbia *42°30′N 22°16′E*
137 N16 **Besni** Adıyaman, S Turkey *37°42′N 37°53′E*
Besontium *see* Besançon
121 Q2 **Beşparmak Dağları** *Eng.* Kyrenia Mountains. ▲▲ N Cyprus
Bessarabka *see* Basarabeasca
92 O2 **Bessels, Kapp** *headland* C Svalbard *78°36′N 21°43′E*
23 P4 **Bessemer** Alabama, S USA *33°24′N 86°57′W*
30 K3 **Bessemer** Michigan, N USA *46°28′N 90°03′W*
21 Q10 **Bessemer City** North Carolina, SE USA *35°16′N 81°16′W*
102 M10 **Bessines-sur-Gartempe** Haute-Vienne, C France *46°06′N 01°22′E*
99 K15 **Best** Noord-Brabant, S Netherlands *51°31′N 05°24′E*
25 N9 **Best** Texas, SW USA *31°13′N 101°34′W*
125 O11 **Bestuzhevo** Arkhangel'skaya Oblast', NW Russian Federation *61°36′N 43°54′E*
123 M11 **Bestyakh** Respublika Sakha (Yakutiya), NE Russian Federation *61°25′N 129°05′E*
Beszterce *see* Bistriţa
Besztercebánya *see* Banská Bystrica
172 I5 **Betafo** Antananarivo, C Madagascar *19°50′S 46°50′E*
104 H2 **Betanzos** Galicia, NW Spain *43°17′N 08°17′W*
104 G2 **Betanzos, Ría de** *estuary* NW Spain
79 G15 **Bétaré Oya** Est, E Cameroon *05°34′N 14°09′E*
105 S9 **Bétera** País Valenciano, E Spain *39°35′N 00°28′W*
77 R15 **Bétérou** C Benin *09°13′N 02°18′E*
83 K21 **Bethal** Mpumalanga, NE South Africa *26°27′S 29°28′E*
30 K15 **Bethalto** Illinois, N USA *38°54′N 90°02′W*
83 D21 **Bethanie** *var.* Bethanien, Bethany. Karas, S Namibia *26°32′S 17°11′E*
Bethanien *see* Bethanie
27 S2 **Bethany** Missouri, C USA *40°15′N 94°03′W*
27 N10 **Bethany** Oklahoma, C USA *35°31′N 97°37′W*
Bethany *see* Bethanie
39 N12 **Bethel** Alaska, USA *60°47′N 161°45′W*
19 P7 **Bethel** Maine, NE USA *44°24′N 70°47′W*
21 W9 **Bethel** North Carolina, SE USA *35°46′N 77°21′W*
18 B15 **Bethel Park** Pennsylvania, NE USA *40°21′N 80°03′W*
21 W3 **Bethesda** Maryland, NE USA *39°00′N 77°05′W*
83 J22 **Bethlehem** Free State, C South Africa *28°12′S 28°16′E*
18 I14 **Bethlehem** Pennsylvania, NE USA *40°36′N 75°22′W*
138 F10 **Bethlehem** *var.* Beit Lekhem, *Ar.* Bayt Laḩm, *Heb.* Bet Leḩem. C West Bank *31°43′N 35°12′E*
Bethlen *see* Beclean
83 I24 **Bethulie** Free State, C South Africa *30°30′S 25°59′E*
103 O1 **Béthune** Pas-de-Calais, N France *50°32′N 02°38′E*
102 M3 **Béthune** ⛆ N France
104 M14 **Béticos, Sistemas** *var.* Sistema Penibético, *Eng.* Baetic Cordillera, Baetic Mountains. ▲▲ S Spain
54 I6 **Betijoque** Trujillo, NW Venezuela *09°25′N 70°45′W*
59 M20 **Betim** Minas Gerais, SE Brazil *19°56′S 44°10′W*
190 H3 **Betio** Tarawa, W Kiribati *01°21′N 172°56′E*
172 H7 **Betioky** Toliara, S Madagascar *23°42′S 44°22′E*
Bet Leḩem *see* Bethlehem
Betlen *see* Beclean
167 O17 **Betong** Yala, SW Thailand *05°45′N 101°05′E*
79 I16 **Bétou** Likouala, N Congo *03°08′N 18°31′E*
145 P14 **Betpak-Dala** *Kaz.* Betpaqdala. *plateau* S Kazakhstan
Betpaqdala *see* Betpak-Dala
172 H7 **Betroka** Toliara, S Madagascar *23°15′S 46°07′E*
Betschau *see* Bečva
Bet She'an *see* Beit She'an
15 T6 **Betsiamites** Québec, SE Canada *48°56′N 68°40′W*
15 T6 **Betsiamites** ⛆ Québec, SE Canada
172 I4 **Betsiboka** ⛆ N Madagascar
Betsukai *see* Bekkai
99 M25 **Bettembourg** Luxembourg, S Luxembourg *49°31′N 06°06′E*
99 M23 **Bettendorf** Diekirch, NE Luxembourg *49°53′N 06°13′E*
29 Z14 **Bettendorf** Iowa, C USA *41°31′N 90°31′W*
75 R13 **Bette, Picco** *var.* Bikkū Bītti, *It.* Picco Bette. ▲ S Libya *22°02′N 19°07′E*
Bette, Picco *see* Bette, Picco
153 P12 **Bettiah** Bihār, N India *26°49′N 84°30′E*
39 Q7 **Bettles** Alaska, USA *66°54′N 151°40′W*
95 N17 **Bettna** Södermanland, C Sweden *58°52′N 16°40′E*
154 H11 **Betūl** *prev.* Badnur. Madhya Pradesh, C India *21°55′N 77°54′E*
154 H9 **Betwa** ⛆ C India
101 F16 **Betzdorf** Rheinland-Pfalz, W Germany *50°47′N 07°50′E*
82 C9 **Béu** Uíge, NW Angola *06°15′S 15°32′E*
31 P6 **Beulah** Michigan, N USA *43°35′N 83°52′W*
28 L5 **Beulah** North Dakota, N USA *47°16′N 101°48′W*
98 M8 **Beulakerwijde** ◎ N Netherlands
98 L13 **Beuningen** Gelderland, SE Netherlands *51°52′N 05°47′E*
Beuthen *see* Bytom
103 N7 **Beuvron** ⛆ C France
99 F16 **Beveren** Oost-Vlaanderen, N Belgium *51°13′N 04°15′E*
21 T9 **B. Everett Jordan Reservoir** *var.* Jordan Lake. ⊠ North Carolina, SE USA
97 N17 **Beverley** E England, United Kingdom *53°51′N 00°26′W*
Beverley *see* Beverly
99 J17 **Beverlo** Limburg, NE Belgium *51°06′N 05°14′E*
19 P11 **Beverly** Massachusetts, NE USA *42°33′N 70°49′W*
32 J9 **Beverly** *var.* Beverley. Washington, NW USA *46°50′N 119°57′W*
35 S15 **Beverly Hills** California, W USA *34°02′N 118°25′W*
101 I14 **Beverungen** Nordrhein-Westfalen, C Germany *51°39′N 09°22′E*
98 H9 **Beverwijk** Noord-Holland, W Netherlands *52°29′N 04°40′E*
108 C10 **Bex** Vaud, W Switzerland *46°15′N 07°00′E*
97 P23 **Bexhill** *var.* Bexhill-on-Sea. SE England, United Kingdom *50°50′N 00°28′E*
Bexhill-on-Sea *see* Bexhill
136 E17 **Bey Dağları** ▲▲ SW Turkey
Beyj *see* Belyy
136 E10 **Beykoz** İstanbul, NW Turkey *41°09′N 29°06′E*
76 K15 **Beyla** SE Guinea *08°43′N 08°41′W*
137 X12 **Beyläqan** *prev.* Zhdanov. SW Azerbaijan *39°43′N 47°38′E*
80 L10 **Beylul** *var.* Beilul. SE Eritrea *13°10′N 42°27′E*
144 H14 **Beyneu** *Kaz.* Beyneū. Mangistau, SW Kazakhstan *45°20′N 55°11′E*
Beyneū *see* Beyneu
165 X14 **Beyonēsu-retsugan** *Eng.* Bayonnaise Rocks. *island group* SE Japan
136 G12 **Beypazarı** Ankara, NW Turkey *40°10′N 31°56′E*
155 F21 **Beypore** Kerala, SW India *11°10′N 75°49′E*
138 G7 **Beyrouth** *var.* Bayrūt, *Eng.* Beirut; *anc.* Berytus. ● (Lebanon) W Lebanon *33°55′N 35°31′E*
138 G7 **Beyrouth** ✈ W Lebanon *33°52′N 35°30′E*
136 G15 **Beyşehir** Konya, SW Turkey *37°40′N 31°43′E*
136 G15 **Beyşehir Gölü** ◎ C Turkey
108 J7 **Bezau** Vorarlberg, NW Austria *47°24′N 09°55′E*
112 J8 **Bezdan** *Ger.* Besdan, *Hung.* Bezdán. Vojvodina, NW Serbia *45°51′N 19°00′E*
Bezdezh *see* Byezdzyezh
124 G15 **Bezhanitsy** Pskovskaya Oblast', W Russian Federation *56°57′N 29°53′E*
124 K15 **Bezhetsk** Tverskaya Oblast', W Russian Federation *57°47′N 36°42′E*
103 P16 **Béziers** *anc.* Baeterrae, Baeterrae Septimanorum, Julia Beterrae. Hérault, S France *43°21′N 03°13′E*
Bezmein *see* Abadan
Bezwada *see* Vijayawāda
154 P12 **Bhadrak** *var.* Bhadrakh. Orissa, E India *21°04′N 86°30′N*
Bhadrakh *see* Bhadrak
155 F19 **Bhadra Reservoir** ⊠ SW India
155 F18 **Bhadrāvati** Karnātaka, SW India *13°52′N 75°43′E*
153 R14 **Bhāgalpur** Bihār, NE India *25°14′N 86°59′E*
Bhairab *see* Bhairab Bazar
153 U14 **Bhairab Bazar** *var.* Bhairab. Dhaka, C Bangladesh *24°04′N 91°00′E*
153 O11 **Bhairahawā** Western, S Nepal *27°31′N 83°27′E*
149 S8 **Bhakkar** Punjab, E Pakistan *31°40′N 71°08′E*
153 P11 **Bhaktapur** Central, C Nepal *27°47′N 85°21′E*
167 N3 **Bhamo** *var.* Banmo. Kachin State, N Myanmar (Burma) *24°15′N 97°15′E*
Bhāmragad *see* Bhāmragarh
154 K13 **Bhāmragarh** *var.* Bhāmragad. Mahārāshtra, C India *19°28′N 80°39′E*
154 J12 **Bhandāra** Mahārāshtra, C India *21°10′N 79°41′E*
Bhārat *see* India
152 J12 **Bharatpur** *prev.* Bhurtpore. Rājasthān, N India *27°14′N 77°29′E*
154 D11 **Bharūch** Gujarāt, W India *21°48′N 72°55′E*
155 E18 **Bhatkal** Karnātaka, W India *13°59′N 74°34′E*
153 O13 **Bhatni** *var.* Bhatni Junction. Uttar Pradesh, N India *26°23′N 83°56′E*
Bhatni Junction *see* Bhatni
153 S16 **Bhātpāra** West Bengal, NE India *22°55′N 88°30′E*
149 U7 **Bhaun** Punjab, E Pakistan *32°53′N 72°48′E*
Bhaunagar *see* Bhāvnagar
154 M13 **Bhavānīpātna** *var.* Bhawanipatna. Orissa, E India *19°56′N 83°09′E*
155 H21 **Bhavānīsāgar** ⊠ S India
154 D11 **Bhāvnagar** *prev.* Bhaunagar. Gujarāt, W India *21°46′N 72°14′E*
Bhawanipatna *see* Bhavānīpātna
Bheanntraí, Bá *see* Bantry Bay
Bheara, Béal an *see* Gweebarra Bay
154 K12 **Bhilai** Chhattīsgarh, C India *21°12′N 81°26′E*
152 G13 **Bhīlwāra** Rājasthān, N India *25°23′N 74°39′E*
155 E14 **Bhīma** ⛆ S India
155 K16 **Bhīmavaram** Andhra Pradesh, E India *16°34′N 81°35′E*
154 I7 **Bhind** Madhya Pradesh, C India *26°33′N 78°47′E*
152 E13 **Bhīnmāl** Rājasthān, N India *25°01′N 72°22′E*
Bhir *see* Bīd
154 D13 **Bhiwandi** Mahārāshtra, W India *19°21′N 73°08′E*
152 H10 **Bhiwāni** Haryāna, N India *28°50′N 76°10′E*
152 L13 **Bhognīpur** Uttar Pradesh, N India *26°12′N 79°48′E*
153 U16 **Bhola** Barisal, S Bangladesh *22°40′N 91°36′E*
154 H10 **Bhopāl** *state capital* Madhya Pradesh, C India *23°17′N 77°25′E*
155 J14 **Bhopālpatnam** Chhattīsgarh, C India *18°51′N 80°22′E*
155 E14 **Bhor** Mahārāshtra, W India *18°10′N 73°55′E*
154 O12 **Bhubaneshwar** *prev.* Bhubaneswar, Bhuvaneshwar. *state capital* Orissa, E India *20°16′N 85°51′E*
Bhubaneswar *see* Bhubaneshwar
154 B9 **Bhuj** Gujarāt, W India *23°16′N 69°40′E*
Bhuket *see* Phuket
Bhurtpore *see* Bharatpur
Bhusaval *see* Bhusāwal
154 G12 **Bhusāwal** *prev.* Bhusaval. Mahārāshtra, C India *21°01′N 75°50′E*
153 T12 **Bhutan** *off.* Kingdom of Bhutan, *var.* Druk-yul. ◆ *monarchy* S Asia
Bhutan, Kingdom of *see* Bhutan
Bhuvaneshwar *see* Bhubaneshwar
143 T15 **Bīābān, Kūh-e** ▲▲ S Iran
77 V18 **Biafra, Bight of** *var.* Bight of Bonny. *bay* W Africa
171 W12 **Biak** Papua, E Indonesia *01°10′S 136°05′E*
171 W12 **Biak, Pulau** *island* E Indonesia
110 P12 **Biała Podlaska** Lubelskie, E Poland *52°03′N 23°08′E*
110 F7 **Białogard** *Ger.* Belgard. Zachodnio-pomorskie, NW Poland *54°01′N 15°59′E*
110 P10 **Białowieska, Puszcza** *Bel.* Byelavyezhskaya Pushcha, *Rus.* Belovezhskaya Pushcha. *physical region* Belarus/Poland *see also* Byelavyezhskaya, Pushcha
Białowieska, Puszcza *see* Byelavyezhskaya Pushcha
110 G8 **Biały Bór** *Ger.* Baldenburg. Zachodnio-pomorskie, NW Poland *53°53′N 16°49′E*
110 P9 **Białystok** *Rus.* Belostok, Bielostok. Podlaskie, NE Poland *53°08′N 23°09′E*
107 L24 **Biancavilla** *prev.* Inessa. Sicilia, Italy, C Mediterranean Sea *37°38′N 14°52′E*
Bianco, Monte *see* Blanc, Mont
Bianjing *see* Xunke
76 L15 **Biankouma** W Ivory Coast *07°44′N 07°37′W*
167 R7 **Bia, Phou** *var.* Pou Bia. ▲ C Laos *18°59′N 103°09′E*
Bia, Pou *see* Bia, Phou
143 R5 **Biārjmand** Semnān, N Iran *36°05′N 55°50′E*
105 P4 **Biarra** ⛆ NE Spain
102 I15 **Biarritz** Pyrénées-Atlantiques, SW France *43°25′N 01°40′W*
108 H10 **Biasca** Ticino, S Switzerland *46°22′N 08°59′E*
61 E17 **Biassini** Salto, N Uruguay *31°18′S 57°05′W*
Biasteri *see* Laguardia
165 S3 **Bibai** Hokkaidō, NE Japan *43°21′N 141°53′E*
83 B15 **Bibala** *Port.* Vila Arriaga. Namibe, SW Angola *14°46′S 13°21′E*
104 I4 **Bibei** ⛆ NW Spain
Biberach *see* Biberach an der Riss
101 I23 **Biberach an der Riss** *var.* Biberach, *Ger.* Biberach an der Riß. Baden-Württemberg, S Germany *48°06′N 09°48′E*
108 E7 **Biberist** Solothurn, NW Switzerland *47°11′N 07°34′E*
77 O16 **Bibiani** SW Ghana *06°28′N 02°20′W*
112 C13 **Bibinje** Zadar, SW Croatia *44°04′N 15°17′E*
Biblical Gebal *see* Jbail
116 I5 **Bibrka** *Pol.* Bóbrka, *Rus.* Bobrka. L'vivs'ka Oblast', NW Ukraine *49°39′N 24°16′E*
117 N10 **Bic** ⛆ S Moldova
113 M18 **Bicaj** Kukës, NE Albania *42°00′N 20°24′E*
116 K10 **Bicaz** *Hung.* Békás. Neamţ, NE Romania *46°53′N 26°05′E*
183 Q16 **Bicheno** Tasmania, SE Australia *41°56′S 148°15′E*
Bichiş *see* Békés
Bichiş-Ciaba *see* Békéscsaba
137 P8 **Bichvint'a** *Rus.* Pitsunda. NW Georgia *43°12′N 40°21′E*
15 T7 **Bic, Île du** *island* Québec, SE Canada
32 J10 **Bickleton** Washington, NW USA *46°00′N 120°16′W*
36 L6 **Bicknell** Utah, W USA *38°20′N 111°32′W*
171 S11 **Bicoli** Pulau Halmahera, E Indonesia *0°34′N 128°33′E*
111 J22 **Bicske** Fejér, C Hungary *47°30′N 18°36′E*
155 F14 **Bīd** *prev.* Bhir. Mahārāshtra, W India *19°17′N 75°22′E*
77 U15 **Bida** Niger, C Nigeria *09°06′N 06°02′E*
155 H15 **Bīdar** Karnātaka, C India *17°56′N 77°35′E*
141 Y8 **Bidbid** NE Oman *23°25′N 58°08′E*
19 P9 **Biddeford** Maine, NE USA *43°29′N 70°27′W*
98 L9 **Biddinghuizen** Flevoland, C Netherlands *52°28′N 05°41′E*
33 X11 **Biddle** Montana, NW USA *45°04′N 105°21′W*
97 J23 **Bideford** SW England, United Kingdom *51°01′N 04°12′W*
82 D13 **Bié** ◈ *province* C Angola
35 O2 **Bieber** California, W USA *41°07′N 121°09′W*
110 O9 **Biebrza** ⛆ NE Poland
165 T3 **Biei** Hokkaidō, NE Japan *43°33′N 142°28′E*
108 D8 **Biel** *Fr.* Bienne. Bern, W Switzerland *47°09′N 07°16′E*
100 G13 **Bielefeld** Nordrhein-Westfalen, NW Germany *52°01′N 08°32′E*
108 D8 **Bieler See** *Fr.* Lac de Bienne. ◎ W Switzerland
Bielitz/Bielitz-Biala *see* Bielsko-Biała
106 C7 **Biella** Piemonte, N Italy *45°34′N 08°04′E*
Bielostok *see* Białystok
111 J17 **Bielsko-Biała** *Ger.* Bielitz, Bielitz-Biala. Śląskie, S Poland *49°49′N 19°01′E*
110 P10 **Bielsk Podlaski** Białystok, E Poland *52°45′N 23°11′E*
Bien Bien *see* Điện Biên
Bien Dong *see* South China Sea
11 V17 **Bienfait** Saskatchewan, S Canada *49°06′N 102°47′W*
167 T14 **Biên Hoa** Đông Nai, S Vietnam *10°58′N 106°50′E*
Bienne *see* Biel
Bienne, Lac de *see* Bieler See
12 K8 **Bienville, Lac** ◎ Québec, C Canada
82 D13 **Bié, Planalto do** *var.* Bié Plateau. *plateau* C Angola
Bié Plateau *see* Bié, Planalto do
108 B9 **Bière** Vaud, W Switzerland *46°32′N 06°19′E*
98 O4 **Bierum** Groningen, NE Netherlands *53°25′N 06°51′E*
98 I13 **Biesbos** *var.* Biesbosch. *wetland* S Netherlands
Biesbosch *see* Biesbos
99 H21 **Biesme** Namur, S Belgium *50°19′N 04°43′E*
101 H21 **Bietigheim-Bissingen** Baden-Württemberg, SW Germany *48°57′N 09°07′E*
99 I23 **Bièvre** Namur, SE Belgium *49°56′N 05°01′E*
79 D18 **Bifoun** Moyen-Ogooué, NW Gabon *0°15′S 10°24′E*
165 T2 **Bifuka** Hokkaidō, NE Japan *44°28′N 142°20′E*
136 C11 **Biga** Çanakkale, NW Turkey *40°13′N 27°14′E*
136 C13 **Bigadiç** Balıkesir, W Turkey *39°24′N 28°08′E*
26 J7 **Big Basin** *basin* Kansas, C USA
185 B20 **Big Bay** *bay* South Island, New Zealand
31 O5 **Big Bay de Noc** ◎ Michigan, N USA
31 N3 **Big Bay Point** *headland* Michigan, N USA *46°51′N 87°40′W*
33 R10 **Big Belt Mountains** ▲▲ Montana, NW USA
29 N10 **Big Bend Dam** *dam* South Dakota, N USA
24 K12 **Big Bend National Park** *national park* Texas, S USA
22 K5 **Big Black River** ⛆ Mississippi, S USA
27 O3 **Big Blue River** ⛆ Kansas/Nebraska, C USA
24 M10 **Big Canyon** ⛆ Texas, SW USA
33 N12 **Big Creek** Idaho, NW USA *45°05′N 115°20′W*
23 N8 **Big Creek Lake** ⊠ Alabama, S USA
23 X15 **Big Cypress Swamp** *wetland* Florida, SE USA
39 S9 **Big Delta** Alaska, USA *64°09′N 145°50′W*
30 K6 **Big Eau Pleine Reservoir** ⊠ Wisconsin, N USA
19 P5 **Bigelow Mountain** ▲ Maine, NE USA *45°09′N 70°17′W*
162 G9 **Biger** *var.* Jargalant. Govĭ-Altay, W Mongolia *45°39′N 97°10′E*
29 U3 **Big Falls** Minnesota, N USA *48°13′N 93°48′W*
33 P8 **Bigfork** Montana, NW USA *48°03′N 114°04′W*
29 U3 **Big Fork River** ⛆ Minnesota, N USA
11 S15 **Biggar** Saskatchewan, S Canada *52°03′N 107°59′W*
180 L3 **Bigge Island** *island* Western Australia
35 O5 **Biggs** California, W USA *39°24′N 121°44′W*
32 I11 **Biggs** Oregon, NW USA *45°39′N 120°49′W*
14 K13 **Big Gull Lake** ◎ Ontario, SE Canada
37 P16 **Big Hachet Peak** ▲ New Mexico, SW USA *31°38′N 108°24′W*
33 P11 **Big Hole River** ⛆ Montana, NW USA
33 V13 **Bighorn Basin** *basin* Wyoming, C USA
33 U11 **Bighorn Lake** ◎ Montana/Wyoming, N USA
33 W13 **Bighorn Mountains** ▲▲ Wyoming, C USA
36 J13 **Big Horn Peak** ▲ Arizona, SW USA *33°40′N 113°01′W*
33 V11 **Bighorn River** ⛆ Montana/Wyoming, NW USA
9 S7 **Big Island** *island* Nunavut, NE Canada
39 O16 **Big Koniuji Island** *island* Shumagin Islands, Alaska, USA
25 N9 **Big Lake** Texas, SW USA *31°12′N 101°29′W*
19 T5 **Big Lake** ◎ Maine, NE USA
30 I3 **Big Manitou Falls** *waterfall* Wisconsin, N USA
35 R2 **Big Mountain** ▲ Nevada, W USA *41°18′N 119°03′W*
108 G10 **Bignasco** Ticino, S Switzerland *46°21′N 08°37′E*
29 R16 **Big Nemaha River** ⛆ Nebraska, C USA
76 G12 **Bignona** SW Senegal *12°49′N 16°16′W*
Bigorra *see* Tarbes
Bigosovo *see* Bihosava
35 S10 **Big Pine** California, W USA *37°09′N 118°18′W*
35 Q14 **Big Pine Mountain** ▲ California, W USA *34°41′N 119°37′W*
27 V6 **Big Piney Creek** ⛆ Missouri, C USA
65 M24 **Big Point** *headland* N Tristan da Cunha *37°10′S 12°18′W*
31 P8 **Big Rapids** Michigan, N USA *43°42′N 85°28′W*
30 K6 **Big Rib River** ⛆ Wisconsin, N USA
14 L14 **Big Rideau Lake** ◎ Ontario, SE Canada
11 T14 **Big River** Saskatchewan, C Canada *53°48′N 106°55′W*
27 X5 **Big River** ⛆ Missouri, C USA
31 N7 **Big Sable Point** *headland* Michigan, N USA *44°03′N 86°30′W*
33 S7 **Big Sandy** Montana, NW USA *48°08′N 110°09′W*
25 W6 **Big Sandy** Texas, SW USA *32°34′N 95°06′W*
37 V5 **Big Sandy Creek** ⛆ Colorado, C USA
29 Q16 **Big Sandy Creek** ⛆ Nebraska, C USA
29 V5 **Big Sandy Lake** ◎ Minnesota, N USA
36 J11 **Big Sandy River** ⛆ Arizona, SW USA
21 P5 **Big Sandy River** ⛆ S USA
23 V6 **Big Satilla Creek** ⛆ Georgia, SE USA
29 R12 **Big Sioux River** ⛆ Iowa/South Dakota, N USA
35 U7 **Big Smoky Valley** *valley* Nevada, W USA
25 N7 **Big Spring** Texas, SW USA *32°15′N 101°30′W*
19 Q5 **Big Squaw Mountain** ▲ Maine, NE USA *45°28′N 69°42′W*
21 O7 **Big Stone Gap** Virginia, NE USA *36°52′N 82°45′W*
29 Q8 **Big Stone Lake** ◎ Minnesota/South Dakota, N USA
22 K4 **Big Sunflower River** ⛆ Mississippi, S USA
33 T11 **Big Timber** Montana, NW USA *45°50′N 109°57′W*
12 D8 **Big Trout Lake** Ontario, C Canada *53°40′N 90°00′W*
14 I12 **Big Trout Lake** ◎ Ontario, SE Canada
35 O2 **Big Valley Mountains** ▲ California, W USA
25 Q13 **Big Wells** Texas, SW USA *28°34′N 99°34′W*
14 F11 **Bigwood** Ontario, S Canada *46°03′N 80°37′W*
112 D11 **Bihać** ◈ Federacija Bosna I Hercegovina, NW Bosnia and Herzegovina
153 P14 **Bihār** *prev.* Behar. ◈ *state* N India
Bihār *see* Bihār Sharīf
81 F20 **Biharamulo** Kagera, NW Tanzania *02°37′S 31°20′E*
153 R13 **Bihārīganj** Bihār, NE India *25°44′N 86°59′E*
153 P14 **Bihār Sharīf** *var.* Bihār. Bihār, N India *25°13′N 85°31′E*
116 F10 **Bihor** ◈ *county* NW Romania
165 V3 **Bihoro** Hokkaidō, NE Japan *43°50′N 144°05′E*
118 K11 **Bihosava** *Rus.* Bigosovo. Vitsyebskaya Voblasts', NW Belarus *55°50′N 27°46′E*
Bijagos Archipelago *see* Bijagós, Arquipélago dos
76 G13 **Bijagós, Arquipélago dos** *var.* Bijagos Archipelago. *island group* W Guinea-Bissau
155 F16 **Bījāpur** Karnātaka, C India *16°50′N 75°42′E*
142 K5 **Bījār** Kordestān, W Iran *35°52′N 47°39′E*

◆ Country
● Country Capital
◇ Dependent Territory
○ Dependent Territory Capital
◈ Administrative Regions
✈ International Airport
▲ Mountain
▲▲ Mountain Range
⛰ Volcano
⛆ River
◎ Lake
⊠ Reservoir

BIJELJINA – BLUE MOUNTAIN

112 J11 **Bijeljina** Republika Srpska, NE Bosnia and Herzegovina 44°46′N 19°13′E
113 K15 **Bijelo Polje** E Montenegro 43°03′N 19°44′E
160 I11 **Bijie** Guizhou, S China 27°15′N 105°16′E
152 J10 **Bijnor** Uttar Pradesh, N India 29°22′N 78°09′E
152 F11 **Bīkāner** Rājasthān, NW India 28°01′N 73°22′E
189 V3 **Bikar Atoll** *var.* Pikaar. *atoll* Ratak Chain, N Marshall Islands
190 H3 **Bikeman** *atoll* Tungaru, W Kiribati
190 I3 **Bikenebu** Tarawa, W Kiribati
123 S14 **Bikin** Khabarovskiy Kray, SE Russian Federation 46°45′N 134°06′E
123 S14 **Bikin** ≈ SE Russian Federation
189 R3 **Bikini Atoll** *var.* Pikinni. *atoll* Ralik Chain, NW Marshall Islands
83 L17 **Bikita** Masvingo, E Zimbabwe 20°06′S 31°41′E
Bikkū Bitti *see* Bette, Picco
79 I19 **Bikoro** Equateur, W Dem. Rep. Congo 0°45′S 18°09′E
141 Z9 **Bilād Banī Bū ʿAlī** NE Oman 22°02′N 59°18′E
141 Z9 **Bilād Banī Bū Ḥasan** NE Oman 22°09′N 59°14′E
141 X9 **Bilād Manaḥ** *var.* Manaḥ. NE Oman 22°44′N 57°36′E
77 Q12 **Bilanga** C Burkina 12°35′N 00°08′W
152 F12 **Bilāra** Rājasthān, N India 26°10′N 73°48′E
152 K10 **Bilāri** Uttar Pradesh, N India 28°37′N 78°48′E
138 J5 **Bil'ās, Jabal al** ▲▲ C Syria
154 L11 **Bilāspur** Chhattīsgarh, C India 22°06′N 82°08′E
152 I8 **Bilāspur** Himāchal Pradesh, N India 31°18′N 76°48′E
168 J9 **Bila, Sungai** ≈ Sumatera, W Indonesia
137 Y13 **Biläsuvar** *Rus.* Bilyasuvar; *prev.* Pushkino. SE Azerbaijan 39°26′N 48°34′E
117 O5 **Bila Tserkva** *Rus.* Belaya Tserkov'. Kyyivs'ka Oblast', N Ukraine 49°49′N 30°08′E
167 N11 **Bilauktaung Range** *var.* Thanintari Taungdan. ▲▲ Myanmar (Burma)/Thailand
105 O2 **Bilbao** *Basq.* Bilbo. País Vasco, N Spain 43°15′N 02°56′W
Bilbo *see* Bilbao
92 H2 **Bíldudalur** Vestfirdhir, NW Iceland 65°40′N 23°35′W
113 I16 **Bileća** ◆ Republika Srpska, S Bosnia and Herzegovina
136 E12 **Bilecik** Bilecik, NW Turkey 39°59′N 29°54′E
136 F12 **Bilecik** ◆ *province* NW Turkey
116 E11 **Biled** *Ger.* Billed, *Hung.* Billéd. Timiş, W Romania 45°55′N 20°55′E
111 O15 **Biłgoraj** Lubelskie, E Poland 50°31′N 22°41′E
117 P11 **Bilhorod-Dnistrovs'kyy** *Rus.* Belgorod-Dnestrovskiy, *Rom.* Cetatea Albă, *prev.* Akkerman; *anc.* Tyras. Odes'ka Oblast', SW Ukraine 46°10′N 30°19′E
79 M16 **Bili** Orientale, N Dem. Rep. Congo 04°07′N 25°09′E
123 T6 **Bilibino** Chukotskiy Avtonomnyy Okrug, NE Russian Federation 67°56′N 166°45′E
166 M8 **Bilin** Mon State, S Myanmar (Burma) 17°14′N 97°12′E
113 N21 **Bilisht** *var.* Bilishti. Korçë, SE Albania 40°36′N 21°00′E
Bilishti *see* Bilisht
183 N10 **Billabong Creek** *var.* Moulamein Creek. *seasonal river* New South Wales, SE Australia
182 G4 **Billa Kalina** South Australia 29°57′S 136°13′E
197 Q17 **Bill Baileys Bank** *undersea feature* N Atlantic Ocean 60°35′N 10°15′W
Billed/Billéd *see* Biled
153 N14 **Billi** Uttar Pradesh, N India 24°30′N 82°59′E
97 M15 **Billingham** N England, United Kingdom 54°36′N 01°17′W
33 U11 **Billings** Montana, NW USA 45°47′N 108°32′W
95 J16 **Billingsfors** Västra Götaland, S Sweden 58°57′N 12°14′E
Bill of Cape Clear, The *see* Clear, Cape
28 L9 **Billsburg** South Dakota, N USA 44°22′N 101°40′W
95 F23 **Billund** Ribe, W Denmark 55°44′N 09°07′E
36 L11 **Bill Williams Mountain** ▲ Arizona, SW USA 35°12′N 112°12′W
36 I12 **Bill Williams River** ≈ Arizona, SW USA
77 Y8 **Bilma** Agadez, NE Niger 18°22′N 13°01′E
77 Y8 **Bilma, Grand Erg de** *desert* NE Niger
181 Y9 **Biloela** Queensland, E Australia 24°27′S 150°31′E
112 G8 **Bilo Gora** ▲▲ N Croatia
117 U13 **Bilohirs'k** *Rus.* Belogorsk; *prev.* Karasubazar. Respublika Krym, S Ukraine 45°04′N 34°35′E
Bilokurakine *see* Bilokurakyne
117 X5 **Bilokurakyne** *var.* Bilokurakine. Luhans'ka Oblast', E Ukraine 49°32′N 38°44′E
117 T3 **Bilopillya** *Rus.* Belopol'ye. Sums'ka Oblast', NE Ukraine 51°09′N 34°17′E
117 Y6 **Bilovods'k** *Rus.* Belovodsk. Luhans'ka Oblast', E Ukraine 49°11′N 39°34′E
22 M9 **Biloxi** Mississippi, S USA 30°24′N 88°53′W
117 R10 **Bilozerka** Khersons'ka Oblast', S Ukraine 46°36′N 32°23′E
117 W7 **Bilozers'ke** Donets'ka Oblast', E Ukraine 48°29′N 37°03′E
98 J11 **Bilthoven** Utrecht, C Netherlands 52°07′N 05°12′E
78 K9 **Biltine** Biltine, E Chad 14°30′N 20°53′E
78 J9 **Biltine** *off.* Préfecture de Biltine. ◆ *prefecture* E Chad
Biltine, Préfecture de *see* Biltine
Bilüü *see* Ulaanhus
Bilwi *see* Puerto Cabezas
Bilyasuvar *see* Biläsuvar
117 O11 **Bilyayivka** Odes'ka Oblast', SW Ukraine 46°28′N 30°11′E
99 K18 **Bilzen** Limburg, NE Belgium 50°52′N 05°31′E
Bimbéréké *see* Bembèrèkè
183 R10 **Bimberi Peak** ▲ New South Wales, SE Australia 35°42′S 148°46′E
77 Q15 **Bimbila** E Ghana 08°54′N 00°05′E
79 I15 **Bimbo** Ombella-Mpoko, SW Central African Republic 04°19′N 18°27′E
44 F2 **Bimini Islands** *island group* W Bahamas
154 I9 **Bina** Madhya Pradesh, C India 24°09′N 78°10′E
143 T4 **Bīnālūd, Kūh-e** ▲▲ NE Iran
99 F20 **Binche** Hainaut, S Belgium 50°25′N 04°10′E
Bindloe Island *see* Marchena, Isla
83 L16 **Bindura** Mashonaland Central, NE Zimbabwe 17°20′S 31°21′E
105 T5 **Binefar** Aragón, NE Spain 41°51′N 00°17′E
83 J16 **Binga** Matabeleland North, W Zimbabwe 17°40′S 27°22′E
183 T5 **Bingara** New South Wales, SE Australia 29°54′S 150°36′E
101 F18 **Bingen am Rhein** Rheinland-Pfalz, SW Germany 49°58′N 07°54′E
26 M11 **Binger** Oklahoma, C USA 35°19′N 98°19′W
Bingerau *see* Węgrów
Bin Ghalfān, Jazā'ir *see* Ḥalāniyāt, Juzur al
19 Q6 **Bingham** Maine, NE USA 45°01′N 69°51′W
18 H11 **Binghamton** New York, NE USA 42°06′N 75°55′W
Bin Ghanīmah, Jabal *see* Bin Ghunaymah, Jabal
75 P11 **Bin Ghunaymah, Jabal** *var.* Jabal Bin Ghanīmah. ▲▲ C Libya
139 U3 **Bingird** As Sulaymānīyah, NE Iraq 36°03′N 45°03′E
Bingmei *see* Congjiang
137 P14 **Bingöl** Bingöl, E Turkey 38°54′N 40°29′E
137 P14 **Bingöl** ◆ *province* E Turkey
161 R6 **Binhai** *var.* Dongkan. Jiangsu, E China 34°00′N 119°51′E
167 V11 **Binh Đinh** *var.* An Nhon. Binh Đinh, C Vietnam 13°53′N 109°07′E
167 U10 **Binh Sơn** *var.* Châu Ô. Quang Ngai, C Vietnam 15°18′N 108°45′E
Binimani *see* Bintimani
168 I8 **Binjai** Sumatera, W Indonesia 03°37′N 98°30′E
183 R6 **Binnaway** New South Wales, SE Australia 31°34′S 149°24′E
108 E6 **Binningen** Basel-Land, NW Switzerland 47°32′N 07°35′E
80 H12 **Bīnshangul Gumuz** ◆ *federal region* W Ethiopia
168 J8 **Bintang, Banjaran** ▲▲ Peninsular Malaysia
168 M10 **Bintan, Pulau** *island* Kepulauan Riau, W Indonesia
76 J14 **Bintimani** *var.* Binimani. ▲ NE Sierra Leone 09°21′N 11°09′W
Bint Jubayl *see* Bent Jbaïl
169 S9 **Bintulu** Sarawak, East Malaysia 03°12′N 113°01′E
169 S9 **Bintuni** *prev.* Steenkool. Papua, E Indonesia 02°03′S 133°45′E
163 W8 **Binxian** Heilongjiang, NE China 45°44′N 127°28′E
160 K14 **Binyang** *var.* Binzhou. Guangxi Zhuangzu Zizhiqu, S China 23°15′N 108°40′E
161 Q4 **Binzhou** Shandong, E China 37°23′N 118°03′E
Binzhou *see* Binyang
63 G14 **Bío Bío** *var.* Región del Bío Bío. ◆ *region* C Chile
Bío Bío, Región del *see* Bío Bío
63 G14 **Bío Bío, Río** ≈ C Chile
79 C16 **Bioco, Isla de** *var.* Bioko, *Eng.* Fernando Po, *Sp.* Fernando Póo; *prev.* Macías Nguema Biyogo. *island* NW Equatorial Guinea
112 D13 **Biograd na Moru** *It.* Zaravecchia. Zadar, SW Croatia 43°57′N 15°27′E
Bioko *see* Bioco, Isla de
113 F14 **Biokovo** ▲▲ S Croatia
Biorra *see* Birr
Bipontium *see* Zweibrücken
143 W13 **Bīrag, Kūh-e** ▲▲ SE Iran
75 O10 **Birāk** *var.* Brak. C Libya 27°32′N 14°17′E
139 S10 **Bi'r al Islām** Karbalā', C Iraq 32°15′N 43°40′E
154 N11 **Biramitrapur** *var.* Birmitrapur. Orissa, E India 22°24′N 84°42′E
139 T11 **Bi'r an Niṣf** An Najaf, S Iraq 31°22′N 44°07′E
78 L12 **Birao** Vakaga, NE Central African Republic 10°14′N 22°49′E
146 J10 **Birata** *Rus.* Darganata, Dargan-Ata. Lebap Welaýaty, NE Turkmenistan 40°30′N 62°09′E
158 M6 **Biratar Bulak** *well* NW China
153 R12 **Birātnagar** Eastern, SE Nepal 26°28′N 87°16′E
165 R5 **Biratori** Hokkaidō, NE Japan 42°35′N 142°07′E
39 S8 **Birch Creek** Alaska, USA 66°17′N 145°54′W
38 M11 **Birch Creek** ≈ Alaska, USA
11 T14 **Birch Hills** Saskatchewan, S Canada 52°58′N 105°22′W
182 M10 **Birchip** Victoria, SE Australia 36°01′S 142°55′E
29 X4 **Birch Lake** ◎ Minnesota, N USA
11 Q11 **Birch Mountains** ▲ Alberta, W Canada
11 V15 **Birch River** Manitoba, S Canada 52°22′N 101°03′W
44 H12 **Birchs Hill** *hill* W Jamaica
39 R11 **Birchwood** Alaska, USA 61°24′N 149°28′W
188 I5 **Bird Island** *island* S Northern Mariana Islands
137 N16 **Birecik** Şanlıurfa, S Turkey 37°03′N 37°59′E
152 M10 **Birendranagar** *var.* Surkhet. Mid Western, W Nepal 28°35′N 81°36′E
Bir es Saba *see* Be'er Sheva
74 A12 **Bir-Gandouz** SW Western Sahara 21°35′N 16°27′W
153 P12 **Birganj** Central, C Nepal 27°03′N 84°53′E
81 B14 **Biri** ≈ W Sudan
Bi'r Ibn Hirmās *see* Al Bi'r
143 U8 **Bīrjand** Khorāsān-e Janūbī, E Iran 32°54′N 59°14′E
139 T11 **Birkat Ḥāmid** *well* S Iraq
95 F18 **Birkeland** Aust-Agder, S Norway 58°18′N 08°13′E
101 E19 **Birkenfeld** Rheinland-Pfalz, SW Germany 49°39′N 07°10′E
97 K18 **Birkenhead** NW England, United Kingdom 53°24′N 03°02′W
109 W7 **Birkfeld** Steiermark, SE Austria 47°21′N 15°40′E
182 A2 **Birksgate Range** ▲▲ South Australia
Birlad *see* Bârlad
97 K20 **Birmingham** C England, United Kingdom 52°30′N 01°50′W
23 P4 **Birmingham** Alabama, S USA 33°30′N 86°47′W
97 M20 **Birmingham** ✈ C England, United Kingdom 52°27′N 01°46′W
Birmitrapur *see* Biramitrapur
Bir Moghrein *see* Bîr Mogreïn
76 J4 **Bîr Mogreïn** *var.* Bir Moghrein; *prev.* Fort-Trinquet. Tiris Zemmour, N Mauritania 25°10′N 11°35′W
191 S4 **Birnie Island** *atoll* Phoenix Islands, C Kiribati
77 S12 **Birnin Gaouré** *var.* Birni-Ngaouré. Dosso, SW Niger 12°59′N 03°02′E
Birni-Ngaouré *see* Birnin Gaouré
77 S12 **Birnin Kebbi** Kebbi, NW Nigeria 12°28′N 04°08′E
77 T12 **Birnin Konni** *var.* Birni-Nkonni. Tahoua, SW Niger 13°51′N 05°15′E
Birni-Nkonni *see* Birnin Konni
77 W13 **Birnin Kudu** Jigawa, N Nigeria 11°28′N 09°29′E
123 S16 **Birobidzhan** Yevreyskaya Avtonomnaya Oblast', SE Russian Federation 48°42′N 132°55′E
97 D18 **Birr** *var.* Parsonstown, *Ir.* Biorra. C Ireland 53°06′N 07°55′W
183 P4 **Birrie River** ≈ New South Wales/Queensland, SE Australia
108 D7 **Birse** ≈ NW Switzerland
Birsen *see* Biržai
108 E6 **Birsfelden** Basel-Land, NW Switzerland 47°33′N 07°37′E
127 U4 **Birsk** Respublika Bashkortostan, W Russian Federation 55°24′N 55°33′E
119 F14 **Birštonas** Kaunas, C Lithuania 54°37′N 24°00′E
159 P14 **Biru** Xinjiang Uygur Zizhiqu, W China 31°30′N 93°56′E
Biruni *see* Beruniy
122 L12 **Biryusa** ≈ C Russian Federation
122 L12 **Biryusinsk** Irkutskaya Oblast', C Russian Federation 55°52′N 97°48′E
118 G10 **Biržai** *Ger.* Birsen. Panevėžys, NE Lithuania 56°12′N 24°47′E
121 P16 **Birżebbuġa** SE Malta 35°50′N 14°32′E
Bisanthe *see* Tekirdağ
171 R12 **Bisa, Pulau** *island* Maluku, E Indonesia
37 N17 **Bisbee** Arizona, SW USA 31°27′N 109°55′W
29 O2 **Bisbee** North Dakota, N USA 48°36′N 99°21′W
Biscaia, Baía de *see* Biscay, Bay of
102 I13 **Biscarrosse et de Parentis, Étang de** ◎ SW France
104 M1 **Biscay, Bay of** *Sp.* Golfo de Vizcaya, *Port.* Baía de Biscaia. *bay* France/Spain
23 Z16 **Biscayne Bay** *bay* Florida, SE USA
64 M7 **Biscay Plain** *undersea feature* SE Bay of Biscay 07°15′W 45°00′N
107 N17 **Bisceglie** Puglia, SE Italy 41°14′N 16°31′E
Bischoflack *see* Škofja Loka
Bischofsburg *see* Biskupiec
109 Q7 **Bischofshofen** Salzburg, NW Austria 47°25′N 13°13′E
101 P15 **Bischofswerda** Sachsen, E Germany 51°07′N 14°13′E
103 V5 **Bischwiller** Bas-Rhin, NE France 48°46′N 07°52′E
21 T10 **Biscoe** North Carolina, SE USA 35°20′N 79°46′W
194 G5 **Biscoe Islands** *island group* Antarctica
14 E9 **Biscotasi Lake** ◎ Ontario, S Canada
14 E9 **Biscotasing** Ontario, S Canada 47°16′N 82°04′W
54 J6 **Biscucuy** Portuguesa, NW Venezuela 09°22′N 69°59′W
99 M24 **Bissen** Luxembourg, C Luxembourg 49°47′N 06°04′E
114 K11 **Biser** Khaskovo, S Bulgaria 41°52′N 25°59′E
113 D15 **Biševo** *It.* Busi. *island* SW Croatia
141 N12 **Bishah, Wādī** *dry watercourse* C Saudi Arabia
147 U7 **Bishkek** *var.* Pishpek; *prev.* Frunze. ● (Kyrgyzstan) Chuyskaya Oblast', N Kyrgyzstan 42°54′N 74°27′E
147 U7 **Bishkek** ✈ Chuyskaya Oblast', N Kyrgyzstan 42°55′N 74°37′E
153 R16 **Bishnupur** West Bengal, NE India 23°05′N 87°20′E
83 J25 **Bisho** Eastern Cape, S South Africa 32°46′S 27°21′E
35 S9 **Bishop** California, W USA 37°22′N 118°24′W
25 S15 **Bishop** Texas, SW USA 27°36′N 97°49′W
97 L15 **Bishop Auckland** N England, United Kingdom 54°41′N 01°41′W
Bishop's Lynn *see* King's Lynn
97 O21 **Bishop's Stortford** E England, United Kingdom 51°45′N 00°11′E
21 S12 **Bishopville** South Carolina, SE USA 34°18′N 80°15′W
138 M5 **Bishrī, Jabal** ▲▲ E Syria
163 U4 **Bishui** Heilongjiang, NE China 52°06′N 123°42′E
81 G17 **Bisina, Lake** *prev.* Lake Salisbury. ◎ E Uganda
Biskara *see* Biskra
74 L6 **Biskra** *var.* Beskra, Biskara. NE Algeria 34°51′N 05°44′E
110 M8 **Biskupiec** *Ger.* Bischofsburg. Warmińsko-Mazurskie, NE Poland 53°52′N 20°57′E
171 R7 **Bislig** Mindanao, S Philippines 08°10′N 126°19′E
27 X6 **Bismarck** Missouri, C USA 37°46′N 90°37′W
28 M5 **Bismarck** *state capital* North Dakota, N USA 46°49′N 100°47′W
186 D5 **Bismarck Archipelago** *island group* NE Papua New Guinea
129 Z16 **Bismarck Plate** *tectonic feature* W Pacific Ocean
186 D7 **Bismarck Range** ▲▲ N Papua New Guinea
186 E6 **Bismarck Sea** *sea* W Pacific Ocean
137 P15 **Bismil** Dıyarbakır, SE Turkey 37°53′N 40°38′E
43 N6 **Bismuna, Laguna** *lagoon* NE Nicaragua
Bisnulok *see* Phitsanulok
171 R10 **Bisoa, Tanjung** *headland* Pulau Halmahera, N Indonesia 02°15′N 127°57′E
28 K7 **Bison** South Dakota, N USA 45°31′N 102°27′W
93 H17 **Bispgården** Jämtland, C Sweden 63°00′N 16°40′E
76 G13 **Bissau** ● (Guinea-Bissau) W Guinea-Bissau 11°52′N 15°39′W
76 G13 **Bissau** ✈ W Guinea-Bissau 11°53′N 15°41′W
Bissojohka *see* Børselv
76 G12 **Bissorã** W Guinea-Bissau 12°16′N 15°35′W
11 O10 **Bistcho Lake** ◎ Alberta, W Canada
22 G5 **Bistineau, Lake** ▣ Louisiana, S USA
Bistrica *see* Ilirska Bistrica
116 I9 **Bistriţa** *Ger.* Bistritz, *Hung.* Beszterce; *prev.* Nösen. Bistriţa-Năsăud, N Romania 47°10′N 24°31′E
116 K10 **Bistriţa** *Ger.* Bistritz. ≈ NE Romania
116 I9 **Bistriţa-Năsăud** ◆ *county* N Romania
Bistritz *see* Bistriţa
Bistritz ober Pernstein *see* Bystřice nad Pernštejnem
152 L11 **Biswān** Uttar Pradesh, N India 27°30′N 81°00′E
110 M7 **Bisztynek** Warmińsko-Mazurskie, NE Poland 54°05′N 20°53′E
79 E17 **Bitam** Woleu-Ntem, N Gabon 02°05′N 11°30′E
101 D18 **Bitburg** Rheinland-Pfalz, SW Germany 49°58′N 06°31′E
103 U4 **Bitche** Moselle, NE France 49°01′N 07°27′E
78 I11 **Bitkine** Guéra, C Chad 11°59′N 18°13′E
137 R15 **Bitlis** Bitlis, SE Turkey 38°23′N 42°04′E
137 R14 **Bitlis** ◆ *province* E Turkey
Bitoeng *see* Bitung
113 N20 **Bitola** *Turk.* Monastir; *prev.* Bitolj. S FYR Macedonia 41°01′N 21°22′E
Bitolj *see* Bitola
107 O17 **Bitonto** *anc.* Butuntum. Puglia, SE Italy 41°07′N 16°41′E
77 Q13 **Bitou** *var.* Bittou. SE Burkina 11°19′N 00°17′W
155 C20 **Bitra Island** *island* Lakshadweep, India, N Indian Ocean
101 M14 **Bitterfeld** Sachsen-Anhalt, E Germany 51°37′N 12°18′E
32 O9 **Bitterroot Range** ▲▲ Idaho/Montana, NW USA
33 P10 **Bitterroot River** ≈ Montana, NW USA
107 D18 **Bitti** Sardegna, Italy, C Mediterranean Sea 40°30′N 09°31′E
Bittou *see* Bitou
171 Q11 **Bitung** *prev.* Bitoeng. Sulawesi, C Indonesia 01°28′N 125°13′E
60 I12 **Bituruna** Paraná, S Brazil 26°11′S 51°34′W
77 Y13 **Biu** Borno, E Nigeria 10°35′N 12°13′E
Biumba *see* Byumba
164 J13 **Biwa-ko** ◎ Honshū, SW Japan
171 X14 **Biwarlaut** Papua, E Indonesia 05°44′S 138°14′E
27 P10 **Bixby** Oklahoma, C USA 35°56′N 95°52′W
122 J13 **Biya** ≈ S Russian Federation
122 J13 **Biysk** Altayskiy Kray, S Russian Federation 52°34′N 85°09′E
164 H13 **Bizen** Okayama, Honshū, SW Japan 34°45′N 134°10′E
Bizerta *see* Bizerte
120 K10 **Bizerte** *Ar.* Banzart, *Eng.* Bizerta. N Tunisia 37°18′N 09°48′E
Bizkaia *see* Vizcaya
92 G2 **Bjargtangar** *headland* W Iceland 63°30′N 24°29′W
Bjärnå *see* Perniö
95 K22 **Bjärnum** Skåne, S Sweden 56°15′N 13°45′E
93 I16 **Bjästa** Västernorrland, C Sweden 63°12′N 18°30′E
113 I14 **Bjelašnica** ▲▲ SE Bosnia and Herzegovina 43°13′N 18°18′E
112 C10 **Bjelolasica** ▲▲ NW Croatia 45°13′N 14°56′E
112 F8 **Bjelovar** *Hung.* Belovár. Bjelovar-Bilogora, N Croatia 45°54′N 16°49′E
112 F8 **Bjelovar-Bilogora** *off.* Bjelovarsko-Bilogorska Županija. ◆ *province* NE Croatia
Bjelovarsko-Bilogorska Županija *see* Bjelovar-Bilogora
92 H10 **Bjerkvik** Nordland, C Norway 68°31′N 16°08′E
95 G21 **Bjerringbro** Viborg, NW Denmark 56°23′N 09°40′E
Bjeshkët e Namuna *see* North Albanian Alps
95 L14 **Björbo** Dalarna, C Sweden 60°28′N 14°44′E
95 I15 **Bjørkelangen** Akershus, S Norway 59°54′N 11°33′E
95 O14 **Björklinge** Uppsala, C Sweden 60°03′N 17°33′E
93 I14 **Björksele** Västerbotten, N Sweden 64°58′N 18°30′E
93 I16 **Björna** Västernorrland, C Sweden 63°34′N 18°38′E
95 C14 **Bjørnafjorden** *fjord* S Norway
95 L16 **Björneborg** Värmland, C Sweden 59°13′N 14°15′E
Björneborg *see* Pori
95 E14 **Bjornesfjorden** ◎ S Norway
92 M9 **Bjørnevatn** Finnmark, N Norway 69°40′N 29°57′E
197 T13 **Bjørnøya** *Eng.* Bear Island. *island* N Norway
93 I15 **Bjurholm** Västerbotten, N Sweden 63°57′N 19°16′E
95 J22 **Bjuv** Skåne, S Sweden 56°05′N 12°57′E
76 M12 **Bla** Ségou, W Mali 12°58′N 05°45′W
181 W8 **Blackall** Queensland, E Australia 24°26′S 145°32′E
29 V2 **Black Bay** *lake bay* Minnesota, N USA
27 N9 **Black Bear Creek** ≈ Oklahoma, C USA
97 K17 **Blackburn** NW England, United Kingdom 53°45′N 02°29′W
45 W10 **Blackburne** ✈ (Plymouth) E Montserrat 16°45′N 62°09′W
39 T11 **Blackburn, Mount** ▲ Alaska, USA 61°43′N 143°25′W
35 N5 **Black Butte Lake** ▣ California, W USA
194 J5 **Black Coast** *physical region* Antarctica
11 Q16 **Black Diamond** Alberta, SW Canada 50°42′N 114°09′W
18 K11 **Black Dome** ▲ New York, NE USA 42°16′N 74°07′W
113 L18 **Black Drin** *Alb.* Lumi i Drinit të Zi, *SCr.* Crni Drim. ≈ Albania/FYR Macedonia
29 U4 **Blackduck** Minnesota, N USA 47°45′N 94°33′W
12 D6 **Black Duck** ≈ Ontario, C Canada
33 R14 **Blackfoot** Idaho, NW USA 43°11′N 112°20′W
33 P9 **Blackfoot River** ≈ Montana, NW USA
Black Forest *see* Schwarzwald
28 J10 **Blackhawk** South Dakota, N USA 44°09′N 103°18′W
28 I10 **Black Hills** ▲▲ South Dakota/Wyoming, N USA
11 T10 **Black Lake** ◎ Saskatchewan, C Canada
22 G6 **Black Lake** ▣ Louisiana, S USA
31 Q5 **Black Lake** ◎ Michigan, N USA
18 I7 **Black Lake** ◎ New York, NE USA
26 F7 **Black Mesa** ▲ Oklahoma, C USA 37°00′N 103°07′W
21 P10 **Black Mountain** North Carolina, SE USA 35°37′N 82°19′W
35 P13 **Black Mountain** ▲ California, W USA 35°22′N 120°21′W
37 Q2 **Black Mountain** ▲ Colorado, C USA 40°47′N 107°23′W
96 K1 **Black Mountains** ▲▲ SE Wales, United Kingdom
36 H10 **Black Mountains** ▲▲ Arizona, SW USA
21 O7 **Black Mountains** ▲ Kentucky, E USA 36°54′N 82°53′W
33 Q16 **Black Pine Peak** ▲ Idaho, NW USA 42°07′N 113°07′W
97 K17 **Blackpool** NW England, United Kingdom 53°50′N 03°03′W
37 Q14 **Black Range** ▲▲ New Mexico, SW USA
44 I12 **Black River** W Jamaica 18°02′N 77°52′W
14 J14 **Black River** ≈ Ontario, SE Canada
129 U12 **Black River** *Chin.* Babian Jiang, Lixian Jiang, *Fr.* Rivière Noire, *Vtn.* Sông Đa. ≈ China/Vietnam
44 I12 **Black River** ≈ W Jamaica
39 T7 **Black River** ≈ Alaska, USA
37 N13 **Black River** ≈ Arizona, SW USA
27 X7 **Black River** ≈ Arkansas/Missouri, C USA
22 I7 **Black River** ≈ Louisiana, S USA
31 Q5 **Black River** ≈ Michigan, N USA
31 S8 **Black River** ≈ Michigan, N USA
18 I8 **Black River** ≈ New York, NE USA
21 T13 **Black River** ≈ South Carolina, SE USA
30 J7 **Black River** ≈ Wisconsin, N USA
30 J7 **Black River Falls** Wisconsin, N USA 44°18′N 90°51′W
35 R3 **Black Rock Desert** *desert* Nevada, W USA
Black Sand Desert *see* Garagum
21 S7 **Blacksburg** Virginia, NE USA 37°15′N 80°25′W
136 H10 **Black Sea** *var.* Euxine Sea, *Bul.* Cherno More, *Rom.* Marea Neagră, *Rus.* Chernoye More, *Turk.* Karadeniz, *Ukr.* Chorne More. *sea* Asia/Europe
117 Q10 **Black Sea Lowland** *Ukr.* Prychornomor'ska Nyzovyna. *depression* SE Europe
33 S17 **Blacks Fork** ≈ Wyoming, C USA
23 V7 **Blackshear** Georgia, SE USA 31°18′N 82°14′W
23 S6 **Blackshear, Lake** ▣ Georgia, SE USA
97 A16 **Blacksod Bay** *Ir.* Cuan an Fhóid Duibh. *inlet* W Ireland
21 V7 **Blackstone** Virginia, NE USA 37°04′N 78°00′W
77 O14 **Black Volta** *var.* Borongo, Mouhoun, Moun Hou, *Fr.* Volta Noire. ≈ W Africa
23 O5 **Black Warrior River** ≈ Alabama, S USA
181 X8 **Blackwater** Queensland, E Australia 23°34′S 148°51′E
97 D20 **Blackwater** *Ir.* An Abhainn Mhór. ≈ S Ireland
27 T4 **Blackwater River** ≈ Missouri, C USA
21 W7 **Blackwater River** ≈ Virginia, NE USA
Blackwater State *see* Nebraska
27 N8 **Blackwell** Oklahoma, C USA 36°48′N 97°16′W
25 P7 **Blackwell** Texas, SW USA 32°05′N 100°19′W
99 J15 **Bladel** Noord-Brabant, S Netherlands 51°22′N 05°13′E
Bladenmarkt *see* Bălăuşeri
127 O14 **Blagodarnyy** Stavropol'skiy Kray, SW Russian Federation 45°06′N 43°26′E
114 G11 **Blagoevgrad** *prev.* Gorna Dzhumaya. Blagoevgrad, W Bulgaria 42°01′N 23°05′E
114 G11 **Blagoevgrad** ◆ *province* SW Bulgaria
123 Q14 **Blagoveshchensk** Amurskaya Oblast', SE Russian Federation 50°19′N 127°30′E
127 V4 **Blagoveshchensk** Respublika Bashkortostan, W Russian Federation 55°03′N 56°01′E
102 I7 **Blain** Loire-Atlantique, NW France 47°26′N 01°47′W
29 V8 **Blaine** Minnesota, N USA 45°09′N 93°13′W
32 H6 **Blaine** Washington, NW USA 48°59′N 122°45′W
11 T15 **Blaine Lake** Saskatchewan, S Canada 52°49′N 106°48′W
29 S14 **Blair** Nebraska, C USA 41°32′N 96°07′W
96 J10 **Blairgowrie** C Scotland, United Kingdom 56°19′N 03°25′W
18 C15 **Blairsville** Pennsylvania, NE USA 40°25′N 79°12′W
116 H11 **Blaj** *Ger.* Blasendorf, *Hung.* Balázsfalva. Alba, SW Romania 46°10′N 23°57′E
64 F9 **Blake-Bahama Ridge** *undersea feature* W Atlantic Ocean 29°00′N 73°30′W
23 S7 **Blakely** Georgia, SE USA 31°22′N 84°55′W
64 E10 **Blake Plateau** *var.* Blake Terrace. *undersea feature* W Atlantic Ocean 31°00′N 79°00′W
30 M1 **Blake Point** *headland* Michigan, N USA 48°11′N 88°25′W
Blake Terrace *see* Blake Plateau
61 B24 **Blanca, Bahía** *bay* E Argentina
56 C12 **Blanca, Cordillera** ▲▲ W Peru
105 T12 **Blanca, Costa** *physical region* SE Spain
37 S7 **Blanca Peak** ▲ Colorado, C USA 37°34′N 105°29′W
24 I9 **Blanca, Sierra** ▲ Texas, SW USA 31°15′N 105°26′W
120 K9 **Blanc, Cap** *headland* N Tunisia 37°20′N 09°41′E
Blanc, Cap *see* Nouâdhibou, Râs
31 R12 **Blanchard River** ≈ Ohio, N USA
182 E8 **Blanche, Cape** *headland* South Australia 33°03′S 134°10′E
182 J4 **Blanche, Lake** ◎ South Australia
31 R14 **Blanchester** Ohio, N USA 39°17′N 83°59′W
182 J9 **Blanchetown** South Australia 34°21′S 139°36′E
45 U13 **Blanchisseuse** Trinidad, Trinidad and Tobago 10°47′N 61°18′W
103 T11 **Blanc, Mont** *It.* Monte Bianco. ▲ France/Italy 45°45′N 06°51′E
25 R11 **Blanco** Texas, SW USA 30°06′N 98°25′W
42 K14 **Blanco, Cabo** *headland* NW Costa Rica 09°34′N 85°06′W
32 D14 **Blanco, Cape** *headland* Oregon, NW USA 42°49′N 124°33′W
62 H10 **Blanco, Río** ≈ W Argentina
56 F10 **Blanco, Río** ≈ NE Peru
15 O9 **Blanc, Réservoir** ▣ Québec, SE Canada
21 R7 **Bland** Virginia, NE USA 37°06′N 81°08′W
92 I2 **Blanda** ≈ N Iceland
37 O7 **Blanding** Utah, W USA 37°37′N 109°28′W
105 X5 **Blanes** Cataluña, NE Spain 41°41′N 02°48′E
103 N3 **Blangy-sur-Bresle** Seine-Maritime, N France 49°55′N 01°37′E
111 C18 **Blanice** *Ger.* Blanitz. ≈ SE Czech Republic
Blanitz *see* Blanice
99 C16 **Blankenberge** West-Vlaanderen, NW Belgium 51°19′N 03°08′E
101 D17 **Blankenheim** Nordrhein-Westfalen, W Germany 50°26′N 06°41′E
25 R8 **Blanket** Texas, SW USA 31°49′N 98°47′W
55 O3 **Blanquilla, Isla** *var.* La Blanquilla. *island* N Venezuela
Blanquilla, La *see* Blanquilla, Isla
61 F18 **Blanquillo** Durazno, C Uruguay 32°53′S 55°37′W
111 G18 **Blansko** *Ger.* Blanz. Jihomoravský Kraj, SE Czech Republic 49°22′N 16°39′E
83 N15 **Blantyre** *var.* Blantyre-Limbe. Southern, S Malawi 15°45′S 35°04′E
83 N15 **Blantyre** ✈ Southern, S Malawi 15°34′S 35°03′E
Blantyre-Limbe *see* Blantyre
Blanz *see* Blansko
98 J10 **Blaricum** Noord-Holland, C Netherlands 52°16′N 05°15′E
Blasendorf *see* Blaj
Blatnitsa *see* Durankulak
113 F15 **Blato** *It.* Blatta. Dubrovnik-Neretva, S Croatia 42°57′N 16°47′E
Blatta *see* Blato
108 E10 **Blatten** Valais, SW Switzerland 46°22′N 08°00′E
101 J20 **Blaufelden** Baden-Württemberg, SW Germany 49°21′N 10°01′E
95 E23 **Blåvands Huk** *headland* W Denmark 55°33′N 08°04′E
102 G6 **Blavet** ≈ NW France
102 J12 **Blaye** Gironde, SW France 45°08′N 00°40′W
183 R8 **Blayney** New South Wales, SE Australia 33°33′S 149°13′E
65 D25 **Bleaker Island** *island* SE Falkland Islands
109 T10 **Bled** *Ger.* Veldes. NW Slovenia 46°23′N 14°06′E
99 D20 **Bléharies** Hainaut, SW Belgium 50°31′N 03°25′E
109 U9 **Bleiburg** *Slvn.* Pliberk. Kärnten, S Austria 46°36′N 14°49′E
101 L17 **Bleiloch-stausee** ▣ C Germany
98 H12 **Bleiswijk** Zuid-Holland, W Netherlands 52°01′N 04°32′E
95 L22 **Blekinge** ◆ *county* S Sweden
14 D17 **Blenheim** Ontario, S Canada 42°20′N 81°59′W
185 K15 **Blenheim** Marlborough, South Island, New Zealand 41°32′S 174°E
99 M15 **Blerick** Limburg, SE Netherlands 51°22′N 06°10′E
Blesae *see* Blois
25 V13 **Blessing** Texas, SW USA 28°52′N 96°12′W
14 I10 **Bleu, Lac** ◎ Québec, SE Canada
Blibba *see* Blitta
120 H10 **Blida** *var.* El Boulaida, El Boulaïda. N Algeria 36°30′N 02°50′E
95 P15 **Blidö** Stockholm, C Sweden 59°37′N 18°55′E
95 K18 **Blidsberg** Västra Götaland, S Sweden 57°55′N 13°30′E
185 A21 **Bligh Sound** *sound* South Island, New Zealand
187 X14 **Bligh Water** *strait* NW Fiji
14 D11 **Blind River** Ontario, S Canada 46°12′N 82°59′W
31 R11 **Blissfield** Michigan, N USA 41°49′N 83°51′W
77 R15 **Blitta** *prev.* Blibba. C Togo 08°19′N 00°59′E
19 O13 **Block Island** *island* Rhode Island, NE USA
19 O13 **Block Island Sound** *sound* Rhode Island, NE USA
98 H10 **Bloemendaal** Noord-Holland, W Netherlands 52°23′N 04°39′E
83 H23 **Bloemfontein** *var.* Mangaung. ● (South Africa-judicial capital) Free State, C South Africa 29°07′S 26°14′E
83 I22 **Bloemhof** North-West, NW South Africa 27°39′S 25°37′E
102 M7 **Blois** *anc.* Blesae. Loir-et-Cher, C France 47°36′N 01°20′E
98 L8 **Blokzijl** Overijssel, N Netherlands 52°46′N 05°58′E
95 N20 **Blomstermåla** Kalmar, S Sweden 56°58′N 16°19′E
92 I2 **Blönduós** Nordhurland Vestra, N Iceland 65°39′N 20°15′W
110 L11 **Błonie** Mazowieckie, C Poland 52°13′N 20°36′E
97 C14 **Bloody Foreland** *Ir.* Cnoc Fola. *headland* NW Ireland 55°09′N 08°18′W
31 N15 **Bloomfield** Indiana, N USA 39°01′N 86°58′W
29 X16 **Bloomfield** Iowa, C USA 40°45′N 92°24′W
27 Y8 **Bloomfield** Missouri, C USA 36°54′N 89°58′W
37 P9 **Bloomfield** New Mexico, SW USA 36°42′N 108°00′W
25 U7 **Blooming Grove** Texas, SW USA 32°05′N 96°43′W
29 W10 **Blooming Prairie** Minnesota, N USA 43°52′N 93°03′W
30 L13 **Bloomington** Illinois, N USA 40°28′N 88°59′W
31 O15 **Bloomington** Indiana, N USA 39°10′N 86°31′W
29 V9 **Bloomington** Minnesota, N USA 44°50′N 93°18′W
25 U13 **Bloomington** Texas, SW USA 28°39′N 96°53′W
18 H14 **Bloomsburg** Pennsylvania, NE USA 40°59′N 76°27′W
181 X7 **Bloomsbury** Queensland, NE Australia 20°47′S 148°35′E
169 R16 **Blora** Jawa, C Indonesia 06°55′S 111°29′E
18 G12 **Blossburg** Pennsylvania, NE USA 41°38′N 77°00′W
25 V5 **Blossom** Texas, SW USA 33°39′N 95°23′W
123 T5 **Blossom, Mys** *headland* Ostrov Vrangelya, NE Russian Federation 70°49′N 178°49′E
23 R8 **Blountstown** Florida, SE USA 30°26′N 85°03′W
21 P8 **Blountville** Tennessee, S USA 36°31′N 82°19′W
21 Q9 **Blowing Rock** North Carolina, SE USA 36°15′N 81°53′W
108 J8 **Bludenz** Vorarlberg, W Austria 47°10′N 09°50′E
36 L6 **Blue Bell Knoll** ▲ Utah, W USA 38°11′N 111°31′W
23 Y12 **Blue Cypress Lake** ◎ Florida, SE USA
29 U11 **Blue Earth** Minnesota, N USA 43°38′N 94°06′W
21 Q7 **Bluefield** Virginia, NE USA 37°15′N 81°16′W
21 R7 **Bluefield** West Virginia, NE USA 37°16′N 81°13′W
43 N10 **Bluefields** Región Autónoma Atlántico Sur, SE Nicaragua 12°01′N 83°47′W
43 N10 **Bluefields, Bahía de** *bay* W Caribbean Sea
29 Z14 **Blue Grass** Iowa, C USA 41°30′N 90°46′W
Bluegrass State *see* Kentucky
Blue Hen State *see* Delaware
19 S7 **Blue Hill** Maine, NE USA 44°25′N 68°36′W
29 P16 **Blue Hill** Nebraska, C USA 40°19′N 98°27′W
30 J5 **Blue Hills** *hill range* Wisconsin, N USA
34 L3 **Blue Lake** California, W USA 40°52′N 124°00′W
Blue Law State *see* Connecticut
37 Q6 **Blue Mesa Reservoir** ▣ Colorado, C USA
27 S12 **Blue Mountain** ▲ Arkansas, C USA 34°42′N 94°04′W
19 O6 **Blue Mountain** ▲ New Hampshire, NE USA 44°48′N 71°26′W
18 K8 **Blue Mountain** ▲ New York, NE USA 43°52′N 74°24′W

◆ Country ● Country Capital ◇ Dependent Territory ○ Dependent Territory Capital ◆ Administrative Regions ✈ International Airport ▲ Mountain ▲▲ Mountain Range ⛰ Volcano ≈ River ◎ Lake ▣ Reservoir

BLUE MOUNTAIN – BORBA

18 H15 **Blue Mountain** *ridge* Pennsylvania, NE USA
44 H10 **Blue Mountain Peak** ▲ E Jamaica 18°02′N 76°34′W
183 S8 **Blue Mountains** ▲▲ New South Wales, SE Australia
32 L11 **Blue Mountains** ▲▲ Oregon/ Washington, NW USA
80 G12 **Blue Nile** ◈ *state* E Sudan
80 H12 **Blue Nile** *var.* Abai, Bahr el, Azraq, *Amh.* Ābay Wenz, *Ar.* An Nīl al Azraq. ≈ Ethiopia/ Sudan
8 J7 **Bluenose Lake** ◎ Nunavut, NW Canada
27 O3 **Blue Rapids** Kansas, C USA 39°39′N 96°38′W
23 S1 **Blue Ridge** Georgia, SE USA 34°51′N 84°19′W
17 S11 **Blue Ridge** *var.* Blue Ridge Mountains. ▲▲ North Carolina/Virginia, USA
23 S1 **Blue Ridge Lake** ▣ Georgia, SE USA
Blue Ridge Mountains *see* Blue Ridge
11 N15 **Blue River** British Columbia, SW Canada 52°03′N 119°21′W
27 O12 **Blue River** ≈ Oklahoma, C USA
27 R4 **Blue Springs** Missouri, C USA 39°01′N 94°16′W
21 R6 **Bluestone Lake** ▣ West Virginia, NE USA
185 C25 **Bluff** Southland, South Island, New Zealand 46°36′S 168°22′E
37 O8 **Bluff** Utah, W USA 37°15′N 109°36′W
21 P8 **Bluff City** Tennessee, S USA 36°28′N 82°15′W
65 E24 **Bluff Cove** East Falkland, Falkland Islands 51°45′S 58°11′W
25 S7 **Bluff Dale** Texas, SW USA 32°18′N 98°01′W
183 N15 **Bluff Hill Point** *headland* Tasmania, SE Australia 41°03′S 144°35′E
31 Q12 **Bluffton** Indiana, N USA 40°44′N 85°10′W
31 R12 **Bluffton** Ohio, N USA 40°54′N 83°53′W
25 T7 **Blum** Texas, SW USA 32°08′N 97°24′W
101 G24 **Blumberg** Baden-Württemberg, SW Germany 47°48′N 08°31′E
60 K13 **Blumenau** Santa Catarina, S Brazil 26°55′S 49°07′W
29 N9 **Blunt** South Dakota, N USA 44°30′N 99°58′E
32 H15 **Bly** Oregon, NW USA 42°22′N 121°04′W
39 R13 **Blying Sound** *sound* Alaska, USA
97 M14 **Blyth** N England, United Kingdom 55°07′N 01°30′W
35 Y16 **Blythe** California, W USA 33°35′N 114°36′W
27 Y9 **Blytheville** Arkansas, C USA 35°56′N 89°55′W
117 V7 **Blyznyuky** Kharkivs'ka Oblast', E Ukraine 48°51′N 36°32′E
95 G16 **Bø** Telemark, S Norway 59°24′N 09°04′E
76 I15 **Bo** S Sierra Leone 07°58′N 11°45′W
171 O4 **Boac** Marinduque, N Philippines 13°26′N 121°50′E
42 K10 **Boaco** Boaco, S Nicaragua 12°28′N 85°45′W
42 J10 **Boaco** ◈ *department* C Nicaragua
79 I15 **Boali** Ombella-Mpoko, SW Central African Republic 04°52′N 18°00′E
Boalsert *see* Bolsward
31 V12 **Boardman** Ohio, N USA 41°01′N 80°39′W
32 J11 **Boardman** Oregon, NW USA 45°50′N 119°42′W
14 F13 **Boat Lake** ◎ Ontario, S Canada
58 F10 **Boa Vista** *state capital* Roraima, NW Brazil 02°51′N 60°43′W
76 D9 **Boa Vista** *island* Ilhas de Barlavento, E Cape Verde
23 Q2 **Boaz** Alabama, S USA 34°12′N 86°10′W
160 L15 **Bobai** Guangxi Zhuangzu Zizhiqu, S China 22°09′N 109°57′E
172 J1 **Bobaomby, Tanjona** *Fr.* Cap d'Ambre. *headland* N Madagascar 11°58′S 49°13′E
155 M14 **Bobbili** Andhra Pradesh, E India 18°32′N 83°29′E
106 D9 **Bobbio** Emilia-Romagna, C Italy 44°48′N 09°27′E
14 I14 **Bobcaygeon** Ontario, SE Canada 44°32′N 78°33′W
Bober *see* Bóbr
103 O5 **Bobigny** Seine-St-Denis, N France 48°55′N 02°27′E
77 N13 **Bobo-Dioulasso** SW Burkina 11°12′N 04°21′W
110 G8 **Bobolice** *Ger.* Bublitz. Zachodnio-pomorskie, NW Poland 53°56′N 16°37′E
83 J19 **Bobonong** Central, E Botswana 21°58′S 28°26′E
171 R11 **Bobopayo** Pulau Halmahera, E Indonesia 01°07′N 127°26′E
113 J15 **Bobotov Kuk** ▲ N Montenegro 43°06′N 19°00′E
114 G10 **Bobovdol** Kyustendil, W Bulgaria 42°21′N 22°59′E
119 M15 **Bobr** Minskaya Voblasts', NW Belarus 54°20′N 29°16′E
119 M15 **Bobr** ≈ C Belarus
111 E14 **Bóbr** *Eng.* Bobrawa, *Ger.* Bober. ≈ SW Poland
Bobrawa *see* Bóbr
Bobrik *see* Bobryk
Bobrinets *see* Bobrynets'
Bobrka/Bóbrka *see* Bibrka
126 L8 **Bobrov** Voronezhskaya Oblast', W Russian Federation 51°10′N 40°03′E
117 Q4 **Bobrovytsya** Chernihivs'ka Oblast', N Ukraine 50°43′N 31°24′E
Bobruysk *see* Babruysk
119 J19 **Bobryk** *Rus.* Bobrik. ≈ SW Belarus
117 Q8 **Bobrynets'** *Rus.* Bobrinets. Kirovohrads'ka Oblast', C Ukraine 48°02′N 32°10′E
14 K14 **Bobs Lake** ◎ Ontario, SE Canada
54 I6 **Bobures** Zulia, NW Venezuela 09°15′N 71°10′W
42 H1 **Boca Bacalar Chico** *headland* N Belize 15°05′N 82°12′W
112 G11 **Bočac** ◈ Republika Srpska, NW Bosnia and Herzegovina
41 R14 **Boca del Río** Veracruz-Llave, S Mexico 19°08′N 96°08′W
55 O4 **Boca de Pozo** Nueva Esparta, NE Venezuela 11°00′N 64°23′W
59 C15 **Boca do Acre** Amazonas, N Brazil 08°45′S 67°23′W
55 N12 **Boca Mavaca** Amazonas, S Venezuela 02°30′N 65°11′W
79 G14 **Bocaranga** Ouham-Pendé, W Central African Republic 07°07′N 15°40′E
23 Z15 **Boca Raton** Florida, SE USA 26°22′N 80°05′W
43 P14 **Bocas del Toro** Bocas del Toro, NW Panama 09°20′N 82°15′W
43 P15 **Bocas del Toro** *off.* Provincia de Bocas del Toro. ◈ *province* NW Panama
43 P15 **Bocas del Toro, Archipiélago de** *island group* NW Panama
Bocas del Toro, Provincia de *see* Bocas del Toro
42 L7 **Bocay** Jinotega, N Nicaragua 14°19′N 85°08′W
105 N6 **Boceguillas** Castilla-León, N Spain 41°20′N 03°39′W
Bocheykovo *see* Bacheykava
111 L17 **Bochnia** Małopolskie, SE Poland 49°58′N 20°27′E
99 K16 **Bocholt** Limburg, NE Belgium 51°10′N 05°37′E
101 D14 **Bocholt** Nordrhein-Westfalen, W Germany 51°50′N 06°37′E
101 E15 **Bochum** Nordrhein-Westfalen, W Germany 51°29′N 07°13′E
103 Y15 **Bocognano** Corse, France, C Mediterranean Sea 42°04′N 09°03′E
54 I6 **Boconó** Trujillo, NW Venezuela 09°17′N 70°17′W
116 F12 **Bocşa** *Ger.* Bokschen, *Hung.* Boksánbánya. Caraş-Severin, SW Romania 45°23′N 21°47′E
79 H15 **Boda** Lobaye, SW Central African Republic 04°17′N 17°25′E
94 L12 **Boda** Dalarna, C Sweden 61°00′N 15°15′E
95 O20 **Böda** Kalmar, S Sweden 57°16′N 17°04′E
95 L19 **Bodafors** Jönköping, S Sweden 57°30′N 14°40′E
123 O12 **Bodaybo** Irkutskaya Oblast', E Russian Federation 57°52′N 114°05′E
22 G5 **Bodcau, Bayou** *var.* Bodcau Creek. ≈ Louisiana, S USA
Bodcau Creek *see* Bodcau, Bayou
44 D8 **Bodden Town** *var.* Boddentown. Grand Cayman, SW Cayman Islands 19°20′N 81°14′W
Boddentown *see* Bodden Town
101 K14 **Bode** ≈ C Germany
34 L7 **Bodega Head** *headland* California, W USA 38°16′N 123°04′W
Bodegas *see* Babahoyo
98 H11 **Bodegraven** Zuid-Holland, C Netherlands 52°05′N 04°45′E
78 H8 **Bodélé** *depression* W Chad
92 J13 **Boden** Norrbotten, N Sweden 65°50′N 21°44′E
Bodensee *see* Constance, Lake, C Europe
65 M15 **Bode Verde Fracture Zone** *tectonic feature* E Atlantic Ocean
155 H14 **Bodhan** Andhra Pradesh, C India 18°40′N 77°51′E
Bodī *see* Jinst
155 H22 **Bodināyakkanūr** Tamil Nādu, SE India 10°02′N 77°18′E
108 H10 **Bodio** Ticino, S Switzerland 46°23′N 08°55′E
Bodjonegoro *see* Bojonegoro
97 I24 **Bodmin** SW England, United Kingdom 50°29′N 04°43′W
97 I24 **Bodmin Moor** *moorland* SW England, United Kingdom
92 G12 **Bodø** Nordland, C Norway 67°17′N 14°22′E
59 H20 **Bodoquena, Serra da** ▲▲ SW Brazil
136 B16 **Bodrum** Muğla, SW Turkey 37°01′N 27°28′E
Bodzafordulő *see* Întorsura Buzăului
99 L14 **Boekel** Noord-Brabant, SE Netherlands 51°35′N 05°42′E
Boeloekoemba *see* Bulukumba
103 Q11 **Boën** Loire, E France 45°45′N 04°01′E
79 K18 **Boende** Equateur, C Dem. Rep. Congo 0°12′S 20°54′E
25 R11 **Boerne** Texas, SW USA 29°47′N 98°44′W
Boeroe *see* Buru, Pulau
Boetoeng *see* Buton, Pulau
22 I5 **Boeuf River** ≈ Arkansas/ Louisiana, S USA
76 H14 **Boffa** W Guinea 10°12′N 14°02′W
Bó Finne, Inis *see* Inishbofin
Boga *see* Bogë
166 L9 **Bogale** Ayeyarwady, SW Myanmar (Burma) 16°16′N 95°21′E
22 L8 **Bogalusa** Louisiana, S USA 30°47′N 89°51′W
77 Q12 **Bogandé** C Burkina 13°02′N 00°08′W
79 I15 **Bogangolo** Ombella-Mpoko, C Central African Republic 05°36′N 18°17′E
183 Q7 **Bogan River** ≈ New South Wales, SE Australia
25 W5 **Bogata** Texas, SW USA 33°28′N 95°12′W
111 D14 **Bogatynia** *Ger.* Reichenau. Dolnośląskie, SW Poland 50°53′N 14°55′E
136 K13 **Boğazlıyan** Yozgat, C Turkey 39°13′N 35°17′E
79 J17 **Bogbonga** Equateur, NW Dem. Rep. Congo 01°36′N 19°24′E
158 J14 **Bogcang Zangbo** ≈ W China
162 I9 **Bogd** *var.* Horiult. Bayanhongor, C Mongolia 45°09′N 100°50′E
162 J10 **Bogd** *var.* Hovd. Övörhangay, C Mongolia 44°43′N 102°08′E
158 L5 **Bogda Feng** ▲ NW China 43°51′N 88°14′E
114 I9 **Bogdan** ▲ C Bulgaria 42°37′N 24°28′E
113 Q20 **Bogdanci** SE FYR Macedonia 41°12′N 22°34′E
158 M5 **Bogda Shan** *var.* Po-ko-to Shan. ▲▲ NW China
113 K17 **Bogë** *var.* Boga. Shkodër, N Albania 42°25′N 19°38′E
Bogeda'er *see* Wenquan
Bogendorf *see* Łuków
95 G23 **Bogense** Fyn, C Denmark 55°34′N 10°06′E
183 T3 **Boggabilla** New South Wales, SE Australia 28°37′S 150°21′E
183 S6 **Boggabri** New South Wales, SE Australia 30°44′S 150°00′E
186 D6 **Bogia** Madang, N Papua New Guinea 04°16′S 144°56′E
97 N23 **Bognor Regis** SE England, United Kingdom 50°47′N 00°41′W
Bogodukhov *see* Bohodukhiv
181 V15 **Bogong, Mount** ▲ Victoria, SE Australia 36°43′S 147°19′E
169 O16 **Bogor** *Dut.* Buitenzorg. Jawa, C Indonesia 06°34′S 106°45′E
126 L5 **Bogoroditsk** Tul'skaya Oblast', W Russian Federation 53°46′N 38°09′E
127 O3 **Bogorodsk** Nizhegorodskaya Oblast', W Russian Federation 56°06′N 43°29′E
Bogorodskoje *see* Bogorodskoye
123 S12 **Bogorodskoye** Khabarovskiy Kray, SE Russian Federation 52°22′N 140°33′E
125 R15 **Bogorodskoye** *var.* Bogorodskoje. Kirovskaya Oblast', NW Russian Federation 57°50′N 50°41′E
54 F10 **Bogotá** *prev.* Santa Fe, Santa Fe de Bogotá. ● (Colombia) Cundinamarca, C Colombia 04°38′N 74°05′W
153 T14 **Bogra** Rajshahi, N Bangladesh 24°52′N 89°28′E
Bogschan *see* Boldu
122 L12 **Boguchany** Krasnoyarskiy Kray, C Russian Federation 58°20′N 97°20′E
126 M9 **Boguchar** Voronezhskaya Oblast', W Russian Federation 49°57′N 40°34′E
76 H10 **Bogué** Brakna, SW Mauritania 16°36′N 14°15′W
22 K8 **Bogue Chitto** ≈ Louisiana/ Mississippi, S USA
Bogushëvsk *see* Bahushewsk
Boguslav *see* Bohuslav
44 K12 **Bog Walk** C Jamaica 18°06′N 77°01′W
161 Q3 **Bo Hai** *var.* Gulf of Chihli. *gulf* NE China
161 R3 **Bohai Haixia** *strait* NE China
161 Q3 **Bohai Wan** *bay* NE China
111 C17 **Bohemia** *Cz.* Čechy, *Ger.* Böhmen. W Czech Republic
111 B18 **Bohemian Forest** *Cz.* Ceský Les, Šumava, *Ger.* Böhmerwald. ▲▲ C Europe
Bohemian-Moravian Highlands *see* Českomoravská Vrchovina
77 R16 **Bohicon** S Benin 07°14′N 02°04′E
109 S11 **Bohinjska Bistrica** *Ger.* Wocheiner Feistritz. NW Slovenia 46°16′N 13°55′E
Bohkká *see* Pokka
Böhmen *see* Bohemia
Böhmerwald *see* Bohemian Forest
Böhmisch-Krumau *see* Český Krumlov
Böhmisch-Leipa *see* Česká Lípa
Böhmisch-Mährische Höhe *see* Českomoravská Vrchovina
Böhmisch-Trübau *see* Česká Třebová
117 U5 **Bohodukhiv** *Rus.* Bogodukhov. Kharkivs'ka Oblast', E Ukraine 50°10′N 35°32′E
171 Q6 **Bohol** *island* C Philippines
171 Q7 **Bohol Sea** *var.* Mindanao Sea. *sea* S Philippines
116 I7 **Bohorodchany** Ivano-Frankivs'ka Oblast', W Ukraine 48°46′N 24°31′E
Böhöt *see* Öndörshil
158 K6 **Bohu** *var.* Bagrax. Xinjiang Uygur Zizhiqu, NW China 42°00′N 86°28′E
111 I17 **Bohumín** *Ger.* Oderberg; *prev.* Neuoderberg, Nový Bohumín. Moravskoslezský Kraj, E Czech Republic 49°55′N 18°20′E
117 P6 **Bohuslav** *Rus.* Boguslav. Kyyivs'ka Oblast', N Ukraine 49°33′N 30°53′E
58 F11 **Boiaçu** Roraima, N Brazil 0°27′S 61°46′W
107 K16 **Boiano** Molise, C Italy 41°28′N 14°28′E
15 R8 **Boilleau** Québec, SE Canada 48°06′N 70°49′W
59 O17 **Boipeba, Ilha de** *island* SE Brazil
104 G3 **Boiro** Galicia, NW Spain 42°39′N 08°53′W
31 Q5 **Bois Blanc Island** *island* Michigan, N USA
29 R7 **Bois de Sioux River** ≈ Minnesota, N USA
33 N14 **Boise** *var.* Boise City. *state capital* Idaho, NW USA 43°39′N 116°14′W
26 G8 **Boise City** Oklahoma, C USA 36°44′N 102°31′W
Boise City *see* Boise
33 N14 **Boise River, Middle Fork** ≈ Idaho, NW USA
Bois, Lac des *see* Woods, Lake of the
Bois-le-Duc *see* 's-Hertogenbosch
11 W17 **Boissevain** Manitoba, S Canada 49°14′N 100°02′W
15 T7 **Boisvert, Pointe au** *headland* Québec, SE Canada 48°34′N 69°07′W
100 K10 **Boizenburg** Mecklenburg-Vorpommern, N Germany 53°23′N 10°43′E
Bojador *see* Boujdour
113 K18 **Bojana** *Alb.* Bunë. ≈ Albania/Montenegro *see also* Bunë
Bojana *see* Bunë
143 S3 **Bojnūrd** *var.* Bujnurd. Khorāsān-e Shemālī, N Iran 37°31′N 57°24′E
169 R16 **Bojonegoro** *prev.* Bodjonegoro. Jawa, C Indonesia 07°06′S 111°50′E
189 T1 **Bokaak Atoll** *var.* Bokak, Taongi. *atoll* Ratak Chain, NE Marshall Islands
Bokak *see* Bokaak Atoll
146 K8 **Bo'kantov Tog'lari** *Rus.* Gory Bukantau. ▲▲ N Uzbekistan
153 Q15 **Bokāro** Jhārkhand, N India 23°46′N 85°55′E
79 I18 **Bokatola** Equateur, NW Dem. Rep. Congo 0°37′S 18°45′E
76 H13 **Boké** W Guinea 10°56′N 14°18′W
Bokhara *see* Buxoro
183 Q4 **Bokharra River** ≈ New South Wales/Queensland, SE Australia
95 C16 **Boknafjorden** *fjord* S Norway
78 H11 **Bokoro** Chari-Baguirmi, W Chad 12°23′N 17°03′E
79 K19 **Bokota** Equateur, NW Dem. Rep. Congo 0°56′S 22°24′E
167 N13 **Bokpyin** Tanintharyi, S Myanmar (Burma) 11°16′N 98°47′E
Boksánbánya/Bokschen *see* Bocşa
124 I13 **Boksitogorsk** Leningradskaya Oblast', NW Russian Federation 59°27′N 33°51′E
83 F21 **Bokspits** Kgalagadi, SW Botswana 26°50′S 20°41′E
79 K18 **Bokungu** Equateur, C Dem. Rep. Congo 0°41′S 22°19′E
146 F12 **Bokurdak** *Rus.* Bakhardok. Ahal Welaýaty, C Turkmenistan 38°51′N 58°34′E
78 G10 **Bol** Lac, W Chad 13°27′N 14°40′E
76 G13 **Bolama** SW Guinea-Bissau 11°35′N 15°30′W
Bolangir *see* Balāngīr
Bolanos *see* Bolanos, Mount, Guam
Bolaños *see* Bolaños de Calatrava, Spain
105 N11 **Bolaños de Calatrava** *var.* Bolaños. Castilla-La Mancha, C Spain 38°55′N 03°39′W
188 B17 **Bolanos, Mount** *var.* Bolanos. ▲ S Guam 13°18′N 144°41′E
40 L12 **Bolaños, Río** ≈ C Mexico
115 M14 **Bolayır** Çanakkale, NW Turkey 40°31′N 26°46′E
102 L3 **Bolbec** Seine-Maritime, N France 49°34′N 00°31′E
116 L13 **Boldu** *var.* Bogschan. Buzău, SE Romania 45°18′N 27°15′E
146 H8 **Boldumsaz** *prev.* Kalinin, Kalininsk, Porsy. Daşoguz Welaýaty, N Turkmenistan 42°12′N 59°33′E
158 I4 **Bole** *var.* Bortala. Xinjiang Uygur Zizhiqu, NW China 44°52′N 82°06′E
77 O15 **Bole** NW Ghana 09°02′N 02°29′W
79 J19 **Boleko** Equateur, W Dem. Rep. Congo 01°27′S 19°52′E
111 E14 **Bolesławiec** *Ger.* Bunzlau. Dolnośląskie, SW Poland 51°16′N 15°34′E
127 R4 **Bolgar** *prev.* Kuybyshev. Respublika Tatarstan, W Russian Federation 54°58′N 49°03′E
77 P14 **Bolgatanga** N Ghana 10°45′N 00°52′W
Bolgrad *see* Bolhrad
117 N12 **Bolhrad** *Rus.* Bolgrad. Odes'ka Oblast', SW Ukraine 45°42′N 28°35′E
163 Y8 **Boli** Heilongjiang, NE China 45°45′N 130°32′E
79 I19 **Bolia** Bandundu, W Dem. Rep. Congo 01°34′S 18°24′E
93 J14 **Boliden** Västerbotten, N Sweden 64°52′N 20°20′E
171 T13 **Bolifar** Pulau Seram, E Indonesia 03°08′S 130°34′E
171 N2 **Bolinao** Luzon, N Philippines 16°22′N 119°52′E
54 C12 **Bolívar** Cauca, SW Colombia 01°52′N 76°56′W
27 T6 **Bolivar** Missouri, C USA 37°37′N 93°25′W
20 F10 **Bolivar** Tennessee, S USA 35°17′N 88°59′W
54 F7 **Bolívar** *off.* Departmento de Bolívar. ◈ *province* N Colombia
56 A13 **Bolívar** ◈ *province* C Ecuador
55 N9 **Bolívar** *off.* Estado Bolívar. ◈ *state* SE Venezuela
Bolívar, Departmento de *see* Bolívar
Bolívar, Estado *see* Bolívar
25 X12 **Bolivar Peninsula** *headland* Texas, SW USA 29°26′N 94°41′W
54 I6 **Bolívar, Pico** ▲ W Venezuela 08°33′N 71°05′W
57 K17 **Bolivia** *off.* Republic of Bolivia. ◆ *republic* W South America
Bolivia, Republic of *see* Bolivia
112 O13 **Boljevac** Serbia, E Serbia 43°50′N 21°57′E
Bolkenhain *see* Bolków
126 J5 **Bolkhov** Orlovskaya Oblast', W Russian Federation 53°28′N 36°00′E
111 F14 **Bolków** *Ger.* Bolkenhain. Dolnośląskie, SW Poland 50°55′N 15°49′E
182 K3 **Bollards Lagoon** South Australia 28°58′S 140°52′E
103 R14 **Bollène** Vaucluse, SE France 44°16′N 04°45′E
94 N12 **Bollnäs** Gävleborg, C Sweden 61°18′N 16°27′E
181 W10 **Bollon** Queensland, C Australia 28°07′S 147°28′E
192 L12 **Bollons Tablemount** *undersea feature* S Pacific Ocean 49°40′S 176°10′W
93 H17 **Bollstabruk** Västernorrland, C Sweden 63°00′N 17°41′E
Bolluilos de Par del Condado *see* Bollulos Par del Condado
104 J14 **Bollulos Par del Condado** *var.* Bolluilos de Par del Condado. Andalucía, S Spain 37°20′N 06°32′W
95 K21 **Bolmen** ◎ S Sweden
137 T10 **Bolnisi** S Georgia 41°28′N 44°34′E
79 H19 **Bolobo** Bandundu, W Dem. Rep. Congo 02°10′S 16°17′E
106 G10 **Bologna** Emilia-Romagna, N Italy 44°30′N 11°20′E
124 I15 **Bologoye** Tverskaya Oblast', W Russian Federation 57°54′N 34°04′E
79 J18 **Bolomba** Equateur, NW Dem. Rep. Congo 0°27′N 19°13′E
41 X13 **Bolónchén de Rejón** *var.* Bolonchén de Rejón. Campeche, SE Mexico 20°00′N 89°34′W
114 J13 **Boloústra, Akrotírio** *headland* NE Greece 40°56′N 24°58′E
167 L8 **Bolovens, Plateau des** *plateau* S Laos
106 H13 **Bolsena** Lazio, C Italy 42°39′N 11°59′E
107 G14 **Bolsena, Lago di** ◎ C Italy
126 B3 **Bol'shakovo** *Ger.* Kreuzingen; *prev.* Gross-Skaisgirren. Kaliningradskaya Oblast', W Russian Federation 54°53′N 21°38′E
Bol'shaya Berëstovitsa *see* Vyalikaya Byerastavitsa
127 S7 **Bol'shaya Chernigovka** Samarskaya Oblast', W Russian Federation 52°07′N 50°49′E
127 S7 **Bol'shaya Glushitsa** Samarskaya Oblast', W Russian Federation 52°22′N 50°29′E
124 J4 **Bol'shaya Imandra, Ozero** ◎ NW Russian Federation
144 H9 **Bol'shaya Khobda** *Kaz.* Ülkenqobda. ≈ Kazakhstan/ Russian Federation
126 M12 **Bol'shaya Martynovka** Rostovskaya Oblast', SW Russian Federation 47°19′N 41°40′E
122 K12 **Bol'shaya Murta** Krasnoyarskiy Kray, C Russian Federation 56°51′N 93°10′E
125 V4 **Bol'shaya Rogovaya** ≈ NW Russian Federation
125 U7 **Bol'shaya Synya** ≈ NW Russian Federation
145 V9 **Bol'shaya Vladimirovka** Vostochnyy Kazakhstan, E Kazakhstan 50°53′N 79°29′E
123 V11 **Bol'sheretsk** Kamchatskaya Oblast', E Russian Federation 52°20′N 156°24′E
127 W3 **Bol'sheust'ikinskoye** Respublika Bashkortostan, W Russian Federation 56°00′N 58°13′E
Bol'shevik *see* Bal'shavik
122 L5 **Bol'shevik, Ostrov** *island* Severnaya Zemlya, N Russian Federation
125 U4 **Bol'shezemel'skaya Tundra** *physical region* NW Russian Federation
144 J13 **Bol'shiye Barsuki, Peski** *desert* SW Kazakhstan
123 T7 **Bol'shoy Anyuy** ≈ NE Russian Federation
123 N7 **Bol'shoy Begichev, Ostrov** *island* NE Russian Federation
123 S15 **Bol'shoye Kamen'** Primorskiy Kray, SE Russian Federation 43°06′N 132°21′E
127 O4 **Bol'shoye Murashkino** Nizhegorodskaya Oblast', W Russian Federation 55°46′N 44°48′E
127 W4 **Bol'shoy Iremel'** ▲ W Russian Federation 54°31′N 58°47′E
127 R7 **Bol'shoy Irgiz** ≈ W Russian Federation
123 Q6 **Bol'shoy Lyakhovskiy, Ostrov** *island* NE Russian Federation
123 Q11 **Bol'shoy Nimnyr** Respublika Sakha (Yakutiya), NE Russian Federation 57°55′N 125°34′E
Bol'shoy Rozhan *see* Vyaliki Rozhan
144 E10 **Bol'shoy Uzen'** *Kaz.* Ülkenözen. ≈ Kazakhstan/ Russian Federation
40 K6 **Bolson de Mapimi** ▲▲ NW Mexico
98 K6 **Bolsward** *Fris.* Boalsert. Friesland, N Netherlands 53°04′N 05°31′E
105 T4 **Boltaña** Aragón, NE Spain 42°28′N 00°02′E
14 G15 **Bolton** Ontario, S Canada 43°52′N 79°45′W
97 K17 **Bolton** *prev.* Bolton-le-Moors. NW England, United Kingdom 53°35′N 02°26′W
21 V12 **Bolton** North Carolina, SE USA 34°22′N 78°26′W
Bolton-le-Moors *see* Bolton
136 G11 **Bolu** Bolu, NW Turkey 40°45′N 31°38′E
136 G11 **Bolu** ◈ *province* NW Turkey
186 G9 **Bolubolu** Goodenough Island, S Papua New Guinea 09°22′S 150°22′E
92 H1 **Bolungarvík** Vestfirdhir, NW Iceland 66°09′N 23°17′W
159 O10 **Boluntay** Qinghai, W China 36°30′N 92°11′E
159 P8 **Boluozhuanjing**, Aksay Kazakzu Zizhixian. Gansu, N China 39°25′N 94°09′E
136 F14 **Bolvadin** Afyon, W Turkey 38°43′N 31°02′E
114 M10 **Bolyarovo** *prev.* Pashkeni. Yambol, E Bulgaria 42°09′N 26°49′E
106 G6 **Bolzano** *Ger.* Bozen; *anc.* Bauzanum. Trentino-Alto Adige, N Italy 46°30′N 11°22′E
79 F22 **Boma** Bas-Congo, W Dem. Rep. Congo 05°42′S 13°05′E
183 R12 **Bombala** New South Wales, SE Australia 36°54′S 149°15′E
104 F10 **Bombarral** Leiria, C Portugal 39°15′N 09°09′W
Bombay *see* Mumbai
171 U13 **Bomberai, Semenanjung** *cape* Papua, E Indonesia
81 F18 **Bombo** S Uganda 0°36′N 32°33′E
162 I8 **Bömbögör** *var.* Dzadgay. Bayanhongor, C Mongolia 46°12′N 99°29′E
79 I17 **Bomboma** Equateur, NW Dem. Rep. Congo 02°23′N 19°03′E
59 I14 **Bom Futuro** Pará, N Brazil 06°27′S 54°44′W
159 Q15 **Bomi** *var.* Bowo, Zhamo. Xizang Zizhiqu, W China 29°43′N 96°12′E
79 N17 **Bomili** Orientale, NE Dem. Rep. Congo 01°45′N 27°01′E
59 N17 **Bom Jesus da Lapa** Bahia, E Brazil 13°16′S 43°23′W
60 Q8 **Bom Jesus do Itabapoana** Rio de Janeiro, SE Brazil 21°07′S 41°43′W
95 C15 **Bømlafjorden** *fjord* S Norway
95 B15 **Bømlo** *island* S Norway
12 Q12 **Bomnak** Amurskaya Oblast', SE Russian Federation 54°43′N 128°50′E
79 I17 **Bomongo** Equateur, NW Dem. Rep. Congo 01°22′N 18°21′E
61 K14 **Bom Retiro** Santa Catarina, S Brazil 27°45′S 49°31′W
79 L15 **Bomu** *var.* Mbomou, Mbomu, M'Bomu. ≈ Central African Republic/ Dem. Rep. Congo
142 J3 **Bonāb** *var.* Benāb, Bunab. Āzarbāyjān-e Sharqī, N Iran 37°30′N 46°03′E
45 Q16 **Bonaire** *island* E Netherlands Antilles
39 U11 **Bona, Mount** ▲ Alaska, USA 61°22′N 141°45′W
183 Q12 **Bonang** Victoria, SE Australia 37°13′S 148°43′E
42 L7 **Bonanza** Región Autónoma Atlántico Norte, NE Nicaragua 13°59′N 84°30′W
37 O4 **Bonanza** Utah, W USA 40°01′N 109°12′W
45 O9 **Bonao** C Dominican Republic 18°55′N 70°25′W
180 L3 **Bonaparte Archipelago** *island group* Western Australia
32 K6 **Bonaparte, Mount** ▲ Washington, NW USA 48°47′N 119°07′W
39 N11 **Bonasila Dome** ▲ Alaska, USA 62°24′N 160°28′W
45 T15 **Bonasse** Trinidad, Trinidad and Tobago 10°02′N 61°48′W
15 X7 **Bonaventure** Québec, SE Canada 48°03′N 65°30′W
15 X7 **Bonaventure** ≈ Québec, SE Canada
13 V11 **Bonavista** Newfoundland, Newfoundland and Labrador, SE Canada 48°38′N 53°08′W
13 U11 **Bonavista Bay** *inlet* NW Atlantic Ocean
79 E19 **Bonda** Ogooué-Lolo, C Gabon 0°50′S 12°28′E
127 N6 **Bondari** Tambovskaya Oblast', W Russian Federation 52°58′N 42°02′E
106 G9 **Bondeno** Emilia-Romagna, C Italy 44°53′N 11°24′E
30 L4 **Bond Falls Flowage** ◎ Michigan, N USA
79 L16 **Bondo** Orientale, N Dem. Rep. Congo 03°52′N 23°41′E
171 N17 **Bondokodi** Pulau Sumba, S Indonesia 09°36′S 119°01′E
77 O15 **Bondoukou** E Ivory Coast 08°03′N 02°45′W
Bondoukui/Bondoukuy *see* Boundoukui
169 T17 **Bondowoso** Jawa, C Indonesia 07°54′S 113°50′E
33 S14 **Bondurant** Wyoming, C USA 43°14′N 110°26′W
Bône *see* Annaba, Algeria
Bone *see* Watampone, Indonesia
30 I5 **Bone Lake** ◎ Wisconsin, N USA
171 P14 **Bonelipu** Pulau Buton, C Indonesia 04°42′S 123°09′E
171 O15 **Bonerate, Kepulauan** *var.* Macan. *island group* C Indonesia
29 O12 **Bonesteel** South Dakota, N USA 43°01′N 98°55′W
62 I8 **Bonete, Cerro** ▲ N Argentina 27°58′S 68°22′W
171 O14 **Bone, Teluk** *bay* Sulawesi, C Indonesia
108 D6 **Bonfol** Jura, NW Switzerland 47°28′N 07°08′E
153 U12 **Bongaigaon** Assam, NE India 26°30′N 90°31′E
79 K17 **Bongandanga** Equateur, NW Dem. Rep. Congo 01°28′N 21°03′E
78 L13 **Bongo, Massif des** *var.* Chaîne des Mongos. ▲▲ NE Central African Republic
78 G12 **Bongor** Mayo-Kébbi, SW Chad 10°18′N 15°20′E
77 N16 **Bongouanou** E Ivory Coast 06°39′N 04°12′W
167 V11 **Bông Sơn** *var.* Hoai Nhơn. Binh Đinh, C Vietnam 14°28′N 109°00′E
25 U5 **Bonham** Texas, SW USA 33°36′N 96°12′W
Bonhard *see* Bonyhád
103 U6 **Bonhomme, Col du** *pass* NE France
103 Y16 **Bonifacio** Corse, France, C Mediterranean Sea 41°24′N 09°09′E
Bonifacio, Bocche de/ Bonifacio, Bouches de *see* Bonifacio, Strait of
103 Y16 **Bonifacio, Strait of** *Fr.* Bouches de Bonifacio, *It.* Bocche di Bonifacio. *strait* C Mediterranean Sea
23 Q8 **Bonifay** Florida, SE USA 30°49′N 85°42′W
Bonin Islands *see* Ogasawara-shotō
192 H5 **Bonin Trench** *undersea feature* NW Pacific Ocean
23 W15 **Bonita Springs** Florida, SE USA 26°19′N 81°48′W
42 I5 **Bonito, Pico** ▲ N Honduras 15°33′N 86°55′W
101 E17 **Bonn** Nordrhein-Westfalen, W Germany 50°44′N 07°06′E
92 H11 **Bonnåsjøen** Nordland, C Norway 67°35′N 15°39′E
14 J12 **Bonnechere** Ontario, SE Canada 45°39′N 77°36′W
14 J12 **Bonnechere** ≈ Ontario, SE Canada
33 N7 **Bonners Ferry** Idaho, NW USA 48°41′N 116°19′W
27 R4 **Bonner Springs** Kansas, C USA 39°03′N 94°52′W
102 L6 **Bonnétable** Sarthe, NW France 48°09′N 00°24′E
27 X6 **Bonne Terre** Missouri, C USA 37°55′N 90°33′W
10 J5 **Bonnet Plume** ≈ Yukon Territory, NW Canada
102 M6 **Bonneval** Eure-et-Loir, C France 48°12′N 01°23′E
103 T10 **Bonneville** Haute-Savoie, E France 46°05′N 06°25′E
36 J3 **Bonneville Salt Flats** *salt flat* Utah, W USA
77 U18 **Bonny** Rivers, S Nigeria 04°25′N 07°13′E
Bonny, Bight of *see* Biafra, Bight of
37 W4 **Bonny Reservoir** ▣ Colorado, C USA
11 R14 **Bonnyville** Alberta, SW Canada 54°16′N 110°46′W
107 C18 **Bono** Sardegna, Italy, C Mediterranean Sea 40°24′N 09°01′E
Bononia *see* Vidin, Bulgaria
Bononia *see* Boulogne-sur-Mer, France
107 B18 **Bonorva** Sardegna, Italy, C Mediterranean Sea 40°27′N 08°46′E
30 M15 **Bonpas Creek** ≈ Illinois, N USA
190 I3 **Bonriki** Tarawa, W Kiribati 01°23′N 173°09′E
183 T4 **Bonshaw** New South Wales, SE Australia 29°06′S 151°15′E
76 I16 **Bonthe** SW Sierra Leone 07°32′N 12°30′W
171 N2 **Bontoc** Luzon, N Philippines 17°04′N 120°58′E
25 Y9 **Bon Wier** Texas, SW USA 30°43′N 93°40′W
111 J25 **Bonyhád** *Ger.* Bonhard. Tolna, S Hungary 46°20′N 18°31′E
Bonzabaai *see* Bonza Bay
83 J25 **Bonza Bay** *Afr.* Bonzabaai. Eastern Cape, S South Africa 32°58′S 27°58′E
182 D7 **Bookabie** South Australia 31°49′S 132°41′E
182 H6 **Bookaloo** South Australia 31°56′S 137°21′E
37 P5 **Book Cliffs** *cliff* Colorado/ Utah, W USA
25 P1 **Booker** Texas, SW USA 36°27′N 100°32′W
76 K15 **Boola** SE Guinea 08°22′N 08°41′W
183 O8 **Booligal** New South Wales, SE Australia 33°56′S 144°54′E
99 G17 **Boom** Antwerpen, N Belgium 51°05′N 04°24′E
43 N6 **Boom** *var.* Boon. Región Autónoma Atlántico Norte, NE Nicaragua 14°52′N 83°36′W
183 S3 **Boomi** New South Wales, SE Australia 28°43′S 149°35′E
Boon *see* Boom
162 H9 **Bööncagaan Nuur** ◎ S Mongolia
29 V13 **Boone** Iowa, C USA 42°04′N 93°52′W
21 Q8 **Boone** North Carolina, SE USA 36°13′N 81°41′W
27 S11 **Booneville** Arkansas, C USA 35°09′N 93°57′W
21 N6 **Booneville** Kentucky, S USA 37°26′N 83°45′W
23 N2 **Booneville** Mississippi, S USA 34°39′N 88°34′W
21 V3 **Boonsboro** Maryland, NE USA 39°30′N 77°39′W
34 L6 **Boonville** California, W USA 38°58′N 123°21′W
31 N16 **Boonville** Indiana, N USA 38°03′N 87°16′W
27 U4 **Boonville** Missouri, C USA 38°58′N 92°43′W
18 I9 **Boonville** New York, NE USA 43°28′N 75°17′W
80 M12 **Boorama** Awdal, NW Somalia 09°58′N 43°15′E
183 O6 **Booroondarra, Mount** *hill* New South Wales, SE Australia
183 N9 **Booroorban** New South Wales, SE Australia 34°55′S 144°45′E
183 R9 **Boorowa** New South Wales, SE Australia 34°26′S 148°42′E
99 H17 **Boortmeerbeek** Vlaams Brabant, C Belgium 50°58′N 04°27′E
80 P11 **Boosaaso** *var.* Bandar Kassim, Bender Qaasim, Bosaso, *It.* Bender Cassim. Bari, N Somalia 11°26′N 49°37′E
19 Q8 **Boothbay Harbor** Maine, NE USA 43°52′N 69°35′W
Boothia Felix *see* Boothia Peninsula
9 N6 **Boothia, Gulf of** *gulf* Nunavut, NE Canada
9 N6 **Boothia Peninsula** *prev.* Boothia Felix. *peninsula* Nunavut, NE Canada
79 E18 **Booué** Ogooué-Ivindo, NE Gabon 0°03′S 11°58′E
101 J21 **Bopfingen** Baden-Württemberg, S Germany 48°51′N 10°21′E
101 F18 **Boppard** Rheinland-Pfalz, W Germany 50°13′N 07°36′E
62 M4 **Boquerón** *off.* Departamento de Boquerón. ◈ *department* W Paraguay
Boquerón, Departamento de *see* Boquerón
43 P15 **Boquete** *var.* Bajo Boquete. Chiriquí, W Panama 08°45′N 82°26′W
40 J6 **Boquilla, Presa de la** ▣ N Mexico
40 L5 **Boquillas** *var.* Boquillas del Carmen. Coahuila, NE Mexico 29°10′N 102°55′W
Boquillas del Carmen *see* Boquillas
127 O3 **Bor** Nizhegorodskaya Oblast', W Russian Federation 56°21′N 44°03′E
112 P12 **Bor** Serbia, E Serbia 44°05′N 22°07′E
81 F15 **Bor** Jonglei, S Sudan 06°12′N 31°33′E
95 L20 **Bor** Jönköping, S Sweden 57°04′N 14°10′E
136 J15 **Bor** Niğde, S Turkey 37°49′N 35°00′E
191 S10 **Bora-Bora** *island* Îles Sous le Vent, W French Polynesia
167 Q9 **Borabu** Maha Sarakham, E Thailand 16°01′N 103°06′E
172 K4 **Boraha, Nosy** *island* E Madagascar
33 P13 **Borah Peak** ▲ Idaho, NW USA 44°21′N 113°53′W
145 U16 **Boralday** *prev.* Burunday. Almaty, SE Kazakhstan 43°21′N 76°48′E
144 G13 **Borankul** *prev.* Opornyy. Mangistau, SW Kazakhstan 46°09′N 54°32′E
95 J19 **Borås** Västra Götaland, S Sweden 57°44′N 12°55′E
143 N11 **Borāzjān** *var.* Borazjān. Būshehr, S Iran 29°19′N 51°12′E
Borazjān *see* Borāzjān
58 G13 **Borba** Amazonas, N Brazil 04°39′S 59°35′W
104 H11 **Borba** Évora, S Portugal 38°48′N 07°28′W

◆ Country
● Country Capital
◇ Dependent Territory
○ Dependent Territory Capital
◈ Administrative Regions
✈ International Airport
▲ Mountain
▲▲ Mountain Range
Volcano
≈ River
◎ Lake
▣ Reservoir

BORBETOMAGUS – BRECON

Borbetomagus *see* Worms
55 O7 **Borbón** Bolívar, E Venezuela 07°55′N 64°03′W
59 Q15 **Borborema, Planalto da** *plateau* NE Brazil
116 M14 **Borcea, Brațul** ≈ S Romania
Borchalo *see* Marneuli
195 R15 **Borchgrevink Coast** *physical region* Antarctica
137 Q11 **Borçka** Artvin, NE Turkey 41°24′N 41°38′E
98 N11 **Borculo** Gelderland, E Netherlands 52°07′N 06°31′E
182 G10 **Borda, Cape** *headland* South Australia 35°45′S 136°34′E
102 K13 **Bordeaux** *anc.* Burdigala. Gironde, SW France 44°49′N 00°33′W
11 T15 **Borden** Saskatchewan, S Canada 52°23′N 107°10′W
14 D8 **Borden Lake** ◎ Ontario, S Canada
9 N4 **Borden Peninsula** *peninsula* Baffin Island, Nunavut, NE Canada
182 K11 **Bordertown** South Australia 36°21′S 140°48′E
92 H2 **Bordheyri** Vestfirdhir, NW Iceland 65°12′N 21°09′W
95 B18 **Bordhoy** *Dan.* Bordø. *island* NE Faeroe Islands
106 B11 **Bordighera** Liguria, NW Italy 43°48′N 07°40′E
74 K5 **Bordj-Bou-Arreridj** *var.* Bordj Bou Arreridj, Bordj Bou Arréridj. N Algeria 36°02′N 04°49′E
74 L10 **Bordj Omar Driss** E Algeria 28°09′N 06°52′E
143 N13 **Bord Khūn** Hormozgān, S Iran
Bordø *see* Bordhoy
147 V7 **Bordunskiy** Chuyskaya Oblast', N Kyrgyzstan 42°37′N 75°31′E
95 M17 **Borensberg** Östergötland, S Sweden 58°33′N 15°15′E
Borgå *see* Porvoo
92 L2 **Borgarfjördhur** Austurland, NE Iceland 65°32′N 13°46′W
92 H3 **Borgarnes** Vesturland, W Iceland 64°33′N 21°55′W
93 G14 **Børgefjelt** ▲▲ C Norway
98 O7 **Borger** Drenthe, NE Netherlands 52°54′N 06°48′E
25 N2 **Borger** Texas, SW USA 35°40′N 101°24′W
95 N20 **Borgholm** Kalmar, S Sweden 56°50′N 16°41′E
107 N22 **Borgia** Calabria, SW Italy 38°48′N 16°28′E
99 J18 **Borgloon** Limburg, NE Belgium 50°48′N 05°21′E
195 P2 **Borgmassivet** ▲▲ Antarctica
22 L9 **Borgne, Lake** ◎ Louisiana, S USA
106 C7 **Borgomanero** Piemonte, NE Italy 45°42′N 08°33′E
106 G10 **Borgo Panigale** ✈ (Bologna) Emilia-Romagna, N Italy 44°33′N 11°16′E
107 J15 **Borgorose** Lazio, C Italy 42°10′N 13°15′E
106 A9 **Borgo San Dalmazzo** Piemonte, N Italy 44°19′N 07°29′E
106 G11 **Borgo San Lorenzo** Toscana, C Italy 43°58′N 11°22′E
106 C7 **Borgosesia** Piemonte, NE Italy 45°41′N 08°21′E
106 E9 **Borgo Val di Taro** Emilia-Romagna, C Italy 44°29′N 09°48′E
106 G6 **Borgo Valsugana** Trentino-Alto Adige, N Italy 46°04′N 11°31′E
Borhoyn Tal *see* Dzamïn-Üüd
167 R8 **Borikhan** *var.* Borikhane. Bolikhamxai, C Laos 18°36′N 103°43′E
Borikhane *see* Borikhan
Borislav *see* Boryslav
127 N8 **Borisoglebsk** Voronezhskaya Oblast', W Russian Federation 51°23′N 42°00′E
Borisov *see* Barysaw
Borisovgrad *see* Pŭrvomay
Borispol' *see* Boryspil'
172 I3 **Boriziny** *Fr.* Port-Bergé. Mahajanga, NW Madagascar 15°31′S 47°40′E
105 Q5 **Borja** Aragón, NE Spain 41°50′N 01°32′W
Borjas Blancas *see* Les Borges Blanques
137 S10 **Borjomi** *Rus.* Borzhomi. C Georgia 41°50′N 43°24′E
118 L12 **Borkavichy** *Rus.* Borkovichi. Vitsyebskaya Voblasts', N Belarus 55°40′N 28°20′E
101 H16 **Borken** Hessen, C Germany 51°01′N 09°16′E
101 E14 **Borken** Nordrhein-Westfalen, W Germany 51°51′N 06°51′E
92 H10 **Borkenes** Troms, N Norway 68°46′N 16°10′E
78 H7 **Borkou-Ennedi-Tibesti** *off.* Préfecture du Borkou-Ennedi-Tibesti. ◈ *prefecture* N Chad
Borkou-Ennedi-Tibesti, Préfecture du *see* Borkou-Ennedi-Tibesti
Borkovichi *see* Borkavichy
100 E9 **Borkum** *island* NW Germany
81 K17 **Bor, Lagh** *var.* Lak Bor. *dry watercourse* NE Kenya
Bor, Lak *see* Bor, Lagh
95 M14 **Borlänge** Dalarna, C Sweden 60°29′N 15°25′E
106 C9 **Bormida** ≈ NW Italy
106 F6 **Bormio** Lombardia, N Italy 46°27′N 10°24′E
101 M16 **Borna** Sachsen, E Germany 51°07′N 12°30′E
98 O10 **Borne** Overijssel, E Netherlands 52°18′N 06°45′E
99 F17 **Bornem** Antwerpen, N Belgium 51°06′N 04°14′E
169 S10 **Borneo** *island* Brunei/Indonesia/Malaysia
101 E16 **Bornheim** Nordrhein-Westfalen, W Germany 50°46′N 06°58′E
95 L24 **Bornholm** ◈ *county* E Denmark
95 L24 **Bornholm** *island* E Denmark
77 Y13 **Borno** ◈ *state* NE Nigeria
104 K15 **Bornos** Andalucía, S Spain 36°50′N 05°42′W
162 L7 **Bornuur** Töv, C Mongolia 48°28′N 106°15′E
117 O4 **Borodyanka** Kyyivs'ka Oblast', N Ukraine 50°40′N 29°54′E
158 I5 **Borohoro Shan** ▲▲ NW China
77 O13 **Boromo** SW Burkina 11°47′N 02°54′W
35 T13 **Boron** California, W USA 35°00′N 117°42′W
Borongo *see* Black Volta
Boron'ki *see* Baron'ki
Borosjenő *see* Ineu
Borossebes *see* Sebiș
76 L15 **Borotou** NW Ivory Coast 08°46′N 07°30′W
117 W6 **Borova** Kharkivs'ka Oblast', E Ukraine 49°22′N 37°39′E
114 H8 **Borovan** Vratsa, NW Bulgaria 43°25′N 23°45′E
124 I14 **Borovichi** Novgorodskaya Oblast', W Russian Federation 58°24′N 33°56′E
Borovlje *see* Ferlach
114 K8 **Borovo** Ruse, N Bulgaria 43°28′N 25°46′E
112 J9 **Borovo** Vukovar-Srijem, NE Croatia 45°22′N 18°57′E
145 Q7 **Borovoye** *Kaz.* Būrabay. Akmola, N Kazakhstan 53°07′N 70°20′E
126 K4 **Borovsk** Kaluzhskaya Oblast', W Russian Federation 55°12′N 36°22′E
145 N7 **Borovskoy** Kostanay, N Kazakhstan 53°48′N 64°17′E
Borovukha *see* Baravukha
95 L23 **Borrby** Skåne, S Sweden 55°27′N 14°10′E
181 R3 **Borroloola** Northern Territory, N Australia 16°09′S 136°18′E
116 F9 **Borș** Bihor, NW Romania 47°07′N 21°49′E
116 I9 **Borșa** *Hung.* Borsa. Maramureș, N Romania 47°40′N 24°37′E
116 J10 **Borsec** *Ger.* Bad Borseck, *Hung.* Borszék. Harghita, C Romania 46°58′N 25°32′E
92 K8 **Børselv** *Lapp.* Bissojohka. Finnmark, N Norway 70°18′N 25°35′E
113 L23 **Borsh** *var.* Borshi. Vlorë, S Albania 40°04′N 19°51′E
Borshchev *see* Borshchiv
116 K7 **Borshchiv** *Pol.* Borszczów, *Rus.* Borshchev. Ternopil's'ka Oblast', W Ukraine 48°48′N 26°00′E
Borshi *see* Borsh
111 L20 **Borsod-Abaúj-Zemplén** *off.* Borsod-Abaúj-Zemplén Megye. ◈ *county* NE Hungary
Borsod-Abaúj-Zemplén Megye *see* Borsod-Abaúj-Zemplén
99 E15 **Borssele** Zeeland, SW Netherlands 51°26′N 03°45′E
Borszczów *see* Borshchiv
Borszék *see* Borsec
Bortala *see* Bole
103 O12 **Bort-les-Orgues** Corrèze, C France 45°28′N 02°31′E
Bor u České Lípy *see* Nový Bor
Bor-Üdzüür *see* Altay
143 N9 **Borūjen** Chahār Maḩall va Bakhtīārī, C Iran 32°N 51°09′E
142 L7 **Borūjerd** *var.* Burujird. Lorestān, W Iran 33°55′N 48°46′E
116 H6 **Boryslav** *Pol.* Borysław, *Rus.* Borislav. L'vivs'ka Oblast', NW Ukraine 49°18′N 23°28′E
Borysław *see* Boryslav
117 P4 **Boryspil'** *Rus.* Borispol'. Kyyivs'ka Oblast', N Ukraine 50°21′N 30°59′E
117 P4 **Boryspil'** *Rus.* Borispol'. ✈ (Kyyiv) Kyyivs'ka Oblast', N Ukraine 50°21′N 30°46′E
Borzhomi *see* Borjomi
117 R3 **Borzna** Chernihivs'ka Oblast', NE Ukraine 51°15′N 32°25′E
123 O14 **Borzya** Chitinskaya Oblast', S Russian Federation 50°18′N 116°24′E
107 B18 **Bosa** Sardegna, Italy, C Mediterranean Sea 40°18′N 08°28′E
112 F10 **Bosanska Dubica** *var.* Kozarska Dubica. ◈ Republika Srpska, NW Bosnia and Herzegovina
112 G10 **Bosanska Gradiška** *var.* Gradiška. ◈ Republika Srpska, N Bosnia and Herzegovina
112 F10 **Bosanska Kostajnica** *var.* Srpska Kostajnica. ◈ Republika Srpska, NW Bosnia and Herzegovina
112 E11 **Bosanska Krupa** *var.* Krupa, Krupa na Uni. ◈ Federacija Bosna I Hercegovina, NW Bosnia and Herzegovina
112 H10 **Bosanski Brod** *var.* Srpski Brod. ◈ Republika Srpska, N Bosnia and Herzegovina
112 E10 **Bosanski Novi** *var.* Novi Grad. Republika Srpska, NW Bosnia and Herzegovina 45°03′N 16°23′E
112 E11 **Bosanski Petrovac** *var.* Petrovac. Federacija Bosna I Hercegovina, NW Bosnia and Herzegovina 44°34′N 16°21′E
112 I10 **Bosanski Šamac** *var.* Šamac. Republika Srpska, N Bosnia and Herzegovina 45°03′N 18°27′E
112 E12 **Bosansko Grahovo** *var.* Grahovo, Hrvatsko Grahovi. Federacija Bosna I Hercegovina, W Bosnia and Herzegovina 44°10′N 16°22′E
Bosaso *see* Boosaaso
186 B7 **Bosavi, Mount** 🌋 W Papua New Guinea 06°33′S 142°50′E
160 J14 **Bose** Guangxi Zhuangzu Zizhiqu, S China 23°55′N 106°32′E
161 Q5 **Boshan** Shandong, E China 36°32′N 117°47′E
113 P16 **Bosilegrad** *prev.* Bosiljgrad. Serbia, SE Serbia 42°30′N 22°30′E
Bosiljgrad *see* Bosilegrad
Bösing *see* Pezinok
98 H12 **Boskoop** Zuid-Holland, C Netherlands 52°04′N 04°40′E
111 G18 **Boskovice** *Ger.* Boskowitz. Jihomoravský Kraj, SE Czech Republic 49°30′N 16°39′E
Boskowitz *see* Boskovice
112 I10 **Bosna** ≈ N Bosnia and Herzegovina
113 G14 **Bosna I Hercegovina, Federacija** ◈ *republic* Bosnia and Herzegovina
112 H12 **Bosnia and Herzegovina** *off.* Republic of Bosnia and Herzegovina. ◆ *republic* SE Europe
Bosnia and Herzegovina, Republic of *see* Bosnia and Herzegovina
79 J16 **Bosobolo** Equateur, NW Dem. Rep. Congo 04°11′N 19°55′E
165 O14 **Bōsō-hantō** *peninsula* Honshū, S Japan
Bosora *see* Buşrá ash Shām
Bosphorus/Bosporus *see* İstanbul Boğazı
Bosporus Cimmerius *see* Kerch Strait
Bosporus Thracius *see* İstanbul Boğazı
Bosra *see* Buşrá ash Shām
79 H14 **Bossangoa** Ouham, C Central African Republic 06°32′N 17°25′E
Bossé Bangou *see* Bossey Bangou
79 I15 **Bossembélé** Ombella-Mpoko, C Central African Republic 05°13′N 17°39′E
79 H15 **Bossentélé** Ouham-Pendé, W Central African Republic 05°36′N 16°37′E
77 R12 **Bossey Bangou** *var.* Bossé Bangou. Tillabéri, SW Niger 13°22′N 01°18′E
22 G5 **Bossier City** Louisiana, S USA 32°31′N 93°43′W
83 D20 **Bossiesvlei** Hardap, S Namibia 25°02′S 16°48′E
77 Y11 **Bosso** Diffa, SE Niger 13°42′N 13°18′E
61 F15 **Bossoroca** Rio Grande do Sul, S Brazil 28°45′S 54°54′W
158 J10 **Bostan** Xinjiang Uygur Zizhiqu, W China 41°20′N 83°15′E
142 K3 **Bostānābād** Āžarbāyjān-e Sharqī, N Iran 37°52′N 46°51′E
158 K6 **Bosten Hu** *var.* Bagrax Hu. ◎ NW China
97 O18 **Boston** *prev.* St.Botolph's Town. E England, United Kingdom 52°59′N 00°01′W
19 O11 **Boston** *state capital* Massachusetts, NE USA 42°22′N 71°04′W
146 I9 **Bo'ston** *Rus.* Bustan. Qoraqalpog'iston Respublikasi, W Uzbekistan 41°49′N 60°51′E
10 M17 **Boston Bar** British Columbia, SW Canada 49°54′N 121°22′W
27 T10 **Boston Mountains** ▲▲ Arkansas, C USA
15 P8 **Bostonnais** ≈ Québec, SE Canada
Bostyn' *see* Bastyn'
112 J10 **Bosut** ≈ E Croatia
154 C11 **Botād** Gujarāt, W India 22°12′N 71°44′E
183 T9 **Botany Bay** *inlet* New South Wales, SE Australia
83 G18 **Boteti** *var.* Botletle. ≈ N Botswana
114 J9 **Botev** ▲ C Bulgaria 42°45′N 24°57′E
114 H9 **Botevgrad** *prev.* Orkhaniye. Sofiya, W Bulgaria 42°55′N 23°47′E
93 J16 **Bothnia, Gulf of** *Fin.* Pohjanlahti, *Swe.* Bottniska Viken. *gulf* N Baltic Sea
183 P17 **Bothwell** Tasmania, SE Australia 42°24′S 147°01′E
104 H5 **Boticas** Vila Real, N Portugal 41°41′N 07°40′W
55 W10 **Boti-Pasi** Sipaliwini, C Suriname 04°15′N 55°27′W
Botletle *see* Boteti
127 P16 **Botlikh** Chechenskaya Respublika, SW Russian Federation 42°39′N 46°12′E
117 N10 **Botna** ≈ E Moldova
116 I9 **Botoșani** *Hung.* Botosány. Botoșani, NE Romania 47°44′N 26°41′E
116 K8 **Botoșani** ◈ *county* NE Romania
Botosány *see* Botoșani
147 P12 **Bototog', Tizmasi** *Rus.* Khrebet Babatag. ▲▲ Tajikistan/Uzbekistan
161 P4 **Botou** *prev.* Bozhen. Hebei, E China 38°09′N 116°37′E
99 M20 **Botrange** ▲ E Belgium 50°30′N 06°03′E
107 O21 **Botricello** Calabria, SW Italy 38°56′N 16°51′E
83 I23 **Botshabelo** Free State, C South Africa 29°15′S 26°51′E
93 J15 **Botsmark** Västerbotten, N Sweden 64°15′N 20°15′E
83 G19 **Botswana** *off.* Republic of Botswana. ◆ *republic* S Africa
Botswana, Republic of *see* Botswana
29 N2 **Bottineau** North Dakota, N USA 48°50′N 100°28′W
Bottniska Viken *see* Bothnia, Gulf of
60 L9 **Botucatu** São Paulo, S Brazil 22°52′S 48°30′W
76 M16 **Bouaflé** C Ivory Coast 06°59′N 05°45′W
77 N16 **Bouaké** *var.* Bwake. C Ivory Coast 07°42′N 05°00′W
79 G14 **Bouar** Nana-Mambéré, W Central African Republic 05°58′N 15°38′E
74 H7 **Bouarfa** NE Morocco 32°33′N 01°54′W
111 B19 **Boubín** ▲ SW Czech Republic 49°00′N 13°51′E
79 I14 **Bouca** Ouham, W Central African Republic 06°57′N 18°18′E
15 T5 **Boucher** ≈ Québec, SE Canada
103 R15 **Bouches-du-Rhône** ◈ *department* SE France
74 C9 **Bou Craa** *var.* Bu Craa. NW Western Sahara 26°32′N 12°52′W
77 O9 **Boû Djébéha** *oasis* C Mali
108 C8 **Boudry** Neuchâtel, W Switzerland 46°57′N 06°46′E
79 F21 **Bouenza** ◈ *province* S Congo
180 L2 **Bougainville, Cape** *cape* Western Australia
Bougainville, Détroit de *see* Bougainville Strait
186 J7 **Bougainville Island** *island* NE Papua New Guinea
186 I8 **Bougainville Strait** *strait* N Solomon Islands
187 Q13 **Bougainville Strait** *Fr.* Détroit de Bougainville. *strait* C Vanuatu
120 I9 **Bougaroun, Cap** *headland* NE Algeria 37°07′N 06°18′E
77 R8 **Boughessa** Kidal, NE Mali 20°05′N 02°13′E
Bougie *see* Béjaïa
76 L13 **Bougouni** Sikasso, SW Mali 11°25′N 07°28′W
99 J24 **Bouillon** Luxembourg, SE Belgium 49°47′N 05°04′E
74 K5 **Bouira** *var.* Bouïra. N Algeria 36°22′N 03°55′E
74 D8 **Bou-Izakarn** SW Morocco 29°12′N 09°43′W
74 B9 **Boujdour** *var.* Bojador. W Western Sahara 26°06′N 14°29′W
74 G5 **Boukhalef** ✈ (Tanger) N Morocco 35°45′N 05°53′W
Boukombé *see* Boukoumbé
77 R14 **Boukoumbé** *var.* Boukombé. C Benin 10°13′N 01°09′E
76 G6 **Boû Lanouâr** Dakhlet Nouâdhibou, W Mauritania 21°17′N 16°29′W
37 T4 **Boulder** Colorado, C USA 40°02′N 105°18′W
33 R10 **Boulder** Montana, NW USA 46°14′N 112°07′W
35 X12 **Boulder City** Nevada, W USA 35°58′N 114°49′W
181 T7 **Boulia** Queensland, C Australia 23°02′S 139°58′E
15 N10 **Boullé** ≈ Québec, SE Canada
102 J9 **Boulogne** ≈ NW France
Boulogne *see* Boulogne-sur-Mer
102 L16 **Boulogne-sur-Gesse** Haute-Garonne, S France 43°18′N 00°38′E
103 N1 **Boulogne-sur-Mer** *var.* Boulogne; *anc.* Bononia, Gesoriacum, Gessoriacum. Pas-de-Calais, N France 50°43′N 01°36′E
77 Q12 **Boulsa** C Burkina 12°41′N 00°29′W
77 W11 **Boultoum** Zinder, C Niger 14°43′N 10°22′E
187 Y14 **Bouma** Taveuni, N Fiji 16°49′S 179°50′W
79 G16 **Boumba** ≈ SE Cameroon
76 J9 **Boûmdeïd** *var.* Boumdeït. Assaba, S Mauritania 17°26′N 11°21′W
Boumdeït *see* Boûmdeïd
115 C17 **Boumistós** ▲ W Greece 38°48′N 20°59′E
77 O15 **Bouna** NE Ivory Coast 09°16′N 03°00′W
19 P4 **Boundary Bald Mountain** ▲ Maine, NE USA 45°45′N 70°10′W
35 S8 **Boundary Peak** ▲ Nevada, W USA 37°50′N 118°21′W
76 M14 **Boundiali** N Ivory Coast 09°30′N 06°31′W
79 G19 **Boundji** Cuvette, C Congo 01°05′S 15°18′E
77 O13 **Boundoukui** *var.* Bondoukui, Bondoukuy. W Burkina 11°51′N 03°47′W
36 L2 **Bountiful** Utah, W USA 40°53′N 111°52′W
Bounty Basin *see* Bounty Trough
191 Q16 **Bounty Bay** *bay* Pitcairn Island, C Pacific Ocean
192 L12 **Bounty Islands** *island group* S New Zealand
175 Q13 **Bounty Trough** *var.* Bounty Basin. *undersea feature* S Pacific Ocean
187 P17 **Bourail** Province Sud, C New Caledonia 21°35′S 165°29′E
27 V5 **Bourbeuse River** ≈ Missouri, C USA
103 Q9 **Bourbon-Lancy** Saône-et-Loire, C France 46°39′N 03°48′E
31 N11 **Bourbonnais** Illinois, N USA 41°08′N 87°52′W
103 O10 **Bourbonnais** *cultural region* C France
103 S7 **Bourbonne-les-Bains** Haute-Marne, N France 48°00′N 05°43′E
Bourbon Vendée *see* la Roche-sur-Yon
74 M8 **Bourdj Messaouda** E Algeria 30°18′N 09°19′E
77 Q10 **Bourem** Gao, C Mali 16°56′N 00°21′W
Bourg *see* Bourg-en-Bresse
103 N11 **Bourganeuf** Creuse, C France 45°57′N 01°47′E
Bourgas *see* Burgas
Bourge-en-Bresse *see* Bourg-en-Bresse
103 S10 **Bourg-en-Bresse** *var.* Bourg, Bourge-en-Bresse. Ain, E France 46°12′N 05°13′E
103 O8 **Bourges** *anc.* Avaricum. Cher, C France 47°06′N 02°24′E
103 T11 **Bourget, Lac du** ◎ E France
103 P8 **Bourgogne** *Eng.* Burgundy. ◈ *region* E France
103 S11 **Bourgoin-Jallieu** Isère, E France 45°34′N 05°16′E
103 R14 **Bourg-St-Andéol** Ardèche, E France 44°24′N 04°36′E
103 U11 **Bourg-St-Maurice** Savoie, E France 45°37′N 06°49′E
108 C11 **Bourg St. Pierre** Valais, SW Switzerland 45°54′N 07°10′E
76 H8 **Boû Rjeimât** *well* W Mauritania
183 P5 **Bourke** New South Wales, SE Australia 30°08′S 145°57′E
97 M24 **Bournemouth** S England, United Kingdom 50°43′N 01°54′W
99 M23 **Bourscheid** Diekirch, NE Luxembourg 49°55′N 06°04′E
74 K6 **Bou Saâda** *var.* Bou Saada. N Algeria 35°10′N 04°09′E
36 I13 **Bouse Wash** ≈ Arizona, SW USA
103 N10 **Boussac** Creuse, C France 46°20′N 02°12′E
102 M16 **Boussens** Haute-Garonne, S France 43°11′N 00°58′E
78 H12 **Bousso** *prev.* Fort-Bretonnet. Chari-Baguirmi, S Chad 10°32′N 16°45′E
76 H9 **Boutilimit** Trarza, SW Mauritania 17°33′N 14°42′W
65 D21 **Bouvet Island** ◇ *Norwegian dependency* S Atlantic Ocean
77 U11 **Bouza** Tahoua, SW Niger 14°25′N 06°09′E
109 R10 **Bovec** *Ger.* Flitsch, *It.* Plezzo. NW Slovenia 46°21′N 13°33′E
98 J8 **Bovenkarspel** Noord-Holland, NW Netherlands 52°33′N 05°03′E
29 V5 **Bovey** Minnesota, N USA 47°18′N 93°25′W
32 M9 **Bovill** Idaho, NW USA 46°50′N 116°24′W
24 L4 **Bovina** Texas, SW USA 34°30′N 102°52′W
107 M17 **Bovino** Puglia, SE Italy 41°14′N 15°19′E
61 C17 **Bovril** Entre Ríos, E Argentina 31°24′S 59°25′W
28 L2 **Bowbells** North Dakota, N USA 48°48′N 102°15′W
11 Q16 **Bow City** Alberta, SW Canada 50°27′N 112°16′W
29 O8 **Bowdle** South Dakota, N USA 45°27′N 99°39′W
181 X6 **Bowen** Queensland, NE Australia 20°S 148°10′E
192 L2 **Bowers Ridge** *undersea feature* S Bering Sea 50°00′N 180°00′W
25 S5 **Bowie** Texas, SW USA 33°33′N 97°51′W
11 R17 **Bow Island** Alberta, SW Canada 49°53′N 111°24′W
Bowkān *see* Būkān
20 J7 **Bowling Green** Kentucky, S USA 37°00′N 86°29′W
27 V3 **Bowling Green** Missouri, C USA 39°21′N 91°11′W
31 R11 **Bowling Green** Ohio, N USA 41°22′N 83°40′W
21 W5 **Bowling Green** Virginia, NE USA 38°02′N 77°22′W
28 J6 **Bowman** North Dakota, N USA 46°11′N 103°26′W
9 Q7 **Bowman Bay** *bay* NW Atlantic Ocean
194 I5 **Bowman Coast** *physical region* Antarctica
28 J7 **Bowman-Haley Lake** ⊠ North Dakota, N USA
195 Z11 **Bowman Island** *island* Antarctica
Bowo *see* Bomi
183 S9 **Bowral** New South Wales, SE Australia 34°28′S 150°52′E
186 E8 **Bowutu Mountains** ▲▲ C Papua New Guinea
83 I16 **Bowwood** Southern, S Zambia 17°09′S 26°16′E
28 I12 **Box Butte Reservoir** ⊠ Nebraska, C USA
28 J10 **Box Elder** South Dakota, N USA 44°06′N 103°04′W
95 M18 **Boxholm** Östergötland, S Sweden 58°12′N 15°05′E
Bo Xian/Boxian *see* Bozhou
161 Q4 **Boxing** Shandong, E China 37°06′N 118°05′E
99 L14 **Boxmeer** Noord-Brabant, SE Netherlands 51°39′N 05°57′E
99 J14 **Boxtel** Noord-Brabant, S Netherlands 51°36′N 05°20′E
136 J10 **Boyabat** Sinop, N Turkey 41°27′N 34°45′E
54 F9 **Boyacá** *off.* Departamento de Boyacá. ◈ *province* C Colombia
Boyacá, Departamento de *see* Boyacá
117 O4 **Boyarka** Kyyivs'ka Oblast', N Ukraine 50°19′N 30°20′E
22 H7 **Boyce** Louisiana, S USA 31°23′N 92°40′W
114 H8 **Boychinovtsi** Montana, NW Bulgaria 43°28′N 23°20′E
33 U11 **Boyd** Montana, NW USA 45°27′N 109°03′W
25 S6 **Boyd** Texas, SW USA 33°01′N 97°33′W
21 V8 **Boydton** Virginia, NE USA 36°40′N 78°26′W
Boyer Ahmadī va Kohkīlūyeh *see* Kohgīlūyeh va Būyer Aḩmad
29 T13 **Boyer River** ≈ Iowa, C USA
21 W8 **Boykins** Virginia, NE USA 36°35′N 77°11′W
11 Q13 **Boyle** Alberta, SW Canada 54°38′N 112°45′W
97 D16 **Boyle** *Ir.* Mainistirna Búille. C Ireland 53°58′N 08°18′W
97 F17 **Boyne** *Ir.* An Bhóinn. ≈ E Ireland
31 Q5 **Boyne City** Michigan, N USA 45°13′N 85°00′W
23 Z14 **Boynton Beach** Florida, SE USA 26°31′N 80°04′W
147 O13 **Boysun** *Rus.* Baysun. Surkhondaryo Viloyati, S Uzbekistan 38°14′N 67°08′E
Bozau *see* Întorsura Buzăului
136 B12 **Bozcaada** *Island* Çanakkale, NW Turkey
136 C14 **Boz Dağları** ▲▲ W Turkey
33 S11 **Bozeman** Montana, NW USA 45°40′N 111°02′W
Bozen *see* Bolzano
79 J16 **Bozene** Equateur, NW Dem. Rep. Congo 02°56′N 19°15′E
Bozhen *see* Botou
161 P7 **Bozhou** *var.* Boxian, Bo Xian. Anhui, E China 33°46′N 115°44′E
136 H16 **Bozkır** Konya, S Turkey 37°10′N 32°15′E
136 K13 **Bozok Yaylası** *plateau* C Turkey
79 H14 **Bozoum** Ouham-Pendé, W Central African Republic 06°17′N 16°26′E
137 N16 **Bozova** Sanlıurfa, S Turkey 37°23′N 38°33′E
Bozrah *see* Buşrá ash Shām
136 E12 **Bozüyük** Bilecik, NW Turkey 39°55′N 30°02′E
106 B9 **Bra** Piemonte, NW Italy 44°42′N 07°51′E
194 G4 **Brabant Island** *island* Antarctica
99 I20 **Brabant Walloon** ◈ *province* C Belgium
113 F15 **Brač** *var.* Brach, *It.* Brazza; *anc.* Brattia. *island* S Croatia
Bracara Augusta *see* Braga
107 H15 **Bracciano** Lazio, C Italy 42°04′N 12°12′E
107 H14 **Bracciano, Lago di** ◎ C Italy
14 H13 **Bracebridge** Ontario, S Canada 45°02′N 79°19′W
Brach *see* Brač
93 G17 **Bräcke** Jämtland, C Sweden 62°43′N 15°30′E
25 P12 **Brackettville** Texas, SW USA 29°19′N 100°27′W
97 N22 **Bracknell** S England, United Kingdom 51°26′N 00°46′W
61 K14 **Braço do Norte** Santa Catarina, S Brazil 28°16′S 49°11′W
116 G11 **Brad** *Hung.* Brád. Hunedoara, SW Romania 45°52′N 23°00′E
107 N18 **Bradano** ≈ S Italy
23 V13 **Bradenton** Florida, SE USA 27°30′N 82°34′W
14 H14 **Bradford** Ontario, S Canada 44°09′N 79°34′W
97 L17 **Bradford** N England, United Kingdom 53°48′N 01°45′W
27 W10 **Bradford** Arkansas, C USA 35°25′N 91°27′W
18 D12 **Bradford** Pennsylvania, NE USA 41°57′N 78°38′W
27 T15 **Bradley** Arkansas, C USA 33°06′N 93°39′W
25 P7 **Bradshaw** Texas, SW USA 32°06′N 99°52′W
25 Q9 **Brady** Texas, SW USA 31°08′N 99°22′W
25 Q9 **Brady Creek** ≈ Texas, SW USA
95 G22 **Brædstrup** Vejle, C Denmark 55°58′N 09°38′E
96 J10 **Braemar** NE Scotland, United Kingdom 57°12′N 02°52′W
116 K8 **Brăești** Botoșani, NW Romania 47°50′N 26°26′E
104 G5 **Braga** *anc.* Bracara Augusta. Braga, NW Portugal 41°32′N 08°26′W
104 G5 **Braga** ◈ *district* N Portugal
116 J15 **Bragadiru** Teleorman, S Romania 43°43′N 25°32′E
61 C20 **Bragado** Buenos Aires, E Argentina 35°10′S 60°29′W
104 J5 **Bragança** *Eng.* Braganza; *anc.* Julio Briga. Bragança, NE Portugal 41°47′N 06°46′W
104 I5 **Bragança** ◈ *district* N Portugal
60 N9 **Bragança Paulista** São Paulo, S Brazil 22°55′S 46°30′W
Braganza *see* Bragança
Bragin *see* Brahin
29 V7 **Braham** Minnesota, N USA 45°43′N 93°10′W
Brahe *see* Brda
Brahestad *see* Raahe
119 O20 **Brahin** *Rus.* Bragin. Homyel'skaya Voblasts', SE Belarus 51°47′N 30°16′E
153 U15 **Brahmanbaria** Chittagong, E Bangladesh 23°58′N 91°04′E
154 O12 **Brāhmani** ≈ E India
154 N13 **Brahmapur** Orissa, E India 19°21′N 84°51′E
129 S10 **Brahmaputra** *var.* Padma, Tsangpo, *Ben.* Jamuna, *Chin.* Yarlung Zangbo Jiang, *Ind.* Bramaputra, Dihang, Siang. ≈ S Asia
97 H19 **Braich y Pwll** *headland* NW Wales, United Kingdom 52°47′N 04°46′W
183 R10 **Braidwood** New South Wales, SE Australia 35°26′S 149°48′E
30 M11 **Braidwood** Illinois, N USA 41°16′N 88°12′W
116 M13 **Brăila** Brăila, E Romania 45°17′N 27°57′E
116 L13 **Brăila** ◈ *county* SE Romania
99 G19 **Braine-l'Alleud** Brabant Walloon, C Belgium 50°41′N 04°22′E
99 F19 **Braine-le-Comte** Hainaut, SW Belgium 50°37′N 04°08′E
29 U6 **Brainerd** Minnesota, N USA 46°22′N 94°10′W
99 J19 **Braives** Liège, E Belgium 50°37′N 05°09′E
83 H23 **Brak** ≈ C South Africa
Brak *see* Birāk
99 E18 **Brakel** Oost-Vlaanderen, SW Belgium 50°50′N 03°48′E
98 J13 **Brakel** Gelderland, C Netherlands 51°49′N 05°05′E
76 H9 **Brakna** ◈ *region* S Mauritania
95 J17 **Brålanda** Västra Götaland, S Sweden 58°32′N 12°18′E
Bramaputra *see* Brahmaputra
95 F23 **Bramming** Ribe, W Denmark 55°28′N 08°42′E
14 G15 **Brampton** Ontario, S Canada 43°42′N 79°46′W
100 F12 **Bramsche** Niedersachsen, NW Germany 52°25′N 07°58′E
116 J12 **Bran** *Ger.* Törzburg, *Hung.* Törcsvár. Brașov, S Romania 45°31′N 25°23′E
29 W8 **Branch** Minnesota, N USA 45°29′N 92°57′W
21 R14 **Branchville** South Carolina, SE USA 33°15′N 80°49′W
47 Y6 **Branco, Cabo** *headland* E Brazil 07°08′S 34°45′W
58 F11 **Branco, Rio** ≈ N Brazil
108 J8 **Brand** Vorarlberg, W Austria 47°07′N 09°45′E
83 B18 **Brandberg** ▲ NW Namibia 21°20′S 14°22′E
95 H14 **Brandbu** Oppland, S Norway 60°24′N 10°30′E
95 F22 **Brande** Ringkøbing, W Denmark 55°57′N 09°08′E
Brandebourg *see* Brandenburg
100 M12 **Brandenburg** *var.* Brandenburg an der Havel. Brandenburg, NE Germany 52°25′N 12°34′E
20 K5 **Brandenburg** Kentucky, S USA 38°00′N 86°11′W
100 N12 **Brandenburg** *off.* Freie und Hansestadt Hamburg, *Fr.* Brandebourg. ◈ *state* NE Germany
Brandenburg an der Havel *see* Brandenburg
83 I23 **Brandfort** Free State, C South Africa 28°42′S 26°28′E
11 W16 **Brandon** Manitoba, S Canada 49°50′N 99°57′W
23 V12 **Brandon** Florida, SE USA 27°56′N 82°17′W
22 L6 **Brandon** Mississippi, S USA 32°16′N 90°01′W
97 A20 **Brandon Mountain** *Ir.* Cnoc Bréanainn. ▲ SW Ireland 52°13′N 10°16′W
Brandsen *see* Coronel Brandsen
95 I14 **Brandval** Hedmark, S Norway 60°18′N 12°01′E
83 F24 **Brandvlei** Northern Cape, W South Africa 30°27′S 20°29′E
23 U9 **Branford** Florida, SE USA 29°57′N 82°54′W
110 K7 **Braniewo** *Ger.* Braunsberg. Warmińsko-mazurskie, N Poland 54°24′N 19°50′E
194 H3 **Bransfield Strait** *strait* Antarctica
37 U8 **Branson** Colorado, C USA 37°01′N 103°52′W
27 T8 **Branson** Missouri, C USA 36°38′N 93°13′W
14 G16 **Brantford** Ontario, S Canada 43°09′N 80°17′W
102 L12 **Brantôme** Dordogne, SW France 45°21′N 00°37′E
182 L12 **Branxholme** Victoria, SE Australia 37°51′S 141°48′E
Brasil *see* Brazil
59 C16 **Brasiléia** Acre, W Brazil 10°59′S 48°45′W
59 K18 **Brasília** ● (Brazil) Distrito Federal, C Brazil 15°45′S 47°57′W
Brasil, Repùblica Federativa do *see* Brazil
Braslav *see* Braslaw
118 J12 **Braslaw** *Pol.* Brasław, *Rus.* Braslav. Vitsyebskaya Voblasts', N Belarus 55°38′N 27°02′E
116 J12 **Brașov** *Ger.* Kronstadt, *Hung.* Brassó; *prev.* Orașul Stalin. Brașov, C Romania 45°40′N 25°35′E
116 I12 **Brașov** ◈ *county* C Romania
77 U18 **Brass** Bayelsa, S Nigeria 04°19′N 06°21′E
99 H16 **Brasschaat** *var.* Brasschaet. Antwerpen, N Belgium 51°17′N 04°30′E
Brasschaet *see* Brasschaat
169 V8 **Brassey, Banjaran** *var.* Brassey Range. ▲▲ East Malaysia
Brassey Range *see* Brassey, Banjaran
Brassó *see* Brașov
23 T1 **Brasstown Bald** ▲ Georgia, SE USA 34°52′N 83°48′W
113 K22 **Brataj** Vlorë, SW Albania 40°18′N 19°37′E
114 J10 **Bratan** *var.* Morozov. ▲ C Bulgaria 42°31′N 25°08′E
111 F21 **Bratislava** *Ger.* Pressburg, *Hung.* Pozsony. ● (Slovakia) Bratislavský Kraj, W Slovakia 48°10′N 17°10′E
111 H21 **Bratislavský Kraj** ◈ *region* W Slovakia
114 H10 **Bratiya** ▲ C Bulgaria 42°36′N 24°08′E
122 M12 **Bratsk** Irkutskaya Oblast', C Russian Federation 56°20′N 101°50′E
117 Q8 **Brats'ke** Mykolayivs'ka Oblast', S Ukraine 47°52′N 31°34′E
122 M13 **Bratskoye Vodokhranilishche** *Eng.* Bratsk Reservoir. ⊠ S Russian Federation
Bratsk Reservoir *see* Bratskoye Vodokhranilishche
Brattia *see* Brač
94 D9 **Brattvåg** Møre og Romsdal, S Norway 62°36′N 06°21′E
112 K12 **Bratunac** ◈ Republika Srpska, E Bosnia and Herzegovina
114 J10 **Bratya Daskalovi** *prev.* Grozdovo. Stara Zagora, C Bulgaria 42°13′N 25°21′E
109 U2 **Braunau** ≈ N Austria
Braunau *see* Braunau am Inn
109 Q4 **Braunau am Inn** *var.* Braunau. Oberösterreich, N Austria 48°16′N 13°03′E
Braunsberg *see* Braniewo
100 J13 **Braunschweig** *Eng./Fr.* Brunswick. Niedersachsen, N Germany 52°16′N 10°32′E
Brava *see* Baraawe
105 Y6 **Brava, Costa** *coastal region* NE Spain
43 V16 **Brava, Punta** *headland* E Panama 08°21′N 78°22′W
95 N17 **Bråviken** *inlet* S Sweden
56 B10 **Bravo, Cerro** ▲ N Peru 05°33′S 79°10′W
Bravo del Norte, Río/Bravo, Río *see* Grande, Rio
35 X17 **Brawley** California, W USA 32°58′N 115°31′W
97 G18 **Bray** *Ir.* Bré. E Ireland 53°12′N 06°06′W
59 G16 **Brazil** *off.* Federative Republic of Brazil, *Port.* Repùblica Federativa do Brasil, *Sp.* Brasil; *prev.* United States of Brazil. ◆ *federal republic* South America
65 K15 **Brazil Basin** *var.* Brazilian Basin, Brazil'skaya Kotlovina. *undersea feature* W Atlantic Ocean 15°00′S 25°00′W
Brazil, Federative Republic of *see* Brazil
Brazilian Basin *see* Brazil Basin
Brazilian Highlands *see* Central, Planalto
Brazil'skaya Kotlovina *see* Brazil Basin
Brazil, United States of *see* Brazil
25 U10 **Brazos River** ≈ Texas, SW USA
Brazza *see* Brač
79 G21 **Brazzaville** ● (Congo) Capital District, S Congo 04°14′S 15°14′E
79 G21 **Brazzaville** ✈ Pool, S Congo 04°15′S 15°15′E
112 J11 **Brčko** ◈ Republika Srpska, NE Bosnia and Herzegovina
110 H8 **Brda** *Ger.* Brahe. ≈ N Poland
Bré *see* Bray
185 A23 **Breaksea Sound** *sound* South Island, New Zealand
184 L4 **Bream Bay** *bay* North Island, New Zealand
184 L4 **Bream Head** *headland* North Island, New Zealand 35°51′S 174°35′E
Bréanainn, Cnoc *see* Brandon Mountain
45 S6 **Brea, Punta** *headland* W Puerto Rico 17°56′N 66°55′W
22 I9 **Breaux Bridge** Louisiana, S USA 30°16′N 91°54′W
116 J13 **Breaza** Prahova, SE Romania 45°13′N 25°38′E
169 P16 **Brebes** Jawa, C Indonesia 06°54′S 109°00′E
96 K10 **Brechin** E Scotland, United Kingdom 56°45′N 02°38′W
99 H15 **Brecht** Antwerpen, N Belgium 51°21′N 04°33′E
37 S4 **Breckenridge** Colorado, C USA 39°28′N 106°02′W
29 R6 **Breckenridge** Minnesota, N USA 46°15′N 96°35′W
25 R6 **Breckenridge** Texas, SW USA 32°45′N 98°56′W
97 J21 **Brecknock** *cultural region* SE Wales, United Kingdom
63 G25 **Brecknock, Península** *headland* S Chile 54°39′S 71°48′W
111 G19 **Břeclav** *Ger.* Lundenburg. Jihomoravský Kraj, SE Czech Republic 49°05′N 16°51′E
97 J21 **Brecon** E Wales, United Kingdom 51°58′N 03°26′W

◆ Country
● Country Capital
◇ Dependent Territory
○ Dependent Territory Capital
◈ Administrative Regions
✈ International Airport
▲ Mountain
▲▲ Mountain Range
🌋 Volcano
≈ River
◎ Lake
⊠ Reservoir

BRECON BEACONS – BUFORD

97 J21 **Brecon Beacons** ▲▲ S Wales, United Kingdom
99 I14 **Breda** Noord-Brabant, S Netherlands 51°35′N 04°46′E
95 K20 **Bredaryd** Jönköping, S Sweden 57°10′N 13°45′E
83 F26 **Bredasdorp** Western Cape, SW South Africa 34°32′S 20°02′E
93 H16 **Bredbyn** Västernorrland, N Sweden 63°28′N 18°04′E
122 F11 **Bredy** Chelyabinskaya Oblast′, C Russian Federation 52°23′N 60°24′E
99 K17 **Bree** Limburg, NE Belgium 51°08′N 05°36′E
67 T15 **Breede** ≈ S South Africa
98 I7 **Breezand** Noord-Holland, NW Netherlands 52°52′N 04°47′E
113 P18 **Bregalnica** ≈ E FYR Macedonia
108 I6 **Bregenz** anc. Brigantium. Vorarlberg, W Austria 47°31′N 09°46′E
108 J7 **Bregenzer Wald** ▲▲ W Austria
114 F6 **Bregovo** Vidin, NW Bulgaria 44°07′N 22°40′E
102 H5 **Bréhat, Île de** island NW France
92 H2 **Breidhafjördhur** bay W Iceland
92 L3 **Breidhdalsvík** Austurland, E Iceland 64°48′N 14°02′W
108 H9 **Breil** Ger. Brigels. Graubünden, S Switzerland 46°46′N 09°04′E
92 J8 **Breivikbotn** Finnmark, N Norway 70°36′N 22°19′E
94 I9 **Brekken** Sør-Trøndelag, S Norway 62°39′N 11°49′E
94 G7 **Brekstad** Sør-Trøndelag, S Norway 63°42′N 09°40′E
94 B10 **Bremangerlandet** island S Norway
Brême see Bremen
100 H11 **Bremen** Fr. Brême. Bremen, NW Germany 53°06′N 08°48′E
23 R3 **Bremen** Georgia, SE USA 33°43′N 85°09′W
31 O11 **Bremen** Indiana, N USA 41°24′N 86°07′W
100 H10 **Bremen** off. Freie Hansestadt Bremen, Fr. Brême. ◈ state N Germany
100 G9 **Bremerhaven** Bremen, NW Germany 53°33′N 08°35′E
Bremersdorp see Manzini
32 G8 **Bremerton** Washington, NW USA 47°34′N 122°37′W
100 H10 **Bremervörde** Niedersachsen, NW Germany 53°29′N 09°06′E
25 U9 **Bremond** Texas, SW USA 31°10′N 96°40′W
25 U10 **Brenham** Texas, SW USA 30°09′N 96°24′W
108 M8 **Brenner** Tirol, W Austria 47°10′N 11°51′E
Brenner, Col du/Brennero, Passo del see Brenner Pass
108 M8 **Brenner Pass** var. Brenner Sattel, Fr. Col du Brenner, Ger. Brennerpass, It. Passo del Brennero. pass Austria/Italy
Brennerpass see Brenner Pass
Brenner Sattel see Brenner Pass
108 G10 **Brenno** ≈ SW Switzerland
106 F7 **Breno** Lombardia, N Italy 45°58′N 10°18′E
23 O5 **Brent** Alabama, S USA 32°54′N 87°10′W
106 H7 **Brenta** ≈ NE Italy
97 P21 **Brentwood** E England, United Kingdom 51°38′N 00°21′E
18 L14 **Brentwood** Long Island, New York, NE USA 40°46′N 73°12′W
106 F7 **Brescia** anc. Brixia. Lombardia, N Italy 45°33′N 10°13′E
99 D15 **Breskens** Zeeland, SW Netherlands 51°24′N 03°33′E
Breslau see Wrocław
106 H5 **Bressanone** Ger. Brixen. Trentino-Alto Adige, N Italy 46°44′N 11°41′E
96 M2 **Bressay** island NE Scotland, United Kingdom
102 K9 **Bressuire** Deux-Sèvres, W France 46°50′N 00°29′W
119 F20 **Brest** Pol. Brześć nad Bugiem, Rus. Brest-Litovsk; prev. Brześć Litewski. Brestskaya Voblasts′, SW Belarus 52°06′N 23°42′E
102 F5 **Brest** Finistère, NW France 48°24′N 04°31′W
Brest-Litovsk see Brest
112 A10 **Brestova** Istra, NW Croatia 45°09′N 14°13′E
Brestskaya Oblast′ see Brestskaya Voblasts′
119 G19 **Brestskaya Voblasts′** prev. Rus. Brestskaya Oblast′. ◈ province SW Belarus
102 G6 **Bretagne** Eng. Brittany, Lat. Britannia Minor. ◈ region NW France
116 G12 **Bretea-Română** Hung. Oláhbrettye; prev. Bretea-Romînă. Hunedoara, W Romania 45°39′N 23°00′E
Bretea-Romînă see Bretea-Română
103 O3 **Breteuil** Oise, N France 49°37′N 02°18′E
102 I10 **Breton, Pertuis** inlet W France
22 L10 **Breton Sound** sound Louisiana, S USA
184 K2 **Brett, Cape** headland North Island, New Zealand 35°11′S 174°21′E
101 G21 **Bretten** Baden-Württemberg, SW Germany 49°01′N 08°42′E
99 K15 **Breugel** Noord-Brabant, S Netherlands 51°30′N 05°30′E
106 B6 **Breuil-Cervinia** It. Cervinia. Valle d′Aosta, NW Italy 45°57′N 07°37′E
98 I11 **Breukelen** Utrecht, C Netherlands 52°11′N 05°01′E
21 P10 **Brevard** North Carolina, SE USA 35°13′N 82°46′W
38 L9 **Brevig Mission** Alaska, USA 65°19′N 166°29′W
95 G16 **Brevik** Telemark, S Norway 59°05′N 09°42′E
183 P5 **Brewarrina** New South Wales, SE Australia 30°01′S 146°50′E
19 R6 **Brewer** Maine, NE USA 44°46′N 68°44′W
29 T11 **Brewster** Minnesota, N USA 43°43′N 95°28′W
29 N14 **Brewster** Nebraska, C USA 41°57′N 99°52′W
31 U12 **Brewster** Ohio, N USA 40°42′N 81°36′W
Brewster, Kap see Kangikajik
183 O8 **Brewster, Lake** ◎ New South Wales, SE Australia
23 P7 **Brewton** Alabama, S USA 31°06′N 87°04′W
Brezhnev see Naberezhnyye Chelny
109 W12 **Brežice** Ger. Rann. E Slovenia 45°54′N 15°35′E
114 G9 **Breznik** Pernik, W Bulgaria 42°45′N 22°54′E
111 K19 **Brezno** Ger. Bries, Briesen, Hung. Breznóbánya; prev. Brezno nad Hronom. Banskobystrický Kraj, C Slovakia 48°49′N 19°40′E
Breznóbánya/Brezno nad Hronom see Brezno
116 I12 **Brezoi** Vâlcea, SW Romania 45°18′N 24°15′E
114 J10 **Brezovo** prev. Abrashlare. Plovdiv, C Bulgaria 42°19′N 25°05′E
79 K14 **Bria** Haute-Kotto, C Central African Republic 06°30′N 22°00′E
103 U13 **Briançon** anc. Brigantio. Hautes-Alpes, SE France 44°55′N 06°37′E
36 K7 **Brian Head** ▲ Utah, W USA 37°40′N 112°49′W
103 O7 **Briare** Loiret, C France 47°35′N 02°46′E
183 V2 **Bribie Island** island Queensland, E Australia
43 O14 **Bribri** Limón, E Costa Rica 09°37′N 82°51′W
116 L8 **Briceni** var. Brinceni, Rus. Brichany. N Moldova 48°21′N 27°02′E
Bricgstow see Bristol
Brichany see Briceni
99 M24 **Bridel** Luxembourg, C Luxembourg 49°40′N 06°03′E
97 J22 **Bridgend** S Wales, United Kingdom 51°30′N 03°37′W
14 I14 **Bridgenorth** Ontario, SE Canada 44°21′N 78°22′W
23 Q1 **Bridgeport** Alabama, S USA 34°57′N 85°42′W
35 R8 **Bridgeport** California, W USA 38°14′N 119°15′W
18 L13 **Bridgeport** Connecticut, NE USA 41°10′N 73°12′W
31 N15 **Bridgeport** Illinois, N USA 38°42′N 87°45′W
28 J14 **Bridgeport** Nebraska, C USA 41°37′N 103°07′W
25 S6 **Bridgeport** Texas, SW USA 33°12′N 97°45′W
21 S3 **Bridgeport** West Virginia, NE USA 39°17′N 80°15′W
25 S5 **Bridgeport, Lake** ⊠ Texas, SW USA
33 U11 **Bridger** Montana, NW USA 45°16′N 108°55′W
18 I17 **Bridgeton** New Jersey, NE USA 39°24′N 75°10′W
180 J14 **Bridgetown** Western Australia 34°01′S 116°07′E
45 Y14 **Bridgetown** ● (Barbados) SW Barbados 13°05′N 59°36′W
183 P17 **Bridgewater** Tasmania, SE Australia 42°47′S 147°15′E
13 P16 **Bridgewater** Nova Scotia, SE Canada 44°19′N 64°30′W
19 P12 **Bridgewater** Massachusetts, NE USA 41°59′N 70°58′W
29 Q11 **Bridgewater** South Dakota, N USA 43°33′N 97°30′W
21 U5 **Bridgewater** Virginia, NE USA 38°22′N 78°58′W
19 P8 **Bridgton** Maine, NE USA 44°04′N 70°43′W
97 K23 **Bridgwater** SW England, United Kingdom 51°08′N 03°W
97 K22 **Bridgwater Bay** bay SW England, United Kingdom
97 O16 **Bridlington** E England, United Kingdom 54°05′N 00°12′W
97 O16 **Bridlington Bay** bay E England, United Kingdom
183 P15 **Bridport** Tasmania, SE Australia 41°03′S 147°26′E
97 K24 **Bridport** S England, United Kingdom 50°44′N 02°43′W
103 O5 **Brie** cultural region N France
Brieg see Brzeg
Briel see Brielle
98 G12 **Brielle** var. Briel, Bril, Eng. The Brill. Zuid-Holland, SW Netherlands 51°54′N 04°10′E
108 E9 **Brienz** Bern, C Switzerland 46°45′N 08°00′E
108 E9 **Brienzer See** ◎ SW Switzerland
Bries/Briesen see Brezno
Brietzig see Brzesko
103 S4 **Briey** Meurthe-et-Moselle, NE France 49°15′N 05°57′E
108 E10 **Brig** Fr. Brigue, It. Briga. Valais, SW Switzerland 46°19′N 08°E
Briga see Brig
101 G24 **Brigach** ≈ S Germany
18 K17 **Brigantine** New Jersey, NE USA 39°23′N 74°21′W
Brigantio see Briançon
Brigantium see Bregenz
Brigels see Breil
25 S9 **Briggs** Texas, SW USA 30°52′N 97°55′W
36 L1 **Brigham City** Utah, W USA 41°30′N 112°00′W
14 J15 **Brighton** Ontario, SE Canada 44°01′N 77°44′W
97 O23 **Brighton** SE England, United Kingdom 50°50′N 00°10′W
37 T4 **Brighton** Colorado, C USA 39°58′N 104°46′W
30 K15 **Brighton** Illinois, N USA 39°01′N 90°09′W
103 T16 **Brignoles** Var, W France 43°25′N 06°03′E
Brigue see Brig
105 O7 **Brihuega** Castilla-La Mancha, C Spain 40°45′N 02°52′W
112 A10 **Brijuni** It. Brioni. island group NW Croatia
76 G12 **Brikama** W Gambia 13°13′N 16°37′W
Bril see Brielle
Brill, The see Brielle
101 G15 **Brilon** Nordrhein-Westfalen, W Germany 51°24′N 08°34′E
Brinceni see Briceni
107 Q18 **Brindisi** anc. Brundisium, Brundusium. Puglia, SE Italy 40°39′N 17°55′E
27 W11 **Brinkley** Arkansas, C USA 34°53′N 91°11′W
Brioni see Brijuni
103 P12 **Brioude** anc. Brivas. Haute-Loire, C France 45°18′N 03°23′E
Briovera see St-Lô
183 U2 **Brisbane** state capital Queensland, E Australia 27°30′S 153°E
183 V2 **Brisbane** ✈ Queensland, E Australia 27°30′S 153°00′E
25 P2 **Briscoe** Texas, SW USA 35°34′N 100°17′W
106 H10 **Brisighella** Emilia-Romagna, C Italy 44°12′N 11°45′E
108 G11 **Brissago** Ticino, S Switzerland 46°07′N 08°40′E
97 K22 **Bristol** anc. Bricgstow. SW England, United Kingdom 51°27′N 02°35′W
18 M12 **Bristol** Connecticut, NE USA 41°40′N 72°56′W
23 R9 **Bristol** Florida, SE USA 30°25′N 84°58′W
19 N9 **Bristol** New Hampshire, NE USA 43°34′N 71°42′W
29 Q8 **Bristol** South Dakota, N USA 45°18′N 97°45′W
21 P8 **Bristol** Tennessee, S USA 36°36′N 82°11′W
18 M8 **Bristol** Vermont, NE USA 44°07′N 73°00′W
39 N14 **Bristol Bay** bay Alaska, USA
97 I22 **Bristol Channel** inlet England/Wales, United Kingdom
35 W14 **Bristol Lake** ◎ California, W USA
27 P10 **Bristow** Oklahoma, C USA 35°49′N 96°23′W
86 C10 **Britain** var. Great Britain. island United Kingdom
Britannia Minor see Bretagne
10 L12 **British Columbia** Fr. Colombie-Britannique. ◈ province SW Canada
British Guiana see Guyana
British Honduras see Belize
173 Q7 **British Indian Ocean Territory** ◇ UK dependent territory C Indian Ocean
86 B9 **British Isles** island group NW Europe
10 I1 **British Mountains** ▲▲ Yukon Territory, NW Canada
British North Borneo see Sabah
British Solomon Islands Protectorate see Solomon Islands
45 S8 **British Virgin Islands** var. Virgin Islands. ◇ UK dependent territory E West Indies
83 J21 **Brits** North-West, N South Africa 25°39′S 27°47′E
83 H24 **Britstown** Northern Cape, W South Africa 30°36′S 23°30′E
14 F12 **Britt** Ontario, S Canada 45°46′N 80°34′W
29 V12 **Britt** Iowa, C USA 43°06′N 93°48′W
Brittany see Bretagne
29 Q7 **Britton** South Dakota, N USA 45°47′N 97°45′W
Briva Curretia see Brive-la-Gaillarde
Briva Isarae see Pontoise
Brivas see Brioude
Brive see Brive-la-Gaillarde
102 M12 **Brive-la-Gaillarde** prev. Brive; anc. Briva Curretia. Corrèze, C France 45°09′N 01°31′E
105 O4 **Briviesca** Castilla-León, N Spain 42°33′N 03°19′W
Brixen see Bressanone
Brixia see Brescia
145 S15 **Brlik** var. Novotroickoje, Novotroitskoye. Zhambyl, SE Kazakhstan 43°39′N 73°45′E
Brněnský Kraj see Jihomoravský Kraj
111 G18 **Brno** Ger. Brünn. Jihomoravský Kraj, SE Czech Republic 49°11′N 16°35′E
96 G7 **Broad Bay** bay NW Scotland, United Kingdom
25 X8 **Broaddus** Texas, SW USA 31°18′N 94°16′W
183 O12 **Broadford** Victoria, SE Australia 37°07′S 145°04′E
96 G9 **Broadford** N Scotland, United Kingdom 57°14′N 05°54′W
96 J13 **Broad Law** ▲ S Scotland, United Kingdom 55°30′N 03°22′W
23 U3 **Broad River** ≈ Georgia, SE USA
21 N8 **Broad River** ≈ North Carolina/South Carolina, SE USA
181 Y8 **Broadsound Range** ▲▲ Queensland, E Australia
33 X11 **Broadus** Montana, NW USA 45°28′N 105°22′W
21 U4 **Broadway** Virginia, NE USA 38°36′N 78°48′W
118 E9 **Brocēni** Saldus, SW Latvia 56°41′N 22°31′E
11 U11 **Brochet** Manitoba, C Canada 57°55′N 101°40′W
11 U10 **Brochet, Lac** ◎ Manitoba, C Canada
15 S5 **Brochet, Lac au** ◎ Québec, SE Canada
101 K14 **Brocken** ▲ C Germany 51°48′N 10°38′E
19 O12 **Brockton** Massachusetts, NE USA 42°04′N 71°01′W
14 L14 **Brockville** Ontario, SE Canada 44°35′N 75°44′W
18 D13 **Brockway** Pennsylvania, NE USA 41°14′N 78°45′W
Brod/Bród see Slavonski Brod
9 N5 **Brodeur Peninsula** peninsula Baffin Island, Nunavut, NE Canada
96 H13 **Brodick** W Scotland, United Kingdom 55°34′N 05°10′W
Brod na Savi see Slavonski Brod
110 K9 **Brodnica** Ger. Buddenbrock. Kujawski-pomorskie, C Poland 53°15′N 19°23′E
112 G10 **Brod-Posavina** off. Brodsko-Posavska Županija, var. Slavonski Brod-Posavina. ◈ province NE Croatia
Brodsko-Posavska Županija see Brod-Posavina
116 J5 **Brody** L′vivs′ka Oblast′, NW Ukraine 50°05′N 25°08′E
98 I10 **Broek-in-Waterland** Noord-Holland, C Netherlands 52°27′N 04°59′E
32 L13 **Brogan** Oregon, NW USA 44°15′N 117°34′W
110 N10 **Brok** Mazowieckie, C Poland 52°42′N 21°53′E
27 P9 **Broken Arrow** Oklahoma, C USA 36°03′N 95°47′W
183 T9 **Broken Bay** bay New South Wales, SE Australia
29 N15 **Broken Bow** Nebraska, C USA 41°24′N 99°38′W
27 R13 **Broken Bow** Oklahoma, C USA 34°01′N 94°44′W
27 R12 **Broken Bow Lake** ⊠ Oklahoma, C USA
182 L6 **Broken Hill** New South Wales, SE Australia 31°58′S 141°27′E
173 S10 **Broken Ridge** undersea feature S Indian Ocean 31°30′S 95°00′E
186 C6 **Broken Water Bay** bay W Bismarck Sea
55 W10 **Brokopondo** Brokopondo, NE Suriname 05°04′N 55°00′W
55 W10 **Brokopondo** ◈ district C Suriname
Bromberg see Bydgoszcz
95 L22 **Bromölla** Skåne, S Sweden 56°04′N 14°28′E
97 L20 **Bromsgrove** W England, United Kingdom 52°20′N 02°03′W
95 G20 **Brønderslev** Nordjylland, N Denmark 57°16′N 09°58′E
106 D8 **Broni** Lombardia, N Italy 45°04′N 09°18′E
10 K11 **Bronlund Peak** ▲ British Columbia, W Canada 57°27′N 126°43′W
93 F14 **Brønnøysund** Nordland, C Norway 65°38′N 12°15′E
23 V10 **Bronson** Florida, SE USA 29°25′N 82°38′W
31 Q11 **Bronson** Michigan, N USA 41°52′N 85°11′W
25 X8 **Bronson** Texas, SW USA 31°20′N 94°00′W
107 L24 **Bronte** Sicilia, Italy, C Mediterranean Sea 37°47′N 14°50′E
25 P8 **Bronte** Texas, SW USA 31°53′N 100°17′W
25 Y9 **Brookeland** Texas, SW USA 31°05′N 93°57′W
170 M7 **Brooke′s Point** Palawan, W Philippines 08°54′N 117°54′E
27 T3 **Brookfield** Missouri, C USA 39°46′N 93°04′W
22 K7 **Brookhaven** Mississippi, S USA 31°34′N 90°26′W
32 E16 **Brookings** Oregon, NW USA 42°03′N 124°16′W
29 R10 **Brookings** South Dakota, N USA 44°15′N 96°46′W
29 W14 **Brooklyn** Iowa, C USA 41°43′N 92°27′W
29 U8 **Brooklyn Park** Minnesota, N USA 45°06′N 93°18′W
21 U7 **Brookneal** Virginia, NE USA 37°03′N 78°56′W
11 R16 **Brooks** Alberta, SW Canada 50°35′N 111°54′W
25 V11 **Brookshire** Texas, SW USA 29°47′N 95°57′W
38 L8 **Brooks Mountain** ▲ Alaska, USA 65°31′N 167°24′W
38 M11 **Brooks Range** ▲▲ Alaska, USA
31 O12 **Brookston** Indiana, N USA 40°34′N 86°53′W
23 V11 **Brooksville** Florida, SE USA 28°33′N 82°23′W
23 N4 **Brooksville** Mississippi, S USA 33°13′N 88°34′W
180 J13 **Brookton** Western Australia 32°24′S 117°04′E
31 Q14 **Brookville** Indiana, N USA 39°25′N 85°00′W
18 D13 **Brookville** Pennsylvania, NE USA 41°07′N 79°05′W
31 Q14 **Brookville Lake** ⊠ Indiana, N USA
180 K5 **Broome** Western Australia 17°58′S 122°15′E
37 S4 **Broomfield** Colorado, C USA 39°55′N 105°05′W
Broos see Orăştie
96 J7 **Brora** N Scotland, United Kingdom 57°59′N 04°00′W
96 I7 **Brora** ≈ N Scotland, United Kingdom
95 F23 **Brørup** Ribe, W Denmark 55°29′N 09°01′E
95 L23 **Brösarp** Skåne, S Sweden 55°43′N 14°10′E
116 J9 **Broşteni** Suceava, NE Romania 47°14′N 25°43′E
102 M6 **Brou** Eure-et-Loir, C France 48°12′N 01°10′E
Broucsella see Brussel/Bruxelles
Broughton Bay see Tongjosŏn-man
Broughton Island see Qikiqtarjuaq
138 G7 **Broummâna** C Lebanon 33°53′N 35°39′E
22 I9 **Broussard** Louisiana, S USA 30°09′N 91°57′W
98 E13 **Brouwersdam** dam SW Netherlands
98 E13 **Brouwershaven** Zeeland, SW Netherlands 51°44′N 03°50′E
117 P4 **Brovary** Kyyivs′ka Oblast′, N Ukraine 50°30′N 30°45′E
95 G20 **Brovst** Nordjylland, N Denmark 57°06′N 09°32′E
31 S8 **Brown City** Michigan, N USA 43°12′N 82°50′W
24 M6 **Brownfield** Texas, SW USA 33°11′N 102°16′W
33 Q7 **Browning** Montana, NW USA 48°33′N 113°00′W
33 R6 **Brown, Mount** ▲ Montana, NW USA 48°52′N 111°08′W
0 M9 **Browns Bank** undersea feature NW Atlantic Ocean 42°40′N 66°05′W
31 O14 **Brownsburg** Indiana, N USA 39°50′N 86°24′W
18 J16 **Browns Mills** New Jersey, NE USA 39°58′N 74°33′W
44 J12 **Browns Town** C Jamaica 18°28′N 77°22′W
31 P15 **Brownstown** Indiana, N USA 38°52′N 86°02′W
29 R8 **Browns Valley** Minnesota, N USA 45°36′N 96°49′W
20 K7 **Brownsville** Kentucky, S USA 37°10′N 86°18′W
20 F9 **Brownsville** Tennessee, S USA 35°35′N 89°15′W
25 T17 **Brownsville** Texas, SW USA 25°56′N 97°28′W
55 W10 **Brownsweg** Brokopondo, C Suriname
29 U9 **Brownton** Minnesota, N USA 44°43′N 94°21′W
19 R5 **Brownville Junction** Maine, NE USA 45°20′N 69°04′W
25 R8 **Brownwood** Texas, SW USA 31°42′N 98°59′W
25 R8 **Brownwood Lake** ⊠ Texas, SW USA
104 I9 **Brozas** Extremadura, W Spain 39°37′N 06°48′W
119 M18 **Brozha** Mahilyowskaya Voblasts′, E Belarus 52°57′N 29°07′E
103 O2 **Bruay-en-Artois** Pas-de-Calais, N France 50°31′N 02°30′E
103 P2 **Bruay-sur-l′Escaut** Nord, N France 50°24′N 03°33′E
14 F13 **Bruce Peninsula** peninsula Ontario, S Canada
20 H9 **Bruceton** Tennessee, S USA 36°02′N 88°14′W
25 T9 **Bruceville** Texas, SW USA 31°17′N 97°15′W
101 G21 **Bruchsal** Baden-Württemberg, SW Germany 49°07′N 08°35′E
109 Q7 **Bruck** Salzburg, NW Austria 47°18′N 12°51′E
Bruck see Bruck an der Mur
109 Y4 **Bruck an der Leitha** Niederösterreich, NE Austria 48°02′N 16°47′E
109 V7 **Bruck an der Mur** var. Bruck. Steiermark, C Austria 47°25′N 15°17′E
101 M24 **Bruckmühl** Bayern, SE Germany 47°52′N 11°54′E
168 E7 **Brueuh, Pulau** island NW Indonesia
Bruges see Brugge
108 F6 **Brugg** Aargau, NW Switzerland 47°29′N 08°13′E
99 C16 **Brugge** Fr. Bruges. West-Vlaanderen, NW Belgium 51°13′N 03°14′E
109 R9 **Bruggen** Kärnten, S Austria 46°46′N 13°13′E
101 E16 **Brühl** Nordrhein-Westfalen, W Germany 50°50′N 06°55′E
99 F14 **Bruinisse** Zeeland, SW Netherlands 51°40′N 04°04′E
169 R9 **Bruit, Pulau** island East Malaysia
14 K10 **Brûlé, Lac** ◎ Québec, SE Canada
30 M4 **Brule River** ≈ Michigan/Wisconsin, N USA
99 H23 **Brûly** Namur, S Belgium 49°55′N 04°31′E
59 N17 **Brumado** Bahia, E Brazil 14°14′S 41°38′W
98 M11 **Brummen** Gelderland, E Netherlands 52°05′N 06°10′E
94 H13 **Brumunddal** Hedmark, S Norway 60°54′N 11°00′E
23 Q6 **Brundidge** Alabama, S USA 31°43′N 85°49′W
Brundisium/Brundusium see Brindisi
33 N15 **Bruneau River** ≈ Idaho, NW USA
Bruneck see Brunico
169 T8 **Brunei** off. Brunei Darussalam, Mal. Negara Brunei Darussalam. ◆ monarchy SE Asia
169 T7 **Brunei Bay** var. Teluk Brunei. bay N Brunei
Brunei Darussalam see Brunei
Brunei, Teluk see Brunei Bay
Brunei Town see Bandar Seri Begawan
106 H5 **Brunico** Ger. Bruneck. Trentino-Alto Adige, N Italy 46°49′N 11°57′E
Brünn see Brno
185 G17 **Brunner, Lake** ◎ South Island, New Zealand
99 M18 **Brunssum** Limburg, SE Netherlands 50°57′N 05°59′E
23 W7 **Brunswick** Georgia, SE USA 31°09′N 81°30′W
19 Q8 **Brunswick** Maine, NE USA 43°54′N 69°58′W
21 V3 **Brunswick** Maryland, NE USA 39°18′N 77°37′W
27 T3 **Brunswick** Missouri, C USA 39°25′N 93°07′W
31 T11 **Brunswick** Ohio, N USA 41°14′N 81°50′W
Brunswick see Braunschweig
63 H24 **Brunswick, Península** headland S Chile 53°30′S 71°27′W
111 H17 **Bruntál** Ger. Freudenthal. Moravskoslezský Kraj, E Czech Republic 50°00′N 17°27′E
195 N3 **Brunt Ice Shelf** ice shelf Antarctica
Brusa see Bursa
114 G7 **Brusartsi** Montana, NW Bulgaria 43°39′N 23°04′E
37 U3 **Brush** Colorado, C USA 40°15′N 103°37′W
42 M5 **Brus Laguna** Gracias a Dios, E Honduras 15°46′N 84°32′W
60 K13 **Brusque** Santa Catarina, S Brazil 27°07′S 48°54′W
Brussa see Bursa
99 E18 **Brussel** var. Brussels, Fr. Bruxelles, Ger. Brüssel; anc. Broucsella. ● (Belgium) Brussels, C Belgium 50°52′N 04°21′E see also Bruxelles
Brussel see Bruxelles
Brüssel/Brussels see Brussel/Bruxelles
117 O5 **Brusyliv** Zhytomyrs′ka Oblast′, N Ukraine 50°16′N 29°31′E
183 Q12 **Bruthen** Victoria, SE Australia 37°43′S 147°49′E
Bruttium see Calabria
Brüx see Most
99 E18 **Bruxelles** var. Brussels, Dut. Brussel, Ger. Brüssel; anc. Broucsella. ● Brussels, C Belgium 50°52′N 04°21′E see also Brussel
Bruxelles see Brussel
54 J7 **Bruzual** Apure, W Venezuela 07°59′N 69°18′W
31 Q11 **Bryan** Ohio, N USA 41°30′N 84°34′W
25 U10 **Bryan** Texas, SW USA 30°40′N 96°23′W
194 J4 **Bryan Coast** physical region Antarctica
122 L11 **Bryanka** Krasnoyarskiy Kray, C Russian Federation 59°01′N 93°13′E
117 Y7 **Bryanka** Luhans′ka Oblast′, E Ukraine 48°30′N 38°45′E
182 J8 **Bryan, Mount** ▲ South Australia 33°25′S 138°59′E
126 I6 **Bryansk** Bryanskaya Oblast′, W Russian Federation 53°16′N 34°07′E
126 H6 **Bryanskaya Oblast′** ◈ province W Russian Federation
194 J5 **Bryant, Cape** headland Antarctica
27 U8 **Bryant Creek** ≈ Missouri, C USA
36 K8 **Bryce Canyon** canyon Utah, W USA
119 O15 **Bryli** Mahilyowskaya Voblasts′, E Belarus 53°54′N 30°33′E
95 C17 **Bryne** Rogaland, S Norway 58°43′N 05°40′E
25 R6 **Bryson** Texas, SW USA 33°09′N 98°23′W
21 N10 **Bryson City** North Carolina, SE USA 35°26′N 83°27′W
14 K11 **Bryson, Lac** ◎ Québec, SE Canada
126 K13 **Bryukhovetskaya** Krasnodarskiy Kray, SW Russian Federation 45°49′N 38°01′E
111 H15 **Brzeg** Ger. Brieg; anc. Civitas Altae Ripae. Opolskie, S Poland 50°52′N 17°27′E
111 G14 **Brzeg Dolny** Ger. Dyhernfurth. Dolnośląskie, SW Poland 51°15′N 16°40′E
Brześć Litewski/Brześć nad Bugiem see Brest
111 L17 **Brzesko** Ger. Brietzig. Małopolskie, SE Poland 49°59′N 20°34′E
Brzeżany see Berezhany
110 K12 **Brzeziny** Łódzkie, C Poland 51°49′N 19°41′E
Brzostowica Wielka see Vyalikaya Byerastavitsa
111 O17 **Brzozów** Podkarpackie, SE Poland 49°38′N 22°00′E
Bsharrī/Bsherri see Bcharré
187 X14 **Bua** Vanua Levu, N Fiji 16°48′S 178°36′E
95 J20 **Bua** Halland, S Sweden 57°14′N 12°07′E
82 M13 **Bua** ≈ C Malawi
Bua see Čiovo
81 L18 **Bu′aale** It. Buale. Jubbada Dhexe, SW Somalia 0°52′N 42°37′E
Buache, Mount see Mutunte, Mount
189 Q8 **Buada Lagoon** lagoon Nauru, C Pacific Ocean
186 M8 **Buala** Santa Isabel, E Solomon Islands 08°06′S 159°31′E
Buale see Bu′aale
190 H1 **Buariki** atoll Tungaru, W Kiribati
167 Q10 **Bua Yai** var. Ban Bua Yai. Nakhon Ratchasima, E Thailand 15°35′N 102°25′E
75 P8 **Bu′ayrāt al Ḩasūn** var. Buwayrāt al Hasūn. C Libya 31°22′N 15°41′E
76 H13 **Buba** S Guinea-Bissau 11°36′N 14°55′W
171 P11 **Bubaa** Sulawesi, N Indonesia 0°32′N 122°27′E
81 D20 **Bubanza** NW Burundi 03°04′S 29°22′E
83 K18 **Bubi** prev. Bubye. ≈ S Zimbabwe
142 L11 **Būbīyan, Jazīrat** island E Kuwait
Bublitz see Bobolice
Bubye see Bubi
187 Y13 **Buca** prev. Mbutha. Vanua Levu, N Fiji 16°39′S 179°51′E
136 F16 **Bucak** Burdur, SW Turkey 37°28′N 30°37′E
54 G8 **Bucaramanga** Santander, N Colombia 07°08′N 73°10′W
107 M18 **Buccino** Campania, S Italy 40°37′N 15°25′E
116 K9 **Bucecea** Botoşani, NE Romania 47°45′N 26°30′E
116 J6 **Buchach** Pol. Buczacz. Ternopil′s′ka Oblast′, W Ukraine 49°04′N 25°23′E
183 Q12 **Buchan** Victoria, SE Australia 37°26′S 148°11′E
76 J17 **Buchanan** prev. Grand Bassa. SW Liberia 05°53′N 10°03′W
23 R3 **Buchanan** Georgia, SE USA 33°48′N 85°11′W
31 O11 **Buchanan** Michigan, N USA 41°49′N 86°21′W
21 T6 **Buchanan** Virginia, NE USA 37°31′N 79°40′W
25 R10 **Buchanan Dam** Texas, SW USA 30°42′N 98°24′W
25 R10 **Buchanan, Lake** ⊠ Texas, SW USA
96 L8 **Buchan Ness** headland NE Scotland, United Kingdom 57°28′N 01°46′W
13 T12 **Buchans** Newfoundland and Labrador, SE Canada 48°49′N 56°53′W
Bucharest see Bucureşti
101 H20 **Buchen** Baden-Württemberg, SW Germany 49°31′N 09°18′E
100 I10 **Buchholz in der Nordheide** Niedersachsen, NW Germany 53°19′N 09°52′E
108 F7 **Buchs** Aargau, N Switzerland 47°24′N 08°04′E
108 I8 **Buchs** Sankt Gallen, NE Switzerland 47°10′N 09°28′E
100 H13 **Bückeburg** Niedersachsen, NW Germany 52°16′N 09°03′E
36 K14 **Buckeye** Arizona, SW USA 33°22′N 112°34′W
Buckeye State see Ohio
21 S4 **Buckhannon** West Virginia, NE USA 38°59′N 80°14′W
25 T9 **Buckholts** Texas, SW USA 30°52′N 97°07′W
96 K8 **Buckie** NE Scotland, United Kingdom 57°39′N 02°56′W
14 M12 **Buckingham** Québec, SE Canada 45°35′N 75°25′W
21 U6 **Buckingham** Virginia, NE USA 37°33′N 78°34′W
97 N21 **Buckinghamshire** cultural region SE England, United Kingdom
39 N8 **Buckland** Alaska, USA 65°58′N 161°07′W
182 G7 **Buckleboo** South Australia 32°55′S 136°11′E
26 K7 **Bucklin** Kansas, C USA 37°33′N 99°37′W
27 T3 **Bucklin** Missouri, C USA 39°46′N 92°53′W
36 I12 **Buckskin Mountains** ▲▲ Arizona, SW USA
19 R7 **Bucksport** Maine, NE USA 44°34′N 68°46′W
82 A9 **Buco Zau** Cabinda, NW Angola 04°45′S 12°34′E
Bu Craa see Bou Craa
116 K14 **Bucureşti** Eng. Bucharest, Ger. Bukarest, prev. Altenburg; anc. Cetatea Damboviţei. ● (Romania) Bucureşti, S Romania 44°27′N 26°06′E
31 S12 **Bucyrus** Ohio, N USA 40°47′N 82°57′W
Buczacz see Buchach
94 E9 **Bud** Møre og Romsdal, S Norway 62°55′N 06°55′E
25 S11 **Buda** Texas, SW USA 30°05′N 97°50′W
119 O18 **Buda-Kashalyova** Rus. Buda-Koshelëvo. Homyel′skaya Voblasts′, SE Belarus 52°43′N 30°34′E
Buda-Koshelëvo see Buda-Kashalyova
166 L4 **Budalin** Sagaing, C Myanmar (Burma) 22°24′N 95°08′E
111 J22 **Budapest** off. Budapest Főváros, SCr. Budimpešta. ● (Hungary) Pest, N Hungary 47°30′N 19°03′E
Budapest Főváros see Budapest
152 K11 **Budaun** Uttar Pradesh, N India 28°02′N 79°07′E
141 O9 **Budayyi‘ah** oasis C Saudi Arabia
195 Y12 **Budd Coast** physical region Antarctica
Buddenbrock see Brodnica
107 C17 **Budduso** Sardegna, Italy, C Mediterranean Sea 40°37′N 09°19′E
97 I23 **Bude** SW England, United Kingdom 50°50′N 04°33′W
22 J7 **Bude** Mississippi, S USA 31°27′N 90°51′W
Budějovický Kraj see Jihočeský Kraj
99 K16 **Budel** Noord-Brabant, SE Netherlands 51°17′N 05°35′E
100 I8 **Büdelsdorf** Schleswig-Holstein, N Germany 54°20′N 09°40′E
127 O14 **Budënnovsk** Stavropol′skiy Kray, SW Russian Federation 44°46′N 44°07′E
116 K14 **Budeşti** Călăraşi, SE Romania 44°13′N 26°30′E
Budge-Budge see Baj Baj
Budgewoi see Budgewoi Lake
183 T8 **Budgewoi Lake** var. Budgewoi. New South Wales, SE Australia 33°14′S 151°34′E
92 I2 **Búdhardalur** Vesturland, W Iceland 65°07′N 21°45′W
Budimpešta see Budapest
79 J16 **Budjala** Equateur, NW Dem. Rep. Congo 02°39′N 19°42′E
106 G10 **Budrio** Emilia-Romagna, C Italy 44°33′N 11°34′E
Budslav see Budslaw
119 K14 **Budslaw** Rus. Budslav. Minskaya Voblasts′, N Belarus 54°47′N 27°27′E
Budua see Budva
169 R9 **Budu, Tanjung** headland East Malaysia 02°51′N 111°42′E
113 J17 **Budva** It. Budua. W Montenegro 42°17′N 18°49′E
Budweis see České Budějovice
Budyšin see Bautzen
79 D16 **Buea** Sud-Ouest, SW Cameroon 04°09′N 09°13′E
103 S13 **Buëch** ≈ SE France
18 J17 **Buena** New Jersey, NE USA 39°30′N 74°55′W
62 K12 **Buena Esperanza** San Luis, C Argentina 34°45′S 65°15′W
54 C11 **Buenaventura** Valle del Cauca, W Colombia 03°54′N 77°02′W
40 I4 **Buenaventura** Chihuahua, N Mexico 29°50′N 107°30′W
57 M18 **Buena Vista** Santa Cruz, C Bolivia 17°28′S 63°37′W
40 G10 **Buenavista** Baja California Sur, NW Mexico 23°39′N 109°41′W
37 S5 **Buena Vista** Colorado, C USA 38°50′N 106°07′W
23 S5 **Buena Vista** Georgia, SE USA 32°19′N 84°31′W
21 T6 **Buena Vista** Virginia, NE USA 37°44′N 79°22′W
44 F5 **Buena Vista, Bahia de** bay N Cuba
35 R13 **Buena Vista Lake Bed** ◎ California, W USA
105 P8 **Buendía, Embalse de** ⊠ C Spain
63 F16 **Bueno, Río** ≈ S Chile
62 N12 **Buenos Aires** hist. Santa Maria del Buen Aire. ● (Argentina) Buenos Aires, E Argentina 34°40′S 58°30′W
43 O15 **Buenos Aires** Puntarenas, SE Costa Rica 09°10′N 83°23′W
61 C20 **Buenos Aires** off. Provincia de Buenos Aires. ◈ province E Argentina
63 H19 **Buenos Aires, Lago** var. Lago General Carrera. ◎ Argentina/Chile
Buenos Aires, Provincia de see Buenos Aires
54 C13 **Buesaco** Nariño, SW Colombia 01°22′N 77°07′W
29 U8 **Buffalo** Minnesota, N USA 45°11′N 93°50′W
26 T6 **Buffalo** Missouri, C USA 37°38′N 93°05′W
18 D10 **Buffalo** New York, NE USA 42°53′N 78°53′W
27 K8 **Buffalo** Oklahoma, C USA 36°51′N 99°38′W
28 J7 **Buffalo** South Dakota, N USA 45°25′N 103°35′W
25 V8 **Buffalo** Texas, SW USA 31°25′N 96°04′W
33 W12 **Buffalo** Wyoming, C USA 44°21′N 106°40′W
29 U11 **Buffalo Center** Iowa, C USA 43°23′N 93°57′W
24 M3 **Buffalo Lake** ⊠ Texas, SW USA
30 K7 **Buffalo Lake** ⊠ Wisconsin, N USA
11 S12 **Buffalo Narrows** Saskatchewan, C Canada 55°52′N 108°28′W
27 U9 **Buffalo River** ≈ Arkansas, C USA
29 R5 **Buffalo River** ≈ Minnesota, N USA
20 I10 **Buffalo River** ≈ Tennessee, S USA
30 J6 **Buffalo River** ≈ Wisconsin, N USA
44 L12 **Buff Bay** E Jamaica 18°18′N 76°40′W
23 T3 **Buford** Georgia, SE USA 34°07′N 84°00′W

◆ Country
● Country Capital
◇ Dependent Territory
○ Dependent Territory Capital
◈ Administrative Regions
✈ International Airport
▲ Mountain
▲▲ Mountain Range
Volcano
≈ River
◎ Lake
⊠ Reservoir

BUFORD – CAÁLA

28 *J3* **Buford** North Dakota, N USA *48°00′N 103°58′W*
33 *Y17* **Buford** Wyoming, C USA *41°05′N 105°17′W*
116 *J14* **Buftea** Ilfov, S Romania *44°34′N 25°58′E*
84 *I9* **Bug** ***Bel.*** Zakhodni Buh, ***Eng.*** Western Bug, ***Rus.*** Zapadnyy Bug, ***Ukr.*** Zakhidnyy Buh. ≈ E Europe
54 *D11* **Buga** Valle del Cauca, W Colombia *03°53′N 76°17′W*
Buga *see* Dörvöljin
103 *O17* **Bugarach, Pic du** ▲ S France *42°52′N 02°23′E*
162 *F8* **Bugat** ***var.*** Bayangol. Govĭ-Altay, SW Mongolia *45°33′N 94°22′E*
146 *B12* **Bugdaýly** ***Rus.*** Bugdayly. Balkan Welaýaty, W Turkmenistan *38°42′N 54°14′E*
Bugdayly *see* Bugdaýly
Buggs Island Lake *see* John H. Kerr Reservoir
Bughotu *see* Santa Isabel
171 *O14* **Bugingkalo** Sulawesi, C Indonesia *04°49′S 121°42′E*
64 *P6* **Bugio** *island* Madeira, Portugal, NE Atlantic Ocean
92 *M8* **Bugøynes** Finnmark, N Norway *69°57′N 29°34′E*
125 *Q3* **Bugrino** Nenetskiy Avtonomnyy Okrug, NW Russian Federation *68°48′N 49°12′E*
127 *T5* **Bugul'ma** Respublika Tatarstan, W Russian Federation *54°31′N 52°45′E*
Bügür *see* Luntai
127 *T6* **Buguruslan** Orenburgskaya Oblast', W Russian Federation *53°38′N 52°30′E*
159 *R9* **Buh He** ≈ C China
101 *F22* **Bühl** Baden-Württemberg, SW Germany *48°42′N 08°07′E*
33 *O15* **Buhl** Idaho, NW USA *42°36′N 114°45′W*
116 *K10* **Buhuşi** Bacău, E Romania *46°41′N 26°45′E*
Buie d'Istria *see* Buje
97 *J20* **Builth Wells** E Wales, United Kingdom *52°07′N 03°28′W*
186 *J8* **Buin** Bougainville Island, NE Papua New Guinea *06°52′S 155°42′E*
108 *J9* **Buin, Piz** ▲ Austria/Switzerland *46°51′N 10°07′E*
127 *Q4* **Buinsk** Chuvashskaya Respublika, W Russian Federation *55°09′N 47°00′E*
127 *Q4* **Buinsk** Respublika Tatarstan, W Russian Federation *54°58′N 48°16′E*
163 *R8* **Buir Nur** ***Mong.*** Buyr Nuur. ◎ China/Mongolia ***see also*** Buyr Nuur
Buir Nur *see* Buyr Nuur
98 *M5* **Buitenpost** ***Fris.*** Bûtenpost. Friesland, N Netherlands *53°15′N 06°09′E*
Buitenzorg *see* Bogor
83 *F19* **Buitepos** Omaheke, E Namibia *22°17′S 19°59′E*
105 *N7* **Buitrago del Lozoya** Madrid, C Spain *41°00′N 03°38′W*
Buj *see* Buy
104 *M13* **Bujalance** Andalucía, S Spain *37°54′N 04°23′W*
113 *O17* **Bujanovac** SE Serbia *42°29′N 21°44′E*
105 *S6* **Bujaraloz** Aragón, NE Spain *41°29′N 00°10′W*
112 *A9* **Buje** ***It.*** Buie d'Istria. Istra, NW Croatia *45°23′N 13°40′E*
Bujnurd *see* Bojnūrd
81 *D21* **Bujumbura** ***prev.*** Usumbura. ● (Burundi) W Burundi *03°25′S 29°24′E*
81 *D20* **Bujumbura** ✈ W Burundi *03°21′S 29°19′E*
159 *N11* **Buka Daban** ***var.*** Bukadaban Feng. ▲ C China *36°09′N 90°52′E*
Bukadaban Feng *see* Buka Daban
186 *J6* **Buka Island** *island* NE Papua New Guinea
81 *F18* **Bukakata** S Uganda *0°18′S 31°57′E*
79 *N24* **Bukama** Katanga, SE Dem. Rep. Congo *09°13′S 25°52′E*
142 *J4* **Būkān** ***var.*** Bowkān. Āzarbāyjān-e Gharbī, NW Iran *36°31′N 46°10′E*
Bukantau, Gory *see* Bo'kantov Tog'lari
Bukarest *see* Bucureşti
79 *O19* **Bukavu** ***prev.*** Costermansville. Sud-Kivu, E Dem. Rep. Congo *02°19′S 28°49′E*
81 *F21* **Bukene** Tabora, NW Tanzania *04°15′S 32°51′E*
141 *W8* **Bū Khābī** ***var.*** Bakhābī. NW Oman *23°29′N 56°06′E*
Bukhara *see* Buxoro
Bukharskaya Oblast' *see* Buxoro Viloyati
168 *M14* **Bukitkemuning** Sumatera, W Indonesia *04°43′S 104°27′E*
168 *I11* **Bukittinggi** ***prev.*** Fort de Kock. Sumatera, W Indonesia *0°18′S 100°20′E*
111 *L21* **Bükk** ▲▲ NE Hungary
81 *F19* **Bukoba** Kagera, NW Tanzania *01°19′S 31°49′E*
113 *N20* **Bukovo** S FYR Macedonia *40°59′N 21°20′E*
108 *G6* **Bülach** Zürich, NW Switzerland *47°31′N 08°30′E*
Būlaevo *see* Bulayevo
Bulag *see* Tünel, Hövsgöl, Mongolia
Bulag *see* Möngönmorĭt, Töv, Mongolia
Bulagiyn Denj *see* Bulgan
183 *U7* **Bulahdelah** New South Wales, SE Australia *32°24′S 152°13′E*
171 *P4* **Bulan** Luzon, N Philippines *12°40′N 123°55′E*
137 *N11* **Bulancak** Giresun, N Turkey *40°57′N 38°14′E*
152 *J10* **Bulandshahr** Uttar Pradesh, N India *28°30′N 77°49′E*
137 *R14* **Bulanık** Muş, E Turkey *39°04′N 42°16′E*
127 *V7* **Bulanovo** Orenburgskaya Oblast', W Russian Federation *52°27′N 55°08′E*
83 *J17* **Bulawayo** ***var.*** Buluwayo. Bulawayo, SW Zimbabwe *20°08′S 28°37′E*
83 *J17* **Bulawayo** ✈ Matabeleland North, SW Zimbabwe *20°00′S 28°36′E*
145 *Q6* **Bulayevo** ***Kaz.*** Būlaevo. Severnyy Kazakhstan, N Kazakhstan *54°55′N 70°29′E*
136 *D15* **Buldan** Denizli, SW Turkey *38°03′N 28°50′E*
154 *G12* **Buldāna** Mahārāshtra, C India *20°31′N 76°18′E*
38 *E16* **Buldir Island** *island* Aleutian Islands, Alaska, USA
Buldur *see* Burdur
162 *I8* **Bulgan** ***var.*** Bulagiyn Denj. Arhangay, C Mongolia *47°14′N 100°56′E*
162 *D7* **Bulgan** ***var.*** Jargalant. Bayan-Ölgiy, W Mongolia *46°56′N 91°07′E*
162 *K6* **Bulgan** Bulgan, N Mongolia *50°31′N 101°30′E*
162 *F7* **Bulgan** ***var.*** Bürenhayrhan. Hovd, W Mongolia *46°04′N 91°34′E*
162 *J10* **Bulgan** Ömnögovĭ, S Mongolia *44°07′N 103°28′E*
162 *J7* **Bulgan** ◈ *province* N Mongolia
Bulgan *see* Bayan-Öndör, Bayanhongor, C Mongolia
Bulgan *see* Darvi, Hovd, Mongolia
Bulgan *see* Tsagaan-Üür, Hövsgöl, Mongolia
114 *H10* **Bulgaria** ***off.*** Republic of Bulgaria, ***Bul.*** Bŭlgariya; ***prev.*** People's Republic of Bulgaria. ◆ *republic* SE Europe
Bulgaria, People's Republic of *see* Bulgaria
Bulgaria, Republic of *see* Bulgaria
Bŭlgariya *see* Bulgaria
114 *L9* **Bŭlgarka** ▲ E Bulgaria *42°43′N 26°19′E*
171 *S11* **Buli** Pulau Halmahera, E Indonesia *0°56′N 128°17′E*
171 *S11* **Buli, Teluk** *bay* Pulau Halmahera, E Indonesia
160 *J13* **Buliu He** ≈ S China
Bullange *see* Büllingen
Bulla, Ostrov *see* Xärä Zirä Adası
104 *M11* **Bullaque** ≈ C Spain
105 *Q13* **Bullas** Murcia, SE Spain *38°02′N 01°40′W*
80 *M12* **Bullaxaar** Woqooyi Galbeed, NW Somalia *10°28′N 44°15′E*
108 *C9* **Bulle** Fribourg, SW Switzerland *46°37′N 07°04′E*
185 *G15* **Buller** ≈ South Island, New Zealand
183 *P12* **Buller, Mount** ▲ Victoria, SE Australia *37°10′S 146°31′E*
36 *H11* **Bullhead City** Arizona, SW USA *35°07′N 114°32′W*
99 *N21* **Büllingen** ***Fr.*** Bullange. Liège, E Belgium *50°23′N 06°15′E*
Bullion State *see* Missouri
21 *T14* **Bull Island** *island* South Carolina, SE USA
182 *M4* **Bulloo River Overflow** *wetland* New South Wales, SE Australia
184 *M12* **Bulls** Manawatu-Wanganui, North Island, New Zealand *40°10′S 175°22′E*
21 *T14* **Bulls Bay** *bay* South Carolina, SE USA
27 *U9* **Bull Shoals Lake** ⊠ Arkansas/Missouri, C USA
181 *Q2* **Bulman** Northern Territory, N Australia *13°39′S 134°21′E*
162 *I6* **Bulnayn Nuruu** ▲▲ N Mongolia
171 *O11* **Bulowa, Gunung** ▲ Sulawesi, N Indonesia *0°33′N 123°39′E*
Bulqiza *see* Bulqizë
113 *L19* **Bulqizë** ***var.*** Bulqiza. Dibër, C Albania *41°30′N 20°16′E*
Bulsar *see* Valsād
171 *N14* **Bulukumba** ***prev.*** Boeloekoemba. Sulawesi, C Indonesia *05°35′S 120°13′E*
147 *O11* **Bulungh'ur** ***Rus.*** Bulungur; ***prev.*** Krasnogvardeysk. Samarqand Viloyati, C Uzbekistan *39°46′N 67°18′E*
79 *I21* **Bulungu** Bandundu, SW Dem. Rep. Congo *04°36′S 18°34′E*
Bulungur *see* Bulungh'ur
Buluwayo *see* Bulawayo
79 *K17* **Bumba** Equateur, N Dem. Rep. Congo *02°14′N 22°25′E*
121 *R12* **Bumbah, Khalīj al** *gulf* N Libya
Bumbat *see* Bayan-Öndör
81 *F19* **Bumbire Island** *island* N Tanzania
169 *V8* **Bum Bun, Pulau** *island* East Malaysia
81 *J17* **Buna** North Eastern, NE Kenya *02°40′N 39°34′E*
25 *Y10* **Buna** Texas, SW USA *30°25′N 94°00′W*
Bunab *see* Bonāb
Bunai *see* M'bunai
147 *S13* **Bunay** S Tajikistan *38°29′N 71°41′E*
180 *I13* **Bunbury** Western Australia *33°24′S 115°44′E*
97 *E14* **Buncrana** ***Ir.*** Bun Cranncha. NW Ireland *55°08′N 07°27′W*
Bun Cranncha *see* Buncrana
181 *Z9* **Bundaberg** Queensland, E Australia *24°50′S 152°16′E*
183 *T5* **Bundarra** New South Wales, SE Australia *30°12′S 151°06′E*
100 *G13* **Bünde** Nordrhein-Westfalen, NW Germany *52°12′N 08°34′E*
152 *H13* **Būndi** Rājasthān, N India *25°28′N 75°42′E*
Bun Dobhráin *see* Bundoran
97 *D15* **Bundoran** ***Ir.*** Bun Dobhráin. NW Ireland *54°30′N 08°11′W*
113 *K18* **Bunë** ***SCr.*** Bojana. ≈ Albania/Montenegro ***see also*** Bojana
Bunë *see* Bojana
171 *Q8* **Bunga** ≈ Mindanao, S Philippines
168 *I12* **Bungalaut, Selat** *strait* W Indonesia
167 *R8* **Bung Kan** Nong Khai, E Thailand *18°19′N 103°39′E*
181 *N4* **Bungle Bungle Range** ▲▲ Western Australia
82 *C10* **Bungo** Uíge, NW Angola *07°30′S 15°24′E*
81 *G18* **Bungoma** Western, W Kenya *0°34′N 34°34′E*
164 *F15* **Bungo-suidō** *strait* SW Japan
164 *E14* **Bungo-Takada** Ōita, Kyūshū, SW Japan *33°34′N 131°28′E*
100 *K8* **Bungsberg** *hill* N Germany
Bungur *see* Bunyu
79 *P17* **Bunia** Orientale, NE Dem. Rep. Congo *01°33′N 30°16′E*
35 *U6* **Bunker Hill** ▲ Nevada, W USA *39°16′N 117°06′W*
22 *I7* **Bunkie** Louisiana, S USA *30°58′N 92°12′W*
23 *X10* **Bunnell** Florida, SE USA *29°28′N 81°15′W*
105 *S10* **Buñol** País Valenciano, E Spain *39°25′N 00°47′W*
98 *K11* **Bunschoten** Utrecht, C Netherlands *52°15′N 05°23′E*
136 *K14* **Bünyan** Kayseri, C Turkey *38°51′N 35°50′E*
169 *W8* **Bunyu** ***var.*** Bungur. Borneo, N Indonesia *03°33′N 117°50′E*
169 *W8* **Bunyu, Pulau** *island* N Indonesia
Bunzlau *see* Bolesławiec
Buoddobohki *see* Patoniva
123 *P7* **Buor-Khaya, Guba** *bay* N Russian Federation
123 *P7* **Buor-Khaya, Guba** *bay* N Russian Federation
171 *Z15* **Bupul** Papua, E Indonesia *07°24′S 140°57′E*
81 *K19* **Bura** Coast, SE Kenya *01°06′S 40°01′E*
80 *P12* **Buraan** Bari, N Somalia *10°03′N 49°08′E*
Būrabay *see* Borovoye
Buraida *see* Buraydah
Buraimi *see* Al Buraymī
145 *Y11* **Buran** Vostochnyy Kazakhstan, E Kazakhstan *48°00′N 85°09′E*
158 *G15* **Burang** Xizang Zizhiqu, W China *30°28′N 81°13′E*
Burao *see* Burco
138 *H8* **Burāq** Dar'ā, S Syria *33°11′N 36°28′E*
141 *O6* **Buraydah** ***var.*** Buraida. Al Qaşīm, N Saudi Arabia *26°50′N 44°E*
35 *S15* **Burbank** California, W USA *34°10′N 118°25′W*
31 *N11* **Burbank** Illinois, N USA *41°45′N 87°48′W*
183 *Q8* **Burcher** New South Wales, SE Australia *33°29′S 147°16′E*
80 *N13* **Burco** ***var.*** Burao, Bur'o. Togdheer, NW Somalia *09°29′N 45°31′E*
162 *K8* **Bürd** ***var.*** Ongon. Övörhangay, C Mongolia *46°58′N 103°45′E*
146 *L13* **Burdalyk** Lebap Welaýaty, E Turkmenistan *38°31′N 64°21′E*
181 *W6* **Burdekin River** ≈ Queensland, NE Australia
27 *O7* **Burden** Kansas, C USA *37°18′N 96°45′W*
Burdigala *see* Bordeaux
136 *E15* **Burdur** ***var.*** Buldur. Burdur, SW Turkey *37°44′N 30°17′E*
136 *E15* **Burdur** ***var.*** Buldur. ◈ *province* SW Turkey
136 *E15* **Burdur Gölü** *salt lake* SW Turkey
65 *H21* **Burdwood Bank** *undersea feature* SW Atlantic Ocean
80 *I12* **Burē** Āmara, N Ethiopia *10°43′N 37°09′E*
80 *H13* **Burē** Oromīya, C Ethiopia *08°13′N 35°09′E*
93 *J15* **Bureå** Västerbotten, N Sweden *64°36′N 21°15′E*
162 *K7* **Büreghangay** ***var.*** Darhan. Bulgan, C Mongolia *48°07′N 103°54′E*
101 *G14* **Büren** Nordrhein-Westfalen, W Germany *51°34′N 08°34′E*
162 *L8* **Büren** ***var.*** Bayantöhöm. Töv, C Mongolia *46°57′N 105°09′E*
162 *K6* **Bürengiyn Nuruu** ▲▲ N Mongolia
Bürenhayrhan *see* Bulgan
162 *I6* **Bürentogtoh** ***var.*** Bayan. Hövsgol, C Mongolia *49°36′N 99°36′E*
Būrewāla *see* Mandi Būrewāla
92 *J9* **Burfjord** Troms, N Norway *69°55′N 21°54′E*
100 *L13* **Burg** ***var.*** Burg an der Ihle, Burg bei Magdeburg. Sachsen-Anhalt, C Germany *52°17′N 11°51′E*
Burg an der Ihle *see* Burg
114 *N10* **Burgas** ***var.*** Bourgas. Burgas, E Bulgaria *42°31′N 27°30′E*
114 *M10* **Burgas** ◈ *province* E Bulgaria
114 *N9* **Burgas** ✈ Burgas, E Bulgaria *42°35′N 27°33′E*
114 *N10* **Burgaski Zaliv** *gulf* E Bulgaria
114 *M10* **Burgasko Ezero** *lagoon* E Bulgaria
21 *V11* **Burgaw** North Carolina, SE USA *34°33′N 77°56′W*
Burg bei Magdeburg *see* Burg
108 *E8* **Burgdorf** Bern, NW Switzerland *47°03′N 07°38′E*
109 *Y7* **Burgenland** ***off.*** Land Burgenland. ◈ *state* SE Austria
13 *S13* **Burgeo** Newfoundland, Newfoundland and Labrador, SE Canada *47°37′N 57°38′W*
83 *I24* **Burgersdorp** Eastern Cape, SE South Africa *31°00′S 26°20′E*
83 *K20* **Burgersfort** Mpumalanga, NE South Africa *24°39′S 30°18′E*
101 *N23* **Burghausen** Bayern, SE Germany *48°10′N 12°48′E*
139 *O5* **Burghūth, Sabkhat al** ◎ E Syria
101 *M20* **Burglengenfeld** Bayern, SE Germany *49°11′N 12°01′E*
41 *P9* **Burgos** Tamaulipas, C Mexico *24°55′N 98°46′W*
105 *N4* **Burgos** Castilla-León, N Spain *42°21′N 03°41′W*
105 *N4* **Burgos** ◈ *province* Castilla-León, N Spain
Burgstadlberg *see* Hradiště
95 *P20* **Burgsvik** Gotland, SE Sweden *57°01′N 18°18′E*
Burgum *see* Bergum
Burgundy *see* Bourgogne
159 *Q11* **Burhan Budai Shan** ▲▲ C China
136 *B12* **Burhaniye** Balıkesir, W Turkey *39°29′N 26°59′E*
154 *G12* **Burhānpur** Madhya Pradesh, C India *21°18′N 76°14′E*
127 *W7* **Buribay** Respublika Bashkortostan, W Russian Federation *51°57′N 58°11′E*
43 *O17* **Burica, Punta** *headland* Costa Rica/Panama *08°02′N 82°53′W*
167 *Q10* **Buriram** ***var.*** Buri Ram, Puriramya. Buri Ram, E Thailand *15°01′N 103°06′E*
Buri Ram *see* Buriram
105 *S10* **Burjassot** País Valenciano, E Spain *39°33′N 00°26′W*
81 *N16* **Burka Giibi** Hiiraan, C Somalia *03°52′N 45°07′E*
147 *X8* **Burkan** ≈ E Kyrgyzstan
25 *R4* **Burkburnett** Texas, SW USA *34°06′N 98°34′W*
29 *O12* **Burke** South Dakota, N USA *43°09′N 99°18′W*
10 *K15* **Burke Channel** *channel* British Columbia, W Canada
194 *J10* **Burke Island** *island* Antarctica
20 *L7* **Burkesville** Kentucky, S USA *36°48′N 85°21′W*
181 *T4* **Burketown** Queensland, NE Australia *17°49′S 139°28′E*
25 *Q8* **Burkett** Texas, SW USA *32°01′N 99°17′W*
25 *Y9* **Burkeville** Texas, SW USA *30°58′N 93°41′W*
21 *V7* **Burkeville** Virginia, NE USA *37°11′N 78°12′W*
77 *O12* **Burkina** ***off.*** Burkina Faso; ***prev.*** Upper Volta. ◆ *republic* W Africa
Burkina *see* Burkina
Burkina Faso *see* Burkina
194 *L13* **Burks, Cape** *headland* Antarctica
14 *H12* **Burk's Falls** Ontario, S Canada *45°38′N 79°25′W*
101 *H23* **Burladingen** Baden-Württemberg, S Germany *48°18′N 09°05′E*
25 *T7* **Burleson** Texas, SW USA *32°32′N 97°19′W*
33 *P15* **Burley** Idaho, NW USA *42°32′N 113°47′W*
144 *G8* **Burlin** Zapadnyy Kazakhstan, NW Kazakhstan *51°25′N 52°42′E*
14 *G16* **Burlington** Ontario, S Canada *42°19′N 79°48′W*
37 *W4* **Burlington** Colorado, C USA *39°17′N 102°17′W*
29 *Y15* **Burlington** Iowa, C USA *40°48′N 91°05′W*
27 *P5* **Burlington** Kansas, C USA *38°11′N 95°46′W*
21 *T9* **Burlington** North Carolina, SE USA *36°05′N 79°27′W*
28 *M3* **Burlington** North Dakota, N USA *48°16′N 101°25′W*
18 *L7* **Burlington** Vermont, NE USA *44°28′N 73°14′W*
30 *M9* **Burlington** Wisconsin, N USA *42°38′N 88°12′W*
27 *Q1* **Burlington Junction** Missouri, C USA *40°27′N 95°04′W*
166 *M4* **Burma** *see* Myanmar
10 *L17* **Burnaby** British Columbia, SW Canada *49°16′N 122°58′W*
117 *O12* **Burnas, Ozero** ◎ SW Ukraine
25 *S10* **Burnet** Texas, SW USA *30°46′N 98°14′W*
35 *O3* **Burney** California, W USA *40°52′N 121°42′W*
183 *O16* **Burnie** Tasmania, SE Australia *41°07′S 145°52′E*
97 *L17* **Burnley** NW England, United Kingdom *53°48′N 02°14′W*
Burnoye *see* Bauyrzhan Momyshuly
153 *R15* **Burnpur** West Bengal, NE India *23°39′N 86°55′E*
32 *K14* **Burns** Oregon, NW USA *43°35′N 119°03′W*
26 *K11* **Burns Flat** Oklahoma, C USA *35°21′N 99°10′W*
20 *M7* **Burnside** Kentucky, S USA *36°55′N 84°34′W*
8 *K8* **Burnside** ≈ Nunavut, NW Canada
32 *L15* **Burns Junction** Oregon, NW USA *42°46′N 117°51′W*
10 *L13* **Burns Lake** British Columbia, SW Canada *54°14′N 125°45′W*
29 *V9* **Burnsville** Minnesota, N USA *44°49′N 93°14′W*
21 *P9* **Burnsville** North Carolina, SE USA *35°56′N 82°18′W*
21 *R4* **Burnsville** West Virginia, NE USA *38°50′N 80°39′W*
14 *I13* **Burnt River** ≈ Ontario, SE Canada
14 *I11* **Burntroot Lake** ◎ Ontario, SE Canada
11 *W12* **Burntwood** ≈ Manitoba, C Canada
Bur'o *see* Burco
158 *L2* **Burqin** Xinjiang Uygur Zizhiqu, NW China *47°42′N 86°50′E*
182 *J8* **Burra** South Australia *33°41′S 138°54′E*
183 *S9* **Burragorang, Lake** ⊠ New South Wales, SE Australia
96 *K5* **Burray** *island* NE Scotland, United Kingdom
113 *L19* **Burrel** ***var.*** Burreli. Dibër, C Albania *41°36′N 20°00′E*
Burreli *see* Burrel
183 *R8* **Burrendong Reservoir** ⊠ New South Wales, SE Australia
183 *R5* **Burren Junction** New South Wales, SE Australia *30°06′S 149°01′E*
105 *T9* **Burriana** País Valenciano, E Spain *39°54′N 00°05′W*
183 *R10* **Burrinjuck Reservoir** ⊠ New South Wales, SE Australia
36 *J12* **Burro Creek** ≈ Arizona, SW USA
40 *M5* **Burro, Serranías del** ▲▲ NW Mexico
62 *K7* **Burruyacú** Tucumán, N Argentina *26°30′S 64°45′W*
136 *E12* **Bursa** ***var.*** Brussa, ***prev.*** Brusa; ***anc.*** Prusa. Bursa, NW Turkey *40°12′N 29°04′E*
136 *D12* **Bursa** ***var.*** Brusa, Brussa. ◈ *province* NW Turkey
75 *Y9* **Bûr Safâga** ***var.*** Būr Safājah. E Egypt *26°43′N 33°55′E*
Būr Safājah *see* Bûr Safâga
75 *W7* **Būr Sa'īd** ***var.*** Port Said. N Egypt *31°17′N 32°18′E*
81 *O14* **Bur Tinle** Nugaal, C Somalia *07°50′N 48°01′E*
31 *Q5* **Burt Lake** ◎ Michigan, N USA
118 *H7* **Burtnieks** ***var.*** Burtnieks Ezers. ◎ N Latvia
Burtnieks Ezers *see* Burtnieks
31 *Q9* **Burton** Michigan, N USA *43°00′N 84°16′W*
Burton on Trent *see* Burton upon Trent
97 *M19* **Burton upon Trent** ***var.*** Burton on Trent, Burton-upon-Trent. C England, United Kingdom *52°48′N 01°36′W*
93 *J15* **Burträsk** Västerbotten, N Sweden *64°31′N 20°40′E*
145 *S14* **Burubaytal** ***prev.*** Burylbaytal. Zhambyl, SE Kazakhstan *44°56′N 73°59′E*
Burujird *see* Borūjerd
Burultokay *see* Fuhai
141 *R15* **Burūm** SE Yemen *14°22′N 48°53′E*
Burunday *see* Boralday
81 *D21* **Burundi** ***off.*** Republic of Burundi; ***prev.*** Kingdom of Burundi, Urundi. ◆ *republic* C Africa
Burundi, Kingdom of *see* Burundi
Burundi, Republic of *see* Burundi
171 *R13* **Buru, Pulau** ***prev.*** Boeroe. *island* E Indonesia
77 *T17* **Burutu** Delta, S Nigeria *05°18′N 05°32′E*
10 *G7* **Burwash Landing** Yukon Territory, W Canada *61°26′N 139°12′W*
29 *O14* **Burwell** Nebraska, C USA *41°46′N 99°04′W*
97 *L17* **Bury** NW England, United Kingdom *53°36′N 02°17′W*
123 *N13* **Buryatiya, Respublika** ***prev.*** Buryatskaya ASSR. ◈ *autonomous republic* S Russian Federation
Buryatskaya ASSR *see* Buryatiya, Respublika
Burylbaytal *see* Burubaytal
117 *S3* **Buryn'** Sums'ka Oblast', NE Ukraine *51°13′N 33°50′E*
97 *P20* **Bury St Edmunds** ***hist.*** Beodericsworth. E England, United Kingdom *52°15′N 00°43′E*
114 *G8* **Bŭrziya** ≈ NW Bulgaria
106 *D9* **Busalla** Liguria, NW Italy *44°35′N 08°55′E*
Busan *see* Pusan
139 *N5* **Buşayrah** Dayr az Zawr, E Syria *35°10′N 40°25′E*
Buševa *see* Baba
143 *N12* **Būshehr** ***off.*** Ostān-e Būshehr. ◈ *province* SW Iran
Būshehr/Bushire *see* Bandar-e Būshehr
Būshehr, Ostān-e *see* Būshehr
25 *N2* **Bushland** Texas, SW USA *35°11′N 102°04′W*
30 *J12* **Bushnell** Illinois, N USA *40°33′N 90°30′W*
Busi *see* Biševo
81 *G18* **Busia** SE Uganda *01°20′N 34°48′E*
Busiasch *see* Buziaş
79 *K16* **Businga** Equateur, NW Dem. Rep. Congo *03°20′N 20°53′E*
79 *J18* **Busira** ≈ NW Dem. Rep. Congo
116 *I5* **Bus'k** ***Rus.*** Busk. L'vivs'ka Oblast', W Ukraine *49°59′N 24°34′E*
95 *E14* **Buskerud** ◈ *county* S Norway
113 *F14* **Buško Jezero** ⊠ SW Bosnia and Herzegovina
111 *M15* **Busko-Zdrój** Świętokrzyskie, C Poland *50°28′N 20°44′E*
Busra *see* Al Başrah, Iraq
Buşrá *see* Buşrá ash Shām, Syria
138 *H9* **Buşrá ash Shām** ***var.*** Bosora, Bosra, Bozrah, Buşrá. Dar'ā, S Syria *32°31′N 36°29′E*
180 *I13* **Busselton** Western Australia *33°43′S 115°15′E*
81 *C14* **Busseri** ≈ W Sudan
106 *E9* **Busseto** Emilia-Romagna, C Italy *45°00′N 10°06′E*
106 *A8* **Bussoleno** Piemonte, NE Italy *45°11′N 07°07′E*
Bussora *see* Al Başrah
41 *N7* **Bustamante** Nuevo León, NE Mexico *26°29′N 100°30′W*
63 *I23* **Bustamante, Punta** *headland* S Argentina *51°35′S 68°58′W*
Bustan *see* Bo'ston
116 *J12* **Buşteni** Prahova, SE Romania *45°23′N 25°32′E*
106 *D7* **Busto Arsizio** Lombardia, N Italy *45°37′N 08°51′E*
147 *Q10* **Bŭston** ***Rus.*** Buston. NW Tajikistan *40°31′N 69°21′E*
100 *H8* **Büsum** Schleswig-Holstein, N Germany *54°08′N 08°52′E*
98 *J10* **Bussum** Noord-Holland, C Netherlands *52°17′N 05°10′E*
79 *M16* **Buta** Orientale, N Dem. Rep. Congo *02°50′N 24°41′E*
81 *E20* **Butare** ***prev.*** Astrida. S Rwanda *02°39′S 29°44′E*
191 *O2* **Butaritari** *atoll* Tungaru, W Kiribati
Butawal *see* Butwal
96 *H13* **Bute** *cultural region* SW Scotland, United Kingdom
162 *K6* **Büteeliyn Nuruu** ▲▲ N Mongolia
10 *L16* **Bute Inlet** *fjord* British Columbia, W Canada
96 *H12* **Bute, Island of** *island* SW Scotland, United Kingdom
79 *P18* **Butembo** Nord-Kivu, NE Dem. Rep. Congo *0°09′N 29°17′E*
Bûtenpost *see* Buitenpost
107 *K25* **Butera** Sicilia, Italy, C Mediterranean Sea *37°12′N 14°12′E*
99 *M20* **Bütgenbach** Liège, E Belgium *50°25′N 06°12′E*
Butha Qi *see* Zalantun
166 *J5* **Buthidaung** Rakhine State, W Myanmar (Burma) *20°50′N 92°25′E*
61 *I16* **Butiá** Rio Grande do Sul, S Brazil *30°09′S 51°55′W*
81 *F17* **Butiaba** NW Uganda *01°48′N 31°21′E*
23 *N6* **Butler** Alabama, S USA *32°05′N 88°13′W*
23 *S5* **Butler** Georgia, SE USA *32°33′N 84°14′W*
31 *Q11* **Butler** Indiana, N USA *41°25′N 84°52′W*
27 *R5* **Butler** Missouri, C USA *38°17′N 94°21′W*
18 *B14* **Butler** Pennsylvania, NE USA *40°51′N 79°52′W*
194 *K5* **Butler Island** *island* Antarctica
21 *U8* **Butner** North Carolina, SE USA *36°07′N 78°45′W*
171 *P14* **Buton, Pulau** ***var.*** Pulau Butung; ***prev.*** Boetoeng. *island* C Indonesia
Bütow *see* Bytów
113 *L23* **Butrintit, Liqeni i** ◎ S Albania
23 *N3* **Buttahatchee River** ≈ Alabama/Mississippi, S USA
33 *Q10* **Butte** Montana, NW USA *46°01′N 112°33′W*
29 *O12* **Butte** Nebraska, C USA *42°54′N 98°51′W*
168 *J7* **Butterworth** Pinang, Peninsular Malaysia *05°24′N 100°22′E*
83 *J25* **Butterworth** ***var.*** Gcuwa. Eastern Cape, SE South Africa *32°20′S 28°09′E*
13 *O3* **Button Islands** *island group* Nunavut, NE Canada
35 *R13* **Buttonwillow** California, W USA *35°24′N 119°26′W*
171 *Q7* **Butuan** ***off.*** Butuan City. Mindanao, S Philippines *08°57′N 125°33′E*
Butuan City *see* Butuan
Butung, Pulau *see* Buton, Pulau
Butuntum *see* Bitonto
126 *M8* **Buturlinovka** Voronezhskaya Oblast', W Russian Federation *50°48′N 40°33′E*
153 *O11* **Butwal** ***var.*** Butawal. Western, C Nepal *27°41′N 83°28′E*
101 *G17* **Butzbach** Hessen, W Germany *50°26′N 08°40′E*
100 *L9* **Bützow** Mecklenburg-Vorpommern, N Germany *53°49′N 11°58′E*
80 *N13* **Buuhoodle** Togdheer, N Somalia *08°18′N 46°15′E*
81 *N16* **Buulobarde** ***var.*** Buulo Berde. Hiiraan, C Somalia *03°52′N 45°37′E*
Buulo Berde *see* Buulobarde
80 *P12* **Buuraha Cal Miskaat** ▲▲ NE Somalia
81 *L19* **Buur Gaabo** Jubbada Hoose, S Somalia *01°14′S 41°48′E*
99 *M22* **Buurgplaatz** ▲ N Luxembourg *50°09′N 06°02′E*
162 *H8* **Buutsagaan** ***var.*** Buyant. Bayanhongor, C Mongolia *46°07′N 98°45′E*
Buwayrāt al Hasūn *see* Bu'ayrāt al Ḩasūn
146 *L11* **Buxoro** ***var.*** Bokhara, ***Rus.*** Bukhara. Buxoro Viloyati, C Uzbekistan *39°51′N 64°23′E*
146 *J11* **Buxoro Viloyati** ***Rus.*** Bukharskaya Oblast'. ◈ *province* C Uzbekistan
100 *I10* **Buxtehude** Niedersachsen, NW Germany *53°29′N 09°42′E*
97 *L18* **Buxton** C England, United Kingdom *53°18′N 01°52′W*
124 *M14* **Buy** ***var.*** Buj. Kostromskaya Oblast', NW Russian Federation *58°27′N 41°31′E*
Buyanbat *see* Jargalant
162 *D6* **Buyant** Bayan-Ölgiy, W Mongolia *48°31′N 89°36′E*
Buyant *see* Buutsagaan, Bayanhongor, Mongolia
Buyant *see* Otgon, Dzavhan, Mongolia
Buyant *see* Galshar, Hentiy, Mongolia
163 *N10* **Buyant-Uhaa** Dornogovĭ, SE Mongolia *44°52′N 110°12′E*
162 *M7* **Buyant Ukha** ✈ (Ulaanbaatar) Töv, N Mongolia
127 *Q16* **Buynaksk** Respublika Dagestan, SW Russian Federation *42°53′N 47°03′E*
119 *L20* **Buynavichy** ***Rus.*** Buynovichi. Homyel'skaya Voblasts', SE Belarus *51°52′N 28°33′E*
Buynovichi *see* Buynavichy
76 *L16* **Buyo** SW Ivory Coast *06°16′N 07°03′W*
76 *L16* **Buyo, Lac de** ⊠ W Ivory Coast
163 *R7* **Buyr Nuur** ***var.*** Buir Nur. ◎ China/Mongolia ***see also*** Buir Nur
Buyr Nuur *see* Buir Nur
137 *T13* **Büyükağrı Dağı** ***var.*** Aghri Dagh, Agri Dagi, Koh I Noh, Masis, ***Eng.*** Great Ararat, Mount Ararat. ▲ E Turkey *39°43′N 44°19′E*
137 *R15* **Büyük Çayı** ≈ NE Turkey
114 *O13* **Büyük Çekmece** İstanbul, NW Turkey *41°02′N 28°35′E*
114 *N12* **Büyükkarıştıran** Kırklareli, NW Turkey *41°17′N 27°33′E*
115 *L14* **Büyükkemikli Burnu** *cape* NW Turkey
136 *E15* **Büyükmenderes Nehri** ≈ SW Turkey
Büyükzap Suyu *see* Great Zab
102 *M9* **Buzançais** Indre, C France *46°53′N 01°25′E*
116 *K13* **Buzău** Buzău, SE Romania *45°08′N 26°51′E*
116 *K13* **Buzău** ◈ *county* SE Romania
116 *L12* **Buzău** ≈ E Romania
75 *S11* **Buzaymah** ***var.*** Bzīmah. SE Libya *24°53′N 22°01′E*
164 *E13* **Buzen** Fukuoka, Kyūshū, SW Japan *33°37′N 131°06′E*
116 *F12* **Buziaş** ***Ger.*** Busiasch, ***Hung.*** Buziásfürdő; ***prev.*** Buziás. Timiş, W Romania *45°38′N 21°36′E*
Buziás *see* Buziaş
Buziásfürdő *see* Buziaş
83 *M18* **Búzi, Rio** ≈ C Mozambique
117 *Q10* **Buz'kyy Lyman** *bay* S Ukraine
Büzmeýin *see* Abadan
145 *O8* **Buzuluk** Akmola, C Kazakhstan *51°53′N 66°09′E*
127 *T6* **Buzuluk** Orenburgskaya Oblast', W Russian Federation *52°47′N 52°16′E*
127 *N8* **Buzuluk** ≈ SW Russian Federation
19 *P12* **Buzzards Bay** Massachusetts, NE USA *41°45′N 70°37′W*
19 *P13* **Buzzards Bay** *bay* Massachusetts, NE USA
83 *G16* **Bwabata** Caprivi, NE Namibia *17°52′S 22°39′E*
186 *H10* **Bwagaoia** Misima Island, SE Papua New Guinea *10°39′S 152°48′E*
Bwake *see* Bouaké
187 *R13* **Bwatnapne** Pentecost, C Vanuatu *15°42′S 168°07′E*
119 *K14* **Byahoml'** ***Rus.*** Begoml'. Vitsyebskaya Voblasts', N Belarus *54°44′N 28°04′E*
114 *K8* **Byala** Ruse, N Bulgaria *43°27′N 25°44′E*
114 *N9* **Byala** ***prev.*** Ak-Dere. Varna, E Bulgaria *42°52′N 27°53′E*
Byala Reka *see* Erythropótamos
114 *H8* **Byala Slatina** Vratsa, NW Bulgaria *43°28′N 23°56′E*
119 *N15* **Byalynichy** ***Rus.*** Belynichi. Mahilyowskaya Voblasts', E Belarus *54°00′N 29°42′E*
Byan Tumen *see* Choybalsan
119 *G19* **Byaroza** ***Pol.*** Bereza Kartuska, ***Rus.*** Berëza. Brestskaya Voblasts', SW Belarus *52°32′N 24°59′E*
119 *H16* **Byarozawka** ***Rus.*** Berëzovka. Hrodzyenskaya Voblasts', W Belarus *53°45′N 25°30′E*
Bybles *see* Jbaïl
111 *O14* **Bychawa** Lubelskie, SE Poland *51°06′N 22°34′E*
Bychikha *see* Bychykha
118 *N11* **Bychykha** ***Rus.*** Bychikha. Vitsyebskaya Voblasts', NE Belarus *55°41′N 29°59′E*
111 *I14* **Byczyna** ***Ger.*** Pitschen. Opolskie, S Poland *51°06′N 18°13′E*
110 *I10* **Bydgoszcz** ***Ger.*** Bromberg. Kujawski-pomorskie, C Poland *53°06′N 18°00′E*
119 *H19* **Byelaazyorsk** ***Rus.*** Beloozersk. Brestskaya Voblasts', SW Belarus *52°28′N 25°10′E*
119 *I17* **Byelaruskaya Hrada** ***Rus.*** Belorusskaya Gryada. *ridge* N Belarus
119 *G18* **Byelavyezhskaya Pushcha** ***Pol.*** Puszcza Białowieska, ***Rus.*** Belovezhskaya Pushcha. *forest* Belarus/Poland ***see also*** Białowieska, Puszcza
Byelavyezhskaya, Pushcha *see* Białowieska, Puszcza
119 *H15* **Byenyakoni** ***Rus.*** Benyakoni. Hrodzyenskaya Voblasts', W Belarus *54°15′N 25°22′E*
119 *M16* **Byerazino** ***Rus.*** Berezino. Minskaya Voblasts', C Belarus *53°50′N 29°00′E*
118 *L13* **Byerazino** ***Rus.*** Berezino. Vitsyebskaya Voblasts', N Belarus *54°54′N 28°12′E*
119 *L14* **Byerezino** ***Rus.*** Berezina. ≈ C Belarus
118 *M13* **Byeshankovichy** ***Rus.*** Beshenkovichi. Vitsyebskaya Voblasts', N Belarus *55°03′N 29°27′E*
31 *U13* **Byesville** Ohio, N USA *39°58′N 81°32′W*
119 *P18* **Byesyedz'** ***Rus.*** Besed'. ≈ SE Belarus
119 *H19* **Byezdzyezh** ***Rus.*** Bezdezh. Brestskaya Voblasts', SW Belarus *52°19′N 25°18′E*
93 *J15* **Bygdeå** Västerbotten, N Sweden *64°03′N 20°49′E*
94 *F12* **Bygdin** ◎ S Norway
93 *J15* **Bygdsiljum** Västerbotten, N Sweden *64°20′N 20°31′E*
95 *E17* **Bygland** Aust-Agder, S Norway *58°46′N 07°50′E*
95 *E17* **Byglandsfjord** Aust-Agder, S Norway *58°42′N 07°51′E*
119 *N16* **Bykhaw** ***Rus.*** Bykhov. Mahilyowskaya Voblasts', E Belarus *53°31′N 30°15′E*
Bykhov *see* Bykhaw
127 *P9* **Bykovo** Volgogradskaya Oblast', SW Russian Federation *49°52′N 45°24′E*
123 *P7* **Bykovskiy** Respublika Sakha (Yakutiya), NE Russian Federation *71°57′N 129°07′E*
195 *R12* **Byrd Glacier** *glacier* Antarctica
14 *K10* **Byrd, Lac** ◎ Québec, SE Canada
183 *P5* **Byrock** New South Wales, SE Australia *30°40′S 146°24′E*
30 *L10* **Byron** Illinois, N USA *42°06′N 89°15′W*
183 *V4* **Byron Bay** New South Wales, SE Australia *28°39′S 153°34′E*
183 *V4* **Byron, Cape** *headland* New South Wales, E Australia *28°37′S 153°40′E*
63 *F21* **Byron, Isla** *island* S Chile
Byron Island *see* Nikunau
65 *B24* **Byron Sound** *sound* NW Falkland Islands
122 *M6* **Byrranga, Gora** ▲▲ N Russian Federation
93 *J14* **Byske** Västerbotten, N Sweden *64°58′N 21°10′E*
111 *K18* **Bystrá** ▲ N Slovakia *49°10′N 19°49′E*
111 *F18* **Bystřice nad Pernštejnem** ***Ger.*** Bistritz ober Pernstein. Vysočina, C Czech Republic *49°32′N 16°16′E*
Bystrovka *see* Kemin
111 *G16* **Bystrzyca Kłodzka** ***Ger.*** Habelschwerdt. Wałbrzych, SW Poland *50°19′N 16°39′E*
111 *I18* **Bytča** Žilinský Kraj, N Slovakia *49°15′N 18°32′E*
119 *L15* **Bytcha** Minskaya Voblasts', NE Belarus *54°19′N 28°24′E*
Byteń/Byten' *see* Bytsyen'
111 *J16* **Bytom** ***Ger.*** Beuthen. Śląskie, S Poland *50°21′N 18°51′E*
110 *H7* **Bytów** ***Ger.*** Bütow. Pomorskie, N Poland *54°10′N 17°30′E*
119 *H18* **Bytsyen'** ***Pol.*** Byteń, ***Rus.*** Byten'. Brestskaya Voblasts', SW Belarus *52°53′N 25°30′E*
81 *E19* **Byumba** ***var.*** Biumba. N Rwanda *01°37′S 30°05′E*
Byuzmeyin *see* Abadan
119 *O20* **Byval'ki** Homyel'skaya Voblasts', SE Belarus *51°51′N 30°38′E*
95 *O20* **Byxelkrok** Kalmar, S Sweden *57°18′N 17°01′E*
Byzantium *see* İstanbul
Bzīmah *see* Buzaymah

C

62 *O6* **Caacupé** Cordillera, S Paraguay *25°23′S 57°05′W*
62 *P6* **Caaguazú** ***off.*** Departamento de Caaguazú. ◈ *department* C Paraguay
Caaguazú, Departamento de *see* Caaguazú
82 *C13* **Caála** ***var.*** Kaala, Robert Williams, ***Port.*** Vila Robert Williams. Huambo, C Angola *12°51′S 15°33′E*

◆ Country
● Country Capital
◇ Dependent Territory
○ Dependent Territory Capital
◈ Administrative Regions
✈ International Airport
▲ Mountain
▲▲ Mountain Range
Volcano
≈ River
◎ Lake
⊠ Reservoir

CAAZAPÁ – CANANDAIGUA

62 P7 **Caazapá** Caazapá, S Paraguay 26°09′S 56°21′W
62 P7 **Caazapá** *off.* Departamento de Caazapá. ⬖ *department* SE Paraguay
Caazapá, Departamento de *see* Caazapá
81 P15 **Cabaad, Raas** *headland* C Somalia 06°13′N 49°01′E
55 N10 **Cabadisocaña** Amazonas, S Venezuela 04°28′N 64°45′W
44 F5 **Cabaiguán** Sancti Spíritus, C Cuba 22°04′N 79°32′W
Caballeria, Cabo *see* Cavalleria, Cap de
37 Q14 **Caballo Reservoir** ⊠ New Mexico, SW USA
40 L6 **Caballos Mesteños, Llano de los** *plain* N Mexico
104 L2 **Cabañaquinta** Asturias, N Spain 43°10′N 05°37′W
42 B9 **Cabañas** ⬖ *department* E El Salvador
171 O3 **Cabanatuan** *off.* Cabanatuan City. Luzon, N Philippines 15°27′N 120°57′E
Cabanatuan City *see* Cabanatuan
15 T8 **Cabano** Québec, SE Canada 47°40′N 68°56′W
104 L11 **Cabeza del Buey** Extremadura, W Spain 38°44′N 05°13′W
45 V5 **Cabezas de San Juan** *headland* E Puerto Rico 18°23′N 65°37′W
105 N2 **Cabezón de la Sal** Cantabria, N Spain 43°19′N 04°14′W
Cabhán *see* Cavan
61 B23 **Cabildo** Buenos Aires, E Argentina 38°28′S 61°50′W
Cabillonum *see* Chalon-sur-Saône
54 H5 **Cabimas** Zulia, NW Venezuela 10°26′N 71°27′W
82 A9 **Cabinda** *var.* Kabinda. Cabinda, NW Angola 05°34′S 12°12′E
82 A9 **Cabinda** *var.* Kabinda. ⬖ *province* NW Angola
33 N7 **Cabinet Mountains** ▲▲ Idaho/Montana, NW USA
82 B11 **Cabiri** Bengo, NW Angola 08°50′S 13°42′E
63 J20 **Cabo Blanco** Santa Cruz, SE Argentina 47°13′S 65°43′W
82 P13 **Cabo Delgado** *off.* Província de Capo Delgado. ⬖ *province* NE Mozambique
14 L9 **Cabonga, Réservoir** ⊠ Québec, SE Canada
27 V7 **Cabool** Missouri, C USA 37°07′N 92°06′W
183 V2 **Caboolture** Queensland, E Australia 27°05′S 152°50′E
Cabora Bassa, Lake *see* Cahora Bassa, Albufeira de
40 F3 **Caborca** Sonora, NW Mexico 30°44′N 112°06′W
Cabo San Lucas *see* San Lucas
27 V11 **Cabot** Arkansas, C USA 34°58′N 92°01′W
14 F12 **Cabot Head** *headland* Ontario, S Canada 45°13′N 81°17′W
13 R13 **Cabot Strait** *strait* E Canada
Cabo Verde, Ilhas do *see* Cape Verde
104 M14 **Cabra** Andalucía, S Spain 37°28′N 04°28′W
107 B19 **Cabras** Sardegna, Italy, C Mediterranean Sea 39°55′N 08°30′E
188 A15 **Cabras Island** *island* W Guam
45 O8 **Cabrera** N Dominican Republic 19°40′N 69°54′W
104 J4 **Cabrera** ≈ NW Spain
105 X10 **Cabrera, Illa de** *anc.* Capraria. *island* Islas Baleares, Spain, W Mediterranean Sea
105 Q15 **Cabrera, Sierra** ▲▲ S Spain
11 S16 **Cabri** Saskatchewan, S Canada 50°38′N 108°28′W
105 R10 **Cabriel** ≈ E Spain
54 M7 **Cabruta** Guárico, C Venezuela 07°39′N 66°19′W
171 N2 **Cabugao** Luzon, N Philippines 17°55′N 120°29′E
54 G10 **Cabuyaro** Meta, C Colombia 04°21′N 72°47′W
60 I13 **Caçador** Santa Catarina, S Brazil 26°47′S 51°00′W
42 G8 **Cacaguatique, Cordillera** *var.* Cordillera. ▲▲ NE El Salvador
112 L13 **Čačak** Serbia, C Serbia 43°52′N 20°23′E
55 Y10 **Cacao** NE French Guiana 04°37′N 52°29′W
61 H16 **Caçapava do Sul** Rio Grande do Sul, S Brazil 30°28′S 53°29′W
21 U3 **Cacapon River** ≈ West Virginia, NE USA
107 J23 **Caccamo** Sicilia, Italy, C Mediterranean Sea 37°56′N 13°40′E
107 A17 **Caccia, Capo** *headland* Sardegna, Italy, C Mediterranean Sea 40°34′N 08°09′E
146 H15 **Çäçe** *var.* Chäche, *Rus.* Chaacha. Ahal Welaýaty, S Turkmenistan 36°49′N 60°33′E
59 G18 **Cáceres** Mato Grosso, W Brazil 16°05′S 57°40′W
104 J10 **Cáceres** *Ar.* Qazris. Extremadura, W Spain 39°29′N 06°23′W
104 J9 **Cáceres** ⬖ *province* Extremadura, W Spain
Cachacrou *see* Scotts Head Village
61 C21 **Cacharí** Buenos Aires, E Argentina 36°24′S 59°32′W
26 L12 **Cache** Oklahoma, C USA 34°37′N 98°37′W
10 M16 **Cache Creek** British Columbia, SW Canada 50°49′N 121°20′W
35 N6 **Cache Creek** ≈ California, W USA
37 S3 **Cache La Poudre River** ≈ Colorado, C USA
Cacheo *see* Cacheu
27 W11 **Cache River** ≈ Arkansas, C USA
30 L17 **Cache River** ≈ Illinois, N USA
76 G12 **Cacheu** *var.* Cacheo. W Guinea-Bissau 12°12′N 16°10′W
59 I15 **Cachimbo** Pará, NE Brazil 09°21′S 54°58′W
59 H15 **Cachimbo, Serra do** ▲▲ C Brazil
82 D13 **Cachingues** Bié, C Angola 13°05′S 16°48′E
54 G7 **Cáchira** Norte de Santander, N Colombia 07°44′N 73°07′W
61 H16 **Cachoeira do Sul** Rio Grande do Sul, S Brazil 29°58′S 52°54′W
59 O20 **Cachoeiro de Itapemirim** Espírito Santo, SE Brazil 20°51′S 41°07′W
82 E12 **Cacolo** Lunda Sul, NE Angola 10°09′S 19°21′E
83 C14 **Caconda** Huíla, C Angola 13°43′S 15°03′E
82 A9 **Cacongo** Cabinda, NW Angola 05°13′S 12°08′E
35 U9 **Cactus Peak** ▲ Nevada, W USA 37°42′N 116°51′W
82 A11 **Cacuaco** Luanda, NW Angola 08°47′S 13°21′E
83 B14 **Cacula** Huíla, SW Angola 14°33′S 14°04′E
67 R12 **Caculuvar** ≈ SW Angola
59 O19 **Caçumba, Ilha** *island* SE Brazil
55 N10 **Cacuri** Amazonas, S Venezuela
81 N17 **Cadale** Shabeellaha Dhexe, E Somalia 02°48′N 46°19′E
105 X4 **Cadaqués** Cataluña, NE Spain 42°17′N 03°16′E
111 J18 **Čadca** *Hung.* Csaca. Žilinský Kraj, N Slovakia 49°27′N 18°46′E
27 P13 **Caddo** Oklahoma, C USA 34°07′N 96°15′W
25 R6 **Caddo** Texas, SW USA 32°42′N 98°40′W
25 X6 **Caddo Lake** ⊠ Louisiana/Texas, SW USA
27 S12 **Caddo Mountains** ▲▲ Arkansas, C USA
41 O8 **Cadereyta** Nuevo León, NE Mexico 25°35′N 99°54′W
97 J19 **Cader Idris** ▲ NW Wales, United Kingdom 52°43′N 03°57′W
182 F3 **Cadibarrawirracanna, Lake** *salt lake* South Australia
14 I7 **Cadillac** Québec, SE Canada 48°12′N 78°23′W
11 T17 **Cadillac** Saskatchewan, S Canada 49°43′N 107°41′W
102 K13 **Cadillac** Gironde, SW France 44°37′N 00°16′W
31 P7 **Cadillac** Michigan, N USA 44°15′N 85°23′W
105 V4 **Cadí, Torre de** ▲ NE Spain 42°16′N 01°38′E
171 P5 **Cadiz** *off.* Cadiz City. Negros, C Philippines 10°58′N 123°18′E
104 J15 **Cádiz** *anc.* Gades, Gadier, Gadir, Gadire. Andalucía, SW Spain 36°32′N 06°18′W
20 H7 **Cadiz** Kentucky, S USA 36°52′N 87°50′W
31 U13 **Cadiz** Ohio, N USA 40°16′N 81°00′W
104 K15 **Cádiz** ⬖ *province* Andalucía, SW Spain
104 I15 **Cadiz, Bahía de** *bay* SW Spain
Cadiz City *see* Cadiz
104 H15 **Cádiz, Golfo de** *Eng.* Gulf of Cadiz. *gulf* Portugal/Spain
Cadiz, Gulf of *see* Cádiz, Golfo de
35 X14 **Cadiz Lake** ◎ California, W USA
182 E2 **Cadney Homestead** South Australia 27°52′S 134°03′E
Cadurcum *see* Cahors
Caecae *see* Xaixai
102 K4 **Caen** Calvados, N France 49°10′N 00°20′W
Caene/Caenepolis *see* Qinā
Caerdydd *see* Cardiff
Caer Glou *see* Gloucester
Caer Gybi *see* Holyhead
Caerleon *see* Chester
Caer Luel *see* Carlisle
97 I18 **Caernarfon** *var.* Caernarvon, Carnarvon. NW Wales, United Kingdom 53°08′N 04°16′W
97 H18 **Caernarfon Bay** *bay* NW Wales, United Kingdom
97 I19 **Caernarvon** *cultural region* NW Wales, United Kingdom
Caernarvon *see* Caernarfon
Caesaraugusta *see* Zaragoza
Caesarea Mazaca *see* Kayseri
Caesarobriga *see* Talavera de la Reina
Caesarodunum *see* Tours
Caesaromagus *see* Beauvais
Caesena *see* Cesena
59 N17 **Caetité** Bahia, E Brazil 14°04′S 42°29′W
62 J6 **Cafayate** Salta, N Argentina 26°02′S 66°00′W
171 O2 **Cagayan** ≈ Luzon, N Philippines
171 Q7 **Cagayan de Oro** *off.* Cagayan de Oro City. Mindanao, S Philippines 08°29′N 124°38′E
Cagayan de Oro City *see* Cagayan de Oro
170 M8 **Cagayan de Tawi Tawi** *island* S Philippines
171 N6 **Cagayan Islands** *island group* C Philippines
31 O14 **Cagles Mill Lake** ⊠ Indiana, N USA
106 I12 **Cagli** Marche, C Italy 43°33′N 12°39′E
107 C20 **Cagliari** *anc.* Caralis. Sardegna, Italy, C Mediterranean Sea 39°15′N 09°06′E
107 C20 **Cagliari, Golfo di** *gulf* Sardegna, Italy, C Mediterranean Sea
103 U15 **Cagnes-sur-Mer** Alpes-Maritimes, SE France 43°40′N 07°09′E
54 L5 **Cagua** Aragua, N Venezuela 10°09′N 67°27′W
171 O1 **Cagua, Mount** ▲ Luzon, N Philippines 18°10′N 122°03′E
54 F13 **Caguán, Río** ≈ SW Colombia
45 U6 **Caguas** E Puerto Rico 18°14′N 66°02′W
146 C9 **Çagyl** *Rus.* Chagyl. Balkan Welaýaty, NW Turkmenistan 40°48′N 55°21′E
23 P5 **Cahaba River** ≈ Alabama, S USA
42 E5 **Cahabón, Río** ≈ C Guatemala
83 B15 **Cahama** Cunene, SW Angola 16°16′S 14°23′E
97 B21 **Caha Mountains** *Ir.* An Cheacha. ▲▲ SW Ireland
97 D20 **Caher** *Ir.* An Cathair. S Ireland 52°21′N 07°58′W
97 A21 **Caherciveen** *Ir.* Cathair Saidhbhín. SW Ireland 51°56′N 10°12′W
30 K15 **Cahokia** Illinois, N USA 38°34′N 90°11′W
83 L15 **Cahora Bassa, Albufeira de** *var.* Lake Cabora Bassa. ⊠ NW Mozambique
97 G20 **Cahore Point** *Ir.* Rinn Chathóir. *headland* SE Ireland 52°33′N 06°11′W
102 M14 **Cahors** *anc.* Cadurcum. Lot, S France 44°26′N 01°27′E
56 D9 **Cahuapanas, Río** ≈ N Peru
116 M12 **Cahul** *Rus.* Kagul. S Moldova 45°53′N 28°13′E
Cahul, Lacul *see* Kahul, Ozero
83 N16 **Caia** Sofala, C Mozambique 17°50′S 35°21′E
59 J19 **Caiapó, Serra do** ▲▲ C Brazil
44 F5 **Caibarién** Villa Clara, C Cuba 22°31′N 79°29′W
55 O5 **Caicara** Monagas, NE Venezuela 09°52′N 63°38′W
54 L5 **Caicara del Orinoco** Bolívar, C Venezuela 07°38′N 66°10′W
59 P14 **Caicó** Rio Grande do Norte, E Brazil 06°25′S 37°04′W
44 M6 **Caicos Islands** *island group* W Turks and Caicos Islands
44 L5 **Caicos Passage** *strait* Bahamas/Turks and Caicos Islands
161 O9 **Caidian** *prev.* Hanyang. Hubei, C China 30°37′N 114°02′E
Caiffa *see* Hefa
180 M12 **Caiguna** Western Australia 32°14′S 125°33′E
Caillí, Ceann *see* Hag's Head
40 J11 **Caimanero, Laguna del** *var.* Laguna del Camaronero. *lagoon* E Pacific Ocean
117 N10 **Căinari** *Rus.* Kaynary. C Moldova 46°43′N 29°00′E
57 L19 **Caine, Río** ≈ C Bolivia
Caiphas *see* Hefa
195 N4 **Caird Coast** *physical region* Antarctica
96 J9 **Cairn Gorm** ▲ C Scotland, United Kingdom 57°07′N 03°38′W
96 J9 **Cairngorm Mountains** ▲▲ C Scotland, United Kingdom
39 P12 **Cairn Mountain** ▲ Alaska, USA 61°07′N 155°23′W
181 W4 **Cairns** Queensland, NE Australia 16°51′S 145°43′E
121 V13 **Cairo** *var.* El Qâhira, *Ar.* Al Qāhirah. ● (Egypt) N Egypt 30°01′N 31°18′E
23 T8 **Cairo** Georgia, SE USA 30°52′N 84°12′W
30 L17 **Cairo** Illinois, N USA 37°00′N 89°10′W
75 V8 **Cairo** ✈ C Egypt 30°06′N 31°36′E
Caiseal *see* Cashel
Caisleán an Bharraigh *see* Castlebar
Caisleán na Finne *see* Castlefinn
96 J6 **Caithness** *cultural region* N Scotland, United Kingdom
83 D15 **Caiundo** Cuando Cubango, S Angola 15°41′S 17°28′E
56 C11 **Cajamarca** *prev.* Caxamarca. Cajamarca, NW Peru 07°09′S 78°32′W
56 B11 **Cajamarca** *off.* Departamento de Cajamarca. ⬖ *department* N Peru
Cajamarca, Departamento de *see* Cajamarca
103 N14 **Cajarc** Lot, S France 44°28′N 01°51′E
42 G6 **Cajón, Represa El** ⊠ NW Honduras
58 N12 **Caju, Ilha do** *island* NE Brazil
159 R10 **Caka Yanhu** ◎ C China
112 E7 **Čakovec** *Ger.* Csakathurn, *Hung.* Csáktornya; *prev. Ger.* Tschakathurn. Medimurje, N Croatia 46°24′N 16°29′E
77 V17 **Calabar** Cross River, S Nigeria 04°56′N 08°25′E
14 K13 **Calabogie** Ontario, SE Canada 45°18′N 76°46′W
54 L6 **Calabozo** Guárico, C Venezuela 08°58′N 67°28′W
107 N20 **Calabria** *anc.* Bruttium. ⬖ *region* SW Italy
104 M16 **Calaburra, Punta de** *headland* S Spain 36°30′N 04°38′W
116 G14 **Calafat** Dolj, SW Romania 43°59′N 22°57′E
Calafate *see* El Calafate
105 Q4 **Calahorra** La Rioja, N Spain 42°19′N 01°58′W
103 N1 **Calais** Pas-de-Calais, N France 51°N 01°54′E
19 T5 **Calais** Maine, NE USA 45°09′N 67°15′W
Calais, Pas de *see* Dover, Strait of
Calalen *see* Kallalen
62 H4 **Calama** Antofagasta, N Chile 22°26′S 68°54′W
Calamianes *see* Calamian Group
170 M5 **Calamian Group** *var.* Calamianes. *island group* W Philippines
105 R7 **Calamocha** Aragón, NE Spain 40°54′N 01°18′W
29 N14 **Calamus River** ≈ Nebraska, C USA
116 G12 **Călan** *Ger.* Kalan, *Hung.* Pusztakalán. Hunedoara, SW Romania 45°45′N 22°59′E
105 S7 **Calanda** Aragón, NE Spain 40°56′N 00°15′W
168 F9 **Calang** Sumatera, W Indonesia 04°37′N 95°37′E
171 N4 **Calapan** Mindoro, N Philippines 13°24′N 121°08′E
Călăras *see* Călărași
116 M9 **Călărași** *var.* Călăras, *Rus.* Kalarash. C Moldova 47°19′N 28°13′E
116 L14 **Călărași** Călărași, SE Romania 44°18′N 26°52′E
116 K14 **Călărași** ⬖ *county* SE Romania
54 E10 **Calarca** Quindío, W Colombia 04°31′N 75°38′W
105 Q12 **Calasparra** Murcia, SE Spain 38°14′N 01°41′W
107 I23 **Calatafimi** Sicilia, Italy, C Mediterranean Sea 37°54′N 12°52′E
105 Q6 **Calatayud** Aragón, NE Spain 41°21′N 01°39′W
171 O4 **Calauag** Luzon, N Philippines 13°57′N 122°18′E
35 P8 **Calaveras River** ≈ California, W USA
171 N4 **Calavite, Cape** *headland* Mindoro, N Philippines 13°25′N 120°16′E
171 Q8 **Calbayog** *off.* Calbayog City. Samar, C Philippines 12°08′N 124°36′E
Calbayog City *see* Calbayog
22 G9 **Calcasieu Lake** ◎ Louisiana, S USA
22 H8 **Calcasieu River** ≈ Louisiana, S USA
56 B6 **Calceta** Manabí, W Ecuador 0°51′S 80°07′W
61 B16 **Calchaquí** Santa Fe, C Argentina 29°56′S 60°14′W
62 J6 **Calchaquí, Río** ≈ NW Argentina
58 J10 **Calçoene** Amapá, NE Brazil 02°29′N 51°01′W
153 S16 **Calcutta** ✈ West Bengal, N India 22°30′N 88°20′E
Calcutta *see* Kolkata
54 E9 **Caldas** *off.* Departamento de Caldas. ⬖ *province* W Colombia
104 F10 **Caldas da Rainha** Leiria, W Portugal 39°24′N 09°08′W
Caldas, Departamento de *see* Caldas
104 G3 **Caldas de Reis** *var.* Caldas de Reyes. Galicia, NW Spain 42°36′N 08°39′W
Caldas de Reyes *see* Caldas de Reis
58 F13 **Caldeirão** Amazonas, NW Brazil 03°18′S 60°22′W
62 G7 **Caldera** Atacama, N Chile 27°05′S 70°48′W
42 L14 **Caldera** Puntarenas, W Costa Rica 09°55′N 84°51′W
105 N10 **Calderina** ▲ C Spain 39°18′N 03°49′W
137 T13 **Çaldıran** Van, E Turkey 39°10′N 43°52′E
32 M14 **Caldwell** Idaho, NW USA 43°39′N 116°41′W
27 N8 **Caldwell** Kansas, C USA 37°01′N 97°36′W
14 G15 **Caledon** Ontario, S Canada 43°51′N 79°58′W
83 I23 **Caledon** *var.* Mohokare. ≈ Lesotho/South Africa
42 G1 **Caledonia** Corozal, N Belize 18°14′N 88°29′W
14 G16 **Caledonia** Ontario, S Canada 43°04′N 79°57′W
29 X11 **Caledonia** Minnesota, N USA 43°37′N 91°30′W
105 X5 **Calella** *var.* Calella de la Costa. Cataluña, NE Spain 41°37′N 02°40′E
Calella de la Costa *see* Calella
23 P4 **Calera** Alabama, S USA 33°06′N 86°45′W
63 I19 **Caleta Olivia** Santa Cruz, SE Argentina 46°21′S 67°37′W
35 X17 **Calexico** California, W USA 32°39′N 115°28′W
97 H16 **Calf of Man** *island* SW Isle of Man
11 Q16 **Calgary** Alberta, SW Canada 51°05′N 114°05′W
11 Q16 **Calgary** ✈ Alberta, SW Canada 51°15′N 114°03′W
37 U5 **Calhan** Colorado, C USA 39°00′N 104°18′W
64 O5 **Calheta** Madeira, Portugal, NE Atlantic Ocean 32°42′N 17°12′W
23 R2 **Calhoun** Georgia, SE USA 34°30′N 84°57′W
20 I6 **Calhoun** Kentucky, S USA 37°32′N 87°15′W
22 M3 **Calhoun City** Mississippi, S USA 33°51′N 89°18′W
21 P12 **Calhoun Falls** South Carolina, SE USA 34°05′N 82°36′W
54 D11 **Cali** Valle del Cauca, W Colombia 03°24′N 76°30′W
27 V9 **Calico Rock** Arkansas, C USA 36°07′N 92°08′W
155 F21 **Calicut** *var.* Kozhikode. Kerala, SW India 11°17′N 75°49′E *see also* Kozhikode
35 Y9 **Caliente** Nevada, W USA 37°37′N 114°30′W
27 U5 **California** Missouri, C USA 38°39′N 92°35′W
18 B15 **California** Pennsylvania, NE USA 40°02′N 79°52′W
35 Q12 **California** *off.* State of California, *also known as* El Dorado, The Golden State. ⬖ *state* W USA
35 P11 **California Aqueduct** *aqueduct* California, W USA
35 T13 **California City** California, W USA 35°06′N 117°55′W
40 F6 **California, Golfo de** *Eng.* Gulf of California; *prev.* Sea of Cortez. *gulf* W Mexico
California, Gulf of *see* California, Golfo de
137 Y13 **Cälilabad** *Rus.* Dzhalilabad; *prev.* Astrakhan-Bazar. S Azerbaijan 39°15′N 48°30′E
116 I12 **Călimănești** Vâlcea, SW Romania 45°14′N 24°20′E
116 J9 **Călimani, Munții** ▲▲ N Romania
Calinisc *see* Cupcina
35 X17 **Calipatria** California, W USA 33°07′N 115°30′W
Calisia *see* Kalisz
34 M7 **Calistoga** California, W USA 38°34′N 122°37′W
83 G25 **Calitzdorp** Western Cape, SW South Africa 33°32′S 21°41′E
41 W12 **Calkiní** Campeche, E Mexico 20°21′N 90°03′W
182 K4 **Callabonna Creek** *var.* Tilcha Creek. *seasonal river* New South Wales/South Australia
182 J4 **Callabonna, Lake** ◎ South Australia
102 G5 **Callac** Côtes d'Armor, NW France 48°28′N 03°22′W
35 U5 **Callaghan, Mount** ▲ Nevada, W USA 39°38′N 116°57′W
Callain *see* Callan
97 E19 **Callan** *Ir.* Callain. S Ireland 52°33′N 07°23′W
14 H11 **Callander** Ontario, S Canada 46°14′N 79°21′W
96 I11 **Callander** C Scotland, United Kingdom 56°15′N 04°16′W
98 H7 **Callantsoog** Noord-Holland, NW Netherlands 52°51′N 04°41′E
57 D14 **Callao** Callao, W Peru 12°03′S 77°10′W
57 D15 **Callao** *off.* Departamento del Callao. ⬖ *constitutional province* W Peru
Callao, Departamento del *see* Callao
56 F11 **Callaria, Río** ≈ E Peru
Callatis *see* Mangalia
11 Q13 **Calling Lake** Alberta, W Canada 55°12′N 113°07′W
Callosa de Ensarriá *see* Callosa d'En Sarrià
105 T11 **Callosa d'En Sarrià** *var.* Callosa de Ensarriá. País Valenciano, E Spain 38°40′N 00°08′W
105 S12 **Callosa de Segura** País Valenciano, E Spain 38°07′N 00°53′W
29 X11 **Calmar** Iowa, C USA 43°10′N 91°51′W
Calmar *see* Kalmar
43 R16 **Calobre** Veraguas, C Panama 08°18′N 80°49′W
23 X14 **Caloosahatchee River** ≈ Florida, SE USA
183 V2 **Caloundra** Queensland, E Australia 26°48′S 153°08′E
Calp *see* Calpe
105 T11 **Calpe** *Cat.* Calp. País Valenciano, E Spain 38°39′N 00°03′E
41 P14 **Calpulalpan** Tlaxcala, S Mexico 19°36′N 98°26′W
107 K25 **Caltagirone** Sicilia, Italy, C Mediterranean Sea 37°14′N 14°31′E
107 J24 **Caltanissetta** Sicilia, Italy, C Mediterranean Sea 37°30′N 14°01′E
82 E11 **Caluango** Lunda Norte, NE Angola 08°16′S 19°36′E
82 C12 **Calucinga** Bié, W Angola 11°18′S 16°12′E
82 B12 **Calulo** Cuanza Sul, NW Angola 09°58′S 14°56′E
83 B14 **Caluquembe** Huíla, W Angola 13°47′S 14°40′E
80 Q11 **Caluula** Bari, NE Somalia 11°55′N 50°51′E
102 K4 **Calvados** ⬖ *department* N France
186 I10 **Calvados Chain, The** *island group* SE Papua New Guinea
25 U9 **Calvert** Texas, SW USA 30°58′N 96°40′W
20 H7 **Calvert City** Kentucky, S USA 37°01′N 88°21′W
103 X14 **Calvi** Corse, France, C Mediterranean Sea 42°34′N 08°44′E
40 L12 **Calvillo** Aguascalientes, C Mexico 21°51′N 102°18′W
83 F24 **Calvinia** Northern Cape, W South Africa 31°25′S 19°47′E
104 K8 **Calvitero** ▲ W Spain 40°16′N 05°48′W
101 G22 **Calw** Baden-Württemberg, SW Germany 48°43′N 08°43′E
Calydon *see* Kalydón
105 N11 **Calzada de Calatrava** Castilla-La Mancha, C Spain 38°42′N 03°46′W
Cama *see* Kama
82 C11 **Camabatela** Cuanza Norte, NW Angola 08°13′S 15°23′E
64 Q5 **Camacha** Porto Santo, Madeira, Portugal, NE Atlantic Ocean 32°41′N 16°52′W
14 L8 **Camachigama, Lac** ◎ Québec, SE Canada
40 M9 **Camacho** Zacatecas, C Mexico 24°23′N 102°20′W
82 D13 **Camacupa** *var.* General Machado, *Port.* Vila General Machado. Bié, C Angola 12°S 17°31′E
54 L7 **Camaguán** Guárico, C Venezuela 08°09′N 67°37′W
44 G6 **Camagüey** *prev.* Puerto Príncipe. Camagüey, C Cuba 21°24′N 77°55′W
44 G5 **Camagüey, Archipiélago de** *island group* C Cuba
40 D5 **Camalli, Sierra de** ▲ NW Mexico 28°21′N 113°26′W
57 G18 **Camana** *var.* Camaná. Arequipa, SW Peru 16°37′S 72°42′W
29 Z14 **Camanche** Iowa, C USA 41°47′N 90°15′W
35 P8 **Camanche Reservoir** ⊠ California, W USA
61 I16 **Camaquã** Rio Grande do Sul, S Brazil 30°50′S 51°47′W
61 H16 **Camaquã, Rio** ≈ S Brazil
64 P6 **Câmara de Lobos** Madeira, Portugal, NE Atlantic Ocean 32°38′N 16°59′W
103 U16 **Camarat, Cap** *headland* SE France 43°12′N 06°42′E
41 O8 **Camargo** Tamaulipas, C Mexico 26°16′N 98°49′W
103 R15 **Camargue** *physical region* SE France
104 F2 **Camariñas** Galicia, NW Spain 43°07′N 09°10′W
Camaronero, Laguna del *see* Caimanero, Laguna del
63 J18 **Camarones** Chubut, S Argentina 44°48′S 65°42′W
63 J18 **Camarones, Bahía** *bay* S Argentina
104 J14 **Camas** Andalucía, S Spain 37°24′N 06°01′W
167 S15 **Ca Mau** *var.* Quan Long. Minh Hai, S Vietnam 09°11′N 105°09′E
82 E11 **Camaxilo** Lunda Norte, NE Angola 08°19′S 18°53′E
104 G3 **Cambados** Galicia, NW Spain 42°31′N 08°49′W
Cambay, Gulf of *see* Khambhāt, Gulf of
Camberia *see* Chambéry
97 N22 **Camberley** SE England, United Kingdom 51°21′N 00°45′W
167 R12 **Cambodia** *off.* Kingdom of Cambodia, *var.* Democratic Kampuchea, Roat Kampuchea, *Cam.* Kampuchea; *prev.* People's Democratic Republic of Kampuchea. ◆ *republic* SE Asia
Cambodia, Kingdom of *see* Cambodia
102 I16 **Cambo-les-Bains** Pyrénées-Atlantiques, SW France 43°22′N 01°24′W
103 P2 **Cambrai** *Flem.* Kambryk, *prev.* Cambray; *anc.* Cameracum. Nord, N France 50°10′N 03°14′E
Cambray *see* Cambrai
104 H2 **Cambre** Galicia, NW Spain 43°18′N 08°21′W
35 O12 **Cambria** California, W USA 35°33′N 121°04′W
97 J20 **Cambrian Mountains** ▲▲ C Wales, United Kingdom
14 G16 **Cambridge** Ontario, S Canada 43°22′N 80°20′W
44 I12 **Cambridge** W Jamaica 18°18′N 77°54′W
184 M8 **Cambridge** Waikato, North Island, New Zealand 37°53′S 175°28′E
97 O20 **Cambridge** *Lat.* Cantabrigia. E England, United Kingdom 52°12′N 00°07′E
32 M12 **Cambridge** Idaho, NW USA 44°34′N 116°42′W
30 K11 **Cambridge** Illinois, N USA 41°18′N 90°11′W
21 Y4 **Cambridge** Maryland, NE USA 38°34′N 76°04′W
19 O11 **Cambridge** Massachusetts, NE USA 42°21′N 71°05′W
29 V7 **Cambridge** Minnesota, N USA 45°34′N 93°13′W
29 N16 **Cambridge** Nebraska, C USA 40°18′N 100°10′W
31 U13 **Cambridge** Ohio, NE USA 40°00′N 81°34′W
8 L7 **Cambridge Bay** *var.* Ikaluktutiak. Victoria Island, Nunavut, NW Canada 68°56′N 105°09′W
97 O20 **Cambridgeshire** *cultural region* E England, United Kingdom
105 U6 **Cambrils de Mar** Cataluña, NE Spain 41°06′N 01°02′E
Cambundi-Catembo *see* Nova Gaia
137 N11 **Çam Burnu** *headland* N Turkey 41°07′N 37°48′E
183 S9 **Camden** New South Wales, SE Australia 34°04′S 150°40′E
23 O6 **Camden** Alabama, S USA 31°59′N 87°17′W
27 U14 **Camden** Arkansas, C USA 33°32′N 92°49′W
21 Y3 **Camden** Delaware, NE USA 39°06′N 75°30′W
19 R7 **Camden** Maine, NE USA 44°12′N 69°04′W
18 I16 **Camden** New Jersey, NE USA 39°55′N 75°07′W
18 I9 **Camden** New York, NE USA 43°21′N 75°45′W
21 R12 **Camden** South Carolina, SE USA 34°16′N 80°36′W
20 H8 **Camden** Tennessee, S USA 36°03′N 88°07′W
25 X9 **Camden** Texas, SW USA 30°55′N 94°43′W
39 S5 **Camden Bay** *bay* S Beaufort Sea
27 U6 **Camdenton** Missouri, C USA 38°01′N 92°44′W
Camellia State *see* Alabama
18 M7 **Camels Hump** ▲ Vermont, NE USA 44°18′N 72°50′W
117 N8 **Camenca** *Rus.* Kamenka. N Moldova 48°01′N 28°43′E
Cameracum *see* Cambrai
22 G9 **Cameron** Louisiana, S USA 29°48′N 93°19′W
25 T9 **Cameron** Texas, SW USA 30°51′N 96°58′W
30 J5 **Cameron** Wisconsin, N USA 45°25′N 91°42′W
10 M12 **Cameron** ≈ British Columbia, W Canada
185 A24 **Cameron Mountains** ▲▲ South Island, New Zealand
79 D15 **Cameroon** *off.* Republic of Cameroon, *Fr.* Cameroun. ◆ *republic* W Africa
79 D15 **Cameroon Mountain** ▲ SW Cameroon 04°12′N 09°00′E
Cameroon, Republic of *see* Cameroon
Cameroon Ridge *see* Camerounaise, Dorsale
Cameroun *see* Cameroon
79 E14 **Camerounaise, Dorsale** *Eng.* Cameroon Ridge. *ridge* NW Cameroon
136 B15 **Çamiçi Gölü** ◎ SW Turkey
171 N3 **Camiling** Luzon, N Philippines 15°41′N 120°22′E
23 T7 **Camilla** Georgia, SE USA 31°13′N 84°12′W
104 G5 **Caminha** Viana do Castelo, N Portugal 41°52′N 08°50′W
35 P7 **Camino** California, W USA 38°43′N 120°39′W
107 J24 **Cammarata** Sicilia, Italy, C Mediterranean Sea 37°36′N 13°39′E
42 K10 **Camoapa** Boaco, S Nicaragua 12°25′N 85°30′W
58 O13 **Camocim** Ceará, E Brazil 02°55′S 40°50′W
106 D10 **Camogli** Liguria, NW Italy 44°21′N 09°10′E
181 S5 **Camooweal** Queensland, C Australia 19°57′S 138°14′E
55 Y11 **Camopi** E French Guiana 03°12′N 52°19′W
151 Q22 **Camorta** *island* Nicobar Islands, India, NE Indian Ocean
42 I6 **Campamento** Olancho, C Honduras 14°36′N 86°38′W
61 D19 **Campana** Buenos Aires, E Argentina 34°10′S 58°57′W
63 F21 **Campana, Isla** *island* S Chile
104 K11 **Campanario** Extremadura, W Spain 38°52′N 05°36′W
107 L17 **Campania** *Eng.* Champagne. ⬖ *region* S Italy
27 Y8 **Campbell** Missouri, C USA 36°29′N 90°04′W
185 K15 **Campbell, Cape** *headland* South Island, New Zealand 41°44′S 174°16′E
14 J14 **Campbellford** Ontario, SE Canada 44°18′N 77°48′W
31 R13 **Campbell Hill** *hill* Ohio, N USA
192 K13 **Campbell Island** *island* S New Zealand
175 P13 **Campbell Plateau** *undersea feature* SW Pacific Ocean 51°00′S 170°00′E
10 K17 **Campbell River** Vancouver Island, British Columbia, SW Canada 49°59′N 125°18′W
20 L6 **Campbellsville** Kentucky, S USA 37°20′N 85°21′W
13 O13 **Campbellton** New Brunswick, SE Canada 48°00′N 66°41′W
183 S9 **Campbelltown** New South Wales, SE Australia 34°04′S 150°46′E
183 P16 **Campbell Town** Tasmania, SE Australia 41°57′S 147°30′E
96 G13 **Campbeltown** W Scotland, United Kingdom 55°26′N 05°38′W
41 W13 **Campeche** Campeche, SE Mexico 19°47′N 90°29′W
41 W14 **Campeche** ⬖ *state* SE Mexico
41 T14 **Campeche, Bahía de** *Eng.* Bay of Campeche. *bay* E Mexico
Campeche, Banco de *see* Campeche Bank
64 C11 **Campeche Bank** *Sp.* Banco de Campeche, Sonda de Campeche. *undersea feature* S Gulf of Mexico 22°00′N 90°00′W
Campeche, Bay of *see* Campeche, Bahía de
Campeche, Sonda de *see* Campeche Bank
44 H7 **Campechuela** Granma, E Cuba 20°15′N 77°17′W
182 M13 **Camperdown** Victoria, SE Australia 38°16′S 143°10′E
167 U6 **Câm Pha** Quang Ninh, N Vietnam 21°04′N 107°20′E
116 H10 **Câmpia Turzii** *Ger.* Jerischmarkt, *Hung.* Aranyosgyéres; *prev.* Cîmpia Turzii, Ghiriș, Gyéres. Cluj, NW Romania 46°33′N 23°53′E
104 K12 **Campillo de Llerena** Extremadura, W Spain 38°30′N 05°48′W
104 L15 **Campillos** Andalucía, S Spain 37°04′N 04°51′W
116 J13 **Câmpina** *prev.* Cîmpina. Prahova, SE Romania 45°08′N 25°44′E
59 Q15 **Campina Grande** Paraíba, E Brazil 07°15′S 35°50′W
60 L9 **Campinas** São Paulo, S Brazil 22°54′S 47°06′W
38 L10 **Camp Kulowiye** Saint Lawrence Island, Alaska, USA 63°15′N 168°45′W
79 D17 **Campo** *var.* Kampo. Sud, SW Cameroon 02°22′N 09°50′E
Campo *see* Ntem
59 N15 **Campo Alegre de Lourdes** Bahia, E Brazil 09°28′S 43°01′W
107 L16 **Campobasso** Molise, C Italy 41°34′N 14°40′E
107 H24 **Campobello di Mazara** Sicilia, Italy, C Mediterranean Sea 37°38′N 12°45′E
Campo Criptana *see* Campo de Criptana
105 O10 **Campo de Criptana** *var.* Campo Criptana. Castilla-La Mancha, C Spain 39°25′N 03°07′W
59 I16 **Campo de Diauarum** *var.* Pôsto Diuarum. Mato Grosso, W Brazil 11°08′S 53°16′W
54 E5 **Campo de la Cruz** Atlántico, N Colombia 10°23′N 74°52′W
105 P11 **Campo de Montiel** *physical region* C Spain
Campo dos Goitacazes *see* Campos
60 H12 **Campo Erê** Santa Catarina, S Brazil 26°24′S 53°04′W
62 L7 **Campo Gallo** Santiago del Estero, N Argentina 26°32′S 62°51′W
59 I20 **Campo Grande** *state capital* Mato Grosso do Sul, SW Brazil 20°24′S 54°35′W
60 K12 **Campo Largo** Paraná, S Brazil 25°27′S 49°29′W
58 N13 **Campo Maior** Piauí, E Brazil 04°50′S 42°12′W
104 I10 **Campo Maior** Portalegre, C Portugal 39°01′N 07°04′W
60 H10 **Campo Mourão** Paraná, S Brazil 24°01′S 52°24′W
60 Q9 **Campos** *var.* Campo dos Goitacazes. Rio de Janeiro, SE Brazil 21°46′S 41°21′W
59 L17 **Campos Belos** Goiás, S Brazil 13°11′S 46°47′W
60 N9 **Campos do Jordão** São Paulo, S Brazil 22°45′S 45°36′W
60 I13 **Campos Novos** Santa Catarina, S Brazil 27°22′S 51°11′W
59 O14 **Campos Sales** Ceará, E Brazil 07°01′S 40°21′W
25 Q9 **Camp San Saba** Texas, SW USA 30°57′N 99°16′W
21 N6 **Campton** Kentucky, S USA 37°44′N 83°35′W
116 I13 **Câmpulung** *prev.* Câmpulung-Mușcel, Cîmpulung. Argeș, S Romania 45°16′N 25°03′E
116 J9 **Câmpulung Moldovenesc** *var.* Cîmpulung Moldovenesc, *Ger.* Kimpolung, *Hung.* Hosszúmezjő. Suceava, NE Romania 47°32′N 25°34′E
Câmpulung-Mușcel *see* Câmpulung
Campus Stellae *see* Santiago
36 L12 **Camp Verde** Arizona, SW USA 34°33′N 111°52′W
25 P11 **Camp Wood** Texas, SW USA 29°40′N 100°00′W
167 V13 **Cam Ranh** Khanh Hoa, S Vietnam 11°54′N 109°14′E
11 Q15 **Camrose** Alberta, SW Canada 53°01′N 112°48′W
Camulodunum *see* Colchester
136 B12 **Çan** Çanakkale, NW Turkey 40°03′N 27°03′E
18 L12 **Canaan** Connecticut, NE USA 42°00′N 73°17′W
11 O13 **Canada** ◆ *commonwealth republic* N North America
197 P6 **Canada Basin** *undersea feature* Arctic Ocean 80°00′N 145°00′W
61 B18 **Cañada de Gómez** Santa Fe, C Argentina 32°50′S 61°23′W
197 P6 **Canada Plain** *undersea feature* Arctic Ocean
61 A18 **Cañada Rosquín** Santa Fe, C Argentina 32°04′S 61°35′W
25 P1 **Canadian** Texas, SW USA 35°54′N 100°23′W
16 K12 **Canadian River** ≈ SW USA
8 L12 **Canadian Shield** *physical region* Canada
63 I18 **Cañadón Grande, Sierra** ▲▲ S Argentina
55 P9 **Canaima** Bolívar, SE Venezuela 09°41′N 72°33′W
136 B11 **Çanakkale** *var.* Dardanelli; *prev.* Chanak, Kale Sultanie. Çanakkale, W Turkey 40°09′N 26°25′E
136 B12 **Çanakkale** ⬖ *province* NW Turkey
136 B11 **Çanakkale Boğazı** *Eng.* Dardanelles. *strait* NW Turkey
187 Q17 **Canala** Province Nord, C New Caledonia 21°31′S 165°57′E
59 A15 **Canamari** Amazonas, W Brazil 07°37′S 72°33′W
18 G10 **Canandaigua** New York, NE USA 42°52′N 77°14′W

◆ Country
● Country Capital
◇ Dependent Territory
○ Dependent Territory Capital
⬖ Administrative Regions
✈ International Airport
▲ Mountain
▲▲ Mountain Range
Volcano
≈ River
◎ Lake
⊠ Reservoir

CANANDAIGUA LAKE – CARTHAGE

18 F10 Canandaigua Lake ◎ New York, NE USA
40 G3 Cananea Sonora, NW Mexico 30°59′N 110°20′W
56 B8 Cañar ◐ province C Ecuador
64 N10 Canarias, Islas Eng. Canary Islands. ◐ autonomous community Spain, NE Atlantic Ocean
Canaries Basin see Canary Basin
44 C6 Canarreos, Archipiélago de los island group W Cuba
Canary Islands see Canarias, Islas
66 K3 Canary Basin var. Canaries Basin, Monaco Basin. undersea feature E Atlantic Ocean 30°00′N 25°00′W
42 L13 Cañas Guanacaste, NW Costa Rica 10°25′N 85°07′W
18 I10 Canastota New York, NE USA 43°04′N 75°45′W
40 K9 Canatlán Durango, C Mexico 24°33′N 104°45′W
104 J9 Cañaveral Extremadura, W Spain 39°47′N 06°24′W
23 Y11 Canaveral, Cape headland Florida, SE USA 28°27′N 80°31′W
59 O18 Canavieiras Bahia, E Brazil 15°44′S 38°58′W
43 R16 Cañazas Veraguas, W Panama 08°25′N 81°10′W
106 H6 Canazei Trentino-Alto Adige, N Italy 46°29′N 11°50′E
183 P6 Canbelego New South Wales, SE Australia 31°36′S 146°20′E
183 R10 Canberra ● (Australia) Australian Capital Territory, SE Australia 35°21′S 149°08′E
183 R10 Canberra ✈ Australian Capital Territory, SE Australia 35°19′S 149°12′E
35 P2 Canby California, W USA 41°27′N 120°51′W
29 S9 Canby Minnesota, N USA 44°42′N 96°17′W
103 N2 Canche ≈ N France
102 L13 Cancon Lot-et-Garonne, SW France 44°33′N 00°37′E
41 Z11 Cancún Quintana Roo, SE Mexico 21°05′N 86°48′W
104 K2 Candás Asturias, N Spain 43°35′N 05°45′W
102 J7 Cande Maine-et-Loire, NW France 47°33′N 01°03′W
41 W14 Candelaria Campeche, SE Mexico 18°10′N 91°00′W
24 J11 Candelaria Texas, SW USA 30°05′N 104°40′W
41 W15 Candelaria, Río ≈ Guatemala/Mexico
104 L8 Candeleda Castilla-León, N Spain 40°10′N 05°14′W
Candia see Irákleio
41 P8 Cándido Aguilar Tamaulipas, C Mexico 25°30′N 97°57′W
39 N8 Candle Alaska, USA 65°54′N 161°55′W
11 T14 Candle Lake Saskatchewan, C Canada 53°43′N 105°09′W
18 L13 Candlewood, Lake ◎ Connecticut, NE USA
29 O3 Cando North Dakota, N USA 48°29′N 99°12′W
Canea see Chaniá
45 O12 Canefield ✈ (Roseau) SW Dominica 15°20′N 61°24′W
61 F20 Canelones prev. Guadalupe. Canelones, S Uruguay 34°32′S 56°17′W
61 E20 Canelones ◐ department S Uruguay
Canendiyú see Canindeyú
63 F14 Cañete Bío Bío, C Chile 37°48′S 73°25′W
105 Q9 Cañete Castilla-La Mancha, C Spain 40°03′N 01°39′W
Cañete see San Vicente de Cañete
27 P8 Caney Kansas, C USA 37°00′N 95°56′W
27 P8 Caney River ≈ Kansas/Oklahoma, C USA
105 S3 Canfranc-Estación Aragón, NE Spain 42°42′N 00°31′W
83 E14 Cangamba Port. Vila de Aljustrel. Moxico, E Angola 13°40′S 19°47′E
82 C12 Cangandala Malanje, NW Angola 09°47′S 16°27′E
104 G4 Cangas Galicia, NW Spain 42°16′N 08°46′W
104 J2 Cangas del Narcea Asturias, N Spain 43°10′N 06°32′W
104 L2 Cangas de Onís Asturias, N Spain 43°21′N 05°08′W
161 S11 Cangnan var. Lingxi. Zhejiang, SE China 27°29′N 120°23′E
82 C10 Cangola Uíge, NW Angola 07°54′S 15°57′E
83 E14 Cangombe Moxico, E Angola 14°27′S 20°05′E
63 H21 Cangrejo, Cerro ▲ S Argentina 49°19′S 72°18′W
61 H17 Canguçu Rio Grande do Sul, S Brazil 31°25′S 52°37′W
161 P3 Cangzhou Hebei, E China 38°19′N 116°54′E
12 M7 Caniapiscau ≈ Québec, E Canada
12 M8 Caniapiscau, Réservoir de ⊠ Québec, C Canada
107 J24 Canicattì Sicilia, Italy, C Mediterranean Sea 37°22′N 13°51′E
136 L11 Canik Dağları ▲▲ N Turkey
105 P14 Caniles Andalucía, S Spain 37°24′N 02°41′W
59 B16 Canindé Acre, W Brazil 10°55′S 69°45′W
62 P6 Canindeyú var. Canendiyú, Canindiyú. ◐ department E Paraguay
Canindiyú see Canindeyú
194 J10 Canisteo Peninsula peninsula Antarctica
18 F11 Canisteo River ≈ New York, NE USA
40 M10 Cañitas var. Cañitas de Felipe Pescador. Zacatecas, C Mexico 23°35′N 102°39′W
Cañitas de Felipe Pescador see Cañitas
105 P15 Canjáyar Andalucía, S Spain 37°00′N 02°45′W
136 I12 Çankırı var. Chankiri; anc. Gangra, Germanicopolis. Çankin, N Turkey 40°36′N 33°35′E
136 I11 Çankırı var. Chankiri. ◐ province N Turkey
171 P6 Canlaon Volcano ⛰ Negros, C Philippines 10°24′N 123°05′E
11 P16 Canmore Alberta, SW Canada 51°07′N 115°18′W
96 F9 Canna island NW Scotland, United Kingdom
155 F20 Cannanore var. Kannur. Kerala, SW India 11°53′N 75°23′E see also Kannur
31 O17 Cannelton Indiana, N USA 37°54′N 86°44′W
103 U15 Cannes Alpes-Maritimes, SE France 43°33′N 06°59′E
39 R5 Canning River ≈ Alaska, USA
106 C6 Cannobio Piemonte, NE Italy 46°04′N 08°39′E
97 L19 Cannock C England, United Kingdom 52°41′N 02°03′W
28 M6 Cannonball River ≈ North Dakota, N USA
29 W9 Cannon Falls Minnesota, N USA 44°30′N 92°54′W
18 I11 Cannonsville Reservoir ⊠ New York, NE USA
183 R12 Cann River Victoria, SE Australia 37°34′S 149°11′E
61 I16 Canoas Rio Grande do Sul, S Brazil 29°42′S 51°07′W
61 I14 Canoas, Rio ≈ S Brazil
14 I12 Canoe Lake ◎ Ontario, SE Canada
60 J12 Canoinhas Santa Catarina, S Brazil 26°12′S 50°24′W
37 T6 Canon City Colorado, C USA 38°25′N 105°14′W
55 P8 Caño Negro Bolívar, SE Venezuela
173 X15 Canonniers Point headland N Mauritius
23 W6 Canoochee River ≈ Georgia, SE USA
11 V15 Canora Saskatchewan, S Canada 51°38′N 102°28′W
45 Y14 Canouan island S Saint Vincent and the Grenadines
13 R15 Canso Nova Scotia, SE Canada 45°20′N 61°00′W
104 M3 Cantabria ◐ autonomous community N Spain
104 K3 Cantábrica, Cordillera ▲▲ N Spain
Cantabrigia see Cambridge
103 O12 Cantal ◐ department C France
105 N6 Cantalejo Castilla-León, N Spain 41°15′N 03°57′W
103 O12 Cantal, Monts du ▲▲ C France
104 G8 Cantanhede Coimbra, C Portugal 40°21′N 08°37′W
Cantaño see Cataño
55 O6 Cantaura Anzoátegui, NE Venezuela 09°22′N 64°24′W
116 M11 Cantemir Rus. Kantemir. S Moldova 46°17′N 28°12′E
97 Q22 Canterbury hist. Cantwaraburh; anc. Durovernum, Lat. Cantuaria. SE England, United Kingdom 51°17′N 01°05′E
185 F19 Canterbury off. Canterbury Region. ◐ region South Island, New Zealand
185 H20 Canterbury Bight bight South Island, New Zealand
185 H19 Canterbury Plains plain South Island, New Zealand
Canterbury Region see Canterbury
167 S14 Cần Thơ Cần Thơ, S Vietnam 10°03′N 105°46′E
104 K13 Cantillana Andalucía, S Spain 37°34′N 05°48′W
59 N15 Canto do Buriti Piauí, NE Brazil 08°07′S 43°00′W
23 S2 Canton Georgia, SE USA 34°14′N 84°29′W
30 K12 Canton Illinois, N USA 40°33′N 90°02′W
22 L5 Canton Mississippi, S USA 32°36′N 90°02′W
27 V2 Canton Missouri, C USA 40°07′N 91°31′W
18 J7 Canton New York, NE USA 44°36′N 75°10′W
21 O10 Canton North Carolina, SE USA 35°31′N 82°50′W
31 U12 Canton Ohio, N USA 40°48′N 81°23′W
26 L9 Canton Oklahoma, C USA 36°03′N 98°35′W
18 G12 Canton Pennsylvania, NE USA 41°38′N 76°49′W
29 R11 Canton South Dakota, N USA 43°19′N 96°33′W
25 V7 Canton Texas, SW USA 32°33′N 95°51′W
Canton see Guangzhou
Canton Island see Kanton
26 L9 Canton Lake ◎ Oklahoma, C USA
106 D7 Cantù Lombardia, N Italy 45°44′N 09°08′E
Cantuaria/Cantwaraburh see Canterbury
39 R10 Cantwell Alaska, USA 63°23′N 148°57′W
59 O16 Canudos Bahia, E Brazil 09°51′S 39°08′W
47 T7 Canumã, Rio ≈ N Brazil
Canusium see Puglia, Canosa di
24 G7 Canutillo Texas, SW USA 31°53′N 106°34′W
25 N3 Canyon Texas, SW USA 34°58′N 101°56′W
33 S12 Canyon Wyoming, C USA 44°44′N 110°30′W
32 K13 Canyon City Oregon, NW USA 44°24′N 118°58′W
33 R10 Canyon Ferry Lake ◎ Montana, NW USA
25 S11 Canyon Lake ⊠ Texas, SW USA
167 T5 Cao Bằng var. Caobang. Cao Bằng, N Vietnam 22°40′N 106°16′E
Caobang see Cao Bằng
160 J12 Caodu He ≈ S China
Caohai see Weining
167 S14 Cao Lanh Đông Thap, S Vietnam 10°35′N 105°25′E
82 C11 Caombo Malanje, NW Angola 08°42′S 16°33′E
Caorach, Cuan na g see Sheep Haven
Caozhou see Heze
171 Q12 Capalulu Pulau Mangole, E Indonesia 01°51′S 125°53′E
54 K8 Capanaparo, Río ≈ Colombia/Venezuela
58 L12 Capanema Pará, NE Brazil 01°08′S 47°07′W
60 L10 Capão Bonito São Paulo, S Brazil 24°01′S 48°23′W
60 I13 Capão Doce, Morro do ▲ S Brazil 26°37′S 51°28′W
54 I4 Capatárida Falcón, N Venezuela 11°11′N 70°37′W
102 I15 Capbreton Landes, SW France 43°40′N 01°25′W
Cap-Breton, Île du see Cape Breton Island
15 W6 Cap-Chat Québec, SE Canada 49°04′N 66°43′W
15 P11 Cap-de-la-Madeleine Québec, SE Canada 46°22′N 72°31′W
103 N13 Capdenac Aveyron, S France 44°35′N 02°06′E
Cap des Palmès see Palmas, Cape
183 Q15 Cape Barren Island island Furneaux Group, Tasmania, SE Australia
65 O18 Cape Basin undersea feature S Atlantic Ocean 37°00′S 07°00′E
13 R14 Cape Breton Island Fr. Île du Cap-Breton. island Nova Scotia, SE Canada
23 Y11 Cape Canaveral Florida, SE USA 28°24′N 80°36′W
21 Y6 Cape Charles Virginia, NE USA 37°16′N 76°01′W
77 P17 Cape Coast prev. Cape Coast Castle. S Ghana 05°10′N 01°13′W
Cape Coast Castle see Cape Coast
19 Q12 Cape Cod Bay bay Massachusetts, NE USA
23 W15 Cape Coral Florida, SE USA 26°33′N 81°57′W
181 R4 Cape Crawford Roadhouse Northern Territory, N Australia 16°39′S 135°44′E
9 Q7 Cape Dorset Baffin Island, Nunavut, NE Canada 76°14′N 76°32′W
21 N8 Cape Fear River ≈ North Carolina, SE USA
27 Y7 Cape Girardeau Missouri, C USA 37°19′N 89°31′W
21 T14 Cape Island island South Carolina, SE USA
186 A6 Capella ▲ NW Papua New Guinea 05°00′S 141°09′E
98 H12 Capelle aan den IJssel Zuid-Holland, SW Netherlands 51°56′N 04°36′E
83 C15 Capelongo Huíla, C Angola 14°45′S 15°02′E
18 J17 Cape May New Jersey, NE USA 38°54′N 74°54′W
18 J17 Cape May Court House New Jersey, NE USA 39°03′N 74°46′W
Cape Palmas see Harper
8 I16 Cape Parry Northwest Territories, N Canada 70°10′N 124°33′W
65 P19 Cape Rise undersea feature SW Indian Ocean 42°00′S 15°00′E
Cape Saint Jacques see Vung Tau
Capesterre see Capesterre-Belle-Eau
45 Y6 Capesterre-Belle-Eau var. Capesterre. Basse Terre, S Guadeloupe 16°03′N 61°34′W
83 D26 Cape Town var. Ekapa, Afr. Kaapstad, Kapstad. ● (South Africa-legislative capital) Western Cape, SW South Africa 33°56′S 18°28′E
83 E26 Cape Town ✈ Western Cape, SW South Africa 31°51′S 21°06′E
76 D9 Cape Verde off. Republic of Cape Verde, Port. Cabo Verde, Ilhas do Cabo Verde. ◆ republic E Atlantic Ocean
64 L11 Cape Verde Basin undersea feature E Atlantic Ocean 15°00′N 30°00′W
66 K5 Cape Verde Islands island group E Atlantic Ocean
64 L10 Cape Verde Plain undersea feature E Atlantic Ocean 23°00′N 26°00′W
Cape Verde Plateau/Cape Verde Rise see Cape Verde Terrace
Cape Verde, Republic of see Cape Verde
64 L11 Cape Verde Terrace var. Cape Verde Plateau, Cape Verde Rise. undersea feature E Atlantic Ocean 18°00′N 20°00′W
181 V2 Cape York Peninsula peninsula Queensland, N Australia
44 M8 Cap-Haïtien var. Le Cap. N Haiti 19°44′N 72°12′W
43 T15 Capira Panamá, C Panama 08°48′N 79°51′W
14 K8 Capitachouane ≈ Québec, SE Canada
14 L8 Capitachouane, Lac ◎ Québec, SE Canada
37 T13 Capitan New Mexico, SW USA 33°33′N 105°34′W
194 G3 Capitán Arturo Prat Chilean research station South Shetland Islands, Antarctica 62°24′S 59°42′W
37 S13 Capitan Mountains ▲▲ New Mexico, SW USA
62 M3 Capitán Pablo Lagerenza var. Mayor Pablo Lagerenza. Chaco, N Paraguay 19°55′S 60°46′W
37 T13 Capitan Peak ▲ New Mexico, SW USA 33°35′N 105°15′W
188 H5 Capitol Hill ● (Northern Mariana Islands-legislative capital) Saipan, S Northern Mariana Islands
60 I9 Capivara, Represa ⊠ S Brazil
61 J16 Capivari Rio Grande do Sul, S Brazil 30°08′S 50°32′W
113 H15 Čapljina Federicija Bosna I Hercegovina, S Bosnia and Herzegovina 43°07′N 17°42′E
83 M15 Capoche var. Kapoche. ≈ Mozambique/Zambia
Capo Delgado, Província de see Cabo Delgado
107 K17 Capodichino ✈ (Napoli) Campania, S Italy 40°53′N 14°15′E
Capodistria see Koper
106 E12 Capraia, Isola di island Arcipelago Toscano, C Italy
107 B16 Caprara, Punta var. Punta dello Scorno. headland Isola Asinara, W Italy 41°07′N 08°19′E
Capraria see Cabrera, Illa de
14 F10 Capreol Ontario, S Canada 46°43′N 80°56′W
107 K18 Capri Campania, S Italy 40°33′N 14°14′E
175 S9 Capricorn Tablemount undersea feature W Pacific Ocean 18°34′S 172°12′W
107 J18 Capri, Isola di island S Italy
83 G16 Caprivi ◐ district NE Namibia
Caprivi Concession see Caprivi Strip
83 F16 Caprivi Strip Ger. Caprivizipfel; prev. Caprivi Concession. cultural region NE Namibia
Caprivizipfel see Caprivi Strip
25 O5 Cap Rock Escarpment cliffs Texas, SW USA
15 R10 Cap-Rouge Québec, SE Canada 46°45′N 71°18′W
Cap Saint-Jacques see Vung Tau
38 F12 Captain Cook Hawaii, USA, C Pacific Ocean 19°30′N 155°55′W
183 R10 Captains Flat New South Wales, SE Australia 35°37′S 149°28′E
102 K14 Captieux Gironde, SW France 44°16′N 00°15′W
107 K17 Capua Campania, S Italy 41°06′N 14°13′E
54 F14 Caquetá off. Departamento del Caquetá. ◐ province S Colombia
Caquetá, Departamento del see Caquetá
54 E13 Caquetá, Río var. Rio Japurá, Yapurá. ≈ Brazil/Colombia see also Japurá, Rio
Caquetá, Río see Japurá, Rio
CAR see Central African Republic
Cara see Kara
57 I16 Carabaya, Cordillera ▲▲ E Peru
54 K5 Carabobo off. Estado Carabobo. ◐ state N Venezuela
Carabobo, Estado see Carabobo
116 I14 Caracal Olt, S Romania 44°07′N 24°18′E
58 F10 Caracaraí Rondônia, W Brazil 01°47′N 51°11′W
54 L5 Caracas ● (Venezuela) Distrito Federal, N Venezuela 10°29′N 66°54′W
54 I5 Carache Trujillo, N Venezuela 09°40′N 70°15′W
60 N10 Caraguatatuba São Paulo, S Brazil 23°37′S 45°24′W
48 I7 Carajás, Serra dos ▲▲ N Brazil
Caralis see Cagliari
54 E9 Caramanta Antioquia, W Colombia 05°36′N 75°38′W
171 P4 Caramoan Catanduanes Island, N Philippines 13°47′N 123°49′E
Caramurat see Mihail Kogălniceanu
116 F12 Caransebeş Ger. Karansebesch, Hung. Karánsebes. Caraş-Severin, SW Romania 45°23′N 22°13′E
Carapella see Carapelle
107 M16 Carapelle var. Carapella. ≈ SE Italy
55 O9 Carapo Bolívar, SE Venezuela
13 P13 Caraquet New Brunswick, SE Canada 47°48′N 64°59′W
Caras see Caraz
116 F12 Caraşova Hung. Krassóvár. Caraş-Severin, SW Romania 45°11′N 21°51′E
116 F12 Caraş-Severin ◐ county SW Romania
42 M5 Caratasca, Laguna de lagoon NE Honduras
58 C13 Carauari Amazonas, NW Brazil 04°55′S 66°57′W
Caravaca see Caravaca de la Cruz
105 Q12 Caravaca de la Cruz var. Caravaca. Murcia. SE Spain 38°06′N 01°51′W
106 E7 Caravaggio Lombardia, N Italy 45°31′N 09°39′E
107 C18 Caravai, Passo di pass Sardegna, Italy, C Mediterranean Sea
59 O19 Caravelas Bahia, E Brazil 17°45′S 39°15′W
56 C12 Caraz var. Caras. Ancash, W Peru 09°03′S 77°47′W
61 H14 Carazinho Rio Grande do Sul, S Brazil 28°16′S 52°46′W
42 J11 Carazo ◐ department SW Nicaragua
Carballiño see O Carballiño
104 G2 Carballo Galicia, NW Spain 43°13′N 08°41′W
11 W16 Carberry Manitoba, S Canada 49°52′N 99°20′W
40 F4 Carbó Sonora, NW Mexico 29°41′N 111°00′W
107 C20 Carbonara, Capo headland Sardegna, Italy, C Mediterranean Sea 39°06′N 09°31′E
37 Q5 Carbondale Colorado, C USA 39°24′N 107°12′W
30 L17 Carbondale Illinois, N USA 37°43′N 89°13′W
27 Q4 Carbondale Kansas, C USA 38°49′N 95°41′W
18 I13 Carbondale Pennsylvania, NE USA 41°34′N 75°30′W
13 V12 Carbonear Newfoundland, Newfoundland and Labrador, SE Canada 47°45′N 53°16′W
105 Q9 Carboneras de Guadazaón var. Carboneras de Guadazón. Castilla-La Mancha, C Spain 39°54′N 01°50′W
Carboneras de Guadazón see Carboneras de Guadazaón
23 O3 Carbon Hill Alabama, S USA 33°53′N 87°31′W
107 B20 Carbonia var. Carbonia Centro. Sardegna, Italy, C Mediterranean Sea 39°11′N 08°31′E
Carbonia Centro see Carbonia
105 S10 Carcaixent País Valenciano, E Spain 39°08′N 00°28′W
Carcaso see Carcassonne
65 B24 Carcass Island island NW Falkland Islands
103 O16 Carcassonne anc. Carcaso. Aude, S France 43°13′N 02°21′E
105 R12 Carche ▲ S Spain 38°24′N 01°11′W
56 A13 Carchi ◐ province N Ecuador
10 I8 Carcross Yukon Territory, W Canada 60°11′N 134°41′W
Cardamomes, Chaîne des see Krâvanh, Chuŏr Phnum
155 G22 Cardamom Hills ▲▲ SW India
Cardamom Mountains see Krâvanh, Chuŏr Phnum
104 M12 Cardeña Andalucía, S Spain 38°16′N 04°20′W
44 D4 Cárdenas Matanzas, W Cuba 23°02′N 81°12′W
41 O11 Cárdenas San Luis Potosí, C Mexico 22°03′N 99°30′W
41 U15 Cárdenas Tabasco, SE Mexico 18°00′N 93°21′W
63 H21 Cardiel, Lago ◎ S Argentina
97 K22 Cardiff Wel. Caerdydd. ◐ S Wales, United Kingdom 51°30′N 03°13′W
97 J22 Cardiff-Wales ✈ S Wales, United Kingdom 51°24′N 03°22′W
97 I21 Cardigan Wel. Aberteifi. SW Wales, United Kingdom 52°06′N 04°40′W
97 I20 Cardigan cultural region W Wales, United Kingdom
97 I20 Cardigan Bay bay W Wales, United Kingdom
19 N8 Cardigan, Mount ▲ New Hampshire, NE USA 43°39′N 71°52′W
14 M13 Cardinal Ontario, SE Canada 44°48′N 75°22′W
105 V5 Cardona Cataluña, NE Spain 41°55′N 01°41′E
61 E19 Cardona Soriano, SW Uruguay 33°53′S 57°18′W
105 V4 Cardoner ≈ NE Spain
11 Q17 Cardston Alberta, SW Canada 49°14′N 113°19′W
181 W5 Cardwell Queensland, NE Australia 18°24′S 146°06′E
116 G8 Carei Ger. Gross-Karol, Karol, Hung. Nagykároly; prev. Careii-Mari. Satu Mare, NW Romania 47°40′N 22°28′E
Careii-Mari see Carei
58 F13 Careiro Amazonas, NW Brazil 03°40′S 60°23′W
102 J4 Carentan Manche, N France 49°18′N 01°15′W
104 M2 Cares ≈ N Spain
33 P14 Carey Idaho, NW USA 43°17′N 113°58′W
31 S12 Carey Ohio, N USA 40°57′N 83°22′W
25 P4 Carey Texas, SW USA 34°28′N 100°18′W
180 L11 Carey, Lake ◎ Western Australia
173 O8 Cargados Carajos Bank undersea feature C Indian Ocean
102 G6 Carhaix-Plouguer Finistère, NW France 48°16′N 03°35′W
61 A22 Carhué Buenos Aires, E Argentina 37°10′S 62°45′W
55 O5 Cariaco Sucre, NE Venezuela 10°33′N 63°37′W
107 O20 Cariati Calabria, SW Italy 39°30′N 16°57′E
2 H17 Caribbean Plate tectonic feature
44 I11 Caribbean Sea sea W Atlantic Ocean
11 N15 Cariboo Mountains ▲▲ British Columbia, SW Canada
11 W9 Caribou Manitoba, C Canada 59°27′N 97°43′W
19 S2 Caribou Maine, NE USA 46°51′N 68°00′W
11 P10 Caribou Mountains ▲▲ Alberta, SW Canada
Caribrod see Dimitrovgrad
40 I6 Carichic Chihuahua, N Mexico 27°57′N 107°01′W
103 R3 Carignan Ardennes, N France 49°38′N 05°08′E
183 Q5 Carinda New South Wales, SE Australia 30°26′S 147°45′E
105 R6 Cariñena Aragón, NE Spain 41°20′N 01°13′W
107 I23 Carini Sicilia, Italy, C Mediterranean Sea 38°06′N 13°09′E
107 K17 Carinola Campania, S Italy 41°14′N 14°03′E
Carinthi see Kärnten
55 O5 Caripe Monagas, NE Venezuela 10°13′N 63°30′W
55 P5 Caripito Monagas, NE Venezuela 10°03′N 63°05′W
15 W7 Carleton Québec, SE Canada 48°07′N 66°07′W
31 S10 Carleton Michigan, N USA 42°03′N 83°23′W
13 O14 Carleton, Mount ▲ New Brunswick, SE Canada 47°10′N 66°54′W
14 L13 Carleton Place Ontario, SE Canada 45°08′N 76°09′W
35 V3 Carlin Nevada, W USA 40°40′N 116°09′W
30 K14 Carlinville Illinois, N USA 39°16′N 89°52′W
97 K14 Carlisle anc. Caer Luel, Luguvallium, Luguvallum. NW England, United Kingdom 54°54′N 02°55′W
27 V11 Carlisle Arkansas, C USA 34°46′N 91°45′W
31 N15 Carlisle Indiana, N USA 38°57′N 87°23′W
29 V14 Carlisle Iowa, C USA 41°30′N 93°29′W
21 N5 Carlisle Kentucky, S USA 38°19′N 84°02′W
18 F15 Carlisle Pennsylvania, NE USA 40°10′N 77°10′W
21 Q11 Carlisle South Carolina, SE USA 34°35′N 81°27′W
38 J17 Carlisle Island island Aleutian Islands, Alaska, USA
27 R7 Carl Junction Missouri, C USA 37°10′N 94°34′W
107 A20 Carloforte Sardegna, Italy, C Mediterranean Sea 39°10′N 08°17′E
Carlopago see Karlobag
61 B21 Carlos Casares Buenos Aires, E Argentina 35°39′S 61°28′W
61 E18 Carlos Reyles Durazno, C Uruguay 33°00′S 56°30′W
61 A21 Carlos Tejedor Buenos Aires, E Argentina 35°25′S 62°25′W
97 F19 Carlow Ir. Ceatharlach. SE Ireland 52°50′N 06°55′W
97 F19 Carlow Ir. Ceatharlach. cultural region SE Ireland
96 F7 Carloway NW Scotland, United Kingdom 58°17′N 06°48′W
35 U17 Carlsbad California, W USA 33°09′N 117°21′W
37 U15 Carlsbad New Mexico, SW USA 32°24′N 104°15′W
Carlsbad see Karlovy Vary
129 N13 Carlsberg Ridge undersea feature S Arabian Sea 06°00′N 61°00′E
Carlsruhe see Karlsruhe
29 W6 Carlton Minnesota, N USA 46°39′N 92°25′W
11 V17 Carlyle Saskatchewan, S Canada 49°39′N 102°18′W
30 L15 Carlyle Illinois, N USA 38°36′N 89°22′W
30 L15 Carlyle Lake ⊠ Illinois, N USA
10 H7 Carmacks Yukon Territory, W Canada 62°04′N 136°21′W
106 B9 Carmagnola Piemonte, NW Italy 44°50′N 07°43′E
11 X16 Carman Manitoba, S Canada 49°32′N 97°59′W
Carmana/Carmania see Kermān
97 I21 Carmarthen SW Wales, United Kingdom 51°52′N 04°19′W
97 I21 Carmarthen cultural region SW Wales, United Kingdom
97 I22 Carmarthen Bay inlet SW Wales, United Kingdom
103 N14 Carmaux Tarn, S France 44°03′N 02°09′E
35 N11 Carmel California, W USA 36°32′N 121°54′W
31 O13 Carmel Indiana, N USA 39°58′N 86°07′W
18 L13 Carmel New York, NE USA 41°25′N 73°40′W
97 H18 Carmel Head headland NW Wales, United Kingdom 53°24′N 04°35′W
42 E2 Carmelita Petén, N Guatemala 17°33′N 90°11′W
61 D19 Carmelo Colonia, SW Uruguay 34°00′S 58°20′W
41 V14 Carmen var. Ciudad del Carmen. Campeche, SE Mexico 18°38′N 91°50′W
61 A25 Carmen de Patagones Buenos Aires, E Argentina 40°45′S 63°00′W
40 F8 Carmen, Isla island NW Mexico
40 M5 Carmen, Sierra del ▲▲ NW Mexico
30 M16 Carmi Illinois, N USA 38°05′N 88°09′W
35 O7 Carmichael California, W USA 38°36′N 121°21′W
Carmiel see Karmi'el
25 U11 Carmine Texas, SW USA 30°07′N 96°40′W
104 K14 Carmona Andalucía, S Spain 37°28′N 05°38′W
Carmona see Uíge
Carnaro see Kvarner
180 G9 Carnarvon Western Australia 24°57′S 113°38′E
14 I13 Carnarvon Ontario, SE Canada 45°03′N 78°41′W
83 G24 Carnarvon Northern Cape, W South Africa 30°59′S 22°08′E
Carnarvon see Caernarfon
180 K9 Carnarvon Range ▲▲ Western Australia
Carn Domhnach see Carndonagh
96 E13 Carndonagh Ir. Carn Domhnach. NW Ireland 55°15′N 07°15′W
11 V17 Carnduff Saskatchewan, S Canada 49°11′N 101°50′W
26 L11 Carnegie Oklahoma, C USA 35°06′N 98°36′W
180 L9 Carnegie, Lake salt lake Western Australia
193 U8 Carnegie Ridge undersea feature E Pacific Ocean 01°00′S 85°00′W
96 H9 Carn Eige ▲ N Scotland, United Kingdom 57°18′N 05°04′W
182 F5 Carnes South Australia 30°12′S 134°31′E
194 J12 Carney Island island Antarctica
18 H16 Carneys Point New Jersey, NE USA 39°38′N 75°29′W
Carniche, Alpi see Karnische Alpen
151 Q21 Car Nicobar island Nicobar Islands, India, NE Indian Ocean
79 H15 Carnot Mambéré-Kadéï, W Central African Republic 04°58′N 15°55′E
182 F10 Carnot, Cape headland South Australia 34°57′S 135°39′E
96 K11 Carnoustie E Scotland, United Kingdom 56°30′N 02°42′W
97 F20 Carnsore Point Ir. Ceann an Chairn. headland SE Ireland 52°10′N 06°22′W
8 H7 Carnwath ≈ Northwest Territories, NW Canada
31 R8 Caro Michigan, N USA 43°29′N 83°24′W
23 Z15 Carol City Florida, SE USA 25°56′N 80°15′W
59 L14 Carolina Maranhão, E Brazil 07°20′S 47°25′W
45 U5 Carolina E Puerto Rico 18°22′N 65°57′W
21 V12 Carolina Beach North Carolina, SE USA 34°02′N 77°53′W
Caroline Island see Millennium Island
189 N15 Caroline Islands island group C Micronesia
129 Z14 Caroline Plate tectonic feature
192 H7 Caroline Ridge undersea feature E Philippine Sea 08°00′N 150°00′E
Carolopois see Châlons-en-Champagne
45 V14 Caroni Arena Dam ⊠ Trinidad, Trinidad and Tobago
Caronie, Monti see Nebrodi, Monti
55 P7 Caroní, Río ≈ E Venezuela
45 U14 Caroni River ≈ Trinidad, Trinidad and Tobago
Caronium see A Coruña
54 J5 Carora Lara, N Venezuela 10°12′N 70°07′W
86 F12 Carpathian Mountains var. Carpathians, Cz./Pol. Karpaty, Ger. Karpaten. ▲▲ E Europe
Carpathians see Carpathian Mountains
Carpathos/Carpathus see Kárpathos
116 H12 Carpaţii Meridionalii var. Alpi Transilvaniei, Carpaţii Sudici, Eng. South Carpathians, Transylvanian Alps, Ger. Südkarpaten, Transsylvanische Alpen, Hung. Déli-Kárpátok, Erdélyi-Havasok. ▲▲ C Romania
Carpaţii Sudici see Carpaţii Meridionalii
174 L7 Carpentaria, Gulf of gulf N Australia
Carpentoracte see Carpentras
103 R14 Carpentras anc. Carpentoracte. Vaucluse, SE France 44°03′N 05°03′E
106 F9 Carpi Emilia-Romagna, N Italy 44°47′N 10°53′E
116 E11 Cărpiniş Hung. Gyertyámos. Timiş, W Romania 45°46′N 20°53′E
35 R14 Carpinteria California, W USA 34°24′N 119°30′W
23 S9 Carrabelle Florida, SE USA 29°51′N 84°39′W
Carraig Aonair see Fastnet Rock
Carraig Fhearghais see Carrickfergus
Carraig Mhachaire Rois see Carrickmacross
Carraig na Siúire see Carrick-on-Suir
Carrantual see Carrauntoohil
106 E10 Carrara Toscana, C Italy 44°05′N 10°07′E
61 F20 Carrasco ✈ (Montevideo) Canelones, S Uruguay 34°51′S 56°00′W
105 P9 Carrascosa del Campo Castilla-La Mancha, C Spain 40°02′N 02°35′W
54 H4 Carrasquero Zulia, NW Venezuela 11°00′N 72°01′W
183 O9 Carrathool New South Wales, SE Australia 34°25′S 145°30′E
Carrauntohil see Carrauntoohil
97 B21 Carrauntoohil Ir. Carrantual, Carrauntohil, Corrán Tuathail. ▲ SW Ireland 51°98′N 09°53′W
45 Y15 Carriacou island N Grenada
97 G15 Carrickfergus Ir. Carraig Fhearghais. NE Northern Ireland, United Kingdom 54°43′N 05°49′W
97 F16 Carrickmacross Ir. Carraig Mhachaire Rois. N Ireland 53°58′N 06°43′W
97 D16 Carrick-on-Shannon Ir. Cora Droma Rúisc. NW Ireland 53°37′N 08°05′W
97 E20 Carrick-on-Suir Ir. Carraig na Siúire. S Ireland 52°21′N 07°25′W
182 I7 Carrieton South Australia 32°27′S 138°33′E
40 L7 Carrillo Chihuahua, N Mexico 25°53′N 103°54′W
29 O4 Carrington North Dakota, N USA 47°27′N 99°07′W
104 M4 Carrión ≈ N Spain
104 M4 Carrión de los Condes Castilla-León, N Spain 42°20′N 04°37′W
25 P13 Carrizo Springs Texas, SW USA 28°33′N 99°54′W
37 S13 Carrizozo New Mexico, SW USA 33°38′N 105°52′W
29 T13 Carroll Iowa, C USA 42°04′N 94°52′W
23 N4 Carrollton Alabama, S USA 33°13′N 88°05′W
23 R3 Carrollton Georgia, SE USA 33°33′N 85°04′W
30 K14 Carrollton Illinois, N USA 39°18′N 90°24′W
20 L4 Carrollton Kentucky, S USA 38°41′N 85°09′W
31 R8 Carrollton Michigan, N USA 43°27′N 83°55′W
27 T3 Carrollton Missouri, C USA 39°20′N 93°30′W
31 U12 Carrollton Ohio, N USA 40°34′N 81°05′W
25 T6 Carrollton Texas, SW USA 32°57′N 96°53′W
11 U14 Carrot ≈ Saskatchewan, S Canada
11 U14 Carrot River Saskatchewan, C Canada 53°18′N 103°32′W
18 J7 Carry Falls Reservoir ⊠ New York, NE USA
136 L11 Çarşamba Samsun, N Turkey 41°13′N 36°43′E
28 L6 Carson North Dakota, N USA 46°26′N 101°34′W
35 Q6 Carson City state capital Nevada, W USA 39°10′N 119°46′W
35 R6 Carson River ≈ Nevada, W USA
35 S5 Carson Sink salt flat Nevada, W USA
11 Q16 Carstairs Alberta, SW Canada 51°35′N 114°02′W
Carstensz, Puntjak see Jaya, Puncak
54 E5 Cartagena var. Cartagena de los Indes. Bolívar, NW Colombia 10°24′N 75°33′W
105 R13 Cartagena anc. Carthago Nova. Murcia, SE Spain 37°36′N 00°59′W
54 E13 Cartagena de Chaira Caquetá, S Colombia 01°19′N 74°52′W
Cartagena de los Indes see Cartagena
54 D10 Cartago Valle del Cauca, W Colombia 04°45′N 75°55′W
43 N14 Cartago Cartago, C Costa Rica 09°50′N 83°54′W
42 M14 Cartago off. Provincia de Cartago. ◐ province C Costa Rica
Cartago, Provincia de see Cartago
25 O11 Carta Valley Texas, SW USA 29°46′N 100°37′W
104 F10 Cartaxo Santarém, C Portugal 39°10′N 08°47′W
104 I14 Cartaya Andalucía, S Spain 37°16′N 07°09′W
Carteret Islands see Tulun Islands
29 S15 Carter Lake Iowa, C USA 41°17′N 95°55′W
23 S3 Cartersville Georgia, SE USA 34°10′N 84°48′W
185 M14 Carterton Wellington, North Island, New Zealand 41°01′S 175°30′E
30 J13 Carthage Illinois, N USA 40°25′N 91°09′W
22 L5 Carthage Mississippi, S USA 32°43′N 89°31′W
27 R7 Carthage Missouri, C USA 37°10′N 94°20′W
18 I8 Carthage New York, NE USA 43°58′N 75°36′W
21 T10 Carthage North Carolina, SE USA 35°21′N 79°27′W
20 K8 Carthage Tennessee, S USA 36°14′N 85°59′W
25 X7 Carthage Texas, SW USA 32°10′N 94°21′W

◆ Country
● Country Capital
◇ Dependent Territory
○ Dependent Territory Capital
◐ Administrative Regions
✈ International Airport
▲ Mountain
▲▲ Mountain Range
⛰ Volcano
≈ River
◎ Lake
⊠ Reservoir

CARTHAGE – CERMEI

74 M5 **Carthage** ✈ (Tunis) N Tunisia 36°51′N 10°12′E
Carthago Nova *see* Cartagena
14 E10 **Cartier** Ontario, S Canada 46°40′N 81°31′W
13 S8 **Cartwright** Newfoundland and Labrador, E Canada 53°40′N 57°W
55 P9 **Caruana de Montaña** Bolívar, SE Venezuela 05°16′N 63°12′W
59 Q15 **Caruaru** Pernambuco, E Brazil 08°15′S 35°55′W
55 P5 **Carúpano** Sucre, NE Venezuela 10°39′N 63°14′W
Carusbur *see* Cherbourg
58 M12 **Carutapera** Maranhão, E Brazil 01°12′S 45°57′W
27 Y9 **Caruthersville** Missouri, C USA 36°11′N 89°40′W
103 O1 **Carvin** Pas-de-Calais, N France 50°31′N 03°00′E
58 E12 **Carvoeiro** Amazonas, NW Brazil 01°24′S 61°59′W
104 E10 **Carvoeiro, Cabo** *headland* C Portugal 39°19′N 09°27′W
21 U9 **Cary** North Carolina, SE USA 35°47′N 78°46′W
182 M3 **Caryapundy Swamp** *wetland* New South Wales/ Queensland, SE Australia
74 F6 **Casablanca** *Ar.* Dar-el-Beida. NW Morocco 33°39′N 07°31′W
60 M8 **Casa Branca** São Paulo, S Brazil 21°47′S 47°05′W
36 L14 **Casa Grande** Arizona, SW USA 32°52′N 111°45′W
106 C8 **Casale Monferrato** Piemonte, NW Italy 45°08′N 08°27′E
106 E8 **Casalpusterlengo** Lombardia, N Italy 45°10′N 09°37′E
54 H10 **Casanare** *off.* Intendencia de Casanare. ◈ *province* C Colombia
Casanare, Intendencia de *see* Casanare
55 P5 **Casanay** Sucre, NE Venezuela 10°30′N 63°25′W
24 K11 **Casa Piedra** Texas, SW USA 29°43′N 104°03′W
107 Q19 **Casarano** Puglia, SE Italy 40°01′N 18°10′E
42 J11 **Casares** Carazo, W Nicaragua 11°37′N 86°19′W
105 R10 **Casas Ibáñez** Castilla-La Mancha, C Spain 39°17′N 01°28′W
61 I14 **Casca** Rio Grande do Sul, S Brazil 28°39′S 51°55′W
172 I17 **Cascade** Mahé, NE Seychelles 04°39′S 55°29′E
33 N13 **Cascade** Idaho, NW USA 44°31′N 116°02′W
29 Y13 **Cascade** Iowa, C USA 42°18′N 91°00′W
33 R9 **Cascade** Montana, NW USA 47°15′N 111°46′W
185 B20 **Cascade Point** *headland* South Island, New Zealand 44°00′S 168°23′E
32 G13 **Cascade Range** ⛰ Oregon/ Washington, NW USA
33 N12 **Cascade Reservoir** ⊠ Idaho, NW USA
0 E8 **Cascadia Basin** *undersea feature* NE Pacific Ocean 47°00′N 127°30′W
104 E11 **Cascais** Lisboa, C Portugal 38°41′N 09°25′W
15 W7 **Cascapédia** ≈ Québec, SE Canada
59 I22 **Cascavel** Ceará, E Brazil 04°10′S 38°15′W
60 G11 **Cascavel** Paraná, S Brazil 24°56′S 53°28′W
106 I13 **Cascia** Umbria, C Italy 42°45′N 13°01′E
106 F11 **Cascina** Toscana, C Italy 43°40′N 10°33′E
19 Q8 **Casco Bay** *bay* Maine, NE USA
194 J7 **Case Island** *island* Antarctica
106 B8 **Caselle** ✈ (Torino) Piemonte, NW Italy 45°06′N 07°41′E
107 K17 **Caserta** Campania, S Italy 41°05′N 14°20′E
15 N8 **Casey** Québec, SE Canada 47°50′N 74°09′W
30 M14 **Casey** Illinois, N USA 39°18′N 87°59′W
195 Y12 **Casey** *Australian research station* Antarctica 65°58′S 111°04′E
195 W3 **Casey Bay** *bay* Antarctica
80 Q11 **Caseyr, Raas** *headland* NE Somalia 11°51′S 51°16′E
97 D20 **Cashel** *Ir.* Caiseal. S Ireland 52°31′N 07°53′W
54 G6 **Casigua** Zulia, W Venezuela 08°46′N 72°30′W
61 B19 **Casilda** Santa Fe, C Argentina 33°05′S 61°10′W
Casim *see* General Toshevo
183 V4 **Casino** New South Wales, SE Australia 28°50′S 153°02′E
107 J16 **Cassino** *prev.* San Germano; *anc.* Casinum. Lazio, C Italy 41°29′N 13°50′E
Casinum *see* Cassino
111 E17 **Čáslav** *Ger.* Tschaslau. Střední Čechy, C Czech Republic 49°54′N 15°23′E
56 C13 **Casma** Ancash, C Peru 09°30′S 78°18′W
167 S7 **Ca, Sông** ≈ N Vietnam
107 K17 **Casoria** Campania, S Italy 40°54′N 14°28′E
105 T6 **Caspe** Aragón, NE Spain 41°14′N 00°03′W
33 X15 **Casper** Wyoming, C USA 42°48′N 106°22′W
84 M10 **Caspian Depression** *Kaz.* Kaspīy Mangy Oypaty, *Rus.* Prikaspiyskaya Nizmennost'. *depression* Kazakhstan/Russian Federation
130 D10 **Caspian Sea** *Az.* Xäzär Dänizi, *Kaz.* Kaspīy Tengizi, *Per.* Bahr-e Khazar, Daryā-ye Khazar, *Rus.* Kaspiyskoye More. *inland sea* Asia/Europe
83 L14 **Cassacatiza** Tete, NW Mozambique 14°20′S 32°24′E
Cassai *see* Kasai
82 F13 **Cassamba** Moxico, E Angola 13°07′S 20°22′E
107 N20 **Cassano allo Ionio** Calabria, SE Italy 39°46′N 16°16′E
31 S8 **Cass City** Michigan, N USA 43°36′N 83°10′W
Cassel *see* Kassel
14 M13 **Casselman** Ontario, SE Canada 45°18′N 75°05′W
29 R5 **Casselton** North Dakota, N USA 46°53′N 97°10′W
59 M16 **Cássia** *var.* Santa Rita de Cassia. Bahia, E Brazil 11°03′S 44°16′W
10 J9 **Cassiar** British Columbia, W Canada 59°16′N 129°40′W
10 K10 **Cassiar Mountains** ⛰ British Columbia, W Canada
83 C15 **Cassinga** Huíla, SW Angola 15°08′S 16°05′E
29 T4 **Cass Lake** Minnesota, N USA 47°22′N 94°36′W
29 T4 **Cass Lake** ◎ Minnesota, N USA
31 P10 **Cassopolis** Michigan, N USA 41°56′N 86°00′W
31 S8 **Cass River** ≈ Michigan, N USA
27 S8 **Cassville** Missouri, C USA 36°42′N 93°52′W
Castamoni *see* Kastamonu
58 L12 **Castanhal** Pará, NE Brazil 01°16′S 47°55′W
104 G8 **Castanheira de Pêra** Leiria, C Portugal 40°01′N 08°12′W
41 N7 **Castaños** Coahuila, NE Mexico 26°48′N 101°26′W
108 I10 **Castasegna** Graubünden, SE Switzerland 46°21′N 09°30′E
106 D8 **Casteggio** Lombardia, N Italy 45°02′N 09°10′E
107 K23 **Castelbuono** Sicilia, Italy, C Mediterranean Sea 37°56′N 14°05′E
107 K15 **Castel di Sangro** Abruzzo, C Italy 41°46′N 14°03′E
106 H7 **Castelfranco Veneto** Veneto, NE Italy 45°40′N 11°55′E
102 K14 **Casteljaloux** Lot-et-Garonne, SW France 44°19′N 00°03′E
107 L18 **Castellabate** *var.* Santa Maria di Castellabate. Campania, S Italy 40°16′N 14°57′E
107 I23 **Castellammare del Golfo** Sicilia, Italy, C Mediterranean Sea 38°02′N 12°53′E
107 H22 **Castellammare, Golfo di** *gulf* Sicilia, Italy, C Mediterranean Sea
103 U15 **Castellane** Alpes-de-Haute-Provence, SE France 43°49′N 06°34′E
107 O18 **Castellaneta** Puglia, SE Italy 40°38′N 16°57′E
106 E9 **Castell'Arquato** Emilia-Romagna, C Italy 44°52′N 09°51′E
61 E21 **Castelli** Buenos Aires, E Argentina 36°07′S 57°47′W
Castelló de la Plana *see* Castellón de la Plana
105 S8 **Castellón** ◈ *province* País Valenciano, E Spain
Castellón *see* Castellón de la Plana
105 T9 **Castellón de la Plana** *var.* Castellón, *Cat.* Castelló de la Plana. País Valenciano, E Spain 39°59′N 00°03′W
105 S7 **Castellote** Aragón, NE Spain 40°46′N 00°18′W
103 N16 **Castelnaudary** Aude, S France 43°18′N 01°57′E
102 L16 **Castelnau-Magnoac** Hautes-Pyrénées, S France 43°18′N 00°30′E
106 F10 **Castelnovo ne' Monti** Emilia-Romagna, C Italy 44°26′N 10°24′E
Castelnuovo *see* Herceg-Novi
104 H9 **Castelo Branco** Castelo Branco, C Portugal 39°50′N 07°30′W
104 H8 **Castelo Branco** ◈ *district* C Portugal
104 I10 **Castelo de Vide** Portalegre, C Portugal 39°25′N 07°27′W
104 G9 **Castelo do Bode, Barragem do** ⊠ C Portugal
106 G10 **Castel San Pietro Terme** Emilia-Romagna, C Italy 44°22′N 11°34′E
107 B17 **Castelsardo** Sardegna, Italy, C Mediterranean Sea 40°54′N 08°42′E
102 M14 **Castelsarrasin** Tarn-et-Garonne, S France 44°02′N 01°06′E
107 I24 **Casteltermini** Sicilia, Italy, C Mediterranean Sea 37°33′N 13°38′E
107 H24 **Castelvetrano** Sicilia, Italy, C Mediterranean Sea 37°40′N 12°46′E
182 L12 **Casterton** Victoria, SE Australia 37°37′S 141°22′E
102 J15 **Castets** Landes, SW France 43°55′N 01°08′W
106 H12 **Castiglione del Lago** Umbria, C Italy 43°07′N 12°02′E
106 F13 **Castiglione della Pescaia** Toscana, C Italy 42°46′N 10°53′E
106 F8 **Castiglione delle Stiviere** Lombardia, N Italy 45°24′N 10°31′E
104 M9 **Castilla-La Mancha** ◈ *autonomous community* NE Spain
104 L5 **Castilla-León** *var.* Castillia y Leon. ◈ *autonomous community* NW Spain
105 N10 **Castilla Nueva** *cultural region* C Spain
105 N6 **Castilla Vieja** ◈ *cultural region* N Spain
Castilla y Leon *see* Castilla-León
Castillo de Locubim *see* Castillo de Locubín
105 N14 **Castillo de Locubín** *var.* Castillo de Locubim. Andalucía, S Spain 37°32′N 03°56′W
102 K13 **Castillon-la-Bataille** Gironde, SW France 44°51′N 00°01′W
63 I19 **Castillo, Pampa del** *plain* S Argentina
61 G19 **Castillos** Rocha, SE Uruguay 34°12′S 53°52′W
97 B16 **Castlebar** *Ir.* Caisleán an Bharraigh. W Ireland 53°52′N 09°17′W
97 F16 **Castleblayney** *Ir.* Baile na Lorgan. N Ireland 54°07′N 06°44′W
45 O11 **Castle Bruce** E Dominica 15°24′N 61°26′W
36 M5 **Castle Dale** Utah, W USA 39°10′N 111°02′W
36 I14 **Castle Dome Peak** ▲ Arizona, SW USA 33°04′N 114°08′W
97 J14 **Castle Douglas** S Scotland, United Kingdom 54°56′N 03°56′W
97 E14 **Castlefinn** *Ir.* Caisleán na Finne. NW Ireland 54°47′N 07°35′W
97 M17 **Castleford** N England, United Kingdom 53°44′N 01°21′W
11 O17 **Castlegar** British Columbia, SW Canada 49°18′N 117°48′W
64 B12 **Castle Harbour** *inlet* Bermuda, NW Atlantic Ocean
21 V12 **Castle Hayne** North Carolina, SE USA 34°23′N 78°07′W
97 B20 **Castleisland** *Ir.* Oileán Ciarral. SW Ireland 52°12′N 09°30′W
183 N12 **Castlemaine** Victoria, SE Australia 37°06′S 144°13′E
37 R5 **Castle Peak** ▲ Colorado, C USA 39°00′N 106°51′W
33 O13 **Castle Peak** ▲ Idaho, NW USA 44°02′N 114°42′W
184 N13 **Castlepoint** Wellington, North Island, New Zealand 40°54′S 176°13′E
97 D17 **Castlerea** *Ir.* An Caisleán Riabhach. W Ireland 53°45′N 08°32′W
97 G15 **Castlereagh** *Ir.* An Caisleán Riabhach. N Northern Ireland, United Kingdom 54°33′N 05°53′W
183 R6 **Castlereagh River** ≈ New South Wales, SE Australia
37 T5 **Castle Rock** Colorado, C USA 39°22′N 104°51′W
30 K7 **Castle Rock Lake** ⊠ Wisconsin, N USA
65 G25 **Castle Rock Point** *headland* S Saint Helena 16°02′S 05°45′W
97 I16 **Castletown** SE Isle of Man 54°05′N 04°39′W
29 R9 **Castlewood** South Dakota, N USA 44°43′N 97°01′W
11 R15 **Castor** Alberta, SW Canada 52°14′N 111°54′W
14 M13 **Castor** ≈ Ontario, SE Canada
27 X7 **Castor River** ≈ Missouri, C USA
Castra Albiensium *see* Castres
Castra Regina *see* Regensburg
103 N15 **Castres** *anc.* Castra Albiensium. Tarn, S France 43°36′N 02°15′E
98 H9 **Castricum** Noord-Holland, W Netherlands 52°33′N 04°40′E
45 S11 **Castries** ● (Saint Lucia) N Saint Lucia 14°01′N 60°59′W
60 J11 **Castro** Paraná, S Brazil 24°46′S 50°03′W
63 F17 **Castro** Los Lagos, W Chile 42°27′S 73°48′W
104 H7 **Castro Daire** Viseu, N Portugal 40°54′N 07°55′W
104 M13 **Castro del Río** Andalucía, S Spain 37°41′N 04°29′W
Castrogiovanni *see* Enna
104 H14 **Castro Marim** Faro, S Portugal 37°13′N 07°26′W
104 J2 **Castropol** Asturias, N Spain 43°30′N 07°01′W
105 O2 **Castro-Urdiales** *var.* Castro Urdiales. Cantabria, N Spain 43°23′N 03°11′W
104 G13 **Castro Verde** Beja, S Portugal 37°42′N 08°05′W
107 N19 **Castrovillari** Calabria, SW Italy 39°48′N 16°12′E
35 N10 **Castroville** California, W USA 36°46′N 121°46′W
25 R12 **Castroville** Texas, SW USA 29°21′N 98°52′W
104 K11 **Castuera** Extremadura, W Spain 38°44′N 05°33′W
61 F19 **Casupá** Florida, S Uruguay 34°09′S 55°38′W
185 A22 **Caswell Sound** *sound* South Island, New Zealand
137 Q13 **Çat** Erzurum, NE Turkey 39°40′N 41°03′E
42 K6 **Catacamas** Olancho, C Honduras 14°55′N 85°54′W
56 A10 **Catacaos** Piura, NW Peru 05°22′S 80°40′W
22 I7 **Catahoula Lake** ◎ Louisiana, S USA
137 S15 **Çatak** Van, SE Turkey 38°02′N 43°05′E
137 S15 **Çatak Çayi** ≈ SE Turkey
114 O12 **Çatalca** İstanbul, NW Turkey 41°09′N 28°28′E
114 O12 **Çatalca Yarimadasi** *physical region* NW Turkey
62 H6 **Catalina** Antofagasta, N Chile 25°19′S 69°37′W
Catalonia *see* Cataluña
105 U5 **Cataluña** *Cat.* Catalunya, *Eng.* Catalonia. ◈ *autonomous community* N Spain
Catalunya *see* Cataluña
62 I7 **Catamarca** *off.* Provincia de Catamarca. ◈ *province* NW Argentina
Catamarca *see* San Fernando del Valle de Catamarca
Catamarca, Provincia de *see* Catamarca
83 M16 **Catandica** Manica, C Mozambique 18°05′S 33°10′E
171 P4 **Catanduanes Island** *island* N Philippines
60 K8 **Catanduva** São Paulo, S Brazil 21°05′S 49°00′W
107 L24 **Catania** Sicilia, Italy, C Mediterranean Sea 37°31′N 15°04′E
107 M24 **Catania, Golfo di** *gulf* Sicilia, Italy, C Mediterranean Sea
45 U5 **Cataño** *var.* Cantaño. E Puerto Rico 18°26′N 66°06′W
107 O21 **Catanzaro** Calabria, SW Italy 38°53′N 16°36′E
107 O22 **Catanzaro Marina** *var.* Marina di Catanzaro. Calabria, S Italy 38°48′N 16°33′E
Marina di Catanzaro *see* Catanzaro Marina
25 Q14 **Catarina** Texas, SW USA 28°19′N 99°36′W
171 Q5 **Catarman** Samar, C Philippines 12°29′N 124°34′E
105 S10 **Catarroja** País Valenciano, E Spain 39°24′N 00°24′W
21 R11 **Catawba River** ≈ North Carolina/South Carolina, SE USA
171 Q5 **Catbalogan** Samar, C Philippines 11°49′N 124°55′E
14 I14 **Catchacoma** Ontario, SE Canada 44°43′N 78°19′W
41 S15 **Catemaco** Veracruz-Llave, SE Mexico 18°28′N 95°10′W
Cathair na Mart *see* Westport
Cathair Saidhbhín *see* Cahersiveen
31 P5 **Cat Head Point** *headland* Michigan, N USA 45°11′N 85°37′W
23 Q2 **Cathedral Caverns** *cave* Alabama, S USA
35 V16 **Cathedral City** California, W USA 33°45′N 116°27′W
24 K10 **Cathedral Mountain** ▲ Texas, SW USA 30°10′N 103°39′W
32 G10 **Cathlamet** Washington, NW USA 46°12′N 123°24′W
76 G13 **Catió** S Guinea-Bissau 11°13′N 15°10′W
55 O10 **Catisimiña** Bolívar, SE Venezuela 04°07′N 63°40′W
44 J3 **Cat Island** *island* C Bahamas
12 B9 **Cat Lake** Ontario, S Canada 51°47′N 91°52′W
21 P5 **Catlettsburg** Kentucky, S USA 38°24′N 82°37′W
185 D24 **Catlins** ≈ South Island, New Zealand
35 R1 **Catnip Mountain** ▲ Nevada, W USA 41°53′N 119°19′W
41 Z11 **Catoche, Cabo** *headland* SE Mexico 21°36′N 87°04′W
27 P9 **Catoosa** Oklahoma, C USA 36°11′N 95°45′W
41 N10 **Catorce** San Luis Potosí, C Mexico 23°42′N 100°49′W
63 I14 **Catriel** Río Negro, C Argentina 37°54′S 67°52′W
62 K13 **Catriló** La Pampa, C Argentina 36°28′S 63°20′W
58 F11 **Catrimani** Roraima, N Brazil 0°24′N 61°30′W
58 E10 **Catrimani, Rio** ≈ N Brazil
18 K11 **Catskill** New York, NE USA 42°13′N 73°52′W
18 K11 **Catskill Creek** ≈ New York, NE USA
18 J11 **Catskill Mountains** ⛰ New York, NE USA
18 D11 **Cattaraugus Creek** ≈ New York, NE USA
Cattaro *see* Kotor
Cattaro, Bocche di *see* Kotorska, Boka
107 K24 **Cattolica Eraclea** Sicilia, Italy, C Mediterranean Sea 37°27′N 13°24′E
83 B14 **Catumbela** ≈ W Angola
83 N14 **Catur** Niassa, N Mozambique 13°50′S 35°43′E
82 C10 **Cauale** ≈ NE Angola
171 O2 **Cauayan** Luzon, N Philippines 16°55′N 121°46′E
54 C12 **Cauca** *off.* Departamento del Cauca. ◈ *province* SW Colombia
47 P5 **Cauca** ≈ SE Venezuela
Cauca, Departamento del *see* Cauca
58 P13 **Caucaia** Ceará, E Brazil 03°44′S 38°45′W
54 E7 **Cauca, Río** ≈ N Colombia
54 E7 **Caucasia** Antioquia, NW Colombia 07°59′N 75°13′W
137 Q8 **Caucasus** *Rus.* Kavkaz. ⛰ Georgia/Russian Federation
62 I10 **Caucete** San Juan, W Argentina 31°38′S 68°16′W
105 R11 **Caudete** Castilla-La Mancha, C Spain 38°42′N 01°00′W
103 P2 **Caudry** Nord, N France 50°07′N 03°24′E
82 D11 **Caungula** Lunda Norte, NE Angola 08°22′S 18°37′E
62 G13 **Cauquenes** Maule, C Chile 35°58′S 72°22′W
55 N8 **Caura, Río** ≈ C Venezuela
15 V7 **Causapscal** Québec, SE Canada 48°22′N 67°14′W
117 N10 **Căuşeni** *Rus.* Kaushany. E Moldova 46°37′N 29°21′E
102 M14 **Caussade** Tarn-et-Garonne, S France 44°10′N 01°31′E
102 K17 **Cauterets** Hautes-Pyrénées, S France 42°53′N 00°08′W
10 J15 **Caution, Cape** *headland* British Columbia, SW Canada 51°10′N 127°43′W
44 H7 **Cauto** ≈ E Cuba
Cauvery *see* Kāveri
102 L3 **Caux, Pays de** *physical region* N France
107 L18 **Cava de' Tirreni** Campania, S Italy 40°42′N 14°42′E
104 G6 **Cávado** ≈ N Portugal
Cavaia *see* Kavajë
103 R15 **Cavaillon** Vaucluse, SE France 43°51′N 05°01′E
103 U16 **Cavalaire-sur-Mer** Var, SE France 43°10′N 06°31′E
106 G6 **Cavalese** *Ger.* Gablös. Trentino-Alto Adige, N Italy 46°18′N 11°29′E
29 Q2 **Cavalier** North Dakota, N USA 48°47′N 97°37′W
76 L17 **Cavalla** *var.* Cavally, Cavally Fleuve. ≈ Ivory Coast/ Liberia
105 Y8 **Cavalleria, Cap de** *var.* Cabo Caballeria. *headland* Menorca, Spain, W Mediterranean Sea 40°04′N 04°06′E
184 K2 **Cavalli Islands** *island group* N New Zealand
Cavally/Cavally Fleuve *see* Cavalla
97 E16 **Cavan** *Ir.* Cabhán. N Ireland 54°N 07°21′W
97 E16 **Cavan** *Ir.* An Cabhán. *cultural region* N Ireland
106 H8 **Cavarzere** Veneto, NE Italy 45°08′N 12°05′E
27 W9 **Cave City** Arkansas, C USA 35°56′N 91°33′W
20 K7 **Cave City** Kentucky, S USA 37°08′N 85°57′W
65 M25 **Cave Point** *headland* S Tristan da Cunha
21 N5 **Cave Run Lake** ⊠ Kentucky, S USA
58 K11 **Caviana de Fora, Ilha** *var.* Ilha Caviana. *island* N Brazil
Caviana, Ilha *see* Caviana de Fora, Ilha
113 I16 **Cavtat** *It.* Ragusavecchia. Dubrovnik-Neretva, SE Croatia 42°36′N 18°13′E
Cawnpore *see* Kānpur
Caxamarca *see* Cajamarca
58 A13 **Caxias** Amazonas, W Brazil 04°27′S 71°27′W
58 N13 **Caxias** Maranhão, E Brazil 04°53′S 43°20′W
61 I15 **Caxias do Sul** Rio Grande do Sul, S Brazil 29°14′S 51°10′W
42 J4 **Caxinas, Punta** *headland* N Honduras 16°01′N 86°02′W
82 B11 **Caxito** Bengo, NW Angola 08°34′S 13°38′E
136 F14 **Çay** Afyon, W Turkey 38°35′N 31°01′E
40 L15 **Cayacal, Punta** *var.* Punta Mongrove. *headland* S Mexico 17°55′N 102°09′W
56 C6 **Cayambe** Pichincha, N Ecuador 0°02′N 78°08′W
56 C6 **Cayambe** ▲ N Ecuador 0°00′S 77°58′W
21 R12 **Cayce** South Carolina, SE USA 33°58′N 81°04′W
55 Y10 **Cayenne** ○ (French Guiana) NE French Guiana 04°55′N 52°18′W
55 Y10 **Cayenne** ✈ NE French Guiana 04°55′N 52°18′W
44 K10 **Cayes** *var.* Les Cayes. SW Haiti 18°10′N 73°48′W
45 U6 **Cayey** C Puerto Rico 18°06′N 66°11′W
45 U6 **Cayey, Sierra de** ⛰ E Puerto Rico
103 N14 **Caylus** Tarn-et-Garonne, S France 44°13′N 01°42′E
44 E8 **Cayman Brac** *island* E Cayman Islands
44 D8 **Cayman Islands** ◇ *UK dependent territory* W West Indies
64 D11 **Cayman Trench** *undersea feature* NW Caribbean Sea 19°00′N 80°00′W
47 O3 **Cayman Trough** *undersea feature* NW Caribbean Sea 18°00′N 81°00′W
80 O13 **Caynabo** Sool, N Somalia 08°55′N 46°28′E
42 F3 **Cayo** ◈ *district* SW Belize
Cayo *see* San Ignacio
43 N9 **Cayos Guerrero** *reef* E Nicaragua
43 O9 **Cayos King** *reef* E Nicaragua
44 E4 **Cay Sal** *islet* SW Bahamas
14 G16 **Cayuga** Ontario, S Canada 42°57′N 79°49′W
25 V8 **Cayuga** Texas, SW USA 31°55′N 95°57′W
18 G10 **Cayuga Lake** ◎ New York, NE USA
104 K13 **Cazalla de la Sierra** Andalucía, S Spain 37°56′N 05°46′W
116 L14 **Căzănești** Ialomița, SE Romania 44°36′N 27°03′E
102 M16 **Cazères** Haute-Garonne, S France 43°15′N 01°11′E
112 E10 **Cazin** ◈ Federacija Bosna I Hercegovina, NW Bosnia and Herzegovina
82 G13 **Cazombo** Moxico, E Angola 11°54′S 22°56′E
105 O13 **Cazorla** Andalucía, S Spain 37°55′N 03°W
Cazza *see* Sušac
104 L4 **Cea** ≈ NW Spain
Ceadâr-Lunga *see* Ciadîr-Lunga
Ceanannas *see* Kells
Ceann Toirc *see* Kanturk
58 O13 **Ceará** *off.* Estado do Ceará. ◈ *state* C Brazil
Ceará *see* Fortaleza
Ceara Abyssal Plain *see* Ceará Plain
Ceará, Estado do *see* Ceará
59 Q14 **Ceará Mirim** Rio Grande do Norte, E Brazil 05°30′S 35°51′W
64 J13 **Ceará Plain** *var.* Ceara Abyssal Plain. *undersea feature* W Atlantic Ocean 0°00′36°30′W
64 I13 **Ceará Ridge** *undersea feature* C Atlantic Ocean
Ceatharlach *see* Carlow
43 Q17 **Cébaco, Isla** *island* SW Panama
40 K7 **Ceballos** Durango, C Mexico 26°33′N 104°07′W
61 G19 **Cebollatí** Rocha, E Uruguay 33°15′S 53°46′W
61 G19 **Cebollatí, Río** ≈ E Uruguay
105 P5 **Cebollera** ▲ N Spain 42°01′N 02°40′W
104 M8 **Cebreros** Castilla-León, N Spain 40°27′N 04°28′W
171 P6 **Cebu** *off.* Cebu City. Cebu, C Philippines 10°17′N 123°46′E
171 P6 **Cebu** *island* C Philippines
Cebu City *see* Cebu
107 J16 **Ceccano** Lazio, C Italy 41°34′N 13°20′E
Čechy *see* Bohemia
106 F12 **Cecina** Toscana, C Italy 43°19′N 10°31′E
26 K4 **Cedar Bluff Reservoir** ⊠ Kansas, C USA
30 M8 **Cedarburg** Wisconsin, N USA 43°18′N 87°58′W
36 J7 **Cedar City** Utah, W USA 37°40′N 113°03′W
25 T11 **Cedar Creek** Texas, SW USA 30°04′N 97°30′W
28 L7 **Cedar Creek** ≈ North Dakota, N USA
25 U7 **Cedar Creek Reservoir** ⊠ Texas, SW USA
29 W13 **Cedar Falls** Iowa, C USA 42°31′N 92°27′W
31 N8 **Cedar Grove** Wisconsin, N USA 43°31′N 87°48′W
21 Y6 **Cedar Island** *island* Virginia, NE USA
23 U11 **Cedar Key** Cedar Keys, Florida, SE USA 29°08′N 83°03′W
23 U11 **Cedar Keys** *island group* Florida, SE USA
11 V14 **Cedar Lake** ◎ Manitoba, C Canada
14 I11 **Cedar Lake** ◎ Ontario, SE Canada
24 M6 **Cedar Lake** ◎ Texas, SW USA
29 X13 **Cedar Rapids** Iowa, C USA 41°58′N 91°40′W
29 X14 **Cedar River** ≈ Iowa/ Minnesota, C USA
29 O14 **Cedar River** ≈ Nebraska, C USA
31 P8 **Cedar Springs** Michigan, N USA 43°13′N 85°33′W
23 R3 **Cedartown** Georgia, SE USA 34°00′N 85°16′W
27 O7 **Cedar Vale** Kansas, C USA 37°06′N 96°30′W
35 Q2 **Cedarville** California, W USA 41°30′N 120°10′W
104 H1 **Cedeira** Galicia, NW Spain 43°40′N 08°03′W
42 H8 **Cedeño** Choluteca, S Honduras 13°10′N 87°25′W
41 N10 **Cedral** San Luis Potosí, C Mexico 23°47′N 100°40′W
42 I6 **Cedros** Francisco Morazán, C Honduras 14°38′N 86°42′W
40 M9 **Cedros** Zacatecas, C Mexico 24°39′N 101°47′W
40 B5 **Cedros, Isla** *island* W Mexico
193 R5 **Cedros Trench** *undersea feature* E Pacific Ocean 27°45′N 115°45′W
182 E7 **Ceduna** South Australia 32°09′S 133°43′E
110 D10 **Cedynia** *Ger.* Zehden. Zachodnio-pomorskie, W Poland 52°54′N 14°15′E
80 P12 **Ceelaayo** Sanaag, N Somalia 11°18′N 49°20′E
81 O16 **Ceel Buur** *It.* El Bur. Galguduud, C Somalia 04°36′N 46°33′E
81 N15 **Ceel Dheere** *var.* Ceel Dher, *It.* El Dere. Galguduud, C Somalia 05°18′N 46°07′E
Ceel Dher *see* Ceel Dheere
81 P14 **Ceel Xamure** Mudug, E Somalia 07°15′N 48°55′E
80 O12 **Ceerigaabo** *var.* Erigabo, Erigavo. Sanaag, N Somalia 10°34′N 47°22′E
107 J23 **Cefalù** *anc.* Cephaloedium. Sicilia, Italy, C Mediterranean Sea 38°02′N 14°02′E
105 N6 **Cega** ≈ N Spain
111 K23 **Cegléd** *prev.* Czegléd. Pest, C Hungary 47°10′N 19°47′E
113 N18 **Čegrane** W FYR Macedonia 41°50′N 20°59′E
105 Q13 **Cehegín** Murcia, SE Spain 38°04′N 01°48′W
136 K12 **Çekerek** Yozgat, N Turkey 40°04′N 35°30′E
146 B13 **Çekiçler** *Rus.* Chekishlyar, *Turkm.* Chekichler. Balkan Welaýaty, W Turkmenistan 37°35′N 53°52′E
107 J15 **Celano** Abruzzo, C Italy 42°06′N 13°33′E
104 H4 **Celanova** Galicia, NW Spain 42°09′N 07°58′W
42 F6 **Celaque, Cordillera de** ⛰ W Honduras
41 N13 **Celaya** Guanajuato, C Mexico 20°32′N 100°48′W
Celebes *see* Sulawesi
192 F7 **Celebes Basin** *undersea feature* SE South China Sea 04°00′N 122°00′E
192 F7 **Celebes Sea** *Ind.* Laut Sulawesi. *sea* Indonesia/ Philippines
41 W12 **Celestún** Yucatán, E Mexico 20°50′N 90°22′W
31 Q12 **Celina** Ohio, N USA 40°34′N 84°35′W
20 L8 **Celina** Tennessee, S USA 36°32′N 85°30′W
25 U5 **Celina** Texas, SW USA 33°19′N 96°46′W
112 G11 **Čelinac Donji** Republika Srpska, N Bosnia and Herzegovina 44°43′N 17°19′E
109 V10 **Celje** *Ger.* Cilli. C Slovenia 46°16′N 15°14′E
111 G23 **Celldömölk** Vas, W Hungary 47°16′N 17°10′E
100 J12 **Celle** *var.* Zelle. Niedersachsen, N Germany 52°38′N 10°05′E
99 D19 **Celles** Hainaut, SW Belgium 50°42′N 03°25′E
104 I7 **Celorico da Beira** Guarda, N Portugal 40°38′N 07°24′W
Celovec *see* Klagenfurt
64 M7 **Celtic Sea** *Ir.* An Mhuir Cheilteach. *sea* SW British Isles
64 N7 **Celtic Shelf** *undersea feature* E Atlantic Ocean 07°00′W 49°15′N
114 L13 **Çeltik Gölu** ◎ NW Turkey
146 J17 **Çemenibit** *prev. Rus.* Chemenibit. Mary Welaýaty, S Turkmenistan 35°27′N 62°19′E
113 M14 **Čemerno** ▲ C Serbia
105 Q12 **Cenajo, Embalse del** ⊠ S Spain
171 V13 **Cenderawasih, Teluk** *var.* Teluk Irian, Teluk Sarera. *bay* W Pacific Ocean
105 P4 **Cenicero** La Rioja, N Spain 42°29′N 02°38′W
106 E9 **Ceno** ≈ NW Italy
102 K13 **Cenon** Gironde, SW France 44°51′N 00°33′W
14 K13 **Centennial Lake** ◎ Ontario, SE Canada
Centennial State *see* Colorado
37 S7 **Center** Colorado, C USA 37°45′N 106°06′W
29 Q13 **Center** Nebraska, C USA 42°33′N 97°51′W
28 M5 **Center** North Dakota, N USA 47°07′N 101°18′W
25 X8 **Center** Texas, SW USA 31°49′N 94°10′W
29 W8 **Center City** Minnesota, N USA 45°25′N 92°48′W
36 L5 **Centerfield** Utah, W USA 39°07′N 111°49′W
20 K9 **Center Hill Lake** ⊠ Tennessee, S USA
29 X13 **Center Point** Iowa, C USA 42°11′N 91°47′W
25 R11 **Center Point** Texas, SW USA 29°56′N 99°01′W
29 W16 **Centerville** Iowa, C USA 40°43′N 92°51′W
27 W7 **Centerville** Missouri, C USA 37°27′N 91°01′W
29 R12 **Centerville** South Dakota, N USA 43°07′N 96°57′W
20 I9 **Centerville** Tennessee, S USA 35°45′N 87°29′W
25 V9 **Centerville** Texas, SW USA 31°17′N 95°59′W
40 M5 **Centinela, Picacho del** ▲ NE Mexico 29°07′N 102°40′W
106 G9 **Cento** Emilia-Romagna, N Italy 44°43′N 11°16′E
Centrafricaine, République *see* Central African Republic
39 S8 **Central** Alaska, USA 65°34′N 144°48′W
37 P15 **Central** New Mexico, SW USA 32°46′N 108°09′W
83 H18 **Central** ◈ *district* E Botswana
138 E10 **Central** ◈ *district* C Israel
81 I19 **Central** ◈ *province* C Kenya
82 M13 **Central** ◈ *region* C Malawi
153 P12 **Central** ◈ *zone* C Nepal
186 E9 **Central** ◈ *province* S Papua New Guinea
63 I21 **Central** ◈ *department* C Paraguay
186 E9 **Central** *off.* Central Province. ◈ *province* S Solomon Islands
155 K25 **Central** ◈ *province* C Sri Lanka
83 J14 **Central** ◈ *province* C Zambia
117 P11 **Central** ✈ (Odesa) Odes'ka Oblast', SW Ukraine 46°26′N 30°41′E
Central *see* Centre
79 H14 **Central African Republic** *var.* République Centrafricaine, *abbrev.* CAR; *prev.* Ubangi-Shari, Oubangui-Chari, Territoire de l'Oubangui-Chari. ◆ *republic* C Africa
192 C6 **Central Basin Trough** *undersea feature* W Pacific Ocean 16°45′N 130°00′E
Central Borneo *see* Kalimantan Tengah
149 P12 **Central Brāhui Range** ⛰ W Pakistan
Central Celebes *see* Sulawesi Tengah
29 Y13 **Central City** Iowa, C USA 42°12′N 91°31′W
20 I6 **Central City** Kentucky, S USA 37°17′N 87°07′W
29 P15 **Central City** Nebraska, C USA 41°04′N 97°59′W
48 D6 **Central, Cordillera** ⛰ W Bolivia
54 D11 **Central, Cordillera** ⛰ W Colombia
42 M13 **Central, Cordillera** ⛰ C Costa Rica
45 N9 **Central, Cordillera** ⛰ C Dominican Republic
43 R16 **Central, Cordillera** ⛰ C Panama
45 S6 **Central, Cordillera** ⛰ Puerto Rico
42 H7 **Central District** *var.* Tegucigalpa. ◈ *district* C Honduras
81 E16 **Central Equatoria** *var.* Bahr el Gebel, Bahr el Jebel. ◈ *state* S Sudan
Central Group *see* Inner Islands
30 L15 **Centralia** Illinois, N USA 38°31′N 89°07′W
27 U4 **Centralia** Missouri, C USA 39°12′N 92°08′W
32 G9 **Centralia** Washington, NW USA 46°43′N 122°57′W
Central Indian Ridge *see* Mid-Indian Ridge
Central Java *see* Jawa Tengah
Central Kalimantan *see* Kalimantan Tengah
148 L14 **Central Makrān Range** ⛰ W Pakistan
192 K7 **Central Pacific Basin** *undersea feature* C Pacific Ocean 05°00′N 175°00′W
59 M19 **Central, Planalto** *var.* Brazilian Highlands. ⛰ E Brazil
32 F15 **Central Point** Oregon, NW USA 42°22′N 122°55′W
Central Province *see* Central
Central Provinces and Berar *see* Madhya Pradesh
186 B6 **Central Range** ⛰ NW Papua New Guinea
Central Russian Upland *see* Srednerusskaya Vozvyshennost'
Central Siberian Plateau/ Central Siberian Uplands *see* Srednesibirskoye Ploskogor'ye
104 K8 **Central, Sistema** ⛰ C Spain
Central Sulawesi *see* Sulawesi Tengah
35 N3 **Central Valley** California, W USA 40°39′N 122°21′W
35 P8 **Central Valley** *valley* California, W USA
23 Q3 **Centre** Alabama, S USA 34°09′N 85°40′W
79 E15 **Centre** *Eng.* Central. ◈ *province* C Cameroon
102 M8 **Centre** ◈ *region* N France
173 Y16 **Centre de Flacq** E Mauritius 20°12′S 57°43′E
55 Y9 **Centre Spatial Guyanais** *space station* N French Guiana
23 O5 **Centreville** Alabama, S USA 32°58′N 87°08′W
21 X3 **Centreville** Maryland, NE USA 39°03′N 76°04′W
22 J7 **Centreville** Mississippi, S USA 31°05′N 91°04′W
Centum Cellae *see* Civitavecchia
160 M14 **Cenxi** Guangxi Zhuangzu Zizhiqu, S China 22°58′N 111°00′E
Ceos *see* Tziá
Cephaloedium *see* Cefalù
112 I9 **Čepin** *Hung.* Csepén. Osijek-Baranja, E Croatia 45°32′N 18°33′E
Ceram *see* Seram, Pulau
171 R13 **Ceram Sea** *Ind.* Laut Seram. *sea* E Indonesia
192 G8 **Ceram Trough** *undersea feature* W Pacific Ocean
Cerasus *see* Giresun
36 I10 **Cerbat Mountains** ⛰ Arizona, SW USA
103 P17 **Cerbère, Cap** *headland* S France 42°28′N 03°15′E
104 F13 **Cercal do Alentejo** Setúbal, S Portugal 37°48′N 08°40′W
111 A18 **Čerchov** *Ger.* Czerkow. ▲ W Czech Republic 49°24′N 12°47′E
103 O13 **Cère** ≈ C France
61 A16 **Ceres** Santa Fe, C Argentina 29°55′S 61°55′W
59 K18 **Ceres** Goiás, C Brazil 15°21′S 49°34′W
Ceresio *see* Lugano, Lago di
103 O17 **Céret** Pyrénées-Orientales, S France 42°30′N 02°44′E
54 E6 **Cereté** Córdoba, NW Colombia 08°54′N 75°51′W
172 I17 **Cerf, Île au** *island* Inner Islands, NE Seychelles
99 G22 **Cerfontaine** Namur, S Belgium 50°08′N 04°25′E
Cergy-Pontoise *see* Pontoise
107 N16 **Cerignola** Puglia, SE Italy 41°17′N 15°53′E
Cerigo *see* Kýthira
103 O9 **Cérilly** Allier, C France 46°38′N 02°51′E
136 I11 **Çerkeş** Çankırı, N Turkey 40°51′N 32°52′E
136 D10 **Çerkezköy** Tekirdağ, NW Turkey 41°17′N 28°00′E
109 T12 **Cerknica** *Ger.* Zirknitz. SW Slovenia 45°48′N 14°21′E
109 S11 **Cerkno** W Slovenia 46°07′N 13°58′E
116 F10 **Cermei** *Hung.* Csermő. Arad, W Romania 46°33′N 21°51′E

◆ Country
● Country Capital
◇ Dependent Territory
○ Dependent Territory Capital
◈ Administrative Regions
✈ International Airport
▲ Mountain
⛰ Mountain Range
Volcano
≈ River
◎ Lake
⊠ Reservoir

ÇERMIK – CHATHAM STRAIT

137 O15 Çermik Diyarbakır, SE Turkey 38°09′N 39°27′E
112 I10 Cerna Vukovar-Srijem, E Croatia 45°10′N 18°36′E
Cernăuţi see Chernivtsi
116 M14 Cernavodă Constanţa, SW Romania 44°20′N 28°03′E
103 U7 Cernay Haut-Rhin, NE France 47°49′N 07°11′E
Černice see Schwarzach
41 O8 Cerralvo Nuevo León, NE Mexico 26°10′N 99°40′W
40 G9 Cerralvo, Isla island NW Mexico
107 L16 Cerreto Sannita Campania, S Italy 41°17′N 14°39′E
113 L20 Cërrik var. Cerriku. Elbasan, C Albania 41°01′N 19°55′E
Cerriku see Cërrik
41 O11 Cerritos San Luis Potosí, C Mexico 22°25′N 100°16′W
60 K11 Cerro Azul Paraná, S Brazil 24°48′S 49°14′W
61 F18 Cerro Chato Treinta y Tres, E Uruguay 33°04′S 55°08′W
61 F19 Cerro Colorado Florida, S Uruguay 33°52′S 55°33′W
56 E13 Cerro de Pasco Pasco, C Peru 10°43′S 76°15′W
61 G14 Cêrro Largo Rio Grande do Sul, S Brazil 28°10′S 54°43′W
61 G18 Cerro Largo ◈ department NE Uruguay
42 E7 Cerrón Grande, Embalse ⊠ N El Salvador
63 I14 Cerros Colorados, Embalse ◎ W Argentina
105 V5 Cervera Cataluña, NE Spain 41°40′N 01°16′E
104 M3 Cervera del Pisuerga Castilla-León, N Spain 42°51′N 04°30′W
105 Q5 Cervera del Río Alhama La Rioja, N Spain 42°01′N 01°58′W
107 H15 Cerveteri Lazio, C Italy 42°00′N 12°06′E
106 H10 Cervia Emilia-Romagna, N Italy 44°14′N 12°22′E
106 J7 Cervignano del Friuli Friuli-Venezia Giulia, NE Italy 45°49′N 13°18′E
107 L17 Cervinara Campania, S Italy 41°02′N 14°36′E
Cervinia see Breuil-Cervinia
106 B6 Cervino, Monte var. Matterhorn. ▲ Italy/Switzerland 46°00′N 07°39′E see also Matterhorn
Cervino, Monte see Matterhorn
103 Y14 Cervione Corse, France, C Mediterranean Sea 42°22′N 09°28′E
104 I1 Cervo Galicia, NW Spain 43°39′N 07°25′W
54 F5 Cesar off. Departamento del Cesar. ◈ province N Colombia
Cesar, Departamento del see Cesar
106 H10 Cesena anc. Caesena. Emilia-Romagna, N Italy 44°09′N 12°14′E
106 I10 Cesenatico Emilia-Romagna, N Italy 44°12′N 12°24′E
118 H8 Cēsis Ger. Wenden. Cēsis, C Latvia 57°19′N 25°17′E
111 D15 Česká Lípa Ger. Böhmisch-Leipa. Liberecký Kraj, N Czech Republic 50°43′N 14°35′E
Česká Republika see Czech Republic
111 F17 Česká Třebová Ger. Böhmisch-Trübau. Pardubický Kraj, C Czech Republic 49°54′N 16°27′E
111 D19 České Budějovice Ger. Budweis. Jihočeský Kraj, S Czech Republic 48°58′N 14°29′E
111 D19 České Velenice Jihočeský Kraj, S Czech Republic 48°49′N 14°57′E
111 E18 Českomoravská Vrchovina var. Českomoravská Vysočina, Eng. Bohemian-Moravian Highlands, Ger. Böhmisch-Mährische Höhe. ▲▲ S Czech Republic
Českomoravská Vysočina see Českomoravská Vrchovina
111 C19 Český Krumlov var. Böhmisch-Krumau, Ger. Krummau. Jihočeský Kraj, S Czech Republic 48°48′N 14°18′E
Český Les see Bohemian Forest
112 F8 Česma ∽ N Croatia
136 A14 Çeşme İzmir, W Turkey 38°19′N 26°20′E
Cess see Cestos
183 T8 Cessnock New South Wales, SE Australia 32°51′S 151°21′E
76 K17 Cestos var. Cess. ∽ S Liberia
118 I9 Cesvaine Madona, E Latvia 56°58′N 26°15′E
116 G14 Cetate Dolj, SW Romania 44°06′N 23°01′E
Cetatea Albă see Bilhorod-Dnistrovs'kyy
Cetatea Damboviţei see Bucureşti
113 J17 Cetinje It. Cettigne. S Montenegro 42°23′N 18°55′E
107 N20 Cetraro Calabria, S Italy 39°30′N 15°59′E
Cette see Sète
188 A17 Cetti Bay bay SW Guam
Cettigne see Cetinje
104 L17 Ceuta var. Sebta. Ceuta, Spain, N Africa 35°53′N 05°19′W
88 C16 Ceuta enclave Spain, N Africa
106 B9 Ceva Piemonte, NE Italy 44°24′N 08°01′E
103 P14 Cévennes ▲▲ S France
108 G10 Cevio Ticino, S Switzerland 46°18′N 08°36′E
136 K16 Ceyhan Adana, S Turkey 37°02′N 35°48′E
136 K17 Ceyhan Nehri ∽ S Turkey
137 P17 Ceylanpınar Şanlıurfa, SE Turkey 36°53′N 40°02′E
Ceylon see Sri Lanka
173 R6 Ceylon Plain undersea feature N Indian Ocean 04°00′S 82°00′E
Ceyre to the Caribs see Marie-Galante
103 Q14 Cèze ∽ S France
Chaacha see Çäçe
127 P6 Chaadayevka Penzenskaya Oblast', W Russian Federation 53°07′N 45°55′E
167 O12 Cha-Am Phetchaburi, SW Thailand 12°48′N 99°58′E
143 W15 Chābahār var. Chāh Bahār, Chahbar. Sīstān va Balūchestān, SE Iran 25°21′N 60°38′E
Chabaricha see Khabarikha
61 B19 Chabas Santa Fe, C Argentina 33°16′S 61°23′W
103 T10 Chablais physical region E France
61 B20 Chacabuco Buenos Aires, E Argentina 34°40′S 60°27′W
42 K8 Chachagón, Cerro ▲ N Nicaragua 13°18′N 85°39′W
56 C10 Chachapoyas Amazonas, NW Peru 06°13′S 77°54′W
Chäche see Çäçe
119 O18 Chachersk Rus. Chechersk. Homyel'skaya Voblasts', SE Belarus 52°54′N 30°54′E
119 N16 Chachevichy Rus. Chechevichi. Mahilyowskaya Voblasts', E Belarus 53°31′N 29°51′E
61 B14 Chaco off. Provincia de Chaco. ◈ province NE Argentina
Chaco see Gran Chaco
62 M6 Chaco Austral physical region N Argentina
62 M3 Chaco Boreal physical region N Paraguay
62 M6 Chaco Central physical region N Argentina
39 Y15 Chacon, Cape headland Prince of Wales Island, Alaska, USA 54°41′N 132°00′W
Chaco, Provincia de see Chaco
78 H9 Chad off. Republic of Chad, Fr. Tchad. ◆ republic C Africa
122 K14 Chadan Respublika Tyva, S Russian Federation 51°16′N 91°25′E
21 U12 Chadbourn North Carolina, SE USA 34°19′N 78°49′W
83 L14 Chadiza Eastern, E Zambia 14°04′S 32°27′E
67 Q7 Chad, Lake Fr. Lac Tchad. ◎ C Africa
Chad, Republic of see Chad
28 J12 Chadron Nebraska, C USA 42°48′N 102°57′W
Chadyr-Lunga see Ciadîr-Lunga
163 W14 Chaeryŏng SW North Korea 38°22′N 125°35′E
105 P17 Chafarinas, Islas island group S Spain
27 Y7 Chaffee Missouri, C USA 37°10′N 89°39′W
148 L12 Chāgai Hills var. Chāh Gay. ▲▲ Afghanistan/Pakistan
123 Q11 Chagda Respublika Sakha (Yakutiya), NE Russian Federation 58°43′N 130°38′E
Chaghasarāy see Asadābād
149 N5 Chaghcharān var. Chakhcharan, Cheghcheran, Qala Āhangarān. Ghowr, C Afghanistan 34°28′N 65°18′E
103 R9 Chagny Saône-et-Loire, C France 46°54′N 04°45′E
173 Q7 Chagos Archipelago var. Oil Islands. island group British Indian Ocean Territory
129 O15 Chagos Bank undersea feature C Indian Ocean 06°15′S 72°00′E
129 O14 Chagos-Laccadive Plateau undersea feature N Indian Ocean 03°00′S 73°00′E
173 Q7 Chagos Trench undersea feature N Indian Ocean 07°00′S 73°30′E
43 T14 Chagres, Río ∽ C Panama
45 U14 Chaguanas Trinidad, Trinidad and Tobago 10°31′N 61°25′W
54 M6 Chaguaramas Guárico, N Venezuela 09°23′N 66°18′W
Chagyl see Çagyl
Chahārmahāl and Bakhtiyārī see Chahār Maḩall va Bakhtiārī
142 M9 Chahār Maḩall va Bakhtiārī off. Ostān-e Chahār Maḩall va Bakhtiārī, var. Chahārmahāl and Bakhtiyārī. ◈ province SW Iran
Chahār Maḩall va Bakhtiārī, Ostān-e see Chahār Maḩall va Bakhtiārī
Chāh Bahār/Chahbar see Chābahār
143 V13 Chāh Derāz Sīstān va Balūchestān, SE Iran 27°07′N 60°01′E
Chāh Gay see Chāgai Hills
167 P10 Chai Badan Lop Buri, C Thailand 15°08′N 101°03′E
153 Q16 Chāībāsa Jhārkhand, N India 22°31′N 85°50′E
79 E19 Chaillu, Massif du ▲ C Gabon
167 O10 Chai Nat var. Chainat, Jainat, Jayanath. Chai Nat, C Thailand 15°10′N 100°10′E
Chainat see Chai Nat
65 M14 Chain Fracture Zone tectonic feature E Atlantic Ocean
173 N5 Chain Ridge undersea feature W Indian Ocean 06°00′N 54°00′E
Chairn, Ceann an see Carnsore Point
158 L5 Chaiwopu Xinjiang Uygur Zizhiqu, W China 43°32′N 87°55′E
167 Q10 Chaiyaphum var. Jayabum. Chaiyaphum, C Thailand 15°46′N 101°55′E
62 N10 Chajarí Entre Ríos, E Argentina 30°45′S 57°57′W
42 C5 Chajul Quiché, W Guatemala 15°28′N 91°02′W
83 K16 Chakari Mashonaland West, N Zimbabwe 18°05′S 29°51′E
81 K22 Chake Chake Pemba South, E Tanzania 05°12′S 39°44′E
148 J9 Chakhānsūr Nīmrūz, SW Afghanistan 31°11′N 62°06′E
Chakhānsūr see Nīmrūz
Chakhcharan see Chaghcharān
149 V8 Chak Jhumra var. Jhumra. Punjab, E Pakistan 31°33′N 73°14′E
146 I16 Chaknakdysonga Ahal Welaýaty, S Turkmenistan 35°39′N 61°24′E
153 P16 Chakradharpur Jhārkhand, N India 22°42′N 85°38′E
152 J8 Chakrāta Uttarakhand, N India 30°42′N 77°52′E
149 U7 Chakwāl Punjab, NE Pakistan 32°56′N 72°53′E
57 F17 Chala Arequipa, SW Peru 15°52′S 74°13′W
102 K12 Chalais Charente, W France 45°16′N 00°02′E
108 D10 Chalais Valais, SW Switzerland 46°18′N 07°37′E
115 J20 Chalándri var. Halandri; prev. Khalándrion. prehistoric site Sýros, Kykládes, Greece, Aegean Sea
188 H6 Chalan Kanoa Saipan, S Northern Mariana Islands 15°08′S 145°43′E
188 C16 Chalan Pago C Guam
Chalap Dalam/Chalap Dalan see Chehel Abdālān, Kūh-e
42 F7 Chalatenango Chalatenango, N El Salvador 14°04′N 88°53′W
42 A9 Chalatenango ◈ department NW El Salvador
83 P15 Chalaua Nampula, NE Mozambique 16°04′S 39°08′E
81 I16 Chalbi Desert desert N Kenya
42 D7 Chalchuapa Santa Ana, W El Salvador 13°55′N 89°41′W
Chalcidice see Chalkidikí
Chalcis see Chalkída
Chālderān see Sīāh Chashmeh
103 N6 Châlette-sur-Loing Loiret, C France 48°01′N 02°45′E
15 X8 Chaleur Bay Fr. Baie des Chaleurs. bay New Brunswick/Québec, E Canada
Chaleurs, Baie des see Chaleur Bay
57 G16 Chalhuanca Apurímac, S Peru 14°17′S 73°15′W
154 F12 Chālīsgaon Mahārāshtra, C India 20°29′N 75°10′E
115 N23 Chálki island Dodekánisa, Greece, Aegean Sea
115 F16 Chalkiádes Thessalía, C Greece 39°24′N 22°25′E
115 H18 Chalkída var. Halkida, prev. Khalkís; anc. Chalcis. Evvoia, E Greece 38°27′N 23°38′E
115 G14 Chalkidikí var. Khalkidhikí; anc. Chalcidice. peninsula NE Greece
185 A24 Chalky Inlet inlet South Island, New Zealand
39 S7 Chalkyitsik Alaska, USA 66°39′N 143°43′W
102 I9 Challans Vendée, NW France 46°51′N 01°52′W
57 K19 Challapata Oruro, SW Bolivia 18°50′S 66°45′W
192 H6 Challenger Deep undersea feature W Pacific Ocean 11°20′N 142°12′E
Challenger Deep see Mariana Trench
193 S11 Challenger Fracture Zone tectonic feature SE Pacific Ocean
192 K11 Challenger Plateau undersea feature E Tasman Sea
33 P13 Challis Idaho, NW USA 44°31′N 114°14′W
22 L9 Chalmette Louisiana, S USA 29°56′N 89°57′W
124 J11 Chalna Respublika Kareliya, NW Russian Federation 61°53′N 33°59′E
103 Q5 Châlons-en-Champagne prev. Châlons-sur-Marne, hist. Arcae Remorum; anc. Carolopois. Marne, NE France 48°58′N 04°22′E
Châlons-sur-Marne see Châlons-en-Champagne
103 R9 Chalon-sur-Saône anc. Cabillonum. Saône-et-Loire, C France 46°47′N 04°51′E
Chaltel, Cerro see Fitzroy, Monte
102 M11 Châlus Haute-Vienne, C France 45°38′N 01°00′E
143 N4 Chālūs Māzandarān, N Iran 36°40′N 51°25′E
101 N20 Cham Bayern, SE Germany 49°13′N 12°40′E
108 F7 Cham Zug, N Switzerland 47°11′N 08°28′E
37 R8 Chama New Mexico, SW USA 36°54′N 106°34′W
Cha Mai see Thung Song
83 E22 Chamaites Karas, S Namibia 27°15′S 17°52′E
149 O9 Chaman Baluchistān, SW Pakistan 30°55′N 66°27′E
37 R9 Chama, Rio ∽ New Mexico, SW USA
152 I6 Chamba Himāchal Pradesh, N India 32°33′N 76°10′E
81 I25 Chamba Ruvuma, S Tanzania 11°33′S 37°01′E
150 H12 Chambal ∽ C India
11 U16 Chamberlain Saskatchewan, S Canada 50°49′N 105°29′W
29 O11 Chamberlain South Dakota, N USA 43°48′N 99°19′W
19 R3 Chamberlain Lake ◎ Maine, NE USA
39 S5 Chamberlin, Mount ▲ Alaska, USA 69°16′N 144°54′W
37 O11 Chambers Arizona, SW USA 35°11′N 109°25′W
18 F16 Chambersburg Pennsylvania, NE USA 39°54′N 77°39′W
31 N5 Chambers Island island Wisconsin, N USA
103 T11 Chambéry anc. Camberia. Savoie, E France 45°34′N 05°56′E
82 L12 Chambeshi Northern, NE Zambia 10°55′S 31°07′E
82 L12 Chambeshi ∽ NE Zambia
74 M6 Chambi, Jebel var. Jabal ash Sha'nabī. ▲ W Tunisia 35°16′N 08°39′E
15 Q7 Chambord Québec, SE Canada 48°25′N 72°02′W
139 U11 Chamcham Al Muthanná, S Iraq 31°17′N 45°05′E
139 T4 Chamchamāl At Ta'mīn, N Iraq 35°32′N 44°50′E
Chamdmanī see Altanshiree
40 J14 Chamela Jalisco, SW Mexico 19°31′N 105°02′W
42 G5 Chamelecón, Río ∽ NW Honduras
62 J9 Chamical La Rioja, C Argentina 30°21′S 66°19′W
115 L23 Chamili island Kykládes, Greece, Aegean Sea
167 Q13 Châmnar Kaôh Kŏng, SW Cambodia 11°45′N 103°32′E
152 K9 Chamoli Uttarakhand, N India 30°22′N 79°19′E
103 U11 Chamonix-Mont-Blanc Haute-Savoie, E France 45°55′N 06°52′E
154 L11 Chāmpa Chhattīsgarh, C India 22°02′N 82°42′E
10 H8 Champagne Yukon Territory, W Canada 60°48′N 136°22′W
103 Q5 Champagne cultural region N France
Champagne see Campania
103 Q5 Champagne-Ardenne ◈ region N France
103 S9 Champagnole Jura, E France 46°44′N 05°55′E
30 M13 Champaign Illinois, N USA 40°07′N 88°15′W
167 S10 Champasak Champasak, S Laos 14°50′N 105°51′E
152 L9 Champāwat Uttarakhand, N India 29°20′N 80°06′E
103 U6 Champ de Feu ▲ NE France 48°24′N 07°15′E
13 O7 Champdoré, Lac ◎ Québec, NE Canada
42 B6 Champerico Retalhuleu, SW Guatemala 14°18′N 91°54′W
108 C11 Champéry Valais, SW Switzerland 46°12′N 06°52′E
18 L6 Champlain New York, NE USA 44°58′N 73°25′W
18 L9 Champlain Canal canal New York, NE USA
15 P13 Champlain, Lac ◎ Québec, Canada/USA see also Champlain, Lake
18 L7 Champlain, Lake ◎ Canada/USA see also Champlain, Lac
103 S7 Champlitte Haute-Saône, E France 47°36′N 05°31′E
41 W13 Champotón Campeche, SE Mexico 19°18′N 90°43′W
155 G21 Chāmrājnagar var. Chamrajnagar. Karnātaka, SW India 11°58′N 76°54′E
Chamrajnagar see Chāmrājnagar
104 G10 Chamusca Santarém, C Portugal 39°21′N 08°29′W
119 O20 Chamyarysy Rus. Chemerisy. Homyel'skaya Voblasts', SE Belarus 51°42′N 30°27′E
127 P5 Chamzinka Respublika Mordoviya, W Russian Federation 54°22′N 45°22′E
Chanáil Mhór, An see Grand Canal
Chanak see Çanakkale
62 G7 Chañaral Atacama, N Chile 26°19′S 70°34′W
104 H13 Chança, Rio var. Chanza. ∽ Portugal/Spain
57 D14 Chancay Lima, W Peru 11°36′S 77°14′W
Chan-chiang/Chanchiang see Zhanjiang
62 G13 Chanco Maule, C Chile 35°43′S 72°35′W
39 R7 Chandalar Alaska, USA 67°30′N 148°29′W
39 R6 Chandalar River ∽ Alaska, USA
152 L10 Chandan Chauki Uttar Pradesh, N India 28°32′N 80°43′E
153 S16 Chandannagar prev. Chandernagore. West Bengal, E India 22°52′N 88°21′E
152 K10 Chandausi Uttar Pradesh, N India 28°27′N 78°43′E
22 M10 Chandeleur Islands island group Louisiana, S USA
22 M9 Chandeleur Sound sound N Gulf of Mexico
Chandernagore see Chandannagar
152 I8 Chandīgarh state capital Punjab, N India 30°41′N 76°51′E
153 Q16 Chāndil Jhārkhand, NE India 22°58′N 86°04′E
182 D2 Chandler South Australia 26°59′S 133°22′E
15 Y7 Chandler Québec, SE Canada 48°21′N 64°41′W
36 L14 Chandler Arizona, SW USA 33°18′N 111°50′W
27 O10 Chandler Oklahoma, C USA 35°43′N 96°54′W
25 V7 Chandler Texas, SW USA 32°18′N 95°28′W
39 Q6 Chandler River ∽ Alaska, USA
56 H13 Chandles, Río ∽ E Peru
162 H9 Chandmanĭ var. Talshand. Govĭ-Altayĭ, C Mongolia 45°21′N 98°00′E
162 E7 Chandmanĭ var. Urdgol. Hovd, W Mongolia 47°39′N 92°46′E
14 J13 Chandos Lake ◎ Ontario, SE Canada
153 U16 Chandpur Chittagong, C Bangladesh 23°13′N 90°43′E
154 I13 Chandrapur Mahārāshtra, C India 19°58′N 79°21′E
83 J15 Changa Southern, S Zambia 16°24′S 28°27′E
Chang'an see Rong'an, Guangxi Zhuangzu Zizhiqu, S China
Changan see Xi'an, Shaanxi, C China
155 G23 Changanācheri var. Changannassery. Kerala, SW India 09°26′N 76°31′E see also Changannassery
83 M19 Changane ∽ S Mozambique
155 G23 Changannassery var. Changanācheri. Kerala, SW India 09°26′N 76°31′E see also Changanācheri
83 M16 Changara Tete, NW Mozambique 16°54′S 33°15′E
163 X11 Changbai var. Changbai Chosenzu Zizhixian. Jilin, NE China 41°25′N 128°08′E
Changbai Chosenzu Zizhixian see Changbai
163 X11 Changbai Shan ▲▲ NE China
163 V10 Changchun var. Ch'ang-ch'un, Ch'ang-ch'un; prev. Hsinking. province capital Jilin, NE China 43°53′N 125°18′E
Ch'angch'un/Ch'ang-ch'un see Changchun
160 M10 Changde Hunan, S China 29°04′N 111°42′E
161 S13 Changhua Jap. Shōka. C Taiwan 24°06′N 120°31′E
168 L10 Changi ✈ (Singapore) E Singapore 01°22′N 103°58′E
158 L5 Changji Xinjiang Uygur Zizhiqu, NW China 44°02′N 87°12′E
160 L17 Changjiang var. Changjiang Lizu Zizhixian, Shiliu. Hainan, S China 19°16′N 109°09′E
157 R11 Chang Jiang var. Yangtze Kiang, Eng. Yangtze. ∽ C China
161 S8 Changjiang Kou delta E China
Changjiang Lizu Zizhixian see Changjiang
Changkiakow see Zhangjiakou
167 F12 Chang, Ko island S Thailand
161 Q2 Changli Hebei, E China 39°44′N 119°13′E
163 V10 Changling Jilin, NE China 44°15′N 124°03′E
Changning see Xunwu
161 N11 Changsha var. Ch'angsha, Ch'ang-sha. province capital Hunan, S China 28°10′N 113°E
Ch'angsha/Ch'ang-sha see Changsha
161 Q10 Changshan Zhejiang, SE China 28°54′N 118°30′E
163 V14 Changshan Qundao island group NE China
161 S8 Changshu var. Ch'ang-shu. Jiangsu, E China 31°39′N 120°45′E
Ch'ang-shu see Changshu
163 V11 Changtu Liaoning, NE China 42°50′N 123°59′E
43 P14 Changuinola Bocas del Toro, NW Panama 09°28′N 82°31′W
159 N9 Changweiliang Qinghai, W China 38°24′N 92°08′E
160 K6 Changwu var. Zhaoren. Shaanxi, C China 35°12′N 107°46′E
163 U13 Changxing Dao island N China
160 M9 Changyang var. Longzhouping. Hubei, C China 30°45′N 111°13′E
163 W14 Changyŏn SW North Korea 38°19′N 125°15′E
161 N5 Changzhi Shanxi, C China 36°10′N 113°02′E
161 R8 Changzhou Jiangsu, E China 31°45′N 119°58′E
115 H24 Chaniá var. Hania, Khaniá, Eng. Canea; anc. Cydonia. Kríti, Greece, E Mediterranean Sea 35°31′N 24°00′E
62 J5 Chañi, Nevado de ▲ NW Argentina 24°09′S 65°44′W
115 H24 Chanión, Kólpos gulf Kríti, Greece, E Mediterranean Sea
Chankiri see Çankırı
30 M11 Channahon Illinois, N USA 41°25′N 88°13′W
155 H20 Channapatna Karnātaka, E India 12°43′N 77°14′E
97 K26 Channel Islands Fr. Iles Normandes. island group S English Channel
35 R16 Channel Islands island group California, W USA
13 S13 Channel-Port aux Basques Newfoundland and Labrador, SE Canada 47°35′N 59°02′W
Channel, The see English Channel
97 Q23 Channel Tunnel tunnel France/United Kingdom
24 M2 Channing Texas, SW USA 35°41′N 102°21′W
Chantabun/Chantaburi see Chanthaburi
104 H3 Chantada Galicia, NW Spain 42°36′N 07°46′W
167 P12 Chanthaburi var. Chantabun, Chantaburi. Chantaburi, S Thailand 12°35′N 102°08′E
103 O4 Chantilly Oise, N France 49°12′N 02°28′E
139 V12 Chanūn as Saʻūdī Dhī Qār, S Iraq 31°04′N 46°00′E
27 Q6 Chanute Kansas, C USA 37°40′N 95°27′W
Chanza see Chança, Rio
Ch'ao-an/Chaochow see Chaozhou
161 Q8 Chaohu Anhui, E China 31°36′N 117°55′E
161 P8 Chao Hu ◎ E China
167 P11 Chao Phraya, Mae Nam ∽ C Thailand
Chaor He see Qulin Gol
Chaouèn see Chefchaouen
161 P14 Chaoyang Guangdong, S China 23°17′N 116°33′E
163 T12 Chaoyang Liaoning, NE China 41°34′N 120°29′E
Chaoyang see Jiayin, Heilongjiang, China
Chaoyang see Huinan, Jilin China
161 Q14 Chaozhou var. Chaoan, Chao'an, Ch'ao-an; prev. Chaochow. Guangdong, SE China 23°42′N 116°36′E
58 N13 Chapadinha Maranhão, E Brazil 03°45′S 43°23′W
12 K12 Chapais Québec, SE Canada 49°47′N 74°54′W
40 L13 Chapala Jalisco, SW Mexico 20°20′N 103°10′W
40 L13 Chapala, Lago de ◎ C Mexico
146 F13 Chapan, Gora ▲ C Turkmenistan 37°48′N 58°03′E
57 M18 Chapare, Río ∽ C Bolivia
54 E11 Chaparral Tolima, C Colombia 03°45′N 75°30′W
144 F9 Chapayev Zapadnyy Kazakhstan, NW Kazakhstan 50°12′N 51°09′E
123 O11 Chapayevo Respublika Sakha (Yakutiya), NE Russian Federation 60°03′N 117°19′E
127 R6 Chapayevsk Samarskaya Oblast', W Russian Federation 52°57′N 49°42′E
60 H13 Chapecó Santa Catarina, S Brazil 27°14′S 52°41′W
60 I13 Chapecó, Rio ∽ S Brazil
20 J9 Chapel Hill Tennessee, S USA 35°38′N 86°40′W
44 J12 Chapelton C Jamaica 18°05′N 77°16′W
14 C8 Chapleau Ontario, SE Canada 47°50′N 83°24′W
14 D7 Chapleau ∽ Ontario, S Canada
11 T16 Chaplin Saskatchewan, S Canada 50°27′N 106°37′W
126 M6 Chaplygin Lipetskaya Oblast', W Russian Federation 53°13′N 39°58′E
117 S11 Chaplynka Khersons'ka Oblast', S Ukraine 46°20′N 33°34′E
9 O6 Chapman, Cape headland Nunavut, NE Canada 69°15′N 89°09′W
25 T15 Chapman Ranch Texas, SW USA 27°32′N 97°25′W
Chapman's see Okwa
21 P5 Chapmanville West Virginia, NE USA 37°58′N 82°01′W
28 K15 Chappell Nebraska, C USA 41°05′N 102°28′W
Chapra see Chhapra
56 D9 Chapuli, Río ∽ N Peru
76 I6 Châr well N Mauritania
123 P12 Chara Chitinskaya Oblast', S Russian Federation 56°57′N 118°05′E
123 O11 Chara ∽ C Russian Federation
54 G8 Charala Santander, C Colombia 06°17′N 73°09′W
41 N10 Charcas San Luis Potosí, C Mexico 23°09′N 101°10′W
25 T13 Charco Texas, SW USA 28°42′N 97°35′E
194 H7 Charcot Island island Antarctica
64 M8 Charcot Seamounts undersea feature E Atlantic Ocean 11°30′W 45°00′N
Chardara see Shardara
145 P17 Chardarinskoye Vodokhranilishche ⊠ S Kazakhstan
31 U11 Chardon Ohio, N USA 41°34′N 81°12′W
44 K9 Chardonnières SW Haiti 18°16′N 74°10′W
Chardzhev see Türkmenabat
Chardzhevskaya Oblast see Lebap Welaýaty
Chardzhou/Chardzhui see Türkmenabat
102 L11 Charente ◈ department W France
102 J11 Charente ∽ W France
102 J10 Charente-Maritime ◈ department W France
137 U12 Ch'arents'avan C Armenia 40°23′N 44°41′E
78 I12 Chari var. Shari. ∽ Central African Republic/Chad
78 G11 Chari-Baguirmi off. Préfecture du Chari-Baguirmi. ◈ prefecture SW Chad
Chari-Baguirmi, Préfecture du see Chari-Baguirmi
149 Q4 Chārīkār Parvān, NE Afghanistan 35°01′N 69°11′E
29 V15 Chariton Iowa, C USA 41°00′N 93°18′W
27 U3 Chariton River ∽ Missouri, C USA
55 T7 Charity NW Guyana 07°22′N 58°34′W
31 R7 Charity Island island Michigan, N USA
Chärjew see Türkmenabat
Chärjew Oblasty see Lebap Welaýaty
Charkhlik/Charkhliq see Ruoqiang
99 G20 Charleroi Hainaut, S Belgium 50°25′N 04°27′E
11 V12 Charles Manitoba, C Canada 55°27′N 100°58′W
15 R10 Charlesbourg Québec, SE Canada 46°50′N 71°15′W
21 Y7 Charles, Cape headland Virginia, NE USA 37°09′N 75°57′W
29 W12 Charles City Iowa, C USA 43°04′N 92°40′W
21 W6 Charles City Virginia, NE USA 37°21′N 77°05′W
103 O5 Charles de Gaulle ✈ (Paris) Seine-et-Marne, N France 49°04′N 02°36′E
12 K1 Charles Island island Nunavut, NE Canada
Charles Island see Santa María, Isla
30 K9 Charles Mound hill Illinois, N USA
185 A22 Charles Sound sound South Island, New Zealand
185 G15 Charleston West Coast, South Island, New Zealand 41°54′S 171°25′E
27 S11 Charleston Arkansas, C USA 35°19′N 94°02′W
30 M14 Charleston Illinois, N USA 39°30′N 88°10′W
22 L3 Charleston Mississippi, S USA 34°00′N 90°03′W
27 Z7 Charleston Missouri, C USA 36°54′N 89°22′W
21 T15 Charleston South Carolina, SE USA 32°48′N 79°57′W
21 Q5 Charleston state capital West Virginia, NE USA 38°21′N 81°38′W
14 L14 Charleston Lake ◎ Ontario, SE Canada
35 W11 Charleston Peak ▲ Nevada, W USA 36°16′N 115°40′W
45 W10 Charlestown Nevis, Saint Kitts and Nevis 17°08′N 62°37′W
31 P16 Charlestown Indiana, N USA 38°27′N 85°40′W
18 M9 Charlestown New Hampshire, NE USA 43°14′N 72°23′W
21 V3 Charles Town West Virginia, NE USA 39°18′N 77°54′W
181 W9 Charleville Queensland, E Australia 26°25′S 146°18′E
103 R3 Charleville-Mézières Ardennes, N France 49°45′N 04°43′E
31 P5 Charlevoix Michigan, N USA 45°19′N 85°15′W
31 Q6 Charlevoix, Lake ◎ Michigan, N USA
39 T9 Charley River ∽ Alaska, USA
64 J6 Charlie-Gibbs Fracture Zone tectonic feature N Atlantic Ocean
103 Q10 Charlieu Loire, E France 46°11′N 04°10′E
31 Q9 Charlotte Michigan, N USA 42°33′N 84°50′W
21 R10 Charlotte North Carolina, SE USA 35°14′N 80°51′W
20 I8 Charlotte Tennessee, S USA 36°11′N 87°18′W
25 R13 Charlotte Texas, SW USA 28°51′N 98°42′W
21 R10 Charlotte ✈ North Carolina, SE USA 35°12′N 80°54′W
45 T9 Charlotte Amalie prev. Saint Thomas. ○ (Virgin Islands (US)) Saint Thomas, N Virgin Islands (US) 18°22′N 64°56′W
21 U7 Charlotte Court House Virginia, NE USA 37°04′N 78°37′W
23 W14 Charlotte Harbor inlet Florida, SE USA
Charlotte Island see Abaiang
95 J15 Charlottenberg Värmland, C Sweden 59°53′N 12°17′E
Charlottenhof see Aegviidu
21 U5 Charlottesville Virginia, NE USA 38°02′N 78°29′W
13 Q14 Charlottetown province capital Prince Edward Island, Prince Edward Island, SE Canada 46°14′N 63°09′W
Charlotte Town see Roseau, Dominica
Charlotte Town see Gouyave, Grenada
45 Z16 Charlotteville Tobago, Trinidad and Tobago 11°16′N 60°33′W
182 M11 Charlton Victoria, SE Australia 36°18′S 143°19′E
12 H10 Charlton Island island Northwest Territories, C Canada
103 T6 Charmes Vosges, NE France 48°19′N 06°19′E
119 F19 Charnawchytsy Rus. Chernavchitsy. Brestskaya Voblasts', SW Belarus 52°13′N 23°44′E
15 R10 Charny Québec, SE Canada 46°43′N 71°15′W
149 T5 Chārsadda North-West Frontier Province, NW Pakistan 34°12′N 71°46′E
Charshanga/Charshangngy/Charshangy see Köýtendag
Charsk see Shar
181 W6 Charters Towers Queensland, NE Australia 20°02′S 146°20′E
15 R12 Chartierville Québec, SE Canada 45°19′N 71°13′W
102 M6 Chartres anc. Autricum, Civitas Carnutum. Eure-et-Loir, C France 48°27′N 01°27′E
145 W15 Charyn Kaz. Sharyn. Almaty, SE Kazakhstan 43°48′N 79°22′E
Charyn see Sharyn
61 D21 Chascomús Buenos Aires, E Argentina 35°34′S 58°01′W
11 N16 Chase British Columbia, SW Canada 50°49′N 119°41′W
21 U7 Chase City Virginia, NE USA 36°48′N 78°27′W
19 S4 Chase, Mount ▲ Maine, NE USA 46°06′N 68°30′W
118 M13 Chashniki Vitsyebskaya Voblasts', N Belarus 54°52′N 29°10′E
115 D15 Chásia ▲ C Greece
29 V9 Chaska Minnesota, N USA 44°47′N 93°36′W
185 D25 Chaslands Mistake headland South Island, New Zealand 46°37′S 169°21′E
125 R11 Chasovo Respublika Komi, NW Russian Federation 61°58′N 50°34′E
Chasovo see Vazhgort
124 H14 Chastova Novgorodskaya Oblast', NW Russian Federation 58°37′N 32°05′E
143 R3 Chāt Golestān, N Iran 37°52′N 55°27′E
Chatak see Chhatak
Chatang see Zhanang
39 R9 Chatanika Alaska, USA 65°06′N 147°28′W
39 R9 Chatanika River ∽ Alaska, USA
147 T8 Chat-Bazar Talasskaya Oblast', NW Kyrgyzstan 42°29′N 72°37′E
45 Y14 Chateaubelair Saint Vincent, W Saint Vincent and the Grenadines 13°15′N 61°05′W
102 J7 Châteaubriant Loire-Atlantique, NW France 47°43′N 01°22′W
103 Q8 Château-Chinon Nièvre, C France 47°04′N 03°50′E
108 C10 Château d'Oex Vaud, W Switzerland 46°28′N 07°09′E
102 L7 Château-du-Loir Sarthe, NW France 47°40′N 00°25′E
102 M6 Châteaudun Eure-et-Loir, C France 48°04′N 01°20′E
102 K7 Château-Gontier Mayenne, NW France 47°49′N 00°42′W
15 O13 Châteauguay Québec, SE Canada 45°20′N 73°44′W
102 F6 Châteaulin Finistère, NW France 48°12′N 04°07′W
103 N9 Châteaumeillant Cher, C France 46°33′N 02°10′E
102 K11 Châteauneuf-sur-Charente Charente, W France 45°34′N 00°33′W
102 M7 Château-Renault Indre-et-Loire, C France 47°34′N 00°52′E
103 N9 Châteauroux prev. Indreville. Indre, C France 46°50′N 01°43′E
103 T5 Château-Salins Moselle, NE France 48°50′N 06°29′E
103 P4 Château-Thierry Aisne, N France 49°03′N 03°24′E
99 H21 Châtelet Hainaut, S Belgium 50°24′N 04°32′E
Châtelherault see Châtellerault
102 L9 Châtellerault var. Châtelherault. Vienne, W France 46°49′N 00°33′E
29 X10 Chatfield Minnesota, N USA 43°51′N 92°11′W
13 O14 Chatham New Brunswick, SE Canada 47°02′N 65°30′W
14 D17 Chatham Ontario, S Canada 42°24′N 82°11′W
97 P22 Chatham SE England, United Kingdom 51°23′N 00°31′E
30 K14 Chatham Illinois, N USA 39°40′N 89°42′W
21 T7 Chatham Virginia, NE USA 36°49′N 79°26′W
63 F22 Chatham, Isla island S Chile
175 R12 Chatham Island island Chatham Islands, New Zealand
Chatham Island see San Cristóbal, Isla
Chatham Island Rise see Chatham Rise
175 R12 Chatham Islands island group New Zealand, SW Pacific Ocean
175 Q12 Chatham Rise var. Chatham Island Rise. undersea feature S Pacific Ocean
39 X13 Chatham Strait strait Alaska, USA

◆ Country ● Country Capital ◇ Dependent Territory ○ Dependent Territory Capital ◈ Administrative Regions ✈ International Airport ▲ Mountain ▲▲ Mountain Range Volcano ∽ River ◎ Lake ⊠ Reservoir
235

Chathóir, Rinn see Cahore Point
102 M9 **Châtillon-sur-Indre** Indre, C France 46°58′N 01°10′E
103 Q7 **Châtillon-sur-Seine** Côte d'Or, C France 47°51′N 04°30′E
147 S8 **Chatkal** Uzb. Chotqol. ≈ Kyrgyzstan/Uzbekistan
147 R9 **Chatkal Range** Rus. Chatkal'skiy Khrebet. ▲▲ Kyrgyzstan/Uzbekistan
Chatkal'skiy Khrebet see Chatkal Range
23 N7 **Chatom** Alabama, S USA 31°28′N 88°15′W
153 P14 **Chatra** Jhārkhand, N India 24°12′N 84°52′E
Chatrapur see Chhatrapur
143 S10 **Chatrūd** Kermān, C Iran 30°39′N 56°57′E
23 S2 **Chatsworth** Georgia, SE USA 34°46′N 84°46′W
Chāttagām see Chittagong
23 S8 **Chattahoochee** Florida, SE USA 30°40′N 84°51′W
23 R8 **Chattahoochee River** ≈ SE USA
20 L10 **Chattanooga** Tennessee, S USA 35°05′N 85°16′W
147 V10 **Chatyr-Kël', Ozero** ◎ C Kyrgyzstan
147 W9 **Chatyr-Tash** Narynskaya Oblast', C Kyrgyzstan 40°54′N 76°22′E
15 R12 **Chaudière** ≈ Québec, SE Canada
167 S14 **Châu Đôc** var. Chauphu, Chau Phu. An Giang, S Vietnam 10°53′N 105°07′E
152 D13 **Chauhtan** prev. Chohtan. Rājasthān, NW India 25°27′N 71°08′E
166 L5 **Chauk** Magway, W Myanmar (Burma) 20°52′N 94°50′E
103 R6 **Chaumont** prev. Chaumont-en-Bassigny. Haute-Marne, N France 48°07′N 05°08′E
Chaumont-en-Bassigny see Chaumont
123 T5 **Chaunskaya Guba** bay NE Russian Federation
103 P3 **Chauny** Aisne, N France 49°37′N 03°13′E
Châu Ô see Binh Sơn
Chau Phu see Châu Đôc
102 I5 **Chausey, Îles** island group N France
Chausy see Chavusy
18 C11 **Chautauqua Lake** ◎ New York, NE USA
ChâuThanh see Ba Ria
102 L9 **Chauvigny** Vienne, W France 46°35′N 00°37′E
124 L6 **Chavan'ga** Murmanskaya Oblast', NW Russian Federation 66°07′N 37°44′E
14 K10 **Chavannes, Lac** ◎ Québec, SE Canada
Chavantes, Represa de see Xavantes, Represa de
61 D15 **Chavarría** Corrientes, NE Argentina 28°57′S 58°35′W
Chavash Respubliki see Chuvashskaya Respublika
104 I5 **Chaves** anc. Aquae Flaviae. Vila Real, N Portugal 41°44′N 07°28′W
Chávez, Isla see Santa Cruz, Isla
82 G13 **Chavuma** North Western, NW Zambia 13°04′S 22°43′E
119 O16 **Chavusy** Rus. Chausy. Mahilyowskaya Voblasts', E Belarus 53°48′N 30°58′E
Chayan see Shayan
147 U8 **Chayek** Narynskaya Oblast', C Kyrgyzstan 41°54′N 74°28′E
139 T6 **Chāy Khānah** Diyālá, E Iraq 34°19′N 44°33′E
125 T16 **Chaykovskiy** Permskaya Oblast', NW Russian Federation 56°45′N 54°09′E
167 T12 **Chbar** Môndól Kiri, E Cambodia 12°46′N 107°10′E
23 Q4 **Cheaha Mountain** ▲ Alabama, S USA 33°29′N 85°48′W
Cheatharlach see Carlow
21 S2 **Cheat River** ≈ NE USA
111 A16 **Cheb** Ger. Eger. Karlovarský Kraj, W Czech Republic 50°05′N 12°23′E
127 Q3 **Cheboksary** Chuvashskaya Respublika, W Russian Federation 56°06′N 47°15′E
31 Q5 **Cheboygan** Michigan, N USA 45°40′N 84°28′W
Chechaouèn see Chefchaouen
Chechenia see Chechenskaya Respublika
127 O15 **Chechenskaya Respublika** Eng. Chechenia, Chechnia, Rus. Chechnya. ⬖ autonomous republic SW Russian Federation
67 N4 **Chech, Erg** desert Algeria/Mali
Chechevichi see Chachevichy
Che-chiang see Zhejiang
Chechnia/Chechnya see Chechenskaya Respublika
163 Y15 **Chech'ŏn** Jap. Teisen. N South Korea 37°06′N 128°15′E
111 L15 **Chęciny** Świętokrzyskie, S Poland 50°51′N 20°31′E
27 Q10 **Checotah** Oklahoma, C USA 35°28′N 95°31′W
13 R15 **Chedabucto Bay** inlet Nova Scotia, E Canada
166 J7 **Cheduba Island** island W Myanmar (Burma)
37 T5 **Cheesman Lake** ⊠ Colorado, C USA
195 S16 **Cheetham, Cape** headland Antarctica 70°26′S 162°40′E
74 G5 **Chefchaouen** var. Chaouèn, Chechaouèn, Sp. Xauen. N Morocco 35°10′N 05°16′W
Chefoo see Yantai
38 M12 **Chefornak** Alaska, USA 60°09′N 164°09′W
123 R13 **Chegdomyn** Khabarovskiy Kray, SE Russian Federation 51°09′N 132°58′E
76 M4 **Chegga** Tiris Zemmour, NE Mauritania 25°27′N 05°49′W
Cheghcheran see Chaghcharān
32 G9 **Chehalis** Washington, NW USA 46°39′N 122°57′W
32 G9 **Chehalis River** ≈ Washington, NW USA
148 M6 **Chehel Abdālān, Kūh-e** var. Chalap Dalam, Pash. Chalap Dalan. ▲▲ C Afghanistan
115 D14 **Cheimadítis, Límni** var. Límni Cheimadítis. ◎ N Greece
Cheimadítis, Límni see Cheimadítis, Límni
103 U15 **Cheiron, Mont** ▲ SE France 43°49′N 07°00′E
163 X17 **Cheju** Jap. Saishū. S South Korea 33°31′N 126°34′E
163 Y17 **Cheju** ✕ S South Korea 33°31′N 126°29′E
163 Y17 **Cheju-do** Jap. Saishū; prev. Quelpart. island S South Korea
163 Y17 **Cheju-haehyŏp** Eng. Cheju Strait. strait S South Korea
Cheju Strait see Cheju-haehyŏp
Chekiang see Zhejiang
Chekichler/Chekishlyar see Çekiçler
188 F8 **Chelab** Babeldaob, N Palau
147 N11 **Chelak** Rus. Chelek. Samarqand Viloyati, C Uzbekistan 39°55′N 66°45′E
32 J7 **Chelan, Lake** ⊠ Washington, NW USA
Chelek see Chelak
Cheleken see Hazar
Chélif/Chéliff see Chelif, Oued
74 J5 **Chelif, Oued** var. Chélif, Chéliff, Chellif, Shellif. ≈ N Algeria
Chelkar see Shalkar
Chelkar Ozero see Shalkar, Ozero
Chellif see Chelif, Oued
111 P14 **Chelm** Rus. Kholm. Lubelskie, SE Poland 51°08′N 23°29′E
110 I9 **Chełmno** Ger. Culm, Kulm. Kujawski-pomorskie, C Poland 53°21′N 18°27′E
115 E19 **Chelmós** var. Aroania. ▲ S Greece
14 F10 **Chelmsford** Ontario, S Canada 46°33′N 81°16′W
97 P21 **Chelmsford** E England, United Kingdom 51°44′N 00°28′E
110 J9 **Chełmża** Ger. Culmsee, Kulmsee. Kujawski-pomorskie, C Poland 53°11′N 18°34′E
27 Q8 **Chelsea** Oklahoma, C USA 36°32′N 95°25′W
18 M8 **Chelsea** Vermont, NE USA 43°58′N 72°29′W
97 L21 **Cheltenham** C England, United Kingdom 51°54′N 02°04′W
105 R9 **Chelva** País Valenciano, E Spain 39°45′N 01°00′W
122 G11 **Chelyabinsk** Chelyabinskaya Oblast', C Russian Federation 55°12′N 61°25′E
122 F11 **Chelyabinskaya Oblast'** ⬖ province C Russian Federation
123 N5 **Chelyuskin, Mys** headland N Russian Federation 77°42′N 104°13′E
41 Y12 **Chemax** Yucatán, SE Mexico 20°41′N 87°54′W
83 N16 **Chemba** Sofala, C Mozambique 17°11′S 34°53′E
82 J13 **Chembe** Luapula, NE Zambia 11°58′S 28°45′E
Chemenibit see Çemenibit
Chemerisy see Chamyarysy
116 K7 **Chemerivtsi** Khmel'nyts'ka Oblast', W Ukraine 49°00′N 26°21′E
102 J8 **Chemillé** Maine-et-Loire, NW France 47°15′N 00°42′W
173 X17 **Chemin Grenier** S Mauritius 20°29′S 57°28′E
101 N16 **Chemnitz** prev. Karl-Marx-Stadt. Sachsen, E Germany 50°50′N 12°55′E
Chemulpo see Inch'ŏn
32 H14 **Chemult** Oregon, NW USA 43°14′N 121°48′W
18 G12 **Chemung River** ≈ New York/Pennsylvania, NE USA
149 U8 **Chenāb** ≈ India/Pakistan
39 S9 **Chena Hot Springs** Alaska, USA 65°06′N 146°02′W
18 I11 **Chenango River** ≈ New York, NE USA
168 J7 **Chenderoh, Tasik** ◎ Peninsular Malaysia
15 Q11 **Chêne, Rivière du** ≈ Québec, SE Canada
32 L8 **Cheney** Washington, NW USA 47°29′N 117°34′W
26 M6 **Cheney Reservoir** ⊠ Kansas, C USA
Chengchiatun see Liaoyuan
Ch'eng-chou/Chengchow see Zhengzhou
161 P1 **Chengde** var. Jehol. Hebei, E China 41°N 117°57′E
160 I9 **Chengdu** var. Chengtu, Ch'eng-tu. province capital Sichuan, C China 30°41′N 104°03′E
161 Q14 **Chenghai** Guangdong, S China 23°30′N 116°42′E
Chenghsien see Zhengzhou
160 H13 **Chengjiang** Yunnan, SW China 24°40′N 102°55′E
Chengjiang see Taihe
160 L17 **Chengmai** var. Jinjiang. Hainan, S China 19°45′N 109°56′E
Chengtu/Ch'eng-tu see Chengdu
Chengwen see Chindu
159 W12 **Chengxian** var. Cheng Xiang. Gansu, C China 33°42′N 105°45′E
Cheng Xiang see Chengxian
Chengyang see Juxian
Chengzhong see Ningming
Chenkiang see Zhenjiang
155 J19 **Chennai** prev. Madras. state capital Tamil Nādu, S India 13°05′N 80°18′E
155 J19 **Chennai** ✕ Tamil Nādu, S India 13°07′N 80°13′E
103 R8 **Chenôve** Côte d'Or, C France 47°16′N 05°00′E
Chenstokhov see Częstochowa
160 L11 **Chenxi** var. Chenyang. Hunan, S China 28°02′N 110°15′E
Chen Xian/Chenxian/Chen Xiang see Chenzhou
Chenyang see Chenxi
161 N12 **Chenzhou** var. Chenxian, Chen Xian, Chen Xiang. Hunan, S China 25°51′N 113°01′E
167 U12 **Cheo Reo** var. A Yun Pa. Gia Lai, S Vietnam 13°19′N 108°27′E
114 I11 **Chepelare** Smolyan, S Bulgaria 41°44′N 24°41′E
114 I11 **Chepelarska Reka** ≈ S Bulgaria
56 B11 **Chepén** La Libertad, C Peru 07°15′S 79°23′W
62 J10 **Chepes** La Rioja, C Argentina 31°19′S 66°40′W
161 O15 **Chep Lap Kok** ✕ S China 22°23′N 114°11′E
43 U14 **Chepo** Panamá, C Panama 09°09′N 79°03′W
Chepping Wycombe see High Wycombe
125 R14 **Cheptsa** ≈ NW Russian Federation
30 K3 **Chequamegon Point** headland Wisconsin, N USA 46°42′N 90°45′W
103 O8 **Cher** ⬖ department C France
102 M8 **Cher** ≈ C France
Cherangani Hills see Cherangany Hills
81 H17 **Cherangany Hills** var. Cherangani Hills. ▲▲ W Kenya
21 S11 **Cheraw** South Carolina, SE USA 34°42′N 79°52′W
102 I3 **Cherbourg** anc. Carusbur. Manche, N France 49°40′N 01°36′W
127 R5 **Cherdakly** Ul'yanovskaya Oblast', W Russian Federation 54°21′N 48°54′E
125 U12 **Cherdyn'** Permskaya Oblast', NW Russian Federation 60°21′N 56°39′E
124 J14 **Cherekha** ≈ W Russian Federation
122 M13 **Cheremkhovo** Irkutskaya Oblast', S Russian Federation 53°16′N 102°44′E
Cheren see Keren
124 K14 **Cherepovets** Vologodskaya Oblast', NW Russian Federation 59°09′N 37°50′E
125 O11 **Cherevkovo** Arkhangel'skaya Oblast', NW Russian Federation 61°45′N 45°16′E
74 I6 **Chergui, Chott ech** salt lake NW Algeria
Cherikov see Cherykaw
117 P6 **Cherkas'ka Oblast'** var. Cherkasy, Rus. Cherkasskaya Oblast'. ⬖ province C Ukraine
Cherkasskaya Oblast' see Cherkas'ka Oblast'
Cherkassy see Cherkasy
117 Q6 **Cherkasy** Rus. Cherkassy. Cherkas'ka Oblast', C Ukraine 49°26′N 32°05′E
Cherkasy see Cherkas'ka Oblast'
126 M15 **Cherkessk** Karachayevo-Cherkesskaya Respublika, SW Russian Federation 44°12′N 42°06′E
122 H12 **Cherlak** Omskaya Oblast', C Russian Federation 54°06′N 74°59′E
122 H12 **Cherlakskoye** Omskaya Oblast', C Russian Federation 53°42′N 74°23′E
125 U13 **Chermoz** Permskaya Oblast', NW Russian Federation 58°49′N 56°07′E
Chernavchitsy see Charnawchytsy
125 T3 **Chernaya** Nenetskiy Avtonomnyy Okrug, NW Russian Federation 68°36′N 56°34′E
125 T4 **Chernaya** ≈ NW Russian Federation
Chernigov see Chernihiv
Chernigovskaya Oblast' see Chernihivs'ka Oblast'
117 Q2 **Chernihiv** Rus. Chernigov. Chernihivs'ka Oblast', NE Ukraine 51°28′N 31°19′E
Chernihiv see Chernihivs'ka Oblast'
117 V9 **Chernihivka** Zaporiz'ka Oblast', SE Ukraine 47°11′N 36°10′E
117 P2 **Chernihivs'ka Oblast'** var. Chernihiv, Rus. Chernigovskaya Oblast'. ⬖ province NE Ukraine
114 I9 **Cherni Osŭm** ≈ N Bulgaria
116 J8 **Chernivets'ka Oblast'** var. Chernivtsi, Rus. Chernovitskaya Oblast'. ⬖ province W Ukraine
114 I9 **Cherni Vit** ≈ NW Bulgaria
114 G10 **Cherni Vrŭkh** ▲ W Bulgaria 42°33′N 23°18′E
116 K8 **Chernivtsi** Ger. Czernowitz, Rom. Cernăuţi, Rus. Chernovtsy. Chernivets'ka Oblast', W Ukraine 48°18′N 25°55′E
116 M7 **Chernivtsi** Vinnyts'ka Oblast', C Ukraine 48°33′N 28°06′E
Chernivtsi see Chernivets'ka Oblast'
Chernobyl' see Chornobyl'
Cherno More see Black Sea
Chernomorskoye see Chornomors'ke
145 T7 **Chernoretskoye** Pavlodar, NE Kazakhstan 52°51′N 76°37′E
Chernovitskaya Oblast' see Chernivets'ka Oblast'
Chernovtsy see Chernivtsi
145 U8 **Chernoye** Pavlodar, NE Kazakhstan 51°40′N 77°33′E
Chernoye More see Black Sea
125 U16 **Chernushka** Permskaya Oblast', NW Russian Federation 56°30′N 56°07′E
117 N4 **Chernyakhiv** Rus. Chernyakhov. Zhytomyrs'ka Oblast', N Ukraine 50°30′N 28°38′E
Chernyakhov see Chernyakhiv
119 C14 **Chernyakhovsk** Ger. Insterburg. Kaliningradskaya Oblast', W Russian Federation 54°36′N 21°49′E
126 K8 **Chernyanka** Belgorodskaya Oblast', W Russian Federation 50°59′N 37°54′E
125 V5 **Chernyshëva, Gryada** ▲▲ NW Russian Federation
144 J14 **Chernyshëva, Zaliv** gulf SW Kazakhstan
123 O10 **Chernyshevskiy** Respublika Sakha (Yakutiya), NE Russian Federation 62°57′N 112°29′E
127 P13 **Chernyye Zemli** plain SW Russian Federation
Chërnyy Irtysh see Ertix He, China/Kazakhstan
Chërnyy Irtysh see Kara Irtysh, Kazakhstan
127 V7 **Chernyy Otrog** Orenburgskaya Oblast', W Russian Federation 52°03′N 56°09′E
29 T12 **Cherokee** Iowa, C USA 42°45′N 95°33′W
26 M8 **Cherokee** Oklahoma, C USA 36°45′N 98°22′W
25 R9 **Cherokee** Texas, SW USA 30°56′N 98°42′W
21 O8 **Cherokee Lake** ⊠ Tennessee, S USA
Cherokees, Lake O' The see Grand Lake O' The Cherokees
44 H1 **Cherokee Sound** Great Abaco, N Bahamas 26°16′N 77°03′W
153 V13 **Cherrapunji** Meghālaya, NE India 25°16′N 91°42′E
28 L9 **Cherry Creek** ≈ South Dakota, N USA
18 J16 **Cherry Hill** New Jersey, NE USA 39°55′N 75°01′W
27 Q7 **Cherryvale** Kansas, C USA 37°16′N 95°33′W
21 Q10 **Cherryville** North Carolina, SE USA 35°22′N 81°22′W
Cherski Range see Cherskogo, Khrebet
123 T6 **Cherskiy** Respublika Sakha (Yakutiya), NE Russian Federation 68°45′N 161°15′E
123 R8 **Cherskogo, Khrebet** var. Cherski Range. ▲▲ NE Russian Federation
Cherso see Cres
126 L10 **Chertkovo** Rostovskaya Oblast', SW Russian Federation 49°22′N 40°10′E
Cherven' see Chervyen'
114 H8 **Cherven Bryag** Pleven, N Bulgaria 43°16′N 24°06′E
116 M4 **Chervonoarmiys'k** Zhytomyrs'ka Oblast', N Ukraine 50°27′N 28°15′E
Chervonograd see Chervonohrad
116 I4 **Chervonohrad** Rus. Chervonograd. L'vivs'ka Oblast', NW Ukraine 50°25′N 24°10′E
117 W6 **Chervonooskil's'ke Vodoskhovyshche** Rus. Krasnooskol'skoye Vodokhranilishche. ⊠ NE Ukraine
Chervonoye, Ozero see Chyrvonaye, Vozyera
117 S4 **Chervonozavods'ke** Poltavs'ka Oblast', C Ukraine 50°24′N 33°22′E
119 L16 **Chervyen'** Rus. Cherven'. Minskaya Voblasts', C Belarus 53°42′N 28°26′E
119 P16 **Cherykaw** Rus. Cherikov. Mahilyowskaya Voblasts', E Belarus 53°34′N 31°23′E
31 R9 **Chesaning** Michigan, N USA 43°10′N 84°07′W
21 X5 **Chesapeake Bay** inlet NE USA
Chesha Bay see Chëshskaya Guba
Cheshevlya see Tsyeshawlya
97 K18 **Cheshire** cultural region C England, United Kingdom
125 P5 **Chëshskaya Guba** var. Archangel Bay, Chesha Bay, Dvina Bay. bay NW Russian Federation
14 F14 **Chesley** Ontario, S Canada 44°17′N 81°06′W
21 Q10 **Chesnee** South Carolina, SE USA 35°09′N 81°51′W
97 K18 **Chester** Wel. Caerleon, hist. Legaceaster, Lat. Deva, Devana Castra. C England, United Kingdom 53°12′N 02°54′W
35 O4 **Chester** California, W USA 40°18′N 121°14′W
30 K16 **Chester** Illinois, N USA 37°54′N 89°49′W
33 S7 **Chester** Montana, NW USA 48°30′N 110°59′W
18 I16 **Chester** Pennsylvania, NE USA 39°51′N 75°21′W
21 R1 **Chester** South Carolina, SE USA 34°43′N 81°14′W
25 X9 **Chester** Texas, SW USA 30°55′N 94°36′W
21 W6 **Chester** Virginia, NE USA 37°22′N 77°27′W
21 R11 **Chester** West Virginia, NE USA 40°34′N 80°33′W
97 M18 **Chesterfield** C England, United Kingdom 53°15′N 01°25′W
21 S11 **Chesterfield** South Carolina, SE USA 34°44′N 80°04′W
21 W6 **Chesterfield** Virginia, NE USA 37°22′N 77°31′W
192 J9 **Chesterfield, Îles** island group NW New Caledonia
9 O9 **Chesterfield Inlet** Nunavut, NW Canada 63°19′N 90°57′W
9 O9 **Chesterfield Inlet** inlet Nunavut, N Canada
21 Y3 **Chester River** ≈ Delaware/Maryland, NE USA
21 X3 **Chestertown** Maryland, NE USA 39°13′N 76°04′W
19 R4 **Chesuncook Lake** ◎ Maine, NE USA
30 J5 **Chetek** Wisconsin, N USA 45°19′N 91°37′W
13 R14 **Chéticamp** Nova Scotia, SE Canada 46°14′N 61°19′W
27 Q8 **Chetopa** Kansas, C USA 37°02′N 95°05′W
41 Y14 **Chetumal** var. Payo Obispo. Quintana Roo, SE Mexico 18°32′N 88°16′W
Chetumal, Bahia/Chetumal, Bahía de see Chetumal Bay
42 G1 **Chetumal Bay** var. Bahia Chetumal, Bahía de Chetumal. bay Belize/Mexico
10 M13 **Chetwynd** British Columbia, W Canada 55°42′N 121°36′W
38 M11 **Chevak** Alaska, USA 61°31′N 165°35′W
36 M12 **Chevelon Creek** ≈ Arizona, SW USA
185 J17 **Cheviot** Canterbury, South Island, New Zealand 42°48′S 173°17′E
96 L13 **Cheviot Hills** hill range England/Scotland, United Kingdom
96 L13 **Cheviot, The** ▲ NE England, United Kingdom 55°28′N 02°10′W
14 M11 **Chevreuil, Lac du** ◎ Québec, SE Canada
81 I16 **Ch'ew Bahir** var. Lake Stefanie. ◎ Ethiopia/Kenya
32 L7 **Chewelah** Washington, NW USA 48°16′N 117°42′W
26 K10 **Cheyenne** Oklahoma, C USA 35°37′N 99°43′W
33 Z17 **Cheyenne** state capital Wyoming, C USA 41°08′N 104°46′W
26 L5 **Cheyenne Bottoms** ◎ Kansas, C USA
16 J8 **Cheyenne River** ≈ South Dakota/Wyoming, N USA
37 W5 **Cheyenne Wells** Colorado, C USA 38°49′N 102°21′W
108 C9 **Cheyres** Vaud, W Switzerland 46°48′N 06°48′E
Chezdi-Oşorheiu see Târgu Secuiesc
153 P13 **Chhapra** prev. Chapra. Bihār, N India 25°50′N 84°42′E
153 V13 **Chhatak** var. Chatak. Sylhet, NE Bangladesh 25°02′N 91°33′E
154 J9 **Chhatarpur** Madhya Pradesh, C India 24°54′N 79°35′E
154 N13 **Chhatrapur** prev. Chatrapur. Orissa, E India 19°26′N 85°02′E
154 K2 **Chhattīsgarh** ⬖ state E India
154 L12 **Chhattīsgarh** plain C India
154 I11 **Chhindwāra** Madhya Pradesh, C India 22°04′N 78°58′E
153 T12 **Chhukha** SW Bhutan 27°02′N 89°36′E
161 S14 **Chiai** var. Chia-i, Chiayi, Kiayi, Jiayi, Jap. Kagi. C Taiwan 23°29′N 120°27′E
Chia-i see Chiai
Chia-mu-ssu see Jiamusi
83 B15 **Chiange** Port. Vila de Almoster. Huíla, SW Angola 15°44′S 13°54′E
Chiang-hsi see Jiangxi
161 S12 **Chiang Kai-shek** ✕ (T'aipei) N Taiwan 25°09′N 121°20′E
167 P8 **Chiang Khan** Loei, E Thailand 17°51′N 101°43′E
167 O7 **Chiang Mai** var. Chiangmai, Chiengmai, Kiangmai. Chiang Mai, NW Thailand 18°48′N 98°59′E
167 O7 **Chiang Mai** ✕ Chiang Mai, NW Thailand 18°44′N 98°53′E
Chiangmai see Chiang Mai
167 O6 **Chiang Rai** var. Chianpai, Chienrai, Muang Chiang Rai. Chiang Rai, NW Thailand 19°56′N 99°51′E
Chiang-su see Jiangsu
Chianning/Chian-ning see Nanjing
Chianpai see Chiang Rai
106 G12 **Chianti** cultural region C Italy
Chiapa see Chiapa de Corzo
41 U16 **Chiapa de Corzo** var. Chiapa. Chiapas, SE Mexico 16°42′N 92°59′W
41 V16 **Chiapas** ⬖ state SE Mexico
106 J12 **Chiaravalle** Marche, C Italy 43°36′N 13°19′E
107 N22 **Chiaravalle Centrale** Calabria, SW Italy 38°40′N 16°25′E
106 E7 **Chiari** Lombardia, N Italy 45°33′N 10°00′E
108 H12 **Chiasso** Ticino, S Switzerland 45°51′N 09°02′E
137 S9 **Chiat'ura** C Georgia 42°13′N 43°11′E
41 P15 **Chiautla** var. Chiautla de Tapia. Puebla, S Mexico 18°16′N 98°31′W
Chiautla de Tapia see Chiautla
106 D10 **Chiavari** Liguria, NW Italy 44°19′N 09°19′E
106 E6 **Chiavenna** Lombardia, N Italy 46°19′N 09°22′E
Chiayi see Chiai
Chiazza see Piazza Armerina
165 O14 **Chiba** var. Tiba. Chiba, Honshū, S Japan 35°37′N 140°06′E
165 O13 **Chiba** off. Chiba-ken, var. Tiba. ⬖ prefecture Honshū, S Japan
83 M18 **Chibabava** Sofala, C Mozambique 20°17′S 33°39′E
Chiba-ken see Chiba
161 O10 **Chibi** prev. Puqi. Hubei, C China 29°45′N 113°55′E
83 B15 **Chibia** Port. João de Almeida, Vila João de Almeida. Huíla, SW Angola 15°11′S 13°41′E
83 M18 **Chiboma** Sofala, C Mozambique 20°06′S 33°54′E
82 J12 **Chibondo** Luapula, N Zambia 10°42′S 28°42′E
82 K11 **Chibote** Luapula, NE Zambia 09°52′S 29°33′E
12 K12 **Chibougamau** Québec, SE Canada 49°56′N 74°24′W
164 H11 **Chiburi-jima** island Oki-shotō, SW Japan
83 M20 **Chibuto** Gaza, S Mozambique 24°40′S 33°33′E
31 N11 **Chicago** Illinois, N USA 41°51′N 87°39′W
31 N11 **Chicago Heights** Illinois, N USA 41°30′N 87°38′W
15 W6 **Chic-Chocs, Monts** Eng. Shickshock Mountains. ▲▲ Québec, SE Canada
39 W13 **Chichagof Island** island Alexander Archipelago, Alaska, USA
57 K20 **Chichas, Cordillera de** ▲▲ SW Bolivia
41 X12 **Chichén-Itzá, Ruinas** ruins Yucatán, SE Mexico
97 N23 **Chichester** SE England, United Kingdom 50°50′N 00°48′W
42 C5 **Chichicastenango** Quiché, W Guatemala 14°55′N 91°06′W
42 I9 **Chichigalpa** Chinandega, NW Nicaragua 12°35′N 87°04′W
Ch'i-ch'i-ha-erh see Qiqihar
165 X16 **Chichijima-rettō** Eng. Beechy Group. island group SE Japan
54 K4 **Chichiriviche** Falcón, N Venezuela 10°58′N 68°17′W
39 R11 **Chickaloon** Alaska, USA 61°48′N 148°27′W
20 L10 **Chickamauga Lake** ⊠ Tennessee, S USA
23 N7 **Chickasawhay River** ≈ Mississippi, S USA
26 M11 **Chickasha** Oklahoma, C USA 35°03′N 97°57′W
39 T9 **Chicken** Alaska, USA 64°04′N 141°56′W
104 J16 **Chiclana de la Frontera** Andalucía, S Spain 36°26′N 06°09′W
56 B11 **Chiclayo** Lambayeque, NW Peru 06°47′S 79°47′W
35 N5 **Chico** California, W USA 39°42′N 121°51′W
83 L15 **Chicoa** Tete, NW Mozambique 15°45′S 32°25′E
83 M20 **Chicomo** Gaza, S Mozambique 24°29′S 34°15′E
18 M11 **Chicopee** Massachusetts, NE USA 42°08′N 72°34′W
63 I19 **Chico, Río** ≈ SE Argentina
63 I21 **Chico, Río** ≈ S Argentina
27 W14 **Chicot, Lake** ◎ Arkansas, C USA
15 R7 **Chicoutimi** Québec, SE Canada 48°24′N 71°04′W
15 Q8 **Chicoutimi** ≈ Québec, SE Canada
83 L19 **Chicualacuala** Gaza, SW Mozambique 22°06′S 31°42′E
83 B14 **Chicuma** Benguela, C Angola 13°33′S 14°41′E
155 J21 **Chidambaram** Tamil Nādu, SE India 11°25′N 79°42′E
196 K13 **Chidley, Cape** headland Newfoundland and Labrador, E Canada 60°25′N 64°39′W
101 N24 **Chiemsee** ◎ SE Germany
Chiengmai see Chiang Mai
Chienrai see Chiang Rai
106 B8 **Chieri** Piemonte, NW Italy 45°01′N 07°49′E
106 F8 **Chiese** ≈ N Italy
107 K14 **Chieti** var. Teate. Abruzzo, C Italy 42°22′N 14°10′E
99 E19 **Chièvres** Hainaut, SW Belgium 50°34′N 03°49′E
163 S12 **Chifeng** var. Ulanhad. Nei Mongol Zizhiqu, N China 42°17′N 118°56′E
82 F13 **Chifumage** ≈ E Angola
82 M13 **Chifunda** Eastern, NE Zambia 11°57′S 32°36′E
145 S14 **Chiganak** var. Čiganak, Kaz. Shyghanaq. Zhambyl, SE Kazakhstan 45°10′N 73°55′E
39 P15 **Chiginagak, Mount** ▲ Alaska, USA 57°10′N 157°00′W
Chigirin see Chyhyryn
41 P13 **Chignahuapan** Puebla, S Mexico 19°52′N 98°03′W
39 O15 **Chignik** Alaska, USA 56°18′N 158°24′W
83 M19 **Chigombe** ≈ S Mozambique
54 D7 **Chigorodó** Antioquia, NW Colombia 07°42′N 76°45′W
83 M19 **Chigubo** Gaza, S Mozambique 22°50′S 33°30′E
Chihertey see Altay
Chih-fu see Yantai
Chihli see Hebei
Chihli, Gulf of see Bo Hai
40 J6 **Chihuahua** Chihuahua, NW Mexico 28°40′N 106°06′W
40 I6 **Chihuahua** ⬖ state N Mexico
145 O15 **Chiili** Kaz. Shīeli. Kzylorda, S Kazakhstan 44°13′N 66°46′E
26 M7 **Chikaskia River** ≈ Kansas/Oklahoma, C USA
155 H19 **Chik Ballāpur** Karnātaka, W India 13°28′N 77°42′E
124 G15 **Chikhachevo** Pskovskaya Oblast', W Russian Federation 57°17′N 29°51′E
155 F19 **Chikmagalūr** Karnātaka, W India 13°20′N 75°46′E
129 V7 **Chikoy** ≈ C Russian Federation
83 J15 **Chikumbi** Lusaka, C Zambia 15°11′S 28°20′E
82 M13 **Chikwa** Eastern, NE Zambia 11°39′S 32°45′E
Chikwana see Chikwawa
83 N15 **Chikwawa** var. Chikwana. Southern, S Malawi 16°03′S 34°48′E
155 J16 **Chilakalūrupet** Andhra Pradesh, E India 16°09′N 80°13′E
146 L14 **Chilan** Lebap Welaýaty, E Turkmenistan 37°57′N 64°58′E
Chilapa see Chilapa de Alvarez
41 P16 **Chilapa de Alvarez** var. Chilapa. Guerrero, S Mexico 17°38′N 99°11′W
155 J25 **Chilaw** North Western Province, W Sri Lanka 07°34′N 79°48′E
57 D15 **Chilca** Lima, W Peru 12°35′S 76°41′W
23 Q4 **Childersburg** Alabama, S USA 33°16′N 86°21′W
25 P4 **Childress** Texas, SW USA 34°25′N 100°14′W
63 G14 **Chile** off. Republic of Chile. ◆ republic SW South America
47 R10 **Chile Basin** undersea feature E Pacific Ocean 33°00′S 80°00′W
63 H20 **Chile Chico** Aisén, W Chile 46°34′S 71°44′W
62 I9 **Chilecito** La Rioja, NW Argentina 29°10′S 67°30′W
62 H12 **Chilecito** Mendoza, W Argentina 33°53′S 69°03′W
83 L14 **Chilembwe** Eastern, E Zambia 13°54′S 31°38′E
Chile, Republic of see Chile
193 S11 **Chile Rise** undersea feature SE Pacific Ocean 40°00′S 90°00′W
117 N13 **Chilia, Braţul** ≈ SE Romania
Chilia-Nouă see Kiliya
145 V15 **Chilik** Kaz. Shelek. Almaty, SE Kazakhstan 43°35′N 78°12′E
145 V15 **Chilik** ≈ SE Kazakhstan
154 O13 **Chilika Lake** var. Chilka Lake. ◎ E India
82 J13 **Chililabombwe** Copperbelt, C Zambia 12°20′S 27°52′E
Chi-lin see Jilin
Chilka Lake see Chilika Lake
10 H9 **Chilkoot Pass** pass British Columbia, W Canada
Chill Ala, Cuan see Killala Bay
62 G13 **Chillán** Bío Bío, C Chile 36°37′S 72°10′W
61 C22 **Chillar** Buenos Aires, E Argentina 37°16′S 59°58′W
Chill Chiaráin, Cuan see Kilkieran Bay
30 K12 **Chillicothe** Illinois, N USA 40°55′N 89°29′W
27 S3 **Chillicothe** Missouri, C USA 39°47′N 93°33′W
31 S14 **Chillicothe** Ohio, N USA 39°20′N 83°00′W
25 Q4 **Chillicothe** Texas, SW USA 34°15′N 99°31′W
10 M17 **Chilliwack** British Columbia, SW Canada 49°09′N 121°54′W
Chill Mhantáin, Ceann see Wicklow Head
Chill Mhantáin, Sléibhte see Wicklow Mountains
108 C10 **Chillon** Vaud, W Switzerland 46°24′N 06°56′E
Chil'mamedkum, Peski/Chilmämetgum see Çilmämmetgum
63 F17 **Chiloé, Isla de** var. Isla Grande de Chiloé. island W Chile
32 H15 **Chiloquin** Oregon, NW USA 42°33′N 121°33′W
41 O16 **Chilpancingo** var. Chilpancingo de los Bravos. Guerrero, S Mexico 17°33′N 99°30′W
Chilpancingo de los Bravos see Chilpancingo
97 N21 **Chiltern Hills** hill range S England, United Kingdom
30 M7 **Chilton** Wisconsin, N USA 44°04′N 88°10′W
82 F11 **Chiluage** Lunda Sul, NE Angola 09°32′S 21°48′E
82 N12 **Chilumba** prev. Deep Bay. Northern, N Malawi 10°27′S 34°12′E
161 T12 **Chilung** var. Keelung, Jap. Kirun, Kirun'; prev. Sp. Santissima Trinidad. N Taiwan 25°10′N 121°43′E
83 N15 **Chilwa, Lake** var. Lago Chirua, Lake Shirwa. ◎ SE Malawi
167 R10 **Chi, Mae Nam** ≈ E Thailand
42 C6 **Chimaltenango** Chimaltenango, C Guatemala 14°40′N 90°48′W
42 A2 **Chimaltenango** off. Departamento de Chimaltenango. ⬖ department S Guatemala
Chimaltenango, Departamento de see Chimaltenango
43 V15 **Chimán** Panamá, E Panama 08°42′N 78°35′W
83 M17 **Chimanimani** prev. Mandidzudzure, Melsetter. Manicaland, E Zimbabwe 19°48′S 32°52′E
99 G22 **Chimay** Hainaut, S Belgium 50°03′N 04°20′E
37 S10 **Chimayo** New Mexico, SW USA 36°00′N 105°55′W
Chimbay see Chimboy
56 A13 **Chimborazo** ⬖ province C Ecuador
56 C7 **Chimborazo** ⛰ C Ecuador 01°29′S 78°50′W
56 C12 **Chimbote** Ancash, W Peru 09°04′S 78°34′W
146 H7 **Chimboy** Rus. Chimbay. Qoraqalpog'iston Respublikasi, NW Uzbekistan 43°03′N 59°52′E
186 D7 **Chimbu** ⬖ province C Papua New Guinea
54 F6 **Chimichagua** Cesar, N Colombia 09°19′N 73°51′W
Chimishliya see Cimişlia
Chimkent see Shymkent
Chimkentskaya Oblast' see Yuzhnyy Kazakhstan
28 I14 **Chimney Rock** rock Nebraska, C USA
83 M17 **Chimoio** Manica, C Mozambique 19°08′S 33°29′E
82 K11 **Chimpembe** Northern, NE Zambia 09°31′S 29°33′E
41 O8 **China** Nuevo León, NE Mexico 25°42′N 99°15′W
156 M9 **China** off. People's Republic of China, Chin. Chung-hua Jen-min Kung-ho-kuo, Zhonghua Renmin Gongheguo; prev. Chinese Empire. ◆ republic E Asia
19 Q7 **China Lake** ◎ Maine, NE USA
42 F8 **Chinameca** San Miguel, E El Salvador 13°30′N 88°20′W
Chi-nan/Chinan see Jinan
42 H9 **Chinandega** Chinandega, NW Nicaragua 12°37′N 87°08′W
42 H9 **Chinandega** ⬖ department NW Nicaragua
China, People's Republic of see China
China, Republic of see Taiwan
24 J11 **Chinati Mountains** ▲▲ Texas, SW USA
Chinaz see Chinoz
57 E15 **Chincha Alta** Ica, SW Peru 13°25′S 76°07′W
11 N11 **Chinchaga** ≈ Alberta, SW Canada
Chin-chiang see Quanzhou
Chinchilla see Chinchilla de Monte Aragón
105 Q11 **Chinchilla de Monte Aragón** var. Chinchilla. Castilla-La Mancha, C Spain 38°56′N 01°44′W
54 D10 **Chinchiná** Caldas, W Colombia 04°59′N 75°37′W
105 O8 **Chinchón** Madrid, C Spain 40°08′N 03°26′W
41 Z14 **Chinchorro, Banco** island SE Mexico
Chin-chou/Chinchow see Jinzhou
21 Z5 **Chincoteague** Assateague Island, Virginia, NE USA 37°55′N 75°22′W
83 O17 **Chinde** Zambézia, NE Mozambique 18°35′S 36°28′E
163 X17 **Chin-do** Jap. Chin-tō. island SW South Korea
159 R13 **Chindu** var. Chengwen; prev. Chuqung. Qinghai, C China 33°19′N 97°08′E
Chindwin see Chindwinn
166 M2 **Chindwinn** var. Chindwin. ≈ N Myanmar (Burma)
Chinese Empire see China
Chinghai see Qinghai
Ch'ing Hai see Qinghai Hu, China
Chingildi see Shengeldi
144 H9 **Chingirlau** Kaz. Shyngghyrlaū. Zapadnyy Kazakhstan, W Kazakhstan 51°10′N 53°44′E
82 J13 **Chingola** Copperbelt, C Zambia 12°31′S 27°53′E
Ching-Tao/Ch'ing-tao see Qingdao
82 C13 **Chinguar** Huambo, C Angola 12°33′S 16°25′E
76 I7 **Chinguețti** var. Chinguetti. Adrar, C Mauritania 20°25′N 12°24′W

◆ Country ● Country Capital ◇ Dependent Territory ○ Dependent Territory Capital ⬖ Administrative Regions ✕ International Airport ▲ Mountain ▲▲ Mountain Range ⛰ Volcano ≈ River ◎ Lake ⊠ Reservoir

CHINHAE – CIRO MARINO

163 Z16 **Chinhae** *Jap.* Chinkai. S South Korea 35°06′N 128°48′E
166 K4 **Chin Hills** ▲▲ W Myanmar (Burma)
83 K16 **Chinhoyi** *prev.* Sinoia. Mashonaland West, N Zimbabwe 17°22′S 30°12′E
Chinhsien *see* Jinzhou
39 Q14 **Chiniak, Cape** *headland* Kodiak Island, Alaska, USA 57°37′N 152°10′W
14 G10 **Chiniguchi Lake** ◎ Ontario, S Canada
149 U8 **Chiniot** Punjab, NE Pakistan 31°40′N 73°00′E
163 Y16 **Chinju** *Jap.* Shinshū. S South Korea 35°12′N 128°06′E
Chinkai *see* Chinhae
78 M13 **Chinko** ≈ E Central African Republic
37 O9 **Chinle** Arizona, SW USA 36°09′N 109°33′W
161 R13 **Chinmen Tao** *var.* Jinmen Dao, Quemoy. *island* W Taiwan
Chinnchâr *see* Shinshâr
Chinnereth *see* Tiberias, Lake
164 C12 **Chino** *var.* Tino. Nagano, Honshū, S Japan 36°00′N 138°10′E
102 L8 **Chinon** Indre-et-Loire, C France 47°10′N 00°15′E
33 T7 **Chinook** Montana, NW USA 48°35′N 109°13′W
Chinook State *see* Washington
192 L4 **Chinook Trough** *undersea feature* N Pacific Ocean
36 K11 **Chino Valley** Arizona, SW USA 34°45′N 112°27′W
147 P10 **Chinoz** *Rus.* Chinaz. Toshkent Viloyati, E Uzbekistan 40°58′N 68°46′E
82 L12 **Chinsali** Northern, NE Zambia 10°33′S 32°05′E
166 K5 **Chin State** ◈ *state* W Myanmar (Burma)
Chinsura *see* Chunchura
Chin-tō *see* Chin-do
54 E6 **Chinú** Córdoba, NW Colombia 09°07′N 75°25′W
99 K24 **Chiny, Forêt de** *forest* SE Belgium
83 M15 **Chioco** Tete, NW Mozambique 16°22′S 32°50′E
106 H8 **Chioggia** *anc.* Fossa Claudia. Veneto, NE Italy 45°14′N 12°17′E
114 H12 **Chionótrypa** ▲ NE Greece 41°16′N 24°06′E
115 L18 **Chíos** *var.* Hios, Khíos, *It.* Scio, *Turk.* Sakiz-Adasi. Chíos, E Greece 38°23′N 26°07′E
115 K18 **Chíos** *var.* Khíos. *island* E Greece
83 M14 **Chipata** *prev.* Fort Jameson. Eastern, E Zambia 13°40′S 32°42′E
83 C14 **Chipindo** Huíla, C Angola 13°53′S 15°47′E
23 R8 **Chipley** Florida, SE USA 30°46′N 85°32′W
155 D15 **Chiplūn** Mahārāshtra, W India 17°32′N 73°32′E
81 H22 **Chipogolo** Dodoma, C Tanzania 06°52′S 36°03′E
23 R8 **Chipola River** ≈ Florida, SE USA
97 L22 **Chippenham** S England, United Kingdom 51°28′N 02°07′W
30 J6 **Chippewa Falls** Wisconsin, N USA 44°56′N 91°25′W
30 J4 **Chippewa, Lake** ⊠ Wisconsin, N USA
31 Q8 **Chippewa River** ≈ Michigan, N USA
30 I6 **Chippewa River** ≈ Wisconsin, N USA
Chipping Wycombe *see* High Wycombe
114 G8 **Chiprovtsi** Montana, NW Bulgaria 43°23′N 22°53′E
19 T4 **Chiputneticook Lakes** *lakes* Canada/USA
56 D13 **Chiquián** Ancash, W Peru 10°09′S 78°08′W
41 Y11 **Chiquilá** Quintana Roo, SE Mexico 21°25′N 87°20′W
42 E6 **Chiquimula** Chiquimula, SE Guatemala 14°46′N 89°32′W
42 A3 **Chiquimula** *off.* Departamento de Chiquimula. ◈ *department* SE Guatemala
Chiquimula, Departamento de *see* Chiquimula
42 D7 **Chiquimulilla** Santa Rosa, S Guatemala 14°06′N 90°23′W
54 F9 **Chiquinquirá** Boyacá, C Colombia 05°37′N 73°51′W
155 J17 **Chīrāla** Andhra Pradesh, E India 15°49′N 80°21′E
149 N4 **Chīras** Ghowr, N Afghanistan 35°15′N 65°39′E
152 H11 **Chirāwa** Rājasthān, N India 28°12′N 75°42′E
Chirchik *see* Chirchiq
147 Q9 **Chirchiq** *Rus.* Chirchik. Toshkent Viloyati, E Uzbekistan 41°30′N 69°32′E
147 P10 **Chirchiq** ≈ E Uzbekistan
Chire *see* Shire
83 L18 **Chiredzi** Masvingo, SE Zimbabwe 21°00′S 31°38′E
25 X8 **Chireno** Texas, SW USA 31°30′N 94°21′W
77 X7 **Chirfa** Agadez, NE Niger 21°01′N 12°41′E
37 O16 **Chiricahua Mountains** ▲▲ Arizona, SW USA
37 O16 **Chiricahua Peak** ▲ Arizona, SW USA 31°51′N 109°17′W
54 F6 **Chiriguaná** Cesar, N Colombia 09°24′N 73°38′W
39 P15 **Chirikof Island** *island* Alaska, USA
43 P16 **Chiriquí** *off.* Provincia de Chiriquí. ◈ *province* SW Panama
43 P17 **Chiriquí, Golfo de** *Eng.* Chiriqui Gulf. *gulf* SW Panama
43 P15 **Chiriquí Grande** Bocas del Toro, W Panama 08°58′N 82°08′W
Chiriqui Gulf *see* Chiriquí, Golfo de
43 P15 **Chiriquí, Laguna de** *lagoon* NW Panama
Chiriquí, Provincia de *see* Chiriquí
43 O16 **Chiriquí Viejo, Río** ≈ W Panama
Chiriquí, Volcán de *see* Barú, Volcán
83 N15 **Chiromo** Southern, S Malawi 16°32′S 35°07′E
114 J10 **Chirpan** Stara Zagora, C Bulgaria 42°12′N 25°20′E
43 N14 **Chirripó Atlántico, Río** ≈ E Costa Rica
Chirripó, Cerro *see* Chirripó Grande, Cerro
Chirripó del Pacífico, Río *see* Chirripó, Río
43 N14 **Chirripó Grande, Cerro** *var.* Cerro Chirripó. ▲ SE Costa Rica 09°31′N 83°28′W
43 N13 **Chirripó, Río** *var.* Río Chirripó del Pacífico. ≈ NE Costa Rica
Chirua, Lago *see* Chilwa, Lake
83 J15 **Chirundu** Southern, S Zambia 16°03′S 28°50′E
29 W8 **Chisago City** Minnesota, N USA 45°22′N 92°53′W
83 J14 **Chisamba** Central, C Zambia 15°00′S 28°22′E
39 T10 **Chisana** Alaska, USA 62°09′N 142°07′W
82 I13 **Chisasa** North Western, NW Zambia 12°09′S 25°30′E
12 I9 **Chisasibi** *prev.* Fort George. Québec, C Canada 53°50′N 79°01′W
42 D4 **Chisec** Alta Verapaz, C Guatemala 15°50′N 90°18′W
127 U5 **Chishmy** Respublika Bashkortostan, W Russian Federation 54°33′N 55°21′E
29 V4 **Chisholm** Minnesota, N USA 47°29′N 92°52′W
149 U10 **Chishtiān Mandi** Punjab, E Pakistan 29°44′N 72°54′E
160 I11 **Chishui He** ≈ C China
Chisimaio/Chisimayu *see* Kismaayo
117 N10 **Chişinău** *Rus.* Kishinev. ● (Moldova) C Moldova 47°N 28°51′E
117 N10 **Chişinău** ✈ S Moldova 46°54′N 28°56′E
Chişinău-Criş *see* Chişineu-Criş
116 F10 **Chişineu-Criş** *Hung.* Kisjenő; *prev.* Chişinău-Criş. Arad, W Romania 46°33′N 21°30′E
83 K14 **Chisomo** Central, C Zambia 13°30′S 30°37′E
106 A8 **Chisone** ≈ NW Italy
24 K12 **Chisos Mountains** ▲▲ Texas, SW USA
39 T10 **Chistochina** Alaska, USA 62°34′N 144°39′W
127 R4 **Chistopol'** Respublika Tatarstan, W Russian Federation 55°20′N 50°39′E
145 O8 **Chistopol'ye** Severnyy Kazakhstan, N Kazakhstan 52°37′N 67°14′E
123 O13 **Chita** Chitinskaya Oblast', S Russian Federation 52°03′N 113°35′E
83 B16 **Chitado** Cunene, SW Angola 17°16′S 13°54′E
Chitaldroog/Chitaldrug *see* Chitradurga
83 C15 **Chitanda** ≈ S Angola
Chitangwiza *see* Chitungwiza
82 F10 **Chitato** Lunda Norte, NE Angola 07°23′S 20°46′E
83 C14 **Chitembo** Bié, C Angola 13°33′S 16°47′E
39 T11 **Chitina** Alaska, USA 61°31′N 144°26′W
39 T11 **Chitina River** ≈ Alaska, USA
123 O12 **Chitinskaya Oblast'** ◈ *province* S Russian Federation
82 M11 **Chitipa** Northern, NW Malawi 09°41′S 33°19′E
165 S4 **Chitose** *var.* Titose. Hokkaidō, NE Japan 42°51′N 141°40′E
155 G18 **Chitradurga** *prev.* Chitaldroog, Chitaldrug. Karnātaka, W India 14°16′N 76°23′E
149 T3 **Chitrāl** North-West Frontier Province, NW Pakistan 35°51′N 71°47′E
43 S16 **Chitré** Herrera, S Panama 07°57′N 80°26′W
153 V16 **Chittagong** *Ben.* Chāttagām. Chittagong, SE Bangladesh 22°20′N 91°48′E
153 U16 **Chittagong** ◈ *division* E Bangladesh
153 Q15 **Chittaranjan** West Bengal, NE India 23°52′N 86°40′E
152 G14 **Chittaurgarh** *var.* Chittorgarh. Rājasthān, N India 24°54′N 74°42′E
155 I19 **Chittoor** Andhra Pradesh, E India 13°13′N 79°06′E
Chittorgarh *see* Chittaurgarh
155 G21 **Chittūr** Kerala, SW India 10°42′N 76°46′E
83 K16 **Chitungwiza** *prev.* Chitangwiza. Mashonaland East, NE Zimbabwe 18°S 31°06′E
62 H4 **Chiuchíu** Antofagasta, N Chile 22°13′S 68°34′W
82 F12 **Chiumbe** *var.* Tshiumbe. ≈ Angola/Dem. Rep. Congo
83 F15 **Chiume** Moxico, E Angola 15°08′S 21°09′E
82 K13 **Chiundaponde** Northern, NE Zambia 12°14′S 30°40′E
106 H13 **Chiusi** Toscana, C Italy 43°00′N 11°56′E
54 J5 **Chivacoa** Yaracuy, N Venezuela 10°10′N 68°54′W
106 B8 **Chivasso** Piemonte, NW Italy 45°13′N 07°54′E
83 L17 **Chivhu** *prev.* Enkeldoorn. Midlands, C Zimbabwe 19°01′S 30°54′E
61 C20 **Chivilcoy** Buenos Aires, E Argentina 34°55′S 60°00′W
82 N12 **Chiweta** Northern, N Malawi 10°36′S 34°09′E
42 D4 **Chixoy, Río** *var.* Río Negro, Río Salinas. ≈ Guatemala/Mexico
82 H13 **Chizela** North Western, NW Zambia 13°11′S 24°59′E
125 O5 **Chizha** Nenetskiy Avtonomnyy Okrug, NW Russian Federation 67°04′N 44°19′E
161 Q9 **Chizhou** *var.* Guichi. Anhui, E China 30°39′N 117°29′E
164 I12 **Chizu** Tottori, Honshū, SW Japan 35°15′N 134°14′E
Chkalov *see* Orenburg
127 N3 **Chkalovsk** Nizhegorodskaya Oblast', W Russian Federation 56°45′N 43°15′E
74 J5 **Chlef** *var.* Ech Cheliff, Ech Chleff; *prev.* Al-Asnam, El Asnam, Orléansville. NW Algeria 36°11′N 01°21′E
115 G18 **Chlómo** ▲ C Greece 38°36′N 22°57′E
111 M15 **Chmielnik** Świętokrzyskie, C Poland 50°37′N 20°43′E
167 S11 **Chŏâm Khsant** Preăh Vihéar, N Cambodia 14°13′N 104°56′E
62 G10 **Choapa, Río** *var.* Choapo. ≈ C Chile
Choapas *see* Las Choapas
Choapo *see* Choapa, Río
Choarta *see* Chwārtā
67 T13 **Chobe** ≈ N Botswana
14 K8 **Chochocouane** ≈ Québec, SE Canada
110 E13 **Chocianów** *Ger.* Kotzenan. Dolnośląskie, SW Poland 51°23′N 15°55′E
54 C9 **Chocó** *off.* Departamento del Chocó. ◈ *province* W Colombia
Chocó, Departamento del *see* Chocó
35 X16 **Chocolate Mountains** ▲▲ California, W USA
21 W9 **Chocowinity** North Carolina, SE USA 35°33′N 77°03′W
27 N10 **Choctaw** Oklahoma, C USA 35°30′N 97°16′W
23 Q8 **Choctawhatchee Bay** *bay* Florida, SE USA
23 Q8 **Choctawhatchee River** ≈ Florida, SE USA
Chodau *see* Chodov
163 V14 **Ch'o-do** *island* SW North Korea
Chodorów *see* Khodoriv
111 A16 **Chodov** *Ger.* Chodau. Karlovarský Kraj, W Czech Republic 50°15′N 12°45′E
110 G10 **Chodzież** Wielkopolskie, C Poland 53°N 16°55′E
63 J15 **Choele Choel** Río Negro, C Argentina 39°19′S 65°42′W
83 L14 **Chofombo** Tete, NW Mozambique 14°43′S 31°48′E
Chohtan *see* Chauhtan
11 U14 **Choiceland** Saskatchewan, C Canada 53°28′N 104°26′W
186 K8 **Choiseul** *var.* Lauru. *island* NW Solomon Islands
63 M23 **Choiseul Sound** *sound* East Falkland, Falkland Islands
40 H7 **Choix** Sinaloa, C Mexico 26°43′N 108°20′W
110 D10 **Chojna** Zachodnio-pomorskie, W Poland 52°56′N 14°25′E
110 H8 **Chojnice** *Ger.* Konitz. Pomorskie, N Poland 53°41′N 17°34′E
111 F14 **Chojnów** *Ger.* Hainau, Haynau. Dolnośląskie, SW Poland 51°16′N 15°55′E
167 Q10 **Chok Chai** Nakhon Ratchasima, C Thailand 14°45′N 102°10′E
80 I12 **Ch'ok'ē** *var.* Choke Mountains. ▲▲ NW Ethiopia
25 R13 **Choke Canyon Lake** ⊠ Texas, SW USA
Choke Mountains *see* Ch'ok'ē
145 T15 **Chokpar** *Kaz.* Shocpar. Zhambyl, S Kazakhstan 43°49′N 74°25′E
147 W7 **Chok-Tal** *var.* Choktal. Issyk-Kul'skaya Oblast', E Kyrgyzstan 42°37′N 76°45′E
Choktal *see* Chok-Tal
Chókué *see* Chokwè
123 R7 **Chokurdakh** Respublika Sakha (Yakutiya), NE Russian Federation 70°38′N 148°18′E
83 L20 **Chokwè** *var.* Chókué. Gaza, S Mozambique 24°27′S 32°55′E
188 F8 **Chol** Babeldaob, N Palau
160 E8 **Chola Shan** ▲▲ C China
102 J8 **Cholet** Maine-et-Loire, NW France 47°03′N 00°52′W
63 H17 **Cholila** Chubut, W Argentina 42°33′S 71°28′W
Cholo *see* Thyolo
147 V8 **Cholpon** Narynskaya Oblast', C Kyrgyzstan 42°07′N 75°25′E
147 X7 **Cholpon-Ata** Issyk-Kul'skaya Oblast', E Kyrgyzstan 42°39′N 77°05′E
41 P14 **Cholula** Puebla, S Mexico 19°03′N 98°19′W
42 I8 **Choluteca** Choluteca, S Honduras 13°15′N 87°10′W
42 H8 **Choluteca** ◈ *department* S Honduras
42 H8 **Choluteca, Río** ≈ SW Honduras
83 I15 **Choma** Southern, S Zambia 16°48′S 26°58′E
158 L17 **Chomo** *var.* Xarsingma. Xizang Zizhiqu, W China 27°31′N 88°58′E *see also* Yadong
153 T11 **Chomo Lhari** ▲ NW Bhutan 27°59′N 89°24′E
167 N7 **Chom Thong** Chiang Mai, NW Thailand 18°25′N 98°44′E
111 B15 **Chomutov** *Ger.* Komotau. Ústecký Kraj, NW Czech Republic 50°28′N 13°24′E
123 N11 **Chona** ≈ C Russian Federation
163 X15 **Ch'ŏnan** *Jap.* Tenan. W South Korea 36°51′N 127°11′E
167 P11 **Chon Buri** *prev.* Bang Pla Soi. Chon Buri, S Thailand 13°24′N 100°59′E
56 B6 **Chone** Manabí, W Ecuador 0°44′S 80°04′W
Chong'an *see* Wuyishan
163 W13 **Ch'ŏngch'ŏn-gang** ≈ W North Korea
163 Y11 **Ch'ŏngjin** NE North Korea 41°48′N 129°44′E
163 W13 **Chŏngju** W North Korea 39°44′N 125°13′E
161 S8 **Chongming Dao** *island* E China
160 J10 **Chongqing** *var.* Ch'ung-ching, Ch'ung-ch'ing, Chungking, Pahsien, Tchongking, Yuzhou. Chongqing Shi, C China 29°34′N 106°27′E
160 K10 **Chongqing Shi** ◈ *municipality* Chongqing Shi, C China
Chŏngup *see* Chŏnju
161 O10 **Chongyang** *var.* Tiancheng. Hubei, C China 29°35′N 114°03′E
160 J15 **Chongzuo** *prev.* Taiping. Guangxi Zhuangzu Zizhiqu, S China 22°18′N 107°23′E
163 Y16 **Chŏnju** *prev.* Chŏngup, *Jap.* Seiyu. SW South Korea 35°51′N 127°08′E
163 Y15 **Chŏnju** *Jap.* Zenshū. SW South Korea 35°51′N 127°08′E
Chonnacht *see* Connaught
Chonogol *see* Erdenetsagaan
63 F19 **Chonos, Archipiélago de los** *island group* S Chile
42 K10 **Chontales** ◈ *department* S Nicaragua
167 T13 **Chơn Thanh** Sông Be, S Vietnam 11°25′N 106°38′E
158 K17 **Cho Oyu** *var.* Qowowuyag. ▲ China/Nepal 28°07′N 86°37′E
116 G7 **Chop** *Cz.* Čop, *Hung.* Csap. Zakarpats'ka Oblast', W Ukraine 48°25′N 22°13′E
21 Y3 **Choptank River** ≈ Maryland, NE USA
115 J22 **Chóra** *prev.* Íos. Íos, Kykládes, Greece, Aegean Sea 36°42′N 25°16′E
115 H25 **Chóra Sfakíon** *var.* Sfákia. Kríti, Greece, E Mediterranean Sea 35°12′N 24°05′E
Chorcaí, Cuan *see* Cork Harbour
43 P15 **Chorcha, Cerro** ▲ W Panama 08°39′N 82°07′W
Chorku *see* Chorkŭh
147 R11 **Chorkŭh** *Rus.* Chorku. N Tajikistan 40°04′N 70°30′E
97 K17 **Chorley** NW England, United Kingdom 53°40′N 02°38′W
Chorne More *see* Black Sea
117 R5 **Chornobay** Cherkas'ka Oblast', C Ukraine 49°40′N 32°20′E
117 O3 **Chornobyl'** *Rus.* Chernobyl'. Kyyivs'ka Oblast', N Ukraine 51°17′N 30°15′E
117 R12 **Chornomors'ke** *Rus.* Chernomorskoye. Respublika Krym, S Ukraine 45°29′N 32°45′E
117 R4 **Chornukhy** Poltavs'ka Oblast', C Ukraine 50°15′N 32°57′E
Chorokh/Chorokhi *see* Çoruh Nehri
110 O9 **Choroszcz** Podlaskie, NE Poland 53°10′N 23°E
116 K6 **Chortkiv** *Rus.* Chortkov. Ternopil's'ka Oblast', W Ukraine 49°01′N 25°46′E
Chortkov *see* Chortkiv
Chorum *see* Çorum
110 M9 **Chorzele** Mazowieckie, C Poland 53°16′N 20°53′E
111 J16 **Chorzów** *Ger.* Königshütte; *prev.* Królewska Huta. Śląskie, S Poland 50°17′N 18°58′E
163 W12 **Ch'osan** N North Korea 40°45′N 125°52′E
Choșebuz *see* Cottbus
Chōsen-kaikyō *see* Korea Strait
164 P14 **Chōshi** *var.* Tyôsi. Chiba, Honshū, S Japan 35°44′N 140°48′E
63 H14 **Chos Malal** Neuquén, W Argentina 37°23′S 70°16′W
Chosŏn-minjujuŭi-inmin-kanghwaguk *see* North Korea
110 E9 **Choszczno** *Ger.* Arnswalde. Zachodnio-pomorskie, NW Poland 53°10′N 15°24′E
153 O15 **Chota Nāgpur** *plateau* N India
33 R8 **Choteau** Montana, NW USA 47°48′N 112°40′W
Chotqol *see* Chatkal
14 M8 **Chouart** ≈ Québec, SE Canada
76 I7 **Choûm** Adrar, C Mauritania 21°19′N 12°59′W
27 Q9 **Chouteau** Oklahoma, C USA 36°11′N 95°20′W
21 X8 **Chowan River** ≈ North Carolina, SE USA
35 Q10 **Chowchilla** California, W USA 37°06′N 120°15′W
163 P7 **Choybalsan** *prev.* Byan Tumen. Dornod, E Mongolia 48°03′N 114°32′E
163 Q7 **Choybalsan** *var.* Hulstay. Dornod, NE Mongolia 48°25′N 114°56′E
162 M9 **Choyr** Govĭ Sumber, C Mongolia 46°20′N 108°21′E
185 I19 **Christchurch** Canterbury, South Island, New Zealand 43°31′S 172°39′E
97 M24 **Christchurch** S England, United Kingdom 50°44′N 01°45′W
185 I18 **Christchurch** ✈ Canterbury, South Island, New Zealand 43°28′S 172°33′E
44 J12 **Christiana** C Jamaica 18°13′N 77°29′W
83 H22 **Christiana** Free State, C South Africa 27°55′S 25°10′E
115 J23 **Christiána** *var.* Christiani. *island* Kykládes, Greece, Aegean Sea
Christiani *see* Christiána
Christiania *see* Oslo
14 G13 **Christian Island** *island* Ontario, S Canada
191 P16 **Christian, Point** *headland* Pitcairn Island, Pitcairn Islands 25°04′S 130°08′E
38 M11 **Christian River** ≈ Alaska, USA
Christiansand *see* Kristiansand
21 S7 **Christiansburg** Virginia, NE USA 37°07′N 80°26′W
95 G23 **Christiansfeld** Sønderjylland, SW Denmark 55°21′N 09°30′E
Christianshåb *see* Qasigiannguit
39 X14 **Christian Sound** *inlet* Alaska, USA
45 T9 **Christiansted** Saint Croix, S Virgin Islands (US) 17°43′N 64°42′W
Christiansund *see* Kristiansund
25 R13 **Christine** Texas, SW USA 28°47′N 98°30′W
173 U7 **Christmas Island** ◇ *Australian external territory* E Indian Ocean
129 T17 **Christmas Island** *island* E Indian Ocean
Christmas Island *see* Kiritimati
192 M7 **Christmas Ridge** *undersea feature* C Pacific Ocean
30 L16 **Christopher** Illinois, N USA 37°58′N 89°03′W
25 P9 **Christoval** Texas, SW USA 31°09′N 100°30′W
111 F17 **Chrudim** Pardubický Kraj, C Czech Republic 49°58′N 15°49′E
115 K25 **Chrýsi** *island* SE Greece
121 N2 **Chrysochoú, Kólpos** *var.* Khrysokhou Bay. *bay* E Mediterranean Sea
114 I13 **Chrysoúpoli** *var.* Hrisoupoli; *prev.* Khrisoúpolis. Anatolikí Makedonía kai Thráki, NE Greece 40°59′N 24°42′E
111 K16 **Chrzanów** *var.* Chrzanow, *Ger.* Zaumgarten. Śląskie, S Poland 50°10′N 19°21′E
129 Q7 **Chu** *Kaz.* Shū. ≈ Kazakhstan/Kyrgyzstan
42 C5 **Chuacús, Sierra de** ▲▲ W Guatemala
153 S15 **Chuadanga** Khulna, W Bangladesh 23°38′N 88°52′E
Chuan *see* Sichuan
Ch'uan-chou *see* Quanzhou
Chuankou *see* Minhe
39 O11 **Chuathbaluk** Alaska, USA 61°36′N 159°14′W
Chubek *see* Moskva
63 I17 **Chubut** *off.* Provincia de Chubut. ◈ *province* S Argentina
Chubut, Provincia de *see* Chubut
63 I17 **Chubut, Río** ≈ SE Argentina
43 V15 **Chucanti, Cerro** ▲ E Panama 08°48′N 78°27′W
Ch'u-chiang *see* Shaoguan
43 W15 **Chucunaque, Río** ≈ E Panama
Chudin *see* Chudzin
116 M5 **Chudniv** Zhytomyrs'ka Oblast', N Ukraine 50°02′N 28°06′E
124 H13 **Chudovo** Novgorodskaya Oblast', W Russian Federation 59°07′N 31°42′E
Chudskoye Ozero *see* Peipus, Lake
119 J18 **Chudzin** *Rus.* Chudin. Brestskaya Voblasts', SW Belarus 52°44′N 26°59′E
39 Q13 **Chugach Islands** *island group* Alaska, USA
39 S11 **Chugach Mountains** ▲▲ Alaska, USA
164 G12 **Chūgoku-sanchi** ▲▲ Honshū, SW Japan
Chugqênsumdo *see* Jigzhi
Chuguyev *see* Chuhuyiv
117 V5 **Chuhuyiv** *var.* Chuguyev. Kharkivs'ka Oblast', E Ukraine 49°51′N 36°44′E
61 H19 **Chuí** Rio Grande do Sul, S Brazil 33°45′S 53°23′W
Chuí *see* Chuy
145 S15 **Chu-Iliyskiye Gory** *Kaz.* Shū-Ile Taūlary. ▲▲ S Kazakhstan
Chukai *see* Cukai
Chukchi Avtonomnyy Okrug *see* Chukotskiy Avtonomnyy Okrug
Chukchi Peninsula *see* Chukotskiy Poluostrov
197 R6 **Chukchi Plain** *undersea feature* Arctic Ocean
197 R6 **Chukchi Plateau** *undersea feature* Arctic Ocean
197 R4 **Chukchi Sea** *Rus.* Chukotskoye More. *sea* Arctic Ocean
125 N14 **Chukhloma** Kostromskaya Oblast', NW Russian Federation 58°42′N 42°39′E
Chukotka *see* Chukotskiy Avtonomnyy Okrug
Chukot Range *see* Anadyrskiy Khrebet
123 V6 **Chukotskiy Avtonomnyy Okrug** *var.* Chukchi Avtonomnyy Okrug, Chukotka. ◈ *autonomous district* NE Russian Federation
123 W5 **Chukotskiy, Mys** *headland* NE Russian Federation 64°15′N 173°03′W
123 V5 **Chukotskiy Poluostrov** *Eng.* Chukchi Peninsula. *peninsula* NE Russian Federation
Chukotskoye More *see* Chukchi Sea
Chukurkak *see* Chuqurqoq
Chulakkurgan *see* Sholakkorgan
35 U17 **Chula Vista** California, W USA 32°38′N 117°04′W
123 Q12 **Chul'man** Respublika Sakha (Yakutiya), NE Russian Federation 56°50′N 124°47′E
56 B9 **Chulucanas** Piura, NW Peru 05°08′S 80°10′W
122 J12 **Chulym** ≈ C Russian Federation
152 K6 **Chumar** Jammu and Kashmir, N India 32°38′N 78°36′E
114 K9 **Chumerna** ▲ C Bulgaria 42°45′N 25°58′E
123 R12 **Chumikan** Khabarovskiy Kray, E Russian Federation 54°41′N 135°12′E
167 Q9 **Chum Phae** Khon Kaen, C Thailand 16°31′N 102°09′E
167 N13 **Chumphon** *var.* Jumporn. Chumphon, SW Thailand 10°30′N 99°11′E
167 O9 **Chumsaeng** *var.* Chum Saeng. Nakhon Sawan, C Thailand 15°52′N 100°18′E
Chum Saeng *see* Chumsaeng
122 L12 **Chuna** ≈ C Russian Federation
161 R9 **Chun'an** *var.* Qiandaohu; *prev.* Pailing. Zhejiang, SE China 29°37′N 118°59′E
161 S13 **Chunan** N Taiwan 24°44′N 120°51′E
Chuncheng *see* Yangchun
163 Y14 **Ch'unch'ŏn** *Jap.* Shunsen. N South Korea 37°52′N 127°48′E
153 S16 **Chunchura** *prev.* Chinsura. West Bengal, NE India 22°54′N 88°20′E
145 W15 **Chundzha** *Kaz.* Shonzhy. Almaty, SE Kazakhstan 43°32′N 79°28′E
Ch'ung-ch'ing/Ch'ung-ching *see* Chongqing
Chung-hua Jen-min Kung-ho-kuo *see* China
163 Y15 **Ch'ungju** *Jap.* Chūshū. C South Korea 36°57′N 127°50′E
Chungking *see* Chongqing
161 T14 **Chungyang Shanmo** *Chin.* Taiwan Shan. ▲▲ C Taiwan
149 V9 **Chūniān** Punjab, E Pakistan 30°57′N 74°01′E
122 L12 **Chunskiy** Irkutskaya Oblast', S Russian Federation 56°10′N 99°15′E
122 M11 **Chunya** ≈ C Russian Federation
124 J6 **Chupa** Respublika Kareliya, NW Russian Federation 66°15′N 33°02′E
125 P8 **Chuprovo** Respublika Komi, NW Russian Federation 64°16′N 46°27′E
57 G17 **Chuquibamba** Arequipa, SW Peru 15°47′S 72°44′W
62 H4 **Chuquicamata** Antofagasta, N Chile 22°20′S 68°56′W
57 L21 **Chuquisaca** ◈ *department* S Bolivia
Chuquisaca *see* Sucre
Chuqung *see* Chindu
146 I8 **Chuqurqoq** *Rus.* Chukurkak. Qoraqalpog'iston Respublikasi, NW Uzbekistan 42°44′N 61°33′E
127 T2 **Chur** Udmurtskaya Respublika, NW Russian Federation 57°06′N 52°57′E
108 I9 **Chur** *Fr.* Coire, *It.* Coira, *Rmsch.* Cuera, Quera; *anc.* Curia Rhaetorum. Graubünden, E Switzerland 46°52′N 09°32′E
123 Q10 **Churapcha** Respublika Sakha (Yakutiya), NE Russian Federation 61°59′N 132°06′E
11 V16 **Churchbridge** Saskatchewan, S Canada 50°55′N 101°53′W
21 O8 **Church Hill** Tennessee, S USA 36°31′N 82°42′W
11 X9 **Churchill** Manitoba, C Canada 58°46′N 94°10′W
11 X10 **Churchill** ≈ Manitoba/Saskatchewan, C Canada
13 P9 **Churchill** ≈ Newfoundland and Labrador, E Canada
11 Y9 **Churchill, Cape** *headland* Manitoba, C Canada 58°42′N 93°12′W
13 P9 **Churchill Falls** Newfoundland and Labrador, E Canada 53°38′N 64°00′W
11 S12 **Churchill Lake** ◎ Saskatchewan, C Canada
19 Q3 **Churchill Lake** ⊠ Maine, NE USA
194 I5 **Churchill Peninsula** *peninsula* Antarctica
22 H8 **Church Point** Louisiana, S USA 30°24′N 92°13′W
29 O3 **Churchs Ferry** North Dakota, N USA 48°15′N 99°12′W
146 G12 **Churchuri** Ahal Welaýaty, C Turkmenistan 38°55′N 59°13′E
21 T5 **Churchville** Virginia, NE USA 38°13′N 79°10′W
152 G10 **Chūru** Rājasthān, NW India 28°18′N 75°00′E
54 J4 **Churuguara** Falcón, N Venezuela 10°52′N 69°35′W
167 U11 **Chư Sê** Gia Lai, C Vietnam 13°38′N 108°06′E
144 J12 **Chushkakul, Gory** ▲▲ SW Kazakhstan
Chūshū *see* Ch'ungju
37 O9 **Chuska Mountains** ▲▲ Arizona/New Mexico, SW USA
Chu, Sông *see* Sam, Nam
125 V14 **Chusovoy** Permskaya Oblast', NW Russian Federation 58°17′N 57°54′E
147 R10 **Chust** Namangan Viloyati, E Uzbekistan 40°58′N 71°12′E
Chust *see* Khust
15 U6 **Chute-aux-Outardes** Québec, SE Canada 49°07′N 68°25′W
117 U5 **Chutove** Poltavs'ka Oblast', C Ukraine 49°45′N 35°11′E
189 O15 **Chuuk** *var.* Truk. ◈ *state* C Micronesia
189 P15 **Chuuk Islands** *var.* Hogoley Islands; *prev.* Truk Islands. *island group* Caroline Islands, C Micronesia
Chuvashia *see* Chuvashskaya Respublika
Chuvashiya *see* Chuvashskaya Respublika
127 P4 **Chuvashskaya Respublika** *var.* Chuvashiya, *Eng.* Chuvashia. ◈ *autonomous republic* W Russian Federation
Chuwārtah *see* Chwārtā
Chu Xian/Chuxian *see* Chuzhou
160 G13 **Chuxiong** Yunnan, SW China 25°02′N 101°32′E
147 V7 **Chuy** Chuyskaya Oblast', N Kyrgyzstan 42°45′N 75°11′E
61 H19 **Chuy** *var.* Chuí. Rocha, E Uruguay 33°42′S 53°27′W
123 O11 **Chuya** Respublika Sakha (Yakutiya), NE Russian Federation 59°30′N 112°26′E
Chüy Oblasty *see* Chuyskaya Oblast'
147 U8 **Chuyskaya Oblast'** *Kir.* Chüy Oblasty. ◈ *province* N Kyrgyzstan
161 Q7 **Chuzhou** *var.* Chuxian, Chu Xian. Anhui, E China 32°20′N 118°18′E
139 U3 **Chwārtā** *var.* Choarta, Chuwārtah. As Sulaymānīyah, NE Iraq 35°11′N 45°59′E
119 N16 **Chyhirynskaye Vodaskhovishcha** ⊠ E Belarus
117 R6 **Chyhyryn** *Rus.* Chigirin. Cherkas'ka Oblast', N Ukraine 49°03′N 32°40′E
119 J18 **Chyrvonaya Slabada** *Rus.* Krasnaya Slabada, Krasnaya Sloboda. Minskaya Voblasts', S Belarus 52°51′N 27°10′E
119 L19 **Chyrvonaye, Vozyera** *Rus.* Ozero Chervonoye. ◎ SE Belarus
117 N11 **Ciadîr-Lunga** *var.* Ceadâr-Lunga, *Rus.* Chadyr-Lunga. S Moldova 46°03′N 28°50′E
169 P16 **Ciamis** *prev.* Tjiamis. Jawa, C Indonesia 07°20′S 108°21′E
107 I16 **Ciampino** ✈ Lazio, C Italy 41°48′N 12°36′E
169 N16 **Cianjur** *prev.* Tjiandjoer. Jawa, C Indonesia 06°50′S 107°09′E
60 H10 **Cianorte** Paraná, S Brazil 23°42′S 52°31′W
Ciarraí *see* Kerry
112 N13 **Ćićevac** Serbia, E Serbia 43°44′N 21°25′E
187 Z14 **Cicia** *prev.* Thithia. *island* Lau Group, E Fiji
105 P4 **Cidacos** ≈ N Spain
136 I10 **Cide** Kastamonu, N Turkey 41°53′N 33°01′E
110 L10 **Ciechanów** *prev.* Zichenau. Mazowieckie, C Poland 52°53′N 20°37′E
110 O10 **Ciechanowiec** *Ger.* Rudelstadt. Podlaskie, E Poland 52°43′N 22°30′E
110 J10 **Ciechocinek** Kujawskio-pomorskie, C Poland 52°53′N 18°49′E
44 F6 **Ciego de Ávila** Ciego de Ávila, C Cuba 21°50′N 78°44′W
54 F4 **Ciénaga** Magdalena, N Colombia 11°01′N 74°15′W
54 E6 **Ciénaga de Oro** Córdoba, NW Colombia 08°54′N 75°39′W
44 E5 **Cienfuegos** Cienfuegos, C Cuba 22°10′N 80°27′W
104 F4 **Cíes, Illas** *island group* NW Spain
111 P16 **Cieszanów** Podkarpackie, SE Poland 50°15′N 23°09′E
111 J17 **Cieszyn** *Cz.* Těšín, *Ger.* Teschen. Śląskie, S Poland 49°45′N 18°35′E
105 R12 **Cieza** Murcia, SE Spain 38°14′N 01°25′W
136 F13 **Çifteler** Eskişehir, W Turkey 39°25′N 31°00′E
105 P7 **Cifuentes** Castilla-La Mancha, C Spain 40°47′N 02°37′W
Čiganak *see* Chiganak
105 P9 **Cigüela** ≈ C Spain
136 H14 **Cihanbeyli** Konya, C Turkey 38°40′N 32°55′E
136 H14 **Cihanbeyli Yaylası** *plateau* C Turkey
104 L10 **Cíjara, Embalse de** ⊠ C Spain
169 P16 **Cikalong** Jawa, S Indonesia 07°46′S 108°13′E
169 N16 **Cikawung** Jawa, S Indonesia 06°49′S 105°29′E
187 Y13 **Cikobia** *prev.* Thikombia. *island* N Fiji
169 P17 **Cilacap** *prev.* Tjilatjap. Jawa, C Indonesia 07°44′S 109°E
173 O16 **Cilaos** C Réunion 21°08′S 55°28′E
137 S11 **Çıldır** Ardahan, NE Turkey 41°08′N 43°08′E
137 S11 **Çıldır Gölü** ◎ NE Turkey
160 M10 **Cili** Hunan, S China 29°24′N 110°59′E
Cilician Gates *see* Gülek Boğazı
121 V10 **Cilicia Trough** *undersea feature* E Mediterranean Sea
Cill Airne *see* Killarney
Cill Chainnigh *see* Kilkenny
Cill Chaoi *see* Kilkee
Cill Choca *see* Kilcock
Cill Dara *see* Kildare
105 N3 **Cilleruelo de Bezana** Castilla-León, N Spain 42°58′N 03°50′W
Cilli *see* Celje
Cill Mhantáin *see* Wicklow
Cill Rois *see* Kilrush
146 C11 **Çilmämmetgum** *Rus.* Peski Chil'mamedkum, *Turkm.* Chilmämetgum. *desert* Balkan Welaýaty, W Turkmenistan
137 Z11 **Çiloy Adası** *Rus.* Ostrov Zhiloy. *island* E Azerbaijan
26 J6 **Cimarron** Kansas, C USA 37°49′N 100°20′W
37 T9 **Cimarron** New Mexico, SW USA 36°30′N 104°55′W
26 M9 **Cimarron River** ≈ Kansas/Oklahoma, C USA
117 N11 **Cimişlia** *Rus.* Chimishliya. S Moldova 46°31′N 28°45′E
Cîmpia Turzii *see* Câmpia Turzii
Cîmpina *see* Câmpina
Cîmpulung *see* Câmpulung
Cîmpulung Moldovenesc *see* Câmpulung Moldovenesc
137 P15 **Çınar** Dıyarbakır, SE Turkey 37°45′N 40°22′E
54 J8 **Cinaruco, Río** ≈ Colombia/Venezuela
Cina Selatan, Laut *see* South China Sea
105 T5 **Cinca** ≈ NE Spain
112 G13 **Cincar** ▲ SW Bosnia and Herzegovina 43°55′N 17°05′E
31 Q15 **Cincinnati** Ohio, N USA 39°04′N 84°34′W
21 M4 **Cincinnati** ✈ Kentucky, S USA 39°03′N 84°39′W
Cinco de Outubro *see* Xá-Muteba
136 C15 **Çine** Aydın, SW Turkey 37°37′N 28°03′E
99 J21 **Ciney** Namur, SE Belgium 50°17′N 05°06′E
104 H6 **Cinfães** Viseu, N Portugal 41°04′N 08°06′W
106 J12 **Cingoli** Marche, C Italy 43°25′N 13°09′E
41 U16 **Cintalapa** *var.* Cintalapa de Figueroa. Chiapas, SE Mexico 16°42′N 93°40′W
Cintalapa de Figueroa *see* Cintalapa
103 X14 **Cinto, Monte** ▲ Corse, France, C Mediterranean Sea 42°22′N 08°57′E
Cintra *see* Sintra
105 Q5 **Cintruénigo** Navarra, N Spain 42°05′N 01°50′W
Cionn tSáile *see* Kinsale
116 K13 **Ciorani** Prahova, SE Romania 44°49′N 26°25′E
113 E14 **Čiovo** *It.* Bua. *island* S Croatia
Cipiúr *see* Kippure
63 I15 **Cipolletti** Río Negro, C Argentina 38°55′S 68°W
120 L7 **Circeo, Capo** *headland* C Italy 41°15′N 13°03′E
39 S8 **Circle** *var.* Circle City. Alaska, USA 65°51′N 144°04′W
33 X8 **Circle** Montana, NW USA 47°25′N 105°32′W
Circle City *see* Circle
31 S14 **Circleville** Ohio, N USA 39°36′N 82°57′W
36 K6 **Circleville** Utah, W USA 38°10′N 112°16′W
169 P16 **Cirebon** *prev.* Tjirebon. Jawa, S Indonesia 06°46′S 108°33′E
97 L21 **Cirencester** *anc.* Corinium, Corinium Dobunorum. C England, United Kingdom 51°44′N 01°59′W
Cirkvenica *see* Crikvenica
107 O20 **Ciro** Calabria, SW Italy 39°22′N 17°02′E
107 O20 **Ciro Marino** Calabria, S Italy 39°21′N 17°07′E

◆ Country
● Country Capital
◇ Dependent Territory
○ Dependent Territory Capital
◈ Administrative Regions
✈ International Airport
▲ Mountain
▲▲ Mountain Range
Ѫ Volcano
≈ River
◎ Lake
⊠ Reservoir

Ciron – Colmenar de Oreja

102 *K14* **Ciron** ≈ SW France
Cirquenizza *see* Crikvenica
25 *R7* **Cisco** Texas, SW USA *32°23′N 98°58′W*
116 *I12* **Cisnădie** *Ger.* Heltau, *Hung.* Nagydisznód. Sibiu, SW Romania *45°42′N 24°09′E*
63 *G18* **Cisnes, Río** ≈ S Chile
25 *T11* **Cistern** Texas, SW USA *29°46′N 97°12′W*
104 *L3* **Cistierna** Castilla-León, N Spain *42°47′N 05°08′W*
Citharista *see* la Ciotat
Citlaltépetl *see* Orizaba, Volcán Pico de
55 *X10* **Citron** NW French Guiana *04°49′N 53°55′W*
23 *N7* **Citronelle** Alabama, S USA *31°05′N 88°13′W*
35 *O7* **Citrus Heights** California, W USA *38°42′N 121°18′W*
106 *H7* **Cittadella** Veneto, NE Italy *45°37′N 11°46′E*
106 *H13* **Città della Pieve** Umbria, C Italy *42°57′N 12°01′E*
106 *H12* **Città di Castello** Umbria, C Italy *43°27′N 12°13′E*
107 *I14* **Cittaducale** Lazio, C Italy *42°24′N 12°55′E*
107 *N22* **Cittanova** Calabria, SW Italy *38°21′N 16°05′E*
Cittavecchia *see* Stari Grad
116 *G10* **Ciucea** *Hung.* Csucsa. Cluj, NW Romania *46°58′N 22°50′E*
116 *M13* **Ciucurova** Tulcea, SE Romania *44°57′N 28°24′E*
Ciudad Acuña *see* Villa Acuña
41 *N15* **Ciudad Altamirano** Guerrero, S Mexico *18°20′N 100°40′W*
42 *G7* **Ciudad Barrios** San Miguel, NE El Salvador *13°46′N 88°13′W*
54 *I7* **Ciudad Bolívar** Barinas, NW Venezuela *08°22′N 70°37′W*
55 *N7* **Ciudad Bolívar** *prev.* Angostura. Bolívar, E Venezuela *08°08′N 63°31′W*
40 *K6* **Ciudad Camargo** Chihuahua, N Mexico *27°42′N 105°10′W*
40 *E8* **Ciudad Constitución** Baja California Sur, NW Mexico *25°09′N 111°43′W*
Ciudad Cortés *see* Cortés
41 *V17* **Ciudad Cuauhtémoc** Chiapas, SE Mexico *15°38′N 91°59′W*
42 *J9* **Ciudad Darío** *var.* Dario. Matagalpa, W Nicaragua *12°42′N 86°10′W*
Ciudad de Dolores Hidalgo *see* Dolores Hidalgo
42 *C6* **Ciudad de Guatemala** *Eng.* Guatemala City; *prev.* Santiago de los Caballeros. ● (Guatemala) Guatemala, C Guatemala *14°38′N 90°29′W*
Ciudad del Carmen *see* Carmen
62 *Q6* **Ciudad del Este** *prev.* Ciudad Presidente Stroessner, Presidente Stroessner, Puerto Presidente Stroessner. Alto Paraná, SE Paraguay *25°34′S 54°40′W*
62 *K5* **Ciudad de Libertador General San Martín** *var.* Libertador General San Martín. Jujuy, C Argentina *23°50′S 64°45′W*
Ciudad Delicias *see* Delicias
41 *O11* **Ciudad del Maíz** San Luis Potosí, C Mexico *22°26′N 99°36′W*
Ciudad de México *see* México
54 *J7* **Ciudad de Nutrias** Barinas, NW Venezuela *08°03′N 69°17′W*
Ciudad de Panama *see* Panamá
55 *P7* **Ciudad Guayana** *prev.* San Tomé de Guayana, Santo Tomé de Guayana. Bolívar, NE Venezuela *08°22′N 62°37′W*
40 *K14* **Ciudad Guzmán** Jalisco, SW Mexico *19°40′N 103°30′W*
41 *V17* **Ciudad Hidalgo** Chiapas, SE Mexico *14°40′N 92°11′W*
41 *N14* **Ciudad Hidalgo** Michoacán, SW Mexico *19°40′N 100°34′W*
40 *J3* **Ciudad Juárez** Chihuahua, N Mexico *31°39′N 105°26′W*
40 *L8* **Ciudad Lerdo** Durango, C Mexico *25°34′N 103°30′W*
41 *Q11* **Ciudad Madero** *var.* Villa Cecilia. Tamaulipas, C Mexico *22°18′N 97°56′W*
41 *P11* **Ciudad Mante** Tamaulipas, C Mexico *22°43′N 99°02′W*
42 *F2* **Ciudad Melchor de Mencos** *var.* Melchor de Mencos. Petén, NE Guatemala *17°03′N 89°12′W*
41 *P8* **Ciudad Miguel Alemán** Tamaulipas, C Mexico *26°20′N 98°56′W*
Ciudad Mutis *see* Bahía Solano
40 *G6* **Ciudad Obregón** Sonora, NW Mexico *27°32′N 109°53′W*
54 *I5* **Ciudad Ojeda** Zulia, NW Venezuela *10°12′N 71°17′W*
55 *P7* **Ciudad Piar** Bolívar, E Venezuela *07°25′N 63°19′W*
Ciudad Porfirio Díaz *see* Piedras Negras
Ciudad Presidente Stroessner *see* Ciudad del Este
Ciudad Quesada *see* Quesada
105 *N11* **Ciudad Real** Castilla-La Mancha, C Spain *38°59′N 03°55′W*
105 *N11* **Ciudad Real** ◈ *province* Castilla-La Mancha, C Spain
104 *J7* **Ciudad-Rodrigo** Castilla-León, N Spain *40°36′N 06°33′W*
42 *A6* **Ciudad Tecún Umán** San Marcos, SW Guatemala *14°40′N 92°06′W*
Ciudad Trujillo *see* Santo Domingo
41 *P12* **Ciudad Valles** San Luis Potosí, C Mexico *21°59′N 99°01′W*
41 *O10* **Ciudad Victoria** Tamaulipas, C Mexico *23°44′N 99°07′W*
42 *C6* **Ciudad Vieja** Suchitepéquez, S Guatemala *14°30′N 90°46′W*
116 *L8* **Ciuhuru** *var.* Reuţel. ≈ N Moldova
105 *Z8* **Ciutadella** *var.* Ciutadella de Menorca. Menorca, Spain, W Mediterranean Sea *40°N 03°50′E*
Ciutadella Ciutadella de Menorca *see* Ciutadella
136 *L11* **Civa Burnu** *headland* N Turkey *41°22′N 36°39′E*
106 *J7* **Cividale del Friuli** Friuli-Venezia Giulia, NE Italy *46°06′N 13°25′E*
107 *H14* **Civita Castellana** Lazio, C Italy *42°16′N 12°24′E*
106 *J12* **Civitanova Marche** Marche, C Italy *43°18′N 13°41′E*
Civitas Altae Ripae *see* Brzeg
Civitas Carnutum *see* Chartres
Civitas Eburovicum *see* Évreux
Civitas Nemetum *see* Speyer
107 *G15* **Civitavecchia** *anc.* Centum Cellae, Trajani Portus. Lazio, C Italy *42°05′N 11°47′E*
102 *L10* **Civray** Vienne, W France *46°10′N 00°18′E*
136 *E14* **Çivril** Denizli, W Turkey *38°18′N 29°43′E*
161 *O5* **Cixian** Hebei, E China *36°19′N 114°22′E*
137 *R16* **Cizre** Şırnak, SE Turkey *37°21′N 42°11′E*
Clacton *see* Clacton-on-Sea
97 *Q21* **Clacton-on-Sea** *var.* Clacton. E England, United Kingdom *51°48′N 01°09′E*
22 *H5* **Claiborne, Lake** ⊠ Louisiana, S USA
102 *L10* **Clain** ≈ W France
11 *Q11* **Claire, Lake** ◎ Alberta, C Canada
25 *O6* **Clairemont** Texas, SW USA *33°09′N 100°45′W*
34 *M3* **Clair Engle Lake** ⊠ California, W USA
18 *B15* **Clairton** Pennsylvania, NE USA *40°17′N 79°52′W*
32 *F7* **Clallam Bay** Washington, NW USA *48°13′N 124°16′W*
103 *P8* **Clamecy** Nièvre, C France *47°28′N 03°30′E*
23 *P5* **Clanton** Alabama, S USA *32°50′N 86°37′W*
61 *D17* **Clara** Entre Ríos, E Argentina *31°50′S 58°48′W*
97 *E18* **Clara** *Ir.* Clóirtheach. C Ireland *53°20′N 07°36′W*
29 *T9* **Clara City** Minnesota, N USA *44°57′N 95°22′W*
61 *D23* **Claraz** Buenos Aires, E Argentina *37°56′S 59°18′W*
Clár Chlainne Mhuiris *see* Claremorris
182 *I8* **Clare** South Australia *33°49′S 138°35′E*
97 *C19* **Clare** *Ir.* An Clár. *cultural region* W Ireland
97 *C18* **Clare** ≈ W Ireland
97 *A16* **Clare Island** *Ir.* Cliara. *island* W Ireland
44 *J12* **Claremont** C Jamaica *18°23′N 77°11′W*
29 *W10* **Claremont** Minnesota, N USA *44°01′N 93°00′W*
19 *N9* **Claremont** New Hampshire, NE USA *43°21′N 72°18′W*
27 *Q9* **Claremore** Oklahoma, C USA *36°20′N 95°37′W*
97 *C17* **Claremorris** *Ir.* Clár Chlainne Mhuiris. W Ireland *53°47′N 09°W*
185 *J16* **Clarence** Canterbury, South Island, New Zealand *42°08′S 173°54′E*
185 *J16* **Clarence** ≈ South Island, New Zealand
65 *F15* **Clarence Bay** *bay* Ascension Island, C Atlantic Ocean
63 *H25* **Clarence, Isla** *island* S Chile
194 *H2* **Clarence Island** *island* South Shetland Islands, Antarctica
183 *V5* **Clarence River** ≈ New South Wales, SE Australia
44 *J5* **Clarence Town** Long Island, C Bahamas *23°03′N 74°57′W*
27 *W12* **Clarendon** Arkansas, C USA *34°41′N 91°19′W*
25 *O3* **Clarendon** Texas, SW USA *34°57′N 100°54′W*
13 *U12* **Clarenville** Newfoundland, Newfoundland and Labrador, SE Canada *48°10′N 54°00′W*
11 *Q17* **Claresholm** Alberta, SW Canada *50°02′N 113°33′W*
29 *T16* **Clarinda** Iowa, C USA *40°44′N 95°02′W*
55 *N5* **Clarines** Anzoátegui, NE Venezuela *09°56′N 65°11′W*
29 *V12* **Clarion** Iowa, C USA *42°43′N 93°43′W*
18 *C13* **Clarion** Pennsylvania, NE USA *41°11′N 79°21′W*
193 *O6* **Clarion Fracture Zone** *tectonic feature* NE Pacific Ocean
18 *D13* **Clarion River** ≈ Pennsylvania, NE USA
29 *Q9* **Clark** South Dakota, N USA *44°50′N 97°44′W*
36 *K11* **Clarkdale** Arizona, SW USA *34°46′N 112°03′W*
15 *W4* **Clarke City** Québec, SE Canada *50°09′N 66°36′W*
183 *Q15* **Clarke Island** *island* Furneaux Group, Tasmania, SE Australia
181 *X6* **Clarke Range** ▲▲ Queensland, E Australia
23 *T2* **Clarkesville** Georgia, SE USA *34°36′N 83°31′W*
29 *S9* **Clarkfield** Minnesota, N USA *44°48′N 95°49′W*
33 *N7* **Clark Fork** Idaho, NW USA *48°06′N 116°10′W*
33 *N8* **Clark Fork** ≈ Idaho/Montana, NW USA
21 *P13* **Clark Hill Lake** *var.* J.Storm Thurmond Reservoir. ⊠ Georgia/South Carolina, SE USA
39 *Q12* **Clark, Lake** ◎ Alaska, USA
35 *W12* **Clark Mountain** ▲ California, W USA *35°30′N 115°34′W*
37 *S3* **Clark Peak** ▲ Colorado, C USA *40°36′N 105°57′W*
14 *D14* **Clark, Point** *headland* Ontario, S Canada *44°04′N 81°45′W*
21 *S3* **Clarksburg** West Virginia, NE USA *39°16′N 80°22′W*
22 *K2* **Clarksdale** Mississippi, S USA *34°12′N 90°34′W*
33 *U12* **Clarks Fork Yellowstone River** ≈ Montana/Wyoming, NW USA
29 *R14* **Clarkson** Nebraska, C USA *41°42′N 97°07′W*
39 *O13* **Clarks Point** Alaska, USA *58°50′N 158°33′W*
18 *I13* **Clarks Summit** Pennsylvania, NE USA *41°29′N 75°42′W*
32 *M10* **Clarkston** Washington, NW USA *46°25′N 117°02′W*
44 *J12* **Clark's Town** C Jamaica *18°25′N 77°32′W*
27 *T10* **Clarksville** Arkansas, C USA *35°29′N 93°29′W*
31 *P13* **Clarksville** Indiana, N USA *40°01′N 85°54′W*
20 *I8* **Clarksville** Tennessee, S USA *36°32′N 87°22′W*
25 *W5* **Clarksville** Texas, SW USA *33°37′N 95°04′W*
21 *U8* **Clarksville** Virginia, NE USA *36°36′N 78°36′W*
21 *U11* **Clarkton** North Carolina, SE USA *34°28′N 78°39′W*
61 *C24* **Claromecó** *var.* Balneario Claromecó. Buenos Aires, E Argentina *38°51′S 60°01′W*
25 *N3* **Claude** Texas, SW USA *35°06′N 101°22′W*
Clausentum *see* Southampton
171 *O1* **Claveria** Luzon, N Philippines *18°36′N 121°04′E*
99 *J20* **Clavier** Liège, E Belgium *50°27′N 05°21′E*
23 *W6* **Claxton** Georgia, SE USA *32°09′N 81°54′W*
21 *R4* **Clay** West Virginia, NE USA *38°28′N 81°17′W*
27 *N3* **Clay Center** Kansas, C USA *39°22′N 97°08′W*
29 *P16* **Clay Center** Nebraska, C USA *40°31′N 98°03′W*
21 *Y2* **Claymont** Delaware, NE USA *39°48′N 75°27′W*
36 *M14* **Claypool** Arizona, SW USA *33°24′N 110°50′W*
23 *R6* **Clayton** Alabama, S USA *31°52′N 85°27′W*
23 *T1* **Clayton** Georgia, SE USA *34°52′N 83°24′W*
22 *J5* **Clayton** Louisiana, S USA *31°43′N 91°32′W*
27 *X5* **Clayton** Missouri, C USA *38°39′N 90°21′W*
37 *V9* **Clayton** New Mexico, SW USA *36°27′N 103°12′W*
21 *V9* **Clayton** North Carolina, SE USA *35°39′N 78°27′W*
27 *Q12* **Clayton** Oklahoma, C USA *34°35′N 95°21′W*
182 *I4* **Clayton River** *seasonal river* South Australia
21 *R7* **Claytor Lake** ⊠ Virginia, NE USA
27 *P13* **Clear Boggy Creek** ≈ Oklahoma, C USA
97 *B22* **Clear, Cape** *var.* The Bill of Cape Clear, *Ir.* Ceann Cléire. *headland* SW Ireland *51°25′N 09°31′W*
36 *M12* **Clear Creek** ≈ Arizona, SW USA
39 *S12* **Cleare, Cape** *headland* Montague Island, Alaska, USA *59°46′N 147°54′W*
18 *E13* **Clearfield** Pennsylvania, NE USA *41°02′N 78°27′W*
36 *L2* **Clearfield** Utah, W USA *41°06′N 112°03′W*
25 *Q6* **Clear Fork Brazos River** ≈ Texas, SW USA
31 *T12* **Clear Fork Reservoir** ⊠ Ohio, N USA
11 *N12* **Clear Hills** ▲▲ Alberta, SW Canada
34 *M6* **Clearlake** California, W USA *38°57′N 122°38′W*
29 *V12* **Clear Lake** Iowa, C USA *43°07′N 93°27′W*
29 *R9* **Clear Lake** South Dakota, N USA *44°45′N 96°40′W*
34 *M6* **Clear Lake** ◎ California, W USA
22 *G6* **Clear Lake** ⊠ Louisiana, S USA
35 *P1* **Clear Lake Reservoir** ⊠ California, W USA
11 *N16* **Clearwater** British Columbia, SW Canada *51°38′N 120°02′W*
23 *U12* **Clearwater** Florida, SE USA *27°58′N 82°46′W*
11 *R12* **Clearwater** ≈ Alberta/Saskatchewan, C Canada
27 *W7* **Clearwater Lake** ⊠ Missouri, C USA
33 *N10* **Clearwater Mountains** ▲▲ Idaho, NW USA
33 *N10* **Clearwater River** ≈ Idaho, NW USA
29 *S4* **Clearwater River** ≈ Minnesota, N USA
25 *T7* **Cleburne** Texas, SW USA *32°21′N 97°24′W*
32 *I9* **Cle Elum** Washington, NW USA *47°12′N 120°56′W*
97 *O17* **Cleethorpes** E England, United Kingdom *53°34′N 00°02′W*
Cléire, Ceann *see* Clear, Cape
21 *O11* **Clemson** South Carolina, SE USA *34°40′N 82°50′W*
21 *Q4* **Clendenin** West Virginia, NE USA *38°29′N 81°21′W*
26 *M9* **Cleo Springs** Oklahoma, C USA *36°25′N 98°25′W*
Clerk Island *see* Onotoa
181 *X8* **Clermont** Queensland, E Australia *22°47′S 147°41′E*
15 *S8* **Clermont** Québec, SE Canada *47°41′N 70°15′W*
103 *O4* **Clermont** Oise, N France *49°23′N 02°26′E*
29 *X12* **Clermont** Iowa, C USA *43°00′N 91°39′W*
103 *P11* **Clermont-Ferrand** Puy-de-Dôme, C France *45°47′N 03°05′E*
103 *Q15* **Clermont-l'Hérault** Hérault, S France *43°37′N 03°25′E*
99 *M22* **Clervaux** Diekirch, N Luxembourg *50°03′N 06°02′E*
106 *G6* **Cles** Trentino-Alto Adige, N Italy *46°22′N 11°04′E*
182 *H8* **Cleve** South Australia *33°43′S 136°30′E*
Cleve *see* Kleve
23 *T2* **Cleveland** Georgia, SE USA *34°36′N 83°45′W*
22 *K3* **Cleveland** Mississippi, S USA *33°45′N 90°43′W*
31 *T11* **Cleveland** Ohio, N USA *41°30′N 81°42′W*
27 *O9* **Cleveland** Oklahoma, C USA *36°18′N 96°27′W*
20 *L10* **Cleveland** Tennessee, S USA *35°10′N 84°51′W*
25 *W10* **Cleveland** Texas, SW USA *30°19′N 95°06′W*
31 *N7* **Cleveland** Wisconsin, N USA *43°58′N 87°45′W*
31 *O4* **Cleveland Cliffs Basin** ◎ Michigan, N USA
31 *U11* **Cleveland Heights** Ohio, N USA *41°30′N 81°34′W*
33 *P6* **Cleveland, Mount** ▲ Montana, NW USA *48°55′N 113°51′W*
Cleves *see* Kleve
97 *B16* **Clew Bay** *Ir.* Cuan Mó. *inlet* W Ireland
23 *Y14* **Clewiston** Florida, SE USA *26°45′N 80°55′W*
Cliara *see* Clare Island
97 *A17* **Clifden** *Ir.* An Clochán. Galway, W Ireland *53°29′N 10°14′W*
37 *O14* **Clifton** Arizona, SW USA *33°03′N 109°18′W*
18 *K14* **Clifton** New Jersey, NE USA *40°50′N 74°28′W*
25 *S8* **Clifton** Texas, SW USA *31°43′N 97°36′W*
21 *S6* **Clifton Forge** Virginia, NE USA *37°49′N 79°50′W*
182 *I1* **Clifton Hills** South Australia *27°03′S 138°49′E*
11 *S17* **Climax** Saskatchewan, S Canada *49°12′N 108°22′W*
21 *O8* **Clinch River** ≈ Tennessee/Virginia, S USA
25 *P12* **Cline** Texas, SW USA *29°14′N 100°07′W*
21 *N10* **Clingmans Dome** ▲ North Carolina/Tennessee, SE USA *35°33′N 83°30′W*
24 *H8* **Clint** Texas, SW USA *31°35′N 106°13′W*
10 *M16* **Clinton** British Columbia, SW Canada *51°06′N 121°31′W*
14 *E15* **Clinton** Ontario, S Canada *43°36′N 81°33′W*
27 *U10* **Clinton** Arkansas, C USA *35°34′N 92°28′W*
30 *L10* **Clinton** Illinois, N USA *40°09′N 88°57′W*
29 *Z14* **Clinton** Iowa, C USA *41°50′N 90°11′W*
20 *G7* **Clinton** Kentucky, S USA *36°39′N 89°00′W*
22 *J8* **Clinton** Louisiana, S USA *30°52′N 91°01′W*
19 *N11* **Clinton** Massachusetts, NE USA *42°25′N 71°40′W*
31 *R10* **Clinton** Michigan, N USA *42°04′N 83°58′W*
22 *K5* **Clinton** Mississippi, S USA *32°22′N 90°22′W*
27 *S5* **Clinton** Missouri, C USA *38°22′N 93°51′W*
21 *V10* **Clinton** North Carolina, SE USA *35°00′N 78°19′W*
26 *L10* **Clinton** Oklahoma, C USA *35°31′N 98°58′W*
21 *Q12* **Clinton** South Carolina, SE USA *34°28′N 81°52′W*
21 *M9* **Clinton** Tennessee, S USA *36°07′N 84°08′W*
8 *L9* **Clinton-Colden Lake** ◎ Northwest Territories, NW Canada
10 *H5* **Clinton Creek** Yukon Territory, NW Canada *64°24′N 140°35′W*
30 *L13* **Clinton Lake** ⊠ Illinois, N USA
27 *Q4* **Clinton Lake** ⊠ Kansas, N USA
21 *T11* **Clio** South Carolina, SE USA *34°34′N 79°33′W*
193 *O7* **Clipperton Fracture Zone** *tectonic feature* E Pacific Ocean
193 *Q7* **Clipperton Island** ◇ *French dependency of French Polynesia* E Pacific Ocean
46 *K6* **Clipperton Island** *island* E Pacific Ocean
0 *F16* **Clipperton Seamounts** *undersea feature* E Pacific Ocean *08°00′N 111°00′W*
102 *J8* **Clisson** Loire-Atlantique, NW France *47°06′N 01°19′W*
62 *K7* **Clodomira** Santiago del Estero, N Argentina *27°35′S 64°14′W*
Cloich na Coillte *see* Clonakilty
Clóirtheach *see* Clara
97 *C21* **Clonakilty** *Ir.* Cloich na Coillte. SW Ireland *51°37′N 08°54′W*
181 *T6* **Cloncurry** Queensland, C Australia *20°45′S 140°30′E*
97 *F18* **Clondalkin** *Ir.* Cluain Dolcáin. E Ireland *53°19′N 06°24′W*
97 *E16* **Clones** *Ir.* Cluain Eois. N Ireland *54°11′N 07°14′W*
97 *D20* **Clonmel** *Ir.* Cluain Meala. S Ireland *52°21′N 07°42′W*
100 *G11* **Cloppenburg** Niedersachsen, NW Germany *52°51′N 08°03′E*
29 *W6* **Cloquet** Minnesota, N USA *46°43′N 92°27′W*
37 *S14* **Cloudcroft** New Mexico, SW USA *32°57′N 105°44′W*
33 *W12* **Cloud Peak** ▲ Wyoming, C USA *44°22′N 107°10′W*
185 *K14* **Cloudy Bay** *inlet* South Island, New Zealand
21 *R10* **Clover** South Carolina, SE USA *35°06′N 81°13′W*
34 *M6* **Cloverdale** California, W USA *38°49′N 123°03′W*
20 *J5* **Cloverport** Kentucky, S USA *37°50′N 86°37′W*
35 *Q10* **Clovis** California, W USA *36°48′N 119°43′W*
37 *W12* **Clovis** New Mexico, SW USA *34°22′N 103°12′W*
14 *K13* **Cloyne** Ontario, SE Canada *44°48′N 77°09′W*
Cluain Dolcáin *see* Clondalkin
Cluain Eois *see* Clones
Cluainín *see* Manorhamilton
Cluain Meala *see* Clonmel
116 *H10* **Cluj** ◈ *county* NW Romania
Cluj *see* Cluj-Napoca
116 *H10* **Cluj-Napoca** *Ger.* Klausenburg, *Hung.* Kolozsvár; *prev.* Cluj. Cluj, NW Romania *46°47′N 23°36′E*
Clunia *see* Feldkirch
103 *R10* **Cluny** Saône-et-Loire, C France *46°25′N 04°38′E*
103 *T10* **Cluses** Haute-Savoie, E France *46°04′N 06°34′E*
106 *E7* **Clusone** Lombardia, N Italy *45°56′N 10°00′E*
25 *W12* **Clute** Texas, SW USA *29°01′N 95°24′W*
185 *D23* **Clutha** ≈ South Island, New Zealand
97 *J18* **Clwyd** *cultural region* NE Wales, United Kingdom
185 *D22* **Clyde** Otago, South Island, New Zealand *45°12′S 169°21′E*
27 *N3* **Clyde** Kansas, C USA *39°35′N 97°24′W*
29 *P2* **Clyde** North Dakota, N USA *48°44′N 98°51′W*
31 *S11* **Clyde** Ohio, N USA *41°18′N 82°58′W*
25 *Q7* **Clyde** Texas, SW USA *32°24′N 99°29′W*
14 *K13* **Clyde** ≈ Ontario, SE Canada
96 *J13* **Clyde** ≈ W Scotland, United Kingdom
96 *H12* **Clydebank** S Scotland, United Kingdom *55°54′N 04°24′W*
96 *H13* **Clyde, Firth of** *inlet* S Scotland, United Kingdom
33 *S11* **Clyde Park** Montana, NW USA *45°56′N 110°39′W*
35 *W16* **Coachella** California, W USA *33°38′N 116°10′W*
35 *W16* **Coachella Canal** *canal* California, W USA
40 *I9* **Coacoyole** Durango, C Mexico *24°30′N 106°33′W*
25 *N7* **Coahoma** Texas, SW USA *32°18′N 101°18′W*
10 *K8* **Coal** ≈ Yukon Territory, NW Canada
40 *L14* **Coalcomán** *var.* Coalcomán de Matamoros. Michoacán, S Mexico *18°49′N 103°13′W*
Coalcomán de Matamoros *see* Coalcomán
39 *T8* **Coal Creek** Alaska, USA *65°21′N 143°08′W*
11 *Q17* **Coaldale** Alberta, SW Canada *49°42′N 112°36′W*
27 *P12* **Coalgate** Oklahoma, C USA *34°33′N 96°15′W*
35 *P11* **Coalinga** California, W USA *36°08′N 120°21′W*
10 *L9* **Coal River** British Columbia, W Canada *59°38′N 126°45′W*
21 *Q6* **Coal River** ≈ West Virginia, NE USA
36 *M2* **Coalville** Utah, W USA *40°56′N 111°22′W*
58 *E13* **Coari** Amazonas, N Brazil *04°08′S 63°07′W*
104 *I7* **Côa, Rio** ≈ N Portugal
59 *D14* **Coari, Rio** ≈ NW Brazil
81 *J20* **Coast** ◈ *province* SE Kenya
Coast *see* Pwani
10 *G12* **Coast Mountains** *Fr.* Chaîne Côtière. ▲▲ Canada/USA
16 *C7* **Coast Ranges** ▲▲ W USA
96 *I12* **Coatbridge** S Scotland, United Kingdom *55°52′N 04°01′W*
42 *B6* **Coatepeque** Quezaltenango, SW Guatemala *14°42′N 91°50′W*
18 *H16* **Coatesville** Pennsylvania, NE USA *39°58′N 75°47′W*
15 *Q13* **Coaticook** Québec, SE Canada *45°07′N 71°46′W*
9 *P9* **Coats Island** *island* Nunavut, NE Canada
195 *O4* **Coats Land** *physical region* Antarctica
41 *T14* **Coatzacoalcos** *var.* Quetzalcoalco; *prev.* Puerto México. Veracruz-Llave, E Mexico *18°06′N 94°26′W*
41 *S14* **Coatzacoalcos, Río** ≈ SE Mexico
116 *M15* **Cobadin** Constanţa, SW Romania *44°05′N 28°13′E*
14 *H9* **Cobalt** Ontario, S Canada *47°24′N 79°41′W*
42 *D5* **Cobán** Alta Verapaz, C Guatemala *15°28′N 90°20′W*
183 *O6* **Cobar** New South Wales, SE Australia *31°31′S 145°51′E*
18 *F12* **Cobb Hill** ▲ Pennsylvania, NE USA *41°52′N 77°52′W*
0 *D8* **Cobb Seamount** *undersea feature* E Pacific Ocean *47°00′N 131°00′W*
14 *K12* **Cobden** Ontario, SE Canada *45°36′N 76°54′W*
97 *D21* **Cobh** *Ir.* An Cóbh; *prev.* Cove of Cork, Queenstown. SW Ireland *51°51′N 08°17′W*
57 *J14* **Cobija** Pando, NW Bolivia *11°04′S 68°49′W*
Coblence/Coblenz *see* Koblenz
18 *J10* **Cobleskill** New York, NE USA *42°40′N 74°29′W*
14 *I15* **Cobourg** Ontario, SE Canada *43°57′N 78°06′W*
181 *P1* **Cobourg Peninsula** *headland* Northern Territory, N Australia *11°27′S 132°33′E*
183 *O10* **Cobram** Victoria, SE Australia *35°56′S 145°36′E*
82 *N13* **Cóbuè** Niassa, N Mozambique *12°08′S 34°46′E*
101 *K18* **Coburg** Bayern, SE Germany *50°16′N 10°58′E*
19 *Q5* **Coburn Mountain** ▲ Maine, NE USA *45°28′N 70°07′W*
57 *H18* **Cocachacra** Arequipa, SW Peru *17°05′S 71°45′W*
59 *J17* **Cocalinho** Mato Grosso, W Brazil *14°22′S 51°00′W*
Cocanada *see* Kākināda
105 *S11* **Cocentaina** País Valenciano, E Spain *38°44′N 00°27′W*
57 *L18* **Cochabamba** *hist.* Oropeza. Cochabamba, C Bolivia *17°23′S 66°10′W*
57 *K18* **Cochabamba** ◈ *department* C Bolivia
57 *L18* **Cochabamba, Cordillera de** ▲▲ C Bolivia
101 *E18* **Cochem** Rheinland-Pfalz, W Germany *50°09′N 07°09′E*
37 *R6* **Cochetopa Hills** ▲▲ Colorado, C USA
155 *G22* **Cochin** *var.* Kochchi, Kochi. Kerala, SW India *09°56′N 76°15′E* *see also* Kochi
44 *D5* **Cochinos, Bahía de** *Eng.* Bay of Pigs. *bay* SE Cuba
37 *O16* **Cochise Head** ▲ Arizona, SW USA *32°03′N 109°19′W*
23 *U5* **Cochran** Georgia, SE USA *32°23′N 83°21′W*
11 *P16* **Cochrane** Alberta, SW Canada *51°15′N 114°25′W*
12 *G12* **Cochrane** Ontario, S Canada *49°04′N 81°02′W*
63 *G20* **Cochrane** Aisén, S Chile *47°16′S 72°33′W*
11 *U10* **Cochrane** ≈ Manitoba/Saskatchewan, C Canada
Cochrane, Lago *see* Pueyrredón, Lago
Cocibolca *see* Nicaragua, Lago de
Cockade State *see* Maryland
44 *M6* **Cockburn Harbour** South Caicos, S Turks and Caicos Islands *21°28′N 71°30′W*
14 *C11* **Cockburn Island** *island* Ontario, S Canada
44 *J3* **Cockburn Town** San Salvador, E Bahamas *24°01′N 74°31′W*
21 *X2* **Cockeysville** Maryland, NE USA *39°29′N 76°34′W*
181 *N12* **Cocklebiddy** Western Australia *32°02′S 125°54′E*
44 *I12* **Cockpit Country, The** *physical region* W Jamaica
43 *S16* **Coclé** *off.* Provincia de Coclé. ◈ *province* C Panama
43 *S15* **Coclé del Norte** Colón, C Panama *09°04′N 80°32′W*
Coclé, Provincia de *see* Coclé
23 *Y12* **Cocoa** Florida, SE USA *28°23′N 80°44′W*
23 *Y12* **Cocoa Beach** Florida, SE USA *28°19′N 80°36′W*
79 *D17* **Cocobeach** Estuaire, NW Gabon *0°59′N 09°34′E*
44 *G5* **Coco, Cayo** *island* C Cuba
151 *Q19* **Coco Channel** *strait* Andaman Sea/Bay of Bengal
173 *N6* **Coco-de-Mer Seamounts** *undersea feature* W Indian Ocean *0°30′N 56°00′E*
36 *K10* **Coconino Plateau** *plain* Arizona, SW USA
43 *N6* **Coco, Río** *var.* Río Wanki, Segoviao Wangkí. ≈ Honduras/Nicaragua
173 *T7* **Cocos Basin** *undersea feature* E Indian Ocean *05°00′S 94°00′E*
188 *B17* **Cocos Island** *island* S Guam
Cocos Island Ridge *see* Cocos Ridge
129 *S17* **Cocos Islands** *island group* E Indian Ocean
173 *T8* **Cocos (Keeling) Islands** ◇ *Australian external territory* E Indian Ocean
0 *G15* **Cocos Plate** *tectonic feature*
193 *T7* **Cocos Ridge** *var.* Cocos Island Ridge. *undersea feature* E Pacific Ocean *05°30′N 86°00′W*
40 *K13* **Cocula** Jalisco, SW Mexico *20°22′N 103°50′W*
107 *D17* **Coda Cavallo, Capo** *headland* Sardegna, Italy, C Mediterranean Sea *40°49′N 09°43′E*
58 *E13* **Codajás** Amazonas, N Brazil *03°50′S 62°12′W*
Codazzi *see* Agustín Codazzi
19 *Q12* **Cod, Cape** *headland* Massachusetts, NE USA *41°50′N 69°56′W*
185 *B25* **Codfish Island** *island* SW New Zealand
106 *H9* **Codigoro** Emilia-Romagna, N Italy *44°50′N 12°07′E*
13 *P5* **Cod Island** *island* Newfoundland and Labrador, E Canada
116 *J12* **Codlea** *Ger.* Zeiden, *Hung.* Feketehalom. Braşov, C Romania *45°43′N 25°27′E*
58 *M13* **Codó** Maranhão, E Brazil *04°28′S 43°51′W*
106 *E8* **Codogno** Lombardia, N Italy *45°10′N 09°42′E*
116 *M10* **Codrii** *hill range* C Moldova
45 *W9* **Codrington** Barbuda, Antigua and Barbuda *17°43′N 61°49′W*
106 *J7* **Codroipo** Friuli-Venezia Giulia, NE Italy *45°58′N 13°00′E*
28 *M12* **Cody** Nebraska, C USA *42°54′N 101°13′W*
33 *U12* **Cody** Wyoming, C USA *43°31′N 109°04′W*
21 *P7* **Coeburn** Virginia, NE USA *36°56′N 82°27′W*
54 *E10* **Coello** Tolima, W Colombia *04°15′N 74°52′W*
Coemba *see* Cuemba
181 *V2* **Coen** Queensland, NE Australia *14°03′S 143°16′E*
101 *E14* **Coesfeld** Nordrhein-Westfalen, W Germany *51°55′N 07°10′E*
32 *M8* **Coeur d'Alene** Idaho, NW USA *47°40′N 116°46′W*
32 *M8* **Coeur d'Alene Lake** ⊠ Idaho, NW USA
98 *O8* **Coevorden** Drenthe, NE Netherlands *52°39′N 06°45′E*
10 *H6* **Coffee Creek** Yukon Territory, W Canada *62°52′N 139°05′W*
30 *L15* **Coffeen Lake** ⊠ Illinois, N USA
22 *L3* **Coffeeville** Mississippi, S USA *33°58′N 89°40′W*
27 *Q8* **Coffeyville** Kansas, C USA *37°02′N 95°37′W*
182 *G9* **Coffin Bay** South Australia *34°39′S 135°30′E*
182 *F9* **Coffin Bay Peninsula** *peninsula* South Australia
183 *V5* **Coffs Harbour** New South Wales, SE Australia *30°18′S 153°08′E*
105 *R10* **Cofrentes** País Valenciano, E Spain *39°14′N 01°04′W*
117 *N10* **Cogîlnic** *Ukr.* Kohyl'nyk. ≈ Moldova/Ukraine
102 *K11* **Cognac** *anc.* Compniacum. Charente, W France *45°42′N 00°19′W*
106 *B7* **Cogne** Valle d'Aosta, NW Italy *45°37′N 07°27′E*
103 *U16* **Cogolin** Var, SE France *43°15′N 06°30′E*
105 *O7* **Cogolludo** Castilla-La Mancha, C Spain *40°58′N 03°05′W*
Cohalm *see* Rupea
92 *K8* **Čohkarášša** *var.* Cuokkarašša. ▲ N Norway *69°57′N 24°38′E*
Čohkkiras *see* Jukkasjärvi
18 *F11* **Cohocton River** ≈ New York, NE USA
18 *L10* **Cohoes** New York, NE USA *42°46′N 73°42′W*
183 *N10* **Cohuna** Victoria, SE Australia *35°51′S 144°15′E*
43 *P17* **Coiba, Isla de** *island* SW Panama
63 *H23* **Coig, Río** ≈ S Argentina
63 *G19* **Coihaique** *var.* Coyhaique. Aisén, S Chile *45°32′S 72°00′W*
155 *G21* **Coimbatore** Tamil Nādu, S India *11°N 76°57′E*
104 *G8* **Coimbra** *anc.* Conimbria, Conimbriga. Coimbra, W Portugal *40°12′N 08°25′W*
104 *G8* **Coimbra** ◈ *district* N Portugal
104 *L15* **Coín** Andalucía, S Spain *36°40′N 04°45′W*
Coin de Mire *see* Gunner's Quoin
57 *J20* **Coipasa, Laguna** ◎ W Bolivia
57 *J20* **Coipasa, Salar de** *salt lake* W Bolivia
Coira/Coire *see* Chur
Coirib, Loch *see* Corrib, Lough
54 *K6* **Cojedes** *off.* Estado Cojedes. ◈ *state* N Venezuela
Cojedes, Estado *see* Cojedes
42 *F7* **Cojutepeque** Cuscatlán, C El Salvador *13°43′N 88°56′W*
Coka *see* Banbar
33 *S16* **Cokeville** Wyoming, C USA *42°03′N 110°55′W*
182 *M13* **Colac** Victoria, SE Australia *38°22′S 143°38′E*
59 *O20* **Colatina** Espírito Santo, SE Brazil *19°35′S 40°37′W*
27 *O13* **Colbert** Oklahoma, C USA *33°51′N 96°30′W*
100 *L12* **Colbitz-Letzinger Heide** *heathland* N Germany
26 *I3* **Colby** Kansas, C USA *39°24′N 101°04′W*
57 *H17* **Colca, Río** ≈ SW Peru
97 *P21* **Colchester** *hist.* Colneceaste; *anc.* Camulodunum. E England, United Kingdom *51°54′N 00°54′E*
19 *N13* **Colchester** Connecticut, NE USA *41°34′N 72°17′W*
38 *M16* **Cold Bay** Alaska, USA *55°11′N 162°43′W*
11 *R14* **Cold Lake** Alberta, SW Canada *54°26′N 110°16′W*
11 *R13* **Cold Lake** ◎ Alberta/Saskatchewan, S Canada
29 *U8* **Cold Spring** Minnesota, N USA *45°27′N 94°25′W*
25 *W10* **Coldspring** Texas, SW USA *30°34′N 95°10′W*
11 *N17* **Coldstream** British Columbia, SW Canada *50°13′N 119°09′W*
96 *L13* **Coldstream** SE Scotland, United Kingdom *55°39′N 02°19′W*
14 *H13* **Coldwater** Ontario, S Canada *44°43′N 79°36′W*
26 *K7* **Coldwater** Kansas, C USA *37°16′N 99°20′W*
31 *Q10* **Coldwater** Michigan, N USA *41°56′N 85°00′W*
25 *N1* **Coldwater Creek** ≈ Oklahoma/Texas, SW USA
22 *K2* **Coldwater River** ≈ Mississippi, S USA
183 *O9* **Coleambally** New South Wales, SE Australia *34°48′S 145°54′E*
19 *O6* **Colebrook** New Hampshire, NE USA *44°52′N 71°27′W*
27 *T5* **Cole Camp** Missouri, C USA *38°27′N 93°12′W*
39 *T6* **Coleen River** ≈ Alaska, USA
11 *P17* **Coleman** Alberta, SW Canada *49°36′N 114°26′W*
25 *Q8* **Coleman** Texas, SW USA *31°50′N 99°27′W*
Çölemerik *see* Hakkâri
83 *K22* **Colenso** KwaZulu/Natal, E South Africa *28°44′S 29°50′E*
182 *L12* **Coleraine** Victoria, SE Australia *37°39′S 141°42′E*
97 *F14* **Coleraine** *Ir.* Cúil Raithin. N Northern Ireland, United Kingdom *55°08′N 06°40′W*
185 *G18* **Coleridge, Lake** ◎ South Island, New Zealand
83 *H24* **Colesberg** Northern Cape, C South Africa *30°41′S 25°08′E*
22 *H7* **Colfax** Louisiana, S USA *31°31′N 92°42′W*
32 *L9* **Colfax** Washington, NW USA *46°52′N 117°21′W*
30 *J6* **Colfax** Wisconsin, N USA *45°00′N 91°44′W*
63 *I19* **Colhué Huapí, Lago** ◎ S Argentina
45 *Z6* **Colibris, Pointe des** *headland* Grande Terre, E Guadeloupe *16°15′N 61°10′W*
106 *D6* **Colico** Lombardia, N Italy *46°08′N 09°24′E*
99 *E14* **Colijnsplaat** Zeeland, SW Netherlands *51°36′N 03°47′E*
40 *L14* **Colima** Colima, S Mexico *19°13′N 103°46′W*
40 *K14* **Colima** ◈ *state* SW Mexico
40 *L14* **Colima, Nevado de** ◭ C Mexico *19°36′N 103°36′W*
59 *M14* **Colinas** Maranhão, E Brazil *06°02′S 44°15′W*
96 *F10* **Coll** *island* W Scotland, United Kingdom
105 *N7* **Collado Villalba** *var.* Villalba. Madrid, C Spain *40°38′N 04°00′W*
183 *R4* **Collarenebri** New South Wales, SE Australia *29°31′S 148°33′E*
37 *P5* **Collbran** Colorado, C USA *39°14′N 107°57′W*
106 *G12* **Colle di Val d'Elsa** Toscana, C Italy *43°26′N 11°06′E*
39 *R9* **College** Alaska, USA *64°49′N 148°06′W*
32 *K10* **College Place** Washington, NW USA *46°03′N 118°23′W*
25 *U10* **College Station** Texas, SW USA *30°38′N 96°21′W*
183 *P4* **Collerina** New South Wales, SE Australia *29°41′S 146°36′E*
180 *I13* **Collie** Western Australia *33°20′S 116°06′E*
180 *L4* **Collier Bay** *bay* Western Australia
21 *F10* **Collierville** Tennessee, S USA *35°02′N 89°39′W*
106 *F11* **Collina, Passo della** *pass* C Italy
14 *G14* **Collingwood** Ontario, S Canada *44°30′N 80°14′W*
184 *I13* **Collingwood** Tasman, South Island, New Zealand *40°40′S 172°40′E*
22 *L7* **Collins** Mississippi, S USA *31°39′N 89°33′W*
30 *K15* **Collinsville** Illinois, N USA *38°40′N 89°58′W*
27 *P9* **Collinsville** Oklahoma, C USA *36°21′N 95°50′W*
20 *H10* **Collinwood** Tennessee, S USA *35°10′N 87°44′W*
Collipo *see* Leiria
63 *G14* **Collipulli** Araucanía, C Chile *37°55′S 72°30′W*
97 *D16* **Collooney** *Ir.* Cúil Mhuine. NW Ireland *54°11′N 08°29′W*
29 *R10* **Colman** South Dakota, N USA *43°58′N 96°48′W*
103 *U6* **Colmar** *Ger.* Kolmar. Haut-Rhin, NE France *48°05′N 07°21′E*
104 *M15* **Colmenar** Andalucía, S Spain *36°54′N 04°20′W*
Colmenar *see* Colmenar de Oreja
105 *O9* **Colmenar de Oreja** *var.* Colmenar. Madrid, C Spain *40°06′N 03°25′W*

◆ Country
● Country Capital
◇ Dependent Territory
○ Dependent Territory Capital
◈ Administrative Regions
✈ International Airport
▲ Mountain
▲▲ Mountain Range
◭ Volcano
≈ River
◎ Lake
⊠ Reservoir

COLMENAR VIEJO – CORONEL OVIEDO

105 N7 **Colmenar Viejo** Madrid, C Spain 40°39′N 03°46′W
25 X9 **Colmesneil** Texas, SW USA 30°54′N 94°25′W
Cöln see Köln
Colneceaste see Colchester
59 G15 **Colniza** Mato Grosso, W Brazil 09°16′S 59°25′W
Cologne see Köln
42 B6 **Colomba** Quezaltenango, SW Guatemala 14°45′N 91°39′W
Colomb-Béchar see Béchar
54 E11 **Colombia** Huila, C Colombia 03°24′N 74°49′W
54 G10 **Colombia** off. Republic of Colombia. ◆ republic N South America
64 E12 **Colombian Basin** undersea feature SW Caribbean Sea 13°00′N 76°00′W
Colombia, Republic of see Colombia
Colombie-Britannique see British Columbia
15 T6 **Colombier** Québec, SE Canada 48°51′N 68°52′W
155 J25 **Colombo** ● (Sri Lanka) Western Province, W Sri Lanka 06°55′N 79°52′E
155 J25 **Colombo** ✈ Western Province, SW Sri Lanka 06°50′N 79°59′E
29 N11 **Colome** South Dakota, N USA 43°13′N 99°42′W
61 B19 **Colón** Buenos Aires, E Argentina 33°53′S 61°06′W
61 D18 **Colón** Entre Ríos, E Argentina 32°10′S 58°16′W
44 D5 **Colón** Matanzas, C Cuba 22°43′N 80°54′W
43 T14 **Colón** prev. Aspinwall. Colón, C Panama 09°04′N 80°33′W
42 K5 **Colón** ◈ department NE Honduras
43 S15 **Colón** off. Provincia de Colón. ◈ province N Panama
57 A16 **Colón, Archipiélago de** var. Islas de los Galápagos, Eng. Galapagos Islands, Tortoise Islands. island group Ecuador, E Pacific Ocean
44 K5 **Colonel Hill** Crooked Island, SE Bahamas 22°43′N 74°12′W
40 C3 **Colonet** Baja California Norte, NW Mexico 31°00′N 116°1′W
40 B3 **Colonet, Cabo** headland NW Mexico 30°57′N 116°19′W
188 G14 **Colonia** Yap, W Micronesia 09°29′N 138°06′E
61 D19 **Colonia** ◈ department SW Uruguay
Colonia see Kolonia, Micronesia
Colonia see Colonia del Sacramento, Uruguay
Colonia Agrippina see Köln
61 D20 **Colonia del Sacramento** var. Colonia. Colonia, SW Uruguay 34°29′S 57°48′W
62 L8 **Colonia Dora** Santiago del Estero, N Argentina 28°34′S 62°59′W
Colonia Julia Fanestris see Fano
21 W5 **Colonial Beach** Virginia, NE USA 38°15′N 76°57′W
21 V6 **Colonial Heights** Virginia, NE USA 37°15′N 77°24′W
Colón, Provincia de see Colón
193 S7 **Colón Ridge** undersea feature E Pacific Ocean 02°00′N 96°00′W
96 F12 **Colonsay** island W Scotland, United Kingdom
57 K22 **Colorada, Laguna** ◎ SW Bolivia
37 R6 **Colorado** off. State of Colorado, also known as Centennial State, Silver State. ◈ state C USA
63 H22 **Colorado, Cerro** ▲ S Argentina 49°58′S 71°38′W
25 O7 **Colorado City** Texas, SW USA 32°24′N 100°51′W
36 M7 **Colorado Plateau** plateau W USA
61 A24 **Colorado, Río** ≈ E Argentina
43 N12 **Colorado, Río** ≈ NE Costa Rica
Colorado, Río see Colorado River
16 F12 **Colorado River** var. Río Colorado. ≈ Mexico/USA
16 K14 **Colorado River** ≈ Texas, SW USA
35 W15 **Colorado River Aqueduct** aqueduct California, W USA
44 A4 **Colorados, Archipiélago de los** island group NW Cuba
62 J9 **Colorados, Desagües de los** ◎ W Argentina
37 T5 **Colorado Springs** Colorado, C USA 38°50′N 104°47′W
40 L11 **Colotlán** Jalisco, SW Mexico 22°08′N 103°15′W
57 L19 **Colquechaca** Potosí, C Bolivia 18°40′S 66°00′W
23 S7 **Colquitt** Georgia, SE USA 31°10′N 84°43′W
29 R11 **Colton** South Dakota, N USA 43°47′N 96°55′W
32 M10 **Colton** Washington, NW USA 46°34′N 117°10′W
35 P8 **Columbia** California, W USA 38°01′N 120°22′W
30 K16 **Columbia** Illinois, N USA 38°26′N 90°12′W
20 L7 **Columbia** Kentucky, S USA 37°05′N 85°15′W
22 I6 **Columbia** Louisiana, S USA 32°05′N 92°03′W
21 W3 **Columbia** Maryland, NE USA 39°13′N 76°51′W
22 L7 **Columbia** Mississippi, S USA 31°15′N 89°56′W
27 U4 **Columbia** Missouri, C USA 38°56′N 92°19′W
21 Y9 **Columbia** North Carolina, SE USA 35°55′N 76°15′W
18 G16 **Columbia** Pennsylvania, NE USA 40°01′N 76°30′W
21 Q12 **Columbia** state capital South Carolina, SE USA 34°00′N 81°02′W
20 I9 **Columbia** Tennessee, S USA 35°37′N 87°02′W
0 F9 **Columbia** ≈ Canada/USA
32 K9 **Columbia Basin** basin Washington, NW USA
197 Q10 **Columbia, Cape** headland Ellesmere Island, Nunavut, NE Canada
31 Q12 **Columbia City** Indiana, N USA 41°09′N 85°29′W
21 W3 **Columbia, District of** ◈ federal district NE USA
33 P7 **Columbia Falls** Montana, NW USA 48°22′N 114°10′W
11 O15 **Columbia Icefield** ice field Alberta/British Columbia, S Canada
11 O15 **Columbia, Mount** ▲ Alberta/British Columbia, SW Canada 52°07′N 117°30′W
11 N15 **Columbia Mountains** ▲▲ British Columbia, SW Canada
23 P4 **Columbiana** Alabama, S USA 33°10′N 86°36′W
31 V12 **Columbiana** Ohio, N USA 40°53′N 80°41′W
32 M14 **Columbia Plateau** plateau Idaho/Oregon, NW USA
29 P7 **Columbia Road Reservoir** ⊠ South Dakota, N USA
65 K16 **Columbia Seamount** undersea feature C Atlantic Ocean 20°30′S 32°00′W
83 D25 **Columbine, Cape** headland SW South Africa 32°50′S 17°39′E
105 U9 **Columbretes, Islas** island group E Spain
23 R5 **Columbus** Georgia, SE USA 32°29′N 84°58′W
31 P14 **Columbus** Indiana, N USA 39°12′N 85°55′W
27 R7 **Columbus** Kansas, C USA 37°09′N 94°52′W
23 N4 **Columbus** Mississippi, S USA 33°30′N 88°25′W
33 U11 **Columbus** Montana, NW USA 45°38′N 109°15′W
29 Q15 **Columbus** Nebraska, C USA 41°25′N 97°22′W
37 Q16 **Columbus** New Mexico, SW USA 31°49′N 107°38′W
21 P10 **Columbus** North Carolina, SE USA 35°15′N 82°09′W
28 K2 **Columbus** North Dakota, N USA 48°52′N 102°47′W
31 S13 **Columbus** state capital Ohio, N USA 39°58′N 83°W
25 U11 **Columbus** Texas, SW USA 29°42′N 96°35′W
30 L8 **Columbus** Wisconsin, N USA 43°21′N 89°00′W
31 R12 **Columbus Grove** Ohio, N USA 40°55′N 84°03′W
29 Y15 **Columbus Junction** Iowa, C USA 41°16′N 91°21′W
44 J3 **Columbus Point** headland Cat Island, C Bahamas 24°07′N 75°19′W
35 T8 **Columbus Salt Marsh** salt marsh Nevada, W USA
35 N6 **Colusa** California, W USA 39°10′N 122°03′W
32 L7 **Colville** Washington, NW USA 48°33′N 117°54′W
184 M5 **Colville, Cape** headland North Island, New Zealand 36°28′S 175°20′E
184 M5 **Colville Channel** channel North Island, New Zealand
39 P6 **Colville River** ≈ Alaska, USA
97 J18 **Colwyn Bay** N Wales, United Kingdom 53°18′N 03°43′W
106 H9 **Comacchio** var. Commachio; anc. Comactium. Emilia-Romagna, N Italy 44°41′N 12°10′E
106 H9 **Comacchio, Valli di** lagoon Adriatic Sea, N Mediterranean Sea
Comactium see Comacchio
159 N16 **Comai** var. Damxoi. Xizang Zizhiqu, W China 28°29′N 91°25′E
41 V17 **Comalapa** Chiapas, SE Mexico 15°42′N 92°06′W
41 U15 **Comalcalco** Tabasco, SE Mexico 18°16′N 93°05′W
63 H16 **Comallo** Río Negro, SW Argentina 40°58′S 70°13′W
26 M12 **Comanche** Oklahoma, C USA 34°22′N 97°57′W
25 R8 **Comanche** Texas, SW USA 31°55′N 98°36′W
194 H2 **Comandante Ferraz** Brazilian research station Antarctica 61°57′S 58°23′W
62 N6 **Comandante Fontana** Formosa, N Argentina 25°19′S 59°42′W
63 I22 **Comandante Luis Peidra Buena** Santa Cruz, S Argentina 50°04′S 68°55′W
59 O18 **Comandatuba** Bahia, SE Brazil 15°13′S 39°00′W
116 K11 **Comănești** Hung. Kománfalva. Bacău, SW Romania 46°25′N 26°29′E
57 M19 **Comarapa** Santa Cruz, C Bolivia 17°53′S 64°30′W
116 J13 **Comarnic** Prahova, SE Romania 45°18′N 25°37′E
42 H6 **Comayagua** Comayagua, W Honduras 14°30′N 87°39′W
42 H6 **Comayagua** ◈ department W Honduras
42 I6 **Comayagua, Montañas de** ▲▲ C Honduras
21 R15 **Combahee River** ≈ South Carolina, SE USA
62 G10 **Combarbalá** Coquimbo, C Chile 31°15′S 71°03′W
103 S7 **Combeaufontaine** Haute-Saône, E France 47°43′N 05°52′E
97 G15 **Comber** Ir. An Comar. E Northern Ireland, United Kingdom 54°33′N 05°45′W
99 K20 **Comblain-au-Pont** Liège, E Belgium 50°29′N 05°36′E
102 I6 **Combourg** Ille-et-Vilaine, NW France 48°21′N 01°44′W
44 M9 **Comendador** prev. Elías Piña. W Dominican Republic 18°53′N 71°42′W
Comer See see Como, Lago di
25 R11 **Comfort** Texas, SW USA 29°58′N 98°54′W
153 V15 **Comilla** Ben. Kumillā. Chittagong, E Bangladesh 23°28′N 91°10′E
99 B18 **Comines** Hainaut, W Belgium 50°46′N 02°58′E
121 O15 **Comino** Malt. Kemmuna island C Malta
107 D18 **Comino, Capo** headland Sardegna, Italy, C Mediterranean Sea 40°32′N 09°49′E
107 K25 **Comiso** Sicilia, Italy, C Mediterranean Sea 36°57′N 14°37′E
41 V16 **Comitán** var. Comitán de Domínguez. Chiapas, SE Mexico 16°15′N 92°06′W
Comitán de Domínguez see Comitán
Commachio see Comacchio
Commander Islands see Komandorskiye Ostrova
103 O10 **Commentry** Allier, C France 46°18′N 02°46′E
23 T2 **Commerce** Georgia, SE USA 34°12′N 83°27′W
27 R8 **Commerce** Oklahoma, C USA 36°55′N 94°52′W
25 V5 **Commerce** Texas, SW USA 33°16′N 95°52′W
37 T4 **Commerce City** Colorado, C USA 39°45′N 104°54′W
103 S5 **Commercy** Meuse, NE France 48°46′N 05°36′E
55 W9 **Commewijne** var. Commewyne. ◈ district NE Suriname
Commewyne see Commewijne
15 P8 **Commissaires, Lac des** ◎ Québec, SE Canada
64 A12 **Commissioner's Point** headland W Bermuda
9 O7 **Committee Bay** bay Nunavut, N Canada
106 D7 **Como** anc. Comum. Lombardia, N Italy 45°48′N 09°05′E
63 J19 **Comodoro Rivadavia** Chubut, SE Argentina 45°50′S 67°30′W
106 D6 **Como, Lago di** var. Lario, Eng. Lake Como, Ger. Comer See. ◎ N Italy
Como, Lake see Como, Lago di
40 E7 **Comondú** Baja California Sur, NW Mexico 26°01′N 111°50′W
116 F12 **Comorâște** Hung. Komornok. Caraș-Severin, SW Romania 45°13′N 21°34′E
Comores, République Fédérale Islamique des see Comoros
155 G24 **Comorin, Cape** headland SE India 08°00′N 77°10′E
172 M8 **Comoro Basin** undersea feature SW Indian Ocean 14°00′S 44°00′E
172 K14 **Comoro Islands** island group W Indian Ocean
172 H13 **Comoros** off. Federal Islamic Republic of the Comoros, Fr. République Fédérale Islamique des Comores. ◆ republic W Indian Ocean
Comoros, Federal Islamic Republic of the see Comoros
10 L17 **Comox** Vancouver Island, British Columbia, SW Canada 49°40′N 124°55′W
103 O4 **Compiègne** Oise, N France 49°25′N 02°50′E
Complutum see Alcalá de Henares
Compniacum see Cognac
40 K12 **Compostela** Nayarit, C Mexico 21°12′N 104°52′W
Compostella see Santiago
60 L11 **Comprida, Ilha** island S Brazil
117 N11 **Comrat** Rus. Komrat. S Moldova 46°18′N 28°40′E
25 O11 **Comstock** Texas, SW USA 29°39′N 101°10′W
31 P9 **Comstock Park** Michigan, N USA 43°00′N 85°40′W
193 N3 **Comstock Seamount** undersea feature N Pacific Ocean 48°15′N 156°55′W
Comum see Como
159 N17 **Cona** Xizang Zizhiqu, W China 27°59′N 91°54′E
76 H14 **Conakry** ● (Guinea) SW Guinea 09°31′N 13°43′W
76 H14 **Conakry** ✈ SW Guinea 09°37′N 13°32′W
Conamara see Connemara
Conca see Cuenca
25 Q12 **Concan** Texas, SW USA 29°27′N 99°43′W
102 F6 **Concarneau** Finistère, NW France 47°53′N 03°55′W
83 O17 **Conceição** Sofala, C Mozambique 18°47′S 36°18′E
59 K15 **Conceição do Araguaia** Pará, NE Brazil 08°15′S 49°15′W
58 F10 **Conceição do Maú** Roraima, W Brazil 03°35′N 59°52′W
61 D14 **Concepción** var. Concepcion. Corrientes, NE Argentina 28°25′S 57°54′W
62 J8 **Concepción** Tucumán, N Argentina 27°20′S 65°35′W
57 O17 **Concepción** Santa Cruz, E Bolivia 16°15′S 62°08′W
62 G13 **Concepción** Bío Bío, C Chile 36°47′S 73°01′W
54 E14 **Concepción** Putumayo, S Colombia 0°03′N 75°35′W
62 O5 **Concepción** var. Villa Concepción. Concepción, C Paraguay 23°26′S 57°24′W
62 O5 **Concepción** off. Departamento de Concepción. ◈ department E Paraguay
Concepción see La Concepción
Concepción de la Vega see La Vega
41 N9 **Concepción del Oro** Zacatecas, C Mexico 24°38′N 101°25′W
61 D18 **Concepción del Uruguay** Entre Ríos, E Argentina 32°30′S 58°15′W
Concepción, Departamento de see Concepción
42 K11 **Concepción, Volcán** ⛰ SW Nicaragua 11°31′N 85°37′W
44 J4 **Conception Island** island C Bahamas
35 P14 **Conception, Point** headland California, W USA 34°27′N 120°28′W
54 H6 **Concha** Zulia, W Venezuela 09°02′N 71°45′W
60 L9 **Conchas** São Paulo, S Brazil 23°00′S 47°58′W
37 U11 **Conchas Dam** New Mexico, SW USA 35°21′N 104°11′W
37 U10 **Conchas Lake** ⊠ New Mexico, SW USA
102 M5 **Conches-en-Ouche** Eure, N France 49°00′N 01°00′E
37 N12 **Concho** Arizona, SW USA 34°28′N 109°33′W
40 J5 **Conchos, Río** ≈ NW Mexico
41 O8 **Conchos, Río** ≈ C Mexico
108 C8 **Concise** Vaud, W Switzerland 46°52′N 06°40′E
35 N8 **Concord** California, W USA 37°58′N 122°01′W
19 O9 **Concord** state capital New Hampshire, NE USA 43°10′N 71°32′W
21 R10 **Concord** North Carolina, SE USA 35°25′N 80°34′W
61 D17 **Concordia** Entre Ríos, E Argentina 31°25′S 58°W
60 I13 **Concórdia** Santa Catarina, S Brazil 27°14′S 52°01′W
54 D9 **Concordia** Antioquia, W Colombia 06°03′N 75°57′W
40 J10 **Concordia** Sinaloa, C Mexico 23°18′N 106°02′W
57 I19 **Concordia** Tacna, SW Peru 18°12′S 70°19′W
27 N3 **Concordia** Kansas, C USA 39°35′N 97°39′W
27 S4 **Concordia** Missouri, C USA 38°58′N 93°34′W
167 S7 **Con Cuông** Nghệ An, N Vietnam 19°02′N 104°54′E
167 T15 **Côn Đao** var. Con Son. island S Vietnam
Condate see Rennes, Ille-et-Vilaine, France
Condate see St-Claude, Jura, France
Condate see Montereau-Faut-Yonne, Seine-St-Denis, France
29 P8 **Conde** South Dakota, N USA 45°08′N 98°07′W
42 J8 **Condega** Estelí, NW Nicaragua 13°19′N 86°26′W
103 P2 **Condé-sur-l'Escaut** Nord, N France 50°27′N 03°36′E
102 K5 **Condé-sur-Noireau** Calvados, N France 48°52′N 00°31′W
Condivincum see Nantes
183 P8 **Condobolin** New South Wales, SE Australia 33°04′S 147°08′E
102 L15 **Condom** Gers, S France 43°56′N 00°23′E
32 J11 **Condon** Oregon, NW USA 45°15′N 120°10′W
54 D9 **Condoto** Chocó, W Colombia 05°06′N 76°37′W
23 P7 **Conecuh River** ≈ Alabama/Florida, SE USA
106 H7 **Conegliano** Veneto, NE Italy 45°53′N 12°18′E
61 C19 **Conesa** Buenos Aires, E Argentina 33°36′S 60°21′W
14 F15 **Conestogo** ≈ Ontario, S Canada
Confluentes see Koblenz
102 L10 **Confolens** Charente, W France 46°00′N 00°40′E
36 J4 **Confusion Range** ▲▲ Utah, W USA
62 N6 **Confuso, Río** ≈ C Paraguay
21 R12 **Congaree River** ≈ South Carolina, SE USA
Công Hoa Xa Hôi Chu Nghia Viêt Nam see Vietnam
160 K12 **Congjiang** var. Bingmei. Guizhou, S China 25°48′N 108°55′E
79 G18 **Congo** off. Republic of the Congo, Fr. Moyen-Congo; prev. Middle Congo. ◆ republic C Africa
79 K19 **Congo** off. Democratic Republic of Congo; prev. Zaire, Belgian Congo, Congo (Kinshasa). ◆ republic C Africa
67 T11 **Congo** var. Kongo, Fr. Zaire. ≈ C Africa
Congo see Zaire (province) Angola
68 G12 **Congo Basin** drainage basin W Dem. Rep. Congo
67 Q11 **Congo Canyon** var. Congo Seavalley, Congo Submarine Canyon. undersea feature E Atlantic Ocean 06°00′S 11°50′E
Congo Cone see Congo Fan
Congo/Congo (Kinshasa) see Congo (Democratic Republic of)
65 P15 **Congo Fan** var. Congo Cone. undersea feature E Atlantic Ocean 06°00′S 09°00′E
Congo Seavalley see Congo Canyon
Congo Submarine Canyon see Congo Canyon
Coni see Cuneo
63 H18 **Cónico, Cerro** ▲ SW Argentina 43°12′S 71°42′W
Conimbria/Conimbriga see Coimbra
Conjeeveram see Kānchipuram
11 R13 **Conklin** Alberta, C Canada 55°36′N 111°06′W
24 M1 **Conlen** Texas, SW USA 36°16′N 102°10′W
Con, Loch see Conn, Lough
Connacht see Connaught
97 B17 **Connaught** var. Connacht, Ir. Chonnacht, Cúige. cultural region W Ireland
31 V10 **Conneaut** Ohio, N USA 41°56′N 80°32′W
18 L13 **Connecticut** off. State of Connecticut, also known as Blue Law State, Constitution State, Land of Steady Habits, Nutmeg State. ◈ state NE USA
19 N8 **Connecticut** ≈ Canada/USA
19 O6 **Connecticut Lakes** lakes New Hampshire, NE USA
32 K9 **Connell** Washington, NW USA 46°39′N 118°51′W
97 B17 **Connemara** Ir. Conamara. physical region W Ireland
31 Q14 **Connersville** Indiana, N USA 39°38′N 85°15′W
97 B16 **Conn, Lough** Ir. Loch Con. ◎ W Ireland
35 X6 **Connors Pass** pass Nevada, W USA
181 X7 **Connors Range** ▲▲ Queensland, E Australia
56 E7 **Cononaco, Río** ≈ E Ecuador
29 W13 **Conrad** Iowa, C USA 42°13′N 92°52′W
33 R7 **Conrad** Montana, NW USA 48°10′N 111°58′W
25 W10 **Conroe** Texas, SW USA 30°19′N 95°28′W
25 V10 **Conroe, Lake** ⊠ Texas, SW USA
61 C17 **Conscripto Bernardi** Entre Ríos, E Argentina 31°03′S 59°05′W
59 M20 **Conselheiro Lafaiete** Minas Gerais, SE Brazil 20°40′S 43°48′W
Consentia see Cosenza
97 L14 **Consett** N England, United Kingdom 54°50′N 01°53′W
44 B5 **Consolación del Sur** Pinar del Río, W Cuba 22°32′N 83°32′W
Con Son see Côn Đao
11 R15 **Consort** Alberta, SW Canada 51°58′N 110°44′W
Constance see Konstanz
108 I6 **Constance, Lake** Ger. Bodensee. ◎ C Europe
104 G9 **Constância** Santarém, C Portugal 39°29′N 08°22′W
117 N14 **Constanța** var. Küstendje, Eng. Constanza, Ger. Konstanza, Turk. Küstence. Constanța, SE Romania 44°09′N 28°37′E
116 L14 **Constanța** ◈ county SE Romania
Constantia see Coutances
Constantia see Konstanz
104 K13 **Constantina** Andalucía, S Spain 37°54′N 05°36′W
74 L5 **Constantine** var. Qacentina, Ar. Qoussantîna. NE Algeria 36°23′N 06°44′E
39 O14 **Constantine, Cape** headland Alaska, USA 58°23′N 158°53′W
Constantinople see İstanbul
Constantiola see Oltenița
Constanz see Konstanz
Constanza see Constanța
62 G13 **Constitución** Maule, C Chile 35°20′S 72°28′W
61 D17 **Constitución** Salto, N Uruguay 31°05′S 57°51′W
Constitution State see Connecticut
105 N10 **Consuegra** Castilla-La Mancha, C Spain 39°28′N 03°36′W
181 X9 **Consuelo Peak** ▲ Queensland, E Australia 24°45′S 148°01′E
56 E11 **Contamana** Loreto, N Peru 07°19′S 75°04′W
Contrasto, Colle del see Contrasto, Portella del
107 K23 **Contrasto, Portella del** var. Colle del Contrasto. pass Sicilia, Italy, C Mediterranean Sea
54 G8 **Contratación** Santander, C Colombia 06°18′N 73°27′W
102 M8 **Contres** Loir-et-Cher, C France 47°24′N 01°30′E
107 O17 **Conversano** Puglia, SE Italy 40°58′N 17°07′E
27 U11 **Conway** Arkansas, C USA 35°05′N 92°27′W
19 O8 **Conway** New Hampshire, NE USA 43°58′N 71°05′W
21 U13 **Conway** South Carolina, SE USA 33°51′N 79°04′W
25 N2 **Conway** Texas, SW USA 35°10′N 101°23′W
27 U11 **Conway, Lake** ⊠ Arkansas, C USA
27 N7 **Conway Springs** Kansas, C USA 37°23′N 97°38′W
97 J18 **Conwy** N Wales, United Kingdom 53°17′N 03°51′W
23 T3 **Conyers** Georgia, SE USA 33°40′N 84°01′W
Coo see Kos
182 F4 **Coober Pedy** South Australia 29°01′S 134°47′E
181 P2 **Cooinda** Northern Territory, N Australia 12°54′S 132°31′E
182 B6 **Cook** South Australia 30°37′S 130°26′E
29 W4 **Cook** Minnesota, N USA 47°51′N 92°41′W
191 N6 **Cook, Baie de** bay Moorea, W French Polynesia
10 J16 **Cook, Cape** headland Vancouver Island, British Columbia, SW Canada 50°04′N 127°52′W
37 Q15 **Cookes Peak** ▲ New Mexico, SW USA 32°32′N 107°43′W
20 L8 **Cookeville** Tennessee, S USA 36°10′N 85°30′W
175 P9 **Cook Fracture Zone** tectonic feature S Pacific Ocean
Cook, Grand Récif de see Cook, Récif de
39 Q12 **Cook Inlet** inlet Alaska, USA
191 X2 **Cook Island** island Line Islands, E Kiribati
190 J14 **Cook Islands** ◇ territory in free association with New Zealand S Pacific Ocean
Cook, Mount see Aoraki
187 O15 **Cook, Récif de** var. Grand Récif de Cook. reef S New Caledonia
14 G14 **Cookstown** Ontario, S Canada 44°12′N 79°39′W
97 F15 **Cookstown** Ir. An Chorr Chríochach. C Northern Ireland, United Kingdom 54°39′N 06°45′W
185 K14 **Cook Strait** var. Raukawa. strait New Zealand
181 W3 **Cooktown** Queensland, NE Australia 15°28′S 145°15′E
183 P6 **Coolabah** New South Wales, SE Australia 31°03′S 146°42′E
182 J11 **Coola Coola Swamp** wetland South Australia
183 S7 **Coolah** New South Wales, SE Australia 31°49′S 149°43′E
183 P9 **Coolamon** New South Wales, SE Australia 34°49′S 147°13′E
183 T4 **Coolatai** New South Wales, SE Australia 29°16′S 150°45′E
180 K12 **Coolgardie** Western Australia 31°01′S 121°12′E
36 L14 **Coolidge** Arizona, SW USA 32°58′N 111°29′W
25 U8 **Coolidge** Texas, SW USA 31°45′N 96°39′W
183 Q11 **Cooma** New South Wales, SE Australia 36°16′S 149°09′E
Coomassie see Kumasi
183 R6 **Coonabarabran** New South Wales, SE Australia 31°19′S 149°18′E
182 J10 **Coonalpyn** South Australia 35°43′S 139°50′E
183 R6 **Coonamble** New South Wales, SE Australia 30°56′S 148°22′E
Coondapoor see Kundāpura
155 G21 **Coonoor** Tamil Nādu, SE India 11°21′N 76°46′E
29 U14 **Coon Rapids** Iowa, C USA 41°52′N 94°40′W
29 V8 **Coon Rapids** Minnesota, N USA 45°12′N 93°18′W
25 V5 **Cooper** Texas, SW USA 33°23′N 95°42′W
181 U9 **Cooper Creek** var. Barcoo, Cooper's Creek. seasonal river Queensland/South Australia
39 R12 **Cooper Landing** Alaska, USA 60°27′N 149°59′W
21 T14 **Cooper River** ≈ South Carolina, SE USA
Cooper's Creek see Cooper Creek
44 H1 **Coopers Town** Great Abaco, N Bahamas 26°46′N 77°27′W
18 J10 **Cooperstown** New York, NE USA 42°43′N 74°56′W
29 P4 **Cooperstown** North Dakota, N USA 47°26′N 98°07′W
31 P9 **Coopersville** Michigan, N USA 43°03′N 85°55′W
182 D7 **Coorabie** South Australia 31°57′S 132°18′E
23 Q3 **Coosa River** ≈ Alabama/Georgia, S USA
32 E14 **Coos Bay** Oregon, NW USA 43°22′N 124°13′W
183 Q9 **Cootamundra** New South Wales, SE Australia 34°41′S 148°03′E
97 E16 **Cootehill** Ir. Muinchille. N Ireland 54°04′N 07°05′W
Čop see Chop
57 J17 **Copacabana** La Paz, W Bolivia 16°11′S 69°02′W
63 H14 **Copahué, Volcán** ⛰ C Chile 37°56′S 71°04′W
41 U16 **Copainalá** Chiapas, SE Mexico 17°04′N 93°13′W
32 F8 **Copalis Beach** Washington, NW USA 47°05′N 124°11′W
42 F6 **Copán** ◈ department W Honduras
Copán see Copán Ruinas
25 T14 **Copano Bay** bay NW Gulf of Mexico
42 F6 **Copán Ruinas** var. Copán. Copán, W Honduras 14°52′N 89°10′W
Copenhagen see København
107 Q19 **Copertino** Puglia, SE Italy 40°16′N 18°03′E
62 H7 **Copiapó** Atacama, N Chile 27°17′S 70°25′W
62 G8 **Copiapó, Bahía** bay N Chile
62 G7 **Copiapó, Río** ≈ N Chile
114 M12 **Çöpköy** Edirne, NW Turkey 41°14′N 26°51′E
182 I5 **Copley** South Australia 30°36′S 138°26′E
106 H9 **Copparo** Emilia-Romagna, C Italy 44°53′N 11°53′E
55 V10 **Coppename Rivier** var. Koppename. ≈ C Suriname
25 S9 **Copperas Cove** Texas, SW USA 31°07′N 97°54′W
82 J13 **Copperbelt** ◈ province C Zambia
39 S11 **Copper Center** Alaska, USA 61°57′N 145°21′W
8 K8 **Coppermine** ≈ Northwest Territories/Nunavut, N Canada
Coppermine see Kugluktuk
39 T11 **Copper River** ≈ Alaska, USA
Copper State see Arizona
116 I11 **Copșa Mică** Ger. Kleinkopisch, Hung. Kiskapus. Sibiu, C Romania 46°06′N 24°15′E
158 J14 **Coqên** Xizang Zizhiqu, W China 31°13′N 85°12′E
Coquilhatville see Mbandaka
32 E14 **Coquille** Oregon, NW USA 43°11′N 124°12′W
62 G9 **Coquimbo** Coquimbo, N Chile 30°S 71°18′W
62 G9 **Coquimbo** off. Región de Coquimbo. ◈ region C Chile
Coquimbo, Región de see Coquimbo
116 I15 **Corabia** Olt, S Romania 43°46′N 24°31′E
57 F17 **Coracora** Ayacucho, SW Peru 15°03′S 73°45′W
Cora Droma Rúisc see Carrick-on-Shannon
44 K9 **Corail** SW Haiti 18°34′N 73°53′W
183 V4 **Coraki** New South Wales, SE Australia 29°01′S 153°15′E
180 G8 **Coral Bay** Western Australia 23°02′S 113°51′E
23 Y16 **Coral Gables** Florida, SE USA 25°43′N 80°16′W
9 P8 **Coral Harbour** Southampton Island, Nunavut, NE Canada 64°10′N 83°15′W
192 I9 **Coral Sea** sea SW Pacific Ocean
174 M7 **Coral Sea Basin** undersea feature N Coral Sea
192 H9 **Coral Sea Islands** ◇ Australian external territory SW Pacific Ocean
182 M12 **Corangamite, Lake** ◎ Victoria, SE Australia
Corantijn Rivier see Courantyne River
18 B14 **Coraopolis** Pennsylvania, NE USA 40°28′N 80°08′W
107 N17 **Corato** Puglia, SE Italy 41°09′N 16°25′E
103 O17 **Corbières** ▲▲ S France
103 P8 **Corbigny** Nièvre, C France 47°15′N 03°42′E
21 N7 **Corbin** Kentucky, S USA 36°57′N 84°06′W
104 L14 **Corbones** ≈ SW Spain
Corcaigh see Cork
35 R11 **Corcoran** California, W USA 36°06′N 119°33′W
47 T14 **Corcovado, Golfo** gulf S Chile
63 G18 **Corcovado, Volcán** ⛰ S Chile 43°13′S 72°45′W
104 F3 **Corcubión** Galicia, NW Spain 42°56′N 09°12′W
Corcyra Nigra see Korčula
60 Q9 **Cordeiro** Rio de Janeiro, SE Brazil 22°01′S 42°20′W
23 T6 **Cordele** Georgia, SE USA 31°55′N 83°49′W
26 L11 **Cordell** Oklahoma, C USA 35°17′N 98°59′W
103 N14 **Cordes** Tarn, S France 44°03′N 01°57′E
62 O6 **Cordillera** off. Departamento de la Cordillera. ◈ department C Paraguay
Cordillera see Cacaguatique, Cordillera
Cordillera, Departamento de la see Cordillera
182 K1 **Cordillo Downs** South Australia 26°44′S 140°37′E
62 K10 **Córdoba** Córdoba, C Argentina 31°25′S 64°11′W
41 R14 **Córdoba** Veracruz-Llave, E Mexico 18°55′N 96°55′W
104 M13 **Córdoba** var. Cordoba, Eng. Cordova; anc. Corduba. Andalucía, SW Spain 37°53′N 04°46′W
62 K11 **Córdoba** off. Provincia de Córdoba. ◈ province C Argentina
54 D7 **Córdoba** off. Departamento de Córdoba. ◈ province NW Colombia
104 L13 **Córdoba** ◈ province Andalucía, S Spain
Córdoba, Departamento de see Córdoba
Córdoba, Provincia de see Córdoba
62 K10 **Córdoba, Sierras de** ▲▲ C Argentina
23 O3 **Cordova** Alabama, S USA 33°45′N 87°10′W
39 S12 **Cordova** Alaska, USA 60°32′N 145°45′W
Cordova/Cordoba see Córdoba
Corduba see Córdoba
Corentyne River see Courantyne River
Corfu see Kérkyra
104 J9 **Coria** Extremadura, W Spain 39°59′N 06°32′W
104 J14 **Coria del Río** Andalucía, S Spain 37°18′N 06°04′W
183 S8 **Coricudgy, Mount** ▲ New South Wales, SE Australia 32°49′S 150°28′E
107 N20 **Corigliano Calabro** Calabria, SW Italy 39°36′N 16°32′E
Corinium/Corinium Dobunorum see Cirencester
23 N1 **Corinth** Mississippi, S USA 34°56′N 88°29′W
Corinth see Kórinthos
Corinth Canal see Dióryga Korinthou
Corinth, Gulf of/Corinthiacus Sinus see Korinthiakós Kólpos
Corinthus see Kórinthos
42 I9 **Corinto** Chinandega, NW Nicaragua 12°29′N 87°14′W
97 C21 **Cork** Ir. Corcaigh. S Ireland 51°54′N 08°06′W
97 C21 **Cork** Ir. Corcaigh. cultural region SW Ireland
97 C21 **Cork** ✈ Cork, SW Ireland 51°52′N 08°25′W
97 D21 **Cork Harbour** Ir. Cuan Chorcaí. inlet SW Ireland
107 I23 **Corleone** Sicilia, Italy, C Mediterranean Sea 37°49′N 13°18′E
114 N13 **Çorlu** Tekirdağ, NW Turkey 41°11′N 27°48′E
114 N12 **Çorlu Çayı** ≈ NW Turkey
Cormaiore see Courmayeur
11 V13 **Cormorant** Manitoba, C Canada 54°12′N 100°33′W
23 T2 **Cornelia** Georgia, SE USA 34°30′N 83°31′W
60 J10 **Cornélio Procópio** Paraná, S Brazil 23°07′S 50°40′W
55 V9 **Corneliskondre** Sipaliwini, N Suriname 05°21′N 56°10′W
30 J5 **Cornell** Wisconsin, N USA 45°09′N 91°10′W
13 S12 **Corner Brook** Newfoundland, Newfoundland and Labrador, E Canada 48°58′N 57°58′W
Corner Rise Seamounts see Corner Seamounts
64 I9 **Corner Seamounts** var. Corner Rise Seamounts. undersea feature NW Atlantic Ocean 35°30′N 51°30′W
116 M9 **Cornești** Rus. Korneshty. C Moldova 47°23′N 28°00′E
Corneto see Tarquinia
Cornhusker State see Nebraska
27 X8 **Corning** Arkansas, C USA 36°26′N 90°35′W
35 N5 **Corning** California, W USA 39°54′N 122°12′W
29 U15 **Corning** Iowa, C USA 40°58′N 94°46′W
18 G11 **Corning** New York, NE USA 42°08′N 77°03′W
Corn Islands see Maíz, Islas del
107 J14 **Corno Grande** ▲ C Italy 42°26′N 13°29′E
15 N13 **Cornwall** Ontario, SE Canada 45°02′N 74°45′W
97 H25 **Cornwall** cultural region SW England, United Kingdom
97 G25 **Cornwall, Cape** headland SW England, United Kingdom 50°11′N 05°39′W
54 J4 **Coro** prev. Santa Ana de Coro. Falcón, NW Venezuela 11°27′N 69°41′W
57 J18 **Corocoro** La Paz, W Bolivia 17°10′S 68°28′W
57 K17 **Coroico** La Paz, W Bolivia 16°09′S 67°45′W
184 M5 **Coromandel** Waikato, North Island, New Zealand 36°47′S 175°30′E
155 K20 **Coromandel Coast** coast E India
184 M5 **Coromandel Peninsula** peninsula North Island, New Zealand
184 M6 **Coromandel Range** ▲▲ North Island, New Zealand
171 N5 **Coron** Busuanga Island, W Philippines 12°02′N 120°10′E
35 T15 **Corona** California, W USA 33°52′N 117°34′W
37 T12 **Corona** New Mexico, SW USA 34°15′N 105°36′W
11 U17 **Coronach** Saskatchewan, S Canada 49°07′N 105°33′W
35 U17 **Coronado** California, W USA 32°41′N 117°10′W
43 N15 **Coronado, Bahía de** bay S Costa Rica
11 R15 **Coronation** Alberta, SW Canada 52°06′N 111°25′W
8 K7 **Coronation Gulf** gulf Nunavut, N Canada
194 I1 **Coronation Island** island Antarctica
39 X14 **Coronation Island** island Alexander Archipelago, Alaska, USA
61 B18 **Coronda** Santa Fe, C Argentina 31°58′S 60°56′W
63 F14 **Coronel** Bío Bío, C Chile 37°01′S 73°08′W
61 D20 **Coronel Brandsen** var. Brandsen. Buenos Aires, E Argentina 35°08′S 58°15′W
62 K4 **Coronel Cornejo** Salta, N Argentina 22°46′S 63°49′W
61 B24 **Coronel Dorrego** Buenos Aires, E Argentina 38°38′S 61°15′W
62 P6 **Coronel Oviedo** Caaguazú, SE Paraguay 25°24′S 56°30′W

◆ Country
● Country Capital
◇ Dependent Territory
○ Dependent Territory Capital
◈ Administrative Regions
✈ International Airport
▲ Mountain
▲▲ Mountain Range
⛰ Volcano
≈ River
◎ Lake
⊠ Reservoir

61 B23 **Coronel Pringles** Buenos Aires, E Argentina 37°56′S 61°25′W

61 B23 **Coronel Suárez** Buenos Aires, E Argentina 37°30′S 61°52′W

61 E22 **Coronel Vidal** Buenos Aires, E Argentina 37°28′S 57°45′W

55 V9 **Coronie** ◈ district NW Suriname

57 G17 **Coropuna, Nevado** ▲ S Peru 15°31′S 72°31′W

Çorovoda see Çorovodë

113 L22 **Çorovodë** var. Çorovoda. Berat, S Albania 40°29′N 20°15′E

183 P11 **Corowa** New South Wales, SE Australia 36°01′S 146°22′E

42 G1 **Corozal** Corozal, N Belize 18°23′N 88°23′W

54 E6 **Corozal** Sucre, NW Colombia 09°18′N 75°19′W

42 G1 **Corozal** ◈ district N Belize

25 T14 **Corpus Christi** Texas, SW USA 27°48′N 97°24′W

25 T14 **Corpus Christi Bay** inlet Texas, SW USA

25 R14 **Corpus Christi, Lake** ⊠ Texas, SW USA

63 F16 **Corral** Los Lagos, C Chile 39°55′S 73°30′W

105 O9 **Corral de Almaguer** Castilla-La Mancha, C Spain 39°45′N 03°10′W

104 K6 **Corrales** Castilla-León, N Spain 41°22′N 05°44′W

37 R11 **Corrales** New Mexico, SW USA 35°11′N 106°37′W

Corrán Tuathail see Carrauntoohil

106 F9 **Correggio** Emilia-Romagna, C Italy 44°47′N 10°46′E

59 M16 **Corrente** Piauí, E Brazil 10°29′S 45°11′W

59 I19 **Correntes, Rio** ≈ SW Brazil

103 N12 **Corrèze** ◈ department C France

97 C17 **Corrib, Lough** Ir. Loch Coirib. ◎ W Ireland

61 C14 **Corrientes** Corrientes, NE Argentina 27°29′S 58°42′W

61 D15 **Corrientes** off. Provincia de Corrientes. ◈ province NE Argentina

44 A5 **Corrientes, Cabo** headland W Cuba 21°48′N 84°30′W

40 I13 **Corrientes, Cabo** headland SW Mexico 20°25′N 105°42′W

Corrientes, Provincia de see Corrientes

61 C16 **Corrientes, Río** ≈ NE Argentina

56 E8 **Corrientes, Río** ≈ Ecuador/Peru

25 W9 **Corrigan** Texas, SW USA 31°00′N 94°49′W

55 U9 **Corriverton** E Guyana 05°55′N 57°09′W

Corriza see Korçë

183 Q11 **Corryong** Victoria, SE Australia 36°14′S 147°54′E

103 F2 **Corse** Eng. Corsica. ◈ region France, C Mediterranean Sea

101 X13 **Corse** Eng. Corsica. island France, C Mediterranean Sea

103 Y12 **Corse, Cap** headland Corse, France, C Mediterranean Sea 43°01′N 09°25′E

103 X15 **Corse-du-Sud** ◈ department Corse, France, C Mediterranean Sea

29 P11 **Corsica** South Dakota, N USA 43°25′N 98°24′W

Corsica see Corse

25 U7 **Corsicana** Texas, SW USA 32°05′N 96°27′W

103 Y15 **Corte** Corse, France, C Mediterranean Sea 42°18′N 09°08′E

63 G16 **Corte Alto** Los Lagos, S Chile 40°58′S 73°04′W

104 I13 **Cortegana** Andalucía, S Spain 37°55′N 06°49′W

43 N15 **Cortés** var. Ciudad Cortés. Puntarenas, SE Costa Rica 08°59′N 83°32′W

42 G5 **Cortés** ◈ department NW Honduras

37 P8 **Cortez** Colorado, C USA 37°22′N 108°36′W

Cortez, Sea of see California, Golfo de

106 H6 **Cortina d'Ampezzo** Veneto, NE Italy 46°33′N 12°09′E

18 H11 **Cortland** New York, NE USA 42°34′N 76°09′W

31 V11 **Cortland** Ohio, N USA 41°19′N 80°43′W

106 H12 **Cortona** Toscana, C Italy 43°15′N 12°01′E

76 H13 **Corubal, Rio** ≈ E Guinea-Bissau

104 G10 **Coruche** Santarém, C Portugal 38°58′N 08°31′W

Çoruh see Rize

137 R11 **Çoruh Nehri** Geor. Chorokh, Rus. Chorokhi. ≈ Georgia/Turkey

136 K12 **Çorum** var. Chorum. Çorum, N Turkey 40°31′N 34°57′E

136 J12 **Çorum** var. Chorum. ◈ province N Turkey

59 H19 **Corumbá** Mato Grosso do Sul, S Brazil 19°S 57°35′W

14 D16 **Corunna** Ontario, S Canada 42°49′N 82°25′W

Corunna see A Coruña

32 F12 **Corvallis** Oregon, NW USA 44°35′N 122°36′W

64 M1 **Corvo** var. Ilha do Corvo. island Azores, Portugal, NE Atlantic Ocean

Corvo, Ilha do see Corvo

31 O16 **Corydon** Indiana, N USA 38°12′N 86°07′W

29 V16 **Corydon** Iowa, C USA 40°45′N 93°19′W

Cos see Kos

40 I9 **Cosalá** Sinaloa, C Mexico 24°25′N 106°39′W

41 R15 **Cosamaloapan** var. Cosamaloapan de Carpio. Veracruz-Llave, E Mexico 18°23′N 95°50′W

Cosamaloapan de Carpio see Cosamaloapan

107 N21 **Cosenza** anc. Consentia. Calabria, SW Italy 39°17′N 16°15′E

31 T13 **Coshocton** Ohio, N USA 40°16′N 81°53′W

42 H9 **Cosigüina, Punta** headland NW Nicaragua 12°53′N 87°42′W

29 T9 **Cosmos** Minnesota, N USA 44°56′N 94°42′W

103 O8 **Cosne-Cours-sur-Loire** Nièvre, C France 47°25′N 02°56′E

108 B9 **Cossonay** Vaud, W Switzerland 46°37′N 06°28′E

Cossyra see Pantelleria

47 R4 **Costa, Cordillera de la** var. Cordillera de Venezuela. ▲▲ N Venezuela

42 K13 **Costa Rica** off. Republic of Costa Rica. ◆ republic Central America

Costa Rica, Republic of see Costa Rica

43 N15 **Costeña, Fila** ▲▲ S Costa Rica

Costermansville see Bukavu

116 I14 **Costeşti** Argeş, SW Romania 44°40′N 24°53′E

37 S8 **Costilla** New Mexico, SW USA 36°58′N 105°31′W

35 O7 **Cosumnes River** ≈ California, W USA

101 O16 **Coswig** Sachsen, E Germany 51°07′N 13°36′E

101 M14 **Coswig** Sachsen-Anhalt, E Germany 51°53′N 12°26′E

Cosyra see Pantelleria

171 Q7 **Cotabato** Mindanao, S Philippines 07°13′N 124°12′E

56 C5 **Cotacachi** ▲ N Ecuador 0°29′N 78°17′W

57 L21 **Cotagaita** Potosí, S Bolivia 20°47′S 65°40′W

103 V15 **Côte d'Azur** prev. Nice. ✈ (Nice) Alpes-Maritimes, SE France 43°40′N 07°12′E

Côte d'Ivoire see Ivory Coast

Côte d'Ivoire, République de la see Ivory Coast

103 R7 **Côte d'Or** ◈ department E France

103 R8 **Côte d'Or** cultural region C France

Côte Française des Somalis see Djibouti

102 J4 **Cotentin** peninsula N France

102 G6 **Côtes d'Armor** prev. Côtes-du-Nord. ◈ department NW France

Côtes-du-Nord see Côtes d'Armor

Cöthen see Köthen

Côtière, Chaîne see Coast Mountains

40 M13 **Cotija** var. Cotija de la Paz. Michoacán, SW Mexico 19°49′N 102°39′W

Cotija de la Paz see Cotija

77 R16 **Cotonou** var. Kotonu. S Benin 06°24′N 02°26′E

77 R16 **Cotonou** ✈ S Benin 06°31′N 02°18′E

56 B6 **Cotopaxi** prev. León. ◈ province C Ecuador

56 C6 **Cotopaxi** ⛰ N Ecuador 0°42′S 78°24′W

Cotrone see Crotone

97 L21 **Cotswold Hills** var. Cotswolds. hill range S England, United Kingdom

Cotswolds see Cotswold Hills

32 F13 **Cottage Grove** Oregon, NW USA 43°48′N 123°03′W

21 S14 **Cottageville** South Carolina, SE USA 32°55′N 80°28′W

101 P14 **Cottbus** Lus. Chośebuz; prev. Kottbus. Brandenburg, E Germany 51°42′N 14°22′E

27 U9 **Cotter** Arkansas, C USA 36°16′N 92°30′W

106 A9 **Cottian Alps** Fr. Alpes Cottiennes, It. Alpi Cozie. ▲▲ France/Italy

Cottiennes, Alpes see Cottian Alps

Cotton State, The see Alabama

22 G4 **Cotton Valley** Louisiana, S USA 32°49′N 93°25′W

36 L12 **Cottonwood** Arizona, SW USA 34°43′N 112°00′W

32 M10 **Cottonwood** Idaho, NW USA 46°01′N 116°20′W

29 S9 **Cottonwood** Minnesota, N USA 44°37′N 95°41′W

25 Q7 **Cottonwood** Texas, SW USA 32°12′N 99°14′W

27 O5 **Cottonwood Falls** Kansas, C USA 38°21′N 96°33′W

36 L3 **Cottonwood Heights** Utah, W USA 40°37′N 111°48′W

29 S10 **Cottonwood River** ≈ Minnesota, N USA

45 O9 **Cotuí** C Dominican Republic 19°04′N 70°10′W

25 Q13 **Cotulla** Texas, SW USA 28°27′N 99°15′W

Cotyora see Ordu

102 I11 **Coubre, Pointe de la** headland W France 45°39′N 01°23′W

18 E12 **Coudersport** Pennsylvania, NE USA 41°45′N 78°00′W

15 S9 **Coudres, Île aux** island Québec, SE Canada

182 G11 **Couedic, Cape de** headland South Australia 36°04′S 136°43′E

Couentrey see Coventry

102 I6 **Couesnon** ≈ NW France

32 H10 **Cougar** Washington, NW USA 46°03′N 122°18′W

102 L10 **Couhé** Vienne, W France 46°18′N 00°10′E

32 K8 **Coulee City** Washington, NW USA 47°36′N 119°18′W

195 Q15 **Coulman Island** island Antarctica

103 P5 **Coulommiers** Seine-et-Marne, N France 48°49′N 03°04′E

14 K11 **Coulonge** ≈ Québec, SE Canada

14 K11 **Coulonge Est** ≈ Québec, SE Canada

35 Q9 **Coulterville** California, W USA 37°41′N 120°10′W

38 M9 **Council** Alaska, USA 64°54′N 163°40′W

32 M12 **Council** Idaho, NW USA 44°45′N 116°26′W

29 S15 **Council Bluffs** Iowa, C USA 41°16′N 95°52′W

27 O5 **Council Grove** Kansas, C USA 38°41′N 96°29′W

27 O5 **Council Grove Lake** ⊠ Kansas, C USA

32 G7 **Coupeville** Washington, NW USA 48°13′N 122°41′W

55 U12 **Courantyne River** var. Corantijn Rivier, Corentyne River. ≈ Guyana/Suriname

99 G21 **Courcelles** Hainaut, S Belgium 50°28′N 04°23′E

108 C7 **Courgenay** Jura, NW Switzerland 47°24′N 07°09′E

126 B2 **Courland Lagoon** Ger. Kurisches Haff, Rus. Kurskiy Zaliv. lagoon Lithuania/Russian Federation

118 B12 **Courland Spit** Lith. Kuršių Nerija, Rus. Kurshskaya Kosa. spit Lithuania/Russian Federation

106 A6 **Courmayeur** prev. Cormaiore. Valle d'Aosta, NW Italy 45°48′N 07°00′E

108 D7 **Courroux** Jura, NW Switzerland 47°22′N 07°23′E

10 K17 **Courtenay** Vancouver Island, British Columbia, SW Canada 49°40′N 124°58′W

21 W7 **Courtland** Virginia, NE USA 36°44′N 77°06′W

25 V10 **Courtney** Texas, SW USA 30°16′N 96°04′W

30 J4 **Court Oreilles, Lac** ◎ Wisconsin, N USA

Courtrai see Kortrijk

99 H19 **Court-Saint-Étienne** Walloon Brabant, C Belgium 50°38′N 04°34′E

22 G6 **Coushatta** Louisiana, S USA 32°00′N 93°20′W

172 I16 **Cousin** island Inner Islands, NE Seychelles

172 I16 **Cousine** island Inner Islands, NE Seychelles

102 J4 **Coutances** anc. Constantia. Manche, N France 49°04′N 01°27′W

102 K12 **Coutras** Gironde, SW France 45°01′N 00°07′W

45 U14 **Couva** Trinidad, Trinidad and Tobago 10°25′N 61°27′W

108 B8 **Couvet** Neuchâtel, W Switzerland 46°57′N 06°41′E

99 H22 **Couvin** Namur, S Belgium 50°03′N 04°30′E

116 K12 **Covasna** Ger. Kowasna, Hung. Kovászna. Covasna, E Romania 45°51′N 26°11′E

116 J11 **Covasna** ◈ county E Romania

14 E12 **Cove Island** island Ontario, S Canada

34 M5 **Covelo** California, W USA 39°46′N 123°16′W

97 M20 **Coventry** anc. Couentrey. C England, United Kingdom 52°25′N 01°30′W

Cove of Cork see Cobh

21 U5 **Covesville** Virginia, NE USA 37°52′N 78°41′W

104 I8 **Covilhã** Castelo Branco, E Portugal 40°17′N 07°30′W

23 T3 **Covington** Georgia, SE USA 33°34′N 83°52′W

31 N13 **Covington** Indiana, N USA 40°08′N 87°23′W

20 M3 **Covington** Kentucky, S USA 39°04′N 84°30′W

22 K8 **Covington** Louisiana, S USA 30°28′N 90°06′W

31 Q13 **Covington** Ohio, N USA 40°07′N 84°21′W

20 F9 **Covington** Tennessee, S USA 35°32′N 89°40′W

21 S6 **Covington** Virginia, NE USA 37°48′N 80°01′W

183 Q8 **Cowal, Lake** seasonal lake New South Wales, SE Australia

11 W15 **Cowan** Manitoba, S Canada 51°59′N 100°36′W

18 F12 **Cowanesque River** ≈ New York/Pennsylvania, NE USA

180 L12 **Cowan, Lake** ◎ Western Australia

15 P13 **Cowansville** Québec, SE Canada 45°13′N 72°44′W

182 H8 **Cowell** South Australia 33°43′S 136°53′E

97 M23 **Cowes** S England, United Kingdom 50°45′N 01°19′W

27 Q10 **Coweta** Oklahoma, C USA 35°57′N 95°39′W

0 D6 **Cowie Seamount** undersea feature NE Pacific Ocean 54°15′N 149°30′W

32 G10 **Cowlitz River** ≈ Washington, NW USA

21 Q11 **Cowpens** South Carolina, SE USA 35°01′N 81°48′W

183 R8 **Cowra** New South Wales, SE Australia 33°50′S 148°45′E

Coxen Hole see Roatán

59 I19 **Coxim** Mato Grosso do Sul, S Brazil 18°28′S 54°45′W

59 I19 **Coxim, Rio** ≈ SW Brazil

Coxin Hole see Roatán

153 V17 **Cox's Bazar** Chittagong, S Bangladesh 21°25′N 91°59′E

76 H14 **Coyah** Conakry, W Guinea 09°45′N 13°26′W

40 K5 **Coyame** Chihuahua, N Mexico 29°29′N 105°07′W

24 L9 **Coyanosa Draw** ≈ Texas, SW USA

Coyhaique see Coihaique

42 C7 **Coyolate, Río** ≈ S Guatemala

Coyote State, The see South Dakota

40 I10 **Coyotitán** Sinaloa, C Mexico 23°48′N 106°37′W

41 N15 **Coyuca** var. Coyuca de Catalán. Guerrero, S Mexico 18°21′N 100°39′W

41 O16 **Coyuca** var. Coyuca de Benítez. Guerrero, S Mexico 17°01′N 100°08′W

Coyuca de Benítez/Coyuca de Catalán see Coyuca

29 N15 **Cozad** Nebraska, C USA 40°52′N 99°58′W

158 L14 **Cozhê** Xizang Zizhiqu, W China 31°53′N 87°51′E

Cozie, Alpi see Cottian Alps

Cozmeni see Kitsman'

40 E3 **Cozón, Cerro** ▲ NW Mexico 31°16′N 112°29′W

41 Z12 **Cozumel** Quintana Roo, E Mexico 20°29′N 86°54′W

41 Z12 **Cozumel, Isla** island SE Mexico

32 K8 **Crab Creek** ≈ Washington, NW USA

44 H12 **Crab Pond Point** headland W Jamaica 18°07′N 78°01′W

Cracovia/Cracow see Kraków

83 I25 **Cradock** Eastern Cape, S South Africa 32°07′S 25°38′E

39 Y14 **Craig** Prince of Wales Island, Alaska, USA 55°29′N 133°04′W

37 Q3 **Craig** Colorado, C USA 40°31′N 107°33′W

97 F15 **Craigavon** C Northern Ireland, United Kingdom 54°28′N 06°25′W

21 T5 **Craigsville** Virginia, NE USA 38°07′N 79°21′W

101 J21 **Crailsheim** Baden-Württemberg, S Germany 49°07′N 10°04′E

116 H14 **Craiova** Dolj, SW Romania 44°19′N 23°49′E

10 K12 **Cranberry Junction** British Columbia, SW Canada 55°35′N 128°21′W

18 J8 **Cranberry Lake** ◎ New York, NE USA

11 V13 **Cranberry Portage** Manitoba, C Canada 54°34′N 101°22′W

11 P17 **Cranbrook** British Columbia, SW Canada 49°29′N 115°48′W

30 M5 **Crandon** Wisconsin, N USA 45°34′N 88°54′W

32 K14 **Crane** Oregon, NW USA 43°24′N 118°35′W

24 M9 **Crane** Texas, SW USA 31°23′N 102°22′W

Crane see The Crane

25 S8 **Cranfills Gap** Texas, SW USA 31°46′N 97°49′W

19 O12 **Cranston** Rhode Island, NE USA 41°46′N 71°26′W

Cranz see Zelenogradsk

59 L15 **Craolândia** Tocantins, E Brazil 07°17′S 47°23′W

102 J7 **Craon** Mayenne, NW France 47°52′N 00°57′W

195 V16 **Crary, Cape** headland Antarctica

Crasna see Kraszna

32 G14 **Crater Lake** ◎ Oregon, NW USA

33 P14 **Craters of the Moon National Monument** national park Idaho, NW USA

59 O14 **Crateús** Ceará, E Brazil 05°10′S 40°39′W

Crathis see Crati

107 N20 **Crati** anc. Crathis. ≈ S Italy

11 U16 **Craven** Saskatchewan, S Canada 50°44′N 104°50′W

54 I8 **Cravo Norte** Arauca, E Colombia 06°17′N 70°15′W

28 J12 **Crawford** Nebraska, C USA 42°40′N 103°24′W

25 T8 **Crawford** Texas, SW USA 31°31′N 97°26′W

11 O17 **Crawford Bay** British Columbia, SW Canada 49°39′N 116°44′W

65 M19 **Crawford Seamount** undersea feature S Atlantic Ocean 40°30′S 10°00′W

31 O13 **Crawfordsville** Indiana, N USA 40°02′N 86°52′W

23 S9 **Crawfordville** Florida, SE USA 30°10′N 84°22′W

97 O23 **Crawley** SE England, United Kingdom 51°07′N 00°12′W

33 S10 **Crazy Mountains** ▲▲ Montana, NW USA

11 T11 **Cree** ≈ Saskatchewan, C Canada

37 R7 **Creede** Colorado, C USA 37°51′N 106°55′W

40 I6 **Creel** Chihuahua, N Mexico 27°45′N 107°36′W

11 S11 **Cree Lake** ◎ Saskatchewan, C Canada

11 V13 **Creighton** Saskatchewan, C Canada 54°46′N 101°54′W

29 Q13 **Creighton** Nebraska, C USA 42°28′N 97°54′W

103 O4 **Creil** Oise, N France 49°16′N 02°29′E

106 E8 **Crema** Lombardia, N Italy 45°22′N 09°40′E

106 E8 **Cremona** Lombardia, N Italy 45°08′N 10°02′E

Creole State see Louisiana

112 M10 **Crepaja** Hung. Cserépalja. Vojvodina, N Serbia 45°02′N 20°36′E

103 O4 **Crépy-en-Valois** Oise, N France 49°13′N 02°54′E

112 B10 **Cres** It. Cherso. Primorje-Gorski Kotar, NW Croatia 44°57′N 14°24′E

112 A11 **Cres** It. Cherso; anc. Crexa. island W Croatia

32 H14 **Crescent** Oregon, NW USA 43°27′N 121°40′W

34 K1 **Crescent City** California, W USA 41°45′N 124°14′W

23 W10 **Crescent City** Florida, SE USA 29°25′N 81°30′W

167 X10 **Crescent Group** island group C Paracel Islands

23 W10 **Crescent Lake** ◎ Florida, SE USA

29 X11 **Cresco** Iowa, C USA 43°22′N 92°06′W

61 B18 **Crespo** Entre Ríos, E Argentina 32°05′S 60°20′W

54 E5 **Crespo** ✈ (Cartagena) Bolívar, NW Colombia 10°27′N 75°31′W

103 R13 **Crest** Drôme, E France 44°45′N 05°00′E

37 R5 **Crested Butte** Colorado, C USA 38°52′N 106°59′W

31 S12 **Crestline** Ohio, N USA 40°47′N 82°44′W

11 O17 **Creston** British Columbia, SW Canada 49°05′N 116°32′W

29 U15 **Creston** Iowa, C USA 41°03′N 94°21′W

33 V16 **Creston** Wyoming, C USA 41°40′N 107°43′W

37 S7 **Crestone Peak** ▲ Colorado, C USA 37°58′N 105°34′W

23 P8 **Crestview** Florida, SE USA 30°44′N 86°34′W

121 R10 **Cretan Trough** undersea feature Aegean Sea, C Mediterranean Sea

29 R16 **Crete** Nebraska, C USA 40°36′N 96°58′W

Crete see Kríti

103 O5 **Créteil** Val-de-Marne, N France 48°47′N 02°28′E

Crete, Sea of/Creticum, Mare see Kritikó Pélagos

105 X4 **Creus, Cap de** headland NE Spain 42°18′N 03°18′E

103 N10 **Creuse** ◈ department C France

102 L9 **Creuse** ≈ C France

103 T4 **Creutzwald** Moselle, NE France 49°13′N 06°41′E

105 S12 **Crevillente** País Valenciano, E Spain 38°15′N 00°48′W

97 L18 **Crewe** C England, United Kingdom 53°05′N 02°27′W

21 V7 **Crewe** Virginia, NE USA 37°10′N 78°07′W

Crexa see Cres

43 Q15 **Cricamola, Río** ≈ NW Panama

61 K14 **Criciúma** Santa Catarina, S Brazil 28°39′S 49°23′W

96 J11 **Crieff** C Scotland, United Kingdom 56°22′N 03°49′W

112 B10 **Crikvenica** It. Cirquenizza; prev. Cirkvenica, Crjkvenica. Primorje-Gorski Kotar, NW Croatia 45°12′N 14°40′E

Crimea/Crimean Oblast see Krym, Avtonomna Respublika

101 M16 **Crimmitschau** var. Krimmitschau. Sachsen, E Germany 50°48′N 12°23′E

116 G11 **Crişcior** Hung. Kristyor. Hunedoara, W Romania 46°09′N 22°54′E

21 Y5 **Crisfield** Maryland, NE USA 37°58′N 75°51′W

31 P3 **Crisp Point** headland Michigan, N USA 46°45′N 85°15′W

59 L19 **Cristalina** Goiás, C Brazil 16°43′S 47°37′W

44 J7 **Cristal, Sierra del** ▲▲ E Cuba

43 T14 **Cristóbal** Colón, C Panama 09°18′N 79°52′W

54 F4 **Cristóbal Colón, Pico** ▲ N Colombia 10°52′N 73°46′W

106 C10 **Cristoforo Colombo** ✈ Liguria, NW Italy

Cristur/Cristuru Săcuiesc see Cristuru Secuiesc

116 I11 **Cristuru Secuiesc** prev. Cristur, Cristuru Săcuiesc, Sitaş Cristuru, Ger. Kreutz, Hung. Székelykeresztúr, Szitás-Keresztúr. Harghita, C Romania 46°17′N 25°02′E

116 F10 **Crişul Alb** var. Weisse Kreisch, Ger. Weisse Körös, Hung. Fehér-Körös. ≈ Hungary/Romania

116 F10 **Crişul Negru** Ger. Schwarze Körös, Hung. Fekete-Körös. ≈ Hungary/Romania

116 G10 **Crişul Repede** var. Schnelle Kreisch, Ger. Schnelle Körös, Hung. Sebes-Körös. ≈ Hungary/Romania

117 N10 **Criuleni** Rus. Kriulyany. C Moldova 47°12′N 29°09′E

Crivadia Vulcanului see Vulcan

Crjkvenica see Crikvenica

113 O17 **Crna Gora** ▲▲ FYR Macedonia/Serbia

Crna Gora see Montenegro

113 O20 **Crna Reka** ≈ S FYR Macedonia

Crni Drim see Black Drin

109 V10 **Črni vrh** ▲ NE Slovenia 46°28′N 15°14′E

109 V13 **Črnomelj** Ger. Tschernembl. SE Slovenia 45°32′N 15°12′E

97 A17 **Croagh Patrick** Ir. Cruach Phádraig. ▲ W Ireland 53°45′N 09°39′W

112 D9 **Croatia** off. Republic of Croatia, Ger. Kroatien, SCr. Hrvatska. ◆ republic SE Europe

Croatia, Republic of see Croatia

Croce, Picco di see Wilde Kreuzspitze

15 P8 **Croche** ≈ Québec, SE Canada

169 V7 **Crocker, Banjaran** var. Crocker Range. ▲▲ East Malaysia

Crocker Range see Crocker, Banjaran

25 V9 **Crockett** Texas, SW USA 31°21′N 95°30′W

67 V14 **Crocodile** var. Krokodil. ≈ N South Africa

Crocodile see Limpopo

20 I7 **Crofton** Kentucky, S USA 37°01′N 87°25′W

29 Q12 **Crofton** Nebraska, C USA 42°43′N 97°30′W

Croia see Krujë

103 R16 **Croisette, Cap** headland SE France 43°12′N 05°21′E

102 G8 **Croisic, Pointe du** headland NW France 47°16′N 02°42′W

103 S13 **Croix Haute, Col de la** pass E France

15 U5 **Croix, Pointe à la** headland Québec, SE Canada 49°16′N 67°46′W

14 F13 **Croker, Cape** headland Ontario, S Canada 44°56′N 80°57′W

181 P1 **Croker Island** island Northern Territory, N Australia

96 I8 **Cromarty** N Scotland, United Kingdom 57°40′N 04°02′W

99 M21 **Crombach** Liège, E Belgium 50°14′N 06°07′E

97 Q18 **Cromer** E England, United Kingdom 52°56′N 01°06′E

185 D22 **Cromwell** Otago, South Island, New Zealand 45°03′S 169°14′E

185 H16 **Cronadun** West Coast, South Island, New Zealand 42°03′S 171°52′E

39 O11 **Crooked Creek** Alaska, USA 61°52′N 158°06′W

44 K5 **Crooked Island** island SE Bahamas

44 J5 **Crooked Island Passage** channel SE Bahamas

32 I13 **Crooked River** ≈ Oregon, NW USA

29 R4 **Crookston** Minnesota, N USA 47°47′N 96°36′W

28 I10 **Crooks Tower** ▲ South Dakota, N USA 44°09′N 103°55′W

31 T14 **Crooksville** Ohio, N USA 39°46′N 82°05′W

183 R9 **Crookwell** New South Wales, SE Australia 34°28′S 149°27′E

14 L14 **Crosby** Ontario, SE Canada 44°39′N 76°13′W

97 K17 **Crosby** var. Great Crosby. NW England, United Kingdom 53°30′N 03°02′W

29 U6 **Crosby** Minnesota, N USA 46°30′N 93°58′W

28 K2 **Crosby** North Dakota, N USA 48°54′N 103°17′W

25 O5 **Crosbyton** Texas, SW USA 33°40′N 101°16′W

77 V16 **Cross** ≈ Cameroon/Nigeria

23 U10 **Cross City** Florida, SE USA 29°37′N 83°08′W

Crossen see Krosno Odrzańskie

27 V14 **Crossett** Arkansas, C USA 33°08′N 91°58′W

97 K15 **Cross Fell** ▲ N England, United Kingdom 54°42′N 02°30′W

11 P16 **Crossfield** Alberta, SW Canada 51°24′N 114°03′W

21 Q12 **Cross Hill** South Carolina, SE USA 34°18′N 81°58′W

19 U6 **Cross Island** island Maine, NE USA

11 X13 **Cross Lake** Manitoba, C Canada 54°38′N 97°35′W

22 F5 **Cross Lake** ⊠ Louisiana, S USA

36 I12 **Crossman Peak** ▲ Arizona, SW USA 34°33′N 114°09′W

25 Q7 **Cross Plains** Texas, SW USA 32°07′N 99°10′W

77 V17 **Cross River** ◈ state SE Nigeria

20 L9 **Crossville** Tennessee, S USA 35°57′N 85°02′W

31 S8 **Croswell** Michigan, N USA 43°16′N 82°37′W

14 K13 **Crotch Lake** ◎ Ontario, SE Canada

Croton/Crotona see Crotone

107 O21 **Crotone** var. Cotrone; anc. Croton, Crotona. Calabria, SW Italy 39°05′N 17°07′E

33 V11 **Crow Agency** Montana, NW USA 45°35′N 107°28′W

183 U7 **Crowdy Head** headland New South Wales, SE Australia 31°52′S 152°45′E

25 Q4 **Crowell** Texas, SW USA 33°59′N 99°45′W

183 O6 **Crowl Creek** seasonal river New South Wales, SE Australia

22 H9 **Crowley** Louisiana, S USA 30°11′N 92°21′W

35 S9 **Crowley, Lake** ⊠ California, W USA

27 X10 **Crowleys Ridge** hill range Arkansas, C USA

31 N11 **Crown Point** Indiana, N USA 41°25′N 87°22′W

37 P10 **Crownpoint** New Mexico, SW USA 35°40′N 108°09′W

33 R10 **Crow Peak** ▲ Montana, NW USA 46°17′N 111°54′W

11 P17 **Crowsnest Pass** pass Alberta/British Columbia, SW Canada

29 T6 **Crow Wing River** ≈ Minnesota, N USA

97 O22 **Croydon** SE England, United Kingdom 51°21′N 00°06′W

Crozer, Mount see Finkol, Mount

173 P11 **Crozet Basin** undersea feature S Indian Ocean 39°00′S 60°00′E

173 O12 **Crozet Islands** island group French Southern and Antarctic Territories

173 N12 **Crozet Plateau** var. Crozet Plateaus. undersea feature SW Indian Ocean 46°00′S 51°00′E

Crozet Plateaus see Crozet Plateau

102 E6 **Crozon** Finistère, NW France 48°14′N 04°31′W

Cruacha Dubha, Na see Macgillycuddy's Reeks

Cruach Phádraig see Croagh Patrick

116 M14 **Crucea** Constanţa, SE Romania 44°30′N 28°18′E

44 E5 **Cruces** Cienfuegos, C Cuba 22°20′N 80°17′W

107 O20 **Crucoli Torretta** Calabria, SW Italy 39°26′N 17°03′E

41 P9 **Cruillas** Tamaulipas, C Mexico 24°43′N 98°26′W

64 K9 **Cruiser Tablemount** undersea feature E Atlantic Ocean 32°00′N 28°00′W

61 G14 **Cruz Alta** Rio Grande do Sul, S Brazil 28°38′S 53°38′W

44 G8 **Cruz, Cabo** headland S Cuba 19°50′N 77°43′W

60 N9 **Cruzeiro** São Paulo, S Brazil 22°33′S 44°59′W

60 H10 **Cruzeiro do Oeste** Paraná, S Brazil 23°45′S 53°03′W

59 A15 **Cruzeiro do Sul** Acre, W Brazil 07°40′S 72°39′W

23 U11 **Crystal Bay** bay Florida, SE USA NE Gulf of Mexico Atlantic Ocean

182 I8 **Crystal Brook** South Australia 33°24′S 138°10′E

11 X17 **Crystal City** Manitoba, S Canada 49°07′N 98°54′W

27 X5 **Crystal City** Missouri, C USA 38°13′N 90°22′W

25 P13 **Crystal City** Texas, SW USA 28°43′N 99°51′W

30 M4 **Crystal Falls** Michigan, N USA 46°06′N 88°20′W

23 Q8 **Crystal Lake** Florida, SE USA 30°26′N 85°41′W

31 O6 **Crystal Lake** ◎ Michigan, N USA

23 V11 **Crystal River** Florida, SE USA 28°54′N 82°35′W

37 Q5 **Crystal River** ≈ Colorado, C USA

22 K6 **Crystal Springs** Mississippi, S USA 31°59′N 90°21′W

Csaca see Čadca

Csakathurn/Csáktornya see Čakovec

Csap see Chop

Csepén see Čepin

Cserépalja see Crepaja

Csermő see Cermei

Csíkszereda see Miercurea-Ciuc

111 L24 **Csongrád** Csongrád, SE Hungary 46°42′N 20°09′E

111 L24 **Csongrád** off. Csongrád Megye. ◈ county SE Hungary

Csongrád Megye see Csongrád

111 H22 **Csorna** Győr-Moson-Sopron, NW Hungary 47°37′N 17°14′E

Csucsa see Ciucea

111 G25 **Csurgó** Somogy, SW Hungary 46°16′N 17°09′E

Csurog see Čurug

54 L5 **Cúa** Miranda, N Venezuela 10°14′N 66°58′W

82 C11 **Cuale** Malanje, NW Angola 08°22′S 16°10′E

67 T12 **Cuando** var. Kwando. ≈ S Africa

83 E15 **Cuando Cubango** var. Kuando-Kubango. ◈ province SE Angola

83 E16 **Cuangar** Cuando Cubango, S Angola 17°34′S 18°39′E

82 D11 **Cuango** Lunda Norte, NE Angola 09°10′S 17°59′E

82 C10 **Cuango** Uíge, NW Angola 06°20′S 16°42′E

82 C10 **Cuango** var. Kwango. ≈ Angola/Dem. Rep. Congo see also Kwango

Cuango see Kwango

Cuan, Loch see Strangford Lough

82 C12 **Cuanza** var. Kwanza. ≈ C Angola

82 B11 **Cuanza Norte** var. Kuanza Norte. ◈ province NE Angola

82 B12 **Cuanza Sul** var. Kuanza Sul. ◈ province NE Angola

61 E16 **Cuareim, Río** var. Río Quaraí. ≈ Brazil/Uruguay see also Quaraí, Rio

Cuareim, Río see Quaraí, Rio

83 D15 **Cuatir** ≈ S Angola

40 M7 **Cuatro Ciénegas** var. Cuatro Ciénegas de Carranza. Coahuila, NE Mexico 27°00′N 102°03′W

Cuatro Ciénegas de Carranza see Cuatro Ciénegas

40 I6 **Cuauhtémoc** Chihuahua, N Mexico 28°22′N 106°52′W

41 P14 **Cuautla** Morelos, S Mexico 18°48′N 98°56′W

104 H12 **Cuba** Beja, S Portugal 38°10′N 07°54′W

27 W6 **Cuba** Missouri, C USA 38°03′N 91°24′W

37 R10 **Cuba** New Mexico, SW USA 36°01′N 106°57′W

44 E6 **Cuba** off. Republic of Cuba. ◆ republic W West Indies

47 O2 **Cuba** island W West Indies

82 B13 **Cubal** Benguela, W Angola 12°58′S 14°16′E

83 C15 **Cubango** var. Kuvango, Port. Vila Artur de Paiva, Vila da Ponte. Huíla, SW Angola 14°27′S 16°18′E

83 D16 **Cubango** var. Kavango, Kavengo, Kubango, Okavango, Okavanggo. ≈ S Africa see also Okavango

Cubango see Okavango

54 H8 **Cubará** Boyacá, N Colombia 07°01′N 72°07′W

Cuba, Republic of see Cuba

136 I12 **Çubuk** Ankara, N Turkey 40°13′N 33°02′E

83 D14 **Cuchi** Cuando Cubango, C Angola 14°40′S 16°58′E

42 C5 **Cuchumatanes, Sierra de los** ▲▲ W Guatemala

Cuculaya, Rio see Kukalaya, Rio

82 E12 **Cucumbi** prev. Trás-os-Montes. Lunda Sul, NE Angola 10°13′S 19°04′E

54 G7 **Cúcuta** var. San José de Cúcuta. Norte de Santander, N Colombia 07°55′N 72°31′W

31 N9 **Cudahy** Wisconsin, N USA 42°54′N 87°51′W

155 J21 **Cuddalore** Tamil Nādu, SE India 11°43′N 79°46′E

155 I18 **Cuddapah** Andhra Pradesh, S India 14°30′N 78°50′E

104 M6 **Cuéllar** Castilla-León, N Spain 41°24′N 04°19′W

82 D13 **Cuemba** var. Coemba. Bié, C Angola 12°09′S 18°07′E

56 B8 **Cuenca** Azuay, S Ecuador 02°54′S 79°W

105 Q9 **Cuenca** anc. Conca. Castilla-La Mancha, C Spain 40°04′N 02°07′W

105 P9 **Cuenca** ◈ province Castilla-La Mancha, C Spain

40 L9 **Cuencamé** var. Cuencamé de Ceniceros. Durango, C Mexico 24°53′N 103°41′W

Cuencamé de Ceniceros see Cuencamé

105 Q8 **Cuenca, Serrania de** ▲▲ C Spain

Cuera see Chur

105 P5 **Cuerda del Pozo, Embalse de la** ⊠ N Spain

41 O14 **Cuernavaca** Morelos, S Mexico 18°57′N 99°15′W

25 T12 **Cuero** Texas, SW USA 29°06′N 97°19′W

44 I7 **Cueto** Holguín, E Cuba 20°43′N 75°54′W

41 Q13 **Cuetzalán** var. Cuetzalán del Progreso. Puebla, S Mexico 20°00′N 97°27′W

Cuetzalán del Progreso see Cuetzalán

105 Q14 **Cuevas de Almanzora** Andalucía, S Spain 37°19′N 01°52′W

Cuevas de Vinromá see Les Coves de Vinromá

116 H12 **Cugir** Hung. Kudzsir. Alba, SW Romania 45°48′N 23°25′E

59 H18 **Cuiabá** prev. Cuyabá. state capital Mato Grosso, SW Brazil 15°32′S 56°05′W

59 H19 **Cuiabá, Rio** ≈ SW Brazil

41 R15 **Cuicatlán** var. San Juan Bautista Cuicatlán. Oaxaca, SE Mexico 17°49′N 96°59′W

191 W16 **Cuidado, Punta** headland Easter Island, Chile, E Pacific Ocean 27°08′S 109°18′W

Cúige see Connaught

Cúige Laighean see Leinster

Cúige Mumhan see Munster

Cuihua see Daguan

98 L13 **Cuijck** Noord-Brabant, SE Netherlands 51°41′N 05°56′E

Cúil an tSúdaire see Portarlington

42 D7 **Cuilapa** Santa Rosa, S Guatemala 14°16′N 90°18′W

42 B5 **Cuilco, Río** ≈ W Guatemala

Cúil Mhuine see Collooney

Cúil Raithin see Coleraine

83 C14 **Cuima** Huambo, C Angola 13°16′S 15°39′E

83 E16 **Cuito** var. Kwito. ≈ SE Angola

83 E15 **Cuíto Cuanavale** Cuando Cubango, E Angola 15°01′S 19°07′E

41 N14 **Cuitzeo, Lago de** ◎ C Mexico

27 W4 **Cuivre River** ≈ Missouri, C USA

Çuka see Çukë

168 L8 **Cukai** var. Chukai, Kemaman. Terengganu, Peninsular Malaysia 04°15′N 103°25′E

113 L23 **Çukë** var. Çuka. Vlorë, S Albania 39°50′N 20°01′E

Cularo see Grenoble

33 Y7 **Culbertson** Montana, NW USA 48°09′N 104°30′W

28 M16 **Culbertson** Nebraska, C USA 40°13′N 100°50′W

183 P10 **Culcairn** New South Wales, SE Australia 35°41′S 147°01′E

45 W5 **Culebra** var. Dewey. E Puerto Rico 18°19′N 65°17′W

45 W6 **Culebra, Isla de** island E Puerto Rico

37 T8 **Culebra Peak** ▲ Colorado, C USA 37°07′N 105°11′W

104 J5 **Culebra, Sierra de la** ▲▲ NW Spain

98 J12 **Culemborg** Gelderland, C Netherlands 51°57′N 05°17′E

137 V14 **Culfa** Rus. Dzhul'fa. SW Azerbaijan 38°58′N 45°37′E

183 P4 **Culgoa River** ≈ New South Wales/Queensland, SE Australia

◆ Country ● Country Capital ◇ Dependent Territory ○ Dependent Territory Capital ◈ Administrative Regions ✈ International Airport ▲ Mountain ▲▲ Mountain Range ⛰ Volcano ≈ River ◎ Lake ⊠ Reservoir

CULIACÁN – DARENDE

40 I9 **Culiacán** var. Culiacán Rosales, Culiacán-Rosales. Sinaloa, C Mexico 24°48′N 107°25′W
Culiacán-Rosales/Culiacán Rosales see Culiacán
105 P14 **Cúllar-Baza** Andalucía, S Spain 37°35′N 02°34′W
105 S10 **Cullera** País Valenciano, E Spain 39°10′N 00°15′W
23 P3 **Cullman** Alabama, S USA 34°10′N 86°50′W
108 B10 **Cully** Vaud, W Switzerland 46°58′N 06°46′E
Culm see Chełmno
Culmsee see Chełmża
21 V4 **Culpeper** Virginia, NE USA 38°28′N 78°00′W
185 I17 **Culverden** Canterbury, South Island, New Zealand 42°46′S 172°51′E
83 H18 **Cum** var. Xhumo. Central, C Botswana 21°13′S 24°38′E
55 N5 **Cumaná** Sucre, NE Venezuela 10°29′N 64°12′W
55 O5 **Cumanacoa** Sucre, NE Venezuela 10°17′N 63°58′W
54 C13 **Cumbal, Nevado de** elevation S Colombia
21 O7 **Cumberland** Kentucky, S USA 36°55′N 83°00′W
21 U2 **Cumberland** Maryland, NE USA 39°40′N 78°47′W
21 V6 **Cumberland** Virginia, NE USA 37°31′N 78°16′W
187 P12 **Cumberland, Cape** var. Cape Nahoi. headland Espiritu Santo, N Vanuatu 14°39′S 166°35′E
11 V14 **Cumberland House** Saskatchewan, C Canada 53°57′N 102°21′W
23 W8 **Cumberland Island** island Georgia, SE USA
20 L7 **Cumberland, Lake** ⊠ Kentucky, S USA
9 R5 **Cumberland Peninsula** peninsula Baffin Island, Nunavut, NE Canada
2 N9 **Cumberland Plateau** plateau E USA
30 L1 **Cumberland Point** headland Michigan, N USA 47°51′N 89°14′W
21 O7 **Cumberland River** ⁓ Kentucky/Tennessee, S USA
9 S6 **Cumberland Sound** inlet Baffin Island, Nunavut, NE Canada
96 I12 **Cumbernauld** S Scotland, United Kingdom 55°57′N 04°W
97 K15 **Cumbria** cultural region NW England, United Kingdom
97 K15 **Cumbrian Mountains** ▲▲ NW England, United Kingdom
23 S2 **Cumming** Georgia, SE USA 34°12′N 84°08′W
Cummin in Pommern see Kamień Pomorski
182 G9 **Cummins** South Australia 34°17′S 135°43′E
96 I13 **Cumnock** W Scotland, United Kingdom 55°32′N 04°28′W
40 G4 **Cumpas** Sonora, NW Mexico 30°N 109°48′W
136 H16 **Çumra** Konya, C Turkey 37°34′N 32°38′E
63 G15 **Cunco** Araucanía, C Chile 38°55′S 72°02′W
54 E9 **Cundinamarca** off. Departamento de Cundinamarca. ◈ province C Colombia
Cundinamarca, Departamento de see Cundinamarca
41 U15 **Cunduacán** Tabasco, SE Mexico 18°00′N 93°07′W
83 C16 **Cunene** ◈ province S Angola
83 A16 **Cunene** var. Kunene. ⁓ Angola/Namibia see also Kunene
Cunene see Kunene
106 A9 **Cuneo** Fr. Coni. Piemonte, NW Italy 44°23′N 07°32′E
83 E15 **Cunjamba** Cuando Cubango, E Angola 15°22′S 20°07′E
181 V10 **Cunnamulla** Queensland, E Australia 28°09′S 145°44′E
Čunusavvon see Junosuando
Cuokkarašša see Čohkarášša
106 B7 **Cuorgnè** Piemonte, NE Italy 45°23′N 07°34′E
96 K11 **Cupar** E Scotland, United Kingdom 56°19′N 03°01′W
116 L8 **Cupcina** Rus. Kupchino; prev. Calinisc, Kalinisk. N Moldova 48°07′N 27°22′E
54 C8 **Cupica** Chocó, W Colombia 06°43′N 77°31′W
54 C8 **Cupica, Golfo de** gulf W Colombia
112 N13 **Ćuprija** Serbia, E Serbia 43°57′N 21°21′E
Cura see Villa de Cura
45 P16 **Curaçao** island Netherlands Antilles
56 H13 **Curanja, Río** ⁓ E Peru
56 F7 **Curaray, Río** ⁓ Ecuador/Peru
116 K14 **Curcani** Călăraşi, SE Romania 44°11′N 26°39′E
182 H4 **Curdimurka** South Australia 29°27′S 136°56′E
103 P7 **Cure** ⁓ C France
173 Y16 **Curepipe** C Mauritius 20°19′S 57°31′E
55 R6 **Curiapo** Delta Amacuro, NE Venezuela 10°03′N 63°05′W
Curia Rhaetorum see Chur
62 G12 **Curicó** Maule, C Chile 35°00′S 71°15′W
Curieta see Krk
172 I15 **Curieuse** island Inner Islands, NE Seychelles
59 C16 **Curitiba** Acre, W Brazil 10°08′S 69°00′W
60 K12 **Curitiba** prev. Curytiba. state capital Paraná, S Brazil 25°25′S 49°25′W
60 J13 **Curitibanos** Santa Catarina, S Brazil 27°18′S 50°35′W
183 S6 **Curlewis** New South Wales, SE Australia 31°09′S 150°18′E
182 J6 **Curnamona** South Australia 31°39′S 139°35′E
83 A15 **Curoca** ⁓ SW Angola
183 T6 **Currabubula** New South Wales, SE Australia 31°17′S 150°43′E
59 Q14 **Currais Novos** Rio Grande do Norte, E Brazil 06°12′S 36°30′W
35 W7 **Currant** Nevada, W USA 38°43′N 115°27′W
35 W6 **Currant Mountain** ▲ Nevada, W USA 38°56′N 115°19′W
44 H2 **Current** Eleuthera Island, C Bahamas 25°24′N 76°44′W
27 W8 **Current River** ⁓ Arkansas/Missouri, C USA
182 M14 **Currie** Tasmania, SE Australia 39°59′S 143°51′E
21 Y8 **Currituck** North Carolina, SE USA 36°29′N 76°02′W
21 Y8 **Currituck Sound** sound North Carolina, SE USA
39 R11 **Curry** Alaska, USA 62°36′N 150°00′W
Curtbunar see Tervel
116 I13 **Curtea de Argeş** var. Curtea-de-Arges. Argeş, S Romania 45°06′N 24°40′E
Curtea-de-Arges see Curtea de Argeş
116 E10 **Curtici** Ger. Kurtitsch, Hung. Kürtös. Arad, W Romania 46°21′N 21°17′E
28 M16 **Curtis** Nebraska, C USA 40°36′N 100°27′W
104 H2 **Curtis-Estación** Galicia, NW Spain 43°09′N 08°10′W
183 O14 **Curtis Group** island group Tasmania, SE Australia
181 Y8 **Curtis Island** island Queensland, SE Australia
58 K11 **Curuá, Ilha do** island NE Brazil
47 U7 **Curuá, Rio** ⁓ N Brazil
59 A14 **Curuçá, Rio** ⁓ NW Brazil
112 L9 **Čurug** Hung. Csurog. Vojvodina, N Serbia 45°30′N 20°02′E
61 D16 **Curuzú Cuatiá** Corrientes, NE Argentina 29°50′S 58°05′W
59 M19 **Curvelo** Minas Gerais, SE Brazil 18°45′S 44°27′W
18 E14 **Curwensville** Pennsylvania, NE USA 40°57′N 78°29′W
30 M3 **Curwood, Mount** ▲ Michigan, N USA 46°42′N 88°14′W
Curytiba see Curitiba
Curzola see Korčula
42 A10 **Cuscatlán** ◈ department C El Salvador
57 H15 **Cusco** var. Cuzco. Cusco, C Peru 13°35′S 72°02′W
57 H15 **Cusco** off. Departamento de Cusco, var. Cuzco. ◈ department C Peru
Cusco, Departamento de see Cusco
27 O9 **Cushing** Oklahoma, C USA 36°01′N 96°46′W
25 W8 **Cushing** Texas, SW USA 31°48′N 94°50′W
40 I6 **Cusihuiriachic** Chihuahua, N Mexico 28°16′N 106°46′W
103 P10 **Cusset** Allier, C France 46°08′N 03°27′E
23 S6 **Cusseta** Georgia, SE USA 32°18′N 84°46′W
28 J10 **Custer** South Dakota, N USA 43°46′N 103°36′W
Cüstrin see Kostrzyn
33 Q7 **Cut Bank** Montana, NW USA 48°38′N 112°20′W
Cutch, Gulf of see Kachchh, Gulf of
23 S6 **Cuthbert** Georgia, SE USA 31°46′N 84°47′W
11 S15 **Cut Knife** Saskatchewan, S Canada 52°40′N 108°54′W
23 Y16 **Cutler Ridge** Florida, SE USA 25°34′N 80°21′W
22 K10 **Cut Off** Louisiana, S USA 29°32′N 90°20′W
63 I15 **Cutral-Có** Neuquén, C Argentina 38°56′S 69°13′W
107 O21 **Cutro** Calabria, SW Italy 39°01′N 16°59′E
183 O4 **Cuttaburra Channels** seasonal river New South Wales, SE Australia
154 O12 **Cuttack** Orissa, E India 20°28′N 85°53′E
83 C15 **Cuvelai** Cunene, SW Angola 15°40′S 15°48′E
79 G18 **Cuvette** var. Région de la Cuvette. ◈ province C Congo
79 G18 **Cuvette-Ouest** ◈ province C Congo
Cuvette, Région de la see Cuvette
173 V9 **Cuvier Basin** undersea feature E Indian Ocean
173 U9 **Cuvier Plateau** undersea feature E Indian Ocean
82 B12 **Cuvo** ⁓ W Angola
100 H9 **Cuxhaven** Niedersachsen, NW Germany 53°51′N 08°43′E
Cuyabá see Cuiabá
Cuyuni, Río see Cuyuni River
55 S8 **Cuyuni River** var. Río Cuyuni. ⁓ Guyana/Venezuela
Cuzco see Cusco
97 K22 **Cwmbran** Wel. Cwmbrân. SW Wales, United Kingdom 51°39′N 03°W
Cwmbrân see Cwmbran
28 K15 **C. W. McConaughy, Lake** ⊠ Nebraska, C USA
81 D20 **Cyangugu** SW Rwanda 02°27′S 29°00′E
110 D11 **Cybinka** Ger. Ziebingen. Lubuskie, W Poland 52°11′N 14°46′E
Cyclades see Kykládes
Cydonia see Chaniá
Cymru see Wales
20 M5 **Cynthiana** Kentucky, S USA 38°22′N 84°18′W
11 S17 **Cypress Hills** ▲▲ Alberta/Saskatchewan, SW Canada
Cypro-Syrian Basin see Cyprus Basin
121 U11 **Cyprus** off. Republic of Cyprus, Gk. Kypros, Turk. Kıbrıs, Kıbrıs Cumhuriyeti. ◆ republic E Mediterranean Sea
84 L14 **Cyprus** Gk. Kypros, Turk. Kıbrıs. island E Mediterranean Sea
121 W11 **Cyprus Basin** var. Cypro-Syrian Basin. undersea feature E Mediterranean Sea 34°00′N 34°00′E
Cyprus, Republic of see Cyprus
75 S8 **Cyrenaica** ◈ cultural region NE Libya
Cythera see Kýthira
Cythnos see Kýthnos
110 F9 **Czaplinek** Ger. Tempelburg. Zachodnio-pomorskie, NW Poland 53°33′N 16°14′E
Czarna Woda see Wda
110 G8 **Czarne** Pomorskie, N Poland 53°40′N 17°00′E
110 G10 **Czarnków** Wielkopolskie, C Poland 52°53′N 16°32′E
111 E17 **Czech Republic** Cz. Česká Republika. ◆ republic C Europe
Czegléd see Cegléd
110 G12 **Czempiń** Wielkopolskie, C Poland 52°10′N 16°46′E
Czenstochau see Częstochowa
Czerkow see Čerchov
Czernowitz see Chernivtsi
110 I8 **Czersk** Pomorskie, N Poland 53°48′N 17°58′E
111 J15 **Częstochowa** Ger. Czenstochau, Tschenstochau, Rus. Chenstokhov. Śląskie, S Poland 50°49′N 19°07′E
110 F10 **Człopa** Ger. Schloppe. Zachodnio-pomorskie, NW Poland 53°05′N 16°05′E
110 H8 **Człuchów** Ger. Schlochau. Pomorskie, NW Poland 53°41′N 17°20′E

D

163 V9 **Da'an** var. Dalai. Jilin, NE China 45°28′N 124°18′E
15 S10 **Daaquam** Québec, SE Canada 46°36′N 70°03′W
Daawo, Webi see Dawa Wenz
54 I4 **Dabajuro** Falcón, NW Venezuela 11°00′N 70°41′W
77 N15 **Dabakala** NE Ivory Coast 08°19′N 04°24′W
163 S11 **Daban** var. Bairin Youqi. Nei Mongol Zizhiqu, N China 43°33′N 118°40′E
158 L5 **Dabancheng** Xinjiang Uygur Zizhiqu, W China 43°21′N 88°19′E
111 K23 **Dabas** Pest, C Hungary 47°36′N 19°22′E
160 L8 **Daba Shan** ▲▲ C China
Dabba see Daocheng
140 J5 **Dabbāgh, Jabal** ▲ NW Saudi Arabia 27°52′N 35°48′E
54 D8 **Dabeiba** Antioquia, NW Colombia 07°01′N 76°18′W
149 P11 **Dābhar** Baluchistān, SW Pakistan 29°28′N 67°39′E
154 E11 **Dabhoi** Gujarāt, W India 22°08′N 73°28′E
161 P8 **Dabie Shan** ▲▲ C China
76 J13 **Dabola** C Guinea 10°48′N 11°02′W
77 N17 **Dabou** S Ivory Coast 05°20′N 04°23′W
162 M15 **Dabqig** prev. Uxin Qi. Nei Mongol Zizhiqu, N China 38°29′N 108°48′E
110 P8 **Dąbrowa Białostocka** Podlaskie, NE Poland 53°38′N 23°18′E
111 M16 **Dąbrowa Tarnowska** Małopolskie, S Poland 50°10′N 21°E
119 M20 **Dabryn'** Rus. Dobryn'. Homyel'skaya Voblasts', SE Belarus 51°46′N 29°12′E
159 P10 **Dabsan Hu** ◎ C China
161 Q13 **Dabu** var. Huliao. Guangdong, S China 24°19′N 116°07′E
116 H15 **Dăbuleni** Dolj, SW Romania 43°48′N 24°05′E
Dacca see Dhaka
101 L23 **Dachau** Bayern, SE Germany 48°15′N 11°26′E
Dachuan see Dazhou
Dacia Bank see Dacia Seamount
64 M10 **Dacia Seamount** var. Dacia Bank. undersea feature E Atlantic Ocean 31°10′N 13°42′W
37 T3 **Dacono** Colorado, C USA 40°04′N 104°56′W
Đắc Tô see Đak Tô
Dacura see Dákura
23 W12 **Dade City** Florida, SE USA 28°21′N 82°12′W
152 L10 **Dadeldhurā** var. Dandeldhura. Far Western, W Nepal 29°12′N 80°31′E
23 Q5 **Dadeville** Alabama, S USA 32°49′N 85°45′W
Dadong see Donggang
103 N15 **Dadou** ⁓ S France
154 D12 **Dādra and Nagar Haveli** ◈ union territory W India
149 P14 **Dādu** Sind, SE Pakistan 26°42′N 67°48′E
167 U11 **Da Du Boloc** Kon Tum, C Vietnam 14°06′N 107°40′E
160 G9 **Dadu He** ⁓ C China
Daegu see Taegu
Daerah Istimewa Aceh see Aceh
171 P4 **Daet** Luzon, N Philippines 14°06′N 122°57′E
160 I11 **Dafang** Guizhou, S China 27°07′N 105°40′E
Dafeng see Shanglin
153 W11 **Dafla Hills** ▲▲ NE India
11 U15 **Dafoe** Saskatchewan, S Canada 51°46′N 104°11′W
76 G10 **Dagana** N Senegal 16°28′N 15°35′W
Dagana see Massakory, Chad
Dagana see Dahana, Tajikistan
Dagcagoin see Zoigê
118 K11 **Dagda** Krāslava, SE Latvia 56°06′N 27°36′E
Dagden see Hiiumaa
Dagden-Sund see Soela Väin
127 P16 **Dagestan, Respublika** prev. Dagestanskaya ASSR, Eng. Daghestan. ◈ autonomous republic SW Russian Federation
Dagestanskaya ASSR see Dagestan, Respublika
127 R17 **Dagestanskiye Ogni** Respublika Dagestan, SW Russian Federation 42°09′N 48°08′E
Dagezhen see Fengning
149 U5 **Daggar** North-West Frontier Province, N Pakistan 34°30′N 72°28′E
185 A23 **Dagg Sound** sound South Island, New Zealand
Daghestan see Dagestan, Respublika
141 Y8 **Daghmar** NE Oman 23°09′N 59°01′E
Dağliq Quarabağ see Nagorno-Karabakh
Dagö see Hiiumaa
54 D11 **Dagua** Valle del Cauca, W Colombia 03°39′N 76°40′W
160 H11 **Daguan** var. Cuihua. Yunnan, SW China 27°42′N 103°51′E
171 N3 **Dagupan** off. Dagupan City. Luzon, N Philippines 16°05′N 120°21′E
Dagupan City see Dagupan
159 N16 **Dagzê** var. Dêqên. Xizang Zizhiqu, W China 29°38′N 91°15′E
147 Q13 **Dahana** Rus. Dagana, Dakhana. SW Tajikistan 38°03′N 69°51′E
163 V10 **Dahei Shan** ▲▲ N China
163 T7 **Da Hinggan Ling** Eng. Great Khingan Range. ▲▲ NE China
Dahlac Archipelago see Dahlak Archipelago
80 K9 **Dahlak Archipelago** var. Dahlac Archipelago. island group E Eritrea
23 T2 **Dahlonega** Georgia, SE USA 34°31′N 83°59′W
100 O14 **Dahme** Brandenburg, E Germany 52°10′N 13°47′E
100 O13 **Dahme** ⁓ E Germany
141 O14 **Dahm, Ramlat** desert NW Yemen
154 E10 **Dāhod** prev. Dohad. Gujarāt, W India 22°48′N 74°18′E
Dahomey see Benin
158 G10 **Dahongliutan** Xinjiang Uygur Zizhiqu, NW China 35°59′N 79°12′E
Dahra see Dara
Dahuaishu see Hongtong
139 R2 **Dahūk** var. Dohuk, Kurd. Dihōk. ◈ governorate N Iraq
139 R2 **Dahūk** var. Dohuk, Kurd. Dihōk. Dahūk, N Iraq 36°52′N 43°01′E
116 J15 **Daia** Giurgiu, S Romania 44°00′N 25°59′E
165 P12 **Daigo** Ibaraki, Honshū, S Japan 36°43′N 140°22′E
163 O13 **Dai Hai** ◎ N China
Daihoku see T'aipei
186 M8 **Dai Island** island N Solomon Islands
166 M8 **Daik-u** Bago, SW Myanmar (Burma) 17°46′N 96°40′E
138 H9 **Dā'il** Dar'ā, S Syria 32°45′N 36°08′E
167 U12 **Đai Lanh** Khanh Hoa, S Vietnam 12°49′N 109°20′E
161 Q13 **Daimao Shan** ▲▲ SE China
105 N11 **Daimiel** Castilla-La Mancha, C Spain 39°04′N 03°37′W
115 F22 **Daimoniá** Pelopónnisos, S Greece 36°38′N 22°54′E
Dainan see T'ainan
25 W6 **Daingerfield** Texas, SW USA 33°03′N 94°42′W
Daingin, Bá an see Dingle Bay
159 R13 **Dainkognubma** Xizang Zizhiqu, W China 32°26′N 97°58′E
164 K14 **Daiō-zaki** headland Honshū, SW Japan 34°15′N 136°50′E
Dairbhre see Valencia Island
61 B22 **Daireaux** Buenos Aires, E Argentina 36°34′S 61°40′W
Dairen see Dalian
Dairût see Dayrūt
25 X10 **Daisetta** Texas, SW USA 30°06′N 94°38′W
192 G5 **Daitō-jima** island group SW Japan
192 G5 **Daitō Ridge** undersea feature N Philippine Sea 25°30′N 133°00′E
161 N3 **Daixian** var. Dai Xian, Shangguan. Shanxi, C China 39°10′N 112°57′E
Dai Xian see Daixian
Daiyue see Shanyin
161 Q12 **Daiyun Shan** ▲▲ SE China
44 M8 **Dajabón** NW Dominican Republic 19°35′N 71°41′W
160 G8 **Dajin Chuan** ⁓ C China
148 J6 **Dak** ◎ W Afghanistan
76 F11 **Dakar** ● (Senegal) W Senegal 14°44′N 17°27′W
76 F11 **Dakar** ✈ W Senegal 14°42′N 17°27′W
167 U10 **Đak Glây** Kon Tum, C Vietnam 15°05′N 107°42′E
Dakhana see Dahana
153 U16 **Dakhin Shahbazpur Island** island S Bangladesh
Dakhla see Ad Dakhla
76 F7 **Dakhlet Nouâdhibou** ◈ region NW Mauritania
Đak Lap see Kiên Đuc
Đak Nông see Gia Nghia
77 U11 **Dakoro** Maradi, S Niger 14°29′N 06°45′E
29 U12 **Dakota City** Iowa, C USA 42°42′N 94°13′W
29 R13 **Dakota City** Nebraska, C USA 42°25′N 96°25′W
Đakovica see Gjakovë
112 I10 **Đakovo** var. Djakovo, Hung. Diakovár. Osijek-Baranja, E Croatia 45°18′N 18°24′E
Dakshin see Deccan
167 U11 **Đak Tô** var. Đắc Tô. Kon Tum, C Vietnam 14°35′N 107°55′E
43 N7 **Dákura** var. Dacura. Región Autónoma Atlántico Norte, NE Nicaragua 14°22′N 83°13′W
95 I14 **Dal** Akershus, S Norway 60°19′N 11°16′E
82 E12 **Dala** Lunda Sul, E Angola 11°04′S 20°15′E
108 J8 **Dalaas** Vorarlberg, W Austria 47°08′N 10°03′E
76 I13 **Dalaba** W Guinea 10°47′N 12°12′W
Dalai see Da'an
162 I12 **Dalain Hob** var. Ejin Qi. Nei Mongol Zizhiqu, N China 41°59′N 101°04′E
Dalai Nor see Hulun Nur
163 Q11 **Dalai Nur** salt lake N China
Dala-Jarna see Järna
95 M14 **Dalälven** ⁓ C Sweden
136 C16 **Dalaman** Muğla, SW Turkey 36°47′N 28°47′E
136 C16 **Dalaman** ✈ Muğla, SW Turkey 36°37′N 28°51′E
136 D16 **Dalaman Çayı** ⁓ SW Turkey
162 K11 **Dalandzadgad** Ömnögovĭ, S Mongolia 43°35′N 104°23′E
95 D17 **Dalane** physical region S Norway
189 Z2 **Dalap-Uliga-Djarrit** var. Delap-Uliga-Darrit, D-U-D. island group Ratak Chain, SE Marshall Islands
94 J12 **Dalarna** prev. Kopparberg. ◈ county C Sweden
94 L13 **Dalarna** prev. Eng. Dalecarlia. cultural region C Sweden
95 P16 **Dalarö** Stockholm, C Sweden 59°07′N 18°25′E
167 U13 **Đa Lat** Lâm Đông, S Vietnam 11°56′N 108°25′E
Dalay see Bayandalay
148 L12 **Dālbandīn** var. Dāl Bandin. Baluchistān, SW Pakistan 28°48′N 64°08′E
95 J17 **Dalbosjön** lake bay S Sweden
181 Y10 **Dalby** Queensland, E Australia 27°11′S 151°12′E
94 D13 **Dale** Hordaland, S Norway 60°35′N 05°48′E
94 C12 **Dale** Sogn Og Fjordane, S Norway 61°22′N 05°24′E
32 K12 **Dale** Oregon, NW USA 44°58′N 118°56′W
25 T11 **Dale** Texas, SW USA 29°56′N 97°34′W
Dalecarlia see Dalarna
21 W4 **Dale City** Virginia, NE USA 38°38′N 77°18′W
20 L8 **Dale Hollow Lake** ⊠ Kentucky/Tennessee, S USA
98 O8 **Dalen** Drenthe, NE Netherlands 52°42′N 06°45′E
95 E15 **Dalen** Telemark, S Norway 59°25′N 07°58′E
166 K14 **Daletme** Chin State, W Myanmar (Burma) 21°44′N 92°48′E
23 Q7 **Daleville** Alabama, S USA 31°18′N 85°42′W
98 M9 **Dalfsen** Overijssel, E Netherlands 52°31′N 06°16′E
24 M1 **Dalhart** Texas, SW USA 36°05′N 102°31′W
13 O13 **Dalhousie** New Brunswick, SE Canada 48°03′N 66°22′W
152 I6 **Dalhousie** Himāchal Pradesh, N India 32°32′N 76°01′E
160 F12 **Dali** var. Xiaguan. Yunnan, SW China 25°34′N 100°11′E
Dali see Idálion
163 U14 **Dalian** var. Dairen, Dalien, Jay Dairen, Lüda, Ta-lien, Rus. Dalny. Liaoning, NE China 38°53′N 121°37′E
105 O15 **Dalías** Andalucía, S Spain 36°49′N 02°50′W
Dalien see Dalian
Dalijan see Delījān
112 J9 **Dalj** Hung. Dalja. Osijek-Baranja, E Croatia 45°29′N 19°00′E
Dalja see Dalj
32 F12 **Dallas** Oregon, NW USA 44°56′N 123°20′W
25 U6 **Dallas** Texas, SW USA 32°47′N 96°48′W
25 T7 **Dallas-Fort Worth** ✈ Texas, SW USA 32°37′N 97°16′W
154 K12 **Dalli Rājhara** var. Dhalli Rajhara. Chhattīsgarh, C India 20°32′N 81°10′E
39 X15 **Dall Island** island Alexander Archipelago, Alaska, USA
38 M12 **Dall Lake** ◎ Alaska, USA
Dállogilli see Korpilombolo
77 S12 **Dallol Bosso** seasonal river W Niger
141 U7 **Dalmā** island W United Arab Emirates
113 E14 **Dalmacija** Eng. Dalmatia, Ger. Dalmatien, It. Dalmazia. cultural region S Croatia
Dalmatia/Dalmatien/Dalmazia see Dalmacija
123 S15 **Dal'negorsk** Primorskiy Kray, SE Russian Federation 44°27′N 135°30′E
Dalny see Dalian
76 M16 **Daloa** C Ivory Coast 06°56′N 06°28′W
160 J11 **Dalou Shan** ▲▲ S China
181 X7 **Dalrymple Lake** ◎ Queensland, E Australia
14 H14 **Dalrymple Lake** ◎ Ontario, S Canada
181 X7 **Dalrymple, Mount** ▲ Queensland, E Australia 21°01′S 148°34′E
93 K20 **Dalsbruk** Fin. Taalintehdas. Länsi-Suomi, W Finland 60°02′N 22°31′E
95 K19 **Dalsjöfors** Västra Götaland, S Sweden 57°43′N 13°05′E
95 J17 **Dals Långed** var. Långed. Västra Götaland, S Sweden 58°54′N 12°20′E
153 O15 **Dāltenganj** prev. Daltonganj. Jhārkhand, N India 24°02′N 84°07′E
23 R2 **Dalton** Georgia, SE USA 34°46′N 84°58′W
Daltonganj see Dāltenganj
195 X14 **Dalton Iceberg Tongue** ice feature Antarctica
92 J1 **Dalvík** Nordhurland Eystra, N Iceland 65°58′N 18°31′W
Dálvvadis see Jokkmokk
35 N8 **Daly City** California, W USA 37°44′N 122°27′W
181 P2 **Daly River** ⁓ Northern Territory, N Australia
181 Q3 **Daly Waters** Northern Territory, N Australia 16°21′S 133°22′E
119 F20 **Damachava** var. Damachova, Pol. Domaczewo, Rus. Domachëvo. Brestskaya Voblasts', SW Belarus 51°45′N 23°36′E
Damachova see Damachava
77 W11 **Damagaram Takaya** Zinder, S Niger 14°02′N 09°28′E
154 D12 **Damān** Damān and Diu, W India 20°25′N 72°58′E
154 B12 **Damān and Diu** ◈ union territory W India
75 V7 **Damanhûr** anc. Hermopolis Parva. N Egypt 31°03′N 30°28′E
161 O1 **Damaqun Shan** ▲▲ E China
79 I15 **Damara** Ombella-Mpoko, S Central African Republic 05°00′N 18°45′E
83 D18 **Damaraland** physical region C Namibia
171 S15 **Damar, Kepulauan** var. Baraf Daja Islands, Kepulauan Barat Daya. island group C Indonesia
168 J8 **Damar Laut** Perak, Peninsular Malaysia 04°13′N 100°36′E
171 S15 **Damar, Pulau** island Maluku, E Indonesia
Damas see Dimashq
77 Y12 **Damasak** Borno, NE Nigeria 13°10′N 12°40′E
Damasco see Dimashq
21 Q8 **Damascus** Virginia, NE USA 36°37′N 81°46′W
Damascus see Dimashq
77 X13 **Damaturu** Yobe, NE Nigeria 11°44′N 11°58′E
171 R9 **Damau** Pulau Kaburuang, N Indonesia 03°46′N 126°49′E
143 O5 **Damāvand, Qolleh-ye** ▲ N Iran 35°56′N 52°08′E
82 B10 **Damba** Uíge, NW Angola 06°44′S 15°20′E
114 M12 **Dambaslar** Tekirdağ, NW Turkey 41°13′N 27°13′E
116 J13 **Dâmboviţa** prev. Dîmboviţa. ◈ county SE Romania
116 J13 **Dâmboviţa** prev. Dîmboviţa. ⁓ S Romania
173 Y15 **D'Ambre, Île** island NE Mauritius
155 K24 **Dambulla** Central Province, C Sri Lanka 07°51′N 80°40′E
44 K9 **Dame-Marie** SW Haiti 18°36′N 74°26′W
44 J9 **Dame Marie, Cap** headland SW Haiti 18°37′N 74°24′W
143 Q4 **Dāmghān** Semnān, N Iran 36°13′N 54°22′E
Damietta see Dumyāt
138 G10 **Dāmiyā** Al Balqā', NW Jordan 32°07′N 35°33′E
146 G11 **Damla** Daşoguz Welaýaty, N Turkmenistan 40°05′N 59°15′E
Dammām see Ad Dammān
100 G12 **Damme** Niedersachsen, NW Germany 52°31′N 08°12′E
153 R15 **Dāmodar** ⁓ NE India
154 J9 **Damoh** Madhya Pradesh, C India 23°50′N 79°30′E
77 P15 **Damongo** NW Ghana 09°05′N 01°49′W
138 G7 **Damoûr** var. Ad Dāmūr. W Lebanon 33°36′N 35°30′E
171 N11 **Dampal, Teluk** bay Sulawesi, C Indonesia
180 H7 **Dampier** Western Australia 20°40′S 116°40′E
180 H6 **Dampier Archipelago** island group Western Australia
141 U14 **Damqawt** var. Damqut. E Yemen 16°35′N 52°39′E
159 O13 **Dam Qu** ⁓ C China
Damqut see Damqawt
167 R13 **Dâmrei, Chuŏr Phmun** Fr. Chaîne de l'Éléphant. ▲▲ SW Cambodia
108 C7 **Damvant** Jura, NW Switzerland 47°22′N 06°55′E
Damwâld see Damwoude
98 L5 **Damwoude** Fris. Damwâld. Friesland, N Netherlands 53°18′N 05°59′E
Damxoi see Comai
159 N15 **Damxung** var. Gongtang. Xizang Zizhiqu, W China 30°29′N 91°02′E
80 K11 **Danakil Desert** var. Afar Depression, Danakil Plain. desert E Africa
Danakil Plain see Danakil Desert
35 R8 **Dana, Mount** ▲ California, W USA 37°54′N 119°13′W
76 L16 **Danané** W Ivory Coast 07°16′N 08°09′W
167 U10 **Đa Năng** prev. Tourane. Quang Nam-Da Nang, C Vietnam 16°04′N 108°14′E
160 G9 **Danba** var. Zhanggu, Tib. Rongzhag. Sichuan, C China 30°54′N 101°49′E
Danborg see Daneborg
18 L13 **Danbury** Connecticut, NE USA 41°21′N 73°27′W
25 W12 **Danbury** Texas, SW USA 29°13′N 95°20′W
35 X15 **Danby Lake** ◎ California, W USA
194 H4 **Danco Coast** physical region Antarctica
82 B11 **Dande** ⁓ NW Angola
Dandeldhura see Dadeldhurā
155 E17 **Dandeli** Karnātaka, W India 15°18′N 74°42′E
183 O12 **Dandenong** Victoria, SE Australia 38°01′S 145°13′E
163 V13 **Dandong** var. Tan-tung; prev. An-tung. Liaoning, NE China 40°10′N 124°23′E
197 Q14 **Daneborg** var. Danborg. ◈ Tunu, N Greenland
25 V12 **Danevang** Texas, SW USA 29°03′N 96°11′W
Dänew see Galkynyş
Danfeng see Shizong
14 L12 **Danford Lake** Québec, SE Canada 45°55′N 76°12′W
19 T4 **Danforth** Maine, NE USA 45°39′N 67°54′W
37 P3 **Danforth Hills** ▲▲ Colorado, C USA
Dangara see Danghara
159 V12 **Dangchang** Gansu, C China 34°01′N 104°19′E
159 P8 **Dangchengwan** var. Subei, Subei Mongolzu Zizhixian. Gansu, N China 39°33′N 94°50′E
82 B10 **Dange** Uíge, NW Angola 07°55′S 15°01′E
Dangerous Archipelago see Tuamotu, Îles
83 E26 **Danger Point** headland SW South Africa 34°37′S 19°20′E
147 Q13 **Danghara** Rus. Dangara. SW Tajikistan 38°05′N 69°14′E
159 P8 **Danghe Nanshan** ▲▲ W China
80 I12 **Dangila** var. Dānglā. Āmara, NW Ethiopia 11°08′N 36°51′E
159 P8 **Dangjin Shankou** pass N China
Dangla see Tanggula Shan, China
Dang La see Tanggula Shankou, China
Dānglā see Dangila, Ethiopia
Dangme Chu see Manās
153 Y11 **Dāngori** Assam, NE India 27°40′N 95°35′E
159 N14 **Dangqên** Xizang Zizhiqu, W China 31°43′N 91°52′E
Dang Raek, Phanom/ Dangrek, Chaîne des see Dângrêk, Chuŏr Phnum
167 S11 **Dângrêk, Chuŏr Phnum** var. Phanom Dang Raek, Phanom Dong Rak, Fr. Chaîne des Dangrek. ▲▲ Cambodia/Thailand
42 G3 **Dangriga** prev. Stann Creek. Stann Creek, E Belize 16°59′N 88°13′W
161 P6 **Dangshan** Anhui, E China 34°22′N 116°21′E
33 T15 **Daniel** Wyoming, C USA 42°49′N 110°04′W
83 H22 **Daniëlskuil** Northern Cape, N South Africa 28°11′S 23°33′E
19 N12 **Danielson** Connecticut, NE USA 41°48′N 71°53′W
124 M15 **Danilov** Yaroslavskaya Oblast', W Russian Federation 58°11′N 40°11′E
127 O9 **Danilovka** Volgogradskaya Oblast', SW Russian Federation 50°21′N 44°03′E
Danish West Indies see Virgin Islands (US)
160 L7 **Dan Jiang** ⁓ C China
160 M7 **Danjiangkou Shuiku** ⊠ C China
141 W8 **Dank** var. Dhank. NW Oman 23°34′N 56°16′E
152 J7 **Dankhar** Himāchal Pradesh, N India 32°08′N 78°12′E
126 L6 **Dankov** Lipetskaya Oblast', W Russian Federation 53°17′N 39°07′E
42 J7 **Danlí** El Paraíso, S Honduras 14°02′N 86°34′W
Danmark see Denmark
Danmarksstraedet see Denmark Strait
95 O14 **Dannemora** Uppsala, C Sweden 60°13′N 17°49′E
18 L6 **Dannemora** New York, NE USA 44°42′N 73°42′W
100 K11 **Dannenberg** Niedersachsen, N Germany 53°05′N 11°06′E
184 N12 **Dannevirke** Manawatu-Wanganui, North Island, New Zealand 40°14′S 176°05′E
21 U8 **Dan River** ⁓ Virginia, NE USA
167 P8 **Dan Sai** Loei, C Thailand 17°15′N 101°04′E
18 F10 **Dansville** New York, NE USA 42°34′N 77°40′W
155 K14 **Dantewāra** Chhattīsgarh, E India 18°53′N 81°20′E
Dantzig see Gdańsk
86 E12 **Danube** Bul. Dunav, Cz. Dunaj, Ger. Donau, Hung. Duna, Rom. Dunărea. ⁓ C Europe
Danubian Plain see Dunavska Ravnina
166 L8 **Danubyu** Ayeyarwady, SW Myanmar (Burma) 17°15′N 95°35′E
Danum see Doncaster
19 P11 **Danvers** Massachusetts, NE USA 42°34′N 70°54′W
27 T11 **Danville** Arkansas, C USA 35°03′N 93°22′W
31 N13 **Danville** Illinois, N USA 40°10′N 87°37′W
31 O14 **Danville** Indiana, N USA 39°45′N 86°31′W
29 Y15 **Danville** Iowa, C USA 40°52′N 91°18′W
20 M6 **Danville** Kentucky, S USA 37°40′N 84°49′W
18 G14 **Danville** Pennsylvania, NE USA 40°57′N 76°36′W
21 T6 **Danville** Virginia, NE USA 36°34′N 79°25′W
Danxian/Dan Xian see Danzhou
160 L17 **Danzhou** prev. Danxian, Dan Xian, Nada. Hainan, S China 19°31′N 109°31′E
Danzhou see Yichuan
Danzig see Gdańsk
Danziger Bucht see Danzig, Gulf of
110 J6 **Danzig, Gulf of** var. Gulf of Gdańsk, Ger. Danziger Bucht, Pol. Zakota Gdańska, Rus. Gdan'skaya Bukhta. gulf N Poland
160 F10 **Daocheng** var. Jinzhu, Tib. Dabba. Sichuan, C China 29°05′N 100°14′E
Daojiang see Daoxian
Daokou see Huaxian
104 H7 **Dão, Rio** ⁓ N Portugal
Daosa see Dausa
77 Y7 **Dao Timmi** Agadez, NE Niger 20°31′N 13°34′E
160 M13 **Daoxian** var. Daojiang. Hunan, S China 25°30′N 111°37′E
77 Q14 **Dapaong** N Togo 10°52′N 00°12′E
23 N8 **Daphne** Alabama, S USA 30°36′N 87°54′W
171 P7 **Dapitan** Mindanao, S Philippines 08°39′N 123°26′E
159 P9 **Da Qaidam** Qinghai, C China 37°50′N 95°18′E
163 V8 **Daqing** var. Sartu. Heilongjiang, NE China 46°29′N 125°07′E
163 O13 **Daqing Shan** ▲▲ N China
163 T11 **Daqin Tal** var. Naiman Qi. Nei Mongol Zizhiqu, N China 42°51′N 120°41′E
Daqm see Duqm
160 G8 **Da Qu** var. Do Qu. ⁓ C China
139 T5 **Dāqūq** var. Tāwūq. At Ta'mīn, N Iraq 35°08′N 44°27′E
76 G10 **Dara** var. Dahra. NW Senegal 15°20′N 15°28′W
138 H9 **Dar'ā** var. Der'a, Fr. Déraa. Dar'ā, SW Syria 32°37′N 36°06′E
138 H8 **Dar'ā** off. Muḥāfaẓat Dar'ā, var. Darā, Der'a, Derrá. ◈ governorate S Syria
143 Q12 **Dārāb** Fārs, S Iran 28°52′N 54°25′E
116 K8 **Darabani** Botoşani, NW Romania 48°10′N 26°39′E
Daraj see Dirj
Dar'ā, Muḥāfaẓat see Dar'ā
142 M8 **Dārān** Eşfahān, W Iran 33°00′N 50°27′E
167 U12 **Da Răng, Sông** var. Ba. ⁓ S Vietnam
Darautt-Kurgan see Daroot-Korgon
77 W13 **Darazo** Bauchi, E Nigeria 11°01′N 10°27′E
139 S3 **Darband** Arbil, N Iraq 36°15′N 44°17′E
139 V4 **Darband-i Khān, Sadd** dam NE Iraq
139 N1 **Darbāsīyah** var. Derbisīye. Al Ḩasakah, N Syria 37°06′N 40°42′E
118 C11 **Darbėnai** Klaipėda, NW Lithuania 56°02′N 21°16′E
153 Q13 **Darbhanga** Bihār, N India 26°10′N 85°54′E
38 M9 **Darby, Cape** headland Alaska, USA 64°19′N 162°46′W
112 I9 **Darda** Hung. Dárda. Osijek-Baranja, E Croatia 45°37′N 18°41′E
Dárda see Darda
27 T11 **Dardanelle** Arkansas, C USA 35°11′N 93°09′W
27 S11 **Dardanelle, Lake** ⊠ Arkansas, C USA
Dardanelles see Çanakkale Boğazı
Dardanelli see Çanakkale
Dardo see Kangding
Dar-el-Beida see Casablanca
136 M14 **Darende** Malatya, C Turkey 38°34′N 37°29′E

◆ Country
● Country Capital
◇ Dependent Territory
○ Dependent Territory Capital
◈ Administrative Regions
✈ International Airport
▲ Mountain
▲▲ Mountain Range
✷ Volcano
⁓ River
◎ Lake
⊠ Reservoir
241

DAR ES SALAAM – DEN HAAG

81 J22 **Dar es Salaam** Dar es Salaam, E Tanzania 06°51´S 39°18´E
81 J22 **Dar es Salaam** ✈ Pwani, E Tanzania 06°57´S 39°17´E
185 H18 **Darfield** Canterbury, South Island, New Zealand 43°29´S 172°07´E
106 F7 **Darfo** Lombardia, N Italy 45°54´N 10°12´E
80 B10 **Darfur** *var.* Darfur Massif. *cultural region* W Sudan
Darfur Massif *see* Darfur
Darganata/Dargan-Ata *see* Birata
143 T3 **Dargaz** *var.* Darreh Gaz; *prev.* Moḩammadābād. Khorāsān-Razavī, NE Iran 37°28´N 59°08´E
139 U4 **Dargazayn** As Sulaymānīyah, NE Iraq 35°39´N 45°00´E
183 P12 **Dargo** Victoria, SE Australia 37°29´S 147°15´E
162 L6 **Darhan** Darhan Uul, N Mongolia 49°24´N 105°57´E
163 N8 **Darhan** Hentiy, C Mongolia 46°38´N 109°25´E
Darhan *see* Büreghangay
Darhan Muminggan Lianheqi *see* Bailingmiao
162 L6 **Darhan Uul** ◐ *province* N Mongolia
23 W7 **Darien** Georgia, SE USA 31°22´N 81°25´W
43 W16 **Darién** *off.* Provincia del Darién. ◐ *province* SE Panama
Darién, Golfo del *see* Darien, Gulf of
43 X14 **Darien, Gulf of** *Sp.* Golfo del Darién. *gulf* S Caribbean Sea
Darien, Isthmus of *see* Panama, Istmo de
Darién, Provincia del *see* Darién
42 K9 **Dariense, Cordillera** ▲ C Nicaragua
43 W15 **Darién, Serranía del** ▲ Colombia/Panama
163 P10 **Dariganga** *var.* Ovoot. Sühbaatar, SE Mongolia 45°08´N 113°51´E
Dario *see* Ciudad Darío
Dariorigum *see* Vannes
Dariv *see* Darvi
Darj *see* Dirj
Darjeeling *see* Dārjiling
153 S12 **Dārjiling** *prev.* Darjeeling. West Bengal, NE India 27°00´N 88°13´E
Darkehnen *see* Ozersk
159 S12 **Darlag** *var.* Gümai. Qinghai, C China 33°43´N 99°42´E
183 T3 **Darling Downs** *hill range* Queensland, E Australia
28 M2 **Darling, Lake** ☒ North Dakota, N USA
180 I12 **Darling Range** ▲ Western Australia
182 L8 **Darling River** ~ New South Wales, SE Australia
97 M15 **Darlington** N England, United Kingdom 54°31´N 01°34´W
21 T12 **Darlington** South Carolina, SE USA 34°19´N 79°53´W
30 K9 **Darlington** Wisconsin, N USA 42°41´N 90°08´W
110 G7 **Darłowo** Zachodnio-pomorskie, NW Poland 54°24´N 16°21´E
101 G19 **Darmstadt** Hessen, SW Germany 49°52´N 08°39´E
75 S7 **Darnah** *var.* Dérna. NE Libya 32°46´N 22°39´E
103 S6 **Darney** Vosges, NE France 48°06´N 05°58´E
182 M7 **Darnick** New South Wales, SE Australia 32°52´S 143°38´E
195 Y6 **Darnley, Cape** *cape* Antarctica
105 R7 **Daroca** Aragón, NE Spain 41°07´N 01°25´W
147 S11 **Daroot-Korgon** *var.* Daraut-Kurgan. Oshskaya Oblast', SW Kyrgyzstan 39°35´N 72°13´E
61 A23 **Darragueira** *var.* Darregueira. Buenos Aires, E Argentina 37°40´S 63°12´W
Darregueira *see* Darragueira
Darreh Gaz *see* Dargaz
142 K7 **Darreh Shahr** *var.* Darreh-ye Shahr. Īlām, W Iran 33°10´N 47°18´E
Darreh-ye Shahr *see* Darreh Shahr
32 I7 **Darrington** Washington, NW USA 48°15´N 121°36´W
25 P1 **Darrouzett** Texas, SW USA 36°27´N 100°19´W
153 S15 **Darsana** *var.* Darshana. Khulna, N Bangladesh 23°32´N 88°49´E
Darshana *see* Darsana
100 M7 **Darss** *peninsula* NE Germany
100 M7 **Darsser Ort** *headland* NE Germany 54°28´N 12°31´E
97 J24 **Dart** ~ SW England, United Kingdom
Dartang *see* Baqên
97 P22 **Dartford** SE England, United Kingdom 51°27´N 00°13´E
182 L12 **Dartmoor** Victoria, SE Australia 37°56´S 141°18´E
97 I24 **Dartmoor** *moorland* SW England, United Kingdom
13 Q15 **Dartmouth** Nova Scotia, SE Canada 44°40´N 63°35´W
97 J24 **Dartmouth** SW England, United Kingdom 50°21´N 03°34´W
15 Y6 **Dartmouth** ~ Québec, SE Canada
183 Q11 **Dartmouth Reservoir** ◎ Victoria, SE Australia
Dartuch, Cabo *see* Artrutx, Cap d'
186 C9 **Daru** Western, SW Papua New Guinea 09°05´S 143°10´E
112 G9 **Daruvar** *Hung.* Daruvár. Bjelovar-Bilogora, NE Croatia 45°34´N 17°12´E
Daruvár *see* Daruvar
Darvaza *see* Derweze, Turkmenistan
Darvaza *see* Darvoza, Uzbekistan
Darvazskiy Khrebet *see* Darvoz, Qatorkŭhi
Darvel Bay *see* Lahad Datu, Teluk
Darvel, Teluk *see* Lahad Datu, Teluk
162 F8 **Darvi** *var.* Dariv. Govĭ-Altay, W Mongolia 46°20´N 94°11´E
162 F7 **Darvi** *var.* Bulgan. Hovd, W Mongolia 46°57´N 93°40´E
148 L9 **Darvishān** *var.* Darweshan, Garmser. Helmand, S Afghanistan 31°02´N 64°12´E
147 O10 **Darvoza** *Rus.* Darvaza. Jizzax Viloyati, C Uzbekistan 40°59´N 67°19´E
147 R13 **Darvoz, Qatorkŭhi** *Rus.* Darvazskiy Khrebet. ▲ C Tajikistan
Darweshan *see* Darvishān
63 J15 **Darwin** Río Negro, S Argentina 39°13´S 65°41´W
181 O1 **Darwin** *prev.* Palmerston, Port Darwin. *territory capital* Northern Territory, N Australia 12°28´S 130°52´E
65 D24 **Darwin** *var.* Darwin Settlement. East Falkland, Falkland Islands 51°51´S 58°55´W
62 H8 **Darwin, Cordillera** ▲ N Chile
Darwin Settlement *see* Darwin
57 B17 **Darwin, Volcán** ⚠ Galápagos Islands, Ecuador, E Pacific Ocean 0°12´S 91°17´W
149 S8 **Darya Khān** Punjab, E Pakistan 31°47´N 71°10´E
145 O15 **Dar'yalyktakyr, Ravnina** *plain* S Kazakhstan
143 T11 **Dārzīn** Kermān, S Iran 29°11´N 58°09´E
Dashhowuz *see* Daşoguz
Dashhowuz Welayaty *see* Daşoguz Welaýaty
162 K7 **Dashinchilen** *var.* Süüj. Bulgan, C Mongolia 47°49´N 104°06´E
119 O16 **Dashkawka** *Rus.* Dashkovka. Mahilyowskaya Voblasts', E Belarus 53°44´N 30°16´E
Dashkhovuz *see* Daşoguz Welaýaty
Dashkhovuzskiy Velayat *see* Daşoguz Welaýaty
Dashköpri *see* Daşköpri
Dashkovka *see* Dashkawka
148 J15 **Dasht** ~ SW Pakistan
Dasht-i *see* Bābūs, Dasht-e
Dashtidzhum *see* Dashtijum
147 R13 **Dashtijum** *Rus.* Dashtidzhum. SW Tajikistan 38°06´N 70°11´E
149 W7 **Daska** Punjab, NE Pakistan 32°15´N 74°23´E
146 J16 **Daşköpri** *var.* Dashköpri, *Rus.* Tashkepri. Mary Welaýaty, S Turkmenistan 36°15´N 62°37´E
146 H8 **Daşoguz** *Rus.* Dashkhovuz, *Turkm.* Dashhowuz; *prev.* Tashauz. Daşoguz Welaýaty, N Turkmenistan 41°51´N 59°53´E
146 E9 **Daşoguz Welaýaty** *var.* Dashhowuz Welayaty, *Rus.* Dashkhovuz, Dashkhovuzskiy Velayat. ◐ *province* N Turkmenistan
Đa, Sông *see* Black River
77 R15 **Dassa** *var.* Dassa-Zoumé. S Benin 07°46´N 02°15´E
Dassa-Zoumé *see* Dassa
29 U8 **Dassel** Minnesota, N USA 45°06´N 94°18´W
152 H3 **Dastegil Sar** ▲ N India
149 U4 **Dasu** North-West Frontier Province, N Pakistan 35°18´N 73°2´E
136 C16 **Datça** Muğla, SW Turkey 36°46´N 27°40´E
165 R4 **Date** Hokkaidō, NE Japan 42°28´N 140°51´E
154 I8 **Datia** *prev.* Duttia. Madhya Pradesh, C India 25°41´N 78°28´E
Dåtnejaevrie *see* Tunnsjøen
159 T10 **Datong** *var.* Datong Huizu Tuzu Zizhixian, Qiaotou. Qinghai, C China 37°01´N 101°33´E
161 N2 **Datong** *var.* Tatung, Ta-t'ung. Shanxi, C China 40°09´N 113°17´E
Datong *see* Tong'an
159 S8 **Datong He** ~ C China
Datong Huizu Tuzu Zizhixian *see* Datong
159 S9 **Datong Shan** ▲ C China
169 O10 **Datu, Tanjung** *headland* Indonesia/Malaysia 02°01´N 109°37´E
Datu, Teluk *see* Lahad Datu, Teluk
Daua *see* Dawa Wenz
172 H16 **Dauban, Mount** ▲ Silhouette, NE Seychelles
149 T7 **Dāūd Khel** Punjab, E Pakistan 32°52´N 71°35´E
119 G15 **Daugai** Alytus, S Lithuania 54°22´N 24°20´E
Daugava *see* Western Dvina
118 J11 **Daugavpils** *Ger.* Dünaburg; *prev. Rus.* Dvinsk. Daugvapils, SE Latvia 55°53´N 26°34´E
Dauka *see* Dawkah
Daulatabad *see* Malāyer
Daulpur *see* Dhaulpur
101 D18 **Daun** Rheinland-Pfalz, W Germany 50°13´N 06°50´E
155 E14 **Daund** *prev.* Dhond. Mahārāshtra, W India 18°28´N 74°38´E
166 M12 **Daung Kyun** *island* S Myanmar (Burma)
11 W15 **Dauphin** Manitoba, S Canada 51°09´N 100°05´W
103 S13 **Dauphiné** *cultural region* E France
23 N9 **Dauphin Island** *island* Alabama, S USA
11 X15 **Dauphin River** Manitoba, S Canada 51°55´N 98°03´W
77 V12 **Daura** Katsina, N Nigeria 13°03´N 08°18´E
152 H12 **Dausa** *prev.* Daosa. Rājasthān, N India 26°51´N 76°21´E
Dauwa *see* Dawwah
137 Y10 **Däväçi** *Rus.* Divichi. NE Azerbaijan 41°15´N 48°58´E
155 F18 **Dāvangere** Karnātaka, W India 14°30´N 75°52´E
171 Q8 **Davao** *off.* Davao City. Mindanao, S Philippines 07°06´N 125°36´E
Davao City *see* Davao
171 Q8 **Davao Gulf** *gulf* Mindanao, S Philippines
15 Q11 **Daveluyville** Québec, SE Canada 46°12´N 72°07´W
29 Z14 **Davenport** Iowa, C USA 41°31´N 90°35´W
32 L8 **Davenport** Washington, NW USA 47°39´N 118°09´W
43 P16 **David** Chiriquí, W Panama 08°26´N 82°26´W
15 O11 **David** ~ Québec, SE Canada
29 R15 **David City** Nebraska, C USA 41°15´N 97°07´W
David-Gorodok *see* Davyd-Haradok
11 T16 **Davidson** Saskatchewan, S Canada 51°15´N 105°59´W
21 R10 **Davidson** North Carolina, SE USA 35°29´N 80°49´W
26 K12 **Davidson** Oklahoma, C USA 34°15´N 99°06´W
39 S6 **Davidson Mountains** ▲ Alaska, USA
172 M8 **Davie Ridge** *undersea feature* W Indian Ocean 17°10´S 41°45´E
182 A1 **Davies, Mount** ▲ South Australia 26°14´S 129°14´E
35 O7 **Davis** California, W USA 38°31´N 121°46´W
27 N12 **Davis** Oklahoma, C USA 34°30´N 97°07´W
195 Y7 **Davis** *Australian research station* Antarctica 68°30´S 78°15´E
194 H3 **Davis Coast** *physical region* Antarctica
18 C16 **Davis, Mount** ▲ Pennsylvania, NE USA 39°47´N 79°10´W
24 K9 **Davis Mountains** ▲ Texas, SW USA
195 Z9 **Davis Sea** *sea* Antarctica
65 O20 **Davis Seamounts** *undersea feature* S Atlantic Ocean
196 M13 **Davis Strait** *strait* Baffin Bay/ Labrador Sea
127 U5 **Davlekanovo** Respublika Bashkortostan, W Russian Federation 54°13´N 55°06´E
108 J9 **Davos** *Rmsch.* Tavau. Graubünden, E Switzerland 46°48´N 09°50´E
119 J20 **Davyd-Haradok** *Pol.* Dawidgródek, *Rus.* David-Gorodok. Brestskaya Voblasts', SW Belarus 52°03´N 27°13´E
163 U12 **Dawa** Liaoning, NE China 40°55´N 122°02´E
141 O11 **Dawāsir, Wādī ad** *dry watercourse* S Saudi Arabia
81 K15 **Dawa Wenz** *var.* Daua, Webi Daawo. ~ E Africa
Dawaymah, Birkat ad *see* Umm al Baqar, Hawr
167 N10 **Dawei** *var.* Tavoy, Htawei. Tanintharyi, S Myanmar (Burma) 14°02´N 98°12´E
119 K14 **Dawhinava** *Rus.* Dolginovo. Minskaya Voblasts', N Belarus 54°39´N 27°29´E
Dawidgródek *see* Davyd-Haradok
141 V12 **Dawkah** *var.* Dauka. SW Oman 18°32´N 54°03´E
Dawlat Qaţar *see* Qatar
24 M3 **Dawn** Texas, SW USA 34°54´N 102°10´W
Dawo *see* Maqên
140 M11 **Daws** Al Bāḩah, SW Saudi Arabia 20°19´N 41°12´E
10 H5 **Dawson** *var.* Dawson City. Yukon Territory, NW Canada 64°04´N 139°24´W
23 S6 **Dawson** Georgia, SE USA 31°46´N 84°27´W
29 S9 **Dawson** Minnesota, N USA 44°55´N 96°03´W
Dawson City *see* Dawson
11 N13 **Dawson Creek** British Columbia, W Canada 55°45´N 120°07´W
10 H7 **Dawson Range** ▲ Yukon Territory, W Canada
181 Y9 **Dawson River** ~ Queensland, E Australia
10 J15 **Dawsons Landing** British Columbia, SW Canada 51°33´N 127°38´W
20 I7 **Dawson Springs** Kentucky, S USA 37°10´N 87°41´W
23 S2 **Dawsonville** Georgia, SE USA 34°28´N 84°07´W
160 G8 **Dawu** *var.* Xianshui. Sichuan, C China 30°55´N 101°08´E
Dawu *see* Maqên
Dawukou *see* Shizuishan
141 Y10 **Dawwah** *var.* Dauwa. W Oman 20°36´N 58°52´E
102 J15 **Dax** *var.* Ax; *anc.* Aquae Augustae, Aquae Tarbelicae. Landes, SW France 43°43´N 01°03´W
Daxian *see* Dazhou
Daxiangshan *see* Gangu
Daxue *see* Wencheng
160 G9 **Daxue Shan** ▲ C China
Dayan *see* Lijiang
160 G12 **Dayao** *var.* Jinbi. Yunnan, SW China 25°41´N 101°23´E
Dayishan *see* Gaoyou
149 O6 **Dāykundī** *province* C Afghanistan
183 N12 **Daylesford** Victoria, SE Australia 37°24´S 144°07´E
35 U10 **Daylight Pass** *pass* California, W USA
61 D17 **Daymán, Río** ~ N Uruguay
Dayong *see* Zhangjiajie
Dayr *see* Ad Dayr
138 G10 **Dayr 'Allā** *var.* Deir 'Alla. Al Balqā', N Jordan 32°39´N 36°06´E
139 N4 **Dayr az Zawr** *var.* Deir ez Zor. Dayr az Zawr, E Syria 35°12´N 40°12´E
138 M5 **Dayr az Zawr** *off.* Muḩāfaẓat Dayr az Zawr, *var.* Dayr Az-Zor. ◐ *governorate* E Syria
Dayr az Zawr, Muḩāfaẓat *see* Dayr az Zawr
Dayr Az-Zor *see* Dayr az Zawr
75 W9 **Dayrūţ** *var.* Dairûţ. C Egypt 27°34´N 30°48´E
11 Q15 **Daysland** Alberta, SW Canada 52°53´N 112°19´W
31 R14 **Dayton** Ohio, N USA 39°46´N 84°12´W
20 L10 **Dayton** Tennessee, S USA 35°30´N 85°01´W
25 W11 **Dayton** Texas, SW USA 30°03´N 94°53´W
32 L10 **Dayton** Washington, NW USA 46°19´N 117°58´W
23 X10 **Daytona Beach** Florida, SE USA 29°12´N 81°03´W
169 U12 **Dayu** Borneo, C Indonesia 01°59´S 115°04´E
161 O13 **Dayu Ling** ▲ S China
161 R7 **Da Yunhe** *Eng.* Grand Canal. *canal* E China
161 S11 **Dayu Shan** *island* SE China
160 K8 **Dazhou** *prev.* Dachuan, Daxian. Sichuan, C China 31°16´N 107°31´E
160 J9 **Dazhu** *var.* Zhuyang. Sichuan, C China 30°45´N 107°11´E
160 J9 **Dazu** *var.* Longgang. Chongqing Shi, C China 29°47´N 106°30´E
83 H24 **De Aar** Northern Cape, C South Africa 30°40´S 24°01´E
194 K5 **Deacon, Cape** *headland* Antarctica
39 R5 **Deadhorse** Alaska, USA 70°15´N 148°28´W
33 T12 **Dead Indian Peak** ▲ Wyoming, C USA 44°36´N 109°45´W
23 R9 **Dead Lake** ◎ Florida, SE USA
44 J4 **Deadman's Cay** Long Island, C Bahamas 23°09´N 75°06´W
138 G11 **Dead Sea** *var.* Bahret Lut, Lacus Asphaltites, *Ar.* Al Baḩr al Mayyit, Baḩrat Lūṭ, *Heb.* Yam HaMelaḥ. *salt lake* Israel/ Jordan
28 J9 **Deadwood** South Dakota, N USA 44°22´N 103°43´W
97 Q22 **Deal** SE England, United Kingdom 51°14´N 01°23´E
83 I22 **Dealesville** Free State, C South Africa 28°40´S 25°46´E
161 P10 **De'an** *var.* Puting. Jiangxi, S China 29°24´N 115°46´E
62 K9 **Deán Funes** Córdoba, C Argentina 30°25´S 64°22´W
194 L12 **Dean Island** *island* Antarctica
Deanuvuotna *see* Tanafjorden
31 S10 **Dearborn** Michigan, N USA 42°16´N 83°13´W
27 R3 **Dearborn** Missouri, C USA 39°31´N 94°46´W
Dearrget *see* Tärendö
32 K9 **Deary** Idaho, NW USA 46°46´N 116°33´W
32 M9 **Deary** Washington, NW USA 46°42´N 116°36´W
10 J10 **Dease** ~ British Columbia, W Canada
10 J10 **Dease Lake** British Columbia, W Canada 58°28´N 130°04´W
35 U11 **Death Valley** California, W USA 36°25´N 116°50´W
35 U11 **Death Valley** *valley* California, W USA
92 M8 **Deatnu** *Fin.* Tenojoki, *Nor.* Tana. ~ Finland/Norway *see also* Tenojoki
102 L4 **Deauville** Calvados, N France 49°21´N 00°06´E
117 X7 **Debal'tseve** *Rus.* Debal'tsevo. Donets'ka Oblast', SE Ukraine 48°21´N 38°26´E
Debal'tsevo *see* Debal'tseve
113 M19 **Debar** *Ger.* Dibra, *Turk.* Debre. W FYR Macedonia 41°32´N 20°33´E
39 O9 **Debauch Mountain** ▲ Alaska, USA 64°31´N 159°52´W
De Behagle *see* Laï
25 X7 **De Berry** Texas, SW USA 32°18´N 94°09´W
127 T2 **Debessy** Udmurtskaya Respublika, NW Russian Federation 57°41´N 53°56´E
111 N16 **Dębica** Podkarpackie, SE Poland 50°04´N 21°24´E
De Bildt *see* De Bilt
98 J11 **De Bilt** *var.* De Bildt. Utrecht, C Netherlands 52°06´N 05°11´E
123 T9 **Debin** Magadanskaya Oblast', E Russian Federation 62°18´N 150°42´E
110 N13 **Dęblin** *Rus.* Ivangorod. Lubelskie, E Poland 51°34´N 21°50´E
110 D10 **Dębno** Zachodnio-pomorskie, NW Poland 52°43´N 14°42´E
39 S10 **Deborah, Mount** ▲ Alaska, USA 63°38´N 147°13´W
33 N8 **De Borgia** Montana, NW USA 47°23´N 115°24´W
Debra Birhan *see* Debre Birhan
Debra Marcos *see* Debre Mark'os
Debra Tabor *see* Debre Tabor
Debre *see* Debar
80 J13 **Debre Birhan** *var.* Debra Birhan. Āmara, N Ethiopia 09°45´N 39°40´E
111 N22 **Debrecen** *Ger.* Debreczin, *Rom.* Debreţin; *prev.* Debreczen. Hajdú-Bihar, E Hungary 47°32´N 21°38´E
Debreczen/Debreczin *see* Debrecen
80 I12 **Debre Mark'os** *var.* Debra Marcos. Āmara, N Ethiopia 10°18´N 37°48´E
113 N19 **Debrešte** SW FYR Macedonia 41°29´N 21°20´E
80 J11 **Debre Tabor** *var.* Debra Tabor. Āmara, N Ethiopia 11°46´N 38°06´E
Debreţin *see* Debrecen
80 J13 **Debre Zeyt** Oromīya, C Ethiopia 08°41´N 39°00´E
113 L16 **Deçan** *Serb.* Dečane; *prev.* Dečani. W Kosovo 42°33´N 20°18´E
Dečane *see* Deçan
Dečani *see* Deçan
23 P2 **Decatur** Alabama, S USA 34°36´N 86°58´W
23 S3 **Decatur** Georgia, SE USA 33°46´N 84°18´W
30 L13 **Decatur** Illinois, N USA 39°50´N 88°57´W
31 Q12 **Decatur** Indiana, N USA 40°40´N 84°57´W
22 M5 **Decatur** Mississippi, S USA 32°26´N 89°06´W
29 S14 **Decatur** Nebraska, C USA 42°00´N 96°19´W
25 S6 **Decatur** Texas, SW USA 33°14´N 97°35´W
20 H9 **Decaturville** Tennessee, S USA 35°35´N 88°08´W
103 O13 **Decazeville** Aveyron, S France 44°34´N 02°18´E
155 H17 **Deccan** *Hind.* Dakshin. *plateau* C India
14 J8 **Decelles, Réservoir** ☒ Québec, SE Canada
12 K2 **Déception** Québec, NE Canada 62°06´N 74°36´W
160 G11 **Dechang** *var.* Dezhou. Sichuan, C China 27°24´N 102°09´E
111 C15 **Děčín** *Ger.* Tetschen. Ústecký Kraj, NW Czech Republic 50°48´N 14°15´E
103 P9 **Decize** Nièvre, C France 46°51´N 03°25´E
98 I6 **De Cocksdorp** Noord-Holland, NW Netherlands 53°09´N 04°52´E
29 X11 **Decorah** Iowa, C USA 43°18´N 91°47´W
Dedeagaç/Dedeagach *see* Alexandroúpoli
188 C15 **Dededo** N Guam 13°30´N 144°51´E
98 N9 **Dedemsvaart** Overijssel, E Netherlands 52°36´N 06°28´E
19 O11 **Dedham** Massachusetts, NE USA 42°14´N 71°10´W
63 H19 **Dedo, Cerro** ▲ SW Argentina 44°46´S 71°48´W
77 O13 **Dédougou** W Burkina 12°29´N 03°25´W
124 G15 **Dedovichi** Pskovskaya Oblast', W Russian Federation 57°31´N 29°53´E
Dedu *see* Wudalianchi
155 J24 **Deduru Oya** ~ W Sri Lanka
83 N14 **Dedza** Central, S Malawi 14°20´S 34°24´E
83 N14 **Dedza Mountain** ▲ C Malawi 14°22´S 34°16´E
96 K9 **Dee** ~ NE Scotland, United Kingdom
97 J19 **Dee** *Wel.* Afon Dyfrdwy. ~ England/Wales, United Kingdom
Deep Bay *see* Chilumba
21 T3 **Deep Creek Lake** ☒ Maryland, NE USA
36 J4 **Deep Creek Range** ▲ Utah, W USA
27 P10 **Deep Fork River** ~ Oklahoma, C USA
14 J11 **Deep River** Ontario, SE Canada 46°04´N 77°29´W
21 T10 **Deep River** ~ North Carolina, SE USA
183 U4 **Deepwater** New South Wales, SE Australia 29°27´S 151°52´E
31 S14 **Deer Creek Lake** ◎ Ohio, N USA
23 Z15 **Deerfield Beach** Florida, SE USA 26°19´N 80°06´W
39 N8 **Deering** Alaska, USA 66°04´N 162°43´W
38 M16 **Deer Island** *island* Alaska, USA
19 S7 **Deer Isle** *island* Maine, NE USA
13 S11 **Deer Lake** Newfoundland and Labrador, SE Canada 49°11´N 57°27´W
99 D18 **Deerlijk** West-Vlaanderen, W Belgium 50°52´N 03°21´E
33 Q10 **Deer Lodge** Montana, NW USA 46°24´N 112°43´W
32 L8 **Deer Park** Washington, NW USA 47°55´N 117°28´W
29 U5 **Deer River** Minnesota, N USA 47°19´N 93°47´W
Deés *see* Dej
Defeng *see* Liping
31 R11 **Defiance** Ohio, N USA 41°17´N 84°21´W
23 Q8 **De Funiak Springs** Florida, SE USA 30°43´N 86°07´W
95 L23 **Degeberga** Skåne, S Sweden 55°48´N 14°06´E
104 H12 **Degebe, Ribeira** ~ S Portugal
80 M13 **Degeh Bur** Sumalē, E Ethiopia 08°08´N 43°35´E
15 U9 **Dégelis** Québec, SE Canada 47°30´N 68°38´W
77 U17 **Degema** Rivers, S Nigeria 04°46´N 06°47´E
95 L16 **Degerfors** Örebro, C Sweden 59°14´N 14°26´E
193 R14 **De Gerlache Seamounts** *undersea feature* SE Pacific Ocean
101 N21 **Deggendorf** Bayern, SE Germany 48°50´N 12°58´E
80 I11 **Degoma** Āmara, N Ethiopia 12°22´N 37°36´E
De Gordyk *see* Gorredijk
27 T12 **De Gray Lake** ☒ Arkansas, C USA
180 J6 **De Grey River** ~ Western Australia
126 M10 **Degtevo** Rostovskaya Oblast', SW Russian Federation 49°12´N 40°39´E
Dehbārez *see* Rūdān
Deh Bīd *see* Şafāshahr
142 M10 **Deh Dasht** Kohkīlūyeh va Būyer Aḩmad, SW Iran 30°49´N 50°36´E
75 N8 **Dehibat** SE Tunisia 31°58´N 10°43´E
Dehli *see* Delhi
142 K8 **Dehlorān** Īlām, W Iran 32°41´N 47°18´E
147 N13 **Dehqonobod** *Rus.* Dekhkanabad. Qashqadaryo Viloyati, S Uzbekistan 38°24´N 66°31´E
152 J9 **Dehra Dūn** Uttararanchal, N India 30°19´N 78°04´E
153 O14 **Dehri** Bihār, N India 24°55´N 84°11´E
148 K10 **Deh Shū** *var.* Deshu. Helmand, S Afghanistan 30°28´N 63°21´E
163 W9 **Dehui** Jilin, NE China 44°23´N 125°42´E
99 D17 **Deinze** Oost-Vlaanderen, NW Belgium 50°59´N 03°32´E
Deir 'Alla *see* Dayr 'Allā
Deir ez Zor *see* Dayr az Zawr
Deirgeirt, Loch *see* Derg, Lough
116 H9 **Dej** *Hung.* Dés; *prev.* Deés. Cluj, NW Romania 47°08´N 23°55´E
95 K15 **Deje** Värmland, C Sweden 59°35´N 13°29´E
171 Y15 **De Jongs, Tanjung** *headland* Papua, SE Indonesia 06°56´S 138°32´E
De Jouwer *see* Joure
30 M10 **De Kalb** Illinois, N USA 41°55´N 88°45´W
22 M5 **De Kalb** Mississippi, S USA 32°46´N 88°39´W
25 W5 **De Kalb** Texas, SW USA 33°30´N 94°34´W
83 G18 **Dekar** *var.* D'Kar. Ghanzi, NW Botswana 21°31´S 21°55´E
Dekéleia *see* Dhekéleia
79 K20 **Dekese** Kasai-Occidental, C Dem. Rep. Congo 03°28´S 21°24´E
Dekhkanabad *see* Dehqonobod
79 I14 **Dékoa** Kémo, C Central African Republic 06°17´N 19°07´E
98 H6 **De Koog** Noord-Holland, NW Netherlands 53°06´N 04°43´E
30 M9 **Delafield** Wisconsin, N USA 43°03´N 88°22´W
61 C23 **De La Garma** Buenos Aires, E Argentina 37°58´S 60°25´W
14 K10 **Delahey, Lac** ◎ Québec, SE Canada
80 E11 **Delami** Southern Kordofan, C Sudan 11°51´N 30°30´E
23 X11 **De Land** Florida, SE USA 29°01´N 81°18´W
35 R12 **Delano** California, W USA 35°46´N 119°15´W
29 V8 **Delano** Minnesota, N USA 45°03´N 93°46´W
36 K6 **Delano Peak** ▲ Utah, W USA 38°22´N 112°21´W
Delap-Uliga-Darrit *see* Dalap-Uliga-Djarrit
148 L7 **Delārām** Nīmrūz, SW Afghanistan 32°11´N 63°27´E
38 F17 **Delarof Islands** *island group* Aleutian Islands, Alaska, USA
30 M9 **Delavan** Wisconsin, N USA 42°37´N 88°37´W
31 S13 **Delaware** Ohio, N USA 40°18´N 83°06´W
18 I17 **Delaware** *off.* State of Delaware, *also known as* Blue Hen State, Diamond State, First State. ◐ *state* NE USA
18 I17 **Delaware Bay** *bay* NE USA
24 J8 **Delaware Mountains** ▲ Texas, SW USA
18 I12 **Delaware River** ~ NE USA
27 Q3 **Delaware River** ~ Kansas, C USA
18 J14 **Delaware Water Gap** *valley* New Jersey/Pennsylvania, NE USA
101 G14 **Delbrück** Nordrhein-Westfalen, W Germany 51°46´N 08°34´E
11 Q15 **Delburne** Alberta, SW Canada 52°09´N 113°11´W
172 M12 **Del Cano Rise** *undersea feature* SW Indian Ocean 45°15´S 44°15´E
113 Q18 **Delčevo** NE FYR Macedonia 41°57´N 22°45´E
Delcommune, Lac *see* Nzilo, Lac
98 O10 **Delden** Overijssel, E Netherlands 52°16´N 06°41´E
183 R12 **Delegate** New South Wales, SE Australia 37°04´S 148°57´E
De Lemmer *see* Lemmer
108 D7 **Delémont** *Ger.* Delsberg. Jura, NW Switzerland 47°22´N 07°21´E
25 R7 **De Leon** Texas, SW USA 32°06´N 98°33´W
115 F18 **Delfoí** Stereá Ellás, C Greece 38°28´N 22°31´E
98 G12 **Delft** Zuid-Holland, W Netherlands 52°01´N 04°22´E
155 J23 **Delft** *island* NW Sri Lanka
98 O5 **Delfzijl** Groningen, NE Netherlands 53°20´N 06°55´E
0 E9 **Delgada Fan** *undersea feature* NE Pacific Ocean 39°15´N 126°00´W
42 F7 **Delgado** San Salvador, SW El Salvador 13°44´N 89°07´W
82 Q12 **Delgado, Cabo** *headland* N Mozambique 10°41´S 40°40´E
162 G8 **Delger** *var.* Taygan. Govĭ-Altay, C Mongolia 46°20´N 97°22´E
163 O9 **Delgereh** *var.* Hongor. Dornogovĭ, SE Mongolia 45°49´N 111°20´E
162 J8 **Delgerhaan** *var.* Hujirt. Töv, C Mongolia 46°41´N 104°40´E
162 K9 **Delgerhangay** *var.* Hashaat. Dundgovĭ, C Mongolia 45°09´N 104°51´E
162 L9 **Delgertsogt** *var.* Amardalay. Dundgovĭ, C Mongolia 46°09´N 106°24´E
80 E6 **Delgo** Northern, N Sudan 20°08´N 30°35´E
159 R10 **Delhi** *var.* Delingha. Qinghai, C China 37°19´N 97°22´E
152 I10 **Delhi** *var.* Dehli, *Hind.* Dilli, *hist.* Shahjahanabad. *union territory capital* Delhi, N India 28°40´N 77°11´E
22 J5 **Delhi** Louisiana, S USA 32°28´N 91°29´W
18 J11 **Delhi** New York, NE USA 42°16´N 74°55´W
152 I10 **Delhi** ◐ *union territory* NW India
136 J17 **Deli Burnu** *headland* S Turkey 36°43´N 34°55´E
136 J12 **Delice Çayı** ~ C Turkey
55 X10 **Délices** C French Guiana 04°45´N 53°45´W
40 J6 **Delicias** *var.* Ciudad Delicias. Chihuahua, N Mexico 28°09´N 105°22´W
143 N7 **Delījān** *var.* Dalijan, Diljan. Markazī, W Iran 34°02´N 50°39´E
112 P12 **Deli Jovan** ▲ E Serbia
Déli-Kárpátok *see* Carpaţii Meridionalii
8 I8 **Déljne** *prev.* Fort Franklin. Northwest Territories, NW Canada 65°10´N 123°30´W
Delingha *see* Delhi
15 Q7 **Delisle** Québec, SE Canada 48°39´N 71°42´W
11 T15 **Delisle** Saskatchewan, S Canada 51°54´N 107°01´W
101 M15 **Delitzsch** Sachsen, E Germany 51°31´N 12°19´E
33 Q12 **Dell** Montana, NW USA 44°41´N 112°42´W
24 I7 **Dell City** Texas, SW USA 31°56´N 105°12´W
103 U7 **Delle** Territoire-de-Belfort, E France 47°30´N 07°00´E
36 J9 **Dellenbaugh, Mount** ▲ Arizona, SW USA 36°06´N 113°32´W
29 R11 **Dell Rapids** South Dakota, N USA 43°50´N 96°42´W
21 Y4 **Delmar** Maryland, NE USA 38°26´N 75°32´W
18 K11 **Delmar** New York, NE USA 42°37´N 73°49´W
100 G11 **Delmenhorst** Niedersachsen, NW Germany 53°03´N 08°38´E
112 C9 **Delnice** Primorje-Gorski Kotar, NW Croatia 45°24´N 14°49´E
37 R7 **Del Norte** Colorado, C USA 37°40´N 106°21´W
39 N6 **De Long Mountains** ▲ Alaska, USA
183 P16 **Deloraine** Tasmania, SE Australia 41°34´S 146°43´E
11 W17 **Deloraine** Manitoba, S Canada 49°12´N 100°28´W
31 O12 **Delphi** Indiana, N USA 40°35´N 86°40´W
31 Q12 **Delphos** Ohio, N USA 40°49´N 84°20´W
23 Z15 **Delray Beach** Florida, SE USA 26°27´N 80°04´W
25 O12 **Del Rio** Texas, SW USA 29°23´N 100°56´W
Delsberg *see* Delémont
94 N11 **Delsbo** Gävleborg, C Sweden 61°49´N 16°34´E
37 P6 **Delta** Colorado, C USA 38°44´N 108°04´W
36 K5 **Delta** Utah, W USA 39°21´N 112°34´W
77 T17 **Delta** ◐ *state* S Nigeria
55 Q6 **Delta Amacuro** *off.* Territorio Delta Amacuro. ◐ *federal district* NE Venezuela
Delta Amacuro, Territorio *see* Delta Amacuro
39 S9 **Delta Junction** Alaska, USA 64°02´N 145°43´W
23 X11 **Deltona** Florida, SE USA 28°54´N 81°15´W
183 T5 **Delungra** New South Wales, SE Australia 29°40´S 150°49´E
162 D6 **Delüün** *var.* Rashaant. Bayan-Ölgiy, W Mongolia 47°48´N 90°45´E
154 C12 **Delvāda** Gujarāt, W India 20°46´N 71°02´E
61 B21 **Del Valle** Buenos Aires, E Argentina 35°55´S 60°42´W
Delvina *see* Delvinë
115 C15 **Delvináki** *var.* Dhelvinákion; *prev.* Pogónion. Ípeiros, W Greece 39°57´N 20°28´E
113 L23 **Delvinë** *var.* Delvina, *It.* Delvino. Vlorë, S Albania 39°56´N 20°07´E
Delvino *see* Delvinë
116 I7 **Delyatyn** Ivano-Frankivs'ka Oblast', W Ukraine 48°32´N 24°38´E
127 U5 **Dëma** ~ W Russian Federation
105 O5 **Demanda, Sierra de la** ▲ W Spain
39 T5 **Demarcation Point** *headland* Alaska, USA 69°40´N 141°19´W
79 K21 **Demba** Kasai-Occidental, C Dem. Rep. Congo 05°24´S 22°16´E
172 H13 **Dembéni** Grande Comore, NW Comoros 11°50´S 43°25´E
79 M15 **Dembia** Mbomou, SE Central African Republic 05°08´N 24°25´E
Dembidollo *see* Dembī Dolo
80 H13 **Dembī Dolo** *var.* Dembidollo. Oromīya, C Ethiopia 08°33´N 34°49´E
152 K6 **Demchok** *var.* Dêmqog. China/India 32°30´N 79°42´E *see also* Dêmqog
152 L6 **Demchok** *var.* Dêmqog. *disputed region* China/India *see also* Dêmqog
98 I12 **De Meern** Utrecht, C Netherlands 52°06´N 05°00´E
99 I17 **Demer** ~ C Belgium
64 H12 **Demerara Plain** *undersea feature* W Atlantic Ocean 10°00´N 48°00´W
64 H12 **Demerara Plateau** *undersea feature* W Atlantic Ocean
55 T9 **Demerara River** ~ NE Guyana
126 H3 **Demidov** Smolenskaya Oblast', W Russian Federation 55°15´N 31°30´E
37 Q15 **Deming** New Mexico, SW USA 32°17´N 107°46´W
32 H6 **Deming** Washington, NW USA 48°49´N 122°13´W
58 E10 **Demini, Rio** ~ NW Brazil
136 D13 **Demirci** Manisa, W Turkey 39°03´N 28°40´E
113 P19 **Demir Kapija** *prev.* Železna Vrata. SE FYR Macedonia 41°25´N 22°15´E
114 N11 **Demirköy** Kırklareli, NW Turkey 41°48´N 27°49´E
100 N9 **Demmin** Mecklenburg-Vorpommern, NE Germany 53°53´N 13°03´E
23 O5 **Demopolis** Alabama, S USA 32°31´N 87°50´W
31 N11 **Demotte** Indiana, N USA 41°13´N 87°07´W
158 F13 **Dêmqog** *var.* Demchok. China/India 32°36´N 79°29´E *see also* Demchok
152 L6 **Dêmqog** *var.* Demchok. *disputed region* China/India *see also* Demchok
171 Y13 **Demta** Papua, E Indonesia 02°19´S 140°06´E
121 K11 **Dem'yanka** ~ C Russian Federation
124 H15 **Demyansk** Novgorodskaya Oblast', W Russian Federation 57°39´N 32°31´E
122 H10 **Dem'yanskoye** Tyumenskaya Oblast', C Russian Federation 59°39´N 69°15´E
103 P2 **Denain** Nord, N France 50°19´N 03°24´E
39 S10 **Denali** Alaska, USA 63°08´N 147°33´W
Denali *see* McKinley, Mount
81 M14 **Denan** Sumalē, E Ethiopia 06°40´N 43°31´E
Denau *see* Denov
97 J18 **Denbigh** *Wel.* Dinbych. NE Wales, United Kingdom 53°11´N 03°25´W
97 J18 **Denbigh** *cultural region* N Wales, United Kingdom
98 I6 **Den Burg** Noord-Holland, NW Netherlands 53°03´N 04°47´E
99 F18 **Dender** *Fr.* Dendre. ~ W Belgium
99 F18 **Denderleeuw** Oost-Vlaanderen, NW Belgium 50°53´N 04°05´E
99 F17 **Dendermonde** *Fr.* Termonde. Oost-Vlaanderen, NW Belgium 51°02´N 04°08´E
Dendre *see* Dender
194 I9 **Dendtler Island** *island* Antarctica
98 P10 **Denekamp** Overijssel, E Netherlands 52°23´N 07°00´E
77 W12 **Dengas** Zinder, S Niger 13°15´N 09°43´E
Dêngka *see* Têwo
Dêngkagoin *see* Têwo
162 L13 **Dengkou** *var.* Bayan Gol. Nei Mongol Zizhiqu, N China 40°15´N 106°59´E
159 Q14 **Dêngqên** *var.* Gyamotang. Xizang Zizhiqu, W China 31°28´N 95°28´E
Deng Xian *see* Dengzhou
160 M7 **Dengzhou** *prev.* Deng Xian. Henan, C China 32°48´N 111°59´E
Dengzhou *see* Penglai
Den Haag *see* 's-Gravenhage

◆ Country
● Country Capital
◇ Dependent Territory
○ Dependent Territory Capital
◐ Administrative Regions
✈ International Airport
▲ Mountain
▲ Mountain Range
⚠ Volcano
~ River
◎ Lake
☒ Reservoir

DENHAM – DIU

180 H10 **Denham** Western Australia 25°56′S 113°35′E
98 N9 **Den Ham** Overijssel, E Netherlands 52°30′N 06°31′E
44 J12 **Denham, Mount** ▲ C Jamaica 18°13′N 77°33′W
22 J8 **Denham Springs** Louisiana, S USA 30°29′N 90°57′W
98 I7 **Den Helder** Noord-Holland, NW Netherlands 52°54′N 04°45′E
105 T11 **Dénia** País Valenciano, E Spain 38°51′N 00°07′E
189 Q8 **Denig** W Nauru
183 N10 **Deniliquin** New South Wales, SE Australia 35°33′S 144°58′E
29 T14 **Denison** Iowa, C USA 42°00′N 95°22′W
25 U5 **Denison** Texas, SW USA 33°45′N 96°32′W
144 L8 **Denisovka** *prev.* Ordzhonikidze. Kostanay, N Kazakhstan 52°27′N 61°42′E
136 D15 **Denizli** Denizli, SW Turkey 37°46′N 29°05′E
136 D15 **Denizli** ◈ *province* SW Turkey
Denjong *see* Sikkim
183 S7 **Denman** New South Wales, SE Australia 32°24′S 150°43′E
195 Y10 **Denman Glacier** *glacier* Antarctica
21 R14 **Denmark** South Carolina, SE USA 33°19′N 81°08′W
95 G23 **Denmark** *off.* Kingdom of Denmark, *Dan.* Danmark; *anc.* Hafnia. ◆ *monarchy* N Europe
Denmark, Kingdom of *see* Denmark
92 H1 **Denmark Strait** *var.* Danmarksstraedet. *strait* Greenland/Iceland
45 T11 **Dennery** E Saint Lucia 13°55′N 60°53′W
98 I7 **Den Oever** Noord-Holland, NW Netherlands 52°56′N 05°01′E
147 O13 **Denov** *Rus.* Denau. Surkhondaryo Viloyati, S Uzbekistan 38°20′N 67°48′E
169 U17 **Denpasar** *prev.* Paloe. Bali, C Indonesia 08°40′S 115°14′E
116 E12 **Denta** Timiş, W Romania 45°20′N 21°15′E
21 Y3 **Denton** Maryland, NE USA 38°53′N 75°50′W
25 T6 **Denton** Texas, SW USA 33°11′N 97°08′W
186 G9 **D'Entrecasteaux Islands** *island group* SE Papua New Guinea
37 T4 **Denver** *state capital* Colorado, C USA 39°45′N 105°W
37 T4 **Denver** ✈ Colorado, C USA 39°57′N 104°38′W
24 L6 **Denver City** Texas, SW USA 32°57′N 102°49′W
152 J9 **Deoband** Uttar Pradesh, N India 29°41′N 77°40′E
154 N12 **Deogarh** Orissa, SW India 21°32′N 84°44′E
Deoghar *see* Devghar
154 E13 **Deolāli** Mahārāshtra, W India 19°55′N 73°49′E
154 I10 **Deori** Madhya Pradesh, C India 23°09′N 78°39′E
153 O12 **Deoria** Uttar Pradesh, N India 26°31′N 83°48′E
99 A17 **De Panne** West-Vlaanderen, W Belgium 51°06′N 02°35′E
Departamento del Quindío *see* Quindío
Departamento de Narino, *see* Nariño
54 M5 **Dependencia Federal** *off.* Territorio Dependencia Federal. ◈ *federal dependency* N Venezuela
Dependencia Federal, Territorio *see* Dependencia Federal
30 M7 **De Pere** Wisconsin, N USA 44°26′N 88°03′W
18 D10 **Depew** New York, NE USA 42°54′N 78°41′W
99 E17 **De Pinte** Oost-Vlaanderen, NW Belgium 51°00′N 03°37′E
25 V5 **Deport** Texas, SW USA 33°31′N 95°19′W
123 Q8 **Deputatskiy** Respublika Sakha (Yakutiya), NE Russian Federation 69°18′N 139°48′E
Dêqên *see* Dagzê
27 S13 **De Queen** Arkansas, C USA 34°02′N 94°20′W
22 G8 **De Quincy** Louisiana, S USA 30°27′N 93°25′W
81 J20 **Dera** *spring/well* S Kenya 02°39′S 39°52′E
149 V11 **Dera Bugti** Baluchistān, SW Pakistan 28°35′N 65°25′E
Der'a/Derá/Déraa *see* Dar'ā
149 S10 **Dera Ghāzi Khān** *var.* Dera Ghāzikhān. Punjab, C Pakistan 30°01′N 70°37′E
Dera Ghāzikhān *see* Dera Ghāzi Khān
149 S8 **Dera Ismāīl Khān** North-West Frontier Province, C Pakistan 31°51′N 70°56′E
149 Q12 **Dera Murād Jamāli** Baluchistān, SW Pakistan 28°34′N 68°12′E
113 L16 **Đeravica** ▲ S Serbia 42°33′N 20°08′E
116 L6 **Derazhnya** Khmel'nyts'ka Oblast', W Ukraine 49°16′N 27°24′E
127 R17 **Derbent** Respublika Dagestan, SW Russian Federation 42°01′N 48°16′E
147 N13 **Derbent** Surkhondaryo Viloyati, S Uzbekistan 38°15′N 66°59′E
Derbisîye *see* Darbāsīyah
79 M15 **Derbissaka** Mbomou, SE Central African Republic 05°43′N 24°48′E
180 L4 **Derby** Western Australia 17°18′S 123°37′E
97 M19 **Derby** C England, United Kingdom 52°55′N 01°30′W
27 N7 **Derby** Kansas, C USA 37°33′N 97°16′W
97 L18 **Derbyshire** *cultural region* C England, United Kingdom
112 O11 **Đerdap** *physical region* E Serbia
Derelí *see* Gónnoi
162 L9 **Deren** *var.* Tsant. Dundgovĭ, C Mongolia 46°16′N 106°55′E
171 W13 **Derew** ∼ Papua, E Indonesia
127 R8 **Dergachi** Saratovskaya Oblast', W Russian Federation 51°15′N 48°58′E
Dergachi *see* Derhachi
97 C19 **Derg, Lough** *Ir.* Loch Deirgeirt. ⊚ W Ireland
117 V5 **Derhachi** *Rus.* Dergachi. Kharkivs'ka Oblast', E Ukraine 50°09′N 36°11′E
22 G8 **De Ridder** Louisiana, S USA 30°51′N 93°18′W
137 P16 **Derik** Mardin, SE Turkey 37°22′N 40°16′E
83 E20 **Derm** Hardap, C Namibia 23°38′S 18°12′E
144 M14 **Dermentobe** *prev.* Dyurment'yube. Kzyl-Orda, S Kazakhstan 45°46′N 63°42′E
27 W14 **Dermott** Arkansas, C USA 33°31′N 91°26′W
Dérna *see* Darnah
Dernberg, Cape *see* Dolphin Head
22 J11 **Dernieres, Isles** *island group* Louisiana, S USA
102 I4 **Déroute, Passage de la** *strait* Channel Islands/France
Derrá *see* Dar'ā
Derry *see* Londonderry
Dertona *see* Tortona
Dertosa *see* Tortosa
80 H8 **Derudeb** Red Sea, NE Sudan 17°31′N 36°07′E
112 H10 **Derventa** Republika Srpska, N Bosnia and Herzegovina 44°57′N 17°55′E
183 O16 **Derwent Bridge** Tasmania, SE Australia 42°10′S 146°13′E
183 O17 **Derwent, River** ∼ Tasmania, SE Australia
146 F10 **Derweze** *Rus.* Darvaza. Ahal Welaýaty, C Turkmenistan 40°10′N 58°27′E
Deržavinsk *see* Derzhavinsk
145 O9 **Derzhavinsk** *var.* Deržavinsk. ◈ Akmola, C Kazakhstan
Dés *see* Dej
57 J18 **Desaguadero** Puno, S Peru 16°35′S 69°05′W
57 J18 **Desaguadero, Río** ∼ Bolivia/Peru
191 W9 **Désappointement, Îles du** *island group* Îles Tuamotu, C French Polynesia
27 W11 **Des Arc** Arkansas, C USA 34°58′N 91°30′W
14 C10 **Desbarats** Ontario, S Canada 46°20′N 83°52′W
62 H13 **Descabezado Grande, Volcán** ⩚ C Chile 35°34′S 70°40′W
40 B2 **Descanso** Baja California Norte, NW Mexico 32°08′N 116°51′W
102 L9 **Descartes** Indre-et-Loire, C France 46°58′N 00°40′E
11 T13 **Deschambault Lake** ⊚ Saskatchewan, C Canada
Deschnaer Koppe *see* Velká Deštná
32 I11 **Deschutes River** ∼ Oregon, NW USA
80 J12 **Desē** *var.* Desse, *It.* Dessie. Āmara, N Ethiopia 11°02′N 39°39′E
63 I20 **Deseado, Río** ∼ S Argentina
106 F8 **Desenzano del Garda** Lombardia, N Italy 45°28′N 10°31′E
36 K3 **Deseret Peak** ▲ Utah, W USA 40°27′N 112°37′W
64 P6 **Deserta Grande** *island* Madeira, Portugal, NE Atlantic Ocean
64 P6 **Desertas, Ilhas** *island group* Madeira, Portugal, NE Atlantic Ocean
35 X16 **Desert Center** California, W USA 33°42′N 115°22′W
35 V15 **Desert Hot Springs** California, W USA 33°57′N 116°33′W
14 K10 **Désert, Lac** ⊚ Québec, SE Canada
36 J2 **Desert Peak** ▲ Utah, W USA 41°03′N 113°22′W
31 R11 **Deshler** Ohio, N USA 41°12′N 83°55′W
Deshu *see* Deh Shū
Desiderii Fanum *see* St-Dizier
106 D7 **Desio** Lombardia, N Italy 45°37′N 09°12′E
115 E15 **Deskáti** *var.* Dheskáti. Dytikí Makedonía, N Greece 39°55′N 21°49′E
28 L2 **Des Lacs River** ∼ North Dakota, N USA
27 X6 **Desloge** Missouri, C USA 37°52′N 90°31′W
11 Q12 **Desmarais** Alberta, W Canada 55°58′N 113°56′W
29 Q10 **De Smet** South Dakota, N USA 44°23′N 97°33′W
29 V14 **Des Moines** *state capital* Iowa, C USA 41°36′N 93°37′W
17 N9 **Des Moines River** ∼ C USA
117 P4 **Desna** ∼ Russian Federation/Ukraine
116 G14 **Desnăţui** ∼ S Romania
63 F24 **Desolación, Isla** *island* S Chile
29 V14 **De Soto** Iowa, C USA 41°31′N 94°00′W
23 Q4 **De Soto Falls** *waterfall* Alabama, S USA
83 I25 **Despatch** Eastern Cape, S South Africa 33°48′S 25°28′E
105 N12 **Despeñaperros, Desfiladero de** *pass* S Spain
31 N10 **Des Plaines** Illinois, N USA 42°01′N 87°52′W
115 J21 **Despotikó** *island* Kykládes, Greece, Aegean Sea
112 N12 **Despotovac** Serbia, E Serbia 44°06′N 21°25′E
101 M14 **Dessau** Sachsen-Anhalt, E Germany 51°51′N 12°15′E
Desse *see* Desē
99 J16 **Dessel** Antwerpen, N Belgium 51°15′N 05°07′E
Dessie *see* Desē
Destêrro *see* Florianópolis
23 P9 **Destin** Florida, SE USA 30°23′N 86°30′W
Deštná *see* Velká Deštná
193 T10 **Desventurados, Islas de los** *island group* W Chile
103 N1 **Desvres** Pas-de-Calais, N France 50°41′N 01°48′E
116 E12 **Deta** *Ger.* Detta. Timiş, W Romania 45°24′N 21°14′E
101 H14 **Detmold** Nordrhein-Westfalen, W Germany 51°55′N 08°52′E
31 S10 **Detroit** Michigan, N USA 42°20′N 83°03′W
25 W5 **Detroit** Texas, SW USA 33°39′N 95°16′W
31 S10 **Detroit** ∼ Canada/USA
29 S6 **Detroit Lakes** Minnesota, N USA 46°49′N 95°49′W
31 S10 **Detroit Metropolitan** ✈ Michigan, N USA 42°12′N 83°16′W
Detta *see* Deta
167 S10 **Det Udom** Ubon Ratchathani, E Thailand 14°54′N 105°03′E
111 K20 **Detva** *Hung.* Gyeva. Bankobýstricky Kraj, C Slovakia 48°35′N 19°25′E
154 G13 **Deūlgaon Rāja** Mahārāshtra, C India 20°04′N 76°08′E
99 L15 **Deurne** Noord-Brabant, SE Netherlands 51°28′N 05°47′E
99 H16 **Deurne** ✈ (Antwerpen) Antwerpen, N Belgium 51°10′N 04°28′E
Deutsch-Brod *see* Havlíčkův Brod
Deutschendorf *see* Poprad
Deutsch-Eylau *see* Iława
109 Y6 **Deutschkreutz** Burgenland, E Austria 47°37′N 16°37′E
Deutsch Krone *see* Wałcz
Deutschland/Deutschland, Bundesrepublik *see* Germany
109 V9 **Deutschlandsberg** Steiermark, SE Austria 46°52′N 15°13′E
Deutsch-Südwestafrika *see* Namibia
109 Y3 **Deutsch-Wagram** Niederösterreich, E Austria 48°19′N 16°33′E
Deux-Ponts *see* Zweibrücken
14 I11 **Deux Rivieres** Ontario, SE Canada 46°13′N 78°16′W
102 K9 **Deux-Sèvres** ◈ *department* W France
116 G11 **Deva** *Ger.* Diemrich, *Hung.* Déva. Hunedoara, W Romania 45°55′N 22°55′E
Déva *see* Deva
Deva *see* Chester
Devana *see* Aberdeen
Devana Castra *see* Chester
Đevđelija *see* Gevgelija
136 L12 **Deveci Dağları** ▲▲ N Turkey
137 P15 **Devegeçidi Barajı** ⊞ SE Turkey
136 K15 **Develi** Kayseri, C Turkey 38°22′N 35°28′E
98 M11 **Deventer** Overijssel, E Netherlands 52°15′N 06°10′E
15 O10 **Devenyns, Lac** ⊚ Québec, SE Canada
96 K8 **Deveron** ∼ NE Scotland, United Kingdom
153 R14 **Devghar** *prev.* Deoghar. Jhārkhand, NE India
27 R10 **Devil's Den** *plateau* Arkansas, C USA
35 R7 **Devils Gate** *pass* California, W USA
30 J2 **Devils Island** *island* Apostle Islands, Wisconsin, N USA
Devil's Island *see* Diable, Île du
29 P3 **Devils Lake** North Dakota, N USA 48°08′N 98°50′W
31 R10 **Devils Lake** ⊚ Michigan, N USA
29 O3 **Devils Lake** ⊚ North Dakota, N USA
35 W13 **Devils Playground** *desert* California, W USA
25 O11 **Devils River** ∼ Texas, SW USA
33 Y12 **Devils Tower** ▲ Wyoming, C USA 44°33′N 104°45′W
114 I11 **Devin** *prev.* Dovlen. Smolyan, S Bulgaria 41°45′N 24°24′E
25 R12 **Devine** Texas, SW USA 29°08′N 98°54′W
152 H13 **Devli** Rājasthān, N India 25°47′N 75°23′E
Devne *see* Devnya
114 N8 **Devnya** *prev.* Devne. Varna, E Bulgaria 43°15′N 27°35′E
31 U14 **Devola** Ohio, N USA 39°28′N 81°28′W
Devoll *see* Devollit, Lumi i
113 M21 **Devollit, Lumi i** *var.* Devoll. ∼ SE Albania
11 Q14 **Devon** Alberta, SW Canada 53°21′N 113°47′W
97 I23 **Devon** *cultural region* SW England, United Kingdom
197 N10 **Devon Island** *prev.* North Devon Island. *island* Parry Islands, Nunavut, NE Canada
183 O16 **Devonport** Tasmania, SE Australia 41°14′S 146°21′E
136 H11 **Devrek** Zonguldak, N Turkey 41°14′N 31°57′E
154 G10 **Dewās** Madhya Pradesh, C India 22°59′N 76°03′E
De Westerein *see* Zwaagwesteinde
27 P8 **Dewey** Oklahoma, C USA 36°48′N 95°56′W
Dewey *see* Culebra
98 M8 **De Wijk** Drenthe, NE Netherlands 52°41′N 06°13′E
27 W12 **De Witt** Arkansas, C USA 34°17′N 91°21′W
29 Z14 **De Witt** Iowa, C USA 41°49′N 90°32′W
29 R16 **De Witt** Nebraska, C USA 40°23′N 96°55′W
97 M17 **Dewsbury** N England, United Kingdom 53°42′N 01°37′W
161 Q10 **Dexing** Jiangxi, S China 28°51′N 117°36′E
27 Y8 **Dexter** Missouri, C USA 36°48′N 89°57′W
37 U14 **Dexter** New Mexico, SW USA 33°12′N 104°25′W
160 I8 **Deyang** Sichuan, C China 31°08′N 104°23′E
182 C4 **Dey-Dey, Lake** *salt lake* South Australia
143 S7 **Deyhūk** Yazd, E Iran 33°18′N 57°30′E
Deynau *see* Galkynyş
Deyyer *see* Bandar-e Dayyer
142 L8 **Dezfūl** *var.* Dizful. Khūzestān, SW Iran 32°23′N 48°28′E
129 X4 **Dezhneva, Mys** *headland* NE Russian Federation 66°08′N 69°40′W
161 P4 **Dezhou** Shandong, E China 37°28′N 116°18′E
Dezhou *see* Dechang
Dezh Shāhpūr *see* Marīvān
Dhaalu Atoll *see* South Nilandhe Atoll
Dhahran *see* Aẓ Ẓahrān
Dhahran Al Khobar *see* Aẓ Ẓahrān al Khubar
153 U14 **Dhaka** *prev.* Dacca. ● (Bangladesh) Dhaka, C Bangladesh 23°42′N 90°22′E
153 T15 **Dhaka** ◈ *division* C Bangladesh
Dhali *see* Idálion
Dhalli Rajhara *see* Dalli Rājhara
141 O15 **Dhamār** W Yemen 14°31′N 44°25′E
154 K12 **Dhamtari** Chhattīsgarh, C India 20°43′N 81°36′E
153 Q15 **Dhanbād** Jhārkhand, NE India 23°48′N 86°27′E
152 L10 **Dhangaḍhi** *var.* Dhangarhi. Far Western, W Nepal 28°45′N 80°38′E
Dhangarhi *see* Dhangaḍhi
Dhank *see* Ḍank
153 R12 **Dhankuṭā** Eastern, E Nepal 27°06′N 87°21′E
152 I6 **Dhaola Dhār** ▲▲ NE India
154 F10 **Dhār** Madhya Pradesh, C India 22°32′N 75°24′E
153 R12 **Dharān** *var.* Dharan Bazar. Eastern, E Nepal 26°51′N 87°18′E
Dharan Bazar *see* Dharān
155 H21 **Dhārāpuram** Tamil Nādu, SE India 10°45′N 77°33′E
155 H20 **Dharmapuri** Tamil Nādu, SE India 12°11′N 78°07′E
155 H18 **Dharmavaram** Andhra Pradesh, E India 14°27′N 77°44′E
154 M11 **Dharmjaygarh** Chhattīsgarh, C India 22°27′N 83°16′E
Dharmsāla *see* Dharmshāla
152 I7 **Dharmshāla** *prev.* Dharmsāla. Himāchal Pradesh, N India 32°14′N 76°24′E
155 F17 **Dhārwād** *prev.* Dharwar. Karnātaka, SW India 15°30′N 75°04′E
Dharwar *see* Dhārwād
Dhaulagiri *see* Dhawalāgiri
152 J12 **Dhaulpur** *var.* Daulpur, Dholpur. Rājasthān, N India 26°43′N 77°54′E
153 O10 **Dhawalāgiri** *var.* Dhaulagiri. ▲ C Nepal 28°45′N 83°27′E
81 L18 **Dheere Laaq** *var.* Lak Dera, *It.* Lach Dera. *seasonal river* Kenya/Somalia
121 Q3 **Dhekeleia Sovereign Base Area** *UK military installation* E Cyprus 34°59′N 33°45′E
121 Q3 **Dhekélia** *Eng.* Dhekelia, *Gk.* Dekéleia. *UK air base* SE Cyprus 35°00′N 33°45′E *see* Dhekélia
Dhelvinákion *see* Delvináki
113 M22 **Dhëmbelit, Majae** ▲ S Albania 40°10′N 20°22′E
154 O12 **Dhenkānāl** Orissa, E India 20°40′N 85°36′E
Dheskáti *see* Deskáti
138 G11 **Dhībān** Ma'dabā, NW Jordan 31°30′N 35°47′E
Dhidhimótikhon *see* Didymóteicho
Dhíkti Ori *see* Díkti
153 V12 **Dhing** Assam, NE India 26°26′N 92°29′E
139 W12 **Dhī Qār** ◈ *governorate* SE Iraq
138 I12 **Dhirwah, Wādī adh** *dry watercourse* C Jordan
Dhístomon *see* Dístomo
Dhodhekánisos *see* Dodekánisa
Dhodhóni *see* Dodóni
Dhofar *see* Ẓufār
Dholpur *see* Dhaulpur
Dhomokós *see* Domokós
Dhond *see* Daund
155 H17 **Dhone** Andhra Pradesh, C India 15°25′N 77°52′E
154 B11 **Dhorāji** Gujarāt, W India 21°44′N 70°27′E
Dhráma *see* Dráma
154 C10 **Dhrāngadhra** Gujarāt, W India 22°59′N 71°32′E
Dhrepanon, Akrotírio *see* Drépano, Akrotírio
153 T13 **Dhuburi** Assam, NE India 26°06′N 89°55′E
154 F12 **Dhule** *prev.* Dhulia. Mahārāshtra, C India 20°54′N 74°47′E
Dhulia *see* Dhule
Dhún Dealgan, Cuan *see* Dundalk Bay
Dhún Droma, Cuan *see* Dundrum Bay
Dhún na nGall, Bá *see* Donegal Bay
Dhū Shaykh *see* Qazānīyah
80 Q13 **Dhuudo** Bari, NE Somalia 09°21′N 50°19′E
81 N15 **Dhuusa Marreeb** *var.* Dusa Marreb, *It.* Dusa Mareb. Galguduud, C Somalia 05°33′N 46°24′E
115 J24 **Día** *island* SE Greece
55 Y9 **Diable, Île du** *var.* Devil's Island. *island* N French Guiana
15 N12 **Diable, Rivière du** ∼ Québec, SE Canada
35 N8 **Diablo, Mount** ▲ California, W USA 37°52′N 121°57′W
35 O9 **Diablo Range** ▲▲ California, W USA
24 I8 **Diablo, Sierra** ▲▲ Texas, SW USA
45 O11 **Diablotins, Morne** ▲ N Dominica 15°30′N 61°23′W
77 N11 **Diafarabé** Mopti, C Mali 14°09′N 05°01′W
77 N11 **Diaka** ∼ SW Mali
Diakovár *see* Đakovo
76 I12 **Dialakoto** S Senegal 13°21′N 13°19′W
61 B18 **Diamante** Entre Ríos, E Argentina 32°05′S 60°40′W
62 I12 **Diamante, Río** ∼ C Argentina
59 M19 **Diamantina** Minas Gerais, SE Brazil 18°17′S 43°37′W
59 N17 **Diamantina, Chapada** ▲▲ E Brazil
173 U11 **Diamantina Fracture Zone** *tectonic feature* E Indian Ocean
181 T8 **Diamantina River** ∼ Queensland/South Australia
38 D9 **Diamond Head** *headland* O'ahu, Hawai'i, USA 21°15′N 157°48′W
37 P2 **Diamond Peak** ▲ Colorado, C USA 40°56′N 108°56′W
35 W5 **Diamond Peak** ▲ Nevada, W USA 39°34′N 115°46′W
Diamond State *see* Delaware
76 J11 **Diamou** Kayes, SW Mali 14°04′N 11°16′W
95 I23 **Dianalund** Vestsjælland, C Denmark 55°32′N 11°30′E
65 G25 **Diana's Peak** ▲ C Saint Helena
160 M16 **Dianbai** *var.* Shuidong. Guangdong, S China 21°30′N 111°05′E
160 G13 **Dian Chi** ⊞ SW China
106 B10 **Diano Marina** Liguria, NW Italy 43°55′N 08°06′E
163 V11 **Diaobingshan** *var.* Tiefa. Liaoning, NE China 42°25′N 123°39′E
77 R13 **Diapaga** E Burkina 12°09′N 01°48′E
Diarbekr *see* Diyarbakır
107 J15 **Diavolo, Passo del** *pass* C Italy
61 B18 **Díaz** Santa Fe, C Argentina 32°22′S 61°05′W
141 W6 **Dibā al Ḩiṣn** *var.* Dibāh, Dibba. Ash Shāriqah, NE United Arab Emirates 25°35′N 56°16′E
139 S3 **Dībaga** Arbīl, N Iraq 35°51′N 43°49′E
Dibāh *see* Dibā al Ḩiṣn
79 L22 **Dibaya** Kasai-Occidental, S Dem. Rep. Congo 06°31′S 22°57′E
Dibba *see* Dibā al Ḩiṣn
195 W15 **Dibble Iceberg Tongue** *ice feature* Antarctica
113 L19 **Dibër** ◈ *district* E Albania
83 I20 **Dibete** Central, SE Botswana 23°45′S 26°26′E
Dibio *see* Dijon
25 W9 **Diboll** Texas, SW USA 31°11′N 94°46′W
Dibra *see* Debar
153 X11 **Dibrugarh** Assam, NE India 27°29′N 94°49′E
54 G4 **Dibulla** La Guajira, N Colombia 11°14′N 73°22′W
25 O5 **Dickens** Texas, SW USA 33°38′N 100°51′W
19 R2 **Dickey** Maine, NE USA 47°04′N 69°05′W
30 K9 **Dickeyville** Wisconsin, N USA 42°37′N 90°36′W
28 K5 **Dickinson** North Dakota, N USA 46°54′N 102°48′W
0 E6 **Dickins Seamount** *undersea feature* NE Pacific Ocean 54°30′N 137°00′W
27 O13 **Dickson** Oklahoma, C USA 34°11′N 96°58′W
20 I9 **Dickson** Tennessee, S USA 36°04′N 87°23′W
Dicle *see* Tigris
Dicsőszentmárton *see* Târnăveni
98 M12 **Didam** Gelderland, E Netherlands 51°56′N 06°08′E
163 Y8 **Didao** Heilongjiang, NE China 45°22′N 130°48′E
76 L12 **Didiéni** Koulikoro, W Mali 13°48′N 08°01′W
Didimo *see* Dídymo
Didimotiho *see* Didymóteicho
81 K17 **Didimtu** *spring/well* NE Kenya 02°58′N 40°07′E
67 U9 **Didinga Hills** ▲▲ S Sudan
11 Q16 **Didsbury** Alberta, SW Canada 51°39′N 114°09′W
152 G11 **Dīdwāna** Rājasthān, N India 27°23′N 74°36′E
115 G20 **Dídymo** *var.* Didimo. ▲ S Greece 37°28′N 23°12′E
114 L12 **Didymóteicho** *var.* Dhidhimótikhon, Didimotiho. Anatolikí Makedonía kai Thráki, NE Greece 41°22′N 26°29′E
103 S13 **Die** Drôme, E France 44°46′N 05°21′E
77 O13 **Diébougou** SW Burkina 11°00′N 03°12′W
Diedenhofen *see* Thionville
11 S16 **Diefenbaker, Lake** ⊞ Saskatchewan, S Canada
62 H7 **Diego de Almagro** Atacama, N Chile 26°24′S 70°10′W
63 F23 **Diego de Almagro, Isla** *island* S Chile
61 A20 **Diego de Alvear** Santa Fe, C Argentina 34°25′S 62°10′W
173 Q7 **Diego Garcia** *island* S British Indian Ocean Territory
Diégo-Suarez *see* Antsirañana
99 M23 **Diekirch** Diekirch, C Luxembourg 49°52′N 06°10′E
99 L23 **Diekirch** ◈ *district* N Luxembourg
76 K11 **Diéma** Kayes, W Mali 14°30′N 09°12′W
101 H15 **Diemel** ∼ W Germany
98 I10 **Diemen** Noord-Holland, C Netherlands 52°21′N 04°58′E
Diemrich *see* Deva
167 R6 **Điện Biên** *var.* Bien Bien, Dien Bien Phu. Lai Châu, N Vietnam 21°23′N 103°02′E
Dien Bien Phu *see* Điện Biên
167 S7 **Diễn Châu** Nghệ An, N Vietnam 18°54′N 105°35′E
99 K18 **Diepenbeek** Limburg, NE Belgium 50°54′N 05°25′E
98 N11 **Diepenheim** Overijssel, E Netherlands 52°10′N 06°37′E
98 M10 **Diepenveen** Overijssel, E Netherlands 52°18′N 06°09′E
100 G12 **Diepholz** Niedersachsen, NW Germany 52°36′N 08°23′E
102 M3 **Dieppe** Seine-Maritime, N France 49°55′N 01°05′E
98 M12 **Dieren** Gelderland, E Netherlands 52°03′N 06°06′E
27 S13 **Dierks** Arkansas, C USA 34°07′N 94°01′W
99 J17 **Diest** Vlaams Brabant, C Belgium 50°58′N 05°03′E
108 F7 **Dietikon** Zürich, NW Switzerland 47°24′N 08°25′E
103 R13 **Dieulefit** Drôme, E France 44°30′N 05°01′E
103 T5 **Dieuze** Moselle, NE France 48°49′N 06°41′E
119 H15 **Dieveniškės** Vilnius, SE Lithuania 54°12′N 25°38′E
98 N7 **Diever** Drenthe, NE Netherlands 52°49′N 06°19′E
101 F17 **Diez** Rheinland-Pfalz, W Germany 50°22′N 08°01′E
77 Y12 **Diffa** Diffa, SE Niger 13°19′N 12°37′E
77 Y10 **Diffa** ◈ *department* SE Niger
99 L25 **Differdange** Luxembourg, SW Luxembourg 49°32′N 05°53′E
13 O16 **Digby** Nova Scotia, SE Canada 44°37′N 65°47′W
26 J5 **Dighton** Kansas, C USA 38°28′N 100°28′W
Dignano d'Istria *see* Vodnjan
103 T14 **Digne** *var.* Digne-les-Bains. Alpes-de-Haute-Provence, SE France 44°05′N 06°14′E
Digne-les-Bains *see* Digne
Digoel *see* Digul, Sungai
103 Q10 **Digoin** Saône-et-Loire, C France 46°30′N 04°E
171 Q8 **Digos** Mindanao, S Philippines 06°46′N 125°21′E
149 Q16 **Digri** Sind, SE Pakistan 25°11′N 69°10′E
171 Y14 **Digul Barat, Sungai** ∼ Papua, E Indonesia
171 Y15 **Digul, Sungai** *prev.* Digoel. ∼ Papua, E Indonesia
171 Z14 **Digul Timur, Sungai** ∼ Papua, E Indonesia
153 X10 **Dihāng** ∼ NE India
Dihang *see* Brahmaputra
Dihōk *see* Dahūk
81 L17 **Diinsoor** Bay, S Somalia 02°28′N 43°00′E
Dijlah *see* Tigris
99 H17 **Dijle** ∼ C Belgium
103 R8 **Dijon** *anc.* Dibio. Côte d'Or, C France 47°21′N 05°04′E
93 H14 **Dikanäs** Västerbotten, N Sweden 65°15′N 16°00′E
80 L12 **Dikhil** SW Djibouti 11°08′N 42°19′E
136 B13 **Dikili** İzmir, W Turkey 39°05′N 26°52′E
99 B17 **Diksmuide** *var.* Dixmuide, *Fr.* Dixmude. West-Vlaanderen, W Belgium 51°02′N 02°52′E
122 K7 **Dikson** Taymyrskiy (Dolgano-Nenetskiy) Avtonomnyy Okrug, N Russian Federation 73°30′N 80°35′E
115 K25 **Díkti** *var.* Dhíkti Ori. ▲▲ Kríti, Greece, E Mediterranean Sea
77 Z13 **Dikwa** Borno, NE Nigeria 12°00′N 13°57′E
81 J15 **Dīla** Southern Nationalities, S Ethiopia 06°19′N 38°16′E
99 G18 **Dilbeek** Vlaams Brabant, C Belgium 50°51′N 04°16′E
171 Q16 **Dili** *var.* Dilli, Dilly. ● (East Timor) N East Timor 08°33′S 125°34′E
77 Y11 **Dilia** *var.* Dillia. ∼ SE Niger
Dilijan *see* Delījān
167 U13 **Di Linh** Lâm Đông, S Vietnam 11°38′N 108°07′E
101 G16 **Dillenburg** Hessen, W Germany 50°45′N 08°16′E
25 Q13 **Dilley** Texas, SW USA 28°40′N 99°10′W
Dilli *see* Dili, East Timor
Dilli *see* Delhi, India
Dillia *see* Dilia
80 E11 **Dilling** *var.* Ad Dalanj. Southern Kordofan, C Sudan 12°02′N 29°41′E
101 D20 **Dillingen** Saarland, SW Germany 49°20′N 06°43′E
Dillingen *see* Dillingen an der Donau
101 J22 **Dillingen an der Donau** *var.* Dillingen. Bayern, S Germany 48°34′N 10°29′E
39 O13 **Dillingham** Alaska, USA 59°03′N 158°30′W
33 Q12 **Dillon** Montana, NW USA 45°14′N 112°38′W
21 T12 **Dillon** South Carolina, SE USA 34°25′N 79°22′W
31 T13 **Dillon Lake** ⊞ Ohio, N USA
Dilly *see* Dili
Dilman *see* Salmās
79 K24 **Dilolo** Katanga, S Dem. Rep. Congo 10°42′S 22°21′E
115 J20 **Dílos** *island* Kykládes, Greece, Aegean Sea
141 Y11 **Ḑil', Ra's aḑ** *headland* E Oman 19°12′N 57°53′E
29 R5 **Dilworth** Minnesota, N USA 46°53′N 96°38′W
138 H7 **Dimashq** *var.* Ash Shām, Esh Sham, *Eng.* Damascus, *Fr.* Damas, *It.* Damasco. ● Dimashq, SW Syria 33°30′N 36°19′E
138 I8 **Dimashq** *off.* Muḩāfaẓat Dimashq, *var.* Damascus, *Ar.* Ash Sham, Ash Shām, Damasco, Esh Sham, *Fr.* Damas. ◈ *governorate* S Syria
138 I7 **Dimashq** ✈ Dimashq, S Syria 33°30′N 36°19′E
Dimashq, Muḩāfaẓat *see* Dimashq
79 L21 **Dimbelenge** Kasai-Occidental, C Dem. Rep. Congo 05°36′S 23°04′E
77 N16 **Dimbokro** E Ivory Coast 06°43′N 04°46′W
182 L11 **Dimboola** Victoria, SE Australia 36°29′S 142°03′E
Dîmboviţa *see* Dâmboviţa
Dimitrov *see* Dymytrov
114 K11 **Dimitrovgrad** Khaskovo, S Bulgaria 42°03′N 25°36′E
127 R5 **Dimitrovgrad** Ul'yanovskaya Oblast', W Russian Federation 54°14′N 49°37′E
113 Q15 **Dimitrovgrad** *prev.* Caribrod. Serbia, SE Serbia 43°01′N 22°46′E
Dimitrovo *see* Pernik
Dimlang *see* Vogel Peak
24 M3 **Dimmitt** Texas, SW USA 34°32′N 102°20′W
114 F7 **Dimovo** Vidin, NW Bulgaria 43°46′N 22°47′E
59 A16 **Dimpolis** Acre, W Brazil 09°52′S 71°51′W
115 O23 **Dimyliá** Ródos, Dodekánisa, Greece, Aegean Sea 36°17′N 27°59′E
171 Q6 **Dinagat Island** *island* S Philippines
153 S13 **Dinajpur** Rajshahi, NW Bangladesh 25°38′N 88°40′E
102 I6 **Dinan** Côtes d'Armor, NW France 48°27′N 02°02′W
99 I21 **Dinant** Namur, S Belgium 50°16′N 04°55′E
136 E15 **Dinar** Afyon, SW Turkey 38°05′N 30°09′E
112 F13 **Dinara** ▲ W Croatia 43°49′N 16°42′E
Dinara *see* Dinaric Alps
102 I5 **Dinard** Ille-et-Vilaine, NW France 48°38′N 02°04′W
112 F13 **Dinaric Alps** *var.* Dinara. ▲▲ Bosnia and Herzegovina/Croatia
143 N10 **Dīnār, Kūh-e** ▲ C Iran 30°51′N 51°36′E
Dinbych *see* Denbigh
155 H22 **Dindigul** Tamil Nādu, SE India 10°23′N 78°E
83 M19 **Dindiza** Gaza, S Mozambique 23°22′S 33°28′E
79 H21 **Dinga** Bandundu, SW Dem. Rep. Congo 05°00′S 16°29′E
149 V7 **Dinga** Punjab, E Pakistan 32°38′N 73°45′E
Dingchang *see* Qinxian
158 L16 **Dinggyê** *var.* Gyangkar. Xizang Zizhiqu, W China 28°18′N 88°06′E
97 A20 **Dingle** *Ir.* An Daingean. SW Ireland 52°09′N 10°16′W
97 A20 **Dingle Bay** *Ir.* Bá an Daingin. *bay* SW Ireland
18 I13 **Dingmans Ferry** Pennsylvania, NE USA 41°12′N 74°51′W
101 N22 **Dingolfing** Bayern, SE Germany 48°37′N 12°28′E
171 O1 **Dingras** Luzon, N Philippines 18°06′N 120°43′E
76 J13 **Dinguiraye** N Guinea 11°19′N 10°49′W
96 I8 **Dingwall** N Scotland, United Kingdom 57°36′N 04°26′W
159 V10 **Dingxi** Gansu, C China 35°36′N 104°33′E
Ding Xian *see* Dingzhou
161 Q7 **Dingyuan** Anhui, E China 32°30′N 117°40′E
161 O3 **Dingzhou** *prev.* Ding Xian. Hebei, E China 38°31′N 114°52′E
167 U6 **Đinh Lập** Lang Sơn, N Vietnam 21°33′N 107°03′E
167 T13 **Đinh Quan** *var.* Tân Phu. Đông Nai, S Vietnam 11°11′N 107°20′E
100 E13 **Dinkel** ∼ Germany/Netherlands
101 J21 **Dinkelsbühl** Bayern, S Germany 49°06′N 10°18′E
101 D14 **Dinslaken** Nordrhein-Westfalen, W Germany 51°34′N 06°43′E
35 R11 **Dinuba** California, W USA 36°32′N 119°23′W
21 W7 **Dinwiddie** Virginia, NE USA 37°02′N 77°40′W
98 N13 **Dinxperlo** Gelderland, E Netherlands 51°51′N 06°30′E
Dio *see* Díon
Diófás *see* Nucet
76 M12 **Dioïla** Koulikoro, W Mali 12°28′N 06°43′W
115 F14 **Díon** *var.* Dio; *anc.* Dium. *site of ancient city* Kentrikí Makedonía, N Greece
115 G19 **Dióryga Korinthou** *Eng.* Corinth Canal. *canal* S Greece
76 G12 **Diouloulou** SW Senegal 13°00′N 16°34′W
77 N11 **Dioura** Mopti, W Mali 14°48′N 05°20′W
76 G11 **Diourbel** W Senegal 14°39′N 16°12′W
152 L10 **Dipāyal** Far Western, W Nepal 29°09′N 80°46′E
121 R1 **Dipkarpaz** *Gk.* Rizokarpaso, Rizokárpason. NE Cyprus 35°36′N 34°23′E
149 R17 **Diplo** Sind, SE Pakistan 24°29′N 69°36′E
171 P7 **Dipolog** *var.* Dipolog City. Mindanao, S Philippines 08°31′N 123°20′E
Dipolog City *see* Dipolog
185 C23 **Dipton** Southland, South Island, New Zealand 45°55′S 168°21′E
149 T4 **Dīr** North-West Frontier Province, N Pakistan 35°12′N 71°53′E
77 O10 **Diré** Tombouctou, C Mali 16°12′N 03°31′W
80 L13 **Dirē Dawa** Dirē Dawa, E Ethiopia 09°35′N 41°53′E
Dirfis *see* Dírfys
115 H18 **Dírfys** *var.* Dirfis. ▲▲ Évvioa, C Greece
75 N9 **Dirj** *var.* Daraj, Darj. W Libya 30°09′N 10°26′E
180 G10 **Dirk Hartog Island** *island* Western Australia
77 Y8 **Dirkou** Agadez, NE Niger 18°45′N 13°00′E
181 X11 **Dirranbandi** Queensland, E Australia 28°37′S 148°13′E
81 O16 **Dirri** Galguduud, C Somalia 04°15′N 46°31′E
Dirschau *see* Tczew
37 N6 **Dirty Devil River** ∼ Utah, W USA
32 E10 **Disappointment, Cape** *headland* Washington, NW USA 46°16′N 124°06′W
180 L8 **Disappointment, Lake** *salt lake* Western Australia
183 R12 **Disaster Bay** *bay* New South Wales, SE Australia
44 J11 **Discovery Bay** C Jamaica 18°27′N 77°24′W
182 K13 **Discovery Bay** *inlet* SE Australia
67 Y15 **Discovery II Fracture Zone** *tectonic feature* SW Indian Ocean
Discovery Seamount/Discovery Seamounts *see* Discovery Tablemounts
65 O19 **Discovery Tablemounts** *var.* Discovery Seamount, Discovery Seamounts. *undersea feature* SW Atlantic Ocean 42°00′S 00°10′E
108 G9 **Disentis** *Rmsch.* Mustér. Graubünden, S Switzerland 46°43′N 08°52′E
39 O10 **Dishna River** ∼ Alaska, USA
Disko Bugt *see* Qeqertarsuup Tunua
195 X4 **Dismal Mountains** ▲▲ Antarctica
28 M14 **Dismal River** ∼ Nebraska, C USA
Disna *see* Dzisna
99 L19 **Dison** Liège, E Belgium 50°37′N 05°52′E
153 V12 **Dispur** *state capital* Assam, NE India 26°03′N 91°52′E
15 R11 **Disraeli** Québec, SE Canada 45°58′N 71°21′W
115 F18 **Dístomo** *prev.* Dhístomon. Stereá Ellás, C Greece 38°25′N 22°40′E
Dístos, Límni *see* Dýstos, Límni
59 L18 **Distrito Federal** *Eng.* Federal District. ◈ *federal district* C Brazil
41 P14 **Distrito Federal** ◈ *federal district* S Mexico
54 L4 **Distrito Federal** *off.* Territorio Distrito Federal. ◈ *federal district* N Venezuela
Distrito Federal, Territorio *see* Distrito Federal
116 J10 **Ditrău** *Hung.* Ditró. Harghita, C Romania 46°49′N 25°31′E
Ditró *see* Ditrău
154 B12 **Diu** Damān and Diu, W India 20°42′N 70°59′E

◆ Country
● Country Capital
◇ Dependent Territory
○ Dependent Territory Capital
◈ Administrative Regions
✈ International Airport
▲ Mountain
▲▲ Mountain Range
⩚ Volcano
∼ River
⊚ Lake
⊞ Reservoir

Dium see Díon
109 S13 **Divača** SW Slovenia 45°40′N 13°58′E
142 J5 **Divāndarreh** Kordestān, NW Iran 35°55′N 47°02′E
102 K5 **Dives** ≈ N France
Divichi see Dəvəçi
33 Q11 **Divide** Montana, NW USA 45°44′N 112°47′W
Divin see Dzivin
83 N18 **Divinhe** Sofala, E Mozambique 20°41′S 34°46′E
59 L20 **Divinópolis** Minas Gerais, SE Brazil 20°08′S 44°55′W
127 N13 **Divnoye** Stavropol'skiy Kray, SW Russian Federation 45°54′N 43°18′E
76 M17 **Divo** S Ivory Coast 05°50′N 05°22′W
Divodurum Mediomatricum see Metz
137 N13 **Divriği** Sivas, C Turkey 39°23′N 38°06′E
Diwaniyah see Ad Dīwānīyah
14 J10 **Dix Milles, Lac** ◎ Québec, SE Canada
14 M8 **Dix Milles, Lac des** ◎ Québec, SE Canada
Dixmude/Dixmuide see Diksmuide
35 N7 **Dixon** California, W USA 38°19′N 121°49′W
30 L10 **Dixon** Illinois, N USA 41°51′N 89°26′W
20 I6 **Dixon** Kentucky, S USA 37°30′N 87°39′W
27 V6 **Dixon** Missouri, C USA 37°59′N 92°05′W
37 S9 **Dixon** New Mexico, SW USA 36°10′N 105°49′W
39 Y15 **Dixon Entrance** strait Canada/USA
18 D14 **Dixonville** Pennsylvania, NE USA 40°43′N 79°01′W
137 T13 **Diyadin** Ağrı, E Turkey 39°33′N 43°41′E
Diyālá, Nahr see Sīrvān, Rūdkhāneh-ye
139 V5 **Diyālá, Sīrwan Nahr** var. Rudkhaneh-ye Sīrvān, Sīrwān. ≈ Iran/Iraq see also Sīrvān, Rudkhaneh-ye
137 P15 **Diyarbakır** var. Diarbekr; anc. Amida. Diyarbakır, SE Turkey 37°55′N 40°14′E
137 P15 **Diyarbakır** var. Diarbekr. ◈ province SE Turkey
Dizful see Dezfūl
79 F16 **Dja** ≈ SE Cameroon
Djadié see Zadié
77 X7 **Djado** Agadez, NE Niger 21°00′N 12°11′E
77 X6 **Djado, Plateau du** ▲▲ NE Niger
Djailolo see Halmahera, Pulau
Djajapura see Jayapura
Djakarta see Jakarta
Djakovo see Đakovo
79 G20 **Djambala** Plateaux, C Congo 02°32′S 14°43′E
Djambi see Jambi
Djambi see Hari, Batang
74 M9 **Djanet** E Algeria 28°43′N 08°57′E
74 M11 **Djanet** prev. Fort Charlet. SE Algeria 24°34′N 09°33′E
Djaul see Dyaul Island
Djawa see Jawa
Djéblé see Jablah
78 I10 **Djédaa** Batha, C Chad 13°31′N 18°34′E
74 J6 **Djelfa** var. El Djelfa. N Algeria 34°43′N 03°14′E
79 M14 **Djéma** Haut-Mbomou, E Central African Republic 06°04′N 25°20′E
Djember see Jember
Djeneponto see Jeneponto
77 N12 **Djenné** var. Jenné. Mopti, C Mali 13°55′N 04°31′W
Djérablous see Jarābulus
Djerba see Jerba, Île de
79 F15 **Djérem** ≈ C Cameroon
Djevdjelija see Gevgelija
77 P11 **Djibo** N Burkina 14°09′N 01°38′W
80 L12 **Djibouti** var. Jibuti. ● (Djibouti) E Djibouti 11°33′N 42°55′E
80 L12 **Djibouti** off. Republic of Djibouti, var. Jibuti; prev. French Somaliland, French Territory of the Afars and Issas, Fr. Côte Française des Somalis, Territoire Français des Afars et des Issas. ◆ republic E Africa
80 L12 **Djibouti** ✈ C Djibouti 11°29′N 42°54′E
Djibouti, Republic of see Djibouti
Djidjel/Djidjelli see Jijel
55 W10 **Djoemoe** Sipaliwini, C Suriname 04°00′N 55°27′W
Djokjakarta see Yogyakarta
79 K21 **Djoku-Punda** Kasai-Occidental, S Dem. Rep. Congo 05°27′S 20°58′E
79 K18 **Djolu** Equateur, N Dem. Rep. Congo 0°35′N 22°30′E
Djombang see Jombang
Djorče Petrov see Đorče Petrov
79 F17 **Djoua** ≈ Congo/Gabon
77 R14 **Djougou** W Benin 09°42′N 01°38′E
79 F16 **Djoum** Sud, S Cameroon 02°38′N 12°51′E
78 I8 **Djourab, Erg du** desert N Chad
79 P17 **Djugu** Orientale, NE Dem. Rep. Congo 01°55′N 30°31′E
Djumbir see Ďumbier
92 L3 **Djúpivogur** Austurland, SE Iceland 64°40′N 14°18′W
94 L13 **Djura** Dalarna, C Sweden 60°37′N 15°00′E
Djurdjevac see Đurđevac
D'Kar see Dekar
197 U6 **Dmitriya Lapteva, Proliv** strait N Russian Federation
126 J7 **Dmitriyev-L'govskiy** Kurskaya Oblast', W Russian Federation 52°08′N 35°09′E
Dmitriyevsk see Makiyivka
126 K3 **Dmitrov** Moskovskaya Oblast', W Russian Federation 56°23′N 37°30′E
Dmitrovichi see Dzmitravichy
126 J6 **Dmitrovsk-Orlovskiy** Orlovskaya Oblast', W Russian Federation 52°28′N 35°01′E
117 R3 **Dmytrivka** Chernihivs'ka Oblast', N Ukraine 50°56′N 32°57′E
Dnepr see Dnieper
Dneprodzerzhinsk see Romaniv
Dneprodzerzhinskoye Vodokhranilishche see Dniprodzerzhyns'ke Vodoskhovyshche
Dnepropetrovsk see Dnipropetrovs'k
Dnepropetrovskaya Oblast' see Dnipropetrovs'ka Oblast'
Dneprorudnoye see Dniprorudne
Dneprovskiy Liman see Dniprovs'kyy Lyman
Dneprovsko-Bugskiy Kanal see Dnyaprowska-Buhski Kanal
Dnestr see Dniester
Dnestrovskiy Liman see Dnistrovs'kyy Lyman
86 H11 **Dnieper** Bel. Dnyapro, Rus. Dnepr, Ukr. Dnipro. ≈ E Europe
117 P3 **Dnieper Lowland** Bel. Prydnyaprowskaya Nizina, Ukr. Prydniprovs'ka Nyzovyna. lowlands Belarus/Ukraine
116 M8 **Dniester** Rom. Nistru, Rus. Dnestr, Ukr. Dnister; anc. Tyras. ≈ Moldova/Ukraine
Dnipro see Dnieper
Dniprodzerzhyns'k see Romaniv
117 T7 **Dniprodzerzhyns'ke Vodoskhovyshche** Rus. Dneprodzerzhinskoye Vodokhranilishche. ⊞ C Ukraine
117 U7 **Dnipropetrovs'k** Rus. Dnepropetrovsk; prev. Yekaterinoslav. Dnipropetrovs'ka Oblast', E Ukraine 48°28′N 35°E
117 U8 **Dnipropetrovs'k** ✈ Dnipropetrovs'ka Oblast', S Ukraine 48°20′N 35°04′E
Dnipropetrovs'k see Dnipropetrovs'ka Oblast'
117 T7 **Dnipropetrovs'ka Oblast'** var. Dnipropetrovs'k, Rus. Dnepropetrovskaya Oblast'. ◈ province E Ukraine
117 U9 **Dniprorudne** Rus. Dneprorudnoye. Zaporiz'ka Oblast', SE Ukraine 47°21′N 35°00′E
117 Q11 **Dniprovs'kyy Lyman** Rus. Dneprovskiy Liman. bay S Ukraine
Dnister see Dniester
117 O11 **Dnistrovs'kyy Lyman** Rus. Dnestrovskiy Liman. inlet S Ukraine
124 G14 **Dno** Pskovskaya Oblast', W Russian Federation 57°48′N 29°58′E
Dnyapro see Dnieper
119 H20 **Dnyaprowska-Buhski Kanal** Rus. Dneprovsko-Bugskiy Kanal. canal SW Belarus
13 O14 **Doaktown** New Brunswick, SE Canada 46°34′N 66°06′W
78 H13 **Doba** Logone-Oriental, S Chad 08°40′N 16°50′E
118 E9 **Dobele** Ger. Doblen. Dobele, W Latvia 56°36′N 23°14′E
101 N16 **Döbeln** Sachsen, E Germany 51°07′N 13°07′E
171 U12 **Doberai, Jazirah** Dut. Vogelkop. peninsula Papua, E Indonesia
110 F10 **Dobiegniew** Ger. Lubuskie, Woldenberg Neumark. Lubuskie, W Poland 52°58′N 15°43′E
Doblen see Dobele
81 K18 **Dobli** spring/well SW Somalia 0°24′N 41°18′E
112 H11 **Doboj** Republika Srpska, N Bosnia and Herzegovina 44°45′N 18°03′E
143 R12 **Doborji** var. Fūrg. Fārs, S Iran 28°16′N 55°13′E
110 L8 **Dobre Miasto** Ger. Guttstadt. Warmińsko-mazurskie, NE Poland 53°59′N 20°25′E
114 N7 **Dobrich** Rom. Bazargic; prev. Tolbukhin. Dobrich, NE Bulgaria 43°35′N 27°49′E
114 N7 **Dobrich** ◈ province NE Bulgaria
126 M8 **Dobrinka** Lipetskaya Oblast', W Russian Federation 52°10′N 40°30′E
126 M7 **Dobrinka** Volgogradskaya Oblast', SW Russian Federation 50°52′N 41°48′E
Dobrla Vas see Eberndorf
111 I15 **Dobrodzień** Ger. Guttentag. Opolskie, S Poland 50°43′N 18°24′E
Dobrogea see Dobruja
117 W7 **Dobropillya** Rus. Dobropol'ye. Donets'ka Oblast', SE Ukraine 48°25′N 37°02′E
Dobropol'ye see Dobropillya
117 P8 **Dobrovelychkivka** Kirovohrads'ka Oblast', C Ukraine 48°22′N 31°12′E
Dobrudja/Dobrudzha see Dobruja
114 O7 **Dobruja** var. Dobrudja, Bul. Dobrudzha, Rom. Dobrogea. physical region Bulgaria/Romania
119 P19 **Dobrush** Homyel'skaya Voblasts', SE Belarus 52°25′N 31°19′E
125 U14 **Dobryanka** Permskaya Oblast', NW Russian Federation 58°28′N 56°27′E
117 P2 **Dobryanka** Chernihivs'ka Oblast', N Ukraine 52°03′N 31°09′E
Dobryn' see Dabryn'
21 R8 **Dobson** North Carolina, SE USA 36°25′N 80°45′W
59 N20 **Doce, Rio** ≈ SE Brazil
93 I16 **Docksta** Västernorrland, C Sweden 63°06′N 18°22′E
41 N10 **Doctor Arroyo** Nuevo León, NE Mexico 23°40′N 100°09′W
62 L4 **Doctor Pedro P. Peña** Boquerón, W Paraguay 22°22′S 62°23′W
171 S11 **Dodaga** Pulau Halmahera, E Indonesia 01°06′N 128°10′E
155 G21 **Dodda Betta** ▲ S India 11°28′N 76°44′E
Dodecanese see Dodekánisa
115 M22 **Dodekánisa** var. Nóties Sporádes, Eng. Dodecanese; prev. Dhodhekánisos, Dodekanisos. island group SE Greece
Dodekanisos see Dodekánisa
26 J6 **Dodge City** Kansas, C USA 37°45′N 100°01′W
30 K9 **Dodgeville** Wisconsin, N USA 42°57′N 90°08′W
97 H25 **Dodman Point** headland SW England, United Kingdom 50°13′N 04°47′W
81 J14 **Dodola** Oromīya, C Ethiopia 07°00′N 39°15′E
81 H22 **Dodoma** ● (Tanzania) Dodoma, C Tanzania 06°11′S 35°45′E
81 H22 **Dodoma** ◈ region C Tanzania
115 C16 **Dodóni** var. Dhodhóni. site of ancient city Ípeiros, W Greece
33 U7 **Dodson** Montana, NW USA 48°25′N 108°18′W
25 P3 **Dodson** Texas, SW USA 34°46′N 100°01′W
98 M12 **Doesburg** Gelderland, E Netherlands 52°01′N 06°08′E
98 N12 **Doetinchem** Gelderland, E Netherlands 51°58′N 06°17′E
158 L12 **Dogai Coring** var. Lake Montcalm. ◎ W China
137 N15 **Doğanşehir** Malatya, C Turkey 38°07′N 37°54′E
84 E9 **Dogger Bank** undersea feature C North Sea 55°00′N 03°00′E
23 S10 **Dog Island** island Florida, SE USA
14 C7 **Dog Lake** ◎ Ontario, S Canada
106 B9 **Dogliani** Piemonte, NE Italy 44°33′N 07°55′E
164 H11 **Dōgo** island Oki-shotō, SW Japan
143 N10 **Do Gonbadān** var. Dow Gonbadān, Gonbadān. Kohkīlūyeh va Būyer AHmad, SW Iran 30°12′N 50°48′E
77 S12 **Dogondoutchi** Dosso, SW Niger 13°36′N 04°03′E
137 T13 **Doğubayazıt** Ağrı, E Turkey 39°33′N 44°07′E
137 P12 **Doğu Karadeniz Dağları** var. Anadolu Dağları. ▲▲ NE Turkey
158 K16 **Dogxung Zangbo** ≈ W China
Doha see Ad Dawḥah
Doha see Ad Dawḥah
Dohad see Dāhod
Dohuk see Dahūk
159 N16 **Doilungdêqên** var. Namka. Xizang Zizhiqu, W China 29°41′N 90°58′E
114 F12 **Doïrani, Límnis** var. Limni Doïranis, Bul. Ezero Doyransko. ◎ N Greece
Doire see Londonderry
99 H22 **Doische** Namur, S Belgium 50°09′N 04°43′E
59 P17 **Dois de Julho** ✈ (Salvador) Bahia, NE Brazil 12°04′S 38°58′W
60 H12 **Dois Vizinhos** Paraná, S Brazil 25°47′S 53°03′W
80 H10 **Doka** Gedaref, E Sudan 13°30′N 35°47′E
Doka see Kéita, Bahr
139 T3 **Dokan** var. Dūkān. As Sulaymānīyah, E Iraq 35°55′N 44°58′E
94 H13 **Dokka** Oppland, S Norway 60°49′N 10°04′E
98 L5 **Dokkum** Friesland, N Netherlands 53°20′N 06°E
98 L5 **Dokkumer Ee** ≈ N Netherlands
76 K13 **Doko** NE Guinea 11°46′N 08°58′W
Dokshitsy see Dokshytsy
118 K13 **Dokshytsy** Rus. Dokshitsy. Vitsyebskaya Voblasts', N Belarus 54°54′N 27°46′E
117 X8 **Dokuchayevs'k** var. Dokuchayevsk. Donets'ka Oblast', SE Ukraine 47°43′N 37°41′E
Dokuchayevsk see Dokuchayevs'k
Dolak, Pulau see Yos Sudarso, Pulau
29 P9 **Doland** South Dakota, N USA 44°51′N 98°06′W
63 J18 **Dolavón** Chaco, S Argentina 43°16′S 65°44′W
15 P6 **Dolbeau** Québec, SE Canada 48°52′N 72°15′W
102 I5 **Dol-de-Bretagne** Ille-et-Vilaine, NW France 48°33′N 01°45′W
64 J13 **Doldrums Fracture Zone** tectonic feature W Atlantic Ocean
103 S8 **Dôle** Jura, E France 47°05′N 05°30′E
97 J19 **Dolgellau** NW Wales, United Kingdom 52°45′N 03°54′W
Dolginovo see Dawhinava
Dolgi, Ostrov see Dolgiy, Ostrov
125 U2 **Dolgiy, Ostrov** var. Ostrov Dolgi. island NW Russian Federation
162 J9 **Dölgöön** Övörhangay, C Mongolia 45°57′N 103°14′E
107 C20 **Dolianova** Sardegna, Italy, C Mediterranean Sea 39°23′N 09°08′E
Dolina see Dolyna
123 T13 **Dolinsk** Ostrov Sakhalin, Sakhalinskaya Oblast', SE Russian Federation 47°20′N 142°52′E
Dolinskaya see Dolyns'ka
79 F21 **Dolisie** prev. Loubomo. Niari, S Congo 04°12′S 12°41′E
116 G14 **Dolj** ◈ county SW Romania
98 P5 **Dollard** bay NW Germany
194 J5 **Dolleman Island** island Antarctica
114 K8 **Dolna Oryakhovitsa** Veliko Tŭrnovo, N Bulgaria 43°09′N 25°44′E
114 N9 **Dolni Chiflik** Varna, E Bulgaria 42°59′N 27°43′E
114 I8 **Dolni Dŭbnik** Pleven, N Bulgaria 43°24′N 24°25′E
114 F8 **Dolni Lom** Vidin, NW Bulgaria 43°31′N 22°46′E
Dolnja Lendava see Lendava
129 F14 **Dolnośląskie** ◈ province SW Poland
111 K18 **Dolný Kubín** Hung. Alsókubin. Žilinský Kraj, N Slovakia 49°12′N 19°17′E
106 H8 **Dolo** Veneto, NE Italy 45°25′N 12°06′E
Dolomites/Dolomiti see Dolomitiche, Alpi
106 H6 **Dolomitiche, Alpi** var. Dolomiti, Eng. Dolomites. ▲▲ NE Italy
Dolonnur see Duolun
Doloon see Tsogt-Ovoo
61 E21 **Dolores** Buenos Aires, E Argentina 36°21′S 57°39′W
42 E3 **Dolores** Petén, N Guatemala 16°33′N 89°26′W
171 Q5 **Dolores** Samar, C Philippines 12°01′N 125°27′E
105 S12 **Dolores** País Valenciano, E Spain 38°09′N 00°45′W
61 D19 **Dolores** Soriano, SW Uruguay 33°34′S 58°15′W
41 N12 **Dolores Hidalgo** var. Ciudad de Dolores Hidalgo. Guanajuato, C Mexico 21°10′N 100°55′W
8 J7 **Dolphin and Union Strait** strait Northwest Territories/Nunavut, N Canada
65 D23 **Dolphin, Cape** headland East Falkland, Falkland Islands 51°15′S 58°57′W
44 H12 **Dolphin Head** hill W Jamaica
83 B21 **Dolphin Head** var. Cape Dernberg. headland SW Namibia 25°33′S 14°36′E
110 G12 **Dolsk** Ger. Dolzig. Weilkopolskie, C Poland 51°59′N 17°03′E
167 S8 **Đô Lương** Nghê An, N Vietnam 18°51′N 105°19′E
116 I6 **Dolyna** Rus. Dolina. Ivano-Frankivs'ka Oblast', W Ukraine 48°58′N 24°01′E
117 R8 **Dolyns'ka** Rus. Dolinskaya. Kirovohrads'ka Oblast', S Ukraine 48°06′N 32°46′E
Dolzig see Dolsk
Domachëvo/Domaczewo see Damachava
117 P9 **Domanivka** Mykolayivs'ka Oblast', S Ukraine 47°40′N 30°56′E
153 S13 **Domar** Rajshahi, N Bangladesh 26°08′N 88°57′E
158 G12 **Domar** prev. Zangkaxa. Xizang Zizhiqu, W China 33°42′N 80°21′E
108 I9 **Domat/Ems** Graubünden, SE Switzerland 46°50′N 09°28′E
111 A18 **Domažlice** Ger. Taus. Plzeňský Kraj, W Czech Republic 49°26′N 12°54′E
127 X8 **Dombarovskiy** Orenburgskaya Oblast', W Russian Federation 50°53′N 59°18′E
94 G10 **Dombås** Oppland, S Norway 62°04′N 09°07′E
83 M17 **Dombe** Manica, C Mozambique 19°59′S 33°24′E
82 A13 **Dombe Grande** Benguela, C Angola 12°57′S 13°07′E
103 R10 **Dombes** physical region E France
111 I25 **Dombóvár** Tolna, S Hungary 46°24′N 18°09′E
99 D14 **Domburg** Zeeland, SW Netherlands 51°34′N 03°30′E
58 L13 **Dom Eliseu** Pará, NE Brazil 04°02′S 47°31′W
Domel Island see Letsôk-aw Kyun
103 O11 **Dôme, Puy de** ▲ C France 45°46′N 03°00′E
36 H13 **Dome Rock Mountains** ▲▲ Arizona, SW USA
Domesnes, Cape see Kolkasrags
62 G8 **Domeyko** Atacama, N Chile 28°58′S 70°54′W
62 H5 **Domeyko, Cordillera** ▲▲ N Chile
102 K5 **Domfront** Orne, N France 48°35′N 00°39′W
171 X13 **Dom, Gunung** ▲ Papua, E Indonesia 02°41′S 137°00′E
45 X11 **Dominica** off. Commonwealth of Dominica. ◆ republic E West Indies
47 S3 **Dominica** island Dominica
Dominica Channel see Martinique Passage
Dominica, Commonwealth of see Dominica
43 N15 **Dominical** Puntarenas, SE Costa Rica 09°16′N 83°52′W
45 Q8 **Dominican Republic** ◆ republic C West Indies
45 X11 **Dominica Passage** passage E Caribbean Sea
99 K14 **Dommel** ≈ S Netherlands
81 O14 **Domo** Somalē, E Ethiopia 07°53′N 46°55′E
126 L4 **Domodedovo** ✈ (Moskva) Moskovskaya Oblast', W Russian Federation 55°19′N 37°55′E
106 C6 **Domodossola** Piemonte, NE Italy 46°07′N 08°20′E
115 F17 **Domokós** var. Dhomokós. Stereá Ellás, C Greece 39°07′N 22°18′E
172 I14 **Domoni** Anjouan, SE Comoros 12°15′S 44°39′E
61 G16 **Dom Pedrito** Rio Grande do Sul, S Brazil 31°00′S 54°40′W
Dompoe see Dompu
170 M16 **Dompu** prev. Dompoe. Sumbawa, C Indonesia 08°30′S 118°28′E
Domschale see Domžale
62 H13 **Domuyo, Volcán** △ W Argentina 36°36′S 70°22′W
109 U11 **Domžale** Ger. Domschale. C Slovenia 46°09′N 14°33′E
127 O10 **Don** var. Duna, Tanais. ≈ SW Russian Federation
96 K9 **Don** ≈ NE Scotland, United Kingdom
182 M11 **Donald** Victoria, SE Australia 36°27′S 143°03′E
22 J9 **Donaldsonville** Louisiana, S USA 30°06′N 90°59′W
23 S8 **Donalsonville** Georgia, SE USA 31°02′N 84°52′W
Donau see Danube
101 G23 **Donaueschingen** Baden-Württemberg, SW Germany 47°57′N 08°30′E
101 K22 **Donaumoos** wetland S Germany
101 K22 **Donauwörth** Bayern, S Germany 48°43′N 10°46′E
109 U7 **Donawitz** Steiermark, SE Austria 47°23′N 15°00′E
117 X7 **Donbass** industrial region Russian Federation/Ukraine
104 K11 **Don Benito** Extremadura, W Spain 38°57′N 05°52′W
97 M17 **Doncaster** anc. Danum. N England, United Kingdom 53°32′N 01°07′W
44 K12 **Don Christophers Point** headland C Jamaica 18°19′N 76°48′W
55 V9 **Donderkamp** Sipaliwini, NW Suriname 05°18′N 56°22′W
82 B12 **Dondo** Cuanza Norte, NW Angola 09°40′S 14°24′E
171 O12 **Dondo** Sulawesi, N Indonesia 0°54′S 121°33′E
83 N17 **Dondo** Sofala, C Mozambique 19°41′S 34°45′E
155 K26 **Dondra Head** headland S Sri Lanka 05°57′N 80°33′E
Donduşani see Donduşeni
116 M8 **Donduşeni** var. Donduşani, Rus. Dondyushany. N Moldova 48°13′N 27°38′E
Dondyushany see Donduşeni
97 D15 **Donegal** Ir. Dún na nGall. Donegal, NW Ireland 54°39′N 08°06′W
97 D14 **Donegal** Ir. Dún na nGall. cultural region NW Ireland
97 C15 **Donegal Bay** Ir. Bá Dhún na nGall. bay NW Ireland
84 K10 **Donets** ≈ Russian Federation/Ukraine
117 X8 **Donets'k** ✈ Rus. Donetsk; prev. Stalino. Donets'ka Oblast', E Ukraine 47°58′N 37°50′E
117 W8 **Donets'k** ✈ Donets'ka Oblast', E Ukraine 48°03′N 37°44′E
Donets'k see Donets'ka Oblast'
117 W8 **Donets'ka Oblast'** var. Donets'k, Rus. Donetskaya Oblast'; prev. Rus. Stalins'kaya Oblast'. ◈ province SE Ukraine
Donetskaya Oblast' see Donets'ka Oblast'
67 P8 **Donga** ≈ Cameroon/Nigeria
157 O13 **Dongchuan** Yunnan, SW China 26°09′N 103°10′E
99 I14 **Dongen** Noord-Brabant, S Netherlands 51°38′N 04°56′E
160 K17 **Dongfang** var. Basuo. Hainan, S China 19°05′N 108°40′E
163 Z7 **Dongfanghong** Heilongjiang, NE China 46°13′N 133°13′E
163 W11 **Dongfeng** Jilin, NE China 42°39′N 125°33′E
171 N12 **Donggala** Sulawesi, C Indonesia 0°40′S 119°44′E
163 V13 **Donggang** var. Dadong; prev. Donggou. Liaoning, NE China 39°52′N 124°08′E
Donggou see Donggang
161 O14 **Dongguan** Guangdong, S China 23°03′N 113°43′E
167 T9 **Đông Ha** Quang Tri, C Vietnam 16°45′N 107°10′E
Dong Hai see East China Sea
160 M16 **Donghai Dao** island S China
162 I12 **Dong He** Mong. Narin Gol. ≈ N China
Donghe see Wangcang
167 T9 **Đông Hơi** Quang Binh, C Vietnam 17°32′N 106°35′E
Donghua see Huating
Donghuang see Xishui
108 H10 **Dongio** Ticino, S Switzerland 46°27′N 08°58′E
159 P15 **Dongjug** Xizang Zizhiqu, W China 29°58′N 94°51′E
Dongkan see Binhai
160 L11 **Dongkou** Hunan, S China 27°06′N 110°35′E
Dongliao see Liaoyuan
Dong-nai see Đông Nai, Sông
167 U13 **Đông Nai, Sông** var. Dong-nai, Dong Noi, Donnai. ≈ S Vietnam
161 N14 **Dongnan Qiuling** plateau SE China
163 Y9 **Dongning** Heilongjiang, NE China 44°01′N 131°03′E
Dong Noi see Đông Nai, Sông
83 C14 **Dongo** Huíla, C Angola 14°35′S 15°51′E
80 E7 **Dongola** var. Donqola, Dunqulah. Northern, N Sudan 19°10′N 30°27′E
79 I17 **Dongou** Likouala, NE Congo 02°05′N 18°E
Đông Phu see Đông Xoai
Dongping see Anhua
Dong Rak, Phanom see Dângrêk, Chuŏr Phnum
161 Q14 **Dongshan Dao** island SE China
Dongsha Qundao see Tungsha Tao
Dongsheng see Ordos
161 R7 **Dongtai** Jiangsu, E China 32°50′N 120°22′E
161 N10 **Dongting Hu** var. Tung-t'ing Hu. ◎ S China
161 P10 **Dongxiang** var. Xiaogang. Jiangxi, S China 28°16′N 116°32′E
167 T13 **Đông Xoai** var. Đông Phu. Sông Be, S Vietnam 11°31′N 106°55′E
161 Q4 **Dongying** Shandong, E China 37°27′N 118°01′E
27 X8 **Doniphan** Missouri, C USA 36°39′N 90°51′W
Donja Łužica see Niederlausitz
10 G7 **Donjek** ≈ Yukon Territory, W Canada
112 E11 **Donji Lapac** Lika-Senj, W Croatia 44°33′N 15°58′E
112 H8 **Donji Miholjac** Osijek-Baranja, NE Croatia 45°45′N 18°10′E
112 P12 **Donji Milanovac** Serbia, E Serbia 44°27′N 22°06′E
112 G12 **Donji Vakuf** var. Srbobran. ◈ Federacija Bosna I Hercegovina, C Bosnia and Herzegovina
98 M6 **Donkerbroek** Friesland, N Netherlands 52°58′N 05°15′E
167 P11 **Don Muang** ✈ (Krung Thep) Nonthaburi, C Thailand 13°51′N 100°40′E
25 S17 **Donna** Texas, SW USA 26°10′N 98°03′W
15 Q10 **Donnacona** Québec, SE Canada 46°41′N 71°46′W
Donnai see Đông Nai, Sông
29 Y16 **Donnellson** Iowa, C USA 40°38′N 91°33′W
11 O13 **Donnelly** Alberta, W Canada 55°42′N 117°06′W
35 P6 **Donner Pass** Pass California, W USA
101 F19 **Donnersberg** ▲ W Germany 49°37′N 07°54′E
Donoso see Miguel de la Borda
105 P2 **Donostia-San Sebastián** País Vasco, N Spain 43°19′N 01°59′W
115 K21 **Donoúsa** var. Donoússa. island Kykládes, Greece, Aegean Sea
Donoússa see Donoúsa
35 P8 **Don Pedro Reservoir** ⊞ California, W USA
Donqola see Dongola
126 L5 **Donskoy** Tul'skaya Oblast', W Russian Federation 54°02′N 38°27′E
81 L16 **Doolow** Somalē, E Ethiopia 04°10′N 42°05′E
39 Q7 **Doonerak, Mount** ▲ Alaska, USA 67°54′N 150°33′W
98 J12 **Doorn** Utrecht, C Netherlands 52°02′N 05°21′E
Doornik see Tournai
31 N6 **Door Peninsula** peninsula Wisconsin, N USA
80 P13 **Dooxo Nugaaleed** var. Nogal Valley. valley E Somalia
Do Qu see Da Qu
106 B7 **Dora Baltea** anc. Duria Major. ≈ NW Italy
180 K7 **Dora, Lake** salt lake Western Australia
106 A8 **Dora Riparia** anc. Duria Minor. ≈ NW Italy
Dorbiljin see Emin
Dorbod/Dorbod Mongolzu Zizhixian see Taikang
Dorbod Mongolzu Zizhixian see Taikang
113 N18 **Đorče Petrov** var. Djorče Petrov, Gorče Petrov. N Macedonia 42°01′N 21°21′E
14 F16 **Dorchester** Ontario, S Canada 43°00′N 81°04′W
97 L24 **Dorchester** anc. Durnovaria. S England, United Kingdom 50°43′N 02°26′W
9 P7 **Dorchester, Cape** headland Baffin Island, Nunavut, NE Canada 65°25′N 77°25′W
83 D19 **Dordabis** Khomas, C Namibia 22°57′S 17°39′E
102 L12 **Dordogne** ◈ department SW France
103 N12 **Dordogne** ≈ W France
98 H13 **Dordrecht** var. Dordt, Dort. Zuid-Holland, SW Netherlands 51°48′N 04°40′E
Dordt see Dordrecht
103 P11 **Dore** ≈ C France
11 S13 **Doré Lake** Saskatchewan, C Canada 54°37′N 107°36′W
103 O12 **Dore, Monts** ▲▲ C France
101 M23 **Dorfen** Bayern, SE Germany 48°16′N 12°06′E
107 D18 **Dorgali** Sardegna, Italy, C Mediterranean Sea 40°18′N 09°34′E
159 N11 **Dorgê Co** var. Elsen Nur. ◎ C China
162 E6 **Dörgön** var. Seer. Hovd, W Mongolia 48°18′N 92°37′E
162 F7 **Dörgön Nuur** ◎ NW Mongolia
77 Q12 **Dori** N Burkina 14°03′N 00°02′W
83 E24 **Doring** ≈ S South Africa
101 E16 **Dormagen** Nordrhein-Westfalen, W Germany 51°06′N 06°49′E
103 P4 **Dormans** Marne, N France 49°03′N 03°44′E
108 E6 **Dornach** Solothurn, NW Switzerland 47°29′N 07°37′E
Dorna Watra see Vatra Dornei
108 J7 **Dornbirn** Vorarlberg, W Austria 47°25′N 09°46′E
96 I7 **Dornoch** N Scotland, United Kingdom 57°52′N 04°01′W
96 J7 **Dornoch Firth** inlet N Scotland, United Kingdom
163 P7 **Dornod** ◈ province E Mongolia
163 N10 **Dornogovĭ** ◈ province SE Mongolia
77 P10 **Doro** Tombouctou, S Mali 16°07′N 00°57′W
116 L14 **Dorobanţu** Călăraşi, S Romania 44°15′N 26°55′E
111 J22 **Dorog** Komárom-Esztergom, N Hungary 47°43′N 18°42′E
126 I4 **Dorogobuzh** Smolenskaya Oblast', W Russian Federation 54°56′N 33°16′E
116 K8 **Dorohoi** Botoşani, NE Romania 47°57′N 26°24′E
93 H15 **Dorotea** Västerbotten, N Sweden 64°17′N 16°30′E
Dorpat see Tartu
180 G10 **Dorre Island** island Western Australia
183 U5 **Dorrigo** New South Wales, SE Australia 30°22′S 152°43′E
35 N1 **Dorris** California, W USA 41°58′N 121°54′W
14 H13 **Dorset** Ontario, SE Canada 45°12′N 78°52′W
97 K23 **Dorset** cultural region S England, United Kingdom
101 E14 **Dorsten** Nordrhein-Westfalen, W Germany 51°38′N 06°58′E
Dort see Dordrecht
101 F15 **Dortmund** Nordrhein-Westfalen, W Germany 51°31′N 07°28′E
100 F12 **Dortmund-Ems-Kanal** canal W Germany
136 L17 **Dörtyol** Hatay, S Turkey 36°51′N 36°11′E
142 L7 **Do Rūd** var. Dow Rūd, Durud. Lorestān, W Iran 33°28′N 49°04′E
79 O15 **Doruma** Orientale, N Dem. Rep. Congo 04°35′N 27°43′E
15 O12 **Dorval** ✈ (Montréal) Québec, SE Canada 45°27′N 73°46′W
162 F7 **Dörvöljin** var. Buga. Dzavhan, W Mongolia 47°42′N 94°53′E
45 T5 **Dos Bocas, Lago** ◎ C Puerto Rico
104 K14 **Dos Hermanas** Andalucía, S Spain 37°16′N 05°55′W
Dospad Dagh see Rhodope Mountains
35 P10 **Dos Palos** California, W USA 37°00′N 120°39′W
114 I11 **Dospat** Smolyan, S Bulgaria 41°39′N 24°10′E
114 H11 **Dospat, Yazovir** ⊞ SW Bulgaria
100 M11 **Dosse** ≈ NE Germany
77 S12 **Dosso** Dosso, SW Niger 13°03′N 03°10′E
77 S12 **Dosso** ◈ department SW Niger
144 G12 **Dossor** Atyrau, SW Kazakhstan 47°31′N 53°01′E
147 O10 **Do'stlik** Jizzax Viloyati, C Uzbekistan 40°37′N 67°59′E
147 V9 **Dostuk** Narynskaya Oblast', C Kyrgyzstan 41°19′N 75°40′E
145 X13 **Dostyk** prev. Druzhba. Almaty, SE Kazakhstan 45°15′N 82°29′E
23 R7 **Dothan** Alabama, S USA 31°13′N 85°23′W
39 T9 **Dot Lake** Alaska, USA 63°39′N 144°10′W
118 F12 **Dotnuva** Kaunas, C Lithuania 55°23′N 23°53′E
99 D19 **Dottignies** Hainaut, W Belgium 50°43′N 03°16′E
103 P2 **Douai** prev. Douay; anc. Duacum. Nord, N France 50°22′N 03°04′E
14 L9 **Douaire, Lac** ◎ Québec, SE Canada
79 D16 **Douala** var. Duala. Littoral, W Cameroon 04°04′N 09°43′E
79 D16 **Douala** ✈ Littoral, W Cameroon 03°57′N 09°48′E
102 F6 **Douarnenez** Finistère, NW France 48°05′N 04°20′W
102 E6 **Douarnenez, Baie de** bay NW France
Douay see Douai
25 O6 **Double Mountain Fork Brazos River** ≈ Texas, SW USA
23 O3 **Double Springs** Alabama, S USA 34°09′N 87°24′W
103 T8 **Doubs** ◈ department E France
108 C8 **Doubs** ≈ France/Switzerland
185 A22 **Doubtful Sound** sound South Island, New Zealand
184 J2 **Doubtless Bay** bay North Island, New Zealand
25 X9 **Doucette** Texas, SW USA 30°48′N 94°25′W
102 K8 **Doué-la-Fontaine** Maine-et-Loire, NW France 47°12′N 00°16′W
77 O11 **Douentza** Mopti, S Mali 14°59′N 02°57′W
97 I16 **Douglas** ○ (Isle of Man) E Isle of Man 54°09′N 04°28′W
83 H23 **Douglas** Northern Cape, C South Africa 29°04′S 23°47′E
39 X13 **Douglas** Alexander Archipelago, Alaska, USA 58°12′N 134°18′W
37 O17 **Douglas** Arizona, SW USA 31°20′N 109°32′W
23 U7 **Douglas** Georgia, SE USA 31°30′N 82°51′W
33 Y15 **Douglas** Wyoming, C USA 42°48′N 105°23′W
21 O7 **Douglas Cape** headland Alaska, USA 64°59′N 166°41′W
10 J14 **Douglas Channel** channel British Columbia, W Canada
182 G3 **Douglas Creek** seasonal river South Australia
31 P5 **Douglas Lake** ◎ Michigan, N USA
21 O9 **Douglas Lake** ⊞ Tennessee, S USA
39 Q13 **Douglas, Mount** ▲ Alaska, USA 58°51′N 153°31′W
194 I6 **Douglas Range** ▲▲ Alexander Island, Antarctica
103 O2 **Doullens** Somme, N France 50°09′N 02°21′E
Douma see Dūmā
79 F15 **Doumé** Est, E Cameroon 04°14′N 13°27′E
99 E21 **Dour** Hainaut, S Belgium 50°24′N 03°47′E
59 K18 **Dourada, Serra** ▲▲ S Brazil
59 I21 **Dourados** Mato Grosso do Sul, S Brazil 22°09′S 54°52′W
103 N5 **Dourdan** Essonne, N France 48°33′N 01°58′E
104 I6 **Douro** Sp. Duero. ≈ Portugal/Spain see also Duero
Douro see Duero
104 G6 **Douro Litoral** former province N Portugal
Douvres see Dover
102 K15 **Douze** ≈ SW France
183 P17 **Dover** Tasmania, SE Australia 43°19′S 147°01′E
97 Q22 **Dover** Fr. Douvres, Lat. Dubris Portus. SE England, United Kingdom 51°08′N 01°E
21 Y3 **Dover** state capital Delaware, NE USA 39°09′N 75°31′W
19 P9 **Dover** New Hampshire, NE USA 43°10′N 70°50′W
18 J14 **Dover** New Jersey, NE USA 40°51′N 74°33′W
31 U12 **Dover** Ohio, N USA 40°31′N 81°28′W
20 H8 **Dover** Tennessee, S USA 36°30′N 87°50′W
97 Q23 **Dover, Strait of** var. Straits of Dover, Fr. Pas de Calais. strait England, United Kingdom/France
Dover, Straits of see Dover, Strait of
Dovlen see Devin
94 G11 **Dovre** Oppland, S Norway 61°59′N 09°16′E
94 G10 **Dovrefjell** plateau S Norway
Dovsk see Dowsk
83 M14 **Dowa** Central, C Malawi 13°40′S 33°55′E
31 O10 **Dowagiac** Michigan, N USA 41°58′N 86°06′W
Dow Gonbadān see Do Gonbadān
148 M2 **Dowlatābād** Fāryāb, N Afghanistan 36°30′N 64°51′E
97 G16 **Down** cultural region SE Northern Ireland, United Kingdom
33 R16 **Downey** Idaho, NW USA 42°25′N 112°06′W
35 P5 **Downieville** California, W USA 39°34′N 120°49′W
97 G16 **Downpatrick** Ir. Dún Pádraig. SE Northern Ireland, United Kingdom 54°20′N 05°43′W
26 M3 **Downs** Kansas, C USA 39°30′N 98°33′W
18 J12 **Downsville** New York, NE USA 42°03′N 74°59′W
Dow Rūd see Do Rūd
29 V12 **Dows** Iowa, C USA 42°39′N 93°30′W
119 O17 **Dowsk** Rus. Dovsk. Homyel'skaya Voblasts', SE Belarus 53°09′N 30°28′E
35 Q4 **Doyle** California, W USA 40°00′N 120°06′W
18 I15 **Doylestown** Pennsylvania, NE USA 40°18′N 75°08′W
Doyransko, Ezero see Doïrani, Límnis
114 I8 **Doyrentsi** Lovech, N Bulgaria 43°13′N 24°46′E
164 G11 **Dōzen** island Oki-shotō, SW Japan
14 K9 **Dozois, Réservoir** ⊞ Québec, SE Canada
74 D9 **Drâa** seasonal river S Morocco
Drâa, Hammada du see Dra, Hamada du

◆ Country
● Country Capital
◇ Dependent Territory
○ Dependent Territory Capital
◈ Administrative Regions
✈ International Airport
▲ Mountain
▲▲ Mountain Range
△ Volcano
≈ River
◎ Lake
⊞ Reservoir

DRABBLE – DYHERNFURTH

Drabble *see* José Enrique Rodó
117 *Q5* **Drabiv** Cherkas'ka Oblast', C Ukraine *49°57′N 32°10′E*
Drable *see* José Enrique Rodó
103 *S13* **Drac** ∽ E France
Drač/Drac *see* Durrës
60 *I8* **Dracena** São Paulo, S Brazil *21°27′S 51°30′W*
98 *M6* **Drachten** Friesland, N Netherlands *53°07′N 06°06′E*
92 *H11* **Drag** *Lapp.* Ájluokta. Nordland, C Norway *68°02′N 16°E*
116 *L14* **Dragalina** Călărași, SE Romania *44°26′N 27°19′E*
116 *I14* **Draganesti-Olt** Olt, S Romania *44°06′N 25°00′E*
116 *J14* **Drăgănești-Vlașca** Teleorman, S Romania *44°05′N 25°39′E*
116 *I13* **Drăgășani** Vâlcea, SW Romania *44°40′N 24°16′E*
114 *G9* **Dragoman** Sofiya, W Bulgaria *42°32′N 22°56′E*
115 *L25* **Dragonáda** *island* SE Greece
Dragonera, Isla *see* Sa Dragonera
45 *T14* **Dragon's Mouths, The** *strait* Trinidad and Tobago/Venezuela
95 *J23* **Dragør** København, E Denmark *55°36′N 12°42′E*
114 *F10* **Dragovishtitsa** Kyustendil, W Bulgaria *42°22′N 22°39′E*
103 *U15* **Draguignan** Var, SE France *43°31′N 06°31′E*
74 *E9* **Dra, Hamada du** *var.* Hammada du Drâa, Haut Plateau du Dra. *plateau* W Algeria
Dra, Haut Plateau du *see* Dra, Hamada du
119 *H19* **Drahichyn** *Pol.* Drohiczyn Poleski, *Rus.* Drogichin. Brestskaya Voblasts', SW Belarus *52°11′N 25°10′E*
29 *N4* **Drake** North Dakota, N USA *47°54′N 100°23′W*
83 *K23* **Drakensberg** ⛰ Lesotho/South Africa
194 *F3* **Drake Passage** *passage* Atlantic Ocean/Pacific Ocean
114 *L8* **Dralfa** Tŭrgovishte, N Bulgaria *43°17′N 26°25′E*
114 *I12* **Dráma** *var.* Dhráma. Anatolikí Makedonía kai Thráki, NE Greece *41°09′N 24°10′E*
Dramburg *see* Drawsko Pomorskie
95 *H15* **Drammen** Buskerud, S Norway *59°44′N 10°12′E*
95 *H15* **Drammensfjorden** *fjord* S Norway
92 *H1* **Drangajökull** ▲ NW Iceland *66°13′N 22°18′W*
95 *F16* **Drangedal** Telemark, S Norway *59°05′N 09°05′E*
92 *I2* **Drangsnes** Vestfirdhir, NW Iceland *65°42′N 21°27′W*
Drann *see* Dravinja
109 *T10* **Drau** *var.* Drava, *Eng.* Drave, *Hung.* Dráva. ∽ C Europe *see also* Drava
Drau *see* Drava
84 *I11* **Drava** *var.* Drau, *Eng.* Drave, *Hung.* Dráva. ∽ C Europe *see also* Drau
Dráva/Drave *see* Drau/Drava
109 *W10* **Dravinja** *Ger.* Drann. ∽ NE Slovenia
109 *V9* **Dravograd** *Ger.* Unterdrauburg; *prev.* Spodnji Dravograd. N Slovenia *46°36′N 15°00′E*
110 *F10* **Drawa** ∽ NW Poland
110 *F9* **Drawno** Zachodnio-pomorskie, NW Poland *53°12′N 15°44′E*
110 *F9* **Drawsko Pomorskie** *Ger.* Dramburg. Zachodnio-pomorskie, NW Poland *53°32′N 15°48′E*
29 *R3* **Drayton** North Dakota, N USA *48°34′N 97°10′W*
11 *P14* **Drayton Valley** Alberta, SW Canada *53°15′N 115°00′W*
186 *B6* **Dreikikir** East Sepik, NW Papua New Guinea *03°42′S 142°46′E*
Dreikirchen *see* Teiuș
98 *N7* **Drenthe** ◐ *province* NE Netherlands
115 *H15* **Drépano, Akrotírio** *var.* Akrotírio Dhrepanon. *headland* N Greece *39°56′N 23°57′E*
Drepanum *see* Trapani
14 *D17* **Dresden** Ontario, S Canada *42°34′N 82°09′W*
101 *O16* **Dresden** Sachsen, E Germany *51°03′N 13°43′E*
20 *G8* **Dresden** Tennessee, S USA *36°17′N 88°42′W*
118 *M11* **Dretun'** Vitsyebskaya Voblasts', N Belarus *55°41′N 29°13′E*
102 *M5* **Dreux** *anc.* Drocae, Durocasses. Eure-et-Loir, C France *48°44′N 01°23′E*
94 *I11* **Drevsjø** Hedmark, S Norway *61°52′N 12°01′E*
22 *K3* **Drew** Mississippi, S USA *33°48′N 90°31′W*
110 *F10* **Drezdenko** *Ger.* Driesen. Lubuskie, W Poland *52°51′N 15°50′E*
98 *J12* **Driebergen** *var.* Driebergen-Rijsenburg. Utrecht, C Netherlands *52°03′N 05°17′E*
Driebergen-Rijsenburg *see* Driebergen
Driesen *see* Drezdenko
97 *N16* **Driffield** E England, United Kingdom *54°00′N 00°28′W*
33 *S14* **Driggs** Idaho, NW USA *43°44′N 111°06′W*
Drin *see* Drinit, Lumi i
112 *K12* **Drina** ∽ Bosnia and Herzegovina/Serbia
Drin, Gulf of *see* Drinit, Gjiri i
113 *K18* **Drinit, Gjiri i** *var.* Pellg i Drinit, *Eng.* Gulf of Drin. *gulf* NW Albania
113 *L17* **Drinit, Lumi i** *var.* Drin. ∽ NW Albania
Drinit, Pellg i *see* Drinit, Gjiri i
Drinit të Zi, Lumi i *see* Black Drin
113 *L22* **Drino** *var.* Drino, Drinos Pótamos, *Alb.* Lumi i Drinos. ∽ Albania/Greece
Drinos, Lumi i/Drinos Pótamos *see* Drino
25 *S11* **Dripping Springs** Texas, SW USA *30°11′N 98°04′W*
25 *S15* **Driscoll** Texas, SW USA *27°40′N 97°45′W*
22 *H5* **Driskill Mountain** ▲ Louisiana, S USA *32°25′N 92°54′W*
Drissa *see* Drysa
94 *G10* **Driva** ∽ S Norway
112 *E13* **Drniš** *It.* Šibenik-Knin. Šibenik-Knin, S Croatia *43°51′N 16°10′E*
95 *H15* **Drøbak** Akershus, S Norway *59°40′N 10°40′E*
116 *G13* **Drobeta-Turnu Severin** *prev.* Turnu Severin. Mehedinți, SW Romania *44°39′N 22°40′E*
Drocae *see* Dreux
116 *M8* **Drochia** *Rus.* Drokiya. N Moldova *48°02′N 27°46′E*
97 *F17* **Drogheda** *Ir.* Droichead Átha. NE Ireland *53°43′N 06°21′W*
Drogichin *see* Drahichyn
Drogobych *see* Drohobych
Drohiczyn Poleski *see* Drahichyn
116 *H6* **Drohobych** *Pol.* Drohobycz, *Rus.* Drogobych. L'vivs'ka Oblast', NW Ukraine *49°22′N 23°33′E*
Drohobycz *see* Drohobych
Droichead Átha *see* Drogheda
Droicheadh Bandan *see* Bandon
Droichead na Banna *see* Banbridge
97 *F18* **Droichead Nua** E Ireland *52°12′N 06°40′W*
Droim Mór *see* Dromore
Drokiya *see* Drochia
103 *R13* **Drôme** ◐ *department* E France
103 *S13* **Drôme** ∽ E France
97 *G15* **Dromore** *Ir.* Droim Mór. SE Northern Ireland, United Kingdom *54°25′N 06°09′W*
106 *A9* **Dronero** Piemonte, NE Italy *44°28′N 07°25′E*
102 *L12* **Dronne** ∽ SW France
195 *Q3* **Dronning Maud Land** *physical region* Antarctica
98 *K6* **Dronrijp** *Fris.* Dronryp. Friesland, N Netherlands *53°12′N 05°37′E*
Dronryp *see* Dronrijp
98 *L9* **Dronten** Flevoland, C Netherlands *52°31′N 05°41′E*
Drontheim *see* Trondheim
102 *L13* **Dropt** ∽ SW France
149 *T4* **Drosh** North-West Frontier Province, NW Pakistan *35°33′N 71°48′E*
Drossen *see* Ośno Lubuskie
Drug *see* Durg
Drujba *see* Pitnak
118 *I12* **Drūkšiai** ◎ NE Lithuania
Druk-yul *see* Bhutan
11 *Q16* **Drumheller** Alberta, SW Canada *51°28′N 112°42′W*
33 *Q10* **Drummond** Montana, NW USA *46°39′N 113°12′W*
31 *R4* **Drummond Island** *island* Michigan, N USA
Drummond Island *see* Tabiteuea
21 *X7* **Drummond, Lake** ◎ Virginia, NE USA
15 *P12* **Drummondville** Québec, SE Canada *45°52′N 72°28′W*
39 *T11* **Drum, Mount** ▲ Alaska, USA *62°11′N 144°37′W*
27 *O9* **Drumright** Oklahoma, C USA *35°59′N 96°36′W*
99 *J14* **Drunen** Noord-Brabant, S Netherlands *51°41′N 05°08′E*
Druskieniki *see* Druskininkai
119 *F15* **Druskininkai** *Pol.* Druskienniki. Alytus, S Lithuania *54°00′N 24°00′E*
98 *K13* **Druten** Gelderland, SE Netherlands *51°53′N 05°37′E*
118 *K11* **Druya** Vitsyebskaya Voblasts', NW Belarus *55°47′N 27°27′E*
117 *S2* **Druzhba** Sums'ka Oblast', NE Ukraine *52°01′N 33°56′E*
Druzhba *see* Dostyk, Kazakhstan
Druzhba *see* Pitnak, Uzbekistan
123 *R7* **Druzhina** Respublika Sakha (Yakutiya), NE Russian Federation *68°01′N 144°58′E*
117 *X7* **Druzhkivka** Donets'ka Oblast', E Ukraine *48°38′N 37°31′E*
112 *E12* **Drvar** Federacija Bosna I Hercegovina, W Bosnia and Herzegovina *44°21′N 16°24′E*
113 *G15* **Drvenik** Split-Dalmacija, SE Croatia *43°10′N 17°13′E*
114 *K9* **Dryanovo** Gabrovo, N Bulgaria *42°58′N 25°28′E*
26 *G7* **Dry Cimarron River** ∽ Kansas/Oklahoma, C USA
12 *B11* **Dryden** Ontario, C Canada *49°48′N 92°48′W*
24 *M11* **Dryden** Texas, SW USA *30°01′N 102°06′W*
195 *Q14* **Drygalski Ice Tongue** *ice feature* Antarctica
118 *L11* **Drysa** *Rus.* Drissa. ∽ N Belarus
23 *V17* **Dry Tortugas** *island* Florida, SE USA
79 *D15* **Dschang** Ouest, W Cameroon *05°28′N 10°02′E*
54 *J5* **Duaca** Lara, N Venezuela *10°22′N 69°08′W*
Duacum *see* Douai
Duala *see* Douala
45 *N9* **Duarte, Pico** ▲ C Dominican Republic *19°02′N 70°57′W*
140 *J5* **Ḍubā** Tabūk, NW Saudi Arabia *27°26′N 35°42′E*
Dubai *see* Dubayy
117 *N9* **Dubăsari** *Rus.* Dubossary. NE Moldova *47°16′N 29°07′E*
117 *N9* **Dubăsari Reservoir** ⊡ NE Moldova
8 *M10* **Dubawnt** ∽ Nunavut, NW Canada
8 *L9* **Dubawnt Lake** ◎ Northwest Territories/Nunavut, N Canada
30 *L6* **Du Bay, Lake** ⊡ Wisconsin, N USA
141 *U7* **Dubayy** *Eng.* Dubai. Dubayy, NE United Arab Emirates *25°11′N 55°18′E*
141 *W7* **Dubayy** *Eng.* Dubai. ✈ Dubayy, NE United Arab Emirates *25°15′N 55°22′E*
183 *R7* **Dubbo** New South Wales, SE Australia *32°16′S 148°41′E*
108 *G7* **Dübendorf** Zürich, NW Switzerland *47°23′N 08°37′E*
97 *F18* **Dublin** *Ir.* Baile Átha Cliath; *anc.* Eblana. ● (Ireland) Dublin, E Ireland *53°20′N 06°15′W*
23 *U5* **Dublin** Georgia, SE USA *32°32′N 82°54′W*
25 *R7* **Dublin** Texas, SW USA *32°05′N 98°20′W*
97 *G18* **Dublin** *Ir.* Baile Átha Cliath; *anc.* Eblana. *cultural region* E Ireland
97 *G18* **Dublin Airport** ✈ Dublin, E Ireland *53°25′N 06°18′W*
189 *V12* **Dublon** *var.* Tonoas. *island* Chuuk Islands, C Micronesia
126 *K2* **Dubna** Moskovskaya Oblast', W Russian Federation *56°45′N 37°09′E*
111 *G19* **Dubňany** *Ger.* Dubnian. Jihomoravský Kraj, SE Czech Republic *48°54′N 17°00′E*
Dubnian *see* Dubňany
111 *I19* **Dubnica nad Váhom** *Hung.* Máriatölgyes; *prev.* Dubnicz. Trenčiansky Kraj, W Slovakia *48°58′N 18°10′E*
Dubnicz *see* Dubnica nad Váhom
116 *K4* **Dubno** Rivnens'ka Oblast', NW Ukraine *50°28′N 25°40′E*
33 *R13* **Dubois** Idaho, NW USA *44°10′N 112°13′W*
18 *D13* **Du Bois** Pennsylvania, NE USA *41°07′N 78°45′W*
33 *T14* **Dubois** Wyoming, C USA *43°31′N 109°37′W*
Dubossary *see* Dubăsari
127 *O10* **Dubovka** Volgogradskaya Oblast', SW Russian Federation *49°10′N 44°49′E*
76 *H14* **Dubréka** SW Guinea *09°48′N 13°31′W*
14 *B7* **Dubreuilville** Ontario, S Canada *48°21′N 84°31′W*
Dubris Portus *see* Dover
119 *L20* **Dubrova** Homyel'skaya Voblasts', SE Belarus *51°47′N 28°13′E*
Dubrovačko-Neretvanska Županija *see* Dubrovnik-Neretva
126 *I5* **Dubrovka** Bryanskaya Oblast', W Russian Federation *53°44′N 33°27′E*
113 *H16* **Dubrovnik** *It.* Ragusa. Dubrovnik-Neretva, SE Croatia *42°40′N 18°06′E*
113 *I16* **Dubrovnik** ✈ Dubrovnik-Neretva, SE Croatia *42°34′N 18°17′E*
113 *F16* **Dubrovnik-Neretva** *off.* Dubrovačko-Neretvanska Županija. ◐ *province* SE Croatia
Dubrovno *see* Dubrowna
116 *L2* **Dubrovytsya** Rivnens'ka Oblast', NW Ukraine *51°34′N 26°37′E*
119 *O14* **Dubrowna** *Rus.* Dubrovno. Vitsyebskaya Voblasts', N Belarus *54°35′N 30°41′E*
29 *Z13* **Dubuque** Iowa, C USA *42°30′N 90°40′W*
118 *E12* **Dubysa** ∽ C Lithuania
167 *U11* **Đưc Cơ** Gia Lai, C Vietnam *13°48′N 107°41′E*
191 *V12* **Duc de Gloucester, Îles du** *Eng.* Duke of Gloucester Islands. *island group* C French Polynesia
111 *C15* **Duchcov** *Ger.* Dux. Ústecký Kraj, NW Czech Republic *50°37′N 13°45′E*
37 *N3* **Duchesne** Utah, W USA *40°09′N 110°24′W*
191 *P17* **Ducie Island** *atoll* E Pitcairn Islands
11 *W15* **Duck Bay** Manitoba, S Canada *52°11′N 100°08′W*
23 *X17* **Duck Key** *island* Florida Keys, Florida, SE USA
11 *T14* **Duck Lake** Saskatchewan, S Canada *52°52′N 106°12′W*
11 *V15* **Duck Mountain** ⛰ Manitoba, S Canada
20 *I9* **Duck River** ∽ Tennessee, S USA
20 *M10* **Ducktown** Tennessee, S USA *35°01′N 84°24′W*
167 *U10* **Đưc Phô** Quang Ngai, C Vietnam *14°56′N 108°55′E*
Duc Tho *see* Lin Camh
167 *U13* **Đưc Trong** *var.* Liên Nghia. Lâm Đông, S Vietnam *11°45′N 108°24′E*
D-U-D *see* Dalap-Uliga-Djarrit
99 *M25* **Dudelange** *var.* Forge du Sud, *Ger.* Dudelingen. Luxembourg, S Luxembourg *49°28′N 06°05′E*
Dudelingen *see* Dudelange
101 *J15* **Duderstadt** Niedersachsen, C Germany *51°31′N 10°16′E*
153 *N15* **Dūdhi** Uttar Pradesh, N India *24°09′N 83°16′E*
122 *K8* **Dudinka** Taymyrskiy (Dolgano-Nenetskiy) Avtonomnyy Okrug, N Russian Federation *69°27′N 86°13′E*
97 *L20* **Dudley** C England, United Kingdom *52°30′N 02°05′W*
154 *G13* **Dudna** ∽ C India
76 *L16* **Duékoué** W Ivory Coast *06°50′N 05°22′W*
104 *M5* **Dueñas** Castilla-León, N Spain *41°52′N 04°33′W*
104 *K4* **Duerna** ∽ NW Spain
105 *O6* **Duero** *Port.* Douro. ∽ Portugal/Spain *see also* Douro
Duero *see* Douro
Duesseldorf *see* Düsseldorf
21 *P12* **Due West** South Carolina, SE USA *34°19′N 82°23′W*
195 *P11* **Dufek Coast** *physical region* Antarctica
99 *H17* **Duffel** Antwerpen, C Belgium *51°06′N 04°30′E*
35 *S2* **Duffer Peak** ▲ Nevada, W USA *41°40′N 118°45′W*
187 *Q9* **Duff Islands** *island group* E Solomon Islands
Dufour, Pizzo/Dufour, Punta *see* Dufour Spitze
108 *E12* **Dufour Spitze** *It.* Pizzo Dufour, Punta Dufour. ▲ Italy/Switzerland *45°54′N 07°50′E*
112 *D9* **Duga Resa** Karlovac, C Croatia *45°25′N 15°30′E*
22 *H5* **Dugdemona River** ∽ Louisiana, S USA
154 *J12* **Duggipar** Mahārāshtra, C India *21°06′N 80°10′E*
112 *B13* **Dugi Otok** *var.* Isola Grossa, *It.* Isola Lunga. *island* W Croatia
113 *F14* **Dugopolje** Split-Dalmacija, S Croatia *43°35′N 16°35′E*
160 *L8* **Du He** ∽ C China
54 *M11* **Duida, Cerro** ▲ S Venezuela *03°21′N 65°45′W*
Duinekerke *see* Dunkerque
101 *E15* **Duisburg** *prev.* Duisburg-Hamborn. Nordrhein-Westfalen, W Germany *51°25′N 06°47′E*
Duisburg-Hamborn *see* Duisburg
99 *F14* **Duiveland** *island* SW Netherlands
98 *M12* **Duiven** Gelderland, E Netherlands *51°57′N 06°02′E*
139 *W10* **Dujaylah, Hawr ad** ◎ S Iraq
160 *H9* **Dujiangyan** *var.* Guanxian, Guan Xian. Sichuan, C China *31°01′N 103°40′E*
81 *L18* **Dujuuma** Shabeellaha Hoose, S Somalia *01°04′N 42°37′E*
Dūkān *see* Dokan
39 *Z14* **Duke Island** *island* Alexander Archipelago, Alaska, USA
Dukelský Priesmy/Dukelský Průsmyk *see* Dukla Pass
Duke of Gloucester Islands *see* Duc de Gloucester, Îles du
81 *F14* **Duk Faiwil** Jonglei, SE Sudan *07°30′N 31°27′E*
141 *T7* **Dukhān** C Qatar *25°29′N 50°48′E*
Dukhan Heights *see* Dukhān, Jabal
143 *N16* **Dukhān, Jabal** *var.* Dukhan Heights. *hill range* S Qatar
127 *Q7* **Dukhovnitskoye** Saratovskaya Oblast', W Russian Federation *52°31′N 48°32′E*
126 *H4* **Dukhovshchina** Smolenskaya Oblast', W Russian Federation *55°15′N 32°22′E*
Dukielska, Przełęcz *see* Dukla Pass
111 *N17* **Dukla** Podkarpackie, SE Poland *49°33′N 21°40′E*
Duklai Hág *see* Dukla Pass
111 *N18* **Dukla Pass** *Cz.* Dukelský Průsmyk, *Ger.* Dukla-Pass, *Hung.* Duklai Hág, *Pol.* Przełęcz Dukielska, *Slvk.* Dukelský Priesmy. *pass* Poland/Slovakia
Dukla-Pass *see* Dukla Pass
Dukou *see* Panzhihua
118 *I12* **Dūkštas** Utena, E Lithuania *55°32′N 26°21′E*
Dulaan *see* Herlenbayan-Ulaan
159 *R10* **Dulan** *var.* Qagan Us. Qinghai, C China *36°11′N 97°51′E*
37 *R8* **Dulce** New Mexico, SW USA *36°55′N 107°00′W*
43 *N16* **Dulce, Golfo** *gulf* S Costa Rica
Dulce, Golfo *see* Izabal, Lago de
42 *K6* **Dulce Nombre de Culmí** Olancho, C Honduras *15°09′N 85°37′W*
62 *L9* **Dulce, Río** ∽ C Argentina
123 *Q9* **Dulgalakh** ∽ NE Russian Federation
114 *M8* **Dŭlgopol** Varna, E Bulgaria *43°05′N 27°24′E*
153 *V14* **Dullabchara** Assam, NE India *24°25′N 92°22′E*
20 *D3* **Dulles** ✈ (Washington DC)Virginia, NE USA *39°00′N 77°27′W*
101 *E14* **Dülmen** Nordrhein-Westfalen, W Germany *51°51′N 07°17′E*
114 *M7* **Dulovo** Silistra, NE Bulgaria *43°51′N 27°10′E*
29 *W5* **Duluth** Minnesota, N USA *46°47′N 92°06′W*
138 *H7* **Dūmā** *Fr.* Douma. Dimashq, SW Syria *33°33′N 36°24′E*
171 *O8* **Dumagasa Point** *headland* Mindanao, S Philippines *07°01′N 121°54′E*
171 *P6* **Dumaguete** *var.* Dumaguete City. Negros, C Philippines *09°16′N 123°17′E*
Dumaguete City *see* Dumaguete
168 *J10* **Dumai** Sumatera, W Indonesia *01°39′N 101°28′E*
183 *T4* **Dumaresq River** ∽ New South Wales/Queensland, SE Australia
27 *W13* **Dumas** Arkansas, C USA *33°53′N 91°29′W*
25 *N1* **Dumas** Texas, SW USA *35°51′N 101°57′W*
138 *I7* **Ḍumayr** Dimashq, W Syria *33°36′N 36°28′E*
96 *I12* **Dumbarton** W Scotland, United Kingdom *55°57′N 04°35′W*
96 *I12* **Dumbarton** *cultural region* C Scotland, United Kingdom
187 *Q17* **Dumbéa** Province Sud, S New Caledonia *22°11′S 166°27′E*
111 *K19* **Ďumbier** *Ger.* Djumbir, *Hung.* Gyömbér. ▲ C Slovakia *48°54′N 19°36′E*
116 *I11* **Dumbrăveni** *Ger.* Elisabethstedt, *Hung.* Erzsébetváros; *prev.* Ebesfalva, Eppeschdorf, Ibașfalău. Sibiu, C Romania *46°14′N 24°34′E*
116 *L12* **Dumbrăveni** Vrancea, E Romania *45°31′N 27°09′E*
97 *J14* **Dumfries** S Scotland, United Kingdom *55°04′N 03°37′W*
97 *J14* **Dumfries** *cultural region* SW Scotland, United Kingdom
153 *R15* **Dumka** Jhārkhand, NE India *24°17′N 87°15′E*
Dümmer *see* Dümmersee
100 *G12* **Dümmersee** *var.* Dümmer. ◎ NW Germany
14 *J11* **Dumoine** ∽ Québec, SE Canada
14 *J10* **Dumoine, Lac** ◎ Québec, SE Canada
195 *V16* **Dumont d'Urville** *French research station* Antarctica *66°24′S 139°38′E*
195 *W15* **Dumont d'Urville Sea** *sea* S Pacific Ocean
14 *K11* **Dumont, Lac** ◎ Québec, SE Canada
75 *W7* **Dumyāṭ** *var.* Dumyât, *Eng.* Damietta. N Egypt *31°26′N 31°48′E*
Duna *see* Danube, C Europe
Düna *see* Western Dvina
Duna *see* Don, Russian Federation
Dünaburg *see* Daugavpils
111 *J24* **Dunaföldvár** Tolna, C Hungary *46°48′N 18°55′E*
Dunaj *see* Wien, Austria
Dunaj *see* Danube, C Europe
111 *L18* **Dunajec** ∽ S Poland
111 *H21* **Dunajská Streda** *Hung.* Dunaszerdahely. Trnavský Kraj, W Slovakia *48°N 17°28′E*
Dunapentele *see* Dunaújváros
Dunărea *see* Danube
116 *M13* **Dunărea Veche, Brațul** ∽ SE Romania
117 *N13* **Dunării, Delta** *delta* SE Romania
Dunaszerdahely *see* Dunajská Streda
111 *J23* **Dunaújváros** *prev.* Dunapentele, Sztálinváros. Fejér, C Hungary *47°N 18°55′E*
Dunav *see* Danube
114 *J8* **Dunavska Ravnina** *Eng.* Danubian Plain. *lowlands* N Bulgaria
114 *G7* **Dunavtsi** Vidin, NW Bulgaria *43°54′N 22°49′E*
123 *S15* **Dunay** Primorskiy Kray, SE Russian Federation *42°53′N 132°20′E*
Dunayevtsy *see* Dunayivtsi
116 *L7* **Dunayivtsi** *Rus.* Dunayevtsy. Khmel'nyts'ka Oblast', NW Ukraine *48°56′N 26°50′E*
185 *F22* **Dunback** Otago, South Island, New Zealand *45°22′S 170°37′E*
10 *L17* **Duncan** Vancouver Island, British Columbia, SW Canada *48°46′N 123°10′W*
37 *O15* **Duncan** Arizona, SW USA *32°43′N 109°06′W*
26 *M12* **Duncan** Oklahoma, C USA *34°30′N 97°57′W*
Duncan Island *see* Pinzón, Isla
151 *Q20* **Duncan Passage** *strait* Andaman Sea/Bay of Bengal
96 *K6* **Duncansby Head** *headland* N Scotland, United Kingdom *58°37′N 03°01′W*
14 *G12* **Dunchurch** Ontario, S Canada *45°36′N 79°54′W*
118 *D7* **Dundaga** Talsi, NW Latvia *57°29′N 22°19′E*
14 *G14* **Dundalk** Ontario, S Canada *44°11′N 80°22′W*
97 *F16* **Dundalk** *Ir.* Dún Dealgan. Louth, NE Ireland *54°01′N 06°25′W*
21 *X3* **Dundalk** Maryland, NE USA *39°15′N 76°31′W*
97 *F16* **Dundalk Bay** *Ir.* Cuan Dhún Dealgan. *bay* NE Ireland
14 *G16* **Dundas** Ontario, S Canada *43°16′N 79°55′W*
180 *L12* **Dundas, Lake** *salt lake* Western Australia
Dundbürd *see* Batnorov
Dún Dealgan *see* Dundalk
15 *N13* **Dundee** Québec, SE Canada *45°01′N 74°27′W*
83 *K22* **Dundee** KwaZulu/Natal, E South Africa *28°09′S 30°12′E*
96 *K11* **Dundee** E Scotland, United Kingdom *56°28′N 03°W*
31 *R10* **Dundee** Michigan, N USA *41°57′N 83°39′W*
25 *R5* **Dundee** Texas, SW USA *33°43′N 98°52′W*
194 *H3* **Dundee Island** *island* Antarctica
162 *L9* **Dundgovĭ** ◐ *province* C Mongolia
97 *G16* **Dundrum Bay** *Ir.* Cuan Dhún Droma. *inlet* NW Irish Sea
11 *T15* **Dundurn** Saskatchewan, S Canada *51°43′N 106°27′W*
Dund-Us *see* Hovd
Dund-Us *see* Hovd
185 *F23* **Dunedin** Otago, South Island, New Zealand *45°52′S 170°31′E*
183 *R7* **Dunedoo** New South Wales, SE Australia *32°04′S 149°23′E*
97 *D14* **Dunfanaghy** *Ir.* Dún Fionnachaidh. NW Ireland *55°11′N 07°59′W*
96 *J12* **Dunfermline** C Scotland, United Kingdom *56°04′N 03°29′W*
Dún Fionnachaidh *see* Dunfanaghy
149 *V10* **Dunga Bunga** Punjab, E Pakistan *29°51′N 73°19′E*
97 *F15* **Dungannon** *Ir.* Dún Geanainn. C Northern Ireland, United Kingdom *54°31′N 06°46′W*
Dun Garbháin *see* Dungarvan
152 *F15* **Dūngarpur** Rājasthān, N India *23°50′N 73°43′E*
97 *E21* **Dungarvan** *Ir.* Dun Garbháin. Waterford, S Ireland *52°05′N 07°37′W*
101 *N21* **Dungau** *cultural region* SE Germany
Dún Geanainn *see* Dungannon
97 *P23* **Dungeness** *headland* SE England, United Kingdom *50°55′N 00°58′E*
63 *I23* **Dungeness, Punta** *headland* S Argentina *52°25′S 68°25′W*
Dungloe *see* Dunglow
97 *D14* **Dunglow** *var.* Dungloe, *Ir.* An Clochán Liath. Donegal, NW Ireland *54°57′N 08°22′W*
183 *T7* **Dungog** New South Wales, SE Australia *32°24′S 151°45′E*
79 *O16* **Dungu** Orientale, NE Dem. Rep. Congo *03°40′N 28°32′E*
168 *L8* **Dungun** *var.* Kuala Dungun. Terengganu, Peninsular Malaysia *04°47′N 103°26′E*
80 *I6* **Dungunab** Red Sea, NE Sudan *21°10′N 37°09′E*
15 *P13* **Dunham** Québec, SE Canada *45°08′N 72°48′W*
Dunheved *see* Launceston
Dunholme *see* Durham
163 *X10* **Dunhua** Jilin, NE China *43°22′N 128°12′E*
159 *P8* **Dunhuang** Gansu, N China *40°10′N 94°40′E*
182 *L12* **Dunkeld** Victoria, SE Australia *37°41′S 142°19′E*
103 *O1* **Dunkerque** *Eng.* Dunkirk, *Flem.* Duinekerke; *prev.* Dunquerque. Nord, N France *51°06′N 02°34′E*
97 *K23* **Dunkery Beacon** ▲ SW England, United Kingdom *51°10′N 03°36′W*
18 *C11* **Dunkirk** New York, NE USA *42°28′N 79°19′W*
Dunkirk *see* Dunkerque
77 *P17* **Dunkwa** SW Ghana *05°59′N 01°45′W*
97 *G18* **Dún Laoghaire** *Eng.* Dunleary; *prev.* Kingstown. E Ireland *53°17′N 06°08′W*
29 *S14* **Dunlap** Iowa, C USA *41°51′N 95°36′W*
20 *L10* **Dunlap** Tennessee, S USA *35°22′N 85°23′W*
Dunleary *see* Dún Laoghaire
Dún Mánmhaí *see* Dunmanway
97 *B21* **Dunmanway** *Ir.* Dún Mánmhaí. Cork, SW Ireland *51°43′N 09°07′W*
18 *I13* **Dunmore** Pennsylvania, NE USA *41°25′N 75°37′W*
21 *U10* **Dunn** North Carolina, SE USA *35°18′N 78°36′W*
Dún na nGall *see* Donegal
23 *V11* **Dunnellon** Florida, SE USA *29°03′N 82°27′W*
96 *J6* **Dunnet Head** *headland* N Scotland, United Kingdom *58°40′N 03°27′W*
29 *N14* **Dunning** Nebraska, C USA *41°49′N 100°04′W*
14 *G17* **Dunnville** Ontario, S Canada *42°54′N 79°36′W*
Dún Pádraig *see* Downpatrick
Dunquerque *see* Dunkerque
Dunqulah *see* Dongola
96 *L12* **Duns** SE Scotland, United Kingdom *55°46′N 02°13′W*
29 *N2* **Dunseith** North Dakota, N USA *48°48′N 100°03′W*
35 *N2* **Dunsmuir** California, W USA *41°12′N 122°19′W*
97 *N21* **Dunstable** *Lat.* Durocobrivae. E England, United Kingdom *51°53′N 00°32′W*
185 *D21* **Dunstan Mountains** ⛰ South Island, New Zealand
103 *O9* **Dun-sur-Auron** Cher, C France *46°52′N 02°40′E*
185 *F21* **Duntroon** Canterbury, South Island, New Zealand *44°52′S 170°40′E*
149 *T10* **Dunyāpur** Punjab, E Pakistan *29°48′N 71°48′E*
163 *U5* **Duobukur He** ∽ NE China
163 *R12* **Duolun** *var.* Dolonnur. Nei Mongol Zizhiqu, N China *42°11′N 116°30′E*
167 *R14* **Dương Đông** Kiên Giang, S Vietnam *10°15′N 103°58′E*
114 *G10* **Dupnitsa** *prev.* Marek, Stanke Dimitrov. Kyustendil, W Bulgaria *42°16′N 23°07′E*
28 *L8* **Dupree** South Dakota, N USA *45°03′N 101°36′W*
33 *Q7* **Dupuyer** Montana, NW USA *48°13′N 112°34′W*
141 *Y11* **Duqm** *var.* Daqm. E Oman *19°42′N 57°40′E*
63 *F23* **Duque de York, Isla** *island* S Chile
181 *N4* **Durack Range** ⛰ Western Australia
136 *K10* **Durağan** Sinop, N Turkey *41°26′N 35°03′E*
103 *S15* **Durance** ∽ SE France
31 *R9* **Durand** Michigan, N USA *42°54′N 83°58′W*
30 *I6* **Durand** Wisconsin, N USA *44°37′N 91°56′W*
40 *K10* **Durango** *var.* Victoria de Durango. Durango, W Mexico *24°03′N 104°38′W*
105 *P3* **Durango** País Vasco, N Spain *43°10′N 02°38′W*
37 *Q8* **Durango** Colorado, C USA *37°13′N 107°51′W*
40 *J9* **Durango** ◐ *state* C Mexico
114 *O7* **Durankulak** *Rom.* Răcari; *prev.* Blatnitsa, Duranulac. Dobrich, NE Bulgaria *43°41′N 28°31′E*
22 *L4* **Durant** Mississippi, S USA *33°04′N 89°51′W*
27 *P13* **Durant** Oklahoma, C USA *33°59′N 96°24′W*
Duranulac *see* Durankulak
105 *N6* **Duratón** ∽ N Spain
61 *E19* **Durazno** *var.* San Pedro de Durazno. Durazno, C Uruguay *33°22′S 56°31′W*
61 *E19* **Durazno** ◐ *department* C Uruguay
Durazzo *see* Durrës
83 *K23* **Durban** *var.* Port Natal. KwaZulu/Natal, E South Africa *29°51′S 31°E*
83 *K23* **Durban** ✈ KwaZulu/Natal, E South Africa *29°55′S 31°01′E*
118 *C9* **Durbe** *Ger.* Durben. Liepāja, W Latvia *56°34′N 21°22′E*
Durben *see* Durbe
99 *K21* **Durbuy** Luxembourg, SE Belgium *50°21′N 05°27′E*
105 *N15* **Dúrcal** Andalucía, S Spain *37°00′N 03°24′W*
112 *F8* **Đurđevac** *Ger.* Sankt Georgen, *Hung.* Szentgyörgy; *prev.* Djurdjevac, Gjurgjevac. Koprivnica-Križevci, N Croatia *46°02′N 17°03′E*
113 *K15* **Đurđevica Tara** N Montenegro *43°09′N 19°18′E*
97 *L24* **Durdle Door** *natural arch* S England, United Kingdom
158 *L3* **Düre** Xinjiang Uygur Zizhiqu, W China *46°30′N 88°26′E*
101 *D16* **Düren** *anc.* Marcodurum. Nordrhein-Westfalen, W Germany *50°48′N 06°30′E*
154 *K12* **Durg** *prev.* Drug. Chhattisgarh, C India *21°12′N 81°20′E*
153 *U13* **Durgapur** Dhaka, N Bangladesh *25°10′N 90°41′E*
153 *R15* **Durgāpur** West Bengal, NE India *23°30′N 87°20′E*
14 *F14* **Durham** Ontario, S Canada *44°10′N 80°48′W*
97 *M14* **Durham** *hist.* Dunholme. N England, United Kingdom *54°47′N 01°34′W*
21 *U9* **Durham** North Carolina, SE USA *36°N 78°54′W*
97 *L15* **Durham** *cultural region* N England, United Kingdom
168 *J10* **Duri** Sumatera, W Indonesia *01°13′N 101°13′E*
Duria Major *see* Dora Baltea
Duria Minor *see* Dora Riparia
Durlas *see* Thurles
141 *P8* **Ḍurmā** Ar Riyāḍ, C Saudi Arabia *24°37′N 46°06′E*
113 *J15* **Durmitor** ▲ N Montenegro
96 *H6* **Durness** N Scotland, United Kingdom *58°34′N 04°46′W*
109 *Y3* **Dürnkrut** Niederösterreich, E Austria *48°28′N 16°50′E*
Durnovaria *see* Dorchester
Durobrivae *see* Rochester
Durocasses *see* Dreux
Durocobrivae *see* Dunstable
Durocortorum *see* Reims
Durostorum *see* Silistra
Durovernum *see* Canterbury
113 *K20* **Durrës** *var.* Durrësi, Dursi, *It.* Durazzo, *SCr.* Drač, *Turk.* Draç. Durrës, W Albania *41°20′N 19°26′E*
113 *K19* **Durrës** ◐ *district* W Albania
Durrësi *see* Durrës
97 *A21* **Dursey Island** *Ir.* Oileán Baoi. *island* SW Ireland
Dursi *see* Durrës
Duru *see* Wuchuan
Durud *see* Do Rūd
114 *P12* **Durusu** İstanbul, NW Turkey *41°18′N 28°41′E*
114 *O12* **Durusu Gölü** ◎ NW Turkey
138 *I9* **Durūz, Jabal ad** ▲ SW Syria *37°00′N 32°30′E*
184 *K13* **D'Urville Island** *island* C New Zealand
171 *X12* **D'Urville, Tanjung** *headland* Papua, E Indonesia *01°26′S 137°52′E*
146 *H14* **Duşak** *Rus.* Dushak. Ahal Welaýaty, S Turkmenistan *37°15′N 59°57′E*
Dusa Mareb/Dusa Marreb *see* Dhuusa Marreeb
118 *I11* **Dusetos** Utena, NE Lithuania *55°44′N 25°49′E*
Dushak *see* Duşak
160 *K12* **Dushan** Guizhou, S China *25°50′N 107°36′E*
147 *P13* **Dushanbe** *var.* Dyushambe; *prev.* Stalinabad, *Taj.* Stalinobod. ● (Tajikistan) W Tajikistan *38°35′N 68°44′E*
147 *P13* **Dushanbe** ✈ W Tajikistan *38°31′N 68°49′E*
158 *J5* **Dushanzi** Xinjiang Uygur Zizhiqu, NW China *44°20′N 84°51′E*
137 *T9* **Dushet'i** E Georgia *42°07′N 44°44′E*
18 *H13* **Dushore** Pennsylvania, NE USA *41°30′N 76°23′W*
185 *A23* **Dusky Sound** *sound* South Island, New Zealand
101 *E15* **Düsseldorf** *var.* Duesseldorf. Nordrhein-Westfalen, W Germany *51°14′N 06°49′E*
147 *P14* **Dŭstí** *Rus.* Dusti. SW Tajikistan *37°22′N 68°41′E*
194 *I9* **Dustin Island** *island* Antarctica
Dutch East Indies *see* Indonesia
Dutch Guiana *see* Suriname
38 *L17* **Dutch Harbor** Unalaska Island, Alaska, USA *53°51′N 166°33′W*
36 *J3* **Dutch Mount** ▲ Utah, W USA *40°16′N 113°56′W*
Dutch New Guinea *see* Papua
Dutch West Indies *see* Netherlands Antilles
83 *H20* **Dutlwe** Kweneng, S Botswana *23°58′S 23°56′E*
67 *V16* **Du Toit Fracture Zone** *tectonic feature* SW Indian Ocean
125 *U8* **Dutovo** Respublika Komi, NW Russian Federation *63°45′N 56°38′E*
77 *V13* **Dutsan Wai** *var.* Dutsen Wai. Kaduna, C Nigeria *10°49′N 08°15′E*
77 *W13* **Dutse** Jigawa, N Nigeria *11°43′N 09°25′E*
Dutsen Wai *see* Dutsan Wai
Duttia *see* Datia
14 *E17* **Dutton** Ontario, S Canada *42°40′N 81°28′W*
36 *L7* **Dutton, Mount** ▲ Utah, W USA *38°00′N 112°10′W*
162 *E7* **Duut** Hovd, W Mongolia *47°28′N 91°52′E*
14 *K11* **Duval, Lac** ◎ Québec, SE Canada
127 *W3* **Duvan** Respublika Bashkortostan, W Russian Federation *55°42′N 57°56′E*
138 *L9* **Duwaykhilat Satih ar Ruwayshid** *seasonal river* SE Jordan
Dux *see* Duchcov
160 *J13* **Duyang Shan** ⛰ S China
167 *T14* **Duyên Hai** Tra Vinh, S Vietnam *09°39′N 106°28′E*
160 *K12* **Duyun** Guizhou, S China *26°16′N 107°29′E*
136 *G11* **Düzce** Düzce, NW Turkey *40°51′N 31°09′E*
136 *K14* **Düzce** ◐ *province* NW Turkey
Duzdab *see* Zāhedān
Duzenkyr, Khrebet *see* Duzkyr, Khrebet
146 *I16* **Duzkyr, Khrebet** *prev.* Khrebet Duzenkyr. ⛰ S Turkmenistan
114 *K8* **Dve Mogili** Ruse, N Bulgaria *43°35′N 25°51′E*
Dvina Bay *see* Chëshskaya Guba
Dvinsk *see* Daugavpils
124 *L7* **Dvinskaya Guba** *bay* NW Russian Federation
112 *E10* **Dvor** Sisak-Moslavina, C Croatia *45°05′N 16°22′E*
117 *W5* **Dvorichna** Kharkivs'ka Oblast', E Ukraine *49°52′N 37°43′E*
111 *F16* **Dvůr Králové nad Labem** *Ger.* Königinhof an der Elbe. Královéhradecký Kraj, N Czech Republic *50°27′N 15°50′E*
154 *A10* **Dwārka** Gujarāt, W India *22°14′N 68°58′E*
30 *M12* **Dwight** Illinois, N USA *41°05′N 88°25′W*
98 *N8* **Dwingeloo** Drenthe, NE Netherlands *52°49′N 06°20′E*
33 *N10* **Dworshak Reservoir** ⊡ Idaho, NW USA
Dyal *see* Dyaul Island
Dyanev *see* Galkynyş
Dyatlovo *see* Dzyatlava
186 *G5* **Dyaul Island** Dyal. *island* NE Papua New Guinea
20 *G8* **Dyer** Tennessee, S USA *36°04′N 88°59′W*
9 *S5* **Dyer, Cape** *headland* Baffin Island, Nunavut, NE Canada *66°37′N 61°13′W*
20 *F8* **Dyersburg** Tennessee, S USA *36°02′N 89°21′W*
29 *Y13* **Dyersville** Iowa, C USA *42°29′N 91°07′W*
97 *I21* **Dyfed** *cultural region* SW Wales, United Kingdom
Dyfrdwy, Afon *see* Dee
Dyhernfurth *see* Brzeg Dolny

◆ Country ◇ Dependent Territory ◐ Administrative Regions ▲ Mountain Volcano ◎ Lake
● Country Capital ○ Dependent Territory Capital ✈ International Airport ⛰ Mountain Range ∽ River ⊡ Reservoir
245

DYJE – EIŠIŠKES

111 E19 Dyje var. Thaya. ≋ Austria/Czech Republic see also Thaya
Dyje see Thaya
117 T5 Dykan'ka Poltavs'ka Oblast', C Ukraine 49°48'N 34°33'E
127 N16 Dykhtau ▲ SW Russian Federation 43°01'N 42°56'E
111 A16 Dyleń Ger. Tillenberg. ▲ NW Czech Republic 49°58'N 12°31'E
110 K9 Dylewska Góra ▲ N Poland 53°33'N 19°57'E
117 O4 Dymer Kyyivs'ka Oblast', N Ukraine 50°50'N 30°20'E
117 W7 Dymytrov Rus. Dimitrov. Donets'ka Oblast', SE Ukraine 48°18'N 37°19'E
111 O17 Dynów Podkarpackie, SE Poland 49°49'N 22°14'E
29 X13 Dysart Iowa, C USA 42°10'N 92°18'W
Dysna see Dzisna
115 H18 Dýstos, Límni var. Límni Dístos. ◎ Évvoia, C Greece
115 D18 Dytikí Ellás Eng. Greece West. ◈ region C Greece
115 C14 Dytikí Makedonía Eng. Macedonia West. ◈ region N Greece
Dyurment'yube see Dermentobe
127 U4 Dyurtyuli Respublika Bashkortostan, W Russian Federation 55°31'N 54°49'E
Dyushambe see Dushanbe
162 K7 Dzaamar var. Bat-Öldziyt. Töv, C Mongolia 48°10'N 104°49'E
Dzaanhushuu see Ihtamir
Dza Chu see Mekong
Dzadgay see Bömbögör
162 H8 Dzag Bayanhongor, C Mongolia 46°54'N 99°11'E
Dzalaa see Shinejinst
163 O11 Dzamïn-Üüd var. Borhoyn Tal. Dornogovĭ, SE Mongolia 43°43'N 111°53'E
172 J14 Dzaoudzi E Mayotte 12°48'S 45°18'E
Dzaudzhikau see Vladikavkaz
162 G7 Dzavhan ◈ province NW Mongolia
162 G7 Dzavhan Gol ≋ NW Mongolia
162 G6 Dzavhanmandal var. Nuga. Dzavhan, W Mongolia 48°17'N 95°07'E
Dzegstey see Ögiynuur
162 E7 Dzereg var. Altanteel. Hovd, W Mongolia 47°05'N 92°57'E
127 O3 Dzerzhinsk Nizhegorodskaya Oblast', W Russian Federation 56°20'N 43°22'E
Dzerzhinsk see Dzyarzhynsk Belarus
Dzerzhinsk see Dzerzhyns'k
Dzerzhinskiy see Nar'yan-Mar
Dzerzhinskoye see Tokzhaylau
Dzerzhinskoye see Tokzhaylau
117 X7 Dzerzhyns'k Rus. Dzerzhinsk. Donets'ka Oblast', SE Ukraine 48°21'N 37°50'E
116 M5 Dzerzhyns'k Zhytomyrs'ka Oblast', N Ukraine 50°07'N 27°56'E
Dzhetygara see Zhitikara
Dzhailgan see Jayilgan
145 N14 Dzhalagash Kaz. Zhalaghash. Kzylorda, S Kazakhstan 45°06'N 64°40'E
147 T10 Dzhalal-Abad Kir. Jalal-Abad. Dzhalal-Abadskaya Oblast', W Kyrgyzstan 40°56'N 73°00'E
147 S9 Dzhalal-Abadskaya Oblast' Kir. Jalal-Abad Oblasty. ◈ province W Kyrgyzstan
Dzhalilabad see Cälilabad
Dzhambeyty see Zhympity
Dzhambul see Taraz
Dzhambulskaya Oblast' see Zhambyl
144 D9 Dzhanibek var. Dzhanybek, Kaz. Zhänibek. Zapadnyy Kazakhstan, W Kazakhstan 49°27'N 46°51'E
Dzhankel'dy see Jongeldi
117 T12 Dzhankoy Respublika Krym, S Ukraine 45°40'N 34°20'E
145 V14 Dzhansugurov Kaz. Zhansügirov. Almaty, SE Kazakhstan 45°23'N 79°29'E
147 R9 Dzhany-Bazar var. Yangibazar. Dzhalal-Abadskaya Oblast', W Kyrgyzstan 41°40'N 70°49'E
Dzhanybek see Dzhanibek
123 P8 Dzhardzhan Respublika Sakha (Yakutiya), NE Russian Federation 68°47'N 123°51'E
Dzharkurgan see Jarqo'rg'on
117 S11 Dzharylhats'ka Zatoka gulf S Ukraine
Dzhayilgan see Jayilgan
Dzhebel see Jebel
147 T14 Dzhelandy SE Tajikistan 37°34'N 72°35'E
147 Y7 Dzhergalan Kir. Jyrgalan. Issyk-Kul'skaya Oblast', NE Kyrgyzstan 42°37'N 78°56'E
Dzhetysay see Zhetysay
Dzhezkazgan see Zhezkazgan
Dzhigirbent see Jigerbent
Dzhirgatal' see Jirgatol
Dzhizak see Jizzax
Dzhizakskaya Oblast' see Jizzax Viloyati
123 P8 Dzhugdzhur, Khrebet ▲▲ E Russian Federation
Dzhul'fa see Culfa
Dzhuma see Juma
145 W14 Dzhungarskiy Alatau ▲▲ China/Kazakhstan
144 M14 Dzhusaly Kaz. Zhosaly. Kzylorda, SW Kazakhstan 45°29'N 64°04'E
146 J12 Dzhynlykum, Peski desert E Turkmenistan
110 L9 Działdowo Warmińsko-Mazurskie, C Poland 53°13'N 20°12'E
111 L16 Działoszyce Świętokrzyskie, C Poland 50°21'N 20°19'E
41 X11 Dzidzantún Yucatán, E Mexico
111 G15 Dzierżoniów Ger. Reichenbach. Dolnośląskie, SW Poland 50°43'N 16°40'E
41 X11 Dzilam de Bravo Yucatán, E Mexico 21°24'N 88°52'W
118 L12 Dzisna Rus. Disna. Vitsyebskaya Voblasts', N Belarus 55°33'N 28°13'E
118 K12 Dzisna Lith. Dysna, Rus. Disna. ≋ Belarus/Lithuania
119 G20 Dzivin Rus. Divin. Brestskaya Voblasts', SW Belarus 51°58'N 24°33'E
119 M15 Dzmitravichy Rus. Dmitrovichi. Minskaya Voblasts', C Belarus 53°58'N 29°14'E
Dzogsool see Bayantsagaan
162 I5 Dzöölön var. Rinchinlhümbe. Hövsgöl, N Mongolia 51°06'N 99°40'E
129 S8 Dzungaria var. Sungaria, Zungaria. physical region W China
Dzungarian Basin see Junggar Pendi
Dzür see Tes
162 J8 Dzüünbayan-Ulaan var. Bayan-Ulaan. Övörhangay, C Mongolia 46°38'N 102°30'E
Dzüünbulag see Matad, Dornod, Mongolia
Dzüünbulag see Uulbayan, Sühbaatar, Mongolia
162 L8 Dzuunmod Töv, C Mongolia 47°45'N 107°00'E
Dzuunmod see Ider
Dzüün Soyonï Nuruu see Eastern Sayans
Dzüyl see Tonhil
Dzvina see Western Dvina
119 J16 Dzyarzhynsk Belarus Rus. Dzerzhinsk; prev. Kaydanovo. Minskaya Voblasts', C Belarus 53°41'N 27°09'E
119 H17 Dzyatlava Pol. Zdzięciół, Rus. Dyatlovo. Hrodzyenskaya Voblasts', W Belarus 53°27'N 25°23'E

E

E see Hubei
Éadan Doire see Edenderry
37 W6 Eads Colorado, C USA 38°28'N 102°46'W
37 O13 Eagar Arizona, SW USA 34°05'N 109°17'W
39 T8 Eagle Alaska, USA 64°47'N 141°12'W
13 S8 Eagle ≋ Newfoundland and Labrador, E Canada
10 I3 Eagle ≋ Yukon Territory, NW Canada
29 T7 Eagle Bend Minnesota, N USA 46°10'N 95°02'W
28 M8 Eagle Butte South Dakota, N USA 44°58'N 101°13'W
29 V12 Eagle Grove Iowa, C USA 42°39'N 93°54'W
19 R2 Eagle Lake Maine, NE USA 47°01'N 68°35'W
25 U11 Eagle Lake Texas, SW USA 29°35'N 96°19'W
12 A11 Eagle Lake ◎ Ontario, S Canada
35 P3 Eagle Lake ◎ California, W USA
19 R3 Eagle Lake ◎ Maine, NE USA
29 Y3 Eagle Mountain ▲ Minnesota, N USA 47°54'N 90°33'W
25 T6 Eagle Mountain Lake ⊠ Texas, SW USA
37 S9 Eagle Nest Lake ⊠ New Mexico, SW USA
25 P13 Eagle Pass Texas, SW USA 28°44'N 100°31'W
65 C25 Eagle Passage passage SW Atlantic Ocean
35 R8 Eagle Peak ▲ California, W USA 38°11'N 119°22'W
35 Q2 Eagle Peak ▲ California, W USA 41°16'N 120°12'W
37 P13 Eagle Peak ▲ New Mexico, SW USA 33°39'N 109°36'W
10 I4 Eagle Plain Yukon Territory, NW Canada 66°23'N 136°42'W
32 G15 Eagle Point Oregon, NW USA 42°28'N 122°48'W
186 P10 Eagle Point headland SE Papua New Guinea 10°31'S 149°53'E
39 R11 Eagle River Alaska, USA 61°18'N 149°38'W
30 M2 Eagle River Michigan, N USA 47°24'N 88°18'W
30 L4 Eagle River Wisconsin, N USA 45°56'N 89°15'W
21 S6 Eagle Rock Virginia, NE USA 37°40'N 79°46'W
36 J13 Eagletail Mountains ▲▲ Arizona, SW USA
167 U12 Ea Hleo Đăc Lăc, S Vietnam 13°09'N 108°14'E
167 U12 Ea Kar Đăc Lăc, S Vietnam 12°47'N 108°26'E
Eanjum see Anjum
Eanodat see Enontekiö
12 B10 Ear Falls Ontario, C Canada 50°38'N 93°13'W
27 X10 Earle Arkansas, C USA 35°16'N 90°28'W
35 R12 Earlimart California, W USA 35°52'N 119°17'W
20 I6 Earlington Kentucky, S USA 37°16'N 87°30'W
14 H8 Earlton Ontario, S Canada 47°41'N 79°46'W
29 T13 Early Iowa, C USA 42°27'N 95°09'W
96 J11 Earn ≋ N Scotland, United Kingdom
185 C21 Earnslaw, Mount ▲ South Island, New Zealand 44°34'S 168°26'E
24 M4 Earth Texas, SW USA 34°13'N 102°24'W
21 P11 Easley South Carolina, SE USA 34°49'N 82°36'W
East see Est
East Açores Fracture Zone see East Azores Fracture Zone
97 P19 East Anglia physical region E England, United Kingdom
15 Q12 East Angus Québec, SE Canada 45°29'N 71°39'W
195 V8 East Antarctica var. Greater Antarctica. physical region Antarctica
18 E10 East Aurora New York, NE USA 42°44'N 78°36'W
East Australian Basin see Tasman Basin
East Azerbaijan see Āžarbāyjān-e Sharqī
64 L9 East Azores Fracture Zone var. East Açores Fracture Zone. tectonic feature E Atlantic Ocean
22 M11 East Bay bay Louisiana, S USA
25 V11 East Bernard Texas, SW USA 29°32'N 96°04'W
29 V8 East Bethel Minnesota, N USA 45°24'N 93°14'W
East Borneo see Kalimantan Timur
97 P23 Eastbourne SE England, United Kingdom 50°46'N 00°16'E
15 R11 East-Broughton Québec, SE Canada 46°14'N 71°05'W
44 M6 East Caicos island E Turks and Caicos Islands
184 R7 East Cape headland North Island, New Zealand 37°40'S 178°31'E
174 M4 East Caroline Basin undersea feature SW Pacific Ocean 04°00'N 146°45'E
192 P4 East China Sea Chin. Dong Hai. sea W Pacific Ocean
97 P19 East Dereham E England, United Kingdom 52°41'N 00°55'E
30 J9 East Dubuque Illinois, N USA 42°29'N 90°38'W
11 S17 Eastend Saskatchewan, S Canada 49°29'N 108°48'W
193 S10 Easter Fracture Zone tectonic feature E Pacific Ocean
Easter Island see Pascua, Isla de
81 J18 Eastern ◈ province Kenya
153 Q12 Eastern ◈ zone E Nepal
155 K25 Eastern ◈ province E Sri Lanka
82 L13 Eastern ◈ province E Zambia
83 H24 Eastern Cape off. Eastern Cape Province, Afr. Oos-Kaap. ◈ province SE South Africa
Eastern Cape Province see Eastern Cape
Eastern Desert see Sahara el Sharqîya
81 F15 Eastern Equatoria ◈ state SE Sudan
Eastern Euphrates see Murat Nehri
155 J17 Eastern Ghats ▲▲ SE India
186 E7 Eastern Highlands ◈ province C Papua New Guinea
Eastern Region see Ash Sharqīyah
122 L13 Eastern Sayans Mong. Dzüün Soyonï Nuruu, Rus. Vostochnyy Sayan. ▲▲ Mongolia/Russian Federation
Eastern Scheldt see Oosterschelde
Eastern Sierra Madre see Madre Oriental, Sierra
Eastern Transvaal see Mpumalanga
11 W14 Easterville Manitoba, C Canada 53°06'N 99°53'W
Easterwâlde see Oosterwolde
63 M23 East Falkland var. Isla Soledad. island E Falkland Islands
19 P12 East Falmouth Massachusetts, NE USA 41°34'N 70°31'W
East Fayu see Fayu
East Flanders see Oost-Vlaanderen
39 S6 East Fork Chandalar River ≋ Alaska, USA
29 U12 East Fork Des Moines River ≋ Iowa/Minnesota, C USA
East Frisian Islands see Ostfriesische Inseln
18 K10 East Glenville New York, NE USA 42°53'N 73°55'W
29 R4 East Grand Forks Minnesota, N USA 47°54'N 97°59'W
97 O23 East Grinstead SE England, United Kingdom 51°08'N 00°00'W
18 M12 East Hartford Connecticut, NE USA 41°45'N 72°36'W
18 M13 East Haven Connecticut, NE USA 41°16'N 72°52'W
173 T9 East Indiaman Ridge undersea feature E Indian Ocean
129 V16 East Indies island group SE Asia
East Java see Jawa Timur
31 Q6 East Jordan Michigan, N USA 45°09'N 85°07'W
East Kalimantan see Kalimantan Timur
East Kazakhstan see Vostochnyy Kazakhstan
96 I12 East Kilbride S Scotland, United Kingdom 55°46'N 04°10'W
25 R7 Eastland Texas, SW USA 32°23'N 98°50'W
31 Q9 East Lansing Michigan, N USA 42°44'N 84°28'W
35 X11 East Las Vegas Nevada, W USA 36°05'N 115°02'W
97 M23 Eastleigh S England, United Kingdom 50°58'N 01°22'W
31 V12 East Liverpool Ohio, N USA 40°37'N 80°34'W
83 J25 East London Afr. Oos-Londen; prev. Emonti, Port Rex. Eastern Cape, S South Africa 33°S 27°54'E
96 K12 East Lothian cultural region SE Scotland, United Kingdom
12 I10 Eastmain Québec, E Canada 52°11'N 78°27'W
12 J10 Eastmain ≋ Québec, C Canada
15 P13 Eastman Québec, SE Canada 45°19'N 72°18'W
23 U6 Eastman Georgia, SE USA 32°12'N 83°10'W
175 O3 East Mariana Basin undersea feature W Pacific Ocean
30 K11 East Moline Illinois, N USA 41°30'N 90°26'W
186 H7 East New Britain ◈ province E Papua New Guinea
29 T15 East Nishnabotna River ≋ Iowa, C USA
197 V12 East Novaya Zemlya Trough var. Novaya Zemlya Trough. undersea feature W Kara Sea
East Nusa Tenggara see Nusa Tenggara Timur
21 X4 Easton Maryland, NE USA 38°46'N 76°04'W
18 I14 Easton Pennsylvania, NE USA 40°41'N 75°13'W
193 R16 East Pacific Rise undersea feature E Pacific Ocean 20°00'S 115°00'W
East Pakistan see Bangladesh
31 V12 East Palestine Ohio, N USA 40°49'N 80°32'W
30 L12 East Peoria Illinois, N USA 40°40'N 89°34'W
23 S3 East Point Georgia, SE USA 33°40'N 84°26'W
19 U6 Eastport Maine, NE USA 44°54'N 66°59'W
27 Z8 East Prairie Missouri, C USA 36°46'N 89°23'W
19 O12 East Providence Rhode Island, NE USA 41°48'N 71°20'W
20 L11 East Ridge Tennessee, S USA 35°00'N 85°15'W
97 N16 East Riding cultural region N England, United Kingdom
18 F9 East Rochester New York, NE USA 43°06'N 77°29'W
30 K15 East Saint Louis Illinois, N USA 38°35'N 90°07'W
65 K21 East Scotia Basin undersea feature SE Scotia Sea
129 Y8 East Sea var. Sea of Japan, Rus. Yapanskoye More. Sea NW Pacific Ocean see also Japan, Sea of
186 B6 East Sepik ◈ province NW Papua New Guinea
173 N4 East Sheba Ridge undersea feature W Arabian Sea 14°30'N 56°15'E
East Siberian Sea see Vostochno-Sibirskoye More
18 I14 East Stroudsburg Pennsylvania, NE USA 41°00'N 75°10'W
East Tasmanian Rise/East Tasmania Plateau/East Tasmania Rise see East Tasman Plateau
192 I12 East Tasman Plateau var. East Tasmanian Rise, East Tasmania Plateau, East Tasmania Rise. undersea feature SW Tasman Sea
64 L7 East Thulean Rise undersea feature N Atlantic Ocean
171 R16 East Timor var. Loro Sae; prev. Portuguese Timor, Timor Timur. ◆ country S Indonesia
21 Y6 Eastville Virginia, NE USA 37°22'N 75°58'W
35 R7 East Walker River ≋ California/Nevada, W USA
182 D1 Eateringinna Creek ≋ South Australia
37 T3 Eaton Colorado, C USA 40°31'N 104°42'W
15 Q12 Eaton ≋ Québec, SE Canada
11 S16 Eatonia Saskatchewan, S Canada 51°13'N 109°22'W
31 Q10 Eaton Rapids Michigan, N USA 42°30'N 84°39'W
23 U4 Eatonton Georgia, SE USA 33°19'N 83°23'W
32 H9 Eatonville Washington, NW USA 46°51'N 122°19'W
30 J6 Eau Claire Wisconsin, N USA 44°50'N 91°30'W
12 J7 Eau Claire, Lac à l' ◎ Québec, SE Canada
Eau Claire, Lac à L' see St. Clair, Lake
30 L6 Eau Claire River ≋ Wisconsin, N USA
188 J16 Eauripik Atoll atoll Caroline Islands, C Micronesia
192 H7 Eauripik Rise undersea feature W Pacific Ocean 03°00'N 142°00'E
102 K15 Eauze Gers, S France 43°52'N 00°06'E
41 P11 Ébano San Luis Potosí, C Mexico 22°16'N 98°26'W
97 K21 Ebbw Vale SE Wales, United Kingdom 51°48'N 03°13'W
79 E17 Ebebiyin NE Equatorial Guinea 02°08'N 11°15'E
95 H22 Ebeltoft Århus, C Denmark 56°11'N 10°42'E
109 X5 Ebenfurth Niederösterreich, E Austria 47°53'N 16°22'E
18 D14 Ebensburg Pennsylvania, NE USA 40°28'N 78°44'W
109 S5 Ebensee Oberösterreich, N Austria 47°48'N 13°46'E
101 H20 Eberbach Baden-Württemberg, SW Germany 49°28'N 08°58'E
121 U8 Eber Gölü salt lake C Turkey
109 U9 Eberndorf Slvn. Dobrla Vas. Kärnten, S Austria 46°33'N 14°35'E
109 R4 Eberschwang Oberösterreich, N Austria 48°09'N 13°37'E
100 O11 Eberswalde-Finow Brandenburg, E Germany 52°50'N 13°48'E
Ebesfalva see Dumbrăveni
165 T4 Ebetsu var. Ebetu. Hokkaidō, NE Japan 43°08'N 141°37'E
Ebetu see Ebetsu
Ebinayon see Evinayong
158 I4 Ebinur Hu ◎ NW China
138 I3 Ebla Ar. Tell Mardikh. site of ancient city Idlib, NW Syria
Eblana see Dublin
108 H7 Ebnat Sankt Gallen, NE Switzerland 47°16'N 09°07'E
107 L18 Eboli Campania, S Italy 40°37'N 15°03'E
79 E16 Ebolowa Sud, S Cameroon 02°56'N 11°11'E
79 N21 Ebombo Kasai-Oriental, C Dem. Rep. Congo 05°42'S 26°07'E
189 T9 Ebon Atoll var. Epoon. atoll Ralik Chain, S Marshall Islands
77 U16 Ebonyi ◈ state SE Nigeria
Ebora see Évora
Eboracum see York
Eborodunum see Yverdon
101 J19 Ebrach Bayern, C Germany 49°49'N 10°30'E
109 X5 Ebreichsdorf Niederösterreich, E Austria 47°58'N 16°24'E
105 S6 Ebro ≋ NE Spain
105 N3 Ebro, Embalse del ⊠ N Spain
120 G7 Ebro Fan undersea feature W Mediterranean Sea
Eburacum see York
Ebusus see Ibiza
Ebusus see Eivissa
99 F20 Écaussinnes-d'Enghien Hainaut, SW Belgium 50°34'N 04°10'E
Ecbatana see Hamadān
21 Q6 Eccles West Virginia, NE USA 37°46'N 81°16'W
115 L14 Eceabat Çanakkale, NW Turkey 40°12'N 26°22'E
171 O2 Echague Luzon, N Philippines 16°42'N 121°37'E
Ech Cheliff/Ech Chleff see Chlef
Echeng see Ezhou
115 C18 Echinádes island group W Greece
114 J12 Echínos var. Ehinos, Ekhínos. Anatolikí Makedonía kai Thráki, NE Greece 41°16'N 25°00'E
Echizen see Takefu
164 J12 Echizen-misaki headland Honshū, SW Japan 35°59'N 135°57'E
Echmiadzin see Vagharshapat
8 J8 Echo Bay Northwest Territories, NW Canada 66°04'N 118°W
35 Y11 Echo Bay Nevada, W USA 36°19'N 114°27'W
36 L9 Echo Cliffs cliff Arizona, SW USA
14 C10 Echo Lake ◎ Ontario, S Canada
35 Q7 Echo Summit ▲ California, W USA 38°47'N 120°06'W
14 L8 Échouani, Lac ◎ Québec, SE Canada
99 L17 Echt Limburg, SE Netherlands 51°07'N 05°52'E
101 H22 Echterdingen ✕ (Stuttgart) Baden-Württemberg, SW Germany 48°40'N 09°13'E
99 N24 Echternach Grevenmacher, E Luxembourg 49°49'N 06°25'E
183 N11 Echuca Victoria, SE Australia 36°10'S 144°20'E
104 L14 Écija anc. Astigi. Andalucía, SW Spain 37°33'N 05°04'W
Eckengraf see Viesīte
100 I7 Eckernförde Schleswig-Holstein, N Germany 54°28'N 09°49'E
100 J7 Eckernförder Bucht inlet N Germany
102 L7 Écommoy Sarthe, NW France 47°51'N 00°15'E
14 L10 Écorce, Lac de l' ◎ Québec, SE Canada
15 Q8 Écorces, Rivière aux ≋ Québec, SE Canada
56 C7 Ecuador off. Republic of Ecuador. ◆ republic NW South America
Ecuador, Republic of see Ecuador
95 I17 Ed Västra Götaland, S Sweden 58°55'N 11°55'E
Ed see 'Īdī
98 I9 Edam Noord-Holland, C Netherlands 52°30'N 05°02'E
96 K4 Eday island NE Scotland, United Kingdom
25 S17 Edcouch Texas, SW USA 26°17'N 97°57'W
80 C11 Ed Da'ein Southern Darfur, W Sudan 11°25'N 26°08'E
80 G11 Ed Damazin var. Ad Damazīn. Blue Nile, E Sudan 11°45'N 34°20'E
80 G8 Ed Damer var. Ad Dāmir, Ad Damar. River Nile, NE Sudan 17°37'N 33°59'E
80 E8 Ed Debba Northern, N Sudan 18°02'N 30°56'E
80 F10 Ed Dueim var. Ad Duwaym, Ad Duwēm. White Nile, C Sudan 13°38'N 32°36'E
183 Q16 Eddystone Point headland Tasmania, SE Australia 41°01'S 148°18'E
97 I25 Eddystone Rocks rocks SW England, United Kingdom
29 W15 Eddyville Iowa, C USA 41°09'N 92°37'W
20 H7 Eddyville Kentucky, S USA 37°03'N 88°02'W
98 L12 Ede Gelderland, C Netherlands 52°03'N 05°40'E
77 T16 Ede Osun, SW Nigeria 07°40'N 04°21'E
79 D16 Edéa Littoral, SW Cameroon 03°47'N 10°08'E
111 M20 Edelény Borsod-Abaúj-Zemplén, NE Hungary 48°18'N 20°40'E
183 R12 Eden New South Wales, SE Australia 37°04'S 149°51'E
21 T8 Eden North Carolina, SE USA 36°29'N 79°46'W
25 P9 Eden Texas, SW USA 31°13'N 99°51'W
97 K14 Eden ≋ NW England, United Kingdom
83 I23 Edenburg Free State, C South Africa 29°45'S 25°57'E
185 D24 Edendale Southland, South Island, New Zealand 46°18'S 168°48'E
97 E18 Edenderry Ir. Éadan Doire. Offaly, C Ireland 53°21'N 07°03'W
182 L11 Edenhope Victoria, SE Australia 37°04'S 141°15'E
21 X8 Edenton North Carolina, SE USA 36°04'N 76°39'W
101 G16 Eder ≋ NW Germany
101 H15 Edersee ◎ W Germany
114 E13 Édessa var. Édhessa. Kentrikí Makedonía, N Greece 40°48'N 22°03'E
Edessa see Şanlıurfa
Edfu see Idfu
29 P16 Edgar Nebraska, C USA 40°22'N 97°58'W
19 P13 Edgartown Martha's Vineyard, Massachusetts, NE USA 41°23'N 70°30'W
39 X13 Edgecumbe, Mount ▲ Baranof Island, Alaska, USA 57°03'N 135°45'W
21 Q13 Edgefield South Carolina, SE USA 33°50'N 81°57'W
29 P6 Edgeley North Dakota, N USA 46°19'N 98°42'W
28 I11 Edgemont South Dakota, N USA 43°18'N 103°49'W
92 O3 Edgeøya island S Svalbard
27 Q4 Edgerton Kansas, C USA 38°45'N 95°00'W
29 S10 Edgerton Minnesota, N USA 43°52'N 96°07'W
21 X3 Edgewood Maryland, NE USA 39°20'N 76°21'W
25 V6 Edgewood Texas, SW USA 32°42'N 95°53'W
Édhessa see Édessa
29 V9 Edina Minnesota, N USA 44°53'N 93°21'W
27 U2 Edina Missouri, C USA 40°10'N 92°10'W
25 S17 Edinburg Texas, SW USA 26°18'N 98°10'W
65 M24 Edinburgh var. Settlement of Edinburgh. ○ (Tristan da Cunha) NW Tristan da Cunha 37°03'S 12°18'W
96 J12 Edinburgh ● S Scotland, United Kingdom 55°57'N 03°13'W
31 P14 Edinburgh Indiana, N USA 39°19'N 86°00'W
96 J12 Edinburgh ✕ S Scotland, United Kingdom 55°57'N 03°22'W
116 L8 Edineţ var. Edineţi, Rus. Yedintsy. NW Moldova 48°10'N 27°18'E
Edineţi see Edineţ
Edingen see Enghien
136 B9 Edirne Eng. Adrianople; anc. Adrianopolis, Hadrianopolis. Edirne, NW Turkey 41°40'N 26°34'E
136 B11 Edirne ◈ province NW Turkey
18 K15 Edison New Jersey, NE USA 40°31'N 74°24'W
21 S15 Edisto Island South Carolina, SE USA 32°34'N 80°17'W
21 R14 Edisto River ≋ South Carolina, SE USA
33 S10 Edith, Mount ▲ Montana, NW USA 46°25'N 111°10'W
27 N10 Edmond Oklahoma, C USA 35°40'N 97°30'W
32 H8 Edmonds Washington, NW USA 47°48'N 122°22'W
11 Q14 Edmonton province capital Alberta, SW Canada 53°34'N 113°25'W
20 K7 Edmonton Kentucky, S USA 36°59'N 85°39'W
11 Q14 Edmonton ✕ Alberta, SW Canada 53°22'N 113°43'W
29 P3 Edmore North Dakota, N USA 48°22'N 98°26'W
13 N13 Edmundston New Brunswick, SE Canada 47°22'N 68°20'W
25 U12 Edna Texas, SW USA 29°00'N 96°41'W
39 X14 Edna Bay Kosciusko Island, Alaska, USA 55°54'N 133°40'W
77 U16 Edo ◈ state S Nigeria
106 F6 Edolo Lombardia, N Italy 46°13'N 10°20'E
64 L6 Edoras Bank undersea feature C Atlantic Ocean
96 G7 Edrachillis Bay bay NW Scotland, United Kingdom
136 B12 Edremit Balıkesir, NW Turkey 39°34'N 27°01'E
136 B12 Edremit Körfezi gulf NW Turkey
95 P14 Edsbro Stockholm, C Sweden 59°54'N 18°30'E
95 N18 Edsbruk Kalmar, S Sweden 58°01'N 16°30'E
94 M12 Edsbyn Gävleborg, C Sweden 61°22'N 15°45'E
11 O14 Edson Alberta, SW Canada 53°36'N 116°28'W
62 K13 Eduardo Castex La Pampa, C Argentina 35°55'S 64°18'W
58 F12 Eduardo Gomes ✕ (Manaus) Amazonas, NW Brazil 05°55'S 35°15'W
Edwardesabad see Bannu
67 U9 Edward, Lake var. Albert Edward Nyanza, Edward Nyanza, Lac Idi Amin, Lake Rutanzige. ◎ Uganda/Dem. Rep. Congo
Edward Nyanza see Edward, Lake
22 K5 Edwards Mississippi, S USA 32°19'N 90°36'W
25 O10 Edwards Plateau plain Texas, SW USA
30 J11 Edwards River ≋ Illinois, N USA
30 K15 Edwardsville Illinois, N USA 38°48'N 89°57'W
195 X4 Edward VIII Gulf bay Antarctica
195 O13 Edward VII Peninsula peninsula Antarctica
10 J11 Edziza, Mount ▲ British Columbia, W Canada 57°43'N 130°39'W
23 H16 Edzo prev. Rae-Edzo. Northwest Territories, NW Canada 62°44'N 115°55'W
39 N12 Eek Alaska, USA 60°13'N 162°01'W
99 D16 Eeklo var. Eekloo. Oost-Vlaanderen, NW Belgium 51°11'N 03°34'E
Eekloo see Eeklo
39 N12 Eek River ≋ Alaska, USA
98 N6 Eelde Drenthe, NE Netherlands 53°07'N 06°30'E
34 L5 Eel River ≋ California, W USA
31 P12 Eel River ≋ Indiana, N USA
Eems see Ems
98 O4 Eemshaven Groningen, NE Netherlands 53°28'N 06°50'E
98 O5 Eems Kanaal canal NE Netherlands
98 M11 Eerbeek Gelderland, E Netherlands 52°07'N 06°04'E
99 C17 Eernegem West-Vlaanderen, W Belgium 51°08'N 03°03'E
99 J15 Eersel Noord-Brabant, S Netherlands 51°22'N 05°19'E
Eesti Vabariik see Estonia
187 R14 Efate var. Efaté, Fr. Vaté; prev. Sandwich Island. island C Vanuatu
Efate see Efate
109 S4 Eferding Oberösterreich, N Austria 48°18'N 14°00'E
30 M15 Effingham Illinois, N USA 39°07'N 88°32'W
117 N15 Eforie-Nord Constanţa, SE Romania 44°04'N 28°37'E
117 N15 Eforie Sud Constanţa, E Romania 44°00'N 28°38'E
Efyrnwy, Afon see Vyrnwy
Eg see Hentiy
107 G23 Egadi, Isole island group S Italy
35 X6 Egan Range ▲▲ Nevada, W USA
14 K12 Eganville Ontario, SE Canada 45°33'N 77°03'W
Ege Denizi see Aegean Sea
39 O14 Egegik Alaska, USA 58°13'N 157°22'W
111 L21 Eger Ger. Erlau. Heves, NE Hungary 47°54'N 20°22'E
Eger see Cheb, Czech Republic
Eger see Ohre, Czech Republic/Germany
173 P8 Egeria Fracture Zone tectonic feature W Indian Ocean
95 C17 Egersund Rogaland, S Norway 58°27'N 06°01'E
108 J7 Egg Vorarlberg, NW Austria 47°27'N 09°55'E
101 H14 Egge-gebirge ▲▲ C Germany
109 Q4 Eggelsberg Oberösterreich, N Austria 48°04'N 13°00'E
109 W2 Eggenburg Niederösterreich, NE Austria 48°29'N 15°49'E
101 N22 Eggenfelden Bayern, SE Germany 48°24'N 12°45'E
18 J17 Egg Harbor City New Jersey, NE USA 39°31'N 74°39'W
65 G25 Egg Island island W Saint Helena
183 N14 Egg Lagoon Tasmania, SE Australia 39°42'S 143°57'E
99 I20 Éghezèe Namur, C Belgium 50°36'N 04°55'E
92 L2 Egilsstadhir Austurland, E Iceland 65°14'N 14°21'W
Egina see Aígina
Egindibulaq see Yegindybulak
Egio see Aígio
103 N12 Égletons Corrèze, C France 45°24'N 02°01'E
98 H9 Egmond aan Zee Noord-Holland, NW Netherlands 52°37'N 04°37'E
Egmont see Taranaki, Mount
184 J10 Egmont, Cape headland North Island, New Zealand 39°18'S 173°44'E
Egoli see Johannesburg
136 I15 Eğridir Gölü ◎ W Turkey
Egri Palanka see Kriva Palanka
95 G23 Egtved Vejle, C Denmark 55°34'N 09°18'E
123 U5 Egvekinot Chukotskiy Avtonomnyy Okrug, NE Russian Federation 66°13'N 178°55'W
75 V9 Egypt off. Arab Republic of Egypt, Ar. Jumhūrīyah Miṣr al 'Arabīyah, prev. United Arab Republic; anc. Aegyptus. ◆ republic NE Africa
30 L17 Egypt, Lake Of ⊠ Illinois, N USA
162 I14 Ehen Hudag var. Alx Youqi. Nei Mongol Zizhiqu, N China 39°12'N 101°40'E
164 F14 Ehime off. Ehime-ken. ◈ prefecture Shikoku, SW Japan
Ehime-ken see Ehime
101 I23 Ehingen Baden-Württemberg, S Germany 48°16'N 09°43'E
Ehinos see Echínos
21 R14 Ehrhardt South Carolina, SE USA 33°06'N 81°00'W
108 L7 Ehrwald Tirol, W Austria 47°24'N 10°52'E
191 W6 Eiao island Îles Marquises, NE French Polynesia
105 P2 Eibar País Vasco, N Spain 43°11'N 02°28'W
98 O11 Eibergen Gelderland, E Netherlands 52°06'N 06°39'E
109 V9 Eibiswald Steiermark, SE Austria 46°40'N 15°15'E
109 P8 Eichham ▲ SW Austria 47°04'N 12°24'E
101 J15 Eichsfeld hill range C Germany
101 K21 Eichstätt Bayern, SE Germany 48°53'N 11°11'E
100 H8 Eider ≋ N Germany
94 E13 Eidfjord Hordaland, S Norway 60°26'N 07°05'E
94 D13 Eidfjorden fjord S Norway
94 F9 Eidsvåg Møre og Romsdal, S Norway 62°46'N 08°00'E
95 I14 Eidsvoll Akershus, S Norway 60°19'N 11°14'E
92 N2 Eidsvollfjellet ▲ NW Svalbard 79°13'N 13°23'E
Eier-Berg see Suur Munamägi
101 D18 Eifel plateau W Germany
108 E9 Eiger ▲ C Switzerland 46°33'N 08°02'E
96 G10 Eigg island W Scotland, United Kingdom
155 D24 Eight Degree Channel channel India/Maldives
44 G1 Eight Mile Rock Grand Bahama Island, N Bahamas 26°28'N 78°43'W
194 J9 Eights Coast physical region Antarctica
180 K6 Eighty Mile Beach beach Western Australia
99 L18 Eijsden Limburg, SE Netherlands 50°47'N 05°41'E
95 G15 Eikeren ◎ S Norway
Eil see Eyl
Eilat see Elat
183 O12 Eildon Victoria, SE Australia 37°17'S 145°57'E
183 O12 Eildon, Lake ◎ Victoria, SE Australia
80 E8 Eilei Northern Kordofan, C Sudan 16°33'N 30°54'E
101 N15 Eilenburg Sachsen, E Germany 51°28'N 12°37'E
Eil Malk see Mecherchar
94 H13 Eina Oppland, S Norway 60°37'N 10°37'E
138 E12 Ein Avdat prev. En 'Avedat. well S Israel
101 I14 Einbeck Niedersachsen, C Germany 51°49'N 09°52'E
99 K15 Eindhoven Noord-Brabant, S Netherlands 51°26'N 05°30'E
138 F11 Ein Gedi prev. 'En Gedi. Southern, E Israel 31°23'N 35°21'E
108 G8 Einsiedeln Schwyz, NE Switzerland 47°07'N 08°45'E
Eipel see Ipel'
Éire see Ireland
Éireann, Muir see Irish Sea
Eirik Outer Ridge see Eirik Ridge
64 I6 Eirik Ridge var. Eirik Outer Ridge. undersea feature E Labrador Sea
92 I3 Eiríksjökull ▲ C Iceland 64°47'N 20°23'W
59 B14 Eirunepé Amazonas, N Brazil 06°38'S 69°53'W
99 L17 Eisden Limburg, NE Belgium 51°05'N 05°42'E
83 F18 Eiseb ≋ Botswana/Namibia
Eisen see Yŏngch'ŏn
101 J16 Eisenach Thüringen, C Germany 50°59'N 10°19'E
Eisenburg see Vasvár
109 U6 Eisenerz Steiermark, SE Austria 47°33'N 14°53'E
100 Q13 Eisenhüttenstadt Brandenburg, E Germany 52°09'N 14°36'E
109 U10 Eisenkappel Slvn. Železna Kapela. Kärnten, S Austria 46°27'N 14°33'E
Eisenmarkt see Hunedoara
109 Y5 Eisenstadt Burgenland, E Austria 47°50'N 16°32'E
Eishū see Yŏngju
119 H15 Eišiškes Vilnius, SE Lithuania 54°10'N 24°59'E

◆ Country ● Country Capital ◇ Dependent Territory ○ Dependent Territory Capital ◈ Administrative Regions ✕ International Airport ▲ Mountain ▲▲ Mountain Range 🌋 Volcano ≋ River ◎ Lake ⊠ Reservoir

Eisleben – Enånger

101 L15 **Eisleben** Sachsen-Anhalt, C Germany 51°32′N 11°33′E
190 I3 **Eita** Tarawa, W Kiribati 01°21′N 173°05′E
Eitape see Aitape
105 V11 **Eivissa** var. Iviza, Cast. Ibiza; anc. Ebusus. Ibiza, Spain, W Mediterranean Sea 38°54′N 01°26′E
Eivissa see Ibiza
105 R4 **Ejea de los Caballeros** Aragón, NE Spain 42°07′N 01°09′W
40 E8 **Ejido Insurgentes** Baja California Sur, NW Mexico 25°18′N 111°51′W
Ejin Qi see Dalain Hob
Ejmiadzin/Ejmiatsin see Vagharshapat
77 P16 **Ejura** C Ghana 07°23′N 01°22′W
41 R16 **Ejutla** var. Ejutla de Crespo. Oaxaca, SE Mexico 16°33′N 96°40′W
Ejutla de Crespo see Ejutla
33 Y10 **Ekalaka** Montana, NW USA 45°52′N 104°32′W
Ekapa see Cape Town
Ekaterinodar see Krasnodar
93 L20 **Ekenäs** Fin. Tammisaari. Etelä-Suomi, SW Finland 60°00′N 23°30′E
146 B13 **Ekerem** Rus. Okarem. Balkan Welaýaty, W Turkmenistan 38°06′N 53°52′E
184 M13 **Eketahuna** Manawatu-Wanganui, North Island, New Zealand 40°41′S 175°40′E
Ekhínos see Echínos
145 T8 **Ekibastuz** Pavlodar, NE Kazakhstan 51°42′N 75°22′E
123 R13 **Ekimchan** Amurskaya Oblast', SE Russian Federation 53°04′N 132°56′E
77 T15 **Ekiti** ◈ state S Nigeria
95 O15 **Ekoln** ◎ C Sweden
80 I7 **Ekowit** Red Sea, NE Sudan 18°46′N 37°07′E
95 L19 **Eksjö** Jönköping, S Sweden 57°40′N 15°00′E
93 I15 **Ekträsk** Västerbotten, N Sweden 64°28′N 19°49′E
39 O13 **Ekuk** Alaska, USA 58°48′N 158°25′W
123 U5 **Ekvyvatapskiy Khrebet** ▲▲ NE Russian Federation
12 F9 **Ekwan** ≈ Ontario, C Canada
39 O13 **Ekwok** Alaska, USA 59°21′N 157°28′W
166 M6 **Ela** Mandalay, C Myanmar (Burma) 19°37′N 96°15′E
El Aaiun see El Ayoun
81 N15 **Ēl Ābrēd** Sumalē, E Ethiopia 05°33′N 45°12′E
115 F22 **Elafónisos** island S Greece
115 F22 **Elafonísou, Porthmós** strait S Greece
El-Aïoun see El Ayoun
El 'Alamein see Al 'Alamayn
41 Q12 **El Alazán** Veracruz-Llave, C Mexico 21°06′N 97°43′W
57 J18 **El Alto** var. La Paz. ✈ (La Paz) La Paz, W Bolivia 16°31′S 68°07′W
Elam see Īlām
El Amparo see El Amparo de Apure
54 I8 **El Amparo de Apure** var. El Amparo. Apure, C Venezuela 07°07′N 70°47′W
171 R13 **Elara** Pulau Ambelau, E Indonesia 03°49′S 127°10′E
El Araïch/El Araïche see Larache
40 D6 **El Arco** Baja California Norte, NW Mexico 28°03′N 113°25′W
El 'Arîsh see Al 'Arīsh
115 L25 **Elása** island SE Greece
El Asnam see Chlef
Elassón see Elassóna
115 E15 **Elassóna** prev. Elassón. Thessalía, C Greece 39°53′N 22°10′E
105 N2 **El Astillero** Cantabria, N Spain 43°23′N 03°45′W
138 F14 **Elat** var. Eilat, Elath. Southern, S Israel 29°33′N 34°57′E
Elat, Gulf of see Aqaba, Gulf of
Elath see Elat, Israel
Elath see Al 'Aqabah, Jordan
115 C17 **Eláti** ▲ Lefkáda, Iónia Nisiá, Greece, C Mediterranean Sea 38°43′N 20°38′E
188 L16 **Elato Atoll** atoll Caroline Islands, C Micronesia
80 C7 **El'Atrun** Northern Darfur, NW Sudan 18°11′N 26°40′E
74 H6 **El Ayoun** var. El Aaiun, El-Aïoun, La Youne. NE Morocco 34°39′N 02°29′W
137 N14 **Elâzīğ** var. Elâzig, Elâziz. Elâzığ, E Turkey 38°41′N 39°14′E
137 O14 **Elâzīğ** var. Elâzig, Elâziz. ◈ province C Turkey
Elâzig/Elâziz see Elâzīğ
23 Q7 **Elba** Alabama, S USA 31°24′N 86°04′W
106 E13 **Elba, Isola d'** island Archipelago Toscano, C Italy
123 S13 **El'ban** Khabarovskiy Kray, E Russian Federation 50°03′N 136°34′E
54 F6 **El Banco** Magdalena, N Colombia 09°00′N 74°01′W
El Barco see O Barco
104 L8 **El Barco de Ávila** Castilla-León, N Spain 40°21′N 05°31′W
El Barco de Valdeorras see O Barco
138 H7 **El Barouk, Jabal** ▲▲ C Lebanon
113 L20 **Elbasan** var. Elbasani. Elbasan, C Albania 41°07′N 20°04′E
113 L20 **Elbasan** ◈ district C Albania
Elbasani see Elbasan
54 K6 **El Baúl** Cojedes, C Venezuela 08°59′N 68°16′W
86 D11 **Elbe** Cz. Labe. ≈ Czech Republic/Germany
100 L13 **Elbe-Havel-Kanal** canal E Germany
100 K9 **Elbe-Lübeck-Kanal** canal N Germany
El Beni see Beni
138 H7 **El Beqaa** var. Al Biqā', Bekaa Valley. valley E Lebanon
25 R6 **Elbert** Texas, SW USA 33°15′N 98°58′W
37 R5 **Elbert, Mount** ▲ Colorado, C USA 39°07′N 106°26′W
23 U3 **Elberton** Georgia, SE USA 34°06′N 82°52′W
100 K11 **Elbe-Seiten-Kanal** canal N Germany
102 M4 **Elbeuf** Seine-Maritime, N France 49°16′N 01°01′E
Elbing see Elbląg
136 M15 **Elbistan** Kahramanmaraş, S Turkey 38°14′N 37°11′E
110 K7 **Elbląg** var. Elblag, Ger. Elbing. Warmińsko-Mazurskie, NE Poland 54°10′N 19°25′E
43 N10 **El Bluff** Región Autónoma Atlántico Sur, SE Nicaragua 12°00′N 83°40′W
63 H17 **El Bolsón** Río Negro, W Argentina 41°59′S 71°35′W
105 P11 **El Bonillo** Castilla-La Mancha, C Spain 38°57′N 02°32′W
El Bordo see Patía
El Boulaida/El Boulaïda see Blida
11 T16 **Elbow** Saskatchewan, S Canada 51°07′N 106°30′W
29 S7 **Elbow Lake** Minnesota, N USA 45°59′N 95°58′W
127 N16 **El'brus** var. Gora El'brus. ▲ SW Russian Federation 42°29′E 43°21′N
El'brus, Gora see El'brus
126 M15 **El'brusskiy** Karachayevo-Cherkesskaya Respublika, SW Russian Federation 43°36′N 42°06′E
81 D14 **El Buhayrat** var. Lakes State. ◈ state S Sudan
El Bur see Ceel Buur
98 L10 **Elburg** Gelderland, E Netherlands 52°27′N 05°46′E
105 O6 **El Burgo de Osma** Castilla-León, C Spain 41°36′N 03°04′W
Elburz Mountains see Alborz, Reshteh-ye Kūhhā-ye
35 V17 **El Cajon** California, W USA 32°46′N 116°52′W
63 H22 **El Calafate** var. Calafate. Santa Cruz, S Argentina 50°20′S 72°13′W
55 Q8 **El Callao** Bolívar, E Venezuela 07°18′N 61°48′W
25 U12 **El Campo** Texas, SW USA 29°12′N 96°16′W
54 I7 **El Cantón** Barinas, W Venezuela 07°23′N 71°10′W
35 Q8 **El Capitan** ▲ California, W USA 37°46′N 119°39′W
54 H5 **El Carmelo** Zulia, NW Venezuela 10°20′N 71°48′W
62 J5 **El Carmen** Jujuy, NW Argentina 24°24′S 65°16′W
54 E5 **El Carmen de Bolívar** Bolívar, NW Colombia 09°43′N 75°07′W
55 O8 **El Casabe** Bolívar, SE Venezuela 06°26′N 63°35′W
42 M12 **El Castillo de La Concepción** Río San Juan, SE Nicaragua 11°01′N 84°24′W
El Cayo see San Ignacio
35 X17 **El Centro** California, W USA 32°47′N 115°33′W
55 N6 **El Chaparro** Anzoátegui, NE Venezuela 09°12′N 65°03′W
105 S12 **Elche** Cat. Elx; anc. Ilici, Lat. Illicis. País Valenciano, E Spain 38°16′N 00°41′W
105 Q12 **Elche de la Sierra** Castilla-La Mancha, C Spain 38°27′N 02°03′W
41 U15 **El Chichónal, Volcán** ⛰ SE Mexico 17°20′N 93°12′W
40 C2 **El Chinero** Baja California Norte, NW Mexico
181 R1 **Elcho Island** island Wessel Islands, Northern Territory, N Australia
63 H18 **El Corcovado** Chubut, SW Argentina 43°31′S 71°30′W
105 R12 **Elda** País Valenciano, E Spain 38°29′N 00°47′W
100 M10 **Elde** ≈ NE Germany
98 L12 **Elden** Gelderland, E Netherlands 51°57′N 05°53′E
81 J16 **El Der** spring/well S Ethiopia 03°55′N 39°48′E
El Dere see Ceel Dheere
40 E3 **El Desemboque** Sonora, NW Mexico 30°33′N 112°59′W
54 F5 **El Difícil** var. Ariguaní. Magdalena, N Colombia 09°55′N 74°12′W
123 R10 **El'dikan** Respublika Sakha (Yakutiya), NE Russian Federation 60°46′N 135°04′E
El Djazaïr see Alger
El Djelfa see Djelfa
29 X15 **Eldon** Iowa, C USA 40°55′N 92°13′W
27 U5 **Eldon** Missouri, C USA 38°21′N 92°34′W
54 E13 **El Doncello** Caquetá, S Colombia 01°43′N 75°17′W
29 W13 **Eldora** Iowa, C USA 42°21′N 93°06′W
60 G12 **Eldorado** Misiones, NE Argentina 26°24′S 54°38′W
40 I9 **El Dorado** Sinaloa, C Mexico 24°19′N 107°23′W
27 U14 **El Dorado** Arkansas, C USA 33°12′N 92°40′W
30 M17 **Eldorado** Illinois, N USA 37°48′N 88°26′W
27 O6 **El Dorado** Kansas, C USA 37°51′N 96°52′W
26 K12 **Eldorado** Oklahoma, C USA 34°28′N 99°39′W
25 O9 **Eldorado** Texas, SW USA 30°53′N 100°37′W
55 Q8 **El Dorado** Bolívar, E Venezuela 06°45′N 61°37′W
54 F10 **El Dorado** ✈ (Bogotá) Cundinamarca, C Colombia 01°15′N 71°52′W
El Dorado see California
27 O6 **El Dorado Lake** ▣ Kansas, C USA
27 S6 **El Dorado Springs** Missouri, C USA 37°53′N 94°01′W
81 H18 **Eldoret** Rift Valley, W Kenya 0°31′N 35°17′E
29 Z14 **Eldridge** Iowa, C USA 41°39′N 90°34′W
95 J21 **Eldsberga** Halland, S Sweden 56°36′N 13°00′E
25 R4 **Electra** Texas, SW USA 34°01′N 98°55′W
37 Q7 **Electra Lake** ▣ Colorado, C USA
38 B8 **'Ele'ele** var. Eleele. Kaua'i, Hawaii, USA, C Pacific Ocean 21°54′N 159°35′W
Eleele see 'Ele'ele
Elefantes see Olifants
115 H19 **Elefsína** prev. Elevsís. Attikí, C Greece 38°02′N 23°33′E
115 G19 **Eléftheres** anc. Eleutherae. site of ancient city Attikí/Stereá Ellás, C Greece
114 I13 **Eleftheroúpoli** prev. Elevtheroúpolis. Anatolikí Makedonía kai Thráki, NE Greece 40°55′N 24°15′E
74 F10 **El Eglab** ▲▲ SW Algeria
118 F10 **Eleja** Jelgava, C Latvia 56°24′N 23°41′E
Elek see Ilek
119 G14 **Elektrėnai** Vilnius, SE Lithuania 54°47′N 24°35′E
126 L3 **Elektrostal'** Moskovskaya Oblast', W Russian Federation 55°47′N 38°24′E
81 H15 **Elemi Triangle** disputed region Kenya/Sudan
114 K9 **Elena** Veliko Tŭrnovo, N Bulgaria 42°55′N 25°53′E
54 G16 **El Encanto** Amazonas, S Colombia 01°45′S 73°12′W
37 R14 **Elephant Butte Reservoir** ▣ New Mexico, SW USA
Éléphant, Chaîne de l' see Dâmrei, Chuŏr Phnum
194 G2 **Elephant Island** island South Shetland Islands, Antarctica
Elephant River see Olifants
El Escorial see San Lorenzo de El Escorial
Élesd see Aleşd
114 F11 **Eleshnitsa** ≈ W Bulgaria
137 S13 **Eleşkirt** Ağrı, E Turkey 39°22′N 42°48′E
42 F5 **El Estor** Izabal, E Guatemala 15°37′N 89°22′W
Eleutherae see Eléftheres
44 I2 **Eleuthera Island** island N Bahamas
37 S5 **Elevenmile Canyon Reservoir** ▣ Colorado, C USA
27 W8 **Eleven Point River** ≈ Arkansas/Missouri, C USA
Elevsís see Elefsína
Elevtheroúpolis see Eleftheroúpoli
80 B10 **El Fasher** var. Al Fāshir. Northern Darfur, W Sudan 13°37′N 25°22′E
El Fashn see Al Fashn
El Ferrol/El Ferrol del Caudillo see Ferrol
39 W13 **Elfin Cove** Chichagof Island, Alaska, USA 58°09′N 136°16′W
105 W4 **El Fluvià** ≈ NE Spain
40 H7 **El Fuerte** Sinaloa, W Mexico 26°28′N 108°35′W
80 D11 **El Fula** Western Kordofan, C Sudan 11°44′N 28°20′E
El Gedaref see Gedaref
80 A10 **El Geneina** var. Ajjinena, Al-Genain, Al Junaynah. Western Darfur, W Sudan 13°27′N 22°30′E
96 J8 **Elgin** NE Scotland, United Kingdom 57°39′N 03°20′W
30 M10 **Elgin** Illinois, N USA 42°02′N 88°16′W
29 P14 **Elgin** Nebraska, C USA 41°58′N 98°04′W
35 Y9 **Elgin** Nevada, W USA 37°19′N 114°30′W
28 L6 **Elgin** North Dakota, N USA 46°24′N 101°51′W
26 M12 **Elgin** Oklahoma, C USA 34°46′N 98°17′W
25 T10 **Elgin** Texas, SW USA 30°21′N 97°22′W
123 R9 **El'ginskiy** Respublika Sakha (Yakutiya), NE Russian Federation 64°27′N 141°57′E
El Gîza see Gîza
74 J8 **El Goléa** var. Al Golea. C Algeria 30°35′N 02°59′E
40 D2 **El Golfo de Santa Clara** Sonora, NW Mexico 31°48′N 114°40′W
81 G18 **Elgon, Mount** ▲ E Uganda 01°07′N 34°29′E
94 I10 **Elgpiggen** ▲ S Norway 62°13′N 11°18′E
105 T4 **El Grado** Aragón, NE Spain 42°09′N 00°13′E
40 L6 **El Guaje, Laguna** ▣ NE Mexico
54 H6 **El Guayabo** Zulia, W Venezuela 08°37′N 72°20′W
77 O6 **El Gueṭṭâra** oasis N Mali
76 J6 **El Ḥammâmi** desert N Mauritania
76 M5 **El Ḥank** cliff N Mauritania
El Haseke see Al Ḥasakah
80 H10 **El Hawata** Gedaref, E Sudan 13°25′N 34°42′E
El Higo see Higos
171 T16 **Eliase** Pulau Selaru, E Indonesia 08°16′S 130°49′E
Elías Piña see Comendador
25 R6 **Eliasville** Texas, SW USA 32°55′N 98°46′W
Elichpur see Achalpur
37 V13 **Elida** New Mexico, SW USA 33°57′N 103°39′W
115 F18 **Elikónas** ▲▲ C Greece
67 T10 **Elila** ≈ W Dem. Rep. Congo
39 N9 **Elim** Alaska, USA 64°37′N 162°15′W
Elimberrum see Auch
Eliocroca see Lorca
61 B16 **Elisa** Santa Fe, C Argentina 30°42′S 61°04′W
Elisabethstedt see Dumbrăveni
Élisabethville see Lubumbashi
127 O13 **Elista** Respublika Kalmykiya, SW Russian Federation 46°18′N 44°09′E
182 I9 **Elizabeth** South Australia 34°44′S 138°39′E
21 Q3 **Elizabeth** West Virginia, NE USA 39°04′N 81°24′W
19 Q9 **Elizabeth, Cape** headland Maine, NE USA 43°34′N 70°12′W
21 Y8 **Elizabeth City** North Carolina, SE USA 36°18′N 76°16′W
21 P8 **Elizabethton** Tennessee, S USA 36°22′N 82°15′W
30 M17 **Elizabethtown** Illinois, N USA 37°24′N 88°21′W
20 K6 **Elizabethtown** Kentucky, S USA 37°41′N 85°51′W
18 L7 **Elizabethtown** New York, NE USA 44°13′N 73°38′W
21 U11 **Elizabethtown** North Carolina, SE USA 34°36′N 78°36′W
18 G15 **Elizabethtown** Pennsylvania, NE USA 40°08′N 76°36′W
74 E6 **El-Jadida** prev. Mazagan. W Morocco 33°15′N 08°27′W
El Jafr see Jafr, Qā' al
80 F11 **El Jebelein** White Nile, E Sudan 12°38′N 32°51′E
110 N8 **Ełk** Ger. Lyck. Warmińsko-mazurskie, NE Poland 53°51′N 22°20′E
110 O8 **Ełk** ≈ NE Poland
29 Y12 **Elkader** Iowa, C USA 42°51′N 91°24′W
80 G9 **El Kamlin** Gezira, C Sudan 15°03′N 33°11′E
33 N11 **Elk City** Idaho, NW USA 45°50′N 115°28′W
26 K10 **Elk City** Oklahoma, C USA 35°24′N 99°24′W
27 P7 **Elk City Lake** ▣ Kansas, C USA
34 M5 **Elk Creek** California, W USA 39°34′N 122°34′W
28 J10 **Elk Creek** ≈ South Dakota, N USA
74 M5 **El Kef** var. Al Kāf, Le Kef. NW Tunisia 36°13′N 08°44′E
74 F7 **El Kelâa Srarhna** var. Kal al Sraghna. C Morocco 32°05′N 07°20′W
El Kerak see Al Karak
11 P17 **Elkford** British Columbia, SW Canada 49°58′N 114°57′W
El Khalil see Hebron
80 E7 **El Khandaq** Northern, N Sudan 18°34′N 30°34′E
El Khârga see Al Khārijah
31 P11 **Elkhart** Indiana, N USA 41°40′N 85°58′W
26 H7 **Elkhart** Kansas, C USA 37°00′N 101°51′W
25 V8 **Elkhart** Texas, SW USA 31°37′N 95°34′W
30 M7 **Elkhart Lake** ◎ Wisconsin, N USA
El Khartûm see Khartoum
37 Q3 **Elkhead Mountains** ▲▲ Colorado, C USA
18 I12 **Elk Hill** ▲ Pennsylvania, NE USA 41°42′N 75°33′W
138 G8 **El Khiyam** var. Al Khiyām, Khiam. S Lebanon 33°12′N 35°42′E
29 S15 **Elkhorn** Nebraska, C USA 41°17′N 96°13′W
30 M9 **Elkhorn** Wisconsin, N USA 42°40′N 88°34′W
29 R14 **Elkhorn River** ≈ Nebraska, C USA
127 O16 **El'khotovo** Respublika Severnaya Osetiya, SW Russian Federation 43°18′N 44°17′E
114 L10 **Elkhovo** prev. Kizilagach. Yambol, E Bulgaria 42°10′N 26°34′E
21 R8 **Elkin** North Carolina, SE USA 36°14′N 80°51′W
21 S4 **Elkins** West Virginia, NE USA 38°56′N 79°53′W
195 X3 **Elkins, Mount** ▲ Antarctica 66°25′S 53°54′E
14 G8 **Elk Lake** Ontario, S Canada 47°44′N 80°19′W
31 P6 **Elk Lake** ◎ Michigan, N USA
18 F12 **Elkland** Pennsylvania, NE USA 41°59′N 77°16′W
35 W3 **Elko** Nevada, W USA 40°48′N 115°46′W
11 R14 **Elk Point** Alberta, SW Canada 53°52′N 110°49′W
29 R12 **Elk Point** South Dakota, N USA 42°42′N 96°37′W
29 V8 **Elk River** Minnesota, N USA 45°18′N 93°34′W
20 J10 **Elk River** ≈ Alabama/Tennessee, S USA
21 R4 **Elk River** ≈ West Virginia, NE USA
20 I7 **Elkton** Kentucky, S USA 36°49′N 87°11′W
21 Y2 **Elkton** Maryland, NE USA 39°37′N 75°50′W
29 R10 **Elkton** South Dakota, N USA 44°14′N 96°28′W
20 I10 **Elkton** Tennessee, S USA 35°01′N 86°51′W
21 U5 **Elkton** Virginia, NE USA 38°22′N 78°35′W
El Kuneitra see Al Qunayṭirah
81 L15 **El Kure** Somali, E Ethiopia 05°37′N 42°05′E
80 D12 **El Lagowa** Western Kordofan, C Sudan 11°23′N 29°10′E
39 S12 **Ellamar** Alaska, USA 60°54′N 146°37′W
Ellás see Greece
23 S6 **Ellaville** Georgia, SE USA 32°14′N 84°18′W
197 P9 **Ellef Ringnes Island** island Nunavut, N Canada
29 V10 **Ellendale** Minnesota, N USA 43°53′N 93°19′W
29 P7 **Ellendale** North Dakota, N USA 45°57′N 98°33′W
36 M6 **Ellen, Mount** ▲ Utah, W USA 38°06′N 110°48′W
32 I9 **Ellensburg** Washington, NW USA 47°00′N 124°34′W
18 K12 **Ellenville** New York, NE USA 41°43′N 74°24′W
Ellep see Lib
21 T10 **Ellerbe** North Carolina, SE USA 35°04′N 79°45′W
197 P10 **Ellesmere Island** island Queen Elizabeth Islands, Nunavut, N Canada
185 H19 **Ellesmere, Lake** ◎ South Island, New Zealand
97 K18 **Ellesmere Port** C England, United Kingdom 53°17′N 02°54′W
31 O14 **Ellettsville** Indiana, N USA 39°13′N 86°37′W
99 E19 **Ellezelles** Hainaut, SW Belgium 50°44′N 03°40′E
8 L7 **Ellice** ≈ Nunavut, NE Canada
Ellice Islands see Tuvalu
Ellichpur see Achalpur
21 W3 **Ellicott City** Maryland, NE USA 39°16′N 76°48′W
23 S2 **Ellijay** Georgia, SE USA 34°42′N 84°28′W
27 W7 **Ellington** Missouri, C USA 37°14′N 90°58′W
26 L5 **Ellinwood** Kansas, C USA 38°21′N 98°34′W
83 J24 **Elliot** Eastern Cape, SE South Africa 31°20′S 27°51′E
14 D10 **Elliot Lake** Ontario, S Canada 46°24′N 82°38′W
181 X6 **Elliot, Mount** ▲ Queensland, E Australia 19°36′S 147°02′E
21 T5 **Elliott Knob** ▲ Virginia, NE USA 38°10′N 79°18′W
26 K4 **Ellis** Kansas, C USA 38°56′N 99°33′W
182 F8 **Elliston** South Australia 33°40′S 134°56′E
22 M7 **Ellisville** Mississippi, S USA 31°36′N 89°12′W
105 V5 **El Llobregat** ≈ NE Spain
96 L9 **Ellon** NE Scotland, United Kingdom 57°22′N 02°06′W
Ellore see Elūru
21 S13 **Elloree** South Carolina, SE USA 33°34′N 80°37′W
26 M4 **Ellsworth** Kansas, C USA 38°45′N 98°15′W
19 S7 **Ellsworth** Maine, NE USA 44°32′N 68°25′W
30 I6 **Ellsworth** Wisconsin, N USA 44°44′N 92°29′W
26 M11 **Ellsworth, Lake** ▣ Oklahoma, C USA
194 K9 **Ellsworth Land** physical region Antarctica
194 L9 **Ellsworth Mountains** ▲▲ Antarctica
101 J21 **Ellwangen** Baden-Württemberg, S Germany 48°58′N 10°07′E
18 B14 **Ellwood City** Pennsylvania, NE USA 40°49′N 80°15′W
108 H8 **Elm** Glarus, NE Switzerland 46°55′N 09°09′E
32 G9 **Elma** Washington, NW USA 47°00′N 123°24′W
121 V13 **El Maḥalla el Kubra** var. Al Maḥallah al Kubrá, Mahalla el Kubra. N Egypt 30°59′N 31°10′E
74 E9 **El Mahbas** var. Mahbés. SW Western Sahara 27°26′N 09°09′W
63 H17 **El Maitén** Chubut, W Argentina 42°03′S 71°10′W
136 E16 **Elmalı** Antalya, SW Turkey 36°43′N 29°19′E
80 G10 **El Manaqil** Gezira, C Sudan 14°12′N 33°01′E
54 M12 **El Mango** Amazonas, S Venezuela 01°55′N 66°35′W
El Manṣûra see Al Manṣūrah
55 P8 **El Manteco** Bolívar, E Venezuela 07°27′N 62°32′W
29 O16 **Elm Creek** Nebraska, C USA 40°43′N 99°22′W
El Mediyya see Médéa
77 V9 **Elméki** Agadez, C Niger 17°52′N 08°07′E
108 K7 **Elmen** Tirol, W Austria 47°22′N 10°34′E
18 I16 **Elmer** New Jersey, NE USA 39°34′N 75°09′W
138 G6 **El Mina** var. Al Mīnā'. N Lebanon 34°28′N 35°49′E
El Minya see Al Minyā
14 F15 **Elmira** Ontario, S Canada 43°35′N 80°34′W
18 G11 **Elmira** New York, NE USA 42°06′N 76°50′W
36 K13 **El Mirage** Arizona, SW USA 33°36′N 112°19′W
29 O7 **Elm Lake** ▣ South Dakota, N USA
El Moján see San Rafael
105 N7 **El Molar** Madrid, C Spain 40°43′N 03°35′W
76 L7 **El Mrâyer** well C Mauritania
76 L5 **El Mreiti** well N Mauritania
76 L8 **El Mreyyé** desert E Mauritania
29 P8 **Elm River** ≈ North Dakota/South Dakota, N USA
100 I9 **Elmshorn** Schleswig-Holstein, N Germany 53°45′N 09°39′E
80 D12 **El Muglad** Western Kordofan, C Sudan 11°02′N 27°44′E
El Muwaqqar see Al Muwaqqar
14 G14 **Elmvale** Ontario, S Canada 44°34′N 79°53′W
30 K12 **Elmwood** Illinois, N USA 40°46′N 89°58′W
26 J8 **Elmwood** Oklahoma, C USA 36°37′N 100°31′W
103 P17 **Elne** anc. Illiberis. Pyrénées-Orientales, S France 42°36′N 02°58′E
54 F11 **El Nevado, Cerro** elevation C Colombia
171 N5 **El Nido** Palawan, W Philippines 11°10′N 119°25′E
62 I12 **El Nihuil** Mendoza, W Argentina 34°58′S 68°40′W
75 W7 **El Nouzha** ✈ (Alexandria) N Egypt 31°06′N 29°58′E
80 E10 **El Obeid** var. Al Obayyid, Al Ubayyiḍ. Northern Kordofan, C Sudan 13°11′N 30°10′E
41 O13 **El Oro** México, S Mexico 19°51′N 100°07′W
56 B8 **El Oro** ◈ province SW Ecuador
61 B19 **Elortondo** Santa Fe, C Argentina 33°42′S 61°37′W
54 J8 **Elorza** Apure, C Venezuela 07°02′N 69°30′W
El Ouâdi see El Oued
74 L7 **El Oued** var. Al Oued, El Ouâdi, El Wad. NE Algeria 33°20′N 06°53′E
36 L15 **Eloy** Arizona, SW USA 32°47′N 111°33′W
55 Q7 **El Palmar** Bolívar, E Venezuela 08°01′N 61°53′W
40 K8 **El Palmito** Durango, W Mexico 25°40′N 104°59′W
55 P7 **El Pao** Bolívar, E Venezuela 08°03′N 62°40′W
54 K5 **El Pao** Cojedes, N Venezuela 09°40′N 68°08′W
42 J7 **El Paraíso** El Paraíso, S Honduras 13°51′N 86°31′W
42 I7 **El Paraíso** ◈ department SE Honduras
30 L12 **El Paso** Illinois, N USA 40°44′N 89°01′W
24 G8 **El Paso** Texas, SW USA 31°45′N 106°30′W
24 G8 **El Paso** ✈ Texas, SW USA 31°48′N 106°24′W
105 U7 **El Perello** Cataluña, NE Spain 40°53′N 00°43′E
55 P5 **El Pilar** Sucre, NE Venezuela 10°31′N 63°12′W
42 F7 **El Pital, Cerro** ▲ El Salvador/Honduras 14°19′N 89°06′W
35 Q9 **El Portal** California, W USA 37°40′N 119°46′W
40 J3 **El Porvenir** Chihuahua, N Mexico 31°15′N 105°48′W
43 U14 **El Porvenir** Kuna Yala, N Panama 09°33′N 78°56′W
105 W6 **El Prat de Llobregat** Cataluña, NE Spain 41°20′N 02°05′E
42 H5 **El Progreso** Yoro, NW Honduras 15°25′N 87°49′W
42 A2 **El Progreso** off. Departamento de El Progreso. ◈ department C Guatemala
El Progreso see Guastatoya
El Progreso, Departamento de see El Progreso
104 L9 **El Puente del Arzobispo** Castilla-La Mancha, C Spain 39°48′N 05°10′W
104 J15 **El Puerto de Santa María** Andalucía, S Spain 36°36′N 06°13′W
62 I8 **El Puesto** Catamarca, NW Argentina 27°57′S 67°37′W
El Qâhira see Cairo
El Qaṣr see Al Qaṣr
El Qatrani see Al Qaṭrānah
40 I10 **El Quelite** Sinaloa, C Mexico 23°37′N 106°26′W
62 G9 **Elqui, Río** ≈ N Chile
El Q'unayṭirah see Al Qunayṭirah
El Quneitra see Al Qunayṭirah
El Quseir see Al Quṣayr
El Quweira see Al Quwayrah
141 O15 **El-Rahaba** ✈ (Ṣan'ā') W Yemen 15°28′N 44°12′E
42 M10 **El Rama** Región Autónoma Atlántico Sur, SE Nicaragua 12°09′N 84°15′W
43 W16 **El Real** var. El Real de Santa María. Darién, SE Panama 08°06′N 77°42′W
El Real de Santa María see El Real
26 M10 **El Reno** Oklahoma, C USA 35°32′N 95°57′W
40 K9 **El Rodeo** Durango, C Mexico 25°12′N 104°35′W
104 J13 **El Ronquillo** Andalucía, S Spain 37°43′N 06°09′W
11 S16 **Elrose** Saskatchewan, S Canada 51°07′N 107°59′W
30 K8 **Elroy** Wisconsin, N USA 43°43′N 90°16′W
25 S17 **Elsa** Texas, SW USA 26°17′N 97°59′W
El Ṣaff see Aş Şaff
40 J10 **El Salto** Durango, C Mexico 23°47′N 105°22′W
42 D8 **El Salvador** off. Republica de El Salvador. ◆ republic Central America
El Salvador, Republica de see El Salvador
54 K7 **El Samán de Apure** Apure, C Venezuela 07°54′N 68°44′W
14 D7 **Elsas** Ontario, S Canada 48°31′N 82°53′W
40 F3 **El Sásabe** var. Aduana del Sásabe. Sonora, NW Mexico 31°27′N 111°31′W
Elsass see Alsace
40 J5 **El Sáuz** Chihuahua, N Mexico 29°03′N 106°15′W
27 W4 **Elsberry** Missouri, C USA 39°10′N 90°46′W
45 P9 **El Seibo** var. Santa Cruz de El Seibo, Santa Cruz del Seibo. E Dominican Republic 18°45′N 69°04′W
42 B7 **El Semillero Barra Nahualate** Escuintla, SW Guatemala 14°01′N 91°28′W
Elsene see Ixelles
Elsen Nur see Dorgê Co
36 L6 **Elsinore** Utah, W USA 38°40′N 112°09′W
Elsinore see Helsingør
99 L18 **Elsloo** Limburg, SE Netherlands 50°57′N 05°46′E
60 G13 **El Soberbio** Misiones, NE Argentina 27°15′S 54°05′W
55 N6 **El Socorro** Guárico, C Venezuela 09°00′N 65°42′W
54 L6 **El Sombrero** Guárico, N Venezuela 09°25′N 67°06′W
98 L10 **Elspeet** Gelderland, E Netherlands 52°19′N 05°47′E
98 L12 **Elst** Gelderland, E Netherlands 51°55′N 05°51′E
101 O15 **Elsterwerda** Brandenburg, E Germany 51°27′N 13°32′E
40 J4 **El Sueco** Chihuahua, N Mexico 29°53′N 106°24′W
El Suweida see As Suwaydā'
El Suweis see Suez
54 D12 **El Tambo** Cauca, SW Colombia 02°25′N 76°50′W
175 T13 **Eltanin Fracture Zone** tectonic feature SE Pacific Ocean
105 X5 **El Ter** ≈ NE Spain
184 K11 **Eltham** Taranaki, North Island, New Zealand 39°26′S 174°25′E
55 O6 **El Tigre** Anzoátegui, NE Venezuela 08°55′N 64°15′W
El Tigrito see San José de Guanipa
54 J5 **El Tocuyo** Lara, N Venezuela 09°48′N 69°51′W
127 Q10 **El'ton** Volgogradskaya Oblast', SW Russian Federation 49°07′N 46°50′E
32 K10 **Eltopia** Washington, NW USA 46°33′N 118°59′W
El Toro see Mare de Déu del Toro
61 A18 **El Trébol** Santa Fe, C Argentina 32°12′S 61°40′W
40 J13 **El Tuito** Jalisco, SW Mexico 20°19′N 105°22′W
El Ṭûr see Aṭ Ṭūr
155 K16 **Elūru** prev. Ellore. Andhra Pradesh, E India 16°45′N 81°10′E
118 H13 **Elva** Ger. Elwa. Tartumaa, SE Estonia 58°13′N 26°25′E
37 R9 **El Vado Reservoir** ▣ New Mexico, SW USA
43 S15 **El Valle** Coclé, C Panama 08°39′N 80°08′W
104 I11 **Elvas** Portalegre, C Portugal 38°53′N 07°10′W
54 K7 **El Venado** Apure, C Venezuela 07°25′N 68°46′W
105 V6 **El Vendrell** Cataluña, NE Spain 41°13′N 01°32′E
94 I13 **Elverum** Hedmark, S Norway 60°54′N 11°33′E
42 I9 **El Viejo** Chinandega, NW Nicaragua 12°39′N 87°11′W
54 G7 **El Viejo, Cerro** ▲ C Colombia 07°31′N 72°56′W
54 H6 **El Vigía** Mérida, NW Venezuela 08°38′N 71°39′W
105 Q4 **El Villar de Arnedo** La Rioja, N Spain 42°19′N 02°05′W
59 A14 **Elvira** Amazonas, W Brazil 07°12′S 69°56′W
Elwa see Elva
El Wad see El Oued
81 K17 **El Wak** North Eastern, NE Kenya 02°46′N 40°57′E
33 R7 **Elwell, Lake** ▣ Montana, NW USA
31 P13 **Elwood** Indiana, N USA 40°16′N 85°50′W
27 R3 **Elwood** Kansas, C USA 39°43′N 94°52′W
29 N16 **Elwood** Nebraska, C USA 40°35′N 99°51′W
Elx see Elche
97 O20 **Ely** E England, United Kingdom 52°24′N 00°15′E
29 X4 **Ely** Minnesota, N USA 47°54′N 91°52′W
35 X6 **Ely** Nevada, W USA 39°15′N 114°53′W
El Yopal see Yopal
31 T11 **Elyria** Ohio, N USA 41°22′N 82°06′W
45 S9 **El Yunque** ▲ E Puerto Rico 18°15′N 65°46′W
101 F23 **Elz** ≈ SW Germany
187 R14 **Emae** island Shepherd Islands, C Vanuatu
118 I5 **Emajõgi** Ger. Embach. ≈ SE Estonia
Emāmrūd see Shāhrūd
149 Q2 **Emām Ṣāḥeb** var. Emam Saheb, Hazarat Imam. Kunduz, NE Afghanistan 37°11′N 68°55′E
Emam Saheb see Emām Ṣāḥeb
Emāmshahr see Shāhrūd
95 M20 **Emån** ≈ S Sweden
144 J11 **Emba** Kaz. Embi. Aktyubinsk, W Kazakhstan 48°50′N 58°10′E
144 H12 **Emba** Kaz. Zhem. ≈ W Kazakhstan
Embach see Emajõgi
62 K5 **Embarcación** Salta, N Argentina 23°15′S 64°05′W
30 M15 **Embarras River** ≈ Illinois, N USA
Embi see Emba
81 I19 **Embu** Eastern, C Kenya 0°32′N 37°28′E
100 E10 **Emden** Niedersachsen, NW Germany 53°22′N 07°12′E
160 H9 **Emei Shan** ▲ Sichuan, C China 29°32′N 103°21′E
29 Q4 **Emerado** North Dakota, N USA 47°55′N 97°21′W
181 X8 **Emerald** Queensland, E Australia 23°33′S 148°11′E
Emerald Isle see Montserrat
57 J15 **Emero, Río** ≈ W Bolivia
11 Y17 **Emerson** Manitoba, S Canada 49°01′N 97°07′W
29 T15 **Emerson** Iowa, C USA 41°00′N 95°22′W
29 R13 **Emerson** Nebraska, C USA 42°16′N 96°43′W
36 M5 **Emery** Utah, W USA 38°54′N 111°16′W
Emesa see Ḥimş
136 E13 **Emet** Kütahya, W Turkey 39°22′N 29°15′E
186 B8 **Emeti** Western, SW Papua New Guinea 07°54′S 143°18′E
35 V3 **Emigrant Pass** pass Nevada, W USA
78 I6 **Emi Koussi** ▲ N Chad 19°52′N 18°34′E
Emilia see Emilia-Romagna
41 V15 **Emiliano Zapata** Chiapas, SE Mexico 17°42′N 91°46′W
106 E9 **Emilia-Romagna** prev. Emilia; anc. Æmilia. ◈ region N Italy
158 J3 **Emin** var. Dorbiljin. Xinjiang Uygur Zizhiqu, NW China 46°30′N 83°42′E
149 W8 **Eminābād** Punjab, E Pakistan 32°02′N 73°51′E
21 L5 **Eminence** Kentucky, S USA 38°22′N 85°10′W
27 W7 **Eminence** Missouri, C USA 37°09′N 91°22′W
114 N9 **Emine, Nos** headland E Bulgaria 42°43′N 27°53′E
158 I3 **Emin He** ≈ NW China
186 G4 **Emirau Island** island N Papua New Guinea
136 F13 **Emirdağ** Afyon, W Turkey 39°01′N 31°09′E
95 M21 **Emmaboda** Kalmar, S Sweden 56°36′N 15°30′E
118 E5 **Emmaste** Hiiumaa, W Estonia 58°43′N 22°36′E
18 I15 **Emmaus** Pennsylvania, NE USA 40°32′N 75°28′W
183 U4 **Emmaville** New South Wales, SE Australia 29°26′S 151°38′E
108 E9 **Emme** ≈ W Switzerland
98 L8 **Emmeloord** Flevoland, N Netherlands 52°43′N 05°46′E
98 O8 **Emmen** Drenthe, NE Netherlands 52°48′N 06°57′E
108 F8 **Emmen** Luzern, C Switzerland 47°03′N 08°14′E
101 F23 **Emmendingen** Baden-Württemberg, SW Germany 48°07′N 07°51′E
98 P8 **Emmer-Compascuum** Drenthe, NE Netherlands 52°47′N 07°03′E
101 D14 **Emmerich** Nordrhein-Westfalen, W Germany 51°49′N 06°16′E
29 U12 **Emmetsburg** Iowa, C USA 43°06′N 94°40′W
32 M14 **Emmett** Idaho, NW USA 43°52′N 116°30′W
38 M10 **Emmonak** Alaska, USA 62°46′N 164°31′W
Emona see Ljubljana
Emonti see East London
24 L12 **Emory Peak** ▲ Texas, SW USA 29°15′N 103°18′W
40 F6 **Empalme** Sonora, NW Mexico 27°57′N 110°49′W
83 L23 **Empangeni** KwaZulu/Natal, E South Africa 28°45′S 31°54′E
61 C14 **Empedrado** Corrientes, NE Argentina 27°59′S 58°47′W
192 K3 **Emperor Seamounts** undersea feature NW Pacific Ocean 42°00′N 170°00′E
192 L3 **Emperor Trough** undersea feature N Pacific Ocean
35 R4 **Empire** Nevada, W USA 40°26′N 119°21′W
Empire State of the South see Georgia
Emplawas see Amplawas
106 F11 **Empoli** Toscana, C Italy 43°43′N 10°57′E
27 P5 **Emporia** Kansas, C USA 38°24′N 96°10′W
21 W7 **Emporia** Virginia, NE USA 36°42′N 77°33′W
18 E13 **Emporium** Pennsylvania, NE USA 41°31′N 78°14′W
Empty Quarter see Ar Rub 'al Khālī
100 E10 **Ems** Dut. Eems. ≈ NW Germany
100 F13 **Emsdetten** Nordrhein-Westfalen, NW Germany 52°11′N 07°32′E
Ems-Hunte Canal see Küstenkanal
100 F10 **Ems-Jade-Kanal** canal NW Germany
100 F11 **Emsland** cultural region NW Germany
182 D3 **Emu Junction** South Australia 28°39′S 132°13′E
163 T3 **Emur He** ≈ NE China
55 R8 **Enachu Landing** NW Guyana 06°09′N 60°02′W
93 F16 **Enafors** Jämtland, C Sweden 63°17′N 12°24′E
94 N11 **Enånger** Gävleborg, C Sweden 61°30′N 17°10′E

◆ Country
● Country Capital
◇ Dependent Territory
○ Dependent Territory Capital
◈ Administrative Regions
✈ International Airport
▲ Mountain
▲▲ Mountain Range
⛰ Volcano
≈ River
◎ Lake
▣ Reservoir

ENARD BAY – ETNA, MOUNT

96 G7 **Enard Bay** *bay* NW Scotland, United Kingdom
Enareträsk *see* Inarijärvi
171 X14 **Enarotali** Papua, E Indonesia 03°55′S 136°21′E
En 'Avedat *see* Ein Avdat
165 T2 **Enbetsu** Hokkaidō, NE Japan 44°44′N 141°47′E
61 H16 **Encantadas, Serra das** ▲▲ S Brazil
40 E7 **Encantado, Cerro** ▲ NW Mexico 26°46′N 112°33′W
62 P7 **Encarnación** Itapúa, S Paraguay 27°20′S 55°50′W
40 M12 **Encarnación de Díaz** Jalisco, SW Mexico 21°33′N 102°13′W
77 O17 **Enchi** SW Ghana 05°53′N 02°48′W
25 Q14 **Encinal** Texas, SW USA 28°02′N 99°21′W
35 U17 **Encinitas** California, W USA 33°02′N 117°17′W
25 S16 **Encino** Texas, SW USA 26°58′N 98°06′W
54 H6 **Encontrados** Zulia, NW Venezuela 09°04′N 72°16′W
182 I10 **Encounter Bay** *inlet* South Australia
61 F15 **Encruzilhada** Rio Grande do Sul, S Brazil 28°58′S 55°31′W
61 H16 **Encruzilhada do Sul** Rio Grande do Sul, S Brazil 30°30′S 52°32′W
111 M20 **Encs** Borsod-Abaúj-Zemplén, NE Hungary 48°21′N 21°09′E
193 P3 **Endeavour Seamount** *undersea feature* N Pacific Ocean 48°15′N 129°04′W
181 V1 **Endeavour Strait** *strait* Queensland, NE Australia
171 O16 **Endeh** Flores, S Indonesia 08°48′S 121°37′E
95 G23 **Endelave** *island* C Denmark
191 T4 **Enderbury Island** *atoll* Phoenix Islands, C Kiribati
11 N16 **Enderby** British Columbia, SW Canada 50°34′N 119°09′W
195 W4 **Enderby Land** *physical region* Antarctica
173 N14 **Enderby Plain** *undersea feature* S Indian Ocean
29 Q6 **Enderlin** North Dakota, N USA 46°37′N 97°36′W
Endersdorf *see* Jędrzejów
28 K16 **Enders Reservoir** ⊠ Nebraska, C USA
18 H11 **Endicott** New York, NE USA 42°06′N 76°03′W
39 P7 **Endicott Mountains** ▲▲ Alaska, USA
118 I5 **Endla Raba** *wetland* C Estonia
127 X7 **Energetik** Orenburgskaya Oblast', W Russian Federation 51°37′N 58°44′E
117 T9 **Enerhodar** Zaporiz'ka Oblast', SE Ukraine 47°30′N 34°40′E
57 F14 **Ene, Río** ≈ C Peru
189 N4 **Enewetak Atoll** *var.* Ānewetak, Eniwetok. *atoll* Ralik Chain, W Marshall Islands
114 L13 **Enez** Edirne, NW Turkey 40°44′N 26°05′E
21 W8 **Enfield** North Carolina, SE USA 36°10′N 77°40′W
186 B7 **Enga** ◈ *province* W Papua New Guinea
45 Q9 **Engaño, Cabo** *headland* E Dominican Republic 18°36′N 68°19′W
164 U3 **Engaru** Hokkaidō, NE Japan 44°06′N 143°30′E
'En Gedi *see* Ein Gedi
108 F9 **Engelberg** Unterwalden, C Switzerland 46°51′N 08°25′E
21 Y9 **Engelhard** North Carolina, SE USA 35°30′N 76°00′W
127 P8 **Engel's** Saratovskaya Oblast', W Russian Federation 51°27′N 46°09′E
101 G24 **Engen** Baden-Württemberg, SW Germany 47°52′N 08°46′E
Engeten *see* Aiud
168 K15 **Enggano, Pulau** *island* W Indonesia
80 J8 **Enghershatu** ▲ N Eritrea 16°41′N 38°21′E
99 F19 **Enghien** *Dut.* Edingen. Hainaut, SW Belgium 50°42′N 04°03′E
27 V12 **England** Arkansas, C USA 34°32′N 91°58′W
97 M20 **England** *Lat.* Anglia. ◈ *national region* England, United Kingdom
14 H8 **Englehart** Ontario, S Canada 47°50′N 79°52′W
37 T4 **Englewood** Colorado, C USA 39°39′N 104°59′W
31 O16 **English** Indiana, N USA 38°20′N 86°28′W
39 Q13 **English Bay** Alaska, USA 59°21′N 151°55′W
English Bazar *see* Ingrāj Bāzār
97 N25 **English Channel** *var.* The Channel, *Fr.* la Manche. *channel* NW Europe
194 J7 **English Coast** *physical region* Antarctica
105 S11 **Enguera** País Valenciano, E Spain 38°58′N 00°42′W
118 E8 **Engure** Tukums, W Latvia 57°09′N 23°13′E
118 E8 **Engures Ezers** ◎ NW Latvia
137 R9 **Enguri** *Rus.* Inguri. ≈ NW Georgia
Engyum *see* Gangi
26 M9 **Enid** Oklahoma, C USA 36°25′N 97°53′W
22 L3 **Enid Lake** ⊠ Mississippi, S USA
189 Y2 **Enigu** *island* Ratak Chain, SE Marshall Islands
Enikale Strait *see* Kerch Strait
147 Z8 **Enil'chek** Issyk-Kul'skaya Oblast', E Kyrgyzstan 42°04′N 79°01′E
115 F17 **Enipéfs** ≈ C Greece
165 S4 **Eniwa** Hokkaidō, NE Japan 42°53′N 141°14′E
Eniwetok *see* Enewetak Atoll
Enjiang *see* Yongfeng
Enkeldoorn *see* Chivhu
98 J8 **Enkhuizen** Noord-Holland, NW Netherlands 52°34′N 05°03′E
109 Q4 **Enknach** ≈ N Austria
95 N15 **Enköping** Uppsala, C Sweden 59°38′N 17°07′E
107 K24 **Enna** *var.* Castrogiovanni, Henna. Sicilia, Italy, C Mediterranean Sea 37°34′N 14°16′E
80 D11 **En Nahud** Western Kordofan, C Sudan 12°41′N 28°28′E
138 F8 **En Nâqoûra** *var.* An Nāqūrah. SW Lebanon 33°06′N 33°30′E
En Nazira *see* Natzrat
78 K8 **Ennedi** *plateau* E Chad
101 E15 **Ennepetal** Nordrhein-Westfalen, W Germany 51°18′N 07°23′E
183 P4 **Enngonia** New South Wales, SE Australia 29°19′S 145°52′E
97 C19 **Ennis** *Ir.* Inis. Clare, W Ireland 52°50′N 08°59′W
33 R11 **Ennis** Montana, NW USA 45°21′N 111°45′W
25 U7 **Ennis** Texas, SW USA 32°19′N 96°37′W
97 F20 **Enniscorthy** *Ir.* Inis Córthaidh. SE Ireland 52°30′N 06°34′W
97 E15 **Enniskillen** *var.* Inniskilling, *Ir.* Inis Ceithleann. SW Northern Ireland, United Kingdom 54°21′N 07°38′W
97 B19 **Ennistimon** *Ir.* Inis Díomáin. Clare, W Ireland 52°57′N 09°17′W
109 T4 **Enns** Oberösterreich, N Austria 48°13′N 14°28′E
109 T4 **Enns** ≈ C Austria
93 O16 **Eno** Itä-Suomi, SE Finland 62°45′N 30°15′E
24 M5 **Enochs** Texas, SW USA 33°51′N 102°46′W
93 N17 **Enonkoski** Itä-Suomi, E Finland 62°04′N 28°53′E
92 K10 **Enontekiö** *Lapp.* Eanodat. Lappi, N Finland 68°25′N 23°40′E
21 Q11 **Enoree** South Carolina, SE USA 34°39′N 81°58′W
21 P11 **Enoree River** ≈ South Carolina, SE USA
18 M6 **Enosburg Falls** Vermont, NE USA 44°54′N 72°50′W
171 N13 **Enrekang** Sulawesi, C Indonesia 03°33′S 119°46′E
45 N10 **Enriquillo** SW Dominican Republic 17°57′N 71°13′W
45 N9 **Enriquillo, Lago** ◎ SW Dominican Republic
98 L9 **Ens** Flevoland, N Netherlands 52°39′N 05°49′E
98 P11 **Enschede** Overijssel, E Netherlands 52°13′N 06°55′E
40 B2 **Ensenada** Baja California Norte, NW Mexico 31°52′N 116°32′W
101 E20 **Ensheim** ✈ (Saarbrücken) Saarland, W Germany 49°13′N 07°09′E
160 L9 **Enshi** Hubei, C China 30°16′N 109°26′E
164 L14 **Enshū-nada** *gulf* SW Japan
23 O8 **Ensley** Florida, SE USA 30°31′N 87°16′W
Enso *see* Svetogorsk
81 F18 **Entebbe** S Uganda 0°07′N 32°30′E
81 F18 **Entebbe** ✈ C Uganda 0°04′N 32°29′E
101 M18 **Entenbühl** ▲ Czech Republic/Germany 50°09′N 12°10′E
98 N10 **Enter** Overijssel, E Netherlands 52°19′N 06°34′E
23 Q7 **Enterprise** Alabama, S USA 31°19′N 85°50′W
32 L11 **Enterprise** Oregon, NW USA 45°25′N 117°18′W
36 J7 **Enterprise** Utah, W USA 37°33′N 113°42′W
32 J8 **Entiat** Washington, NW USA 47°39′N 120°15′W
105 P15 **Entinas, Punta de las** *headland* S Spain 36°40′N 02°44′W
108 F8 **Entlebuch** Luzern, W Switzerland 47°02′N 08°04′E
108 F8 **Entlebuch** *valley* C Switzerland
63 I22 **Entrada, Punta** *headland* S Argentina
103 O13 **Entraygues-sur-Truyère** Aveyron, S France 44°39′N 02°36′E
187 O14 **Entrecasteaux, Récifs d'** *reef* N New Caledonia
61 C17 **Entre Ríos** *off.* Provincia de Entre Ríos. ◈ *province* NE Argentina
42 K7 **Entre Ríos, Cordillera** ▲▲ Honduras/Nicaragua
Entre Ríos, Provincia de *see* Entre Ríos
104 G9 **Entroncamento** Santarém, C Portugal 39°28′N 08°28′W
77 V16 **Enugu** Enugu, S Nigeria 06°24′N 07°24′E
77 U16 **Enugu** ◈ *state* SE Nigeria
123 V5 **Enurmino** Chukotskiy Avtonomnyy Okrug, NE Russian Federation 66°46′N 171°40′W
54 E9 **Envigado** Antioquia, W Colombia 06°09′N 75°38′W
59 B15 **Envira** Amazonas, W Brazil 07°12′S 69°59′W
Enyélé *see* Enyellé
79 I16 **Enyellé** *var.* Enyélé. Likouala, NE Congo 02°49′N 18°02′E
101 H21 **Enz** ≈ SW Germany
165 N13 **Enzan** *var.* Kōshū. Yamanashi, Honshū, S Japan 35°44′N 138°43′E
104 I2 **Eo** ≈ NW Spain
Eochaill *see* Youghal
Eochaille, Cuan *see* Youghal Bay
107 K22 **Eolie, Isole** *var.* Isole Lipari, *Eng.* Aeolian Islands, Lipari Islands. *island group* S Italy
189 U12 **Eot** *island* Chuuk, C Micronesia
Epáno Archánes/Epáno Arkhánai *see* Archánes
115 G14 **Epanomí** Kentrikí Makedonía, N Greece 40°25′N 22°57′E
98 M10 **Epe** Gelderland, E Netherlands 52°21′N 05°59′E
77 S16 **Epe** Lagos, S Nigeria 06°37′N 04°01′E
79 I17 **Epéna** Likouala, NE Congo 01°28′N 17°29′E
Eperies/Eperjes *see* Prešov
103 Q4 **Épernay** *anc.* Sparnacum. Marne, N France 49°02′N 03°58′E
36 L5 **Ephraim** Utah, W USA 39°21′N 111°35′W
18 H15 **Ephrata** Pennsylvania, NE USA 40°09′N 76°08′W
32 J8 **Ephrata** Washington, NW USA 47°19′N 119°33′W
187 R14 **Epi** *var.* Épi. *island* C Vanuatu
Épi *see* Epi
105 R6 **Épila** Aragón, NE Spain 41°34′N 01°19′W
103 T6 **Épinal** Vosges, NE France 48°10′N 06°28′E
Epiphania *see* Ḩamāh
Epirus *see* Ípeiros
121 P3 **Episkopí** SW Cyprus 34°37′N 32°53′E
Episkopi Bay *see* Episkopí, Kólpos
121 P3 **Episkopí, Kólpos** *var.* Episkopi Bay. *bay* SE Cyprus
Epitoli *see* Tshwane
Epoon *see* Ebon Atoll
Eporedia *see* Ivrea
Eppeschdorf *see* Dumbrăveni
101 H21 **Eppingen** Baden-Württemberg, SW Germany 49°09′N 08°54′E
83 E18 **Epukiro** Omaheke, E Namibia 21°40′S 19°09′E
29 Y13 **Epworth** Iowa, C USA 42°27′N 90°55′W
143 O10 **Eqlīd** *var.* Iqlid. Fārs, C Iran 30°54′N 52°40′E
Equality State *see* Wyoming
79 J18 **Equateur** *off.* Région de l' Equateur. ◈ *region* N Dem. Rep. Congo
Equateur, Région de l' *see* Equateur
151 K22 **Equatorial Channel** *channel* S Maldives
79 B17 **Equatorial Guinea** *off.* Equatorial Guinea, Republic of. ◆ *republic* C Africa
Equatorial Guinea, Republic of *see* Equatorial Guinea
121 V11 **Eratosthenes Tablemount** *undersea feature* E Mediterranean Sea 33°48′N 32°53′E
Erautini *see* Johannesburg
136 L12 **Erbaa** Tokat, N Turkey 40°42′N 36°37′E
101 E19 **Erbeskopf** ▲ W Germany 49°43′N 07°04′E
Erbil *see* Arbīl
121 P2 **Ercan** ✈ (Nicosia) N Cyprus 35°07′N 33°30′E
Ercegnovi *see* Herceg-Novi
137 T14 **Erçek Gölü** ◎ E Turkey
137 S14 **Erciş** Van, E Turkey 39°02′N 43°21′E
136 K14 **Erciyes Dağı** *anc.* Argaeus. ▲ C Turkey 38°32′N 35°28′E
111 J22 **Érd** *Ger.* Hanselbeck. Pest, C Hungary 47°22′N 18°56′E
163 X11 **Erdaobaihe** *prev.* Baihe. Jilin, NE China 42°24′N 128°09′E
159 O12 **Erdaogou** Qinghai, W China 34°30′N 92°50′E
163 X11 **Erdao Jiang** ▲▲ NE China
Erdăt-Sângeorz *see* Sângeorgiu de Pădure
136 C11 **Erdek** Balıkesir, NW Turkey 40°24′N 27°47′E
Erdély *see* Transylvania
Erdélyi-Havasok *see* Carpaţii Meridionalii
136 J17 **Erdemli** İçel, S Turkey 36°35′N 34°19′E
163 O10 **Erdene** *var.* Ulaan-Uul. Dornogovĭ, SE Mongolia 44°21′N 111°06′E
162 H9 **Erdene** *var.* Sangiyn Dalay. Govĭ-Altay, C Mongolia 45°12′N 97°51′E
162 E6 **Erdenebüren** *var.* Har-Us. Hovd, W Mongolia 48°30′N 91°25′E
162 K9 **Erdenedalay** *var.* Sangiyn Dalay. Dundgovĭ, C Mongolia 45°59′N 104°58′E
162 G7 **Erdenehayrhan** *var.* Altan. Dzavhan, W Mongolia 48°05′N 95°48′E
162 J7 **Erdenemandal** *var.* Öldziyt. Arhangay, C Mongolia 48°30′N 101°25′E
162 K6 **Erdenet** Orhon, N Mongolia 49°01′N 104°07′E
163 Q9 **Erdenetsagaan** *var.* Chonogol. Sühbaatar, E Mongolia 45°55′N 115°19′E
162 I8 **Erdenetsogt** Bayanhongor, C Mongolia 46°27′N 100°53′E
Erdenetsogt *see* Bayan-Ovoo
78 K7 **Erdi** *plateau* NE Chad
78 L7 **Erdi Ma** *desert* NE Chad
101 M23 **Erding** Bayern, SE Germany 48°18′N 11°54′E
Erdőszáda *see* Ardusat
Erdőszentgyörgy *see* Sângeorgiu de Pădure
102 I7 **Erdre** ≈ NW France
195 R13 **Erebus, Mount** ⛰ Ross Island, Antarctica 78°11′S 165°09′E
61 H14 **Erechim** Rio Grande do Sul, S Brazil 27°35′S 52°15′W
163 O7 **Ereen Davaanĭ Nuruu** ▲▲ NE Mongolia
163 Q6 **Ereentsav** Dornod, NE Mongolia 49°51′N 115°41′E
136 I16 **Ereğli** Konya, S Turkey 37°30′N 34°02′E
115 A15 **Ereíkoussa** *island* Iónia Nisiá, Greece, C Mediterranean Sea
163 O11 **Erenhot** *var.* Erlian. Nei Mongol Zizhiqu, NE China 43°35′N 112°E
104 M6 **Eresma** ≈ N Spain
115 K17 **Eresós** *var.* Eressós. Lésvos, E Greece 39°11′N 25°57′E
Eressós *see* Eresós
Ereymentaū *see* Yereymentau
99 K21 **Érezée** Luxembourg, SE Belgium 50°16′N 05°34′E
74 G7 **Erfoud** SE Morocco 31°29′N 04°18′W
101 D16 **Erft** ≈ W Germany
101 K16 **Erfurt** Thüringen, C Germany 50°59′N 11°02′E
137 P15 **Ergani** Dıyarbakır, SE Turkey 38°17′N 39°44′E
Ergel *see* Hatanbulag
Ergene Çayı *see* Ergene Irmaği
136 C10 **Ergene Irmaği** *var.* Ergene Çayı. ≈ NW Turkey
118 I9 **Ērgļi** Madona, C Latvia 56°55′N 25°38′E
78 H11 **Erguig, Bahr** ≈ SW Chad
163 S5 **Ergun** *var.* Labudalin; *prev.* Ergun Youqi. Nei Mongol Zizhiqu, N China 50°13′N 120°09′E
Ergun He *see* Argun
Ergun Youqi *see* Ergun
Ergun Zuoqi *see* Genhe
160 F12 **Er Hai** ⊠ SW China
104 K4 **Ería** ≈ NW Spain
80 H8 **Eriba** Kassala, NE Sudan 16°37′N 36°04′E
96 I6 **Eriboll, Loch** *inlet* NW Scotland, United Kingdom
65 Q18 **Erica Seamount** *undersea feature* SW Indian Ocean 38°15′S 14°30′E
107 H23 **Erice** Sicilia, Italy, C Mediterranean Sea 38°02′N 12°35′E
104 E10 **Ericeira** Lisboa, C Portugal 38°58′N 09°25′W
96 H10 **Ericht, Loch** ◎ C Scotland, United Kingdom
26 J11 **Erick** Oklahoma, C USA 35°13′N 99°52′W
18 B11 **Erie** Pennsylvania, NE USA 42°07′N 80°04′W
18 E9 **Erie Canal** *canal* New York, NE USA
Érié, Lac *see* Erie, Lake
31 T10 **Erie, Lake** *Fr.* Lac Érié. ◎ Canada/USA
Erigabo *see* Ceerigaabo
77 N8 **'Erîgât** *desert* N Mali
Erigavo *see* Ceerigaabo
92 P2 **Erik Eriksenstretet** *strait* E Svalbard
11 X15 **Eriksdale** Manitoba, S Canada 50°52′N 98°07′W
189 V6 **Erikub Atoll** *var.* Ādkup. *atoll* Ratak Chain, C Marshall Islands
102 G4 **Er, Îles d'** *Island group* NW France
Erimanthos *see* Erýmanthos
165 T6 **Erimo** Hokkaidō, NE Japan 42°01′N 143°07′E
165 T6 **Erimo-misaki** *headland* Hokkaidō, NE Japan 41°57′N 143°12′E
20 H8 **Erin** Tennessee, S USA 36°19′N 87°42′W
96 E9 **Eriskay** *island* NW Scotland, United Kingdom
Erithraí *see* Erythrés
80 I9 **Eritrea** *off.* State of Eritrea, Ērtra. ◆ *transitional government* E Africa
Eritrea, State of *see* Eritrea
Erivan *see* Yerevan
101 D16 **Erkelenz** Nordrhein-Westfalen, W Germany 51°04′N 06°19′E
95 P15 **Erken** ◎ C Sweden
101 K19 **Erlangen** Bayern, S Germany 49°36′N 11°E
160 G9 **Erlang Shan** ▲ C China 29°56′N 102°24′E
Erlau *see* Eger
109 V5 **Erlauf** ≈ NE Austria
181 Q8 **Erldunda Roadhouse** Northern Territory, N Australia 25°13′S 133°13′E
Erlian *see* Erenhot
27 T15 **Erling, Lake** ⊠ Arkansas, USA
109 O8 **Erlsbach** Tirol, W Austria 46°54′N 12°15′E
Ermak *see* Aksu
98 K10 **Ermelo** Gelderland, C Netherlands 52°18′N 05°38′E
83 K21 **Ermelo** Mpumalanga, NE South Africa 26°32′S 29°59′E
136 H17 **Ermenek** Karaman, S Turkey 36°38′N 32°55′E
Érmihályfalva *see* Valea lui Mihai
115 G20 **Ermióni** Pelopónnisos, S Greece 37°24′N 23°15′E
115 J20 **Ermoúpoli** *var.* Hermoupolis; *prev.* Ermoúpolis. Sýyros, Kykládes, Greece, Aegean Sea 37°26′N 24°55′E
Ermoúpolis *see* Ermoúpoli
Ernabella *see* Pukatja
155 G22 **Ernākulam** Kerala, SW India 10°04′N 76°18′E
102 J6 **Ernée** Mayenne, NW France 48°18′N 00°54′W
61 H14 **Ernestina, Barragem** ⊠ S Brazil
54 E4 **Ernesto Cortissoz** ✈ (Barranquilla) Atlántico, N Colombia
155 H21 **Erode** Tamil Nādu, SE India 11°21′N 77°43′E
Eroj *see* Iroj
83 C19 **Erongo** ◈ *district* W Namibia
99 F21 **Erquelinnes** Hainaut, S Belgium 50°18′N 04°08′E
74 G7 **Er-Rachidia** *var.* Ksar al Soule. E Morocco 31°58′N 04°22′W
80 E11 **Er Rahad** *var.* Ar Rahad. Northern Kordofan, C Sudan 12°43′N 30°39′E
Er Ramle *see* Ramla
83 O15 **Errego** Zambézia, NE Mozambique 16°02′S 37°11′E
105 Q2 **Errenteria** *Cast.* Rentería. País Vasco, N Spain 43°17′N 01°54′W
Er Rif/Er Riff *see* Rif
97 D14 **Errigal Mountain** *Ir.* An Earagail. ▲ N Ireland 55°03′N 08°09′W
97 A15 **Erris Head** *Ir.* Ceann Iorrais. *headland* W Ireland 54°18′N 10°01′W
187 S15 **Erromango** *island* S Vanuatu
Error Guyot *see* Error Tablemount
173 O4 **Error Tablemount** *var.* Error Guyot. *undersea feature* W Indian Ocean 10°20′N 56°05′E
80 G11 **Er Roseires** Blue Nile, E Sudan 11°52′N 34°23′E
Erseka *see* Ersekë
113 M22 **Ersekë** *var.* Erseka, Kolonjë. Korçë, SE Albania 40°19′N 20°39′E
Érsekújvár *see* Nové Zámky
29 S4 **Erskine** Minnesota, N USA 47°42′N 96°00′W
103 V6 **Erstein** Bas-Rhin, NE France 48°24′N 07°39′E
108 G9 **Erstfeld** Uri, C Switzerland 46°49′N 08°41′E
158 M3 **Ertai** Xinjiang Uygur Zizhiqu, NW China 46°04′N 90°06′E
126 M7 **Ertil'** Voronezhskaya Oblast', W Russian Federation 51°51′N 40°46′E
Ertis *see* Irtysh, C Asia
Ertis *see* Irtyshsk, Kazakhstan
158 K2 **Ertix He** *Rus.* Chërnyy Irtysh. ≈ China/Kazakhstan
Ērtra *see* Eritrea
21 P9 **Erwin** North Carolina, SE USA 35°19′N 78°40′W
Erydropótamos *see* Erythropótamos
115 E19 **Erýmanthos** *var.* Erimanthos. ▲ S Greece 37°57′N 21°51′E
115 G19 **Erythrés** *prev.* Erithraí. Stereá Ellás, C Greece 38°18′N 23°20′E
114 L12 **Erythropótamos** *Bul.* Byala Reka, *var.* Erydropótamos. ≈ Bulgaria/Greece
160 F12 **Eryuan** *var.* Yuhu. Yunnan, SW China 26°09′N 100°01′E
109 U6 **Erzbach** ≈ W Austria
Erzerum *see* Erzurum
101 N17 **Erzgebirge** *Cz.* Krušné Hory, *Eng.* Ore Mountains. ▲ Czech Republic/Germany *see also* Krušné Hory
Erzgebirge *see* Krušné Hory
122 L14 **Erzin** Respublika Tyva, S Russian Federation 50°17′N 95°03′E
137 O13 **Erzincan** *var.* Erzinjan. Erzincan, E Turkey 39°44′N 39°30′E
137 N13 **Erzincan** *var.* Erzinjan. ◈ *province* NE Turkey
Erzinjan *see* Erzincan
Erzsébetváros *see* Dumbrăveni
137 Q13 **Erzurum** *prev.* Erzerum. Erzurum, NE Turkey 39°57′N 41°17′E
137 Q12 **Erzurum** *prev.* Erzerum. ◈ *province* NE Turkey
186 G9 **Esa'ala** Normanby Island, SE Papua New Guinea 09°45′S 150°47′E
165 T2 **Esashi** Hokkaidō, NE Japan 44°57′N 142°32′E
165 Q9 **Esashi** *var.* Esasi. Iwate, Honshū, C Japan 39°13′N 141°11′E
165 Q5 **Esasho** Hokkaidō, N Japan
Esasi *see* Esashi
95 F23 **Esbjerg** Ribe, W Denmark 55°28′N 08°28′E
Esbo *see* Espoo
36 L7 **Escalante** Utah, W USA 37°46′N 111°36′W
36 M7 **Escalante River** ≈ Utah, W USA
14 L12 **Escalier, Réservoir l'** ⊠ Québec, SE Canada
40 K7 **Escalón** Chihuahua, N Mexico 26°43′N 104°20′W
104 M8 **Escalona** Castilla-La Mancha, C Spain 40°10′N 04°24′W
23 O8 **Escambia River** ≈ Florida, SE USA
31 N5 **Escanaba** Michigan, N USA 45°45′N 87°03′W
31 N4 **Escanaba River** ≈ Michigan, N USA
105 R8 **Escandón, Puerto de** *pass* E Spain
41 W14 **Escárcega** Campache, SE Mexico 18°33′N 90°41′W
171 O1 **Escarpada Point** *headland* Luzon, N Philippines 18°28′N 122°10′E
23 N8 **Escatawpa River** ≈ Alabama/Mississippi, S USA
103 P2 **Escaut** ≈ N France
Escaut *see* Scheldt
99 M25 **Esch-sur-Alzette** Luxembourg, S Luxembourg 49°30′N 05°59′E
101 J15 **Eschwege** Hessen, C Germany 51°10′N 10°03′E
101 D16 **Eschweiler** Nordrhein-Westfalen, W Germany 50°49′N 06°16′E
Esclaves, Grand Lac des *see* Great Slave Lake
45 O8 **Escocesa, Bahía** *bay* N Dominican Republic
43 W15 **Escocés, Punta** *headland* NE Panama 08°50′N 77°37′W
35 U17 **Escondido** California, W USA 33°07′N 117°05′W
42 M10 **Escondido, Río** ≈ SE Nicaragua
15 S7 **Escoumins, Rivière des** ≈ Québec, SE Canada
37 O13 **Escudilla Mountain** ▲ Arizona, SW USA 33°57′N 109°07′W
40 J11 **Escuinapa** *var.* Escuinapa de Hidalgo. Sinaloa, C Mexico 22°50′N 105°46′W
Escuinapa de Hidalgo *see* Escuinapa
42 C6 **Escuintla** Escuintla, S Guatemala 14°17′N 90°46′W
41 V17 **Escuintla** Chiapas, SE Mexico 15°20′N 92°40′W
42 A2 **Escuintla** *off.* Departamento de Escuintla. ◈ *department* S Guatemala
Escuintla, Departamento de *see* Escuintla
15 W7 **Escuminac** ≈ Québec, SE Canada
79 D16 **Eséka** Centre, SW Cameroon 03°40′N 10°48′E
136 I12 **Esenboğa** ✈ (Ankara) Ankara, C Turkey 40°05′N 33°01′E
136 D17 **Eşen Çayı** ≈ SW Turkey
146 B13 **Esenguly** *Rus.* Gasan-Kuli. Balkan Welaýaty, W Turkmenistan 37°29′N 53°57′E
105 T4 **Ésera** ≈ NE Spain
143 N8 **Eşfahān** *Eng.* Isfahan; *anc.* Aspadana. Eşfahān, C Iran 32°41′N 51°41′E
143 O7 **Eşfahān** *off.* Ostān-e Eşfahān. ◈ *province* C Iran
Eşfahān, Ostān-e *see* Eşfahān
105 N5 **Esgueva** ≈ N Spain
149 Q3 **Eshkamesh** Takhār, NE Afghanistan 36°25′N 69°11′E
149 T2 **Eshkāshem** Badakhshān, NE Afghanistan 36°43′N 71°34′E
83 L23 **Eshowe** KwaZulu/Natal, E South Africa 28°53′S 31°28′E
143 T5 **'Eshqābād** Khorāsān, NE Iran 36°00′N 59°01′E
Esh Sham *see* Dimashq
Esh Sharā *see* Ash Sharāh
Esik *see* Yesik
Esil *see* Yesil'
Esil *see* Ishim, Kazakhstan/Russian Federation
183 V2 **Esk** Queensland, E Australia 27°15′S 152°23′E
184 O11 **Eskdale** Hawke's Bay, North Island, New Zealand 39°24′S 176°51′E
Eski Dzhumaya *see* Tŭrgovishte
92 L2 **Eskifjördhur** Austurland, E Iceland 65°04′N 14°01′W
139 S3 **Eski Kaļak** *var.* Askī Kalak, Kalak. Arbīl, N Iraq 36°16′N 43°40′E
95 N16 **Eskilstuna** Södermanland, C Sweden 59°22′N 16°31′E
8 H6 **Eskimo Lakes** ◎ Northwest Territories, NW Canada
9 O10 **Eskimo Point** *headland* Nunavut, E Canada 61°19′N 93°49′W
Eskimo Point *see* Arviat
139 Q2 **Eski Mosul** Nīnawá, N Iraq 36°31′N 42°45′E
147 T10 **Eski-Nookat** *var.* Iski-Nauket. Oshskaya Oblast', SW Kyrgyzstan 40°18′N 72°29′E
136 F12 **Eskişehir** *var.* Eskishehr. Eskişehir, W Turkey 39°46′N 30°30′E
136 F13 **Eskişehir** *var.* Eski shehr. ◈ *province* NW Turkey
Eskishehr *see* Eskişehir
104 K5 **Esla** ≈ NW Spain
142 J6 **Eslāmābād** *var.* Eslāmābād-e Gharb; *prev.* Harunabad, Shāhābād. Kermānshāhān, W Iran 34°08′N 46°35′E
Eslāmābād-e Gharb *see* Eslāmābād
148 J4 **Eslām Qal'eh** *Pash.* Islam Qala. Herāt, W Afghanistan 34°41′N 61°03′E
95 K23 **Eslöv** Skåne, S Sweden 55°50′N 13°20′E
143 S12 **Esmā'īlābād** Kermān, S Iran 28°48′N 56°39′E
143 U8 **Esmā'īlābād** Khorāsān, E Iran 35°20′N 60°30′E
136 D14 **Eşme** Uşak, W Turkey 38°26′N 28°59′E
44 G6 **Esmeralda** Camagüey, E Cuba 21°51′N 78°10′W
63 F21 **Esmeralda, Isla** *island* S Chile
56 B5 **Esmeraldas** Esmeraldas, N Ecuador 0°55′N 79°40′W
56 B5 **Esmeraldas** ◈ *province* NW Ecuador
Esna *see* Isnā
14 B6 **Esnagi Lake** ◎ Ontario, S Canada
143 V14 **Espakeh** Sīstān va Balūchestān, SE Iran 26°54′N 60°09′E
103 O13 **Espalion** Aveyron, S France 44°31′N 02°45′E
España *see* Spain
14 E11 **Espanola** Ontario, S Canada 46°15′N 81°46′W
37 S10 **Espanola** New Mexico, SW USA 35°59′N 106°04′W
57 C18 **Española, Isla** *var.* Hood Island. *island* Galapagos Islands, Ecuador, E Pacific Ocean
104 M13 **Espejo** Andalucía, S Spain 37°40′N 04°34′W
94 C13 **Espeland** Hordaland, S Norway 60°22′N 05°27′E
100 G12 **Espelkamp** Nordrhein-Westfalen, NW Germany 52°22′N 08°37′E
38 M8 **Espenberg, Cape** *headland* Alaska, USA 66°33′N 163°36′W
180 L13 **Esperance** Western Australia 33°49′S 121°52′E
186 L9 **Esperance, Cape** *headland* Guadacanal, C Solomon Islands 09°09′S 159°38′E
57 P18 **Esperancita** Santa Cruz, E Bolivia
61 B17 **Esperanza** Santa Fe, C Argentina 31°29′S 61°00′W
40 G6 **Esperanza** Sonora, NW Mexico 27°37′N 109°51′W
24 H9 **Esperanza** Texas, SW USA 31°09′N 105°40′W
194 H3 **Esperanza** *Argentinian research station* Antarctica 63°29′S 56°53′W
104 E12 **Espichel, Cabo** *headland* S Portugal 38°25′N 09°15′W
54 E10 **Espinal** Tolima, C Colombia 04°08′N 74°53′W
48 K10 **Espinhaço, Serra do** ▲▲ SE Brazil
104 G6 **Espinho** Aveiro, N Portugal 41°01′N 08°38′W
59 N18 **Espinosa** Minas Gerais, SE Brazil 14°58′S 42°49′W
103 O15 **Espinouse** ▲▲ S France
60 Q8 **Espírito Santo** *off.* Estado do Espírito Santo. ◈ *state* E Brazil
Espírito Santo, Estado do *see* Espírito Santo
187 P13 **Espiritu Santo** *var.* Santo. *island* W Vanuatu
41 Z13 **Espíritu Santo, Bahía del** *bay* SE Mexico
40 F9 **Espíritu Santo, Isla del** *island* NW Mexico
41 Y12 **Espita** Yucatán, SE Mexico 21°00′N 88°17′W
15 Y7 **Espoir, Cap d'** *headland* Québec, SE Canada 48°24′N 64°21′W
Esponsede/Esponsende *see* Esposende
93 L20 **Espoo** *Swe.* Esbo. Etelä-Suomi, S Finland 60°10′N 24°42′E
104 G5 **Esposende** *var.* Esponsede, Esponsende. Braga, N Portugal 41°32′N 08°47′W
83 M18 **Espungabera** Manica, SW Mozambique 20°29′S 32°48′E
63 H17 **Esquel** Chubut, SW Argentina 42°55′S 71°20′W
10 L17 **Esquimalt** Vancouver Island, British Columbia, SW Canada 48°26′N 123°27′W
61 C16 **Esquina** Corrientes, NE Argentina 30°00′S 59°30′W
42 E6 **Esquipulas** Chiquimula, SE Guatemala 14°36′N 89°22′W
42 K9 **Esquipulas** Matagalpa, C Nicaragua 12°30′N 85°55′W
94 I8 **Essandjøen** ◎ S Norway
74 E7 **Essaouira** *prev.* Mogador. W Morocco 31°33′N 09°40′W
Esseg *see* Osijek
Es Semara *see* Smara
99 G15 **Essen** Antwerpen, N Belgium 51°28′N 04°28′E
101 E15 **Essen** *var.* Essen an der Ruhr. Nordrhein-Westfalen, W Germany 51°28′N 07°01′E
Essen an der Ruhr *see* Essen
74 I5 **Es Senia** ✈ (Oran) NW Algeria 35°34′N 00°42′W
55 T8 **Essequibo Islands** *island group* N Guyana
55 T11 **Essequibo River** ≈ C Guyana
14 C18 **Essex** Ontario, S Canada 42°10′N 82°50′W
29 T16 **Essex** Iowa, C USA 40°49′N 95°18′W
97 P21 **Essex** *cultural region* E England, United Kingdom
31 R8 **Essexville** Michigan, N USA 43°37′N 83°50′W
101 H22 **Esslingen** *var.* Esslingen am Neckar. Baden-Württemberg, SW Germany 48°45′N 09°19′E
Esslingen am Neckar *see* Esslingen
103 N6 **Essonne** ◈ *department* N France
Es Suweida *see* As Suwaydā'
79 F16 **Est** *Eng.* East. ◈ *province* SE Cameroon
104 I1 **Estaca de Bares, Punta da** *point* NW Spain
24 M5 **Estacado, Llano** *plain* New Mexico/Texas, SW USA
63 K25 **Estados, Isla de los** *prev. Eng.* Staten Island. *island* S Argentina
Estado Vargas *see* Vargas
143 P12 **Eşţahbān** Fārs, S Iran
14 F11 **Estaire** Ontario, S Canada 46°19′N 80°47′W
59 P16 **Estância** Sergipe, E Brazil 11°15′S 37°28′W
37 S12 **Estancia** New Mexico, SW USA 34°45′N 106°03′W
104 G7 **Estarreja** Aveiro, N Portugal 40°45′N 08°35′W
102 M17 **Estats, Pic d'** *Sp.* Pico d'Estats. ▲ France/Spain 42°39′N 01°24′E
Estats, Pico d' *see* Estats, Pic d'
83 K23 **Estcourt** KwaZulu/Natal, E South Africa 29°00′S 29°53′E
106 H8 **Este** *anc.* Ateste. Veneto, NE Italy 45°14′N 11°40′E
42 J9 **Estelí** Estelí, NW Nicaragua 13°05′N 86°21′W
42 J9 **Estelí** ◈ *department* NW Nicaragua
105 Q4 **Estella** *Bas.* Lizarra. Navarra, N Spain 42°41′N 02°02′W
29 R9 **Estelline** South Dakota, N USA 44°34′N 96°54′W
25 P4 **Estelline** Texas, SW USA 34°33′N 100°26′W
104 L14 **Estepa** Andalucía, S Spain 37°17′N 04°52′W
104 L16 **Estepona** Andalucía, S Spain 36°26′N 05°09′W
39 R9 **Ester** Alaska, USA 64°49′N 148°03′W
11 V16 **Esterhazy** Saskatchewan, S Canada 50°40′N 102°02′W
37 S3 **Estes Park** Colorado, C USA 40°22′N 105°31′W
43 Q7 **Este Sudesre, Cayos del** NW Colombia, Caribbean Sea
11 V17 **Estevan** Saskatchewan, S Canada 49°07′N 103°05′W
29 T11 **Estherville** Iowa, C USA 43°24′N 94°49′W
21 R15 **Estill** South Carolina, SE USA 32°45′N 81°14′W
103 Q6 **Estissac** Aube, N France 48°17′N 03°51′E
15 T9 **Est, Lac de l'** ◎ Québec, SE Canada
Estland *see* Estonia
11 S16 **Eston** Saskatchewan, S Canada 51°09′N 198°42′W
118 G5 **Estonia** *off.* Republic of Estonia, *Est.* Eesti Vabariik, *Ger.* Estland, *Latv.* Igaunija; *prev.* Estonian SSR, *Rus.* Estonskaya SSR. ◆ *republic* NE Europe
Estonian SSR *see* Estonia
Estonia, Republic of *see* Estonia
Estonskaya SSR *see* Estonia
104 E11 **Estoril** Lisboa, W Portugal 38°42′N 09°23′W
59 L14 **Estreito** Maranhão, E Brazil 06°34′S 47°22′W
104 I8 **Estrela, Serra da** ▲▲ C Portugal
40 D3 **Estrella, Punta** *headland* NW Mexico 30°53′N 114°45′W
104 F10 **Estremadura** *cultural and historical region* W Portugal
Estremadura *see* Extremadura
104 H11 **Estremoz** Évora, S Portugal 38°50′N 07°35′W
79 D18 **Estuaire** *off.* Province de l'Estuaire, *var.* L'Estuaire. ◈ *province* NW Gabon
Estuaire, Province de l' *see* Estuaire
Eszék *see* Osijek
111 I22 **Esztergom** *Ger.* Gran; *anc.* Strigonium. Komárom-Esztergom, N Hungary 47°47′N 18°44′E
152 K11 **Etah** Uttar Pradesh, N India 27°33′N 78°39′E
189 R17 **Etal Atoll** *atoll* Mortlock Islands, C Micronesia
99 K24 **Étalle** Luxembourg, SE Belgium 49°41′N 05°36′E
103 N6 **Étampes** Essonne, N France 48°26′N 02°10′E
182 J1 **Etamunbanie, Lake** *salt lake* South Australia
103 N1 **Étaples** Pas-de-Calais, N France 50°31′N 01°39′E
152 K12 **Etāwah** Uttar Pradesh, N India 26°46′N 79°01′E
15 R10 **Etchemin** ≈ Québec, SE Canada
Etchmiadzin *see* Vagharshapat
40 G7 **Etchojoa** Sonora, NW Mexico 26°54′N 109°37′W
93 L19 **Etelä-Suomi** ◈ *province* S Finland
83 B16 **Etengua** Kunene, NW Namibia 17°24′S 13°05′E
99 K25 **Éthe** Luxembourg, SE Belgium 49°34′N 05°32′E
11 W15 **Ethelbert** Manitoba, S Canada 51°30′N 100°22′W
80 H12 **Ethiopia** *off.* Federal Democratic Republic of Ethiopia; *prev.* Abyssinia, People's Democratic Republic of Ethiopia. ◆ *republic* E Africa
Ethiopia, Federal Democratic Republic of *see* Ethiopia
80 I13 **Ethiopian Highlands** *var.* Ethiopian Plateau. *plateau* N Ethiopia
Ethiopian Plateau *see* Ethiopian Highlands
Ethiopia, People's Democratic Republic of *see* Ethiopia
34 M2 **Etna** California, W USA 41°25′N 122°53′W
18 B14 **Etna** Pennsylvania, NE USA 40°29′N 79°55′W
94 G12 **Etna** ≈ S Norway
107 L24 **Etna, Monte** *Eng.* Mount Etna. ⛰ Sicilia, Italy, C Mediterranean Sea 37°46′N 15°00′E
Etna, Mount *see* Etna, Monte

◆ Country
● Country Capital
◇ Dependent Territory
○ Dependent Territory Capital
◈ Administrative Regions
✈ International Airport
▲ Mountain
▲▲ Mountain Range
⛰ Volcano
≈ River
◎ Lake
⊠ Reservoir

ETNE – FEATHERSTON

95 C15 Etne Hordaland, S Norway 59°40′N 05°55′E
Etoliko see Aitolikó
39 Y14 Etolin Island island Alexander Archipelago, Alaska, USA
38 L12 Etolin Strait strait Alaska, USA
83 C17 Etosha Pan salt lake N Namibia
79 G18 Etoumbi Cuvette Ouest, NW Congo 0°01′N 14°57′E
20 M10 Etowah Tennessee, S USA 35°19′N 84°31′W
23 S2 Etowah River Georgia, SE USA
146 B13 Etrek var. Gyzyletrek, Rus. Kizyl-Atrek. Balkan Welaýaty, W Turkmenistan 37°40′N 54°44′E
146 C13 Etrek Per. Rūd-e Atrak, Rus. Atrak, Atrek. Iran/Turkmenistan
102 L3 Étretat Seine-Maritime, N France 49°46′N 00°23′E
114 H9 Etropole Sofiya, W Bulgaria 42°50′N 24°00′E
Etsch see Adige
Et Tafila see Aţ Ţafīlah
99 M23 Ettelbrück Diekirch, C Luxembourg 49°51′N 06°06′E
189 V12 Etten atoll Chuuk Islands, C Micronesia
99 H14 Etten-Leur Noord-Brabant, S Netherlands 51°34′N 04°37′E
76 G7 Et Tîdra var. Ile Tîdra. island Dakhlet Nouâdhibou, NW Mauritania
101 G21 Ettlingen Baden-Württemberg, SW Germany 48°57′N 08°25′E
102 M2 Eu Seine-Maritime, N France 50°01′N 01°24′E
193 W16 'Eua prev. Middleburg Island. island Tongatapu Group, SE Tonga
193 W15 Eua Iki island Tongatapu Group, S Tonga
Euboea see Évvoia
181 O12 Eucla Western Australia 31°41′S 128°51′E
31 U11 Euclid Ohio, N USA 41°34′N 81°33′W
27 W14 Eudora Arkansas, C USA 33°06′N 91°15′W
27 Q4 Eudora Kansas, C USA 38°56′N 95°06′W
182 J9 Eudunda South Australia 34°11′S 139°03′E
23 R6 Eufaula Alabama, S USA 31°53′N 85°09′W
27 Q11 Eufaula Oklahoma, C USA 35°16′N 95°36′W
27 Q11 Eufaula Lake var. Eufaula Reservoir. ⊠ Oklahoma, C USA
Eufaula Reservoir see Eufaula Lake
32 F13 Eugene Oregon, NW USA 44°03′N 123°05′W
40 B6 Eugenia, Punta headland NW Mexico 27°48′N 115°03′W
183 Q8 Eugowra New South Wales, SE Australia 33°28′S 148°21′E
104 I2 Eume NW Spain
104 H2 Eume, Embalse do ⊠ NW Spain
Eumolpias see Plovdiv
59 O18 Eunápolis Bahia, SE Brazil 16°20′S 39°36′W
22 H8 Eunice Louisiana, S USA 30°29′N 92°25′W
37 W15 Eunice New Mexico, SW USA 32°26′N 103°09′W
99 M19 Eupen Liège, E Belgium 50°38′N 06°02′E
130 B10 Euphrates Ar. Al-Furāt, Turk. Firat Nehri. SW Asia
138 L3 Euphrates Dam dam N Syria
22 M4 Eupora Mississippi, S USA 33°32′N 89°16′W
93 K19 Eura Länsi-Suomi, SW Finland 61°07′N 22°12′E
93 K19 Eurajoki Länsi-Suomi, SW Finland 61°13′N 21°45′E
0-1 Eurasian Plate tectonic feature
102 L4 Eure ◆ department N France
102 L4 Eure N France
102 M6 Eure-et-Loir ◆ department C France
34 K3 Eureka California, W USA 40°47′N 124°12′W
27 P6 Eureka Kansas, C USA 37°51′N 96°17′W
33 O6 Eureka Montana, NW USA 48°52′N 115°03′W
35 V5 Eureka Nevada, W USA 39°31′N 115°58′W
29 O7 Eureka South Dakota, N USA 45°46′N 99°37′W
36 L4 Eureka Utah, W USA 39°57′N 112°07′W
32 K10 Eureka Washington, NW USA 46°21′N 118°41′W
27 S9 Eureka Springs Arkansas, C USA 36°25′N 93°45′W
182 K6 Eurinilla Creek seasonal river South Australia
183 O11 Euroa Victoria, SE Australia 36°46′S 145°35′E
172 M9 Europa, Île island W Madagascar
104 L3 Europa, Picos de ▲ N Spain
104 L16 Europa Point headland S Gibraltar 36°07′N 05°20′W
84-85 Europe continent
98 F12 Europoort Zuid-Holland, W Netherlands 51°59′N 04°08′E
Euskadi see País Vasco
101 D17 Euskirchen Nordrhein-Westfalen, W Germany 50°40′N 06°47′E
23 W11 Eustis Florida, SE USA 28°51′N 81°41′W
182 M9 Euston New South Wales, SE Australia 34°34′S 142°45′E
23 N5 Eutaw Alabama, S USA 32°50′N 87°53′W
100 K8 Eutin Schleswig-Holstein, N Germany 54°08′N 10°38′E
10 K14 Eutsuk Lake ⊠ British Columbia, SW Canada
Euxine Sea see Black Sea
83 C16 Evale Cunene, SW Angola 16°36′S 15°46′E
37 T3 Evans Colorado, C USA 40°22′N 104°41′W
11 P14 Evansburg Alberta, SW Canada 53°34′N 114°57′W
29 X13 Evansdale Iowa, C USA 42°28′N 92°16′W
183 V4 Evans Head New South Wales, SE Australia 29°07′S 153°27′E
12 J11 Evans, Lac ◎ Québec, SE Canada
37 S5 Evans, Mount ▲ Colorado, C USA 39°15′N 106°10′W
9 Q6 Evans Strait strait Nunavut, N Canada
31 N10 Evanston Illinois, N USA 42°02′N 87°41′W
33 S17 Evanston Wyoming, C USA 41°16′N 110°57′W
14 D11 Evansville Manitoulin Island, Ontario, S Canada 45°48′N 82°34′W
31 N16 Evansville Indiana, N USA 37°58′N 87°33′W
30 L9 Evansville Wisconsin, N USA 42°46′N 89°16′W
25 S8 Evant Texas, SW USA 31°28′N 98°09′W
143 P13 Evaz Fārs, S Iran 27°48′N 53°58′E
29 W4 Eveleth Minnesota, N USA 47°27′N 92°32′W
182 E3 Evelyn Creek seasonal river South Australia
181 Q2 Evelyn, Mount ▲ Northern Territory, N Australia 13°28′S 132°50′E
122 K10 Evenkiyskiy Avtonomnyy Okrug ◆ autonomous district Krasnoyarskiy Kray, N Russian Federation
183 R13 Everard, Cape headland Victoria, SE Australia 37°48′S 149°21′E
182 F6 Everard, Lake salt lake South Australia
182 C2 Everard Ranges ▲ South Australia
153 R11 Everest, Mount Chin. Qomolangma Feng, Nep. Sagarmāthā. ▲ China/Nepal 27°59′N 86°57′E
18 E15 Everett Pennsylvania, NE USA 40°00′N 78°22′W
32 H7 Everett Washington, NW USA 47°59′N 122°12′W
99 E17 Evergem Oost-Vlaanderen, NW Belgium 51°07′N 03°43′E
23 X16 Everglades City Florida, SE USA 25°51′N 81°22′W
23 Y16 Everglades, The wetland Florida, SE USA
23 P7 Evergreen Alabama, S USA 31°25′N 86°55′W
37 T4 Evergreen Colorado, C USA 39°37′N 105°19′W
Evergreen State see Washington
97 L21 Evesham C England, United Kingdom 52°06′N 01°57′W
103 T10 Évian-les-Bains Haute-Savoie, E France 46°22′N 06°34′E
93 K16 Evijärvi Länsi-Suomi, W Finland 63°22′N 23°30′E
79 D17 Evinayong var. Ebinayon, Evinayoung. C Equatorial Guinea 01°28′N 10°17′E
Evinayoung see Evinayong
115 E18 Évinos C Greece
95 E17 Evje Aust-Agder, S Norway 58°35′N 07°49′E
Evmolpia see Plovdiv
104 H11 Évora anc. Ebora, Lat. Liberalitas Julia. Évora, C Portugal 38°34′N 07°54′W
104 G11 Évora ◆ district S Portugal
102 M4 Évreux anc. Civitas Eburovicum. Eure, N France 49°02′N 01°10′E
102 K6 Évron Mayenne, NW France 48°10′N 00°24′W
114 L13 Évros Bul. Maritsa, Turk. Meriç; anc. Hebrus. SE Europe see also Maritsa/Meriç
Évros see Meriç
Évros see Maritsa
115 F21 Evrótas S Greece
103 O5 Évry Essonne, N France 48°38′N 02°34′E
25 O8 E. V. Spence Reservoir ⊠ Texas, SW USA
115 I18 Évvoia Lat. Euboea. island C Greece
38 D9 'Ewa Beach var. Ewa Beach. O'ahu, Hawaii, USA, C Pacific Ocean 21°19′N 158°00′W
Ewa Beach see 'Ewa Beach
32 L9 Ewan Washington, NW USA 47°06′N 117°46′W
44 K12 Ewarton C Jamaica 18°11′N 77°06′W
81 J18 Ewaso Ng'iro var. Nyiro. C Kenya
29 P13 Ewing Nebraska, C USA 42°13′N 98°20′W
194 J5 Ewing Island island Antarctica
65 P17 Ewing Seamount undersea feature E Atlantic Ocean 23°20′S 08°45′E
158 L6 Ewirgol Xinjiang Uygur Zizhiqu, W China 42°56′N 87°39′E
79 G19 Ewo Cuvette, W Congo 0°55′S 14°49′E
27 S3 Excelsior Springs Missouri, C USA 39°20′N 94°13′W
97 J23 Exe SW England, United Kingdom
194 L12 Executive Committee Range ▲ Antarctica
14 E16 Exeter Ontario, S Canada 43°19′N 81°26′W
97 J24 Exeter anc. Isca Damnoniorum. SW England, United Kingdom 50°43′N 03°31′W
35 R11 Exeter California, W USA 36°17′N 119°08′W
19 P10 Exeter New Hampshire, NE USA 42°57′N 70°55′W
Exin see Kcynia
29 T14 Exira Iowa, C USA 41°36′N 94°55′W
97 J23 Exmoor moorland SW England, United Kingdom
21 Y6 Exmore Virginia, NE USA 37°31′N 75°48′W
180 G8 Exmouth Western Australia 22°01′S 114°06′E
97 J24 Exmouth SW England, United Kingdom 50°36′N 03°25′W
180 G8 Exmouth Gulf gulf Western Australia
173 V8 Exmouth Plateau undersea feature E Indian Ocean
115 J20 Exompourgo ancient monument Tínos, Kykládes, Greece, Aegean Sea
104 I10 Extremadura var. Estremadura. ◆ autonomous community W Spain
78 F12 Extrême-Nord Eng. Extreme North. ◆ province N Cameroon
Extreme North see Extrême-Nord
44 I3 Exuma Cays islets C Bahamas
44 I3 Exuma Sound sound C Bahamas
81 H20 Eyasi, Lake ◎ N Tanzania
95 F17 Eydehavn Aust-Agder, S Norway 58°31′N 08°53′E
96 L12 Eyemouth SE Scotland, United Kingdom 55°52′N 02°07′W
96 G7 Eye Peninsula peninsula NW Scotland, United Kingdom
80 Q13 Eyl It. Eil. Nugaal, E Somalia 08°03′N 49°49′E
103 N11 Eymoutiers Haute-Vienne, C France 45°45′N 01°43′E
Eyo (lower course) see Uolo, Río
29 X10 Eyota Minnesota, N USA 44°00′N 92°13′W
182 H2 Eyre Basin, Lake salt lake South Australia
182 I1 Eyre Creek seasonal river Northern Territory/South Australia
174 L9 Eyre, Lake salt lake South Australia
185 C22 Eyre Mountains ▲ South Island, New Zealand
182 H3 Eyre North, Lake salt lake South Australia
182 G7 Eyre Peninsula peninsula South Australia
182 H4 Eyre South, Lake salt lake South Australia
95 B18 Eysturoy Dan. Østerø. island N Faeroe Islands
142 J7 Eyvān Īlām, W Iran 33°50′N 46°18′E
61 D20 Ezeiza ✕ (Buenos Aires) Buenos Aires, E Argentina 34°49′S 58°30′W
Ezeres see Ezeriş
116 F12 Ezeriş Hung. Ezeres. Caraş-Severin, W Romania 45°21′N 21°55′E
161 O9 Ezhou prev. Echeng. Hubei, C China 30°23′N 114°52′E
125 R11 Ezhva Respublika Komi, NW Russian Federation 61°45′N 50°43′E
136 B12 Ezine Çanakkale, NW Turkey 39°46′N 26°20′E
Ezo see Hokkaidō
Ezra/Ezraa see Izra'

F

191 P7 Faaa Tahiti, W French Polynesia 17°32′S 149°36′W
191 P7 Faaa ✕ (Papeete) Tahiti, W French Polynesia 17°31′S 149°36′W
95 H24 Faaborg var. Fåborg. Fyn, C Denmark 55°06′N 10°10′E
151 K19 Faadhippolhu Atoll var. Fadiffolu, Lhaviyani Atoll. atoll N Maldives
191 U10 Faaite atoll Îles Tuamotu, C French Polynesia
191 Q8 Faaone Tahiti, W French Polynesia 17°39′S 149°13′W
24 H8 Fabens Texas, SW USA 31°30′N 106°09′W
94 H12 Fåberg Oppland, S Norway 61°15′N 10°21′E
Fåborg see Faaborg
106 I12 Fabriano Marche, C Italy 43°20′N 12°54′E
145 U16 Fabrichnyy Almaty, SE Kazakhstan 43°12′N 76°19′E
54 F10 Facatativá Cundinamarca, C Colombia 04°49′N 74°22′W
77 X9 Fachi Agadez, C Niger 18°01′N 11°36′E
188 B16 Facpi Point headland W Guam
18 I13 Factoryville Pennsylvania, NE USA 41°34′N 75°45′W
78 K8 Fada Borkou-Ennedi-Tibesti, E Chad 17°14′N 21°32′E
77 Q13 Fada-Ngourma E Burkina 12°05′N 00°26′E
123 N6 Faddeya, Zaliv bay N Russian Federation
123 Q5 Faddeyevskiy, Ostrov island Novosibirskiye Ostrova, NE Russian Federation
141 W12 Fadhī S Oman 17°54′N 55°30′E
Fadiffolu see Faadhippolhu Atoll
106 H10 Faenza anc. Faventia. Emilia-Romagna, N Italy 44°17′N 11°53′E
64 M5 Faeroe-Iceland Ridge undersea feature NW Norwegian Sea 64°00′N 10°00′W
64 M5 Faeroe Islands Dan. Færøerne, Faer. Føroyar. ◇ Danish external territory N Atlantic Ocean
86 C8 Faeroe Islands island group N Atlantic Ocean
Færøerne see Faeroe Islands
64 N6 Faeroe-Shetland Trough undersea feature NE Atlantic Ocean
104 H6 Fafe Braga, N Portugal 41°27′N 08°11′W
80 K13 Fafen Shet' E Ethiopia
193 V15 Fafo island Tongatapu Group, S Tonga
192 I16 Fagaloa Bay bay Upolu, E Samoa
192 H15 Fagamālo Savai'i, N Samoa 13°27′S 172°22′W
116 I12 Făgăraş Ger. Fogarasch, Hung. Fogaras. Braşov, C Romania 45°50′N 24°59′E
95 M20 Fagerhult Kalmar, S Sweden 57°07′N 15°40′E
94 G13 Fagernes Oppland, S Norway 60°59′N 09°14′E
92 I9 Fagernes Troms, N Norway 69°31′N 19°16′E
95 M14 Fagersta Västmanland, C Sweden 59°59′N 15°49′E
77 W13 Faggo var. Foggo. Bauchi, N Nigeria 11°22′N 09°55′E
Faghman see Fughmah
Fagibina, Lake see Faguibine, Lac
63 J25 Fagnano, Lago ◎ S Argentina
99 G22 Fagne hill range S Belgium
77 N10 Faguibine, Lac var. Lake Fagibina. ◎ NW Mali
Fahaheel see Al Fuḩayḩīl
Fahlun see Falun
143 U12 Fahraj Kermān, SE Iran 29°00′N 59°00′E
64 P5 Faial Madeira, Portugal, NE Atlantic Ocean 32°47′N 16°53′W
64 N2 Faial var. Ilha do Faial. island Azores, Portugal, NE Atlantic Ocean
Faial, Ilha do see Faial
108 G10 Faido Ticino, S Switzerland 46°30′N 08°48′E
Faifo see Hôi An
Failaka Island see Faylakah
190 G12 Faioa, Île island N Wallis and Futuna
181 W8 Fairbairn Reservoir ⊠ Queensland, E Australia
39 R9 Fairbanks Alaska, USA 64°48′N 147°47′W
21 U12 Fair Bluff North Carolina, SE USA 34°18′N 79°02′W
31 R14 Fairborn Ohio, N USA 39°48′N 84°03′W
23 S3 Fairburn Georgia, SE USA 33°34′N 84°34′W
30 M12 Fairbury Illinois, N USA 40°45′N 88°30′W
29 Q17 Fairbury Nebraska, C USA 40°08′N 97°10′W
29 T9 Fairfax Minnesota, N USA 44°31′N 94°43′W
27 O8 Fairfax Oklahoma, C USA 36°34′N 96°42′W
21 R14 Fairfax South Carolina, SE USA 32°57′N 81°14′W
35 N8 Fairfield California, W USA 38°14′N 122°03′W
33 O14 Fairfield Idaho, NW USA 43°20′N 114°45′W
30 M16 Fairfield Illinois, N USA 38°22′N 88°23′W
29 X15 Fairfield Iowa, C USA 41°00′N 91°57′W
33 R8 Fairfield Montana, NW USA 47°36′N 111°59′W
31 Q14 Fairfield Ohio, N USA 39°21′N 84°34′W
25 U8 Fairfield Texas, SW USA 31°43′N 96°10′W
27 T7 Fair Grove Missouri, C USA 37°22′N 93°09′W
19 P12 Fairhaven Massachusetts, NE USA 41°38′N 70°51′W
23 N8 Fairhope Alabama, S USA 30°31′N 87°54′W
96 L4 Fair Isle island NE Scotland, United Kingdom
185 F20 Fairlie Canterbury, South Island, New Zealand 44°06′S 170°50′E
29 U11 Fairmont Minnesota, N USA 43°40′N 94°27′W
29 Q16 Fairmont Nebraska, C USA 40°37′N 97°36′W
21 S3 Fairmont West Virginia, NE USA 39°28′N 80°08′W
31 P13 Fairmount Indiana, N USA 40°25′N 85°39′W
18 H10 Fairmount New York, NE USA 43°03′N 76°14′W
29 R7 Fairmount North Dakota, N USA 46°02′N 96°36′W
37 S5 Fairplay Colorado, C USA 39°13′N 106°00′W
18 F9 Fairport New York, NE USA 43°06′N 77°26′W
11 O12 Fairview Alberta, W Canada 56°03′N 118°28′W
26 L9 Fairview Oklahoma, C USA 36°16′N 98°29′W
36 L4 Fairview Utah, W USA 39°37′N 111°26′W
35 T6 Fairview Peak ▲ Nevada, W USA 39°13′N 118°09′W
188 H14 Fais atoll Caroline Islands, W Micronesia
149 U8 Faisalābād prev. Lyallpur. Punjab, NE Pakistan 31°26′N 73°06′E
Faisaliya see Fayşalīyah
28 L8 Faith South Dakota, N USA 45°01′N 102°02′W
153 N12 Faizābād Uttar Pradesh, N India 26°46′N 82°08′E
Faizabad/Faizābād see Feyzābād
45 S9 Fajardo E Puerto Rico 18°20′N 65°39′W
139 R9 Fajj, Wādī al dry watercourse S Iraq
140 K4 Fajr, Bi'r well NW Saudi Arabia
191 W10 Fakahina atoll Îles Tuamotu, C French Polynesia
190 L10 Fakaofo Atoll island SE Tokelau
191 U10 Fakarava atoll Îles Tuamotu, C French Polynesia
127 T2 Fakel Udmurtskaya Respublika, NW Russian Federation 57°35′N 53°00′E
97 P19 Fakenham E England, United Kingdom 52°50′N 00°51′E
171 U13 Fakfak Papua, E Indonesia 02°55′S 132°17′E
153 T12 Fakiragrām Assam, NE India 26°22′N 90°15′E
114 M10 Fakiyska Reka SE Bulgaria
95 J24 Fakse Storstrøm, SE Denmark 55°16′N 12°08′E
95 J24 Fakse Bugt bay SE Denmark
95 J24 Fakse Ladeplads Storstrøm, SE Denmark 55°14′N 12°11′E
163 V11 Faku Liaoning, NE China 42°30′N 123°27′E
76 J14 Falaba N Sierra Leone 09°54′N 11°22′W
102 K5 Falaise Calvados, N France 48°52′N 00°12′W
114 H12 Falakró ▲ NE Greece
189 T12 Falalu island Chuuk, C Micronesia
166 L4 Falam Chin State, W Myanmar (Burma) 22°58′N 93°45′E
143 N8 Falāvarjān Eşfahān, C Iran 32°33′N 51°28′E
116 M11 Fălciu Vaslui, E Romania 46°19′N 28°10′E
54 I4 Falcón off. Estado Falcón. ◆ state NW Venezuela
106 J12 Falconara Marittima Marche, C Italy 43°37′N 13°23′E
Falcone, Capo del see Falcone, Punta del
107 A16 Falcone, Punta del var. Capo del Falcone. headland Sardegna, Italy, C Mediterranean Sea 40°57′N 08°12′E
Falcón, Estado see Falcón
11 Y16 Falcon Lake Manitoba, S Canada 49°44′N 95°18′W
Falcon Lake see Falcón, Presa/Falcon Reservoir
41 O7 Falcón, Presa var. Falcon Lake, Falcon Reservoir. ⊠ Mexico/USA see also Falcon Reservoir
Falcón, Presa see Falcon Reservoir
25 Q16 Falcon Reservoir var. Falcon Lake, Presa Falcón. ⊠ Mexico/USA see also Falcón, Presa
Falcon Reservoir see Falcón, Presa
190 L10 Fale island Fakaofo Atoll, SE Tokelau
192 F15 Faleālupo Savai'i, NW Samoa 13°30′S 172°46′W
190 B10 Falefatu island Funafuti Atoll, C Tuvalu
192 G15 Fālelima Savai'i, NW Samoa 13°30′S 172°41′W
95 N18 Falerum Östergötland, S Sweden 58°07′N 16°15′E
Faleshty see Făleşti
116 M9 Făleşti Rus. Faleshty. NW Moldova 47°33′N 27°43′E
25 S15 Falfurrias Texas, SW USA 27°17′N 98°10′W
11 O13 Falher Alberta, W Canada 55°45′N 117°18′W
Falkenau an der Eger see Sokolov
95 J21 Falkenberg Halland, S Sweden 56°55′N 12°30′E
Falkenberg see Niemodlin
Falkenburg in Pommern see Złocieniec
100 N12 Falkensee Brandenburg, NE Germany 52°34′N 13°04′E
96 J12 Falkirk C Scotland, United Kingdom 56°00′N 03°48′W
65 I20 Falkland Escarpment undersea feature SW Atlantic Ocean 50°00′S 45°00′W
63 K24 Falkland Islands var. Falklands, Islas Malvinas. ◇ UK dependent territory SW Atlantic Ocean
47 W14 Falkland Islands island group SW Atlantic Ocean
65 I20 Falkland Plateau var. Argentine Rise. undersea feature SW Atlantic Ocean 51°00′S 50°00′W
Falklands see Falkland Islands
63 M23 Falkland Sound var. Estrecho de San Carlos. strait C Falkland Islands
Falknov nad Ohří see Sokolov
115 H21 Falkonéra island S Greece
95 K18 Falköping Västra Götaland, S Sweden 58°10′N 13°31′E
139 U8 Fallāh Wāsiţ, E Iraq 32°58′N 45°09′E
35 U16 Fallbrook California, W USA 33°22′N 117°15′W
189 U12 Falleallej Pass passage Chuuk Islands, C Micronesia
93 J14 Fällfors Västerbotten, N Sweden 65°07′N 20°46′E
194 I6 Fallières Coast physical region Antarctica
100 I11 Fallingbostel Niedersachsen, NW Germany 52°52′N 09°42′E
33 X9 Fallon Montana, NW USA 46°49′N 105°07′W
35 S5 Fallon Nevada, W USA 39°29′N 118°47′W
19 O12 Fall River Massachusetts, NE USA 41°42′N 71°09′W
27 P6 Fall River Lake ⊠ Kansas, C USA
35 O3 Fall River Mills California, W USA 41°00′N 121°28′W
21 W4 Falls Church Virginia, NE USA 38°53′N 77°11′W
29 S17 Falls City Nebraska, C USA 40°03′N 95°36′W
25 S12 Falls City Texas, SW USA 28°58′N 98°01′W
Falluja see Al Fallūjah
77 S12 Falmey Dosso, SW Niger 12°29′N 02°58′E
45 W10 Falmouth Antigua, Antigua and Barbuda 17°02′N 61°47′W
44 J11 Falmouth W Jamaica 18°28′N 77°39′W
97 H25 Falmouth SW England, United Kingdom 50°08′N 05°04′W
20 M4 Falmouth Kentucky, S USA 38°40′N 84°20′W
19 P13 Falmouth Massachusetts, NE USA 41°31′N 70°36′W
21 W5 Falmouth Virginia, NE USA 38°19′N 77°28′W
189 U12 Falos island Chuuk, C Micronesia
83 E26 False Bay Afr. Valsbaai. bay SW South Africa
155 K17 False Divi Point headland E India 15°46′N 80°43′E
38 M16 False Pass Unimak Island, Alaska, USA 54°52′N 163°15′W
154 P12 False Point headland E India 20°23′N 86°52′E
105 U6 Falset Cataluña, NE Spain 41°08′N 00°49′E
95 I25 Falster island SE Denmark
116 K9 Fălticeni Hung. Falticsén. Suceava, NE Romania 47°27′N 26°20′E
Falticsén see Fălticeni
94 M13 Falun var. Fahlun. Kopparberg, C Sweden 60°36′N 15°36′E
Famagusta see Gazimağusa
Famagusta Bay see Gazimağusa Körfezi
62 I8 Famatina La Rioja, NW Argentina 28°58′S 67°46′W
99 J21 Famenne physical region SE Belgium
113 D22 Fan var. Fani. N Albania
77 X15 Fan ▲ E Nigeria
76 M12 Fana Koulikoro, SW Mali 12°45′N 06°55′W
115 K19 Fána ancient harbor Chíos, SE Greece
189 V13 Fanan island Chuuk, C Micronesia
189 U12 Fanapanges island Chuuk, C Micronesia
115 L20 Fanári, Akrotírio headland Ikaría, Dodekánisa, Greece, Aegean Sea 37°40′N 26°21′E
45 Q13 Fancy Saint Vincent, Saint Vincent and the Grenadines 13°22′N 61°10′W
172 I5 Fandriana Fianarantsoa, SE Madagascar 20°14′S 47°21′E
167 O6 Fang Chiang Mai, NW Thailand 19°56′N 99°14′E
80 E13 Fangak Jonglei, SE Sudan 09°05′N 30°52′E
191 W10 Fangatau atoll Îles Tuamotu, C French Polynesia
191 X12 Fangataufa island Îles Tuamotu, SE French Polynesia
193 V15 Fanga Uta bay S Tonga
161 N7 Fangcheng Henan, C China 33°18′N 113°03′E
Fangcheng see Fangchenggang
160 K15 Fangchenggang var. Fangcheng Gezu Zizhixian; prev. Fangcheng. Guangxi Zhuangzu Zizhiqu, S China 21°49′N 108°21′E
Fangcheng Gezu Zizhixian see Fangchenggang
161 S15 Fangshan S Taiwan 22°19′N 120°41′E
163 X8 Fangzheng Heilongjiang, NE China 45°50′N 128°50′E
119 K16 Fanipal' Rus. Fanipol'. Minskaya Voblasts', C Belarus 53°45′N 27°20′E
Fanipol' see Fanipal'
25 T13 Fannin Texas, SW USA 28°41′N 97°13′W
Fanning Island see Tabuaeran
94 G8 Fannrem Sør-Trøndelag, S Norway 63°16′N 09°48′E
106 I11 Fano anc. Colonia Julia Fanestris, Fanum Fortunae. Marche, C Italy 43°50′N 13°E
95 E23 Fanø island W Denmark
167 R5 Fan Si Pan ▲ N Vietnam 22°18′N 103°36′E
Fanum Fortunae see Fano
Fao see Al Fāw
141 W7 Faq' var. Al Faqa. Dubayy, E United Arab Emirates 24°42′N 55°37′E
Farab see Farap
185 G16 Faraday, Mount ▲ South Island, New Zealand 42°01′S 171°37′E
79 P16 Faradje Orientale, NE Dem. Rep. Congo 03°45′N 29°43′E
Faradofay see Tôlañaro
172 I7 Farafangana Fianarantsoa, SE Madagascar 22°50′S 47°50′E
148 J7 Farāh var. Farah, Fararud. Farāh, W Afghanistan 32°22′N 62°07′E
148 K7 Farāh ◆ province W Afghanistan
148 J7 Farāh Rūd W Afghanistan
188 K7 Farallon de Medinilla island C Northern Mariana Islands
188 J2 Farallon de Pajaros var. Uracas. island N Northern Mariana Islands
76 J14 Faranah Haute-Guinée, S Guinea 10°02′N 10°44′W
146 K12 Farap Rus. Farab. Lebap Welaýaty, NE Turkmenistan 39°15′N 63°32′E
Fararud see Farāh
140 M13 Farasān, Jazā'ir island group SW Saudi Arabia
172 I5 Faratsiho Antananarivo, C Madagascar 19°24′S 46°57′E
188 K15 Faraulep Atoll atoll Caroline Islands, C Micronesia
99 H20 Farciennes Hainaut, S Belgium 50°26′N 04°33′E
105 O14 Fardes S Spain
191 S10 Fare Huahine, W French Polynesia 16°42′S 151°01′W
97 M23 Fareham S England, United Kingdom 50°51′N 01°10′W
39 P11 Farewell Alaska, USA 62°35′N 153°59′W
184 H13 Farewell, Cape headland South Island, New Zealand 40°30′S 172°39′E
Farewell, Cape see Nunap Isua
184 I13 Farewell Spit spit South Island, New Zealand
95 I17 Färgelanda Västra Götaland, S Sweden 58°34′N 11°59′E
Farghona, Wodii/Farghona Valley see Fergana Valley
Farghona Wodiysi see Fergana Valley
23 V8 Fargo Georgia, SE USA 30°42′N 82°33′W
29 R5 Fargo North Dakota, N USA 46°53′N 96°47′W
147 S10 Farg'ona Rus. Fergana; prev. Novyy Margilan. Farg'ona Viloyati, E Uzbekistan 40°28′N 71°44′E
147 R10 Farg'ona Viloyati Rus. Ferganskaya Oblast'. ◆ province E Uzbekistan
29 V10 Faribault Minnesota, N USA 44°18′N 93°16′W
152 J11 Farīdābād Haryāna, N India 28°26′N 77°19′E
152 H8 Farīdkot Punjab, NW India 30°42′N 74°47′E
153 T15 Faridpur Dhaka, C Bangladesh 23°29′N 89°50′E
121 P14 Fārigh, Wādī al N Libya
172 I4 Farihy Alaotra ◎ C Madagascar
94 M11 Färila Gävleborg, C Sweden 61°48′N 15°55′E
104 E9 Farilhões island C Portugal
76 G12 Farim NW Guinea-Bissau 12°30′N 15°09′W
Farish see Forish
141 T11 Fāris, Qalamat well SE Saudi Arabia
95 N21 Färjestaden Kalmar, S Sweden 56°38′N 16°30′E
149 R2 Farkhār Takhār, NE Afghanistan 36°39′N 69°43′E
147 Q14 Farkhor Rus. Parkhar. SW Tajikistan 37°32′N 69°22′E
116 F12 Fârliug prev. Fîrliug, Hung. Furluk. Caraş-Severin, SW Romania 45°21′N 21°55′E
115 M21 Farmakonísi island Dodekánisa, Greece, Aegean Sea
30 M13 Farmer City Illinois, N USA 40°14′N 88°38′W
31 N14 Farmersburg Indiana, N USA 39°14′N 87°21′W
25 U6 Farmersville Texas, SW USA 33°09′N 96°21′W
22 H5 Farmerville Louisiana, S USA 32°46′N 92°24′W
29 X16 Farmington Iowa, C USA 40°37′N 91°43′W
19 Q6 Farmington Maine, NE USA 44°40′N 70°09′W
29 V9 Farmington Minnesota, N USA 44°39′N 93°09′W
27 X6 Farmington Missouri, C USA 37°46′N 90°26′W
19 O9 Farmington New Hampshire, NE USA 43°23′N 71°04′W
37 P9 Farmington New Mexico, SW USA 36°44′N 108°13′W
36 L2 Farmington Utah, W USA 40°58′N 111°53′W
21 W9 Farmville North Carolina, SE USA 35°37′N 77°36′W
21 U6 Farmville Virginia, NE USA 37°17′N 78°25′W
97 N22 Farnborough S England, United Kingdom 51°17′N 00°46′W
97 N22 Farnham S England, United Kingdom 51°13′N 00°49′W
10 J7 Faro Yukon Territory, W Canada 62°15′N 133°30′W
104 G14 Faro Faro, S Portugal 37°01′N 07°56′W
95 Q18 Fårö Gotland, SE Sweden 57°55′N 19°10′E
104 G14 Faro ◆ district S Portugal
78 F13 Faro Cameroon/Nigeria
104 G14 Faro ✕ Faro, S Portugal 37°02′N 08°01′W
Faro, Punta del see Peloro, Capo
95 Q18 Fårösund Gotland, SE Sweden 57°51′N 19°02′E
173 N7 Farquhar Group island group S Seychelles
18 B13 Farrell Pennsylvania, NE USA 41°12′N 80°28′W
152 K11 Farrukhābād Uttar Pradesh, N India 27°24′N 79°34′E
143 P11 Fārs off. Ostān-e Fārs; anc. Persis. ◆ province S Iran
115 F16 Fársala Thessalía, C Greece 39°17′N 22°23′E
143 R4 Fārsīān Golestān, N Iran
Fars, Khalīj-e see Gulf, The
95 G21 Farsø Nordjylland, N Denmark 56°47′N 09°21′E
Fārs, Ostān-e see Fārs
95 D18 Farsund Vest-Agder, S Norway 58°05′N 06°49′E
141 U14 Fartak, Ra's headland E Yemen 15°34′N 52°19′E
60 H13 Fartura, Serra da ▲ S Brazil
Farvel, Kap see Nunap Isua
24 L4 Farwell Texas, SW USA 34°23′N 103°03′W
194 I9 Farwell Island island Antarctica
152 L9 Far Western ◆ zone W Nepal
148 M3 Fāryāb ◆ province N Afghanistan
143 P12 Fasā Fārs, S Iran 28°55′N 53°39′E
141 U12 Fasad, Ramlat desert SW Oman
107 P17 Fasano Puglia, SE Italy 40°50′N 17°21′E
92 L3 Fáskrúdhsfjördhur Austurland, E Iceland 64°55′N 14°01′W
117 O5 Fastiv Rus. Fastov. Kyyivs'ka Oblast', NW Ukraine 50°08′N 29°59′E
97 B22 Fastnet Rock Ir. Carraig Aonair. island SW Ireland
Fastov see Fastiv
190 C9 Fatato island Funafuti Atoll, C Tuvalu
152 H10 Fatehābād Haryāna, N India 29°31′N 75°27′E
152 K12 Fatehgarh Uttar Pradesh, N India 27°22′N 79°38′E
149 U6 Fatehjang Punjab, E Pakistan 33°33′N 72°43′E
152 G11 Fatehpur Rājasthān, N India 27°59′N 74°58′E
152 L13 Fatehpur Uttar Pradesh, N India 25°56′N 80°55′E
126 J7 Fatezh Kurskaya Oblast', W Russian Federation 52°01′N 35°51′E
76 G11 Fatick W Senegal 14°19′N 16°27′W
104 G9 Fátima Santarém, W Portugal 39°37′N 08°39′W
136 M11 Fatsa Ordu, N Turkey 41°02′N 37°31′E
Fatshan see Foshan
190 D12 Fatua, Pointe var. Pointe Nord. headland Île Futuna, S Wallis and Futuna
191 X7 Fatu Hiva island Îles Marquises, NE French Polynesia
Fatunda see Fatundu
79 H21 Fatundu var. Fatunda. Bandundu, W Dem. Rep. Congo 04°08′S 17°13′E
29 O8 Faulkton South Dakota, N USA 45°02′N 99°07′W
116 L13 Făurei prev. Filimon Sîrbu. Brăila, SE Romania 45°05′N 27°15′E
92 G12 Fauske Nordland, C Norway 67°15′N 15°27′E
11 P13 Faust Alberta, W Canada 55°19′N 115°33′W
99 L23 Fauvillers Luxembourg, SE Belgium 49°52′N 05°40′E
107 J24 Favara Sicilia, Italy, C Mediterranean Sea 37°19′N 13°40′E
Faventia see Faenza
107 G23 Favignana, Isola island Isole Egadi, S Italy
12 D8 Fawn Ontario, SE Canada
Faxa Bay see Faxaflói
92 H3 Faxaflói Eng. Faxa Bay. bay W Iceland
78 I7 Faya prev. Faya-Largeau, Largeau. Borkou-Ennedi-Tibesti, N Chad 17°58′N 19°06′E
Faya-Largeau see Faya
187 Q16 Fayaoué Province des Îles Loyauté, C New Caledonia 20°41′S 166°31′E
138 M5 Fayḑāt hill range E Syria
23 O3 Fayette Alabama, S USA 33°40′N 87°49′W
29 X12 Fayette Iowa, C USA 42°50′N 91°48′W
22 J6 Fayette Mississippi, S USA 31°42′N 91°03′W
27 U4 Fayette Missouri, C USA 39°09′N 92°40′W
27 S9 Fayetteville Arkansas, C USA 36°04′N 94°10′W
21 U10 Fayetteville North Carolina, SE USA 35°03′N 78°53′W
20 J10 Fayetteville Tennessee, S USA 35°08′N 86°33′W
25 U11 Fayetteville Texas, SW USA 29°52′N 96°40′W
21 R5 Fayetteville West Virginia, NE USA 38°03′N 81°09′W
141 R4 Faylakah var. Failaka Island. island E Kuwait
139 T10 Fayşalīyah var. Faisaliya. Al Qādisīyah, S Iraq 31°48′N 44°36′E
189 P15 Fayu var. East Fayu. island Hall Islands, C Micronesia
152 G8 Fāzilka Punjab, NW India 30°26′N 74°04′E
Fdérick see Fdérik
76 I6 Fdérik var. Fdérick, Fr. Fort Gouraud. Tiris Zemmour, NW Mauritania 22°40′N 12°41′W
Feabhail, Loch see Foyle, Lough
97 B20 Feale SW Ireland
21 V12 Fear, Cape headland Bald Head Island, North Carolina, SE USA 33°50′N 77°57′W
35 O6 Feather River California, W USA
185 M14 Featherston Wellington, North Island, New Zealand 41°07′S 175°28′E

◆ Country
● Country Capital
◇ Dependent Territory
○ Dependent Territory Capital
◆ Administrative Regions
✕ International Airport
▲ Mountain
▲ Mountain Range
Volcano
River
◎ Lake
⊠ Reservoir

FÉCAMP – FOREST GROVE

102 L3 **Fécamp** Seine-Maritime, N France 49°45´N 00°22´E
Fédala *see* Mohammedia
61 D17 **Federación** Entre Ríos, E Argentina 31°00´S 57°55´W
61 D17 **Federal** Entre Ríos, E Argentina 30°55´S 58°45´W
77 T15 **Federal Capital District** ◆ *capital territory* C Nigeria
Federal Capital Territory *see* Australian Capital Territory
Federal District *see* Distrito Federal
21 Y4 **Federalsburg** Maryland, NE USA 38°41´N 75°46´W
74 M6 **Fedjaj, Chott el** *var.* Chott el Fejaj, Shaṭṭ al Fijāj. *salt lake* C Tunisia
94 B13 **Fedje** *island* S Norway
144 M7 **Fedorovka** Kostanay, N Kazakhstan 51°12´N 52°00´E
127 U6 **Fedorovka** Respublika Bashkortostan, W Russian Federation 53°09´N 55°07´E
Fëdory *see* Fyadory
117 U11 **Fedotova Kosa** *spit* SE Ukraine
189 V13 **Fefan** *atoll* Chuuk Islands, C Micronesia
111 O21 **Fehérgyarmat** Szabolcs-Szatmár-Bereg, E Hungary 47°59´N 22°29´E
Fehér-Körös *see* Crişul Alb
Fehértemplom *see* Bela Crkva
Fehérvölgy *see* Albac
100 L7 **Fehmarn** *island* N Germany
95 H25 **Fehmarn Belt** *Dan.* Femern Bælt, *Ger.* Fehmarnbelt. *strait* Denmark /Germany *see also* Femern Bælt
Fehmarnbelt *see* Fehmarn Belt/Femer Bælt
109 X8 **Fehring** Steiermark, SE Austria 46°56´N 16°00´E
59 B15 **Feijó** Acre, W Brazil 08°07´S 70°27´W
184 M12 **Feilding** Manawatu-Wanganui, North Island, New Zealand 40°15´S 175°34´E
Feira *see* Feira de Santana
59 O17 **Feira de Santana** *var.* Feira. Bahia, E Brazil 12°17´S 38°53´W
109 X7 **Feistritz** ∽ SE Austria
Feistritz *see* Ilirska Bistrica
161 P8 **Feixi** *var.* Shangpai; *prev.* Shangpaihe. Anhui, E China 31°40´N 117°08´E
Fejaj, Chott el *see* Fedjaj, Chott el
111 I23 **Fejér** *off.* Fejér Megye. ◆ *county* W Hungary
Fejér Megye *see* Fejér
95 I24 **Fejø** *island* SE Denmark
136 K15 **Feke** Adana, S Turkey 37°49´N 35°55´E
Feketehalom *see* Codlea
Fekete-Körös *see* Crişul Negru
105 Y9 **Felanitx** Mallorca, Spain, W Mediterranean Sea 39°28´N 03°08´E
109 T3 **Feldaist** ∽ N Austria
109 W8 **Feldbach** Steiermark, SE Austria 46°58´N 15°53´E
101 F24 **Feldberg** ▲ SW Germany 47°52´N 08°01´E
116 J12 **Feldioara** *Ger.* Marienburg, *Hung.* Földvár. Braşov, C Romania 45°49´N 25°36´E
108 I7 **Feldkirch** *anc.* Clunia. Vorarlberg, W Austria 47°15´N 09°38´E
109 S9 **Feldkirchen in Kärnten** *Slvn.* Trg. Kärnten, S Austria 46°42´N 14°01´E
Félegyháza *see* Kiskunfélegyháza
192 H16 **Feleolo** ✈ (Āpia) Upolu, C Samoa 13°49´S 171°59´W
104 H6 **Felgueiras** Porto, N Portugal 41°22´N 08°12´W
Felicitas Julia *see* Lisboa
172 J16 **Félicité** *island* Inner Islands, NE Seychelles
151 K20 **Felidhu Atoll** *atoll* C Maldives
41 Y13 **Felipe Carrillo Puerto** Quintana Roo, SE Mexico 19°34´N 88°02´W
97 Q21 **Felixstowe** E England, United Kingdom 51°58´N 01°20´E
103 N11 **Felletin** Creuse, C France 45°53´N 02°12´E
Fellin *see* Viljandi
Felsőbánya *see* Baia Sprie
Felsőmuzslya *see* Mužlja
Felsővisó *see* Vişeu de Sus
35 N10 **Felton** California, W USA 37°03´N 122°04´W
106 H7 **Feltre** Veneto, NE Italy 46°01´N 11°55´E
95 H25 **Femer Bælt** *Dan.* Fehmarn Belt, *Ger.* Fehmarnbelt. *strait* Denmark/Germany *see also* Fehmarn Belt
95 I24 **Femø** *island* SE Denmark
94 I10 **Femunden** ◎ S Norway
104 H2 **Fene** Galicia, NW Spain 43°28´N 08°10´W
14 I14 **Fenelon Falls** Ontario, SE Canada 44°34´N 78°43´W
189 U13 **Feneppi** *atoll* Chuuk Islands, C Micronesia
137 O11 **Fener Burnu** *headland* N Turkey 41°07´N 39°26´E
Fénérive *see* Fenoarivo Atsinanana
115 J14 **Fengári** ▲ Samothráki, E Greece 40°27´N 25°37´E
163 V13 **Fengcheng** *var.* Feng-cheng, Fenghwangcheng. Liaoning, NE China 40°28´N 124°01´E
Fengcheng *see* Lianjiang
Feng-cheng *see* Fengcheng
160 K11 **Fenggang** *var.* Longquan. Guizhou, S China 27°57´N 107°42´E
161 S9 **Fenghua** Zhejiang, SE China 29°40´N 121°25´E
Fenghwangcheng *see* Fengcheng
Fengjiaba *see* Wangcang
160 L9 **Fengjie** *var.* Yong'an. Sichuan, C China 31°06´N 109°30´E
160 M14 **Fengkai** *var.* Jiangkou. Guangdong, S China 23°26´N 111°28´E
161 T13 **Fenglin** *Jap.* Hōrin. C Taiwan 23°52´N 121°30´E
161 P1 **Fengning** *prev.* Dagezhen. Hebei, E China 41°12´N 116°37´E
160 E13 **Fengqing** *var.* Fengshan. Yunnan, SW China 24°38´N 99°54´E
161 O6 **Fengqiu** Henan, C China 35°02´N 114°24´E
161 Q2 **Fengrun** Hebei, E China 39°50´N 118°10´E
Fengshan *see* Luoyuan, Fujian, China
Fengshan *see* Fengqing, Yunnan, China
163 T4 **Fengshui Shan** ▲ NE China 52°20´N 123°22´E
161 P14 **Fengshun** Guangdong, S China 23°51´N 116°11´E
Fengtien *see* Liaoning, China
Fengtien *see* Shenyang, China
160 J7 **Fengxian** *var.* Feng Xian; *prev.* Shuangshipu. Shaanxi, C China 33°50´N 106°33´E
Feng Xian *see* Fengxian
Fengxiang *see* Luobei
Fengyizhen *see* Maoxian
163 P13 **Fengzhen** Nei Mongol Zizhiqu, N China 40°25´N 113°09´E
160 M6 **Fen He** ∽ C China
153 V15 **Feni** Chittagong, E Bangladesh 23°00´N 91°24´E
186 I6 **Feni Islands** *island group* NE Papua New Guinea
38 H17 **Fenimore Pass** *strait* Aleutian Islands, Alaska, USA
84 B9 **Feni Ridge** *undersea feature* N Atlantic Ocean 53°45´N 18°00´W
Fennern *see* Vändra
30 J9 **Fennimore** Wisconsin, N USA 42°58´N 90°39´W
172 J4 **Fenoarivo Atsinanana** *Fr.* Fénérive. Toamasina, E Madagascar 20°52´S 46°52´E
95 I24 **Fensmark** Storstrøm, SE Denmark 55°17´N 11°48´E
97 O19 **Fens, The** *wetland* E England, United Kingdom
31 R9 **Fenton** Michigan, N USA 42°48´N 83°42´W
190 K10 **Fenua Fala** *island* SE Tokelau
190 F12 **Fenuafo'ou, Île** *island* E Wallis and Futuna
190 L10 **Fenua Loa** *island* Fakaofo Atoll, E Tokelau
160 M4 **Fenyang** Shanxi, C China 37°14´N 111°40´E
117 U13 **Feodosiya** *var.* Kefe, *It.* Kaffa; *anc.* Theodosia. Respublika Krym, S Ukraine 45°03´N 35°24´E
94 I10 **Feragen** ◎ S Norway
74 L5 **Fer, Cap de** *headland* NE Algeria 37°05´N 07°10´E
31 O16 **Ferdinand** Indiana, N USA 38°13´N 86°51´W
Ferdinand *see* Montana, Bulgaria
Ferdinand *see* Mihail Kogălniceanu, Romania
Ferdinandsberg *see* Oţelu Roşu
143 T7 **Ferdows** *var.* Firdaus; *prev.* Tūn. Khorāsān-Razavī, E Iran 34°00´N 58°09´E
103 Q5 **Fère-Champenoise** Marne, N France 48°45´N 03°59´E
Ferencz-József Csúcs *see* Gerlachovský štít
107 J16 **Ferentino** Lazio, C Italy 41°40´N 13°16´E
114 L13 **Féres** Anatolikí Makedonía kai Thrakí, NE Greece 40°54´N 26°12´E
Fergana *see* Farg'ona
147 S10 **Fergana Valley** *var.* Farghona Valley, *Rus.* Ferganskaya Dolina, *Taj.* Wodii Farghona, *Uzb.* Farghona Wodiysi. *basin* Tajikistan/Uzbekistan
Ferganskaya Dolina *see* Fergana Valley
Ferganskaya Oblast' *see* Farg'ona Viloyati
147 U9 **Ferganskiy Khrebet** ▲▲ C Kyrgyzstan
14 F15 **Fergus** Ontario, S Canada 43°42´N 80°22´W
29 S6 **Fergus Falls** Minnesota, N USA 46°15´N 96°02´W
186 G9 **Fergusson Island** *var.* Kaluwawa. *island* SE Papua New Guinea
111 K22 **Ferihegy** ✈ (Budapest) Budapest, C Hungary 47°25´N 19°13´E
113 N17 **Ferizaj** *Serb.* Uroševac. C Kosovo 42°23´N 21°09´E
77 N14 **Ferkessédougou** N Ivory Coast 09°36´N 05°12´W
109 T10 **Ferlach** *Slvn.* Borovlje. Kärnten, S Austria 46°31´N 14°18´E
97 E16 **Fermanagh** *cultural region* SW Northern Ireland, United Kingdom
106 J13 **Fermo** *anc.* Firmum Picenum. Marche, C Italy 43°09´N 13°44´E
104 J6 **Fermoselle** Castilla-León, N Spain 41°19´N 06°24´W
97 D20 **Fermoy** *Ir.* Mainistir Fhear Maí. SW Ireland 52°08´N 08°16´W
23 W8 **Fernandina Beach** Amelia Island, Florida, SE USA 30°40´N 81°27´W
57 A17 **Fernandina, Isla** *var.* Narborough Island. *island* Galapagos Islands, Ecuador, E Pacific Ocean
47 Y5 **Fernando de Noronha** *island* E Brazil
Fernando Po/Fernando Póo *see* Bioco, Isla de
60 J7 **Fernandópolis** São Paulo, S Brazil 20°18´S 50°13´W
104 M13 **Fernán Núñez** Andalucía, S Spain 37°40´N 04°44´W
83 Q14 **Fernão Veloso, Baia de** *bay* NE Mozambique
34 K3 **Ferndale** California, W USA 40°34´N 124°16´W
32 H6 **Ferndale** Washington, NW USA 48°51´N 122°35´W
11 P17 **Fernie** British Columbia, SW Canada 49°30´N 115°00´W
35 R5 **Fernley** Nevada, W USA 39°35´N 119°15´W
Ferozepore *see* Firozpur
107 N18 **Ferrandina** Basilicata, S Italy 40°30´N 16°25´E
106 G9 **Ferrara** *anc.* Forum Alieni. Emilia-Romagna, N Italy 44°50´N 11°36´E
120 F9 **Ferrat, Cap** *headland* NW Algeria 35°52´N 00°24´W
107 D20 **Ferrato, Capo** *headland* Sardegna, Italy, C Mediterranean Sea 39°18´N 09°37´E
104 G12 **Ferreira do Alentejo** Beja, S Portugal 38°04´N 08°06´W
56 B11 **Ferreñafe** Lambayeque, W Peru 06°42´S 79°45´W
108 C12 **Ferret** Valais, SW Switzerland 45°57´N 07°04´E
102 I13 **Ferret, Cap** *headland* W France 44°37´N 01°15´W
22 I6 **Ferriday** Louisiana, S USA 31°37´N 91°33´W
Ferro *see* Hierro
107 D16 **Ferro, Capo** *headland* Sardegna, Italy, C Mediterranean Sea 41°09´N 09°31´E
104 H2 **Ferrol** *var.* El Ferrol; *prev.* El Ferrol del Caudillo. Galicia, NW Spain 43°29´N 08°14´W
56 B12 **Ferrol, Península de** *peninsula* W Peru
36 M5 **Ferron** Utah, W USA 39°05´N 111°07´W
21 S7 **Ferrum** Virginia, NE USA 36°54´N 80°01´W
23 O8 **Ferry Pass** Florida, SE USA 30°30´N 87°12´W
Ferryville *see* Menzel Bourguiba
29 S4 **Fertile** Minnesota, N USA 47°32´N 96°16´W
Fertő *see* Neusiedler See
98 L5 **Ferwerd** *Fris.* Ferwert. Friesland, N Netherlands 53°21´N 05°47´E
Ferwert *see* Ferwerd
74 G6 **Fès** *Eng.* Fez. N Morocco 34°06´N 04°57´W
79 I22 **Feshi** Bandundu, SW Dem. Rep. Congo 06°08´S 18°12´E
29 O4 **Fessenden** North Dakota, N USA 47°36´N 99°37´W
Festenberg *see* Twardogóra
27 X5 **Festus** Missouri, C USA 38°13´N 90°24´W
116 M14 **Feteşti** Ialomiţa, SE Romania 44°22´N 27°51´E
136 D17 **Fethiye** Muğla, SW Turkey 36°37´N 29°08´E
96 M1 **Fetlar** *island* NE Scotland, United Kingdom
95 I15 **Fetsund** Akershus, S Norway 59°55´N 11°03´E
12 L5 **Feuilles, Lac aux** ◎ Québec, E Canada
12 L5 **Feuilles, Rivière aux** ∽ Québec, E Canada
99 M23 **Feulen** Diekirch, C Luxembourg 49°52´N 06°03´E
103 Q11 **Feurs** Loire, E France 45°44´N 04°14´E
95 F18 **Fevik** Aust-Agder, S Norway 58°22´N 08°40´E
123 R13 **Fevral'sk** Amurskaya Oblast', SE Russian Federation 52°25´N 131°06´E
149 S2 **Feyzābād** *var.* Faizabad, Faizābād, Feyzabad, Fyzabad. Badakhshān, NE Afghanistan 37°06´N 70°34´E
Feyzābād *see* Feyzābād
Fez *see* Fès
75 Q10 **Fezzan** ◆ *cultural region* C Libya
97 J19 **Ffestiniog** NW Wales, United Kingdom 52°55´N 03°54´W
Fhóid Duibh, Cuan an *see* Blacksod Bay
62 I8 **Fiambalá** Catamarca, NW Argentina 27°45´S 67°37´W
172 I6 **Fianarantsoa** Fianarantsoa, C Madagascar 21°27´S 47°05´E
172 H6 **Fianarantsoa** ◆ *province* SE Madagascar
78 G12 **Fianga** Mayo-Kébbi, SW Chad 09°57´N 15°09´E
Ficce *see* Fichē
80 J12 **Fichē** *It.* Ficce. Oromīya, C Ethiopia 09°48´N 38°43´E
101 N17 **Fichtelberg** ▲ Czech Republic/Germany 50°26´N 12°57´E
101 M18 **Fichtelgebirge** ▲▲ SE Germany
101 M19 **Fichtelnaab** ∽ SE Germany
106 E9 **Fidenza** Emilia-Romagna, N Italy 44°52´N 10°04´E
113 K21 **Fier** *var.* Fieri. Fier, SW Albania 40°44´N 19°34´E
113 K21 **Fier** ◆ *district* W Albania
Fieri *see* Fier
Fierza *see* Fierzë
113 L17 **Fierzë** *var.* Fierza. Shkodër, N Albania 42°15´N 20°02´E
113 L17 **Fierzës, Liqeni i** ⊠ N Albania
108 F10 **Fiesch** Valais, SW Switzerland 46°25´N 08°09´E
106 G11 **Fiesole** Toscana, C Italy 43°50´N 11°18´E
138 G12 **Fīfah** At Ṭafīlah, W Jordan 30°55´N 35°25´E
96 K11 **Fife** *var.* Kingdom of Fife. *cultural region* E Scotland, United Kingdom
Fife, Kingdom of *see* Fife
96 K11 **Fife Ness** *headland* E Scotland, United Kingdom 56°16´N 02°35´W
Fifteen Twenty Fracture Zone *see* Barracuda Fracture Zone
103 N13 **Figeac** Lot, S France 44°37´N 02°01´E
95 N19 **Figeholm** Kalmar, SE Sweden 57°12´N 16°34´E
Figig *see* Figuig
83 J18 **Figtree** Matabeleland South, SW Zimbabwe 20°24´S 28°21´E
104 F8 **Figueira da Foz** Coimbra, W Portugal 40°09´N 08°51´W
105 X4 **Figueres** Cataluña, E Spain 42°16´N 02°57´E
74 H7 **Figuig** *var.* Figig. E Morocco 32°09´N 01°13´W
Fijāj, Shaṭṭ al *see* Fedjaj, Chott el
187 Y15 **Fiji** *off.* Sovereign Democratic Republic of Fiji, *Fij.* Viti. ◆ *republic* SW Pacific Ocean
192 K9 **Fiji** *island group* SW Pacific Ocean
175 Q8 **Fiji Plate** *tectonic feature*
Fiji, Sovereign Democratic Republic of *see* Fiji
105 P14 **Filabres, Sierra de los** ▲▲ SE Spain
83 K18 **Filabusi** Matabeleland South, S Zimbabwe 20°34´S 29°20´E
42 K13 **Filadelfia** Guanacaste, W Costa Rica 10°28´N 85°33´W
111 K20 **Fil'akovo** *Hung.* Fülek. Banskobystrický Kraj, C Slovakia 48°15´N 19°53´E
195 N5 **Filchner Ice Shelf** *ice shelf* Antarctica
14 J11 **Fildegrand** ∽ Québec, SE Canada
33 O15 **Filer** Idaho, NW USA 42°34´N 114°36´W
Filevo *see* Vŭrbitsa
116 H14 **Filiaşi** Dolj, SW Romania 44°32´N 23°31´E
115 B16 **Filiátes** Ípeiros, W Greece 39°38´N 20°16´E
115 D21 **Filiatrá** Pelopónnisos, S Greece 37°09´N 21°35´E
107 K22 **Filicudi, Isola** *island* Isole Eolie, S Italy
141 Y10 **Filim** E Oman 20°37´N 58°11´E
Filimon Sîrbu *see* Făurei
77 S11 **Filingué** Tillabéri, W Niger 14°21´N 03°22´E
Filiouri *see* Líssos
114 I13 **Filippoi** *anc.* Philippi. *site of ancient city* Anatolikí Makedonía kai Thrakí, NE Greece
95 L15 **Filipstad** Värmland, C Sweden 59°44´N 14°10´E
108 I9 **Filisur** Graubünden, S Switzerland 46°40´N 09°43´E
94 E12 **Fillefjell** ▲▲ S Norway
35 R14 **Fillmore** California, W USA 34°23´N 118°56´W
36 K5 **Fillmore** Utah, W USA 38°57´N 112°19´W
14 J10 **Fils, Lac du** ◎ Québec, SE Canada
Filyos Çayı *see* Yenice Çayı
195 Q1 **Fimbulisen** *ice shelf* Antarctica
195 Q2 **Fimbulheimen** *physical region* Antarctica
106 G9 **Finale Emilia** Emilia-Romagna, C Italy 44°50´N 11°17´E
106 C10 **Finale Ligure** Liguria, NW Italy 44°11´N 08°22´E
105 P14 **Fiñana** Andalucía, S Spain 37°09´N 02°47´W
21 S6 **Fincastle** Virginia, NE USA 37°30´N 79°54´W
99 M25 **Findel** ✈ (Luxembourg) Luxembourg, C Luxembourg 49°39´N 06°16´E
96 J9 **Findhorn** ∽ N Scotland, United Kingdom
31 R12 **Findlay** Ohio, N USA 41°02´N 83°40´W
18 G11 **Finger Lakes** ◎ New York, NE USA
83 L14 **Fingoè** Tete, NW Mozambique 15°10´S 31°51´E
136 E17 **Finike** Antalya, SW Turkey 36°18´N 30°08´E
102 F6 **Finistère** ◆ *department* NW France
186 D7 **Finisterre Range** ▲▲ N Papua New Guinea
181 Q8 **Finke** Northern Territory, N Australia 25°37´S 134°35´E
109 S10 **Finkenstein** Kärnten, S Austria 46°34´N 13°53´E
189 Y15 **Finkol, Mount** *var.* Mount Crozer. ▲ Kosrae, E Micronesia 05°18´N 163°00´E
93 L17 **Finland** *off.* Republic of Finland, *Fin.* Suomen Tasavalta, Suomi. ◆ *republic* N Europe
124 F12 **Finland, Gulf of** *Est.* Soome Laht, *Fin.* Suomenlahti, *Ger.* Finnischer Meerbusen, *Rus.* Finskiy Zaliv, *Swe.* Finska Viken. *gulf* E Baltic Sea
Finland, Republic of *see* Finland
10 L11 **Finlay** ∽ British Columbia, W Canada
183 O10 **Finley** New South Wales, SE Australia 35°41´S 145°33´E
29 Q4 **Finley** North Dakota, N USA 47°30´N 97°50´W
Finnischer Meerbusen *see* Finland, Gulf of
92 K9 **Finnmark** ◆ *county* N Norway
92 K9 **Finnmarksvidda** *physical region* N Norway
92 I9 **Finnsnes** Troms, N Norway 69°16´N 18°00´E
186 E7 **Finschhafen** Morobe, C Papua New Guinea 06°35´S 147°51´E
94 E13 **Finse** Hordaland, S Norway 60°35´N 07°33´E
Finska Viken/Finskiy Zaliv *see* Finland, Gulf of
95 M17 **Finspång** Östergötland, S Sweden 58°42´N 15°45´E
108 F10 **Finsteraarhorn** ▲ S Switzerland 46°33´N 08°07´E
101 O14 **Finsterwalde** Brandenburg, E Germany 51°38´N 13°43´E
185 A23 **Fiordland** *physical region* South Island, New Zealand
106 E9 **Fiorenzuola d'Arda** Emilia-Romagna, C Italy 44°57´N 09°53´E
Firat Nehri *see* Euphrates
Firdaus *see* Ferdows
18 M14 **Fire Island** *island* New York, NE USA
106 G11 **Firenze** *Eng.* Florence; *anc.* Florentia. Toscana, C Italy 43°47´N 11°15´E
106 G10 **Firenzuola** Toscana, C Italy 44°07´N 11°22´E
14 C6 **Fire River** Ontario, S Canada 48°46´N 83°34´W
Fîrliug *see* Fârliug
61 B19 **Firmat** Santa Fe, C Argentina 33°29´S 61°29´W
103 Q12 **Firminy** Loire, E France 45°22´N 04°18´E
Firmum Picenum *see* Fermo
152 J12 **Fīrozābād** Uttar Pradesh, N India 27°09´N 78°24´E
152 G8 **Fīrozpur** *var.* Ferozepore. Punjab, NW India 30°55´N 74°38´E
First State *see* Delaware
143 O12 **Fīrūzābād** Fārs, S Iran 28°51´N 52°35´E
Fischamend *see* Fischamend Markt
109 Y4 **Fischamend Markt** *var.* Fischamend. Niederösterreich, NE Austria 48°08´N 16°37´E
109 W6 **Fischbacher Alpen** ▲▲ E Austria
Fischhausen *see* Primorsk
83 D21 **Fish** *var.* Vis. ∽ S Namibia
83 F24 **Fish** *Afr.* Vis. ∽ SW South Africa
11 X15 **Fisher Branch** Manitoba, S Canada 51°09´N 97°34´W
11 X15 **Fisher River** Manitoba, S Canada 51°25´N 97°23´W
19 N13 **Fishers Island** *island* New York, NE USA
37 U8 **Fishers Peak** ▲ Colorado, C USA 37°06´N 104°27´W
9 P9 **Fisher Strait** *strait* Nunavut, N Canada
97 H21 **Fishguard** *Wel.* Abergwaun. SW Wales, United Kingdom 51°59´N 04°49´W
19 R2 **Fish River Lake** ◎ Maine, NE USA
194 K6 **Fiske, Cape** *headland* Antarctica 74°27´S 60°28´W
103 P4 **Fismes** Marne, N France 49°19´N 03°41´E
104 F3 **Fisterra, Cabo** *headland* NW Spain 42°53´N 09°16´W
19 N11 **Fitchburg** Massachusetts, NE USA 42°34´N 71°48´W
96 L3 **Fitful Head** *headland* NE Scotland, United Kingdom 59°57´N 01°24´W
95 C14 **Fitjar** Hordaland, S Norway 59°55´N 05°19´E
192 H16 **Fito, Mauga** ▲ Upolu, C Samoa 13°57´S 171°42´W
23 U6 **Fitzgerald** Georgia, SE USA 31°42´N 83°15´W
180 M5 **Fitzroy Crossing** Western Australia 18°10´S 125°40´E
63 G21 **Fitzroy, Monte** *var.* Cerro Chaltel. ▲ S Argentina 49°18´S 73°06´W
181 Y8 **Fitzroy River** ∽ Queensland, E Australia
180 L5 **Fitzroy River** ∽ Western Australia
14 E12 **Fitzwilliam Island** *island* Ontario, S Canada
107 J15 **Fiuggi** Lazio, C Italy 41°47´N 13°16´E
Fiume *see* Rijeka
107 H15 **Fiumicino** Lazio, C Italy 41°46´N 12°13´E
Fiumicino *see* Leonardo da Vinci
106 E10 **Fivizzano** Toscana, C Italy 44°13´N 10°06´E
79 O21 **Fizi** Sud-Kivu, E Dem. Rep. Congo 04°15´S 28°57´E
Fizuli *see* Füzuli
92 I11 **Fjällåsen** Norrbotten, N Sweden 67°31´N 20°08´E
95 G20 **Fjerritslev** Nordjylland, N Denmark 57°06´N 09°17´E
F.J.S. *see* Franz Josef Strauss
95 L16 **Fjugesta** Örebro, C Sweden 59°10´N 14°50´E
Fladstrand *see* Frederikshavn
37 V5 **Flagler** Colorado, C USA 39°17´N 103°04´W
23 X10 **Flagler Beach** Florida, SE USA 29°28´N 81°07´W
36 L11 **Flagstaff** Arizona, SW USA 35°12´N 111°39´W
65 H24 **Flagstaff Bay** *bay* N Saint Helena, C Atlantic Ocean
19 P5 **Flagstaff Lake** ◎ Maine, NE USA
94 E13 **Flåm** Sogn Og Fjordane, S Norway 60°51´N 07°06´E
15 O8 **Flamand** ∽ Québec, SE Canada
30 J5 **Flambeau River** ∽ Wisconsin, N USA
97 O16 **Flamborough Head** *headland* E England, United Kingdom 54°06´N 00°03´W
100 N13 **Fläming** *hill range* NE Germany
16 H8 **Flaming Gorge Reservoir** ⊠ Utah/Wyoming, NW USA
99 B18 **Flanders** *Dut.* Vlaanderen, *Fr.* Flandre. *cultural region* Belgium/France
Flandre *see* Flanders
29 R10 **Flandreau** South Dakota, N USA 44°03´N 96°36´W
96 D6 **Flannan Isles** *island group* NW Scotland, United Kingdom
28 M6 **Flasher** North Dakota, N USA 46°25´N 101°12´W
93 G15 **Flåsjön** ◎ N Sweden
39 O11 **Flat** Alaska, USA 62°27´N 158°00´W
92 H1 **Flateyri** Vestfirdhir, NW Iceland 66°03´N 23°28´W
33 P8 **Flathead Lake** ◎ Montana, NW USA
173 Y15 **Flat Island** *Fr.* Île Plate. *island* N Mauritius
25 T11 **Flatonia** Texas, SW USA 29°41´N 97°06´W
185 M14 **Flat Point** *headland* North Island, New Zealand 41°12´S 176°03´E
27 X6 **Flat River** Missouri, C USA 37°51´N 90°31´W
31 P8 **Flat River** ∽ Michigan, N USA
31 P14 **Flatrock River** ∽ Indiana, N USA
32 E6 **Flattery, Cape** *headland* Washington, NW USA 48°22´N 124°43´W
64 B12 **Flatts Village** *var.* The Flatts Village. C Bermuda 32°19´N 64°44´W
108 H7 **Flawil** Sankt Gallen, NE Switzerland 47°25´N 09°12´E
97 N22 **Fleet** S England, United Kingdom 51°16´N 00°50´W
97 K16 **Fleetwood** NW England, United Kingdom 53°55´N 03°02´W
18 H15 **Fleetwood** Pennsylvania, NE USA 40°27´N 75°49´W
95 D18 **Flekkefjord** Vest-Agder, S Norway 58°17´N 06°40´E
21 N5 **Flemingsburg** Kentucky, S USA 38°26´N 83°43´W
18 J15 **Flemington** New Jersey, NE USA 40°30´N 74°51´W
64 I7 **Flemish Cap** *undersea feature* NW Atlantic Ocean 47°00´N 45°00´W
95 N16 **Flen** Södermanland, C Sweden 59°04´N 16°39´E
100 I6 **Flensburg** Schleswig-Holstein, N Germany 54°47´N 09°26´E
100 J6 **Flensburger Förde** *inlet* Denmark/Germany
102 K5 **Flers** Orne, N France 48°45´N 00°34´W
95 C14 **Flesland** ✈ (Bergen) Hordaland, S Norway 60°18´N 05°15´E
Flessingue *see* Vlissingen
21 P10 **Fletcher** North Carolina, SE USA 35°24´N 82°29´W
31 R6 **Fletcher Pond** ◎ Michigan, N USA
102 L15 **Fleurance** Gers, S France 43°50´N 00°39´E
108 B8 **Fleurier** Neuchâtel, W Switzerland 46°55´N 06°37´E
99 H20 **Fleurus** Hainaut, S Belgium 50°28´N 04°33´E
103 N7 **Fleury-les-Aubrais** Loiret, C France 47°55´N 01°55´E
98 K10 **Flevoland** ◆ *province* C Netherlands
Flickertail State *see* North Dakota
108 H9 **Flims** Glarus, NE Switzerland 46°50´N 09°16´E
182 F8 **Flinders Island** *island* Investigator Group, South Australia
183 P14 **Flinders Island** *island* Furneaux Group, Tasmania, SE Australia
182 I6 **Flinders Ranges** ▲▲ South Australia
181 U5 **Flinders River** ∽ Queensland, NE Australia
11 V13 **Flin Flon** Manitoba, C Canada 54°47´N 101°51´W
97 K18 **Flint** NE Wales, United Kingdom 53°15´N 03°10´W
31 R9 **Flint** Michigan, N USA 43°01´N 83°41´W
97 J18 **Flint** *cultural region* NE Wales, United Kingdom
27 O7 **Flint Hills** *hill range* Kansas, C USA
191 Y6 **Flint Island** *island* Line Islands, E Kiribati
23 S4 **Flint River** ∽ Georgia, SE USA
31 R9 **Flint River** ∽ Michigan, N USA
189 X12 **Flipper Point** *headland* C Wake Island 19°18´N 166°37´E
94 I13 **Flisa** Hedmark, S Norway 60°36´N 12°02´E
94 I13 **Flisa** ∽ S Norway
122 J5 **Flissingskiy, Mys** *headland* Novaya Zemlya, NW Russian Federation 76°43´N 69°01´E
Flitsch *see* Bovec
105 U6 **Flix** Cataluña, NE Spain 41°13´N 00°32´E
95 J19 **Floda** Västra Götaland, S Sweden 57°47´N 12°20´E
101 O16 **Flöha** ∽ E Germany
25 O4 **Flomot** Texas, SW USA 34°13´N 100°58´W
29 V5 **Floodwood** Minnesota, N USA 46°55´N 92°55´W
30 M15 **Flora** Illinois, N USA 38°40´N 88°29´W
103 P14 **Florac** Lozère, S France 44°18´N 03°35´E
23 Q8 **Florala** Alabama, S USA 31°00´N 86°19´W
103 S4 **Florange** Moselle, NE France 49°21´N 06°06´E
Floreana, Isla *see* Santa María, Isla
23 O2 **Florence** Alabama, S USA 34°48´N 87°40´W
36 L14 **Florence** Arizona, SW USA 33°01´N 111°23´W
37 T6 **Florence** Colorado, C USA 38°20´N 105°06´W
27 O5 **Florence** Kansas, C USA 38°13´N 96°56´W
20 M4 **Florence** Kentucky, S USA 39°00´N 84°37´W
32 E13 **Florence** Oregon, NW USA 43°58´N 124°06´W
21 T12 **Florence** South Carolina, SE USA 34°12´N 79°44´W
25 S9 **Florence** Texas, SW USA 30°50´N 97°47´W
Florence *see* Firenze
54 E13 **Florencia** Caquetá, S Colombia 01°37´N 75°37´W
99 H21 **Florennes** Namur, S Belgium 50°15´N 04°36´E
Florentia *see* Firenze
63 J18 **Florentino Ameghino, Embalse** ⊠ S Argentina
99 J24 **Florenville** Luxembourg, SE Belgium 49°42´N 05°19´E
42 E3 **Flores** Petén, N Guatemala 16°55´N 89°56´W
61 E19 **Flores** ◆ *department* S Uruguay
171 O16 **Flores** *island* Nusa Tenggara, C Indonesia
64 M1 **Flores** *island* Azores, Portugal, NE Atlantic Ocean
Floreshty *see* Floreşti
Flores, Lago de *see* Petén Itzá, Lago
Flores, Laut *see* Flores Sea
171 N15 **Flores Sea** *Ind.* Laut Flores. *sea* C Indonesia
116 M8 **Floreşti** *Rus.* Floreshty. N Moldova 47°52´N 28°19´E
25 S12 **Floresville** Texas, SW USA 29°10´N 98°10´W
59 N14 **Floriano** Piauí, E Brazil 06°45´S 43°00´W
61 K14 **Florianópolis** *prev.* Destêrro. *state capital* Santa Catarina, S Brazil 27°35´S 48°32´W
44 G6 **Florida** Camagüey, C Cuba 21°32´N 78°14´W
61 F19 **Florida** Florida, S Uruguay 34°04´S 56°14´W
61 F19 **Florida** ◆ *department* S Uruguay
23 U9 **Florida** *off.* State of Florida, *also known as* Peninsular State, Sunshine State. ◆ *state* SE USA
23 Y17 **Florida Bay** *bay* Florida, SE USA
54 G8 **Floridablanca** Santander, N Colombia 07°04´N 73°06´W
23 Y17 **Florida Keys** *island group* Florida, SE USA
37 Q16 **Florida Mountains** ▲▲ New Mexico, SW USA
64 D10 **Florida, Straits of** *strait* Atlantic Ocean/Gulf of Mexico
114 D13 **Flórina** *var.* Phlórina. Dytikí Makedonía, N Greece 40°48´N 21°26´E
27 X4 **Florissant** Missouri, C USA 38°47´N 90°19´W
94 C11 **Florø** Sogn Og Fjordane, S Norway 61°36´N 05°04´E
115 L22 **Floúda, Akrotírio** *headland* Astypálaia, Kykládes, Greece, Aegean Sea 36°38´N 26°23´E
21 S7 **Floyd** Virginia, NE USA 36°55´N 80°22´W
25 N4 **Floydada** Texas, SW USA 33°58´N 101°20´W
Flúela Wisshorn *see* Weisshorn
98 K7 **Fluessen** ◎ N Netherlands
105 S5 **Flúmen** ∽ NE Spain
107 C20 **Flumendosa** ∽ Sardegna, Italy, C Mediterranean Sea
31 R9 **Flushing** Michigan, N USA 43°03´N 83°51´W
Flushing *see* Vlissingen
25 O6 **Fluvanna** Texas, SW USA 32°54´N 101°06´W
186 B8 **Fly** ∽ Indonesia/Papua New Guinea
194 I10 **Flying Fish, Cape** *headland* Thurston Island, Antarctica 72°00´S 102°25´W
Flylân *see* Vlieland
193 Y15 **Foa** *island* Ha'apai Group, C Tonga
11 U15 **Foam Lake** Saskatchewan, S Canada 51°38´N 103°31´W
113 J14 **Foča** *var.* Srbinje. SE Bosnia and Herzegovina 43°32´N 18°46´E
116 L12 **Focşani** Vrancea, E Romania 45°45´N 27°13´E
Fogaras/Fogarasch *see* Făgăraş
107 M16 **Foggia** Puglia, SE Italy 41°28´N 15°31´E
Foggo *see* Faggo
76 D10 **Fogo** *island* Ilhas de Sotavento, SW Cape Verde
13 U11 **Fogo Island** *island* Newfoundland and Labrador, E Canada
109 U7 **Fohnsdorf** Steiermark, SE Austria 47°13´N 14°40´E
100 G7 **Föhr** *island* NW Germany
104 F14 **Fóia** ▲ S Portugal 37°19´N 08°39´W
14 I10 **Foins, Lac aux** ◎ Québec, SE Canada
103 N17 **Foix** Ariège, S France 42°58´N 01°39´E
126 I5 **Fokino** Bryanskaya Oblast', W Russian Federation 53°22´N 34°22´E
123 S15 **Fokino** Primorskiy Kray, SE Russian Federation 42°58´N 132°25´E
Fola, Cnoc *see* Bloody Foreland
94 E13 **Folarskardnuten** ▲ S Norway 60°34´N 07°18´E
92 G11 **Folda** *fjord* C Norway
93 F14 **Foldereid** Nord-Trøndelag, C Norway 64°58´N 12°09´E
Földvár *see* Feldioara
115 J22 **Folégandros** *island* Kykládes, Greece, Aegean Sea
23 O9 **Foley** Alabama, S USA 30°24´N 87°40´W
29 U7 **Foley** Minnesota, N USA 45°39´N 93°54´W
14 E7 **Foleyet** Ontario, S Canada 48°15´N 82°26´W
95 D14 **Folgefonni** *glacier* S Norway
106 I13 **Foligno** Umbria, C Italy 42°58´N 12°40´E
97 Q23 **Folkestone** SE England, United Kingdom 51°05´N 01°11´E
23 W8 **Folkston** Georgia, SE USA 30°49´N 82°00´W
94 H10 **Folldal** Hedmark, S Norway 62°08´N 10°00´E
25 P1 **Follett** Texas, SW USA 36°25´N 100°08´W
106 F13 **Follonica** Toscana, C Italy 42°55´N 10°45´E
21 T15 **Folly Beach** South Carolina, SE USA 32°39´N 79°56´W
35 O7 **Folsom** California, W USA 38°40´N 121°11´W
116 M12 **Folteşti** Galaţi, E Romania 45°45´N 28°00´E
172 H14 **Fomboni** Mohéli, S Comoros 12°18´S 43°46´E
18 K10 **Fonda** New York, NE USA 42°57´N 74°24´W
11 S10 **Fond-du-Lac** Saskatchewan, C Canada 59°20´N 107°09´W
30 M8 **Fond du Lac** Wisconsin, N USA 43°48´N 88°27´W
11 T10 **Fond-du-Lac** ∽ Saskatchewan, C Canada
190 C9 **Fongafale** *var.* Funafuti. ● (Tuvalu) Funafuti Atoll, SE Tuvalu 08°31´N 179°11´E
190 G8 **Fongafale** *atoll* C Tuvalu
107 C18 **Fonni** Sardegna, Italy, C Mediterranean Sea 40°07´N 09°17´E
189 V12 **Fono** *island* Chuuk, C Micronesia
54 G4 **Fonseca** La Guajira, N Colombia 10°53´N 72°51´W
Fonseca, Golfo de *see* Fonseca, Gulf of
42 H8 **Fonseca, Gulf of** *Sp.* Golfo de Fonseca. *gulf* C Central America
103 O6 **Fontainebleau** Seine-et-Marne, N France 48°24´N 02°42´E
63 G19 **Fontana, Lago** ◎ W Argentina
21 N10 **Fontana Lake** ⊠ North Carolina, SE USA
107 L24 **Fontanarossa** ✈ (Catania) Sicilia, Italy, C Mediterranean Sea 37°28´N 15°04´E
11 N11 **Fontas** ∽ British Columbia, W Canada
58 D12 **Fonte Boa** Amazonas, N Brazil 02°32´S 66°01´W
102 J10 **Fontenay-le-Comte** Vendée, NW France 46°28´N 00°48´W
33 T16 **Fontenelle Reservoir** ⊠ Wyoming, C USA
193 Y14 **Fonualei** *island* Vava'u Group, N Tonga
111 H24 **Fonyód** Somogy, W Hungary 46°43´N 17°32´E
Foochow *see* Fuzhou
39 Q10 **Foraker, Mount** ▲ Alaska, USA 62°57´N 151°24´W
187 R14 **Forari** Éfaté, C Vanuatu 17°42´S 168°33´E
103 U4 **Forbach** Moselle, NE France 49°11´N 06°54´E
183 Q8 **Forbes** New South Wales, SE Australia 33°24´S 148°00´E
77 T17 **Forcados** Delta, S Nigeria 05°16´N 05°25´E
103 S14 **Forcalquier** Alpes-de-Haute-Provence, SE France 43°57´N 05°46´E
101 K19 **Forchheim** Bayern, SE Germany 49°43´N 11°07´E
35 R13 **Ford City** California, W USA 35°09´N 119°27´W
94 D11 **Førde** Sogn Og Fjordane, S Norway 61°27´N 05°51´E
31 N4 **Ford River** ∽ Michigan, N USA
183 O4 **Fords Bridge** New South Wales, SE Australia 29°44´S 145°25´E
20 J6 **Fordsville** Kentucky, S USA 37°36´N 86°39´W
27 U13 **Fordyce** Arkansas, C USA 33°49´N 92°23´W
76 I14 **Forécariah** SW Guinea 09°28´N 13°06´W
197 O14 **Forel, Mont** ▲ SE Greenland 66°55´N 36°45´W
11 R17 **Foremost** Alberta, SW Canada 49°30´N 111°34´W
14 D16 **Forest** Ontario, S Canada 43°05´N 82°00´W
22 L5 **Forest** Mississippi, S USA 32°22´N 89°30´W
31 S12 **Forest** Ohio, N USA 40°47´N 83°26´W
29 V11 **Forest City** Iowa, C USA 43°15´N 93°38´W
21 Q10 **Forest City** North Carolina, SE USA 35°19´N 81°52´W
32 G11 **Forest Grove** Oregon, NW USA 45°31´N 123°06´W

◆ Country ● Country Capital ◇ Dependent Territory ○ Dependent Territory Capital ◆ Administrative Regions ✈ International Airport ▲ Mountain ▲▲ Mountain Range Volcano ∽ River ◎ Lake ⊠ Reservoir

FORESTIER PENINSULA – FROST

183 P17 **Forestier Peninsula** *peninsula* Tasmania, SE Australia
29 V8 **Forest Lake** Minnesota, N USA *45°16′N 92°59′W*
23 S3 **Forest Park** Georgia, SE USA *33°37′N 84°22′W*
29 Q3 **Forest River** ⇝ North Dakota, N USA
15 T6 **Forestville** Québec, SE Canada *48°45′N 69°04′W*
103 Q11 **Forez, Monts du** ▲ C France
96 K10 **Forfar** E Scotland, United Kingdom *56°38′N 02°54′W*
26 J8 **Forgan** Oklahoma, C USA *36°54′N 100°32′W*
Forge du Sud *see* Dudelange
101 J24 **Forggensee** ⊚ S Germany
147 N10 **Forish** *Rus.* Farish. Jizzax Viloyati, C Uzbekistan *40°33′N 66°52′E*
20 F9 **Forked Deer River** ⇝ Tennessee, S USA
32 F7 **Forks** Washington, NW USA *47°57′N 124°22′W*
92 N2 **Forlandsundet** *sound* W Svalbard
106 H10 **Forlì** *anc.* Forum Livii. Emilia-Romagna, N Italy *44°14′N 12°02′E*
29 Q7 **Forman** North Dakota, N USA *46°07′N 97°39′W*
97 K17 **Formby** NW England, United Kingdom *53°34′N 03°05′W*
105 V11 **Formentera** *anc.* Ophiusa, *Lat.* Frumentum. *island* Islas Baleares, Spain, W Mediterranean Sea
Formentor, Cabo de *see* Formentor, Cap de
105 Y9 **Formentor, Cap de** *var.* Cabo de Formentor, Cape Formentor. *headland* Mallorca, Spain, W Mediterranean Sea *39°57′N 03°12′E*
Formentor, Cape *see* Formentor, Cap de
107 J16 **Formia** Lazio, C Italy *41°16′N 13°37′E*
62 O7 **Formosa** Formosa, NE Argentina *26°07′S 58°14′W*
62 M6 **Formosa** *off.* Provincia de Formosa. ◈ *province* NE Argentina
Formosa/Formo'sa *see* Taiwan
Formosa, Provincia de *see* Formosa
59 I17 **Formosa, Serra** ▲▲ C Brazil
Formosa Strait *see* Taiwan Strait
95 H21 **Fornæs** *headland* C Denmark *56°26′N 10°57′E*
25 U6 **Forney** Texas, SW USA *32°45′N 96°28′W*
106 E9 **Fornovo di Taro** Emilia-Romagna, C Italy *44°42′N 10°07′E*
117 T14 **Foros** Respublika Krym, S Ukraine *44°24′N 33°47′E*
Føroyar *see* Faeroe Islands
96 J8 **Forres** NE Scotland, United Kingdom *57°32′N 03°38′W*
27 X11 **Forrest City** Arkansas, C USA *35°01′N 90°48′W*
39 Y15 **Forrester Island** *island* Alexander Archipelago, Alaska, USA
25 N7 **Forsan** Texas, SW USA *32°06′N 101°22′W*
181 V5 **Forsayth** Queensland, NE Australia *18°31′S 143°37′E*
95 L19 **Forserum** Jönköping, S Sweden *57°42′N 14°28′E*
95 K15 **Forshaga** Värmland, C Sweden *59°33′N 13°29′E*
93 L19 **Forssa** Etelä-Suomi, S Finland *60°49′N 23°40′E*
101 Q14 **Forst** *Lus.* Baršć Łužyca. Brandenburg, E Germany *51°43′N 14°38′E*
183 U7 **Forster-Tuncurry** New South Wales, SE Australia *32°11′S 152°30′E*
23 T4 **Forsyth** Georgia, SE USA *33°00′N 83°57′W*
27 T8 **Forsyth** Missouri, C USA *36°41′N 93°07′W*
33 W10 **Forsyth** Montana, NW USA *46°16′N 106°40′W*
149 U11 **Fort Abbās** Punjab, E Pakistan *29°12′N 73°00′E*
12 G10 **Fort Albany** Ontario, C Canada *52°15′N 81°35′W*
56 L13 **Fortaleza** Pando, N Bolivia *09°48′S 65°29′W*
58 P13 **Fortaleza** *prev.* Ceará. *state capital* Ceará, NE Brazil *03°45′S 38°35′W*
59 D16 **Fortaleza** Rondônia, W Brazil *08°45′S 64°06′W*
56 C13 **Fortaleza, Río** ⇝ W Peru
Fort-Archambault *see* Sarh
21 U3 **Fort Ashby** West Virginia, NE USA *39°30′N 78°46′W*
96 I9 **Fort Augustus** N Scotland, United Kingdom *57°14′N 04°38′W*
Fort-Bayard *see* Zhanjiang
33 S8 **Fort Benton** Montana, NW USA *47°49′N 110°40′W*
35 Q1 **Fort Bidwell** California, W USA *41°50′N 120°07′W*
34 L5 **Fort Bragg** California, W USA *39°25′N 123°48′W*
31 N16 **Fort Branch** Indiana, N USA *38°15′N 87°34′W*
Fort-Bretonnet *see* Bousso
33 T17 **Fort Bridger** Wyoming, C USA *41°18′N 110°19′W*
Fort-Cappolani *see* Tidjikja
Fort-Carnot *see* Ikongo
Fort Charlet *see* Djanet
Fort-Chimo *see* Kuujjuaq
11 R10 **Fort Chipewyan** Alberta, C Canada *58°42′N 111°08′W*
Fort Cobb Lake *see* Fort Cobb Reservoir
26 L11 **Fort Cobb Reservoir** *var.* Fort Cobb Lake. ⊠ Oklahoma, C USA
37 T3 **Fort Collins** Colorado, C USA *40°35′N 105°05′W*
14 K12 **Fort-Coulonge** Québec, SE Canada *45°50′N 76°45′W*
Fort-Crampel *see* Kaga Bandoro
Fort-Dauphin *see* Tôlañaro
24 K10 **Fort Davis** Texas, SW USA *30°35′N 103°54′W*
37 O10 **Fort Defiance** Arizona, SW USA *35°44′N 109°04′W*
45 Q12 **Fort-de-France** *prev.* Fort-Royal. ○ (Martinique) W Martinique *14°36′N 61°05′W*
45 P12 **Fort-de-France, Baie de** *bay* W Martinique
Fort de Kock *see* Bukittinggi
23 P6 **Fort Deposit** Alabama, S USA *31°58′N 86°34′W*
29 U13 **Fort Dodge** Iowa, C USA *42°30′N 94°10′W*
13 S10 **Forteau** Québec, E Canada *51°30′N 56°55′W*
106 E11 **Forte dei Marmi** Toscana, C Italy *43°59′N 10°10′E*
14 H17 **Fort Erie** Ontario, S Canada *42°55′N 78°56′W*
180 H7 **Fortescue River** ⇝ Western Australia
19 S2 **Fort Fairfield** Maine, NE USA *46°45′N 67°51′W*
Fort-Foureau *see* Kousséri
12 A11 **Fort Frances** Ontario, S Canada *48°37′N 93°23′W*
Fort Franklin *see* Déline
23 R7 **Fort Gaines** Georgia, SE USA *31°36′N 85°03′W*
37 T8 **Fort Garland** Colorado, C USA *37°22′N 105°24′W*
21 P5 **Fort Gay** West Virginia, NE USA *38°06′N 82°35′W*
Fort George *see* La Grande Rivière
Fort George *see* Chisasibi
27 Q10 **Fort Gibson** Oklahoma, C USA *35°48′N 95°15′W*
27 Q9 **Fort Gibson Lake** ⊠ Oklahoma, C USA
8 H7 **Fort Good Hope** *var.* Rádeyilikóé. Northwest Territories, NW Canada *66°16′N 128°37′W*
23 V4 **Fort Gordon** Georgia, SE USA *33°25′N 82°09′W*
Fort Gouraud *see* Fdérik
96 I11 **Forth** ⇝ C Scotland, United Kingdom
Fort Hall *see* Murang'a
24 H8 **Fort Hancock** Texas, SW USA *31°18′N 105°49′W*
Fort Hertz *see* Putao
96 K12 **Forth, Firth of** *estuary* E Scotland, United Kingdom
14 L14 **Forthton** Ontario, SE Canada *44°43′N 75°31′W*
14 M8 **Fortier** ⇝ Québec, SE Canada
Fortín General Eugenio Garay *see* General Eugenio A. Garay
Fort Jameson *see* Chipata
Fort Johnston *see* Mangochi
19 R1 **Fort Kent** Maine, NE USA *47°15′N 68°33′W*
Fort-Lamy *see* Ndjamena
23 Z15 **Fort Lauderdale** Florida, SE USA *26°07′N 80°09′W*
21 R11 **Fort Lawn** South Carolina, SE USA *34°43′N 80°46′W*
8 H10 **Fort Liard** *var.* Liard. Northwest Territories, W Canada *60°14′N 123°28′W*
44 M8 **Fort-Liberté** NE Haiti *19°42′N 71°51′W*
21 N9 **Fort Loudoun Lake** ⊠ Tennessee, S USA
37 T3 **Fort Lupton** Colorado, C USA *40°04′N 104°48′W*
11 R12 **Fort MacKay** Alberta, C Canada *57°12′N 111°41′W*
11 Q17 **Fort Macleod** *var.* MacLeod. Alberta, SW Canada *49°44′N 113°24′W*
29 Y16 **Fort Madison** Iowa, C USA *40°37′N 91°15′W*
Fort Manning *see* Mchinji
25 P9 **Fort McKavett** Texas, SW USA *30°50′N 100°07′W*
11 R12 **Fort McMurray** Alberta, C Canada *56°44′N 111°23′W*
8 G7 **Fort McPherson** *var.* McPherson. Northwest Territories, NW Canada *67°29′N 134°50′W*
21 R11 **Fort Mill** South Carolina, SE USA *35°00′N 80°57′W*
Fort-Millot *see* Ngouri
37 U3 **Fort Morgan** Colorado, C USA *40°14′N 103°48′W*
23 W14 **Fort Myers** Florida, SE USA *26°39′N 81°52′W*
23 W15 **Fort Myers Beach** Florida, SE USA *26°27′N 81°57′W*
10 M10 **Fort Nelson** British Columbia, W Canada *58°48′N 122°44′W*
10 M10 **Fort Nelson** ⇝ British Columbia, W Canada
Fort Norman *see* Tulita
23 Q2 **Fort Payne** Alabama, S USA *34°23′N 85°43′W*
33 W7 **Fort Peck** Montana, NW USA *48°00′N 106°28′W*
33 V8 **Fort Peck Lake** ⊠ Montana, NW USA
23 Y13 **Fort Pierce** Florida, SE USA *27°28′N 80°20′W*
29 N10 **Fort Pierre** South Dakota, N USA *44°21′N 100°22′W*
81 E18 **Fort Portal** SW Uganda *0°39′N 30°17′E*
8 J10 **Fort Providence** *var.* Providence. Northwest Territories, W Canada *61°21′N 117°39′W*
11 U16 **Fort Qu'Appelle** Saskatchewan, S Canada *50°50′N 103°52′W*
Fort-Repoux *see* Akjoujt
8 K10 **Fort Resolution** *var.* Resolution. Northwest Territories, W Canada *61°10′N 113°39′W*
33 T13 **Fortress Mountain** ▲ Wyoming, C USA *44°20′N 109°51′W*
Fort Rosebery *see* Mansa
Fort Rousset *see* Owando
Fort-Royal *see* Fort-de-France
Fort Rupert *see* Waskaganish
8 H13 **Fort St. James** British Columbia, SW Canada *54°26′N 124°15′W*
11 N12 **Fort St. John** British Columbia, W Canada *56°16′N 120°52′W*
Fort Sandeman *see* Zhob
11 Q14 **Fort Saskatchewan** Alberta, SW Canada *53°42′N 113°12′W*
27 R6 **Fort Scott** Kansas, C USA *37°52′N 94°43′W*
12 E6 **Fort Severn** Ontario, C Canada *56°N 87°40′W*
31 R12 **Fort Shawnee** Ohio, N USA *40°41′N 84°08′W*
144 E14 **Fort-Shevchenko** Mangistau, W Kazakhstan *44°29′N 50°16′E*
Fort-Sibut *see* Sibut
8 I10 **Fort Simpson** *var.* Simpson. Northwest Territories, W Canada *61°52′N 121°23′W*
8 I10 **Fort Smith** Northwest Territories, W Canada *60°01′N 111°55′W*
27 R10 **Fort Smith** Arkansas, C USA *35°23′N 94°24′W*
37 T13 **Fort Stanton** New Mexico, SW USA *33°28′N 105°31′W*
24 L9 **Fort Stockton** Texas, SW USA *30°54′N 102°54′W*
37 U12 **Fort Sumner** New Mexico, SW USA *34°28′N 104°15′W*
26 K8 **Fort Supply** Oklahoma, C USA *36°34′N 99°34′W*
26 K8 **Fort Supply Lake** ⊠ Oklahoma, C USA
29 O10 **Fort Thompson** South Dakota, N USA *44°01′N 99°22′W*
Fort-Trinquet *see* Bîr Mogreïn
105 R12 **Fortuna** Murcia, SE Spain *38°11′N 01°07′W*
34 K3 **Fortuna** California, W USA *40°35′N 124°07′W*
28 J2 **Fortuna** North Dakota, N USA *48°53′N 103°46′W*
23 T5 **Fort Valley** Georgia, SE USA *32°33′N 83°53′W*
11 P11 **Fort Vermilion** Alberta, W Canada *58°22′N 115°59′W*
Fort Victoria *see* Masvingo
31 P13 **Fortville** Indiana, N USA *39°55′N 85°51′W*
23 P9 **Fort Walton Beach** Florida, SE USA *30°24′N 86°37′W*
31 P12 **Fort Wayne** Indiana, N USA *41°08′N 85°08′W*
96 H10 **Fort William** N Scotland, United Kingdom *56°49′N 05°07′W*
25 T6 **Fort Worth** Texas, SW USA *32°44′N 97°19′W*
28 M7 **Fort Yates** North Dakota, N USA *46°05′N 100°37′W*
39 S7 **Fort Yukon** Alaska, USA *66°35′N 145°05′W*
Forum Alieni *see* Ferrara
Forum Julii *see* Fréjus
Forum Livii *see* Forlì
143 Q15 **Forūr-e Bozorg, Jazīreh-ye** *island* S Iran
94 H7 **Fosen** *physical region* S Norway
161 N14 **Foshan** *var.* Fatshan, Foshan, Namhoi. Guangdong, S China *23°03′N 113°08′E*
Fo-shan *see* Foshan
194 J6 **Fossil Bluff** *UK research station* Antarctica *71°30′S 68°30′W*
Fossa Claudia *see* Chioggia
106 B9 **Fossano** Piemonte, NW Italy *44°33′N 07°43′E*
99 H21 **Fosses-la-Ville** Namur, S Belgium *50°24′N 04°42′E*
32 J12 **Fossil** Oregon, NW USA *45°01′N 120°14′W*
Foss Lake *see* Foss Reservoir
106 I11 **Fossombrone** Marche, C Italy *43°42′N 12°48′E*
26 K10 **Foss Reservoir** *var.* Foss Lake. ⊠ Oklahoma, C USA
29 S4 **Fosston** Minnesota, N USA *47°34′N 95°45′W*
183 O13 **Foster** Victoria, SE Australia *38°40′S 146°15′E*
11 T12 **Foster Lakes** ⊚ Saskatchewan, C Canada
31 S12 **Fostoria** Ohio, N USA *41°09′N 83°25′W*
79 D19 **Fougamou** Ngounié, C Gabon *01°16′S 10°36′E*
102 J6 **Fougères** Ille-et-Vilaine, NW France *48°21′N 01°12′W*
Fou-hsin *see* Fuxin
27 S14 **Fouke** Arkansas, C USA *33°15′N 93°53′W*
96 K2 **Foula** *island* NE Scotland, United Kingdom
Foul Bay *bay* East Falkland, Falkland Islands
97 P21 **Foulness Island** *island* SE England, United Kingdom
185 F15 **Foulwind, Cape** *headland* South Island, New Zealand *41°45′S 171°28′E*
79 E15 **Foumban** Ouest, NW Cameroon *05°43′N 10°50′E*
172 H13 **Foumbouni** Grande Comore, NW Comoros *11°49′S 43°30′E*
195 N8 **Foundation Ice Stream** *glacier* Antarctica
37 T6 **Fountain** Colorado, C USA *38°40′N 104°42′W*
36 L4 **Fountain Green** Utah, W USA *39°37′N 111°37′W*
21 P11 **Fountain Inn** South Carolina, SE USA *34°41′N 82°12′W*
27 S11 **Fourche LaFave River** ⇝ Arkansas, C USA
33 Z13 **Four Corners** Wyoming, C USA *44°04′N 104°08′W*
103 Q2 **Fourmies** Nord, N France *50°01′N 04°03′E*
38 J17 **Four Mountains, Islands of** *island group* Aleutian Islands, Alaska, USA
173 P17 **Fournaise, Piton de la** ▲ SE Réunion *21°14′S 55°43′E*
14 J8 **Fournière, Lac** ⊚ Québec, SE Canada
115 L20 **Foúrnoi** *island* Dodekánisa, Greece, Aegean Sea
64 K13 **Four North Fracture Zone** *tectonic feature* W Atlantic Ocean
Fouron-Saint-Martin *see* Sint-Martens-Voeren
30 L3 **Fourteen Mile Point** *headland* Michigan, N USA *46°59′N 89°07′W*
Fou-shan *see* Fushun
76 I13 **Fouta Djallon** *var.* Futa Jallon. ▲▲ W Guinea
185 C25 **Foveaux Strait** *strait* S New Zealand
35 Q11 **Fowler** California, W USA *36°35′N 119°40′W*
37 U6 **Fowler** Colorado, C USA *38°07′N 104°01′W*
31 N12 **Fowler** Indiana, N USA *40°36′N 87°20′W*
182 D7 **Fowlers Bay** *bay* South Australia
25 R13 **Fowlerton** Texas, SW USA *28°27′N 98°48′W*
142 M3 **Fowman** *var.* Fuman, Fumen. Gīlān, NW Iran *37°15′N 49°19′E*
65 C25 **Fox Bay East** West Falkland, Falkland Islands
14 J14 **Foxboro** Ontario, SE Canada *44°16′N 77°23′W*
11 O14 **Fox Creek** Alberta, W Canada *54°25′N 116°57′W*
64 G5 **Foxe Basin** *sea* Nunavut, N Canada
64 G5 **Foxe Channel** *channel* Nunavut, N Canada
95 I16 **Foxen** ⊚ C Sweden
9 Q7 **Foxe Peninsula** *peninsula* Baffin Island, Nunavut, NE Canada
185 E19 **Fox Glacier** West Coast, South Island, New Zealand *43°28′S 170°00′E*
38 L17 **Fox Islands** *island* Aleutian Islands, Alaska, USA
30 M10 **Fox Lake** Illinois, N USA *42°24′N 88°10′W*
9 V12 **Fox Mine** Manitoba, C Canada *56°36′N 101°48′W*
35 R3 **Fox Mountain** ▲ Nevada, W USA *41°01′N 119°30′W*
65 E25 **Fox Point** *headland* East Falkland, Falkland Islands *51°55′S 58°24′W*
30 M11 **Fox River** ⇝ Illinois/Wisconsin, N USA
30 L7 **Fox River** ⇝ Wisconsin, N USA
184 L13 **Foxton** Manawatu-Wanganui, North Island, New Zealand *40°27′S 175°18′E*
11 S16 **Fox Valley** Saskatchewan, S Canada *50°29′N 109°29′W*
11 W16 **Foxwarren** Manitoba, S Canada *50°30′N 101°09′W*
97 E14 **Foyle, Lough** *inlet* N Ireland
194 H5 **Foyn Coast** *physical region* Antarctica
104 I2 **Foz** Galicia, NW Spain *43°33′N 07°16′W*
60 I12 **Foz do Areia, Represa de** ⊠ S Brazil
59 A16 **Foz do Breu** Acre, W Brazil *09°21′S 72°41′W*
83 A16 **Foz do Cunene** Namibe, SW Angola *17°11′S 11°52′E*
60 G12 **Foz do Iguaçu** Paraná, S Brazil *25°33′S 54°31′W*
58 C12 **Foz do Mamoriá** Amazonas, NW Brazil *02°28′S 66°06′W*
105 T6 **Fraga** Aragón, NE Spain *41°32′N 00°21′E*
44 F5 **Fragoso, Cayo** *island* C Cuba
61 G18 **Fraile Muerto** Cerro Largo, NE Uruguay *32°30′S 54°30′W*
99 H21 **Fraire** Namur, S Belgium *50°16′N 04°30′E*
99 L21 **Fraiture, Baraque de** *hill* SE Belgium
Frakštát *see* Hlohovec
197 S10 **Fram Basin** *var.* Amundsen Basin. *undersea feature* Arctic Ocean *88°00′N 90°00′E*
99 F20 **Frameries** Hainaut, S Belgium *50°25′N 03°41′E*
19 O11 **Framingham** Massachusetts, NE USA *42°15′N 71°24′W*
60 L7 **Franca** São Paulo, S Brazil *20°33′S 47°27′W*
187 O15 **Français, Récif des** *reef* W New Caledonia
107 K14 **Francavilla al Mare** Abruzzo, C Italy *42°25′N 14°16′E*
107 P18 **Francavilla Fontana** Puglia, SE Italy *40°32′N 17°35′E*
102 M8 **France** *off.* French Republic, *It./Sp.* Francia; *prev.* Gaul, Gaule, *Lat.* Gallia. ◆ *republic* W Europe
45 O8 **Francés Viejo, Cabo** *headland* NE Dominican Republic *19°39′N 69°57′W*
79 F19 **Franceville** *var.* Massoukou, Masuku. Haut-Ogooué, E Gabon *01°40′S 13°31′E*
79 F19 **Franceville** ✈ Haut-Ogooué, E Gabon *01°38′S 13°24′E*
Francfort *see* Frankfurt am Main
103 T8 **Franche-Comté** ◈ *region* E France
Francia *see* France
29 O11 **Francis Case, Lake** ⊠ South Dakota, N USA
60 H12 **Francisco Beltrão** Paraná, S Brazil *26°05′S 53°04′W*
Francisco l. Madero *see* Villa Madero
61 A21 **Francisco Madero** Buenos Aires, E Argentina *35°52′S 62°03′W*
42 H6 **Francisco Morazán** *prev.* Tegucigalpa. ◈ *department* C Honduras
83 J18 **Francistown** North East, NE Botswana *21°08′S 27°31′E*
Franconian Forest *see* Frankenwald
Franconian Jura *see* Fränkische Alb
98 K6 **Franeker** *Fris.* Frjentsjer. Friesland, N Netherlands *53°11′N 05°33′E*
Frankenalb *see* Fränkische Alb
101 H16 **Frankenberg** Hessen, C Germany *51°04′N 08°49′E*
101 J20 **Frankenhöhe** *hill range* C Germany
31 R8 **Frankenmuth** Michigan, N USA *43°19′N 83°44′W*
101 F20 **Frankenstein** *hill* W Germany
Frankenstein/Frankenstein in Schlesien *see* Ząbkowice Śląskie
101 G20 **Frankenthal** Rheinland-Pfalz, W Germany *49°32′N 08°22′E*
101 L18 **Frankenwald** *Eng.* Franconian Forest. ▲▲ C Germany
44 J12 **Frankfield** C Jamaica *18°08′N 77°22′W*
14 J14 **Frankford** Ontario, SE Canada *44°12′N 77°36′W*
31 O13 **Frankfort** Indiana, N USA *40°16′N 86°30′W*
27 O3 **Frankfort** Kansas, C USA *39°42′N 96°25′W*
20 L5 **Frankfort** *state capital* Kentucky, S USA *38°12′N 84°52′W*
Frankfort on the Main *see* Frankfurt am Main
Frankfurt *see* Frankfurt am Main, Germany
Frankfurt *see* Słubice, Poland
101 G18 **Frankfurt am Main** *var.* Frankfurt, *Fr.* Francfort; *prev. Eng.* Frankfort on the Main. Hessen, SW Germany *50°07′N 08°41′E*
100 Q12 **Frankfurt an der Oder** Brandenburg, E Germany *52°20′N 14°32′E*
101 L21 **Fränkische Alb** *var.* Frankenalb, *Eng.* Franconian Jura. ▲▲ S Germany
101 I18 **Fränkische Saale** ⇝ C Germany
101 L19 **Fränkische Schweiz** *hill range* C Germany
23 R4 **Franklin** Georgia, SE USA *33°15′N 85°06′W*
31 P14 **Franklin** Indiana, N USA *39°29′N 86°02′W*
20 J7 **Franklin** Kentucky, S USA *36°42′N 86°35′W*
22 I9 **Franklin** Louisiana, S USA *29°48′N 91°30′W*
29 O17 **Franklin** Nebraska, C USA *40°06′N 98°57′W*
21 N10 **Franklin** North Carolina, SE USA *35°12′N 83°23′W*
18 C13 **Franklin** Pennsylvania, NE USA *41°24′N 79°49′W*
20 J9 **Franklin** Tennessee, S USA *35°55′N 86°52′W*
25 U9 **Franklin** Texas, SW USA *31°02′N 96°30′W*
21 X7 **Franklin** Virginia, NE USA *36°41′N 76°58′W*
21 T4 **Franklin** West Virginia, NE USA *38°39′N 79°21′W*
30 M9 **Franklin** Wisconsin, N USA *42°53′N 88°00′W*
8 I6 **Franklin Bay** *inlet* Northwest Territories, N Canada
32 K7 **Franklin D. Roosevelt Lake** ⊠ Washington, NW USA
35 W4 **Franklin Lake** ⊚ Nevada, W USA
185 B22 **Franklin Mountains** ▲▲ South Island, New Zealand
39 R5 **Franklin Mountains** ▲▲ Alaska, USA
39 N4 **Franklin, Point** *headland* Alaska, USA *70°54′N 158°48′W*
183 O17 **Franklin River** ⇝ Tasmania, SE Australia
22 K8 **Franklinton** Louisiana, S USA *30°51′N 90°09′W*
21 U9 **Franklinton** North Carolina, SE USA *36°06′N 78°27′W*
Frankstadt *see* Frenštát pod Radhoštěm
25 V7 **Frankston** Texas, SW USA *32°03′N 95°30′W*
33 U12 **Frannie** Wyoming, C USA *44°57′N 108°37′W*
15 U5 **Franquelin** Québec, SE Canada *49°17′N 67°52′W*
15 U5 **Franquelin** ⇝ Québec, SE Canada
83 C18 **Fransfontein** Kunene, NW Namibia *20°12′S 15°01′E*
93 H17 **Fränsta** Västernorrland, C Sweden *62°30′N 16°06′E*
122 J3 **Frantsa-Iosifa, Zemlya** *Eng.* Franz Josef Land. *island group* N Russian Federation
185 E18 **Franz Josef Glacier** West Coast, South Island, New Zealand *43°22′S 170°11′E*
Franz Josef Land *see* Frantsa-Iosifa, Zemlya
Franz-Josef-Spitze *see* Gerlachovský štít
101 L23 **Franz Josef Strauss** *abbrev.* F.J.S.. ✈ (München) Bayern, SE Germany *48°07′N 11°43′E*
107 A19 **Frasca, Capo della** *headland* Sardegna, Italy, C Mediterranean Sea *39°46′N 08°27′E*
107 I15 **Frascati** Lazio, C Italy *41°48′N 12°41′E*
11 N14 **Fraser** ⇝ British Columbia, SW Canada
83 G24 **Fraserburg** Western Cape, SW South Africa *31°55′S 21°31′E*
96 L8 **Fraserburgh** NE Scotland, United Kingdom *57°42′N 02°20′W*
181 Z9 **Fraser Island** *var.* Great Sandy Island. *island* Queensland, E Australia
10 L14 **Fraser Lake** British Columbia, SW Canada *54°00′N 124°45′W*
10 L15 **Fraser Plateau** *plateau* British Columbia, SW Canada
184 P10 **Frasertown** Hawke's Bay, North Island, New Zealand *38°58′S 177°25′E*
99 E19 **Frasnes-lez-Buissenal** Hainaut, SW Belgium *50°40′N 03°37′E*
108 I7 **Frastanz** Vorarlberg, NW Austria *47°13′N 09°38′E*
14 B8 **Frater** Ontario, S Canada *47°19′N 84°28′W*
Frauenbach *see* Baia Mare
Frauenburg *see* Saldus, Latvia
Frauenburg *see* Frombork, Poland
108 H6 **Frauenfeld** Thurgau, NE Switzerland *47°34′N 08°54′E*
109 Z5 **Frauenkirchen** Burgenland, E Austria *47°50′N 16°57′E*
61 D19 **Fray Bentos** Río Negro, W Uruguay *33°09′S 58°14′W*
61 F19 **Fray Marcos** Florida, S Uruguay *34°13′S 55°43′W*
29 S6 **Frazee** Minnesota, N USA *46°42′N 95°40′W*
104 M5 **Frechilla** Castilla-León, N Spain *42°08′N 04°50′W*
30 I4 **Frederic** Wisconsin, N USA *45°42′N 92°30′W*
95 G23 **Fredericia** Vejle, C Denmark *55°34′N 09°47′E*
21 W3 **Frederick** Maryland, NE USA *39°25′N 77°25′W*
26 L12 **Frederick** Oklahoma, C USA *34°24′N 99°03′W*
29 P7 **Frederick** South Dakota, N USA *45°49′N 98°31′W*
29 X12 **Fredericksburg** Iowa, C USA *42°58′N 92°12′W*
25 R10 **Fredericksburg** Texas, SW USA *30°17′N 98°52′W*
21 W5 **Fredericksburg** Virginia, NE USA *38°16′N 77°27′W*
39 X13 **Frederick Sound** *sound* Alaska, USA
27 X6 **Fredericktown** Missouri, C USA *37°33′N 90°19′W*
60 H13 **Frederico Westphalen** Rio Grande do Sul, S Brazil *27°22′S 53°20′W*
13 O15 **Fredericton** *province capital* New Brunswick, SE Canada *45°57′N 66°40′W*
95 I22 **Frederiksborg** *off.* Frederiksborgs Amt. ◈ *county* E Denmark
Frederiksborgs Amt *see* Frederiksborg
Frederikshåb *see* Paamiut
95 H19 **Frederikshavn** *prev.* Fladstrand. Nordjylland, N Denmark *57°28′N 10°33′E*
95 J22 **Frederikssund** Frederiksborg, E Denmark *55°51′N 12°05′E*
45 T9 **Frederiksted** Saint Croix, S Virgin Islands (US) *17°41′N 64°51′W*
95 I22 **Frederiksværk** *var.* Frederiksværk og Hanehoved. Frederiksborg, E Denmark *55°58′N 12°02′E*
Frederiksværk og Hanehoved *see* Frederiksværk
54 E9 **Fredonia** Antioquia, W Colombia *05°57′N 75°42′W*
36 K8 **Fredonia** Arizona, SW USA *36°57′N 112°31′W*
27 P7 **Fredonia** Kansas, C USA *37°32′N 95°50′W*
18 C11 **Fredonia** New York, NE USA *42°26′N 79°19′W*
35 P4 **Fredonyer Pass** *pass* California, W USA
93 I15 **Fredrika** Västerbotten, N Sweden *64°03′N 18°25′E*
95 L14 **Fredriksberg** Dalarna, C Sweden *60°07′N 14°23′E*
Fredrikshald *see* Halden
Fredrikshamn *see* Hamina
95 H16 **Fredrikstad** Østfold, S Norway *59°12′N 10°57′E*
30 K16 **Freeburg** Illinois, N USA *38°25′N 89°54′W*
18 K15 **Freehold** New Jersey, NE USA *40°14′N 74°14′W*
18 H14 **Freeland** Pennsylvania, NE USA *41°01′N 75°54′W*
182 J5 **Freeling Heights** ▲ South Australia *30°09′S 139°24′E*
35 Q7 **Freel Peak** ▲ California, W USA *38°52′N 119°52′W*
11 Z9 **Freels, Cape** *headland* Newfoundland and Labrador, E Canada *49°16′N 53°30′W*
29 Q11 **Freeman** South Dakota, N USA *43°21′N 97°26′W*
44 G1 **Freeport** Grand Bahama Island, N Bahamas *26°28′N 78°43′W*
30 L10 **Freeport** Illinois, N USA *42°18′N 89°37′W*
25 W12 **Freeport** Texas, SW USA *28°57′N 95°21′W*
44 G1 **Freeport** ✈ Grand Bahama Island, N Bahamas *26°31′N 78°48′W*
25 R14 **Freer** Texas, SW USA *27°52′N 98°37′W*
83 I22 **Free State** *off.* Free State Province; *prev.* Orange Free State, *Afr.* Oranje Vrystaat. ◈ *province* C South Africa
Free State *see* Maryland
Free State Province *see* Free State
76 G15 **Freetown** ● (Sierra Leone) W Sierra Leone *08°27′N 13°16′W*
172 J16 **Frégate** *island* Inner Islands, NE Seychelles
104 J12 **Fregenal de la Sierra** Extremadura, W Spain *38°10′N 06°39′W*
182 C2 **Fregon** South Australia *26°44′S 132°03′E*
102 H5 **Fréhel, Cap** *headland* NW France *48°41′N 02°21′W*
94 F8 **Frei** Møre og Romsdal, S Norway *63°02′N 07°47′E*
101 O16 **Freiberg** Sachsen, E Germany *50°55′N 13°21′E*
101 O16 **Freiberger Mulde** ⇝ E Germany
Freiburg *see* Freiburg im Breisgau, Germany
Freiburg *see* Fribourg, Switzerland
101 F23 **Freiburg im Breisgau** *var.* Freiburg, *Fr.* Fribourg-en-Brisgau. Baden-Württemberg, SW Germany *48°N 07°52′E*
Freiburg in Schlesien *see* Świebodzice
Freie Hansestadt Bremen *see* Bremen
Freie und Hansestadt Hamburg *see* Brandenburg
101 L22 **Freising** Bayern, SE Germany *48°24′N 11°45′E*
109 T3 **Freistadt** Oberösterreich, N Austria *48°31′N 14°31′E*
Freistadtl *see* Hlohovec
101 O16 **Freital** Sachsen, E Germany *51°00′N 13°40′E*
Freiwaldau *see* Jeseník
104 J6 **Freixo de Espada à Cinta** Bragança, N Portugal *41°05′N 06°49′W*
103 U15 **Fréjus** *anc.* Forum Julii. Var, SE France *43°26′N 06°44′E*
180 I13 **Fremantle** Western Australia *32°07′S 115°44′E*
35 N9 **Fremont** California, W USA *37°34′N 122°01′W*
31 Q11 **Fremont** Indiana, N USA *41°43′N 84°54′W*
29 W15 **Fremont** Iowa, C USA *41°12′N 92°26′W*
31 P8 **Fremont** Michigan, N USA *43°28′N 85°56′W*
29 R15 **Fremont** Nebraska, C USA *41°25′N 96°30′W*
31 S11 **Fremont** Ohio, N USA *41°21′N 83°08′W*
33 T14 **Fremont Peak** ▲ Wyoming, C USA *43°07′N 109°37′W*
36 M6 **Fremont River** ⇝ Utah, W USA
21 O9 **French Broad River** ⇝ Tennessee, S USA
21 N5 **Frenchburg** Kentucky, S USA *37°58′N 83°37′W*
18 C12 **French Creek** ⇝ Pennsylvania, NE USA
32 K15 **Frenchglen** Oregon, NW USA *42°49′N 118°55′W*
55 Y10 **French Guiana** *var.* Guiana, Guyane. ◇ *French overseas department* N South America
French Guinea *see* Guinea
31 O15 **French Lick** Indiana, N USA *38°33′N 86°37′W*
185 J14 **French Pass** Marlborough, South Island, New Zealand *40°57′S 173°49′E*
191 T11 **French Polynesia** ◇ *French overseas territory* S Pacific Ocean
French Republic *see* France
14 F11 **French River** ⇝ Ontario, S Canada
French Somaliland *see* Djibouti
173 P12 **French Southern and Antarctic Territories** *Fr.* Terres Australes et Antarctiques Françaises. ◇ *French overseas territory* S Indian Ocean
French Sudan *see* Mali
French Territory of the Afars and Issas *see* Djibouti
French Togoland *see* Togo
74 J6 **Frenda** NW Algeria *35°04′N 01°03′E*
111 I18 **Frenštát pod Radhoštěm** *Ger.* Frankstadt. Moravskoslezský Kraj, E Czech Republic *49°33′N 18°10′E*
76 M17 **Fresco** S Ivory Coast *05°03′N 05°31′W*
195 U16 **Freshfield, Cape** *headland* Antarctica
40 L10 **Fresnillo** *var.* Fresnillo de González Echeverría. Zacatecas, C Mexico *23°11′N 102°53′W*
Fresnillo de González Echeverría *see* Fresnillo
35 Q10 **Fresno** California, W USA *36°45′N 119°48′W*
Freu, Cabo del *see* Freu, Cap des
105 Y9 **Freu, Cap des** *var.* Cabo del Freu. *cape* Mallorca, Spain, W Mediterranean Sea
101 G22 **Freudenstadt** Baden-Württemberg, SW Germany *48°28′N 08°25′E*
Freudenthal *see* Bruntál
183 Q17 **Freycinet Peninsula** *peninsula* Tasmania, SE Australia
76 H14 **Fria** W Guinea *10°27′N 13°38′W*
83 A17 **Fria, Cape** *headland* NW Namibia *18°32′S 12°00′E*
35 Q10 **Friant** California, W USA *36°56′N 119°44′W*
62 K8 **Frías** Catamarca, N Argentina *28°41′S 65°00′W*
108 D9 **Fribourg** *Ger.* Freiburg. Fribourg, W Switzerland *46°50′N 07°10′E*
108 C9 **Fribourg** *Ger.* Freiburg. ◈ *canton* W Switzerland
Fribourg-en-Brisgau *see* Freiburg im Breisgau
32 G7 **Friday Harbor** San Juan Islands, Washington, NW USA *48°31′N 123°01′W*
Friedau *see* Ormož
101 K23 **Friedberg** Bayern, S Germany *48°21′N 10°58′E*
101 H18 **Friedberg** Hessen, W Germany *50°19′N 08°46′E*
Friedeberg Neumark *see* Strzelce Krajeńskie
Friedek-Mistek *see* Frýdek-Místek
Friedland *see* Pravdinsk
101 I24 **Friedrichshafen** Baden-Württemberg, S Germany *47°39′N 09°29′E*
Friedrichstadt *see* Jaunjelgava
29 Q16 **Friend** Nebraska, C USA *40°37′N 97°16′W*
Friendly Islands *see* Tonga
55 V9 **Friendship** Coronie, N Suriname *05°50′N 56°16′W*
30 L7 **Friendship** Wisconsin, N USA *43°58′N 89°48′W*
109 T8 **Friesach** Kärnten, S Austria *46°58′N 14°24′E*
Friesche Eilanden *see* Frisian Islands
101 F22 **Friesenheim** Baden-Württemberg, SW Germany *48°27′N 07°56′E*
Friesische Inseln *see* Frisian Islands
98 K6 **Friesland** ◈ *province* N Netherlands
60 Q10 **Frio, Cabo** *headland* SE Brazil *23°01′S 41°59′W*
24 M3 **Friona** Texas, SW USA *34°38′N 102°43′W*
42 L12 **Frío, Río** ⇝ N Costa Rica
25 R13 **Frio River** ⇝ Texas, SW USA
99 M25 **Frisange** Luxembourg, S Luxembourg *49°31′N 06°12′E*
Frisches Haff *see* Vistula Lagoon
36 J6 **Frisco Peak** ▲ Utah, W USA *38°31′N 113°17′W*
84 F9 **Frisian Islands** *Dut.* Friesche Eilanden, *Ger.* Friesische Inseln. *island group* N Europe
18 L12 **Frissell, Mount** ▲ Connecticut, NE USA *42°01′N 73°25′W*
95 J19 **Fristad** Västra Götaland, S Sweden *57°50′N 13°01′E*
25 N2 **Fritch** Texas, SW USA *35°38′N 101°36′W*
95 J19 **Fritsla** Västra Götaland, S Sweden *57°33′N 12°47′E*
101 H16 **Fritzlar** Hessen, C Germany *51°09′N 09°16′E*
106 H6 **Friuli-Venezia Giulia** ◈ *region* NE Italy
Frjentsjer *see* Franeker
196 L13 **Frobisher Bay** *inlet* Baffin Island, Nunavut, NE Canada
Frobisher Bay *see* Iqaluit
11 S12 **Frobisher Lake** ⊚ Saskatchewan, C Canada
94 G7 **Frohavet** *sound* C Norway
Frohenbruck *see* Veselí nad Lužnicí
109 V7 **Frohnleiten** Steiermark, SE Austria *47°17′N 15°20′E*
99 G22 **Froidchapelle** Hainaut, S Belgium *50°10′N 04°18′E*
127 O9 **Frolovo** Volgogradskaya Oblast', SW Russian Federation *49°46′N 43°38′E*
110 K7 **Frombork** *Ger.* Frauenburg. Warmińsko-Mazurskie, NE Poland *54°21′N 19°40′E*
97 L22 **Frome** SW England, United Kingdom *51°15′N 02°22′W*
182 I4 **Frome Creek** *seasonal river* South Australia
182 J6 **Frome Downs** South Australia *31°17′S 139°48′E*
182 J5 **Frome, Lake** *salt lake* South Australia
Fronicken *see* Wronki
104 H10 **Fronteira** Portalegre, C Portugal *39°03′N 07°39′W*
40 M7 **Frontera** Coahuila, NE Mexico *26°55′N 101°27′W*
41 U14 **Frontera** Tabasco, SE Mexico *18°32′N 92°39′W*
40 G3 **Fronteras** Sonora, NW Mexico *30°51′N 109°33′W*
103 Q16 **Frontignan** Hérault, S France *43°27′N 03°45′E*
54 D8 **Frontino** Antioquia, NW Colombia *06°46′N 76°10′W*
21 V4 **Front Royal** Virginia, NE USA *38°56′N 78°13′W*
107 J16 **Frosinone** *anc.* Frusino. Lazio, C Italy *41°38′N 13°22′E*
107 K16 **Frosolone** Molise, C Italy *41°34′N 14°25′E*
25 U7 **Frost** Texas, SW USA *32°04′N 96°48′W*

◆ Country ● Country Capital ◇ Dependent Territory ○ Dependent Territory Capital ◈ Administrative Regions ✈ International Airport ▲ Mountain ▲▲ Mountain Range Volcano ⇝ River ⊚ Lake ⊠ Reservoir

FROSTBURG – GARDELEGEN

21 U2 **Frostburg** Maryland, NE USA 39°39′N 78°55′W
23 X13 **Frostproof** Florida, SE USA 27°45′N 81°31′W
Frostviken *see* Kvarnbergsvattnet
95 M15 **Frövi** Örebro, C Sweden 59°28′N 15°24′E
94 F7 **Frøya** *island* W Norway
37 P5 **Fruita** Colorado, C USA 39°10′N 108°42′W
28 J9 **Fruitdale** South Dakota, N USA 44°39′N 103°38′W
23 W11 **Fruitland Park** Florida, SE USA 28°51′N 81°54′W
Frumentum *see* Formentera
147 S11 **Frunze** Batkenskaya Oblast', SW Kyrgyzstan 40°07′N 71°40′E
Frunze *see* Bishkek
117 O9 **Frunzivka** Odes'ka Oblast', SW Ukraine 47°19′N 29°46′E
Frusino *see* Frosinone
108 E9 **Frutigen** Bern, W Switzerland 46°35′N 07°38′E
111 I17 **Frýdek-Místek** ***Ger.*** Friedek-Mistek. Moravskoslezský Kraj, E Czech Republic 49°40′N 18°22′E
193 V16 **Fua'amotu** Tongatapu, S Tonga 21°15′S 175°08′W
190 A9 **Fuafatu** *island* Funafuti Atoll, C Tuvalu
190 A9 **Fuagea** *island* Funafuti Atoll, C Tuvalu
190 B8 **Fualifeke** *atoll* C Tuvalu
190 A8 **Fualopa** *island* Funafuti Atoll, C Tuvalu
151 K22 **Fuammulah** ***var.*** Fuammulah, Gnaviyani. *atoll* S Maldives
Fuammulah *see* Fuammulah
161 R11 **Fu'an** Fujian, SE China 27°11′N 119°42′E
Fu-chien *see* Fujian
Fu-chou *see* Fuzhou
164 G13 **Fuchū** ***var.*** Hutyû. Hiroshima, Honshū, SW Japan 34°35′N 133°12′E
160 M13 **Fuchuan** ***var.*** Fuyang. Guangxi Zhuangzu Zizhiqu, S China 24°56′N 111°15′E
165 R8 **Fudai** Iwate, Honshū, C Japan 39°59′N 141°50′E
161 S11 **Fuding** ***var.*** Tongshan. Fujian, SE China 27°21′N 120°10′E
81 J20 **Fudua** *spring/well* S Kenya 02°13′S 39°43′E
104 M16 **Fuengirola** Andalucía, S Spain 36°32′N 04°38′W
104 J12 **Fuente de Cantos** Extremadura, W Spain 38°15′N 06°18′W
104 J11 **Fuente del Maestre** Extremadura, W Spain 38°31′N 06°26′W
104 L12 **Fuente Obejuna** Andalucía, S Spain 38°15′N 05°25′W
104 L6 **Fuentesaúco** Castilla-León, N Spain 41°14′N 05°30′W
62 O3 **Fuerte Olimpo** ***var.*** Olimpo. Alto Paraguay, NE Paraguay 21°02′S 57°51′W
40 H8 **Fuerte, Río** ≈ C Mexico
64 Q11 **Fuerteventura** *island* Islas Canarias, Spain, NE Atlantic Ocean
141 S14 **Fughmah** ***var.*** Faghman, Fugma. C Yemen 16°08′N 49°23′E
92 M2 **Fuglehuken** *headland* W Svalbard 78°54′N 10°30′E
Fuglø *see* Fugloy
95 B18 **Fugloy** ***Dan.*** Fuglø. *island* NE Faeroe Islands
197 T15 **Fugløya Bank** *undersea feature* E Norwegian Sea 71°00′N 19°20′E
Fugma *see* Fughmah
160 E11 **Fugong** Yunnan, SW China 27°00′N 98°48′E
81 K16 **Fugugo** *spring/well* NE Kenya 03°19′N 39°39′E
158 L2 **Fuhai** ***var.*** Burultokay. Xinjiang Uygur Zizhiqu, NW China 47°15′N 87°39′E
161 P10 **Fu He** ≈ S China
Fuhkien *see* Fujian
100 J9 **Fuhlsbüttel** ✈ (Hamburg) Hamburg, N Germany 53°37′N 09°57′E
101 L14 **Fuhne** ≈ C Germany
Fu-hsin *see* Fuxin
Fujairah *see* Al Fujayrah
164 M14 **Fuji** ***var.*** Huzi. Shizuoka, Honshū, S Japan 35°08′N 138°39′E
161 Q12 **Fujian** ***var.*** Fu-chien, Fuhkien, Fukien, Min, Fujian Sheng. ⬖ *province* SE China
160 I9 **Fu Jiang** ≈ C China
Fujian Sheng *see* Fujian
164 M14 **Fujieda** ***var.*** Huzieda. Shizuoka, Honshū, S Japan 34°54′N 138°15′E
Fuji, Mount/Fujiyama *see* Fuji-san
163 Y7 **Fujin** Heilongjiang, NE China 47°12′N 132°01′E
164 M13 **Fujinomiya** ***var.*** Huzinomiya. Shizuoka, Honshū, S Japan 35°16′N 138°33′E
164 N13 **Fuji-san** ***var.*** Fujiyama, ***Eng.*** Mount Fuji. ▲ Honshū, SE Japan 35°23′N 138°44′E
165 N14 **Fujisawa** ***var.*** Huzisawa. Kanagawa, Honshū, S Japan 35°22′N 139°29′E
165 T3 **Fukagawa** ***var.*** Hukagawa. Hokkaidō, NE Japan 43°44′N 142°03′E
158 L5 **Fukang** Xinjiang Uygur Zizhiqu, W China 44°07′N 87°55′E
165 P7 **Fukaura** Aomori, Honshū, C Japan 40°38′N 139°55′E
193 W15 **Fukave** *island* Tongatapu Group, S Tonga
Fukien *see* Fujian
164 J13 **Fukuchiyama** ***var.*** Hukutiyama. Kyōto, Honshū, SW Japan 35°19′N 135°08′E
164 A14 **Fukue** ***var.*** Hukue. Nagasaki, Fukue-jima, SW Japan 32°41′N 128°52′E
164 A13 **Fukue-jima** *island* Gotō-rettō, SW Japan
164 K12 **Fukui** ***var.*** Hukui. Fukui, Honshū, SW Japan 36°03′N 136°12′E
164 K12 **Fukui** ***off.*** Fukui-ken, ***var.*** Hukui. ⬖ *prefecture* Honshū, SW Japan
Fukui-ken *see* Fukui
164 D13 **Fukuoka** ***var.*** Hukuoka, ***hist.*** Najima. Fukuoka, Kyūshū, SW Japan 33°36′N 130°24′E
164 D13 **Fukuoka** ***off.*** Fukuoka-ken, ***var.*** Hukuoka. ⬖ *prefecture* Kyūshū, SW Japan
Fukuoka-ken *see* Fukuoka
165 Q6 **Fukushima** Hokkaidō, NE Japan 41°27′N 140°14′E
165 Q12 **Fukushima** ***off.*** Fukushima-ken, ***var.*** Hukusima. ⬖ *prefecture* Honshū, C Japan
Fukushima-ken *see* Fukushima
164 G13 **Fukuyama** ***var.*** Hukuyama. Hiroshima, Honshū, SW Japan 34°29′N 133°21′E
76 G13 **Fulacunda** C Guinea-Bissau 11°44′N 15°03′W
129 P8 **Fūlādī, Kūh-e** ▲ E Afghanistan 34°38′N 67°32′E
187 Z15 **Fulaga** *island* Lau Group, E Fiji
101 I17 **Fulda** Hessen, C Germany 50°33′N 09°41′E
29 S10 **Fulda** Minnesota, N USA 43°52′N 95°36′W
101 I16 **Fulda** ≈ C Germany
Fülek *see* Fil'akovo
Fulin *see* Hanyuan
160 K10 **Fuling** Chongqing Shi, C China 29°45′N 107°23′E
35 T15 **Fullerton** California, SE USA 33°53′N 117°55′W
29 P15 **Fullerton** Nebraska, C USA 41°21′N 97°58′W
108 M8 **Fulpmes** Tirol, W Austria 47°11′N 11°22′E
20 G8 **Fulton** Kentucky, S USA 36°31′N 88°52′W
23 N2 **Fulton** Mississippi, S USA 34°16′N 88°24′W
27 V4 **Fulton** Missouri, C USA 38°50′N 91°57′W
18 H9 **Fulton** New York, NE USA 43°18′N 76°22′W
Fuman/Fumen *see* Fowman
103 R3 **Fumay** Ardennes, N France 49°58′N 04°42′E
102 M13 **Fumel** Lot-et-Garonne, SW France 44°31′N 00°58′E
190 B10 **Funafara** *atoll* C Tuvalu
190 C9 **Funafuti** ✈ Funafuti Atoll, C Tuvalu 08°30′S 179°12′E
Funafuti *see* Fongafale
190 F8 **Funafuti Atoll** *atoll* C Tuvalu
Funan *see* Fusui
190 B9 **Funangongo** *atoll* C Tuvalu
93 F17 **Funäsdalen** Jämtland, C Sweden 62°33′N 12°33′E
64 O6 **Funchal** Madeira, Portugal, NE Atlantic Ocean 32°40′N 16°55′W
64 P5 **Funchal** ✈ Madeira, Portugal, NE Atlantic Ocean 32°38′N 16°53′W
54 F5 **Fundación** Magdalena, N Colombia 10°31′N 74°09′W
104 I8 **Fundão** ***var.*** Fundáo. Castelo Branco, C Portugal 40°08′N 07°30′W
Fundáo *see* Fundão
13 O16 **Fundy, Bay of** *bay* Canada/USA
Fünen *see* Fyn
54 C13 **Fúnes** Nariño, SW Colombia 0°59′N 77°27′W
Fünfkirchen *see* Pécs
83 M19 **Funhalouro** Inhambane, S Mozambique 23°04′S 34°24′E
161 R6 **Funing** Jiangsu, E China 33°43′N 119°47′E
160 I14 **Funing** ***var.*** Xinhua. Yunnan, SW China 23°39′N 105°41′E
160 M7 **Funiu Shan** ▲▲ C China
77 U13 **Funtua** Katsina, N Nigeria 11°31′N 07°19′E
161 R12 **Fuqing** Fujian, SE China 25°40′N 119°23′E
83 M14 **Furancungo** Tete, NW Mozambique 14°51′S 33°39′E
116 I15 **Furculești** Teleorman, S Romania 43°51′N 25°07′E
Füred *see* Balatonfüred
165 W4 **Füren-ko** ◎ Hokkaidō, NE Japan
Fürg *see* Doborjī
Furluk *see* Fârliug
Fürmanov/Furmanovka *see* Moyynkum
Furmanovo *see* Zhalpaktal
59 L20 **Furnas, Represa de** ⊠ SE Brazil
183 Q14 **Furneaux Group** *island group* Tasmania, SE Australia
Furnes *see* Veurne
160 J10 **Furong Jiang** ≈ S China
138 I5 **Furqlus** Ḥimṣ, W Syria 34°40′N 37°02′E
100 F12 **Fürstenau** Niedersachsen, NW Germany 52°30′N 07°40′E
109 X8 **Fürstenfeld** Steiermark, SE Austria 47°03′N 16°05′E
101 L23 **Fürstenfeldbruck** Bayern, S Germany 48°10′N 11°16′E
100 P12 **Fürstenwalde** Brandenburg, NE Germany 52°22′N 14°04′E
101 K20 **Fürth** Bayern, S Germany 49°29′N 10°59′E
109 W3 **Furth bei Göttweig** Niederösterreich, NW Austria 48°22′N 15°33′E
165 R3 **Furubira** Hokkaidō, NE Japan 43°14′N 140°38′E
94 L12 **Furudal** Dalarna, C Sweden 61°10′N 15°07′E
164 L12 **Furukawa** ***var.*** Hida. Gifu, Honshū, SW Japan 36°13′N 137°11′E
165 Q10 **Furukawa** ***var.*** Hurukawa, Ōsaki. Miyagi, Honshū, C Japan 38°36′N 140°57′E
54 F10 **Fusagasugá** Cundinamarca, C Colombia 04°22′N 74°21′W
Fusan *see* Pusan
Fushë-Arëzi/Fushë-Arrësi *see* Fushë-Arrëz
113 L18 **Fushë-Arrëz** ***var.*** Fushë-Arëzi, Fushë-Arrësi. Shkodër, N Albania 42°05′N 20°01′E
113 N16 **Fushë Kosovë** ***Serb.*** Kosovo Polje. C Kosovo 42°40′N 21°07′E
Fushë-Kruja *see* Fushë-Krujë
113 K19 **Fushë-Krujë** ***var.*** Fushë-Kruja. Durrës, C Albania 41°30′N 19°43′E
163 V12 **Fushun** ***var.*** Fou-shan, Fu-shun. Liaoning, NE China 41°50′N 123°54′E
Fu-shun *see* Fushun
Fusin *see* Fuxin
108 G10 **Fusio** Ticino, S Switzerland 46°27′N 08°39′E
163 X11 **Fusong** Jilin, NE China 42°20′N 127°17′E
101 K24 **Füssen** Bayern, S Germany 47°34′N 10°43′E
160 K15 **Fusui** ***var.*** Xinning; ***prev.*** Funan. Guangxi Zhuangzu Zizhiqu, S China 22°39′N 107°49′E
Futa Jallon *see* Fouta Djallon
63 G18 **Futaleufú** Los Lagos, S Chile 43°14′S 71°50′W
112 K10 **Futog** Vojvodina, NW Serbia 45°15′N 19°43′E
165 O14 **Futtsu** ***var.*** Huttu. Chiba, Honshū, S Japan 35°11′N 139°52′E
187 S15 **Futuna** *island* S Vanuatu
190 D12 **Futuna, Île** *island* S Wallis and Futuna
161 Q11 **Futun Xi** ≈ SE China
160 L5 **Fuxian** ***var.*** Fu Xian. Shaanxi, C China 36°03′N 109°19′E
Fuxian *see* Wafangdian
Fu Xian *see* Fuxian
160 G13 **Fuxian Hu** ⊠ SW China
163 U12 **Fuxin** ***var.*** Fou-hsin, Fu-hsin, Fusin. Liaoning, NE China 41°59′N 121°40′E
Fuxing *see* Wangmo
161 P7 **Fuyang** Anhui, E China 32°52′N 115°51′E
Fuyang *see* Fuchuan
161 O4 **Fuyang He** ≈ E China
163 U7 **Fuyu** Heilongjiang, NE China 47°48′N 124°26′E
163 Z6 **Fuyuan** Heilongjiang, NE China 48°20′N 134°22′E
Fuyu/Fu-yü *see* Songyuan
158 M3 **Fuyun** ***var.*** Koktokay. Xinjiang Uygur Zizhiqu, NW China 46°58′N 89°30′E
111 L22 **Füzesabony** Heves, E Hungary 47°46′N 20°25′E
161 R12 **Fuzhou** ***var.*** Foochow, Fu-chou. *province capital* Fujian, SE China 26°09′N 119°17′E
161 P11 **Fuzhou** Jiangxi, S China 27°58′N 116°20′E
137 W13 **Füzuli** ***Rus.*** Fizuli. SW Azerbaijan 39°33′N 47°09′E
119 I20 **Fyadory** ***Rus.*** Fëdory. Brestskaya Voblasts', SW Belarus 51°57′N 26°24′E
95 G24 **Fyn** ***off.*** Fyns Amt, ***var.*** Fünen. ⬖ *county* C Denmark
95 G23 **Fyn** ***Ger.*** Fünen. *island* C Denmark
96 H12 **Fyne, Loch** *inlet* W Scotland, United Kingdom
Fyns Amt *see* Fyn
95 E16 **Fyresvatnet** ◎ S Norway
FYR Macedonia/FYROM *see* Macedonia, FYR
Fyzabad *see* Feyẕābād

G

Gaafu Alifu Atoll *see* North Huvadhu Atoll
81 O14 **Gaalkacyo** ***var.*** Galka'yo, ***It.*** Galcaio. Mudug, C Somalia 06°42′N 47°24′E
146 J11 **Gabakly** ***Rus.*** Kabakly. Lebap Welaýaty, NE Turkmenistan 39°45′N 62°30′E
114 H8 **Gabare** Vratsa, NW Bulgaria 43°20′N 23°57′E
102 K15 **Gabas** ≈ SW France
Gabasumdo *see* Tongde
35 T7 **Gabbs** Nevada, W USA 38°51′N 117°55′W
82 B12 **Gabela** Cuanza Sul, W Angola 10°50′S 14°21′E
Gaberones *see* Gaborone
189 X14 **Gabert** *island* Caroline Islands, E Micronesia
74 M7 **Gabès** ***var.*** Qābis. E Tunisia 33°53′N 10°03′E
74 M6 **Gabès, Golfe de** ***Ar.*** Khalīj Qābis. *gulf* E Tunisia
Gablonz an der Neisse *see* Jablonec nad Nisou
Gablös *see* Cavalese
79 E18 **Gabon** ***off.*** Gabonese Republic. ◆ *republic* C Africa
Gabonese Republic *see* Gabon
83 I20 **Gaborone** ***prev.*** Gaberones. ● (Botswana) South East, SE Botswana 24°42′S 25°50′E
83 I20 **Gaborone** ✈ South East, SE Botswana 24°45′S 25°49′E
104 K8 **Gabriel y Galán, Embalse de** ⊠ W Spain
143 U15 **Gābrīk, Rūd-e** ≈ SE Iran
114 J9 **Gabrovo** Gabrovo, N Bulgaria 42°54′N 25°19′E
114 J9 **Gabrovo** ⬖ *province* N Bulgaria
76 H12 **Gabú** ***prev.*** Nova Lamego. E Guinea-Bissau 12°16′N 14°09′W
29 O6 **Gackle** North Dakota, N USA 46°34′N 99°07′W
113 I15 **Gacko** Repulika Srpska, S Bosnia and Herzegovina 43°08′N 18°29′E
155 F17 **Gadag** Karnātaka, W India 15°25′N 75°37′E
93 G15 **Gäddede** Jämtland, C Sweden 64°30′N 14°15′E
159 S12 **Gadê** ***var.*** Kequ; ***prev.*** Pagqên. Qinghai, C China 33°56′N 99°49′E
Gades/Gadier/Gadir/Gadire *see* Cádiz
105 P15 **Gádor, Sierra de** ▲▲ S Spain
149 S15 **Gadra** Sind, SE Pakistan 25°39′N 70°28′E
23 Q3 **Gadsden** Alabama, S USA 34°00′N 86°00′W
36 H15 **Gadsden** Arizona, SW USA 32°33′N 114°45′W
Gadyach *see* Hadyach
124 J3 **Gadzhiyevo** Murmanskaya Oblast', NW Russian Federation 69°16′N 33°20′E
79 H15 **Gadzi** Mambéré-Kadéï, SW Central African Republic 04°46′N 16°42′E
116 J13 **Găești** Dâmbovița, S Romania 44°42′N 25°19′E
107 J17 **Gaeta** Lazio, C Italy 41°12′N 13°35′E
107 J17 **Gaeta, Golfo di** ***var.*** Gulf of Gaeta. *gulf* C Italy
Gaeta, Gulf of *see* Gaeta, Golfo di
188 L14 **Gaferut** *atoll* Caroline Islands, W Micronesia
21 Q10 **Gaffney** South Carolina, SE USA 35°03′N 81°40′W
Gäfle *see* Gävle
Gäfleborg *see* Gävleborg
74 M6 **Gafsa** ***var.*** Qafşah. W Tunisia 34°25′N 08°52′E
Gafurov *see* Ghafurov
126 J3 **Gagarin** ***prev.*** Gzhatsk. Smolenskaya Oblast', W Russian Federation 53°33′N 35°00′E
147 O10 **Gagarin** Jizzax Viloyati, C Uzbekistan 40°40′N 68°04′E
101 G21 **Gaggenau** Baden-Württemberg, SW Germany 48°48′N 08°19′E
188 F16 **Gagil Tamil** ***var.*** Gagil-Tomil. *island* Caroline Islands, W Micronesia
Gagil-Tomil *see* Gagil Tamil
127 O4 **Gagino** Nizhegorodskaya Oblast', W Russian Federation 55°18′N 45°01′E
107 Q19 **Gagliano del Capo** Puglia, SE Italy 39°49′N 18°22′E
94 L13 **Gagnef** Dalarna, C Sweden 60°34′N 15°04′E
76 M17 **Gagnoa** C Ivory Coast 06°11′N 05°56′W
13 N10 **Gagnon** Québec, E Canada 51°56′N 68°16′W
Gago Coutinho *see* Lumbala N'Guimbo
137 P8 **Gagra** NW Georgia 43°17′N 40°18′E
31 S13 **Gahanna** Ohio, N USA 40°01′N 82°52′W
143 R13 **Gahkom** Hormozgān, S Iran 28°14′N 55°48′E
Gahnpa *see* Ganta
57 Q19 **Gaíba, Laguna** ◎ E Bolivia
153 T13 **Gaibandha** ***var.*** Gaibanda. Rajshahi, NW Bangladesh 25°21′N 89°36′E
Gaibhlte, Cnoc Mór na n *see* Galtymore Mountain
109 R9 **Gail** ≈ S Austria
101 I21 **Gaildorf** Baden-Württemberg, S Germany 48°41′N 10°08′E
103 N15 **Gaillac** ***var.*** Gaillac-sur-Tarn. Tarn, S France 43°54′N 01°54′E
Gaillac-sur-Tarn *see* Gaillac
Gaillimh *see* Galway
Gaillimhe, Cuan na *see* Galway Bay
109 Q9 **Gailtaler Alpen** ▲▲ S Austria
63 J17 **Gaimán** Chaco, S Argentina 43°15′S 65°30′W
20 K8 **Gainesboro** Tennessee, S USA 36°20′N 85°41′W
23 V10 **Gainesville** Florida, SE USA 29°39′N 82°19′W
23 T2 **Gainesville** Georgia, SE USA 34°18′N 83°49′W
27 U8 **Gainesville** Missouri, C USA 36°37′N 92°28′W
25 T5 **Gainesville** Texas, SW USA 33°39′N 97°08′W
109 X5 **Gainfarn** Niederösterreich, NE Austria 47°59′N 16°11′E
97 N18 **Gainsborough** E England, United Kingdom 53°24′N 00°48′W
182 G6 **Gairdner, Lake** *salt lake* South Australia
Gaissane *see* Gáissát
92 L8 **Gáissát** ***var.*** Gaissane. ▲▲ N Norway
43 T15 **Gaital, Cerro** ▲ C Panama 08°37′N 80°04′W
21 W3 **Gaithersburg** Maryland, NE USA 39°08′N 77°13′W
163 U13 **Gaizhou** Liaoning, NE China 40°24′N 122°17′E
Gaizina Kalns *see* Gaiziņkalns
118 H7 **Gaiziņkalns** ***var.*** Gaizina Kalns. ▲ E Latvia 56°51′N 25°58′E
Gajac *see* Villeneuve-sur-Lot
39 S10 **Gakona** Alaska, USA 62°21′N 145°16′W
158 M16 **Gala** Xizang Zizhiqu, China 28°17′N 89°21′E
Galaassiya *see* Galaosiyo
Ğalāğıl *see* Jalājil
Galam, Pulau *see* Gelam, Pulau
62 J6 **Galán, Cerro** ▲ NW Argentina 25°54′S 66°45′W
111 H21 **Galanta** ***Hung.*** Galánta. Trnavský Kraj, W Slovakia 48°12′N 17°45′E
146 L11 **Galaosiyo** ***Rus.*** Galaassiya. Buxoro Viloyati, C Uzbekistan 39°53′N 64°25′E
57 B17 **Galápagos** ***off.*** Provincia de Galápagos. ⬖ *province* W Ecuador, E Pacific Ocean
193 P8 **Galapagos Fracture Zone** *tectonic feature* E Pacific Ocean
Galapagos Islands *see* Colón, Archipiélago de
Galápagos, Islas de los *see* Colón, Archipiélago de
Galápagos, Provincia de *see* Galápagos
193 S9 **Galapagos Rise** *undersea feature* E Pacific Ocean 15°00′S 97°00′W
96 K13 **Galashiels** SE Scotland, United Kingdom 55°37′N 02°49′W
116 M12 **Galați** ***Ger.*** Galatz. Galați, E Romania 45°27′N 28°00′E
116 L12 **Galați** ⬖ *county* E Romania
107 Q19 **Galatina** Puglia, SE Italy 40°10′N 18°10′E
107 Q19 **Galatone** Puglia, SE Italy 40°09′N 18°05′E
Galatz *see* Galați
21 R8 **Galax** Virginia, NE USA 36°40′N 88°56′W
146 J16 **Galaýmor** ***Rus.*** Kala-i-Mor. Mary Welaýaty, S Turkmenistan 35°40′N 62°28′E
Galcaio *see* Gaalkacyo
64 P11 **Gáldar** Gran Canaria, Islas Canarias, NE Atlantic Ocean 28°09′N 15°40′W
94 F11 **Galdhøpiggen** ▲ S Norway 61°30′N 08°08′E
40 I4 **Galeana** Chihuahua, N Mexico 30°08′N 107°38′W
41 O9 **Galeana** Nuevo León, NE Mexico 24°45′N 99°59′W
60 P9 **Galeão** ✈ (Rio de Janeiro) Rio de Janeiro, SE Brazil 22°48′S 43°16′W
171 R10 **Galela** Pulau Halmahera, E Indonesia 01°52′N 127°48′E
39 O9 **Galena** Alaska, USA 64°43′N 156°55′W
30 K10 **Galena** Illinois, N USA 42°25′N 90°25′W
27 R7 **Galena** Kansas, C USA 37°04′N 94°38′W
27 T8 **Galena** Missouri, C USA 36°45′N 93°30′W
45 V15 **Galeota Point** *headland* Trinidad, Trinidad and Tobago 10°07′N 60°59′W
105 P13 **Galera** Andalucía, S Spain 37°45′N 02°33′W
45 Y16 **Galera Point** *headland* Trinidad, Trinidad and Tobago 10°49′N 60°54′W
56 A5 **Galera, Punta** *headland* NW Ecuador 0°49′N 80°03′W
30 K12 **Galesburg** Illinois, N USA 40°57′N 90°22′W
30 J7 **Galesville** Wisconsin, N USA 44°04′N 91°21′W
18 F12 **Galeton** Pennsylvania, NE USA 41°43′N 77°38′W
116 H9 **Gâlgău** ***Hung.*** Galgó; ***prev.*** Gîlgău. Sălaj, NW Romania 47°17′N 23°43′E
Galgó *see* Gâlgău
Galgóc *see* Hlohovec
81 N15 **Galguduud** ***off.*** Gobolka Galguduud. ⬖ *region* E Somalia
Galguduud, Gobolka *see* Galguduud
137 Q9 **Gali** W Georgia 42°40′N 41°39′E
125 N14 **Galich** Kostromskaya Oblast', NW Russian Federation 58°21′N 42°21′E
114 H7 **Galiche** Vratsa, NW Bulgaria 43°36′N 23°53′E
104 H3 **Galicia** ***anc.*** Gallaecia. ⬖ *autonomous community* NW Spain
64 M8 **Galicia Bank** *undersea feature* E Atlantic Ocean 11°45′W 42°40′N
Galilee *see* HaGalil
181 W7 **Galilee, Lake** ◎ Queensland, NE Australia
Galilee, Sea of *see* Tiberias, Lake
106 E11 **Galileo Galilei** ✈ (Pisa) Toscana, C Italy 43°40′N 10°22′E
31 S12 **Galion** Ohio, N USA 40°43′N 82°47′W
Galka'yo *see* Gaalkacyo
146 K12 **Galkynyş** ***prev. Rus.*** Deynau, Dyanev, ***Turkm.*** Dänew. Lebap Welaýaty, NE Turkmenistan 39°16′N 63°10′E
80 H11 **Gallabat** Gedaref, E Sudan 12°57′N 36°10′E
Gallaecia *see* Galicia
147 O11 **G'allaorol** Jizzax Viloyati, C Uzbekistan 40°01′N 67°30′E
106 C7 **Gallarate** Lombardia, NW Italy 45°39′N 08°47′E
27 S2 **Gallatin** Missouri, C USA 39°54′N 93°57′W
20 J8 **Gallatin** Tennessee, S USA 36°22′N 86°28′W
33 R11 **Gallatin Peak** ▲ Montana, NW USA 45°22′N 111°21′W
33 R12 **Gallatin River** ≈ Montana/Wyoming, NW USA
155 J26 **Galle** ***prev.*** Point de Galle. Southern Province, SW Sri Lanka 06°04′N 80°12′E
105 S5 **Gállego** ≈ NE Spain
193 Q8 **Gallego Rise** *undersea feature* E Pacific Ocean 02°00′S 115°00′W
Gallegos *see* Río Gallegos
63 H23 **Gallegos, Río** ≈ Argentina/Chile
Gallia *see* France
22 K10 **Galliano** Louisiana, S USA 29°26′N 90°18′W
114 G13 **Gallikós** ≈ N Greece
37 S12 **Gallinas Peak** ▲ New Mexico, SW USA 34°14′N 105°47′W
54 H3 **Gallinas, Punta** *headland* NE Colombia 12°27′N 71°44′W
37 T11 **Gallinas River** ≈ New Mexico, SW USA
107 Q19 **Gallipoli** Puglia, SE Italy 40°08′N 18°E
Gallipoli *see* Gelibolu
Gallipoli Peninsula *see* Gelibolu Yarımadası
31 T15 **Gallipolis** Ohio, N USA 38°49′N 82°14′W
92 J12 **Gällivare** ***Lapp.*** Váhtjer. Norrbotten, N Sweden 67°08′N 20°39′E
109 T4 **Gallneukirchen** Oberösterreich, N Austria 48°22′N 14°25′E
93 G17 **Gällö** Jämtland, C Sweden 62°57′N 15°15′E
105 Q7 **Gallo** ≈ C Spain
107 I23 **Gallo, Capo** *headland* Sicilia, Italy, C Mediterranean Sea 38°13′N 13°18′E
37 P13 **Gallo Mountains** ▲▲ New Mexico, SW USA
18 G8 **Galloo Island** *island* New York, NE USA
97 H15 **Galloway, Mull of** *headland* S Scotland, United Kingdom 54°37′N 04°54′W
37 P10 **Gallup** New Mexico, SW USA 35°32′N 108°45′W
105 R5 **Gallur** Aragón, NE Spain 41°51′N 01°21′W
Gâlma *see* Guelma
163 N9 **Galshar** ***var.*** Buyant. Hentiy, C Mongolia 46°15′N 110°50′E
162 I6 **Galt** ***var.*** Ider. Hövsgöl, C Mongolia 48°45′N 99°52′E
35 O8 **Galt** California, W USA 38°13′N 121°19′W
74 C10 **Galtat-Zemmour** C Western Sahara 25°07′N 12°21′W
95 G22 **Galten** Århus, C Denmark 56°09′N 09°54′E
97 D20 **Galtymore Mountain** ***Ir.*** Cnoc Mór na nGaibhlte. ▲ S Ireland 52°21′N 08°09′W
97 D20 **Galty Mountains** ***Ir.*** Na Gaibhlte. ▲▲ S Ireland
30 K11 **Galva** Illinois, N USA 41°10′N 90°02′W
25 X12 **Galveston** Texas, SW USA 29°17′N 94°48′W
25 W11 **Galveston Bay** *inlet* Texas, SW USA
25 W12 **Galveston Island** *island* Texas, SW USA
61 B18 **Gálvez** Santa Fe, C Argentina 32°03′S 61°14′W
97 C18 **Galway** ***Ir.*** Gaillimh. W Ireland 53°16′N 09°03′W
97 B18 **Galway** ***Ir.*** Gaillimh. *cultural region* W Ireland
97 B18 **Galway Bay** ***Ir.*** Cuan na Gaillimhe. *bay* W Ireland
83 F18 **Gam** Otjozondjupa, NE Namibia 20°10′S 20°51′E
164 L14 **Gamagōri** Aichi, Honshū, SW Japan 34°49′N 137°15′E
54 F7 **Gamarra** Cesar, N Colombia 08°21′N 73°46′W
Gámas *see* Kaamanen
158 L17 **Gamba** Xizang Zizhiqu, W China 28°13′N 88°32′E
Gamba *see* Zamtang
77 P14 **Gambaga** NE Ghana 10°32′N 00°28′W
80 G13 **Gambēla** Gambēla Hizboch, W Ethiopia 08°09′N 34°15′E
81 H14 **Gambēla** ⬖ *federal region* W Ethiopia
38 K10 **Gambell** Saint Lawrence Island, Alaska, USA 63°44′N 171°41′W
76 E12 **Gambia** ***off.*** Republic of The Gambia, The Gambia. ◆ *republic* W Africa
76 I12 **Gambia** ***Fr.*** Gambie. ≈ W Africa
64 K12 **Gambia Plain** *undersea feature* E Atlantic Ocean
Gambia, Republic of The *see* Gambia
Gambia, The *see* Gambia
Gambie *see* Gambia
31 T13 **Gambier** Ohio, N USA 40°22′N 82°24′W
191 Y13 **Gambier, Îles** *island group* E French Polynesia
182 G10 **Gambier Islands** *island group* South Australia
79 H19 **Gamboma** Plateaux, E Congo 01°53′S 15°51′E
79 G16 **Gamboula** Mambéré-Kadéï, SW Central African Republic 04°09′N 15°12′E
37 P10 **Gamerco** New Mexico, SW USA 35°34′N 108°45′W
137 V12 **Gamış Dağı** ▲ W Azerbaijan 40°18′N 46°15′E
Gamlakarleby *see* Kokkola
95 N18 **Gamleby** Kalmar, S Sweden 57°54′N 16°25′E
Gammelstad *see* Gammelstaden
93 J14 **Gammelstaden** ***var.*** Gammelstad. Norrbotten, N Sweden 65°38′N 22°05′E
Gammouda *see* Sidi Bouzid
155 J25 **Gampaha** Western Province, W Sri Lanka 07°05′N 80°00′E
155 K25 **Gampola** Central Province, C Sri Lanka 07°10′N 80°34′E
167 S5 **Gâm, Sông** ≈ N Vietnam
92 L7 **Gamvik** Finnmark, N Norway 71°04′N 28°08′E
150 H13 **Gan** Addu Atoll, C Maldives
Gan *see* Gansu, China
Gan *see* Jiangxi, China
Ganaane *see* Juba
37 O10 **Ganado** Arizona, SW USA 35°42′N 109°31′W
25 U12 **Ganado** Texas, SW USA 29°02′N 96°30′W
14 L14 **Gananoque** Ontario, SE Canada 44°21′N 76°11′W
Ganāveh *see* Bandar-e Gonāveh
137 V11 **Gäncä** ***Rus.*** Gyandzha; ***prev.*** Kirovabad, Yelisavetpol. W Azerbaijan 40°42′N 46°23′E
Ganchi *see* Ghonchí
Gand *see* Gent
82 B13 **Ganda** ***var.*** Mariano Machado, ***Port.*** Vila Mariano Machado. Benguela, W Angola 13°02′S 14°40′E
79 L22 **Gandajika** Kasai-Oriental, S Dem. Rep. Congo 06°42′S 24°01′E
153 O12 **Gandak** ***Nep.*** Nārāyāni. ≈ India/Nepal
149 P12 **Gandāva** Baluchistān, SW Pakistan 28°37′N 67°29′E
13 U11 **Gander** Newfoundland and Labrador, SE Canada 48°56′N 54°33′W
13 U11 **Gander** ✈ Newfoundland and Labrador, E Canada 49°03′N 54°49′W
100 G11 **Ganderkesee** Niedersachsen, NW Germany 53°01′N 08°33′E
105 T7 **Gandesa** Cataluña, NE Spain 41°03′N 00°26′E
154 B10 **Gāndhīdhām** Gujarāt, W India 23°08′N 70°05′E
154 D10 **Gāndhīnagar** *state capital* Gujarāt, W India 23°12′N 72°37′E
154 F9 **Gāndhi Sāgar** ◎ C India
105 T11 **Gandía** País Valenciano, E Spain 38°59′N 00°11′W
159 O10 **Gang** Qinghai, W China
152 G9 **Gangānagar** Rājasthān, NW India 29°54′N 73°56′E
152 I12 **Gangāpur** Rājasthān, N India 26°30′N 76°49′E
153 S17 **Ganga Sāgar** West Bengal, NE India 21°39′N 88°05′E
Gangavathi *see* Gangāwati
155 G17 **Gangāwati** ***var.*** Gangavathi. Karnātaka, C India 15°26′N 76°35′E
159 S9 **Gangca** ***var.*** Shaliuhe. Qinghai, C China 37°21′N 100°09′E
158 H14 **Gangdisê Shan** ***Eng.*** Kailas Range. ▲▲ W China
103 Q15 **Ganges** Hérault, S France 43°57′N 03°42′E
153 P13 **Ganges** ***Ben.*** Padma. ≈ Bangladesh/India *see also* Padma
Ganges *see* Padma
Ganges Cone *see* Ganges Fan
173 S3 **Ganges Fan** ***var.*** Ganges Cone. *undersea feature* N Bay of Bengal 12°00′N 87°00′E
153 U17 **Ganges, Mouths of the** *delta* Bangladesh/India
107 K23 **Gangi** ***anc.*** Engyum. Sicilia, Italy, C Mediterranean Sea 37°48′N 14°13′E
152 K8 **Gangotri** Uttarakhand, N India 30°56′N 79°02′E
Gangra *see* Çankırı
153 S11 **Gangtok** *state capital* Sikkim, N India 27°20′N 88°39′E
159 W11 **Gangu** ***var.*** Daxiangshan. Gansu, C China 34°38′N 105°18′E
163 U5 **Gan He** ≈ NE China
171 S12 **Gani** Pulau Halmahera, E Indonesia 0°45′S 128°13′E
161 O12 **Gan Jiang** ≈ S China
163 U11 **Ganjig** ***var.*** Horqin Zuoyi Houqi. Nei Mongol Zizhiqu, N China 42°53′N 122°22′E
146 H15 **Gannaly** Ahal Welaýaty, S Turkmenistan 37°02′N 60°43′E
163 U7 **Gannan** Heilongjiang, NE China 47°58′N 123°36′E
103 P10 **Gannat** Allier, C France 46°06′N 03°12′E
33 T14 **Gannett Peak** ▲ Wyoming, C USA 43°10′N 109°39′W
29 O10 **Gannvalley** South Dakota, N USA 44°01′N 98°59′W
Ganqu *see* Lhünzhub
109 Y3 **Gänserndorf** Niederösterreich, NE Austria 48°21′N 16°43′E
Gansos, Lago dos *see* Goose Lake
159 T9 **Gansu** ***var.*** Gan, Gansu Sheng, Kansu. ⬖ *province* N China
Gansu Sheng *see* Gansu
76 K16 **Ganta** ***var.*** Gahnpa. NE Liberia 07°15′N 08°59′W
182 H11 **Gantheaume, Cape** *headland* South Australia 36°04′S 137°28′E
Gantsevichi *see* Hantsavichy
161 Q6 **Ganyu** ***var.*** Qingkou. Jiangsu, E China 34°52′N 119°11′E
144 D12 **Ganyushkino** Atyrau, SW Kazakhstan 46°38′N 49°12′E
161 O12 **Ganzhou** Jiangxi, S China 25°51′N 114°59′E
Ganzhou *see* Zhangye
77 Q10 **Gao** Gao, E Mali 16°16′N 00°03′E
77 R10 **Gao** ⬖ *region* SE Mali
161 O10 **Gao'an** Jiangxi, S China 28°24′N 115°27′E
Gaocheng *see* Litang
Gaoleshan *see* Xianfeng
161 R5 **Gaomi** Shandong, C China 36°23′N 119°45′E
161 N5 **Gaoping** Shanxi, C China 35°51′N 112°55′E
159 S8 **Gaotai** Gansu, N China 39°22′N 99°44′E
Gaoth Dobhair *see* Gweedore
77 O14 **Gaoua** SW Burkina 10°18′N 03°12′W
76 I13 **Gaoual** N Guinea 11°44′N 13°14′W
Gaoxiong *see* Kaohsiung
161 R7 **Gaoyou** ***var.*** Dayishan. Jiangsu, E China 32°48′N 119°26′E
161 R7 **Gaoyou Hu** ◎ E China
160 M15 **Gaozhou** Guangdong, S China 21°56′N 110°49′E
103 T13 **Gap** ***anc.*** Vapincum. Hautes-Alpes, SE France 44°33′N 06°05′E
146 E9 **Gaplaňgyr Platosy** ***Rus.*** Plato Kaplangky. *ridge* Turkmenistan/Uzbekistan
158 G13 **Gar** Xizang Zizhiqu, W China 32°50′N 79°46′E
Gar *see* Gar Xincun
Garabekevyul *see* Garabekewül
146 L13 **Garabekewül** ***Rus.*** Garabekevyul, Karabekaul. Lebap Welaýaty, E Turkmenistan 38°31′N 64°04′E
146 K15 **Garabil Belentligi** ***Rus.*** Vozvyshennost' Karabil'. ▲▲ S Turkmenistan
146 A8 **Garabogaz** ***Rus.*** Bekdash. Balkan Welaýaty, NW Turkmenistan 41°33′N 52°33′E
146 B9 **Garabogaz Aylagy** ***Rus.*** Zaliv Kara-Bogaz-Gol. *bay* NW Turkmenistan
146 A9 **Garabogazköl** ***Rus.*** Kara-Bogaz-Gol. Balkan Welaýaty, NW Turkmenistan 41°03′N 52°52′E
43 V16 **Garachiné** Darién, SE Panama 08°03′N 78°22′W
43 V16 **Garachiné, Punta** *headland* SE Panama 08°05′N 78°23′W
146 K12 **Garagan** ***Rus.*** Karagan. Ahal Welaýaty, C Turkmenistan 38°16′N 57°34′E
54 G10 **Garagoa** Boyacá, C Colombia 05°05′N 73°20′W
146 A11 **Garagöl'** ***Rus.*** Karagel'. Balkan Welaýaty, W Turkmenistan 39°24′N 53°13′E
146 F12 **Garagum** ***var.*** Garagumy, Qara Qum, ***Eng.*** Black Sand Desert, Kara Kum; ***prev.*** Peski Karakumy. *desert* C Turkmenistan
146 E12 **Garagum Kanaly** ***var.*** Kara Kum Canal, ***Rus.*** Karagumskiy Kanal, Karakumskiy Kanal. *canal* C Turkmenistan
Garagumy *see* Garagum
183 S4 **Garah** New South Wales, SE Australia 29°07′S 149°37′E
64 O11 **Garajonay** ▲ Gomera, Islas Canarias, NE Atlantic Ocean 28°07′N 17°14′W
114 M8 **Gara Khitrino** Shumen, NE Bulgaria 43°26′N 26°55′E
76 L13 **Garalo** Sikasso, SW Mali 10°58′N 07°26′W
Garam *see* Hron, Slovakia
146 L14 **Garamätnyýaz** ***Rus.*** Karamet-Niyaz. Lebap Welaýaty, E Turkmenistan 37°45′N 64°28′E
Garamszentkereszt *see* Žiar nad Hronom
77 Q13 **Garango** S Burkina 11°45′N 00°30′W
59 Q15 **Garanhuns** Pernambuco, E Brazil 08°53′S 36°28′W
188 H5 **Garapan** Saipan, S Northern Mariana Islands 15°12′S 145°43′E
Gárasavvon *see* Karesuando
Gárassavon *see* Kaaresuvanto
78 J13 **Garba** Bamingui-Bangoran, N Central African Republic 09°09′N 20°24′E
Garba *see* Jiulong
81 L16 **Garbahaarrey** ***It.*** Garba Harre. Gedo, SW Somalia 03°14′N 42°18′E
Garba Harre *see* Garbahaarrey
81 J18 **Garba Tula** Eastern, C Kenya 0°31′N 38°35′E
27 N9 **Garber** Oklahoma, C USA 36°26′N 97°35′W
34 L4 **Garberville** California, W USA 40°07′N 123°48′W
Garbo *see* Lhozhag
100 I12 **Garbsen** Niedersachsen, N Germany 52°25′N 09°36′E
60 K9 **Garça** São Paulo, S Brazil 22°14′S 49°36′W
104 L10 **García de Solá, Embalse de** ⊠ C Spain
103 Q14 **Gard** ⬖ *department* S France
103 Q14 **Gard** ≈ S France
106 F7 **Garda, Lago di** ***var.*** Benaco, ***Eng.*** Lake Garda, ***Ger.*** Gardasee. ◎ NE Italy
Garda, Lake *see* Garda, Lago di
Gardan Divāl *see* Gardan Dīwāl
149 Q5 **Gardan Dīwāl** ***var.*** Gardan Divāl. Vardak, C Afghanistan 34°30′N 68°15′E
103 S15 **Gardanne** Bouches-du-Rhône, SE France 43°27′N 05°28′E
Gardasee *see* Garda, Lago di
100 L12 **Gardelegen** Sachsen-Anhalt, C Germany 52°31′N 11°25′E

◆ Country
● Country Capital
◇ Dependent Territory
○ Dependent Territory Capital
⬖ Administrative Regions
✈ International Airport
▲ Mountain
▲▲ Mountain Range
⛰ Volcano
≈ River
◎ Lake
⊠ Reservoir

Garden ~ Ontario, S Canada

GHUND – GOODHOPE BAY

147 S14 Ghund Rus. Gunt. SE Tajikistan
Ghurābīyah, Sha'īb al see Gharbīyah, Sha'īb al
Ghurdaqah see Hurghada
148 J5 Ghūrīān Herāt, W Afghanistan 34°20′N 61°26′E
141 T8 Ghuwayfāt var. Gheweifat. Abū Ẓaby, W United Arab Emirates 24°06′N 51°40′E
121 O14 Ghuzayyil, Sabkhat salt lake N Libya
126 J3 Ghzatsk Smolenskaya Oblast', W Russian Federation 55°33′N 35°00′E
115 G17 Giáltra Évvoia, C Greece 38°21′N 22°58′E
Giamame see Jamaame
167 U13 Gia Nghia var. Đak Nông. Đặc Lắc, S Vietnam 11°58′N 107°42′E
114 F13 Giannitsá var. Yiannitsá. Kentrikí Makedonía, N Greece 40°49′N 22°24′E
107 F14 Giannutri, Isola di island Archipelago Toscano, C Italy
96 F13 Giant's Causeway Ir. Clochán an Aifir. lava flow N Northern Ireland, United Kingdom
167 S15 Gia Rai Minh Hai, S Vietnam 09°14′N 105°28′E
107 L24 Giarre Sicilia, Italy, C Mediterranean Sea 37°44′N 15°12′E
44 I7 Gibara Holguín, E Cuba 21°09′N 76°11′W
29 O16 Gibbon Nebraska, C USA 40°45′N 98°50′W
32 K11 Gibbon Oregon, NW USA 45°40′N 118°22′W
33 P11 Gibbonsville Idaho, NW USA 45°33′N 113°55′W
64 A13 Gibbs Hill hill S Bermuda
92 I9 Gibostad Troms, N Norway 69°21′N 18°01′E
104 I14 Gibraleón Andalucía, S Spain 37°23′N 06°58′W
104 L16 Gibraltar ○ (Gibraltar) S Gibraltar 36°08′N 05°21′W
104 L16 Gibraltar ◇ UK dependent territory SW Europe
Gibraltar, Détroit de/Gibraltar, Estrecho de see Gibraltar, Strait of
104 J17 Gibraltar, Strait of Fr. Détroit de Gibraltar, Sp. Estrecho de Gibraltar. strait Atlantic Ocean/Mediterranean Sea
31 S11 Gibsonburg Ohio, N USA 41°22′N 83°19′W
30 M13 Gibson City Illinois, N USA 40°27′N 88°24′W
180 L8 Gibson Desert desert Western Australia
10 L17 Gibsons British Columbia, SW Canada 49°24′N 123°32′W
149 N12 Gīdār Baluchistān, SW Pakistan 28°16′N 66°00′E
155 I17 Giddalūr Andhra Pradesh, E India 15°24′N 78°54′E
25 U10 Giddings Texas, SW USA 30°12′N 96°59′W
27 Y8 Gideon Missouri, C USA 36°27′N 89°55′W
81 I15 Gīdolē Southern Nationalities, S Ethiopia 05°31′N 37°26′E
118 H13 Giedraičiai Utena, E Lithuania 55°05′N 25°16′E
103 O7 Gien Loiret, C France 47°40′N 02°37′E
101 G17 Giessen Hessen, W Germany 50°35′N 08°41′E
98 O6 Gieten Drenthe, NE Netherlands 53°00′N 06°43′E
23 Y13 Gifford Florida, SE USA 27°40′N 80°24′W
9 O5 Gifford Baffin Island, Nunavut, NE Canada
100 J12 Gifhorn Niedersachsen, N Germany 52°28′N 10°33′E
11 P13 Gift Lake Alberta, W Canada 55°49′N 115°57′W
164 L13 Gifu var. Gihu. Gifu, Honshū, SW Japan 35°24′N 136°46′E
164 K13 Gifu off. Gifu-ken, var. Gihu. ◐ prefecture Honshū, SW Japan
Gifu-ken see Gifu
126 M13 Gigant Rostovskaya Oblast', SW Russian Federation 46°29′N 41°18′E
40 E8 Giganta, Sierra de la ▲▲ NW Mexico
54 E12 Gigante Huila, S Colombia 02°24′N 75°34′W
114 I7 Gigen Pleven, N Bulgaria 43°40′N 24°31′E
Gîggiga see Jijiga
96 G12 Gigha Island island SW Scotland, United Kingdom
107 E14 Giglio, Isola del island Archipelago Toscano, C Italy
Gihu see Gifu
146 L11 G'ijduvon Rus. Gizhduvon. Buxoro Viloyati, C Uzbekistan 40°06′N 64°38′E
104 L2 Gijón var. Xixón. Asturias, NW Spain 43°32′N 05°40′W
81 D20 Gikongoro SW Rwanda 02°30′S 29°32′E
36 K14 Gila Bend Arizona, SW USA 32°57′N 112°43′W
36 J14 Gila Bend Mountains ▲▲ Arizona, SW USA
37 N14 Gila Mountains ▲▲ Arizona, SW USA
36 I15 Gila Mountains ▲▲ Arizona, SW USA
142 M4 Gīlān off. Ostān-e Gīlān, var. Ghilan, Guilan. ◐ province NW Iran
Gīlān, Ostān-e see Gīlān
36 L14 Gila River Arizona, SW USA
29 W4 Gilbert Minnesota, N USA 47°29′N 92°27′W
Gilbert Islands see Tungaru
10 L16 Gilbert, Mount ▲ British Columbia, SW Canada 50°49′N 124°03′W
181 U4 Gilbert River Queensland, NE Australia
0 C6 Gilbert Seamounts undersea feature NE Pacific Ocean 52°50′N 150°10′W
33 S7 Gildford Montana, NW USA 48°34′N 110°21′W
83 P15 Gilé Zambézia, NE Mozambique 16°10′S 38°17′E
30 K4 Gile Flowage ◎ Wisconsin, N USA
182 G7 Giles, Lake salt lake South Australia
Gilf Kebir Plateau see Haḍabat al Jilf al Kabīr
183 R6 Gilgandra New South Wales, SE Australia 31°43′S 148°39′E
Gilgâu see Gâlgău
81 I19 Gilgil Rift Valley, SW Kenya 0°29′S 36°19′E
183 S4 Gil Gil Creek New South Wales, SE Australia
149 V3 Gilgit Jammu and Kashmir, NE Pakistan 35°54′N 74°20′E
149 V3 Gilgit N Pakistan
11 X11 Gillam Manitoba, C Canada 56°25′N 94°45′W
95 J22 Gilleleje Frederiksborg, E Denmark 56°05′N 12°17′E
30 K14 Gillespie Illinois, N USA 39°07′N 89°49′W
27 W13 Gillett Arkansas, C USA 34°07′N 91°22′W
33 X12 Gillette Wyoming, C USA 44°17′N 105°30′W
97 P22 Gillingham SE England, United Kingdom 51°24′N 00°33′E
195 X6 Gillock Island island Antarctica
173 O16 Gillot ✈ (St-Denis) N Réunion 20°53′S 55°31′E
65 H25 Gill Point headland E Saint Helena 15°59′S 05°38′W
30 M12 Gilman Illinois, N USA 40°44′N 87°58′W
25 W6 Gilmer Texas, SW USA 32°44′N 94°58′W
Gilolo see Halmahera, Pulau
81 G14 Gilo Wenz SW Ethiopia
35 O10 Gilroy California, W USA 37°00′N 121°34′W
123 Q12 Gilyuy SE Russian Federation
99 I14 Gilze Noord-Brabant, S Netherlands 51°33′N 04°56′E
165 R16 Gima Okinawa, Kume-jima, SW Japan
80 H13 Gīmbī It. Ghimbi. Oromīya, C Ethiopia 09°13′N 35°39′E
45 T12 Gimie, Mount ▲ C Saint Lucia 13°51′N 61°00′W
11 X16 Gimli Manitoba, S Canada 50°39′N 97°00′W
Gimma see Jīma
95 O14 Gimo Uppsala, C Sweden 60°11′N 18°12′E
102 L15 Gimone S France
Gimpoe see Gimpu
171 N12 Gimpu prev. Gimpoe. Sulawesi, C Indonesia 01°38′S 120°00′E
182 F5 Gina South Australia 29°56′S 134°33′E
Ginevra see Genève
99 J19 Gingelom Limburg, NE Belgium 50°46′N 05°09′E
180 I12 Gingin Western Australia 31°22′S 115°51′E
171 Q7 Gingoog Mindanao, S Philippines 08°47′N 125°05′E
81 K14 Ginīr Oromīya, C Ethiopia 07°12′N 40°43′E
Giohar see Jawhar
107 O17 Gióia del Colle Puglia, SE Italy 40°47′N 16°56′E
107 M22 Gioia, Golfo di gulf S Italy
Giona see Gkióna
115 I16 Gioúra island Vóreies Sporádes, Greece, Aegean Sea
107 O17 Giovinazzo Puglia, SE Italy 41°11′N 16°40′E
Gipeswic see Ipswich
Gipuzkoa see Guipúzcoa
Giran see Ilan
30 K14 Girard Illinois, N USA 39°27′N 89°46′W
27 R7 Girard Kansas, C USA 37°30′N 94°50′W
25 O6 Girard Texas, SW USA 33°18′N 100°38′W
54 E10 Girardot Cundinamarca, C Colombia 04°19′N 74°47′W
172 M7 Giraud Seamount undersea feature SW Indian Ocean 09°57′S 46°55′E
83 A15 Giraul SW Angola
96 L9 Girdle Ness headland NE Scotland, United Kingdom 57°09′N 02°04′W
137 N11 Giresun var. Kerasunt; anc. Cerasus, Pharnacia. Giresun, NE Turkey 40°55′N 38°35′E
137 N12 Giresun var. Kerasunt. ◐ province NE Turkey
137 N12 Giresun Dağları ▲▲ N Turkey
Girga see Jirjā
Girgeh see Jirjā
Girgenti see Agrigento
153 Q15 Girīdīh Jhārkhand, NE India 24°10′N 86°20′E
183 P6 Girilambone New South Wales, SE Australia 31°19′S 146°57′E
Girin see Jilin
121 W10 Girne Gk. Kerýneia, Kyrenia. N Cyprus 35°20′N 33°20′E
Giron see Kiruna
105 X5 Girona var. Gerona; anc. Gerunda. Cataluña, NE Spain 41°59′N 02°49′E
105 W5 Girona var. Gerona. ◐ province Cataluña, NE Spain
102 J12 Gironde ◐ department SW France
102 J11 Gironde estuary SW France
105 V5 Gironella Cataluña, NE Spain 42°02′N 01°53′E
103 N15 Girou S France
97 H14 Girvan W Scotland, United Kingdom 55°14′N 04°53′W
24 M9 Girvin Texas, SW USA 31°05′N 102°24′W
184 Q9 Gisborne Gisborne, North Island, New Zealand 38°41′S 178°01′E
184 P9 Gisborne off. Gisborne District. ◐ unitary authority North Island, New Zealand
Gisborne District see Gisborne
Giseifu see Üijŏngbu
Gisenye see Gisenyi
81 D19 Gisenyi var. Gisenye. NW Rwanda 01°42′S 29°18′E
95 K20 Gislaved Jönköping, S Sweden 57°19′N 13°30′E
103 N4 Gisors Eure, N France 49°18′N 01°46′E
Gissar see Hisor
147 P12 Gissar Range Rus. Gissarskiy Khrebet. ▲▲ Tajikistan/Uzbekistan
Gissarskiy Khrebet see Gissar Range
99 B16 Gistel West-Vlaanderen, W Belgium 51°09′N 02°58′E
108 F9 Giswil Unterwalden, C Switzerland 46°49′N 08°11′E
115 B16 Gitánes ancient monument Ípeiros, W Greece
81 E20 Gitarama C Rwanda 02°05′S 29°45′E
81 E20 Gitega C Burundi 03°20′S 29°56′E
Githio see Gýtheio
108 H11 Giubiasco Ticino, S Switzerland 46°11′N 09°01′E
106 K13 Giulianova Abruzzi, C Italy 42°45′N 13°58′E
Giulie, Alpi see Julian Alps
Giumri see Gyumri
116 M13 Giurgeni Ialomiţa, SE Romania 44°45′N 27°48′E
116 J15 Giurgiu Giurgiu, S Romania 43°54′N 25°58′E
116 J14 Giurgiu ◐ county SE Romania
95 F22 Give Vejle, C Denmark 55°51′N 09°15′E
103 R2 Givet Ardennes, N France 50°08′N 04°50′E
103 R11 Givors Rhône, E France 45°35′N 04°47′E
83 K19 Giyani Limpopo, NE South Africa 23°20′S 30°37′E
80 I13 Giyon Oromīya, C Ethiopia 08°31′N 37°56′E
75 W8 Gîza var. Al Jīzah, El Gîza, Gizeh. N Egypt 30°01′N 31°13′E
75 V8 Giza, Pyramids of ancient monument N Egypt
Gizhduvon see G'ijduvon
123 U8 Gizhiga Magadanskaya Oblast', E Russian Federation 61°58′N 160°16′E
123 T9 Gizhiginskaya Guba bay E Russian Federation
186 K8 Gizo Gizo, NW Solomon Islands 08°03′S 156°49′E
110 N7 Giżycko Ger. Lötzen. Warmińsko-Mazurskie, NE Poland 54°03′N 21°48′E
Gízymałów see Hrymayliv
113 M17 Gjakovë Serb. Đakovica. W Kosovo 42°22′N 20°30′E
94 F12 Gjende ◎ S Norway
95 F17 Gjerstad Aust-Agder, S Norway 58°54′N 09°03′E
113 O17 Gjilan Serb. Gnjilane. E Kosovo 42°27′N 21°28′E
Gjinokastër see Gjirokastër
113 L23 Gjirokastër var. Gjirokastra; prev. Gjinokastër, Gk. Argyrokastron, It. Argirocastro. Gjirokastër, S Albania 40°04′N 20°09′E
113 L22 Gjirokastër ◐ district S Albania
Gjirokastra see Gjirokastër
9 N7 Gjoa Haven var. Uqsuqtuuq. King William Island, Nunavut, NW Canada 68°38′N 95°57′W
94 H13 Gjøvik Oppland, S Norway 60°47′N 10°40′E
113 J22 Gjuhëzës, Kepi i headland SW Albania 40°25′N 19°19′E
Gjurgjevac see Đurđevac
115 E18 Gkióna var. Giona. ▲ C Greece
121 R3 Gkréko, Akrotíri var. Cape Greco, Pidálion. cape E Cyprus
99 I18 Glabbeek-Zuurbemde Vlaams Brabant, C Belgium 50°54′N 04°58′E
13 R14 Glace Bay Cape Breton Island, Nova Scotia, SE Canada 46°12′N 59°57′W
11 O16 Glacier British Columbia, SW Canada 51°12′N 117°33′W
39 W12 Glacier Bay inlet Alaska, USA
32 I7 Glacier Peak ▲ Washington, NW USA 48°06′N 121°06′W
21 Q7 Glade Spring Virginia, NE USA 36°47′N 81°46′W
43 W7 Gladewater Texas, SW USA 32°32′N 94°57′W
181 Y8 Gladstone Queensland, E Australia 23°52′S 151°16′E
182 I8 Gladstone South Australia 33°16′S 138°21′E
11 X16 Gladstone Manitoba, S Canada 50°12′N 98°56′W
31 O5 Gladstone Michigan, N USA 45°51′N 87°01′W
27 R4 Gladstone Missouri, C USA 39°12′N 94°33′W
31 Q7 Gladwin Michigan, N USA 43°58′N 84°29′W
95 J15 Glafsfjorden ◎ C Sweden
92 H2 Gláma physical region NW Iceland
94 I12 Gláma var. Glommen. S Norway
112 F13 Glamoč Federacija Bosna I Hercegovina, NE Bosnia and Herzegovina 44°01′N 16°51′E
97 J22 Glamorgan cultural region S Wales, United Kingdom
95 G24 Glamsbjerg Fyn, C Denmark 55°17′N 10°07′E
171 Q8 Glan Mindanao, S Philippines 05°49′N 125°11′E
109 T9 Glan SE Austria
101 F19 Glan W Germany
95 M17 Glan ◎ S Sweden
Glaris see Glarus
108 H9 Glarner Alpen Eng. Glarus Alps. ▲▲ E Switzerland
108 H8 Glarus Glarus, E Switzerland 47°03′N 09°04′E
108 H9 Glarus Fr. Glaris. ◐ canton C Switzerland
Glarus Alps see Glarner Alpen
27 N3 Glasco Kansas, C USA 39°21′N 97°50′W
96 I12 Glasgow S Scotland, United Kingdom 55°53′N 04°15′W
20 K7 Glasgow Kentucky, S USA 37°00′N 85°54′W
27 T4 Glasgow Missouri, C USA 39°13′N 92°51′W
33 W7 Glasgow Montana, NW USA 48°12′N 106°37′W
21 T6 Glasgow Virginia, NE USA 37°37′N 79°27′W
96 I12 Glasgow ✈ W Scotland, United Kingdom 55°52′N 04°27′W
11 S14 Glaslyn Saskatchewan, S Canada 53°20′N 108°18′W
18 I16 Glassboro New Jersey, NE USA 39°40′N 75°05′W
24 L10 Glass Mountains ▲▲ Texas, SW USA
97 K23 Glastonbury SW England, United Kingdom 51°09′N 02°43′W
Glatz see Kłodzko
101 N16 Glauchau Sachsen, E Germany 50°48′N 12°32′E
114 M7 Glavinitsa Silistra, NE Bulgaria 43°55′N 26°50′E
Glavn'a Morava see Velika Morava
Glavnik see Gllamnik
127 T1 Glazov Udmurtskaya Respublika, NW Russian Federation 58°06′N 52°38′E
Głda see Gwda
109 U8 Gleinalpe ▲▲ SE Austria
109 W8 Gleisdorf Steiermark, SE Austria 47°07′N 15°43′E
Gleiwitz see Gliwice
39 S11 Glenallen Alaska, USA 62°06′N 145°33′W
102 F7 Glénan, Îles island group NW France
185 G21 Glenavy Canterbury, South Island, New Zealand 44°53′S 171°04′E
10 H5 Glenboyle Yukon Territory, NW Canada 63°55′N 138°43′W
21 X3 Glen Burnie Maryland, NE USA 39°09′N 76°37′W
36 L8 Glen Canyon canyon Utah, W USA
36 L8 Glen Canyon Dam dam Arizona, SW USA
30 K15 Glen Carbon Illinois, N USA 38°45′N 89°58′W
14 E17 Glencoe Ontario, S Canada 42°44′N 81°42′W
83 K22 Glencoe KwaZulu/Natal, E South Africa 28°10′S 30°15′E
29 U9 Glencoe Minnesota, N USA 44°46′N 94°09′W
96 H10 Glen Coe valley N Scotland, United Kingdom
36 K13 Glendale Arizona, SW USA 33°32′N 112°11′W
35 S15 Glendale California, W USA 34°09′N 118°20′W
182 G5 Glendambo South Australia 30°59′S 135°45′E
33 Y8 Glendive Montana, NW USA 47°08′N 104°42′W
33 Y15 Glendo Wyoming, C USA 42°27′N 105°01′W
55 S10 Glendor Mountains C Guyana
182 K12 Glenelg River South Australia/Victoria, SE Australia
29 P4 Glenfield North Dakota, N USA 47°25′N 98°33′W
25 V12 Glen Flora Texas, SW USA 29°22′N 96°12′W
181 P7 Glen Helen Northern Territory, N Australia 23°45′S 132°46′E
183 U5 Glen Innes New South Wales, SE Australia 29°42′S 151°45′E
31 P6 Glen Lake ◎ Michigan, N USA
10 I7 Glenlyon Peak ▲ Yukon Territory, W Canada 62°32′N 134°51′W
37 N16 Glenn, Mount ▲ Arizona, SW USA 31°55′N 110°00′W
33 N15 Glenns Ferry Idaho, NW USA 42°57′N 115°18′W
23 W6 Glennville Georgia, SE USA 31°56′N 81°55′W
10 J10 Glenora British Columbia, W Canada 57°52′N 131°16′W
182 M11 Glenorchy Victoria, SE Australia 36°56′S 142°39′E
183 V5 Glenreagh New South Wales, SE Australia 30°04′S 153°00′E
33 X15 Glenrock Wyoming, C USA 42°51′N 105°52′W
96 K11 Glenrothes E Scotland, United Kingdom 56°11′N 03°09′W
18 L9 Glens Falls New York, NE USA 43°18′N 73°38′W
97 D14 Glenties Ir. Na Gleannta. Donegal, NW Ireland 54°47′N 08°17′W
28 L5 Glen Ullin North Dakota, N USA 46°49′N 101°49′W
21 R4 Glenville West Virginia, NE USA 38°57′N 80°51′W
27 T12 Glenwood Arkansas, C USA 34°19′N 93°33′W
29 S15 Glenwood Iowa, C USA 41°03′N 95°44′W
29 T7 Glenwood Minnesota, N USA 45°39′N 95°23′W
36 L5 Glenwood Utah, W USA 38°45′N 111°59′W
30 I5 Glenwood City Wisconsin, N USA 45°04′N 92°11′W
37 Q4 Glenwood Springs Colorado, C USA 39°33′N 107°21′W
108 F10 Gletsch Valais, S Switzerland 46°34′N 08°21′E
Glevum see Gloucester
29 U14 Glidden Iowa, C USA 42°03′N 94°43′W
112 E9 Glina var. Banijska Palanka. Sisak-Moslavina, NE Croatia 45°19′N 16°07′E
94 F11 Glittertind ▲ S Norway 61°24′N 08°19′E
111 J16 Gliwice Ger. Gleiwitz. Śląskie, S Poland 50°19′N 18°49′E
113 N16 Gllamnik Serb. Glavnik. N Kosovo 42°53′N 21°10′E
36 M14 Globe Arizona, SW USA 33°24′N 110°47′W
Globino see Hlobyne
108 L9 Glockturm ▲ SW Austria 46°54′N 10°42′E
116 L9 Glodeni Rus. Glodyany. N Moldova 47°47′N 27°33′E
109 S9 Glödnitz Kärnten, S Austria 46°57′N 14°03′E
Glodyany see Glodeni
Glogau see Głogów
109 W6 Gloggnitz Niederösterreich, E Austria 47°41′N 15°57′E
110 F13 Głogów Ger. Glogau, Glogow. Dolnośląskie, SW Poland 51°40′N 16°04′E
Glogow see Głogów
111 I16 Głogówek Ger. Oberglogau. Opolskie, S Poland 50°21′N 17°51′E
92 G12 Glomfjord Nordland, C Norway 66°49′N 14°00′E
Glomma see Gláma
Glommen see Gláma
93 I14 Glommersträsk Norrbotten, N Sweden 65°17′N 19°40′E
172 I1 Glorieuses, Îles Eng. Glorioso Islands. island (to France) N Madagascar
Glorioso Islands see Glorieuses, Îles
38 J12 Glory of Russia Cape headland Saint Matthew Island, Alaska, USA 60°36′N 172°57′W
22 J7 Gloster Mississippi, S USA 31°12′N 91°01′W
183 U7 Gloucester New South Wales, SE Australia 32°01′S 152°00′E
186 F7 Gloucester New Britain, E Papua New Guinea 05°30′S 148°30′E
97 L21 Gloucester hist. Caer Glou, Lat. Glevum. C England, United Kingdom 51°53′N 02°14′W
19 P10 Gloucester Massachusetts, NE USA 42°36′N 70°36′W
21 X6 Gloucester Virginia, NE USA 37°26′N 76°33′W
97 K21 Gloucestershire cultural region C England, United Kingdom
31 T14 Glouster Ohio, N USA 39°30′N 82°04′W
42 H3 Glovers Reef reef E Belize
18 K10 Gloversville New York, NE USA 43°03′N 74°20′W
110 K12 Głowno Łódź, C Poland 51°58′N 19°43′E
111 H16 Głubczyce Ger. Leobschütz. Opolskie, S Poland 50°13′N 17°50′E
126 L11 Glubokiy Rostovskaya Oblast', SW Russian Federation 48°34′N 40°16′E
145 W9 Glubokoye Vostochnyy Kazakhstan, E Kazakhstan 50°08′N 82°16′E
Glubokoye see Hlybokaye
111 H16 Głuchołazy Ger. Ziegenhais. Opolskie, S Poland 50°20′N 17°23′E
100 I9 Glückstadt Schleswig-Holstein, N Germany 53°47′N 09°26′E
Glukhov see Hlukhiv
Glushkevichi see Hlushkavichy
Glusk/Glussk see Hlusk
Glybokaya see Hlyboka
95 F21 Glyngøre Viborg, NW Denmark 56°45′N 08°55′E
127 Q9 Gmelinka Volgogradskaya Oblast', SW Russian Federation 50°50′N 46°51′E
109 R8 Gmünd Kärnten, S Austria 46°56′N 13°32′E
109 U2 Gmünd Niederösterreich, N Austria 48°47′N 14°59′E
Gmünd see Schwäbisch Gmünd
109 S5 Gmunden Oberösterreich, N Austria 47°56′N 13°48′E
Gmundner See see Traunsee
94 N10 Gnarp Gävleborg, C Sweden 62°03′N 17°19′E
109 W8 Gnas Steiermark, SE Austria 46°53′N 15°48′E
Gnaviyani see Fuammulah
Gnesen see Gniezno
95 O16 Gnesta Södermanland, C Sweden 59°05′N 17°20′E
110 H11 Gniezno Ger. Gnesen. Weilkopolskie, C Poland 52°33′N 17°35′E
Gnjilane see Gjilan
95 K20 Gnosjö Jönköping, S Sweden 57°22′N 13°44′E
155 E17 Goa prev. Old Goa, Vela Goa, Velha Goa. Goa, W India 15°31′N 73°56′E
155 E17 Goa var. Old Goa. ◐ state W India
Goabddális see Kåbdalis
153 U12 Goalpāra Assam, NE India 26°11′N 90°37′E
42 H7 Goascorán, Río El Salvador/Honduras
77 O16 Goaso var. Gawso. W Ghana 06°49′N 02°27′W
81 K14 Goba It. Oromo. Binishangul Gumuz, C Ethiopia 07°02′N 39°58′E
83 C20 Gobabed Erongo, W Namibia 23°36′S 15°03′E
83 E19 Gobabis Omaheke, E Namibia 22°25′S 18°58′E
Gobannium see Abergavenny
64 M7 Goban Spur undersea feature NW Atlantic Ocean
63 H21 Gobernador Gregores Santa Cruz, S Argentina 48°43′S 70°21′W
61 F14 Gobernador Ingeniero Virasoro Corrientes, NE Argentina 28°06′S 56°00′W
162 L12 Gobi desert China/Mongolia
164 I14 Gobō Wakayama, Honshū, SW Japan 33°52′N 135°09′E
Gobolka Awdal see Awdal
Gobolka Sahil see Sahil
Gobolka Sool see Sool
101 D14 Goch Nordrhein-Westfalen, W Germany 51°41′N 06°10′E
83 E20 Gochas Hardap, S Namibia 24°54′S 18°43′E
155 I14 Godāvari var. Godavari. C India
Godavari see Godāvari
155 L16 Godāvari, Mouths of the delta E India
15 V5 Godbout Québec, SE Canada 49°19′N 67°37′W
15 U5 Godbout Québec, SE Canada
15 U5 Godbout Est Québec, SE Canada
153 R14 Godda Jharkhand, India 24°50′N 87°13′E
27 N6 Goddard Kansas, C USA 37°39′N 97°34′W
14 E15 Goderich Ontario, S Canada 43°43′N 81°43′W
Godhavn see Qeqertarsuaq
154 E10 Godhra Gujarāt, W India 22°49′N 73°40′E
Göding see Hodonín
111 K22 Gödöllő Pest, N Hungary 47°36′N 19°20′E
62 H11 Godoy Cruz Mendoza, W Argentina 32°59′S 68°49′W
11 Y11 Gods Manitoba, C Canada
11 Y13 Gods Lake Manitoba, C Canada 54°29′N 94°21′W
11 X13 Gods Lake ◎ Manitoba, C Canada
Godthaab/Godthåb see Nuuk
Godwin Austen, Mount see K2
Goede Hoop, Kaap de see Good Hope, Cape of
Goedgegun see Nhlangano
Goeie Hoop, Kaap die see Good Hope, Cape of
13 O7 Goélands, Lac aux ◎ Québec, SE Canada
98 E13 Goeree island SW Netherlands
99 F15 Goes Zeeland, SW Netherlands 51°30′N 03°55′E
Goettingen see Göttingen
19 O10 Goffstown New Hampshire, NE USA 43°01′N 71°34′W
14 E8 Gogama Ontario, S Canada 47°42′N 81°44′W
30 L3 Gogebic, Lake ◎ Michigan, N USA
30 K3 Gogebic Range hill range Michigan/Wisconsin, N USA
Gogi Lerr see Gogi, Mount
137 V13 Gogi, Mount Arm. Gogi Lerr, Az. Küküdağ. ▲ Armenia/Azerbaijan 39°33′N 45°35′E
124 F12 Gogland, Ostrov island NW Russian Federation
111 I15 Gogolin Opolskie, S Poland 50°28′N 18°04′E
Gogonou see Gogounou
77 S14 Gogounou var. Gogonou. N Benin 10°50′N 02°50′E
152 I10 Gohāna Haryāna, N India 29°06′N 76°43′E
59 K18 Goianésia Goiás, C Brazil 15°21′S 49°02′W
59 K18 Goiânia prev. Goyania. state capital Goiás, C Brazil 16°43′S 49°18′W
59 K18 Goiás Goiás, C Brazil 15°57′S 50°07′W
59 J18 Goiás off. Estado de Goiás; prev. Goiaz, Goyaz. ◐ state C Brazil
Goiás, Estado de see Goiás
Goiaz see Goiás
Goidhoo Atoll see Horsburgh Atoll
159 R14 Goinsargoin Xizang Zizhiqu, W China 31°56′N 98°04′E
60 H10 Goio-Erê Paraná, SW Brazil 24°08′S 53°07′W
99 I15 Goirle Noord-Brabant, S Netherlands 51°31′N 05°04′E
104 H8 Góis Coimbra, N Portugal 40°10′N 08°06′W
165 Q8 Gojōme Akita, Honshū, NW Japan 39°55′N 140°07′E
149 U9 Gojra Punjab, E Pakistan 31°10′N 72°43′E
136 A11 Gökçeada var. Imroz Adasī, Gk. Imbros. island NW Turkey
Gökçeada see İmroz
146 F13 Gökdepe Rus. Gëkdepe, Geok-Tepe. Ahal Welaýaty, C Turkmenistan 38°05′N 58°08′E
136 I10 Gökırmak N Turkey
Goklenkuy, Solonchak see Geklengkui, Solonchak
136 C16 Gökova Körfezi gulf SW Turkey
136 K15 Göksu S Turkey
136 L15 Göksun Kahramanmaraş, C Turkey 38°03′N 36°30′E
136 I17 Göksu Nehri S Turkey
83 J16 Gokwe Midlands, NW Zimbabwe 18°13′S 28°55′E
94 F13 Gol Buskerud, S Norway 60°42′N 08°57′E
153 X12 Golāghāt Assam, NE India 26°31′N 93°54′E
110 H10 Gołańcz Wielkopolskie, C Poland 52°57′N 17°17′E
138 G8 Golan Heights Ar. Al Jawlān, Heb. HaGolan. ▲▲ SW Syria
Golārā see Ārān
Golaya Pristan see Hola Prystan'
143 T11 Golbāf Kermān, C Iran 29°51′N 57°44′E
136 M15 Gölbaşı Adıyaman, S Turkey 37°46′N 37°40′E
109 P9 Gölbner ▲ SW Austria 46°51′N 12°31′E
30 M17 Golconda Illinois, N USA 37°20′N 88°29′W
35 T3 Golconda Nevada, W USA 40°56′N 117°29′W
136 E11 Gölcük Kocaeli, NW Turkey 40°44′N 29°50′E
108 I7 Goldach Sankt Gallen, NE Switzerland 47°28′N 09°28′E
110 N7 Gołdap Ger. Goldap. Warmińsko-Mazurskie, NE Poland 54°19′N 22°23′E
32 E15 Gold Beach Oregon, NW USA 42°25′N 124°27′W
Goldberg see Złotoryja
183 V3 Gold Coast cultural region Queensland, E Australia
68 D12 Gold Coast coastal region S Ghana
39 R10 Gold Creek Alaska, USA 62°48′N 149°40′W
11 O16 Golden British Columbia, SW Canada 51°19′N 116°58′W
37 T4 Golden Colorado, C USA 39°40′N 105°12′W
184 I13 Golden Bay bay South Island, New Zealand
27 R7 Golden City Missouri, C USA 37°23′N 94°05′W
32 I11 Goldendale Washington, NW USA 45°49′N 120°49′W
Goldener Tisch see Zlatý Stôl
44 L13 Golden Grove E Jamaica 17°56′N 76°17′W
14 J12 Golden Lake ◎ Ontario, SE Canada
22 K10 Golden Meadow Louisiana, S USA 29°22′N 90°15′W
45 V10 Golden Rock ✈ (Basseterre) Saint Kitts, Saint Kitts and Nevis 17°16′N 62°43′W
Golden State, The see California
83 K16 Golden Valley Mashonaland West, N Zimbabwe 18°11′S 29°50′E
35 U9 Goldfield Nevada, W USA 37°42′N 117°15′W
Goldingen see Kuldīga
Goldmarkt see Zlatna
10 K17 Gold River Vancouver Island, British Columbia, SW Canada 49°41′N 126°05′W
21 V10 Goldsboro North Carolina, SE USA 35°23′N 78°00′W
24 M8 Goldsmith Texas, SW USA 31°58′N 102°36′W
25 R8 Goldthwaite Texas, SW USA 31°28′N 98°35′W
137 R11 Göle Ardahan, NE Turkey 40°47′N 42°36′E
Golema Ada see Ostrovo
114 H9 Golema Planina ▲▲ W Bulgaria
114 F9 Golemi Vrŭkh ▲ W Bulgaria 42°41′N 22°38′E
110 D8 Goleniów Ger. Gollnow. Zachodnio-pomorskie, NW Poland 53°34′N 14°48′E
143 R3 Golestān ◐ province N Iran
35 Q14 Goleta California, W USA 34°26′N 119°50′W
43 O16 Golfito Puntarenas, SE Costa Rica 08°42′N 83°10′W
25 T13 Goliad Texas, SW USA 28°40′N 97°26′W
113 L14 Golija ▲▲ SW Serbia
Golinka see Gongbo'gyamda
113 O16 Goljak ▲▲ SE Serbia
136 M12 Gölköy Ordu, N Turkey 40°42′N 37°37′E
Gollel see Lavumisa
109 X3 Göllersbach NE Austria
Gollnow see Goleniów
Golmo see Golmud
159 P10 Golmud var. Ge'e'mu, Golmo, Chin. Ko-erh-mu. Qinghai, C China 36°23′N 94°56′E
103 Y14 Golo Corse, France, C Mediterranean Sea
Golovanevsk see Holovanivs'k
Golovchin see Halowchyn
39 N9 Golovin Alaska, USA 64°33′N 162°54′W
142 M7 Golpāyegān var. Gulpaigan. Eşfahān, W Iran 33°23′N 50°18′E
Golshan see Ṭabas
Gol'shany see Hal'shany
96 J7 Golspie N Scotland, United Kingdom 57°59′N 03°56′W
112 O11 Golubac Serbia, NE Serbia 44°38′N 21°36′E
110 J9 Golub-Dobrzyń Kujawski-pomorskie, C Poland 53°07′N 19°03′E
145 S7 Golubovka Pavlodar, N Kazakhstan 53°07′N 74°11′E
82 B11 Golungo Alto Cuanza Norte, NW Angola 09°10′S 14°45′E
114 M8 Golyama Kamchiya E Bulgaria
114 L8 Golyama Reka N Bulgaria
114 H11 Golyama Syutkya ▲ SW Bulgaria 41°55′N 24°03′E
114 I12 Golyam Perelik ▲ S Bulgaria 41°37′N 24°34′E
114 I11 Golyam Persenk ▲ S Bulgaria 41°50′N 24°33′E
79 P19 Goma Nord-Kivu, NE Dem. Rep. Congo 01°36′S 29°08′E
153 N13 Gomati var. Gumti. N India
77 X14 Gombe Gombe, E Nigeria 10°19′N 11°02′E
67 U10 Gombe var. Igombe. E Tanzania
77 Y14 Gombi Adamawa, E Nigeria 10°07′N 12°45′E
Gombroon see Bandar-e 'Abbās
Gomel' see Homyel'
Gomel'skaya Oblast' see Homyel'skaya Voblasts'
64 N11 Gomera island Islas Canarias, Spain, NE Atlantic Ocean
40 I5 Gómez Farias Chihuahua, N Mexico 29°25′N 107°46′W
40 L8 Gómez Palacio Durango, C Mexico 25°39′N 103°30′W
158 J13 Gomo Xizang Zizhiqu, W China 33°37′N 86°40′E
143 T6 Gonābād var. Gunabad. Khorāsān-Razavī, NE Iran 36°30′N 59°18′E
44 L8 Gonaïves var. Les Gonaïves. N Haiti 19°26′N 72°41′W
123 Q12 Gonam NE Russian Federation
44 L9 Gonâve, Canal de la var. Canal de Sud. channel N Caribbean Sea
44 K9 Gonâve, Golfe de la gulf N Caribbean Sea
Gonāveh see Bandar-e Gonāveh
44 K9 Gonâve, Île de la island C Haiti
Gonbadān see Do Gonbadān
143 Q3 Gonbad-e Kāvūs var. Gunbad-i-Qawus. Golestān, N Iran 37°15′N 55°11′E
152 M12 Gonda Uttar Pradesh, N India 27°08′N 81°58′E
Gondar see Gonder
80 I11 Gonder var. Gondar. Āmara, NW Ethiopia 12°36′N 37°27′E
78 J13 Gondey Moyen-Chari, S Chad 09°07′N 19°10′E
154 J12 Gondia Mahārāshtra, C India 21°27′N 80°12′E
104 G6 Gondomar Porto, NW Portugal 41°10′N 08°35′W
136 C12 Gönen Balıkesir, W Turkey 40°06′N 27°39′E
136 C12 Gönen Çayı NW Turkey
159 O15 Gongbo'gyamda var. Golinka. Xizang Zizhiqu, W China 30°03′N 93°10′E
Gongchang see Longxi
159 N16 Gonggar var. Gyixong. Xizang Zizhiqu, W China 29°18′N 90°56′E
160 G9 Gongga Shan ▲ C China 29°50′N 101°55′E
159 T10 Gonghe var. Qabqa. Qinghai, C China 36°20′N 100°46′E
Gongjiang see Yudu
158 I5 Gongliu var. Tokkuztara. Xinjiang Uygur Zizhiqu, NW China 43°29′N 82°16′E
77 W14 Gongola E Nigeria
Gongoleh State see Jonglei
183 P5 Gongolgon New South Wales, SE Australia 30°19′S 146°57′E
159 Q6 Gongpoquan Gansu, N China 41°45′N 100°27′E
Gongquan see Gongxian
Gongtang see Damxung
160 I10 Gongxian var. Gongquan, Gong Xian. Sichuan, C China 28°25′N 104°51′E
Gong Xian see Gongxian
157 V10 Gongzhuling prev. Huaide. Jilin, NE China 43°30′N 124°48′E
159 S14 Gonjo Xizang Zizhiqu, W China 30°51′N 98°16′E
107 B20 Gonnesa Sardegna, Italy, C Mediterranean Sea 39°15′N 08°27′E
Gonni/Gónnos see Gónnoi
115 F15 Gónnoi var. Gonni, Gónnos; prev. Dereli. Thessalía, C Greece 39°52′N 22°27′E
164 C13 Gōnoura Nagasaki, Iki, SW Japan 33°44′N 129°41′E
35 O11 Gonzales California, W USA 36°30′N 121°26′W
22 J9 Gonzales Louisiana, S USA 30°14′N 90°55′W
25 T12 Gonzales Texas, SW USA 29°31′N 97°29′W
41 P11 González Tamaulipas, C Mexico 22°50′N 98°25′W
21 V6 Goochland Virginia, NE USA 37°42′N 77°54′W
195 X14 Goodenough, Cape headland Antarctica 66°15′S 126°35′E
186 F9 Goodenough Island var. Morata. island SE Papua New Guinea
39 N8 Goodhope Bay bay Alaska, USA

◆ Country
● Country Capital
◇ Dependent Territory
○ Dependent Territory Capital
◐ Administrative Regions
✈ International Airport
▲ Mountain
▲▲ Mountain Range
Volcano
River
◎ Lake
Reservoir

GOOD HOPE, CAPE OF – GRAYLAND

83 D26 Good Hope, Cape of Afr. Kaap de Goede Hoop, Kaap die Goeie Hoop. headland SW South Africa 34°19′S 18°25′E
10 K10 Good Hope Lake British Columbia, W Canada 59°15′N 129°18′W
83 E23 Goodhouse Northern Cape, W South Africa 28°54′S 18°13′E
33 O15 Gooding Idaho, NW USA 42°56′N 114°42′W
26 H3 Goodland Kansas, C USA 39°20′N 101°43′W
173 Y15 Goodlands NW Mauritius 20°02′S 57°39′E
20 J8 Goodlettsville Tennessee, S USA 36°19′N 86°42′W
39 N13 Goodnews Alaska, USA 59°07′N 161°35′W
25 O3 Goodnight Texas, SW USA 35°00′N 101°07′W
183 Q4 Goodooga New South Wales, SE Australia 29°09′S 147°30′E
29 N4 Goodrich North Dakota, N USA 47°24′N 100°07′W
25 W10 Goodrich Texas, SW USA 30°36′N 94°57′W
29 X10 Goodview Minnesota, N USA 44°04′N 91°42′W
26 H8 Goodwell Oklahoma, C USA 36°36′N 101°38′W
97 N17 Goole E England, United Kingdom 53°43′N 00°46′W
183 O8 Goolgowi New South Wales, SE Australia 34°00′S 145°43′E
182 I10 Goolwa South Australia 35°31′S 138°43′E
181 Y11 Goondiwindi Queensland, E Australia 28°33′S 150°22′E
98 O11 Goor Overijssel, E Netherlands 52°13′N 06°33′E
Goose Bay see Happy Valley-Goose Bay
33 V13 Gooseberry Creek Wyoming, C USA
21 S14 Goose Creek South Carolina, SE USA 32°58′N 80°01′W
63 M23 Goose Green var. Prado del Ganso. East Falkland, Falkland Islands 51°52′S 59°W
16 D8 Goose Lake var. Lago dos Gansos. ◎ California/Oregon, W USA
29 Q4 Goose River North Dakota, N USA
153 T16 Gopalganj Dhaka, S Bangladesh 23°00′N 89°48′E
153 O12 Gopālganj Bihār, N India 26°28′N 84°26′E
Gopher State see Minnesota
101 I22 Göppingen Baden-Württemberg, SW Germany 48°42′N 09°39′E
110 G13 Góra Ger. Guhrau. Dolnośląskie, SW Poland 51°40′N 16°03′E
110 M12 Góra Kalwaria Mazowieckie, C Poland 52°00′N 21°14′E
153 O12 Gorakhpur Uttar Pradesh, N India 26°45′N 83°23′E
Gora Kyuren see Kürendag
Gorany see Harany
113 J14 Goražde Federacija Bosna I Hercegovina, SE Bosnia and Herzegovina 43°39′N 18°58′E
Gorbovichi see Harbavichy
Gorče Petrov see Đorče Petrov
0 E9 Gorda Ridges undersea feature NE Pacific Ocean 41°30′N 128°00′W
Gordiaz see Gardīz
78 K12 Gordil Vakaga, N Central African Republic 09°37′N 21°42′E
23 U5 Gordon Georgia, SE USA 32°52′N 83°19′W
28 K12 Gordon Nebraska, C USA 42°48′N 102°12′W
25 R7 Gordon Texas, SW USA 32°32′N 98°21′W
28 L13 Gordon Creek Nebraska, C USA
63 I25 Gordon, Isla island S Chile
183 O17 Gordon, Lake ◎ Tasmania, SE Australia
183 O17 Gordon River Tasmania, SE Australia
21 V5 Gordonsville Virginia, NE USA 38°08′N 78°11′W
78 H13 Goré Logone-Oriental, S Chad 07°55′N 16°38′E
80 H13 Gorē Oromīya, C Ethiopia 08°08′N 35°33′E
185 D24 Gore Southland, South Island, New Zealand 46°06′S 168°58′E
14 D11 Gore Bay Manitoulin Island, Ontario, S Canada 45°54′N 82°28′W
25 Q5 Goree Texas, SW USA 33°28′N 99°31′W
137 O11 Görele Giresun, NE Turkey 41°00′N 39°00′E
19 N6 Gore Mountain ▲ Vermont, NE USA 44°55′N 71°47′W
39 R13 Gore Point headland Alaska, USA 59°12′N 150°57′W
37 R4 Gore Range ▲▲ Colorado, C USA
97 F19 Gorey Ir. Guaire. Wexford, SE Ireland 52°40′N 06°18′W
143 R12 Gorgāb Kermān, S Iran
143 Q4 Gorgān var. Astarabad, Astrabad, Gurgan, prev. Asterābād; anc. Hyrcania. Golestān, N Iran 36°53′N 54°28′E
143 Q4 Gorgān, Rūd-e N Iran
76 I10 Gorgol ◐ region S Mauritania
106 D12 Gorgona, Isola di island Archipelago Toscano, C Italy
19 P8 Gorham Maine, NE USA 43°41′N 70°27′W
137 T10 Gori C Georgia 42°00′N 44°07′E
98 I13 Gorinchem var. Gorkum. Zuid-Holland, C Netherlands 51°50′N 04°59′E
137 V13 Goris SE Armenia 39°31′N 46°20′E
124 K16 Goritsy Tverskaya Oblast', W Russian Federation 57°09′N 36°44′E
106 J7 Gorizia Ger. Görz. Friuli-Venezia Giulia, NE Italy 45°57′N 13°37′E
116 G13 Gorj ◐ county SW Romania
109 W12 Gorjanci var. Uskočke Planine, Žumberak, Žumberačko Gorje, Ger. Uskokengebirge; prev. Sichelburger Gerbirge. ▲ Croatia/Slovenia Europe see also Žumberačko Gorje
Görkau see Jirkov
Gorki see Horki
Gor'kiy see Nizhniy Novgorod
127 O11 Gor'kovskiy Volgogradskaya Oblast', SW Russian Federation 48°41′N 44°20′E
Gorkum see Gorinchem
95 I23 Gørlev Vestsjælland, E Denmark 55°33′N 11°14′E
111 M17 Gorlice Małopolskie, S Poland 49°40′N 21°09′E
101 Q15 Görlitz Sachsen, E Germany 51°09′N 14°58′E
Görlitz see Zgorzelec
Gorlovka see Horlivka
25 R7 Gorman Texas, SW USA 32°12′N 98°40′W
21 T3 Gormania West Virginia, NE USA 39°16′N 79°18′W
Gorna Dzhumaya see Blagoevgrad
114 K8 Gorna Oryakhovitsa Veliko Tŭrnovo, N Bulgaria 43°07′N 25°40′E
114 J8 Gorna Studena Veliko Tŭrnovo, N Bulgaria 43°26′N 25°21′E
Gornja Mužlja see Mužlja
109 X9 Gornja Radgona Ger. Oberradkersburg. NE Slovenia 46°39′N 16°00′E
112 M13 Gornji Milanovac Serbia, C Serbia 44°01′N 20°26′E
112 G13 Gornji Vakuf var. Uskoplje. Federacija Bosna I Hercegovina, SW Bosnia and Herzegovina 43°55′N 17°34′E
122 J13 Gorno-Altaysk Respublika Altay, S Russian Federation 51°59′N 85°56′E
Gorno-Altayskaya Respublika see Altay, Respublika
123 N12 Gorno-Chuyskiy Irkutskaya Oblast', C Russian Federation 57°33′N 111°38′E
125 V14 Gornozavodsk Permskaya Oblast', NW Russian Federation 58°21′N 58°24′E
125 V14 Gornozavodsk Ostrov Sakhalin, Sakhalinskaya Oblast', SE Russian Federation 46°34′N 141°52′E
122 I13 Gornyak Altayskiy Kray, S Russian Federation 50°58′N 81°24′E
123 O14 Gornyy Chitunskaya Oblast', Russian Federation 51°42′N 114°16′E
127 R8 Gornyy Saratovskaya Oblast', W Russian Federation 51°42′N 48°26′E
Gornyy Altay see Altay, Respublika
127 O10 Gornyy Balykley Volgogradskaya Oblast', SW Russian Federation 49°37′N 45°03′E
80 I13 Goroch'an ▲ W Ethiopia 09°09′N 37°16′E
116 J7 Gorodenka var. Horodenka. Ivano-Frankivs'ka Oblast', W Ukraine 48°41′N 25°28′E
127 O3 Gorodets Nizhegorodskaya Oblast', W Russian Federation 56°36′N 43°27′E
Gorodets see Haradzyets
Gorodeya see Haradzyeya
127 P6 Gorodishche Penzenskaya Oblast', W Russian Federation 53°17′N 45°39′E
Gorodishche see Horodyshche
Gorodnya see Horodnya
Gorodok see Haradok
Gorodok/Gorodok Yagellonski see Horodok
126 M13 Gorodovikovsk Respublika Kalmykiya, SW Russian Federation 46°07′N 41°56′E
186 D7 Goroka Eastern Highlands, C Papua New Guinea 06°02′S 145°22′E
Gorokhov see Horokhiv
127 N3 Gorokhovets Vladimirskaya Oblast', W Russian Federation 56°12′N 42°40′E
77 Q11 Gorom-Gorom NE Burkina 14°27′N 00°14′W
171 U13 Gorong, Kepulauan island group E Indonesia
83 M17 Gorongosa Sofala, C Mozambique 18°40′S 34°03′E
171 P11 Gorontalo Sulawesi, C Indonesia 00°33′N 123°05′E
171 O11 Gorontalo off. Propinsi Gorontalo. ◐ province N Indonesia
Propinsi Gorontalo see Gorontalo
Gorontalo, Teluk see Tomini, Gulf of
110 L7 Górowo Iławeckie Ger. Landsberg. Warmińsko-Mazurskie, NE Poland 54°18′N 20°30′E
98 M7 Gorredijk Fris. De Gordyk. Friesland, N Netherlands 53°00′N 06°04′E
84 C14 Gorringe Ridge undersea feature E Atlantic Ocean 36°40′N 11°35′W
98 M11 Gorssel Gelderland, E Netherlands 52°12′N 06°13′E
109 T8 Görtschitz S Austria
Goryn see Horyn'
Görz see Gorizia
110 E10 Gorzów Wielkopolski Ger. Landsberg, Landsberg an der Warthe. Lubuskie, W Poland 52°44′N 15°12′E
146 B10 Goşabo var. Goshoba, Rus. Koshoba. Balkan Welaýaty, NW Turkmenistan 40°28′N 54°11′E
108 G9 Göschenen Uri, C Switzerland 46°40′N 08°36′E
165 O11 Gosen Niigata, Honshū, C Japan 37°45′N 139°11′E
183 T8 Gosford New South Wales, SE Australia 33°25′S 151°18′E
31 P11 Goshen Indiana, N USA 41°34′N 85°49′W
18 K13 Goshen New York, NE USA 41°24′N 74°17′W
Goshoba see Goşabo
Goshoba see Goşoba
165 Q7 Goshogawara var. Gosyogawara. Aomori, Honshū, C Japan 40°47′N 140°24′E
Goshquduq Qum see Tosquduq Qumlari
101 J14 Goslar Niedersachsen, C Germany 51°55′N 10°25′E
27 Y9 Gosnell Arkansas, C USA 35°57′N 89°58′W
146 B10 Goşoba var. Goshoba, Rus. Koshoba. Balkanskiy Velayat, NW Turkmenistan 40°28′N 54°11′E
112 C11 Gospić Lika-Senj, C Croatia 44°32′N 15°21′E
97 N23 Gosport S England United Kingdom 50°48′N 01°08′W
94 D9 Gossa island S Norway
108 H7 Gossau Sankt Gallen, NE Switzerland 47°25′N 09°16′E
99 G20 Gosselies var. Goss'lies. Hainaut, S Belgium 50°28′N 04°26′E
77 P10 Gossi Tombouctou, C Mali 15°44′N 01°19′W
Goss'lies see Gosselies
113 N18 Gostivar W FYR Macedonia 41°48′N 20°55′E
Gostomel' see Hostomel'
110 G12 Gostyń var. Gostyn. Wielkopolskie, C Poland 51°52′N 17°00′E
Gostyn see Gostyń
110 K11 Gostynin Mazowieckie, C Poland 52°25′N 19°27′E
Gosyogawara see Goshogawara
95 J18 Göta Älv S Sweden
95 N17 Göta kanal canal S Sweden
95 K18 Götaland cultural region S Sweden
95 H17 Göteborg Eng. Gothenburg. Västra Götaland, S Sweden 57°43′N 11°58′E
77 X16 Gotel Mountains ▲ E Nigeria
95 K17 Götene Västra Götaland, S Sweden 58°32′N 13°29′E
Gotera see San Francisco
101 K16 Gotha Thüringen, C Germany 50°57′N 10°43′E
29 N15 Gothenburg Nebraska, C USA 40°57′N 100°09′W
Gothenburg see Göteborg
77 R12 Gothèye Tillabéri, SW Niger 13°52′N 01°27′E
Gothland see Gotland
95 P19 Gotland var. Gothland, Gottland. ◐ county SE Sweden
95 O18 Gotland island SE Sweden
164 B13 Gotō-rettō island group SW Japan
114 H12 Gotse Delchev prev. Nevrokop. Blagoevgrad, SW Bulgaria 41°33′N 23°42′E
95 P17 Gotska Sandön island SE Sweden
101 I15 Göttingen var. Goettingen. Niedersachsen, C Germany 51°33′N 09°55′E
Gottland see Gotland
93 I16 Gottne Västernorrland, C Sweden 63°27′N 18°25′E
Gottschee see Kočevje
Gottwaldov see Zlín
146 B11 Goturdepe Rus. Koturdepe. Balkan Welaýaty, W Turkmenistan 39°32′N 53°39′E
108 I7 Götzis Vorarlberg, NW Austria 47°21′N 09°40′E
98 H12 Gouda Zuid-Holland, C Netherlands 52°01′N 04°42′E
76 I11 Goudiri var. Goudiry. E Senegal 14°12′N 12°41′W
Goudiry see Goudiri
77 X12 Goudoumaria Diffa, S Niger 13°28′N 11°15′E
15 R9 Gouffre, Rivière du Québec, SE Canada
65 M19 Gough Fracture Zone tectonic feature S Atlantic Ocean
65 M19 Gough Island island Tristan da Cunha, S Atlantic Ocean
15 N8 Gouin, Réservoir ⊠ Québec, SE Canada
14 B10 Goulais River Ontario, S Canada 46°41′N 84°22′W
183 R9 Goulburn New South Wales, SE Australia 34°45′S 149°44′E
183 O11 Goulburn River Victoria, SE Australia
195 O10 Gould Coast physical region Antarctica
Goulimime see Guelmime
114 F13 Gouménissa Kentrikí Makedonía, N Greece 40°56′N 22°27′E
77 O10 Goundam Tombouctou, NW Mali 16°27′N 03°39′W
78 H12 Goundi Moyen-Chari, S Chad 09°22′N 17°21′E
78 G12 Gounou-Gaya Mayo-Kébbi, SW Chad 09°37′N 15°30′E
Gourci see Goursi
Gourcy see Goursi
102 M13 Gourdon Lot, S France 44°45′N 01°22′E
77 W11 Gouré Zinder, SE Niger 13°59′N 10°16′E
102 G6 Gourin Morbihan, NW France 48°07′N 03°37′W
77 P10 Gourma-Rharous Tombouctou, C Mali 16°54′N 01°55′W
103 N4 Gournay-en-Bray Seine-Maritime, N France 49°29′N 01°42′E
78 J6 Gouro Borkou-Ennedi-Tibesti, N Chad 19°26′N 19°36′E
77 O12 Goursi var. Gourci, Gourcy. NW Burkina 13°13′N 02°20′W
104 H8 Gouveia Guarda, N Portugal 40°29′N 07°35′W
18 I7 Gouverneur New York, NE USA 44°20′N 75°27′W
99 L21 Gouvy Luxembourg, E Belgium 50°10′N 05°55′E
45 R14 Gouyave var. Charlotte Town. NW Grenada 12°10′N 61°44′W
Goverla, Gora see Hoverla, Hora
59 N20 Governador Valadares Minas Gerais, SE Brazil 18°51′S 41°57′W
171 R8 Governor Generoso Mindanao, S Philippines 06°36′N 126°06′E
44 I2 Governor's Harbour Eleuthera Island, C Bahamas 25°11′N 76°15′W
162 F9 Govĭ-Altay ◐ province SW Mongolia
162 I10 Govĭ Altayn Nuruu ▲ S Mongolia
154 L9 Govind Ballabh Pant Sāgar ⊠ C India
152 I7 Govind Sāgar ⊠ NE India
162 M8 Govĭ-Sumber ◐ province C Mongolia
Govurdak see Magdanly
18 D11 Gowanda New York, NE USA 42°25′N 78°55′W
148 J10 Gowd-e Zereh, Dasht-e var. Guad-i-Zirreh. marsh SW Afghanistan
14 F8 Gowganda Ontario, S Canada 47°41′N 80°46′W
14 G8 Gowganda Lake ◎ Ontario, S Canada
29 U13 Gowrie Iowa, C USA 42°16′N 94°17′W
Gowurdak see Magdanly
61 C15 Goya Corrientes, NE Argentina 29°10′S 59°15′W
Goyania see Goiânia
Goyaz see Goiás
137 X11 Göyçay Rus. Geokchay. C Azerbaijan 40°38′N 47°44′E
146 D10 Goymat Rus. Koymat. Balkan Welaýaty, NW Turkmenistan 40°23′N 55°45′E
146 D10 Goymatdag, Gory Rus. Gory Koymatdag. hill range Balkan Welaýaty, NW Turkmenistan
136 F12 Göynük Bolu, NW Turkey 40°24′N 30°45′E
165 R9 Goyō-san ▲ Honshū, C Japan 39°12′N 141°40′E
78 K11 Goz Beïda Ouaddaï, SE Chad 12°06′N 21°22′E
146 M10 G'ozg'on Rus. Gazgan. Navoiy Viloyati, C Uzbekistan 40°36′N 65°29′E
158 H11 Gozha Co ◎ W China
121 O15 Gozo var. Ghawdex. island N Malta
80 H9 Göz Regeb Kassala, NE Sudan 16°03′N 35°33′E
83 H25 Graaff-Reinet Eastern Cape, S South Africa 32°15′S 24°32′E
Graasten see Gråsten
76 L17 Grabo SW Ivory Coast 04°57′N 07°30′W
112 P11 Grabovica Serbia, E Serbia 44°30′N 22°29′E
110 I13 Grabów nad Prosną Wielkopolskie, C Poland 51°30′N 18°06′E
108 I8 Grabs Sankt Gallen, NE Switzerland 47°10′N 09°27′E
112 D12 Gračac Zadar, SW Croatia 44°18′N 15°52′E
112 I11 Gračanica Federacija Bosna I Hercegovina, NE Bosnia and Herzegovina 44°41′N 18°20′E
14 L11 Gracefield Québec, SE Canada 46°06′N 76°03′W
99 K19 Grâce-Hollogne Liège, E Belgium 50°38′N 05°30′E
23 R8 Graceville Florida, SE USA 30°57′N 85°31′W
29 R8 Graceville Minnesota, N USA 45°34′N 96°25′W
42 G6 Gracias Lempira, W Honduras 14°35′N 88°35′W
Gracias see Lempira
42 L5 Gracias a Dios ◐ department E Honduras
43 O6 Gracias a Dios, Cabo de headland Honduras/Nicaragua 15°00′N 83°10′W
64 O2 Graciosa var. Ilha Graciosa. island Azores, Portugal, NE Atlantic Ocean
64 Q11 Graciosa island Islas Canarias, Spain, NE Atlantic Ocean
Graciosa, Ilha see Graciosa
112 I11 Gradačac Federacija Bosna I Hercegovina, N Bosnia and Herzegovina 44°51′N 18°24′E
59 J15 Gradaús, Serra dos ▲▲ C Brazil
104 L3 Gradefes Castilla-León, N Spain 42°37′N 05°14′W
Gradiška see Bosanska Gradiška
Gradizhsk see Hradyz'k
106 J7 Grado Friuli-Venezia Giulia, NE Italy 45°41′N 13°24′E
104 K2 Grado Asturias, N Spain 43°23′N 06°04′W
113 P19 Gradsko C FYR Macedonia 41°34′N 21°56′E
37 V11 Grady New Mexico, SW USA 34°49′N 103°19′W
Grad Zagreb see Zagreb
29 T12 Graettinger Iowa, C USA 43°14′N 94°45′W
101 M23 Grafing Bayern, SE Germany 48°01′N 11°57′E
25 S6 Graford Texas, SW USA 32°56′N 98°15′W
183 V5 Grafton New South Wales, SE Australia 29°41′S 152°55′E
29 Q3 Grafton North Dakota, N USA 48°24′N 97°24′W
21 S3 Grafton West Virginia, NE USA 39°21′N 80°03′W
21 T9 Graham North Carolina, SE USA 36°05′N 79°25′W
25 R6 Graham Texas, SW USA 33°07′N 98°36′W
Graham Bell Island see Greem-Bell, Ostrov
10 I13 Graham Island island Queen Charlotte Islands, British Columbia, SW Canada
19 S6 Graham Lake ◎ Maine, NE USA
194 H4 Graham Land physical region Antarctica
37 N15 Graham, Mount ▲ Arizona, SW USA 32°42′N 109°52′W
Grahamstad see Grahamstown
83 I25 Grahamstown Afr. Grahamstad. Eastern Cape, S South Africa 33°18′S 26°32′E
Grahovo see Bosansko Grahovo
68 C12 Grain Coast coastal region S Liberia
169 S17 Grajagan, Teluk bay Jawa, S Indonesia
59 L14 Grajaú Maranhão, E Brazil 05°50′S 46°12′W
58 M13 Grajaú, Rio NE Brazil
110 O8 Grajewo Podlaskie, NE Poland 53°38′N 22°26′E
95 F24 Gram Sønderjylland, SW Denmark 55°18′N 09°03′E
103 N13 Gramat Lot, S France 44°45′N 01°45′E
22 H5 Grambling Louisiana, S USA 32°31′N 92°43′W
115 C14 Grámmos ▲ Albania/Greece
96 I9 Grampian Mountains ▲ C Scotland, United Kingdom
182 L12 Grampians, The ▲ Victoria, SE Australia
98 O9 Gramsbergen Overijssel, E Netherlands 52°37′N 06°39′E
113 L21 Gramsh var. Gramshi. Elbasan, C Albania 40°52′N 20°12′E
Gramshi see Gramsh
Gran see Esztergom, Hungary
Gran see Hron
54 F11 Granada Meta, C Colombia 03°33′N 73°44′W
42 J10 Granada Granada, SW Nicaragua 11°55′N 85°58′W
105 N14 Granada Andalucía, S Spain 37°13′N 03°41′W
37 W6 Granada Colorado, C USA 38°00′N 102°18′W
42 J11 Granada ◐ department SW Nicaragua
105 N14 Granada ◐ province Andalucía, S Spain
63 I21 Gran Antiplanicie Central plain S Argentina
97 E17 Granard Ir. Gránard. C Ireland 53°47′N 07°30′W
Gránard see Granard
63 J20 Gran Bajo basin S Argentina
63 J15 Gran Bajo del Gualicho basin E Argentina
63 I21 Gran Bajo de San Julián basin SE Argentina
25 S7 Granbury Texas, SW USA 32°27′N 97°47′W
15 P12 Granby Québec, SE Canada 45°23′N 72°44′W
27 S8 Granby Missouri, C USA 36°55′N 94°14′W
37 S3 Granby, Lake ⊠ Colorado, C USA
64 O12 Gran Canaria var. Grand Canary. island Islas Canarias, Spain, NE Atlantic Ocean
47 T11 Gran Chaco var. Chaco. lowland plain South America
45 R14 Grand Anse SW Grenada 12°01′N 61°45′W
Grand-Anse see Portsmouth
44 G1 Grand Bahama Island island N Bahamas
Grand Balé see Tui
103 U7 Grand Ballon Ger. Ballon de Guebwiller. ▲ NE France 47°53′N 07°06′E
13 T13 Grand Bank Newfoundland, Newfoundland and Labrador, SE Canada 47°06′N 55°48′W
64 I7 Grand Banks of Newfoundland undersea feature NW Atlantic Ocean 45°00′N 40°00′W
Grand Bassa see Buchanan
77 N17 Grand-Bassam var. Bassam. SE Ivory Coast 05°14′N 03°45′W
14 E16 Grand Bend Ontario, S Canada 43°17′N 81°46′W
76 L17 Grand-Bérébi var. Grand-Béréby. SW Ivory Coast 04°38′N 06°55′W
Grand-Béréby see Grand-Bérébi
45 X11 Grand-Bourg Marie-Galante, SE Guadeloupe 15°53′N 61°19′W
44 M6 Grand Caicos var. Middle Caicos. island C Turks and Caicos Islands
14 K12 Grand Calumet, Île du island Québec, SE Canada
97 E18 Grand Canal Ir. An Chanáil Mhór. canal C Ireland
Grand Canal see Da Yunhe
Grand Canary see Gran Canaria
36 K10 Grand Canyon Arizona, SW USA 36°01′N 112°10′W
36 J9 Grand Canyon canyon Arizona, SW USA
Grand Canyon State see Arizona
44 D8 Grand Cayman island SW Cayman Islands
11 R14 Grand Centre Alberta, SW Canada 54°25′N 110°13′W
76 L17 Grand Cess SE Liberia 04°36′N 08°12′W
108 D12 Grand Combin ▲ S Switzerland 45°58′N 07°27′E
32 K8 Grand Coulee Washington, NW USA 47°56′N 119°00′W
32 J8 Grand Coulee valley Washington, NW USA
45 X5 Grand Cul-de-Sac Marin bay N Guadeloupe
Grand Duchy of Luxembourg see Luxembourg
63 I22 Grande, Bahía bay S Argentina
11 N14 Grande Cache Alberta, W Canada 53°53′N 119°07′W
103 U12 Grande Casse ▲ E France 45°22′N 06°50′E
Grande-Comore see Ngazidja
61 G18 Grande, Cuchilla hill range E Uruguay
45 S5 Grande de Añasco, Río W Puerto Rico
Grande de Chiloé, Isla see Chiloé, Isla de
58 J12 Grande de Gurupá, Ilha river island NE Brazil
57 K21 Grande de Lipez, Río SW Bolivia
45 U6 Grande de Loíza, Río E Puerto Rico
45 T5 Grande de Manatí, Río C Puerto Rico
42 L9 Grande de Matagalpa, Río C Nicaragua
40 K12 Grande de Santiago, Río var. Santiago. C Mexico
43 O15 Grande de Térraba, Río var. Río Térraba. SE Costa Rica
12 J9 Grande Deux, Réservoir la ⊠ Québec, E Canada
60 O10 Grande, Ilha island SE Brazil
11 O13 Grande Prairie Alberta, W Canada 55°10′N 118°52′W
74 I8 Grand Erg Occidental desert W Algeria
74 L9 Grand Erg Oriental desert Algeria/Tunisia
57 M18 Grande, Río C Bolivia
59 J20 Grande, Rio S Brazil
2 F15 Grande, Rio var. Río Bravo, Sp. Río Bravo del Norte, Bravo del Norte. Mexico/USA
15 Y7 Grande-Rivière Québec, SE Canada 48°27′N 64°37′W
15 Y6 Grande Rivière Québec, SE Canada
44 M8 Grande-Rivière-du-Nord N Haiti 19°36′N 72°10′W
62 K9 Grande, Salina var. Gran Salitral. salt lake C Argentina
15 S7 Grandes-Bergeronnes Québec, SE Canada 48°16′N 69°32′W
47 W6 Grande, Serra ▲ W Brazil
40 K4 Grande, Sierra ▲ N Mexico
103 S12 Grandes Rousses ▲▲ E France
63 K17 Grandes, Salinas salt lake E Argentina
45 Y5 Grande Terre island E West Indies
15 X5 Grande-Vallée Québec, SE Canada 49°14′N 65°08′W
45 Y5 Grande Vigie, Pointe de la headland Grande Terre, N Guadeloupe 16°31′N 61°27′W
13 N14 Grand Falls New Brunswick, SE Canada 47°02′N 67°46′W
13 T11 Grand Falls Newfoundland, Newfoundland and Labrador, SE Canada 48°57′N 55°48′W
24 L9 Grandfalls Texas, SW USA 31°20′N 102°51′W
21 P9 Grandfather Mountain ▲ North Carolina, SE USA 36°06′N 81°48′W
26 L13 Grandfield Oklahoma, C USA 34°15′N 98°40′W
11 N17 Grand Forks British Columbia, SW Canada 49°02′N 118°30′W
29 R4 Grand Forks North Dakota, N USA 47°54′N 97°03′W
31 O9 Grand Haven Michigan, N USA 43°03′N 86°13′W
Grandichi see Hrandzichy
29 P15 Grand Island Nebraska, C USA 40°55′N 98°20′W
31 O3 Grand Island island Michigan, N USA
22 K10 Grand Isle Louisiana, S USA 29°12′N 90°00′W
65 A23 Grand Jason island Jason Islands, NW Falkland Islands
37 P5 Grand Junction Colorado, C USA 39°03′N 108°33′W
20 F10 Grand Junction Tennessee, S USA 35°03′N 89°11′W
14 J9 Grand-Lac-Victoria Québec, SE Canada 47°33′N 77°28′W
14 J9 Grand lac Victoria ◎ Québec, SE Canada
77 N17 Grand-Lahou var. Grand Lahu. S Ivory Coast 05°09′N 05°01′W
Grand Lahu see Grand-Lahou
37 S3 Grand Lake Colorado, C USA 40°15′N 105°49′W
13 S11 Grand Lake ◎ Newfoundland and Labrador, E Canada
22 G9 Grand Lake ◎ Louisiana, S USA
31 R5 Grand Lake ◎ Michigan, N USA
31 Q13 Grand Lake ⊠ Ohio, N USA
27 R9 Grand Lake O' The Cherokees var. Lake O' The Cherokees. ⊠ Oklahoma, C USA
31 Q9 Grand Ledge Michigan, N USA 42°45′N 84°45′W
102 I8 Grand-Lieu, Lac de ◎ NW France
19 U6 Grand Manan Channel channel Canada/USA
13 O15 Grand Manan Island island New Brunswick, SE Canada
29 Y4 Grand Marais Minnesota, N USA 47°45′N 90°19′W
15 P10 Grand-Mère Québec, SE Canada 46°36′N 72°41′W
37 P5 Grand Mesa ▲ Colorado, C USA
108 C10 Grand Muveran ▲ W Switzerland 46°16′N 07°12′E
104 G12 Grândola Setúbal, S Portugal 38°10′N 08°34′W
Grand Paradis see Gran Paradiso
187 O15 Grand Passage passage N New Caledonia
77 R16 Grand-Popo S Benin 06°19′N 01°50′E
29 Z3 Grand Portage Minnesota, N USA 48°00′N 89°36′W
25 T6 Grand Prairie Texas, SW USA 32°45′N 97°00′W
11 W14 Grand Rapids Manitoba, C Canada 53°12′N 99°19′W
31 P9 Grand Rapids Michigan, N USA 42°57′N 86°40′W
29 V5 Grand Rapids Minnesota, N USA 47°14′N 93°31′W
14 L10 Grand-Remous Québec, SE Canada 46°36′N 75°53′W
14 F15 Grand River Ontario, S Canada
31 P9 Grand River Michigan, N USA
27 T3 Grand River Missouri, C USA
28 M7 Grand River South Dakota, N USA
45 Q11 Grand' Rivière N Martinique 14°52′N 61°11′W
32 F11 Grand Ronde Oregon, NW USA 45°03′N 123°43′W
32 L11 Grand Ronde River Oregon/Washington, NW USA
Grand-Saint-Bernard, Col du see Great Saint Bernard Pass
25 V6 Grand Saline Texas, SW USA 32°40′N 95°42′W
55 X10 Grand-Santi W French Guiana 04°19′N 54°24′W
Grandsee see Grandson
172 J16 Grand Sœur island Les Sœurs, NE Seychelles
108 B9 Grandson prev. Grandsee. Vaud, W Switzerland 46°49′N 06°39′E
33 S14 Grand Teton ▲ Wyoming, C USA 43°44′N 110°48′W
31 P5 Grand Traverse Bay lake bay Michigan, N USA
45 N6 Grand Turk ○ (Turks and Caicos Islands) Grand Turk Island, S Turks and Caicos Islands 21°24′N 71°08′W
45 N6 Grand Turk Island island SE Turks and Caicos Islands
103 S13 Grand Veymont ▲ E France 44°51′N 05°32′E
11 W15 Grandview Manitoba, S Canada 51°11′N 100°41′W
27 R4 Grandview Missouri, C USA 38°53′N 94°31′W
36 I10 Grand Wash Cliffs cliff Arizona, SW USA
14 J8 Granet, Lac ◎ Québec, SE Canada
95 L14 Grangärde Dalarna, C Sweden 60°15′N 15°00′E
44 H12 Grange Hill W Jamaica 18°19′N 78°11′W
96 J12 Grangemouth C Scotland, United Kingdom 56°01′N 03°44′W
25 T10 Granger Texas, SW USA 30°43′N 97°26′W
32 J10 Granger Washington, NW USA 46°20′N 120°11′W
33 T17 Granger Wyoming, C USA 41°37′N 109°58′W
Granges see Grenchen
95 L14 Grängesberg Dalarna, C Sweden 60°06′N 15°00′E
33 N11 Grangeville Idaho, NW USA 45°55′N 116°07′W
10 K13 Granisle British Columbia, SW Canada 54°55′N 126°14′W
30 K15 Granite City Illinois, N USA 38°42′N 90°09′W
29 S9 Granite Falls Minnesota, N USA 44°48′N 95°33′W
21 Q9 Granite Falls North Carolina, SE USA 35°48′N 81°25′W
36 K12 Granite Mountain ▲ Arizona, SW USA 34°38′N 112°34′W
33 T12 Granite Peak ▲ Montana, NW USA 45°09′N 109°48′W
35 T2 Granite Peak ▲ Nevada, W USA 41°40′N 117°35′W
36 J3 Granite Peak ▲ Utah, W USA 40°09′N 113°18′W
Granite State see New Hampshire
107 H24 Granitola, Capo headland Sicilia, Italy, C Mediterranean Sea 37°33′N 12°39′E
185 H15 Granity West Coast, South Island, New Zealand 41°37′S 171°53′E
Gran Lago see Nicaragua, Lago de
63 J18 Gran Laguna Salada ◎ S Argentina
Gran Malvina see West Falkland
95 L18 Gränna Jönköping, S Sweden 58°02′N 14°30′E
105 W5 Granollers var. Granollérs. Cataluña, NE Spain 41°37′N 02°18′E
Granollérs see Granollers
106 A7 Gran Paradiso Fr. Grand Paradis. ▲ NW Italy 45°31′N 07°13′E
Gran Pilastro see Hochfeiler
Gran Salitral see Grande, Salina
Gran San Bernardo, Passo di see Great Saint Bernard Pass
Gran Santiago see Santiago
107 J14 Gran Sasso d'Italia ▲▲ C Italy
100 N11 Gransee Brandenburg, NE Germany 53°00′N 13°10′E
28 L15 Grant Nebraska, C USA 40°50′N 101°43′W
27 R1 Grant City Missouri, C USA 40°29′N 94°25′W
97 N19 Grantham E England, United Kingdom 52°55′N 00°39′W
194 K13 Grant Island island Antarctica
45 Z14 Grantley Adams ✈ (Bridgetown) SE Barbados 13°04′N 59°29′W
35 S7 Grant, Mount ▲ Nevada, W USA 38°34′N 118°47′W
96 J9 Grantown-on-Spey N Scotland, United Kingdom 57°11′N 03°53′W
35 W8 Grant Range ▲▲ Nevada, W USA
37 Q11 Grants New Mexico, SW USA 35°09′N 107°50′W
30 I4 Grantsburg Wisconsin, N USA 45°47′N 92°40′W
32 F15 Grants Pass Oregon, NW USA 42°26′N 123°20′W
36 K3 Grantsville Utah, W USA 40°36′N 112°27′W
21 R4 Grantsville West Virginia, NE USA 38°55′N 81°07′W
102 I5 Granville Manche, N France 48°50′N 01°35′W
11 V12 Granville Lake ◎ Manitoba, C Canada
25 V8 Grapeland Texas, SW USA 31°29′N 95°28′W
25 T6 Grapevine Texas, SW USA 32°55′N 97°04′W
83 K20 Graskop Mpumalanga, NE South Africa 24°58′S 30°49′E
95 P14 Gräsö Uppsala, C Sweden 60°22′N 18°30′E
93 I19 Gräsö island C Sweden
103 U15 Grasse Alpes-Maritimes, SE France 43°42′N 06°52′E
18 E14 Grassflat Pennsylvania, NE USA 41°00′N 78°04′W
33 U9 Grassrange Montana, NW USA 47°02′N 108°48′W
18 J6 Grass River New York, NE USA
35 P6 Grass Valley California, W USA 39°12′N 121°04′W
183 N14 Grassy Tasmania, SE Australia 40°03′S 144°04′E
28 K4 Grassy Butte North Dakota, N USA 47°20′N 103°13′W
21 R5 Grassy Knob ▲ West Virginia, NE USA 38°04′N 80°31′W
95 G24 Gråsten var. Graasten. Sønderjylland, SW Denmark 54°55′N 09°37′E
95 J18 Grästorp Västra Götaland, S Sweden 58°20′N 12°40′E
Gratianopolis see Grenoble
109 V8 Gratwein Steiermark, SE Austria 47°08′N 15°20′E
Gratz see Graz
108 I9 Graubünden Fr. Grisons, It. Grigioni. ◐ canton SE Switzerland
Graudenz see Grudziądz
103 N15 Graulhet Tarn, S France 43°45′N 01°58′E
105 T4 Graus Aragón, NE Spain 42°11′N 00°21′E
61 I16 Gravataí Rio Grande do Sul, S Brazil 29°55′S 51°00′W
98 L13 Grave Noord-Brabant, SE Netherlands 51°45′N 05°45′E
11 T17 Gravelbourg Saskatchewan, S Canada 49°53′N 106°33′W
103 N1 Gravelines Nord, N France 51°00′N 02°07′E
Graven see Grez-Doiceau
14 H13 Gravenhurst Ontario, S Canada 44°55′N 79°22′W
33 O10 Grave Peak ▲ Idaho, NW USA 46°24′N 114°43′W
102 I11 Grave, Pointe de headland W France 45°33′N 01°24′W
183 S4 Gravesend New South Wales, SE Australia 29°37′S 150°15′E
97 P22 Gravesend SE England, United Kingdom 51°27′N 00°24′E
107 N17 Gravina in Puglia Puglia, SE Italy 40°48′N 16°25′E
103 S8 Gray Haute-Saône, E France 47°28′N 05°34′E
23 T4 Gray Georgia, SE USA 33°00′N 83°31′W
195 V16 Gray, Cape headland Antarctica 67°30′S 143°30′E
32 F9 Grayland Washington, NW USA 46°46′N 124°07′W

◆ Country
● Country Capital
◇ Dependent Territory
○ Dependent Territory Capital
◐ Administrative Regions
✈ International Airport
▲ Mountain
▲▲ Mountain Range
Volcano
River
◎ Lake
⊠ Reservoir

GRAYLING – GUANGSHUI

39 N10 **Grayling** Alaska, USA 62°55′N 160°07′W
31 Q6 **Grayling** Michigan, N USA 44°40′N 84°43′W
32 F9 **Grays Harbor** inlet Washington, NW USA
21 O5 **Grayson** Kentucky, S USA 38°21′N 82°59′W
37 S4 **Grays Peak** ▲ Colorado, C USA 39°37′N 105°49′W
30 M16 **Grayville** Illinois, N USA 38°15′N 87°59′W
109 V8 **Graz** prev. Gratz. Steiermark, SE Austria 47°05′N 15°23′E
104 L15 **Grazalema** Andalucía, S Spain 36°46′N 05°23′W
113 P15 **Grdelica** Serbia, SE Serbia 42°54′N 22°05′E
44 H1 **Great Abaco** var. Abaco Island. island N Bahamas
Great Admiralty Island see Manus Island
Great Alfold see Great Hungarian Plain
Great Ararat see Büyükağrı Dağı
181 U8 **Great Artesian Basin** lowlands Queensland, C Australia
181 O12 **Great Australian Bight** bight S Australia
64 E11 **Great Bahama Bank** undersea feature E Gulf of Mexico 23°15′N 78°00′W
184 M4 **Great Barrier Island** island N New Zealand
181 X4 **Great Barrier Reef** reef Queensland, NE Australia
18 L11 **Great Barrington** Massachusetts, NE USA 42°11′N 73°20′W
0 F10 **Great Basin** basin W USA
8 I8 **Great Bear Lake** Fr. Grand Lac de l'Ours. ◎ Northwest Territories, NW Canada
Great Belt see Storebælt
26 L5 **Great Bend** Kansas, C USA 38°22′N 98°47′W
Great Bermuda see Bermuda
97 A20 **Great Blasket Island** Ir. An Blascaod Mór. island SW Ireland
Great Britain see Britain
151 Q23 **Great Channel** channel Andaman Sea/Indian Ocean
166 J10 **Great Coco Island** island SW Myanmar (Burma)
Great Crosby see Crosby
21 X7 **Great Dismal Swamp** wetland North Carolina/Virginia, SE USA
33 V16 **Great Divide Basin** basin Wyoming, C USA
181 W7 **Great Dividing Range** ▲▲ NE Australia
14 D12 **Great Duck Island** island Ontario, S Canada
Great Elder Reservoir see Waconda Lake
44 G8 **Greater Antilles** island group West Indies
129 V16 **Greater Sunda Islands** var. Sunda Islands. island group Indonesia
184 I1 **Great Exhibition Bay** inlet North Island, New Zealand
44 H4 **Great Exuma Island** island C Bahamas
33 R8 **Great Falls** Montana, NW USA 47°30′N 111°18′W
21 R11 **Great Falls** South Carolina, SE USA 34°34′N 80°54′W
84 F9 **Great Fisher Bank** undersea feature C North Sea 57°00′N 04°00′E
Great Glen see Mor, Glen
Great Grimsby see Grimsby
44 I4 **Great Guana Cay** island C Bahamas
64 I5 **Great Hellefiske Bank** undersea feature N Atlantic Ocean
111 L24 **Great Hungarian Plain** var. Great Alfold, Plain of Hungary, Hung. Alföld. plain SE Europe
44 L7 **Great Inagua** var. Inagua Islands. island S Bahamas
Great Indian Desert see Thar Desert
83 G25 **Great Karoo** var. Great Karroo, High Veld, Afr. Groot Karoo, Hoë Karoo. plateau region S South Africa
Great Karroo see Great Karoo
Great Kei see Nciba
Great Khingan Range see Da Hinggan Ling
14 E11 **Great La Cloche Island** island Ontario, S Canada
183 P16 **Great Lake** ◎ Tasmania, SE Australia
Great Lake see Tônlé Sap
11 R15 **Great Lakes** lakes Ontario, Canada/USA
Great Lakes State see Michigan
97 L20 **Great Malvern** W England, United Kingdom 52°07′N 02°19′W
184 M5 **Great Mercury Island** island N New Zealand
Great Meteor Seamount see Great Meteor Tablemount
64 K10 **Great Meteor Tablemount** var. Great Meteor Seamount. undersea feature E Atlantic Ocean 30°00′N 28°30′W
31 Q14 **Great Miami River** ≈ Ohio, N USA
151 Q24 **Great Nicobar** island Nicobar Islands, India, NE Indian Ocean
97 O19 **Great Ouse** var. Ouse. ≈ E England, United Kingdom
183 Q17 **Great Oyster Bay** bay Tasmania, SE Australia
44 I13 **Great Pedro Bluff** headland W Jamaica 17°51′N 77°44′W
21 T12 **Great Pee Dee River** ≈ North Carolina/South Carolina, SE USA
129 W9 **Great Plain of China** plain E China
0 F12 **Great Plains** var. High Plains. plains Canada/USA
37 W6 **Great Plains Reservoirs** ▨ Colorado, C USA
19 Q13 **Great Point** headland Nantucket Island, Massachusetts, NE USA 41°23′N 70°03′W
68 I13 **Great Rift Valley** var. Rift Valley. depression Asia/Africa
81 I23 **Great Ruaha** ≈ S Tanzania
18 K10 **Great Sacandaga Lake** ▨ New York, NE USA
108 C12 **Great Saint Bernard Pass** Fr. Col du Grand-Saint-Bernard, It. Passo del Gran San Bernardo. pass Italy/Switzerland
44 F1 **Great Sale Cay** island N Bahamas
Great Salt Desert see Kavīr, Dasht-e
36 K1 **Great Salt Lake** salt lake Utah, W USA
36 J3 **Great Salt Lake Desert** plain Utah, W USA
26 M8 **Great Salt Plains Lake** ▨ Oklahoma, C USA
75 T9 **Great Sand Sea** desert Egypt/Libya
180 L6 **Great Sandy Desert** desert Western Australia
Great Sandy Desert see Ar Rub 'al Khālī
Great Sandy Island see Fraser Island
187 Y13 **Great Sea Reef** reef Vanua Levu, N Fiji
38 H17 **Great Sitkin Island** island Aleutian Islands, Alaska, USA
8 J10 **Great Slave Lake** Fr. Grand Lac des Esclaves. ◎ Northwest Territories, NW Canada
21 O10 **Great Smoky Mountains** ▲▲ North Carolina/Tennessee, SE USA
10 L11 **Great Snow Mountain** ▲ British Columbia, W Canada 57°22′N 124°08′W
Great Socialist People's Libyan Arab Jamahiriya see Libya
64 A12 **Great Sound** sound Bermuda, NW Atlantic Ocean
180 M10 **Great Victoria Desert** desert South Australia/Western Australia
194 H2 **Great Wall** Chinese research station South Shetland Islands, Antarctica 61°57′S 58°23′W
19 T7 **Great Wass Island** island Maine, NE USA
97 Q19 **Great Yarmouth** var. Yarmouth. E England, United Kingdom 52°37′N 01°44′E
139 S1 **Great Zab** Ar. Az Zāb al Kabīr, Kurd. Zē-i Bādīnān, Turk. Büyükzap Suyu. ≈ Iraq/Turkey
95 I17 **Grebbestad** Västra Götaland, S Sweden 58°42′N 11°15′E
Grebenka see Hrebinka
42 M13 **Grecia** Alajuela, C Costa Rica 10°04′N 84°19′W
61 E18 **Greco** Río Negro, W Uruguay 32°49′S 57°03′W
Greco, Cape see Gkréko, Akrotíri
104 L8 **Gredos, Sierra de** ▲▲ W Spain
18 F9 **Greece** New York, NE USA 43°12′N 77°41′W
115 E17 **Greece** off. Hellenic Republic, Gk. Ellás; anc. Hellas ◆ republic SE Europe
Greece Central see Stereá Ellás
Greece West see Dytikí Ellás
37 T3 **Greeley** Colorado, C USA 40°21′N 104°41′W
29 P14 **Greeley** Nebraska, C USA 41°33′N 98°31′W
122 K3 **Greem-Bell, Ostrov** Eng. Graham Bell Island. island Zemlya Frantsa-Iosifa, N Russian Federation
30 M6 **Green Bay** Wisconsin, N USA 44°32′N 88°W
31 N6 **Green Bay** lake bay Michigan/Wisconsin, N USA
21 S5 **Greenbrier River** ≈ West Virginia, NE USA
29 S2 **Greenbush** Minnesota, N USA 48°42′N 96°10′W
183 R12 **Green Cape** headland New South Wales, SE Australia 37°15′S 150°03′E
31 O14 **Greencastle** Indiana, N USA 39°38′N 86°51′W
18 F16 **Greencastle** Pennsylvania, NE USA 39°47′N 77°43′W
27 T2 **Green City** Missouri, C USA 40°16′N 92°57′W
21 O9 **Greeneville** Tennessee, S USA 36°10′N 82°50′W
35 O11 **Greenfield** California, W USA 36°19′N 121°15′W
31 P14 **Greenfield** Indiana, N USA 39°47′N 85°46′W
29 U15 **Greenfield** Iowa, C USA 41°18′N 94°27′W
18 M11 **Greenfield** Massachusetts, NE USA 42°33′N 72°34′W
27 S7 **Greenfield** Missouri, C USA 37°25′N 93°50′W
31 S14 **Greenfield** Ohio, N USA 39°21′N 83°22′W
20 G8 **Greenfield** Tennessee, S USA 36°09′N 88°48′W
30 M9 **Greenfield** Wisconsin, N USA 42°55′N 87°59′W
27 T9 **Green Forest** Arkansas, C USA 36°19′N 93°24′W
37 T7 **Greenhorn Mountain** ▲ Colorado, C USA 37°50′N 104°59′W
Green Island see Lü Tao
186 I6 **Green Islands** var. Nissan Islands. island group NE Papua New Guinea
11 S14 **Green Lake** Saskatchewan, C Canada 54°15′N 107°51′W
30 L8 **Green Lake** ◎ Wisconsin, N USA
197 O14 **Greenland** Dan. Grønland, Inuit Kalaallit Nunaat. ◇ Danish external territory NE North America
84 D4 **Greenland** island NE North America
197 R13 **Greenland Plain** undersea feature N Greenland Sea
197 R14 **Greenland Sea** sea Arctic Ocean
37 R4 **Green Mountain Reservoir** ▨ Colorado, C USA
18 M8 **Green Mountains** ▲▲ Vermont, NE USA
Green Mountain State see Vermont
96 H12 **Greenock** W Scotland, United Kingdom 55°57′N 04°45′W
39 T5 **Greenough, Mount** ▲ Alaska, USA 69°15′N 141°37′W
186 A6 **Green River** Sandaun, NW Papua New Guinea 03°54′S 141°08′E
37 N5 **Green River** Utah, W USA 39°00′N 110°07′W
33 U17 **Green River** Wyoming, C USA 41°33′N 109°27′W
16 H9 **Green River** ≈ W USA
30 K11 **Green River** ≈ Illinois, N USA
20 J7 **Green River** ≈ Kentucky, C USA
28 K5 **Green River** ≈ North Dakota, N USA
37 N6 **Green River** ≈ Utah, W USA
33 T16 **Green River** ≈ Wyoming, C USA
20 L7 **Green River Lake** ▨ Kentucky, S USA
23 O5 **Greensboro** Alabama, S USA 32°42′N 87°36′W
23 U3 **Greensboro** Georgia, SE USA 33°34′N 83°10′W
21 T9 **Greensboro** North Carolina, SE USA 36°04′N 79°48′W
31 P14 **Greensburg** Indiana, N USA 39°20′N 85°28′W
26 K6 **Greensburg** Kansas, C USA 37°36′N 99°17′W
20 L7 **Greensburg** Kentucky, S USA 37°14′N 85°30′W
18 C15 **Greensburg** Pennsylvania, NE USA 40°18′N 79°32′W
37 O13 **Greens Peak** ▲ Arizona, SW USA 34°06′N 109°34′W
21 V12 **Green Swamp** wetland North Carolina, SE USA
21 O4 **Greenup** Kentucky, S USA 38°34′N 82°49′W
36 M16 **Green Valley** Arizona, SW USA 31°49′N 111°00′W
76 K17 **Greenville** var. Sino, Sinoe. SE Liberia 05°01′N 09°03′W
23 P6 **Greenville** Alabama, S USA 31°49′N 86°37′W
23 T8 **Greenville** Florida, SE USA 30°28′N 83°37′W
23 S4 **Greenville** Georgia, SE USA 33°03′N 84°42′W
30 L15 **Greenville** Illinois, N USA 38°53′N 89°24′W
20 I7 **Greenville** Kentucky, S USA 37°11′N 87°11′W
19 Q5 **Greenville** Maine, NE USA 45°26′N 69°36′W
31 P9 **Greenville** Michigan, N USA 43°10′N 85°15′W
22 J4 **Greenville** Mississippi, S USA 33°24′N 91°03′W
21 W9 **Greenville** North Carolina, SE USA 35°36′N 77°23′W
31 Q13 **Greenville** Ohio, N USA 40°06′N 84°37′W
19 O12 **Greenville** Rhode Island, NE USA 41°52′N 71°33′W
21 P11 **Greenville** South Carolina, SE USA 34°51′N 82°24′W
25 U6 **Greenville** Texas, SW USA 33°09′N 96°07′W
31 T12 **Greenwich** Ohio, N USA 41°01′N 82°31′W
27 S11 **Greenwood** Arkansas, C USA 35°13′N 94°15′W
31 O14 **Greenwood** Indiana, N USA 39°38′N 86°06′W
22 K4 **Greenwood** Mississippi, S USA 33°30′N 90°11′W
21 P12 **Greenwood** South Carolina, SE USA 34°11′N 82°10′W
21 Q12 **Greenwood, Lake** ▨ South Carolina, SE USA
21 P11 **Greer** South Carolina, SE USA 34°56′N 82°13′W
27 V10 **Greers Ferry Lake** ▨ Arkansas, C USA
27 S13 **Greeson, Lake** ▨ Arkansas, C USA
29 O12 **Gregory** South Dakota, N USA 43°11′N 99°26′W
182 J3 **Gregory, Lake** salt lake South Australia
180 J9 **Gregory Lake** ◎ Western Australia
181 V5 **Gregory Range** ▲▲ Queensland, E Australia
Greifenberg/Greifenberg in Pommern see Gryfice
Greifenhagen see Gryfino
100 O8 **Greifswald** Mecklenburg-Vorpommern, NE Germany 54°04′N 13°24′E
100 O8 **Greifswalder Bodden** bay NE Germany
109 U4 **Grein** Oberösterreich, N Austria 48°14′N 14°50′E
101 M17 **Greiz** Thüringen, C Germany 50°40′N 12°11′E
125 V14 **Gremyachinsk** Permskaya Oblast', NW Russian Federation 58°33′N 57°52′E
Grenå see Grenaa
95 H21 **Grenaa** var. Grenå. Århus, C Denmark 56°25′N 10°53′E
22 L3 **Grenada** Mississippi, S USA 33°46′N 89°48′W
45 W15 **Grenada** ◆ commonwealth republic SE West Indies
47 S4 **Grenada** island Grenada
47 R4 **Grenada Basin** undersea feature W Atlantic Ocean 13°30′N 62°00′W
22 L3 **Grenada Lake** ▨ Mississippi, S USA
45 Y14 **Grenadines, The** island group Grenada/St Vincent and the Grenadines
108 D7 **Grenchen** Fr. Granges. Solothurn, NW Switzerland 47°13′N 07°24′E
183 Q9 **Grenfell** New South Wales, SE Australia 33°54′S 148°09′E
11 V16 **Grenfell** Saskatchewan, S Canada 50°24′N 102°56′W
92 J1 **Grenivík** Nordhurland Eystra, N Iceland 65°57′N 18°10′W
103 S12 **Grenoble** anc. Cularo, Gratianopolis. Isère, E France 45°11′N 05°42′E
28 J2 **Grenora** North Dakota, N USA 48°36′N 103°57′W
92 N8 **Grense-Jakobselv** Finnmark, N Norway 69°46′N 30°39′E
45 S14 **Grenville** E Grenada 12°07′N 61°37′W
32 G11 **Gresham** Oregon, NW USA 45°30′N 122°25′W
Gresk see Hresk
106 B7 **Gressoney-St-Jean** Valle d'Aosta, NW Italy 45°48′N 07°49′E
22 K9 **Gretna** Louisiana, S USA 29°54′N 90°03′W
21 T7 **Gretna** Virginia, NE USA 36°57′N 79°21′W
98 F13 **Grevelingen** inlet S North Sea
100 F13 **Greven** Nordrhein-Westfalen, NW Germany 52°07′N 07°38′E
115 D15 **Grevená** Dytikí Makedonía, N Greece 40°05′N 21°26′E
101 D16 **Grevenbroich** Nordrhein-Westfalen, W Germany 51°06′N 06°34′E
99 N24 **Grevenmacher** Grevenmacher, E Luxembourg 49°41′N 06°27′E
99 M24 **Grevenmacher** ◈ district E Luxembourg
100 K9 **Grevesmülhen** Mecklenburg-Vorpommern, N Germany 53°52′N 11°12′E
185 H16 **Grey** ≈ South Island, New Zealand
33 V12 **Greybull** Wyoming, C USA 44°29′N 108°03′W
33 U13 **Greybull River** ≈ Wyoming, C USA
65 A24 **Grey Channel** sound Falkland Islands
Greyerzer See see Gruyère, Lac de la
13 T10 **Grey Islands** island group Newfoundland and Labrador, E Canada
18 L10 **Greylock, Mount** ▲ Massachusetts, NE USA 42°38′N 73°09′W
185 G17 **Greymouth** West Coast, South Island, New Zealand 42°29′S 171°14′E
181 U10 **Grey Range** ▲▲ New South Wales/Queensland, E Australia
97 G18 **Greystones** Ir. Na Clocha Liatha. E Ireland 53°08′N 06°05′W
185 M14 **Greytown** Wellington, North Island, New Zealand 41°04′S 175°29′E
83 K23 **Greytown** KwaZulu/Natal, E South Africa 29°04′S 30°35′E
Greytown see San Juan del Norte
99 H19 **Grez-Doiceau** Dut. Graven. Walloon Brabant, C Belgium 50°43′N 04°41′E
115 J19 **Griá, Akrotírio** headland Ándros, Kykládes, Greece, Aegean Sea 37°54′N 24°57′E
127 N8 **Gribanovskiy** Voronezhskaya Oblast', W Russian Federation 51°27′N 41°53′E
78 I13 **Gribingui** ≈ N Central African Republic
35 O6 **Gridley** California, W USA 39°21′N 121°41′W
83 G23 **Griekwastad** Northern Cape, C South Africa 28°50′S 23°16′E
23 S4 **Griffin** Georgia, SE USA 33°15′N 84°17′W
183 O9 **Griffith** New South Wales, SE Australia 34°18′S 146°04′E
14 F13 **Griffith Island** island Ontario, S Canada
21 W10 **Grifton** North Carolina, SE USA 35°22′N 77°26′W
Grigioni see Graubünden
119 H14 **Grigiškes** Vilnius, SE Lithuania 54°42′N 25°00′E
117 N10 **Grigoriopol** C Moldova 47°09′N 29°18′E
147 X7 **Grigor'yevka** Issyk-Kul'skaya Oblast', E Kyrgyzstan 42°43′N 77°27′E
193 U8 **Grijalva Ridge** undersea feature E Pacific Ocean
41 U15 **Grijalva, Río** var. Tabasco. ≈ Guatemala/Mexico
98 N5 **Grijpskerk** Groningen, NE Netherlands 53°15′N 06°18′E
83 C22 **Grillenthal** Karas, SW Namibia 26°55′S 15°24′E
79 J15 **Grimari** Ouaka, C Central African Republic 05°44′N 20°02′E
Grimaylov see Hrymayliv
99 G18 **Grimbergen** Vlaams Brabant, C Belgium 50°56′N 04°22′E
183 N15 **Grim, Cape** headland Tasmania, SE Australia 40°42′S 144°42′E
100 N8 **Grimmen** Mecklenburg-Vorpommern, NE Germany 54°06′N 13°03′E
14 G16 **Grimsby** Ontario, S Canada 43°12′N 79°35′W
97 O17 **Grimsby** prev. Great Grimsby. E England, United Kingdom 53°35′N 00°05′W
92 J1 **Grímsey** var. Grimsey. island N Iceland
Grimsey see Grímsey
11 O12 **Grimshaw** Alberta, W Canada 56°11′N 117°37′W
95 F18 **Grimstad** Aust-Agder, S Norway 58°20′N 08°35′E
92 H4 **Grindavík** Reykjanes, W Iceland 65°57′N 18°10′W
108 F9 **Grindelwald** Bern, S Switzerland 46°37′N 08°04′E
95 F23 **Grindsted** Ribe, W Denmark 55°46′N 08°56′E
29 W14 **Grinnell** Iowa, C USA 41°44′N 92°43′W
109 U10 **Grintovec** ▲ N Slovenia 46°21′N 14°31′E
9 N4 **Grise Fiord** var. Ausuitoq. Northwest Territories, Ellesmere Island, N Canada 76°10′N 83°15′W
182 H1 **Griselda, Lake** salt lake South Australia
Grisons see Graubünden
95 P14 **Grisslehamn** Stockholm, C Sweden 60°04′N 18°50′E
29 T15 **Griswold** Iowa, C USA 41°14′N 95°08′W
102 M1 **Griz Nez, Cap** headland N France 50°51′N 01°34′E
112 P13 **Grljan** Serbia, E Serbia 43°52′N 22°18′E
112 E11 **Grmeč** ▲▲ NW Bosnia and Herzegovina
99 H16 **Grobbendonk** Antwerpen, N Belgium 51°12′N 04°41′E
Grobin see Grobiņa
118 C10 **Grobiņa** Ger. Grobin. Liepāja, W Latvia 56°32′N 21°12′E
83 K20 **Groblersdal** Mpumalanga, NE South Africa 25°15′S 29°25′E
83 G23 **Groblershoop** Northern Cape, W South Africa 28°51′S 22°01′E
Gródek Jagielloński see Horodok
109 Q6 **Grödig** Salzburg, W Austria 47°42′N 13°06′E
111 H15 **Grodków** Opolskie, S Poland 50°42′N 17°23′E
Grodnenskaya Oblast' see Hrodzyenskaya Voblasts'
Grodno see Hrodna
110 L12 **Grodzisk Mazowiecki** Mazowieckie, C Poland 52°09′N 20°38′E
110 F12 **Grodzisk Wielkopolski** Wielkopolskie, C Poland 52°13′N 16°21′E
Grodzyanka see Hradzyanka
98 O12 **Groenlo** Gelderland, E Netherlands 52°02′N 06°36′E
83 E22 **Groenrivier** Karas, SE Namibia 27°27′S 18°52′E
25 U8 **Groesbeck** Texas, SW USA 31°31′N 96°35′W
98 L13 **Groesbeek** Gelderland, SE Netherlands 51°47′N 05°56′E
102 G7 **Groix, Îles de** island group NW France
110 M12 **Grójec** Mazowieckie, C Poland 51°51′N 20°52′E
65 K15 **Gröll Seamount** undersea feature C Atlantic Ocean 12°54′S 33°24′W
100 E13 **Gronau** var. Gronau in Westfalen. Nordrhein-Westfalen, NW Germany 52°13′N 07°02′E
Gronau in Westfalen see Gronau
93 F15 **Grong** Nord-Trøndelag, C Norway 64°29′N 12°19′E
95 N22 **Grönhögen** Kalmar, S Sweden 56°16′N 16°09′E
98 N5 **Groningen** Groningen, NE Netherlands 53°13′N 06°35′E
55 W9 **Groningen** Saramacca, N Suriname 05°45′N 55°31′W
98 N5 **Groningen** ◈ province NE Netherlands
Grønland see Greenland
108 H11 **Grono** Graubünden, S Switzerland 46°15′N 09°07′E
95 M20 **Grönskåra** Kalmar, S Sweden 57°04′N 15°45′E
25 O2 **Groom** Texas, SW USA 35°12′N 101°06′W
35 W9 **Groom Lake** ◎ Nevada, W USA
83 H25 **Groot** ≈ S South Africa
181 S2 **Groote Eylandt** island Northern Territory, N Australia
98 M6 **Grootegast** Groningen, NE Netherlands 53°11′N 06°12′E
83 D17 **Grootfontein** Otjozondjupa, N Namibia 19°32′S 18°05′E
83 E22 **Groot Karasberge** ▲▲ S Namibia
Groot Karoo see Great Karoo
Groot-Kei see Nciba
15 V6 **Grosses-Roches** Québec, SE Canada 48°55′N 67°06′W
109 V2 **Gross-Siegharts** Niederösterreich, N Austria 48°48′N 15°25′E
45 T10 **Gros Islet** N Saint Lucia 14°04′N 60°57′W
44 L8 **Gros-Morne** NW Haiti 19°45′N 72°46′W
13 S11 **Gros Morne** ▲ Newfoundland, Newfoundland and Labrador, E Canada 49°38′N 57°45′W
103 R9 **Grosne** ≈ C France
45 S12 **Gros Piton** ▲ SW Saint Lucia 13°48′N 61°04′W
Grossa, Isola see Dugi Otok
Grossbetschkerek see Zrenjanin
Grosse Isper see Grosse Ysper
Grosse Kokel see Târnava Mare
101 M21 **Grosse Laaber** var. Grosse Laber. ≈ SE Germany
Grosse Laber see Grosse Laaber
Grosse Morava see Velika Morava
101 O15 **Grossenhain** Sachsen, E Germany 51°18′N 13°31′E
109 Y4 **Grossenzersdorf** Niederösterreich, NE Austria 48°12′N 16°33′E
101 O21 **Grosser Arber** ▲ SE Germany 49°07′N 13°10′E
101 K17 **Grosser Beerberg** ▲ C Germany 50°39′N 10°45′E
101 G18 **Grosser Feldberg** ▲ W Germany 50°13′N 08°28′E
109 O8 **Grosser Löffler** It. Monte Lovello. ▲ Austria/Italy 47°02′N 11°56′E
109 N8 **Grosser Möseler** var. Mesule. ▲ Austria/Italy 47°01′N 11°52′E
100 J8 **Grosser Plöner See** ◎ N Germany
101 O21 **Grosser Rachel** ▲ SE Germany 48°59′N 13°23′E
Grosser Sund see Suur Väin
109 P8 **Grosses Weiesbachhorn** var. Wiesbachhorn. ▲ W Austria 47°09′N 12°44′E
106 F13 **Grosseto** Toscana, C Italy 42°45′N 11°07′E
101 M22 **Grosse Vils** ≈ SE Germany
109 U4 **Grosse Ysper** var. Grosse Isper. ≈ N Austria
101 G19 **Gross-Gerau** Hessen, W Germany 49°55′N 08°28′E
109 U3 **Gross Gerungs** Niederösterreich, N Austria 48°33′N 14°58′E
109 P8 **Grossglockner** ▲ W Austria 47°05′N 12°39′E
Grosskanizsa see Nagykanizsa
Gross-Karol see Carei
Grosskikinda see Kikinda
109 W9 **Grossklein** Steiermark, SE Austria 46°43′N 15°24′E
Grosskoppe see Velká Deštná
Grossmeseritsch see Velké Meziříčí
Grossmichel see Michalovce
101 H19 **Grossostheim** Bayern, C Germany 49°54′N 09°03′E
109 X7 **Grosspetersdorf** Burgenland, SE Austria 47°15′N 16°19′E
109 T5 **Grossraming** Oberösterreich, C Austria 47°54′N 14°34′E
101 P14 **Grossräschen** Brandenburg, E Germany 51°34′N 14°00′E
Grossrauschenbach see Revúca
Gross-Sankt-Johannis see Suure-Jaani
Gross-Schlatten see Abrud
Gross-Skaisgirren see Bol'shakovo
Gross-Steffelsdorf see Rimavská Sobota
Gross Strehlitz see Strzelce Opolskie
109 O8 **Grossvenediger** ▲ W Austria 47°07′N 12°19′E
Grosswardein see Oradea
Gross Wartenberg see Syców
109 U11 **Grosuplje** C Slovenia 46°00′N 14°36′E
99 H17 **Grote Nete** ≈ N Belgium
94 E10 **Grotli** Oppland, S Norway 62°02′N 07°36′E
19 N13 **Groton** Connecticut, NE USA 41°20′N 72°03′W
29 P8 **Groton** South Dakota, N USA 45°27′N 98°06′W
107 P18 **Grottaglie** Puglia, SE Italy 40°32′N 17°26′E
107 L17 **Grottaminarda** Campania, S Italy 41°04′N 15°02′E
106 K13 **Grottammare** Marche, C Italy 43°00′N 13°52′E
21 U5 **Grottoes** Virginia, NE USA 38°16′N 78°49′W
Grou see Grouw
13 N10 **Groulx, Monts** ▲▲ Québec, E Canada
14 E7 **Groundhog** ≈ Ontario, S Canada
36 J1 **Grouse Creek** Utah, W USA 41°41′N 113°52′W
36 J1 **Grouse Creek Mountains** ▲▲ Utah, W USA
98 L6 **Grouw** Fris. Grou. Friesland, N Netherlands 53°07′N 05°51′E
27 R8 **Grove** Oklahoma, C USA 36°35′N 94°46′W
31 S13 **Grove City** Ohio, N USA 39°52′N 83°05′W
18 B13 **Grove City** Pennsylvania, NE USA 41°09′N 80°02′W
23 O6 **Grove Hill** Alabama, S USA 31°42′N 87°46′W
33 S15 **Grover** Wyoming, C USA 42°48′N 110°57′W
35 P13 **Grover City** California, W USA 35°08′N 120°37′W
25 Y11 **Groves** Texas, SW USA 29°57′N 93°55′W
19 O7 **Groveton** New Hampshire, NE USA 44°35′N 71°28′W
25 W9 **Groveton** Texas, SW USA 31°04′N 95°08′W
36 J15 **Growler Mountains** ▲▲ Arizona, SW USA
Grozdovo see Bratya Daskalovi
127 P16 **Groznyy** Chechenskaya Respublika, SW Russian Federation 43°20′N 45°43′E
Grubeshov see Hrubieszów
112 G9 **Grubišno Polje** Bjelovar-Bilogora, NE Croatia 45°42′N 17°09′E
Grudovo see Sredets
110 J9 **Grudziądz** Ger. Graudenz. Kujawsko-pomorskie, C Poland 53°29′N 18°45′E
25 R17 **Grulla** var. La Grulla. Texas, SW USA 26°15′N 98°37′W
40 K14 **Grullo** Jalisco, SW Mexico 19°45′N 104°15′W
67 V10 **Grumeti** ≈ N Tanzania
95 K16 **Grums** Värmland, C Sweden 59°22′N 13°11′E
109 S5 **Grünau im Almtal** Oberösterreich, N Austria 47°51′N 13°56′E
101 H17 **Grünberg** Hessen, W Germany 50°36′N 08°57′E
Grünberg/Grünberg in Schlesien see Zielona Góra
92 H3 **Grundarfjördhur** Vestfirdhir, W Iceland 64°55′N 23°15′W
21 P7 **Grundy** Virginia, NE USA 37°17′N 82°06′W
29 W13 **Grundy Center** Iowa, C USA 42°21′N 92°46′W
Grüneberg see Zielona Góra
25 N1 **Gruver** Texas, SW USA 36°16′N 101°24′W
108 C9 **Gruyère, Lac de la** Ger. Greyerzer See. ◎ SW Switzerland
108 C9 **Gruyères** Fribourg, W Switzerland 46°34′N 07°04′E
118 E11 **Gruzdiai** Šiauliai, N Lithuania 56°06′N 23°15′E
Gruzinskaya SSR/Gruziya see Georgia
Gryada Akkyr see Akgyr Erezi
126 L7 **Gryazi** Lipetskaya Oblast', W Russian Federation 52°27′N 39°56′E
124 M14 **Gryazovets** Vologodskaya Oblast', NW Russian Federation 58°52′N 40°12′E
111 M17 **Grybów** Małopolskie, SE Poland 49°35′N 20°54′E
94 M13 **Grycksbo** Dalarna, C Sweden 60°40′N 15°30′E
110 E8 **Gryfice** Ger. Greifenberg, Greifenberg in Pommern. Zachodnio-pomorskie, NW Poland 53°55′N 15°11′E
110 D9 **Gryfino** Ger. Greifenhagen. Zachodnio-pomorskie, NW Poland 53°15′N 14°30′E
92 H9 **Gryllefjord** Troms, N Norway 69°21′N 17°07′E
95 L15 **Grythyttan** Örebro, C Sweden 59°52′N 14°31′E
108 D10 **Gstaad** Bern, W Switzerland 46°30′N 07°16′E
43 P14 **Guabito** Bocas del Toro, NW Panama 09°30′N 82°35′W
44 G7 **Guacanayabo, Golfo de** gulf S Cuba
40 I7 **Guachochi** Chihuahua, N Mexico
104 J11 **Guadajira** ≈ SW Spain
104 M13 **Guadajoz** ≈ S Spain
40 L13 **Guadalajara** Jalisco, C Mexico 20°43′N 103°24′W
105 O8 **Guadalajara** Ar. Wad Al-Hajarah; anc. Arriaca. Castilla-La Mancha, C Spain 40°37′N 03°10′W
105 O7 **Guadalajara** ◈ province Castilla-La Mancha, C Spain
104 K12 **Guadalcanal** Andalucía, S Spain 38°06′N 05°49′W
186 L10 **Guadalcanal** off. Guadalcanal Province. ◈ province C Solomon Islands
186 M9 **Guadalcanal** island C Solomon Islands
Guadalcanal Province see Guadalcanal
105 O12 **Guadalén** ≈ S Spain
105 R13 **Guadalentín** ≈ SE Spain
104 K15 **Guadalete** ≈ SW Spain
105 O13 **Guadalimar** ≈ S Spain
105 P12 **Guadalmena** ≈ S Spain
104 L11 **Guadalmez** ≈ W Spain
105 S7 **Guadalope** ≈ E Spain
104 K13 **Guadalquivir** ≈ W Spain
104 J14 **Guadalquivir, Marismas del** var. Las Marismas. wetland SW Spain
40 M11 **Guadalupe** Zacatecas, C Mexico 22°47′N 102°30′W
57 E16 **Guadalupe** Ica, W Peru 13°59′S 75°49′W
104 L10 **Guadalupe** Extremadura, W Spain 39°26′N 05°18′W
36 L14 **Guadalupe** Arizona, SW USA 33°20′N 111°57′W
35 P13 **Guadalupe** California, W USA 34°55′N 120°34′W
Guadalupe see Canelones
40 J3 **Guadalupe Bravos** Chihuahua, N Mexico 31°22′N 106°04′W
40 A4 **Guadalupe, Isla** island NW Mexico
37 U15 **Guadalupe Mountains** ▲▲ New Mexico/Texas, SW USA
24 J8 **Guadalupe Peak** ▲ Texas, SW USA 31°53′N 104°51′W
25 R11 **Guadalupe River** ≈ SW USA
104 K10 **Guadalupe, Sierra de** ▲▲ W Spain
40 K9 **Guadalupe Victoria** Durango, C Mexico 24°30′N 104°08′W
40 I8 **Guadalupe y Calvo** Chihuahua, N Mexico 26°04′N 106°58′W
105 N7 **Guadarrama** Madrid, C Spain 40°40′N 04°06′W
105 N7 **Guadarrama** ≈ C Spain
104 M7 **Guadarrama, Puerto de** pass C Spain
105 N9 **Guadarrama, Sierra de** ▲▲ C Spain
105 Q9 **Guadazaón** ≈ C Spain
45 X10 **Guadeloupe** ◇ French overseas department E West Indies
47 S3 **Guadeloupe** island group E West Indies
45 W10 **Guadeloupe Passage** passage E Caribbean Sea
104 H13 **Guadiana** ≈ Portugal/Spain
105 O13 **Guadiana Menor** ≈ S Spain
105 Q8 **Guadiela** ≈ C Spain
105 O14 **Guadix** Andalucía, S Spain 37°19′N 03°08′W
Guad-i-Zirreh see Gowd-e Zereh, Dasht-e
193 T12 **Guafo Fracture Zone** tectonic feature SE Pacific Ocean
63 F18 **Guafo, Isla** island S Chile
42 I6 **Guaimaca** Francisco Morazán, C Honduras 14°34′N 86°49′W
54 J12 **Guainía** off. Comisaría del Guainía. ◈ province E Colombia
Guainía, Comisaría del see Guainía
54 K12 **Guainía, Río** ≈ Colombia/Venezuela
55 O9 **Guaiquinima, Cerro** elevation SE Venezuela
60 G10 **Guaíra** Paraná, S Brazil 24°05′S 54°15′W
60 L7 **Guaíra** São Paulo, S Brazil 20°17′S 48°21′W
62 O7 **Guairá** off. Departamento del Guairá. ◈ department S Paraguay
Guairá, Departamento del see Guairá
Guaire see Gorey
63 F18 **Guaiteca, Isla** island S Chile
44 G6 **Guajaba, Cayo** headland C Cuba 21°50′N 77°33′W
59 D16 **Guajará-Mirim** Rondônia, W Brazil 10°50′S 65°21′W
Guajira see La Guajira
Guajira, Departamento de La see La Guajira
54 H3 **Guajira, Península de la** peninsula N Colombia
42 J6 **Gualaco** Olancho, C Honduras 15°00′N 86°03′W
34 L7 **Gualala** California, W USA 38°45′N 123°33′W
42 E5 **Gualán** Zacapa, C Guatemala 15°06′N 89°22′W
61 C19 **Gualeguay** Entre Ríos, E Argentina 33°09′S 59°20′W
61 D18 **Gualeguaychú** Entre Ríos, E Argentina 33°03′S 58°31′W
61 C18 **Gualeguay, Río** ≈ E Argentina
63 K16 **Gualicho, Salina del** salt lake E Argentina
188 B15 **Guam** ◇ US unincorporated territory W Pacific Ocean
63 F19 **Guamblin, Isla** island Archipiélago de los Chonos, S Chile
61 A22 **Guaminí** Buenos Aires, E Argentina 37°01′S 62°28′W
40 H8 **Guamúchil** Sinaloa, C Mexico 25°23′N 108°01′W
54 H4 **Guana** var. Misión de Guana. Zulia, NW Venezuela 11°07′N 72°17′W
44 C4 **Guanabacoa** La Habana, W Cuba 23°02′N 82°12′W
42 K13 **Guanacaste** off. Provincia de Guanacaste. ◈ province NW Costa Rica
42 K12 **Guanacaste, Cordillera de** ▲▲ NW Costa Rica
Guanacaste, Provincia de see Guanacaste
40 J8 **Guanaceví** Durango, C Mexico 25°55′N 105°51′W
44 A5 **Guanahacabibes, Golfo de** gulf W Cuba
42 K4 **Guanaja, Isla de** island Islas de la Bahía, N Honduras
44 C4 **Guanajay** La Habana, W Cuba 22°56′N 82°42′W
41 N12 **Guanajuato** Guanajuato, C Mexico 21°N 101°19′W
40 M12 **Guanajuato** ◈ state C Mexico
54 J6 **Guanare** Portuguesa, N Venezuela 09°04′N 69°45′W
54 K7 **Guanare, Río** ≈ W Venezuela
54 J6 **Guanarito** Portuguesa, NW Venezuela 08°43′N 69°12′W
160 M3 **Guancen Shan** ▲▲ C China
62 I9 **Guandacol** La Rioja, W Argentina 29°32′S 68°37′W
44 A5 **Guane** Pinar del Río, W Cuba 22°12′N 84°05′W
160 J9 **Guang'an** Sichuan, C China 30°18′N 106°22′E
161 N14 **Guangdong** var. Guangdong Sheng, Kuang-tung, Kwangtung, Yue. ◈ province S China
Guangdong Sheng see Guangdong
Guanghua see Laohekou
Guangju see Kwangju
160 I13 **Guangnan** var. Liancheng. Yunnan, SW China 24°07′N 104°54′E
161 N8 **Guangshui** prev. Yingshan. Hubei, C China 31°41′N 113°53′E

◆ Country
● Country Capital
◇ Dependent Territory
○ Dependent Territory Capital
◈ Administrative Regions
✈ International Airport
▲ Mountain
▲▲ Mountain Range
Volcano
≈ River
◎ Lake
▨ Reservoir

GUANGXI – HAFNIA

Guangxi *see* Guangxi Zhuangzu Zizhiqu
160 *K14* **Guangxi Zhuangzu Zizhiqu** *var.* Guangxi, Gui, Kuang-hsi, Kwangsi, *Eng.* Kwangsi Chuang Autonomous Region. ◆ *autonomous region* S China
160 *J8* **Guangyuan** *var.* Kuang-yuan, Kwangyuan. Sichuan, C China *32°27′N 105°49′E*
161 *N14* **Guangzhou** *var.* Kuang-chou, Kwangchow, *Eng.* Canton. *province capital* Guangdong, S China *23°11′N 113°19′E*
59 *N19* **Guanhães** Minas Gerais, SE Brazil *18°46′S 42°58′W*
160 *I12* **Guanling** *var.* Guanling Bouyeizu Miaozu Zizhixian. Guizhou, S China *26°00′N 105°40′E*
Guanling Bouyeizu Miaozu Zizhixian *see* Guanling
55 *N5* **Guanta** Anzoátegui, NE Venezuela *10°15′N 64°38′W*
44 *J8* **Guantánamo** Guantánamo, SE Cuba *20°06′N 75°16′W*
44 *J8* **Guantánamo, Bahía de** *Eng.* Guantanamo Bay. *US military base* SE Cuba *20°06′N 75°16′W*
Guantanamo Bay *see* Guantánamo, Bahía de
Guanxian/Guan Xian *see* Dujiangyan
161 *Q6* **Guanyun** *var.* Yishan. Jiangsu, E China *34°18′N 119°14′E*
54 *C12* **Guapí** Cauca, SW Colombia *02°36′N 77°54′W*
43 *N13* **Guápiles** Limón, NE Costa Rica *10°15′N 83°46′W*
61 *I15* **Guaporé** Rio Grande do Sul, S Brazil *28°55′S 51°53′W*
47 *S8* **Guaporé, Rio** *var.* Río Iténez. ⚡ Bolivia/Brazil *see also* Río Iténez
Guaporé, Rio *see* Iténez, Río
56 *B7* **Guaranda** Bolívar, C Ecuador *01°35′S 78°59′W*
60 *H11* **Guaraniaçu** Paraná, S Brazil *25°05′S 52°52′W*
59 *O20* **Guarapari** Espírito Santo, SE Brazil *20°39′S 40°31′W*
60 *I12* **Guarapuava** Paraná, S Brazil *25°22′S 51°28′W*
60 *J8* **Guararapes** São Paulo, S Brazil *21°16′S 50°37′W*
105 *S4* **Guara, Sierra de** ▲ NE Spain
60 *N10* **Guaratinguetá** São Paulo, S Brazil *22°44′S 45°16′W*
104 *I7* **Guarda** Guarda, N Portugal *40°32′N 07°17′W*
104 *I7* **Guarda** ◆ *district* N Portugal
Guardak *see* Magdanly
104 *M3* **Guardo** Castilla-León, N Spain *42°48′N 04°50′W*
104 *K11* **Guareña** Extremadura, W Spain *38°51′N 06°06′W*
60 *J11* **Guaricana, Pico** ▲ S Brazil *25°13′S 48°50′W*
54 *L6* **Guárico** *off.* Estado Guárico. ◆ *state* N Venezuela
Guárico, Estado *see* Guárico
44 *J7* **Guarico, Punta** *headland* E Cuba *20°36′N 74°43′W*
54 *L7* **Guárico, Río** ⚡ C Venezuela
60 *M10* **Guarujá** São Paulo, SE Brazil *23°50′S 46°27′W*
61 *L22* **Guarulhos** ✈ (São Paulo) São Paulo, S Brazil *23°23′S 46°32′W*
43 *R17* **Guarumal** Veraguas, S Panama *07°48′N 81°15′W*
Guasapa *see* Guasopa
40 *H8* **Guasave** Sinaloa, C Mexico *25°33′N 108°29′W*
54 *I8* **Guasdualito** Apure, C Venezuela *07°15′N 70°40′W*
55 *Q7* **Guasipati** Bolívar, E Venezuela *07°28′N 61°58′W*
186 *I9* **Guasopa** *var.* Guasapa. Woodlark Island, SE Papua New Guinea *09°12′S 152°58′E*
106 *F9* **Guastalla** Emilia-Romagna, C Italy *44°54′N 10°38′E*
42 *D6* **Guastatoya** *var.* El Progreso. El Progreso, C Guatemala *14°51′N 90°01′W*
42 *D5* **Guatemala** *off.* Republic of Guatemala. ◆ *republic* Central America
42 *A2* **Guatemala** *off.* Departamento de Guatemala. ◆ *department* S Guatemala
193 *S7* **Guatemala Basin** *undersea feature* E Pacific Ocean *11°00′N 95°00′W*
Guatemala City *see* Ciudad de Guatemala
Guatemala, Departamento de *see* Guatemala
Guatemala, Republic of *see* Guatemala
45 *V14* **Guatuaro Point** *headland* Trinidad, Trinidad and Tobago *10°19′N 60°58′W*
186 *B8* **Guavi** ⚡ SW Papua New Guinea
54 *G13* **Guaviare** *off.* Comisaría Guaviare. ◆ *province* S Colombia
Guaviare, Comisaría *see* Guaviare
54 *J11* **Guaviare, Río** ⚡ E Colombia
61 *E15* **Guaviravi** Corrientes, NE Argentina *29°20′S 56°50′W*
54 *G12* **Guayabero, Río** ⚡ SW Colombia
45 *U6* **Guayama** E Puerto Rico *17°59′N 66°07′W*
42 *J7* **Guayambre, Río** ⚡ S Honduras
Guayanas, Macizo de las *see* Guiana Highlands
45 *V6* **Guayanés, Punta** *headland* E Puerto Rico *18°03′N 65°48′W*
42 *J6* **Guayape, Río** ⚡ C Honduras
56 *B7* **Guayaquil** *var.* Santiago de Guayaquil. Guayas, SW Ecuador *02°13′S 79°54′W*
Guayaquil *see* Simon Bolivar
56 *A8* **Guayaquil, Golfo de** *var.* Gulf of Guayaquil. *gulf* SW Ecuador
Guayaquil, Gulf of *see* Guayaquil, Golfo de
56 *A7* **Guayas** ◆ *province* W Ecuador
62 *N7* **Guaycurú, Río** ⚡ NE Argentina
40 *F6* **Guaymas** Sonora, NW Mexico *27°56′N 110°54′W*
45 *U5* **Guaynabo** E Puerto Rico *18°19′N 66°05′W*
80 *H12* **Guba** Binishangul Gumuz, W Ethiopia *11°11′N 35°21′E*
146 *H8* **Gubadag** *Turkm.* Tel'man; *prev.* Tel'mansk. Daşoguz Welaýaty, N Turkmenistan *42°07′N 59°55′E*
125 *T1* **Guba Dolgaya** Nenetskiy Avtonomnyy Okrug, NW Russian Federation *70°16′N 58°45′E*
125 *V13* **Gubakha** Permskaya Oblast', NW Russian Federation *58°52′N 57°35′E*
106 *I12* **Gubbio** Umbria, C Italy *43°27′N 12°34′E*
100 *Q13* **Guben** *var.* Wilhelm-Pieck-Stadt. Brandenburg, E Germany *51°59′N 14°42′E*
Guben *see* Gubin
110 *D12* **Gubin** *Ger.* Guben. Lubuskie, W Poland *51°59′N 14°43′E*
126 *K8* **Gubkin** Belgorodskaya Oblast', W Russian Federation *51°16′N 37°32′E*
162 *J9* **Guchin-Us** *var.* Arguut. Övörhangay, C Mongolia *45°27′N 102°25′E*
Gudara *see* Ghŭdara
105 *S8* **Gúdar, Sierra de** ▲ E Spain
137 *P8* **Gudaut'a** NW Georgia *43°07′N 40°35′E*
94 *G12* **Gudbrandsdalen** *valley* S Norway
95 *G21* **Gudenå** *var.* Gudenaa. ⚡ C Denmark
Gudenaa *see* Gudenå
127 *P16* **Gudermes** Chechenskaya Respublika, SW Russian Federation *43°23′N 46°06′E*
155 *J18* **Gūdūr** Andhra Pradesh, E India *14°10′N 79°51′E*
146 *B13* **Gudurolum** Balkan Welaýaty, W Turkmenistan *37°28′N 54°30′E*
94 *D13* **Gudvangen** Sogn Og Fjordane, S Norway *60°54′N 06°49′E*
103 *U7* **Guebwiller** Haut-Rhin, NE France *47°55′N 07°13′E*
Guéckédou *see* Guékédou
14 *K8* **Guéguen, Lac** ◎ Québec, SE Canada
76 *J15* **Guékédou** *var.* Guéckédou. Guinée-Forestière, S Guinea *08°33′N 10°08′W*
41 *R16* **Guelatao** Oaxaca, SE Mexico
Guelders *see* Gelderland
78 *G11* **Guélengdeng** Mayo-Kébbi, W Chad *10°55′N 15°31′E*
74 *L5* **Guelma** *var.* Gâlma. NE Algeria *36°29′N 07°25′E*
74 *D8* **Guelmime** *var.* Goulimime. SW Morocco *28°59′N 10°10′W*
14 *G15* **Guelph** Ontario, S Canada *43°34′N 80°16′W*
102 *I7* **Gueméné-Penfao** Loire-Atlantique, NW France *47°37′N 01°49′W*
102 *I7* **Guer** Morbihan, NW France *47°54′N 02°07′W*
78 *I11* **Guéra** *off.* Préfecture du Guéra. ◆ *prefecture* S Chad
102 *H8* **Guérande** Loire-Atlantique, NW France *47°20′N 02°25′W*
Guéra, Préfecture du *see* Guéra
78 *K9* **Guéréda** Biltine, E Chad *14°30′N 22°05′E*
103 *N10* **Guéret** Creuse, C France *46°10′N 01°52′E*
Guernica/Guernica y Lumo *see* Gernika-Lumo
33 *Z15* **Guernsey** Wyoming, C USA *42°16′N 104°44′W*
97 *K25* **Guernsey** *island* Channel Islands, NW Europe
76 *J10* **Guérou** Assaba, S Mauritania *16°48′N 11°40′W*
25 *R16* **Guerra** Texas, SW USA *26°54′N 98°53′W*
41 *O15* **Guerrero** ◆ *state* S Mexico
40 *D6* **Guerrero Negro** Baja California Sur, NW Mexico *27°56′N 114°04′W*
103 *P9* **Gueugnon** Saône-et-Loire, C France *46°36′N 04°03′E*
76 *M17* **Guéyo** S Ivory Coast *05°25′N 06°04′W*
107 *L15* **Guglionesi** Molise, C Italy *41°54′N 14°54′E*
188 *K5* **Guguan** *island* C Northern Mariana Islands
Guhrau *see* Góra
Gui *see* Guangxi Zhuangzu Zizhiqu
Guiana *see* French Guiana
47 *V4* **Guiana Basin** *undersea feature* W Atlantic Ocean *11°00′N 52°00′W*
48 *G6* **Guiana Highlands** *var.* Macizo de las Guayanas. ▲ N South America
Guiba *see* Juba
102 *I7* **Guichen** Ille-et-Vilaine, NW France *47°57′N 01°47′W*
Guichi *see* Chizhou
61 *E18* **Guichón** Paysandú, W Uruguay *32°30′S 57°13′W*
77 *U12* **Guidan-Roumji** Maradi, S Niger *13°40′N 06°41′E*
Guidder *see* Guider
159 *T10* **Guide** *var.* Heyin. Qinghai, C China *36°06′N 101°25′E*
78 *F12* **Guider** *var.* Guidder. Nord, N Cameroon *09°55′N 13°59′E*
76 *I11* **Guidimaka** ◆ *region* S Mauritania
77 *W12* **Guidimouni** Zinder, S Niger *13°40′N 09°31′E*
76 *G10* **Guier, Lac de** *var.* Lac de Guiers. ◎ N Senegal
Guiers, Lac de *see* Guier, Lac de
160 *L14* **Guigang** *var.* Guixian, Gui Xian. Guangxi Zhuangzu Zizhiqu, S China *23°06′N 109°36′E*
76 *L16* **Guiglo** W Ivory Coast *06°33′N 07°29′W*
54 *L5* **Güigüe** Carabobo, N Venezuela *10°05′N 67°45′W*
83 *M20* **Guijá** Gaza, S Mozambique *24°31′S 33°02′E*
42 *E7* **Güija, Lago de** ◎ El Salvador/Guatemala
160 *L14* **Gui Jiang** *var.* Gui Shui. ⚡ S China
104 *K8* **Guijuelo** Castilla-León, N Spain *40°34′N 05°40′W*
Guilan *see* Gīlān
97 *N22* **Guildford** SE England, United Kingdom *51°14′N 00°35′W*
19 *R5* **Guildford** Maine, NE USA *45°10′N 69°22′W*
19 *O7* **Guildhall** Vermont, NE USA *44°34′N 71°36′W*
103 *R13* **Guilherand** Ardèche, E France *44°57′N 04°49′E*
160 *L13* **Guilin** *var.* Kuei-lin, Kweilin. Guangxi Zhuangzu Zizhiqu, S China *25°15′N 110°16′E*
12 *J6* **Guillaume-Delisle, Lac** ◎ Québec, NE Canada
103 *U13* **Guillestre** Hautes-Alpes, SE France *44°41′N 06°39′E*
104 *H6* **Guimarães** *var.* Guimaráes. Braga, N Portugal *41°26′N 08°19′W*
Guimaráes *see* Guimarães
58 *D11* **Guimarães Rosas, Pico** ▲ NW Brazil
23 *N3* **Guin** Alabama, S USA *33°58′N 87°54′W*
Güina *see* Wina
76 *I14* **Guinea** *off.* Republic of Guinea, *var.* Guinée; *prev.* French Guinea, People's Revolutionary Republic of Guinea. ◆ *republic* W Africa
64 *N13* **Guinea Basin** *undersea feature* E Atlantic Ocean *0°00′N 05°00′W*
76 *E12* **Guinea-Bissau** *off.* Republic of Guinea-Bissau, *Fr.* Guinée-Bissau, *Port.* Guiné-Bissau; *prev.* Portuguese Guinea. ◆ *republic* W Africa
Guinea-Bissau, Republic of *see* Guinea-Bissau
66 *K7* **Guinea Fracture Zone** *tectonic feature* E Atlantic Ocean
64 *O13* **Guinea, Gulf of** *Fr.* Golfe de Guinée. *gulf* E Atlantic Ocean
Guinea, People's Revolutionary Republic of *see* Guinea
Guinea, Republic of *see* Guinea
Guiné-Bissau *see* Guinea-Bissau
Guinée *see* Guinea
Guinée-Bissau *see* Guinea-Bissau
Guinée, Golfe de *see* Guinea, Gulf of
44 *C4* **Güines** La Habana, W Cuba *22°50′N 82°02′W*
102 *G5* **Guingamp** Côtes d'Armor, NW France *48°34′N 03°09′W*
105 *P3* **Guipúzcoa** *Basq.* Gipuzkoa. ◆ *province* País Vasco, N Spain
44 *C5* **Güira de Melena** La Habana, W Cuba *22°47′N 82°33′W*
74 *G8* **Guir, Hamada du** *desert* Algeria/Morocco
55 *P5* **Güiria** Sucre, NE Venezuela *10°37′N 62°21′W*
Gui Shui *see* Gui Jiang
104 *H2* **Guitiriz** Galicia, NW Spain *43°10′N 07°52′W*
77 *N17* **Guitri** S Ivory Coast *05°31′N 05°14′W*
171 *Q5* **Guiuan** Samar, C Philippines *11°02′N 125°45′E*
Gui Xian/Guixian *see* Guigang
160 *J12* **Guiyang** *var.* Kuei-Yang, Kuei-yang, Kueyang, Kweiyang; *prev.* Kweichu. *province capital* Guizhou, S China *26°33′N 106°45′E*
160 *J12* **Guizhou** *var.* Guizhou Sheng, Kuei-chou, Kweichow, Qian. ◆ *province* S China
Guizhou Sheng *see* Guizhou
102 *J13* **Gujan-Mestras** Gironde, SW France *44°39′N 01°04′W*
154 *B10* **Gujarāt** *var.* Gujerat. ◆ *state* W India
149 *V6* **Gūjar Khān** Punjab, E Pakistan *33°19′N 73°23′E*
Gujerat *see* Gujarāt
149 *V7* **Gujrānwāla** Punjab, NE Pakistan *32°11′N 74°09′E*
149 *V7* **Gujrāt** Punjab, E Pakistan *32°34′N 74°04′E*
146 *B8* **Gulandag** *Rus.* Gory Kulandag. ▲ Balkan Welaýaty, W Turkmenistan
159 *U9* **Gulang** Gansu, C China *37°31′N 102°55′E*
183 *R6* **Gulargambone** New South Wales, SE Australia *31°19′S 148°31′E*
155 *G15* **Gulbarga** Karnātaka, C India *17°22′N 76°47′E*
118 *J8* **Gulbene** *Ger.* Alt-Schwanenburg. Gulbene, NE Latvia *57°10′N 26°44′E*
147 *U10* **Gul'cha** *Kir.* Gülchö. Oshskaya Oblast', SW Kyrgyzstan *40°16′N 73°27′E*
Gülchö *see* Gul'cha
173 *T10* **Gulden Draak Seamount** *undersea feature* E Indian Ocean *33°45′S 101°00′E*
136 *J16* **Gülek Boğazı** *var.* Cilician Gates. *pass* S Turkey
186 *D8* **Gulf** ◆ *province* S Papua New Guinea
23 *O9* **Gulf Breeze** Florida, SE USA *30°21′N 87°09′W*
Gulf of Liaotung *see* Liaodong Wan
23 *V13* **Gulfport** Florida, SE USA *27°45′N 82°42′W*
22 *M9* **Gulfport** Mississippi, S USA *30°22′N 89°06′W*
23 *O9* **Gulf Shores** Alabama, S USA *30°15′N 87°40′W*
141 *T5* **Gulf, The** *var.* Persian Gulf, *Ar.* Khalīj al 'Arabī, *Per.* Khalīj-e Fars. *gulf* SW Asia *see also* Persian Gulf
183 *R7* **Gulgong** New South Wales, SE Australia *32°22′S 149°31′E*
160 *I11* **Gulin** Sichuan, C China *28°06′N 105°47′E*
171 *U14* **Gulir** Pulau Kasiui, E Indonesia *04°27′S 131°41′E*
Gulistan *see* Guliston
147 *P10* **Guliston** *Rus.* Gulistan. Sirdaryo Viloyati, E Uzbekistan *40°29′N 68°46′E*
163 *T6* **Guliya Shan** ▲ NE China *49°42′N 122°22′E*
Gulja *see* Yining
39 *S11* **Gulkana** Alaska, USA *62°17′N 145°25′W*
11 *S17* **Gull Lake** Saskatchewan, S Canada *50°05′N 108°30′W*
31 *P10* **Gull Lake** ◎ Michigan, N USA
29 *T6* **Gull Lake** ◎ Minnesota, N USA
95 *L16* **Gullspång** Västra Götaland, S Sweden *58°58′N 14°04′E*
136 *B15* **Güllük Körfezi** *prev.* Akbük Limanı. *bay* W Turkey
152 *H5* **Gulmarg** Jammu and Kashmir, NW India *34°04′N 74°25′E*
Gulpaigan *see* Golpāyegān
99 *L18* **Gulpen** Limburg, SE Netherlands *50°48′N 05°53′E*
Gul'shad *see* Gul'shat
145 *S13* **Gul'shat** *var.* Gul'shad. Karaganda, E Kazakhstan *46°37′N 74°22′E*
81 *F17* **Gulu** N Uganda *02°46′N 32°21′E*
114 *K10* **Gŭlŭbovo** Stara Zagora, C Bulgaria *42°08′N 25°51′E*
114 *I7* **Gulyantsi** Pleven, N Bulgaria *43°37′N 24°40′E*
Gulyaypole *see* Hulyaypole
Guma *see* Pishan
Gümai *see* Darlag
79 *K16* **Gumba** Equateur, NW Dem. Rep. Congo *02°58′N 21°23′E*
Gumbinnen *see* Gusev
81 *H24* **Gumbiro** Ruvuma, S Tanzania *10°19′S 35°40′E*
146 *B11* **Gumdag** *prev.* Kum-Dag. Balkan Welaýaty, W Turkmenistan *39°13′N 54°35′E*
77 *W12* **Gumel** Jigawa, N Nigeria *12°37′N 09°23′E*
105 *N5* **Gumiel de Hizán** Castilla-León, N Spain *41°46′N 03°42′W*
153 *P16* **Gumla** Jhārkhand, N India *23°03′N 84°36′E*
Gumma *see* Gunma
101 *F16* **Gummersbach** Nordrhein-Westfalen, W Germany *51°01′N 07°34′E*
77 *T13* **Gummi** Zamfara, NW Nigeria *12°07′N 05°07′E*
Gumpolds *see* Humpolec
Gumti *see* Gomati
Gümülcine/Gümüljina *see* Komotiní
Gümüşane *see* Gümüşhane
137 *O12* **Gümüşhane** *var.* Gümüşane, Gumushkhane. Gümüşhane, NE Turkey *40°31′N 39°27′E*
137 *O12* **Gümüşhane** *var.* Gümüşane, Gumushkhane. ◆ *province* NE Turkey
Gumushkhane *see* Gümüşhane
171 *V14* **Gumzai** Pulau Kola, E Indonesia *05°27′S 134°38′E*
154 *H9* **Guna** Madhya Pradesh, C India *24°39′N 77°18′E*
Gunabad *see* Gonābād
Gunan *see* Qij ang
Gunbad-i-Qawus *see* Gonbad-e Kāvūs
183 *O9* **Gunbar** New South Wales, SE Australia *34°03′S 145°32′E*
183 *O9* **Gun Creek** *seasonal river* New South Wales, SE Australia
183 *Q10* **Gundagai** New South Wales, SE Australia *35°06′S 148°03′E*
79 *K17* **Gundji** Equateur, N Dem. Rep. Congo *02°03′N 21°31′E*
155 *G20* **Gundlupet** Karnātaka, W India *11°48′N 76°42′E*
136 *G16* **Gündoğmuş** Antalya, S Turkey *36°50′N 32°07′E*
137 *O14* **Güney Doğu Toroslar** ▲ SE Turkey
79 *J21* **Gungu** Bandundu, SW Dem. Rep. Congo *05°43′S 19°20′E*
127 *P17* **Gunib** Respublika Dagestan, SW Russian Federation *42°24′N 46°55′E*
112 *J11* **Gunja** Vukovar-Srijem, E Croatia *44°53′N 18°51′E*
31 *P9* **Gun Lake** ◎ Michigan, N USA
165 *N12* **Gunma** *off.* Gunma-ken, *var.* Gumma. ◆ *prefecture* Honshū, S Japan
Gunma-ken *see* Gunma
197 *P15* **Gunnbjørn Fjeld** *var.* Gunnbjörns Bjerge. ▲ C Greenland *69°03′N 29°36′W*
Gunnbjörns Bjerge *see* Gunnbjørn Fjeld
183 *S6* **Gunnedah** New South Wales, SE Australia *30°59′S 150°15′E*
173 *Y15* **Gunner's Quoin** *var.* Coin de Mire. *island* N Mauritius
37 *R6* **Gunnison** Colorado, C USA *38°33′N 106°55′W*
36 *L5* **Gunnison** Utah, W USA *39°09′N 111°49′W*
37 *P5* **Gunnison River** ⚡ Colorado, C USA
21 *X2* **Gunpowder River** ⚡ Maryland, NE USA
Güns *see* Kőszeg
Gunsan *see* Kunsan
109 *S4* **Gunskirchen** Oberösterreich, N Austria *48°07′N 13°54′E*
Gunt *see* Ghund
155 *H17* **Guntakal** Andhra Pradesh, C India *15°11′N 77°24′E*
23 *Q2* **Guntersville** Alabama, S USA *34°21′N 86°17′W*
23 *Q2* **Guntersville Lake** ⊠ Alabama, S USA
109 *X4* **Guntramsdorf** Niederösterreich, E Austria *48°03′N 16°19′E*
155 *J16* **Guntūr** *var.* Guntur. Andhra Pradesh, SE India *16°20′N 80°27′E*
168 *H10* **Gunungsitoli** Pulau Nias, W Indonesia *01°11′N 97°35′E*
155 *M14* **Gunupur** Orissa, E India *19°04′N 83°52′E*
101 *J23* **Günz** ⚡ S Germany
Gunzan *see* Kunsan
101 *J22* **Günzburg** Bayern, S Germany *48°25′N 10°18′E*
101 *K21* **Gunzenhausen** Bayern, S Germany *49°07′N 10°45′E*
Guolüezhen *see* Lingbao
Guovdageaidnu *see* Kautokeino
161 *P7* **Guoyang** Anhui, E China *33°30′N 116°12′E*
116 *G11* **Gurahonț** *Hung.* Honctő. Arad, W Romania *46°16′N 22°21′E*
Gurahumora *see* Gura Humorului
116 *K9* **Gura Humorului** *Ger.* Gurahumora. Suceava, NE Romania *47°31′N 26°00′E*
146 *H8* **Gurbansoltan Eje** *prev.* Yylanly, *Rus.* Il'yaly. Daşoguz Welaýaty, N Turkmenistan *41°57′N 59°42′E*
158 *K4* **Gurbantünggüt Shamo** *desert* W China
152 *H7* **Gurdāspur** Punjab, N India *32°04′N 75°28′E*
27 *T13* **Gurdon** Arkansas, C USA *33°55′N 93°09′W*
Gurdzhaani *see* Gurjaani
Gurgan *see* Gorgān
152 *I10* **Gurgaon** Haryāna, N India *28°27′N 77°01′E*
59 *M15* **Gurguéia, Rio** ⚡ NE Brazil
55 *Q7* **Guri, Embalse de** ⊠ E Venezuela
137 *V10* **Gurjaani** *Rus.* Gurdzhaani. E Georgia *41°42′N 45°47′E*
109 *T8* **Gurk** Kärnten, S Austria *46°52′N 14°17′E*
109 *T9* **Gurk** *Slvn.* Krka. ⚡ S Austria
Gurkfeld *see* Krško
114 *K9* **Gurkovo** *prev.* Kolupchii. Stara Zagora, C Bulgaria *42°42′N 25°46′E*
109 *S9* **Gurktaler Alpen** ▲ S Austria
146 *H8* **Gurlan** *Rus.* Gurlen. Xorazm Viloyati, W Uzbekistan *41°54′N 60°18′E*
Gurlen *see* Gurlan
83 *M16* **Guro** Manica, C Mozambique *17°28′S 33°18′E*
136 *M14* **Gürün** Sivas, C Turkey *38°44′N 37°15′E*
59 *K16* **Gurupi** Tocantins, C Brazil *11°44′S 49°01′W*
58 *L12* **Gurupi, Rio** ⚡ NE Brazil
152 *E14* **Guru Sikhar** ▲ NW India *24°45′N 72°51′E*
162 *H8* **Gurvanbulag** *var.* Höviyn Am. Bayanhongor, C Mongolia *47°08′N 98°41′E*
162 *K7* **Gurvanbulag** *var.* Avdzaga. Bulgan, C Mongolia *47°43′N 103°30′E*
162 *I11* **Gurvantes** *var.* Urt. Ömnögovĭ, S Mongolia *43°16′N 101°00′E*
Gur'yev/Gur'yevskaya Oblast' *see* Atyrau
77 *U13* **Gusau** Zamfara, NW Nigeria *12°18′N 06°27′E*
126 *C3* **Gusev** *Ger.* Gumbinnen. Kaliningradskaya Oblast', W Russian Federation *54°36′N 22°14′E*
146 *J17* **Gushgy** *Rus.* Kushka. ⚡ Mary Welaýaty, S Turkmenistan
Gushiago *see* Gushiegu
77 *Q14* **Gushiegu** *var.* Gushiago. NE Ghana *09°54′N 00°12′W*
165 *S17* **Gushikawa** Okinawa, Okinawa, SW Japan *26°21′N 127°50′E*
113 *L16* **Gusinje** E Montenegro *42°34′N 19°51′E*
126 *M4* **Gus'-Khrustal'nyy** Vladimirskaya Oblast', W Russian Federation *55°39′N 40°42′E*
107 *B19* **Guspini** Sardegna, Italy, C Mediterranean Sea *39°33′N 08°39′E*
109 *X8* **Güssing** Burgenland, SE Austria *47°03′N 16°19′E*
109 *V6* **Gusswerk** Steiermark, E Austria *47°43′N 15°18′E*
92 *O2* **Gustav Adolf Land** *physical region* NE Svalbard
195 *X5* **Gustav Bull Mountains** ▲ Antarctica
39 *W13* **Gustavus** Alaska, USA *58°24′N 135°44′W*
92 *O1* **Gustav V Land** *physical region* NE Svalbard
35 *P9* **Gustine** California, W USA *37°14′N 121°00′W*
25 *R8* **Gustine** Texas, SW USA *31°51′N 98°24′W*
100 *M9* **Güstrow** Mecklenburg-Vorpommern, NE Germany *53°48′N 12°12′E*
95 *N18* **Gusum** Östergötland, S Sweden *58°15′N 16°30′E*
Guta/Gúta *see* Kolárovo
Gutenstein *see* Ravne na Koroškem
101 *G14* **Gütersloh** Nordrhein-Westfalen, W Germany *51°54′N 08°23′E*
27 *N10* **Guthrie** Oklahoma, C USA *35°53′N 97°26′W*
25 *P5* **Guthrie** Texas, SW USA *33°38′N 100°21′W*
29 *U14* **Guthrie Center** Iowa, C USA *41°40′N 94°30′W*
41 *Q13* **Gutiérrez Zamora** Veracruz-Llave, E Mexico *20°29′N 97°07′W*
Gutta *see* Kolárovo
29 *Y12* **Guttenberg** Iowa, C USA *42°47′N 91°06′W*
Guttentag *see* Dobrodzień
Guttstadt *see* Dobre Miasto
162 *G8* **Guulin** Govĭ-Altay, C Mongolia *46°33′N 97°21′E*
153 *V12* **Guwāhāti** *prev.* Gauhāti. Assam, NE India *26°09′N 91°42′E*
139 *R3* **Guwër** *var.* Al Kuwayr, Al Quwayr, Quwair. Arbīl, N Iraq *36°03′N 43°30′E*
146 *A10* **Guwlumaýak** *Rus.* Kuuli-Mayak. Balkan Welaýaty, NW Turkmenistan *40°14′N 52°43′E*
55 *R9* **Guyana** *off.* Co-operative Republic of Guyana; *prev.* British Guiana. ◆ *republic* N South America
Guyana, Co-operative Republic of *see* Guyana
21 *P5* **Guyandotte River** ⚡ West Virginia, NE USA
Guyane *see* French Guiana
Guyi *see* Sanjiang
26 *H8* **Guymon** Oklahoma, C USA *36°42′N 101°30′W*
146 *K12* **Guynuk** Lebap Welaýaty, NE Turkmenistan *39°18′N 63°00′E*
Guyong *see* Jiangle
21 *O9* **Guyot, Mount** ▲ North Carolina/Tennessee, SE USA *35°42′N 83°15′W*
183 *U5* **Guyra** New South Wales, SE Australia *30°13′S 151°42′E*
159 *W10* **Guyuan** Ningxia, N China *35°57′N 106°13′E*
Guzar *see* G'uzor
121 *P2* **Güzelyurt** *Gk.* Kólpos Mórfu, Morphou. W Cyprus *35°12′N 33°E*
121 *N2* **Güzelyurt Körfezi** *var.* Morfou Bay, Morphou Bay, *Gk.* Kólpos Mórfou. *bay* W Cyprus
Guzhou *see* Rongjiang
40 *I3* **Guzmán** Chihuahua, N Mexico *31°13′N 107°27′W*
147 *N13* **G'uzor** *Rus.* Guzar. Qashqadaryo Viloyati, S Uzbekistan *38°41′N 66°12′E*
119 *B14* **Gvardeysk** *Ger.* Tapaiu. Kaliningradskaya Oblast', W Russian Federation *54°39′N 21°02′E*
Gvardeyskoye *see* Hvardiys'ke
183 *R5* **Gwabegar** New South Wales, SE Australia *30°34′S 148°58′E*
148 *J16* **Gwādar** *var.* Gwadur. Baluchistān, SW Pakistan *25°09′N 62°21′E*
148 *J16* **Gwādar East Bay** *bay* SW Pakistan
148 *J16* **Gwādar West Bay** *bay* SW Pakistan
Gwadur *see* Gwādar
83 *J17* **Gwai** Matabeleland North, W Zimbabwe *19°17′S 27°37′E*
154 *I7* **Gwalior** Madhya Pradesh, C India *26°16′N 78°12′E*
83 *J18* **Gwanda** Matabeleland South, SW Zimbabwe *20°56′S 29°E*
79 *N15* **Gwane** Orientale, N Dem. Rep. Congo *04°40′N 25°51′E*
83 *I17* **Gwayi** ⚡ W Zimbabwe
110 *G8* **Gwda** *var.* Glda, *Ger.* Küddow. ⚡ NW Poland
97 *C14* **Gweebarra Bay** *Ir.* Béal an Bheara. *inlet* W Ireland
97 *D14* **Gweedore** *Ir.* Gaoth Dobhair. Donegal, NW Ireland *55°03′N 08°14′W*
Gwelo *see* Gweru
97 *K21* **Gwent** *cultural region* S Wales, United Kingdom
83 *K17* **Gweru** *prev.* Gwelo. Midlands, C Zimbabwe *19°27′S 29°49′E*
29 *Q7* **Gwinner** North Dakota, N USA *46°10′N 97°42′W*
77 *Y13* **Gwoza** Borno, NE Nigeria *11°07′N 13°40′E*
Gwy *see* Wye
183 *R4* **Gwydir River** ⚡ New South Wales, SE Australia
97 *I19* **Gwynedd** *var.* Gwyneth. *cultural region* NW Wales, United Kingdom
Gwyneth *see* Gwynedd
159 *O16* **Gyaca** *var.* Ngarrab. Xizang Zizhiqu, W China *29°06′N 92°37′E*
Gya'gya *see* Saga
Gyaijêpozhanggê *see* Zhidoi
Gyaisi *see* Jiulong
115 *M22* **Gyalí** *var.* Yialí. *island* Dodekánisa, Greece, Aegean Sea
Gyamotang *see* Dêngqên
Gyandzha *see* Gäncä
Gyangkar *see* Dinggyê
158 *M16* **Gyangzê** Xizang Zizhiqu, W China *28°50′N 89°38′E*
158 *L14* **Gyaring Co** ◎ W China
159 *Q12* **Gyaring Hu** ◎ C China
115 *I20* **Gyáros** *var.* Yioúra. *island* Kykládes, Greece, Aegean Sea
122 *J7* **Gyda** Yamalo-Nenetskiy Avtonomnyy Okrug, N Russian Federation *70°55′N 78°34′E*
122 *J7* **Gydanskiy Poluostrov** *Eng.* Gyda Peninsula. *peninsula* N Russian Federation
Gyda Peninsula *see* Gydanskiy Poluostrov
Gyêgu *see* Yushu
Gyéres *see* Câmpia Turzii
Gyergyószentmiklós *see* Gheorgheni
Gyergyótölgyes *see* Tulgheş
Gyertyámos *see* Cărpiniş
Gyeva *see* Detva
Gyigang *see* Zayü
158 *J16* **Gyirong** Xizang Zizhiqu, W China *28°51′N 85°16′E*
Gyixong *see* Gonggar
95 *I23* **Gyldenløveshøy** *hill range* C Denmark
181 *Z10* **Gympie** Queensland, E Australia *26°05′S 152°40′E*
166 *L7* **Gyobingauk** Bago, SW Myanmar (Burma) *18°14′N 95°39′E*
111 *M23* **Gyomaendrőd** Békés, SE Hungary *45°56′N 20°50′E*
Gyömbér *see* Ďumbier
111 *L22* **Gyöngyös** Heves, NE Hungary *47°44′N 19°49′E*
111 *H22* **Győr** *Ger.* Raab, *Lat.* Arrabona. Győr-Moson-Sopron, NW Hungary *47°41′N 17°40′E*
111 *G22* **Győr-Moson-Sopron** *off.* Győr-Moson-Sopron Megye. ◆ *county* NW Hungary
Győr-Moson-Sopron Megye *see* Győr-Moson-Sopron
11 *X15* **Gypsumville** Manitoba, S Canada *51°47′N 98°38′W*
12 *M4* **Gyrfalcon Islands** *island group* Northwest Territories, NE Canada
95 *N14* **Gysinge** Gävleborg, C Sweden *60°16′N 16°55′E*
115 *F22* **Gýtheio** *var.* Githio; *prev.* Yíthion. Pelopónnisos, S Greece *36°46′N 22°34′E*
146 *L13* **Gyuichbirleshik** Lebap Welaýaty, E Turkmenistan *38°10′N 64°33′E*
111 *N24* **Gyula** *Rom.* Jula. Békés, SE Hungary *46°39′N 21°17′E*
Gyulafehérvár *see* Alba Iulia
Gyulovo *see* Roza
137 *T11* **Gyumri** *var.* Giumri, *Rus.* Kumayri; *prev.* Aleksandropol', Leninakan. W Armenia *40°48′N 43°51′E*
146 *D13* **Gyunuzyndag, Gora** ▲ Balkan Welaýaty, W Turkmenistan *38°15′N 56°25′E*
146 *J15* **Gyzylbaýdak** *Rus.* Krasnoye Znamya. Mary Welaýaty, S Turkmenistan *36°51′N 62°24′E*
Gyzyletrek *see* Etrek
146 *D10* **Gyzylgaýa** *Rus.* Kizyl-Kaya. Balkan Welaýaty, NW Turkmenistan *40°37′N 55°15′E*
146 *A10* **Gyzylsuw** *Rus.* Kizyl-Su. Balkan Welaýaty, W Turkmenistan *39°49′N 53°00′E*
Gyzyrlabat *see* Serdar
Gzhatsk *see* Gagarin

H

153 *T12* **Ha** W Bhutan *27°17′N 89°22′E*
Haabai *see* Ha'apai Group
99 *H17* **Haacht** Vlaams Brabant, C Belgium *50°58′N 04°38′E*
109 *T4* **Haag** Niederösterreich, NE Austria *48°07′N 14°32′E*
194 *L8* **Haag Nunataks** ▲ Antarctica
92 *N2* **Haakon VII Land** *physical region* NW Svalbard
98 *O11* **Haaksbergen** Overijssel, E Netherlands *52°09′N 06°45′E*
99 *E14* **Haamstede** Zeeland, SW Netherlands *51°43′N 03°45′E*
193 *Y15* **Ha'ano** *island* Ha'apai Group, C Tonga
193 *Y15* **Ha'apai Group** *var.* Haabai. *island group* C Tonga
93 *L15* **Haapajärvi** Oulu, C Finland *63°45′N 25°20′E*
93 *L17* **Haapamäki** Länsi-Suomi, C Finland *62°11′N 24°32′E*
93 *L15* **Haapavesi** Oulu, C Finland *64°09′N 25°25′E*
191 *N7* **Haapiti** Moorea, W French Polynesia *17°33′S 149°52′W*
118 *F4* **Haapsalu** *Ger.* Hapsal. Läänemaa, W Estonia *58°58′N 23°32′E*
Ha'Arava *see* 'Arabah, Wādī al
95 *G24* **Haarby** *var.* Hårby. Fyn, C Denmark *55°13′N 10°07′E*
98 *H10* **Haarlem** *prev.* Harlem. Noord-Holland, W Netherlands *52°23′N 04°39′E*
185 *D19* **Haast** West Coast, South Island, New Zealand *43°53′S 169°02′E*
185 *C20* **Haast** ⚡ South Island, New Zealand
185 *D20* **Haast Pass** *pass* South Island, New Zealand
193 *W16* **Ha'atua** 'Eua, E Tonga *21°23′S 174°57′W*
149 *P15* **Hab** ⚡ SW Pakistan
141 *W7* **Haba** *var.* Al Haba. Dubayy, NE United Arab Emirates *25°01′N 55°37′E*
158 *K2* **Habahe** *var.* Kaba. Xinjiang Uygur Zizhiqu, NW China *48°04′N 86°20′E*
141 *U13* **Ḩabarūt** *var.* Habrut. SW Oman *17°19′N 52°45′E*
81 *J18* **Habaswein** North Eastern, NE Kenya *01°01′N 39°27′E*
99 *L24* **Habay-la-Neuve** Luxembourg, SE Belgium *49°43′N 05°38′E*
139 *S8* **Ḩabbānīyah, Buḩayrat** ◎ C Iraq
Habelschwerdt *see* Bystrzyca Kłodzka
153 *V14* **Habiganj** Sylhet, NE Bangladesh *24°23′N 91°25′E*
163 *Q12* **Habirag** Nei Mongol Zizhiqu, N China *42°18′N 115°40′E*
95 *L19* **Habo** Västra Götaland, S Sweden *57°55′N 14°05′E*
123 *V14* **Habomai Islands** *island group* Kuril'skiye Ostrova, SE Russian Federation
165 *S2* **Haboro** Hokkaidō, NE Japan *44°19′N 141°42′E*
153 *S16* **Habra** West Bengal, NE India *22°39′N 88°17′E*
Habrut *see* Ḩabarūt
143 *P17* **Ḩabshān** Abū Ẓaby, C United Arab Emirates *23°51′N 53°34′E*
54 *E14* **Hacha** Putumayo, S Colombia *0°02′S 75°30′W*
165 *X13* **Hachijō** Tōkyō, Hachijō-jima, SE Japan *33°40′N 139°20′E*
165 *X13* **Hachijō-jima** *island* Izu-shotō, SE Japan
164 *L12* **Hachiman** Gifu, Honshū, SW Japan *35°46′N 136°57′E*
165 *P7* **Hachimori** Akita, Honshū, C Japan *40°22′N 139°59′E*
165 *R7* **Hachinohe** Aomori, Honshū, C Japan *40°30′N 141°29′E*
93 *G17* **Hackås** Jämtland, C Sweden *62°55′N 14°31′E*
18 *K14* **Hackensack** New Jersey, NE USA *40°51′N 73°57′W*
75 *U12* **Ḩadabat al Jilf al Kabīr** *var.* Gilf Kebir Plateau. *plateau* SW Egypt
Hadama *see* Nazrēt
141 *W13* **Ḩadbaram** S Oman *17°27′N 55°13′E*
139 *U13* **Ḩaddānīyah** *well* S Iraq
96 *K12* **Haddington** SE Scotland, United Kingdom *55°59′N 02°46′W*
141 *Z8* **Ḩadd, Ra's al** *headland* NE Oman *22°28′N 59°54′E*
Haded *see* Xadeed
77 *W12* **Hadejia** Jigawa, N Nigeria *12°22′N 10°02′E*
77 *W12* **Hadejia** ⚡ N Nigeria
138 *F9* **Hadera** *var.* Khadera; *prev.* Hadera. Haifa, C Israel *32°26′N 34°55′E*
Ḩadera *see* Hadera
Hadersleben *see* Haderslev
95 *G24* **Haderslev** *Ger.* Hadersleben. Sønderjylland, SW Denmark *55°15′N 09°30′E*
151 *J21* **Hadhdhunmathi Atoll** *atoll* S Maldives
141 *W17* **Ḩadīboh** Suquţrā, SE Yemen *12°38′N 54°05′E*
158 *K9* **Hadilik** Xinjiang Uygur Zizhiqu, W China *37°51′N 86°10′E*
136 *H16* **Hadım** Konya, S Turkey *36°58′N 32°27′E*
140 *K7* **Ḩadīyah** Al Madīnah, W Saudi Arabia *25°36′N 38°31′E*
8 *L5* **Hadley Bay** *bay* Victoria Island, Nunavut, N Canada
167 *S6* **Ha Đông** *var.* Hadong. Ha Tây, N Vietnam *20°58′N 105°46′E*
Hadong *see* Ha Đông
Hadramaut *see* Ḩaḑramawt
141 *R15* **Ḩaḑramawt** *Eng.* Hadramaut. ▲ S Yemen
Hadria *see* Adria
Hadrianopolis *see* Edirne
Hadria Picena *see* Apricena
95 *G22* **Hadsten** Århus, C Denmark *56°19′N 10°03′E*
95 *G21* **Hadsund** Nordjylland, N Denmark *56°43′N 10°08′E*
117 *S4* **Hadyach** *Rus.* Gadyach. Poltavs'ka Oblast', NE Ukraine *50°21′N 34°00′E*
112 *I13* **Hadžići** Federacija Bosna I Hercegovina, SE Bosnia and Herzegovina *43°49′N 18°12′E*
163 *W14* **Haeju** S North Korea *38°04′N 125°40′E*
Haerbin/Haerhpin/Ha-erh-pin *see* Harbin
141 *P5* **Ḩafar al Bāţin** Ash Sharqīyah, N Saudi Arabia *28°25′N 45°59′E*
11 *T15* **Hafford** Saskatchewan, S Canada *52°43′N 107°19′W*
136 *M13* **Hafik** Sivas, N Turkey *39°53′N 37°24′E*
149 *V8* **Hāfizābād** Punjab, E Pakistan *32°03′N 73°42′E*
153 *W13* **Hāflong** Assam, NE India *25°10′N 93°01′E*
92 *H4* **Hafnarfjördhur** Reykjanes, W Iceland *64°03′N 21°57′W*
Hafnia *see* Denmark
Hafnia *see* København

◆ Country ● Country Capital ◇ Dependent Territory ○ Dependent Territory Capital ◆ Administrative Regions ✈ International Airport ▲ Mountain ▲ Mountain Range ⚡ Volcano ⚡ River ◎ Lake ⊠ Reservoir

HAFREN – HARMONY

Hafren see Severn
Hafun see Xaafuun
Hafun, Ras see Xaafuun, Raas
80 G10 Hag 'Abdullah Sinnar, E Sudan 13°59′N 33°35′E
81 K18 Hagadera North Eastern, E Kenya 0°06′N 40°23′E
138 G8 HaGalil Eng. Galilee. ▲▲ N Israel
14 G10 Hagar Ontario, S Canada 46°27′N 80°22′W
155 G18 Hagari var. Vedāvati. ≈ W India
188 B16 Hagåtña, var. Agaña. ○ (Guam) NW Guam 13°27′N 144°45′E
100 M13 Hagelberg hill NE Germany
39 N14 Hagemeister Island island Alaska, USA
101 F15 Hagen Nordrhein-Westfalen, W Germany 51°22′N 07°27′E
100 K10 Hagenow Mecklenburg-Vorpommern, N Germany 53°27′N 11°10′E
10 K15 Hagensborg British Columbia, SW Canada 52°24′N 126°24′W
80 I13 Hägere Hiywet var. Agere Hiywet, Ambo. Oromīya, C Ethiopia 09°00′N 37°55′E
33 O15 Hagerman Idaho, NW USA 42°48′N 114°53′W
37 U14 Hagerman New Mexico, SW USA 33°07′N 104°19′W
21 V2 Hagerstown Maryland, NE USA 39°39′N 77°44′W
14 G16 Hagersville Ontario, S Canada 42°58′N 80°03′W
102 J15 Hagetmau Landes, SW France 43°40′N 00°36′W
95 K14 Hagfors Värmland, C Sweden 60°03′N 13°45′E
93 G16 Häggenås Jämtland, C Sweden 63°24′N 14°53′E
164 E12 Hagi Yamaguchi, Honshū, SW Japan 34°25′N 131°22′E
167 S5 Ha Giang Ha Giang, N Vietnam 22°50′N 104°58′E
Hagios Evstrátios see Ágios Efstrátios
HaGolan see Golan Heights
103 T4 Hagondange Moselle, NE France 49°16′N 06°06′E
97 B18 Hag's Head Ir. Ceann Caillí. headland W Ireland 52°56′N 09°29′W
102 I3 Hague, Cap de la headland N France 49°43′N 01°56′W
103 V5 Haguenau Bas-Rhin, NE France 48°49′N 07°47′E
165 X16 Hahajima-rettō island group SE Japan
15 R8 Há Há, Lac ◎ Québec, SE Canada
172 H13 Hahaya ✕ (Moroni) Grande Comore, NW Comoros
22 K9 Hahnville Louisiana, S USA 29°58′N 90°24′W
83 E22 Haib Karas, S Namibia 28°12′S 18°19′E
Haibak see Āybak
149 N15 Haibo ≈ SW Pakistan
Haibowan see Wuhai
163 U12 Haicheng Liaoning, NE China 40°53′N 122°45′E
Haicheng see Haifeng
Haicheng see Haiyuan
Haida see Nový Bor
Haidarabad see Hyderābād
Haidenschaft see Ajdovščina
167 T6 Hai Dương Hai Hưng, N Vietnam 20°56′N 106°21′E
138 F9 Haifa ◈ district NW Israel
Haifa see Hefa
Haifa, Bay of see Mifrats Hefa
161 P14 Haifeng var. Haicheng. Guangdong, S China 22°56′N 115°19′E
Haifong see Hai Phong
161 P3 Hai He ≈ E China
Haikang see Leizhou
160 L17 Haikou var. Hai-k'ou, Hoihow, Fr. Hoï-Hao. province capital Hainan, S China 20°N 110°17′E
Hai-k'ou see Haikou
140 M6 Ḩā'il Ḩā'il, NW Saudi Arabia 27°N 42°50′E
141 N5 Ḩā'il off. Minţaqah Ḩā'il. ◈ province N Saudi Arabia
163 S6 Hailar He ≈ NE China
33 P14 Hailey Idaho, NW USA 43°31′N 114°18′W
14 H9 Haileybury Ontario, S Canada 47°27′N 79°39′W
163 X9 Hailin Heilongjiang, NE China 44°37′N 129°24′E
Ḩā'il, Minţaqah see Ḩā'il
Hailong see Meihekou
93 K14 Hailuoto Swe. Karlö. island W Finland
Haima see Haymā'
Haimen see Taizhou
160 M17 Hainan var. Hainan Sheng, Qiong. ◈ province S China
160 K17 Hainan Dao island S China
Hainan Sheng see Hainan
Hainan Strait see Qiongzhou Haixia
Hainasch see Ainaži
Hainau see Chojnów
99 E20 Hainaut ◈ province SW Belgium
Hainburg see Hainburg an der Donau
109 Z4 Hainburg an der Donau var. Hainburg. Niederösterreich, NE Austria 48°09′N 16°57′E
39 W12 Haines Alaska, USA 59°13′N 135°27′W
32 L12 Haines Oregon, NW USA 44°53′N 117°56′W
23 W12 Haines City Florida, SE USA 28°06′N 81°37′W
10 H8 Haines Junction Yukon Territory, W Canada 60°45′N 137°30′W
109 W4 Hainfeld Niederösterreich, NE Austria 48°03′N 15°47′E
101 N16 Hainichen Sachsen, E Germany 50°58′N 13°08′E
Hai Ninh see Mong Cai
167 T6 Hai Phong var. Haifong, Haiphong. N Vietnam 20°50′N 106°41′E
Haiphong see Hai Phong
161 S12 Haitan Dao island SE China
44 K8 Haiti off. Republic of Haiti. ◆ republic C West Indies
Haiti, Republic of see Haiti
35 T11 Haiwee Reservoir ⊠ California, W USA
80 I7 Haiya Red Sea, NE Sudan 18°17′N 36°21′E
159 T10 Haiyan var. Sanjiaocheng. Qinghai, W China 36°55′N 100°54′E
160 M13 Haiyang Shan ▲▲ S China
159 V10 Haiyuan Ningxia, N China 36°32′N 105°31′E
Hajda see Nový Bor
111 M22 Hajdú-Bihar off. Hajdú-Bihar Megye. ◈ county E Hungary
Hajdú-Bihar Megye see Hajdú-Bihar
111 N22 Hajdúböszörmény Hajdú-Bihar, E Hungary 47°39′N 21°32′E
111 N22 Hajdúhadház Hajdú-Bihar, E Hungary 47°40′N 21°40′E
111 N21 Hajdúnánás Hajdú-Bihar, E Hungary 47°50′N 21°26′E
111 N22 Hajdúszoboszló Hajdú-Bihar, E Hungary 47°27′N 21°24′E
142 I3 Ḩājī Ebrāhīm, Kūh-e ▲ Iran/Iraq 36°53′N 44°56′E
165 O9 Hajiki-zaki headland Sado, C Japan 38°19′N 138°28′E
Hajîne see Abū Ḩardān
153 P13 Hājīpur Bihār, N India 25°41′N 85°13′E
141 N14 Ḩajjah W Yemen 15°43′N 43°33′E
139 U11 Hajjama Al Muthanná, S Iraq 31°24′N 45°20′E
143 Q13 Ḩājjīābād Fārs, S Iran 28°21′N 54°27′E
143 R12 Ḩājjīābād Hormozgān, C Iran
139 U14 Ḩājj, Thaqb al well S Iraq
113 L16 Hajla ▲▲ E Montenegro
110 P10 Hajnówka Ger. Hermhausen. Podlaskie, NE Poland 52°45′N 23°32′E
Haka see Hakha
Hakapehi see Punaauia
Hakâri see Hakkâri
138 F12 HaKatan, HaMakhtesh prev. HaMakhtesh HaQatan. ▲▲ S Israel
166 K4 Hakha var. Haka. Chin State, W Myanmar (Burma) 22°42′N 93°41′E
137 T16 Hakkâri var. Çölemerik, Hakâri. Hakkâri, SE Turkey 37°36′N 43°45′E
137 T16 Hakkâri var. Hakkari. ◈ province SE Turkey
Hakkari see Hakkâri
92 J12 Hakkas Norrbotten, N Sweden 66°53′N 21°36′E
164 J14 Hakken-zan ▲ Honshū, SW Japan 34°11′N 135°57′E
165 R7 Hakkōda-san ▲ Honshū, C Japan 40°40′N 140°49′E
165 T2 Hako-dake ▲ Hokkaidō, NE Japan 44°40′N 142°22′E
165 R5 Hakodate Hokkaidō, NE Japan 41°46′N 140°43′E
164 L11 Hakui Ishikawa, Honshū, SW Japan 36°55′N 136°46′E
190 B16 Hakupu SE Niue 19°06′S 169°50′E
164 L12 Haku-san ▲ Honshū, SW Japan 36°07′N 136°45′E
Hakusan see Mattō
Hal see Halle
149 Q15 Hāla Sind, SE Pakistan 25°47′N 68°28′E
138 J3 Ḩalab Eng. Aleppo, Fr. Alep; anc. Beroea. Ḩalab, NW Syria 36°14′N 37°10′E
138 J3 Ḩalab off. Muḩāfaẓat Ḩalab, var. Aleppo, Halab. ◈ governorate NW Syria
138 J3 Ḩalab ✕ Ḩalab, NW Syria 36°12′N 37°10′E
Halab see Ḩalab
141 O8 Ḩalabān var. Halibān. Ar Riyāḑ, C Saudi Arabia 23°29′N 44°20′E
139 V4 Ḩalabja As Sulaymānīyah, NE Iraq 35°11′N 45°59′E
Ḩalab, Muḩāfaẓat see Ḩalab
146 L13 Halaç Rus. Khalach. Lebap Welaýaty, E Turkmenistan 38°05′N 64°46′E
190 A16 Halagigie Point headland W Niue
75 Z11 Halaib SE Egypt 22°10′N 36°33′E
190 G12 Halalo Île Uvea, N Wallis and Futuna 13°21′S 176°11′W
Halandri see Chalándri
141 X13 Ḩalāniyāt, Juzur al var. Jazā'ir Bin Ghalfān, Eng. Kuria Muria Islands. island group S Oman
141 W13 Ḩalāniyāt, Khalīj al Eng. Kuria Muria Bay. bay S Oman
Halas see Kiskunhalas
38 G11 Hālawa var. Halawa. Hawaii, USA, C Pacific Ocean 20°13′N 155°46′W
Halawa see Hālawa
38 F9 Hālawa, Cape var. Cape Halawa. headland Moloka'i, Hawai'i, USA 21°09′N 156°43′W
Cape Halawa see Hālawa, Cape
Halban see Tsetserleg
101 K14 Halberstadt Sachsen-Anhalt, C Germany 51°54′N 11°04′E
184 M12 Halcombe Manawatu-Wanganui, North Island, New Zealand 40°09′S 175°30′E
95 I16 Halden prev. Fredrikshald. Østfold, S Norway 59°08′N 11°20′E
100 L13 Haldensleben Sachsen-Anhalt, C Germany 52°18′N 11°25′E
Háldi see Halti
153 S17 Haldia West Bengal, NE India 22°04′N 88°02′E
152 K10 Haldwāni Uttarakhand, N India 29°13′N 79°31′E
163 P9 Haldzan Sühbaatar, E Mongolia 46°10′N 112°57′E
163 P9 Haldzan var. Hatavch. Sühbaatar, E Mongolia 46°10′N 112°57′E
38 F10 Haleakalā var. Haleakala. crater Maui, Hawai'i, USA
Haleakala see Haleakalā
25 N4 Hale Center Texas, SW USA 34°03′N 101°50′W
99 J18 Halen Limburg, NE Belgium 50°35′N 05°08′E
23 O2 Haleyville Alabama, S USA 34°13′N 87°37′W
77 O17 Half Assini SW Ghana 05°03′N 02°57′W
35 R8 Half Dome ▲ California, W USA 37°46′N 119°27′W
185 C25 Halfmoon Bay var. Oban. Stewart Island, Southland, New Zealand 46°53′S 168°08′E
182 E5 Half Moon Lake salt lake South Australia
163 R7 Halhgol Dornod, E Mongolia 47°57′N 118°07′E
163 S8 Halhgol var. Tsagaannuur. Dornod, E Mongolia 47°30′N 118°45′E
Haliacmon see Aliákmonas
Halibān see Ḩalabān
14 I13 Haliburton Ontario, SE Canada 45°03′N 78°20′W
14 I12 Haliburton Highlands var. Madawaska Highlands. hill range Ontario, SE Canada
13 Q15 Halifax province capital Nova Scotia, SE Canada 44°38′N 63°35′W
97 L17 Halifax N England, United Kingdom 53°44′N 01°52′W
21 W8 Halifax North Carolina, SE USA 36°19′N 77°37′W
21 U7 Halifax Virginia, NE USA 36°46′N 78°55′W
13 Q15 Halifax ✕ Nova Scotia, SE Canada 44°33′N 63°48′W
143 T13 Halīl Rūd seasonal river SE Iran
138 I6 Ḩalīmah ▲ Lebanon/Syria 34°12′N 36°37′E
162 G8 Haliun Govĭ-Altay, W Mongolia 45°55′N 96°06′E
118 I3 Haljala Ger. Halljal. Lääne-Virumaa, N Estonia 59°25′N 26°18′E
39 Q4 Halkett, Cape headland Alaska, USA 70°48′N 152°11′W
Halkida see Chalkída
96 J6 Halkirk N Scotland, United Kingdom 58°30′N 03°29′W
15 X7 Hall ≈ Québec, SE Canada
Hall see Schwäbisch Hall
93 H15 Hälla Västerbotten, N Sweden 63°56′N 17°20′E
96 J6 Halladale ≈ N Scotland, United Kingdom
95 J21 Halland ◈ county S Sweden
23 Z15 Hallandale Florida, SE USA 25°58′N 80°09′W
95 K22 Hallandsås physical region S Sweden
9 P6 Hall Beach Nunavut, N Canada 68°10′N 81°56′W
99 G19 Halle Fr. Hal. Vlaams Brabant, C Belgium 50°44′N 04°14′E
101 M15 Halle var. Halle an der Saale. Sachsen-Anhalt, C Germany 51°28′N 11°58′E
Halle an der Saale see Halle
35 W3 Halleck Nevada, W USA 40°57′N 115°27′W
95 L15 Hällefors Örebro, C Sweden 59°46′N 14°30′E
95 N16 Hälleforsnäs Södermanland, C Sweden 59°10′N 16°30′E
109 Q6 Hallein Salzburg, N Austria 47°41′N 13°06′E
101 L15 Halle-Neustadt Sachsen-Anhalt, C Germany 51°29′N 11°54′E
25 U12 Hallettsville Texas, SW USA 29°27′N 96°57′W
195 N4 Halley UK research station Antarctica 75°42′S 26°30′W
28 L4 Halliday North Dakota, N USA 47°19′N 102°19′W
37 S2 Halligan Reservoir ⊠ Colorado, C USA
100 G7 Halligen island group N Germany
94 G13 Hallingdal valley S Norway
38 J12 Hall Island island Alaska, USA
Hall Island see Maiana
189 P15 Hall Islands island group C Micronesia
118 H6 Halliste ≈ S Estonia
Halljal see Haljala
93 I15 Hällnäs Västerbotten, N Sweden 64°20′N 19°41′E
29 R2 Hallock Minnesota, N USA 48°47′N 96°56′W
9 S6 Hall Peninsula peninsula Baffin Island, Nunavut, NE Canada
20 F9 Halls Tennessee, S USA 35°52′N 89°24′W
95 M16 Hallsberg Örebro, C Sweden 59°05′N 15°07′E
181 N5 Halls Creek Western Australia 18°17′S 127°39′E
182 L12 Halls Gap Victoria, SE Australia 37°09′S 142°30′E
95 N15 Hallstahammar Västmanland, C Sweden 59°37′N 16°13′E
109 R6 Hallstatt Salzburg, W Austria 47°32′N 13°39′E
109 R6 Hallstätter See ◎ C Austria
95 P14 Hallstavik Stockholm, C Sweden 60°12′N 18°45′E
25 X7 Hallsville Texas, SW USA 32°31′N 94°30′W
103 P1 Halluin Nord, N France 50°46′N 03°07′E
Halmahera, Laut see Halmahera Sea
171 R11 Halmahera, Pulau prev. Djailolo, Gilolo, Jailolo. island E Indonesia
171 S12 Halmahera Sea Ind. Laut Halmahera. sea E Indonesia
95 J21 Halmstad Halland, S Sweden 56°41′N 12°49′E
119 N15 Halowchyn Rus. Golovchin. Mahilyowskaya Voblasts', E Belarus 54°04′N 29°55′E
95 H20 Hals Nordjylland, N Denmark 57°00′N 10°19′E
94 F8 Halsa Møre og Romsdal, S Norway 63°04′N 08°13′E
119 I15 Hal'shany Rus. Gol'shany. Hrodzyenskaya Voblasts', W Belarus 54°15′N 26°01′E
Hälsingborg see Helsingborg
29 R5 Halstad Minnesota, N USA 47°21′N 96°49′W
27 N6 Halstead Kansas, C USA 38°00′N 97°30′W
99 G15 Halsteren Noord-Brabant, S Netherlands 51°32′N 04°16′E
93 L16 Halsua Länsi-Suomi, W Finland 63°28′N 24°10′E
101 E14 Haltern Nordrhein-Westfalen, W Germany 51°45′N 07°10′E
92 J9 Halti var. Haltiatunturi, Lapp. Háldi. ▲ Finland/Norway 69°18′N 21°19′E
Haltiatunturi see Halti
116 J6 Halych Ivano-Frankivs'ka Oblast', W Ukraine 49°08′N 24°44′E
Halycus see Platani
103 P3 Ham Somme, N France 49°46′N 03°03′E
Hama see Ḩamāh
164 F12 Hamada Shimane, Honshū, SW Japan 34°54′N 132°07′E
142 L6 Hamadān anc. Ecbatana. Hamadān, W Iran 34°51′N 48°31′E
142 L6 Hamadān off. Ostān-e Hamadān. ◈ province W Iran
Hamadān, Ostān-e see Hamadān
138 I5 Ḩamāh var. Hama; anc. Epiphania, Bibl. Hamath. Ḩamāh, W Syria 35°09′N 36°44′E
138 I5 Ḩamāh off. Muḩāfaẓat Ḩamāh, var. Hama. ◈ governorate C Syria
Ḩamāh, Muḩāfaẓat see Ḩamāh
1665 S3 Hamamasu Hokkaidō, NE Japan 43°37′N 141°24′E
164 L14 Hamamatsu var. Hamamatu. Shizuoka, Honshū, S Japan 34°43′N 137°46′E
Hamamatu see Hamamatsu
165 W14 Hamanaka Hokkaidō, NE Japan 43°05′N 145°05′E
164 L14 Hamana-ko ◎ Honshū, S Japan
94 I13 Hamar prev. Storhammer. Hedmark, S Norway 60°57′N 10°55′E
141 U10 Ḩamārīr al Kidan, Qalamat well E Saudi Arabia
164 I12 Hamasaka Hyōgo, Honshū, SW Japan 35°37′N 134°27′E
Hamath see Ḩamāh
165 T1 Hamatonbetsu Hokkaidō, NE Japan 45°07′N 142°21′E
155 K26 Hambantota Southern Province, SE Sri Lanka 06°07′N 81°07′E
Hambourg see Hamburg
100 J9 Hamburg Hamburg, N Germany 53°33′N 10°03′E
27 V14 Hamburg Arkansas, C USA 33°13′N 91°50′W
29 S16 Hamburg Iowa, C USA 40°36′N 95°39′W
18 D10 Hamburg New York, NE USA 42°40′N 78°49′W
100 I10 Hamburg Fr. Hambourg. ◈ state N Germany
148 K5 Hamdam Āb, Dasht-e Pash. Dasht-i Hamdamab. ▲▲ W Afghanistan
Hamdamab, Dasht-i see Hamdam Āb, Dasht-e
18 M13 Hamden Connecticut, NE USA 41°23′N 72°55′W
140 K6 Ḩamḑ, Wādī al dry watercourse W Saudi Arabia
93 K18 Hämeenkyrö Länsi-Suomi, W Finland 61°39′N 23°10′E
93 L19 Hämeenlinna Swe. Tavastehus. Etelä-Suomi, S Finland 61°N 24°25′E
HaMela h, Yam see Dead Sea
Hamelin see Hameln
100 I13 Hameln Eng. Hamelin. Niedersachsen, N Germany 52°07′N 09°22′E
180 I8 Hamersley Range ▲▲ Western Australia
163 Y12 Hamgyŏng-sanmaek ▲▲ N North Korea
163 X13 Hamhŭng C North Korea 39°53′N 127°31′E
159 O6 Hami var. Ha-mi, Uigh. Kumul, Qomul. Xinjiang Uygur Zizhiqu, NW China 42°48′N 93°27′E
Ha-mi see Hami
139 X10 Ḩāmid Amīn Maysān, E Iraq 32°06′N 46°53′E
141 W11 Hamīdān, Khawr oasis SE Saudi Arabia
138 H5 Ḩamīdīyah var. Hamīdīyé. Ţarţūs, W Syria 34°43′N 35°58′E
114 L12 Hamidiye Edirne, NW Turkey 41°09′N 26°40′E
Hamīdīyé see Ḩamīdīyah
182 L12 Hamilton Victoria, SE Australia 37°45′S 142°04′E
64 B12 Hamilton ○ (Bermuda) C Bermuda 32°18′N 64°48′W
14 G16 Hamilton Ontario, S Canada 43°15′N 79°50′W
184 M7 Hamilton Waikato, North Island, New Zealand 37°49′S 175°16′E
96 I12 Hamilton S Scotland, United Kingdom 55°47′N 04°03′W
23 N3 Hamilton Alabama, S USA 34°08′N 87°59′W
38 M10 Hamilton Alaska, USA 62°54′N 163°53′W
30 J13 Hamilton Illinois, N USA 40°24′N 91°20′W
27 S3 Hamilton Missouri, C USA 39°44′N 94°00′W
33 P10 Hamilton Montana, NW USA 46°15′N 114°09′W
25 S8 Hamilton Texas, SW USA 31°42′N 98°08′W
14 G16 Hamilton ✕ Ontario, SE Canada 43°12′N 79°54′W
64 I6 Hamilton Bank undersea feature SE Labrador Sea
182 E1 Hamilton Creek seasonal river South Australia
13 R8 Hamilton Inlet inlet Newfoundland and Labrador, E Canada
27 T12 Hamilton, Lake ⊠ Arkansas, C USA
35 W6 Hamilton, Mount ▲ Nevada, W USA 39°15′N 115°30′W
75 S8 Ḩamīm, Wādī al ≈ NE Libya
93 N19 Hamina Swe. Fredrikshamn. Kymi, S Finland 60°33′N 27°15′E
11 W16 Hamiota Manitoba, S Canada 50°13′N 100°37′W
152 L13 Hamīrpur Uttar Pradesh, N India 25°57′N 80°08′E
Hamīs Musait see Khamīs Mushayt
21 T11 Hamlet North Carolina, SE USA 34°52′N 79°41′W
25 P6 Hamlin Texas, SW USA 32°52′N 100°07′W
21 P5 Hamlin West Virginia, NE USA 38°16′N 82°07′W
31 O7 Hamlin Lake ◎ Michigan, N USA
101 F14 Hamm var. Hamm in Westfalen. Nordrhein-Westfalen, W Germany 51°39′N 07°49′E
Ḩammāmāt, Khalīj al see Hammamet, Golfe de
75 N5 Hammamet, Golfe de Ar. Khalīj al Ḩammāmāt. gulf NE Tunisia
139 R3 Ḩammān al 'Alīl Nīnawé, N Iraq 36°07′N 43°15′E
139 X12 Ḩammār, Hawr al ◎ SE Iraq
93 J20 Hammarland Åland, SW Finland 60°13′N 19°45′E
93 H16 Hammarstrand Jämtland, C Sweden 63°07′N 16°27′E
93 O17 Hammaslahti Itä-Suomi, SE Finland 62°26′N 29°58′E
99 F17 Hamme Oost-Vlaanderen, NW Belgium 51°06′N 04°08′E
100 H10 Hamme ≈ NW Germany
95 G22 Hammel Århus, C Denmark 56°15′N 09°53′E
101 I18 Hammelburg Bayern, C Germany 50°06′N 09°50′E
99 H18 Hamme-Mille Walloon Brabant, C Belgium 50°48′N 04°42′E
100 H10 Hamme-Oste-Kanal canal NW Germany
93 G16 Hammerdal Jämtland, C Sweden 63°34′N 15°19′E
92 K8 Hammerfest Finnmark, N Norway 70°40′N 23°44′E
101 D14 Hamminkeln Nordrhein-Westfalen, W Germany 51°43′N 06°36′E
Hamm in Westfalen see Hamm
26 K10 Hammon Oklahoma, C USA 35°37′N 99°22′W
31 N11 Hammond Indiana, N USA 41°35′N 87°30′W
22 K8 Hammond Louisiana, S USA 30°30′N 90°27′W
99 K20 Hamoir Liège, E Belgium 50°28′N 05°35′E
99 J21 Hamois Namur, SE Belgium 50°21′N 05°09′E
99 K16 Hamont Limburg, NE Belgium 51°15′N 05°33′E
185 F22 Hampden Otago, South Island, New Zealand 45°18′S 170°49′E
19 R6 Hampden Maine, NE USA 44°44′N 68°51′W
97 M23 Hampshire cultural region S England, United Kingdom
13 O15 Hampton New Brunswick, SE Canada 45°30′N 65°50′W
27 U14 Hampton Arkansas, C USA 33°33′N 92°28′W
29 V12 Hampton Iowa, C USA 42°44′N 93°12′W
19 P10 Hampton New Hampshire, NE USA 42°55′N 70°48′W
21 R14 Hampton South Carolina, SE USA 32°52′N 81°06′W
21 P8 Hampton Tennessee, S USA 36°16′N 82°10′W
21 X7 Hampton Virginia, NE USA 37°02′N 76°23′W
94 L11 Hamra Gävleborg, C Sweden 61°40′N 15°00′E
80 D10 Hamrat esh Sheikh Northern Kordofan, C Sudan 14°38′N 27°56′E
139 S5 Ḩamrīn, Jabal ▲▲ N Iraq
121 P16 Ḩamrun C Malta 35°53′N 14°28′E
167 U14 Ham Thuân Nam Binh Thuân, S Vietnam 10°49′N 107°49′E
Hāmūn, Daryācheh-ye see Şāberī, Hāmūn-e/Sīstān, Daryācheh-ye
Hamwih see Southampton
38 G10 Hāna var. Hana. Maui, Hawaii, USA, C Pacific Ocean 20°45′N 155°59′W
Hana see Hāna
21 S14 Hanahan South Carolina, SE USA 32°55′N 80°01′W
38 B8 Hanalei Kaua'i, Hawaii, USA, C Pacific Ocean 22°12′N 159°30′W
167 U10 Ha Nam Quang Nam-Đa Nẵng, C Vietnam 15°42′N 108°24′E
165 Q9 Hanamaki Iwate, Honshū, C Japan 39°25′N 141°04′E
38 F10 Hanamanioa, Cape headland Maui, Hawai'i, USA 20°34′N 156°22′W
190 B16 Hanan ✕ (Alofi) SW Niue
101 H18 Hanau Hessen, W Germany 50°06′N 08°56′E
162 M11 Hanbogd var. Ih Bulag. Ömnögovĭ, S Mongolia 43°04′N 107°43′E
8 L9 Hanbury ≈ Northwest Territories, NW Canada
Hânceşti see Hînceşti
10 M15 Hanceville British Columbia, SW Canada 51°54′N 122°56′W
23 P3 Hanceville Alabama, S USA 34°03′N 86°46′W
Hancewicze see Hantsavichy
160 L6 Hancheng Shaanxi, C China 35°22′N 110°27′E
21 V2 Hancock Maryland, NE USA 39°42′N 78°10′W
30 M3 Hancock Michigan, N USA 47°07′N 88°34′W
29 S8 Hancock Minnesota, N USA 45°30′N 95°47′W
18 I12 Hancock New York, NE USA 41°57′N 75°15′W
80 Q12 Handa Bari, NE Somalia 10°35′N 51°09′E
161 O5 Handan var. Han-tan. Hebei, E China 36°35′N 114°28′E
95 P16 Handen Stockholm, C Sweden 59°12′N 18°09′E
81 J22 Handeni Tanga, E Tanzania 05°25′S 38°04′E
37 Q7 Handies Peak ▲ Colorado, C USA 37°54′N 107°30′W
111 J19 Handlová Ger. Krickerhäu, Hung. Nyitrabánya; prev. Kriegerhaj. Trenčiansky Kraj, C Slovakia 48°45′N 18°45′E
165 O13 Haneda ✕ (Tōkyō) Tōkyō, Honshū, S Japan 35°33′N 139°45′E
138 F13 HaNegev Eng. Negev. desert S Israel
Hanfeng see Kaixian
35 Q11 Hanford California, W USA 36°19′N 119°39′W
191 V16 Hanga Roa Easter Island, Chile, E Pacific Ocean 27°09′S 109°26′W
162 I7 Hangay var. Hunt. Arhangay, C Mongolia 47°49′N 99°24′E
162 H7 Hangayn Nuruu ▲▲ C Mongolia
Hang-chou/Hangchow see Hangzhou
95 K20 Hånger Jönköping, S Sweden 57°06′N 13°58′E
Hangö see Hanko
149 T6 Hangu North-West Frontier Province, N Pakistan 33°32′N 71°04′E
161 R9 Hangzhou var. Hang-chou, Hangchow. province capital Zhejiang, SE China 30°18′N 120°07′E
162 J4 Hanh var. Turt. Hövsgöl, N Mongolia 51°30′N 100°40′E
162 F5 Hanhöhiy Uul ▲▲ NW Mongolia
162 K10 Hanhongor var. Ögöömör. Ömnögovĭ, S Mongolia 43°47′N 104°31′E
146 I14 Hanhowuz Rus. Khauz-Khan. Ahal Welaýaty, S Turkmenistan 37°15′N 61°12′E
146 I14 Hanhowuz Suw Howdany Rus. Khauzkhanskoye Vodoranilishche. ⊠ S Turkmenistan
137 P15 Hani Diyarbakır, SE Turkey 38°26′N 40°23′E
Hania see Chaniá
141 R11 Ḩanīsh al Kabīr, Jazīrat al island SW Yemen
Hanka, Lake see Khanka, Lake
93 M17 Hankasalmi Länsi-Suomi, C Finland 62°25′N 26°27′E
29 R7 Hankinson North Dakota, N USA 46°04′N 96°54′W
93 K20 Hanko Swe. Hangö. Etelä-Suomi, SW Finland 59°50′N 23°E
Han-kou/Han-k'ou/Hankow see Wuhan
36 M6 Hanksville Utah, W USA 38°21′N 110°43′W
152 K6 Hanle Jammu and Kashmir, NW India 32°46′N 79°01′E
185 I17 Hanmer Springs Canterbury, South Island, New Zealand 42°31′S 172°49′E
11 R16 Hanna Alberta, SW Canada 51°38′N 111°56′W
27 V3 Hannibal Missouri, C USA 39°42′N 91°23′W
180 M3 Hann, Mount ▲ Western Australia 15°53′S 125°46′E
100 I12 Hannover Eng. Hanover. Niedersachsen, NW Germany 52°23′N 09°43′E
99 J19 Hannut Liège, C Belgium 50°40′N 05°05′E
95 L22 Hanöbukten bay S Sweden
167 T6 Ha Nôi Eng. Hanoi, Fr. Hanoï. ● (Vietnam) N Vietnam 21°01′N 105°52′E
14 F14 Hanover Ontario, S Canada 44°10′N 81°03′W
31 P15 Hanover Indiana, N USA 38°42′N 85°28′W
18 G16 Hanover Pennsylvania, NE USA 39°46′N 76°57′W
21 W6 Hanover Virginia, NE USA 37°44′N 77°21′W
Hanover see Hannover
63 G23 Hanover, Isla island S Chile
Hanselbeck see Érd
195 X5 Hansen Mountains ▲▲ Antarctica
160 M8 Han Shui ≈ C China
152 H10 Hānsi Haryāna, NW India 29°06′N 76°01′E
95 F20 Hanstholm Viborg, NW Denmark 57°05′N 08°39′E
Han-tan see Handan
158 H6 Hantengri Feng var. Pik Khan-Tengri. ▲ China/Kazakhstan 42°17′N 80°11′E see also Khan-Tengri, Pik
119 I18 Hantsavichy Pol. Hancewicze, Rus. Gantsevichi. Brestskaya Voblasts', SW Belarus 52°45′N 26°27′E
9 Q6 Hantzsch ≈ Baffin Island, Nunavut, NE Canada
152 G9 Hanumāngarh Rājasthān, NW India 29°33′N 74°21′E
183 O9 Hanwood New South Wales, SE Australia 34°19′S 146°03′E
Hanyang see Wuhan
Hanyang see Caidian
160 H10 Hanyuan var. Fulin. Sichuan, C China 29°29′N 102°45′E
Hanyuan see Xihe
160 J7 Hanzhong Shaanxi, C China 33°12′N 107°E
191 W11 Hao atoll Îles Tuamotu, C French Polynesia
153 S16 Hāora prev. Howrah. West Bengal, NE India 22°35′N 88°20′E
78 K8 Haouach, Ouadi dry watercourse E Chad
92 K13 Haparanda Norrbotten, N Sweden 65°49′N 24°05′E
25 N3 Happy Texas, SW USA 34°44′N 101°51′W
34 M1 Happy Camp California, W USA 41°48′N 123°24′W
13 Q9 Happy Valley-Goose Bay prev. Goose Bay. Newfoundland and Labrador, E Canada 53°19′N 60°24′W
Hapsal see Haapsalu
152 J10 Hāpur Uttar Pradesh, N India 28°43′N 77°47′E
HaQatan, HaMakhtesh see HaKatan, HaMakhtesh
140 I4 Ḩaql Tabūk, NW Saudi Arabia 29°18′N 34°58′E
171 U14 Har Pulau Kai Besar, E Indonesia 05°21′S 133°09′E
Haraat see Tsagaandelger
141 R8 Ḩaraḑ var. Haradh. Ash Sharqīyah, E Saudi Arabia 24°08′N 49°02′E
Haradh see Ḩaraḑ
118 N12 Haradok Rus. Gorodok. Vitsyebskaya Voblasts', N Belarus 55°28′N 30°00′E
92 J13 Harads Norrbotten, N Sweden 66°04′N 21°04′E
119 G19 Haradzyets Rus. Gorodets. Brestskaya Voblasts', SW Belarus 52°12′N 24°40′E
119 J17 Haradzyeya Rus. Gorodeya. Minskaya Voblasts', C Belarus 53°19′N 26°32′E
191 V10 Haraiki atoll Îles Tuamotu, C French Polynesia
165 Q11 Haramachi Fukushima, Honshū, E Japan 37°40′N 140°55′E
118 M12 Harany Rus. Gorany. Vitsyebskaya Voblasts', N Belarus 55°25′N 29°03′E
83 L16 Harare prev. Salisbury. ● (Zimbabwe) Mashonaland East, NE Zimbabwe 17°47′S 31°04′E
83 L16 Harare ✕ Mashonaland East, NE Zimbabwe 17°51′S 31°06′E
78 J10 Haraz-Djombo Batha, C Chad 14°10′N 19°35′E
119 O16 Harbavichy Rus. Gorbovichi. Mahilyowskaya Voblasts', E Belarus 53°49′N 30°42′E
76 J16 Harbel W Liberia 06°19′N 10°20′W
163 W8 Harbin var. Haerbin, Ha-erh-pin, Kharbin; prev. Haerhpin, Pingkiang, Pinkiang. province capital Heilongjiang, NE China 45°45′N 126°41′E
31 S7 Harbor Beach Michigan, N USA 43°50′N 82°39′W
13 T13 Harbour Breton Newfoundland, Newfoundland and Labrador, E Canada 47°29′N 55°50′W
65 D25 Harbours, Bay of bay East Falkland, Falkland Islands
Hårby see Haarby
36 I13 Harcuvar Mountains ▲▲ Arizona, SW USA
108 I7 Hard Vorarlberg, NW Austria 47°29′N 09°42′E
154 H11 Harda Khas Madhya Pradesh, C India 22°22′N 77°06′E
95 D14 Hardanger physical region S Norway
95 D14 Hardangerfjorden fjord S Norway
94 E13 Hardangerjøkulen glacier S Norway
95 E14 Hardangervidda plateau S Norway
83 D20 Hardap ◈ district S Namibia
21 R15 Hardeeville South Carolina, SE USA 32°18′N 81°04′W
98 L5 Hardegarijp Fris. Hurdegaryp. Friesland, N Netherlands 53°13′N 05°57′E
98 O9 Hardenberg Overijssel, E Netherlands 52°34′N 06°38′E
183 Q9 Harden-Murrumburrah New South Wales, SE Australia 34°33′S 148°22′E
98 K10 Harderwijk Gelderland, C Netherlands 52°21′N 05°37′E
30 J14 Hardin Illinois, N USA 39°10′N 90°38′W
33 V11 Hardin Montana, NW USA 45°44′N 107°35′W
23 R5 Harding, Lake ⊠ Alabama/Georgia, SE USA
20 J6 Hardinsburg Kentucky, S USA 37°46′N 86°29′W
98 I13 Hardinxveld-Giessendam Zuid-Holland, C Netherlands 51°52′N 04°49′E
11 R15 Hardisty Alberta, SW Canada 52°42′N 111°22′W
152 L12 Hardoi Uttar Pradesh, N India 27°23′N 80°06′E
Hardwar see Haridwār
23 U4 Hardwick Georgia, SE USA 33°03′N 83°13′W
27 W9 Hardy Arkansas, C USA 36°19′N 91°29′W
94 D10 Hareid Møre og Romsdal, S Norway 62°22′N 06°02′E
8 H7 Hare Indian ≈ Northwest Territories, NW Canada
99 D18 Harelbeke var. Harlebeke. West-Vlaanderen, W Belgium 50°51′N 03°19′E
Harem see Ḩārim
100 E11 Haren Niedersachsen, NW Germany 52°47′N 07°16′E
98 N6 Haren Groningen, NE Netherlands 53°10′N 06°37′E
80 L13 Hārer E Ethiopia 09°17′N 42°19′E
95 P14 Harg Uppsala, C Sweden 60°13′N 18°25′E
Hargeisa see Hargeysa
80 M13 Hargeysa var. Hargeisa. Woqooyi Galbeed, NW Somalia 09°32′N 44°07′E
116 J10 Harghita ◈ county NE Romania
25 S17 Hargill Texas, SW USA 26°26′N 98°00′W
162 J8 Harhorin Övörhangay, C Mongolia 47°13′N 102°48′E
159 Q9 Har Hu ◎ C China
Hariana see Haryāna
141 P15 Ḩarīb W Yemen 15°08′N 45°35′E
168 M12 Hari, Batang prev. Djambi. ≈ Sumatera, W Indonesia
152 J9 Haridwār prev. Hardwar. Uttarakhand, N India 29°58′N 78°09′E
155 F18 Harihar Karnātaka, W India 14°33′N 75°44′E
185 F18 Harihari West Coast, South Island, New Zealand 43°09′S 170°35′E
138 I3 Ḩārim var. Harem. Idlib, W Syria 36°30′N 36°30′E
98 F13 Haringvliet channel SW Netherlands
98 F13 Haringvlietdam dam SW Netherlands
149 U5 Harīpur North-West Frontier Province, NW Pakistan 34°00′N 73°01′E
148 J4 Harīrūd var. Tedzhen, Turkm. Tejen. ≈ Afghanistan/Iran see also Tejen
Harīrūd see Tejen
94 J11 Härjåhågnen Swe. Härjahågnen, var. Härjehågna. ▲ Norway/Sweden 61°43′N 12°07′E
Härjahågnen see Østrehogna
Härjahågnen see Härjåhågnen
93 K18 Harjavalta Länsi-Suomi, W Finland 61°19′N 22°10′E
Härjehågna see Østrehogna
Härjehågna see Härjåhågnen
118 G4 Harjumaa var. Harju Maakond. ◈ province NW Estonia
Harju Maakond see Harjumaa
21 X11 Harkers Island North Carolina, SE USA 34°42′N 76°33′W
139 S1 Harki Dahūk, N Iraq 37°03′N 43°39′E
29 T14 Harlan Iowa, C USA 41°40′N 95°19′W
21 O7 Harlan Kentucky, S USA 36°50′N 83°19′W
29 N17 Harlan County Lake ⊠ Nebraska, C USA
116 L9 Hârlău var. Hîrlău. Iaşi, NE Romania 47°26′N 26°54′E
Harlebeke see Harelbeke
33 U7 Harlem Montana, NW USA 48°31′N 108°46′W
Harlem see Haarlem
95 G22 Harlev Århus, C Denmark 56°08′N 10°00′E
98 K6 Harlingen Fris. Harns. Friesland, N Netherlands 53°10′N 05°25′E
25 T17 Harlingen Texas, SW USA 26°12′N 97°43′W
97 O21 Harlow E England, United Kingdom 51°47′N 00°07′E
33 T10 Harlowton Montana, NW USA 46°26′N 109°49′W
94 N11 Harmånger Gävleborg, C Sweden 61°55′N 17°19′E
98 I11 Harmelen Utrecht, C Netherlands 52°06′N 04°58′E
29 X11 Harmony Minnesota, N USA 43°33′N 92°00′W

◆ Country
● Country Capital
◇ Dependent Territory
○ Dependent Territory Capital
◈ Administrative Regions
✕ International Airport
▲ Mountain
▲▲ Mountain Range
▲ Volcano
≈ River
◎ Lake
⊠ Reservoir

HARNEY BASIN – HELVECIA

32 J14 **Harney Basin** *basin* Oregon, NW USA
32 J14 **Harney Lake** ◎ Oregon, NW USA
28 J10 **Harney Peak** ▲ South Dakota, N USA 43°52′N 103°31′W
93 H17 **Härnösand** *var.* Hernösand. Västernorrland, C Sweden 62°37′N 17°55′E
Harns *see* Harlingen
162 F6 **Har Nuur** ◎ NW Mongolia
105 P4 **Haro** La Rioja, N Spain 42°34′N 02°52′W
40 F6 **Haro, Cabo** *headland* NW Mexico 27°50′N 110°55′W
94 D9 **Harøy** *island* S Norway
97 N21 **Harpenden** E England, United Kingdom 51°49′N 00°22′W
76 L18 **Harper** *var.* Cape Palmas. NE Liberia 04°25′N 07°43′W
26 M7 **Harper** Kansas, C USA 37°17′N 98°01′W
32 L13 **Harper** Oregon, NW USA 43°51′N 117°37′W
25 Q10 **Harper** Texas, SW USA 30°18′N 99°18′W
35 U13 **Harper Lake** *salt flat* California, W USA
39 T9 **Harper, Mount** ▲ Alaska, USA 64°14′N 143°54′W
95 J21 **Harplinge** Halland, S Sweden 56°45′N 12°45′E
36 J13 **Harquahala Mountains** ▲▲ Arizona, SW USA
141 T15 **Harrah** SE Yemen 15°02′N 50°23′E
12 H11 **Harricana** ⚔ Québec, SE Canada
20 M9 **Harriman** Tennessee, S USA 35°57′N 84°33′W
13 R11 **Harrington Harbour** Québec, E Canada 50°34′N 59°29′W
64 B12 **Harrington Sound** *bay* Bermuda, NW Atlantic Ocean
96 F8 **Harris** *physical region* NW Scotland, United Kingdom
27 X10 **Harrisburg** Arkansas, C USA 35°33′N 90°43′W
30 M17 **Harrisburg** Illinois, N USA 37°44′N 88°32′W
28 I14 **Harrisburg** Nebraska, C USA 41°33′N 103°46′W
32 F12 **Harrisburg** Oregon, NW USA 44°16′N 123°10′W
18 G15 **Harrisburg** *state capital* Pennsylvania, NE USA 40°16′N 76°53′W
182 F6 **Harris, Lake** ◎ South Australia
23 W11 **Harris, Lake** ◎ Florida, SE USA
83 J22 **Harrismith** Free State, E South Africa 28°16′S 29°08′E
27 T9 **Harrison** Arkansas, C USA 36°13′N 93°07′W
31 Q7 **Harrison** Michigan, N USA 44°02′N 84°46′W
28 I12 **Harrison** Nebraska, C USA 42°42′N 103°53′W
39 Q5 **Harrison Bay** *inlet* Alaska, USA
22 I6 **Harrisonburg** Louisiana, S USA 31°44′N 91°51′W
21 U4 **Harrisonburg** Virginia, NE USA 38°27′N 78°54′W
13 R7 **Harrison, Cape** *headland* Newfoundland and Labrador, E Canada 54°55′N 57°48′W
27 R5 **Harrisonville** Missouri, C USA 38°43′N 94°21′W
Harris Ridge *see* Lomonosov Ridge
192 M3 **Harris Seamount** *undersea feature* N Pacific Ocean 46°09′N 161°25′W
96 F8 **Harris, Sound of** *strait* NW Scotland, United Kingdom
31 R6 **Harrisville** Michigan, N USA 44°41′N 83°19′W
21 R3 **Harrisville** West Virginia, NE USA 39°13′N 81°04′W
20 M6 **Harrodsburg** Kentucky, S USA 37°45′N 84°51′W
97 M16 **Harrogate** N England, United Kingdom 54°N 01°33′W
25 Q4 **Harrold** Texas, SW USA 34°05′N 99°02′W
27 S5 **Harry S. Truman Reservoir** ⊠ Missouri, C USA
100 G13 **Harsewinkel** Nordrhein-Westfalen, W Germany 51°58′N 08°13′E
116 M14 **Hârşova** *prev.* Hîrşova. Constanţa, SE Romania 44°41′N 27°56′E
92 H10 **Harstad** Troms, N Norway 68°48′N 16°31′E
31 O8 **Hart** Michigan, N USA 43°43′N 86°22′W
24 M4 **Hart** Texas, SW USA 34°23′N 102°07′W
10 I5 **Hart** ⚔ Yukon Territory, NW Canada
83 F23 **Hartbees** ⚔ C South Africa
109 X7 **Hartberg** Steiermark, SE Austria 47°18′N 15°58′E
182 I10 **Hart, Cape** *headland* South Australia 35°54′S 138°01′E
95 E14 **Hårteigen** ▲ S Norway 60°11′N 07°01′E
23 Q7 **Hartford** Alabama, S USA 31°06′N 85°42′W
27 R11 **Hartford** Arkansas, C USA 35°01′N 94°22′W
18 M12 **Hartford** *state capital* Connecticut, NE USA 41°46′N 72°41′W
20 J6 **Hartford** Kentucky, S USA 37°26′N 86°57′W
31 P10 **Hartford** Michigan, N USA 42°12′N 85°54′W
29 R11 **Hartford** South Dakota, N USA 43°37′N 96°56′W
30 M8 **Hartford** Wisconsin, N USA 43°19′N 88°25′W
31 P13 **Hartford City** Indiana, N USA 40°27′N 85°22′W
29 Q13 **Hartington** Nebraska, C USA 42°37′N 97°15′W
13 N14 **Hartland** New Brunswick, SE Canada 46°18′N 67°31′W
97 H23 **Hartland Point** *headland* SW England, United Kingdom 51°01′N 04°33′W
97 M15 **Hartlepool** N England, United Kingdom 54°41′N 01°13′W
29 T12 **Hartley** Iowa, C USA 43°10′N 95°28′W
24 M1 **Hartley** Texas, SW USA 35°52′N 102°24′W
32 J15 **Hart Mountain** ▲ Oregon, NW USA 42°24′N 119°46′W
173 U10 **Hartog Ridge** *undersea feature* W Indian Ocean
93 M18 **Hartola** Etelä-Suomi, S Finland 61°34′N 26°04′E
67 U14 **Harts** *var.* Hartz. ⚔ N South Africa
23 P2 **Hartselle** Alabama, S USA 34°26′N 86°56′W
23 S3 **Hartsfield Atlanta** ✈ Georgia, SE USA 33°38′N 84°24′W
27 Q11 **Hartshorne** Oklahoma, C USA 34°51′N 95°33′W
21 S12 **Hartsville** South Carolina, SE USA 34°22′N 80°04′W
20 K8 **Hartsville** Tennessee, S USA 36°23′N 86°11′W
27 U7 **Hartville** Missouri, C USA 37°15′N 92°30′W
23 U2 **Hartwell** Georgia, SE USA 34°21′N 82°55′W
21 O11 **Hartwell Lake** ⊠ Georgia/South Carolina, SE USA
Hartz *see* Harts
Harunabad *see* Eslāmābād
Har-Us *see* Erdenebüren
162 F6 **Har Us Gol** ◎ Hovd, W Mongolia
162 E6 **Har Us Nuur** ◎ NW Mongolia
30 M10 **Harvard** Illinois, N USA 42°25′N 88°36′W
29 P16 **Harvard** Nebraska, C USA 40°37′N 98°06′W
37 R5 **Harvard, Mount** ▲ Colorado, C USA 38°55′N 106°19′W
31 N11 **Harvey** Illinois, N USA 41°36′N 87°39′W
29 N4 **Harvey** North Dakota, N USA 47°43′N 99°55′W
97 Q21 **Harwich** E England, United Kingdom 51°56′N 01°16′E
152 H10 **Haryāna** *var.* Hariana. ◆ *state* N India
141 Y9 **Ḩaryān, Ţawī al** *spring/well* NE Oman 21°56′N 58°33′E
101 J14 **Harz** ▲▲ C Germany
Ḩasakah, Muḩāfaẓat al *see* Al Ḩasakah
165 Q9 **Hasama** Miyagi, Honshū, C Japan 38°42′N 141°09′E
136 J15 **Hasan Dağı** ▲ C Turkey 38°09′N 34°15′E
139 T9 **Ḩasan Ibn Ḩassūn** An Najaf, C Iraq 32°24′N 44°13′E
149 R6 **Ḩasan Khēl** *var.* Ahmad Khel. Paktīā, SE Afghanistan 33°46′N 69°37′E
100 F12 **Hase** ⚔ NW Germany
Haselberg *see* Krasnoznamensk
100 F12 **Haselünne** Niedersachsen, NW Germany 52°40′N 07°28′E
Hashaat *see* Delgerhangay
Hashemite Kingdom of Jordan *see* Jordan
139 V8 **Hāshimah** Wāsiţ, E Iraq 33°22′N 45°56′E
142 K3 **Hashtrūd** *var.* Azaran. Āžarbāyjān-e Khāvarī, N Iran 37°34′N 47°10′E
141 W13 **Ḩāsik** S Oman 17°22′N 55°18′E
149 U10 **Hāsilpur** Punjab, E Pakistan 29°42′N 72°40′E
27 Q10 **Haskell** Oklahoma, C USA 35°49′N 95°40′W
25 Q6 **Haskell** Texas, SW USA 33°10′N 99°45′W
114 M11 **Hasköy** Edirne, NW Turkey 41°37′N 26°51′E
95 L24 **Hasle** Bornholm, E Denmark 55°12′N 14°43′E
97 N23 **Haslemere** SE England, United Kingdom 51°06′N 00°45′W
102 I16 **Hasparren** Pyrénées-Atlantiques, SW France 43°23′N 01°18′W
Hassakeh *see* Al Ḩasakah
155 G19 **Hassan** Karnātaka, W India 13°01′N 76°03′E
36 J13 **Hassayampa River** ⚔ Arizona, SW USA
101 J18 **Hassberge** *hill range* C Germany
94 N10 **Hassela** Gävleborg, C Sweden 62°06′N 16°45′E
99 J18 **Hasselt** Limburg, NE Belgium 50°56′N 05°20′E
98 M9 **Hasselt** Overijssel, E Netherlands 52°36′N 06°05′E
Hassetché *see* Al Ḩasakah
101 J18 **Hassfurt** Bayern, C Germany 50°02′N 10°32′E
74 L9 **Hassi Bel Guebbour** E Algeria 28°41′N 06°29′E
74 L8 **Hassi Messaoud** E Algeria 31°41′N 06°10′E
95 K22 **Hässleholm** Skåne, S Sweden 56°09′N 13°45′E
Hasta Colonia/Hasta Pompeia *see* Asti
183 O13 **Hastings** Victoria, SE Australia 38°18′S 145°12′E
184 O11 **Hastings** Hawke's Bay, North Island, New Zealand 39°39′S 176°51′E
97 P23 **Hastings** SE England, United Kingdom 50°51′N 00°36′E
31 P9 **Hastings** Michigan, N USA 42°38′N 85°17′W
29 W9 **Hastings** Minnesota, N USA 44°44′N 92°51′W
29 P16 **Hastings** Nebraska, C USA 40°35′N 98°23′W
95 K22 **Hästveda** Skåne, S Sweden 56°16′N 13°55′E
92 J8 **Hasvik** Finnmark, N Norway 70°29′N 22°08′E
37 V6 **Haswell** Colorado, C USA 38°27′N 103°09′W
163 N11 **Hatanbulag** *var.* Ergel. Dornogovĭ, SE Mongolia 43°10′N 109°13′E
Hatansuudal *see* Bayanlig
Hatavch *see* Haldzan
136 K17 **Hatay** ◆ *province* S Turkey
37 R15 **Hatch** New Mexico, SW USA 32°40′N 107°10′W
36 K7 **Hatch** Utah, W USA 37°39′N 112°25′W
20 F9 **Hatchie River** ⚔ Tennessee, S USA
116 G12 **Haţeg** *Ger.* Wallenthal, *Hung.* Hátszeg; *prev.* Hatzeg, Hötzing. Hunedoara, SW Romania 45°35′N 22°57′E
165 O17 **Hateruma-jima** *island* Yaeyama-shotō, SW Japan
183 N8 **Hatfield** New South Wales, SE Australia 33°54′S 143°43′E
162 I5 **Hatgal** Hövsgöl, N Mongolia 50°24′N 100°12′E
153 V16 **Hathazari** Chittagong, SE Bangladesh 22°30′N 91°46′E
141 T13 **Hathūt, Hiṣā'** *oasis* NE Yemen
167 R14 **Ha Tiên** Kiên Giang, S Vietnam 10°24′N 104°30′E
167 T8 **Ha Tinh** Ha Tinh, N Vietnam 18°21′N 105°55′E
Ḩatira, Haré *see* Hatira, Harei
138 F12 **Hatira, Harei** *prev.* Haré Ḩatira. *hill range* S Israel
167 R6 **Hat Lot** *var.* Mai Son. Son La, N Vietnam 21°07′N 104°10′E
45 P16 **Hato Airport** ✈ (Willemstad) Curaçao, SW Netherlands Antilles 12°10′N 68°56′W
54 H9 **Hato Corozal** Casanare, C Colombia 06°08′N 71°45′W
Hato del Volcán *see* Volcán
45 P9 **Hato Mayor** E Dominican Republic 18°49′N 68°16′W
Hatra *see* Al Ḩaḑr
Hatria *see* Adria
Hátszeg *see* Haţeg
143 R16 **Ḩattā** Dubayy, NE United Arab Emirates 24°50′N 56°06′E
182 L9 **Hattah** Victoria, SE Australia 34°49′S 142°18′E
98 M9 **Hattem** Gelderland, E Netherlands 52°29′N 06°04′E
21 Z10 **Hatteras** Hatteras Island, North Carolina, SE USA 35°13′N 75°39′W
21 R10 **Hatteras, Cape** *headland* North Carolina, SE USA 35°29′N 75°33′W
21 Z9 **Hatteras Island** *island* North Carolina, SE USA
64 F10 **Hatteras Plain** *undersea feature* W Atlantic Ocean 31°00′N 71°00′W
93 G14 **Hattfjelldal** Troms, N Norway 65°37′N 13°58′E
22 M7 **Hattiesburg** Mississippi, S USA 31°20′N 89°17′W
29 Q4 **Hatton** North Dakota, N USA 47°38′N 97°27′W
Hatton Bank *see* Hatton Ridge
64 L6 **Hatton Ridge** *var.* Hatton Bank. *undersea feature* N Atlantic Ocean 59°00′N 17°30′W
191 W6 **Hatutu** *island* Îles Marquises, NE French Polynesia
111 K22 **Hatvan** Heves, NE Hungary 47°40′N 19°39′E
167 O16 **Hat Yai** *var.* Ban Hat Yai. Songkhla, SW Thailand 07°01′N 100°27′E
Hatzeg *see* Haţeg
Hatzfeld *see* Jimbolia
80 N13 **Haud** *plateau* Ethiopia/Somalia
95 D18 **Hauge** Rogaland, S Norway 58°20′N 06°17′E
95 C15 **Haugesund** Rogaland, S Norway 59°24′N 05°17′E
109 X2 **Haugsdorf** Niederösterreich, NE Austria 48°41′N 15°04′E
184 M9 **Hauhungaroa Range** ▲▲ North Island, New Zealand
95 E15 **Haukeligrend** Telemark, S Norway 59°45′N 07°33′E
93 L14 **Haukipudas** Oulu, C Finland 65°11′N 25°21′E
93 M17 **Haukivesi** ◎ SE Finland
93 M17 **Haukivuori** Itä-Suomi, E Finland 62°02′N 27°11′E
Hauptkanal *see* Havelländ Grosse
187 N10 **Hauraha** San Cristobal, SE Solomon Islands 10°47′S 162°00′E
184 L5 **Hauraki Gulf** *gulf* North Island, N New Zealand
185 B24 **Hauroko, Lake** ◎ South Island, New Zealand
167 S14 **Hâu, Sông** ⚔ S Vietnam
92 N12 **Hautajärvi** Lappi, NE Finland 66°30′N 29°01′E
74 F7 **Haut Atlas** *Eng.* High Atlas. ▲▲ C Morocco
79 M17 **Haut-Congo** *off.* Région du Haut-Congo; *prev.* Haut-Zaïre. ◆ *region* NE Dem. Rep. Congo
103 Y14 **Haute-Corse** ◆ *department* Corse, France, C Mediterranean Sea
102 L16 **Haute-Garonne** ◆ *department* S France
79 K14 **Haute-Kotto** ◆ *prefecture* E Central African Republic
103 P12 **Haute-Loire** ◆ *department* C France
103 R6 **Haute-Marne** ◆ *department* N France
102 M3 **Haute-Normandie** ◆ *region* N France
15 U6 **Hauterive** Québec, SE Canada 49°11′N 68°16′W
103 T13 **Hautes-Alpes** ◆ *department* SE France
103 S7 **Haute-Saône** ◆ *department* E France
103 T10 **Haute-Savoie** ◆ *department* E France
99 M20 **Hautes Fagnes** *Ger.* Hohes Venn. ▲ E Belgium
102 K16 **Hautes-Pyrénées** ◆ *department* S France
99 L23 **Haute Sûre, Lac de la** ⊠ NW Luxembourg
102 M11 **Haute-Vienne** ◆ *department* C France
19 S8 **Haut, Isle au** *island* Maine, NE USA
79 M14 **Haut-Mbomou** ◆ *prefecture* SE Central African Republic
103 Q2 **Hautmont** Nord, N France 50°15′N 03°55′E
79 F19 **Haut-Ogooué** *off.* Province du Haut-Ogooué, *var.* Le Haut-Ogooué. ◆ *province* SE Gabon
Haut-Ogooué, Le *see* Haut-Ogooué
Haut-Ogooué, Province du *see* Haut-Ogooué
103 U7 **Haut-Rhin** ◆ *department* NE France
74 I6 **Hauts Plateaux** *plateau* Algeria/Morocco
Haut-Zaïre *see* Haut-Congo
38 D9 **Hau'ula** *var.* Hauula. O'ahu, Hawaii, USA, C Pacific Ocean 21°36′N 157°54′W
Hauula *see* Hau'ula
101 O22 **Hauzenberg** Bayern, SE Germany 48°39′N 13°37′E
30 K13 **Havana** Illinois, N USA 40°18′N 90°03′W
Havana *see* La Habana
97 N23 **Havant** S England, United Kingdom 50°51′N 00°59′W
35 Y14 **Havasu, Lake** ⊠ Arizona/California, W USA
95 J23 **Havdrup** Roskilde, E Denmark 55°33′N 12°08′E
100 N10 **Havel** ⚔ NE Germany
99 J21 **Havelange** Namur, SE Belgium 50°23′N 05°14′E
100 M11 **Havelberg** Sachsen-Anhalt, NE Germany 52°49′N 12°05′E
149 U5 **Haveliān** North-West Frontier Province, NW Pakistan 34°05′N 73°14′E
100 N12 **Havelländ Grosse** *var.* Hauptkanal. *canal* NE Germany
14 J14 **Havelock** Ontario, SE Canada 44°22′N 77°57′W
185 J14 **Havelock** Marlborough, South Island, New Zealand 41°17′S 173°46′E
21 X11 **Havelock** North Carolina, SE USA 34°52′N 76°54′W
184 O11 **Havelock North** Hawke's Bay, North Island, New Zealand 39°40′S 176°53′E
98 M8 **Havelte** Drenthe, NE Netherlands 52°46′N 06°14′E
27 N6 **Haven** Kansas, C USA 37°54′N 97°46′W
97 H21 **Haverfordwest** SW Wales, United Kingdom 51°50′N 04°57′W
97 P20 **Haverhill** E England, United Kingdom 52°05′N 00°26′E
19 O10 **Haverhill** Massachusetts, NE USA 42°46′N 71°02′W
155 F18 **Hāveri** Karnātaka, SW India 14°47′N 75°24′E
93 G17 **Haverö** Västernorrland, C Sweden 62°25′N 15°04′E
111 I17 **Havířov** Moravskoslezský Kraj, E Czech Republic 49°47′N 18°30′E
111 E17 **Havlíčkův Brod** *Ger.* Deutsch-Brod; *prev.* Německý Brod. Vysočina, C Czech Republic 49°38′N 15°46′E
92 K7 **Havøysund** Finnmark, N Norway 70°59′N 24°39′E
99 F20 **Havré** Hainaut, S Belgium 50°29′N 04°03′E
33 T7 **Havre** Montana, NW USA 48°33′N 109°41′W
Havre *see* le Havre
13 P11 **Havre-St-Pierre** Québec, E Canada 50°16′N 63°36′W
136 B10 **Havsa** Edirne, NW Turkey 41°32′N 26°49′E
38 D8 **Hawai'i** *off.* State of Hawai'i, *also known as* Aloha State, Paradise of the Pacific, *var.* Hawaii. ◆ *state* USA, C Pacific Ocean
38 G12 **Hawai'i** *var.* Hawaii. *island* Hawaiian Islands, USA, C Pacific Ocean
192 M5 **Hawaiian Islands** *prev.* Sandwich Islands. *island group* Hawaii, USA
192 L5 **Hawaiian Ridge** *undersea feature* N Pacific Ocean 24°00′N 165°00′W
193 N6 **Hawaiian Trough** *undersea feature* N Pacific Ocean
29 R12 **Hawarden** Iowa, C USA 43°00′N 96°29′W
Hawash *see* Āwash
139 P6 **Ḩawbayn al Gharbīyah** Al Anbār, C Iraq 34°24′N 42°06′E
185 D21 **Hawea, Lake** ◎ South Island, New Zealand
184 K11 **Hawera** Taranaki, North Island, New Zealand 39°36′S 174°16′E
20 J5 **Hawesville** Kentucky, S USA 37°53′N 86°47′W
38 G11 **Hawi** Hawaii, USA, C Pacific Ocean 20°14′N 155°50′W
38 G11 **Hāwī** *var.* Hawi. Hawaii, USA, C Pacific Ocean 20°13′N 155°49′W
Hawi *see* Hāwī
96 K13 **Hawick** SE Scotland, United Kingdom 55°24′N 02°49′W
139 S4 **Ḩawījah** At Ta'mīn, C Iraq 35°15′N 43°54′E
139 Y10 **Ḩawīzah, Hawr al** ◎ S Iraq
185 E21 **Hawkdun Range** ▲▲ South Island, New Zealand
184 P10 **Hawke Bay** *bay* North Island, New Zealand
182 I6 **Hawker** South Australia 31°54′S 138°25′E
184 N11 **Hawke's Bay** *off.* Hawkes Bay Region. ◆ *region* North Island, New Zealand
149 O16 **Hawkes Bay** *bay* SE Pakistan
Hawkes Bay Region *see* Hawke's Bay
15 N12 **Hawkesbury** Ontario, SE Canada 45°36′N 74°38′W
Hawkeye State *see* Iowa
23 T5 **Hawkinsville** Georgia, SE USA 32°16′N 83°28′W
14 B7 **Hawk Junction** Ontario, S Canada 48°05′N 84°34′W
21 N10 **Haw Knob** ▲ North Carolina/Tennessee, SE USA 35°18′N 84°01′W
21 Q9 **Hawksbill Mountain** ▲ North Carolina, SE USA 35°54′N 81°53′W
33 Z16 **Hawk Springs** Wyoming, C USA 41°48′N 104°17′W
Hawlēr *see* Arbīl
29 S5 **Hawley** Minnesota, N USA 46°53′N 96°18′W
25 P7 **Hawley** Texas, SW USA 32°36′N 99°47′W
141 R14 **Ḩawrā'** C Yemen 15°39′N 48°21′E
139 P7 **Ḩawrān, Wadi** *dry watercourse* W Iraq
21 T9 **Haw River** ⚔ North Carolina, SE USA
139 U5 **Ḩawshqūrah** Diyālá, E Iraq 34°34′N 45°33′E
35 S7 **Hawthorne** Nevada, W USA 38°30′N 118°38′W
37 W3 **Haxtun** Colorado, C USA 40°36′N 102°38′W
183 N9 **Hay** New South Wales, SE Australia 34°31′S 144°51′E
11 O10 **Hay** ⚔ W Canada
171 S13 **Haya** Pulau Seram, E Indonesia 03°22′S 129°31′E
165 R9 **Hayachine-san** ▲ Honshū, C Japan 39°31′N 141°28′E
103 S4 **Hayange** Moselle, NE France 49°19′N 06°04′E
HaYarden *see* Jordan
Hayastani Hanrapetut'yun *see* Armenia
Hayasui-seto *see* Hōyo-kaikyō
39 N9 **Haycock** Alaska, USA 65°12′N 161°10′W
36 M14 **Hayden** Arizona, SW USA 33°00′N 110°46′W
37 Q3 **Hayden** Colorado, C USA 40°29′N 107°15′W
28 M10 **Hayes** South Dakota, N USA 44°20′N 101°01′W
9 X13 **Hayes** ⚔ Manitoba, C Canada
11 P12 **Hayes** ⚔ Nunavut, NE Canada
28 M16 **Hayes Center** Nebraska, C USA 40°30′N 101°02′W
39 S10 **Hayes, Mount** ▲ Alaska, USA 63°37′N 146°43′W
21 N11 **Hayesville** North Carolina, SE USA 35°03′N 83°49′W
35 X10 **Hayford Peak** ▲ Nevada, W USA 36°40′N 115°10′W
34 M3 **Hayfork** California, W USA 40°33′N 123°10′W
Hayir, Qasr al *see* Ḩayr al Gharbī, Qaşr al
Haylaastay *see* Sühbaatar
14 I12 **Hay Lake** ◎ Ontario, SE Canada
141 X11 **Haymā'** *var.* Haima. C Oman 19°59′N 56°20′E
136 H13 **Haymana** Ankara, C Turkey 39°26′N 32°30′E
138 J7 **Ḩaymūr, Jabal** ▲▲ W Syria
Haynau *see* Chojnów
22 G4 **Haynesville** Louisiana, S USA 32°57′N 93°08′W
23 P6 **Hayneville** Alabama, S USA 32°13′N 86°34′W
114 M12 **Hayrabolu** Tekirdağ, NW Turkey 41°14′N 27°04′E
136 C10 **Hayrabolu Deresi** ⚔ NW Turkey
138 J6 **Ḩayr al Gharbī, Qaşr al** *var.* Qasr al Hayir, Qasr al Hir al Gharbi. *ruins* Ḩimş, C Syria
138 L5 **Ḩayr ash Sharqī, Qaşr al** *var.* Qasr al Hir Ash Sharqī. *ruins* Ḩimş, C Syria
162 J7 **Hayrhan** *var.* Uubulan. Arhangay, C Mongolia 48°37′N 101°58′E
162 J9 **Hayrhandulaan** *var.* Mardzad. Övörhangay, C Mongolia 45°58′N 102°06′E
8 J10 **Hay River** Northwest Territories, W Canada 60°51′N 115°42′W
26 K4 **Hays** Kansas, C USA 38°53′N 99°20′W
28 K12 **Hay Springs** Nebraska, C USA 42°40′N 102°41′W
65 H25 **Haystack, The** ▲ NE Saint Helena 15°55′S 05°40′W
27 N7 **Haysville** Kansas, C USA 37°34′N 97°21′W
117 O7 **Haysyn** *Rus.* Gaysin. Vinnyts'ka Oblast', C Ukraine 48°50′N 29°29′E
27 Y9 **Hayti** Missouri, C USA 36°13′N 89°45′W
29 Q9 **Hayti** South Dakota, N USA 44°40′N 97°22′W
117 O8 **Hayvoron** *Rus.* Gayvorno. Kirovohrads'ka Oblast', C Ukraine 48°20′N 29°52′E
35 N9 **Hayward** California, W USA 37°40′N 122°07′W
30 J4 **Hayward** Wisconsin, N USA 46°02′N 91°26′W
97 O23 **Haywards Heath** SE England, United Kingdom 51°N 00°06′W
146 A11 **Hazar** *prev. Rus.* Cheleken. Balkan Welaýaty, W Turkmenistan 39°26′N 53°07′E
143 S11 **Hazārān, Kūh-e** *var.* Kūh-e ā Hazr. ▲ SE Iran 29°26′N 57°15′E
Hazarat Imam *see* Emām Şāḩeb
21 O7 **Hazard** Kentucky, S USA 37°14′N 83°11′W
137 O15 **Hazar Gölü** ◎ C Turkey
153 P15 **Hazārībāg** *var.* Hazārībāgh. Jhārkhand, N India 24°00′N 85°23′E
Hazārībāgh *see* Hazārībāg
103 O1 **Hazebrouck** Nord, N France 50°43′N 02°33′E
30 K9 **Hazel Green** Wisconsin, N USA 42°33′N 90°26′W
192 K9 **Hazel Holme Bank** *undersea feature* S Pacific Ocean 12°49′S 174°30′E
10 K13 **Hazelton** British Columbia, SW Canada 55°15′N 127°38′W
29 N6 **Hazelton** North Dakota, N USA 46°27′N 100°17′W
35 R5 **Hazen** Nevada, W USA 39°33′N 119°02′W
28 L5 **Hazen** North Dakota, N USA 47°18′N 101°37′W
38 L12 **Hazen Bay** *bay* E Bering Sea
9 N1 **Hazen, Lake** ◎ Nunavut, N Canada
139 S5 **Hazīm, Bi'r** *well* C Iraq
23 V6 **Hazlehurst** Georgia, SE USA 31°51′N 82°35′W
22 K6 **Hazlehurst** Mississippi, S USA 31°51′N 90°24′W
18 K15 **Hazlet** New Jersey, NE USA 40°24′N 74°10′W
146 I9 **Hazorasp** *Rus.* Khazarosp. Xorazm Viloyati, W Uzbekistan 41°21′N 61°01′E
147 R13 **Hazratishoh, Qatorkŭhi** *var.* Khrebet Khazretishi, *Rus.* Khrebet Khozretishi. ▲▲ S Tajikistan
Hazr, Kūh-e ā *see* Hazārān, Kūh-e
149 U6 **Hazro** Punjab, E Pakistan 33°55′N 72°33′E
23 R7 **Headland** Alabama, S USA 31°21′N 85°20′W
182 C6 **Head of Bight** *headland* South Australia 31°33′S 131°05′E
33 N10 **Headquarters** Idaho, NW USA 46°38′N 115°52′W
34 M7 **Healdsburg** California, W USA 38°36′N 122°52′W
27 N13 **Healdton** Oklahoma, C USA 34°13′N 97°29′W
183 O12 **Healesville** Victoria, SE Australia 37°41′S 145°31′E
39 R10 **Healy** Alaska, USA 63°51′N 148°58′W
173 R13 **Heard and McDonald Islands** ◇ *Australian external territory* S Indian Ocean
173 R13 **Heard Island** *island* Heard and McDonald Islands, S Indian Ocean
25 U9 **Hearne** Texas, SW USA 30°52′N 96°35′W
12 F12 **Hearst** Ontario, S Canada 49°42′N 83°40′W
194 J5 **Hearst Island** *island* Antarctica
Heart of Dixie *see* Alabama
28 L5 **Heart River** ⚔ North Dakota, N USA
31 T13 **Heath** Ohio, N USA 40°01′N 82°26′W
183 N11 **Heathcote** Victoria, SE Australia 36°57′S 144°43′E
97 N22 **Heathrow** ✈ (London) SE England, United Kingdom 51°28′N 00°27′W
21 X5 **Heathsville** Virginia, NE USA 37°55′N 76°29′W
27 R11 **Heavener** Oklahoma, C USA 34°53′N 94°36′W
25 R15 **Hebbronville** Texas, SW USA 27°19′N 98°41′W
163 Q13 **Hebei** *var.* Hebei Sheng, Hopeh, Hopei, Ji; *prev.* Chihli. ◆ *province* E China
Hebei Sheng *see* Hebei
36 M3 **Heber City** Utah, W USA 40°31′N 111°25′W
27 V10 **Heber Springs** Arkansas, C USA 35°30′N 92°01′W
161 N5 **Hebi** Henan, C China 35°57′N 114°08′E
32 F11 **Hebo** Oregon, NW USA 45°10′N 123°55′W
96 F9 **Hebrides, Sea of the** *sea* NW Scotland, United Kingdom
13 P5 **Hebron** Newfoundland and Labrador, E Canada 58°15′N 62°45′W
31 N11 **Hebron** Indiana, N USA 41°19′N 87°12′W
29 Q17 **Hebron** Nebraska, C USA 40°10′N 97°35′W
28 L5 **Hebron** North Dakota, N USA 46°54′N 102°03′W
138 F11 **Hebron** *var.* Al Khalīl, El Khalil, *Heb.* Hevron; *anc.* Kiriath-Arba. S West Bank 31°30′N 35°E
Hebrus *see* Évros/Maritsa/Meriç
95 N14 **Heby** Västmanland, C Sweden 59°56′N 16°53′E
10 I14 **Hecate Strait** *strait* British Columbia, W Canada
41 W12 **Hecelchakán** Campeche, SE Mexico 20°09′N 90°04′W
160 K13 **Hechi** *var.* Jinchengjiang. Guangxi Zhuangzu Zizhiqu, S China 24°39′N 108°02′E
101 H23 **Hechingen** Baden-Württemberg, S Germany 48°20′N 08°58′E
99 K17 **Hechtel** Limburg, NE Belgium 51°07′N 05°24′E
160 J9 **Hechuan** *var.* Heyang. Chongqing Shi, C China 30°02′N 106°15′E
29 P7 **Hecla** South Dakota, N USA 45°52′N 98°09′W
9 N1 **Hecla, Cape** *headland* Nunavut, N Canada 82°00′N 64°00′W
29 T9 **Hector** Minnesota, N USA 44°44′N 94°43′W
93 F17 **Hede** Jämtland, C Sweden 62°25′N 13°33′E
Hede *see* Sheyang
95 M14 **Hedemora** Dalarna, C Sweden 60°18′N 15°58′E
92 K13 **Hedenäset** Norrbotten, N Sweden 66°12′N 23°40′E
95 G23 **Hedensted** Vejle, C Denmark 55°47′N 09°43′E
95 N14 **Hedesunda** Gävleborg, C Sweden 60°25′N 17°00′E
95 N14 **Hedesundafjord** ◎ C Sweden
25 O3 **Hedley** Texas, SW USA 34°52′N 100°39′W
94 I12 **Hedmark** ◆ *county* S Norway
165 T16 **Hedo-misaki** *headland* Okinawa, SW Japan 26°55′N 128°15′E
29 X15 **Hedrick** Iowa, C USA 41°10′N 92°18′W
99 L16 **Heel** Limburg, SE Netherlands 51°12′N 06°01′E
189 Y12 **Heel Point** *point* Wake Island
98 H9 **Heemskerk** Noord-Holland, W Netherlands 52°31′N 04°40′E
98 M10 **Heerde** Gelderland, E Netherlands 52°24′N 06°02′E
98 L7 **Heerenveen** *Fris.* It Hearrenfean. Friesland, N Netherlands 52°57′N 05°55′E
98 I8 **Heerhugowaard** Noord-Holland, NW Netherlands 52°40′N 04°50′E
92 O3 **Heer Land** *physical region* C Svalbard
99 M18 **Heerlen** Limburg, SE Netherlands 50°55′N 06°E
99 J19 **Heers** Limburg, NE Belgium 50°46′N 05°17′E
Heerwegen *see* Polkowice
98 K13 **Heesch** Noord-Brabant, S Netherlands 51°44′N 05°32′E
99 K15 **Heeze** Noord-Brabant, SE Netherlands 51°23′N 05°35′E
138 F8 **Hefa** *var.* Haifa, *hist.* Caiffa, Caiphas; *anc.* Sycaminum. Haifa, N Israel 32°49′N 34°59′E
Hefa, Mifraz *see* Mifrats Hefa
161 Q8 **Hefei** *var.* Hofei, *hist.* Luchow. *province capital* Anhui, E China 31°51′N 117°20′E
23 R3 **Heflin** Alabama, S USA 33°39′N 85°35′W
163 X7 **Hegang** Heilongjiang, NE China 47°18′N 130°16′E
164 L10 **Hegura-jima** *island* SW Japan
Heguri-jima *see* Heigun-tō
Hei *see* Heilongjiang
100 H8 **Heide** Schleswig-Holstein, N Germany 54°12′N 09°06′E
101 G20 **Heidelberg** Baden-Württemberg, SW Germany 49°24′N 08°41′E
83 J21 **Heidelberg** Gauteng, NE South Africa 26°31′S 28°21′E
22 M6 **Heidelberg** Mississippi, S USA 31°53′N 88°58′W
Heidenheim *see* Heidenheim an der Brenz
101 J22 **Heidenheim an der Brenz** *var.* Heidenheim. Baden-Württemberg, S Germany 48°41′N 10°09′E
109 U2 **Heidenreichstein** Niederösterreich, N Austria 48°53′N 15°07′E
164 F14 **Heigun-tō** *var.* Heguri-jima. *island* SW Japan
163 W5 **Heihe** *prev.* Ai-hun. Heilongjiang, NE China 50°13′N 127°29′E
162 S8 **Hei He** ⚔ C China
Hei-ho *see* Nagqu
83 J22 **Heilbron** Free State, N South Africa 27°17′S 27°58′E
101 H21 **Heilbronn** Baden-Württemberg, SW Germany 49°09′N 09°13′E
Heiligenbeil *see* Mamonovo
109 Q8 **Heiligenblut** Tirol, W Austria 47°04′N 12°50′E
100 K7 **Heiligenhafen** Schleswig-Holstein, N Germany 54°22′N 10°57′E
Heiligenkreuz *see* Žiar nad Hronom
101 J15 **Heiligenstadt** Thüringen, C Germany 51°22′N 10°09′E
163 W8 **Heilongjiang** *var.* Hei, Heilongjiang Sheng, Hei-lung-chiang, Heilungkiang. ◆ *province* NE China
Heilong Jiang *see* Amur
Heilongjiang Sheng *see* Heilongjiang
98 H9 **Heiloo** Noord-Holland, NW Netherlands 52°36′N 04°43′E
Heilsberg *see* Lidzbark Warmiński
Hei-lung-chiang/Heilungkiang *see* Heilongjiang
Heimaæy *see* Heimaey
92 I4 **Heimaey** *var.* Heimaæy. *island* S Iceland
94 H8 **Heimdal** Sør-Trøndelag, S Norway 63°21′N 10°23′E
Heinaste *see* Ainaži
93 N17 **Heinävesi** Itä-Suomi, E Finland 62°22′N 28°42′E
99 M22 **Heinerscheid** Diekirch, N Luxembourg 50°06′N 06°05′E
98 M10 **Heino** Overijssel, E Netherlands 52°26′N 06°13′E
93 M18 **Heinola** Etelä-Suomi, S Finland 61°13′N 26°05′E
101 C16 **Heinsberg** Nordrhein-Westfalen, W Germany 51°02′N 06°01′E
163 U12 **Heishan** Liaoning, NE China 41°43′N 122°12′E
160 H8 **Heishui** *var.* Luhua. Sichuan, C China 32°08′N 102°54′E
99 H17 **Heist-op-den-Berg** Antwerpen, C Belgium 51°04′N 04°43′E
Heitō *see* P'ingtung
171 X15 **Heitske** Papua, E Indonesia 07°02′S 138°45′E
Hejanah *see* Al Hījānah
Hejaz *see* Al Ḩijāz
160 M14 **He Jiang** ⚔ S China
Hejiayan *see* Lüeyang
158 K6 **Hejing** Xinjiang Uygur Zizhiqu, NW China 42°21′N 86°19′E
Héjjasfalva *see* Vânători
Heka *see* Hoika
137 N14 **Hekimhan** Malatya, C Turkey 38°50′N 37°56′E
92 J4 **Hekla** ▲ S Iceland 63°56′N 19°42′W
Hekou *see* Yanshan, Jiangxi, China
Hekou *see* Yajiang, Sichuan, China
110 J6 **Hel** *Ger.* Hela. Pomorskie, N Poland 54°35′N 18°48′E
Hela *see* Hel
93 F17 **Helagsfjället** ▲ C Sweden 62°57′N 12°31′E
159 W8 **Helan** *var.* Xigang. Ningxia, N China 38°33′N 106°21′E
162 K14 **Helan Shan** ▲▲ N China
99 M16 **Helden** Limburg, SE Netherlands 51°20′N 06°00′E
27 X12 **Helena** Arkansas, C USA 34°32′N 90°34′W
33 R10 **Helena** *state capital* Montana, NW USA 46°36′N 112°02′W
96 H12 **Helensburgh** W Scotland, United Kingdom 56°00′N 04°45′W
184 K5 **Helensville** Auckland, North Island, New Zealand 36°42′S 174°26′E
95 L20 **Helgasjön** ◎ S Sweden
100 G8 **Helgoland** *Eng.* Heligoland. *island* NW Germany
Helgoland Bay *see* Helgoländer Bucht
100 G8 **Helgoländer Bucht** *var.* Helgoland Bay, Heligoland Bight. *bay* NW Germany
Heligoland *see* Helgoland
Heligoland Bight *see* Helgoländer Bucht
Heliopolis *see* Baalbek
92 I4 **Hella** Sudhurland, SW Iceland 63°51′N 20°24′W
Hellas *see* Greece
143 N11 **Ḩelleh, Rūd-e** ⚔ S Iran
98 N10 **Hellendoorn** Overijssel, E Netherlands 52°22′N 06°27′E
Hellenic Republic *see* Greece
121 Q10 **Hellenic Trough** *undersea feature* Aegean Sea, C Mediterranean Sea 22°00′E 35°30′N
94 E10 **Hellesylt** Møre og Romsdal, S Norway 62°06′N 06°51′E
98 F13 **Hellevoetsluis** Zuid-Holland, SW Netherlands 51°49′N 04°08′E
105 Q12 **Hellín** Castilla-La Mancha, C Spain 38°31′N 01°43′W
115 H19 **Hellinikon** ✈ (Athína) Attikí, C Greece 37°53′N 23°43′E
32 M12 **Hells Canyon** *valley* Idaho/Oregon, NW USA
148 L9 **Helmand** ◆ *province* S Afghanistan
148 K10 **Helmand, Daryā-ye** *var.* Rūd-e Hirmand. ⚔ Afghanistan/Iran *see also* Hirmand, Rūd-e
Helmand, Daryā-ye *see* Hirmand, Rūd-e
Helmantica *see* Salamanca
101 K15 **Helme** ⚔ C Germany
99 L15 **Helmond** Noord-Brabant, S Netherlands 51°29′N 05°41′E
96 J7 **Helmsdale** N Scotland, United Kingdom 58°06′N 03°36′W
100 K13 **Helmstedt** Niedersachsen, N Germany 52°14′N 11°01′E
163 Y10 **Helong** Jilin, NE China 42°38′N 129°01′E
36 M4 **Helper** Utah, W USA 39°40′N 110°52′W
100 O10 **Helpter Berge** *hill* NE Germany
95 J22 **Helsingborg** *prev.* Hälsingborg. Skåne, S Sweden 56°N 12°48′E
Helsingfors *see* Helsinki
95 J22 **Helsingør** *Eng.* Elsinore. Frederiksborg, E Denmark 56°03′N 12°38′E
93 M20 **Helsinki** *Swe.* Helsingfors. ● (Finland) Etelä-Suomi, S Finland 60°18′N 24°58′E
97 H25 **Helston** SW England, United Kingdom 50°04′N 05°17′W
Heltau *see* Cisnădie
61 C17 **Helvecia** Santa Fe, C Argentina 31°09′S 60°09′W

◆ Country ◇ Dependent Territory ◆ Administrative Regions ▲ Mountain Volcano ◎ Lake
● Country Capital ○ Dependent Territory Capital ✈ International Airport ▲▲ Mountain Range ⚔ River ⊠ Reservoir

HELVELLYN – HOFMARKT

97 K15 **Helvellyn** ▲ NW England, United Kingdom *54°31′N 03°00′W*
Helvetia *see* Switzerland
Helwân *see* Hilwān
97 N21 **Hemel Hempstead** E England, United Kingdom *51°46′N 00°28′W*
35 U16 **Hemet** California, W USA *33°45′N 116°58′W*
28 J13 **Hemingford** Nebraska, C USA *42°18′N 103°02′W*
21 T13 **Hemingway** South Carolina, SE USA *33°45′N 79°25′W*
92 G13 **Hemnesberget** Nordland, C Norway *66°14′N 13°40′E*
25 Y8 **Hemphill** Texas, SW USA *31°21′N 93°50′W*
25 V11 **Hempstead** Texas, SW USA *30°06′N 96°06′W*
95 P20 **Hemse** Gotland, SE Sweden *57°12′N 18°22′E*
94 F13 **Hemsedal** *valley* S Norway
161 N6 **Henan** *var.* Henan Sheng, Honan, Yu. ◈ *province* C China
184 L4 **Hen and Chickens** *island group* N New Zealand
Henan Mongolzu Zizhixian/Henan Sheng *see* Yêgainnyin
105 O7 **Henares** ≈ C Spain
165 P7 **Henashi-zaki** *headland* Honshū, C Japan *40°37′N 139°51′E*
102 I16 **Hendaye** Pyrénées-Atlantiques, SW France *43°22′N 01°46′W*
136 F11 **Hendek** Sakarya, NW Turkey *40°47′N 30°45′E*
61 B21 **Henderson** Buenos Aires, E Argentina *36°18′S 61°43′W*
20 I5 **Henderson** Kentucky, S USA *37°50′N 87°35′W*
35 X11 **Henderson** Nevada, W USA *36°02′N 114°58′W*
21 V8 **Henderson** North Carolina, SE USA *36°20′N 78°26′W*
20 G10 **Henderson** Tennessee, S USA *35°27′N 88°40′W*
25 W7 **Henderson** Texas, SW USA *32°11′N 94°48′W*
30 J12 **Henderson Creek** ≈ Illinois, N USA
186 M9 **Henderson Field** ✈ (Honiara) Guadalcanal, C Solomon Islands *09°28′S 160°02′E*
191 O17 **Henderson Island** *atoll* N Pitcairn Islands
21 O10 **Hendersonville** North Carolina, SE USA *35°19′N 82°28′W*
20 J8 **Hendersonville** Tennessee, S USA *36°18′N 86°37′W*
143 O14 **Hendorābī, Jazīreh-ye** *island* S Iran
55 V10 **Hendrik Top** *var.* Hendriktop. *elevation* C Suriname
Hendriktop *see* Hendrik Top
Hendū Kosh *see* Hindu Kush
14 L12 **Heney, Lac** ◎ Québec, SE Canada
Hengchow *see* Hengyang
161 S15 **Hengchun** S Taiwan *22°09′N 120°43′E*
159 R16 **Hengduan Shan** ▲▲ SW China
98 N12 **Hengelo** Gelderland, E Netherlands *52°03′N 06°19′E*
98 O10 **Hengelo** Overijssel, E Netherlands *52°16′N 06°46′E*
Hengnan *see* Hengyang
161 N11 **Hengshan** Hunan, S China *27°17′N 112°51′E*
160 L4 **Hengshan** Shaanxi, C China *37°57′N 109°17′E*
161 O4 **Hengshui** Hebei, E China *37°42′N 115°39′E*
161 N12 **Hengyang** *var.* Hengnan, Heng-yang; *prev.* Hengchow. Hunan, S China *26°55′N 112°34′E*
Heng-yang *see* Hengyang
117 U11 **Heniches'k** *Rus.* Genichesk. Khersons'ka Oblast', S Ukraine *46°10′N 34°49′E*
21 Z4 **Henlopen, Cape** *headland* Delaware, NE USA *38°48′N 75°06′W*
Henna *see* Enna
94 M10 **Hennan** Gävleborg, C Sweden *62°01′N 15°55′E*
102 G7 **Hennebont** Morbihan, NW France *47°48′N 03°17′W*
30 L11 **Hennepin** Illinois, N USA *41°14′N 89°21′W*
26 M9 **Hennessey** Oklahoma, C USA *36°06′N 97°54′W*
100 N12 **Hennigsdorf** *var.* Hennigsdorf bei Berlin. Brandenburg, NE Germany *52°37′N 13°13′E*
Hennigsdorf bei Berlin *see* Hennigsdorf
19 N9 **Henniker** New Hampshire, NE USA *43°10′N 71°47′W*
25 S5 **Henrietta** Texas, SW USA *33°49′N 98°13′W*
Henrique de Carvalho *see* Saurimo
30 L12 **Henry** Illinois, N USA *41°06′N 89°21′W*
21 Y7 **Henry, Cape** *headland* Virginia, NE USA *36°55′N 76°01′W*
27 P10 **Henryetta** Oklahoma, C USA *35°26′N 95°58′W*
194 M7 **Henry Ice Rise** *ice cap* Antarctica
9 R5 **Henry Kater, Cape** *headland* Baffin Island, Nunavut, NE Canada *69°09′N 66°45′W*
33 R13 **Henrys Fork** ≈ Idaho, NW USA
14 E15 **Hensall** Ontario, S Canada *43°25′N 81°28′W*
100 J9 **Henstedt-Ulzburg** Schleswig-Holstein, N Germany *53°45′N 09°59′E*
163 N7 **Hentiy** *var.* Batshireet, Eg. ◈ *province* N Mongolia
162 M7 **Hentiyn Nuruu** ▲▲ N Mongolia
183 P10 **Henty** New South Wales, SE Australia *35°33′S 147°03′E*
Henzada *see* Hinthada
Heping *see* Huishui
101 G19 **Heppenheim** Hessen, W Germany *49°39′N 08°38′E*
32 J11 **Heppner** Oregon, NW USA *45°21′N 119°32′W*
160 L15 **Hepu** *var.* Lianzhou. Guangxi Zhuangzu Zizhiqu, S China *21°40′N 109°12′E*
Heracleum *see* Irákleio
92 J2 **Heradhsvötn** ≈ C Iceland
Herakleion *see* Irákleio
148 K5 **Herāt** *var.* Herat; *anc.* Aria. Herāt, W Afghanistan *34°23′N 62°11′E*
148 J5 **Herāt** ◈ *province* W Afghanistan
103 P14 **Hérault** ◈ *department* S France
103 P15 **Hérault** ≈ S France
11 T16 **Herbert** Saskatchewan, S Canada *50°27′N 107°09′W*
185 F22 **Herbert** Otago, South Island, New Zealand *45°14′S 170°48′E*
38 J17 **Herbert Island** *island* Aleutian Islands, Alaska, USA
Herbertshöhe *see* Kokopo
15 Q7 **Hérbertville** Québec, SE Canada *48°23′N 71°42′W*
101 G17 **Herborn** Hessen, W Germany *50°40′N 08°18′E*
113 I17 **Herceg-Novi** *It.* Castelnuovo; *prev.* Ercegnovi. SW Montenegro *42°28′N 18°35′E*
11 X10 **Herchmer** Manitoba, C Canada *57°25′N 94°12′W*
186 E8 **Hercules Bay** *bay* E Papua New Guinea
92 K2 **Herdhubreidh** ▲ C Iceland *65°12′N 16°26′W*
42 M13 **Heredia** Heredia, C Costa Rica *10°N 84°06′W*
42 M12 **Heredia** *off.* Provincia de Heredia. ◈ *province* N Costa Rica
Heredia, Provincia de *see* Heredia
97 K21 **Hereford** W England, United Kingdom *52°04′N 02°43′W*
24 M3 **Hereford** Texas, SW USA *34°49′N 102°25′W*
15 Q13 **Hereford, Mont** ▲ Québec, SE Canada *45°04′N 71°38′W*
97 K21 **Herefordshire** *cultural region* W England, United Kingdom
191 U11 **Hereheretue** *atoll* Îles Tuamotu, C French Polynesia
105 N10 **Herencia** Castilla-La Mancha, C Spain *39°22′N 03°12′W*
99 H18 **Herent** Vlaams Brabant, C Belgium *50°54′N 04°40′E*
99 I16 **Herentals** *var.* Herenthals. Antwerpen, N Belgium *51°11′N 04°50′E*
Herenthals *see* Herentals
99 H17 **Herenthout** Antwerpen, N Belgium *51°09′N 04°45′E*
95 J23 **Herfølge** Roskilde, E Denmark *55°25′N 12°09′E*
100 G13 **Herford** Nordrhein-Westfalen, NW Germany *52°07′N 08°41′E*
27 O5 **Herington** Kansas, C USA *38°37′N 96°55′W*
108 H7 **Herisau** *Fr.* Hérisau. Appenzell Ausser Rhoden, NE Switzerland *47°23′N 09°17′E*
Hérisau *see* Herisau
Héristal *see* Herstal
99 J18 **Herk-de-Stad** Limburg, NE Belgium *50°57′N 05°12′E*
Herkulesbad/Herkulesfürdő *see* Băile Herculane
162 M8 **Herlenbayan-Ulaan** *var.* Dulaan. Hentiy, C Mongolia *47°09′N 108°48′E*
Herlen Gol/Herlen He *see* Kerulen
35 Q4 **Herlong** California, W USA *40°07′N 120°06′W*
97 L26 **Herm** *island* Channel Islands
109 R9 **Hermagor** *Slvn.* Šmohor. Kärnten, S Austria *46°37′N 13°24′E*
29 S7 **Herman** Minnesota, N USA *45°49′N 96°08′W*
96 L1 **Herma Ness** *headland* NE Scotland, United Kingdom *60°51′N 00°55′W*
27 V4 **Hermann** Missouri, C USA *38°43′N 91°26′W*
181 Q8 **Hermannsburg** Northern Territory, N Australia *23°59′S 132°55′E*
Hermannstadt *see* Sibiu
94 E12 **Hermansverk** Sogn Og Fjordane, S Norway *61°11′N 06°52′E*
138 H6 **Hermel** *var.* Hirmil. NE Lebanon *34°23′N 36°19′E*
Hermhausen *see* Hajnówka
183 P6 **Hermidale** New South Wales, SE Australia *31°36′S 146°42′E*
55 X9 **Herminadorp** Sipaliwini, NE Suriname *05°05′N 54°22′W*
32 K11 **Hermiston** Oregon, NW USA *45°50′N 119°17′W*
27 T6 **Hermitage** Missouri, C USA *37°57′N 93°21′W*
186 D4 **Hermit Islands** *island group* N Papua New Guinea
25 O7 **Hermleigh** Texas, SW USA *32°37′N 100°44′W*
138 G7 **Hermon, Mount** *Ar.* Jabal ash Shaykh. ▲ S Syria *35°30′N 33°30′E*
Hermopolis Parva *see* Damanhûr
28 J10 **Hermosa** South Dakota, N USA *43°49′N 103°12′W*
40 F5 **Hermosillo** Sonora, NW Mexico *28°59′N 110°53′W*
Hermoupolis *see* Ermoúpoli
111 N20 **Hernád** *var.* Hornád, *Ger.* Kundert. ≈ Hungary/Slovakia
61 C18 **Hernández** Entre Ríos, E Argentina *32°21′S 60°02′W*
23 V11 **Hernando** Florida, SE USA *28°54′N 82°22′W*
22 L1 **Hernando** Mississippi, S USA *34°49′N 89°59′W*
105 Q2 **Hernani** País Vasco, N Spain *43°16′N 01°59′W*
99 F19 **Herne** Vlaams Brabant, C Belgium *50°45′N 04°03′E*
101 E14 **Herne** Nordrhein-Westfalen, W Germany *51°32′N 07°12′E*
95 F22 **Herning** Ringkøbing, W Denmark *56°08′N 08°59′E*
Hernösand *see* Härnösand
121 U11 **Herodotus Basin** *undersea feature* E Mediterranean Sea
121 Q12 **Herodotus Trough** *undersea feature* C Mediterranean Sea
29 T11 **Heron Lake** Minnesota, N USA *43°48′N 95°18′W*
Herowābād *see* Khalkhāl
95 G16 **Herre** Telemark, S Norway *59°06′N 09°34′E*
29 N7 **Herreid** South Dakota, N USA *45°49′N 100°04′W*
101 H22 **Herrenberg** Baden-Württemberg, S Germany *48°36′N 08°52′E*
104 L14 **Herrera** Andalucía, S Spain *37°22′N 04°50′W*
43 R17 **Herrera** *off.* Provincia de Herrera. ◈ *province* S Panama
104 L10 **Herrera del Duque** Extremadura, W Spain *39°10′N 05°03′W*
104 M4 **Herrera de Pisuerga** Castilla-León, N Spain *42°35′N 04°20′W*
Herrera, Provincia de *see* Herrera
41 Z13 **Herrero, Punta** *headland* SE Mexico *19°15′N 87°28′W*
183 P16 **Herrick** Tasmania, SE Australia *41°07′S 147°53′E*
30 L17 **Herrin** Illinois, N USA *37°48′N 89°01′W*
20 M6 **Herrington Lake** ⊠ Kentucky, S USA
95 K18 **Herrljunga** Västra Götaland, S Sweden *58°05′N 13°02′E*
103 N16 **Hers** ≈ S France
10 I1 **Herschel Island** *island* Yukon Territory, NW Canada
99 I17 **Herselt** Antwerpen, C Belgium *51°04′N 04°53′E*
18 G15 **Hershey** Pennsylvania, NE USA *40°17′N 76°39′W*
99 K19 **Herstal** *Fr.* Héristal. Liège, E Belgium *50°40′N 05°38′E*
97 O21 **Hertford** E England, United Kingdom *51°48′N 00°05′W*
21 X8 **Hertford** North Carolina, SE USA *36°11′N 76°30′W*
97 O21 **Hertfordshire** *cultural region* E England, United Kingdom
181 Z9 **Hervey Bay** Queensland, E Australia *25°17′S 152°48′E*
101 O14 **Herzberg** Brandenburg, E Germany *51°42′N 13°15′E*
99 E18 **Herzele** Oost-Vlaanderen, NW Belgium *50°52′N 03°52′E*
101 K20 **Herzogenaurach** Bayern, SE Germany *49°34′N 10°52′E*
109 W4 **Herzogenburg** Niederösterreich, NE Austria *48°18′N 15°43′E*
Herzogenbusch *see* 's-Hertogenbosch
103 N2 **Hesdin** Pas-de-Calais, N France *50°21′N 02°00′E*
160 K14 **Heshan** Guangxi Zhuangzu Zizhiqu, S China *23°45′N 108°58′E*
159 X10 **Heshui** *var.* Xihuachi. Gansu, C China *35°42′N 108°06′E*
99 M25 **Hespérange** Luxembourg, SE Luxembourg *49°34′N 06°10′E*
35 U14 **Hesperia** California, W USA *34°25′N 117°17′W*
37 P7 **Hesperus Mountain** ▲ Colorado, C USA *37°27′N 108°05′W*
10 J6 **Hess** ≈ Yukon Territory, NW Canada
Hesse *see* Hessen
101 J21 **Hesselberg** ▲ S Germany *49°04′N 10°32′E*
95 I22 **Hesselo** *island* E Denmark
101 H17 **Hessen** *Eng./Fr.* Hesse. ◈ *state* C Germany
192 L6 **Hess Tablemount** *undersea feature* C Pacific Ocean *17°49′N 174°15′W*
27 N6 **Hesston** Kansas, C USA *38°08′N 97°25′W*
93 G15 **Hestkjøltoppen** ▲ C Norway *64°21′N 13°57′E*
97 K18 **Heswall** NW England, United Kingdom *53°20′N 03°06′W*
153 P12 **Hetaudā** Central, C Nepal
Hétfalu *see* Săcele
28 K7 **Hettinger** North Dakota, N USA *46°00′N 102°38′W*
101 L14 **Hettstedt** Sachsen-Anhalt, C Germany *51°39′N 11°31′E*
92 P3 **Heuglin, Kapp** *headland* SE Svalbard *78°15′N 22°49′E*
187 N10 **Heuru** San Cristobal, SE Solomon Islands *10°13′S 161°25′E*
99 J17 **Heusden** Limburg, NE Belgium *51°02′N 05°17′E*
98 J13 **Heusden** Noord-Brabant, S Netherlands *51°43′N 05°05′E*
102 K3 **Hève, Cap de la** *headland* N France *49°28′N 00°13′W*
99 H18 **Heverlee** Vlaams Brabant, C Belgium *50°52′N 04°41′E*
111 L22 **Heves** Heves, NE Hungary *47°36′N 20°17′E*
111 L22 **Heves** *off.* Heves Megye. ◈ *county* NE Hungary
Heves Megye *see* Heves
Hevron *see* Hebron
45 Y13 **Hewanorra** ✈ (Saint Lucia) S Saint Lucia *13°44′N 60°57′W*
Hexian *see* Hezhou
160 L6 **Heyang** Shaanxi, C China *35°14′N 110°02′E*
Heyang *see* Hechuan
Heydebrech *see* Kędzierzyn-Kozle
Heydekrug *see* Šilutė
Heyin *see* Guide
97 K16 **Heysham** NW England, United Kingdom *54°02′N 02°54′W*
161 O14 **Heyuan** *var.* Yuancheng. Guangdong, S China *23°41′N 114°45′E*
182 L12 **Heywood** Victoria, SE Australia *38°09′S 141°38′E*
180 K3 **Heywood Islands** *island group* Western Australia
161 O6 **Heze** *var.* Caozhou. Shandong, E China *35°16′N 115°27′E*
159 U11 **Hezheng** Gansu, C China *35°29′N 103°36′E*
160 M13 **Hezhou** *var.* Babu; *prev.* Hexian. Guangxi Zhuangzu Zizhiqu, S China *24°33′N 11°30′E*
159 U11 **Hezuo** Gansu, C China *34°55′N 102°49′E*
23 Z16 **Hialeah** Florida, SE USA *25°51′N 80°16′W*
27 Q3 **Hiawatha** Kansas, C USA *39°51′N 95°34′W*
36 M4 **Hiawatha** Utah, W USA *39°28′N 111°00′W*
29 V4 **Hibbing** Minnesota, N USA *47°24′N 92°55′W*
183 N17 **Hibbs, Point** *headland* Tasmania, SE Australia *42°37′S 145°15′E*
Hibernia *see* Ireland
20 F8 **Hickman** Kentucky, S USA *36°33′N 89°11′W*
21 Q9 **Hickory** North Carolina, SE USA *35°44′N 81°20′W*
21 Q9 **Hickory, Lake** ◎ North Carolina, SE USA
184 Q7 **Hicks Bay** Gisborne, North Island, New Zealand *37°36′S 178°18′E*
25 S8 **Hico** Texas, SW USA *31°58′N 98°01′W*
Hida *see* Furukawa
165 T4 **Hidaka** Hokkaidō, NE Japan *42°53′N 142°24′E*
164 I12 **Hidaka** Hyōgo, Honshū, SW Japan *35°27′N 134°43′E*
165 T5 **Hidaka-sanmyaku** ▲▲ Hokkaidō, NE Japan
41 O6 **Hidalgo** *var.* Villa Hidalgo. Coahuila, NE Mexico *27°46′N 99°54′W*
41 N8 **Hidalgo** Nuevo León, NE Mexico *29°59′N 100°27′W*
41 O10 **Hidalgo** Tamaulipas, C Mexico *24°16′N 99°28′W*
41 O13 **Hidalgo** ◈ *state* C Mexico
40 J7 **Hidalgo del Parral** *var.* Parral. Chihuahua, N Mexico *26°58′N 105°40′W*
100 N7 **Hiddensee** *island* NE Germany
80 G6 **Hidiglib, Wadi** ≈ NE Sudan
109 U6 **Hieflau** Salzburg, E Austria *47°36′N 14°34′E*
187 P16 **Hienghène** Province Nord, C New Caledonia *20°43′S 164°54′E*
Hierosolyma *see* Jerusalem
64 N12 **Hierro** *var.* Ferro. *island* Islas Canarias, Spain, NE Atlantic Ocean
164 G13 **Higashi-Hiroshima** *var.* Higasihirosima. Hiroshima, Honshū, SW Japan *34°27′N 132°43′E*
164 C12 **Higashi-suidō** *strait* SW Japan
Higasihirosima *see* Higashi-Hiroshima
25 P1 **Higgins** Texas, SW USA *36°06′N 100°01′W*
31 P7 **Higgins Lake** ◎ Michigan, N USA
27 S4 **Higginsville** Missouri, C USA *39°04′N 93°43′W*
High Atlas *see* Haut Atlas
30 M5 **High Falls Reservoir** ⊠ Wisconsin, N USA
44 K12 **Highgate** C Jamaica *18°16′N 76°53′W*
25 X11 **High Island** Texas, SW USA *29°35′N 94°24′W*
31 O5 **High Island** *island* Michigan, N USA
30 K15 **Highland** Illinois, N USA *38°44′N 89°40′W*
31 N10 **Highland Park** Illinois, N USA *42°10′N 87°48′W*
21 O10 **Highlands** North Carolina, SE USA *35°04′N 83°10′W*
11 O11 **High Level** Alberta, W Canada *58°31′N 117°08′W*
29 O9 **Highmore** South Dakota, N USA *44°29′N 99°26′W*
171 N3 **High Peak** ▲ Luzon, N Philippines *15°28′N 120°07′E*
High Plains *see* Great Plains
21 S9 **High Point** North Carolina, SE USA *35°58′N 80°00′W*
18 J13 **High Point** *hill* New Jersey, NE USA
11 P13 **High Prairie** Alberta, W Canada *55°27′N 116°28′W*
11 Q16 **High River** Alberta, SW Canada *50°35′N 113°50′W*
21 S9 **High Rock Lake** ⊠ North Carolina, SE USA
23 V9 **High Springs** Florida, SE USA *29°49′N 82°36′W*
High Veld *see* Great Karoo
97 J24 **High Willhays** ▲ SW England, United Kingdom *50°39′N 03°58′W*
97 N22 **High Wycombe** *prev.* Chepping Wycombe, Chipping Wycombe. SE England, United Kingdom *51°38′N 00°46′W*
41 P12 **Higos** *var.* El Higo. Veracruz-Llave, E Mexico *21°48′N 98°25′W*
102 I16 **Higuer, Cap** *headland* NE Spain *43°23′N 01°46′W*
45 R5 **Higüero, Punta** *headland* W Puerto Rico *18°21′N 67°15′W*
45 P9 **Higüey** *var.* Salvaleón de Higüey. E Dominican Republic *18°40′N 68°43′W*
190 G11 **Hihifo** ✈ (Matā'utu) Île Uvea, N Wallis and Futuna
81 N16 **Hiiraan** *off.* Gobolka Hiiraan. ◈ *region* C Somalia
Hiiraan, Gobolka *see* Hiiraan
118 E4 **Hiiumaa** *var.* Hiiumaa Maakond. ◈ *province* W Estonia
118 D4 **Hiiumaa** *Ger.* Dagden, *Swe.* Dagö. *island* W Estonia
Hiiumaa Maakond *see* Hiiumaa
Hijanah *see* Al Hījānah
105 S6 **Híjar** Aragón, NE Spain *41°10′N 00°27′W*
191 V10 **Hikueru** *atoll* Îles Tuamotu, C French Polynesia
184 K3 **Hikurangi** Northland, North Island, New Zealand *35°37′S 174°16′E*
184 Q8 **Hikurangi** ▲ North Island, New Zealand *37°55′S 177°59′E*
192 L11 **Hikurangi Trench** *var.* Hikurangi Trough. *undersea feature* SW Pacific Ocean
Hikurangi Trough *see* Hikurangi Trench
190 B15 **Hikutavake** NW Niue
121 Q12 **Hilāl, Ra's al** *headland* N Libya *32°55′N 22°09′E*
61 A24 **Hilario Ascasubi** Buenos Aires, E Argentina *39°22′S 62°39′W*
101 K17 **Hildburghausen** Thüringen, C Germany *50°26′N 10°44′E*
101 E15 **Hilden** Nordrhein-Westfalen, W Germany *51°12′N 06°56′E*
100 I13 **Hildesheim** Niedersachsen, N Germany *52°09′N 09°57′E*
33 T9 **Hilger** Montana, NW USA *47°15′N 109°18′W*
153 S13 **Hili** *var.* Hilli. Rajshahi, NW Bangladesh *25°16′N 89°04′E*
Hilla *see* Al Ḥillah
45 O14 **Hillaby, Mount** ▲ N Barbados *13°12′N 59°34′W*
95 K19 **Hillared** Västra Götaland, S Sweden *57°37′N 13°10′E*
195 R12 **Hillary Coast** *physical region* Antarctica
42 G2 **Hill Bank** Orange Walk, N Belize *17°36′N 88°43′W*
33 O14 **Hill City** Idaho, NW USA *43°18′N 115°03′W*
26 K3 **Hill City** Kansas, C USA *39°23′N 99°51′W*
29 V5 **Hill City** Minnesota, N USA *46°59′N 93°36′W*
28 J10 **Hill City** South Dakota, N USA *43°54′N 103°33′W*
98 H10 **Hillegom** Zuid-Holland, W Netherlands *52°18′N 04°35′E*
95 J22 **Hillerød** Frederiksborg, E Denmark *55°56′N 12°19′E*
36 M7 **Hillers, Mount** ▲ Utah, W USA *37°53′N 110°42′W*
Hilli *see* Hili
29 R11 **Hills** Minnesota, N USA *43°31′N 96°21′W*
30 L14 **Hillsboro** Illinois, N USA *39°09′N 89°29′W*
27 N5 **Hillsboro** Kansas, C USA *38°21′N 97°12′W*
27 X5 **Hillsboro** Missouri, C USA *38°13′N 90°33′W*
19 N10 **Hillsboro** New Hampshire, NE USA *43°06′N 71°52′W*
37 Q14 **Hillsboro** New Mexico, SW USA *32°55′N 107°33′W*
29 R4 **Hillsboro** North Dakota, N USA *47°25′N 97°03′W*
31 R14 **Hillsboro** Ohio, N USA *39°12′N 83°36′W*
32 G11 **Hillsboro** Oregon, NW USA *45°32′N 122°59′W*
25 T8 **Hillsboro** Texas, SW USA *32°01′N 97°08′W*
30 K8 **Hillsboro** Wisconsin, N USA *43°40′N 90°21′W*
23 Y14 **Hillsboro Canal** *canal* Florida, SE USA
45 Y15 **Hillsborough** Carriacou, N Grenada *12°28′N 61°28′W*
97 G15 **Hillsborough** E Northern Ireland, United Kingdom *54°27′N 06°06′W*
21 U9 **Hillsborough** North Carolina, SE USA *36°04′N 79°06′W*
31 Q10 **Hillsdale** Michigan, N USA *41°55′N 84°37′W*
183 O8 **Hillston** New South Wales, SE Australia *33°30′S 145°33′E*
21 R7 **Hillsville** Virginia, NE USA *36°46′N 80°44′W*
96 L2 **Hillswick** NE Scotland, United Kingdom *60°28′N 01°37′W*
Hill Tippera *see* Tripura
38 H11 **Hilo** Hawaii, USA, C Pacific Ocean *19°42′N 155°04′W*
18 F9 **Hilton** New York, NE USA *43°17′N 77°47′W*
14 C10 **Hilton Beach** Ontario, S Canada *46°14′N 83°51′W*
21 R16 **Hilton Head Island** South Carolina, SE USA *32°13′N 80°45′W*
21 R16 **Hilton Head Island** *island* South Carolina, SE USA
99 J15 **Hilvarenbeek** Noord-Brabant, S Netherlands *51°29′N 05°08′E*
98 J11 **Hilversum** Noord-Holland, C Netherlands *52°14′N 05°10′E*
75 W8 **Hilwān** *var.* Helwân, Hulwan, Hulwān. N Egypt *29°51′N 31°20′E*
Hilwân *see* Hilwān
152 J7 **Himāchal Pradesh** ◈ *state* NW India
Himalaya/Himalaya Shan *see* Himalayas
152 M9 **Himalayas** *var.* Himalaya, *Chin.* Himalaya Shan. ▲▲ S Asia
171 P6 **Himamaylan** Negros, C Philippines *10°04′N 122°52′E*
93 K15 **Himanka** Länsi-Suomi, W Finland *64°04′N 23°40′E*
Himara *see* Himarë
113 L23 **Himarë** *var.* Himara. Vlorë, S Albania *40°06′N 19°45′E*
138 M2 **Ḩimār, Wādī al** *dry watercourse* N Syria
154 D9 **Himatnagar** Gujarāt, W India *23°38′N 73°02′E*
109 Y4 **Himberg** Niederösterreich, E Austria *48°05′N 16°27′E*
164 I13 **Himeji** *var.* Himezi. Hyōgo, Honshū, SW Japan *34°47′N 134°32′E*
164 E14 **Hime-jima** *island* SW Japan
Himezi *see* Himeji
164 L13 **Himi** Toyama, Honshū, SW Japan *36°54′N 136°59′E*
109 S9 **Himmelberg** Kärnten, S Austria *46°45′N 14°01′E*
138 I5 **Ḩimş** *var.* Homs; *anc.* Emesa. Ḩimş, C Syria *34°44′N 36°43′E*
138 K6 **Ḩimş** *off.* Muḩāfaẓat Ḩims, *var.* Homs. ◈ *governorate* C Syria
138 I5 **Ḩimş, Buḩayrat** *var.* Buḩayrat Qaṭṭinah. ◎ W Syria
171 R7 **Hinatuan** Mindanao, S Philippines *08°21′N 126°19′E*
117 N10 **Hînceşti** *var.* Hânceşti; *prev.* Kotovsk. C Moldova *46°48′N 28°33′E*
44 M9 **Hinche** C Haiti *19°07′N 72°00′W*
181 X5 **Hinchinbrook Island** *island* Queensland, NE Australia
39 S12 **Hinchinbrook Island** *island* Alaska, USA
97 M19 **Hinckley** C England, United Kingdom *52°33′N 01°21′W*
29 V7 **Hinckley** Minnesota, N USA *46°01′N 92°57′W*
36 K5 **Hinckley** Utah, W USA *39°21′N 112°39′W*
18 J9 **Hinckley Reservoir** ⊠ New York, NE USA
152 I12 **Hindaun** Rājasthān, N India *26°44′N 77°02′E*
Hindenburg/Hindenburg in Oberschlesien *see* Zabrze
Hindiya *see* Al Hindīyah
21 O6 **Hindman** Kentucky, S USA *37°20′N 82°58′W*
182 L10 **Hindmarsh, Lake** ◎ Victoria, SE Australia
185 G19 **Hinds** Canterbury, South Island, New Zealand *44°01′S 171°33′E*
185 G19 **Hinds** ≈ South Island, New Zealand
95 H23 **Hindsholm** *island* C Denmark
149 S4 **Hindu Kush** *Per.* Hendū Kosh. ▲▲ Afghanistan/Pakistan
155 H19 **Hindupur** Andhra Pradesh, E India *13°46′N 77°33′E*
11 O12 **Hines Creek** Alberta, W Canada *56°14′N 118°36′W*
23 W6 **Hinesville** Georgia, SE USA *31°51′N 81°36′W*
154 I12 **Hinganghāt** Mahārāshtra, C India *20°32′N 78°52′E*
149 N15 **Hingol** ≈ SW Pakistan
154 H13 **Hingoli** Mahārāshtra, C India *19°45′N 77°08′E*
137 R13 **Hınıs** Erzurum, E Turkey *39°22′N 41°44′E*
92 O2 **Hinlopenstretet** *strait* N Svalbard
92 G10 **Hinnøya** *Lapp.* Iinnasuolu. *island* C Norway
108 H10 **Hinterrhein** ≈ SW Switzerland
166 L8 **Hinthada** *var.* Henzada. Ayeyarwady, SW Myanmar (Burma) *17°36′N 95°26′E*
11 O14 **Hinton** Alberta, SW Canada *53°24′N 117°35′W*
26 M10 **Hinton** Oklahoma, C USA *35°28′N 98°21′W*
21 R6 **Hinton** West Virginia, NE USA *37°42′N 80°54′W*
Hios *see* Chíos
41 N8 **Hipolito** Coahuila, NE Mexico *25°42′N 101°22′W*
Hipponium *see* Vibo Valentia
164 B13 **Hirado** Nagasaki, Hirado-shima, SW Japan *33°22′N 129°31′E*
164 B13 **Hirado-shima** *island* SW Japan
165 P16 **Hirakubo-saki** *headland* Ishigaki-jima, SW Japan *24°36′N 124°19′E*
154 M11 **Hīrākud Reservoir** ⊠ E India
Hir al Gharbi, Qasr al *see* Ḩayr al Gharbī, Qaşr al
165 Q16 **Hirara** Okinawa, Miyako-jima, SW Japan *24°48′N 125°17′E*
Hir Ash Sharqi, Qasr al *see* Ḩayr ash Sharqī, Qaşr al
164 G12 **Hirata** Shimane, Honshū, SW Japan *35°25′N 132°45′E*
136 I13 **Hirfanlı Barajı** ⊠ C Turkey
155 G18 **Hiriyūr** Karnātaka, W India *13°58′N 76°33′E*
Hîrlău *see* Hârlău
148 K10 **Hīrmand, Rūd-e** *var.* Daryā-ye Helmand. ≈ Afghanistan/Iran *see also* Helmand, Daryā-ye
Hīrmand, Rūd-e *see* Helmand, Daryā-ye
Hirmil *see* Hermel
165 T5 **Hiroo** Hokkaidō, NE Japan *42°16′N 143°16′E*
165 Q7 **Hirosaki** Aomori, Honshū, C Japan *40°34′N 140°28′E*
164 G13 **Hiroshima** *var.* Hirosima. Hiroshima, Honshū, SW Japan *34°23′N 132°26′E*
164 F13 **Hiroshima** *off.* Hiroshima-ken, *var.* Hirosima. ◈ *prefecture* Honshū, SW Japan
Hiroshima-ken *see* Hiroshima
Hirosima *see* Hiroshima
Hirschberg/Hirschberg im Riesengebirge/Hirschberg in Schlesien *see* Jelenia Góra
103 Q3 **Hirson** Aisne, N France *49°56′N 04°05′E*
Hîrşova *see* Hârşova
95 G19 **Hirtshals** Nordjylland, N Denmark *57°34′N 09°58′E*
152 H10 **Hisār** Haryāna, NW India *29°10′N 75°45′E*
162 K7 **Hishig Öndör** *var.* Maanĭt. Bulgan, C Mongolia *48°17′N 103°29′E*
186 E9 **Hisiu** Central, SW Papua New Guinea *09°20′S 146°48′E*
147 P13 **Hisor** *Rus.* Gissar. W Tajikistan *38°34′N 68°29′E*
Hispalis *see* Sevilla
Hispana/Hispania *see* Spain
44 M7 **Hispaniola** *island* Dominion Republic/Haiti
64 F11 **Hispaniola Basin** *var.* Hispaniola Trough. *undersea feature* SW Atlantic Ocean
Hispaniola Trough *see* Hispaniola Basin
Histonium *see* Vasto
139 R7 **Hīt** Al Anbār, SW Iraq *33°38′N 42°50′E*
165 P14 **Hita** Ōita, Kyūshū, SW Japan *33°19′N 130°55′E*
165 P12 **Hitachi** *var.* Hitati. Ibaraki, Honshū, S Japan *36°40′N 140°42′E*
165 P12 **Hitachi-Ōta** *var.* Hitatiôta. Ibaraki, Honshū, S Japan *36°32′N 140°31′E*
Hitati *see* Hitachi
Hitatiôta *see* Hitachi-Ōta
97 O21 **Hitchin** E England, United Kingdom *51°57′N 00°17′W*
191 Q7 **Hitiaa** Tahiti, W French Polynesia *17°35′S 149°17′W*
164 D15 **Hitoyoshi** *var.* Hitoyosi. Kumamoto, Kyūshū, SW Japan *32°12′N 130°48′E*
Hitoyosi *see* Hitoyoshi
94 F7 **Hitra** *prev.* Hitteren. *island* S Norway
Hitteren *see* Hitra
187 Q11 **Hiu** *island* Torres Islands, N Vanuatu
165 O11 **Hiuchiga-take** ▲ Honshū, C Japan *36°57′N 139°18′E*
191 X7 **Hiva Oa** *island* Îles Marquises, N French Polynesia
20 M10 **Hiwassee Lake** ⊠ North Carolina, SE USA
20 M10 **Hiwassee River** ≈ SE USA
95 H20 **Hjallerup** Nordjylland, N Denmark *57°10′N 10°10′E*
95 M16 **Hjälmaren** *Eng.* Lake Hjalmar. ◎ C Sweden
Hjalmar, Lake *see* Hjälmaren
95 C14 **Hjellestad** Hordaland, S Norway *60°15′N 05°13′E*
95 D16 **Hjelmeland** Rogaland, S Norway *59°12′N 06°07′E*
94 G10 **Hjerkinn** Oppland, S Norway *62°13′N 09°37′E*
95 L18 **Hjo** Västra Götaland, S Sweden *58°18′N 14°17′E*
95 G19 **Hjørring** Nordjylland, N Denmark *57°28′N 09°59′E*
167 O1 **Hkakabo Razi** ▲ Myanmar (Burma)/China *28°17′N 97°28′E*
167 N1 **Hkring Bum** ▲ N Myanmar (Burma) *27°05′N 97°16′E*
83 L21 **Hlathikulu** *var.* Hlatikulu. S Swaziland *26°58′S 31°19′E*
Hlatikulu *see* Hlathikulu
Hliboka *see* Hlyboka
111 F17 **Hlinsko** *var.* Hlinsko v Čechách. Pardubický Kraj, C Czech Republic *49°46′N 15°54′E*
Hlinsko v Čechách *see* Hlinsko
117 S6 **Hlobyne** *Rus.* Globino. Poltavs'ka Oblast', NE Ukraine *49°24′N 33°16′E*
111 H20 **Hlohovec** *Ger.* Freistadtl, *Hung.* Galgóc; *prev.* Frakštát. Trnavský Kraj, W Slovakia *48°26′N 17°49′E*
83 J23 **Hlotse** *var.* Leribe. NW Lesotho *28°55′S 28°01′E*
111 I17 **Hlučín** *Ger.* Hultschin, *Pol.* Hulczyn. Moravskoslezský Kraj, E Czech Republic *49°54′N 18°11′E*
117 S2 **Hlukhiv** *Rus.* Glukhov. Sums'ka Oblast', NE Ukraine *51°40′N 33°53′E*
119 K21 **Hlushkavichy** *Rus.* Glushkevichi. Homyel'skaya Voblasts', SE Belarus *51°34′N 27°47′E*
119 L18 **Hlusk** *Rus.* Glusk, Glussk. Mahilyowskaya Voblasts', E Belarus *52°54′N 28°41′E*
116 K8 **Hlyboka** *Ger.* Hliboka, *Rus.* Glybokaya. Chernivets'ka Oblast', W Ukraine *48°04′N 25°56′E*
118 K13 **Hlybokaye** *Rus.* Glubokoye. Vitsyebskaya Voblasts', N Belarus *55°08′N 27°41′E*
77 Q16 **Ho** SE Ghana *06°36′N 00°28′E*
167 S6 **Hoa Binh** Hoa Binh, N Vietnam *20°49′N 105°20′E*
83 E20 **Hoachanas** Hardap, C Namibia *23°55′S 18°04′E*
Hoai Nhơn *see* Bồng Sơn
167 T8 **Hoa Lac** Quang Binh, C Vietnam *17°54′N 106°24′E*
167 S5 **Hoang Liên Sơn** ▲▲ N Vietnam
83 B17 **Hoanib** ≈ NW Namibia
33 S15 **Hoback Peak** ▲ Wyoming, C USA *43°04′N 110°34′W*
183 P17 **Hobart** *prev.* Hobarton, Hobart Town. *state capital* Tasmania, SE Australia *42°54′S 147°18′E*
26 L11 **Hobart** Oklahoma, C USA *35°03′N 99°04′W*
183 P17 **Hobart** ✈ Tasmania, SE Australia *42°52′S 147°28′E*
Hobarton/Hobart Town *see* Hobart
37 W14 **Hobbs** New Mexico, SW USA *32°42′N 103°08′W*
194 L12 **Hobbs Coast** *physical region* Antarctica
23 Z14 **Hobe Sound** Florida, SE USA *27°03′N 80°08′W*
Hobicaurikány *see* Uricani
54 E12 **Hobo** Huila, S Colombia *02°34′N 75°28′W*
99 G16 **Hoboken** Antwerpen, N Belgium *51°12′N 04°22′E*
158 K3 **Hoboksar** *var.* Hoboksar Mongol Zizhixian. Xinjiang Uygur Zizhiqu, NW China *46°48′N 85°42′E*
Hoboksar Mongol Zizhixian *see* Hoboksar
95 G21 **Hobro** Nordjylland, N Denmark *56°39′N 09°51′E*
21 X10 **Hobucken** North Carolina, SE USA *35°15′N 76°31′W*
95 O20 **Hoburgen** *headland* SE Sweden *56°54′N 18°07′E*
81 P15 **Hobyo** *It.* Obbia. Mudug, E Somalia *05°16′N 48°24′E*
109 R8 **Hochalmspitze** ▲ SW Austria *47°00′N 13°19′E*
109 Q4 **Hochburg** Oberösterreich, N Austria *48°10′N 12°57′E*
108 F8 **Hochdorf** Luzern, N Switzerland *47°10′N 08°16′E*
109 N8 **Hochfeiler** *It.* Gran Pilastro. ▲ Austria/Italy *46°59′N 11°42′E*
167 T14 **Hô Chi Minh** *var.* Ho Chi Minh City; *prev.* Saigon. S Vietnam *10°46′N 106°43′E*
Ho Chi Minh City *see* Hô Chi Minh
108 I7 **Höchst** Vorarlberg, NW Austria *47°28′N 09°40′E*
Höchstadt *see* Höchstadt an der Aisch
101 K19 **Höchstadt an der Aisch** *var.* Höchstadt. Bayern, C Germany *49°43′N 10°48′E*
108 L9 **Hochwilde** *It.* L'Altissima. ▲ Austria/Italy *46°45′N 11°00′E*
109 S7 **Hochwildstelle** ▲ C Austria *47°21′N 13°53′E*
31 T14 **Hocking River** ≈ Ohio, N USA
Hoctūm *see* Hoctún
41 X12 **Hoctún** *var.* Hoctúm. Yucatán, E Mexico *20°48′N 89°14′W*
Hodeida *see* Al Ḩudaydah
20 K6 **Hodgenville** Kentucky, S USA *37°34′N 85°45′W*
11 T17 **Hodgeville** Saskatchewan, S Canada *50°06′N 106°55′W*
76 L9 **Hodh ech Chargui** ◈ *region* E Mauritania
Hodh el Garbi *see* Hodh el Gharbi
76 J10 **Hodh el Gharbi** *var.* Hodh el Garbi. ◈ *region* S Mauritania
111 L25 **Hódmezővásárhely** Csongrád, SE Hungary *46°27′N 20°18′E*
74 J6 **Hodna, Chott El** *var.* Chott el-Hodna, *Ar.* Shatt al-Hodna. *salt lake* N Algeria
Hodna, Chott el-/Hodna, Shatt al- *see* Hodna, Chott El
111 G19 **Hodonín** *Ger.* Göding. Jihomoravský Kraj, SE Czech Republic *48°52′N 17°07′E*
Hödrögö *see* Nömrög
Hodság/Hodschag *see* Odžaci
39 R7 **Hodzana River** ≈ Alaska, USA
Hoei *see* Huy
99 H19 **Hoeilaart** Vlaams Brabant, C Belgium *50°46′N 04°28′E*
Hoë Karoo *see* Great Karoo
98 F12 **Hoek van Holland** *Eng.* Hook of Holland. Zuid-Holland, W Netherlands *52°00′N 04°07′E*
98 L11 **Hoenderloo** Gelderland, E Netherlands *52°08′N 05°46′E*
99 L18 **Hoensbroek** Limburg, SE Netherlands *50°55′N 05°55′E*
163 Y11 **Hoeryŏng** NE North Korea *42°23′N 129°46′E*
99 K18 **Hoeselt** Limburg, NE Belgium *50°50′N 05°30′E*
98 K11 **Hoevelaken** Gelderland, C Netherlands *52°10′N 05°27′E*
Hoey *see* Huy
101 M18 **Hof** Bayern, SE Germany *50°19′N 11°55′E*
Höfdhakaupstadhur *see* Skagaströnd
Hofei *see* Hefei
101 G18 **Hofheim am Taunus** Hessen, W Germany *50°04′N 08°27′E*
Hofmarkt *see* Odorheiu Secuiesc

◆ Country
● Country Capital
◇ Dependent Territory
○ Dependent Territory Capital
◈ Administrative Regions
✈ International Airport
▲ Mountain
▲▲ Mountain Range
Volcano
≈ River
◎ Lake
⊠ Reservoir

HÖFN – HSÜEH SHAN

92 L3 **Höfn** Austurland, SE Iceland 64°14′N 15°17′W
94 N13 **Hofors** Gävleborg, C Sweden 60°33′N 16°21′E
92 J6 **Hofsjökull** *glacier* C Iceland
92 J1 **Hofsós** Nordhurland Vestra, N Iceland 65°54′N 19°25′W
164 E13 **Hōfu** Yamaguchi, Honshū, SW Japan 34°01′N 131°34′E
Hofuf *see* Al Hufūf
95 J22 **Höganäs** Skåne, S Sweden 56°11′N 12°39′E
183 P14 **Hogan Group** *island group* Tasmania, SE Australia
23 R4 **Hogansville** Georgia, SE USA 33°10′N 84°55′W
39 P8 **Hogatza River** ⟿ Alaska, USA
28 I14 **Hogback Mountain** ▲ Nebraska, C USA 41°40′N 103°44′W
95 G14 **Høgevarde** ▲ S Norway 60°19′N 09°27′E
Högfors *see* Karkkila
31 P5 **Hog Island** *island* Michigan, N USA
21 Y6 **Hog Island** *island* Virginia, NE USA
Hogoley Islands *see* Chuuk Islands
95 N20 **Högsby** Kalmar, S Sweden 57°10′N 16°03′E
36 K1 **Hogup Mountains** ⛰ Utah, W USA
101 E17 **Hohe Acht** ▲ W Germany 50°23′N 07°00′E
Hohenelbe *see* Vrchlabí
108 I7 **Hohenems** Vorarlberg, W Austria 47°23′N 09°43′E
Hohenmauth *see* Vysoké Mýto
Hohensalza *see* Inowrocław
Hohenstadt *see* Zábřeh
Hohenstein in Ostpreussen *see* Olsztynek
20 I9 **Hohenwald** Tennessee, S USA 35°33′N 87°31′W
101 L17 **Hohenwarte-Stausee** ☒ C Germany
Hohes Venn *see* Hautes Fagnes
109 Q8 **Hohe Tauern** ⛰ W Austria
163 O13 **Hohhot** *var.* Huhehot, Huhohaote, *Mong.* Kukukhoto; *prev.* Kweisui, Kwesui. Nei Mongol Zizhiqu, N China 40°49′N 111°37′E
162 F7 **Hohmorït** *var.* Sayn-Ust. Govĭ-Altay, W Mongolia 47°23′N 94°.9′E
103 U6 **Hohneck** ▲ NE France 48°04′N 07°01′E
77 Q16 **Hohoe** E Ghana 07°08′N 00°:2′E
164 E12 **Hōhoku** Yamaguchi, Honshū, SW Japan 34°15′N 130°56′E
159 O11 **Hoh Sai Hu** ◎ C China
159 N11 **Hoh Xil Hu** ◎ C China
158 L11 **Hoh Xil Shan** ⛰ W China
167 U10 **Hôi An** *prev.* Faifo. Quang Nam-Đa Nang, C Vietnam 15°54′N 108°19′E
Hoï-Hao/Hoihow *see* Haikou
159 S11 **Hoika** *prev.* Heka. Qinghai, W China 35°49′N 99°50′E
81 F17 **Hoima** W Uganda 01°25′N 31°22′E
26 L5 **Hoisington** Kansas, C USA 38°31′N 98°46′W
146 D12 **Hojagala** *Rus.* Khodzhakala. Balkan Welaýaty, W Turkmenistan 38°46′N 56°14′E
146 M13 **Hojambaz** *Rus.* Khodzhambas. Lebap Welaýaty, E Turkmenistan 38°11′N 64°33′E
95 H23 **Højby** Fyn, C Denmark 55°20′N 10°27′E
95 F24 **Højer** Sønderjylland, SW Denmark 54°57′N 08°43′E
164 E14 **Hōjō** *var.* Hôzyô. Ehime, Shikoku, SW Japan 33°58′N 132°47′E
184 J3 **Hokianga Harbour** *inlet* SE Tasman Sea
185 F17 **Hokitika** West Coast, South Island, New Zealand 42°44′S 170°58′E
165 U4 **Hokkai-dō** ◐ *territory* Hokkaidō, NE Japan
165 T3 **Hokkaidō** *prev.* Ezo, Yeso, Yezo. *island* NE Japan
95 G15 **Hokksund** Buskerud, S Norway 59°45′N 09°55′E
143 S4 **Hokmābād** Khorāsān-Razavī, N Iran 36°37′N 57°34′E
Hokō *see* P'ohang
Hoko-guntō/Hoko-shotō *see* P'enghu Liehtao
Hoktemberyan *see* Armavir
94 F13 **Hol** Buskerud, S Norway 60°36′N 08°18′E
117 R11 **Hola Prystan'** *Rus.* Golaya Pristan. Khersons'ka Oblast', S Ukraine 46°31′N 32°31′E
95 I23 **Holbæk** Vestsjælland, E Denmark 55°42′N 11°42′E
Holboo *see* Santmargats
183 P10 **Holbrook** New South Wales, SE Australia 35°45′S 147°18′E
37 N11 **Holbrook** Arizona, SW USA 34°54′N 110°09′W
27 S5 **Holden** Missouri, C USA 38°42′N 93°59′W
36 K5 **Holden** Utah, W USA 39°06′N 112°16′W
27 O11 **Holdenville** Oklahoma, C USA 35°05′N 96°25′W
29 O16 **Holdrege** Nebraska, C USA 40°28′N 99°28′W
35 X3 **Hole in the Mountain Peak** ▲ Nevada, W USA 40°54′N 115°06′W
155 G20 **Hole Narsipur** Karnātaka, W India 12°46′N 76°14′E
111 H18 **Holešov** *Ger.* Holleschau. Zlínský Kraj, E Czech Republic 49°20′N 17°35′E
45 N14 **Holetown** *prev.* Jamestown. W Barbados 13°11′N 59°38′W
31 Q12 **Holgate** Ohio, N USA 41°12′N 84°06′W
44 I7 **Holguín** Holguín, SE Cuba 20°51′N 76°16′W
23 V12 **Holiday** Florida, SE USA 28°11′N 82°44′W
39 O12 **Holitna River** ⟿ Alaska, USA
94 J13 **Höljes** Värmland, C Sweden 60°54′N 12°34′E
109 X3 **Hollabrunn** Niederösterreich, NE Austria 48°33′N 16°06′E
36 L3 **Holladay** Utah, W USA 40°39′N 111°49′W
11 X16 **Holland** Manitoba, S Canada 49°36′N 98°52′W
31 O9 **Holland** Michigan, N USA 42°47′N 86°06′W
25 T9 **Holland** Texas, SW USA 30°52′N 97°24′W
Holland *see* Netherlands
22 K4 **Hollandale** Mississippi, S USA 33°10′N 90°51′W
Hollandia *see* Jayapura
Hollandsch Diep *see* Hollands Diep
99 H14 **Hollands Diep** *var.* Hollandsch Diep. *channel* SW Netherlands
Holleschau *see* Holešov
25 R5 **Holliday** Texas, SW USA 33°49′N 98°41′W
18 E15 **Hollidaysburg** Pennsylvania, NE USA 40°24′N 78°22′W
21 S6 **Hollins** Virginia, NE USA 37°20′N 79°56′W
26 J12 **Hollis** Oklahoma, C USA 34°42′N 99°56′W
35 O10 **Hollister** California, W USA 36°51′N 121°25′W
27 T8 **Hollister** Missouri, C USA 36°37′N 93°13′W
93 M19 **Hollola** Etelä-Suomi, S Finland 61°N 25°32′E
98 K4 **Hollum** Friesland, N Netherlands 53°27′N 05°38′E
95 J23 **Höllviksnäs** Skåne, S Sweden 55°25′N 12°57′E
37 W6 **Holly** Colorado, C USA 38°03′N 102°07′W
31 R9 **Holly** Michigan, N USA 42°47′N 83°37′W
21 S14 **Holly Hill** South Carolina, SE USA 33°19′N 80°24′W
21 W11 **Holly Ridge** North Carolina, SE USA 34°31′N 77°31′W
22 L1 **Holly Springs** Mississippi, S USA 34°47′N 89°25′W
23 Z15 **Hollywood** Florida, SE USA 26°00′N 80°09′W
8 J6 **Holman** Victoria Island, Northwest Territories, N Canada 70°42′N 117°45′W
92 I2 **Hólmavík** Vestfirdhir, NW Iceland 65°42′N 21°43′W
30 J7 **Holmen** Wisconsin, N USA 43°57′N 91°14′W
23 R8 **Holmes Creek** ⟿ Alabama/Florida, SE USA
95 H16 **Holmestrand** Vestfold, S Norway 59°29′N 10°20′E
93 J16 **Holmön** *island* N Sweden
95 E22 **Holmsland Klit** *beach* W Denmark
93 J16 **Holmsund** Västerbotten, N Sweden 63°42′N 20°26′E
95 Q18 **Holmudden** *headland* SE Sweden 57°59′N 19°14′E
138 F10 **Holon** *var.* Kholon; *prev.* Holon. Tel Aviv, C Israel 32°01′N 34°46′E
Holon *see* Holon
163 P7 **Hölönbuyr** *var.* Bayan. Dornod, E Mongolia 47°56′N 112°58′E
117 P8 **Holovanivs'k** *Rus.* Golovanevsk. Kirovohrads'ka Oblast', C Ukraine 48°21′N 30°26′E
95 F21 **Holstebro** Ringkøbing, W Denmark 56°22′N 08°38′E
95 F23 **Holsted** Ribe, W Denmark 55°30′N 08°54′E
29 T13 **Holstein** Iowa, C USA 42°29′N 95°32′W
Holsteinborg/Holsteinsborg/Holstenborg/Holstensborg *see* Sisimiut
21 O8 **Holston River** ⟿ Tennessee, S USA
31 Q9 **Holt** Michigan, N USA 42°38′N 84°31′W
98 N10 **Holten** Overijssel, E Netherlands 52°16′N 06°25′E
27 P3 **Holton** Kansas, C USA 39°27′N 95°44′W
27 U5 **Holts Summit** Missouri, C USA 38°38′N 92°07′W
35 X17 **Holtville** California, W USA 32°48′N 115°22′W
98 L5 **Holwerd** *Fris.* Holwert. Friesland, N Netherlands 53°22′N 05°51′E
Holwert *see* Holwerd
39 O11 **Holy Cross** Alaska, USA 62°12′N 159°46′W
37 R4 **Holy Cross, Mount Of The** ▲ Colorado, C USA 39°28′N 106°28′W
97 I18 **Holyhead** *Wel.* Caer Gybi. NW Wales, United Kingdom 53°19′N 04°38′W
97 H18 **Holy Island** *island* NW Wales, United Kingdom
96 L12 **Holy Island** *island* NE England, United Kingdom
37 W3 **Holyoke** Colorado, C USA 40°31′N 102°18′W
18 M11 **Holyoke** Massachusetts, NE USA 42°12′N 72°37′W
101 I14 **Holzminden** Niedersachsen, C Germany 51°49′N 09°27′E
81 G19 **Homa Bay** Nyanza, W Kenya 0°31′S 34°30′E
Homāyūnshahr *see* Khomeynīshahr
77 P11 **Hombori** Mopti, S Mali 15°13′N 01°39′W
101 E20 **Homburg** Saarland, SW Germany 49°20′N 07°20′E
9 S5 **Home Bay** *bay* Baffin Bay, Nunavut, NE Canada
Homenau *see* Humenné
39 Q13 **Homer** Alaska, USA 59°38′N 151°33′W
22 H4 **Homer** Louisiana, S USA 32°47′N 93°03′W
18 H10 **Homer** New York, NE USA 42°38′N 76°10′W
23 V7 **Homerville** Georgia, SE USA 31°02′N 82°45′W
23 Y16 **Homestead** Florida, SE USA 25°28′N 80°28′W
27 O9 **Hominy** Oklahoma, C USA 36°24′N 96°24′W
94 H8 **Hommelvik** Sør-Trøndelag, S Norway 63°24′N 10°48′E
95 C16 **Hommersåk** Rogaland, S Norway 58°55′N 05°51′E
155 H15 **Homnābād** Karnātaka, C India 17°46′N 77°08′E
22 J7 **Homochitto River** ⟿ Mississippi, S USA
83 N20 **Homoine** Inhambane, SE Mozambique 23°51′S 35°04′E
112 O12 **Homoljske Planine** ⛰ E Serbia
Homonna *see* Humenné
Homs *see* Al Khums, Libya
Homs *see* Ḥimṣ
119 P19 **Homyel'** *Rus.* Gomel'. Homyel'skaya Voblasts', SE Belarus 52°25′N 31°E
118 L12 **Homyel'** Vitsyebskaya Voblasts', N Belarus 55°20′N 28°52′E
119 L19 **Homyel'skaya Voblasts'** *prev. Rus.* Gomel'skaya Oblast'. ◐ *province* SE Belarus
Honan *see* Luoyang, China
Honan *see* Henan, China
164 U4 **Honbetsu** Hokkaidō, NE Japan 43°09′N 143°46′E
Honctő *see* Gurahonţ
54 E9 **Honda** Tolima, C Colombia 05°12′N 74°45′W
83 D24 **Hondeklip** *Afr.* Hondeklipbaai. Northern Cape, W South Africa 30°15′S 17°17′E
Hondeklipbaai *see* Hondeklip
11 Q13 **Hondo** Alberta, W Canada 54°43′N 113°14′W
164 C15 **Hondo** Kumamoto, Shimo-jima, SW Japan 32°28′N 130°12′E
25 Q12 **Hondo** Texas, SW USA 29°21′N 99°09′W
42 G1 **Hondo** ⟿ Central America
Hondo *see* Honshū
42 G6 **Honduras** *off.* Republic of Honduras. ◆ *republic* Central America
Honduras, Golfo de *see* Honduras, Gulf of
42 H4 **Honduras, Gulf of** *Sp.* Golfo de Honduras. *gulf* W Caribbean Sea
Honduras, Republic of *see* Honduras
11 V12 **Hone** Manitoba, C Canada 56°13′N 101°12′W
21 P12 **Honea Path** South Carolina, SE USA 34°27′N 82°23′W
95 H14 **Hønefoss** Buskerud, S Norway 60°10′N 10°15′E
31 S12 **Honey Creek** ⟿ Ohio, N USA
25 V5 **Honey Grove** Texas, SW USA 33°34′N 95°54′W
35 Q4 **Honey Lake** ◎ California, W USA
102 L4 **Honfleur** Calvados, N France 49°25′N 00°14′E
Hon Gai *see* Hông Gai
161 O8 **Hong'an** *prev.* Huang'an. Hubei, C China 31°20′N 114°43′E
Hongay *see* Hông Gai
167 T6 **Hông Gai** *var.* Hon Gai, Hongay. Quang Ninh, N Vietnam 20°57′N 107°06′E
161 O15 **Honghai Wan** *bay* N South China Sea
Hông Hà, Sông *see* Red River
161 O7 **Hong He** ⟿ C China
161 N9 **Hong Hu** ◎ C China
160 L11 **Hongjiang** Hunan, S China 27°09′N 109°58′E
Hongjiang *see* Wangcang
161 O15 **Hong Kong** *Chin.* Xianggang. Hong Kong, S China 22°17′N 114°09′E
160 L4 **Hongliu He** ⟿ C China
160 L4 **Hongliu He** ⟿ C China
159 P8 **Hongliuwan** *var.* Aksay, Aksay Kazakzu Zizhixian. Gansu, N China 39°25′N 94°09′E
159 P7 **Hongliuyuan** Gansu, N China 41°02′N 95°24′E
Hongor *see* Delgerekh
161 S8 **Hongqiao** ✕ (Shanghai) Shanghai Shi, E China 31°28′N 121°08′E
Hongshui *see* Minle
160 K14 **Hongshui He** ⟿ S China
160 M5 **Hongtong** *var.* Dahuaishu. Shanxi, C China 36°30′N 111°42′E
164 J15 **Hongū** Wakayama, Honshū, SW Japan 33°50′N 135°42′E
Honguedo, Détroit d' *see* Honguedo Passage
15 Y5 **Honguedo Passage** *var.* Honguedo Strait, *Fr.* Détroit d'Honguedo. *strait* Québec, E Canada
Honguedo Strait *see* Honguedo Passage
Hongwan *see* Hongwansi
159 S8 **Hongwansi** *var.* Sunan, Sunan Yugurzu Zizhixian; *prev.* Hongwan. Gansu, N China 38°55′N 99°29′E
163 X13 **Hongwŏn** E North Korea 40°03′N 127°54′E
160 H7 **Hongyuan** *var.* Qiongxi; *prev.* Hurama. Sichuan, C China 32°49′N 102°40′E
161 Q7 **Hongze Hu** *var.* Hung-tse Hu. ◎ E China
186 L9 **Honiara** ● (Solomon Islands) Guadalcanal, C Solomon Islands 09°27′S 159°56′E
165 P8 **Honjō** *var.* Honzyô, Yurihonjō. Akita, Honshū, C Japan 39°23′N 140°03′E
93 K18 **Honkajoki** Länsi-Suomi, SW Finland 62°00′N 22°15′E
92 K7 **Honningsvåg** Finnmark, N Norway 70°58′N 25°59′E
95 I19 **Hönö** Västra Götaland, S Sweden 57°42′N 11°39′E
38 G11 **Honoka'a** Hawaii, USA, C Pacific Ocean 20°04′N 155°27′W
38 G11 **Honoka'a** *var.* Honokaa. Hawaii, USA, C Pacific Ocean 20°04′N 155°27′W
Honokaa *see* Honoka'a
38 D9 **Honolulu** *state capital* O'ahu, Hawaii, USA, C Pacific Ocean 21°18′N 157°52′W
38 H11 **Honomū** *var.* Honomu. Hawaii, USA, C Pacific Ocean 19°51′N 155°06′W
105 P10 **Honrubia** Castilla-La Mancha, C Spain 39°36′N 02°17′W
164 M12 **Honshū** *var.* Hondo, Honsyû. *island* SW Japan
Honsyû *see* Honshū
Honte *see* Westerschelde
Honzyô *see* Honjō
8 K8 **Hood** ⟿ Nunavut, NW Canada
Hood Island *see* Española, Isla
32 H11 **Hood, Mount** ▲ Oregon, NW USA 45°22′N 121°41′W
32 H11 **Hood River** Oregon, NW USA 45°44′N 121°31′W
98 H10 **Hoofddorp** Noord-Holland, W Netherlands 52°18′N 04°41′E
99 G15 **Hoogerheide** Noord-Brabant, S Netherlands 51°25′N 04°19′E
98 N8 **Hoogeveen** Drenthe, NE Netherlands 52°44′N 06°30′E
98 O6 **Hoogezand-Sappemeer** Groningen, NE Netherlands 53°10′N 06°47′E
98 J8 **Hoogkarspel** Noord-Holland, NW Netherlands 52°42′N 04°59′E
98 N5 **Hoogkerk** Groningen, NE Netherlands 53°13′N 06°30′E
98 G13 **Hoogvliet** Zuid-Holland, SW Netherlands 51°51′N 04°23′E
26 I8 **Hooker** Oklahoma, C USA 36°51′N 101°12′W
97 E21 **Hook Head** *Ir.* Rinn Duáin. *headland* SE Ireland 52°07′N 06°55′W
Hook of Holland *see* Hoek van Holland
Hoolt *see* Tögrög
39 W13 **Hoonah** Chichagof Island, Alaska, USA 58°05′N 135°21′W
38 L11 **Hooper Bay** Alaska, USA 61°31′N 166°06′W
31 N13 **Hoopeston** Illinois, N USA 40°28′N 87°40′W
95 K22 **Höör** Skåne, S Sweden 55°55′N 13°33′E
98 I9 **Hoorn** Noord-Holland, NW Netherlands 52°38′N 05°04′E
18 L10 **Hoosic River** ⟿ New York, NE USA
Hoosier State *see* Indiana
35 Y11 **Hoover Dam** *dam* Arizona/Nevada, W USA
Höövör *see* Baruunbayan-Ulaan
Hope *see* Hope
137 Q11 **Hopa** Artvin, NE Turkey 41°23′N 41°28′E
18 J14 **Hopatcong** New Jersey, NE USA 40°55′N 74°39′W
10 M17 **Hope** British Columbia, SW Canada 49°21′N 121°28′W
39 R12 **Hope** Alaska, USA 60°55′N 149°38′W
27 T14 **Hope** Arkansas, C USA 33°40′N 93°36′W
31 P14 **Hope** Indiana, N USA 39°18′N 85°46′W
29 Q5 **Hope** North Dakota, N USA 47°18′N 97°42′W
13 Q7 **Hopedale** Newfoundland and Labrador, NE Canada 55°26′N 60°14′W
Hopeh/Hopei *see* Hebei
180 K13 **Hope, Lake** *salt lake* Western Australia
41 X13 **Hopelchén** Campeche, SE Mexico 19°46′N 89°50′W
21 U11 **Hope Mills** North Carolina, SE USA 34°58′N 78°57′W
183 O7 **Hope, Mount** New South Wales, SE Australia 32°49′S 145°55′E
92 P4 **Hopen** *island* SE Svalbard
197 Q4 **Hope, Point** *headland* Alaska, USA
12 M3 **Hopes Advance, Cap** *cape* Québec, NE Canada
182 L10 **Hopetoun** Victoria, SE Australia 35°46′S 142°23′E
83 H23 **Hopetown** Northern Cape, W South Africa 29°37′S 24°05′E
21 W6 **Hopewell** Virginia, NE USA 37°16′N 77°15′W
109 O7 **Hopfgarten im Brixental** Tirol, W Austria 47°28′N 12°14′E
181 N8 **Hopkins Lake** *salt lake* Western Australia
182 M12 **Hopkins River** ⟿ Victoria, SE Australia
20 I7 **Hopkinsville** Kentucky, S USA 36°50′N 87°30′W
34 M6 **Hopland** California, W USA 38°58′N 123°09′W
95 G24 **Hoptrup** Sønderjylland, SW Denmark 55°09′N 09°27′E
Hoqin Zuoyi Zhongji *see* Baokang
32 F9 **Hoquiam** Washington, NW USA 46°58′N 123°53′W
29 R6 **Horace** North Dakota, N USA 46°44′N 96°54′W
117 T14 **Hora Roman-Kash** ▲ S Ukraine 44°37′N 34°13′E
137 R12 **Horasan** Erzurum, NE Turkey 40°03′N 42°10′E
101 G22 **Horb am Neckar** Baden-Württemberg, S Germany 48°27′N 08°42′E
95 K23 **Hörby** Skåne, S Sweden 55°51′N 13°42′E
43 P16 **Horconcitos** Chiriquí, W Panama 08°20′N 82°10′W
95 C14 **Hordaland** ◐ *county* S Norway
116 H13 **Horezu** Vâlcea, SW Romania 45°06′N 24°00′E
108 G7 **Horgen** Zürich, N Switzerland 47°16′N 08°36′E
Horgo *see* Tariat
Horin *see* Fenglin
163 O13 **Horinger** Nei Mongol Zizhiqu, N China 40°23′N 111°48′E
Horiult *see* Bogd
11 U17 **Horizon** Saskatchewan, S Canada 49°33′N 105°05′W
192 K9 **Horizon Bank** *undersea feature* S Pacific Ocean
192 L10 **Horizon Deep** *undersea feature* W Pacific Ocean
95 L14 **Hörken** Örebro, S Sweden 60°03′N 14°55′E
119 O15 **Horki** *Rus.* Gorki. Mahilyowskaya Voblasts', E Belarus 54°18′N 31°E
195 O10 **Horlick Mountains** ⛰ Antarctica
117 X7 **Horlivka** *Rom.* Adâncata, *Rus.* Gorlovka. Donets'ka Oblast', E Ukraine 48°19′N 38°04′E
143 V11 **Hormak** Sīstān va Balūchestān, SE Iran 30°00′N 60°50′E
143 R13 **Hormozgān** *off.* Ostān-e Hormozgān. ◐ *province* S Iran
Hormozgān, Ostān-e *see* Hormozgān
Hormoz, Tangeh-ye *see* Hormuz, Strait of
141 W6 **Hormuz, Strait of** *var.* Strait of Ormuz, *Per.* Tangeh-ye Hormoz. *strait* Iran/Oman
109 W2 **Horn** Niederösterreich, NE Austria 48°40′N 15°40′E
95 M18 **Horn** Östergötland, S Sweden 57°54′N 15°49′E
8 J9 **Horn** ⟿ Northwest Territories, NW Canada
Hornád *see* Hernád
8 I6 **Hornaday** ⟿ Northwest Territories, NW Canada
92 H13 **Hornavan** ◎ N Sweden
65 C24 **Hornby Mountains** *hill range* West Falkland, Falkland Islands
Horn, Cape *see* Hornos, Cabo de
97 O18 **Horncastle** E England, United Kingdom 53°12′N 00°07′W
95 N14 **Horndal** Dalarna, C Sweden 60°16′N 16°25′E
93 I16 **Hörnefors** Västerbotten, N Sweden 63°37′N 19°54′E
18 F11 **Hornell** New York, NE USA 42°19′N 77°38′W
Horné Mesto *see* Kysucké Nové Mesto
12 F12 **Hornepayne** Ontario, S Canada 49°14′N 84°48′W
94 D10 **Hornindalsvatnet** ◎ S Norway
101 G22 **Hornisgrinde** ▲ SW Germany 48°37′N 08°13′E
22 M9 **Horn Island** *island* Mississippi, S USA
Hornja Łužica *see* Oberlausitz
63 J26 **Hornos, Cabo de** *Eng.* Cape Horn. *headland* S Chile 55°52′S 67°00′W
117 S10 **Hornostayivka** Khersons'ka Oblast', S Ukraine 47°00′N 33°42′E
183 T9 **Hornsby** New South Wales, SE Australia 33°44′S 151°08′E
97 O16 **Hornsea** E England, United Kingdom 53°54′N 00°10′W
94 O11 **Hornslandet** *peninsula* C Sweden
95 H22 **Hornslet** Århus, C Denmark 56°19′N 10°20′E
92 O4 **Hornsundtind** ▲ S Svalbard 76°54′N 16°07′E
Horochów *see* Horokhiv
Horodenka *see* Gorodenka
117 Q2 **Horodnya** *Rus.* Gorodnya. Chernihivs'ka Oblast', NE Ukraine 51°54′N 31°30′E
116 K6 **Horodok** Khmel'nyts'ka Oblast', W Ukraine 49°10′N 26°34′E
116 H5 **Horodok** *Pol.* Gródek Jagielloński, *Rus.* Gorodok, Gorodok Yagellonski. L'vivs'ka Oblast', NW Ukraine 49°48′N 23°39′E
117 Q6 **Horodyshche** *Rus.* Gorodishche. Cherkas'ka Oblast', C Ukraine 49°19′N 31°27′E
165 T3 **Horokanai** Hokkaidō, NE Japan 44°02′N 142°08′E
116 J4 **Horokhiv** *Pol.* Horochów, *Rus.* Gorokhov. Volyns'ka Oblast', NW Ukraine 50°31′N 24°50′E
165 T4 **Horoshiri-dake** *var.* Horosiri Dake. ▲ Hokkaidō, N Japan 42°43′N 142°41′E
Horosiri Dake *see* Horoshiri-dake
111 C17 **Hořovice** *Ger.* Horowitz. Střední Čechy, W Czech Republic 49°49′N 13°53′E
Horowitz *see* Hořovice
Horqin Zuoyi Houqi *see* Ganjig
Horqin Zuoyi Zhongqi *see* Bayan Huxu
62 O5 **Horqueta** Concepción, C Paraguay 23°24′S 56°53′W
55 O12 **Horqueta Minas** Amazonas, S Venezuela 02°20′N 63°32′W
95 J20 **Horred** Västra Götaland, S Sweden 57°22′N 12°25′E
151 J19 **Horsburgh Atoll** *var.* Goidhoo Atoll. *atoll* N Maldives
20 K7 **Horse Cave** Kentucky, S USA 37°10′N 85°54′W
37 V6 **Horse Creek** ⟿ Colorado, C USA
27 S6 **Horse Creek** ⟿ Missouri, C USA
18 G11 **Horseheads** New York, NE USA 42°10′N 76°49′W
37 P13 **Horse Mount** ▲ New Mexico, SW USA 33°58′N 108°10′W
95 G22 **Horsens** Vejle, C Denmark 55°53′N 09°53′E
65 F25 **Horse Pasture Point** *headland* W Saint Helena 15°57′S 05°46′W
33 N13 **Horseshoe Bend** Idaho, NW USA 43°55′N 116°11′W
36 L13 **Horseshoe Reservoir** ☒ Arizona, SW USA
64 M9 **Horseshoe Seamounts** *undersea feature* E Atlantic Ocean 36°30′N 15°00′W
182 L11 **Horsham** Victoria, SE Australia 36°44′S 142°13′E
97 O23 **Horsham** SE England, United Kingdom 51°01′N 00°21′W
99 M15 **Horst** Limburg, SE Netherlands 51°30′N 06°05′E
64 N2 **Horta** Faial, Azores, Portugal, NE Atlantic Ocean 38°32′N 28°39′W
95 H16 **Horten** Vestfold, S Norway 59°25′N 10°25′E
111 M23 **Hortobágy-Berettyó** ⟿ E Hungary
27 Q3 **Horton** Kansas, C USA 39°39′N 95°31′W
8 I7 **Horton** ⟿ Northwest Territories, NW Canada
95 I23 **Hørve** Vestsjælland, E Denmark 55°46′N 11°28′E
95 L22 **Hörvik** Blekinge, S Sweden 56°01′N 14°45′E
Horvot Haluza *see* Horvot Halutsa
14 E7 **Horwood Lake** ◎ Ontario, S Canada
116 K4 **Horyn'** *Rus.* Goryn. ⟿ NW Ukraine
81 I14 **Hosa'ina** *var.* Hosseina, *It.* Hosanna. Southern Nationalities, S Ethiopia 07°38′N 37°58′E
Hosanna *see* Hosa'ina
101 H18 **Hösbach** Bayern, C Germany 50°00′N 09°12′E
Hose Mountains *see* Hose, Pegunungan
169 T9 **Hose, Pegunungan** *var.* Hose Mountains. ⛰ East Malaysia
148 L15 **Hoshāb** Baluchistān, SW Pakistan 26°01′N 63°51′E
154 H10 **Hoshangābād** Madhya Pradesh, C India 22°44′N 77°45′E
116 L4 **Hoshcha** Rivnens'ka Oblast', NW Ukraine 50°37′N 26°38′E
152 I7 **Hoshiārpur** Punjab, NW India 31°30′N 75°59′E
Höshööt *see* Öldziyt
99 M23 **Hosingen** Diekirch, NE Luxembourg 50°01′N 06°05′E
186 G7 **Hoskins** New Britain, E Papua New Guinea 05°28′S 150°25′E
155 G17 **Hospet** Karnātaka, C India 15°16′N 76°20′E
104 K4 **Hospital de Orbigo** Castilla-León, N Spain 42°27′N 05°53′W
Hospitalet *see* L'Hospitalet de Llobregat
92 N13 **Hossa** Oulu, E Finland 65°28′N 29°36′E
Hosseina *see* Hosa'ina
Hosszúmezjő *see* Câmpulung Moldovenesc
63 I25 **Hoste, Isla** *island* S Chile
117 O4 **Hostomel'** *Rus.* Gostomel'. Kyyivs'ka Oblast', N Ukraine 50°41′N 30°15′E
155 H20 **Hosūr** Tamil Nādu, SE India 12°45′N 77°51′E
167 N8 **Hot** Chiang Mai, NW Thailand 18°07′N 98°34′E
158 G10 **Hotan** *var.* Khotan, *Chin.* Ho-t'ien. Xinjiang Uygur Zizhiqu, NW China 37°10′N 79°51′E
158 H9 **Hotan He** ⟿ NW China
83 G22 **Hotazel** Northern Cape, N South Africa 27°12′S 22°58′E
37 Q5 **Hotchkiss** Colorado, C USA 38°47′N 107°43′W
35 V7 **Hot Creek Range** ⛰ Nevada, W USA
Hote *see* Hoti
171 T13 **Hoti** *var.* Hote. Pulau Seram, E Indonesia 02°58′S 130°19′E
Ho-t'ien *see* Hotan
Hotin *see* Khotyn
93 H15 **Hoting** Jämtland, C Sweden 64°07′N 16°14′E
162 L14 **Hotong Qagan Nur** ◎ N China
162 J8 **Hotont** Arhangay, C Mongolia 47°21′N 102°27′E
27 T12 **Hot Springs** Arkansas, C USA 34°31′N 93°03′W
28 J11 **Hot Springs** South Dakota, N USA 43°26′N 103°29′W
21 S5 **Hot Springs** Virginia, NE USA 38°00′N 79°50′W
35 Q4 **Hot Springs Peak** ▲ California, W USA 40°23′N 120°06′W
27 T12 **Hot Springs Village** Arkansas, C USA 34°39′N 93°03′W
Hotspur Bank *see* Hotspur Seamount
65 J16 **Hotspur Seamount** *var.* Hotspur Bank. *undersea feature* C Atlantic Ocean 18°00′S 35°00′W
8 J8 **Hottah Lake** ◎ Northwest Territories, NW Canada
44 K9 **Hotte, Massif de la** ⛰ SW Haiti
99 K21 **Hotton** Luxembourg, SE Belgium 50°18′N 05°25′E
Hötzing *see* Hațeg
187 P17 **Houaïlou** Province Nord, C New Caledonia 21°17′S 165°37′E
74 K5 **Houari Boumediène** ✕ (Alger) N Algeria 36°38′N 03°15′E
167 P6 **Houayxay** *var.* Ban Houayxay. Bokèo, N Laos 20°17′N 100°27′E
103 N5 **Houdan** Yvelines, N France 48°48′N 01°36′E
99 F20 **Houdeng-Goegnies** *var.* Houdeng-Gœgnies. Hainaut, S Belgium 50°29′N 04°10′E
102 K14 **Houeillès** Lot-et-Garonne, SW France 44°15′N 00°02′E
99 L22 **Houffalize** Luxembourg, SE Belgium 50°08′N 05°47′E
30 M3 **Houghton** Michigan, N USA 47°07′N 88°34′W
31 Q7 **Houghton Lake** Michigan, N USA 44°18′N 84°45′W
31 Q7 **Houghton Lake** ◎ Michigan, N USA
19 T3 **Houlton** Maine, NE USA 46°09′N 67°50′W
160 M5 **Houma** Shanxi, C China 35°36′N 111°23′E
193 U16 **Houma** Tongatapu, S Tonga 21°18′S 174°55′W
22 J10 **Houma** Louisiana, S USA 29°35′N 90°44′W
196 V16 **Houma Taloa** *headland* Tongatapu, S Tonga 21°16′S 175°08′W
77 O13 **Houndé** SW Burkina 11°34′N 03°31′W
102 J12 **Hourtin-Carcans, Lac d'** ◎ SW France
36 J5 **House Range** ⛰ Utah, W USA
10 K13 **Houston** British Columbia, SW Canada 54°24′N 126°39′W
39 R11 **Houston** Alaska, USA 61°37′N 149°50′W
29 X10 **Houston** Minnesota, N USA 43°45′N 91°34′W
22 M3 **Houston** Mississippi, S USA 33°54′N 89°00′W
27 V7 **Houston** Missouri, C USA 37°19′N 91°59′W
25 W11 **Houston** Texas, SW USA 29°46′N 95°22′W
25 W11 **Houston** ✕ Texas, SW USA 30°03′N 95°18′W
98 J12 **Houten** Utrecht, C Netherlands 52°02′N 05°10′E
99 K17 **Houthalen** Limburg, NE Belgium 51°02′N 05°22′E
99 I22 **Houyet** Namur, SE Belgium 50°10′N 05°00′E
95 H22 **Hov** Århus, C Denmark 55°54′N 10°13′E
95 L17 **Hova** Västra Götaland, S Sweden 58°52′N 14°13′E
162 E6 **Hovd** *var.* Khovd, Kobdo; *prev.* Jirgalanta. Hovd, W Mongolia 47°59′N 91°41′E
162 J10 **Hovd** *var.* Dund-Us. Hovd, W Mongolia 48°06′N 91°22′E
162 E6 **Hovd** *var.* Dund-Us. Hovd, W Mongolia 48°06′N 91°22′E
162 E7 **Hovd** ◐ *province* W Mongolia
Hovd *see* Bogd
162 C5 **Hovd Gol** ⟿ NW Mongolia
97 O23 **Hove** SE England, United Kingdom 50°49′N 00°11′W
29 N8 **Hoven** South Dakota, N USA 45°12′N 99°47′W
116 I8 **Hoverla, Hora** *Rus.* Gora Goverla. ▲ W Ukraine 48°09′N 24°30′E
Höviyn Am *see* Gurvanbulag
95 M21 **Hovmantorp** Kronoberg, S Sweden 56°47′N 15°08′E
163 N11 **Hövsgöl** Dornogovĭ, SE Mongolia 43°35′N 109°40′E
162 I5 **Hövsgöl** ◐ *province* N Mongolia
Hovsgol, Lake *see* Hövsgöl Nuur
162 J5 **Hövsgöl Nuur** *var.* Lake Hovsgol. ◎ N Mongolia
78 L9 **Howa, Ouadi** *var.* Wādi Howar. ⟿ Chad/Sudan *see also* Howar, Wādi
Howa, Ouadi *see* Howar, Wādi
27 P7 **Howard** Kansas, C USA 37°27′N 96°16′W
29 Q10 **Howard** South Dakota, N USA 43°58′N 97°31′W
25 N10 **Howard Draw** *valley* Texas, SW USA
29 U8 **Howard Lake** Minnesota, N USA 45°03′N 94°03′W
80 B8 **Howar, Wādi** *var.* Ouadi Howa. ⟿ Chad/Sudan *see also* Howa, Ouadi
Howar, Wādi *see* Howa, Ouadi
25 U5 **Howe** Texas, SW USA 33°29′N 96°38′W
183 R12 **Howe, Cape** *headland* New South Wales/Victoria, SE Australia 37°30′S 149°58′E
31 R9 **Howell** Michigan, N USA 42°36′N 83°55′W
28 L9 **Howes** South Dakota, N USA 44°34′N 102°03′W
83 K23 **Howick** KwaZulu/Natal, E South Africa 29°29′S 30°13′E
Howrah *see* Hāora
27 W9 **Hoxie** Arkansas, C USA 36°03′N 90°58′W
26 J3 **Hoxie** Kansas, C USA 39°21′N 100°27′W
101 I14 **Höxter** Nordrhein-Westfalen, W Germany 51°46′N 09°22′E
158 K6 **Hoxud** *var.* Tewulike. Xinjiang Uygur Zizhiqu, NW China 42°18′N 86°51′E
96 J5 **Hoy** *island* N Scotland, United Kingdom
43 S17 **Hoya, Cerro** ▲ S Panama 07°22′N 80°38′W
94 D12 **Høyanger** Sogn Og Fjordane, S Norway 61°13′N 06°05′E
101 P15 **Hoyerswerda** *Lus.* Wojerecy. Sachsen, E Germany 51°27′N 14°18′E
164 R14 **Hōyo-kaikyō** *var.* Hayasui-seto. *strait* SW Japan
104 J8 **Hoyos** Extremadura, W Spain 40°10′N 06°43′W
29 W4 **Hoyt Lakes** Minnesota, N USA 47°31′N 92°08′W
87 V2 **Hoyvík** Streymoy, N Faeroe Islands
137 O14 **Hozat** Tunceli, E Turkey 39°09′N 39°13′E
Hôzyô *see* Hōjō
167 N8 **Hpa-an** *var.* Pa-an. Kayin State, S Myanmar (Burma) 16°51′N 97°37′E
Hpyu *see* Phyu
111 F16 **Hradec Králové** *Ger.* Königgrätz. Královéhradecký Kraj, N Czech Republic 50°13′N 15°50′E
Hradecký Kraj *see* Královehradecký Kraj
111 B16 **Hradiště** *Ger.* Burgstadlberg. ▲ NW Czech Republic 50°12′N 13°04′E
117 R6 **Hradyz'k** *Rus.* Gradizhsk. Poltavs'ka Oblast', NE Ukraine 49°14′N 33°07′E
119 M16 **Hradzyanka** *Rus.* Grodzyanka. Mahilyowskaya Voblasts', E Belarus 53°33′N 28°45′E
119 F16 **Hrandzichy** *Rus.* Grandichi. Hrodzyenskaya Voblasts', W Belarus 53°43′N 23°49′E
111 H18 **Hranice** *Ger.* Mährisch-Weisskirchen. Olomoucký Kraj, E Czech Republic 49°34′N 17°45′E
112 I13 **Hrasnica** Federacija Bosna I Hercegovina, SE Bosnia and Herzegovina 43°48′N 18°19′E
109 V11 **Hrastnik** C Slovenia 46°09′N 15°08′E
137 U12 **Hrazdan** *Rus.* Razdan. C Armenia 40°30′N 44°50′E
137 T12 **Hrazdan** *var.* Zanga, *Rus.* Razdan. ⟿ C Armenia
117 R5 **Hrebinka** *Rus.* Grebenka. Poltavs'ka Oblast', NE Ukraine 50°08′N 32°27′E
119 K17 **Hresk** *Rus.* Gresk. Minskaya Voblasts', C Belarus 53°10′N 27°29′E
Hrisoupoli *see* Chrysoúpoli
119 F16 **Hrodna** *Pol.* Grodno. Hrodzyenskaya Voblasts', W Belarus 53°40′N 23°50′E
119 F16 **Hrodzyenskaya Voblasts'** *prev. Rus.* Grodnenskaya Oblast'. ◐ *province* W Belarus
111 J21 **Hron** *Ger.* Gran, *Hung.* Garam. ⟿ C Slovakia
111 Q14 **Hrubieszów** *Rus.* Grubeshov. Lubelskie, E Poland 50°49′N 23°53′E
112 F13 **Hrvace** Split-Dalmacija, SE Croatia 43°46′N 16°35′E
Hrvatska *see* Croatia
112 F10 **Hrvatska Kostanjnica** *var.* Kostajnica. Sisak-Moslavina, C Croatia 45°14′N 16°35′E
Hrvatsko Grahovi *see* Bosansko Grahovo
116 K6 **Hrymayliv** *Pol.* Gizymałów, *Rus.* Grimaylov. Ternopil's'ka Oblast', W Ukraine 49°18′N 26°02′E
167 N4 **Hsenwi** Shan State, E Myanmar (Burma) 23°20′N 97°59′E
Hsia-men *see* Xiamen
Hsiang-t'an *see* Xiangtan
Hsi Chiang *see* Xi Jiang
167 N6 **Hsihseng** Shan State, C Myanmar (Burma) 20°07′N 97°17′E
161 S13 **Hsinchu** N Taiwan 24°48′N 120°59′E
Hsing-K'ai Hu *see* Khanka, Lake
Hsi-ning/Hsining *see* Xining
Hsinking *see* Changchun
Hsin-yang *see* Xinyang
161 S14 **Hsinying** *var.* Sinying, *Jap.* Shinei. C Taiwan 23°12′N 120°15′E
167 N4 **Hsipaw** Shan State, C Myanmar (Burma) 22°32′N 97°12′E
Hsu-chou *see* Xuzhou
161 S13 **Hsüeh Shan** ▲ N Taiwan

◆ Country ◇ Dependent Territory ◐ Administrative Regions ▲ Mountain ⛰ Volcano ◎ Lake
● Country Capital ○ Dependent Territory Capital ✕ International Airport ⛰ Mountain Range ⟿ River ☒ Reservoir

HTAWEI – IDER

Htawei see Dawei
Hu see Shanghai Shi
83 B18 Huab W Namibia
57 M21 Huacaya Chuquisaca, S Bolivia 20°45´S 63°42´W
57 J19 Huachacalla Oruro, SW Bolivia 18°47´S 68°23´W
159 X9 Huachi var. Rouyuan, Rouyuanchengzi. Gansu, C China 36°24´N 107°58´E
57 N16 Huachi, Laguna ◎ N Bolivia
57 D14 Huacho Lima, W Peru 11°05´S 77°36´W
163 Y7 Huachuan Heilongjiang, NE China 46°57´S 130°48´E
163 P12 Huade Nei Mongol Zizhiqu, N China 41°52´N 113°58´E
163 W10 Huadian Jilin, NE China 42°59´N 126°38´E
56 E13 Huagaruncho, Cordillera ▲ C Peru
Hua Hin see Ban Hua Hin
191 S10 Huahine island Îles Sous le Vent, W French Polynesia
Huahua, Rio see Wawa, Río
167 R8 Huai E Thailand
161 Q7 Huai'an var. Qingjiang; prev. Huaiyin. Jiangsu, E China 33°33´N 119°03´E
161 P6 Huaibei Anhui, E China 34°00´N 116°48´E
Huaide see Gongzhuling
157 T10 Huai He C China
160 L11 Huaihua Hunan, S China 27°36´N 109°57´E
161 N14 Huaiji Guangdong, S China 23°54´N 112°12´E
161 O2 Huailai var. Shacheng. Hebei, E China 40°22´N 115°34´E
161 P7 Huainan var. Huai-nan, Hwainan. Anhui, E China 32°37´N 116°57´E
Huai-nan see Huainan
161 N2 Huairen var. Yunzhong. Shanxi, C China 35°28´N 110°29´E
161 O7 Huaiyang Henan, C China 33°44´N 114°55´E
161 Q7 Huaiyin Jiangsu, E China 33°31´N 119°03´E
Huaiyin see Huai'an
167 N16 Huai Yot Trang, SW Thailand 07°45´N 99°36´E
41 Q15 Huajuapan var. Huajuapan de León. Oaxaca, SE Mexico 17°50´N 97°48´W
Huajuapan de León see Huajuapan
41 O9 Hualahuises Nuevo León, NE Mexico 24°56´N 99°42´W
36 I11 Hualapai Mountains ▲▲ Arizona, SW USA
36 I11 Hualapai Peak ▲ Arizona, SW USA 35°04´N 113°54´W
62 J7 Hualfín Catamarca, N Argentina 27°15´S 66°53´W
161 T13 Hualien var. Hwalien, Jap. Karen. C Taiwan 23°58´N 121°35´E
56 E10 Huallaga, Río N Peru
159 U10 Hualong Qinghai, C China 36°06´N 102°16´E
56 C11 Huamachuco La Libertad, C Peru 07°50´S 78°01´W
41 Q14 Huamantla Tlaxcala, S Mexico 19°18´N 97°57´W
82 C13 Huambo Port. Nova Lisboa. Huambo, C Angola 12°48´S 15°45´E
82 B13 Huambo ◆ province C Angola
41 P15 Huamuxtitlán Guerrero, S Mexico 17°49´N 98°34´W
163 Y8 Huanan Heilongjiang, NE China 46°21´N 130°43´E
63 H17 Huancache, Sierra ▲▲ SW Argentina
57 I17 Huancané Puno, SE Peru 15°10´S 69°44´W
57 F16 Huancapi Ayacucho, C Peru 13°40´S 74°05´W
57 E15 Huancavelica Huancavelica, SW Peru 12°45´S 75°03´W
57 E15 Huancavelica off. Departamento de Huancavelica. ◆ department W Peru
Huancavelica, Departamento de see Huancavelica
57 E14 Huancayo Junín, C Peru 12°03´S 75°14´W
57 K20 Huanchaca, Cerro ▲ S Bolivia 20°12´S 66°35´W
Huancheng see Huanxian
56 C12 Huandoy, Nevado ▲ W Peru 08°48´S 77°33´W
Huang'an see Hong'an
161 O8 Huangchuan Henan, C China 32°00´N 115°02´E
161 O9 Huanggang Hubei, C China 30°27´N 114°48´E
Huang Hai see Yellow Sea
157 Q8 Huang He var. Yellow River. C China
Huanghe see Madoi
161 Q4 Huanghe Kou delta E China
Huangheyan see Madoi
160 L5 Huangling Shaanxi, C China 35°40´N 109°14´E
161 O9 Huangpi Hubei, C China 30°53´N 114°22´E
163 P13 Huangqi Hai ◎ N China
161 Q9 Huangshan var. Tunxi. Anhui, E China 29°43´N 118°20´E
161 Q9 Huangshan ▲ Anhui, China 30°06´N 118°04´E
161 O9 Huangshi var. Huang-shih, Hwangshih. Hubei, C China 30°14´N 115E
Huang-shih see Huangshi
160 L5 Huangtu Gaoyuan plateau C China
61 B22 Huanguelén Buenos Aires, E Argentina 37°02´S 61°57´W
161 S10 Huangyan Zhejiang, SE China 28°39´N 121°19´E
159 T10 Huangyuan Qinghai, C China 36°40´N 101°12´E
159 T10 Huangzhong var. Lushar. Qinghai, C China 36°31´N 101°32´E
163 W12 Huanren var. Huanren Manzu Zizhixian. Liaoning, NE China 41°16´N 125°25´E
Huanren Manzu Zizhixian see Huanren
57 F15 Huanta Ayacucho, C Peru 12°54´S 74°13´W
56 E13 Huánuco Huánuco, C Peru 09°58´S 76°16´W
56 D13 Huánuco off. Departamento de Huánuco. ◆ department C Peru
Huánuco, Departamento de see Huánuco
57 K19 Huanuni Oruro, W Bolivia 18°15´S 66°48´W
159 X9 Huanxian var. Huancheng. Gansu, C China 36°30´N 107°20´E
161 S12 Huap'ing Yu island N Taiwan
62 H3 Huara Tarapacá, N Chile 19°59´S 69°42´W
57 D14 Huaral Lima, W Peru 11°31´S 77°10´W
Huarás see Huaraz
56 D13 Huaraz var. Huarás. Ancash, W Peru 09°31´S 77°32´W
57 I16 Huari Huari, Río S Peru
56 C13 Huarmey Ancash, W Peru 10°03´S 78°08´W
40 H4 Huásabas Sonora, NW Mexico 29°47´N 109°18´W
56 D8 Huasaga, Río Ecuador/Peru
167 O15 Hua Sai Nakhon Si Thammarat, SW Thailand 08°02´N 100°18´E
56 D12 Huascarán, Nevado ▲ W Peru 09°01´S 77°27´W
62 G8 Huasco Atacama, N Chile 28°30´S 71°15´W
62 G8 Huasco, Río C Chile
159 S11 Huashikia Qinghai, W China
40 G7 Huatabampo Sonora, NW Mexico 26°49´N 109°40´W
159 W10 Huating var. Donghua. Gansu, C China 35°13´N 106°39´E
167 S7 Huatt, Phou ▲ N Vietnam 19°45´N 104°48´E
41 Q14 Huatusco var. Huatusco de Chicuellar. Veracruz-Llave, C Mexico 19°13´N 96°57´W
Huatusco de Chicuellar see Huatusco
41 P13 Huauchinango Puebla, S Mexico 20°11´N 98°04´W
Huaunta see Wounta
41 R15 Huautla var. Huautla de Jiménez. Oaxaca, SE Mexico 18°10´N 96°51´W
Huautla de Jiménez see Huautla
161 O5 Huaxian var. Daokou, Hua Xian. Henan, C China 35°33´N 114°30´E
Hua Xian see Huaxian
Huazangsi see Tianzhu
29 V13 Hubbard Iowa, C USA 42°18´N 93°18´W
25 U8 Hubbard Texas, SW USA 31°52´N 96°43´W
25 Q6 Hubbard Creek Lake ◎ Texas, SW USA
31 R6 Hubbard Lake ◎ Michigan, N USA
160 M9 Hubei var. E, Hubei Sheng, Hupeh, Hupei. ◆ province C China
Hubei Sheng see Hubei
109 P8 Huben Tirol, W Austria 46°55´N 12°35´E
31 R13 Huber Heights Ohio, N USA 39°50´N 84°07´W
155 F17 Hubli Karnātaka, SW India 15°20´N 75°14´E
163 X12 Huch'ang N North Korea 41°25´N 127°04´E
97 M18 Hucknall C England, United Kingdom 53°02´N 01°11´W
97 L17 Huddersfield N England, United Kingdom 53°39´N 01°47´W
95 O16 Huddinge Stockholm, C Sweden 59°15´N 17°57´E
94 N11 Hudiksvall Gävleborg, C Sweden 61°45´N 17°12´E
29 W13 Hudson Iowa, C USA 42°24´N 92°27´W
19 O11 Hudson Massachusetts, NE USA 42°24´N 71°34´W
31 Q11 Hudson Michigan, N USA 41°51´N 84°21´W
30 H6 Hudson Wisconsin, N USA 44°59´N 92°43´W
11 V14 Hudson Bay Saskatchewan, S Canada 52°51´N 102°23´W
12 G6 Hudson Bay bay NE Canada
195 T16 Hudson, Cape headland Antarctica 68°15´S 154°00´E
Hudson, Détroit d' see Hudson Strait
27 Q9 Hudson, Lake ⊠ Oklahoma, C USA
18 K9 Hudson River New Jersey/New York, NE USA
10 M12 Hudson's Hope British Columbia, W Canada 56°03´N 121°59´W
12 L2 Hudson Strait Fr. Détroit d'Hudson. strait Northwest Territories/Québec, NE Canada
Hudūd ash Shamālīyah, Minṭaqat al see Al Ḥudūd ash Shamālīyah
Hudur see Xuddur
167 U9 Huê Thưa Thiên-Huê, C Vietnam 16°28´N 107°35´E
104 J7 Huebra W Spain
24 H8 Hueco Mountains ▲▲ Texas, SW USA
116 G10 Huedin Hung. Bánffyhunyad. Cluj, NW Romania 46°52´N 23°02´E
40 J10 Huehuento, Cerro ▲ C Mexico 24°04´N 105°42´W
42 B5 Huehuetenango Huehuetenango, W Guatemala 15°19´N 91°26´W
42 B4 Huehuetenango off. Departamento de Huehuetenango. ◆ department W Guatemala
Huehuetenango, Departamento de see Huehuetenango
40 L11 Huejuquilla Jalisco, SW Mexico 22°40´N 103°52´W
41 P12 Huejutla var. Huejutla de Reyes. Hidalgo, C Mexico 21°10´N 98°25´W
Huejutla de Reyes see Huejutla
102 G6 Huelgoat Finistère, NW France 48°22´N 03°45´W
105 O13 Huelma Andalucía, S Spain 37°39´N 03°28´W
104 I14 Huelva anc. Onuba. Andalucía, SW Spain 37°15´N 06°56´W
104 I13 Huelva ◆ province Andalucía, SW Spain
104 J13 Huelva SW Spain
105 Q14 Huércal-Overa Andalucía, S Spain 37°23´N 01°56´W
37 Q9 Huerfano Mountain ▲ New Mexico, SW USA 36°25´N 107°50´W
37 T7 Huerfano River Colorado, C USA
105 S12 Huertas, Cabo headland SE Spain 38°21´N 00°25´W
105 R6 Huerva N Spain
105 S4 Huesca anc. Osca. Aragón, NE Spain 42°08´N 00°25´W
105 T4 Huesca ◆ province Aragón, NE Spain
105 P13 Huéscar Andalucía, S Spain 37°39´N 02°32´W
41 N15 Huetamo var. Huetamo de Núñez. Michoacán, SW Mexico 18°36´N 100°54´W
Huetamo de Núñez see Huetamo
105 P8 Huete Castilla-La Mancha, C Spain 40°09´N 02°42´W
23 P4 Hueytown Alabama, S USA 33°27´N 87°00´W
28 L16 Hugh Butler Lake ⊠ Nebraska, C USA
181 V6 Hughenden Queensland, NE Australia 20°57´S 144°16´E
182 A6 Hughes South Australia 30°41´S 129°31´E
39 P8 Hughes Alaska, USA 66°03´N 154°15´W
27 X11 Hughes Arkansas, C USA 34°57´N 90°28´W
25 W6 Hughes Springs Texas, SW USA 33°00´N 94°37´W
153 S17 Hugli N India
37 V5 Hugo Colorado, C USA 39°08´N 103°28´W
27 Q13 Hugo Oklahoma, C USA 34°01´N 95°31´W
27 Q13 Hugo Lake ⊠ Oklahoma, C USA
26 H7 Hugoton Kansas, C USA 37°11´N 101°22´W
Huhehot/Huhohaote see Hohhot
Huhttán see Kvikkjokk
161 R13 Hui'an var. Luocheng. Fujian, SE China 25°06´N 118°45´E
184 O9 Huiarau Range ▲▲ North Island, New Zealand
83 D22 Huib-Hoch Plateau plateau S Namibia
41 O13 Huichapán Hidalgo, C Mexico 20°24´N 99°40´W
Huicheng see Shexian
163 W13 Hŭich'ŏn C North Korea 40°09´N 126°17´E
83 B15 Huíla ◆ province SW Angola
54 E12 Huila off. Departamento del Huila. ◆ province S Colombia
Huila, Departamento del see Huila
54 D11 Huila, Nevado del elevation C Colombia
83 B15 Huíla Plateau plateau S Angola
160 G12 Huili Sichuan, C China 26°39´N 102°13´E
161 P4 Huimin Shandong, E China 37°29´N 117°30´E
163 W11 Huinan var. Chaoyang. Jilin, NE China 42°40´N 126°03´E
62 K12 Huinca Renancó Córdoba, C Argentina 34°51´S 64°22´W
159 V10 Huining var. Huishi. Gansu, C China 35°42´N 105°01´E
Huishi see Huining
160 J12 Huishui var. Heping. Guizhou, S China 26°07´N 106°39´E
102 L6 Huisne NW France
98 L12 Huissen Gelderland, SE Netherlands 51°57´N 05°57´E
159 N11 Huiten Nur ◎ C China
93 K19 Huittinen Länsi-Suomi, SW Finland 61°11´N 22°40´E
41 O15 Huitzuco var. Huitzuco de los Figueroa. Guerrero, S Mexico 18°18´N 99°22´W
Huitzuco de los Figueroa see Huitzuco
159 W11 Huixian var. Hui Xian. Gansu, C China 33°48´N 106°02´E
Hui Xian see Huixian
41 V17 Huixtla Chiapas, SE Mexico 15°09´N 92°30´W
160 H12 Huize var. Zhongping. Yunnan, SW China 26°28´N 103°18´E
98 J10 Huizen Noord-Holland, C Netherlands 52°17´N 05°15´E
161 O14 Huizhou Guangdong, S China 23°02´N 114°28´E
162 J6 Hujirt Arhangay, C Mongolia 48°49´N 101°20´E
Hujirt see Tsetserleg, Övörhangay, Mongolia
Hujirt see Delgerhaan, Töv, Mongolia
Hukagawa see Fukagawa
163 W17 Hŭksan-chedo var. Hŭksan-chedo. island group SW South Korea
Hŭksan-chedo see Hŭksan-chedo
Hukue see Fukue
Hukui see Fukui
83 G20 Hukuntsi Kgalagadi, SW Botswana 23°59´S 21°44´E
Hukuoka see Fukuoka
Hukusima see Fukushima
Hukutiyama see Fukuchiyama
Hukuyama see Fukuyama
163 W8 Hulan Heilongjiang, NE China 45°59´N 126°37´E
163 W8 Hulan He NE China
31 Q4 Hulbert Lake ◎ Michigan, N USA
Hulczyn see Hlučín
Huliao see Dabu
163 Z8 Hulin Heilongjiang, NE China 45°48´N 133°06´E
163 S9 Hulingol prev. Huolin Gol. Nei Mongol Zizhiqu, N China 45°36´N 119°54´E
14 L12 Hull Québec, SE Canada 45°26´N 75°45´W
29 S12 Hull Iowa, C USA 43°11´N 96°07´W
Hull see Kingston upon Hull
Hull Island see Orona
99 F16 Hulst Zeeland, SW Netherlands 51°17´N 04°03´E
Hulstay see Choybalsan
Hultschin see Hlučín
95 M19 Hultsfred Kalmar, S Sweden 57°30´N 15°50´E
163 T13 Huludao prev. Jinxi, Lianshan. Liaoning, NE China 40°46´N 120°47´E
Hulun see Hulun Buir
163 S6 Hulun Buir var. Hailar; prev. Hulun. Nei Mongol Zizhiqu, N China 49°15´N 119°41´E
Hu-lun Ch'ih see Hulun Nur
163 Q6 Hulun Nur var. Hu-lun Ch'ih; prev. Dalai Nor. ◎ NE China
Hulwan/Hulwân see Hilwān
117 V8 Hulyaypole Rus. Gulyaypole. Zaporiz'ka Oblast', SE Ukraine 47°41´N 36°10´E
163 V4 Huma Heilongjiang, NE China 51°40´N 126°38´E
45 V6 Humacao E Puerto Rico 18°09´N 65°50´W
163 U4 Huma He NE China
62 J5 Humahuaca Jujuy, N Argentina 23°13´S 65°20´W
59 E14 Humaitá Amazonas, N Brazil 07°33´S 63°01´W
62 N7 Humaitá Ñeembucú, S Paraguay 27°02´S 58°31´W
83 H26 Humansdorp Eastern Cape, S South Africa 34°01´S 24°45´E
27 S6 Humansville Missouri, C USA 37°47´N 93°34´W
40 I8 Humaya, Río C Mexico
83 C16 Humbe Cunene, SW Angola 16°37´S 14°52´E
97 N17 Humber estuary E England, United Kingdom
97 N17 Humberside cultural region E England, United Kingdom
Humberto see Umberto
25 W11 Humble Texas, SW USA 29°58´N 95°15´W
11 U15 Humboldt Saskatchewan, S Canada 52°13´N 105°09´W
29 U12 Humboldt Iowa, C USA 42°42´N 94°13´W
27 Q6 Humboldt Kansas, C USA 37°48´N 95°26´W
29 S17 Humboldt Nebraska, C USA 40°09´N 95°56´W
35 S3 Humboldt Nevada, W USA 40°36´N 118°15´W
20 G9 Humboldt Tennessee, S USA 35°49´N 88°55´W
34 K3 Humboldt Bay bay California, W USA
35 S4 Humboldt Lake ◎ Nevada, W USA
35 S4 Humboldt River Nevada, W USA
35 T5 Humboldt Salt Marsh wetland Nevada, W USA
183 P11 Hume, Lake ◎ New South Wales/Victoria, SE Australia
111 N19 Humenné Ger. Homenau, Hung. Homonna. Prešovský Kraj, E Slovakia 48°57´N 21°54´E
29 V15 Humeston Iowa, C USA 40°51´N 93°30´W
54 J5 Humocaro Bajo Lara, N Venezuela 09°41´N 70°00´W
29 Q14 Humphrey Nebraska, C USA 41°38´N 97°29´W
35 S9 Humphreys, Mount ▲ California, W USA 37°11´N 118°39´W
36 L11 Humphreys Peak ▲ Arizona, SW USA 35°18´N 111°40´W
111 E17 Humpolec Ger. Gumpolds, Humpoletz. Vysočina, C Czech Republic 49°33´N 15°23´E
Humpoletz see Humpolec
93 K19 Humppila Etelä-Suomi, S Finland 60°54´N 23°21´E
32 F8 Humptulips Washington, NW USA 47°13´N 123°57´W
42 H7 Humuya, Río W Honduras
75 P9 Hūn N Libya 29°06´N 15°56´E
92 I1 Húnaflói bay NW Iceland
160 M11 Hunan var. Hunan Sheng, Xiang. ◆ province S China
Hunan Sheng see Hunan
163 Y10 Hunchun Jilin, NE China 42°51´N 130°21´E
95 I22 Hundested Frederiksborg, E Denmark 55°58´N 11°53´E
Hundred Mile House see 100 Mile House
116 G12 Hunedoara Ger. Eisenmarkt, Hung. Vajdahunyad. Hunedoara, SW Romania 45°45´N 22°54´E
116 G12 Hunedoara ◆ county W Romania
101 I17 Hünfeld Hessen, C Germany 50°41´N 09°46´E
Hungarian People's Republic see Hungary
111 H23 Hungary off. Republic of Hungary, Ger. Ungarn, Hung. Magyarország, Rom. Ungaria, SCr. Mađarska, Ukr. Uhorshchyna; prev. Hungarian People's Republic. ◆ republic C Europe
Hungary, Plain of see Great Hungarian Plain
Hungary, Republic of see Hungary
Hungiy see Urgamal
163 X13 Hŭngnam E North Korea 39°50´N 127°36´E
33 P8 Hungry Horse Reservoir ⊠ Montana, NW USA
Hungt'ou see Lan Yü
Hung-tse Hu see Hongze Hu
167 T6 Hưng Yên Hai Hưng, N Vietnam 20°38´N 106°05´E
Hunjiang see Baishan
95 I18 Hunnebostrand Västra Götaland, S Sweden 58°26´N 11°19´E
101 E19 Hunsrück ▲▲ W Germany
97 P18 Hunstanton E England, United Kingdom 52°57´N 00°27´E
155 G20 Hunsūr Karnātaka, E India 12°18´N 76°15´E
Hunt see Hangay
100 G12 Hunte NW Germany
29 Q5 Hunter North Dakota, N USA 47°10´N 97°11´W
25 S11 Hunter Texas, SW USA 29°47´N 98°01´W
185 D20 Hunter South Island, New Zealand
183 N15 Hunter Island island Tasmania, SE Australia
18 K11 Hunter Mountain ▲ New York, NE USA 42°10´N 74°13´W
185 B23 Hunter Mountains ▲▲ South Island, New Zealand
183 S7 Hunter River New South Wales, SE Australia
32 L7 Hunters Washington, NW USA 48°07´N 118°13´W
185 F20 Hunters Hills, The hill range South Island, New Zealand
184 M12 Hunterville Manawatu-Wanganui, North Island, New Zealand 39°55´S 175°34´E
31 N16 Huntingburg Indiana, N USA 38°18´N 86°57´W
97 O20 Huntingdon E England, United Kingdom 52°20´N 00°12´W
18 E15 Huntingdon Pennsylvania, NE USA 40°28´N 78°00´W
20 G9 Huntingdon Tennessee, S USA 36°00´N 88°25´W
97 O20 Huntingdonshire cultural region C England, United Kingdom
31 P12 Huntington Indiana, N USA 40°52´N 85°30´W
32 L13 Huntington Oregon, NW USA 44°22´N 117°18´W
25 X9 Huntington Texas, SW USA 31°16´N 94°34´W
36 M5 Huntington Utah, W USA 39°19´N 110°57´W
21 P5 Huntington West Virginia, NE USA 38°25´N 82°27´W
35 T16 Huntington Beach California, W USA 33°39´N 118°00´W
35 W4 Huntington Creek Nevada, W USA
184 L7 Huntly Waikato, North Island, New Zealand 37°34´S 175°09´E
96 K8 Huntly NE Scotland, United Kingdom 57°25´N 02°48´W
10 K8 Hunt, Mount ▲ Yukon Territory, NW Canada 61°29´N 129°10´W
14 H12 Huntsville Ontario, S Canada 45°20´N 79°14´W
23 P2 Huntsville Alabama, S USA 34°44´N 86°35´W
27 S9 Huntsville Arkansas, C USA 36°04´N 93°46´W
27 U3 Huntsville Missouri, C USA 39°27´N 92°31´W
20 M8 Huntsville Tennessee, S USA 36°25´N 84°30´W
25 V10 Huntsville Texas, SW USA 30°43´N 95°34´W
36 L2 Huntsville Utah, W USA 41°16´N 111°47´W
41 W12 Hunucmá Yucatán, SE Mexico 20°59´N 89°55´W
149 W3 Hunza var. Karīmābād. Jammu and Kashmir, NE Pakistan 36°23´N 74°43´E
149 W3 Hunza NE Pakistan
Hunze see Oostermoers Vaart
158 H4 Huocheng var. Shuiding. Xinjiang Uygur Zizhiqu, NW China 44°03´N 80°49´E
161 N6 Huojia Henan, C China 35°14´N 113°38´E
Huolin Gol see Hulingol
186 N14 Huon reef N New Caledonia
186 E7 Huon Peninsula headland C Papua New Guinea 06°24´S 147°50´E
Huoshao Dao see Lü Tao
Huoshao Tao see Lan Yü
Hupeh/Hupei see Hubei
Hurama see Hongyuan
95 H14 Hurdalssjøen ◎ S Norway
14 E13 Hurd, Cape headland Ontario, S Canada 45°12´N 81°43´W
Hurdegaryp see Hardegarijp
29 N4 Hurdsfield North Dakota, N USA 47°24´N 99°55´W
Hüremt see Sayhan, Bulgan, Mongolia
Hüremt see Taragt, Övörhangay, Mongolia
75 X9 Hurghada var. Al Ghurdaqah, Ghurdaqah. E Egypt 27°17´N 33°47´E
81 I17 Huri Hills ▲▲ NW Kenya
37 P15 Hurley New Mexico, SW USA 32°42´N 108°07´W
30 K4 Hurley Wisconsin, N USA 46°25´N 90°15´W
21 Y4 Hurlock Maryland, NE USA 38°37´N 75°51´W
162 K11 Hürmen var. Tsoohor. Ömnögovĭ, S Mongolia 43°15´N 104°04´E
29 P10 Huron South Dakota, N USA 44°19´N 98°13´W
31 S6 Huron, Lake ◎ Canada/USA
31 N3 Huron Mountains hill range Michigan, N USA
36 J8 Hurricane Utah, W USA 37°10´N 113°18´W
21 P5 Hurricane West Virginia, NE USA 38°25´N 82°01´W
36 J8 Hurricane Cliffs cliff Arizona, SW USA
23 V6 Hurricane Creek Georgia, SE USA
94 E12 Hurrungane ▲ S Norway 61°25´N 07°48´E
101 E16 Hürth Nordrhein-Westfalen, W Germany 50°52´N 06°49´E
Hurukawa see Furukawa
185 I17 Hurunui South Island, New Zealand
95 F21 Hurup Viborg, NW Denmark 56°46´N 08°26´E
117 T14 Hurzuf Respublika Krym, S Ukraine 44°33´N 34°18´E
Huş see Huşi
95 B19 Húsavík Dan. Husevig. Sandoy, C Faeroe Islands 65°24´N 06°38´W
92 K1 Húsavík Nordhurland Eystra, NE Iceland 66°03´N 17°20´W
Husevig see Húsavík
116 M10 Huşi var. Huş. Vaslui, E Romania 46°40´N 28°05´E
95 L19 Huskvarna Jönköping, S Sweden 57°47´N 14°15´E
39 P8 Huslia Alaska, USA 65°42´N 156°24´W
Husn see Al Ḥuṣn
95 C15 Husnes Hordaland, S Norway 59°52´N 05°46´E
94 D8 Hustadvika sea area S Norway
Husté see Khust
100 H7 Husum Schleswig-Holstein, N Germany 54°29´N 09°04´E
93 I16 Husum Västernorrland, C Sweden 63°21´N 19°12´E
116 K6 Husyatyn Ternopil's'ka Oblast', W Ukraine 49°04´N 26°10´E
Huszt see Khust
Hutag see Hutag-Öndör
162 K6 Hutag-Öndör var. Hutag. Bulgan, N Mongolia 49°22´N 102°50´E
26 M6 Hutchinson Kansas, C USA 38°03´N 97°56´W
29 U9 Hutchinson Minnesota, N USA 44°53´N 94°22´W
23 Y13 Hutchinson Island island Florida, SE USA
36 L11 Hutch Mountain ▲ Arizona, SW USA 34°49´N 111°22´W
141 O14 Ḥūth NW Yemen 16°14´N 44°E
186 I7 Hutjena Buka Island, NE Papua New Guinea 05°19´S 154°40´E
109 T8 Hüttenberg Kärnten, S Austria 46°58´N 14°33´E
25 T10 Hutto Texas, SW USA 30°32´N 97°33´W
Huttu see Futtsu
108 E8 Huttwil Bern, W Switzerland 47°06´N 07°48´E
158 K5 Hutubi Xinjiang Uygur Zizhiqu, NW China 44°10´N 86°51´E
161 N4 Hutuo He C China
Hutyû see Fuchū
185 E20 Huxley, Mount ▲ South Island, New Zealand 44°02´S 169°42´E
99 J20 Huy Dut. Hoei, Hoey. Liège, E Belgium 50°32´N 05°14´E
161 R8 Huzhou var. Wuxing. Zhejiang, SE China 30°54´N 120°05´E
159 T10 Huzhu Qinghai, China 36°40´N 101°58´E
Huzi see Fuji
Huzieda see Fujieda
Huzinomiya see Fujinomiya
Huzisawa see Fujisawa
92 I2 Hvammstangi Nordhurland Vestra, N Iceland 65°22´N 20°54´W
92 K4 Hvannadalshnúkur S Iceland 64°01´N 16°39´W
113 E15 Hvar It. Lesina. Split-Dalmacija, S Croatia 43°10´N 16°27´E
113 F15 Hvar It. Lesina; anc. Pharus. island S Croatia
117 T13 Hvardiys'ke Rus. Gvardeyskoye. Respublika Krym, S Ukraine 45°08´N 34°01´E
92 I4 Hveragerdhi Sudhurland, SW Iceland 64°00´N 21°13´W
95 E22 Hvide Sande Ringkøbing, W Denmark 56°00´N 08°08´E
92 I3 Hvítá C Iceland
95 G15 Hvittingfoss Buskerud, S Norway 59°28´N 10°00´E
92 I4 Hvolsvöllur Sudhurland, SW Iceland 63°44´N 20°12´W
Hwach'ŏn-chŏsuji see P'aro-ho
Hwainan see Huainan
Hwalien see Hualien
83 I16 Hwange prev. Wankie. Matabeleland North, W Zimbabwe 18°18´S 26°31´E
Hwang-Hae see Yellow Sea
Hwangshih see Huangshi
83 L17 Hwedza Mashonaland East, E Zimbabwe 18°35´S 31°35´E
63 G20 Hyades, Cerro ▲ S Chile 46°57´S 73°09´W
162 K6 Hyalganat var. Selenge. Bulgan, N Mongolia 49°34´N 104°18´E
19 Q12 Hyannis Massachusetts, NE USA 41°38´N 70°15´W
28 L13 Hyannis Nebraska, C USA 42°00´N 101°45´W
162 F6 Hyargas Nuur ◎ NW Mongolia
Hybla/Hybla Major see Paternò
39 Y14 Hydaburg Prince of Wales Island, Alaska, USA 55°10´N 132°44´W
185 F22 Hyde Otago, South Island, New Zealand 45°17´S 170°17´E
21 O7 Hyden Kentucky, S USA 37°08´N 83°23´W
18 K12 Hyde Park New York, NE USA 41°46´N 73°52´W
39 Z14 Hyder Alaska, USA 55°55´N 130°01´W
155 I15 Hyderābād var. Haidarabad. state capital Andhra Pradesh, C India 17°22´N 78°26´E
149 Q16 Hyderābād var. Haidarabad. Sind, SE Pakistan 25°26´N 68°22´E
103 T16 Hyères Var, SE France 43°07´N 06°08´E
103 T16 Hyères, Îles d' island group S France
118 K12 Hyermanavichy Rus. Germanovichi. Vitsyebskaya Voblasts', N Belarus 55°24´N 27°48´E
163 X12 Hyesan NE North Korea 41°18´N 128°13´E
10 K8 Hyland Yukon Territory, NW Canada
95 K20 Hyltebruk Halland, S Sweden 57°N 13°14´E
18 D16 Hyndman Pennsylvania, NE USA 39°49´N 78°42´W
33 P14 Hyndman Peak ▲ Idaho, NW USA 43°45´N 114°07´W
164 I13 Hyōgo off. Hyōgo-ken. ◆ prefecture Honshū, SW Japan
Hyōgo-ken see Hyōgo
Hypsas see Belice
Hyrcania see Gorgān
36 L1 Hyrum Utah, W USA 41°37´N 111°51´W
93 N14 Hyrynsalmi Oulu, C Finland 64°41´N 28°30´E
33 V10 Hysham Montana, NW USA 46°16´N 107°14´W
11 N13 Hythe Alberta, W Canada 55°18´N 119°44´W
97 Q23 Hythe SE England, United Kingdom 51°05´N 01°04´E
Hyvinge see Hyvinkää
93 L19 Hyvinkää Swe. Hyvinge. Etelä-Suomi, S Finland 60°37´N 24°50´E

I

116 J9 Iacobeni Ger. Jakobeny. Suceava, NE Romania 47°24´N 25°20´E
Iader see Zadar
172 I7 Iakora Fianarantsoa, SE Madagascar 23°04´S 46°40´E
116 K14 Ialomiţa var. Jalomitsa. ◆ county SE Romania
116 K14 Ialomiţa SE Romania
117 N10 Ialoveni Rus. Yaloveny. C Moldova 46°57´N 28°47´E
117 N11 Ialpug var. Ialpugul Mare, Rus. Yalpug. Moldova/Ukraine
Ialpugul Mare see Ialpug
23 T8 Iamonia, Lake ◎ Florida, SE USA
116 L13 Ianca Brăila, SE Romania 45°06´N 27°29´E
116 M10 Iaşi Ger. Jassy. Iaşi, NE Romania 47°08´N 27°38´E
116 L9 Iaşi Ger. Jassy, Yassy. ◆ county NE Romania
114 J13 Íasmos Anatolikí Makedonía kai Thráki, NE Greece 41°07´N 25°12´E
22 H6 Iatt, Lake ⊠ Louisiana, S USA
58 B11 Iauretê Amazonas, NW Brazil 0°37´N 69°10´W
171 N3 Iba Luzon, N Philippines 15°25´N 119°55´E
77 S16 Ibadan Oyo, SW Nigeria 07°22´N 04°01´E
54 E10 Ibagué Tolima, C Colombia 04°27´N 75°14´W
60 J10 Ibaiti Paraná, S Brazil 23°49´S 50°15´W
36 J4 Ibapah Peak ▲ Utah, W USA 39°51´N 113°55´W
113 M15 Ibar Alb. Ibër. C Serbia
165 P13 Ibaraki off. Ibaraki-ken. ◆ prefecture Honshū, S Japan
Ibaraki-ken see Ibaraki
56 C5 Ibarra var. San Miguel de Ibarra. Imbabura, N Ecuador 0°23´S 78°08´W
Ibaşfalău see Dumbrăveni
141 O16 Ibb W Yemen 13°55´N 44°10´E
100 F13 Ibbenbüren Nordrhein-Westfalen, NW Germany 52°17´N 07°43´E
79 H16 Ibenga N Congo
Ibër see Ibar
57 I14 Iberia Madre de Dios, E Peru 11°21´S 69°36´W
Iberia see Spain
66 M1 Iberian Basin undersea feature E Atlantic Ocean 39°00´N 16°00´W
Iberian Mountains see Ibérico, Sistema
84 D12 Iberian Peninsula physical region Portugal/Spain
64 M8 Iberian Plain undersea feature E Atlantic Ocean 13°30´W 43°45´N
Ibérica, Cordillera see Ibérico, Sistema
105 P6 Ibérico, Sistema var. Cordillera Ibérica, Eng. Iberian Mountains. ▲▲ NE Spain
12 K7 Iberville Lac d' ◎ Québec, NE Canada
77 T14 Ibeto Niger, W Nigeria 10°30´N 05°07´E
77 W15 Ibi Taraba, C Nigeria 08°13´N 09°46´E
105 S11 Ibi País Valenciano, E Spain 38°38´N 00°35´W
59 L20 Ibiá Minas Gerais, SE Brazil 19°30´S 46°31´W
61 F15 Ibicuí, Rio S Brazil
61 C19 Ibicuy Entre Ríos, E Argentina 33°44´S 59°10´W
61 F16 Ibirapuitã S Brazil
105 V10 Ibiza var. Iviza, Cast. Eivissa; anc. Ebusus. island Islas Baleares, Spain, W Mediterranean Sea
Ibiza see Eivissa
138 J4 Ibn Wardān, Qaşr ruins Ḥamāh, C Syria
Ibo see Sassandra
188 E9 Ibobang Babeldaob, N Palau
171 V13 Ibonma Papua, E Indonesia 03°27´S 133°30´E
59 N17 Ibotirama Bahia, E Brazil 12°13´S 43°12´W
141 Y8 Ibrā NE Oman 22°45´N 58°30´E
127 Q4 Ibresi Chuvashskaya Respublika, W Russian Federation 55°22´N 47°04´E
141 X8 'Ibrī NW Oman 23°12´N 56°28´E
164 C16 Ibusuki Kagoshima, Kyūshū, SW Japan 31°15´N 130°40´E
57 E16 Ica Ica, SW Peru 14°02´S 75°48´W
57 E16 Ica off. Departamento de Ica. ◆ department SW Peru
Ica, Departamento de see Ica
58 C11 Içana Amazonas, NW Brazil 0°22´N 67°25´W
Icaria see Ikaría
58 B13 Içá, Rio var. Río Putumayo. NW South America
see also Putumayo, Río
Içá, Rio see Putumayo, Río
136 I17 İçel prev. Ichili; prev. Mersin. ◆ province S Turkey
İçel see Mersin
92 I3 Iceland off. Republic of Iceland, Dan. Island, Icel. Ísland. ◆ republic N Atlantic Ocean
86 B6 Iceland island N Atlantic Ocean
64 L5 Iceland Basin undersea feature N Atlantic Ocean 61°00´N 19°00´W
Icelandic Plateau see Iceland Plateau
197 Q15 Iceland Plateau var. Icelandic Plateau. undersea feature S Greenland Sea 12°00´W 69°30´N
Iceland, Republic of see Iceland
155 E16 Ichalkaranji Mahārāshtra, W India 16°42´N 74°28´E
164 D15 Ichifusa-yama ▲ Kyūshū, SW Japan 32°18´N 131°05´E
Ichili see İçel
164 K13 Ichinomiya var. Itinomiya. Aichi, Honshū, SW Japan 35°18´N 136°48´E
165 Q9 Ichinoseki var. Itinoseki. Iwate, Honshū, C Japan 38°56´N 141°08´E
117 R3 Ichnya Chernihivs'ka Oblast', NE Ukraine 50°52´N 32°24´E
57 L17 Ichoa, Río C Bolivia
Iconium see Konya
Iculisma see Angoulême
39 U12 Icy Bay inlet Alaska, USA
39 N5 Icy Cape headland Alaska, USA 70°19´N 161°52´W
39 W13 Icy Strait strait Alaska, USA
27 R13 Idabel Oklahoma, C USA 33°54´N 94°50´W
29 T13 Ida Grove Iowa, C USA 42°21´N 95°28´W
77 U16 Idah Kogi, S Nigeria 07°06´N 06°45´E
33 N13 Idaho off. State of Idaho, also known as Gem of the Mountains, Gem State. ◆ state NW USA
33 N14 Idaho City Idaho, NW USA 43°48´N 115°51´W
33 R14 Idaho Falls Idaho, NW USA 43°28´N 112°01´W
121 P2 Idálion var. Dali, Dhali. C Cyprus 35°00´N 33°25´E
25 N5 Idalou Texas, SW USA 33°40´N 101°40´W
104 I9 Idanha-a-Nova Castelo Branco, C Portugal 39°55´N 07°15´W
101 E19 Idar-Oberstein Rheinland-Pfalz, SW Germany 49°43´N 07°19´E
118 J3 Ida-Virumaa var. Ida-Viru Maakond. ◆ province NE Estonia
Ida-Viru Maakond see Ida-Virumaa
124 J8 Idel' Respublika Kareliya, NW Russian Federation 64°08´N 34°12´E
79 C15 Idenao Sud-Ouest, SW Cameroon 04°04´N 09°01´E
Idensalmi see Iisalmi
162 I6 Ider var. Dzuunmod. Hövsgöl, C Mongolia 48°09´N 97°22´E

◆ Country
● Country Capital
◇ Dependent Territory
○ Dependent Territory Capital
◆ Administrative Regions
✕ International Airport
▲ Mountain
▲▲ Mountain Range
Volcano
River
◎ Lake
⊠ Reservoir

IDER – INVESTIGATOR RIDGE

Ider *see* Galt
75 X10 **Idfū** *var.* Edfu. SE Egypt 24°55′N 32°52′E
Ídhi Óros *see* Ídi
Ídhra *see* Ýdra
80 L10 **ʿĪdi** *var.* Ed. SE Eritrea 13°54′N 41°39′E
168 H7 **Idi** Sumatera, W Indonesia 05°00′N 98°00′E
115 I25 **Ídi** *var.* Ídhi Óros. ▲▲ Kríti, Greece, E Mediterranean Sea
Idi Amin, Lac *see* Edward, Lake
106 G10 **Idice** ≈ N Italy
76 G9 **Idîni** Trarza, W Mauritania 17°58′N 15°40′W
79 J21 **Idiofa** Bandundu, SW Dem. Rep. Congo 05°00′S 19°38′E
39 O10 **Iditarod River** ≈ Alaska, USA
95 M14 **Idkerberget** Dalarna, C Sweden 60°22′N 15°15′E
138 I3 **Idlib** Idlib, NW Syria 35°57′N 36°38′E
138 I4 **Idlib** *off.* Muḩāfaẓat Idlib. ◈ *governorate* NW Syria
Idlib, Muḩāfaẓat *see* Idlib
Idra *see* Ýdra
94 J11 **Idre** Dalarna, C Sweden 61°52′N 12°45′E
Idria *see* Idrija
109 S11 **Idrija** *It.* Idria. W Slovenia 46°00′N 14°59′E
101 G18 **Idstein** Hessen, W Germany 50°10′N 08°16′E
83 J25 **Idutywa** Eastern Cape, SE South Africa 32°06′S 28°20′E
Idzhevan *see* Ijevan
118 G9 **Iecava** Bauska, S Latvia 56°36′N 24°10′E
165 T16 **Ie-jima** *var.* Ii-shima. *island* Nansei-shotō, SW Japan
99 B18 **Ieper** *Fr.* Ypres. West-Vlaanderen, W Belgium 50°51′N 02°53′E
115 K25 **Ierápetra** Kríti, Greece, E Mediterranean Sea 35°00′N 25°45′E
115 G22 **Iérax, Akrotírio** *headland* S Greece 36°45′N 23°06′E
Ierisós *see* Ierissós
115 H14 **Ierissós** *var.* Ierisós. Kentrikí Makedonía, N Greece 40°24′N 23°53′E
116 I11 **Iernut** *Hung.* Radnót. Mureş, C Romania 46°27′N 24°15′E
106 J12 **Iesi** *var.* Jesi. Marche, C Italy 43°33′N 13°16′E
92 K9 **Iešjávri** ◎ N Norway
Iesolo *see* Jesolo
188 K16 **Ifalik Atoll** *atoll* Caroline Islands, C Micronesia
172 I6 **Ifanadiana** Fianarantsoa, SE Madagascar 21°19′S 47°39′E
77 T16 **Ife** Osun, SW Nigeria 07°25′N 04°31′E
77 V8 **Iferouâne** Agadez, N Niger 19°05′N 08°24′E
Iferten *see* Yverdon
92 L8 **Ifjord** Finnmark, N Norway 70°27′N 27°06′E
77 R8 **Ifôghas, Adrar des** *var.* Adrar des Iforas. ▲▲ NE Mali
Iforas, Adrar des *see* Ifôghas, Adrar des
182 D6 **Ifould lake** *salt lake* South Australia
74 G6 **Ifrane** C Morocco 33°31′N 05°09′W
171 S11 **Iga** Pulau Halmahera, E Indonesia 01°23′N 128°17′E
81 G18 **Iganga** SE Uganda 0°34′N 33°27′E
60 L7 **Igarapava** São Paulo, S Brazil 20°01′S 47°46′W
122 K9 **Igarka** Krasnoyarskiy Kray, N Russian Federation 67°31′N 86°33′E
Igaunija *see* Estonia
137 T12 **Iğdir** E Turkey 39°50′N 44°00′E
I.G.Duca *see* General Toshevo
Igel *see* Jihlava
94 N11 **Iggesund** Gävleborg, C Sweden 61°38′N 17°04′E
39 P7 **Igikpak, Mount** ▲ Alaska, USA 67°28′N 154°55′W
39 P13 **Igiugig** Alaska, USA 59°19′N 155°53′W
Iglau/Iglawa/Igława *see* Jihlava
107 B20 **Iglesias** Sardegna, Italy, C Mediterranean Sea 39°20′N 08°34′E
127 V4 **Iglino** Respublika Bashkortostan, W Russian Federation 54°51′N 56°29′E
Igló *see* Spišská Nová Ves
9 O6 **Igloolik** Nunavut, N Canada 69°24′N 81°55′W
12 B11 **Ignace** Ontario, S Canada 49°26′N 91°40′W
118 I12 **Ignalina** Utena, E Lithuania 55°20′N 26°10′E
127 Q5 **Ignatovka** Ul'yanovskaya Oblast', W Russian Federation 53°56′N 47°40′E
124 K12 **Ignatovo** Vologodskaya Oblast', NW Russian Federation 60°47′N 37°51′E
114 N11 **İğneada** Kırklareli, NW Turkey 41°54′N 27°58′E
121 S7 **İğneada Burnu** *headland* NW Turkey 41°54′N 28°03′E
Igombe *see* Gombe
115 B16 **Igoumenítsa** Ípeiros, W Greece 39°30′N 20°16′E
127 T2 **Igra** Udmurtskaya Respublika, NW Russian Federation 57°30′N 53°01′E
122 H9 **Igrim** Khanty-Mansiyskiy Avtonomnyy Okrug-Yugra, N Russian Federation 63°09′N 64°33′E
60 G12 **Iguaçu, Rio** *Sp.* Río Iguazú. ≈ Argentina/Brazil *see also* Iguazú, Río
Iguaçu, Rio *see* Iguazú, Río
59 I22 **Iguaçu, Salto do** *Sp.* Cataratas del Iguazú; *prev.* Victoria Falls. *waterfall* Argentina/Brazil *see also* Iguazú, Cataratas del
Iguaçu, Salto do *see* Iguazú, Cataratas del
41 O15 **Iguala** *var.* Iguala de la Independencia. Guerrero, S Mexico 18°21′N 99°31′W
105 V5 **Igualada** Cataluña, NE Spain 41°35′N 01°37′E
Iguala de la Independencia *see* Iguala
60 G12 **Iguazú, Cataratas del** *Port.* Salto do Iguaçu; *prev.* Victoria Falls. *waterfall* Argentina/Brazil *see also* Iguaçu, Salto do
Iguazú, Cataratas del *see* Iguaçu, Salto do
62 Q6 **Iguazú, Río** *var.* Río Iguaçu. ≈ Argentina/Brazil *see also* Iguaçu, Rio
Iguazú, Río *see* Iguaçu, Rio
79 D19 **Iguéla** Ogooué-Maritime, SW Gabon 02°00′S 09°23′E
Iguid, Erg *see* Iguîdi, 'Erg
67 M5 **Iguîdi, 'Erg** *var.* Erg Iguid. *desert* Algeria/Mauritania
172 K2 **Iharaña** *prev.* Vohémar. Antsiranana, NE Madagascar 13°22′S 50°00′E
151 K18 **Ihavandhippolhu Atoll** *var.* Ihavandiffulu Atoll. *atoll* N Maldives
Ihavandiffulu Atoll *see* Ihavandhippolhu Atoll
Ih Bulag *see* Hanbogd
165 T16 **Iheya-jima** *island* Nansei-shotō, SW Japan
Ihhayrhan *see* Bayan-Önjüül
163 N9 **Ihhet** *var.* Bayan. Dornogovĭ, SE Mongolia 46°15′N 110°16′E
172 I6 **Ihosy** Fianarantsoa, S Madagascar 22°23′S 46°09′E
Ihsüüj *see* Bayanchandmanĭ
162 I7 **Ihtamir** *var.* Dzaanhushuu. Arhangay, C Mongolia 47°36′N 101°06′E
162 H6 **Ih-Uul** *var.* Bayan-Uhaa. Dzavhan, C Mongolia 48°41′N 98°46′E
162 J6 **Ih-Uul** *var.* Selenge. Hövsgöl, N Mongolia 49°25′N 101°30′E
93 L14 **Ii** Oulu, C Finland 65°18′N 25°23′E
164 M13 **Iida** Nagano, Honshū, S Japan 35°32′N 137°48′E
93 M14 **Iijoki** ≈ C Finland
Iinnasuolu *see* Hinnøya
118 J4 **Iisaku** *Ger.* Isaak. Ida-Virumaa, NE Estonia 59°06′N 27°19′E
93 M16 **Iisalmi** *var.* Idensalmi. Itä-Suomi, C Finland 63°32′N 27°10′E
Ii-shima *see* Ie-jima
165 N11 **Iiyama** Nagano, Honshū, S Japan 36°52′N 138°22′E
77 S16 **Ijebu-Ode** Ogun, SW Nigeria 06°46′N 03°57′E
137 U11 **Ijevan** *Rus.* Idzhevan. N Armenia 40°53′N 45°07′E
98 H9 **IJmuiden** Noord-Holland, W Netherlands 52°28′N 04°38′E
98 M12 **IJssel** *var.* Yssel. ≈ Netherlands
98 J8 **IJsselmeer** *prev.* Zuider Zee. ◎ N Netherlands
98 L9 **IJsselmuiden** Overijssel, E Netherlands 52°34′N 05°55′E
98 I12 **IJsselstein** Utrecht, C Netherlands 52°01′N 05°02′E
61 G14 **Ijuí** Rio Grande do Sul, S Brazil 28°23′S 53°55′W
61 G14 **Ijuí, Rio** ≈ S Brazil
189 R8 **Ijuw** NE Nauru 0°30′S 166°57′E
99 E16 **IJzendijke** Zeeland, SW Netherlands 51°20′N 03°36′E
99 A18 **Ijzer** ≈ W Belgium
Ikaahuk *see* Sachs Harbour
93 K18 **Ikaalinen** Länsi-Suomi, W Finland 61°46′N 23°05′E
172 I6 **Ikalamavony** Fianarantsoa, SE Madagascar 21°10′S 46°35′E
Ikaluktutiak *see* Cambridge Bay
185 G16 **Ikamatua** West Coast, South Island, New Zealand 42°16′S 171°42′E
77 U16 **Ikare** Ondo, SW Nigeria 07°36′N 05°52′E
115 L20 **Ikaría** *var.* Kariot, Nicaria, Nikaria; *anc.* Icaria. *island* Dodekánisa, Greece, Aegean Sea
95 F22 **Ikast** Ringkøbing, W Denmark 56°09′N 09°10′E
184 O9 **Ikawhenua Range** ▲▲ North Island, New Zealand
165 U4 **Ikeda** Hokkaidō, NE Japan 42°54′N 143°25′E
164 H14 **Ikeda** Tokushima, Shikoku, SW Japan 34°00′N 133°47′E
77 S16 **Ikeja** Lagos, SW Nigeria 06°36′N 03°16′E
79 L19 **Ikela** Equateur, C Dem. Rep. Congo 01°11′S 23°16′E
114 H10 **Ikhtiman** Sofiya, W Bulgaria 42°26′N 23°49′E
164 C13 **Iki** *island* SW Japan
127 O13 **Iki Burul** Respublika Kalmykiya, SW Russian Federation 45°48′N 44°44′E
137 P11 **İkizdere** Rize, NE Turkey 40°47′N 40°34′E
39 P14 **Ikolik, Cape** *headland* Kodiak Island, Alaska, USA 57°12′N 154°46′W
77 V17 **Ikom** Cross River, SE Nigeria 05°57′N 08°43′E
172 I6 **Ikongo** *prev.* Fort-Carnot. Fianarantsoa, SE Madagascar 21°52′S 47°27′E
39 P5 **Ikpikpuk River** ≈ Alaska, USA
190 H1 **Iku** *prev.* Lone Tree Islet *atoll* Tungaru, W Kiribati
164 I12 **Ikuno** Hyōgo, Honshū, SW Japan 35°13′N 134°48′E
190 H16 **Ikurangi** ▲ Rarotonga, S Cook Islands 21°12′S 159°45′W
171 X14 **Ilaga** Papua, E Indonesia 03°54′S 137°30′E
171 O2 **Ilagan** Luzon, N Philippines 17°08′N 121°54′E
142 J7 **Īlām** *var.* Elam. Īlām, W Iran 33°37′N 46°27′E
153 R12 **Ilām** Eastern, E Nepal 26°52′N 87°58′E
142 J8 **Īlām** *off.* Ostān-e Īlām. ◈ *province* W Iran
Īlām, Ostān-e *see* Īlām
161 T13 **Ilan** *Jap.* Giran. N Taiwan 24°45′N 121°44′E
146 G9 **Ilanly Obvodnitel'nyy Kanal** *canal* N Turkmenistan
122 L12 **Ilanskiy** Krasnoyarskiy Kray, S Russian Federation 56°16′N 95°59′E
108 H9 **Ilanz** Graubünden, S Switzerland 46°46′N 09°10′E
77 S16 **Ilaro** Ogun, SW Nigeria 06°52′N 03°01′E
57 I17 **Ilave** Puno, S Peru 16°07′S 69°40′W
110 K8 **Iława** *Ger.* Deutsch-Eylau. Warmińsko-Mazurskie, NE Poland 53°36′N 19°35′E
123 P10 **Il'benge** Respublika Sakha (Yakutiya), NE Russian Federation 62°52′N 124°13′E
129 R7 **Ile** *var.* Ili, *Chin.* Ili He, *Rus.* Reka Ili. ≈ China/Kazakhstan *see also* Ili He
Ile *see* Ili He
11 S13 **Île-à-la-Crosse** Saskatchewan, C Canada 55°29′N 108°00′W
79 J21 **Ilebo** *prev.* Port-Francqui. Kasai-Occidental, W Dem. Rep. Congo 04°19′S 20°32′E
103 N5 **Île-de-France** ◈ *region* N France
144 I9 **Ilek** *Kaz.* Elek. ≈ Kazakhstan/Russian Federation
Ilerda *see* Lleida
77 T16 **Ilesha** Osun, SW Nigeria 07°35′N 04°49′E
187 Q16 **Îles Loyauté, Province des** ◈ *province* E New Caledonia
11 X12 **Ilford** Manitoba, C Canada 56°02′N 95°48′W
116 K14 **Ilfov** ◈ *county* S Romania
97 I23 **Ilfracombe** SW England, United Kingdom 51°12′N 04°10′W
136 I11 **Ilgaz Dağları** ▲▲ N Turkey
136 G15 **Ilgın** Konya, W Turkey 38°16′N 31°57′E
60 I7 **Ilha Solteira** São Paulo, S Brazil 20°28′S 51°19′W
104 G7 **Ílhavo** Aveiro, N Portugal 40°36′N 08°40′W
59 O18 **Ilhéus** Bahia, E Brazil 14°50′S 39°06′W
Ili *see* Ile/Ili He
116 G11 **Ilia** *Hung.* Marosillye. Hunedoara, SW Romania 45°57′N 22°40′E
39 P13 **Iliamna** Alaska, USA 59°42′N 154°49′W
39 P13 **Iliamna Lake** ◎ Alaska, USA
137 N13 **Iliç** Erzincan, C Turkey 39°27′N 38°34′E
Il'ichevsk *see* Şärur, Azerbaijan
Il'ichevsk *see* Illichivs'k, Ukraine
Ilici *see* Elche
37 V2 **Iliff** Colorado, C USA 40°46′N 103°04′W
171 Q7 **Iligan** *off.* Iligan City. Mindanao, S Philippines 08°12′N 124°16′E
171 Q7 **Iligan Bay** *bay* S Philippines
Iligan City *see* Iligan
158 I5 **Ili He** *var.* Ili, *Kaz.* Ile, *Rus.* Reka Ili. ≈ China/Kazakhstan *see also* Ile
Ili He *see* Ile
56 C6 **Iliniza** ▲ N Ecuador 0°37′S 78°41′W
Ilinski *see* Il'inskiy
125 U14 **Il'inskiy** *var.* Ilinski. Permskaya Oblast', NW Russian Federation 58°33′N 55°31′E
125 U14 **Il'inskiy** Ostrov Sakhalin, Sakhalinskaya Oblast', SE Russian Federation 47°59′N 142°14′E
18 I10 **Ilion** New York, NE USA 43°01′N 75°02′W
38 E9 **'Ilio Point** *var.* Ilio Point. *headland* Moloka'i, Hawai'i, USA 21°13′N 157°15′W
Ilio Point *see* 'Ilio Point
109 T13 **Ilirska Bistrica** *prev.* Bistrica, *Ger.* Feistritz, Illyrisch-Feistritz, *It.* Villa del Nevoso. SW Slovenia 45°34′N 14°12′E
137 Q16 **Ilisu Barajı** ⊠ SE Turkey
155 G17 **Ilkal** Karnātaka, C India 15°59′N 76°08′E
97 M19 **Ilkeston** C England, United Kingdom 52°59′N 01°18′W
121 O16 **Il-Kullana** *headland* SW Malta 35°49′N 14°26′E
108 J8 **Ill** ≈ W Austria
103 U6 **Ill** ≈ NE France
62 G10 **Illapel** Coquimbo, C Chile 31°40′S 71°13′W
Illaue Fartak Trench *see* Alula-Fartak Trench
182 C2 **Illbillee, Mount** ▲ South Australia 27°01′S 132°13′E
102 I6 **Ille-et-Vilaine** ◈ *department* NW France
77 T11 **Illéla** Tahoua, SW Niger 14°25′N 05°10′E
101 J24 **Iller** ≈ S Germany
101 J23 **Illertissen** Bayern, S Germany 48°13′N 10°08′E
105 X9 **Illes Baleares** ◈ *autonomous community* E Spain
105 N8 **Illescas** Castilla-La Mancha, C Spain 40°08′N 03°51′W
Ille-sur-la-Têt *see* Ille-sur-Têt
103 O17 **Ille-sur-Têt** *var.* Ille-sur-la-Têt. Pyrénées-Orientales, S France 42°40′N 02°37′E
Illiberis *see* Elne
117 P11 **Illichivs'k** *Rus.* Il'ichevsk. Odes'ka Oblast', SW Ukraine 46°18′N 30°36′E
Illicis *see* Elche
102 M6 **Illiers-Combray** Eure-et-Loir, C France 48°18′N 01°15′E
30 K12 **Illinois** *off.* State of Illinois, *also known as* Prairie State, Sucker State. ◈ *state* C USA
30 J13 **Illinois River** ≈ Illinois, N USA
117 N6 **Illintsi** Vinnyts'ka Oblast', C Ukraine 49°07′N 29°13′E
Illiturgis *see* Andújar
74 M10 **Illizi** SE Algeria 26°30′N 08°28′E
27 Y7 **Illmo** Missouri, C USA 37°13′N 89°30′W
Illurco *see* Lorca
Illuro *see* Mataró
Illyrisch-Feistritz *see* Ilirska Bistrica
101 K16 **Ilm** ≈ C Germany
101 K17 **Ilmenau** Thüringen, C Germany 50°40′N 10°55′E
124 H14 **Il'men', Ozero** ◎ NW Russian Federation
57 H18 **Ilo** Moquegua, SW Peru 17°42′S 71°20′W
171 O6 **Iloilo** *off.* Iloilo City. Panay Island, C Philippines 10°42′N 122°34′E
Iloilo City *see* Iloilo
112 K10 **Ilok** *Hung.* Újlak. Vojvodina, NW Serbia 45°12′N 19°22′E
93 O16 **Ilomantsi** Itä-Suomi, SE Finland 62°40′N 30°55′E
42 F8 **Ilopango, Lago de** *volcanic lake* C El Salvador
77 T15 **Ilorin** Kwara, W Nigeria 08°32′N 04°35′E
117 X8 **Ilovays'k** *Rus.* Ilovaysk. Donets'ka Oblast', SE Ukraine 47°55′N 38°14′E
Ilovaysk *see* Ilovays'k
127 O10 **Ilovlya** Volgogradskaya Oblast', SW Russian Federation 49°45′N 44°19′E
127 O10 **Ilovlya** ≈ SW Russian Federation
126 K14 **Il'skiy** Krasnodarskiy Kray, SW Russian Federation 44°52′N 38°26′E
182 B2 **Iltur** South Australia 27°33′S 130°31′E
171 Y13 **Ilugwa** Papua, E Indonesia 03°42′S 139°09′E
Iluh *see* Batman
118 I11 **Ilūkste** Daugvapils, SE Latvia 55°58′N 26°21′E
171 Y13 **Ilur** Pulau Gorong, E Indonesia 04°00′S 131°25′E
32 F10 **Ilwaco** Washington, NW USA 46°19′N 124°03′W
Il'yaly *see* Gurbansoltan Eje
İlyasbaba Burnu *see* Tekke Burnu
125 U9 **Ilych** ≈ NW Russian Federation
101 O21 **Ilz** ≈ SE Germany
111 M14 **Iłża** Radom, SE Poland 51°09′N 21°15′E
164 G13 **Imabari** *var.* Imaharu. Ehime, Shikoku, SW Japan 34°04′N 132°59′E
Imaharu *see* Imabari
165 O12 **Imaichi** *var.* Imaiti. Tochigi, Honshū, S Japan 36°43′N 139°41′E
Imaiti *see* Imaichi
164 K12 **Imajō** Fukui, Honshū, SW Japan 35°45′N 136°10′E
139 R9 **Imām Ibn Hāshim** Karbalā', C Iraq 32°46′N 43°21′E
139 T11 **Imān 'Abd Allāh** Al Qādisīyah, S Iraq 31°36′N 44°34′E
164 F15 **Imano-yama** ▲ Shikoku, SW Japan 32°51′N 132°48′E
164 C13 **Imari** Saga, Kyūshū, SW Japan 33°18′N 129°51′E
Imarssuak Mid-Ocean Seachannel *see* Imarssuak Seachannel
64 J6 **Imarssuak Seachannel** *var.* Imarssuak Mid-Ocean Seachannel. *channel* N Atlantic Ocean
93 N18 **Imatra** Etelä-Suomi, SE Finland 61°14′N 28°50′E
164 K13 **Imazu** Shiga, Honshū, SW Japan 35°25′N 136°00′E
56 C6 **Imbabura** ◈ *province* N Ecuador
55 R9 **Imbaimadai** W Guyana 05°44′N 60°23′W
61 K14 **Imbituba** Santa Catarina, S Brazil 28°15′S 48°44′W
27 W9 **Imboden** Arkansas, C USA 36°12′N 91°10′W
Imbros *see* Gökçeada
Imeni 26 Bakinskikh Komissarov *see* 26 Bakı Komissarı
Imeni 26 Bakinskikh Komissarov *see* Uzboý
125 N13 **Imeni Babushkina** Vologodskaya Oblast', NW Russian Federation 59°40′N 43°04′E
126 J7 **Imeni Karla Libknekhta** Kurskaya Oblast', W Russian Federation 51°36′N 35°28′E
Imeni Mollanepesa *see* Mollanepes Adyndaky
Imeni S. A. Niyazova *see* S. A.Nyýazow Adyndaky
Imeni Sverdlova Rudnik *see* Sverdlovs'k
188 E9 **Imeong** Babeldaob, N Palau
81 L14 **Īmī** Sumalē, E Ethiopia 06°27′N 42°10′E
115 M21 **Imia** *Turk.* Kardak. *island* Dodekánisa, Greece, Aegean Sea
Imishli *see* İmişli
137 X12 **İmişli** *Rus.* Imishli. C Azerbaijan 39°54′N 48°04′E
163 X14 **Imjin-gang** ≈ North Korea/South Korea
35 S3 **Imlay** Nevada, W USA 40°39′N 118°10′W
31 S9 **Imlay City** Michigan, N USA 43°01′N 83°04′W
23 X15 **Immokalee** Florida, SE USA 26°24′N 81°25′W
77 U17 **Imo** ◈ *state* SE Nigeria
106 G10 **Imola** Emilia-Romagna, N Italy 44°22′N 11°43′E
186 A5 **Imonda** Sandaun, NW Papua New Guinea 03°21′S 141°10′E
Imoschi *see* Imotski
113 G14 **Imotski** *It.* Imoschi. Split-Dalmacija, SE Croatia 43°28′N 17°13′E
59 L14 **Imperatriz** Maranhão, NE Brazil 05°32′S 47°28′W
106 B10 **Imperia** Liguria, NW Italy 43°53′N 08°03′E
57 E15 **Imperial** Lima, W Peru 13°04′S 76°21′W
35 X17 **Imperial** California, W USA 32°51′N 115°34′W
28 L16 **Imperial** Nebraska, C USA 40°30′N 101°37′W
24 M9 **Imperial** Texas, SW USA 31°15′N 102°40′W
35 Y17 **Imperial Dam** *dam* California, W USA
79 I17 **Impfondo** Likouala, NE Congo 01°37′N 18°04′E
153 X14 **Imphāl** *state capital* Manipur, NE India 24°47′N 93°55′E
103 P9 **Imphy** Nièvre, C France 46°55′N 03°16′E
106 G11 **Impruneta** Toscana, C Italy 43°42′N 11°16′E
115 K15 **İmroz** *var.* Gökçeada. Çanakkale, NW Turkey 40°06′N 25°50′E
Imroz Adası *see* Gökçeada
108 L7 **Imst** Tirol, W Austria 47°14′N 10°45′E
40 F3 **Imuris** Sonora, NW Mexico 30°48′N 110°52′W
164 M13 **Ina** Nagano, Honshū, S Japan 35°52′N 137°58′E
65 M18 **Inaccessible Island** *island* W Tristan da Cunha
115 F20 **Ínachos** ≈ S Greece
188 H6 **I Naftan, Puntan** *headland* Saipan, S Northern Mariana Islands
Inagua Islands *see* Great Inagua
Inagua Islands *see* Little Inagua
185 H15 **Inangahua** West Coast, South Island, New Zealand 41°51′S 171°58′E
57 I14 **Iñapari** Madre de Dios, E Peru 11°00′S 69°34′W
188 B17 **Inarajan** SE Guam 13°16′N 144°45′E
92 L10 **Inari** *Lapp.* Anár, Aanaar. Lappi, N Finland 68°54′N 27°06′E
92 L10 **Inarijärvi** *Lapp.* Aanaarjävri, *Swe.* Enareträsk. ◎ N Finland
92 L9 **Inarijoki** *Lapp.* Anárjohka. ≈ Finland/Norway
Inău *see* Ineu
165 P11 **Inawashiro-ko** *var.* Inawasiro Ko. ◎ Honshū, C Japan
Inawasiro Ko *see* Inawashiro-ko
105 X9 **Inca** Mallorca, Spain, W Mediterranean Sea 39°43′N 02°54′E
62 H7 **Inca de Oro** Atacama, N Chile 26°45′S 69°54′W
115 J15 **İnce Burnu** *cape* NW Turkey
136 K9 **İnce Burnu** *headland* N Turkey 42°06′N 34°57′E
136 I17 **İncekum Burnu** *headland* S Turkey 36°13′N 33°57′E
76 G7 **Inchiri** ◈ *region* NW Mauritania
163 X15 **Inch'ŏn** *off.* Inch'ŏn-gwangyŏksi, *Jap.* Jinsen; *prev.* Chemulpo. NW South Korea 37°27′N 126°41′E
161 X15 **Inch'on** ✈ (Sŏul) NW South Korea 37°37′N 126°42′E
Inch'ŏn-gwangyŏksi *see* Inch'ŏn
83 M17 **Inchope** Manica, C Mozambique 19°09′S 33°54′E
Incoronata *see* Kornat
103 Y15 **Incudine, Monte** ▲ Corse, France, C Mediterranean Sea 41°52′N 09°13′E
60 M10 **Indaiatuba** São Paulo, S Brazil 23°03′S 47°14′W
93 H17 **Indal** Västernorrland, C Sweden 62°36′N 17°06′E
93 H17 **Indalsälven** ≈ C Sweden
40 K8 **Inde** Durango, C Mexico 25°55′N 105°10′W
Indefatigable Island *see* Santa Cruz, Isla
35 S10 **Independence** California, W USA 36°48′N 118°14′W
29 X13 **Independence** Iowa, C USA 42°28′N 91°42′W
27 P7 **Independence** Kansas, C USA 37°13′N 95°43′W
20 M4 **Independence** Kentucky, S USA 38°56′N 84°32′W
27 R4 **Independence** Missouri, C USA 39°04′N 94°27′W
21 R8 **Independence** Virginia, NE USA 36°38′N 81°11′W
30 J7 **Independence** Wisconsin, N USA 44°21′N 91°25′W
197 R12 **Independence Fjord** *fjord* N Greenland
Independence Island *see* Malden Island
35 W2 **Independence Mountains** ▲▲ Nevada, W USA
57 K18 **Independencia** Cochabamba, C Bolivia 17°08′S 66°52′W
57 E16 **Independencia, Bahía de la** *bay* W Peru
Independencia, Monte *see* Adam, Mount
116 M12 **Independenţa** Galaţi, SE Romania 45°29′N 27°45′E
Inderagiri *see* Indragiri, Sungai
Inderbor *see* Inderborskiy
144 F11 **Inderborskiy** *Kaz.* Inderbor. Atyrau, W Kazakhstan 48°35′N 51°45′E
151 I14 **India** *off.* Republic of India, *var.* Indian Union, Union of India, *Hind.* Bhārat. ◆ *republic* S Asia
India *see* Inđija
18 D14 **Indiana** Pennsylvania, NE USA 40°37′N 79°09′W
31 N13 **Indiana** *off.* State of Indiana, *also known as* Hoosier State. ◈ *state* N USA
31 O14 **Indianapolis** *state capital* Indiana, N USA 39°46′N 86°09′W
11 O10 **Indian Cabins** Alberta, W Canada 59°51′N 117°06′W
42 G1 **Indian Church** Orange Walk, N Belize 17°47′N 88°39′W
Indian Desert *see* Thar Desert
11 U16 **Indian Head** Saskatchewan, S Canada 50°32′N 103°41′W
31 O4 **Indian Lake** ◎ Michigan, N USA
18 K9 **Indian Lake** ◎ New York, NE USA
31 R13 **Indian Lake** ⊠ Ohio, N USA
172-173 **Indian Ocean** *ocean*
29 V15 **Indianola** Iowa, C USA 41°21′N 93°33′W
22 K4 **Indianola** Mississippi, S USA 33°27′N 90°39′W
36 J6 **Indian Peak** ▲ Utah, W USA 38°18′N 113°52′W
23 Y13 **Indian River** *lagoon* Florida, SE USA
35 W10 **Indian Springs** Nevada, W USA 36°33′N 115°40′W
23 Y14 **Indiantown** Florida, SE USA 27°01′N 80°29′W
Indian Union *see* India
59 K19 **Indiara** Goiás, S Brazil 17°12′S 50°09′W
India, Republic of *see* India
India, Union of *see* India
125 Q4 **Indiga** Nenetskiy Avtonomnyy Okrug, NW Russian Federation 67°40′N 49°01′E
123 R9 **Indigirka** ≈ NE Russian Federation
112 L10 **Inđija** *Hung.* India; *prev.* Indjija. Vojvodina, N Serbia 45°03′N 20°04′E
35 V16 **Indio** California, W USA 33°42′N 116°13′W
42 M12 **Indio, Río** ≈ SE Nicaragua
152 I10 **Indira Gandhi** ✈ (Delhi) Delhi, N India
151 Q23 **Indira Point** *headland* Andaman and Nicobar Island, India, NE Indian Ocean 6°54′N 93°54′E
Indjija *see* Inđija
129 Q13 **Indo-Australian Plate** *tectonic feature*
173 N11 **Indomed Fracture Zone** *tectonic feature* SW Indian Ocean
170 L12 **Indonesia** *off.* Republic of Indonesia, *Ind.* Republik Indonesia; *prev.* Dutch East Indies, Netherlands East Indies, United States of Indonesia. ◆ *republic* SE Asia
Indonesian Borneo *see* Kalimantan
Indonesia, Republic of *see* Indonesia
Indonesia, Republik *see* Indonesia
Indonesia, United States of *see* Indonesia
154 G10 **Indore** Madhya Pradesh, C India 22°42′N 75°51′E
168 L11 **Indragiri, Sungai** *var.* Batang Kuantan, Inderagiri. ≈ Sumatera, W Indonesia
Indramajoe/Indramaju *see* Indramayu
169 P15 **Indramayu** *prev.* Indramajoe, Indramaju. Jawa, C Indonesia 06°22′S 108°20′E
155 K14 **Indrāvati** ≈ S India
103 N9 **Indre** ◈ *department* C France
102 M8 **Indre** ≈ C France
94 D13 **Indre Ålvik** Hordaland, S Norway 60°26′N 06°27′E
102 L8 **Indre-et-Loire** ◈ *department* C France
Indreville *see* Châteauroux
152 G3 **Indus** *Chin.* Yindu He; *prev.* Yin-tu Ho. ≈ S Asia
Indus Cone *see* Indus Fan
173 P3 **Indus Fan** *var.* Indus Cone. *undersea feature* N Arabian Sea 16°00′N 65°30′E
149 P17 **Indus, Mouths of the** *delta* S Pakistan
83 I24 **Indwe** Eastern Cape, SE South Africa 31°28′S 27°20′E
136 I10 **İnebolu** Kastamonu, N Turkey 41°57′N 33°45′E
77 P8 **I-n-Échaï** *oasis* C Mali
114 M13 **İnecik** Tekirdağ, NW Turkey 40°55′N 27°16′E
136 E12 **İnegöl** Bursa, NW Turkey 40°06′N 29°31′E
Inessa *see* Biancavilla
116 F10 **Ineu** *Hung.* Borosjenő; *prev.* Inău. Arad, W Romania 46°26′N 21°51′E
Ineul/Ineu, Vîrful *see* Ineu, Vârful
116 J9 **Ineu, Vârful** *var.* Ineul; *prev.* Vîrful Ineu. ▲ N Romania 47°31′N 24°52′E
21 P6 **Inez** Kentucky, S USA 37°53′N 82°33′W
74 E8 **Inezgane** ✈ (Agadir) W Morocco 30°35′N 09°27′W
41 T17 **Inferior, Laguna** *lagoon* S Mexico
40 M15 **Infiernillo, Presa del** ⊠ S Mexico
104 L2 **Infiesto** Asturias, N Spain 43°21′N 05°21′W
93 L20 **Ingå** *Fin.* Inkoo. Etelä-Suomi, S Finland 60°01′N 24°05′E
77 U10 **Ingal** *var.* I-n-Gall. Agadez, C Niger 16°52′N 06°57′E
I-n-Gall *see* Ingal
99 C18 **Ingelmunster** West-Vlaanderen, W Belgium 50°12′N 03°15′E
79 I18 **Ingende** Equateur, W Dem. Rep. Congo 0°15′S 18°58′E
62 L5 **Ingeniero Guillermo Nueva Juárez** Formosa, N Argentina 23°55′S 61°50′W
63 H16 **Ingeniero Jacobacci** Río Negro, C Argentina 41°18′S 69°35′W
14 F16 **Ingersoll** Ontario, S Canada 43°03′N 80°53′W
Ingettolgoy *see* Selenge
181 W5 **Ingham** Queensland, NE Australia 18°35′S 146°12′E
146 M11 **Ingichka** Samarqand Viloyati, C Uzbekistan 39°46′N 65°56′E
97 L16 **Ingleborough** ▲ N England, United Kingdom 54°07′N 02°22′W
25 T14 **Ingleside** Texas, SW USA 27°52′N 97°12′W
184 K10 **Inglewood** Taranaki, North Island, New Zealand 39°07′S 174°13′E
35 S15 **Inglewood** California, W USA 33°57′N 118°21′W
101 L21 **Ingolstadt** Bayern, S Germany 48°46′N 11°26′E
33 V9 **Ingomar** Montana, NW USA 46°34′N 107°21′W
13 R14 **Ingonish Beach** Cape Breton Island, Nova Scotia, SE Canada 46°42′N 60°22′W
153 S14 **Ingrāj Bāzār** *prev.* English Bazar. West Bengal, NE India 25°00′N 88°10′E
25 Q11 **Ingram** Texas, SW USA 30°04′N 99°14′W
195 X7 **Ingrid Christensen Coast** *physical region* Antarctica
74 K14 **I-n-Guezzam** S Algeria 19°35′N 05°49′E
Ingulets *see* Inhulets'
Inguri *see* Enguri
Ingushetia/Ingushetiya, Respublika *see* Ingushetiya, Respublika
127 O15 **Ingushetiya, Respublika** *var.* Respublika Ingushetiya, *Eng.* Ingushetia. ◈ *autonomous republic* SW Russian Federation
83 N20 **Inhambane** Inhambane, SE Mozambique 23°52′S 35°31′E
83 M20 **Inhambane** *off.* Província de Inhambane. ◈ *province* S Mozambique
Inhambane, Província de *see* Inhambane
83 N17 **Inhaminga** Sofala, C Mozambique 18°24′S 35°00′E
83 N20 **Inharrime** Inhambane, SE Mozambique 24°29′S 35°01′E
83 M18 **Inhassoro** Inhambane, E Mozambique 21°32′S 35°13′E
117 S9 **Inhulets'** *Rus.* Ingulets. Dnipropetrovs'ka Oblast', E Ukraine 47°43′N 33°16′E
117 R10 **Inhulets'** *Rus.* Ingulets. ≈ S Ukraine
105 Q10 **Iniesta** Castilla-La Mancha, C Spain 39°27′N 01°45′W
I-ning *see* Yining
54 K11 **Inírida, Río** ≈ E Colombia
Inis *see* Ennis
Inis Ceithleann *see* Enniskillen
Inis Córthaidh *see* Enniscorthy
Inis Díomáin *see* Ennistimon
97 A17 **Inishbofin** *Ir.* Inis Bó Finne. *island* W Ireland
97 B18 **Inisheer** *var.* Inishere, *Ir.* Inis Oírr. *island* W Ireland
Inishere *see* Inisheer
97 B18 **Inishmaan** *Ir.* Inis Meáin. *island* W Ireland
97 A18 **Inishmore** *Ir.* Árainn. *island* W Ireland
96 E13 **Inishtrahull** *Ir.* Inis Trá Tholl. *island* NW Ireland
97 A17 **Inishturk** *Ir.* Inis Toirc. *island* W Ireland
Inkoo *see* Ingå
185 J16 **Inland Kaikoura Range** ▲▲ South Island, New Zealand
Inland Sea *see* Seto-naikai
21 P11 **Inman** South Carolina, SE USA 35°03′N 82°05′W
108 L7 **Inn** ≈ C Europe
197 O11 **Innaanganeq** *var.* Kap York. *headland* NW Greenland 75°54′N 66°27′W
182 K2 **Innamincka** South Australia 27°47′S 140°45′E
92 G12 **Inndyr** Nordland, C Norway 67°01′N 14°00′E
42 G3 **Inner Channel** *inlet* SE Belize
96 F11 **Inner Hebrides** *island group* W Scotland, United Kingdom
172 H15 **Inner Islands** *var.* Central Group. *island group* NE Seychelles
Inner Mongolia/Inner Mongolian Autonomous Region *see* Nei Mongol Zizhiqu
96 G8 **Inner Sound** *strait* NW Scotland, United Kingdom
100 J13 **Innerste** ≈ C Germany
181 W5 **Innisfail** Queensland, NE Australia 17°29′S 146°03′E
11 Q15 **Innisfail** Alberta, SW Canada 52°01′N 113°59′W
Inniskilling *see* Enniskillen
39 O11 **Innoko River** ≈ Alaska, USA
Innsbruch *see* Innsbruck
108 M7 **Innsbruck** *var.* Innsbruch. Tirol, W Austria 47°17′N 11°25′E
79 I19 **Inongo** Bandundu, W Dem. Rep. Congo 01°55′S 18°20′E
Inoucdjouac *see* Inukjuak
Inowrazlaw *see* Inowrocław
110 I10 **Inowrocław** *Ger.* Hohensalza; *prev.* Inowrazlaw. Kujawski-pomorskie, C Poland 52°47′N 18°15′E
57 K18 **Inquisivi** La Paz, W Bolivia 16°55′S 67°10′W
Inrin *see* Yüanlin
77 O8 **I-n-Sâkâne, 'Erg** *desert* N Mali
77 O8 **I-n-Sâkâne, 'Erg** *desert* N Mali
74 J10 **I-n-Salah** *var.* In Salah. C Algeria 27°11′N 02°31′E
127 O5 **Insar** Respublika Mordoviya, W Russian Federation 53°52′N 44°26′E
189 X15 **Insiaf** Kosrae, E Micronesia
94 L13 **Insjön** Dalarna, C Sweden 60°40′N 15°05′E
Insterburg *see* Chernyakhovsk
Insula *see* Lille
116 L13 **Însurăţei** Brăila, SE Romania 44°55′N 27°40′E
125 V6 **Inta** Respublika Komi, NW Russian Federation 66°00′N 60°10′E
77 R9 **I-n-Tebezas** Kidal, E Mali 17°58′N 01°51′E
Interamna *see* Teramo
Interamna Nahars *see* Terni
28 L11 **Interior** South Dakota, N USA 43°42′N 101°57′W
108 E9 **Interlaken** Bern, SW Switzerland 46°41′N 07°51′E
29 V2 **International Falls** Minnesota, N USA 48°33′N 93°26′W
167 O7 **Inthanon, Doi** ▲ NW Thailand 18°33′N 98°29′E
42 G7 **Intibucá** ◈ *department* SW Honduras
42 G8 **Intipucá** La Unión, SE El Salvador 13°10′N 88°03′W
61 B15 **Intiyaco** Santa Fe, C Argentina 28°43′S 60°04′W
116 K12 **Întorsura Buzăului** *Ger.* Bozau, *Hung.* Bodzafordulő. Covasna, E Romania 45°40′N 26°02′E
22 H9 **Intracoastal Waterway** *inland waterway system* Louisiana, S USA
25 V13 **Intracoastal Waterway** *inland waterway system* Texas, SW USA
108 G11 **Intragna** Ticino, S Switzerland 46°12′N 08°42′E
165 P14 **Inubō-zaki** *headland* Honshū, S Japan 35°42′N 140°51′E
164 E14 **Inukai** Ōita, Kyūshū, SW Japan 33°05′N 131°37′E
12 I5 **Inukjuak** *var.* Inoucdjouac; *prev.* Port Harrison. Québec, NE Canada 58°28′N 77°58′W
63 I24 **Inútil, Bahía** *bay* S Chile
Inuuvik *see* Inuvik
11 R8 **Inuvik** *var.* Inuuvik. Northwest Territories, NW Canada 68°25′N 133°35′W
164 L13 **Inuyama** Aichi, Honshū, SW Japan 35°23′N 136°55′E
56 G13 **Inuya, Río** ≈ E Peru
125 U13 **In'va** ≈ NW Russian Federation
96 H11 **Inveraray** W Scotland, United Kingdom 56°13′N 05°05′W
185 C24 **Invercargill** Southland, South Island, New Zealand 46°25′S 168°22′E
183 T5 **Inverell** New South Wales, SE Australia 29°46′S 151°10′E
96 I8 **Invergordon** N Scotland, United Kingdom 57°42′N 04°02′W
11 P16 **Invermere** British Columbia, SW Canada 50°30′N 116°00′W
13 R14 **Inverness** Cape Breton Island, Nova Scotia, SE Canada 46°14′N 61°19′W
96 I8 **Inverness** N Scotland, United Kingdom 57°27′N 04°15′W
23 V11 **Inverness** Florida, SE USA 28°50′N 82°19′W
96 I9 **Inverness** *cultural region* NW Scotland, United Kingdom
96 K9 **Inverurie** NE Scotland, United Kingdom 57°14′N 02°14′W
182 F8 **Investigator Group** *island group* South Australia
173 T7 **Investigator Ridge** *undersea feature* E Indian Ocean 11°30′S 98°10′E

◆ Country
● Country Capital
◇ Dependent Territory
C Dependent Territory Capital
◈ Administrative Regions
✈ International Airport
▲ Mountain
▲▲ Mountain Range
Volcano
≈ River
◎ Lake
⊠ Reservoir

◆ Country | ◇ Dependent Territory | ◆ Administrative Regions | ▲ Mountain | ✲ Volcano | ☐ Lake
● Country Capital | ○ Dependent Territory Capital | ✗ International Airport | ▲ Mountain Range | ✲ River | ☐ Reservoir

IZOLA – JHANG/JHANG SADAR

109 S13 **Izola** *It.* Isola d'Istria. SW Slovenia 45°31′N 13°40′E
138 H9 **Izra'** *var.* Ezra, Ezraa. Dar'ā, S Syria 32°52′N 36°15′E
41 P14 **Iztaccíhuatl, Volcán** *var.* Volcán Ixtaccíhuatal. S Mexico 19°07′N 98°37′W
42 C7 **Iztapa** Escuintla, SE Guatemala 13°58′N 90°42′W
Izúcar de Matamoros *see* Matamoros
165 N14 **Izu-hantō** *peninsula* Honshū, S Japan
164 C12 **Izuhara** Nagasaki, Tsushima, SW Japan 34°11′N 129°16′E
164 J14 **Izumiōtsu** Ōsaka, Honshū, SW Japan 34°29′N 135°25′E
164 I14 **Izumi-Sano** Ōsaka, Honshū, SW Japan 34°23′N 135°18′E
164 G12 **Izumo** Shimane, Honshū, SW Japan 35°22′N 132°46′E
192 H5 **Izu Trench** *undersea feature* NW Pacific Ocean
122 K6 **Izvestiy TsIK, Ostrova** *island* N Russian Federation
114 G10 **Izvor** Pernik, W Bulgaria 42°27′N 22°53′E
116 L5 **Izyaslav** Khmel'nyts'ka Oblast', W Ukraine 50°08′N 26°53′E
117 W6 **Izyum** Kharkivs'ka Oblast', E Ukraine 49°12′N 37°19′E

J

93 M18 **Jaala** Etelä-Suomi, S Finland 61°04′N 26°30′E
Jaanilinn *see* Ivangorod
140 J5 **Jabal ash Shifā** *desert* NW Saudi Arabia
141 U8 **Jabal az Ẕannah** *var.* Jebel Dhanna. Abū Ẓaby, W United Arab Emirates 24°10′N 52°36′E
138 E11 **Jabalīya** *var.* Jabāliyah. NE Gaza Strip 31°32′N 34°29′E
Jabāliyah *see* Jabalīya
105 N11 **Jabalón** ~ C Spain
154 J10 **Jabalpur** *prev.* Jubbulpore. Madhya Pradesh, C India 23°10′N 79°59′E
141 N15 **Jabal Zuqar, Jazīrat** *var.* Az Zuqur. *island* SW Yemen
Jabat *see* Jabwot
138 J3 **Jabbūl, Sabkhat al** *sabkha* NW Syria
181 P1 **Jabiru** Northern Territory, N Australia 12°44′S 132°48′E
138 H4 **Jablah** *var.* Jeble, *Fr.* Djéblé. Al Lādhiqīyah, W Syria 35°00′N 36°00′E
112 C11 **Jablanac** Lika-Senj, W Croatia 44°43′N 14°54′E
113 H14 **Jablanica** Federacija Bosna I Hercegovina, SW Bosnia and Herzegovina 43°39′N 17°43′E
113 M20 **Jablanica** *Alb.* Mali i Jabllanicës, *var.* Malet e Jabllanicës. ▲ Albania/FYR Macedonia *see also* Jabllanicës, Mali i
Jabllanicës, Malet e *see* Jablanica/Jabllanicës, Mali i
113 M20 **Jabllanicës, Mali i**, *Mac.* Jablanica. ▲ Albania/FYR Macedonia *see also* Jablanica
111 E15 **Jablonec nad Nisou** *Ger.* Gablonz an der Neisse. Liberecký Kraj, N Czech Republic 50°44′N 15°10′E
Jabłonków/Jablunkau *see* Jablunkov
110 J9 **Jabłonowo Pomorskie** Kujawski-pomorskie, C Poland 53°24′N 19°08′E
111 J17 **Jablunkov** *Ger.* Jablunkau, *Pol.* Jabłonków. Moravskoslezský Kraj, E Czech Republic 49°35′N 18°46′E
59 Q15 **Jaboatão** Pernambuco, E Brazil 08°05′S 35°W
60 L8 **Jaboticabal** São Paulo, S Brazil 21°15′S 48°17′W
189 U7 **Jabwot** *var* Jabat, Jebat, Jōwat. *island* Ralik Chain, S Marshall Islands
105 S4 **Jaca** Aragón, NE Spain 42°34′N 00°33′W
42 B4 **Jacaltenango** Huehuetenango, W Guatemala 15°39′N 91°46′W
59 G14 **Jacaré-a-Canga** Pará, NE Brazil 05°59′S 57°32′W
60 N10 **Jacareí** São Paulo, S Brazil 23°18′S 45°55′W
59 I18 **Jaciara** Mato Grosso, W Brazil 15°59′S 54°57′W
59 E15 **Jaciparaná** Rondônia, W Brazil 09°20′S 64°28′W
19 P5 **Jackman** Maine, NE USA 45°35′N 70°14′W
35 X1 **Jackpot** Nevada, W USA 41°57′N 114°41′W
20 M8 **Jacksboro** Tennessee, S USA 36°19′N 84°11′W
25 S6 **Jacksboro** Texas, SW USA 33°13′N 98°11′W
23 N7 **Jackson** Alabama, S USA 31°30′N 87°53′W
35 P7 **Jackson** California, W USA 38°19′N 120°45′W
23 T4 **Jackson** Georgia, SE USA 33°17′N 83°58′W
21 O6 **Jackson** Kentucky, S USA 37°32′N 83°24′W
22 J8 **Jackson** Louisiana, S USA 30°50′N 91°13′W
31 Q10 **Jackson** Michigan, N USA 42°15′N 84°24′W
29 T11 **Jackson** Minnesota, N USA 43°38′N 95°00′W
22 K5 **Jackson** *state capital* Mississippi, S USA 32°19′N 90°12′W
27 Y7 **Jackson** Missouri, C USA 37°23′N 89°40′W
21 W8 **Jackson** North Carolina, SE USA 36°24′N 77°25′W
31 T15 **Jackson** Ohio, NE USA 39°03′N 82°40′W
20 G9 **Jackson** Tennessee, S USA 35°37′N 88°50′W
33 S14 **Jackson** Wyoming, C USA 43°28′N 110°45′W
185 C19 **Jackson Bay** *bay* South Island, New Zealand
186 E9 **Jackson Field** ✈ (Port Moresby) Central/National Capital District, S Papua New Guinea 09°28′S 147°12′E
185 C20 **Jackson Head** *headland* South Island, New Zealand 43°57′S 168°38′E
23 S8 **Jackson, Lake** ◎ Florida, SE USA
33 S13 **Jackson Lake** ◎ Wyoming, C USA
194 J6 **Jackson, Mount** ▲ Antarctica 71°43′S 63°45′W
37 U3 **Jackson Reservoir** ◎ Colorado, C USA
23 Q3 **Jacksonville** Alabama, S USA 33°48′N 85°45′W
27 V11 **Jacksonville** Arkansas, C USA 34°52′N 92°08′W
23 W8 **Jacksonville** Florida, SE USA 30°20′N 81°39′W
30 K14 **Jacksonville** Illinois, N USA 39°43′N 90°13′W
21 W11 **Jacksonville** North Carolina, SE USA 34°45′N 77°26′W
25 W7 **Jacksonville** Texas, SW USA 31°57′N 95°16′W
23 X9 **Jacksonville Beach** Florida, SE USA 30°17′N 81°23′W
44 L9 **Jacmel** *var.* Jaquemel. S Haiti 18°13′N 72°33′W
Jacob *see* Nkayi
149 Q12 **Jacobābād** Sind, SE Pakistan 28°16′N 68°30′E
55 T11 **Jacobs Ladder Falls** *waterfall* S Guyana
45 O11 **Jaco, Pointe** *headland* N Dominica 15°38′N 61°25′W
15 Q9 **Jacques-Cartier** ~ Québec, SE Canada
13 P11 **Jacques-Cartier, Détroit de** *var.* Jacques-Cartier Passage. *strait* Gulf of St. Lawrence/St. Lawrence River, Canada
15 W6 **Jacques-Cartier, Mont** ▲ Québec, SE Canada 48°58′N 66°00′W
Jacques-Cartier Passage *see* Jacques-Cartier, Détroit de
61 H16 **Jacuí, Rio** ~ S Brazil
60 L11 **Jacupiranga** São Paulo, S Brazil 24°42′S 48°00′W
100 G10 **Jade** ~ NW Germany
100 G10 **Jadebusen** *bay* NW Germany
Jadotville *see* Likasi
Jadransko More/Jadransko Morje *see* Adriatic Sea
105 O7 **Jadraque** Castilla-La Mancha, C Spain 40°55′N 02°55′W
95 I22 **Jægerspris** Frederiksborg, E Denmark 55°52′N 11°59′E
56 C10 **Jaén** Cajamarca, N Peru 05°45′S 78°51′W
105 N13 **Jaén** Andalucía, SW Spain 37°46′N 03°48′W
105 N13 **Jaén** ◐ *province* Andalucía, S Spain
95 C17 **Jæren** *physical region* S Norway
155 J23 **Jaffna** Northern Province, N Sri Lanka 09°42′N 80°03′E
155 K23 **Jaffna Lagoon** *lagoon* N Sri Lanka
19 N10 **Jaffrey** New Hampshire, NE USA 42°46′N 72°00′W
138 H13 **Jafr, Qā' al** *var.* El Jafr. *salt pan* S Jordan
152 J9 **Jagādhri** Haryāna, N India 30°11′N 77°18′E
118 H4 **Jägala** *var.* Jägala Jōgi, *Ger.* Jaggowal. ~ NW Estonia
Jägala Jōgi *see* Jägala
Jagannath *see* Puri
154 P13 **httt†t** Orissa, SE India 20°15′N 86°10′E
155 L14 **Jagdalpur** Chhattīsgarh, C India 19°07′N 82°04′E
163 U5 **Jagdaqi** Nei Mongol Zizhiqu, N China 50°26′N 124°03′E
Jägerndorf *see* Krnov
Jaggowal *see* Jägala
139 O2 **Jaghjaghah, Nahr** ~ N Syria
112 N13 **Jagodina** *prev.* Svetozarevo. Serbia, C Serbia 43°59′N 21°15′E
112 K12 **Jagodnja** ▲▲ W Serbia
101 I20 **Jagst** ~ SW Germany
155 I14 **Jagtiāl** Andhra Pradesh, C India 18°49′N 78°53′E
61 H18 **Jaguarão** Rio Grande do Sul, S Brazil 32°30′S 53°25′W
61 H18 **Jaguarão, Rio** *var.* Río Yaguarón. ~ Brazil/Uruguay
60 K11 **Jaguariaíva** Paraná, S Brazil 24°15′S 49°44′W
44 D5 **Jagüey Grande** Matanzas, W Cuba 22°31′N 81°07′W
153 P14 **Jahānābād** Bihār, N India 25°13′N 84°59′E
Jahra *see* Al Jahrā'
143 P12 **Jahrom** *var.* Jahrum. Fārs, S Iran 28°35′N 53°32′E
Jahrum *see* Jahrom
Jailolo *see* Halmahera, Pulau
Jainat *see* Chai Nat
Jainti *see* Jayanti
152 H12 **Jaipur** *prev.* Jeypore. *state capital* Rājasthān, N India 26°54′N 75°47′E
153 T14 **Jaipurhat** *var.* Joypurhat. Rajshahi, NW Bangladesh 25°04′N 89°06′E
152 D11 **Jaisalmer** Rājasthān, NW India 26°55′N 70°56′E
154 O12 **Jājapur** *var.* Jajpur, Panikoilli. Orissa, E India 18°54′N 82°36′E
143 R4 **Jājarm** Khorāsān-e Shemālī, NE Iran 36°58′N 56°26′E
112 G12 **Jajce** Federacija Bosna I Hercegovina, W Bosnia and Herzegovina 44°20′N 17°16′E
Jajı *see* 'Alī Kheyl
Jajpur *see* Jājapur
83 D17 **Jakalsberg** Otjozondjupa, N Namibia 19°23′S 17°28′E
169 O15 **Jakarta** *prev.* Djakarta, *Dut.* Batavia. ● (Indonesia) Jawa, C Indonesia 06°08′S 106°45′E
10 I8 **Jakes Corner** Yukon Territory, W Canada 60°18′N 134°00′W
152 H9 **Jākhal** Haryāna, NW India 29°46′N 75°51′E
Jakobeny *see* Iacobeni
93 K16 **Jakobstad** *Fin.* Pietarsaari. Länsi-Suomi, W Finland 63°41′N 22°40′E
Jakobstadt *see* Jēkabpils
113 O18 **Jakupica** ▲▲ C FYR Macedonia
37 W15 **Jal** New Mexico, SW USA 32°07′N 103°10′W
141 P7 **Jalājil** *var.* Ğalāğıl. Ar Riyāḍ, C Saudi Arabia 25°43′N 45°22′E
149 S5 **Jalālābād** *var.* Jalalabad, Jelalabad. Nangarhār, E Afghanistan 34°26′N 70°28′E
Jalal-Abad *see* Dzhalal-Abad, Dzhalal-Abadskaya Oblast', Kyrgyzstan
Jalal-Abad Oblasty *see* Dzhalal-Abadskaya Oblast'
149 V7 **Jalālpur** Punjab, E Pakistan 32°39′N 74°11′E
149 T11 **Jalālpur Pīrwāla** Punjab, E Pakistan 29°30′N 71°20′E
152 H8 **Jalandhar** *prev.* Jullundur. Punjab, N India 31°20′N 75°37′E
42 J7 **Jalán, Río** ~ S Honduras
42 E6 **Jalapa** Jalapa, C Guatemala 14°39′N 89°59′W
42 J7 **Jalapa** Nueva Segovia, NW Nicaragua 13°56′N 86°11′W
42 A3 **Jalapa** *off.* Departamento de Jalapa. ◐ *department* SE Guatemala
Jalapa, Departamento de *see* Jalapa
42 E6 **Jalapa, Río** ~ SE Guatemala
143 X13 **Jālaq** Sīstān va Balūchestān, SE Iran
93 K17 **Jalasjärvi** Länsi-Suomi, W Finland 62°30′N 22°50′E
149 O8 **Jaldak** Zābol, SE Afghanistan 32°00′N 66°45′E
60 J7 **Jales** São Paulo, S Brazil 20°15′S 50°34′W
154 P11 **Jaleshwar** *var.* Jaleswar. Orissa, NE India 21°51′N 87°15′E
Jaleswar *see* Jaleshwar
154 F12 **Jalgaon** Mahārāshtra, C India 21°01′N 75°34′E
139 W12 **Jalībah** Dhī Qār, S Iraq 30°37′N 46°31′E
139 W13 **Jalīb Shahāb** Al Muthanná, S Iraq 30°26′N 46°09′E
77 X15 **Jalingo** Taraba, E Nigeria 08°54′N 11°22′E
40 K13 **Jalisco** ◐ *state* SW Mexico
154 G13 **Jālna** Mahārāshtra, W India 19°50′N 75°53′N
Jalomitsa *see* Ialomiţa
105 R5 **Jalón** ~ N Spain
152 E13 **Jālor** Rājasthān, N India 25°21′N 72°43′E
112 K11 **Jalovik** Serbia, W Serbia 44°37′N 19°48′E
40 L12 **Jalpa** Zacatecas, C Mexico 21°40′N 103°W
153 S12 **Jalpāiguri** West Bengal, NE India 26°43′N 88°24′E
41 O12 **Jalpán** *var.* Jalpan. Querétaro de Arteaga, C Mexico 21°13′N 99°28′W
Jalpan *see* Jalpán
67 P2 **Jalta** *island* N Tunisia
75 S9 **Jālū** *var.* Jūlā. NE Libya 29°02′N 21°33′E
189 U8 **Jaluit Atoll** *var.* Jālwōj. *atoll* Ralik Chain, S Marshall Islands
Jālwōj *see* Jaluit Atoll
81 L18 **Jamaame** *It.* Giamame; *prev.* Margherita. Jubbada Hoose, S Somalia 0°00′N 42°43′E
77 W13 **Jamaare** ~ NE Nigeria
44 G9 **Jamaica** ◆ *commonwealth republic* W West Indies
47 P3 **Jamaica** *island* W West Indies
44 I9 **Jamaica Channel** *channel* Haiti/Jamaica
153 T14 **Jamalpur** Dhaka, N Bangladesh 24°54′N 89°57′E
153 Q14 **Jamālpur** Bihār, NE India 25°19′N 86°30′E
168 L9 **Jamaluang** *var.* Jemaluang. Johor, Peninsular Malaysia 02°15′N 103°50′E
59 I14 **Jamanxim, Rio** ~ C Brazil
56 B8 **Jambeli, Canal de** *channel* S Ecuador
99 I20 **Jambes** Namur, SE Belgium 50°26′N 04°51′E
168 L12 **Jambi** *var.* Telanaipura; *prev.* Djambi. Sumatera, W Indonesia 01°34′S 103°37′E
168 K12 **Jambi** *off.* Propinsi Jambi, *var.* Djambi. ◐ *province* W Indonesia
Jambi, Propinsi *see* Jambi
Jamdena *see* Yamdena, Pulau
12 H8 **James Bay** *bay* Ontario/Québec, E Canada
63 F19 **James, Isla** *island* Archipiélago de los Chonos, S Chile
181 Q8 **James Ranges** ▲▲ Northern Territory, C Australia
29 P8 **James River** ~ North Dakota/South Dakota, N USA
21 X7 **James River** ~ Virginia, NE USA
194 H4 **James Ross Island** *island* Antarctica
182 I8 **Jamestown** South Australia 33°13′S 138°36′E
65 G25 **Jamestown** ○ (Saint Helena) NW Saint Helena 15°56′S 05°44′W
35 P8 **Jamestown** California, W USA 37°57′N 120°25′W
20 L7 **Jamestown** Kentucky, S USA 36°58′N 85°03′W
18 D11 **Jamestown** New York, NE USA 42°05′N 79°15′W
29 P5 **Jamestown** North Dakota, N USA 46°54′N 98°42′W
20 L8 **Jamestown** Tennessee, S USA 36°24′N 84°58′W
Jamestown *see* Holetown
15 N10 **Jamet** ~ Québec, SE Canada
41 Q17 **Jamiltepec** *var.* Santiago Jamiltepec. Oaxaca, SE Mexico 16°18′N 97°51′W
95 F20 **Jammerbugten** *bay* Skagerrak, E North Sea
152 H6 **Jammu** *prev.* Jummoo. *state capital* Jammu and Kashmir, NW India 32°43′N 74°54′E
152 I5 **Jammu and Kashmir** *var.* Jammu-Kashmir, Kashmir. ◐ *state* NW India
149 V4 **Jammu and Kashmīr** *disputed region* India/Pakistan
Jammu-Kashmir *see* Jammu and Kashmir
154 B10 **Jāmnagar** *prev.* Navanagar. Gujarāt, W India 22°28′N 70°06′E
149 S11 **Jāmpur** Punjab, E Pakistan 29°38′N 70°40′E
93 L18 **Jämsä** Länsi-Suomi, C Finland 61°51′N 25°10′E
93 L18 **Jämsänkoski** Länsi-Suomi, C Finland 61°54′N 25°10′E
153 Q16 **Jamshedpur** Jhārkhand, NE India 22°47′N 86°12′E
94 K9 **Jämtland** ◐ *county* C Sweden
153 Q14 **Jamūi** Bihār, NE India 24°57′N 86°14′E
Jamuna *see* Brahmaputra
153 T14 **Jamuna Nadi** ~ N Bangladesh
Jamundá *see* Nhamundá, Rio
54 D11 **Jamundí** Valle del Cauca, SW Colombia 03°16′N 76°31′W
153 Q12 **Janakpur** Central, C Nepal 26°45′N 85°55′E
59 N18 **Janaúba** Minas Gerais, SE Brazil 15°47′S 43°16′W
58 K11 **Janaucu, Ilha** *island* NE Brazil
143 Q7 **Jandaq** Eşfahān, C Iran 34°04′N 54°26′E
54 Q11 **Jandia, Punta de** *headland* Fuerteventura, Islas Canarias, Spain, NE Atlantic Ocean 28°03′N 14°32′W
59 B14 **Jandiatuba, Rio** ~ NW Brazil
105 N12 **Jándula** ~ S Spain
29 V10 **Janesville** Minnesota, N USA 44°07′N 93°43′W
30 L9 **Janesville** Wisconsin, N USA 42°42′N 89°02′W
83 N20 **Jangamo** Inhambane, SE Mozambique 24°04′S 35°25′E
155 J14 **Jangaon** Andhra Pradesh, C India 18°47′N 79°25′E
153 S14 **Jangīpur** West Bengal, NE India 24°31′N 88°03′E
Janina *see* Ioánnina
Janischken *see* Joniškis
112 J11 **Janja** NE Bosnia and Herzegovina 44°40′N 19°15′E
154 L12 **Jānjgir** Chhattīsgarh, SW India 22°02′N 82°30′E
Jankovac *see* Jánoshalma
197 Q15 **Jan Mayen** ◇ *Norwegian dependency* N Atlantic Ocean
84 D5 **Jan Mayen** *island* N Atlantic Ocean
197 R15 **Jan Mayen Fracture Zone** *tectonic feature* Greenland Sea/Norwegian Sea
197 R15 **Jan Mayen Ridge** *undersea feature* Greenland Sea/Norwegian Sea 69°00′N 08°00′W
40 H3 **Janos** Chihuahua, N Mexico 30°50′N 108°10′W
111 K25 **Jánoshalma** *SCr.* Jankovac. Bács-Kiskun, S Hungary 46°19′N 19°16′E
Janów *see* Ivanava, Belarus
110 H10 **Janowiec Wielkopolski** *Ger.* Janowitz. Kujawski-pomorskie, C Poland 52°47′N 17°30′E
Janowitz *see* Janowiec Wielkopolski
Janow/Janów *see* Jonava, Lithuania
111 O15 **Janów Lubelski** Lubelski, E Poland 50°42′N 22°24′E
Janów Poleski *see* Ivanava
83 H25 **Jansenville** Eastern Cape, S South Africa 32°56′S 24°40′E
59 M18 **Januária** Minas Gerais, SE Brazil 15°28′S 44°23′W
Janūbīyah, Al Bādiyah al *see* Ash Shāmīyah
102 I7 **Janzé** Ille-et-Vilaine, NW France 47°55′N 01°28′W
154 F10 **Jaora** Madhya Pradesh, C India 23°40′N 75°10′E
131 Y9 **Japan** *var.* Nippon, *Jap.* Nihon. ◆ *monarchy* E Asia
129 Y9 **Japan** *island group* E Asia
192 H4 **Japan Basin** *undersea feature* N Sea of Japan 40°00′N 135°00′E
129 Y8 **Japan, Sea of** *var.* East Sea, *Rus.* Yapanskoye More. *sea* NW Pacific Ocean *see also* East Sea
192 H4 **Japan Trench** *undersea feature* NW Pacific Ocean 37°00′N 143°00′E
Japen *see* Yapen, Pulau
59 A15 **Japiim** *var.* Máncio Lima. Acre, W Brazil 08°00′S 73°39′W
58 D12 **Japurá** Amazonas, N Brazil 01°43′S 66°14′W
58 C12 **Japurá, Rio** *var.* Río Caquetá, Yapurá. ~ Brazil/Colombia *see also* Caquetá, Río
Japurá, Rio *see* Caquetá, Río
43 W17 **Jaqué** Darién, SE Panama 07°31′N 78°09′W
Jaquemel *see* Jacmel
Jarablos *see* Jarābulus
138 K2 **Jarābulus** *var.* Jarablos, Jerablus, *Fr.* Djérablous. Ḥalab, N Syria 36°51′N 38°02′E
60 K13 **Jaraguá do Sul** Santa Catarina, S Brazil 26°29′S 49°07′W
104 K9 **Jaraicejo** Extremadura, W Spain 39°40′N 05°49′W
104 K9 **Jaráiz de la Vera** Extremadura, W Spain 40°04′N 05°45′W
105 O7 **Jarama** ~ C Spain
63 J20 **Jaramillo** Santa Cruz, SE Argentina 47°10′S 67°07′W
Jarandilla de la Vega *see* Jarandilla de la Vera
104 K8 **Jarandilla de la Vera** *var.* Jarandilla de la Vega. Extremadura, W Spain 40°08′N 05°39′W
149 V9 **Jarānwāla** Punjab, E Pakistan 31°20′N 73°26′E
138 G9 **Jarash** *var.* Jerash; *anc.* Gerasa. Irbid, NW Jordan 32°17′N 35°54′E
Jarbah, Jazīrat *see* Jerba, Île de
94 N13 **Järbo** Gävleborg, C Sweden 60°43′N 16°40′E
Jardan *see* Yordon
44 F7 **Jardines de la Reina, Archipiélago de los** *island group* C Cuba
162 I8 **Jargalant** Bayanhongor, C Mongolia 47°14′N 99°43′E
162 K6 **Jargalant** Bulgan, N Mongolia 49°09′N 104°19′E
162 G7 **Jargalant** *var.* Buyanbat. Govĭ-Altay, W Mongolia 47°00′N 95°57′E
162 I6 **Jargalant** *var.* Orgil. Hövsgöl, C Mongolia 48°31′N 99°19′E
Jargalant *see* Battsengel
Jargalant *see* Bulgan, Bayan-Ölgiy, Mongolia
Jargalant *see* Biger, Govĭ-Altay, Mongolia
Jarīd, Shaţţ al *see* Jerid, Chott el
58 I11 **Jari, Rio** *var.* Jary. ~ N Brazil
141 N7 **Jarīr, Wādī al** *dry watercourse* C Saudi Arabia
Jarja *see* Yur'ya
94 L13 **Järna** *var.* Dala-Jarna. Dalarna, C Sweden 60°31′N 14°22′E
95 O16 **Järna** Stockholm, C Sweden 59°05′N 17°35′E
102 K11 **Jarnac** Charente, W France 45°41′N 00°10′W
110 H12 **Jarocin** Wielkopolskie, C Poland 51°59′N 17°30′E
111 F16 **Jaroměř** *Ger.* Jermer. Královéhradecký Kraj, N Czech Republic 50°22′N 15°55′E
Jaroslau *see* Jarosław
111 O16 **Jarosław** *Ger.* Jaroslau, *Rus.* Yaroslav. Podkarpackie, SE Poland 50°01′N 22°41′E
93 F16 **Järpen** Jämtland, C Sweden 63°21′N 13°30′E
147 O14 **Jarqo'rg'on** *Rus.* Dzharkurgan. Surkhondaryo Viloyati, S Uzbekistan 37°31′N 67°20′E
139 P2 **Jarrāh, Wadi** *dry watercourse* NE Syria
Jars, Plain of *see* Xiangkhoang, Plateau de
162 K14 **Jartai Yanchi** ◎ N China
59 E16 **Jaru** Rondônia, W Brazil 10°24′S 62°45′W
Jarud Qi *see* Lubei
118 I4 **Järva-Jaani** *Ger.* Sankt-Johannis. Järvamaa, N Estonia 59°03′N 25°54′E
118 G5 **Järvakandi** *Ger.* Jerwakant. Raplamaa, NW Estonia 58°45′N 24°49′E
118 H4 **Järvamaa** *var.* Järva Maakond. ◐ *province* N Estonia
Järva Maakond *see* Järvamaa
93 L19 **Järvenpää** Etelä-Suomi, S Finland 60°29′N 25°06′E
14 G17 **Jarvis** Ontario, S Canada 42°53′N 80°06′W
177 R8 **Jarvis Island** ◇ *US unincorporated territory* C Pacific Ocean
94 M11 **Järvsö** Gävleborg, C Sweden 61°43′N 16°25′E
Jary *see* Jari, Rio
112 M9 **Jaša Tomić** Vojvodina, NE Serbia 45°27′N 20°51′E
112 D12 **Jasenice** Zadar, SW Croatia 44°15′N 15°33′E
154 L12 **Jashpurnagar** Chhattīsgarh, SW India 22°53′N 84°09′E
138 I11 **Jashshat al 'Adlah, Wādī al** *dry watercourse* C Jordan
77 Q16 **Jasikan** E Ghana 07°24′N 00°28′E
Jāsk *see* Bandar-e Jāsk
146 F6 **Jasliq** *Rus.* Zhaslyk. Qoraqalpog'iston Respublikasi, NW Uzbekistan 43°57′N 57°30′E
111 N17 **Jasło** Podkarpackie, SE Poland 49°45′N 21°28′E
11 U16 **Jasmin** Saskatchewan, S Canada 51°11′N 103°34′W
65 A23 **Jason Islands** *island group* NW Falkland Islands
194 I4 **Jason Peninsula** *peninsula* Antarctica
31 N15 **Jasonville** Indiana, N USA 39°09′N 87°12′W
11 O15 **Jasper** Alberta, SW Canada 52°55′N 118°05′W
14 L13 **Jasper** Ontario, SE Canada 44°50′N 75°57′W
23 O3 **Jasper** Alabama, S USA 33°49′N 87°16′W
27 T9 **Jasper** Arkansas, C USA 36°00′N 93°11′W
23 U8 **Jasper** Florida, SE USA 30°31′N 82°57′W
31 N16 **Jasper** Indiana, N USA 38°22′N 86°57′W
29 R11 **Jasper** Minnesota, N USA 43°51′N 96°24′W
27 S7 **Jasper** Missouri, C USA 37°20′N 94°18′W
20 K10 **Jasper** Tennessee, S USA 35°04′N 85°36′W
25 Y9 **Jasper** Texas, SW USA 30°55′N 94°00′W
11 O15 **Jasper National Park** *national park* Alberta/British Columbia, SW Canada
Jassy *see* Iaşi
113 N14 **Jastrebac** ▲▲ SE Serbia
112 D9 **Jastrebarsko** Zagreb, N Croatia 45°40′N 15°40′E
Jastrow *see* Jastrowie
110 G9 **Jastrowie** *Ger.* Jastrow. Wielkopolskie, C Poland 53°25′N 16°48′E
111 J17 **Jastrzębie-Zdrój** Śląskie, S Poland 49°58′N 18°34′E
111 L22 **Jászapáti** Jász-Nagykun-Szolnok, E Hungary 47°30′N 20°10′E
111 L22 **Jászberény** Jász-Nagykun-Szolnok, E Hungary 47°30′N 19°56′E
111 L23 **Jász-Nagykun-Szolnok** *off.* Jász-Nagykun-Szolnok Megye. ◐ *county* E Hungary
Jász-Nagykun-Szolnok Megye *see* Jász-Nagykun-Szolnok
59 J19 **Jataí** Goiás, C Brazil 17°58′S 51°45′W
58 G12 **Jatapu, Serra do** ▲▲ N Brazil
41 W16 **Jatate, Río** ~ SE Mexico
149 P17 **Jāti** Sind, SE Pakistan 24°20′N 68°18′E
44 F6 **Jatibonico** Sancti Spíritus, C Cuba 21°56′N 79°11′W
169 O16 **Jatiluhur, Danau** ◎ Jawa, S Indonesia
Jativa *see* Xàtiva
149 S11 **Jattoi** Punjab, E Pakistan 29°29′N 70°58′E
60 L9 **Jaú** São Paulo, S Brazil 22°11′S 48°35′W
58 F11 **Jauaperi, Rio** ~ N Brazil
99 I19 **Jauche** Walloon Brabant, C Belgium 50°42′N 04°55′E
Jauer *see* Jawor
Jauf *see* Al Jawf
149 U7 **Jauharābād** Punjab, E Pakistan 32°16′N 72°17′E
57 E14 **Jauja** Junín, C Peru 11°48′S 75°30′W
41 O10 **Jaumave** Tamaulipas, C Mexico 23°28′N 99°22′W
118 H10 **Jaunjelgava** *Ger.* Friedrichstadt. Aizkraukle, S Latvia 56°38′N 25°03′E
Jaunlatgale *see* Pytalovo
118 I8 **Jaunpiebalga** Gulbene, NE Latvia 57°10′N 26°02′E
118 E9 **Jaunpils** Tukums, C Latvia 56°45′N 23°03′E
153 N13 **Jaunpur** Uttar Pradesh, N India 25°44′N 82°41′E
29 N8 **Java** South Dakota, N USA 45°29′N 99°54′W
Java *see* Jawa
105 R9 **Javalambre** ▲ E Spain 40°02′N 01°06′W
173 V7 **Java Ridge** *undersea feature* E Indian Ocean
59 A14 **Javari, Rio** *var.* Yavarí. ~ Brazil/Peru
Javarthushuu *see* Bayan-Uul
169 Q15 **Java Sea** *Ind.* Laut Jawa. *sea* W Indonesia
173 U7 **Java Trench** *var.* Sunda Trench. *undersea feature* E Indian Ocean
143 Q10 **Javazm** *var.* Jowzam. Kermān, C Iran 30°31′N 55°01′E
105 T11 **Jávea** *Cat.* Xàbia. País Valenciano, E Spain 38°48′N 00°10′E
Javhlant *see* Bayan-Ovoo
63 G20 **Javier, Isla** *island* S Chile
113 L14 **Javor** ▲▲ Bosnia and Herzegovina/Serbia
111 K20 **Javorie** *Hung.* Jávoros. ▲ S Slovakia 48°26′N 19°16′E
Jávoros *see* Javorie
93 J14 **Jävre** Norrbotten, N Sweden 65°07′N 21°31′E
192 E8 **Jawa** *Eng.* Java; *prev.* Djawa. *island* C Indonesia
169 O16 **Jawa Barat** *off.* Propinsi Jawa Barat, *Eng.* West Java. ◐ *province* S Indonesia
Jawa Barat, Propinsi *see* Jawa Barat
Jawa, Laut *see* Java Sea
139 R3 **Jawān** Nīnawýa, NW Iraq 35°57′N 43°03′E
169 P16 **Jawa Tengah** *off.* Propinsi Jawa Tengah, *Eng.* Central Java. ◐ *province* S Indonesia
Jawa Tengah, Propinsi *see* Jawa Tengah
169 R16 **Jawa Timur** *off.* Propinsi Jawa Timur, *Eng.* East Java. ◐ *province* S Indonesia
Jawa Timur, Propinsi *see* Jawa Timur
81 N17 **Jawhar** *var.* Jowhar, *It.* Giohar. Shabeellaha Dhexe, S Somalia 02°37′N 45°30′E
111 F14 **Jawor** *Ger.* Jauer. Dolnośląskie, SW Poland 51°01′N 16°11′E
Jaworów *see* Yavoriv
111 J16 **Jaworzno** Śląskie, S Poland 50°13′N 19°11′E
Jaxartes *see* Syr Darya
27 R9 **Jay** Oklahoma, C USA 36°25′N 94°49′W
Jayabum *see* Chaiyaphum
Jayanath *see* Chai Nat
153 T12 **Jayanti** *prev.* Jainti. West Bengal, NE India 26°45′N 89°40′E
171 X14 **Jaya, Puncak** *prev.* Puntjak Carstensz, Puntjak Sukarno. ▲ Papua, E Indonesia 04°00′S 137°10′E
171 Z13 **Jayapura** *var.* Djajapura, *Dut.* Hollandia; *prev.* Kotabaru, Sukarnapura. Papua, E Indonesia 02°37′S 140°39′E
Jay Dairen *see* Dalian
Jayhawker State *see* Kansas
147 S12 **Jayilgan** *Rus.* Dzhailgan, Dzhayilgan. C Tajikistan 39°17′N 71°32′E
155 L14 **Jaypur** *var.* Jeypore, Jeypur. Orissa, E India 18°54′N 82°36′E
25 O6 **Jayton** Texas, SW USA 33°16′N 100°35′W
143 U13 **Jaz Mūrīān, Hāmūn-e** ◎ SE Iran
138 M4 **Jazrah** Ar Raqqah, C Syria 35°56′N 39°02′E
138 G6 **Jbaïl** *var.* Jebeil, Jubayl, Jubeil; *anc.* Biblical Gebal, Bybles. W Lebanon 34°00′N 35°45′E
25 O7 **J. B. Thomas, Lake** ▣ Texas, SW USA
Jdaïdé *see* Judaydah
35 X12 **Jean** Nevada, W USA 35°45′N 115°20′W
22 I9 **Jeanerette** Louisiana, S USA 29°54′N 91°39′W
44 L8 **Jean-Rabel** NW Haiti 19°48′N 73°05′W
143 T12 **Jebāl Bārez, Kūh-e** ▲▲ SE Iran
Jebat *see* Jabwot
77 T15 **Jebba** Kwara, W Nigeria 09°04′N 04°50′E
Jebeil *see* Jbaïl
116 E12 **Jebel** *Hung.* Széphely; *prev. Hung.* Zsebely. Timiş, W Romania 45°33′N 21°14′E
146 B11 **Jebel** *Rus.* Dzhebel. Balkan Welaýaty, W Turkmenistan 39°42′N 54°10′E
Jebel, Bahr el *see* White Nile
Jebel Dhanna *see* Jabal az Ẕannah
Jeble *see* Jablah
96 K13 **Jedburgh** SE Scotland, United Kingdom 55°29′N 02°34′W
Jedda *see* Jiddah
111 L15 **Jędrzejów** *Ger.* Endersdorf. Świętokrzyskie, C Poland 50°39′N 20°18′E
100 K12 **Jeetze** *var.* Jeetzel. ~ C Germany
Jeetzel *see* Jeetze
29 U14 **Jefferson** Iowa, C USA 42°01′N 94°22′W
21 Q8 **Jefferson** North Carolina, SE USA 36°24′N 81°33′W
25 X6 **Jefferson** Texas, SW USA 32°45′N 94°21′W
30 M9 **Jefferson** Wisconsin, N USA 43°01′N 88°48′W
27 U5 **Jefferson City** *state capital* Missouri, C USA 38°33′N 92°13′W
33 R10 **Jefferson City** Montana, NW USA 46°24′N 112°01′W
21 N9 **Jefferson City** Tennessee, S USA 36°07′N 83°29′W
35 U7 **Jefferson, Mount** ▲ Nevada, W USA 38°49′N 116°54′W
32 H12 **Jefferson, Mount** ▲ Oregon, NW USA 44°40′N 121°48′W
20 L5 **Jeffersontown** Kentucky, S USA 38°11′N 85°33′W
31 P16 **Jeffersonville** Indiana, N USA 38°16′N 85°45′W
33 V15 **Jeffrey City** Wyoming, C USA 42°29′N 107°49′W
77 T13 **Jega** Kebbi, NW Nigeria 12°15′N 04°21′E
Jehol *see* Chengde
62 P5 **Jejui-Guazú, Río** ~ E Paraguay
118 I10 **Jēkabpils** *Ger.* Jakobstadt. Jēkabpils, S Latvia 56°30′N 25°56′E
23 W7 **Jekyll Island** *island* Georgia, SE USA
169 R13 **Jelai, Sungai** ~ Borneo, N Indonesia
Jelalabad *see* Jalālābād
111 H14 **Jelcz-Laskowice** Dolnośląskie, SW Poland 51°01′N 17°24′E
111 E14 **Jelenia Góra** *Ger.* Hirschberg, Hirschberg im Riesengebirge, Hirschberg in Riesengebirge, Hirschberg in Schlesien. Dolnośląskie, SW Poland 50°54′N 15°48′E
153 S11 **Jelep La** *pass* N India
118 F9 **Jelgava** *Ger.* Mitau. Jelgava, C Latvia 56°38′N 23°47′E
112 L13 **Jelica** ▲▲ C Serbia
20 M8 **Jellico** Tennessee, S USA 36°33′N 84°06′W
95 G23 **Jelling** Vejle, C Denmark 55°45′N 09°24′E
169 N9 **Jemaja, Pulau** *island* W Indonesia
Jemaluang *see* Jamaluang
99 E20 **Jemappes** Hainaut, S Belgium 50°27′N 03°53′E
169 S17 **Jember** *prev.* Djember. Jawa, C Indonesia 08°07′S 113°45′E
99 I20 **Jemeppe-sur-Sambre** Namur, S Belgium 50°27′N 04°41′E
37 R10 **Jemez Pueblo** New Mexico, SW USA 35°36′N 106°43′W
158 K2 **Jeminay** *var.* Tuotiereke. Xinjiang Uygur Zizhiqu, NW China 47°28′N 85°49′E
189 U5 **Jemo Island** *atoll* Ratak Chain, C Marshall Islands
169 U11 **Jempang, Danau** ◎ Borneo, N Indonesia
101 L16 **Jena** Thüringen, C Germany 50°55′N 11°35′E
22 I6 **Jena** Louisiana, S USA 31°40′N 92°07′W
108 I8 **Jenaz** Graubünden, SE Switzerland 46°56′N 09°43′E
109 N7 **Jenbach** Tirol, W Austria 47°24′N 11°47′E
171 N15 **Jeneponto** *prev.* Djeneponto. Sulawesi, C Indonesia 05°41′S 119°42′E
138 F9 **Jenin** N West Bank 32°28′N 35°17′E
21 P7 **Jenkins** Kentucky, S USA 37°10′N 82°37′W
27 P9 **Jenks** Oklahoma, C USA 36°01′N 95°58′W
Jenné *see* Djenné
109 X8 **Jennersdorf** Burgenland, SE Austria 46°57′N 16°08′E
22 H9 **Jennings** Louisiana, S USA 30°13′N 92°39′W
11 N7 **Jenny Lind Island** *island* Nunavut, N Canada
23 Y13 **Jensen Beach** Florida, SE USA 27°15′N 80°13′W
9 P6 **Jens Munk Island** *island* Nunavut, NE Canada
59 O17 **Jequié** Bahia, E Brazil 13°52′S 40°06′W
59 O18 **Jequitinhonha, Rio** ~ E Brazil
Jerablus *see* Jarābulus
74 H6 **Jerada** NE Morocco 34°16′N 02°07′W
Jerash *see* Jarash
75 N7 **Jerba, Île de** *var.* Djerba, Jazīrat Jarbah. *island* E Tunisia
44 K9 **Jérémie** SW Haiti 18°39′N 74°11′W
Jeréz *see* Jerez de García Salinas, Mexico
Jerez *see* Jeréz de la Frontera, Spain
40 L11 **Jerez de García Salinas** *var.* Jeréz. Zacatecas, C Mexico 22°40′N 103°00′W
104 J15 **Jeréz de la Frontera** *var.* Jerez; *prev.* Xeres. Andalucía, SW Spain 36°41′N 06°08′W
104 I12 **Jeréz de los Caballeros** Extremadura, W Spain 38°20′N 06°45′W
Jergucati *see* Jorgucat
138 G10 **Jericho** *Ar.* Arīḩā, *Heb.* Yeriḩo. E West Bank 31°51′N 35°27′E
74 M7 **Jerid, Chott el** *var.* Shaţţ al Jarīd. *salt lake* SW Tunisia
183 O10 **Jerilderie** New South Wales, SE Australia 35°24′S 145°43′E
Jerischmarkt *see* Câmpia Turzii
92 K11 **Jerisjärvi** ◎ NW Finland
Jermak *see* Aksu
Jermentau *see* Yereymentau
Jermer *see* Jaroměř
36 K11 **Jerome** Arizona, SW USA 34°45′N 112°06′W
33 O15 **Jerome** Idaho, NW USA 42°43′N 114°31′W
97 L26 **Jersey** *island* NW Europe
18 K14 **Jersey City** New Jersey, NE USA 40°42′N 74°01′W
18 F13 **Jersey Shore** Pennsylvania, NE USA 41°12′N 77°13′W
30 K14 **Jerseyville** Illinois, N USA 39°07′N 90°19′W
104 K8 **Jerte** ~ W Spain
138 F10 **Jerusalem** *Ar.* Al Quds, Al Quds ash Sharīf, *Heb.* Yerushalayim; *anc.* Hierosolyma. ● (Israel) Jerusalem, NE Israel 31°47′N 35°13′E
138 G10 **Jerusalem** ◐ *district* E Israel
183 S10 **Jervis Bay** New South Wales, SE Australia 35°09′S 150°42′E
183 S10 **Jervis Bay Territory** ◐ *territory* SE Australia
Jerwakant *see* Järvakandi
109 S10 **Jesenice** *Ger.* Assling. NW Slovenia 46°26′N 14°01′E
111 H16 **Jeseník** *Ger.* Freiwaldau. Olomoucký Kraj, E Czech Republic 50°14′N 17°12′E
Jesi *see* Iesi
106 I8 **Jesolo** *var.* Iesolo. Veneto, NE Italy 45°32′N 12°37′E
Jesselton *see* Kota Kinabalu
95 I14 **Jessheim** Akershus, S Norway 60°07′N 11°10′E
153 T15 **Jessore** Khulna, W Bangladesh 23°10′N 89°12′E
23 W6 **Jesup** Georgia, SE USA 31°36′N 81°54′W
41 S15 **Jesús Carranza** Veracruz-Llave, SE Mexico 17°30′N 95°01′W
62 K10 **Jesús María** Córdoba, C Argentina 30°59′S 64°05′W
26 K6 **Jetmore** Kansas, C USA 38°05′N 99°55′W
103 Q2 **Jeumont** Nord, N France 50°18′N 04°06′E
95 H14 **Jevnaker** Oppland, S Norway 60°15′N 10°25′E
Jewe *see* Jõhvi
25 V9 **Jewett** Texas, SW USA 31°21′N 96°08′W
19 N12 **Jewett City** Connecticut, NE USA 41°36′N 71°58′W
Jeypore *see* Jaipur, Rājasthān, India
Jeypore/Jeypur *see* Jaypur, Orissa, India
113 L17 **Jezercës, Maja e** ▲ N Albania 42°27′N 19°49′E
111 B18 **Jezerní Hora** ▲ SW Czech Republic 49°10′N 13°11′E
154 F10 **Jhābua** Madhya Pradesh, C India 22°44′N 74°37′E
152 H10 **Jhajjar** Haryāna, N India 28°35′N 76°39′E
152 H14 **Jhālāwār** Rājasthān, N India 24°37′N 76°12′E
Jhang/Jhang Sadar *see* Jhang Sadr

◆ Country
● Country Capital
◇ Dependent Territory
○ Dependent Territory Capital
◐ Administrative Regions
✈ International Airport
▲ Mountain
▲▲ Mountain Range
Volcano
~ River
◎ Lake
▣ Reservoir

◆ Country   ◇ Dependent Territory   ◆ Administrative Regions   ▲ Mountain   ℞ Volcano   ◉ Lake
● Country Capital   ○ Dependent Territory Capital   × International Airport   ▲ Mountain Range   ∠ River   ⊠ Reservoir

◆ Country ◇ Dependent Territory ◉ Administrative Regions ▲ Mountain ☒ Volcano ◎ Lake
○ Country Capital ○ Dependent Territory Capital ✕ International Airport ▲ Mountain Range ◢ River ◙ Reservoir

Kaminoyama – Karkinits'ka Zatoka

165 *P10* **Kaminoyama** Yamagata, Honshū, C Japan *38°10′N 140°16′E*
39 *Q13* **Kamishak Bay** *bay* Alaska, USA
165 *U4* **Kami-Shihoro** Hokkaidō, NE Japan *43°14′N 143°18′E*
Kamishli *see* Al Qāmishlī
Kamissar *see* Kamsar
164 *C11* **Kami-Tsushima** Nagasaki, Tsushima, SW Japan *34°40′N 129°27′E*
79 *O20* **Kamituga** Sud-Kivu, E Dem. Rep. Congo *03°07′S 28°10′E*
164 *B17* **Kamiyaku** Kagoshima, Yaku-shima, SW Japan *30°24′N 130°32′E*
11 *N16* **Kamloops** British Columbia, SW Canada *50°39′N 120°24′W*
107 *G25* **Kamma** Sicilia, Italy, C Mediterranean Sea *36°46′N 12°03′E*
192 *K4* **Kammu Seamount** *undersea feature* N Pacific Ocean *32°09′N 173°00′E*
109 *U11* **Kamnik** *Ger.* Stein. C Slovenia *46°13′N 14°34′E*
Kamniške Alpe *see* Kamniško-Savinjske Alpe
109 *T10* **Kamniško-Savinjske Alpe** *var.* Kamniške Alpe, Sanntaler Alpen, *Ger.* Steiner Alpen. ▲▲ N Slovenia
Kamo *see* Gavarr
165 *R3* **Kamoenai** *var.* Kamuenai. Hokkaidō, NE Japan *43°07′N 140°25′E*
165 *O14* **Kamogawa** Chiba, Honshū, S Japan *35°05′N 140°04′E*
149 *W8* **Kāmoke** Punjab, E Pakistan *31°58′N 74°15′E*
82 *L13* **Kamoto** Eastern, E Zambia *13°16′S 32°04′E*
109 *V3* **Kamp** ≈ N Austria
81 *F18* **Kampala** ● (Uganda) S Uganda *0°20′N 32°28′E*
168 *K11* **Kampar, Sungai** ≈ Sumatera, W Indonesia
98 *L9* **Kampen** Overijssel, E Netherlands *52°33′N 05°55′E*
79 *N20* **Kampene** Maniema, E Dem. Rep. Congo *03°35′S 26°40′E*
29 *Q9* **Kampeska, Lake** ◎ South Dakota, N USA
167 *O9* **Kamphaeng Phet** *var.* Kambaeng Petch. Kamphaeng Phet, W Thailand *16°28′N 99°31′E*
Kampo *see* Campo, Cameroon
Kampo *see* Ntem, Cameroon/Equatorial Guinea
167 *S12* **Kâmpóng Cham** *prev.* Kompong Cham. Kâmpóng Cham, C Cambodia *12°N 105°27′E*
167 *R12* **Kâmpóng Chhnăng** *prev.* Kompong. Kâmpóng Chhnăng, C Cambodia *12°15′N 104°40′E*
167 *R12* **Kâmpóng Khleăng** *prev.* Kompong Kleang. Siĕmréab, NW Cambodia *13°04′N 104°07′E*
167 *Q14* **Kâmpóng Saôm** *prev.* Kompong Som, Sihanoukville. Kâmpóng Saôm, SW Cambodia *10°38′N 103°30′E*
167 *R13* **Kâmpóng Spoe** *prev.* Kompong Speu. Kâmpóng Spœ, S Cambodia *11°28′N 104°29′E*
121 *O2* **Kámpos** *var.* Kambos. NW Cyprus *35°03′N 32°44′E*
167 *R14* **Kâmpôt** Kâmpôt, SW Cambodia *10°37′N 104°11′E*
Kamptee *see* Kāmthi
77 *O14* **Kampti** SW Burkina *10°07′N 03°22′W*
Kampuchea *see* Cambodia
Kampuchea, Democratic *see* Cambodia
Kampuchea, People's Democratic Republic of *see* Cambodia
169 *Q9* **Kampung Sirik** Sarawak, East Malaysia *02°42′N 111°28′E*
11 *V15* **Kamsack** Saskatchewan, S Canada *51°34′N 101°51′W*
76 *H13* **Kamsar** *var.* Kamissar. Guinée-Maritime, W Guinea *10°33′N 14°34′W*
127 *R4* **Kamskoye Ust'ye** Respublika Tatarstan, W Russian Federation *55°13′N 49°11′E*
125 *U14* **Kamskoye Vodokhranilishche** *var.* Kama Reservoir. ⊠ NW Russian Federation
154 *I12* **Kāmthi** *prev.* Kamptee. Mahārāshtra, C India *21°19′N 79°11′E*
Kamuela *see* Waimea
Kamuenai *see* Kamoenai
165 *T5* **Kamui-dake** ⛰ Hokkaidō, NE Japan *42°24′N 142°57′E*
165 *R3* **Kamui-misaki** *headland* Hokkaidō, NE Japan *43°20′N 140°20′E*
43 *O15* **Kámuk, Cerro** ▲ SE Costa Rica *09°15′N 83°01′W*
116 *K7* **Kam"yanets'-Podil's'kyy** *Rus.* Kamenets-Podol'skiy. Khmel'nyts'ka Oblast', W Ukraine *48°43′N 26°36′E*
117 *Q6* **Kam"yanka** *Rus.* Kamenka. Cherkas'ka Oblast', C Ukraine *49°03′N 32°06′E*
116 *I5* **Kam"yanka-Buz'ka** *Rus.* Kamenka-Bugskaya. L'vivs'ka Oblast', NW Ukraine *50°04′N 24°21′E*
117 *T9* **Kam"yanka-Dniprovs'ka** *Rus.* Kamenka Dneprovskaya. Zaporiz'ka Oblast', SE Ukraine *47°28′N 34°24′E*
119 *F19* **Kamyanyets** *Rus.* Kamenets. Brestskaya Voblasts', SW Belarus *52°24′N 23°49′E*
127 *P9* **Kamyshin** Volgogradskaya Oblast', SW Russian Federation *50°07′N 45°20′E*
127 *Q13* **Kamyzyak** Astrakhanskaya Oblast', SW Russian Federation *46°07′N 48°03′E*
12 *K8* **Kanaaupscow** ≈ Québec, C Canada
36 *K8* **Kanab** Utah, W USA *37°03′N 112°31′W*
36 *K9* **Kanab Creek** ≈ Arizona/Utah, SW USA
187 *Y14* **Kanacea** *prev.* Kanathea. Taveuni, N Fiji *16°59′S 179°54′E*
38 *G17* **Kanaga Island** *island* Aleutian Islands, Alaska, USA
38 *G17* **Kanaga Volcano** ▲ Kanaga Island, Alaska, USA *51°55′N 177°09′W*
164 *N14* **Kanagawa** *off.* Kanagawa-ken. ◈ *prefecture* Honshū, S Japan
Kanagawa-ken *see* Kanagawa
13 *Q8* **Kanairiktok** ≈ Newfoundland and Labrador, E Canada
Kanaky *see* New Caledonia
79 *K22* **Kananga** *prev.* Luluabourg. Kasai-Occidental, S Dem. Rep. Congo *05°51′S 22°22′E*
Kanara *see* Karnātaka
36 *J7* **Kanarraville** Utah, W USA *37°32′N 113°10′W*
127 *Q4* **Kanash** Chuvashskaya Respublika, W Russian Federation *55°30′N 47°27′E*
Kanathea *see* Kanacea
21 *Q4* **Kanawha River** ≈ West Virginia, NE USA
164 *L13* **Kanayama** Gifu, Honshū, SW Japan *35°46′N 137°15′E*
164 *L11* **Kanazawa** Ishikawa, Honshū, SW Japan *36°35′N 136°40′E*
166 *M4* **Kanbalu** Sagaing, C Myanmar (Burma) *23°10′N 95°31′E*
166 *L8* **Kanbe** Yangon, SW Myanmar (Burma) *16°40′N 96°01′E*
167 *O11* **Kanchanaburi** Kanchanaburi, W Thailand *14°02′N 99°32′E*
Kanchanjańghā/Kānchenjunga *see* Kangchenjunga
145 *V11* **Kanchingiz, Khrebet** ▲▲ E Kazakhstan
155 *J19* **Kānchīpuram** *prev.* Conjeeveram. Tamil Nādu, SE India *12°50′N 79°44′E*
149 *N8* **Kandahār** *Per.* Qandahār. Kandahār, S Afghanistan *31°36′N 65°48′E*
149 *N9* **Kandahār** *Per.* Qandahār. ◈ *province* SE Afghanistan
Kandalakša *see* Kandalaksha
124 *I5* **Kandalaksha** *var.* Kandalakša, *Fin.* Kantalahti. Murmanskaya Oblast', NW Russian Federation *67°09′N 32°14′E*
Kandalaksha Gulf/Kandalakshskaya Guba *see* Kandalakshskiy Zaliv
124 *K6* **Kandalakshskiy Zaliv** *var.* Kandalakshskaya Guba, *Eng.* Kandalaksha Gulf. *bay* NW Russian Federation
83 *G17* **Kandalengoti** *var.* Kandalengoti. Ngamiland, NW Botswana *19°25′S 22°12′E*
Kandalengoti *see* Kandalengoti
169 *U13* **Kandangan** Borneo, C Indonesia *02°50′S 115°15′E*
Kandau *see* Kandava
118 *E8* **Kandava** *Ger.* Kandau. Tukums, W Latvia *57°02′N 22°48′E*
Kandavu *see* Kadavu
77 *R14* **Kandé** *var.* Kanté. NE Togo *09°55′N 01°01′E*
101 *F23* **Kandel** ▲ SW Germany *48°03′N 08°00′E*
186 *C7* **Kandep** Enga, W Papua New Guinea *05°54′S 143°34′E*
149 *R12* **Kandh Kot** Sind, SE Pakistan *28°15′N 69°18′E*
77 *S13* **Kandi** N Benin *11°05′N 02°59′E*
149 *P14* **Kandiāro** Sind, SE Pakistan *27°02′N 68°16′E*
136 *F11* **Kandıra** Kocaeli, NW Turkey *41°05′N 30°08′E*
183 *S8* **Kandos** New South Wales, SE Australia *32°52′S 149°58′E*
148 *M16* **Kandrāch** *var.* Kanrach. Baluchistān, SW Pakistan *25°26′N 65°28′E*
172 *I4* **Kandreho** Mahajanga, C Madagascar *17°27′S 46°06′E*
186 *F7* **Kandrian** New Britain, E Papua New Guinea *06°14′S 149°32′E*
Kandukur *see* Kondukūr
155 *K25* **Kandy** Central Province, C Sri Lanka *07°17′N 80°40′E*
144 *I10* **Kandyagash** *Kaz.* Qandyaghash; *prev.* Oktyab'rsk. Aktyubinsk, W Kazakhstan *49°25′N 57°24′E*
18 *D12* **Kane** Pennsylvania, NE USA *41°39′N 78°47′W*
64 *I11* **Kane Fracture Zone** *tectonic feature* NW Atlantic Ocean
Kanëka *see* Kanëvka
78 *G9* **Kanem** *off.* Préfecture du Kanem. ◈ *prefecture* W Chad
Kanem, Préfecture du *see* Kanem
38 *D9* **Kāne'ohe** *var.* Kaneohe. O'ahu, Hawaii, USA, C Pacific Ocean *21°25′N 157°48′W*
Kanestron, Akrotírio *see* Palioúri, Akrotírio
Kanëv *see* Kaniv
124 *M5* **Kanëvka** *var.* Kanëka. Murmanskaya Oblast', NW Russian Federation *67°07′N 39°43′E*
126 *K13* **Kanevskaya** Krasnodarskiy Kray, SW Russian Federation *46°07′N 38°57′E*
Kanevskoye Vodokhranilishche *see* Kanivs'ke Vodoskhovyshche
165 *P9* **Kaneyama** Yamagata, Honshū, C Japan *38°54′N 140°20′E*
83 *G20* **Kang** Kgalagadi, C Botswana *23°41′S 22°50′E*
76 *L13* **Kangaba** Koulikoro, SW Mali *11°57′N 08°24′W*
136 *M13* **Kangal** Sivas, C Turkey *39°15′N 37°23′E*
143 *S15* **Kangān** Hormozgān, SE Iran *27°49′N 52°04′E*
Kangān *see* Bandar-e Kangān
168 *J6* **Kangar** Perlis, Peninsular Malaysia *06°28′N 100°10′E*
76 *L13* **Kangaré** Sikasso, S Mali *11°39′N 08°10′W*
182 *F10* **Kangaroo Island** *island* South Australia
93 *M17* **Kangasniemi** Itä-Suomi, E Finland *61°58′N 26°37′E*
142 *K6* **Kangāvar** *var.* Kangāwar. Kermānshāhān, W Iran *34°29′N 47°55′E*
Kangāwar *see* Kangāvar
153 *S11* **Kangchenjunga** *var.* Kānchenjunga, *Nep.* Kanchanjańghā. ▲ NE India *27°36′N 88°06′E*
160 *G9* **Kangding** *var.* Lucheng, *Tib.* Dardo. Sichuan, C China *30°03′N 101°56′E*
169 *U16* **Kangean, Kepulauan** *island group* S Indonesia
169 *T16* **Kangean, Pulau** *island* Kepulauan Kangean, S Indonesia
67 *U8* **Kangen** *var.* Kengen. ≈ SE Sudan
197 *N14* **Kangerlussuaq** *Dan.* Sondre Strømfjord. ✈ Kitaa, W Greenland *66°59′N 50°28′E*
197 *Q15* **Kangertittivaq** *Dan.* Scoresby Sund. *fjord* E Greenland
167 *O2* **Kangfang** Kachin State, N Myanmar (Burma) *26°09′N 98°36′E*
163 *X12* **Kanggye** N North Korea *40°58′N 126°37′E*
197 *P15* **Kangikajik** *var.* Kap Brewster. *headland* E Greenland *70°10′N 22°00′W*
13 *N5* **Kangiqsualujjuaq** *prev.* George River, Port-Nouveau-Québec. Québec, E Canada *58°35′N 65°59′W*
12 *L2* **Kangiqsujuaq** *prev.* Maricourt, Wakeham Bay. Québec, NE Canada *61°35′N 72°00′W*
12 *M4* **Kangirsuk** *prev.* Bellin, Payne. Québec, E Canada *60°00′N 70°01′W*
159 *V11* **Kangle** Gansu, C China *35°22′N 103°42′E*
Kangle *see* Wanzai
158 *M16* **Kangmar** Xizang Zizhiqu, W China *28°34′N 89°40′E*
163 *Y14* **Kangnŭng** *Jap.* Kōryō. NE South Korea *37°47′N 128°51′E*
79 *D18* **Kango** Estuaire, NW Gabon *0°17′N 10°00′E*
152 *I7* **Kāngra** Himāchal Pradesh, NW India *32°04′N 76°16′E*
153 *Q16* **Kangsabati Reservoir** ⊠ N India
159 *O17* **Kangto** ▲ China/India *27°54′N 92°33′E*
159 *W12* **Kangxian** *var.* Kang Xian, Zuitai, Zuitaizi. Gansu, C China *33°21′N 105°40′E*
Kang Xian *see* Kangxian
76 *M15* **Kani** NW Ivory Coast *08°29′N 06°36′W*
166 *L4* **Kani** Sagaing, C Myanmar (Burma) *22°24′N 94°55′E*
79 *M23* **Kaniama** Katanga, S Dem. Rep. Congo *07°32′S 24°11′E*
Kanibadam *see* Konibodom
169 *V6* **Kanibongan** Sabah, East Malaysia *06°40′N 117°12′E*
185 *F17* **Kaniere** West Coast, South Island, New Zealand *42°45′S 171°00′E*
185 *G17* **Kaniere, Lake** ◎ South Island, New Zealand
188 *E17* **Kanifaay** Yap, W Micronesia
125 *O4* **Kanin Kamen'** ▲▲ NW Russian Federation
125 *N3* **Kanin Nos** Nenetskiy Avtonomnyy Okrug, NW Russian Federation *68°38′N 43°19′E*
125 *N3* **Kanin Nos, Mys** *cape* NW Russian Federation
125 *O5* **Kanin, Poluostrov** *peninsula* NW Russian Federation
139 *V8* **Kānī Sakht** Wāsiţ, E Iraq *33°19′N 46°04′E*
139 *T3* **Kānī Sulaymān** Arbīl, N Iraq *35°54′N 44°35′E*
165 *Q6* **Kanita** Aomori, Honshū, C Japan *41°04′N 140°36′E*
117 *Q5* **Kaniv** *Rus.* Kanëv. Cherkas'ka Oblast', C Ukraine *49°46′N 31°28′E*
182 *K11* **Kaniva** Victoria, SE Australia *36°25′S 141°13′E*
117 *Q5* **Kanivs'ke Vodoskhovyshche** *Rus.* Kanevskoye Vodokhranilishche. ⊠ C Ukraine
112 *L8* **Kanjiža** *Ger.* Altkanischa, *Hung.* Magyarkanizsa, Ókanizsa; *prev.* Stara Kanjiža. Vojvodina, N Serbia *46°03′N 20°03′E*
93 *K18* **Kankaanpää** Länsi-Suomi, SW Finland *61°47′N 22°25′E*
30 *M12* **Kankakee** Illinois, N USA *41°07′N 87°51′W*
31 *O11* **Kankakee River** ≈ Illinois/Indiana, N USA
76 *K14* **Kankan** E Guinea *10°25′N 09°19′W*
154 *K13* **Kānker** Chhattīsgarh, C India *20°19′N 81°29′E*
76 *J10* **Kankossa** Assaba, S Mauritania *15°54′N 11°31′W*
169 *N12* **Kanmaw Kyun** *var.* Kisseraing, Kithareng. *island* Mergui Archipelago, S Myanmar (Burma)
164 *F12* **Kanmuri-yama** ▲ Kyūshū, SW Japan *34°28′N 132°03′E*
21 *R10* **Kannapolis** North Carolina, SE USA *35°30′N 80°36′W*
93 *L16* **Kannonkoski** Länsi-Suomi, C Finland *62°59′N 25°20′E*
155 *F20* **Kannur** *var.* Cannanore. Kerala, SW India *11°53′N 75°23′E* *see also* Cannanore
93 *K15* **Kannus** Länsi-Suomi, W Finland *63°55′N 23°55′E*
77 *V13* **Kano** Kano, N Nigeria *11°56′N 08°31′E*
77 *V13* **Kano** ◈ *state* N Nigeria
77 *V13* **Kano** ✈ Kano, N Nigeria *11°56′N 08°26′E*
164 *G14* **Kan'onji** *var.* Kanonzi. Kagawa, Shikoku, SW Japan *34°08′N 133°38′E*
Kanonzi *see* Kan'onji
26 *M5* **Kanopolis Lake** ⊠ Kansas, C USA
36 *K5* **Kanosh** Utah, W USA *38°48′N 112°26′W*
169 *R9* **Kanowit** Sarawak, East Malaysia *02°03′N 112°15′E*
164 *C16* **Kanoya** Kagoshima, Kyūshū, SW Japan *31°22′N 130°50′E*
152 *L13* **Kānpur** *Eng.* Cawnpore. Uttar Pradesh, N India *26°28′N 80°21′E*
Kanrach *see* Kandrāch
164 *I14* **Kansai** ✈ (Ōsaka) Ōsaka, Honshū, SW Japan *34°25′N 135°13′E*
27 *R9* **Kansas** Oklahoma, C USA *36°14′N 94°46′W*
26 *L5* **Kansas** *off.* State of Kansas, *also known as* Jayhawker State, Sunflower State. ◈ *state* C USA
27 *R4* **Kansas City** Kansas, C USA *39°07′N 94°38′W*
27 *R4* **Kansas City** Missouri, C USA *39°06′N 94°35′W*
27 *R3* **Kansas City** ✈ Missouri, C USA *39°18′N 94°45′W*
27 *P4* **Kansas River** ≈ Kansas, C USA
122 *L14* **Kansk** Krasnoyarskiy Kray, S Russian Federation *56°11′N 95°32′E*
Kansu *see* Gansu
147 *V7* **Kant** Chuyskaya Oblast', N Kyrgyzstan *42°54′N 74°47′E*
Kantalahti *see* Kandalaksha
167 *N16* **Kantang** *var.* Ban Kantang. Trang, SW Thailand *07°25′N 99°30′E*
115 *H25* **Kántanos** Kríti, Greece, E Mediterranean Sea *35°20′N 23°42′E*
77 *R12* **Kantchari** E Burkina *12°47′N 01°37′E*
Kanté *see* Kandé
Kantemir *see* Cantemir
126 *L9* **Kantemirovka** Voronezhskaya Oblast', W Russian Federation *49°44′N 39°53′E*
167 *R11* **Kantharalak** Si Sa Ket, E Thailand *14°32′N 104°37′E*
Kantipur *see* Kathmandu
39 *Q9* **Kantishna River** ≈ Alaska, USA
191 *S3* **Kanton** *var.* Abariringa, Canton Island; *prev.* Mary Island. *atoll* Phoenix Islands, C Kiribati
97 *C20* **Kanturk** *Ir.* Ceann Toirc. Cork, SW Ireland *52°12′N 08°54′W*
55 *T11* **Kanuku Mountains** ▲▲ S Guyana
165 *O12* **Kanuma** Tochigi, Honshū, S Japan *36°34′N 139°44′E*
83 *H20* **Kanye** Southern, SE Botswana *24°55′S 25°14′E*
83 *H17* **Kanyu** North-West, C Botswana *20°04′S 24°36′E*
166 *M7* **Kanyutkwin** Bago, C Myanmar (Burma) *18°19′N 96°30′E*
79 *M24* **Kanzenze** Katanga, SE Dem. Rep. Congo *10°33′S 25°28′E*
193 *Y15* **Kao** *island* Kotu Group, W Tonga
161 *S14* **Kaohsiung** *var.* Gaoxiong, *Jap.* Takao, Takow. S Taiwan *22°36′N 120°17′E*
161 *S14* **Kaohsiung** ✈ S Taiwan *22°26′N 120°32′E*
Kaokaona *see* Kirakira
83 *B17* **Kaoko Veld** ▲▲ N Namibia
76 *G11* **Kaolack** *var.* Kaolak. W Senegal *14°09′N 16°08′W*
Kaolak *see* Kaolack
Kaolan *see* Lanzhou
114 *M7* **Kaolinovo** Shumen, NE Bulgaria *43°36′N 27°04′E*
186 *M8* **Kaolo** San Jorge, N Solomon Islands *08°24′S 159°35′E*
83 *H14* **Kaoma** Western, W Zambia *14°50′S 24°48′E*
38 *B8* **Kapa'a** *var.* Kapaa. Kaua'i, Hawaii, USA, C Pacific Ocean *22°04′N 159°19′W*
Kapaa *see* Kapa'a
113 *J16* **Kapa Moračka** ▲ C Montenegro *42°53′N 19°01′E*
137 *V13* **Kapan** *Rus.* Kafan; *prev.* Ghap'an. SE Armenia *39°13′N 46°25′E*
82 *L13* **Kapandashila** Northern, NE Zambia *12°43′S 31°00′E*
79 *L23* **Kapanga** Katanga, S Dem. Rep. Congo *08°22′S 22°37′E*
145 *U15* **Kapchagay** *Kaz.* Qapshaghay. Almaty, SE Kazakhstan *43°52′N 77°05′E*
145 *V15* **Kapchagayskoye Vodokhranilishche** *Kaz.* Qapshagay Böyeni. ⊠ SE Kazakhstan
99 *F15* **Kapelle** Zeeland, SW Netherlands *51°29′N 03°58′E*
99 *G16* **Kapellen** Antwerpen, N Belgium *51°19′N 04°25′E*
95 *P15* **Kapellskär** Stockholm, C Sweden *59°43′N 19°03′E*
81 *H18* **Kapenguria** Rift Valley, W Kenya *01°14′N 35°08′E*
109 *V6* **Kapfenberg** Steiermark, C Austria *47°27′N 15°18′E*
83 *J14* **Kapiri Mposhi** Central, C Zambia *13°59′S 28°40′E*
149 *R4* **Kāpīsā** ◈ *province* E Afghanistan
12 *G10* **Kapiskau** ≈ Ontario, C Canada
184 *K13* **Kapiti Island** *island* C New Zealand
78 *K9* **Kapka, Massif du** ▲▲ E Chad
Kaplamada *see* Kaubalatmada, Gunung
22 *H9* **Kaplan** Louisiana, S USA *30°00′N 92°16′W*
Kaplangky, Plato *see* Gaplaňgyr Platosy
111 *D19* **Kaplice** *Ger.* Kaplitz. Jihočeský Kraj, S Czech Republic *48°42′N 14°27′E*
Kaplitz *see* Kaplice
Kapoche *see* Capoche
171 *T12* **Kapocol** Papua, E Indonesia *01°59′S 130°11′E*
167 *N14* **Kapoe** Ranong, SW Thailand *09°33′N 98°37′E*
Kapoeas *see* Kapuas, Sungai
81 *G15* **Kapoeta** Eastern Equatoria, SE Sudan *04°50′N 33°35′E*
111 *I25* **Kapos** ≈ S Hungary
111 *H25* **Kaposvár** Somogy, SW Hungary *46°23′N 17°54′E*
94 *H13* **Kapp** Oppland, S Norway *60°42′N 10°49′E*
100 *I7* **Kappeln** Schleswig-Holstein, N Germany *54°41′N 09°56′E*
Kapronca *see* Koprivnica
109 *P7* **Kaprun** Salzburg, C Austria *47°15′N 12°48′E*
Kapstad *see* Cape Town
Kapsukas *see* Marijampolė
171 *Y13* **Kaptiau** Papua, E Indonesia *02°23′S 139°51′E*
119 *L19* **Kaptsevichy** *Rus.* Koptsevichi. Homyel'skaya Voblasts', SE Belarus *52°14′N 28°19′E*
Kapuas Hulu, Banjaran/Kapuas Hulu, Pegunungan *see* Kapuas Mountains
169 *S10* **Kapuas Mountains** *Ind.* Banjaran Kapuas Hulu, Pegunungan Kapuas Hulu. ▲▲ Indonesia/Malaysia
169 *P11* **Kapuas, Sungai** ≈ Borneo, N Indonesia
169 *T13* **Kapuas, Sungai** *prev.* Kapoeas. ≈ Borneo, C Indonesia
182 *J9* **Kapunda** South Australia *34°23′S 138°51′E*
152 *H8* **Kapūrthala** Punjab, N India *31°20′N 75°26′E*
12 *G12* **Kapuskasing** Ontario, S Canada *49°25′N 82°26′W*
14 *D6* **Kapuskasing** ≈ Ontario, S Canada
127 *P11* **Kapustin Yar** Astrakhanskaya Oblast', SW Russian Federation *48°36′N 45°49′E*
82 *K11* **Kaputa** Northern, NE Zambia *08°28′S 29°41′E*
111 *G22* **Kapuvár** Győr-Moson-Sopron, NW Hungary *47°35′N 17°01′E*
Kapydzhik, Gora *see* Qazangödağ
119 *J17* **Kapyl'** *Rus.* Kopyl'. Minskaya Voblasts', C Belarus *53°09′N 27°05′E*
43 *N9* **Kara** *var.* Cara. Región Autónoma Atlántico Sur, E Nicaragua *12°50′N 83°35′W*
77 *R14* **Kara** *var.* Lama-Kara. NE Togo *09°33′N 01°12′E*
77 *Q14* **Kara** ≈ N Togo
147 *U7* **Kara-Balta** Chuyskaya Oblast', N Kyrgyzstan *42°51′N 73°51′E*
144 *L7* **Karabalyk** *var.* Komsomolets, *Kaz.* Komsomol. Kostanay, N Kazakhstan *53°47′N 61°58′E*
144 *G11* **Karabau** *Kaz.* Qarabaū. Atyrau, W Kazakhstan *48°29′N 53°05′E*
146 *E7* **Karabaur', Uval** *Kaz.* Korabavur Pastligi, *Uzb.* Qorabowur Kirlari. *physical region* Kazakhstan/Uzbekistan
Karabekaul *see* Garabekewül
Karabil', Vozvyshennost' *see* Garabil Belentligi
Kara-Bogaz-Gol *see* Garabogazköl
Kara-Bogaz-Gol, Zaliv *see* Garabogaz Aylagy
145 *R15* **Karaboget** *Kaz.* Qaraböget. Zhambyl, S Kazakhstan *44°36′N 72°03′E*
136 *H11* **Karabük** Karabük, NW Turkey *41°12′N 32°36′E*
136 *H11* **Karabük** ◈ *province* NW Turkey
122 *L12* **Karabula** Krasnoyarskiy Kray, C Russian Federation *58°01′N 97°17′E*
145 *V14* **Karabulak** *Kaz.* Qarabulaq. Taldykorgan, SE Kazakhstan *44°53′N 78°29′E*
145 *Y11* **Karabulak** *Kaz.* Qarabulaq. Vostochnyy Kazakhstan, E Kazakhstan *47°34′N 84°40′E*
145 *Q17* **Karabulak** *Kaz.* Qarabulaq. Yuzhnyy Kazakhstan, S Kazakhstan *42°31′N 69°47′E*
Karabura *see* Yumin
136 *C17* **Kara Burnu** *headland* SW Turkey *36°34′N 28°00′E*
144 *K10* **Karabutak** *Kaz.* Qarabutaq. Aktyubinsk, W Kazakhstan *49°55′N 60°05′E*
136 *D12* **Karacabey** Bursa, NW Turkey *40°14′N 28°22′E*
114 *O12* **Karacaköy** İstanbul, NW Turkey *41°24′N 28°21′E*
114 *M12* **Karacaoğlan** Kırklareli, NW Turkey *41°30′N 27°06′E*
Karachay-Cherkessia *see* Karachayevo-Cherkesskaya Respublika
126 *L15* **Karachayevo-Cherkesskaya Respublika** *Eng.* Karachay-Cherkessia. ◈ *autonomous republic* SW Russian Federation
126 *M15* **Karachayevsk** Karachayevo-Cherkesskaya Respublika, SW Russian Federation *43°43′N 41°53′E*
126 *J6* **Karachev** Bryanskaya Oblast', W Russian Federation *53°07′N 35°56′E*
149 *O16* **Karāchi** Sind, SE Pakistan *24°51′N 67°02′E*
149 *O16* **Karāchi** ✈ Sind, S Pakistan *24°51′N 67°02′E*
Karácsonkő *see* Piatra-Neamţ
155 *E15* **Karād** Mahārāshtra, W India *17°19′N 74°15′E*
136 *H16* **Karadağ** ▲ S Turkey *37°00′N 33°00′E*
147 *T10* **Karadar'ya** *Uzb.* Qoradaryo. ≈ Kyrgyzstan/Uzbekistan
Karadeniz *see* Black Sea
Karadeniz Boğazi *see* İstanbul Boğazı
146 *B13* **Karadepe** Balkan Welaýaty, W Turkmenistan *38°04′N 54°01′E*
Karadzhar *see* Qorajar
Karaferiye *see* Véroia
Karagan *see* Garagan
145 *R10* **Karaganda** *Kaz.* Qaraghandy. Karaganda, C Kazakhstan *49°53′N 73°07′E*
145 *R10* **Karaganda** *off.* Karagandinskaya Oblast', *Kaz.* Qaraghandy Oblysy. ◈ *province* C Kazakhstan
Karagandinskaya Oblast' *see* Karaganda
145 *T10* **Karagayly** *Kaz.* Qaraghayly. Karaganda, C Kazakhstan *49°25′N 75°31′E*
Karagel' *see* Garagöl'
123 *U9* **Karaginskiy, Ostrov** *island* E Russian Federation
197 *T1* **Karaginskiy Zaliv** *bay* E Russian Federation
137 *P13* **Karagöl Dağları** ▲▲ NE Turkey
Karagumskiy Kanal *see* Garagum Kanaly
114 *L13* **Karahisar** Edirne, NW Turkey *40°47′N 26°34′E*
127 *V3* **Karaidel'** Respublika Bashkortostan, W Russian Federation *55°50′N 56°55′E*
114 *L13* **Karaidemir Barajı** ⊠ NW Turkey
155 *J21* **Kāraikāl** Pondicherry, SE India *10°58′N 79°50′E*
155 *I22* **Kāraikkudi** Tamil Nādu, SE India *10°04′N 78°46′E*
145 *Y11* **Kara Irtysh** *Rus.* Chërnyy Irtysh. ≈ NE Kazakhstan
143 *N5* **Karaj** Tehrān, N Iran *35°44′N 51°26′E*
168 *K8* **Karak** Pahang, Peninsular Malaysia *03°24′N 101°59′E*
149 *T7* **Karak** North-West Frontier Province, N Pakistan *33°07′N 71°06′E*
Karak *see* Al Karak
147 *T11* **Kara-Kabak** Oshskaya Oblast', SW Kyrgyzstan *39°40′N 72°45′E*
Kara-Kala *see* Magtymguly
Karakala *see* Oqqal'a
Karakalpakstan, Respublika *see* Qoraqalpog'iston Respublikasi
Karakalpakya *see* Qoraqalpog'iston
Karakax *see* Moyu
158 *G10* **Karakax He** ≈ NW China
121 *X8* **Karakaya Barajı** ⊠ C Turkey
171 *Q9* **Karakelong, Pulau** *island* N Indonesia
Karakılısse *see* Ağrı
Karak, Muḩāfaẓat al *see* Al Karak
147 *X8* **Karakol** *var.* Karakolka. Issyk-Kul'skaya Oblast', NE Kyrgyzstan *41°30′N 77°18′E*
147 *Y7* **Karakol** *prev.* Przheval'sk. Issyk-Kul'skaya Oblast', NE Kyrgyzstan *42°32′N 78°21′E*
Kara-Köl *see* Kara-Kul'
Karakolka *see* Karakol
149 *W2* **Karakoram Highway** *road* China/Pakistan
149 *Z3* **Karakoram Pass** *Chin.* Karakoram Shankou. *pass* C Asia
152 *I3* **Karakoram Range** ▲▲ C Asia
Karakoram Shankou *see* Karakoram Pass
Karaköse *see* Ağrı
145 *P14* **Karakoyyn, Ozero** *Kaz.* Qaraqoyyn. ◎ C Kazakhstan
83 *F19* **Karakubis** Ghanzi, W Botswana *22°03′S 20°36′E*
147 *T9* **Kara-Kul'** *Kir.* Kara-Köl. Dzhalal-Abadskaya Oblast', W Kyrgyzstan *40°35′N 73°36′E*
Karakul' *see* Qarokŭl, Tajikistan
Karakul' *see* Qorako'l, Uzbekistan
147 *U10* **Kara-Kul'dzha** Oshskaya Oblast', SW Kyrgyzstan *40°32′N 73°50′E*
127 *T3* **Karakulino** Udmurtskaya Respublika, NW Russian Federation *56°02′N 53°45′E*
Karakul', Ozero *see* Qarokŭl
Kara Kum *see* Garagum
Kara Kum Canal/Karakumskiy Kanal *see* Garagum Kanaly
Karakumy, Peski *see* Garagum
83 *E17* **Karakuwisa** Okavango, NE Namibia *18°56′S 19°40′E*
122 *M13* **Karam** Irkutskaya Oblast', S Russian Federation *55°07′N 107°21′E*
Karamai *see* Karamay
169 *T14* **Karamain, Pulau** *island* N Indonesia
136 *I16* **Karaman** Karaman, S Turkey *37°11′N 33°13′E*
136 *H16* **Karaman** ◈ *province* S Turkey
114 *M8* **Karamandere** ≈ NE Bulgaria
158 *J4* **Karamay** *var.* Karamai, Kelamayi; *prev. Chin.* K'o-la-ma-i. Xinjiang Uygur Zizhiqu, NW China *45°33′N 84°45′E*
169 *U14* **Karambu** Borneo, N Indonesia *03°48′S 116°06′E*
185 *H14* **Karamea** West Coast, South Island, New Zealand *41°15′S 172°07′E*
185 *H14* **Karamea** ≈ South Island, New Zealand
185 *G15* **Karamea Bight** *gulf* South Island, New Zealand
Karamet-Niyaz *see* Garamätnyýaz
158 *K10* **Karamiran He** ≈ NW China
147 *S11* **Karamyk** Oshskaya Oblast', SW Kyrgyzstan *39°28′N 71°45′E*
169 *U17* **Karangasem** Bali, S Indonesia *08°24′S 115°40′E*
154 *H12* **Kāranja** Mahārāshtra, C India *20°30′N 77°26′E*
Karanpur *see* Karanpura
152 *F9* **Karanpura** *var.* Karanpur. Rājasthān, NW India *29°46′N 73°30′E*
Karánsebes/Karansebesch *see* Caransebeş
145 *T14* **Karaoy** *Kaz.* Qaraoy. Almaty, SE Kazakhstan *45°52′N 74°44′E*
114 *N7* **Karapelit** *Rom.* Stejarul. Dobrich, NE Bulgaria *43°40′N 27°33′E*
136 *I15* **Karapınar** Konya, C Turkey *37°43′N 33°34′E*
83 *D22* **Karas** ◈ *district* S Namibia
147 *Y8* **Kara-Say** Issyk-Kul'skaya Oblast', NE Kyrgyzstan *41°34′N 77°56′E*
83 *E22* **Karasburg** Karas, S Namibia *27°59′S 18°46′E*
Kara Sea *see* Karskoye More
92 *K9* **Kárášjohka** *var.* Karašjokka. ≈ N Norway
Kárášjohka *see* Karasjok
92 *L9* **Karasjok** *Fin.* Kaarasjoki, *Lapp.* Kárášjohka. Finnmark, N Norway *69°27′N 25°28′E*
Karašjokka *see* Kárášjohka
Kara Strait *see* Karskiye Vorota, Proliv
145 *N8* **Karasu** *Kaz.* Qarasū. Kostanay, N Kazakhstan *52°44′N 65°29′E*
136 *F11* **Karasu** Sakarya, NW Turkey *41°07′N 30°37′E*
Kara Su *see* Mesta/Néstos
Karasubazar *see* Bilohirs'k
122 *I12* **Karasuk** Novosibirskaya Oblast', C Russian Federation *53°41′N 78°04′E*
145 *U13* **Karatal** *Kaz.* Qaratal. ≈ SE Kazakhstan
136 *K17* **Karataş** Adana, S Turkey *36°32′N 35°22′E*
145 *Q16* **Karatau** *Kaz.* Qarataū. Zhambyl, S Kazakhstan *43°09′N 70°28′E*
Karatau *see* Karatau, Khrebet
145 *P16* **Karatau, Khrebet** *var.* Karatau, *Kaz.* Qarataū. ▲▲ S Kazakhstan
144 *G13* **Karaton** *Kaz.* Qaraton. Atyrau, W Kazakhstan *46°33′N 53°31′E*
164 *C13* **Karatsu** *var.* Karatu. Saga, Kyūshū, SW Japan *33°28′N 129°48′E*
Karatu *see* Karatsu
122 *K8* **Karaul** Taymyrskiy (Dolgano-Nenetskiy) Avtonomnyy Okrug, N Russian Federation *70°07′N 83°12′E*
Karaulbazar *see* Qorowulbozor
152 *I13* **Karauli** Rājasthān, N India *26°29′N 77°01′E*
Karauzyak *see* Qorao'zak
115 *D16* **Karáva** ▲ C Greece *39°19′N 21°33′E*
Karavanke *see* Karawanken
115 *F22* **Karavás** Kýthira, S Greece *36°21′N 22°57′E*
113 *J20* **Karavastasë, Laguna e** *var.* Kënet' e Karavastas, Kravasta Lagoon. *lagoon* W Albania
Karavastas, Kënet' e *see* Karavastasë, Laguna e
118 *I5* **Käravere** Tartumaa, E Estonia *58°25′N 26°29′E*
115 *L23* **Karavonísia** *island* Kykládes, Greece, Aegean Sea
169 *O15* **Karawang** *prev.* Krawang. Jawa, C Indonesia *06°13′S 107°16′E*
109 *T10* **Karawanken** *Slvn.* Karavanke. ▲▲ Austria/Serbia
Karaxahar *see* Kaidu He
137 *R13* **Karayazı** Erzurum, NE Turkey *39°40′N 42°09′E*
145 *Q12* **Karazhal** *Kaz.* Qarazhal. Karaganda, C Kazakhstan *48°002′N 70°52′E*
139 *T10* **Karbalā'** ◈ *governorate* S Iraq
139 *S9* **Karbalā'** *var.* Kerbala, Kerbela. Karbalā', S Iraq *32°37′N 44°03′E*
94 *L11* **Kårböle** Gävleborg, C Sweden *61°59′N 15°16′E*
111 *M23* **Karcag** Jász-Nagykun-Szolnok, E Hungary *47°22′N 20°51′E*
Kardak *see* Imia
114 *N7* **Kardam** Dobrich, NE Bulgaria *43°45′N 28°06′E*
Kardamila *see* Kardámyla
115 *L18* **Kardámyla** *var.* Kardamila, Kardhámila. Chíos, E Greece *38°33′N 26°04′E*
Kardeljevo *see* Ploče
Kardh *see* Qardho
Kardhámila *see* Kardámyla
Kardhítsa *see* Kardítsa
115 *E16* **Kardítsa** *var.* Kardhítsa. Thessalía, C Greece *39°22′N 21°56′E*
118 *E4* **Kärdla** *Ger.* Kertel. Hiiumaa, W Estonia *59°00′N 22°42′E*
Karelia *see* Kareliya, Respublika
119 *I16* **Karelichy** *Pol.* Korelicze, *Rus.* Korelichi. Hrodzyenskaya Voblasts', W Belarus *53°34′N 26°08′E*
124 *I10* **Kareliya, Respublika** *prev.* Karel'skaya ASSR, *Eng.* Karelia. ◈ *autonomous republic* NW Russian Federation
Karel'skaya ASSR *see* Kareliya, Respublika
81 *E22* **Karema** Rukwa, W Tanzania *06°50′S 30°25′E*
Karen *see* Hualien
83 *I14* **Karenda** Central, C Zambia *14°42′S 26°52′E*
167 *N8* **Karen State** *var.* Kawthule State, Kayin State. ◈ *state* S Myanmar (Burma)
92 *J10* **Karesuando** *Fin.* Kaaresuanto, *Lapp.* Gárasavvon. Norrbotten, N Sweden *68°25′N 22°28′E*
Karet *see* Kâgheț
Kareyz-e-Elyās/Kārez Iliās *see* Kārīz-e Elyās
122 *J11* **Kargasok** Tomskaya Oblast', C Russian Federation *59°01′N 80°34′E*
122 *I12* **Kargat** Novosibirskaya Oblast', C Russian Federation *55°07′N 80°19′E*
136 *J11* **Kargı** Çorum, N Turkey *41°09′N 34°32′E*
152 *I5* **Kargil** Jammu and Kashmir, NW India *34°34′N 76°06′E*
Kargilik *see* Yecheng
124 *L11* **Kargopol'** Arkhangel'skaya Oblast', NW Russian Federation *61°30′N 38°53′E*
110 *F12* **Kargowa** *Ger.* Unruhstadt. Lubuskie, W Poland *52°05′N 15°50′E*
77 *X13* **Kari** Bauchi, E Nigeria *11°13′N 10°34′E*
83 *J15* **Kariba** Mashonaland West, N Zimbabwe *16°29′S 28°48′E*
83 *J16* **Kariba, Lake** ⊠ Zambia/Zimbabwe
165 *Q4* **Kariba-yama** ▲ Hokkaidō, NE Japan *42°36′N 139°55′E*
83 *C19* **Karibib** Erongo, C Namibia *21°56′S 15°51′E*
Karies *see* Karyés
92 *L9* **Karigasniemi** *Lapp.* Garegegasnjárga. Lappi, N Finland *69°24′N 25°52′E*
184 *J2* **Karikari, Cape** *headland* North Island, New Zealand *34°47′S 173°24′E*
Karīmābād *see* Hunza
169 *P12* **Karimata, Kepulauan** *island group* N Indonesia
169 *P12* **Karimata, Pulau** *island* Kepulauan Karimata, N Indonesia
169 *O11* **Karimata, Selat** *strait* W Indonesia
155 *I14* **Karīmnagar** Andhra Pradesh, C India *18°28′N 79°09′E*
186 *C7* **Karimui** Chimbu, C Papua New Guinea *06°19′S 144°48′E*
169 *Q15* **Karimunjawa, Pulau** *island* S Indonesia
80 *N12* **Karin** Sahil, N Somalia *10°48′N 45°46′E*
Kariot *see* Ikaría
93 *L20* **Karis** *Fin.* Karjaa. Etelä-Suomi, SW Finland *60°05′N 23°39′E*
Káristos *see* Kárystos
148 *J4* **Kārīz-e Elyās** *var.* Kareyz-e-Elyās, Kārez Iliās. Herāt, NW Afghanistan *35°26′N 61°24′E*
Karjaa *see* Karis
145 *T10* **Karkaralinsk** *Kaz.* Qarqaraly. Karaganda, E Kazakhstan *49°31′N 75°53′E*
186 *D6* **Karkar Island** *island* N Papua New Guinea
143 *N7* **Karkas, Kūh-e** ▲▲ C Iran
142 *K8* **Karkheh, Rūd-e** ≈ SW Iran
115 *L20* **Karkinágri** *var.* Karkinagrio. Ikaría, Dodekánisa, Greece, Aegean Sea *37°31′N 26°01′E*
Karkinagrio *see* Karkinágri
117 *R12* **Karkinits'ka Zatoka** *Rus.* Karkinitskiy Zaliv. *gulf* S Ukraine

◆ Country
● Country Capital
◇ Dependent Territory
○ Dependent Territory Capital
◈ Administrative Regions
✈ International Airport
▲ Mountain
▲▲ Mountain Range
⛰ Volcano
≈ River
◎ Lake
⊠ Reservoir

KARKINITSKIY ZALIV – KELLETT, CAPE

Karkinitskiy Zaliv see Karkinits'ka Zatoka
93 L19 Karkkila Swe. Högfors. Uusimaa, S Finland 60°32'N 24°10'E
93 M19 Kärkölä Etelä-Suomi, S Finland 60°52'N 25°17'E
182 G9 Karkoo South Australia 34°03'S 135°45'E
Karkūk see Kirkūk
118 D5 Kärla Ger. Kergel. Saaremaa, W Estonia 58°20'N 22°15'E
Karleby see Kokkola
110 F7 Karlino Ger. Körlin an der Persante. Zachodnio-pomorskie, NW Poland 54°02'N 15°52'E
137 Q13 Karlıova Bingöl, E Turkey 39°16'N 41°01'E
117 U6 Karlivka Poltavs'ka Oblast', C Ukraine 49°27'N 35°08'E
Karl-Marx-Stadt see Chemnitz
Karlö see Hailuoto
112 C11 Karlobag It. Carlopago. Lika-Senj, W Croatia 44°31'N 15°06'E
112 D9 Karlovac Ger. Karlstadt, Hung. Károlyváros. Karlovac, C Croatia 45°29'N 15°31'E
112 C10 Karlovac off. Karlovačka Županija. ◆ province C Croatia
Karlovačka Županija see Karlovac
111 A16 Karlovarský Kraj ◆ W Czech Republic
115 M19 Karlovási var. Néon Karlovásion, Néon Karlovasi. Sámos, Dodekánisa, Greece, Aegean Sea 37°47'N 26°40'E
114 J9 Karlovo prev. Levskigrad. Plovdiv, C Bulgaria 42°38'N 24°49'E
111 A16 Karlovy Vary Ger. Karlsbad; prev. Eng. Carlsbad. Karlovarský Kraj, W Czech Republic 50°13'N 12°51'E
Karlsbad see Karlovy Vary
95 L17 Karlsborg Västra Götaland, S Sweden 58°32'N 14°32'E
Karlsburg see Alba Iulia
95 L22 Karlshamn Blekinge, S Sweden 56°10'N 14°50'E
95 L16 Karlskoga Örebro, C Sweden 59°19'N 14°33'E
95 M22 Karlskrona Blekinge, S Sweden 56°11'N 15°39'E
101 G21 Karlsruhe var. Carlsruhe. Baden-Württemberg, SW Germany 49°01'N 08°24'E
95 K16 Karlstad Värmland, C Sweden 59°22'N 13°36'E
29 R3 Karlstad Minnesota, N USA 48°34'N 96°31'W
101 I18 Karlstadt Bayern, C Germany 49°58'N 09°46'E
Karlstadt see Karlovac
39 Q14 Karluk Kodiak Island, Alaska, USA 57°34'N 154°27'W
Karluk see Qarluq
119 O17 Karma Rus. Korma. Homyel'skaya Voblasts', SE Belarus 53°07'N 30°48'E
155 F14 Karmāla Mahārāshtra, W India 18°26'N 75°08'E
146 M11 Karmana Navoiy Viloyati, C Uzbekistan 40°09'N 65°18'E
138 G8 Karmi'el var. Carmiel. Northern, N Israel 32°55'N 35°18'E
95 B16 Karmøy island S Norway
152 I9 Karnāl Haryāna, N India 29°41'N 76°58'E
153 W15 Karnaphuli Reservoir ⊠ NE India
155 F17 Karnātaka var. Kanara; prev. Maisur, Mysore. ◆ state W India
25 S13 Karnes City Texas, SW USA 28°54'N 97°55'W
109 P9 Karnische Alpen It. Alpi Carniche. ▲▲ Austria/Italy
114 M9 Karnobat Burgas, E Bulgaria 42°39'N 26°59'E
109 Q9 Kärnten off. Land Kärnten, Eng. Carinthia, Slvn. Koroška. ◆ state S Austria
Karnul see Kurnool
83 K16 Karoi Mashonaland West, N Zimbabwe 16°50'S 29°40'E
Karol see Carei
Károly-Fehérvár see Alba Iulia
Károlyváros see Karlovac
82 M12 Karonga Northern, N Malawi 09°54'S 33°55'E
147 W10 Karool-Tëbë Narynskaya Oblast', C Kyrgyzstan 40°33'N 75°52'E
182 J9 Karoonda South Australia 35°04'S 139°58'E
149 S9 Karor Lāl Esan Punjab, E Pakistan 31°15'N 70°58'E
149 T11 Karor Pacca var. Kahror, Kahror Pakka. Punjab, E Pakistan 29°38'N 71°59'E
Karosa see Karossa
171 N12 Karossa var. Karosa. Sulawesi, C Indonesia 01°38'S 119°21'E
Karpaten see Carpathian Mountains
115 L22 Karpáthio Pélagos sea Dodekánisa, Greece, Aegean Sea
115 N24 Kárpathos Kárpathos, SE Greece 35°30'N 27°13'E
115 N24 Kárpathos It. Scarpanto; anc. Carpathos, Carpathus. island SE Greece
Karpathos Strait see Karpathou, Stenó
115 N24 Karpathou, Stenó var. Karpathos Strait, Scarpanto Strait. strait Dodekánisa, Greece, Aegean Sea
Karpaty see Carpathian Mountains
115 E17 Karpenísi prev. Karpenísion. Stereá Ellás, C Greece 38°55'N 21°46'E
Karpenísion see Karpenísi
Karpilovka see Aktsyabrski
125 O8 Karpogory Arkhangel'skaya Oblast', NW Russian Federation 64°01'N 44°22'E
180 I7 Karratha Western Australia 20°44'S 116°52'E
137 S12 Kars var. Qars. Kars, NE Turkey 40°35'N 43°05'E
137 S12 Kars var. Qars. ◆ province NE Turkey
145 O12 Karsakpay Kaz. Qarsaqbay. Karaganda, C Kazakhstan 47°51'N 66°42'E
93 L15 Kärsämäki Oulu, C Finland 63°58'N 25°49'E
Karsau see Kārsava
118 K9 Kārsava Ger. Karsau; prev. Rus. Korsovka. Ludza, E Latvia 56°46'N 27°39'E
Karshi see Garşy, Turkmenistan
Karshi see Qarshi, Uzbekistan
Karshinskaya Step see Qarshi Choʻli
Karshinskiy Kanal see Qarshi Kanali
84 I5 Karskiye Vorota, Proliv Eng. Kara Strait. strait N Russian Federation
122 J6 Karskoye More Eng. Kara Sea. sea Arctic Ocean
93 L17 Karstula Länsi-Suomi, C Finland 62°52'N 24°48'E
127 Q5 Karsun Ul'yanovskaya Oblast', W Russian Federation 54°12'N 47°00'E
122 F11 Kartaly Chelyabinskaya Oblast', C Russian Federation 53°02'N 60°42'E
18 E13 Karthaus Pennsylvania, NE USA 41°06'N 78°03'W
110 I7 Kartuzy Pomorskie, NW Poland 54°21'N 18°11'E
165 R8 Karumai Iwate, Honshū, C Japan 40°19'N 141°27'E
181 U4 Karumba Queensland, NE Australia 17°31'S 140°51'E
142 L10 Kārūn var. Rūd-e Kārūn. ≈ SW Iran
92 K13 Karungi Norrbotten, N Sweden 66°03'N 23°55'E
92 K13 Karunki Lappi, N Finland 66°01'N 24°06'E
Kārūn, Rūd-e see Kārūn
155 H21 Karūr Tamil Nādu, SE India 10°58'N 78°03'E
93 K17 Karvia Länsi-Suomi, SW Finland 62°07'N 22°34'E
111 J17 Karviná Ger. Karwin, Pol. Karwina; prev. Nová Karvinná. Moravskoslezský Kraj, E Czech Republic 49°50'N 18°30'E
155 E17 Kārwār Karnātaka, W India 14°50'N 74°09'E
108 M7 Karwendelgebirge ▲▲ Austria/Germany
Karwin/Karwina see Karviná
115 I14 Karyés var. Karies. Ágion Óros, N Greece 40°15'N 24°15'E
115 I19 Kárystos var. Káristos. Évvoia, C Greece 38°01'N 24°25'E
136 E17 Kaş Antalya, SW Turkey 36°12'N 29°38'E
39 Y14 Kasaan Prince of Wales Island, Alaska, USA 55°32'N 132°24'W
164 I13 Kasai Hyōgo, Honshū, SW Japan 34°56'N 134°49'E
79 K21 Kasai var. Cassai, Kassai. ≈ Angola/Dem. Rep. Congo
79 K22 Kasai-Occidental off. Région Kasai Occidental. ◆ region S Dem. Rep. Congo
Kasai Occidental, Région see Kasai-Occidental
79 L21 Kasai-Oriental off. Région Kasai Oriental. ◆ region C Dem. Rep. Congo
Kasai Oriental, Région see Kasai-Oriental
79 L24 Kasaji Katanga, S Dem. Rep. Congo 10°22'S 23°29'E
82 L12 Kasama Northern, N Zambia 10°14'S 31°12'E
Kasan see Koson
83 H16 Kasane North-West, NE Botswana 17°48'S 20°06'E
81 E23 Kasanga Rukwa, W Tanzania 08°27'S 31°10'E
79 G21 Kasangulu Bas-Congo, W Dem. Rep. Congo 04°33'S 15°12'E
Kasansay see Kosonsoy
155 E20 Kāsaragod Kerala, SW India 12°30'N 74°59'E
Kasargen see Kasari
118 P13 Kasari var. Kasari Jõgi, Ger. Kasargen. ≈ W Estonia
Kasari Jõgi see Kasari
8 L11 Kasba Lake ⊚ Northwest Territories, Nunavut N Canada
Kaschau see Košice
164 B16 Kaseda var. Minami-Satsuma. Kagoshima, Kyūshū, SW Japan 31°25'N 130°17'E
83 I14 Kasempa North Western, NW Zambia 13°27'S 25°49'E
79 O24 Kasenga Katanga, SE Dem. Rep. Congo 10°22'S 28°37'E
79 P17 Kasenye var. Kasenyi. Orientale, NE Dem. Rep. Congo 01°23'N 30°25'E
Kasenyi see Kasenye
79 O19 Kasese Maniema, E Dem. Rep. Congo 01°36'S 27°31'E
81 E18 Kasese SW Uganda 0°10'N 30°06'E
152 J11 Kāsganj Uttar Pradesh, N India 27°48'N 78°38'E
143 U4 Kashaf Rūd ≈ NE Iran
143 N7 Kāshān Eşfahān, C Iran 33°57'N 51°31'E
126 M10 Kashary Rostovskaya Oblast', SW Russian Federation 49°02'N 40°58'E
39 O12 Kashegelok Alaska, USA 60°57'N 157°46'W
Kashgar see Kashi
158 E7 Kashi Chin. Kaxgar, K'o-shih, Uigh. Kashgar. Xinjiang Uygur Zizhiqu, NW China 39°32'N 75°58'E
164 J14 Kashihara var. Kasihara. Nara, Honshū, SW Japan 34°28'N 135°46'E
165 P13 Kashima-nada gulf S Japan
124 K15 Kashin Tverskaya Oblast', W Russian Federation 57°20'N 37°34'E
152 K10 Kāshīpur Uttarakhand, N India 29°13'N 78°58'E
126 L4 Kashira Moskovskaya Oblast', W Russian Federation 54°53'N 38°13'E
165 N11 Kashiwazaki var. Kasiwazaki. Niigata, Honshū, C Japan 37°22'N 138°33'E
Kashkadar'inskaya Oblast' see Qashqadaryo Viloyati
143 T5 Kāshmar var. Turshiz; prev. Solṭānābād, Torshiz. Khorāsān, NE Iran 35°13'N 58°25'E
Kashmir see Jammu and Kashmir
149 R12 Kashmor Sind, SE Pakistan 28°24'N 69°42'E
149 S5 Kashmūnd Ghar Eng. Kashmund Range. ▲▲ E Afghanistan
Kashmund Range see Kashmūnd Ghar
Kasi see Vārānasi
153 O12 Kasia Uttar Pradesh, N India 26°45'N 83°55'E
39 N12 Kasigluk Alaska, USA 60°54'N 162°31'W
Kasihara see Kashihara
39 R12 Kasilof Alaska, USA 60°20'N 151°16'W
Kasimköj see General Toshevo
126 M4 Kasimov Ryazanskaya Oblast', W Russian Federation 54°59'N 41°22'E
79 P18 Kasindi Nord-Kivu, E Dem. Rep. Congo 0°03'N 29°43'E
82 M12 Kasitu ≈ N Malawi
Kasiwazaki see Kashiwazaki
30 L14 Kaskaskia River ≈ Illinois, N USA
93 J17 Kaskinen Swe. Kaskö. Länsi-Suomi, W Finland 62°23'N 21°10'E
Kaskö see Kaskinen
Kas Kong see Kŏng, Kaôh
11 O17 Kaslo British Columbia, SW Canada 49°54'N 116°57'W
Käsmark see Kežmarok
169 T12 Kasongan Borneo, C Indonesia 02°01'S 113°21'E
79 N21 Kasongo Maniema, E Dem. Rep. Congo 04°22'S 26°42'E
79 H22 Kasongo-Lunda Bandundu, SW Dem. Rep. Congo 06°30'S 16°51'E
115 M24 Kásos island S Greece
Kasos Strait see Kasou, Stenó
115 M25 Kasou, Stenó var. Kasos Strait. strait Dodekánisos/Kríti, Greece, Aegean Sea
137 T10 Kaspi C Georgia 41°54'N 44°25'E
114 M8 Kaspichan Shumen, NE Bulgaria 43°18'N 27°09'E
Kaspiy Mangy Oypaty see Caspian Depression
127 Q16 Kaspiysk Respublika Dagestan, SW Russian Federation 42°52'N 47°40'E
Kaspiyskiy see Lagan'
Kaspiyskoye More/Kaspiy Tengizi see Caspian Sea
Kassa see Košice
Kassai see Kasai
80 I9 Kassala Kassala, E Sudan 15°24'N 36°25'E
80 H9 Kassala ◆ state NE Sudan
115 G15 Kassándra prev. Pallíni; anc. Pallene. peninsula NE Greece
115 G15 Kassándra headland N Greece 39°58'N 23°22'E
115 H15 Kassándras, Kólpos var. Kólpos Toronaíos. gulf N Greece
139 Y11 Kassārah Maysān, E Iraq 31°21'N 47°25'E
101 I15 Kassel prev. Cassel. Hessen, C Germany 51°19'N 09°30'E
74 M6 Kasserine var. Al Qaşrayn. W Tunisia 35°15'N 08°52'E
14 J14 Kasshabog Lake ⊚ Ontario, SE Canada
139 O5 Kassīr, Sabkhat al ⊚ E Syria
29 W10 Kasson Minnesota, N USA 44°00'N 92°42'W
115 C17 Kassópeia Var. Kassópi. site of ancient city Ípeiros, W Greece
Kassópi see Kassópeia
115 N24 Kastállou, Akrotírio headland Kárpathos, SE Greece 35°24'N 27°08'E
136 I11 Kastamonu var. Castamoni, Kastamuni. Kastamonu, N Turkey 41°22'N 33°47'E
136 I10 Kastamonu var. Kastamuni. ◆ province N Turkey
Kastamuni see Kastamonu
115 E14 Kastaneá Kentrikí Makedonía, N Greece 40°25'N 22°09'E
Kastélli see Kíssamos
Kastellórizon see Megísti
95 N21 Kastlösa Kalmar, S Sweden 56°25'N 16°25'E
115 D14 Kastoría Dytikí Makedonía, N Greece 40°33'N 21°15'E
126 K7 Kastornoye Kurskaya Oblast', W Russian Federation 51°49'N 38°07'E
115 I21 Kástro Sífnos, Kykládes, Greece, Aegean Sea 36°58'N 24°45'E
95 J23 Kastrup ✈ (København) København, E Denmark 55°36'N 12°39'E
119 Q17 Kastsyukovichy Rus. Kostyukovichi. Mahilyowskaya Voblasts', E Belarus 53°20'N 32°03'E
119 O18 Kastsyukowka Rus. Kostyukovka. Homyel'skaya Voblasts', SE Belarus 52°32'N 30°54'E
164 D13 Kasuga Fukuoka, Kyūshū, SW Japan 33°31'N 130°27'E
164 L13 Kasugai Aichi, Honshū, SW Japan 35°15'N 136°57'E
81 E21 Kasulu Kigoma, W Tanzania 04°33'S 30°06'E
164 I12 Kasumi Hyōgo, Honshū, SW Japan 35°36'N 134°37'E
127 R17 Kasumkent Respublika Dagestan, SW Russian Federation 41°39'N 48°09'E
82 M13 Kasungu Central, C Malawi 13°04'S 33°29'E
149 W9 Kasūr Punjab, E Pakistan 31°07'N 74°30'E
83 G15 Kataba Western, W Zambia 15°28'S 23°25'E
19 R4 Katahdin, Mount ▲ Maine, NE USA 45°55'N 68°52'W
79 M20 Katako-Kombe Kasai-Oriental, C Dem. Rep. Congo 03°24'S 24°25'E
39 T12 Katalla Alaska, USA 60°12'N 144°31'W
Katana see Qaṭanā
79 L24 Katanga off. Région du Katanga; prev. Shaba. ◆ region SE Dem. Rep. Congo
122 M11 Katanga ≈ C Russian Federation
Katanga, Région du see Katanga
154 J11 Katāngi Madhya Pradesh, C India 21°46'N 79°50'E
180 J13 Katanning Western Australia 33°45'S 117°33'E
181 P8 Kata Tjuta var. Mount Olga. ▲ Northern Territory, C Australia 25°20'S 130°47'E
Katawaz see Zarghūn Shahr
151 Q22 Katchall Island island Nicobar Islands, India, NE Indian Ocean
115 F14 Kateríni Kentrikí Makedonía, N Greece 40°15'N 22°30'E
117 P7 Katerynopil' Cherkas'ka Oblast', C Ukraine 49°00'N 30°59'E
166 M3 Katha Sagaing, N Myanmar (Burma) 24°11'N 96°20'E
181 P2 Katherine Northern Territory, N Australia 14°29'S 132°20'E
154 B11 Kāthiāwār Peninsula peninsula W India
153 P11 Kathmandu prev. Kantipur. ● (Nepal) Central, C Nepal 27°46'N 85°17'E
152 H7 Kathua Jammu and Kashmir, NW India 32°23'N 75°34'E
76 L12 Kati Koulikoro, SW Mali 12°41'N 08°04'W
153 R13 Katihār Bihār, NE India 25°33'N 87°34'E
184 N7 Katikati Bay of Plenty, North Island, New Zealand 37°34'S 175°55'E
83 H16 Katima Mulilo Caprivi, NE Namibia 17°31'S 24°20'E
77 N15 Katiola C Ivory Coast 08°11'N 05°04'W
191 V10 Katiu atoll Îles Tuamotu, C French Polynesia
117 N12 Katlabukh, Ozero ⊚ SW Ukraine
39 P14 Katmai, Mount ▲ Alaska, USA 58°16'N 154°57'W
154 J9 Katni Madhya Pradesh, C India 23°47'N 80°29'E
115 D19 Káto Achaïa var. Kato Ahaia, Káto Akhaía. Dytikí Ellás, S Greece 38°08'N 21°33'E
Kato Ahaia/Káto Akhaía see Káto Achaïa
121 P2 Kato Lakatámeia var. Kato Lakatamia. C Cyprus 35°07'N 33°20'E
Kato Lakatamia see Kato Lakatámeia
79 N22 Katompi Katanga, SE Dem. Rep. Congo 06°10'S 26°19'E
83 K14 Katondwe Lusaka, C Zambia 15°08'S 30°10'E
114 H12 Káto Nevrokópi prev. Káto Nevrokópion. Anatolikí Makedonía kai Thráki, NE Greece 41°21'N 23°51'E
Káto Nevrokópion see Káto Nevrokópi
81 E18 Katonga ≈ S Uganda
115 F15 Káto Ólympos ▲▲ C Greece
115 D17 Katoúna Dytikí Ellás, C Greece 38°47'N 21°07'E
115 E19 Káto Vlasiá Dytikí Makedonía, S Greece 38°02'N 21°54'E
111 J16 Katowice Ger. Kattowitz. Śląskie, S Poland 50°15'N 19°01'E
153 S15 Kātoya West Bengal, NE India 23°39'N 88°11'E
136 E16 Katrançık Dağı ▲▲ SW Turkey
95 N16 Katrineholm Södermanland, C Sweden 58°59'N 16°15'E
96 I11 Katrine, Loch ⊚ C Scotland, United Kingdom
77 V12 Katsina Katsina, N Nigeria 12°59'N 07°33'E
77 U12 Katsina ◆ state N Nigeria
67 P8 Katsina Ala ≈ S Nigeria
164 C13 Katsumoto Nagasaki, Iki, SW Japan 33°49'N 129°42'E
165 P13 Katsuta var. Katuta. Ibaraki, Honshū, S Japan 36°24'N 140°32'E
165 O14 Katsuura var. Katuura. Chiba, Honshū, S Japan 35°09'N 140°16'E
164 K12 Katsuyama var. Katuyama. Fukui, Honshū, SW Japan 36°00'N 136°30'E
164 H12 Katsuyama Okayama, Honshū, SW Japan 35°06'N 133°43'E
Kattakurgan see Kattaqoʻrgʻon
147 N11 Kattaqoʻrgʻon Rus. Kattakurgan. Samarqand Viloyati, C Uzbekistan 39°56'N 66°11'E
115 O23 Kattavía Ródos, Dodekánisa, Greece, Aegean Sea 35°56'N 27°47'E
95 I21 Kattegat Dan. Kattegatt. strait N Europe
Kattegatt see Kattegat
95 P19 Katthammarsvik Gotland, SE Sweden 57°27'N 18°54'E
Kattowitz see Katowice
122 J13 Katun' ≈ S Russian Federation
Katuta see Katsuta
Katuura see Katsuura
Katuyama see Katsuyama
Katwijk see Katwijk aan Zee
98 G11 Katwijk aan Zee var. Katwijk. Zuid-Holland, W Netherlands 52°12'N 04°24'E
38 B8 Kaua'i var. Kauai. island Hawaiian Islands, Hawai'i, USA, C Pacific Ocean
Kauai see Kaua'i
38 C8 Kaua'i Channel var. Kauai Channel. channel Hawai'i, USA, C Pacific Ocean
Kauai Channel see Kaua'i Channel
171 R13 Kaubalatmada, Gunung var. Kaplamada. ▲ Pulau Buru, E Indonesia 03°16'S 126°17'E
191 U10 Kauehi atoll Îles Tuamotu, C French Polynesia
Kauen see Kaunas
101 K24 Kaufbeuren Bayern, S Germany 47°53'N 10°37'E
25 U7 Kaufman Texas, SW USA 32°35'N 96°18'W
101 I15 Kaufungen Hessen, C Germany 51°16'N 09°39'E
93 K17 Kauhajoki Länsi-Suomi, W Finland 62°26'N 22°10'E
93 K16 Kauhava Länsi-Suomi, W Finland 63°06'N 23°08'E
30 M7 Kaukauna Wisconsin, N USA 44°18'N 88°18'W
92 L11 Kaukonen Lappi, N Finland 67°28'N 24°49'E
38 A8 Kaulakahi Channel channel Hawai'i, USA, C Pacific Ocean
38 E9 Kaunakakai Moloka'i, Hawaii, USA, C Pacific Ocean 21°05'N 157°01'W
38 F12 Kaunā Point var. Kauna Point. headland Hawai'i, USA, C Pacific Ocean 19°02'N 155°52'W
Kauna Point see Kaunā Point
118 F13 Kaunas Ger. Kauen, Pol. Kowno; prev. Rus. Kovno. Kaunas, C Lithuania 54°54'N 23°57'E
118 F13 Kaunas ◆ province C Lithuania
186 C6 Kaup East Sepik, NW Papua New Guinea 03°50'S 144°01'E
77 U12 Kaura Namoda Zamfara, NW Nigeria 12°43'N 06°17'E
Kaushany see Căuşeni
93 K16 Kaustinen Länsi-Suomi, W Finland 63°33'N 23°40'E
99 M23 Kautenbach Diekirch, NE Luxembourg 49°57'N 06°01'E
92 K10 Kautokeino Lapp. Guovdageaidnu. Finnmark, N Norway 69°N 23°01'E
Kavadar see Kavadarci
113 P19 Kavadarci Turk. Kavadar. C Macedonia 41°25'N 22°00'E
Kavaja see Kavajë
113 K20 Kavajë It. Cavaia, Kavaja. Tiranë, W Albania 41°11'N 19°33'E
114 M13 Kavak Çayı ≈ NW Turkey
Kavakli see Topolovgrad
114 I13 Kavála prev. Kaválla. Anatolikí Makedonía kai Thráki, NE Greece 40°57'N 24°26'E
114 I13 Kaválas, Kólpos gulf Aegean Sea, NE Mediterranean Sea
155 J17 Kāvali Andhra Pradesh, E India 15°05'N 80°02'E
Kaválla see Kavála
Kavango see Cubango/Okavango
155 C21 Kavaratti Lakshadweep, SW India 10°33'N 72°38'E
114 O8 Kavarna Dobrich, NE Bulgaria 43°27'N 28°21'E
118 G12 Kavarskas Utena, E Lithuania 55°27'N 24°55'E
76 I13 Kavendou ▲ C Guinea 10°49'N 12°14'W
Kavengo see Cubango/Okavango
155 F20 Kāveri var. Cauvery. ≈ S India
186 G5 Kavieng var. Kaewieng. New Ireland, NE Papua New Guinea 02°34'S 152°11'E
83 H16 Kavimba North-West, NE Botswana 18°02'S 24°38'E
83 I15 Kavingu Southern, S Zambia 15°39'S 26°03'E
143 Q6 Kavīr, Dasht-e var. Great Salt Desert. salt pan N Iran
Kavirondo Gulf see Winam Gulf
Kavkaz see Caucasus
95 K23 Kävlinge Skåne, S Sweden 55°47'N 13°05'E
82 G12 Kavungo Moxico, E Angola 11°31'S 22°59'E
165 Q8 Kawabe Akita, Honshū, C Japan 39°39'N 140°14'E
165 R9 Kawai Iwate, Honshū, C Japan 39°36'N 141°40'E
38 A8 Kawaihoa Point headland Ni'ihau, Hawai'i, USA, C Pacific Ocean 21°47'N 160°12'W
184 K3 Kawakawa Northland, North Island, New Zealand 35°23'S 174°06'E
82 I13 Kawama North Western, NW Zambia 13°04'S 25°59'E
82 K11 Kawambwa Luapula, N Zambia 09°45'S 29°10'E
154 K11 Kawardha Chhattīsgarh, C India 21°59'N 81°12'E
14 I14 Kawartha Lakes ⊚ Ontario, SE Canada
165 O13 Kawasaki Kanagawa, Honshū, S Japan 35°32'N 139°41'E
171 R12 Kawassi Pulau Obi, E Indonesia 01°32'S 127°25'E
165 R6 Kawauchi Aomori, Honshū, C Japan 41°11'N 141°00'E
184 L5 Kawau Island island N New Zealand
184 N10 Kaweka Range ▲▲ North Island, New Zealand
Kawelecht see Puhja
184 O8 Kawerau Bay of Plenty, North Island, New Zealand 38°06'S 176°43'E
184 L8 Kawhia Waikato, North Island, New Zealand 38°04'S 174°49'E
184 K8 Kawhia Harbour inlet North Island, New Zealand
35 V8 Kawich Peak ▲ Nevada, W USA 38°00'N 116°27'W
35 V9 Kawich Range ▲▲ Nevada, W USA
14 G12 Kawigamog Lake ⊚ Ontario, S Canada
171 P9 Kawio, Kepulauan island group N Indonesia
167 N9 Kawkareik Kayin State, S Myanmar (Burma) 16°33'N 98°18'E
27 O8 Kaw Lake ⊠ Oklahoma, C USA
166 M3 Kawlin Sagaing, N Myanmar (Burma) 23°48'N 95°41'E
Kawm Umbū see Kom Ombo
Kawthule State see Karen State
Kaxgar see Kashi
158 D7 Kaxgar He ≈ NW China
158 I5 Kax He ≈ NW China
77 P12 Kaya C Burkina 13°04'N 01°09'W
167 N6 Kayah State ◆ state C Myanmar (Burma)
39 T12 Kayak Island island Alaska, USA
114 M11 Kayalıköy Barajı ⊠ NW Turkey
166 M8 Kayan Yangon, SW Myanmar (Burma) 16°54'N 96°35'E
Kayangel Islands see Ngcheangel
155 G23 Kāyankulam Kerala, SW India 09°10'N 76°31'E
169 V9 Kayan, Sungai prev. Kajan. ≈ Borneo, C Indonesia
144 F14 Kaydak, Sor salt flat SW Kazakhstan
Kaydanovo see Dzyarzhynsk Belarus
37 N9 Kayenta Arizona, SW USA 36°43'N 110°15'W
76 J11 Kayes Kayes, W Mali 14°26'N 11°22'W
76 J11 Kayes ◆ region SW Mali
Kayin State see Karen State
145 U10 Kaynar Kaz. Qaynar, var. Kajnar. Vostochnyy Kazakhstan, E Kazakhstan 49°13'N 77°27'E
Kaynary see Căinari
83 H15 Kayoya Western, W Zambia 16°13'S 24°09'E
Kayrakkum see Qayroqqum
Kayrakkumskoye Vodokhranilishche see Qayroqqum, Obanbori
136 K14 Kayseri var. Kaisaria; anc. Caesarea Mazaca, Mazaca. Kayseri, C Turkey 38°42'N 35°28'E
136 K14 Kayseri var. Kaisaria. ◆ province C Turkey
36 L2 Kaysville Utah, W USA 41°10'N 111°55'W
Kayyngdy see Kaindy
14 L11 Kazabazua Québec, SE Canada 45°58'N 76°00'W
14 L12 Kazabazua ≈ Québec, SE Canada
123 Q7 Kazach'ye Respublika Sakha (Yakutiya), NE Russian Federation 70°38'N 135°54'E
Kazakdar'ya see Qozoqdaryo
146 E9 Kazakhlyshor, Solonchak var. Solonchak Shorkazakhly. salt marsh NW Turkmenistan
Kazakhskaya SSR/Kazakh Soviet Socialist Republic see Kazakhstan
145 R9 Kazakhskiy Melkosopochnik Eng. Kazakh Uplands, Kirghiz Steppe, Kaz. Saryarqa. uplands C Kazakhstan
144 L12 Kazakhstan off. Republic of Kazakhstan, var. Kazakstan, Kaz. Qazaqstan, Qazaqstan Respublikasy; prev. Kazakh Soviet Socialist Republic, Rus. Kazakhskaya SSR. ◆ republic C Asia
Kazakhstan, Republic of see Kazakhstan
Kazakh Uplands see Kazakhskiy Melkosopochnik
Kazakstan see Kazakhstan
144 L14 Kazalinsk Kzyl-Orda, S Kazakhstan 45°45'N 62°01'E
127 R4 Kazan' Respublika Tatarstan, W Russian Federation 55°43'N 49°07'E
8 M10 Kazan ≈ Nunavut, NW Canada
127 R4 Kazan' ✈ Respublika Tatarstan, W Russian Federation 55°46'N 49°21'E
Kazandzhik see Bereket
117 R8 Kazanka Mykolayivs'ka Oblast', S Ukraine 47°49'N 32°50'E
Kazanketken see Qozonketkan
Kazanlik see Kazanlŭk
114 J9 Kazanlŭk prev. Kazanlik. Stara Zagora, C Bulgaria 42°38'N 25°24'E
165 Y16 Kazan-rettō Eng. Volcano Islands. island group SE Japan
117 V12 Kazantip, Mys headland S Ukraine 45°27'N 35°50'E
147 U9 Kazarman Narynskaya Oblast', C Kyrgyzstan 41°21'N 74°03'E
Kazatin see Kozyatyn
Kazbegi see Qazbegi
Kazbegi see Kazbek
137 T9 Kazbek var. Kazbegi, Geor. Mqinvartsveri. ▲ N Georgia 42°43'N 44°28'E
82 M13 Kazembe Eastern, NE Zambia 12°06'S 32°45'E
143 N11 Kāzerūn Fārs, S Iran 29°41'N 51°38'E
125 R12 Kazhym Respublika Komi, NW Russian Federation 60°19'N 51°26'E
Kazi Ahmad see Qāzi Ahmad
Kazi Magomed see Qazimämmäd
136 H16 Kazımkarabekir Karaman, S Turkey 37°13'N 32°58'E
111 M20 Kazincbarcika Borsod-Abaúj-Zemplén, NE Hungary 48°15'N 20°40'E
119 H17 Kazlowshchyna Pol. Kozlowszczyzna, Rus. Kozlovshchina. Hrodzyenskaya Voblasts', W Belarus 53°19'N 25°18'E
119 E14 Kazlų Rūda Marijampolė, S Lithuania 54°45'N 23°28'E
144 E9 Kaztalovka Zapadnyy Kazakhstan, W Kazakhstan 49°45'N 48°42'E
79 K22 Kazumba Kasai-Occidental, S Dem. Rep. Congo 06°25'S 22°02'E
165 Q8 Kazuno Akita, Honshū, C Japan 40°14'N 140°48'E
Kazvin see Qazvīn
118 J12 Kaz'yany Rus Koz'yany. Vitsyebskaya Voblasts', NW Belarus 55°18'N 26°52'E
122 H9 Kazym ≈ N Russian Federation
110 H10 Kcynia Ger. Exin. Kujawsko-pomorskie, C Poland 53°00'N 17°29'E
Kéa see Tziá
Kéa see Ioulís
38 H11 Kea'au var. Keaau. Hawaii, USA, C Pacific Ocean 19°36'N 155°01'W
Keaau see Kea'au
38 F11 Keāhole Point var. Keahole Point. headland Hawai'i, USA, C Pacific Ocean 19°43'N 156°03'W
38 G12 Kealakekua Hawaii, USA, C Pacific Ocean 19°31'N 155°56'W
38 H11 Kea, Mauna ▲ Hawai'i, USA 19°50'N 155°30'W
37 N10 Keams Arizona, SW USA 35°47'N 110°09'W
Kéamu see Aneityum
29 O16 Kearney Nebraska, C USA 40°42'N 99°06'W
36 L3 Kearns Utah, W USA 40°39'N 112°00'W
115 H20 Kéas, Stenó strait SE Greece
137 O14 Keban Barajı dam C Turkey
137 O14 Keban Barajı ⊠ C Turkey
77 S13 Kebbi ◆ state NW Nigeria
76 G10 Kébémèr NW Senegal 15°24'N 16°25'W
74 M7 Kebili var. Qibilī. C Tunisia 33°42'N 09°06'E
138 H4 Kebir, Nahr el ≈ NW Syria
80 A10 Kebkabiya Northern Darfur, W Sudan 13°39'N 24°05'E
92 I11 Kebnekaise ▲ N Sweden 68°01'N 18°24'E
81 M14 K'ebrī Dehar Sumalē, E Ethiopia 06°43'N 44°15'E
148 K15 Kech ≈ SW Pakistan
10 K10 Kechika ≈ British Columbia, W Canada
111 K23 Kecskemét Bács-Kiskun, C Hungary 46°54'N 19°42'E
168 J6 Kedah ◆ state Peninsular Malaysia
118 F12 Kėdainiai Kaunas, C Lithuania 55°19'N 24°00'E
152 K8 Kedārnāth Uttarakhand, N India 30°44'N 79°03'E
Kedder see Kehra
13 N13 Kedgwick New Brunswick, SE Canada 47°38'N 67°21'W
169 R16 Kediri Jawa, C Indonesia 07°45'S 112°01'E
171 Y13 Kedir Sarmi Papua, E Indonesia 02°00'S 139°01'E
163 V7 Kedong Heilongjiang, NE China 48°00'N 126°15'E
76 I12 Kédougou SE Senegal 12°35'N 12°09'W
122 I11 Kedrovyy Tomskaya Oblast', C Russian Federation 57°31'N 79°45'E
111 H16 Kędzierzyn-Koźle Ger. Heydebrech. Opolskie, S Poland 50°20'N 18°12'E
8 H8 Keele ≈ Northwest Territories, NW Canada
10 K6 Keele Peak ▲ Yukon Territory, NW Canada 63°31'N 130°21'W
Keelung see Chilung
19 N10 Keene New Hampshire, NE USA 42°56'N 72°14'W
99 H17 Keerbergen Vlaams Brabant, C Belgium 51°01'N 04°39'E
83 E21 Keetmanshoop Karas, S Namibia 26°36'S 18°08'E
12 A11 Keewatin Ontario, S Canada 49°47'N 94°30'W
29 V4 Keewatin Minnesota, N USA 47°24'N 93°04'W
Kefallinía see Kefallonía
115 B18 Kefallonía var. Kefallinía. island Iónia Nisiá, Greece, C Mediterranean Sea
115 M22 Kéfalos Kos, Dodekánisa, Greece, Aegean Sea 36°44'N 26°58'E
171 Q17 Kefamenanu Timor, C Indonesia 09°31'S 124°29'E
Kefar Sava see Kfar Saba
Kefe see Feodosiya
77 V15 Keffi Nassarawa, C Nigeria 08°52'N 07°54'E
92 H4 Keflavík Reykjanes, W Iceland 64°01'N 22°35'W
92 H4 Keflavík ✈ (Reykjavík) Reykjanes, W Iceland 63°58'N 22°37'W
Kegalee see Kegalla
155 J25 Kegalla var. Kegalee, Kegalle. Sabaragamuwa Province, C Sri Lanka 07°14'N 80°21'E
Kegalle see Kegalla
Kegayli see Kegeyli
Kegel see Keila
145 W16 Kegen Almaty, SE Kazakhstan 42°58'N 79°12'E
146 H7 Kegeyli prev. Kegayli. Qoraqalpogʻiston Respublikasi, W Uzbekistan 42°46'N 59°49'E
101 F22 Kehl Baden-Württemberg, SW Germany 48°34'N 07°49'E
118 H3 Kehra Ger. Kedder. Harjumaa, NW Estonia 59°19'N 25°21'E
117 U6 Kehychivka Kharkivs'ka Oblast', E Ukraine 49°18'N 35°46'E
97 L17 Keighley N England, United Kingdom 53°51'N 01°58'W
Kei Islands see Kai, Kepulauan
Keijō see Sŏul
118 G3 Keila Ger. Kegel. Harjumaa, NW Estonia 59°18'N 24°29'E
Keilberg see Klínovec
83 F23 Keimoes Northern Cape, W South Africa 28°41'S 20°59'E
Keina/Keinis see Käina
Keishū see Kyŏngju
77 T11 Keïta Tahoua, C Niger 14°45'N 05°40'E
78 J12 Kéita, Bahr var. Doka. ≈ S Chad
182 K10 Keith South Australia 36°01'S 140°22'E
96 K8 Keith NE Scotland, United Kingdom 57°33'N 02°57'W
26 K3 Keith Sebelius Lake ⊠ Kansas, C USA
32 G11 Keizer Oregon, NW USA 44°59'N 123°01'W
38 A8 Kekaha Kaua'i, Hawaii, USA, C Pacific Ocean 21°58'N 159°43'W
147 U10 Këk-Art prev. Alaykel', Alay-Kuu. Oshskaya Oblast', SW Kyrgyzstan 40°16'N 74°21'E
147 W10 Këk-Aygyr var. Keyaygyr. Narynskaya Oblast', C Kyrgyzstan 40°42'N 75°37'E
147 V9 Këk-Dzhar Narynskaya Oblast', C Kyrgyzstan 41°28'N 74°48'E
14 L8 Kekek ≈ Québec, SE Canada
185 K15 Kekerengu Canterbury, South Island, New Zealand 41°55'S 174°05'E
111 L21 Kékes ▲ N Hungary 47°53'N 19°59'E
171 P17 Kekneno, Gunung ▲ Timor, S Indonesia
147 S9 Këk-Tash Kir. Kök-Tash. Dzhalal-Abadskaya Oblast', W Kyrgyzstan 41°08'N 72°25'E
81 M15 K'elafo Sumalē, E Ethiopia 05°36'N 44°12'E
169 U10 Kelai, Sungai ≈ Borneo, N Indonesia
Kelamayi see Karamay
Kelang see Klang
168 K7 Kelantan ◆ state Peninsular Malaysia
Kelantan see Kelantan, Sungai
168 K7 Kelantan, Sungai var. Kelantan. ≈ Peninsular Malaysia
Kelat see Kālat
Këlcyra see Këlcyrë
113 L22 Këlcyrë var. Këlcyra. Gjirokastër, S Albania 40°19'N 20°10'E
Kelifskiy Uzboy see Kelif Uzboýy
146 L14 Kelif Uzboýy Rus. Kelifskiy Uzboy. salt marsh E Turkmenistan
137 O12 Kelkit Gümüşhane, NE Turkey 40°07'N 39°28'E
136 M12 Kelkit Çayı ≈ N Turkey
79 G18 Kellé Cuvette-Ouest, W Congo 0°04'S 14°33'E
77 W11 Kellé Zinder, S Niger 14°10'N 10°10'E
145 P7 Kellerovka Severnyy Kazakhstan, N Kazakhstan 53°51'N 69°15'E
8 I5 Kellett, Cape headland Banks Island, Northwest Territories, NW Canada 71°57'N 125°55'W

◆ Country ● Country Capital ◇ Dependent Territory ○ Dependent Territory Capital ◆ Administrative Regions ✈ International Airport ▲ Mountain ▲▲ Mountain Range ▲ Volcano ≈ River ⊚ Lake ⊠ Reservoir

KELLEYS ISLAND – KHONG SEDONE

31 S11 **Kelleys Island** *island* Ohio, N USA
33 N8 **Kellogg** Idaho, NW USA 47°30′N 116°07′W
92 M12 **Kelloselkä** Lappi, N Finland 66°56′N 28°52′E
97 F17 **Kells** *Ir.* Ceanannas. Meath, E Ireland 53°44′N 06°53′W
118 E12 **Kelmė** Šiaulai, C Lithuania 55°39′N 22°57′E
99 M19 **Kelmis** *var.* La Calamine. Liège, E Belgium 50°43′N 06°01′E
78 H12 **Kélo** Tandjilé, SW Chad 09°21′N 15°50′E
83 I14 **Kelongwa** North Western, NW Zambia 13°41′S 26°19′E
11 N17 **Kelowna** British Columbia, SW Canada 49°50′N 119°29′W
11 X12 **Kelsey** Manitoba, C Canada 56°02′N 96°31′W
34 M6 **Kelseyville** California, W USA 38°58′N 122°51′W
96 K13 **Kelso** SE Scotland, United Kingdom 55°36′N 02°27′W
32 G10 **Kelso** Washington, NW USA 46°09′N 122°54′W
195 W15 **Keltie, Cape** *headland* Antarctica
Keltsy *see* Kielce
168 L9 **Keluang** *var.* Kluang. Johor, Peninsular Malaysia 02°01′N 103°18′E
168 M11 **Kelume** Pulau Lingga, W Indonesia 0°12′S 104°27′E
11 U15 **Kelvington** Saskatchewan, S Canada 52°10′N 103°30′W
124 J7 **Kem'** Respublika Kareliya, NW Russian Federation 64°55′N 34°18′E
124 I7 **Kem'** ≈ NW Russian Federation
137 O13 **Kemah** Erzincan, E Turkey 39°35′N 39°02′E
137 N13 **Kemaliye** Erzincan, C Turkey 39°16′N 38°29′E
Kemaman *see* Cukai
Kemanlar *see* Isperikh
10 K14 **Kemano** British Columbia, SW Canada 53°39′N 127°58′W
Kemarat *see* Khemmarat
171 P12 **Kembani** Pulau Peleng, N Indonesia 01°32′S 122°57′E
136 F17 **Kemer** Antalya, SW Turkey 36°39′N 30°33′E
122 J12 **Kemerovo** *prev.* Shcheglovsk. Kemerovskaya Oblast', C Russian Federation 55°25′N 86°05′E
122 K12 **Kemerovskaya Oblast'** ◆ *province* S Russian Federation
92 L13 **Kemi** Lappi, NW Finland 65°46′N 24°34′E
92 M12 **Kemijärvi** *Swe.* Kemiträsk. Lappi, N Finland 66°41′N 27°24′E
92 M12 **Kemijärvi** ◎ N Finland
92 L13 **Kemijoki** ≈ NW Finland
147 V7 **Kemin** *prev.* Bystrovka. Chuyskaya Oblast', N Kyrgyzstan
92 L13 **Keminmaa** Lappi, NW Finland 65°49′N 24°34′E
Kemins Island *see* Nikumaroro
Kemiö *see* Kimito
Kemiträsk *see* Kemijärvi
127 P5 **Kemlya** Respublika Mordoviya, W Russian Federation 54°42′N 45°16′E
99 B18 **Kemmel** West-Vlaanderen, W Belgium 50°42′N 02°51′E
33 S16 **Kemmerer** Wyoming, C USA 41°47′N 110°32′W
Kemmuna *see* Comino
79 I14 **Kémo** ◆ *prefecture* S Central African Republic
25 U7 **Kemp** Texas, SW USA 32°26′N 96°13′W
93 L14 **Kempele** Oulu, C Finland 64°56′N 25°26′E
101 D15 **Kempen** Nordrhein-Westfalen, W Germany 51°22′N 06°25′E
25 Q5 **Kemp, Lake** ◎ Texas, SW USA
195 W5 **Kemp Land** *physical region* Antarctica
25 S9 **Kempner** Texas, SW USA 31°03′N 98°01′W
44 H3 **Kemp's Bay** Andros Island, W Bahamas 24°02′N 77°32′W
183 U6 **Kempsey** New South Wales, SE Australia 31°05′S 152°50′E
101 J24 **Kempten** Bayern, S Germany 47°44′N 10°19′E
15 N9 **Kempt, Lac** ◎ Québec, SE Canada
183 P17 **Kempton** Tasmania, SE Australia 42°34′S 147°13′E
154 J9 **Ken** ≈ C India
39 R12 **Kenai** Alaska, USA 60°33′N 151°15′W
0 D5 **Kenai Mountains** ▲▲ Alaska, USA
39 R12 **Kenai Peninsula** *peninsula* Alaska, USA
21 V11 **Kenansville** North Carolina, SE USA 34°57′N 77°54′W
146 A10 **Kenar** *prev. Rus.* Ufra. Balkan Welaýaty, NW Turkmenistan 40°00′N 53°05′E
121 U13 **Kenâyis, Râs el-** *headland* N Egypt 31°13′N 27°53′E
97 K16 **Kendal** NW England, United Kingdom 54°20′N 02°45′W
23 Y16 **Kendall** Florida, SE USA 25°39′N 80°18′W
9 O8 **Kendall, Cape** *headland* Nunavut, E Canada 63°31′N 87°09′W
18 J15 **Kendall Park** New Jersey, NE USA 40°25′N 74°33′W
31 Q11 **Kendallville** Indiana, N USA 41°24′N 85°10′W
171 P14 **Kendari** Sulawesi, C Indonesia 03°57′S 122°36′E
169 Q13 **Kendawangan** Borneo, C Indonesia 02°32′S 110°13′E
154 O12 **Kendrāpāra** *var.* Kendrāparha. Orissa, E India 20°29′N 86°25′E
Kendrāparha *see* Kendrāpāra
154 O11 **Kendujhargarh** *prev.* Keonjhargarh. Orissa, E India 21°38′N 85°40′E
25 S13 **Kenedy** Texas, SW USA 28°49′N 97°51′W
76 J15 **Kenema** SE Sierra Leone 07°55′N 11°12′W
29 P16 **Kenesaw** Nebraska, C USA 40°37′N 98°39′W
Këneurgench *see* Köneürgenç
79 H21 **Kenge** Bandundu, SW Dem. Rep. Congo 04°52′S 16°59′E
Kengen *see* Kangen
167 O5 **Keng Tung** *var.* Kentung. Shan State, E Myanmar (Burma) 21°18′N 99°36′E
83 F23 **Kenhardt** Northern Cape, W South Africa 29°19′S 21°08′E
76 J12 **Kéniéba** Kayes, W Mali 12°47′N 11°16′W
Kenimekh *see* Konimex
169 U7 **Keningau** Sabah, East Malaysia 05°21′N 116°11′E
74 F6 **Kénitra** *prev.* Port-Lyautey. NW Morocco 34°20′N 06°29′W
21 V9 **Kenly** North Carolina, SE USA 35°39′N 78°16′W
97 B21 **Kenmare** *Ir.* Neidín. S Ireland 51°53′N 09°35′W
28 L2 **Kenmare** North Dakota, N USA 48°40′N 102°04′W
97 A21 **Kenmare River** *Ir.* An Ribhéar. *inlet* NE Atlantic Ocean
18 D10 **Kenmore** New York, NE USA 42°58′N 78°52′W
25 W8 **Kennard** Texas, SW USA 31°21′N 95°10′W
29 N10 **Kennebec** South Dakota, N USA 43°53′N 99°51′W
19 Q7 **Kennebec River** ≈ Maine, NE USA
19 P9 **Kennebunk** Maine, NE USA 43°22′N 70°33′W
39 R13 **Kennedy Entrance** *strait* Alaska, USA
166 L3 **Kennedy Peak** ▲ W Myanmar (Burma) 23°18′N 93°52′E
22 K9 **Kenner** Louisiana, S USA 29°57′N 90°15′W
180 I8 **Kenneth Range** ▲▲ Western Australia
27 Y9 **Kennett** Missouri, C USA 36°15′N 90°04′W
18 I16 **Kennett Square** Pennsylvania, NE USA 39°50′N 75°40′W
32 K10 **Kennewick** Washington, NW USA 46°12′N 119°08′W
12 E11 **Kenogami** ≈ Ontario, S Canada
15 Q7 **Kénogami, Lac** ◎ Québec, SE Canada
14 G8 **Kenogami Lake** Ontario, S Canada 48°04′N 80°10′W
14 F7 **Kenogamissi Lake** ◎ Ontario, S Canada
10 I6 **Keno Hill** Yukon Territory, NW Canada 63°54′N 135°18′W
12 A11 **Kenora** Ontario, S Canada 49°47′N 94°26′W
31 N9 **Kenosha** Wisconsin, N USA 42°34′N 87°50′W
13 P14 **Kensington** Prince Edward Island, SE Canada 46°26′N 63°39′W
26 L3 **Kensington** Kansas, C USA 39°46′N 99°01′W
32 I11 **Kent** Oregon, NW USA 45°14′N 120°43′W
24 J9 **Kent** Texas, SW USA 31°03′N 104°13′W
32 H8 **Kent** Washington, NW USA 47°22′N 122°13′W
97 P22 **Kent** *cultural region* SE England, United Kingdom
145 P16 **Kentau** Yuzhnyy Kazakhstan, S Kazakhstan 43°28′N 68°41′E
183 P14 **Kent Group** *island group* Tasmania, SE Australia
31 N12 **Kentland** Indiana, N USA 40°46′N 87°26′W
31 R12 **Kenton** Ohio, N USA 40°39′N 83°36′W
8 K7 **Kent Peninsula** *peninsula* Nunavut, N Canada
115 F14 **Kentrikí Makedonía** *Eng.* Macedonia Central. ◆ *region* N Greece
20 J6 **Kentucky** *off.* Commonwealth of Kentucky, *also known as* Bluegrass State. ◆ *state* C USA
20 H8 **Kentucky Lake** ⊠ Kentucky/Tennessee, S USA
Kentung *see* Keng Tung
13 P15 **Kentville** Nova Scotia, SE Canada 45°04′N 64°30′W
22 K8 **Kentwood** Louisiana, S USA 30°56′N 90°30′W
31 P9 **Kentwood** Michigan, N USA 42°52′N 85°33′W
81 H17 **Kenya** *off.* Republic of Kenya. ◆ *republic* E Africa
Kenya, Mount *see* Kirinyaga
Kenya, Republic of *see* Kenya
168 L7 **Kenyir, Tasik** *var.* Tasek Kenyir. ◎ Peninsular Malaysia
29 W10 **Kenyon** Minnesota, N USA 44°16′N 92°59′W
29 Y16 **Keokuk** Iowa, C USA 40°24′N 91°22′W
Keonjhargarh *see* Kendujhargarh
Kéos *see* Tziá
29 X16 **Keosauqua** Iowa, C USA 40°43′N 91°58′W
29 X15 **Keota** Iowa, C USA 41°21′N 91°57′W
21 O11 **Keowee, Lake** ⊠ South Carolina, SE USA
124 I7 **Kepa** *var.* Kepe. Respublika Kareliya, NW Russian Federation 65°09′N 32°15′E
Kepe *see* Kepa
189 O13 **Kepirohi Falls** *waterfall* Pohnpei, E Micronesia
185 B22 **Kepler Mountains** ▲▲ South Island, New Zealand
111 I14 **Kępno** Wielkopolskie, C Poland 51°17′N 17°57′E
65 C24 **Keppel Island** *island* N Falkland Islands
Keppel Island *see* Niuatoputapu
65 C23 **Keppel Sound** *sound* N Falkland Islands
136 D12 **Kepsut** Balıkesir, NW Turkey 39°41′N 28°09′E
168 M11 **Kepulauan Riau** *off.* Propinsi Kepulauan Riau. ◆ *province* NW Indonesia
Kequ *see* Gadê
171 V13 **Kerai** Papua, E Indonesia 03°53′S 134°30′E
Kerak *see* Al Karak
155 F22 **Kerala** ◆ *state* S India
165 R16 **Kerama-rettō** *island group* SW Japan
183 N10 **Kerang** Victoria, SE Australia 35°46′S 144°01′E
Kerasunt *see* Giresun
115 H19 **Keratéa** *var.* Keratea. Attikí, C Greece 37°48′N 23°58′E
Keratea *see* Keratéa
93 M19 **Kerava** *Swe.* Kervo. Etelä-Suomi, S Finland 60°25′N 25°10′E
Kerbala/Kerbela *see* Karbalā'
32 F15 **Kerby** Oregon, NW USA 42°10′N 123°39′W
117 W12 **Kerch** *Rus.* Kerch'. Respublika Krym, SE Ukraine 45°22′N 36°30′E
Kerch' *see* Kerch
Kerchens'ka Protska/Kerchenskiy Proliv *see* Kerch Strait
117 V13 **Kerchens'kyy Pivostriv** *peninsula* S Ukraine
121 V4 **Kerch Strait** *var.* Bosporus Cimmerius, Enikale Strait, *Rus.* Kerchenskiy Proliv, *Ukr.* Kerchens'ka Protska. *strait* Black Sea/Sea of Azov
Kerdilio *see* Kerdýlio
114 H13 **Kerdýlio** *var.* Kerdilio. ▲ N Greece 40°46′N 23°37′E
186 D8 **Kerema** Gulf, S Papua New Guinea 07°59′S 145°46′E
Keremitlik *see* Lyulyakovo
136 I9 **Kerempe Burnu** *headland* N Turkey 42°01′N 33°20′E
80 J9 **Keren** *var.* Cheren. C Eritrea 15°45′N 38°22′E
25 U7 **Kerens** Texas, SW USA 32°07′N 96°13′W
184 M6 **Kerepehi** Waikato, North Island, New Zealand 37°18′S 175°33′E
145 P10 **Kerey, Ozero** ◎ C Kazakhstan
Kergel *see* Kärla
173 Q12 **Kerguelen** *island* C French Southern and Antarctic Territories
173 Q13 **Kerguelen Plateau** *undersea feature* S Indian Ocean
115 C20 **Kerí** Zákynthos, Iónia Nisiá, Greece, C Mediterranean Sea 37°40′N 20°48′E
81 H19 **Kericho** Rift Valley, W Kenya 0°22′S 35°19′E
184 K2 **Kerikeri** Northland, North Island, New Zealand 35°14′S 173°58′E
93 O17 **Kerimäki** Itä-Suomi, E Finland 61°56′N 29°18′E
168 K12 **Kerinci, Gunung** ▲ Sumatera, W Indonesia 02°00′S 101°40′E
Keriya *see* Yutian
158 H9 **Keriya He** ≈ NW China
98 J9 **Kerkbuurt** Noord-Holland, C Netherlands 52°29′N 05°08′E
98 J13 **Kerkdriel** Gelderland, C Netherlands 51°46′N 05°21′E
75 N6 **Kerkenah, Îles de** *var.* Kerkenna Islands, *Ar.* Juzur Qarqannah. *island group* E Tunisia
Kerkenna Islands *see* Kerkenah, Îles de
115 M20 **Kerketévs** ▲ Sámos, Dodekánisa, Greece, Aegean Sea 37°44′N 26°39′E
29 T8 **Kerkhoven** Minnesota, N USA 45°12′N 95°18′W
Kerki *see* Atamyrat
Kerkichi *see* Kerkiçi
146 M14 **Kerkiçi** *Rus.* Kerkichi. Lebap Welaýaty, E Turkmenistan 37°46′N 65°18′E
115 F16 **Kerkíneo** *prehistoric site* Thessalía, C Greece
114 G12 **Kerkíni, Límni** *var.* Límni Kerkinitis. ◎ N Greece
Kerkinitis Límni *see* Kerkíni, Límni
Kérkira *see* Kérkyra
99 M18 **Kerkrade** Limburg, SE Netherlands 50°53′N 06°04′E
Kerkuk *see* Kirkūk
115 B16 **Kérkyra** *var.* Kérkira, *Eng.* Corfu. Kérkyra, Iónia Nisiá, Greece, C Mediterranean Sea 39°37′N 19°56′E
115 B16 **Kérkyra** ✕ Kérkyra, Iónia Nisiá, Greece, C Mediterranean Sea 39°36′N 19°55′E
115 A16 **Kérkyra** *var.* Kérkira, *Eng.* Corfu. *island* Iónia Nisiá, Greece, C Mediterranean Sea
192 K10 **Kermadec Islands** *island group* New Zealand, SW Pacific Ocean
175 R10 **Kermadec Ridge** *undersea feature* SW Pacific Ocean 30°30′S 178°30′W
175 R11 **Kermadec Trench** *undersea feature* SW Pacific Ocean
143 S10 **Kermān** *var.* Kirman; *anc.* Carmana. Kermān, C Iran 30°18′N 57°05′E
143 R11 **Kermān** *off.* Ostān-e Kermān, *var.* Kirman; *anc.* Carmania. ◆ *province* SE Iran
143 U12 **Kermān, Biābān-e** *desert* SE Iran
Kermān, Ostān-e *see* Kermān
142 K6 **Kermānshāh** *var.* Qahremānshahr; *prev.* Bākhtarān. Kermānshāhān, W Iran 34°19′N 47°04′E
143 Q9 **Kermānshāh** Yazd, C Iran 34°19′N 47°04′E
142 J6 **Kermānshāh** *off.* Ostān-e Kermānshāhān; *prev.* Bākhtarān. ◆ *province* W Iran
Kermānshāhān, Ostān-e *see* Kermānshāh
114 L10 **Kermen** Sliven, C Bulgaria 42°30′N 26°12′E
24 L8 **Kermit** Texas, SW USA 31°49′N 103°07′W
21 P6 **Kermit** West Virginia, NE USA 37°51′N 82°24′W
21 S9 **Kernersville** North Carolina, SE USA 36°12′N 80°13′W
35 S12 **Kern River** ≈ California, W USA
35 S12 **Kernville** California, W USA 35°44′N 118°25′W
115 K21 **Kéros** *island* Kykládes, Greece, Aegean Sea
76 K14 **Kérouané** SE Guinea 09°16′N 09°00′W
101 D16 **Kerpen** Nordrhein-Westfalen, W Germany 50°51′N 06°40′E
146 I11 **Kerpichli** Lebap Welaýaty, NE Turkmenistan 40°12′N 61°09′E
24 M1 **Kerrick** Texas, SW USA 36°29′N 102°14′W
Kerr Lake *see* John H. Kerr Reservoir
11 S15 **Kerrobert** Saskatchewan, S Canada 51°56′N 109°09′W
25 Q11 **Kerrville** Texas, SW USA 30°03′N 99°09′W
97 B20 **Kerry** *Ir.* Ciarraí. *cultural region* SW Ireland
21 S11 **Kershaw** South Carolina, SE USA 34°33′N 80°34′W
Kertel *see* Kärdla
95 H23 **Kerteminde** Fyn, C Denmark 55°27′N 10°40′E
163 Q7 **Kerulen** *Chin.* Herlen He, *Mong.* Herlen Gol. ≈ China/Mongolia
Kervo *see* Kerava
Kerýneia *see* Girne
12 H11 **Kesagami Lake** ◎ Ontario, SE Canada
93 O17 **Kesälahti** Itä-Suomi, SE Finland 61°54′N 29°49′E
136 B11 **Keşan** Edirne, NW Turkey 40°52′N 26°37′E
165 R9 **Kesennuma** Miyagi, Honshū, C Japan 38°55′N 141°35′E
163 V7 **Keshan** Heilongjiang, NE China 48°00′N 125°46′E
30 M6 **Keshena** Wisconsin, N USA 44°54′N 88°37′W
136 I13 **Keskin** Kırıkkale, C Turkey 39°41′N 33°36′E
Késmárk *see* Kežmarok
124 I6 **Kesten'ga** *var.* Kest Enga. Respublika Kareliya, NW Russian Federation 65°53′N 31°47′E
Kest Enga *see* Kesten'ga
98 K12 **Kesteren** Gelderland, C Netherlands 51°55′N 05°34′E
14 H14 **Keswick** Ontario, S Canada 44°15′N 79°26′W
97 K15 **Keswick** NW England, United Kingdom 54°30′N 03°04′W
111 H24 **Keszthely** Zala, SW Hungary 46°47′N 17°16′E
122 K11 **Ket'** ≈ C Russian Federation
77 R17 **Keta** SE Ghana 05°55′N 00°59′E
169 Q12 **Ketapang** Borneo, C Indonesia 01°50′S 109°59′E
127 O12 **Ketchenery** *prev.* Sovetskoye. Respublika Kalmykiya, SW Russian Federation 47°18′N 44°31′E
39 Y14 **Ketchikan** Revillagigedo Island, Alaska, USA 55°21′N 131°39′W
33 O14 **Ketchum** Idaho, NW USA 43°40′N 114°24′W
Kete/Kete Krakye *see* Kete-Krachi
77 Q15 **Kete-Krachi** *var.* Kete, Kete Krakye. E Ghana 07°50′N 00°03′W
98 L9 **Ketelmeer** *channel* E Netherlands
149 P17 **Keti Bandar** Sind, SE Pakistan 23°55′N 67°31′E
145 W16 **Ketmen', Khrebet** ▲▲ SE Kazakhstan
77 S16 **Kétou** SE Benin 07°25′N 02°36′E
110 M7 **Kętrzyn** *Ger.* Rastenburg. Warmińsko-Mazurskie, NE Poland 54°05′N 21°24′E
97 N20 **Kettering** C England, United Kingdom 52°24′N 00°44′W
31 R14 **Kettering** Ohio, N USA 39°41′N 84°10′W
18 F13 **Kettle Creek** ≈ Pennsylvania, NE USA
32 L7 **Kettle Falls** Washington, NW USA 48°36′N 118°03′W
14 D16 **Kettle Point** *headland* Ontario, S Canada 43°12′N 82°01′W
29 V6 **Kettle River** ≈ Minnesota, N USA
186 B7 **Ketu** ≈ W Papua New Guinea
18 G10 **Keuka Lake** ◎ New York, NE USA
Keupriya *see* Primorsko
93 L17 **Keuruu** Länsi-Suomi, C Finland 62°15′N 24°34′E
Kevevára *see* Kovin
92 L9 **Kevo** *Lapp.* Geavvú. Lappi, N Finland 69°42′N 27°08′E
44 M6 **Kew** North Caicos, N Turks and Caicos Islands 21°52′N 71°57′W
30 K11 **Kewanee** Illinois, N USA 41°15′N 89°55′W
31 N7 **Kewaunee** Wisconsin, N USA 44°27′N 87°31′W
30 M3 **Keweenaw Bay** ◎ Michigan, N USA
31 N2 **Keweenaw Peninsula** *peninsula* Michigan, N USA
31 N2 **Keweenaw Point** *peninsula* Michigan, N USA
29 N12 **Keya Paha River** ≈ Nebraska/South Dakota, N USA
Keyaygyr *see* Këk-Aygyr
23 Z16 **Key Biscayne** Florida, SE USA 25°41′N 80°09′W
26 G8 **Keyes** Oklahoma, C USA 36°48′N 102°15′W
23 Y17 **Key Largo** Key Largo, Florida, SE USA 25°06′N 80°25′W
21 U3 **Keyser** West Virginia, NE USA 39°25′N 78°59′W
27 O9 **Keystone Lake** ⊠ Oklahoma, C USA
36 L16 **Keystone Peak** ▲ Arizona, SW USA 31°52′N 111°12′W
Keystone State *see* Pennsylvania
21 U7 **Keysville** Virginia, NE USA 37°02′N 78°28′W
27 T3 **Keytesville** Missouri, C USA 39°25′N 92°56′W
23 W17 **Key West** Florida Keys, Florida, SE USA 24°34′N 81°48′W
127 T1 **Kez** Udmurtskaya Respublika, NW Russian Federation 57°55′N 53°42′E
Kezdivásárhely *see* Târgu Secuiesc
122 M12 **Kezhma** Krasnoyarskiy Kray, C Russian Federation 58°57′N 101°00′E
111 L18 **Kežmarok** *Ger.* Käsmark, *Hung.* Késmárk. Prešovský Kraj, E Slovakia 49°09′N 20°25′E
Kfar Saba *see* Kfar Sava
138 F10 **Kfar Sava** *var.* Kfar Saba; *prev.* Kefar Sava. Central, C Israel 32°11′N 34°58′E
83 F20 **Kgalagadi** ◆ *district* SW Botswana
83 I20 **Kgatleng** ◆ *district* SE Botswana
188 F8 **Kgkeklau** Babeldaob, N Palau
125 R6 **Khabarikha** *var.* Chabaricha. Respublika Komi, NW Russian Federation 65°52′N 52°19′E
123 S14 **Khabarovsk** Khabarovskiy Kray, SE Russian Federation 48°32′N 135°08′E
123 R11 **Khabarovskiy Kray** ◆ *territory* E Russian Federation
141 W7 **Khabb** Abū Ẓaby, E United Arab Emirates 24°39′N 55°43′E
Khabour, Nahr al *see* Khābūr, Nahr al
Khabura *see* Al Khābūrah
139 N2 **Khābūr, Nahr al** *var.* Nahr al Khabour. ≈ Syria/Turkey
Khachmas *see* Xaçmaz
80 B12 **Khadari** ≈ W Sudan
Khadera *see* Hadera
141 X12 **Khādhil** *var.* Khudal. SE Oman 18°48′N 56°48′E
155 E14 **Khadki** *prev.* Kirkee. Mahārāshtra, W India 18°34′N 73°52′E
126 L14 **Khadyzhensk** Krasnodarskiy Kray, SW Russian Federation 44°26′N 39°31′E
114 N9 **Khadzhiyska Reka** ≈ E Bulgaria
117 P10 **Khadzhybeys'kyy Lyman** ◎ SW Ukraine
138 K3 **Khafsah** Ḥalab, N Syria 36°16′N 38°03′E
152 M13 **Khāga** Uttar Pradesh, N India 25°47′N 81°05′E
153 Q13 **Khagaria** Bihār, NE India 25°31′N 86°27′E
149 Q13 **Khairpur** Sind, SE Pakistan 27°30′N 68°50′E
122 K13 **Khakasiya, Respublika** *prev.* Khakasskaya Avtonomnaya Oblast', *Eng.* Khakassia. ◆ *autonomous republic* C Russian Federation
Khakassia/Khakasskaya Avtonomnaya Oblast' *see* Khakasiya, Respublika
167 N9 **Kha Khaeng, Khao** ▲ W Thailand 16°13′N 99°03′E
83 G20 **Khakhea** *var.* Kakia. Southern, S Botswana 24°41′S 23°29′E
Khalach *see* Halaç
Khalándrion *see* Chalándri
75 T7 **Khalīj as Sallūm** *Ar.* Gulf of Salûm. *gulf* Egypt/Libya
75 X8 **Khalīj as Suways** *var.* Suez, Gulf of. *gulf* NE Egypt
127 W7 **Khalilovo** Orenburgskaya Oblast', W Russian Federation 51°25′N 58°13′E
Khalkabad *see* Xalqobod
142 L3 **Khalkhāl** *prev.* Herowābād. Ardabīl, NW Iran 37°36′N 48°36′E
Khalkidhikí *see* Chalkidikí
Khalkís *see* Chalkída
125 W3 **Khal'mer-Yu** Respublika Komi, NW Russian Federation 68°00′N 64°45′E
119 M14 **Khalopyenichy** *Rus.* Kholopenichi. Minskaya Voblasts', NE Belarus 54°31′N 28°58′E
Khalturin *see* Orlov
141 Y10 **Khalūf** *var.* Al Khaluf. E Oman 20°27′N 57°59′E
154 K10 **Khamaria** Madhya Pradesh, C India 23°07′N 80°54′E
154 D11 **Khambhāt** Gujarāt, W India 22°19′N 72°39′E
154 C12 **Khambhāt, Gulf of** *Eng.* Gulf of Cambay. *gulf* W India
167 U10 **Khâm Đưc** *var.* Phươc Sơn. Quang Nam-Đa Năng, C Vietnam 15°28′N 107°49′E
154 G12 **Khāmgaon** Mahārāshtra, C India 20°41′N 76°34′E
141 O14 **Khamir** *var.* Khamr. W Yemen 16°N 43°56′E
141 N12 **Khamīs Mushayt** *var.* Hamīs Musait. 'Asīr, SW Saudi Arabia 18°19′N 42°41′E
155 I18 **Khammam** Andhra Pradesh, India 17°16′N 80°13′E
123 P10 **Khampa** Respublika Sakha (Yakutiya), NE Russian Federation 63°43′N 123°02′E
Khamr *see* Khamir
83 C19 **Khan** ≈ W Namibia
149 Q2 **Khānābād** Kunduz, NE Afghanistan 36°42′N 69°08′E
Khân Abou Châmâte/Khan Abou Ech Cham *see* Khān Abū Shāmāt
138 I7 **Khān Abū Shāmāt** *var.* Khân Abou Châmâte, Khan Abou Ech Cham. Dimashq, W Syria 33°43′N 36°56′E
Khān al Baghdādī *see* Al Baghdādī
Khān al Maḩāwīl *see* Al Maḩāwīl
139 T7 **Khān al Mashāhidah** Baghdād, C Iraq 33°40′N 44°15′E
139 T10 **Khān al Muşallá** An Najaf, S Iraq 32°09′N 44°20′E
139 U6 **Khānaqīn** Diyālá, E Iraq 34°22′N 45°22′E
139 T11 **Khān ar Ruḩbah** An Najaf, S Iraq 31°42′N 44°18′E
139 P2 **Khān as Sūr** Nīnawá, N Iraq 36°28′N 41°36′E
139 T8 **Khān Āzād** Baghdād, C Iraq 33°08′N 44°21′E
154 N13 **Khandaparha** *prev.* Khandpara. Orissa, E India 20°15′N 85°11′E
Khandpara *see* Khandaparha
149 T2 **Khandūd** *var.* Khandud, Wakhan. Badakhshān, NE Afghanistan 36°57′N 72°19′E
Khandud *see* Khandūd
154 G11 **Khandwa** Madhya Pradesh, C India 21°49′N 76°23′E
123 R10 **Khandyga** Respublika Sakha (Yakutiya), NE Russian Federation 62°39′N 135°30′E
149 T10 **Khānewāl** Punjab, NE Pakistan 30°18′N 71°56′E
149 S10 **Khāngarh** Punjab, E Pakistan 29°57′N 71°14′E
Khanh Hung *see* Soc Trăng
Khaniá *see* Chaniá
Khanka *see* Xonqa
163 Z8 **Khanka, Lake** *var.* Hsing-K'ai Hu, Lake Hanka, *Chin.* Xingkai Hu, *Rus.* Ozero Khanka. ◎ China/Russian Federation
Khanka, Ozero *see* Khanka, Lake
Khankendi *see* Xankändi
Khanlar *see* Xanlar
123 O9 **Khannya** ≈ NE Russian Federation
149 S12 **Khānpur** Punjab, E Pakistan 28°31′N 70°30′E
138 I4 **Khān Shaykhūn** *var.* Khan Sheikhun. Idlib, NW Syria 35°27′N 36°38′E
Khan Sheikhun *see* Khān Shaykhūn
145 S15 **Khantau** Zhambyl, S Kazakhstan 44°13′N 73°47′E
145 W16 **Khan Tengri, Pik** ▲ SE Kazakhstan 42°17′N 80°11′E
Khan-Tengri, Pik *see* Hantengri Feng
167 S9 **Khanthabouli** *prev.* Savannakhét. Savannakhét, S Laos 16°38′N 104°49′E
127 V8 **Khanty-Mansiysk** *prev.* Ostyako-Voguls'k. Khanty-Mansiyskiy Avtonomnyy Okrug-Yugra, C Russian Federation 61°01′N 69°E
125 V8 **Khanty-Mansiyskiy Avtonomnyy Okrug-Yugra** ◆ *autonomous district* C Russian Federation
139 R4 **Khānūqah** Nīnawýé, C Iraq 35°25′N 43°15′E
138 E11 **Khān Yūnis** *var.* Khān Yūnus. S Gaza Strip 31°21′N 34°18′E
Khān Yūnus *see* Khān Yūnis
Khanzi *see* Ghanzi
139 U5 **Khān Zūr** As Sulaymānīyah, E Iraq 35°03′N 45°08′E
167 N10 **Khao Laem Reservoir** ⊠ W Thailand
123 O14 **Khapcheranga** Chitinskaya Oblast', S Russian Federation 49°46′N 112°21′E
127 Q12 **Kharabali** Astrakhanskaya Oblast', SW Russian Federation 47°28′N 47°14′E
153 R16 **Kharagpur** West Bengal, NE India 22°30′N 87°19′E
139 V11 **Kharā'ib 'Abd al Karīm** Al Muthannā, S Iraq 31°07′N 45°33′E
149 N12 **Khārān** Baluchistān, SW Pakistan 28°35′N 65°25′E
143 Q8 **Kharānaq** Yazd, C Iran 31°54′N 54°21′E
Kharbin *see* Harbin
Kharchi *see* Mārwār
146 H13 **Khardzhagaz** Ahal Welaýaty, C Turkmenistan 37°54′N 60°10′E
154 F11 **Khargon** Madhya Pradesh, C India 21°49′N 75°39′E
149 V7 **Khāriān** Punjab, NE Pakistan 32°52′N 73°52′E
117 X8 **Kharisyz'k** Donets'ka Oblast', E Ukraine 48°01′N 38°10′E
117 V5 **Kharkiv** *Rus.* Khar'kov. Kharkivs'ka Oblast', NE Ukraine 50°N 36°14′E
117 V5 **Kharkiv** ✕ Kharkivs'ka Oblast', E Ukraine 49°54′N 36°20′E
Kharkiv *see* Kharkivs'ka Oblast'
117 U5 **Kharkivs'ka Oblast'** *var.* Kharkiv, *Rus.* Khar'kovskaya Oblast'. ◆ *province* E Ukraine
Khar'kov *see* Kharkiv
Khar'kovskaya Oblast' *see* Kharkivs'ka Oblast'
124 L3 **Kharlovka** Murmanskaya Oblast', NW Russian Federation 68°47′N 37°09′E
114 K11 **Kharmanli** Khaskovo, S Bulgaria 41°56′N 25°54′E
114 K11 **Kharmanliyska Reka** ≈ S Bulgaria
124 M13 **Kharovsk** Vologodskaya Oblast', NW Russian Federation 59°57′N 40°05′E
80 F9 **Khartoum** *var.* El Khartûm, Khartum. ● (Sudan) Khartoum, C Sudan 15°33′N 32°32′E
80 F9 **Khartoum** ◆ *state* NE Sudan
80 F9 **Khartoum** ✕ Khartoum, C Sudan 15°36′N 32°37′E
80 F9 **Khartoum North** Khartoum, C Sudan 15°38′N 32°33′E
117 X8 **Khartsyz'k** *Rus.* Khartsyzsk. Donets'ka Oblast', SE Ukraine 48°01′N 38°10′E
Khartsyzsk *see* Khartsyz'k
Khartum *see* Khartoum
154 G12 **Khās** Madhya Pradesh, C India 22°12′N 77°30′E
Khasab *see* Al Khaşab
123 S15 **Khasan** Primorskiy Kray, SE Russian Federation 42°24′N 130°45′E
127 P16 **Khasavyurt** Respublika Dagestan, SW Russian Federation 43°16′N 46°33′E
143 W12 **Khāsh** *prev.* Vāsht. Sīstān va Balūchestān, SE Iran 28°15′N 61°11′E
148 K8 **Khāsh, Dasht-e** *Eng.* Khash Desert. *desert* SW Afghanistan
Khash Desert *see* Khāsh, Dasht-e
Khashim Al Qirba/Khashm al Qirbah *see* Khashm el Girba
80 H9 **Khashm el Girba** *var.* Khashim Al Qirba, Khashm al Qirbah. Kassala, E Sudan 15°00′N 35°59′E
138 G14 **Khashsh, Jabal al** ▲ S Jordan
137 S10 **Khashuri** C Georgia 41°59′N 43°36′E
153 V13 **Khāsi Hills** *hill range* NE India
114 K11 **Khaskovo** Khaskovo, S Bulgaria 41°56′N 25°35′E
114 K11 **Khaskovo** ◆ *province* S Bulgaria
122 M7 **Khatanga** ≈ N Russian Federation
Khatanga, Gulf of *see* Khatangskiy Zaliv
123 N7 **Khatangskiy Zaliv** *var.* Gulf of Khatanga. *bay* N Russian Federation
141 W7 **Khatmat al Malāḩah** N Oman 24°58′N 56°22′E
143 S16 **Khaṭmat al Malāḩah** Ash Shāriqah, E United Arab Emirates
123 V7 **Khatyrka** Chukotskiy Avtonomnyy Okrug, NE Russian Federation 62°03′N 175°09′E
Khauz-Khan *see* Hanhowuz
Khauzkhanskoye Vodoranilishche *see* Hanhowuz Suw Howdany
Khavaling *see* Khovaling
Khavast *see* Xovos
139 W10 **Khawrah, Nahr al** ≈ S Iraq
Khawr Barakah *see* Barka
141 W7 **Khawr Fakkān** *var.* Khor Fakkan. Ash Shāriqah, NE United Arab Emirates 25°22′N 56°19′E
140 L6 **Khaybar** Al Madīnah, NW Saudi Arabia 25°53′N 39°16′E
Khaybar, Kowtal-e *see* Khyber Pass
147 S11 **Khaydarkan** *var.* Khaydarken. Batkenskaya Oblast', SW Kyrgyzstan 39°56′N 71°17′E
Khaydarken *see* Khaydarkan
125 U2 **Khaypudyrskaya Guba** *bay* NW Russian Federation
139 S1 **Khayrūzuk** Arbīl, E Iraq 36°58′N 44°19′E
Khazar, Baḩr-e/Khazar, Daryā-ye *see* Caspian Sea
Khazarosp *see* Hazorasp
Khazretishi, Khrebet *see* Hazratishoh, Qatorkŭhi
75 X11 **Khazzān Aswān** *var.* Aswān Dam. *dam* SE Egypt
Khelat *see* Kālat
74 F6 **Khemisset** NW Morocco 33°52′N 06°04′W
167 R10 **Khemmarat** *var.* Kemarat. Ubon Ratchathani, E Thailand 16°03′N 105°11′E
74 L6 **Khenchela** *var.* Khenchla. NE Algeria 35°22′N 07°09′E
Khenchla *see* Khenchela
74 G7 **Khénifra** C Morocco 32°59′N 05°37′W
152 L12 **Kheri** Uttar Pradesh, N India 27°54′N 80°47′E
Khersān, Rūd-e *see* Garm, Āb-e
117 R10 **Kherson** Khersons'ka Oblast', S Ukraine 46°39′N 32°38′E
Kherson *see* Khersons'ka Oblast'
117 S14 **Khersones, Mys** *Rus.* Mys Khersonesskiy. *headland* S Ukraine 44°34′N 33°24′E
Khersonesskiy, Mys *see* Khersones, Mys
117 R10 **Khersons'ka Oblast'** *var.* Kherson, *Rus.* Khersonskaya Oblast'. ◆ *province* S Ukraine
Khersonskaya Oblast' *see* Khersons'ka Oblast'
122 L8 **Kheta** ≈ N Russian Federation
167 S8 **Khe Ve** Quang Binh, C Vietnam 17°52′N 105°49′E
149 U7 **Khewra** Punjab, E Pakistan 32°41′N 73°04′E
Khiam *see* El Khiyam
124 J4 **Khibiny** ▲▲ NW Russian Federation
126 K3 **Khimki** Moskovskaya Oblast', W Russian Federation 55°57′N 37°48′E
147 S12 **Khingov** *Rus.* Obi-Khingou. ≈ C Tajikistan
Khíos *see* Chíos
149 R15 **Khipro** Sind, SE Pakistan 25°50′N 69°24′E
139 S10 **Khirr, Wādī al** *dry watercourse* S Iraq
114 I10 **Khisarya** Plovdiv, C Bulgaria 42°33′N 24°43′E
Khiva/Khiwa *see* Xiva
167 N9 **Khlong Khlung** Kamphaeng Phet, W Thailand 16°15′N 99°41′E
167 N15 **Khlong Thom** Krabi, SW Thailand 07°55′N 99°09′E
167 P12 **Khlung** Chantaburi, S Thailand 12°25′N 102°12′E
Khmel'nik *see* Khmil'nyk
Khmel'nitskaya Oblast' *see* Khmel'nyts'ka Oblast'
Khmel'nitskiy *see* Khmel'nyts'kyy
116 K5 **Khmel'nyts'ka Oblast'** *var.* Khmel'nyts'kyy, *Rus.* Khmel'nitskaya Oblast'; *prev.* Kamenets-Podol'skaya Oblast'. ◆ *province* NW Ukraine
116 L6 **Khmel'nyts'kyy** *Rus.* Khmel'nitskiy; *prev.* Proskurov. Khmel'nyts'ka Oblast', W Ukraine 49°24′N 26°59′E
Khmel'nyts'kyy *see* Khmel'nyts'ka Oblast'
116 M6 **Khmil'nyk** *Rus.* Khmel'nik. Vinnyts'ka Oblast', C Ukraine 49°36′N 27°59′E
144 I10 **Khobda** *prev.* Novoalekseyevka. Aktyubinsk, W Kazakhstan 50°09′N 55°39′E
137 R9 **Khobi** W Georgia 42°20′N 41°54′E
119 P15 **Khodasy** *Rus.* Khodosy. Mahilyowskaya Voblasts', E Belarus 53°56′N 31°29′E
116 I6 **Khodoriv** *Pol.* Chodorów, *Rus.* Khodorov. L'vivs'ka Oblast', NW Ukraine 49°20′N 24°19′E
Khodorov *see* Khodoriv
Khodosy *see* Khodasy
Khodzhakala *see* Hojagala
Khodzhambas *see* Hojambaz
Khodzhent *see* Khujand
Khodzheyli *see* Xo'jayli
Khoi *see* Khvoy
Khojend *see* Khujand
Khokand *see* Qo'qon
126 L8 **Khokhol'skiy** Voronezhskaya Oblast', W Russian Federation 51°33′N 38°43′E
167 P10 **Khok Samrong** Lop Buri, C Thailand 15°03′N 100°44′E
149 P2 **Kholm** *var.* Tashqurghan, *Pash.* Khulm. Balkh, N Afghanistan 36°42′N 67°41′E
124 H15 **Kholm** Novgorodskaya Oblast', W Russian Federation 57°10′N 31°06′E
Kholm *see* Chełm
Kholmech' *see* Kholmyech
123 T13 **Kholmsk** Ostrov Sakhalin, Sakhalinskaya Oblast', SE Russian Federation 46°57′N 142°10′E
119 O19 **Kholmyech** *Rus.* Kholmech'. Homyel'skaya Voblasts', SE Belarus 52°09′N 30°37′E
Kholon *see* Holon
Kholopenichi *see* Khalopyenichy
83 D19 **Khomas** ◆ *district* C Namibia
83 D19 **Khomas Hochland** *var.* Khomasplato. *plateau* C Namibia
Khomasplato *see* Khomas Hochland
Khomein *see* Khomeyn
142 M7 **Khomeyn** *var.* Khomein, Khumain. Markazī, W Iran 33°38′N 50°03′E
143 N8 **Khomeynīshahr** *prev.* Homāyūnshahr. Eşfahān, C Iran 32°42′N 51°28′E
Khoms *see* Al Khums
Khong Sedone *see* Muang Khôngxédôn

◆ Country
● Country Capital
◇ Dependent Territory
○ Dependent Territory Capital
◆ Administrative Regions
✕ International Airport
▲ Mountain
▲▲ Mountain Range
Volcano
≈ River
◎ Lake
⊠ Reservoir

KHON KAEN – KISHANGARH

167 Q9 **Khon Kaen** var. Muang Khon Kaen. Khon Kaen, E Thailand 16°25'N 102°50'E
Khonqa see Xonqa
153 Y11 **Khonsa** Arunāchal Pradesh, NE India 27°01'N 95°95'E
167 Q9 **Khon San** Khon Kaen, E Thailand 16°40'N 101°51'E
123 R8 **Khonuu** Respublika Sakha (Yakutiya), NE Russian Federation 66°24'N 143°15'E
127 N8 **Khopër** var. Khoper. ≈ SW Russian Federation
Khoper see Khopër
123 S14 **Khor** Khabarovskiy Kray, SE Russian Federation 47°44'N 134°48'E
143 U9 **Khorāsān-e Janūbī** off. Ostan-e Khorāsān-e Janūbī. ◈ province E Iran
143 U5 **Khorāsān-e Razavī** off. Ostān-e Khorāsān, var. Khorassan, Khurasan. ◈ province NE Iran
143 S3 **Khorāsān-e Shemālī** off. Ostan-e Khorāsān-e Shemālī. ◈ province NE Iran
Khorāsān, Ostān-e see Khorāsān-e Razavī
Khorassan see Khorāsān-e Razavī
Khorat see Nakhon Ratchasima
154 O13 **Khordha** prev. Khurda. Orissa, E India 20°10'N 85°42'E
125 U4 **Khorey-Ver** Nenetskiy Avtonomnyy Okrug, NW Russian Federation 67°25'N 58°05'E
Khorezmskaya Oblast' see Xorazm Viloyati
Khor Fakkan see Khawr Fakkān
145 W15 **Khorgos** Almaty, SE Kazakhstan 44°13'N 80°22'E
123 N13 **Khorinsk** Respublika Buryatiya, S Russian Federation 52°13'N 109°52'E
83 C18 **Khorixas** Kunene, NW Namibia 20°23'S 14°55'E
141 O17 **Khormaksar** var. Aden. ✈ ('Adan) SW Yemen 12°56'N 45°00'E
Khormal see Khurmāl
Khormuj see Khvormūj
Khorog see Khorugh
117 S5 **Khorol** Poltavs'ka Oblast', NE Ukraine 49°49'N 33°17'E
142 L7 **Khorramābād** var. Khurramabad. Lorestān, W Iran 33°29'N 48°21'E
143 R9 **Khorramdasht** Kermān, C Iran 31°41'N 56°10'E
142 K10 **Khorramshahr** var. Khurramshahr, Muhammerah; prev. Mohammerah. Khūzestān, SW Iran 30°30'N 48°09'E
147 S14 **Khorugh** Rus. Khorog. S Tajikistan 37°30'N 71°31'E
Khorvot Khalutsa see Horvot Halutsa
127 Q12 **Khosheutovo** Astrakhanskaya Oblast', SW Russian Federation 47°04'N 47°49'E
Khotan see Hotan
Khotimsk see Khotsimsk
Khotin see Khotyn
119 R16 **Khotsimsk** Rus. Khotimsk. Mahilyowskaya Voblasts', E Belarus 53°24'N 32°35'E
116 K7 **Khotyn** Rom. Hotin, Rus. Khotin. Chernivets'ka Oblast', W Ukraine 48°29'N 26°30'E
74 F7 **Khouribga** C Morocco 32°55'N 06°51'W
147 Q13 **Khovaling** Rus. Khavaling. SW Tajikistan 38°22'N 69°54'E
Khovd see Hovd
149 R6 **Khowst** Khowst, E Afghanistan 33°22'N 69°57'E
149 S6 **Khowst** ◈ province E Afghanistan
Khoy see Khvoy
119 N20 **Khoyniki** Homyel'skaya Voblasts', SE Belarus 51°54'N 29°58'E
Khozretishi, Khrebet see Hazratishoh, Qatorkŭhi
Khrisoúpolis see Chrysoúpoli
144 J10 **Khromtau** Kaz. Khromtaū. Aktyubinsk, W Kazakhstan 50°14'N 58°22'E
Khromtaū see Khromtau
Khrysokhou Bay see Chrysochoú, Kólpos
117 O7 **Khrystynivka** Cherkas'ka Oblast', C Ukraine 48°49'N 29°55'E
167 R10 **Khuang Nai** Ubon Ratchathani, E Thailand 15°22'N 104°33'E
Khudal see Khādhil
Khudat see Xudat
149 W9 **Khudiān** Punjab, E Pakistan 30°59'N 74°19'E
Khudzhand see Khujand
83 G21 **Khuis** Kgalagadi, SW Botswana 26°37'S 21°50'E
147 Q11 **Khujand** var. Khodzhent, Khojend, Rus. Khudzhand; prev. Leninabad, Taj. Leninobod. N Tajikistan 40°17'N 69°37'E
167 R11 **Khukhan** Si Sa Ket, E Thailand 14°38'N 104°12'E
Khulm see Kholm
153 T16 **Khulna** Khulna, SW Bangladesh 22°48'N 89°32'E
153 T16 **Khulna** ◈ division SW Bangladesh
Khumain see Khomeyn
Khums see Al Khums
149 W2 **Khunjerāb Pass** pass China/Pakistan
Khūnjerāb Pass see Kunjirap Daban
153 P16 **Khunti** Jhārkhand, N India 23°02'N 85°19'E
167 N7 **Khun Yuam** Mae Hong Son, NW Thailand 18°54'N 97°54'E
Khurais see Khurayş
Khurasan see Khorāsān-e Razavī
141 R7 **Khurayş** var. Khurais. Ash Sharqīyah, C Saudi Arabia 25°06'N 48°03'E
Khurda see Khordha
152 J11 **Khurja** Uttar Pradesh, N India 28°15'N 77°51'E
139 V4 **Khurmāl** var. Khormal. As Sulaymānīyah, NE Iraq 35°19'N 46°06'E
Khurramabad see Khorramābād
Khurramshahr see Khorramshahr
149 U7 **Khushāb** Punjab, NE Pakistan 32°16'N 72°18'E
116 H8 **Khust** var. Husté, Cz. Chust, Hung. Huszt. Zakarpats'ka Oblast', W Ukraine 48°11'N 23°19'E
80 D11 **Khuwei** Western Kordofan, C Sudan 13°02'N 29°13'E
149 O13 **Khuzdār** Baluchistān, SW Pakistan 27°49'N 66°39'E
142 L9 **Khūzestān** off. Ostān-e Khūzestān, var. Khuzistan, prev. Arabistan; anc. Susiana. ◈ province SW Iran
Khūzestān, Ostān-e see Khūzestān
Khuzistan see Khūzestān
149 R2 **Khvājeh Ghār** var. Khwajaghar, Khwaja-i-Ghar. Takhār, NE Afghanistan 37°08'N 69°24'E
127 Q7 **Khvalynsk** Saratovskaya Oblast', W Russian Federation 52°30'N 48°06'E
143 N12 **Khvormūj** var. Khormuj. Būshehr, S Iran 28°32'N 51°22'E
142 I2 **Khvoy** var. Khoi, Khoy. Āžarbāyjān-e Bākhtarī, NW Iran 38°36'N 45°04'E
Khwajaghar/Khwaja-i-Ghar see Khvājeh Ghār
149 S5 **Khyber Pass** var. Kowtal-e Khaybar. pass Afghanistan/Pakistan
186 L8 **Kia** Santa Isabel, N Solomon Islands 07°34'S 158°31'E
183 S10 **Kiama** New South Wales, SE Australia 34°41'S 150°49'E
79 O22 **Kiambi** Katanga, SE Dem. Rep. Congo 07°15'S 28°01'E
27 Q12 **Kiamichi Mountains** ⛰ Oklahoma, C USA
27 Q12 **Kiamichi River** ≈ Oklahoma, C USA
14 M10 **Kiamika, Réservoir** ⊠ Québec, SE Canada
Kiamusze see Jiamusi
39 N7 **Kiana** Alaska, USA 66°58'N 160°25'W
Kiangmai see Chiang Mai
Kiang-ning see Nanjing
Kiangsi see Jiangxi
Kiangsu see Jiangsu
93 M14 **Kiantajärvi** ◎ E Finland
115 F19 **Kiáto** prev. Kiáton. Pelopónnisos, S Greece 38°01'N 22°45'E
Kiáton see Kiáto
Kiayi see Chiai
95 F22 **Kibæk** Ringkøbing, W Denmark 56°03'N 08°52'E
67 T9 **Kibali** var. Uele (upper course). ≈ NE Dem. Rep. Congo
79 E20 **Kibangou** Niari, SW Congo 03°27'S 12°21'E
Kibarty see Kybartai
92 M8 **Kiberg** Finnmark, N Norway 70°17'N 30°47'E
79 N20 **Kibombo** Maniema, E Dem. Rep. Congo 03°52'S 25°59'E
81 E20 **Kibondo** Kigoma, NW Tanzania 03°34'S 30°41'E
81 J15 **Kibre Mengist** var. Adola. Oromīya, C Ethiopia 05°50'N 39°06'E
Kıbrıs see Cyprus
Kıbrıs/Kıbrıs Cumhuriyeti see Cyprus
81 E20 **Kibungo** var. Kibungu. SE Rwanda 02°09'S 30°30'E
Kibungu see Kibungo
113 N19 **Kičevo** SW FYR Macedonia 41°31'N 20°57'E
125 P13 **Kichmengskiy Gorodok** Vologodskaya Oblast', NW Russian Federation 60°00'N 45°52'E
30 J8 **Kickapoo River** ≈ Wisconsin, N USA
11 P16 **Kicking Horse Pass** pass Alberta/British Columbia, SW Canada
77 R9 **Kidal** Kidal, C Mali 18°22'N 01°21'E
77 Q8 **Kidal** ◈ region NE Mali
171 Q7 **Kidapawan** Mindanao, S Philippines 07°02'N 125°04'E
97 L20 **Kidderminster** C England, United Kingdom 52°23'N 02°14'W
76 I11 **Kidira** E Senegal 14°28'N 12°13'W
184 O11 **Kidnappers, Cape** headland North Island, New Zealand 41°13'S 175°15'E
100 J8 **Kiel** Schleswig-Holstein, N Germany 54°21'N 10°05'E
111 L15 **Kielce** Rus. Keltsy. Świętokrzyskie, C Poland 50°53'N 20°39'E
100 K7 **Kieler Bucht** bay N Germany
100 J7 **Kieler Förde** inlet N Germany
167 U13 **Kiên Đuc** var. Đak Lap. Đăc Lăc, S Vietnam 11°59'N 107°30'E
79 N24 **Kienge** Katanga, SE Dem. Rep. Congo 10°33'S 27°33'E
100 Q12 **Kietz** Brandenburg, NE Germany 52°33'N 14°36'E
Kiev see Kyyiv
Kiev Reservoir see Kyyivs'ke Vodoskhovyshche
76 J10 **Kiffa** Assaba, S Mauritania 16°38'N 11°23'W
115 H19 **Kifisiá** Attikí, C Greece 38°04'N 23°49'E
115 F18 **Kifisós** ≈ C Greece
139 U5 **Kifrī** At Ta'mīn, N Iraq 34°44'N 44°58'E
81 D20 **Kigali** ● (Rwanda) C Rwanda 01°59'S 30°02'E
81 E20 **Kigali** ✈ C Rwanda 01°43'S 30°01'E
137 P13 **Kiğı** Bingöl, E Turkey 39°19'N 40°20'E
81 E21 **Kigoma** Kigoma, W Tanzania 04°52'S 29°36'E
81 E21 **Kigoma** ◈ region W Tanzania
38 F10 **Kīhei** var. Kihei. Maui, Hawaii, USA, C Pacific Ocean 20°47'N 156°28'W
93 K17 **Kihniö** Länsi-Suomi, W Finland 62°11'N 23°10'E
118 F6 **Kihnu** var. Kihnu Saar, Ger. Kühnö. island SW Estonia
Kihnu Saar see Kihnu
38 A8 **Kii Landing** Ni'ihau, Hawaii, USA, C Pacific Ocean 21°58'N 160°03'W
93 L14 **Kiiminki** Oulu, C Finland 65°05'N 25°47'E
164 J14 **Kii-Nagashima** var. Nagashima. Mie, Honshū, SW Japan 34°10'N 136°18'E
164 J14 **Kii-sanchi** ⛰ Honshū, SW Japan
92 L11 **Kiistala** Lappi, N Finland 67°52'N 25°19'E
164 I15 **Kii-suidō** strait S Japan
165 V16 **Kikai-shima** island Nansei-shotō, SW Japan
112 M8 **Kikinda** Ger. Grosskikinda, Hung. Nagykikinda; prev. Velika Kikinda. Vojvodina, N Serbia 45°48'N 20°29'E
Kikládhes see Kykládes
165 Q5 **Kikonai** Hokkaidō, NE Japan 41°40'N 140°25'E
186 C8 **Kikori** Gulf, S Papua New Guinea 07°25'S 144°13'E
186 C8 **Kikori** ≈ W Papua New Guinea
165 O14 **Kikuchi** var. Kikuti. Kumamoto, Kyūshū, SW Japan 33°00'N 130°49'E
Kikuti see Kikuchi
127 N8 **Kikvidze** Volgogradskaya Oblast', SW Russian Federation 50°47'N 42°58'E
14 I10 **Kikwissi, Lac** ◎ Québec, SE Canada
79 I21 **Kikwit** Bandundu, W Dem. Rep. Congo 05°S 18°53'E
95 K15 **Kil** Värmland, C Sweden 59°30'N 13°20'E
94 N12 **Kilafors** Gävleborg, C Sweden 61°13'N 16°34'E
38 B8 **Kilauea** Kaua'i, Hawaii, USA, C Pacific Ocean 22°12'N 159°24'W
38 H12 **Kīlauea Caldera** var. Kilauea Caldera. crater Hawai'i, USA, C Pacific Ocean
Kilauea Caldera see Kīlauea Caldera
109 V4 **Kilb** Niederösterreich, C Austria 48°06'N 15°21'E
39 O12 **Kilbuck Mountains** ⛰ Alaska, USA
163 Y12 **Kilchu** NE North Korea 40°58'N 129°22'E
97 F18 **Kilcock** Ir. Cill Choca. Kildare, E Ireland 53°25'N 06°40'W
183 V2 **Kilcoy** Queensland, E Australia 26°58'S 152°30'E
97 F18 **Kildare** Ir. Cill Dara. E Ireland 53°10'N 06°55'W
97 F18 **Kildare** Ir. Cill Dara. cultural region E Ireland
124 K2 **Kil'din, Ostrov** island NW Russian Federation
25 W7 **Kilgore** Texas, SW USA 32°23'N 94°52'W
Kilien Mountains see Qilian Shan
114 K9 **Kilifarevo** Veliko Tŭrnovo, N Bulgaria 43°00'N 25°36'E
81 K20 **Kilifi** Coast, SE Kenya 03°37'S 39°50'E
189 U9 **Kili Island** var. Kōle. island Ralik Chain, S Marshall Islands
149 V2 **Kilik Pass** pass Afghanistan/China
Kilimane see Quelimane
81 I21 **Kilimanjaro** ◈ region E Tanzania
81 I20 **Kilimanjaro** var. Uhuru Peak. △ NE Tanzania 03°01'S 37°14'E
Kilimbangara see Kolombangara
Kilinailau Islands see Tulun Islands
81 K23 **Kilindoni** Pwani, E Tanzania 07°56'S 39°40'E
118 H6 **Kilingi-Nõmme** Ger. Kurkund. Pärnumaa, SW Estonia 58°07'N 24°00'E
136 M17 **Kilis** Kilis, S Turkey 36°43'N 37°07'E
136 M16 **Kilis** ◈ province S Turkey
117 N12 **Kiliya** Rom. Chilia-Nouă. Odes'ka Oblast', SW Ukraine 45°30'N 29°16'E
97 B19 **Kilkee** Ir. Cill Chaoi. Clare, W Ireland 52°41'N 09°38'W
97 E19 **Kilkenny** Ir. Cill Chainnigh. Kilkenny, S Ireland 52°39'N 07°15'W
97 E19 **Kilkenny** Ir. Cill Chainnigh. cultural region S Ireland
97 B18 **Kilkieran Bay** Ir. Cuan Chill Chiaráin. bay W Ireland
114 G13 **Kilkís** Kentrikí Makedonía, N Greece 40°59'N 22°55'E
97 C15 **Killala Bay** Ir. Cuan Chill Ala. inlet NW Ireland
11 R15 **Killam** Alberta, SW Canada 52°45'N 111°46'W
183 U3 **Killarney** Queensland, E Australia 28°18'S 152°15'E
11 W17 **Killarney** Manitoba, S Canada 49°12'N 99°40'W
14 E11 **Killarney** Ontario, S Canada 45°58'N 81°27'W
97 B20 **Killarney** Ir. Cill Airne. Kerry, SW Ireland 52°03'N 09°30'W
28 K4 **Killdeer** North Dakota, N USA 47°21'N 102°45'W
28 J4 **Killdeer Mountains** ⛰ North Dakota, N USA
45 V15 **Killdeer River** ≈ Trinidad, Trinidad and Tobago
25 S9 **Killeen** Texas, SW USA 31°07'N 97°44'W
39 P6 **Killik River** ≈ Alaska, USA
11 T7 **Killinek Island** island Nunavut, NE Canada
Killini see Kyllíni
115 C19 **Killinis, Akrotírio** headland S Greece 37°55'N 21°07'E
97 D15 **Killybegs** Ir. Na Cealla Beaga. NW Ireland 54°38'N 08°27'W
Kilmain see Quelimane
96 I13 **Kilmarnock** W Scotland, United Kingdom 55°37'N 04°30'W
21 X6 **Kilmarnock** Virginia, NE USA 37°42'N 76°22'W
125 S16 **Kil'mez'** Kirovskaya Oblast', NW Russian Federation 56°55'N 51°03'E
127 S2 **Kil'mez'** Udmurtskaya Respublika, NW Russian Federation 57°04'N 51°22'E
125 R16 **Kil'mez'** ≈ NW Russian Federation
67 V11 **Kilombero** ≈ S Tanzania
92 J10 **Kilpisjärvi** Lappi, N Finland 69°03'N 20°50'E
97 B19 **Kilrush** Ir. Cill Rois. Clare, W Ireland 52°39'N 09°29'W
79 O24 **Kilwa** Katanga, SE Dem. Rep. Congo 09°22'S 28°19'E
Kilwa see Kilwa Kivinje
81 J24 **Kilwa Kivinje** var. Kilwa. Lindi, SE Tanzania 08°45'S 39°21'E
81 J24 **Kilwa Masoko** Lindi, SE Tanzania 08°55'S 39°31'E
171 T13 **Kilwo** Pulau Seram, E Indonesia 03°36'S 130°48'E
114 P12 **Kilyos** İstanbul, NW Turkey 41°15'N 29°01'E
37 V8 **Kim** Colorado, C USA 37°12'N 103°22'W
169 U7 **Kimanis, Teluk** bay Sabah, East Malaysia
182 H8 **Kimba** South Australia 33°09'S 136°26'E
28 I15 **Kimball** Nebraska, C USA 41°16'N 103°40'W
29 O11 **Kimball** South Dakota, N USA 43°45'N 98°57'W
79 I21 **Kimbao** Bandundu, SW Dem. Rep. Congo 05°27'S 17°40'E
186 F7 **Kimbe** New Britain, E Papua New Guinea 05°36'S 150°10'E
186 G7 **Kimbe Bay** inlet New Britain, E Papua New Guinea
11 P17 **Kimberley** British Columbia, SW Canada 49°40'N 115°58'W
83 H23 **Kimberley** Northern Cape, C South Africa 28°45'S 24°46'E
180 M4 **Kimberley Plateau** plateau Western Australia
33 P15 **Kimberly** Idaho, NW USA 42°31'N 114°21'W
163 Y12 **Kimch'aek** prev. Sŏngjin. E North Korea 40°42'N 129°13'E
163 Y15 **Kimch'ŏn** C South Korea 36°08'N 128°06'E
163 Z16 **Kim Hae** var. Pusan. ✈ (Pusan) SE South Korea 35°10'N 128°57'E
Kími see Kými
93 K20 **Kimito** Swe. Kemiö. Länsi-Suomi, SW Finland 60°10'N 22°45'E
9 R7 **Kimmirut** prev. Lake Harbour. Baffin Island, Nunavut, NE Canada 62°48'N 69°49'W
165 R4 **Kimobetsu** Hokkaidō, NE Japan 42°47'N 140°55'E
115 I21 **Kímolos** island Kykládes, Greece, Aegean Sea
115 I21 **Kímolou Sífnou, Stenó** strait Kykládes, Greece, Aegean Sea
126 L5 **Kimovsk** Tul'skaya Oblast', W Russian Federation 53°59'N 38°34'E
Kimpolung see Câmpulung Moldovenesc
124 K16 **Kimry** Tverskaya Oblast', W Russian Federation 56°52'N 37°21'E
79 H21 **Kimvula** Bas-Congo, SW Dem. Rep. Congo 05°44'S 15°58'E
169 U6 **Kinabalu, Gunung** ▲ East Malaysia 05°52'N 116°08'E
Kinabatangan see Kinabatangan, Sungai
169 V7 **Kinabatangan, Sungai** var. Kinabatangan. ≈ East Malaysia
115 L21 **Kínaros** island Kykládes, Greece, Aegean Sea
11 O15 **Kinbasket Lake** ⊠ British Columbia, SW Canada
96 I7 **Kinbrace** N Scotland, United Kingdom 58°16'N 02°59'W
14 E14 **Kincardine** Ontario, S Canada 44°11'N 81°38'W
95 K10 **Kincardine** cultural region E Scotland, United Kingdom
79 K21 **Kinda** Kasai-Occidental, SE Dem. Rep. Congo 04°48'S 21°50'E
79 M24 **Kinda** Katanga, SE Dem. Rep. Congo 09°20'S 25°06'E
166 L3 **Kindat** Sagaing, N Myanmar (Burma) 23°42'N 94°29'E
109 V6 **Kindberg** Steiermark, C Austria 47°31'N 15°27'E
22 H8 **Kinder** Louisiana, S USA 30°29'N 92°51'W
98 H13 **Kinderdijk** Zuid-Holland, SW Netherlands 51°52'N 04°37'E
97 M17 **Kinder Scout** ▲ C England, United Kingdom 53°25'N 01°52'W
11 S16 **Kindersley** Saskatchewan, S Canada 51°29'N 109°08'W
76 I14 **Kindia** Guinée-Maritime, SW Guinea 10°12'N 12°26'W
64 B11 **Kindley Field** air base E Bermuda
29 R6 **Kindred** North Dakota, N USA 46°39'N 97°01'W
79 N20 **Kindu** prev. Kindu-Port-Empain. Maniema, C Dem. Rep. Congo 02°57'S 25°54'E
Kindu-Port-Empain see Kindu
127 S6 **Kinel'** Samarskaya Oblast', W Russian Federation 53°14'N 50°40'E
125 N15 **Kineshma** Ivanovskaya Oblast', W Russian Federation 57°28'N 42°08'E
King see King William's Town
140 K10 **King Abdul Aziz** ✈ (Makkah) Makkah, W Saudi Arabia 21°44'N 39°08'E
21 X6 **King and Queen Court House** Virginia, NE USA 37°40'N 76°49'W
King Charles Islands see Kong Karls Land
King Christian IX Land see Kong Christian IX Land
King Christian X Land see Kong Christian X Land
35 O11 **King City** California, W USA 36°12'N 121°09'W
27 R2 **King City** Missouri, C USA 40°03'N 94°31'W
38 M16 **King Cove** Alaska, USA 55°03'N 162°19'W
26 M10 **Kingfisher** Oklahoma, C USA 35°53'N 97°56'W
King Frederik VI Coast see Kong Frederik VI Kyst
King Frederik VIII Land see Kong Frederik VIII Land
65 B24 **King George Bay** bay West Falkland, Falkland Islands
194 G3 **King George Island** var. King George Land. island South Shetland Islands, Antarctica
12 I6 **King George Islands** island group Northwest Territories, C Canada
King George Land see King George Island
124 G13 **Kingisepp** Leningradskaya Oblast', NW Russian Federation 59°23'N 28°37'E
183 N14 **King Island** island Tasmania, SE Australia
10 J15 **King Island** island British Columbia, SW Canada
King Island see Kadan Kyun
Kingissepp see Kuressaare
141 Q7 **King Khalid** ✈ (Ar Riyāḍ) Ar Riyāḍ, C Saudi Arabia 25°00'N 46°40'E
35 S2 **King Lear Peak** ▲ Nevada, W USA 41°13'N 118°30'W
195 Y8 **King Leopold and Queen Astrid Land** physical region Antarctica
180 M4 **King Leopold Ranges** ⛰ Western Australia
36 I11 **Kingman** Arizona, SW USA 35°12'N 114°02'W
26 M6 **Kingman** Kansas, C USA 37°39'N 98°07'W
192 L7 **Kingman Reef** ◇ US territory C Pacific Ocean
79 N20 **Kingombe** Maniema, E Dem. Rep. Congo 02°37'S 26°39'E
182 F5 **Kingoonya** South Australia 30°56'S 135°20'E
194 J10 **King Peninsula** peninsula Antarctica
39 P13 **King Salmon** Alaska, USA 58°41'N 156°39'W
35 Q6 **Kings Beach** California, W USA 39°13'N 120°02'W
35 R11 **Kingsburg** California, W USA 36°30'N 119°33'W
182 I10 **Kingscote** South Australia 35°41'S 137°36'E
King's County see Offaly
194 H2 **King Sejong** South Korean research station Antarctica 61°57'S 58°23'W
183 T9 **Kingsford Smith** ✈ (Sydney) New South Wales, SE Australia 33°58'S 151°09'E
11 P17 **Kingsgate** British Columbia, SW Canada 48°58'N 116°09'W
23 W8 **Kingsland** Georgia, SE USA 30°48'N 81°41'W
29 S13 **Kingsley** Iowa, C USA 42°35'N 95°58'W
97 O19 **King's Lynn** var. Bishop's Lynn, Kings Lynn, Lynn, Lynn Regis. E England, United Kingdom 52°45'N 00°24'E
Kings Lynn see King's Lynn
21 Q10 **Kings Mountain** North Carolina, SE USA 35°15'N 81°20'W
180 K4 **King Sound** sound Western Australia
37 N2 **Kings Peak** ▲ Utah, W USA 40°43'N 110°27'W
21 O8 **Kingsport** Tennessee, S USA 36°32'N 82°33'W
35 R11 **Kings River** ≈ California, W USA
183 P17 **Kingston** Tasmania, SE Australia 42°57'S 147°18'E
14 K14 **Kingston** Ontario, SE Canada 44°14'N 76°30'W
44 K13 **Kingston** ● (Jamaica) E Jamaica 17°58'N 76°48'W
185 C22 **Kingston** Otago, South Island, New Zealand 45°20'S 168°45'E
19 P12 **Kingston** Massachusetts, NE USA 41°59'N 70°43'W
27 S3 **Kingston** Missouri, C USA 39°36'N 94°02'W
18 K12 **Kingston** New York, NE USA 41°55'N 74°00'W
31 S14 **Kingston** Ohio, N USA 39°28'N 82°54'W
19 O13 **Kingston** Rhode Island, NE USA 41°28'N 71°31'W
20 M9 **Kingston** Tennessee, S USA 35°52'N 84°30'W
35 W12 **Kingston Peak** ▲ California, W USA 35°43'N 115°54'W
182 J11 **Kingston Southeast** South Australia 36°51'S 139°53'E
97 N17 **Kingston upon Hull** var. Hull. E England, United Kingdom 53°45'N 00°20'W
97 N22 **Kingston upon Thames** SE England, United Kingdom 51°26'N 00°18'W
45 P14 **Kingstown** ● (Saint Vincent and the Grenadines) Saint Vincent, Saint Vincent and the Grenadines 13°09'N 61°14'W
Kingstown see Dún Laoghaire
21 T13 **Kingstree** South Carolina, SE USA 33°40'N 79°50'W
64 L8 **Kings Trough** undersea feature E Atlantic Ocean 22°00'W 43°48'N
14 C18 **Kingsville** Ontario, S Canada 42°03'N 82°43'W
25 S15 **Kingsville** Texas, SW USA 27°32'N 97°53'W
21 W6 **King William** Virginia, NE USA 37°42'N 77°03'W
9 N7 **King William Island** island Nunavut, N Canada
83 I25 **King William's Town** var. King, Kingwilliamstown. Eastern Cape, S South Africa 32°53'S 27°24'E
Kingwilliamstown see King William's Town
21 T3 **Kingwood** West Virginia, NE USA 39°27'N 79°43'W
136 C13 **Kınık** İzmir, W Turkey 39°05'N 27°25'E
79 G21 **Kinkala** Pool, S Congo 04°18'S 14°49'E
165 R10 **Kinka-san** headland Honshū, C Japan 38°17'N 141°34'E
184 M8 **Kinleith** Waikato, North Island, New Zealand 38°16'S 175°53'E
95 J19 **Kinna** Västra Götaland, S Sweden 57°32'N 12°42'E
96 L8 **Kinnaird Head** var. Kinnairds Head. headland NE Scotland, United Kingdom 58°39'N 03°22'W
Kinnairds Head see Kinnaird Head
95 K20 **Kinnared** Halland, S Sweden 57°01'N 13°04'E
Kinneret, Yam see Tiberias, Lake
155 K24 **Kinniyai** Eastern Province, NE Sri Lanka 08°30'N 81°11'E
93 L16 **Kinnula** Länsi-Suomi, C Finland 63°24'N 25°E
14 I8 **Kinojévis** ≈ Québec, SE Canada
164 I14 **Kino-kawa** ≈ Honshū, SW Japan
11 U11 **Kinoosao** Saskatchewan, C Canada 57°06'N 101°02'W
99 L17 **Kinrooi** Limburg, NE Belgium 51°09'N 05°48'E
96 J11 **Kinross** C Scotland, United Kingdom 56°14'N 03°27'W
96 J11 **Kinross** cultural region C Scotland, United Kingdom
97 C21 **Kinsale** Ir. Cionn tSáile. Cork, SW Ireland 51°42'N 08°32'W
95 D14 **Kinsarvik** Hordaland, S Norway 60°22'N 06°43'E
79 G21 **Kinshasa** prev. Léopoldville. ● Kinshasa, W Dem. Rep. Congo 04°21'S 15°16'E
79 G21 **Kinshasa** off. Ville de Kinshasa, var. Kinshasa City. ◈ region (Dem. Rep. Congo) SW Dem. Rep. Congo
79 G21 **Kinshasa** ✈ Kinshasa, SW Dem. Rep. Congo 04°23'S 15°30'E
Kinshasa City see Kinshasa
117 U9 **Kins'ka** ≈ SE Ukraine
26 K6 **Kinsley** Kansas, C USA 37°55'N 99°26'W
21 W10 **Kinston** North Carolina, SE USA 35°16'N 77°35'W
77 P15 **Kintampo** W Ghana 08°06'N 01°40'W
182 B1 **Kintore, Mount** ▲ South Australia 26°30'S 130°24'E
96 G13 **Kintyre** peninsula W Scotland, United Kingdom
96 G13 **Kintyre, Mull of** headland W Scotland, United Kingdom 55°16'N 05°46'W
166 M4 **Kin-u** Sagaing, C Myanmar (Burma) 22°47'N 95°36'E
12 G8 **Kinushseo** ≈ Ontario, C Canada
11 P13 **Kinuso** Alberta, W Canada 55°19'N 115°23'W
154 I13 **Kinwat** Mahārāshtra, C India 19°37'N 78°12'E
81 F16 **Kinyeti** ▲ S Sudan 03°56'N 32°52'E
101 I17 **Kinzig** ≈ SW Germany
Kioga, Lake see Kyoga, Lake
26 M8 **Kiowa** Kansas, C USA 37°01'N 98°29'W
27 P12 **Kiowa** Oklahoma, C USA 34°43'N 95°54'W
Kiparissia see Kyparissía
14 H10 **Kipawa, Lac** ◎ Québec, SE Canada
81 G24 **Kipengere Range** ⛰ SW Tanzania
81 E23 **Kipili** Rukwa, W Tanzania 07°30'S 30°39'E
81 K20 **Kipini** Coast, SE Kenya 02°30'S 40°30'E
11 V16 **Kipling** Saskatchewan, S Canada 50°04'N 102°45'W
38 M13 **Kipnuk** Alaska, USA 59°56'N 164°02'W
97 F18 **Kippure** Ir. Cipiúr. ▲ E Ireland 53°10'N 06°22'W
79 N25 **Kipushi** Katanga, SE Dem. Rep. Congo 11°45'S 27°20'E
187 N10 **Kirakira** var. Kaokaona. San Cristobal, SE Solomon Islands 10°28'S 161°54'E
155 K14 **Kirandul** var. Bailādila. Chhattīsgarh, C India 18°46'N 81°18'E
155 I21 **Kīranūr** Tamil Nādu, SE India 11°37'N 79°10'E
119 N21 **Kiraw** Rus. Kirovo. Homyel'skaya Voblasts', SE Belarus 51°30'N 29°25'E
119 M17 **Kirawsk** Rus. Kirovsk; prev. Startsy. Mahilyowskaya Voblasts', E Belarus 53°16'N 29°29'E
118 F5 **Kirbla** Läänemaa, W Estonia 58°45'N 23°57'E
25 Y9 **Kirbyville** Texas, SW USA 30°39'N 93°53'W
114 M12 **Kırcasalih** Edirne, NW Turkey 41°24'N 26°48'E
109 W8 **Kirchbach** var. Kirchbach in Steiermark. Steiermark, SE Austria 46°55'N 15°40'E
Kirchbach in Steiermark see Kirchbach
108 H7 **Kirchberg** Sankt Gallen, NE Switzerland 47°24'N 09°03'E
109 S5 **Kirchdorf an der Krems** Oberösterreich, N Austria 47°55'N 14°08'E
Kirchheim see Kirchheim unter Teck
101 I22 **Kirchheim unter Teck** var. Kirchheim. Baden-Württemberg, SW Germany 48°39'N 09°28'E
Kirdzhali see Kŭrdzhali
123 N13 **Kirenga** ≈ S Russian Federation
123 N12 **Kirensk** Irkutskaya Oblast', C Russian Federation 57°37'N 107°54'E
Kirghizia see Kyrgyzstan
145 S16 **Kirghiz Range** Rus. Kirgizskiy Khrebet; prev. Alexander Range. ⛰ Kazakhstan/Kyrgyzstan
Kirghiz SSR see Kyrgyzstan
Kirghiz Steppe see Kazakhskiy Melkosopochnik
Kirgizskaya SSR see Kyrgyzstan
Kirgizskiy Khrebet see Kirghiz Range
79 I19 **Kiri** Bandundu, W Dem. Rep. Congo 01°29'S 19°00'E
Kiriath-Arba see Hebron
191 R3 **Kiribati** off. Republic of Kiribati. ◆ republic C Pacific Ocean
Kiribati, Republic of see Kiribati
136 L17 **Kırıkhan** Hatay, S Turkey 36°30'N 36°20'E
136 I13 **Kırıkkale** Kırıkkale, C Turkey 39°50'N 33°31'E
136 C10 **Kırıkkale** ◈ province C Turkey
124 L13 **Kirillov** Vologodskaya Oblast', NW Russian Federation 59°52'N 38°24'E
Kirin see Jilin
81 I18 **Kirinyaga** prev. Mount Kenya. △ C Kenya 0°02'S 37°19'E
124 H13 **Kirishi** var. Kirisi. Leningradskaya Oblast', NW Russian Federation 59°28'N 32°02'E
164 C16 **Kirishima-yama** ▲ Kyūshū, SW Japan 31°58'N 130°51'E
Kirisi see Kirishi
191 Y2 **Kiritimati** ✈ Kiritimati, E Kiribati 02°00'N 157°30'W
191 Y2 **Kiritimati** prev. Christmas Island. atoll Line Islands, E Kiribati
186 G9 **Kiriwina Island** Eng. Trobriand Island. island SE Papua New Guinea
186 G9 **Kiriwina Islands** var. Trobriand Islands. island group S Papua New Guinea
96 K12 **Kirkcaldy** E Scotland, United Kingdom 56°07'N 03°10'W
97 I14 **Kirkcudbright** S Scotland, United Kingdom 54°50'N 04°03'W
97 I14 **Kirkcudbright** cultural region S Scotland, United Kingdom
Kirkee see Khadki
95 I14 **Kirkenær** Hedmark, S Norway 60°27'N 12°04'E
92 M8 **Kirkenes** Fin. Kirkkoniemi. Finnmark, N Norway 69°43'N 30°02'E
92 J4 **Kirkjubæjarklaustur** Sudhurland, S Iceland 63°46'N 18°03'W
Kirk-Kilissa see Kırklareli
Kirkkoniemi see Kirkenes
93 L20 **Kirkkonummi** Swe. Kyrkslätt. Uusimaa, S Finland 60°06'N 24°20'E
14 G7 **Kirkland Lake** Ontario, S Canada 48°10'N 80°02'W
136 C9 **Kırklareli** prev. Kirk-Kilissa. Kırklareli, NW Turkey 41°45'N 27°12'E
136 I13 **Kırklareli** ◈ province NW Turkey
185 F20 **Kirkliston Range** ⛰ South Island, New Zealand
14 D10 **Kirkpatrick Lake** ◎ Ontario, S Canada
195 Q11 **Kirkpatrick, Mount** ▲ Antarctica 84°37'S 164°36'E
27 U2 **Kirksville** Missouri, C USA 40°12'N 92°35'W
139 T4 **Kirkūk** var. Karkūk, Kerkuk. At Ta'mīn, N Iraq 35°28'N 44°26'E
139 U7 **Kir Kush** Diyālá, E Iraq 33°42'N 45°15'E
96 K5 **Kirkwall** NE Scotland, United Kingdom 58°59'N 02°58'W
83 H25 **Kirkwood** Eastern Cape, S South Africa 33°23'S 25°19'E
27 X5 **Kirkwood** Missouri, C USA 38°35'N 90°24'W
Kirman see Kermān
Kir Moab/Kir of Moab see Al Karak
126 I5 **Kirov** Kaluzhskaya Oblast', W Russian Federation 54°02'N 34°17'E
125 R14 **Kirov** prev. Vyatka. Kirovskaya Oblast', NW Russian Federation 58°35'N 49°39'E
Kirov see Balpyk Bi/Ust'yevoye
Kirovabad see Gäncä
Kirovabad see Panj, Tajikistan
Kirovakan see Vanadzor
Kirov/Kirova see Kopbirlik, Kazakhstan
Kirovo see Kiraw, Belarus
Kirovo see Beshariq, Uzbekistan
125 R14 **Kirovo-Chepetsk** Kirovskaya Oblast', NW Russian Federation 58°33'N 50°06'E
Kirovogradskaya Oblast'/Kirovohrad see Kirovohrads'ka Oblast'
117 R7 **Kirovohrad** Rus. Kirovograd; prev. Kirovo, Yelizavetgrad, Zinov'yevsk. Kirovohrads'ka Oblast', C Ukraine 48°30'N 31°17'E
117 P7 **Kirovohrads'ka Oblast'** var. Kirovohrad, Rus. Kirovogradskaya Oblast'. ◈ province C Ukraine
Kirovo/Kirovograd see Kirovohrad
124 J4 **Kirovsk** Murmanskaya Oblast', NW Russian Federation 67°37'N 33°38'E
117 X7 **Kirovs'k** Luhans'ka Oblast', E Ukraine 48°40'N 38°39'E
Kirovsk see Kirawsk, Belarus
Kirovsk see Babadaýhan, Turkmenistan
122 E9 **Kirovskaya Oblast'** ◈ province NW Russian Federation
117 X8 **Kirovs'ke** Donets'ka Oblast', E Ukraine 48°12'N 38°20'E
117 U13 **Kirovs'ke** Rus. Kirovskoye. Respublika Krym, S Ukraine 45°13'N 35°12'E
Kirovskiy see Balpyk Bi
Kirovskoye see Kyzyl-Adyr
Kirovskoye see Kirovs'ke
146 E11 **Kirpili** Ahal Welaýaty, C Turkmenistan 39°31'N 57°13'E
96 K10 **Kirriemuir** E Scotland, United Kingdom 56°38'N 03°01'W
125 S13 **Kirs** Kirovskaya Oblast', NW Russian Federation 59°22'N 52°20'E
127 N7 **Kirsanov** Tambovskaya Oblast', W Russian Federation 52°40'N 42°48'E
136 J14 **Kırşehir** anc. Justinianopolis. Kırşehir, C Turkey 39°09'N 34°08'E
136 I13 **Kırşehir** ◈ province C Turkey
149 P4 **Kirthar Range** ⛰ S Pakistan
37 P9 **Kirtland** New Mexico, SW USA 36°43'N 108°21'W
92 J11 **Kiruna** Lapp. Giron. Norrbotten, N Sweden 67°50'N 20°16'E
79 M18 **Kirundu** Orientale, NE Dem. Rep. Congo 0°45'S 25°28'E
Kirun/Kirun' see Chilung
26 L3 **Kirwin Reservoir** ⊠ Kansas, C USA
127 Q4 **Kirya** Chuvashskaya Respublika, W Russian Federation 55°04'N 46°50'E
138 G8 **Kiryat Shmona** prev. Qiryat Shemona. Northern, N Israel 33°13'N 35°35'E
95 M18 **Kisa** Östergötland, S Sweden 58°N 15°39'E
165 P9 **Kisakata** Akita, Honshū, C Japan 39°12'N 139°55'E
Kisalföld see Little Alföld
79 L18 **Kisangani** prev. Stanleyville. Orientale, NE Dem. Rep. Congo 0°30'N 25°14'E
39 N12 **Kisaralik River** ≈ Alaska, USA
165 O14 **Kisarazu** Chiba, Honshū, S Japan 35°23'N 139°57'E
111 I22 **Kisbér** Komárom-Esztergom, NW Hungary 47°30'N 18°00'E
11 V17 **Kisbey** Saskatchewan, S Canada 49°41'N 102°39'W
122 J13 **Kiselevsk** Kemerovskaya Oblast', S Russian Federation 54°00'N 86°38'E
153 R13 **Kishanganj** Bihār, NE India 26°06'N 87°57'E
152 G12 **Kishangarh** Rājasthān, N India 26°33'N 74°52'E

◆ Country
● Country Capital
◇ Dependent Territory
○ Dependent Territory Capital
◈ Administrative Regions
✈ International Airport
▲ Mountain
⛰ Mountain Range
△ Volcano
≈ River
◎ Lake
⊠ Reservoir

KISHEGYES – KOMI-PERMYATSKIY AVTONOMNYY OKRUG

Kishegyes *see* Mali Iđoš
77 *S15* **Kishi** Oyo, W Nigeria *09°01′N 03°53′E*
Kishinev *see* Chişinău
Kishiözen *see* Malyy Uzen'
164 *I14* **Kishiwada** *var.* Kisiwada. Ōsaka, Honshū, SW Japan *34°28′N 135°22′E*
143 *P14* **Kīsh, Jazīreh-ye** *var.* Qey. *island* S Iran
145 *R7* **Kishkenekol'** *prev.* Kzyltu, *Kaz.* Qyzyltū. Kokshetau, N Kazakhstan *53°39′N 72°22′E*
138 *G9* **Kishon, Nahal** *prev.* Nahal Qishon. ≈ N Israel
152 *I6* **Kishtwār** Jammu and Kashmir, NW India *33°20′N 75°49′E*
81 *H19* **Kisii** Nyanza, SW Kenya *0°40′S 34°47′E*
81 *J23* **Kisiju** Pwani, E Tanzania *07°25′S 39°20′E*
Kisiwada *see* Kishiwada
Kisjenő *see* Chişineu-Criş
38 *E17* **Kiska Island** *island* Aleutian Islands, Alaska, USA
Kiskapus *see* Copşa Mică
111 *M22* **Kiskörei-víztároló** ⊠ E Hungary
Kis-Küküllo *see* Târnava Mică
111 *L24* **Kiskunfélegyháza** *var.* Félegyháza. Bács-Kiskun, C Hungary *46°42′N 19°52′E*
111 *K25* **Kiskunhalas** *var.* Halas. Bács-Kiskun, S Hungary *46°26′N 19°29′E*
111 *K24* **Kiskunmajsa** Bács-Kiskun, S Hungary *46°30′N 19°46′E*
127 *N15* **Kislovodsk** Stavropol'skiy Kray, SW Russian Federation *43°55′N 42°45′E*
81 *L18* **Kismaayo** *var.* Chisimayu, Kismayu, *It.* Chisimaio. Jubbada Hoose, S Somalia *0°05′S 42°35′E*
Kismayu *see* Kismaayo
164 *M13* **Kiso-sanmyaku** ▲▲ Honshū, S Japan
115 *H24* **Kíssamos** *prev.* Kastélli. Kríti, Greece, E Mediterranean Sea *35°30′N 23°39′E*
Kisseraing *see* Kanmaw Kyun
76 *K14* **Kissidougou** Guinée-Forestière, S Guinea *09°15′N 10°08′W*
23 *X12* **Kissimmee** Florida, SE USA *28°17′N 81°24′W*
23 *X12* **Kissimmee, Lake** ◎ Florida, SE USA
23 *X13* **Kissimmee River** ≈ Florida, SE USA
11 *V13* **Kississing Lake** ◎ Manitoba, C Canada
111 *L24* **Kistelek** Csongrád, SE Hungary *46°27′N 19°58′E*
Kistna *see* Krishna
111 *M23* **Kisújszállás** Jász-Nagykun-Szolnok, E Hungary *47°14′N 20°45′E*
164 *G12* **Kisuki** *var.* Unnan. Shimane, Honshū, SW Japan *35°25′N 133°15′E*
81 *H18* **Kisumu** *prev.* Port Florence. Nyanza, W Kenya *0°02′N 34°42′E*
Kisutzaneustadtl *see* Kysucké Nové Mesto
111 *O20* **Kisvárda** *Ger.* Kleinwardein. Szabolcs-Szatmár-Bereg, E Hungary *48°13′N 22°03′E*
81 *J24* **Kiswere** Lindi, SE Tanzania *09°24′S 39°37′E*
Kiszucaújhely *see* Kysucké Nové Mesto
76 *K12* **Kita** Kayes, W Mali *13°00′N 09°28′W*
197 *N14* **Kitaa** ◈ *province* W Greenland
Kita-Akita *see* Takanosu
Kitab *see* Kitob
165 *Q4* **Kitahiyama** Hokkaidō, NE Japan *42°25′N 139°55′E*
165 *P12* **Kita-Ibaraki** Ibaraki, Honshū, S Japan *36°46′N 140°45′E*
165 *X16* **Kita-Iō-jima** *Eng.* San Alessandro. *island* SE Japan
165 *Q9* **Kitakami** Iwate, Honshū, C Japan *39°18′N 141°05′E*
165 *P11* **Kitakata** Fukushima, Honshū, C Japan *37°38′N 139°52′E*
164 *D13* **Kitakyūshū** *var.* Kitakyûsyû. Fukuoka, Kyūshū, SW Japan *33°51′N 130°49′E*
Kitakyûsyû *see* Kitakyūshū
81 *H18* **Kitale** Rift Valley, W Kenya *01°01′N 35°01′E*
165 *U3* **Kitami** Hokkaidō, NE Japan *43°52′N 143°51′E*
165 *T2* **Kitami-sanchi** ▲▲ Hokkaidō, NE Japan
37 *W5* **Kit Carson** Colorado, C USA *38°45′N 102°47′W*
180 *M12* **Kitchener** Western Australia *31°03′S 124°00′E*
14 *F16* **Kitchener** Ontario, S Canada *43°28′N 80°27′W*
93 *O17* **Kitee** Itä-Suomi, SE Finland *62°06′N 30°09′E*
81 *G16* **Kitgum** N Uganda *03°17′N 32°54′E*
Kithareng *see* Kanmaw Kyun
Kíthira *see* Kýthira
Kíthnos *see* Kýthnos
10 *J13* **Kitimat** British Columbia, SW Canada *54°05′N 128°38′W*
92 *L11* **Kitinen** ≈ N Finland
147 *N12* **Kitob** *Rus.* Kitab. Qashqadaryo Viloyati, S Uzbekistan *39°06′N 66°47′E*
116 *K7* **Kitsman'** *Ger.* Kotzman, *Rom.* Cozmeni, *Rus.* Kitsman. Chernivets'ka Oblast', W Ukraine *48°30′N 25°50′E*
164 *E14* **Kitsuki** *var.* Kituki. Ōita, Kyūshū, SW Japan *33°24′N 131°36′E*
18 *C14* **Kittanning** Pennsylvania, NE USA *40°48′N 79°28′W*
19 *P10* **Kittery** Maine, NE USA *43°05′N 70°44′W*
92 *L11* **Kittilä** Lappi, N Finland *67°39′N 24°53′E*
109 *Z4* **Kittsee** Burgenland, E Austria *48°06′N 17°03′E*
81 *J19* **Kitui** Eastern, S Kenya *01°25′S 38°00′E*
Kituki *see* Kitsuki
81 *G22* **Kitunda** Tabora, C Tanzania *06°47′S 33°13′E*
10 *K13* **Kitwanga** British Columbia, SW Canada *55°07′N 128°03′W*
82 *J13* **Kitwe** *var.* Kitwe-Nkana. Copperbelt, C Zambia *12°48′S 28°13′E*
Kitwe-Nkana *see* Kitwe
109 *O7* **Kitzbühel** Tirol, W Austria *47°27′N 12°23′E*
109 *O7* **Kitzbüheler Alpen** ▲▲ W Austria
101 *J19* **Kitzingen** Bayern, SE Germany *49°45′N 10°11′E*
153 *Q14* **Kiul** Bihār, NE India *25°10′N 86°06′E*
186 *A7* **Kiunga** Western, SW Papua New Guinea *06°10′S 141°15′E*
93 *M16* **Kiuruvesi** Itä-Suomi, C Finland *63°38′N 26°40′E*
38 *M7* **Kivalina** Alaska, USA *67°44′N 164°32′W*
92 *L13* **Kivalo** *ridge* C Finland
116 *J3* **Kivertsi** *Pol.* Kiwerce, *Rus.* Kivertsy. Volyns'ka Oblast', NW Ukraine *50°50′N 25°31′E*
Kivertsy *see* Kivertsi
93 *L16* **Kivijärvi** Länsi-Suomi, C Finland *63°09′N 25°04′E*
95 *L23* **Kivik** Skåne, S Sweden *55°40′N 14°15′E*
118 *J3* **Kiviõli** Ida-Virumaa, NE Estonia *59°20′N 27°00′E*
Kivu, Lac *see* Kivu, Lake
67 *U10* **Kivu, Lake** *Fr.* Lac Kivu. ◎ Rwanda/Dem. Rep. Congo
186 *C9* **Kiwai Island** *island* SW Papua New Guinea
39 *N8* **Kiwalik** Alaska, USA *66°01′N 161°50′W*
Kiwerce *see* Kivertsi
Kiyev *see* Kyyiv
145 *R10* **Kiyevka** Karaganda, C Kazakhstan *50°15′N 71°33′E*
Kiyevskaya Oblast' *see* Kyyivs'ka Oblast'
Kiyevskoye Vodokhranilishche *see* Kyyivs'ke Vodoskhovyshche
136 *D10* **Kıyıköy** Kırklareli, NW Turkey *41°37′N 28°07′E*
145 *O9* **Kiyma** Akmola, C Kazakhstan *51°37′N 67°31′E*
125 *V13* **Kizel** Permskaya Oblast', NW Russian Federation *58°59′N 57°37′E*
125 *O12* **Kizema** *var.* Kizëma. Arkhangel'skaya Oblast', NW Russian Federation *61°06′N 44°51′E*
Kizëma *see* Kizema
Kizilagach *see* Elkhovo
136 *H12* **Kızılcahamam** Ankara, N Turkey *40°28′N 32°37′E*
136 *J10* **Kızıl Irmak** ≈ C Turkey
Kizil Kum *see* Kyzyl Kum
137 *P16* **Kızıltepe** Mardin, SE Turkey *37°12′N 40°36′E*
Ki Zil Uzen *see* Qezel Owzan, Rūd-e
127 *Q16* **Kizilyurt** Respublika Dagestan, SW Russian Federation *43°13′N 46°54′E*
127 *Q15* **Kizlyar** Respublika Dagestan, SW Russian Federation *43°51′N 46°39′E*
127 *S3* **Kizner** Udmurtskaya Respublika, NW Russian Federation *56°19′N 51°37′E*
Kizyl-Arvat *see* Serdar
Kizyl-Atrek *see* Etrek
Kizyl-Kaya *see* Gyzylgaýa
Kizyl-Su *see* Gyzylsuw
95 *H16* **Kjerkøy** *island* S Norway
Kjølen *see* Kölen
92 *L7* **Kjøllefjord** Finnmark, N Norway *70°55′N 27°19′E*
92 *H11* **Kjøpsvik** Nordland, C Norway *68°06′N 16°21′E*
169 *N12* **Klabat, Teluk** *bay* Pulau Bangka, W Indonesia
112 *I12* **Kladanj** ◈ Fedederacijia Bosna I Hercegovina, E Bosnia and Herzegovina
171 *X16* **Kladar** Papua, E Indonesia *08°14′S 137°46′E*
111 *C16* **Kladno** Středočeský, NW Czech Republic *50°10′N 14°05′E*
112 *P11* **Kladovo** Serbia, E Serbia *44°37′N 22°36′E*
167 *P12* **Klaeng** Rayong, S Thailand *12°48′N 101°41′E*
109 *T9* **Klagenfurt** *Slvn.* Celovec. Kärnten, S Austria *46°38′N 14°20′E*
118 *B11* **Klaipėda** *Ger.* Memel. Klaipeda, NW Lithuania *55°42′N 21°09′E*
118 *C11* **Klaipėda** ◈ *province* W Lithuania
Klaksvig *see* Klaksvík
95 *B18* **Klaksvík** *Dan.* Klaksvig. Faeroe Islands *62°13′N 06°34′W*
34 *L2* **Klamath** California, W USA *41°31′N 124°02′W*
32 *H16* **Klamath Falls** Oregon, NW USA *42°14′N 121°47′W*
34 *M1* **Klamath Mountains** ▲▲ California/Oregon, W USA
34 *L2* **Klamath River** ≈ California/Oregon, W USA
168 *K9* **Klang** *var.* Kelang; *prev.* Port Swettenham. Selangor, Peninsular Malaysia *03°02′N 101°27′E*
94 *J13* **Klarälven** ≈ Norway/Sweden
111 *B15* **Klášterec nad Ohří** *Ger.* Klösterle an der Eger. Ústecky Kraj, NW Czech Republic *50°24′N 13°10′E*
111 *B18* **Klatovy** *Ger.* Klattau. Plzeňský Kraj, W Czech Republic *49°24′N 13°16′E*
Klattau *see* Klatovy
Klausenburg *see* Cluj-Napoca
39 *Y14* **Klawock** Prince of Wales Island, Alaska, USA *55°33′N 133°06′W*
98 *P8* **Klazienaveen** Drenthe, NE Netherlands *52°43′N 07°E*
Kleck *see* Klyetsk
110 *H11* **Kłecko** Weilkopolskie, C Poland *52°37′N 17°27′E*
110 *I11* **Kleczew** Wielkopolskie, C Poland *52°22′N 18°12′E*
10 *L15* **Kleena Kleene** British Columbia, SW Canada *51°55′N 124°54′W*
83 *D20* **Klein Aub** Hardap, C Namibia *23°48′S 16°39′E*
Kleine Donau *see* Mosoni-Duna
101 *O14* **Kleine Elster** ≈ E Germany
Kleine Kokel *see* Târnava Mică
99 *I16* **Kleine Nete** ≈ N Belgium
Kleines Ungarisches Tiefland *see* Little Alföld
83 *E22* **Klein Karas** Karas, S Namibia *27°36′S 18°05′E*
Kleinkopisch *see* Copşa Mică
Klein-Marien *see* Väike-Maarja
Kleinschlatten *see* Zlatna
83 *D23* **Kleinsee** Northern Cape, W South Africa *29°43′S 17°03′E*
Kleinwardein *see* Kisvárda
115 *C16* **Kleisoúra** Ípeiros, W Greece *39°21′N 20°52′E*
95 *C17* **Klepp** Rogaland, S Norway *58°46′N 05°39′E*
83 *I22* **Klerksdorp** North-West, N South Africa *26°52′S 26°39′E*
126 *I5* **Kletnya** Bryanskaya Oblast', W Russian Federation *53°25′N 32°58′E*
Kletsk *see* Klyetsk
101 *D14* **Kleve** *Eng.* Cleves, *Fr.* Clèves; *prev.* Cleve. Nordrhein-Westfalen, W Germany *51°47′N 06°11′E*
113 *J16* **Kličevo** C Montenegro *42°45′N 18°58′E*
119 *M16* **Klichaw** *Rus.* Klichev. Mahilyowskaya Voblasts', E Belarus *53°29′N 29°21′E*
Klichev *see* Klichaw
119 *Q16* **Klimavichy** *Rus.* Klimovichi. Mahilyowskaya Voblasts', E Belarus *53°37′N 31°58′E*
114 *M7* **Kliment** Shumen, NE Bulgaria *43°37′N 27°00′E*
Klimovichi *see* Klimavichy
93 *G14* **Klimpfjäll** Västerbotten, N Sweden *65°05′N 14°50′E*
126 *K3* **Klin** Moskovskaya Oblast', W Russian Federation *56°19′N 36°45′E*
Klina *see* Klinë
113 *M16* **Klinë** *Serb.* Klina. W Kosovo *42°38′N 20°35′E*
111 *B15* **Klínovec** *Ger.* Keilberg. ▲ NW Czech Republic *50°23′N 12°57′E*
95 *P19* **Klintehamn** Gotland, SE Sweden *57°22′N 18°15′E*
127 *R8* **Klintsovka** Saratovskaya Oblast', W Russian Federation *51°42′N 49°17′E*
126 *H6* **Klintsy** Bryanskaya Oblast', W Russian Federation *52°46′N 32°21′E*
95 *K22* **Klippan** Skåne, S Sweden *56°08′N 13°10′E*
92 *G13* **Klippen** Västerbotten, N Sweden *65°50′N 15°07′E*
121 *P2* **Klírou** W Cyprus *35°01′N 33°11′E*
114 *I9* **Klisura** Plovdiv, C Bulgaria *42°40′N 24°28′E*
95 *F20* **Klitmøller** Viborg, NW Denmark *57°01′N 08°29′E*
112 *F11* **Ključ** Federacija Bosna I Hercegovina, NW Bosnia and Herzegovina *44°32′N 16°46′E*
111 *J14* **Kłobuck** Śląskie, S Poland *50°56′N 18°55′E*
110 *J11* **Kłodawa** Wielkopolskie, C Poland *52°14′N 18°55′E*
111 *G16* **Kłodzko** *Ger.* Glatz. Dolnośląskie, SW Poland *50°27′N 16°37′E*
95 *I14* **Kløfta** Akershus, S Norway *60°04′N 11°06′E*
112 *P12* **Klokočevac** Serbia, E Serbia *44°19′N 22°11′E*
118 *G3* **Klooga** *Ger.* Lodensee. Harjumaa, NW Estonia *59°18′N 24°10′E*
99 *F15* **Kloosterzande** Zeeland, SW Netherlands *51°22′N 04°01′E*
113 *L19* **Klos** *var.* Klosi. Dibër, C Albania *41°30′N 20°07′E*
Klosi *see* Klos
Klösterle an der Eger *see* Klášterec nad Ohří
109 *X3* **Klosterneuburg** Niederösterreich, NE Austria *48°19′N 16°20′E*
108 *J9* **Klosters** Graubünden, SE Switzerland *46°54′N 09°52′E*
108 *G7* **Kloten** Zürich, N Switzerland *47°27′N 08°35′E*
108 *G7* **Kloten** ✈ (Zürich) Zürich, N Switzerland *47°25′N 08°36′E*
100 *K12* **Klötze** Sachsen-Anhalt, C Germany *52°37′N 11°09′E*
12 *K3* **Klotz, Lac** ◎ Québec, NE Canada
101 *O15* **Klotzsche** ✈ (Dresden) Sachsen, E Germany *51°06′N 13°44′E*
10 *H7* **Kluane Lake** ◎ Yukon Territory, W Canada
Kluang *see* Keluang
111 *I14* **Kluczbork** *Ger.* Kreuzburg, Kreuzburg in Oberschlesien. Opolskie, S Poland *50°59′N 18°13′E*
39 *W12* **Klukwan** Alaska, USA *59°24′N 135°49′W*
Klyastitsy *see* Klyastsitsy
118 *L11* **Klyastsitsy** *Rus.* Klyastitsy. Vitsyebskaya Voblasts', N Belarus *55°53′N 28°36′E*
127 *T5* **Klyavlino** Samarskaya Oblast', W Russian Federation *54°21′N 52°12′E*
84 *K9* **Klyaz'in** ≈ W Russian Federation
127 *N3* **Klyaz'ma** ≈ W Russian Federation
119 *J17* **Klyetsk** *Pol.* Kleck, *Rus.* Kletsk. Minskaya Voblasts', SW Belarus *53°04′N 26°38′E*
147 *S8* **Klyuchevka** Talasskaya Oblast', NW Kyrgyzstan *42°34′N 71°45′E*
123 *V10* **Klyuchevskaya Sopka, Vulkan** ✶ E Russian Federation *56°03′N 160°38′E*
95 *D17* **Knaben** Vest-Agder, S Norway *58°46′N 07°04′E*
95 *K21* **Knäred** Halland, S Sweden *56°30′N 13°21′E*
97 *M16* **Knaresborough** N England, United Kingdom *54°01′N 01°35′W*
114 *H8* **Knezha** Vratsa, NW Bulgaria *43°29′N 24°04′E*
25 *O9* **Knickerbocker** Texas, SW USA *31°18′N 100°35′W*
28 *K5* **Knife River** ≈ North Dakota, N USA
10 *K16* **Knight Inlet** *inlet* British Columbia, W Canada
39 *S12* **Knight Island** *island* Alaska, USA
97 *K20* **Knighton** E Wales, United Kingdom *52°20′N 03°01′W*
35 *O7* **Knights Landing** California, W USA *38°47′N 121°43′W*
112 *E13* **Knin** Šibenik-Knin, S Croatia *44°03′N 16°12′E*
25 *Q12* **Knippal** Texas, SW USA
109 *U7* **Knittelfeld** Steiermark, C Austria *47°14′N 14°50′E*
95 *O15* **Knivsta** Uppsala, C Sweden *59°43′N 17°49′E*
113 *P14* **Knjaževac** Serbia, E Serbia *43°34′N 22°16′E*
27 *S4* **Knob Noster** Missouri, C USA *38°47′N 93°33′W*
99 *D15* **Knokke-Heist** West-Vlaanderen, NW Belgium *51°21′N 03°19′E*
95 *H20* **Knøsen** *hill* N Denmark
Knosós *see* Knossos
115 *J25* **Knossos** *Gk.* Knosós. *prehistoric site* Kríti, Greece, E Mediterranean Sea
25 *N7* **Knott** Texas, SW USA *32°21′N 101°35′W*
194 *K5* **Knowles, Cape** *headland* Antarctica *71°45′S 60°20′W*
31 *O11* **Knox** Indiana, N USA *41°17′N 86°37′W*
29 *O3* **Knox** North Dakota, N USA *48°19′N 99°43′W*
18 *C13* **Knox** Pennsylvania, NE USA *41°13′N 79°33′W*
189 *X8* **Knox Atoll** *var.* Nadikdik, Narikrik. *atoll* Ratak Chain, SE Marshall Islands
10 *H13* **Knox, Cape** *headland* Graham Island, British Columbia, SW Canada *54°05′N 133°02′W*
25 *P5* **Knox City** Texas, SW USA *33°25′N 99°49′W*
195 *Y11* **Knox Coast** *physical region* Antarctica
31 *T12* **Knox Lake** ⊠ Ohio, N USA
23 *T5* **Knoxville** Georgia, SE USA *32°44′N 83°58′W*
30 *K12* **Knoxville** Illinois, N USA *40°54′N 90°16′W*
29 *W15* **Knoxville** Iowa, C USA *41°19′N 93°06′W*
21 *N9* **Knoxville** Tennessee, S USA *35°58′N 83°55′W*
197 *P11* **Knud Rasmussen Land** *physical region* N Greenland
Knüll *see* Knüllgebirge
101 *I16* **Knüllgebirge** *var.* Knüll. ▲▲ C Germany
124 *I5* **Knyazhegubskoye Vodokhranilishche** ◎ NW Russian Federation
Knyazhevo *see* Sredishte
Knyazhitsy *see* Knyazhytsy
119 *O15* **Knyazhytsy** *Rus.* Knyazhitsy. Mahilyowskaya Voblasts', E Belarus *54°10′N 30°28′E*
83 *G26* **Knysna** Western Cape, SW South Africa *34°03′S 23°03′E*
Koartac *see* Quaqtaq
81 *J23* **Koani** Zanzibar South, E Tanzania *06°08′S 39°18′E*
169 *N13* **Koba** Pulau Bangka, W Indonesia *02°30′S 106°26′E*
164 *D16* **Kobayashi** *var.* Kobayasi. Miyazaki, Kyūshū, SW Japan *32°00′N 130°58′E*
Kobayasi *see* Kobayashi
Kobdo *see* Hovd
164 *I13* **Kōbe** Hyōgo, Honshū, SW Japan *34°40′N 135°10′E*
Kobelyaki *see* Kobelyaky
117 *T6* **Kobelyaky** *Rus.* Kobelyaki. Poltavs'ka Oblast', NE Ukraine *49°10′N 34°13′E*
95 *J22* **København** *Eng.* Copenhagen; *anc.* Hafnia. ● (Denmark) Sjælland, København, E Denmark *55°43′N 12°34′E*
95 *J23* **København** *off.* Københavns Amt. ◈ *county* E Denmark
Københavns Amt *see* København
76 *K10* **Kobenni** Hodh el Gharbi, S Mauritania *15°58′N 09°24′W*
171 *T13* **Kobi** Pulau Seram, E Indonesia *02°56′S 129°53′E*
101 *F17* **Koblenz** *prev.* Coblenz, *Fr.* Coblence; *anc.* Confluentes. Rheinland-Pfalz, W Germany *50°21′N 07°36′E*
108 *F6* **Koblenz** Aargau, N Switzerland *47°34′N 08°16′E*
Kobrin *see* Kobryn
171 *V15* **Kobroor, Pulau** *island* Kepulauan Aru, E Indonesia
119 *G19* **Kobryn** *Rus.* Kobrin. Brestskaya Voblasts', SW Belarus *52°13′N 24°21′E*
39 *O7* **Kobuk** Alaska, USA *66°54′N 156°52′W*
39 *O7* **Kobuk River** ≈ Alaska, USA
137 *Q10* **K'obulet'i** W Georgia *41°47′N 41°47′E*
123 *P10* **Kobyay** Respublika Sakha (Yakutiya), NE Russian Federation *63°36′N 126°33′E*
136 *E11* **Kocaeli** ◈ *province* NW Turkey
113 *P18* **Kočani** NE FYR Macedonia *41°55′N 22°25′E*
112 *K12* **Koceljevo** Serbia, W Serbia *44°28′N 19°49′E*
109 *U12* **Kočevje** *Ger.* Gottschee. S Slovenia *45°41′N 14°48′E*
153 *T12* **Koch Bihār** West Bengal, NE India *26°19′N 89°26′E*
Kochchi *see* Cochin/Kochi
122 *M9* **Kochechum** ≈ N Russian Federation
101 *I20* **Kocher** ≈ SW Germany
125 *T13* **Kochevo** Komi-Permyatskiy Avtonomnyy Okrug, NW Russian Federation *59°37′N 54°16′E*
155 *G22* **Kochi** *var.* Cochin, Kochchi. Kerala, SW India *09°56′N 76°15′E* **see also** Cochin
164 *G14* **Kōchi** *var.* Kôti. Kōchi, Shikoku, SW Japan *33°31′N 133°30′E*
164 *G14* **Kōchi** *off.* Kōchi-ken, *var.* Kôti. ◈ *prefecture* Shikoku, SW Japan
Kōchi-ken *see* Kōchi
Kochiu *see* Gejiu
Kochkor *see* Kochkorka
147 *V8* **Kochkorka** *Kir.* Kochkor. Narynskaya Oblast', C Kyrgyzstan *42°09′N 75°42′E*
125 *V5* **Kochmes** Respublika Komi, NW Russian Federation *66°10′N 60°46′E*
127 *P15* **Kochubey** Respublika Dagestan, SW Russian Federation *44°25′N 46°33′E*
115 *I17* **Kochýlas** ▲ Skńyros, Vóreies Sporádes, Greece, Aegean Sea *38°50′N 24°35′E*
110 *O13* **Kock** Lubelskie, E Poland *51°39′N 22°26′E*
81 *J19* **Kodacho** *spring/well* S Kenya *01°52′S 39°22′E*
153 *Q14* **Kodarma** Jharkhand, N India *24°26′N 85°31′E*
155 *K24* **Koddiyar Bay** *bay* NE Sri Lanka
39 *Q14* **Kodiak** Kodiak Island, Alaska, USA *57°47′N 152°24′W*
39 *Q14* **Kodiak Island** *island* Alaska, USA
154 *B12* **Kodīnār** Gujarāt, W India *20°44′N 70°46′E*
124 *M9* **Kodino** Arkhangel'skaya Oblast', NW Russian Federation *63°36′N 39°54′E*
122 *M12* **Kodinsk** Krasnoyarskiy Kray, C Russian Federation *58°37′N 99°18′E*
80 *F12* **Kodok** Upper Nile, SE Sudan *09°51′N 32°07′E*
117 *N8* **Kodyma** Odes'ka Oblast', SW Ukraine *48°05′N 29°09′E*
Koedoes *see* Kudus
99 *B17* **Koekelare** West-Vlaanderen, W Belgium *51°07′N 02°58′E*
Koeln *see* Köln
Koepang *see* Kupang
Ko-erh-mu *see* Golmud
99 *J17* **Koersel** Limburg, NE Belgium *51°04′N 05°17′E*
83 *E21* **Koës** Karas, SE Namibia *25°59′S 19°08′E*
Koetai *see* Mahakam, Sungai
Koetaradja *see* Bandaaceh
36 *I14* **Kofa Mountains** ▲▲ Arizona, SW USA
171 *Y15* **Kofarau** Papua, E Indonesia *07°29′S 140°28′E*
147 *P13* **Kofarnihon** *Rus.* Kofarnikhon; *prev.* Ordzhonikidzeabad, *Taj.* Orjonikidzeobod, Yangi-Bazar. W Tajikistan *38°32′N 68°56′E*
147 *P14* **Kofarnihon** *Rus.* Kafirnigan. ≈ SW Tajikistan
Kofarnikhon *see* Kofarnihon
114 *M11* **Kofçaz** Kırklareli, NW Turkey *41°58′N 27°12′E*
115 *J25* **Kófinas** ▲ Kríti, Greece, E Mediterranean Sea *34°58′N 25°03′E*
121 *P3* **Kofínou** *var.* Kophinou. S Cyprus *34°49′N 33°24′E*
109 *V8* **Köflach** Steiermark, SE Austria *47°04′N 15°04′E*
77 *Q17* **Koforidua** SE Ghana *06°01′N 00°12′W*
164 *H12* **Kōfu** Tottori, Honshū, SW Japan *35°16′N 133°31′E*
164 *M13* **Kōfu** *var.* Kôhu. Yamanashi, Honshū, S Japan *35°41′N 138°33′E*
81 *F22* **Koga** Tabora, C Tanzania *06°08′S 32°20′E*
Kogălniceanu *see* Mihail Kogălniceanu
13 *P6* **Kogaluk** ≈ Newfoundland and Labrador, E Canada
12 *J4* **Kogaluk** ≈ Québec, NE Canada
122 *I10* **Kogalym** Khanty-Mansiyskiy Avtonomnyy Okrug-Yugra, C Russian Federation *62°13′N 74°34′E*
95 *J23* **Køge** Roskilde, E Denmark *55°28′N 12°12′E*
95 *J23* **Køge Bugt** *bay* E Denmark
77 *U16* **Kogi** ◈ *state* C Nigeria
146 *L11* **Kogon** *Rus.* Kagan. Buxoro Viloyati, C Uzbekistan *39°47′N 64°29′E*
163 *Y17* **Kōgŭm-do** *island* S South Korea
Kőhalom *see* Rupea
149 *T6* **Kohāt** North-West Frontier Province, NW Pakistan *33°37′N 71°30′E*
142 *L10* **Kohgīlūyeh va Būyer Aḩmad** *off.* Ostān-e Kohkīlūyeh va Būyer Aḩmadī, *var.* Boyer Ahmadī va Kohkīlūyeh. ◈ *province* SW Iran
118 *G4* **Kohila** *Ger.* Koil. Raplamaa, NW Estonia *59°09′N 24°45′E*
153 *X13* **Kohīma** *state capital* Nāgāland, E India *25°40′N 94°08′E*
Koh I Noh *see* Büyükağrı Dağı
Kohkīlūyeh va Būyer Aḩmadī, Ostān-e *see* Kohgīlūyeh va Būyer Aḩmad
149 *R10* **Kohlu** Baluchistān, SW Pakistan *29°54′N 69°15′E*
Kohsān *see* Kūhestān
118 *J3* **Kohtla-Järve** Ida-Virumaa, NE Estonia *59°22′N 27°21′E*
Kôhu *see* Kōfu
Kohyl'nyk *see* Cogîlnic
165 *N11* **Koide** Niigata, Honshū, C Japan *37°13′N 138°58′E*
10 *G7* **Koidern** Yukon Territory, W Canada *61°55′N 140°22′W*
76 *J15* **Koidu** E Sierra Leone *08°40′N 11°01′W*
118 *I4* **Koigi** Järvamaa, C Estonia *58°51′N 25°45′E*
Koil *see* Kohila
172 *H13* **Koimbani** Grande Comore, NW Comoros *11°37′S 43°23′E*
139 *T3* **Koi Sanjaq** *var.* Koysanjaq, Kūysanjaq. Arbīl, N Iraq *36°05′N 44°38′E*
93 *O16* **Koitere** ◎ E Finland
Koivisto *see* Primorsk
163 *Z16* **Kŏje-do** *Jap.* Kyōsai-tō. *island* S South Korea
80 *J13* **K'ok'a Hāyk'** ◎ C Ethiopia
Kokand *see* Qo'qon
182 *F6* **Kokatha** South Australia *31°17′S 135°16′E*
146 *M10* **Ko'kcha** *Rus.* Kokcha. Buxoro Viloyati, C Uzbekistan *40°30′N 64°58′E*
Kokcha *see* Ko'kcha
Kokchetav *see* Kokshetau
93 *K18* **Kokemäenjoki** ≈ SW Finland
171 *W14* **Kokenau** *var.* Kokonau. Papua, E Indonesia *04°38′S 136°24′E*
83 *E22* **Kokerboom** Karas, SE Namibia *28°11′S 19°25′E*
119 *N14* **Kokhanava** *Rus.* Kokhanovo. Vitsyebskaya Voblasts', NE Belarus *54°28′N 29°59′E*
Kokhanovichi *see* Kakhanavichy
Kokhanovo *see* Kokhanava
Kök-Janggak *see* Kok-Yangak
93 *K16* **Kokkola** *Swe.* Karleby; *prev. Swe.* Gamlakarleby. Länsi-Suomi, W Finland *63°50′N 23°10′E*
158 *L3* **Kok Kuduk** *spring/well* N China *46°03′N 87°34′E*
118 *H9* **Koknese** Aizkraukle, C Latvia *56°38′N 25°27′E*
77 *T13* **Koko** Kebbi, W Nigeria *11°25′N 04°33′E*
186 *E9* **Kokoda** Northern, S Papua New Guinea *08°52′S 147°44′E*
76 *K12* **Kokofata** Kayes, W Mali *12°48′N 09°56′W*
39 *N6* **Kokolik River** ≈ Alaska, USA
31 *O13* **Kokomo** Indiana, N USA *40°29′N 86°07′W*
Kokonau *see* Kokenau
Koko Nor *see* Qinghai Hu, China
Koko Nor *see* Qinghai, China
186 *H6* **Kokopo** *var.* Kopopo; *prev.* Herbertshöhe. New Britain, E Papua New Guinea *04°18′S 152°17′E*
145 *X10* **Kokpekti** *Kaz.* Kökpekti. Vostochnyy Kazakhstan, E Kazakhstan *48°47′N 82°28′E*
145 *X11* **Kokpekti** ≈ E Kazakhstan
Kökpekti *see* Kokpekti
153 *T12* **Kokrajhar** Assam, NE India *26°24′N 90°16′E*
39 *P9* **Kokrines** Alaska, USA *64°58′N 154°42′W*
39 *P9* **Kokrines Hills** ▲▲ Alaska, USA
145 *P17* **Koksaray** Yuzhnyy Kazakhstan, S Kazakhstan *42°34′N 68°06′E*
147 *X9* **Kokshaal-Tau** *Rus.* Khrebet Kakshaal-Too. ▲▲ China/Kyrgyzstan
145 *P7* **Kokshetau** *Kaz.* Kökshetaū; *prev.* Kokchetav. Kokshetau, N Kazakhstan *53°18′N 69°25′E*
Kökshetaū *see* Kokshetau
99 *A17* **Koksijde** West-Vlaanderen, W Belgium *51°07′N 02°40′E*
12 *M5* **Koksoak** ≈ Québec, E Canada
83 *K24* **Kokstad** KwaZulu/Natal, E South Africa *30°23′S 29°23′E*
145 *V14* **Koksu** *Kaz.* Rūdnīchnyy. Almaty, SE Kazakhstan *44°39′N 78°57′E*
145 *W15* **Koktal** *Kaz.* Köktal. Almaty, SE Kazakhstan *44°05′N 79°44′E*
145 *Q12* **Koktas** ≈ C Kazakhstan
Kök-Tash *see* Këk-Tash
Koktokay *see* Fuyun
147 *T9* **Kok-Yangak** *Kir.* Kök-Janggak. Dzhalal-Abadskaya Oblast', W Kyrgyzstan *41°02′N 73°11′E*
158 *F9* **Kokyar** Xinjiang Uygur Zizhiqu, W China *37°24′N 77°15′E*
124 *J3* **Kola** Murmanskaya Oblast', NW Russian Federation *68°52′N 33°03′E*
149 *O13* **Kolāchi** *var.* Kulachi. ≈ SW Pakistan
76 *J15* **Kolahun** N Liberia *08°24′N 10°02′W*
171 *O14* **Kolaka** Sulawesi, C Indonesia *04°04′S 121°38′E*
K'o-la-ma-i *see* Karamay
Kola Peninsula *see* Kol'skiy Poluostrov
155 *H19* **Kolār** Karnātaka, E India *13°10′N 78°10′E*
155 *H19* **Kolār Gold Fields** Karnātaka, E India *12°56′N 78°16′E*
92 *K11* **Kolari** Lappi, NW Finland *67°20′N 23°51′E*
111 *I21* **Kolárovo** *Ger.* Gutta; *prev.* Guta, *Hung.* Gúta. Nitriansky Kraj, SW Slovakia *47°54′N 18°01′E*
113 *K16* **Kolašin** E Montenegro *42°49′N 19°32′E*
152 *F11* **Kolāyat** Rājasthān, NW India *27°56′N 73°02′E*
95 *N15* **Kolbäck** Västmanland, C Sweden *59°33′N 16°15′E*
Kolbcha *see* Kowbcha
197 *Q15* **Kolbeinsey Ridge** *undersea feature* Denmark Strait/Norwegian Sea *69°00′N 17°30′W*
Kolberg *see* Kołobrzeg
95 *H15* **Kolbotn** Akershus, S Norway *62°15′N 10°24′E*
111 *N16* **Kolbuszowa** Podkarpackie, SE Poland *50°12′N 22°07′E*
126 *L3* **Kol'chugino** Vladimirskaya Oblast', W Russian Federation *56°19′N 39°24′E*
76 *H12* **Kolda** S Senegal *12°58′N 14°58′W*
95 *G23* **Kolding** Vejle, C Denmark *55°29′N 09°30′E*
79 *K20* **Kole** Kasai-Oriental, SW Dem. Rep. Congo *03°30′S 22°28′E*
79 *M17* **Kole** Orientale, N Dem. Rep. Congo *02°08′N 25°25′E*
Kōle *see* Kili Island
84 *F6* **Kölen** *Nor.* Kjølen. ▲▲ Norway/Sweden
Kolepom, Pulau *see* Yos Sudarso, Pulau
118 *H3* **Kolga Laht** *Ger.* Kolko-Wiek. *bay* N Estonia
125 *Q3* **Kolguyev, Ostrov** *island* NW Russian Federation
155 *E16* **Kolhāpur** Mahārāshtra, SW India *16°42′N 74°13′E*
151 *K21* **Kolhumadulu** *var.* Thaa Atoll. *atoll* S Maldives
93 *O16* **Koli** *var.* Kolinkylä. Itä-Suomi, E Finland *63°06′N 29°46′E*
39 *O13* **Koliganek** Alaska, USA *59°43′N 157°16′W*
111 *E16* **Kolín** *Ger.* Kolin. Střední Čechy, C Czech Republic *50°02′N 15°10′E*
Kolinkylä *see* Koli
190 *E12* **Koliu** Île Futuna, W Wallis and Futuna
118 *E7* **Kolka** Talsi, NW Latvia *57°44′N 22°34′E*
118 *E7* **Kolkasrags** *prev. Eng.* Cape Domesnes. *headland* NW Latvia *57°45′N 22°35′E*
153 *S16* **Kolkata** *prev.* Calcutta. *state capital* West Bengal, NE India *22°30′N 88°20′E*
Kolkhozabad *see* Kolkhozobod
147 *P14* **Kolkhozobod** *Rus.* Kolkhozabad; *prev.* Kaganovichabad, Tugalan. SW Tajikistan *37°33′N 68°34′E*
Kolki/Kołki *see* Kolky
Kolko-Wiek *see* Kolga Laht
116 *K3* **Kolky** *Pol.* Kołki, *Rus.* Kolki. Volyns'ka Oblast', NW Ukraine *51°05′N 25°40′E*
155 *G23* **Kollam** *var.* Quilon. Kerala, SW India *08°57′N 76°37′E* *see also* Quilon
155 *G20* **Kollegāl** Karnātaka, W India *12°08′N 77°06′E*
98 *M5* **Kollum** Friesland, N Netherlands *53°17′N 06°09′E*
Kolmar *see* Colmar
101 *E16* **Köln** *var.* Koeln, *Eng./Fr.* Cologne, *prev.* Cöln; *anc.* Colonia Agrippina, Oppidum Ubiorum. Nordrhein-Westfalen, W Germany *50°57′N 06°57′E*
110 *N9* **Kolno** Podlaskie, NE Poland *53°24′N 21°57′E*
110 *J12* **Koło** Wielkopolskie, C Poland *52°11′N 18°39′E*
38 *B8* **Kōloa** *var.* Koloa. Kaua'i, Hawaii, USA, C Pacific Ocean *21°54′N 159°28′W*
Koloa *see* Kōloa
110 *E7* **Kołobrzeg** *Ger.* Kolberg. Zachodnio-pomorskie, NW Poland *54°11′N 15°34′E*
126 *H4* **Kolodnya** Smolenskaya Oblast', W Russian Federation *54°57′N 32°22′E*
190 *E13* **Kolofau, Mont** ✶ Île Alofi, S Wallis and Futuna *14°21′S 178°02′W*
125 *O14* **Kologriv** Kostromskaya Oblast', NW Russian Federation *58°49′N 44°22′E*
76 *L12* **Kolokani** Koulikoro, W Mali *13°35′N 08°01′W*
77 *N13* **Koloko** W Burkina *11°06′N 05°18′W*
186 *K8* **Kolombangara** *var.* Kilimbangara, Nduke. *island* New Georgia Islands, NW Solomon Islands
Kolomea *see* Kolomyya
126 *L4* **Kolomna** Moskovskaya Oblast', W Russian Federation *55°03′N 38°52′E*
116 *J7* **Kolomyya** *Ger.* Kolomea. Ivano-Frankivs'ka Oblast', W Ukraine *48°31′N 25°00′E*
76 *M13* **Kolondiéba** Sikasso, SW Mali *11°04′N 06°55′W*
193 *V15* **Kolonga** Tongatapu, S Tonga *21°07′S 175°05′W*
189 *U16* **Kolonia** *var.* Colonia. Pohnpei, E Micronesia *06°57′N 158°12′E*
Kolonja *see* Kolonjë
113 *K21* **Kolonjë** *var.* Kolonja. Fier, C Albania *40°49′N 19°37′E*
Kolonjë *see* Ersekë
Kolosjoki *see* Nikel'
Kolotambu *see* Avuavu
193 *U15* **Kolovai** Tongatapu, S Tonga *21°05′S 175°20′W*
Kolozsvár *see* Cluj-Napoca
112 *C9* **Kolpa** *Ger.* Kulpa, *SCr.* Kupa. ≈ Croatia/Slovenia
122 *J11* **Kolpashevo** Tomskaya Oblast', C Russian Federation *58°21′N 82°44′E*
124 *H13* **Kolpino** Leningradskaya Oblast', NW Russian Federation *59°44′N 30°39′E*
100 *M10* **Kölpinsee** ◎ NE Germany
Kólpos Mórfu *see* Güzelyurt
146 *K8* **Ko'lquduq** *Rus.* Kulkuduk. Navoiy Viloyati, N Uzbekistan *42°36′N 63°24′E*
124 *K5* **Kol'skiy Poluostrov** *Eng.* Kola Peninsula. *peninsula* NW Russian Federation
127 *T6* **Koltubanovskiy** Orenburgskaya Oblast', W Russian Federation *53°00′N 52°00′E*
112 *L11* **Kolubara** ≈ C Serbia
Kolupchii *see* Gurkovo
110 *K13* **Koluszki** Łódźskie, C Poland *51°44′N 19°50′E*
125 *T6* **Kolva** ≈ NW Russian Federation
93 *E14* **Kolvereid** Nord-Trøndelag, W Norway *64°47′N 11°22′E*
79 *M24* **Kolwezi** Katanga, S Dem. Rep. Congo *10°43′S 25°29′E*
123 *S7* **Kolyma** ≈ NE Russian Federation
Kolyma Lowland *see* Kolymskaya Nizmennost'
Kolyma Range/Kolymskiy, Khrebet *see* Kolymskoye Nagor'ye
123 *S7* **Kolymskaya Nizmennost'** *Eng.* Kolyma Lowland. *lowlands* NE Russian Federation
123 *S7* **Kolymskoye** Respublika Sakha (Yakutiya), NE Russian Federation *68°42′N 158°46′E*
123 *U8* **Kolymskoye Nagor'ye** *var.* Khrebet Kolymskiy, *Eng.* Kolyma Range. ▲▲ E Russian Federation
123 *V5* **Kolyuchinskaya Guba** *bay* NE Russian Federation
145 *W15* **Kol'zhat** *Kaz.* Qalzhat. Almaty, SE Kazakhstan *43°29′N 80°37′E*
114 *G8* **Kom** ▲ NW Bulgaria *43°10′N 23°02′E*
80 *I13* **Koma** Oromīya, C Ethiopia *08°19′N 36°48′E*
77 *X12* **Komadugu Gana** ≈ NE Nigeria
164 *M13* **Komagane** Nagano, Honshū, S Japan *35°44′N 137°54′E*
79 *P17* **Komanda** Orientale, NE Dem. Rep. Congo *01°25′N 29°43′E*
197 *U1* **Komandorskaya Basin** *var.* Kamchatka Basin. *undersea feature* SW Bering Sea *57°00′N 168°00′E*
125 *Pp9* **Komandorskiye Ostrova** *Eng.* Commander Islands. *island group* E Russian Federation
Kománfalva *see* Comăneşti
111 *I22* **Komárno** *Ger.* Komorn, *Hung.* Komárom. Nitriansky Kraj, SW Slovakia *47°46′N 18°07′E*
111 *I22* **Komárom** Komárom-Esztergom, NW Hungary *47°43′N 18°06′E*
Komárom *see* Komárno
111 *I22* **Komárom-Esztergom** *off.* Komárom-Esztergom Megye. ◈ *county* N Hungary
Komárom-Esztergom Megye *see* Komárom-Esztergom
164 *K11* **Komatsu** *var.* Komatu. Ishikawa, Honshū, SW Japan *36°25′N 136°27′E*
Komatu *see* Komatsu
83 *D17* **Kombat** Otjozondjupa, N Namibia *19°42′S 17°45′E*
Kombissiguiri *see* Kombissiri
77 *P13* **Kombissiri** *var.* Kombissiguiri. C Burkina *12°01′N 01°27′W*
188 *E10* **Komebail Lagoon** *lagoon* N Palau
81 *F20* **Kome Island** *island* N Tanzania
Komeyo *see* Wandai
117 *P10* **Kominternivs'ke** Odes'ka Oblast', SW Ukraine *46°52′N 30°56′E*
125 *S12* **Komi-Permyatskiy Avtonomnyy Okrug** ◈ *autonomous district* Permskiy Kray, W Russian Federation

272
◆ Country ● Country Capital ◇ Dependent Territory ○ Dependent Territory Capital ◈ Administrative Regions ✈ International Airport ▲ Mountain ▲▲ Mountain Range ✶ Volcano ≈ River ◎ Lake ⊠ Reservoir

KOMI, RESPUBLIKA – KOZHIKODE

125 R8 **Komi, Respublika** ◆ *autonomous republic* NW Russian Federation
111 I25 **Komló** Baranya, SW Hungary *46°11′N 18°15′E*
Kommunarsk *see* Alchevs'k
Kommunizm, Qullai *see* Ismoili Somoní, Qullai
186 B7 **Komo** Southern Highlands, W Papua New Guinea *06°06′S 142°52′E*
170 M16 **Komodo, Pulau** *island* Nusa Tenggara, S Indonesia
77 N15 **Komoé** *var.* Komoé Fleuve. ⛐ E Ivory Coast
Komoé Fleuve *see* Komoé
75 X11 **Kom Ombo** *var.* Kôm Ombo, Kawm Umbū. SE Egypt *24°26′N 32°57′E*
79 F20 **Komono** Lékoumou, SW Congo *03°15′S 13°14′E*
171 Y16 **Komoran** Papua, E Indonesia *08°14′S 138°51′E*
171 Y16 **Komoran, Pulau** *island* E Indonesia
Komorn *see* Komárno
Komornok *see* Comorâşte
Komosolabad *see* Komsomolobod
Komotau *see* Chomutov
114 K13 **Komotiní** *var.* Gümüljina, *Turk.* Gümülcine. Anatolikí Makedonía kai Thráki, NE Greece *41°07′N 25°27′E*
113 K16 **Komovi** ▲ E Montenegro
117 R8 **Kompaniyivka** Kirovohrads'ka Oblast', C Ukraine *48°16′N 32°12′E*
Kompong *see* Kâmpóng Chhnăng
Kompong Cham *see* Kâmpóng Cham
Kompong Kleang *see* Kâmpóng Khleăng
Kompong Som *see* Kâmpóng Saôm
Kompong Speu *see* Kâmpóng Spoe
Komrat *see* Comrat
Komsomol *see* Komsomol'skiy
122 K14 **Komsomolets, Ostrov** *island* Severnaya Zemlya, N Russian Federation
144 F13 **Komsomolets, Zaliv** *lake gulf* SW Kazakhstan
Komsomol/Komsomolets *see* Karabalyk, Kostanay, Kazakhstan
147 Q12 **Komsomolobod** *Rus.* Komosolabad. C Tajikistan *38°51′N 69°54′E*
124 M16 **Komsomol'sk** Ivanovskaya Oblast', W Russian Federation *56°58′N 40°15′E*
117 S6 **Komsomol's'k** Poltavs'ka Oblast', C Ukraine *49°01′N 33°37′E*
146 M11 **Komsomol'sk** Navoiy Viloyati, N Uzbekistan *40°14′N 65°10′E*
144 G12 **Komsomol'skiy** *Kaz.* Komsomol. Atyrau, W Kazakhstan *47°18′N 53°37′E*
127 P5 **Komsomol'skiy** Respublika Mordoviya, W Russian Federation *54°26′N 45°50′E*
125 W4 **Komsomol'skiy** Respublika Komi, NW Russian Federation *67°33′N 64°00′E*
123 S13 **Komsomol'sk-na-Amure** Khabarovskiy Kray, SE Russian Federation *50°32′N 136°59′E*
Komsomol'sk-na-Ustyurte *see* Kubla-Ustyurt
144 K10 **Komsomol'skoye** Aktyubinsk, NW Kazakhstan
127 Q8 **Komsomol'skoye** Saratovskaya Oblast', W Russian Federation *50°45′N 47°00′E*
145 P10 **Kon** ⛐ C Kazakhstan
Kona *see* Kailua-Kona
124 K16 **Konakovo** Tverskaya Oblast', W Russian Federation *56°42′N 36°44′E*
149 S4 **Konar** *Per.* Konarhā, *Pash.* Kunar. ◆ *province* E Afghanistan
143 V15 **Konārak** Sīstān va Balūchestān, SE Iran *25°26′N 60°23′E*
Konarhā *see* Konar
27 O11 **Konawa** Oklahoma, C USA *34°57′N 96°45′W*
122 H10 **Konda** ⛐ C Russian Federation
154 L13 **Kondagaon** Chhattīsgarh, C India *19°33′N 81°41′E*
14 K10 **Kondiaronk, Lac** ◎ Québec, SE Canada
180 J13 **Kondinin** Western Australia *32°31′S 118°15′E*
81 H21 **Kondoa** Dodoma, C Tanzania *04°54′S 35°46′E*
127 P6 **Kondol'** Penzenskaya Oblast', W Russian Federation *52°49′N 45°03′E*
114 N10 **Kondolovo** Burgas, E Bulgaria *42°07′N 27°43′E*
171 Z16 **Kondomirat** Papua, E Indonesia *08°57′S 140°55′E*
124 J10 **Kondopoga** Respublika Kareliya, NW Russian Federation *62°13′N 34°17′E*
149 Q2 **Kondoz** *var.* Kondūz, Qondūz, *Pash.* Kunduz, Kundūz. Kunduz, NE Afghanistan *36°49′N 68°50′E*
149 Q2 **Kondoz** *Pash.* Kunduz. ◆ *province* NE Afghanistan
155 J17 **Kondukūr** *var.* Kandukur. Andhra Pradesh, E India *15°17′N 79°45′E*
Kondūz *see* Kondoz
187 P16 **Koné** Province Nord, W New Caledonia *21°04′S 164°51′E*
Konechnaya *see* Kurchatov
146 E13 **Könekesir** Balkan Welaýaty, W Turkmenistan *38°16′N 56°51′E*
146 G8 **Köneürgenç** *var.* Köneürgench, *Rus.* Këneurgench; *prev.* Kunya-Urgench. Daşoguz Welaýaty, N Turkmenistan *42°21′N 59°09′E*
77 N15 **Kong** N Ivory Coast *09°10′N 04°33′W*
39 S5 **Kongakut River** ⛐ Alaska, USA
197 O14 **Kong Christian IX Land** *Eng.* King Christian IX Land. *physical region* SE Greenland
197 P13 **Kong Christian X Land** *Eng.* King Christian X Land. *physical region* E Greenland
197 N13 **Kong Frederik IX Land** *physical region* SW Greenland
197 Q12 **Kong Frederik VIII Land** *Eng.* King Frederik VIII Land. *physical region* NE Greenland
197 N15 **Kong Frederik VI Kyst** *Eng.* King Frederik VI Coast. *physical region* SE Greenland
167 P13 **Kŏng, Kaôh** *prev.* Kas Kong. *island* SW Cambodia
92 P2 **Kong Karls Land** *Eng.* King Charles Islands. *island group* SE Svalbard
81 G14 **Kong Kong** ⛐ SE Sudan
Kongo *see* Congo (river)
83 G16 **Kongola** Caprivi, NE Namibia *17°47′S 23°24′E*
79 N21 **Kongolo** Katanga, E Dem. Rep. Congo *05°20′S 26°58′E*
81 F14 **Kongor** Jonglei, SE Sudan *07°09′N 31°44′E*
197 Q14 **Kong Oscar Fjord** *fjord* E Greenland
77 P12 **Kongoussi** N Burkina *13°19′N 01°31′W*
95 G15 **Kongsberg** Buskerud, S Norway *59°39′N 09°38′E*
92 Q2 **Kongsøya** *island* Kong Karls Land, E Svalbard
95 I14 **Kongsvinger** Hedmark, S Norway *60°10′N 12°00′E*
Kongtong *see* Pingliang
167 T11 **Kông, Tônle** *var.* Xê Kong. ⛐ Cambodia/Laos
158 E8 **Kongur Shan** ▲ NW China *38°39′N 75°21′E*
81 I22 **Kongwa** Dodoma, C Tanzania *06°13′S 36°28′E*
Kong, Xê *see* Kông, Tônle
Konia *see* Konya
147 R11 **Konibodom** *Rus.* Kanibadam. N Tajikistan *40°16′N 70°20′E*
111 K15 **Koniecpol nad Pilicą** Śląskie, S Poland *50°47′N 19°45′E*
Konieh *see* Konya
Königgrätz *see* Hradec Králové
Königinhof an der Elbe *see* Dvůr Králové nad Labem
101 K23 **Königsbrunn** Bayern, S Germany *48°16′N 10°52′E*
101 O24 **Königssee** ◎ SE Germany
Königshütte *see* Chorzów
109 S8 **Königstuhl** ▲ S Austria *46°57′N 13°47′E*
109 U3 **Königswiesen** Oberösterreich, N Austria *48°25′N 14°48′E*
101 E17 **Königswinter** Nordrhein-Westfalen, W Germany *50°40′N 07°12′E*
146 M11 **Konimex** *Rus.* Kenimekh. Navoiy Viloyati, N Uzbekistan *40°14′N 65°10′E*
110 I12 **Konin** *Ger.* Kuhnau. Weilkopolskie, C Poland *52°13′N 18°17′E*
Koninkrijk der Nederlanden *see* Netherlands
113 L24 **Konispol** *var.* Konispoli. Vlorë, S Albania *39°40′N 20°10′E*
Konispoli *see* Konispol
115 C15 **Kónitsa** Ípeiros, W Greece *40°04′N 20°48′E*
Konitz *see* Chojnice
108 D8 **Köniz** Bern, W Switzerland *46°56′N 07°25′E*
113 H14 **Konjic** ◆ Federacija Bosna I Hercegovina, S Bosnia and Herzegovina
92 J10 **Könkämäälven** ⛐ Finland/Sweden
155 D14 **Konkan** *plain* W India
83 D22 **Konkiep** ⛐ S Namibia
76 I14 **Konkouré** ⛐ W Guinea
77 O11 **Konna** Mopti, S Mali *14°58′N 03°49′W*
186 H6 **Konogaiang, Mount** ▲ New Ireland, NE Papua New Guinea *04°05′S 152°43′E*
186 H5 **Konogogo** New Ireland, NE Papua New Guinea *03°25′S 152°09′E*
108 E9 **Konolfingen** Bern, W Switzerland *46°53′N 07°36′E*
77 P16 **Konongo** C Ghana *06°39′N 01°06′W*
186 H5 **Konos** New Ireland, NE Papua New Guinea *03°09′S 151°47′E*
124 M12 **Konosha** Arkhangel'skaya Oblast', NW Russian Federation *60°58′N 40°09′E*
117 R3 **Konotop** Sums'ka Oblast', NE Ukraine *51°15′N 33°14′E*
158 L7 **Konqi He** ⛐ NW China
111 L14 **Końskie** Siętokrzyskie, C Poland *51°12′N 20°23′E*
Konstantinovka *see* Kostyantynivka
126 M11 **Konstantinovsk** Rostovskaya Oblast', SW Russian Federation *47°37′N 41°07′E*
101 H24 **Konstanz** *var.* Constanz, *Eng.* Constance, *hist.* Kostnitz; *anc.* Constantia. Baden-Württemberg, S Germany *47°40′N 09°10′E*
Konstanza *see* Constanţa
77 T14 **Kontagora** Niger, W Nigeria *10°25′N 05°29′E*
78 E13 **Kontcha** Nord, N Cameroon *08°00′N 12°13′E*
99 G17 **Kontich** Antwerpen, N Belgium *51°08′N 04°27′E*
93 O16 **Kontiolahti** Itä-Suomi, SE Finland *62°46′N 29°51′E*
93 M15 **Kontiomäki** Oulu, C Finland *64°20′N 28°09′E*
167 U11 **Kon Tum** *var.* Kontum. Kon Tum, C Vietnam *14°23′N 108°00′E*
Kontum *see* Kon Tum
Konur *see* Sulakyurt
136 H15 **Konya** *var.* Konieh, *prev.* Konia; *anc.* Iconium. Konya, C Turkey *37°51′N 32°30′E*
136 H15 **Konya** *var.* Konia, Konieh. ◆ *province* C Turkey
151 E15 **Konya Reservoir** *var.* Shivāji Sāgar. ⊠ W India
145 T13 **Konyrat** *var.* Kounradskiy, *Kaz.* Qongyrat. Karaganda, SE Kazakhstan *46°57′N 75°01′E*
145 W15 **Konyrolen** Almaty, SE Kazakhstan *44°16′N 79°18′E*
81 I19 **Konza** Eastern, S Kenya *01°44′S 37°07′E*
98 I9 **Koog aan den Zaan** Noord-Holland, C Netherlands *52°28′N 04°49′E*
182 E7 **Koonibba** South Australia *31°55′S 133°23′E*
31 O11 **Koontz Lake** Indiana, N USA *41°25′N 86°24′W*
171 U12 **Koor** Papua, E Indonesia *0°21′S 132°28′E*
183 R9 **Koorawatha** New South Wales, SE Australia *34°03′S 148°33′E*
118 J5 **Koosa** Tartumaa, E Estonia *58°31′N 27°06′E*
33 N7 **Kootenai** *var.* Kootenay. ⛐ Canada/USA *see also* Kootenay
Kootenai *see* Kootenay
11 P17 **Kootenay** *var.* Kootenai. ⛐ Canada/USA *see also* Kootenai
Kootenay *see* Kootenai
83 F24 **Kootjieskolk** Northern Cape, W South Africa *31°16′S 20°21′E*
Kopal *see* Koppal
113 M15 **Kopaonik** ▲ S Serbia
Kopar *see* Koper
92 K1 **Kópasker** Nordhurland Eystra, N Iceland *66°15′N 16°23′W*
92 H4 **Kópavogur** Reykjanes, W Iceland *64°06′N 21°47′W*
145 U13 **Kopbirlik** *prev.* Kirov, Kirova. Almaty, SE Kazakhstan *46°24′N 77°16′E*
109 S13 **Koper** *It.* Capodistria; *prev.* Kopar. SW Slovenia *45°32′N 13°43′E*
95 C16 **Kopervik** Rogaland, S Norway *59°17′N 05°20′E*
Köpetdag Gershi/ Kopetdag, Khrebet *see* Koppeh Dāgh
Kophinou *see* Kofinou
182 G8 **Kopi** South Australia *33°24′S 135°40′E*
153 W12 **Kopili** ⛐ NE India
95 M15 **Köping** Västmanland, C Sweden *59°31′N 16°00′E*
113 K17 **Koplik** *var.* Kopliku. Shkodër, NW Albania *42°12′N 19°26′E*
Kopliku *see* Koplik
Kopopo *see* Kokopo
155 G18 **Koppal** *var.* Kopal. Karnātaka, SW India *14°20′N 76°09′E*
94 I11 **Koppang** Hedmark, S Norway *61°34′N 11°04′E*
Kopparberg *see* Dalarna
143 S3 **Koppeh Dāgh** *Rus.* Khrebet Kopetdag, *Turkm.* Köpetdag Gershi. ▲▲ Iran/Turkmenistan
Koppename *see* Coppename Rivier
95 J15 **Koppom** Värmland, C Sweden *59°42′N 12°07′E*
Kopreinitz *see* Koprivnica
114 K9 **Koprinka, Yazovir** *prev.* Yazovir Georgi Dimitrov. ⊠ C Bulgaria
112 F7 **Koprivnica** *Ger.* Kopreinitz, *Hung.* Kaproncza. Koprivnica-Križevci, N Croatia *46°10′N 16°49′E*
112 F8 **Koprivnica-Križevci** *off.* Koprivničko-Križevačka Županija. ◆ *province* N Croatia
111 I17 **Kopřivnice** *Ger.* Nesselsdorf. Moravskoslezský Kraj, E Czech Republic *49°36′N 18°09′E*
Koprivničko-Križevačka Županija *see* Koprivnica-Križevci
Köprülü *see* Veles
Koptsevichi *see* Kaptsevichy
Kopyl' *see* Kapyl'
119 O14 **Kopys'** Vitsyebskaya Voblasts', NE Belarus *54°19′N 30°18′E*
113 M18 **Korab** ▲ Albania/FYR Macedonia *41°48′N 20°33′E*
Korabavur Pastligi *see* Karabaur', Uval
81 M14 **K'orahē** Sumalē, E Ethiopia *06°36′N 44°21′E*
115 L16 **Kórakas, Akrotírio** *cape* Lésvos, E Greece
112 D9 **Korana** ⛐ C Croatia
155 L14 **Korāput** Orissa, E India *18°48′N 82°41′E*
Korat *see* Nakhon Ratchasima
167 Q9 **Korat Plateau** *plateau* E Thailand
139 T1 **Korāwa, Sar-i** ▲ NE Iraq *37°08′N 44°39′E*
154 L11 **Korba** Chhattīsgarh, C India *22°25′N 82°43′E*
101 H15 **Korbach** Hessen, C Germany *51°16′N 08°52′E*
Korça *see* Korçë
113 M21 **Korçë** *var.* Korça, *Gk.* Korytsa, *It.* Corriza; *prev.* Koritsa. Korçë, SE Albania *40°38′N 20°47′E*
113 M21 **Korçë** ◆ *district* SE Albania
113 G15 **Korčula** *It.* Curzola. Dubrovnik-Neretva, S Croatia *42°57′N 17°08′E*
113 F15 **Korčula** *It.* Curzola; *anc.* Corcyra Nigra. *island* S Croatia
113 F15 **Korčulanski Kanal** *channel* S Croatia
145 T6 **Korday** *prev.* Georgiyevka. Zhambyl, SE Kazakhstan *43°03′N 74°43′E*
142 J5 **Kordestān** *off.* Ostān-e Kordestān, *var.* Kurdestan. ◆ *province* W Iran
Kordestān, Ostān-e *see* Kordestān
143 P4 **Kord Kūy** *var.* Kurd Kui. Golestān, N Iran *36°49′N 54°05′E*
163 V13 **Korea Bay** *bay* China/North Korea
Korea, Democratic People's Republic of *see* North Korea
171 T15 **Koreare** Pulau Yamdena, E Indonesia *07°33′S 131°13′E*
Korea, Republic of *see* South Korea
163 Z17 **Korea Strait** *Jap.* Chōsen-kaikyō, *Kor.* Taehan-haehyŏp. *channel* Japan/South Korea
Korelichi/Korelicze *see* Karelichy
80 J11 **Korem** Tigrai, N Ethiopia *12°32′N 39°29′E*
77 U11 **Korén Adoua** ⛐ C Niger
127 O8 **Korenevo** Kurskaya Oblast', W Russian Federation *51°21′N 34°53′E*
126 L13 **Korenovsk** Krasnodarskiy Kray, SW Russian Federation *45°28′N 39°25′E*
116 L4 **Korets'** *Pol.* Korzec, *Rus.* Korets. Rivnens'ka Oblast', NW Ukraine *50°38′N 27°12′E*
194 L7 **Korff Ice Rise** *ice cap* Antarctica
145 Q10 **Korgalzhyn** *var.* Kurgal'dzhino, Kurgal'dzhinsky, *Kaz.* Qorghalzhyn. Akmola, C Kazakhstan *50°33′N 69°58′E*
92 G13 **Korgen** Troms, N Norway *66°04′N 13°51′E*
147 R9 **Korgon-Dĕbĕ** Dzhalal-Abadskaya Oblast', W Kyrgyzstan *41°51′N 70°52′E*
76 M14 **Korhogo** N Ivory Coast *09°29′N 05°39′W*
115 F19 **Korinthiakós Kólpos** *Eng.* Gulf of Corinth; *anc.* Corinthiacus Sinus. *gulf* C Greece
115 F19 **Kórinthos** *anc.* Corinthus *Eng.* Corinth. Pelopónnisos, S Greece *37°56′N 22°55′E*
113 M18 **Koritnik** ▲ S Serbia *42°06′N 20°34′E*
Koritsa *see* Korçë
165 P11 **Kōriyama** Fukushima, Honshū, C Japan *37°25′N 140°20′E*
136 E16 **Korkuteli** Antalya, SW Turkey *37°07′N 30°11′E*
158 K6 **Korla** *Chin.* K'u-erh-lo. Xinjiang Uygur Zizhiqu, NW China *41°48′N 86°10′E*
122 J10 **Korliki** Khanty-Mansiyskiy Avtonomnyy Okrug-Yugra, C Russian Federation *61°28′N 82°12′E*
Körlin an der Persante *see* Karlino
Korma *see* Karma
14 D8 **Kormak** Ontario, S Canada *47°38′N 83°00′W*
Kormakiti, Akrotíri/ Kormakiti, Cape/ Kormakítis *see* Koruçam Burnu
111 G23 **Körmend** Vas, W Hungary *47°02′N 16°35′E*
139 T5 **Kōrmōr** Şalāḩ ad Dīn, E Iraq *35°06′N 44°47′E*
112 C13 **Kornat** *It.* Incoronata. *island* W Croatia
Korneshty *see* Corneşti
109 X3 **Korneuburg** Niederösterreich, NE Austria *48°22′N 16°20′E*
145 P7 **Korneyevka** Severnyy Kazakhstan, N Kazakhstan *54°01′N 68°30′E*
95 I17 **Kornsjø** Østfold, S Norway *58°55′N 11°40′E*
77 O11 **Koro** Mopti, S Mali *14°05′N 03°06′W*
187 Y14 **Koro** *island* C Fiji
186 B7 **Koroba** Southern Highlands, W Papua New Guinea *05°46′S 142°48′E*
126 K8 **Korocha** Belgorodskaya Oblast', W Russian Federation *50°49′N 37°08′E*
136 H12 **Köroğlu Dağları** ▲▲ C Turkey
183 V6 **Korogoro Point** *headland* New South Wales, SE Australia *31°03′S 153°04′E*
81 J21 **Korogwe** Tanga, E Tanzania *05°10′S 38°30′E*
182 L13 **Koroit** Victoria, SE Australia *38°17′S 142°22′E*
187 X15 **Korolevu** Viti Levu, W Fiji *18°12′S 177°44′E*
190 I17 **Koromiri** *island* S Cook Islands
171 Q8 **Koronadal** Mindanao, S Philippines *06°23′N 124°54′E*
114 G13 **Koróneia, Límni** *var.* Límni Korónia. ◎ N Greece
115 E22 **Koróni** Pelopónnisos, S Greece *36°47′N 21°57′E*
Korónia, Límni *see* Koróneia, Límni
110 I9 **Koronowo** *Ger.* Krone an der Brahe. Kujawski-pomorskie, C Poland *53°18′N 17°56′E*
117 R2 **Korop** Chernihivs'ka Oblast', N Ukraine *51°35′N 32°57′E*
115 H19 **Koropí** Attikí, C Greece *37°54′N 23°52′E*
188 C8 **Koror** (Palau) Oreor, N Palau *07°21′N 134°28′E*
Koror *see* Oreor
111 L23 **Körös** ⛐ E Hungary
Kőrös *see* Križevci
Körösbánya *see* Baia de Criş
187 Y14 **Koro Sea** *sea* C Fiji
Koroška *see* Kärnten
117 N3 **Korosten'** Zhytomyrs'ka Oblast', NW Ukraine *50°56′N 28°39′E*
Korostyshev *see* Korostyshiv
117 N4 **Korostyshiv** *Rus.* Korostyshev. Zhytomyrs'ka Oblast', N Ukraine *50°18′N 29°05′E*
125 V3 **Korotaikha** ⛐ NW Russian Federation
122 J9 **Korotchayevo** Yamalo-Nenetskiy Avtonomnyy Okrug, N Russian Federation *66°00′N 78°11′E*
78 I8 **Koro Toro** Borkou-Ennedi-Tibesti, N Chad *16°01′N 18°27′E*
39 N16 **Korovin Island** *island* Shumagin Islands, Alaska, USA
187 X14 **Korovou** Viti Levu, W Fiji *17°48′S 178°32′E*
93 M17 **Korpilahti** Länsi-Suomi, C Finland *62°02′N 25°34′E*
92 K12 **Korpilombolo** *Lapp.* Dállogilli. Norrbotten, N Sweden *66°51′N 23°00′E*
123 T13 **Korsakov** Ostrov Sakhalin, Sakhalinskaya Oblast', SE Russian Federation *46°41′N 142°45′E*
93 J16 **Korsholm** *Fin.* Mustasaari. Länsi-Suomi, W Finland *63°05′N 21°43′E*
95 I23 **Korsør** Vestsjælland, E Denmark *55°19′N 11°09′E*
Korsovka *see* Kārsava
117 P6 **Korsun'-Shevchenkivs'kyy** *Rus.* Korsun'-Shevchenkovskiy. Cherkas'ka Oblast', C Ukraine *49°26′N 31°15′E*
Korsun'-Shevchenkovskiy *see* Korsun'-Shevchenkivs'kyy
99 C17 **Kortemark** West-Vlaanderen, W Belgium *51°03′N 03°03′E*
99 H18 **Kortenberg** Vlaams Brabant, C Belgium *50°53′N 04°33′E*
99 K18 **Kortessem** Limburg, NE Belgium *50°52′N 05°22′E*
99 E14 **Kortgene** Zeeland, SW Netherlands *51°34′N 03°48′E*
80 F8 **Korti** Northern, N Sudan *18°06′N 31°33′E*
99 C18 **Kortrijk** *Fr.* Courtrai. West-Vlaanderen, W Belgium *50°50′N 03°17′E*
121 O2 **Koruçam Burnu** *var.* Cape Kormakiti, Kormakítis, *Gk.* Akrotíri Kormakíti. *headland* N Cyprus *35°24′N 32°55′E*
183 O13 **Korumburra** Victoria, SE Australia *38°27′S 145°48′E*
Koryak Range *see* Koryakskoye Nagor'ye
123 V8 **Koryakskiy Avtonomnyy Okrug** ◆ *autonomous district* E Russian Federation
Koryakskiy Khrebet *see* Koryakskoye Nagor'ye
123 V7 **Koryakskoye Nagor'ye** *var.* Koryakskiy Khrebet, *Eng.* Koryak Range. ▲▲ NE Russian Federation
125 P11 **Koryazhma** Arkhangel'skaya Oblast', NW Russian Federation *61°16′N 47°07′E*
Koryŏ *see* Kangnŭng
Korytsa *see* Korçë
117 Q2 **Koryukivka** Chernihivs'ka Oblast', N Ukraine *51°45′N 32°16′E*
Korzec *see* Korets'
115 N21 **Kos** Kos, Dodekánisa, Greece, Aegean Sea *36°53′N 27°19′E*
115 M21 **Kos** *It.* Coo; *anc.* Cos. *island* Dodekánisa, Greece, Aegean Sea
125 T12 **Kosa** Komi-Permyatskiy Avtonomnyy Okrug, NW Russian Federation *59°55′N 54°54′E*
125 T13 **Kosa** ⛐ NW Russian Federation
164 B12 **Kō-saki** *headland* Nagasaki, Tsushima, SW Japan *34°06′N 129°13′E*
163 X13 **Kosan** SE North Korea *38°50′N 127°26′E*
119 H18 **Kosava** *Rus.* Kosovo. Brestskaya Voblasts', SW Belarus *52°45′N 25°16′E*
Kosch *see* Kose
144 G12 **Koschagyl** *Kaz.* Qosshaghyl. Atyrau, W Kazakhstan *46°52′N 53°46′E*
110 G12 **Kościan** *Ger.* Kosten. Wielkopolskie, C Poland *52°05′N 16°38′E*
110 I7 **Kościerzyna** Pomorskie, NW Poland *54°07′N 17°55′E*
22 L4 **Kosciusko** Mississippi, S USA *33°03′N 89°35′W*
Kosciusko, Mount *see* Kosciuszko, Mount
183 R11 **Kosciuszko, Mount** *prev.* Mount Kosciusko. ▲ New South Wales, SE Australia *36°28′S 148°15′E*
118 H4 **Kose** *Ger.* Kosch. Harjumaa, NW Estonia *59°11′N 25°10′E*
25 U9 **Kosse** Texas, SW USA *31°16′N 96°38′W*
114 G6 **Koshava** Vidin, NW Bulgaria *44°03′N 23°00′E*
147 U9 **Kosh-Dĕbĕ** *var.* Koshtebë. Narynskaya Oblast', C Kyrgyzstan *41°03′N 74°08′E*
K'o-shih *see* Kashi
164 B12 **Koshikijima-rettō** *var.* Kosikizima Rettô. *island group* SW Japan
145 W13 **Koshkarkol', Ozero** ◎ SE Kazakhstan
30 L9 **Koshkonong, Lake** ◎ Wisconsin, N USA
Koshoba *see* Goşabo
Koshoba *see* Goşoba
164 M12 **Kōshoku** *var.* Kôsyoku. Nagano, Honshū, S Japan *36°33′N 138°09′E*
Koshtebë *see* Kosh-Dĕbĕ
Kōshū *see* Enzan
Kōshū *see* Kwangju
111 N19 **Košice** *Ger.* Kaschau, *Hung.* Kassa. Košický Kraj, E Slovakia *48°44′N 21°15′E*
111 M20 **Košický Kraj** ◆ *region* E Slovakia
Kosikizima Rettô *see* Koshikijima-rettō
153 R12 **Kosi Reservoir** ⊠ E Nepal
116 J8 **Kosiv** Ivano-Frankivs'ka Oblast', W Ukraine *48°19′N 25°04′E*
145 O11 **Koskol'** *Kaz.* Qosköl. Karaganda, C Kazakhstan *49°32′N 67°08′E*
125 Q9 **Koslan** Respublika Komi, NW Russian Federation *63°27′N 48°52′E*
Köslin *see* Koszalin
146 M12 **Koson** *Rus.* Kasan. Qashqadaryo Viloyati, S Uzbekistan *39°04′N 65°35′E*
163 Y13 **Kosŏng** SE North Korea *38°41′N 128°14′E*
147 S9 **Kosonsoy** *Rus.* Kasansay. Namangan Viloyati, E Uzbekistan *41°15′N 71°28′E*
113 M16 **Kosovo** *prev.* Autonomous Province of Kosovo and Metohija. ◆ *republic* SE Europe
Kosovo *see* Kosava
Kosovo and Metohija, Autonomous Province of *see* Kosovo
Kosovo Polje *see* Fushë Kosovë
Kosovska Kamenica *see* Kamenicë
Kosovska Mitrovica *see* Mitrovicë
189 X17 **Kosrae** ◆ *state* E Micronesia
189 Y14 **Kosrae** *prev.* Kusaie. *island* Caroline Islands, E Micronesia
109 P6 **Kössen** Tirol, W Austria *47°40′N 12°24′E*
76 M16 **Kossou, Lac de** ◎ C Ivory Coast
Kossukavak *see* Krumovgrad
Kostajnica *see* Hrvatska Kostajnica
Kostamus *see* Kostomuksha
144 M7 **Kostanay** *var.* Kustanay, *Kaz.* Qostanay. Kostanay, N Kazakhstan *53°16′N 63°34′E*
144 L8 **Kostanay** *var.* Kostanayskaya Oblast', *Kaz.* Qostanay Oblysy. ◆ *province* N Kazakhstan
Kostanayskaya Oblast' *see* Kostanay
Kosten *see* Kościan
114 H10 **Kostenets** *prev.* Georgi Dimitrov. Sofiya, W Bulgaria *42°15′N 23°48′E*
80 F10 **Kosti** White Nile, C Sudan *13°11′N 32°38′E*
Kostnitz *see* Konstanz
124 H7 **Kostomuksha** *Fin.* Kostamus. Respublika Kareliya, NW Russian Federation *64°33′N 30°28′E*
116 K3 **Kostopil'** *Rus.* Kostopol'. Rivnens'ka Oblast', NW Ukraine *50°20′N 26°29′E*
Kostopol' *see* Kostopil'
124 M15 **Kostroma** Kostromskaya Oblast', NW Russian Federation *57°46′N 41°E*
125 N14 **Kostroma** ⛐ NW Russian Federation
125 N14 **Kostromskaya Oblast'** ◆ *province* NW Russian Federation
110 D11 **Kostrzyn** *Ger.* Cüstrin, Küstrin. Lubuskie, W Poland *52°35′N 14°40′E*
110 H11 **Kostrzyn** Wielkopolskie, C Poland *52°23′N 17°13′E*
117 X7 **Kostyantynivka** *Rus.* Konstantinovka. Donets'ka Oblast', SE Ukraine
Kostyukovichi *see* Kastsyukovichy
Kostyukovka *see* Kastsyukowka
Kôsyoku *see* Kōshoku
125 U6 **Kos'yu** Respublika Komi, NW Russian Federation *65°39′N 59°01′E*
125 U6 **Kos'yu** ⛐ NW Russian Federation
110 F7 **Koszalin** *Ger.* Köslin. Zachodnio-pomorskie, NW Poland *54°12′N 16°10′E*
111 F22 **Kőszeg** *Ger.* Güns. Vas, W Hungary *47°23′N 16°33′E*
152 H13 **Kota** *prev.* Kotah. Rājasthān, N India *25°14′N 75°52′E*
Kota Baharu *see* Kota Bharu
Kota Bahru *see* Kota Bharu
169 U13 **Kotabaru** Pulau Laut, C Indonesia *03°15′S 116°15′E*
168 K12 **Kota Baru** Sumatera, W Indonesia *01°07′S 101°43′E*
Kotabaru *see* Jayapura
168 K6 **Kota Bharu** *var.* Kota Baharu, Kota Bahru. Kelantan, Peninsular Malaysia *06°07′N 102°15′E*
Kotaboemi *see* Kotabumi
168 M14 **Kotabumi** *prev.* Kotaboemi. Sumatera, W Indonesia *04°50′S 104°54′E*
149 S10 **Kot Addu** Punjab, E Pakistan *30°28′N 70°58′E*
Kotah *see* Kota
169 U7 **Kota Kinabalu** *prev.* Jesselton. Sabah, East Malaysia *05°59′N 116°04′E*
169 U7 **Kota Kinabalu** ✈ Sabah, East Malaysia *05°59′N 116°04′E*
92 M12 **Kotala** Lappi, N Finland *67°01′N 29°00′E*
Kotamobagoe *see* Kotamobagu
171 Q11 **Kotamobagu** *prev.* Kotamobagoe. Sulawesi, C Indonesia *0°46′N 124°21′E*
155 L14 **Kotapad** *var.* Kotapārh. Orissa, E India *19°10′N 82°23′E*
Kotapārh *see* Kotapad
166 N17 **Ko Ta Ru Tao** *island* SW Thailand
169 R13 **Kotawaringin, Teluk** *bay* Borneo, C Indonesia
149 Q13 **Kot Diji** Sind, SE Pakistan *27°16′N 68°44′E*
152 K9 **Kotdwāra** Uttarakhand, N India *29°44′N 78°33′E*
125 Q14 **Kotel'nich** Kirovskaya Oblast', NW Russian Federation *58°19′N 48°12′E*
127 N12 **Kotel'nikovo** Volgogradskaya Oblast', SW Russian Federation *47°37′N 43°07′E*
123 Q6 **Kotel'nyy, Ostrov** *island* Novosibirskiye Ostrova, N Russian Federation
117 T5 **Kotel'va** Poltavs'ka Oblast', C Ukraine *50°04′N 34°46′E*
101 M14 **Köthen** *var.* Cöthen. Sachsen-Anhalt, C Germany *51°46′N 11°59′E*
Kôti *see* Kōchi
81 G17 **Kotido** NE Uganda *03°03′N 34°07′E*
93 N19 **Kotka** Etelä-Suomi, S Finland *60°28′N 26°55′E*
125 P11 **Kotlas** Arkhangel'skaya Oblast', NW Russian Federation *61°14′N 46°43′E*
38 M10 **Kotlik** Alaska, USA *63°01′N 163°33′W*
77 Q17 **Kotoka** ✈ (Accra) S Ghana *05°41′N 00°10′W*
Kotonu *see* Cotonou
113 J17 **Kotor** *It.* Cattaro. SW Montenegro *42°25′N 18°47′E*
Kotor *see* Kotoriba
112 F7 **Kotoriba** *Hung.* Kotor. Medimurje, N Croatia *46°20′N 16°47′E*
113 I17 **Kotorska, Boka** *It.* Bocche di Cattaro. *bay* SW Montenegro
112 H11 **Kotorsko** ◆ Republika Srpska, N Bosnia and Herzegovina
112 G11 **Kotor Varoš** ◆ Republika Srpska, N Bosnia and Herzegovina
Koto Sho/Kotosho *see* Lan Yü
126 M7 **Kotovsk** Tambovskaya Oblast', W Russian Federation *52°39′N 41°31′E*
117 O9 **Kotovs'k** *Rus.* Kotovsk. Odes'ka Oblast', SW Ukraine *47°42′N 29°30′E*
Kotovsk *see* Hînceşti
119 G16 **Kotra** ⛐ W Belarus
149 P16 **Kotri** Sind, SE Pakistan *25°22′N 68°18′E*
109 Q9 **Kötschach** Kärnten, S Austria *46°41′N 12°57′E*
155 K15 **Kottagūdem** Andhra Pradesh, E India *17°36′N 80°40′E*
155 F21 **Kottappadi** Kerala, SW India *11°38′N 76°03′E*
155 G23 **Kottayam** Kerala, SW India *09°34′N 76°31′E*
Kottbus *see* Cottbus
79 K15 **Kotto** ⛐ Central African Republic/Dem. Rep. Congo
193 X15 **Kotu Group** *island group* W Tonga
Koturdepe *see* Goturdepe
122 M9 **Kotuy** ⛐ N Russian Federation
83 M16 **Kotwa** Mashonaland East, NE Zimbabwe *16°58′S 32°46′E*
39 N7 **Kotzebue** Alaska, USA *66°54′N 162°36′W*
38 M7 **Kotzebue Sound** *inlet* Alaska, USA
Kotzenan *see* Chocianów
Kotzman *see* Kitsman'
77 R14 **Kouandé** NW Benin *10°20′N 01°42′E*
79 J15 **Kouango** Ouaka, S Central African Republic *05°00′N 20°01′E*
77 O13 **Koudougou** C Burkina *12°15′N 02°23′W*
98 K7 **Koudum** Friesland, N Netherlands *52°55′N 05°26′E*
115 L25 **Koufonísi** *island* SE Greece
115 K21 **Koufonísi** *island* Kykládes, Greece, Aegean Sea
38 M8 **Kougarok Mountain** ▲ Alaska, USA *65°41′N 165°29′W*
79 E21 **Kouilou** ◆ *province* SW Congo
79 E20 **Kouilou** ⛐ S Congo
121 O3 **Koúklia** SW Cyprus *34°42′N 32°35′E*
79 E19 **Koulamoutou** Ogooué-Lolo, C Gabon *01°07′S 12°27′E*
76 L12 **Koulikoro** Koulikoro, SW Mali *12°55′N 07°31′W*
76 L11 **Koulikoro** ◆ *region* SW Mali
187 P16 **Koumac** Province Nord, W New Caledonia *20°34′S 164°18′E*
165 N12 **Koumi** Nagano, Honshū, S Japan *36°06′N 138°27′E*
78 I13 **Koumra** Moyen-Chari, S Chad *08°56′N 17°32′E*
Kounadougou *see* Koundougou
76 M15 **Kounahiri** C Ivory Coast *07°47′N 05°51′W*
76 I12 **Koundâra** Moyenne-Guinée, NW Guinea *12°28′N 13°15′W*
77 N13 **Koundougou** *var.* Kounadougou. C Burkina *11°43′N 04°40′W*
76 H11 **Koungheul** C Senegal *14°00′N 14°48′W*
Kounradskiy *see* Konyrat
25 X10 **Kountze** Texas, SW USA *30°22′N 94°20′W*
77 Q13 **Koupéla** C Burkina *12°07′N 00°21′W*
77 N13 **Kouri** Sikasso, SW Mali *12°09′N 04°46′W*
55 Y9 **Kourou** N French Guiana *05°08′N 52°37′W*
114 J12 **Kouroú** ⛐ NE Greece
76 K14 **Kouroussa** C Guinea *10°40′N 09°50′W*
Kousseir *see* Al Quşayr
78 G11 **Kousséri** *prev.* Fort-Foureau. Extrême-Nord, NE Cameroon *12°05′N 14°56′E*
Kouteifé *see* Al Quţayfah
76 M13 **Koutiala** Sikasso, S Mali *12°20′N 05°23′W*
76 M14 **Kouto** NW Ivory Coast *09°51′N 06°25′W*
93 M19 **Kouvola** Etelä-Suomi, S Finland *60°50′N 26°48′E*
79 G18 **Kouyou** ⛐ C Congo
112 M10 **Kovačica** *Hung.* Antalfalva; *prev.* Kovacsicza. Vojvodina, N Serbia *45°08′N 20°36′E*
Kovacsicza *see* Kovačica
Kővárhosszúfalu *see* Satulung
Kovászna *see* Covasna
124 I4 **Kovdor** Murmanskaya Oblast', NW Russian Federation *67°32′N 30°27′E*
116 J3 **Kovel'** *Pol.* Kowel. Volyns'ka Oblast', NW Ukraine *51°14′N 24°43′E*
112 M11 **Kovin** *Hung.* Kevevára; *prev.* Temes-Kubin. Vojvodina, NE Serbia *44°45′N 20°59′E*
Kovno *see* Kaunas
127 N3 **Kovrov** Vladimirskaya Oblast', W Russian Federation *56°24′N 41°21′E*
127 O5 **Kovylkino** Respublika Mordoviya, W Russian Federation *54°03′N 43°52′E*
110 J11 **Kowal** Kujawsko-pomorskie, C Poland *52°31′N 19°09′E*
110 J9 **Kowalewo Pomorskie** *Ger.* Schönsee. Kujawsko-pomorskie, N Poland *53°07′N 18°48′E*
Kowasna *see* Covasna
119 M16 **Kowbcha** *Rus.* Kolbcha. Mahilyowskaya Voblasts', E Belarus *53°39′N 29°14′E*
Koweit *see* Kuwait
Kowel *see* Kovel'
185 F17 **Kowhitirangi** West Coast, South Island, New Zealand *42°54′S 171°01′E*
161 O15 **Kowloon** Hong Kong, S China
Kowno *see* Kaunas
159 N7 **Kox Kuduk** *well* NW China
136 D16 **Köyceğiz** Muğla, SW Turkey *36°57′N 28°40′E*
125 N6 **Koyda** Arkhangel'skaya Oblast', NW Russian Federation *66°22′N 42°42′E*
Koymat *see* Goymat
Koymatdag, Gory *see* Goymatdag, Gory
151 E15 **Koyna Reservoir** ⊠ W India
165 P9 **Koyoshi-gawa** ⛐ Honshū, C Japan
Koysanjaq *see* Koi Sanjaq
Koytash *see* Qo'ytosh
146 M14 **Köýtendag** *prev.* *Rus.* Charshanga, Charshangy, *Turkm.* Charshangngy. Lebap Welaýaty, E Turkmenistan *37°31′N 65°58′E*
39 N9 **Koyuk** Alaska, USA *64°55′N 161°09′W*
39 N9 **Koyuk River** ⛐ Alaska, USA
39 O9 **Koyukuk** Alaska, USA *64°52′N 157°42′W*
39 O9 **Koyukuk River** ⛐ Alaska, USA
136 J13 **Kozaklı** Nevşehir, C Turkey *39°12′N 34°48′E*
136 K16 **Kozan** Adana, S Turkey *37°27′N 35°47′E*
115 E14 **Kozáni** Dytikí Makedonía, N Greece *40°19′N 21°48′E*
112 F10 **Kozara** ▲▲ NW Bosnia and Herzegovina
Kozarska Dubica *see* Bosanska Dubica
117 P3 **Kozelets'** *Rus.* Kozelets. Chernihivs'ka Oblast', NE Ukraine *50°54′N 31°06′E*
Kozelets *see* Kozelets'
117 S6 **Kozel'shchyna** Poltavs'ka Oblast', C Ukraine *49°13′N 33°49′E*
126 J5 **Kozel'sk** Kaluzhskaya Oblast', W Russian Federation *54°04′N 35°51′E*
151 F21 **Kozhikode** *var.* Calicut. Kerala, SW India *11°17′N 75°49′E* *see also* Calicut

◆ Country
● Country Capital
◇ Dependent Territory
○ Dependent Territory Capital
◆ Administrative Regions
✈ International Airport
▲ Mountain
▲▲ Mountain Range
⛰ Volcano
⛐ River
◎ Lake
⊠ Reservoir

Kozhim – Kumamoto

125 U6 **Kozhim** Respublika Komi, NW Russian Federation 65°43′N 59°25′E
124 L9 **Kozhozero, Ozero** ◎ NW Russian Federation
125 T7 **Kozhva** Respublika Komi, NW Russian Federation 65°06′N 57°00′E
125 T7 **Kozhva** ≈ NW Russian Federation
125 V9 **Kozhymiz, Gora** ▲ NW Russian Federation 63°13′N 58°54′E
110 N13 **Kozienice** Mazowieckie, C Poland 51°35′N 21°31′E
109 S13 **Kozina** SW Slovenia 45°36′N 13°56′E
114 H7 **Kozloduy** Vratsa, NW Bulgaria 43°48′N 23°42′E
127 Q3 **Kozlovka** Chuvashskaya Respublika, W Russian Federation 55°53′N 48°07′E
Kozlovshchina/ Kozlowszczyzna *see* Kazlowshchyna
127 P3 **Koz'modem'yansk** Respublika Mariy El, W Russian Federation 56°19′N 46°33′E
116 J6 **Kozova** Ternopil's'ka Oblast', W Ukraine 49°25′N 25°09′E
113 P20 **Kožuf** ▲▲ Greece/Macedonia
165 N15 **Kōzu-shima** *island* E Japan
Koz'yany *see* Kaz'yany
117 N5 **Kozyatyn** *Rus.* Kazatin. Vinnyts'ka Oblast', C Ukraine 49°41′N 28°49′E
77 Q16 **Kpalimé** *var.* Palimé. SW Togo 06°54′N 00°38′E
77 Q16 **Kpandu** E Ghana 07°00′N 00°18′E
99 F15 **Krabbendijke** Zeeland, SW Netherlands 51°25′N 04°07′E
167 N15 **Krabi** *var.* Muang Krabi. Krabi, SW Thailand 08°04′N 98°52′E
167 N13 **Kra Buri** Ranong, SW Thailand 10°25′N 98°48′E
167 S12 **Krâchéh** *prev.* Kratie. Krâchéh, E Cambodia 12°29′N 106°01′E
95 G17 **Kragerø** Telemark, S Norway 58°54′N 09°25′E
112 M13 **Kragujevac** Serbia, C Serbia 44°01′N 20°55′E
Krainburg *see* Kranj
166 N13 **Kra, Isthmus of** *isthmus* Malaysia/Thailand
112 D12 **Krajina** *cultural region* SW Croatia
Krakatau, Pulau *see* Rakata, Pulau
Krakau *see* Kraków
111 L16 **Kraków** *Eng.* Cracow, *Ger.* Krakau; *anc.* Cracovia. Małopolskie, S Poland 50°03′N 19°58′E
100 L9 **Krakower See** ◎ NE Germany
167 Q11 **Krâlănh** Siĕmréab, NW Cambodia 13°35′N 103°27′E
45 Q16 **Kralendijk** Bonaire, E Netherlands Antilles 12°07′N 68°13′W
112 B10 **Kraljevica** *It.* Porto Re. Primorje-Gorski Kotar, NW Croatia 45°15′N 14°36′E
112 M13 **Kraljevo** *prev.* Rankovićevo. Serbia, C Serbia 43°44′N 20°40′E
111 E16 **Královehradecký Kraj** *prev.* Hradecký Kraj. ◐ *region* N Czech Republic
Kralup an der Moldau *see* Kralupy nad Vltavou
111 C16 **Kralupy nad Vltavou** *Ger.* Kralup an der Moldau. Středočeský Kraj, NW Czech Republic 50°15′N 14°20′E
117 W7 **Kramators'k** *Rus.* Kramatorsk. Donets'ka Oblast', SE Ukraine 48°43′N 37°34′E
Kramatorsk *see* Kramators'k
93 H17 **Kramfors** Västernorrland, C Sweden 62°55′N 17°50′E
Kranéa *see* Kraniá
108 M7 **Kranebitten** ✈ (Innsbruck) Tirol, W Austria 47°18′N 11°21′E
115 D15 **Kraniá** *var.* Kranéa. Dytikí Makedonía, N Greece 39°54′N 21°21′E
115 G20 **Kranídi** Pelopónnisos, S Greece 37°21′N 23°09′E
109 T11 **Kranj** *Ger.* Krainburg. NW Slovenia 46°17′N 14°16′E
115 F16 **Krannón** *battleground* Thessalía, C Greece
Kranz *see* Zelenogradsk
112 D7 **Krapina** Krapina-Zagorje, N Croatia 46°12′N 15°52′E
112 E8 **Krapina** ≈ N Croatia
112 D8 **Krapina-Zagorje** *off.* Krapinsko-Zagorska Županija. ◐ *province* N Croatia
114 L7 **Krapinets** ≈ NE Bulgaria
Krapinsko-Zagorska Županija *see* Krapina-Zagorje
111 I15 **Krapkowice** *Ger.* Krappitz. Opolskie, SW Poland 50°29′N 17°56′E
Krappitz *see* Krapkowice
125 O12 **Krasavino** Vologodskaya Oblast', NW Russian Federation 60°56′N 46°27′E
122 H6 **Krasino** Novaya Zemlya, Arkhangel'skaya Oblast', N Russian Federation 70°45′N 54°16′E
123 S15 **Kraskino** Primorskiy Kray, SE Russian Federation 42°40′N 130°51′E
118 J11 **Krāslava** Krāslava, SE Latvia 55°56′N 27°08′E
119 M14 **Krasnaluki** *Rus.* Krasnoluki. Vitsyebskaya Voblasts', N Belarus 54°37′N 28°50′E
119 P17 **Krasnapollye** *Rus.* Krasnopol'ye. Mahilyowskaya Voblasts', E Belarus 53°20′N 31°24′E
126 L15 **Krasnaya Polyana** Krasnodarskiy Kray, SW Russian Federation 43°40′N 40°13′E
Krasnaya Slabada / Krasnaya Sloboda *see* Chyrvonaya Slabada
119 J15 **Krasnaye** *Rus.* Krasnoye. Minskaya Voblasts', C Belarus 54°14′N 27°05′E
111 O14 **Kraśnik** *Ger.* Kratznick. Lubelskie, E Poland 50°56′N 22°14′E
117 O9 **Krasni Okny** Odes'ka Oblast', SW Ukraine 47°33′N 29°28′E
127 P8 **Krasnoarmeysk** Saratovskaya Oblast', W Russian Federation 51°02′N 45°42′E
Krasnoarmeysk *see* Tayynsha
Krasnoarmeysk *see* Krasnoarmiys'k/Tayynsha
123 T6 **Krasnoarmeyskiy** Chukotskiy Avtonomnyy Okrug, NE Russian Federation 69°30′N 171°44′E
117 W7 **Krasnoarmiys'k** *Rus.* Krasnoarmeysk. Donets'ka Oblast', SE Ukraine 48°17′N 37°14′E
125 P11 **Krasnoborsk** Arkhangel'skaya Oblast', NW Russian Federation 61°31′N 45°57′E
126 K14 **Krasnodar** *prev.* Ekaterinodar, Yekaterinodar. Krasnodarskiy Kray, SW Russian Federation 45°06′N 39°01′E
126 K13 **Krasnodarskiy Kray** ◐ *territory* SW Russian Federation
117 Z7 **Krasnodon** Luhans'ka Oblast', E Ukraine 48°17′N 39°44′E
Krasnogor *see* Kallaste
127 T2 **Krasnogorskoye** *Latv.* Sarkaņi. Udmurtskaya Respublika, NW Russian Federation 57°42′N 52°29′E
Krasnograd *see* Krasnohrad
Krasnogvardeysk *see* Bulungh'ur
126 M13 **Krasnogvardeyskoye** Stavropol'skiy Kray, SW Russian Federation 45°49′N 41°31′E
Krasnogvardeyskoye *see* Krasnohvardiys'ke
117 U6 **Krasnohrad** *Rus.* Krasnograd. Kharkivs'ka Oblast', E Ukraine 49°22′N 35°28′E
117 S12 **Krasnohvardiys'ke** *Rus.* Krasnogvardeyskoye. Respublika Krym, S Ukraine 45°30′N 34°19′E
123 P14 **Krasnokamensk** Chitinskaya Oblast', S Russian Federation 50°03′N 118°01′E
125 U14 **Krasnokamsk** Permskaya Oblast', W Russian Federation 58°08′N 55°48′E
127 U8 **Krasnokholm** Orenburgskaya Oblast', W Russian Federation 51°34′N 54°11′E
117 U5 **Krasnokuts'k** *Rus.* Krasnokutsk. Kharkivs'ka Oblast', E Ukraine 50°01′N 35°03′E
Krasnokutsk *see* Krasnokuts'k
126 L7 **Krasnolesnyy** Voronezhskaya Oblast', W Russian Federation 51°53′N 39°37′E
Krasnoluki *see* Krasnaluki
Krasnoosol'skoye Vodokhranilishche *see* Chervonooskil's'ke Vodoskhovyshche
117 S11 **Krasnoperekops'k** *Rus.* Krasnoperekopsk. Respublika Krym, S Ukraine 45°56′N 33°47′E
Krasnoperekopsk *see* Krasnoperekops'k
117 U4 **Krasnopillya** Sums'ka Oblast', NE Ukraine 50°46′N 35°17′E
Krasnopol'ye *see* Krasnapollye
124 L5 **Krasnoshchel'ye** Murmanskaya Oblast', NW Russian Federation 67°22′N 37°03′E
127 O5 **Krasnoslobodsk** Respublika Mordoviya, W Russian Federation 54°24′N 43°51′E
127 T2 **Krasnoslobodsk** Volgogradskaya Oblast', SW Russian Federation 48°41′N 44°34′E
Krasnostav *see* Krasnystaw
127 V5 **Krasnousol'skiy** Respublika Bashkortostan, W Russian Federation 53°55′N 56°22′E
125 U12 **Krasnovishersk** Permskaya Oblast', NW Russian Federation 60°22′N 57°04′E
Krasnovodsk *see* Türkmenbaşy
Krasnovodskiy Zaliv *see* Türkmenbasy Aylagy
146 B10 **Krasnovodskoye Plato** *Turkm.* Krasnowodsk Platosy. *plateau* NW Turkmenistan
Krasnowodsk Aylagy *see* Türkmenbasy Aylagy
Krasnowodsk Platosy *see* Krasnovodskoye Plato
122 K12 **Krasnoyarsk** Krasnoyarskiy Kray, S Russian Federation 56°05′N 92°46′E
127 X7 **Krasnoyarskiy** Orenburgskaya Oblast', W Russian Federation 51°56′N 59°54′E
122 K11 **Krasnoyarskiy Kray** ◐ *territory* C Russian Federation
Krasnoye *see* Krasnaye
Krasnoye Znamya *see* Gyzylbaydak
125 R11 **Krasnozatonskiy** Respublika Komi, NW Russian Federation 61°39′N 51°00′E
118 D13 **Krasnoznamensk** *prev.* Lasdehnen, *Ger.* Haselberg. Kaliningradskaya Oblast', W Russian Federation 54°57′N 22°28′E
126 K3 **Krasnoznamensk** Moskovskaya Oblast', W Russian Federation 55°40′N 37°05′E
117 R11 **Krasnoznam"yans'kyy Kanal** *canal* S Ukraine
111 P14 **Krasnystaw** *Rus.* Krasnostav. Lubelskie, SE Poland 51°N 23°10′E
126 H4 **Krasnyy** Smolenskaya Oblast', W Russian Federation 54°36′N 31°27′E
127 P2 **Krasnyye Baki** Nizhegorodskaya Oblast', W Russian Federation 57°07′N 45°12′E
127 Q13 **Krasnyye Barrikady** Astrakhanskaya Oblast', SW Russian Federation 46°14′N 47°48′E
124 K15 **Krasnyy Kholm** Tverskaya Oblast', W Russian Federation 58°04′N 37°05′E
127 Q8 **Krasnyy Kut** Saratovskaya Oblast', W Russian Federation 50°54′N 46°58′E
Krasnyy Liman *see* Krasnyy Lyman
117 Y7 **Krasnyy Luch** *prev.* Krindachevka. Luhans'ka Oblast', E Ukraine 48°09′N 38°52′E
117 X6 **Krasnyy Lyman** *Rus.* Krasnyy Liman. Donets'ka Oblast', SE Ukraine 49°00′N 37°50′E
127 R3 **Krasnyy Steklovar** Respublika Mariy El, W Russian Federation 56°14′N 48°49′E
127 P8 **Krasnyy Tekstil'shchik** Saratovskaya Oblast', W Russian Federation 51°35′N 45°49′E
127 R13 **Krasnyy Yar** Astrakhanskaya Oblast', SW Russian Federation 46°33′N 48°21′E
Krassóvár *see* Caraşova
116 L5 **Krasyliv** Khmel'nyts'ka Oblast', W Ukraine 49°38′N 26°59′E
111 O21 **Kraszna** *Rom.* Crasna. ≈ Hungary/Romania
Kratie *see* Krâchéh
113 P17 **Kratovo** NE FYR Macedonia 42°04′N 22°08′E
Kratznick *see* Kraśnik
171 Y13 **Krau** Papua, E Indonesia 03°15′S 140°07′E
167 Q13 **Krâvanh, Chuŏr Phnum** *Eng.* Cardamom Mountains, *Fr.* Chaîne des Cardamomes. ▲▲ W Cambodia
Kravasta Lagoon *see* Karavastasë, Laguna e
Krawang *see* Karawang
127 Q15 **Kraynovka** Respublika Dagestan, SW Russian Federation 43°58′N 47°24′E
118 D12 **Kražiai** Šiaulai, C Lithuania 55°36′N 22°41′E
27 P11 **Krebs** Oklahoma, C USA 34°55′N 95°43′W
101 D15 **Krefeld** Nordrhein-Westfalen, W Germany 51°20′N 06°34′E
Kreisstadt *see* Krosno Odrzańskie
115 D17 **Kremastón, Technití Límni** ▣ C Greece
Kremenchug *see* Kremenchuk
Kremenchugskoye Vodokhranilishche/ Kremenchuk Reservoir *see* Kremenchuts'ke Vodoskhovyshche
117 S6 **Kremenchuk** *Rus.* Kremenchug. Poltavs'ka Oblast', NE Ukraine 49°04′N 33°27′E
117 R6 **Kremenchuts'ke Vodoskhovyshche** *Eng.* Kremenchuk Reservoir, *Rus.* Kremenchugskoye Vodokhranilishche. ▣ C Ukraine
116 K5 **Kremenets'** *Pol.* Krzemieniec, *Rus.* Kremenets. Ternopil's'ka Oblast', W Ukraine 50°06′N 25°43′E
Kremennaya *see* Kreminna
117 X6 **Kreminna** *Rus.* Kremennaya. Luhans'ka Oblast', E Ukraine 49°03′N 38°15′E
37 R4 **Kremmling** Colorado, C USA 40°03′N 106°23′W
109 V3 **Krems** ≈ NE Austria
Krems *see* Krems an der Donau
109 W3 **Krems an der Donau** *var.* Krems. Niederösterreich, N Austria 48°25′N 15°36′E
Kremsier *see* Kroměříž
109 S4 **Kremsmünster** Oberösterreich, N Austria 48°04′N 14°08′E
38 M17 **Krenitzin Islands** *island* Aleutian Islands, Alaska, USA
Kresena *see* Kresna
114 G11 **Kresna** *var.* Kresena. Blagoevgrad, SW Bulgaria 41°43′N 23°10′E
112 O12 **Krespoljin** Serbia, E Serbia 44°22′N 21°36′E
25 N4 **Kress** Texas, SW USA 34°21′N 101°43′W
123 V6 **Kresta, Zaliv** *bay* E Russian Federation
115 D20 **Kréstena** *prev.* Selinoús. Dytikí Ellás, S Greece 37°36′N 21°36′E
124 H14 **Kresttsy** Novgorodskaya Oblast', W Russian Federation 58°15′N 32°28′E
Kretikon Delagos *see* Kritikó Pélagos
118 C11 **Kretinga** *Ger.* Krottingen. Klaipėda, NW Lithuania 55°53′N 21°13′E
Kreutz *see* Cristuru Secuiesc
Kreuz *see* Križevci, Croatia
Kreuz *see* Risti, Estonia
Kreuzburg/Kreuzburg in Oberschlesien *see* Kluczbork
Kreuzingen *see* Bol'shakovo
108 H6 **Kreuzlingen** Thurgau, NE Switzerland 47°38′N 09°12′E
101 K25 **Kreuzspitze** ▲ S Germany 47°30′N 10°55′E
101 F16 **Kreuztal** Nordrhein-Westfalen, W Germany 50°58′N 08°00′E
119 I15 **Kreva** *Rus.* Krevo. Hrodzyenskaya Voblasts', W Belarus 54°19′N 26°17′E
Krevo *see* Kreva
Kría Vrísi *see* Krýa Vrýsi
79 D16 **Kribi** Sud, SW Cameroon 02°53′N 09°57′E
Krichëv *see* Krychaw
Krickerhäu/Kriegerhaj *see* Handlová
109 W6 **Krieglach** Steiermark, E Austria 47°33′N 15°37′E
108 F8 **Kriens** Luzern, W Switzerland 47°03′N 08°17′E
Krievija *see* Russian Federation
Krimmitschau *see* Crimmitschau
98 H12 **Krimpen aan den IJssel** Zuid-Holland, SW Netherlands 51°56′N 04°39′E
Krindachevka *see* Krasnyy Luch
115 G25 **Kríos, Akrotírio** *headland* Kríti, Greece, E Mediterranean Sea 35°17′N 23°31′E
155 J16 **Krishna** *prev.* Kistna. ≈ C India
155 H20 **Krishnagiri** Tamil Nādu, SE India 12°33′N 78°11′E
155 K17 **Krishna, Mouths of the** *delta* SE India
153 S15 **Krishnanagar** West Bengal, N India 23°22′N 88°32′E
155 G20 **Krishnarājāsāgara Reservoir** ▣ W India
95 N19 **Kristdala** Kalmar, S Sweden 57°24′N 16°12′E
Kristiania *see* Oslo
95 E18 **Kristiansand** *var.* Christiansand. Vest-Agder, S Norway 58°08′N 07°52′E
95 L22 **Kristianstad** Skåne, S Sweden 56°02′N 14°10′E
94 F8 **Kristiansund** *var.* Christiansund. Møre og Romsdal, S Norway 63°07′N 07°45′E
Kristiinankaupunki *see* Kristinestad
93 I14 **Kristineberg** Västerbotten, N Sweden 65°07′N 18°36′E
95 L16 **Kristinehamn** Värmland, C Sweden 59°17′N 14°09′E
93 J17 **Kristinestad** *Fin.* Kristiinankaupunki. Länsi-Suomi, W Finland 62°15′N 21°24′E
Kristyor *see* Crişcior
115 J25 **Kríti** *Eng.* Crete. ◐ *region* Greece, Aegean Sea
115 J24 **Kríti** *Eng.* Crete. *island* Greece, Aegean Sea
115 J23 **Kritikó Pélagos** *var.* Kretikon Delagos, *Eng.* Sea of Crete; *anc.* Mare Creticum. *sea* Greece, Aegean Sea
Kriulyany *see* Criuleni
112 I12 **Krivaja** ≈ NE Bosnia and Herzegovina
Krivaja *see* Mali Iđoš
113 P17 **Kriva Palanka** *Turk.* Eğri Palanka. NE Macedonia 42°13′N 22°19′E
Krivichi *see* Kryvychy
114 H8 **Krivodol** Vratsa, NW Bulgaria 43°23′N 23°30′E
126 M10 **Krivorozh'ye** Rostovskaya Oblast', SW Russian Federation 48°51′N 40°49′E
Krivoshin *see* Kryvoshyn
Krivoy Rog *see* Kryvyy Rih
112 F7 **Križevci** *Ger.* Kreuz, *Hung.* Kőrös. Varaždin, NE Croatia 46°02′N 16°32′E
112 B10 **Krk** *It.* Veglia. Primorje-Gorski Kotar, NW Croatia 45°01′N 14°36′E
112 B10 **Krk** *It.* Veglia; *anc.* Curieta. *island* NW Croatia
109 V12 **Krka** ≈ SE Slovenia
Krka *see* Gurk
109 R11 **Krn** ▲ NW Slovenia 46°15′N 13°37′E
111 H16 **Krnov** *Ger.* Jägerndorf. Moravskoslezský Kraj, E Czech Republic 50°05′N 17°40′E
Kroatien *see* Croatia
95 G14 **Krøderen** Buskerud, S Norway 60°06′N 09°48′E
95 G14 **Krøderen** ◎ S Norway
Kroi *see* Krui
95 N17 **Krokek** Östergötland, S Sweden 58°40′N 16°25′E
Krokodil *see* Crocodile
93 G16 **Krokom** Jämtland, C Sweden 63°20′N 14°30′E
117 S2 **Krolevets'** *Rus.* Krolevets. Sums'ka Oblast', NE Ukraine 51°34′N 33°24′E
Krolevets *see* Krolevets'
Królewska Huta *see* Chorzów
111 H18 **Kroměříž** *Ger.* Kremsier. Zlínský Kraj, E Czech Republic 49°18′N 17°24′E
98 I9 **Krommenie** Noord-Holland, C Netherlands 52°30′N 04°46′E
126 J6 **Kromy** Orlovskaya Oblast', W Russian Federation 52°41′N 35°45′E
101 L18 **Kronach** Bayern, E Germany 50°14′N 11°19′E
Krone an der Brahe *see* Koronowo
167 Q13 **Krŏng Kaôh Kŏng** Kaôh Kông, SW Cambodia 11°37′N 102°59′E
95 K21 **Kronoberg** ◐ *county* S Sweden
123 V10 **Kronotskiy Zaliv** *bay* E Russian Federation
195 O2 **Kronprinsesse Märtha Kyst** *physical region* Antarctica
195 V3 **Kronprins Olav Kyst** *physical region* Antarctica
124 G12 **Kronshtadt** Leningradskaya Oblast', NW Russian Federation 60°01′N 29°42′E
Kronstadt *see* Braşov
83 I22 **Kroonstad** Free State, C South Africa 27°40′S 27°15′E
123 O12 **Kropotkin** Irkutskaya Oblast', C Russian Federation 58°30′N 115°21′E
126 L14 **Kropotkin** Krasnodarskiy Kray, SW Russian Federation 45°29′N 40°31′E
110 J11 **Krośniewice** Łódzskie, C Poland 52°14′N 19°10′E
111 N17 **Krosno** *Ger.* Krossen. Podkarpackie, SE Poland 49°40′N 21°46′E
110 E12 **Krosno Odrzańskie** *Ger.* Crossen, Kreisstadt. Lubuskie, W Poland 52°02′N 15°06′E
Krossen *see* Krosno
Krotoschin *see* Krotoszyn
110 H13 **Krotoszyn** *Ger.* Krotoschin. Wielkopolskie, C Poland 51°43′N 17°24′E
Krottingen *see* Kretinga
Krousón *see* Krousónas
115 J25 **Krousónas** *prev.* Krousón, Kroussón. Kríti, Greece, E Mediterranean Sea 35°14′N 24°59′E
Kroussón *see* Krousónas
Krraba *see* Krrabë
113 L20 **Krrabë** *var.* Krraba. Tiranë, C Albania 41°15′N 19°56′E
113 L17 **Krrabit, Mali i** ▲▲ N Albania
109 W12 **Krško** *Ger.* Gurkfeld; *prev.* Videm-Krško. E Slovenia 45°57′N 15°31′E
83 K19 **Kruger National Park** *national park* Northern, N South Africa
83 J21 **Krugersdorp** Gauteng, NE South Africa 26°06′S 27°46′E
38 D16 **Krugloi Point** *headland* Agattu Island, Alaska, USA 52°30′N 173°46′E
Krugloye *see* Kruhlaye
119 N15 **Kruhlaye** *Rus.* Krugloye. Mahilyowskaya Voblasts', E Belarus 54°15′N 29°48′E
168 L15 **Krui** *var.* Kroi. Sumatera, SW Indonesia 05°11′S 103°55′E
99 G16 **Kruibeke** Oost-Vlaanderen, N Belgium 51°10′N 04°18′E
83 G25 **Kruidfontein** Western Cape, SW South Africa 32°50′S 21°59′E
99 F15 **Kruiningen** Zeeland, SW Netherlands 51°28′N 04°01′E
Kruja *see* Krujë
113 L19 **Krujë** *var.* Kruja, *It.* Croia. Durrës, C Albania 41°30′N 19°48′E
Krulevshchina/ Krulewshchyna *see* Krulyewshchyna
118 K13 **Krulyewshchyna** *Rus.* Krulevshchina, Krulewshchyna. Vitsyebskaya Voblasts', N Belarus 55°02′N 27°45′E
25 T6 **Krum** Texas, SW USA 33°15′N 97°14′W
101 J23 **Krumbach** Bayern, S Germany 48°12′N 10°21′E
113 M17 **Krumë** Kukës, NE Albania 42°11′N 20°25′E
Krummau *see* Český Krumlov
114 K12 **Krumovgrad** *prev.* Kossukavak. Yambol, E Bulgaria 41°27′N 25°40′E
114 K12 **Krumovitsa** ≈ S Bulgaria
114 L10 **Krumovo** Yambol, E Bulgaria 42°16′N 26°25′E
167 O11 **Krung Thep, Ao** *var.* Bight of Bangkok. *bay* S Thailand
Krung Thep Mahanakhon *see* Ao Krung Thep
Krupa/Krupa na Uni *see* Bosanska Krupa
119 M15 **Krupki** Minskaya Voblasts', C Belarus 54°19′N 29°08′E
95 G24 **Kruså** *var.* Krusaa. Sønderjylland, SW Denmark 54°50′N 09°25′E
Krusaa *see* Kruså
113 N14 **Kruševac** Serbia, C Serbia 43°37′N 21°20′E
113 N19 **Kruševo** SW FYR Macedonia 41°22′N 21°15′E
111 A15 **Krušné Hory** *Eng.* Ore Mountains, *Ger.* Erzgebirge. ▲ Czech Republic/Germany *see also* Erzgebirge
Krušné Hory *see* Erzgebirge
39 W13 **Kruzof Island** *island* Alexander Archipelago, Alaska, USA
114 F13 **Krýa Vrýsi** *var.* Kría Vrísi. Kentrikí Makedonía, N Greece 40°41′N 22°18′E
119 P16 **Krychaw** *Rus.* Krichëv. Mahilyowskaya Voblasts', E Belarus 53°42′N 31°43′E
64 K11 **Krylov Seamount** *undersea feature* E Atlantic Ocean 17°35′N 30°07′W
Krym *see* Krym, Avtonomna Respublika
117 S13 **Krym, Avtonomna Respublika** *var.* Krym, *Eng.* Crimea, Crimean Oblast; *prev. Rus.* Krymskaya ASSR, Krymskaya Oblast'. ◐ *province* SE Ukraine
126 K14 **Krymsk** Krasnodarskiy Kray, SW Russian Federation 44°56′N 38°02′E
Krymskaya ASSR/ Krymskaya Oblast' *see* Krym, Avtonomna Respublika
117 T13 **Kryms'ki Hory** ▲▲ S Ukraine
117 T13 **Kryms'kyy Pivostriv** *peninsula* S Ukraine
111 M18 **Krynica** *Ger.* Tannenhof. Małopolskie, S Poland 49°25′N 20°56′E
117 P8 **Kryve Ozero** Odes'ka Oblast', SW Ukraine 47°54′N 30°19′E
119 I18 **Kryvoshyn** *Rus.* Krivoshin. Brestskaya Voblasts', SW Belarus 52°52′N 26°08′E
119 K14 **Kryvychy** *Rus.* Krivichi. Minskaya Voblasts', C Belarus 54°43′N 27°17′E
117 S8 **Kryvyy Rih** *Rus.* Krivoy Rog. Dnipropetrovs'ka Oblast', SE Ukraine 47°53′N 33°24′E
117 N8 **Kryzhopil'** Vinnyts'ka Oblast', C Ukraine 48°22′N 28°51′E
Krzemieniec *see* Kremenets'
111 J14 **Krzepice** Śląskie, S Poland 50°58′N 18°42′E
110 F10 **Krzyż Wielkopolskie** Wielkopolskie, W Poland 52°52′N 16°03′E
Ksar al Kabir *see* Ksar-el-Kebir
Ksar al Soule *see* Er-Rachidia
74 J5 **Ksar El Boukhari** N Algeria 35°55′N 02°47′E
74 G5 **Ksar-el-Kebir** *var.* Alcázar, Ksar al Kabir, Ksar-el-Kébir, *Ar.* Al-Kasr al-Kebir, Al-Qsar al-Kbir, *Sp.* Alcazarquivir. NW Morocco 35°04′N 05°56′W
Ksar-el-Kébir *see* Ksar-el-Kebir
110 H12 **Książ Wielkopolski** *Ger.* Xions. Weilkopolskie, W Poland 52°03′N 17°10′E
127 O3 **Kstovo** Nizhegorodskaya Oblast', W Russian Federation 56°07′N 44°12′E
169 T8 **Kuala Belait** W Brunei 04°48′N 114°12′E
Kuala Dungun *see* Dungun
169 S10 **Kualakeriau** Borneo, C Indonesia
169 S12 **Kualakuayan** Borneo, C Indonesia 02°01′S 112°35′E
168 K8 **Kuala Lipis** Pahang, Peninsular Malaysia 04°11′N 102°00′E
168 K9 **Kuala Lumpur** ● (Malaysia) Kuala Lumpur, Peninsular Malaysia 03°08′N 101°42′E
168 K9 **Kuala Lumpur International** ✈ Selangor, Peninsular Malaysia 02°51′N 101°45′E
Kuala Pelabohan Kelang *see* Pelabuhan Klang
169 U7 **Kuala Penyu** Sabah, East Malaysia 05°37′N 115°36′E
38 E9 **Kualapu'u** *var.* Kualapuu. Moloka'i, Hawaii, USA, C Pacific Ocean 21°09′N 157°02′W
Kualapuu *see* Kualapu'u
168 L7 **Kuala Terengganu** *var.* Kuala Trengganu. Terengganu, Peninsular Malaysia 05°20′N 103°07′E
168 L11 **Kualatungkal** Sumatera, W Indonesia 0°49′S 103°22′E
171 P11 **Kuandang** Sulawesi, N Indonesia 0°50′N 122°55′E
163 V12 **Kuandian** *var.* Kuandian Manzu Zizhixian. Liaoning, NE China 40°41′N 124°46′E
Kuandian Manzu Zizhixian *see* Kuandian
Kuando-Kubango *see* Cuando Cubango
Kuang-chou *see* Guangzhou
Kuang-hsi *see* Guangxi Zhuangzu Zizhiqu
Kuang-tung *see* Guangdong
Kuang-yuan *see* Guangyuan
Kuantan, Batang *see* Indragiri, Sungai
Kuanza Norte *see* Cuanza Norte
Kuanza Sul *see* Cuanza Sul
Kuanzhou *see* Qingjian
Kuba *see* Quba
Kubango *see* Cubango/ Okavango
141 X8 **Kubārah** NW Oman 23°03′N 56°52′E
93 H16 **Kubbe** Västernorrland, C Sweden 63°31′N 18°04′E
80 A11 **Kubbum** Southern Darfur, W Sudan 11°47′N 23°47′E
124 L13 **Kubenskoye, Ozero** ◎ NW Russian Federation
146 G6 **Kubla-Ustyurt** *Rus.* Komsomol'sk-na-Ustyurte. Qoraqalpog'iston Respublikasi, NW Uzbekistan 44°06′N 58°14′E
164 G15 **Kubokawa** Kōchi, Shikoku, SW Japan 33°22′N 133°14′E
114 L7 **Kubrat** *prev.* Balbunar. Razgrad, N Bulgaria 43°48′N 26°31′E
112 O13 **Kučajske Planine** ▲▲ E Serbia
165 T1 **Kuccharo-ko** ◎ Hokkaidō, N Japan
112 O11 **Kučevo** Serbia, NE Serbia 44°29′N 21°42′E
Kuchan *see* Qūchān
169 Q10 **Kuching** *prev.* Sarawak. Sarawak, East Malaysia 01°32′N 110°20′E
169 Q10 **Kuching** ✈ Sarawak, East Malaysia 01°32′N 110°20′E
164 B17 **Kuchinoerabu-jima** *island* Nansei-shotō, SW Japan
164 C14 **Kuchinotsu** Nagasaki, Kyūshū, SW Japan 32°36′N 130°11′E
109 Q6 **Kuchl** Salzburg, NW Austria 47°37′N 13°12′E
148 L9 **Kūchnay Darweyshān** Helmand, S Afghanistan 31°02′N 64°10′E
Kuchurgan *see* Kuchurhan
117 O9 **Kuchurhan** *Rus.* Kuchurgan. ≈ NE Ukraine
Kuçova *see* Kuçovë
113 L21 **Kuçovë** *var.* Kuçova; *prev.* Qyteti Stalin. Berat, C Albania 40°48′N 19°55′E
136 D11 **Küçük Çekmece** İstanbul, NW Turkey 41°01′N 28°47′E
164 F14 **Kudamatsu** *var.* Kudamatu. Yamaguchi, Honshū, SW Japan 34°00′N 131°53′E
Kudamatu *see* Kudamatsu
Kudara *see* Ghŭdara
169 V6 **Kudat** Sabah, East Malaysia 06°54′N 116°47′E
Küddow *see* Gwda
155 G17 **Kūdligi** Karnātaka, W India 14°58′N 76°24′E
Kudowa *see* Kudowa-Zdrój
111 F16 **Kudowa-Zdrój** *Ger.* Kudowa. Wałbrzych, SW Poland 50°27′N 16°20′E
117 P9 **Kudryavtsivka** Mykolayivs'ka Oblast', S Ukraine 47°18′N 31°02′E
169 R16 **Kudus** *prev.* Koedoes. Jawa, C Indonesia 06°46′S 110°48′E
125 T13 **Kudymkar** Komi-Permyatskiy Avtonomnyy Okrug, NW Russian Federation 59°01′N 54°40′E
Kudzsir *see* Cugir
Kuei-chou *see* Guizhou
Kuei-lin *see* Guilin
Kuei-Yang/Kuei-yang *see* Guiyang
K'u-erh-lo *see* Korla
Kueyang *see* Guiyang
Kufa *see* Al Kūfah
136 E14 **Küfiçayı** ≈ C Turkey
109 O6 **Kufstein** Tirol, W Austria 47°36′N 12°10′E
9 N7 **Kugaaruk** *prev.* Pelly Bay. Nunavut, N Canada 68°38′N 89°45′W
145 V14 **Kugaly** *Kaz.* Qoghaly. Almaty, SE Kazakhstan 44°30′N 78°40′E
8 K8 **Kugluktuk** *var.* Qurlurtuuq; *prev.* Coppermine. Nunavut, NW Canada 67°49′N 115°12′W
143 Y13 **Kūhak** Sīstān va Balūchestān, SE Iran 27°10′N 63°15′E
143 R9 **Kūhbonān** Kermān, C Iran 31°23′N 56°16′E
148 J5 **Kūhestān** *var.* Kohsān. Herāt, W Afghanistan 34°40′N 61°11′E
Kūhīrī *see* Kahīrī
93 N15 **Kuhmo** Oulu, E Finland 64°04′N 29°34′E
93 L18 **Kuhmoinen** Länsi-Suomi, C Finland 61°32′N 25°09′E
Kuhnau *see* Konin
Kühnö *see* Kihnu
143 O8 **Kūhpāyeh** Eşfahān, C Iran 32°42′N 52°25′E
167 O12 **Kui Buri** *var.* Ban Kui Nua. Prachuap Khiri Khan, SW Thailand 12°10′N 99°49′E
Kuibyshev *see* Kuybyshevskoye Vodokhranilishche
82 D13 **Kuito** *Port.* Silva Porto. Bié, C Angola 12°21′S 16°55′E
39 X14 **Kuiu Island** *island* Alexander Archipelago, Alaska, USA
92 L13 **Kuivaniemi** Oulu, C Finland 65°34′N 25°13′E
77 V14 **Kujama** Kaduna, C Nigeria 10°27′N 07°39′E
110 I10 **Kujawsko-pomorskie** ◐ *province* C Poland
165 R8 **Kuji** *var.* Kuzi. Iwate, Honshū, C Japan 40°12′N 141°47′E
Kujto, Ozero *see* Yushkozerskoye Vodokhranilishche
Kujū-renzan *see* Kujū-san
164 D14 **Kujū-san** *var.* Kujū-renzan. ▲ Kyūshū, SW Japan 33°07′N 131°13′E
43 N7 **Kukalaya, Rio** *var.* Rio Cuculaya, Rio Kukulaya. ≈ NE Nicaragua
113 O16 **Kukavica** *var.* Vlajna. ▲ SE Serbia 42°46′N 21°58′E
113 M18 **Kukës** *var.* Kukësi. Kukës, NE Albania 42°03′N 20°25′E
113 L18 **Kukës** ◐ *district* NE Albania
Kukësi *see* Kukës
186 D8 **Kukipi** Gulf, S Papua New Guinea 08°11′S 146°09′E
127 S3 **Kukmor** Respublika Tatarstan, W Russian Federation 56°11′N 50°56′E
Kukong *see* Shaoguan
39 N6 **Kukpowruk River** ≈ Alaska, USA
38 M6 **Kukpuk River** ≈ Alaska, USA
Kükýdağ *see* Gogi, Mount
Kukukhoto *see* Hohhot
Kukulaya, Rio *see* Kukalaya, Rio
189 W12 **Kuku Point** *headland* NW Wake Island 19°19′N 166°36′E
146 G11 **Kukurtli** Ahal Welaýaty, C Turkmenistan 39°58′N 58°47′E
Kül *see* Kül, Rūd-e
114 F7 **Kula** Vidin, NW Bulgaria 43°55′N 22°32′E
112 K9 **Kula** Vojvodina, NW Serbia 45°37′N 19°31′E
136 D14 **Kula** Manisa, W Turkey 38°33′N 28°38′E
149 S8 **Kulāchi** North-West Frontier Province, NW Pakistan 31°58′N 70°30′E
Kulachi *see* Kolāchi
144 F11 **Kulagino** *Kaz.* Kūlagīno. Atyrau, W Kazakhstan 48°30′N 51°33′E
Kūlagīno *see* Kulagino
168 L10 **Kulai** Johor, Peninsular Malaysia 01°41′N 103°33′E
114 M7 **Kulak** ≈ NE Bulgaria
153 T11 **Kula Kangri** *var.* Kulhakangri. ▲ Bhutan/ China 28°06′N 90°19′E
144 E13 **Kulaly, Ostrov** *island* SW Kazakhstan
145 S16 **Kulan** *Kaz.* Qulan; *prev.* Lugovoy, Lugovoye. Zhambyl, S Kazakhstan 42°54′N 72°45′E
147 V9 **Kulanak** Narynskaya Oblast', C Kyrgyzstan 41°18′N 75°38′E
Gory Kulandag *see* Gulandag
153 V14 **Kulaura** Sylhet, NE Bangladesh 24°32′N 92°02′E
118 D9 **Kuldīga** *Ger.* Goldingen. Kuldīga, W Latvia 56°57′N 21°59′E
Kuldja *see* Yining
Kul'dzhuktau, Gory *see* QuljuqtovTog'lari
127 N4 **Kulebaki** Nizhegorodskaya Oblast', W Russian Federation 55°25′N 42°31′E
112 E11 **Kulen Vakuf** *var.* Spasovo. ◐ Federacija Bosna I Hercegovina, NW Bosnia and Herzegovina
181 Q9 **Kulgera Roadhouse** Northern Territory, N Australia 25°49′S 133°30′E
Kulhakangri *see* Kula Kangri
127 T1 **Kuliga** Udmurtskaya Respublika, NW Russian Federation 58°14′N 53°49′E
Kulkuduk *see* Ko'lquduq
118 G4 **Kullamaa** Läänemaa, W Estonia 58°52′N 24°05′E
197 O12 **Kullorsuaq** *var.* Kuvdlorssuak. ◐ Kitaa, C Greenland
29 O6 **Kulm** North Dakota, N USA 46°18′N 98°57′W
Kulm *see* Chełmno
146 D12 **Kul'mach** *prev. Turkm.* Isgender. Balkan Welaýaty, W Turkmenistan 39°04′N 55°49′E
101 L18 **Kulmbach** Bayern, SE Germany 50°07′N 11°27′E
Kulmsee *see* Chełmża
147 Q14 **Kŭlob** *Rus.* Kulyab. SW Tajikistan 37°55′N 68°46′E
92 M13 **Kuloharju** Lappi, N Finland 65°51′N 28°10′E
125 N7 **Kuloy** Arkhangel'skaya Oblast', NW Russian Federation 64°55′N 43°35′E
125 N7 **Kuloy** ≈ NW Russian Federation
137 Q14 **Kulp** Dıyarbakır, SE Turkey 38°32′N 41°01′E
Kulpa *see* Kolpa
77 P14 **Kulpawn** ≈ N Ghana
143 R13 **Kūl, Rūd-e** *var.* Kül. ≈ S Iran
144 G12 **Kul'sary** *Kaz.* Qulsary. Atyrau, W Kazakhstan 46°59′N 54°02′E
153 R15 **Kulti** West Bengal, NE India 23°45′N 86°50′E
93 G14 **Kultsjön** ◎ N Sweden
136 I14 **Kulu** Konya, W Turkey 39°06′N 33°02′E
123 S9 **Kulu** ≈ E Russian Federation
122 I13 **Kulunda** Altayskiy Kray, S Russian Federation 52°33′N 79°04′E
145 T7 **Kulunda Steppe** *Kaz.* Qulyndy Zhazyghy, *Rus.* Kulundinskaya Ravnina. *grassland* Kazakhstan/Russian Federation
Kulundinskaya Ravnina *see* Kulunda Steppe
182 M9 **Kulwin** Victoria, SE Australia 35°04′S 142°37′E
Kulyab *see* Kŭlob
117 Q3 **Kulykivka** Chernihivs'ka Oblast', N Ukraine 51°23′N 31°39′E
Kum *see* Qom
164 F14 **Kuma** Ehime, Shikoku, SW Japan 33°36′N 132°53′E
127 P14 **Kuma** ≈ SW Russian Federation
165 O12 **Kumagaya** Saitama, Honshū, S Japan 36°09′N 139°22′E
165 Q5 **Kumaishi** Hokkaidō, NE Japan 42°08′N 139°57′E
169 R13 **Kumai, Teluk** *bay* Borneo, C Indonesia
127 Y7 **Kumak** Orenburgskaya Oblast', W Russian Federation 51°16′N 60°06′E
164 C14 **Kumamoto** Kumamoto, Kyūshū, SW Japan 32°49′N 130°41′E

◆ Country
● Country Capital
◇ Dependent Territory
○ Dependent Territory Capital
◐ Administrative Regions
✈ International Airport
▲ Mountain
▲▲ Mountain Range
Volcano
≈ River
◎ Lake
▣ Reservoir

Kumamoto – Labrador City

164 D15 **Kumamoto** *off.* Kumamoto-ken. ◈ *prefecture* Kyūshū, SW Japan
Kumamoto-ken *see* Kumamoto
164 J15 **Kumano** Mie, Honshū, SW Japan 33°54′N 136°08′E
Kumanova *see* Kumanovo
113 O17 **Kumanovo** *Turk.* Kumanova. N Macedonia 42°08′N 21°43′E
185 G17 **Kumara** West Coast, South Island, New Zealand 42°39′S 171°12′E
180 J8 **Kumarina Roadhouse** Western Australia 24°46′S 119°39′E
153 T15 **Kumarkhali** Khulna, W Bangladesh 23°54′N 89°16′E
77 P16 **Kumasi** *prev.* Coomassie. C Ghana 06°41′N 01°40′W
Kumayri *see* Gyumri
79 D15 **Kumba** Sud-Ouest, W Cameroon 04°39′N 09°26′E
114 N13 **Kumbağ** Tekirdağ, NW Turkey 40°51′N 27°26′E
155 J21 **Kumbakonam** Tamil Nādu, SE India 10°59′N 79°24′E
Kum-Dag *see* Gumdag
165 R16 **Kume-jima** *island* Nansei-shotō, SW Japan
127 V6 **Kumertau** Respublika Bashkortostan, W Russian Federation 52°48′N 55°48′E
Kumillā *see* Comilla
35 R4 **Kumiva Peak** ▲ Nevada, W USA 40°24′N 119°16′W
159 N7 **Kum Kuduk** Xinjiang Uygur Zizhiqu, W China 40°15′N 91°55′E
159 N8 **Kum Kuduk** *well* NW China
Kumkurgan *see* Qumqo'rg'on
95 M16 **Kumla** Örebro, C Sweden 59°08′N 15°09′E
136 E17 **Kumluca** Antalya, SW Turkey 36°23′N 30°17′E
100 N9 **Kummerower See** ◎ NE Germany
77 X14 **Kumo** Gombe, E Nigeria 10°03′N 11°14′E
145 O13 **Kumola** ~ C Kazakhstan
167 N1 **Kumon Range** ▲ N Myanmar (Burma)
83 F22 **Kums** Karas, SE Namibia 28°07′S 19°40′E
124 I7 **Kumskoye Vodokhranilishche** ☒ NW Russian Federation
155 E18 **Kumta** Karnātaka, W India 14°25′N 74°24′E
158 L6 **Kümük** Xinjiang Uygur Zizhiqu, W China
38 H12 **Kumukahi, Cape** *headland* Hawai'i, USA, C Pacific Ocean 19°31′N 154°48′W
127 Q17 **Kumukh** Respublika Dagestan, SW Russian Federation 42°10′N 47°07′E
Kumul *see* Hami
127 N9 **Kumylzhenskaya** Volgogradskaya Oblast', SW Russian Federation 49°54′N 42°35′E
141 W6 **Kumzār** N Oman
43 W15 **Kuna de Madungandí** ◈ *special territory* NE Panama
Kunar *see* Konar
Kunashiri *see* Kunashir, Ostrov
123 U14 **Kunashir, Ostrov** *var.* Kunashiri. *island* Kuril'skiye Ostrova, SE Russian Federation
43 V14 **Kuna Yala** *prev.* San Blas. ◈ *special territory* NE Panama
118 I3 **Kunda** Lääne-Virumaa, NE Estonia 59°31′N 26°33′E
152 M13 **Kunda** Uttar Pradesh, N India 25°43′N 81°31′E
155 E19 **Kundāpura** *var.* Coondapoor. Karnātaka, W India 13°39′N 74°41′E
79 O24 **Kundelungu, Monts** ▲ S Dem. Rep. Congo
Kundert *see* Hernád
186 D7 **Kundiawa** Chimbu, W Papua New Guinea 06°00′S 144°57′E
Kundla *see* Sāvarkundla
Kunduk, Ozero *see* Sasyk, Ozero
168 L10 **Kundur, Pulau** *island* W Indonesia
Kunduz *see* Kondoz
Kunduz/Kundūz *see* Kondoz
Kuneitra *see* Al Qunayṭirah
83 B18 **Kunene** ◈ *district* NE Namibia
83 A16 **Kunene** *var.* Cunene. ~ Angola/Namibia *see also* Cunene
Kunene *see* Cunene
Künes *see* Xinyuan
158 J5 **Künes He** ~ NW China
95 I19 **Kungälv** Västra Götaland, S Sweden 57°54′N 12°00′E
147 W7 **Kungei Ala-Tau** *Rus.* Khrebet Kyungëy Ala-Too, *Kir.* Küngöy Ala-Too. ▲ Kazakhstan/Kyrgyzstan
Küngöy Ala-Too *see* Kungei Ala-Tau
Kungrad *see* Qo'ng'irot
95 J19 **Kungsbacka** Halland, S Sweden 57°30′N 12°05′E
95 I18 **Kungshamn** Västra Götaland, S Sweden 58°21′N 11°15′E
95 M16 **Kungsör** Västmanland, C Sweden 59°25′N 16°05′E
79 J16 **Kungu** Equateur, NW Dem. Rep. Congo 02°47′N 19°12′E
125 V15 **Kungur** Permskaya Oblast', NW Russian Federation 57°24′N 56°56′E
166 L9 **Kungyangon** Yangon, SW Myanmar (Burma) 16°27′N 96°00′E
111 M22 **Kunhegyes** Jász-Nagykun-Szolnok, E Hungary 47°22′N 20°36′E
167 O5 **Kunhing** Shan State, E Myanmar (Burma) 21°17′N 98°26′E
158 D9 **Kunjirap Daban** *var.* Khūnjerāb Pass. *pass* China/Pakistan *see also* Khūnjerāb Pass
Kunjirap Daban *see* Khunjerab Pass
Kunlun Mountains *see* Kunlun Shan
158 H10 **Kunlun Shan** *Eng.* Kunlun Mountains. ▲ NW China
159 P11 **Kunlun Shankou** *pass* C China
160 G13 **Kunming** *var.* K'un-ming; *prev.* Yunnan. *province capital* Yunnan, SW China 25°04′N 102°41′E
K'un-ming *see* Kunming
95 B18 **Kunoy** *Dan.* Kunø. *island* N Faeroe Islands
163 X16 **Kunsan** *var.* Gunsan, *Jap.* Gunzan. W South Korea 35°58′N 126°42′E
111 L24 **Kunszentmárton** Jász-Nagykun-Szolnok, E Hungary 46°50′N 20°19′E
111 J23 **Kunszentmiklós** Bács-Kiskun, C Hungary 47°00′N 19°07′E
181 N3 **Kununurra** Western Australia 15°50′S 128°44′E
Kunyang *see* Pingyang
Kunya-Urgench *see* Köneürgenç
Kunyé *see* Pins, Île des
169 T11 **Kunyi** Borneo, C Indonesia 03°23′S 119°20′E
101 I20 **Künzelsau** Baden-Württemberg, S Germany 49°22′N 09°43′E
161 S10 **Kuocang Shan** ▲ SE China
Kuolajärvi *see* Kuoloyarvi
124 H5 **Kuoloyarvi** *Finn.* Kuolajärvi, *var.* Luolajarvi. Murmanskaya Oblast', NW Russian Federation 66°58′N 29°13′E
93 N16 **Kuopio** Itä-Suomi, C Finland 62°54′N 27°41′E
93 K17 **Kuortane** Länsi-Suomi, W Finland 62°48′N 23°30′E
93 M18 **Kuortti** Itä-Suomi, E Finland 61°25′N 26°25′E
112 E9 **Kupa** ~ Croatia/Slovenia
Kupa *see* Kolpa
171 P17 **Kupang** *prev.* Koepang. Timor, C Indonesia 10°13′S 123°38′E
39 Q5 **Kuparuk River** ~ Alaska, USA
Kupchino *see* Cupcina
186 E9 **Kupiano** Central, S Papua New Guinea 10°06′S 148°12′E
180 M4 **Kupingarri** Western Australia 16°46′S 125°57′E
122 I12 **Kupino** Novosibirskaya Oblast', C Russian Federation 54°22′N 77°09′E
118 H11 **Kupiškis** Panevėžys, NE Lithuania 55°51′N 24°58′E
114 L13 **Küplü** Edirne, NW Turkey 41°06′N 26°23′E
39 X13 **Kupreanof Island** *island* Alexander Archipelago, Alaska, USA
39 O16 **Kupreanof Point** *headland* Alaska, USA 55°34′N 159°36′W
112 G13 **Kupres** ◈ Federacija Bosna I Hercegovina, SW Bosnia and Herzegovina
117 W5 **Kup"yans'k** *Rus.* Kupyansk. Kharkivs'ka Oblast', E Ukraine 49°42′N 37°36′E
Kupyansk *see* Kup"yans'k
117 W5 **Kup"yans'k-Vuzlovyy** Kharkivs'ka Oblast', E Ukraine 49°40′N 37°41′E
158 I6 **Kuqa** Xinjiang Uygur Zizhiqu, NW China 41°43′N 82°58′E
Kür *see* Kura
137 W11 **Kura** *Az.* Kür, *Geor.* Mtkvari, *Turk.* Kura Nehri. ~ SW Asia
55 R8 **Kuracki** NW Guyana 06°52′N 60°13′W
Kura Kurk *see* Irbe Strait
147 Q10 **Kurama Range** *Rus.* Kuraminskiy Khrebet. ▲ Tajikistan/Uzbekistan
Kuraminskiy Khrebet *see* Kurama Range
Kura Nehri *see* Kura
119 J14 **Kuranyets** *Rus.* Kurenets. Minskaya Voblasts', C Belarus 54°33′N 26°57′E
164 H13 **Kurashiki** *var.* Kurasiki. Okayama, Honshū, SW Japan 34°35′N 133°44′E
154 L10 **Kurasia** Chhattīsgarh, C India 23°11′N 82°16′E
Kurasiki *see* Kurashiki
164 H12 **Kurayoshi** *var.* Kurayosi. Tottori, Honshū, SW Japan 35°27′N 133°52′E
Kurayosi *see* Kurayoshi
163 X6 **Kurbin He** ~ NE China
145 U9 **Kurchatov** *prev.* Konechnaya. Pavlodar, NE Kazakhstan 50°45′N 78°32′E
145 X10 **Kurchum** *Kaz.* Kürshim. Vostochnyy Kazakhstan, E Kazakhstan 48°35′N 83°37′E
145 Y10 **Kurchum** ~ E Kazakhstan
137 X11 **Kürdämir** *Rus.* Kyurdamir. C Azerbaijan 40°21′N 48°08′E
Kurdestan *see* Kordestān
139 S1 **Kurdistan** *cultural region* SW Asia
Kurd Kui *see* Kord Küy
155 F15 **Kurduvādi** Mahārāshtra, W India 18°06′N 75°31′E
114 J11 **Kŭrdzhali** *var.* Kirdzhali. Kŭrdzhali, S Bulgaria 41°39′N 25°23′E
114 K11 **Kŭrdzhali** ◈ *province* S Bulgaria
114 J11 **Kŭrdzhali, Yazovir** ☒ S Bulgaria
164 F13 **Kure** Hiroshima, Honshū, SW Japan 34°15′N 132°33′E
192 K5 **Kure Atoll** *var.* Ocean Island. *atoll* Hawaiian Islands, Hawaii, USA
136 J10 **Küre Dağları** ▲ N Turkey
146 C11 **Kürendag** *Rus.* Gora Kyuren. ▲ W Turkmenistan 39°05′N 55°09′E
Kurenets *see* Kuranyets
118 E6 **Kuressaare** *Ger.* Arensburg; *prev.* Kingissepp. Saaremaa, W Estonia 58°17′N 22°29′E
122 K9 **Kureyka** Krasnoyarskiy Kray, N Russian Federation 66°22′N 87°21′E
122 K9 **Kureyka** ~ N Russian Federation
Kurgal'dzhino/Kurgal'dzhinsky *see* Korgalzhyn
122 G11 **Kurgan** Kurganskaya Oblast', C Russian Federation 55°30′N 65°20′E
126 L14 **Kurganinsk** Krasnodarskiy Kray, SW Russian Federation 44°55′N 40°45′E
122 G11 **Kurganskaya Oblast'** ◈ *province* C Russian Federation
Kurgan-Tyube *see* Qŭrghonteppa
191 O2 **Kuria** *prev.* Woodle Island. *island* Tungaru, W Kiribati
Kuria Muria Bay *see* Ḥalāniyāt, Khalīj al
Kuria Muria Islands *see* Ḥalāniyāt, Juzur al
153 T13 **Kurigram** Rajshahi, N Bangladesh 25°49′N 89°39′E
93 K17 **Kurikka** Länsi-Suomi, W Finland 62°36′N 22°25′E
192 I3 **Kurile Basin** *undersea feature* NW Pacific Ocean 47°00′N 150°00′E
Kurile Islands *see* Kuril'skiye Ostrova
Kurile-Kamchatka Depression *see* Kurile Trench
192 J3 **Kurile Trench** *var.* Kurile-Kamchatka Depression. *undersea feature* NW Pacific Ocean 47°00′N 155°00′E
127 Q9 **Kurilovka** Saratovskaya Oblast', W Russian Federation 50°39′N 48°02′E
123 U13 **Kuril'sk** *Jap.* Shana. Kuril'skiye Ostrova, Sakhalinskaya Oblats', SE Russian Federation 45°10′N 147°51′E
122 G11 **Kuril'skiye Ostrova** *Eng.* Kurile Islands. *island group* SE Russian Federation
42 M9 **Kurinwas, Río** ~ E Nicaragua
Kurisches Haff *see* Courland Lagoon
Kurkund *see* Kilingi-Nõmme
126 M4 **Kurlovskiy** Vladimirskaya Oblast', W Russian Federation 55°25′N 40°39′E
80 G12 **Kurmuk** Blue Nile, SE Sudan 10°36′N 34°16′E
Kurna *see* Al Qurnah
155 H17 **Kurnool** *var.* Karnul. Andhra Pradesh, S India 15°51′N 78°01′E
164 M11 **Kurobe** Toyama, Honshū, SW Japan 36°55′N 137°24′E
165 Q7 **Kuroishi** *var.* Kuroisi. Aomori, Honshū, C Japan 40°37′N 140°34′E
Kuroisi *see* Kuroishi
165 O12 **Kuroiso** Tochigi, Honshū, S Japan 36°58′N 140°02′E
165 Q4 **Kuromatsunai** Hokkaidō, NE Japan 42°40′N 140°18′E
164 B17 **Kuro-shima** *island* SW Japan
185 F21 **Kurow** Canterbury, South Island, New Zealand 44°44′S 170°29′E
127 N15 **Kursavka** Stavropol'skiy Kray, SW Russian Federation 44°28′N 42°31′E
118 E11 **Kuršėnai** Šiauliai, N Lithuania 56°00′N 22°56′E
Kürshim *see* Kurchum
Kurshskaya Kosa/Kuršių Nerija *see* Courland Spit
126 J7 **Kursk** Kurskaya Oblast', W Russian Federation 51°44′N 36°47′E
126 I7 **Kurskaya Oblast'** ◈ *province* W Russian Federation
Kurskiy Zaliv *see* Courland Lagoon
113 N15 **Kuršumlija** Serbia, S Serbia 43°09′N 21°16′E
137 R15 **Kurtalan** Siirt, SE Turkey 37°58′N 41°36′E
Kurtbunar *see* Tervel
Kurt-Dere *see* Vŭlchidol
Kurtitsch/Kürtös *see* Curtici
145 U15 **Kurtty** ~ SE Kazakhstan
93 L18 **Kuru** Länsi-Suomi, W Finland 61°51′N 23°46′E
80 C13 **Kuru** ~ W Sudan
114 M13 **Kuru Dağı** ▲ NW Turkey
158 L7 **Kuruktag** ▲ NW China
83 G22 **Kuruman** Northern Cape, N South Africa 27°28′S 23°27′E
67 T14 **Kuruman** ~ W South Africa
164 D14 **Kurume** Fukuoka, Kyūshū, SW Japan 33°15′N 130°27′E
123 N13 **Kurumkan** Respublika Buryatiya, S Russian Federation 54°13′N 110°21′E
155 J25 **Kurunegala** North Western Province, C Sri Lanka 07°28′N 80°23′E
55 T10 **Kurupukari** C Guyana 04°39′N 58°39′W
125 U10 **Kur"ya** Respublika Komi, NW Russian Federation 61°38′N 57°12′E
144 E15 **Kuryk** *var.* Yeraliyev, *Kaz.* Quryq. Mangistau, SW Kazakhstan 43°12′N 51°43′E
136 B15 **Kuşadası** Aydın, SW Turkey 37°50′N 27°16′E
115 M19 **Kuşadası Körfezi** *gulf* SW Turkey
164 A17 **Kusagaki-guntō** *island* SW Japan
Kusaie *see* Kosrae
145 T12 **Kusak** ~ C Kazakhstan
Kusary *see* Qusar
167 P7 **Ku Sathan, Doi** ▲ NW Thailand 18°22′N 100°31′E
164 J13 **Kusatsu** *var.* Kusatu. Shiga, Honshū, SW Japan 35°02′N 136°00′E
Kusatu *see* Kusatsu
138 F11 **Kuseifa** Southern, C Israel 31°15′N 35°01′E
136 C12 **Kuş Gölü** ◎ NW Turkey
126 L12 **Kushchevskaya** Krasnodarskiy Kray, SW Russian Federation 46°35′N 39°40′E
164 D16 **Kushima** *var.* Kusima. Miyazaki, Kyūshū, SW Japan 31°28′N 131°14′E
164 I15 **Kushimoto** Wakayama, Honshū, SW Japan 33°28′N 135°45′E
165 V4 **Kushiro** *var.* Kusiro. Hokkaidō, NE Japan 42°58′N 144°24′E
148 K4 **Kūshk** Herāt, W Afghanistan 34°55′N 62°20′E
Kushka *see* Serhetabat
Kushka *see* Gushgy/Serhetabat
145 N8 **Kushmurun** *Kaz.* Qusmuryn. Kostanay, N Kazakhstan 52°27′N 64°31′E
145 N8 **Kushmurun, Ozero** *Kaz.* Qusmuryn. ◎ N Kazakhstan
127 U4 **Kushnarenkovo** Respublika Bashkortostan, W Russian Federation 55°07′N 55°24′E
Kushrabat *see* Qo'shrabot
Kushtia *see* Kustia
Kusima *see* Kushima
Kusiro *see* Kushiro
38 M13 **Kuskokwim Bay** *bay* Alaska, USA
39 P11 **Kuskokwim Mountains** ▲ Alaska, USA
39 N12 **Kuskokwim River** ~ Alaska, USA
108 G7 **Küsnacht** Zürich, N Switzerland 47°19′N 08°34′E
165 V4 **Kussharo-ko** *var.* Kussyaro. ◎ Hokkaidō, NE Japan
Küssnacht *see* Küssnacht am Rigi
108 F8 **Küssnacht am Rigi** *var.* Küssnacht. Schwyz, C Switzerland 47°03′N 08°25′E
Kussyaro *see* Kussharo-ko
Kustanay *see* Kostanay
Küstence/Küstendje *see* Constanța
100 F11 **Küstenkanal** *var.* Ems-Hunte Canal. *canal* NW Germany
153 T15 **Kustia** *var.* Kushtia. Khulna, W Bangladesh 23°54′N 89°07′E
Küstrin *see* Kostrzyn
171 R11 **Kusu** Pulau Halmahera, E Indonesia 0°51′N 127°41′E
170 L16 **Kuta** Pulau Lombok, S Indonesia 08°53′S 116°15′E
139 T4 **Kutabān** At Ta'mīn, N Iraq 35°21′N 44°45′E
136 E13 **Kütahya** *prev.* Kutaia. Kütahya, W Turkey 39°25′N 29°56′E
136 E13 **Kütahya** *var.* Kutaia. ◈ *province* W Turkey
Kutai *see* Mahakam, Sungai
Kutaia *see* Kütahya
137 R9 **K'ut'aisi** W Georgia 42°16′N 42°42′E
Kūt al 'Amārah *see* Al Kūt
Kut al Hai/Kūt al Ḥayy *see* Al Ḥayy
Kūt al Imara *see* Al Kūt
123 Q11 **Kutana** Respublika Sakha (Yakutiya), NE Russian Federation 59°05′N 131°43′E
Kutaradja/Kutaraja *see* Bandaaceh
165 R4 **Kutchan** Hokkaidō, NE Japan 42°54′N 140°46′E
Kutch, Gulf of *see* Kachchh, Gulf of
Kutch, Rann of *see* Kachchh, Rann of
112 F9 **Kutina** Sisak-Moslavina, NE Croatia 45°29′N 16°45′E
112 H9 **Kutjevo** Požega-Slavonija, NE Croatia 45°26′N 17°54′E
111 E17 **Kutná Hora** *Ger.* Kuttenberg. Střední Čechy, C Czech Republic 49°58′N 15°18′E
110 K12 **Kutno** Łódzkie, C Poland 52°14′N 19°23′E
Kuttenberg *see* Kutná Hora
79 I20 **Kutu** Bandundu, W Dem. Rep. Congo 02°42′S 18°10′E
153 V17 **Kutubdia Island** *island* SE Bangladesh
80 B10 **Kutum** Northern Darfur, W Sudan 14°10′N 24°40′E
147 Y7 **Kuturgu** Issyk-Kul'skaya Oblast', E Kyrgyzstan 42°45′N 78°04′E
12 M5 **Kuujjuaq** *prev.* Fort-Chimo. Québec, E Canada 58°10′N 68°15′W
12 I7 **Kuujjuarapik** Québec, C Canada 55°07′N 78°09′W
Kuuli-Mayak *see* Guwlumaýak
118 I6 **Kuulsemägi** ▲ S Estonia
92 N13 **Kuusamo** Oulu, E Finland 65°57′N 29°15′E
93 M19 **Kuusankoski** Etelä-Suomi, S Finland 60°51′N 26°40′E
127 W7 **Kuvandyk** Orenburgskaya Oblast', W Russian Federation 51°27′N 57°18′E
Kuvango *see* Cubango
Kuvasay *see* Quvasoy
Kuvdlorssuak *see* Kullorsuaq
124 I16 **Kuvshinovo** Tverskaya Oblast', W Russian Federation 57°03′N 34°09′E
141 Q4 **Kuwait** *off.* State of Kuwait, *var.* Dawlat al Kuwait, Koweit, Kuweit. ◆ *monarchy* SW Asia
Kuwait *see* Al Kuwayt
Kuwait Bay *see* Kuwayt, Jūn al
Kuwait City *see* Al Kuwayt
Kuwait, Dawlat al *see* Kuwait
Kuwait, State of *see* Kuwait
Kuwajleen *see* Kwajalein Atoll
164 K13 **Kuwana** Mie, Honshū, SW Japan 35°04′N 136°40′E
139 X9 **Kuwayt** Maysān, E Iraq 32°26′N 47°12′E
142 K11 **Kuwayt, Jūn al** *var.* Kuwait Bay. *bay* E Kuwait
Kuweit *see* Kuwait
117 P10 **Kuyal'nyts'kyy Lyman** ◎ SW Ukraine
122 I12 **Kuybyshev** Novosibirskaya Oblast', C Russian Federation 55°28′N 77°55′E
Kuybyshev *see* Bolgar, Respublika Tatarstan, Russian Federation
Kuybyshev *see* Samara
117 W9 **Kuybysheve** *Rus.* Kuybyshevo. Zaporiz'ka Oblast', SE Ukraine 47°20′N 36°41′E
Kuybyshevo *see* Kuybysheve
Kuybyshev Reservoir *see* Kuybyshevskoye Vodokhranilishche
Kuybyshevskaya Oblast' *see* Samarskaya Oblast'
Kuybyshevskiy *see* Novoishimskiy
127 R4 **Kuybyshevskoye Vodokhranilishche** *var.* Kuibyshev, *Eng.* Kuybyshev Reservoir. ☒ W Russian Federation
123 S9 **Kuydusun** Respublika Sakha (Yakutiya), NE Russian Federation 63°15′N 143°10′E
125 U16 **Kuyeda** Permskaya Oblast', NW Russian Federation 56°23′N 55°19′E
Küysanjaq *see* Koi Sanjaq
158 J4 **Kuytun** Xinjiang Uygur Zizhiqu, NW China 44°25′N 84°55′E
122 M13 **Kuytun** Irkutskaya Oblast', S Russian Federation 54°18′N 101°28′E
55 S12 **Kuyuwini Landing** S Guyana 02°06′N 59°14′W
Kuzi *see* Kuji
38 M9 **Kuzitrin River** ~ Alaska, USA
127 P6 **Kuznetsk** Penzenskaya Oblast', W Russian Federation 53°06′N 46°27′E
116 K3 **Kuznetsovs'k** Rivnens'ka Oblast', NW Ukraine 51°21′N 25°51′E
165 R8 **Kuzumaki** Iwate, Honshū, C Japan 40°04′N 141°26′E
95 H24 **Kværndrup** Fyn, C Denmark 55°10′N 10°31′E
92 H9 **Kvaløya** *island* N Norway
92 K8 **Kvalsund** Finnmark, N Norway 70°30′N 23°56′E
94 G11 **Kvam** Oppland, S Norway 61°42′N 09°43′E
127 X7 **Kvarkeno** Orenburgskaya Oblast', W Russian Federation 52°09′N 59°44′E
93 G15 **Kvarnbergsvattnet** *var.* Frostviken. ◎ N Sweden
112 A11 **Kvarner** *var.* Carnaro, *It.* Quarnero. *gulf* W Croatia
112 B11 **Kvarnerić** *channel* W Croatia
39 O14 **Kvichak Bay** *bay* Alaska, USA
92 H12 **Kvikkjokk** *Lapp.* Huhttán. Norrbotten, N Sweden 66°58′N 17°45′E
95 D17 **Kvina** ~ S Norway
92 Q1 **Kvitøya** *island* NE Svalbard
95 F16 **Kvitseid** Telemark, S Norway 59°23′N 08°31′E
79 H20 **Kwa** ~ W Dem. Rep. Congo
77 Q15 **Kwadwokurom** C Ghana 07°49′N 00°15′W
186 M8 **Kwailibesi** Malaita, N Solomon Islands 08°25′S 160°48′E
189 S6 **Kwajalein Atoll** *var.* Kuwajleen. *atoll* Ralik Chain, C Marshall Islands
55 W9 **Kwakoegron** Brokopondo, N Suriname 05°14′N 55°20′W
81 J21 **Kwale** Coast, S Kenya 04°10′S 39°27′E
77 U17 **Kwale** Delta, S Nigeria 05°51′N 06°29′E
79 H20 **Kwamouth** Bandundu, W Dem. Rep. Congo 03°11′S 16°16′E
Kwando *see* Cuando
Kwangchow *see* Guangzhou
Kwangchu *see* Kwangju
163 X16 **Kwangju** *off.* Kwangju-gwangyŏksi, *var.* Guangju, Kwangchu, *Jap.* Kōshū. SW South Korea 35°09′N 126°53′E
Kwangju-gwangyŏksi *see* Kwangju
79 H20 **Kwango** *Port.* Cuango. ~ Angola/Dem. Rep. Congo *see also* Cuango
Kwango *see* Cuango
Kwangsi/Kwangsi Chuang Autonomous Region *see* Guangxi Zhuangzu Zizhiqu
Kwangtung *see* Guangdong
Kwangyuan *see* Guangyuan
81 F17 **Kwania, Lake** ◎ C Uganda
Kwanza *see* Cuanza
77 S15 **Kwara** ◈ *state* SW Nigeria
83 K22 **KwaZulu/Natal** *off.* KwaZulu/Natal Province; *prev.* Natal. ◈ *province* E South Africa
KwaZulu/Natal Province *see* KwaZulu/Natal
Kweichow *see* Guizhou
Kweichu *see* Guiyang
Kweilin *see* Guilin
Kweisui *see* Hohhot
Kweiyang *see* Guiyang
83 K17 **Kwekwe** *prev.* Que Que. Midlands, C Zimbabwe 18°56′S 29°49′E
83 G20 **Kweneng** ◈ *district* S Botswana
Kwesui *see* Hohhot
39 N12 **Kwethluk** Alaska, USA 60°48′N 161°26′W
39 N12 **Kwethluk River** ~ Alaska, USA
110 J8 **Kwidzyń** *Ger.* Marienwerder. Pomorskie, N Poland 53°44′N 18°55′E
38 M13 **Kwigillingok** Alaska, USA 59°52′N 163°08′W
186 E9 **Kwikila** Central, S Papua New Guinea 09°51′S 147°43′E
79 I20 **Kwilu** ~ W Dem. Rep. Congo
Kwito *see* Cuito
171 U12 **Kwoka, Gunung** ▲ Papua, E Indonesia 0°34′S 132°25′E
78 I12 **Kyabé** Moyen-Chari, S Chad 09°28′N 18°54′E
183 O11 **Kyabram** Victoria, SE Australia 36°21′S 145°05′E
166 M9 **Kyaikkami** *prev.* Amherst. Mon State, S Myanmar (Burma) 16°03′N 97°36′E
166 L9 **Kyaiklat** Ayeyarwady, SW Myanmar (Burma) 16°25′N 95°42′E
166 M8 **Kyaikto** Mon State, S Myanmar (Burma) 17°16′N 97°01′E
123 N14 **Kyakhta** Respublika Buryatiya, S Russian Federation 50°25′N 106°13′E
182 G8 **Kyancutta** South Australia 33°10′S 135°33′E
167 T8 **Ky Anh** Ha Tinh, N Vietnam 18°05′N 106°16′E
166 L5 **Kyaukpadaung** Mandalay, C Myanmar (Burma) 20°50′N 95°08′E
166 J6 **Kyaukpyu** Rakhine State, W Myanmar (Burma) 19°27′N 93°33′E
166 M5 **Kyaukse** Mandalay, C Myanmar (Burma) 21°33′N 96°06′E
166 L8 **Kyaunggon** Ayeyarwady, SW Myanmar (Burma) 17°04′N 95°12′E
119 E14 **Kybartai** *Pol.* Kibarty. Marijampolė, S Lithuania 54°37′N 22°44′E
152 I7 **Kyelang** Himāchal Pradesh, NW India 32°33′N 77°03′E
111 G19 **Kyjov** *Ger.* Gaya. Jihomoravský Kraj, SE Czech Republic 49°00′N 17°07′E
115 J21 **Kykládes** *var.* Kikládhes, *Eng.* Cyclades. *island group* SE Greece
25 S11 **Kyle** Texas, SW USA 29°59′N 97°52′W
96 G9 **Kyle of Lochalsh** N Scotland, United Kingdom 57°18′N 05°39′W
101 D18 **Kyll** ~ W Germany
115 F19 **Kyllíni** *var.* Killini. ▲ S Greece
93 M19 **Kymijoki** ~ S Finland
115 H18 **Kými** *prev.* Kími. Évvoia, C Greece 38°38′N 24°06′E
115 H18 **Kýmis, Akrotírio** *headland* Évvoia, C Greece 38°39′N 24°08′E
125 W14 **Kyn** Permskaya Oblast', NW Russian Federation 57°48′N 58°38′E
183 N12 **Kyneton** Victoria, SE Australia 37°14′S 144°28′E
81 G17 **Kyoga, Lake** *var.* Lake Kioga. ◎ C Uganda
164 J12 **Kyōga-misaki** *headland* Honshū, SW Japan 35°46′N 135°13′E
183 V4 **Kyogle** New South Wales, SE Australia 28°37′S 153°00′E
163 W15 **Kyŏnggi-man** *bay* NW South Korea
163 Z16 **Kyŏngju** *Jap.* Keishū. SE South Korea 35°49′N 129°09′E
Kyŏngsŏng *see* Sŏul
Kyōsai-tō *see* Kŏje-do
81 F19 **Kyotera** S Uganda 0°38′S 31°34′E
164 J13 **Kyōto** Kyōto, Honshū, SW Japan 35°01′N 135°46′E
164 J13 **Kyōto** *off.* Kyōto-fu, *var.* Kyōto Hu. ◈ *urban prefecture* Honshū, SW Japan
Kyōto-fu/Kyōto Hu *see* Kyōto
115 D21 **Kyparissía** *var.* Kiparissía. Pelopónnisos, S Greece 37°15′N 21°40′E
115 D20 **Kyparissiakós Kólpos** *gulf* S Greece
Kyperounda *see* Kyperoúnta
121 P3 **Kyperoúnta** *var.* Kyperounda. C Cyprus 34°57′N 33°02′E
Kypros *see* Cyprus
115 H16 **Kyrá Panagía** *island* Vóreies Sporádes, Greece, Aegean Sea
Kyrenia *see* Girne
Kyrenia Mountains *see* Beşparmak Dağları
Kyrgyz Republic *see* Kyrgyzstan
147 U9 **Kyrgyzstan** *off.* Kyrgyz Republic, *var.* Kirghizia; *prev.* Kirgizskaya SSR, Kirghiz SSR, Republic of Kyrgyzstan. ◆ *republic* C Asia
Kyrgyzstan, Republic of *see* Kyrgyzstan
138 F11 **Kyriat Gat** *prev.* Qiryat Gat. Southern, C Israel 31°37′N 34°47′E
100 M11 **Kyritz** Brandenburg, NE Germany 52°56′N 12°24′E
94 G8 **Kyrksæterøra** Sør-Trøndelag, S Norway 63°17′N 09°06′E
Kyrkslätt *see* Kirkkonummi
125 U8 **Kyrta** Respublika Komi, NW Russian Federation 64°03′N 57°41′E
111 J18 **Kysucké Nové Mesto** *prev.* Horné Nové Mesto, *Ger.* Kisutzaneustadtl, Oberneustadtl, *Hung.* Kiszucaújhely. Žilinský Kraj, N Slovakia 49°18′N 18°48′E
117 N12 **Kytay, Ozero** ◎ SW Ukraine
115 F23 **Kýthira** *var.* Kíthira, *It.* Cerigo, *Lat.* Cythera. Kýthira, S Greece 41°39′N 26°30′E
115 F23 **Kýthira** *var.* Kíthira, *It.* Cerigo, *Lat.* Cythera. *island* S Greece
115 I20 **Kýthnos** Kýthnos, Kykládes, Greece, Aegean Sea 37°24′N 24°28′E
115 I20 **Kýthnos** *var.* Kíthnos, Thermiá, *It.* Termia; *anc.* Cythnos. *island* Kykládes, Greece, Aegean Sea
115 I20 **Kýthnou, Stenó** *strait* Kykládes, Greece, Aegean Sea
Kyungëy Ala-Too, Khrebet *see* Kungei Ala-Tau
Kyurdamir *see* Kürdämir
164 D15 **Kyūshū** *var.* Kyûsyû. *island* SW Japan
192 H6 **Kyushu-Palau Ridge** *var.* Kyusyu-Palau Ridge. *undersea feature* W Pacific Ocean 20°00′N 136°00′E
114 F10 **Kyustendil** *anc.* Pautalia. Kyustendil, W Bulgaria 42°17′N 22°42′E
114 G11 **Kyustendil** ◈ *province* W Bulgaria
Kyûsyû *see* Kyūshū
Kyusyu-Palau Ridge *see* Kyushu-Palau Ridge
123 P8 **Kyusyur** Respublika Sakha (Yakutiya), NE Russian Federation 70°36′N 127°19′E
183 P10 **Kywong** New South Wales, SE Australia 34°59′S 146°42′E
117 P4 **Kyyiv** *Eng.* Kiev, *Rus.* Kiyev. ● (Ukraine) Kyyivs'ka Oblast', N Ukraine 50°26′N 30°32′E
Kyyiv *see* Kyyivs'ka Oblast'
117 O4 **Kyyivs'ka Oblast'** *var.* Kyyiv, *Rus.* Kiyevskaya Oblast'. ◈ *province* N Ukraine
117 P3 **Kyyivs'ke Vodoskhovyshche** *Eng.* Kiev Reservoir, *Rus.* Kiyevskoye Vodokhranilishche. ☒ N Ukraine
93 L16 **Kyyjärvi** Länsi-Suomi, C Finland 63°02′N 24°34′E
122 K14 **Kyzyl** Respublika Tyva, C Russian Federation 51°45′N 94°28′E
147 S8 **Kyzyl-Adyr** *var.* Kirovskoye. Talasskaya Oblast', NW Kyrgyzstan 42°37′N 71°34′E
145 V14 **Kyzylagash** *Kaz.* Qyzylaghash. Almaty, SE Kazakhstan 45°20′N 78°45′E
146 C13 **Kyzylbair** Balkan Welaýaty, W Turkmenistan 38°13′N 55°38′E
Kyzyl-Dzhiik, Pereval *see* Uzbel Shankou
145 S7 **Kyzylkak, Ozero** ◎ NE Kazakhstan
145 X11 **Kyzylkesek** Vostochnyy Kazakhstan, E Kazakhstan 47°56′N 82°02′E
147 S10 **Kyzyl-Kiya** *Kir.* Kyzyl-Kyya. Batkenskaya Oblast', SW Kyrgyzstan 40°15′N 72°07′E
144 L11 **Kyzylkol', Ozero** ◎ C Kazakhstan
142 K14 **Kyzyl Kum** *var.* Kizil Kum, Qizil Qum, *Uzb.* Qizilqum. *desert* Kazakhstan/Uzbekistan
Kyzyl-Kyya *see* Kyzyl-Kiya
144 L14 **Kyzylorda** *off.* Kyzylordinskaya Oblysy, *Kaz.* Qyzylorda Oblysy. ◈ *province* S Kazakhstan
Kyzylordinskaya Oblast' *see* Kyzylorda
Kyzylrabat *see* Qizilravote
Kyzylrabot *see* Qizilrabot
Kyzylsu *see* Kyzyl-Suu
147 X7 **Kyzyl-Suu** *prev.* Pokrovka. Issyk-Kul'skaya Oblast', NE Kyrgyzstan 42°20′N 77°55′E
147 S12 **Kyzyl-Suu** *var.* Kyzylsu. ~ Kyrgyzstan/Tajikistan
147 X8 **Kyzyl-Tuu** Issyk-Kul'skaya Oblast', E Kyrgyzstan 42°06′N 76°54′E
145 Q12 **Kyzylzhar** *Kaz.* Qyzylzhar. Karaganda, C Kazakhstan 48°22′N 70°00′E
145 N15 **Kzylorda** *var.* Kzyl-Orda, Qizil Orda, Qyzylorda; *prev.* Perovsk. Kyzylorda, S Kazakhstan 44°54′N 65°31′E
Kzyl-Orda *see* Kzylorda
Kzyltu *see* Kishkenekol'

L

109 X2 **Laa an der Thaya** Niederösterreich, NE Austria 48°44′N 16°23′E
63 K15 **La Adela** La Pampa, SE Argentina 38°57′S 64°02′W
Laagen *see* Numedalslågen
109 S5 **Laakirchen** Oberösterreich, N Austria 47°59′N 13°49′E
Laaland *see* Lolland
104 I11 **La Albuera** Extremadura, W Spain 38°43′N 06°49′W
105 O7 **La Alcarria** *physical region* C Spain
104 K14 **La Algaba** Andalucía, S Spain 37°27′N 06°01′W
105 P9 **La Almarcha** Castilla-La Mancha, C Spain 39°41′N 02°23′W
105 R6 **La Almunia de Doña Godina** Aragón, NE Spain 41°28′N 01°23′W
41 N5 **La Amistad, Presa** ☒ NW Mexico
118 F4 **Läänemaa** *var.* Lääne Maakond. ◈ *province* NW Estonia
Lääne Maakond *see* Läänemaa
118 I3 **Lääne-Virumaa** *off.* Lääne-Viru Maakond. ◈ *province* NE Estonia
Lääne-Viru Maakond *see* Lääne-Virumaa
62 J9 **La Antigua, Salina** *salt lake* W Argentina
99 E17 **Laarne** Oost-Vlaanderen, NW Belgium 51°03′N 03°50′E
80 O13 **Laas Caanood** Sool, N Somalia 08°33′N 47°44′E
41 O9 **La Ascensión** Nuevo León, NE Mexico 24°15′N 99°53′W
80 N12 **Laas Dhaareed** Sanaag, N Somalia 10°12′N 46°09′E
55 O4 **La Asunción** Nueva Esparta, NE Venezuela 11°06′N 63°53′W
Laatokka *see* Ladozhskoye, Ozero
100 I13 **Laatzen** Niedersachsen, NW Germany 52°19′N 09°46′E
38 E9 **La'au Point** *var.* Laau Point. *headland* Moloka'i, Hawai'i, USA 21°06′N 157°18′W
Laau Point *see* La'au Point
42 D6 **La Aurora** ✈ (Ciudad de Guatemala) Guatemala, C Guatemala 14°33′N 90°30′W
74 C9 **Laâyoune** *var.* Aaiún. ● (Western Sahara) NW Western Sahara 27°10′N 13°11′W
126 L14 **Laba** ~ SW Russian Federation
40 M6 **La Babia** Coahuila, NE Mexico 28°39′N 102°00′W
15 R7 **La Baie** Québec, SE Canada 48°20′N 70°54′W
171 P16 **Labala** Pulau Lomblen, S Indonesia 08°30′S 123°27′E
62 K8 **La Banda** Santiago del Estero, N Argentina 27°44′S 64°14′W
La Banda Oriental *see* Uruguay
104 K4 **La Bañeza** Castilla-León, N Spain 42°18′N 05°54′W
40 M13 **La Barca** Jalisco, SW Mexico 20°20′N 102°33′W
40 K14 **La Barra de Navidad** Jalisco, C Mexico 19°12′N 104°38′W
187 Y13 **Labasa** *prev.* Lambasa. Vanua Levu, N Fiji 16°25′S 179°24′E
102 H8 **la Baule-Escoublac** Loire-Atlantique, NW France 47°17′N 02°24′W
76 I13 **Labé** NW Guinea 11°19′N 12°17′W
Labe *see* Elbe
15 N11 **Labelle** Québec, SE Canada 46°15′N 74°43′W
23 X14 **La Belle** Florida, SE USA 26°45′N 81°26′W
10 H7 **Laberge, Lake** ◎ Yukon Territory, W Canada
Labes *see* Łobez
Labiau *see* Polessk
112 A10 **Labin** *It.* Albona. Istra, NW Croatia 45°05′N 14°10′E
126 L14 **Labinsk** Krasnodarskiy Kray, SW Russian Federation 44°39′N 40°43′E
105 X5 **La Bisbal d'Empordà** Cataluña, NE Spain 41°58′N 03°02′E
119 P16 **Labkovichy** *Rus.* Lobkovichi. Mahilyowskaya Voblasts', E Belarus 53°50′N 31°45′E
15 S4 **La Blache, Lac de** ◎ Québec, SE Canada
171 P4 **Labo** Luzon, N Philippines 14°10′N 122°47′E
Laboehanbadjo *see* Labuhanbajo
Laborca *see* Laborec
111 N18 **Laborec** *Hung.* Laborca. ~ E Slovakia
108 D11 **La Borgne** ~ S Switzerland
45 T12 **Laborie** SW Saint Lucia 13°45′N 61°00′W
102 J14 **Labouheyre** Landes, SW France 44°12′N 00°55′W
62 L12 **Laboulaye** Córdoba, C Argentina 34°05′S 63°20′W
13 Q7 **Labrador** *cultural region* Newfoundland and Labrador, SW Canada
64 I6 **Labrador Basin** *var.* Labrador Sea Basin. *undersea feature* Labrador Sea 53°00′N 48°00′W
13 N9 **Labrador City** Newfoundland and Labrador, E Canada 52°56′N 66°52′W

◆ Country ● Country Capital ◇ Dependent Territory ○ Dependent Territory Capital ◈ Administrative Regions ✈ International Airport ▲ Mountain ▲ Mountain Range Volcano ~ River ◎ Lake ☒ Reservoir

LABRADOR SEA – LANDEN

13 Q5 **Labrador Sea** *sea* NW Atlantic Ocean
Labrador Sea Basin *see* Labrador Basin
Labrang *see* Xiahe
54 G9 **Labranzagrande** Boyacá, C Colombia *05°34′N 72°34′W*
59 D14 **Lábrea** Amazonas, N Brazil *07°20′S 64°46′W*
45 U15 **La Brea** Trinidad, Trinidad and Tobago *10°14′N 61°37′W*
15 S6 **Labrieville** Québec, SE Canada *49°15′N 69°31′W*
102 K14 **Labrit** Landes, SW France *44°03′N 00°29′W*
108 C9 **La Broye** ≈ SW Switzerland
103 N15 **Labruguière** Tarn, S France *43°32′N 02°15′E*
168 M11 **Labu** Pulau Singkep, W Indonesia *0°34′S 104°24′E*
169 T7 **Labuan** *var.* Victoria. Labuan, East Malaysia *05°20′N 115°14′E*
169 T7 **Labuan** ◈ *federal territory* East Malaysia
Labuan *see* Labuan, Pulau
169 T7 **Labuan, Pulau** *var.* Labuan. *island* East Malaysia
Labudalin *see* Ergun
171 N16 **Labuhanbajo** *prev.* Laboehanbadjo. Flores, S Indonesia *08°33′S 119°55′E*
168 J9 **Labuhanbilik** Sumatera, N Indonesia *02°30′N 100°10′E*
168 G8 **Labuhanhaji** Sumatera, W Indonesia *03°31′N 97°00′E*
Labuk *see* Labuk, Sungai
Labuk Bay *see* Labuk, Teluk
169 V7 **Labuk, Sungai** *var.* Labuk. ≈ East Malaysia
169 W6 **Labuk, Teluk** *var.* Labuk Bay, Telukan Labuk. *bay* S Sulu Sea
Labuk, Telukan *see* Labuk, Teluk
166 K9 **Labutta** Ayeyarwady, SW Myanmar (Burma) *16°08′N 94°45′E*
122 I8 **Labytnangi** Yamalo-Nenetskiy Avtonomnyy Okrug, N Russian Federation *66°39′N 66°26′E*
113 K19 **Laç** *var.* Laci. Lezhë, C Albania *41°37′N 19°37′E*
78 F10 **Lac** *off.* Préfecture du Lac. ◈ *prefecture* W Chad
57 K19 **Lacajahuira, Rio** ≈ W Bolivia
La Calamine *see* Kelmis
62 G11 **La Calera** Valparaíso, C Chile *32°47′S 71°16′W*
13 P11 **Lac-Allard** Québec, E Canada *50°37′N 63°26′W*
104 L13 **La Campana** Andalucía, S Spain *37°35′N 05°24′W*
102 J12 **Lacanau** Gironde, SW France *44°59′N 01°04′W*
42 C2 **Lacandón, Sierra del** ▲▲ Guatemala/Mexico
La Cañiza *see* A Cañiza
41 W16 **Lacantún, Río** ≈ SE Mexico
103 Q3 **la Capelle** Aisne, N France *49°58′N 03°55′E*
112 K10 **Laćarak** Vojvodina, NW Serbia *45°00′N 19°34′E*
62 L11 **La Carlota** Córdoba, C Argentina *33°30′S 63°15′W*
104 L13 **La Carlota** Andalucía, S Spain *37°40′N 04°56′W*
105 N12 **La Carolina** Andalucía, S Spain *38°15′N 03°37′W*
103 O15 **Lacaune** Tarn, S France *43°42′N 02°42′E*
15 P7 **Lac-Bouchette** Québec, SE Canada *48°14′N 72°11′W*
Laccadive Islands/Laccadive Minicoy and Amindivi Islands, the *see* Lakshadweep
11 Y16 **Lac du Bonnet** Manitoba, S Canada *50°13′N 96°04′W*
30 L4 **Lac du Flambeau** Wisconsin, N USA *45°58′N 89°51′W*
15 P8 **Lac-Édouard** Québec, SE Canada *47°39′N 72°16′W*
42 I4 **La Ceiba** Atlántida, N Honduras *15°45′N 86°29′W*
54 E9 **La Ceja** Antioquia, W Colombia *06°02′N 75°30′W*
182 J11 **Lacepede Bay** *bay* South Australia
32 G9 **Lacey** Washington, NW USA *47°01′N 122°49′W*
103 P12 **la Chaise-Dieu** Haute-Loire, C France *45°19′N 03°41′E*
114 G13 **Lachanás** Kentrikí Makedonía, N Greece *40°57′N 23°15′E*
124 L11 **Lacha, Ozero** ◎ NW Russian Federation
103 O8 **la Charité-sur-Loire** Nièvre, C France *47°10′N 02°59′E*
103 N9 **la Châtre** Indre, C France *46°35′N 01°59′E*
108 C8 **La Chaux-de-Fonds** Neuchâtel, W Switzerland *47°07′N 06°51′E*
Lach Dera *see* Dheere Laaq
108 G8 **Lachen** Schwyz, C Switzerland *47°12′N 08°51′E*
183 Q8 **Lachlan River** ≈ New South Wales, SE Australia
43 T15 **La Chorrera** Panamá, C Panama *08°51′N 79°46′W*
15 V7 **Lac-Humqui** Québec, SE Canada *48°21′N 67°32′W*
15 N12 **Lachute** Québec, SE Canada *45°39′N 74°21′W*
Lachyn *see* Laçın
Laci *see* Laç
137 W13 **Laçın** *Rus.* Lachyn. SW Azerbaijan *39°35′N 46°34′E*
103 S16 **la Ciotat** *anc.* Citharista. Bouches-du-Rhône, SE France *43°10′N 05°36′E*
18 D10 **Lackawanna** New York, NE USA *42°49′N 78°49′W*
11 Q13 **Lac La Biche** Alberta, SW Canada *54°46′N 111°59′W*
Lac la Martre *see* Wha Ti
15 R12 **Lac-Mégantic** *var.* Mégantic. Québec, SE Canada *45°35′N 70°53′W*
Lacobriga *see* Lagos
40 G5 **La Colorada** Sonora, NW Mexico *28°49′N 110°32′W*
11 Q15 **Lacombe** Alberta, SW Canada *52°30′N 113°42′W*
30 L12 **Lacon** Illinois, N USA *41°01′N 89°24′W*
43 P16 **La Concepción** *var.* Concepción. Chiriquí, W Panama *08°31′N 82°39′W*
54 H5 **La Concepción** Zulia, NW Venezuela *10°48′N 71°46′W*
107 C19 **Laconi** Sardegna, Italy, C Mediterranean Sea *39°52′N 09°02′E*
19 O9 **Laconia** New Hampshire, NE USA *43°32′N 71°29′W*
61 H19 **La Coronilla** Rocha, E Uruguay *33°44′S 53°31′W*
La Coruña *see* A Coruña
103 O11 **la Courtine** Creuse, C France *45°42′N 02°18′E*
Lac, Préfecture du *see* Lac
102 J16 **Lacq** Pyrénées-Atlantiques, SW France *43°25′N 00°37′W*
15 P9 **La Croche** Québec, SE Canada *47°38′N 72°42′W*
29 X3 **la Croix, Lac** ◎ Canada/USA
26 K5 **La Crosse** Kansas, C USA *38°32′N 99°19′W*
21 V7 **La Crosse** Virginia, NE USA *36°41′N 78°03′W*
32 L9 **La Crosse** Washington, NW USA *46°48′N 117°51′W*
30 J7 **La Crosse** Wisconsin, N USA *43°46′N 91°12′W*
54 C13 **La Cruz** Nariño, SW Colombia *01°33′N 76°58′W*
42 K12 **La Cruz** Guanacaste, NW Costa Rica *11°05′N 85°39′W*
40 I10 **La Cruz** Sinaloa, W Mexico *23°53′N 106°53′W*
61 F19 **La Cruz** Florida, S Uruguay *33°54′S 56°11′W*
42 M9 **La Cruz de Río Grande** Región Autónoma Atlántico Sur, E Nicaragua *13°04′N 84°12′W*
54 J4 **La Cruz de Taratara** Falcón, N Venezuela *11°03′N 69°44′W*
15 Q10 **Lac-St-Charles** Québec, SE Canada *46°56′N 71°24′W*
40 M6 **La Cuesta** Coahuila, NE Mexico *28°45′N 102°26′W*
57 A17 **La Cumbra, Volcán** Ѫ Galápagos Islands, Ecuador, E Pacific Ocean *0°21′S 91°30′W*
152 J5 **Ladākh Range** ▲▲ NE India
26 J5 **Ladder Creek** ≈ Kansas, C USA
45 X10 **la Désirade** *atoll* E Guadeloupe
Lādhiqīyah, Muḥāfaẓat al *see* Al Lādhiqīyah
172 J16 **La Digue** *island* Inner Islands, NE Seychelles
83 F25 **Ladismith** Western Cape, SW South Africa *33°30′S 21°15′E*
152 G11 **Lādnūn** Rājasthān, NW India *27°36′N 74°26′E*
Ladoga, Lake *see* Ladozhskoye, Ozero
115 E19 **Ládon** ≈ S Greece
54 E9 **La Dorada** Caldas, C Colombia *05°28′N 74°41′W*
124 H11 **Ladozhskoye, Ozero** *Eng.* Lake Ladoga, *Fin.* Laatokka. ◎ NW Russian Federation
37 R12 **Ladron Peak** ▲ New Mexico, SW USA *34°25′N 107°04′W*
124 J11 **Ladva-Vetka** Respublika Kareliya, NW Russian Federation *61°18′N 34°24′E*
183 Q15 **Lady Barron** Tasmania, SE Australia *40°12′S 148°12′E*
14 G9 **Lady Evelyn Lake** ◎ Ontario, S Canada
23 W11 **Lady Lake** Florida, SE USA *28°55′N 81°55′W*
10 L17 **Ladysmith** Vancouver Island, British Columbia, SW Canada *48°55′N 123°45′W*
83 J22 **Ladysmith** KwaZulu/Natal, E South Africa *28°34′S 29°47′E*
30 J5 **Ladysmith** Wisconsin, N USA *45°27′N 91°07′W*
145 P9 **Ladyzhenka** Akmola, C Kazakhstan *50°58′N 68°44′E*
186 E7 **Lae** Morobe, W Papua New Guinea *06°45′S 147°00′E*
189 R6 **Lae Atoll** *atoll* Ralik Chain, W Marshall Islands
40 C3 **La Encantada, Cerro de** ▲ NW Mexico *31°03′N 115°25′W*
55 N11 **La Esmeralda** Amazonas, S Venezuela *03°11′N 65°33′W*
42 G7 **La Esperanza** Intibucá, SW Honduras *14°19′N 88°09′W*
30 K8 **La Farge** Wisconsin, N USA *43°36′N 90°39′W*
23 R5 **Lafayette** Alabama, S USA *32°54′N 85°24′W*
37 T4 **Lafayette** Colorado, C USA *39°59′N 105°06′W*
23 R2 **La Fayette** Georgia, SE USA *34°42′N 85°16′W*
31 O13 **Lafayette** Indiana, N USA *40°25′N 86°52′W*
22 I9 **Lafayette** Louisiana, S USA *30°13′N 92°01′W*
20 K8 **Lafayette** Tennessee, S USA *36°31′N 86°01′W*
19 N7 **Lafayette, Mount** ▲ New Hampshire, NE USA *44°09′N 71°37′W*
La Fe *see* Santa Fé
103 P3 **la Fère** Aisne, N France *49°41′N 03°20′E*
102 L6 **la Ferté-Bernard** Sarthe, NW France *48°13′N 00°40′E*
102 K5 **la Ferté-Macé** Orne, N France *48°35′N 00°21′W*
103 N7 **la Ferté-St-Aubin** Loiret, C France *47°42′N 01°57′E*
103 P5 **la Ferté-sous-Jouarre** Seine-et-Marne, N France *48°57′N 03°08′E*
77 V15 **Lafia** Nassarawa, C Nigeria *08°29′N 08°34′E*
77 T15 **Lafiagi** Kwara, W Nigeria *08°52′N 05°25′E*
11 T17 **Lafleche** Saskatchewan, S Canada *49°40′N 106°28′W*
102 K7 **la Flèche** Sarthe, NW France *47°42′N 00°04′W*
109 X7 **Lafnitz** *Hung.* Lapines. ≈ Austria/Hungary
187 P17 **La Foa** Province Sud, S New Caledonia *21°46′S 165°49′E*
20 M8 **La Follette** Tennessee, S USA *36°22′N 84°07′W*
15 N12 **Lafontaine** Québec, SE Canada *45°52′N 74°01′W*
22 K10 **Lafourche, Bayou** ≈ Louisiana, S USA
62 K6 **La Fragua** Santiago del Estero, N Argentina *26°06′S 64°06′W*
54 H7 **La Fría** Táchira, NW Venezuela *08°13′N 72°15′W*
104 J7 **La Fuente de San Esteban** Castilla-León, N Spain *40°48′N 06°14′W*
186 C7 **Lagaip** ≈ W Papua New Guinea
61 B15 **La Gallareta** Santa Fe, C Argentina *29°34′S 60°23′W*
127 Q14 **Lagan'** *prev.* Kaspiyskiy. Respublika Kalmykiya, SW Russian Federation *45°25′N 47°19′E*
95 L20 **Lagan** Kronoberg, S Sweden *56°55′N 14°01′E*
95 K21 **Lagan** ≈ S Sweden
92 L2 **Lagarfljót** *var.* Lögurinn. ◎ E Iceland
37 R7 **La Garita Mountains** ▲▲ Colorado, C USA
171 O2 **Lagawe** Luzon, N Philippines *16°46′N 121°06′E*
78 F13 **Lagdo** Nord, N Cameroon *09°12′N 13°43′E*
78 F13 **Lagdo, Lac de** ◎ N Cameroon
100 H13 **Lage** Nordrhein-Westfalen, W Germany *52°00′N 08°48′E*
94 H12 **Lågen** ≈ S Norway
61 J14 **Lages** Santa Catarina, S Brazil *27°45′S 50°16′W*
Lágesvuotna *see* Laksefjorden
149 R4 **Laghmān** ◈ *province* E Afghanistan
74 J6 **Laghouat** N Algeria *33°49′N 02°59′E*
105 Q10 **La Gineta** Castilla-La Mancha, C Spain *39°08′N 02°00′W*
115 E21 **Lagkáda** *var.* Langada. Pelopónnisos, S Greece *36°49′N 22°19′E*
114 G13 **Lagkadás** *var.* Langades, Langadhás. Kentrikí Makedonía, N Greece *40°45′N 23°04′E*
115 E20 **Lagkádia** *var.* Langádhia, *cont.* Langadia. Pelopónnisos, S Greece *37°40′N 22°01′E*
54 F6 **La Gloria** Cesar, N Colombia *08°37′N 73°51′W*
41 O7 **La Gloria** Nuevo León, NE Mexico
92 N3 **Lågneset** *headland* W Svalbard *77°46′N 13°44′E*
104 G14 **Lagoa** Faro, S Portugal *37°07′N 08°27′W*
La Goagira *see* La Guajira
Lago Agrio *see* Nueva Loja
61 I14 **Lagoa Vermelha** Rio Grande do Sul, S Brazil *28°13′S 51°32′W*
137 V10 **Lagodekhi** SE Georgia *41°49′N 46°15′E*
42 C7 **La Gomera** Escuintla, S Guatemala *14°05′N 91°03′W*
Lagone *see* Logone
107 M19 **Lagonegro** Basilicata, S Italy *40°06′N 15°42′E*
63 G16 **Lago Ranco** Los Lagos, S Chile *40°21′S 72°29′W*
77 S16 **Lagos** Lagos, SW Nigeria *06°24′N 03°17′E*
104 F14 **Lagos** *anc.* Lacobriga. Faro, S Portugal *37°05′N 08°40′W*
77 S16 **Lagos** ◈ *state* SW Nigeria
40 M12 **Lagos de Moreno** Jalisco, SW Mexico *21°21′N 101°55′W*
Lagosta *see* Lastovo
74 A12 **Lagouira** SW Western Sahara *20°55′N 17°05′W*
92 O1 **Lågøya** *island* N Svalbard
32 L11 **La Grande** Oregon, NW USA *45°21′N 118°05′W*
103 Q14 **la Grande-Combe** Gard, S France *44°13′N 04°01′E*
12 K9 **La Grande Rivière** *var.* Fort George. ≈ Québec, SE Canada
23 R4 **La Grange** Georgia, SE USA *33°02′N 85°02′W*
31 P11 **Lagrange** Indiana, N USA *41°38′N 85°25′W*
20 L5 **La Grange** Kentucky, S USA *38°24′N 85°23′W*
27 V2 **La Grange** Missouri, C USA *40°00′N 91°31′W*
21 V10 **La Grange** North Carolina, SE USA *35°18′N 77°47′W*
25 U11 **La Grange** Texas, SW USA *29°55′N 96°54′W*
105 N7 **La Granja** Castilla-León, N Spain *40°53′N 04°01′W*
55 Q9 **La Gran Sabana** *grassland* E Venezuela
54 H7 **La Grita** Táchira, NW Venezuela *08°09′N 71°58′W*
La Grulla *see* Grulla
15 R11 **La Guadeloupe** Québec, SE Canada *45°57′N 70°56′W*
65 L6 **La Guaira** Distrito Federal, N Venezuela *10°35′N 66°52′W*
54 G4 **La Guajira** *off.* Departamento de La Guajira, *var.* Guajira, La Goagira. ◈ *province* NE Colombia
188 I4 **Lagua Lichan, Punta** *headland* Saipan, S Northern Mariana Islands
105 P4 **Laguardia** *Basq.* Biasteri. País Vasco, N Spain *42°32′N 02°31′W*
18 K14 **La Guardia** ✕ (New York) Long Island, New York, NE USA *40°44′N 73°51′W*
La Guardia/Laguardia *see* A Guarda
La Gudiña *see* A Gudiña
103 O9 **la Guerche-sur-l'Aubois** Cher, C France *46°55′N 03°00′E*
103 O13 **Laguiole** Aveyron, S France *44°42′N 02°51′E*
83 F26 **L'Agulhas** *var.* Agulhas. Western Cape, SW South Africa *34°49′S 20°01′E*
61 K14 **Laguna** Santa Catarina, S Brazil *28°29′S 48°45′W*
37 Q11 **Laguna** New Mexico, SW USA *35°03′N 107°30′W*
35 T16 **Laguna Beach** California, W USA *33°32′N 117°46′W*
35 Y17 **Laguna Dam** *dam* Arizona/California, W USA
40 L7 **Laguna El Rey** Coahuila, N Mexico
35 V17 **Laguna Mountains** ▲▲ California, W USA
61 B17 **Laguna Paiva** Santa Fe, C Argentina *31°21′S 60°40′W*
62 H3 **Lagunas** Tarapacá, N Chile *21°01′S 69°36′W*
56 E9 **Lagunas** Loreto, N Peru *05°15′S 75°24′W*
57 M20 **Lagunillas** Santa Cruz, SE Bolivia *19°38′S 63°39′W*
54 H6 **Lagunillas** Mérida, NW Venezuela *08°31′N 71°24′W*
44 C4 **La Habana** *var.* Havana. ● (Cuba) Ciudad de La Habana, W Cuba *23°07′N 82°25′W*
169 W7 **Lahad Datu** Sabah, East Malaysia *05°01′N 118°20′E*
169 W7 **Lahad Datu, Teluk** *var.* Telukan Lahad Datu, Teluk Darvel, Teluk Datu; *prev.* Darvel Bay. *bay* Sabah, East Malaysia, C Pacific Ocean
Lahad Datu, Telukan *see* Lahad Datu, Teluk
38 F10 **Lahaina** Maui, Hawaii, USA, C Pacific Ocean *20°52′N 156°40′W*
168 L14 **Lahat** Sumatera, W Indonesia *03°46′S 103°32′E*
La Haye *see* 's-Gravenhage
Lahej *see* Laḥij
62 G9 **La Higuera** Coquimbo, N Chile *29°33′S 71°15′W*
141 S13 **Laḥī, Ḥisā' al** *spring/well* NE Yemen *17°28′N 50°05′E*
141 O16 **Laḥij** *var.* Laḥj, *Eng.* Lahej. SW Yemen *13°04′N 44°55′E*
142 M3 **Lāhījān** Gīlān, NW Iran *37°12′N 50°00′E*
119 I19 **Lahishyn** *Pol.* Lohiszyn, *Rus.* Logishin. Brestskaya Voblasts', SW Belarus *52°20′N 25°59′E*
Laḥj *see* Laḥij
101 F18 **Lahn** ≈ W Germany
Lähn *see* Wleń
95 J21 **Laholm** Halland, S Sweden *56°30′N 13°05′E*
95 J21 **Laholmsbukten** *bay* S Sweden
35 R6 **Lahontan Reservoir** ⊠ Nevada, W USA
149 W8 **Lahore** Punjab, NE Pakistan *31°36′N 74°18′E*
149 W8 **Lahore** ✕ Punjab, E Pakistan *31°34′N 74°22′E*
55 Q6 **La Horqueta** Delta Amacuro, NE Venezuela *09°13′N 62°02′W*
119 K15 **Lahoysk** *Rus.* Logoysk. Minskaya Voblasts', C Belarus *54°12′N 27°53′E*
101 F22 **Lahr** Baden-Württemberg, S Germany *48°21′N 07°52′E*
93 M19 **Lahti** *Swe.* Lahtis. Etelä-Suomi, S Finland *61°N 25°40′E*
Lahtis *see* Lahti
40 M14 **La Huacana** Michoacán, SW Mexico *18°56′N 101°52′W*
40 K14 **La Huerta** Jalisco, SW Mexico *19°29′N 104°40′W*
78 H12 **Laï** *prev.* Behagle, De Behagle. Tandjilé, S Chad *09°22′N 16°14′E*
Laibach *see* Ljubljana
160 K14 **Laibin** Guangxi Zhuangzu Zizhiqu, China *23°26′N 109°09′E*
167 Q5 **Lai Châu** Lai Châu, N Vietnam *22°04′N 103°10′E*
Laichow Bay *see* Laizhou Wan
38 D9 **Lā'ie** *var.* Laie. O'ahu, Hawaii, USA, C Pacific Ocean *21°39′N 157°55′W*
Laie *see* Lā'ie
102 L5 **l'Aigle** Orne, N France *48°46′N 00°37′E*
103 Q7 **Laignes** Côte d'Or, C France *47°51′N 04°24′E*
93 K17 **Laihia** Länsi-Suomi, W Finland *62°58′N 22°00′E*
Laila *see* Laylā
83 F25 **Laingsburg** Western Cape, SW South Africa *33°12′S 20°51′E*
109 U2 **Lainsitz** *Cz.* Lužnice. ≈ Austria/Czech Republic
96 I7 **Lairg** N Scotland, United Kingdom *58°02′N 04°23′W*
81 I17 **Laisamis** Eastern, N Kenya *01°35′N 37°49′E*
Laisberg *see* Leisi
127 R4 **Laishevo** Respublika Tatarstan, W Russian Federation *55°26′N 49°27′E*
Laisholm *see* Jõgeva
92 H13 **Laisvall** Norrbotten, N Sweden *66°07′N 17°10′E*
93 K19 **Laitila** Länsi-Suomi, SW Finland *60°52′N 21°40′E*
161 P5 **Laiwu** Shandong, E China *36°14′N 117°40′E*
161 R4 **Laixi** *var.* Shuiji. Shandong, E China *36°50′N 120°40′E*
161 R4 **Laiyang** Shandong, E China *36°58′N 120°40′E*
161 O3 **Laiyuan** Hebei, E China *39°19′N 114°44′E*
161 R4 **Laizhou** *var.* Ye Xian. Shandong, E China *37°12′N 120°01′E*
161 Q4 **Laizhou Wan** *var.* Laichow Bay. *bay* E China
37 S8 **La Jara** Colorado, C USA *37°16′N 105°57′W*
61 I15 **Lajeado** Rio Grande do Sul, S Brazil *29°28′S 52°00′W*
112 L12 **Lajkovac** Serbia, C Serbia *44°22′N 20°12′E*
111 K23 **Lajosmizse** Bács-Kiskun, C Hungary *47°02′N 19°31′E*
Lajta *see* Leitha
40 I6 **La Junta** Chihuahua, N Mexico *28°30′N 107°20′W*
37 V7 **La Junta** Colorado, C USA *37°59′N 103°34′W*
92 J13 **Lakaträsk** Norrbotten, N Sweden *66°16′N 21°10′E*
Lak Dera *see* Dheere Laaq
Lakeamu *see* Lakekamu
29 P12 **Lake Andes** South Dakota, N USA *43°08′N 98°33′W*
22 H9 **Lake Arthur** Louisiana, S USA *30°04′N 92°40′W*
187 Z15 **Lakeba** *prev.* Lakemba. *island* Lau Group, E Fiji
187 Z14 **Lakeba Passage** *channel* E Fiji
29 S10 **Lake Benton** Minnesota, N USA *44°15′N 96°17′W*
23 U9 **Lake Butler** Florida, SE USA *30°01′N 82°20′W*
183 P8 **Lake Cargelligo** New South Wales, SE Australia *33°21′S 146°25′E*
22 G9 **Lake Charles** Louisiana, S USA *30°14′N 93°13′W*
27 X9 **Lake City** Arkansas, C USA *35°50′N 90°28′W*
37 Q7 **Lake City** Colorado, C USA *38°01′N 107°18′W*
23 V9 **Lake City** Florida, SE USA *30°12′N 82°39′W*
29 U13 **Lake City** Iowa, C USA *42°16′N 94°43′W*
31 P7 **Lake City** Michigan, N USA *44°22′N 85°12′W*
29 W9 **Lake City** Minnesota, N USA *44°27′N 92°16′W*
21 T13 **Lake City** South Carolina, SE USA *33°52′N 79°45′W*
29 Q7 **Lake City** South Dakota, N USA *45°42′N 97°22′W*
20 M8 **Lake City** Tennessee, S USA *36°13′N 84°09′W*
10 L17 **Lake Cowichan** Vancouver Island, British Columbia, SW Canada *48°50′N 124°04′W*
29 U10 **Lake Crystal** Minnesota, N USA *44°07′N 94°13′W*
25 T6 **Lake Dallas** Texas, SW USA *33°06′N 97°01′W*
97 K15 **Lake District** *physical region* NW England, United Kingdom
18 D10 **Lake Erie Beach** New York, NE USA *42°37′N 79°04′W*
29 T11 **Lakefield** Minnesota, N USA *43°40′N 95°10′W*
25 V6 **Lake Fork Reservoir** ⊠ Texas, SW USA
30 M9 **Lake Geneva** Wisconsin, N USA *42°36′N 88°25′W*
18 L9 **Lake George** New York, NE USA *43°25′N 73°45′W*
Lake Harbour *see* Kimmirut
36 I12 **Lake Havasu City** Arizona, SW USA *34°26′N 114°20′W*
25 W12 **Lake Jackson** Texas, SW USA *29°01′N 95°25′W*
186 D8 **Lakekamu** *var.* Lakeamu. ≈ S Papua New Guinea
180 K13 **Lake King** Western Australia *33°09′S 119°46′E*
23 V12 **Lakeland** Florida, SE USA *28°03′N 81°57′W*
23 U7 **Lakeland** Georgia, SE USA *31°02′N 83°04′W*
181 W4 **Lakeland Downs** Queensland, NE Australia *15°54′S 144°54′E*
11 P16 **Lake Louise** Alberta, SW Canada *51°26′N 116°10′W*
Lakemba *see* Lakeba
29 V11 **Lake Mills** Iowa, C USA *43°25′N 93°31′W*
39 Q10 **Lake Minchumina** Alaska, USA *63°55′N 152°25′W*
Lakemti *see* Nek'emtē
186 A7 **Lake Murray** Western, SW Papua New Guinea *06°35′S 141°28′E*
31 R9 **Lake Orion** Michigan, N USA *42°46′N 83°14′W*
190 B16 **Lakepa** NE Niue *18°59′S 169°48′E*
29 T11 **Lake Park** Iowa, C USA *43°27′N 95°19′W*
18 K7 **Lake Placid** New York, NE USA *44°16′N 73°57′W*
18 K9 **Lake Pleasant** New York, NE USA *43°27′N 74°24′W*
34 M6 **Lakeport** California, W USA *39°04′N 122°56′W*
29 Q10 **Lake Preston** South Dakota, N USA *44°21′N 97°22′W*
22 J5 **Lake Providence** Louisiana, S USA *32°48′N 91°10′W*
185 E20 **Lake Pukaki** Canterbury, South Island, New Zealand *44°12′S 170°10′E*
183 Q12 **Lakes Entrance** Victoria, SE Australia *37°52′S 147°58′E*
37 N12 **Lakeside** Arizona, SW USA *34°09′N 109°58′W*
35 V17 **Lakeside** California, W USA *32°50′N 116°55′W*
23 S9 **Lakeside** Florida, SE USA *30°22′N 84°18′W*
28 K13 **Lakeside** Nebraska, C USA *42°01′N 102°27′W*
32 E13 **Lakeside** Oregon, NW USA *43°34′N 124°10′W*
21 W6 **Lakeside** Virginia, NE USA *37°36′N 77°28′W*
Lakes State *see* El Buhayrat
Lake State *see* Michigan
185 F20 **Lake Tekapo** Canterbury, South Island, New Zealand *44°01′S 170°29′E*
21 O10 **Lake Toxaway** North Carolina, SE USA *35°06′N 82°57′W*
29 T13 **Lake View** Iowa, C USA *42°18′N 95°04′W*
32 I16 **Lakeview** Oregon, NW USA *42°13′N 120°21′W*
25 O3 **Lakeview** Texas, SW USA *34°38′N 100°36′W*
27 W14 **Lake Village** Arkansas, C USA *33°20′N 91°19′W*
23 W12 **Lake Wales** Florida, SE USA *27°54′N 81°35′W*
37 T4 **Lakewood** Colorado, C USA *39°38′N 105°07′W*
18 K15 **Lakewood** New Jersey, NE USA *40°04′N 74°11′W*
18 C11 **Lakewood** New York, NE USA *42°03′N 79°19′W*
31 T11 **Lakewood** Ohio, N USA *41°28′N 81°48′W*
23 Y13 **Lakewood Park** Florida, SE USA *27°32′N 80°24′W*
23 Z14 **Lake Worth** Florida, SE USA *26°37′N 80°03′W*
124 H11 **Lakhdenpokh'ya** Respublika Kareliya, NW Russian Federation *61°25′N 30°05′E*
152 L11 **Lakhīmpur** Uttar Pradesh, N India *27°57′N 80°47′E*
154 J11 **Lakhnādon** Madhya Pradesh, C India *22°34′N 79°38′E*
Lakhnau *see* Lucknow
154 A9 **Lakhpat** Gujarāt, W India *23°49′N 68°54′E*
119 K19 **Lakhva** Brestskaya Voblasts', SW Belarus *52°13′N 27°06′E*
26 I6 **Lakin** Kansas, C USA *37°57′N 101°16′W*
149 S7 **Lakki Marwat** North-West Frontier Province, NW Pakistan *32°35′N 70°58′E*
115 F21 **Lakonía** *historical region* S Greece
115 F22 **Lakonikós Kólpos** *gulf* S Greece
76 M17 **Lakota** S Ivory Coast *05°50′N 05°40′W*
29 U11 **Lakota** Iowa, C USA *43°22′N 94°04′W*
29 P3 **Lakota** North Dakota, N USA *48°02′N 98°20′W*
Lak Sao *see* Ban Lakxao
92 L8 **Laksefjorden** *Lapp.* Lágesvuotna. *fjord* N Norway
92 K8 **Lakselv** *Lapp.* Leavdnja. Finnmark, N Norway *70°02′N 24°57′E*
155 B21 **Lakshadweep** *prev.* the Laccadive Minicoy and Amindivi Islands. ◈ *union territory* India, N Indian Ocean
155 C22 **Lakshadweep** *Eng.* Laccadive Islands. *island group* India, N Indian Ocean
153 S17 **Lakshmikāntapur** West Bengal, NE India *22°05′N 88°19′E*
112 G11 **Laktaši** ◈ Republika Srpska, N Bosnia and Herzegovina
149 V7 **Lāla Mūsa** Punjab, NE Pakistan *32°41′N 74°01′E*
la Laon *see* Laon
114 M11 **Lalapaşa** Edirne, NW Turkey *41°52′N 26°44′E*
83 P14 **Lalaua** Nampula, N Mozambique *14°21′S 38°16′E*
105 S9 **L'Alcora** *var.* Alcora. País Valenciano, E Spain *40°05′N 00°14′W*
105 S10 **L'Alcúdia** *var.* L'Alcudia. País Valenciano, E Spain *39°10′N 00°30′W*
80 J11 **Lalibela** Āmara, Ethiopia *12°01′N 39°05′E*
42 E8 **La Libertad** La Libertad, SW El Salvador *13°28′N 89°20′W**
42 E3 **La Libertad** Petén, N Guatemala *16°49′N 90°08′W*
42 H6 **La Libertad** Comayagua, SW Honduras *14°43′N 87°36′W*
40 E4 **La Libertad** *var.* Puerto Libertad. Sonora, NW Mexico *29°52′N 112°39′W*
42 K10 **La Libertad** Chontales, S Nicaragua *12°12′N 85°10′W*
42 A9 **La Libertad** ◈ *department* SW El Salvador
56 B11 **La Libertad** *off.* Departamento de La Libertad. ◈ *department* W Peru
La Libertad, Departamento de *see* La Libertad
62 G11 **La Ligua** Valparaíso, C Chile *31°30′S 71°16′W*
139 U5 **La'lī Khān** As Sulaymānīyah, E Iraq *34°58′N 45°36′E*
104 H3 **Lalín** Galicia, NW Spain *42°40′N 08°06′W*
102 L13 **Lalinde** Dordogne, SW France *44°52′N 00°42′E*
104 K16 **La Línea** *var.* La Línea de la Concepción. Andalucía, S Spain *36°10′N 05°21′W*
La Línea de la Concepción *see* La Línea
152 J14 **Lalitpur** Uttar Pradesh, N India *24°42′N 78°24′E*
153 P11 **Lalitpur** Central, C Nepal *27°45′N 85°18′E*
152 K10 **Lālkua** Uttaranchal, N India *29°04′N 79°31′E*
153 T12 **Lalmanirhat** Rājshāhi, N Bangladesh *25°51′N 89°34′E*
11 R12 **La Loche** Saskatchewan, C Canada *56°31′N 109°27′W*
102 M6 **la Loupe** Eure-et-Loir, C France *48°30′N 01°04′E*
99 G20 **La Louvière** Hainaut, S Belgium *50°29′N 04°15′E*
L'Altissima *see* Hochwilde
104 L14 **La Luisiana** Andalucía, S Spain *37°30′N 05°14′W*
37 S14 **La Luz** New Mexico, SW USA *32°58′N 105°56′W*
107 D16 **la Maddalena** Sardegna, Italy, C Mediterranean Sea *41°13′N 09°25′E*
62 J7 **La Madrid** Tucumán, N Argentina *27°37′S 65°16′W*
Lama-Kara *see* Kara
15 S8 **La Malbaie** Québec, SE Canada *47°39′N 70°11′W*
167 T10 **Lamam** Xékong, S Laos *15°22′N 106°40′E*
105 P10 **La Mancha** *physical region* C Spain
la Manche *see* English Channel
187 R13 **Lamap** Malekula, C Vanuatu *16°26′S 167°47′E*
37 W6 **Lamar** Colorado, C USA *38°40′N 102°37′W*
27 S7 **Lamar** Missouri, C USA *37°30′N 94°18′W*
21 S12 **Lamar** South Carolina, SE USA *34°10′N 80°03′W*
Lamard *see* Lāmerd
107 C19 **La Marmora, Punta** ▲ Sardegna, Italy, C Mediterranean Sea *39°58′N 09°20′E*
8 I9 **La Martre, Lac** ◎ Northwest Territories, NW Canada
56 D10 **Lamas** San Martín, N Peru *06°28′S 76°31′W*
42 I5 **La Masica** Atlántida, NW Honduras *15°38′N 87°08′W*
103 R12 **Lamastre** Ardèche, E France *45°00′N 04°32′E*
La Matepec *see* Santa Ana, Volcán de
44 I7 **La Maya** Santiago de Cuba, E Cuba *20°11′N 75°40′W*
109 S5 **Lambach** Oberösterreich, N Austria *48°06′N 13°51′E*
168 I11 **Lambak** Pulau Pini, W Indonesia *0°08′N 98°36′E*
102 H5 **Lamballe** Côtes d'Armor, NW France *48°28′N 02°31′W*
79 D18 **Lambaréné** Moyen-Ogooué, W Gabon *0°41′S 10°13′E*
Lambasa *see* Labasa
56 B11 **Lambayeque** Lambayeque, W Peru *06°42′S 79°55′W*
56 A10 **Lambayeque** *off.* Departamento de Lambayeque. ◈ *department* NW Peru
Lambayeque, Departamento de *see* Lambayeque
97 G17 **Lambay Island** *Ir.* Reachrainn. *island* E Ireland
186 G6 **Lambert, Cape** *headland* New Britain, E Papua New Guinea *04°15′S 151°31′E*
195 W6 **Lambert Glacier** *glacier* Antarctica
29 T10 **Lamberton** Minnesota, N USA *44°14′N 95°15′W*
27 X4 **Lambert-Saint Louis** ✕ Missouri, C USA *38°43′N 90°19′W*
31 R11 **Lambertville** Michigan, N USA *41°46′N 83°37′W*
18 J15 **Lambertville** New Jersey, NE USA *40°20′N 74°55′W*
171 N12 **Lambogo** Sulawesi, N Indonesia *0°57′S 120°23′E*
106 D8 **Lambro** ≈ N Italy
33 W11 **Lame Deer** Montana, NW USA *45°37′N 106°37′W*
104 H6 **Lamego** Viseu, N Portugal *41°05′N 07°49′W*
187 Q14 **Lamen Bay** Épi, C Vanuatu *16°36′S 168°10′E*
45 X6 **Lamentin** Basse Terre, N Guadeloupe *16°16′N 61°38′W*
Lamentin *see* le Lamentin
143 P14 **Lāmerd** *var.* Lamard. Fārs, S Iran *27°22′N 53°08′E*
182 K10 **Lameroo** South Australia *35°22′S 140°30′E*
54 F10 **La Mesa** Cundinamarca, C Colombia *04°37′N 74°30′W*
35 U17 **La Mesa** California, W USA *32°44′N 117°00′W*
37 R16 **La Mesa** New Mexico, SW USA *32°03′N 106°41′W*
25 N6 **Lamesa** Texas, SW USA *32°43′N 101°57′W*
107 N21 **Lamezia Terme** Calabria, SE Italy *38°54′N 16°13′E*
115 F17 **Lamía** Stereá Ellás, C Greece *38°54′N 22°27′E*
171 O8 **Lamitan** Basilan Island, SW Philippines *06°40′N 122°07′E*
187 Y14 **Lamiti** Gau, C Fiji *18°00′S 179°20′E*
171 T11 **Lamlam** Papua, E Indonesia *0°03′S 130°46′E*
188 B16 **Lamlam, Mount** ▲ SW Guam *13°20′N 144°40′E*
109 Q6 **Lammer** ≈ E Austria
185 E23 **Lammerlaw Range** ▲▲ South Island, New Zealand
95 L20 **Lammhult** Kronoberg, S Sweden *57°09′N 14°35′E*
93 L18 **Lammi** Etelä-Suomi, S Finland *61°06′N 25°00′E*
189 U11 **Lamoil** *island* Chuuk, C Micronesia
35 W3 **Lamoille** Nevada, W USA *40°47′N 115°37′W*
18 M7 **Lamoille River** ≈ Vermont, NE USA
30 J13 **La Moine River** ≈ Illinois, N USA
171 P4 **Lamon Bay** *bay* Luzon, N Philippines
29 V16 **Lamoni** Iowa, C USA *40°37′N 93°56′W*
35 R13 **Lamont** California, W USA *35°15′N 118°54′W*
27 N8 **Lamont** Oklahoma, C USA *36°41′N 97°33′W*
54 E13 **La Montañita** *var.* Montañita. Caquetá, S Colombia *01°22′N 75°25′W*
43 N8 **La Mosquitia** *var.* Miskito Coast, *Eng.* Mosquito Coast. *coastal region* E Nicaragua
102 I9 **la Mothe-Achard** Vendée, NW France *46°37′N 01°37′W*
188 L15 **Lamotrek Atoll** *atoll* Caroline Islands, C Micronesia
29 P6 **La Moure** North Dakota, N USA *46°21′N 98°17′W*
167 O8 **Lampang** *var.* Muang Lampang. Lampang, NW Thailand *18°16′N 99°30′E*
167 R9 **Lam Pao Reservoir** ⊠ E Thailand
25 S9 **Lampasas** Texas, SW USA *31°04′N 98°12′W*
25 S9 **Lampasas River** ≈ Texas, SW USA
41 N7 **Lampazos** *var.* Lampazos de Naranjo. Nuevo León, NE Mexico *27°00′N 100°28′W*
Lampazos de Naranjo *see* Lampazos
115 E19 **Lámpeia** Dytikí Ellás, S Greece *37°51′N 21°48′E*
101 G19 **Lampertheim** Hessen, W Germany *49°36′N 08°28′E*
97 I20 **Lampeter** SW Wales, United Kingdom *52°08′N 04°04′W*
167 O7 **Lamphun** *var.* Lampun, Muang Lamphun. Lamphun, NW Thailand *18°36′N 99°02′E*
11 X10 **Lamprey** Manitoba, C Canada *58°18′N 94°06′W*
Lampun *see* Lamphun
168 M15 **Lampung** *off.* Propinsi Lampung. ◈ *province* SW Indonesia
Lampung, Propinsi *see* Lampung
126 K6 **Lamskoye** Lipetskaya Oblast', W Russian Federation *52°57′N 38°04′E*
81 K20 **Lamu** Coast, SE Kenya *02°17′S 40°54′E*
43 N14 **La Muerte, Cerro** ▲ C Costa Rica *09°33′N 83°47′W*
103 S13 **la Mure** Isère, E France *44°54′N 05°48′E*
37 S10 **Lamy** New Mexico, SW USA *35°27′N 105°52′W*
119 J18 **Lan'** *Rus.* Lan'. ≈ C Belarus
38 E10 **Lāna'i** *var.* Lanai. *island* Hawai'i, USA, C Pacific Ocean
38 E10 **Lāna'i City** *var.* Lanai City. Lanai, Hawaii, USA, C Pacific Ocean *20°49′N 156°55′W*
Lanai City *see* Lāna'i City
99 L18 **Lanaken** Limburg, NE Belgium *50°53′N 05°39′E*
171 Q7 **Lanao, Lake** *var.* Lake Sultan Alonto. ◎ Mindanao, S Philippines
96 J12 **Lanark** S Scotland, United Kingdom *55°38′N 04°25′W*
96 I13 **Lanark** *cultural region* C Scotland, United Kingdom
104 L9 **La Nava de Ricomalillo** Castilla-La Mancha, C Spain *39°40′N 04°59′W*
166 M13 **Lanbi Kyun** *prev.* Sullivan Island. *island* Mergui Archipelago, S Myanmar (Burma)
Lancang Jiang *see* Mekong
97 K17 **Lancashire** *cultural region* N England, United Kingdom
15 N13 **Lancaster** Ontario, SE Canada *45°10′N 74°31′W*
97 K16 **Lancaster** NW England, United Kingdom *54°03′N 02°48′W*
35 T14 **Lancaster** California, W USA *34°42′N 118°08′W*
20 M6 **Lancaster** Kentucky, S USA *37°35′N 84°34′W*
27 U1 **Lancaster** Missouri, C USA *40°32′N 92°31′W*
19 O7 **Lancaster** New Hampshire, NE USA *44°29′N 71°34′W*
18 D10 **Lancaster** New York, NE USA *42°54′N 78°40′W*
31 T14 **Lancaster** Ohio, N USA *39°42′N 82°36′W*
18 H16 **Lancaster** Pennsylvania, NE USA *40°03′N 76°18′W*
21 R11 **Lancaster** South Carolina, SE USA *34°43′N 80°47′W*
25 U7 **Lancaster** Texas, SW USA *32°35′N 96°45′W*
21 X5 **Lancaster** Virginia, NE USA *37°48′N 76°30′W*
30 J9 **Lancaster** Wisconsin, N USA *42°52′N 90°43′W*
197 N10 **Lancaster Sound** *sound* Nunavut, N Canada
Lan-chou/Lan-chow/Lanchow *see* Lanzhou
107 K14 **Lanciano** Abruzzo, C Italy *42°13′N 14°23′E*
111 O16 **Łańcut** Podkarpackie, SE Poland *50°04′N 22°14′E*
169 Q11 **Landak, Sungai** ≈ Borneo, N Indonesia
Landao *see* Lantau Island
Landau *see* Landau an der Isar
Landau *see* Landau in der Pfalz
101 N22 **Landau an der Isar** *var.* Landau. Bayern, SE Germany *48°40′N 12°41′E*
101 F20 **Landau in der Pfalz** *var.* Landau. Rheinland-Pfalz, SW Germany *49°12′N 08°07′E*
Land Burgenland *see* Burgenland
108 K8 **Landeck** Tirol, W Austria *47°09′N 10°35′E*
99 J19 **Landen** Vlaams Brabant, C Belgium *50°45′N 05°05′E*

◆ Country
● Country Capital
◇ Dependent Territory
○ Dependent Territory Capital
◈ Administrative Regions
✕ International Airport
▲ Mountain
▲▲ Mountain Range
Ѫ Volcano
≈ River
◎ Lake
⊠ Reservoir

Lander – La Vall d'Uixó

33 U15 Lander Wyoming, C USA 42°49′N 108°43′W
102 F5 Landerneau Finistère, NW France 48°27′N 04°16′W
95 K20 Landeryd Halland, S Sweden 57°04′N 13°15′E
102 J15 Landes ◈ department SW France
Landeshut/Landeshut in Schlesien see Kamienna Góra
105 R9 Landete Castilla-La Mancha, C Spain 39°54′N 01°22′W
99 M18 Landgraaf Limburg, SE Netherlands 50°55′N 06°04′E
102 F5 Landivisiau Finistère, NW France 48°31′N 04°03′W
Land Kärten see Kärnten
Land of Enchantment see New Mexico
The Land of Opportunity see Arkansas
Land of Steady Habits see Connecticut
Land of the Midnight Sun see Alaska
108 I8 Landquart Graubünden, SE Switzerland 46°58′N 09°35′E
108 J9 Landquart ≈ Austria/Switzerland
21 P10 Landrum South Carolina, SE USA 35°10′N 82°11′W
Landsberg see Gorzów Wielkopolski, Lubuskie, Poland
Landsberg see Górowo Iławeckie, Warmińsko-Mazurskie, NE Poland
101 K23 Landsberg am Lech Bayern, S Germany 48°03′N 10°52′E
Landsberg an der Warthe see Gorzów Wielkopolski
97 G25 Land's End headland SW England, United Kingdom 50°02′N 05°41′W
101 M22 Landshut Bayern, SE Germany 48°32′N 12°09′E
Landskron see Lanškroun
95 J22 Landskrona Skåne, S Sweden 55°52′N 12°52′E
98 I10 Landsmeer Noord-Holland, C Netherlands 52°26′N 04°55′E
95 J19 Landvetter ✈ (Göteborg) Västra Götaland, S Sweden 57°39′N 12°22′E
Landwarów see Lentvaris
23 R5 Lanett Alabama, S USA 32°52′N 85°11′W
108 C8 La Neuveville var. Neuveville, Ger. Neuenstadt. Neuchâtel, W Switzerland 47°05′N 07°03′E
95 G21 Langå var. Langaa. Århus, C Denmark 56°23′N 09°55′E
Langaa see Langå
158 G14 La'nga Co ◎ W China
Langada see Lagkáda
Langades/Langadhás see Lagkadás
Langádhia/ see Lagkádia
147 T14 Langar Rus. Lyangar. SE Tajikistan 37°04′N 72°39′E
146 M10 Langar Rus. Lyangar. Navoiy Viloyati, C Uzbekistan 40°27′N 65°54′E
142 M3 Langarūd Gīlān, NW Iran 37°10′N 50°09′E
11 V16 Langbank Saskatchewan, S Canada 50°01′N 102°16′W
29 P2 Langdon North Dakota, N USA 48°45′N 98°22′W
103 P12 Langeac Haute-Loire, C France 45°06′N 03°31′E
102 L8 Langeais Indre-et-Loire, C France 47°22′N 00°27′E
80 I8 Langeb, Wadi ≈ NE Sudan
Långed see Dals Långed
95 G25 Langeland island S Denmark
99 B18 Langemark West-Vlaanderen, W Belgium 50°55′N 02°55′E
101 G18 Langen Hessen, W Germany 49°58′N 08°40′E
101 J22 Langenau Baden-Württemberg, S Germany 48°30′N 10°08′E
11 V16 Langenburg Saskatchewan, S Canada 50°50′N 101°43′W
108 L8 Langenfeld Tirol, W Austria 47°04′N 10°59′E
101 E16 Langenfeld Nordrhein-Westfalen, W Germany 51°06′N 06°57′E
100 I12 Langenhagen Niedersachsen, N Germany 52°26′N 09°45′E
100 I12 Langenhagen ✈ (Hannover) Niedersachsen, NW Germany 52°28′N 09°40′E
109 W3 Langenlois Niederösterreich, NE Austria 48°29′N 15°42′E
108 E7 Langenthal Bern, NW Switzerland 47°13′N 07°48′E
109 W6 Langenwang Steiermark, E Austria 47°34′N 15°39′E
109 X3 Langenzersdorf Niederösterreich, E Austria 48°20′N 16°22′E
100 F9 Langeoog island NW Germany
95 H23 Langeskov Fyn, C Denmark 55°22′N 10°36′E
95 G16 Langesund Telemark, S Norway 59°00′N 09°43′E
95 G17 Langesundsfjorden fjord S Norway
94 D10 Langevågen Møre og Romsdal, S Norway 62°26′N 06°15′E
161 P3 Langfang Hebei, E China 39°30′N 116°39′E
94 E9 Langfjorden fjord S Norway
29 Q8 Langford South Dakota, N USA 45°35′N 97°48′W
168 I10 Langgapayung Sumatera, W Indonesia 01°42′N 99°57′E
106 E9 Langhirano Emilia-Romagna, C Italy 44°37′N 10°16′E
97 K14 Langholm S Scotland, United Kingdom 55°14′N 03°11′W
92 I3 Langjökull glacier C Iceland
168 I6 Langkawi, Pulau island Peninsular Malaysia
166 M14 Langkha Tuk, Khao ▲ SW Thailand 09°19′N 98°39′E
14 L8 Langlade Québec, SE Canada 48°13′N 75°58′W
10 M17 Langley British Columbia, SW Canada 49°07′N 122°39′W
167 S7 Lang Mô Thanh Hoa, N Vietnam 19°36′N 105°30′E
Langnau see Langnau im Emmental
108 E8 Langnau im Emmental var. Langnau. Bern, W Switzerland 46°57′N 07°47′E
103 Q13 Langogne Lozère, S France 44°40′N 03°52′E
102 K13 Langon Gironde, SW France 44°33′N 00°14′W
La Ngounié see Ngounié
92 G10 Langøya island C Norway
158 G14 Langqên Zangbo ≈ China/India
104 K2 Langreo var. Sama de Langreo. Asturias, N Spain 43°18′N 05°40′W
103 S7 Langres Haute-Marne, N France 47°53′N 05°20′E
103 R8 Langres, Plateau de plateau C France
168 H8 Langsa Sumatera, W Indonesia 04°30′N 97°53′E
93 H16 Långsele Västernorrland, C Sweden 63°11′N 17°05′E
162 L12 Lang Shan ▲▲ N China
95 M14 Långshyttan Dalarna, C Sweden 60°26′N 16°02′E
167 T5 Lang Sơn var. Langson. Lang Sơn, N Vietnam 21°50′N 106°45′E
Langson see Lang Sơn
167 N14 Lang Suan Chumphon, SW Thailand 09°55′N 99°07′E
93 J14 Långträsk Norrbotten, N Sweden 65°22′N 20°19′E
25 N11 Langtry Texas, SW USA 29°46′N 101°25′W
103 P16 Languedoc cultural region S France
103 P15 Languedoc-Roussillon ◈ region S France
27 X10 L'Anguille River ≈ Arkansas, C USA
93 I16 Långviksmon Västernorrland, N Sweden 63°39′N 18°45′E
101 K22 Langweid Bayern, S Germany 48°29′N 10°50′E
160 J8 Langzhong Sichuan, C China 31°46′N 105°55′E
Lan Hsü see Lan Yü
11 U15 Lanigan Saskatchewan, S Canada 51°50′N 105°01′W
116 K5 Lanivtsi Ternopil's'ka Oblast', W Ukraine 49°52′N 26°05′E
137 Y13 Länkäran Rus. Lenkoran'. S Azerbaijan 38°46′N 48°51′E
102 L16 Lannemezan Hautes-Pyrénées, S France 43°08′N 00°22′E
102 G5 Lannion Côtes d'Armor, NW France 48°44′N 03°27′W
14 M11 L'Annonciation Québec, SE Canada 46°22′N 74°51′W
105 V5 L'Anoia ≈ NE Spain
18 I15 Lansdale Pennsylvania, NE USA 40°14′N 75°13′W
14 L14 Lansdowne Ontario, SE Canada 44°25′N 76°00′W
152 K9 Lansdowne Uttarakhand, N India 29°50′N 78°42′E
30 M3 L'Anse Michigan, N USA 46°45′N 88°27′W
15 S7 L'Anse-St-Jean Québec, SE Canada 48°14′N 70°13′W
29 Y11 Lansing Iowa, C USA 43°22′N 91°11′W
27 R4 Lansing Kansas, C USA 39°15′N 94°54′W
31 Q9 Lansing state capital Michigan, N USA 42°44′N 84°33′W
93 K18 Länsi-Suomi ◈ province W Finland
92 J12 Lansjärv Norrbotten, N Sweden 66°39′N 22°10′E
111 G17 Lanškroun Ger. Landskron. Pardubický Kraj, E Czech Republic 49°55′N 16°38′E
167 N16 Lanta, Ko island S Thailand
161 O15 Lantau Island Cant. Tai Yue Shan, Chin. Landao. island Hong Kong, S China
Lantian see Lianyuan
Lan-ts'ang Chiang see Mekong
Lantung, Gulf of see Liaodong Wan
171 O11 Lanu Sulawesi, N Indonesia 01°00′N 121°33′E
107 D19 Lanusei Sardegna, Italy, C Mediterranean Sea 39°55′N 09°31′E
102 H7 Lanvaux, Landes de physical region NW France
163 W8 Lanxi Heilongjiang, NE China 46°18′N 126°15′E
161 R10 Lanxi Zhejiang, SE China 29°12′N 119°27′E
La Nyanga see Nyanga
161 T15 Lan Yü var. Huoshao Tao, Hungt'ou, Lan Hsü, Lanyü, Eng. Orchid Island; prev. Kotosho, Koto Sho. island SE Taiwan
Lanyü see Lan Yü
64 P11 Lanzarote island Islas Canarias, Spain, NE Atlantic Ocean
159 V10 Lanzhou var. Lan-chou, Lanchow, Lan-chow; prev. Kaolan. province capital Gansu, C China 36°01′N 103°52′E
106 B8 Lanzo Torinese Piemonte, NE Italy 45°18′N 07°26′E
171 O11 Laoag Luzon, N Philippines 18°11′N 120°34′E
171 Q5 Laoang Samar, C Philippines 12°29′N 125°01′E
167 R5 Lao Cai Lao Cai, N Vietnam 22°29′N 104°00′E
Laodicea/Laodicea ad Mare see Al Lādhiqīyah
Laoet see Laut, Pulau
163 T11 Laoha He ≈ NE China
160 M8 Laohekou var. Guanghua. Hubei, C China 32°20′N 111°42′E
Laoi, An see Lee
97 E19 Laois prev. Leix, Queen's County. cultural region C Ireland
159 R8 Laojunmiao prev. Yumen. Gansu, N China 39°49′N 97°47′E
163 W12 Lao Ling ▲▲ N China
64 Q11 La Oliva var. Oliva. Fuerteventura, Islas Canarias, Spain, NE Atlantic Ocean 28°36′N 13°53′W
Lao, Loch see Belfast Lough
Laolong see Longchuan
Lao Mangnai see Mangnai
103 P3 Laon var. la Laon; anc. Laudunum. Aisne, N France 49°34′N 03°37′E
Lao People's Democratic Republic see Laos
54 M3 La Orchila, Isla island N Venezuela
64 O11 La Orotava Tenerife, Islas Canarias, Spain, NE Atlantic Ocean 28°23′N 16°32′W
57 E14 La Oroya Junín, C Peru 11°36′S 75°54′W
167 Q7 Laos off. Lao People's Democratic Republic. ◆ republic SE Asia
161 R5 Laoshan Wan bay E China
163 Y10 Laoye Ling ▲▲ NE China
60 J12 Lapa Paraná, S Brazil 25°46′S 49°44′W
103 P10 Lapalisse Allier, C France 46°13′N 03°39′E
54 F9 La Palma Cundinamarca, C Colombia 05°23′N 74°24′W
42 F7 La Palma Chalatenango, N El Salvador 14°19′N 89°10′W
43 W16 La Palma Darién, SE Panama 08°24′N 78°09′W
64 N11 La Palma island Islas Canarias, Spain, NE Atlantic Ocean
104 J14 La Palma del Condado Andalucía, S Spain 37°23′N 06°33′W
61 F18 La Paloma Durazno, C Uruguay 32°54′S 55°36′W
61 G20 La Paloma Rocha, E Uruguay 34°37′S 54°08′W
61 A21 La Pampa off. Provincia de La Pampa. ◈ province C Argentina
La Pampa, Provincia de see La Pampa
55 P8 La Paragua Bolívar, E Venezuela 06°53′N 63°16′W
119 O16 Lapatsichy Rus. Lapatichi. Mahilyowskaya Voblasts', E Belarus 53°34′N 30°53′E
61 C16 La Paz Entre Ríos, E Argentina 30°45′S 59°36′W
62 I11 La Paz Mendoza, C Argentina 33°30′S 67°36′W
57 J18 La Paz var. La Paz de Ayacucho. ● (Bolivia-legislative and administrative capital) La Paz, W Bolivia 16°30′S 68°13′W
42 H6 La Paz La Paz, SW Honduras 14°20′N 87°40′W
40 F9 La Paz Baja California Sur, NW Mexico 24°07′N 110°18′W
61 F20 La Paz Canelones, S Uruguay 34°46′S 56°13′W
57 J16 La Paz ◈ department W Bolivia
42 B9 La Paz ◈ department S El Salvador
42 G7 La Paz ◈ department SW Honduras
La Paz see El Alto, Bolivia
La Paz see Robles, Colombia
La Paz see La Paz Centro
40 F9 La Paz, Bahía de bay NW Mexico
42 I10 La Paz Centro var. La Paz. León, W Nicaragua 12°20′N 86°41′W
La Paz de Ayacucho see La Paz
54 J15 La Pedrera Amazonas, SE Colombia 01°19′S 69°31′W
31 S9 Lapeer Michigan, N USA 43°03′N 83°19′W
40 K6 La Perla Chihuahua, N Mexico 28°18′N 104°34′W
165 T1 La Perouse Strait Jap. Sōya-kaikyō, Rus. Proliv Laperuza. strait Japan/Russian Federation
63 I14 La Perra, Salitral de salt lake C Argentina
Laperuza, Proliv see La Perouse Strait
41 Q10 La Pesca Tamaulipas, C Mexico 23°49′N 97°45′W
40 M13 La Piedad Cavadas Michoacán, C Mexico 20°20′N 102°01′W
Lapines see Lafnitz
93 M16 Lapinlahti Itä-Suomi, C Finland 63°21′N 27°25′E
Lápithos see Lapta
22 K9 Laplace Louisiana, S USA 30°04′N 90°28′W
45 X12 La Plaine SE Dominica 15°20′N 61°15′W
173 P16 La Plaine-des-Palmistes C Réunion
92 K11 Lapland Fin. Lappi, Swe. Lappland. cultural region N Europe
28 M8 La Plant South Dakota, N USA 45°06′N 100°40′W
61 D20 La Plata Buenos Aires, E Argentina 34°56′S 57°55′W
54 D12 La Plata Huila, SW Colombia 02°33′N 75°55′W
21 W4 La Plata Maryland, NE USA 38°32′N 76°59′W
La Plata see Sucre
45 U6 la Plata, Río de ≈ C Puerto Rico
105 W4 La Pobla de Lillet Cataluña, NE Spain 42°15′N 01°57′E
105 U4 La Pobla de Segur Cataluña, NE Spain 42°15′N 00°58′E
15 S9 La Pocatière Québec, SE Canada 47°21′N 70°04′W
104 L3 La Pola de Gordón Castilla-León, N Spain 42°50′N 05°38′W
31 O11 La Porte Indiana, N USA 41°36′N 86°43′W
18 H13 Laporte Pennsylvania, NE USA 41°25′N 76°29′W
29 X13 La Porte City Iowa, C USA 42°19′N 92°11′W
62 J8 La Posta Catamarca, C Argentina 27°59′S 65°32′W
40 E8 La Poza Grande Baja California Sur, NW Mexico 25°50′N 112°00′W
93 K16 Lappajärvi Länsi-Suomi, W Finland 63°13′N 23°40′E
93 L16 Lappajärvi ◎ W Finland
93 N18 Lappeenranta Swe. Villmanstrand. Etelä-Suomi, SE Finland 61°04′N 28°15′E
93 J17 Lappfjärd Fin. Lapväärtti. Länsi-Suomi, W Finland 62°14′N 21°30′E
92 L12 Lappi Swe. Lappland. ◈ province N Finland
Lappi/Lappland see Lapland
Lappo see Lapua
61 C23 Laprida Buenos Aires, E Argentina 37°34′S 60°45′W
25 P13 La Pryor Texas, SW USA 28°56′N 99°51′W
136 B11 Lâpseki Çanakkale, NW Turkey 40°22′N 26°42′E
121 P2 Lapta Gk. Lápithos. NW Cyprus 35°20′N 33°11′E
Laptev Sea see Laptevykh, More
122 N6 Laptevykh, More Eng. Laptev Sea. sea Arctic Ocean
93 K16 Lapua Swe. Lappo. Länsi-Suomi, W Finland 62°57′N 23°E
105 P3 La Puebla de Arganzón País Vasco, N Spain 42°45′N 02°49′W
104 L14 La Puebla de Cazalla Andalucía, S Spain 37°14′N 05°18′W
104 M9 La Puebla de Montalbán Castilla-La Mancha, C Spain 39°52′N 04°22′W
54 I6 La Puerta Trujillo, NW Venezuela 09°08′N 70°46′W
Lapurdum see Bayonne
40 E7 La Purísima Baja California Sur, NW Mexico 26°10′N 112°05′W
Lapväärtti see Lappfjärd
110 O10 Łapy Podlaskie, NE Poland 53°N 22°54′E
80 D6 Laqiya Arba'in Northern, NW Sudan 20°01′N 28°01′E
62 J4 La Quiaca Jujuy, N Argentina 22°12′S 65°36′W
107 J14 L'Aquila var. Aquila, Aquila degli Abruzzi. Abruzzo, C Italy 42°21′N 13°24′E
143 Q13 Lār Fārs, S Iran 27°42′N 54°19′E
54 J5 Lara off. Estado Lara. ◈ state NW Venezuela
104 G2 Laracha Galicia, NW Spain 43°14′N 08°34′W
74 G5 Larache var. al Araïch, El Araïch, prev. El Araïche; anc. Lixus. NW Morocco 35°12′N 06°10′W
Lara, Estado see Lara
103 T14 Laragne-Montéglin Hautes-Alpes, SE France 44°21′N 05°46′E
104 M13 La Rambla Andalucía, S Spain 37°37′N 04°44′W
33 Y17 Laramie Wyoming, C USA 41°18′N 105°35′W
33 X15 Laramie Mountains ▲▲ Wyoming, C USA
33 Y16 Laramie River ≈ Wyoming, C USA
Larang see Zhongdian
60 H12 Laranjeiras do Sul Paraná, S Brazil 25°23′S 52°23′W
Larantoeka see Larantuka
171 P16 Larantuka prev. Larantoeka. Flores, C Indonesia 08°20′S 123°00′E
171 U15 Larat Pulau Larat, E Indonesia 07°07′S 131°46′E
171 U15 Larat, Pulau island Kepulauan Tanimbar, E Indonesia
95 P19 Lärbro Gotland, SE Sweden 57°46′N 18°49′E
106 A9 Larche, Col de pass France/Italy
14 H8 Larder Lake Ontario, S Canada 48°06′N 79°44′W
105 O2 Laredo Cantabria, N Spain 43°23′N 03°22′W
25 Q15 Laredo Texas, SW USA 27°30′N 99°30′W
40 H9 La Reforma Sinaloa, W Mexico 25°05′N 108°03′W
98 N11 Laren Gelderland, E Netherlands 52°12′N 06°22′E
98 J11 Laren Noord-Holland, C Netherlands 52°15′N 05°13′E
102 K13 la Réole Gironde, SW France 44°34′N 00°00′W
La Réunion see Réunion
Largeau see Faya
103 U13 l'Argentière-la-Bessée Hautes-Alpes, SE France 44°49′N 06°34′E
149 O4 Lar Gerd var. Largird. Balkh, N Afghanistan 35°36′N 66°48′E
Largird see Lar Gerd
23 V12 Largo Florida, SE USA 27°55′N 82°47′W
37 Q9 Largo, Canon valley New Mexico, SW USA
44 D6 Largo, Cayo island W Cuba
23 Z17 Largo, Key island Florida Keys, Florida, SE USA
96 H12 Largs W Scotland, United Kingdom 55°48′N 04°50′W
102 I16 la Rhune var. Larrún. ▲ France/Spain 43°19′N 01°36′W see also Larrún
la Rhune see Larrún
la Riege see Ariège
29 Q4 Larimore North Dakota, N USA 47°54′N 97°37′W
107 L15 Larino Molise, C Italy 41°46′N 14°50′E
Lario see Como, Lago di
62 J9 La Rioja La Rioja, NW Argentina 29°26′S 66°50′W
62 I9 La Rioja off. Provincia de La Rioja. ◈ province NW Argentina
105 O4 La Rioja ◈ autonomous community N Spain
La Rioja, Provincia de see La Rioja
115 F16 Lárisa var. Larissa. Thessalía, C Greece 39°38′N 22°27′E
Larissa see Lárisa
149 Q13 Lārkāna var. Larkhana. Sind, SE Pakistan 27°32′N 68°18′E
Larkhana see Lārkāna
Larnaca see Lárnaka
121 Q3 Lárnaka var. Larnaca, Larnax. SE Cyprus 34°55′N 33°39′E
121 Q3 Lárnaka ✈ SE Cyprus 34°52′N 33°38′E
Larnax see Lárnaka
97 G14 Larne Ir. Latharna. E Northern Ireland, United Kingdom 54°51′N 05°49′W
26 L5 Larned Kansas, C USA 38°12′N 99°05′W
104 L3 La Robla Castilla-León, N Spain 42°48′N 05°37′W
104 J10 La Roca de la Sierra Extremadura, W Spain 39°06′N 06°41′W
99 K22 La Roche-en-Ardenne Luxembourg, SE Belgium 50°11′N 05°35′E
102 L11 la Rochefoucauld Charente, W France 45°43′N 00°23′E
102 J10 la Rochelle anc. Rupella. Charente-Maritime, W France 46°09′N 01°07′W
102 I9 la Roche-sur-Yon prev. Bourbon Vendée, Napoléon-Vendée. Vendée, NW France 46°40′N 01°26′W
105 Q10 La Roda Castilla-La Mancha, C Spain 39°13′N 02°10′W
104 L14 La Roda de Andalucía Andalucía, S Spain 37°12′N 04°45′W
45 P9 La Romana E Dominican Republic 18°25′N 69°00′W
11 T13 La Ronge Saskatchewan, C Canada 55°07′N 105°18′W
11 U13 La Ronge, Lac ◎ Saskatchewan, C Canada
22 K10 Larose Louisiana, S USA 29°34′N 90°22′W
42 M7 La Rosita Región Autónoma Atlántico Norte, NE Nicaragua 13°55′N 84°23′W
181 Q3 Larrimah Northern Territory, N Australia 15°30′S 133°12′E
62 N11 Larroque Entre Ríos, E Argentina 33°05′S 59°06′W
105 Q2 Larrún Fr. la Rhune. ▲ France/Spain 43°18′N 01°35′W see also la Rhune
Larrún see la Rhune
195 X6 Lars Christensen Coast physical region Antarctica
39 Q14 Larsen Bay Kodiak Island, Alaska, USA 57°32′N 153°58′W
194 I5 Larsen Ice Shelf ice shelf Antarctica
8 M6 Larsen Sound sound Nunavut, N Canada
La Rúa see A Rúa de Valdeorras
102 K16 Laruns Pyrénées-Atlantiques, SW France 43°00′N 00°25′W
95 G16 Larvik Vestfold, S Norway 59°04′N 10°02′E
La-sa see Lhasa
171 S13 Lasahata Pulau Seram, E Indonesia 02°52′S 128°27′E
Lasahau see Lasihao
37 O6 La Sal Utah, W USA 38°19′N 109°14′W
14 C17 La Salle Ontario, S Canada 42°13′N 83°05′W
30 L11 La Salle Illinois, N USA 41°19′N 89°06′W
45 O9 Las Americas ✈ (Santo Domingo) S Dominican Republic 18°24′N 69°38′W
37 V6 Las Animas Colorado, C USA 38°04′N 103°13′W
108 D10 La Sarine var. Sarine. ≈ SW Switzerland
108 B9 La Sarraz Vaud, W Switzerland 46°40′N 06°32′E
12 H12 La Sarre Québec, SE Canada 48°49′N 79°12′W
54 L3 Las Aves, Islas var. Islas de Aves. island group N Venezuela
55 N7 Las Bonitas Bolívar, C Venezuela 07°50′N 65°40′W
104 K15 Las Cabezas de San Juan Andalucía, S Spain 36°59′N 05°56′W
61 G19 Lascano Rocha, E Uruguay 33°40′S 54°12′W
62 I5 Lascar, Volcán ⛰ N Chile 23°22′S 67°33′W
41 T15 Las Choapas var. Choapas. Veracruz-Llave, SE Mexico 17°51′N 94°00′W
37 R15 Las Cruces New Mexico, SW USA 32°19′N 106°49′W
Lasdehnen see Krasnoznamensk
105 V4 La See d'Urgel var. La Seu d'Urgell, Seo de Urgel. Cataluña, NE Spain 42°22′N 01°27′E
La Selle see Selle, Pic de la
62 G9 La Serena Coquimbo, C Chile 29°54′S 71°18′W
104 K11 La Serena physical region W Spain
La Seu d'Urgell see La See d'Urgel
103 T16 la Seyne-sur-Mer Var, SE France 43°07′N 05°53′E
61 D21 Las Flores Buenos Aires, E Argentina 36°03′S 59°08′W
62 H9 Las Flores San Juan, W Argentina 30°14′S 69°10′W
11 S14 Lashburn Saskatchewan, S Canada 53°09′N 109°37′W
62 I11 Las Heras Mendoza, W Argentina 32°48′S 68°50′W
148 M8 Lashkar Gāh var. Lash-Kar-Gar'. Helmand, S Afghanistan 31°35′N 64°21′E
Lash-Kar-Gar' see Lashkar Gāh
171 P14 Lasihao var. Lasahau. Pulau Muna, C Indonesia 05°01′S 122°23′E
107 N21 La Sila ▲▲ SW Italy
63 H23 La Silueta, Cerro ▲ S Chile 52°22′S 72°09′W
42 L9 La Sirena Región Autónoma Atlántico Sur, E Nicaragua 12°59′N 84°35′W
110 J13 Łask Łódzkie, C Poland 51°36′N 19°06′E
109 V11 Laško Ger. Tüffer. C Slovenia 46°08′N 15°13′E
63 H14 Las Lajas Neuquén, W Argentina 38°31′S 70°22′W
63 H15 Las Lajas, Cerro ▲ W Argentina 38°49′S 70°42′W
62 M6 Las Lomitas Formosa, N Argentina 24°45′S 60°35′W
41 V16 Las Margaritas Chiapas, SE Mexico 16°15′N 91°58′W
Las Marismas see Guadalquivir, Marismas del
54 M6 Las Mercedes Guárico, N Venezuela 09°08′N 66°27′W
42 F6 Las Minas, Cerro ▲ W Honduras 14°33′N 88°41′W
105 O11 La Solana Castilla-La Mancha, C Spain 38°56′N 03°14′W
45 Q14 La Soufrière ▲ Saint Vincent, Saint Vincent and the Grenadines 13°20′N 61°11′W
102 M10 la Souterraine Creuse, C France 46°15′N 01°28′E
62 N7 Las Palmas Chaco, N Argentina 27°08′S 58°45′W
43 Q16 Las Palmas Veraguas, W Panama 08°09′N 81°28′W
64 P12 Las Palmas var. Las Palmas de Gran Canaria. Gran Canaria, Islas Canarias, Spain, NE Atlantic Ocean 28°08′N 15°27′W
64 P12 Las Palmas ◈ province Islas Canarias, Spain, NE Atlantic Ocean
64 Q12 Las Palmas ✈ Gran Canaria, Islas Canarias, Spain, NE Atlantic Ocean
Las Palmas de Gran Canaria see Las Palmas
40 D6 Las Palomas Baja California Norte, W Mexico 31°44′N 107°37′W
105 P10 Las Pedroñeras Castilla-La Mancha, C Spain 39°27′N 02°41′W
106 E10 La Spezia Liguria, NW Italy 44°08′N 09°50′E
61 F20 Las Piedras Canelones, S Uruguay 34°42′S 56°14′W
63 J18 Las Plumas Chubut, S Argentina 43°46′S 67°15′W
61 B18 Las Rosas Santa Fe, C Argentina 32°27′S 61°30′W
Lassa see Lhasa
35 O4 Lassen Peak ▲ California, W USA 40°27′N 121°28′W
194 K6 Lassiter Coast physical region Antarctica
109 V9 Lassnitz ≈ SE Austria
15 O12 L'Assomption Québec, SE Canada 45°48′N 73°27′W
15 N11 L'Assomption ≈ Québec, SE Canada
43 S17 Las Tablas Los Santos, S Panama 07°45′N 80°17′W
Lastarria, Volcán see Azufre, Volcán
37 V4 Last Chance Colorado, C USA 39°41′N 103°34′W
Last Frontier, The see Alaska
11 U16 Last Mountain Lake ◎ Saskatchewan, S Canada
62 H9 Las Tórtolas, Cerro ▲ W Argentina 29°57′S 69°49′W
61 C14 Las Toscas Santa Fe, C Argentina 28°22′S 59°20′W
79 F19 Lastoursville Ogooué-Lolo, E Gabon 00°50′S 12°43′E
113 F16 Lastovo It. Lagosta. island SW Croatia
113 F16 Lastovski Kanal channel SW Croatia
40 E6 Las Tres Vírgenes, Volcán ⛰ NW Mexico 27°27′N 112°34′W
40 F4 Las Trincheras Sonora, NW Mexico 30°21′N 111°27′W
55 N8 Las Trincheras Bolívar, E Venezuela 06°57′N 64°49′W
44 H7 Las Tunas var. Victoria de las Tunas. Las Tunas, E Cuba 20°58′N 76°59′W
La Suisse see Switzerland
40 I5 Las Varas Chihuahua, N Mexico 29°35′N 108°01′W
40 J12 Las Varas Nayarit, C Mexico 21°12′N 105°10′W
62 L10 Las Varillas Córdoba, E Argentina 31°54′S 62°45′W
35 X11 Las Vegas Nevada, W USA 36°09′N 115°10′W
37 T10 Las Vegas New Mexico, SW USA 35°35′N 105°15′W
187 P10 Lata Nendö, Solomon Islands 10°45′S 165°43′E
13 R10 La Tabatière Québec, E Canada 50°51′N 58°59′W
56 C6 Latacunga Cotopaxi, C Ecuador 00°58′S 78°36′W
194 I7 Latady Island island Antarctica
54 E14 La Tagua Putumayo, S Colombia 0°05′S 74°39′W
Latakia see Al Lādhiqīyah
92 J10 Lätäseno ≈ NW Finland
14 H9 Latchford Ontario, S Canada 47°20′N 79°45′W
14 J13 Latchford Bridge Ontario, SE Canada 45°16′N 77°29′W
193 Y14 Late island Vava'u Group, N Tonga
153 P15 Lātehār Jhārkhand, N India 23°48′N 84°28′E
15 R7 Laterrière Québec, SE Canada 48°17′N 71°10′W
102 J13 la Teste Gironde, SW France 44°38′N 01°04′W
25 V8 Latexo Texas, SW USA 31°24′N 95°28′W
18 L10 Latham New York, NE USA 42°45′N 73°45′W
Latharna see Larne
108 B9 La Thielle var. Thièle. ≈ W Switzerland
27 R3 Lathrop Missouri, C USA 39°33′N 94°19′W
107 I16 Latina prev. Littoria. Lazio, C Italy 41°28′N 12°53′E
41 R14 La Tinaja Veracruz-Llave, S Mexico
106 J7 Latisana Friuli-Venezia Giulia, NE Italy 45°47′N 13°01′E
Latium see Lazio
115 K25 Lató site of ancient city Kríti, Greece, E Mediterranean Sea
187 Q17 La Tontouta ✈ (Noumea) Province Sud, S New Caledonia 22°06′S 166°12′E
55 N4 La Tortuga, Isla var. Isla Tortuga. island N Venezuela
108 C10 La Tour-de-Peilz var. La Tour de Peilz. Vaud, SW Switzerland 46°28′N 06°52′E
La Tour de Peilz see La Tour-de-Peilz
103 S11 la Tour-du-Pin Isère, E France 45°34′N 05°25′E
102 J11 la Tremblade Charente-Maritime, W France 45°45′N 01°07′W
102 L10 la Trimouille Vienne, W France 46°27′N 01°02′E
42 J9 La Trinidad Estelí, NW Nicaragua 12°57′N 86°15′W
41 V16 La Trinitaria Chiapas, SE Mexico 16°02′N 92°00′W
45 Q11 la Trinité E Martinique 14°44′N 60°58′W
15 U7 La Trinité-des-Monts Québec, SE Canada 48°07′N 68°31′W
18 C15 Latrobe Pennsylvania, NE USA 40°18′N 79°19′W
183 P13 La Trobe River ≈ Victoria, SE Australia
Lattakia/Lattaquié see Al Lādhiqīyah
171 S13 Latu Pulau Seram, E Indonesia 03°24′S 128°37′E
15 P9 La Tuque Québec, SE Canada 47°26′N 72°47′W
155 G14 Lātūr Mahārāshtra, C India 18°24′N 76°34′E
118 G8 Latvia off. Republic of Latvia, Ger. Lettland, Latv. Latvija, Latvijas Republika; prev. Latvian SSR, Rus. Latviyskaya SSR. ◆ republic NE Europe
Latvian SSR/Latvija/Latvijas Republika/Latviyskaya SSR see Latvia
Latvia, Republic of see Latvia
186 H7 Lau New Britain, E Papua New Guinea 05°46′S 151°21′E
175 R9 Lau Basin undersea feature S Pacific Ocean
101 O15 Lauchhammer Brandenburg, E Germany 51°30′N 13°48′E
Laudunum see Laon
Laudus see St-Lô
Lauenburg/Lauenburg in Pommern see Lębork
101 L20 Lauf an der Pegnitz Bayern, SE Germany 49°31′N 11°16′E
108 D7 Laufen Basel, NW Switzerland 47°26′N 07°31′E
109 P5 Lauffen Salzburg, NW Austria 47°54′N 12°57′E
92 I2 Laugarbakki Nordhurland Vestra, N Iceland 65°18′N 20°51′W
92 I4 Laugarvatn Sudhurland, SW Iceland 64°09′N 20°43′W
31 O3 Laughing Fish Point headland Michigan, N USA 46°31′N 87°01′W
187 Z14 Lau Group island group E Fiji
Lauis see Lugano
93 M17 Laukaa Länsi-Suomi, C Finland 62°27′N 25°58′E
118 D12 Laukuva Tauragė, W Lithuania 55°37′N 22°12′E
Laun see Louny
183 P16 Launceston Tasmania, SE Australia 41°25′S 147°07′E
97 I24 Launceston anc. Dunheved. SW England, United Kingdom 50°38′N 04°21′W
54 C13 La Unión Nariño, SW Colombia 01°35′N 77°09′W
42 H8 La Unión La Unión, SE El Salvador 13°20′N 87°50′W
42 I6 La Unión Olancho, C Honduras 15°02′N 86°40′W
40 M15 La Unión Guerrero, S Mexico 17°58′N 101°49′W
41 Y14 La Unión Quintana Roo, E Mexico 18°00′N 101°48′W
105 S13 La Unión Murcia, SE Spain 37°37′N 00°54′W
54 L7 La Unión Barinas, C Venezuela 08°15′N 67°46′W
42 B10 La Unión ◈ department E El Salvador
38 H11 Laupāhoehoe var. Laupahoehoe. Hawaii, USA, C Pacific Ocean 20°00′N 155°15′W
Laupahoehoe see Laupāhoehoe
101 I23 Laupheim Baden-Württemberg, S Germany 48°13′N 09°54′E
181 W3 Laura Queensland, NE Australia 15°37′S 144°34′E
189 X2 Laura atoll Majuro Atoll, SE Marshall Islands
Laurana see Lovran
54 L8 La Urbana Bolívar, C Venezuela 07°05′N 66°58′W
21 Y4 Laurel Delaware, NE USA 38°33′N 75°34′W
23 V14 Laurel Florida, SE USA 27°07′N 82°27′W
21 W3 Laurel Maryland, NE USA 39°06′N 76°51′W
22 M6 Laurel Mississippi, S USA 31°41′N 89°10′W
33 U11 Laurel Montana, NW USA 45°40′N 108°46′W
29 R13 Laurel Nebraska, C USA 42°25′N 97°04′W
18 H15 Laureldale Pennsylvania, NE USA 40°24′N 75°52′W
18 C16 Laurel Hill ridge Pennsylvania, NE USA
29 T12 Laurens Iowa, C USA 42°51′N 94°51′W
21 P11 Laurens South Carolina, SE USA 34°29′N 82°01′W
Laurentian Highlands see Laurentian Mountains
15 P10 Laurentian Mountains var. Laurentian Highlands, Fr. Les Laurentides. plateau Newfoundland and Labrador/Québec, Canada
15 O12 Laurentides Québec, SE Canada 45°51′N 73°49′W
Laurentides, Les see Laurentian Mountains
107 M19 Lauria Basilicata, S Italy 40°03′N 15°50′E
194 I1 Laurie Island island Antarctica
21 T11 Laurinburg North Carolina, SE USA 34°46′N 79°29′W
30 M2 Laurium Michigan, N USA 47°14′N 88°26′W
Lauru see Choiseul
108 B9 Lausanne It. Losanna. Vaud, SW Switzerland 46°32′N 06°39′E
101 Q16 Lausche var. Luže. ▲ Czech Republic/Germany 50°52′N 14°39′E see also Luže
Lausche see Luže
101 Q16 Lausitzer Bergland var. Lausitzer Gebirge, Cz. Gory Lužické, Lužické Hory, Eng. Lusatian Mountains. ▲▲ E Germany
Lausitzer Gebirge see Lausitzer Bergland
Lausitzer Neisse see Neisse
103 T12 Lautaret, Col du pass SE France
63 G15 Lautaro Araucanía, C Chile 38°30′S 71°30′W
101 F21 Lauter ≈ W Germany
108 I7 Lauterach Vorarlberg, NW Austria 47°29′N 09°44′E
101 I17 Lauterbach Hessen, C Germany 50°37′N 09°24′E
108 E9 Lauterbrunnen Bern, C Switzerland 46°36′N 07°52′E
169 U14 Laut Kecil, Kepulauan island group N Indonesia
187 X14 Lautoka Viti Levu, W Fiji 17°36′S 177°28′E
169 O8 Laut, Pulau prev. Laoet. island Borneo, C Indonesia
169 V14 Laut, Pulau island Kepulauan Natuna, W Indonesia
169 U13 Laut, Selat strait Borneo, C Indonesia
168 H8 Laut Tawar, Danau ◎ Sumatera, NW Indonesia
189 V14 Lauvergne Island island Chuuk, C Micronesia
98 M5 Lauwers Meer ◎ N Netherlands
98 M4 Lauwersoog Groningen, NE Netherlands 53°25′N 06°14′E
102 M14 Lauzerte Tarn-et-Garonne, S France 44°15′N 01°08′E
25 U12 Lavaca Bay bay Texas, SW USA
25 U12 Lavaca River ≈ Texas, SW USA
15 O12 Laval Québec, SE Canada 45°32′N 73°44′W
102 J6 Laval Mayenne, NW France 48°04′N 00°46′W
15 T6 Laval ≈ Québec, SE Canada
105 S9 La Vall d'Uixó var. Vall D'Uxó. País Valenciano, E Spain 39°49′N 00°15′W

◆ Country
● Country Capital
◇ Dependent Territory
○ Dependent Territory Capital
◈ Administrative Regions
✈ International Airport
▲ Mountain
▲▲ Mountain Range
⛰ Volcano
≈ River
◎ Lake
⊠ Reservoir

LAVALLEJA – LES STES-MARIES-DE-LA-MER

61 F19 **Lavalleja** ◈ *department* S Uruguay
15 O12 **Lavaltrie** Québec, SE Canada 45°56′N 73°14′W
186 M10 **Lavanggu** Rennell, S Solomon Islands 11°39′S 160°13′E
143 O14 **Lāvān, Jazīreh-ye** *island* S Iran
109 U8 **Lavant** ≈ S Austria
118 G5 **Lavassaare** *Ger.* Lawassaar. Pärnumaa, SW Estonia 58°29′N 24°22′E
104 L3 **La Vecilla de Curueño** Castilla-León, N Spain 42°51′N 05°24′W
45 N8 **La Vega** *var.* Concepción de la Vega. C Dominican Republic 19°15′N 70°33′W
La Vela *see* La Vela de Coro
54 J4 **La Vela de Coro** *var.* La Vela. Falcón, N Venezuela 11°30′N 69°33′W
103 N17 **Lavelanet** Ariège, S France 42°56′N 01°50′E
107 M17 **Lavello** Basilicata, S Italy 41°03′N 15°48′E
36 J8 **La Verkin** Utah, W USA 37°12′N 113°16′W
26 J8 **Laverne** Oklahoma, C USA 36°42′N 99°53′W
25 S12 **La Vernia** Texas, SW USA 29°19′N 98°07′W
93 K18 **Lavia** Länsi-Suomi, SW Finland 61°36′N 22°34′E
14 I12 **Lavieille, Lake** ◎ Ontario, SE Canada
94 C12 **Lavik** Sogn Og Fjordane, S Norway 61°06′N 05°25′E
La Vila Joiosa *see* Villajoyosa
33 U10 **Lavina** Montana, NW USA 46°18′N 108°55′W
194 H5 **Lavoisier Island** *island* Antarctica
23 U2 **Lavonia** Georgia, SE USA 34°26′N 83°06′W
103 R13 **la Voulte-sur-Rhône** Ardèche, E France 44°49′N 04°46′E
123 W5 **Lavrentiya** Chukotskiy Avtonomnyy Okrug, NE Russian Federation 65°33′N 171°12′W
115 H20 **Lávrio** *prev.* Lávrion. Attikí, C Greece 37°43′N 24°03′E
Lávrion *see* Lávrio
83 L22 **Lavumisa** *prev.* Gollel. SE Swaziland 27°18′S 31°55′E
149 T4 **Lawarai Pass** *pass* N Pakistan
Lawassaar *see* Lavassaare
141 P16 **Lawdar** SW Yemen 13°49′N 45°55′E
25 Q7 **Lawn** Texas, SW USA 32°07′N 99°45′W
195 Y4 **Law Promontory** *headland* Antarctica
77 O14 **Lawra** NW Ghana 10°40′N 02°49′W
185 E23 **Lawrence** Otago, South Island, New Zealand 45°53′S 169°43′E
31 P14 **Lawrence** Indiana, N USA 39°49′N 86°01′W
27 Q4 **Lawrence** Kansas, C USA 38°58′N 95°15′W
19 O10 **Lawrence** Massachusetts, NE USA 42°42′N 71°09′W
20 L5 **Lawrenceburg** Kentucky, S USA 38°02′N 84°53′W
20 I10 **Lawrenceburg** Tennessee, S USA 35°16′N 87°20′W
23 T3 **Lawrenceville** Georgia, SE USA 33°57′N 83°59′W
31 N15 **Lawrenceville** Illinois, N USA 38°43′N 87°40′W
21 V7 **Lawrenceville** Virginia, NE USA 36°45′N 77°50′W
27 S3 **Lawson** Missouri, C USA 39°26′N 94°12′W
26 L12 **Lawton** Oklahoma, C USA 34°35′N 98°20′W
140 I4 **Lawz, Jabal al** ▲ NW Saudi Arabia 28°45′N 35°20′E
95 L16 **Laxå** Örebro, C Sweden 59°00′N 14°37′E
125 T5 **Laya** ≈ NW Russian Federation
57 I19 **La Yarada** Tacna, SW Peru 18°14′S 70°30′W
141 S15 **Layjūn** C Yemen 15°27′N 49°16′E
141 Q9 **Laylā** *var.* Laila. Ar Riyāḍ, C Saudi Arabia 22°14′N 46°40′E
23 P4 **Lay Lake** ⊠ Alabama, S USA
45 P14 **Layou** Saint Vincent, Saint Vincent and the Grenadines 13°11′N 61°16′W
La Youne *see* El Ayoun
192 L5 **Laysan Island** *island* Hawaiian Islands, Hawai'i, USA
36 L2 **Layton** Utah, W USA 41°03′N 112°00′W
34 L5 **Laytonville** California, W USA 39°39′N 123°30′W
172 H17 **Lazare, Pointe** *headland* Mahé, NE Seychelles 04°46′S 55°28′E
123 T12 **Lazarev** Khabarovskiy Kray, SE Russian Federation 52°11′N 141°18′E
112 L12 **Lazarevac** Serbia, C Serbia 44°25′N 20°17′E
65 N22 **Lazarev Sea** *sea* Antarctica
40 M15 **Lázaro Cárdenas** Michoacán, SW Mexico 17°56′N 102°13′W
119 F15 **Lazdijai** Alytus, S Lithuania 54°13′N 23°33′E
107 H15 **Lazio** *anc.* Latium. ◈ *region* C Italy
111 A16 **Lázně Kynžvart** *Ger.* Bad Königswart. Karlovarský Kraj, W Czech Republic 50°00′N 12°40′E
Lazovsk *see* Sîngerei
167 R12 **Leach** Poŭthĭsăt, W Cambodia 12°19′N 103°45′E
27 X9 **Leachville** Arkansas, C USA 35°56′N 90°15′W
28 I9 **Lead** South Dakota, N USA 44°21′N 103°45′W
11 S16 **Leader** Saskatchewan, S Canada 50°55′N 109°31′W
19 S6 **Lead Mountain** ▲ Maine, NE USA 44°53′N 68°07′W
37 R5 **Leadville** Colorado, C USA 39°15′N 106°17′W
11 V12 **Leaf Rapids** Manitoba, C Canada 56°30′N 100°02′W
22 M7 **Leaf River** ≈ Mississippi, S USA
25 W11 **League City** Texas, SW USA 29°30′N 95°05′W
92 K8 **Leaibevuotna** *Nor.* Olderfjord. Finnmark, N Norway 70°29′N 24°58′E
23 N7 **Leakesville** Mississippi, S USA 31°09′N 88°33′W
25 Q11 **Leakey** Texas, SW USA 29°44′N 99°48′W
Leal *see* Lihula
83 G15 **Lealui** Western, W Zambia 15°12′S 22°59′E
Leamhcán *see* Lucan
14 C18 **Leamington** Ontario, S Canada 42°03′N 82°35′W
Leamington/Leamington Spa *see* Royal Leamington Spa
Leammi *see* Lemmenjoki
25 S10 **Leander** Texas, SW USA 30°34′N 97°51′W
60 F13 **Leandro N. Alem** Misiones, NE Argentina 27°34′S 55°15′W
97 A20 **Leane, Lough** *Ir.* Loch Léin. ◎ SW Ireland
180 G8 **Learmonth** Western Australia 22°17′S 114°03′E
Leau *see* Zoutleeuw
L'Eau d'Heure *see* Plate Taille, Lac de la
190 D12 **Leava** Île Futuna, S Wallis and Futuna
Leavdnja *see* Lakselv
27 R3 **Leavenworth** Kansas, C USA 39°19′N 94°55′W
32 I8 **Leavenworth** Washington, NW USA 47°36′N 120°39′W
92 L8 **Leavvajohka** *var.* Levajok. Finnmark, N Norway 69°57′N 26°18′E
27 R4 **Leawood** Kansas, C USA 38°57′N 94°37′W
110 H6 **Łeba** *Ger.* Leba. Pomorskie, N Poland 54°45′N 17°32′E
110 I6 **Łeba** *Ger.* Leba. ≈ N Poland
Leba *see* Łeba
101 D20 **Lebach** Saarland, SW Germany 49°25′N 06°54′E
Łeba, Jezioro *see* Łebsko, Jezioro
171 P8 **Lebak** Mindanao, S Philippines 06°28′N 124°03′E
Lebanese Republic *see* Lebanon
31 O13 **Lebanon** Indiana, N USA 40°03′N 86°28′W
20 L6 **Lebanon** Kentucky, S USA 37°33′N 85°15′W
27 U6 **Lebanon** Missouri, C USA 37°40′N 92°40′W
19 N9 **Lebanon** New Hampshire, NE USA 43°40′N 72°15′W
32 G12 **Lebanon** Oregon, NW USA 44°32′N 122°54′W
18 H15 **Lebanon** Pennsylvania, NE USA 40°20′N 76°24′W
20 J8 **Lebanon** Tennessee, S USA 36°11′N 86°19′W
21 P7 **Lebanon** Virginia, NE USA 36°52′N 82°07′W
138 G6 **Lebanon** *off.* Lebanese Republic, *Ar.* Al Lubnān, *Fr.* Liban. ◆ *republic* SW Asia
20 K6 **Lebanon Junction** Kentucky, S USA 37°49′N 85°43′W
Lebanon, Mount *see* Liban, Jebel
146 J10 **Lebap** Lebapskiy Velayat, NE Turkmenistan 41°04′N 61°49′E
Lebapskiy Velayat *see* Lebap Welayaty
146 J11 **Lebap Welayaty** *Rus.* Lebapskiy Velayat; *prev. Rus.* Chardzhevskaya Oblast, *Turkm.* Chärjew Oblasty. ◈ *province* E Turkmenistan
Lebasee *see* Łebsko, Jezioro
99 F17 **Lebbeke** Oost-Vlaanderen, NW Belgium 51°00′N 04°08′E
35 S14 **Lebec** California, W USA 34°51′N 118°52′W
Lebedin *see* Lebedyn
123 Q11 **Lebedinyy** Respublika Sakha (Yakutiya), NE Russian Federation 58°23′N 125°24′E
126 L6 **Lebedyan'** Lipetskaya Oblast', W Russian Federation 53°00′N 39°11′E
117 T4 **Lebedyn** *Rus.* Lebedin. Sums'ka Oblast', NE Ukraine 50°36′N 34°30′E
12 I12 **Lebel-sur-Quévillon** Québec, SE Canada 49°01′N 76°56′W
92 L8 **Lebesby** Finnmark, N Norway 70°31′N 27°00′E
102 M9 **le Blanc** Indre, C France 46°38′N 01°04′E
79 L15 **Lebo** Orientale, N Dem. Rep. Congo 04°30′N 23°58′E
27 P5 **Lebo** Kansas, C USA 38°22′N 95°50′W
110 H6 **Lębork** *var.* Lębórk, *Ger.* Lauenburg, Lauenburg in Pommern. Pomorskie, N Poland 54°32′N 17°43′E
103 O17 **le Boulou** Pyrénées-Orientales, S France 42°32′N 02°50′E
108 A9 **Le Brassus** Vaud, W Switzerland 46°35′N 06°14′E
104 J15 **Lebrija** Andalucía, S Spain 36°55′N 06°04′W
110 G6 **Łebsko, Jezioro** *Ger.* Lebasee; *prev.* Jezioro Łeba. ◎ N Poland
63 F14 **Lebu** Bío Bío, C Chile 37°38′S 73°43′W
Lebyazh'ye *see* Akku
104 F6 **Leça da Palmeira** Porto, N Portugal 41°12′N 08°43′W
103 U15 **le Cannet** Alpes-Maritimes, SE France 43°35′N 07°E
Le Cap *see* Cap-Haïtien
103 P2 **le Cateau-Cambrésis** Nord, N France 50°05′N 03°32′E
107 Q18 **Lecce** Puglia, SE Italy 40°23′N 18°11′E
106 D7 **Lecco** Lombardia, N Italy 45°51′N 09°23′E
29 V10 **Le Center** Minnesota, N USA 44°23′N 93°43′W
108 J7 **Lech** Vorarlberg, W Austria 47°14′N 10°10′E
101 K22 **Lech** ≈ Austria/Germany
115 D19 **Lechainá** *var.* Lehena, Lechaina. Dytikí Ellás, S Greece 37°57′N 21°16′E
102 J11 **le Château d'Oléron** Charente-Maritime, W France 45°53′N 01°12′W
103 R3 **le Chesne** Ardennes, N France 49°33′N 04°42′E
103 R13 **le Cheylard** Ardèche, E France 44°55′N 04°27′E
108 K7 **Lechtaler Alpen** ▲▲ W Austria
100 H6 **Leck** Schleswig-Holstein, N Germany 54°45′N 09°00′E
14 L9 **Lecointre, Lac** ◎ Québec, SE Canada
22 H7 **Lecompte** Louisiana, S USA 31°05′N 92°24′W
103 Q9 **le Creusot** Saône-et-Loire, C France 46°48′N 04°27′E
Lecumberri *see* Lekunberri
110 P13 **Łęczna** Lubelskie, E Poland 51°20′N 22°52′E
110 J12 **Łęczyca** *Ger.* Lentschiza, *Rus.* Lenchitsa. Łódzkie, C Poland 52°04′N 19°10′E
100 F10 **Leda** ≈ NW Germany
109 Y9 **Ledava** ≈ NE Slovenia
99 F17 **Lede** Oost-Vlaanderen, NW Belgium 50°58′N 03°59′E
104 K6 **Ledesma** Castilla-León, N Spain 41°05′N 06°00′W
45 Q12 **le Diamant** SW Martinique 14°29′N 61°02′W
172 J16 **Le Digue** *island* Inner Islands, NE Seychelles
103 Q10 **le Donjon** Allier, C France 46°19′N 03°50′E
102 M10 **le Dorat** Haute-Vienne, C France 46°14′N 01°05′E
Ledo Salinarius *see* Lons-le-Saunier
159 U10 **Ledu** Qinghai, China 36°18′N 102°13′E
11 Q14 **Leduc** Alberta, SW Canada 53°17′N 113°30′W
123 V7 **Ledyanaya, Gora** ▲ E Russian Federation 61°51′N 171°03′E
97 C21 **Lee** *Ir.* An Laoi. ≈ SW Ireland
29 U5 **Leech Lake** ◎ Minnesota, N USA
26 K10 **Leedey** Oklahoma, C USA 35°54′N 99°21′W
97 M17 **Leeds** N England, United Kingdom 53°50′N 01°35′W
23 P4 **Leeds** Alabama, S USA 33°33′N 86°32′W
29 O3 **Leeds** North Dakota, N USA 48°19′N 99°43′W
98 N6 **Leek** Groningen, NE Netherlands 53°10′N 06°24′E
99 K15 **Leende** Noord-Brabant, SE Netherlands 51°21′N 05°34′E
100 F10 **Leer** Niedersachsen, NW Germany 53°14′N 07°26′E
98 J13 **Leerdam** Zuid-Holland, C Netherlands 51°54′N 05°06′E
98 K12 **Leersum** Utrecht, C Netherlands 52°01′N 05°26′E
23 W11 **Leesburg** Florida, SE USA 28°48′N 81°52′W
21 V3 **Leesburg** Virginia, NE USA 39°09′N 77°34′W
27 R4 **Lees Summit** Missouri, C USA 38°55′N 94°21′W
22 G7 **Leesville** Louisiana, S USA 31°08′N 93°15′W
25 S12 **Leesville** Texas, SW USA 29°22′N 97°45′W
31 U13 **Leesville Lake** ⊠ Ohio, N USA
Leesville Lake *see* Smith Mountain Lake
183 P9 **Leeton** New South Wales, SE Australia 34°33′S 146°24′E
98 L6 **Leeuwarden** *Fris.* Ljouwert. Friesland, N Netherlands 53°15′N 05°48′E
180 I14 **Leeuwin, Cape** *headland* Western Australia 34°18′S 115°03′E
35 R8 **Lee Vining** California, W USA 37°57′N 119°07′W
45 V8 **Leeward Islands** *island group* E West Indies
Leeward Islands *see* Sotavento, Ilhas de
Leeward Islands *see* Vent, Îles Sous le
79 G20 **Léfini** ≈ SE Congo
115 C17 **Lefkáda** *prev.* Levkás. Lefkáda, Iónia Nisiá, Greece, C Mediterranean Sea 38°50′N 20°42′E
115 B17 **Lefkáda** *It.* Santa Maura, *prev.* Levkás; *anc.* Leucas. *island* Iónia Nisiá, Greece, C Mediterranean Sea
115 H25 **Lefká Óri** ▲ Kríti, Greece, E Mediterranean Sea
115 B16 **Lefkímmi** *var.* Levkímmi. Kérkyra, Iónia Nisiá, Greece, C Mediterranean Sea 39°26′N 20°05′E
Lefkosía/Lefkoşa *see* Nicosia
25 O2 **Lefors** Texas, SW USA 35°26′N 100°48′W
45 R12 **le François** E Martinique 14°36′N 60°59′W
180 L12 **Lefroy, Lake** *salt lake* Western Australia
Legaceaster *see* Chester
105 N8 **Leganés** Madrid, C Spain 40°20′N 03°46′W
Legaspi *see* Legazpi City
Leghorn *see* Livorno
110 M11 **Legionowo** Mazowieckie, C Poland 52°25′N 20°56′E
99 K24 **Léglise** Luxembourg, SE Belgium 49°48′N 05°31′E
106 G8 **Legnago** Lombardia, NE Italy 45°13′N 11°18′E
106 D7 **Legnano** Veneto, NE Italy 45°36′N 08°54′E
111 F14 **Legnica** *Ger.* Liegnitz. Dolnośląskie, SW Poland 51°12′N 16°11′E
35 Q9 **Le Grand** California, W USA 37°12′N 120°15′W
103 Q15 **le Grau-du-Roi** Gard, S France 43°32′N 04°10′E
183 U3 **Legume** New South Wales, SE Australia 28°24′S 152°20′E
102 L4 **le Havre** *Eng.* Havre; *prev.* le Havre-de-Grâce. Seine-Maritime, N France 49°30′N 00°06′E
le Havre-de-Grâce *see* le Havre
Lehena *see* Lechainá
36 L3 **Lehi** Utah, W USA 40°23′N 111°51′W
18 I14 **Lehighton** Pennsylvania, NE USA 40°49′N 75°42′W
29 O6 **Lehr** North Dakota, N USA 46°15′N 99°21′W
38 A8 **Lehua Island** *island* Hawaiian Islands, Hawai'i, USA
149 S9 **Leiāh** Punjab, NE Pakistan 30°59′N 70°58′E
109 W9 **Leibnitz** Steiermark, SE Austria 46°48′N 15°33′E
97 M19 **Leicester** *Lat.* Batae Coritanorum. C England, United Kingdom 52°38′N 01°05′W
97 M19 **Leicestershire** *cultural region* C England, United Kingdom
Leicheng *see* Leizhou
98 H11 **Leiden** *prev.* Leyden; *anc.* Lugdunum Batavorum. Zuid-Holland, W Netherlands 52°09′N 04°30′E
98 H11 **Leiderdorp** Zuid-Holland, W Netherlands 52°08′N 04°32′E
98 G11 **Leidschendam** Zuid-Holland, W Netherlands 52°05′N 04°24′E
99 D18 **Leie** *Fr.* Lys. ≈ Belgium/France
Leifear *see* Lifford
184 L4 **Leigh** Auckland, North Island, New Zealand 36°17′S 174°48′E
97 K17 **Leigh** NW England, United Kingdom 53°30′N 02°33′W
182 I5 **Leigh Creek** South Australia 30°27′S 138°23′E
23 O2 **Leighton** Alabama, S USA 34°42′N 87°31′W
97 M21 **Leighton Buzzard** E England, United Kingdom 51°55′N 00°41′W
Léim an Bhradáin *see* Leixlip
Léim An Mhadaidh *see* Limavady
Léime, Ceann *see* Loop Head, Ireland
Léime, Ceann *see* Slyne Head, Ireland
101 G20 **Leimen** Baden-Württemberg, SW Germany 49°21′N 08°40′E
100 I13 **Leine** ≈ NW Germany
101 J15 **Leinefelde** Thüringen, C Germany 51°22′N 10°19′E
Léin, Loch *see* Leane, Lough
97 D19 **Leinster** *Ir.* Cúige Laighean. *cultural region* E Ireland
97 F19 **Leinster, Mount** *Ir.* Stua Laighean. ▲ SE Ireland 52°36′N 06°45′W
119 F15 **Leipalingis** Alytus, S Lithuania 54°05′N 23°52′E
92 J12 **Leipojärvi** Norrbotten, N Sweden 67°03′N 21°15′E
31 R12 **Leipsic** Ohio, N USA 41°06′N 83°58′W
Leipsic *see* Leipzig
115 M20 **Leipsoí** *island* Dodekánisa, Greece, Aegean Sea
101 M15 **Leipzig** *Pol.* Lipsk, *hist.* Leipsic; *anc.* Lipsia. Sachsen, E Germany 51°19′N 12°24′E
101 M15 **Leipzig Halle** ✈ Sachsen, E Germany 51°26′N 12°14′E
104 G9 **Leiria** *anc.* Collipo. Leiria, C Portugal 39°45′N 08°49′W
104 F9 **Leiria** ◈ *district* C Portugal
95 C15 **Leirvik** Hordaland, S Norway 59°49′N 05°27′E
118 E5 **Leisi** *Ger.* Laisberg. Saaremaa, W Estonia 58°33′N 22°41′E
104 J3 **Leitariegos, Puerto de** *pass* NW Spain
20 J6 **Leitchfield** Kentucky, S USA 37°28′N 86°19′W
109 Y5 **Leitha** *Hung.* Lajta. ≈ Austria/Hungary
Leitir Ceanainn *see* Letterkenny
Leitmeritz *see* Litoměřice
Leitomischl *see* Litomyšl
97 D16 **Leitrim** *Ir.* Liatroim. *cultural region* NW Ireland
Leix *see* Laois
97 F18 **Leixlip** *Eng.* Salmon Leap, *Ir.* Léim an Bhradáin. Kildare, E Ireland 53°23′N 06°32′W
64 N8 **Leixões** Porto, N Portugal 41°11′N 08°41′W
161 N12 **Leiyang** Hunan, S China 26°23′N 112°49′E
160 L16 **Leizhou** *var.* Haikang, Leicheng. Guangdong, S China 20°54′N 110°05′E
160 L16 **Leizhou Bandao** *var.* Luichow Peninsula. *peninsula* S China
98 H13 **Lek** ≈ SW Netherlands
114 I13 **Lekánis** ▲ NE Greece
172 H13 **Le Kartala** ▲ Grande Comore, NW Comoros
Le Kef *see* El Kef
79 G20 **Lékéti, Monts de la** ▲ S Congo
Lekhainá *see* Lechainá
92 G11 **Leknes** Nordland, C Norway 68°07′N 13°36′E
79 F20 **Lékoumou** ◈ *province* SW Congo
94 L13 **Leksand** Dalarna, C Sweden 60°44′N 15°E
124 H8 **Leksozero, Ozero** ◎ NW Russian Federation
105 Q3 **Lekunberri** *var.* Lecumberri. Navarra, N Spain 43°00′N 01°54′W
171 S11 **Lelai, Tanjung** *headland* Pulau Halmahera, N Indonesia 01°32′N 128°43′E
45 Q12 **le Lamentin** *var.* Lamentin. C Martinique 14°37′N 61°01′W
45 Q12 **le Lamentin** ✈ (Fort-de-France) C Martinique 14°34′N 61°00′W
31 P6 **Leland** Michigan, N USA 45°01′N 85°44′W
22 J4 **Leland** Mississippi, S USA 33°24′N 90°54′W
95 J16 **Lelång** *var.* Lelången. ◎ S Sweden
Lelången *see* Lelång
Lel'chitsy *see* Lyel'chytsy
le Léman *see* Geneva, Lake
Leli *see* Tianlin
25 O3 **Lelia Lake** Texas, SW USA 34°52′N 100°42′W
113 I14 **Lelija** ▲ SE Bosnia and Herzegovina 43°25′N 18°31′E
108 C8 **Le Locle** Neuchâtel, W Switzerland 47°04′N 06°45′E
189 Y14 **Lelu** Kosrae, E Micronesia
Lelu *see* Lelu Island
189 Y14 **Lelu Island** *var.* Lelu. *island* Kosrae, E Micronesia
55 W9 **Lelydorp** Wanica, N Suriname 05°36′N 55°04′W
98 K9 **Lelystad** Flevoland, C Netherlands 52°30′N 05°26′E
63 K25 **Le Maire, Estrecho de** *strait* S Argentina
168 L10 **Lemang** Pulau Rangsang, W Indonesia 01°04′N 102°44′E
186 I7 **Lemankoa** Buka Island, NE Papua New Guinea 05°06′S 154°23′E
Léman, Lac *see* Geneva, Lake
102 L6 **le Mans** Sarthe, NW France 48°00′N 00°12′E
29 S12 **Le Mars** Iowa, C USA 42°47′N 96°10′W
109 S3 **Lembach im Mühlkreis** Oberösterreich, N Austria 48°28′N 13°53′E
101 G23 **Lemberg** ▲ SW Germany 48°09′N 08°47′E
Lemberg *see* L'viv
Lemdiyya *see* Médéa
121 P3 **Lemesós** *var.* Limassol. SW Cyprus 34°41′N 33°02′E
100 H13 **Lemgo** Nordrhein-Westfalen, W Germany 52°02′N 08°54′E
33 P13 **Lemhi Range** ▲▲ Idaho, NW USA
9 S6 **Lemieux Islands** *island group* Nunavut, NE Canada
171 O11 **Lemito** Sulawesi, N Indonesia 0°34′N 121°31′E
92 L10 **Lemmenjoki** *Lapp.* Leammi. ≈ NE Finland
98 L7 **Lemmer** *Fris.* De Lemmer. Friesland, N Netherlands 52°50′N 05°43′E
28 L7 **Lemmon** South Dakota, N USA 45°54′N 102°08′W
36 M15 **Lemmon, Mount** ▲ Arizona, SW USA 32°26′N 110°47′W
Lemnos *see* Límnos
31 O14 **Lemon, Lake** ◎ Indiana, N USA
102 J5 **le Mont St-Michel** *castle* Manche, N France
35 Q11 **Lemoore** California, W USA 36°16′N 119°48′W
189 T13 **Lemotol Bay** *bay* Chuuk Islands, C Micronesia
45 Y5 **le Moule** *var.* Moule. Grande Terre, NE Guadeloupe 16°20′N 61°21′W
Lemovices *see* Limoges
Le Moyen-Ogooué *see* Moyen-Ogooué
12 M6 **le Moyne, Lac** ◎ Québec, E Canada
93 L18 **Lempäälä** Länsi-Suomi, W Finland 61°14′N 23°47′E
42 E7 **Lempa, Río** ≈ Central America
42 F7 **Lempira** *prev.* Gracias. ◈ *department* SW Honduras
Lemsalu *see* Limbaži
107 N17 **Le Murge** ▲ SE Italy
125 V6 **Lemva** ≈ NW Russian Federation
95 F21 **Lemvig** Ringkøbing, W Denmark 56°31′N 08°19′E
166 K8 **Lemyethna** Ayeyarwady, SW Myanmar (Burma) 17°36′N 95°08′E
30 K10 **Lena** Illinois, N USA 42°22′N 89°49′W
129 V4 **Lena** ≈ NE Russian Federation
173 N13 **Lena Tablemount** *undersea feature* S Indian Ocean 51°06′S 56°54′E
Lenchitsa *see* Łęczyca
59 N17 **Lençóis** Bahia, E Brazil 12°36′S 41°24′W
60 K9 **Lençóis Paulista** São Paulo, S Brazil 22°35′S 48°51′W
109 Y9 **Lendava** *Hung.* Lendva, *Ger.* Unterlimbach; *prev.* Dolnja Lendava. NE Slovenia 46°33′N 16°27′E
83 F20 **Lendepas** Hardap, SE Namibia 24°41′S 19°58′E
124 H9 **Lendery** *Finn.* Lentiira. Respublika Kareliya, NW Russian Federation 63°20′N 31°18′E
Lendum *see* Lens
Lendva *see* Lendava
27 R4 **Lenexa** Kansas, C USA 38°57′N 94°43′W
109 Q5 **Lengau** Oberösterreich, N Austria 48°01′N 13°17′E
145 Q17 **Lenger** Yuzhnyy Kazakhstan, S Kazakhstan 42°10′N 69°54′E
Lenghu *see* Lenghuzhen
159 O9 **Lenghuzhen** *var.* Lenghu. Qinghai, C China 38°50′N 93°25′E
159 T9 **Lenglong Ling** ▲ N China 37°40′N 102°13′E
108 D7 **Lengnau** Bern, W Switzerland 47°12′N 07°23′E
Lengshuitan *see* Yongzhou
95 M20 **Lenhovda** Kronoberg, S Sweden 57°00′N 15°16′E
Lenīn *see* Uzynkol', Kazakhstan
Lenin *see* Akdepe, Turkmenistan
Leninabad *see* Khujand
Leninakan *see* Gyumri
Lenina, Pik *see* Lenin Peak
117 V12 **Lenine** *Rus.* Lenino. Respublika Krym, S Ukraine 45°18′N 35°47′E
Leningor *see* Ridder
147 Q13 **Leningrad** *Rus.* Leningradskiy; *prev.* Mü'minobod, *Rus.* Muminabad. SW Tajikistan 38°03′N 69°50′E
Leningrad *see* Sankt-Peterburg
126 L13 **Leningradskaya** Krasnodarskiy Kray, SW Russian Federation 46°19′N 39°23′E
195 S16 **Leningradskaya** *Russian research station* Antarctica 69°30′S 159°51′E
124 H12 **Leningradskaya Oblast'** ◈ *province* NW Russian Federation
Leningradskiy *see* Leningrad
Lenino *see* Lyenina, Belarus
Lenino *see* Lenine, Ukraine
Leninobod *see* Khujand
127 T5 **Leninogorsk** Respublika Tatarstan, W Russian Federation 54°34′N 52°27′E
147 T12 **Lenin Peak** *Rus.* Pik Lenina, *Taj.* Qullai Lenin. ▲ Kyrgyzstan/Tajikistan 39°20′N 72°50′E
147 S8 **Leninpol'** Talasskaya Oblast', NW Kyrgyzstan 42°29′N 71°54′E
Lenin, Qullai *see* Lenin Peak
127 P11 **Leninsk** Volgogradskaya Oblast', SW Russian Federation 48°41′N 45°18′E
Leninsk *see* Baykonyr, Kazakhstan
Leninsk *see* Akdepe, Turkmenistan
Leninsk *see* Asaka, Uzbekistan
145 T8 **Leninskiy** Pavlodar, E Kazakhstan 52°13′N 76°50′E
122 I13 **Leninsk-Kuznetskiy** Kemerovskaya Oblast', S Russian Federation 54°42′N 86°16′E
125 P15 **Leninskoje** Kirovskaya Oblast', NW Russian Federation 58°19′N 47°03′E
Leninskoye *see* Uzynkol'
Lenin-Turkmenski *see* Türkmenabat
Leninváros *see* Tiszaújváros
Lenkoran' *see* Länkäran
101 F15 **Lenne** ≈ W Germany
101 G16 **Lennestadt** Nordrhein-Westfalen, W Germany 51°07′N 08°04′E
29 R11 **Lennox** South Dakota, N USA 43°21′N 96°53′W
63 J25 **Lennox, Isla** *Eng.* Lennox Island. *island* S Chile
Lennox Island *see* Lennox, Isla
21 Q9 **Lenoir** North Carolina, SE USA 35°56′N 81°31′W
20 M9 **Lenoir City** Tennessee, S USA 35°48′N 84°15′W
108 C7 **Le Noirmont** Jura, NW Switzerland 47°14′N 06°57′E
14 L9 **Lenôtre, Lac** ◎ Québec, SE Canada
29 U15 **Lenox** Iowa, C USA 40°52′N 94°33′W
103 O2 **Lens** *anc.* Lendum, Lentium. Pas-de-Calais, N France 50°26′N 02°50′E
123 O11 **Lensk** Respublika Sakha (Yakutiya), NE Russian Federation 60°43′N 115°16′E
111 F24 **Lenti** Zala, SW Hungary 46°38′N 16°30′E
Lentia *see* Linz
93 N14 **Lentiira** Oulu, E Finland 64°22′N 29°52′E
Lentiira *see* Lendery
107 L25 **Lentini** *anc.* Leontini. Sicilia, Italy, C Mediterranean Sea 37°17′N 15°00′E
Lentium *see* Lens
Lentschiza *see* Łęczyca
93 N15 **Lentua** ◎ E Finland
119 H14 **Lentvaris** *Pol.* Landwarów. Vilnius, SE Lithuania 54°39′N 24°58′E
108 F7 **Lenzburg** Aargau, N Switzerland 47°23′N 08°11′E
109 R5 **Lenzing** Oberösterreich, N Austria 47°58′N 13°34′E
77 P13 **Léo** SW Burkina 11°07′N 02°08′W
109 V7 **Leoben** Steiermark, C Austria 47°23′N 15°06′E
Leobschütz *see* Głubczyce
44 L9 **Léogâne** S Haiti 18°32′N 72°37′W
171 O11 **Leok** Sulawesi, N Indonesia 01°10′N 121°20′E
29 O7 **Leola** South Dakota, N USA 45°41′N 98°58′W
97 K20 **Leominster** W England, United Kingdom 52°09′N 02°18′W
19 N11 **Leominster** Massachusetts, NE USA 42°29′N 71°43′W
102 I15 **Léon** Landes, SW France 43°54′N 01°17′W
40 M12 **León** *var.* León de los Aldamas. Guanajuato, C Mexico 21°05′N 101°43′W
42 I10 **León** León, NW Nicaragua 12°24′N 86°52′W
104 L4 **León** Castilla-León, NW Spain 42°34′N 05°34′W
29 V16 **Leon** Iowa, C USA 40°44′N 93°45′W
42 I9 **León** ◈ *department* W Nicaragua
104 K4 **León** ◈ *province* Castilla-León, NW Spain
León *see* Cotopaxi
25 V9 **Leona** Texas, SW USA 31°09′N 95°58′W
180 K11 **Leonara** Western Australia 28°52′S 121°16′E
25 U5 **Leonard** Texas, SW USA 33°22′N 96°15′W
107 H15 **Leonardo da Vinci** *prev.* Fiumicino. ✈ (Roma) Lazio, C Italy 41°48′N 12°15′E
21 X5 **Leonardtown** Maryland, NE USA 38°17′N 76°35′W
25 Q13 **Leona River** ≈ Texas, SW USA
41 Z11 **Leona Vicario** Quintana Roo, SE Mexico 20°57′N 87°06′W
101 H21 **Leonberg** Baden-Württemberg, SW Germany 48°48′N 09°01′E
62 M3 **León, Cerro** ▲ NW Paraguay 20°21′S 60°16′W
León de los Aldamas *see* León
109 T4 **Leonding** Oberösterreich, N Austria 48°17′N 14°15′E
107 I14 **Leonessa** Lazio, C Italy 42°36′N 12°56′E
107 K24 **Leonforte** Sicilia, Italy, C Mediterranean Sea 37°38′N 14°23′E
183 O13 **Leongatha** Victoria, SE Australia 38°30′S 145°56′E
Leonídi *see* Leonídio
115 F21 **Leonídio** *var.* Leonídi. Pelopónnisos, S Greece 37°11′N 22°50′E
104 J4 **León, Montes de** ▲▲ NW Spain
25 S8 **Leon River** ≈ Texas, SW USA
Leontini *see* Lentini
Léopold II, Lac *see* Mai-Ndombe, Lac
99 J17 **Leopoldsburg** Limburg, NE Belgium 51°07′N 05°16′E
Léopoldville *see* Kinshasa
26 I5 **Leoti** Kansas, C USA 38°28′N 101°22′W
116 M11 **Leova** *Rus.* Leovo. SW Moldova 46°31′N 28°16′E
Leovo *see* Leova
102 G8 **le Palais** Morbihan, NW France 47°20′N 03°08′W
27 X10 **Lepanto** Arkansas, C USA 35°34′N 90°21′W
169 N13 **Lepar, Pulau** *island* W Indonesia
104 I14 **Lepe** Andalucía, S Spain 37°15′N 07°12′W
Lepel' *see* Lyepyel'
83 I20 **Lephepe** *var.* Lephephe. Kweneng, SE Botswana 23°20′S 25°50′E
Lephephe *see* Lephepe
161 Q10 **Leping** Jiangxi, S China 28°57′N 117°07′E
Lépontiennes, Alpes/Lepontine, Alpi *see* Lepontine Alps
108 G10 **Lepontine Alps** *Fr.* Alpes Lépontiennes, *It.* Alpi Lepontine. ▲▲ Italy/Switzerland
79 G20 **Le Pool** ◈ *province* S Congo
173 O16 **Le Port** NW Réunion
103 N1 **le Portel** Pas-de-Calais, N France 50°42′N 01°35′E
93 N17 **Leppävirta** Itä-Suomi, C Finland 62°30′N 27°50′E
45 Q11 **le Prêcheur** NW Martinique 14°48′N 61°14′W
Lepsi *see* Lepsy
145 V13 **Lepsy** *Kaz.* Lepsi. Taldykorgan, SE Kazakhstan 46°14′N 78°56′E
145 V13 **Lepsy** *Kaz.* Lepsi. ≈ SE Kazakhstan
Le Puglie *see* Puglia
103 Q12 **le Puy** *prev.* le Puy-en-Velay, *hist.* Anicium, Podium Anicensis. Haute-Loire, C France 45°03′N 03°53′E
le Puy-en-Velay *see* le Puy
45 X11 **le Raizet** *var.* Le Raizet. ✈ (Pointe-à-Pitre) Grande Terre, C Guadeloupe 16°16′N 61°31′W
107 J24 **Lercara Friddi** Sicilia, Italy, C Mediterranean Sea 37°45′N 13°37′E
78 G12 **Léré** Mayo-Kébbi, SW Chad 09°41′N 14°17′E
Leribe *see* Hlotse
106 E10 **Lerici** Liguria, NW Italy 44°06′N 09°53′E
54 I14 **Lérida** Vaupés, SE Colombia 0°01′S 70°28′W
105 U5 **Lérida** ◈ *province* Cataluña, NE Spain
Lérida *see* Lleida
105 N5 **Lerma** Castilla-León, N Spain 42°02′N 03°46′W
40 M13 **Lerma, Río** ≈ C Mexico
Lerna *see* Lérni
115 F20 **Lérni** *var.* Lerna. *prehistoric site* Pelopónnisos, S Greece
45 R11 **le Robert** E Martinique 14°41′N 60°57′W
115 M21 **Léros** *island* Dodekánisa, Greece, Aegean Sea
30 L13 **Le Roy** Illinois, N USA 40°21′N 88°45′W
27 Q6 **Le Roy** Kansas, C USA 38°04′N 95°37′W
29 W11 **Le Roy** Minnesota, N USA 43°30′N 92°30′W
18 E10 **Le Roy** New York, NE USA 42°58′N 77°58′W
Lerrnayin Gharabakh *see* Nagorno-Karabakh
95 J19 **Lerum** Västra Götaland, S Sweden 57°46′N 12°12′E
96 M2 **Lerwick** NE Scotland, United Kingdom 60°09′N 01°09′W
45 Y6 **les Abymes** *var.* Abymes. Grande Terre, C Guadeloupe 16°16′N 61°31′W
les Albères *see* Albères, Chaîne des
102 M4 **les Andelys** Eure, N France 49°15′N 01°26′E
45 Q12 **les Anses-d'Arlets** SW Martinique 14°29′N 61°05′W
105 U6 **Les Borges Blanques** *var.* Borjas Blancas. Cataluña, NE Spain 41°31′N 00°52′E
Lesbos *see* Lésvos
Les Cayes *see* Cayes
31 Q4 **Les Cheneaux Islands** *island* Michigan, N USA
105 T8 **Les Coves de Vinromá** *Cast.* Cuevas de Vinromá. País Valenciano, E Spain 40°18′N 00°07′E
103 T12 **les Écrins** ▲ E France 44°54′N 06°25′E
108 C10 **Le Sépey** Vaud, W Switzerland 46°21′N 07°04′E
15 T7 **Les Escoumins** Québec, SE Canada 48°21′N 69°26′W
Les Gonaïves *see* Gonaïves
160 H9 **Leshan** Sichuan, C China 29°42′N 103°43′E
108 D11 **Les Haudères** Valais, SW Switzerland 46°02′N 07°27′E
102 J9 **les Herbiers** Vendée, NW France 46°52′N 01°01′W
Lesh/Leshi *see* Lezhë
125 O8 **Leshukonskoye** Arkhangel'skaya Oblast', NW Russian Federation 64°54′N 45°48′E
Lesina *see* Hvar
107 M15 **Lesina, Lago di** ◎ SE Italy
114 K13 **Lesítse** ▲ NE Greece
94 G10 **Lesja** Oppland, S Norway 62°07′N 08°56′E
95 L15 **Lesjöfors** Värmland, C Sweden 59°57′N 14°12′E
111 O18 **Lesko** Podkarpackie, SE Poland 49°28′N 22°19′E
113 O15 **Leskovac** Serbia, SE Serbia 43°00′N 21°58′E
113 M22 **Leskovik** *var.* Leskoviku. Korçë, S Albania 40°09′N 20°39′E
Leskoviku *see* Leskovik
33 P14 **Leslie** Idaho, NW USA 43°51′N 113°28′W
31 Q10 **Leslie** Michigan, N USA 42°27′N 84°25′W
Lesna/Lesnaya *see* Lyasnaya
Lesnaya *see* Lyasnaya
102 F5 **Lesneven** Finistère, NW France 48°35′N 04°19′W
112 J11 **Lešnica** Serbia, W Serbia 44°40′N 19°18′E
125 S13 **Lesnoy** Kirovskaya Oblast', NW Russian Federation 59°49′N 52°07′E
122 G10 **Lesnoy** Sverdlovskaya Oblast', C Russian Federation 58°40′N 59°48′E
122 K12 **Lesosibirsk** Krasnoyarskiy Kray, C Russian Federation 58°13′N 92°23′E
83 J23 **Lesotho** *off.* Kingdom of Lesotho; *prev.* Basutoland. ◆ *monarchy* S Africa
Lesotho, Kingdom of *see* Lesotho
102 J12 **Lesparre-Médoc** Gironde, SW France 45°18′N 00°57′W
108 C8 **Les Ponts-de-Martel** Neuchâtel, W Switzerland 47°00′N 06°45′E
103 P1 **Lesquin** ✈ Nord, N France 50°34′N 03°07′E
102 I9 **les Sables-d'Olonne** Vendée, NW France 46°30′N 01°47′W
109 S7 **Lessach** *var.* Lessachbach. ≈ E Austria
Lessachbach *see* Lessach
45 W11 **les Saintes** *var.* Îles des Saintes. *island group* S Guadeloupe
74 L5 **Les Salines** ✈ (Annaba) NE Algeria 36°45′N 07°57′E
99 J22 **Lesse** ≈ SE Belgium
95 M21 **Lessebo** Kronoberg, S Sweden 56°45′N 15°19′E
Lesser Antarctica *see* West Antarctica
45 P15 **Lesser Antilles** *island group* E West Indies
137 T10 **Lesser Caucasus** *Rus.* Malyy Kavkaz. ▲▲ SW Asia
Lesser Khingan Range *see* Xiao Hinggan Ling
11 P13 **Lesser Slave Lake** ◎ Alberta, W Canada
99 E19 **Lessines** Hainaut, SW Belgium 50°43′N 03°50′E
172 I16 **Les Sœurs** *island* Les Sœurs, NE Seychelles
103 R16 **les Stes-Maries-de-la-Mer** Bouches-du-Rhône, SE France 43°27′N 04°26′E

◆ Country
● Country Capital
◇ Dependent Territory
○ Dependent Territory Capital
◈ Administrative Regions
✈ International Airport
▲ Mountain
▲▲ Mountain Range
Volcano
≈ River
◎ Lake
⊠ Reservoir

◆ Country　　◇ Dependent Territory　　◆ Administrative Regions　　▲ Mountain　　🌋 Volcano　　◎ Lake
● Country Capital　　○ Dependent Territory Capital　　✈ International Airport　　▲ Mountain Range　　≈ River　　▨ Reservoir

LIPING – LONGPING

160 L12 **Liping** var. Defeng. Guizhou, S China 26°16′N 109°08′E
Lipkany see Lipcani
119 H15 **Lipnishki** Hrodzyenskaya Voblasts', W Belarus 54°00′N 25°37′E
110 J10 **Lipno** Kujawsko-pomorskie, C Poland 52°52′N 19°11′E
116 F11 **Lipova** Hung. Lippa. Arad, W Romania 46°05′N 21°42′E
Lipovets see Lypovets'
Lippa see Lipova
101 E14 **Lippe** W Germany
Lippehne see Lipiany
101 G14 **Lippstadt** Nordrhein-Westfalen, W Germany 51°41′N 08°20′E
25 P1 **Lipscomb** Texas, SW USA 36°14′N 100°16′W
Lipsia/Lipsk see Leipzig
Liptau-Sankt-Nikolaus/ Liptószentmiklós see Liptovský Mikuláš
111 K19 **Liptovský Mikuláš** Ger. Liptau-Sankt-Nikolaus, Hung. Liptószentmiklós. Žilinský Kraj, N Slovakia 49°06′N 19°36′E
183 O13 **Liptrap, Cape** headland Victoria, SE Australia 38°55′S 145°58′E
160 L13 **Lipu** var. Licheng. Guangxi Zhuangzu Zizhiqu, S China 24°25′N 110°15′E
81 G17 **Lira** N Uganda 02°15′N 32°55′E
57 F15 **Lircay** Huancavelica, C Peru 12°59′S 74°44′W
107 K17 **Liri** C Italy
144 M8 **Lisakovsk** Kostanay, NW Kazakhstan 52°32′N 62°32′E
79 K17 **Lisala** Equateur, N Dem. Rep. Congo 02°10′N 21°29′E
104 F11 **Lisboa** Eng. Lisbon; anc. Felicitas Julia, Olisipo. ● (Portugal) Lisboa, W Portugal 38°44′N 09°08′W
104 F10 **Lisboa** Eng. Lisbon. ◆ district C Portugal
19 N7 **Lisbon** New Hampshire, NE USA 44°11′N 71°52′W
29 Q6 **Lisbon** North Dakota, N USA 46°27′N 97°42′W
Lisbon see Lisboa
19 Q8 **Lisbon Falls** Maine, NE USA 44°00′N 70°03′W
97 G15 **Lisburn** Ir. Lios na gCearrbhach. E Northern Ireland, United Kingdom 54°31′N 06°03′W
38 L6 **Lisburne, Cape** headland Alaska, USA 68°52′N 166°13′W
97 B19 **Liscannor Bay** Ir. Bá Lios Ceannúir. inlet W Ireland
113 Q18 **Lisec** ▲ E FYR Macedonia 41°46′N 22°30′E
160 F13 **Lishe Jiang** SW China
Lishi see Lüliang
163 V10 **Lishu** Jilin, NE China 43°25′N 124°19′E
161 R10 **Lishui** Zhejiang, SE China 28°27′N 119°25′E
192 L5 **Lisianski Island** island Hawaiian Islands, Hawai'i, USA
Lisichansk see Lysychans'k
102 L4 **Lisieux** anc. Noviomagus. Calvados, N France 49°09′N 00°13′E
126 L8 **Liski** prev. Georgiu-Dezh. Voronezhskaya Oblast', W Russian Federation 51°00′N 39°36′E
103 N4 **l'Isle-Adam** Val-d'Oise, N France 49°07′N 02°13′E
Lisle/l'Isle see Lille
103 R15 **l'Isle-sur-la-Sorgue** Vaucluse, SE France 43°55′N 05°03′E
15 S9 **L'Islet** Québec, SE Canada 47°07′N 70°18′W
183 V4 **Lismore** New South Wales, SE Australia 28°48′S 153°12′E
182 M12 **Lismore** Victoria, SE Australia 37°59′S 143°18′E
97 D20 **Lismore** Ir. Lios Mór. S Ireland 52°10′N 07°10′W
Lissa see Vis, Croatia
Lissa see Leszno, Poland
98 H11 **Lisse** Zuid-Holland, W Netherlands 52°15′N 04°33′E
114 K13 **Líssos** var. Filiouri. NE Greece
95 D18 **Lista** peninsula S Norway
95 D18 **Listafjorden** fjord S Norway
195 R13 **Lister, Mount** ▲ Antarctica 78°12′S 161°46′E
126 M8 **Listopadovka** Voronezhskaya Oblast', W Russian Federation 51°54′N 41°08′E
14 F15 **Listowel** Ontario, S Canada 43°44′N 80°57′W
97 B20 **Listowel** Ir. Lios Tuathail. Kerry, SW Ireland 52°27′N 09°29′W
160 L14 **Litang** Guangxi Zhuangzu Zizhiqu, S China 23°09′N 109°08′E
160 F9 **Litang** var. Gaocheng. Sichuan, C China 30°03′N 100°12′E
160 F10 **Litang Qu** C China
55 X12 **Litani** var. Itany. French Guiana/Suriname
138 G8 **Līṭāni, Nahr el** var. Nahr al Litant. C Lebanon
Litant, Nahr al see Līṭāni, Nahr el
Litauen see Lithuania
30 K14 **Litchfield** Illinois, N USA 39°17′N 89°52′W
29 U8 **Litchfield** Minnesota, N USA 45°09′N 94°31′W
36 K13 **Litchfield Park** Arizona, SW USA 33°29′N 112°21′W
183 S8 **Lithgow** New South Wales, SE Australia 33°30′S 150°09′E
115 I26 **Líthino, Akrotírio** headland Kríti, Greece, E Mediterranean Sea 34°55′N 24°43′E
118 D12 **Lithuania** off. Republic of Lithuania, Ger. Litauen, Lith. Lietuva, Pol. Litwa, Rus. Litva; prev. Lithuanian SSR, Rus. Litovskaya SSR. ◆ republic NE Europe
Lithuanian SSR see Lithuania
Lithuania, Republic of see Lithuania
109 U11 **Litija** Ger. Littai. C Slovenia 46°03′N 14°50′E
18 H15 **Lititz** Pennsylvania, NE USA 40°09′N 76°18′W
115 F15 **Litóchoro** var. Litohoro, Litókhoron. Kentrikí Makedonía, N Greece 40°06′N 22°30′E
Litohoro/Litókhoron see Litóchoro
111 C15 **Litoměřice** Ger. Leitmeritz. Ústecký Kraj, NW Czech Republic 50°33′N 14°10′E
111 F17 **Litomyšl** Ger. Leitomischl. Pardubický Kraj, C Czech Republic 49°54′N 16°18′E
111 G17 **Litovel** Ger. Littau. Olomoucký Kraj, E Czech Republic 49°42′N 17°05′E
123 S13 **Litovko** Khabarovskiy Kray, SE Russian Federation 49°22′N 135°10′E
Litovskaya SSR see Lithuania
Littai see Litija
Littau see Litovel
44 G1 **Little Abaco** var. Abaco Island. island N Bahamas
111 I21 **Little Alföld** Ger. Kleines Ungarisches Tiefland, Hung. Kisalföld, Slvk. Podunajská Rovina. plain Hungary/Slovakia
151 Q20 **Little Andaman** island Andaman Islands, India, NE Indian Ocean
26 M5 **Little Arkansas River** Kansas, C USA
184 L4 **Little Barrier Island** island N New Zealand
Little Belt see Lillebælt
38 M11 **Little Black River** Alaska, USA
27 O2 **Little Blue River** Kansas/Nebraska, C USA
44 D8 **Little Cayman** island E Cayman Islands
11 X11 **Little Churchill** Manitoba, C Canada
166 J10 **Little Coco Island** island SW Myanmar (Burma)
36 L10 **Little Colorado River** Arizona, SW USA
14 E11 **Little Current** Manitoulin Island, Ontario, S Canada 45°57′N 81°56′W
12 E11 **Little Current** Ontario, S Canada
38 L8 **Little Diomede Island** island Alaska, USA
44 I4 **Little Exuma** island C Bahamas
29 U7 **Little Falls** Minnesota, N USA 45°59′N 94°21′W
18 J10 **Little Falls** New York, NE USA 43°02′N 74°51′W
24 M5 **Littlefield** Texas, SW USA 33°56′N 102°20′W
29 V3 **Littlefork** Minnesota, N USA 48°24′N 93°33′W
29 V3 **Little Fork River** Minnesota, N USA
11 N16 **Little Fort** British Columbia, SW Canada 51°27′N 120°15′W
11 Y14 **Little Grand Rapids** Manitoba, C Canada 52°06′N 95°29′W
97 N23 **Littlehampton** SE England, United Kingdom 50°48′N 00°33′W
35 T2 **Little Humboldt River** Nevada, W USA
44 K6 **Little Inagua** var. Inagua Islands. island S Bahamas
21 Q4 **Little Kanawha River** West Virginia, NE USA
83 F25 **Little Karoo** plateau S South Africa
39 O16 **Little Koniuji Island** island Shumagin Islands, Alaska, USA
44 H12 **Little London** W Jamaica 18°15′N 78°13′W
13 R10 **Little Mecatina** Fr. Rivière du Petit Mécatina. Newfoundland and Labrador/Québec, E Canada
96 F8 **Little Minch, The** strait NW Scotland, United Kingdom
27 T13 **Little Missouri River** Arkansas, USA
28 J7 **Little Missouri River** NW USA
28 J3 **Little Muddy River** North Dakota, N USA
151 Q22 **Little Nicobar** island Nicobar Islands, India, NE Indian Ocean
27 R6 **Little Osage River** Missouri, C USA
97 P20 **Little Ouse** E England, United Kingdom
149 V2 **Little Pamir** Pash. Pāmīr-e Khord, Rus. Malyy Pamir. ▲▲ Afghanistan/Tajikistan
21 U12 **Little Pee Dee River** North Carolina/South Carolina, SE USA
27 V10 **Little Red River** Arkansas, C USA
Little Rhody see Rhode Island
185 I19 **Little River** Canterbury, South Island, New Zealand 43°45′S 172°49′E
21 U12 **Little River** South Carolina, SE USA 33°52′N 78°36′W
27 Y9 **Little River** Arkansas/Missouri, C USA
27 R13 **Little River** Arkansas/Oklahoma, USA
23 T7 **Little River** Georgia, SE USA
22 H6 **Little River** Louisiana, S USA
25 T10 **Little River** Texas, SW USA
27 V12 **Little Rock** state capital Arkansas, C USA 34°45′N 92°17′W
31 N8 **Little Sable Point** headland Michigan, N USA 43°38′N 86°32′W
103 U11 **Little Saint Bernard Pass** Fr. Col du Petit St-Bernard, It. Colle del Piccolo San Bernardo. pass France/Italy
36 K7 **Little Salt Lake** ◎ Utah, W USA
180 K8 **Little Sandy Desert** desert Western Australia
29 S13 **Little Sioux River** Iowa, C USA
38 E17 **Little Sitkin Island** island Aleutian Islands, Alaska, USA
11 O13 **Little Smoky** Alberta, W Canada 54°35′N 117°06′W
11 O14 **Little Smoky** Alberta, W Canada
37 P3 **Little Snake River** Colorado, C USA
64 A12 **Little Sound** bay Bermuda, NW Atlantic Ocean
37 T4 **Littleton** Colorado, C USA 39°36′N 105°01′W
19 N7 **Littleton** New Hampshire, NE USA 44°18′N 71°46′W
18 D11 **Little Valley** New York, NE USA 42°15′N 78°47′W
30 M15 **Little Wabash River** Illinois, N USA
14 D10 **Little White River** Ontario, S Canada
28 M12 **Little White River** South Dakota, N USA
25 R5 **Little Wichita River** Texas, SW USA
142 I4 **Little Zab** Ar. Nahraz Zāb aş Şaghīr, Kurd. Zē-i Kōya, Per. Rūdkhāneh-ye Zāb-e Kūchek. Iran/Iraq
79 D15 **Littoral** ◆ province W Cameroon
Littoria see Latina
Litva/Litwa see Lithuania
111 B15 **Litvínov** Ger. Leutensdorf. Ústecký Kraj, NW Czech Republic 50°38′N 13°30′E
116 M6 **Lityn** Vinnyts'ka Oblast', C Ukraine 49°19′N 28°06′E
Liu-chou/Liuchow see Liuzhou
163 W11 **Liuhe** Jilin, NE China 42°15′N 125°49′E
Liujiaxia see Yongjing
Liulin see Jonê
83 Q15 **Liúpo** Nampula, NE Mozambique 15°36′S 39°57′E
83 G14 **Liuwa Plain** plain W Zambia
160 L13 **Liuzhou** var. Liu-chou, Liuchow. Guangxi Zhuangzu Zizhiqu, S China 24°09′N 108°55′E
116 H8 **Livada** Hung. Sárköz. Satu Mare, NW Romania 47°52′N 23°04′E
115 J20 **Liváda, Akrotírio** headland Tínos, Kykládes, Greece, Aegean Sea 37°36′N 25°15′E
115 F18 **Livádeia** prev. Levádia. Stereá Ellás, C Greece 38°24′N 22°51′E
Livádi see Liádi
Livanátai see Livanátes
115 G18 **Livanátes** prev. Livanátai. Stereá Ellás, C Greece 38°43′N 23°03′E
118 I10 **Līvāni** Ger. Lievenhof. Preiļi, SE Latvia 56°22′N 26°12′E
65 E25 **Lively Island** island SE Falkland Islands
65 D25 **Lively Sound** sound SE Falkland Islands
39 R8 **Livengood** Alaska, USA 65°31′N 148°32′W
106 I7 **Livenza** NE Italy
35 O6 **Live Oak** California, W USA 39°17′N 121°41′W
23 U9 **Live Oak** Florida, SE USA 30°18′N 82°59′W
35 O9 **Livermore** California, W USA 37°40′N 121°46′W
20 I6 **Livermore** Kentucky, S USA 37°31′N 87°08′W
19 Q7 **Livermore Falls** Maine, NE USA 44°30′N 70°09′W
24 J10 **Livermore, Mount** ▲ Texas, SW USA 30°37′N 104°10′W
13 P16 **Liverpool** Nova Scotia, SE Canada 44°03′N 64°43′W
97 K17 **Liverpool** NW England, United Kingdom 53°25′N 02°55′W
183 S7 **Liverpool Range** ▲▲ New South Wales, SE Australia
42 F4 **Lívingston** Izabal, E Guatemala 15°50′N 88°44′W
96 J12 **Livingston** C Scotland, United Kingdom 55°51′N 03°31′W
23 N5 **Livingston** Alabama, S USA 32°35′N 88°12′W
35 P9 **Livingston** California, W USA 37°22′N 120°45′W
22 J8 **Livingston** Louisiana, S USA 30°30′N 90°45′W
33 S11 **Livingston** Montana, NW USA 45°40′N 110°33′W
20 L8 **Livingston** Tennessee, S USA 36°22′N 85°20′W
25 W9 **Livingston** Texas, SW USA 30°42′N 94°58′W
83 I16 **Livingstone** var. Maramba. Southern, S Zambia 17°51′S 25°48′E
185 B22 **Livingstone Mountains** ▲▲ South Island, New Zealand
80 K13 **Livingstone Mountains** ▲▲ S Tanzania
82 N12 **Livingstonia** Northern, N Malawi 10°29′S 34°06′E
194 G4 **Livingston Island** island Antarctica
25 W9 **Livingston, Lake** ⊠ Texas, SW USA
112 F13 **Livno** ◆ Federicija Bosna I Hercegovina, SW Bosnia and Herzegovina
126 K7 **Livny** Orlovskaya Oblast', W Russian Federation 52°25′N 37°42′E
93 M14 **Livojoki** C Finland
31 R10 **Livonia** Michigan, N USA 42°22′N 83°22′W
106 E11 **Livorno** Eng. Leghorn. Toscana, C Italy 43°32′N 10°18′E
Livramento see Santana do Livramento
141 U8 **Līwā** var. Al Liwā'. oasis region S United Arab Emirates
81 I24 **Liwale** Lindi, SE Tanzania 09°46′S 37°56′E
159 W9 **Liwangbu** Ningxia, N China 36°42′N 106°05′E
83 N15 **Liwonde** Southern, S Malawi 15°01′S 35°15′E
159 V11 **Lixian** var. Li Xian. Gansu, C China 34°15′N 105°07′E
160 H8 **Lixian** var. Li Xian, Zagunao. Sichuan, C China 31°27′N 103°06′E
Li Xian see Lixian
Lixian Jiang see Black River
115 B18 **Lixoúri** prev. Lixoúrion. Kefallinía, Iónia Nisiá, Greece, C Mediterranean Sea 38°14′N 20°24′E
Lixoúrion see Lixoúri
Lixus see Larache
33 U15 **Lizard Head Peak** ▲ Wyoming, C USA 42°47′N 109°12′W
97 H25 **Lizard Point** headland SW England, United Kingdom 49°57′N 05°12′W
Lizarra see Estella
112 L12 **Ljig** Serbia, C Serbia 44°14′N 20°16′E
Ljouwert see Leeuwarden
Ljubelj see Loibl Pass
109 U11 **Ljubljana** Ger. Laibach, It. Lubiana; anc. Aemona, Emona. ● (Slovenia) C Slovenia 46°03′N 14°29′E
109 T11 **Ljubljana** ✈ C Slovenia 46°14′N 14°26′E
113 N17 **Ljuboten** ▲ S Serbia 42°12′N 21°06′E
95 P19 **Ljugarn** Gotland, SE Sweden 57°23′N 18°45′E
84 G7 **Ljungan** N Sweden
93 F17 **Ljungan** C Sweden
95 K21 **Ljungby** Kronoberg, S Sweden 56°49′N 13°55′E
95 M17 **Ljungsbro** Östergötland, S Sweden 58°31′N 15°30′E
95 I18 **Ljungskile** Västra Götaland, S Sweden 58°14′N 11°55′E
94 M11 **Ljusdal** Gävleborg, C Sweden 61°50′N 16°10′E
94 M11 **Ljusnan** C Sweden
94 N12 **Ljusne** Gävleborg, C Sweden 61°11′N 17°07′E
95 P15 **Ljusterö** Stockholm, C Sweden 59°31′N 18°40′E
109 X9 **Ljutomer** Ger. Luttenberg. NE Slovenia 46°31′N 16°12′E
63 G15 **Llaima, Volcán** S Chile 39°01′S 71°38′W
105 X4 **Llançà** var. Llansá. Cataluña, NE Spain 42°23′N 03°08′E
97 J21 **Llandovery** C Wales, United Kingdom 52°01′N 03°47′W
97 J20 **Llandrindod Wells** E Wales, United Kingdom 52°15′N 03°23′W
97 J18 **Llandudno** N Wales, United Kingdom 53°19′N 03°49′W
97 I21 **Llanelli** prev. Llanelly. SW Wales, United Kingdom 51°41′N 04°12′W
Llanelly see Llanelli
104 M2 **Llanes** Asturias, N Spain 43°25′N 04°46′W
97 K19 **Llangollen** NE Wales, United Kingdom 52°58′N 03°10′W
25 R10 **Llano** Texas, SW USA 30°49′N 98°42′W
25 Q10 **Llano River** Texas, SW USA
54 I9 **Llanos** physical region Colombia/Venezuela
63 G16 **Llanquihue, Lago** ◎ S Chile
Llansá see Llançà
105 U5 **Lleida** Cast. Lérida; anc. Ilerda. Cataluña, NE Spain 41°38′N 00°35′E
104 K12 **Llerena** Extremadura, W Spain 38°13′N 06°00′W
105 S9 **Llíria** País Valenciano, E Spain 39°38′N 00°36′W
105 W4 **Llivia** Cataluña, NE Spain 42°27′N 02°00′E
105 O3 **Llodio** País Vasco, N Spain 43°08′N 02°59′W
105 X5 **Lloret de Mar** Cataluña, NE Spain 41°42′N 02°51′E
Llorri see Tossal de l'Orri
10 L11 **Lloyd George, Mount** ▲ British Columbia, W Canada 57°46′N 124°57′W
11 R14 **Lloydminster** Alberta/Saskatchewan, SW Canada 53°18′N 110°00′W
105 X9 **Llucmajor** Mallorca, Spain, W Mediterranean Sea 39°29′N 02°53′E
36 L6 **Loa** Utah, W USA 38°24′N 111°38′W
169 S8 **Loagan Bunut** ◎ East Malaysia
38 G12 **Loa, Mauna** ▲ Hawai'i, USA 19°28′N 155°39′W
Loanda see Luanda
79 J22 **Loange** S Dem. Rep. Congo
79 E21 **Loango** Kouilou, S Congo 04°38′S 11°50′E
106 B10 **Loano** Liguria, NW Italy 44°07′N 08°15′E
62 H4 **Loa, Río** N Chile
83 I20 **Lobatse** var. Lobatsi. Kgatleng, SE Botswana 25°11′S 25°40′E
Lobatsi see Lobatse
101 Q15 **Löbau** Sachsen, E Germany 51°07′N 14°40′E
79 H16 **Lobaye** ◆ prefecture SW Central African Republic
79 I16 **Lobaye** SW Central African Republic
99 G21 **Lobbes** Hainaut, S Belgium 50°21′N 04°16′E
61 D23 **Lobería** Buenos Aires, E Argentina 38°08′S 58°48′W
110 F8 **Łobez** Ger. Labes. Zacodniopomorskie, NW Poland 53°38′N 15°39′E
82 A13 **Lobito** Benguela, W Angola 12°20′S 13°34′E
Lobkovichi see Labkovichy
Lob Nor see Lop Nur
171 V13 **Lobo** Papua, E Indonesia 03°41′S 134°06′E
104 J11 **Lobón** Extremadura, W Spain 38°51′N 06°38′W
61 D20 **Lobos** Buenos Aires, E Argentina 35°11′S 59°08′W
40 E4 **Lobos, Cabo** headland NW Mexico 29°53′N 112°43′W
40 F6 **Lobos, Isla** island NW Mexico
Lobositz see Lovosice
Lobsens see Łobżenica
Loburi see Lop Buri
110 H9 **Łobżenica** Ger. Lobsens. Wielkopolskie, C Poland 53°19′N 17°11′E
108 G11 **Locarno** Ger. Luggarus. Ticino, S Switzerland 46°11′N 08°48′E
96 E9 **Lochboisdale** NW Scotland, United Kingdom 57°08′N 07°17′W
98 N11 **Lochem** Gelderland, E Netherlands 52°10′N 06°25′E
102 M8 **Loches** Indre-et-Loire, C France 47°08′N 01°00′E
Loch Garman see Wexford
96 H12 **Lochgilphead** W Scotland, United Kingdom 56°02′N 05°27′W
96 H7 **Lochinver** N Scotland, United Kingdom 58°10′N 05°15′W
96 F8 **Lochmaddy** NW Scotland, United Kingdom 57°35′N 07°10′W
96 J10 **Lochnagar** ▲ C Scotland, United Kingdom 56°58′N 03°09′W
99 E17 **Lochristi** Oost-Vlaanderen, NW Belgium 51°07′N 03°49′E
96 H9 **Lochy, Loch** ◎ N Scotland, United Kingdom
182 G8 **Lock** South Australia 33°37′S 135°45′E
97 J14 **Lockerbie** S Scotland, United Kingdom 55°11′N 03°27′W
27 S13 **Lockesburg** Arkansas, C USA 33°58′N 94°10′W
183 P10 **Lockhart** New South Wales, SE Australia 35°15′S 146°43′E
25 S11 **Lockhart** Texas, SW USA 29°54′N 97°41′W
18 F13 **Lock Haven** Pennsylvania, NE USA 41°08′N 77°27′W
25 N4 **Lockney** Texas, SW USA 34°06′N 101°27′W
100 O12 **Löcknitz** NE Germany
18 E9 **Lockport** New York, NE USA 43°09′N 78°40′W
167 T13 **Lôc Ninh** Sông Be, S Vietnam 11°51′N 106°35′E
107 N23 **Locri** Calabria, SW Italy 38°16′N 16°16′E
Locse see Levoča
27 T2 **Locust Creek** Missouri, C USA
23 P3 **Locust Fork** Alabama, S USA
27 Q9 **Locust Grove** Oklahoma, C USA 36°12′N 95°10′W
94 E11 **Lodalskåpa** ▲ S Norway 61°47′N 07°10′E
183 N10 **Loddon River** Victoria, SE Australia
Lodensee see Klooga
103 P15 **Lodève** anc. Luteva. Hérault, S France 43°44′N 03°19′E
124 I12 **Lodeynoye Pole** Leningradskaya Oblast', NW Russian Federation 60°41′N 33°29′E
33 V11 **Lodge Grass** Montana, NW USA 45°19′N 107°20′W
28 J15 **Lodgepole Creek** Nebraska/Wyoming, C USA
149 T11 **Lodhrān** Punjab, E Pakistan 29°32′N 71°40′E
106 D8 **Lodi** Lombardia, NW Italy 45°19′N 09°30′E
35 O8 **Lodi** California, W USA 38°07′N 121°17′W
31 T12 **Lodi** Ohio, N USA 41°00′N 82°01′W
92 H10 **Lødingen** Nordland, C Norway 68°25′N 16°00′E
79 L20 **Lodja** Kasai-Oriental, C Dem. Rep. Congo 03°29′S 23°25′E
37 O3 **Lodore, Canyon of** canyon Colorado, C USA
105 Q4 **Lodosa** Navarra, N Spain 42°26′N 02°05′W
81 H16 **Lodwar** Rift Valley, NW Kenya 03°06′N 35°38′E
110 K13 **Łódź** Rus. Lodz. Łódź, C Poland 51°51′N 19°26′E
110 E12 **Łódzkie** ◆ province C Poland
167 P8 **Loei** var. Loey, Muang Loei. Loei, C Thailand 17°32′N 101°40′E
98 I11 **Loenen** Utrecht, C Netherlands 52°13′N 05°01′E
167 R9 **Loeng Nok Tha** Yasothon, E Thailand 16°12′N 104°31′E
83 F24 **Loeriesfontein** Northern Cape, W South Africa 30°59′S 19°29′E
Loewoek see Luwuk
Loey see Loei
76 J16 **Lofa** N Liberia
109 P6 **Lofer** Salzburg, C Austria 47°37′N 12°42′E
92 F11 **Lofoten** var. Lofoten Islands. island group C Norway
Lofoten Islands see Lofoten
95 N18 **Loftahammar** Kalmar, S Sweden 57°55′N 16°45′E
127 O10 **Log** Volgogradskaya Oblast', SW Russian Federation 49°32′N 43°52′E
77 S12 **Loga** Dosso, SW Niger 13°40′N 03°15′E
29 S14 **Logan** Iowa, C USA 41°38′N 95°47′W
26 K3 **Logan** Kansas, C USA 39°39′N 99°34′W
31 T14 **Logan** Ohio, N USA 39°32′N 82°24′W
36 L1 **Logan** Utah, W USA 41°45′N 111°50′W
21 P6 **Logan** West Virginia, NE USA 37°52′N 82°00′W
35 Y10 **Logandale** Nevada, W USA 36°36′N 114°28′W
19 O11 **Logan International** ✈ (Boston) Massachusetts, NE USA 42°22′N 71°00′W
11 N16 **Logan Lake** British Columbia, SW Canada 50°28′N 120°42′W
23 Q4 **Logan Martin Lake** ⊠ Alabama, S USA
10 G8 **Logan, Mount** ▲ Yukon Territory, W Canada 60°32′N 140°34′W
32 I7 **Logan, Mount** ▲ Washington, NW USA 48°32′N 120°57′W
33 P7 **Logan Pass** pass Montana, NW USA
31 O12 **Logansport** Indiana, N USA 40°44′N 86°25′W
22 F6 **Logansport** Louisiana, S USA 31°58′N 94°00′W
Logar see Lowgar
67 R11 **Loge** NW Angola
Logishin see Lahishyn
Log na Coille see Lugnaquillia Mountain
78 G11 **Logone** var. Lagone. Cameroon/Chad
78 G13 **Logone-Occidental** off. Préfecture du Logone-Occidental. ◆ prefecture SW Chad
78 H13 **Logone Occidental** SW Chad
Logone-Occidental, Préfecture du see Logone-Occidental
78 G13 **Logone-Oriental** off. Préfecture du Logone-Oriental. ◆ prefecture SW Chad
78 H13 **Logone Oriental** SW Chad
Logone Oriental see Pendé
Logone-Oriental, Préfecture du see Logone-Oriental
L'Ogooué-Ivindo see Ogooué-Ivindo
L'Ogooué-Lolo see Ogooué-Lolo
L'Ogooué-Maritime see Ogooué-Maritime
Logoysk see Lahoysk
105 P4 **Logroño** anc. Vareia, Lat. Juliobriga. La Rioja, N Spain 42°28′N 02°26′W
104 L10 **Logrosán** Extremadura, W Spain 39°21′N 05°29′W
95 G20 **Løgstør** Nordjylland, N Denmark 56°57′N 09°19′E
95 H22 **Løgten** Århus, C Denmark 56°17′N 10°20′E
95 F24 **Løgumkloster** Sønderjylland, SW Denmark 55°04′N 08°58′E
Lögurinn see Lagarfljót
153 P15 **Lohārdaga** Jhārkhand, N India 23°27′N 84°42′E
152 H10 **Lohāru** Haryāna, N India 28°28′N 75°50′E
101 D15 **Lohausen** ✈ (Düsseldorf) Nordrhein-Westfalen, W Germany 51°18′N 06°51′E
189 O14 **Lohd** Pohnpei, E Micronesia
92 L12 **Lohiniva** Lappi, N Finland 67°09′N 25°04′E
Lohiszyn see Lahishyn
93 L20 **Lohja** var. Lojo. Etelä-Suomi, S Finland 60°14′N 24°07′E
169 V11 **Lohjanan** Borneo, C Indonesia
25 Q9 **Lohn** Texas, SW USA 31°15′N 99°22′W
100 G12 **Lohne** Niedersachsen, NW Germany 52°40′N 08°13′E
Lohr see Lohr am Main
101 I18 **Lohr am Main** var. Lohr. Bayern, C Germany 50°00′N 09°30′E
109 T10 **Loibl Pass** Ger. Loiblpass, Slvn. Ljubelj. pass Austria/Slovenia
Loiblpass see Loibl Pass
167 N6 **Loikaw** Kayah State, C Myanmar (Burma) 19°40′N 97°17′E
93 K19 **Loimaa** Länsi-Suomi, SW Finland 60°51′N 23°03′E
103 O6 **Loing** C France
167 R6 **Loi, Phou** ▲ N Laos 20°18′N 103°14′E
102 L7 **Loir** C France
103 Q11 **Loire** ◆ department E France
102 M7 **Loire** var. Liger. C France
102 I7 **Loire-Atlantique** ◆ department NW France
103 O7 **Loiret** ◆ department C France
102 M8 **Loir-et-Cher** ◆ department C France
101 L24 **Loisach** SE Germany
56 B9 **Loja** Loja, S Ecuador 03°59′S 79°16′W
104 M14 **Loja** Andalucía, S Spain 37°10′N 04°09′W
56 B9 **Loja** ◆ province S Ecuador
Lojo see Lohja
116 J4 **Lokachi** Volyns'ka Oblast', NW Ukraine 50°44′N 24°39′E
79 M20 **Lokandu** Maniema, C Dem. Rep. Congo 02°34′S 25°44′E
92 M11 **Lokan Tekojärvi** ◎ NE Finland
137 Z11 **Lökbatan** Rus. Lokbatan. E Azerbaijan 40°21′N 49°43′E
Lokbatan see Lökbatan
99 F17 **Lokeren** Oost-Vlaanderen, NW Belgium 51°06′N 03°59′E
Lokhvitsa see Lokhvytsya
117 S4 **Lokhvytsya** Rus. Lokhvitsa. Poltavs'ka Oblast', NE Ukraine 50°22′N 33°16′E
81 H17 **Lokichar** Rift Valley, NW Kenya 02°23′N 35°40′E
81 G16 **Lokichokio** Rift Valley, NW Kenya 04°16′N 34°22′E
81 H16 **Lokitaung** Rift Valley, NW Kenya 04°15′N 35°45′E
92 M11 **Lokka** Lappi, N Finland 67°48′N 27°41′E
94 G8 **Løkken Verk** Sør-Trøndelag, S Norway 63°06′N 09°43′E
124 G16 **Loknya** Pskovskaya Oblast', W Russian Federation 56°48′N 30°08′E
77 V15 **Loko** Nassarawa, C Nigeria 08°00′N 07°48′E
77 U15 **Lokoja** Kogi, C Nigeria 07°48′N 06°45′E
81 H17 **Lokori** Rift Valley, W Kenya 01°56′N 36°03′E
77 R16 **Lokossa** S Benin 06°38′N 01°43′E
118 I3 **Loksa** Ger. Loxa. Harjumaa, NW Estonia 59°32′N 25°42′E
9 T7 **Loks Land** island Nunavut, NE Canada
80 C13 **Lol** S Sudan
76 K15 **Lola** SE Guinea 07°52′N 08°29′W
35 Q5 **Lola, Mount** ▲ California, W USA 39°27′N 120°20′W
81 H20 **Loliondo** Arusha, NE Tanzania 02°03′S 35°46′E
95 H25 **Lolland** prev. Laaland. island S Denmark
186 G6 **Lolobau Island** island E Papua New Guinea
79 E16 **Lolodorf** Sud, SW Cameroon 03°17′N 10°50′E
114 G7 **Lom** prev. Lom-Palanka. Montana, NW Bulgaria 43°49′N 23°16′E
114 G7 **Lom** NW Bulgaria
79 M19 **Lomami** C Dem. Rep. Congo
57 F17 **Lomas** Arequipa, SW Peru 15°29′S 74°54′W
63 I23 **Lomas, Bahía** bay S Chile
61 D20 **Lomas de Zamora** Buenos Aires, E Argentina 34°53′S 58°26′W
61 D20 **Loma Verde** Buenos Aires, E Argentina 35°16′S 58°24′W
180 K4 **Lombadina** Western Australia 16°39′S 122°54′E
106 E6 **Lombardia** Eng. Lombardy. ◆ region N Italy
Lombardy see Lombardia
102 M15 **Lombez** Gers, S France 43°29′N 00°54′E
171 Q16 **Lomblen, Pulau** island Nusa Tenggara, S Indonesia
173 W7 **Lombok Basin** undersea feature E Indian Ocean 09°50′S 116°00′E
170 L16 **Lombok, Pulau** island Nusa Tenggara, C Indonesia
77 Q16 **Lomé** ● (Togo) S Togo 06°08′N 01°13′E
77 Q16 **Lomé** ✈ S Togo 06°08′N 01°13′E
79 L19 **Lomela** Kasai-Oriental, C Dem. Rep. Congo 02°19′S 23°15′E
25 R9 **Lometa** Texas, SW USA 31°13′N 98°23′W
79 F16 **Lomié** Est, SE Cameroon 03°09′N 13°35′E
30 M8 **Lomira** Wisconsin, N USA 43°36′N 88°26′W
95 K23 **Lomma** Skåne, S Sweden 55°41′N 13°05′E
99 J16 **Lommel** Limburg, N Belgium 51°14′N 05°19′E
96 I11 **Lomond, Loch** ◎ C Scotland, United Kingdom
197 R9 **Lomonosov Ridge** var. Harris Ridge, Rus. Khrebet Homonsova. undersea feature Arctic Ocean 88°00′N 140°00′E
Lomonsova, Khrebet see Lomonosov Ridge
Lom-Palanka see Lom
Lomphat see Lumphăt
35 P14 **Lompoc** California, W USA 34°39′N 120°29′W
167 P9 **Lom Sak** var. Muang Lom Sak. Phetchabun, C Thailand 16°45′N 101°12′E
110 N9 **Łomża** Rus. Lomzha. Podlaskie, NE Poland 53°11′N 22°04′E
Lomzha see Łomża
Lonaula see Lonāvale
155 D14 **Lonāvale** prev. Lonaula. Mahārāshtra, W India 18°45′N 73°27′E
63 G15 **Loncoche** Araucanía, C Chile 39°22′S 72°34′W
63 H14 **Loncopue** Neuquén, W Argentina 38°04′S 70°43′W
99 G17 **Londerzeel** Vlaams Brabant, C Belgium 51°00′N 04°19′E
Londinium see London
14 E16 **London** Ontario, S Canada 42°59′N 81°13′W
191 Y2 **London** Kiritimati, E Kiribati 02°00′N 157°28′W
97 O22 **London** anc. Augusta, Lat. Londinium. ● (United Kingdom) SE England, United Kingdom 51°30′N 00°10′W
21 N7 **London** Kentucky, S USA 37°07′N 84°05′W
31 S13 **London** Ohio, NE USA 39°52′N 83°27′W
25 Q10 **London** Texas, SW USA 30°40′N 99°33′W
97 O22 **London City** ✈ SE England, United Kingdom 51°31′N 00°07′E
97 E14 **Londonderry** var. Derry, Ir. Doire. NW Northern Ireland, United Kingdom 55°N 07°19′W
97 F14 **Londonderry** cultural region NW Northern Ireland, United Kingdom
180 M2 **Londonderry, Cape** cape Western Australia
63 H25 **Londonderry, Isla** island S Chile
43 O7 **Londres, Cayos** reef NE Nicaragua
60 I10 **Londrina** Paraná, S Brazil 23°18′S 51°13′W
27 N13 **Lone Grove** Oklahoma, C USA 34°11′N 97°15′W
14 E12 **Lonely Island** island Ontario, S Canada
35 T8 **Lone Mountain** ▲ Nevada, W USA 38°01′N 117°28′W
25 V6 **Lone Oak** Texas, SW USA 33°02′N 95°58′W
35 T11 **Lone Pine** California, W USA 36°36′N 118°04′W
Lone Star State see Texas
Lone Tree Islet see Iku
83 D14 **Longa** Cuando Cubango, C Angola 14°44′S 18°36′E
82 B12 **Longa** W Angola
83 E15 **Longa** SE Angola
Long'an see Pingwu
163 W11 **Longang Shan** ▲▲ NE China
197 S4 **Longa, Proliv** Eng. Long Strait. strait NE Russian Federation
44 J13 **Long Bay** bay W Jamaica
21 V13 **Long Bay** bay North Carolina/South Carolina, E USA
35 T16 **Long Beach** California, W USA 33°46′N 118°11′W
22 M9 **Long Beach** Mississippi, S USA 30°21′N 89°09′W
18 L14 **Long Beach** Long Island, New York, NE USA 40°34′N 73°38′W
32 F9 **Long Beach** Washington, NW USA 46°21′N 124°03′W
18 K16 **Long Beach Island** island New Jersey, NE USA
65 M25 **Longbluff** headland SW Tristan da Cunha
23 U13 **Longboat Key** island Florida, SE USA
18 K15 **Long Branch** New Jersey, NE USA 40°18′N 73°59′W
44 J5 **Long Cay** island SE Bahamas
Longcheng see Xiaoxian
161 P14 **Longchuan** var. Laolong. Guangdong, S China 24°07′N 115°10′E
Longchuan see Nanhua
Longchuan Jiang see Shweli
32 K12 **Long Creek** Oregon, NW USA 44°40′N 119°07′W
159 W10 **Longde** Ningxia, N China 35°37′N 106°07′E
183 P16 **Longford** Tasmania, SE Australia 41°41′S 147°03′E
97 D17 **Longford** Ir. An Longfort. Longford, C Ireland 53°45′N 07°50′W
97 E17 **Longford** Ir. An Longfort. cultural region C Ireland
Longgang see Dazu
161 P1 **Longhua** Hebei, E China 41°18′N 117°44′E
169 U11 **Longiram** Borneo, C Indonesia 0°02′S 115°36′E
44 J4 **Long Island** island C Bahamas
12 H8 **Long Island** island Nunavut, C Canada
186 D7 **Long Island** var. Arop Island. island N Papua New Guinea
18 L14 **Long Island** island New York, NE USA
Long Island see Bermuda
18 M14 **Long Island Sound** sound NE USA
163 U7 **Longjiang** Heilongjiang, NE China 47°20′N 123°09′E
160 K13 **Long Jiang** S China
163 Y10 **Longjing** var. Yanji. Jilin, NE China 42°48′N 129°26′E
161 R4 **Longkou** Shandong, E China 37°40′N 120°21′E
12 E11 **Longlac** Ontario, S Canada 49°47′N 86°34′W
19 S1 **Long Lake** ◎ Maine, NE USA
31 R5 **Long Lake** ◎ Michigan, N USA
31 O6 **Long Lake** ◎ Michigan, N USA
29 N6 **Long Lake** ◎ North Dakota, N USA
30 J4 **Long Lake** ⊠ Wisconsin, N USA
99 K23 **Longlier** Luxembourg, SE Belgium 49°51′N 05°27′E
160 I13 **Longlin** var. Longlin Gezu Zizhixian, Xinzhou. Guangxi Zhuangzu Zizhiqu, S China 24°46′N 105°19′E
Longlin Gezu Zizhixian see Longlin
37 T3 **Longmont** Colorado, C USA 40°09′N 105°07′W
157 P10 **Longnan** var. Wudu. Gansu, C China 33°27′N 104°57′E
29 N13 **Long Pine** Nebraska, C USA 42°32′N 99°42′W
Longping see Luodian

◆ Country
● Country Capital
◇ Dependent Territory
○ Dependent Territory Capital
◆ Administrative Regions
✈ International Airport
▲ Mountain
▲▲ Mountain Range
Volcano
River
◎ Lake
⊠ Reservoir

LONG POINT – LUKRANSAR

14 F17 **Long Point** *headland* Ontario, S Canada 42°33′N 80°15′W
14 K15 **Long Point** *headland* Ontario, SE Canada 45°56′N 76°53′W
184 P10 **Long Point** *headland* North Island, New Zealand 39°07′S 177°41′E
30 L2 **Long Point** *headland* Michigan, N USA 47°50′N 89°09′W
14 G17 **Long Point Bay** *lake bay* Ontario, S Canada
29 T7 **Long Prairie** Minnesota, N USA 45°58′N 94°52′W
Longquan *see* Fenggang
Longquan *see* Yanggao
13 S11 **Long Range Mountains** *hill range* Newfoundland and Labrador, E Canada
65 H25 **Long Range Point** *headland* SE Saint Helena 16°00′S 05°41′W
181 V8 **Longreach** Queensland, E Australia 23°31′S 144°18′E
160 H7 **Longriba** Sichuan, C China 32°32′N 102°20′E
160 L10 **Longshan** *var.* Min'an. Hunan, S China 29°25′N 109°28′E
37 S3 **Longs Peak** ▲ Colorado, C USA 40°15′N 105°37′W
Long Strait *see* Longa, Proliv
102 K8 **Longué** Maine-et-Loire, NW France 47°23′N 00°07′W
13 P11 **Longue-Pointe** Québec, E Canada 50°20′N 64°13′W
103 S4 **Longuyon** Meurthe-et-Moselle, NE France 49°25′N 05°37′E
25 W7 **Longview** Texas, SW USA 32°30′N 94°45′W
32 G10 **Longview** Washington, NW USA 46°08′N 122°56′W
65 H25 **Longwood** C Saint Helena
25 P7 **Longworth** Texas, SW USA 32°37′N 100°20′W
103 S3 **Longwy** Meurthe-et-Moselle, NE France 49°31′N 05°46′E
159 V11 **Longxi** *var.* Gongchang. Gansu, C China 35°00′N 104°34′E
Longxian *see* Wengyuan
167 S14 **Long Xuyên** *var.* Longxuyen. An Giang, S Vietnam 10°23′N 105°25′E
Longxuyen *see* Long Xuyên
161 Q13 **Longyan** Fujian, SE China 25°06′N 117°02′E
92 O3 **Longyearbyen** ○ (Svalbard) Spitsbergen, W Svalbard 78°12′N 15°39′E
160 J15 **Longzhou** Guangxi Zhuangzu Zizhiqu, S China 22°22′N 106°46′E
Longzhouping *see* Changyang
100 F12 **Löningen** Niedersachsen, NW Germany 52°43′N 07°42′E
27 V11 **Lonoke** Arkansas, C USA 34°46′N 91°56′W
95 L21 **Lönsboda** Skåne, S Sweden 56°24′N 14°19′E
103 S9 **Lons-le-Saunier** *anc.* Ledo Salinarius. Jura, E France 46°41′N 05°33′E
31 O15 **Loogootee** Indiana, N USA 38°40′N 86°54′W
31 Q9 **Looking Glass River** ~ Michigan, N USA
21 X11 **Lookout, Cape** *headland* North Carolina, SE USA 34°36′N 76°31′W
39 O6 **Lookout Ridge** *ridge* Alaska, USA
Lookransar *see* Lūnkaransar
181 N11 **Loongana** Western Australia 30°53′S 127°15′E
99 I14 **Loon op Zand** Noord-Brabant, S Netherlands 51°38′N 05°05′E
97 A19 **Loop Head** *Ir.* Ceann Léime. *promontory* W Ireland
109 V4 **Loosdorf** Niederösterreich, NE Austria 48°13′N 15°25′E
158 G10 **Lop** Xinjiang Uygur Zizhiqu, NW China 37°06′N 80°12′E
112 J11 **Lopare** ◈ Republika Srpska, NE Bosnia and Herzegovina
Lopatichi *see* Lapatsichy
127 P7 **Lopatino** Penzenskaya Oblast', W Russian Federation 52°38′N 45°46′E
167 P10 **Lop Buri** *var.* Loburi. Lop Buri, C Thailand 14°49′N 100°37′E
25 R16 **Lopeno** Texas, SW USA 26°42′N 99°06′W
79 C18 **Lopez, Cap** *headland* W Gabon 0°39′S 08°44′E
98 I12 **Lopik** Utrecht, C Netherlands 51°58′N 04°57′E
Lop Nor *see* Lop Nur
158 M7 **Lop Nur** *var.* Lob Nor, Lop Nor, Lo-pu Po. *seasonal lake* NW China
Lopnur *see* Yuli
79 K17 **Lopori** ~ NW Dem. Rep. Congo
98 O5 **Loppersum** Groningen, NE Netherlands 53°20′N 06°45′E
92 I8 **Lopphavet** *sound* N Norway
Lo-pu Po *see* Lop Nur
Lora *see* Lowrah
182 F3 **Lora Creek** *seasonal river* South Australia
104 K13 **Lora del Río** Andalucía, S Spain 37°39′N 05°32′W
148 M11 **Lora, Hāmūn-i** *wetland* SW Pakistan
31 T11 **Lorain** Ohio, N USA 41°27′N 82°10′W
25 O7 **Loraine** Texas, SW USA 32°24′N 100°42′W
149 Q10 **Loralai** Baluchistān, SW Pakistan 30°22′N 68°36′E
31 R13 **Loramie, Lake** ▣ Ohio, N USA
105 Q13 **Lorca** *Ar.* Lurka; *anc.* Eliocroca, *Lat.* Illurco. Murcia, S Spain 37°40′N 01°41′W
143 N11 **Lordegān** Chahār Mahall va Bakhtīārī, C Iran 31°31′N 50°48′E
192 I10 **Lord Howe Island** *island* E Australia
Lord Howe Island *see* Ontong Java Atoll
175 O10 **Lord Howe Rise** *undersea feature* SW Pacific Ocean
192 J10 **Lord Howe Seamounts** *undersea feature* W Pacific Ocean
37 P15 **Lordsburg** New Mexico, SW USA 32°19′N 108°42′W
186 E5 **Lorengau** *var.* Lorungau. Manus Island, N Papua New Guinea 02°01′S 147°15′E
25 N5 **Lorenzo** Texas, SW USA 33°40′N 101°31′W
142 K7 **Lorestān** *off.* Ostān-e Lorestān, *var.* Luristan. ◈ *province* W Iran
Lorestān, Ostān-e *see* Lorestān
57 M17 **Loreto** Beni, N Bolivia 15°13′S 64°44′W
106 J12 **Loreto** Marche, C Italy 43°25′N 13°37′E
40 F8 **Loreto** Baja California Sur, NW Mexico 25°59′N 111°22′W
40 M11 **Loreto** Zacatecas, C Mexico 22°15′N 102°00′W
56 E9 **Loreto** *off.* Departamento de Loreto. ◈ *department* NE Peru
Loreto, Departamento de *see* Loreto
81 K18 **Lorian Swamp** *swamp* E Kenya
54 E6 **Lorica** Córdoba, NW Colombia 09°14′N 75°50′W
102 G7 **Lorient** *prev.* l'Orient. Morbihan, NW France 47°45′N 03°22′W
l'Orient *see* Lorient
111 K22 **Lőrinci** Heves, NE Hungary 47°46′N 19°40′E
14 G11 **Loring** Ontario, S Canada 45°55′N 79°59′W
33 V6 **Loring** Montana, NW USA 48°49′N 107°48′W
103 R13 **Loriol-sur-Drôme** Drôme, E France 44°46′N 04°51′E
21 U12 **Loris** South Carolina, SE USA 34°03′N 78°53′W
57 I18 **Loriscota, Laguna** ◎ S Peru
183 N13 **Lorne** Victoria, SE Australia 38°33′S 143°57′E
96 G11 **Lorn, Firth of** *inlet* W Scotland, United Kingdom
Loro Sae *see* East Timor
101 F24 **Lörrach** Baden-Württemberg, S Germany 47°38′N 07°40′E
103 T5 **Lorraine** ◈ *region* NE France
Lorungau *see* Lorengau
94 L11 **Los** Gävleborg, C Sweden 61°43′N 15°15′E
35 P14 **Los Alamos** California, W USA 34°44′N 120°16′W
37 S10 **Los Alamos** New Mexico, SW USA 35°52′N 106°17′W
42 F5 **Los Amates** Izabal, E Guatemala 15°14′N 89°06′W
63 G14 **Los Ángeles** Bío Bío, C Chile 37°30′S 72°18′W
35 S15 **Los Angeles** California, W USA 34°03′N 118°15′W
35 S15 **Los Angeles** ✈ California, W USA 33°54′N 118°24′W
35 T13 **Los Angeles Aqueduct** *aqueduct* California, W USA
Losanna *see* Lausanne
63 H20 **Los Antiguos** Santa Cruz, SW Argentina 46°36′S 71°31′W
189 Q16 **Losap Atoll** *atoll* C Micronesia
35 P10 **Los Banos** California, W USA 37°00′N 120°39′W
104 K16 **Los Barrios** Andalucía, S Spain 36°11′N 05°30′W
62 L5 **Los Blancos** Salta, N Argentina 23°36′S 62°35′W
42 L12 **Los Chiles** Alajuela, NW Costa Rica 11°00′N 84°42′W
105 O2 **Los Corrales de Buelna** Cantabria, N Spain 43°15′N 04°04′W
25 T17 **Los Fresnos** Texas, SW USA 26°03′N 97°28′W
35 N9 **Los Gatos** California, W USA 37°13′N 121°58′W
127 P10 **Loshchina** Volgogradskaya Oblast', SW Russian Federation 48°58′N 46°14′E
110 O11 **Łosice** Mazowieckie, C Poland 52°13′N 22°42′E
112 B11 **Lošinj** *Ger.* Lussin, *It.* Lussino. *island* W Croatia
Los Jardines *see* Ngetik Atoll
63 G15 **Los Lagos** Los Lagos, C Chile 39°50′S 72°50′W
63 F17 **Los Lagos** *off.* Región de los Lagos. ◈ *region* C Chile
los Lagos, Región de *see* Los Lagos
Loslau *see* Wodzisław Śląski
64 N11 **Los Llanos de Aridane** *var.* Los Llanos de Aridane. La Palma, Islas Canarias, Spain, NE Atlantic Ocean 28°39′N 17°54′W
Los Llanos de Aridane *see* Los Llanos de Aridane
37 R11 **Los Lunas** New Mexico, SW USA 34°48′N 106°43′W
63 I16 **Los Menucos** Río Negro, C Argentina 40°52′S 68°07′W
40 H8 **Los Mochis** Sinaloa, C Mexico 25°48′N 108°58′W
35 N4 **Los Molinos** California, W USA 40°00′N 122°05′W
104 M9 **Los Navalmorales** Castilla-La Mancha, C Spain 39°43′N 04°38′W
25 S15 **Los Olmos Creek** ~ Texas, SW USA
Losonc/Losontz *see* Lučenec
167 S5 **Lô, Sông** *var.* Panlong Jiang. ~ China/Vietnam
44 B5 **Los Palacios** Pinar del Río, W Cuba 22°35′N 83°16′W
104 K14 **Los Palacios y Villafranca** Andalucía, S Spain 37°10′N 05°55′W
37 R12 **Los Pinos Mountains** ▲▲ New Mexico, SW USA
37 R11 **Los Ranchos de Albuquerque** New Mexico, SW USA 35°09′N 106°37′W
40 M14 **Los Reyes** Michoacán, SW Mexico 19°36′N 102°29′W
56 B7 **Los Ríos** ◈ *province* C Ecuador
64 O11 **Los Rodeos** ✈ (Santa Cruz de Tenerife) Tenerife, Islas Canarias, Spain, NE Atlantic Ocean 28°27′N 16°20′W
54 L4 **Los Roques, Islas** *island group* N Venezuela
43 S17 **Los Santos** Los Santos, S Panama 07°56′N 80°23′W
43 S17 **Los Santos** *off.* Provincia de Los Santos. ◈ *province* S Panama
Los Santos *see* Los Santos de Maimona
104 J12 **Los Santos de Maimona** *var.* Los Santos. Extremadura, W Spain 38°27′N 06°22′W
Los Santos, Provincia de *see* Los Santos
98 P10 **Losser** Overijssel, E Netherlands 52°16′N 06°25′E
96 J8 **Lossiemouth** NE Scotland, United Kingdom 57°43′N 03°18′W
61 B14 **Los Tábanos** Santa Fe, C Argentina 28°27′S 59°57′W
54 J4 **Los Taques** Falcón, N Venezuela 11°50′N 70°16′W
14 G11 **Lost Channel** Ontario, S Canada 45°54′N 80°20′W
54 L5 **Los Teques** Miranda, N Venezuela 10°25′N 67°01′W
35 Q12 **Lost Hills** California, W USA 35°35′N 119°40′W
36 I7 **Lost Peak** ▲ Utah, W USA 37°30′N 113°57′W
33 P11 **Lost Trail Pass** *pass* Montana, NW USA
186 G9 **Losuia** Kiriwina Island, SE Papua New Guinea 08°29′S 151°03′E
62 G10 **Los Vilos** Coquimbo, C Chile 31°56′S 71°35′W
105 N10 **Los Yébenes** Castilla-La Mancha, C Spain 39°35′N 03°52′W
103 N13 **Lot** ◈ *department* S France
103 N13 **Lot** ~ S France
63 F14 **Lota** Bío Bío, C Chile 37°07′S 73°10′W
81 G15 **Lotagipi Swamp** *wetland* Kenya/Sudan
102 K14 **Lot-et-Garonne** ◈ *department* SW France
83 K21 **Lothair** Mpumalanga, NE South Africa 26°23′S 30°26′E
33 R7 **Lothair** Montana, NW USA 48°28′N 111°15′W
79 L20 **Loto** Kasai-Oriental, C Dem. Rep. Congo 02°48′S 22°30′E
108 E10 **Lötschbergtunnel** *tunnel* Valais, SW Switzerland
25 T9 **Lott** Texas, SW USA 31°12′N 97°02′W
124 H3 **Lotta** *var.* Lutto. ~ Finland/Russian Federation
184 Q7 **Lottin Point** *headland* North Island, New Zealand 37°26′S 178°07′E
Lötzen *see* Giżycko
Loualaba *see* Lualaba
167 P6 **Louangnamtha** *var.* Luong Nam Tha. Louang Namtha, N Laos 20°55′N 101°24′E
167 Q7 **Louangphabang** *var.* Louangphrabang, Luang Prabang. Louangphabang, N Laos 19°51′N 102°08′E
Louangphrabang *see* Louangphabang
194 H5 **Loubet Coast** *physical region* Antarctica
Loubomo *see* Dolisie
Louch *see* Loukhi
102 H6 **Loudéac** Côtes d'Armor, NW France 48°11′N 02°45′W
160 M11 **Loudi** Hunan, S China 27°51′N 111°59′E
79 F21 **Loudima** Bouenza, S Congo 04°06′S 13°05′E
20 M9 **Loudon** Tennessee, S USA 35°43′N 84°19′W
31 T12 **Loudonville** Ohio, N USA 40°38′N 82°13′W
102 L8 **Loudun** Vienne, W France 47°01′N 00°05′E
102 K7 **Loué** Sarthe, NW France 48°00′N 00°14′W
76 G10 **Louga** NW Senegal 15°36′N 16°15′W
97 M19 **Loughborough** C England, United Kingdom 52°47′N 01°11′W
97 C18 **Loughrea** *Ir.* Baile Locha Riach. Galway, W Ireland 53°12′N 08°34′W
103 S9 **Louhans** Saône-et-Loire, C France 46°38′N 05°12′E
21 P5 **Louisa** Kentucky, S USA 38°06′N 82°37′W
21 V5 **Louisa** Virginia, NE USA 38°02′N 78°00′W
21 V9 **Louisburg** North Carolina, SE USA 36°05′N 78°18′W
25 U12 **Louise** Texas, SW USA 29°07′N 96°22′W
15 P11 **Louiseville** Québec, SE Canada 46°15′N 72°54′W
27 W3 **Louisiana** Missouri, C USA 39°25′N 91°03′W
22 G8 **Louisiana** *off.* State of Louisiana, *also known as* Creole State, Pelican State. ◈ *state* S USA
Louis Trichardt *see* Makhado
23 V4 **Louisville** Georgia, SE USA 33°00′N 82°24′W
30 M15 **Louisville** Illinois, N USA 38°46′N 88°32′W
20 K5 **Louisville** Kentucky, S USA 38°15′N 85°46′W
22 M4 **Louisville** Mississippi, S USA 33°07′N 89°03′W
29 S15 **Louisville** Nebraska, C USA 41°00′N 96°09′W
192 L11 **Louisville Ridge** *undersea feature* S Pacific Ocean
124 J6 **Loukhi** *var.* Louch. Respublika Kareliya, NW Russian Federation 66°05′N 33°04′E
79 H19 **Loukoléla** Cuvette, E Congo 01°04′S 17°10′E
104 G14 **Loulé** Faro, S Portugal 37°08′N 08°02′W
111 C16 **Louny** *Ger.* Laun. Ústecký Kraj, NW Czech Republic 50°22′N 13°50′E
29 O15 **Loup City** Nebraska, C USA 41°16′N 98°58′W
29 P15 **Loup River** ~ Nebraska, C USA
15 S9 **Loup, Rivière du** ~ Québec, SE Canada
12 K7 **Loups Marins, Lacs des** ◎ Québec, NE Canada
102 K16 **Lourdes** Hautes-Pyrénées, S France 43°06′N 00°03′W
Lourenço Marques *see* Maputo
104 F11 **Loures** Lisboa, C Portugal 38°50′N 09°10′W
104 F10 **Lourinhã** Lisboa, C Portugal 39°14′N 09°19′W
115 C16 **Loúros** ~ W Greece
104 G8 **Lousã** Coimbra, N Portugal 40°07′N 08°15′W
Loushanguan *see* Tongzi
160 M10 **Lou Shui** ~ C China
183 O5 **Louth** New South Wales, SE Australia 30°34′S 145°07′E
97 O18 **Louth** E England, United Kingdom 53°19′N 00°00′E
97 F17 **Louth** *Ir.* Lú. *cultural region* NE Ireland
115 H15 **Loutrá** Kentrikí Makedonía, N Greece 39°55′N 23°37′E
115 G19 **Loutráki** Pelopónnisos, S Greece 37°55′N 22°55′E
Louvain *see* Leuven
99 H19 **Louvain-la Neuve** Walloon Brabant, C Belgium 50°39′N 04°36′E
14 J8 **Louvicourt** Québec, SE Canada 48°04′N 77°22′W
102 M4 **Louviers** Eure, N France 49°13′N 01°11′E
30 K14 **Lou Yaeger, Lake** ▣ Illinois, N USA
93 J15 **Lövånger** Västerbotten, N Sweden 64°22′N 21°19′E
124 J14 **Lovat'** ~ NW Russian Federation
113 J17 **Lovćen** ▲ SW Montenegro 42°22′N 18°49′E
114 I8 **Lovech** Lovech, N Bulgaria 43°08′N 24°45′E
114 I9 **Lovech** ◈ *province* N Bulgaria
25 V9 **Lovelady** Texas, SW USA 31°07′N 95°27′W
37 T3 **Loveland** Colorado, C USA 40°24′N 105°04′W
33 U12 **Lovell** Wyoming, C USA 44°50′N 108°23′W
Lovello, Monte *see* Grosser Löffler
35 S4 **Lovelock** Nevada, W USA 40°11′N 118°30′W
106 E7 **Lovere** Lombardia, N Italy 45°51′N 10°06′E
30 L10 **Loves Park** Illinois, N USA 42°19′N 89°03′W
26 M2 **Lovewell Reservoir** ▣ Kansas, C USA
93 M19 **Loviisa** *Swe.* Lovisa. Etelä-Suomi, S Finland 60°27′N 26°15′E
37 V15 **Loving** New Mexico, SW USA 32°17′N 104°06′W
21 U6 **Lovingston** Virginia, NE USA 37°46′N 78°54′W
37 V14 **Lovington** New Mexico, SW USA 32°56′N 103°21′W
Lovisa *see* Loviisa
111 C15 **Lovosice** *Ger.* Lobositz. Ústecký Kraj, NW Czech Republic 50°30′N 14°02′E
124 K4 **Lovozero** Murmanskaya Oblast', NW Russian Federation 68°00′N 35°03′E
124 K4 **Lovozero, Ozero** ◎ NW Russian Federation
112 B9 **Lovran** *It.* Laurana. Primorje-Gorski Kotar, NW Croatia 45°16′N 14°15′E
116 E11 **Lovrin** *Ger.* Lowrin. Timiș, W Romania 45°58′N 20°49′E
82 E10 **Lóvua** Lunda Norte, NE Angola 07°21′S 20°09′E
82 G12 **Lóvua** Moxico, E Angola 11°33′S 23°35′E
65 D25 **Low Bay** *bay* East Falkland, Falkland Islands
9 P9 **Low, Cape** *headland* Nunavut, E Canada 63°05′N 85°27′W
33 N10 **Lowell** Idaho, NW USA 46°07′N 115°36′W
19 O10 **Lowell** Massachusetts, NE USA 42°38′N 71°19′W
Löwen *see* Leuven
Löwenberg in Schlesien *see* Lwówek Śląski
Lower Austria *see* Niederösterreich
Lower Bann *see* Bann
Lower California *see* Baja California
Lower Danube *see* Niederösterreich
185 L14 **Lower Hutt** Wellington, North Island, New Zealand 41°13′S 174°51′E
39 N11 **Lower Kalskag** Alaska, USA 61°30′N 160°28′W
35 O1 **Lower Klamath Lake** ◎ California, W USA
35 Q2 **Lower Lake** ◎ California/Nevada, W USA
97 E15 **Lower Lough Erne** ◎ SW Northern Ireland, United Kingdom
Lower Lusatia *see* Niederlausitz
Lower Normandy *see* Basse-Normandie
10 K9 **Lower Post** British Columbia, W Canada 59°53′N 128°19′W
29 T4 **Lower Red Lake** ◎ Minnesota, N USA
Lower Rhine *see* Neder Rijn
Lower Saxony *see* Niedersachsen
97 Q19 **Lowestoft** E England, United Kingdom 52°29′N 01°45′E
149 Q5 **Lowgar** *var.* Logar. ◈ *province* E Afghanistan
182 H7 **Low Hill** South Australia 32°17′S 136°46′E
110 K12 **Łowicz** Łódzkie, C Poland 52°06′N 19°55′E
33 N13 **Lowman** Idaho, NW USA 44°04′N 115°37′W
149 P8 **Lowrah** *var.* Lora. ~ SE Afghanistan
Lowrin *see* Lovrin
183 N17 **Low Rocky Point** *headland* Tasmania, SE Australia 42°59′S 145°28′E
18 I8 **Lowville** New York, NE USA 43°47′N 75°29′W
Loxa *see* Loksa
182 K9 **Loxton** South Australia 34°30′S 140°36′E
81 G21 **Loya** Tabora, C Tanzania 04°57′S 33°53′E
30 K6 **Loyal** Wisconsin, N USA 44°45′N 90°30′W
18 G13 **Loyalsock Creek** ~ Pennsylvania, NE USA
35 Q5 **Loyalton** California, W USA 39°39′N 120°16′W
Lo-yang *see* Luoyang
187 Q16 **Loyauté, Îles** *island group* S New Caledonia
Loyev *see* Loyew
119 O20 **Loyew** *Rus.* Loyev. Homyel'skaya Voblasts', SE Belarus 51°56′N 30°48′E
125 S13 **Loyno** Kirovskaya Oblast', NW Russian Federation 59°44′N 52°42′E
103 P13 **Lozère** ◈ *department* S France
103 Q14 **Lozère, Mont** ▲ S France 44°27′N 03°44′E
112 J11 **Loznica** Serbia, W Serbia 44°32′N 19°13′E
114 L8 **Loznitsa** Razgrad, N Bulgaria 43°22′N 26°36′E
117 V7 **Lozova** *Rus.* Lozovaya. Kharkivs'ka Oblast', E Ukraine 48°54′N 36°23′E
Lozovaya *see* Lozova
105 N7 **Lozoyuela** Madrid, C Spain 40°55′N 03°36′W
Lu *see* Shandong, China
Lú *see* Louth, Ireland
82 F12 **Luacano** Moxico, E Angola 11°19′S 21°30′E
79 N21 **Lualaba** *Fr.* Loualaba. ~ SE Dem. Rep. Congo
83 H14 **Luampa** Western, NW Zambia 15°02′S 24°27′E
83 H15 **Luampa Kuta** Western, W Zambia 15°22′S 24°40′E
161 P8 **Lu'an** Anhui, E China 31°46′N 116°31′E
104 K2 **Luanco** Asturias, N Spain 43°36′N 05°48′W
82 A11 **Luanda** *var.* Loanda, *Port.* São Paulo de Loanda. ● Luanda, NW Angola 08°48′S 13°17′E
82 A11 **Luanda** ◈ *province* (Angola) NW Angola
82 A11 **Luanda** ✈ Luanda, NW Angola 08°49′S 13°16′E
82 D12 **Luando** ~ C Angola
Luang *see* Tapi, Mae Nam
83 G14 **Luanginga** *var.* Luanguinga. ~ Angola/Zambia
167 N15 **Luang, Khao** ▲ SW Thailand 08°21′N 99°46′E
Luang Prabang *see* Louangphabang
167 P8 **Luang Prabang Range** *Th.* Thiukhaoluang Phrahang. ▲▲ Laos/Thailand
167 N16 **Luang, Thale** *lagoon* S Thailand
Luangua, Rio *see* Luangwa
82 E11 **Luangue** ~ NE Angola
Luanguinga *see* Luanginga
83 K15 **Luangwa** *var.* Aruângua. Lusaka, C Zambia 15°36′S 30°27′E
83 K14 **Luangwa** *var.* Aruângua, Rio Luangua. ~ Mozambique/Zambia
161 Q2 **Luan He** ~ E China
190 G11 **Luaniva, Île** *island* E Wallis and Futuna
161 P2 **Luanping** *var.* Anjiangying. Hebei, E China 40°55′N 117°19′E
82 J13 **Luanshya** Copperbelt, C Zambia 13°09′S 28°24′E
62 K13 **Luan Toro** La Pampa, C Argentina 36°14′S 64°15′W
161 Q2 **Luanxian** *var.* Luan Xian. Hebei, E China 39°46′N 118°46′E
Luan Xian *see* Luanxian
82 J12 **Luapula** ◈ *province* N Zambia
79 O25 **Luapula** ~ Dem. Rep. Congo/Zambia
104 J2 **Luarca** Asturias, N Spain 43°33′N 06°31′W
169 R10 **Luar, Danau** ◎ Borneo, N Indonesia
79 L25 **Luashi** Katanga, S Dem. Rep. Congo 10°54′S 23°55′E
82 G12 **Luau** *Port.* Vila Teixeira de Sousa. Moxico, NE Angola 10°42′S 22°12′E
79 C16 **Luba** *prev.* San Carlos. Isla de Bioco, NW Equatorial Guinea 03°26′N 08°36′E
42 F4 **Lubaantun** *ruins* Toledo, S Belize
111 P16 **Lubaczów** *var.* Lúbaczów. Podkarpackie, SE Poland 50°10′N 23°08′E
Lubale *see* Lubalo
82 E11 **Lubalo** Lunda Norte, NE Angola 09°02′S 19°11′E
82 E11 **Lubalo** *var.* Lubale. ~ Angola/Dem. Rep. Congo
118 J9 **Lubāna** Madona, E Latvia 56°55′N 29°43′E
Lubānas Ezers *see* Lubāns
171 N4 **Lubang Island** *island* N Philippines
83 B15 **Lubango** *Port.* Sá da Bandeira. Huíla, SW Angola 14°55′S 13°33′E
118 J9 **Lubāns** *var.* Lubānas Ezers. ◎ E Latvia
79 M21 **Lubao** Kasai-Oriental, C Dem. Rep. Congo 05°21′S 25°42′E
110 O13 **Lubartów** *Ger.* Qumälisch. Lublin, E Poland 51°29′N 22°38′E
100 G13 **Lübbecke** Nordrhein-Westfalen, NW Germany 52°18′N 08°37′E
100 O13 **Lübben** Brandenburg, E Germany 51°56′N 13°52′E
101 P14 **Lübbenau** Brandenburg, E Germany 51°52′N 13°57′E
25 N5 **Lubbock** Texas, SW USA 33°35′N 101°51′W
Lubcz *see* Lyubcha
19 U6 **Lubec** Maine, NE USA 44°49′N 67°00′W
100 K9 **Lübeck** Schleswig-Holstein, N Germany 53°52′N 10°41′E
100 K8 **Lübecker Bucht** *bay* N Germany
79 M21 **Lubefu** Kasai-Oriental, C Dem. Rep. Congo 04°43′S 24°25′E
163 T10 **Lubei** *var.* Jarud Qi. Nei Mongol Zizhiqu, N China 44°25′N 121°12′E
111 O14 **Lubelska, Wyżyna** *plateau* SE Poland
110 O13 **Lubelskie** ◈ *province* E Poland
Lubembe *see* Luembe
Lüben *see* Lubin
144 H9 **Lubenka** Zapadnyy Kazakhstan, W Kazakhstan 50°27′N 54°07′E
79 P18 **Lubero** Nord-Kivu, E Dem. Rep. Congo 0°10′S 29°12′E
79 L22 **Lubi** ~ S Dem. Rep. Congo
Lubiana *see* Ljubljana
110 J11 **Lubień Kujawski** Kujawsko-pomorskie, C Poland 52°25′N 19°10′E
67 T11 **Lubilandji** ~ S Dem. Rep. Congo
110 F13 **Lubin** *Ger.* Lüben. Dolnośląskie, SW Poland 51°23′N 16°12′E
111 O14 **Lublin** *Rus.* Lyublin. Lubelskie, E Poland 51°15′N 22°33′E
111 J15 **Lubliniec** Śląskie, S Poland 50°41′N 18°41′E
Lubnān, Jabal *see* Liban, Jebel
117 R5 **Lubny** Poltavs'ka Oblast', NE Ukraine 50°00′N 33°00′E
Luboml *see* Lyuboml'
110 G11 **Luboń** *Ger.* Peterhof. Wielkopolskie, C Poland 52°23′N 16°54′E
110 D12 **Lubsko** *Ger.* Sommerfeld. Lubuskie, W Poland 51°47′N 14°57′E
79 N24 **Lubudi** Katanga, SE Dem. Rep. Congo 09°57′S 25°59′E
168 L13 **Lubuklinggau** Sumatera, W Indonesia 03°10′S 102°52′E
79 N25 **Lubumbashi** *prev.* Élisabethville. Shaba, SE Dem. Rep. Congo 11°40′S 27°31′E
83 I14 **Lubungu** Central, C Zambia 14°28′S 26°30′E
110 E12 **Lubuskie** ◈ *province* W Poland
Lubuskie *see* Dobiegniew
79 N18 **Lubutu** Maniema, E Dem. Rep. Congo 0°48′S 26°39′E
Luca *see* Lucca
82 C11 **Lucala** ~ W Angola
14 E16 **Lucan** Ontario, S Canada 43°10′N 81°22′W
97 F18 **Lucan** *Ir.* Leamhcán. Dublin, E Ireland 53°22′N 06°27′W
Lucanian Mountains *see* Lucano, Appennino
107 M18 **Lucano, Appennino** *Eng.* Lucanian Mountains. ▲▲ S Italy
82 F11 **Lucapa** *var.* Lukapa. Lunda Norte, NE Angola 08°24′S 20°42′E
29 V15 **Lucas** Iowa, C USA 41°01′N 93°26′W
61 C18 **Lucas González** Entre Ríos, E Argentina 32°25′S 59°33′W
31 S15 **Lucasville** Ohio, N USA 38°52′N 83°00′W
106 F11 **Lucca** *anc.* Luca. Toscana, C Italy 43°50′N 10°30′E
44 H12 **Lucea** W Jamaica 18°26′N 78°11′W
97 H15 **Luce Bay** *inlet* SW Scotland, United Kingdom
22 M8 **Lucedale** Mississippi, S USA 30°55′N 88°35′W
171 O4 **Lucena** *off.* Lucena City. Luzon, N Philippines 13°57′N 121°38′E
104 M14 **Lucena** Andalucía, S Spain 37°25′N 04°29′W
Lucena City *see* Lucena
105 S8 **Lucena del Cid** País Valenciano, E Spain 40°07′N 00°15′W
111 D15 **Lučenec** *Ger.* Losontz, *Hung.* Losonc. Banskobystrický Kraj, C Slovakia 48°21′N 19°37′E
Lucentum *see* Alicante
107 M16 **Lucera** Puglia, SE Italy 41°30′N 15°19′E
Lucerna/Lucerne *see* Luzern
Lucerne, Lake of *see* Vierwaldstätter See
40 J4 **Lucero** Chihuahua, N Mexico 30°50′N 106°30′W
123 S14 **Luchegorsk** Primorskiy Kray, SE Russian Federation 46°26′N 134°10′E
105 Q13 **Luchena** ~ SE Spain
Lucheng *see* Kangding
82 N13 **Lucheringo** *var.* Luchulingo. ~ N Mozambique
Luchesa *see* Luchosa
Luchin *see* Luchyn
118 N13 **Luchosa** *Rus.* Luchesa. ~ N Belarus
100 K11 **Lüchow** Mecklenburg-Vorpommern, N Germany 52°57′N 11°10′E
Luchow *see* Hefei
Luchulingo *see* Lucheringo
119 N17 **Luchyn** *Rus.* Luchin. Homyel'skaya Voblasts', SE Belarus 53°01′N 30°01′E
55 U11 **Lucie Rivier** ~ W Suriname
182 K11 **Lucindale** South Australia 36°57′S 140°20′E
83 A14 **Lucira** Namibe, SW Angola 13°51′S 12°35′E
Łuck *see* Luts'k
101 O14 **Luckau** Brandenburg, E Germany 51°50′N 13°42′E
100 N13 **Luckenwalde** Brandenburg, E Germany 52°05′N 13°11′E
14 E15 **Lucknow** Ontario, S Canada 43°58′N 81°30′W
152 L12 **Lucknow** *var.* Lakhnau. *state capital* Uttar Pradesh, N India 26°50′N 80°54′E
102 J10 **Luçon** Vendée, NW France 46°27′N 01°10′W
44 I7 **Lucrecia, Cabo** *headland* E Cuba 21°00′N 75°34′W
82 F13 **Lucusse** Moxico, E Angola 12°32′S 20°46′E
Lüda *see* Dalian
114 M9 **Luda Kamchiya** ~ E Bulgaria
Ludasch *see* Luduș
114 I10 **Luda Yana** ~ C Bulgaria
112 F7 **Ludbreg** Varaždin, N Croatia 46°15′N 16°36′E
29 P7 **Ludden** North Dakota, N USA 45°58′N 98°07′W
101 F15 **Lüdenscheid** Nordrhein-Westfalen, W Germany 51°13′N 07°38′E
83 C21 **Lüderitz** *prev.* Angra Pequena. Karas, SW Namibia 26°38′S 15°10′E
152 H8 **Ludhiāna** Punjab, N India 30°56′N 75°52′E
31 O7 **Ludington** Michigan, N USA 43°58′N 86°27′W
97 K20 **Ludlow** W England, United Kingdom 52°20′N 02°28′W
35 W14 **Ludlow** California, W USA 34°43′N 116°07′W
28 J7 **Ludlow** South Dakota, N USA 45°48′N 103°21′W
18 M9 **Ludlow** Vermont, NE USA 43°24′N 72°39′W
114 L7 **Ludogorie** *physical region* NE Bulgaria
23 W6 **Ludowici** Georgia, SE USA 31°42′N 81°44′W
Ludsan *see* Ludza
116 I10 **Luduș** *Ger.* Ludasch, *Hung.* Marosludas. Mureș, C Romania 46°28′N 24°05′E
95 M14 **Ludvika** Dalarna, C Sweden 60°08′N 15°14′E
101 H21 **Ludwigsburg** Baden-Württemberg, SW Germany 48°54′N 09°12′E
100 O13 **Ludwigsfelde** Brandenburg, NE Germany 52°17′N 13°15′E
101 G20 **Ludwigshafen** *var.* Ludwigshafen am Rhein. Rheinland-Pfalz, W Germany 49°29′N 08°24′E
Ludwigshafen am Rhein *see* Ludwigshafen
101 L20 **Ludwigskanal** *canal* SE Germany
100 L10 **Ludwigslust** Mecklenburg-Vorpommern, N Germany 53°19′N 11°29′E
118 K10 **Ludza** *Ger.* Ludsan. Ludza, E Latvia 56°32′N 27°41′E
79 K21 **Luebo** Kasai-Occidental, SW Dem. Rep. Congo 05°19′S 21°21′E
25 Q6 **Lueders** Texas, SW USA 32°46′N 99°38′W
79 N20 **Lueki** Maniema, C Dem. Rep. Congo 03°25′S 25°50′E
82 F10 **Luembe** *var.* Lubembe. ~ Angola/Dem. Rep. Congo
82 E13 **Luena** *var.* Lwena, *Port.* Luso. Moxico, E Angola 11°47′S 19°52′E
79 M24 **Luena** Katanga, SE Dem. Rep. Congo 09°28′S 25°45′E
82 K12 **Luena** Northern, NE Zambia 10°40′S 30°21′E
82 F13 **Luena** ~ E Angola
83 F16 **Luengue** ~ SE Angola
67 V13 **Luenha** ~ W Mozambique
83 G15 **Lueti** ~ Angola/Zambia
160 J7 **Lüeyang** *var.* Hejiayan. Shaanxi, C China 33°12′N 106°31′E
161 P14 **Lufeng** Guangdong, S China 22°59′N 115°40′E
79 N24 **Lufira** ~ SE Dem. Rep. Congo
79 N25 **Lufira, Lac de Retenue de la** *var.* Lac Tshangalele. ◎ SE Dem. Rep. Congo
25 W8 **Lufkin** Texas, SW USA 31°21′N 94°47′W
82 L11 **Lufubu** ~ N Zambia
124 G14 **Luga** Leningradskaya Oblast', NW Russian Federation 58°43′N 29°46′E
124 G13 **Luga** ~ NW Russian Federation
Luganer See *see* Lugano, Lago di
108 H11 **Lugano** *Ger.* Lauis. Ticino, S Switzerland 46°01′N 08°57′E
108 H12 **Lugano, Lago di** *var.* Ceresio, *Ger.* Luganer See. ◎ S Switzerland
Lugansk *see* Luhans'k
187 Q13 **Luganville** Espiritu Santo, C Vanuatu 15°31′S 167°12′E
Lugdunum *see* Lyon
Lugdunum Batavorum *see* Leiden
83 O15 **Lugela** Zambézia, NE Mozambique 16°27′S 36°47′E
83 O16 **Lugela** ~ C Mozambique
82 P13 **Lugenda, Rio** ~ N Mozambique
Luggarus *see* Locarno
Lugh Ganana *see* Luuq
97 G19 **Lugnaquillia Mountain** *Ir.* Log na Coille. ▲ E Ireland 52°58′N 06°27′W
106 H10 **Lugo** Emilia-Romagna, N Italy 44°25′N 11°53′E
104 I3 **Lugo** *anc.* Lugus Augusti. Galicia, NW Spain 43°N 07°33′W
104 I3 **Lugo** ◈ *province* Galicia, NW Spain
21 R12 **Lugoff** South Carolina, SE USA 34°13′N 80°41′W
116 F12 **Lugoj** *Ger.* Lugosch, *Hung.* Lugos. Timiș, W Romania 45°41′N 21°56′E
Lugos/Lugosch *see* Lugoj
Lugovoy/Lugovoye *see* Kulan
158 I13 **Lugu** Xizang Zizhiqu, W China 33°26′N 84°10′E
Lugus Augusti *see* Lugo
Luguvallium/Luguvallum *see* Carlisle
117 Y7 **Luhans'k** *Rus.* Lugansk; *prev.* Voroshilovgrad. Luhans'ka Oblast', E Ukraine 48°32′N 39°21′E
117 Y7 **Luhans'k** ✈ Luhans'ka Oblast', E Ukraine 48°25′N 39°24′E
Luhans'k *see* Luhans'ka Oblast'
117 X6 **Luhans'ka Oblast'** *var.* Luhans'k; *prev.* Voroshilovgrad, *Rus.* Voroshilovgradskaya Oblast'. ◈ *province* E Ukraine
161 Q7 **Luhe** Jiangsu, E China 32°20′N 118°52′E
171 S13 **Luhu** Pulau Seram, E Indonesia 03°20′S 127°58′E
Luhua *see* Heishui
160 G8 **Luhuo** *var.* Xindu, *Tib.* Zhaggo. Sichuan, C China 31°18′N 100°39′E
116 M3 **Luhyny** Zhytomyrs'ka Oblast', N Ukraine 51°06′N 28°24′E
83 G15 **Lui** ~ W Zambia
83 G16 **Luiana** ~ SE Angola
83 L15 **Luia, Rio** *var.* Ruya. ~ Mozambique/Zimbabwe
Luichow Peninsula *see* Leizhou Bandao
Luik *see* Liège
82 C13 **Luimbale** Huambo, C Angola 12°15′S 15°19′E
Luimneach *see* Limerick
106 D6 **Luino** Lombardia, N Italy 46°00′N 08°45′E
82 E13 **Luio** ~ E Angola
92 L11 **Luiro** ~ NE Finland
79 N25 **Luishia** Katanga, SE Dem. Rep. Congo 11°18′S 27°08′E
59 M19 **Luislândia do Oeste** Minas Gerais, SE Brazil 17°59′S 45°35′W
40 K5 **Luis L. León, Presa** ▣ N Mexico
Luis Muñoz Marin *see* San Juan
195 N5 **Luitpold Coast** *physical region* Antarctica
79 K22 **Luiza** Kasai-Occidental, S Dem. Rep. Congo 07°11′S 22°27′E
61 D20 **Luján** Buenos Aires, E Argentina 34°34′S 59°07′W
79 N24 **Lukafu** Katanga, SE Dem. Rep. Congo 10°28′S 27°32′E
Lukapa *see* Lucapa
112 I11 **Lukavac** ◈ Federacija Bosna I Hercegovina, NE Bosnia and Herzegovina
79 I20 **Lukenie** ~ C Dem. Rep. Congo
114 J11 **Lŭki** Plovdiv, C Bulgaria 41°50′N 24°49′E
79 H19 **Lukolela** Equateur, W Dem. Rep. Congo 01°10′S 17°11′E
119 M14 **Lukoml'skaye, Vozyera** *Rus.* Ozero Lukoml'skoye. ◎ N Belarus
Lukoml'skoye, Ozero *see* Lukoml'skaye, Vozyera
114 I8 **Lukovit** Lovech, N Bulgaria 43°11′N 24°10′E
110 O12 **Łuków** *Ger.* Bogendorf. Lubelskie, E Poland 51°57′N 22°22′E
127 O4 **Lukoyanov** Nizhegorodskaya Oblast', W Russian Federation 55°02′N 44°26′E
Lukransar *see* Lūnkaransar

◆ Country ◇ Dependent Territory ◈ Administrative Regions ▲ Mountain ⛰ Volcano ◎ Lake
● Country Capital ○ Dependent Territory Capital ✈ International Airport ▲▲ Mountain Range ~ River ▣ Reservoir
281

LUKUGA – MADENIYET

79 N22 **Lukuga** ≈ SE Dem. Rep. Congo
79 F21 **Lukula** Bas-Congo, SW Dem. Rep. Congo 05°23′S 12°57′E
83 G14 **Lukulu** Western, NW Zambia 14°24′S 23°12′E
189 R17 **Lukunor Atoll** atoll Mortlock Islands, C Micronesia
82 J12 **Lukwesa** Luapula, NE Zambia 10°03′S 28°42′E
93 K14 **Luleå** Norrbotten, N Sweden 65°35′N 22°10′E
92 J13 **Luleälven** ≈ N Sweden
136 C10 **Lüleburgaz** Kırklareli, NW Turkey 41°25′N 27°22′E
160 M4 **Lüliang** var. Lishi. Shanxi, C China 37°27′N 111°05′E
160 M4 **Lüliang Shan** ▲▲ C China
79 O21 **Lulimba** Maniema, E Dem. Rep. Congo 04°42′S 28°38′E
22 K9 **Luling** Louisiana, S USA 29°55′N 90°22′W
25 T11 **Luling** Texas, SW USA 29°40′N 97°39′W
79 I18 **Lulonga** ≈ NW Dem. Rep. Congo
79 K22 **Lulua** ≈ S Dem. Rep. Congo
Luluabourg see Kananga
192 L17 **Luma** Ta'ū, E American Samoa 14°15′S 169°30′W
169 S17 **Lumajang** Jawa, C Indonesia 08°06′S 113°13′E
158 G12 **Lumajangdong Co** ◎ W China
82 G13 **Lumbala Kaquengue** Moxico, E Angola 12°40′S 22°34′E
83 F14 **Lumbala N'Guimbo** var. Nguimbo, Gago Coutinho, Port. Vila Gago Coutinho. Moxico, E Angola 14°08′S 21°25′E
21 T11 **Lumber River** ≈ North Carolina/South Carolina, SE USA
Lumber State see Maine
22 L8 **Lumberton** Mississippi, S USA 31°00′N 89°27′W
21 U11 **Lumberton** North Carolina, SE USA 34°37′N 79°00′W
105 R4 **Lumbier** Navarra, N Spain 42°39′N 01°19′W
83 Q15 **Lumbo** Nampula, NE Mozambique 15°S 40°40′E
124 M4 **Lumbovka** Murmanskaya Oblast', NW Russian Federation 67°41′N 40°31′E
104 J7 **Lumbrales** Castilla-León, N Spain 40°57′N 06°43′W
153 W13 **Lumding** Assam, NE India 25°46′N 93°10′E
82 F12 **Lumege** var. Lumeje. Moxico, E Angola 11°30′S 20°57′E
Lumeje see Lumege
99 J17 **Lummen** Limburg, NE Belgium 50°58′N 05°12′E
93 J20 **Lumparland** Åland, SW Finland 60°06′N 20°15′E
167 T11 **Lumphăt** prev. Lomphat. Rôtânôkiri, NE Cambodia 13°30′N
11 U16 **Lumsden** Saskatchewan, S Canada 50°39′N 104°52′W
185 C23 **Lumsden** Southland, South Island, New Zealand 45°43′S 168°26′E
169 N14 **Lumut, Tanjung** headland Sumatera, W Indonesia 03°47′S 105°55′E
157 P4 **Lün** Töv, C Mongolia 47°51′N 105°11′E
116 I13 **Lunca Corbului** Argeş, S Romania 44°41′N 24°46′E
95 K23 **Lund** Skåne, S Sweden 55°42′N 13°10′E
35 X6 **Lund** Nevada, W USA 38°50′N 115°00′W
82 D11 **Lunda Norte** ◈ province NE Angola
82 E12 **Lunda Sul** ◈ province NE Angola
82 M13 **Lundazi** Eastern, NE Zambia 12°19′S 33°11′E
95 G16 **Lunde** Telemark, S Norway 61°31′N 06°38′E
Lundenburg see Břeclav
95 C17 **Lundevatnet** ◎ S Norway
Lundi see Runde
97 I23 **Lundy** island SW England, United Kingdom
100 J10 **Lüneburg** Niedersachsen, N Germany 53°15′N 10°25′E
100 J11 **Lüneburger Heide** heathland NW Germany
103 Q15 **Lunel** Hérault, S France 43°40′N 04°08′E
101 F14 **Lünen** Nordrhein-Westfalen, W Germany 51°37′N 07°31′E
13 P16 **Lunenburg** Nova Scotia, SE Canada 44°23′N 64°21′W
21 V7 **Lunenburg** Virginia, NE USA 36°56′N 78°15′W
103 T5 **Lunéville** Meurthe-et-Moselle, NE France 48°35′N 06°30′E
83 I14 **Lunga** ≈ C Zambia
Lunga, Isola see Dugi Otok
158 H12 **Lungdo** Xizang Zizhiqu, W China 33°45′N 82°09′E
158 I14 **Lunggar** Xizang Zizhiqu, W China 31°10′N 84°01′E
76 I15 **Lungi** ✈ (Freetown) W Sierra Leone 08°36′N 13°10′W
Lungkiang see Qiqihar
Lungleh see Lunglei
153 W15 **Lunglei** prev. Lungleh. Mizoram, NE India 22°55′N 92°49′E
158 L15 **Lungsang** Xizang Zizhiqu, W China 29°50′N 88°27′E
82 E13 **Lungué-Bungo** var. Lungwebungu. ≈ Angola/Zambia see also Lungwebungu
Lungué-Bungo see Lungwebungu
83 G14 **Lungwebungu** var. Lungué-Bungo. ≈ Angola/Zambia see also Lungué-Bungo
Lungwebungu see Lungué-Bungo
152 F12 **Lūni** Rājasthān, N India 26°03′N 73°00′E
152 F12 **Lūni** ≈ N India
Luninets see Luninyets
35 S7 **Luning** Nevada, W USA 38°29′N 118°10′W
Łuniniec see Luninyets
127 P6 **Lunino** Penzenskaya Oblast', W Russian Federation 53°35′N 45°12′E
119 J19 **Luninyets** Pol. Łuniniec, Rus. Luninets. Brestskaya Voblasts', SW Belarus 52°15′N 26°48′E
152 F10 **Lūnkaransar** var. Lookransar, Lukransar. Rājasthān, NW India 28°32′N 73°50′E
119 G17 **Lunna** Pol. Łunna. Hrodzyenskaya Voblasts', W Belarus 53°27′N 24°16′E
76 I15 **Lunsar** W Sierra Leone 08°41′N 12°32′W
83 K14 **Lunsemfwa** ≈ C Zambia
158 J6 **Luntai** var. Bügür. Xinjiang Uygur Zizhiqu, NW China 41°48′N 84°14′E
98 K11 **Lunteren** Gelderland, C Netherlands 52°05′N 05°38′E
109 U5 **Lunz am See** Niederösterreich, C Austria 47°54′N 15°01′E
163 Y7 **Luobei** var. Fengxiang. Heilongjiang, NE China 47°35′N 130°51′E
Luocheng see Hui'an, Fujian, China
Luocheng see Luoding, Guangdong, China
160 J13 **Luodian** var. Longping. Guizhou, S China 25°25′N 106°49′E
160 M15 **Luoding** var. Luocheng. Guangdong, S China 22°44′N 111°28′E
161 N7 **Luohe** Henan, C China 33°37′N 114°00′E
160 M6 **Luo He** ≈ C China
160 L5 **Luo He** ≈ C China
Luolajarvi see Kuoloyarvi
Luong Nam Tha see Louangnamtha
160 L13 **Luoqing Jiang** ≈ S China
161 O8 **Luoshan** Henan, C China 32°12′N 114°30′E
161 O12 **Luoxiao Shan** ▲▲ S China
161 N6 **Luoyang** var. Honan, Lo-yang. Henan, C China 34°41′N 112°25′E
161 R12 **Luoyuan** var. Fengshan. Fujian, SE China 26°29′N 119°32′E
79 F21 **Luozi** Bas-Congo, W Dem. Rep. Congo 04°57′S 14°08′E
83 J17 **Lupane** Matabeleland North, W Zimbabwe 18°54′S 27°44′E
160 I12 **Lupanshui** prev. Shuicheng. Guizhou, S China 26°38′N 104°49′E
169 R10 **Lupar, Batang** ≈ East Malaysia
Lupatia see Altamura
116 G12 **Lupeni** Hung. Lupény. Hunedoara, SW Romania 45°20′N 23°10′E
Lupény see Lupeni
82 N13 **Lupiliche** Niassa, N Mozambique 11°36′S 35°15′E
83 E14 **Lupire** Cuando Cubango, E Angola 14°39′S 19°39′E
79 L22 **Luputa** Kasai-Oriental, S Dem. Rep. Congo 07°07′S 23°43′E
121 P16 **Luqa** ✈ (Valletta) S Malta 35°53′N 14°27′E
159 U11 **Luqu** var. Ma'ai. Gansu, C China 34°34′N 102°27′E
45 U5 **Luquillo, Sierra de** ▲▲ E Puerto Rico
26 L4 **Luray** Kansas, C USA 39°06′N 98°41′W
21 U4 **Luray** Virginia, NE USA 38°40′N 78°28′W
103 T7 **Lure** Haute-Saône, E France 47°42′N 06°30′E
82 D11 **Luremo** Lunda Norte, NE Angola 08°32′S 17°55′E
97 F15 **Lurgan** Ir. An Lorgain. S Northern Ireland, United Kingdom 54°28′N 06°20′W
57 K18 **Luribay** La Paz, W Bolivia 17°05′S 67°37′W
Luring see Gêrzê
83 Q14 **Lúrio** Nampula, NE Mozambique 13°32′S 40°34′E
83 P14 **Lúrio, Rio** ≈ NE Mozambique
Luristan see Lorestān
Lurka see Lorca
83 J15 **Lusaka** ● (Zambia) Lusaka, SE Zambia 15°24′S 28°17′E
83 J15 **Lusaka** ◈ province C Zambia
83 J15 **Lusaka** ✈ Lusaka, C Zambia 15°10′S 28°22′E
79 L21 **Lusambo** Kasai-Oriental, C Dem. Rep. Congo 04°59′S 23°26′E
186 F8 **Lusancay Islands and Reefs** island group SE Papua New Guinea
79 I21 **Lusanga** Bandundu, SW Dem. Rep. Congo 04°55′S 18°40′E
79 N21 **Lusangi** Maniema, E Dem. Rep. Congo 04°39′S 27°10′E
Lusatian Mountains see Lausitzer Bergland
Lushar see Huangzhong
Lushnja see Lushnjë
113 K21 **Lushnjë** var. Lushnja. Fier, C Albania 40°54′N 19°43′E
81 J21 **Lushoto** Tanga, E Tanzania 04°48′S 38°20′E
102 L10 **Lusignan** Vienne, W France 46°25′N 00°06′E
33 Z15 **Lusk** Wyoming, C USA 42°45′N 104°27′W
Luso see Luena
102 L10 **Lussac-les-Châteaux** Vienne, W France 46°23′N 00°44′E
Lussin/Lussino see Lošinj
Lussinpiccolo see Mali Lošinj
108 I7 **Lustenau** Vorarlberg, W Austria 47°26′N 09°42′E
161 T14 **Lü Tao** var. Huoshao Dao, Lütao, Eng. Green Island. island SE Taiwan
Lütao see Lü Tao
Lūt, Baḩrat/Lut, Bahret see Dead Sea
22 K9 **Lutcher** Louisiana, S USA 30°02′N 90°42′W
143 T9 **Lūt, Dasht-e** var. Kavīr-e Lūt. desert E Iran
83 F14 **Lutembo** Moxico, E Angola 13°30′S 21°21′E
Lutetia/Lutetia Parisiorum see Paris
Luteva see Lodève
14 G15 **Luther Lake** ◎ Ontario, S Canada
186 K8 **Luti** Choiseul Island, NW Solomon Islands 07°13′S 157°01′E
Lūt, Kavīr-e see Lūt, Dasht-e
97 N21 **Luton** E England, United Kingdom 51°53′N 00°25′W
97 N21 **Luton** ✈ (London) SE England, United Kingdom 51°54′N 00°24′W
108 B10 **Lutry** Vaud, SW Switzerland 46°31′N 06°32′E
8 K10 **Łutselk'e** prev. Snowdrift. Northwest Territories, W Canada 62°24′N 110°42′W
29 Y4 **Lutsen** Minnesota, N USA 47°39′N 90°37′W
116 J4 **Luts'k** Pol. Łuck, Rus. Lutsk. Volyns'ka Oblast', NW Ukraine 50°45′N 25°23′E
Lutsk see Luts'k
Luttenberg see Ljutomer
Lüttich see Liège
83 G25 **Luttig** Western Cape, SW South Africa 32°33′S 22°13′E
Lutto see Lotta
82 E13 **Lutuai** Moxico, E Angola 12°38′S 20°06′E
117 Y7 **Lutuhyne** Luhans'ka Oblast', E Ukraine 48°24′N 39°12′E
171 V14 **Lutur, Pulau** island Kepulauan Aru, E Indonesia
23 V12 **Lutz** Florida, SE USA 28°09′N 82°27′W
Lutzow-Holm Bay see Lützow Holmbukta
195 V2 **Lützow Holmbukta** var. Lutzow-Holm Bay. bay Antarctica
81 L16 **Luuq** It. Lugh Ganana. Gedo, SW Somalia 03°42′N 42°34′E
92 M12 **Luusua** Lappi, NE Finland 66°28′N 27°16′E
23 Q6 **Luverne** Alabama, S USA 31°43′N 86°15′W
29 S11 **Luverne** Minnesota, N USA 43°39′N 96°12′W
79 O22 **Luvua** ≈ SE Dem. Rep. Congo
82 F13 **Luvuei** Moxico, E Angola 13°08′S 21°09′E
81 H24 **Luwego** ≈ S Tanzania
82 K12 **Luwingu** Northern, NE Zambia 10°13′S 29°58′E
171 P12 **Luwuk** prev. Loewoek. Sulawesi, C Indonesia 0°56′S 122°47′E
23 N3 **Luxapallila Creek** ≈ Alabama/Mississippi, S USA
99 M25 **Luxembourg** ● (Luxembourg) Luxembourg, S Luxembourg 49°37′N 06°08′E
99 M25 **Luxembourg** off. Grand Duchy of Luxembourg, var. Lëtzebuerg, Luxemburg. ◆ monarchy NW Europe
99 J23 **Luxembourg** ◈ province SE Belgium
99 L24 **Luxembourg** ◈ district S Luxembourg
31 N6 **Luxemburg** Wisconsin, N USA 44°32′N 87°42′W
Luxemburg see Luxembourg
103 U7 **Luxeuil-les-Bains** Haute-Saône, E France 47°49′N 06°22′E
160 E13 **Luxi** prev. Mangshi. Yunnan, SW China 24°27′N 98°31′E
82 E10 **Luxico** ≈ Angola/Dem. Rep. Congo
75 X10 **Luxor** Ar. Al Uqşur. E Egypt 25°39′N 32°39′E
75 X10 **Luxor** ✈ C Egypt 25°39′N 32°48′E
160 M4 **Luya Shan** ▲▲ C China
102 J15 **Luy de Béarn** ≈ SW France
102 J15 **Luy de France** ≈ SW France
125 P12 **Luza** Kirovskaya Oblast', NW Russian Federation 60°38′N 47°13′E
125 Q12 **Luza** ≈ NW Russian Federation
104 I16 **Luz, Costa de la** coastal region SW Spain
111 K20 **Luže** var. Lausche. ▲ Czech Republic/Germany 50°51′N 14°40′E see also Lausche
Luže see Lausche
108 F8 **Luzern** Fr. Lucerne, It. Lucerna. Luzern, C Switzerland 47°03′N 08°17′E
108 E8 **Luzern** Fr. Lucerne. ◈ canton C Switzerland
160 L13 **Luzhai** Guangxi Zhuangzu Zizhiqu, S China 24°31′N 109°46′E
118 K12 **Luzhki** Vitsyebskaya Voblasts', N Belarus 55°21′N 27°52′E
160 I10 **Luzhou** Sichuan, C China 28°55′N 105°25′E
Lužická Nisa see Neisse
Lužické Hory' see Lausitzer Bergland
Lužnice see Lainsitz
171 O2 **Luzon** island N Philippines
171 N1 **Luzon Strait** strait Philippines/Taiwan
Łużyckie, Gory see Lausitzer Bergland
116 I5 **L'viv** Ger. Lemberg, Pol. Lwów, Rus. L'vov. L'vivs'ka Oblast', W Ukraine 49°49′N 24°05′E
L'viv see L'vivs'ka Oblast'
116 I4 **L'vivs'ka Oblast'** var. L'viv, Rus. L'vovskaya Oblast'. ◈ province NW Ukraine
L'vov see L'viv
L'vovskaya Oblast' see L'vivs'ka Oblast'
Lwena see Luena
Lwów see L'viv
110 F11 **Lwówek** Ger. Neustadt bei Pinne. Wielkopolskie, C Poland 52°27′N 16°10′E
111 E14 **Lwówek Śląski** Ger. Löwenberg in Schlesien. Jelenia Góra, SW Poland 51°06′N 15°35′E
119 I18 **Lyakhavichy** Rus. Lyakhovichi. Brestskaya Voblasts', SW Belarus 53°02′N 26°16′E
Lyakhovichi see Lyakhavichy
185 B22 **Lyall, Mount** ▲ South Island, New Zealand 45°14′S 167°31′E
Lyallpur see Faisalābād
Lyangar see Langar
124 H11 **Lyaskelya** Respublika Kareliya, NW Russian Federation 61°42′N 31°06′E
119 I18 **Lyasnaya** Rus. Lesnaya. Brestskaya Voblasts', SW Belarus 52°59′N 25°46′E
119 F19 **Lyasnaya** Pol. Leśna, Rus. Lesnaya. ≈ SW Belarus
124 H15 **Lychkovo** Novgorodskaya Oblast', W Russian Federation 57°55′N 32°24′E
Lyck see Ełk
93 I15 **Lycksele** Västerbotten, N Sweden 64°34′N 18°40′E
18 G13 **Lycoming Creek** ≈ Pennsylvania, NE USA
Lycopolis see Asyūţ
195 N3 **Lyddan Island** island Antarctica
83 K20 **Lydenburg** Mpumalanga, NE South Africa 25°10′S 30°29′E
119 L20 **Lyel'chytsy** Rus. Lel'chitsy. Homyel'skaya Voblasts', SE Belarus 51°47′N 28°20′E
119 P14 **Lyenina** Rus. Lenino. Mahilyowskaya Voblasts', E Belarus 54°25′N 31°08′E
118 L13 **Lyepyel'** Rus. Lepel'. Vitsyebskaya Voblasts', N Belarus 54°54′N 28°44′E
25 S17 **Lyford** Texas, SW USA 26°24′N 97°47′W
95 E17 **Lygna** ≈ S Norway
18 G14 **Lykens** Pennsylvania, NE USA 40°33′N 76°42′W
115 E21 **Lykódimo** ▲ S Greece 36°56′N 21°49′E
97 K24 **Lyme Bay** bay S England, United Kingdom
97 K24 **Lyme Regis** S England, United Kingdom 50°44′N 02°56′W
110 L7 **Łyna** Ger. Alle. ≈ N Poland
29 P12 **Lynch** Nebraska, C USA 42°49′N 98°27′W
20 J10 **Lynchburg** Tennessee, S USA 35°17′N 86°22′W
21 T6 **Lynchburg** Virginia, NE USA 37°24′N 79°09′W
21 T12 **Lynches River** ≈ South Carolina, SE USA
32 H6 **Lynden** Washington, NW USA 48°57′N 122°27′W
182 I5 **Lyndhurst** South Australia 30°19′S 138°20′E
27 Q5 **Lyndon** Kansas, C USA 38°37′N 95°40′W
19 N7 **Lyndonville** Vermont, NE USA 44°31′N 71°58′W
95 D18 **Lyngdal** Vest-Agder, S Norway 58°10′N 07°08′E
92 I9 **Lyngen** Lapp. Ivgovuotna. inlet Arctic Ocean
95 G17 **Lyngør** Aust-Agder, S Norway 58°38′N 09°05′E
92 I9 **Lyngseidet** Troms, N Norway 69°36′N 20°07′E
19 P11 **Lynn** Massachusetts, NE USA 42°28′N 70°57′W
Lynn see King's Lynn
23 R9 **Lynn Haven** Florida, SE USA 30°15′N 85°39′W
11 V11 **Lynn Lake** Manitoba, C Canada 56°51′N 101°01′W
Lynn Regis see King's Lynn
118 I13 **Lyntupy** Vitsyebskaya Voblasts', NW Belarus 55°03′N 26°19′E
103 R11 **Lyon** Eng. Lyons; anc. Lugdunum. Rhône, E France 45°46′N 04°50′E
8 I6 **Lyon, Cape** headland Northwest Territories, NW Canada 69°47′N 123°10′W
18 K6 **Lyon Mountain** ▲ New York, NE USA 44°42′N 73°52′W
103 Q11 **Lyonnais, Monts du** ▲▲ C France
65 N25 **Lyon Point** headland SE Tristan da Cunha 37°06′S 12°13′W
182 E5 **Lyons** South Australia 30°40′S 133°50′E
37 T3 **Lyons** Colorado, C USA 40°13′N 105°16′W
23 V6 **Lyons** Georgia, SE USA 32°12′N 82°19′W
26 M5 **Lyons** Kansas, C USA 38°22′N 98°13′W
29 R14 **Lyons** Nebraska, C USA 41°56′N 96°28′W
18 G10 **Lyons** New York, NE USA 43°03′N 76°58′W
Lyons see Lyon
118 O13 **Lyozna** Rus. Liozno. Vitsyebskaya Voblasts', NE Belarus 55°02′N 30°48′E
117 S4 **Lypova Dolyna** Sums'ka Oblast', NE Ukraine 50°36′N 33°50′E
117 N6 **Lypovets'** Rus. Lipovets. Vinnyts'ka Oblast', C Ukraine 49°13′N 29°06′E
Lys see Leie
111 I18 **Lysá Hora** ▲ E Czech Republic 49°31′N 18°27′E
95 D16 **Lysefjorden** fjord S Norway
95 I18 **Lysekil** Västra Götaland, S Sweden 58°16′N 11°26′E
Lýsi see Akdoğan
33 V14 **Lysite** Wyoming, C USA 43°16′N 107°42′W
127 P3 **Lyskovo** Nizhegorodskaya Oblast', W Russian Federation 56°04′N 45°01′E
108 D8 **Lyss** Bern, W Switzerland 47°04′N 07°19′E
95 H22 **Lystrup** Århus, C Denmark 56°14′N 10°14′E
125 V14 **Lys'va** Permskaya Oblast', NW Russian Federation 58°04′N 57°48′E
117 P6 **Lysyanka** Cherkas'ka Oblast', C Ukraine 49°15′N 30°50′E
117 X6 **Lysychans'k** Rus. Lisichansk. Luhans'ka Oblast', E Ukraine 48°52′N 38°27′E
97 K17 **Lytham St Anne's** NW England, United Kingdom 53°45′N 03°01′W
185 I19 **Lyttelton** South Island, New Zealand 43°35′S 172°44′E
10 M17 **Lytton** British Columbia, SW Canada 50°12′N 121°34′W
119 L18 **Lyuban'** Minskaya Voblasts', S Belarus 52°48′N 28°00′E
119 L18 **Lyubanskaye Vodaskhovishcha** ⊠ C Belarus
116 M5 **Lyubar** Zhytomyrs'ka Oblast', N Ukraine 49°54′N 27°48′E
Lyubashëvka see Lyubashivka
117 O8 **Lyubashivka** Rus. Lyubashëvka. Odes'ka Oblast', SW Ukraine 47°49′N 30°18′E
119 I16 **Lyubcha** Pol. Lubcz. Hrodzyenskaya Voblasts', W Belarus 53°45′N 26°04′E
126 L4 **Lyubertsy** Moskovskaya Oblast', W Russian Federation 55°37′N 38°02′E
116 K2 **Lyubeshiv** Volyns'ka Oblast', NW Ukraine 51°46′N 25°33′E
124 M14 **Lyubim** Yaroslavskaya Oblast', NW Russian Federation 58°21′N 40°46′E
114 K11 **Lyubimets** Khaskovo, S Bulgaria 41°51′N 26°03′E
Lyublin see Lublin
116 I3 **Lyuboml'** Pol. Luboml. Volyns'ka Oblast', NW Ukraine 51°12′N 24°01′E
Lyubotin see Lyubotyn
117 U5 **Lyubotyn** Rus. Lyubotin. Kharkivs'ka Oblast', E Ukraine 49°57′N 35°57′E
126 I5 **Lyudinovo** Kaluzhskaya Oblast', W Russian Federation 53°52′N 34°28′E
127 T2 **Lyuk** Udmurtskaya Respublika, NW Russian Federation 56°55′N 52°45′E
114 M9 **Lyulyakovo** prev. Keremitlik. Burgas, E Bulgaria 42°53′N 27°05′E
119 I18 **Lyusina** Rus. Lyusino. Brestskaya Voblasts', SW Belarus 52°38′N 26°31′E
Lyusino see Lyusina

M

138 G9 **Ma'ād** Irbid, N Jordan 32°37′N 35°36′E
Ma'ai see Luqu
Maalahti see Malax
Maale see Male'
138 G13 **Ma'ān** Ma'ān, SW Jordan 30°11′N 35°45′E
138 H13 **Ma'ān** off. Muḩāfaẓat Ma'ān, var. Ma'an, Ma'ān. ◈ governorate S Jordan
93 M16 **Maaninka** Itä-Suomi, C Finland 63°10′N 27°19′E
Maanīt see Bayan, Töv, Mongolia
Maanīt see Hishig Öndör, Bulgan, Mongolia
Ma'ān, Muḩāfaẓat see Ma'ān
93 N15 **Maanselkä** Oulu, C Finland 63°54′N 28°28′E
161 Q8 **Ma'anshan** Anhui, E China 31°45′N 118°32′E
188 F16 **Maap** island Caroline Islands, W Micronesia
118 H3 **Maardu** Ger. Maart. Harjumaa, NW Estonia 59°28′N 24°56′E
Ma'aret-en-Nu'man see Ma'arrat an Nu'mān
99 K16 **Maarheeze** Noord-Brabant, SE Netherlands 51°19′N 05°37′E
Maarianhamina see Mariehamn
138 I4 **Ma'arrat an Nu'mān** var. Ma'aret-en-Nu'man, Fr. Maarret enn Naamâne. Idlib, NW Syria 35°40′N 36°40′E
Maarret enn Naamâne see Ma'arrat an Nu'mān
98 I11 **Maarssen** Utrecht, C Netherlands 52°08′N 05°03′E
Maart see Maardu
99 L17 **Maas** Fr. Meuse. ≈ W Europe see also Meuse
Maas see Meuse
99 M15 **Maasbree** Limburg, SE Netherlands 51°22′N 06°03′E
99 L17 **Maaseik** prev. Maeseyck. Limburg, NE Belgium 51°05′N 05°48′E
171 Q6 **Maasin** Leyte, C Philippines 10°10′N 124°55′E
99 L17 **Maasmechelen** Limburg, NE Belgium 50°58′N 05°42′E
98 G12 **Maassluis** Zuid-Holland, SW Netherlands 51°55′N 04°15′E
99 L18 **Maastricht** var. Maestricht; anc. Traiectum ad Mosam, Traiectum Tungorum. Limburg, SE Netherlands 50°51′N 05°42′E
183 N18 **Maatsuyker Group** island group Tasmania, SE Australia
Maba see Qujiang
83 L20 **Mabalane** Gaza, S Mozambique 23°43′S 32°37′E
25 V7 **Mabank** Texas, SW USA 32°22′N 96°06′W
97 O18 **Mablethorpe** E England, United Kingdom 53°21′N 00°14′E
171 V12 **Maboi** Papua, E Indonesia 01°00′S 134°02′E
83 M19 **Mabote** Inhambane, S Mozambique 22°03′S 34°09′E
32 J10 **Mabton** Washington, NW USA 46°13′N 120°00′W
83 H20 **Mabutsane** Southern, S Botswana 24°24′S 23°34′E
63 G19 **Macá, Cerro** ▲ S Chile 45°07′S 73°11′W
60 Q9 **Macaé** Rio de Janeiro, SE Brazil 22°21′S 41°48′W
82 N13 **Macaloge** Niassa, N Mozambique 12°27′S 35°25′E
Macan see Bonerate, Kepulauan
161 N15 **Macao** Chin. Aomen, Port. Macau. Guangdong, SE China 22°06′N 113°30′E
104 H9 **Mação** Santarém, C Portugal 39°33′N 08°00′W
58 J11 **Macapá** state capital Amapá, N Brazil 0°04′N 51°04′W
43 S17 **Macaracas** Los Santos, S Panama 07°46′N 80°31′W
55 P6 **Macare, Caño** ≈ NE Venezuela
55 Q6 **Macareo, Caño** ≈ NE Venezuela
Macarsca see Makarska
182 L12 **Macarthur** Victoria, SE Australia 38°04′S 142°02′E
MacArthur see Ormoc
56 C7 **Macas** Morona Santiago, SE Ecuador 02°22′S 78°08′W
Macassar see Makassar
59 Q14 **Macau** Rio Grande do Norte, E Brazil 05°05′S 36°37′W
Macău see Makó, Hungary
Macau see Macao
65 E24 **Macbride Head** headland East Falkland, Falkland Islands 51°25′S 57°55′W
23 V9 **Macclenny** Florida, SE USA 30°16′N 82°07′W
97 L18 **Macclesfield** C England, United Kingdom 53°16′N 02°07′W
192 F6 **Macclesfield Bank** undersea feature N South China Sea 15°50′N 114°20′E
MacCluer Gulf see Berau, Teluk
181 N7 **Macdonald, Lake** salt lake Western Australia
181 Q7 **Macdonnell Ranges** ▲▲ Northern Territory, C Australia
96 K8 **Macduff** NE Scotland, United Kingdom 57°40′N 02°29′W
104 I6 **Macedo de Cavaleiros** Bragança, N Portugal 41°31′N 06°57′W
Macedonia see Macedonia, FYR
Macedonia Central see Kentrikí Makedonía
Macedonia East and Thrace see Anatolikí Makedonía kai Thráki
113 O19 **Macedonia, FYR** off. the Former Yugoslav Republic of Macedonia, var. Macedonia, Mac. Makedonija, abbrev. FYR Macedonia, FYROM. ◆ republic SE Europe
Macedonia, the Former Yugoslav Republic of see Macedonia, FYR
Macedonia West see Dytikí Makedonía
59 Q16 **Maceió** state capital Alagoas, E Brazil 09°40′S 35°44′W
76 K15 **Macenta** SE Guinea 08°31′N 09°32′W
106 J12 **Macerata** Marche, C Italy 43°18′N 13°27′E
11 S11 **MacFarlane** ≈ Saskatchewan, C Canada
182 H7 **Macfarlane, Lake** var. Lake Mcfarlane. ◎ South Australia
Macgillicuddy's Reeks Mountains see Macgillycuddy's Reeks
97 B21 **Macgillycuddy's Reeks** var. Macgillicuddy's Reeks Mountains, Ir. Na Cruacha Dubha. ▲▲ SW Ireland
11 X16 **MacGregor** Manitoba, S Canada 49°58′N 98°49′W
149 O10 **Mach** Baluchistān, SW Pakistan 29°52′N 67°20′E
56 C6 **Machachi** Pichincha, C Ecuador 0°33′S 78°34′W
83 M19 **Machaila** Gaza, S Mozambique 22°15′S 32°57′E
Machaire Fíolta see Magherafelt
Machaire Rátha see Maghera
81 I19 **Machakos** Eastern, S Kenya 01°31′S 37°16′E
56 B8 **Machala** El Oro, SW Ecuador 03°20′S 79°57′W
83 J19 **Machaneng** Central, SE Botswana 23°12′S 27°30′E
83 M18 **Machanga** Sofala, E Mozambique 20°56′S 35°04′E
80 G13 **Machar Marshes** wetland SE Sudan
102 I8 **Machecoul** Loire-Atlantique, NW France 46°59′N 01°51′W
161 O8 **Macheng** Hubei, C China 31°10′N 115°00′E
155 J16 **Mācherla** Andhra Pradesh, C India 16°29′N 79°25′E
153 O11 **Māchhāpuchhre** ▲ C Nepal 28°30′N 83°57′E
19 T6 **Machias** Maine, NE USA 44°44′N 67°28′W
19 R3 **Machias River** ≈ Maine, NE USA
19 T6 **Machias River** ≈ Maine, NE USA
64 P5 **Machico** Madeira, Portugal, NE Atlantic Ocean 32°43′N 16°47′W
155 K16 **Machilīpatnam** var. Bandar Masulipatnam. Andhra Pradesh, E India 16°12′N 81°11′E
54 G5 **Machiques** Zulia, NW Venezuela 10°04′N 72°37′W
57 G15 **Machu Picchu** Cusco, C Peru 13°08′S 72°30′W
83 M20 **Macia** var. Vila de Macia. Gaza, S Mozambique 25°02′S 33°08′E
Macías Nguema Biyogo see Bioco, Isla de
116 M13 **Măcin** Tulcea, SE Romania 45°15′N 28°09′E
183 T4 **Macintyre River** ≈ New South Wales/Queensland, SE Australia
181 Y7 **Mackay** Queensland, NE Australia 21°10′S 149°10′E
181 O7 **Mackay, Lake** salt lake Northern Territory/Western Australia
10 M13 **Mackenzie** British Columbia, W Canada 55°18′N 123°09′W
8 I9 **Mackenzie** ≈ Northwest Territories, NW Canada
195 Y6 **Mackenzie Bay** bay Antarctica
10 J1 **Mackenzie Bay** bay NW Canada
2 D9 **Mackenzie Delta** delta Northwest Territories, NW Canada
197 P8 **Mackenzie King Island** island Queen Elizabeth Islands, Northwest Territories, N Canada
8 H8 **Mackenzie Mountains** ▲▲ Northwest Territories, NW Canada
31 Q5 **Mackinac, Straits of** ◎ Michigan, N USA
194 K5 **Mackintosh, Cape** headland Antarctica 72°52′S 60°00′W
11 R15 **Macklin** Saskatchewan, S Canada 52°19′N 109°51′W
183 V6 **Macksville** New South Wales, SE Australia 30°39′S 152°54′E
183 V5 **Maclean** New South Wales, SE Australia 29°30′S 153°15′E
83 J24 **Maclear** Eastern Cape, SE South Africa 31°05′S 28°22′E
183 U6 **Macleay River** ≈ New South Wales, SE Australia
MacLeod see Fort Macleod
180 G9 **Macleod, Lake** ◎ Western Australia
10 I6 **Macmillan** ≈ Yukon Territory, NW Canada
30 J12 **Macomb** Illinois, N USA 40°27′N 90°40′W
107 B18 **Macomer** Sardegna, Italy, C Mediterranean Sea 40°15′N 08°47′E
82 Q13 **Macomia** Cabo Delgado, NE Mozambique 12°15′S 40°06′E
103 R10 **Mâcon** anc. Matisco, Matisco Ædourum. Saône-et-Loire, C France 46°19′N 04°49′E
23 T5 **Macon** Georgia, SE USA 32°49′N 83°41′W
23 N4 **Macon** Mississippi, S USA 33°06′N 88°33′W
27 U3 **Macon** Missouri, C USA 39°44′N 92°27′W
22 J6 **Macon, Bayou** ≈ Arkansas/Louisiana, S USA
82 G13 **Macondo** Moxico, E Angola 12°31′S 23°45′E
83 M16 **Macossa** Manica, C Mozambique 17°51′S 33°54′E
11 T12 **Macoun Lake** ◎ Saskatchewan, C Canada
30 K14 **Macoupin Creek** ≈ Illinois, N USA
Macouria see Tonate
83 N18 **Macovane** Inhambane, SE Mozambique 21°30′S 35°07′E
183 N17 **Macquarie Harbour** inlet Tasmania, SE Australia
192 J13 **Macquarie Island** island New Zealand, SW Pacific Ocean
183 T8 **Macquarie, Lake** lagoon New South Wales, SE Australia
183 Q6 **Macquarie Marshes** wetland New South Wales, SE Australia
175 O13 **Macquarie Ridge** undersea feature SW Pacific Ocean 57°00′S 159°00′E
183 Q6 **Macquarie River** ≈ New South Wales, SE Australia
183 P17 **Macquarie River** ≈ Tasmania, SE Australia
195 V5 **Mac. Robertson Land** physical region Antarctica
97 C21 **Macroom** Ir. Maigh Chromtha. Cork, SW Ireland 51°54′N 08°57′W
42 G5 **Macuelizo** Santa Bárbara, NW Honduras 15°21′N 88°31′W
182 G2 **Macumba River** ≈ South Australia
57 I16 **Macusani** Puno, S Peru 14°05′S 70°24′W
56 E8 **Macusari, Río** ≈ N Peru
41 U15 **Macuspana** Tabasco, SE Mexico 17°43′N 92°36′W
138 G10 **Ma'dabā** var. Mādabā, Madeba; anc. Medeba. Ma'dabā, NW Jordan 31°44′N 35°48′E
138 G11 **Ma'dabā** off. Muḩāfazat Ma'dabā. ◈ governorate C Jordan
Mādabā see Ma'dabā
172 G2 **Madagascar** off. Democratic Republic of Madagascar, Malg. Madagasikara; prev. Malagasy Republic. ◆ republic W Indian Ocean
172 I5 **Madagascar** island W Indian Ocean
128 L17 **Madagascar Basin** undersea feature W Indian Ocean 27°00′S 53°00′E
Madagascar, Democratic Republic of see Madagascar
128 L16 **Madagascar Plain** undersea feature W Indian Ocean 19°00′S 52°00′E
67 Y14 **Madagascar Plateau** var. Madagascar Ridge, Madagascar Rise, Rus. Madagaskarskiy Khrebet. undersea feature W Indian Ocean 30°00′S 45°00′E
Madagascar Rise/Madagascar Ridge see Madagascar Plateau
Madagasikara see Madagascar
Madagaskarskiy Khrebet see Madagascar Plateau
64 N2 **Madalena** Pico, Azores, Portugal, NE Atlantic Ocean 38°32′N 28°15′W
77 Y6 **Madama** Agadez, NE Niger 21°54′N 13°43′E
114 J12 **Madan** Smolyan, S Bulgaria 41°29′N 24°56′E
155 I19 **Madanapalle** Andhra Pradesh, E India 13°33′N 78°31′E
186 D7 **Madang** Madang, N Papua New Guinea 05°14′S 145°45′E
186 C6 **Madang** ◈ province N Papua New Guinea
146 G7 **Madaniyat** Rus. Madeniyet. Qoraqalpog'iston Respublikasi, W Uzbekistan 42°48′N 59°00′E
Madanīyīn see Médenine
77 U11 **Madaoua** Tahoua, SW Niger 14°06′N 06°01′E
Madaras see Vtáčnik
153 U15 **Madaripur** Dhaka, C Bangladesh 23°09′N 90°11′E
77 U12 **Madarounfa** Maradi, S Niger 13°16′N 07°07′E
Madarska see Hungary
146 B13 **Madau** Balkan Welaýaty, W Turkmenistan 38°11′N 54°46′E
186 H9 **Madau Island** island SE Papua New Guinea
19 S1 **Madawaska** Maine, NE USA 47°19′N 68°19′W
14 J13 **Madawaska** ≈ Ontario, SE Canada
Madawaska Highlands see Haliburton Highlands
166 M4 **Madaya** Mandalay, C Myanmar (Burma) 22°12′N 96°05′E
107 K17 **Maddaloni** Campania, S Italy 41°03′N 14°23′E
29 O3 **Maddock** North Dakota, N USA 47°57′N 99°31′W
99 I14 **Made** Noord-Brabant, S Netherlands 51°41′N 04°48′E
Madeba see Ma'dabā
64 L9 **Madeira** var. Ilha de Madeira. island Madeira, Portugal, NE Atlantic Ocean
Madeira, Ilha de see Madeira
64 O5 **Madeira Islands** Port. Região Autoónoma da Madeira. ◈ autonomous region Madeira, Portugal, NE Atlantic Ocean
64 L9 **Madeira Plain** undersea feature E Atlantic Ocean
Madeira, Região Autoónoma da see Madeira Islands
64 L9 **Madeira Ridge** undersea feature E Atlantic Ocean 35°30′N 15°45′W
59 F14 **Madeira, Rio** var. Río Madera. ≈ Bolivia/Brazil see also Madera, Río
Madeira, Rio see Madera, Río
101 J25 **Mädelegabel** ▲ Austria/Germany 47°18′N 10°19′E
15 X6 **Madeleine** ≈ Québec, SE Canada
15 X5 **Madeleine, Cap de la** headland Québec, SE Canada 49°13′N 65°20′W
13 Q13 **Madeleine, Îles de la** Eng. Magdalen Islands. island group Québec, E Canada
29 U10 **Madelia** Minnesota, N USA 44°03′N 94°26′W
35 P3 **Madeline** California, W USA 41°02′N 120°28′W
30 K3 **Madeline Island** island Apostle Islands, Wisconsin, N USA
137 O15 **Maden** Elazığ, SE Turkey 38°24′N 39°42′E
145 V12 **Madeniyet** Vostochnyy Kazakhstan, E Kazakhstan 47°51′N 78°37′E

◆ Country
● Country Capital
◇ Dependent Territory
○ Dependent Territory Capital
◈ Administrative Regions
✈ International Airport
▲ Mountain
▲▲ Mountain Range
Volcano
≈ River
◎ Lake
⊠ Reservoir

◆ Country   ◇ Dependent Territory   ◆ Administrative Regions   ▲ Mountain   🌋 Volcano   ◎ Lake
● Country Capital   ○ Dependent Territory Capital   ◆ province   ✕ International Airport   ▲ Mountain Range   ≈ River   ▨ Reservoir

MALAY PENINSULA – MANTORVILLE

168 J7 Malay Peninsula *peninsula* Malaysia/Thailand
168 L7 Malaysia *off.* Malaysia, *var.* Federation of Malaysia; *prev.* the separate territories of Federation of Malaya, Sarawak and Sabah (North Borneo) and Singapore. ◆ *monarchy* SE Asia
Malaysia, Federation of *see* Malaysia
137 R14 Malazgirt Muş, E Turkey 39°09′N 42°30′E
15 R8 Malbaie ∽ Québec, SE Canada
77 T12 Malbaza Tahoua, S Niger 13°57′N 05°32′E
110 J7 Malbork *Ger.* Marienburg, Marienburg in Westpreussen. Pomorskie, N Poland 54°01′N 19°03′E
100 N9 Malchin Mecklenburg-Vorpommern, N Germany 53°43′N 12°46′E
100 M9 Malchiner See ◎ NE Germany
99 D16 Maldegem Oost-Vlaanderen, NW Belgium 51°12′N 03°27′E
98 L13 Malden Gelderland, SE Netherlands 51°47′N 05°51′E
19 O11 Malden Massachusetts, NE USA 42°25′N 71°04′W
27 Y8 Malden Missouri, C USA 36°33′N 89°58′W
191 X4 Malden Island *prev.* Independence Island. *atoll* E Kiribati
173 Q6 Maldives *off.* Maldivian Divehi, Republic of Maldives. ◆ *republic* N Indian Ocean
Maldives, Republic of *see* Maldives
Maldivian Divehi *see* Maldives
97 P21 Maldon E England, United Kingdom 51°44′N 00°40′E
61 G20 Maldonado Maldonado, S Uruguay 34°57′S 54°59′W
61 G20 Maldonado ◈ *department* S Uruguay
41 P17 Maldonado, Punta *headland* S Mexico 16°18′N 98°31′W
106 G6 Malè Trentino-Alto Adige, N Italy 46°21′N 10°51′E
151 K19 Male' *Div.* Maale. ● (Maldives) Male' Atoll, C Maldives 04°10′N 73°29′E
76 K13 Maléa *var.* Maléya. NE Guinea 11°46′N 09°43′W
Maléas, Ákra *see* Agriliá, Akrotírio
115 G22 Maléas, Akrotírio *headland* S Greece 36°25′N 23°11′E
151 K19 Male' Atoll *var.* Kaafu Atoll. *atoll* C Maldives
Malebo, Pool *see* Stanley Pool
154 E12 Mālegaon Mahārāshtra, W India 20°33′N 74°32′E
81 F15 Malek Jonglei, S Sudan 06°04′N 31°36′E
187 Q13 Malekula *var.* Malakula; *prev.* Mallicolo. *island* W Vanuatu
189 Y15 Malem Kosrae, E Micronesia 05°16′N 163°01′E
83 O15 Malema Nampula, N Mozambique 14°57′S 37°28′E
79 N23 Malemba-Nkulu Katanga, SE Dem. Rep. Congo 08°01′S 26°48′E
124 K9 Malen'ga Respublika Kareliya, NW Russian Federation 63°50′N 36°21′E
95 M20 Målerås Kalmar, S Sweden 56°55′N 15°34′E
103 O6 Malesherbes Loiret, C France 48°18′N 02°25′E
115 G18 Malesína Stereá Ellás, E Greece 38°37′N 23°15′E
Maléya *see* Maléa
127 O15 Malgobek Respublika Ingushetiya, SW Russian Federation 43°34′N 44°34′E
105 X5 Malgrat de Mar Cataluña, NE Spain 41°39′N 02°45′E
80 C9 Malha Northern Darfur, W Sudan 15°07′N 26°00′E
139 Q5 Malḩah *var.* Malḩāt. Şalāḩ ad Dīn, C Iraq 34°44′N 42°41′E
Malḩāt *see* Malḩah
32 K14 Malheur Lake ◎ Oregon, NW USA
32 L14 Malheur River ∽ Oregon, NW USA
76 I13 Mali NW Guinea 12°08′N 12°29′W
77 O9 Mali *off.* Republic of Mali, *Fr.* République du Mali; *prev.* French Sudan, Sudanese Republic. ◆ *republic* W Africa
171 Q16 Maliana W East Timor 08°57′S 125°25′E
167 O2 Mali Hka ∽ N Myanmar (Burma)
Mali Idjoš *see* Mali Idoš
112 K8 Mali Idoš *var.* Mali Idjoš, *Hung.* Kishegyes; *prev.* Krivaja. Vojvodina, N Serbia 45°43′N 19°40′E
112 K9 Mali Kanal *canal* N Serbia
171 P12 Maliku Sulawesi, N Indonesia 0°36′S 123°13′E
Malik, Wadi al *see* Milk, Wadi el
Mālikwāla *see* Malakwāl
167 N11 Mali Kyun *var.* Tavoy Island. *island* Mergui Archipelago, S Myanmar (Burma)
95 M19 Målilla Kalmar, S Sweden 57°24′N 15°49′E
112 B11 Mali Lošinj *It.* Lussinpiccolo. Primorje-Gorski Kotar, W Croatia 44°31′N 14°28′E
Malin *see* Malyn
171 P7 Malindang, Mount ▲ Mindanao, S Philippines 08°12′N 123°37′E
81 K20 Malindi Coast, SE Kenya 03°14′S 40°05′E
Malines *see* Mechelen
96 E13 Malin Head *Ir.* Cionn Mhálanna. *headland* NW Ireland 55°37′N 07°37′W
171 O11 Malino, Gunung ▲ Sulawesi, N Indonesia 0°44′N 120°45′E
113 M21 Maliq *var.* Maliqi. Korçë, SE Albania 40°45′N 20°45′E
Maliqi *see* Maliq
149 O16 Malir Sind, SE Pakistan 24°52′N 67°11′E
Mali, Republic of *see* Mali
Mali, République du *see* Mali
171 Q8 Malita Mindanao, S Philippines 06°13′N 125°39′E
155 L15 Malkangiri *var.* Malakanagiri. Orissa, E India 18°21′N 81°53′E
154 G12 Malkāpur Mahārāshtra, C India 20°52′N 76°18′E
136 B10 Malkara Tekirdağ, NW Turkey 40°54′N 26°54′E
119 J19 Mal'kavichy *Rus.* Mal'kovichi. Brestskaya Voblasts', SW Belarus 52°31′N 26°36′E
Malkiye *see* Al Mālikīyah
114 L11 Malko Sharkovo, Yazovir ⊠ SE Bulgaria
114 N11 Malko Tŭrnovo Burgas, E Bulgaria 42°00′N 27°33′E
Mal'kovichi *see* Mal'kavichy
183 R12 Mallacoota Victoria, SE Australia 37°34′S 149°45′E
96 G10 Mallaig N Scotland, United Kingdom 57°04′N 05°48′W
182 I9 Mallala South Australia 34°29′S 138°30′E
75 W9 Mallawī *var.* Mallawi. C Egypt 27°44′N 30°50′E
Mallawi *see* Mallawī
105 R5 Mallén Aragón, NE Spain 41°53′N 01°25′W
106 F5 Malles Venosta *Ger.* Mals im Vinschgau. Trentino-Alto Adige, N Italy 46°40′N 10°37′E
Mallicolo *see* Malekula
109 Q8 Mallnitz Salzburg, S Austria 46°58′N 13°09′E
105 W9 Mallorca *Eng.* Majorca; *anc.* Baleares Major. *island* Islas Baleares, Spain, W Mediterranean Sea
97 C20 Mallow *Ir.* Mala. SW Ireland 52°08′N 08°39′W
93 E15 Malm Nord-Trøndelag, C Norway 64°04′N 11°12′E
95 L19 Malmbäck Jönköping, S Sweden 57°34′N 14°30′E
92 J12 Malmberget *Lapp.* Malmivaara. Norrbotten, N Sweden 67°09′N 20°39′E
99 M20 Malmédy Liège, E Belgium 50°26′N 06°02′E
83 E25 Malmesbury Western Cape, SW South Africa 33°28′S 18°43′E
Malmivaara *see* Malmberget
95 N16 Malmköping Södermanland, C Sweden 59°08′N 16°49′E
95 K23 Malmö Skåne, S Sweden 55°36′N 13°E
95 K23 Malmo ✈ Skåne, S Sweden 55°33′N 13°23′E
45 Q16 Malmok *headland* Bonaire, S Netherlands Antilles 12°16′N 68°21′W
95 M18 Malmslätt Östergötland, S Sweden 58°25′N 15°30′E
125 R16 Malmyzh Kirovskaya Oblast', NW Russian Federation 56°30′N 50°37′E
187 Q13 Malo *island* W Vanuatu
126 J7 Maloarkhangel'sk Orlovskaya Oblast', W Russian Federation 52°25′N 36°37′E
Maloelap *see* Maloelap Atoll
189 V6 Maloelap Atoll *var.* Maloelap. *atoll* E Marshall Islands
Maloenda *see* Malunda
108 I10 Maloja Graubünden, S Switzerland 46°25′N 09°42′E
82 L12 Malole Northern, NE Zambia 10°05′S 31°37′E
171 O3 Malolos Luzon, N Philippines 14°51′N 120°49′E
18 K6 Malone New York, NE USA 44°51′N 74°18′W
79 K25 Malonga Katanga, S Dem. Rep. Congo 10°26′S 23°10′E
111 L17 Małopolskie ◈ *province* SE Poland
Malorita/Maloryta *see* Malaryta
124 K9 Maloshuyka Arkhangel'skaya Oblast', NW Russian Federation 63°43′N 37°20′E
114 G10 Mal'ovitsa ▲ W Bulgaria 42°12′N 23°19′E
145 V15 Malovodnoye Almaty, SE Kazakhstan 43°31′N 77°42′E
94 C10 Måløy Sogn Og Fjordane, S Norway 61°57′N 05°06′E
126 K4 Maloyaroslavets Kaluzhskaya Oblast', W Russian Federation 55°03′N 36°31′E
122 G7 Malozemel'skaya Tundra *physical region* NW Russian Federation
104 J10 Malpartida de Cáceres Extremadura, W Spain 39°26′N 06°30′W
104 K9 Malpartida de Plasencia Extremadura, W Spain 39°59′N 06°03′W
106 C7 Malpensa ✈ (Milano) Lombardia, N Italy 45°41′N 08°40′E
76 J6 Malqteïr *desert* N Mauritania
Mals im Vinschgau *see* Malles Venosta
118 J10 Malta Rēzekne, SE Latvia 56°19′N 27°11′E
33 V7 Malta Montana, NW USA 48°21′N 107°52′W
120 M11 Malta *off.* Republic of Malta. ◆ *republic* C Mediterranean Sea
109 R8 Malta *var.* Maltabach. ∽ S Austria
120 M11 Malta *island* Malta, C Mediterranean Sea
Maltabach *see* Malta
Malta, Canale di *see* Malta Channel
120 M11 Malta Channel *It.* Canale di Malta. *strait* Italy/Malta
83 D20 Maltahöhe Hardap, SW Namibia 24°50′S 17°00′E
Malta, Republic of *see* Malta
97 N16 Malton N England, United Kingdom 54°07′N 00°50′W
171 R13 Maluku *off.* Propinsi Maluku, *Dut.* Molukken, *Eng.* Moluccas. ◈ *province* E Indonesia
171 R13 Maluku *Dut.* Molukken, *Eng.* Moluccas; *prev.* Spice Islands. *island group* E Indonesia
Maluku, Laut *see* Molucca Sea
Maluku, Propinsi *see* Maluku
171 R11 Maluku Utara *off.* Propinsi Maluku Utara. ◈ *province* E Indonesia
Maluku Utara, Propinsi *see* Maluku Utara
77 V13 Malumfashi Katsina, N Nigeria 11°51′N 07°39′E
171 N13 Malunda *prev.* Maloenda. Sulawesi, C Indonesia 02°58′S 118°52′E
94 K13 Malung Dalarna, C Sweden 60°40′N 13°45′E
94 K13 Malungsfors Dalarna, C Sweden 60°43′N 13°34′E
186 M8 Maluu *var.* Malu'u. Malaita, N Solomon Islands 08°22′S 160°39′E
Malu'u *see* Maluu
155 D16 Mālvan Mahārāshtra, W India 16°05′N 73°28′E
Malventum *see* Benevento
27 U12 Malvern Arkansas, C USA 34°21′N 92°50′W
29 S15 Malvern Iowa, C USA 40°59′N 95°36′W
44 I13 Malvern ▲ W Jamaica 17°59′N 77°42′W
Malvina, Isla Gran *see* West Falkland
Malvinas, Islas *see* Falkland Islands
117 N4 Malyn *Rus.* Malin. Zhytomyrs'ka Oblast', N Ukraine 50°46′N 29°14′E
127 O11 Malyye Derbety Respublika Kalmykiya, SW Russian Federation 47°57′N 44°39′E
Malyy Kavkaz *see* Lesser Caucasus
123 Q6 Malyy Lyakhovskiy, Ostrov *island* NE Russian Federation
Malyy Pamir *see* Little Pamir
122 N5 Malyy Taymyr, Ostrov *island* Severnaya Zemlya, N Russian Federation
144 E10 Malyy Uzen' *Kaz.* Kishiözen. ∽ Kazakhstan/Russian Federation
122 L14 Malyy Yenisey *var.* Ka-Krem. ∽ S Russian Federation
127 S3 Mamadysh Respublika Tatarstan, W Russian Federation 55°46′N 51°22′E
117 N14 Mamaia Constanţa, E Romania 44°13′N 28°37′E
187 W14 Mamanuca Group *island group* Yasawa Group, W Fiji
146 L13 Mamash Lebap Welaýaty, E Turkmenistan 38°24′N 64°12′E
79 O17 Mambasa Orientale, NE Dem. Rep. Congo 01°20′N 29°05′E
171 X13 Mamberamo, Sungai ∽ Papua, E Indonesia
79 G15 Mambéré ∽ SW Central African Republic
79 G15 Mambéré-Kadéï ◈ *prefecture* SW Central African Republic
Mambij *see* Manbij
79 H18 Mambili ∽ W Congo
83 N18 Mambone *var.* Nova Mambone. Inhambane, E Mozambique 20°59′S 35°04′E
171 O4 Mamburao Mindoro, N Philippines 13°16′N 120°36′E
172 I16 Mamelles *island* Inner Islands, NE Seychelles
99 M25 Mamer Luxembourg, SW Luxembourg 49°37′N 06°01′E
102 L6 Mamers Sarthe, NW France 48°21′N 00°22′E
79 D15 Mamfe Sud-Ouest, W Cameroon 05°46′N 09°18′E
145 P6 Mamlyutka Severnyy Kazakhstan, N Kazakhstan 54°54′N 68°36′E
36 M15 Mammoth Arizona, SW USA 32°43′N 110°38′W
33 S12 Mammoth Hot Springs Wyoming, C USA 44°57′N 110°40′W
Mamoedjoe *see* Mamuju
119 A14 Mamonovo *Ger.* Heiligenbeil. Kaliningradskaya Oblast', W Russian Federation 54°28′N 19°57′E
57 L14 Mamoré, Río ∽ Bolivia/Brazil
76 I14 Mamou W Guinea 10°24′N 12°05′W
22 H8 Mamou Louisiana, S USA 30°37′N 92°25′W
172 I14 Mamoudzou ○ (Mayotte) C Mayotte 12°48′S 45°E
172 I3 Mampikony Mahajanga, N Madagascar 16°03′S 47°39′E
77 P16 Mampong C Ghana 07°06′N 01°20′W
110 M7 Mamry, Jezioro *Ger.* Mauersee. ◎ NE Poland
171 N13 Mamuju *prev.* Mamoedjoe. Sulawesi, S Indonesia 02°41′S 118°55′E
83 F19 Mamuno Ghanzi, W Botswana 22°15′S 20°02′E
113 K19 Mamuras *var.* Mamurasi, Mamurras. Lezhë, C Albania 41°34′N 19°42′E
Mamurasi/Mamurras *see* Mamuras
76 L16 Man W Ivory Coast 07°24′N 07°33′W
55 X9 Mana NW French Guiana 05°40′N 53°49′W
56 A6 Manabí ◈ *province* W Ecuador
42 G4 Manabique, Punta *var.* Cabo Tres Puntas. *headland* E Guatemala 15°57′N 88°37′W
54 G11 Manacacías, Río ∽ C Colombia
58 F13 Manacapuru Amazonas, N Brazil 03°16′S 60°37′W
105 Y9 Manacor Mallorca, Spain, W Mediterranean Sea 39°35′N 03°12′E
171 Q11 Manado *prev.* Menado. Sulawesi, C Indonesia 01°32′N 124°55′E
188 H5 Managaha *island* S Northern Mariana Islands
99 G20 Manage Hainaut, S Belgium 50°30′N 04°14′E
42 J10 Managua ● (Nicaragua) Managua, W Nicaragua 12°08′N 86°15′W
42 J10 Managua ◈ *department* W Nicaragua
42 J10 Managua ✈ Managua, W Nicaragua 12°07′N 86°11′W
42 J10 Managua, Lago de *var.* Xolotlán. ◎ W Nicaragua
Manah *see* Bilād Manaḩ
18 K16 Manahawkin New Jersey, NE USA 39°39′N 74°12′W
184 K11 Manaia Taranaki, North Island, New Zealand 39°33′S 174°07′E
172 J6 Manakara Fianarantsoa, SE Madagascar 22°09′S 48°E
152 J7 Manāli Himāchal Pradesh, NW India 32°12′N 77°06′E
Ma, Nam *see* Sông Ma
Manama *see* Al Manāmah
186 D6 Manam Island *island* N Papua New Guinea
67 Y13 Mananara Avaratra ∽ SE Madagascar
182 M9 Manangatang Victoria, SE Australia 35°04′S 142°53′E
172 J6 Mananjary Fianarantsoa, SE Madagascar 21°13′S 48°20′E
76 L14 Manankoro Sikasso, SW Mali 10°33′N 07°25′W
76 J12 Manantali, Lac de ⊠ W Mali
Manáos *see* Manaus
185 B23 Manapouri Southland, South Island, New Zealand 45°33′S 167°38′E
185 B23 Manapouri, Lake ◎ South Island, New Zealand
58 F13 Manaquiri Amazonas, NW Brazil 03°27′S 60°37′W
Manar *see* Mannar
158 K5 Manas Xinjiang Uygur Zizhiqu, NW China 44°16′N 86°12′E
153 U12 Manās *var.* Dangme Chu. ∽ Bhutan/India
153 P10 Manāslu *var.* Manaslu. ▲ C Nepal 28°33′N 84°33′E
147 R8 Manas, Gora ▲ Kyrgyzstan/Uzbekistan 42°17′N 71°04′E
158 K3 Manas Hu ◎ NW China
Manaslu *see* Manāslu
37 S8 Manassa Colorado, C USA 37°10′N 105°56′W
21 W4 Manassas Virginia, NE USA 38°45′N 77°28′W
45 T5 Manatí C Puerto Rico 18°26′N 66°29′W
186 E8 Manau Northern, S Papua New Guinea 08°02′S 148°00′E
54 H4 Manaure La Guajira, N Colombia 11°46′N 72°28′W
58 F12 Manaus *prev.* Manáos. *state capital* Amazonas, NW Brazil 03°06′S 60°W
136 G17 Manavgat Antalya, SW Turkey 36°47′N 31°28′E
184 M13 Manawatu ∽ North Island, New Zealand
184 L11 Manawatu-Wanganui *off.* Manawatu-Wanganui Region. ◈ *region* North Island, New Zealand
Manawatu-Wanganui Region *see* Manawatu-Wanganui
171 R7 Manay Mindanao, S Philippines 07°12′N 126°29′E
138 K2 Manbij *var.* Mambij, *Fr.* Membidj. Ḩalab, N Syria 36°32′N 37°55′E
105 N13 Mancha Real Andalucía, S Spain 37°47′N 03°37′W
102 I4 Manche ◈ *department* N France
97 L17 Manchester *Lat.* Mancunium. NW England, United Kingdom 53°30′N 02°15′W
23 S5 Manchester Georgia, SE USA 32°51′N 84°37′W
29 Y13 Manchester Iowa, C USA 42°28′N 91°27′W
21 N7 Manchester Kentucky, S USA 37°09′N 83°46′W
19 O10 Manchester New Hampshire, NE USA 42°59′N 71°26′W
20 K10 Manchester Tennessee, S USA 35°28′N 86°05′W
18 M9 Manchester Vermont, NE USA 43°09′N 73°03′W
97 L18 Manchester ✈ NW England, United Kingdom 53°21′N 02°16′W
149 P15 Manchhar Lake ◎ SE Pakistan
Man-chou-li *see* Manzhouli
129 X7 Manchurian Plain *plain* NE China
Máncio Lima *see* Japiim
Mancunium *see* Manchester
148 J15 Mand Baluchistān, SW Pakistan 26°06′N 61°58′E
Mand *see* Mand, Rūd-e
81 H25 Manda Iringa, SW Tanzania 10°30′S 34°37′E
172 H6 Mandabe Toliara, W Madagascar 21°02′S 44°56′E
162 M10 Mandah *var.* Töhöm. Dornogovĭ, SE Mongolia 44°25′N 108°18′E
95 E18 Mandal Vest-Agder, S Norway 58°02′N 07°30′E
Mandal *see* Arbulag, Hövsgöl, Mongolia
Mandal *see* Batsümber, Töv, Mongolia
166 L5 Mandalay Mandalay, C Myanmar (Burma) 21°57′N 96°04′E
166 M6 Mandalay ◈ *division* C Myanmar (Burma)
162 L9 Mandalgovĭ Dundgovĭ, C Mongolia 45°47′N 106°18′E
139 V7 Mandalī Diyālá, E Iraq 33°43′N 45°33′E
162 K10 Mandal-Ovoo *var.* Sharhulsan. Ömnögovĭ, S Mongolia 44°43′N 104°06′E
95 E18 Mandalselva ∽ S Norway
163 P11 Mandalt *var.* Sonid Zuoqi. Nei Mongol Zizhiqu, N China 43°49′N 113°36′E
28 M5 Mandan North Dakota, N USA 46°49′N 100°53′W
Mandargiri Hill *see* Mandār Hill
153 R14 Mandār Hill *prev.* Mandargiri Hill. Bihār, NE India 24°51′N 87°03′E
170 M13 Mandar, Teluk *bay* Sulawesi, C Indonesia
107 C19 Mandas Sardegna, Italy, C Mediterranean Sea 39°40′N 09°07′E
Mandasor *see* Mandsaur
81 L16 Mandera North Eastern, NE Kenya 03°56′N 41°53′E
33 V13 Manderson Wyoming, C USA 44°13′N 107°55′W
44 J12 Mandeville C Jamaica 18°02′N 77°31′W
22 K9 Mandeville Louisiana, S USA 30°21′N 90°04′W
152 I7 Mandi Himāchal Pradesh, NW India 31°40′N 76°59′E
76 K14 Mandiana E Guinea 10°37′N 08°39′W
149 U10 Mandi Būrewāla *var.* Būrewāla. Punjab, E Pakistan 30°05′N 72°47′E
152 G9 Mandi Dabwāli Haryāna, NW India 29°56′N 74°40′E
Mandidzudzure *see* Chimanimani
83 M15 Mandié Manica, NW Mozambique 16°27′S 33°28′E
83 N14 Mandimba Niassa, N Mozambique 14°21′S 35°40′E
57 Q19 Mandioré, Laguna ◎ E Bolivia
154 J10 Mandla Madhya Pradesh, C India 22°36′N 80°23′E
83 M20 Mandlakazi *var.* Manjacaze. Gaza, S Mozambique 24°47′S 33°50′E
95 E24 Mandø *var.* Manø. *island* W Denmark
Mandoúdhion/Mandoudi *see* Mantoúdi
115 G19 Mándra Attikí, C Greece 38°04′N 23°30′E
172 I7 Mandrare ∽ S Madagascar
114 M10 Mandra, Yazovir *salt lake* SE Bulgaria
107 L23 Mandrazzi, Portella *pass* Sicilia, Italy, C Mediterranean Sea
172 J3 Mandritsara Mahajanga, N Madagascar 15°49′S 48°50′E
143 O13 Mand, Rūd-e *var.* Mand. ∽ S Iran
154 F9 Mandsaur *prev.* Mandasor. Madhya Pradesh, C India 24°03′N 75°10′E
154 F11 Māndu Madhya Pradesh, C India 22°22′N 75°24′E
169 W8 Mandul, Pulau *island* N Indonesia
83 G15 Mandundu Western, W Zambia 16°34′S 22°18′E
180 I13 Mandurah Western Australia 32°31′S 115°41′E
107 P18 Manduria Puglia, SE Italy 40°24′N 17°38′E
155 G20 Mandya Karnātaka, C India 12°34′N 76°55′E
77 P12 Mané C Burkina 12°59′N 01°21′W
106 E8 Manerbio Lombardia, NW Italy 45°22′N 10°09′E
Manevichi *see* Manevychi
116 K3 Manevychi *Pol.* Maniewicze, *Rus.* Manevichi. Volyns'ka Oblast', NW Ukraine 51°18′N 25°29′E
107 N16 Manfredonia Puglia, SE Italy 41°38′N 15°54′E
107 N16 Manfredonia, Golfo di *gulf* Adriatic Sea, N Mediterranean Sea
77 P13 Manga C Burkina 11°41′N 01°04′W
59 L16 Mangabeiras, Chapada das ▲ E Brazil
79 J20 Mangai Bandundu, W Dem. Rep. Congo 03°58′S 19°32′E
190 L17 Mangaia *island group* S Cook Islands
184 M9 Mangakino Waikato, North Island, New Zealand 38°23′S 175°47′E
153 V12 Mangaldai Assam, NE India 26°26′N 92°02′E
116 M15 Mangalia *anc.* Callatis. Constanţa, SE Romania 43°48′N 28°35′E
78 J11 Mangalmé Guéra, SE Chad 12°26′N 19°37′E
155 E19 Mangalore Karnātaka, W India 12°54′N 74°51′E
191 Y13 Mangareva *var.* Magareva. *island* Îles Tuamotu, SE French Polynesia
83 I23 Mangaung Free State, C South Africa 29°10′S 26°19′E
Mangaung *see* Bloemfontein
154 K9 Mangawān Madhya Pradesh, C India 24°39′N 81°33′E
184 M11 Mangaweka Manawatu-Wanganui, North Island, New Zealand 39°49′S 175°47′E
184 N11 Mangaweka ▲ North Island, New Zealand 39°51′S 176°06′E
79 P17 Mangbwalu Orientale, NE Dem. Rep. Congo 02°06′N 30°04′E
101 L24 Mangfall ∽ SE Germany
169 P13 Manggar Pulau Belitung, W Indonesia 02°52′S 108°13′E
166 M2 Mangin Range ▲▲ N Myanmar (Burma)
139 R1 Mangish Dahūk, N Iraq 37°03′N 43°04′E
144 F15 Mangistau *Kaz.* Mangqystaū Oblysy; *prev.* Mangyshlaskaya. ◈ *province* SW Kazakhstan
146 H8 Mang'it *Rus.* Mangit. Qoraqalpog'iston Respublikasi, W Uzbekistan 42°06′N 60°02′E
Mangit *see* Mang'it
54 A13 Manglares, Cabo *headland* SW Colombia 01°36′N 79°02′W
149 V6 Mangla Reservoir ⊠ NE Pakistan
159 N9 Mangnai *var.* Lao Mangnai. Qinghai, C China 37°52′N 91°45′E
Mango *see* Mago, Fiji
Mango *see* Sansanné-Mango, Togo
Mangoche *see* Mangochi
83 N14 Mangochi *var.* Mangoche; *prev.* Fort Johnston. Southern, SE Malawi 14°30′S 35°15′E
77 N14 Mangodara SW Burkina 09°49′N 04°22′W
172 H6 Mangoky ∽ W Madagascar
171 Q12 Mangole, Pulau *island* Kepulauan Sula, E Indonesia
184 J2 Mangonui Northland, North Island, New Zealand 35°00′S 173°30′E
Mangqystaū Oblysy *see* Mangistau
Mangqystaū Shyghanaghy *see* Mangyshlakskiy Zaliv
Mangshi *see* Luxi
104 H7 Mangualde Viseu, N Portugal 40°36′N 07°46′W
61 H18 Mangueira, Lagoa ◎ S Brazil
77 X6 Manguéni, Plateau du ▲ NE Niger
163 T4 Mangui Nei Mongol Zizhiqu, N China 52°02′N 122°13′E
26 K11 Mangum Oklahoma, C USA 34°52′N 99°30′W
79 O18 Mangurdjipa Nord-Kivu, E Dem. Rep. Congo 0°28′N 28°33′E
83 L16 Mangwendi Mashonaland East, E Zimbabwe 18°22′S 31°24′E
144 F15 Mangyshlak, Plato *plateau* SW Kazakhstan
144 E14 Mangyshlakskiy Zaliv *Kaz.* Mangqystaū Shyghanaghy. *gulf* SW Kazakhstan
Mangyshlaskaya *see* Mangistau
162 E7 Manhan *var.* Tögrög. Hovd, W Mongolia 47°24′N 92°06′E
27 O4 Manhattan Kansas, C USA 39°11′N 96°35′W
99 L21 Manhay Luxembourg, SE Belgium 50°13′N 05°43′E
83 L21 Manhiça *prev.* Vila de Manhiça. Maputo, S Mozambique 25°25′S 32°49′E
83 L21 Manhoca Maputo, S Mozambique 26°49′S 32°36′E
59 N20 Manhuaçu Minas Gerais, SE Brazil 20°16′S 42°01′W
117 W9 Manhush *prev.* Pershotravneve. Donets'ka Oblast', E Ukraine 47°03′N 37°20′E
54 H10 Maní Casanare, C Colombia 04°50′N 72°15′W
143 R11 Mānī Kermān, C Iran
83 M17 Manica *var.* Vila de Manica. Manica, W Mozambique 18°56′S 32°52′E
83 M17 Manica *off.* Província de Manica. ◈ *province* W Mozambique
83 L17 Manicaland ◈ *province* E Zimbabwe
Manica, Província de *see* Manica
15 U5 Manic Deux, Réservoir ⊠ Québec, SE Canada
Manich *see* Manych
59 F14 Manicoré Amazonas, N Brazil 05°48′S 61°16′W
13 N11 Manicouagan Québec, SE Canada 50°40′N 68°46′W
13 N11 Manicouagan ∽ Québec, SE Canada
15 U6 Manicouagan, Péninsule de *peninsula* Québec, SE Canada
13 N11 Manicouagan, Réservoir ◎ Québec, E Canada
15 T4 Manic Trois, Réservoir ⊠ Québec, SE Canada
79 M20 Maniema *off.* Région du Maniema. ◈ *region* E Dem. Rep. Congo
Maniema, Région du *see* Maniema
Maniewicze *see* Manevychi
160 F8 Maniganggo Sichuan, C China 32°01′N 99°04′E
11 Y15 Manigotagan Manitoba, S Canada 51°06′N 96°18′W
153 R13 Manihāri Bihār, N India 25°21′N 87°37′E
191 U9 Manihi *island* Îles Tuamotu, C French Polynesia
190 L13 Manihiki *atoll* N Cook Islands
175 U8 Manihiki Plateau *undersea feature* C Pacific Ocean
196 M14 Maniitsoq *var.* Manîtsoq, *Dan.* Sukkertoppen. ◈ Kitaa, S Greenland
153 T15 Manikganj Dhaka, C Bangladesh 23°52′N 90°00′E
152 M14 Mānikpur Uttar Pradesh, N India 25°04′N 81°06′E
171 N4 Manila *off.* City of Manila. ● (Philippines) Luzon, N Philippines 14°34′N 120°59′E
27 Y9 Manila Arkansas, C USA 35°52′N 90°10′W
Manila, City of *see* Manila
189 N16 Manila Reef *reef* W Micronesia
183 T6 Manilla New South Wales, SE Australia 30°44′S 150°43′E
192 P6 Maniloa *island* Tongatapu Group, S Tonga
123 U8 Manily Koryakskiy Avtonomnyy Okrug, E Russian Federation 62°33′N 165°03′E
171 V12 Manim, Pulau *island* E Indonesia
168 I11 Maninjau, Danau ◎ Sumatera, W Indonesia
153 W13 Manipur ◈ *state* NE India
153 X14 Manipur Hills *hill range* E India
136 C14 Manisa *var.* Manissa, *prev.* Saruhan; *anc.* Magnesia. Manisa, W Turkey 38°36′N 27°29′E
136 C13 Manisa *var.* Manissa. ◈ *province* W Turkey
Manissa *see* Manisa
31 O7 Manistee Michigan, N USA 44°14′N 86°19′W
31 P7 Manistee River ∽ Michigan, N USA
31 O4 Manistique Michigan, N USA 45°57′N 86°15′W
31 P4 Manistique Lake ◎ Michigan, N USA
11 W13 Manitoba ◈ *province* S Canada
11 X16 Manitoba, Lake ◎ Manitoba, S Canada
11 X17 Manitou Manitoba, S Canada 49°12′N 98°28′W
31 N2 Manitou Island *island* Michigan, N USA
14 H11 Manitou Lake ◎ Ontario, SE Canada
12 G15 Manitoulin Island *island* Ontario, S Canada
37 T5 Manitou Springs Colorado, C USA 38°51′N 104°56′W
14 G12 Manitouwabing Lake ◎ Ontario, S Canada
12 E12 Manitouwadge Ontario, S Canada 49°14′N 85°51′W
12 G15 Manitowaning Manitoulin Island, Ontario, S Canada 45°44′N 81°50′W
14 B7 Manitowik Lake ◎ Ontario, S Canada
31 N7 Manitowoc Wisconsin, N USA 44°04′N 87°40′W
Manîtsoq *see* Maniitsoq
139 O7 Mānī', Wādī al *dry watercourse* W Iraq
12 J14 Maniwaki Québec, SE Canada 46°22′N 75°58′W
171 W13 Maniwori Papua, E Indonesia 02°49′S 136°00′E
54 E10 Manizales Caldas, W Colombia 05°03′N 73°52′W
112 F11 Manjača ▲ NW Bosnia and Herzegovina
Manjacaze *see* Mandlakazi
180 J14 Manjimup Western Australia 34°18′S 116°14′E
109 V4 Mank Niederösterreich, C Austria 48°06′N 15°13′E
79 I17 Mankanza Equateur, NW Dem. Rep. Congo 01°40′N 19°08′E
153 N12 Mankāpur Uttar Pradesh, N India 27°03′N 82°12′E
26 M3 Mankato Kansas, C USA 39°48′N 98°13′W
29 U10 Mankato Minnesota, N USA 44°10′N 94°00′W
117 O7 Man'kivka Cherkas'ka Oblast', C Ukraine 48°58′N 30°10′E
76 M15 Mankono C Ivory Coast 08°01′N 06°09′W
11 T17 Mankota Saskatchewan, S Canada 49°25′N 107°05′W
155 K23 Mankulam Northern Province, N Sri Lanka 09°07′N 80°27′E
162 L10 Manlay *var.* Üydzen. Ömnögovĭ, S Mongolia 44°08′N 106°48′E
39 Q9 Manley Hot Springs Alaska, USA 65°00′N 150°37′W
18 H10 Manlius New York, NE USA 43°00′N 75°58′W
105 W5 Manlleu Cataluña, NE Spain 41°59′N 02°17′E
29 V11 Manly Iowa, C USA 43°17′N 93°12′W
154 E13 Manmād Mahārāshtra, W India 20°15′N 74°29′E
182 J7 Mannahill South Australia 32°29′S 139°58′E
155 J23 Mannar *var.* Manar. Northern Province, NW Sri Lanka 09°01′N 79°53′E
155 I24 Mannar, Gulf of *gulf* India/Sri Lanka
155 J23 Mannar Island *island* N Sri Lanka
Mannersdorf *see* Mannersdorf am Leithagebirge
109 Y5 Mannersdorf am Leithagebirge *var.* Mannersdorf. Niederösterreich, E Austria 47°59′N 16°36′E
109 Y6 Mannersdorf an der Rabnitz Burgenland, E Austria 47°25′N 16°32′E
101 G20 Mannheim Baden-Württemberg, SW Germany 49°29′N 08°29′E
11 O12 Manning Alberta, W Canada 56°53′N 117°39′W
29 T14 Manning Iowa, C USA 41°54′N 95°03′W
28 K5 Manning North Dakota, N USA 47°15′N 102°48′W
21 S13 Manning South Carolina, SE USA 33°42′N 80°12′W
191 Y2 Manning, Cape *headland* Kiritimati, NE Kiribati 02°02′N 157°26′W
21 S3 Mannington West Virginia, NE USA 39°31′N 80°20′W
182 A1 Mann Ranges ▲▲ South Australia
107 C19 Mannu ∽ Sardegna, Italy, C Mediterranean Sea
11 R14 Mannville Alberta, SW Canada 53°19′N 111°08′W
76 J15 Mano ∽ Liberia/Sierra Leone
Manø *see* Mandø
39 O13 Manokotak Alaska, USA 59°00′N 158°58′W
171 V12 Manokwari Papua, E Indonesia 0°53′S 134°05′E
79 N22 Manono Shaba, SE Dem. Rep. Congo 07°18′S 27°25′E
25 T10 Manor Texas, SW USA 30°20′N 97°33′W
97 D16 Manorhamilton *Ir.* Cluainín. Leitrim, NW Ireland 54°18′N 08°10′W
103 S15 Manosque Alpes-de-Haute-Provence, SE France 43°50′N 05°47′E
12 L11 Manouane, Lac ◎ Québec, SE Canada
163 W12 Manp'o *var.* Manp'ojin. NW North Korea 41°10′N 126°24′E
Manp'ojin *see* Manp'o
191 T4 Manra *prev.* Sydney Island. *atoll* Phoenix Islands, C Kiribati
105 V5 Manresa Cataluña, NE Spain 41°43′N 01°50′E
152 H9 Mānsa Punjab, NW India 30°00′N 75°25′E
82 J12 Mansa *prev.* Fort Rosebery. Luapula, N Zambia 11°14′S 28°55′E
76 G12 Mansa Konko C Gambia 13°26′N 15°29′W
15 Q11 Manseau Québec, SE Canada 46°23′N 71°59′W
149 U5 Mānsehra North-West Frontier Province, NW Pakistan 34°23′N 73°18′E
9 Q9 Mansel Island *island* Nunavut, NE Canada
183 O12 Mansfield Victoria, SE Australia 37°04′S 146°06′E
97 M18 Mansfield C England, United Kingdom 53°09′N 01°11′W
27 S11 Mansfield Arkansas, C USA 35°03′N 94°15′W
22 G6 Mansfield Louisiana, S USA 32°02′N 93°42′W
19 O12 Mansfield Massachusetts, NE USA 42°00′N 71°11′W
31 T12 Mansfield Ohio, N USA 40°45′N 82°31′W
18 G12 Mansfield Pennsylvania, NE USA 41°46′N 77°02′W
18 M7 Mansfield, Mount ▲ Vermont, NE USA 44°31′N 72°49′W
59 M16 Mansidão Bahia, E Brazil 10°46′S 44°04′W
102 L11 Mansle Charente, W France 45°52′N 00°11′E
76 G12 Mansôa C Guinea-Bissau 12°08′N 15°18′W
47 V8 Manso, Rio ∽ C Brazil
Manşūra *see* Al Manşūrah
Mansurabad *see* Mehrān, Rūd-e
56 A6 Manta Manabí, W Ecuador 0°59′S 80°44′W
56 A6 Manta, Bahía de *bay* W Ecuador
57 F14 Mantaro, Río ∽ C Peru
35 O8 Manteca California, W USA 37°48′N 121°13′W
54 J7 Mantecal Apure, C Venezuela 07°34′N 69°07′W
31 N11 Manteno Illinois, N USA 41°15′N 87°49′W
21 Y9 Manteo Roanoke Island, North Carolina, SE USA 35°54′N 75°42′W
Mantes-Gassicourt *see* Mantes-la-Jolie
103 N5 Mantes-la-Jolie *prev.* Mantes-Gassicourt, Mantes-sur-Seine; *anc.* Medunta. Yvelines, N France 48°59′N 01°43′E
Mantes-sur-Seine *see* Mantes-la-Jolie
36 L5 Manti Utah, W USA 39°16′N 111°38′W
Mantinea *see* Mantíneia
115 F20 Mantíneia *anc.* Mantinea. *site of ancient city* Pelopónnisos, S Greece
59 M21 Mantiqueira, Serra da ▲ S Brazil
29 W10 Mantorville Minnesota, N USA 44°04′N 92°45′W

◆ Country ● Country Capital ◇ Dependent Territory ○ Dependent Territory Capital ◈ Administrative Regions ✈ International Airport ▲ Mountain ▲▲ Mountain Range Volcano ∽ River ◎ Lake ⊠ Reservoir

MANTOÚDI – MARTHAGUY CREEK

115 G17 **Mantoúdi** *var.* Mandoudi; *prev.* Mandoúdhion. Évvoia, C Greece 38°47′N 23°29′E
Mantoue *see* Mantova
106 F8 **Mantova** *Eng.* Mantua, *Fr.* Mantoue. Lombardia, NW Italy 45°10′N 10°47′E
93 M19 **Mäntsälä** Etelä-Suomi, S Finland 60°38′N 25°21′E
93 L17 **Mänttä** Länsi-Suomi, W Finland 62°00′N 24°36′E
Mantua *see* Mantova
125 O14 **Manturovo** Kostromskaya Oblast', NW Russian Federation 58°19′N 44°42′E
93 M18 **Mäntyharju** Itä-Suomi, SE Finland 61°25′N 26°53′E
92 M13 **Mäntyjärvi** Lappi, N Finland 66°00′N 27°35′E
190 L16 **Manuae** *island* S Cook Islands
191 Q10 **Manuae** *atoll* Îles Sous le Vent, W French Polynesia
192 L16 **Manu'a Islands** *island group* E American Samoa
40 L5 **Manuel Benavides** Chihuahua, N Mexico 29°07′N 103°52′W
61 D21 **Manuel J. Cobo** Buenos Aires, E Argentina 35°49′S 57°54′W
58 M12 **Manuel Luís, Recife** *reef* E Brazil
61 F15 **Manuel Viana** Rio Grande do Sul, S Brazil 29°33′S 55°28′W
59 I14 **Manuel Zinho** Pará, N Brazil 07°21′S 54°47′W
191 V11 **Manuhangi** *atoll* Îles Tuamotu, C French Polynesia
185 E22 **Manuherikia** ≈ South Island, New Zealand
171 P13 **Manui, Pulau** *island* N Indonesia
Manukau *see* Manurewa
184 L6 **Manukau Harbour** *harbor* North Island, New Zealand
191 Z2 **Manulu Lagoon** ◎ Kiritimati, E Kiribati
182 J7 **Manunda Creek** *seasonal river* South Australia
57 K15 **Manupari, Río** ≈ N Bolivia
184 L6 **Manurewa** *var.* Manukau. Auckland, North Island, New Zealand 37°01′S 174°55′E
57 K15 **Manurimi, Río** ≈ NW Bolivia
186 D5 **Manus** ◈ *province* N Papua New Guinea
186 D5 **Manus Island** *var.* Great Admiralty Island. *island* N Papua New Guinea
171 T16 **Manuwui** Pulau Babar, E Indonesia 07°47′S 129°39′E
29 Q3 **Manvel** North Dakota, N USA 48°07′N 97°15′W
33 Z14 **Manville** Wyoming, C USA 42°45′N 104°38′W
22 G6 **Many** Louisiana, S USA 31°34′N 93°28′W
81 I22 **Manyara** ◈ NE Tanzania
81 H21 **Manyara, Lake** ◎ NE Tanzania
126 L12 **Manych** *var.* Manich. ≈ SW Russian Federation
83 H14 **Manyinga** North Western, NW Zambia 13°28′S 24°18′E
105 O11 **Manzanares** Castilla-La Mancha, C Spain 39°00′N 03°23′W
44 H7 **Manzanillo** Granma, E Cuba 20°21′N 77°07′W
40 K14 **Manzanillo** Colima, SW Mexico 19°00′N 104°19′W
40 K14 **Manzanillo, Bahía** *bay* SW Mexico
37 S11 **Manzano Mountains** ▲▲ New Mexico, SW USA
37 R12 **Manzano Peak** ▲ New Mexico, SW USA 34°35′N 106°27′W
163 R6 **Manzhouli** *var.* Man-chou-li. Nei Mongol Zizhiqu, N China 49°36′N 117°28′E
Manzil Bū Ruqaybah *see* Menzel Bourguiba
139 X9 **Manzilīyah** Maysān, E Iraq 32°26′N 47°01′E
83 L21 **Manzini** *prev.* Bremersdorp. C Swaziland 26°30′S 31°22′E
83 L21 **Manzini** ✕ (Mbabane) C Swaziland 26°36′S 31°25′E
78 G10 **Mao** Kanem, W Chad 14°06′N 15°17′E
45 N8 **Mao** NW Dominican Republic 19°37′N 71°04′W
Maó *see* Mahón
Maoemere *see* Maumere
159 W9 **Maojing** Gansu, N China 36°26′N 106°36′E
171 Y14 **Maoke, Pegunungan** *Dut.* Sneeuw-gebergte, *Eng.* Snow Mountains. ▲▲ Papua, E Indonesia
Maol Réidh, Caoc *see* Mweelrea
160 M15 **Maoming** Guangdong, S China 21°46′N 110°51′E
160 H8 **Maoxian** *var.* Mao Xian; *prev.* Fengyizhen. Sichuan, C China 31°42′N 103°48′E
Mao Xian *see* Maoxian
83 L19 **Mapai** Gaza, SW Mozambique 22°52′S 32°00′E
158 H15 **Mapam Yumco** ◎ W China
83 I15 **Mapanza** Southern, S Zambia 16°16′S 26°54′E
54 J4 **Mapararí** Falcón, N Venezuela 10°52′N 69°27′W
41 U17 **Mapastepec** Chiapas, SE Mexico 15°28′N 93°00′W
169 V9 **Mapat, Pulau** *island* N Indonesia
171 Y15 **Mapi** Papua, E Indonesia 07°02′S 139°24′E
171 V11 **Mapia, Kepulauan** *island group* E Indonesia
40 L8 **Mapimí** Durango, C Mexico 25°50′N 103°50′W
83 N19 **Mapinhane** Inhambane, SE Mozambique 22°14′S 35°07′E
55 N7 **Mapire** Monagas, NE Venezuela 07°48′N 64°40′W
11 S17 **Maple Creek** Saskatchewan, S Canada 49°55′N 109°28′W
31 Q9 **Maple River** ≈ Michigan, N USA
29 P7 **Maple River** ≈ North Dakota/South Dakota, N USA
29 S13 **Mapleton** Iowa, C USA 42°10′N 95°47′W
29 U10 **Mapleton** Minnesota, N USA 43°55′N 93°57′W
29 R5 **Mapleton** North Dakota, N USA 46°51′N 97°04′W
32 F13 **Mapleton** Oregon, NW USA 44°01′N 123°55′W
36 L3 **Mapleton** Utah, W USA 40°07′N 111°37′W
192 K5 **Mapmaker Seamounts** *undersea feature* N Pacific Ocean 25°00′N 165°00′E
186 B6 **Maprik** East Sepik, NW Papua New Guinea 03°38′S 143°02′E
83 L21 **Maputo** *prev.* Lourenço Marques. ● (Mozambique) Maputo, S Mozambique 25°58′S 32°35′E
83 L21 **Maputo** ◈ *province* S Mozambique
67 V14 **Maputo** ≈ S Mozambique
83 L21 **Maputo** ✕ Maputo, S Mozambique 25°47′S 32°36′E
Maqanshy *see* Makanchi
Maqat *see* Makat
113 K19 **Maqë** ≈ NW Albania
113 M19 **Maqellarë** Dibër, C Albania 41°36′N 20°29′E
159 S12 **Maqên** *var.* Dawu; *prev.* Dawu. Qinghai, C China 34°32′N 100°17′E
159 S11 **Maqên Kangri** ▲ C China 34°44′N 99°25′E
141 X7 **Maqiz al Kurbā** N Oman 24°13′N 56°48′E
159 U12 **Maqu** *var.* Nyinma. Gansu, C China 34°02′N 102°00′E
104 M9 **Maqueda** Castilla-La Mancha, C Spain 40°04′N 04°22′W
82 B9 **Maquela do Zombo** Uíge, NW Angola 06°06′S 15°12′E
63 I16 **Maquinchao** Río Negro, C Argentina 41°19′S 68°47′W
29 Z13 **Maquoketa** Iowa, C USA 42°03′N 90°42′W
29 Y13 **Maquoketa River** ≈ Iowa, C USA
14 F13 **Mar** Ontario, S Canada 44°48′N 81°12′W
95 F14 **Mår** ◎ S Norway
81 G19 **Mara** ◈ *region* N Tanzania
58 D12 **Maraã** Amazonas, NW Brazil 01°48′S 65°21′W
191 P8 **Maraa** Tahiti, W French Polynesia 17°44′S 149°34′W
191 O8 **Maraa, Pointe** *headland* Tahiti, W French Polynesia 17°44′S 149°34′W
59 K14 **Marabá** Pará, NE Brazil 05°23′S 49°10′W
54 H5 **Maracaibo** Zulia, NW Venezuela 10°40′N 71°39′W
Maracaibo, Gulf of *see* Venezuela, Golfo de
54 H5 **Maracaibo, Lago de** *var.* Lake Maracaibo. *inlet* NW Venezuela
Maracaibo, Lake *see* Maracaibo, Lago de
58 K10 **Maracá, Ilha de** *island* NE Brazil
59 H20 **Maracaju, Serra de** ▲▲ S Brazil
58 I11 **Maracanaquará, Planalto** ▲▲ NE Brazil
54 L5 **Maracay** Aragua, N Venezuela 10°15′N 67°36′W
Marada *see* Marādah
75 R9 **Marādah** *var.* Marada. N Libya 29°16′N 19°29′E
77 U12 **Maradi** Maradi, S Niger 13°30′N 07°05′E
77 U11 **Maradi** ◈ *department* S Niger
81 E21 **Maragarazi** *var.* Muragarazi. ≈ Burundi/Tanzania
Maragha *see* Marāgheh
142 J3 **Marāgheh** *var.* Maragha. Āžarbāyjān-e Khāvarī, NW Iran 37°21′N 46°14′E
141 P7 **Marāh** *var.* Marrāt. Ar Riyāḍ, C Saudi Arabia 25°04′N 45°30′E
55 N11 **Marahuaca, Cerro** ▲ S Venezuela 03°37′N 65°25′W
27 R5 **Marais des Cygnes River** ≈ Kansas/Missouri, C USA
58 L11 **Marajó, Baía de** *bay* N Brazil
58 K12 **Marajó, Ilha de** *island* N Brazil
191 O2 **Marakei** *atoll* Tungaru, W Kiribati
Marakesh *see* Marrakech
81 I18 **Maralal** Rift Valley, C Kenya 01°05′N 36°42′E
83 G21 **Maralaleng** Kgalagadi, S Botswana 25°42′S 22°39′E
145 U8 **Maraldy, Ozero** ◎ NE Kazakhstan
182 C5 **Maralinga** South Australia 30°16′S 131°35′E
Máramarossziget *see* Sighetu Marmaţiei
187 N9 **Maramasike** *var.* Small Malaita. *island* N Solomon Islands
Maramba *see* Livingstone
194 H3 **Marambio** *Argentinian research station* Antarctica 64°22′S 57°18′W
116 H9 **Maramureş** ◈ *county* NW Romania
36 L15 **Marana** Arizona, SW USA 32°24′N 111°12′W
105 P7 **Maranchón** Castilla-La Mancha, C Spain 41°02′N 02°11′W
142 J2 **Marand** *var.* Merend. Āžarbāyjān-e Sharqī, NW Iran 38°25′N 45°40′E
Marandellas *see* Marondera
58 L13 **Maranhão** *off.* Estado do Maranhão. ◈ *state* E Brazil
104 H10 **Maranhão, Barragem do** ⊠ C Portugal
Maranhão, Estado do *see* Maranhão
149 O11 **Mārān, Koh-i** ▲ SW Pakistan 29°24′N 66°50′E
106 J7 **Marano, Laguna di** *lagoon* NE Italy
56 E9 **Marañón, Río** ≈ N Peru
102 J10 **Marans** Charente-Maritime, W France 46°19′N 00°58′W
83 M20 **Marão** Inhambane, S Mozambique 24°15′S 34°09′E
185 B23 **Mararoa** ≈ South Island, New Zealand
Maraş/Marash *see* Kahramanmaraş
107 M19 **Maratea** Basilicata, S Italy 39°57′N 15°44′E
104 G11 **Marateca** Setúbal, S Portugal 38°34′N 08°40′W
115 B20 **Marathiá, Akrotírio** *headland* Zákynthos, Iónia Nisiá, Greece, C Mediterranean Sea 37°39′N 20°49′E
12 E12 **Marathon** Ontario, S Canada 48°44′N 86°23′W
23 Y17 **Marathon** Florida Keys, Florida, SE USA 24°42′N 81°05′W
24 L10 **Marathon** Texas, SW USA 30°10′N 103°14′W
Marathón *see* Marathónas
115 H19 **Marathónas** *prev.* Marathón. Attikí, C Greece 38°09′N 23°57′E
169 W9 **Maratua, Pulau** *island* N Indonesia
59 O18 **Maraú** Bahia, SE Brazil 14°07′S 39°02′W
143 R3 **Marāveh Tappeh** Golestān, N Iran 37°53′N 55°57′E
24 L11 **Maravillas Creek** ≈ Texas, SW USA
186 D8 **Marawaka** Eastern Highlands, C Papua New Guinea 06°56′S 145°54′E
171 Q7 **Marawi** Mindanao, S Philippines 07°59′N 124°16′E
137 Y11 **Mārāzā** *Rus.* Maraza. E Azerbaijan 40°32′N 48°56′E
Maraza *see* Mārāzā
Marbat *see* Mirbāţ
104 L16 **Marbella** Andalucía, S Spain 36°31′N 04°50′W
180 J7 **Marble Bar** Western Australia 21°13′S 119°48′E
36 L9 **Marble Canyon** *canyon* Arizona, SW USA
25 S10 **Marble Falls** Texas, SW USA 30°34′N 98°16′W
27 Y7 **Marble Hill** Missouri, C USA 37°18′N 89°58′W
33 T15 **Marbleton** Wyoming, C USA 42°31′N 110°06′W
Marburg *see* Marburg an der Lahn, Germany
Marburg *see* Maribor, Slovenia
101 H16 **Marburg an der Lahn** *hist.* Marburg. Hessen, W Germany 50°49′N 08°46′E
111 H23 **Marcal** ≈ W Hungary
42 G7 **Marcala** La Paz, SW Honduras 14°11′N 88°00′W
111 H24 **Marcali** Somogy, SW Hungary 46°33′N 17°29′E
83 A16 **Marca, Ponta da** *headland* SW Angola 16°31′S 11°42′E
59 I16 **Marcelândia** Mato Grosso, W Brazil 11°18′S 54°49′W
27 T3 **Marceline** Missouri, C USA 39°42′N 92°57′W
60 I13 **Marcelino Ramos** Rio Grande do Sul, S Brazil 27°31′S 51°57′W
55 Y12 **Marcel, Mont** ▲ S French Guiana 02°32′N 53°00′W
97 O19 **March** E England, United Kingdom 52°37′N 00°13′E
109 Z3 **March** *var.* Morava. ≈ C Europe *see also* Morava
March *see* Morava
106 I12 **Marche** *Eng.* Marches. ◈ *region* C Italy
103 N11 **Marche** *cultural region* C France
99 J21 **Marche-en-Famenne** Luxembourg, SE Belgium 50°13′N 05°21′E
104 K14 **Marchena** Andalucía, S Spain 37°20′N 05°24′W
57 B17 **Marchena, Isla** *var.* Bindloe Island. *island* Galapagos Islands, Ecuador, E Pacific Ocean
Marches *see* Marche
99 J20 **Marchin** Liège, E Belgium 50°30′N 05°17′E
181 S1 **Marchinbar Island** *island* Wessel Islands, Northern Territory, N Australia
62 L9 **Mar Chiquita, Laguna** ◎ C Argentina
103 Q10 **Marcigny** Saône-et-Loire, C France 46°16′N 04°04′E
23 W16 **Marco** Florida, SE USA 25°56′N 81°43′W
Marcodurum *see* Düren
59 O15 **Marcolândia** Pernambuco, E Brazil 07°21′S 40°40′W
106 I8 **Marco Polo** ✕ (Venezia) Veneto, NE Italy 45°30′N 12°21′E
Marcounda *see* Markounda
Marcq *see* Mark
116 M8 **Mărculeşti** *Rus.* Markulesty. N Moldova 47°54′N 28°14′E
29 S12 **Marcus** Iowa, C USA 42°49′N 95°48′W
39 S11 **Marcus Baker, Mount** ▲ Alaska, USA 61°26′N 147°45′W
192 I5 **Marcus Island** *var.* Minami Tori Shima. *island* E Japan
18 K8 **Marcy, Mount** ▲ New York, NE USA 44°06′N 73°55′W
149 T5 **Mardān** North-West Frontier Province, N Pakistan 34°14′N 71°59′E
63 N14 **Mar del Plata** Buenos Aires, E Argentina 38°S 57°32′W
137 Q16 **Mardin** Mardin, SE Turkey 37°19′N 40°43′E
137 Q16 **Mardin** ◈ *province* SE Turkey
137 Q16 **Mardin Dağları** ▲▲ SE Turkey
Mardzad *see* Hayrhandulaan
187 R17 **Maré** *island* Îles Loyauté, E New Caledonia
Marea Neagră *see* Black Sea
105 Z8 **Mare de Déu del Toro** *var.* El Toro. ▲ Menorca, Spain, W Mediterranean Sea 39°59′N 04°06′E
181 W4 **Mareeba** Queensland, NE Australia 17°03′S 145°30′E
96 G8 **Maree, Loch** ◎ N Scotland, United Kingdom
Mareeq *see* Mereeg
Marek *see* Dupnitsa
76 J11 **Maréna** Kayes, W Mali 14°36′N 10°57′W
190 I2 **Marenanuka** *atoll* Tungaru, W Kiribati
29 X14 **Marengo** Iowa, C USA 41°48′N 92°04′W
102 J11 **Marennes** Charente-Maritime, W France 45°47′N 01°04′W
107 G23 **Marettimo, Isola** *island* Isole Egadi, S Italy
24 K10 **Marfa** Texas, SW USA 30°19′N 104°03′W
57 P17 **Marfil, Laguna** ◎ E Bolivia
Marganets *see* Marhanets'
25 Q4 **Margaret** Texas, SW USA 34°00′N 99°38′W
180 I14 **Margaret River** Western Australia 33°58′S 115°10′E
186 C7 **Margarima** Southern Highlands, W Papua New Guinea 06°00′S 143°23′E
55 N4 **Margarita, Isla de** *island* N Venezuela
115 I25 **Margarítes** Kríti, Greece, E Mediterranean Sea 35°19′N 24°40′E
97 Q22 **Margate** *prev.* Mergate. SE England, United Kingdom 51°24′N 01°24′E
23 Z15 **Margate** Florida, SE USA 26°14′N 80°12′W
Margelan *see* Marg'ilon
103 P13 **Margeride, Montagnes de la** ▲▲ C France
Margherita *see* Jamaame
107 N16 **Margherita di Savoia** Puglia, SE Italy 41°23′N 16°09′E
Margherita, Lake *see* Ābaya Hāyk'
81 E18 **Margherita Peak** *Fr.* Pic Marguerite. ▲ Uganda/Dem. Rep. Congo 0°28′N 29°58′E
149 O4 **Marghī** Bāmīān, N Afghanistan 35°10′N 66°26′E
116 G9 **Marghita** *Hung.* Margitta. Bihor, NW Romania 47°20′N 22°20′E
Margilan *see* Marg'ilon
147 S10 **Marg'ilon** *var.* Margelan, *Rus.* Margilan. Farg'ona Viloyati, E Uzbekistan 40°29′N 71°43′E
116 K8 **Marginea** Suceava, NE Romania 47°49′N 25°47′E
Margitta *see* Marghita
148 K9 **Mārgow, Dasht-e** *desert* SW Afghanistan
99 L18 **Margraten** Limburg, SE Netherlands 50°49′N 05°49′E
10 M15 **Marguerite** British Columbia, SW Canada 52°17′N 122°10′W
15 V3 **Marguerite** ≈ Quebec, SE Canada
194 I6 **Marguerite Bay** *bay* Antarctica
Marguerite, Pic *see* Margherita Peak
117 T9 **Marhanets'** *Rus.* Marganets. Dnipropetrovs'ka Oblast', E Ukraine 47°35′N 34°37′E
186 B9 **Mari** Western, SW Papua New Guinea 09°10′S 141°39′E
191 Y12 **Maria** *atoll* Groupe Actéon, SE French Polynesia
191 R12 **Maria** *island* Îles Australes, SW French Polynesia
40 I12 **María Cleofas, Isla** *island* C Mexico
62 H4 **María Elena** *var.* Oficina María Elena. Antofagasta, N Chile 22°18′S 69°40′W
95 G21 **Mariager** Århus, C Denmark 56°39′N 09°59′E
61 C22 **María Ignacia** Buenos Aires, E Argentina 37°24′S 59°30′W
183 P17 **Maria Island** *island* Tasmania, SE Australia
40 H12 **María Madre, Isla** *island* C Mexico
40 I12 **María Magdalena, Isla** *island* C Mexico
192 H6 **Mariana Islands** *island group* Guam/Northern Mariana Islands
175 N3 **Mariana Trench** *var.* Challenger Deep. *undersea feature* W Pacific Ocean 15°00′N 147°30′E
153 X12 **Mariāni** Assam, NE India 26°39′N 94°18′E
27 X11 **Marianna** Arkansas, C USA 34°46′N 90°49′W
23 R8 **Marianna** Florida, SE USA 30°46′N 85°13′W
172 J16 **Marianne** *island* Inner Islands, NE Seychelles
95 M19 **Mariannelund** Jönköping, S Sweden 57°37′N 15°33′E
61 D15 **Mariano I. Loza** Corrientes, NE Argentina 29°22′S 58°12′W
Mariano Machado *see* Ganda
111 A16 **Mariánské Lázně** *Ger.* Marienbad. Karlovarský Kraj, W Czech Republic 49°57′N 12°43′E
Máriaradna *see* Radna
33 S7 **Marias River** ≈ Montana, NW USA
Maria-Theresiopel *see* Subotica
Máriatölgyes *see* Dubnica nad Váhom
184 H1 **Maria van Diemen, Cape** *headland* North Island, New Zealand 34°27′S 172°38′E
109 V5 **Mariazell** Steiermark, E Austria 47°47′N 15°20′E
141 P15 **Ma'rib** W Yemen 15°28′N 45°25′E
95 I25 **Maribo** Storstrøm, S Denmark 54°47′N 11°30′E
109 W9 **Maribor** *Ger.* Marburg. NE Slovenia 46°34′N 15°40′E
Marica *see* Maritsa
35 R13 **Maricopa** California, W USA 35°03′N 119°24′W
Maricourt *see* Kangiqsujuaq
81 D15 **Maridi** Western Equatoria, SW Sudan 04°55′N 29°30′E
194 M11 **Marie Byrd Land** *physical region* Antarctica
193 P14 **Marie Byrd Seamount** *undersea feature* N Amundsen Sea 70°00′S 118°00′W
45 X11 **Marie-Galante** *var.* Ceyre to the Caribs. *island* SE Guadeloupe
45 Y6 **Marie-Galante, Canal de** *channel* S Guadeloupe
93 J20 **Mariehamn** *Fin.* Maarianhamina. Åland, SW Finland 60°05′N 19°55′E
44 C4 **Mariel** La Habana, W Cuba 23°02′N 82°44′W
99 H22 **Mariembourg** Namur, S Belgium 50°07′N 04°30′E
Marienbad *see* Mariánské Lázně
Marienburg *see* Alūksne, Latvia
Marienburg *see* Malbork, Poland
Marienburg *see* Feldioara, Romania
Marienburg in Westpreussen *see* Malbork
Marienhausen *see* Viļaka
83 D20 **Mariental** Hardap, SW Namibia 24°35′S 17°56′E
18 D13 **Marienville** Pennsylvania, NE USA 41°27′N 79°07′W
Marienwerder *see* Kwidzyń
58 C12 **Marié, Rio** ≈ NW Brazil
95 K17 **Mariestad** Västra Götaland, S Sweden 58°42′N 13°50′E
23 S3 **Marietta** Georgia, SE USA 33°57′N 84°34′W
31 U14 **Marietta** Ohio, N USA 39°25′N 81°27′W
27 N13 **Marietta** Oklahoma, C USA 33°57′N 97°08′W
81 H18 **Marigat** Rift Valley, W Kenya 0°29′S 35°59′E
103 S16 **Marignane** Bouches-du-Rhône, SE France 43°25′N 05°12′E
Marignano *see* Melegnano
45 O11 **Marigot** NE Dominica 15°32′N 61°18′W
122 K12 **Mariinsk** Kemerovskaya Oblast', S Russian Federation 56°13′N 87°27′E
127 Q3 **Mariinskiy Posad** Respublika Mariy El, W Russian Federation 56°07′N 47°44′E
119 E14 **Marijampolė** *prev.* Kapsukas. Marijampolė, S Lithuania 54°33′N 23°21′E
114 G12 **Marikostinovo** Blagoevgrad, SW Bulgaria 41°25′N 23°21′E
60 J9 **Marília** São Paulo, S Brazil 22°13′S 49°58′W
82 D11 **Marimba** Malanje, NW Angola 08°18′S 16°58′E
139 T1 **Marī Mīlā** Arbīl, E Iraq 36°58′N 44°42′E
104 G4 **Marín** Galicia, NW Spain 42°23′N 08°43′W
35 N10 **Marina** California, W USA 36°40′N 121°48′W
Mar''ina Gorka *see* Mar''ina Horka
119 L17 **Mar''ina Horka** *Rus.* Mar'ina Gorka. Minskaya Voblasts', C Belarus 53°31′N 28°09′E
171 O4 **Marinduque** *island* C Philippines
31 S9 **Marine City** Michigan, N USA 42°43′N 82°29′W
31 N6 **Marinette** Wisconsin, N USA 45°06′N 87°38′W
60 I10 **Maringá** Paraná, S Brazil 23°26′S 51°55′W
83 N16 **Maringuè** Sofala, C Mozambique 17°57′S 34°23′E
104 F9 **Marinha Grande** Leiria, C Portugal 39°45′N 08°55′W
107 I15 **Marino** Lazio, C Italy 41°46′N 12°40′E
59 A15 **Mário Lobão** Acre, W Brazil 08°21′S 72°58′W
23 O5 **Marion** Alabama, S USA 32°37′N 87°19′W
27 Y11 **Marion** Arkansas, C USA 35°12′N 90°12′W
30 L17 **Marion** Illinois, N USA 37°43′N 88°55′W
31 P13 **Marion** Indiana, N USA 40°32′N 85°40′W
29 X13 **Marion** Iowa, C USA 42°01′N 91°36′W
27 O5 **Marion** Kansas, C USA 38°22′N 97°02′W
20 H6 **Marion** Kentucky, S USA 37°19′N 88°06′W
21 P9 **Marion** North Carolina, SE USA 35°43′N 82°00′W
31 S12 **Marion** Ohio, N USA 40°35′N 83°08′W
21 T12 **Marion** South Carolina, SE USA 34°11′N 79°23′W
21 Q7 **Marion** Virginia, NE USA 36°51′N 81°30′W
27 O5 **Marion Lake** ⊠ Kansas, C USA
21 S13 **Marion, Lake** ⊠ South Carolina, SE USA
27 S8 **Marionville** Missouri, C USA 37°00′N 93°38′W
55 N7 **Maripa** Bolívar, E Venezuela 07°27′N 65°10′W
55 X11 **Maripasoula** W French Guiana 03°43′N 54°04′W
35 Q9 **Mariposa** California, W USA 37°28′N 119°59′W
61 G19 **Mariscala** Lavalleja, S Uruguay 34°03′S 54°47′W
62 M4 **Mariscal Estigarribia** Boquerón, NW Paraguay 22°03′S 60°39′W
56 C6 **Mariscal Sucre** *var.* Quito. ✕ (Quito) Pichincha, C Ecuador 0°21′S 78°37′W
30 K16 **Marissa** Illinois, N USA 38°15′N 89°45′W
103 U14 **Maritime Alps** *Fr.* Alpes Maritimes, *It.* Alpi Marittime. ▲▲ France/Italy
Maritimes, Alpes *see* Maritime Alps
Maritime Territory *see* Primorskiy Kray
114 K11 **Maritsa** *var.* Marica, *Gk.* Évros, *Turk.* Meriç; *anc.* Hebrus. ≈ SW Europe *see also* Évros/Meriç
Maritsa *see* Simeonovgrad, Bulgaria
Marittime, Alpi *see* Maritime Alps
Maritzburg *see* Pietermaritzburg
117 X9 **Mariupol'** *prev.* Zhdanov. Donets'ka Oblast', SE Ukraine 47°06′N 37°34′E
55 Q6 **Mariusa, Caño** ≈ NE Venezuela
142 J5 **Marīvān** *prev.* Dezh Shāhpūr. Kordestān, W Iran 35°30′N 46°09′E
127 R3 **Mariyets** Respublika Mariy El, W Russian Federation 56°31′N 49°48′E
118 G4 **Märjamaa** *Ger.* Merjama. Raplamaa, NW Estonia 58°54′N 24°21′E
99 I15 **Mark** *Fr.* Marcq. ≈ Belgium/Netherlands
81 N17 **Marka** *var.* Merca. Shabeellaha Hoose, S Somalia 01°43′N 44°45′E
145 Z10 **Markakol', Ozero** *Kaz.* Marqaköl. ◎ E Kazakhstan
76 M12 **Markala** Ségou, W Mali 13°38′N 06°07′W
159 S15 **Markam** *var.* Gartog. Xizang Zizhiqu, W China 29°40′N 98°33′E
95 K21 **Markaryd** Kronoberg, S Sweden 56°26′N 13°35′E
142 L7 **Markazī** *off.* Ostān-e Markazī. ◈ *province* W Iran
Markazī, Ostān-e *see* Markazī
14 F14 **Markdale** Ontario, S Canada 44°19′N 80°37′W
27 X10 **Marked Tree** Arkansas, C USA 35°31′N 90°25′W
98 N11 **Markelo** Overijssel, E Netherlands 52°15′N 06°30′E
98 J9 **Markermeer** ◎ C Netherlands
97 N20 **Market Harborough** C England, United Kingdom 52°30′N 00°57′W
97 N18 **Market Rasen** E England, United Kingdom 53°23′N 00°21′W
123 O10 **Markha** ≈ NE Russian Federation
12 H16 **Markham** Ontario, S Canada 43°54′N 79°16′W
25 V12 **Markham** Texas, SW USA 28°57′N 96°04′W
186 E7 **Markham** ≈ C Papua New Guinea
195 Q11 **Markham, Mount** ▲ Antarctica 82°58′S 163°30′E
110 M11 **Marki** Mazowieckie, C Poland 52°20′N 21°07′E
158 F8 **Markit** Xinjiang Uygur Zizhiqu, NW China 38°55′N 77°40′E
117 Y5 **Markivka** *Rus.* Markovka. Luhans'ka Oblast', E Ukraine 49°34′N 39°35′E
35 Q7 **Markleeville** California, W USA 38°41′N 119°46′W
98 L8 **Marknesse** Flevoland, N Netherlands 52°44′N 05°54′E
79 H14 **Markounda** *var.* Marcounda. Ouham, NW Central African Republic 07°38′N 17°00′E
Markovka *see* Markivka
123 U7 **Markovo** Chukotskiy Avtonomnyy Okrug, NE Russian Federation 64°43′N 170°13′E
127 P8 **Marks** Saratovskaya Oblast', W Russian Federation 51°40′N 46°44′E
22 K2 **Marks** Mississippi, S USA 34°15′N 90°16′W
22 I7 **Marksville** Louisiana, S USA 31°07′N 92°04′W
101 I19 **Marktheidenfeld** Bayern, C Germany 49°50′N 09°36′E
101 J24 **Marktoberdorf** Bayern, S Germany 47°45′N 10°36′E
101 M18 **Marktredwitz** Bayern, E Germany 50°N 12°04′E
Markt-Übelbach *see* Übelbach
27 V3 **Mark Twain Lake** ⊠ Missouri, C USA
Markulesty *see* Mărculeşti
101 E14 **Marl** Nordrhein-Westfalen, W Germany 51°38′N 07°06′E
182 E2 **Marla** South Australia 27°19′S 133°35′E
181 Y8 **Marlborough** Queensland, E Australia 22°55′S 150°07′E
97 M22 **Marlborough** S England, United Kingdom 51°25′N 01°45′W
185 I15 **Marlborough** *off.* Marlborough District. ◈ *unitary authority* South Island, New Zealand
Marlborough District *see* Marlborough
103 P3 **Marle** Aisne, N France 49°44′N 03°47′E
31 S8 **Marlette** Michigan, N USA 43°20′N 83°05′W
25 T9 **Marlin** Texas, SW USA 31°20′N 96°55′W
21 S5 **Marlinton** West Virginia, NE USA 38°14′N 80°06′W
26 M12 **Marlow** Oklahoma, C USA 34°39′N 97°57′W
155 E17 **Marmagao** Goa, W India 15°26′N 73°50′E
Marmanda *see* Marmande
102 L13 **Marmande** *anc.* Marmanda. Lot-et-Garonne, SW France 44°30′N 00°10′E
136 C11 **Marmara** Balıkesir, NW Turkey 40°36′N 27°34′E
136 D11 **Marmara Denizi** *Eng.* Sea of Marmara. *sea* NW Turkey
114 N13 **Marmaraereğlisi** Tekirdağ, NW Turkey 40°59′N 27°57′E
Marmara, Sea of *see* Marmara Denizi
136 C16 **Marmaris** Muğla, SW Turkey 36°52′N 28°17′E
28 J6 **Marmarth** North Dakota, N USA 46°17′N 103°55′W
21 Q5 **Marmet** West Virginia, NE USA 38°12′N 81°31′W
106 H5 **Marmolada, Monte** ▲ N Italy 46°36′N 11°58′E
104 M13 **Marmolejo** Andalucía, S Spain 38°03′N 04°10′W
14 J14 **Marmora** Ontario, SE Canada 44°29′N 77°40′W
39 Q14 **Marmot Bay** *bay* Alaska, USA
103 Q4 **Marne** ◈ *department* N France
103 Q4 **Marne** ≈ N France
137 U10 **Marneuli** *prev.* Borchalo, Sarvani. S Georgia 41°28′N 44°45′E
78 I13 **Maro** Moyen-Chari, S Chad 08°25′N 18°46′E
54 L12 **Maroa** Amazonas, S Venezuela 02°40′N 67°33′W
172 J3 **Maroantsetra** Toamasina, NE Madagascar 15°23′S 49°44′E
191 W11 **Marokau** *atoll* Îles Tuamotu, C French Polynesia
172 J5 **Marolambo** Toamasina, E Madagascar 20°03′S 48°08′E
172 J2 **Maromokotro** ▲ N Madagascar
83 L16 **Marondera** *prev.* Marandellas. Mashonaland East, NE Zimbabwe 18°11′S 31°33′E
55 X9 **Maroni** *Dut.* Marowijne. ≈ French Guiana/Suriname
183 V2 **Maroochydore-Mooloolaba** Queensland, E Australia 26°36′S 153°04′E
171 N14 **Maros** Sulawesi, C Indonesia 04°59′S 119°35′E
116 H11 **Maros** *var.* Mureş, Mureşul, *Ger.* Marosch, Mieresch. ≈ Hungary/Romania *see also* Mureş
Marosch *see* Maros/Mureş
Marosheviz *see* Toplița
Marosillye *see* Ilia
Marosludas *see* Luduş
Marosújvár/ Marosújvárakna *see* Ocna Mureş
Marosvásárhely *see* Târgu Mureş
191 V14 **Marotiri** *var.* Îlots de Bass, Morotiri. *island group* Îles Australes, SW French Polynesia
78 G12 **Maroua** Extrême-Nord, N Cameroon 10°35′N 14°20′E
55 X12 **Marouini Rivier** ≈ SE Suriname
172 I3 **Marovoay** Mahajanga, NW Madagascar 16°05′S 46°40′E
55 W9 **Marowijne** ◈ *district* NE Suriname
Marowijne *see* Maroni
Marqaköl *see* Markakol', Ozero
193 P8 **Marquesas Fracture Zone** *tectonic feature* E Pacific Ocean
Marquesas Islands *see* Marquises, Îles
23 W17 **Marquesas Keys** *island group* Florida, SE USA
29 Y12 **Marquette** Iowa, C USA 43°02′N 91°10′W
31 N3 **Marquette** Michigan, N USA 46°32′N 87°24′W
103 N1 **Marquise** Pas-de-Calais, N France 50°49′N 01°42′E
191 X7 **Marquises, Îles** *Eng.* Marquesas Islands. *island group* N French Polynesia
183 Q6 **Marra Creek** ≈ New South Wales, SE Australia
80 B10 **Marra Hills** *plateau* W Sudan
80 B11 **Marra, Jebel** ▲ W Sudan 12°59′N 24°16′E
74 E7 **Marrakech** *var.* Marakesh, *Eng.* Marrakesh; *prev.* Morocco. W Morocco 31°39′N 07°58′W
Marrakesh *see* Marrakech
Marrāt *see* Marāh
183 N15 **Marrawah** Tasmania, SE Australia 40°56′S 144°41′E
182 J4 **Marree** South Australia 29°40′S 138°06′E
81 L17 **Marrehan** ▲ SW Somalia
83 N17 **Marromeu** Sofala, C Mozambique 18°18′S 35°58′E
104 J17 **Marroquí, Punta** *headland* SW Spain 36°01′N 05°39′W
183 N8 **Marrowie Creek** *seasonal river* New South Wales, SE Australia
83 O14 **Marrupa** Niassa, N Mozambique 13°10′S 37°30′E
182 D1 **Marryat** South Australia 26°22′S 133°22′E
75 Y10 **Marsá al 'Alam** *var.* Marsa 'Alam. SE Egypt 25°03′N 33°44′E
Marsa 'Alam *see* Marsá al 'Alam
75 R8 **Marsá al Burayqah** *var.* Al Burayqah. N Libya 30°21′N 19°37′E
81 J17 **Marsabit** Eastern, N Kenya 02°20′N 37°59′E
107 H23 **Marsala** *anc.* Lilybaeum. Sicilia, Italy, C Mediterranean Sea 37°48′N 12°26′E
121 P16 **Marsaxlokk Bay** *bay* SE Malta
65 G15 **Mars Bay** *bay* Ascension Island, C Atlantic Ocean
101 H15 **Marsberg** Nordrhein-Westfalen, W Germany 51°28′N 08°51′E
11 R15 **Marsden** Saskatchewan, S Canada 52°50′N 109°45′W
98 H7 **Marsdiep** *strait* NW Netherlands
103 R16 **Marseille** *Eng.* Marseilles; *anc.* Massilia. Bouches-du-Rhône, SE France 43°19′N 05°22′E
Marseille-Marigrane *see* Provence
30 M11 **Marseilles** Illinois, N USA 41°19′N 88°42′W
Marseilles *see* Marseille
76 J16 **Marshall** W Liberia 06°10′N 10°23′W
39 N11 **Marshall** Alaska, USA 61°52′N 162°04′W
27 U9 **Marshall** Arkansas, C USA 35°54′N 92°40′W
31 N14 **Marshall** Illinois, N USA 39°23′N 87°41′W
31 Q10 **Marshall** Michigan, N USA 42°16′N 84°57′W
29 S9 **Marshall** Minnesota, N USA 44°26′N 95°48′W
27 T4 **Marshall** Missouri, C USA 39°07′N 93°12′W
21 O9 **Marshall** North Carolina, SE USA 35°48′N 82°43′W
25 X6 **Marshall** Texas, SW USA 32°33′N 94°22′W
189 S4 **Marshall Islands** *off.* Republic of the Marshall Islands. ◆ *republic* W Pacific Ocean
175 Q3 **Marshall Islands** *island group* W Pacific Ocean
Marshall Islands, Republic of the *see* Marshall Islands
192 K6 **Marshall Seamounts** *undersea feature* SW Pacific Ocean 10°00′N 165°00′E
29 W13 **Marshalltown** Iowa, C USA 42°01′N 92°54′W
19 P12 **Marshfield** Massachusetts, NE USA 42°04′N 70°40′W
27 T7 **Marshfield** Missouri, C USA 37°20′N 92°55′W
30 K6 **Marshfield** Wisconsin, N USA 44°41′N 90°12′W
44 H1 **Marsh Harbour** Great Abaco, W Bahamas 26°31′N 77°03′W
19 S3 **Mars Hill** Maine, NE USA 46°31′N 67°51′W
21 P9 **Mars Hill** North Carolina, SE USA 35°49′N 82°33′W
22 H10 **Marsh Island** *island* Louisiana, S USA
21 S11 **Marshville** North Carolina, SE USA 34°59′N 80°22′W
15 W5 **Marsoui** Québec, SE Canada 49°12′N 65°58′W
15 R8 **Mars, Rivière à** ≈ Québec, SE Canada
95 O15 **Märsta** Stockholm, C Sweden 59°37′N 17°52′E
95 H24 **Marstal** Fyn, C Denmark 54°52′N 10°32′E
95 I19 **Marstrand** Västra Götaland, S Sweden 57°54′N 11°31′E
25 U8 **Mart** Texas, SW USA 31°32′N 96°49′W
166 M9 **Martaban** *var.* Moktama. Mon State, S Myanmar (Burma) 16°32′N 97°35′E
166 L9 **Martaban, Gulf of** *gulf* S Myanmar (Burma)
107 Q19 **Martano** Puglia, SE Italy 40°12′N 18°19′E
Martapoera *see* Martapura
169 T13 **Martapura** *prev.* Martapoera. Borneo, C Indonesia 03°25′S 114°51′E
99 L23 **Martelange** Luxembourg, SE Belgium 49°50′N 05°43′E
114 L7 **Marten** Ruse, N Bulgaria 43°57′N 26°08′E
14 H10 **Marten River** Ontario, S Canada 46°43′N 79°45′W
11 T15 **Martensville** Saskatchewan, S Canada 52°15′N 106°42′W
Marteskirch *see* Târnăveni
Martes Tolosane *see* Martres-Tolosane
115 K25 **Mártha** Kríti, Greece, E Mediterranean Sea 35°03′N 25°22′E
183 Q6 **Marthaguy Creek** ≈ New South Wales, SE Australia

◆ Country ● Country Capital ◇ Dependent Territory ○ Dependent Territory Capital ◈ Administrative Regions ✕ International Airport ▲ Mountain ▲▲ Mountain Range ※ Volcano ≈ River ◎ Lake ⊠ Reservoir

MARTHA'S VINEYARD – MAZARRÓN

19 P13 **Martha's Vineyard** *island* Massachusetts, NE USA
108 C11 **Martigny** Valais, SW Switzerland 46°06′N 07°04′E
103 R16 **Martigues** Bouches-du-Rhône, SE France 43°24′N 05°03′E
111 J19 **Martin** *Ger.* Sankt Martin, *Hung.* Turócszentmárton; *prev.* Turčiansky Svätý Martin. Žilinský Kraj, N Slovakia 49°03′N 18°54′E
28 L11 **Martin** South Dakota, N USA 43°10′N 101°43′W
20 G8 **Martin** Tennessee, S USA 36°20′N 88°51′W
105 S7 **Martín** ⚞ E Spain
107 P18 **Martina Franca** Puglia, SE Italy 40°42′N 17°20′E
185 M14 **Martinborough** Wellington, North Island, New Zealand 41°12′S 175°28′E
25 S11 **Martindale** Texas, SW USA 29°49′N 97°49′W
35 N8 **Martinez** California, W USA 38°00′N 122°12′W
23 V3 **Martinez** Georgia, SE USA 33°31′N 82°04′W
41 Q13 **Martínez de La Torre** Veracruz-Llave, E Mexico 20°05′N 97°02′W
45 Y12 **Martinique** ◇ *French overseas department* E West Indies
1 O15 **Martinique** *island* E West Indies
Martinique Channel *see* Martinique Passage
45 X12 **Martinique Passage** *var.* Dominica Channel, Martinique Channel. *channel* Dominica/Martinique
23 Q5 **Martin Lake** ⊠ Alabama, S USA
115 G18 **Martíno** *prev.* Martínon. Stereá Ellás, C Greece 38°34′N 23°13′E
Martínon *see* Martíno
194 J11 **Martin Peninsula** *peninsula* Antarctica
39 S5 **Martin Point** *headland* Alaska, USA 70°06′N 143°04′W
109 V3 **Martinsberg** Niederösterreich, NE Austria 48°23′N 15°09′E
21 V3 **Martinsburg** West Virginia, NE USA 39°28′N 77°59′W
31 V13 **Martins Ferry** Ohio, N USA 40°06′N 80°43′W
Martinskirch *see* Târnăveni
31 O14 **Martinsville** Indiana, N USA 39°25′N 86°25′W
21 S8 **Martinsville** Virginia, NE USA 36°43′N 79°53′W
65 K16 **Martin Vaz, Ilhas** *island group* E Brazil
Martök *see* Martuk
184 M12 **Marton** Manawatu-Wanganui, North Island, New Zealand 40°05′S 175°22′E
105 N13 **Martos** Andalucía, S Spain 37°44′N 03°58′W
102 M16 **Martres-Tolosane** *var.* Martes Tolosane. Haute-Garonne, S France 43°13′N 01°00′E
92 M11 **Martti** Lappi, NE Finland 67°28′N 28°20′E
144 I9 **Martuk** *Kaz.* Martök. Aktyubinsk, NW Kazakhstan 50°45′N 56°30′E
137 U12 **Martuni** E Armenia 40°07′N 45°20′E
58 L11 **Marudá** Pará, E Brazil 05°25′S 49°04′W
169 V6 **Marudu, Teluk** *bay* East Malaysia
148 M4 **Ma'rūf** Kandahār, SE Afghanistan 31°34′N 67°06′E
164 H13 **Marugame** Kagawa, Shikoku, SW Japan 34°17′N 133°46′E
185 H16 **Maruia** ⚞ South Island, New Zealand
98 M6 **Marum** Groningen, NE Netherlands 53°07′N 06°16′E
187 R13 **Marum, Mount** ▲ Ambrym, C Vanuatu 16°15′S 168°07′E
79 P23 **Marungu** ▲▲ SE Dem. Rep. Congo
191 Y12 **Marutea** *atoll* Groupe Actéon, C French Polynesia
143 O11 **Marv Dasht** *var.* Mervdasht. Fārs, S Iran 29°50′N 52°40′E
103 P13 **Marvejols** Lozère, S France 44°35′N 03°16′E
27 X12 **Marvell** Arkansas, C USA 34°33′N 90°52′W
36 L6 **Marvine, Mount** ▲ Utah, W USA 38°40′N 111°38′W
139 Q7 **Marwānīyah** Al Anbār, C Iraq 33°58′N 42°31′E
152 F13 **Mārwār** *var.* Kharchi, Marwar Junction. Rājasthān, N India 25°41′N 73°42′E
Marwar Junction *see* Mārwār
11 R14 **Marwayne** Alberta, SW Canada 53°30′N 110°25′W
146 I14 **Mary** *prev.* Merv. Mary Welaýaty, S Turkmenistan 37°25′N 61°48′E
Mary *see* Mary Welaýaty
181 Z9 **Maryborough** Queensland, E Australia 25°32′S 152°36′E
182 M11 **Maryborough** Victoria, SE Australia 37°05′S 143°47′E
Maryborough *see* Port Laoise
83 G23 **Marydale** Northern Cape, W South Africa 29°25′S 22°06′E
117 W8 **Mar"yinka** Donets'ka Oblast', E Ukraine 47°57′N 37°27′E
Mary Island *see* Kanton
21 W4 **Maryland** *off.* State of Maryland, *also known as* America in Miniature, Cockade State, Free State, Old Line State. ◆ *state* NE USA
Maryland, State of *see* Maryland
25 P7 **Maryneal** Texas, SW USA 32°12′N 100°25′W
97 J15 **Maryport** NW England, United Kingdom 54°45′N 03°28′W
13 U13 **Marystown** Newfoundland, Newfoundland and Labrador, SE Canada 47°10′N 55°10′W
36 K6 **Marysvale** Utah, W USA 38°26′N 112°14′W
35 O6 **Marysville** California, W USA 39°07′N 121°35′W
27 O3 **Marysville** Kansas, C USA 39°48′N 96°37′W
31 S13 **Marysville** Michigan, N USA 42°54′N 82°29′W
31 S9 **Marysville** Ohio, NE USA 40°13′N 83°22′W
32 H7 **Marysville** Washington, NW USA 48°03′N 122°10′W
27 R2 **Maryville** Missouri, C USA 40°20′N 94°53′W
21 N9 **Maryville** Tennessee, S USA 35°45′N 83°59′W
146 I15 **Mary Welaýaty** *var.* Mary, *Rus.* Maryyskiy Velayat. ◆ *province* S Turkmenistan
Maryyskiy Velayat *see* Mary Welaýaty
Marzūq *see* Murzuq
42 J11 **Masachapa** *var.* Puerto Masachapa. Managua, W Nicaragua 11°47′N 86°31′W
81 G19 **Masai Mara National Reserve** *reserve* C Kenya
81 I21 **Masai Steppe** *grassland* NW Tanzania
81 F19 **Masaka** SW Uganda 0°20′S 31°46′E
169 T15 **Masalembo Besar, Pulau** *island* S Indonesia
137 Y13 **Masallı** *Rus.* Masally. S Azerbaijan 39°03′N 48°39′E
Masally *see* Masallı
171 N13 **Masamba** Sulawesi, C Indonesia 02°33′S 120°20′E
Masampo *see* Masan
163 Y16 **Masan** *prev.* Masampo. S South Korea 35°11′N 128°36′E
Masandam Peninsula *see* Musandam Peninsula
81 J25 **Masasi** Mtwara, SE Tanzania 10°43′S 38°48′E
Masawa/Massawa *see* Mits'iwa
42 J10 **Masaya** Masaya, W Nicaragua 11°59′N 86°06′W
42 J10 **Masaya** ◆ *department* W Nicaragua
171 P5 **Masbate** Masbate, N Philippines 12°21′N 123°34′E
171 P5 **Masbate** *island* C Philippines
74 I6 **Mascara** *var.* Mouaskar. NW Algeria 35°20′N 00°09′E
173 O7 **Mascarene Basin** *undersea feature* W Indian Ocean 15°00′S 56°00′E
173 O9 **Mascarene Islands** *island group* W Indian Ocean
173 N9 **Mascarene Plain** *undersea feature* W Indian Ocean 19°00′S 52°00′E
173 O7 **Mascarene Plateau** *undersea feature* W Indian Ocean 10°00′S 60°00′E
194 H5 **Mascart, Cape** *headland* Adelaide Island, Antarctica
62 J10 **Mascasín, Salinas de** *salt lake* C Argentina
40 K13 **Mascota** Jalisco, C Mexico 20°31′N 104°46′W
15 O12 **Mascouche** Québec, SE Canada 45°46′N 73°37′W
124 J9 **Masel'gskaya** Respublika Kareliya, NW Russian Federation 63°09′N 34°22′E
83 J23 **Maseru** ● (Lesotho) W Lesotho 29°21′S 27°35′E
83 J23 **Maseru** ✕ W Lesotho 29°27′S 27°37′E
Mashaba *see* Mashava
160 K14 **Mashan** *var.* Baishan. Guangxi Zhuangzu Zizhiqu, S China 23°40′N 108°20′E
83 K17 **Mashava** *prev.* Mashaba. Masvingo, SE Zimbabwe 20°03′S 30°29′E
143 U4 **Mashhad** *var.* Meshed. Khorāsān-Razavī, NE Iran 36°16′N 59°34′E
165 S3 **Mashike** Hokkaidō, NE Japan 43°51′N 141°30′E
Mashiz *see* Bardsīr
149 N14 **Mashkai** ⚞ SW Pakistan
143 X13 **Māshkel** *var.* Rūd-i Māshkel, Rūd-e Māshkīd. ⚞ Iran/Pakistan
148 K12 **Māshkel, Hāmūn-i** *salt marsh* SW Pakistan
Māshkel, Rūd-i/Māshkīd, Rūd-e *see* Māshkel
83 K15 **Mashonaland Central** ◆ *province* N Zimbabwe
83 K16 **Mashonaland East** ◆ *province* NE Zimbabwe
83 J16 **Mashonaland West** ◆ *province* NW Zimbabwe
Mashtagi *see* Maştağa
141 S14 **Masīlah, Wādī al** *dry watercourse* SE Yemen
79 I21 **Masi-Manimba** Bandundu, SW Dem. Rep. Congo 04°47′S 17°54′E
81 F17 **Masindi** W Uganda 01°41′N 31°45′E
81 I19 **Masinga Reservoir** ⊠ S Kenya
Masīra *see* Maşīrah, Jazīrat
Masīra, Gulf of *see* Maşīrah, Khalīj
141 Y10 **Maşīrah, Jazīrat** *var.* Masīra. *island* E Oman
141 Y10 **Maşīrah, Khalīj** *var.* Gulf of Masira. *bay* E Oman
Masis *see* Büyükağrı Dağı
79 O19 **Masisi** Nord-Kivu, E Dem. Rep. Congo 01°25′S 28°50′E
Masjed-e Soleymān *see* Masjed Soleymān
142 L9 **Masjed Soleymān** *var.* Masjed-e Soleymān, Masjid-i Sulaiman. Khūzestān, SW Iran 31°59′N 49°18′E
Masjid-i Sulaiman *see* Masjed Soleymān
Maskat *see* Masqaţ
139 Q7 **Maskhān** Al Anbār, C Iraq 33°41′N 42°46′E
141 X8 **Maskin** *var.* Miskin. NW Oman 23°28′N 56°46′E
97 B17 **Mask, Lough** *Ir.* Loch Measca. ◎ W Ireland
114 N10 **Maslen Nos** *headland* E Bulgaria 42°19′N 27°47′E
172 K3 **Masoala, Tanjona** *headland* NE Madagascar 15°59′S 50°13′E
Masohi *see* Amahai
31 Q9 **Mason** Michigan, N USA 42°33′N 84°25′W
31 R14 **Mason** Ohio, N USA 39°21′N 84°18′W
25 Q10 **Mason** Texas, SW USA 30°45′N 99°15′W
21 P4 **Mason** West Virginia, NE USA 39°01′N 82°01′W
185 B25 **Mason Bay** *bay* Stewart Island, New Zealand
30 K13 **Mason City** Illinois, N USA 40°12′N 89°42′W
29 V12 **Mason City** Iowa, C USA 43°09′N 93°12′W
18 B16 **Masontown** Pennsylvania, NE USA 39°49′N 79°53′W
141 Y8 **Masqaţ** *var.* Maskat, *Eng.* Muscat. ● (Oman) NE Oman 23°35′N 58°36′E
106 E10 **Massa** Toscana, C Italy 44°02′N 10°07′E
18 M11 **Massachusetts** *off.* Commonwealth of Massachusetts, *also known as* Bay State, Old Bay State, Old Colony State. ◆ *state* NE USA
19 P11 **Massachusetts Bay** *bay* Massachusetts, NE USA
35 R2 **Massacre Lake** ◎ Nevada, W USA
107 O18 **Massafra** Puglia, SE Italy 40°35′N 17°08′E
108 G11 **Massagno** Ticino, S Switzerland 46°01′N 08°55′E
78 G11 **Massaguet** Chari-Baguirmi, W Chad 12°28′N 15°26′E
Massakori *see* Massakory
78 G10 **Massakory** *var.* Massakori; *prev.* Dagana. Chari-Baguirmi, W Chad 13°02′N 15°43′E
78 H11 **Massalassef** Chari-Baguirmi, SW Chad 11°37′N 17°09′E
106 F13 **Massa Marittima** Toscana, C Italy 43°03′N 10°55′E
82 B11 **Massangano** Cuanza Norte, NW Angola 09°40′S 14°13′E
83 M18 **Massangena** Gaza, S Mozambique 21°34′S 32°57′E
80 K9 **Massawa Channel** *channel* E Eritrea
18 J6 **Massena** New York, NE USA 44°55′N 74°53′W
78 H11 **Massenya** Chari-Baguirmi, SW Chad 11°21′N 16°09′E
10 I13 **Masset** Graham Island, British Columbia, SW Canada 54°00′N 132°09′W
102 L16 **Masseube** Gers, S France 43°26′N 00°33′E
14 E11 **Massey** Ontario, S Canada 46°13′N 82°06′W
103 P12 **Massiac** Cantal, C France 45°16′N 03°13′E
103 P12 **Massif Central** *plateau* C France
Massif de L'Isalo *see* Isalo
Massilia *see* Marseille
31 U12 **Massillon** Ohio, N USA 40°48′N 81°31′W
77 N12 **Massina** Ségou, W Mali 13°58′N 05°24′W
83 N19 **Massinga** Inhambane, SE Mozambique 23°20′S 35°25′E
83 L20 **Massingir** Gaza, SW Mozambique 23°51′S 31°58′E
195 Z10 **Masson Island** *island* Antarctica
Massoukou *see* Franceville
137 Z11 **Maştağa** *Rus.* Mashtagi, Mastaga. E Azerbaijan 40°31′N 50°01′E
Mastanli *see* Momchilgrad
184 M13 **Masterton** Wellington, North Island, New Zealand 40°56′S 175°40′E
18 M14 **Mastic** Long Island, New York, NE USA 40°48′N 72°50′W
149 O10 **Mastung** Baluchistān, SW Pakistan 29°44′N 66°56′E
119 J20 **Mastva** *Rus.* Mostva. ⚞ SW Belarus
119 G17 **Masty** *Rus.* Mosty. Hrodzyenskaya Voblasts', W Belarus 53°25′N 24°32′E
164 F12 **Masuda** Shimane, Honshū, SW Japan 34°40′N 131°50′E
92 J11 **Masugnsbyn** Norrbotten, N Sweden 67°28′N 22°01′E
Masuku *see* Franceville
83 K17 **Masvingo** *prev.* Fort Victoria, Nyanda, Victoria. Masvingo, SE Zimbabwe 20°05′S 30°50′E
83 K18 **Masvingo** *prev.* Victoria. ◆ *province* SE Zimbabwe
138 H5 **Maşyāf** *Fr.* Misiaf. Ḩamāh, C Syria 35°04′N 36°21′E
110 E9 **Maszewo** Zachodniopomorskie, NW Poland 53°29′N 15°01′E
83 I17 **Matabeleland North** ◆ *province* W Zimbabwe
83 J18 **Matabeleland South** ◆ *province* S Zimbabwe
82 O13 **Mataca** Niassa, N Mozambique 12°27′S 36°13′E
14 G8 **Matachewan** Ontario, S Canada 47°58′N 80°37′W
163 Q8 **Matad** *var.* Dzüünbulag. Dornod, E Mongolia 46°48′N 115°21′E
79 F22 **Matadi** Bas-Congo, W Dem. Rep. Congo 05°49′S 13°31′E
25 O4 **Matador** Texas, SW USA 34°01′N 100°50′W
42 J9 **Matagalpa** Matagalpa, C Nicaragua 12°53′N 85°56′W
42 K9 **Matagalpa** ◆ *department* W Nicaragua
12 I12 **Matagami** Québec, S Canada 49°47′N 77°38′W
25 U13 **Matagorda** Texas, SW USA 28°40′N 96°57′W
25 U13 **Matagorda Bay** *inlet* Texas, SW USA
25 U14 **Matagorda Island** *island* Texas, SW USA
25 V13 **Matagorda Peninsula** *headland* Texas, SW USA 28°34′N 96°01′W
191 Q8 **Mataiea** Tahiti, W French Polynesia 17°46′S 149°25′W
191 T9 **Mataiva** *atoll* Îles Tuamotu, C French Polynesia
183 O7 **Matakana** New South Wales, SE Australia 32°59′S 145°53′E
184 N7 **Matakana Island** *island* NE New Zealand
83 C15 **Matala** Huíla, SW Angola 14°45′S 15°02′E
190 G12 **Matala'a Pointe** *headland* Île Uvea, N Wallis and Futuna 13°20′S 176°08′W
155 K25 **Matale** Central Province, C Sri Lanka 07°29′N 80°38′E
190 E12 **Matalesina, Pointe** *headland* Île Alofi, W Wallis and Futuna
76 I10 **Matam** NE Senegal 15°40′N 13°18′W
184 M8 **Matamata** Waikato, North Island, New Zealand 37°49′S 175°45′E
77 V12 **Matamey** Zinder, S Niger 13°27′N 08°27′E
40 L8 **Matamoros** Coahuila, NE Mexico 25°34′N 103°13′W
41 P15 **Matamoros** *var.* Izúcar de Matamoros. Puebla, S Mexico 18°38′N 98°30′W
41 Q8 **Matamoros** Tamaulipas, C Mexico 25°50′N 97°31′W
75 S13 **Ma'ţan as Sārah** SE Libya 21°45′N 21°55′E
82 J12 **Matanda** Luapula, N Zambia 11°24′S 28°25′E
81 J24 **Matandu** ⚞ S Tanzania
15 V6 **Matane** Québec, SE Canada 48°50′N 67°31′W
15 V6 **Matane** ⚞ Québec, SE Canada
77 S12 **Matankari** Dosso, SW Niger 13°39′N 04°03′E
39 R11 **Matanuska River** ⚞ Alaska, USA
54 G7 **Matanza** Santander, N Colombia 07°22′N 73°02′W
44 D4 **Matanzas** Matanzas, NW Cuba 23°N 81°32′W
15 V7 **Matapédia** ⚞ Québec, SE Canada
15 V6 **Matapédia, Lac** ◎ Québec, SE Canada
190 B17 **Mata Point** *headland* SE Niue 19°07′S 169°51′E
190 D12 **Matapu, Pointe** *headland* Île Futuna, W Wallis and Futuna
62 G12 **Mataquito, Río** ⚞ C Chile
155 K26 **Matara** Southern Province, S Sri Lanka 05°58′N 80°33′E
115 D18 **Matarágka** *var.* Mataránga. Dytikí Ellás, C Greece 38°32′N 21°28′E
171 K16 **Mataram** Pulau Lombok, C Indonesia 08°36′S 116°07′E
Mataránga *see* Matarágka
181 Q3 **Mataranka** Northern Territory, N Australia 14°55′S 133°03′E
105 W6 **Mataró** *anc.* Illuro. Cataluña, E Spain 41°32′N 02°27′E
184 O8 **Matata** Bay of Plenty, North Island, New Zealand 37°54′S 176°45′E
192 K16 **Matātula, Cape** *headland* Tutuila, W American Samoa 14°15′S 170°35′W
185 D24 **Mataura** Southland, South Island, New Zealand 46°12′S 168°53′E
185 D24 **Mataura** ⚞ South Island, New Zealand
Mata Uta *see* Matā'utu
192 H16 **Matāutu** Upolu, C Samoa 13°57′S 171°55′W
190 G11 **Matā'utu** *var.* Mata Uta. ○ (Wallis and Futuna) Île Uvea, Wallis and Futuna 13°22′S 176°12′W
190 G12 **Matā'utu, Baie de** *bay* Île Uvea, Wallis and Futuna
191 P7 **Mataval, Baie de** *bay* Tahiti, W French Polynesia
190 I16 **Matavera** Rarotonga, S Cook Islands 21°13′S 159°44′W
191 V16 **Mataveri** Easter Island, Chile, E Pacific Ocean 27°10′S 109°27′W
191 V17 **Mataveri** ✕ (Easter Island) Easter Island, Chile, E Pacific Ocean 27°10′S 109°27′W
184 P9 **Matawai** Gisborne, North Island, New Zealand 38°23′S 177°31′E
15 O10 **Matawin** ⚞ Québec, SE Canada
145 V13 **Matay** Almaty, SE Kazakhstan 45°53′N 78°45′E
14 K8 **Matchi-Manitou, Lac** ◎ Québec, SE Canada
41 O10 **Matehuala** San Luis Potosí, C Mexico 23°40′N 100°40′W
45 V13 **Matelot** Trinidad, Trinidad and Tobago 10°48′N 61°06′W
83 M15 **Matenge** Tete, NW Mozambique 15°22′S 33°47′E
107 O18 **Matera** Basilicata, S Italy 40°39′N 16°35′E
111 O21 **Mátészalka** Szabolcs-Szatmár-Bereg, E Hungary 47°58′N 22°17′E
93 H17 **Matfors** Västernorrland, C Sweden 62°21′N 17°02′E
102 K11 **Matha** Charente-Maritime, W France 45°50′N 00°13′W
0 F15 **Mathematicians Seamounts** *undersea feature* E Pacific Ocean 15°00′N 111°00′W
21 X6 **Mathews** Virginia, NE USA 37°26′N 76°20′W
25 S14 **Mathis** Texas, SW USA 28°05′N 97°49′W
152 J11 **Mathura** *prev.* Muttra. Uttar Pradesh, N India 27°30′N 77°42′E
Mathurai *see* Madurai
171 R7 **Mati** Mindanao, S Philippines 06°58′N 126°11′E
Matianus *see* Orūmīyeh, Daryācheh-ye
Matiara *see* Matiāri
149 Q15 **Matiāri** *var.* Matiara. Sind, SE Pakistan 25°38′N 68°29′E
41 S16 **Matías Romero** Oaxaca, SE Mexico 16°53′N 95°02′W
43 O13 **Matina** Limón, E Costa Rica 10°06′N 83°18′W
14 D10 **Matinenda Lake** ◎ Ontario, S Canada
19 R8 **Matinicus Island** *island* Maine, NE USA
Matisco/Matisco Ædourum *see* Mâcon
190 G12 **Mati'utu, Baie de** E Wallis and Futuna
149 Q16 **Mātli** Sind, SE Pakistan 25°06′N 68°37′E
97 M18 **Matlock** C England, United Kingdom 53°08′N 01°32′W
59 F18 **Mato Grosso** *prev.* Vila Bela da Santissima Trindade. Mato Grosso, W Brazil 14°53′S 59°58′W
59 G17 **Mato Grosso** *off.* Estado de Mato Grosso; *prev.* Matto Grosso. ◆ *state* W Brazil
60 H8 **Mato Grosso do Sul** *off.* Estado de Mato Grosso do Sul. ◆ *state* S Brazil
Mato Grosso do Sul, Estado de *see* Mato Grosso do Sul
Mato Grosso, Estado de *see* Mato Grosso
59 I18 **Mato Grosso, Planalto de** *plateau* C Brazil
83 L21 **Matola** Maputo, S Mozambique 25°57′S 32°27′E
104 G6 **Matosinhos** *prev.* Matozinhos. Porto, NW Portugal 41°11′N 08°42′W
191 O7 **Matotea, Mont** ▲ Moorea, W French Polynesia 17°31′S 149°52′W
Matou *see* Pingguo
55 Z10 **Matoury** NE French Guiana 04°49′N 52°17′W
Matozinhos *see* Matosinhos
111 L21 **Mátra** ▲▲ N Hungary
141 Y8 **Maţraḩ** *var.* Mutrah. NE Oman 23°35′N 58°31′E
116 L12 **Mătrașești** Vrancea, E Romania 45°53′N 27°14′E
108 M8 **Matrei am Brenner** Tirol, W Austria 47°09′N 11°28′E
109 P8 **Matrei in Osttirol** Tirol, W Austria 47°04′N 12°31′E
76 I15 **Matru** SW Sierra Leone 07°37′N 12°08′W
Maţrūḩ *see* Mersā Maţrūḩ
165 U16 **Matsubara** *var.* Matubara. Kagoshima, Tokuno-shima, SW Japan 32°58′N 129°56′E
164 G12 **Matsue** *var.* Matsuye, Matue. Shimane, Honshū, SW Japan 35°27′N 133°04′E
165 Q6 **Matsumae** Hokkaidō, NE Japan 41°27′N 140°04′E
164 M12 **Matsumoto** *var.* Matumoto. Nagano, Honshū, S Japan 36°18′N 137°58′E
164 K14 **Matsusaka** *var.* Matsuzaka, Matusaka. Mie, Honshū, SW Japan 34°33′N 136°31′E
161 S12 **Matsu Tao** *Chin.* Mazu Dao. *island* NW Taiwan
Matsutō *see* Mattō
164 F14 **Matsuyama** *var.* Matuyama. Ehime, Shikoku, SW Japan 33°50′N 132°47′E
Matsuye *see* Matsue
Matsuzaka *see* Matsusaka
164 M14 **Matsuzaki** Shizuoka, Honshū, S Japan 34°43′N 138°45′E
14 F8 **Mattagami** ⚞ Ontario, S Canada
14 F8 **Mattagami Lake** ◎ Ontario, S Canada
62 K12 **Mattaldi** Córdoba, C Argentina 34°26′S 64°14′W
21 Y9 **Mattamuskeet, Lake** ◎ North Carolina, SE USA
21 W6 **Mattaponi River** ⚞ Virginia, NE USA
14 I11 **Mattawa** Ontario, SE Canada 46°19′N 78°42′W
14 I11 **Mattawa** ⚞ Ontario, SE Canada
19 S5 **Mattawamkeag** Maine, NE USA 45°30′N 68°20′W
19 S4 **Mattawamkeag Lake** ◎ Maine, NE USA
108 D11 **Matterhorn** *It.* Monte Cervino. ▲ Italy/Switzerland 45°58′N 07°36′E *see also* Cervino, Monte
32 L12 **Matterhorn** *var.* Sacajawea Peak. ▲ Oregon, NW USA 45°12′N 117°18′W
35 W1 **Matterhorn** ▲ Nevada, W USA 41°48′N 115°22′W
Matterhorn *see* Cervino, Monte
35 R8 **Matterhorn Peak** ▲ California, W USA 38°06′N 119°19′W
109 Y5 **Mattersburg** Burgenland, E Austria 47°45′N 16°24′E
108 E11 **Matter Vispa** ⚞ S Switzerland
55 R7 **Matthews Ridge** N Guyana 07°30′N 60°07′W
44 K7 **Matthew Town** Great Inagua, S Bahamas 20°56′N 73°41′W
109 Q4 **Mattighofen** Oberösterreich, NW Austria 48°07′N 13°09′E
107 N16 **Mattinata** Puglia, SE Italy 41°41′N 16°01′E
141 T9 **Maţţī, Sabkhat** *salt flat* Saudi Arabia/United Arab Emirates
18 M14 **Mattituck** Long Island, New York, NE USA 40°59′N 72°31′W
164 L11 **Mattō** *var.* Hakusan, Matsutō. Ishikawa, Honshū, SW Japan 36°31′N 136°34′E
Matto Grosso *see* Mato Grosso
30 M14 **Mattoon** Illinois, N USA 39°28′N 88°22′W
57 L16 **Mattos, Río** ⚞ C Bolivia
Mattu *see* Metu
169 R9 **Matu** Sarawak, East Malaysia 02°39′N 111°31′E
Matubara *see* Matsubara
57 E14 **Matucana** Lima, W Peru 11°54′S 76°25′W
Matue *see* Matsue
187 Y15 **Matuku** *island* S Fiji
112 B9 **Matulji** Primorje-Gorski Kotar, NW Croatia 45°21′N 14°18′E
Matumoto *see* Matsumoto
55 P5 **Maturín** Monagas, NE Venezuela 09°45′N 63°10′W
Matusaka *see* Matsusaka
Matuyama *see* Matsuyama
126 K11 **Matveyev Kurgan** Rostovskaya Oblast', SW Russian Federation 47°31′N 38°55′E
127 O8 **Matyshevo** Volgogradskaya Oblast', SW Russian Federation 50°53′N 44°09′E
153 O13 **Mau** *var.* Maunāth Bhanjan. Uttar Pradesh, N India 25°57′N 83°33′E
83 O14 **Maúa** Niassa, N Mozambique 13°53′S 37°10′E
102 M17 **Maubermé, Pic de** *var.* Tuc de Moubermé, *Sp.* Pico Mauberme; *prev.* Tuc de Maubermé. ▲ France/Spain 42°48′N 00°54′E *see also* Moubermé, Tuc de
Maubermé, Pic de *see* Moubermé, Tuc de
Mauberme, Pico *see* Maubermé, Pic de/Moubermé, Tuc de
Maubermé, Tuc de *see* Maubermé, Pic de/Moubermé, Tuc de
103 Q2 **Maubeuge** Nord, N France 50°16′N 04°00′E
166 L8 **Maubin** Ayeyarwady, SW Myanmar (Burma) 16°44′N 95°37′E
152 L13 **Maudaha** Uttar Pradesh, N India 25°41′N 80°07′E
183 N9 **Maude** New South Wales, SE Australia 34°30′S 144°20′E
195 P3 **Maudheimvidda** *physical region* Antarctica
65 N22 **Maud Rise** *undersea feature* S Atlantic Ocean
109 Q4 **Mauerkirchen** Oberösterreich, NW Austria 48°11′N 13°08′E
Mauersee *see* Mamry, Jezioro
188 K2 **Maug Islands** *island group* N Northern Mariana Islands
103 Q15 **Mauguio** Hérault, S France 43°37′N 04°01′E
193 N5 **Maui** *island* Hawai'i, USA, C Pacific Ocean
190 M16 **Mauke** *atoll* S Cook Islands
62 G13 **Maule** *var.* Región del Maule. ◆ *region* C Chile
102 J9 **Mauléon** Deux-Sèvres, W France 46°55′N 00°45′W
102 J16 **Mauléon-Licharre** Pyrénées-Atlantiques, SW France 43°14′N 00°51′W
Maule, Región del *see* Maule
62 G13 **Maule, Río** ⚞ C Chile
63 G17 **Maullín** Los Lagos, S Chile 41°38′S 73°35′W
31 R11 **Maumee** Ohio, N USA 41°34′N 83°40′W
31 Q12 **Maumee River** ⚞ Indiana/Ohio, N USA
27 U11 **Maumelle** Arkansas, C USA 34°51′N 92°24′W
27 T11 **Maumelle, Lake** ⊠ Arkansas, C USA
171 O16 **Maumere** *prev.* Maoemere. Flores, S Indonesia 08°35′S 122°13′E
83 G17 **Maun** North-West, C Botswana 20°01′S 23°28′E
Maunāth Bhanjan *see* Mau
Maunawai *see* Waimea
190 H16 **Maungaroa** ▲ Rarotonga, S Cook Islands 21°13′S 159°48′W
184 K3 **Maungatapere** Northland, North Island, New Zealand 35°46′S 174°10′E
184 K4 **Maungaturoto** Northland, North Island, New Zealand 36°06′S 174°21′E
191 R10 **Maupiti** *var.* Maurua. *island* Îles Sous le Vent, W French Polynesia
152 K14 **Mau Rānīpur** Uttar Pradesh, N India 25°14′N 79°07′E
22 K9 **Maurepas, Lake** ◎ Louisiana, S USA
103 T16 **Maures** ▲▲ SE France
103 O12 **Mauriac** Cantal, C France 45°13′N 02°21′E
Maurice *see* Mauritius
65 J20 **Maurice Ewing Bank** *undersea feature* SW Atlantic Ocean 51°00′S 43°00′W
182 C4 **Maurice, Lake** *salt lake* South Australia
18 I17 **Maurice River** ⚞ New Jersey, NE USA
25 Y10 **Mauriceville** Texas, SW USA 30°13′N 93°52′W
98 K12 **Maurik** Gelderland, C Netherlands 51°57′N 05°25′E
76 H8 **Mauritania** *off.* Islamic Republic of Mauritania, *Ar.* Mūrītānīyah. ◆ *republic* W Africa
Mauritania, Islamic Republic of *see* Mauritania
173 W15 **Mauritius** *off.* Republic of Mauritius, *Fr.* Maurice. ◆ *republic* W Indian Ocean
128 M17 **Mauritius** *island* W Indian Ocean
Mauritius, Republic of *see* Mauritius
173 N9 **Mauritius Trench** *undersea feature* W Indian Ocean
102 H6 **Mauron** Morbihan, NW France 48°06′N 02°16′W
103 N13 **Maurs** Cantal, C France 44°45′N 02°12′E
Maurua *see* Maupiti
Maury Mid-Ocean Channel *see* Maury Seachannel
64 L6 **Maury Seachannel** *var.* Maury Mid-Ocean Channel. *undersea feature* N Atlantic Ocean 56°33′N 24°00′W
30 K8 **Mauston** Wisconsin, N USA 43°46′N 90°06′W
109 R8 **Mauterndorf** Salzburg, NW Austria 47°09′N 13°39′E
109 T4 **Mauthausen** Oberösterreich, N Austria 48°13′N 14°30′E
109 Q9 **Mauthen** Kärnten, S Austria 46°39′N 12°58′E
83 F15 **Mavinga** Cuando Cubango, SE Angola 15°44′S 20°21′E
83 M17 **Mavita** Manica, W Mozambique 19°31′S 33°09′E
115 K22 **Mavrópetra, Akrotírio** *headland* Santoríni, Kykládes, Greece, Aegean Sea 36°28′N 25°22′E
115 F16 **Mavrovoúni** ▲ C Greece 39°37′N 22°45′E
184 Q8 **Mawhai Point** *headland* North Island, New Zealand 38°08′S 178°24′E
166 L3 **Mawlaik** Sagaing, C Myanmar (Burma) 23°40′N 94°26′E
Mawlamyaing *see* Mawlamyine
166 M9 **Mawlamyine** *var.* Mawlamyaing, Moulmein. Mon State, S Myanmar (Burma) 16°30′N 97°39′E
141 N14 **Mawr, Wādī** *dry watercourse* NW Yemen
195 X5 **Mawson** *Australian research station* Antarctica 67°24′S 63°16′E
195 X5 **Mawson Coast** *physical region* Antarctica
28 M4 **Max** North Dakota, N USA 47°48′N 101°18′W
41 W12 **Maxcanú** Yucatán, SE Mexico 20°35′N 90°00′W
Maxesibebi *see* Mount Ayliff
109 Q5 **Maxglan** ✕ (Salzburg) Salzburg, W Austria 47°46′N 13°00′E
93 K16 **Maxmo** *Fin.* Maksamaa. Länsi-Suomi, W Finland 63°13′N 22°04′E
21 T11 **Maxton** North Carolina, SE USA 34°47′N 79°34′W
25 R8 **May** Texas, SW USA 31°58′N 98°54′W
186 B6 **May** ⚞ NW Papua New Guinea
123 R10 **Maya** ⚞ E Russian Federation
151 Q19 **Māyābandar** Andaman and Nicobar Islands, India, E Indian Ocean 12°43′N 92°52′E
Mayadin *see* Al Mayādīn
44 L5 **Mayaguana** *island* SE Bahamas
44 L5 **Mayaguana Passage** *passage* SE Bahamas
45 S6 **Mayagüez** W Puerto Rico 18°12′N 67°08′W
45 R6 **Mayagüez, Bahía de** *bay* W Puerto Rico
Mayals *see* Maials
79 G20 **Mayama** Pool, SE Congo 03°50′S 14°52′E
37 V8 **Maya, Mesa De** ▲ Colorado, C USA 37°06′N 103°30′W
143 R4 **Mayamey** Semnān, N Iran 36°50′N 55°50′E
42 F3 **Maya Mountains** *Sp.* Montañas Mayas. ▲▲ Belize/Guatemala
44 I7 **Mayarí** Holguín, E Cuba 20°41′N 75°42′W
Mayas, Montañas *see* Maya Mountains
18 I17 **May, Cape** *headland* New Jersey, NE USA 38°55′N 74°57′W
80 J11 **Maych'ew** *var.* Mai Chio, *It.* Mai Ceu. Tigray, N Ethiopia 12°55′N 39°30′E
138 I2 **Maydān Ikbiz** Ḩalab, N Syria 36°51′N 36°40′E
Maydān Shahr *see* Meydān Shahr
80 O12 **Maydh** Sanaag, N Somalia 10°57′N 47°07′E
Maydī *see* Mīdī
Mayebashi *see* Maebashi
Mayence *see* Mainz
102 K6 **Mayenne** Mayenne, NW France 48°18′N 00°37′W
102 J6 **Mayenne** ◆ *department* NW France
102 J7 **Mayenne** ⚞ N France
36 K12 **Mayer** Arizona, SW USA 34°25′N 112°15′W
22 J4 **Mayersville** Mississippi, S USA 32°54′N 91°04′W
11 P14 **Mayerthorpe** Alberta, SW Canada 53°59′N 115°06′W
21 R12 **Mayesville** South Carolina, SE USA 34°00′N 80°10′W
185 G19 **Mayfield** Canterbury, South Island, New Zealand 43°50′S 171°24′E
33 N14 **Mayfield** Idaho, NW USA 43°24′N 115°56′W
20 G7 **Mayfield** Kentucky, S USA 36°45′N 88°40′W
36 L5 **Mayfield** Utah, W USA 39°06′N 111°42′W
Mayhan *see* Sant
37 T14 **Mayhill** New Mexico, SW USA 32°52′N 105°28′W
145 T9 **Maykain** *Kaz.* Mayqayyng. Pavlodar, NE Kazakhstan 51°27′N 75°52′E
126 L14 **Maykop** Respublika Adygeya, SW Russian Federation 44°36′N 40°07′E
Maylibash *see* Maylybas
Mayli-Say *see* Mayluu-Suu
147 T9 **Mayluu-Suu** *prev.* Mayli-Say, *Kir.* Mayly-Say. Dzhalal-Abadskaya Oblast', W Kyrgyzstan 41°16′N 72°27′E
144 L14 **Maylybas** *prev.* Maylibash. Kzylorda, S Kazakhstan 45°51′N 62°37′E
Mayly-Say *see* Mayluu-Suu
Maymana *see* Meymaneh
Maymyo *see* Pyin-Oo-Lwin
123 V7 **Mayn** ⚞ NE Russian Federation
127 Q5 **Mayna** Ul'yanovskaya Oblast', W Russian Federation 54°04′N 47°20′E
21 N8 **Maynardville** Tennessee, S USA 36°15′N 83°48′W
14 J13 **Maynooth** Ontario, SE Canada 45°14′N 77°54′W
10 I6 **Mayo** Yukon Territory, NW Canada 63°37′N 135°48′W
23 U9 **Mayo** Florida, SE USA 30°03′N 83°10′W
97 B16 **Mayo** *Ir.* Maigh Eo. *cultural region* W Ireland
Mayo *see* Maio
78 G12 **Mayo-Kébbi** *off.* Préfecture du Mayo-Kébbi, *var.* Mayo-Kébi. ◆ *prefecture* SW Chad
Mayo-Kébbi, Préfecture du *see* Mayo-Kébbi
Mayo-Kébi *see* Mayo-Kébbi
79 F19 **Mayoko** Niari, SW Congo 02°19′S 12°47′E
171 P4 **Mayon Volcano** ⚡ Luzon, N Philippines 13°15′N 123°41′E
61 A24 **Mayor Buratovich** Buenos Aires, E Argentina 39°15′S 62°35′W
104 L4 **Mayorga** Castilla-León, N Spain 42°10′N 05°16′W
184 N6 **Mayor Island** *island* NE New Zealand
Mayor Pablo Lagerenza *see* Capitán Pablo Lagerenza
173 I14 **Mayotte** ◇ *French territorial collectivity* E Africa
Mayoumba *see* Mayumba
44 J13 **May Pen** C Jamaica 17°58′N 77°15′W
Mayqayyng *see* Maykain
171 O1 **Mayraira Point** *headland* Luzon, N Philippines 18°36′N 120°47′E
109 N8 **Mayrhofen** Tirol, W Austria 47°09′N 11°52′E
186 A6 **May River** East Sepik, NW Papua New Guinea 04°24′S 141°52′E
139 X10 **Maysān** ◆ *governorate* SE Iraq
123 R13 **Mayskiy** Amurskaya Oblast', SE Russian Federation 52°13′N 129°30′E
127 O15 **Mayskiy** Kabardino-Balkarskaya Respublika, SW Russian Federation 43°37′N 44°04′E
145 U9 **Mayskoye** Pavlodar, NE Kazakhstan 50°55′N 78°11′E
18 J17 **Mays Landing** New Jersey, NE USA 39°27′N 74°44′W
21 N4 **Maysville** Kentucky, S USA 38°38′N 83°46′W
27 R2 **Maysville** Missouri, C USA 39°53′N 94°21′W
79 D20 **Mayumba** *var.* Mayoumba. Nyanga, S Gabon 03°23′S 10°38′E
31 S8 **Mayville** Michigan, N USA 43°18′N 83°16′W
18 C11 **Mayville** New York, NE USA 42°15′N 79°32′W
29 Q4 **Mayville** North Dakota, N USA 47°27′N 97°17′W
Mayyali *see* Mahe
Mayyit, Al Baḩr al *see* Dead Sea
83 J15 **Mazabuka** Southern, S Zambia 15°52′S 27°46′E
Mazaca *see* Kayseri
Mazagan *see* El-Jadida
32 J7 **Mazama** Washington, NW USA 48°34′N 120°26′W
103 O15 **Mazamet** Tarn, S France 43°30′N 02°21′E
143 O4 **Māzandarān** *off.* Ostān-e Māzandarān. ◆ *province* N Iran
Māzandarān, Ostān-e *see* Māzandarān
156 F7 **Mazar** Xinjiang Uygur Zizhiqu, NW China 36°28′N 77°00′E
107 H24 **Mazara del Vallo** Sicilia, Italy, C Mediterranean Sea 37°39′N 12°36′E
149 O2 **Mazār-e Sharīf** *var.* Mazār-i Sharif. Balkh, N Afghanistan 36°44′N 67°06′E
Mazār-i Sharif *see* Mazār-e Sharīf
105 R13 **Mazarrón** Murcia, SE Spain 37°36′N 01°19′W

◆ Country
● Country Capital
◇ Dependent Territory
○ Dependent Territory Capital
◆ Administrative Regions
✕ International Airport
▲ Mountain
▲▲ Mountain Range
⚡ Volcano
⚞ River
◎ Lake
⊠ Reservoir

MAZARRÓN, GOLFO DE – MENESJÄRVI

105 R14 **Mazarrón, Golfo de** *gulf* SE Spain
55 S9 **Mazaruni River** ≈ N Guyana
42 B6 **Mazatenango** Suchitepéquez, SW Guatemala 14°31′N 91°30′W
40 I10 **Mazatlán** Sinaloa, C Mexico 23°15′N 106°24′W
36 L12 **Mazatzal Mountains** ▲▲ Arizona, SW USA
118 D10 **Mažeikiai** Telšiai, NW Lithuania 56°19′N 22°22′E
118 D7 **Mazirbe** Talsi, NW Latvia 57°39′N 22°16′E
40 G5 **Mazocahui** Sonora, NW Mexico 29°32′N 110°09′W
57 I18 **Mazocruz** Puno, S Peru 16°41′S 69°42′W
Mazoe, Rio *see* Mazowe
79 N21 **Mazomeno** Maniema, E Dem. Rep. Congo 04°54′S 27°13′E
159 Q6 **Mazong Shan** ▲ N China 41°40′N 97°10′E
83 L16 **Mazowe** *var.* Rio Mazoe. ≈ Mozambique/Zimbabwe
110 M11 **Mazowieckie** ◈ *province* C Poland
Mazra'a *see* Al Mazra'ah
138 G6 **Mazraat Kfar Debiâne** C Lebanon 34°00′N 35°51′E
118 H7 **Mazsalaca** *Est.* Väike-Salatsi, *Ger.* Salisburg. Valmiera, N Latvia 57°52′N 25°03′E
Mazu Dao *see* Matsu Tao
110 L9 **Mazury** *physical region* NE Poland
119 M20 **Mazyr** *Rus.* Mozyr'. Homyel'skaya Voblasts', SE Belarus 52°04′N 29°15′E
107 K25 **Mazzarino** Sicilia, Italy, C Mediterranean Sea 37°18′N 14°13′E
Mba *see* Ba
83 L21 **Mbabane** ● (Swaziland) NW Swaziland 26°24′S 31°13′E
Mbacké *see* Mbaké
77 N16 **Mbahiakro** E Ivory Coast 07°33′N 04°19′W
79 I16 **Mbaïki** *var.* M'Baiki. Lobaye, SW Central African Republic 03°52′N 17°58′E
M'Baiki *see* Mbaïki
79 F14 **Mbakaou, Lac de** ◎ C Cameroon
76 G11 **Mbaké** *var.* Mbacké. W Senegal 14°47′N 15°54′W
82 L11 **Mbala** *prev.* Abercorn. Northern, NE Zambia 08°50′S 31°23′E
83 J18 **Mbalabala** *prev.* Balla Balla. Matabeleland South, SW Zimbabwe 20°27′S 29°03′E
81 G18 **Mbale** E Uganda 01°04′N 34°12′E
79 E16 **Mbalmayo** *var.* M'Balmayo. Centre, S Cameroon 03°30′N 11°31′E
M'Balmayo *see* Mbalmayo
81 H25 **Mbamba Bay** Ruvuma, S Tanzania 11°15′S 34°44′E
79 I18 **Mbandaka** *prev.* Coquilhatville. Equateur, NW Dem. Rep. Congo 0°07′N 18°12′E
82 B9 **M'Banza Congo** *var.* Mbanza Congo; *prev.* São Salvador, São Salvador do Congo. Dem Rep. Congo, NW Angola 06°11′S 14°16′E
79 G21 **Mbanza-Ngungu** Bas-Congo, W Dem. Rep. Congo 05°19′S 14°45′E
67 V11 **Mbarangandu** ≈ E Tanzania
81 E19 **Mbarara** SW Uganda 0°36′S 30°40′E
79 L15 **Mbari** ≈ SE Central African Republic
81 I24 **Mbarika Mountains** ▲▲ S Tanzania
78 F13 **Mbé** Nord, N Cameroon 07°51′N 13°36′E
81 J24 **Mbemkuru** *var.* Mbwemkuru. ≈ S Tanzania
Mbengga *see* Beqa
172 H13 **Mbéni** Grande Comore, NW Comoros
83 K18 **Mberengwa** Midlands, S Zimbabwe 20°29′S 29°55′E
81 G24 **Mbeya** Mbeya, SW Tanzania 08°54′S 33°29′E
81 G23 **Mbeya** ◈ *region* S Tanzania
83 J24 **Mbhashe** *prev.* Mbashe. ≈ S South Africa
79 E19 **Mbigou** Ngounié, C Gabon 01°54′S 12°00′E
Mbilua *see* Vella Lavella
79 F19 **Mbinda** Niari, SW Congo 02°07′S 12°52′E
79 D17 **Mbini** W Equatorial Guinea 01°34′N 09°39′E
Mbini *see* Uolo, Río
83 L18 **Mbizi** Masvingo, SE Zimbabwe 21°23′S 30°54′E
81 G23 **Mbogo** Mbeya, W Tanzania 07°24′S 33°26′E
79 N15 **Mboki** Haut-Mbomou, SE Central African Republic 05°18′N 25°52′E
79 G18 **Mbomo** Cuvette, NW Congo 0°25′N 14°42′E
79 L15 **Mbomou** ◈ *prefecture* SE Central African Republic
Mbomou/M'Bomu/Mbomu *see* Bomu
76 F11 **Mbour** W Senegal 14°22′N 16°54′W
76 I10 **Mbout** Gorgol, S Mauritania 16°02′N 12°38′W
79 J14 **Mbrès** *var.* Mbrés. Nana-Grébizi, C Central African Republic 06°40′N 19°46′E
Mbrés *see* Mbrès
79 L22 **Mbuji-Mayi** *prev.* Bakwanga. Kasai-Oriental, S Dem. Rep. Congo 06°05′S 23°30′E
81 H21 **Mbulu** Manyara, N Tanzania 03°45′S 35°33′E
186 E5 **M'bunai** *var.* Bunai. Manus Island, N Papua New Guinea 02°08′S 147°13′E
62 N8 **Mburucuyá** Corrientes, NE Argentina 28°03′S 58°15′W
Mbutha *see* Buca
Mbwemkuru *see* Mbemkuru
81 G21 **Mbwikwe** Singida, C Tanzania 05°19′S 34°09′E
13 O15 **McAdam** New Brunswick, SE Canada 45°34′N 67°20′W
25 O5 **McAdoo** Texas, SW USA 33°41′N 100°58′W
35 V2 **McAfee Peak** ▲ Nevada, W USA 41°31′N 115°57′W
27 P11 **McAlester** Oklahoma, C USA 34°56′N 95°46′W
25 S17 **McAllen** Texas SW USA 26°12′N 98°14′W
21 S11 **McBee** South Carolina, SE USA 34°30′N 80°12′W
11 N14 **McBride** British Columbia, SW Canada 53°21′N 120°19′W
24 M9 **McCamey** Texas, SW USA 31°08′N 102°13′W
33 R15 **McCammon** Idaho, NW USA 42°38′N 112°10′W
35 X11 **McCarran** ✈ (Las Vegas) Nevada, W USA 36°04′N 115°07′W
39 T11 **McCarthy** Alaska, USA 61°25′N 142°55′W
30 M5 **McCaslin Mountain** *hill* Wisconsin, N USA
25 O2 **McClellan Creek** ≈ Texas, SW USA
21 T14 **McClellanville** South Carolina, SE USA 33°07′N 79°27′W
8 L6 **McClintock Channel** *channel* Nunavut, N Canada
195 R12 **McClintock, Mount** ▲ Antarctica 80°09′S 156°42′E
35 N2 **McCloud** California, W USA 41°15′N 122°09′W
35 N3 **McCloud River** ≈ California, W USA
35 Q9 **McClure, Lake** ⊞ California, W USA
197 O8 **McClure Strait** *strait* Northwest Territories, N Canada
29 N4 **McClusky** North Dakota, N USA 47°27′N 100°25′W
21 T11 **McColl** South Carolina, SE USA 34°40′N 79°33′W
22 K7 **McComb** Mississippi, S USA 31°14′N 90°27′W
18 E16 **McConnellsburg** Pennsylvania, NE USA 39°56′N 78°00′W
31 T14 **McConnelsville** Ohio, N USA 39°39′N 81°51′W
28 M17 **McCook** Nebraska, C USA 40°12′N 100°38′W
21 P13 **McCormick** South Carolina, SE USA 33°55′N 82°19′W
11 W16 **McCreary** Manitoba, S Canada 50°48′N 99°34′W
27 W11 **McCrory** Arkansas, C USA 35°15′N 91°12′W
25 T10 **McDade** Texas, SW USA 30°15′N 97°15′W
23 O8 **McDavid** Florida, SE USA 30°51′N 87°18′W
35 T1 **McDermitt** Nevada, W USA 41°57′N 117°43′W
23 S4 **McDonough** Georgia, SE USA 33°27′N 84°09′W
36 L12 **McDowell Mountains** ▲▲ Arizona, SW USA
20 H8 **McEwen** Tennessee, S USA 36°06′N 87°37′W
35 R12 **McFarland** California, W USA 35°41′N 119°14′W
Mcfarlane, Lake *see* Macfarlane, Lake
27 P12 **McGee Creek Lake** ⊞ Oklahoma, C USA
27 W13 **McGehee** Arkansas, C USA 33°37′N 91°24′W
35 X5 **Mcgill** Nevada, W USA 39°24′N 114°46′W
14 K11 **McGillivray, Lac** ◎ Québec, SE Canada
39 P10 **McGrath** Alaska, USA 62°57′N 155°36′W
25 T8 **McGregor** Texas, SW USA 31°26′N 97°24′W
33 O12 **McGuire, Mount** ▲ Idaho, NW USA 45°10′N 114°36′W
83 M14 **Mchinji** *prev.* Fort Manning. Central, W Malawi 13°48′S 32°55′E
28 M7 **McIntosh** South Dakota, N USA 45°56′N 101°21′W
9 S7 **McKeand** ≈ Baffin Island, Nunavut, NE Canada
191 R4 **McKean Island** *island* Phoenix Islands, C Kiribati
30 J13 **McKee Creek** ≈ Illinois, N USA
18 C15 **Mckeesport** Pennsylvania, NE USA 40°18′N 79°48′W
21 V7 **McKenney** Virginia, NE USA 36°57′N 77°42′W
20 G8 **McKenzie** Tennessee, S USA 36°07′N 88°31′W
185 B20 **McKerrow, Lake** ◎ South Island, New Zealand
39 Q10 **McKinley, Mount** *var.* Denali. ▲ Alaska, USA 63°04′N 151°00′W
39 R10 **McKinley Park** Alaska, USA 63°42′N 149°01′W
34 K3 **McKinleyville** California, W USA 40°56′N 124°06′W
25 U6 **McKinney** Texas, SW USA 33°14′N 96°37′W
26 I5 **McKinney, Lake** ◎ Kansas, C USA
28 M7 **McLaughlin** South Dakota, N USA 45°48′N 100°48′W
25 O2 **McLean** Texas, SW USA 35°13′N 100°36′W
30 M16 **Mcleansboro** Illinois, N USA 38°05′N 88°32′W
11 O13 **McLennan** Alberta, W Canada 55°42′N 116°50′W
14 L9 **McLennan, Lac** ◎ Québec, SE Canada
10 M13 **McLeod Lake** British Columbia, W Canada 55°03′N 123°02′W
27 N10 **McLoud** Oklahoma, C USA 35°26′N 97°05′W
32 G15 **McLoughlin, Mount** ▲ Oregon, NW USA 42°27′N 122°18′W
37 U15 **McMillan, Lake** ⊞ New Mexico, SW USA
32 G11 **McMinnville** Oregon, NW USA 45°14′N 123°12′W
20 K9 **McMinnville** Tennessee, S USA 35°40′N 85°49′W
195 R13 **McMurdo** *US research station* Antarctica 77°40′S 167°16′E
37 N13 **Mcnary** Arizona, SW USA 34°04′N 109°51′W
24 H9 **McNary** Texas, SW USA 31°15′N 105°46′W
27 N5 **McPherson** Kansas, C USA 38°22′N 97°41′W
McPherson *see* Fort McPherson
23 U6 **McRae** Georgia, SE USA 32°04′N 82°54′W
29 P4 **McVille** North Dakota, N USA 47°45′N 98°10′W
83 J25 **Mdantsane** Eastern Cape, SE South Africa 32°55′S 27°39′E
167 T6 **Me** Ninh Binh, N Vietnam 20°21′N 105°49′E
26 J7 **Meade** Kansas, C USA 37°17′N 100°21′W
39 O5 **Meade River** ≈ Alaska, USA
35 Y11 **Mead, Lake** ⊞ Arizona/Nevada, W USA
24 M5 **Meadow** Texas, SW USA 33°20′N 102°12′W
11 S14 **Meadow Lake** Saskatchewan, C Canada 54°90′N 108°30′W
35 Y10 **Meadow Valley Wash** ≈ Nevada, W USA
22 J7 **Meadville** Mississippi, S USA 31°28′N 90°51′W
18 B12 **Meadville** Pennsylvania, NE USA 41°38′N 80°09′W
14 F14 **Meaford** Ontario, S Canada 44°35′N 80°35′W
Meáin, Inis *see* Inishmaan
104 G8 **Mealhada** Aveiro, N Portugal 40°22′N 08°27′W
13 R8 **Mealy Mountains** ▲▲ Newfoundland and Labrador, E Canada
11 O10 **Meander River** Alberta, W Canada 59°02′N 117°42′W
32 E11 **Meares, Cape** *headland* Oregon, NW USA 45°29′N 123°59′W
47 V6 **Mearim, Rio** ≈ NE Brazil
Measca, Loch *see* Mask, Lough
97 F17 **Meath** *Ir.* An Mhí. *cultural region* E Ireland
11 T14 **Meath Park** Saskatchewan, S Canada 53°25′N 105°18′W
103 O5 **Meaux** Seine-et-Marne, N France 48°47′N 02°54′E
21 T9 **Mebane** North Carolina, SE USA 36°06′N 79°16′W
171 U12 **Mebo, Gunung** ▲ Papua, E Indonesia 01°10′S 133°53′E
94 I8 **Mebonden** Sør-Trøndelag, S Norway 63°13′N 11°00′E
82 A10 **Mebridege** ≈ NW Angola
35 W16 **Mecca** California, W USA 33°34′N 116°04′W
Mecca *see* Makkah
29 Y14 **Mechanicsville** Iowa, C USA 41°54′N 91°15′W
18 L10 **Mechanicville** New York, NE USA 42°54′N 73°41′W
99 H17 **Mechelen** *Eng.* Mechlin, *Fr.* Malines. Antwerpen, C Belgium 51°02′N 04°29′E
188 C8 **Mecherchar** *var.* Eil Malk. *island* Palau Islands, Palau
101 D17 **Mechernich** Nordrhein-Westfalen, W Germany 50°36′N 06°39′E
126 L12 **Mechetinskaya** Rostovskaya Oblast', SW Russian Federation 46°46′N 40°30′E
114 J11 **Mechka** ≈ S Bulgaria
Mechlin *see* Mechelen
61 D23 **Mechongué** Buenos Aires, E Argentina 38°09′S 58°13′W
115 L14 **Mecidiye** Edirne, NW Turkey 40°39′N 26°33′E
101 I24 **Meckenbeuren** Baden-Württemberg, S Germany 47°42′N 09°34′E
100 L8 **Mecklenburger Bucht** *bay* N Germany
100 M10 **Mecklenburgische Seenplatte** *wetland* NE Germany
100 L9 **Mecklenburg-Vorpommern** ◈ *state* NE Germany
83 Q15 **Meconta** Nampula, NE Mozambique 15°01′S 39°52′E
111 I25 **Mecsek** ▲▲ SW Hungary
83 P14 **Mecubúri** ≈ N Mozambique
83 Q14 **Mecúfi** Cabo Delgado, NE Mozambique 13°20′S 40°32′E
82 O13 **Mecula** Niassa, N Mozambique 12°03′S 37°37′E
168 I8 **Medan** Sumatera, E Indonesia 03°35′N 98°39′E
61 A24 **Médanos** *var.* Medanos. Buenos Aires, E Argentina 38°52′S 62°45′W
61 C19 **Médanos** Entre Ríos, E Argentina 33°28′S 59°07′W
155 K24 **Medawachchiya** North Central Province, N Sri Lanka 08°32′N 80°30′E
106 C8 **Mede** Lombardia, N Italy 45°06′N 08°43′E
74 J5 **Médéa** *var.* El Mediyya, Lemdiyya. N Algeria 36°15′N 02°48′E
Medeba *see* Ma'dabā
54 E8 **Medellín** Antioquia, NW Colombia 06°15′N 75°36′W
100 H9 **Medem** ≈ NW Germany
98 J8 **Medemblik** Noord-Holland, NW Netherlands 52°47′N 05°06′E
75 N7 **Médenine** *var.* Madanīyīn. SE Tunisia 33°23′N 10°30′E
76 G9 **Mederdra** Trarza, SW Mauritania 16°56′N 15°40′W
Medeshamstede *see* Peterborough
42 F4 **Medesto Mendez** Izabal, NE Guatemala 15°54′N 89°13′W
19 O11 **Medford** Massachusetts, NE USA 42°25′N 71°08′W
27 N8 **Medford** Oklahoma, C USA 36°48′N 97°45′W
32 G15 **Medford** Oregon, NW USA 42°20′N 122°52′W
30 K6 **Medford** Wisconsin, N USA 45°08′N 90°22′W
39 P10 **Medfra** Alaska, USA 63°06′N 154°42′W
116 M14 **Medgidia** Constanța, SE Romania 44°15′N 28°16′E
Medgyes *see* Mediaș
43 O5 **Media Luna, Arrecifes de la** *reef* E Honduras
60 G11 **Medianeira** Paraná, S Brazil 25°15′S 54°07′W
29 Y15 **Mediapolis** Iowa, C USA 41°00′N 91°09′W
116 I11 **Mediaș** *Ger.* Mediasch, *Hung.* Medgyes. Sibiu, C Romania 46°10′N 24°20′E
41 S15 **Medias Aguas** Veracruz-Llave, SE Mexico 17°40′N 95°02′W
Mediasch *see* Mediaș
106 G10 **Medicina** Emilia-Romagna, C Italy 44°29′N 11°41′E
33 X16 **Medicine Bow** Wyoming, C USA 41°52′N 106°11′W
37 S2 **Medicine Bow Mountains** ▲▲ Colorado/Wyoming, C USA
33 X16 **Medicine Bow River** ≈ Wyoming, C USA
11 R17 **Medicine Hat** Alberta, SW Canada 50°03′N 110°41′W
26 L7 **Medicine Lodge** Kansas, C USA 37°18′N 98°35′W
26 L7 **Medicine Lodge River** ≈ Kansas/Oklahoma, C USA
112 E7 **Međimurje** *off.* Međimurska Županija. ◈ *province* N Croatia
Međimurska Županija *see* Međimurje
54 G10 **Medina** Cundinamarca, C Colombia 04°31′N 73°21′W
18 E9 **Medina** New York, NE USA 43°13′N 78°23′W
29 O5 **Medina** North Dakota, N USA 46°53′N 99°18′W
31 T11 **Medina** Ohio, N USA 41°08′N 81°51′W
25 Q11 **Medina** Texas, SW USA 29°46′N 99°14′W
Medina *see* Al Madīnah
105 P6 **Medinaceli** Castilla-León, N Spain 41°10′N 02°26′W
104 L6 **Medina del Campo** Castilla-León, N Spain 41°18′N 04°55′W
104 L5 **Medina de Ríoseco** Castilla-León, N Spain 41°53′N 05°03′W
Médina Gonassé *see* Médina Gounas
76 H12 **Médina Gounas** *var.* Médina Gonassé. S Senegal 13°06′N 13°49′W
25 S12 **Medina River** ≈ Texas, SW USA
104 K16 **Medina Sidonia** Andalucía, S Spain 36°28′N 05°55′W
Medinat Israel *see* Israel
119 H14 **Medininkai** Vilnius, SE Lithuania 54°32′N 25°40′E
153 R16 **Medinīpur** West Bengal, NE India 22°25′N 87°24′E
Mediolanum *see* Saintes, France
Mediolanum *see* Milano, Italy
Mediomatrica *see* Metz
121 Q11 **Mediterranean Ridge** *undersea feature* C Mediterranean Sea 34°00′N 23°00′E
121 O16 **Mediterranean Sea** *Fr.* Mer Méditerranée. *sea* Africa/Asia/Europe
Méditerranée, Mer *see* Mediterranean Sea
79 N17 **Medje** Orientale, NE Dem. Rep. Congo 02°27′N 27°14′E
Medjerda, Oued *see* Mejerda
114 G7 **Medkovets** Montana, NW Bulgaria 43°39′N 23°22′E
93 J15 **Medle** Västerbotten, N Sweden 64°45′N 20°45′E
127 W7 **Mednogorsk** Orenburgskaya Oblast', W Russian Federation 51°24′N 57°37′E
123 W9 **Mednyy, Ostrov** *island* E Russian Federation
102 J12 **Médoc** *cultural region* SW France
159 Q16 **Mêdog** Xizang Zizhiqu, W China 29°26′N 95°26′E
28 J5 **Medora** North Dakota, N USA 46°56′N 103°40′W
79 E17 **Médouneu** Woleu-Ntem, N Gabon 0°58′N 10°50′E
106 I7 **Meduna** ≈ NE Italy
Medunta *see* Mantes-la-Jolie
127 P3 **Medvedevo** Respublika Mariy El, W Russian Federation 56°38′N 47°48′E
Medvedica *see* Medveditsa
124 J16 **Medveditsa** *var.* Medvedica. ≈ W Russian Federation
127 O9 **Medveditsa** ≈ SW Russian Federation
112 E8 **Medvednica** ▲▲ NE Croatia
125 R15 **Medvedok** Kirovskaya Oblast', NW Russian Federation 57°23′N 50°01′E
123 S6 **Medvezh'i, Ostrova** *island group* NE Russian Federation
124 J9 **Medvezh'yegorsk** Respublika Kareliya, NW Russian Federation 62°56′N 34°26′E
109 T11 **Medvode** *Ger.* Zwischenwässern. NW Slovenia 46°09′N 14°21′E
126 J4 **Medyn'** Kaluzhskaya Oblast', W Russian Federation 54°59′N 35°52′E
180 J10 **Meekatharra** Western Australia 26°37′S 118°35′E
37 Q4 **Meeker** Colorado, C USA 40°02′N 107°54′W
13 T12 **Meelpaeg Lake** ◎ Newfoundland, Newfoundland and Labrador, E Canada
Meemu Atoll *see* Mulakatholhu
Meenen *see* Menen
101 M16 **Meerane** Sachsen, E Germany 50°50′N 12°28′E
101 D15 **Meerbusch** Nordrhein-Westfalen, W Germany 51°19′N 06°43′E
98 I12 **Meerkerk** Zuid-Holland, C Netherlands 51°55′N 05°00′E
99 L18 **Meerssen** *var.* Mersen. Limburg, SE Netherlands 50°53′N 05°45′E
152 J10 **Meerut** Uttar Pradesh, N India 29°01′N 77°41′E
33 U13 **Meeteetse** Wyoming, C USA 44°10′N 108°53′W
99 K17 **Meeuwen** Limburg, NE Belgium 51°04′N 05°36′E
81 J16 **Mēga** Oromīya, C Ethiopia 04°03′N 38°15′E
81 J16 **Mēga Escarpment** *escarpment* S Ethiopia
Megála Kalívia *see* Megála Kalývia
115 E16 **Megála Kalývia** *var.* Megála Kalívia. Thessalía, C Greece 39°30′N 21°48′E
115 H14 **Megáli Panagiá** *var.* Megáli Panayía. Kentrikí Makedonía, N Greece 40°24′N 23°42′E
Megáli Panayía *see* Megáli Panagiá
Megáli Préspa, Límni *see* Prespa, Lake
114 K12 **Megálo Livádi** ▲ Bulgaria/Greece 41°18′N 25°51′E
115 E20 **Megalópoli** *prev.* Megalópolis. Pelopónnisos, S Greece 37°24′N 22°08′E
Megalópolis *see* Megalópoli
171 U12 **Megamo** Papua, E Indonesia 0°55′S 131°46′E
115 C18 **Meganísi** *island* Iónia Nisiá, Greece, C Mediterranean Sea
Meganom, Mys *see* Mehanom, Mys
Mégantic *see* Lac-Mégantic
15 R12 **Mégantic, Mont** ▲ Québec, SE Canada 45°27′N 71°09′W
115 G19 **Mégara** Attikí, C Greece 38°00′N 23°20′E
25 R5 **Megargel** Texas, SW USA 33°27′N 98°55′W
98 K13 **Megen** Noord-Brabant, S Netherlands 51°49′N 05°34′E
153 U13 **Meghālaya** ◈ *state* NE India
153 U16 **Meghna Nadi** ≈ S Bangladesh
137 V14 **Meghri** *Rus.* Megri. SE Armenia 38°57′N 46°15′E
115 Q23 **Megísti** *var.* Kastellórizon. *island* SE Greece
Megri *see* Meghri
Mehabad *see* Mahābād
116 F13 **Mehadia** *Hung.* Mehádia. Caraș-Severin, SW Romania 44°53′N 22°20′E
Mehádia *see* Mehadia
92 L7 **Mehamn** Finnmark, N Norway 71°01′N 27°46′E
117 U13 **Mehanom, Mys** *Rus.* Mys Meganom. *headland* S Ukraine 44°48′N 35°04′E
149 P14 **Mehar** Sind, SE Pakistan 27°12′N 67°51′E
180 J8 **Meharry, Mount** ▲ Western Australia 23°17′S 118°48′E
Mehdia *see* Mahdia
116 G14 **Mehedinți** ◈ *county* SW Romania
153 S15 **Meherpur** Khulna, W Bangladesh 23°47′N 88°40′E
21 W8 **Meherrin River** ≈ North Carolina/Virginia, SE USA
Meheso *see* Mī'ēso
191 T11 **Mehetia** *island* Îles du Vent, W French Polynesia
118 K6 **Mehikoorma** Tartumaa, E Estonia 58°14′N 27°29′E
Me Hka *see* Nmai Hka
143 N5 **Mehrabad** ✈ (Tehrān) Tehrān, N Iran 35°46′N 51°07′E
142 J7 **Mehrān** Īlām, W Iran 33°07′N 46°10′E
143 Q14 **Mehrān, Rūd-e** *prev.* Mansurabad. ≈ W Iran
143 Q9 **Mehrīz** Yazd, C Iran 31°32′N 54°28′E
149 R5 **Mehtar Lām** *var.* Mehtarlām, Meterlam, Methariam, Metharlam. Laghmān, E Afghanistan 34°39′N 70°10′E
Mehtarlām *see* Mehtar Lām
103 N8 **Mehun-sur-Yèvre** Cher, C France 47°09′N 02°15′E
79 G14 **Meiganga** Adamaoua, NE Cameroon 06°31′N 14°07′E
160 H10 **Meigu** *var.* Bapu. Sichuan, C China 28°16′N 103°20′E
163 W11 **Meihekou** *var.* Hailong. Jilin, NE China 42°31′N 125°40′E
99 L15 **Meijel** Limburg, SE Netherlands 51°22′N 05°52′E
Meijiang *see* Ningdu
166 M5 **Meiktila** Mandalay, C Myanmar (Burma) 20°53′N 95°54′E
Meilbhe, Loch *see* Melvin, Lough
108 G7 **Meilen** Zürich, N Switzerland 47°17′N 08°39′E
Meilu *see* Wuchuan
161 T12 **Meinhua Yu** *island* N Taiwan
101 J17 **Meiningen** Thüringen, C Germany 50°34′N 10°25′E
108 F9 **Meiringen** Bern, S Switzerland 46°42′N 08°13′E
160 H9 **Meishan** Sichuan, C China 30°02′N 103°29′E
Meishan *see* Jinzhai
101 O15 **Meissen** *Ger.* Meißen. Sachsen, E Germany 51°10′N 13°28′E
Meißen *see* Meissen
101 I15 **Meissner** ▲ C Germany 51°13′N 09°52′E
99 K25 **Meix-devant-Virton** Luxembourg, SE Belgium 49°36′N 05°27′E
Meixian *see* Meizhou
Meixing *see* Xinjin
161 P13 **Meizhou** *var.* Meixian, Mei Xian. Guangdong, S China 24°21′N 116°05′E
67 P2 **Mejerda** *var.* Oued Medjerda, Wādī Majardah. ≈ Algeria/Tunisia *see also* Medjerda, Oued
42 F7 **Mejicanos** San Salvador, C El Salvador 13°50′N 89°13′W
Méjico *see* Mexico
62 G5 **Mejillones** Antofagasta, N Chile 23°03′S 70°25′W
189 V5 **Mejit Island** *var.* Mājeej. *island* Ratak Chain, NE Marshall Islands
79 F17 **Mékambo** Ogooué-Ivindo, NE Gabon 01°03′N 13°50′E
80 J10 **Mek'elē** *var.* Makale. Tigray, N Ethiopia 13°36′N 39°29′E
74 I10 **Mekerrhane, Sebkha** *var.* Sebkha Meqerghane, Sebkra Mekerrhane. *salt flat* C Algeria
Mekerrhane, Sebkra *see* Mekerrhane, Sebkha
76 G10 **Mékhé** NW Senegal 15°02′N 16°40′W
146 G14 **Mekhinli** Ahal Welaýaty, C Turkmenistan 37°28′N 59°20′E
15 P9 **Mékinac, Lac** ◎ Québec, SE Canada
Meklong *see* Samut Songhram
74 G6 **Meknès** N Morocco 33°54′N 05°27′W
129 U12 **Mekong** *var.* Lan-ts'ang Chiang, *Cam.* Mékôngk, *Chin.* Lancang Jiang, *Lao.* Mènam Khong, *Th.* Mae Nam Khong, *Tib.* Dza Chu, *Vtn.* Sông Tiên Giang. ≈ SE Asia
Mékôngk *see* Mekong
167 T15 **Mekong, Mouths of the** *delta* S Vietnam
38 L12 **Mekoryuk** Nunivak Island, Alaska, USA 60°23′N 166°11′W
77 R14 **Mékrou** ≈ N Benin
168 K9 **Melaka** *var.* Malacca. Melaka, Peninsular Malaysia 02°14′N 102°14′E
168 L9 **Melaka** *var.* Malacca. ◈ *state* Peninsular Malaysia
Melaka, Selat *see* Malacca, Strait of
175 O6 **Melanesia** *island group* W Pacific Ocean
175 P5 **Melanesian Basin** *undersea feature* W Pacific Ocean 0°05′N 160°35′E
171 R9 **Melanguane** Pulau Karakelang, N Indonesia 04°02′N 126°43′E
169 R11 **Melawi, Sungai** ≈ Borneo, N Indonesia
183 N12 **Melbourne** *state capital* Victoria, SE Australia 37°51′S 144°56′E
27 V9 **Melbourne** Arkansas, C USA 36°04′N 91°54′W
23 Y12 **Melbourne** Florida, SE USA 28°04′N 80°36′W
29 W14 **Melbourne** Iowa, C USA 41°57′N 93°07′W
92 G10 **Melbu** Nordland, C Norway 68°31′N 14°50′E
Melchor de Mencos *see* Ciudad Melchor de Mencos
63 F19 **Melchor, Isla** *island* Archipiélago de los Chonos, S Chile
40 M9 **Melchor Ocampo** Zacatecas, C Mexico 24°45′N 101°38′W
14 C11 **Meldrum Bay** Manitoulin Island, Ontario, S Canada 45°55′N 83°06′W
Meleda *see* Mljet
106 D8 **Melegnano** *prev.* Marignano. Lombardia, N Italy 45°22′N 09°19′E
Melekeiok *see* Melekeok
188 F9 **Melekeok** *var.* Melekeiok. ● Babeldaob, N Palau 07°30′N 134°39′E
112 L9 **Melenci** *Hung.* Melencze. Vojvodina, N Serbia 45°32′N 20°18′E
Melencze *see* Melenci
127 N4 **Melenki** Vladimirskaya Oblast', W Russian Federation 55°21′N 41°37′E
127 V6 **Meleuz** Respublika Bashkortostan, W Russian Federation 52°55′N 55°54′E
12 L6 **Mélèzes, Rivière aux** ≈ Québec, C Canada
78 I11 **Melfi** Guéra, S Chad 11°05′N 17°57′E
107 M17 **Melfi** Basilicata, S Italy 41°00′N 15°33′E
11 U14 **Melfort** Saskatchewan, S Canada 52°52′N 104°38′W
104 H4 **Melgaço** Viana do Castelo, N Portugal 42°07′N 08°15′W
105 N4 **Melgar de Fernamental** Castilla-León, N Spain 42°24′N 04°15′W
74 L6 **Melghir, Chott** *var.* Chott Melrhir. *salt lake* E Algeria
94 H8 **Melhus** Sør-Trøndelag, S Norway 63°17′N 10°18′E
104 H3 **Melide** Galicia, NW Spain 42°54′N 08°01′W
Meligalá *see* Meligalás
115 E21 **Meligalás** *prev.* Meligalá. Pelopónnisos, S Greece 37°13′N 21°58′E
60 L12 **Mel, Ilha do** *island* S Brazil
120 E10 **Melilla** *anc.* Rusaddir, Russadir. Melilla, Spain, N Africa 35°18′N 02°56′W
71 N1 **Melilla** *enclave* Spain, N Africa
63 G18 **Melimoyu, Monte** ▲ S Chile 44°06′S 72°49′W
169 V11 **Melintang, Danau** ◎ Borneo, N Indonesia
117 U7 **Melioratyvne** Dnipropetrovs'ka Oblast', E Ukraine 48°35′N 35°18′E
62 G11 **Melipilla** Santiago, C Chile 33°42′S 71°15′W
115 I25 **Mélissa, Akrotírio** *headland* Kríti, Greece, E Mediterranean Sea 35°06′N 24°33′E
11 W17 **Melita** Manitoba, S Canada 49°16′N 100°59′W
Melita *see* Mljet
Melitene *see* Malatya
107 M23 **Melito di Porto Salvo** Calabria, SW Italy 37°55′N 15°48′E
117 U10 **Melitopol'** Zaporiz'ka Oblast', SE Ukraine 46°49′N 35°23′E
109 V4 **Melk** Niederösterreich, NE Austria 48°14′N 15°21′E
95 K15 **Mellan-Fryken** ◎ C Sweden
99 E17 **Melle** Oost-Vlaanderen, NW Belgium 51°N 03°48′E
100 G13 **Melle** Niedersachsen, NW Germany 52°12′N 08°19′E
95 J17 **Mellerud** Västra Götaland, S Sweden 58°42′N 12°27′E
102 K10 **Melle-sur-Bretonne** Deux-Sèvres, W France 46°13′N 00°07′W
29 P8 **Mellette** South Dakota, N USA 45°07′N 98°29′W
121 O15 **Mellieħa** E Malta 35°58′N 14°21′E
80 B10 **Mellit** Northern Darfur, W Sudan 14°07′N 25°34′E
75 N7 **Mellita** ✈ SE Tunisia 33°47′N 10°51′E
63 G21 **Mellizo Sur, Cerro** ▲ S Chile 48°27′S 73°10′W
100 G9 **Mellum** *island* NW Germany
83 L22 **Melmoth** KwaZulu/Natal, E South Africa 28°35′S 31°25′E
111 D16 **Mělník** *Ger.* Melnik. Středočeský Kraj, NW Czech Republic 50°21′N 14°30′E
122 J12 **Mel'nikovo** Tomskaya Oblast', C Russian Federation 56°35′N 84°11′E
61 G18 **Melo** Cerro Largo, NE Uruguay 32°22′S 54°10′W
Melodunum *see* Melun
Melrhir, Chott *see* Melghir, Chott
183 P7 **Melrose** New South Wales, SE Australia 32°41′S 146°58′E
182 I7 **Melrose** South Australia 32°52′S 138°16′E
29 T7 **Melrose** Minnesota, N USA 45°40′N 94°46′W
33 Q11 **Melrose** Montana, NW USA 45°33′N 112°41′W
37 V12 **Melrose** New Mexico, SW USA 34°25′N 103°37′W
108 I8 **Mels** Sankt Gallen NE Switzerland 47°03′N 09°26′E
Melsetter *see* Chimanimani
33 V9 **Melstone** Montana, NW USA 46°37′N 107°49′W
101 I16 **Melsungen** Hessen, C Germany 51°08′N 09°33′E
92 L12 **Meltaus** Lappi, NW Finland 66°54′N 25°18′E
97 N19 **Melton Mowbray** C England, United Kingdom 52°46′N 01°04′W
82 Q13 **Meluco** Cabo Delgado, NE Mozambique 12°31′S 39°39′E
103 O5 **Melun** *anc.* Melodunum. Seine-et-Marne, N France 48°32′N 02°40′E
80 F12 **Melut** Upper Nile, SE Sudan 10°27′N 32°13′E
27 P5 **Melvern Lake** ⊞ Kansas, C USA
11 V16 **Melville** Saskatchewan, S Canada 50°57′N 102°49′W
Melville Bay/Melville Bugt *see* Qimusseriarsuaq
45 O11 **Melville Hall** ✈ (Dominica) NE Dominica 15°33′N 61°19′W
181 O1 **Melville Island** *island* Northern Territory, N Australia
197 O8 **Melville Island** *island* Parry Islands, Northwest Territories, NW Canada
11 W9 **Melville, Lake** ◎ Newfoundland and Labrador, E Canada
9 O7 **Melville Peninsula** *peninsula* Nunavut, NE Canada
Melville Sound *see* Viscount Melville Sound
25 Q9 **Melvin** Texas, SW USA 31°12′N 99°34′W
97 D15 **Melvin, Lough** *Ir.* Loch Meilbhe. ◎ S Northern Ireland, United Kingdom/Ireland
169 S12 **Memala** Borneo, C Indonesia 01°44′S 112°36′E
113 L22 **Memaliaj** Gjirokastër, S Albania 40°21′N 19°56′E
83 Q14 **Memba** Nampula, NE Mozambique 14°07′S 40°33′E
83 Q14 **Memba, Baia de** *inlet* NE Mozambique
Membidj *see* Manbij
Memel *see* Neman, NE Europe
Memel *see* Klaipeda, Lithuania
101 J23 **Memmingen** Bayern, S Germany 47°59′N 10°11′E
27 U1 **Memphis** Missouri, C USA 40°28′N 92°11′W
20 E10 **Memphis** Tennessee, S USA 35°09′N 90°03′W
25 P3 **Memphis** Texas, SW USA 34°43′N 100°34′W
20 E10 **Memphis** ✈ Tennessee, S USA 35°02′N 89°57′W
15 Q13 **Memphrémagog, Lac** *var.* Lake Memphremagog. ◎ Canada/USA *see also* Lake Memphremagog
19 N6 **Memphremagog, Lake** *var.* Lac Memphrémagog. ◎ Canada/USA *see also* Memphrémagog, Lac
117 Q2 **Mena** Chernihivs'ka Oblast', NE Ukraine 51°30′N 32°15′E
27 S12 **Mena** Arkansas, C USA 34°40′N 94°15′W
Menaam *see* Menaldum
Menado *see* Manado
106 D6 **Menaggio** Lombardia, N Italy 46°03′N 09°14′E
29 T6 **Menahga** Minnesota, N USA 46°45′N 95°06′W
77 R10 **Ménaka** Goa, E Mali 15°55′N 02°25′E
98 K5 **Menaldum** *Fris.* Menaam. Friesland, N Netherlands 53°14′N 05°38′E
Mènam Khong *see* Mekong
74 E7 **Menara** ✈ (Marrakech) C Morocco 31°36′N 08°00′W
25 Q9 **Menard** Texas, SW USA 30°56′N 99°48′W
193 Q12 **Menard Fracture Zone** *tectonic feature* E Pacific Ocean
30 M7 **Menasha** Wisconsin, N USA 44°13′N 88°25′W
Mencezi Garagum *see* Merkezi Garagumy
193 U9 **Mendaña Fracture Zone** *tectonic feature* E Pacific Ocean
169 S13 **Mendawai, Sungai** ≈ Borneo, C Indonesia
103 P13 **Mende** *anc.* Mimatum. Lozère, S France 44°32′N 03°30′E
81 J14 **Mendebo** ▲▲ C Ethiopia
80 J9 **Mendefera** *prev.* Adi Ugri. S Eritrea 14°53′N 38°51′E
197 S7 **Mendeleyev Ridge** *undersea feature* Arctic Ocean
127 T3 **Mendeleyevsk** Respublika Tatarstan, W Russian Federation 55°54′N 52°19′E
101 F15 **Menden** Nordrhein-Westfalen, W Germany 51°26′N 07°47′E
22 L6 **Mendenhall** Mississippi, S USA 31°57′N 89°52′W
38 L13 **Mendenhall, Cape** *headland* Nunivak Island, Alaska, USA 59°45′N 166°10′W
41 P9 **Méndez** *var.* Villa de Méndez. Tamaulipas, C Mexico 25°06′N 98°32′W
80 H13 **Mendī** Oromīya C Ethiopia 09°43′N 35°07′E
186 C7 **Mendi** Southern Highlands, W Papua New Guinea 06°13′S 143°39′E
97 K22 **Mendip Hills** *var.* Mendips. *hill range* S England, United Kingdom
Mendips *see* Mendip Hills
34 L6 **Mendocino** California, W USA 39°18′N 123°48′W
34 J3 **Mendocino, Cape** *headland* California, W USA 40°26′N 124°24′W
0 B8 **Mendocino Fracture Zone** *tectonic feature* NE Pacific Ocean
35 P10 **Mendota** California, W USA 36°44′N 120°24′W
30 L11 **Mendota** Illinois, N USA 41°32′N 89°04′W
30 K8 **Mendota, Lake** ◎ Wisconsin, N USA
62 I11 **Mendoza** Mendoza, W Argentina 33°00′S 68°47′W
62 I12 **Mendoza** *off.* Provincia de Mendoza. ◈ *province* W Argentina
Mendoza, Provincia de *see* Mendoza
108 H12 **Mendrisio** Ticino, S Switzerland 45°53′N 08°59′E
168 L10 **Mendung** Pulau Mendol, W Indonesia 0°33′N 103°09′E
54 I5 **Mene de Mauroa** Falcón, NW Venezuela 10°39′N 71°04′W
54 I5 **Mene Grande** Zulia, NW Venezuela 09°51′N 70°57′W
136 B14 **Menemen** İzmir, W Turkey 38°34′N 27°03′E
99 C18 **Menen** *var.* Meenen, *Fr.* Menin. West-Vlaanderen, W Belgium 50°48′N 03°07′E
163 Q8 **Menengiyn Tal** *plain* E Mongolia
189 R9 **Meneng Point** *headland* SW Nauru 0°33′S 166°57′E
92 L10 **Menesjärvi** *Lapp.* Menešjávri. Lappi, N Finland 68°39′N 26°22′E

◆ Country
● Country Capital
◇ Dependent Territory
○ Dependent Territory Capital
◈ Administrative Regions
✈ International Airport
▲ Mountain
▲▲ Mountain Range
⩚ Volcano
≈ River
◎ Lake
⊞ Reservoir

MENEŠJÁVRI – MILANGE

Menešjávri *see* Menesjärvi
107 *I24* **Menfi** Sicilia, Italy, C Mediterranean Sea *37°36′N 12°59′E*
161 *P7* **Mengcheng** Anhui, E China *33°15′N 116°33′E*
160 *F15* **Menghai** Yunnan, SW China *22°02′N 100°18′E*
160 *F15* **Mengla** Yunnan, SW China *21°30′N 101°33′E*
160 *M13* **Mengzhu Ling** ▲▲ S China
160 *H14* **Mengzi** Yunnan, SW China *23°20′N 103°32′E*
114 *H13* **Menikio** *var.* Menoíkio. ▲ NE Greece *40°50′N 12°40′E*
Menin *see* Menen
182 *L7* **Menindee** New South Wales, SE Australia *32°24′S 142°25′E*
182 *L7* **Menindee Lake** ◎ New South Wales, SE Australia
182 *J10* **Meningie** South Australia *35°43′S 139°20′E*
103 *O5* **Mennecy** Essonne, N France *48°34′N 02°25′E*
29 *Q12* **Menno** South Dakota, N USA *43°14′N 97°34′W*
114 *H13* **Menoíkio** ▲▲ NE Greece
Menoíkio *see* Menikio
31 *N5* **Menominee** Michigan, N USA *45°06′N 87°35′W*
30 *M5* **Menominee River** ⁓ Michigan/Wisconsin, N USA
30 *M8* **Menomonee Falls** Wisconsin, N USA *43°11′N 88°09′W*
30 *I6* **Menomonie** Wisconsin, N USA *44°52′N 91°55′W*
83 *D14* **Menongue** *var.* Vila Serpa Pinto, *Port.* Serpa Pinto. Cuando Cubango, C Angola *14°38′S 17°39′E*
120 *H8* **Menorca** *Eng.* Minorca; *anc.* Balearis Minor. *island* Islas Baleares, Spain, W Mediterranean Sea
105 *S13* **Menor, Mar** *lagoon* SE Spain
39 *S10* **Mentasta Lake** ◎ Alaska, USA
39 *S10* **Mentasta Mountains** ▲▲ Alaska, USA
168 *I13* **Mentawai, Kepulauan** *island group* W Indonesia
168 *I12* **Mentawai, Selat** *strait* W Indonesia
168 *M12* **Mentok** Pulau Bangka, W Indonesia *02°01′S 105°10′E*
103 *V15* **Menton** *It.* Mentone. Alpes-Maritimes, SE France *43°47′N 07°30′E*
24 *K8* **Mentone** Texas, SW USA *31°42′N 103°36′W*
Mentone *see* Menton
31 *U11* **Mentor** Ohio, N USA *41°40′N 81°20′W*
169 *U10* **Menyapa, Gunung** ▲ Borneo, N Indonesia *01°04′N 116°01′E*
159 *T9* **Menyuan** *var.* Menyuan Huizu Zizhixian. Qinghai, C China *37°27′N 101°33′E*
Menyuan Huizu Zizhixian *see* Menyuan
74 *M5* **Menzel Bourguiba** *var.* Manzil Bū Ruqaybah; *prev.* Ferryville. N Tunisia *37°09′N 09°51′E*
136 *M15* **Menzelet Barajı** ▣ C Turkey
127 *T4* **Menzelinsk** Respublika Tatarstan, W Russian Federation *55°44′N 53°00′E*
180 *K11* **Menzies** Western Australia *29°42′S 121°04′E*
195 *V6* **Menzies, Mount** ▲ Antarctica *73°32′S 61°02′E*
40 *J6* **Meoqui** Chihuahua, N Mexico *28°18′N 105°30′W*
83 *N14* **Meponda** Niassa, NE Mozambique *13°20′S 34°53′E*
98 *M8* **Meppel** Drenthe, NE Netherlands *52°42′N 06°12′E*
100 *E12* **Meppen** Niedersachsen, NW Germany *52°42′N 07°18′E*
Meqerghane, Sebkha *see* Mekerrhane, Sebkha
105 *T6* **Mequinenza, Embalse de** ▣ NE Spain
30 *M8* **Mequon** Wisconsin, N USA *43°13′N 87°57′W*
Mera *see* Maira
182 *D3* **Meramangye, Lake** *salt lake* South Australia
27 *W5* **Meramec River** ⁓ Missouri, C USA
Meran *see* Merano
168 *K13* **Merangin** ⁓ Sumatera, W Indonesia
106 *G5* **Merano** *Ger.* Meran. Trentino-Alto Adige, N Italy *46°40′N 11°10′E*
168 *K8* **Meraphu Lama** Pahang, Peninsular Malaysia *04°37′N 101°58′E*
106 *D7* **Merate** Lombardia, N Italy *45°42′N 09°26′E*
169 *U13* **Meratus, Pegunungan** ▲▲ Borneo, N Indonesia
171 *Y16* **Merauke, Sungai** ⁓ Papua, E Indonesia
182 *L9* **Merbein** Victoria, SE Australia *34°11′S 142°03′E*
99 *F21* **Merbes-le-Château** Hainaut, S Belgium *50°19′N 04°09′E*
Merca *see* Marka
54 *C13* **Mercaderes** Cauca, SW Colombia *01°46′N 77°09′W*
Mercara *see* Madikeri
35 *P9* **Merced** California, W USA *37°17′N 120°30′W*
61 *C20* **Mercedes** Buenos Aires, E Argentina *34°42′S 59°30′W*
61 *D15* **Mercedes** Corrientes, NE Argentina *29°09′S 58°05′W*
61 *D19* **Mercedes** Soriano, SW Uruguay *33°16′S 58°01′W*
25 *S17* **Mercedes** Texas, SW USA *26°09′N 97°54′W*
Mercedes *see* Villa Mercedes
35 *R9* **Merced Peak** ▲ California, W USA *37°34′N 119°30′W*
35 *P9* **Merced River** ⁓ California, W USA
18 *B13* **Mercer** Pennsylvania, NE USA *41°14′N 80°14′W*
99 *G18* **Merchtem** Vlaams Brabant, C Belgium *50°57′N 04°14′E*
15 *O13* **Mercier** Québec, SE Canada *45°15′N 73°45′W*
25 *Q9* **Mercury** Texas, SW USA *31°23′N 99°09′W*
184 *M5* **Mercury Islands** *island group* N New Zealand
19 *O9* **Meredith** New Hampshire, NE USA *43°36′N 71°28′W*
65 *B25* **Meredith, Cape** *var.* Cabo Belgrano. *headland* West Falkland, Falkland Islands *52°15′S 60°40′W*
37 *V6* **Meredith, Lake** ◎ Colorado, C USA
25 *N2* **Meredith, Lake** ▣ Texas, SW USA
81 *O16* **Mereeg** *var.* Mareeq, *It.* Meregh. Galguduud, E Somalia *03°47′N 47°19′E*
117 *V5* **Merefa** Kharkivs'ka Oblast', E Ukraine *49°49′N 36°05′E*
Meregh *see* Mereeg
99 *E17* **Merelbeke** Oost-Vlaanderen, NW Belgium *51°00′N 03°45′E*
Merend *see* Marand
167 *T12* **Mereuch** Môndól Kiri, E Cambodia *13°01′N 107°26′E*
Mergate *see* Margate
Mergui *see* Myeik
166 *M12* **Mergui Archipelago** *island group* S Myanmar (Burma)
114 *L12* **Meriç** Edirne, NW Turkey *41°12′N 26°24′E*
114 *L12* **Meriç** *Bul.* Maritsa, *Gk.* Évros; *anc.* Hebrus. ⁓ SE Europe *see also* Évros/Maritsa
41 *X12* **Mérida** Yucatán, SW Mexico *20°58′N 89°35′W*
104 *J11* **Mérida** *anc.* Augusta Emerita. Extremadura, W Spain *38°55′N 06°20′W*
54 *I6* **Mérida** Mérida, W Venezuela *08°36′N 71°08′W*
54 *H7* **Mérida** *off.* Estado Mérida. ◈ *state* W Venezuela
Mérida, Estado *see* Mérida
18 *M13* **Meriden** Connecticut, NE USA *41°32′N 72°48′W*
22 *M5* **Meridian** Mississippi, S USA *32°24′N 88°43′W*
25 *S8* **Meridian** Texas, SW USA *31°56′N 97°40′W*
102 *J13* **Mérignac** Gironde, SW France *44°50′N 00°40′W*
102 *J13* **Mérignac** ✈ (Bordeaux) Gironde, SW France *44°51′N 00°44′W*
93 *J18* **Merikarvia** Länsi-Suomi, SW Finland *61°51′N 21°30′E*
183 *R12* **Merimbula** New South Wales, SE Australia *36°52′S 149°51′E*
182 *L9* **Meringur** Victoria, SE Australia *34°26′S 141°19′E*
Merín, Laguna *see* Mirim Lagoon
97 *I19* **Merioneth** *cultural region* W Wales, United Kingdom
188 *A11* **Merir** *island* Palau Islands, N Palau
188 *B17* **Merizo** SW Guam *13°15′N 144°40′E*
Merjama *see* Märjamaa
145 *S16* **Merke** Zhambyl, S Kazakhstan *42°48′N 73°10′E*
25 *P7* **Merkel** Texas, SW USA *32°28′N 100°00′W*
146 *E12* **Merkezi Garagumy** *var.* Merkezi Garagum, *Rus.* Tsentral'nyye Nizmennyye Garagumy. *desert* C Turkmenistan
119 *F15* **Merkinė** Alytus, S Lithuania *54°09′N 24°11′E*
99 *G16* **Merksem** Antwerpen, N Belgium *51°17′N 04°26′E*
99 *I15* **Merksplas** Antwerpen, N Belgium *51°22′N 04°54′E*
Merkulovichi *see* Myerkulavichy
119 *G15* **Merkys** ⁓ S Lithuania
32 *F15* **Merlin** Oregon, NW USA *42°34′N 123°23′W*
61 *C20* **Merlo** Buenos Aires, E Argentina *34°39′S 58°45′W*
138 *G8* **Meron, Harei** *prev.* Haré Meron. ▲ N Israel *35°06′N 33°00′E*
74 *K6* **Merouane, Chott** *salt lake* NE Algeria
80 *F7* **Merowe** Northern, N Sudan *18°29′N 31°49′E*
180 *J12* **Merredin** Western Australia *31°31′S 118°18′E*
97 *I14* **Merrick** ▲ S Scotland, United Kingdom *55°09′N 04°28′W*
32 *H16* **Merrill** Oregon, NW USA *42°00′N 121°37′W*
30 *L5* **Merrill** Wisconsin, N USA *45°12′N 89°43′W*
31 *N11* **Merrillville** Indiana, N USA *41°28′N 87°19′W*
19 *O10* **Merrimack River** ⁓ Massachusetts/New Hampshire, NE USA
28 *L12* **Merriman** Nebraska, C USA *42°54′N 101°42′W*
11 *N17* **Merritt** British Columbia, SW Canada *50°09′N 120°49′W*
23 *Y12* **Merritt Island** Florida, SE USA *28°21′N 80°42′W*
23 *Y11* **Merritt Island** *island* Florida, SE USA
28 *M12* **Merritt Reservoir** ▣ Nebraska, C USA
183 *S7* **Merriwa** New South Wales, SE Australia *32°09′S 150°24′E*
183 *O8* **Merriwagga** New South Wales, SE Australia *33°51′S 145°38′E*
22 *G8* **Merryville** Louisiana, S USA *30°45′N 93°32′W*
80 *K9* **Mersa Fat'ma** E Eritrea *14°52′N 40°16′E*
102 *M7* **Mer St-Aubin** Loir-et-Cher, C France *47°42′N 01°31′E*
75 *U7* **Mersá Maṭrūḥ** *var.* Matrūḥ; *anc.* Paraetonium. NW Egypt *31°21′N 27°15′E*
99 *M24* **Mersch** Luxembourg, C Luxembourg *49°45′N 06°06′E*
101 *M15* **Merseburg** Sachsen-Anhalt, C Germany *51°22′N 12°00′E*
Mersen *see* Meerssen
97 *K18* **Mersey** ⁓ NW England, United Kingdom
136 *J17* **Mersin** *var.* İçel. İçel, S Turkey *36°50′N 34°39′E*
Mersin *see* İçel
168 *L9* **Mersing** Johor, Peninsular Malaysia *02°25′N 103°50′E*
118 *E8* **Mērsrags** Talsi, NW Latvia *57°21′N 23°05′E*
152 *G12* **Merta** *var.* Merta City. Rājasthān, N India *26°40′N 74°04′E*
Merta City *see* Merta
152 *F12* **Merta Road** Rājasthān, N India *26°42′N 73°54′E*
97 *J21* **Merthyr Tydfil** S Wales, United Kingdom *51°46′N 03°23′W*
104 *H13* **Mértola** Beja, S Portugal *37°38′N 07°40′W*
144 *G14* **Mertvyy Kultuk, Sor** *salt flat* SW Kazakhstan
195 *V16* **Mertz Glacier** *glacier* Antarctica
99 *M24* **Mertzig** Diekirch, C Luxembourg *49°50′N 06°00′E*
25 *O9* **Mertzon** Texas, SW USA *31°16′N 100°50′W*
103 *N4* **Méru** Oise, N France *49°15′N 02°07′E*
81 *I18* **Meru** Eastern, C Kenya *0°03′N 37°38′E*
81 *I20* **Meru, Mount** ▲ NE Tanzania *03°12′S 36°45′E*
Meru *see* Mary
Mervdasht *see* Marv Dasht
136 *K11* **Merzifon** Amasya, N Turkey *40°52′N 35°28′E*
101 *D20* **Merzig** Saarland, SW Germany *49°27′N 06°39′E*
36 *L14* **Mesa** Arizona, SW USA *33°25′N 111°49′W*
29 *V4* **Mesabi Range** ▲▲ Minnesota, N USA
54 *H6* **Mesa Bolívar** Mérida, NW Venezuela *08°30′N 71°38′W*
107 *Q18* **Mesagne** Puglia, SE Italy *40°33′N 17°49′E*
39 *P12* **Mesa Mountain** ▲ Alaska, USA *60°26′N 155°14′W*
115 *J25* **Mesará** *lowland* Kríti, Greece, E Mediterranean Sea
37 *S14* **Mescalero** New Mexico, SW USA *33°09′N 105°46′W*
101 *G15* **Meschede** Nordrhein-Westfalen, W Germany *51°21′N 08°16′E*
137 *Q12* **Mescit Dağları** ▲▲ NE Turkey
189 *V13* **Mesegon** *island* Chuuk, C Micronesia
Meseritz *see* Międzyrzecz
54 *F11* **Mesetas** Meta, C Colombia *03°14′N 74°09′W*
Meshchera Lowland *see* Meshcherskaya Nizmennost'
Meshcherskaya Nizina *see* Meshcherskaya Nizmennost'
126 *M4* **Meshcherskaya Nizmennost'** *var.* Meshcherskaya Nizina, *Eng.* Meshchera Lowland. *basin* W Russian Federation
126 *J5* **Meshchovsk** Kaluzhskaya Oblast', W Russian Federation *54°21′N 35°23′E*
125 *R9* **Meshchura** Respublika Komi, NW Russian Federation *63°18′N 50°56′E*
Meshed *see* Mashhad
Meshed-i-Sar *see* Bābolsar
80 *E13* **Meshra'er Req** Warab, S Sudan *08°30′N 29°27′E*
37 *R15* **Mesilla** New Mexico, SW USA *32°15′N 106°49′W*
108 *H10* **Mesocco** *Ger.* Misox. Ticino, S Switzerland *46°18′N 09°13′E*
115 *D18* **Mesolóngi** *prev.* Mesolóngion. Dytikí Ellás, W Greece *38°21′N 21°26′E*
Mesolóngion *see* Mesolóngi
14 *E8* **Mesomikenda Lake** ◎ Ontario, S Canada
61 *D15* **Mesopotamia** *var.* Mesopotamia Argentina. *physical region* NE Argentina
Mesopotamia Argentina *see* Mesopotamia
35 *Y10* **Mesquite** Nevada, W USA *36°47′N 114°04′W*
82 *Q13* **Messalo, Rio** *var.* Mualo. ⁓ NE Mozambique
Messana/Messene *see* Messina
99 *L25* **Messancy** Luxembourg, SE Belgium *49°36′N 05°49′E*
107 *M23* **Messina** *var.* Messana, Messene; *anc.* Zancle. Sicilia, Italy, C Mediterranean Sea *38°12′N 15°33′E*
Messina *see* Musina
Messina, Strait of *see* Messina, Stretto di
107 *M23* **Messina, Stretto di** *Eng.* Strait of Messina. *strait* SW Italy
115 *E21* **Messíni** Pelopónnisos, S Greece *37°03′N 22°00′E*
115 *E22* **Messinía** *peninsula* S Greece
115 *E22* **Messiniakós Kólpos** *gulf* S Greece
122 *J8* **Messoyakha** ⁓ N Russian Federation
114 *H11* **Mesta** *Gk.* Néstos, *Turk.* Kara Su. ⁓ Bulgaria/Greece *see also* Néstos
Mesta *see* Néstos
Mestghanem *see* Mostaganem
137 *R8* **Mestia** *var.* Mestiya. N Georgia *43°03′N 42°50′E*
Mestiya *see* Mestia
115 *K18* **Mestón, Akrotírio** *cape* Chíos, E Greece
106 *H8* **Mestre** Veneto, NE Italy *45°30′N 12°14′E*
59 *M16* **Mestre, Espigão** ▲▲ E Brazil
169 *N14* **Mesuji** ⁓ Sumatera, W Indonesia
Mesule *see* Grosser Möseler
10 *J10* **Meszah Peak** ▲ British Columbia, W Canada *58°31′N 131°28′W*
54 *G11* **Meta** *off.* Departamento del Meta. ◈ *province* C Colombia
15 *Q8* **Metabetchouane** ⁓ Québec, SE Canada
Meta, Departamento del *see* Meta
9 *S7* **Meta Incognita Peninsula** *peninsula* Baffin Island, Nunavut, NE Canada
22 *K9* **Metairie** Louisiana, S USA *29°58′N 90°09′W*
32 *M6* **Metaline Falls** Washington, NW USA *48°51′N 117°21′W*
62 *K6* **Metán** Salta, N Argentina *25°29′S 64°57′W*
82 *N13* **Metangula** Niassa, N Mozambique *12°41′S 34°50′E*
42 *E7* **Metapán** Santa Ana, NW El Salvador *14°20′N 89°28′W*
54 *K9* **Meta, Río** ⁓ Colombia/Venezuela
106 *I11* **Metauro** ⁓ C Italy
80 *H11* **Metema** Āmara, N Ethiopia *12°53′N 36°10′E*
115 *D15* **Metéora** *religious building* Thessalía, C Greece
65 *O20* **Meteor Rise** *undersea feature* SW Indian Ocean *46°00′S 05°30′E*
186 *G5* **Meteran** New Hanover, NE Papua New Guinea *02°40′S 150°12′E*
Meterlam *see* Mehtar Lām
115 *G20* **Methanon** *peninsula* S Greece
Methariam/Metharlam *see* Mehtar Lām
32 *J6* **Methow River** ⁓ Washington, NW USA
19 *O10* **Methuen** Massachusetts, NE USA *42°43′N 71°10′W*
185 *G19* **Methven** Canterbury, South Island, New Zealand *43°37′S 171°38′E*
Metis *see* Metz
113 *G15* **Metković** Dubrovnik-Neretva, SE Croatia *43°02′N 17°37′E*
39 *Y14* **Metlakatla** Annette Island, Alaska, USA *55°07′N 131°34′W*
109 *V13* **Metlika** *Ger.* Möttling. SE Slovenia *45°38′N 15°18′E*
109 *T8* **Metnitz** Kärnten, S Austria *46°58′N 14°09′E*
27 *W12* **Meto, Bayou** ⁓ Arkansas, C USA
168 *M15* **Metro** Sumatera, W Indonesia *05°05′S 105°20′E*
30 *M17* **Metropolis** Illinois, N USA *37°09′N 88°43′W*
Metropolitan *see* Santiago
35 *N8* **Metropolitan Oakland** ✈ California, W USA *37°42′N 122°13′W*
115 *D15* **Métsovo** *prev.* Métsovon. Ípeiros, C Greece *39°47′N 21°12′E*
Métsovon *see* Métsovo
23 *V5* **Metter** Georgia, SE USA *32°24′N 82°03′W*
99 *H21* **Mettet** Namur, S Belgium *50°19′N 04°43′E*
101 *D20* **Mettlach** Saarland, SW Germany *49°28′N 06°37′E*
Mettu *see* Metu
80 *H13* **Metu** *var.* Mattu, Mettu. Oromīya, C Ethiopia *08°18′N 35°39′E*
138 *G8* **Metula** *prev.* Metulla. Northern, N Israel *33°16′N 35°35′E*
169 *T10* **Metulang** Borneo, N Indonesia *01°28′N 114°40′E*
Metulla *see* Metula
103 *T4* **Metz** *anc.* Divodurum Mediomatricum, Mediomatrica, Metis. Moselle, NE France *49°07′N 06°09′E*
101 *H22* **Metzingen** Baden-Württemberg, S Germany *48°31′N 09°16′E*
168 *G8* **Meulaboh** Sumatera, W Indonesia *04°10′N 96°09′E*
99 *D18* **Meulebeke** West-Vlaanderen, W Belgium *50°57′N 03°18′E*
103 *U6* **Meurthe** ⁓ NE France
103 *S5* **Meurthe-et-Moselle** ◈ *department* NE France
103 *S4* **Meuse** ◈ *department* NE France
84 *F10* **Meuse** *Dut.* Maas. ⁓ W Europe *see also* Maas
Meuse *see* Maas
Mexcala, Río *see* Balsas, Río
25 *U8* **Mexia** Texas, SW USA *31°40′N 96°28′W*
58 *K11* **Mexiana, Ilha** *island* NE Brazil
40 *C1* **Mexicali** Baja California Norte, NW Mexico *32°34′N 115°26′W*
Mexicanos, Estados Unidos *see* Mexico
41 *O14* **México** *var.* Ciudad de México, *Eng.* Mexico City. ● (Mexico) México, C Mexico *19°26′N 99°08′W*
27 *V4* **Mexico** Missouri, C USA *19°10′N 99°04′W*
18 *H9* **Mexico** New York, NE USA *43°27′N 76°14′W*
40 *L7* **Mexico** *off.* United Mexican States, *var.* Méjico, México, *Sp.* Estados Unidos Mexicanos. ◆ *federal republic* N Central America
41 *O13* **México** ◈ *state* S Mexico
México *see* Mexico
0 *J13* **Mexico Basin** *var.* Sigsbee Deep. *undersea feature* C Gulf of Mexico *25°00′N 92°00′W*
Mexico City *see* México
México, Golfo de *see* Mexico, Gulf of
44 *B4* **Mexico, Gulf of** *Sp.* Golfo de México. *gulf* W Atlantic Ocean
Meyadine *see* Al Mayādīn
143 *Q9* **Meybod** Yazd, C Iran *32°16′N 53°59′E*
149 *Q5* **Meydān Shahr** *var.* Maydān Shahr. Vardak, E Afghanistan *34°27′N 68°48′E*
39 *Y14* **Meyers Chuck** Etolin Island, Alaska, USA *55°44′N 132°15′W*
148 *M3* **Meymaneh** *var.* Maimāna, Maymana. Fāryāb, NW Afghanistan *35°57′N 64°48′E*
143 *N7* **Meymeh** Eşfahān, C Iran *33°29′N 51°09′E*
123 *V7* **Meynypil'gyno** Chukotskiy Avtonomnyy Okrug, NE Russian Federation *62°33′N 177°00′E*
108 *A10* **Meyrin** Genève, SW Switzerland *46°14′N 06°05′E*
166 *L7* **Mezaligon** Ayeyarwady, SW Myanmar (Burma) *17°53′N 95°12′E*
41 *O15* **Mezcala** Guerrero, S Mexico *17°55′N 99°34′W*
114 *H8* **Mezdra** Vratsa, NW Bulgaria *43°08′N 23°42′E*
103 *P16* **Mèze** Hérault, S France *43°26′N 03°37′E*
125 *O6* **Mezen'** Arkhangel'skaya Oblast', NW Russian Federation *65°54′N 44°10′E*
125 *P8* **Mezen'** ⁓ NW Russian Federation
Mezen, Bay of *see* Mezenskaya Guba
103 *Q13* **Mézenc, Mont** ▲ C France *44°57′N 04°15′E*
125 *O8* **Mezenskaya Guba** *var.* Bay of Mezen. *bay* NW Russian Federation
Mezha *see* Myazha
122 *H6* **Mezhdusharskiy, Ostrov** *island* Novaya Zemlya, N Russian Federation
Mezhëvo *see* Myezhava
Mezhgor'ye *see* Mizhhir"ya
117 *V8* **Mezhova** Dnipropetrovs'ka Oblast', E Ukraine *48°15′N 36°44′E*
10 *J12* **Meziadin Junction** British Columbia, W Canada *56°06′N 129°15′W*
111 *G16* **Mezileské Sedlo** *var.* Przełęcz Międzyleska. *pass* Czech Republic/Poland
102 *L14* **Mézin** Lot-et-Garonne, SW France *44°03′N 00°16′E*
111 *M24* **Mezőberény** Békés, SE Hungary *46°49′N 21°00′E*
111 *M25* **Mezőhegyes** Békés, SE Hungary *46°20′N 20°48′E*
111 *M25* **Mezőkovácsháza** Békés, SE Hungary *46°24′N 20°52′E*
111 *M21* **Mezőkövesd** Borsod-Abaúj-Zemplén, NE Hungary *47°49′N 20°32′E*
Mezőtelegd *see* Tileagd
111 *M23* **Mezőtúr** Jász-Nagykun-Szolnok, E Hungary *47°N 20°37′E*
40 *K10* **Mezquital** Durango, C Mexico *23°31′N 104°19′W*
106 *G6* **Mezzolombardo** Trentino-Alto Adige, N Italy *46°13′N 11°08′E*
82 *L13* **Mfuwe** Northern, N Zambia *13°00′S 31°45′E*
121 *O15* **Mġarr** Gozo, N Malta *36°01′N 14°18′E*
126 *H6* **Mglin** Bryanskaya Oblast', W Russian Federation *53°01′N 32°54′E*
Mhálanna, Cionn *see* Malin Head
154 *G10* **Mhow** Madhya Pradesh, C India *22°32′N 75°49′E*
Miadzioł Nowy *see* Myadzyel
171 *O6* **Miagao** Panay Island, C Philippines *10°40′N 122°15′E*
41 *R17* **Miahuatlán** *var.* Miahuatlán de Porfirio Díaz. Oaxaca, SE Mexico *16°21′N 96°36′W*
Miahuatlán de Porfirio Díaz *see* Miahuatlán
104 *K10* **Miajadas** Extremadura, W Spain *39°10′N 05°54′W*
Miajlar *see* Myājlār
36 *M14* **Miami** Arizona, SW USA *33°23′N 110°53′W*
23 *Z16* **Miami** Florida, SE USA *25°46′N 80°12′W*
27 *R8* **Miami** Oklahoma, C USA *36°53′N 94°54′W*
25 *O2* **Miami** Texas, SW USA *35°42′N 100°37′W*
23 *Z16* **Miami** ✈ Florida, SE USA *25°47′N 80°16′W*
23 *Z16* **Miami Beach** Florida, SE USA *25°47′N 80°08′W*
23 *Y15* **Miami Canal** *canal* Florida, SE USA
31 *R14* **Miamisburg** Ohio, N USA *39°38′N 84°17′W*
149 *U10* **Miān Channūn** Punjab, E Pakistan *30°24′N 72°27′E*
142 *J4* **Miāndowāb** *var.* Mianduab, Miyāndoāb. Āžarbāyjān-e Gharbī, NW Iran *36°57′N 46°06′E*
172 *H5* **Miandrivazo** Toliara, C Madagascar *19°31′S 45°29′E*
Mianduab *see* Miāndowāb
142 *K3* **Mīāneh** *var.* Miyāneh. Āžarbāyjān-e Sharqī, NW Iran *37°23′N 47°45′E*
149 *O16* **Miāni Hōr** *lagoon* S Pakistan
160 *G10* **Mianning** Sichuan, C China *28°34′N 102°12′E*
149 *T7* **Miānwāli** Punjab, NE Pakistan *32°32′N 71°33′E*
160 *J7* **Mianxian** *var.* Mian Xian. Shaanxi, C China *33°12′N 106°36′E*
Mian Xian *see* Mianxian
160 *I8* **Mianyang** Sichuan, C China *31°29′N 104°43′E*
Mianyang *see* Xiantao
161 *R3* **Miaodao Qundao** *island group* E China
161 *S13* **Miaoli** N Taiwan *24°33′N 120°48′E*
122 *F11* **Miass** Chelyabinskaya Oblast', C Russian Federation *55°00′N 59°55′E*
110 *G8* **Miastko** *Ger.* Rummelsburg in Pommern. Pomorskie, N Poland *54°N 16°58′E*
Miava *see* Myjava
11 *O15* **Mica Creek** British Columbia, SW Canada *51°58′N 118°29′W*
160 *J7* **Micang Shan** ▲▲ C China
Mi Chai *see* Nong Khai
111 *O19* **Michalovce** *Ger.* Grossmichel, *Hung.* Nagymihály. Košický Kraj, E Slovakia *48°46′N 21°55′E*
99 *M20* **Michel, Baraque** *hill* E Belgium
39 *S5* **Michelson, Mount** ▲ Alaska, USA *69°19′N 144°16′W*
45 *P9* **Miches** E Dominican Republic *18°59′N 69°03′W*
30 *M3* **Michigamme, Lake** ◎ Michigan, N USA
30 *M4* **Michigamme Reservoir** ▣ Michigan, N USA
31 *N4* **Michigamme River** ⁓ Michigan, N USA
31 *O7* **Michigan** *off.* State of Michigan, *also known as* Great Lakes State, Lake State, Wolverine State. ◈ *state* N USA
31 *O11* **Michigan City** Indiana, N USA *41°43′N 86°52′W*
31 *O8* **Michigan, Lake** ◎ N USA
31 *P2* **Michipicoten Bay** *lake bay* Ontario, N Canada
14 *A8* **Michipicoten Island** *island* Ontario, S Canada
14 *B7* **Michipicoten River** Ontario, S Canada *47°56′N 84°48′W*
Michurin *see* Tsarevo
126 *M6* **Michurinsk** Tambovskaya Oblast', W Russian Federation *52°56′N 40°31′E*
Mico, Punta/Mico, Punto *see* Monkey Point
42 *L10* **Mico, Río** ⁓ SE Nicaragua
45 *T12* **Micoud** SE Saint Lucia *13°49′N 60°54′W*
189 *N16* **Micronesia** *off.* Federated States of Micronesia. ◆ *federation* W Pacific Ocean
175 *P4* **Micronesia** *island group* W Pacific Ocean
Micronesia, Federated States of *see* Micronesia
169 *O9* **Midai, Pulau** *island* Kepulauan Natuna, W Indonesia
Mid-Atlantic Cordillera *see* Mid-Atlantic Ridge
65 *M17* **Mid-Atlantic Ridge** *var.* Mid-Atlantic Cordillera, Mid-Atlantic Rise, Mid-Atlantic Swell. *undersea feature* Atlantic Ocean *0°00′N 20°00′W*
Mid-Atlantic Rise/Mid-Atlantic Swell *see* Mid-Atlantic Ridge
99 *E15* **Middelburg** Zeeland, SW Netherlands *51°30′N 03°36′E*
83 *H24* **Middelburg** Eastern Cape, S South Africa *31°28′S 25°01′E*
83 *K21* **Middelburg** Mpumalanga, NE South Africa *25°47′S 29°28′E*
95 *G23* **Middelfart** Fyn, C Denmark *55°30′N 09°44′E*
98 *G13* **Middelharnis** Zuid-Holland, SW Netherlands *51°45′N 04°10′E*
99 *B16* **Middelkerke** West-Vlaanderen, W Belgium *51°12′N 02°51′E*
98 *I9* **Middenbeemster** Noord-Holland, C Netherlands *52°33′N 04°55′E*
98 *I8* **Middenmeer** Noord-Holland, NW Netherlands *52°48′N 04°58′E*
35 *Q2* **Middle Alkali Lake** ◎ California, W USA
193 *S6* **Middle America Trench** *undersea feature* E Pacific Ocean *15°00′N 95°00′W*
151 *P19* **Middle Andaman** *island* Andaman Islands, India, NE Indian Ocean
Middle Atlas *see* Moyen Atlas
21 *R3* **Middlebourne** West Virginia, NE USA *39°30′N 80°53′W*
23 *W9* **Middleburg** Florida, SE USA *30°03′N 81°55′W*
Middleburg Island *see* 'Eua
Middle Caicos *see* Grand Caicos
25 *N8* **Middle Concho River** ⁓ Texas, SW USA
Middle Congo *see* Congo (Republic of)
39 *R6* **Middle Fork Chandalar River** ⁓ Alaska, USA
39 *Q7* **Middle Fork Koyukuk River** ⁓ Alaska, USA
33 *O12* **Middle Fork Salmon River** ⁓ Idaho, NW USA
11 *T15* **Middle Lake** Saskatchewan, S Canada *52°31′N 105°16′W*
28 *L13* **Middle Loup River** ⁓ Nebraska, C USA
185 *E22* **Middlemarch** Otago, South Island, New Zealand *45°30′S 170°07′E*
31 *T15* **Middleport** Ohio, N USA *39°00′N 82°03′W*
29 *U14* **Middle Raccoon River** ⁓ Iowa, C USA
29 *R3* **Middle River** ⁓ Minnesota, N USA
21 *N8* **Middlesboro** Kentucky, S USA *36°37′N 83°42′W*
97 *M15* **Middlesbrough** N England, United Kingdom *54°35′N 01°14′W*
42 *G3* **Middlesex** Stann Creek, C Belize *17°00′N 88°31′W*
97 *N22* **Middlesex** *cultural region* SE England, United Kingdom
13 *P15* **Middleton** Nova Scotia, SE Canada *44°56′N 65°04′W*
20 *F10* **Middleton** Tennessee, S USA *35°05′N 88°57′W*
30 *L9* **Middleton** Wisconsin, N USA *43°06′N 89°30′W*
39 *S13* **Middleton Island** *island* Alaska, USA
34 *M7* **Middletown** California, W USA *38°44′N 122°39′W*
21 *Y2* **Middletown** Delaware, NE USA *39°25′N 75°39′W*
18 *K15* **Middletown** New Jersey, NE USA *40°23′N 74°08′W*
18 *K13* **Middletown** New York, NE USA *41°27′N 74°25′W*
31 *R14* **Middletown** Ohio, N USA *39°33′N 84°19′W*
18 *G15* **Middletown** Pennsylvania, NE USA *40°11′N 76°42′W*
141 *N14* **Midī** *var.* Maydī. NW Yemen *16°18′N 42°51′E*
103 *O16* **Midi, Canal du** *canal* S France
102 *K17* **Midi de Bigorre, Pic du** ▲ S France *42°57′N 00°08′E*
102 *K17* **Midi d'Ossau, Pic du** ▲ SW France *42°51′N 00°27′W*
173 *R7* **Mid-Indian Basin** *undersea feature* N Indian Ocean *10°00′S 80°00′E*
173 *P7* **Mid-Indian Ridge** *var.* Central Indian Ridge. *undersea feature* C Indian Ocean *12°00′S 66°00′E*
103 *N14* **Midi-Pyrénées** ◈ *region* S France
25 *N8* **Midkiff** Texas, SW USA *31°35′N 101°51′W*
14 *G13* **Midland** Ontario, S Canada *44°45′N 79°53′W*
31 *R8* **Midland** Michigan, N USA *43°37′N 84°15′W*
28 *M10* **Midland** South Dakota, N USA *44°04′N 101°07′W*
24 *M8* **Midland** Texas, SW USA *32°N 102°05′W*
83 *K17* **Midlands** ◈ *province* C Zimbabwe
97 *D21* **Midleton** *Ir.* Mainistir na Corann. SW Ireland *51°55′N 08°10′W*
25 *T7* **Midlothian** Texas, SW USA *32°28′N 96°59′W*
96 *K12* **Midlothian** *cultural region* S Scotland, United Kingdom
172 *I7* **Midongy Atsimo** Fianarantsoa, S Madagascar *21°58′S 47°47′E*
102 *K15* **Midou** ⁓ SW France
192 *J6* **Mid-Pacific Mountains** *var.* Mid-Pacific Seamounts. *undersea feature* NW Pacific Ocean *20°00′N 178°00′W*
Mid-Pacific Seamounts *see* Mid-Pacific Mountains
171 *Q7* **Midsayap** Mindanao, S Philippines *07°12′N 124°31′E*
36 *L3* **Midway** Utah, W USA *40°30′N 111°28′W*
192 *L5* **Midway Islands** ◇ *US territory* C Pacific Ocean
33 *X14* **Midwest** Wyoming, C USA *43°24′N 106°15′W*
27 *N10* **Midwest City** Oklahoma, C USA *35°28′N 98°24′W*
152 *M10* **Mid Western** ◈ *zone* W Nepal
98 *P5* **Midwolda** Groningen, NE Netherlands *53°12′N 07°00′E*
137 *Q16* **Midyat** Mardin, SE Turkey *37°25′N 41°20′E*
114 *F8* **Midzhur** *SCr.* Midžor. ▲ Bulgaria/Serbia *43°24′N 22°41′E* *see also* Midžor
Midzhur *see* Midžor
113 *Q14* **Midžor** *Bul.* Midzhur. ▲ Bulgaria/Serbia *43°24′N 22°40′E* *see also* Midzhur
Midžor *see* Midzhur
164 *K14* **Mie** *off.* Mie-ken. ◈ *prefecture* Honshū, SW Japan
111 *L16* **Miechów** Małopolskie, S Poland *50°21′N 20°01′E*
110 *F11* **Międzychód** *Ger.* Mitteldorf. Wielkopolskie, C Poland *52°36′N 15°53′E*
Międzyleska, Przełęcz *see* Mezileské Sedlo
110 *O12* **Międzyrzec Podlaski** Lubelskie, E Poland *52°N 22°47′E*
110 *E11* **Międzyrzecz** *Ger.* Meseritz. Lubuskie, W Poland *52°26′N 15°33′E*
Mie-ken *see* Mie
102 *L16* **Miélan** Gers, S France *43°26′N 00°19′E*
111 *N16* **Mielec** Podkarpackie, SE Poland *50°18′N 21°27′E*
95 *L21* **Mien** ◎ S Sweden
41 *O8* **Mier** Tamaulipas, C Mexico *26°28′N 99°10′W*
116 *J11* **Miercurea-Ciuc** *Ger.* Szeklerburg, *Hung.* Csíkszereda. Harghita, C Romania *46°24′N 25°48′E*
Mieresch *see* Maros/Mureş
Mieres del Camín *see* Mieres del Camino
104 *K2* **Mieres del Camino** *var.* Mieres del Camín. Asturias, NW Spain *43°15′N 05°46′W*
99 *K15* **Mierlo** Noord-Brabant, SE Netherlands *51°27′N 05°37′E*
41 *O10* **Mier y Noriega** Nuevo León, NE Mexico *23°24′N 100°06′W*
Mies *see* Stříbro
80 *K13* **Mī'ēso** *var.* Meheso, Miesso. Oromīya, C Ethiopia *09°13′N 40°47′E*
Miesso *see* Mī'ēso
110 *D10* **Mieszkowice** *Ger.* Bärwalde Neumark. Zachodnio-pomorskie, W Poland *52°45′N 14°24′E*
18 *G14* **Mifflinburg** Pennsylvania, NE USA *40°55′N 77°03′W*
18 *F14* **Mifflintown** Pennsylvania, NE USA *40°34′N 77°24′W*
138 *F8* **Mifrats Hefa** *Eng.* Bay of Haifa; *prev.* MifrazHefa. *bay* N Israel
41 *R15* **Miguel Alemán, Presa** ▣ SE Mexico
40 *L9* **Miguel Asua** *var.* Miguel Auza. Zacatecas, C Mexico *24°17′N 103°29′W*
Miguel Auza *see* Miguel Asua
43 *S15* **Miguel de la Borda** *var.* Donoso. Colón, C Panama *09°09′N 80°20′W*
41 *N13* **Miguel Hidalgo** ✈ (Guadalajara) Jalisco, SW Mexico *20°52′N 101°09′W*
40 *H7* **Miguel Hidalgo, Presa** ▣ W Mexico
116 *J14* **Mihăileşti** Giurgiu, S Romania *44°20′N 25°54′E*
116 *M14* **Mihail Kogălniceanu** *var.* Kogălniceanu; *prev.* Caramurat, Ferdinand. Constanța, SE Romania *44°22′N 28°27′E*
117 *N14* **Mihai Viteazu** Constanța, SE Romania *44°37′N 28°41′E*
136 *G12* **Mihalıççık** Eskişehir, NW Turkey *39°52′N 31°30′E*
164 *G13* **Mihara** Hiroshima, Honshū, SW Japan *34°24′N 133°04′E*
165 *N14* **Mihara-yama** Volcano Miyako-jima, SE Japan *34°43′N 139°23′E*
105 *S8* **Mijares** ⁓ E Spain
98 *I11* **Mijdrecht** Utrecht, C Netherlands *52°12′N 04°52′E*
165 *S4* **Mikasa** Hokkaidō, NE Japan *43°15′N 141°57′E*
Mikashevichi *see* Mikashevichy
119 *K19* **Mikashevichy** *Pol.* Mikaszewicze, *Rus.* Mikashevichi. Brestskaya Voblasts', SW Belarus *52°13′N 27°28′E*
Mikaszewicze *see* Mikashevichy
126 *L5* **Mikhaylov** Ryazanskaya Oblast', W Russian Federation *54°12′N 39°03′E*
Mikhaylovgrad *see* Montana
195 *Z8* **Mikhaylov Island** *island* Antarctica
145 *T6* **Mikhaylovka** Pavlodar, N Kazakhstan *53°49′N 76°31′E*
127 *N9* **Mikhaylovka** Volgogradskaya Oblast', SW Russian Federation *50°06′N 43°17′E*
Mikhaylovka *see* Mykhaylivka
81 *K24* **Mikindani** Mtwara, SE Tanzania *10°16′S 40°05′E*
93 *N18* **Mikkeli** *Swe.* Sankt Michel. Itä-Suomi, SE Finland *61°41′N 27°14′E*
110 *M8* **Mikołajki** *Ger.* Nikolaiken. Warmińsko-Mazurskie, NE Poland *53°49′N 21°31′E*
Míkonos *see* Mýkonos
114 *I9* **Mikre** Lovech, N Bulgaria *43°01′N 24°31′E*
114 *C13* **Mikrí Préspa, Límni** ◎ N Greece
125 *P4* **Mikulkin, Mys** *headland* NW Russian Federation *67°50′N 46°36′E*
81 *I23* **Mikumi** Morogoro, SE Tanzania *07°22′S 37°00′E*
125 *R10* **Mikun'** Respublika Komi, NW Russian Federation *62°20′N 50°02′E*
164 *K13* **Mikuni** Fukui, Honshū, SW Japan *36°12′N 136°09′E*
165 *X13* **Mikura-jima** *island* E Japan
29 *V7* **Milaca** Minnesota, N USA *45°45′N 93°40′W*
62 *J10* **Milagro** La Rioja, C Argentina *31°00′S 66°01′W*
56 *B7* **Milagro** Guayas, SW Ecuador *02°11′S 79°36′W*
31 *P4* **Milakokia Lake** ◎ Michigan, N USA
30 *J1* **Milan** Illinois, N USA *41°27′N 90°33′W*
31 *R10* **Milan** Michigan, N USA *42°05′N 83°40′W*
27 *T2* **Milan** Missouri, C USA *40°12′N 93°08′W*
37 *Q11* **Milan** New Mexico, SW USA *35°10′N 107°53′W*
20 *G9* **Milan** Tennessee, S USA *35°55′N 88°45′W*
Milan *see* Milano
95 *F15* **Miland** Telemark, S Norway *59°57′N 08°48′E*
83 *N15* **Milange** Zambézia, NE Mozambique *16°09′S 35°44′E*

◆ Country ● Country Capital ◇ Dependent Territory ○ Dependent Territory Capital ◈ Administrative Regions ✈ International Airport ▲ Mountain ▲▲ Mountain Range Volcano ◎ Lake ⁓ River ▣ Reservoir

MILANO – MOCKSVILLE

106 D8 **Milano** *Eng.* Milan, *Ger.* Mailand; *anc.* Mediolanum. Lombardia, N Italy 45°28′N 09°10′E
25 U10 **Milano** Texas, SW USA 30°42′N 96°51′W
136 C15 **Milas** Muğla, SW Turkey 37°17′N 27°46′E
119 K21 **Milashavichy** *Rus.* Milashevichi. Homyel'skaya Voblasts', SE Belarus 51°39′N 27°56′E
Milashevichi *see* Milashavichy
119 I18 **Milavidy** *Rus.* Milovidy. Brestskaya Voblasts', SW Belarus 52°54′N 25°51′E
107 L23 **Milazzo** *anc.* Mylae. Sicilia, Italy, C Mediterranean Sea 38°13′N 15°15′E
29 R8 **Milbank** South Dakota, N USA 45°12′N 96°36′W
19 T7 **Milbridge** Maine, NE USA 44°31′N 67°55′W
100 L11 **Milde** ≈ C Germany
14 F14 **Mildmay** Ontario, S Canada 44°03′N 81°07′W
182 L9 **Mildura** Victoria, SE Australia 34°13′S 142°09′E
137 X12 **Mil Düzü** *Rus.* Mil'skaya Ravnina, Mil'skaya Step'. *physical region* C Azerbaijan
160 H13 **Mile** *var.* Miyang. Yunnan, SW China 24°28′N 103°26′E
Mile *see* Mili Atoll
181 Y10 **Miles** Queensland, E Australia 26°41′S 150°15′E
25 P8 **Miles** Texas, SW USA 31°36′N 100°10′W
33 X9 **Miles City** Montana, NW USA 46°24′N 105°48′W
11 U17 **Milestone** Saskatchewan, S Canada 50°00′N 104°24′W
107 N22 **Mileto** Calabria, SW Italy 38°35′N 16°03′E
107 K16 **Miletto, Monte** ▲ C Italy 41°28′N 14°21′E
18 M13 **Milford** Connecticut, NE USA 41°12′N 73°01′W
21 Y3 **Milford** *var.* Milford City. Delaware, NE USA 38°54′N 75°25′W
29 T11 **Milford** Iowa, C USA 43°19′N 95°09′W
19 S6 **Milford** Maine, NE USA 44°57′N 68°37′W
29 R16 **Milford** Nebraska, C USA 40°46′N 97°03′W
19 O10 **Milford** New Hampshire, NE USA 42°49′N 71°38′W
18 J13 **Milford** Pennsylvania, NE USA 41°20′N 74°48′W
25 T7 **Milford** Texas, SW USA 32°07′N 96°57′W
36 K6 **Milford** Utah, W USA 38°22′N 112°57′W
Milford *see* Milford Haven
Milford City *see* Milford
97 H21 **Milford Haven** *prev.* Milford. SW Wales, United Kingdom 51°44′N 05°02′W
27 O4 **Milford Lake** ⊠ Kansas, C USA
185 B21 **Milford Sound** Southland, South Island, New Zealand 44°41′S 167°57′E
185 B21 **Milford Sound** *inlet* South Island, New Zealand
Milhau *see* Millau
Milḩ, Baḩr al *see* Razāzah, Buḩayrat ar
139 T10 **Milḩ, Wādī al** *dry watercourse* S Iraq
189 W8 **Mili Atoll** *var.* Mile. *atoll* Ratak Chain, SE Marshall Islands
110 H13 **Milicz** Dolnośląskie, SW Poland 51°32′N 17°15′E
107 L25 **Militello in Val di Catania** Sicilia, Italy, C Mediterranean Sea 37°17′N 14°47′E
11 R17 **Milk River** Alberta, SW Canada 49°10′N 112°06′W
44 J13 **Milk River** ≈ C Jamaica
33 W7 **Milk River** ≈ Montana, NW USA
80 D9 **Milk, Wadi el** *var.* Wadi al Malik. ≈ C Sudan
99 L14 **Mill** Noord-Brabant, SE Netherlands 51°42′N 05°46′E
103 P14 **Millau** *var.* Milhau; *anc.* Æmilianum. Aveyron, S France 44°06′N 03°05′E
14 I14 **Millbrook** Ontario, SE Canada 44°09′N 78°26′W
23 U4 **Milledgeville** Georgia, SE USA 33°04′N 83°13′W
12 C12 **Mille Lacs, Lac des** ◎ Ontario, S Canada
29 V6 **Mille Lacs Lake** ◎ Minnesota, N USA
23 V4 **Millen** Georgia, SE USA 32°50′N 81°56′W
191 Y5 **Millennium Island** *prev.* Caroline Island, Thornton Island. *atoll* Line Islands, E Kiribati
29 O9 **Miller** South Dakota, N USA 44°31′N 98°59′W
30 K5 **Miller Dam Flowage** ⊠ Wisconsin, N USA
39 U12 **Miller, Mount** ▲ Alaska, USA 60°29′N 142°16′W
126 L10 **Millerovo** Rostovskaya Oblast', SW Russian Federation 48°57′N 40°26′E
37 N17 **Miller Peak** ▲ Arizona, SW USA 31°23′N 110°17′W
31 T12 **Millersburg** Ohio, N USA 40°33′N 81°55′W
18 G15 **Millersburg** Pennsylvania, NE USA 40°31′N 76°56′W
185 D23 **Millers Flat** Otago, South Island, New Zealand 45°42′S 169°25′E
25 Q8 **Millersview** Texas, SW USA 31°26′N 99°44′W
106 B10 **Millesimo** Piemonte, NE Italy 44°24′N 08°09′E
12 C12 **Milles Lacs, Lac des** ◎ Ontario, SW Canada
25 Q13 **Millett** Texas, SW USA 28°33′N 99°10′W
103 N11 **Millevaches, Plateau de** *plateau* C France
182 K12 **Millicent** South Australia 37°29′S 140°01′E
98 M13 **Millingen aan den Rijn** Gelderland, SE Netherlands 51°52′N 06°02′E
20 E10 **Millington** Tennessee, S USA 35°20′N 89°54′W
19 R4 **Millinocket** Maine, NE USA 45°38′N 68°45′W
19 R4 **Millinocket Lake** ◎ Maine, NE USA
195 Z11 **Mill Island** *island* Antarctica
183 T3 **Millmerran** Queensland, E Australia 27°53′S 151°15′E
109 R9 **Millstatt** Kärnten, S Austria 46°45′N 13°36′E
97 B19 **Milltown Malbay** *Ir.* Sráid na Cathrach. W Ireland 52°51′N 09°23′W
18 J17 **Millville** New Jersey, NE USA 39°24′N 75°01′W
27 S13 **Millwood Lake** ⊠ Arkansas, C USA
Milne Bank *see* Milne Seamounts
186 G10 **Milne Bay** ◈ *province* SE Papua New Guinea
64 J8 **Milne Seamounts** *var.* Milne Bank. *undersea feature* N Atlantic Ocean
29 Q6 **Milnor** North Dakota, N USA 46°15′N 97°27′W
19 R5 **Milo** Maine, NE USA 45°15′N 69°01′W
115 I22 **Mílos** *island* Kykládes, Greece, Aegean Sea
Mílos *see* Pláka
110 H11 **Miłosław** Wielkopolskie, C Poland 52°13′N 17°28′E
113 K19 **Milot** *var.* Miloti. Lezhë, C Albania 41°42′N 19°43′E
Miloti *see* Milot
117 Z5 **Milove** Luhans'ka Oblast', E Ukraine 49°22′N 40°09′E
Milovidy *see* Milavidy
182 L4 **Milparinka** New South Wales, SE Australia 29°48′S 141°57′E
35 N9 **Milpitas** California, W USA 37°25′N 121°54′W
Mil'skaya Ravnina/Mil'skaya Step' *see* Mil Düzü
14 G15 **Milton** Ontario, S Canada 43°31′N 79°53′W
185 E24 **Milton** Otago, South Island, New Zealand 46°08′S 169°59′E
21 Y4 **Milton** Delaware, NE USA 38°48′N 75°21′W
23 P8 **Milton** Florida, SE USA 30°37′N 87°02′W
18 G14 **Milton** Pennsylvania, NE USA 41°01′N 76°49′W
18 L7 **Milton** Vermont, NE USA 44°37′N 73°04′W
32 K11 **Milton-Freewater** Oregon, NW USA 45°54′N 118°24′W
97 N21 **Milton Keynes** SE England, United Kingdom 52°N 00°43′W
27 N3 **Miltonvale** Kansas, C USA 39°21′N 97°27′W
161 N10 **Miluo** Hunan, S China 28°52′N 113°00′E
30 M9 **Milwaukee** Wisconsin, N USA 43°03′N 87°56′W
Milyang *see* Miryang
Mimatum *see* Mende
37 Q15 **Mimbres Mountains** ▲▲ New Mexico, SW USA
182 D2 **Mimili** South Australia 27°01′S 132°33′E
102 J14 **Mimizan** Landes, SW France 44°12′N 01°12′W
Mimmaya *see* Minmaya
79 E19 **Mimongo** Ngounié, C Gabon 01°36′S 11°44′E
Min *see* Fujian
35 T7 **Mina** Nevada, W USA 38°23′N 118°07′W
143 S14 **Mīnāb** Hormozgān, SE Iran 27°08′N 57°02′E
Mīnā Barānīs *see* Baranīs
149 R9 **Mīna Bāzār** Baluchistān, SW Pakistan 30°58′N 69°11′E
Minami-Awaji *see* Nandan
165 X17 **Minami-Iō-jima** *Eng.* San Augustine. *island* SE Japan
165 R5 **Minami-Kayabe** Hokkaidō, NE Japan 41°54′N 140°58′E
Minami-Satsuma *see* Kaseda
164 C17 **Minamitane** Kagoshima, Tanega-shima, SW Japan 30°23′N 130°54′E
Minami Tori Shima *see* Marcus Island
Min'an *see* Longshan
62 J4 **Mina Pirquitas** Jujuy, NW Argentina 22°48′S 66°24′W
173 O3 **Mīnā' Qābūs** NE Oman
61 F19 **Minas** Lavalleja, S Uruguay 34°20′S 55°15′W
13 P15 **Minas Basin** *bay* Nova Scotia, SE Canada
61 F17 **Minas de Corrales** Rivera, NE Uruguay 31°35′S 55°20′W
44 A5 **Minas de Matahambre** Pinar del Río, W Cuba 22°34′N 83°57′W
104 J13 **Minas de Ríotinto** Andalucía, S Spain 37°40′N 06°36′W
60 K7 **Minas Gerais** *off.* Estado de Minas Gerais. ◈ *state* E Brazil
Minas Gerais, Estado de *see* Minas Gerais
42 E5 **Minas, Sierra de las** ▲▲ E Guatemala
41 T15 **Minatitlán** Veracruz-Llave, E Mexico 17°59′N 94°32′W
166 L6 **Minbu** Magway, W Myanmar (Burma) 20°09′N 94°52′E
149 V10 **Minchinābād** Punjab, E Pakistan 30°10′N 73°40′E
63 G17 **Minchinmávida, Volcán** ⛰ S Chile 42°51′S 72°23′W
96 G7 **Minch, The** *var.* North Minch. *strait* NW Scotland, United Kingdom
106 F8 **Mincio** *anc.* Mincius. ≈ N Italy
Mincius *see* Mincio
26 M11 **Minco** Oklahoma, C USA 35°18′N 97°56′W
171 Q7 **Mindanao** *island* S Philippines
Mindanao Sea *see* Bohol Sea
101 J23 **Mindel** ≈ S Germany
101 J23 **Mindelheim** Bayern, S Germany 48°03′N 10°30′E
Mindello *see* Mindelo
76 C9 **Mindelo** *var.* Mindello; *prev.* Porto Grande. São Vicente, N Cape Verde 16°54′N 25°01′W
14 I13 **Minden** Ontario, SE Canada 44°54′N 78°41′W
100 H13 **Minden** *anc.* Minthun. Nordrhein-Westfalen, NW Germany 52°18′N 08°55′E
22 G5 **Minden** Louisiana, S USA 32°37′N 93°17′W
29 O16 **Minden** Nebraska, C USA 40°30′N 98°57′W
35 Q6 **Minden** Nevada, W USA 38°58′N 119°47′W
182 L8 **Mindona Lake** *seasonal lake* New South Wales, SE Australia
171 O4 **Mindoro** *island* N Philippines
171 N5 **Mindoro Strait** *strait* W Philippines
159 S9 **Mine** Gansu, N China
97 J23 **Minehead** SW England, United Kingdom 51°13′N 03°29′W
97 E21 **Mine Head** *Ir.* Mionn Ard. *headland* S Ireland 51°58′N 07°36′W
59 J19 **Mineiros** Goiás, C Brazil 17°34′S 52°33′W
25 V6 **Mineola** Texas, SW USA 32°39′N 95°29′W
25 S13 **Mineral** Texas, SW USA 28°32′N 97°54′W
127 N15 **Mineral'nyye Vody** Stavropol'skiy Kray, SW Russian Federation 44°13′N 43°06′E
30 K9 **Mineral Point** Wisconsin, N USA 42°54′N 90°09′W
25 S6 **Mineral Wells** Texas, SW USA 32°48′N 98°06′W
36 K6 **Minersville** Utah, W USA 38°12′N 112°56′W
31 U12 **Minerva** Ohio, N USA 40°43′N 81°06′W
107 N17 **Minervino Murge** Puglia, SE Italy 41°06′N 16°05′E
103 O16 **Minervois** *physical region* S France
158 I10 **Minfeng** *var.* Niya. Xinjiang Uygur Zizhiqu, NW China 37°07′N 82°43′E
79 O25 **Minga** Katanga, SE Dem. Rep. Congo 11°06′S 27°57′E
137 W11 **Mingäçevir** *Rus.* Mingechaur, Mingechevir. C Azerbaijan 40°46′N 47°02′E
137 W11 **Mingäçevir Su Anbarı** *Rus.* Mingechaurskoye Vodokhranilishche, Mingechevirskoye Vodokhranilishche. ⊠ NW Azerbaijan
166 L8 **Mingaladon** ✈ (Yangon) Yangon, SW Myanmar (Burma) 16°55′N 96°11′E
13 P11 **Mingan** Québec, E Canada 50°19′N 64°02′W
146 K8 **Mingbuloq** *Rus.* Mynbulak. Navoiy Viloyati, N Uzbekistan 42°18′N 62°53′E
146 K9 **Mingbuloq Botig'i** *Rus.* Vpadina Mynbulak. *depression* N Uzbekistan
Mingechaur/Mingechevir *see* Mingäçevir
Mingechaurskoye Vodokhranilishche/Mingechevirskoye Vodokhranilishche *see* Mingäçevir Su Anbarı
161 Q7 **Mingguang** *prev.* Jiashan. Anhui, SE China 32°45′N 117°59′E
166 L4 **Mingin** Sagaing, C Myanmar (Burma) 22°51′N 94°30′E
105 Q10 **Minglanilla** Castilla-La Mancha, C Spain 39°32′N 01°36′W
31 V13 **Mingo Junction** Ohio, N USA 40°19′N 80°36′W
Mingora *see* Saidu Sharif
163 V7 **Mingshui** Heilongjiang, NE China 47°10′N 125°53′E
Mingtekl Daban *see* Mintaka Pass
Mingu *see* Zhenfeng
83 Q14 **Minguri** Nampula, NE Mozambique 14°30′S 40°37′E
Mingzhou *see* Suide
159 U10 **Minhe** *var.* Chuankou; *prev.* Minhe Huizu Tuzu Zizhixian, Shangchuankou. Qinghai, C China 36°21′N 102°40′E
Minhe Huizu Tuzu Zizhixian *see* Minhe
166 L6 **Minhla** Magway, W Myanmar (Burma) 19°58′N 95°03′E
167 S14 **Minh Lương** Kiên Giang, S Vietnam 09°52′N 105°10′E
104 G5 **Minho** *former province* N Portugal
104 G5 **Minho, Rio** *Sp.* Miño. ≈ Portugal/Spain *see also* Miño
Minho, Rio *see* Miño
155 C24 **Minicoy Island** *island* SW India
33 P15 **Minidoka** Idaho, NW USA 42°45′N 113°29′W
118 C11 **Minija** ≈ W Lithuania
180 G9 **Minilya** Western Australia 23°45′S 114°03′E
14 E8 **Minisinakwa Lake** ◎ Ontario, S Canada
45 T12 **Ministre Point** *headland* S Saint Lucia 13°42′N 60°57′W
11 V15 **Minitonas** Manitoba, S Canada 52°07′N 101°02′W
Minius *see* Miño
161 R12 **Min Jiang** ≈ SE China
160 H10 **Min Jiang** ≈ C China
182 H9 **Minlaton** South Australia 34°52′S 137°33′E
159 S9 **Minle** *var.* Hongshui. Gansu, N China 38°15′N 100°36′E
165 Q6 **Minmaya** *var.* Mimmaya. Aomori, Honshū, C Japan 41°10′N 140°24′E
77 U14 **Minna** Niger, C Nigeria 09°33′N 06°33′E
165 P16 **Minna-jima** *island* Sakishima-shotō, SW Japan
27 N4 **Minneapolis** Kansas, C USA 39°08′N 97°43′W
29 U9 **Minneapolis** Minnesota, N USA 44°59′N 93°16′W
29 V8 **Minneapolis-Saint Paul** ✈ Minnesota, N USA 44°53′N 93°13′W
11 W16 **Minnedosa** Manitoba, S Canada 50°14′N 99°50′W
26 J7 **Minneola** Kansas, C USA 37°26′N 100°00′W
29 S7 **Minnesota** *off.* State of Minnesota, *also known as* Gopher State, New England of the West, North Star State. ◈ *state* N USA
29 S9 **Minnesota River** ≈ Minnesota/South Dakota, N USA
29 V9 **Minnetonka** Minnesota, N USA 44°55′N 93°28′W
29 O3 **Minnewaukan** North Dakota, N USA 48°04′N 99°14′W
182 F7 **Minnipa** South Australia 32°52′S 135°07′E
104 H2 **Miño** Galicia, NW Spain 43°21′N 08°12′W
104 G5 **Miño** *var.* Mino, Minius, *Port.* Rio Minho. ≈ Portugal/Spain *see also* Minho, Rio
Miño *see* Minho, Rio
30 L4 **Minocqua** Wisconsin, N USA 45°53′N 89°42′W
30 L12 **Minonk** Illinois, N USA 40°54′N 89°01′W
Minorca *see* Menorca
28 M3 **Minot** North Dakota, N USA 48°15′N 101°19′W
159 U8 **Minqin** Gansu, N China 38°35′N 103°07′E
119 J16 **Minsk** ● (Belarus) Minskaya Voblasts', C Belarus 53°52′N 27°34′E
119 L16 **Minsk** ✈ Minskaya Voblasts', C Belarus 53°52′N 27°58′E
Minskaya Oblast' *see* Minskaya Voblasts'
119 K16 **Minskaya Voblasts'** *prev. Rus.* Minskaya Oblast'. ◈ *province* C Belarus
119 J16 **Minskaya Wzvyshsha** ▲▲ C Belarus
110 N12 **Mińsk Mazowiecki** *var.* Nowo-Minsk. Mazowieckie, C Poland 52°10′N 21°31′E
31 Q13 **Minster** Ohio, N USA 40°23′N 84°22′W
79 F15 **Minta** Centre, C Cameroon 04°34′N 12°54′E
149 W2 **Mintaka Pass** *Chin.* Mingtekl Daban. *pass* China/Pakistan
115 D20 **Mínthi** ▲▲ S Greece
Minthun *see* Minden
13 O14 **Minto** New Brunswick, SE Canada 46°05′N 66°05′W
10 H6 **Minto** Yukon Territory, W Canada 62°33′N 136°45′W
39 R9 **Minto** Alaska, USA 65°07′N 149°22′W
29 Q3 **Minto** North Dakota, N USA 48°17′N 97°22′W
12 K6 **Minto, Lac** ◎ Québec, C Canada
195 R16 **Minto, Mount** ▲ Antarctica 71°38′S 169°11′E
11 U17 **Minton** Saskatchewan, S Canada 49°12′N 104°33′W
189 R15 **Minto Reef** *atoll* Caroline Islands, C Micronesia
37 R4 **Minturn** Colorado, C USA 39°34′N 106°21′W
107 J16 **Minturno** Lazio, C Italy 41°15′N 13°47′E
122 K13 **Minusinsk** Krasnoyarskiy Kray, S Russian Federation 53°37′N 91°49′E
108 G11 **Minusio** Ticino, S Switzerland 46°11′N 08°47′E
79 E17 **Minvoul** Woleu-Ntem, N Gabon 02°08′N 12°12′E
141 R13 **Minwakh** N Yemen 16°55′N 48°04′E
159 V11 **Minxian** *var.* Min Xian, Minyang. Gansu, C China 34°20′N 104°09′E
Min Xian *see* Minxian
Minya *see* Al Minyā
Minyang *see* Minxian
31 R6 **Mio** Michigan, N USA 44°40′N 84°09′W
Mionn Ard *see* Mine Head
158 L5 **Miquan** Xinjiang Uygur Zizhiqu, NW China 44°04′N 87°40′E
119 I17 **Mir** Hrodzyenskaya Voblasts', W Belarus 53°25′N 26°28′E
106 H8 **Mira** Veneto, NE Italy 45°25′N 12°07′E
12 K15 **Mirabel** *var.* Montreal. ✈ (Montréal) Québec, SE Canada 45°27′N 73°47′W
60 Q8 **Miracema** Rio de Janeiro, SE Brazil 21°24′S 42°10′W
54 G9 **Miraflores** Boyacá, C Colombia 05°07′N 73°09′W
40 G10 **Miraflores** Baja California Sur, NW Mexico 23°24′N 109°45′W
44 L9 **Miragoâne** S Haiti 18°25′N 73°07′W
155 E16 **Miraj** Mahārāshtra, W India 16°51′N 74°42′E
61 E23 **Miramar** Buenos Aires, E Argentina 38°15′S 57°50′W
103 R15 **Miramas** Bouches-du-Rhône, SE France 43°33′N 05°02′E
102 K12 **Mirambeau** Charente-Maritime, W France 45°23′N 00°33′W
102 L13 **Miramont-de-Guyenne** Lot-et-Garonne, SW France 44°34′N 00°20′E
115 L25 **Mirampéllou Kólpos** *gulf* Kríti, Greece, E Mediterranean Sea
158 L8 **Miran** Xinjiang Uygur Zizhiqu, NW China 39°13′N 88°58′E
54 M5 **Miranda** *off.* Estado Miranda. ◈ *state* N Venezuela
Miranda de Corvo *see* Miranda do Corvo
105 O3 **Miranda de Ebro** La Rioja, N Spain 42°41′N 02°57′W
104 G8 **Miranda do Corvo** *var.* Miranda de Corvo. Coimbra, N Portugal 40°05′N 08°20′W
104 J6 **Miranda do Douro** Bragança, N Portugal 41°30′N 06°16′W
Miranda, Estado *see* Miranda
102 L15 **Mirande** Gers, S France 43°31′N 00°25′E
104 I6 **Mirandela** Bragança, N Portugal 41°28′N 07°10′W
25 R15 **Mirando City** Texas, SW USA 27°24′N 99°00′W
106 G9 **Mirandola** Emilia-Romagna, N Italy 44°52′N 11°04′E
60 I8 **Mirandópolis** São Paulo, S Brazil 21°10′S 51°03′W
104 G13 **Mira, Rio** ≈ S Portugal
60 K8 **Mirassol** São Paulo, S Brazil 20°50′S 49°30′W
104 J3 **Miravalles** ▲ NW Spain 42°52′N 06°45′W
42 L12 **Miravalles, Volcán** ⛰ NW Costa Rica 10°43′N 85°07′W
141 W13 **Mirbāṭ** *var.* Marbat. S Oman 17°03′N 54°44′E
44 M9 **Mirebalais** C Haiti 18°51′N 72°08′W
103 T6 **Mirecourt** Vosges, NE France 48°19′N 06°04′E
103 N16 **Mirepoix** Ariège, S France 43°05′N 01°51′E
Mirgorod *see* Myrhorod
139 W10 **Mīr Ḩājī Khalīl** Wāsiţ, E Iraq 32°11′N 46°19′E
169 T8 **Miri** Sarawak, East Malaysia 04°23′N 113°59′E
77 W12 **Mirria** Zinder, S Niger 13°39′N 09°15′E
182 F5 **Mirikata** South Australia 29°56′S 135°13′E
54 K4 **Mirimire** Falcón, N Venezuela 11°14′N 68°39′W
61 H18 **Mirim Lagoon** *var.* Lake Mirim, *Sp.* Laguna Merín. *lagoon* Brazil/Uruguay
Mirim, Lake *see* Mirim Lagoon
Mírina *see* Mýrina
172 H14 **Miringoni** Mohéli, S Comoros 12°17′S 93°39′E
143 W11 **Mīrjāveh** Sīstān va Balūchestān, SE Iran 29°04′N 61°24′E
195 Z9 **Mirny** *Russian research station* Antarctica 66°25′S 93°09′E
124 M10 **Mirnyy** Arkhangel'skaya Oblast', NW Russian Federation 62°50′N 40°20′E
123 O10 **Mirnyy** Respublika Sakha (Yakutiya), NE Russian Federation 62°30′N 113°58′E
Mironovka *see* Myronivka
110 F9 **Mirosławiec** Zachodnio-pomorskie, NW Poland 53°21′N 16°04′E
Mirovo *see* Vrattsa
100 N10 **Mirow** Mecklenburg-Vorpommern, N Germany 53°16′N 12°48′E
152 G6 **Mīrpur** Jammu and Kashmir, NW India 33°06′N 73°49′E
Mīrpur *see* New Mīrpur
149 P17 **Mīrpur Batoro** Sind, SE Pakistan 24°40′N 68°15′E
149 Q16 **Mīrpur Khās** Sind, SE Pakistan 25°31′N 69°01′E
149 P17 **Mīrpur Sakro** Sind, SE Pakistan 24°32′N 67°38′E
143 T14 **Mīr Shahdād** Hormozgān, S Iran 26°15′N 58°29′E
Mirtoan Sea *see* Mirtóo Pélagos
115 G21 **Mirtóo Pélagos** *Eng.* Mirtoan Sea; *anc.* Myrtoum Mare. *sea* S Greece
163 Z16 **Miryang** *var.* Milyang, *Jap.* Mitsuō. SE South Korea 35°30′N 128°46′E
Mirzachirla *see* Murzechirla
164 E14 **Misaki** Ehime, Shikoku, SW Japan 33°22′N 132°04′E
41 Q13 **Misantla** Veracruz-Llave, E Mexico 19°54′N 96°51′W
165 R7 **Misawa** Aomori, Honshū, C Japan 40°42′N 141°26′E
57 G14 **Mishagua, Río** ≈ C Peru
163 Z8 **Mishan** Heilongjiang, NE China 45°30′N 131°53′E
31 O11 **Mishawaka** Indiana, N USA 41°40′N 86°10′W
39 N6 **Misheguk Mountain** ▲ Alaska, USA 68°13′N 161°11′W
165 N14 **Mishima** *var.* Misima. Shizuoka, Honshū, S Japan 35°08′N 138°54′E
164 E12 **Mi-shima** *island* SW Japan
127 V4 **Mishkino** Respublika Bashkortostan, W Russian Federation 55°31′N 55°57′E
153 Y10 **Mishmi Hills** *hill range* NE India
161 N11 **Mi Shui** ≈ S China
Misiaf *see* Maşyāf
107 J23 **Misilmeri** Sicilia, Italy, C Mediterranean Sea 38°03′N 13°27′E
Misima *see* Mishima
14 C7 **Missinaibi Lake** ◎ Ontario, S Canada
Misión de Guana *see* Guana
60 F13 **Misiones** *off.* Provincia de Misiones. ◈ *province* NE Argentina
62 P8 **Misiones** *off.* Departamento de las Misiones. ◈ *department* S Paraguay
Misiones, Departamento de las *see* Misiones
Misiones, Provincia de *see* Misiones
Misión San Fernando *see* San Fernando
Miskin *see* Maskin
Miskito Coast *see* La Mosquitia
43 O7 **Miskitos, Cayos** *island group* NE Nicaragua
111 M21 **Miskolc** Borsod-Abaúj-Zemplén, NE Hungary 48°05′N 20°46′E
171 T12 **Misool, Pulau** *island* Maluku, E Indonesia
Misox *see* Mesocco
29 Y3 **Misquah Hills** *hill range* Minnesota, N USA
75 P7 **Mişrātah** *var.* Misurata. NW Libya 32°23′N 15°06′E
75 P7 **Mişrātah, Râs** *headland* N Libya 32°22′N 15°16′E
14 C7 **Missanabie** Ontario, S Canada 48°18′N 84°04′W
58 E10 **Missão Catrimani** Roraima, N Brazil 01°26′N 62°05′W
14 D6 **Missinaibi** ≈ Ontario, S Canada
11 T13 **Missinipe** Saskatchewan, C Canada 55°36′N 104°45′W
28 M11 **Mission** South Dakota, N USA 43°16′N 100°38′W
25 S17 **Mission** Texas, SW USA 26°13′N 98°19′W
12 F10 **Missisa Lake** ◎ Ontario, C Canada
18 M6 **Missisquoi Bay** *lake bay* Canada/USA
14 C10 **Mississagi** ≈ Ontario, S Canada
14 G15 **Mississauga** Ontario, S Canada 43°38′N 79°36′W
31 P12 **Mississinewa Lake** ⊠ Indiana, N USA
31 P12 **Mississinewa River** ≈ Indiana/Ohio, N USA
22 K4 **Mississippi** *off.* State of Mississippi, *also known as* Bayou State, Magnolia State. ◈ *state* SE USA
14 K13 **Mississippi** ≈ Ontario, SE Canada
47 N1 **Mississippi Fan** *undersea feature* N Gulf of Mexico 26°45′N 88°30′W
14 L13 **Mississippi Lake** ◎ Ontario, SE Canada
22 M10 **Mississippi Delta** *delta* Louisiana, S USA
0 J11 **Mississippi River** ≈ C USA
22 M9 **Mississippi Sound** *sound* Alabama/Mississippi, S USA
33 P9 **Missoula** Montana, NW USA 46°54′N 114°03′W
27 T5 **Missouri** *off.* State of Missouri, *also known as* Bullion State, Show Me State. ◈ *state* C USA
25 V11 **Missouri City** Texas, SW USA 29°37′N 95°32′W
0 J10 **Missouri River** ≈ C USA
15 Q6 **Mistassibi** ≈ Québec, SE Canada
15 P6 **Mistassini** ≈ Québec, SE Canada
15 P6 **Mistassini** Québec, SE Canada 48°54′N 72°13′W
12 J11 **Mistassini, Lac** ◎ Québec, SE Canada
109 Y3 **Mistelbach an der Zaya** Niederösterreich, NE Austria 48°34′N 16°33′E
107 L24 **Misterbianco** Sicilia, Italy, C Mediterranean Sea 37°31′N 15°01′E
95 N19 **Misterhult** Kalmar, S Sweden 57°28′N 16°34′E
57 H17 **Misti, Volcán** ⛰ S Peru 16°20′S 71°22′W
Mistras *see* Mystrás
107 K23 **Mistretta** *anc.* Amestratus. Sicilia, Italy, C Mediterranean Sea 37°56′N 14°22′E
164 F12 **Misumi** Shimane, Honshū, SW Japan 34°47′N 132°00′E
Misurata *see* Mişrātah
83 O14 **Mitande** Niassa, N Mozambique 14°06′S 36°03′E
40 J13 **Mita, Punta de** *headland* C Mexico 20°46′N 105°31′W
55 W12 **Mitaraka, Massif du** ▲ NE South America 02°18′N 54°31′W
Mitau *see* Jelgava
181 X9 **Mitchell** Queensland, E Australia 26°29′S 148°00′E
14 E15 **Mitchell** Ontario, S Canada 43°28′N 81°11′W
28 I13 **Mitchell** Nebraska, C USA 41°56′N 103°48′W
32 J12 **Mitchell** Oregon, NW USA 44°34′N 120°09′W
29 P11 **Mitchell** South Dakota, N USA 43°42′N 98°01′W
23 P5 **Mitchell Lake** ⊠ Alabama, S USA
31 P7 **Mitchell, Lake** ◎ Michigan, N USA
21 P9 **Mitchell, Mount** ▲ North Carolina, SE USA 35°46′N 82°16′W
181 V3 **Mitchell River** ≈ Queensland, NE Australia
97 D20 **Mitchelstown** *Ir.* Baile Mhistéala. SW Ireland 52°20′N 08°16′W
14 M9 **Mitchinamécus, Lac** ◎ Québec, SE Canada
Mitèmboni *see* Mitemele, Río
79 D17 **Mitemele, Río** *var.* Mitèmboni, Temboni, Utamboni. ≈ S Equatorial Guinea
149 S12 **Mithān Kot** Punjab, E Pakistan 28°53′N 70°25′E
149 T7 **Mitha Tiwāna** Punjab, E Pakistan 32°18′N 72°08′E
149 R17 **Mithi** Sind, SE Pakistan 24°43′N 69°53′E
Míthimna *see* Míthymna
Mi Tho *see* My Tho
115 L16 **Míthymna** *var.* Míthimna. Lésvos, E Greece 39°20′N 26°12′E
190 L16 **Mitiaro** *island* S Cook Islands
Mitilíni *see* Mytilíni
15 U7 **Mitis** ≈ Québec, SE Canada
41 R16 **Mitla** Oaxaca, SE Mexico 16°56′N 96°19′W
165 P13 **Mito** Ibaraki, Honshū, S Japan 36°21′N 140°26′E
92 N2 **Mitra, Kapp** *headland* W Svalbard 79°07′N 11°11′E
184 M13 **Mitre** ▲ North Island, New Zealand 40°46′S 175°27′E
185 B21 **Mitre Peak** ▲ South Island, New Zealand 44°37′S 167°45′E
39 O15 **Mitrofania Island** *island* Alaska, USA
Mitrovica/Mitrovicë *see* Kosovska Mitrovica, Serbia
Mitrovica/Mitrovitz *see* Sremska Mitrovica, Serbia
113 M16 **Mitrovicë** *Serb.* Mitrovica, Kosovska Mitrovica, Titova Mitrovica. N Kosovo 42°54′N 20°52′E
172 H12 **Mitsamiouli** Grande Comore, NW Comoros 11°22′S 43°19′E
172 I3 **Mitsinjo** Mahajanga, NW Madagascar 16°00′S 45°52′E
80 J9 **Mits'iwa** *var.* Masawa, Massawa. E Eritrea 15°37′N 39°27′E
172 H13 **Mitsoudjé** Grande Comore, NW Comoros
138 F12 **Mitspe Ramon** *prev.* Mizpe Ramon. Southern, S Israel 30°38′N 34°47′E
165 T5 **Mitsuishi** Hokkaidō, NE Japan 42°12′N 142°40′E
165 O11 **Mitsuke** *var.* Mituke. Niigata, Honshū, C Japan 37°30′N 138°54′E
Mitsuō *see* Miryang
164 C12 **Mitsushima** Nagasaki, Tsushima, SW Japan 34°16′N 129°18′E
100 G12 **Mittellandkanal** *canal* NW Germany
108 J7 **Mittelberg** Vorarlberg, NW Austria 47°19′N 10°09′E
Mitteldorf *see* Międzychód
Mittelstadt *see* Baia Sprie
Mitterburg *see* Pazin
109 P7 **Mittersill** Salzburg, NW Austria 47°16′N 12°27′E
101 N16 **Mittweida** Sachsen, E Germany 50°59′N 12°57′E
54 J13 **Mitú** Vaupés, SE Colombia 01°07′N 70°05′W
Mituke *see* Mitsuke
Mitumba, Chaîne des/Mitumba Range *see* Mitumba, Monts
79 O22 **Mitumba, Monts** *var.* Chaîne des Mitumba, Mitumba Range. ▲▲ E Dem. Rep. Congo
79 N23 **Mitwaba** Katanga, SE Dem. Rep. Congo 08°37′S 27°20′E
79 E18 **Mitzic** Woleu-Ntem, N Gabon 0°48′N 11°30′E
82 K11 **Miueru Wantipa, Lake** ◎ N Zambia
165 N14 **Miura** Kanagawa, Honshū, S Japan 35°08′N 139°37′E
165 Q10 **Miyagi** *off.* Miyagi-ken. ◈ *prefecture* Honshū, C Japan
Miyagi-ken *see* Miyagi
138 M7 **Miyāh, Wādī al** *dry watercourse* E Syria
165 X13 **Miyake** Tōkyō, Miyako-jima, SE Japan 34°35′N 135°33′E
165 Q16 **Miyake-jima** *island* Sakishima-shotō, SW Japan
165 R8 **Miyako** Iwate, Honshū, C Japan 39°39′N 141°57′E
164 D16 **Miyakonojō** *var.* Miyakonzyô. Miyazaki, Kyūshū, SW Japan 31°42′N 131°04′E
Miyakonzyô *see* Miyakonojō
165 Q16 **Miyako-shotō** *island group* SW Japan
144 G11 **Miyaly** Atyrau, W Kazakhstan 48°52′N 53°55′E
Miyāndoāb *see* Mīāndowāb
Miyāneh *see* Mīāneh
Miyang *see* Mile
164 D16 **Miyazaki** Miyazaki, Kyūshū, SW Japan 31°55′N 131°24′E
164 D16 **Miyazaki** *off.* Miyazaki-ken. ◈ *prefecture* Kyūshū, SW Japan
Miyazaki-ken *see* Miyazaki
164 J12 **Miyazu** Kyōto, Honshū, SW Japan 35°33′N 135°12′E
Miyory *see* Myory
164 G12 **Miyoshi** *var.* Miyosi. Hiroshima, Honshū, SW Japan 34°48′N 132°51′E
Miyosi *see* Miyoshi
Miza *see* Mizë
81 H14 **Mīzan Teferī** Southern Nationalities, S Ethiopia 06°57′N 35°30′E
Mizda *see* Mizdah
75 O8 **Mizdah** *var.* Mizda. NW Libya 31°26′N 12°59′E
113 K20 **Mizë** *var.* Miza. Fier, W Albania 40°58′N 19°32′E
97 A22 **Mizen Head** *Ir.* Carn Uí Néid. *headland* SW Ireland 51°26′N 09°50′W
116 H7 **Mizhhir"ya** *Rus.* Mezhgor'ye. Zakarpats'ka Oblast', W Ukraine 48°30′N 23°30′E
160 L4 **Mizhi** Shaanxi, C China 37°50′N 110°03′E
116 K13 **Mizil** Prahova, SE Romania 45°00′N 26°29′E
114 H7 **Miziya** Vratsa, NW Bulgaria 43°42′N 23°52′E
153 W15 **Mizo Hills** *hill range* E India
153 W15 **Mizoram** ◈ *state* NE India
Mizpe Ramon *see* Mitspe Ramon
57 L19 **Mizque** Cochabamba, C Bolivia 17°57′S 65°10′W
57 M19 **Mizque, Río** ≈ C Bolivia
165 Q9 **Mizusawa** *var.* Ōshū. Iwate, Honshū, C Japan 39°10′N 141°07′E
95 M18 **Mjölby** Östergötland, S Sweden 58°19′N 15°10′E
95 G15 **Mjøndalen** Buskerud, S Norway 59°45′N 09°58′E
95 J19 **Mjörn** ◎ S Sweden
94 I13 **Mjøsa** *var.* Mjøsen. ◎ S Norway
Mjøsen *see* Mjøsa
81 G21 **Mkalama** Singida, C Tanzania 04°09′S 34°35′E
80 K13 **Mkata** ≈ C Tanzania
83 K14 **Mkushi** Central, C Zambia 13°40′S 29°26′E
83 L22 **Mkuze** KwaZulu/Natal, E South Africa 27°37′S 32°03′E
81 J22 **Mkwaja** Tanga, E Tanzania 05°42′S 38°48′E
111 D16 **Mladá Boleslav** *Ger.* Jungbunzlau. Středočeský Kraj, N Czech Republic 50°26′N 14°55′E
112 M12 **Mladenovac** Serbia, C Serbia 44°27′N 20°42′E
114 L11 **Mladinovo** Khaskovo, S Bulgaria 41°57′N 26°13′E
113 O17 **Mlado Nagoričane** N FYR Macedonia 42°11′N 21°49′E
Mlanje *see* Mulanje
112 N12 **Mlava** ≈ E Serbia
110 L9 **Mława** Mazowieckie, C Poland 53°07′N 20°23′E
113 G16 **Mljet** *It.* Meleda; *anc.* Melita. *island* S Croatia
116 K4 **Mlyniv** Rivnens'ka Oblast', NW Ukraine 50°31′N 25°36′E
83 I21 **Mmabatho** North-West, N South Africa 25°51′S 25°37′E
83 I19 **Mmashoro** Central, E Botswana 21°56′S 26°39′E
44 J7 **Moa** Holguín, E Cuba 20°42′N 74°57′W
76 J15 **Moa** ≈ Guinea/Sierra Leone
37 O6 **Moab** Utah, W USA 38°35′N 109°34′W
181 V1 **Moa Island** *island* Queensland, NE Australia
187 Y15 **Moala** *island* S Fiji
83 L21 **Moamba** Maputo, SW Mozambique 25°35′S 32°13′E
79 F19 **Moanda** *var.* Mouanda. Haut-Ogooué, SE Gabon 01°31′S 13°07′E
83 M15 **Moatize** Tete, NW Mozambique 16°04′S 33°43′E
79 P22 **Moba** Katanga, E Dem. Rep. Congo 07°03′S 29°52′E
Mobay *see* Montego Bay
79 K15 **Mobaye** Basse-Kotto, S Central African Republic 04°19′N 21°17′E
79 K15 **Mobayi-Mbongo** Equateur, NW Dem. Rep. Congo 04°21′N 21°10′E
25 P2 **Mobeetie** Texas, SW USA 35°33′N 100°25′W
27 U3 **Moberly** Missouri, C USA 39°25′N 92°26′W
23 N8 **Mobile** Alabama, S USA 30°42′N 88°03′W
23 N9 **Mobile Bay** *bay* Alabama, S USA
23 N8 **Mobile River** ≈ Alabama, S USA
29 N8 **Mobridge** South Dakota, N USA 45°32′N 100°25′W
Mobutu Sese Seko, Lac *see* Albert, Lake
45 N8 **Moca** N Dominican Republic 19°26′N 70°33′W
83 Q15 **Moçambique** Nampula, NE Mozambique 15°00′S 40°44′E
Moçambique *see* Mozambique
167 S6 **Môc Châu** Sơn La, N Vietnam 20°49′N 104°38′E
187 Z15 **Moce** *island* Lau Group, E Fiji
Mocha *see* Al Mukhā
193 T11 **Mocha Fracture Zone** *tectonic feature* SE Pacific Ocean
63 F14 **Mocha, Isla** *island* C Chile
56 C12 **Moche, Río** ≈ W Peru
167 S14 **Mộc Hóa** Long An, S Vietnam 10°46′N 105°56′E
83 I20 **Mochudi** Kgatleng, SE Botswana 24°25′S 26°07′E
82 Q13 **Mocímboa da Praia** *var.* Vila de Mocímboa da Praia. Cabo Delgado, N Mozambique 11°17′S 40°21′E
94 L13 **Mockfjärd** Dalarna, C Sweden 60°30′N 14°57′E
21 R9 **Mocksville** North Carolina, SE USA 35°53′N 80°33′W

◆ Country ● Country Capital ◇ Dependent Territory ○ Dependent Territory Capital ◈ Administrative Regions ✈ International Airport ▲ Mountain ▲▲ Mountain Range ⛰ Volcano ≈ River ◎ Lake ⊠ Reservoir

MOCLIPS – MONTICELLO

32 F8 Moclips Washington, NW USA 47°11′N 124°13′W
82 C13 Môco var. Morro de Môco. ▲ W Angola 12°36′S 15°09′E
54 D13 Mocoa Putumayo, SW Colombia 01°07′N 76°38′W
60 M8 Mococa São Paulo, S Brazil 21°30′S 47°00′W
Môco, Morro de see Môco
40 H8 Mocorito Sinaloa, C Mexico 25°24′N 107°55′W
40 J4 Moctezuma Chihuahua, N Mexico 30°10′N 106°28′W
41 N11 Moctezuma San Luis Potosí, C Mexico 22°46′N 101°06′W
40 G4 Moctezuma Sonora, NW Mexico 29°50′N 109°40′W
41 P12 Moctezuma, Río ≈ C Mexico
Mó, Cuan see Clew Bay
83 O16 Mocuba Zambézia, NE Mozambique 16°50′S 37°02′E
103 U12 Modane Savoie, E France 45°14′N 06°41′E
106 F9 Modena anc. Mutina. Emilia-Romagna, N Italy 44°39′N 10°55′E
36 I7 Modena Utah, W USA 37°46′N 113°54′W
35 O9 Modesto California, W USA 37°38′N 121°02′W
107 L25 Modica anc. Motyca. Sicilia, Italy, C Mediterranean Sea 36°52′N 14°45′E
83 J20 Modimolle prev. Nylstroom. Limpopo, NE South Africa 24°39′N 28°23′E
79 K17 Modjamboli Equateur, N Dem. Rep. Congo 02°27′N 22°03′E
109 X4 Mödling Niederösterreich, NE Austria 48°06′N 16°18′E
Modohn see Madona
Modot see Tsenhermandal
171 V14 Modowi Papua, E Indonesia 04°05′S 134°39′E
112 I12 Modračko Jezero ⊠ NE Bosnia and Herzegovina
112 I10 Modriča Republika Srpska, N Bosnia and Herzegovina 44°57′N 18°17′E
183 O13 Moe Victoria, SE Australia 38°11′S 146°18′E
Moearatewe see Muaratewe
Moei, Mae Nam see Thaungyin
94 H13 Moelv Hedmark, S Norway 60°55′N 10°47′E
92 I10 Moen Troms, N Norway 69°08′N 18°35′E
Möen see Møn, Denmark
Moen see Weno, Micronesia
Moena see Muna, Pulau
36 M10 Moenkopi Wash ≈ Arizona, SW USA
185 F22 Moeraki Point headland South Island, New Zealand 45°23′S 170°52′E
99 F16 Moerbeke Oost-Vlaanderen, NW Belgium 51°11′N 03°57′E
99 H14 Moerdijk Noord-Brabant, S Netherlands 51°42′N 04°37′E
Moero, Lac see Mweru, Lake
101 D15 Moers var. Mörs. Nordrhein-Westfalen, W Germany 51°27′N 06°36′E
Moesi see Musi, Air
Moeskroen see Mouscron
96 J13 Moffat S Scotland, United Kingdom 55°29′N 03°36′W
185 C22 Moffat Peak ▲ South Island, New Zealand 44°57′S 168°10′E
79 N19 Moga Sud-Kivu, E Dem. Rep. Congo 02°16′S 26°54′E
152 H8 Moga Punjab, N India 30°49′N 75°13′E
Mogadiscio/Mogadishu see Muqdisho
Mogador see Essaouira
104 J6 Mogadouro Bragança, N Portugal 41°20′N 06°43′W
167 N2 Mogaung Kachin State, N Myanmar (Burma) 25°20′N 96°54′E
110 L13 Mogielnica Mazowieckie, C Poland 51°40′N 20°42′E
Mogilëv see Mahilyow
Mogilev-Podol'skiy see Mohyliv-Podil's'kyy
Mogilëvskaya Oblast' see Mahilyowskaya Voblasts'
110 I11 Mogilno Kujawsko-pomorskie, C Poland 52°39′N 17°58′E
60 L9 Mogi-Mirim var. Moji-Mirim. São Paulo, S Brazil 22°26′S 46°55′W
83 Q15 Mogincual Nampula, NE Mozambique 15°33′S 40°28′E
114 E13 Moglenítsas ≈ N Greece
106 H8 Mogliano Veneto Veneto, NE Italy 45°34′N 12°14′E
113 M21 Mogliçë Korçë, SE Albania 40°43′N 20°22′E
123 O13 Mogocha Chitinskaya Oblast', S Russian Federation 53°39′N 119°47′E
122 J11 Mogochin Tomskaya Oblast', C Russian Federation 57°42′N 83°24′E
80 F13 Mogogh Jonglei, SE Sudan 08°26′N 31°19′E
171 U12 Mogoi Papua, E Indonesia 01°44′S 133°13′E
166 M4 Mogok Mandalay, C Myanmar (Burma) 22°55′N 96°29′E
37 P14 Mogollon Mountains ▲▲ New Mexico, SW USA
36 M12 Mogollon Rim cliff Arizona, SW USA
61 E23 Mogotes, Punta headland E Argentina 38°03′S 57°31′W
42 J8 Mogotón ▲ NW Nicaragua 13°45′N 86°22′W
104 I14 Moguer Andalucía, S Spain 37°15′N 06°52′W
111 J26 Mohács Baranya, SW Hungary 46°N 18°40′E
185 C20 Mohaka ≈ North Island, New Zealand
28 M2 Mohall North Dakota, N USA 48°45′N 101°30′W
Mohammadābād see Dargaz
143 U12 Mohammadābād-e Rīgān Kermān, SE Iran 28°39′N 59°01′E
74 F6 Mohammedia prev. Fédala. NW Morocco 33°46′N 07°16′W
74 F6 Mohammed V ✕ (Casablanca) W Morocco 33°07′N 08°28′W
Mohammerah see Khorramshahr
36 H10 Mohave, Lake ⊠ Arizona/Nevada, W USA
36 I12 Mohave Mountains ▲▲ Arizona, SW USA
36 I15 Mohawk Mountains ▲▲ Arizona, SW USA
18 J10 Mohawk River ≈ New York, NE USA
163 T3 Mohe var. Xilinji. Heilongjiang, NE China 53°00′N 122°34′E
95 L20 Moheda Kronoberg, S Sweden 57°00′N 14°34′E
Mohéli see Mwali
152 I11 Mohendergarh Haryāna, N India 28°17′N 76°14′E
38 K12 Mohican, Cape headland Nunivak Island, Alaska, USA 60°12′N 167°25′W
Mohn see Muhu
101 G15 Möhne ≈ W Germany
101 G15 Möhne-Stausee ⊠ W Germany
92 P2 Mohn, Kapp headland NW Svalbard 79°26′N 25°44′E
197 S14 Mohns Ridge undersea feature Greenland Sea/Norwegian Sea 72°30′N 05°00′E
57 I17 Moho Puno, SE Peru 15°21′S 69°32′W
Moholkare see Caledon
95 L17 Moholm Västra Götaland, S Sweden 58°37′N 14°04′E
36 J11 Mohon Peak ▲ Arizona, SW USA 34°55′N 113°07′W
81 J23 Mohoro Pwani, E Tanzania 08°09′S 39°10′E
Mohra see Moravice
Mohrungen see Morąg
116 M7 Mohyliv-Podil's'kyy Rus. Mogilev-Podol'skiy. Vinnyts'ka Oblast', C Ukraine 48°29′N 27°49′E
95 D17 Moi Rogaland, S Norway 58°27′N 06°32′E
Moili see Mwali
116 K11 Moinești Hung. Mojnest. Bacău, E Romania 46°27′N 26°31′E
Móinteach Mílic see Mountmellick
14 J14 Moira ≈ Ontario, SE Canada
92 G13 Mo i Rana Nordland, C Norway 66°19′N 14°10′E
153 X14 Moirāng Manipur, NE India 24°29′N 93°45′E
115 J25 Moíres Kríti, Greece, E Mediterranean Sea 35°03′N 24°51′E
118 H6 Mõisaküla Ger. Moiseküll. Viljandimaa, S Estonia 58°05′N 25°12′E
Moiseküll see Mõisaküla
15 W4 Moisie Québec, E Canada 50°12′N 66°06′W
15 W3 Moisie ≈ Québec, SE Canada
102 M14 Moissac Tarn-et-Garonne, S France 44°07′N 01°05′E
78 I13 Moïssala Moyen-Chari, S Chad 08°21′N 17°46′E
55 O7 Moitaco Bolívar, E Venezuela 08°00′N 64°22′W
95 P15 Möja Stockholm, C Sweden 59°25′N 18°55′E
105 Q14 Mojácar Andalucía, S Spain 37°09′N 01°50′W
35 T13 Mojave California, W USA 35°03′N 118°10′W
35 V13 Mojave Desert plain California, W USA
35 V13 Mojave River ≈ California, W USA
Moji-Mirim see Mogi-Mirim
113 K15 Mojkovac E Montenegro 42°57′N 19°34′E
Mojnest see Moinești
Mōka see Mooka
153 Q13 Mokāma prev. Mokameh, Mukama. Bihār, N India 25°24′N 85°55′E
79 O25 Mokambo Katanga, SE Dem. Rep. Congo 12°23′S 28°21′E
Mokameh see Mokāma
38 D9 Mōkapu Point var. Mokapu Point. headland O'ahu, Hawai'i, USA 21°27′N 157°43′W
184 L9 Mokau Waikato, North Island, New Zealand 38°42′S 174°37′E
184 L9 Mokau ≈ North Island, New Zealand
35 P7 Mokelumne River ≈ California, W USA
83 J23 Mokhotlong NE Lesotho 29°19′S 29°06′E
Moki. Atoll see Mwokil Atoll
95 N14 Möklinta Västmanland, C Sweden 60°04′N 16°34′E
184 L4 Mokohinau Islands island group N New Zealand
153 X12 Mokokchūng Nāgāland, NE India 26°20′N 94°30′E
78 F12 Mokolo Extrême-Nord, N Cameroon 10°49′N 13°54′E
83 J20 Mokopane prev. Potgietersrus. Limpopo, NE South Africa 24°09′S 28°58′E
185 D24 Mokoreta ≈ South Island, New Zealand
163 X17 Mokp'o Jap. Moppo. SW South Korea 34°50′N 126°26′E
113 L16 Mokra Gora ▲▲ S Serbia
Mokrany see Makrany
127 O5 Moksha ≈ W Russian Federation
127 O6 Mokshan Penzenskaya Oblast', W Russian Federation 53°26′N 44°38′E
143 X12 Mok Sukhteh-ye Pāyīn Sīstān va Balūchestān, SE Iran
Moktama see Martaban
77 T14 Mokwa Niger, W Nigeria 09°19′N 05°01′E
99 J16 Mol prev. Moll. Antwerpen, N Belgium 51°11′N 05°07′E
107 O17 Mola di Bari Puglia, SE Italy 41°03′N 17°05′E
Molai see Moláoi
41 P13 Molango Hidalgo, C Mexico 20°48′N 98°44′W
115 F22 Moláoi var. Molai. Pelopónnisos, S Greece 36°48′N 22°51′E
41 Z12 Molas del Norte, Punta var. Punta Molas. headland SE Mexico 20°34′N 86°43′W
Molas, Punta see Molas del Norte, Punta
105 R11 Molatón ▲ C Spain 38°58′N 01°19′W
97 K18 Mold NE Wales, United Kingdom 53°10′N 03°08′W
Moldau see Vltava, Czech Republic
Moldau see Moldova
Moldavia see Moldova
Moldavian SSR/Moldavskaya SSR see Moldova
94 E9 Molde Møre og Romsdal, S Norway 62°44′N 07°08′E
Moldotau, Khrebet see Moldo-Too, Khrebet
147 V9 Moldo-Too, Khrebet prev. Khrebet Moldotau. ▲▲ C Kyrgyzstan
116 L9 Moldova off. Republic of Moldova, var. Moldavia; prev. Moldavian SSR, Rus. Moldavskaya SSR. ◆ republic SE Europe
116 K9 Moldova Eng. Moldavia, Ger. Moldau. former province NE Romania
116 K9 Moldova ≈ N Romania
116 F13 Moldova Nouă Ger. Neumoldowa, Hung. Újmoldova. Caraș-Severin, SW Romania 44°45′N 21°39′E
Moldova, Republic of see Moldova
116 F13 Moldova Veche Ger. Altmoldowa, Hung. Ómoldova. Caraș-Severin, SW Romania 44°45′N 21°13′E
Moldoveanul see Vârful Moldoveanu
83 I20 Molepolole Kweneng, SE Botswana 24°25′S 25°30′E
44 L8 Môle-St-Nicolas NW Haiti 19°46′N 73°19′W
118 H13 Molėtai Utena, E Lithuania 55°14′N 25°25′E
107 O17 Molfetta Puglia, SE Italy 41°12′N 16°35′E
171 P11 Molibagu Sulawesi, N Indonesia 0°25′N 123°57′E
62 G12 Molina Maule, C Chile 35°06′S 71°18′W
105 Q7 Molina de Aragón Castilla-La Mancha, C Spain 40°50′N 01°54′W
105 R13 Molina de Segura Murcia, SE Spain 38°03′N 01°11′W
30 J11 Moline Illinois, N USA 41°30′N 90°31′W
27 P7 Moline Kansas, C USA 37°21′N 96°18′W
79 P23 Moliro Katanga, SE Dem. Rep. Congo 08°11′S 30°31′E
107 K16 Molise ◈ region S Italy
95 K15 Molkom Värmland, C Sweden 59°36′N 13°43′E
109 Q9 Möll ≈ S Austria
Moll see Mol
146 I14 Mollanepes Adyndaky Rus. Imeni Mollanepesa. Mary Welaýaty, S Turkmenistan 37°36′N 61°54′E
95 J22 Mölle Skåne, S Sweden 56°15′N 12°19′E
57 H18 Mollendo Arequipa, SW Peru 17°02′S 72°01′W
105 U5 Mollerussa Cataluña, NE Spain 41°37′N 00°53′E
108 H8 Mollis Glarus, NE Switzerland 47°05′N 09°03′E
95 J19 Mölndal Västra Götaland, S Sweden 57°39′N 12°05′E
95 J19 Mölnlycke Västra Götaland, S Sweden 57°39′N 12°09′E
117 U9 Molochans'k Rus. Molochansk. Zaporiz'ka Oblast', SE Ukraine 47°10′N 35°38′E
117 U10 Molochna Rus. Molochnaya. ≈ S Ukraine
Molochnaya see Molochna
117 U10 Molochnyy Lyman bay N Black Sea
Molodechno/Molodeczno see Maladzyechna
195 V3 Molodezhnaya Russian research station Antarctica 67°33′S 46°12′E
124 J14 Mologa ≈ NW Russian Federation
38 E9 Moloka'i var. Molokai. island Hawaiian Islands, Hawai'i, USA
175 X3 Molokai Fracture Zone tectonic feature NE Pacific Ocean
124 K15 Molokovo Tverskaya Oblast', W Russian Federation 58°10′N 36°43′E
125 Q14 Moloma ≈ NW Russian Federation
183 R8 Molong New South Wales, SE Australia 33°07′S 148°52′E
83 H21 Molopo seasonal river Botswana/South Africa
115 F17 Mólos Stereá Ellás, C Greece 38°48′N 22°39′E
171 O11 Molosipat Sulawesi, N Indonesia 0°28′N 121°08′E
Molotov see Severodvinsk, Arkhangel'skaya Oblast', Russian Federation
Molotov see Perm', Permskaya Oblast', Russian Federation
79 G17 Moloundou Est, SE Cameroon 02°03′N 15°14′E
103 U5 Molsheim Bas-Rhin, NE France 48°33′N 07°30′E
11 X13 Molson Lake ◎ Manitoba, C Canada
Moluccas see Maluku
171 Q12 Molucca Sea Ind. Laut Maluku. sea E Indonesia
Molukken see Maluku
83 O15 Molumbo Zambézia, N Mozambique 15°33′S 36°19′E
171 T15 Molu, Pulau island Maluku, E Indonesia
83 P16 Moma Nampula, NE Mozambique 16°42′S 39°12′E
171 X14 Momats ≈ Papua, E Indonesia
42 J11 Mombacho, Volcán ⛰ SW Nicaragua 11°49′N 85°58′W
81 K21 Mombasa Coast, SE Kenya 04°04′S 39°40′E
81 J21 Mombasa ✕ Coast, SE Kenya 04°01′S 39°31′E
Mombetsu see Monbetsu
114 J12 Momchilgrad prev. Mastanli. Kŭrdzhali, S Bulgaria 41°33′N 25°25′E
99 F23 Momignies Hainaut, S Belgium 50°02′N 04°10′E
54 E6 Momil Córdoba, NW Colombia 09°15′N 75°40′W
42 I10 Momotombo, Volcán ⛰ W Nicaragua 12°25′N 86°33′W
56 B5 Mompiche, Ensenada de bay NW Ecuador
79 K18 Mompono Equateur, NW Dem. Rep. Congo 0°11′N 21°31′E
54 F6 Mompós Bolívar, NW Colombia 09°15′N 74°29′W
95 J24 Møn prev. Möen. island SE Denmark
153 Y12 Mon Nāgāland, NE India 26°43′N 95°01′E
36 L4 Mona Utah, W USA 39°49′N 111°52′W
Mona, Canal de la see Mona Passage
96 E8 Monach Islands island group NW Scotland, United Kingdom
103 V14 Monaco var. Monaco-Ville; anc. Monoecus. ● (Monaco) S Monaco 43°46′N 07°23′E
103 V14 Monaco off. Principality of Monaco. ◆ monarchy W Europe
Monaco see München
Monaco Basin see Canary Basin
Monaco, Principality of see Monaco
Monaco-Ville see Monaco
96 I9 Monadhliath Mountains ▲▲ N Scotland, United Kingdom
55 O6 Monagas off. Estado Monagas. ◈ state NE Venezuela
Monagas, Estado see Monagas
97 F16 Monaghan Ir. Muineachán. Monaghan, N Ireland 54°15′N 06°58′W
97 E16 Monaghan Ir. Muineachán. cultural region N Ireland
43 S16 Monagrillo Herrera, S Panama 08°00′N 80°28′W
24 L8 Monahans Texas, SW USA 31°35′N 102°54′W
45 Q9 Mona, Isla island W Puerto Rico
45 Q9 Mona Passage Sp. Canal de la Mona. channel Dominican Republic/Puerto Rico
43 O14 Mona, Punta headland E Costa Rica 09°44′N 82°48′W
155 K25 Monaragala Uva Province, SE Sri Lanka 06°52′N 81°22′E
33 S9 Monarch Montana, NW USA 47°04′N 110°51′W
10 H14 Monarch Mountain ▲ British Columbia, SW Canada 51°59′N 125°56′W
Monasterio see Monesterio
Monasterzyska see Monastyrys'ka
Monastir see Bitola
Monastyriska see Monastyrys'ka
117 O7 Monastyryshche Cherkas'ka Oblast', C Ukraine 48°59′N 29°47′E
116 J6 Monastyrys'ka Pol. Monasterzyska, Rus. Monastyriska. Ternopil's'ka Oblast', W Ukraine 49°05′N 25°10′E
79 E15 Monatélé Centre, SW Cameroon 04°16′N 11°12′E
165 U2 Monbetsu var. Mombetsu, Monbetu. Hokkaidō, NE Japan 44°23′N 143°22′E
Monbetu see Monbetsu
106 B8 Moncalieri Piemonte, NW Italy 45°N 07°41′E
104 G4 Monção Viana do Castelo, N Portugal 42°03′N 08°29′W
105 Q5 Moncayo ▲ N Spain 41°43′N 01°51′W
105 Q5 Moncayo, Sierra del ▲▲ N Spain
124 J4 Monchegorsk Murmanskaya Oblast', NW Russian Federation 67°56′N 32°47′E
101 D15 Mönchengladbach prev. München-Gladbach. Nordrhein-Westfalen, W Germany 51°12′N 06°35′E
104 F14 Monchique Faro, S Portugal 37°19′N 08°33′W
104 G14 Monchique, Serra de ▲▲ S Portugal
21 S14 Moncks Corner South Carolina, SE USA 33°12′N 80°00′W
41 N7 Monclova Coahuila, NE Mexico 26°55′N 101°25′W
Moncorvo see Torre de Moncorvo
13 P14 Moncton New Brunswick, SE Canada 46°04′N 64°50′W
104 F8 Mondego, Cabo headland N Portugal 40°10′N 08°58′W
104 G8 Mondego, Rio ≈ N Portugal
104 I2 Mondoñedo Galicia, NW Spain 43°25′N 07°22′W
99 N25 Mondorf-les-Bains Grevenmacher, SE Luxembourg 49°30′N 06°16′E
102 M7 Mondoubleau Loir-et-Cher, C France 48°00′N 00°49′E
106 B9 Mondovì Piemonte, NW Italy 44°23′N 07°56′E
30 J6 Mondovi Wisconsin, N USA 44°34′N 91°40′W
Mondragón see Arrasate
107 J17 Mondragone Campania, S Italy 41°07′N 13°53′E
109 R5 Mondsee ◎ N Austria
115 G22 Monemvasiá var. Monemvasia. Pelopónnisos, S Greece 36°22′N 23°03′E
18 B15 Monessen Pennsylvania, NE USA 40°07′N 79°51′W
104 J12 Monesterio var. Monasterio. Extremadura, W Spain 38°05′N 06°16′W
14 L8 Monet Québec, SE Canada 48°09′N 75°37′W
27 S8 Monett Missouri, C USA 36°55′N 93°55′W
27 X9 Monette Arkansas, C USA 35°53′N 90°20′W
14 G11 Monetville Ontario, S Canada 46°08′N 80°24′W
106 J7 Monfalcone Friuli-Venezia Giulia, NE Italy 45°49′N 13°32′E
104 H10 Monforte Portalegre, C Portugal 39°03′N 07°26′W
104 I4 Monforte de Lemos Galicia, NW Spain 42°32′N 07°30′W
79 L16 Monga Orientale, N Dem. Rep. Congo 04°12′N 22°49′E
81 I24 Monga Lindi, SE Tanzania 09°05′S 37°51′E
81 F15 Mongalla Bahr el Gabel, S Sudan 05°12′N 31°42′E
153 U11 Mongar E Bhutan 27°16′N 91°07′E
167 U6 Mong Cai var. Hai Ninh. Quang Ninh, N Vietnam 21°33′N 107°56′E
180 I11 Mongers Lake salt lake Western Australia
186 K8 Mongga Kolombangara, NW Solomon Islands 07°51′S 157°00′E
167 O6 Möng Hpayak Shan State, E Myanmar (Burma) 20°56′N 100°00′E
Monghyr see Munger
106 B10 Mongioie ▲ NW Italy 44°13′N 07°46′E
153 T16 Mongla var. Mungla. Khulna, S Bangladesh 22°18′N 89°34′E
188 C15 Mongmong C Guam
167 N6 Möng Nai Shan State, E Myanmar (Burma) 20°28′N 97°51′E
78 I11 Mongo Guéra, C Chad 12°12′N 18°40′E
76 I14 Mongo ≈ N Sierra Leone
163 I8 Mongolia Mong. Mongol Uls. ◆ republic E Asia
129 V8 Mongolia, Plateau of plateau E Mongolia
Mongolküre see Zhaosu
Mongol Uls see Mongolia
79 E17 Mongomo E Equatorial Guinea 01°39′N 11°18′E
162 M7 Mönggönmorĭt var. Bulag. Töv, C Mongolia 48°09′N 108°33′E
77 Y12 Mongonu var. Monguno. Borno, NE Nigeria 12°42′N 13°37′E
Mongora see Saidu Sharif
78 K11 Mongororo Ouaddaï, SE Chad 12°03′N 22°26′E
Mongos, Chaîne des see Bongo, Massif des
79 I16 Mongoumba Lobaye, SW Central African Republic 03°39′N 18°30′E
Mongrove, Punta see Cayacal, Punta
83 G15 Mongu Western, W Zambia 15°13′S 23°09′E
76 I10 Mônguel Gorgol, SW Mauritania 16°25′N 13°08′W
Monguno see Mongonu
167 N4 Möng Yai Shan State, E Myanmar (Burma) 22°25′N 98°02′E
167 O5 Möng Yang Shan State, E Myanmar (Burma) 21°52′N 99°31′E
167 N3 Möng Yu Shan State, E Myanmar (Burma) 24°00′N 97°57′E
Mönhbulag see Yösöndzüyl
163 O8 Mönhhaan var. Bayasgalant. Sühbaatar, E Mongolia 46°55′N 112°11′E
162 E7 Mönhhayrhan var. Tsenher. Hovd, W Mongolia 47°07′N 92°04′E
Mönh Sarĭdag see Munku-Sardyk, Gora
186 P9 Moni ≈ S Papau New Guinea
115 I15 Moní Megístis Lávras monastery Kentrikí Makedonía, N Greece
115 F18 Moní Osíou Loúkas monastery Stereá Ellás, C Greece
54 F9 Moniquirá Boyacá, C Colombia 05°54′N 73°35′W
103 Q12 Monistrol-sur-Loire Haute-Loire, C France 45°19′N 04°12′E
35 V7 Monitor Range ▲▲ Nevada, W USA
115 I14 Moní Vatopedíou monastery Kentrikí Makedonía, N Greece
Monkchester see Newcastle upon Tyne
83 N14 Monkey Bay Southern, SE Malawi 14°09′S 34°53′E
43 N11 Monkey Point var. Punta Mico, Punte Mono, Punto Mico. headland SE Nicaragua 11°37′N 83°39′W
Monkey River see Monkey River Town
42 G3 Monkey River Town var. Monkey River. Toledo, SE Belize 16°22′N 88°29′W
14 M13 Monkland Ontario, SE Canada 45°11′N 74°51′W
79 J19 Monkoto Equateur, NW Dem. Rep. Congo 01°39′S 20°41′E
97 K21 Monmouth Wel. Trefynwy. SE Wales, United Kingdom 51°50′N 02°43′W
30 J12 Monmouth Illinois, N USA 40°54′N 90°39′W
32 F12 Monmouth Oregon, NW USA 44°51′N 123°13′W
97 K21 Monmouth cultural region SE Wales, United Kingdom
98 I10 Monnickendam Noord-Holland, C Netherlands 52°28′N 05°02′E
77 R15 Mono ≈ C Togo
Monoecus see Monaco
35 R8 Mono Lake ◎ California, W USA
115 O23 Monólithos Ródos, Dodekánisa, Greece, Aegean Sea 36°08′N 27°45′E
19 Q12 Monomoy Island island Massachusetts, NE USA
31 O12 Monon Indiana, N USA 40°52′N 86°54′W
29 Y12 Monona Iowa, C USA 43°03′N 91°23′W
30 L9 Monona Wisconsin, N USA 43°03′N 89°18′W
18 B15 Monongahela Pennsylvania, NE USA 40°10′N 79°54′W
18 B16 Monongahela River ≈ NE USA
107 P17 Monopoli Puglia, SE Italy 40°57′N 17°18′E
Mono, Punte see Monkey Point
111 K23 Monor Pest, C Hungary 47°21′N 19°27′E
Monostor see Beli Manastir
78 K8 Monou Borkou-Ennedi-Tibesti, NE Chad 16°22′N 22°15′E
105 S12 Monovar Cat. Monover. País Valenciano, E Spain 38°26′N 00°50′W
Monover see Monovar
105 R7 Monreal del Campo Aragón, NE Spain 40°47′N 01°20′W
107 I23 Monreale Sicilia, Italy, C Mediterranean Sea 38°05′N 13°17′E
23 T3 Monroe Georgia, SE USA 33°47′N 83°42′W
29 W14 Monroe Iowa, C USA 41°31′N 93°06′W
22 I5 Monroe Louisiana, S USA 32°32′N 92°06′W
31 S10 Monroe Michigan, N USA 41°55′N 83°24′W
18 K13 Monroe New York, NE USA 41°18′N 74°09′W
21 S11 Monroe North Carolina, SE USA 35°00′N 80°35′W
36 L6 Monroe Utah, W USA 38°37′N 112°07′W
32 H7 Monroe Washington, NW USA 47°51′N 121°58′W
30 L9 Monroe Wisconsin, N USA 42°35′N 89°39′W
27 V3 Monroe City Missouri, C USA 39°39′N 91°43′W
31 O15 Monroe Lake ⊠ Indiana, N USA
23 O7 Monroeville Alabama, S USA 31°31′N 87°19′W
18 C15 Monroeville Pennsylvania, NE USA 40°24′N 79°44′W
76 J16 Monrovia ● (Liberia) W Liberia 06°18′N 10°48′W
76 J16 Monrovia ✕ W Liberia 06°22′N 10°50′W
105 T7 Monroyo Aragón, NE Spain 40°47′N 00°03′W
99 F20 Mons Dut. Bergen. Hainaut, S Belgium 50°28′N 03°58′E
104 I8 Monsanto Castelo Branco, C Portugal 40°02′N 07°07′W
106 H8 Monselice Veneto, NE Italy 45°15′N 11°47′E
166 M9 Mon State ◈ state S Myanmar (Burma)
98 G12 Monster Zuid-Holland, W Netherlands 52°01′N 04°10′E
95 N20 Mönsterås Kalmar, S Sweden 57°03′N 16°27′E
101 F17 Montabaur Rheinland-Pfalz, W Germany 50°25′N 07°48′E
106 G8 Montagnana Veneto, NE Italy 45°14′N 11°31′E
35 N1 Montague California, W USA 41°43′N 122°31′W
25 S5 Montague Texas, SW USA 33°40′N 97°44′W
183 S11 Montague Island island New South Wales, SE Australia
39 S12 Montague Island island Alaska, USA
39 S13 Montague Strait strait N Gulf of Alaska
102 J8 Montaigu Vendée, NW France 46°58′N 01°18′W
Montaigu see Scherpenheuvel
105 S7 Montalbán Aragón, NE Spain 40°49′N 00°48′W
106 G13 Montalcino Toscana, C Italy 43°01′N 11°34′E
104 H5 Montalegre Vila Real, N Portugal 41°49′N 07°48′W
114 G8 Montana prev. Ferdinand, Mikhaylovgrad. Montana, NW Bulgaria 43°25′N 23°14′E
108 D10 Montana Valais, SW Switzerland 46°23′N 07°29′E
39 R11 Montana Alaska, USA 62°06′N 150°03′W
114 G8 Montana ◈ province NW Bulgaria
33 T9 Montana off. State of Montana, also known as Mountain State, Treasure State. ◈ state NW USA
104 J10 Montánchez Extremadura, W Spain 39°15′N 06°07′W
Montañita see La Montañita
15 Q8 Mont-Apica Québec, SE Canada 47°57′N 71°24′W
104 G10 Montargil Portalegre, C Portugal 39°05′N 08°10′W
104 G10 Montargil, Barragem de ⊠ C Portugal
103 O7 Montargis Loiret, C France 48°N 02°44′E
103 O4 Montataire Oise, N France 49°16′N 02°24′E
102 M14 Montauban Tarn-et-Garonne, S France 44°01′N 01°20′E
19 N14 Montauk Long Island, New York, NE USA 41°01′N 71°58′W
19 N14 Montauk Point headland Long Island, New York, NE USA 41°04′N 71°51′W
103 Q7 Montbard Côte d'Or, C France 47°35′N 04°25′E
103 U7 Montbéliard Doubs, E France 47°31′N 06°49′E
25 W11 Mont Belvieu Texas, SW USA 29°51′N 94°53′W
105 U6 Montblanc var. Montblanch. Cataluña, NE Spain 41°23′N 01°10′E
Montblanch see Montblanc
103 Q11 Montbrison Loire, E France 45°37′N 04°04′E
Montcalm, Lake see Dogai Coring
103 Q9 Montceau-les-Mines Saône-et-Loire, C France 46°40′N 04°19′E
103 U12 Mont Cenis, Col du pass E France
102 K15 Mont-de-Marsan Landes, SW France 43°54′N 00°30′W
103 O3 Montdidier Somme, N France 49°39′N 02°35′E
187 Q17 Mont-Dore Province Sud, S New Caledonia 22°18′S 166°34′E
20 K10 Monteagle Tennessee, S USA 35°15′N 85°47′W
57 M20 Monteagudo Chuquisaca, S Bolivia 19°48′S 63°57′W
41 R16 Monte Albán ruins Oaxaca, S Mexico
105 R11 Montealegre del Castillo Castilla-La Mancha, C Spain 38°48′N 01°18′W
59 N18 Monte Azul Minas Gerais, SE Brazil 15°13′S 42°53′W
14 M12 Montebello Québec, SE Canada 45°40′N 74°56′W
106 H7 Montebelluna Veneto, NE Italy 45°46′N 12°03′E
60 G13 Montecarlo Misiones, NE Argentina 26°38′S 54°45′W
61 D16 Monte Caseros Corrientes, NE Argentina 30°15′S 57°39′W
60 J13 Monte Castelo Santa Catarina, S Brazil 26°34′S 50°12′W
106 F11 Montecatini Terme Toscana, C Italy 43°53′N 10°46′E
42 H7 Montecillos, Cordillera de ▲▲ W Honduras
62 I12 Monte Comén Mendoza, W Argentina 34°35′S 67°53′W
44 M8 Monte Cristi var. San Fernando de Monte Cristi. NW Dominican Republic 19°52′N 71°39′W
58 C13 Monte Cristo Amazonas, W Brazil 03°14′S 68°00′W
107 E14 Montecristo, Isola di island Archipelago Toscano, C Italy
Monte Croce Carnico, Passo di see Plöcken Pass
58 J12 Monte Dourado Pará, NE Brazil 0°48′S 52°32′W
40 L11 Monte Escobedo Zacatecas, C Mexico 22°19′N 103°30′W
106 I13 Montefalco Umbria, C Italy 42°54′N 12°40′E
107 H14 Montefiascone Lazio, C Italy 42°33′N 12°01′E
105 N14 Montefrío Andalucía, S Spain 37°19′N 04°00′W
44 I11 Montego Bay var. Mobay. W Jamaica 18°28′N 77°55′W
Montego Bay see Sangster
104 J8 Montehermoso Extremadura, W Spain 40°05′N 06°20′W
104 F10 Montejunto, Serra de ▲ C Portugal 39°10′N 09°01′W
Monteleone di Calabria see Vibo Valentia
54 E7 Montelíbano Córdoba, NW Colombia 08°02′N 75°29′W
103 R13 Montélimar anc. Acunum Acusio, Montilium Adhemari. Drôme, E France 44°33′N 04°45′E
104 K15 Montellano Andalucía, S Spain 37°00′N 05°34′W
35 Y2 Montello Nevada, W USA 41°18′N 114°10′W
30 L8 Montello Wisconsin, N USA 43°47′N 89°20′W
63 J18 Montemayor, Meseta de plain SE Argentina
41 O9 Montemorelos Nuevo León, NE Mexico 25°10′N 99°52′W
104 G11 Montemor-o-Novo Évora, S Portugal 38°38′N 08°13′W
104 G8 Montemor-o-Velho var. Montemor-o-Vélho. Coimbra, N Portugal 40°11′N 08°41′W
Montemor-o-Vélho see Montemor-o-Velho
104 H7 Montemuro, Serra de ▲ N Portugal 40°59′N 07°59′W
102 K12 Montendre Charente-Maritime, W France 45°17′N 00°24′W
61 I15 Montenegro Rio Grande do Sul, S Brazil 29°40′S 51°32′W
113 J16 Montenegro Serb. Crna Gora. ◆ republic SW Europe
62 G10 Monte Patria Coquimbo, N Chile 30°40′S 71°00′W
45 O9 Monte Plata E Dominican Republic 18°50′N 69°47′W
83 P14 Montepuez Cabo Delgado, N Mozambique 13°09′S 39°00′E
83 P14 Montepuez ≈ N Mozambique
106 G13 Montepulciano Toscana, C Italy 43°02′N 11°51′E
62 L6 Monte Quemado Santiago del Estero, N Argentina 25°48′S 62°52′W
103 O6 Montereau-Faut-Yonne anc. Condate. Seine-St-Denis, N France 48°23′N 02°57′E
35 N11 Monterey California, W USA 36°36′N 121°53′W
20 L9 Monterey Tennessee, S USA 36°09′N 85°16′W
21 T5 Monterey Virginia, NE USA 38°24′N 79°36′W
Monterey see Monterrey
35 N10 Monterey Bay bay California, W USA
54 D6 Montería Córdoba, NW Colombia 08°45′N 75°54′W
57 N18 Montero Santa Cruz, C Bolivia 17°20′S 63°15′W
62 J7 Monteros Tucumán, C Argentina 27°12′S 65°30′W
104 I4 Monterrei Galicia, NW Spain 41°56′N 07°27′W
41 O8 Monterrey var. Monterey. Nuevo León, NE Mexico 25°41′N 100°16′W
32 F9 Montesano Washington, NW USA 46°58′N 123°37′W
107 M19 Montesano sulla Marcellana Campania, S Italy 40°15′N 15°41′E
107 N16 Monte Sant' Angelo Puglia, SE Italy 41°43′N 15°58′E
59 O16 Monte Santo Bahia, E Brazil 10°25′S 39°18′W
107 D18 Monte Santu, Capo di headland Sardegna, Italy, C Mediterranean Sea 40°05′N 09°43′E
59 M19 Montes Claros Minas Gerais, SE Brazil 16°45′S 43°52′W
107 K14 Montesilvano Marina Abruzzo, C Italy 42°28′N 14°07′E
23 P4 Montevallo Alabama, S USA 33°06′N 86°51′W
106 G12 Montevarchi Toscana, C Italy 43°32′N 11°34′E
61 F20 Montevideo ● (Uruguay) Montevideo, S Uruguay 34°55′S 56°10′W
29 S9 Montevideo Minnesota, N USA 44°56′N 95°43′W
37 S7 Monte Vista Colorado, C USA 37°33′N 106°08′W
23 T5 Montezuma Georgia, SE USA 32°18′N 84°01′W
29 W14 Montezuma Iowa, C USA 41°35′N 92°31′W
26 J6 Montezuma Kansas, C USA 37°33′N 100°25′W
103 U12 Montgenèvre, Col de pass France/Italy
97 K20 Montgomery E Wales, United Kingdom 52°38′N 03°05′W
23 Q5 Montgomery state capital Alabama, S USA 32°22′N 86°18′W
29 V9 Montgomery Minnesota, N USA 44°26′N 93°34′W
18 G13 Montgomery Pennsylvania, NE USA 41°08′N 76°52′W
21 Q5 Montgomery West Virginia, NE USA 38°07′N 81°19′W
97 K19 Montgomery cultural region E Wales, United Kingdom
Montgomery see Sāhīwāl
27 V4 Montgomery City Missouri, C USA 38°57′N 91°27′W
35 S8 Montgomery Pass pass Nevada, W USA
102 K12 Montguyon Charente-Maritime, W France 45°12′N 00°13′W
108 C10 Monthey Valais, SW Switzerland 46°15′N 06°56′E
27 V13 Monticello Arkansas, C USA 33°38′N 91°49′W
23 T4 Monticello Florida, SE USA 30°33′N 83°52′W
23 T8 Monticello Georgia, SE USA 33°18′N 83°40′W
30 M13 Monticello Illinois, N USA 40°01′N 88°34′W
31 O12 Monticello Indiana, N USA 40°45′N 86°46′W

◆ Country ● Country Capital ◇ Dependent Territory ○ Dependent Territory Capital ◈ Administrative Regions ✕ International Airport ▲ Mountain ▲▲ Mountain Range ⛰ Volcano ≈ River ◎ Lake ⊠ Reservoir

MONTICELLO – MOUNT PLEASANT

29 Y13 **Monticello** Iowa, C USA 42°14′N 91°11′W
20 L7 **Monticello** Kentucky, S USA 36°50′N 84°50′W
29 V8 **Monticello** Minnesota, N USA 45°19′N 93°45′W
22 K7 **Monticello** Mississippi, S USA 31°33′N 90°06′W
27 V2 **Monticello** Missouri, C USA 40°07′N 91°42′W
18 J12 **Monticello** New York, NE USA 41°39′N 74°41′W
37 O7 **Monticello** Utah, W USA 37°52′N 109°20′W
106 F8 **Montichiari** Lombardia, N Italy 45°24′N 10°27′E
102 M12 **Montignac** Dordogne, SW France 45°24′N 00°54′E
99 G21 **Montignies-le-Tilleul** *var.* Montigny-le-Tilleul. Hainaut, S Belgium 50°22′N 04°23′E
14 J8 **Montigny, Lac de** ◎ Québec, SE Canada
103 S6 **Montigny-le-Roi** Haute-Marne, N France 48°02′N 05°28′E
Montigny-le-Tilleul *see* Montignies-le-Tilleul
43 R16 **Montijo** Veraguas, S Panama 07°59′N 80°58′W
104 F11 **Montijo** Setúbal, W Portugal 38°42′N 08°59′W
104 J11 **Montijo** Extremadura, W Spain 38°55′N 06°38′W
Montilium Adhemari *see* Montélimar
104 M13 **Montilla** Andalucía, S Spain 37°36′N 04°39′W
102 L3 **Montivilliers** Seine-Maritime, N France 49°31′N 00°10′E
15 U7 **Mont-Joli** Québec, SE Canada 48°36′N 68°14′W
14 M10 **Mont-Laurier** Québec, SE Canada 46°33′N 75°31′W
15 X5 **Mont-Louis** Québec, SE Canada 49°15′N 65°46′W
103 N17 **Mont-Louis** *var.* Mont Louis. Pyrénées-Orientales, S France 42°30′N 02°08′E
103 O10 **Montluçon** Allier, C France 46°21′N 02°37′E
15 R10 **Montmagny** Québec, SE Canada 47°00′N 70°31′W
103 S3 **Montmédy** Meuse, NE France 49°31′N 05°21′E
103 P5 **Montmirail** Marne, N France 48°53′N 03°31′E
15 R9 **Montmorency** ≈ Québec, SE Canada
102 M10 **Montmorillon** Vienne, W France 46°26′N 00°52′E
107 J14 **Montorio al Vomano** Abruzzo, C Italy 42°31′N 13°39′E
104 M13 **Montoro** Andalucía, S Spain 38°00′N 04°21′W
33 S16 **Montpelier** Idaho, NW USA 42°19′N 111°18′W
29 P6 **Montpelier** North Dakota, N USA 46°40′N 98°34′W
18 M7 **Montpelier** *state capital* Vermont, NE USA 44°16′N 72°32′W
103 Q15 **Montpellier** Hérault, S France 43°37′N 03°52′E
102 L12 **Montpon-Ménestérol** Dordogne, SW France 45°01′N 00°10′E
12 K15 **Montréal** *Eng.* Montreal. Québec, SE Canada 45°30′N 73°36′W
14 G8 **Montreal** ≈ Ontario, S Canada
Montreal *see* Mirabel
11 T14 **Montreal Lake** ◎ Saskatchewan, C Canada
14 B9 **Montreal River** Ontario, S Canada 47°13′N 84°36′W
103 N2 **Montreuil** Pas-de-Calais, N France 50°28′N 01°46′E
102 K8 **Montreuil-Bellay** Maine-et-Loire, NW France 47°07′N 00°10′W
108 C10 **Montreux** Vaud, SW Switzerland 46°27′N 06°55′E
108 B9 **Montricher** Vaud, W Switzerland 46°37′N 06°24′E
96 K10 **Montrose** E Scotland, United Kingdom 56°43′N 02°29′W
27 W14 **Montrose** Arkansas, C USA 33°18′N 91°29′W
37 Q6 **Montrose** Colorado, C USA 38°29′N 107°53′W
29 Y16 **Montrose** Iowa, C USA 40°31′N 91°24′W
18 H12 **Montrose** Pennsylvania, NE USA 41°49′N 75°53′W
21 X5 **Montross** Virginia, NE USA 38°04′N 76°51′W
15 O12 **Mont-St-Hilaire** Québec, SE Canada 45°34′N 73°10′W
103 S3 **Mont-St-Martin** Meurthe-et-Moselle, NE France 49°31′N 05°51′E
45 V10 **Montserrat** *var.* Emerald Isle. ◇ *UK dependent territory* E West Indies
105 V5 **Montserrat** ▲ NE Spain 41°39′N 01°44′E
104 M7 **Montuenga** Castilla-León, N Spain 41°04′N 04°38′W
99 M19 **Montzen** Liège, E Belgium 50°42′N 05°59′E
37 N8 **Monument Valley** *valley* Arizona/Utah, SW USA
166 L4 **Monywa** Sagaing, C Myanmar (Burma) 22°05′N 95°12′E
106 D7 **Monza** Lombardia, N Italy 45°35′N 09°16′E
83 J15 **Monze** Southern, S Zambia 16°20′S 27°29′E
105 T5 **Monzón** Aragón, NE Spain 41°54′N 00°12′E
25 T9 **Moody** Texas, SW USA 31°18′N 97°21′W
98 L13 **Mook** Limburg, SE Netherlands 51°45′N 05°52′E
165 O12 **Mooka** *var.* Mōka. Tochigi, Honshū, S Japan 36°27′N 139°59′E
182 K3 **Moomba** South Australia 28°07′S 140°12′E
14 G13 **Moon** ≈ Ontario, S Canada
Moon *see* Muhu
181 Y10 **Moonie** Queensland, E Australia 27°46′S 150°22′E
193 O5 **Moonless Mountains** *undersea feature* E Pacific Ocean 30°40′N 140°00′W
182 L13 **Moonlight Head** *headland* Victoria, SE Australia 38°47′S 143°12′E
Moon-Sund *see* Väinameri
182 H8 **Moonta** South Australia 34°03′S 137°36′E
Moor *see* Mór
180 I12 **Moora** Western Australia 30°23′S 116°05′E
98 H12 **Moordrecht** Zuid-Holland, C Netherlands 51°59′N 04°40′E
33 T9 **Moore** Montana, NW USA 47°00′N 109°40′W
27 N11 **Moore** Oklahoma, C USA 35°21′N 97°30′W
25 R12 **Moore** Texas, SW USA 29°03′N 99°01′W
191 S10 **Moorea** *island* Îles du Vent, W French Polynesia
21 U3 **Moorefield** West Virginia, NE USA 39°04′N 78°59′W
23 X14 **Moore Haven** Florida, SE USA 26°49′N 81°05′W
180 J11 **Moore, Lake** ◎ Western Australia
19 N7 **Moore Reservoir** ⊠ New Hampshire/Vermont, NE USA
44 G1 **Moores Island** *island* N Bahamas
21 R10 **Mooresville** North Carolina, SE USA 35°34′N 80°48′W
29 R5 **Moorhead** Minnesota, N USA 46°51′N 96°44′W
22 K4 **Moorhead** Mississippi, S USA 33°27′N 90°30′W
99 F18 **Moorsel** Oost-Vlaanderen, C Belgium 50°58′N 04°06′E
99 C18 **Moorslede** West-Vlaanderen, W Belgium 50°53′N 03°03′E
18 L8 **Moosalamoo, Mount** ▲ Vermont, NE USA 43°55′N 73°03′W
101 M22 **Moosburg in der Isar** Bayern, SE Germany 48°28′N 11°55′E
33 S14 **Moose** Wyoming, C USA 43°38′N 110°42′W
12 H11 **Moose** ≈ Ontario, S Canada
12 H10 **Moose Factory** Ontario, S Canada 51°16′N 80°32′W
19 Q4 **Moosehead Lake** ◎ Maine, NE USA
11 U16 **Moose Jaw** Saskatchewan, S Canada 50°23′N 105°35′W
11 V14 **Moose Lake** Manitoba, C Canada 53°42′N 100°22′W
29 W6 **Moose Lake** Minnesota, N USA 46°28′N 92°46′W
19 P6 **Mooselookmeguntic Lake** ◎ Maine, NE USA
39 R12 **Moose Pass** Alaska, USA 60°28′N 149°21′W
19 P5 **Moose River** ≈ Maine, NE USA
18 J9 **Moose River** ≈ New York, NE USA
11 V16 **Moosomin** Saskatchewan, S Canada 50°09′N 101°41′W
12 H10 **Moosonee** Ontario, SE Canada 51°18′N 80°40′W
19 N12 **Moosup** Connecticut, NE USA 41°42′N 71°51′W
83 N16 **Mopeia** Zambézia, NE Mozambique 17°59′S 35°43′E
83 H18 **Mopipi** Central, C Botswana 21°07′S 24°55′E
Moppo *see* Mokp'o
77 N11 **Mopti** Mopti, C Mali 14°30′N 04°15′W
77 O11 **Mopti** ◈ *region* S Mali
57 H18 **Moquegua** Moquegua, SE Peru 17°07′S 70°55′W
57 H18 **Moquegua** *off.* Departamento de Moquegua. ◈ *department* S Peru
Moquegua, Departamento de *see* Moquegua
111 I23 **Mór** *Ger.* Moor. Fejér, C Hungary 47°21′N 18°12′E
78 G11 **Mora** Extrême-Nord, N Cameroon 11°02′N 14°07′E
104 G11 **Mora** Évora, S Portugal 38°56′N 08°10′W
105 N9 **Mora** Castilla-La Mancha, C Spain 39°40′N 03°46′W
94 L12 **Mora** Dalarna, C Sweden 61°N 14°30′E
29 V7 **Mora** Minnesota, N USA 45°52′N 93°18′W
37 T10 **Mora** New Mexico, SW USA 35°56′N 105°16′W
113 J17 **Morača** ≈ S Montenegro
152 K10 **Morādābād** Uttar Pradesh, N India 28°50′N 78°45′E
105 U6 **Móra d'Ebre** *var.* Mora de Ebro. Cataluña, NE Spain 41°05′N 00°38′E
Mora de Ebro *see* Móra d'Ebre
105 S8 **Mora de Rubielos** Aragón, NE Spain 40°15′N 00°45′W
172 H4 **Morafenobe** Mahajanga, W Madagascar 17°49′S 44°54′E
110 K8 **Morąg** *Ger.* Mohrungen. Warmińsko-Mazurskie, N Poland 53°55′N 19°56′E
111 L25 **Mórahalom** Csongrád, S Hungary 46°14′N 19°52′E
105 N11 **Moral de Calatrava** Castilla-La Mancha, C Spain 38°50′N 03°34′W
63 G19 **Moraleda, Canal** *strait* SE Pacific Ocean
54 J3 **Morales** Bolívar, N Colombia 08°17′N 73°52′W
54 D12 **Morales** Cauca, SW Colombia 02°46′N 76°44′W
42 F5 **Morales** Izabal, E Guatemala 15°28′N 88°46′W
172 J5 **Moramanga** Toamasina, E Madagascar 18°57′S 48°13′E
27 Q6 **Moran** Kansas, C USA 37°55′N 95°10′W
25 Q7 **Moran** Texas, SW USA 32°33′N 99°10′W
181 X7 **Moranbah** Queensland, NE Australia 22°01′S 148°08′E
44 L13 **Morant Bay** E Jamaica 17°53′N 76°25′W
96 G10 **Morar, Loch** ◎ N Scotland, United Kingdom
Morata *see* Goodenough Island
105 Q12 **Moratalla** Murcia, SE Spain 38°11′N 01°53′W
108 C8 **Morat, Lac de** *Ger.* Murtensee. ◎ W Switzerland
84 I11 **Morava** *var.* March. ≈ C Europe *see also* March
Morava *see* March
Morava *see* Moravia, Czech Republic
Morava *see* Velika Morava, Serbia
29 W15 **Moravia** Iowa, C USA 40°53′N 92°49′W
111 F18 **Moravia** *Cz.* Morava, *Ger.* Mähren. *cultural region* E Czech Republic
111 H17 **Moravice** *Ger.* Mohra. ≈ NE Czech Republic
116 E12 **Moravița** Timiș, SW Romania 45°15′N 21°17′E
111 G17 **Moravská Třebová** *Ger.* Mährisch-Trübau. Pardubický Kraj, C Czech Republic 49°47′N 16°40′E
111 E19 **Moravské Budějovice** *Ger.* Mährisch-Budwitz. Vysočina, C Czech Republic 49°03′N 15°48′E
111 H17 **Moravskoslezský Kraj** *prev.* Ostravský Kraj. ◈ *region* E Czech Republic
111 F19 **Moravský Krumlov** *Ger.* Mährisch-Kromau. Jihomoravský Kraj, SE Czech Republic 48°58′N 16°30′E
96 J8 **Moray** *cultural region* N Scotland, United Kingdom
96 J8 **Moray Firth** *inlet* N Scotland, United Kingdom
42 B10 **Morazán** ◈ *department* NE El Salvador
154 C10 **Morbi** Gujarāt, W India 22°51′N 70°49′E
102 G7 **Morbihan** ◈ *department* NW France
Mörbisch *see* Mörbisch am See
109 Y5 **Mörbisch am See** *var.* Mörbisch. Burgenland, E Austria 47°43′N 16°40′E
95 N21 **Mörbylånga** Kalmar, S Sweden 56°31′N 16°25′E
102 J14 **Morcenx** Landes, SW France 44°04′N 00°55′W
Morcheh Khort *see* Mürcheh Khvort
163 T5 **Mordaga** Nei Mongol Zizhiqu, N China 51°15′N 120°47′E
11 X17 **Morden** Manitoba, S Canada 49°12′N 98°05′W
Mordovia *see* Mordoviya, Respublika
127 N5 **Mordoviya, Respublika** *prev.* Mordovskaya ASSR, *Eng.* Mordovia, Mordvinia. ◈ *autonomous republic* W Russian Federation
126 M7 **Mordovo** Tambovskaya Oblast', W Russian Federation 52°05′N 40°49′E
Mordovskaya ASSR/ Mordvinia *see* Mordoviya, Respublika
Morea *see* Pelopónnisos
28 K8 **Moreau River** ≈ South Dakota, N USA
97 K16 **Morecambe** NW England, United Kingdom 54°04′N 02°53′W
97 K16 **Morecambe Bay** *inlet* NW England, United Kingdom
183 S4 **Moree** New South Wales, SE Australia 29°29′S 149°53′E
21 N5 **Morehead** Kentucky, S USA 38°11′N 83°27′W
21 X11 **Morehead City** North Carolina, SE USA 34°43′N 76°43′W
27 Y8 **Morehouse** Missouri, C USA 36°51′N 89°41′W
108 E10 **Mörel** Valais, SW Switzerland 46°22′N 08°03′E
54 D13 **Morelia** Caquetá, S Colombia 01°30′N 75°43′W
41 N14 **Morelia** Michoacán, S Mexico 19°40′N 101°11′W
105 T7 **Morella** País Valenciano, E Spain 40°37′N 00°06′W
40 I7 **Morelos** Chihuahua, N Mexico 26°37′N 107°37′W
41 O15 **Morelos** ◈ *state* S Mexico
154 H7 **Morena** Madhya Pradesh, C India 26°30′N 78°04′E
104 L12 **Morena, Sierra** ▲▲ S Spain
37 O14 **Morenci** Arizona, SW USA 33°05′N 109°21′W
31 R11 **Morenci** Michigan, N USA 41°43′N 84°13′W
116 J13 **Moreni** Dâmbovița, S Romania 44°59′N 25°39′E
94 D9 **Møre og Romsdal** ◈ *county* S Norway
10 I14 **Moresby Island** *island* Queen Charlotte Islands, British Columbia, SW Canada
183 W2 **Moreton Island** *island* Queensland, E Australia
103 O3 **Moreuil** Somme, N France 49°47′N 02°28′E
35 V7 **Morey Peak** ▲ Nevada, W USA 38°40′N 116°16′W
125 U4 **More-Yu** ≈ NW Russian Federation
103 T9 **Morez** Jura, E France 46°33′N 06°01′E
Morfou Bay/Mórfou, Kólpos *see* Güzelyurt Körfezi
182 J8 **Morgan** South Australia 34°02′S 139°39′E
23 S7 **Morgan** Georgia, SE USA 31°31′N 84°34′W
25 S8 **Morgan** Texas, SW USA 32°01′N 97°36′W
22 J10 **Morgan City** Louisiana, S USA 29°42′N 91°12′W
20 H6 **Morganfield** Kentucky, S USA 37°41′N 87°55′W
35 O10 **Morgan Hill** California, W USA 37°05′N 121°38′W
21 Q9 **Morganton** North Carolina, SE USA 35°44′N 81°43′W
20 J7 **Morgantown** Kentucky, S USA 37°12′N 86°42′W
21 S2 **Morgantown** West Virginia, NE USA 39°38′N 79°57′W
108 B10 **Morges** Vaud, SW Switzerland 46°31′N 06°30′E
148 M4 **Morghāb, Daryā-ye** *Rus.* Murgab, Murghab, *Turk.* Murgap, Deryasy Murgap. ≈ Afghanistan/ Turkmenistan *see also* Murgap
Morghāb, Daryā-ye *see* Murgap
96 I9 **Mor, Glen** *var.* Glen Albyn, Great Glen. *valley* N Scotland, United Kingdom
103 T5 **Morhange** Moselle, NE France 48°56′N 06°37′E
158 M5 **Mori** *var.* Mori Kazak Zizhixian. Xinjiang Uygur Zizhiqu, NW China 43°48′N 90°21′E
165 R5 **Mori** Hokkaidō, NE Japan 42°04′N 140°36′E
35 Y6 **Moriah, Mount** ▲ Nevada, W USA 39°16′N 114°10′W
37 S11 **Moriarty** New Mexico, SW USA 34°59′N 106°03′W
54 J12 **Morichal** Guaviare, E Colombia 02°09′N 70°35′W
Mori Kazak Zizhixian *see* Mori
Morin Dawa Daurzu Zizhiqi *see* Nirji
11 Q14 **Morinville** Alberta, SW Canada 53°48′N 113°38′W
165 R8 **Morioka** Iwate, Honshū, C Japan 39°42′N 141°08′E
183 T8 **Morisset** New South Wales, SE Australia 33°07′S 151°32′E
165 Q8 **Moriyoshi-zan** ▲ Honshū, C Japan 39°58′N 140°32′E
92 K13 **Morjärv** Norrbotten, N Sweden 66°03′N 22°45′E
127 R3 **Morki** Respublika Mariy El, W Russian Federation 56°27′N 49°01′E
123 N10 **Morkoka** ≈ NE Russian Federation
102 F5 **Morlaix** Finistère, NW France 48°35′N 03°50′W
95 M20 **Mörlunda** Kalmar, S Sweden 57°19′N 15°52′E
107 N19 **Mormanno** Calabria, SW Italy 39°54′N 15°58′E
36 L11 **Mormon Lake** ◎ Arizona, SW USA
35 Y10 **Mormon Peak** ▲ Nevada, W USA 36°59′N 114°25′W
Mormon State *see* Utah
45 Y5 **Morne-à-l'Eau** Grande Terre, N Guadeloupe 16°20′N 61°31′W
29 Y15 **Morning Sun** Iowa, C USA 41°06′N 91°15′W
193 S12 **Mornington Abyssal Plain** *undersea feature* SE Pacific Ocean 50°00′S 90°00′W
63 F22 **Mornington, Isla** *island* S Chile
181 T4 **Mornington Island** *island* Wellesley Islands, Queensland, N Australia
115 E18 **Mórnos** ≈ C Greece
149 P14 **Moro** Sind, SE Pakistan 26°36′N 67°59′E
32 I11 **Moro** Oregon, NW USA 45°30′N 120°46′W
186 E8 **Morobe** Morobe, C Papua New Guinea 07°45′S 147°35′E
186 E8 **Morobe** ◈ *province* C Papua New Guinea
31 N12 **Morocco** Indiana, N USA 40°57′N 87°27′W
74 E8 **Morocco** *off.* Kingdom of Morocco, *Ar.* Al Mamlakah. ◆ *monarchy* N Africa
Morocco *see* Marrakech
Morocco, Kingdom of *see* Morocco
81 I22 **Morogoro** Morogoro, E Tanzania 06°49′S 37°40′E
81 H24 **Morogoro** ◈ *region* SE Tanzania
171 Q7 **Moro Gulf** *gulf* S Philippines
41 N13 **Moroleón** Guanajuato, C Mexico 20°00′N 101°13′W
172 H6 **Morombe** Toliara, W Madagascar 21°47′S 43°21′E
44 G5 **Morón** Ciego de Ávila, C Cuba 22°08′N 78°39′W
163 N8 **Mörön** Hentiy, C Mongolia 47°21′N 110°21′E
162 I6 **Mörön** Hövsgöl, N Mongolia 49°39′N 100°08′E
54 K5 **Morón** Carabobo, N Venezuela 10°29′N 68°11′W
Morón *see* Morón de la Frontera
56 D8 **Morona, Río** ≈ N Peru
56 C8 **Morona Santiago** ◈ *province* E Ecuador
172 H5 **Morondava** Toliara, W Madagascar 20°19′S 44°17′E
104 K14 **Morón de la Frontera** *var.* Morón. Andalucía, S Spain 37°07′N 05°27′W
172 G13 **Moroni** ● (Comoros) Grande Comore, NW Comoros 11°41′S 43°16′E
171 S10 **Morotai, Pulau** *island* Maluku, E Indonesia
Morotiri *see* Marotiri
81 H17 **Moroto** NE Uganda 02°32′N 34°41′E
Morozov *see* Bratan
126 M11 **Morozovsk** Rostovskaya Oblast', SW Russian Federation 48°21′N 41°54′E
97 L14 **Morpeth** N England, United Kingdom 55°10′N 01°41′W
Morphou *see* Güzelyurt
Morphou Bay *see* Güzelyurt Körfezi
28 I13 **Morrill** Nebraska, C USA 41°57′N 103°55′W
27 U11 **Morrilton** Arkansas, C USA 35°09′N 92°45′W
11 Q16 **Morrin** Alberta, SW Canada 51°40′N 112°45′W
184 M7 **Morrinsville** Waikato, North Island, New Zealand 37°41′S 175°32′E
11 X16 **Morris** Manitoba, S Canada 49°22′N 94°21′W
30 M11 **Morris** Illinois, N USA 41°21′N 88°25′W
29 S8 **Morris** Minnesota, N USA 45°32′N 95°53′W
14 M13 **Morrisburg** Ontario, SE Canada 44°55′N 75°07′W
197 R11 **Morris Jesup, Kap** *headland* N Greenland 83°33′N 32°40′W
182 B1 **Morris, Mount** ▲ South Australia 26°04′S 131°03′E
30 K10 **Morrison** Illinois, N USA 41°48′N 89°58′W
36 K13 **Morristown** Arizona, SW USA 33°48′N 112°34′W
18 J14 **Morristown** New Jersey, NE USA 40°48′N 74°29′W
21 O8 **Morristown** Tennessee, S USA 36°13′N 83°18′W
42 L11 **Morrito** Río San Juan, SW Nicaragua 11°37′N 85°05′W
35 P13 **Morro Bay** California, W USA 35°21′N 120°51′W
95 L22 **Mörrum** Blekinge, S Sweden 56°11′N 14°45′E
83 N16 **Morrumbala** Zambézia, NE Mozambique 17°17′S 35°35′E
83 N20 **Morrumbene** Inhambane, SE Mozambique 23°41′S 35°25′E
95 F21 **Mors** *island* NW Denmark
Mörs *see* Moers
25 N1 **Morse** Texas, SW USA 36°03′N 101°28′W
127 N6 **Morshansk** Tambovskaya Oblast', W Russian Federation 53°27′N 41°46′E
102 L5 **Mortagne-au-Perche** Orne, N France 48°32′N 00°31′E
102 J8 **Mortagne-sur-Sèvre** Vendée, NW France 47°00′N 00°57′W
104 G8 **Mortágua** Viseu, N Portugal 40°24′N 08°14′W
102 J5 **Mortain** Manche, N France 48°39′N 00°51′W
106 C8 **Mortara** Lombardia, N Italy 45°15′N 08°44′E
59 J17 **Mortes, Rio das** ≈ C Brazil
182 M12 **Mortlake** Victoria, SE Australia 38°06′S 142°48′E
Mortlock Group *see* Takuu Islands
189 Q17 **Mortlock Islands** *prev.* Nomoi Islands. *island group* C Micronesia
29 T9 **Morton** Minnesota, N USA 44°33′N 94°58′W
22 L5 **Morton** Mississippi, S USA 32°21′N 89°39′W
24 M5 **Morton** Texas, SW USA 33°40′N 102°45′W
32 H9 **Morton** Washington, NW USA 46°33′N 122°16′W
0 D7 **Morton Seamount** *undersea feature* NE Pacific Ocean 50°15′N 142°45′W
45 U15 **Moruga** Trinidad, Trinidad and Tobago 10°04′N 61°16′W
183 P9 **Morundah** New South Wales, SE Australia 34°57′S 146°18′E
Moruroa *see* Mururoa
183 S11 **Moruya** New South Wales, SE Australia 35°55′S 150°04′E
103 Q8 **Morvan** *physical region* C France
185 G21 **Morven** Canterbury, South Island, New Zealand 44°51′S 171°07′E
183 O13 **Morwell** Victoria, SE Australia 38°14′S 146°25′E
125 N6 **Morzhovets, Ostrov** *island* NW Russian Federation
126 J4 **Mosal'sk** Kaluzhskaya Oblast', W Russian Federation 54°30′N 34°55′E
101 H20 **Mosbach** Baden-Württemberg, SW Germany 49°21′N 09°06′E
95 E18 **Mosby** Vest-Agder, S Norway 58°12′N 07°55′E
33 V9 **Mosby** Montana, NW USA 46°58′N 107°53′W
32 M9 **Moscow** Idaho, NW USA 46°43′N 117°00′W
20 F10 **Moscow** Tennessee, S USA 35°04′N 89°27′W
Moscow *see* Moskva
101 D19 **Mosel** *Fr.* Moselle. ≈ W Europe *see also* Moselle
Mosel *see* Moselle
103 T4 **Moselle** ◈ *department* NE France
103 T6 **Moselle** *Ger.* Mosel. ≈ W Europe *see also* Mosel
Moselle *see* Mosel
32 K9 **Moses Lake** ◎ Washington, NW USA
83 I18 **Mosetse** Central, E Botswana 20°40′S 26°38′E
92 H4 **Mosfellsbær** Sudhurland, SW Iceland 65°09′N 21°43′W
183 N8 **Mossgiel** New South Wales, SE Australia 33°16′S 144°34′E
185 F23 **Mosgiel** Otago, South Island, New Zealand 45°51′S 170°22′E
124 M11 **Mosha** ≈ NW Russian Federation
81 I20 **Moshi** Kilimanjaro, NE Tanzania 03°21′S 37°19′E
110 G12 **Mosina** Wielkolpolskie, C Poland 52°15′N 16°50′E
30 L6 **Mosinee** Wisconsin, N USA 44°45′N 89°39′W
92 F13 **Mosjøen** Nordland, C Norway 65°49′N 13°12′E
123 S12 **Moskal'vo** Ostrov Sakhalin, Sakhalinskaya Oblast', SE Russian Federation 53°36′N 142°31′E
92 I13 **Moskosel** Norrbotten, N Sweden 65°52′N 19°30′E
126 K4 **Moskovskaya Oblast'** ◈ *province* W Russian Federation
Moskovskiy *see* Moskva
126 J3 **Moskva** *Eng.* Moscow. ● (Russian Federation) Gorod Moskva, W Russian Federation 55°45′N 37°42′E
147 Q14 **Moskva** *Rus.* Moskovskiy; *prev.* Chubek. SW Tajikistan 37°41′N 69°33′E
126 L4 **Moskva** ≈ W Russian Federation
83 I20 **Mosomane** Kgatleng, SE Botswana 24°04′S 26°15′E
Moson and Magyaróvár *see* Mosonmagyaróvár
111 H21 **Mosoni-Duna** *Ger.* Kleine Donau. ≈ NW Hungary
111 H21 **Mosonmagyaróvár** *Ger.* Wieselburg-Ungarisch-Altenburg; *prev.* Moson and Magyaróvár, *Ger.* Wieselburg and Ungarisch-Altenburg. Győr-Moson-Sopron, NW Hungary 47°52′N 17°15′E
Mospino *see* Mospyne
117 X8 **Mospyne** *Rus.* Mospino. Donets'ka Oblast', E Ukraine 47°53′N 38°03′E
54 B12 **Mosquera** Nariño, SW Colombia 02°32′N 78°24′W
37 U10 **Mosquero** New Mexico, SW USA 35°46′N 103°57′W
Mosquito Coast *see* La Mosquitia
31 U11 **Mosquito Creek Lake** ⊠ Ohio, N USA
Mosquito Gulf *see* Mosquitos, Golfo de los
23 X11 **Mosquito Lagoon** *wetland* Florida, SE USA
43 N10 **Mosquito, Punta** *headland* E Nicaragua 12°18′N 83°38′W
43 W14 **Mosquito, Punta** *headland* NE Panama 09°06′N 77°52′W
43 Q15 **Mosquitos, Golfo de los** *Eng.* Mosquito Gulf. *gulf* N Panama
95 H16 **Moss** Østfold, S Norway 59°25′N 10°40′E
Mossâmedes *see* Namibe
22 G8 **Moss Bluff** Louisiana, S USA 30°18′N 93°11′W
185 C23 **Mossburn** Southland, South Island, New Zealand 45°40′S 168°15′E
83 G26 **Mosselbaai** *var.* Mosselbai, *Eng.* Mossel Bay. Western Cape, SW South Africa 34°11′S 22°08′E
Mosselbai/Mossel Bay *see* Mosselbaai
79 F20 **Mossendjo** Niari, SW Congo 02°57′S 12°40′E
101 H22 **Mössingen** Baden-Württemberg, S Germany 48°22′N 09°01′E
181 W4 **Mossman** Queensland, NE Australia 16°34′S 145°27′E
59 P14 **Mossoró** Rio Grande do Norte, NE Brazil 05°11′S 37°20′W
23 N9 **Moss Point** Mississippi, S USA 30°24′N 88°31′W
183 S9 **Moss Vale** New South Wales, SE Australia 34°33′S 150°20′E
32 G9 **Mossyrock** Washington, NW USA 46°32′N 122°30′W
111 B15 **Most** *Ger.* Brüx. Ústecký Kraj, NW Czech Republic 50°30′N 13°37′E
162 E7 **Möst** *var.* Ulaantolgoy. Hovd, W Mongolia 46°39′N 92°50′E
121 P16 **Mosta** *var.* Musta. C Malta 35°54′N 14°25′E
74 I5 **Mostaganem** *var.* Mestghanem. NW Algeria 35°54′N 00°05′E
113 H14 **Mostar** Federacija Bosna I Hercegovina, S Bosnia and Herzegovina 43°21′N 17°47′E
61 J17 **Mostardas** Rio Grande do Sul, S Brazil 31°02′S 50°51′W
116 K14 **Mostiștea** ≈ S Romania
Mostva *see* Mastva
Mosty *see* Masty
116 H5 **Mostys'ka** L'vivs'ka Oblast', W Ukraine 49°47′N 23°09′E
Mosul *see* Al Mawșil
95 F15 **Møsvatnet** ◎ S Norway
80 J12 **Mot'a** Āmara, N Ethiopia 11°03′N 38°03′E
79 H16 **Motaba** ≈ N Congo
105 O10 **Mota del Cuervo** Castilla-La Mancha, C Spain 39°30′N 02°52′W
104 L5 **Mota del Marqués** Castilla-León, N Spain 41°38′N 05°11′W
42 F5 **Motagua, Río** ≈ Guatemala/Honduras
119 H19 **Motal'** Brestskaya Voblasts', SW Belarus 52°13′N 25°34′E
95 L17 **Motala** Östergötland, S Sweden 58°34′N 15°05′E
191 X7 **Motane** *island* Îles Marquises, NE French Polynesia
152 K13 **Moth** Uttar Pradesh, N India 25°44′N 78°56′E
Mother of Presidents/ Mother of States *see* Virginia
96 I12 **Motherwell** C Scotland, United Kingdom 55°48′N 04°W
153 P12 **Motīhāri** Bihār, N India 26°40′N 84°55′E
105 Q10 **Motilla del Palancar** Castilla-La Mancha, C Spain 39°34′N 01°55′W
184 N7 **Motiti Island** *island* NE New Zealand
83 J19 **Motloutse** ≈ E Botswana
41 V17 **Motozintla de Mendoza** Chiapas, SE Mexico 15°21′N 92°14′W
105 N15 **Motril** Andalucía, S Spain 36°45′N 03°30′W
116 G13 **Motru** Gorj, SW Romania 44°49′N 22°56′E
165 Q4 **Motsuta-misaki** *headland* Hokkaidō, NE Japan 42°36′N 139°48′E
28 L6 **Mott** North Dakota, N USA 46°21′N 102°17′W
Möttling *see* Metlika
107 O18 **Mottola** Puglia, SE Italy 40°38′N 17°02′E
184 P8 **Motu** ≈ North Island, New Zealand
135 I14 **Motueka** Tasman, South Island, New Zealand 41°08′S 173°00′E
135 I14 **Motueka** ≈ South Island, New Zealand
Motu Iti *see* Tupai
41 X12 **Motul** *var.* Motul de Felipe Carrillo Puerto. Yucatán, SE Mexico 21°06′N 89°17′W
Motul de Felipe Carrillo Puerto *see* Motul
191 U17 **Motu Nui** *island* Easter Island, Chile, E Pacific Ocean
191 Q10 **Motu One** *var.* Bellingshausen. *atoll* Îles Sous le Vent, W French Polynesia
190 I16 **Motutapu** *island* E Cook Islands
193 V15 **Motu Tapu** *island* Tongatapu Group, S Tonga
184 L5 **Motutapu Island** *island* N New Zealand
Motyca *see* Modica
Mouanda *see* Moanda
Mouaskar *see* Mascara
105 U3 **Moubermé, Tuc de** *Fr.* Pic de Maubermé, *Sp.* Pico Mauberme; *prev.* Tuc de Maubermé. ▲ France/ Spain 42°48′N 00°57′E *see also* Maubermé, Pic de
Moubermé, Tuc de *see* Maubermé, Pic de
45 N7 **Mouchoir Passage** *passage* SE Turks and Caicos Islands
76 I9 **Moudjéria** Tagant, SW Mauritania 17°52′N 12°20′W
108 C9 **Moudon** Vaud, W Switzerland 46°41′N 06°49′E
Mouhoun *see* Black Volta
79 E19 **Mouila** Ngounié, C Gabon 01°50′S 11°02′E
79 K14 **Mouka** Haute-Kotto, C Central African Republic 07°12′N 21°52′E
Moukden *see* Shenyang
183 N10 **Moulamein** New South Wales, SE Australia 35°06′S 144°03′E
Moulamein Creek *see* Billabong Creek
74 F6 **Moulay-Bousselham** NW Morocco 35°00′N 06°22′W
Moule *see* le Moule
80 M11 **Moulhoulé** N Djibouti 12°34′N 43°06′E
103 P9 **Moulins** Allier, C France 46°34′N 03°20′E
Moulmein *see* Mawlamyine
166 L8 **Moulmeingyun** Ayeyarwady, SW Myanmar (Burma) 16°24′N 95°15′E
74 G6 **Moulouya** *var.* Mulucha, Muluya, Mulwiya. *seasonal river* NE Morocco
23 O2 **Moulton** Alabama, S USA 34°28′N 87°18′W
29 W16 **Moulton** Iowa, C USA 40°41′N 92°40′W
25 T11 **Moulton** Texas, SW USA 29°34′N 97°08′W
23 T7 **Moultrie** Georgia, SE USA 31°10′N 83°47′W
21 S14 **Moultrie, Lake** ⊠ South Carolina, SE USA
22 K3 **Mound Bayou** Mississippi, S USA 33°52′N 90°43′W
30 L17 **Mound City** Illinois, N USA 37°06′N 89°09′W
27 R6 **Mound City** Kansas, C USA 38°07′N 94°49′W
27 Q2 **Mound City** Missouri, C USA 40°07′N 95°13′W
29 N7 **Mound City** South Dakota, N USA 45°44′N 100°03′W
78 H13 **Moundou** Logone-Occidental, SW Chad 08°35′N 16°01′E
27 P10 **Mounds** Oklahoma, C USA 35°52′N 96°03′W
21 R2 **Moundsville** West Virginia, NE USA 39°54′N 80°44′W
167 Q12 **Moŭng Roessei** Bătdâmbâng, W Cambodia 12°47′N 103°28′E
Moun Hou *see* Black Volta
8 H8 **Mountain** ≈ Northwest Territories, NW Canada
37 S12 **Mountainair** New Mexico, SW USA 34°31′N 106°14′W
35 V1 **Mountain City** Nevada, W USA 41°48′N 115°58′W
21 Q8 **Mountain City** Tennessee, S USA 36°28′N 81°48′W
27 U7 **Mountain Grove** Missouri, C USA 37°07′N 92°15′W
27 U9 **Mountain Home** Arkansas, C USA 36°19′N 92°24′W
33 N15 **Mountain Home** Idaho, NW USA 43°07′N 115°42′W
25 Q11 **Mountain Home** Texas, SW USA 30°11′N 99°19′W
29 W4 **Mountain Iron** Minnesota, N USA 47°31′N 92°37′W
29 T10 **Mountain Lake** Minnesota, N USA 43°57′N 94°54′W
23 S3 **Mountain Park** Georgia, SE USA 34°04′N 84°24′W
35 W12 **Mountain Pass** *pass* California, W USA
27 T12 **Mountain Pine** Arkansas, C USA 34°34′N 93°10′W
39 Y14 **Mountain Point** Annette Island, Alaska, USA 55°17′N 131°31′W
Mountain State *see* Montana
Mountain State *see* West Virginia
27 V7 **Mountain View** Arkansas, C USA 35°52′N 92°07′W
38 H12 **Mountain View** Hawaii, USA, C Pacific Ocean 19°32′N 155°03′W
27 V10 **Mountain View** Missouri, C USA 37°00′N 91°42′W
38 M11 **Mountain Village** Alaska, USA 62°06′N 163°42′W
21 R8 **Mount Airy** North Carolina, SE USA 36°30′N 80°36′W
83 K24 **Mount Ayliff** *Xh.* Maxesibebi. Eastern Cape, SE South Africa 30°48′S 29°23′E
29 U16 **Mount Ayr** Iowa, C USA 40°42′N 94°14′W
182 J9 **Mount Barker** South Australia 35°06′S 138°52′E
180 J14 **Mount Barker** Western Australia 34°42′S 117°40′E
183 P11 **Mount Beauty** Victoria, SE Australia 36°47′S 147°12′E
14 E16 **Mount Brydges** Ontario, S Canada 42°54′N 81°29′W
31 N16 **Mount Carmel** Illinois, N USA 38°23′N 87°46′W
30 K10 **Mount Carroll** Illinois, N USA 42°05′N 89°59′W
31 S9 **Mount Clemens** Michigan, N USA 42°36′N 82°52′W
185 E19 **Mount Cook** Canterbury, South Island, New Zealand 43°47′S 170°06′E
83 L16 **Mount Darwin** Mashonaland Central, NE Zimbabwe 16°45′S 31°39′E
19 S7 **Mount Desert Island** *island* Maine, NE USA
23 W11 **Mount Dora** Florida, SE USA 28°48′N 81°38′W
182 G5 **Mount Eba** South Australia 30°11′S 135°40′E
25 W8 **Mount Enterprise** Texas, SW USA 31°53′N 94°40′W
182 J4 **Mount Fitton** South Australia 29°55′S 139°26′E
83 J24 **Mount Fletcher** Eastern Cape, SE South Africa 30°41′S 28°30′E
14 F15 **Mount Forest** Ontario, S Canada 43°58′N 80°44′W
182 K12 **Mount Gambier** South Australia 37°47′S 140°49′E
181 W5 **Mount Garnet** Queensland, NE Australia 17°41′S 145°07′E
21 P6 **Mount Gay** West Virginia, NE USA 37°49′N 82°00′W
31 S12 **Mount Gilead** Ohio, N USA 40°33′N 82°49′W
186 C7 **Mount Hagen** Western Highlands, C Papua New Guinea 05°54′S 144°13′E
18 J16 **Mount Holly** New Jersey, NE USA 39°59′N 74°46′W
21 R10 **Mount Holly** North Carolina, SE USA 35°18′N 81°01′W
27 T12 **Mount Ida** Arkansas, C USA 34°32′N 93°38′W
181 T6 **Mount Isa** Queensland, C Australia 20°48′S 139°32′E
21 U4 **Mount Jackson** Virginia, NE USA 38°45′N 78°38′W
18 D12 **Mount Jewett** Pennsylvania, NE USA 41°43′N 78°37′W
18 L13 **Mount Kisco** New York, NE USA 41°12′N 73°42′W
18 B15 **Mount Lebanon** Pennsylvania, NE USA 40°21′N 80°03′W
182 J8 **Mount Lofty Ranges** ▲▲ South Australia
180 J10 **Mount Magnet** Western Australia 28°09′S 117°52′E
184 N7 **Mount Maunganui** Bay of Plenty, North Island, New Zealand 37°39′S 176°11′E
97 E18 **Mountmellick** *Ir.* Móinteach Mílic. Laois, C Ireland 53°07′N 07°20′W
30 L10 **Mount Morris** Illinois, N USA 42°03′N 89°25′W
31 R9 **Mount Morris** Michigan, N USA 43°07′N 83°42′W
18 F10 **Mount Morris** New York, NE USA 42°43′N 77°51′W
18 B16 **Mount Morris** Pennsylvania, NE USA 39°43′N 80°06′W
30 K15 **Mount Olive** Illinois, N USA 39°04′N 89°43′W
21 V10 **Mount Olive** North Carolina, SE USA 35°12′N 78°03′W
21 N4 **Mount Olivet** Kentucky, S USA 38°32′N 84°01′W
29 Y15 **Mount Pleasant** Iowa, C USA 40°57′N 91°33′W
31 Q8 **Mount Pleasant** Michigan, N USA 43°36′N 84°46′W
18 C15 **Mount Pleasant** Pennsylvania, NE USA 40°07′N 79°33′W
21 T14 **Mount Pleasant** South Carolina, SE USA 32°47′N 79°51′W
20 I9 **Mount Pleasant** Tennessee, S USA 35°32′N 87°11′W
25 W6 **Mount Pleasant** Texas, SW USA 33°10′N 94°49′W
36 L4 **Mount Pleasant** Utah, W USA 39°33′N 111°27′W

◆ Country
● Country Capital
◇ Dependent Territory
○ Dependent Territory Capital
◈ Administrative Regions
✈ International Airport
▲ Mountain
▲▲ Mountain Range
Volcano
≈ River
◎ Lake
⊠ Reservoir

MOUNT PLEASANT – MURRUPULA

63 N23 **Mount Pleasant** ✈ (Stanley) East Falkland, Falkland Islands
97 G25 **Mount's Bay** *inlet* SW England, United Kingdom
35 N2 **Mount Shasta** California, W USA *41°18′N 122°19′W*
30 J13 **Mount Sterling** Illinois, N USA *39°59′N 90°44′W*
21 N5 **Mount Sterling** Kentucky, S USA *38°03′N 83°56′W*
18 E15 **Mount Union** Pennsylvania, NE USA *40°21′N 77°51′W*
23 V6 **Mount Vernon** Georgia, SE USA *32°10′N 82°35′W*
30 L16 **Mount Vernon** Illinois, N USA *38°19′N 88°54′W*
20 M6 **Mount Vernon** Kentucky, S USA *37°20′N 84°20′W*
27 S7 **Mount Vernon** Missouri, C USA *37°05′N 93°49′W*
31 T13 **Mount Vernon** Ohio, N USA *40°23′N 82°29′W*
32 K13 **Mount Vernon** Oregon, NW USA *44°22′N 119°07′W*
25 W6 **Mount Vernon** Texas, SW USA *33°11′N 95°13′W*
32 H7 **Mount Vernon** Washington, NW USA *48°25′N 122°19′W*
20 L5 **Mount Washington** Kentucky, S USA *38°03′N 85°33′W*
182 F8 **Mount Wedge** South Australia *33°29′S 135°08′E*
30 L14 **Mount Zion** Illinois, N USA *39°46′N 88°52′W*
181 Y9 **Moura** Queensland, NE Australia *24°34′S 149°57′E*
58 F12 **Moura** Amazonas, NW Brazil *01°32′S 61°43′W*
104 H12 **Moura** Beja, S Portugal *38°08′N 07°27′W*
104 I12 **Mourão** Évora, S Portugal *38°22′N 07°20′W*
76 L11 **Mourdiah** Koulikoro, W Mali *14°28′N 07°31′W*
78 K7 **Mourdi, Dépression du** *desert lowland* Chad/Sudan
102 J16 **Mourenx** Pyrénées-Atlantiques, SW France *43°24′N 00°37′W*
Mourgana see Mourgkána
115 C15 **Mourgkána** *var.* Mourgana. ▲ Albania/Greece *39°48′N 20°24′E*
97 G16 **Mourne Mountains** *Ir.* Beanna Boirche. ▲▲ SE Northern Ireland, United Kingdom
115 I15 **Moúrtzeflos, Akrotírio** *headland* Límnos, E Greece *40°00′N 25°02′E*
99 C19 **Mouscron** *Dut.* Moeskroen. Hainaut, W Belgium *50°44′N 03°14′E*
Mouse River see Souris River
78 H10 **Moussoro** Kanem, W Chad *13°41′N 16°31′E*
103 T11 **Moûtiers** Savoie, E France *45°28′N 06°31′E*
172 J14 **Moutsamudou** *var.* Mutsamudu. Anjouan, SE Comoros *12°10′S 44°25′E*
74 K11 **Mouydir, Monts de** ▲ S Algeria
79 F20 **Mouyondzi** Bouenza, S Congo *03°58′S 13°57′E*
115 E16 **Mouzáki** *prev.* Mouzákion. Thessalía, C Greece *39°25′N 21°40′E*
Mouzákion see Mouzáki
29 S13 **Moville** Iowa, C USA *42°30′N 96°04′W*
82 E13 **Moxico** ◈ *province* E Angola
172 I14 **Moya** Anjouan, SE Comoros *12°18′S 44°27′E*
40 L12 **Moyahua** Zacatecas, C Mexico *21°18′N 103°09′W*
81 J16 **Moyalē** Oromīya, C Ethiopia *03°34′N 38°58′E*
76 I15 **Moyamba** W Sierra Leone *08°04′N 12°30′W*
74 G7 **Moyen Atlas** *Eng.* Middle Atlas. ▲▲ N Morocco
78 H13 **Moyen-Chari** *off.* Préfecture du Moyen-Chari. ◈ *prefecture* S Chad
Moyen-Chari, Préfecture du see Moyen-Chari
Moyen-Congo see Congo (Republic of)
83 J24 **Moyeni** *var.* Quthing. SW Lesotho *30°25′S 27°43′E*
79 D18 **Moyen-Ogooué** *off.* Province du Moyen-Ogooué, *var.* Le Moyen-Ogooué. ◈ *province* C Gabon
Moyen-Ogooué, Province du see Moyen-Ogooué
103 S4 **Moyeuvre-Grande** Moselle, NE France *49°15′N 06°03′E*
33 N7 **Moyie Springs** Idaho, NW USA *48°43′N 116°15′W*
146 G6 **Mo'ynoq** *Rus.* Muynak. Qoraqalpog'iston Respublikasi, NW Uzbekistan *43°45′N 59°03′E*
81 F16 **Moyo** NW Uganda *03°38′N 31°43′E*
56 D10 **Moyobamba** San Martín, NW Peru *06°04′S 76°56′W*
78 H10 **Moyto** Chari-Baguirmi, W Chad *12°35′N 16°33′E*
158 G9 **Moyu** *var.* Karakax. Xinjiang Uygur Zizhiqu, NW China *37°16′N 79°39′E*
122 M9 **Moyyero** ≈ N Russian Federation
145 S15 **Moyynkum** *var.* Furmanovka, *Kaz.* Fūrmanov. Zhambyl, S Kazakhstan *44°15′N 72°55′E*
145 Q15 **Moyynkum, Peski** *Kaz.* Moyynqum. *desert* S Kazakhstan
Moyynqum see Moyynkum, Peski
145 S12 **Moyynty** Karaganda, C Kazakhstan *47°10′N 73°24′E*
145 S12 **Moyynty** ≈ Karaganda, C Kazakhstan
Mozambika, Lakandranon' i see Mozambique Channel
83 M18 **Mozambique** *off.* Republic of Mozambique; *prev.* People's Republic of Mozambique, Portuguese East Africa. ◆ *republic* S Africa
Mozambique Basin see Natal Basin
Mozambique, Canal de see Mozambique Channel
83 P17 **Mozambique Channel** *Fr.* Canal de Mozambique, *Mal.* Lakandranon' i Mozambika. *strait* W Indian Ocean
172 L11 **Mozambique Escarpment** *var.* Mozambique Scarp. *undersea feature* SW Indian Ocean *33°00′S 36°30′E*
Mozambique, People's Republic of see Mozambique
172 L10 **Mozambique Plateau** *var.* Mozambique Rise. *undersea feature* SW Indian Ocean *32°00′S 35°00′E*
Mozambique, Republic of see Mozambique
Mozambique Rise see Mozambique Plateau
Mozambique Scarp see Mozambique Escarpment
127 O15 **Mozdok** Respublika Severnaya Osetiya, SW Russian Federation *43°48′N 44°42′E*
57 K17 **Mozetenes, Serranías de** ▲▲ C Bolivia
126 J4 **Mozhaysk** Moskovskaya Oblast', W Russian Federation *55°31′N 36°01′E*
127 T3 **Mozhga** Udmurtskaya Respublika, NW Russian Federation *56°24′N 52°13′E*
Mozyr' see Mazyr
79 P22 **Mpala** Katanga, E Dem. Rep. Congo *06°43′S 29°28′E*
79 G19 **Mpama** ≈ C Congo
81 E22 **Mpanda** Rukwa, W Tanzania *06°21′S 31°01′E*
82 L11 **Mpande** Northern, NE Zambia *09°13′S 31°42′E*
83 J18 **Mphoengs** Matabeleland South, SW Zimbabwe *21°04′S 27°56′E*
81 F18 **Mpigi** S Uganda *0°14′N 32°19′E*
82 L13 **Mpika** Northern, NE Zambia *11°50′S 31°30′E*
83 J14 **Mpima** Central, C Zambia *14°25′S 28°34′E*
82 J13 **Mpongwe** Copperbelt, C Zambia *13°25′S 28°13′E*
82 K11 **Mporokoso** Northern, N Zambia *09°22′S 30°06′E*
79 H20 **Mpouya** Plateaux, SE Congo *02°38′S 16°13′E*
77 P16 **Mpraeso** C Ghana *06°36′N 00°43′W*
82 L11 **Mpulungu** Northern, N Zambia *08°50′S 31°06′E*
83 K21 **Mpumalanga** *prev.* Eastern Transvaal, *Afr.* Oos-Transvaal. ◈ *province* NE South Africa
83 D16 **Mpungu** Okavango, N Namibia *17°36′S 18°16′E*
81 I22 **Mpwapwa** Dodoma, C Tanzania *06°21′S 36°29′E*
Mqinvartsveri see Kazbek
110 M8 **Mrągowo** *Ger.* Sensburg. Warmińsko-Mazurskie, NE Poland *53°53′N 21°19′E*
127 V6 **Mrakovo** Respublika Bashkortostan, W Russian Federation *52°43′N 56°36′E*
172 I13 **Mramani** Anjouan, E Comoros *12°18′N 44°39′E*
166 K5 **Mrauk-oo** *var.* Mrauk U, Myohaung. Rakhine State, W Myanmar (Burma) *20°35′N 93°12′E*
Mrauk U see Mrauk-oo
112 F12 **Mrkonjić Grad** ◈ Republika Srpska, W Bosnia and Herzegovina
110 H9 **Mrocza** Kujawsko-pomorskie, C Poland *53°15′N 17°38′E*
124 I14 **Msta** ≈ NW Russian Federation
Mstislavl' see Mstsislaw
119 P15 **Mstsislaw** *Rus.* Mstislavl'. Mahilyowskaya Voblasts', E Belarus *54°01′N 31°43′E*
Mtkvari see Kura
Mtoko see Mutoko
126 K6 **Mtsensk** Orlovskaya Oblast', W Russian Federation *53°17′N 36°34′E*
81 K24 **Mtwara** Mtwara, SE Tanzania *10°17′S 40°11′E*
81 J25 **Mtwara** ◈ *region* SE Tanzania
104 G14 **Mu** ▲ S Portugal *37°24′N 08°04′W*
193 V15 **Mu'a** Tongatapu, S Tonga *21°11′S 175°07′W*
Muai To see Mae Hong Son
83 P16 **Mualama** Zambézia, NE Mozambique *16°51′S 38°21′E*
Mualo see Messalo, Rio
79 E22 **Muanda** Bas-Congo, SW Dem. Rep. Congo *05°53′S 12°17′E*
Muang Chiang Rai see Chiang Rai
167 R6 **Muang Ham** Houaphan, N Laos *20°19′N 104°00′E*
167 S8 **Muang Hinboun** Khammouan, C Laos *17°37′N 104°37′E*
Muang Kalasin see Kalasin
Muang Khammouan see Thakhèk
167 S11 **Muang Không** Champasak, S Laos *14°08′N 105°48′E*
167 S10 **Muang Khôngxédôn** *var.* Khong Sedone. Salavan, S Laos *15°34′N 105°46′E*
Muang Khon Kaen see Khon Kaen
167 Q6 **Muang Khoua** Phôngsali, N Laos *21°07′N 102°31′E*
Muang Krabi see Krabi
Muang Lampang see Lampang
Muang Lamphun see Lamphun
Muang Loei see Loei
Muang Lom Sak see Lom Sak
Muang Nakhon Sawan see Nakhon Sawan
167 Q6 **Muang Namo** Oudômxai, N Laos *20°58′N 101°46′E*
Muang Nan see Nan
167 Q6 **Muang Ngoy** Louangphabang, N Laos *20°43′N 102°42′E*
167 Q5 **Muang Ou Tai** Phôngsali, N Laos *22°06′N 101°59′E*
Muang Pak Lay see Pak Lay
Muang Pakxan see Pakxan
167 T10 **Muang Pakxong** Champasak, S Laos *15°10′N 106°17′E*
167 S9 **Muang Phalan** *var.* Muang Phalane. Savannakhét, S Laos *16°40′N 105°33′E*
Muang Phalane see Muang Phalan
Muang Phan see Phan
Muang Phayao see Phayao
Muang Phichit see Phichit
167 T9 **Muang Phin** Savannakhét, S Laos *16°31′N 106°01′E*
Muang Phitsanulok see Phitsanulok
Muang Phrae see Phrae
Muang Roi Et see Roi Et
Muang Sakon Nakhon see Sakon Nakhon
Muang Samut Prakan see Samut Prakan
167 P6 **Muang Sing** Louang Namtha, N Laos *21°12′N 101°09′E*
Muang Ubon see Ubon Ratchathani
Muang Uthai Thani see Uthai Thani
167 P7 **Muang Vangviang** Viangchan, C Laos *18°53′N 102°27′E*
Muang Xaignabouri see Xaignabouli
Muang Xay see Xai
167 S9 **Muang Xépôn** *var.* Sepone. Savannakhét, S Laos *16°40′N 106°15′E*
168 K10 **Muar** *var.* Bandar Maharani. Johor, Peninsular Malaysia *02°01′N 102°35′E*
168 J9 **Muara** Sumatera, W Indonesia *02°18′N 98°54′E*
168 L13 **Muarabeliti** Sumatera, W Indonesia *03°13′S 103°00′E*
168 K12 **Muarabungo** Sumatera, W Indonesia *01°28′S 102°06′E*
168 L13 **Muaraenim** Sumatera, W Indonesia *03°40′S 103°48′E*
169 T11 **Muarajuloi** Borneo, C Indonesia *0°12′S 114°03′E*
169 U12 **Muarakaman** Borneo, C Indonesia *0°09′S 116°43′E*
168 H12 **Muarasigep** Pulau Siberut, W Indonesia *01°01′S 98°48′E*
168 L12 **Muaratembesi** Sumatera, W Indonesia *01°40′S 103°08′E*
169 T12 **Muaratewe** *var.* Muarateweh; *prev.* Moearatewe. Borneo, C Indonesia *0°58′S 114°52′E*
Muarateweh see Muaratewe
169 U10 **Muarawahau** Borneo, N Indonesia *01°03′N 116°48′E*
138 G13 **Mubārak, Jabal** ▲ S Jordan *29°19′N 35°13′E*
153 N13 **Mubārakpur** Uttar Pradesh, N India *26°05′N 83°19′E*
Mubarek see Muborak
81 F18 **Mubende** SW Uganda *0°35′N 31°24′E*
77 Y14 **Mubi** Adamawa, NE Nigeria *10°15′N 13°18′E*
146 M12 **Muborak** *Rus.* Mubarek. Qashqadaryo Viloyati, S Uzbekistan *39°17′N 65°10′E*
171 U12 **Mubrani** Papua, E Indonesia *0°42′S 133°25′E*
67 U12 **Muchinga Escarpment** *escarpment* NE Zambia
127 N7 **Muchkapskiy** Tambovskaya Oblast', W Russian Federation *51°51′N 42°25′E*
96 G10 **Muck** *island* W Scotland, United Kingdom
82 Q13 **Mucojo** Cabo Delgado, N Mozambique *12°05′S 40°30′E*
82 F12 **Muconda** Lunda Sul, NE Angola *10°37′S 21°19′E*
54 I10 **Muco, Río** ≈ E Colombia
83 O16 **Mucubela** Zambézia, NE Mozambique *16°51′S 37°48′E*
42 J5 **Mucupina, Monte** ▲ N Honduras *15°07′N 86°36′W*
136 J14 **Mucur** Kirşehir, C Turkey *39°05′N 34°25′E*
143 U8 **Mūd** Khorāsān-e Janūbī, E Iran *32°41′N 59°30′E*
163 Y9 **Mudanjiang** *var.* Mu-tan-chiang. Heilongjiang, NE China *44°33′N 129°40′E*
163 Y10 **Mudan Jiang** ≈ NE China
136 D11 **Mudanya** Bursa, NW Turkey *40°23′N 28°53′E*
28 K8 **Mud Butte** South Dakota, N USA *45°00′N 102°51′W*
155 G16 **Muddebihāl** Karnātaka, C India *16°26′N 76°07′E*
27 P12 **Muddy Boggy Creek** ≈ Oklahoma, C USA
36 M6 **Muddy Creek** ≈ Utah, W USA
37 V7 **Muddy Creek Reservoir** ⊠ Colorado, C USA
33 W15 **Muddy Gap** Wyoming, C USA *42°21′N 107°27′W*
35 Y11 **Muddy Peak** ▲ Nevada, W USA *36°17′N 114°40′W*
183 R7 **Mudgee** New South Wales, SE Australia *32°37′S 149°36′E*
29 S3 **Mud Lake** ◎ Minnesota, N USA
29 P7 **Mud Lake Reservoir** ⊠ South Dakota, N USA
167 N9 **Mudon** Mon State, S Myanmar (Burma) *16°17′N 97°40′E*
81 O14 **Mudug** *off.* Gobolka Mudug. ◈ *region* NE Somalia
81 O14 **Mudug** *var.* Mudugh. *plain* N Somalia
Mudug, Gobolka see Mudug
Mudugh see Mudug
83 Q15 **Muecate** Nampula, NE Mozambique *14°56′S 39°38′E*
82 Q13 **Mueda** Cabo Delgado, NE Mozambique *11°40′S 39°31′E*
42 L10 **Muelle de los Bueyes** Región Autónoma Atlántico Sur, SE Nicaragua *12°03′N 84°34′W*
Muenchen see München
83 M14 **Muende** Tete, NW Mozambique *14°22′S 33°00′E*
25 T5 **Muenster** Texas, SW USA *33°39′N 97°22′W*
Muenster see Münster
43 O6 **Muerto, Cayo** *reef* NE Nicaragua
41 T17 **Muerto, Mar** *lagoon* SE Mexico
64 F11 **Muertos Trough** *undersea feature* N Caribbean Sea
83 H14 **Mufaya Kuta** Western, NW Zambia *14°30′S 24°18′E*
82 J13 **Mufulira** Copperbelt, C Zambia *12°33′S 28°16′E*
161 O10 **Mufu Shan** ▲▲ C China
Mugalla see Yutian
Mugalzhar Taūlary see Mugodzhary, Gory
137 Y12 **Muğan Düzü** *Rus.* Muganskaya Ravnina, Muganskaya Step'. *physical region* S Azerbaijan
Muganskaya Ravnina/Muganskaya Step' see Muğan Düzü
106 K8 **Múggia** Friuli-Venezia Giulia, NE Italy *45°36′N 13°48′E*
153 N14 **Mughal Sarāi** Uttar Pradesh, N India *25°18′N 83°07′E*
Mughla see Muğla
141 W11 **Mughshin** *var.* Muqshin. S Oman *19°26′N 54°38′E*
147 S12 **Mughsu** *Rus.* Muksu. ≈ C Tajikistan
164 H14 **Mugi** Tokushima, Shikoku, SW Japan *33°39′N 134°24′E*
136 C16 **Muğla** *var.* Mughla. Muğla, SW Turkey *37°13′N 28°22′E*
136 C16 **Muğla** *var.* Mughla. ◈ *province* SW Turkey
114 K10 **Müglizh** Stara Zagora, C Bulgaria *42°36′N 25°32′E*
144 J11 **Mugodzhary, Gory** *Kaz.* Mugalzhar Taūlary. ▲▲ W Kazakhstan
83 O15 **Mugulama** Zambézia, NE Mozambique *16°01′S 37°33′E*
Muḩāfazat Hims see Ḩimş
Muḩāfazat Ma'dabā see Ma'dabā
139 U9 **Muḩammad** Wāsiţ, E Iraq *32°46′N 45°14′E*
139 R8 **Muḩammadīyah** Al Anbār, C Iraq *33°22′N 42°48′E*
80 I6 **Muhammad Qol** Red Sea, NE Sudan *20°53′N 37°09′E*
75 Y9 **Muhammad, Râs** *headland* E Egypt *27°45′N 34°18′E*
Muhammerah see Khorramshahr
Muḩāfazat Al 'Aqabah see Al 'Aqabah
140 M12 **Muhāyil** *var.* Mahāil. 'Asīr, SW Saudi Arabia *18°34′N 42°01′E*
139 O7 **Muḩaywīr** Al Anbār, W Iraq *33°35′N 41°06′E*
101 H21 **Mühlacker** Baden-Württemberg, SW Germany *48°57′N 08°51′E*
Mühlbach see Sebeş
Mühldorf see Mühldorf am Inn
101 N23 **Mühldorf am Inn** *var.* Mühldorf. Bayern, SE Germany *48°14′N 12°32′E*
101 J15 **Mühlhausen** *var.* Mühlhausen in Thüringen. Thüringen, C Germany *51°13′N 10°28′E*
Mühlhausen in Thüringen see Mühlhausen
195 Q2 **Mühlig-Hofmanfjella** ▲▲ Antarctica
93 L14 **Muhos** Oulu, C Finland *64°48′N 26°00′E*
138 K6 **Mūḩ, Sabkhat al** ◎ C Syria
118 E5 **Muhu** *Ger.* Mohn, Moon. *island* W Estonia
81 F19 **Muhutwe** Kagera, NW Tanzania *01°31′S 31°41′E*
Muhu Väin see Väinameri
98 J10 **Muiden** Noord-Holland, C Netherlands *52°19′N 05°04′E*
193 W15 **Mui Hopohoponga** *headland* Tongatapu, S Tonga *21°09′S 175°02′W*
Muinchille see Cootehill
Muineachán see Monaghan
97 F19 **Muine Bheag** *Eng.* Bagenalstown. Carlow, SE Ireland *52°42′N 06°57′W*
56 B5 **Muisne** Esmeraldas, NW Ecuador *0°35′N 79°58′W*
83 P14 **Muite** Nampula, NE Mozambique *14°02′S 39°06′E*
41 Z11 **Mujeres, Isla** *island* E Mexico
116 G7 **Mukacheve** *Hung.* Munkács, *Rus.* Mukachevo. Zakarpats'ka Oblast', W Ukraine *48°27′N 22°45′E*
Mukachevo see Mukacheve
169 R9 **Mukah** Sarawak, East Malaysia *02°56′N 112°02′E*
Mukalla see Al Mukallā
Mukama see Mokāma
Mukāshafa/Mukashshafah see Mukayshīfah
139 S6 **Mukayshīfah** *var.* Mukāshafa, Mukashshafah. Şalāḩ ad Dīn, N Iraq *34°24′N 43°44′E*
167 R9 **Mukdahan** Mukdahan, E Thailand *16°31′N 104°43′E*
Mukden see Shenyang
165 Y15 **Mukojima-rettō** *Eng.* Parry group. *island group* SE Japan
146 M14 **Mukry** Lebap Welaýaty, E Turkmenistan *37°39′N 65°37′E*
Muksu see Mughsu
Muktagacha see Muktagachha
153 U14 **Muktagachha** *var.* Muktagacha. N Bangladesh *24°46′N 90°16′E*
82 K13 **Mukuku** Central, C Zambia *12°10′S 29°50′E*
82 K11 **Mukupa Kaoma** Northern, NE Zambia *09°55′S 30°19′E*
81 I18 **Mukutan** Rift Valley, W Kenya *01°06′N 36°16′E*
83 F16 **Mukwe** Caprivi, NE Namibia *18°01′S 21°24′E*
105 R13 **Mula** Murcia, SE Spain *38°02′N 01°29′W*
151 K20 **Mulakatholhu** *var.* Meemu Atoll, Mulaku Atoll. *atoll* C Maldives
Mulaku Atoll see Mulakatholhu
83 J15 **Mulalika** Lusaka, C Zambia *15°37′S 28°48′E*
163 X8 **Mulan** Heilongjiang, NE China *45°57′N 128°00′E*
83 N15 **Mulanje** *var.* Mlanje. Southern, S Malawi *16°05′S 35°29′E*
40 H5 **Mulatos** Sonora, NW Mexico *28°42′N 108°44′W*
23 P3 **Mulberry Fork** ≈ Alabama, S USA
39 P12 **Mulchatna River** ≈ Alaska, USA
125 W4 **Mul'da** Respublika Komi, NW Russian Federation *67°29′N 63°55′E*
101 M14 **Mulde** ≈ E Germany
27 R10 **Muldrow** Oklahoma, C USA *35°25′N 94°34′W*
40 E7 **Mulegé** Baja California Sur, NW Mexico *26°54′N 112°00′W*
108 I10 **Mulegns** Graubünden, S Switzerland *46°30′N 09°36′E*
79 M21 **Mulenda** Kasai-Oriental, C Dem. Rep. Congo *04°19′S 24°55′E*
24 M4 **Muleshoe** Texas, SW USA *34°13′N 102°43′W*
83 O15 **Mulevala** Zambézia, NE Mozambique *16°25′S 37°35′E*
183 P5 **Mulgoa Creek** *seasonal river* New South Wales, SE Australia
105 O15 **Mulhacén** *var.* Cerro de Mulhacén. ▲ S Spain *37°07′N 03°11′W*
Mulhacén, Cerro de see Mulhacén
Mülhausen see Mulhouse
101 E24 **Müllheim** Baden-Württemberg, SW Germany *47°50′N 07°37′E*
101 E15 **Mülheim** *var.* Mulheim an der Ruhr. Nordrhein-Westfalen, W Germany *51°25′N 06°50′E*
Mülheim an der Ruhr see Mülheim
103 U7 **Mulhouse** *Ger.* Mülhausen. Haut-Rhin, NE France *47°45′N 07°20′E*
160 G11 **Muli** *var.* Qiaowa, Muli Zangzu Zizhixian. Sichuan, C China *27°49′N 101°10′E*
171 X15 **Muli** *channel* Papua, E Indonesia
163 Y9 **Muling** Heilongjiang, NE China *44°54′N 130°35′E*
Muli Zangzu Zizhixian see Muli
Mullach Íde see Malahide
Mullaitivu see Mullaittivu
155 K23 **Mullaittivu** *var.* Mullaitivu. Northern Province, N Sri Lanka *09°15′N 80°48′E*
33 N8 **Mullan** Idaho, NW USA *47°28′N 115°48′W*
28 M13 **Mullen** Nebraska, C USA *42°02′N 101°01′W*
183 Q6 **Mullengudgery** New South Wales, SE Australia *31°42′S 147°24′E*
21 Q6 **Mullens** West Virginia, NE USA *37°34′N 81°22′W*
Müller-gerbergte see Muller, Pegunungan
169 T10 **Muller, Pegunungan** *Dut.* Müller-gerbergte. ▲▲ Borneo, C Indonesia
31 Q5 **Mullett Lake** ◎ Michigan, N USA
18 J16 **Mullica River** ≈ New Jersey, NE USA
25 R8 **Mullin** Texas, SW USA *31°33′N 98°40′W*
97 E17 **Mullingar** *Ir.* An Muileann gCearr. C Ireland *53°32′N 07°20′W*
21 T12 **Mullins** South Carolina, SE USA *34°12′N 79°15′W*
96 G11 **Mull, Isle of** *island* W Scotland, United Kingdom
127 R5 **Mullovka** Ul'yanovskaya Oblast', W Russian Federation *54°13′N 49°19′E*
95 K19 **Mullsjö** Västra Götaland, S Sweden *57°56′N 13°55′E*
183 V4 **Mullumbimby** New South Wales, SE Australia *28°34′S 153°28′E*
83 H15 **Mulobezi** Western, SW Zambia *16°48′S 25°11′E*
83 C15 **Mulondo** Huíla, SW Angola *15°41′S 15°09′E*
83 G15 **Mulonga Plain** *plain* W Zambia
79 N23 **Mulongo** Katanga, SE Dem. Rep. Congo *07°44′S 26°57′E*
149 T10 **Multān** Punjab, E Pakistan *30°12′N 71°30′E*
93 L17 **Multia** Länsi-Suomi, C Finland *62°27′N 24°49′E*
Mulucha see Moulouya
83 J14 **Mulungushi** Central, C Zambia *14°15′S 28°27′E*
83 K14 **Mulungwe** Central, C Zambia *13°57′S 29°51′E*
Muluya see Moulouya
27 N7 **Mulvane** Kansas, C USA *37°28′N 97°14′W*
183 O10 **Mulwala** New South Wales, SE Australia *35°59′S 146°00′E*
Mulwiya see Moulouya
182 K6 **Mulyungarie** South Australia *31°29′S 140°45′E*
154 D13 **Mumbai** *prev.* Bombay. *state capital* Mahārāshtra, W India *18°56′N 72°51′E*
154 D13 **Mumbai** ✈ Mahārāshtra, W India *19°10′N 72°51′E*
83 D14 **Mumbué** Bié, C Angola *13°52′S 17°15′E*
186 E8 **Mumeng** Morobe, C Papua New Guinea *06°57′S 146°34′E*
171 V12 **Mumi** Papua, E Indonesia *01°33′S 134°09′E*
Muminabad/Mŭ'minobod see Leningrad
127 Q13 **Mumra** Astrakhanskaya Oblast', SW Russian Federation *45°46′N 47°46′E*
41 X12 **Muna** Yucatán, SE Mexico *20°29′N 89°41′W*
123 O9 **Muna** ≈ NE Russian Federation
152 C12 **Munābāo** Rājasthān, NW India *25°46′N 70°19′E*
Munamägi see Suur Munamägi
171 O14 **Muna, Pulau** *prev.* Moena. *island* C Indonesia
101 L18 **Münchberg** Bayern, E Germany *50°10′N 11°50′E*
101 L23 **München** *var.* Muenchen, *Eng.* Munich, *It.* Monaco. Bayern, SE Germany *48°09′N 11°34′E*
München-Gladbach see Mönchengladbach
108 E6 **Münchenstein** Basel-Land, NW Switzerland *47°31′N 07°38′E*
10 L10 **Muncho Lake** British Columbia, W Canada *58°52′N 125°40′W*
31 P13 **Muncie** Indiana, N USA *40°11′N 85°22′W*
18 G13 **Muncy** Pennsylvania, NE USA *41°10′N 76°46′W*
11 Q14 **Mundare** Alberta, SW Canada *53°34′N 112°20′W*
25 Q5 **Munday** Texas, SW USA *33°27′N 99°37′W*
31 N10 **Mundelein** Illinois, N USA *42°15′N 88°00′W*
101 I15 **Münden** Niedersachsen, C Germany *52°16′N 08°54′E*
105 Q12 **Mundo** ≈ S Spain
82 B12 **Munenga** Cuanza Sul, NW Angola *10°03′S 14°40′E*
105 P11 **Munera** Castilla-La Mancha, C Spain *39°03′N 02°29′W*
20 E9 **Munford** Tennessee, S USA *35°27′N 89°49′W*
20 K7 **Munfordville** Kentucky, S USA *37°17′N 85°55′W*
182 D5 **Mungala** South Australia *30°36′S 132°57′E*
83 M16 **Mungári** Manica, C Mozambique *17°09′S 33°33′E*
79 O16 **Mungbere** Orientale, NE Dem. Rep. Congo *02°38′N 28°30′E*
153 Q13 **Munger** *prev.* Monghyr. Bihār, NE India *25°23′N 86°28′E*
182 J1 **Mungeranie** South Australia *28°02′S 138°42′E*
Mu Nggava see Rennell
169 O10 **Mungguresak, Tanjung** *headland* Borneo, N Indonesia *01°57′N 109°19′E*
Mungiki see Bellona
183 R4 **Mungindi** New South Wales, SE Australia *28°59′S 149°00′E*
Mungkawn see Maingkwan
Mungla see Mongla
82 C13 **Mungo** Huambo, W Angola *11°49′S 16°16′E*
188 F16 **Munguuy Bay** *bay* Yap, W Micronesia
82 E13 **Munhango** Bié, C Angola *12°12′S 18°34′E*
Munich see München
105 S7 **Muniesa** Aragón, NE Spain *41°02′N 00°49′W*
31 O4 **Munising** Michigan, N USA *46°24′N 86°39′W*
Munkács see Mukacheve
95 I17 **Munkedal** Västra Götaland, S Sweden *58°28′N 11°38′E*
95 K15 **Munkfors** Värmland, C Sweden *59°50′N 13°35′E*
122 M14 **Munku-Sardyk, Gora** *var.* Mönh Sarĭdag. ▲ Mongolia/Russian Federation *51°45′N 100°22′E*
99 E18 **Munkzwalm** Oost-Vlaanderen, NW Belgium *50°53′N 03°44′E*
167 R10 **Mun, Mae Nam** ≈ E Thailand
153 U15 **Munshiganj** Dhaka, C Bangladesh *23°32′N 90°32′E*
108 D8 **Münsingen** Bern, W Switzerland *46°53′N 07°34′E*
103 U6 **Munster** Haut-Rhin, NE France *48°03′N 07°09′E*
100 J11 **Munster** Niedersachsen, NW Germany *52°59′N 10°07′E*
100 F13 **Münster** *var.* Muenster, Münster in Westfalen. Nordrhein-Westfalen, W Germany *51°58′N 07°38′E*
108 F10 **Münster** Valais, S Switzerland *46°31′N 08°18′E*
97 B20 **Munster** *Ir.* Cúige Mumhan. *cultural region* S Ireland
Münsterberg in Schlesien see Ziębice
Münster in Westfalen see Münster
100 E13 **Münsterland** *cultural region* NW Germany
100 F13 **Münster-Osnabruck** ✈ Nordrhein-Westfalen, NW Germany *52°08′N 07°41′E*
31 R4 **Munuscong Lake** ◎ Michigan, N USA
83 K17 **Munyati** ≈ C Zimbabwe
109 R3 **Münzkirchen** Oberösterreich, N Austria *48°29′N 13°37′E*
92 K11 **Muodoslompolo** Norrbotten, N Sweden *67°57′N 23°31′E*
92 M13 **Muojärvi** ◎ NE Finland
167 S6 **Mương Khên** Hoa Binh, N Vietnam *20°34′N 105°18′E*
Muong Sai see Xai
167 Q7 **Muong Xiang Ngeun** *var.* Xieng Ngeun. Louangphabang, N Laos *19°43′N 102°09′E*
92 K11 **Muonio** Lappi, N Finland *67°58′N 23°40′E*
Muonioälv/Muoniojoki see Muonionjoki
92 K11 **Muonionjoki** *var.* Muoniojoki, *Swe.* Muonioälv. ≈ Finland/Sweden
83 N17 **Mupa** ≈ C Mozambique
83 E16 **Mupini** Okavango, NE Namibia *17°55′S 19°34′E*
80 F8 **Muqaddam, Wadi** ≈ N Sudan
138 K9 **Muqāṭ** Al Mafraq, E Jordan *32°28′N 38°04′E*
81 N17 **Muqdisho** *Eng.* Mogadishu, *It.* Mogadiscio. ● (Somalia) Banaadir, S Somalia *02°06′N 45°27′E*
81 N17 **Muqdisho** ✈ Banaadir, E Somalia *01°58′N 45°18′E*
Muqshin see Mughshin
109 T8 **Mur** *SCr.* Mura. ≈ C Europe
109 X9 **Mura** ≈ NE Slovenia
Mura see Mur
137 T14 **Muradiye** Van, E Turkey *39°N 43°44′E*
Muragarazi see Maragarazi
165 O10 **Murakami** Niigata, Honshū, C Japan *38°13′N 139°28′E*
63 G22 **Murallón, Cerro** ▲ S Argentina *49°49′S 73°25′W*
81 E20 **Muramvya** C Burundi *03°18′S 29°41′E*
81 I19 **Murang'a** *prev.* Fort Hall. Central, SW Kenya *0°43′S 37°10′E*
81 H16 **Murangering** Rift Valley, NW Kenya *03°48′N 35°29′E*
Murapara see Murupara
140 M5 **Murār, Bi'r al** *well* NW Saudi Arabia
125 Q13 **Murashi** Kirovskaya Oblast', NW Russian Federation *59°27′N 48°02′E*
103 O12 **Murat** Cantal, C France *45°07′N 02°52′E*
114 N12 **Muratlı** Tekirdağ, NW Turkey *41°12′N 27°30′E*
137 R14 **Murat Nehri** *var.* Eastern Euphrates; *anc.* Arsanias. ≈ NE Turkey
107 D20 **Muravera** Sardegna, Italy, C Mediterranean Sea *39°24′N 09°34′E*
165 P10 **Murayama** Yamagata, Honshū, C Japan *38°29′N 140°21′E*
121 R13 **Muraysah, Ra's al** *headland* N Libya *31°58′N 25°00′E*
104 I6 **Murça** Vila Real, N Portugal *41°24′N 07°28′W*
80 Q11 **Murcanyo** Bari, NE Somalia *11°39′N 50°27′E*
143 N8 **Mūrcheh Khvort** *var.* Morcheh Khort. Eşfahān, C Iran *33°07′N 51°26′E*
185 H15 **Murchison** Tasman, South Island, New Zealand *41°48′S 172°19′E*
185 B22 **Murchison Mountains** ▲▲ South Island, New Zealand
180 I10 **Murchison River** ≈ Western Australia
105 R13 **Murcia** Murcia, SE Spain *37°59′N 01°08′W*
105 Q13 **Murcia** ◈ *autonomous community* SE Spain
103 O13 **Mur-de-Barrez** Aveyron, S France *44°48′N 02°39′E*
182 G8 **Murdinga** South Australia *33°46′S 135°46′E*
28 M10 **Murdo** South Dakota, N USA *43°53′N 100°42′W*
15 X6 **Murdochville** Québec, SE Canada *48°57′N 65°30′W*
109 W9 **Mureck** Steiermark, SE Austria *46°42′N 15°46′E*
114 M13 **Mürefte** Tekirdağ, NW Turkey *40°40′N 27°15′E*
116 I10 **Mureş** ◈ *county* N Romania
84 J11 **Mureş** ≈ Hungary/Romania
Mureş see Maros
Mureşul see Maros/Mureş
102 M16 **Muret** Haute-Garonne, S France *43°28′N 01°19′E*
27 T13 **Murfreesboro** Arkansas, C USA *34°04′N 93°42′W*
21 W8 **Murfreesboro** North Carolina, SE USA *36°26′N 77°06′W*
20 J9 **Murfreesboro** Tennessee, S USA *35°50′N 86°25′W*
Murgab see Morghāb, Daryā-ye/Murgap
Murgab see Murghob
146 I14 **Murgap** Mary Welaýaty, S Turkmenistan *37°19′N 61°48′E*
146 J16 **Murgap** *var.* Deryasy Murgap, Murghab, *Pash.* Daryā-ye Morghāb, *Rus.* Murgab. ≈ Afghanistan/Turkmenistan *see also* Morghāb, Daryā-ye
Murgap see Morghāb, Daryā-ye
Murgap, Deryasy see Morghāb, Daryā-ye/Murgap
114 H9 **Murgash** ▲ W Bulgaria *42°51′N 23°58′E*
Murghab see Morghāb, Daryā-ye/Murgap
147 U13 **Murghob** *Rus.* Murgab. SE Tajikistan *38°11′N 74°E*
147 U13 **Murghob** *Rus.* Murgab. ≈ SE Tajikistan
181 Z10 **Murgon** Queensland, E Australia *26°08′S 152°04′E*
190 I16 **Muri** Rarotonga, S Cook Islands *21°15′S 159°44′W*
108 F7 **Muri** Aargau, W Switzerland *47°16′N 08°21′E*
108 D8 **Muri** *var.* Muri bei Bern. Bern, W Switzerland *46°55′N 07°30′E*
104 K3 **Murias de Paredes** Castilla-León, N Spain *42°51′N 06°11′W*
Muri bei Bern see Muri
82 F11 **Muriege** Lunda Sul, NE Angola *09°55′S 21°12′E*
189 P14 **Murilo Atoll** *atoll* Hall Islands, C Micronesia
Mūrītānīyah see Mauritania
100 N10 **Müritz** *var.* Müritzee. ◎ NE Germany
Müritzee see Müritz
100 L10 **Müritz-Elde-Kanal** *canal* N Germany
184 K6 **Muriwai Beach** Auckland, North Island, New Zealand *36°56′S 174°28′E*
92 J13 **Murjek** Norrbotten, N Sweden *66°27′N 20°54′E*
124 J3 **Murmansk** Murmanskaya Oblast', NW Russian Federation *68°59′N 33°08′E*
124 I4 **Murmanskaya Oblast'** ◈ *province* NW Russian Federation
197 V14 **Murmansk Rise** *undersea feature* SW Barents Sea *71°00′N 37°00′E*
124 J3 **Murmashi** Murmanskaya Oblast', NW Russian Federation *68°49′N 32°43′E*
126 M5 **Murmino** Ryazanskaya Oblast', W Russian Federation *54°31′N 40°01′E*
101 K24 **Murnau** Bayern, SE Germany *47°41′N 11°12′E*
103 X16 **Muro, Capo di** *headland* Corse, France, C Mediterranean Sea *41°45′N 08°40′E*
107 M18 **Muro Lucano** Basilicata, S Italy *40°48′N 15°33′E*
127 N4 **Murom** Vladimirskaya Oblast', W Russian Federation *55°33′N 42°03′E*
122 I11 **Muromtsevo** Omskaya Oblast', C Russian Federation *56°18′N 75°15′E*
165 R5 **Muroran** Hokkaidō, NE Japan *42°20′N 140°58′E*
104 G3 **Muros** Galicia, NW Spain *42°47′N 09°04′W*
104 F3 **Muros e Noia, Ría de** *estuary* NW Spain
164 H15 **Muroto** Kōchi, Shikoku, SW Japan *33°16′N 134°10′E*
164 H15 **Muroto-zaki** Shikoku, SW Japan
116 L7 **Murovani Kurylivtsi** Vinnyts'ka Oblast', C Ukraine *48°43′N 27°31′E*
110 G11 **Murowana Goślina** Wielkolpolskie, W Poland *52°33′N 16°59′E*
32 M14 **Murphy** Idaho, NW USA *43°14′N 116°36′W*
21 N10 **Murphy** North Carolina, SE USA *35°05′N 84°02′W*
35 P8 **Murphys** California, W USA *38°07′N 120°27′W*
30 L17 **Murphysboro** Illinois, N USA *37°45′N 89°20′W*
29 V15 **Murray** Iowa, C USA *41°03′N 93°56′W*
20 H8 **Murray** Kentucky, S USA *36°35′N 88°20′W*
182 J10 **Murray Bridge** South Australia *35°10′S 139°17′E*
175 X2 **Murray Fracture Zone** *tectonic feature* NE Pacific Ocean
192 H11 **Murray, Lake** ◎ SW Papua New Guinea
21 P12 **Murray, Lake** ⊠ South Carolina, SE USA
10 K8 **Murray, Mount** ▲ Yukon Territory, NW Canada *60°49′N 128°57′W*
Murray Range see Murray Ridge
173 O3 **Murray Ridge** *var.* Murray Range. *undersea feature* N Arabian Sea *21°45′N 61°50′E*
183 N10 **Murray River** ≈ SE Australia
182 K10 **Murrayville** Victoria, SE Australia *35°17′S 141°12′E*
149 U5 **Murree** Punjab, E Pakistan *33°55′N 73°26′E*
101 I21 **Murrhardt** Baden-Württemberg, S Germany *49°00′N 09°34′E*
183 O9 **Murrumbidgee River** ≈ New South Wales, SE Australia
83 P15 **Murrupula** Nampula, NE Mozambique *15°26′S 38°46′E*

◆ Country ● Country Capital ◇ Dependent Territory ○ Dependent Territory Capital ◈ Administrative Regions ✈ International Airport ▲ Mountain ▲▲ Mountain Range ⋏ Volcano ≈ River ◎ Lake ⊠ Reservoir

MURRURUNDI – NAMHAE-DO

183 *T7* **Murrurundi** New South Wales, SE Australia *31°47′S 150°51′E*
109 *X9* **Murska Sobota** *Ger.* Olsnitz. NE Slovenia *46°41′N 16°09′E*
154 *G12* **Murtajāpur** *prev.* Murtazapur. Mahārāshtra, C India *20°43′N 77°28′E*
77 *S16* **Murtala Muhammed** ✈ (Lagos) Ogun, SW Nigeria *06°31′N 03°12′E*
Murtazapur *see* Murtajāpur
108 *C8* **Murten** Neuchâtel, W Switzerland *46°55′N 07°06′E*
Murtensee *see* Morat, Lac de
182 *L11* **Murtoa** Victoria, SE Australia *36°39′S 142°27′E*
92 *N13* **Murtovaara** Oulu, E Finland *65°40′N 29°25′E*
Murua Island *see* Woodlark Island
155 *D14* **Murud** Mahārāshtra, W India *18°27′N 72°56′E*
184 *O9* **Murupara** *var.* Murapara. Bay of Plenty, North Island, New Zealand *38°27′S 176°41′E*
191 *X12* **Mururoa** *var.* Moruroa. *atoll* Îles Tuamotu, SE French Polynesia
Murviedro *see* Sagunto
154 *J9* **Murwāra** Madhya Pradesh, N India *23°50′N 80°23′E*
183 *V4* **Murwillumbah** New South Wales, SE Australia *28°20′S 153°24′E*
146 *H11* **Murzechirla** *prev.* Mirzachirla. Ahal Welaýaty, C Turkmenistan *39°33′N 60°02′E*
Murzuk *see* Murzuq
75 *O11* **Murzuq** *var.* Marzūq, Murzuk. SW Libya *25°55′N 13°55′E*
Murzuq, Edeyin *see* Murzuq, Idhān
75 *N11* **Murzuq, Ḥammādat** *plateau* W Libya
75 *O11* **Murzuq, Idhān** *var.* Edeyin Murzuq. *desert* SW Libya
109 *W6* **Mürzzuschlag** Steiermark, E Austria *47°35′N 15°41′E*
137 *Q14* **Muş** *var.* Mush. Muş, E Turkey *38°45′N 41°30′E*
137 *Q14* **Muş** *var.* Mush. ◈ *province* E Turkey
118 *G11* **Mūša** ≋ Latvia/Lithuania
186 *F9* **Musa** ≋ S Papua New Guinea
Mûsa, Gebel *see* Mūsá, Jabal
Musaiyib *see* Al Musayyib
75 *X8* **Mūsá, Jabal** *var.* Gebel Mûsa. ▲ NE Egypt *28°33′N 33°51′E*
Musa Khel *see* Mūsa Khel Bāzār
149 *R9* **Mūsa Khel Bāzār** *var.* Musa Khel. Baluchistān, SW Pakistan *30°53′N 69°52′E*
114 *H10* **Musala** ▲ W Bulgaria *42°12′N 23°36′E*
168 *H10* **Musala, Pulau** *island* W Indonesia
83 *I15* **Musale** Southern, S Zambia *15°27′S 26°50′E*
141 *Y9* **Muṣalla** NE Oman *22°20′N 58°03′E*
141 *W6* **Musandam Peninsula** *Ar.* Masandam Peninsula. *peninsula* N Oman
Musay'īd *see* Umm Sa'īd
Muscat *see* Masqaṭ
Muscat and Oman *see* Oman
29 *Y14* **Muscatine** Iowa, C USA *41°25′N 91°03′W*
Muscat Sīb Airport *see* Seeb
31 *O15* **Muscatuck River** ≋ Indiana, N USA
30 *K8* **Muscoda** Wisconsin, N USA *43°11′N 90°27′W*
185 *F19* **Musgrave, Mount** ▲ South Island, New Zealand *43°48′S 170°43′E*
181 *P9* **Musgrave Ranges** ▲▲ South Australia
Mush *see* Muş
138 *H12* **Mushayyish, Qaṣr al** *castle* Ma'ān, C Jordan
79 *H20* **Mushie** Bandundu, W Dem. Rep. Congo *03°00′S 16°55′E*
168 *M13* **Musi, Air** *prev.* Moesi. ≋ Sumatera, W Indonesia
192 *M4* **Musicians Seamounts** *undersea feature* N Pacific Ocean
83 *K19* **Musina** *prev.* Messina. Limpopo, NE South Africa *22°18′S 30°02′E*
54 *D8* **Musinga, Alto** ▲ NW Colombia *06°49′N 76°24′W*
29 *T2* **Muskeg Bay** *lake bay* Minnesota, N USA
31 *O8* **Muskegon** Michigan, N USA *43°13′N 86°15′W*
31 *O8* **Muskegon Heights** Michigan, N USA *43°12′N 86°14′W*
31 *P8* **Muskegon River** ≋ Michigan, N USA
31 *T14* **Muskingum River** ≋ Ohio, N USA
95 *P16* **Muskö** Stockholm, C Sweden *58°58′N 18°10′E*
Muskogean *see* Tallahassee
27 *Q10* **Muskogee** Oklahoma, C USA *35°45′N 95°21′W*
14 *H13* **Muskoka, Lake** ◎ Ontario, S Canada
80 *H8* **Musmar** Red Sea, NE Sudan *18°13′N 35°40′E*
83 *K14* **Musofu** Central, C Zambia *13°31′S 29°02′E*
81 *G19* **Musoma** Mara, N Tanzania *01°31′S 33°49′E*
82 *L13* **Musoro** Central, C Zambia *13°21′S 31°04′E*
186 *F4* **Mussau Island** *island* NE Papua New Guinea
98 *P7* **Musselkanaal** Groningen, NE Netherlands *52°55′N 07°01′E*
33 *V9* **Musselshell River** ≋ Montana, NW USA
82 *C12* **Mussende** Cuanza Sul, NW Angola *10°33′S 16°02′E*
102 *L12* **Mussidan** Dordogne, SW France *45°03′N 00°22′E*
99 *L25* **Musson** Luxembourg, SE Belgium *49°33′N 05°42′E*
152 *J9* **Mussoorie** Uttarakhand, N India *30°25′N 78°04′E*
Musta *see* Mosta
152 *M13* **Mustafābād** Uttar Pradesh, N India *25°54′N 81°17′E*
136 *D12* **Mustafakemalpaşa** Bursa, NW Turkey *40°03′N 28°25′E*
Mustafa-Pasha *see* Svilengrad
81 *M15* **Mustahīl** Sumalē, E Ethiopia *05°18′N 44°34′E*
24 *M7* **Mustang Draw** *valley* Texas, SW USA
25 *T14* **Mustang Island** *island* Texas, SW USA
Mustasaari *see* Korsholm
Mustér *see* Disentis
63 *I19* **Musters, Lago** ◎ S Argentina
45 *Y14* **Mustique** *island* C Saint Vincent and the Grenadines
118 *I6* **Mustla** Viljandimaa, S Estonia *58°12′N 25°50′E*
118 *J4* **Mustvee** *Ger.* Tschorna. Jõgevamaa, E Estonia *58°51′N 26°59′E*
42 *L9* **Musún, Cerro** ▲ NE Nicaragua *13°01′N 85°02′W*
183 *T7* **Muswellbrook** New South Wales, SE Australia *32°17′S 150°55′E*
111 *M18* **Muszyna** Małopolskie, SE Poland *49°21′N 20°54′E*
75 *V10* **Mūṭ** *var.* Mut. C Egypt *25°28′N 28°58′E*
136 *I17* **Mut** İçel, S Turkey *36°38′N 33°27′E*
109 *V9* **Muta** N Slovenia *46°37′N 15°09′E*
190 *B15* **Mutalau** N Niue *18°56′S 169°50′E*
Mu-tan-chiang *see* Mudanjiang
82 *I13* **Mutanda** North Western, NW Zambia *12°24′S 26°13′E*
59 *O17* **Mutá, Ponta do** *headland* E Brazil *13°54′S 38°54′W*
83 *L17* **Mutare** *var.* Mutari; *prev.* Umtali. Manicaland, E Zimbabwe *18°55′S 32°36′E*
Mutari *see* Mutare
54 *D8* **Mutatá** Antioquia, NW Colombia *07°16′N 76°32′W*
Mutina *see* Modena
83 *L16* **Mutoko** *prev.* Mtoko. Mashonaland East, NE Zimbabwe *17°24′S 32°13′E*
81 *J20* **Mutomo** Eastern, S Kenya *01°50′S 38°13′E*
Mutrah *see* Maṭraḥ
Mutsamudu *see* Moutsamudou
79 *M24* **Mutshatsha** Katanga, S Dem. Rep. Congo *10°40′S 24°26′E*
165 *R6* **Mutsu** *var.* Mutu. Aomori, Honshū, N Japan *41°18′N 141°11′E*
165 *R6* **Mutsu-wan** *bay* N Japan
108 *E6* **Muttenz** Basel-Land, NW Switzerland *47°31′N 07°39′E*
185 *A26* **Muttonbird Islands** *island group* SW New Zealand
Muttra *see* Mathura
Mutu *see* Mutsu
83 *O15* **Mutuáli** Nampula, N Mozambique *14°51′S 37°01′E*
82 *D13* **Mutumbo** Bié, C Angola *13°10′S 17°22′E*
189 *Y14* **Mutunte, Mount** *var.* Mount Buache. ▲ Kosrae, E Micronesia *05°21′N 163°00′E*
155 *K24* **Mutur** Eastern Province, E Sri Lanka *08°27′N 81°15′E*
92 *L13* **Muurola** Lappi, NW Finland *66°22′N 25°20′E*
162 *M14* **Mu Us Shadi** *var.* Ordos Desert; *prev.* Mu Us Shamo. *desert* N China
Mu Us Shamo *see* Mu Us Shadi
82 *B11* **Muxima** Bengo, NW Angola *09°33′S 13°58′E*
124 *I8* **Muyezerskiy** Respublika Kareliya, NW Russian Federation *63°54′N 32°00′E*
81 *E20* **Muyinga** NE Burundi *02°54′S 30°19′E*
42 *K9* **Muy Muy** Matagalpa, C Nicaragua *12°43′N 85°35′W*
Muynak *see* Mo'ynoq
79 *N22* **Muyumba** Katanga, SE Dem. Rep. Congo *07°13′S 27°02′E*
149 *V5* **Muzaffarābād** Jammu and Kashmir, NE Pakistan *34°23′N 73°34′E*
149 *S10* **Muzaffargarh** Punjab, E Pakistan *30°04′N 71°15′E*
152 *J9* **Muzaffarnagar** Uttar Pradesh, N India *29°28′N 77°42′E*
153 *P13* **Muzaffarpur** Bihār, N India *26°07′N 85°23′E*
158 *H6* **Muzat He** ≋ W China
83 *L15* **Muze** Tete, NW Mozambique *15°05′S 31°16′E*
122 *H8* **Muzhi** Yamalo-Nenetskiy Avtonomnyy Okrug, N Russian Federation *65°25′N 64°28′E*
102 *H7* **Muzillac** Morbihan, NW France *47°34′N 02°30′W*
Muzkol, Khrebet *see* Muzqŭl, Qatorkŭhi
112 *L9* **Mužlja** *Hung.* Felsőmuzslya; *prev.* Gornja Mužlja. Vojvodina, N Serbia *45°21′N 20°25′E*
54 *F9* **Muzo** Boyacá, C Colombia *05°34′N 74°07′W*
83 *J15* **Muzoka** Southern, S Zambia *16°39′S 27°18′E*
39 *Y15* **Muzon, Cape** *headland* Dall Island, Alaska, USA *54°39′N 132°41′W*
40 *M6* **Múzquiz** Coahuila, NE Mexico *27°54′N 101°30′W*
147 *U13* **Muzqŭl, Qatorkŭhi** *Rus.* Khrebet Muzkol. ▲▲ SE Tajikistan
158 *G10* **Muz Tag** ▲ NW China *36°02′N 80°13′E*
158 *K10* **Muztag** ▲ W China *36°26′N 87°15′E*
158 *D8* **Muztagata** ▲ NW China *38°16′N 75°03′E*
83 *K17* **Mvuma** *prev.* Umvuma. Midlands, C Zimbabwe *19°17′S 30°32′E*
172 *H13* **Mwali** *var.* Moili, *Fr.* Mohéli. *island* S Comoros
82 *L13* **Mwanya** Eastern, E Zambia *12°40′S 32°15′E*
79 *N23* **Mwanza** Katanga, SE Dem. Rep. Congo *07°49′S 26°49′E*
81 *G20* **Mwanza** Mwanza, NW Tanzania *02°31′S 32°56′E*
81 *F20* **Mwanza** ◈ *region* N Tanzania
82 *M13* **Mwase Lundazi** Eastern, E Zambia *12°26′S 33°20′E*
97 *B17* **Mweelrea** *Ir.* Caoc Maol Réidh. ▲ W Ireland *53°37′N 09°47′W*
79 *K21* **Mweka** Kasai-Occidental, C Dem. Rep. Congo *04°52′S 21°38′E*
82 *K12* **Mwenda** Luapula, N Zambia *10°30′S 30°21′E*
79 *L22* **Mwene-Ditu** Kasai-Oriental, S Dem. Rep. Congo *07°06′S 23°34′E*
83 *L18* **Mwenezi** ≋ S Zimbabwe
79 *O20* **Mwenga** Sud-Kivu, E Dem. Rep. Congo *03°00′S 28°28′E*
82 *K11* **Mweru, Lake** *var.* Lac Moero. ◎ Dem. Rep. Congo/Zambia
82 *H13* **Mwinilunga** North Western, NW Zambia *11°44′S 24°24′E*
189 *V16* **Mwokil Atoll** *prev.* Mokil Atoll. *atoll* Caroline Islands, E Micronesia
Myadel' *see* Myadzyel
118 *J13* **Myadzyel** *Pol.* Miadzioł Nowy, *Rus.* Myadel'. Minskaya Voblasts', N Belarus *54°51′N 26°51′E*
152 *C12* **Myājlār** *var.* Miajlar. Rājasthān, NW India *26°16′N 70°21′E*
123 *T9* **Myakit** Magadanskaya Oblast', E Russian Federation *61°23′N 151°58′E*
23 *W13* **Myakka River** ≋ Florida, SE USA
124 *L14* **Myaksa** Vologodskaya Oblast', NW Russian Federation *58°54′N 38°15′E*
183 *U8* **Myall Lake** ◎ New South Wales, SE Australia
166 *L7* **Myanaung** Ayeyarwady, SW Myanmar (Burma) *18°17′N 95°19′E*
Myanmar *off.* Union of Myanmar, Myanmar. ◆ *military dictatorship* SE Asia
166 *K8* **Myaungmya** Ayeyarwady, SW Myanmar (Burma) *16°33′N 94°55′E*
Myaydo *see* Aunglan
118 *N11* **Myazha** *Rus.* Mezha. Vitsyebskaya Voblasts', NE Belarus *55°41′N 30°25′E*
167 *N12* **Myeik** *var.* Mergui. Tanintharyi, S Myanmar (Burma) *12°26′N 98°34′E*
119 *O18* **Myerkulavichy** *Rus.* Merkulovichi. Homyel'skaya Voblasts', SE Belarus *52°58′N 30°36′E*
119 *N14* **Myezhava** *Rus.* Mezhëvo. Vitsyebskaya Voblasts', NE Belarus *54°38′N 30°20′E*
Myggenaes *see* Mykines
166 *L5* **Myingyan** Mandalay, C Myanmar (Burma) *21°25′N 95°20′E*
167 *N12* **Myitkyina** Kachin State, N Myanmar (Burma) *25°24′N 97°25′E*
166 *M5* **Myittha** Mandalay, C Myanmar (Burma) *21°21′N 96°06′E*
111 *H19* **Myjava** *Hung.* Miava. Trenčiansky Kraj, W Slovakia *48°45′N 17°35′E*
Myjeldino *see* Myyëldino
117 *U9* **Mykhaylivka** *Rus.* Mikhaylovka. Zaporiz'ka Oblast', SE Ukraine *47°16′N 35°14′E*
95 *A18* **Mykines** *Dan.* Myggenaes. *island* W Faeroe Islands
116 *I5* **Mykolayiv** L'vivs'ka Oblast', W Ukraine *49°34′N 23°58′E*
117 *Q10* **Mykolayiv** *Rus.* Nikolayev. Mykolayivs'ka Oblast', S Ukraine *46°58′N 31°59′E*
117 *Q10* **Mykolayiv** ✈ Mykolayivs'ka Oblast', S Ukraine *47°02′N 31°54′E*
Mykolayiv *see* Mykolayivs'ka Oblast'
117 *P9* **Mykolayivka** Odes'ka Oblast', SW Ukraine *47°34′N 30°48′E*
117 *S13* **Mykolayivka** Respublika Krym, S Ukraine *44°58′N 33°37′E*
117 *P9* **Mykolayivs'ka Oblast'** *var.* Mykolayiv, *Rus.* Nikolayevskaya Oblast'. ◈ *province* S Ukraine
115 *J20* **Mýkonos** Mýkonos, Kykládes, Greece, Aegean Sea *37°27′N 25°20′E*
115 *K20* **Mýkonos** *var.* Míkonos. *island* Kykládes, Greece, Aegean Sea
125 *R7* **Myla** Respublika Komi, NW Russian Federation *65°24′N 50°51′E*
Mylae *see* Milazzo
93 *M19* **Myllykoski** Etelä-Suomi, S Finland *60°45′N 26°52′E*
153 *U14* **Mymensing** *var.* Mymensingh. Dhaka, N Bangladesh *24°45′N 90°23′E*
Mymensingh *see* Mymensing
93 *K19* **Mynämäki** Länsi-Suomi, SW Finland *60°41′N 22°00′E*
145 *S14* **Mynaral** *Kaz.* Myngaral. Zhambyl, S Kazakhstan *45°25′N 73°37′E*
Mynbulak *see* Mingbuloq
Mynbulak, Vpadina *see* Mingbuloq Botig'I
Myngaral *see* Mynaral
Myohaung *see* Mrauk-oo
163 *W13* **Myohyang-sanmaek** ▲▲ C North Korea
164 *M11* **Myōkō-san** ▲ Honshū, S Japan *36°54′N 138°05′E*
83 *J15* **Myooye** Central, C Zambia *15°11′S 27°10′E*
118 *K12* **Myory** *prev.* Miyory. Vitsyebskaya Voblasts', N Belarus *55°39′N 27°39′E*
92 *J4* **Mýrdalsjökull** *glacier* S Iceland
92 *G10* **Myre** Nordland, C Norway *68°54′N 15°04′E*
117 *S5* **Myrhorod** *Rus.* Mirgorod. Poltavs'ka Oblast', NE Ukraine *49°58′N 33°37′E*
115 *J15* **Mýrina** *var.* Mírina. Límnos, SE Greece *39°52′N 25°04′E*
117 *P5* **Myronivka** *Rus.* Mironovka. Kyyivs'ka Oblast', N Ukraine *49°40′N 30°59′E*
21 *U13* **Myrtle Beach** South Carolina, SE USA *33°41′N 78°53′W*
32 *F14* **Myrtle Creek** Oregon, NW USA *43°01′N 123°19′W*
183 *P11* **Myrtleford** Victoria, SE Australia *36°34′S 146°45′E*
32 *E14* **Myrtle Point** Oregon, NW USA *43°04′N 124°08′W*
115 *K25* **Mýrtos** Kríti, Greece, E Mediterranean Sea *35°00′N 25°34′E*
Myrtoum Mare *see* Mirtóo Pélagos
93 *G17* **Myrviken** Jämtland, C Sweden *62°59′N 14°19′E*
95 *I15* **Mysen** Østfold, S Norway *59°33′N 11°20′E*
124 *L15* **Myshkin** Yaroslavskaya Oblast', NW Russian Federation *57°47′N 38°28′E*
111 *K17* **Myślenice** Małopolskie, S Poland *49°50′N 19°55′E*
110 *D10* **Myślibórz** Zachodnio-pomorskie, NW Poland *52°55′N 14°51′E*
155 *G20* **Mysore** *var.* Maisur. Karnātaka, W India *12°18′N 76°37′E*
Mysore *see* Karnātaka
115 *F21* **Mystrás** *var.* Mistras. Pelopónnisos, S Greece *37°03′N 22°22′E*
111 *K15* **Myszków** Śląskie, S Poland *50°36′N 19°20′E*
167 *T14* **My Tho** *var.* Mi Tho. Tiên Giang, S Vietnam *10°21′N 106°21′E*
Mytilene *see* Mytilíni
115 *L17* **Mytilíni** *var.* Mitilíni; *anc.* Mytilene. Lésvos, E Greece *39°06′N 26°33′E*
126 *K3* **Mytishchi** Moskovskaya Oblast', W Russian Federation *56°00′N 37°51′E*
37 *N3* **Myton** Utah, W USA *40°11′N 110°03′W*
92 *K2* **Mývatn** ◎ C Iceland
125 *T11* **Myyëldino** *var.* Myjeldino. Respublika Komi, NW Russian Federation *61°46′N 54°48′E*
82 *M13* **Mzimba** Northern, NW Malawi *11°56′S 33°36′E*
82 *M12* **Mzuzu** Northern, N Malawi *11°23′S 34°03′E*

N

101 *M19* **Naab** ≋ SE Germany
98 *G12* **Naaldwijk** Zuid-Holland, W Netherlands *52°00′N 04°13′E*
38 *G12* **Nā'ālehu** *var.* Naalehu. Hawaii, USA, C Pacific Ocean *19°04′N 155°36′W*
93 *K19* **Naantali** *Swe.* Nådendal. Länsi-Suomi, SW Finland *60°28′N 22°05′E*
98 *J10* **Naarden** Noord-Holland, C Netherlands *52°18′N 05°10′E*
109 *U4* **Naarn** ≋ N Austria
97 *F18* **Naas** *Ir.* An Nás, Nás na Ríogh. Kildare, C Ireland *53°13′N 06°39′W*
92 *M9* **Näätämöjoki** *Lapp.* Njávdám. ≋ NE Finland
83 *E23* **Nababeep** *var.* Nababiep. Northern Cape, W South Africa *29°36′S 17°46′E*
Nababiep *see* Nababeep
Nabadwip *see* Navadwīp
155 *L14* **Nabarangapur** *var.* Nowrangapur. Orissa, E India *19°13′N 82°33′E*
164 *J14* **Nabari** Mie, Honshū, SW Japan *34°37′N 136°05′E*
Nabatié *see* Nabatîyé
138 *G8* **Nabatîyé** *var.* An Nabatīyah at Taḥtā, Nabatié, Nabatiyet et Tahta. SW Lebanon *33°18′N 35°36′E*
Nabatiyet et Tahta *see* Nabatîyé
187 *X14* **Nabavatu** Vanua Levu, N Fiji *16°35′S 178°55′E*
190 *I2* **Nabeina** *island* Tungaru, W Kiribati
127 *T4* **Naberezhnyye Chelny** *prev.* Brezhnev. Respublika Tatarstan, W Russian Federation *55°43′N 52°21′E*
39 *T10* **Nabesna** Alaska, USA *62°22′N 143°00′W*
39 *T10* **Nabesna River** ≋ Alaska, USA
75 *N5* **Nabeul** *var.* Nābul. NE Tunisia *36°32′N 10°45′E*
152 *I9* **Nābha** Punjab, NW India *30°22′N 76°12′E*
171 *W13* **Nabire** Papua, E Indonesia *03°23′S 135°31′E*
141 *O15* **Nabī Shu'ayb, Jabal an** ▲ W Yemen *15°24′N 44°04′E*
138 *F10* **Nablus** *var.* Nābulus, *Heb.* Shekhem; *anc.* Neapolis, *Bibl.* Shechem. N West Bank *32°13′N 35°16′E*
187 *X14* **Nabouwalu** Vanua Levu, N Fiji *17°00′S 178°43′E*
Nābul *see* Nabeul
Nābulus *see* Nablus
187 *Y13* **Nabuna** Vanua Levu, N Fiji *16°13′S 179°46′E*
83 *Q14* **Nacala** Nampula, NE Mozambique *14°30′S 40°37′E*
42 *H8* **Nacaome** Valle, S Honduras *13°30′N 87°31′W*
Na Cealla Beaga *see* Killybegs
Na-Ch'ii *see* Nagqu
164 *J15* **Nachikatsuura** *var.* Nachi-Katsuura. Wakayama, Honshū, SE Japan *33°37′N 135°54′E*
Nachi-Katsuura *see* Nachikatsuura
81 *J24* **Nachingwea** Lindi, SE Tanzania *10°21′S 38°46′E*
111 *F16* **Náchod** Královéhradecký Kraj, N Czech Republic *50°26′N 16°10′E*
Na Clocha Liatha *see* Greystones
40 *G3* **Naco** Sonora, NW Mexico *31°16′N 109°56′W*
25 *X8* **Nacogdoches** Texas, SW USA *31°36′N 94°40′W*
40 *G4* **Nacozari de García** Sonora, NW Mexico *30°27′N 109°43′W*
Nada *see* Danzhou
77 *O14* **Nadawli** NW Ghana *10°30′N 02°40′W*
104 *I3* **Nadela** Galicia, NW Spain *42°58′N 07°33′W*
Nådendal *see* Naantali
144 *M7* **Nadezhdinka** *prev.* Nadezhdinskiy. Kostanay, N Kazakhstan *53°46′N 63°44′E*
Nadezhdinskiy *see* Nadezhdinka
Nadgan *see* Nadqān, Qalamat
187 *W14* **Nadi** *prev.* Nandi. Viti Levu, W Fiji *17°47′S 177°32′E*
187 *X14* **Nadi** *prev.* Nandi. ✈ Viti Levu, W Fiji *17°46′S 177°28′E*
154 *D10* **Nadiād** Gujarāt, W India *22°42′N 72°55′E*
Nadikdik *see* Knox Atoll
116 *E11* **Nădlac** *Ger.* Nadlak, *Hung.* Nagylak. Arad, W Romania *46°10′N 20°47′E*
Nadlak *see* Nădlac
74 *H6* **Nador** *prev.* Villa Nador. NE Morocco *35°10′N 05°22′W*
141 *S9* **Nadqān, Qalamat** *var.* Nadgan. *well* E Saudi Arabia
111 *N22* **Nádudvar** Hajdú-Bihar, E Hungary *47°36′N 21°09′E*
121 *O15* **Nadur** Gozo, N Malta *36°03′N 14°18′E*
187 *X13* **Naduri** *prev.* Nanduri. Vanua Levu, N Fiji *16°26′S 179°08′E*
116 *I7* **Nadvirna** *Pol.* Nadwórna, *Rus.* Nadvornaya. Ivano-Frankivs'ka Oblast', W Ukraine *48°27′N 24°30′E*
124 *J8* **Nadvoitsy** Respublika Kareliya, NW Russian Federation *63°53′N 34°17′E*
Nadvornaya/Nadwórna *see* Nadvirna
122 *I9* **Nadym** Yamalo-Nenetskiy Avtonomnyy Okrug, N Russian Federation *65°25′N 72°40′E*
122 *I9* **Nadym** ≋ C Russian Federation
186 *E7* **Nadzab** Morobe, C Papua New Guinea *06°36′S 146°46′E*
95 *C17* **Nærbø** Rogaland, S Norway *58°40′N 05°39′E*
95 *I24* **Næstved** Storstrøm, SE Denmark *55°12′N 11°47′E*
77 *X13* **Nafada** Gombe, E Nigeria *11°02′N 11°18′E*
108 *H8* **Näfels** Glarus, NE Switzerland *47°06′N 09°04′E*
115 *E18* **Náfpaktos** *var.* Návpaktos. Dytikí Ellás, C Greece *38°23′N 21°50′E*
115 *F20* **Náfplio** *prev.* Návplion. Pelopónnisos, S Greece *37°34′N 22°50′E*
139 *U6* **Naft Khāneh** Diyālá, E Iraq *34°01′N 45°26′E*
149 *N13* **Nāg** Baluchistān, SW Pakistan *27°43′N 65°31′E*
171 *P4* **Naga** *off.* Naga City; *prev.* Nueva Caceres. Luzon, N Philippines *13°36′N 123°10′E*
Nagaarzê *see* Nagarzê
Naga City *see* Naga
12 *F11* **Nagagami** ≋ Ontario, S Canada
164 *F14* **Nagahama** Ehime, Shikoku, SW Japan *33°36′N 132°29′E*
153 *X12* **Nāga Hills** ▲▲ NE India
165 *P10* **Nagai** Yamagata, Honshū, C Japan *38°08′N 140°00′E*
Na Gaibhlte *see* Galty Mountains
39 *N16* **Nagai Island** *island* Shumagin Islands, Alaska, USA
153 *X12* **Nāgāland** ◈ *state* NE India
164 *M11* **Nagano** Nagano, Honshū, S Japan *36°39′N 138°11′E*
164 *M12* **Nagano** *off.* Nagano-ken. ◈ *prefecture* Honshū, S Japan
Nagano-ken *see* Nagano
165 *N11* **Nagaoka** Niigata, Honshū, C Japan *37°26′N 138°48′E*
153 *W12* **Nagaon** *prev.* Nowgong. Assam, NE India *26°21′N 92°41′E*
155 *J21* **Nāgappattinam** *var.* Negapatam, Negapattinam. Tamil Nādu, SE India *10°45′N 79°50′E*
Nagara Nayok *see* Nakhon Nayok
Nagara Panom *see* Nakhon Phanom
Nagara Pathom *see* Nakhon Pathom
Nagara Sridharmaraj *see* Nakhon Si Thammarat
Nagara Svarga *see* Nakhon Sawan
155 *H16* **Nāgārjuna Sāgar** ⊠ E India
42 *I10* **Nagarote** León, SW Nicaragua *12°15′N 86°35′W*
158 *M16* **Nagarzê** *var.* Nagaarzê. Xizang Zizhiqu, W China *28°57′N 90°26′E*
164 *C14* **Nagasaki** Nagasaki, Kyūshū, SW Japan *32°45′N 129°52′E*
164 *C14* **Nagasaki** *off.* Nagasaki-ken. ◈ *prefecture* Kyūshū, SW Japan
Nagasaki-ken *see* Nagasaki
Nagashima *see* Kii-Nagashima
164 *E12* **Nagato** Yamaguchi, Honshū, SW Japan *34°22′N 131°10′E*
152 *F11* **Nāgaur** Rājasthān, NW India *27°12′N 73°48′E*
154 *F10* **Nāgda** Madhya Pradesh, C India *23°30′N 75°29′E*
98 *L8* **Nagele** Flevoland, N Netherlands *52°39′N 05°43′E*
155 *H24* **Nāgercoil** Tamil Nādu, SE India *08°11′N 77°30′E*
153 *X12* **Nāginimāra** Nāgāland, NE India *26°44′N 94°51′E*
Na Gleannta *see* Glenties
165 *T16* **Nago** Okinawa, Okinawa, SW Japan *26°36′N 127°59′E*
154 *K9* **Nāgod** Madhya Pradesh, C India *24°34′N 80°34′E*
155 *J26* **Nagoda** Southern Province, S Sri Lanka *06°13′N 80°13′E*
101 *G22* **Nagold** Baden-Württemberg, SW Germany *48°33′N 08°43′E*
137 *V12* **Nagorno-Karabakh** *var.* Nagorno- Karabakhskaya Avtonomnaya Oblast, *Arm.* Lerrnayin Gharabakh, *Az.* Dağliq Quarabağ, *Rus.* Nagornyy Karabakh. *former autonomous region* SW Azerbaijan
Nagorno- Karabakhskaya Avtonomnaya Oblast *see* Nagorno-Karabakh
123 *Q12* **Nagornyy** Respublika Sakha (Yakutiya), NE Russian Federation *55°53′N 124°58′E*
Nagornyy Karabakh *see* Nagorno-Karabakh
125 *R13* **Nagorsk** Kirovskaya Oblast', NW Russian Federation *59°18′N 50°49′E*
164 *K13* **Nagoya** Aichi, Honshū, SW Japan *35°10′N 136°53′E*
154 *I12* **Nāgpur** Mahārāshtra, C India *21°09′N 79°06′E*
156 *K10* **Nagqu** *Chin.* Na-Ch'ii; *prev.* Hei-ho. Xizang Zizhiqu, W China *31°30′N 91°57′E*
152 *J8* **Nāg Tibba Range** ▲▲ N India
45 *O8* **Nagua** NE Dominican Republic *19°25′N 69°49′W*
111 *H25* **Nagyatád** Somogy, SW Hungary *46°15′N 17°25′E*
Nagybánya *see* Baia Mare
Nagybecskerek *see* Zrenjanin
Nagydisznód *see* Cisnădie
Nagyenyed *see* Aiud
111 *N21* **Nagykálló** Szabolcs-Szatmár-Bereg, E Hungary *47°50′N 21°47′E*
111 *G25* **Nagykanizsa** *Ger.* Grosskanizsa. Zala, SW Hungary *46°27′N 17°E*
Nagykároly *see* Carei
111 *K22* **Nagykáta** Pest, C Hungary *47°25′N 19°45′E*
Nagykikinda *see* Kikinda
111 *K23* **Nagykőrös** Pest, C Hungary *47°01′N 19°46′E*
Nagy-Küküllő *see* Târnava Mare
Nagylak *see* Nădlac
Nagymihály *see* Michalovce
Nagyrőce *see* Revúca
Nagysomkút *see* Şomcuta Mare
Nagysurány *see* Šurany
Nagyszalonta *see* Salonta
Nagyszeben *see* Sibiu
Nagyszentmiklós *see* Sânnicolau Mare
Nagyszöllös *see* Vynohradiv
Nagyszombat *see* Trnava
Nagytapolcsány *see* Topoľčany
Nagyvárad *see* Oradea
165 *S17* **Naha** Okinawa, Okinawa, SW Japan *26°10′N 127°40′E*
152 *J8* **Nāhan** Himāchal Pradesh, NW India *30°33′N 77°18′E*
Nahang, Rūd-e *see* Nihing
138 *F8* **Nahariya** *prev.* Nahariyya. Northern, N Israel *33°01′N 35°05′E*
Nahariyya *see* Nahariya
142 *L6* **Nahāvand** *var.* Nehavend. Hamadān, W Iran *34°13′N 48°21′E*
101 *F19* **Nahe** ≋ SW Germany
Na H-Iarmhidhe *see* Westmeath
189 *O13* **Nahnalaud** ▲ Pohnpei, E Micronesia
Nahoi, Cape *see* Cumberland, Cape
Nahtavárr *see* Nattavaara
63 *H16* **Nahuel Huapí, Lago** ◎ W Argentina
23 *W7* **Nahunta** Georgia, SE USA *31°11′N 81°58′W*
40 *J6* **Naica** Chihuahua, N Mexico *27°53′N 105°30′W*
11 *U15* **Naicam** Saskatchewan, S Canada *52°26′N 104°30′W*
Naiman Qi *see* Daqin Tal
158 *M4* **Naimin Bulak** *spring* NW China
13 *P6* **Nain** Newfoundland and Labrador, NE Canada *56°33′N 61°46′W*
143 *P8* **Nā'īn** Eşfahān, C Iran *32°52′N 53°05′E*
152 *K10* **Naini Tāl** Uttarakhand, N India *29°22′N 79°26′E*
154 *J11* **Nainpur** Madhya Pradesh, C India *22°26′N 80°10′E*
96 *J8* **Nairn** N Scotland, United Kingdom *57°36′N 03°51′W*
96 *I8* **Nairn** *cultural region* NE Scotland, United Kingdom
81 *I19* **Nairobi** ● (Kenya) Nairobi Area, S Kenya *01°17′S 36°50′E*
81 *I19* **Nairobi** ✈ Nairobi Area, S Kenya *01°21′S 37°01′E*
82 *P13* **Nairoto** Cabo Delgado, NE Mozambique *12°22′S 39°05′E*
118 *G3* **Naissaar** *island* N Estonia
Naissus *see* Niš
187 *Z14* **Naitaba** *var.* Naitauba; *prev.* Naitamba. *island* Lau Group, E Fiji
Naitamba/Naitauba *see* Naitaba
81 *I19* **Naivasha** Rift Valley, SW Kenya *0°44′S 36°26′E*
81 *H19* **Naivasha, Lake** ◎ SW Kenya
Najaf *see* An Najaf
143 *N8* **Najafābād** *var.* Nejafabad. Eşfahān, C Iran *32°38′N 51°23′E*
141 *N7* **Najd** *var.* Nejd. *cultural region* C Saudi Arabia
105 *O4* **Nájera** La Rioja, N Spain *42°25′N 02°45′W*
105 *P4* **Najerilla** ≋ N Spain
163 *U7* **Naji** *var.* Arun Qi. Nei Mongol Zizhiqu, N China *48°05′N 123°28′E*
152 *J9* **Najībābād** Uttar Pradesh, N India *29°37′N 78°19′E*
Najima *see* Fukuoka
163 *Y11* **Najin** NE North Korea *42°13′N 130°16′E*
139 *T9* **Najm al Ḥassūn** Bābil, C Iraq *32°24′N 44°13′E*
141 *O13* **Najrān** *var.* Abā as Su'ūd. Najrān, S Saudi Arabia *17°31′N 44°09′E*
141 *P12* **Najrān** *var.* Minṭaqat al Najrān. ◈ *province* S Saudi Arabia
Najrān, Minṭaqat al *see* Najrān
165 *T2* **Nakagawa** Hokkaidō, NE Japan *44°49′N 142°04′E*
38 *F9* **Nākālele Point** *var.* Nakalele Point. *headland* Maui, Hawai'i, USA *21°01′N 156°35′W*
164 *D13* **Nakama** Fukuoka, Kyūshū, SW Japan *33°53′N 130°48′E*
Nakambé *see* White Volta
Nakamti *see* Nek'emtē
164 *F15* **Nakamura** *var.* Shimanto. Kōchi, Shikoku, SW Japan *33°00′N 132°55′E*
186 *H7* **Nakanai Mountains** ▲▲ New Britain, E Papua New Guinea
164 *H11* **Nakano-shima** *island* Oki-shotō, SW Japan
165 *Q6* **Nakasato** Aomori, Honshū, C Japan *40°58′N 140°26′E*
165 *T5* **Nakasatsunai** Hokkaidō, NE Japan *42°42′N 143°09′E*
165 *W4* **Nakashibetsu** Hokkaidō, NE Japan *43°31′N 144°58′E*
81 *F18* **Nakasongola** C Uganda *01°19′N 32°28′E*
165 *T1* **Nakatonbetsu** Hokkaidō, NE Japan *44°58′N 142°18′E*
164 *L13* **Nakatsugawa** *var.* Nakatugawa. Gifu, Honshū, SW Japan *35°30′N 137°29′E*
Nakatugawa *see* Nakatsugawa
Nakdong *see* Naktong-gang
Nakel *see* Nakło nad Notecią
Nakfa *see* Nakh'fa
80 *J8* **Nakh'fa** *var.* Nakfa. N Eritrea *16°38′N 38°26′E*
Nakhichevan' *see* Naxçıvan
123 *S15* **Nakhodka** Primorskiy Kray, SE Russian Federation *42°46′N 132°48′E*
122 *J8* **Nakhodka** Yamalo-Nenetskiy Avtonomnyy Okrug, N Russian Federation *67°48′N 77°48′E*
Nakhon Navok *see* Nakhon Nayok
167 *P11* **Nakhon Nayok** *var.* Nagara Nayok, Nakhon Navok. Nakhon Nayok, C Thailand *14°15′N 101°12′E*
167 *O11* **Nakhon Pathom** *var.* Nagara Pathom, Nakorn Pathom. Nakhon Pathom, W Thailand *13°49′N 100°06′E*
167 *R8* **Nakhon Phanom** *var.* Nagara Panom. Nakhon Phanom, E Thailand *17°22′N 104°46′E*
167 *Q10* **Nakhon Ratchasima** *var.* Khorat, Korat. Nakhon Ratchasima, E Thailand *15°N 102°06′E*
167 *O9* **Nakhon Sawan** *var.* Muang Nakhon Sawan, Nagara Svarga. Nakhon Sawan, W Thailand *15°42′N 100°06′E*
167 *N15* **Nakhon Si Thammarat** *var.* Nagara Sridharmaraj, Nakhon Sithamnaraj. Nakhon Si Thammarat, SW Thailand *08°24′N 99°58′E*
Nakhon Sithamnaraj *see* Nakhon Si Thammarat
139 *Y11* **Nakhrash** Al Başrah, SE Iraq *31°13′N 47°24′E*
10 *I9* **Nakina** British Columbia, W Canada *59°12′N 132°48′W*
110 *H9* **Nakło nad Notecią** *Ger.* Nakel. Kujawsko-pomorskie, C Poland *53°08′N 17°35′E*
39 *P13* **Naknek** Alaska, USA *58°45′N 157°01′W*
152 *H8* **Nakodar** Punjab, NW India *31°06′N 75°31′E*
82 *M11* **Nakonde** Northern, NE Zambia *09°22′S 42°47′E*
Nakorn Pathom *see* Nakhon Pathom
95 *H24* **Nakskov** Storstrøm, SE Denmark *54°50′N 11°10′E*
163 *Y15* **Naktong-gang** *var.* Nakdong, *Jap.* Rakutō-kō. ≋ C South Korea
81 *H18* **Nakuru** Rift Valley, SW Kenya *0°16′S 36°04′E*
81 *H19* **Nakuru, Lake** ◎ Rift Valley, C Kenya
11 *O17* **Nakusp** British Columbia, SW Canada *50°14′N 117°48′W*
149 *N15* **Nāl** ≋ W Pakistan
162 *M7* **Nalayh** Töv, C Mongolia *47°48′N 107°17′E*
153 *V12* **Nalbāri** Assam, NE India *26°36′N 91°49′E*
63 *G19* **Nalcayec, Isla** *island* Archipiélago de los Chonos, S Chile
127 *N15* **Nal'chik** Kabardino-Balkarskaya Respublika, SW Russian Federation *43°30′N 43°39′E*
155 *I16* **Nalgonda** Andhra Pradesh, C India *17°04′N 79°15′E*
153 *S14* **Nalhāti** West Bengal, NE India *24°19′N 87°53′E*
153 *U14* **Nalitabari** Dhaka, N Bangladesh *25°06′N 90°11′E*
155 *I17* **Nallamala Hills** ▲▲ E India
136 *G12* **Nallıhan** Ankara, NW Turkey *40°12′N 31°22′E*
104 *K2* **Nalón** ≋ NW Spain
167 *N3* **Nalong** Kachin State, N Myanmar (Burma) *24°42′N 97°27′E*
75 *N8* **Nālūt** NW Libya *31°52′N 10°59′E*
171 *T14* **Nama** Pulau Manawoka, E Indonesia *04°07′S 131°22′E*
189 *Q16* **Nama** *island* C Micronesia
83 *O16* **Namacurra** Zambézia, NE Mozambique *17°31′S 37°03′E*
188 *F9* **Namai Bay** *bay* Babeldaob, N Palau
Namakal *see* Nāmakkal
29 *W2* **Namakan Lake** ◎ Canada/USA
143 *O6* **Namak, Daryācheh-ye** *marsh* N Iran
155 *H22* **Nāmakkal** *var.* Namakal. Tamil Nādu, SE India *11°13′N 78°10′E*
143 *T6* **Namak, Kavīr-e** *salt pan* NE Iran
167 *O6* **Namaklwe** Shan State, E Myanmar (Burma) *19°45′N 99°01′E*
Namaksār, Kowl-e/ Namakzār, Daryācheh-ye *see* Namakzar
148 *I5* **Namakzar** *Pash.* Daryācheh-ye Namakzār, Kowl-e Namaksār. *marsh* Afghanistan/Iran
171 *V15* **Namalau** Pulau Jursian, E Indonesia *05°50′S 134°43′E*
81 *I20* **Namanga** Rift Valley, S Kenya *02°33′S 36°48′E*
147 *S10* **Namangan** Namangan Viloyati, E Uzbekistan *40°59′N 71°34′E*
Namanganskaya Oblast' *see* Namangan Viloyati
147 *R10* **Namangan Viloyati** *Rus.* Namanganskaya Oblast'. ◈ *province* E Uzbekistan
83 *Q14* **Namapa** Nampula, NE Mozambique *13°43′S 39°48′E*
83 *C21* **Namaqualand** *physical region* S Namibia
81 *G18* **Namasagali** C Uganda *01°02′N 32°58′E*
186 *H6* **Namatanai** New Ireland, NE Papua New Guinea *03°40′S 152°26′E*
83 *I14* **Nambala** Central, C Zambia *15°04′S 26°56′E*
81 *J23* **Nambanje** Lindi, SE Tanzania *08°37′S 38°21′E*
183 *V2* **Nambour** Queensland, E Australia *26°40′S 152°52′E*
183 *V6* **Nambucca Heads** New South Wales, SE Australia *30°37′S 153°00′E*
159 *N15* **Nam Co** ◎ W China
167 *R5* **Nâm Cum** Lai Châu, N Vietnam *22°37′N 103°12′E*
Namdik *see* Namorik Atoll
167 *T6* **Nam Đinh** Nam Ha, N Vietnam *20°25′N 106°12′E*
99 *I20* **Namêche** Namur, SE Belgium *50°29′N 05°02′E*
30 *J4* **Namekagon Lake** ◎ Wisconsin, N USA
188 *F10* **Namekakl Passage** *passage* Babeldaob, N Palau
Namen *see* Namur
83 *P15* **Nametil** Nampula, NE Mozambique *15°46′S 39°21′E*
163 *X14* **Nam-gang** ≋ C North Korea
163 *Y16* **Nam-gang** ≋ S South Korea
163 *Y17* **Namhae-do** *Jap.* Nankai-tō. *island* S South Korea

◆ Country
● Country Capital
◇ Dependent Territory
○ Dependent Territory Capital
◈ Administrative Regions
✈ International Airport
▲ Mountain
▲▲ Mountain Range
Ѫ Volcano
≋ River
◎ Lake
⊠ Reservoir

NAMHOI – NEÁPOLI

- **Namhoi** *see* Foshan
- 83 C19 **Namib Desert** *desert* W Namibia
- 83 A15 **Namibe** *Port.* Moçâmedes, Mossâmedes. Namibe, SW Angola 15°10′S 12°09′E
- 83 A15 **Namibe** ◈ *province* SE Angola
- 83 C18 **Namibia** *off.* Republic of Namibia, *var.* South West Africa, *Afr.* Suidwes-Afrika, *Ger.* Deutsch-Südwestafrika; *prev.* German Southwest Africa, South-West Africa. ◆ *republic* S Africa
- 65 O17 **Namibia Plain** *undersea feature* S Atlantic Ocean
- **Namibia, Republic of** *see* Namibia
- 165 Q11 **Namie** Fukushima, Honshū, C Japan 37°29′N 140°58′E
- 165 Q7 **Namioka** Aomori, Honshū, C Japan 40°43′N 140°34′E
- 40 I5 **Namiquipa** Chihuahua, N Mexico 29°15′N 107°25′W
- 159 P15 **Namjagbarwa Feng** ▲ W China 29°39′N 95°00′E
- **Namka** *see* Doilungdêqên
- 171 R13 **Namlea** Pulau Buru, E Indonesia 03°12′S 127°06′E
- 158 L16 **Namling** Xizang Zizhiqu, W China 29°40′N 88°58′E
- **Namnetes** *see* Nantes
- 167 R8 **Nam Ngum** ≈ C Laos
- **Namo** *see* Namu Atoll
- 183 R5 **Namoi River** ≈ New South Wales, SE Australia
- 189 Q17 **Namoluk Atoll** *atoll* Mortlock Islands, C Micronesia
- 189 O15 **Namonuito Atoll** *atoll* Caroline Islands, C Micronesia
- 189 T9 **Namorik Atoll** *var.* Namdik. *atoll* Ralik Chain, S Marshall Islands
- 167 Q6 **Nam Ou** ≈ N Laos
- 32 M14 **Nampa** Idaho, NW USA 43°32′N 116°33′W
- 76 M11 **Nampala** Ségou, W Mali 15°21′N 05°32′W
- 163 W14 **Namp'o** SW North Korea 38°46′N 125°25′E
- 83 P15 **Nampula** Nampula, NE Mozambique 15°09′S 39°14′E
- 83 P15 **Nampula** *off.* Província de Nampula. ◈ *province* NE Mozambique
- **Nampula, Província de** *see* Nampula
- 163 W13 **Namsan-ni** NW North Korea 40°25′N 125°01′E
- **Namslau** *see* Namysłów
- 93 E15 **Namsos** Nord-Trøndelag, C Norway 64°28′N 11°31′E
- 93 F14 **Namsskogan** Nord-Trøndelag, C Norway 64°57′N 13°04′E
- 167 O6 **Nam Teng** ≈ E Myanmar (Burma)
- 167 P6 **Nam Tha** ≈ N Laos
- 123 Q10 **Namtsy** Respublika Sakha (Yakutiya), NE Russian Federation 62°42′N 129°30′E
- 167 N4 **Namtu** Shan State, E Myanmar (Burma) 23°04′N 97°26′E
- 10 J15 **Namu** British Columbia, SW Canada 51°46′N 127°49′W
- 189 T7 **Namu Atoll** *var.* Namo. *atoll* Ralik Chain, C Marshall Islands
- 187 Y15 **Namuka-i-lau** *island* Lau Group, E Fiji
- 83 O15 **Namuli, Mont** ▲ NE Mozambique 15°15′S 37°33′E
- 83 P14 **Namuno** Cabo Delgado, N Mozambique 13°39′S 38°50′E
- 99 I20 **Namur** *Dut.* Namen. Namur, SE Belgium 50°28′N 04°52′E
- 99 H21 **Namur** *Dut.* Namen. ◈ *province* S Belgium
- 83 D17 **Namutoni** Kunene, N Namibia 18°49′S 16°55′E
- 163 Y16 **Namwŏn** *Jap.* Nangen. S South Korea 35°24′N 127°20′E
- 111 H14 **Namysłów** *Ger.* Namslau. Opole, SW Poland 51°03′N 17°41′E
- 167 P7 **Nan** *var.* Muang Nan. Nan, NW Thailand 18°47′N 100°50′E
- 79 G15 **Nana** ≈ W Central African Republic
- 165 R5 **Nanae** Hokkaidō, NE Japan 41°55′N 140°40′E
- 79 I14 **Nana-Grébizi** ◈ *prefecture* N Central African Republic
- 10 L17 **Nanaimo** Vancouver Island, British Columbia, SW Canada 49°08′N 123°58′W
- 38 C9 **Nānākuli** *var.* Nanakuli. O'ahu, Hawaii, USA, C Pacific Ocean 21°23′N 158°09′W
- 79 G15 **Nana-Mambéré** ◈ *prefecture* W Central African Republic
- 161 R13 **Nan'an** Fujian, SE China 24°57′N 118°22′E
- 183 U2 **Nanango** Queensland, E Australia 26°42′S 151°58′E
- 164 L11 **Nanao** Ishikawa, Honshū, SW Japan 37°03′N 136°58′E
- 161 Q14 **Nan'ao Dao** *island* S China
- 164 L10 **Nanatsu-shima** *island* SW Japan
- 56 F8 **Nanay, Río** ≈ NE Peru
- 160 J8 **Nanbu** Sichuan, C China 31°19′N 106°02′E
- 163 X7 **Nancha** Heilongjiang, NE China 47°09′N 129°17′E
- 161 P10 **Nanchang** *var.* Nan-ch'ang, Nanch'ang-hsien. *province capital* Jiangxi, S China 28°38′N 115°58′E
- **Nan-ch'ang** *see* Nanchang
- **Nanch'ang-hsien** *see* Nanchang
- 161 P11 **Nancheng** *var.* Jianchang. Jiangxi, S China 27°37′N 116°37′E
- **Nan-ching** *see* Nanjing
- 160 J9 **Nanchong** Sichuan, C China 30°47′N 106°03′E
- 160 J10 **Nanchuan** Chongqing Shi, C China 29°06′N 107°13′E
- 103 T5 **Nancy** Meurthe-et-Moselle, NE France 48°40′N 06°11′E
- 185 A22 **Nancy Sound** *sound* South Island, New Zealand
- 152 L9 **Nanda Devi** ▲ NW India 30°27′N 80°00′E
- 42 J11 **Nandaime** Granada, SW Nicaragua 11°45′N 86°02′W
- 160 K13 **Nandan** *var.* Minami-Awaji. Guangxi Zhuangzu Zizhiqu, S China 25°03′N 107°31′E
- 155 H14 **Nānded** Mahārāshtra, C India 19°11′N 77°21′E
- 183 S5 **Nandewar Range** ▲▲ New South Wales, SE Australia
- **Nandi** *see* Nadi
- 160 E13 **Nanding He** ≈ China/Vietnam
- **Nándorhgy** *see* Oțelu Roșu
- 154 E11 **Nandurbār** Mahārāshtra, W India 21°22′N 74°18′E
- **Nanduri** *see* Naduri
- 155 I17 **Nandyāl** Andhra Pradesh, E India 15°30′N 78°28′E
- 161 P11 **Nanfeng** *var.* Qincheng. Jiangxi, S China 27°15′N 116°16′E
- **Nang** *see* Nangxian
- 79 E15 **Nanga Eboko** Centre, C Cameroon 04°38′N 12°21′E
- **Nangah Serawai** *see* Nangaserawai
- 149 W4 **Nanga Parbat** ▲ India/Pakistan 35°15′N 74°36′E
- 169 R11 **Nangapinoh** Borneo, C Indonesia 0°21′S 111°44′E
- 149 R5 **Nangarhār** ◈ *province* E Afghanistan
- 169 S11 **Nangaserawai** *var.* Nangah Serawai. Borneo, C Indonesia 0°20′S 112°26′E
- 169 Q12 **Nangatayap** Borneo, C Indonesia 01°30′S 110°33′E
- **Nangen** *see* Namwŏn
- 103 P5 **Nangis** Seine-et-Marne, N France 48°36′N 03°02′E
- 163 X13 **Nangnim-sanmaek** ▲▲ C North Korea
- 161 O4 **Nangong** Hebei, E China 37°22′N 115°20′E
- 159 Q14 **Nangqên** *var.* Xangda. Qinghai, C China 32°05′N 96°28′E
- 167 Q10 **Nang Rong** Buri Ram, E Thailand 14°37′N 102°48′E
- 159 O16 **Nangxian** *var.* Nang. Xizang Zizhiqu, W China 29°04′N 93°03′E
- **Nan Hai** *see* South China Sea
- 160 L8 **Nan He** ≈ C China
- 160 F12 **Nanhua** *var.* Longchuan. Yunnan, SW China 25°15′N 101°15′E
- **Naniwa** *see* Ōsaka
- 155 G20 **Nanjangūd** Karnātaka, W India 12°07′N 76°40′E
- 161 Q8 **Nanjing** *var.* Nan-ching, Nanking; *prev.* Chianning, Chian-ning, Kiang-ning, Jiangsu. *province capital* Jiangsu, E China 32°03′N 118°47′E
- **Nankai-tō** *see* Namhae-do
- 161 O12 **Nankang** *var.* Rongjiang. Jiangxi, S China 25°42′N 114°45′E
- **Nanking** *see* Nanjing
- 161 N13 **Nan Ling** ▲▲ S China
- 160 L15 **Nanliu Jiang** ≈ S China
- 189 P13 **Nan Madol** *ruins* Temwen Island, E Micronesia
- 160 K15 **Nanning** *var.* Nan-ning; *prev.* Yung-ning. Guangxi Zhuangzu Zizhiqu, S China 22°50′N 108°19′E
- **Nan-ning** *see* Nanning
- 196 M15 **Nanortalik** Kitaa, S Greenland 60°12′N 44°53′W
- **Nanouki** *see* Aranuka
- 160 H13 **Nanpan Jiang** ≈ S China
- 152 M11 **Nānpāra** Uttar Pradesh, N India 27°51′N 81°30′E
- 161 Q12 **Nanping** *var.* Nan-p'ing; *prev.* Yenping. Fujian, SE China 26°40′N 118°07′E
- **Nan-p'ing** *see* Nanping
- **Nanping** *see* Jiuzhaigou
- **Nanpu** *see* Pucheng
- 161 R12 **Nanri Dao** *island* SE China
- 165 S16 **Nansei-shotō** *Eng.* Ryukyu Islands. *island group* SW Japan
- **Nansei Syotō Trench** *see* Ryukyu Trench
- 197 T10 **Nansen Basin** *undersea feature* Arctic Ocean
- 197 T10 **Nansen Cordillera** *var.* Arctic Mid Oceanic Ridge, Nansen Ridge. *undersea feature* Arctic Ocean 87°00′N 90°00′E
- **Nansen Ridge** *see* Nansen Cordillera
- 129 T9 **Nan Shan** ▲▲ C China
- **Nansha Qundao** *see* Spratly Islands
- 12 K3 **Nantais, Lac** ◎ Québec, NE Canada
- 103 N5 **Nanterre** Hauts-de-Seine, N France 48°53′N 02°13′E
- 102 I8 **Nantes** *Bret.* Naoned; *anc.* Condivincum, Namnetes. Loire-Atlantique, NW France 47°12′N 01°32′W
- 14 G17 **Nanticoke** Ontario, S Canada 42°49′N 80°04′W
- 18 H13 **Nanticoke** Pennsylvania, NE USA 41°12′N 76°00′W
- 21 Y4 **Nanticoke River** ≈ Delaware/Maryland, NE USA
- 11 Q17 **Nanton** Alberta, SW Canada 50°21′N 113°47′W
- 161 S8 **Nantong** Jiangsu, E China 32°00′N 120°52′E
- 161 S13 **Nant'ou** W Taiwan 23°54′N 120°51′E
- 103 S10 **Nantua** Ain, E France 46°10′N 05°34′E
- 19 Q13 **Nantucket** Nantucket Island, Massachusetts, NE USA 41°15′N 70°05′W
- 19 Q13 **Nantucket Island** *island* Massachusetts, NE USA
- 19 Q13 **Nantucket Sound** *sound* Massachusetts, NE USA
- 82 P13 **Nantulo** Cabo Delgado, N Mozambique 12°30′S 39°03′E
- 189 O12 **Nanuh** Pohnpei, E Micronesia
- 190 D6 **Nanumaga** *var.* Nanumanga. *atoll* NW Tuvalu
- **Nanumanga** *see* Nanumaga
- 190 D5 **Nanumea Atoll** *atoll* NW Tuvalu
- 59 O19 **Nanuque** Minas Gerais, SE Brazil 17°49′S 40°21′W
- 171 R10 **Nanusa, Kepulauan** *island group* N Indonesia
- 163 U4 **Nanweng He** ≈ NE China
- 160 I10 **Nanxi** Sichuan, C China 28°54′N 104°59′E
- 161 N10 **Nanxian** *var.* Nan Xian, Nanzhou. Hunan, S China 29°23′N 112°18′E
- **Nan Xian** *see* Nanxian
- 161 N7 **Nanyang** *var.* Nan-yang. Henan, C China 32°59′N 112°29′E
- **Nan-yang** *see* Nanyang
- 161 P6 **Nanyang Hu** ◎ E China
- 165 P10 **Nan'yō** Yamagata, Honshū, C Japan 38°04′N 140°06′E
- 81 I18 **Nanyuki** Central, C Kenya 0°01′N 37°05′E
- 160 M8 **Nanzhang** Hubei, C China 31°47′N 111°48′E
- **Nanzhou** *see* Nanxian
- 105 T11 **Nao, Cabo de La** *headland* E Spain 38°43′N 00°13′E
- 12 M9 **Naococane, Lac** ◎ Québec, E Canada
- 153 S14 **Naogaon** Rajshahi, NW Bangladesh 24°49′N 88°59′E
- **Naokot** *see* Naukot
- 187 R13 **Naone** Maewo, C Vanuatu 15°03′S 168°06′E
- **Naoned** *see* Nantes
- 115 E14 **Náousa** Kentrikí Makedonía, N Greece 40°38′N 22°04′E
- 35 N8 **Napa** California, W USA 38°15′N 122°17′W
- 39 O11 **Napaimiut** Alaska, USA 61°32′N 158°46′W
- 39 N12 **Napakiak** Alaska, USA 60°42′N 161°57′W
- 122 J7 **Napalkovo** Yamalo-Nenetskiy Avtonomnyy Okrug, N Russian Federation 70°06′N 73°43′E
- 12 I16 **Napanee** Ontario, SE Canada 44°13′N 76°57′W
- 39 N12 **Napaskiak** Alaska, USA 60°42′N 161°46′W
- 167 S5 **Na Phac** Cao Băng, N Vietnam 22°24′N 105°54′E
- 184 O11 **Napier** Hawke's Bay, North Island, New Zealand 39°30′S 176°55′E
- 195 X3 **Napier Mountains** ▲▲ Antarctica
- 15 O13 **Napierville** Québec, SE Canada 45°12′N 73°25′W
- 23 W15 **Naples** Florida, SE USA 26°08′N 81°48′W
- 25 W5 **Naples** Texas, SW USA 33°12′N 94°40′W
- **Naples** *see* Napoli
- 160 I14 **Napo** Guangxi Zhuangzu Zizhiqu, S China 23°21′N 105°47′E
- 56 C6 **Napo** ◈ *province* NE Ecuador
- 29 O6 **Napoleon** North Dakota, N USA 46°30′N 99°46′W
- 31 R11 **Napoleon** Ohio, N USA 41°23′N 84°07′W
- **Napoléon-Vendée** *see* la Roche-sur-Yon
- 22 J9 **Napoleonville** Louisiana, S USA 29°55′N 91°01′W
- 107 K17 **Napoli** *Eng.* Naples, *Ger.* Neapel; *anc.* Neapolis. Campania, S Italy 40°52′N 14°15′E
- 107 J18 **Napoli, Golfo di** *gulf* S Italy
- 57 F7 **Napo, Río** ≈ Ecuador/Peru
- 191 W9 **Napuka** *island* Îles Tuamotu, C French Polynesia
- 142 J3 **Naqadeh** Āžarbāyjān-e Bākhtarī, NW Iran 36°57′N 45°24′E
- 139 U6 **Naqnah** Diyālá, E Iraq 34°13′N 45°33′E
- **Nar** *see* Nera
- 164 J14 **Nara** Nara, Honshū, SW Japan 34°41′N 135°49′E
- 76 L11 **Nara** Koulikoro, W Mali 15°04′N 07°19′W
- 149 R14 **Nāra Canal** *irrigation canal* S Pakistan
- 182 K11 **Naracoorte** South Australia 37°02′S 140°45′E
- 183 P8 **Naradhan** New South Wales, SE Australia 33°37′S 146°19′E
- **Naradhivas** *see* Narathiwat
- 56 B8 **Naranjal** Guayas, W Ecuador 02°43′S 79°38′W
- 57 Q19 **Naranjos** Santa Cruz, E Bolivia
- 41 Q12 **Naranjos** Veracruz-Llave, E Mexico 21°21′N 97°41′W
- 159 Q6 **Naran Sebstein Bulag** *spring* NW China
- 164 B14 **Narao** Nagasaki, Nakadōri-jima, SW Japan 32°40′N 129°03′E
- 155 J16 **Narasaraopet** Andhra Pradesh, E India 16°16′N 80°06′E
- 158 J5 **Narat** Xinjiang Uygur Zizhiqu, W China 43°20′N 84°02′E
- 167 P17 **Narathiwat** *var.* Naradhivas. Narathiwat, SW Thailand 06°25′N 101°48′E
- 37 V10 **Nara Visa** New Mexico, SW USA 35°35′N 103°06′W
- **Nārāyāni** *see* Gandak
- **Narbada** *see* Narmada
- **Narbo Martius** *see* Narbonne
- 103 P16 **Narbonne** *anc.* Narbo Martius. Aude, S France 43°11′N 03°E
- **Narborough Island** *see* Fernandina, Isla
- 104 J2 **Narcea** ≈ NW Spain
- 152 J9 **Narendranagar** Uttarakhand, N India 30°10′N 78°21′E
- **Nares Abyssal Plain** *see* Nares Plain
- 64 G11 **Nares Plain** *var.* Nares Abyssal Plain. *undersea feature* NW Atlantic Ocean 23°30′N 63°00′W
- **Nares Stræde** *see* Nares Strait
- 197 P10 **Nares Strait** *Dan.* Nares Stræde. *strait* Canada/Greenland
- 110 O9 **Narew** ≈ E Poland
- 155 F17 **Nargund** Karnātaka, W India 15°43′N 75°23′E
- 83 D20 **Narib** Hardap, S Namibia 24°11′S 17°46′E
- **Narikrik** *see* Knox Atoll
- **Narin Gol** *see* Dong He
- 54 B13 **Nariño** *off.* Departamento de Narino. ◈ *province* SW Colombia
- 165 P13 **Narita** Chiba, Honshū, S Japan 35°46′N 140°20′E
- 165 P13 **Narita** ✈ (Tōkyō) Chiba, Honshū, S Japan 35°45′N 140°23′E
- **Narıya** *see* An Nu'ayrīyah
- 162 F5 **Nariyn Gol** ≈ Mongolia/Russian Federation
- 162 J8 **Nariynteel** *var.* Tsagaan-Ovoo. Övörhangay, C Mongolia 45°57′N 101°25′E
- 152 J8 **Nārkanda** Himāchal Pradesh, NW India 31°14′N 77°27′E
- 92 L13 **Narkaus** Lappi, NW Finland 66°13′N 26°09′E
- 154 E11 **Narmada** *var.* Narbada. ≈ C India
- 152 H11 **Narnaul** *var.* Nārnaul. Haryāna, N India 28°04′N 76°10′E
- 107 I14 **Narni** Umbria, C Italy 42°31′N 12°31′E
- 107 J24 **Naro** Sicilia, Italy, C Mediterranean Sea 37°18′N 13°48′E
- **Narodichi** *see* Narodychi
- 125 V7 **Narodnaya, Gora** ▲ NW Russian Federation 65°04′N 60°12′E
- 117 N3 **Narodychi** *Rus.* Narodichi. Zhytomyrs'ka Oblast', N Ukraine 51°11′N 29°01′E
- 126 J4 **Naro-Fominsk** Moskovskaya Oblast', W Russian Federation 55°25′N 36°41′E
- 81 H19 **Narok** Rift Valley, SW Kenya 01°04′S 35°54′E
- 104 H2 **Narón** Galicia, NW Spain 43°31′N 08°08′W
- 183 S11 **Narooma** New South Wales, SE Australia 36°16′S 150°08′E
- **Narova** *see* Narva
- **Narovlya** *see* Narowlya
- 149 W8 **Nārowāl** Punjab, E Pakistan 32°04′N 74°54′E
- 119 N20 **Narowlya** *Rus.* Narovlya. Homyel'skaya Voblasts', SE Belarus 51°48′N 29°30′E
- 93 J17 **Närpes** *Fin.* Närpiö. Länsi-Suomi, W Finland 62°28′N 21°19′E
- **Närpiö** *see* Närpes
- 183 S5 **Narrabri** New South Wales, SE Australia 30°21′S 149°48′E
- 183 P9 **Narrandera** New South Wales, SE Australia 34°46′S 146°32′E
- 183 Q4 **Narran Lake** ◎ New South Wales, SE Australia
- 183 Q4 **Narran River** ≈ New South Wales/Queensland, SE Australia
- 180 J13 **Narrogin** Western Australia 32°53′S 117°17′E
- 183 Q7 **Narromine** New South Wales, SE Australia 32°16′S 148°15′E
- 21 R6 **Narrows** Virginia, NE USA 37°19′N 80°48′W
- 196 M15 **Narsarsuaq** ✈ Kitaa, S Greenland 61°07′N 45°03′W
- 154 I10 **Narsimhapur** Madhya Pradesh, C India 22°58′N 79°15′E
- 153 U15 **Narsingdi** *var.* Narsinghdi. Dhaka, C Bangladesh 23°56′N 90°40′E
- **Narsinghdi** *see* Narsingdi
- 154 H9 **Narsinghgarh** Madhya Pradesh, C India 23°42′N 77°08′E
- 163 Q11 **Nart** Nei Mongol Zizhiqu, N China 42°54′N 115°55′E
- **Nartës, Gjol i/Nartës, Laguna e** *see* Nartës, Liqeni i
- 113 J22 **Nartës, Liqeni i** *var.* Gjol i Nartës, Laguna e Nartës. ◎ SW Albania
- 115 F17 **Nartháki** ▲ C Greece 39°12′N 22°24′E
- 127 O15 **Nartkala** Kabardino-Balkarskaya Respublika, SW Russian Federation 43°34′N 43°55′E
- 118 K3 **Narva** Ida-Virumaa, NE Estonia 59°23′N 28°12′E
- 118 K4 **Narva** *prev.* Narova. ≈ Estonia/Russian Federation
- 118 J3 **Narva Bay** *Est.* Narva Laht, *Ger.* Narwa-Bucht, *Rus.* Narvskiy Zaliv. *bay* Estonia/Russian Federation
- **Narva Laht** *see* Narva Bay
- 124 F13 **Narva Reservoir** *Est.* Narva Veehoidla, *Rus.* Narvskoye Vodokhranilishche. ⊠ Estonia/Russian Federation
- **Narva Veehoidla** *see* Narva Reservoir
- 92 H10 **Narvik** Nordland, C Norway 68°26′N 17°24′E
- **Narvskiy Zaliv** *see* Narva Bay
- **Narvskoye Vodokhranilishche** *see* Narva Reservoir
- **Narwa-Bucht** *see* Narva Bay
- 152 I9 **Narwāna** Haryāna, NW India 29°36′N 76°11′E
- 125 R4 **Nar'yan-Mar** *prev.* Beloshchel'ye, Dzerzhinskiy. Nenetskiy Avtonomnyy Okrug, NW Russian Federation 67°38′N 53°E
- 122 J12 **Narym** Tomskaya Oblast', C Russian Federation 58°59′N 81°20′E
- 145 Y10 **Narymskiy Khrebet** *Kaz.* Naryn Zhotasy. ▲▲ E Kazakhstan
- 147 W9 **Naryn** Narynskaya Oblast', C Kyrgyzstan 41°24′N 76°E
- 147 U8 **Naryn** ≈ Kyrgyzstan/Uzbekistan
- 145 W16 **Narynkol** *Kaz.* Narynqol. Almaty, SE Kazakhstan 42°45′N 80°12′E
- **Naryn Oblasty** *see* Narynskaya Oblast'
- **Narynqol** *see* Narynkol
- 147 V9 **Narynskaya Oblast'** *Kir.* Naryn Oblasty. ◈ *province* C Kyrgyzstan
- **Naryn Zhotasy** *see* Narymskiy Khrebet
- 126 J6 **Naryshkino** Orlovskaya Oblast', W Russian Federation 53°00′N 35°41′E
- 95 L14 **Nås** Dalarna, C Sweden 60°28′N 14°30′E
- 10 J11 **Nass** ≈ British Columbia, SW Canada
- 92 G13 **Nasafjellet** *Lapp.* Násávárre. ▲ C Norway 66°29′N 15°23′E
- 93 H16 **Näsåker** Västernorrland, C Sweden 63°27′N 16°55′E
- 44 H2 **Nassau** ● (Bahamas) New Providence, N Bahamas 25°03′N 77°21′W
- 187 Y14 **Nasau** Koro, C Fiji 17°20′S 179°26′E
- 44 H2 **Nassau** ✈ New Providence, C Bahamas 25°00′N 77°26′W
- 190 J13 **Nassau** *island* N Cook Islands
- 116 I9 **Năsăud** *Ger.* Nussdorf, *Hung.* Naszód. Bistrița-Năsăud, N Romania 47°16′N 24°24′E
- **Násávárre** *see* Nasafjellet
- 103 P13 **Nasbinals** Lozère, S France 44°40′N 03°03′E
- **Na Sceirí** *see* Skerries
- **Nase** *see* Naze
- 185 E22 **Naseby** Otago, South Island, New Zealand 45°02′S 170°09′E
- 143 R10 **Nāṣerīyeh** Kermān, C Iran
- 25 X5 **Nash** Texas, SW USA 33°26′N 94°04′W
- 154 E13 **Nāshik** *prev.* Nāsik. Mahārāshtra, W India 20°05′N 73°48′E
- 56 E7 **Nashiño, Río** ≈ Ecuador/Peru
- 29 W12 **Nashua** Iowa, C USA 42°57′N 92°32′W
- 33 W7 **Nashua** Montana, NW USA 48°06′N 106°16′W
- 19 O10 **Nashua** New Hampshire, NE USA 42°45′N 71°26′W
- 27 S13 **Nashville** Arkansas, C USA 33°57′N 93°50′W
- 23 U7 **Nashville** Georgia, SE USA 31°12′N 83°15′W
- 30 L16 **Nashville** Illinois, N USA 38°20′N 89°22′W
- 31 O14 **Nashville** Indiana, N USA 39°13′N 86°15′W
- 21 V9 **Nashville** North Carolina, SE USA 35°58′N 78°00′W
- 20 J8 **Nashville** *state capital* Tennessee, S USA 36°11′N 86°48′W
- 20 J9 **Nashville** ✈ Tennessee, S USA 36°06′N 86°44′W
- 64 H10 **Nashville Seamount** *undersea feature* NW Atlantic Ocean 30°00′N 57°20′W
- 112 H9 **Našice** Osijek-Baranja, E Croatia 45°29′N 18°05′E
- 110 M11 **Nasielsk** Mazowieckie, C Poland 52°33′N 20°46′E
- 93 K18 **Näsijärvi** ◎ SW Finland
- **Nāsik** *see* Nāshik
- 80 G13 **Nasir** Upper Nile, SE Sudan 08°37′N 33°06′E
- 148 K15 **Nasīrābād** Baluchistān, SW Pakistan 26°15′N 62°32′E
- **Nasir, Buhayrat/Nâşir,Buḥeiret** *see* Nasser, Lake
- **Nāsiri** *see* Ahvāz
- **Nasiriya** *see* An Nāşirīyah
- **Nás na Ríogh** *see* Naas
- 107 L23 **Naso** Sicilia, Italy, C Mediterranean Sea 38°07′N 14°46′E
- **Nasratabad** *see* Zābol
- 77 V15 **Nassarawa** Nassarawa, C Nigeria 08°33′N 07°42′E
- 23 W8 **Nassau Sound** *sound* Florida, SE USA
- 108 L7 **Nassereith** Tirol, W Austria 47°19′N 10°51′E
- 80 F5 **Nasser, Lake** *var.* Buhayrat Nasir, Buḥayrat Nāşir, Buḥeiret Nâşir. ◎ Egypt/Sudan
- 95 L19 **Nässjö** Jönköping, S Sweden 57°39′N 14°40′E
- 99 K22 **Nassogne** Luxembourg, SE Belgium 50°08′N 05°19′E
- 12 J6 **Nastapoka Islands** *island group* Northwest Territories, C Canada
- 93 M19 **Nastola** Etelä-Suomi, S Finland 60°57′N 25°56′E
- 171 O4 **Nasugbu** Luzon, N Philippines 14°03′N 120°39′E
- 94 N11 **Näsviken** Gävleborg, C Sweden 61°46′N 16°55′E
- **Naszód** *see* Năsăud
- 83 I17 **Nata** Central, NE Botswana 20°11′S 26°10′E
- 54 E11 **Natagaima** Tolima, C Colombia 03°38′N 75°07′W
- 59 Q14 **Natal** *state capital* Rio Grande do Norte, E Brazil 05°46′S 35°15′W
- 168 I11 **Natal** Sumatera, N Indonesia 0°32′N 99°07′E
- **Natal** *see* KwaZulu/Natal
- 173 L10 **Natal Basin** *var.* Mozambique Basin. *undersea feature* W Indian Ocean 30°00′S 40°00′E
- 25 R12 **Natalia** Texas, SW USA 29°11′N 98°51′W
- 67 W15 **Natal Valley** *undersea feature* SW Indian Ocean 31°00′S 33°15′E
- **Natanya** *see* Netanya
- 143 O7 **Naṭanz** Eşfahān, C Iran 33°31′N 51°55′E
- 13 Q11 **Natashquan** Québec, E Canada 50°10′N 61°50′W
- 13 Q10 **Natashquan** ≈ Newfoundland and Labrador/Québec, E Canada
- 22 J7 **Natchez** Mississippi, S USA 31°34′N 91°24′W
- 22 G6 **Natchitoches** Louisiana, S USA 31°45′N 93°05′W
- 108 E10 **Naters** Valais, S Switzerland 46°22′N 08°00′E
- **Nathanya** *see* Netanya
- 92 O3 **Nathorst Land** *physical region* W Svalbard
- 186 E9 **National Capital District** ◈ *province* S Papua New Guinea
- 35 U17 **National City** California, W USA 32°40′N 117°06′W
- 184 M10 **National Park** Manawatu-Wanganui, North Island, New Zealand 39°11′S 175°22′E
- 77 R14 **Natitingou** NW Benin 10°21′N 01°26′E
- 40 B5 **Natividad, Isla** *island* NW Mexico
- 165 Q10 **Natori** Miyagi, Honshū, C Japan 38°12′N 140°51′E
- 18 C14 **Natrona Heights** Pennsylvania, NE USA 40°37′N 79°42′W
- 81 H20 **Natron, Lake** ◎ Kenya/Tanzania
- **Natsrat** *see* Natzrat
- 166 L7 **Nattalin** Bago, C Myanmar (Burma) 18°25′N 95°34′E
- 92 J12 **Nattavaara** *Lapp.* Nahtavárr. Norrbotten, N Sweden 66°45′N 20°58′E
- 109 S3 **Natternbach** Oberösterreich, N Austria 48°26′N 13°44′E
- 95 M22 **Nättraby** Blekinge, S Sweden 56°12′N 15°30′E
- 169 P10 **Natuna Besar, Pulau** *island* Kepulauan Natuna, W Indonesia
- **Natuna Islands** *see* Natuna, Kepulauan
- 169 O9 **Natuna, Kepulauan** *var.* Natuna Islands. *island group* W Indonesia
- 169 N9 **Natuna, Laut** *Eng.* Natuna Sea. *sea* W Indonesia
- **Natuna Sea** *see* Natuna, Laut
- 21 N6 **Natural Bridge** *tourist site* Kentucky, C USA
- 173 V11 **Naturaliste Fracture Zone** *tectonic feature* E Indian Ocean
- 174 J10 **Naturaliste Plateau** *undersea feature* E Indian Ocean
- 138 G9 **Natzrat** *var.* Natsrat, *Ar.* En Nazira, *Eng.* Nazareth; *prev.* Nazerat. Northern, N Israel 32°42′N 35°18′E
- **Nau** *see* Nov
- 103 O14 **Naucelle** Aveyron, S France 44°10′N 02°19′E
- 83 D20 **Nauchas** Hardap, C Namibia 23°40′S 16°19′E
- 108 K9 **Nauders** Tirol, W Austria 46°52′N 10°31′E
- **Naugard** *see* Nowogard
- 153 N12 **Naugarh** Uttar Pradesh, N India 24°50′N 83°17′E
- 118 F12 **Naujamiestis** Panevėžys, C Lithuania 55°42′N 24°10′E
- 118 E10 **Naujoji Akmenė** Šiaulai, NW Lithuania 56°20′N 22°57′E
- 149 R16 **Naukot** *var.* Naokot. Sind, SE Pakistan 24°52′N 69°27′E
- 101 L16 **Naumburg** *var.* Naumburg an der Saale. Sachsen-Anhalt, C Germany 51°09′N 11°48′E
- **Naumburg am Queis** *see* Nowogrodziec
- **Naumburg an der Saale** *see* Naumburg
- 191 W15 **Naunau** *ancient monument* Easter Island, Chile, E Pacific Ocean
- **Nauparha** *see* Nūāparha
- 138 G10 **Nā'ūr** 'Ammān, W Jordan 31°52′N 35°50′E
- 189 Q8 **Nauru** *off.* Republic of Nauru; *prev.* Pleasant Island. ◆ *republic* W Pacific Ocean
- 175 P5 **Nauru** *island* W Pacific Ocean
- 189 Q9 **Nauru International** ✈ S Nauru
- **Nauru, Republic of** *see* Nauru
- **Nausari** *see* Navsāri
- 19 Q12 **Nauset Beach** *beach* Massachusetts, NE USA
- **Naushahra** *see* Nowshera
- 149 P14 **Naushahro Fīroz** Sind, SE Pakistan 26°51′N 68°11′E
- **Naushara** *see* Nowshera
- 187 X14 **Nausori** Viti Levu, W Fiji 18°01′S 178°31′E
- 56 F9 **Nauta** Loreto, N Peru 04°31′S 73°36′W
- 153 O12 **Nautanwa** Uttar Pradesh, N India 27°26′N 83°25′E
- 41 R13 **Nautla** Veracruz-Llave, E Mexico 20°15′N 96°45′W
- **Nauzad** *see* Now Zād
- 41 N6 **Nava** Coahuila, NE Mexico 28°28′N 100°45′W
- **Navabad** *see* Navobod
- 104 L6 **Nava del Rey** Castilla-León, N Spain 41°19′N 05°04′W
- 153 S15 **Navadwīp** *prev.* Nabadwip. West Bengal, NE India 23°24′N 88°23′E
- 104 M9 **Navahermosa** Castilla-La Mancha, C Spain 39°39′N 04°25′W
- 119 I16 **Navahrudak** *Pol.* Nowogródek, *Rus.* Novogrudok. Hrodzyenskaya Voblasts', W Belarus 53°36′N 25°50′E
- 119 I16 **Navahrudskaye Wzvyshsha** ▲▲ W Belarus
- 36 M8 **Navajo Mount** ▲ Utah, W USA 37°00′N 110°52′W
- 37 Q9 **Navajo Reservoir** ⊠ New Mexico, SW USA
- 104 K9 **Navalmoral de la Mata** Extremadura, W Spain 39°54′N 05°33′W
- 104 K10 **Navalvillar de Pelea** Extremadura, W Spain 39°05′N 05°27′W
- 97 F17 **Navan** *Ir.* An Uaimh. E Ireland 53°39′N 06°41′W
- **Navanagar** *see* Jāmnagar
- 118 L12 **Navapolatsk** *Rus.* Novopolotsk. Vitsyebskaya Voblasts', N Belarus 55°34′N 28°35′E
- 149 P6 **Nāvar, Dasht-e** *Pash.* Dasht-i-Nawar. *desert* C Afghanistan
- 123 W6 **Navarin, Mys** *headland* NE Russian Federation 62°18′N 179°06′E
- 63 I25 **Navarino, Isla** *island* S Chile
- 105 Q4 **Navarra** *Eng./Fr.* Navarre. ◈ *autonomous community* N Spain
- **Navarre** *see* Navarra
- 105 P4 **Navarrete** La Rioja, N Spain 42°26′N 02°34′W
- 61 C20 **Navarro** Buenos Aires, E Argentina 35°00′S 59°15′W
- 105 O12 **Navas de San Juan** Andalucía, S Spain 38°11′N 03°19′W
- 127 N4 **Navashino** Nizhegorodskaya Oblast', W Russian Federation 55°33′N 42°11′E
- 25 V10 **Navasota** Texas, SW USA 30°23′N 96°05′W
- 25 U9 **Navasota River** ≈ Texas, SW USA
- 44 I9 **Navassa Island** ◇ *US unincorporated territory* C West Indies
- 119 L19 **Navasyolki** *Rus.* Novosëlki. Homyel'skaya Voblasts', SE Belarus 52°24′N 28°33′E
- 119 H17 **Navayel'nya** *Pol.* Nowojelnia, *Rus.* Novoyel'nya. Hrodzyenskaya Voblasts', W Belarus 53°28′N 25°35′E
- 171 Y13 **Naver** Papua, E Indonesia 03°27′S 139°45′E
- 118 H5 **Navesti** ≈ C Estonia
- 104 J2 **Navia** Asturias, N Spain 43°33′N 06°43′W
- 104 J2 **Navia** ≈ NW Spain
- 59 I21 **Naviraí** Mato Grosso do Sul, SW Brazil 23°01′S 54°09′W
- 126 I6 **Navlya** Bryanskaya Oblast', W Russian Federation 52°47′N 34°28′E
- 187 X13 **Navoalevu** Vanua Levu, N Fiji 16°22′S 179°28′E
- 147 R12 **Navobod** *Rus.* Navabad, Novabad. C Tajikistan 39°00′N 70°06′E
- 147 P13 **Navobod** *Rus.* Navabad. W Tajikistan 38°37′N 68°42′E
- **Navoi** *see* Navoiy
- 146 M11 **Navoiy** *Rus.* Navoi. Navoiy Viloyati, C Uzbekistan 40°05′N 65°23′E
- **Navoiyskaya Oblast'** *see* Navoiy Viloyati
- 146 K8 **Navoiy Viloyati** *Rus.* Navoiyskaya Oblast'. ◈ *province* N Uzbekistan
- 40 G7 **Navojoa** Sonora, NW Mexico 27°04′N 109°28′W
- **Navolat** *see* Navolato
- 40 H9 **Navolato** *var.* Navolat. Sinaloa, C Mexico 24°46′N 107°42′W
- 187 Q13 **Navonda** Ambae, C Vanuatu 15°21′S 167°58′E
- **Návpaktos** *see* Náfpaktos
- **Návplion** *see* Náfplio
- 77 P14 **Navrongo** N Ghana 10°51′N 01°03′W
- 154 D12 **Navsāri** *var.* Nausari. Gujarāt, W India 20°55′N 72°55′E
- 187 X15 **Navua** Viti Levu, W Fiji 18°15′S 178°10′E
- 138 H8 **Nawá** Dar'ā, S Syria 32°53′N 36°03′E
- **Nawabashah** *see* Nawābshāh
- 153 S14 **Nawabganj** Rajshahi, NW Bangladesh 24°35′N 88°21′E
- 153 S14 **Nawābganj** Uttar Pradesh, N India 26°52′N 82°09′E
- 149 Q15 **Nawābshāh** *var.* Nawabashah. Sind, S Pakistan 26°15′N 68°26′E
- 153 P14 **Nawāda** Bihār, N India 24°54′N 85°33′E
- 152 H11 **Nawalgarh** Rājasthān, N India 27°48′N 75°21′E
- **Nawāl, Sabkhat an** *see* Noual, Sebkhet en
- **Nawapara** *see* Nūāparha
- **Nawar, Dasht-i-** *see* Nāvar, Dasht-e
- 167 N4 **Nawnghkio** *var.* Nawngkio. Shan State, C Myanmar (Burma) 22°17′N 96°50′E
- **Nawngkio** *see* Nawnghkio
- 137 U13 **Naxçıvan** *Rus.* Nakhichevan'. SW Azerbaijan 39°14′N 45°24′E
- 160 I10 **Naxi** Sichuan, C China 28°50′N 105°20′E
- 115 K21 **Náxos** *var.* Naxos. Náxos, Kykládes, Greece, Aegean Sea 36°07′N 25°24′E
- 115 K21 **Náxos** *island* Kykládes, Greece, Aegean Sea
- 40 J11 **Nayarit** ◈ *state* C Mexico
- 187 Y14 **Nayau** *island* Lau Group, E Fiji
- 143 S8 **Nāy Band** Yazd, E Iran 32°26′N 57°30′E
- 165 T2 **Nayoro** Hokkaidō, NE Japan 44°22′N 142°27′E
- 104 F9 **Nazaré** *var.* Nazare. Leiria, C Portugal 39°36′N 09°04′W
- **Nazare** *see* Nazaré
- 24 M4 **Nazareth** Texas, SW USA 34°32′N 102°06′W
- **Nazareth** *see* Natzrat
- 173 O8 **Nazareth Bank** *undersea feature* W Indian Ocean
- 40 K9 **Nazas** Durango, C Mexico 25°15′N 104°06′W
- 57 F16 **Nazca** Ica, S Peru 14°53′S 74°54′W
- 0 L17 **Nazca Plate** *tectonic feature*
- 193 U9 **Nazca Ridge** *undersea feature* E Pacific Ocean 22°00′S 82°00′W
- 165 V15 **Naze** *var.* Nase. Kagoshima, Amami-ōshima, SW Japan 28°21′N 129°30′E
- **Naẓerat** *see* Natzrat
- 137 R14 **Nazik Gölü** ◎ E Turkey
- 136 C15 **Nazilli** Aydın, SW Turkey 37°55′N 28°20′E
- 137 P14 **Nazimiye** Tunceli, E Turkey 39°12′N 39°51′E
- **Nazinon** *see* Red Volta
- 10 L15 **Nazko** British Columbia, SW Canada 52°57′N 123°44′W
- 127 O16 **Nazran'** Respublika Ingushetiya, SW Russian Federation 43°14′N 44°47′E
- 80 J13 **Nazrēt** *var.* Adama, Hadama. Oromīya, C Ethiopia 08°31′N 39°20′E
- **Nazwāh** *see* Nizwa
- 82 J13 **Nchanga** Copperbelt, C Zambia 12°30′S 27°53′E
- 82 J11 **Nchelenge** Luapula, N Zambia 09°20′S 28°50′E
- **Ncheu** *see* Ntcheu
- 83 J25 **Nciba** *Eng.* Great Kei; *prev.* Groot-Kei. ≈ S South Africa
- **Ndaghamcha, Sebkra de** *see* Te-n-Dghâmcha, Sebkhet
- 81 G21 **Ndala** Tabora, C Tanzania 04°45′S 33°15′E
- 82 B11 **N'Dalatando** *Port.* Salazar, Vila Salazar. Cuanza Norte, NW Angola 09°19′S 14°48′E
- 77 S14 **Ndali** C Benin 09°50′N 02°46′E
- 81 E18 **Ndeke** SW Uganda 0°11′S 30°04′E
- 78 J13 **Ndélé** Bamingui-Bangoran, N Central African Republic 08°24′N 20°41′E
- 79 E19 **Ndendé** Ngounié, S Gabon 02°21′S 11°20′E
- 79 E20 **Ndindi** Nyanga, S Gabon 03°47′S 11°06′E
- 78 G11 **Ndjamena** *var.* N'Djamena; *prev.* Fort-Lamy. ● (Chad) Chari-Baguirmi, W Chad 12°08′N 15°02′E
- 78 G11 **Ndjamena** ✈ Chari-Baguirmi, W Chad 12°09′N 15°00′E
- **N'Djamena** *see* Ndjamena
- 79 D18 **Ndjolé** Moyen-Ogooué, W Gabon 0°07′S 10°45′E
- 82 J13 **Ndola** Copperbelt, C Zambia 12°59′S 28°35′E
- **Ndrhamcha, Sebkha de** *see* Te-n-Dghâmcha, Sebkhet
- 79 L15 **Ndu** Orientale, N Dem. Rep. Congo 04°36′N 22°49′E
- 81 H21 **Nduguti** Singida, C Tanzania 04°19′S 34°40′E
- 186 M9 **Nduindui** Guadalcanal, C Solomon Islands 09°46′S 159°54′E
- **Nduke** *see* Kolombangara
- **Ndzouani** *see* Anjouan
- 115 F16 **Néa Anchiálos** *var.* Nea Anhialos, Néa Ankhíalos. Thessalía, C Greece 39°16′N 22°49′E
- **Nea Anhialos/Néa Ankhíalos** *see* Néa Anchiálos
- 115 H18 **Néa Artáki** Évvoia, C Greece 38°31′N 23°39′E
- 97 F15 **Neagh, Lough** ◎ E Northern Ireland, United Kingdom
- 32 F7 **Neah Bay** Washington, NW USA 48°21′N 124°39′W
- 115 J22 **Nea Kaméni** *island* Kykládes, Greece, Aegean Sea
- 181 O8 **Neale, Lake** ◎ Northern Territory, C Australia
- 182 G2 **Neales River** *seasonal river* South Australia
- 115 G14 **Néa Moudanía** *var.* Néa Moudhaniá. Kentrikí Makedonía, N Greece 40°14′N 23°17′E
- **Néa Moudhaniá** *see* Néa Moudanía
- 116 K10 **Neamț** ◈ *county* NE Romania
- **Neapel** *see* Napoli
- 115 D14 **Neápoli** *prev.* Neápolis. Dytikí Makedonía, N Greece 40°19′N 21°23′E
- 115 K25 **Neápoli** Kríti, Greece, E Mediterranean Sea 35°15′N 25°37′E

◆ Country ● Country Capital ◇ Dependent Territory ○ Dependent Territory Capital ◈ Administrative Regions ✈ International Airport ▲ Mountain ▲▲ Mountain Range ⛰ Volcano ≈ River ◎ Lake ⊠ Reservoir

NEÁPOLI – NEW PORT RICHEY

115 G22 Neápoli Pelopónnisos, S Greece 36°29′N 23°05′E
Neápolis see Neápoli, Greece
Neapolis see Napoli, Italy
Neapolis see Nablus, West Bank
38 D16 Near Islands island group Aleutian Islands, Alaska, USA
97 J21 Neath S Wales, United Kingdom 51°40′N 03°48′W
114 H13 Néa Zíchni var. Néa Zíkhni; prev. Néa Zíkhna. Kentrikí Makedonía, NE Greece 41°02′N 23°50′E
Néa Zíkhna/Néa Zíkhni see Néa Zíchni
42 C5 Nebaj Quiché, W Guatemala 15°25′N 91°05′W
77 P13 Nebbou S Burkina 11°22′N 01°49′W
Nebitdag see Balkanabat
54 M13 Neblina, Pico da ▲ NW Brazil 0°49′N 66°31′W
124 I13 Nebolchi Novgorodskaya Oblast', W Russian Federation 59°08′N 33°19′E
36 L4 Nebo, Mount ▲ Utah, W USA 39°47′N 111°46′W
28 L14 Nebraska off. State of Nebraska, also known as Blackwater State, Cornhusker State, Tree Planters State. ◈ state C USA
29 S16 Nebraska City Nebraska, C USA 40°38′N 95°52′W
107 K23 Nebrodi, Monti var. Monti Caronie. ▲▲ Sicilia, Italy, C Mediterranean Sea
10 L14 Nechako ~ British Columbia, SW Canada
29 Q2 Neche North Dakota, N USA 48°57′N 97°33′W
25 V8 Neches Texas, SW USA 31°51′N 95°28′W
25 W8 Neches River ~ Texas, SW USA
101 H20 Neckar ~ SW Germany
101 H20 Neckarsulm Baden-Württemberg, SW Germany 49°12′N 09°13′E
192 L5 Necker Island island C British Virgin Islands
175 U3 Necker Ridge undersea feature N Pacific Ocean
61 D23 Necochea Buenos Aires, E Argentina 38°34′S 58°42′W
104 H2 Neda Galicia, NW Spain 43°29′N 08°09′W
115 E20 Néda var. Nédas. ~ S Greece
Nédas see Néda
114 J12 Nedelino Smolyan, S Bulgaria 41°27′N 25°05′E
25 Y11 Nederland Texas, SW USA 29°58′N 93°59′W
Nederland see Netherlands
98 K12 Neder Rijn Eng. Lower Rhine. ~ C Netherlands
99 L16 Nederweert Limburg, SE Netherlands 51°17′N 05°45′E
159 N17 Nêdong var. Zêtang. Xizang Zizhiqu, W China 29°11′N 91°48′E
95 G16 Nedre Tokke ◎ S Norway
Nedrigaylov see Nedryhayliv
117 S3 Nedryhayliv Rus. Nedrigaylov. Sums'ka Oblast', NE Ukraine 50°51′N 33°54′E
98 O11 Neede Gelderland, E Netherlands 52°08′N 06°36′E
33 T13 Needle Mountain ▲ Wyoming, C USA 44°03′N 109°33′W
35 Y14 Needles California, W USA 34°50′N 114°37′W
97 M24 Needles, The rocks S England, United Kingdom
62 O7 Ñeembucú off. Departamento de Ñeembucú. ◈ department SW Paraguay
Ñeembucú, Departamento de see Ñeembucú
30 M7 Neenah Wisconsin, N USA 44°09′N 88°26′W
11 W16 Neepawa Manitoba, S Canada 50°14′N 99°29′W
99 K16 Neerpelt Limburg, NE Belgium 51°13′N 05°26′E
74 M6 Nefta ✈ W Tunisia 34°03′N 08°05′E
126 L15 Neftegorsk Krasnodarskiy Kray, SW Russian Federation 44°21′N 39°40′E
127 S6 Neftegorsk Samarskaya Oblast', W Russian Federation 52°48′N 51°04′E
127 U3 Neftekamsk Respublika Bashkortostan, W Russian Federation 56°07′N 54°13′E
127 O14 Neftekumsk Stavropol'skiy Kray, SW Russian Federation 44°45′N 45°00′E
Neftezavodsk see Seýdi
82 C10 Negage var. N'Gage. Uíge, NW Angola 07°47′S 15°27′E
Negapatam/Negapattinam see Nāgappattinam
169 T17 Negara Bali, Indonesia 08°21′S 114°35′E
169 T13 Negara Borneo, C Indonesia 02°40′S 115°05′E
Negara Brunei Darussalam see Brunei
31 N4 Negaunee Michigan, N USA 46°30′N 87°36′W
81 J15 Negēlē var. Negelli, It. Neghelli. Oromīya, C Ethiopia 05°13′N 39°43′E
Negelli see Negēlē
Negeri Pahang Darul Makmur see Pahang
Negeri Selangor Darul Ehsan see Selangor
168 K9 Negeri Sembilan var. Negri Sembilan. ◈ state Peninsular Malaysia
92 P3 Negerpynten headland S Svalbard 77°15′N 22°40′E
Negev see HaNegev
Neghelli see Negēlē
116 I12 Negoiu var. Negoiul. ▲ S Romania 45°34′N 24°34′E
Negoiul see Negoiu
82 P13 Negomane var. Negomano. Cabo Delgado, N Mozambique 11°22′S 38°32′E
Negomano see Negomane
155 J25 Negombo Western Province, SW Sri Lanka 07°13′N 79°51′E
Negoreloye see Nyeharelaye
112 P12 Negotin Serbia, E Serbia 44°14′N 22°31′E
113 P19 Negotino C Macedonia 41°29′N 22°04′E
56 A10 Negra, Punta headland NW Peru 06°03′S 81°08′W
104 G3 Negreira Galicia, NW Spain 42°54′N 08°46′W
116 L10 Negreşti Vaslui, E Romania 46°50′N 27°28′E
Negreşti see Negreşti-Oaş
116 H8 Negreşti-Oaş Hung. Avasfelsőfalu; prev. Negreşti. Satu Mare, NE Romania 47°56′N 23°22′E
44 H12 Negril W Jamaica 18°16′N 78°21′W
Negri Sembilan see Negeri Sembilan
63 K15 Negro, Río ~ E Argentina
62 N7 Negro, Río ~ NE Argentina
57 N17 Negro, Río ~ E Bolivia
48 F6 Negro, Río ~ N South America
61 E18 Negro, Río ~ Brazil/Uruguay
62 O5 Negro, Río ~ C Paraguay
Negro, Río see Chixoy, Río, Guatemala/Mexico
Negro, Río see Sico Tinto, Río, Honduras
171 P6 Negros island C Philippines
116 M15 Negru Vodă Constanţa, SE Romania 43°49′N 28°12′E
13 P13 Neguac New Brunswick, SE Canada 47°16′N 65°04′W
14 B7 Negwazu, Lake ◎ Ontario, S Canada
Négyfalu see Săcele
32 F10 Nehalem Oregon, NW USA 45°42′N 123°55′W
32 F10 Nehalem River ~ Oregon, NW USA
Nehavend see Nahāvand
143 V9 Nehbandān Khorāsān, E Iran 31°00′N 60°00′E
163 V6 Nehe Heilongjiang, NE China 48°28′N 124°52′E
193 Y14 Neiafu 'Uta Vava'u, N Tonga 18°36′S 173°58′W
45 N9 Neiba var. Neyba. SW Dominican Republic 18°31′N 71°25′W
Néid, Carn Uí see Mizen Head
92 M9 Neiden Finnmark, N Norway 69°41′N 29°23′E
Neidín see Kenmare
Néifinn see Nephin
103 S10 Neige, Crêt de la ▲ E France 46°18′N 05°58′E
173 O16 Neiges, Piton des ▲ C Réunion 21°05′S 55°28′E
15 R9 Neiges, Rivière des ~ Québec, SE Canada
160 I10 Neijiang Sichuan, C China 29°32′N 105°03′E
30 K6 Neillsville Wisconsin, N USA 44°34′N 90°36′W
Nei Monggol Zizhiqu/Nei Mongol see Nei Mongol Zizhiqu
163 Q10 Nei Mongol Gaoyuan plateau NE China
163 O12 Nei Mongol Zizhiqu var. Nei Mongol, Eng. Inner Mongolia, Inner Mongolian Autonomous Region; prev. Nei Monggol Zizhiqu. ◈ autonomous region N China
161 O4 Neiqiu Hebei, E China 37°22′N 114°34′E
Neiriz see Neyrīz
101 Q16 Neisse Cz. Lužická Nisa, Pol. Nisa, Ger. Lausitzer Neisse, Nysa Łużycka. ~ C Europe
Neisse see Nysa
54 E11 Neiva Huila, S Colombia 02°58′N 75°15′W
160 M7 Neixiang Henan, C China 33°08′N 111°50′E
Nejafabad see Najafābād
11 V9 Nejanilini Lake ◎ Manitoba, C Canada
Nejd see Najd
80 I13 Nek'emtē var. Lakemti, Nakamti. Oromīya, C Ethiopia 09°06′N 36°31′E
126 M9 Nekhayevskaya Volgogradskaya Oblast', SW Russian Federation 50°25′N 41°44′E
30 K7 Nekoosa Wisconsin, N USA 44°19′N 89°54′W
Neksø Bornholm see Nexø
104 H7 Nelas Viseu, N Portugal 40°32′N 07°52′W
124 H16 Nelidovo Tverskaya Oblast', W Russian Federation 56°13′N 32°45′E
29 P13 Neligh Nebraska, C USA 42°07′N 98°01′W
123 R11 Nel'kan Khabarovskiy Kray, E Russian Federation 57°44′N 136°09′E
92 M10 Nellim var. Nellimö, Lapp. Njellim. Lappi, N Finland 68°49′N 28°18′E
Nellimö see Nellim
155 J18 Nellore Andhra Pradesh, E India 14°29′N 80°E
61 B17 Nelson Santa Fe, C Argentina 31°16′S 60°45′W
11 O17 Nelson British Columbia, SW Canada 49°29′N 117°17′W
185 I14 Nelson Nelson, South Island, New Zealand 41°17′S 173°17′E
97 L17 Nelson NW England, United Kingdom 53°51′N 02°13′W
29 P17 Nelson Nebraska, C USA 40°12′N 98°04′W
185 J14 Nelson ◈ unitary authority South Island, New Zealand
11 X12 Nelson ~ Manitoba, C Canada
183 U8 Nelson Bay New South Wales, SE Australia 32°48′S 152°10′E
182 K13 Nelson, Cape headland Victoria, SE Australia 38°25′S 141°33′E
63 G23 Nelson, Estrecho strait SE Pacific Ocean
11 W12 Nelson House Manitoba, C Canada 55°49′N 98°51′W
30 J4 Nelson Lake ◎ Wisconsin, N USA
31 T14 Nelsonville Ohio, N USA 39°27′N 82°13′W
27 S2 Nelsoon River ~ Iowa/Missouri, C USA
83 K21 Nelspruit Mpumalanga, NE South Africa 25°28′S 30°58′E
76 L10 Néma Hodh ech Chargui, SE Mauritania 16°32′N 07°12′W
118 D13 Neman Ger. Ragnit. Kaliningradskaya Oblast', W Russian Federation 55°01′N 22°00′E
84 I9 Neman Bel. Nyoman, Ger. Memel, Lith. Nemunas, Pol. Niemen. ~ NE Europe
Nemausus see Nîmes
115 F19 Neméa Pelopónnisos, S Greece 37°49′N 22°40′E
Německý Brod see Havlíčkův Brod
14 D7 Nemegosenda ~ Ontario, S Canada
14 D8 Nemegosenda Lake ◎ Ontario, S Canada
119 H14 Nemenčinė Vilnius, SE Lithuania 54°50′N 25°29′E
Nemetocenna see Arras
Nemirov see Nemyriv
103 O6 Nemours Seine-et-Marne, N France 48°16′N 02°41′E
Nemunas see Neman
165 W4 Nemuro Hokkaidō, NE Japan 43°20′N 145°35′E
165 W4 Nemuro-hantō peninsula Hokkaidō, NE Japan
165 W3 Nemuro-kaikyō strait Japan/Russian Federation
165 W4 Nemuro-wan bay N Japan
116 H5 Nemyriv Rus. Nemirov. L'vivs'ka Oblast', NW Ukraine 50°08′N 23°28′E
117 N7 Nemyriv Rus. Nemirov. Vinnyts'ka Oblast', C Ukraine 48°58′N 28°50′E
97 D19 Nenagh Ir. An tAonach. Tipperary, C Ireland 52°52′N 08°12′W
39 R9 Nenana Alaska, USA 64°33′N 149°05′W
39 R9 Nenana River ~ Alaska, USA
187 P10 Nendö var. Swallow Island. island Santa Cruz Islands, E Solomon Islands
97 O19 Nene ~ E England, United Kingdom
125 R4 Nenetskiy Avtonomnyy Okrug ◈ autonomous district Arkhangel'skaya Oblast', NW Russian Federation
191 W11 Nengonengo atoll Îles Tuamotu, C French Polynesia
163 V6 Nenjiang Heilongjiang, NE China 49°11′N 125°18′E
163 U6 Nen Jiang var. Nonni. ~ NE China
189 P16 Neoch atoll Caroline Islands, C Micronesia
115 D18 Neochóri Dytikí Elláda, C Greece 38°23′N 21°14′E
27 Q7 Neodesha Kansas, C USA 37°25′N 95°40′W
29 S14 Neola Iowa, C USA 41°27′N 95°40′W
115 E16 Néo Monastíri var. Néon Monastiri. Thessalía, C Greece 39°22′N 21°55′E
Néon Karlovasi/Néon Karlovásion see Karlovási
Néon Monastiri see Néo Monastíri
27 R8 Neosho Missouri, C USA 36°53′N 94°24′W
27 Q7 Neosho River ~ Kansas/Oklahoma, C USA
123 N12 Nepa ~ C Russian Federation
153 N10 Nepal off. Nepal. ◆ monarchy S Asia
Nepal see Nepal
152 M11 Nepālganj Mid Western, SW Nepal 28°04′N 81°37′E
14 L13 Nepean Ontario, SE Canada 45°19′N 75°54′W
36 L4 Nephi Utah, W USA 39°43′N 111°50′W
97 B16 Nephin Ir. Néifinn. ▲ W Ireland 54°00′N 09°21′W
67 T9 Nepoko ~ NE Dem. Rep. Congo
18 K15 Neptune New Jersey, NE USA 40°10′N 74°03′W
182 G10 Neptune Islands island group South Australia
107 I14 Nera anc. Nar. ~ C Italy
102 L14 Nérac Lot-et-Garonne, SW France 44°08′N 00°21′E
111 D16 Neratovice Ger. Neratowitz. Středočeský Kraj, C Czech Republic 50°16′N 14°31′E
Neratowitz see Neratovice
123 O13 Nercha ~ S Russian Federation
123 O13 Nerchinsk Chitinskaya Oblast', S Russian Federation 52°01′N 116°25′E
123 P14 Nerchinskiy Zavod Chitinskaya Oblast', S Russian Federation 51°13′N 119°25′E
124 M15 Nerekhta Kostromskaya Oblast', NW Russian Federation 57°27′N 40°33′E
118 H10 Nereta Aizkraukle, S Latvia 56°12′N 25°18′E
106 K13 Nereto Abruzzo, C Italy 42°49′N 13°50′E
113 H15 Neretva ~ Bosnia and Herzegovina/Croatia
115 C17 Nerikós ruins Lefkáda, Iónia Nisiá, Greece, C Mediterranean Sea
83 F15 Neriquinha Cuando Cubango, SE Angola 15°44′S 21°34′E
118 I13 Neris Bel. Viliya, Pol. Wilia; prev. Pol. Wilja. ~ Belarus/Lithuania
Neris see Viliya
105 N15 Nerja Andalucía, S Spain 36°45′N 03°35′W
124 L16 Nerl' ~ W Russian Federation
105 P12 Nerpio Castilla-La Mancha, C Spain 38°08′N 02°18′W
104 J13 Nerva Andalucía, S Spain 37°40′N 06°31′W
98 L4 Nes Friesland, N Netherlands 53°28′N 05°46′E
94 G13 Nesbyen Buskerud, S Norway 60°36′N 09°35′E
114 M9 Nesebŭr Burgas, E Bulgaria 42°40′N 27°43′E
92 L2 Neskaupstadhur Austurland, E Iceland 65°08′N 13°45′W
92 F13 Nesna Nordland, C Norway 66°11′N 12°54′E
26 K5 Ness City Kansas, C USA 38°27′N 99°54′W
Nesselsdorf see Kopřivnice
108 H7 Nesslau Sankt Gallen, NE Switzerland 47°13′N 09°12′E
96 I9 Ness, Loch ◎ N Scotland, United Kingdom
Nesterov see Zhovkva
114 I12 Néstos Bul. Mesta, Turk. Kara Su. ~ Bulgaria/Greece see also Mesta
Néstos see Mesta
95 C14 Nesttun Hordaland, S Norway 60°19′N 05°16′E
Nesvizh see Nyasvizh
138 F9 Netanya var. Natanya, Nathanya. Central, C Israel 32°20′N 34°51′E
98 I9 Netherlands off. Kingdom of the Netherlands, var. Holland, Dut. Koninkrijk der Nederlanden, Nederland. ◆ monarchy NW Europe
45 S9 Netherlands Antilles prev. Dutch West Indies. ◇ Dutch autonomous region S Caribbean Sea
Netherlands East Indies see Indonesia
Netherlands Guiana see Suriname
Netherlands, Kingdom of the see Netherlands
Netherlands New Guinea see Papua
116 L4 Netishyn Khmel'nyts'ka Oblast', W Ukraine 50°20′N 26°38′E
138 E11 Netivot Southern, S Israel 31°26′N 34°36′E
107 O21 Neto ~ S Italy
9 Q6 Nettilling Lake ◎ Baffin Island, Nunavut, N Canada
29 V3 Nett Lake ◎ Minnesota, N USA
107 I16 Nettuno Lazio, C Italy 41°27′N 12°40′E
Netum see Noto
41 U16 Netzahualcóyotl, Presa ⊠ SE Mexico
Netze see Noteć
Neu Amerika see Puławy
Neubetsche see Novi Bečej
Neubidschow see Nový Bydžov
Neubistritz see Nová Bystřice
100 N9 Neubrandenburg Mecklenburg-Vorpommern, NE Germany 53°33′N 13°16′E
101 K22 Neuburg an der Donau Bayern, S Germany 48°43′N 11°10′E
108 C8 Neuchâtel Ger. Neuenburg. Neuchâtel, W Switzerland 46°59′N 06°55′E
108 C8 Neuchâtel Ger. Neuenburg. ◈ canton W Switzerland
108 C8 Neuchâtel, Lac de Ger. Neuenburger See. ◎ W Switzerland
Neudorf see Spišská Nová Ves
100 L10 Neue Elde canal N Germany
Neuenburg see Neuchâtel
Neuenburg an der Elbe see Nymburk
Neuenburger See see Neuchâtel, Lac de
108 F7 Neuenhof Aargau, N Switzerland 47°27′N 08°17′E
100 H11 Neuenland ✈ (Bremen) Bremen, NW Germany 53°03′N 08°46′E
Neuenstadt see La Neuveville
101 C18 Neuerburg Rheinland-Pfalz, W Germany 50°01′N 06°13′E
99 K24 Neufchâteau Luxembourg, SE Belgium 49°50′N 05°26′E
103 S6 Neufchâteau Vosges, NE France 48°21′N 05°42′E
102 M3 Neufchâtel-en-Bray Seine-Maritime, N France 49°44′N 01°26′E
109 S3 Neufelden Oberösterreich, N Austria 48°27′N 14°01′E
Neugradisk see Nova Gradiška
Neuhaus see Jindřichův Hradec
Neuhäusel see Nové Zámky
108 G6 Neuhausen var. Neuhausen am Rheinfall. Schaffhausen, N Switzerland 47°24′N 08°37′E
Neuhausen am Rheinfall see Neuhausen
101 I17 Neuhof Hessen, C Germany 50°26′N 09°34′E
Neuhof see Zgierz
Neukuhren see Pionerskiy
Neu-Langenburg see Tukuyu
109 W4 Neulengbach Niederösterreich, NE Austria 48°10′N 15°53′E
113 G15 Neum Federacija Bosna I Hercegovina, S Bosnia and Herzegovina 42°57′N 17°33′E
Neumark see Nowy Targ, Małopolskie, Poland
Neumark see Nowe Miasto Lubawskie, Warmińsko-Mazurskie, Poland
Neumarkt see Neumarkt im Hausruckkreis, Oberösterreich, Austria
Neumarkt see Neumarkt am Wallersee, Salzburg, Austria
Neumarkt see Środa Śląska, Dolnośląskie, Poland
Neumarkt see Târgu Secuiesc, Covasna, Romania
Neumarkt see Târgu Mureş
109 Q5 Neumarkt am Wallersee var. Neumarkt. Salzburg, NW Austria 47°55′N 13°16′E
109 R4 Neumarkt im Hausruckkreis var. Neumarkt. Oberösterreich, N Austria 48°16′N 13°40′E
101 L20 Neumarkt in der Oberpfalz Bayern, SE Germany 49°16′N 11°28′E
Neumarktl see Tržič
Neumoldowa see Moldova Nouă
100 J8 Neumünster Schleswig-Holstein, N Germany 54°04′N 09°59′E
109 X5 Neunkirchen var. Neunkirchen am Steinfeld. Niederösterreich, E Austria 47°44′N 16°05′E
101 E20 Neunkirchen Saarland, SW Germany 49°21′N 07°11′E
Neunkirchen am Steinfeld see Neunkirchen
Neuoderberg see Bohumín
63 I15 Neuquén Neuquén, SE Argentina 39°03′S 68°36′W
63 H14 Neuquén off. Provincia de Neuquén. ◈ province W Argentina
Neuquén, Provincia de see Neuquén
63 H14 Neuquén, Río ~ W Argentina
Neurode see Nowa Ruda
100 N11 Neuruppin Brandenburg, NE Germany 52°56′N 12°49′E
Neusalz an der Oder see Nowa Sól
Neu Sandec see Nowy Sącz
101 K22 Neusäss Bayern, S Germany 48°24′N 10°49′E
Neusatz see Novi Sad
Neuschliss see Gherla
21 N8 Neuse River ~ North Carolina, SE USA
109 Z5 Neusiedl am See Burgenland, E Austria 47°58′N 16°51′E
111 G22 Neusiedler See Hung. Fertő. ◎ Austria/Hungary
Neusohl see Banská Bystrica
101 D15 Neuss anc. Novaesium, Novesium. Nordrhein-Westfalen, W Germany 51°12′N 06°42′E
Neuss see Nyon
Neustadt see Neustadt bei Coburg, Bayern, Germany
Neustadt see Neustadt an der Aisch, Bayern, Germany
Neustadt see Prudnik, Opole, Poland
Neustadt see Baia Mare, Maramureş, Romania
100 I12 Neustadt am Rübenberge Niedersachsen, N Germany 52°30′N 09°28′E
101 J19 Neustadt an der Aisch var. Neustadt. Bayern, C Germany 49°34′N 10°36′E
Neustadt an der Haardt see Neustadt an der Weinstrasse
101 F20 Neustadt an der Weinstrasse prev. Neustadt an der Haardt, hist. Niewenstat; anc. Nova Civitas. Rheinland-Pfalz, SW Germany 49°21′N 08°09′E
101 K18 Neustadt bei Coburg var. Neustadt. Bayern, C Germany 50°19′N 11°06′E
Neustadt bei Pinne see Lwówek
Neustadt in Oberschlesien see Prudnik
Neustadtl see Novo mesto
Neustadtl in Mähren see Nové Město na Moravě
Neustettin see Szczecinek
108 M8 Neustift im Stubaital var. Stubaital. Tirol, W Austria 47°07′N 11°26′E
100 N10 Neustrelitz Mecklenburg-Vorpommern, NE Germany 53°22′N 13°05′E
Neutitschein see Nový Jičín
Neutra see Nitra
101 J22 Neu-Ulm Bayern, S Germany 48°23′N 10°02′E
Neuveville see La Neuveville
103 N12 Neuvic Corrèze, C France 45°23′N 02°16′E
Neuwarp see Nowe Warpno
100 G9 Neuwerk island NW Germany
101 E17 Neuwied Rheinland-Pfalz, W Germany 50°26′N 07°28′E
Neuzen see Terneuzen
124 H12 Neva ~ NW Russian Federation
29 V14 Nevada Iowa, C USA 42°01′N 93°27′W
27 R6 Nevada Missouri, C USA 37°51′N 94°22′W
35 R5 Nevada off. State of Nevada, also known as Battle Born State, Sagebrush State, Silver State. ◈ state W USA
35 P6 Nevada City California, W USA 39°15′N 121°02′W
105 O14 Nevada, Sierra ▲▲ S Spain
35 P6 Nevada, Sierra ▲▲ W USA
62 I13 Nevado, Sierra del ▲▲ W Argentina
124 G16 Nevel' Pskovskaya Oblast', W Russian Federation 56°01′N 29°54′E
123 T14 Nevel'sk Ostrov Sakhalin, Sakhalinskaya Oblast', SE Russian Federation 46°41′N 141°54′E
123 Q13 Never Amurskaya Oblast', SE Russian Federation 53°58′N 124°04′E
127 Q6 Neverkino Penzenskaya Oblast', W Russian Federation 52°53′N 46°46′E
103 P9 Nevers anc. Noviodunum. Nièvre, C France 47°N 03°09′E
18 J12 Neversink River ~ New York, NE USA
183 Q6 Nevertire New South Wales, SE Australia 31°52′S 147°42′E
113 H15 Nevesinje ◈ Republika Srpska, S Bosnia and Herzegovina
118 G12 Nevėžis ~ C Lithuania
138 F11 Neve Zohar prev. Newé Zohar. Southern, E Israel 31°07′N 35°23′E
126 M14 Nevinnomyssk Stavropol'skiy Kray, SW Russian Federation 44°39′N 41°57′E
45 W10 Nevis island Saint Kitts and Nevis
Nevoso, Monte see Veliki Snežnik
Nevrokop see Gotse Delchev
136 J14 Nevşehir var. Nevshehr. Nevşehir, C Turkey 38°38′N 34°43′E
136 J14 Nevşehir var. Nevshehr. ◈ province C Turkey
Nevshehr see Nevşehir
122 G10 Nev'yansk Sverdlovskaya Oblast', C Russian Federation 57°26′N 60°15′E
81 J25 Newala Mtwara, SE Tanzania 10°59′S 39°18′E
31 P16 New Albany Indiana, N USA 38°17′N 85°50′W
22 M2 New Albany Mississippi, S USA 34°29′N 89°00′W
29 Y11 New Albin Iowa, C USA 43°30′N 91°17′W
55 U8 New Amsterdam E Guyana 06°17′N 57°31′W
183 Q4 New Angledool New South Wales, SE Australia 29°06′S 147°54′E
21 Y2 Newark Delaware, NE USA 39°42′N 75°45′W
18 K14 Newark New Jersey, NE USA 40°42′N 74°12′W
18 G10 Newark New York, NE USA 43°01′N 77°04′W
31 T13 Newark Ohio, N USA 40°03′N 82°24′W
Newark see Newark-on-Trent
35 W5 Newark Lake ◎ Nevada, W USA
97 N18 Newark-on-Trent var. Newark. C England, United Kingdom 53°05′N 00°49′W
22 M7 New Augusta Mississippi, S USA 31°12′N 89°03′W
19 P12 New Bedford Massachusetts, NE USA 41°38′N 70°55′W
32 G11 Newberg Oregon, NW USA 45°18′N 122°58′W
21 X10 New Bern North Carolina, SE USA 35°05′N 77°04′W
20 F8 Newbern Tennessee, S USA 36°06′N 89°15′W
31 P4 Newberry Michigan, N USA 46°21′N 85°30′W
21 Q12 Newberry South Carolina, SE USA 34°17′N 81°39′W
18 F15 New Bloomfield Pennsylvania, NE USA 40°24′N 77°08′W
25 X5 New Boston Texas, SW USA 33°27′N 94°25′W
25 S11 New Braunfels Texas, SW USA 29°43′N 98°09′W
31 Q13 New Bremen Ohio, N USA 40°26′N 84°22′W
97 F18 Newbridge Ir. An Droichead Nua. Kildare, C Ireland 53°11′N 06°48′W
18 B14 New Brighton Pennsylvania, NE USA 40°44′N 80°18′W
18 M12 New Britain Connecticut, NE USA 41°37′N 72°45′W
186 G7 New Britain island E Papua New Guinea
192 I8 New Britain Trench undersea feature W Pacific Ocean
18 J15 New Brunswick New Jersey, NE USA 40°29′N 74°27′W
15 V8 New Brunswick Fr. Nouveau-Brunswick. ◈ province SE Canada
18 K13 Newburgh New York, NE USA 41°30′N 74°00′W
97 M22 Newbury S England, United Kingdom 51°25′N 01°20′W
19 P10 Newburyport Massachusetts, NE USA 42°49′N 70°53′W
77 T14 New Bussa Niger, W Nigeria 09°50′N 04°32′E
187 O17 New Caledonia var. Kanaky, Fr. Nouvelle-Calédonie. ◇ French overseas territory SW Pacific Ocean
187 O15 New Caledonia island SW Pacific Ocean
175 O10 New Caledonia Basin undersea feature W Pacific Ocean
183 T8 Newcastle New South Wales, SE Australia 32°55′S 151°46′E
13 O14 Newcastle New Brunswick, SE Canada 47°01′N 65°36′W
14 I15 Newcastle Ontario, SE Canada 43°55′N 78°35′W
83 K22 Newcastle KwaZulu/Natal, E South Africa 27°45′S 29°55′E
97 G16 Newcastle Ir. An Caisleán Nua. SE Northern Ireland, United Kingdom 54°12′N 05°54′W
31 P13 New Castle Indiana, N USA 39°56′N 85°21′W
20 L5 New Castle Kentucky, S USA 38°28′N 85°10′W
27 N11 Newcastle Oklahoma, C USA 35°15′N 97°36′W
18 B13 New Castle Pennsylvania, NE USA 41°00′N 80°22′W
25 R6 Newcastle Texas, SW USA 33°11′N 98°44′W
36 J7 Newcastle Utah, W USA 37°40′N 113°31′W
21 S6 New Castle Virginia, NE USA 37°31′N 80°09′W
33 Z13 Newcastle Wyoming, C USA 43°52′N 104°14′W
45 W10 Newcastle ✈ Nevis, Saint Kitts and Nevis 17°08′N 62°36′W
97 L14 Newcastle ✈ NE England, United Kingdom 55°03′N 01°42′W
Newcastle see Newcastle upon Tyne
97 L18 Newcastle-under-Lyme C England, United Kingdom 53°N 02°14′W
97 M14 Newcastle upon Tyne var. Newcastle, hist. Monkchester, Lat. Pons Aelii. NE England, United Kingdom 54°59′N 01°35′W
181 Q4 Newcastle Waters Northern Territory, N Australia 17°20′S 133°26′E
Newchwang see Yingkou
18 K13 New City New York, NE USA 41°08′N 73°57′W
31 U13 Newcomerstown Ohio, N USA 40°16′N 81°36′W
18 G15 New Cumberland Pennsylvania, NE USA 40°13′N 76°52′W
21 R1 New Cumberland West Virginia, NE USA 40°30′N 80°35′W
152 I10 New Delhi ● (India) Delhi, N India 28°35′N 77°15′E
11 O17 New Denver British Columbia, SW Canada 49°58′N 117°21′W
28 J9 Newell South Dakota, N USA 44°42′N 103°25′W
21 Q13 New Ellenton South Carolina, SE USA 33°25′N 81°41′W
22 J6 Newellton Louisiana, S USA 32°04′N 91°14′W
28 K6 New England North Dakota, N USA 46°32′N 102°52′W
19 P8 New England cultural region NE USA
New England of the West see Minnesota
183 U5 New England Range ▲▲ New South Wales, SE Australia
64 G9 New England Seamounts var. Bermuda-New England Seamount Arc. undersea feature W Atlantic Ocean 38°00′N 61°00′W
38 M14 Newenham, Cape headland Alaska, USA 58°39′N 162°10′W
Newé Zohar see Neve Zohar
18 D9 Newfane New York, NE USA 43°16′N 78°40′W
97 M23 New Forest physical region S England, United Kingdom
13 T12 Newfoundland Fr. Terre-Neuve. island Newfoundland and Labrador, SE Canada
13 R9 Newfoundland and Labrador Fr. Terre Neuve. ◈ province E Canada
65 J8 Newfoundland Basin undersea feature NW Atlantic Ocean 45°00′N 40°00′W
64 I8 Newfoundland Ridge undersea feature NW Atlantic Ocean
64 J8 Newfoundland Seamounts undersea feature N Sargasso Sea
18 G16 New Freedom Pennsylvania, NE USA 39°43′N 76°41′W
186 K9 New Georgia island New Georgia Islands, NW Solomon Islands
186 K8 New Georgia Islands island group NW Solomon Islands
186 L8 New Georgia Sound var. The Slot. sound E Solomon Sea
30 L9 New Glarus Wisconsin, N USA 42°50′N 89°38′W
13 Q15 New Glasgow Nova Scotia, SE Canada 45°36′N 62°38′W
New Goa see Panaji
186 A6 New Guinea Dut. Nieuw Guinea, Ind. Irian. island Indonesia/Papua New Guinea
192 H8 New Guinea Trench undersea feature SW Pacific Ocean
32 I6 Newhalem Washington, NW USA 48°40′N 121°18′W
39 P13 Newhalen Alaska, USA 59°43′N 154°54′W
29 X13 Newhall Iowa, C USA 42°00′N 91°58′W
14 F16 New Hamburg Ontario, S Canada 43°24′N 80°37′W
19 N9 New Hampshire off. State of New Hampshire, also known as Granite State. ◈ state NE USA
29 W12 New Hampton Iowa, C USA 43°03′N 92°19′W
186 G5 New Hanover island NE Papua New Guinea
97 P23 Newhaven SE England, United Kingdom 50°48′N 00°00′E
18 M13 New Haven Connecticut, NE USA 41°18′N 72°55′W
31 Q12 New Haven Indiana, N USA 41°02′N 84°59′W
27 W5 New Haven Missouri, C USA 38°34′N 91°15′W
10 K13 New Hazelton British Columbia, SW Canada 55°15′N 127°30′W
New Hebrides see Vanuatu
175 P9 New Hebrides Trench undersea feature N Coral Sea
18 H15 New Holland Pennsylvania, NE USA 40°06′N 76°05′W
22 I9 New Iberia Louisiana, S USA 30°00′N 91°51′W
186 G5 New Ireland ◈ province NE Papua New Guinea
186 G5 New Ireland island NE Papua New Guinea
65 A24 New Island island W Falkland Islands
18 J15 New Jersey off. State of New Jersey, also known as The Garden State. ◈ state NE USA
18 C14 New Kensington Pennsylvania, NE USA 40°33′N 79°45′W
21 W6 New Kent Virginia, NE USA 37°32′N 76°59′W
27 O8 Newkirk Oklahoma, C USA 36°54′N 97°03′W
21 Q9 Newland North Carolina, SE USA 36°04′N 81°50′W
28 L6 New Leipzig North Dakota, N USA 46°21′N 101°54′W
14 H9 New Liskeard Ontario, S Canada 47°31′N 79°41′W
22 G7 Newllano Louisiana, S USA 31°06′N 93°16′W
19 N13 New London Connecticut, NE USA 41°21′N 72°04′W
29 Y15 New London Iowa, C USA 40°55′N 91°24′W
29 T8 New London Minnesota, N USA 45°18′N 94°56′W
27 V3 New London Missouri, C USA 39°34′N 91°24′W
30 M7 New London Wisconsin, N USA 44°25′N 88°44′W
27 Y8 New Madrid Missouri, C USA 36°34′N 89°32′W
180 J8 Newman Western Australia 23°18′S 119°45′E
194 M13 Newman Island island Antarctica
14 H15 Newmarket Ontario, S Canada 44°03′N 79°27′W
97 P20 Newmarket E England, United Kingdom 52°18′N 00°28′E
19 P10 Newmarket New Hampshire, NE USA 43°04′N 70°53′W
21 U4 New Market Virginia, NE USA 38°39′N 78°40′W
21 R2 New Martinsville West Virginia, NE USA 39°39′N 80°52′W
31 U14 New Matamoras Ohio, N USA 39°32′N 81°04′W
32 M12 New Meadows Idaho, NW USA 44°57′N 116°16′W
26 R12 New Mexico off. State of New Mexico, also known as Land of Enchantment, Sunshine State. ◈ state SW USA
149 V6 New Mirpur var. Mirpur. Sind, SE Pakistan 33°11′N 73°46′E
151 N15 New Moore Island Island E India
23 S4 Newnan Georgia, SE USA 33°22′N 84°48′W
183 P17 New Norfolk Tasmania, SE Australia 42°46′S 147°02′E
22 K9 New Orleans Louisiana, S USA 30°00′N 90°01′W
22 K9 New Orleans ✈ Louisiana, S USA 29°59′N 90°17′W
18 K12 New Paltz New York, NE USA 41°44′N 74°04′W
31 U12 New Philadelphia Ohio, N USA 40°29′N 81°27′W
184 K10 New Plymouth Taranaki, North Island, New Zealand 39°04′S 174°06′E
97 M24 Newport S England, United Kingdom 50°42′N 01°18′W
97 K22 Newport SE Wales, United Kingdom 51°35′N 03°W
27 W10 Newport Arkansas, C USA 35°36′N 91°16′W
31 N13 Newport Indiana, N USA 39°52′N 87°24′W
20 M3 Newport Kentucky, S USA 39°05′N 84°27′W
29 W9 Newport Minnesota, N USA 44°52′N 93°00′W
32 F12 Newport Oregon, NW USA 44°39′N 124°04′W
19 O13 Newport Rhode Island, NE USA 41°29′N 71°17′W
21 O9 Newport Tennessee, S USA 35°58′N 83°13′W
19 N6 Newport Vermont, NE USA 44°56′N 72°13′W
32 M7 Newport Washington, NW USA 48°08′N 117°05′W
21 X7 Newport News Virginia, NE USA 35°59′N 76°26′W
97 N20 Newport Pagnell SE England, United Kingdom 52°05′N 00°44′W
23 U12 New Port Richey Florida, SE USA 28°14′N 82°42′W

◆ Country ● Country Capital ◇ Dependent Territory ○ Dependent Territory Capital ◈ Administrative Regions ✈ International Airport ▲ Mountain ▲▲ Mountain Range ▲ Volcano ~ River ◎ Lake ⊠ Reservoir

NEW PRAGUE – NOGENT-LE-ROTROU

29 V9 New Prague Minnesota, N USA 44°32′N 93°34′W
44 H3 New Providence island N Bahamas
97 I20 New Quay SW Wales, United Kingdom 52°13′N 04°22′W
97 H24 Newquay SW England, United Kingdom 50°27′N 05°03′W
29 V10 New Richland Minnesota, N USA 43°53′N 93°29′W
15 X7 New-Richmond Québec, SE Canada 48°12′N 65°52′W
31 R15 New Richmond Ohio, N USA 38°57′N 84°16′W
30 I5 New Richmond Wisconsin, N USA 45°09′N 92°31′W
42 G1 New River ≈ N Belize
55 T12 New River ≈ SE Guyana
21 R6 New River ≈ West Virginia, NE USA
42 G1 New River Lagoon ◎ N Belize
22 J8 New Roads Louisiana, S USA 30°42′N 91°26′W
18 L14 New Rochelle New York, NE USA 40°55′N 73°44′W
29 O4 New Rockford North Dakota, N USA 47°40′N 99°08′W
97 P23 New Romney SE England, United Kingdom 50°58′N 00°56′E
97 F20 New Ross Ir. Ros Mhic Thriúin. Wexford, SE Ireland 52°24′N 06°56′W
97 F16 Newry Ir. An tIúr. SE Northern Ireland, United Kingdom 54°11′N 06°20′W
28 M5 New Salem North Dakota, N USA 46°51′N 101°24′W
New Sarum see Salisbury
29 W14 New Sharon Iowa, C USA 41°28′N 92°39′W
New Siberian Islands see Novosibirskiye Ostrova
23 X11 New Smyrna Beach Florida, SE USA 29°01′N 80°55′W
183 O7 New South Wales ◈ state SE Australia
39 O13 New Stuyahok Alaska, USA 59°27′N 157°18′W
21 N8 New Tazewell Tennessee, S USA 36°26′N 83°36′W
New Tehri see Tehri
38 M12 Newtok Alaska, USA 60°56′N 164°37′W
23 S7 Newton Georgia, SE USA 31°18′N 84°20′W
29 W14 Newton Iowa, C USA 41°42′N 93°03′W
27 N6 Newton Kansas, C USA 38°02′N 97°22′W
19 O11 Newton Massachusetts, NE USA 42°19′N 71°10′W
22 M5 Newton Mississippi, S USA 32°19′N 89°09′W
18 J14 Newton New Jersey, NE USA 41°03′N 74°45′W
21 R9 Newton North Carolina, SE USA 35°42′N 81°14′W
25 Y9 Newton Texas, SW USA 30°51′N 93°45′W
97 J24 Newton Abbot SW England, United Kingdom 50°33′N 03°34′W
96 K13 Newton St Boswells SE Scotland, United Kingdom 55°34′N 02°40′W
97 I14 Newton Stewart S Scotland, United Kingdom 54°58′N 04°30′W
92 O2 Newtontoppen ▲ C Svalbard 78°57′N 17°34′E
97 J20 Newtown E Wales, United Kingdom 52°32′N 03°19′W
28 K3 New Town North Dakota, N USA 47°58′N 102°30′W
97 G15 Newtownabbey Ir. Baile na Mainistreach. E Northern Ireland, United Kingdom 54°40′N 05°57′W
97 G15 Newtownards Ir. Baile Nua na hArda. SE Northern Ireland, United Kingdom 54°36′N 05°41′W
29 U10 New Ulm Minnesota, N USA 44°20′N 94°28′W
28 K10 New Underwood South Dakota, N USA 44°05′N 102°46′W
25 V10 New Waverly Texas, SW USA 30°32′N 95°28′W
18 K14 New York New York, NE USA 40°45′N 73°57′W
18 G10 New York ◈ state NE USA
35 X13 New York Mountains ▲▲ California, W USA
184 K12 New Zealand ◆ commonwealth republic SW Pacific Ocean
95 M24 Nexø var. Neksø. Bornholm, E Denmark 55°04′N 15°09′E
125 O15 Neya Kostromskaya Oblast', NW Russian Federation 58°19′N 43°51′E
Neyba see Neiba
143 Q12 Neyrīz var. Neiriz, Niriz. Fārs, S Iran 29°14′N 54°18′E
143 T4 Neyshābūr var. Nishapur. Khorāsān-Razavī, NE Iran 36°15′N 58°47′E
155 J21 Neyveli Tamil Nādu, SE India 11°36′N 79°26′E
Nezhin see Nizhyn
33 N10 Nezperce Idaho, NW USA 46°14′N 116°15′W
22 H8 Nezpique, Bayou ≈ Louisiana, S USA
77 Y13 Ngadda ≈ NE Nigeria
N'Gage see Negage
185 G16 Ngahere West Coast, South Island, New Zealand 42°22′S 171°29′E
77 Z12 Ngala Borno, NE Nigeria 12°19′N 14°11′E
158 K16 Ngamring Xizang Zizhiqu, W China 29°16′N 87°10′E
81 K19 Ngangerabeli Plain plain SE Kenya
158 I14 Ngangla Ringco ◎ W China
158 H13 Nganglong Kangri ▲ W China 32°55′N 81°00′E
158 K15 Ngangzê Co ◎ W China
79 F14 Ngaoundéré var. N'Gaoundéré. Adamaoua, N Cameroon 07°20′N 13°35′E
N'Gaoundéré see Ngaoundéré
81 E20 Ngara Kagera, NW Tanzania 02°30′S 30°40′E
188 F8 Ngardmau Bay bay Babeldaob, N Palau
188 F7 Ngaregur island Palau Islands, N Palau
Ngarrab see Gyaca
184 L7 Ngaruawahia Waikato, North Island, New Zealand 37°41′S 175°10′E
184 N11 Ngaruroro ≈ North Island, New Zealand
190 I16 Ngatangiia Rarotonga, S Cook Islands 21°14′S 159°44′W
184 M6 Ngatea Waikato, North Island, New Zealand 37°16′S 175°29′E
166 L8 Ngathainggyaung Ayeyarwady, SW Myanmar (Burma) 17°22′N 95°04′E
Ngatik see Ngetik Atoll
Ngau see Gau
Ngawa see Aba
172 G12 Ngazidja Fr. Grande-Comore. island NW Comoros
188 C7 Ngcheangel var. Kayangel Islands. island Palau Islands, N Palau
188 E10 Ngchemiangel Babeldaob, N Palau
188 C8 Ngeaur var. Angaur. island Palau Islands, S Palau
188 E10 Ngerkeai Babeldaob, N Palau
188 F9 Ngermechau Babeldaob, N Palau 07°35′N 134°39′E
188 C8 Ngeruktabel prev. Urukthapel. island Palau Islands, S Palau
188 F8 Ngetbong Babeldaob, N Palau 07°37′N 134°35′E
189 T17 Ngetik Atoll var. Ngatik; prev. Los Jardines. atoll Caroline Islands, E Micronesia
188 E10 Ngetkip Babeldaob, N Palau
Nghia Dan see Thai Hoa
83 C16 N'Giva var. Ondjiva, Port. Vila Pereira de Eça. Cunene, S Angola 17°02′S 15°42′E
79 G20 Ngo Plateaux, SE Congo 02°28′S 15°43′E
43 P16 Ngöbe-Buglé ◈ special territory W Panama
167 S7 Ngoc Lac Thanh Hoa, N Vietnam 20°06′N 105°21′E
79 G17 Ngoko ≈ Cameroon/Congo
81 H19 Ngorengore Rift Valley, SW Kenya 01°01′S 35°26′E
159 Q11 Ngoring Hu ◎ C China
Ngorolaka see Banifing
81 H20 Ngorongoro Crater crater N Tanzania
79 D19 Ngounié off. Province de la Ngounié, var. La Ngounié. ◈ province S Gabon
79 D19 Ngounié ≈ Congo/Gabon
Ngounié, Province de la see Ngounié
78 H10 Ngoura var. NGoura. Chari-Baguirmi, W Chad 12°52′N 16°27′E
NGoura see Ngoura
78 G10 Ngouri var. NGouri; prev. Fort-Millot. Lac, W Chad 13°42′N 15°19′E
NGouri see Ngouri
77 Y10 Ngourti Diffa, E Niger 15°22′N 13°13′E
77 Y11 Nguigmi var. N'Guigmi. Diffa, SE Niger 14°17′N 13°07′E
N'Guigmi see Nguigmi
Nguimbo see Lumbala N'Guimbo
188 F15 Ngulu Atoll atoll Caroline Islands, W Micronesia
187 R14 Nguna island C Vanuatu
N'Gunza see Sumbe
169 U17 Ngurah Rai ✕ (Bali) Bali, S Indonesia 08°40′S 115°14′E
77 W12 Nguru Yobe, NE Nigeria 12°55′N 10°31′E
Ngwaketze see Southern
83 I16 Ngweze ≈ S Zambia
83 M17 Nhamatanda Sofala, C Mozambique 19°16′S 34°10′E
58 G12 Nhamundá, Rio var. Jamundá, Yamundá. ≈ N Brazil
60 J7 Nhandeara São Paulo, S Brazil 20°40′S 50°03′W
82 D12 Nharêa var. N'Harea, Nharea. Bié, W Angola 11°38′S 16°58′E
N'Harea see Nharêa
Nharea see Nharêa
167 V12 Nha Trang Khanh Hoa, S Vietnam 12°15′N 109°10′E
182 L11 Nhill Victoria, SE Australia 36°21′S 141°38′E
83 L22 Nhlangano prev. Goedgegun. SW Swaziland 27°06′S 31°12′E
181 S1 Nhulunbuy Northern Territory, N Australia 12°16′S 136°46′E
77 N10 Niafunké Tombouctou, W Mali 15°54′N 03°58′W
31 N5 Niagara Wisconsin, N USA 45°45′N 87°57′W
14 H16 Niagara ≈ Ontario, S Canada
14 G15 Niagara Escarpment hill range Ontario, S Canada
14 H16 Niagara Falls Ontario, S Canada 43°05′N 79°06′W
18 D9 Niagara Falls New York, NE USA 43°06′N 79°04′W
14 H16 Niagara Falls waterfall Canada/USA
76 K12 Niagassola var. Nyagassola. Haute-Guinée, NE Guinea 12°24′N 09°03′W
77 R12 Niamey ● (Niger) Niamey, SW Niger 13°28′N 02°03′E
77 R12 Niamey ✕ Niamey, SW Niger 13°28′N 02°14′E
77 R14 Niamtougou N Togo 09°50′N 01°08′E
79 O16 Niangara Orientale, NE Dem. Rep. Congo 03°45′N 27°54′E
77 O10 Niangay, Lac ◎ E Mali
77 N14 Niangoloko SW Burkina 10°15′N 04°53′W
27 U6 Niangua River ≈ Missouri, C USA
79 O17 Nia-Nia Orientale, NE Dem. Rep. Congo 01°26′N 27°38′E
19 N13 Niantic Connecticut, NE USA 41°19′N 72°11′W
163 U7 Nianzishan Heilongjiang, NE China 47°31′N 122°53′E
79 E20 Niari ◈ province SW Congo
168 H10 Nias, Pulau island W Indonesia
82 O13 Niassa off. Província do Niassa. ◈ province N Mozambique
Niassa, Provincia do see Niassa
191 U10 Niau island Îles Tuamotu, C French Polynesia
95 G20 Nibe Nordjylland, N Denmark 56°59′N 09°39′E
189 Q8 Nibok N Nauru 0°31′S 166°55′E
118 C10 Nīca Liepāja, W Latvia 56°21′N 21°03′E
Nicaea see Nice
42 J9 Nicaragua off. Republic of Nicaragua. ◆ republic Central America
42 K11 Nicaragua, Lago de var. Cocibolca, Gran Lago, Eng. Lake Nicaragua. ◎ S Nicaragua
Nicaragua, Lake see Nicaragua, Lago de
64 D11 Nicaraguan Rise undersea feature NW Caribbean Sea 16°00′N 80°00′W
Nicaragua, Republic of see Nicaragua
Nicaria see Ikaría
107 N21 Nicastro Calabria, SW Italy 38°59′N 16°20′E
103 V15 Nice It. Nizza; anc. Nicaea. Alpes-Maritimes, SE France 43°43′N 07°13′E
Nice see Côte d'Azur
Nicephorium see Ar Raqqah
12 M9 Nichicun, Lac ◎ Québec, E Canada
164 D16 Nichinan var. Nitinan. Miyazaki, Kyūshū, SW Japan 31°36′N 131°23′E
44 E4 Nicholas Channel channel N Cuba
Nicholas II Land see Severnaya Zemlya
149 U2 Nicholas Range Pash. Selselehye Kuhe Vākhān, Taj. Qatorkŭhi Vakhon. ▲▲ Afghanistan/Tajikistan
20 M6 Nicholasville Kentucky, S USA 37°52′N 84°34′W
44 G2 Nicholls Town Andros Island, NW Bahamas 25°07′N 78°01′W
21 U12 Nichols South Carolina, SE USA 34°13′N 79°09′W
55 U9 Nickerie ◈ district NW Suriname
55 V9 Nickerie Rivier ≈ NW Suriname
151 P22 Nicobar Islands island group India, E Indian Ocean
116 L9 Nicolae Bălcescu Botoşani, NE Romania 47°33′N 26°52′E
15 P11 Nicolet Québec, SE Canada 46°13′N 72°37′W
15 Q12 Nicolet ≈ Québec, SE Canada
31 Q4 Nicolet, Lake ◎ Michigan, N USA
29 U10 Nicollet Minnesota, N USA 44°16′N 94°11′W
61 F19 Nico Pérez Florida, S Uruguay 33°30′S 55°10′W
Nicopolis see Nikopol, Bulgaria
Nicopolis see Nikópoli, Greece
121 P2 Nicosia Gk. Lefkosía, Turk. Lefkoşa. ● (Cyprus) C Cyprus 35°10′N 33°23′E
107 K24 Nicosia Sicilia, Italy, C Mediterranean Sea 37°45′N 14°24′E
107 N22 Nicotera Calabria, SW Italy 38°33′N 15°55′E
42 K13 Nicoya Guanacaste, W Costa Rica 10°09′N 85°26′W
42 L14 Nicoya, Golfo de gulf W Costa Rica
42 L14 Nicoya, Península de peninsula NW Costa Rica
Nictheroy see Niterói
118 B12 Nida Ger. Nidden. Klaipėda, SW Lithuania 55°20′N 21°00′E
111 L15 Nida ≈ S Poland
Nidaros see Trondheim
108 D8 Nidau Bern, W Switzerland 47°07′N 07°15′E
101 H17 Nidda ≈ W Germany
Nidden see Nida
95 F17 Nidelva ≈ S Norway
110 L9 Nidzica Ger. Niedenburg. Warmińsko-Mazurskie, NE Poland 53°22′N 20°27′E
100 H6 Niebüll Schleswig-Holstein, N Germany 54°47′N 08°51′E
Niedenburg see Nidzica
99 N25 Niederanven Luxembourg, C Luxembourg 49°39′N 06°15′E
103 V4 Niederbronn-les-Bains Bas-Rhin, NE France 48°57′N 07°37′E
Niederdonau see Niederösterreich
109 S7 Niedere Tauern ▲▲ C Austria
101 P14 Niederlausitz Eng. Lower Lusatia, Lus. Donja Łužica. physical region E Germany
109 U5 Niederösterreich off. Land Niederösterreich, Eng. Lower Austria, Ger. Niederdonau; prev. Lower Danube. ◈ state NE Austria
Niederösterreich, Land see Niederösterreich
100 G12 Niedersachsen Eng. Lower Saxony, Fr. Basse-Saxe. ◈ state NW Germany
79 D17 Niefang var. Sevilla de Niefang. NW Equatorial Guinea 01°52′N 10°12′E
83 G23 Niekerkshoop Northern Cape, W South Africa 29°21′S 22°49′E
99 G17 Niel Antwerpen, N Belgium 51°07′N 04°20′E
Niélé see Niellé
76 M14 Niellé var. Niélé. N Ivory Coast 10°12′N 05°38′W
79 O22 Niemba Katanga, E Dem. Rep. Congo 05°58′S 28°24′E
111 G15 Niemcza Ger. Nimptsch. Dolnośląskie, SW Poland 50°45′N 16°52′E
Niemen see Neman
92 J13 Niemisel Norrbotten, N Sweden 66°00′N 22°00′E
111 H15 Niemodlin Ger. Falkenberg. Opolskie, SW Poland 50°37′N 17°45′E
76 M13 Niéna Sikasso, SW Mali 11°24′N 06°20′W
100 H12 Nienburg Niedersachsen, N Germany 52°37′N 09°12′E
100 N13 Nieplitz ≈ NE Germany
111 L16 Niepołomice Małopolskie, S Poland 50°02′N 20°12′E
101 D14 Niers ≈ Germany/Netherlands
101 Q15 Niesky Lus. Niska. Sachsen, E Germany 51°16′N 14°49′E
Nieśwież see Nyasvizh
Nieuport see Nieuwpoort
98 O8 Nieuw-Amsterdam Drenthe, NE Netherlands 52°43′N 06°52′E
55 W9 Nieuw Amsterdam Commewijne, NE Suriname 05°53′N 55°05′W
99 M14 Nieuw-Bergen Limburg, SE Netherlands 51°36′N 06°04′E
98 O7 Nieuw-Buinen Drenthe, NE Netherlands 52°57′N 06°55′E
98 J12 Nieuwegein Utrecht, C Netherlands 52°03′N 05°06′E
98 P6 Nieuwe Pekela Groningen, NE Netherlands 53°04′N 06°58′E
98 P5 Nieuweschans Groningen, NE Netherlands 53°10′N 07°10′E
Nieuw Guinea see New Guinea
98 I11 Nieuwkoop Zuid-Holland, C Netherlands 52°09′N 04°46′E
98 M9 Nieuwleusen Overijssel, S Netherlands 52°34′N 06°16′E
98 J11 Nieuw-Loosdrecht Noord-Holland, C Netherlands 52°12′N 05°08′E
55 U9 Nieuw Nickerie Nickerie, NW Suriname 05°56′N 57°W
98 P5 Nieuwolda Groningen, NE Netherlands 53°15′N 06°58′E
99 B17 Nieuwpoort var. Nieuport. West-Vlaanderen, W Belgium 51°08′N 02°45′E
99 G14 Nieuw-Vossemeer Noord-Brabant, S Netherlands 51°34′N 04°13′E
98 P7 Nieuw-Weerdinge Drenthe, NE Netherlands 52°51′N 07°00′E
40 L10 Nieves Zacatecas, C Mexico 24°00′N 102°57′W
64 O11 Nieves, Pico de las ▲ Gran Canaria, Islas Canarias, Spain, NE Atlantic Ocean 27°58′N 15°34′W
103 P8 Nièvre ◈ department C France
Niewenstat see Neustadt an der Weinstrasse
136 J15 Niğde Niğde, C Turkey 37°58′N 34°42′E
136 J15 Niğde ◈ province C Turkey
83 J21 Nigel Gauteng, NE South Africa 26°25′S 28°28′E
77 V10 Niger off. Republic of Niger. ◆ republic W Africa
77 T14 Niger ◈ state C Nigeria
67 P8 Niger ≈ W Africa
Niger Cone see Niger Fan
67 P9 Niger Delta delta S Nigeria
67 P9 Niger Fan var. Niger Cone. undersea feature E Atlantic Ocean 04°15′N 05°00′E
77 T13 Nigeria off. Federal Republic of Nigeria. ◆ federal republic W Africa
Nigeria, Federal Republic of see Nigeria
77 T17 Niger, Mouths of the delta S Nigeria
Niger, Republic of see Niger
185 C24 Nightcaps Southland, South Island, New Zealand 45°58′S 168°03′E
14 F7 Night Hawk Lake ◎ Ontario, S Canada
65 M19 Nightingale Island island S Tristan da Cunha, S Atlantic Ocean
38 M12 Nightmute Alaska, USA 60°28′N 164°43′W
114 G13 Nigrita Kentrikí Makedonía, NE Greece 40°54′N 23°29′E
148 J15 Nihing Per. Rūd-e Nahang. ≈ Iran/Pakistan
191 V10 Nihiru atoll Îles Tuamotu, C French Polynesia
Nihommatsu see Nihonmatsu
Nihon see Japan
165 P11 Nihonmatsu var. Nihommatsu, Nihonmatu. Fukushima, Honshū, C Japan 37°34′N 140°25′E
Nihonmatu see Nihonmatsu
62 I12 Nihuil, Embalse del ⊠ W Argentina
165 O10 Niigata Niigata, Honshū, C Japan 37°55′N 139°01′E
165 O11 Niigata off. Niigata-ken. ◈ prefecture Honshū, C Japan
Niigata-ken see Niigata
165 G14 Niihama Ehime, Shikoku, SW Japan 33°57′N 133°15′E
38 A8 Ni'ihau var. Niihau. island Hawai'i, USA, C Pacific Ocean
165 X12 Nii-jima island E Japan
165 H12 Niimi Okayama, Honshū, SW Japan 35°00′N 133°27′E
165 O10 Niitsu var. Niitu. Niigata, Honshū, C Japan 37°48′N 139°09′E
Niitu see Niitsu
105 P15 Níjar Andalucía, S Spain 36°57′N 02°13′W
98 K11 Nijkerk Gelderland, C Netherlands 52°13′N 05°30′E
99 H16 Nijlen Antwerpen, N Belgium 51°10′N 04°40′E
98 L13 Nijmegen Ger. Nimwegen; anc. Noviomagus. Gelderland, SE Netherlands 51°50′N 05°52′E
98 N10 Nijverdal Overijssel, E Netherlands 52°22′N 06°28′E
190 G16 Nikao Rarotonga, S Cook Islands
Nikaria see Ikaría
124 I2 Nikel' Finn. Kolosjoki. Murmanskaya Oblast', NW Russian Federation 69°25′N 30°12′E
171 Q17 Nikiniki Timor, S Indonesia 10°S 124°30′E
129 Q15 Nikitin Seamount undersea feature E Indian Ocean 05°48′S 83°48′E
77 S14 Nikki E Benin 09°55′N 03°12′E
Niklasmarkt see Gheorgheni
39 P10 Nikolai Alaska, USA 63°00′N 154°22′W
Nikolaiken see Mikołajki
Nikolainkaupunki see Vaasa
Nikolayev see Mykolayiv
145 O6 Nikolayevka Severnyy Kazakhstan, N Kazakhstan
Nikolayevka see Zhetigen
127 P9 Nikolayevsk Volgogradskaya Oblast', SW Russian Federation 50°03′N 45°30′E
Nikolayevskaya Oblast' see Mykolayivs'ka Oblast'
123 S12 Nikolayevsk-na-Amure Khabarovskiy Kray, SE Russian Federation 53°04′N 140°39′E
127 P6 Nikol'sk Penzenskaya Oblast', W Russian Federation 53°46′N 46°03′E
125 O13 Nikol'sk Vologodskaya Oblast', NW Russian Federation 59°35′N 45°31′E
Nikol'sk see Ussuriysk
38 K17 Nikolski Umnak Island, Alaska, USA 52°56′N 168°52′W
Nikol'skiy see Satpayev
127 V7 Nikol'skoye Orenburgskaya Oblast', W Russian Federation 52°01′N 55°48′E
Nikol'sk-Ussuriyskiy see Ussuriysk
114 J7 Nikopol anc. Nicopolis. Pleven, N Bulgaria 43°43′N 24°55′E
117 S9 Nikopol' Dnipropetrovs'ka Oblast', SE Ukraine 47°34′N 34°23′E
115 C17 Nikópoli anc. Nicopolis. site of ancient city Ípeiros, W Greece
136 M12 Niksar Tokat, N Turkey 40°35′N 36°59′E
143 V14 Nīkshahr Sīstān va Balūchestān, SE Iran 26°15′N 60°10′E
113 J16 Nikšić C Montenegro 42°47′N 18°56′E
191 R4 Nikumaroro ; prev. Gardner Island. atoll Phoenix Islands, C Kiribati
191 P3 Nikunau var. Nukunau; prev. Byron Island. atoll Tungaru, W Kiribati
155 G21 Nilambūr Kerala, SW India 11°17′N 76°15′E
35 X16 Niland California, W USA 33°14′N 115°31′W
80 G8 Nile former province NW Uganda
67 T3 Nile Ar. Nahr an Nīl. ≈ N Africa
75 W7 Nile Delta delta N Egypt
67 T3 Nile Fan undersea feature E Mediterranean Sea 33°00′N 31°00′E
31 O11 Niles Michigan, N USA 41°49′N 86°15′W
31 V11 Niles Ohio, N USA 41°10′N 80°46′W
155 F20 Nīleswaram Kerala, SW India 12°18′N 75°07′E
14 K10 Nilgaut, Lac ◎ Québec, SE Canada
149 O6 Nīlī Dāykondī, C Afghanistan 33°43′N 66°07′E
158 I5 Nilka Xinjiang Uygur Zizhiqu, NW China 43°46′N 82°33′E
Nīl, Nahr an see Nile
93 N16 Nilsiä Itä-Suomi, C Finland 63°13′N 28°00′E
154 F9 Nīmach Madhya Pradesh, C India 24°27′N 74°56′E
152 G14 Nimbāhera Rājasthān, N India 24°38′N 74°45′E
76 L15 Nimba, Monts var. Nimba Mountains. ▲▲ W Africa
Nimba Mountains see Nimba, Monts
Nimburg see Nymburk
103 Q15 Nîmes anc. Nemausus, Nismes. Gard, S France 43°49′N 04°20′E
152 H11 Nīm ka Thāna Rājasthān, N India 27°42′N 75°50′E
183 R11 Nimmitabel New South Wales, SE Australia 36°34′S 149°18′E
Nimptsch see Niemcza
195 R11 Nimrod Glacier glacier Antarctica
Nimroze see Nīmrūz
148 K8 Nīmrūz var. Nimroze; prev. Chakhānsūr. ◈ province SW Afghanistan
81 F16 Nimule Eastern Equatoria, S Sudan 03°35′N 32°03′E
Nimwegen see Nijmegen
139 P3 Nīnawá ◈ governorate NW Iraq
155 C23 Nine Degree Channel channel India/Maldives
18 G9 Ninemile Point headland New York, NE USA 43°31′N 76°22′W
173 S8 Ninetyeast Ridge undersea feature E Indian Ocean 04°00′S 90°00′E
183 P13 Ninety Mile Beach beach Victoria, SE Australia
184 I2 Ninety Mile Beach beach North Island, New Zealand
21 P12 Ninety Six South Carolina, SE USA 34°10′N 82°01′W
163 Y9 Ning'an Heilongjiang, NE China 44°20′N 129°28′E
161 S9 Ningbo var. Ning-po, Yin-hsien; prev. Ninghsien. Zhejiang, SE China 29°54′N 121°33′E
161 U12 Ningde Fujian, SE China 26°48′N 119°33′E
161 P12 Ningdu var. Meijiang. Jiangxi, S China 26°28′N 115°53′E
Ning'er see Pu'er
186 A7 Ningerum Western, SW Papua New Guinea 05°40′S 141°10′E
161 R9 Ningguo Anhui, E China 30°33′N 118°58′E
161 S9 Ninghai Zhejiang, SE China 29°18′N 121°26′E
Ning-hsia see Ningxia
Ninghsien see Ningbo
159 S15 Ningjing Shan ▲▲ W China
160 J15 Ningming var. Chengzhong. Guangxi Zhuangzu Zizhiqu, S China 22°07′N 106°43′E
160 H11 Ningnan var. Pisha. Sichuan, C China 26°59′N 102°49′E
Ning-po see Ningbo
Ningsia/Ningsia Hui/Ningsia Hui Autonomous Region see Ningxia
160 J5 Ningxia off. Ningxia Huizu Zizhiqu, var. Ning-hsia, Ningsia, Eng. Ningsia Hui, Ningsia Hui Autonomous Region. ◈ autonomous region N China
Ningxia Huizu Zizhiqu see Ningxia
159 X10 Ningxian var. Xinning. Gansu, N China 35°30′N 108°05′E
167 T7 Ninh Binh Ninh Binh, N Vietnam 20°14′N 106°00′E
167 V12 Ninh Hoa Khanh Hoa, S Vietnam 12°28′N 109°07′E
186 C4 Ninigo Group island group N Papua New Guinea
39 Q12 Ninilchik Alaska, USA 60°03′N 151°40′W
27 N7 Ninnescah River ≈ Kansas, C USA
195 U16 Ninnis Glacier glacier Antarctica
165 R8 Ninohe Iwate, Honshū, C Japan 40°16′N 141°18′E
99 F18 Ninove Oost-Vlaanderen, C Belgium 50°50′N 04°02′E
171 O4 Ninoy Aquino ✕ (Manila) Luzon, N Philippines 14°26′N 121°00′E
Nio see Íos
29 P12 Niobrara Nebraska, C USA 42°43′N 97°59′W
28 M12 Niobrara River ≈ Nebraska/Wyoming, C USA
79 I20 Nioki Bandundu, W Dem. Rep. Congo 02°44′S 17°42′E
76 M11 Niono Ségou, C Mali 14°18′N 05°59′W
76 K11 Nioro var. Nioro du Sahel. Kayes, W Mali 15°13′N 09°39′W
76 G11 Nioro du Rip SW Senegal 13°44′N 15°48′W
Nioro du Sahel see Nioro
102 K10 Niort Deux-Sèvres, W France 46°21′N 00°25′W
172 H14 Nioumachoua Mohéli, S Comoros 12°21′S 43°43′E
186 C7 Nipa Southern Highlands, W Papua New Guinea 06°11′S 143°27′E
11 U14 Nipawin Saskatchewan, S Canada 53°23′N 104°01′W
12 D12 Nipigon Ontario, S Canada 49°02′N 88°15′W
12 D11 Nipigon, Lake ◎ Ontario, S Canada
11 S13 Nipin ≈ Saskatchewan, C Canada
14 G11 Nipissing, Lake ◎ Ontario, S Canada
35 P13 Nipomo California, W USA 35°02′N 120°28′W
Nippon see Japan
138 K6 Niqniqīyah, Jabal an ▲ C Syria
62 I9 Niquivil San Juan, W Argentina 30°25′S 68°42′W
171 Y13 Nirabotong Papua, E Indonesia 02°35′S 140°08′E
Niriz see Neyrīz
163 U7 Nirji var. Morin Dawa Daurzu Zizhiqi. Nei Mongol Zizhiqu, N China 48°21′N 124°32′E
155 I14 Nirmal Andhra Pradesh, C India 19°04′N 78°21′E
153 Q13 Nirmāli Bihār, NE India 26°18′N 86°35′E
113 O14 Niš Eng. Nish, Ger. Nisch; anc. Naissus. Serbia, SE Serbia 43°21′N 21°53′E
104 H9 Nisa Portalegre, C Portugal 39°31′N 07°39′W
Nisa see Neisse
141 P4 Niṣab Al Ḥudūd ash Shamālīyah, N Saudi Arabia 29°11′N 44°43′E
141 Q15 Niṣāb var. Anṣāb. SW Yemen 14°24′N 46°47′E
113 P14 Nišava Bul. Nishava. ≈ Bulgaria/Serbia see also Nishava
Nišava see Nishava
107 K25 Niscemi Sicilia, Italy, C Mediterranean Sea 37°09′N 14°23′E
Nisch/Nish see Niš
165 R4 Niseko Hokkaidō, NE Japan 42°50′N 140°43′E
Nishapur see Neyshābūr
114 G9 Nishava var. Nišava. ≈ Bulgaria/Serbia see also Nišava
Nishava see Nišava
118 L11 Nishcha ≈ N Belarus
165 C17 Nishinoomote Kagoshima, Tanega-shima, SW Japan 30°42′N 130°59′E
165 X15 Nishino-shima Eng. Rosario. island Ogasawara-shotō, SE Japan
165 I13 Nishiwaki var. Nisiwaki. Hyōgo, Honshū, SW Japan 34°59′N 134°58′E
141 U14 Nishtūn SE Yemen 15°47′N 52°08′E
Nisibin see Nusaybin
Nisiros see Nísyros
Nisiwaki see Nishiwaki
Niska see Niesky
113 O14 Niška Banja Serbia, SE Serbia 43°18′N 22°01′E
12 D6 Niskibi ≈ Ontario, C Canada
111 O15 Nisko Podkrapackie, SE Poland 50°31′N 22°09′E
10 H7 Nisling ≈ Yukon Territory, W Canada
99 H22 Nismes Namur, S Belgium 50°04′N 04°31′E
Nismes see Nîmes
116 M10 Nisporeni Rus. Nisporeny. W Moldova 47°04′N 28°10′E
Nisporeny see Nisporeni
95 K20 Nissan ≈ S Sweden
Nissan Islands see Green Islands
95 F16 Nisser ◎ S Norway
95 E21 Nissum Bredning inlet NW Denmark
29 U6 Nisswa Minnesota, N USA 46°31′N 94°17′W
Nistru see Dniester
115 M22 Nísyros var. Nisiros. island Dodekánisa, Greece, Aegean Sea
118 H8 Nītaure Cēsis, C Latvia 57°05′N 25°12′E
60 P10 Niterói prev. Nictheroy. Rio de Janeiro, SE Brazil 22°54′S 43°06′W
14 F16 Nith ≈ Ontario, S Canada
96 J13 Nith ≈ S Scotland, United Kingdom
Nitinan see Nichinan
111 I21 Nitra Ger. Neutra, Hung. Nyitra. Nitriansky Kraj, SW Slovakia 48°20′N 18°05′E
111 I20 Nitra Ger. Neutra, Hung. Nyitra. ≈ W Slovakia
111 I21 Nitriansky Kraj ◈ region SW Slovakia
21 Q5 Nitro West Virginia, NE USA 38°24′N 81°50′W
95 H14 Nittedal Akershus, S Norway 60°08′N 10°45′E
Niuatobutabu see Niuatoputapu
193 X13 Niuatoputapu var. Niuatobutabu; prev. Keppel Island. island N Tonga
193 U15 Niu'Aunofa headland Tongatapu, S Tonga 21°03′S 175°19′W
Niuchwang see Yingkou
190 B16 Niue ◇ self-governing territory in free association with New Zealand S Pacific Ocean
190 F10 Niulakita var. Nurakita. atoll S Tuvalu
190 E6 Niutao atoll NW Tuvalu
93 L15 Nivala Oulu, C Finland 63°56′N 25°00′E
102 I15 Nive ≈ SW France
99 G19 Nivelles Walloon Brabant, C Belgium 50°36′N 04°20′E
103 P8 Nivernais cultural region C France
15 N8 Niverville, Lac ◎ Québec, SE Canada
27 T7 Nixa Missouri, C USA 37°02′N 93°17′W
35 R5 Nixon Nevada, W USA 39°48′N 119°24′W
25 S12 Nixon Texas, SW USA 29°16′N 97°45′W
Niya see Minfeng
Niyazov see Nyýazow
155 H15 Nizāmābād Andhra Pradesh, C India 18°40′N 78°05′E
155 H16 Nizām Sāgar ◎ C India
125 N16 Nizhegorodskaya Oblast' ◈ province W Russian Federation
Nizhnegorskiy see Nyzhn'ohirs'kyy
127 S4 Nizhnekamsk Respublika Tatarstan, W Russian Federation 55°36′N 51°45′E
127 U3 Nizhnekamskoye Vodokhranilishche ⊠ W Russian Federation
123 S14 Nizhneleninskoye Yevreyskaya Avtonomnaya Oblast', SE Russian Federation 47°50′N 132°30′E
122 L13 Nizhneudinsk Irkutskaya Oblast', S Russian Federation 54°48′N 98°51′E
122 I10 Nizhnevartovsk Khanty-Mansiyskiy Avtonomnyy Okrug-Yugra, C Russian Federation 60°57′N 76°40′E
123 Q7 Nizhneyansk Respublika Sakha (Yakutiya), NE Russian Federation 71°25′N 135°59′E
127 Q11 Nizhniy Baskunchak Astrakhanskaya Oblast', SW Russian Federation 48°15′N 46°49′E
127 O6 Nizhniy Lomov Penzenskaya Oblast', W Russian Federation 53°32′N 43°39′E
127 P3 Nizhniy Novgorod prev. Gor'kiy. Nizhegorodskaya Oblast', W Russian Federation 56°17′N 44°E
125 T8 Nizhniy Odes Respublika Komi, NW Russian Federation 63°42′N 54°59′E
Nizhniy Pyandzh see Panji Poyon
122 G10 Nizhniy Tagil Sverdlovskaya Oblast', C Russian Federation 57°57′N 59°51′E
127 T4 Nizhnyaya Maktama Respublika Tatarstan, W Russian Federation 54°51′N 52°22′E
125 T9 Nizhnyaya-Omra Respublika Komi, NW Russian Federation 62°46′N 55°54′E
125 P5 Nizhnyaya Pesha Nenetskiy Avtonomnyy Okrug, NW Russian Federation 66°54′N 47°37′E
117 Q3 Nizhyn Rus. Nezhin. Chernihivs'ka Oblast', NE Ukraine 51°03′N 31°54′E
136 M17 Nizip Gaziantep, S Turkey 37°02′N 37°47′E
141 X8 Nizwa var. Nazwāh. NE Oman 23°00′N 57°50′E
Nizza see Nice
106 C9 Nizza Monferrato Piemonte, NE Italy 44°47′N 08°22′E
Njávdám see Näätämöjoki
Njellim see Nellim
81 H24 Njombe Iringa, S Tanzania 09°20′S 34°47′E
81 G23 Njombe ≈ C Tanzania
Njuk, Ozero see Nyuk, Ozero
Njuksenica see Nyuksenitsa
92 I10 Njunis ▲ N Norway 68°47′N 19°24′E
93 H17 Njurunda Västernorrland, C Sweden 62°15′N 17°24′E
94 N11 Njutånger Gävleborg, C Sweden 61°37′N 17°04′E
79 D14 Nkambe Nord-Ouest, NW Cameroon 06°35′N 10°44′E
Nkata Bay see Nkhata Bay
79 F21 Nkayi prev. Jacob. Bouenza, S Congo 04°11′S 13°17′E
83 J17 Nkayi Matabeleland North, W Zimbabwe 19°00′S 28°54′E
82 N13 Nkhata Bay var. Nkata Bay. Northern, N Malawi 11°37′S 34°20′E
81 E22 Nkonde Kigoma, N Tanzania 06°16′S 30°17′E
79 D15 Nkongsamba var. N'Kongsamba. Littoral, W Cameroon 04°59′N 09°53′E
N'Kongsamba see Nkongsamba
83 E16 Nkurenkuru Okavango, N Namibia 17°38′S 18°39′E
77 Q15 Nkwanta E Ghana 08°18′N 00°27′E
167 O2 Nmai Hka var. Me Hka. ≈ N Myanmar (Burma)
Noardwâlde see Noordwolde
39 N7 Noatak Alaska, USA 67°34′N 162°58′W
39 N7 Noatak River ≈ Alaska, USA
164 E15 Nobeoka Miyazaki, Kyūshū, SW Japan 32°34′N 131°37′E
27 N11 Noble Oklahoma, C USA 35°08′N 97°23′W
31 P13 Noblesville Indiana, N USA 40°03′N 86°00′W
165 R5 Noboribetsu var. Noboribetu. Hokkaidō, NE Japan 42°27′N 141°08′E
Noboribetu see Noboribetsu
59 H18 Nobres Mato Grosso, W Brazil 14°44′S 56°15′W
107 N21 Nocera Terinese Calabria, S Italy 39°03′N 16°10′E
41 Q16 Nochixtlán var. Asunción Nochixtlán. Oaxaca, SE Mexico 17°29′N 97°17′W
25 S5 Nocona Texas, SW USA 33°47′N 97°43′W
63 K21 Nodales, Bahía de los bay S Argentina
27 Q2 Nodaway River ≈ Iowa/Missouri, C USA
27 R8 Noel Missouri, C USA 36°33′N 94°29′W
40 H3 Nogales Chihuahua, NW Mexico 18°50′N 97°12′W
40 F3 Nogales Sonora, NW Mexico 31°17′N 110°53′W
36 M17 Nogales Arizona, SW USA 31°20′N 110°55′W
Nogal Valley see Dooxo Nugaaleed
102 K15 Nogaro Gers, S France 43°46′N 00°01′W
110 J7 Nogat ≈ N Poland
164 D12 Nōgata Fukuoka, Kyūshū, SW Japan 33°46′N 130°42′E
127 P15 Nogayskaya Step' steppe SW Russian Federation
102 M6 Nogent-le-Rotrou Eure-et-Loir, C France 48°19′N 00°50′E

◆ Country
● Country Capital
◇ Dependent Territory
○ Dependent Territory Capital
◈ Administrative Regions
✕ International Airport
▲ Mountain
▲▲ Mountain Range
Volcano
◎ Lake
≈ River
⊠ Reservoir

NOGENT-SUR-OISE – NOTRE-DAME-DU-LAC

103 *O4* **Nogent-sur-Oise** Oise, N France 49°16′N 02°28′E
103 *P6* **Nogent-sur-Seine** Aube, N France 48°30′N 03°31′E
122 *L10* **Noginsk** Evenkiyskiy Avtonomnyy Okrug, N Russian Federation 64°28′N 91°09′E
126 *L3* **Noginsk** Moskovskaya Oblast', W Russian Federation 55°51′N 38°23′E
123 *T12* **Nogliki** Ostrov Sakhalin, Sakhalinskaya Oblast', SE Russian Federation 51°44′N 143°14′E
164 *K12* **Nōgōhaku-san** ▲ Honshū, SW Japan 35°46′N 136°30′E
162 *D5* **Nogoonnuur** Bayan-Ölgiy, NW Mongolia 49°31′N 89°48′E
61 *C18* **Nogoyá** Entre Ríos, E Argentina 32°25′S 59°50′W
111 *K21* **Nógrád** *off.* Nógrád Megye. ◆ *county* N Hungary
Nógrád Megye *see* Nógrád
105 *U5* **Noguera Pallaresa** ⛐ NE Spain
105 *U4* **Noguera Ribagorçana** ⛐ NE Spain
101 *E19* **Nohfelden** Saarland, SW Germany 49°35′N 07°08′E
38 *A8* **Nohili Point** *headland* Kaua'i, Hawai'i, USA 22°03′N 159°48′W
104 *G3* **Noia** Galicia, NW Spain 42°48′N 08°52′W
103 *N16* **Noire, Montagne** ▲▲ S France
14 *J10* **Noire, Rivière** ⛐ Québec, SE Canada
15 *P12* **Noire, Rivière** ⛐ Québec, SE Canada
Noire, Rivi`ere *see* Black River
102 *G6* **Noires, Montagnes** ▲▲ NW France
102 *H8* **Noirmoutier-en-l'Île** Vendée, NW France 47°00′N 02°15′W
102 *H8* **Noirmoutier, Île de** *island* NW France
187 *Q10* **Noka** Nendö, E Solomon Islands 10°42′S 165°57′E
83 *G17* **Nokaneng** North West, NW Botswana 19°40′S 22°12′E
93 *L18* **Nokia** Länsi-Suomi, W Finland 61°29′N 23°30′E
148 *K11* **Nok Kundi** Baluchistān, SW Pakistan 28°49′N 62°39′E
30 *L14* **Nokomis** Illinois, N USA 39°18′N 89°17′W
30 *K5* **Nokomis, Lake** ⊠ Wisconsin, N USA
78 *G9* **Nokou** Kanem, W Chad 14°36′N 14°45′E
187 *Q12* **Nokuku** Espiritu Santo, W Vanuatu 14°56′S 166°34′E
95 *J18* **Nol** Västra Götaland, S Sweden 57°55′N 12°03′E
79 *H16* **Nola** Sangha-Mbaéré, SW Central African Republic 03°29′N 16°05′E
25 *P7* **Nolan** Texas, SW USA 32°15′N 100°15′W
125 *R15* **Nolinsk** Kirovskaya Oblast', NW Russian Federation 57°35′N 49°54′E
Nolsø *see* Nólsoy
95 *B19* **Nólsoy** *Dan.* Nolsø. *island* E Faeroe Islands
186 *B7* **Nomad** Western, SW Papau New Guinea 06°11′S 142°13′E
164 *B16* **Noma-zaki** Kyūshū, SW Japan
40 *K10* **Nombre de Dios** Durango, C Mexico 23°51′N 104°14′W
42 *I5* **Nombre de Dios, Cordillera** ▲▲ N Honduras
38 *M9* **Nome** Alaska, USA 64°30′N 165°24′W
29 *Q6* **Nome** North Dakota, N USA 46°39′N 97°49′W
38 *M9* **Nome, Cape** *headland* Alaska, USA 64°25′N 165°00′W
162 *K11* **Nomgon** *var.* Sangiyn Dalay. Ömnögovĭ, S Mongolia 42°50′N 105°04′E
14 *M11* **Nominingue, Lac** ◎ Québec, SE Canada
Nomoi Islands *see* Mortlock Islands
164 *B16* **Nomo-zaki** *headland* Kyūshū, SW Japan 32°34′N 129°45′E
162 *G6* **Nömrög** *var.* Hödrögö. Dzavhan, N Mongolia 48°51′N 96°48′E
193 *X15* **Nomuka** *island* Nomuka Group, C Tonga
193 *X15* **Nomuka Group** *island group* W Tonga
189 *Q15* **Nomwin Atoll** *atoll* Hall Islands, C Micronesia
8 *L10* **Nonacho Lake** ◎ Northwest Territories, NW Canada
Nondaburi *see* Nonthaburi
39 *P12* **Nondalton** Alaska, USA 59°58′N 154°51′W
163 *V10* **Nong'an** Jilin, NE China 44°25′N 125°10′E
169 *P10* **Nong Bua Khok** Nakhon Ratchasima, C Thailand 15°23′N 101°51′E
167 *Q9* **Nong Bua Lamphu** Udon Thani, E Thailand 17°11′N 102°27′E
167 *R7* **Nông Hèt** Xiangkhoang, N Laos 19°27′N 104°02′E
Nongkaya *see* Nong Khai
167 *Q8* **Nong Khai** *var.* Mi Chai, Nongkaya. Nong Khai, E Thailand 17°52′N 102°44′E
167 *N14* **Nong Met** Surat Thani, SW Thailand 09°27′N 99°09′E
83 *L22* **Nongoma** KwaZulu/Natal, E South Africa 27°54′S 31°40′E
167 *P9* **Nong Phai** Phetchabun, C Thailand 15°58′N 101°02′E
153 *U13* **Nongstoin** Meghālaya, NE India 25°24′N 91°19′E
83 *C19* **Nonidas** Erongo, N Namibia 22°36′S 14°40′E
Nonni *see* Nen Jiang
40 *J7* **Nonoava** Chihuahua, N Mexico 27°24′N 106°18′W
191 *O3* **Nonouti** *prev.* Sydenham Island. *atoll* Tungaru, W Kiribati
167 *O11* **Nonthaburi** *var.* Nondaburi, Nontha Buri. Nonthaburi, C Thailand 13°48′N 100°11′E
Nontha Buri *see* Nonthaburi
102 *L11* **Nontron** Dordogne, SW France 45°34′N 00°41′E
181 *P1* **Noonamah** Northern Territory, N Australia 12°46′S 131°08′E
28 *K2* **Noonan** North Dakota, N USA 48°51′N 102°57′W
Noonu *see* South Miladhunmadulu Atoll
99 *E14* **Noord-Beveland** *var.* North Beveland. *island* SW Netherlands
99 *J14* **Noord-Brabant** *Eng.* North Brabant. ◆ *province* S Netherlands
98 *H7* **Noorder Haaks** *spit* NW Netherlands
98 *H9* **Noord-Holland** *Eng.* North Holland. ◆ *province* NW Netherlands
Noordhollandsch Kanaal *see* Noordhollands Kanaal
98 *H8* **Noordhollands Kanaal** *var.* Noordhollandsch Kanaal. *canal* NW Netherlands
Noord-Kaap *see* Northern Cape
98 *L8* **Noordoostpolder** *island* N Netherlands
45 *P16* **Noordpunt** *headland* Curaçao, C Netherlands Antilles 12°21′N 69°08′W
98 *I8* **Noord-Scharwoude** Noord-Holland, NW Netherlands 52°42′N 04°48′E
Noordwes *see* North-West
98 *G11* **Noordwijk aan Zee** Zuid-Holland, W Netherlands 52°15′N 04°25′E
98 *H11* **Noordwijkerhout** Zuid-Holland, W Netherlands 52°16′N 04°30′E
98 *M7* **Noordwolde** *Fris.* Noardwâlde. Friesland, N Netherlands 52°54′N 06°10′E
Noordzee *see* North Sea
98 *H10* **Noordzee-Kanaal** *canal* NW Netherlands
93 *K18* **Noormarkku** *Swe.* Normark. Länsi-Suomi, SW Finland 61°35′N 21°54′E
39 *N8* **Noorvik** Alaska, USA 66°50′N 161°01′W
10 *J17* **Nootka Sound** *inlet* British Columbia, W Canada
82 *A9* **Nóqui** Dem. Rep. Congo, NW Angola 05°54′S 13°30′E
95 *L15* **Nora** Örebro, C Sweden 59°31′N 15°02′E
147 *Q13* **Norak** *Rus.* Nurek. W Tajikistan 38°23′N 69°14′E
13 *I13* **Noranda** Québec, SE Canada 48°16′N 79°03′W
29 *W12* **Nora Springs** Iowa, C USA 43°08′N 93°00′W
95 *M14* **Norberg** Västmanland, C Sweden 60°04′N 15°56′E
14 *K13* **Norcan Lake** ◎ Ontario, SE Canada
197 *R12* **Nord** Avannaarsua, N Greenland 81°38′N 12°51′W
78 *F13* **Nord** *Eng.* North. ◆ *province* N Cameroon
103 *P2* **Nord** ◆ *department* N France
92 *P1* **Nordaustlandet** *island* NE Svalbard
95 *G24* **Nordborg** *Ger.* Nordburg. Sønderjylland, SW Denmark 55°04′N 09°41′E
Nordburg *see* Nordborg
95 *F23* **Nordby** Ribe, W Denmark 55°27′N 08°25′E
11 *P15* **Nordegg** Alberta, SW Canada 52°27′N 116°06′W
100 *E9* **Norden** Niedersachsen, NW Germany 53°36′N 07°12′E
100 *G10* **Nordenham** Niedersachsen, NW Germany 53°30′N 08°29′E
122 *M6* **Nordenshel'da, Arkhipelag** *island group* N Russian Federation
92 *O3* **Nordenskiold Land** *physical region* W Svalbard
100 *E9* **Norderney** *island* NW Germany
100 *J9* **Norderstedt** Schleswig-Holstein, N Germany 53°42′N 09°59′E
94 *D11* **Nordfjord** *fjord* S Norway
94 *C11* **Nordfjord** *physical region* S Norway
94 *D11* **Nordfjordeid** Sogn og Fjordane, S Norway 61°54′N 06°E
92 *G11* **Nordfold** Nordland, C Norway 67°48′N 15°16′E
Nordfriesische Inseln *see* North Frisian Islands
100 *H7* **Nordfriesland** *cultural region* N Germany
101 *K15* **Nordhausen** Thüringen, C Germany 51°31′N 10°48′E
25 *T13* **Nordheim** Texas, SW USA 28°55′N 97°36′W
94 *C13* **Nordhordland** *physical region* S Norway
100 *E12* **Nordhorn** Niedersachsen, NW Germany 52°26′N 07°04′E
92 *I1* **Nordhurfjördhur** Vestfirdhir, NW Iceland 66°01′N 21°33′W
92 *J1* **Nordhurland Eystra** ◆ *region* N Iceland
92 *I2* **Nordhurland Vestra** ◆ *region* N Iceland
172 *H16* **Nord, Île du** *island* Inner Islands, NE Seychelles
95 *F20* **Nordjylland** *var.* Nordjyllands Amt. ◆ *county* N Denmark
Nordjyllands Amt *see* Nordjylland
92 *K7* **Nordkapp** *Eng.* North Cape. *headland* N Norway 25°47′E 71°10′N
92 *O1* **Nordkapp** *headland* N Svalbard 80°31′N 19°58′E
92 *L7* **Nordkinn** *headland* N Norway 71°07′N 27°40′E
79 *N19* **Nord-Kivu** *off.* Région du Nord Kivu. ◆ *region* E Dem. Rep. Congo
Nord Kivu, Région du *see* Nord-Kivu
92 *G12* **Nordland** ◆ *county* C Norway
101 *J21* **Nördlingen** Bayern, S Germany 48°49′N 10°28′E
93 *I16* **Nordmaling** Västerbotten, N Sweden 63°35′N 19°30′E
95 *K15* **Nordmark** Värmland, C Sweden 59°52′N 14°04′E
Nord, Mer du *see* North Sea
94 *F8* **Nordmøre** *physical region* S Norway
100 *I8* **Nord-Ostee-Kanal** *canal* N Germany
0 *J3* **Nordøstrundingen** *cape* NE Greenland
79 *D14* **Nord-Ouest** *Eng.* North-West. ◆ *province* NW Cameroon
Nord-Ouest, Territoires du *see* Northwest Territories
103 *N2* **Nord-Pas-de-Calais** ◆ *region* N France
101 *F19* **Nordpfälzer Bergland** ▲▲ W Germany
Nord, Pointe *see* Fatua, Pointe
187 *P16* **Nord, Province** ◆ *province* C New Caledonia
101 *D14* **Nordrhein-Westfalen** *Eng.* North Rhine-Westphalia, *Fr.* Rhénanie du Nord-Westphalie. ◆ *state* W Germany
Nordsee/Nordsjøen/Nordsøen *see* North Sea
100 *H7* **Nordstrand** *island* N Germany
93 *E15* **Nord-Trøndelag** ◆ *county* C Norway
97 *E19* **Nore** *Ir.* An Fheoir. ⛐ S Ireland
29 *Q14* **Norfolk** Nebraska, C USA 42°01′N 97°25′W
21 *X7* **Norfolk** Virginia, NE USA 36°51′N 76°17′W
97 *P19* **Norfolk** *cultural region* E England, United Kingdom
192 *K10* **Norfolk Island** ◇ *Australian external territory* SW Pacific Ocean
175 *P9* **Norfolk Ridge** *undersea feature* W Pacific Ocean
27 *U8* **Norfork Lake** ⊠ Arkansas/Missouri, C USA
98 *N6* **Norg** Drenthe, NE Netherlands 53°04′N 06°28′E
Norge *see* Norway
95 *D14* **Norheimsund** Hordaland, S Norway 60°22′N 06°09′E
25 *S16* **Norias** Texas, SW USA 26°47′N 97°45′W
164 *L12* **Norikura-dake** ▲ Honshū, S Japan 36°06′N 137°33′E
122 *K8* **Noril'sk** Taymyrskiy (Dolgano-Nenetskiy) Avtonomnyy Okrug, N Russian Federation 69°21′N 88°02′E
14 *I13* **Norland** Ontario, SE Canada 44°46′N 78°48′W
21 *V8* **Norlina** North Carolina, SE USA 36°26′N 78°11′W
30 *L13* **Normal** Illinois, N USA 40°30′N 88°59′W
27 *N11* **Norman** Oklahoma, C USA 35°13′N 97°27′W
Norman *see* Tulita
186 *G9* **Normanby Island** *island* SE Papua New Guinea
Normandes, Îles *see* Channel Islands
58 *G9* **Normandia** Roraima, N Brazil 03°57′N 59°39′W
102 *L5* **Normandie** *Eng.* Normandy. *cultural region* N France
102 *J5* **Normandie, Collines de** *hill range* NW France
Normandy *see* Normandie
25 *V9* **Normangee** Texas, SW USA 31°01′N 96°06′W
21 *Q10* **Norman, Lake** ⊠ North Carolina, SE USA
44 *K13* **Norman Manley** ✈ (Kingston) E Jamaica 17°55′N 76°46′W
181 *U5* **Norman River** ⛐ Queensland, NE Australia
181 *U4* **Normanton** Queensland, NE Australia 17°49′S 141°08′E
8 *I8* **Norman Wells** Northwest Territories, NW Canada 65°18′N 126°42′W
12 *H12* **Normétal** Québec, S Canada 48°59′N 79°23′W
163 *O7* **Norovlin** *var.* Uldz. Hentiy, NE Mongolia 48°47′N 112°01′E
11 *V15* **Norquay** Saskatchewan, S Canada 51°51′N 102°04′W
94 *N11* **Norra Dellen** ◎ C Sweden
93 *G15* **Norråker** Jämtland, C Sweden 64°25′N 15°40′E
94 *N12* **Norrala** Gävleborg, C Sweden 61°22′N 17°04′E
Norra Ny *see* Stöllet
92 *G13* **Norra Storfjället** ▲ N Sweden 65°57′N 15°15′E
92 *I13* **Norrbotten** ◆ *county* N Sweden
95 *G23* **Nørre Aaby** *var.* Nørre Åby. Fyn, C Denmark 55°28′N 09°53′E
Nørre Åby *see* Nørre Aaby
95 *I24* **Nørre Alslev** Storstrøm, SE Denmark 54°54′N 11°53′E
95 *E23* **Nørre Nebel** Ribe, W Denmark 55°45′N 08°16′E
95 *G20* **Nørresundby** Nordjylland, N Denmark 57°05′N 09°55′E
21 *N8* **Norris Lake** ⊠ Tennessee, S USA
18 *I15* **Norristown** Pennsylvania, NE USA 40°07′N 75°20′W
95 *N17* **Norrköping** Östergötland, S Sweden 58°35′N 16°10′E
Norrmark *see* Noormarkku
94 *N13* **Norrsundet** Gävleborg, C Sweden 60°55′N 17°09′E
95 *P15* **Norrtälje** Stockholm, C Sweden 59°46′N 18°42′E
180 *L12* **Norseman** Western Australia 32°16′S 121°46′E
93 *I14* **Norsjö** Västerbotten, N Sweden 64°55′N 19°30′E
95 *G16* **Norsjø** ◎ S Norway
123 *R13* **Norsk** Amurskaya Oblast', SE Russian Federation 52°20′N 129°57′E
Norske Havet *see* Norwegian Sea
187 *Q13* **Norsup** Malekula, C Vanuatu 16°05′S 167°24′E
191 *V15* **Norte, Cabo** *headland* Easter Island, Chile, E Pacific Ocean 27°03′S 109°24′W
54 *F7* **Norte de Santander** *off.* Departamento de Norte de Santander. ◆ *province* N Colombia
Norte de Santander, Departamento de *see* Norte de Santander
61 *E21* **Norte, Punta** *headland* E Argentina 36°17′S 56°46′W
21 *R13* **North** South Carolina, SE USA 33°37′N 81°06′W
North *see* Nord
18 *L10* **North Adams** Massachusetts, NE USA 42°40′N 73°06′W
113 *L17* **North Albanian Alps** *Alb.* Bjeshkët e Namuna, *SCr.* Prokletije. ▲▲ SE Europe
97 *M15* **Northallerton** N England, United Kingdom 54°20′N 01°26′W
180 *J12* **Northam** Western Australia 31°40′S 116°40′E
83 *J20* **Northam** Northern, N South Africa 24°56′S 27°18′E
1 **North America** *continent*
1 *N12* **North American Basin** *undersea feature* W Sargasso Sea 30°00′N 60°00′W
0 *C5* **North American Plate** *tectonic feature*
18 *M11* **North Amherst** Massachusetts, NE USA 42°24′N 72°31′W
97 *N20* **Northampton** C England, United Kingdom 52°14′N 00°54′W
97 *M20* **Northamptonshire** *cultural region* C England, United Kingdom
151 *P18* **North Andaman** *island* Andaman Islands, India, NE Indian Ocean
65 *D25* **North Arm** East Falkland, Falkland Islands 52°06′S 59°21′W
21 *Q13* **North Augusta** South Carolina, SE USA 33°30′N 81°58′W
173 *W8* **North Australian Basin** *Fr.* Bassin Nord de l' Australie. *undersea feature* E Indian Ocean
31 *R11* **North Baltimore** Ohio, N USA 41°10′N 83°40′W
11 *T15* **North Battleford** Saskatchewan, S Canada 52°47′N 108°19′W
14 *H11* **North Bay** Ontario, S Canada 46°20′N 79°28′W
12 *H6* **North Belcher Islands** *island group* Belcher Islands, Nunavut, C Canada
29 *R15* **North Bend** Nebraska, C USA 41°27′N 96°46′W
32 *E14* **North Bend** Oregon, NW USA 43°24′N 124°13′W
96 *K12* **North Berwick** SE Scotland, United Kingdom 56°04′N 02°44′W
North Beveland *see* Noord-Beveland
North Borneo *see* Sabah
183 *P5* **North Bourke** New South Wales, SE Australia 30°03′S 145°56′E
North Brabant *see* Noord-Brabant
182 *F2* **North Branch Neales** *seasonal river* South Australia
44 *M6* **North Caicos** *island* NW Turks and Caicos Islands
26 *L10* **North Canadian River** ⛐ Oklahoma, C USA
31 *U12* **North Canton** Ohio, N USA 40°52′N 81°24′W
13 *R13* **North, Cape** *headland* Cape Breton Island, Nova Scotia, SE Canada 47°06′N 60°24′W
184 *I1* **North Cape** *headland* North Island, New Zealand 34°23′S 173°02′E
186 *G5* **North Cape** *headland* New Ireland, NE Papua New Guinea 02°33′S 150°48′E
North Cape *see* Nordkapp
18 *J17* **North Cape May** New Jersey, NE USA 38°59′N 74°55′W
12 *C9* **North Caribou Lake** ◎ Ontario, C Canada
21 *U10* **North Carolina** *off.* State of North Carolina, *also known as* Old North State, Tar Heel State, Turpentine State. ◆ *state* SE USA
North Celebes *see* Sulawesi Utara
155 *J24* **North Central** ◆ *province* N Sri Lanka
31 *S4* **North Channel** *lake channel* Canada/USA
97 *G14* **North Channel** *strait* Northern Ireland/Scotland, United Kingdom
21 *S14* **North Charleston** South Carolina, SE USA 32°53′N 79°59′W
31 *N10* **North Chicago** Illinois, N USA 42°19′N 87°50′W
195 *Y10* **Northcliffe Glacier** *glacier* Antarctica
31 *Q14* **North College Hill** Ohio, N USA 39°13′N 84°33′W
25 *O8* **North Concho River** ⛐ Texas, SW USA
19 *O8* **North Conway** New Hampshire, NE USA 44°03′N 71°06′W
27 *V14* **North Crossett** Arkansas, C USA 33°10′N 91°56′W
28 *L4* **North Dakota** *off.* State of North Dakota, *also known as* Flickertail State, Peace Garden State, Sioux State. ◆ *state* N USA
North Devon Island *see* Devon Island
97 *O22* **North Downs** *hill range* SE England, United Kingdom
18 *C11* **North East** Pennsylvania, NE USA 42°13′N 79°49′W
83 *I18* **North East** ◆ *district* NE Botswana
65 *G15* **North East Bay** *bay* Ascension Island, C Atlantic Ocean
38 *L10* **Northeast Cape** *headland* Saint Lawrence Island, Alaska, USA 63°16′N 168°50′W
81 *J17* **North Eastern** ◆ *province* Kenya
North East Frontier Agency/North East Frontier Agency of Assam *see* Arunāchal Pradesh
189 *V11* **Northeast Island** *island* Chuuk, C Micronesia
44 *L6* **Northeast Point** *headland* Great Inagua, S Bahamas 21°18′N 73°01′W
44 *K5* **Northeast Point** *headland* Acklins Island, SE Bahamas 22°43′N 73°50′W
44 *L12* **North East Point** *headland* E Jamaica 18°09′N 76°19′W
191 *Z2* **Northeast Point** *headland* Kiritimati, E Kiribati 10°23′S 105°45′E
44 *H2* **Northeast Providence Channel** *channel* N Bahamas
101 *J14* **Northeim** Niedersachsen, C Germany 51°42′N 10°E
29 *X14* **North English** Iowa, C USA 41°30′N 92°04′W
138 *G8* **Northern** ◆ *district* N Israel
82 *M12* **Northern** ◆ *region* N Malawi
186 *F8* **Northern** ◆ *province* S Papua New Guinea
155 *J23* **Northern** ◆ *province* N Sri Lanka
80 *D7* **Northern** ◆ *state* N Sudan
82 *K12* **Northern** ◆ *province* NE Zambia
Northern *see* Limpopo
80 *B13* **Northern Bahr el Ghazal** ◆ *state* SW Sudan
Northern Border Region *see* Al Ḥudūd ash Shamālīyah
83 *F24* **Northern Cape** *off.* Northern Cape Province, *Afr.* Noord-Kaap. ◆ *province* W South Africa
Northern Cape Province *see* Northern Cape
190 *K14* **Northern Cook Islands** *island group* N Cook Islands
80 *B8* **Northern Darfur** ◆ *state* NW Sudan
Northern Dvina *see* Severnaya Dvina
97 *F14* **Northern Ireland** *var.* The Six Counties. *cultural region* Northern Ireland, United Kingdom
97 *F14* **Northern Ireland** *var.* The Six Counties. ◆ *political division* Northern Ireland, United Kingdom
80 *D9* **Northern Kordofan** ◆ *state* C Sudan
187 *Z14* **Northern Lau Group** *island group* Lau Group, NE Fiji
188 *K3* **Northern Mariana Islands** ◇ *US commonwealth territory* W Pacific Ocean
Northern Rhodesia *see* Zambia
Northern Sporades *see* Vóreies Sporádes
182 *D1* **Northern Territory** ◆ *territory* N Australia
Northern Transvaal *see* Limpopo
Northern Ural Hills *see* Severnyye Uvaly
84 *I9* **North European Plain** *plain* N Europe
27 *V2* **North Fabius River** ⛐ Missouri, C USA
65 *D24* **North Falkland Sound** *sound* N Falkland Islands
29 *V9* **Northfield** Minnesota, N USA 44°27′N 93°10′W
19 *O9* **Northfield** New Hampshire, NE USA 43°26′N 71°34′W
175 *Q8* **North Fiji Basin** *undersea feature* N Coral Sea
97 *Q22* **North Foreland** *headland* SE England, United Kingdom 51°22′N 01°26′E
35 *P6* **North Fork American River** ⛐ California, W USA
39 *R7* **North Fork Chandalar River** ⛐ Alaska, USA
28 *K7* **North Fork Grand River** ⛐ North Dakota/South Dakota, N USA
21 *O6* **North Fork Kentucky River** ⛐ Kentucky, S USA
39 *Q7* **North Fork Koyukuk River** ⛐ Alaska, USA
39 *Q10* **North Fork Kuskokwim River** ⛐ Alaska, USA
26 *K11* **North Fork Red River** ⛐ Oklahoma/Texas, SW USA
26 *K3* **North Fork Solomon River** ⛐ Kansas, C USA
23 *W14* **North Fort Myers** Florida, SE USA 26°40′N 81°52′W
31 *P5* **North Fox Island** *island* Michigan, N USA
100 *G6* **North Frisian Islands** *var.* Nordfriesische Inseln. *island group* N Germany
197 *N9* **North Geomagnetic Pole** *pole* Arctic Ocean
18 *M13* **North Haven** Connecticut, NE USA 41°25′N 72°51′W
184 *J5* **North Head** *headland* North Island, New Zealand 36°23′S 174°01′E
18 *L6* **North Hero** Vermont, NE USA 44°49′N 73°14′W
35 *O7* **North Highlands** California, W USA 38°40′N 121°25′W
North Holland *see* Noord-Holland
81 *I16* **North Horr** Eastern, N Kenya 03°17′N 37°08′E
151 *K21* **North Huvadhu Atoll** *var.* Gaafu Alifu Atoll. *atoll* S Maldives
184 *N9* **North Island** *island* N New Zealand
21 *U14* **North Island** *island* South Carolina, SE USA
31 *O11* **North Judson** Indiana, N USA 41°12′N 86°44′W
North Kazakhstan *see* Severnyy Kazakhstan
31 *V10* **North Kingsville** Ohio, N USA 41°54′N 80°41′W
163 *Y13* **North Korea** *off.* Democratic People's Republic of Korea, *Kor.* Chosŏn-minjujuŭi-inmin-kanghwaguk. ◆ *republic* E Asia
153 *X11* **North Lakhimpur** Assam, NE India 27°10′N 94°00′E
184 *J3* **Northland** *off.* Northland Region. ◆ *region* North Island, New Zealand
192 *K11* **Northland Plateau** *undersea feature* S Pacific Ocean
Northland Region *see* Northland
35 *X11* **North Las Vegas** Nevada, W USA 36°12′N 115°07′W
31 *O11* **North Liberty** Indiana, N USA 41°36′N 86°22′W
29 *X14* **North Liberty** Iowa, C USA 41°45′N 91°36′W
27 *V12* **North Little Rock** Arkansas, C USA 34°46′N 92°15′W
28 *M13* **North Loup River** ⛐ Nebraska, C USA
151 *K18* **North Maalhosmadulu Atoll** *var.* North Malosmadulu Atoll, Raa Atoll. *atoll* N Maldives
31 *U10* **North Madison** Ohio, N USA 41°48′N 81°03′W
North Malosmadulu Atoll *see* North Maalhosmadulu Atoll
31 *P12* **North Manchester** Indiana, N USA 41°00′N 85°45′W
31 *P6* **North Manitou Island** *island* Michigan, N USA
29 *U10* **North Mankato** Minnesota, N USA 44°11′N 94°03′W
23 *Z15* **North Miami** Florida, SE USA 25°54′N 80°11′W
151 *K18* **North Miladhunmadulu Atoll** *var.* Shaviyani Atoll. *atoll* N Maldives
North Minch *see* Minch, The
23 *W15* **North Naples** Florida, SE USA 26°13′N 81°47′W
175 *P8* **North New Hebrides Trench** *undersea feature* N Coral Sea
23 *Y15* **North New River Canal** ⛐ Florida, SE USA
151 *K20* **North Nilandhe Atoll** *atoll* C Maldives
36 *L2* **North Ogden** Utah, W USA 41°18′N 111°57′W
North Ossetia *see* Severnaya Osetiya-Alaniya, Respublika
35 *S10* **North Palisade** ▲ California, W USA 37°06′N 118°31′W
189 *U11* **North Pass** *passage* Chuuk Islands, C Micronesia
28 *M15* **North Platte** Nebraska, C USA 41°07′N 100°46′W
33 *X17* **North Platte River** ⛐ C USA
65 *G14* **North Point** *headland* Ascension Island, C Atlantic Ocean
172 *I16* **North Point** *headland* Mahé, NE Seychelles 04°23′S 55°28′E
31 *R5* **North Point** *headland* Michigan, N USA 45°21′N 83°30′W
31 *S6* **North Point** *headland* Michigan, N USA 45°01′N 83°16′W
39 *S9* **North Pole** Alaska, USA 64°42′N 147°09′W
197 *R9* **North Pole** *pole* Arctic Ocean
23 *O4* **Northport** Alabama, S USA 33°13′N 87°34′W
23 *W14* **North Port** Florida, SE USA 27°03′N 82°15′W
32 *L6* **Northport** Washington, NW USA 48°54′N 117°48′W
32 *L12* **North Powder** Oregon, NW USA 45°00′N 117°56′W
29 *U13* **North Raccoon River** ⛐ Iowa, C USA
North Rhine-Westphalia *see* Nordrhein-Westfalen
97 *M16* **North Riding** *cultural region* N England, United Kingdom
96 *G5* **North Rona** *island* NW Scotland, United Kingdom
96 *K4* **North Ronaldsay** *island* NE Scotland, United Kingdom
36 *L2* **North Salt Lake** Utah, W USA 40°51′N 111°54′W
11 *P15* **North Saskatchewan** ⛐ Alberta/Saskatchewan, S Canada
35 *X5* **North Schell Peak** ▲ Nevada, W USA 39°25′N 114°34′W
North Scotia Ridge *see* South Georgia Ridge
86 *D10* **North Sea** *Dan.* Nordsøen, *Dut.* Noordzee, *Fr.* Mer du Nord, *Ger.* Nordsee, *Nor.* Nordsjøen; *prev.* German Ocean, *Lat.* Mare Germanicum. *sea* NW Europe
35 *T6* **North Shoshone Peak** ▲ Nevada, W USA 39°08′N 117°28′W
North Siberian Lowland/North Siberian Plain *see* Severo-Sibirskaya Nizmennost'
29 *R13* **North Sioux City** South Dakota, N USA 42°31′N 96°28′W
96 *K4* **North Sound, The** *sound* N Scotland, United Kingdom
183 *T4* **North Star** New South Wales, SE Australia 28°55′S 150°25′E
North Star State *see* Minnesota
183 *V3* **North Stradbroke Island** *island* Queensland, E Australia
North Sulawesi *see* Sulawesi Utara
North Sumatra *see* Sumatera Utara
14 *D17* **North Sydenham** ⛐ Ontario, S Canada
18 *H9* **North Syracuse** New York, NE USA 43°07′N 76°07′W
184 *K9* **North Taranaki Bight** *gulf* North Island, New Zealand
12 *H9* **North Twin Island** *island* Nunavut, C Canada
96 *E8* **North Uist** *island* NW Scotland, United Kingdom
97 *L14* **Northumberland** *cultural region* N England, United Kingdom
181 *Y7* **Northumberland Isles** *island group* Queensland, NE Australia
13 *Q14* **Northumberland Strait** *strait* SE Canada
32 *G14* **North Umpqua River** ⛐ Oregon, NW USA
45 *Q13* **North Union** Saint Vincent, Saint Vincent and the Grenadines 13°15′N 61°07′W
10 *L17* **North Vancouver** British Columbia, SW Canada 49°21′N 123°05′W
18 *K9* **Northville** New York, NE USA 43°13′N 74°08′W
97 *Q19* **North Walsham** E England, United Kingdom 52°49′N 01°22′E
39 *T10* **Northway** Alaska, USA 62°57′N 141°56′W
149 *R7* **North Wazīristān** ◆ *federally administered tribal area* NW Pakistan
83 *G17* **North-West** ◆ *district* NW Botswana
83 *G21* **North-West** *off.* North-West Province, *Afr.* Noordwes. ◆ *province* N South Africa
North-West *see* Nord-Ouest
64 *I6* **Northwest Atlantic Mid-Ocean Canyon** *undersea feature* N Atlantic Ocean
180 *G8* **North West Cape** *cape* Western Australia
38 *J9* **Northwest Cape** *headland* Saint Lawrence Island, Alaska, USA 63°46′N 171°45′W
155 *J24* **North Western** ◆ *province* W Sri Lanka
82 *H13* **North Western** ◆ *province* W Zambia
149 *U4* **North-West Frontier Province** ◆ *province* NW Pakistan
96 *H8* **North West Highlands** ▲▲ N Scotland, United Kingdom
192 *J4* **Northwest Pacific Basin** *undersea feature* NW Pacific Ocean 40°00′N 150°00′E
191 *Y2* **Northwest Point** *headland* Kiritimati, E Kiribati 10°25′S 105°35′E
44 *G1* **Northwest Providence Channel** *channel* N Bahamas
North-West Province *see* North-West
13 *Q8* **North West River** Newfoundland and Labrador, E Canada 53°30′N 60°10′W
8 *J9* **Northwest Territories** *Fr.* Territoires du Nord-Ouest. ◆ *territory* NW Canada
97 *K18* **Northwich** C England, United Kingdom 53°16′N 02°32′W
25 *Q5* **North Wichita River** ⛐ Texas, SW USA
18 *J17* **North Wildwood** New Jersey, NE USA 39°00′N 74°45′W
21 *R9* **North Wilkesboro** North Carolina, SE USA 36°09′N 81°09′W
19 *P8* **North Windham** Maine, NE USA 43°51′N 70°25′W
197 *Q6* **Northwind Plain** *undersea feature* Arctic Ocean
29 *V11* **Northwood** Iowa, C USA 43°26′N 93°13′W
29 *Q4* **Northwood** North Dakota, N USA 47°43′N 97°34′W
97 *M15* **North York Moors** *moorland* N England, United Kingdom
25 *V9* **North Zulch** Texas, SW USA 30°54′N 96°06′W
26 *K2* **Norton** Kansas, C USA 39°51′N 99°53′W
31 *S13* **Norton** Ohio, N USA 40°25′N 83°04′W
21 *P7* **Norton** Virginia, NE USA 36°56′N 82°37′W
39 *N9* **Norton Bay** *bay* Alaska, USA
Norton de Matos *see* Balombo
31 *O9* **Norton Shores** Michigan, N USA 43°10′N 86°15′W
38 *M10* **Norton Sound** *inlet* Alaska, USA
27 *Q3* **Nortonville** Kansas, C USA 39°25′N 95°19′W
102 *I8* **Nort-sur-Erdre** Loire-Atlantique, NW France 47°27′N 01°30′W
195 *N2* **Norvegia, Cape** *headland* Antarctica 71°16′S 12°25′W
18 *L13* **Norwalk** Connecticut, NE USA 41°08′N 73°28′W
29 *V14* **Norwalk** Iowa, C USA 41°28′N 93°40′W
31 *S11* **Norwalk** Ohio, N USA 41°14′N 82°37′W
19 *P7* **Norway** Maine, NE USA 44°13′N 70°30′W
31 *N5* **Norway** Michigan, N USA 45°47′N 87°54′W
93 *E17* **Norway** *off.* Kingdom of Norway, *Nor.* Norge. ◆ *monarchy* N Europe
11 *X13* **Norway House** Manitoba, C Canada 53°59′N 97°50′W
Norway, Kingdom of *see* Norway
197 *R16* **Norwegian Basin** *undersea feature* NW Norwegian Sea 68°00′N 02°00′W
84 *D6* **Norwegian Sea** *var.* Norske Havet. *sea* NE Atlantic Ocean
197 *S17* **Norwegian Trench** *undersea feature* NE North Sea 59°00′N 04°30′E
14 *F16* **Norwich** Ontario, S Canada 42°57′N 80°37′W
97 *Q19* **Norwich** E England, United Kingdom 52°38′N 01°18′E
19 *N13* **Norwich** Connecticut, NE USA 41°30′N 72°02′W
18 *I11* **Norwich** New York, NE USA 42°31′N 75°31′W
29 *U9* **Norwood** Minnesota, N USA 44°46′N 93°55′W
31 *Q15* **Norwood** Ohio, N USA 39°07′N 84°27′W
14 *H11* **Nosbonsing, Lake** ◎ Ontario, S Canada
Nösen *see* Bistrița
165 *T1* **Noshappu-misaki** *headland* Hokkaidō, NE Japan 45°26′N 141°38′E
165 *P7* **Noshiro** *var.* Nosiro; *prev.* Noshirominato. Akita, Honshū, C Japan 40°11′N 140°02′E
Noshirominato/Nosiro *see* Noshiro
117 *Q3* **Nosivka** *Rus.* Nosovka. Chernihivs'ka Oblast', NE Ukraine 50°55′N 31°37′E
67 *T14* **Nosop** *var.* Nossob, Nossop. ⛐ Botswana/Namibia
83 *E20* **Nossop** ⛐ E Namibia
125 *S4* **Nosovaya** Nenetskiy Avtonomnyy Okrug, NW Russian Federation 68°12′N 54°33′E
Nosovka *see* Nosivka
143 *V11* **Noṣratābād** Sīstān va Balūchestān, E Iran 29°53′N 59°57′E
95 *J18* **Nossebro** Västra Götaland, S Sweden 58°12′N 12°42′E
96 *K6* **Noss Head** *headland* N Scotland, United Kingdom 58°29′N 03°03′W
Nossi-Bé *see* Be, Nosy
81 *E20* **Nossob** ⛐ Namibia
Nossob/Nossop *see* Nosop
172 *J2* **Nosy Be** ✈ Antsirañana, N Madagascar 23°36′S 47°36′E
172 *J6* **Nosy Varika** Fianarantsoa, SE Madagascar 20°36′S 48°31′E
14 *L10* **Notawassi** ⛐ Québec, SE Canada
14 *M9* **Notawassi, Lac** ◎ Québec, SE Canada
36 *J5* **Notch Peak** ▲ Utah, W USA 39°08′N 113°24′W
110 *G10* **Noteć** *Ger.* Netze. ⛐ NW Poland
Nótios Sporádes *see* Dodekánisa
115 *J22* **Nótion Aigaíon** *Eng.* Aegean South. ◆ *region* E Greece
115 *H18* **Nótios Evvoïkós Kólpos** *gulf* E Greece
115 *B16* **Nótio Stenó Kérkyras** *strait* W Greece
107 *L25* **Noto** *anc.* Netum. Sicilia, Italy, C Mediterranean Sea 36°53′N 15°05′E
164 *M10* **Noto** Ishikawa, Honshū, SW Japan 37°18′N 137°11′E
95 *G15* **Notodden** Telemark, S Norway 59°35′N 09°18′E
107 *L25* **Noto, Golfo di** *gulf* Sicilia, Italy, C Mediterranean Sea
164 *L10* **Noto-hantō** *peninsula* Honshū, SW Japan
164 *L11* **Noto-jima** *island* SW Japan
13 *T11* **Notre Dame Bay** *bay* Newfoundland, Newfoundland and Labrador, E Canada
15 *P6* **Notre-Dame-de-Lorette** Québec, SE Canada 49°05′N 72°24′W
14 *L11* **Notre-Dame-de-Pontmain** Québec, SE Canada 46°18′N 75°37′W
15 *T8* **Notre-Dame-du-Lac** Québec, SE Canada 47°36′N 68°48′W

◆ Country ◇ Dependent Territory ◆ Administrative Regions ▲ Mountain Volcano ◎ Lake
● Country Capital ○ Dependent Territory Capital ✈ International Airport ▲▲ Mountain Range ⛐ River ⊠ Reservoir

NOTRE-DAME-DU-ROSAIRE – NYMBOIDA RIVER

15 Q6 **Notre-Dame-du-Rosaire** Québec, SE Canada 48°48′N 71°27′W
15 U8 **Notre-Dame, Monts** ▲▲ Québec, S Canada
77 R16 **Notsé** S Togo 06°59′N 01°12′E
14 G14 **Nottawasaga** ≈ Ontario, S Canada
14 G14 **Nottawasaga Bay** *lake bay* Ontario, S Canada
12 I11 **Nottaway** ≈ Québec, SE Canada
23 S1 **Nottely Lake** ⊠ Georgia, SE USA
95 H16 **Nøtterøy** *island* S Norway
97 M19 **Nottingham** C England, United Kingdom 52°58′N 01°10′W
9 E14 **Nottingham Island** *island* Nunavut, NE Canada
97 N18 **Nottinghamshire** *cultural region* C England, United Kingdom
21 V7 **Nottoway** Virginia, NE USA 37°07′N 78°03′W
21 V7 **Nottoway River** ≈ Virginia, NE USA
76 G7 **Nouâdhibou** *prev.* Port-Étienne. Dakhlet Nouâdhibou, W Mauritania 20°54′N 17°01′W
76 G7 **Nouâdhibou** ✕ Dakhlet Nouâdhibou, W Mauritania 20°59′N 17°02′W
76 F7 **Nouâdhibou, Dakhlet** *prev.* Baie du Lévrier. *bay* W Mauritania
76 F7 **Nouâdhibou, Râs** *prev.* Cap Blanc. *headland* NW Mauritania 20°48′N 17°03′W
76 G9 **Nouakchott** ● (Mauritania) Nouakchott District, SW Mauritania 18°09′N 15°58′W
76 G9 **Nouakchott** ✕ Trarza, SW Mauritania 18°18′N 15°54′W
120 J11 **Noual, Sebkhet en** *var.* Sabkhat an Nawāl. *salt flat* C Tunisia
76 G8 **Nouâmghâr** *var.* Nouamrhar. Dakhlet Nouâdhibou, W Mauritania 19°22′N 16°31′W
Nouamrhar *see* Nouâmghâr
Nouă Sulița *see* Novoselytsya
187 Q17 **Nouméa** ○ (New Caledonia) Province Sud, S New Caledonia 22°13′S 166°29′E
79 E15 **Noun** ≈ C Cameroon
77 N12 **Nouna** W Burkina 12°44′N 03°54′W
83 H24 **Noupoort** Northern Cape, C South Africa 31°11′S 24°57′E
Nouveau-Brunswick *see* New Brunswick
Nouveau-Comptoir *see* Wemindji
15 T4 **Nouvel, Lacs** ◎ Québec, SE Canada
15 W7 **Nouvelle** Québec, SE Canada 48°07′N 66°16′W
15 W7 **Nouvelle** ≈ Québec, SE Canada
Nouvelle-Calédonie *see* New Caledonia
Nouvelle Écosse *see* Nova Scotia
103 R3 **Nouzonville** Ardennes, N France 49°49′N 04°45′E
147 Q11 **Nov** *Rus.* Nau. NW Tajikistan 40°10′N 69°16′E
59 I21 **Nova Alvorada** Mato Grosso do Sul, SW Brazil 21°25′S 54°19′W
Novabad *see* Navobod
111 D19 **Nová Bystřice** *Ger.* Neubistritz. Jihočeský Kraj, S Czech Republic 49°N 15°05′E
116 H13 **Novaci** Gorj, SW Romania 45°07′N 23°37′E
Nova Civitas *see* Neustadt an der Weinstrasse
Novaesium *see* Neuss
60 H10 **Nova Esperança** Paraná, S Brazil 23°09′S 52°13′W
106 H11 **Novafeltria** Marche, C Italy 43°54′N 12°18′E
60 Q9 **Nova Friburgo** Rio de Janeiro, SE Brazil 22°16′S 42°34′W
82 D12 **Nova Gaia** *var.* Cambundi-Catembo. Malanje, NE Angola 10°09′S 17°31′E
109 S12 **Nova Gorica** W Slovenia 45°57′N 13°40′E
112 G10 **Nova Gradiška** *Ger.* Neugradisk, *Hung.* Újgradiska. Brod-Posavina, NE Croatia 45°15′N 17°23′E
60 K7 **Nova Granada** São Paulo, S Brazil 20°33′S 49°19′W
60 O10 **Nova Iguaçu** Rio de Janeiro, SE Brazil 22°31′S 44°05′W
117 S10 **Nova Kakhovka** *Rus.* Novaya Kakhovka. Khersons'ka Oblast', SE Ukraine 46°45′N 33°20′E
Nová Karvinná *see* Karviná
Nova Lamego *see* Gabú
Nova Lisboa *see* Huambo
112 C11 **Novalja** Lika-Senj, W Croatia 44°33′N 14°53′E
119 M14 **Novalukoml'** *Rus.* Novolukoml'. Vitsyebskaya Voblasts', N Belarus 54°40′N 29°09′E
Nova Mambone *see* Mambone
83 P16 **Nova Nabúri** Zambézia, NE Mozambique 16°47′S 38°55′E
117 Q9 **Nova Odesa** *var.* Novaya Odessa. Mykolayivs'ka Oblast', S Ukraine 47°19′N 31°45′E
60 H10 **Nova Olímpia** Paraná, S Brazil 23°28′S 53°12′W
61 I15 **Nova Prata** Rio Grande do Sul, S Brazil 28°45′S 51°37′W
14 H12 **Novar** Ontario, S Canada 45°26′N 79°14′W
106 C7 **Novara** *anc.* Novaria. Piemonte, NW Italy 45°27′N 08°36′E
Novaria *see* Novara
117 P7 **Novarkanels'k** Kirovohrads'ka Oblast', C Ukraine 48°39′N 30°48′E
13 P15 **Nova Scotia** *Fr.* Nouvelle Écosse. ◈ *province* SE Canada
0 M9 **Nova Scotia** *physical region* SE Canada
34 M8 **Novato** California, W USA 38°06′N 122°35′W
192 M7 **Nova Trough** *undersea feature* W Pacific Ocean
116 L7 **Nova Ushtsya** Khmel'nyts'ka Oblast', W Ukraine 48°50′N 27°16′E
83 M17 **Nova Vanduzi** Manica, C Mozambique 18°54′S 33°18′E
117 U5 **Nova Vodolaha** *Rus.* Novaya Vodolaga. Kharkivs'ka Oblast', E Ukraine 49°43′N 35°49′E
123 O12 **Novaya Chara** Chitinskaya Oblast', S Russian Federation 56°45′N 117°58′E
122 M12 **Novaya Igirma** Irkutskaya Oblast', C Russian Federation 57°08′N 103°52′E
Novaya Kakhovka *see* Nova Kakhovka
144 E10 **Novaya Kazanka** Zapadnyy Kazakhstan, W Kazakhstan 48°57′N 49°34′E
124 I12 **Novaya Ladoga** Leningradskaya Oblast', NW Russian Federation 60°03′N 32°15′E
127 R5 **Novaya Malykla** Ul'yanovskaya Oblast', W Russian Federation 54°13′N 49°55′E
Novaya Odessa *see* Nova Odesa
123 Q5 **Novaya Sibir', Ostrov** *island* Novosibirskiye Ostrova, NE Russian Federation
Novaya Vodolaga *see* Nova Vodolaha
119 P17 **Novaya Yel'nya** Mahilyowskaya Voblasts', E Belarus 53°16′N 31°14′E
122 I6 **Novaya Zemlya** *island group* N Russian Federation
Novaya Zemlya Trough *see* East Novaya Zemlya Trough
114 K10 **Nova Zagora** Sliven, C Bulgaria 42°29′N 26°00′E
105 S12 **Novelda** País Valenciano, E Spain 38°24′N 00°45′W
111 H19 **Nové Mesto nad Váhom** *Ger.* Waagneustadtl, *Hung.* Vágújhely. Trenčiansky Kraj, W Slovakia 48°46′N 17°50′E
111 F17 **Nové Město na Moravě** *Ger.* Neustadtl in Mähren. Vysočina, C Czech Republic 49°34′N 16°05′E
Novesium *see* Neuss
111 I21 **Nové Zámky** *Ger.* Neuhäusel, *Hung.* Érsekújvár. Nitriansky Kraj, SW Slovakia 49°00′N 18°10′E
Novgorod *see* Velikiy Novgorod
Novgorod-Severskiy *see* Novhorod-Sivers'kyy
122 C7 **Novgorodskaya Oblast'** ◈ *province* W Russian Federation
117 R8 **Novhorodka** Kirovohrads'ka Oblast', C Ukraine 48°21′N 32°38′E
117 R2 **Novhorod-Sivers'kyy** *Rus.* Novgorod-Severskiy. Chernihivs'ka Oblast', NE Ukraine 52°00′N 33°15′E
31 R10 **Novi** Michigan, N USA 42°28′N 83°28′W
Novi *see* Novi Vinodolski
112 L9 **Novi Bečej** *prev.* Új-Becse, Vološinovo, *Ger.* Neubetsche, *Hung.* Törökbecse. Vojvodina, N Serbia 45°36′N 20°09′E
116 M3 **Novi Bilokorovychi** *Rus.* Belokorovichi. Zhytomyrs'ka Oblast', N Ukraine 51°07′N 28°02′E
25 Q8 **Novice** Texas, SW USA 32°00′N 99°38′W
112 A9 **Novigrad** Istra, NW Croatia 45°19′N 13°33′E
Novi Grad *see* Bosanski Novi
114 G9 **Novi Iskŭr** Sofiya-Grad, W Bulgaria 42°46′N 23°19′E
106 C9 **Novi Ligure** Piemonte, NW Italy 44°46′N 08°47′E
99 L22 **Noville** Luxembourg, SE Belgium 50°04′N 05°46′E
194 I10 **Noville Peninsula** *peninsula* Thurston Island, Antarctica
Noviodunum *see* Soissons, Aisne, France
Noviodunum *see* Nevers, Nièvre, France
Noviodunum *see* Nyon, Vaud, Switzerland
Noviomagus *see* Lisieux, Calvados, France
Noviomagus *see* Nijmegen, Netherlands
114 M8 **Novi Pazar** Shumen, NE Bulgaria 43°20′N 27°12′E
113 M15 **Novi Pazar** *Turk.* Yenipazar. Serbia, S Serbia 43°09′N 20°31′E
112 K10 **Novi Sad** *Ger.* Neusatz, *Hung.* Újvidék. Vojvodina, N Serbia 45°16′N 19°49′E
117 T6 **Novi Sanzhary** Poltavs'ka Oblast', C Ukraine 49°21′N 34°18′E
112 H12 **Novi Travnik** *prev.* Pučarevo. Federacija Bosna I Hercegovina, C Bosnia and Herzegovina 44°12′N 17°39′E
112 B10 **Novi Vinodolski** *var.* Novi. Primorje-Gorski Kotar, NW Croatia 45°08′N 14°46′E
58 F12 **Novo Airão** Amazonas, N Brazil 02°06′S 61°20′W
Novoalekseyevka *see* Khobda
127 N9 **Novoanninskiy** Volgogradskaya Oblast', SW Russian Federation 50°31′N 42°43′E
58 F13 **Novo Aripuanã** Amazonas, N Brazil 05°05′S 60°20′W
117 Y6 **Novoaydar** Luhans'ka Oblast', E Ukraine 49°00′N 39°00′E
117 X9 **Novoazovs'k** *Rus.* Novoazovsk. Donets'ka Oblast', E Ukraine 47°07′N 38°06′E
123 R14 **Novobureyskiy** Amurskaya Oblast', SE Russian Federation 49°42′N 129°46′E
127 Q3 **Novocheboksarsk** Chuvashskaya Respublika, W Russian Federation 56°07′N 47°33′E
127 R5 **Novocheremshansk** Ul'yanovskaya Oblast', W Russian Federation 54°23′N 50°08′E
126 L12 **Novocherkassk** Rostovskaya Oblast', SW Russian Federation 47°23′N 40°00′E
127 R6 **Novodevich'ye** Samarskaya Oblast', W Russian Federation 53°33′N 48°51′E
124 M8 **Novodvinsk** Arkhangel'skaya Oblast', NW Russian Federation 64°22′N 40°49′E
Novograd-Volynskiy *see* Novohrad-Volyns'kyy
Novogrudok *see* Navahrudak
61 I15 **Novo Hamburgo** Rio Grande do Sul, S Brazil 29°42′S 51°07′W
59 H16 **Novo Horizonte** Mato Grosso, W Brazil 11°19′S 57°11′W
60 K8 **Novo Horizonte** São Paulo, S Brazil 21°27′S 49°14′W
116 M4 **Novohrad-Volyns'kyy** *Rus.* Novograd-Volynskiy. Zhytomyrs'ka Oblast', N Ukraine 50°34′N 27°32′E
145 O7 **Novoishimskiy** *prev.* Kuybyshevskiy. Severnyy Kazakhstan, N Kazakhstan 53°15′N 66°51′E
Novokazalinsk *see* Ayteke Bi
126 M8 **Novokhoperskiy** Voronezhskaya Oblast', W Russian Federation 51°09′N 41°34′E
127 R6 **Novokuybyshevsk** Samarskaya Oblast', W Russian Federation 53°06′N 49°56′E
122 J13 **Novokuznetsk** *prev.* Stalinsk. Kemerovskaya Oblast', S Russian Federation 53°45′N 87°12′E
195 R1 **Novolazarevskaya** *Russian research station* Antarctica 70°42′S 11°31′E
Novolukoml' *see* Novalukoml'
109 V12 **Novo mesto** *Ger.* Rudolfswert; *prev. Ger.* Neustadtl. SE Slovenia 45°49′N 15°09′E
126 K15 **Novomikhaylovskiy** Krasnodarskiy Kray, SW Russian Federation 44°18′N 38°49′E
112 L8 **Novo Miloševo** Vojvodina, N Serbia 45°43′N 20°20′E
Novomirgorod *see* Novomyrhorod
126 L5 **Novomoskovsk** Tul'skaya Oblast', W Russian Federation 54°05′N 38°23′E
117 U7 **Novomoskovs'k** *Rus.* Novomoskovsk. Dnipropetrovs'ka Oblast', E Ukraine 48°38′N 35°15′E
117 V8 **Novomykolayivka** Zaporiz'ka Oblast', SE Ukraine 47°58′N 35°54′E
117 Q7 **Novomyrhorod** *Rus.* Novomirgorod. Kirovohrads'ka Oblast', S Ukraine 48°46′N 31°39′E
127 N8 **Novonikolayevskiy** Volgogradskaya Oblast', SW Russian Federation 50°55′N 42°24′E
127 P10 **Novonikol'skoye** Volgogradskaya Oblast', SW Russian Federation 49°23′N 45°06′E
127 X7 **Novoorsk** Orenburgskaya Oblast', W Russian Federation 51°21′N 59°03′E
126 M13 **Novopokrovskaya** Krasnodarskiy Kray, SW Russian Federation 45°58′N 40°43′E
Novopolotsk *see* Navapolatsk
117 Y5 **Novopskov** Luhans'ka Oblast', E Ukraine 49°33′N 39°07′E
Novoradomsk *see* Radomsko
Novo Redondo *see* Sumbe
127 R8 **Novorepnoye** Saratovskaya Oblast', W Russian Federation 51°04′N 48°34′E
126 K14 **Novorossiysk** Krasnodarskiy Kray, SW Russian Federation 44°50′N 37°38′E
Novorossiyskiy/Novorossiyskoye *see* Akzhar
124 F15 **Novorzhev** Pskovskaya Oblast', W Russian Federation 57°01′N 29°19′E
Novoselitsa *see* Novoselytsya
117 S12 **Novoselivs'ke** Respublika Krym, S Ukraine 45°26′N 33°37′E
Novosëlki *see* Navasyolki
114 G6 **Novo Selo** Vidin, NW Bulgaria 44°08′N 22°48′E
113 M14 **Novo Selo** Serbia, C Serbia 43°39′N 20°54′E
116 K8 **Novoselytsya** *Rom.* Nouă Sulița, *Rus.* Novoselitsa. Chernivets'ka Oblast', W Ukraine 48°14′N 26°18′E
127 U7 **Novosergiyevka** Orenburgskaya Oblast', W Russian Federation 52°04′N 53°40′E
126 L11 **Novoshakhtinsk** Rostovskaya Oblast', SW Russian Federation 47°48′N 39°51′E
122 J12 **Novosibirsk** Novosibirskaya Oblast', C Russian Federation 55°04′N 83°05′E
122 J12 **Novosibirskaya Oblast'** ◈ *province* C Russian Federation
122 M4 **Novosibirskiye Ostrova** *Eng.* New Siberian Islands. *island group* N Russian Federation
126 K6 **Novosil'** Orlovskaya Oblast', W Russian Federation 53°00′N 37°59′E
124 G16 **Novosokol'niki** Pskovskaya Oblast', W Russian Federation 56°21′N 30°07′E
127 Q6 **Novospasskoye** Ul'yanovskaya Oblast', W Russian Federation 53°08′N 47°48′E
Novotroickoje *see* Brlik
127 X8 **Novotroitsk** Orenburgskaya Oblast', W Russian Federation 51°10′N 58°18′E
Novotroitskoye *see* Brlik, Kazakhstan
Novotroitskoye *see* Novotroyits'ke, Ukraine
117 T11 **Novotroyits'ke** *Rus.* Novotroitskoye. Khersons'ka Oblast', S Ukraine 46°21′N 34°21′E
Novoukrainka *see* Novoukrayinka
117 Q8 **Novoukrayinka** *Rus.* Novoukrainka. Kirovohrads'ka Oblast', C Ukraine 48°19′N 31°33′E
127 Q5 **Novoul'yanovsk** Ul'yanovskaya Oblast', W Russian Federation 54°10′N 48°19′E
127 W8 **Novoural'sk** Orenburgskaya Oblast', W Russian Federation 51°19′N 56°57′E
Novo-Urgench *see* Urganch
127 Q9 **Novouzensk** Saratovskaya Oblast', W Russian Federation 50°28′N 48°07′E
116 I4 **Novovolyns'k** *Rus.* Novovolynsk. Volyns'ka Oblast', NW Ukraine 50°46′N 24°09′E
117 S9 **Novovorontsovka** Khersons'ka Oblast', S Ukraine 47°28′N 33°55′E
147 Y7 **Novovoznesenovka** Issyk-Kul'skaya Oblast', E Kyrgyzstan 42°36′N 78°44′E
125 R14 **Novovyatsk** Kirovskaya Oblast', NW Russian Federation 58°30′N 49°42′E
Novoyel'nya *see* Navayel'nya
117 O6 **Novozhyvotiv** Vinnyts'ka Oblast', C Ukraine 49°16′N 29°31′E
126 H6 **Novozybkov** Bryanskaya Oblast', W Russian Federation 52°36′N 31°58′E
112 F9 **Novska** Sisak-Moslavina, NE Croatia 45°20′N 16°58′E
Nový Bohumín *see* Bohumín
111 D15 **Nový Bor** *Ger.* Haida; *prev.* Bor u České Lípy, Hajda. Liberecký Kraj, N Czech Republic 50°46′N 14°32′E
111 E16 **Nový Bydžov** *Ger.* Neubidschow. Královéhradecký Kraj, N Czech Republic 50°15′N 15°27′E
119 G18 **Novy Dvor** *Rus.* Novyy Dvor. Hrodzyenskaya Voblasts', W Belarus 53°48′N 24°34′E
111 I17 **Nový Jičín** *Ger.* Neutitschein. Moravskoslezský Kraj, E Czech Republic 49°36′N 18°00′E
118 K12 **Novy Pahost** *Rus.* Novyy Pogost. Vitsyebskaya Voblasts', NW Belarus 55°30′N 27°29′E
Novyy Bug *see* Novyy Buh
117 R9 **Novyy Buh** *Rus.* Novyy Bug. Mykolayivs'ka Oblast', S Ukraine 47°40′N 32°30′E
117 Q4 **Novyy Bykiv** Chernihivs'ka Oblast', N Ukraine 50°36′N 31°39′E
Novyy Dvor *see* Novy Dvor
Novyye Aneny *see* Anenii Noi
127 P7 **Novyye Burasy** Saratovskaya Oblast', W Russian Federation 52°10′N 46°00′E
Novyy Margilan *see* Farg'ona
126 K8 **Novyy Oskol** Belgorodskaya Oblast', W Russian Federation 50°43′N 37°55′E
Novyy Pogost *see* Novy Pahost
127 R2 **Novyy Tor"yal** Respublika Mariy El, W Russian Federation 56°59′N 48°53′E
123 N12 **Novyy Uoyan** Respublika Buryatiya, S Russian Federation 56°06′N 111°27′E
122 J9 **Novyy Urengoy** Yamalo-Nenetskiy Avtonomnyy Okrug, N Russian Federation 66°06′N 76°25′E
Novyy Uzen' *see* Zhanaozen
111 N16 **Nowa Dęba** Podkarpackie, SE Poland 50°31′N 21°53′E
111 G15 **Nowa Ruda** *Ger.* Neurode. Dolnośląskie, SW Poland 50°34′N 16°30′E
110 F12 **Nowa Sól** *var.* Nowasól, *Ger.* Neusalz an der Oder. Lubuskie, W Poland 51°47′N 15°43′E
Nowasól *see* Nowa Sól
27 Q8 **Nowata** Oklahoma, C USA 36°42′N 95°36′W
142 M6 **Nowbarān** Markazī, W Iran 35°07′N 49°51′E
110 J8 **Nowe** Kujawski-pomorskie, N Poland 53°40′N 18°44′E
110 K9 **Nowe Miasto Lubawskie** *Ger.* Neumark. Warmińsko-Mazurskie, NE Poland 53°24′N 19°36′E
110 L13 **Nowe Miasto nad Pilicą** Mazowieckie, C Poland 51°37′N 20°34′E
110 D8 **Nowe Warpno** *Ger.* Neuwarp. Zachodnio-pomorskie, NW Poland 53°52′N 14°12′E
Nowgong *see* Nagaon
110 E8 **Nowogard** *var.* Nowógard, *Ger.* Naugard. Zachodnio-pomorskie, NW Poland 53°41′N 15°09′E
110 N9 **Nowogród** Podlaskie, NE Poland 53°14′N 21°52′E
Nowogródek *see* Navahrudak
111 E14 **Nowogrodziec** *Ger.* Naumburg am Queis. Dolnośląskie, SW Poland 51°12′N 15°24′E
Nowojelnia *see* Navayel'nya
Nowo-Minsk *see* Mińsk Mazowiecki
33 V13 **Nowood River** ≈ Wyoming, C USA
Nowo-Święciany *see* Švenčionėliai
183 S10 **Nowra-Bomaderry** New South Wales, SE Australia 34°51′S 150°41′E
Nowrangapur *see* Nabarangapur
149 T5 **Nowshera** *var.* Naushahra, Naushara. North-West Frontier Province, NE Pakistan 34°00′N 72°00′E
110 J7 **Nowy Dwór Gdański** *Ger.* Tiegenhof. Pomorskie, N Poland 54°12′N 19°03′E
110 L11 **Nowy Dwór Mazowiecki** Mazowieckie, C Poland 52°26′N 20°43′E
111 M17 **Nowy Sącz** *Ger.* Neu Sandec. Małopolskie, S Poland 49°36′N 20°42′E
111 L18 **Nowy Targ** *Ger.* Neumark. Małopolskie, S Poland 49°28′N 20°00′E
110 F11 **Nowy Tomyśl** *var.* Nowy Tomysl. Wielkopolskie, C Poland 52°18′N 16°07′E
Nowy Tomysl *see* Nowy Tomyśl
148 M7 **Now Zād** *var.* Nauzad. Helmand, S Afghanistan 32°22′N 64°32′E
23 N4 **Noxubee River** ≈ Alabama/Mississippi, S USA
122 I10 **Noyabr'sk** Yamalo-Nenetskiy Avtonomnyy Okrug, N Russian Federation 63°08′N 75°19′E
102 L8 **Noyant** Maine-et-Loire, NW France 47°28′N 00°08′W
39 X14 **Noyes Island** *island* Alexander Archipelago, Alaska, USA
103 O3 **Noyon** Oise, N France 49°35′N 03°E
102 I7 **Nozay** Loire-Atlantique, NW France 47°34′N 01°36′W
82 L12 **Nsando** Northern, NE Zambia 10°22′S 31°14′E
83 N16 **Nsanje** Southern, S Malawi 16°57′S 35°10′E
77 Q17 **Nsawam** SE Ghana 05°47′N 00°19′W
79 E16 **Nsimalen** ✕ Centre, C Cameroon 19°15′N 81°22′E
82 K12 **Nsombo** Northern, NE Zambia 10°35′S 29°58′E
82 H13 **Ntambu** North Western, NW Zambia 12°21′S 25°03′E
83 N14 **Ntcheu** *var.* Ncheu. Central, S Malawi 14°49′S 34°37′E
79 D17 **Ntem** *prev.* Campo, Kampo. ≈ Cameroon/Equatorial Guinea
83 I14 **Ntemwa** North Western, NW Zambia 14°03′S 26°13′E
Ntlenyana, Mount *see* Thabana Ntlenyana
79 I19 **Ntomba, Lac** *var.* Lac Tumba. ◎ NW Dem. Rep. Congo
115 I19 **Ntóro, Kávo** *prev.* Akrotírio Kafiréas. *cape* Évvoia, C Greece
81 E19 **Ntungamo** SW Uganda 0°54′S 30°16′E
81 E18 **Ntusi** SW Uganda 0°05′N 31°13′E
83 H18 **Ntwetwe Pan** *salt lake* NE Botswana
154 L13 **Nũāparha** *var.* Nauparha, Nawapara. Orissa, SW India 20°43′N 82°42′E
93 M15 **Nuasjärvi** ◎ C Finland
80 F11 **Nuba Mountains** ▲▲ C Sudan
68 J9 **Nubian Desert** *desert* NE Sudan
116 G10 **Nucet** *Hung.* Diófás. Bihor, W Romania 46°28′N 22°35′E
Nu Chiang *see* Salween
145 U9 **Nuclear Testing Ground** *nuclear site* Pavlodar, E Kazakhstan
56 E9 **Nucuray, Río** ≈ N Peru
25 R14 **Nueces River** ≈ Texas, SW USA
9 V9 **Nueltin Lake** ◎ Manitoba/Northwest Territories, C Canada
99 K15 **Nuenen** Noord-Brabant, S Netherlands 51°29′N 05°36′E
62 G6 **Nuestra Señora, Bahía** *bay* N Chile
61 D14 **Nuestra Señora Rosario de Caa Catí** Corrientes, NE Argentina 27°48′S 57°42′W
54 J9 **Nueva Antioquia** Vichada, E Colombia 06°04′N 69°30′W
Nueva Caceres *see* Naga
41 O7 **Nueva Ciudad Guerrera** Tamaulipas, C Mexico 26°32′N 99°13′W
55 N4 **Nueva Esparta** *off.* Estado Nueva Esparta. ◈ *state* NE Venezuela
Nueva Esparta, Estado *see* Nueva Esparta
44 C5 **Nueva Gerona** Isla de la Juventud, S Cuba 21°49′N 82°49′W
42 H8 **Nueva Guadalupe** San Miguel, E El Salvador 13°30′N 88°21′W
42 M11 **Nueva Guinea** Región Autónoma Atlántico Sur, SE Nicaragua 11°40′N 84°22′W
61 D19 **Nueva Helvecia** Colonia, SW Uruguay 34°16′S 57°53′W
63 J25 **Nueva, Isla** *island* S Chile
40 M14 **Nueva Italia** Michoacán, SW Mexico 19°01′N 102°06′W
56 D6 **Nueva Loja** *var.* Lago Agrio. Sucumbíos, NE Ecuador
42 F6 **Nueva Ocotepeque** *prev.* Ocotepeque. Ocotepeque, W Honduras 14°25′N 89°10′W
61 D19 **Nueva Palmira** Colonia, SW Uruguay 33°53′S 58°25′W
41 N6 **Nueva Rosita** Coahuila, NE Mexico 27°58′N 101°11′W
42 E7 **Nueva San Salvador** *prev.* Santa Tecla. La Libertad, SW El Salvador 13°40′N 89°18′W
42 J8 **Nueva Segovia** ◈ *department* NW Nicaragua
Nueva Tabarca *see* Plana, Isla
Nueva Villa de Padilla *see* Nuevo Padilla
61 B21 **Nueve de Julio** Buenos Aires, E Argentina 35°29′S 60°52′W
44 H6 **Nuevitas** Camagüey, E Cuba 21°34′N 77°18′W
61 D18 **Nuevo Berlín** Río Negro, W Uruguay 32°59′S 58°03′W
40 I4 **Nuevo Casas Grandes** Chihuahua, N Mexico 30°23′N 107°54′W
43 T14 **Nuevo Chagres** Colón, C Panama 09°14′N 80°05′W
41 W15 **Nuevo Coahuila** Campeche, E Mexico 17°53′N 90°46′W
63 K17 **Nuevo, Golfo** *gulf* S Argentina
41 O7 **Nuevo Laredo** Tamaulipas, NE Mexico 27°28′N 99°32′W
41 N8 **Nuevo León** ◈ *state* NE Mexico
41 P10 **Nuevo Padilla** *var.* Nueva Villa de Padilla. Tamaulipas, C Mexico 24°01′N 98°48′W
56 E6 **Nuevo Rocafuerte** Orellana, E Ecuador 0°59′S 75°27′W
Nuga *see* Dzavhanmandal
80 O13 **Nugaal** *off.* Gobolka Nugaal. ◈ *region* N Somalia
Nugaal, Gobolka *see* Nugaal
185 E24 **Nugget Point** *headland* South Island, New Zealand 46°26′S 169°49′E
186 J5 **Nuguria Islands** *island group* E Papua New Guinea
184 P10 **Nuhaka** Hawke's Bay, North Island, New Zealand 39°03′S 177°43′E
138 M10 **Nuhaydayn, Wādī an** *dry watercourse* W Iraq
190 E7 **Nui Atoll** *atoll* W Tuvalu
Nu Jiang *see* Salween
Nûk *see* Nuuk
182 G7 **Nukey Bluff** *hill* South Australia
Nukha *see* Şäki
123 T9 **Nukh Yablonevyy, Gora** ▲ E Russian Federation 60°26′N 151°45′E
186 K7 **Nukiki** Choiseul Island, NW Solomon Islands 06°45′S 156°30′E
186 B6 **Nuku** Sandaun, NW Papua New Guinea 03°48′S 142°23′E
193 W15 **Nuku** *island* Tongatapu Group, NE Tonga
193 Y16 **Nuku'alofa** ● (Tonga) Tongatapu, S Tonga 21°08′S 175°13′W
193 U15 **Nuku'alofa** Tongatapu, S Tonga 21°09′S 175°14′W
190 G12 **Nukuatea** *island* N Wallis and Futuna
190 F7 **Nukufetau Atoll** *atoll* C Tuvalu
190 G12 **Nukuhifala** *island* E Wallis and Futuna
191 W7 **Nuku Hiva** *island* Îles Marquises, NE French Polynesia
191 W7 **Nuku Hiva Island** *island* Îles Marquises, N French Polynesia
190 F9 **Nukulaelae Atoll** *var.* Nukulailai. *atoll* E Tuvalu
Nukulailai *see* Nukulaelae Atoll
190 G11 **Nukuloa** *island* N Wallis and Futuna
186 L6 **Nukumanu Islands** *prev.* Tasman Group. *island group* NE Papua New Guinea
Nukunau *see* Nikunau
190 J9 **Nukunonu Atoll** *island* C Tokelau
190 J9 **Nukunonu Village** Nukunonu Atoll, C Tokelau
189 S18 **Nukuoro Atoll** *atoll* Caroline Islands, S Micronesia
146 H8 **Nukus** Qoraqalpog'iston Respublikasi, W Uzbekistan 42°29′N 59°32′E
190 G11 **Nukutapu** *island* N Wallis and Futuna
39 O9 **Nulato** Alaska, USA 64°43′N 158°06′W
39 O10 **Nulato Hills** ▲▲ Alaska, USA
105 T9 **Nules** País Valenciano, E Spain 39°52′N 00°10′W
Nuling *see* Sultan Kudarat
182 C6 **Nullarbor** South Australia 31°28′S 130°57′E
180 M11 **Nullarbor Plain** *plateau* South Australia/Western Australia
163 S12 **Nulu'erhu Shan** ▲▲ N China
77 X14 **Numan** Adamawa, E Nigeria 09°26′N 11°58′E
165 S3 **Numata** Hokkaidō, NE Japan 43°48′N 141°55′E
81 C15 **Numatinna** ≈ W Sudan
95 F14 **Numedalen** *valley* S Norway
95 G14 **Numedalslågen** *var.* Laagen. ≈ S Norway
93 L19 **Nummela** Etelä-Suomi, S Finland 60°21′N 24°20′E
183 O11 **Numurkah** Victoria, SE Australia 36°04′S 145°28′E
196 L16 **Nunap Isua** *var.* Uummannarsuaq, *Dan.* Kap Farvel, *Eng.* Cape Farewell. *cape* S Greenland
9 N8 **Nunavut** ◈ *territory* N Canada
54 H9 **Nunchía** Casanare, C Colombia 05°37′N 72°13′W
97 M20 **Nuneaton** C England, United Kingdom 52°32′N 01°28′W
153 W14 **Nungba** Manipur, NE India 24°46′N 93°25′E
38 L12 **Nunivak Island** *island* Alaska, USA
152 I5 **Nun Kun** ▲ NW India 34°01′N 76°04′E
98 L10 **Nunspeet** Gelderland, E Netherlands 52°21′N 05°45′E
107 C18 **Nuoro** Sardegna, Italy, C Mediterranean Sea 40°20′N 09°20′E
75 R12 **Nuqayy, Jabal** *hill range* S Libya
54 C9 **Nuquí** Chocó, W Colombia 05°44′N 77°16′W
143 O4 **Nūr** Māzandarān, N Iran 36°32′N 52°00′E
145 Q9 **Nura** ≈ N Kazakhstan
143 N11 **Nūrābād** Fārs, C Iran 30°08′N 51°30′E
Nurakita *see* Niulakita
Nurata *see* Nurota
Nuratau, Khrebet *see* Nurota Tizmasi
136 L17 **Nur Dağları** ▲▲ S Turkey
Nurek *see* Norak
Nuremberg *see* Nürnberg
149 S4 **Nūrestān** ◈ *province* C Afghanistan
136 M15 **Nurhak** Kahramanmaraş, S Turkey 37°57′N 37°21′E
182 J9 **Nuriootpa** South Australia 34°28′S 139°00′E
127 S5 **Nurlat** Respublika Tatarstan, W Russian Federation 54°26′N 50°48′E
93 N15 **Nurmes** Itä-Suomi, E Finland 63°31′N 29°10′E
101 K20 **Nürnberg** *Eng.* Nuremberg. Bayern, S Germany 49°27′N 11°05′E
101 K20 **Nürnberg** ✕ Bayern, SE Germany 49°29′N 11°04′E
146 M10 **Nurota** *Rus.* Nurata. Navoiy Viloyati, C Uzbekistan 40°41′N 65°43′E
147 N10 **Nurota Tizmasi** *Rus.* Khrebet Nuratau. ▲▲ C Uzbekistan
149 T8 **Nūrpur** Punjab, E Pakistan 31°54′N 71°55′E
183 P6 **Nurri, Mount** *hill* New South Wales, SE Australia
25 T13 **Nursery** Texas, SW USA 28°55′N 97°05′W
169 V17 **Nusa Tenggara Barat** *off.* Propinsi Nusa Tenggara Barat, *Eng.* West Nusa Tenggara. ◈ *province* S Indonesia
Nusa Tenggara Barat, Propinsi *see* Nusa Tenggara Barat
171 O16 **Nusa Tenggara Timur** *off.* Propinsi Nusa Tenggara Timur, *Eng.* East Nusa Tenggara. ◈ *province* S Indonesia
Nusa Tenggara Timur, Propinsi *see* Nusa Tenggara Timur
171 U14 **Nusawulan** Papua, E Indonesia 04°03′S 132°56′E
137 Q16 **Nusaybin** *var.* Nisibin. Manisa, SE Turkey 37°08′N 41°11′E
39 O14 **Nushagak Bay** *bay* Alaska, USA
39 O13 **Nushagak Peninsula** *headland* Alaska, USA 58°39′N 159°03′W
39 O13 **Nushagak River** ≈ Alaska, USA
160 E11 **Nu Shan** ▲▲ SW China
149 N11 **Nushki** Baluchistān, SW Pakistan 29°33′N 66°01′E
Nussdorf *see* Năsăud
112 J9 **Nuštar** Vukovar-Srijem, E Croatia 45°20′N 18°48′E
99 L18 **Nuth** Limburg, SE Netherlands 50°55′N 05°52′E
100 N13 **Nuthe** ≈ NE Germany
Nutmeg State *see* Connecticut
39 T10 **Nutzotin Mountains** ▲▲ Alaska, USA
64 I5 **Nuuk** *var.* Nûk, *Dan.* Godthaab, Godthåb. ○ (Greenland) Kitaa, SW Greenland 64°15′N 51°35′W
92 L13 **Nuupas** Lappi, NW Finland 66°01′N 26°19′E
191 O7 **Nuupere, Pointe** *headland* Moorea, W French Polynesia 17°35′S 149°47′W
191 O7 **Nuuroa, Pointe** *headland* Tahiti, W French Polynesia
Nüürst *see* Baganuur
Nuwara *see* Nuwara Eliya
155 K25 **Nuwara Eliya** *var.* Nuwara. Central Province, S Sri Lanka 06°58′N 80°46′E
182 E7 **Nuyts Archipelago** *island group* South Australia
83 F17 **Nxaunxau** North West, NW Botswana 18°57′S 21°18′E
39 N12 **Nyac** Alaska, USA 61°00′N 159°56′W
122 H9 **Nyagan'** Khanty-Mansiyskiy Avtonomnyy Okrug-Yugra, N Russian Federation 62°10′N 65°32′E
Nyagassola *see* Niagassola
Nyagquka *see* Yajiang
81 I18 **Nyahururu** Central, W Kenya 0°04′N 36°22′E
182 M10 **Nyah West** Victoria, SE Australia 35°14′S 143°18′E
158 M15 **Nyainqêntanglha Feng** ▲ W China 30°20′N 90°28′E
159 N15 **Nyainqêntanglha Shan** ▲▲ W China
159 O13 **Nyainrong** Xizang Zizhiqu, W China 32°02′N 92°20′E
80 B11 **Nyala** Southern Darfur, W Sudan 12°01′N 24°50′E
158 J17 **Nyalam** Xizang Zizhiqu, SW China 28°10′N 85°57′E
83 M16 **Nyamapanda** Mashonaland East, NE Zimbabwe 16°59′S 32°52′E
81 H25 **Nyamtumbo** Ruvuma, S Tanzania 10°33′S 36°08′E
Nyanda *see* Masvingo
124 M11 **Nyandoma** Arkhangel'skaya Oblast', NW Russian Federation 61°39′N 40°10′E
83 M16 **Nyanga** *prev.* Inyanga. Manicaland, E Zimbabwe 18°13′S 32°46′E
79 D20 **Nyanga** *off.* Province de la Nyanga, *var.* La Nyanga. ◈ *province* SW Gabon
79 E20 **Nyanga** ≈ Congo/Gabon
Nyanga, Province de la *see* Nyanga
81 F20 **Nyantakara** Kagera, NW Tanzania 03°05′S 31°23′E
81 G19 **Nyanza** ◈ *province* W Kenya
81 E21 **Nyanza-Lac** S Burundi 04°16′S 29°38′E
68 J14 **Nyasa, Lake** *var.* Lake Malawi; *prev.* Lago Nyassa. ◎ E Africa
Nyasaland/Nyasaland Protectorate *see* Malawi
Nyassa, Lago *see* Nyasa, Lake
119 J17 **Nyasvizh** *Pol.* Nieśwież, *Rus.* Nesvizh. Minskaya Voblasts', C Belarus 53°13′N 26°40′E
166 M8 **Nyaunglebin** Bago, SW Myanmar (Burma) 17°59′N 96°44′E
166 M5 **Nyaung-u** Magway, C Myanmar (Burma) 21°03′N 95°44′E
95 H24 **Nyborg** Fyn, C Denmark 55°19′N 10°48′E
95 N21 **Nybro** Kalmar, S Sweden 56°45′N 15°54′E
119 J16 **Nyeharelaye** *Rus.* Negoreloye. Minskaya Voblasts', C Belarus 53°36′N 27°04′E
158 M16 **Nyêmo** *var.* Tarrong. Xizang Zizhiqu, W China 29°25′N 90°10′E
195 W3 **Nye Mountains** ▲▲ Antarctica
81 I19 **Nyeri** Central, C Kenya 0°25′S 36°56′E
118 M11 **Nyeshcharda, Vozyera** ◎ N Belarus
92 O2 **Ny-Friesland** *physical region* N Svalbard
95 L14 **Nyhammar** Dalarna, C Sweden 60°19′N 14°55′E
160 F7 **Nyikog Qu** ≈ C China
158 K14 **Nyima** Xizang Zizhiqu, W China 31°56′N 87°16′E
83 L14 **Nyimba** Eastern, E Zambia 14°33′S 30°49′E
159 P15 **Nyingchi** *var.* Pula. Xizang Zizhiqu, W China 29°34′N 94°33′E
159 P15 **Nyingchi** Xizang Zizhiqu, W China 29°27′N 94°43′E
Nyinma *see* Maqu
111 O21 **Nyírbátor** Szabolcs-Szatmár-Bereg, E Hungary 47°50′N 22°09′E
111 N21 **Nyíregyháza** Szabolcs-Szatmár-Bereg, NE Hungary 47°57′N 21°43′E
Nyiro *see* Ewaso Ng'iro
Nyitra *see* Nitra
Nyitrabánya *see* Handlová
93 K16 **Nykarleby** *Fin.* Uusikaarlepyy. Länsi-Suomi, W Finland 63°22′N 22°30′E
95 I25 **Nykøbing** Storstrøm, SE Denmark 54°47′N 11°53′E
95 I22 **Nykøbing** Vestsjælland, C Denmark 55°56′N 11°41′E
95 F21 **Nykøbing** Viborg, NW Denmark 56°48′N 08°52′E
95 N17 **Nyköping** Södermanland, S Sweden 58°45′N 17°03′E
95 L15 **Nykroppa** Värmland, C Sweden 59°37′N 14°18′E
Nylstroom *see* Modimolle
183 P7 **Nymagee** New South Wales, SE Australia 32°06′S 146°19′E
183 V5 **Nymboida** New South Wales, SE Australia 29°57′S 152°45′E
183 U5 **Nymboida River** ≈ New South Wales, SE Australia

◆ Country ● Country Capital ◇ Dependent Territory ○ Dependent Territory Capital ◈ Administrative Regions ✕ International Airport ▲ Mountain ▲▲ Mountain Range Volcano ≈ River ◎ Lake ⊠ Reservoir

NYMBURK – OLÁHSZENTGYÖRGY

111 D16 **Nymburk** *var.* Neuenburg an der Elbe, *Ger.* Nimburg. Středočesky Kraj, C Czech Republic *50°12′N 15°00′E*
95 O16 **Nynäshamn** Stockholm, C Sweden *58°54′N 17°55′E*
183 Q6 **Nyngan** New South Wales, SE Australia *31°36′S 147°07′E*
Nyoman *see* Neman
108 A10 **Nyon** *Ger.* Neuss; *anc.* Noviodunum. Vaud, SW Switzerland *46°23′N 06°15′E*
79 D16 **Nyong** ~ SW Cameroon
103 S14 **Nyons** Drôme, E France *44°22′N 05°06′E*
79 D14 **Nyos, Lac** *Eng.* Lake Nyos. ◎ NW Cameroon
Nyos, Lake *see* Nyos, Lac
125 U11 **Nyrob** *var.* Nyrov. Permskaya Oblast', NW Russian Federation *60°41′N 56°42′E*
Nyrov *see* Nyrob
111 H15 **Nysa** *Ger.* Neisse. Opolskie, S Poland *50°28′N 17°20′E*
32 M13 **Nyssa** Oregon, NW USA *43°52′N 116°59′W*
Nysa Łużycka *see* Neisse
Nyslott *see* Savonlinna
Nystad *see* Uusikaupunki
95 I25 **Nysted** Storstrøm, SE Denmark *54°40′N 11°41′E*
125 U14 **Nytva** Permskaya Oblast', NW Russian Federation *57°56′N 55°22′E*
165 P8 **Nyūdō-zaki** *headland* Honshū, C Japan *39°59′N 139°40′E*
125 P9 **Nyukhcha** Arkhangel'skaya Oblast', NW Russian Federation *63°24′N 46°34′E*
124 H8 **Nyuk, Ozero** *var.* Ozero Njuk. ◎ NW Russian Federation
125 O12 **Nyuksenitsa** *var.* Njuksenica. Vologodskaya Oblast', NW Russian Federation *60°25′N 44°12′E*
79 O22 **Nyunzu** Katanga, SE Dem. Rep. Congo *05°55′S 28°00′E*
123 O10 **Nyurba** Respublika Sakha (Yakutiya), NE Russian Federation *63°17′N 118°15′E*
123 O11 **Nyuya** Respublika Sakha (Yakutiya), NE Russian Federation *60°33′N 116°10′E*
146 K12 **Nyýazow** *Rus.* Niyazov. Lebap Welaýaty, NE Turkmenistan *39°13′N 63°16′E*
117 T10 **Nyzhni Sirohozy** Khersons'ka Oblast', S Ukraine *46°49′N 34°21′E*
117 U12 **Nyzhn'ohirs'kyy** *Rus.* Nizhnegorskiy. Respublika Krym, S Ukraine *45°26′N 34°42′E*
NZ *see* New Zealand
81 G21 **Nzega** Tabora, C Tanzania *04°13′S 33°11′E*
76 K15 **Nzérékoré** SE Guinea *07°45′N 08°49′W*
82 A10 **N'Zeto** *prev.* Ambrizete. Zaire, NW Angola *07°14′S 12°52′E*
79 M24 **Nzilo, Lac** *prev.* Lac Delcommune. ◎ SE Dem. Rep. Congo
Nzwani *see* Anjouan

O

29 O11 **Oacoma** South Dakota, N USA *43°49′N 99°25′W*
29 N9 **Oahe Dam** *dam* South Dakota, N USA
28 M9 **Oahe, Lake** ⊠ North Dakota/South Dakota, N USA
38 C9 **Oa'hu** *var.* Oahu. *island* Hawai'ian Islands, Hawai'i, USA
165 V4 **O-Akan-dake** ▲ Hokkaidō, NE Japan *43°26′N 144°09′E*
182 K8 **Oakbank** South Australia *33°07′S 140°36′E*
19 P13 **Oak Bluffs** Martha's Vineyard, New York, NE USA *41°25′N 70°32′W*
36 K4 **Oak City** Utah, W USA *39°22′N 112°19′W*
37 R3 **Oak Creek** Colorado, C USA *40°16′N 106°57′W*
35 P8 **Oakdale** California, W USA *37°46′N 120°51′W*
22 H8 **Oakdale** Louisiana, S USA *30°49′N 92°39′W*
29 P7 **Oakes** North Dakota, N USA *46°08′N 98°05′W*
22 J4 **Oak Grove** Louisiana, S USA *32°51′N 91°25′W*
97 N19 **Oakham** C England, United Kingdom *52°41′N 00°45′W*
32 H7 **Oak Harbor** Washington, NW USA *48°17′N 122°38′W*
21 R5 **Oak Hill** West Virginia, NE USA *37°59′N 81°09′W*
35 N8 **Oakland** California, W USA *37°48′N 122°16′W*
29 T15 **Oakland** Iowa, C USA *41°18′N 95°22′W*
19 Q7 **Oakland** Maine, NE USA *44°32′N 69°43′W*
21 T3 **Oakland** Maryland, NE USA *39°24′N 79°25′W*
29 R14 **Oakland** Nebraska, C USA *41°50′N 96°28′W*
31 N11 **Oak Lawn** Illinois, N USA *41°43′N 87°45′W*
33 P16 **Oakley** Idaho, NW USA *42°13′N 113°54′W*
26 I4 **Oakley** Kansas, C USA *39°08′N 100°53′W*
31 N10 **Oak Park** Illinois, N USA *41°53′N 87°46′W*
11 X16 **Oak Point** Manitoba, S Canada *50°23′N 97°00′W*
32 G13 **Oakridge** Oregon, NW USA *43°45′N 122°27′W*
20 M9 **Oak Ridge** Tennessee, S USA *36°02′N 84°12′W*
184 K10 **Oakura** Taranaki, North Island, New Zealand *39°07′S 173°58′E*
22 L7 **Oak Vale** Mississippi, S USA *31°26′N 89°57′W*
14 G16 **Oakville** Ontario, S Canada *43°27′N 79°41′W*
25 V8 **Oakwood** Texas, SW USA *31°34′N 95°51′W*
185 F22 **Oamaru** Otago, South Island, New Zealand *45°10′S 170°51′E*
96 F13 **Oa, Mull of** *headland* W Scotland, United Kingdom *55°35′N 06°20′W*
171 O11 **Oan** Sulawesi, N Indonesia *01°16′N 121°25′E*
185 J17 **Oaro** Canterbury, South Island, New Zealand *42°29′S 173°30′E*
35 X2 **Oasis** Nevada, W USA *41°01′N 114°29′W*
195 S15 **Oates Land** *physical region* Antarctica
183 P17 **Oatlands** Tasmania, SE Australia *42°21′S 147°23′E*
36 I11 **Oatman** Arizona, SW USA *35°03′N 114°19′W*
41 R16 **Oaxaca** *var.* Oaxaca de Juárez; *prev.* Antequera. Oaxaca, SE Mexico *17°04′N 96°41′W*
41 Q16 **Oaxaca** ◆ *state* SE Mexico
Oaxaca de Juárez *see* Oaxaca
122 I19 **Ob'** ~ C Russian Federation
14 G9 **Obabika Lake** ◎ Ontario, S Canada
Obagan *see* Ubagan
118 M12 **Obal'** *Rus.* Obol'. Vitsyebskaya Voblasts', N Belarus *55°22′N 29°17′E*
79 E16 **Obala** Centre, SW Cameroon *04°09′N 11°32′E*
14 C6 **Oba Lake** ◎ Ontario, S Canada
164 J12 **Obama** Fukui, Honshū, SW Japan *35°32′N 135°45′E*
96 H11 **Oban** W Scotland, United Kingdom *56°25′N 05°29′W*
Oban *see* Halfmoon Bay
Obando *see* Puerto Inírida
104 I4 **O Barco** *var.* El Barco, El Barco de Valdeorras, O Barco de Valdeorras. Galicia, NW Spain *42°24′N 07°00′W*
O Barco de Valdeorras *see* O Barco
Obbia *see* Hobyo
93 J16 **Obbola** Västerbotten, N Sweden *63°41′N 20°16′E*
Obbrovazzo *see* Obrovac
Obchuga *see* Abchuha
Obdorsk *see* Salekhard
Óbecse *see* Bečej
118 I11 **Obeliai** Panevėžys, NE Lithuania *55°57′N 25°47′E*
60 F13 **Oberá** Misiones, NE Argentina *27°29′S 55°08′W*
108 E8 **Oberburg** Bern, W Switzerland *47°00′N 07°37′E*
109 Q9 **Oberdrauburg** Salzburg, S Austria *46°45′N 12°59′E*
Oberglogau *see* Głogówek
109 W4 **Ober Grafendorf** Niederösterreich, NE Austria *48°09′N 15°33′E*
101 E15 **Oberhausen** Nordrhein-Westfalen, W Germany *51°27′N 06°50′E*
Oberhollabrunn *see* Tulln
Oberlaibach *see* Vrhnika
101 Q15 **Oberlausitz** *var.* Hornja Łužica. *physical region* E Germany
26 J2 **Oberlin** Kansas, C USA *39°49′N 100°33′W*
22 H8 **Oberlin** Louisiana, S USA *30°37′N 92°45′W*
31 T11 **Oberlin** Ohio, N USA *41°17′N 82°13′W*
103 U5 **Obernai** Bas-Rhin, NE France *48°28′N 07°30′E*
109 R4 **Obernberg am Inn** Oberösterreich, N Austria *48°19′N 13°20′E*
Oberndorf *see* Oberndorf am Neckar
101 G23 **Oberndorf am Neckar** *var.* Oberndorf. Baden-Württemberg, SW Germany *48°18′N 08°32′E*
109 Q5 **Oberndorf bei Salzburg** Salzburg, W Austria *47°57′N 12°57′E*
Oberneustadtl *see* Kysucké Nové Mesto
183 S8 **Oberon** New South Wales, SE Australia *33°42′S 149°56′E*
109 Q4 **Oberösterreich** *off.* Land Oberösterreich, *Eng.* Upper Austria. ◆ *state* NW Austria
Oberösterreich, Land *see* Oberösterreich
Oberpahlen *see* Põltsamaa
101 M19 **Oberpfälzer Wald** ▲▲ SE Germany
109 Y6 **Oberpullendorf** Burgenland, E Austria *47°32′N 16°30′E*
Oberradkersburg *see* Gornja Radgona
101 G18 **Oberursel** Hessen, W Germany *50°12′N 08°34′E*
109 Q8 **Obervellach** Salzburg, S Austria *46°56′N 13°10′E*
109 X7 **Oberwart** Burgenland, SE Austria *47°18′N 16°12′E*
Oberwischau *see* Vişeu de Sus
109 T7 **Oberwölz** *var.* Oberwölz-Stadt. Steiermark, SE Austria *47°12′N 14°20′E*
Oberwölz-Stadt *see* Oberwölz
31 S13 **Obetz** Ohio, N USA *39°52′N 82°57′W*
Ob', Gulf of *see* Obskaya Guba
54 G8 **Obia** Santander, C Colombia *06°16′N 73°18′W*
58 H12 **Óbidos** Pará, NE Brazil *01°52′S 55°30′W*
104 F10 **Óbidos** Leiria, C Portugal *39°21′N 09°09′W*
Obidovichi *see* Abidavichy
147 Q13 **Obigarm** W Tajikistan *38°42′N 69°34′E*
165 T2 **Obihiro** Hokkaidō, NE Japan *42°56′N 143°10′E*
Obi-Khingou *see* Khingov
147 P13 **Obikiik** SW Tajikistan *38°07′N 68°36′E*
Obilić *see* Obiliq
113 N16 **Obiliq** *Serb.* Obilić. N Kosovo *42°50′N 20°57′E*
127 O12 **Obil'noye** Respublika Kalmykiya, SW Russian Federation *47°31′N 44°24′E*
20 F8 **Obion** Tennessee, S USA *36°15′N 89°11′W*
20 F8 **Obion River** ~ Tennessee, S USA
171 S12 **Obi, Pulau** *island* Maluku, E Indonesia
165 S2 **Obira** Hokkaidō, NE Japan *44°01′N 141°39′E*
127 N11 **Oblivskaya** Rostovskaya Oblast', SW Russian Federation *48°34′N 42°31′E*
123 R14 **Obluch'ye** Yevreyskaya Avtonomnaya Oblast', SE Russian Federation *48°59′N 131°18′E*
126 K4 **Obninsk** Kaluzhskaya Oblast', W Russian Federation *55°06′N 36°40′E*
114 J8 **Obnova** Pleven, N Bulgaria *43°26′N 25°04′E*
79 N15 **Obo** Haut-Mbomou, E Central African Republic *05°20′N 26°29′E*
159 T9 **Obo** Qinghai, C China *37°57′N 101°03′E*
80 M11 **Obock** E Djibouti *11°57′N 43°09′E*
Obol' *see* Obal'
Obolyanka *see* Abalyanka
171 V13 **Obome** Papua, E Indonesia *03°42′S 133°21′E*
110 G11 **Oborniki** Wielkolpolskie, W Poland *52°38′N 16°48′E*
79 G19 **Obouya** Cuvette, C Congo *0°56′S 15°41′E*
126 J8 **Oboyan'** Kurskaya Oblast', W Russian Federation *51°12′N 36°15′E*
124 M9 **Obozerskiy** Arkhangel'skaya Oblast', NW Russian Federation *63°26′N 40°20′E*
112 L11 **Obrenovac** Serbia, N Serbia *44°39′N 20°12′E*
112 D12 **Obrovac** *It.* Obbrovazzo. Zadar, SW Croatia *44°12′N 15°40′E*
Obrovo *see* Abrova
35 Q3 **Observation Peak** ▲ California, W USA *40°48′N 120°07′W*
122 J8 **Obskaya Guba** *Eng.* Gulf of Ob. *gulf* N Russian Federation
173 N13 **Ob' Tablemount** *undersea feature* S Indian Ocean *50°16′S 51°59′E*
173 T10 **Ob' Trench** *undersea feature* E Indian Ocean
77 P16 **Obuasi** S Ghana *06°15′N 01°36′W*
117 P5 **Obukhiv** *Rus.* Obukhov. Kyyivs'ka Oblast', N Ukraine *50°05′N 30°37′E*
Obukhov *see* Obukhiv
125 U14 **Obva** ~ NW Russian Federation
117 V10 **Obytichna Kosa** *spit* SE Ukraine
117 V10 **Obytichna Zatoka** *gulf* SE Ukraine
114 N9 **Obzor** Burgas, E Bulgaria *42°52′N 27°53′E*
105 O3 **Oca** ~ N Spain
23 W10 **Ocala** Florida, SE USA *29°11′N 82°08′W*
40 M7 **Ocampo** Coahuila, NE Mexico *27°18′N 102°24′W*
54 G7 **Ocaña** Norte de Santander, N Colombia *08°16′N 73°21′W*
105 N9 **Ocaña** Castilla-La Mancha, C Spain *39°57′N 03°30′W*
104 H4 **O Carballiño** *Cast.* Carballiño. Galicia, NW Spain *42°26′N 08°05′W*
37 T9 **Ocate** New Mexico, SW USA *36°09′N 105°03′W*
Ocavango *see* Okavango
57 D14 **Occidental, Cordillera** ▲▲ W South America
21 Q6 **Oceana** West Virginia, NE USA *37°41′N 81°37′W*
21 Z4 **Ocean City** Maryland, NE USA *38°20′N 75°05′W*
18 J17 **Ocean City** New Jersey, NE USA *39°15′N 74°33′W*
10 K15 **Ocean Falls** British Columbia, SW Canada *52°24′N 127°42′W*
Ocean Island *see* Banaba
Ocean Island *see* Kure Atoll
64 J9 **Oceanographer Fracture Zone** *tectonic feature* NW Atlantic Ocean
35 U17 **Oceanside** California, W USA *33°12′N 117°23′W*
22 M9 **Ocean Springs** Mississippi, S USA *30°24′N 88°49′W*
Ocean State *see* Rhode Island
25 O9 **O C Fisher Lake** ⊠ Texas, SW USA
117 Q10 **Ochakiv** *Rus.* Ochakov. Mykolayivs'ka Oblast', S Ukraine *46°36′N 31°33′E*
Ochakov *see* Ochakiv
Ochamchira *see* Och'amch'ire
137 Q9 **Och'amch'ire** *Rus.* Ochamchira. W Georgia *42°45′N 41°30′E*
Ochansk *see* Okhansk
125 T15 **Ochër** Permskaya Oblast', NW Russian Federation *57°54′N 54°40′E*
115 I19 **Óchi** ▲ Évvoia, C Greece *38°03′N 24°27′E*
165 W4 **Ochiishi-misaki** *headland* Hokkaidō, NE Japan *43°10′N 145°29′E*
23 S9 **Ochlockonee River** ~ Florida/Georgia, SE USA
44 K12 **Ocho Rios** C Jamaica *18°24′N 77°06′W*
Ochrida *see* Ohrid
Ochrida, Lake *see* Ohrid, Lake
101 J19 **Ochsenfurt** Bayern, C Germany *49°39′N 10°03′E*
23 U7 **Ocilla** Georgia, SE USA *31°35′N 83°15′W*
94 N13 **Ockelbo** Gävleborg, C Sweden *60°51′N 16°46′E*
Ocker *see* Oker
95 I19 **Öckerö** Västra Götaland, S Sweden *57°43′N 11°39′E*
23 U6 **Ocmulgee River** ~ Georgia, SE USA
116 H11 **Ocna Mureş** *Hung.* Marosújvár; *prev.* Ocna Mureşului, *prev. Hung.* Marosújvárakna. Alba, C Romania *46°25′N 23°53′E*
Ocna Mureşului *see* Ocna Mureş
116 H11 **Ocna Sibiului** *Ger.* Salzburg, *Hung.* Vizakna. Sibiu, C Romania *45°52′N 23°59′E*
116 H13 **Ocnele Mari** *prev.* Vioara. Vâlcea, S Romania *45°03′N 24°18′E*
116 L7 **Ocniţa** *Rus.* Oknitsa. N Moldova *48°25′N 27°30′E*
23 U4 **Oconee, Lake** ⊠ Georgia, SE USA
23 U5 **Oconee River** ~ Georgia, SE USA
30 M9 **Oconomowoc** Wisconsin, N USA *43°06′N 88°29′W*
30 M6 **Oconto** Wisconsin, N USA *44°55′N 87°52′W*
30 M6 **Oconto Falls** Wisconsin, N USA *44°52′N 88°06′W*
30 M6 **Oconto River** ~ Wisconsin, N USA
104 I3 **O Corgo** Galicia, NW Spain *42°56′N 07°25′W*
41 V16 **Ocosingo** Chiapas, SE Mexico *17°04′N 92°15′W*
42 J8 **Ocotal** Nueva Segovia, NW Nicaragua *13°38′N 86°28′W*
42 F6 **Ocotepeque** ◆ *department* W Honduras
Ocotepeque *see* Nueva Ocotepeque
40 L13 **Ocotlán** Jalisco, SW Mexico *20°21′N 102°42′W*
41 R16 **Ocotlán** *var.* Ocotlán de Morelos. Oaxaca, SE Mexico *16°49′N 96°49′W*
Ocotlán de Morelos *see* Ocotlán
41 U16 **Ocozocuautla** Chiapas, SE Mexico *16°46′N 93°22′W*
21 Y10 **Ocracoke Island** *island* North Carolina, SE USA
102 I3 **Octeville** Manche, N France *49°37′N 01°39′W*
October Revolution Island *see* Oktyabr'skoy Revolyutsii, Ostrov
43 R17 **Ocú** Herrera, S Panama *07°55′N 80°43′W*
83 Q14 **Ocua** Cabo Delgado, NE Mozambique *13°37′S 39°44′E*
Ocumare *see* Ocumare del Tuy
54 M5 **Ocumare del Tuy** *var.* Ocumare. Miranda, N Venezuela *10°07′N 66°47′W*
77 P17 **Oda** SE Ghana *05°55′N 00°56′W*
165 G12 **Ōda** *var.* Oda. Shimane, Honshū, SW Japan *35°10′N 132°29′E*
92 K3 **Ódadhahraun** *lava flow* C Iceland
165 Q7 **Ōdate** Akita, Honshū, C Japan *40°18′N 140°34′E*
165 N14 **Odawara** Kanagawa, Honshū, S Japan *35°15′N 139°08′E*
95 D14 **Odda** Hordaland, S Norway *60°03′N 06°34′E*
95 G22 **Odder** Århus, C Denmark *55°59′N 10°10′E*
Oddur *see* Xuddur
29 T13 **Odebolt** Iowa, C USA *42°18′N 95°15′W*
104 H14 **Odeleite** Faro, S Portugal *37°02′N 07°29′W*
25 Q4 **Odell** Texas, SW USA *34°19′N 99°24′W*
25 T14 **Odem** Texas, SW USA *27°57′N 97°34′W*
104 F13 **Odemira** Beja, S Portugal *37°35′N 08°38′W*
136 C14 **Ödemiş** İzmir, SW Turkey *38°11′N 27°58′E*
Ödenburg *see* Sopron
83 I22 **Odendaalsrus** Free State, C South Africa *27°52′S 26°42′E*
Odenpäh *see* Otepää
95 H23 **Odense** Fyn, C Denmark *55°24′N 10°23′E*
101 H19 **Odenwald** ▲▲ W Germany
84 H10 **Oder** *Cz./Pol.* Odra. ~ C Europe
Oderberg *see* Bohumín
100 P11 **Oderbruch** *wetland* Germany/Poland
Oderhaff *see* Szczeciński, Zalew
100 O11 **Oder-Havel-Kanal** *canal* NE Germany
Oderhellen *see* Odorheiu Secuiesc
100 P13 **Oder-Spree-Kanal** *canal* NE Germany
Odertal *see* Zdzieszowice
106 I7 **Oderzo** Veneto, NE Italy *45°48′N 12°33′E*
177 P10 **Odesa** *Rus.* Odessa. Odes'ka Oblast', SW Ukraine *46°29′N 30°44′E*
24 M8 **Odessa** Texas, SW USA *31°51′N 102°22′W*
32 K8 **Odessa** Washington, NW USA *47°19′N 118°41′W*
Odesa *see* Odes'ka Oblast'
95 L18 **Ödeshög** Östergötland, S Sweden *58°13′N 14°40′E*
117 O9 **Odes'ka Oblast'** *var.* Odesa, *Rus.* Odesskaya Oblast'. ◆ *province* SW Ukraine
Odesskaya Oblast' *see* Odes'ka Oblast'
122 H12 **Odesskoye** Omskaya Oblast', C Russian Federation *54°15′N 72°45′E*
Odessus *see* Varna
102 F6 **Odet** ~ NW France
104 I14 **Odiel** ~ SW Spain
76 L14 **Odienné** NW Ivory Coast *09°32′N 07°35′W*
171 O4 **Odiongan** Tablas Island, C Philippines *12°23′N 122°01′E*
116 L12 **Odobeşti** Vrancea, E Romania *45°46′N 27°06′E*
110 H13 **Odolanów** *Ger.* Adelnau. Wielkopolskie, C Poland *51°35′N 17°42′E*
167 R13 **Ŏdôngk** Kâmpóng Spoe, S Cambodia *11°48′N 104°45′E*
25 N6 **O'donnell** Texas, SW USA *32°57′N 101°49′W*
98 O7 **Odoorn** Drenthe, NE Netherlands *52°52′N 06°49′E*
Odorhei *see* Odorheiu Secuiesc
116 J11 **Odorheiu Secuiesc** *Ger.* Oderhellen, *Hung.* Vámosudvarhely; *prev.* Odorhei, *Ger.* Hofmarkt. Harghita, C Romania *46°18′N 25°19′E*
Odra *see* Oder
112 J9 **Odžaci** *Ger.* Hodschag, *Hung.* Hodság. Vojvodina, NW Serbia *45°31′N 19°15′E*
59 N14 **Oeiras** Piauí, E Brazil *07°00′S 42°07′W*
104 F11 **Oeiras** Lisboa, C Portugal *38°41′N 09°18′W*
101 G14 **Oelde** Nordrhein-Westfalen, W Germany *51°49′N 08°09′E*
28 J11 **Oelrichs** South Dakota, N USA *43°08′N 103°13′W*
101 M17 **Oelsnitz** Sachsen, E Germany *50°22′N 12°12′E*
Oels/Oels in Schlesien *see* Oleśnica
29 X12 **Oelwein** Iowa, C USA *42°40′N 91°54′W*
Oeniadae *see* Oiniádes
191 N17 **Oeno Island** *atoll* Pitcairn Islands, C Pacific Ocean
Oesel *see* Saaremaa
108 L7 **Oetz** *var.* Ötz. Tirol, W Austria *47°15′N 10°56′E*
137 P11 **Of** Trabzon, NE Turkey *40°57′N 40°17′E*
30 K15 **O'Fallon** Illinois, N USA *38°35′N 89°54′W*
27 W4 **O'Fallon** Missouri, C USA *38°54′N 90°31′W*
107 N16 **Ofanto** ~ S Italy
97 D18 **Offaly** *Ir.* Ua Uíbh Fhailí; *prev.* King's County. *cultural region* C Ireland
101 H18 **Offenbach** *var.* Offenbach am Main. Hessen, W Germany *50°06′N 08°46′E*
Offenbach am Main *see* Offenbach
101 F22 **Offenburg** Baden-Württemberg, SW Germany *48°28′N 07°57′E*
182 C2 **Officer Creek** *seasonal river* South Australia
Oficina María Elena *see* María Elena
Oficina Pedro de Valdivia *see* Pedro de Valdivia
115 K22 **Ofidoússa** *island* Kykládes, Greece, Aegean Sea
Ofiral *see* Sharm ash Shaykh
92 H10 **Ofotfjorden** *fjord* N Norway
192 L16 **Ofu** *island* Manua Islands, E American Samoa
165 R9 **Ōfunato** Iwate, Honshū, C Japan *39°04′N 141°43′E*
165 P8 **Oga** Akita, Honshū, C Japan *39°56′N 139°47′E*
Ogaadeen *see* Ogaden
165 Q9 **Ogachi** Akita, Honshū, C Japan *39°03′N 140°26′E*
165 P9 **Ogachi-tōge** *pass* Honshū, C Japan
81 N14 **Ogaden** *Som.* Ogaadeen. *plateau* Ethiopia/Somalia
165 P8 **Oga-hantō** *peninsula* Honshū, C Japan
165 K13 **Ōgaki** Gifu, Honshū, SW Japan *35°22′N 136°35′E*
28 L15 **Ogallala** Nebraska, C USA *41°09′N 101°44′W*
168 M14 **Ogan, Air** ~ Sumatera, W Indonesia
165 Y15 **Ogasawara-shotō** *Eng.* Bonin Islands. *island group* SE Japan
14 I9 **Ogascanane, Lac** ◎ Québec, SE Canada
165 R7 **Ogawara-ko** ◎ Honshū, C Japan
77 T15 **Ogbomosho** *var.* Ogmoboso. Oyo, W Nigeria *08°10′N 04°16′E*
29 U13 **Ogden** Iowa, C USA *42°03′N 94°01′W*
36 L2 **Ogden** Utah, W USA *41°09′N 111°58′W*
18 I6 **Ogdensburg** New York, NE USA *44°42′N 75°25′W*
23 W5 **Ogeechee River** ~ Georgia, SE USA
Oger *see* Ogre
165 N10 **Ogi** Niigata, Sado, C Japan *37°49′N 138°16′E*
10 H5 **Ogilvie** Yukon Territory, NW Canada *63°34′N 139°44′W*
10 H4 **Ogilvie** ~ Yukon Territory, NW Canada
10 H5 **Ogilvie Mountains** ▲▲ Yukon Territory, NW Canada
Oginskiy Kanal *see* Ahinski Kanal
162 J7 **Ögiynuur** *var.* Dzegstey. Arhangay, C Mongolia *47°38′N 102°31′E*
146 F6 **Og'iyon Sho'rxogi** *wetland* NW Uzbekistan
146 B10 **Oglanly** Balkan Welaýaty, W Turkmenistan *39°56′N 54°25′E*
23 T5 **Oglethorpe** Georgia, SE USA *32°17′N 84°03′W*
23 T2 **Oglethorpe, Mount** ▲ Georgia, SE USA *34°29′N 84°19′W*
106 F7 **Oglio** *anc.* Ollius. ~ N Italy
Ogmoboso *see* Ogbomosho
103 T8 **Ognon** ~ E France
123 R13 **Ogodzha** Amurskaya Oblast', S Russian Federation *52°51′N 132°49′E*
77 W16 **Ogoja** Cross River, S Nigeria *06°37′N 08°48′E*
12 C10 **Ogoki** ~ Ontario, S Canada
12 D11 **Ogoki Lake** ◎ Ontario, C Canada
Ögöömör *see* Hanhongor
79 F19 **Ogooué** ~ Congo/Gabon
79 E18 **Ogooué-Ivindo** *off.* Province de l'Ogooué-Ivindo, *var.* L'Ogooué-Ivindo. ◆ *province* N Gabon
Ogooué-Ivindo, Province de l' *see* Ogooué-Ivindo
79 E19 **Ogooué-Lolo** *off.* Province de l'Ogooué-Lolo, *var.* L'Ogooué-Lolo. ◆ *province* C Gabon
Ogooué-Lolo, Province de l' *see* Ogooué-Lolo
79 C19 **Ogooué-Maritime** *off.* Province de l'Ogooué-Maritime, *var.* L'Ogooué-Maritime. ◆ *province* W Gabon
Ogooué-Maritime, Province de l' *see* Ogooué-Maritime
165 D14 **Ogōri** Fukuoka, Kyūshū, SW Japan *33°24′N 130°34′E*
114 H7 **Ogosta** ~ NW Bulgaria
112 Q9 **Ogražden** *Bul.* Ograzhden. ▲ Bulgaria/FYR Macedonia *see also* Ograzhden
114 G12 **Ograzhden** *Mac.* Ogražden. ▲ Bulgaria/FYR Macedonia *see also* Ogražden
Ograzhden *see* Ogražden
118 H9 **Ogre** *Ger.* Oger. Ogre, C Latvia *56°49′N 24°36′E*
118 G9 **Ogre** ~ C Latvia
112 C10 **Ogulin** Karlovac, NW Croatia *45°15′N 15°13′E*
77 S16 **Ogun** ◆ *state* SW Nigeria
Ogurdzhaly, Ostrov *see* Ogurjalyadasy
146 A12 **Ogurjalyadasy** *Rus.* Ogurdzhaly, Ostrov. *island* W Turkmenistan
77 U16 **Ogwashi-Uku** Delta, S Nigeria *06°08′N 06°38′E*
185 B23 **Ohai** Southland, South Island, New Zealand *45°56′S 167°59′E*
147 Q10 **Ohangaron** *Rus.* Akhangaran. Toshkent Viloyati, E Uzbekistan *40°56′N 69°37′E*
147 Q10 **Ohangaron** *Rus.* Akhangaran. ~ E Uzbekistan
83 C16 **Ohangwena** ◆ *district* N Namibia
30 M10 **O'Hare** ✈ (Chicago) Illinois, N USA *41°59′N 87°56′W*
165 R6 **Ōhata** Aomori, Honshū, C Japan *41°23′N 141°09′E*
184 L13 **Ohau** Manawatu-Wanganui, North Island, New Zealand *40°40′S 175°15′E*
185 E20 **Ohau, Lake** ◎ South Island, New Zealand
Ohcejohka *see* Utsjoki
99 J20 **Ohey** Namur, SE Belgium *50°26′N 05°07′E*
191 X15 **O'Higgins, Cabo** *headland* Easter Island, Chile, E Pacific Ocean *27°05′S 109°15′W*
O'Higgins, Lago *see* San Martín, Lago
31 S12 **Ohio** *off.* State of Ohio, *also known as* Buckeye State. ◆ *state* N USA
0 L10 **Ohio River** ~ N USA
Ohlau *see* Oława
101 H16 **Ohm** ~ C Germany
193 W16 **Ohonua** 'Eua, E Tonga *21°20′S 174°57′W*
23 V5 **Ohoopee River** ~ Georgia, SE USA
100 L12 **Ohre** *Ger.* Eger. ~ Czech Republic/Germany
Ohri *see* Ohrid
113 M20 **Ohrid** *Turk.* Ochrida, Ohri. SW FYR Macedonia *41°07′N 20°48′E*
113 M20 **Ohrid, Lake** *var.* Lake Ochrida, *Alb.* Liqeni i Ohrit, *Mac.* Ohridsko Ezero. ◎ Albania/FYR Macedonia
Ohridsko Ezero/Ohrit, Liqeni i *see* Ohrid, Lake
184 L9 **Ohura** Manawatu-Wanganui, North Island, New Zealand *38°51′S 174°58′E*
58 J9 **Oiapoque** Amapá, E Brazil *03°54′N 51°46′W*
58 J10 **Oiapoque, Rio** *var.* Fleuve l'Oyapok, Oyapock. ~ Brazil/French Guiana *see also* Oyapok, Fleuve l'
Oiapoque, Rio *see* Oyapok, Fleuve l'
15 O9 **Oies, Île aux** *island* Québec, SE Canada
92 L13 **Oijärvi** Oulu, C Finland *65°38′N 26°05′E*
92 L12 **Oikarainen** Lappi, N Finland *66°30′N 25°46′E*
188 F10 **Oikuul** Babeldaob, N Palau
18 C13 **Oil City** Pennsylvania, NE USA *41°25′N 79°42′W*
18 C12 **Oil Creek** ~ Pennsylvania, NE USA
35 R13 **Oildale** California, W USA *35°25′N 119°01′W*
Oileán Ciarral *see* Castleisland
Oil Islands *see* Chagos Archipelago
115 D18 **Oiniádes** *anc.* Oeniadae. *site of ancient city* Dytikí Ellás, W Greece
115 L18 **Oinoússes** *island* E Greece
Oírr, Inis *see* Inisheer
99 J15 **Oirschot** Noord-Brabant, S Netherlands *51°30′N 05°18′E*
103 N4 **Oise** ◆ *department* N France
103 P3 **Oise** ~ N France
99 J14 **Oisterwijk** Noord-Brabant, S Netherlands *51°35′N 05°12′E*
45 O14 **Oistins** S Barbados *13°04′N 59°33′W*
165 E4 **Ōita** Ōita, Kyūshū, SW Japan *33°15′N 131°35′E*
165 D14 **Ōita** *off.* Ōita-ken. ◆ *prefecture* Kyūshū, SW Japan
Ōita-ken *see* Ōita
115 E17 **Oíti** ▲ C Greece *38°48′N 22°12′E*
165 S4 **Oiwake** Hokkaidō, NE Japan *42°54′N 141°49′E*
35 R14 **Ojai** California, W USA *34°25′N 119°15′W*
94 K13 **Öje** Dalarna, C Sweden *60°49′N 13°54′E*
93 J14 **Öjebyn** Norrbotten, N Sweden *65°20′N 21°26′E*
165 B13 **Ojika-jima** *island* SW Japan
40 K5 **Ojinaga** Chihuahua, N Mexico *29°31′N 104°26′W*
40 M11 **Ojo Caliente** *var.* Ojocaliente. Zacatecas, C Mexico *22°35′N 102°18′W*
Ojocaliente *see* Ojo Caliente
40 D6 **Ojo de Liebre, Laguna** *var.* Laguna Scammon, Scammon Lagoon. *lagoon* NW Mexico
62 I7 **Ojos del Salado, Cerro** ▲ W Argentina *27°04′S 68°34′W*
105 R7 **Ojos Negros** Aragón, NE Spain *40°43′N 01°30′W*
40 M12 **Ojuelos de Jalisco** Aguascalientes, C Mexico *21°52′N 101°40′W*
127 N4 **Oka** ~ W Russian Federation
83 D19 **Okahandja** Otjozondjupa, C Namibia *21°58′S 16°55′E*
184 L9 **Okahukura** Manawatu-Wanganui, North Island, New Zealand *38°48′S 175°13′E*
184 J3 **Okaihau** Northland, North Island, New Zealand *35°19′S 173°45′E*
83 D18 **Okakarara** Otjozondjupa, N Namibia *20°33′S 17°20′E*
13 P5 **Okak Islands** *island group* Newfoundland and Labrador, E Canada
10 M17 **Okanagan** ~ British Columbia, SW Canada
11 N17 **Okanagan Lake** ◎ British Columbia, SW Canada
Ókanizsa *see* Kanjiža
83 C16 **Okankolo** Otjikoto, N Namibia *17°57′S 16°28′E*
32 K6 **Okanogan River** ~ Washington, NW USA
83 D18 **Okaputa** Otjozondjupa, N Namibia *20°05′S 16°56′E*
149 V9 **Okāra** Punjab, E Pakistan *30°49′N 73°31′E*
26 M10 **Okarche** Oklahoma, C USA *35°43′N 97°58′W*
Okarem *see* Ekerem
189 X14 **Okat Harbor** *harbor* Kosrae, E Micronesia
22 M5 **Okatibbee Creek** ~ Mississippi, S USA
83 C17 **Okaukuejo** Kunene, N Namibia *19°10′S 15°23′E*
Okavanggo *see* Cubango/Okavango
83 E17 **Okavango** ◆ *district* NW Namibia
83 G17 **Okavango** *var.* Cubango, Kavango, Kavengo, Kubango, Okavanggo, *Port.* Ocavango. ~ S Africa *see also* Cubango
Okavango *see* Cubango
83 G17 **Okavango Delta** *wetland* N Botswana
164 M12 **Okaya** Nagano, Honshū, S Japan *36°03′N 138°00′E*
164 H13 **Okayama** Okayama, Honshū, SW Japan *34°40′N 133°54′E*
164 H13 **Okayama** *off.* Okayama-ken. ◆ *prefecture* Honshū, SW Japan
Okayama-ken *see* Okayama
164 L14 **Okazaki** Aichi, Honshū, C Japan *34°58′N 137°10′E*
110 M12 **Okęcie** ✈ (Warszawa) Mazowieckie, C Poland *52°08′N 20°57′E*
23 Y13 **Okeechobee** Florida, SE USA *27°14′N 80°49′W*
23 Y14 **Okeechobee, Lake** ◎ Florida, SE USA
26 M9 **Okeene** Oklahoma, C USA *36°07′N 98°19′W*
23 V8 **Okefenokee Swamp** *wetland* Georgia, SE USA
97 J24 **Okehampton** SW England, United Kingdom *50°44′N 04°W*
27 P10 **Okemah** Oklahoma, C USA *35°25′N 96°20′W*
77 U16 **Okene** Kogi, S Nigeria *07°31′N 06°15′E*
100 K13 **Oker** *var.* Ocker. ~ NW Germany
101 J14 **Oker-Stausee** ◎ C Germany
123 T12 **Okha** Ostrov Sakhalin, Sakhalinskaya Oblast', SE Russian Federation *53°33′N 142°55′E*
125 U15 **Okhansk** *var.* Ochansk. Permskaya Oblast', NW Russian Federation *57°44′N 55°20′E*
123 S10 **Okhotsk** Khabarovskiy Kray, E Russian Federation *59°21′N 143°15′E*
192 J2 **Okhotsk, Sea of** *sea* NW Pacific Ocean
117 T4 **Okhtyrka** *Rus.* Akhtyrka. Sums'ka Oblast', NE Ukraine *50°19′N 34°54′E*
83 E23 **Okiep** Northern Cape, W South Africa *29°39′S 17°53′E*
Oki-guntō *see* Oki-shotō
164 H11 **Oki-kaikyō** *strait* SW Japan
165 P16 **Okinawa** Okinawa, SW Japan *26°20′N 127°47′E*
165 S16 **Okinawa** *off.* Okinawa-ken. ◆ *prefecture* Okinawa, SW Japan
165 S16 **Okinawa** *island* SW Japan
Okinawa-ken *see* Okinawa
165 U16 **Okinoerabu-jima** *island* Nansei-shotō, SW Japan
164 F15 **Okino-shima** *island* SW Japan
164 H11 **Oki-shotō** *var.* Oki-guntō. *island group* SW Japan
77 T16 **Okitipupa** Ondo, SW Nigeria *06°33′N 04°43′E*
166 L8 **Okkan** Bago, SW Myanmar (Burma) *17°30′N 95°52′E*
27 N10 **Oklahoma** *off.* State of Oklahoma, *also known as* The Sooner State. ◆ *state* C USA
27 N11 **Oklahoma City** *state capital* Oklahoma, C USA *35°28′N 97°31′W*
25 Q4 **Oklaunion** Texas, SW USA *34°07′N 99°07′W*
23 W10 **Oklawaha River** ~ Florida, SE USA
27 P10 **Okmulgee** Oklahoma, C USA *35°38′N 95°59′W*
Oknitsa *see* Ocniţa
22 M3 **Okolona** Mississippi, S USA *34°00′N 88°45′W*
165 U2 **Okoppe** Hokkaidō, NE Japan *44°27′N 143°06′E*
11 Q16 **Okotoks** Alberta, SW Canada *50°46′N 113°57′W*
80 H6 **Oko, Wadi** ~ NE Sudan
79 G19 **Okoyo** Cuvette, W Congo *01°28′S 15°04′E*
77 S15 **Okpara** ~ Benin/Nigeria
92 J8 **Øksfjord** Finnmark, N Norway *70°13′N 22°22′E*
125 R4 **Oksino** Nenetskiy Avtonomnyy Okrug, NW Russian Federation *67°33′N 52°15′E*
92 G13 **Oksskolten** ▲ C Norway *66°00′N 14°18′E*
Oksu *see* Oqsu
144 M8 **Oktaybr'skiy** Kostanay, N Kazakhstan
186 B7 **Ok Tedi** Western, W Papua New Guinea
Oktemberyan *see* Armavir
166 M7 **Oktwin** Bago, C Myanmar (Burma) *18°47′N 96°21′E*
127 R6 **Oktyab'rsk** Samarskaya Oblast', W Russian Federation *53°13′N 48°36′E*
Oktyab'rsk *see* Kandyagash
125 N12 **Oktyabr'skiy** Arkhangel'skaya Oblast', NW Russian Federation *61°03′N 43°16′E*
122 E10 **Oktyabr'skiy** Kamchatskaya Oblast', E Russian Federation *52°35′N 156°18′E*
127 T5 **Oktyabr'skiy** Respublika Bashkortostan, W Russian Federation *54°28′N 53°29′E*
127 O11 **Oktyabr'skiy** Volgogradskaya Oblast', SW Russian Federation *48°00′N 43°35′E*
Oktyabr'skiy *see* Aktsyabrski
127 V7 **Oktyabr'skoye** Orenburgskaya Oblast', W Russian Federation *52°22′N 55°39′E*
122 M5 **Oktyabr'skoy Revolyutsii, Ostrov** *Eng.* October Revolution Island. *island* Severnaya Zemlya, N Russian Federation
164 C15 **Ōkuchi** *var.* Ōkuti. Kagoshima, Kyūshū, SW Japan *32°04′N 130°36′E*
124 I14 **Okulovka** *var.* Okulovka. Novgorodskaya Oblast', W Russian Federation *58°24′N 33°16′E*
Okulovka *see* Okulovka
165 Q4 **Okushiri-tō** *var.* Okusiri Tô. *island* NE Japan
Okusiri Tô *see* Okushiri-tō
77 S15 **Okuta** Kwara, W Nigeria *09°18′N 03°09′E*
Ōkuti *see* Ōkuchi
83 F19 **Okwa** *var.* Chapman's. ~ Botswana/Namibia
123 T10 **Ola** Magadanskaya Oblast', E Russian Federation *59°36′N 151°18′E*
27 T11 **Ola** Arkansas, C USA *35°01′N 93°13′W*
Ola *see* Ala
35 T11 **Olacha Peak** ▲ California, W USA *36°15′N 118°07′W*
92 J1 **Ólafsfjördhur** Norðurland Eystra, N Iceland *66°04′N 18°36′W*
92 H3 **Ólafsvík** Vesturland, W Iceland *64°52′N 23°45′W*
Oláhbrettye *see* Bretea-Română
Oláhszentgyörgy *see* Sângeorz-Băi

◆ Country ● Country Capital ◇ Dependent Territory ○ Dependent Territory Capital ◆ Administrative Regions ✈ International Airport ▲ Mountain ▲▲ Mountain Range Volcano ~ River ◎ Lake ⊠ Reservoir
299

Oláh-Toplicza – Orenburg

Oláh-Toplicza see Toplița
35 T11 Olancha California, W USA 36°16′N 118°00′W
42 J5 Olanchito Yoro, C Honduras 15°30′N 86°34′W
42 J6 Olancho ◈ department E Honduras
95 O20 Öland island S Sweden
95 O19 Ölands norra udde headland S Sweden 57°21′N 17°06′E
95 N22 Ölands södra udde headland S Sweden 56°12′N 16°26′E
182 K7 Olary South Australia 32°18′S 140°16′E
27 R4 Olathe Kansas, C USA 38°52′N 94°50′W
61 C22 Olavarría Buenos Aires, E Argentina 36°57′S 60°20′W
92 O2 Olav V Land physical region C Svalbard
111 H14 Oława Ger. Ohlau. Dolnośląskie, SW Poland 50°57′N 17°18′E
107 D17 Olbia prev. Terranova Pausania. Sardegna, Italy, C Mediterranean Sea 40°55′N 09°30′E
44 G5 Old Bahama Channel channel Bahamas/Cuba
Old Bay State/Old Colony State see Massachusetts
10 H2 Old Crow Yukon Territory, NW Canada 67°34′N 139°55′W
Old Dominion see Virginia
Oldeberkeap see Oldeberkoop
98 M7 Oldeberkoop Fris. Oldeberkeap. Friesland, N Netherlands 52°55′N 06°07′E
98 L10 Oldebroek Gelderland, E Netherlands 52°27′N 05°54′E
98 L8 Oldemarkt Overijssel, N Netherlands 52°49′N 05°58′E
94 E11 Olden Sogn Og Fjordane, C Norway 61°52′N 06°44′E
100 G10 Oldenburg Niedersachsen, NW Germany 53°09′N 08°13′E
100 K8 Oldenburg var. Oldenburg in Holstein. Schleswig-Holstein, N Germany 54°17′N 10°55′E
Oldenburg in Holstein see Oldenburg
98 P10 Oldenzaal Overijssel, E Netherlands 52°19′N 06°53′E
Olderfjord see Leaibevuotna
18 J8 Old Forge New York, NE USA 43°42′N 74°59′W
Old Goa see Goa
97 L17 Oldham NW England, United Kingdom 53°36′N 02°W
39 Q14 Old Harbor Kodiak Island, Alaska, USA 57°12′N 153°18′W
44 J13 Old Harbour C Jamaica 17°56′N 77°06′W
97 C22 Old Head of Kinsale Ir. An Seancheann. headland SW Ireland 51°37′N 08°33′W
20 J8 Old Hickory Lake ⊠ Tennessee, S USA
Old Line State see Maryland
Old North State see North Carolina
81 I17 Ol Doinyo Lengeyo ▲▲ C Kenya
11 Q16 Olds Alberta, SW Canada 51°50′N 114°06′W
19 O7 Old Speck Mountain ▲ Maine, NE USA 44°34′N 70°55′W
19 S6 Old Town Maine, NE USA 44°55′N 68°39′W
11 T17 Old Wives Lake ◎ Saskatchewan, S Canada
162 J7 Öldziyt var. Höshööt. Arhangay, C Mongolia 48°06′N 102°34′E
162 I8 Öldziyt var. Ulaan-Uul. Bayanhongor, C Mongolia 46°03′N 100°52′E
162 L10 Öldziyt var. Rashaant. Dundgovĭ, C Mongolia 44°54′N 106°32′E
162 K8 Öldziyt var. Sangiyn Dalay. Övörhangay, C Mongolia 46°35′N 103°18′E
Öldziyt see Erdenemandal, Arhangay, Mongolia
Öldziyt see Sayhandulaan, Dornogovĭ, Mongolia
188 H6 Oleai var. San Jose. Saipan, S Northern Mariana Islands
18 E11 Olean New York, NE USA 42°04′N 78°24′W
110 O7 Olecko Ger. Treuburg. Warmińsko-Mazurskie, NE Poland 54°02′N 22°29′E
106 C7 Oleggio Piemonte, NE Italy 45°36′N 08°37′E
123 P11 Olëkma Amurskaya Oblast', SE Russian Federation 57°00′N 120°27′E
123 P12 Olëkma ⟿ C Russian Federation
123 P11 Olëkminsk Respublika Sakha (Yakutiya), NE Russian Federation 60°25′N 120°25′E
117 W7 Oleksandrivka Donets'ka Oblast', E Ukraine 48°42′N 36°56′E
117 R7 Oleksandrivka Rus. Aleksandrovka. Kirovohrads'ka Oblast', C Ukraine 48°59′N 32°14′E
117 Q9 Oleksandrivka Mykolayivs'ka Oblast', S Ukraine 47°42′N 31°17′E
117 S7 Oleksandriya Rus. Aleksandriya. Kirovohrads'ka Oblast', C Ukraine 48°42′N 33°07′E
93 B20 Ølen Hordaland, S Norway 59°36′N 05°48′E
124 J4 Olenegorsk Murmanskaya Oblast', NW Russian Federation 68°06′N 33°15′E
123 N9 Olenëk Respublika Sakha (Yakutiya), NE Russian Federation 68°28′N 112°18′E
123 N9 Olenëk ⟿ NE Russian Federation
123 O7 Olenëkskiy Zaliv bay N Russian Federation
124 K6 Olenitsa Murmanskaya Oblast', NW Russian Federation 66°27′N 35°21′E
102 I11 Oléron, Île d' island W France
111 H14 Oleśnica Ger. Oels, Oels in Schlesien. Dolnośląskie, SW Poland 51°13′N 17°20′E
111 I15 Olesno Ger. Rosenberg. Opolskie, S Poland 50°53′N 18°23′E
116 M3 Olevs'k Rus. Olevsk. Zhytomyrs'ka Oblast', N Ukraine 51°12′N 27°38′E
Olevsk see Olevs'k
123 S15 Ol'ga Primorskiy Kray, SE Russian Federation 43°41′N 135°06′E
Olga, Mount see Kata Tjuta
92 P2 Olgastretet strait E Svalbard
162 D5 Ölgiy Bayan-Ölgiy, W Mongolia 48°57′N 89°59′E
95 F23 Ølgod Ribe, W Denmark 55°44′N 08°37′E
104 H14 Olhão Faro, S Portugal 37°01′N 07°50′W
93 L14 Olhava Oulu, C Finland 65°28′N 25°25′E
112 B12 Olib It. Ulbo. island W Croatia
83 B16 Olifa Kunene, NW Namibia 17°25′S 14°27′E
83 E20 Olifants var. Elephant River. ⟿ E Namibia
83 E25 Olifants var. Elefantes. ⟿ SW South Africa
83 I20 Olifants Drift var. Oliphants Drift. Kgatleng, SE Botswana 24°13′S 26°52′E
83 G22 Olifantshoek Northern Cape, N South Africa 27°56′S 22°45′E
188 L15 Olimarao Atoll atoll Caroline Islands, C Micronesia
Ólimbos see Ólympos
Olimpo see Fuerte Olimpo
59 Q15 Olinda Pernambuco, E Brazil 08°S 34°51′W
Olinthos see Ólynthos
Oliphants Drift see Olifants Drift
Olisipo see Lisboa
Olita see Alytus
105 Q4 Olite Navarra, N Spain 42°29′N 01°40′W
62 K10 Oliva Córdoba, C Argentina 32°03′S 63°34′W
105 T11 Oliva País Valenciano, E Spain 38°55′N 00°09′W
Oliva see La Oliva
104 I12 Oliva de la Frontera Extremadura, W Spain 38°17′N 06°54′W
Olivares see Olivares de Júcar
62 H9 Olivares, Cerro de ▲ N Chile 30°25′S 69°52′W
105 P9 Olivares de Júcar var. Olivares. Castilla-La Mancha, C Spain 39°45′N 02°21′W
22 L1 Olive Branch Mississippi, S USA 34°58′N 89°49′W
21 O5 Olive Hill Kentucky, S USA 38°18′N 83°10′W
35 O6 Olivehurst California, W USA 39°05′N 121°33′W
104 G7 Oliveira de Azeméis Aveiro, N Portugal 40°49′N 08°29′W
104 I11 Olivenza Extremadura, W Spain 38°41′N 07°06′W
11 N17 Oliver British Columbia, SW Canada 49°10′N 119°37′W
103 N7 Olivet Loiret, C France 47°53′N 01°53′E
29 Q12 Olivet South Dakota, N USA 43°14′N 97°40′W
29 T9 Olivia Minnesota, N USA 44°46′N 94°59′W
185 C20 Olivine Range ▲▲ South Island, New Zealand
108 H10 Olivone Ticino, S Switzerland 46°32′N 08°55′E
Ölkeyek see Ul'kayak
127 O9 Ol'khovka Volgogradskaya Oblast', SW Russian Federation 49°54′N 44°36′E
111 K16 Olkusz Małopolskie, S Poland 50°18′N 19°33′E
22 I6 Olla Louisiana, S USA 31°54′N 92°14′W
62 I4 Ollagüe, Volcán var. Oyahue, Volcán Oyahue. Ѫ N Chile 21°25′S 68°10′W
189 U13 Ollan island Chuuk, C Micronesia
188 F7 Ollei Babeldaob, N Palau 07°43′N 134°37′E
Ollius see Oglio
108 C10 Ollon Vaud, W Switzerland 46°19′N 07°00′E
147 Q10 Olmaliq Rus. Almalyk. Toshkent Viloyati, E Uzbekistan 40°51′N 69°39′E
104 M6 Olmedo Castilla-León, N Spain 41°17′N 04°41′W
56 B10 Olmos Lambayeque, W Peru 06°00′S 79°43′W
Olmütz see Olomouc
30 M15 Olney Illinois, N USA 38°43′N 88°05′W
25 R5 Olney Texas, SW USA 33°22′N 98°45′W
95 L22 Olofström Blekinge, S Sweden 56°16′N 14°33′E
187 N9 Olomburi Malaita, N Solomon Islands 09°00′S 161°09′E
111 H17 Olomouc Ger. Olmütz, Pol. Ołomuniec. Olomoucký Kraj, E Czech Republic 49°36′N 17°13′E
111 H18 Olomoucký Kraj ◈ region E Czech Republic
Ołomuniec see Olomouc
122 D7 Olonets Respublika Kareliya, NW Russian Federation 60°58′N 33°01′E
171 N3 Olongapo off. Olongapo City. Luzon, N Philippines 14°52′N 120°16′E
Olongapo City see Olongapo
102 J16 Oloron-Ste-Marie Pyrénées-Atlantiques, SW France 43°12′N 00°35′W
192 L16 Olosega island Manua Islands, E American Samoa
105 W4 Olot Cataluña, NE Spain 42°11′N 02°30′E
146 K12 Olot Rus. Alat. Buxoro Viloyati, C Uzbekistan 39°22′N 63°42′E
112 I12 Olovo Federacija Bosna I Hercegovina, E Bosnia and Herzegovina 44°08′N 18°35′E
123 O14 Olovyannaya Chitinskaya Oblast', S Russian Federation 50°59′N 115°24′E
123 T7 Oloy ⟿ NE Russian Federation
101 F16 Olpe Nordrhein-Westfalen, W Germany 51°02′N 07°51′E
109 N8 Olperer ▲ SW Austria 47°03′N 11°36′E
Olshanka see Vil'shanka
Ol'shany see Al'shany
Olsnitz see Murska Sobota
98 M10 Olst Overijssel, E Netherlands 52°19′N 06°06′E
110 L8 Olsztyn Ger. Allenstein. Warmińsko-Mazurskie, N Poland 53°46′N 20°28′E
110 L8 Olsztynek Ger. Hohenstein in Ostpreussen. Warmińsko-Mazurskie, N Poland 53°35′N 20°17′E
116 I14 Olt ◈ county SW Romania
116 I14 Olt var. Oltul, Ger. Alt. ⟿ S Romania
108 E7 Olten Solothurn, NW Switzerland 47°22′N 07°55′E
116 K14 Oltenița prev. Eng. Oltenitsa; anc. Constantiola. Călărași, SE Romania 44°05′N 26°40′E
Oltenitsa see Oltenița
116 H14 Olteț ⟿ S Romania
24 M4 Olton Texas, SW USA 34°10′N 102°07′W
137 R12 Oltu Erzurum, NE Turkey 40°34′N 41°59′E
Oltul see Olt
146 G7 Oltynko'l Qoraqalpog'iston Respublikasi, NW Uzbekistan 43°04′N 58°51′E
161 S15 Oluan Pi Eng. Cape Olwanpi. headland S Taiwan 21°57′N 120°48′E
Ólubló see Stará L'ubovňa
137 R11 Olur Erzurum, NE Turkey 40°49′N 42°08′E
104 L15 Olvera Andalucía, S Spain 36°56′N 05°15′W
Ol'viopol' see Pervomays'k
Olwanpi, Cape see Oluan Pi
115 D20 Olympia Dytikí Ellás, S Greece 37°39′N 21°36′E
32 G9 Olympia state capital Washington, NW USA 47°02′N 122°54′W
182 H5 Olympic Dam South Australia 30°25′S 136°56′E
32 F7 Olympic Mountains ▲▲ Washington, NW USA
121 O3 Ólympos var. Troodos, Eng. Mount Olympus. ▲ C Cyprus 34°55′N 32°49′E
115 F15 Ólympos var. Ólimbos, Eng. Mount Olympus. ▲ N Greece 40°04′N 22°24′E
115 L17 Ólympos ▲ Lésvos, E Greece 39°03′N 26°20′E
16 C5 Olympus, Mount ▲ Washington, NW USA 47°48′N 123°42′W
Olympus, Mount see Ólympos
115 G14 Ólynthos var. Olinthos; anc. Olynthus. site of ancient city Kentrikí Makedonía, N Greece
Olynthus see Ólynthos
117 Q3 Olyshivka Chernihivs'ka Oblast', N Ukraine 51°13′N 31°19′E
123 W8 Olyutorskiy, Mys headland E Russian Federation 59°56′N 170°22′E
123 V8 Olyutorskiy Zaliv bay E Russian Federation
186 M10 Om ⟿ W Papua New Guinea
129 S6 Om' ⟿ N Russian Federation
158 I13 Oma Xizang Zizhiqu, W China 32°30′N 83°14′E
165 R6 Ōma Aomori, Honshū, C Japan 41°31′N 140°54′E
125 P6 Oma ⟿ NW Russian Federation
164 M12 Ōmachi var. Ōmati. Nagano, Honshū, S Japan 36°30′N 137°51′E
165 Q8 Ōmagari Akita, Honshū, C Japan 39°29′N 140°29′E
97 E15 Omagh Ir. An Ómaigh. W Northern Ireland, United Kingdom 54°36′N 07°18′W
29 S15 Omaha Nebraska, C USA 41°14′N 95°57′W
83 E19 Omaheke ◈ district W Namibia
141 W10 Oman off. Sultanate of Oman, Ar. Salṭanat 'Umān; prev. Muscat and Oman. ◆ monarchy SW Asia
129 O10 Oman Basin var. Bassin d'Oman. undersea feature N Indian Ocean 23°20′N 63°00′E
Oman, Bassin d' see Oman Basin
129 N10 Oman, Gulf of Ar. Khalīj 'Umān. gulf N Arabian Sea
Oman, Sultanate of see Oman
184 J3 Omapere Northland, North Island, New Zealand 35°32′S 173°24′E
185 E20 Omarama Canterbury, South Island, New Zealand 44°29′S 169°57′E
112 F11 Omarska ◈ Republika Srpska, NW Bosnia and Herzegovina
83 C18 Omaruru Erongo, NW Namibia 21°28′S 15°56′E
83 C19 Omaruru ⟿ W Namibia
83 E17 Omatako ⟿ NE Namibia
Ōmati see Ōmachi
83 E18 Omawewozonyanda Omaheke, E Namibia 21°30′S 19°34′E
165 R6 Ōma-zaki headland Honshū, C Japan 41°32′N 140°53′E
Omba see Ambae
Ombai see Alor, Pulau
83 C16 Ombalantu Omusati, N Namibia 17°33′S 14°58′E
79 H15 Ombella-Mpoko ◈ prefecture S Central African Republic
Ombetsu see Onbetsu
83 B17 Ombombo Kunene, NW Namibia 18°43′S 13°53′E
79 D19 Omboué Ogooué-Maritime, W Gabon 01°38′S 09°20′E
106 G13 Ombrone ⟿ C Italy
80 F9 Omdurman var. Umm Durmān. Khartoum, C Sudan 15°37′N 32°29′E
165 N13 Ōme Tōkyō, Honshū, S Japan 35°48′N 139°17′E
106 C6 Omegna Piemonte, NE Italy 45°54′N 08°25′E
183 P12 Omeo Victoria, SE Australia 37°09′S 147°36′E
138 F11 Omer Southern, C Israel 31°16′N 34°51′E
41 P16 Ometepec Guerrero, S Mexico 16°39′N 98°23′W
42 K11 Ometepe, Isla de island S Nicaragua
Om Hager see Om Hajer
80 I10 Om Hajer var. Om Hager. SW Eritrea 14°19′N 36°46′E
142 L10 Omīdīyeh Khūzestān, SW Iran 30°45′N 49°42′E
165 J13 Ōmi-Hachiman var. Ōmihachiman. Shiga, Honshū, SW Japan 35°08′N 136°04′E
Ōmihachiman see Ōmi-Hachiman
10 L12 Omineca Mountains ▲▲ British Columbia, W Canada
113 F14 Omiš It. Almissa. Split-Dalmacija, S Croatia 43°27′N 16°41′E
112 B10 Omišalj Primorje-Gorski Kotar, NW Croatia 45°10′N 14°33′E
83 D19 Omitara Khomas, C Namibia 22°18′S 18°01′E
41 O16 Omitlán, Río ⟿ S Mexico
39 X14 Ommaney, Cape headland Baranof Island, Alaska, USA 56°10′N 134°40′W
98 N9 Ommen Overijssel, E Netherlands 52°31′N 06°25′E
163 N7 Ömnödelger var. Bayanbulag. Hentiy, C Mongolia 47°54′N 109°51′E
162 K11 Ömnögovĭ ◈ province S Mongolia
191 X7 Omoa Fatu Hira, NE French Polynesia 10°30′S 138°41′E
Omo Botego see Omo Wenz
Ömoldova see Moldova Veche
123 T7 Omolon Chukotskiy Avtonomnyy Okrug, NE Russian Federation 65°11′N 160°33′E
123 T7 Omolon ⟿ NE Russian Federation
123 Q8 Omoloy ⟿ NE Russian Federation
165 P8 Omono-gawa ⟿ Honshū, C Japan
81 I14 Omo Wenz var. Omo Botego. ⟿ Ethiopia/Kenya
122 H12 Omsk Omskaya Oblast', C Russian Federation 55°N 73°22′E
122 H11 Omskaya Oblast' ◈ province C Russian Federation
165 U2 Ōmu Hokkaidō, NE Japan 44°36′N 142°55′E
110 M9 Omulew ⟿ NE Poland
116 J12 Omul, Vârful prev. Vîrful Omu. ▲ C Romania 45°24′N 25°26′E
83 D16 Omundaungilo Ohangwena, N Namibia 17°28′S 16°39′E
164 C14 Ōmura Nagasaki, Kyūshū, SW Japan 32°56′N 129°58′E
83 B17 Omusati ◈ district N Namibia
164 C14 Ōmuta Fukuoka, Kyūshū, SW Japan 33°01′N 130°27′E
125 S14 Omutninsk Kirovskaya Oblast', NW Russian Federation 58°37′N 52°08′E
Omu, Vîrful see Omul, Vârful
29 V7 Onamia Minnesota, N USA 46°04′N 93°40′W
21 Y5 Onancock Virginia, NE USA 37°42′N 75°45′W
14 E10 Onaping Lake ◎ Ontario, S Canada
30 M12 Onarga Illinois, N USA 40°39′N 88°00′W
15 R6 Onatchiway, Lac ◎ Québec, SE Canada
29 S14 Onawa Iowa, C USA 42°01′N 96°06′W
165 U5 Onbetsu var. Ombetsu. Hokkaidō, NE Japan 42°52′N 143°54′E
83 B16 Oncócua Cunene, SW Angola 16°37′S 13°23′E
105 S9 Onda País Valenciano, E Spain 39°58′N 00°17′W
111 N18 Ondava ⟿ NE Slovakia
Ondjiva see N'Giva
77 T16 Ondo Ondo, SW Nigeria 07°07′N 04°50′E
77 T16 Ondo ◈ state SW Nigeria
163 N8 Öndörhaan var. Undur Khan; prev. Tsetsen Khan. Hentiy, E Mongolia 47°21′N 110°42′E
162 M9 Öndörshil var. Böhöt. Dundgovĭ, C Mongolia 45°13′N 108°12′E
162 L8 Öndörshireet var. Bayshint. Töv, C Mongolia 47°22′N 105°04′E
162 I7 Öndör-Ulaan var. Teel. Arhangay, C Mongolia 48°01′N 100°30′E
83 D18 Ondundazongonda Otjozondjupa, N Namibia 20°28′S 18°00′E
151 K21 One and Half Degree Channel channel S Maldives
187 Z15 Oneata island Lau Group, E Fiji
124 L9 Onega Arkhangel'skaya Oblast', NW Russian Federation 63°54′N 37°59′E
124 L9 Onega ⟿ NW Russian Federation
Onega Bay see Onezhskaya Guba
Onega, Lake see Onezhskoye Ozero
18 I10 Oneida New York, NE USA 43°05′N 75°39′W
20 M8 Oneida Tennessee, S USA 36°30′N 84°30′W
18 H9 Oneida Lake ◎ New York, NE USA
29 P13 O'Neill Nebraska, C USA 42°28′N 98°38′W
123 V12 Onekotan, Ostrov island Kuril'skiye Ostrova, SE Russian Federation
23 P3 Oneonta Alabama, S USA 33°57′N 86°28′W
18 J11 Oneonta New York, NE USA 42°27′N 75°03′W
190 I16 Oneroa island S Cook Islands
116 K11 Onești Hung. Onyest; prev. Gheorghe Gheorghiu-Dej. Bacău, E Romania 46°14′N 26°46′E
193 V15 Onevai island Tongatapu Group, S Tonga
108 A11 Onex Genève, SW Switzerland 46°12′N 06°04′E
124 K8 Onezhskaya Guba Eng. Onega Bay. bay NW Russian Federation
122 D7 Onezhskoye Ozero Eng. Lake Onega. ◎ NW Russian Federation
83 C16 Ongandjera Omusati, N Namibia 17°49′S 15°06′E
184 N12 Ongaonga Hawke's Bay, North Island, New Zealand 39°57′S 176°21′E
Ongi see Sayhan-Ovoo, Dundgovĭ, Mongolia
Ongi see Uyanga
163 W14 Ongjin SW North Korea 37°56′N 125°22′E
155 J17 Ongole Andhra Pradesh, E India 15°33′N 80°03′E
Ongon see Bürd
Ongtüstik Qazaqstan Oblysy see Yuzhnyy Kazakhstan
99 I21 Onhaye Namur, S Belgium 50°15′N 04°51′E
166 M8 Onhne Bago, SW Myanmar (Burma) 17°02′N 96°28′E
137 S9 Oni N Georgia 42°36′N 43°13′E
29 N9 Onida South Dakota, N USA 44°42′N 100°03′W
164 F15 Onigajō-yama ▲ Shikoku, SW Japan 33°10′N 132°37′E
172 H7 Onilahy ⟿ S Madagascar
77 U16 Onitsha Anambra, S Nigeria 06°09′N 06°48′E
164 K12 Ōno Fukui, Honshū, SW Japan 35°59′N 136°30′E
164 I13 Ono Hyōgo, Honshū, SW Japan 34°52′N 134°55′E
187 K15 Ono island SW Fiji
164 E13 Onoda Yamaguchi, Honshū, SW Japan 34°00′N 131°11′E
187 Z16 Ono-i-lau island SE Fiji
164 D13 Ōnojō var. Ōnozyô. Fukuoka, Kyūshū, SW Japan 33°34′N 130°29′E
163 O7 Onon Gol ⟿ N Mongolia
Ononte see Orontes
55 N6 Onoto Anzoátegui, NE Venezuela 09°36′N 65°12′W
191 O3 Onotoa prev. Clerk Island. atoll Tungaru, W Kiribati
Ōnozyô see Ōnojō
95 I19 Onsala Halland, S Sweden 57°25′N 12°00′E
83 E23 Onseepkans Northern Cape, W South Africa 28°44′S 19°18′E
104 F4 Ons, Illa de island NW Spain
180 H7 Onslow Western Australia 21°42′S 115°08′E
21 W11 Onslow Bay bay North Carolina, E USA
98 P6 Onstwedde Groningen, NE Netherlands 53°01′N 07°04′E
164 C16 On-take ▲ Kyūshū, SW Japan 31°35′N 130°39′E
35 T15 Ontario California, W USA 34°03′N 117°39′W
32 M13 Ontario Oregon, NW USA 44°01′N 116°57′W
12 D10 Ontario ◈ province S Canada
11 P14 Ontario, Lake ◎ Canada/USA
0 L9 Ontario Peninsula peninsula Canada/USA
Onteniente see Ontinyent
105 S11 Ontinyent var. Onteniente. País Valenciano, E Spain 38°49′N 00°37′W
93 N15 Ontojärvi ◎ E Finland
30 L3 Ontonagon Michigan, N USA 46°52′N 89°18′W
30 L3 Ontonagon River ⟿ Michigan, N USA
186 M7 Ontong Java Atoll prev. Lord Howe Island. atoll N Solomon Islands
175 N5 Ontong Java Rise undersea feature W Pacific Ocean 01°00′N 157°00′E
Onuba see Huelva
55 W9 Onverwacht Para, N Suriname 05°36′N 55°12′W
Onyest see Onești
Oodeypore see Udaipur
182 J7 Oodla Wirra South Australia 32°52′S 139°05′E
182 F2 Oodnadatta South Australia 27°34′S 135°27′E
182 C5 Ooldea South Australia 30°29′S 131°50′E
27 Q8 Oologah Lake ⊠ Oklahoma, C USA
Oos-Kaap see Eastern Cape
Oos-Londen see East London
99 E17 Oostakker Oost-Vlaanderen, NW Belgium 51°06′N 03°46′E
99 D15 Oostburg Zeeland, SW Netherlands 51°20′N 03°30′E
98 K9 Oostelijk-Flevoland polder C Netherlands
99 B16 Oostende Eng. Ostend, Fr. Ostende. West-Vlaanderen, NW Belgium 51°13′N 02°55′E
99 B16 Oostende ✈ West-Vlaanderen, NW Belgium 51°12′N 02°55′E
98 L12 Oosterbeek Gelderland, SE Netherlands 51°59′N 05°51′E
99 I14 Oosterhout Noord-Brabant, S Netherlands 51°38′N 04°51′E
98 O6 Oostermoers Vaart var. Hunze. ⟿ NE Netherlands
99 F14 Oosterschelde Eng. Eastern Scheldt. inlet SW Netherlands
99 E14 Oosterscheldedam dam SW Netherlands
98 M7 Oosterwolde Fris. Easterwâlde. Friesland, N Netherlands 53°01′N 06°15′E
98 I9 Oosthuizen Noord-Holland, NW Netherlands 52°34′N 05°00′E
99 H16 Oostmalle Antwerpen, N Belgium 51°18′N 04°44′E
Oos-Transvaal see Mpumalanga
99 E15 Oost-Souburg Zeeland, SW Netherlands 51°28′N 03°36′E
99 E17 Oost-Vlaanderen Eng. East Flanders. ◈ province NW Belgium
98 J5 Oost-Vlieland Friesland, N Netherlands 53°19′N 05°02′E
98 F12 Oostvoorne Zuid-Holland, SW Netherlands 51°55′N 04°06′E
Ootacamund see Udagamandalam
98 O10 Ootmarsum Overijssel, E Netherlands 52°25′N 06°55′E
10 K14 Ootsa Lake ⊠ British Columbia, SW Canada
Ooty see Udagamandalam
114 L8 Opaka Tŭrgovishte, N Bulgaria 43°26′N 26°12′E
79 M18 Opala Orientale, C Dem. Rep. Congo 0°40′S 24°20′E
125 Q13 Oparino Kirovskaya Oblast', NW Russian Federation 59°52′N 48°14′E
14 H8 Opasatica, Lac ◎ Québec, SE Canada
112 B9 Opatija It. Abbazia. Primorje-Gorski Kotar, NW Croatia 45°18′N 14°15′E
111 N15 Opatów Świętokrzyskie, C Poland 50°45′N 21°27′E
111 I17 Opava Ger. Troppau. Moravskoslezský Kraj, E Czech Republic 49°56′N 17°53′E
111 H16 Opava Ger. Oppa. ⟿ NE Czech Republic
Opazova see Stara Pazova
Opécska see Pecica
14 E8 Opeepeesway Lake ◎ Ontario, S Canada
23 R5 Opelika Alabama, S USA 32°39′N 85°22′W
22 I8 Opelousas Louisiana, S USA 30°31′N 92°04′W
186 G6 Open Bay bay New Britain, E Papua New Guinea
14 I12 Opeongo Lake ◎ Ontario, SE Canada
99 K17 Opglabbeek Limburg, NE Belgium 51°04′N 05°39′E
33 W6 Opheim Montana, NW USA 48°50′N 106°24′W
39 P10 Ophir Alaska, USA 63°08′N 156°31′W
Ophiusa see Formentera
79 N18 Opienge Orientale, E Dem. Rep. Congo 0°15′N 27°25′E
185 G20 Opihi ⟿ South Island, New Zealand
12 J9 Opinaca ⟿ Québec, C Canada
12 J10 Opinaca, Réservoir ⊠ Québec, E Canada
117 T5 Opishnya Rus. Oposhnya. Poltavs'ka Oblast', NE Ukraine 49°58′N 34°37′E
98 I8 Opmeer Noord-Holland, NW Netherlands 52°43′N 04°56′E
77 V17 Opobo Akwa Ibom, S Nigeria 04°36′N 07°37′E
124 F16 Opochka Pskovskaya Oblast', W Russian Federation 56°42′N 28°40′E
110 L13 Opoczno Lodzkie, C Poland 51°24′N 20°18′E
111 I15 Opole Ger. Oppeln. Opolskie, S Poland 50°40′N 17°56′E
111 H15 Opolskie ◈ province S Poland
Opornyy see Borankul
104 G4 O Porriño var. Porriño. Galicia, NW Spain 42°10′N 08°38′W
Oporto see Porto
Oposhnya see Opishnya
184 P8 Opotiki Bay of Plenty, North Island, New Zealand 38°02′S 177°18′E
23 Q7 Opp Alabama, S USA 31°16′N 86°14′W
Oppa see Opava
94 G9 Oppdal Sør-Trøndelag, S Norway 62°36′N 09°41′E
Oppeln see Opole
107 N23 Oppido Mamertina Calabria, SW Italy 38°17′N 15°58′E
Oppidum Ubiorum see Köln
94 F12 Oppland ◈ county S Norway
118 J12 Opsa Vitsyebskaya Voblasts', NW Belarus 55°32′N 26°50′E
26 I8 Optima Lake ⊠ Oklahoma, C USA
184 J11 Opunake Taranaki, North Island, New Zealand 39°27′S 173°52′E
191 N6 Opunohu, Baie d' bay Moorea, W French Polynesia
83 B17 Opuwo Kunene, NW Namibia 18°03′S 13°54′E
146 H6 Oqqal'a var. Akkala, Rus. Karakala. Qoraqalpog'iston Respublikasi, NW Uzbekistan 43°43′N 59°25′E
147 V13 Oqsu Rus. Oksu. ⟿ SE Tajikistan
147 P14 Oqtogh, Qatorkŭhi Rus. Khrebet Aktau. ▲▲ SW Tajikistan
146 M11 Oqtosh Rus. Aktash. Samarqand Viloyati, C Uzbekistan 39°22′N 65°46′E
147 N11 Oqtov Tizmasi var. Khrebet Aktau. ▲▲ C Uzbekistan
30 J12 Oquawka Illinois, N USA 40°56′N 90°56′W
144 J10 Or' Kaz. Or. ⟿ Kazakhstan/Russian Federation
36 M15 Oracle Arizona, SW USA 32°36′N 110°46′W
147 N13 O'radaryo Rus. Uradar'ya. ⟿ S Uzbekistan
116 F9 Oradea prev. Oradea Mare, Ger. Grosswardein, Hung. Nagyvárad. Bihor, NW Romania 47°03′N 21°56′E
Oradea Mare see Oradea
Orahovac see Rahovec
112 H9 Orahovica Virovitica-Podravina, NE Croatia 45°33′N 17°54′E
152 K13 Orai Uttar Pradesh, N India 26°00′N 79°26′E
92 K12 Orajärvi Lappi, NW Finland 66°54′N 24°04′E
138 F9 Or'Akiva prev. Or 'Aqiva. Haifa, W Israel 32°40′N 34°58′E
Oral see Ural'sk
74 I5 Oran var. Ouahran, Wahran. NW Algeria 35°42′N 00°37′W
183 R8 Orange New South Wales, SE Australia 33°16′S 149°06′E
103 R14 Orange anc. Arausio. Vaucluse, SE France 44°06′N 04°52′E
25 Y10 Orange Texas, SW USA 30°05′N 93°43′W
21 V5 Orange Virginia, NE USA 38°14′N 78°07′W
21 R13 Orangeburg South Carolina, SE USA 33°28′N 80°53′W
58 J9 Orange, Cabo headland NE Brazil 04°24′N 51°33′W
29 S12 Orange City Iowa, C USA 43°00′N 96°03′W
Orange Cone see Orange Fan
172 J10 Orange Fan var. Orange Cone. undersea feature SW Indian Ocean 32°00′S 12°00′E
Orange Free State see Free State
25 S14 Orange Grove Texas, SW USA 27°57′N 97°56′W
18 K13 Orange Lake New York, NE USA 41°32′N 74°06′W
23 V10 Orange Lake ◎ Florida, SE USA
Orange Mouth/Orangemund see Oranjemund
23 W9 Orange Park Florida, SE USA 30°10′N 81°42′W
83 E23 Orange River Afr. Oranjerivier. ⟿ S Africa
14 G15 Orangeville Ontario, S Canada 43°55′N 80°06′W
36 M5 Orangeville Utah, W USA 39°14′N 111°03′W
42 G1 Orange Walk Orange Walk, N Belize 18°06′N 88°30′W
42 F1 Orange Walk ◈ district NW Belize
100 N11 Oranienburg Brandenburg, NE Germany 52°46′N 13°15′E
98 O7 Oranjekanaal canal NE Netherlands
83 D23 Oranjemund var. Orangemund; prev. Orange Mouth. Karas, SW Namibia 28°33′S 16°28′E
Oranjerivier see Orange River
45 N16 Oranjestad ○ (Aruba) W Aruba 12°31′N 70°W
Oranje Vrystaat see Free State
Orany see Varėna
83 H18 Orapa Central, C Botswana 21°16′S 25°22′E
Or 'Aqiva see Or'Akiva
112 I10 Orašje ◈ Federacija Bosna I Herecegovina, N Bosnia and Herzegovina
116 G11 Orăștie Ger. Broos, Hung. Szászváros. Hunedoara, W Romania 45°50′N 23°11′E
Orașul Stalin see Brașov
111 K18 Orava Hung. Árva, Pol. Orawa. ⟿ N Slovakia
Oravainen see Oravais
93 K16 Oravais Fin. Oravainen. Länsi-Suomi, W Finland 63°18′N 22°25′E
Oravicabánya see Oravița
116 F13 Oravița Ger. Orawitza, Hung. Oravicabánya. Caraș-Severin, SW Romania 45°02′N 21°43′E
Orawa see Orava
185 B24 Orawia Southland, South Island, New Zealand 46°03′S 167°49′E
Orawitza see Oravița
103 P16 Orb ⟿ S France
106 C9 Orba ⟿ NW Italy
158 H12 Orba Co ◎ W China
108 B9 Orbe Vaud, W Switzerland 46°42′N 06°28′E
107 G14 Orbetello Toscana, C Italy 42°28′N 11°15′E
104 K3 Órbigo ⟿ NW Spain
183 Q12 Orbost Victoria, SE Australia 37°44′S 148°28′E
95 O14 Örbyhus Uppsala, C Sweden 60°15′N 17°43′E
194 I1 Orcadas Argentinian research station South Orkney Islands, Antarctica 60°37′S 44°48′W
105 P12 Orcera Andalucía, S Spain 38°20′N 02°36′W
33 P9 Orchard Homes Montana, NW USA 46°52′N 114°01′W
37 P5 Orchard Mesa Colorado, C USA 39°02′N 108°33′W
18 D10 Orchard Park New York, NE USA 42°46′N 78°44′W
Orchid Island see Lan Yü
115 G18 Orchómenos var. Orhomenos, Orkhómenos, prev. Skripón; anc. Orchomenus. Stereá Ellás, C Greece 38°29′N 22°58′E
Orchomenus see Orchómenos
106 B7 Orco ⟿ NW Italy
103 R8 Or, Côte d' physical region C France
29 O14 Ord Nebraska, C USA 41°36′N 98°55′W
119 O15 Ordats' Rus. Ordat'. Mahilyowskaya Voblasts', E Belarus 54°10′N 30°42′E
36 K8 Orderville Utah, W USA 37°16′N 112°38′W
104 H2 Ordes Galicia, NW Spain 43°04′N 08°25′W
35 V14 Ord Mountain ▲ California, W USA 34°41′N 116°46′W
163 N14 Ordos prev. Dongsheng. Nei Mongol Zizhiqu, N China 39°51′N 110°00′E
Ordos Desert see Mu Us Shadi
188 B16 Ordot C Guam
137 N11 Ordu anc. Cotyora. Ordu, N Turkey 41°N 37°52′E
136 M11 Ordu ◈ province N Turkey
137 V14 Ordubad SW Azerbaijan 38°55′N 46°00′E
Orduña see Urduña
37 U6 Ordway Colorado, C USA 38°13′N 103°45′W
117 T9 Ordzhonikidze Dnipropetrovs'ka Oblast', E Ukraine 47°39′N 34°08′E
Ordzhonikidze see Denisovka, Kazakhstan
Ordzhonikidze see Vladikavkaz, Russian Federation
Ordzhonikidze see Yenakiyeve, Ukraine
Ordzhonikidzeabad see Kofarnihon
55 U9 Orealla E Guyana 05°13′N 57°17′W
113 G15 Orebić It. Sabbioncello. Dubrovnik-Neretva, S Croatia 42°58′N 17°12′E
95 M16 Örebro Örebro, C Sweden 59°18′N 15°12′E
95 L16 Örebro ◈ county C Sweden
25 W6 Ore City Texas, SW USA 32°48′N 94°43′W
30 L10 Oregon Illinois, N USA 42°00′N 89°19′W
27 Q2 Oregon Missouri, C USA 39°59′N 95°08′W
31 R11 Oregon Ohio, N USA 41°38′N 83°29′W
32 H13 Oregon off. State of Oregon, also known as Beaver State, Sunset State, Valentine State, Webfoot State. ◈ state NW USA
32 G11 Oregon City Oregon, NW USA 45°21′N 122°36′W
Oregon, State of see Oregon
95 P14 Öregrund Uppsala, C Sweden 60°19′N 18°30′E
Orekhov see Orikhiv
126 L3 Orekhovo-Zuyevo Moskovskaya Oblast', W Russian Federation 55°46′N 39°01′E
Orekhovsk see Arekhawsk
126 J6 Orël Orlovskaya Oblast', W Russian Federation 52°57′N 36°06′E
Orel see Oril'
56 E11 Orellana Loreto, N Peru 06°53′S 75°10′W
56 E6 Orellana ◈ province NE Ecuador
104 L11 Orellana, Embalse de ⊠ W Spain
36 L3 Orem Utah, W USA 40°18′N 111°42′W
Ore Mountains see Erzgebirge/Krušné Hory
127 V7 Orenburg prev. Chkalov. Orenburgskaya Oblast', W Russian Federation 51°46′N 55°12′E

◆ Country ● Country Capital ◇ Dependent Territory ○ Dependent Territory Capital ◈ Administrative Regions ✈ International Airport ▲ Mountain ▲▲ Mountain Range Ѫ Volcano ⟿ River ◎ Lake ⊠ Reservoir

ORENBURG – OUIDAH

127 V7 **Orenburg** ✈ Orenburgskaya Oblast', W Russian Federation *51°54′N 55°15′E*
127 T7 **Orenburgskaya Oblast'** ◈ *province* W Russian Federation
Orense *see* Ourense
188 C8 **Oreor** *var.* Koror. *island* N Palau
185 B24 **Orepuki** Southland, South Island, New Zealand *46°17′S 167°45′E*
114 L12 **Orestiáda** *prev.* Orestiás. Anatolikí Makedonía kai Thráki, NE Greece *41°30′N 26°31′E*
Orestiás *see* Orestiáda
Öresund/Øresund *see* Sound, The
185 C23 **Oreti** ≈ South Island, New Zealand
184 L5 **Orewa** Auckland, North Island, New Zealand *36°34′S 174°43′E*
65 A25 **Orford, Cape** *headland* West Falkland, Falkland Islands *52°00′S 61°04′W*
44 B5 **Órganos, Sierra de los** ▲▲ W Cuba
37 R15 **Organ Peak** ▲ New Mexico, SW USA *32°17′N 106°35′W*
105 N9 **Orgaz** Castilla-La Mancha, C Spain *39°39′N 03°52′W*
Orgeyev *see* Orhei
Orgil *see* Jargalant
105 O15 **Orgiva** *var.* Orjiva. Andalucía, S Spain *36°54′N 03°25′W*
163 O10 **Örgön** *var.* Senj. Dornogovĭ, SE Mongolia *44°34′N 110°58′E*
Örgön *see* Bayangovĭ
Orgražden *see* Ograzhden
117 N9 **Orhei** *var.* Orheiu, *Rus.* Orgeyev. N Moldova *47°25′N 28°48′E*
Orheiu *see* Orhei
105 R3 **Orhi** *var.* Orhy, Pico de Orhy, Pic d'Orhy. ▲ France/Spain *42°55′N 01°01′W* *see also* Orhy
Orhi *see* Orhy
Orhomenos *see* Orchómenos
162 K6 **Orhon** ◈ *province* N Mongolia
162 L6 **Orhon Gol** ≈ N Mongolia
102 J16 **Orhy** *var.* Orhi, Pico de Orhy, Pic d'Orhy. ▲ France/Spain *43°00′N 01°00′W* *see also* Orhi
Orhy *see* Orhi
Orhy, Pic d'/Orhy, Pico de *see* Orhi/Orhy
34 L2 **Orick** California, W USA *41°16′N 124°03′W*
32 L6 **Orient** Washington, NW USA *48°51′N 118°14′W*
48 D6 **Oriental, Cordillera** ▲▲ Bolivia/Peru
48 D6 **Oriental, Cordillera** ▲▲ C Colombia
57 H16 **Oriental, Cordillera** ▲▲ C Peru
63 M15 **Oriente** Buenos Aires, E Argentina *38°45′S 60°37′W*
105 R12 **Orihuela** País Valenciano, E Spain *38°05′N 00°56′W*
117 V9 **Orikhiv** *Rus.* Orekhov. Zaporiz'ka Oblast', SE Ukraine *47°32′N 35°48′E*
113 K22 **Orikum** *var.* Orikumi. Vlorë, SW Albania *40°20′N 19°28′E*
Orikumi *see* Orikum
117 V6 **Oril'** *Rus.* Orel. ≈ E Ukraine
14 H14 **Orillia** Ontario, S Canada *44°36′N 79°26′W*
93 M19 **Orimattila** Etelä-Suomi, S Finland *60°48′N 25°40′E*
33 Y15 **Orin** Wyoming, C USA *42°39′N 105°10′W*
47 R4 **Orinoco, Río** ≈ Colombia/Venezuela
186 C9 **Oriomo** Western, SW Papua New Guinea *08°53′S 143°13′E*
30 K11 **Orion** Illinois, N USA *41°21′N 90°22′W*
29 Q5 **Oriska** North Dakota, N USA *46°54′N 97°46′W*
153 P17 **Orissa** ◈ *state* NE India
Orissaar *see* Orissaare
118 E5 **Orissaare** *Ger.* Orissaar. Saaremaa, W Estonia *58°34′N 23°05′E*
107 B19 **Oristano** Sardegna, Italy, C Mediterranean Sea *39°54′N 08°35′E*
107 A19 **Oristano, Golfo di** *gulf* Sardegna, Italy, C Mediterranean Sea
54 D13 **Orito** Putumayo, SW Colombia *0°49′N 76°57′W*
93 L18 **Orivesi** Häme, W Finland *61°39′N 24°21′E*
93 N17 **Orivesi** ◎ Länsi-Suomi, SE Finland
58 H12 **Oriximiná** Pará, NE Brazil *01°45′S 55°50′W*
41 Q14 **Orizaba** Veracruz-Llave, E Mexico *18°51′N 97°08′W*
41 Q14 **Orizaba, Volcán Pico de** *var.* Citlaltépetl. ▲ S Mexico *19°00′N 97°15′W*
95 I16 **Ørje** Østfold, S Norway *59°28′N 11°40′E*
113 I16 **Orjen** ▲ Bosnia and Herzegovina/Montenegro
Orjiva *see* Orgiva
Orjonikidzeobod *see* Kofarnihon
94 G8 **Orkanger** Sør-Trøndelag, S Norway *63°17′N 09°52′E*
94 G8 **Orkdalen** *valley* S Norway
95 K22 **Örkelljunga** Skåne, S Sweden *56°17′N 13°20′E*
Orkhaniye *see* Botevgrad
Orkhómenos *see* Orchómenos
94 H9 **Orkla** ≈ S Norway
Orkney *see* Orkney Islands
65 J22 **Orkney Deep** *undersea feature* Scotia Sea/Weddell Sea
96 J4 **Orkney Islands** *var.* Orkney, Orkneys. *island group* N Scotland, United Kingdom
Orkneys *see* Orkney Islands
24 K8 **Orla** Texas, SW USA *31°48′N 103°55′W*
35 N5 **Orland** California, W USA *39°43′N 122°12′W*
23 X11 **Orlando** Florida, SE USA *28°32′N 81°23′W*
23 X12 **Orlando** ✈ Florida, SE USA *28°24′N 81°16′W*
107 K23 **Orlando, Capo d'** *headland* Sicilia, Italy, C Mediterranean Sea *38°10′N 14°44′E*
Orlau *see* Orlová
103 N6 **Orléanais** *cultural region* C France
103 N7 **Orléans** *anc.* Aurelianum. Loiret, C France *47°54′N 01°53′E*
34 L2 **Orleans** California, W USA *41°16′N 123°36′W*
19 Q12 **Orleans** Massachusetts, NE USA *41°48′N 69°57′W*
15 R10 **Orléans, Île d'** *island* Québec, SE Canada
Orléansville *see* Chlef
111 F16 **Orlice** *Ger.* Adler. ≈ NE Czech Republic
122 L13 **Orlik** Respublika Buryatiya, S Russian Federation *52°32′N 99°36′E*
125 Q14 **Orlov** *prev.* Khalturin. Kirovskaya Oblast', NW Russian Federation *58°34′N 48°57′E*
111 I17 **Orlová** *Ger.* Orlau, *Pol.* Orłowa. Moravskoslezský Kraj, E Czech Republic *49°50′N 18°21′E*
Orlov, Mys *see* Orlovskiy, Mys
126 I6 **Orlovskaya Oblast'** ◈ *province* W Russian Federation
124 M5 **Orlovskiy, Mys** *var.* Mys Orlov. *headland* NW Russian Federation *67°14′N 41°17′E*
Orłowa *see* Orlová
103 O5 **Orly** ✈ (Paris) Essonne, N France *48°43′N 02°24′E*
119 G16 **Orlya** Hrodzyenskaya Voblasts', W Belarus *53°30′N 24°59′E*
114 M7 **Orlyak** *prev.* Makenzen, Trubchular, *Rom.* Trupcilar. Dobrich, NE Bulgaria *43°39′N 27°21′E*
148 L16 **Ormāra** Baluchistān, SW Pakistan *25°14′N 64°36′E*
171 P5 **Ormoc** *off.* Ormoc City, *var.* MacArthur. Leyte, C Philippines *11°02′N 124°35′E*
Ormoc City *see* Ormoc
23 X10 **Ormond Beach** Florida, SE USA *29°16′N 81°04′W*
109 X10 **Ormož** *Ger.* Friedau. NE Slovenia *46°24′N 16°09′E*
14 J13 **Ormsby** Ontario, SE Canada *44°52′N 77°45′W*
97 K17 **Ormskirk** NW England, United Kingdom *53°35′N 02°54′W*
Ormsö *see* Vormsi
15 N13 **Ormstown** Québec, SE Canada *45°08′N 73°57′W*
Ormuz, Strait of *see* Hormuz, Strait of
103 T8 **Ornans** Doubs, E France *47°06′N 06°06′E*
102 K5 **Orne** ◈ *department* N France
102 K5 **Orne** ≈ N France
92 G12 **Ørnes** Nordland, C Norway *66°51′N 13°43′E*
110 L7 **Orneta** Warmińsko-Mazurskie, NE Poland *54°07′N 20°10′E*
95 P16 **Ornö** Stockholm, C Sweden *59°03′N 18°28′E*
37 Q3 **Orno Peak** ▲ Colorado, C USA *40°06′N 107°06′W*
93 I16 **Örnsköldsvik** Västernorrland, C Sweden *63°16′N 18°45′E*
163 X13 **Oro** E North Korea *39°59′N 127°27′E*
45 T6 **Orocovis** C Puerto Rico *18°13′N 66°22′W*
54 H10 **Orocué** Casanare, E Colombia *04°51′N 71°21′W*
77 N13 **Orodara** SW Burkina *11°00′N 04°54′W*
105 S4 **Oroel, Peña de** ▲ N Spain *42°30′N 00°31′W*
33 N10 **Orofino** Idaho, NW USA *46°28′N 116°15′W*
162 I9 **Orog Nuur** ◎ S Mongolia
35 U14 **Oro Grande** California, W USA *34°36′N 117°19′W*
37 S15 **Orogrande** New Mexico, SW USA *32°24′N 106°04′W*
191 Q7 **Orohena, Mont** ▲ Tahiti, W French Polynesia *17°37′S 149°27′W*
Orolaunum *see* Arlon
Orol Dengizi *see* Aral Sea
189 S15 **Oroluk Atoll** *atoll* Caroline Islands, C Micronesia
80 J13 **Oromīya** ◈ *federal region* C Ethiopia
Oromo *see* Goba
13 O15 **Oromocto** New Brunswick, SE Canada *45°50′N 66°28′W*
191 S4 **Orona** *prev.* Hull Island. *atoll* Phoenix Islands, C Kiribati
191 V17 **Orongo** *ancient monument* Easter Island, Chile, E Pacific Ocean
138 I3 **Orontes** *var.* Ononte, Nahr el Aassi, *Ar.* Nahr al 'Aṣī. ≈ SW Asia
104 L9 **Oropesa** Castilla-La Mancha, C Spain *39°55′N 05°10′W*
Oropesa *see* Oropesa del Mar
105 T8 **Oropesa del Mar** *var.* Oropesa, *Cat.* Orpes. País Valenciano, E Spain *40°06′N 00°07′E*
Oropeza *see* Cochabamba
Oroqen Zizhiqi *see* Alihe
171 P7 **Oroquieta** *var.* Oroquieta City. Mindanao, S Philippines *08°27′N 123°46′E*
Oroquieta City *see* Oroquieta
40 J8 **Oro, Río del** ≈ C Mexico
59 O14 **Orós, Açude** ⊠ E Brazil
107 D18 **Orosei, Golfo di** *gulf* Tyrrhenian Sea, C Mediterranean Sea
111 M24 **Orosháza** Békés, SE Hungary *46°33′N 20°40′E*
Orosirá Rodhópis *see* Rhodope Mountains
111 I22 **Oroszlány** Komárom-Esztergom, W Hungary *47°28′N 18°16′E*
188 B16 **Orote Peninsula** *peninsula* W Guam
123 T9 **Orotukan** Magadanskaya Oblast', E Russian Federation *62°18′N 150°46′E*
35 O5 **Oroville** California, W USA *39°29′N 121°35′W*
32 K6 **Oroville** Washington, NW USA *48°56′N 119°25′W*
35 O5 **Oroville, Lake** ⊠ California, W USA
0 G15 **Orozco Fracture Zone** *tectonic feature* E Pacific Ocean
Orpes *see* Oropesa del Mar
64 I7 **Orphan Knoll** *undersea feature* NW Atlantic Ocean *51°00′N 47°00′W*
29 V3 **Orr** Minnesota, N USA *48°03′N 92°48′W*
95 M21 **Orrefors** Kalmar, S Sweden *56°48′N 15°45′E*
182 I7 **Orroroo** South Australia *32°46′S 138°38′E*
31 T12 **Orrville** Ohio, N USA *40°50′N 81°45′W*
94 L12 **Orsa** Dalarna, C Sweden *61°07′N 14°40′E*
Orschowa *see* Orşova
Orschütz *see* Orzyc
119 O14 **Orsha** Vitsyebskaya Voblasts', NE Belarus *54°30′N 30°26′E*
127 Q2 **Orshanka** Respublika Mariy El, W Russian Federation *56°54′N 47°54′E*
108 C11 **Orsières** Valais, SW Switzerland *46°00′N 07°09′E*
127 X8 **Orsk** Orenburgskaya Oblast', W Russian Federation *51°13′N 58°35′E*
116 F13 **Orşova** *Ger.* Orschowa, *Hung.* Orsova. Mehedinţi, SW Romania *44°42′N 22°22′E*
94 D10 **Ørsta** Møre og Romsdal, S Norway *62°12′N 06°09′E*
95 O15 **Örsundsbro** Uppsala, C Sweden *59°45′N 17°19′E*
136 D16 **Ortaca** Muğla, SW Turkey *36°49′N 28°43′E*
83 I21 **O.R. Tambo** ✈ (Johannesburg) Gauteng, NE South Africa *26°08′S 28°01′E*
107 M16 **Orta Nova** Puglia, SE Italy *41°20′N 15°43′E*
136 I17 **Orta Toroslar** ▲▲ S Turkey
54 E11 **Ortega** Tolima, W Colombia *03°57′N 75°11′W*
104 H1 **Ortegal, Cabo** *headland* NW Spain *43°46′N 07°54′W*
Ortelsburg *see* Szczytno
102 J15 **Orthez** Pyrénées-Atlantiques, SW France *43°29′N 00°46′W*
57 K14 **Orthon, Río** ≈ N Bolivia
60 J10 **Ortigueira** Paraná, S Brazil *24°10′S 50°55′W*
104 H1 **Ortigueira** Galicia, NW Spain *43°40′N 07°50′W*
106 H5 **Ortisei** *Ger.* Sankt-Ulrich. Trentino-Alto Adige, N Italy *46°35′N 11°42′E*
40 F6 **Ortiz** Sonora, NW Mexico *28°18′N 110°40′W*
54 L5 **Ortiz** Guárico, N Venezuela *09°37′N 67°20′W*
Ortler *see* Ortles
106 F5 **Ortles** *Ger.* Ortler. ▲ N Italy *46°29′N 10°33′E*
107 K14 **Ortona** Abruzzo, C Italy *42°21′N 14°24′E*
29 R8 **Ortonville** Minnesota, N USA *45°18′N 96°26′W*
147 W8 **Orto-Tokoy** Issyk-Kul'skaya Oblast', NE Kyrgyzstan *42°20′N 76°03′E*
93 I15 **Örträsk** Västerbotten, N Sweden *64°10′N 19°00′E*
100 J12 **Örtze** ≈ NW Germany
Oruba *see* Aruba
142 I3 **Orūmīyeh** *var.* Rizaiyeh, Urmia, Urmiyeh; *prev.* Rezā'īyeh. Āžarbāyjān-e Gharbī, NW Iran *37°33′N 45°06′E*
142 J3 **Orūmīyeh, Daryācheh-ye** *var.* Matianus, Sha Hi, Urumi Yeh, *Eng.* Lake Urmia; *prev.* Daryācheh-ye Reẕā'īyeh. ◎ NW Iran
57 K19 **Oruro** Oruro, W Bolivia *17°58′S 67°06′W*
57 J19 **Oruro** ◈ *department* W Bolivia
95 I18 **Orust** *island* S Sweden
149 O7 **Orūzgān** *var.* Oruzgān, *Pash.* Ūrūzgān. Orūzgān, C Afghanistan *32°58′N 66°39′E*
149 N6 **Orūzgān** *Pash.* Urūzgān. ◈ *province* C Afghanistan
106 H13 **Orvieto** *anc.* Velsuna. Umbria, C Italy *42°43′N 12°06′E*
194 K7 **Orville Coast** *physical region* Antarctica
114 H7 **Oryakhovo** Vratsa, NW Bulgaria *43°44′N 23°58′E*
Oryokko *see* Yalu
117 R5 **Orzhytsya** Poltavs'ka Oblast', C Ukraine *49°48′N 32°40′E*
110 M9 **Orzyc** *Ger.* Orschütz. ≈ NE Poland
110 N8 **Orzysz** *Ger.* Arys. Warmińsko-Mazurskie, NE Poland *53°49′N 21°54′E*
98 K13 **Oss** Noord-Brabant, S Netherlands *51°46′N 05°32′E*
94 I10 **Os** Hedmark, S Norway *62°29′N 11°14′E*
125 U15 **Osa** Permskaya Oblast', NW Russian Federation *57°16′N 55°22′E*
115 F15 **Óssa** ▲▲ C Greece
104 H11 **Ossa** ▲ S Portugal *38°43′N 07°33′W*
29 W11 **Osage** Iowa, C USA *43°16′N 92°48′W*
27 U5 **Osage Beach** Missouri, C USA *38°09′N 92°37′W*
27 P5 **Osage City** Kansas, C USA *38°37′N 95°49′W*
27 U7 **Osage Fork River** ≈ Missouri, C USA
27 U5 **Osage River** ≈ Missouri, C USA
164 J13 **Ōsaka** *hist.* Naniwa. Ōsaka, Honshū, SW Japan *34°38′N 135°28′E*
164 I13 **Ōsaka** *off.* Ōsaka-fu, *var.* Ōsaka Hu. ◈ *urban prefecture* Honshū, SW Japan
Ōsaka-fu/Ōsaka Hu *see* Ōsaka
145 R10 **Osakarovka** Karaganda, C Kazakhstan *50°32′N 72°39′E*
Ōsaki *see* Furukawa
29 T7 **Osakis** Minnesota, N USA *45°51′N 95°08′W*
43 N16 **Osa, Península de** *peninsula* S Costa Rica
60 M10 **Osasco** São Paulo, S Brazil *23°32′S 46°46′W*
27 R5 **Osawatomie** Kansas, C USA *38°30′N 94°57′W*
26 L3 **Osborne** Kansas, C USA *39°26′N 98°42′W*
173 S8 **Osborn Plateau** *undersea feature* E Indian Ocean
95 L21 **Osby** Skåne, S Sweden *56°24′N 14°00′E*
Osca *see* Huesca
92 N2 **Oscar II Land** *physical region* W Svalbard
27 Y10 **Osceola** Arkansas, C USA *35°43′N 89°58′W*
29 V15 **Osceola** Iowa, C USA *41°01′N 93°45′W*
27 S6 **Osceola** Missouri, C USA *38°01′N 93°41′W*
29 Q15 **Osceola** Nebraska, C USA *41°09′N 97°28′W*
101 N15 **Oschatz** Sachsen, E Germany *51°17′N 13°10′E*
100 K13 **Oschersleben** Sachsen-Anhalt, C Germany *52°02′N 11°14′E*
31 R7 **Oscoda** Michigan, N USA *44°25′N 83°19′W*
Ösel *see* Saaremaa
94 H6 **Osen** Sør-Trøndelag, S Norway *64°17′N 10°29′E*
94 I12 **Osensjøen** ◎ S Norway
164 A14 **Ōse-zaki** Fukue-jima, SW Japan
147 T10 **Osh** Oshskaya Oblast', SW Kyrgyzstan *40°34′N 72°46′E*
83 C16 **Oshakati** Oshana, N Namibia *17°46′S 15°43′E*
83 C16 **Oshana** ◈ *district* N Namibia
14 H15 **Oshawa** Ontario, SE Canada *43°54′N 78°50′W*
165 R10 **Oshika-hantō** *peninsula* Honshū, C Japan
83 C16 **Oshikango** Ohangwena, N Namibia *17°29′S 15°54′E*
Oshikoto *see* Otjikoto
165 P5 **Ō-shima** *island* NE Japan
165 N14 **Ō-shima** *island* S Japan
165 Q5 **Oshima-hantō** ▲▲ Hokkaidō, NE Japan
83 D17 **Oshivelo** Otjikoto, N Namibia *18°37′S 17°10′E*
28 K14 **Oshkosh** Nebraska, C USA *41°25′N 102°21′W*
30 M7 **Oshkosh** Wisconsin, N USA *44°01′N 88°32′W*
Oshmyany *see* Ashmyany
Osh Oblasty *see* Oshskaya Oblast'
77 T16 **Oshogbo** *var.* Osogbo. Osun, W Nigeria *07°42′N 04°31′E*
147 S11 **Oshskaya Oblast'** *Kir.* Osh Oblasty. ◈ *province* SW Kyrgyzstan
Ōshū *see* Mizusawa
Oshun *see* Osun
79 J20 **Oshwe** Bandundu, C Dem. Rep. Congo *03°24′S 19°32′E*
Osiek *see* Osijek
112 I9 **Osijek** *prev.* Osiek, Osjek, *Ger.* Esseg, *Hung.* Eszék. Osijek-Baranja, E Croatia *45°33′N 18°41′E*
112 I9 **Osijek-Baranja** *off.* Osječko-Baranjska Županija. ◈ *province* E Croatia
106 J12 **Osimo** Marche, C Italy *43°28′N 13°29′E*
122 M12 **Osinovka** Irkutskaya Oblast', C Russian Federation *56°19′N 101°55′E*
Osintorf *see* Asintorf
112 N11 **Osipaonica** Serbia, NE Serbia *44°34′N 21°00′E*
Osipenko *see* Berdyans'k
Osipovichi *see* Asipovichy
Osječko-Baranjska Županija *see* Osijek-Baranja
Osjek *see* Osijek
29 W15 **Oskaloosa** Iowa, C USA *41°17′N 92°38′W*
27 Q4 **Oskaloosa** Kansas, C USA *39°14′N 95°21′W*
95 N20 **Oskarshamn** Kalmar, S Sweden *57°16′N 16°25′E*
95 J21 **Oskarström** Halland, S Sweden *56°48′N 13°00′E*
14 M8 **Oskélanéo** Québec, SE Canada *48°06′N 75°12′W*
Öskemen *see* Ust'-Kamenogorsk
117 W5 **Oskil** *Rus.* Oskil. ≈ Russian Federation/Ukraine
Oskil *see* Oskil
93 D20 **Oslo** *prev.* Christiania, Kristiania. ● (Norway) Oslo, S Norway *59°54′N 10°44′E*
93 D20 **Oslo** ◈ *county* S Norway
93 D21 **Oslofjorden** *fjord* S Norway
155 G15 **Osmānābād** Mahārāshtra, C India *18°09′N 76°06′E*
136 J11 **Osmancık** Çorum, N Turkey *40°58′N 34°50′E*
136 L16 **Osmaniye** Osmaniye, S Turkey *37°04′N 36°15′E*
136 L16 **Osmaniye** ◈ *province* S Turkey
95 O16 **Ösmo** Stockholm, C Sweden *58°58′N 17°55′E*
118 E3 **Osmussaar** *island* W Estonia
100 G13 **Osnabrück** Niedersachsen, NW Germany *52°09′N 07°42′E*
110 D11 **Ośno Lubuskie** *Ger.* Drossen. Lubuskie, W Poland *52°28′N 14°51′E*
Osogbo *see* Oshogbo
113 P19 **Osogov Mountains** *var.* Osogovske Planine, Osogovski Planina, *Mac.* Osogovski Planini. ▲▲ Bulgaria/FYR Macedonia
Osogovske Planine/Osogovski Planina/Osogovski Planini *see* Osogov Mountains
165 R6 **Osore-zan** ▲ Honshū, C Japan *41°18′N 141°06′E*
61 J16 **Osório** Rio Grande do Sul, S Brazil *29°53′S 50°17′W*
63 G16 **Osorno** Los Lagos, C Chile *40°39′S 73°05′W*
104 M4 **Osorno** Castilla-León, N Spain *42°24′N 04°22′W*
11 N17 **Osoyoos** British Columbia, SW Canada *49°02′N 119°31′W*
95 C14 **Osøyro** Hordaland, S Norway *60°11′N 05°30′E*
54 J6 **Ospino** Portuguesa, N Venezuela *09°17′N 69°26′W*
23 X6 **Ossabaw Island** *island* Georgia, SE USA
23 X6 **Ossabaw Sound** *sound* Georgia, SE USA
183 O16 **Ossa, Mount** ▲ Tasmania, SE Australia *41°55′S 146°03′E*
104 H11 **Ossa, Serra d'** ▲ SE Portugal
77 U16 **Osse** ≈ S Nigeria
30 J6 **Osseo** Wisconsin, N USA *44°33′N 91°13′W*
109 S9 **Ossiacher See** ◎ S Austria
18 K13 **Ossining** New York, NE USA *41°10′N 73°50′W*
123 V9 **Ossora** Koryakskiy Avtonomnyy Okrug, E Russian Federation *59°16′N 163°02′E*
124 I15 **Ostashkov** Tverskaya Oblast', W Russian Federation *57°08′N 33°10′E*
100 H9 **Oste** ≈ NW Germany
Ostee *see* Baltic Sea
Ostend/Ostende *see* Oostende
117 P3 **Oster** Chernihivs'ka Oblast', N Ukraine *50°57′N 30°55′E*
95 O14 **Österbybruk** Uppsala, C Sweden *60°13′N 17°55′E*
95 M19 **Österbymo** Östergötland, S Sweden *57°49′N 15°15′E*
94 K12 **Österdalälven** ≈ C Sweden
94 I12 **Østerdalen** *valley* S Norway
95 L18 **Östergötland** ◈ *county* S Sweden
100 H10 **Osterholz-Scharmbeck** Niedersachsen, NW Germany *53°13′N 08°46′E*
Östermark *see* Teuva
Östermyra *see* Seinäjoki
Østerø *see* Eysturoy
101 J14 **Osterode am Harz** Niedersachsen, C Germany *51°43′N 10°15′E*
Osterode/Osterode in Ostpreussen *see* Ostróda
94 C13 **Osterøy** *island* S Norway
Österreich *see* Austria
93 G16 **Östersund** Jämtland, C Sweden *63°10′N 14°44′E*
95 N14 **Östervåla** Västmanland, C Sweden *60°10′N 17°13′E*
101 H22 **Ostfildern** Baden-Württemberg, SW Germany *48°43′N 09°16′E*
95 H16 **Østfold** ◈ *county* S Norway
100 E9 **Ostfriesische Inseln** *Eng.* East Frisian Islands. *island group* NW Germany
100 F10 **Ostfriesland** *historical region* NW Germany
95 P14 **Östhammar** Uppsala, C Sweden *60°15′N 18°25′E*
Ostia Aterni *see* Pescara
106 G8 **Ostiglia** Lombardia, N Italy *45°04′N 11°09′E*
95 J14 **Östmark** Värmland, C Sweden *60°15′N 12°45′E*
95 K22 **Östra Ringsjön** ◎ S Sweden
111 I17 **Ostrava** Moravskoslezský Kraj, E Czech Republic *49°50′N 18°15′E*
Ostravský Kraj *see* Moravskoslezský Kraj
94 J11 **Østrehogna** *Swe.* Härjahågnan, Härjehågna. ▲ Norway/Sweden *61°43′N 12°07′E*
110 K8 **Ostróda** *Ger.* Osterode, Osterode in Ostpreussen. Warmińsko-Mazurskie, NE Poland *53°42′N 19°59′E*
Ostrog/Ostróg *see* Ostroh
126 L8 **Ostrogozhsk** Voronezhskaya Oblast', W Russian Federation *50°52′N 39°00′E*
116 L4 **Ostroh** *Pol.* Ostróg, *Rus.* Ostrog. Rivnens'ka Oblast', NW Ukraine *50°20′N 26°29′E*
110 N9 **Ostrołęka** *Ger.* Wiesenhof, *Rus.* Ostrolenka. Mazowieckie, C Poland *53°06′N 21°34′E*
Ostrolenka *see* Ostrołęka
111 A16 **Ostrov** *Ger.* Schlackenwerth. Karlovarský Kraj, W Czech Republic *50°18′N 12°56′E*
124 F15 **Ostrov** *Latv.* Austrava. Pskovskaya Oblast', W Russian Federation *57°21′N 28°18′E*
Ostrovets *see* Ostrowiec Świętokrzyski
113 M21 **Ostrovicës, Mali i** ▲ SE Albania *40°36′N 20°25′E*
165 Z2 **Ostrov Iturup** *island* NE Russian Federation
124 M4 **Ostrovnoy** Murmanskaya Oblast', NW Russian Federation *68°00′N 39°40′E*
114 L7 **Ostrovo** *prev.* Golema Ada. Razgrad, N Bulgaria *43°40′N 26°37′E*
125 N15 **Ostrovskoye** Kostromskaya Oblast', NW Russian Federation *57°45′N 42°18′E*
Ostrów *see* Ostrów Wielkopolski
Ostrowiec *see* Ostrowiec Świętokrzyski
111 M14 **Ostrowiec Świętokrzyski** *var.* Ostrowiec, *Rus.* Ostrovets. Świętokrzyskie, C Poland *50°55′N 21°23′E*
110 P13 **Ostrów Lubelski** Lubelskie, E Poland *51°29′N 22°57′E*
110 N10 **Ostrów Mazowiecka** *var.* Ostrów Mazowiecki. Mazowieckie, NE Poland *52°49′N 21°53′E*
Ostrów Mazowiecki *see* Ostrów Mazowiecka
Ostrowo *see* Ostrów Wielkopolski
110 H13 **Ostrów Wielkopolski** *var.* Ostrów, *Ger.* Ostrowo. Wielkopolskie, C Poland *51°40′N 17°47′E*
Ostryna *see* Astryna
110 I13 **Ostrzeszów** Wielkopolskie, C Poland *51°25′N 17°55′E*
107 P18 **Ostuni** Puglia, SE Italy *40°44′N 17°35′E*
Ostyako-Voguls'k *see* Khanty-Mansiysk
114 I9 **Osŭm** ≈ N Bulgaria
Osum *see* Osumit, Lumi i
164 C17 **Ōsumi-hantō** ▲ Kyūshū, SW Japan
164 C17 **Ōsumi-kaikyō** *strait* SW Japan
113 L22 **Osumit, Lumi i** *var.* Osum. ≈ SE Albania
77 T16 **Osun** *var.* Oshun. ◈ *state* SW Nigeria
104 L14 **Osuna** Andalucía, S Spain *37°14′N 05°06′W*
60 J8 **Osvaldo Cruz** São Paulo, S Brazil *21°49′S 50°52′W*
Osveya *see* Asveya
18 J7 **Oswegatchie River** ≈ New York, NE USA
27 Q7 **Oswego** Kansas, C USA *37°11′N 95°10′W*
18 H9 **Oswego** New York, NE USA *43°27′N 76°13′W*
97 K19 **Oswestry** W England, United Kingdom *52°51′N 03°06′W*
111 J16 **Oświęcim** *Ger.* Auschwitz. Małopolskie, S Poland *50°02′N 19°11′E*
185 E22 **Otago** *off.* Otago Region. ◈ *region* South Island, New Zealand
185 F23 **Otago Peninsula** *peninsula* South Island, New Zealand
Otago Region *see* Otago
165 F13 **Ōtake** Hiroshima, Honshū, SW Japan *34°13′N 132°12′E*
184 L13 **Otaki** Wellington, North Island, New Zealand *40°46′S 175°08′E*
93 M15 **Otanmäki** Oulu, C Finland *64°07′N 27°04′E*
145 T15 **Otar** Zhambyl, SE Kazakhstan *43°30′N 75°13′E*
165 R4 **Otaru** Hokkaidō, NE Japan *43°14′N 140°59′E*
185 C24 **Otatara** Southland, South Island, New Zealand *46°26′S 168°18′E*
185 C24 **Otautau** Southland, South Island, New Zealand *46°10′S 168°01′E*
93 M18 **Otava** Itä-Suomi, E Finland *61°37′N 27°07′E*
111 B18 **Otava** *Ger.* Wottawa. ≈ SW Czech Republic
56 C6 **Otavalo** Imbabura, N Ecuador *0°13′N 78°15′W*
83 D17 **Otavi** Otjozondjupa, N Namibia *19°35′S 17°25′E*
165 P12 **Ōtawara** Tochigi, Honshū, S Japan *36°52′N 140°01′E*
83 B16 **Otchinjau** Cunene, SW Angola *16°31′S 13°54′E*
116 F12 **Oţelu Roşu** *Ger.* Ferdinandsberg, *Hung.* Nándorhgy. Caras-Severin, SW Romania *45°30′N 22°22′E*
185 E21 **Otematata** Canterbury, South Island, New Zealand *44°37′S 170°12′E*
118 I6 **Otepää** *Ger.* Odenpäh. Valgamaa, SE Estonia *58°01′N 26°30′E*
162 H7 **Otgon** *var.* Buyant. Dzavhan, C Mongolia *47°14′N 97°14′E*
32 K9 **Othello** Washington, NW USA *46°49′N 119°10′W*
115 A15 **Othonoí** *island* Iónia Nisiá, Greece, C Mediterranean Sea
Othris *see* Óthrys
115 F17 **Óthrys** *var.* Othris. ▲ C Greece
77 Q14 **Oti** ≈ N Togo
40 K10 **Otinapa** Durango, C Mexico *24°01′N 104°58′W*
185 G17 **Otira** West Coast, South Island, New Zealand *42°52′S 171°33′E*
37 V3 **Otis** Colorado, C USA *40°09′N 102°57′W*
12 L10 **Otish, Monts** ▲ Québec, E Canada
83 C17 **Otjikondo** Kunene, N Namibia *19°50′S 15°23′E*
83 C17 **Otjikoto** *var.* Oshikoto. ◈ *district* N Namibia
83 E18 **Otjinene** Omaheke, NE Namibia *21°10′S 18°43′E*
83 D18 **Otjiwarongo** Otjozondjupa, N Namibia *20°29′S 16°36′E*
83 D18 **Otjosondu** *var.* Otjosundu. Otjozondjupa, C Namibia *21°19′S 17°51′E*
Otjosundu *see* Otjosondu
83 D18 **Otjozondjupa** ◈ *district* C Namibia
112 C11 **Otočac** Lika-Senj, W Croatia *44°52′N 15°13′E*
Otog Qi *see* Ulan
112 J10 **Otok** Vukovar-Srijem, E Croatia *45°10′N 18°52′E*
116 K14 **Otopeni** ✈ (Bucureşti) Ilfov, S Romania *44°34′N 26°09′E*
184 L8 **Otorohanga** Waikato, North Island, New Zealand *38°10′S 175°14′E*
12 D9 **Otoskwin** ≈ Ontario, C Canada
165 G14 **Ōtoyo** Kōchi, Shikoku, SW Japan *33°45′N 133°42′E*
95 E16 **Otra** ≈ S Norway
107 R19 **Otranto** Puglia, SE Italy *40°08′N 18°28′E*
Otranto, Canale d' *see* Otranto, Strait of
107 Q18 **Otranto, Strait of** *It.* Canale d'Otranto. *strait* Albania/Italy
111 H18 **Otrokovice** *Ger.* Otrokowitz. Zlínský Kraj, E Czech Republic *49°13′N 17°33′E*
Otrokowitz *see* Otrokovice
31 P10 **Otsego** Michigan, N USA *42°27′N 85°42′W*
31 Q6 **Otsego Lake** ◎ Michigan, N USA
18 I11 **Otselic River** ≈ New York, NE USA
164 J14 **Ōtsu** *var.* Ōtu. Shiga, Honshū, SW Japan *35°03′N 135°49′E*
94 G11 **Otta** Oppland, S Norway *61°46′N 09°33′E*
189 U13 **Otta** *island* Chuuk, C Micronesia
94 F11 **Otta** ≈ S Norway
189 U13 **Otta Pass** *passage* Chuuk Islands, C Micronesia
95 J22 **Ottarp** Skåne, S Sweden *55°55′N 12°55′E*
14 L12 **Ottawa** ● (Canada) Ontario, SE Canada *45°24′N 75°41′W*
30 L11 **Ottawa** Illinois, N USA *41°21′N 88°50′W*
27 Q5 **Ottawa** Kansas, C USA *38°35′N 95°16′W*
31 R12 **Ottawa** Ohio, N USA *41°01′N 84°03′W*
14 L12 **Ottawa** *var.* Uplands. ✈ Ontario, SE Canada *45°19′N 75°39′W*
14 M12 **Ottawa** *Fr.* Outaouais. ≈ Ontario/Québec, SE Canada
9 R10 **Ottawa Islands** *island group* Nunavut, C Canada
18 L8 **Otter Creek** ≈ Vermont, NE USA
36 L6 **Otter Creek Reservoir** ⊠ Utah, W USA
98 L11 **Otterlo** Gelderland, E Netherlands *52°06′N 05°46′E*
94 D9 **Otterøya** *island* S Norway
29 S6 **Otter Tail Lake** ◎ Minnesota, C USA
29 R7 **Otter Tail River** ≈ Minnesota, C USA
95 H23 **Otterup** Fyn, C Denmark *55°31′N 10°25′E*
99 H19 **Ottignies** Wallon Brabant, C Belgium *50°40′N 04°34′E*
101 L23 **Ottobrunn** Bayern, SE Germany *48°02′N 11°40′E*
29 X15 **Ottumwa** Iowa, C USA *41°00′N 92°24′W*
Ōtu *see* Ōtsu
83 B16 **Otuazuma** Kunene, NW Namibia *17°52′S 13°16′E*
77 V16 **Oturkpo** Benue, S Nigeria *07°12′N 08°06′E*
193 Y15 **Otu Tolu Group** *island group* SE Tonga
182 M13 **Otway, Cape** *headland* Victoria, SE Australia *38°52′S 143°31′E*
63 H24 **Otway, Seno** *inlet* S Chile
Ötz *see* Oetz
108 L8 **Ötztaler Ache** ≈ W Austria
108 L9 **Ötztaler Alpen** *It.* Alpi Venoste. ▲▲ SW Austria
27 T12 **Ouachita, Lake** ⊠ Arkansas, C USA
27 R11 **Ouachita Mountains** ▲▲ Arkansas/Oklahoma, C USA
27 U13 **Ouachita River** ≈ Arkansas/Louisiana, C USA
Ouadaï *see* Ouaddaï
76 J7 **Ouadâne** *var.* Ouadane. Adrar, C Mauritania *20°57′N 11°35′W*
78 K13 **Ouadda** Haute-Kotto, N Central African Republic *08°02′N 22°22′E*
78 J10 **Ouaddaï** *off.* Préfecture du Ouaddaï, *var.* Ouadaï, Wadai. ◈ *prefecture* SE Chad
Ouaddaï, Préfecture du *see* Ouaddaï
77 P13 **Ouagadougou** *var.* Wagadugu. ● (Burkina) C Burkina *12°20′N 01°32′W*
77 P13 **Ouagadougou** ✈ C Burkina *12°21′N 01°27′W*
77 O12 **Ouahigouya** NW Burkina *13°31′N 02°20′W*
Ouahran *see* Oran
79 J14 **Ouaka** ◈ *prefecture* C Central African Republic
79 J15 **Ouaka** ≈ S Central African Republic
Oualam *see* Ouallam
76 M9 **Oualâta** *var.* Oualata. Hodh ech Chargui, SE Mauritania *17°18′N 07°00′W*
77 R11 **Ouallam** *var.* Oualam. Tillabéri, W Niger *14°23′N 02°09′E*
172 H14 **Ouanani** Mohéli, S Comoros *12°19′S 93°98′E*
55 Z10 **Ouanary** E French Guiana *04°11′N 51°40′W*
78 L13 **Ouanda Djallé** Vakaga, NE Central African Republic *08°53′N 22°47′E*
79 N14 **Ouando** Haut-Mbomou, SE Central African Republic *05°57′N 25°57′E*
79 L15 **Ouango** Mbomou, S Central African Republic *04°19′N 22°30′E*
77 N14 **Ouangolodougou** *var.* Wangolodougou. N Ivory Coast *09°58′N 05°09′W*
172 I13 **Ouani** Anjouan, SE Comoros
79 M15 **Ouara** ≈ E Central African Republic
76 K7 **Ouarâne** *desert* C Mauritania
15 O11 **Ouareau** ≈ Québec, SE Canada
74 K7 **Ouargla** *var.* Wargla. NE Algeria *32°00′N 05°16′E*
74 F8 **Ouarzazate** S Morocco *30°54′N 06°55′W*
77 Q11 **Ouatagouna** Gao, E Mali *15°06′N 00°41′E*
74 G6 **Ouazzane** *var.* Ouezzane, *Ar.* Wazan, Wazzan. N Morocco *34°52′N 05°35′W*
Oubangui *see* Ubangi
Oubangui-Chari *see* Central African Republic
Oubangui-Chari, Territoire de l' *see* Central African Republic
Oubari, Edeyen d' *see* Awbāri, Idhān
98 G13 **Oud-Beijerland** Zuid-Holland, SW Netherlands *51°50′N 04°25′E*
98 F13 **Ouddorp** Zuid-Holland, SW Netherlands *51°49′N 03°55′E*
77 P9 **Oudeïka** *oasis* C Mali
98 G13 **Oude Maas** ≈ SW Netherlands
99 E18 **Oudenaarde** *Fr.* Audenarde. Oost-Vlaanderen, SW Belgium *50°50′N 03°37′E*
99 H14 **Oudenbosch** Noord-Brabant, S Netherlands *51°35′N 04°32′E*
98 P6 **Oude Pekela** Groningen, NE Netherlands *53°06′N 07°00′E*
Ouderkerk *see* Ouderkerk aan den Amstel
98 I10 **Ouderkerk aan den Amstel** *var.* Ouderkerk. Noord-Holland, C Netherlands *52°18′N 04°54′E*
98 I6 **Oudeschild** Noord-Holland, NW Netherlands *53°01′N 04°51′E*
99 G14 **Oude-Tonge** Zuid-Holland, SW Netherlands *51°40′N 04°13′E*
98 I12 **Oudewater** Utrecht, C Netherlands *52°02′N 04°54′E*
Oudjda *see* Oujda
98 L5 **Oudkerk** Friesland, N Netherlands *53°16′N 05°52′E*
102 J7 **Oudon** ≈ NW France
98 I9 **Oudorp** Noord-Holland, NW Netherlands *52°39′N 04°47′E*
83 G25 **Oudtshoorn** Western Cape, SW South Africa *33°35′S 22°14′E*
99 I16 **Oud-Turnhout** Antwerpen, N Belgium *51°19′N 05°01′E*
74 F7 **Oued-Zem** C Morocco *32°53′N 06°30′W*
187 P16 **Ouégoa** Province Nord, C New Caledonia *20°22′S 164°25′E*
76 L13 **Ouélessébougou** *var.* Ouolossébougou. Koulikoro, SW Mali *11°58′N 07°51′W*
77 N16 **Ouellé** E Ivory Coast *07°18′N 04°01′W*
77 R16 **Ouémé** ≈ C Benin
77 O13 **Ouessa** S Burkina *11°02′N 02°44′W*
102 D5 **Ouessant, Île d'** *Eng.* Ushant. *island* NW France
79 H17 **Ouésso** Sangha, NW Congo *01°38′N 16°03′E*
79 D15 **Ouest** *Eng.* West. ◈ *province* W Cameroon
190 G11 **Ouest, Baie de l'** *bay* Îles Wallis, E Wallis and Futuna
15 Y7 **Ouest, Pointe de l'** *headland* Québec, SE Canada *48°08′N 64°57′W*
Ouezzane *see* Ouazzane
99 K20 **Ouffet** Liège, E Belgium *50°30′N 05°31′E*
79 H14 **Ouham** ◈ *prefecture* NW Central African Republic
78 I13 **Ouham** ≈ Central African Republic/Chad
79 G14 **Ouham-Pendé** ◈ *prefecture* W Central African Republic
77 R16 **Ouidah** *Eng.* Whydah, Wida. S Benin *06°23′N 02°08′E*

◆ Country ● Country Capital ◇ Dependent Territory ○ Dependent Territory Capital ◈ Administrative Regions ✈ International Airport ▲ Mountain ▲▲ Mountain Range ⩓ Volcano ≈ River ◎ Lake ⊠ Reservoir

Oujda – Pama

74 H6 Oujda Ar. Oudjda, Ujda. NE Morocco 34°45′N 01°53′W
76 I7 Oujeft Adrar, C Mauritania 20°05′N 13°00′W
93 L15 Oulainen Oulu, C Finland 64°14′N 24°50′E
Ould Yanja see Ould Yenjé
76 J10 Ould Yenjé var. Ould Yanja. Guidimaka, S Mauritania 15°33′N 11°43′W
93 L14 Oulu Swe. Uleåborg. Oulu, C Finland 65°01′N 25°28′E
93 M14 Oulu Swe. Uleåborg. ◈ province N Finland
93 L15 Oulujärvi Swe. Uleträsk. ⊚ C Finland
93 M14 Oulujoki Swe. Uleälv. ↝ C Finland
93 L14 Oulunsalo Oulu, C Finland 64°55′N 25°19′E
106 A8 Oulx Piemonte, NE Italy 45°05′N 06°41′E
78 J9 Oum-Chalouba Borkou-Ennedi-Tibesti, NE Chad 15°48′N 20°46′E
76 M16 Oumé C Ivory Coast 06°25′N 05°23′W
74 F7 Oum er Rbia ↝ C Morocco
78 J10 Oum-Hadjer Batha, E Chad 13°18′N 19°41′E
92 K10 Ounasjoki ↝ N Finland
78 J7 Ounianga Kébir Borkou-Ennedi-Tibesti, N Chad 19°06′N 20°29′E
Ouolossébougou see Ouéléssébougou
Oup see Auob
99 K19 Oupeye Liège, E Belgium 50°42′N 05°38′E
99 N21 Our ↝ NW Europe
37 Q7 Ouray Colorado, C USA 38°01′N 107°40′W
103 R7 Ource ↝ C France
104 G9 Ourém Santarém, C Portugal 39°40′N 08°32′W
104 H4 Ourense Cast. Orense, Lat. Aurium. Galicia, NW Spain 42°20′N 07°52′W
104 I4 Ourense Cast. Orense. ◈ province Galicia, NW Spain
59 O15 Ouricuri Pernambuco, E Brazil 07°51′S 40°05′W
60 J9 Ourinhos São Paulo, S Brazil 22°59′S 49°52′W
104 G13 Ourique Beja, S Portugal 37°38′N 08°13′W
59 M20 Ouro Preto Minas Gerais, NE Brazil 20°25′S 43°30′W
Ours, Grand Lac de l' see Great Bear Lake
99 K20 Ourthe ↝ E Belgium
165 Q9 Ōu-sanmyaku ▲▲ Honshū, C Japan
97 M17 Ouse ↝ N England, United Kingdom
Ouse see Great Ouse
102 H7 Oust ↝ NW France
Outaouais see Ottawa
15 T4 Outardes Quatre, Réservoir ⊞ Québec, SE Canada
15 T5 Outardes, Rivière aux ↝ Québec, SE Canada
96 E8 Outer Hebrides var. Western Isles. island group NW Scotland, United Kingdom
30 K3 Outer Island island Apostle Islands, Wisconsin, N USA
35 S16 Outer Santa Barbara Passage passage California, SW USA
104 G3 Outes Galicia, NW Spain 42°50′N 08°54′W
83 C18 Outjo Kunene, N Namibia 20°08′S 16°08′E
11 T16 Outlook Saskatchewan, S Canada 51°30′N 107°03′W
93 N16 Outokumpu Itä-Suomi, E Finland 62°43′N 29°05′E
96 M2 Out Skerries island group NE Scotland, United Kingdom
187 Q16 Ouvéa island Îles Loyauté, NE New Caledonia
103 S14 Ouvèze ↝ SE France
182 L9 Ouyen Victoria, SE Australia 35°07′S 142°19′E
39 Q14 Ouzinkie Kodiak Island, Alaska, USA 57°54′N 152°27′W
137 O13 Ovacık Tunceli, E Turkey 39°23′N 39°13′E
106 C9 Ovada Piemonte, NE Italy 44°41′N 08°39′E
187 X14 Ovalau island C Fiji
62 G9 Ovalle Coquimbo, N Chile 30°33′S 71°16′W
83 C17 Ovamboland physical region N Namibia
54 L10 Ovana, Cerro ▲ S Venezuela 04°41′N 66°54′W
104 G7 Ovar Aveiro, N Portugal 40°52′N 08°38′W
114 L10 Ovcharitsa, Yazovir ⊞ SE Bulgaria
54 E6 Ovejas Sucre, NW Colombia 09°32′N 75°14′W
101 E16 Overath Nordrhein-Westfalen, W Germany 50°55′N 07°16′E
98 F13 Overflakkee island SW Netherlands
99 H19 Overijse Vlaams Brabant, C Belgium 50°46′N 04°32′E
98 N10 Overijssel ◈ province E Netherlands
98 M9 Overijssels Kanaal canal E Netherlands
92 K13 Överkalix Norrbotten, N Sweden 66°19′N 22°49′E
27 R4 Overland Park Kansas, C USA 38°57′N 94°41′W
99 L14 Overloon Noord-Brabant, SE Netherlands 51°35′N 05°54′E
99 K16 Overpelt Limburg, NE Belgium 51°13′N 05°24′E
35 Y10 Overton Nevada, W USA 36°32′N 114°25′W
25 W7 Overton Texas, SW USA 32°16′N 94°58′W
92 K13 Övertorneå Norrbotten, N Sweden 66°22′N 23°40′E
95 N18 Överum Kalmar, S Sweden 57°58′N 16°20′E
92 G13 Överuman ⊚ N Sweden
117 P11 Ovidiopol' Odes'ka Oblast', SW Ukraine 46°15′N 30°27′E
116 M14 Ovidiu Constanța, SE Romania 44°16′N 28°34′E
45 N10 Oviedo SW Dominican Republic 17°47′N 71°22′W
104 K2 Oviedo anc. Asturias. Asturias, NW Spain 43°21′N 05°50′W
104 K2 Oviedo ✕ Asturias, N Spain 43°21′N 05°50′W
Ovilava see Wels
118 D7 Ovīši Ventspils, W Latvia 57°34′N 21°43′E
146 K10 Ovminzatovo Tog'lari Rus. Gory Auminzatau. ▲▲ N Uzbekistan
Övögdiy see Telmen
Ovoot see Dariganga
157 O4 Övörhangay ◈ province C Mongolia
94 E12 Øvre Årdal Sogn Og Fjordane, S Norway 61°18′N 07°48′E
95 J14 Övre Fryken ⊚ C Sweden
92 J11 Övre Soppero Lapp. Badje-Sohppar. Norrbotten, N Sweden 68°07′N 21°40′E
117 N3 Ovruch Zhytomyrs'ka Oblast', N Ukraine 51°20′N 28°50′E
Övt see Bat-Öldziy
185 E24 Owaka Otago, South Island, New Zealand 46°27′S 169°42′E
79 H18 Owando prev. Fort Rousset. Cuvette, C Congo 0°29′S 15°55′E
164 J14 Owase Mie, Honshū, SW Japan 34°04′N 136°11′E
27 P9 Owasso Oklahoma, C USA 36°16′N 95°51′W
29 V10 Owatonna Minnesota, N USA 44°04′N 93°13′W
173 O4 Owen Fracture Zone tectonic feature W Arabian Sea
185 H15 Owen, Mount ▲ South Island, New Zealand 41°32′S 172°33′E
185 H15 Owen River Tasman, South Island, New Zealand 41°40′S 172°28′E
44 D8 Owen Roberts ✕ Grand Cayman, Cayman Islands 19°15′N 81°22′W
20 I6 Owensboro Kentucky, S USA 37°46′N 87°07′W
35 T11 Owens Lake salt flat California, W USA
14 F14 Owen Sound Ontario, S Canada 44°34′N 80°56′W
14 F13 Owen Sound ⊚ Ontario, S Canada
35 T10 Owens River ↝ California, W USA
186 F9 Owen Stanley Range ▲▲ S Papua New Guinea
27 V5 Owensville Missouri, C USA 38°21′N 91°30′W
20 M4 Owenton Kentucky, S USA 38°33′N 84°50′W
77 U17 Owerri Imo, S Nigeria 05°19′N 07°07′E
184 M10 Owhango Manawatu-Wanganui, North Island, New Zealand 39°01′S 175°22′E
21 N5 Owingsville Kentucky, S USA 38°09′N 83°46′W
77 T16 Owo Ondo, SW Nigeria 07°10′N 05°31′E
31 R9 Owosso Michigan, N USA 43°00′N 84°10′W
35 V1 Owyhee Nevada, W USA 41°57′N 116°07′W
32 L14 Owyhee, Lake ⊚ Oregon, NW USA
32 L15 Owyhee River ↝ Idaho/Oregon, NW USA
92 K1 Öxarfjördhur var. Axarfjördhur. fjord N Iceland
94 K12 Oxberg Dalarna, C Sweden 61°07′N 14°10′E
11 V17 Oxbow Saskatchewan, S Canada 49°16′N 102°12′W
95 O17 Oxelösund Södermanland, S Sweden 58°40′N 17°10′E
185 H18 Oxford Canterbury, South Island, New Zealand 43°18′S 172°10′E
97 M21 Oxford Lat. Oxonia. S England, United Kingdom 51°46′N 01°15′W
23 Q3 Oxford Alabama, S USA 33°36′N 85°50′W
22 L2 Oxford Mississippi, S USA 34°23′N 89°30′W
29 N16 Oxford Nebraska, C USA 40°15′N 99°37′W
18 I11 Oxford New York, NE USA 42°21′N 75°39′W
21 U8 Oxford North Carolina, SE USA 36°22′N 78°37′W
31 Q14 Oxford Ohio, N USA 39°30′N 84°45′W
18 H16 Oxford Pennsylvania, NE USA 39°46′N 75°57′W
11 X12 Oxford House Manitoba, C Canada 54°55′N 95°13′W
29 Y13 Oxford Junction Iowa, C USA 41°58′N 90°57′W
11 X12 Oxford Lake ⊚ Manitoba, C Canada
97 M21 Oxfordshire cultural region S England, United Kingdom
Oxia see Oxyá
41 X12 Oxkutzcab Yucatán, SE Mexico 20°18′N 89°26′W
35 R15 Oxnard California, W USA 34°12′N 119°10′W
Oxonia see Oxford
14 I12 Oxtongue ↝ Ontario, SE Canada
Oxus see Amu Darya
115 E15 Oxyá var. Oxia. ▲ C Greece 39°46′N 21°56′E
164 L11 Oyabe Toyama, Honshū, SW Japan 36°42′N 136°52′E
Oyahue/Oyahue, Volcán see Ollagüe, Volcán
165 O12 Oyama Tochigi, Honshū, S Japan 36°19′N 139°46′E
47 U5 Oyapock ↝ E French Guiana
Oyapock see Oiapoque, Rio/Oyapok, Fleuve l'
55 Z10 Oyapok, Baie de L' bay Brazil/French Guiana South America W Atlantic Ocean
55 Z11 Oyapok, Fleuve l' var. Rio Oiapoque, Oyapock. ↝ Brazil/French Guiana see also Oiapoque, Rio
Oyapok, Fleuve l' see Oiapoque, Rio
79 E17 Oyem Woleu-Ntem, N Gabon 01°34′N 11°31′E
11 R16 Oyen Alberta, SW Canada 51°20′N 110°28′W
95 I15 Øyeren ⊚ S Norway
Oygon see Tüdevtey
96 I7 Oykel ↝ N Scotland, United Kingdom
123 R9 Oymyakon Respublika Sakha (Yakutiya), NE Russian Federation 63°28′N 142°22′E
79 H19 Oyo Cuvette, C Congo 01°17′S 16°00′E
77 S15 Oyo Oyo, W Nigeria 07°51′N 03°57′E
77 S15 Oyo ◈ state SW Nigeria
56 D13 Oyón Lima, C Peru 10°39′S 76°44′W
103 S10 Oyonnax Ain, E France 46°16′N 05°39′E
146 L10 Oyoqog'itma Rus. Ayakagytma. Buxoro Viloyati, C Uzbekistan 40°37′N 64°26′E
146 M9 Oyoqquduq Rus. Ayakkuduk. Navoiy Viloyati, N Uzbekistan 41°16′N 65°12′E
32 F9 Oysterville Washington, NW USA 46°33′N 124°03′W
95 D14 Øystese Hordaland, S Norway 60°23′N 06°13′E
145 S16 Oytal Zhambyl, S Kazakhstan 42°54′N 73°21′E
147 U10 Oy-Tal Oshskaya Oblast', SW Kyrgyzstan 40°23′N 74°04′E
147 T10 Oy-Tal ↝ SW Kyrgyzstan
Oyyl see Uil
Ozarichi see Azarychy
23 R7 Ozark Alabama, S USA 31°27′N 85°38′W
27 S10 Ozark Arkansas, C USA 35°30′N 93°50′W
27 T8 Ozark Missouri, C USA 37°01′N 93°12′W
27 T8 Ozark Plateau plain Arkansas/Missouri, C USA
27 T6 Ozarks, Lake of the ⊞ Missouri, C USA
192 L10 Ozbourn Seamount undersea feature W Pacific Ocean 26°00′S 174°49′W
111 L20 Ózd Borsod-Abaúj-Zemplén, NE Hungary 48°15′N 20°18′E
112 D11 Ozeblin ▲ C Croatia 44°37′N 15°52′E
123 V11 Ozernovskiy Kamchatskaya Oblast', E Russian Federation 51°28′N 156°32′E
144 M7 Ozërnoye var. Ozërnyy. Kostanay, N Kazakhstan 53°29′N 63°14′E
124 J15 Ozërnyy Tverskaya Oblast', W Russian Federation 57°55′N 33°45′E
Ozërnyy see Ozërnoye
115 D18 Ozerós, Límni ⊚ W Greece
122 G11 Ozërsk Chelyabinskaya Oblast', C Russian Federation 55°44′N 60°59′E
119 D14 Ozersk prev. Darkehnen, Ger. Angerapp. Kaliningradskaya Oblast', W Russian Federation 54°23′N 21°59′E
126 L4 Ozery Moskovskaya Oblast', W Russian Federation 54°51′N 38°37′E
Özgön see Uzgen
107 C17 Ozieri Sardegna, Italy, C Mediterranean Sea 40°35′N 09°01′E
111 I15 Ozimek Ger. Malapane. Opolskie, SW Poland 50°41′N 18°16′E
127 R8 Ozinki Saratovskaya Oblast', W Russian Federation 51°16′N 49°45′E
25 O10 Ozona Texas, SW USA 30°43′N 101°13′W
Ozorkov see Ozorków
110 J12 Ozorków Rus. Ozorkov. Łódź, C Poland 52°00′N 19°17′E
164 F14 Ōzu Ehime, Shikoku, SW Japan 33°30′N 132°33′E
137 R10 Ozurget'i prev. Makharadze. W Georgia 41°57′N 42°01′E

P

99 J17 Paal Limburg, NE Belgium 51°03′N 05°08′E
196 M14 Paamiut var. Pâmiut, Dan. Frederikshåb. S Greenland 62°22′N 49°52′W
Pa-an see Hpa-an
101 L22 Paar ↝ SE Germany
83 E26 Paarl Western Cape, SW South Africa 33°45′S 18°58′E
93 L15 Paavola Oulu, C Finland 64°34′N 25°15′E
96 E8 Pabbay island NW Scotland, United Kingdom
153 T15 Pabna Rajshahi, W Bangladesh 24°02′N 89°15′E
109 U4 Pabneukirchen Oberösterreich, N Austria 48°19′N 14°49′E
118 H13 Pabradė Pol. Podbrodzie. Vilnius, SE Lithuania 54°58′N 25°43′E
56 L13 Pacahuaras, Río ↝ N Bolivia
Pacaraima, Sierra/Pacaraim, Serra see Pakaraima Mountains
56 B11 Pacasmayo La Libertad, W Peru 07°27′S 79°33′W
42 D6 Pacaya, Volcán de ℞ S Guatemala 14°19′N 90°36′W
115 K23 Pacheía var. Pachía. island Kykládes, Greece, Aegean Sea
Pachía see Pacheía
107 L26 Pachino Sicilia, Italy, C Mediterranean Sea 36°43′N 15°06′E
56 F12 Pachitea, Río ↝ C Peru
154 I11 Pachmarhi Madhya Pradesh, C India 22°36′N 78°18′E
121 P3 Páchna var. Pakhna. SW Cyprus 34°47′N 32°48′E
115 H25 Páchnes ▲ Kríti, Greece, E Mediterranean Sea 35°19′N 24°00′E
54 F9 Pacho Cundinamarca, C Colombia 05°09′N 74°08′W
154 F12 Pāchora Mahārāshtra, C India 20°52′N 75°28′E
41 P13 Pachuca var. Pachuca de Soto. Hidalgo, C Mexico 20°05′N 98°46′W
Pachuca de Soto see Pachuca
27 W5 Pacific Missouri, C USA 38°28′N 90°44′W
192 L14 Pacific-Antarctic Ridge undersea feature S Pacific Ocean 62°00′S 157°00′W
32 F8 Pacific Beach Washington, NW USA 47°09′N 124°12′W
35 N10 Pacific Grove California, W USA 36°35′N 121°54′W
29 S15 Pacific Junction Iowa, C USA 41°01′N 95°48′W
192-193 Pacific Ocean ocean
129 Z10 Pacific Plate tectonic feature
113 J15 Pačir ▲ N Montenegro 43°19′N 19°07′E
182 L5 Packsaddle New South Wales, SE Australia 30°42′S 141°55′E
32 H9 Packwood Washington, NW USA 46°37′N 121°38′W
Padalung see Phatthalung
168 J12 Padang Sumatera, W Indonesia 01°S 100°21′E
168 L9 Padang Endau Pahang, Peninsular Malaysia 02°38′N 103°37′E
Padangpandjang see Padangpanjang
168 I11 Padangpanjang prev. Padangpandjang. Sumatera, W Indonesia 0°30′S 100°26′E
168 I10 Padangsidempuan prev. Padangsidimpoean. Sumatera, W Indonesia 01°23′N 99°15′E
Padangsidimpoean see Padangsidempuan
124 I9 Padany Respublika Kareliya, NW Russian Federation 63°18′N 33°20′E
93 M18 Padasjoki Etelä-Suomi, S Finland 61°20′N 25°21′E
57 M22 Padcaya Tarija, S Bolivia 21°52′S 64°46′W
101 H14 Paderborn Nordrhein-Westfalen, NW Germany 51°43′N 08°45′E
Padeşul/Padeş, Vîrful see Padeş, Vârful
116 F12 Padeş, Vârful var. Padeşul; prev. Vîrful Padeş. ▲ W Romania 45°39′N 22°19′E
112 L10 Padinska Skela Serbia, N Serbia 44°58′N 20°25′E
153 S14 Padma var. Ganges. ↝ Bangladesh/India see also Ganges
Padma see Brahmaputra
Padma see Ganges
106 H8 Padova Eng. Padua; anc. Patavium. Veneto, NE Italy 45°24′N 11°52′E
82 A10 Padrão, Ponta do headland NW Angola 06°06′S 12°18′E
25 T16 Padre Island island Texas, SW USA
104 G3 Padrón Galicia, NW Spain 42°44′N 08°40′W
118 K13 Padsvillye Rus. Podsvil'ye. Vitsyebskaya Voblasts', N Belarus 55°09′N 27°58′E
182 K11 Padthaway South Australia 36°39′S 140°30′E
Padua see Padova
20 G7 Paducah Kentucky, S USA 37°03′N 88°36′W
25 P4 Paducah Texas, SW USA 34°01′N 100°18′W
105 N15 Padul Andalucía, S Spain 37°02′N 03°37′W
191 P8 Paea Tahiti, W French Polynesia 17°41′S 149°35′W
185 L14 Paekakariki Wellington, North Island, New Zealand 41°00′S 174°58′E
163 X11 Paektu-san var. Baitou Shan. ▲ China/North Korea 42°00′N 128°03′E
163 V15 Paengnyŏng-do island NW South Korea
184 M7 Paeroa Waikato, North Island, New Zealand 37°23′S 175°39′E
54 D12 Páez Cauca, SW Colombia 02°37′N 76°00′W
121 O3 Páfos var. Paphos. W Cyprus 34°46′N 32°26′E
121 O3 Páfos ✕ SW Cyprus 34°46′N 32°25′E
83 L19 Pafúri Gaza, SW Mozambique 22°27′S 31°21′E
112 C12 Pag It. Pago. Lika-Senj, SW Croatia 44°26′N 15°01′E
112 B11 Pag It. Pago. island Zadar, C Croatia
171 P7 Pagadian Mindanao, S Philippines 07°47′N 123°22′E
168 J13 Pagai Selatan, Pulau island Kepulauan Mentawai, W Indonesia
168 J13 Pagai Utara, Pulau island Kepulauan Mentawai, W Indonesia
188 K4 Pagan island C Northern Mariana Islands
115 G16 Pagasitikós Kólpos gulf E Greece
36 L8 Page Arizona, SW USA 36°54′N 111°28′W
29 Q5 Page North Dakota, N USA 47°09′N 97°33′W
118 D13 Pagėgiai Ger. Pogegen. Tauragė, SW Lithuania 55°08′N 21°54′E
21 S11 Pageland South Carolina, SE USA 34°46′N 80°23′W
81 G16 Pager ↝ NE Uganda
149 Q5 Paghmān Kābol, E Afghanistan 34°33′N 68°55′E
Pago see Pag
188 C16 Pago Bay bay E Guam, W Pacific Ocean
115 M20 Pagóndas var. Pagóndhas. Sámos, Dodekánisa, Greece, Aegean Sea 37°41′N 26°50′E
Pagóndhas see Pagóndas
192 J16 Pago Pago ○ (American Samoa) Tutuila, W American Samoa 14°16′S 170°43′W
37 R8 Pagosa Springs Colorado, C USA 37°13′N 107°01′W
Pagqên see Gadê
38 H12 Pāhala var. Pahala. Hawaii, USA, C Pacific Ocean 19°12′N 155°28′W
168 K8 Pahang var. Negeri Pahang Darul Makmur. ◈ state Peninsular Malaysia
Pahang see Pahang, Sungai
168 L8 Pahang, Sungai var. Pahang, Sungei Pahang. ↝ Peninsular Malaysia
149 S8 Pahārpur North-West Frontier Province, NW Pakistan 32°06′N 71°00′E
185 B24 Pahia Point headland South Island, New Zealand 46°19′S 167°42′E
184 M13 Pahiatua Manawatu-Wanganui, North Island, New Zealand 40°30′S 175°49′E
38 H12 Pāhoa var. Pahoa. Hawaii, USA, C Pacific Ocean 19°29′N 154°56′W
23 Y14 Pahokee Florida, SE USA 26°49′N 80°40′W
35 X9 Pahranagat Range ▲▲ Nevada, W USA
35 W11 Pahrump Nevada, W USA 36°11′N 115°58′W
Pahsien see Chongqing
35 V9 Pahute Mesa ▲ Nevada, W USA
167 N7 Pai Mae Hong Son, NW Thailand 19°24′N 98°26′E
38 F10 Pa'ia var. Paia. Maui, Hawaii, USA, C Pacific Ocean 20°54′N 156°22′W
Paia see Pa'ia
Pai-ch'eng see Baicheng
118 H4 Paide Ger. Weissenstein. Järvamaa, N Estonia 58°55′N 25°36′E
97 J24 Paignton SW England, United Kingdom 50°26′N 03°34′W
184 K3 Paihia Northland, North Island, New Zealand 35°18′S 174°06′E
93 M18 Päijänne ⊚ S Finland
114 F13 Páïko ▲ N Greece
57 M17 Paila, Río ↝ C Bolivia
167 Q12 Pailin Bătdâmbâng, W Cambodia 12°51′N 102°34′E
Pailing see Chun'an
54 F6 Pailitas Cesar, N Colombia 08°58′N 73°38′W
38 F9 Pailolo Channel channel Hawai'i, USA, C Pacific Ocean
93 K19 Paimio Swe. Pemar. Länsi-Suomi, SW Finland 60°27′N 22°42′E
165 O16 Paimi-saki var. Yaeme-saki. headland Iriomote-jima, SW Japan 24°18′N 123°40′E
102 G5 Paimpol Côtes d'Armor, NW France 48°47′N 03°03′W
168 J12 Painan Sumatera, W Indonesia 01°22′S 100°33′E
155 G23 Painävu Kerala, SW India 9°50′N 76°56′E
63 G23 Paine, Cerro ▲ S Chile 51°01′S 72°57′W
31 U11 Painesville Ohio, N USA 41°43′N 81°15′W
31 S14 Paint Creek ↝ Ohio, N USA
36 L10 Painted Desert desert Arizona, SW USA
Paint Hills see Wemindji
30 M4 Paint River ↝ Michigan, N USA
25 P8 Paint Rock Texas, SW USA 31°32′N 99°56′W
21 O6 Paintsville Kentucky, S USA 37°48′N 82°48′W
Paisance see Piacenza
96 I12 Paisley W Scotland, United Kingdom 55°50′N 04°26′W
32 I15 Paisley Oregon, NW USA 42°40′N 120°31′W
105 R10 País Valenciano var. Valencia, Cat. València; anc. Valentia. ◈ autonomous community NE Spain
105 O3 País Vasco Basq. Euskadi, Eng. The Basque Country, Sp. Provincias Vascongadas. ◈ autonomous community N Spain
56 A9 Paita Piura, NW Peru 05°11′S 81°09′W
169 V6 Paitan, Teluk bay Sabah, East Malaysia
104 H7 Paiva, Rio ↝ N Portugal
92 K12 Pajala Norrbotten, N Sweden 67°12′N 23°19′E
104 K3 Pajares, Puerto de pass NW Spain
54 G9 Pajarito Boyacá, C Colombia 05°18′N 72°43′W
54 G4 Pajaro La Guajira, S Colombia 11°41′N 72°37′W
Pakanbaru see Pekanbaru
55 Q10 Pakaraima Mountains var. Serra Pacaraim, Sierra Pacaraima. ▲▲ N South America
153 S14 Pakaur var. Pakur. Jharkhand, N India 24°48′N 87°14′E
167 P10 Pak Chong Nakhon Ratchasima, C Thailand 14°38′N 101°22′E
123 V8 Pakhachi Koryakskiy Avtonomnyy Okrug, E Russian Federation 60°36′N 168°59′E
Pakhna see Páchna
189 U16 Pakin Atoll atoll Caroline Islands, E Micronesia
149 Q12 Pakistan off. Islamic Republic of Pakistan, var. Islami Jamhuriya e Pakistan. ◆ republic S Asia
Pakistan, Islamic Republic of see Pakistan
Pakistan, Islami Jamhuriya e see Pakistan
167 P8 Pak Lay var. Muang Pak Lay. Xaignabouli, C Laos 18°06′N 101°21′E
Paknam see Samut Prakan
166 L5 Pakokku Magway, C Myanmar (Burma) 21°20′N 95°05′E
110 I10 Pakość Ger. Pakosch. Kujawski-pomorskie, C Poland 52°47′N 18°03′E
Pakosch see Pakość
149 V10 Pākpattan Punjab, E Pakistan 30°20′N 73°27′E
167 O15 Pak Phanang var. Ban Pak Phanang. Nakhon Si Thammarat, SW Thailand 08°20′N 100°10′E
112 G9 Pakrac Hung. Pakrácz. Požega-Slavonija, NE Croatia 45°26′N 17°09′E
Pakrácz see Pakrac
118 F11 Pakruojis Šiaulai, N Lithuania 56°N 23°51′E
111 J24 Paks Tolna, S Hungary 46°38′N 18°51′E
Pak Sane see Pakxan
Paksé see Pakxé
167 Q10 Pak Thong Chai Nakhon Ratchasima, C Thailand 14°43′N 102°01′E
149 R6 Paktīā ◈ province SE Afghanistan
149 Q7 Paktīkā ◈ province SE Afghanistan
171 N12 Pakuli Sulawesi, C Indonesia 01°14′S 119°55′E
Pakur see Pakaur
81 F17 Pakwach NW Uganda 02°28′N 31°28′E
167 R8 Pakxan var. Muang Pakxan, Pak Sane. Bolikhamxai, C Laos 18°27′N 103°38′E
167 S10 Pakxé var. Paksé. Champasak, S Laos 15°09′N 105°49′E
78 G12 Pala Mayo-Kébbi, SW Chad 09°22′N 14°54′E
61 A17 Palacios Santa Fe, C Argentina 30°43′S 61°37′W
25 V13 Palacios Texas, SW USA 28°42′N 96°13′W
105 X5 Palafrugell Cataluña, NE Spain 41°55′N 03°10′E
107 L24 Palagonia Sicilia, Italy, C Mediterranean Sea 37°20′N 14°45′E
113 E17 Palagruža It. Pelagosa. island SW Croatia
115 G20 Palaiá Epídavros Pelopónnisos, S Greece 37°38′N 23°09′E
121 P3 Palaichóri var. Palekhori. C Cyprus 34°55′N 33°06′E
115 H25 Palaiochóra Kríti, Greece, E Mediterranean Sea 35°14′N 23°37′E
115 A15 Palaiolastrítsa religious building Kérkyra, Iónia Nisiá, Greece, C Mediterranean Sea
115 J19 Palaiópoli Ándros, Kykládes, Greece, Aegean Sea 37°49′N 24°49′E
103 N5 Palaiseau Essonne, N France 48°41′N 02°14′E
155 G21 Palakkad var. Pālghāt. Kerala, SW India 10°46′N 76°42′E see also Pālghāt
154 N11 Pāla Laharha Orissa, E India 21°25′N 85°18′E
83 G19 Palamakoloi Ghanzi, C Botswana 23°10′S 22°22′E
115 E16 Palamás Thessalía, C Greece 39°28′N 22°05′E
105 X5 Palamós Cataluña, NE Spain 41°51′N 03°06′E
118 J5 Palamuse Ger. Sankt-Bartholomäi. Jõgevamaa, E Estonia 58°41′N 26°35′E
183 Q14 Palana Tasmania, SE Australia 39°48′S 147°54′E
123 U9 Palana Koryakskiy Avtonomnyy Okrug, E Russian Federation 59°05′N 159°59′E
118 C11 Palanga Ger. Polangen. Klaipėda, NW Lithuania 55°54′N 21°05′E
143 V10 Palangān, Kūh-e ▲▲ E Iran
Palangkaraja see Palangkaraya
169 T12 Palangkaraya prev. Palangkaraja. Borneo, C Indonesia 02°16′S 113°55′E
155 H22 Palani Tamil Nādu, SE India 10°30′N 77°24′E
Palanka see Bačka Palanka
154 D9 Pālanpur Gujarāt, W India 24°12′N 72°29′E
Palantia see Palencia
83 I19 Palapye Central, SE Botswana 22°37′S 27°06′E
155 J19 Palār ↝ SE India
104 H3 Palas de Rei Galicia, NW Spain 42°52′N 07°51′W
123 T9 Palatka Magadanskaya Oblast', E Russian Federation 60°09′N 150°33′E
23 W10 Palatka Florida, SE USA 29°39′N 81°38′W
188 B9 Palau var. Belau. ◆ republic W Pacific Ocean
Palau see Palau Islands
129 Y14 Palau Islands var. Palau. island group N Palau
192 G16 Palauli Bay bay Savai'i, C Samoa, C Pacific Ocean
167 N11 Palaw Tanintharyi, S Myanmar (Burma) 12°57′N 98°39′E
170 M6 Palawan island W Philippines
171 N6 Palawan Passage passage W Philippines
192 E7 Palawan Trough undersea feature S South China Sea 07°00′N 115°00′E
155 H23 Pālayankottai Tamil Nādu, SE India 08°42′N 77°46′E
107 L25 Palazzola Acreide anc. Acrae. Sicilia, Italy, C Mediterranean Sea 37°04′N 14°54′E
118 G3 Paldiski prev. Baltiski, Eng. Baltic Port, Ger. Baltischport. Harjumaa, NW Estonia 59°22′N 24°08′E
112 I13 Pale Republika Srpska, SE Bosnia and Herzegovina 43°49′N 18°35′E
Palekhori see Palaichóri
168 L13 Palembang Sumatera, W Indonesia 02°59′S 104°45′E
63 G18 Palena Los Lagos, S Chile 43°40′S 71°50′W
63 G18 Palena, Río ↝ S Chile
104 M5 Palencia anc. Palantia, Pallantia. Castilla-León, NW Spain 42°23′N 04°32′W
104 M3 Palencia ◈ province Castilla-León, N Spain
35 X15 Palen Dry Lake ⊚ California, W USA
41 V15 Palenque Chiapas, SE Mexico 17°32′N 91°59′W
41 V15 Palenque var. Ruinas de Palenque. ruins Chiapas, SE Mexico
45 O9 Palenque, Punta headland S Dominican Republic 18°13′N 70°08′W
Palenque, Ruinas de see Palenque
Palerme see Palermo
107 I23 Palermo Fr. Palerme; anc. Panhormus, Panormus. Sicilia, Italy, C Mediterranean Sea 38°08′N 13°23′E
25 V8 Palestine Texas, SW USA 31°45′N 93°39′W
25 V7 Palestine, Lake ⊞ Texas, SW USA
107 I15 Palestrina Lazio, C Italy 41°49′N 12°53′E
166 K5 Paletwa Chin State, W Myanmar (Burma) 21°25′N 92°49′E
155 G21 Pālghāt var. Palakkad. Kerala, SW India 10°46′N 76°42′E see also Palakkad
152 F13 Pāli Rājasthān, N India 25°48′N 73°21′E
167 N16 Palian Trang, SW Thailand 07°11′N 99°41′E
189 O12 Palikir ● (Micronesia) Pohnpei, E Micronesia 06°58′N 158°13′E
Palimé see Kpalimé
107 L19 Palinuro, Capo headland S Italy 40°02′N 15°16′E
115 H15 Palioúri, Akrotírio var. Akrotírio Kanestron. headland N Greece 39°55′N 23°45′E
33 R14 Palisades Reservoir ⊞ Idaho, NW USA
99 J23 Paliseul Luxembourg, SE Belgium 49°55′N 05°09′E
154 C11 Pālitāna Gujarāt, W India 21°30′N 71°50′E
118 F4 Palivere Läänemaa, W Estonia 58°59′N 23°58′E
41 V14 Palizada Campeche, SE Mexico 18°15′N 92°03′W
93 L18 Pälkäne Länsi-Suomi, W Finland 61°22′N 24°16′E
155 J22 Palk Strait strait India/Sri Lanka
155 J23 Pallai Northern Province, NW Sri Lanka 09°35′N 80°20′E
Pallantia see Palencia
106 C6 Pallanza Piemonte, NE Italy 45°57′N 08°32′E
127 Q9 Pallasovka Volgogradskaya Oblast', SW Russian Federation 50°06′N 46°52′E
Pallene/Pallíni see Kassándra
185 L15 Palliser Bay bay North Island, New Zealand
185 L15 Palliser, Cape headland North Island, New Zealand 41°37′S 175°16′E
191 U9 Palliser, Îles island group Îles Tuamotu, C French Polynesia
82 Q12 Palma Cabo Delgado, N Mozambique 10°46′S 40°30′E
105 X9 Palma var. Palma de Mallorca. Mallorca, Spain, W Mediterranean Sea 39°35′N 02°39′E
105 X9 Palma ✕ Mallorca, Spain, W Mediterranean Sea
105 X10 Palma, Badia de bay Mallorca, Spain, W Mediterranean Sea
104 L13 Palma del Río Andalucía, S Spain 37°42′N 05°16′W
Palma de Mallorca see Palma
107 J25 Palma di Montechiaro Sicilia, Italy, C Mediterranean Sea 37°12′N 13°46′E
106 J7 Palmanova Friuli-Venezia Giulia, NE Italy 45°54′N 13°20′E
54 J7 Palmarito Apure, C Venezuela 07°36′N 70°08′W
43 N15 Palmar Sur Puntarenas, SE Costa Rica 08°54′N 83°27′W
60 I12 Palmas Paraná, S Brazil 26°29′S 52°00′W
59 K16 Palmas var. Palmas do Tocantins. Tocantins, C Brazil 10°24′S 48°19′W
76 L18 Palmas, Cape Fr. Cap des Palmès. headland SW Ivory Coast 04°18′N 07°31′W
Palmas do Tocantins see Palmas
54 D11 Palmaseca ✕ (Cali) Valle del Cauca, SW Colombia 03°31′N 76°27′W
107 B21 Palmas, Golfo di gulf Sardegna, Italy, C Mediterranean Sea
44 I7 Palma Soriano Santiago de Cuba, E Cuba 20°10′N 76°00′W
23 Y12 Palm Bay Florida, SE USA 28°01′N 80°35′W
35 T14 Palmdale California, W USA 34°34′N 118°07′W
61 H14 Palmeira das Missões Rio Grande do Sul, S Brazil 27°54′S 53°20′W
82 A11 Palmeirinhas, Ponta das headland NW Angola 09°04′S 13°02′E
39 R11 Palmer Alaska, USA 61°36′N 149°06′W
19 N11 Palmer Massachusetts, NE USA 42°09′N 72°19′W
25 U7 Palmer Texas, SW USA 32°25′N 96°40′W
194 H4 Palmer US research station Antarctica 64°37′S 64°01′W
15 R11 Palmer ↝ Québec, SE Canada
37 T5 Palmer Lake Colorado, C USA 39°07′N 104°55′W
194 J6 Palmer Land physical region Antarctica
14 F15 Palmerston Ontario, SE Canada 43°51′N 80°49′W
185 F22 Palmerston Otago, South Island, New Zealand 45°27′S 170°42′E
190 K15 Palmerston island S Cook Islands
Palmerston see Darwin
184 M12 Palmerston North Manawatu-Wanganui, North Island, New Zealand 40°20′S 175°52′E
23 V13 Palmetto Florida, SE USA 27°31′N 82°34′W
The Palmetto State see South Carolina
107 M22 Palmi Calabria, SW Italy 38°21′N 15°51′E
54 D11 Palmira Valle del Cauca, W Colombia 03°33′N 76°17′W
56 F8 Palmira, Río ↝ N Peru
61 D19 Palmitas Soriano, SW Uruguay 33°27′S 57°48′W
Palmnicken see Yantarnyy
35 V15 Palm Springs California, W USA 33°48′N 116°33′W
27 V2 Palmyra Missouri, C USA 39°48′N 91°31′W
18 G10 Palmyra New York, NE USA 43°02′N 77°13′W
18 G15 Palmyra Pennsylvania, NE USA 40°18′N 76°35′W
21 V5 Palmyra Virginia, NE USA 37°53′N 78°17′W
Palmyra see Tudmur
192 L7 Palmyra Atoll ◇ US privately owned unincorporated territory C Pacific Ocean
154 P12 Palmyras Point headland E India 20°46′N 87°00′E
35 N9 Palo Alto California, W USA 37°26′N 122°08′W
25 O1 Palo Duro Creek ↝ Texas, SW USA
Paloe see Denpasar, Bali, C Indonesia
Paloe see Palu
168 L9 Paloh Johor, Peninsular Malaysia 02°10′N 103°11′E
80 F12 Paloich Upper Nile, SE Sudan 10°29′N 32°31′E
40 I3 Palomas Chihuahua, N Mexico 31°45′N 107°38′W
107 I15 Palombara Sabina Lazio, C Italy 42°04′N 12°45′E
105 S13 Palos, Cabo de headland SE Spain 37°38′N 00°42′W
104 I14 Palos de la Frontera Andalucía, S Spain 37°14′N 06°53′W
60 G11 Palotina Paraná, S Brazil 24°16′S 53°49′W
32 M9 Palouse Washington, NW USA 46°54′N 117°04′W
32 L9 Palouse River ↝ Washington, NW USA
35 Y16 Palo Verde California, W USA 33°25′N 114°43′W
57 E16 Palpa Ica, W Peru 14°35′S 75°09′W
95 M16 Pålsboda Örebro, C Sweden 59°04′N 15°21′E
93 M15 Paltamo Oulu, C Finland 64°25′N 27°50′E
171 N12 Palu prev. Paloe. Sulawesi, C Indonesia 0°54′S 119°52′E
137 P14 Palu Elazığ, E Turkey 38°43′N 39°56′E
152 I11 Palwal Haryāna, N India 28°15′N 77°18′E
123 U6 Palyavaam ↝ NE Russian Federation
77 Q13 Pama SE Burkina 11°13′N 00°46′E

◆ Country
● Country Capital
◇ Dependent Territory
○ Dependent Territory Capital
◈ Administrative Regions
✕ International Airport
▲ Mountain
▲▲ Mountain Range
℞ Volcano
↝ River
⊚ Lake
⊞ Reservoir

PAMANDZI – PATHĀNKOT

172 *J14* **Pamandzi** ✈ (Mamoudzou) Petite-Terre, E Mayotte
Pamangkat *see* Pemangkat
143 *R11* **Pā Mazār** Kermān, C Iran
83 *N19* **Pambarra** Inhambane, SE Mozambique *21°57′S 35°06′E*
171 *X12* **Pamdai** Papua, E Indonesia *01°58′S 137°19′E*
103 *N16* **Pamiers** Ariège, S France *43°07′N 01°37′E*
147 *T14* **Pamir** *var.* Daryā-ye Pāmīr, *Taj.* Dar"yoi Pomir. ≈ Afghanistan/Tajikistan *see also* Pāmīr, Daryā-ye
Pamir *see* Pāmīr, Daryā-ye
149 *U1* **Pāmīr, Daryā-ye** *var.* Pamir, *Taj.* Dar"yoi Pomir. ≈ Afghanistan/Tajikistan *see also* Pamir
Pāmīr, Daryā-ye *see* Pamir
Pāmīr-e Khord *see* Little Pamir
Pamir/Pāmīr, Daryā-ye *see* Pamirs
129 *Q8* **Pamirs** *Pash.* Daryā-ye Pāmīr, *Rus.* Pamir. ▲▲ C Asia
Pâmiut *see* Paamiut
21 *X10* **Pamlico River** ≈ North Carolina, SE USA
21 *Y10* **Pamlico Sound** *sound* North Carolina, SE USA
25 *O2* **Pampa** Texas, SW USA *35°32′N 100°58′W*
Pampa Aullagas, Lago *see* Poopó, Lago
61 *B21* **Pampa Húmeda** *grassland* E Argentina
56 *A10* **Pampa las Salinas** *salt lake* NW Peru
57 *F15* **Pampas** Huancavelica, C Peru *12°22′S 74°53′W*
62 *K13* **Pampas** *plain* C Argentina
55 *O4* **Pampatar** Nueva Esparta, NE Venezuela *11°03′N 63°51′W*
Pampeluna *see* Pamplona
104 *H8* **Pampilhosa da Serra** *var.* Pampilhosa de Serra. Coimbra, N Portugal *40°03′N 07°58′W*
173 *Y15* **Pamplemousses** N Mauritius *20°06′S 57°34′E*
54 *G7* **Pamplona** Norte de Santander, N Colombia *07°24′N 72°38′W*
105 *Q3* **Pamplona** *Basq.* Iruña, *prev.* Pampeluna; *anc.* Pompaelo. Navarra, N Spain *42°49′N 01°39′W*
114 *I11* **Pamporovo** *prev.* Vasil Kolarov. Smolyan, S Bulgaria *41°39′N 24°45′E*
136 *D15* **Pamukkale** Denizli, W Turkey *37°51′N 29°13′E*
21 *W5* **Pamunkey River** ≈ Virginia, NE USA
152 *K5* **Pamzal** Jammu and Kashmir, NW India *34°17′N 78°50′E*
30 *L14* **Pana** Illinois, N USA *39°23′N 89°04′W*
41 *Y11* **Panabá** Yucatán, SE Mexico *21°20′N 88°16′W*
35 *Y8* **Panaca** Nevada, W USA *37°47′N 114°24′W*
115 *E19* **Panachaikó** ▲▲ S Greece
14 *F11* **Panache Lake** ◎ Ontario, S Canada
114 *I10* **Panagyurishte** Pazardzhik, C Bulgaria *42°30′N 24°11′E*
168 *M16* **Panaitan, Pulau** *island* S Indonesia
115 *D18* **Panaitolikó** ▲▲ C Greece
155 *E17* **Panaji** *var.* Pangim, Panjim, New Goa. *state capital* Goa, W India *15°31′N 73°52′E*
43 *T15* **Panamá** *var.* Ciudad de Panama, *Eng.* Panama City. ● (Panama) Panamá, C Panama *08°57′N 79°33′W*
43 *T14* **Panama** *off.* Republic of Panama. ◆ *republic* Central America
43 *U14* **Panamá** *off.* Provincia de Panamá. ◈ *province* E Panama
43 *U15* **Panamá, Bahía de** *bay* N Gulf of Panama
193 *T7* **Panama Basin** *undersea feature* E Pacific Ocean *05°00′N 83°30′W*
43 *T15* **Panama Canal** *canal* E Panama
23 *R9* **Panama City** Florida, SE USA *30°09′N 85°39′W*
43 *T14* **Panama City** ✈ Panamá, C Panama *09°02′N 79°24′W*
Panama City *see* Panamá
23 *Q9* **Panama City Beach** Florida, SE USA *30°10′N 85°48′W*
43 *T17* **Panamá, Golfo de** *var.* Gulf of Panama. *gulf* S Panama
Panama, Gulf of *see* Panamá, Golfo de
Panama, Isthmus of *see* Panama, Istmo de
43 *T15* **Panama, Istmo de** *Eng.* Isthmus of Panama; *prev.* Isthmus of Darien. *isthmus* E Panama
Panamá, Provincia de *see* Panamá
Panama, Republic of *see* Panama
35 *U11* **Panamint Range** ▲▲ California, W USA
107 *L22* **Panarea, Isola** *island* Isole Eolie, S Italy
106 *G9* **Panaro** ≈ N Italy
171 *P5* **Panay Island** *island* C Philippines
35 *W7* **Pancake Range** ▲▲ Nevada, W USA
112 *M11* **Pančevo** *Ger.* Pantschowa, *Hung.* Pancsova. Vojvodina, N Serbia *44°53′N 20°40′E*
113 *M15* **Pančićev Vrh** ▲ SW Serbia *43°16′N 20°49′E*
116 *L12* **Panciu** Vrancea, E Romania *45°54′N 27°08′E*
116 *F10* **Pâncota** *Hung.* Pankota; *prev.* Pîncota. Arad, W Romania *46°20′N 21°45′E*
Pancsova *see* Pančevo
83 *N20* **Panda** Inhambane, SE Mozambique *24°02′S 34°45′E*
171 *X12* **Pandaidori, Kepulauan** *island group* E Indonesia
25 *N11* **Pandale** Texas, SW USA *30°09′N 101°34′W*
169 *P12* **Pandang Tikar, Pulau** *island* N Indonesia
61 *F20* **Pan de Azúcar** Maldonado, S Uruguay *34°45′S 55°14′W*
118 *H11* **Pandėlys** Panevėžys, NE Lithuania *56°04′N 25°18′E*
155 *F15* **Pandharpur** Mahārāshtra, W India *17°42′N 75°24′E*
182 *J1* **Pandie Pandie** South Australia *26°06′S 139°26′E*
171 *O12* **Pandiri** Sulawesi, C Indonesia *01°32′S 120°47′E*
61 *F20* **Pando** Canelones, S Uruguay *34°44′S 55°58′W*
57 *J14* **Pando** ◈ *department* N Bolivia
192 *K9* **Pandora Bank** *undersea feature* W Pacific Ocean
95 *G20* **Pandrup** Nordjylland, N Denmark *57°14′N 09°42′E*
79 *J15* **Pandu** Equateur, NW Dem. Rep. Congo *05°03′N 19°14′E*
153 *V12* **Pandu** Assam, NE India *26°08′N 91°37′E*
Paneas *see* Bāniyās
59 *F15* **Panelas** Mato Grosso, W Brazil *09°06′S 60°41′W*
118 *G12* **Panevėžys** Panevėžys, C Lithuania *55°44′N 24°21′E*
118 *G11* **Panevėžys** ◈ *province* NW Lithuania
Panfilov *see* Zharkent
127 *N9* **Panfilovo** Volgogradskaya Oblast', SW Russian Federation *50°25′N 42°55′E*
79 *N17* **Panga** Orientale, N Dem. Rep. Congo *01°52′N 26°18′E*
193 *Y15* **Pangai** Lifuka, C Tonga *19°50′S 174°23′W*
114 *H13* **Pangaío** ▲▲ N Greece
79 *G20* **Pangala** Pool, S Congo *03°26′S 14°38′E*
81 *J22* **Pangani** Tanga, E Tanzania *05°27′S 39°00′E*
81 *I21* **Pangani** ≈ NE Tanzania
186 *K8* **Panggoe** Choiseul Island, NW Solomon Islands *07°00′S 157°05′E*
79 *N20* **Pangi** Maniema, E Dem. Rep. Congo *03°12′S 26°39′E*
Pangim *see* Panaji
168 *H8* **Pangkalanbrandan** Sumatera, W Indonesia *04°00′N 98°15′E*
Pangkalanbun *see* Pangkalanbuun
169 *R13* **Pangkalanbuun** *var.* Pangkalanbun. Borneo, C Indonesia *02°43′S 111°38′E*
169 *N12* **Pangkalpinang** Pulau Bangka, W Indonesia *02°05′S 106°09′E*
11 *U17* **Pangman** Saskatchewan, S Canada *49°37′N 104°33′W*
Pang-Nga *see* Phang-Nga
9 *S6* **Pangnirtung** Baffin Island, Nunavut, NE Canada *66°05′N 65°45′W*
152 *K6* **Pangong Tso** *var.* Bangong Co. ◎ China/India *see also* Bangong Co
Pangong Tso *see* Banggong Co
36 *K7* **Panguitch** Utah, W USA *37°49′N 112°26′W*
186 *J7* **Panguna** Bougainville Island, NE Papua New Guinea *06°22′S 155°20′E*
171 *N8* **Pangutaran Group** *island group* Sulu Archipelago, SW Philippines
25 *N2* **Panhandle** Texas, SW USA *35°21′N 101°24′W*
Panhormus *see* Palermo
171 *W14* **Paniai, Danau** ◎ Papua, E Indonesia
79 *L21* **Pania-Mutombo** Kasai-Oriental, C Dem. Rep. Congo *05°09′S 23°49′E*
187 *P16* **Panié, Mont** ▲ C New Caledonia *20°33′S 164°41′E*
Panikoilli *see* Jājapur
152 *I10* **Pānīpat** Haryāna, N India *29°18′N 77°00′E*
147 *Q14* **Panj** *Rus.* Pyandzh; *prev.* Kirovabad. SW Tajikistan *37°39′N 69°55′E*
147 *P15* **Panj** *Rus.* Pyandzh. ≈ Afghanistan/Tajikistan
149 *O5* **Panjāb** Bāmīān, C Afghanistan *34°21′N 67°00′E*
147 *O12* **Panjakent** *Rus.* Pendzhikent. W Tajikistan *39°28′N 67°33′E*
148 *L14* **Panjgūr** Baluchistān, SW Pakistan *26°58′N 64°05′E*
Panjim *see* Panaji
163 *U12* **Panjin** Liaoning, NE China *41°11′N 122°05′E*
147 *P14* **Panji Poyon** *Rus.* Nizhniy Pyandzh. SW Tajikistan *37°14′N 68°32′E*
149 *S4* **Panjshīr** ◈ *province* NE Afghanistan
149 *Q4* **Panjshīr** ≈ E Afghanistan
Pankota *see* Pâncota
77 *W14* **Pankshin** Plateau, C Nigeria *09°21′N 09°27′E*
163 *Y10* **Pan Ling** ▲▲ N China
Panlong Jiang *see* Lô, Sông
154 *J9* **Panna** Madhya Pradesh, C India *24°43′N 80°11′E*
99 *M16* **Panningen** Limburg, SE Netherlands *51°20′N 05°59′E*
149 *R13* **Pāno Āqil** Sind, SE Pakistan *27°55′N 69°18′E*
121 *P3* **Páno Léfkara** S Cyprus *34°52′N 33°18′E*
121 *O3* **Páno Panagiá** *var.* Pano Panayia. W Cyprus *34°55′N 32°38′E*
Pano Panayia *see* Páno Panagiá
Panopolis *see* Akhmīm
29 *U14* **Panora** Iowa, C USA *41°41′N 94°21′W*
60 *I8* **Panorama** São Paulo, S Brazil *21°22′S 51°51′W*
115 *I24* **Pánormos** Kríti, Greece, E Mediterranean Sea *35°24′N 24°42′E*
Panormus *see* Palermo
163 *W11* **Panshi** Jilin, NE China *42°56′N 126°02′E*
59 *H19* **Pantanal** *var.* Pantanalmato-Grossense. *swamp* SW Brazil
Pantanalmato-Grossense *see* Pantanal
61 *H16* **Pântano Grande** Rio Grande do Sul, S Brazil *30°12′S 52°24′W*
171 *Q16* **Pantar, Pulau** *island* Kepulauan Alor, S Indonesia
21 *X9* **Pantego** North Carolina, SE USA *35°34′N 76°39′E*
107 *G25* **Pantelleria** *anc.* Cossyra, Cosyra. Sicilia, Italy, C Mediterranean Sea *36°47′N 12°00′E*
107 *G25* **Pantelleria, Isola di** *island* SW Italy
Pante Makasar/Pante Macassar/Pante Makassar *see* Ponte Macassar
152 *K10* **Pantnagar** Uttarakhand, N India *29°00′N 79°28′E*
115 *A15* **Pantokrátoras** ▲ Kérkyra, Iónia Nisiá, Greece, C Mediterranean Sea *39°45′N 19°51′E*
Pantschowa *see* Pančevo
41 *P11* **Pánuco** Veracruz-Llave, E Mexico *22°01′N 98°13′W*
41 *P11* **Pánuco, Río** ≈ C Mexico
160 *I12* **Panxian** Guizhou, S China *25°45′N 104°39′E*
168 *I10* **Panyabungan** Sumatera, N Indonesia *0°55′N 99°30′E*
77 *W14* **Panyam** Plateau, C Nigeria *09°28′N 09°13′E*
157 *N13* **Panzhihua** *prev.* Dukou, Tu-k'ou. Sichuan, C China *26°35′N 101°41′E*
79 *I22* **Panzi** Bandundu, SW Dem. Rep. Congo *07°10′S 17°55′E*
42 *E5* **Panzós** Alta Verapaz, E Guatemala *15°21′N 89°40′W*
Pao-chi/Paoki *see* Baoji
Pao-king *see* Shaoyang
107 *N20* **Paola** Calabria, SW Italy *39°21′N 16°03′E*
121 *P16* **Paola** E Malta *35°52′N 14°30′E*
27 *R5* **Paola** Kansas, C USA *38°34′N 94°54′W*
31 *O15* **Paoli** Indiana, N USA *38°35′N 86°25′W*
187 *R14* **Paonangisu** Éfaté, C Vanuatu *17°33′S 168°23′E*
171 *S13* **Paoni** *var.* Pauni. Pulau Seram, E Indonesia *02°48′S 129°03′E*
37 *Q5* **Paonia** Colorado, C USA *38°52′N 107°35′W*
191 *O7* **Paopao** Moorea, W French Polynesia *17°28′S 149°48′W*
Pao-shan *see* Baoshan
Pao-ting *see* Baoding
Pao-t'ou/Paotow *see* Baotou
79 *H14* **Paoua** Ouham-Pendé, W Central African Republic *07°22′N 16°25′E*
Pap *see* Pop
111 *H23* **Pápa** Veszprém, W Hungary *47°20′N 17°29′E*
42 *J12* **Papagayo, Golfo de** *gulf* NW Costa Rica
38 *H11* **Pāpa'ikou** *var.* Papaikou. Hawaii, USA, C Pacific Ocean *19°45′N 155°06′W*
41 *R15* **Papaloapan, Río** ≈ S Mexico
184 *L6* **Papakura** Auckland, North Island, New Zealand *37°03′S 174°57′E*
41 *Q13* **Papantla** *var.* Papantla de Olarte. Veracruz-Llave, E Mexico *20°30′N 97°21′W*
Papantla de Olarte *see* Papantla
191 *P8* **Papara** Tahiti, W French Polynesia *17°45′S 149°33′W*
184 *K4* **Paparoa** Northland, North Island, New Zealand *36°06′S 174°12′E*
185 *G16* **Paparoa Range** ▲▲ South Island, New Zealand
115 *K20* **Pápas, Akrotírio** *headland* Ikaría, Dodekánisa, Greece, Aegean Sea *37°31′N 25°58′E*
96 *L2* **Papa Stour** *island* NE Scotland, United Kingdom
184 *L6* **Papatoetoe** Auckland, North Island, New Zealand *36°58′S 174°52′E*
185 *E25* **Papatowai** Otago, South Island, New Zealand *46°33′S 169°33′E*
96 *K4* **Papa Westray** *island* NE Scotland, United Kingdom
191 *T10* **Papeete** ○ (French Polynesia) Tahiti, W French Polynesia *17°32′S 149°34′W*
100 *F11* **Papenburg** Niedersachsen, NW Germany *53°04′N 07°24′E*
98 *H13* **Papendrecht** Zuid-Holland, SW Netherlands *51°50′N 04°42′E*
191 *Q7* **Papenoo** Tahiti, W French Polynesia *17°29′S 149°25′W*
191 *Q7* **Papenoo Rivière** ≈ Tahiti, W French Polynesia
191 *N7* **Papetoai** Moorea, W French Polynesia *17°29′S 149°52′W*
92 *L3* **Papey** *island* E Iceland
Paphos *see* Páfos
40 *H5* **Papigochic, Río** ≈ NW Mexico
118 *E10* **Papilė** Šiaulai, NW Lithuania *56°08′N 22°51′E*
29 *S15* **Papillion** Nebraska, C USA *41°09′N 96°02′W*
15 *T5* **Papinachois** ≈ Québec, SE Canada
171 *X13* **Papua** *var.* Irian Barat, West Irian, West New Guinea, West Papua; *prev.* Dutch New Guinea, Irian Jaya, Netherlands New Guinea. ◈ *province* E Indonesia
Papua and New Guinea, Territory of *see* Papua New Guinea
186 *C9* **Papua, Gulf of** *gulf* S Papua New Guinea
186 *C8* **Papua New Guinea** *off.* Independent State of Papua New Guinea; *prev.* Territory of Papua and New Guinea. ◆ *commonwealth republic* NW Melanesia
Papua New Guinea, Independent State of *see* Papua New Guinea
192 *H8* **Papua Plateau** *undersea feature* N Coral Sea
112 *G9* **Papuk** ▲▲ NE Croatia
167 *N8* **Papun** Kayin State, S Myanmar (Burma) *18°05′N 97°26′E*
42 *L14* **Paquera** Puntarenas, W Costa Rica *09°52′N 84°56′W*
58 *I13* **Pará** *off.* Estado do Pará. ◈ *state* NE Brazil
55 *V9* **Para** ◈ *district* N Suriname
Pará *see* Belém
180 *I8* **Paraburdoo** Western Australia *23°07′S 117°40′E*
57 *E16* **Paracas, Península de** *peninsula* W Peru
59 *L19* **Paracatu** Minas Gerais, NE Brazil *17°14′S 46°52′W*
192 *E6* **Paracel Islands** ◇ *disputed territory* SE Asia
182 *I6* **Parachilna** South Australia *31°09′S 138°23′E*
149 *R6* **Pārachinār** North-West Frontier Province, NW Pakistan *33°56′N 70°04′E*
112 *N13* **Paraćin** Serbia, C Serbia *43°51′N 21°25′E*
14 *K8* **Paradis** Québec, SE Canada *48°13′N 76°36′W*
39 *N11* **Paradise** *var.* Paradise Hill. Alaska, USA *62°28′N 160°09′W*
35 *O5* **Paradise** California, W USA *39°42′N 121°39′W*
35 *X11* **Paradise** Nevada, W USA *36°05′N 115°10′W*
Paradise Hill *see* Paradise
37 *R11* **Paradise Hills** New Mexico, SW USA *35°12′N 106°42′W*
Paradise of the Pacific *see* Hawai'i
36 *L13* **Paradise Valley** Arizona, SW USA *33°31′N 111°56′W*
35 *T2* **Paradise Valley** Nevada, W USA *41°30′N 117°30′W*
115 *O22* **Paradisi** ✈ (Ródos) Ródos, Dodekánisa, Greece, Aegean Sea *36°24′N 28°08′E*
154 *P12* **Pārādwīp** Orissa, E India *20°17′N 86°42′E*
Pará, Estado do *see* Pará
Paraetonium *see* Mersá Maṭrûḥ
117 *R4* **Parafiyivka** Chernihivs'ka Oblast', N Ukraine *50°53′N 32°40′E*
36 *K7* **Paragonah** Utah, W USA *37°53′N 112°46′W*
27 *X9* **Paragould** Arkansas, C USA *36°02′N 90°30′W*
47 *X8* **Paraguaçu** *var.* Paraguassú. ≈ E Brazil
60 *J9* **Paraguaçu Paulista** São Paulo, S Brazil *22°22′S 50°35′W*
54 *H4* **Paraguaipoa** Zulia, NW Venezuela *11°21′N 71°58′W*
62 *O6* **Paraguarí** Paraguarí, S Paraguay *25°36′S 57°06′W*
62 *O7* **Paraguarí** *off.* Departamento de Paraguarí. ◈ *department* S Paraguay
Paraguarí, Departamento de *see* Paraguarí
57 *O16* **Paraguá, Río** ≈ NE Bolivia
55 *O8* **Paragua, Río** ≈ SE Venezuela
Paraguassú *see* Paraguaçu
62 *N5* **Paraguay** ◆ *republic* C South America
47 *U10* **Paraguay** *var.* Río Paraguay. ≈ C South America
Paraguay, Río *see* Paraguay
Parahiba/Parahyba *see* Paraíba
59 *P15* **Paraíba** *off.* Estado da Paraíba; *prev.* Parahiba, Parahyba. ◈ *state* E Brazil
Paraíba *see* João Pessoa
60 *P9* **Paraíba do Sul, Rio** ≈ SE Brazil
Paraíba, Estado da *see* Paraíba
Parainen *see* Pargas
43 *N14* **Paraíso** Cartago, C Costa Rica *09°51′N 83°50′W*
41 *U14* **Paraíso** Tabasco, SE Mexico *18°26′N 93°10′W*
57 *O17* **Paraiso, Río** ≈ E Bolivia
Parajd *see* Praid
77 *S14* **Parakou** C Benin *09°23′N 02°40′E*
115 *F20* **Paralía Tyrou** Pelopónnisos, S Greece *37°17′N 22°50′E*
121 *Q2* **Paralímni** E Cyprus *35°02′N 34°00′E*
115 *G18* **Paralímni, Límni** ◎ C Greece
55 *W8* **Paramaribo** ● (Suriname) Paramaribo, N Suriname *05°52′N 55°14′W*
55 *W9* **Paramaribo** ◈ *district* N Suriname
55 *W9* **Paramaribo** ✈ Paramaribo, N Suriname *05°52′N 55°14′W*
Paramithiá *see* Paramythiá
56 *C13* **Paramonga** Lima, W Peru *10°42′S 77°50′W*
123 *V12* **Paramushir, Ostrov** *island* SE Russian Federation
115 *C16* **Paramythiá** *var.* Paramithiá. Ípeiros, W Greece *39°28′N 20°31′E*
62 *M10* **Paraná** Entre Ríos, E Argentina *31°48′S 60°29′W*
60 *H11* **Paraná** *off.* Estado do Paraná. ◈ *state* S Brazil
47 *U11* **Paraná** *var.* Alto Paraná. ≈ C South America
Paraná, Estado do *see* Paraná
60 *K12* **Paranaguá** Paraná, S Brazil *25°32′S 48°36′W*
59 *J20* **Paranaíba, Rio** ≈ E Brazil
61 *C19* **Paraná Ibicuy, Río** ≈ E Argentina
59 *H15* **Paranaíta** Mato Grosso, W Brazil *09°35′S 57°01′W*
60 *H9* **Paranapanema, Rio** ≈ S Brazil
60 *K11* **Paranapiacaba, Serra do** ▲▲ S Brazil
60 *H9* **Paranavaí** Paraná, S Brazil *23°02′S 52°36′W*
143 *N5* **Parandak** Markazī, W Iran *35°19′N 50°40′E*
114 *I12* **Paranésti** *var.* Paranestio. Anatolikí Makedonía kai Thráki, NE Greece *41°16′N 24°31′E*
Paranestio *see* Paranésti
191 *W11* **Paraoa** *atoll* Îles Tuamotu, C French Polynesia
184 *L13* **Paraparaumu** Wellington, North Island, New Zealand *40°55′S 175°01′E*
57 *N20* **Parapetí, Río** ≈ SE Bolivia
54 *L10* **Paraque, Cerro** ▲ W Venezuela *06°00′S 67°00′W*
154 *I11* **Parāsiya** Madhya Pradesh, C India *22°11′N 78°50′E*
115 *M23* **Paraspóri, Akrotírio** *headland* Kárpathos, SE Greece *35°54′N 27°15′E*
60 *O10* **Parati** Rio de Janeiro, SE Brazil *23°15′S 44°42′W*
59 *K14* **Parauapebas** Pará, N Brazil *06°03′S 49°48′W*
103 *Q10* **Paray-le-Monial** Saône-et-Loire, C France *46°27′N 04°07′E*
Parbatsar *see* Parvatsar
154 *G13* **Parbhani** Mahārāshtra, C India *19°16′N 76°51′E*
100 *L10* **Parchim** Mecklenburg-Vorpommern, N Germany *53°26′N 11°51′E*
Parchwitz *see* Prochowice
110 *P13* **Parczew** Lubelskie, E Poland *51°40′N 23°E*
60 *L8* **Pardo, Rio** ≈ S Brazil
111 *E16* **Pardubice** *Ger.* Pardubitz. Pardubický Kraj, C Czech Republic *50°01′N 15°47′E*
111 *E17* **Pardubický Kraj** ◈ *region* N Czech Republic
Pardubitz *see* Pardubice
119 *F16* **Parechcha** *Pol.* Porzecze, *Rus.* Porech'ye. Hrodzyenskaya Voblasts', W Belarus *53°53′N 24°08′E*
59 *F17* **Parecis, Chapada dos** *var.* Serra dos Parecis. ▲▲ W Brazil
Parecis, Serra dos *see* Parecis, Chapada dos
104 *M4* **Paredes de Nava** Castilla-León, N Spain *42°09′N 04°42′W*
189 *U12* **Parem** *island* Chuuk, C Micronesia
189 *O12* **Parem Island** *island* E Micronesia
184 *I1* **Parengarenga Harbour** *inlet* North Island, New Zealand
15 *N8* **Parent** Québec, SE Canada *47°55′N 74°36′W*
102 *J14* **Parentis-en-Born** Landes, SW France *44°22′N 01°04′W*
Parenzo *see* Poreč
185 *G20* **Pareora** Canterbury, South Island, New Zealand *44°28′S 171°12′E*
171 *N14* **Parepare** Sulawesi, C Indonesia *04°S 119°40′E*
115 *B16* **Párga** Ípeiros, W Greece *39°18′N 20°19′E*
93 *K20* **Pargas** *Swe.* Parainen. Länsi-Suomi, SW Finland *60°18′N 22°20′E*
64 *O5* **Pargo, Ponta do** *headland* Madeira, Portugal, NE Atlantic Ocean *32°48′N 17°17′W*
Paria, Golfo de *see* Paria, Gulf of
55 *N6* **Pariaguán** Anzoátegui, NE Venezuela *08°51′N 64°43′W*
45 *X17* **Paria, Gulf of** *var.* Golfo de Paria. *gulf* Trinidad and Tobago/Venezuela
57 *I15* **Pariamanu, Río** ≈ E Peru
36 *L8* **Paria River** ≈ Utah, W USA
Parichi *see* Parychy
40 *M14* **Paricutín, Volcán** ⛰ C Mexico *19°25′N 102°20′W*
43 *P16* **Parida, Isla** *island* SW Panama
55 *T8* **Parika** NE Guyana *06°51′N 58°25′W*
93 *O18* **Parikkala** Etelä-Suomi, SE Finland *61°33′N 29°34′E*
58 *E10* **Parima, Serra** *var.* Sierra Parima. ▲ Brazil/Venezuela *see also* Parima, Sierra
55 *N11* **Parima, Sierra** *var.* Serra Parima. ▲ Brazil/Venezuela *see also* Parima, Serra
57 *F17* **Parinacochas, Laguna** ◎ SW Peru
56 *A9* **Pariñas, Punta** *headland* NW Peru *04°45′S 81°22′W*
58 *H12* **Parintins** Amazonas, N Brazil *02°38′S 56°45′W*
103 *O5* **Paris** *anc.* Lutetia, Lutetia Parisiorum, Parisii. ● (France) Paris, N France *48°52′N 02°19′E*
191 *Y2* **Paris** Kiritimati, E Kiribati *01°55′N 157°30′W*
27 *S11* **Paris** Arkansas, C USA *35°17′N 93°46′W*
33 *S16* **Paris** Idaho, NW USA *42°14′N 111°24′W*
31 *N14* **Paris** Illinois, N USA *39°36′N 87°42′W*
20 *M5* **Paris** Kentucky, S USA *38°13′N 84°15′W*
27 *V3* **Paris** Missouri, C USA *39°28′N 92°00′W*
20 *H8* **Paris** Tennessee, S USA *36°19′N 88°20′W*
25 *V5* **Paris** Texas, SW USA *33°41′N 95°33′W*
Parisii *see* Paris
43 *S16* **Parita** Herrera, S Panama *08°01′N 80°30′W*
43 *S16* **Parita, Bahía de** *bay* S Panama
93 *K18* **Parkano** Länsi-Suomi, W Finland *62°03′N 23°E*
Parkan/Párkány *see* Štúrovo
27 *N6* **Park City** Kansas, C USA *37°48′N 97°19′W*
36 *L3* **Park City** Utah, W USA *40°39′N 111°30′W*
36 *I12* **Parker** Arizona, SW USA *34°07′N 114°16′W*
23 *R9* **Parker** Florida, SE USA *30°07′N 85°36′W*
29 *R11* **Parker** South Dakota, N USA *43°24′N 97°08′W*
35 *Z14* **Parker Dam** California, W USA *34°17′N 114°08′W*
29 *W13* **Parkersburg** Iowa, C USA *42°34′N 92°47′W*
21 *Q3* **Parkersburg** West Virginia, NE USA *39°17′N 81°33′W*
29 *T7* **Parkers Prairie** Minnesota, N USA *46°09′N 95°19′W*
171 *P8* **Parker Volcano** ⛰ Mindanao, S Philippines *06°09′N 124°52′E*
181 *W13* **Parkes** New South Wales, SE Australia *33°10′S 148°10′E*
30 *K4* **Park Falls** Wisconsin, N USA *45°57′N 90°25′W*
Parkhar *see* Farkhor
14 *E16* **Parkhill** Ontario, S Canada *43°11′N 81°39′W*
29 *T5* **Park Rapids** Minnesota, N USA *46°55′N 95°03′W*
29 *Q3* **Park River** North Dakota, N USA *48°24′N 97°44′W*
29 *Q11* **Parkston** South Dakota, N USA *43°24′N 97°58′W*
10 *L17* **Parksville** Vancouver Island, British Columbia, SW Canada *49°13′N 124°13′W*
37 *S3* **Parkview Mountain** ▲ Colorado, C USA *40°19′N 106°08′W*
105 *N8* **Parla** Madrid, C Spain *40°13′N 03°48′W*
155 *N14* **Parlākimidi** Andhra Pradesh, E India *18°46′N 84°05′E*
29 *S8* **Parle, Lac qui** ⊠ Minnesota, N USA
155 *G14* **Parli Vaijnāth** Mahārāshtra, C India *18°53′N 76°36′E*
106 *F9* **Parma** Emilia-Romagna, N Italy *44°50′N 10°20′E*
31 *T11* **Parma** Ohio, N USA *41°24′N 81°43′W*
Parnahyba *see* Parnaíba
58 *N13* **Parnaíba** *var.* Parnahyba. Piauí, E Brazil *02°58′S 41°46′W*
65 *J14* **Parnaíba Ridge** *undersea feature* C Atlantic Ocean
58 *N13* **Parnaíba, Rio** ≈ NE Brazil
115 *F18* **Parnassós** ▲▲ C Greece
185 *J17* **Parnassus** Canterbury, South Island, New Zealand *42°41′S 173°18′E*
182 *H10* **Parndana** South Australia *35°48′S 137°13′E*
115 *H19* **Párnitha** ▲▲ C Greece
Parnon *see* Párnonas
115 *F21* **Párnonas** *var.* Parnon. ▲▲ S Greece
118 *G5* **Pärnu** *Ger.* Pernau, *Latv.* Pērnava; *prev. Rus.* Pernov. Pärnumaa, SW Estonia *58°24′N 24°32′E*
118 *G6* **Pärnu** *var.* Parnu Jõgi, *Ger.* Pernau. ≈ SW Estonia
118 *G5* **Pärnu-Jaagupi** *Ger.* Sankt-Jakobi. Pärnumaa, SW Estonia *58°36′N 24°30′E*
Parnu Jõgi *see* Pärnu
118 *G5* **Pärnu Laht** *Ger.* Pernauer Bucht. *bay* SW Estonia
118 *F5* **Pärnumaa** *var.* Pärnu Maakond. ◈ *province* SW Estonia
Pärnu Maakond *see* Pärnumaa
153 *T11* **Paro** W Bhutan *27°23′N 89°31′E*
153 *T11* **Paro** ✈ (Thimphu) W Bhutan *27°23′N 89°31′E*
185 *G17* **Paroa** West Coast, South Island, New Zealand *42°31′S 171°10′E*
163 *X14* **P'aro-ho** *var.* Hwach'ŏn-chŏsuji. ⊠ N South Korea
115 *J21* **Pároikiá** *prev.* Páros. Páros, Kykládes, Greece, Aegean Sea *37°04′N 25°06′E*
183 *N6* **Paroo River** *seasonal river* New South Wales/Queensland, SE Australia
Paropamisus Range *see* Sefīd Kūh, Selseleh-ye
Paropamisus Range *see* Sefīd Kūh, Selseleh-ye
115 *J21* **Páros** *island* Kykládes, Greece, Aegean Sea
Páros *see* Pároikiá
36 *K7* **Parowan** Utah, W USA *37°50′N 112°49′W*
103 *U13* **Parpaillon** ▲▲ SE France
108 *I9* **Parpan** Graubünden, S Switzerland *46°46′N 09°32′E*
62 *G13* **Parral** Maule, C Chile *36°08′S 71°52′W*
Parral *see* Hidalgo del Parral
183 *T9* **Parramatta** New South Wales, SE Australia *33°49′S 150°59′E*
21 *Y6* **Parramore Island** *island* Virginia, NE USA
40 *M8* **Parras** *var.* Parras de la Fuente. Coahuila, NE Mexico *25°26′N 102°07′W*
Parras de la Fuente *see* Parras
42 *M14* **Parrita** Puntarenas, S Costa Rica *09°30′N 84°20′W*
Parry group *see* Mukojima-rettō
14 *G13* **Parry Island** *island* Ontario, S Canada
197 *O9* **Parry Islands** *island group* Nunavut, NW Canada
14 *G12* **Parry Sound** Ontario, S Canada *45°21′N 80°03′W*
110 *F7* **Parsęta** *Ger.* Persante. ≈ NW Poland
28 *L3* **Parshall** North Dakota, N USA *47°57′N 102°07′W*
27 *Q7* **Parsons** Kansas, C USA *37°20′N 95°15′W*
20 *H9* **Parsons** Tennessee, S USA *35°39′N 88°07′W*
21 *T3* **Parsons** West Virginia, NE USA *39°06′N 79°43′W*
Parsonstown *see* Birr
100 *P11* **Parsteiner See** ◎ NE Germany
107 *I24* **Partanna** Sicilia, Italy, C Mediterranean Sea *37°43′N 12°54′E*
108 *J8* **Partenen** Graubünden, E Switzerland *46°58′N 10°01′E*
102 *K9* **Parthenay** Deux-Sèvres, W France *46°39′N 00°13′W*
95 *J19* **Partille** Västra Götaland, S Sweden *57°43′N 12°12′E*
107 *I23* **Partinico** Sicilia, Italy, C Mediterranean Sea *38°03′N 13°07′E*
111 *I20* **Partizánske** *prev.* Šimonovany, *Hung.* Simony. Trenčiansky Kraj, W Slovakia *48°35′N 18°23′E*
58 *H11* **Paru de Oeste, Rio** ≈ N Brazil
182 *K9* **Paruna** South Australia *34°45′S 140°43′E*
58 *I11* **Paru, Rio** ≈ N Brazil
149 *Q5* **Parvān** *Pash.* Parwān. ◈ *province* E Afghanistan
155 *M14* **Pārvatipuram** Andhra Pradesh, E India *17°01′N 81°47′E*
152 *G12* **Parvatsar** *prev.* Parbatsar. Rājasthān, N India *26°52′N 74°49′E*
Parwān *see* Parvān
158 *I15* **Paryang** Xizang Zizhiqu, W China *30°04′N 83°28′E*
119 *M18* **Parychy** *Rus.* Parichi. Homyel'skaya Voblasts', SE Belarus *52°48′N 29°25′E*
83 *J21* **Parys** Free State, C South Africa *26°55′S 27°28′E*
35 *T15* **Pasadena** California, W USA *34°09′N 118°09′W*
25 *W11* **Pasadena** Texas, SW USA *29°41′N 95°13′W*
56 *B8* **Pasaje** El Oro, SW Ecuador *03°23′S 79°50′W*
137 *T9* **P'asanauri** N Georgia *42°21′N 44°40′E*
168 *I13* **Pasapuat** Pulau Pagai Utara, W Indonesia *02°36′S 99°58′E*
167 *N7* **Pasawng** Kayah State, C Myanmar (Burma) *18°50′N 97°16′E*
114 *L13* **Paşayiğit** Edirne, NW Turkey *40°58′N 26°38′E*
23 *N9* **Pascagoula** Mississippi, S USA *30°21′N 88°32′W*
22 *M8* **Pascagoula River** ≈ Mississippi, S USA
116 *F12* **Paşcani** *Hung.* Páskán. Iaşi, NE Romania *47°14′N 26°46′E*
109 *T4* **Pasching** Oberösterreich, N Austria *48°16′N 14°10′E*
32 *K10* **Pasco** Washington, NW USA *46°13′N 119°06′W*
56 *E13* **Pasco** *off.* Departamento de Pasco. ◈ *department* C Peru
Pasco, Departamento de *see* Pasco
191 *N11* **Pascua, Isla de** *var.* Rapa Nui, Easter Island. *island* E Pacific Ocean
63 *G21* **Pascua, Río** ≈ S Chile
103 *N1* **Pas-de-Calais** ◈ *department* N France
100 *P10* **Pasewalk** Mecklenburg-Vorpommern, NE Germany *53°31′N 13°59′E*
11 *T10* **Pasfield Lake** ◎ Saskatchewan, C Canada
Pa-shih Hai-hsia *see* Bashi Channel
Pashkeni *see* Bolyarovo
Pashmakli *see* Smolyan
153 *X10* **Pāsighāt** Arunāchel Pradesh, NE India *28°08′N 95°13′E*
137 *Q12* **Pasinler** Erzurum, NE Turkey *39°59′N 41°41′E*
Pasi Oloy, Qatorkŭhi *see* Zaalayskiy Khrebet
42 *E3* **Pasión, Río de la** ≈ N Guatemala
168 *J12* **Pasirganting** Sumatera, W Indonesia *02°04′S 100°51′E*
Pasirpangarayan *see* Bagansiapiapi
168 *K6* **Pasir Puteh** *var.* Pasir Putih. Kelantan, Peninsular Malaysia *05°50′N 102°24′E*
Pasir Putih *see* Pasir Puteh
169 *R9* **Pasir, Tanjung** *headland* East Malaysia *02°24′N 111°12′E*
95 *N20* **Påskallavik** Kalmar, S Sweden *57°10′N 16°25′E*
Páskán *see* Paşcani
Paskevicha, Zaliv *see* Tushchybas, Zaliv
110 *K7* **Pasłęk** *Ger.* Preußisch Holland. Warmińsko-Mazurskie, NE Poland *54°03′N 19°40′E*
110 *K7* **Pasłęka** *Ger.* Passarge. ≈ N Poland
148 *K16* **Pasni** Baluchistān, SW Pakistan *25°13′N 63°30′E*
63 *I18* **Paso de Indios** Chubut, S Argentina *43°52′S 69°06′W*
54 *L7* **Paso del Caballo** Guárico, N Venezuela *08°19′N 67°08′W*
61 *E15* **Paso de los Libres** Corrientes, NE Argentina *29°43′S 57°09′W*
61 *E18* **Paso de los Toros** Tacuarembó, C Uruguay *32°45′S 56°30′W*
Pasoeroean *see* Pasuruan
35 *P12* **Paso Robles** California, W USA *35°37′N 120°42′W*
15 *Y7* **Paspébiac** Québec, SE Canada *48°03′N 65°10′W*
11 *U14* **Pasquia Hills** ▲▲ Saskatchewan, S Canada
149 *W7* **Pasrūr** Punjab, E Pakistan *32°12′N 74°42′E*
30 *M1* **Passage Island** *island* Michigan, N USA
65 *B24* **Passage Islands** *island group* W Falkland Islands
8 *K5* **Passage Point** *headland* Banks Island, Northwest Territories, NW Canada *73°31′N 115°12′W*
Passarge *see* Pasłęka
115 *C15* **Passarón** *ancient monument* Ípeiros, W Greece
Passarowitz *see* Požarevac
101 *O22* **Passau** Bayern, SE Germany *48°34′N 13°28′E*
22 *M9* **Pass Christian** Mississippi, S USA *30°19′N 89°15′W*
107 *L26* **Passero, Capo** *headland* Sicilia, Italy, C Mediterranean Sea *36°40′N 15°09′E*
171 *P5* **Passi** Panay Island, C Philippines *11°05′N 122°37′E*
61 *H14* **Passo Fundo** Rio Grande do Sul, S Brazil *28°16′S 52°20′W*
60 *H13* **Passo Fundo, Barragem de** ⊠ S Brazil
61 *H15* **Passo Real, Barragem de** ⊠ S Brazil
59 *L20* **Passos** Minas Gerais, NE Brazil *20°45′S 46°38′W*
167 *X10* **Passu Keah** *island* S Paracel Islands
118 *J13* **Pastavy** *Pol.* Postawy, *Rus.* Postavy. Vitsyebskaya Voblasts', NW Belarus *55°07′N 26°50′E*
56 *D7* **Pastaza** ◈ *province* E Ecuador
56 *D9* **Pastaza, Río** ≈ Ecuador/Peru
61 *A21* **Pasteur** Buenos Aires, E Argentina *35°10′S 62°14′W*
15 *V3* **Pasteur** ≈ Québec, SE Canada
147 *Q12* **Pastigav** *Rus.* Pastigov. W Tajikistan *39°27′N 69°16′E*
Pastigov *see* Pastigav
54 *C13* **Pasto** Nariño, SW Colombia *01°12′N 77°17′W*
38 *M10* **Pastol Bay** *bay* Alaska, USA
37 *O8* **Pastora Peak** ▲ Arizona, SW USA *36°48′N 109°10′W*
105 *O8* **Pastrana** Castilla-La Mancha, C Spain *40°24′N 02°55′W*
169 *S16* **Pasuruan** *prev.* Pasoeroean. Jawa, C Indonesia *07°38′S 112°44′E*
118 *F11* **Pasvalys** Panevėžys, N Lithuania *56°03′N 24°24′E*
111 *K21* **Pásztó** Nógrád, N Hungary *47°57′N 19°41′E*
189 *U12* **Pata** *var.* Patta. *atoll* Chuuk Islands, C Micronesia
36 *M16* **Patagonia** Arizona, SW USA *31°32′N 110°45′W*
63 *H20* **Patagonia** *physical region* Argentina/Chile
Patalung *see* Phatthalung
154 *D9* **Pātan** Gujarāt, W India *23°51′N 72°11′E*
154 *J10* **Pātan** Madhya Pradesh, C India *23°19′N 79°41′E*
171 *S11* **Patani** Pulau Halmahera, E Indonesia *0°19′N 128°46′E*
Patani *see* Pattani
15 *V7* **Patapédia Est** ≈ Québec, SE Canada
116 *K13* **Pătâriagele** *prev.* Pătîriagele. Buzău, SE Romania *45°19′N 26°21′E*
Patavium *see* Padova
182 *I5* **Patawarta Hill** ▲ South Australia *30°57′S 138°42′E*
182 *L10* **Patchewollock** Victoria, SE Australia *35°24′S 142°11′E*
184 *K11* **Patea** Taranaki, North Island, New Zealand *39°48′S 174°35′E*
184 *K11* **Patea** ≈ North Island, New Zealand
77 *U15* **Pategi** Kwara, C Nigeria *08°39′N 05°46′E*
81 *K20* **Pate Island** *var.* Patta Island. *island* SE Kenya
105 *S10* **Paterna** País Valenciano, E Spain *39°30′N 00°24′W*
109 *R9* **Paternion** *Slvn.* Špatrjan. Kärnten, S Austria *46°40′N 13°43′E*
107 *L24* **Paternò** *anc.* Hybla, Hybla Major. Sicilia, Italy, C Mediterranean Sea *37°34′N 14°55′E*
32 *J7* **Pateros** Washington, NW USA *48°01′N 119°55′W*
18 *J14* **Paterson** New Jersey, NE USA *40°55′N 74°12′W*
32 *J10* **Paterson** Washington, NW USA *45°56′N 119°37′W*
185 *C25* **Paterson Inlet** *inlet* Stewart Island, New Zealand
98 *N6* **Paterswolde** Drenthe, NE Netherlands *53°07′N 06°32′E*
155 *G24* **Pathanāmthitta** Kerala, SW India *9°05′N 76°38′E*
152 *H7* **Pathānkot** Himāchal Pradesh, N India *32°16′N 75°43′E*

◆ Country
● Country Capital
◇ Dependent Territory
○ Dependent Territory Capital
◈ Administrative Regions
✈ International Airport
▲ Mountain
▲▲ Mountain Range
⛰ Volcano
≈ River
◎ Lake
⊠ Reservoir

PATHEIN – PERNIÖ

166 K8 **Pathein** var. Bassein. Ayeyarwady, SW Myanmar (Burma) 16°46′N 94°45′E
33 W15 **Pathfinder Reservoir** Wyoming, C USA
167 O11 **Pathum Thani** var. Patumdhani, Prathum Thani. Pathum Thani, C Thailand 14°03′N 100°29′E
54 C12 **Patía** var. El Bordo. Cauca, SW Colombia 02°07′N 76°57′W
152 I9 **Patiāla** var. Puttiala. Punjab, NW India 30°21′N 76°27′E
54 B12 **Patía, Río** SW Colombia
188 D15 **Pati Point** headland NE Guam 13°36′N 144°39′E
Pătîriagele see Pătâriagele
56 C13 **Pativilca** Lima, W Peru 10°44′S 77°45′W
166 M1 **Pātkai Bum** var. Patkai Range. ▲▲ Myanmar (Burma)/India
Patkai Range see Pātkai Bum
115 L20 **Pátmos** Pátmos, Dodekánisa, Greece, Aegean Sea 37°18′N 26°32′E
115 L20 **Pátmos** island Dodekánisa, Greece, Aegean Sea
153 P13 **Patna** var. Azimabad. state capital Bihār, N India 25°36′N 85°11′E
154 M12 **Patnāgarh** Orissa, E India 20°42′N 83°12′E
171 O5 **Patnongon** Panay Island, C Philippines 10°56′N 122°03′E
137 S13 **Patnos** Ağrı, E Turkey 39°14′N 42°52′E
60 H12 **Pato Branco** Paraná, S Brazil 26°20′S 52°40′W
31 O16 **Patoka Lake** Indiana, N USA
92 L9 **Patoniva** Lapp. Buoddobohki. Lappi, N Finland 69°44′N 27°01′E
113 K21 **Patos** var. Patosi. Fier, SW Albania 40°40′N 19°37′E
Patos see Patos de Minas
59 K19 **Patos de Minas** var. Patos. Minas Gerais, NE Brazil 18°35′S 46°32′W
Patosi see Patos
61 I17 **Patos, Lagoa dos** lagoon S Brazil
62 J9 **Patquía** La Rioja, C Argentina 30°02′S 66°54′W
115 E19 **Pátra** Eng. Patras; prev. Pátrai. Dytikí Ellás, S Greece 38°14′N 21°45′E
115 D18 **Patraïkós Kólpos** gulf S Greece
Pátrai/Patras see Pátra
92 G2 **Patreksfjördhur** Vestfirdhir, W Iceland 65°33′N 23°54′W
24 M7 **Patricia** Texas, SW USA 32°34′N 102°00′W
63 F21 **Patricio Lynch, Isla** island S Chile
Patta see Pata
Patta Island see Pate Island
167 O16 **Pattani** var. Patani. Pattani, SW Thailand 06°50′N 101°20′E
167 P12 **Pattaya** Chon Buri, S Thailand 12°57′N 100°53′E
19 S4 **Patten** Maine, NE USA 45°58′N 68°27′W
35 O9 **Patterson** California, W USA 37°27′N 121°07′W
22 J10 **Patterson** Louisiana, S USA 29°41′N 91°18′W
35 R7 **Patterson, Mount** ▲ California, W USA 38°27′N 119°16′W
31 P4 **Patterson, Point** headland Michigan, N USA 45°58′N 85°39′W
107 L23 **Patti** Sicilia, Italy, C Mediterranean Sea 38°08′N 14°58′E
107 L23 **Patti, Golfo di** gulf Sicilia, Italy
93 L14 **Pattijoki** Oulu, W Finland 64°41′N 24°40′E
193 Q4 **Patton Escarpment** undersea feature E Pacific Ocean
27 S2 **Pattonsburg** Missouri, C USA 40°03′N 94°08′W
0 D6 **Patton Seamount** undersea feature NE Pacific Ocean 54°40′N 150°30′W
10 J12 **Pattullo, Mount** ▲ British Columbia, W Canada 56°18′N 129°43′W
153 U16 **Patuakhali** var. Patukhali. Barisal, S Bangladesh 22°20′N 90°20′E
42 M5 **Patuca, Río** E Honduras
Patukhali see Patuakhali
Patumdhani see Pathum Thani
40 M14 **Pátzcuaro** Michoacán, SW Mexico 19°30′N 101°38′W
42 C6 **Patzicía** Chimaltenango, S Guatemala 14°38′N 90°52′W
102 K16 **Pau** Pyrénées-Atlantiques, SW France 43°18′N 00°22′W
102 J12 **Pauillac** Gironde, SW France 45°12′N 00°44′W
166 L5 **Pauk** Magway, W Myanmar (Burma) 21°25′N 94°30′E
8 I6 **Paulatuk** Northwest Territories, NW Canada 69°23′N 124°W
42 K5 **Paulayá, Río** NE Honduras
22 M6 **Paulding** Mississippi, S USA 32°01′N 89°01′W
31 Q12 **Paulding** Ohio, N USA 41°08′N 84°34′W
29 S12 **Paullina** Iowa, C USA 42°58′N 95°41′W
59 P15 **Paulo Afonso** Bahia, E Brazil 09°21′S 38°14′W
38 M16 **Pauloff Harbor** var. Pavlor Harbour. Sanak Island, Alaska, USA 54°26′N 162°43′W
27 N12 **Pauls Valley** Oklahoma, C USA 34°46′N 97°14′W
166 L7 **Paungde** Bago, C Myanmar (Burma) 18°30′N 95°30′E
Pauni see Paoni
152 K9 **Pauri** Uttaranchal, N India 30°08′N 78°48′E
Pautalia see Kyustendil
142 J5 **Pāveh** Kermānshāhān, NW Iran 35°02′N 46°15′E
114 I9 **Pavel Banya** Stara Zagora, C Bulgaria 42°35′N 25°19′E
126 L5 **Pavelets** Ryazanskaya Oblast', W Russian Federation 53°47′N 39°22′E
106 D8 **Pavia** anc. Ticinum. Lombardia, N Italy 45°10′N 09°10′E
118 C9 **Pāvilosta** Liepāja, W Latvia 56°52′N 21°12′E
125 P14 **Pavino** Kostromskaya Oblast', NW Russian Federation 59°10′N 46°09′E
114 J8 **Pavlikeni** Veliko Tŭrnovo, N Bulgaria 43°14′N 25°20′E
145 T8 **Pavlodar** Pavlodar, NE Kazakhstan 52°21′N 76°59′E
145 S9 **Pavlodar** off. Pavlodarskaya Oblast', Kaz. Pavlodar Oblysy. province NE Kazakhstan
Pavlodar Oblysy/Pavlodarskaya Oblast' see Pavlodar
Pavlograd see Pavlohrad
117 U7 **Pavlohrad** Rus. Pavlograd. Dnipropetrovs'ka Oblast', E Ukraine 48°32′N 35°50′E
Pavlor Harbour see Pauloff Harbor
145 R9 **Pavlovka** Akmola, C Kazakhstan 51°22′N 72°35′E
127 V4 **Pavlovka** Respublika Bashkortostan, W Russian Federation 55°28′N 56°36′E
127 Q7 **Pavlovka** Ul'yanovskaya Oblast', W Russian Federation 52°40′N 47°08′E
127 N3 **Pavlovo** Nizhegorodskaya Oblast', W Russian Federation 55°59′N 43°03′E
126 L9 **Pavlovsk** Voronezhskaya Oblast', W Russian Federation 50°26′N 40°08′E
126 L13 **Pavlovskaya** Krasnodarskiy Kray, SW Russian Federation 46°06′N 39°52′E
117 S7 **Pavlysh** Kirovohrads'ka Oblast', C Ukraine 48°54′N 33°20′E
106 F10 **Pavullo nel Frignano** Emilia-Romagna, C Italy 44°19′N 10°52′E
27 P8 **Pawhuska** Oklahoma, C USA 36°42′N 96°21′W
21 U13 **Pawleys Island** South Carolina, SE USA 33°27′N 79°07′W
167 N6 **Pawn** C Myanmar (Burma)
30 K14 **Pawnee** Illinois, N USA 39°35′N 89°34′W
27 O9 **Pawnee** Oklahoma, C USA 36°21′N 96°50′W
37 U2 **Pawnee Buttes** ▲ Colorado, C USA 40°49′N 103°58′W
29 S17 **Pawnee City** Nebraska, C USA 40°06′N 96°09′W
26 K5 **Pawnee River** Kansas, C USA
31 O10 **Paw Paw** Michigan, N USA 42°12′N 86°09′W
31 O10 **Paw Paw Lake** Michigan, N USA 42°12′N 86°16′W
19 O12 **Pawtucket** Rhode Island, NE USA 41°52′N 71°22′W
Pax Augusta see Badajoz
115 I25 **Paximádia** island SE Greece
Pax Julia see Beja
115 B16 **Paxoí** island Iónia Nisiá, Greece, C Mediterranean Sea
39 S10 **Paxson** Alaska, USA 62°58′N 145°27′W
147 O11 **Paxtakor** Jizzax Viloyati, C Uzbekistan 40°21′N 67°54′E
30 M13 **Paxton** Illinois, N USA 40°27′N 88°06′W
124 J11 **Pay** Respublika Kareliya, NW Russian Federation 61°10′N 34°24′E
166 M8 **Payagyi** Bago, SW Myanmar (Burma) 17°28′N 96°32′E
108 C9 **Payerne** Ger. Peterlingen. Vaud, W Switzerland 46°49′N 06°57′E
32 M13 **Payette** Idaho, NW USA 44°04′N 116°55′W
32 M13 **Payette River** Idaho, NW USA
125 V2 **Pay-Khoy, Khrebet** ▲▲ NW Russian Federation
Payne see Kangirsuk
12 K4 **Payne, Lac** Québec, NE Canada
29 T8 **Paynesville** Minnesota, N USA 45°22′N 94°42′W
169 S8 **Payong, Tanjung** cape East Malaysia
Payo Obispo see Chetumal
61 D18 **Paysandú** Paysandú, W Uruguay 32°21′S 58°05′W
61 D17 **Paysandú** department W Uruguay
102 I7 **Pays de la Loire** region NW France
36 L12 **Payson** Arizona, SW USA 34°13′N 111°19′W
36 L4 **Payson** Utah, W USA 40°02′N 111°43′W
125 W4 **Payyer, Gora** ▲ NW Russian Federation 66°49′N 64°33′E
Payzawat see Jiashi
137 Q11 **Pazar** Rize, NE Turkey 41°10′N 40°53′E
136 F10 **Pazarbaşı Burnu** headland NW Turkey 41°12′N 30°18′E
136 M16 **Pazarcık** Kahramanmaraş, S Turkey 37°31′N 37°19′E
114 I10 **Pazardzhik** prev. Tatar Pazardzhik. Pazardzhik, SW Bulgaria 42°11′N 24°21′E
64 H11 **Pazardzhik** province C Bulgaria
54 H9 **Paz de Ariporo** Casanare, E Colombia 05°54′N 71°52′W
112 A10 **Pazin** Ger. Mitterburg, It. Pisino. Istra, NW Croatia 45°14′N 13°56′E
42 D7 **Paz, Río** El Salvador/Guatemala
113 O18 **Pčinja** N Macedonia
193 V15 **Pea** Tongatapu, S Tonga 21°10′S 175°14′W
27 O6 **Peabody** Kansas, C USA 38°10′N 97°06′W
11 O12 **Peace** Alberta/British Columbia, W Canada
Peace Garden State see North Dakota
11 Q10 **Peace Point** Alberta, C Canada 59°11′N 112°12′W
11 O12 **Peace River** Alberta, W Canada 56°15′N 117°18′W
23 W13 **Peace River** Florida, SE USA
11 N17 **Peachland** British Columbia, SW Canada 49°49′N 119°48′W
36 J10 **Peach Springs** Arizona, SW USA 35°33′N 113°27′W
Peach State see Georgia
23 S4 **Peachtree City** Georgia, SE USA 33°24′N 84°36′W
189 Y13 **Peacock Point** point SE Wake Island
97 M18 **Peak District** physical region C England, United Kingdom
183 Q7 **Peak Hill** New South Wales, SE Australia 32°39′S 148°12′E
65 G15 **Peak, The** ▲ C Ascension Island
105 O13 **Peal de Becerro** Andalucía, S Spain 37°55′N 03°08′W
189 X11 **Peale Island** island N Wake Island
37 O6 **Peale, Mount** ▲ Utah, W USA 38°26′N 109°13′W
39 O4 **Peard Bay** bay Alaska, USA
23 Q7 **Pea River** Alabama/Florida, S USA
25 W11 **Pearland** Texas, SW USA 29°33′N 95°17′W
38 D9 **Pearl City** O'ahu, Hawaii, USA, C Pacific Ocean 21°24′N 157°58′W
38 D9 **Pearl Harbor** inlet O'ahu, Hawai'i, USA, C Pacific Ocean
Pearl Islands see Perlas, Archipiélago de las
Pearl Lagoon see Perlas, Laguna de
22 M5 **Pearl River** Louisiana/Mississippi, S USA
25 Q13 **Pearsall** Texas, SW USA 28°54′N 99°07′W
23 U7 **Pearson** Georgia, SE USA 31°18′N 82°51′W
25 P4 **Pease River** Texas, SW USA
12 F7 **Peawanuk** Ontario, C Canada 54°55′N 85°31′W
12 E8 **Peawanuk** Ontario, S Canada
83 P16 **Pebane** Zambézia, NE Mozambique 17°14′S 38°10′E
65 C23 **Pebble Island** island N Falkland Islands
Peć see Pejë
25 R8 **Pecan Bayou** Texas, SW USA
22 H10 **Pecan Island** Louisiana, S USA 29°39′N 92°26′W
60 L12 **Peças, Ilha das** island S Brazil
30 L10 **Pecatonica River** Illinois/Wisconsin, N USA
108 G10 **Peccia** Ticino, S Switzerland 46°24′N 08°39′E
Pechenegi see Pechenihy
Pechenezhskoye Vodokhranilishche see Pecheniz'ke Vodoskhovyshche
124 I2 **Pechenga** Fin. Petsamo. Murmanskaya Oblast', NW Russian Federation 69°34′N 31°14′E
117 V5 **Pechenihy** Rus. Pechenegi. Kharkivs'ka Oblast', E Ukraine 49°49′N 36°57′E
117 V5 **Pecheniz'ke Vodoskhovyshche** Rus. Pechenezhskoye Vodokhranilishche. E Ukraine
125 U7 **Pechora** Respublika Komi, NW Russian Federation 65°09′N 57°09′E
125 R6 **Pechora** NW Russian Federation
Pechora Bay see Pechorskaya Guba
Pechora Sea see Pechorskoye More
125 S3 **Pechorskaya Guba** Eng. Pechora Bay. bay NW Russian Federation
122 H7 **Pechorskoye More** Eng. Pechora Sea. sea NW Russian Federation
124 F14 **Pechory** Est. Petseri. Pskovskaya Oblast', W Russian Federation 57°49′N 27°37′E
116 E11 **Pecica** Ger. Petschka, Hung. Ópécska. Arad, W Romania 46°09′N 21°06′E
24 K8 **Pecos** Texas, SW USA 31°25′N 103°30′W
25 N11 **Pecos River** New Mexico/Texas, SW USA
111 I25 **Pécs** Ger. Fünfkirchen, Lat. Sopianae. Baranya, SW Hungary 46°05′N 18°11′E
43 T17 **Pedasí** Los Santos, S Panama 07°36′N 80°04′W
Pedde see Pedja
183 O17 **Pedder, Lake** Tasmania, SE Australia
44 M10 **Pedernales** SW Dominican Republic 18°02′N 71°41′W
55 Q5 **Pedernales** Delta Amacuro, NE Venezuela 09°58′N 62°15′W
25 R10 **Pedernales River** Texas, SW USA
62 H6 **Pedernales, Salar de** salt lake N Chile
Pedhoulas see Pedoulás
55 X11 **Pédima** var. Malavate. SW French Guiana 03°15′N 54°08′W
182 F1 **Pedirka** South Australia 26°41′S 135°11′E
171 S11 **Pediwang** Pulau Halmahera, E Indonesia 01°29′N 127°57′E
118 I5 **Pedja** var. Pedja Jõgi, Ger. Pedde. E Estonia
Pedja Jõgi see Pedja
121 O3 **Pedoulás** var. Pedhoulas. W Cyprus 34°58′N 32°51′E
59 N18 **Pedra Azul** Minas Gerais, NE Brazil 16°02′S 41°17′W
104 I3 **Pedrafita, Porto de** var. Puerto de Piedrafita. pass NW Spain
76 E9 **Pedra Lume** Sal, NE Cape Verde 16°47′N 22°54′W
43 P16 **Pedregal** Chiriquí, W Panama 09°04′N 79°25′W
54 J4 **Pedregal** Falcón, N Venezuela 11°04′N 70°08′W
40 L9 **Pedriceña** Durango, C Mexico 25°08′N 103°46′W
60 L11 **Pedro Barros** São Paulo, S Brazil 24°12′S 47°22′W
39 Q13 **Pedro Bay** Alaska, USA 59°47′N 154°06′W
62 H4 **Pedro de Valdivia** var. Oficina Pedro de Valdivia. Antofagasta, N Chile 22°33′S 69°38′W
62 P4 **Pedro Juan Caballero** Amambay, E Paraguay 22°34′S 55°41′W
63 L15 **Pedro Luro** Buenos Aires, E Argentina 39°30′S 62°38′W
105 O10 **Pedro Muñoz** Castilla-La Mancha, C Spain 39°25′N 02°56′W
155 J22 **Pedro, Point** headland NW Sri Lanka 09°54′N 80°08′E
182 K9 **Peebinga** South Australia 34°56′S 140°56′E
96 J13 **Peebles** SE Scotland, United Kingdom 55°40′N 03°15′W
31 S15 **Peebles** Ohio, N USA 38°57′N 83°23′W
96 J12 **Peebles** cultural region SE Scotland, United Kingdom
18 K13 **Peekskill** New York, NE USA 41°17′N 73°54′W
97 I16 **Peel** W Isle of Man 54°13′N 04°04′W
8 G7 **Peel** Northwest Territories/Yukon Territory, NW Canada
8 K5 **Peel Point** headland Victoria Island, Northwest Territories, NW Canada 73°22′N 114°33′W
8 M5 **Peel Sound** passage Nunavut, N Canada
100 N9 **Peene** NE Germany
99 K17 **Peer** Limburg, NE Belgium 51°08′N 05°29′E
14 H14 **Pefferlaw** Ontario, S Canada 44°18′N 79°11′W
185 I18 **Pegasus Bay** bay South Island, New Zealand
121 O3 **Pégeia** var. Peyia. SW Cyprus 34°52′N 32°24′E
109 V7 **Peggau** Steiermark, SE Austria 47°10′N 15°20′E
101 L19 **Pegnitz** Bayern, SE Germany 49°45′N 11°33′E
101 L19 **Pegnitz** SE Germany
105 T11 **Pego** País Valenciano, E Spain 38°51′N 00°08′W
Pegu see Bago
Pegu see Bago
189 N13 **Pehleng** Pohnpei, E Micronesia
114 M12 **Pehlivanköy** Kırklareli, NW Turkey 41°21′N 26°55′E
77 R14 **Péhonko** C Benin 10°14′N 01°57′E
61 B21 **Pehuajó** Buenos Aires, E Argentina 35°48′S 61°53′W
Pei-ching see Beijing/Beijing Shi
100 J13 **Peine** Niedersachsen, C Germany 52°19′N 10°14′E
Pei-p'ing see Beijing/Beijing Shi
Peipsi Järv/Peipus-See see Peipus, Lake
118 J5 **Peipus, Lake** Est. Peipsi Järv, Ger. Peipus-See, Rus. Chudskoye Ozero. Estonia/Russian Federation
115 H19 **Peiraías** prev. Piraiévs, Eng. Piraeus. Attikí, C Greece 37°57′N 23°42′E
Peisern see Pyzdry
60 I8 **Peixe, Rio do** S Brazil
59 I16 **Peixoto de Azevedo** Mato Grosso, W Brazil 10°18′S 55°03′W
168 O11 **Pejantan, Pulau** island W Indonesia
113 L16 **Pejë** Serb. Peć. W Kosovo 42°40′N 20°19′E
167 R7 **Pèk** var. Xieng Khouang; prev. Xiangkhoang. Xiangkhoang, N Laos 19°19′N 103°23′E
112 N11 **Pek** E Serbia
169 Q16 **Pekalongan** Jawa, C Indonesia 06°54′S 109°37′E
168 K11 **Pekanbaru** var. Pakanbaru. Sumatera, W Indonesia 0°31′N 101°27′E
30 L12 **Pekin** Illinois, N USA 40°34′N 89°38′W
Peking see Beijing/Beijing Shi
Pelabohan Kelang/Pelabuhan Kelang see Pelabuhan Klang
168 J9 **Pelabuhan Klang** var. Kuala Pelabohan Kelang, Pelabohan Kelang, Pelabuhan Kelang, Port Klang, Port Swettenham. Selangor, Peninsular Malaysia 02°57′N 101°24′E
120 L11 **Pelagie, Isole** island group SW Italy
Pelagosa see Palagruža
22 L5 **Pelahatchie** Mississippi, S USA 32°19′N 89°48′W
169 T14 **Pelaihari** var. Pleihari. Borneo, C Indonesia 03°48′S 114°45′E
103 U14 **Pelat, Mont** ▲ SE France 44°16′N 06°46′E
116 F12 **Peleaga, Vârful** prev. Vîrful Peleaga. ▲ W Romania 45°23′N 22°52′E
Peleaga, Vîrful see Peleaga, Vârful
123 O11 **Peleduy** Respublika Sakha (Yakutiya), NE Russian Federation 59°39′N 112°36′E
14 C18 **Pelee Island** island Ontario, S Canada
45 Q11 **Pelée, Montagne** ▲ N Martinique 14°47′N 61°10′W
14 D18 **Pelee, Point** headland Ontario, S Canada 41°56′N 82°30′W
171 P12 **Pelei** Pulau Peleng, N Indonesia 01°26′S 123°27′E
Peleliu see Beliliou
171 P12 **Peleng, Pulau** island Kepulauan Banggai, N Indonesia
23 T7 **Pelham** Georgia, SE USA 31°07′N 84°09′W
111 E18 **Pelhřimov** Ger. Pilgram. Vysočina, C Czech Republic 49°26′N 15°14′E
39 W13 **Pelican** Chichagof Island, Alaska, USA 57°52′N 136°05′W
191 Z3 **Pelican Lagoon** Kiritimati, E Kiribati
29 U6 **Pelican Lake** Minnesota, N USA
29 V3 **Pelican Lake** Minnesota, N USA
30 L5 **Pelican Lake** Wisconsin, N USA
44 G1 **Pelican Point** Grand Bahama Island, N Bahamas 26°39′N 78°09′W
83 B19 **Pelican Point** headland W Namibia 22°55′S 14°25′E
29 S6 **Pelican Rapids** Minnesota, N USA 46°34′N 96°04′W
Pelican State see Louisiana
11 U13 **Pelikan Narrows** Saskatchewan, C Canada 55°11′N 102°51′W
115 L18 **Pelinaío** ▲ Chíos, E Greece 38°31′N 26°01′E
Pelinnaeum see Pelinnaío
115 E16 **Pelinnaío** anc. Pelinnaeum. ruins Thessalía, C Greece
113 N20 **Pelister** ▲ SW FYR Macedonia 41°00′N 21°12′E
113 G15 **Pelješac** peninsula S Croatia
92 M12 **Pelkosenniemi** Lappi, NE Finland 67°06′N 27°30′E
29 W15 **Pella** Iowa, C USA 41°24′N 92°55′W
114 F13 **Pélla** site of ancient city Kentrikí Makedonía, N Greece
23 Q3 **Pell City** Alabama, S USA 33°35′N 86°17′W
61 A22 **Pellegrini** Buenos Aires, E Argentina 36°16′S 63°07′W
92 K12 **Pello** Lappi, NW Finland 66°47′N 24°E
100 G7 **Pellworm** island N Germany
10 H6 **Pelly** Yukon Territory, NW Canada
Pelly Bay see Kugaaruk
10 I8 **Pelly Mountains** ▲▲ Yukon Territory, W Canada
Pélmonostor see Beli Manastir
37 P13 **Pelona Mountain** ▲ New Mexico, SW USA 33°40′N 108°06′W
Peloponnese/Peloponnesus see Pelopónnisos
115 E20 **Pelopónnisos** Eng. Peloponnese. region S Greece
115 E20 **Pelopónnisos** var. Morea, Eng. Peloponnese; anc. Peloponnesus. peninsula S Greece
107 L23 **Peloritani, Monti** anc. Pelorus and Neptunius. ▲▲ Sicilia, Italy, C Mediterranean Sea
107 M22 **Peloro, Capo** var. Punta del Faro. headland S Italy 38°15′N 15°39′E
Pelorus and Neptunius see Peloritani, Monti
61 H17 **Pelotas** Rio Grande do Sul, S Brazil 31°45′S 52°20′W
61 I14 **Pelotas, Rio** S Brazil
92 K10 **Peltovuoma** Lapp. Bealdovuopmi. Lappi, N Finland 68°23′N 24°12′E
19 R4 **Pemadumcook Lake** Maine, NE USA
169 Q16 **Pemalang** Jawa, C Indonesia 06°53′S 109°07′E
169 P10 **Pemangkat** var. Pamangkat. Borneo, C Indonesia 01°11′N 109°00′E
Pemar see Paimio
168 I9 **Pematangsiantar** Sumatera, W Indonesia 02°59′N 99°01′E
83 Q14 **Pemba** prev. Port Amelia, Porto Amélia. Cabo Delgado, NE Mozambique 13°S 40°35′E
81 J22 **Pemba** region E Tanzania
81 K21 **Pemba** island E Tanzania
83 Q14 **Pemba, Baia de** inlet NE Mozambique
81 J21 **Pemba Channel** channel E Tanzania
81 J22 **Pemba North** region E Tanzania
81 J22 **Pemba South** region E Tanzania
180 J14 **Pemberton** Western Australia 34°27′S 116°09′E
10 M16 **Pemberton** British Columbia, SW Canada 50°19′N 122°49′W
29 Q2 **Pembina** North Dakota, N USA 48°58′N 97°14′W
11 P15 **Pembina** Alberta, SW Canada
29 Q2 **Pembina** Canada/USA
171 X16 **Pembre** Papua, E Indonesia 07°49′S 138°01′E
14 K12 **Pembroke** Ontario, SE Canada 45°49′N 77°08′W
97 H21 **Pembroke** SW Wales, United Kingdom 51°41′N 04°55′W
23 W6 **Pembroke** Georgia, SE USA 32°09′N 81°35′W
21 U11 **Pembroke** North Carolina, SE USA 34°40′N 79°12′W
21 R7 **Pembroke** Virginia, NE USA 37°19′N 80°38′W
97 H21 **Pembroke** cultural region SW Wales, United Kingdom
Pembuang, Sungai see Seruyan, Sungai
43 S15 **Peña Blanca, Cerro** ▲ C Panama 08°39′N 80°39′W
104 K8 **Peña de Francia, Sierra de la** ▲▲ W Spain
104 G6 **Penafiel** var. Peñafiel. Porto, N Portugal 41°12′N 08°17′W
105 N6 **Peñafiel** Castilla-León, N Spain 41°36′N 04°07′W
Peñafiel see Penafiel
105 S8 **Peñagolosa** ▲ E Spain 40°10′N 00°15′W
105 N7 **Peñalara, Pico de** ▲ C Spain 40°52′N 03°55′W
171 X16 **Penambo, Banjaran** var. Banjaran Tama Abu, Penambo Range. ▲▲ Indonesia/Malaysia
Penambo Range see Penambo, Banjaran
41 O10 **Peña Nevada, Cerro** ▲ C Mexico 23°46′N 99°52′W
Penang see Pinang
Penang see George Town
Penang see Pinang, Pulau, Peninsular Malaysia
60 J8 **Penápolis** São Paulo, S Brazil 21°23′S 50°02′W
104 L7 **Peñaranda de Bracamonte** Castilla-León, N Spain 40°54′N 05°13′W
105 S8 **Peñarroya** ▲ E Spain 40°24′N 00°42′W
104 L12 **Peñarroya-Pueblonuevo** Andalucía, S Spain 38°21′N 05°18′W
97 K22 **Penarth** S Wales, United Kingdom 51°27′N 03°11′W
104 K1 **Peñas, Cabo de** headland N Spain 43°39′N 05°52′W
63 F20 **Penas, Golfo de** gulf S Chile
Pen-ch'i see Benxi
79 H14 **Pendé** var. Logone Oriental. Central African Republic/Chad
76 I14 **Pendembu** E Sierra Leone 09°06′N 12°12′W
29 R13 **Pender** Nebraska, C USA 42°06′N 96°42′W
Penderma see Bandırma
32 K11 **Pendleton** Oregon, NW USA 45°40′N 118°47′W
32 M7 **Pend Oreille, Lake** Idaho, NW USA
32 M7 **Pend Oreille River** Idaho/Washington, NW USA
Pendzhikent see Panjakent
Peneius see Pineiós
104 G8 **Penela** Coimbra, N Portugal 40°02′N 08°23′W
14 G13 **Penetanguishene** Ontario, S Canada 44°45′N 79°55′W
151 H15 **Penganga** C India
161 T12 **P'engchia Yu** island N Taiwan
79 M21 **Penge** Kasai-Oriental, C Dem. Rep. Congo 05°29′S 24°38′E
Penghu Archipelago/P'enghu Ch'üntao/Penghu Islands see P'enghu Liehtao
161 R14 **P'enghu Liehtao** var. P'enghu Ch'üntao, Penghu Islands, Eng. Penghu Archipelago, Pescadores, Jap. Hoko-guntō, Hoko-shotō. island group W Taiwan
Penghu Shuidao/P'enghu Shuitao see Pescadores Channel
161 R4 **Penglai** var. Dengzhou. Shandong, E China 37°50′N 120°45′E
Peng-pu see Bengbu
Penhsihu see Benxi
Penibético, Sistema see Béticos, Sistemas
104 F10 **Peniche** Leiria, W Portugal 39°21′N 09°23′W
169 U17 **Penida, Nusa** island S Indonesia
Peninsular State see Florida
105 T8 **Peñíscola** País Valenciano, E Spain 40°22′N 00°24′E
40 M13 **Pénjamo** Guanajuato, C Mexico 20°26′N 101°44′W
Penki see Benxi
102 F7 **Penmarch, Pointe de** headland NW France 47°46′N 04°34′W
107 L15 **Penna, Punta della** headland C Italy 42°10′N 14°43′E
107 K14 **Penne** Abruzzo, C Italy 42°28′N 13°57′E
Penner see Penneru
155 J18 **Penneru** var. Penner. C India
182 I10 **Penneshaw** South Australia 35°45′S 137°57′E
18 C14 **Penn Hills** Pennsylvania, NE USA 40°28′N 79°53′W
Penninae, Alpes/Pennine, Alpi see Pennine Alps
108 D11 **Pennine Alps** Fr. Alpes Pennines, It. Alpi Pennine, Lat. Alpes Penninae. ▲▲ Italy/Switzerland
Pennine Chain see Pennines
97 L15 **Pennines** var. Pennine Chain. ▲▲ N England, United Kingdom
Pennines, Alpes see Pennine Alps
21 O8 **Pennington Gap** Virginia, NE USA 36°45′N 83°01′W
18 I16 **Penns Grove** New Jersey, NE USA 39°42′N 75°27′W
18 I16 **Pennsville** New Jersey, NE USA 39°37′N 75°29′W
18 E14 **Pennsylvania** off. Commonwealth of Pennsylvania, also known as Keystone State. state NE USA
18 G10 **Penn Yan** New York, NE USA 42°39′N 77°02′W
124 H16 **Peno** Tverskaya Oblast', W Russian Federation 56°55′N 32°44′E
19 R7 **Penobscot Bay** bay Maine, NE USA
19 S5 **Penobscot River** Maine, NE USA
182 K12 **Penola** South Australia 37°24′S 140°50′E
40 K9 **Peñón Blanco** Durango, C Mexico 25°12′N 100°50′W
182 E7 **Penong** South Australia 31°57′S 133°01′E
43 S16 **Penonomé** Coclé, C Panama 08°29′N 80°22′W
190 L13 **Penrhyn** atoll N Cook Islands
192 M9 **Penrhyn Basin** undersea feature C Pacific Ocean
183 S9 **Penrith** New South Wales, SE Australia 33°45′S 150°48′E
97 K15 **Penrith** NW England, United Kingdom 54°40′N 02°44′W
23 O9 **Pensacola** Florida, SE USA 30°25′N 87°13′W
23 O9 **Pensacola Bay** bay Florida, SE USA
195 N7 **Pensacola Mountains** ▲▲ Antarctica
182 L12 **Penshurst** Victoria, SE Australia 37°54′S 142°19′E
187 R13 **Pentecost** Fr. Pentecôte. island C Vanuatu
15 V4 **Pentecôte** Québec, SE Canada
Pentecôte see Pentecost
15 V4 **Pentecôte, Lac** Québec, SE Canada
8 H15 **Penticton** British Columbia, SW Canada 49°29′N 119°38′W
96 J6 **Pentland Firth** strait N Scotland, United Kingdom
96 J12 **Pentland Hills** hill range S Scotland, United Kingdom
171 Q12 **Penu** Pulau Taliabu, E Indonesia 01°43′S 125°09′E
155 H18 **Penukonda** Andhra Pradesh, E India 14°04′N 77°38′E
166 L7 **Penwegon** Bago, C Myanmar (Burma) 18°14′N 96°34′E
24 M8 **Penwell** Texas, SW USA 31°45′N 102°32′W
97 J21 **Pen y Fan** ▲ SE Wales, United Kingdom 51°52′N 03°25′W
97 L16 **Pen-y-ghent** ▲ N England, United Kingdom 54°11′N 02°15′W
127 O6 **Penza** Penzenskaya Oblast', W Russian Federation 53°11′N 45°E
97 G25 **Penzance** SW England, United Kingdom 50°08′N 05°33′W
127 N6 **Penzenskaya Oblast'** province W Russian Federation
123 U7 **Penzhina** E Russian Federation
123 U9 **Penzhinskaya Guba** bay E Russian Federation
Penzig see Pieńsk
36 K13 **Peoria** Arizona, SW USA 33°34′N 112°14′W
30 L12 **Peoria** Illinois, N USA 40°42′N 89°35′W
30 L12 **Peoria Heights** Illinois, N USA 40°45′N 89°34′W
31 N11 **Peotone** Illinois, N USA 41°19′N 87°47′W
18 J11 **Pepacton Reservoir** New York, NE USA
76 I15 **Pepel** W Sierra Leone 08°39′N 13°04′W
30 I6 **Pepin, Lake** Minnesota/Wisconsin, N USA
99 L20 **Pepinster** Liège, E Belgium 50°34′N 05°49′E
113 L20 **Peqin** var. Peqini. Elbasan, C Albania 41°03′N 19°46′E
Peqini see Peqin
40 D7 **Pequeña, Punta** headland NW Mexico 26°13′N 112°34′W
168 J8 **Perak** state Peninsular Malaysia
105 R7 **Perales del Alfambra** Aragón, NE Spain 40°38′N 01°00′W
115 C15 **Pérama** var. Perama. Ípeiros, W Greece 39°42′N 20°51′E
Perama see Pérama
155 I22 **Perambalūr** Tamil Nādu, SE India 11°14′N 78°51′E
92 M13 **Perä-Posio** Lappi, NE Finland 66°10′N 27°56′E
15 Z6 **Percé** Québec, SE Canada 48°32′N 64°14′W
15 Z6 **Percé, Rocher** island Québec, S Canada
102 L5 **Perche, Collines de** ▲▲ N France
109 X4 **Perchtoldsdorf** Niederösterreich, NE Austria 48°06′N 16°16′E
180 L6 **Percival Lakes** lakes Western Australia
105 T3 **Perdido, Monte** ▲ NE Spain 42°41′N 00°01′E
23 O8 **Perdido River** Alabama/Florida, S USA
Perece Vela Basin see West Mariana Basin
116 G7 **Perechyn** Zakarpats'ka Oblast', W Ukraine 48°45′N 22°28′E
54 E10 **Pereira** Risaralda, W Colombia 04°47′N 75°46′W
60 I7 **Pereira Barreto** São Paulo, S Brazil 20°37′S 51°07′W
59 G15 **Pereirinha** Pará, N Brazil 08°18′S 57°30′W
127 N10 **Perelazovskiy** Volgogradskaya Oblast', SW Russian Federation 49°10′N 42°30′E
127 S7 **Perelyub** Saratovskaya Oblast', W Russian Federation 51°52′N 50°19′E
31 P7 **Pere Marquette River** Michigan, N USA
Peremyshl see Przemyśl
116 I5 **Peremyshlyany** L'vivs'ka Oblast', W Ukraine 49°42′N 24°33′E
Pereshchepino see Pereshchepyne
116 L9 **Pereshchepyne** Rus. Pereshchepino. Dnipropetrovs'ka Oblast', E Ukraine 48°59′N 35°22′E
124 L16 **Pereslavl'-Zalesskiy** Yaroslavskaya Oblast', W Russian Federation 56°42′N 38°45′E
117 Y7 **Pereval's'k** Luhans'ka Oblast', E Ukraine 48°28′N 38°54′E
127 U7 **Perevolotskiy** Orenburgskaya Oblast', W Russian Federation 51°54′N 54°05′E
Pereyaslav-Khmel'nitskiy see Pereyaslav-Khmel'nyts'kyy
117 Q5 **Pereyaslav-Khmel'nyts'kyy** Rus. Pereyaslav-Khmel'nitskiy. Kyyivs'ka Oblast', N Ukraine 50°05′N 31°28′E
109 U4 **Perg** Oberösterreich, N Austria 48°15′N 14°38′E
61 B19 **Pergamino** Buenos Aires, E Argentina 33°56′S 60°38′W
106 G6 **Pergine Valsugana** Ger. Persen. Trentino-Alto Adige, N Italy 46°04′N 11°13′E
29 S6 **Perham** Minnesota, N USA 46°35′N 95°34′W
93 L16 **Perho** Länsi-Suomi, W Finland 63°15′N 24°25′E
116 E11 **Periam** Ger. Perjamosch, Hung. Perjámos. Timiş, W Romania 46°02′N 20°54′E
15 Q6 **Péribonca** Québec, SE Canada
12 L11 **Péribonca, Lac** Québec, SE Canada
15 Q6 **Péribonca, Petite Rivière** Québec, SE Canada
15 Q7 **Péribonka** Québec, SE Canada 48°45′N 72°01′W
40 I9 **Pericos** Sinaloa, C Mexico 25°03′N 107°42′W
169 Q10 **Perigi** Borneo, C Indonesia
102 L12 **Périgueux** anc. Vesuna. Dordogne, SW France 45°12′N 00°41′E
54 G5 **Perijá, Serranía de** ▲▲ Columbia/Venezuela
115 H17 **Peristéra** island Vóreies Sporádes, Greece, Aegean Sea
63 H20 **Perito Moreno** Santa Cruz, S Argentina 46°35′S 71°W
155 G22 **Periyāl** var. Periyār. SW India
Periyār see Periyāl
155 G23 **Periyār Lake** S India
Perjámos/Perjamosch see Periam
27 O9 **Perkins** Oklahoma, C USA 35°58′N 97°01′W
116 L7 **Perkivtsi** Chernivets'ka Oblast', W Ukraine 48°28′N 26°48′E
43 U15 **Perlas, Archipiélago de las** Eng. Pearl Islands. island group SE Panama
43 O10 **Perlas, Cayos de** reef SE Nicaragua
43 N9 **Perlas, Laguna de** Eng. Pearl Lagoon. lagoon E Nicaragua
43 N10 **Perlas, Punta de** headland E Nicaragua 12°22′N 83°30′W
100 L11 **Perleberg** Brandenburg, N Germany 53°04′N 11°52′E
Perlepe see Prilep
168 I6 **Perlis** state Peninsular Malaysia
125 U14 **Perm'** prev. Molotov. Permskaya Oblast', NW Russian Federation 58°01′N 56°10′E
113 M22 **Përmet** var. Përmeti, Prëmet. Gjirokastër, S Albania 40°12′N 20°24′E
Përmeti see Përmet
125 U15 **Permskaya Oblast'** province NW Russian Federation
59 P15 **Pernambuco** off. Estado de Pernambuco. state E Brazil
Pernambuco see Recife
Pernambuco Abyssal Plain see Pernambuco Plain
Pernambuco, Estado de see Pernambuco
47 Y6 **Pernambuco Plain** var. Pernambuco Abyssal Plain. undersea feature E Atlantic Ocean 07°30′S 27°00′W
65 K15 **Pernambuco Seamounts** undersea feature C Atlantic Ocean
182 H6 **Pernatty Lagoon** salt lake South Australia
Pernau see Pärnu
Pernauer Bucht see Pärnu Laht
Pērnava see Pärnu
114 G9 **Pernik** prev. Dimitrovo. Pernik, W Bulgaria 42°36′N 23°02′E
114 G10 **Pernik** province W Bulgaria
93 K20 **Perniö** Swe. Bjärnå. Länsi-Suomi, SW Finland 60°13′N 23°10′E

◆ Country
● Country Capital
◇ Dependent Territory
○ Dependent Territory Capital
Administrative Regions
International Airport
▲ Mountain
▲▲ Mountain Range
Volcano
River
Lake
Reservoir

Pernitz – Pindus Mountains

109 X5 **Pernitz** Niederösterreich, E Austria 47°54′N 15°58′E
Pernov *see* Pärnu
103 O3 **Péronne** Somme, N France 49°56′N 02°57′E
14 L8 **Péronne, Lac** ◎ Québec, SE Canada
106 A8 **Perosa Argentina** Piemonte, NE Italy 45°02′N 07°10′E
41 Q14 **Perote** Veracruz-Llave, E Mexico 19°32′N 97°16′W
Pérouse *see* Perugia
191 W15 **Pérouse, Bahía de la** *bay* Easter Island, Chile, E Pacific Ocean
Perovsk *see* Kzylorda
103 O17 **Perpignan** Pyrénées-Orientales, S France 42°41′N 02°53′E
113 M20 **Përrenjas** *var.* Përrenjasi, Prenjas, Prenjasi. Elbasan, E Albania 41°04′N 20°34′E
Përrenjasi *see* Përrenjas
92 O2 **Perriertoppen** ▲ C Svalbard 79°10′N 17°01′E
25 S6 **Perrin** Texas, SW USA 32°59′N 98°03′W
23 Y16 **Perrine** Florida, SE USA 25°36′N 80°21′W
37 S12 **Perro, Laguna del** ◎ New Mexico, SW USA
102 G5 **Perros-Guirec** Côtes d'Armor, NW France 48°49′N 03°28′W
23 T9 **Perry** Florida, SE USA 30°07′N 83°34′W
23 T5 **Perry** Georgia, SE USA 32°27′N 83°43′W
29 U14 **Perry** Iowa, C USA 41°50′N 94°06′W
18 E10 **Perry** New York, NE USA 42°43′N 78°00′W
27 N9 **Perry** Oklahoma, C USA 36°17′N 97°18′W
27 Q3 **Perry Lake** ⊠ Kansas, C USA
31 R11 **Perrysburg** Ohio, N USA 41°33′N 83°37′W
25 O1 **Perryton** Texas, SW USA 36°23′N 100°48′W
39 O15 **Perryville** Alaska, USA 55°55′N 159°08′W
27 U11 **Perryville** Arkansas, C USA 35°00′N 92°48′W
27 Y6 **Perryville** Missouri, C USA 37°43′N 89°51′W
Persante *see* Parsęta
Persen *see* Pergine Valsugana
Pershay *see* Pyarshai
117 V7 **Pershotravens'k** Dnipropetrovs'ka Oblast', E Ukraine 48°19′N 36°22′E
Pershotravneve *see* Manhush
Persia *see* Iran
141 T5 **Persian Gulf** *var.* The Gulf, *Ar.* Khalīj al 'Arabī, *Per.* Khalīj-e Fars. *Gulf* SW Asia *see also* Gulf, The
Persis *see* Fārs
95 K22 **Perstorp** Skåne, S Sweden 56°08′N 13°23′E
137 O14 **Pertek** Tunceli, C Turkey 38°53′N 39°19′E
183 P16 **Perth** Tasmania, SE Australia 41°39′S 147°11′E
180 I13 **Perth** *state capital* Western Australia 31°58′S 115°49′E
14 L13 **Perth** Ontario, SE Canada 44°54′N 76°15′W
96 J11 **Perth** C Scotland, United Kingdom 56°24′N 03°28′W
96 J10 **Perth** *cultural region* C Scotland, United Kingdom
180 I12 **Perth** ✈ Western Australia 31°51′S 116°06′E
173 V10 **Perth Basin** *undersea feature* SE Indian Ocean 28°30′S 110°00′E
103 S15 **Pertuis** Vaucluse, SE France 43°42′N 05°30′E
103 Y16 **Pertusato, Capo** *headland* Corse, France, C Mediterranean Sea 41°22′N 09°10′E
30 L11 **Peru** Illinois, N USA 41°18′N 89°09′W
31 P12 **Peru** Indiana, N USA 40°45′N 86°04′W
57 E13 **Peru** *off.* Republic of Peru. ◆ *republic* W South America
Peru *see* Beru
193 T9 **Peru Basin** *undersea feature* E Pacific Ocean 15°00′S 85°00′W
193 U8 **Peru-Chile Trench** *undersea feature* E Pacific Ocean 20°00′S 73°00′W
112 F13 **Perućko Jezero** ◎ S Croatia
106 H13 **Perugia** *Fr.* Pérouse; *anc.* Perusia. Umbria, C Italy 43°06′N 12°24′E
Perugia, Lake of *see* Trasimeno, Lago
61 D15 **Perugorria** Corrientes, NE Argentina 29°21′S 58°35′W
60 M11 **Peruíbe** São Paulo, S Brazil 24°18′S 47°01′W
155 B21 **Perumalpār** *reef* India, N Indian Ocean
Peru, Republic of *see* Peru
Perusia *see* Perugia
99 D20 **Péruwelz** Hainaut, SW Belgium 50°30′N 03°35′E
137 R15 **Pervari** Siirt, SE Turkey 37°55′N 42°32′E
127 O4 **Pervomaysk** Nizhegorodskaya Oblast', W Russian Federation 54°52′N 43°49′E
117 X7 **Pervomays'k** Luhans'ka Oblast', E Ukraine 48°38′N 38°36′E
117 P8 **Pervomays'k** *prev.* Ol'viopol'. Mykolayivs'ka Oblast', S Ukraine 48°02′N 30°51′E
117 S12 **Pervomays'ke** Respublika Krym, S Ukraine 45°43′N 33°49′E
127 V7 **Pervomayskiy** Orenburgskaya Oblast', W Russian Federation 51°32′N 54°58′E
126 M6 **Pervomayskiy** Tambovskaya Oblast', W Russian Federation 53°15′N 40°20′E
117 V6 **Pervomays'kyy** Kharkivs'ka Oblast', E Ukraine 49°24′N 36°12′E
122 F10 **Pervoural'sk** Sverdlovskaya Oblast', C Russian Federation 56°58′N 59°50′E
123 V11 **Pervyy Kuril'skiy Proliv** *strait* E Russian Federation
99 I19 **Perwez** Walloon Brabant, C Belgium 50°39′N 04°49′E
106 I11 **Pesaro** *anc.* Pisaurum. Marche, C Italy 43°55′N 12°53′E
35 N9 **Pescadero** California, W USA 37°15′N 122°23′W
Pescadores *see* P'enghu Liehtao
161 S14 **Pescadores Channel** *var.* Penghu Shuidao, P'enghu Shuitao. *channel* W Taiwan
107 K14 **Pescara** *anc.* Aternum, Ostia Aterni. Abruzzo, C Italy 42°28′N 14°13′E
107 K15 **Pescara** ↝ C Italy
106 F11 **Pescia** Toscana, C Italy 43°54′N 10°41′E
108 C8 **Peseux** Neuchâtel, W Switzerland 46°59′N 06°53′E
125 P6 **Pësha** ↝ NW Russian Federation
149 T5 **Peshāwar** North-West Frontier Province, N Pakistan 34°01′N 71°33′E
149 T6 **Peshāwar** ✈ North-West Frontier Province, N Pakistan 34°01′N 71°40′E
113 M19 **Peshkopi** *var.* Peshkopia, Peshkopija. Dibër, NE Albania 41°40′N 20°25′E
Peshkopia/Peshkopija *see* Peshkopi
114 I11 **Peshtera** Pazardzhik, C Bulgaria 42°02′N 24°18′E
31 N6 **Peshtigo** Wisconsin, N USA 45°04′N 87°43′W
31 N6 **Peshtigo River** ↝ Wisconsin, N USA
Peski *see* Pyeski
125 S13 **Peskovka** Kirovskaya Oblast', NW Russian Federation 59°04′N 52°17′E
103 S8 **Pesmes** Haute-Saône, E France 47°17′N 05°33′E
104 H6 **Peso da Régua** *var.* Pêso da Regua. Vila Real, N Portugal 41°10′N 07°47′W
40 F5 **Pesqueira** Sonora, NW Mexico 29°22′N 110°58′W
102 J13 **Pessac** Gironde, SW France 44°46′N 00°42′W
111 J23 **Pest** *off.* Pest Megye. ◆ *county* C Hungary
Pest Megye *see* Pest
124 J14 **Pestovo** Novgorodskaya Oblast', W Russian Federation 58°37′N 35°48′E
40 M15 **Petacalco, Bahía** *bay* W Mexico
Petach-Tikva *see* Petah Tikva
138 F10 **Petah Tikva** *var.* Petach-Tikva, Petah Tiqva, Petakh Tikva; *prev.* Petah Tiqwa. Tel Aviv, C Israel 32°05′N 34°53′E
Petah Tiqwa *see* Petah Tikva
93 L17 **Petäjävesi** Länsi-Suomi, C Finland 62°17′N 25°10′E
Petakh Tikva/Petah Tiqva *see* Petah Tikva
22 M7 **Petal** Mississippi, S USA 31°21′N 89°15′W
115 I19 **Petalioi** *island* C Greece
115 H19 **Petalión, Kólpos** *gulf* E Greece
115 J19 **Pétalo** ▲ Ándros, Kykládes, Greece, Aegean Sea 37°51′N 24°50′E
34 M8 **Petaluma** California, W USA 38°15′N 122°37′W
99 L25 **Pétange** Luxembourg, SW Luxembourg 49°33′N 05°53′E
54 M5 **Petare** Miranda, N Venezuela 10°31′N 66°50′W
41 N16 **Petatlán** Guerrero, S Mexico 17°31′N 101°16′W
83 L14 **Petauke** Eastern, E Zambia 14°12′S 31°16′E
14 J12 **Petawawa** Ontario, SE Canada 45°54′N 77°18′W
14 J11 **Petawawa** ↝ Ontario, SE Canada
Petchaburi *see* Phetchaburi
42 D2 **Petén** *off.* Departamento del Petén. ◆ *department* N Guatemala
Petén, Departamento del *see* Petén
42 D2 **Petén Itzá, Lago** *var.* Lago de Flores. ◎ N Guatemala
30 K7 **Petenwell Lake** ⊠ Wisconsin, N USA
14 D6 **Peterbell** Ontario, S Canada 48°34′N 83°19′W
182 I7 **Peterborough** South Australia 32°59′S 138°51′E
14 I14 **Peterborough** Ontario, SE Canada 44°19′N 78°20′W
97 N20 **Peterborough** *prev.* Medeshamstede. E England, United Kingdom 52°35′N 00°15′W
19 N10 **Peterborough** New Hampshire, NE USA 42°51′N 71°54′W
96 L8 **Peterhead** NE Scotland, United Kingdom 57°30′N 01°46′W
Peterhof *see* Luboń
Peter I øy *see* Peter I Øy
193 Q14 **Peter I Øy** ◆ *Norwegian dependency* Antarctica
194 H9 **Peter I Øy** *var.* Peter I øy. *island* Antarctica
97 M14 **Peterlee** N England, United Kingdom 54°45′N 01°18′W
Peterlingen *see* Payerne
197 P14 **Petermann Bjerg** ▲ C Greenland 73°16′N 27°59′W
11 S12 **Peter Pond Lake** ◎ Saskatchewan, C Canada
39 X13 **Petersburg** Mytkof Island, Alaska, USA 56°43′N 132°51′W
30 K13 **Petersburg** Illinois, N USA 40°01′N 89°52′W
31 N16 **Petersburg** Indiana, N USA 38°30′N 87°16′W
29 Q3 **Petersburg** North Dakota, N USA 47°59′N 97°59′W
25 N5 **Petersburg** Texas, SW USA 33°52′N 101°36′W
21 V7 **Petersburg** Virginia, NE USA 37°14′N 77°24′W
21 T4 **Petersburg** West Virginia, NE USA 39°01′N 79°09′W
100 H12 **Petershagen** Nordrhein-Westfalen, NW Germany 52°22′N 08°58′E
55 S9 **Peters Mine** *var.* Peter's Mine. N Guyana 06°13′N 59°18′W
107 O21 **Petilia Policastro** Calabria, SW Italy 39°07′N 16°48′E
44 M9 **Pétionville** S Haiti 18°29′N 72°16′W
45 X6 **Petit-Bourg** Basse Terre, C Guadeloupe 16°12′N 61°36′W
15 Y5 **Petit-Cap** Québec, SE Canada 49°00′N 64°26′W
45 Y6 **Petit Cul-de-Sac Marin** *bay* C Guadeloupe
44 M9 **Petite-Rivière-de-l'Artibonite** C Haiti 19°10′N 72°30′W
173 X16 **Petite Rivière Noire, Piton de la** ▲ C Mauritius
15 R9 **Petite-Rivière-St-François** Québec, SE Canada 47°18′N 70°34′W
44 L9 **Petit-Goâve** S Haiti 18°27′N 72°51′W
Petitjean *see* Sidi-Kacem
13 N10 **Petit Lac Manicouagan** ◎ Québec, E Canada
19 T7 **Petit Manan Point** *headland* Maine, NE USA 44°23′N 67°54′W
Petit Mécatina, Rivière du *see* Little Mecatina
11 N10 **Petitot** ↝ Alberta/British Columbia, W Canada
45 S12 **Petit Piton** ▲ SW Saint Lucia 13°49′N 61°03′W
Petit-Popo *see* Aného
Petit St-Bernard, Col du *see* Little Saint Bernard Pass
13 O8 **Petitsikapau Lake** ◎ Newfoundland and Labrador, E Canada
92 L11 **Petkula** Lappi, N Finland 67°41′N 26°44′E
41 X12 **Peto** Yucatán, SE Mexico 20°09′N 88°55′W
62 G10 **Petorca** Valparaíso, C Chile 32°18′S 70°49′W
31 Q5 **Petoskey** Michigan, N USA 45°51′N 88°03′W
138 G14 **Petra** *archaeological site* Ma'ān, W Jordan
Petra *see* Wādī Mūsā
115 F14 **Pétras, Sténa** *pass* N Greece
123 S16 **Petra Velikogo, Zaliv** *bay* SE Russian Federation
Petrel *see* Petrer
14 K15 **Petre, Point** *headland* Ontario, SE Canada 43°49′N 77°07′W
105 S12 **Petrer** *var.* Petrel. País Valenciano, E Spain 38°28′N 00°46′W
125 U11 **Petretsovo** Permskaya Oblast', NW Russian Federation 61°22′N 57°21′E
114 G12 **Petrich** Blagoevgrad, SW Bulgaria 41°25′N 23°12′E
187 P15 **Petrie, Récif** *reef* N New Caledonia
37 N11 **Petrified Forest** *prehistoric site* Arizona, SW USA
Petrikau *see* Piotrków Trybunalski
Petrikov *see* Pyetrykaw
116 H12 **Petrila** *Hung.* Petrilla. Hunedoara, W Romania 45°27′N 23°25′E
Petrilla *see* Petrila
112 E9 **Petrinja** Sisak-Moslavina, C Croatia 45°27′N 16°14′E
Petroaleksandrovsk *see* To'rtko'l
Petrőcz *see* Bački Petrovac
124 G12 **Petrodvorets** *Fin.* Pietarhovi. Leningradskaya Oblast', NW Russian Federation 59°53′N 29°52′E
Petrograd *see* Sankt-Peterburg
Petrokov *see* Piotrków Trybunalski
54 G6 **Petrólea** Norte de Santander, NE Colombia 08°30′N 72°35′W
14 D16 **Petrolia** Ontario, S Canada 42°54′N 82°07′W
25 S4 **Petrolia** Texas, SW USA 34°00′N 98°13′W
59 O15 **Petrolina** Pernambuco, E Brazil 09°22′S 40°30′W
45 T6 **Petrona, Punta** *headland* C Puerto Rico 17°57′N 66°23′W
Petropavl *see* Petropavlovsk
117 V7 **Petropavlivka** Dnipropetrovs'ka Oblast', E Ukraine 48°28′N 36°28′E
145 P6 **Petropavlovsk** *Kaz.* Petropavl. Severnyy Kazakhstan, N Kazakhstan 54°47′N 69°06′E
123 V11 **Petropavlovsk-Kamchatskiy** Kamchatskaya Oblast', E Russian Federation 53°03′N 158°43′E
60 P9 **Petrópolis** Rio de Janeiro, SE Brazil 22°30′S 43°28′W
116 H12 **Petroșani** *var.* Petroșeni, *Ger.* Petroschen, *Hung.* Petrozsény. Hunedoara, W Romania 45°25′N 23°22′E
Petroschen/Petroșeni *see* Petroșani
Petroskoi *see* Petrozavodsk
112 N12 **Petrovac** Serbia, E Serbia 42°22′N 21°25′E
Petrovac *see* Bosanski Petrovac
113 J17 **Petrovac na Moru** S Montenegro 42°11′N 19°00′E
Petrovac/Petrovácz *see* Bački Petrovac
117 S8 **Petrove** Kirovohrads'ka Oblast', C Ukraine 48°22′N 33°12′E
113 O18 **Petrovec** C FYR Macedonia 41°57′N 21°37′E
Petrovgrad *see* Zrenjanin
127 P7 **Petrovsk** Saratovskaya Oblast', W Russian Federation 52°20′N 45°23′E
Petrovsk-Port *see* Makhachkala
127 P9 **Petrov Val** Volgogradskaya Oblast', SW Russian Federation 50°10′N 45°16′E
124 J11 **Petrozavodsk** *Fin.* Petroskoi. Respublika Kareliya, NW Russian Federation 61°46′N 34°19′E
Petrozsény *see* Petroșani
83 D20 **Petrusdal** Hardap, C Namibia 23°42′S 17°23′E
117 T7 **Petrykivka** Dnipropetrovs'ka Oblast', E Ukraine 48°44′N 34°42′E
Petsamo *see* Pechenga
Petschka *see* Pecica
Petseri *see* Pechory
Pettau *see* Ptuj
109 S5 **Pettenbach** Oberösterreich, C Austria 47°58′N 14°03′E
25 S13 **Pettus** Texas, SW USA 28°34′N 97°49′W
122 G12 **Petukhovo** Kurganskaya Oblast', C Russian Federation 55°04′N 67°49′E
Petuna *see* Songyuan
109 R4 **Peuerbach** Oberösterreich, N Austria 48°19′N 13°45′E
62 G12 **Peumo** Libertador, C Chile 34°20′S 71°12′W
123 T6 **Pevek** Chukotskiy Avtonomnyy Okrug, NE Russian Federation 69°41′N 170°19′E
27 X5 **Pevely** Missouri, C USA 38°16′N 90°24′W
Peyia *see* Pégeia
102 J15 **Peyrehorade** Landes, SW France 43°33′N 01°05′W
124 J14 **Peza** ↝ NW Russian Federation
103 P16 **Pézenas** Hérault, S France 43°28′N 03°25′E
111 H20 **Pezinok** *Ger.* Bösing, *Hung.* Bazin. Bratislavský Kraj, W Slovakia 48°17′N 17°15′E
101 L22 **Pfaffenhofen an der Ilm** Bayern, SE Germany 48°31′N 11°30′E
108 G7 **Pfäffikon** Schwyz, C Switzerland 47°11′N 08°46′E
101 F20 **Pfälzer Wald** *hill range* W Germany
101 N22 **Pfarrkirchen** Bayern, SE Germany 48°25′N 12°56′E
101 G21 **Pforzheim** Baden-Württemberg, SW Germany 48°53′N 08°42′E
101 H24 **Pfullendorf** Baden-Württemberg, S Germany 47°55′N 09°16′E
108 K8 **Pfunds** Tirol, W Austria 46°56′N 10°30′E
101 G19 **Pfungstadt** Hessen, W Germany 49°48′N 08°36′E
83 L20 **Phalaborwa** Limpopo, NE South Africa 23°59′S 31°04′E
152 E11 **Phalodi** Rājasthān, NW India 27°06′N 72°22′E
152 E12 **Phalsund** Rājasthān, NW India 26°22′N 71°56′E
155 E15 **Phaltan** Mahārāshtra, W India 18°01′N 74°31′E
167 O7 **Phan** *var.* Muang Phan. Chiang Rai, NW Thailand 19°34′N 99°44′E
167 O14 **Phangan, Ko** *island* SW Thailand
166 M15 **Phang-Nga** *var.* Pang-Nga, Phangnga. Phangnga, SW Thailand 08°29′N 98°31′E
Phangnga *see* Phang-Nga
Phan Rang/Phanrang *see* Phan Rang-Thap Cham
167 V13 **Phan Rang-Thap Cham** *var.* Phanrang, Phan Rang, Phan Rang Thap Cham. Ninh Thuân, S Vietnam 11°34′N 109°00′E
167 U13 **Phan Ri** Binh Thuân, S Vietnam 11°11′N 108°31′E
167 U13 **Phan Thiêt** Binh Thuân, S Vietnam 10°55′N 108°06′E
Pharnacia *see* Giresun
25 S17 **Pharr** Texas, SW USA 26°11′N 98°10′W
Pharus *see* Hvar
167 N16 **Phatthalung** *var.* Padalung, Patalung. Phatthalung, SW Thailand 07°38′N 100°04′E
167 O7 **Phayao** *var.* Muang Phayao. Phayao, NW Thailand 19°10′N 99°55′E
11 U10 **Phelps Lake** ◎ Saskatchewan, C Canada
21 X9 **Phelps Lake** ◎ North Carolina, SE USA
23 R5 **Phenix City** Alabama, S USA 32°28′N 85°00′W
167 T8 **Pheo** Quang Binh, C Vietnam 17°42′N 105°58′E
Phet Buri *see* Phetchaburi
167 O11 **Phetchaburi** *var.* Bejraburi, Petchaburi, Phet Buri. Phetchaburi, SW Thailand 13°05′N 99°58′E
167 O9 **Phichit** *var.* Bichitra, Muang Phichit, Pichit. Phichit, C Thailand 16°29′N 100°21′E
22 M5 **Philadelphia** Mississippi, S USA 32°45′N 89°06′W
18 I7 **Philadelphia** New York, NE USA 44°10′N 75°40′W
18 I16 **Philadelphia** Pennsylvania, NE USA 40°N 75°10′W
18 I16 **Philadelphia** ✈ Pennsylvania, NE USA 39°51′N 75°13′W
Philadelphia *see* 'Ammān
28 L10 **Philip** South Dakota, N USA 44°02′N 101°39′W
99 H22 **Philippeville** Namur, S Belgium 50°12′N 04°33′E
Philippeville *see* Skikda
21 S3 **Philippi** West Virginia, NE USA 39°08′N 80°03′W
Philippi *see* Fílippoi
195 Y9 **Philippi Glacier** *glacier* Antarctica
192 G6 **Philippine Basin** *undersea feature* W Pacific Ocean 17°00′N 132°00′E
129 X12 **Philippine Plate** *tectonic feature*
171 O5 **Philippines** *off.* Republic of the Philippines. ◆ *republic* SE Asia
129 X13 **Philippines** *island group* W Pacific Ocean
171 P3 **Philippine Sea** *sea* W Pacific Ocean
Philippines, Republic of the *see* Philippines
192 F6 **Philippine Trench** *undersea feature* W Philippine Sea
83 H23 **Philippolis** Free State, C South Africa 30°16′S 25°16′E
Philippopolis *see* Plovdiv
Philippopolis *see* Shahbā', Syria
45 V9 **Philipsburg** Sint Maarten, N Netherlands Antilles 17°58′N 63°02′W
33 P10 **Philipsburg** Montana, NW USA 46°19′N 113°17′W
39 R6 **Philip Smith Mountains** ▲▲ Alaska, USA
152 H8 **Phillaur** Punjab, N India 31°02′N 75°50′E
183 N13 **Phillip Island** *island* Victoria, SE Australia
25 N2 **Phillips** Texas, SW USA 35°39′N 101°21′W
30 K5 **Phillips** Wisconsin, N USA 45°42′N 90°23′W
26 K3 **Phillipsburg** Kansas, C USA 39°45′N 99°19′W
18 I14 **Phillipsburg** New Jersey, NE USA 40°39′N 75°09′W
21 S7 **Philpott Lake** ⊠ Virginia, NE USA
Phintias *see* Licata
167 P9 **Phitsanulok** *var.* Bisnulok, Muang Phitsanulok, Pitsanulok. Phitsanulok, C Thailand 16°49′N 100°15′E
Phlórina *see* Flórina
Phnom Penh *see* Phnum Penh
167 S13 **Phnum Penh** *var.* Phnom Penh. ● (Cambodia) Phnum Penh, S Cambodia 11°35′N 104°55′E
167 S11 **Phnum Tbêng Meanchey** Preăh Vihéar, N Cambodia 13°45′N 104°58′E
36 K13 **Phoenix** *state capital* Arizona, SW USA 33°27′N 112°04′W
Phoenix Island *see* Rawaki
191 R3 **Phoenix Islands** *island group* C Kiribati
18 I15 **Phoenixville** Pennsylvania, NE USA 40°07′N 75°31′W
83 K22 **Phofung** *var.* Mont-aux-Sources. ▲ N Lesotho 28°47′S 28°52′E
167 Q10 **Phon** Khon Kaen, E Thailand 15°47′N 102°35′E
167 Q5 **Phôngsali** *var.* Phong Saly. Phôngsali, N Laos 21°40′N 102°04′E
Phong Saly *see* Phôngsali
167 Q8 **Phônhông** C Laos 18°29′N 102°26′E
167 R5 **Phô Rang** *var.* Bao Yèn. Lao Cai, N Vietnam 22°12′N 104°27′E
Phort Láirge, Cuan *see* Waterford Harbour
167 N10 **Phra Chedi Sam Ong** Kanchanaburi, W Thailand 15°18′N 98°26′E
167 O8 **Phrae** *var.* Muang Phrae, Prae. Phrae, NW Thailand 18°07′N 100°09′E
Phra Nakhon Si Ayutthaya *see* Ayutthaya
167 M14 **Phra Thong, Ko** *island* SW Thailand
Phu Cương *see* Thu Dâu Môt
166 M15 **Phuket** *var.* Bhuket, Puket, *Mal.* Ujung Salang; *prev.* Junkseylon, Salang. Phuket, SW Thailand 07°52′N 98°22′E
166 M15 **Phuket** ✈ Phuket, SW Thailand 08°03′N 98°16′E
166 M15 **Phuket, Ko** *island* SW Thailand
154 N12 **Phulabāni** *prev.* Phulbani. Orissa, E India 20°30′N 84°18′E
Phulbani *see* Phulabāni
167 U9 **Phu Lôc** Th,a Thiên-Huê, C Vietnam 16°13′N 107°53′E
167 S13 **Phumĭ Banam** Prey Vêng, S Cambodia 11°14′N 105°18′E
167 R13 **Phumĭ Chŏâm** Kâmpóng Spœ, SW Cambodia 11°42′N 103°58′E
167 T11 **Phumĭ Kalêng** Stœng Trêng, NE Cambodia 13°57′N 106°17′E
167 S12 **Phumĭ Kâmpóng Trâbêk** *prev.* Phum Kompong Trabek. Kâmpóng Thum, C Cambodia 13°06′N 105°16′E
167 Q11 **Phumĭ Koŭk Kduŏch** Bătdâmbâng, NW Cambodia 13°16′N 103°08′E
167 T11 **Phumĭ Labăng** Rôtânôkiri, NE Cambodia 13°51′N 107°01′E
167 S11 **Phumĭ Mlu Prey** Preăh Vihéar, N Cambodia 13°48′N 105°16′E
167 R11 **Phumĭ Moŭng** Siĕmréab, NW Cambodia 13°45′N 103°35′E
167 Q12 **Phumĭ Prâmaôy** Poŭthĭsăt, W Cambodia 12°13′N 103°05′E
167 Q13 **Phumĭ Samĭt** Kaôh Kông, SW Cambodia 10°54′N 103°09′E
167 R11 **Phumĭ Sâmraông** *prev.* Phum Samrong. Siĕmréab, NW Cambodia 14°11′N 103°31′E
167 S12 **Phumĭ Siĕmbok** Stœng Trêng, N Cambodia 13°28′N 105°59′E
167 S11 **Phumĭ Thalabârĭvăt** Stœng Trêng, N Cambodia 13°34′N 105°57′E
167 R13 **Phumĭ Veal Renh** Kâmpôt, SW Cambodia 10°43′N 103°49′E
167 P13 **Phumĭ Yeay Sên** Kaôh Kông, SW Cambodia 11°09′N 103°09′E
Phum Kompong Trabek *see* Phumĭ Kâmpóng Trâbêk
Phum Samrong *see* Phumĭ Sâmraông
167 V11 **Phu My** Binh Đinh, C Vietnam 14°07′N 109°05′E
167 S14 **Phung Hiêp** Cân Thơ, S Vietnam 09°50′N 105°48′E
153 T12 **Phuntsholing** SW Bhutan 26°52′N 89°26′E
167 R15 **Phước Long** Minh Hai, S Vietnam 09°27′N 105°25′E
Phước Sơn *see* Khâm Đuc
167 R14 **Phu Quôc, Đao** *var.* Phu Quoc Island. *island* S Vietnam
Phu Quoc Island *see* Phu Quôc, Đao
167 S6 **Phu Tho** Vinh Phu, N Vietnam 21°23′N 105°13′E
Phu Vinh *see* Tra Vinh
166 M7 **Phyu** *var.* Hpyu, Pyu. Bago, C Myanmar (Burma) 18°29′N 96°28′E
189 T13 **Piaanu Pass** *passage* Chuuk Islands, C Micronesia
106 E8 **Piacenza** *Fr.* Paisance; *anc.* Placentia. Emilia-Romagna, N Italy 45°02′N 09°42′E
107 K14 **Pianella** Abruzzo, C Italy 42°23′N 14°04′E
107 M15 **Pianosa, Isola** *island* Archipelago Toscano, C Italy
171 U13 **Piar** Papua, E Indonesia 02°49′S 132°46′E
45 U14 **Piarco** *var.* Port of Spain. ✈ (Port-of-Spain) Trinidad, Trinidad and Tobago 10°36′N 61°21′W
110 M12 **Piaseczno** Mazowieckie, C Poland 52°03′N 21°00′E
116 I15 **Piatra** Teleorman, S Romania 43°49′N 25°10′E
116 L10 **Piatra-Neamţ** *Hung.* Karácsonkő. Neamţ, NE Romania 46°54′N 26°23′E
Piauhy *see* Piauí
59 N15 **Piauí** *off.* Estado do Piauí; *prev.* Piauhy. ◆ *state* E Brazil
Piauí, Estado do *see* Piauí
106 I7 **Piave** ↝ NE Italy
107 K24 **Piazza Armerina** *var.* Chiazza. Sicilia, Italy, C Mediterranean Sea 37°23′N 14°22′E
81 G14 **Pibor** *Amh.* Pibor Wenz. ↝ Ethiopia/Sudan
81 G14 **Pibor Post** Jonglei, SE Sudan 06°50′N 33°06′E
Pibor Wenz *see* Pibor
Pibrans *see* Příbram
36 K11 **Picacho Butte** ▲ Arizona, SW USA 35°12′N 112°44′W
40 D4 **Picachos, Cerro** ▲ NW Mexico 29°15′N 114°04′W
103 O4 **Picardie** *Eng.* Picardy. ◆ *region* N France
Picardy *see* Picardie
22 L8 **Picayune** Mississippi, S USA 30°31′N 89°40′W
Piccolo San Bernardo, Colle di *see* Little Saint Bernard Pass
PicdeBälaitous *see* Balaïtous
62 K5 **Pichanal** Salta, N Argentina 23°18′S 64°10′W
147 P12 **Pichandar** W Tajikistan 38°44′N 68°51′E
27 R8 **Picher** Oklahoma, C USA 36°59′N 94°49′W
62 G12 **Pichilemu** Libertador, C Chile 34°25′S 72°00′W
40 F9 **Pichilingue** Baja California Sur, NW Mexico 24°20′N 110°17′W
56 B6 **Pichincha** ◆ *province* N Ecuador
56 C6 **Pichincha** ▲ N Ecuador 0°12′S 78°39′W
Pichit *see* Phichit
41 U15 **Pichucalco** Chiapas, SE Mexico 17°32′N 93°07′W
22 L5 **Pickens** Mississippi, S USA 32°52′N 89°58′W
21 O11 **Pickens** South Carolina, SE USA 34°53′N 82°42′W
14 G11 **Pickerel** ↝ Ontario, S Canada
14 H15 **Pickering** Ontario, S Canada 43°50′N 79°03′W
97 N16 **Pickering** N England, United Kingdom 54°14′N 00°47′W
31 S13 **Pickerington** Ohio, N USA 39°52′N 82°45′W
12 C10 **Pickle Lake** Ontario, C Canada 51°30′N 90°10′W
29 P12 **Pickstown** South Dakota, N USA 43°02′N 98°31′W
25 V6 **Pickton** Texas, SW USA 33°01′N 95°19′W
23 N1 **Pickwick Lake** ⊠ S USA
64 N2 **Pico** *var.* Ilha do Pico. *island* Azores, Portugal, NE Atlantic Ocean
63 J19 **Pico de Salamanca** Chubut, SE Argentina 45°26′S 67°26′W
1 P9 **Pico Fracture Zone** *tectonic feature* NW Atlantic Ocean
Pico, Ilha do *see* Pico
59 O14 **Picos** Piauí, E Brazil 07°05′S 41°24′W
63 I20 **Pico Truncado** Santa Cruz, SE Argentina 46°45′S 68°00′W
183 S9 **Picton** New South Wales, SE Australia 34°12′S 150°36′E
14 K15 **Picton** Ontario, SE Canada 43°59′N 77°09′W
185 K14 **Picton** Marlborough, South Island, New Zealand 41°18′S 174°00′E
63 H15 **Picún Leufú, Arroyo** ↝ SW Argentina
Pidálion *see* Gkréko, Akrotíri
155 K25 **Pidurutalagala** ▲ S Sri Lanka 07°03′N 80°47′E
116 K6 **Pidvolochys'k** Ternopil's'ka Oblast', W Ukraine 49°31′N 26°09′E
107 K16 **Piedimonte Matese** Campania, S Italy 41°20′N 14°30′E
27 X7 **Piedmont** Missouri, C USA 37°09′N 90°42′W
21 P11 **Piedmont** South Carolina, SE USA 34°42′N 82°27′W
17 S12 **Piedmont** *escarpment* E USA
Piedmont *see* Piemonte
31 U13 **Piedmont Lake** ⊠ Ohio, N USA
104 M11 **Piedrabuena** Castilla-La Mancha, C Spain 39°02′N 04°10′W
Piedrafita, Puerto de *see* Pedrafita, Porto de
104 L8 **Piedrahita** Castilla-León, N Spain 40°27′N 05°20′W
41 N6 **Piedras Negras** *var.* Ciudad Porfirio Díaz. Coahuila, NE Mexico 28°40′N 100°32′W
61 E21 **Piedras, Punta** *headland* E Argentina 35°27′S 57°04′W
57 I14 **Piedras, Río de las** ↝ E Peru
111 J16 **Piekary Śląskie** Śląskie, S Poland 50°24′N 18°58′E
93 M17 **Pieksämäki** Itä-Suomi, E Finland 62°18′N 27°10′E
109 V5 **Pielach** ↝ NE Austria
93 M16 **Pielavesi** Itä-Suomi, C Finland 63°14′N 26°45′E
93 M16 **Pielavesi** ◎ C Finland
93 N16 **Pielinen** *var.* Pielisjärvi. ◎ E Finland
Pielisjärvi *see* Pielinen
106 A8 **Piemonte** *Eng.* Piedmont. ◆ *region* NW Italy
111 L18 **Pieniny** ▲▲ S Poland
111 E14 **Pieńsk** *Ger.* Penzig. Dolnośląskie, SW Poland 51°14′N 15°03′E
29 Q13 **Pierce** Nebraska, C USA 42°12′N 97°31′W
11 R14 **Pierceland** Saskatchewan, C Canada
115 E14 **Piéria** ▲▲ N Greece
29 N10 **Pierre** *state capital* South Dakota, N USA 44°22′N 100°21′W
102 K16 **Pierrefitte-Nestalas** Hautes-Pyrénées, S France 42°57′N 00°04′W
103 R14 **Pierrelatte** Drôme, E France 44°22′N 04°40′E
15 P11 **Pierreville** Québec, SE Canada 46°05′N 72°48′W
15 O7 **Pierriche** ↝ Québec, SE Canada
111 H20 **Piešťany** *Ger.* Pistyan, *Hung.* Pöstyén. Trnavský Kraj, W Slovakia 48°37′N 17°48′E
109 X5 **Piesting** ↝ E Austria
Pietarhovi *see* Petrodvorets
Pietari *see* Sankt-Peterburg
Pietarsaari *see* Jakobstad
83 K23 **Pietermaritzburg** *var.* Maritzburg. KwaZulu/Natal, E South Africa 29°35′S 30°23′E
Pietersburg *see* Polokwane
107 K24 **Pietraperzia** Sicilia, Italy, C Mediterranean Sea 37°25′N 14°08′E
107 N22 **Pietra Spada, Passo della** *pass* SW Italy
83 K22 **Piet Retief** Mpumalanga, E South Africa 27°00′S 30°49′E
116 J10 **Pietrosul, Vârful** *prev.* Vîrful Pietrosu. ▲ N Romania 47°06′N 25°09′E
106 I6 **Pieve di Cadore** Veneto, NE Italy 46°27′N 12°22′E
14 C18 **Pigeon Bay** *lake bay* Ontario, S Canada
27 X8 **Piggott** Arkansas, C USA 36°22′N 90°11′W
83 L21 **Piggs Peak** NW Swaziland 25°58′S 31°17′E
Pigs, Bay of *see* Cochinos, Bahía de
61 A23 **Pigüé** Buenos Aires, E Argentina 37°38′S 62°27′W
41 O12 **Piguícas** ▲ C Mexico 21°08′N 99°37′W
193 W15 **Piha Passage** *passage* S Tonga
Pihkva Järv *see* Pskov, Lake
93 N18 **Pihlajavesi** ◎ SE Finland
93 J18 **Pihlava** Länsi-Suomi, SW Finland 61°33′N 21°36′E
93 L16 **Pihtipudas** Länsi-Suomi, C Finland 63°20′N 25°37′E
40 L14 **Pihuamo** Jalisco, SW Mexico 19°20′N 103°21′W
189 U11 **Piis Moen** *var.* Pis. *atoll* Chuuk Islands, C Micronesia
41 U17 **Pijijiapán** Chiapas, SE Mexico 15°42′N 93°12′W
98 G12 **Pijnacker** Zuid-Holland, W Netherlands 52°01′N 04°26′E
42 H5 **Pijol, Pico** ▲ NW Honduras 15°07′N 87°39′W
Pikaar *see* Bikar Atoll
124 I13 **Pikalevo** Leningradskaya Oblast', NW Russian Federation 59°33′N 34°04′E
188 M15 **Pikelot** *island* Caroline Islands, C Micronesia
30 M5 **Pike River** ↝ Wisconsin, N USA
37 T5 **Pikes Peak** ▲ Colorado, C USA 38°51′N 105°06′W
21 P6 **Pikeville** Kentucky, S USA 37°29′N 82°33′W
20 L9 **Pikeville** Tennessee, S USA 35°35′N 85°11′W
Pikinni *see* Bikini Atoll
79 H18 **Pikounda** Sangha, C Congo 0°30′N 16°44′E
110 G9 **Piła** *Ger.* Schneidemühl. Wielkopolskie, C Poland 53°09′N 16°44′E
62 N6 **Pilagá, Riacho** ↝ NE Argentina
61 D20 **Pilar** Buenos Aires, E Argentina 34°28′S 58°55′W
62 N7 **Pilar** *var.* Villa del Pilar. Ñeembucú, S Paraguay 26°55′S 58°20′W
62 N6 **Pilcomayo, Río** ↝ C South America
147 R12 **Pildon** *Rus.* Pil'don. C Tajikistan 39°10′N 71°00′E
Piles *see* Pylés
Pilgram *see* Pelhřimov
152 L10 **Pīlībhīt** Uttar Pradesh, N India 28°37′N 79°48′E
110 M13 **Pilica** ↝ C Poland
115 G16 **Pílio** ▲▲ C Greece
111 J22 **Pilisvörösvár** Pest, N Hungary 47°38′N 18°55′E
65 G15 **Pillar Bay** *bay* Ascension Island, C Atlantic Ocean
183 P17 **Pillar, Cape** *headland* Tasmania, SE Australia 43°13′S 147°58′E
Pillau *see* Baltiysk
183 R5 **Pilliga** New South Wales, SE Australia 30°22′S 148°53′E
44 H8 **Pilón** Granma, E Cuba 19°54′N 77°20′W
Pilos *see* Pýlos
11 W17 **Pilot Mound** Manitoba, S Canada 49°12′N 98°49′W
21 S8 **Pilot Mountain** North Carolina, SE USA 36°23′N 80°28′W
39 O14 **Pilot Point** Alaska, USA 57°33′N 157°34′W
25 T5 **Pilot Point** Texas, SW USA 33°24′N 96°57′W
32 K11 **Pilot Rock** Oregon, NW USA 45°28′N 118°49′W
38 M11 **Pilot Station** Alaska, USA 61°56′N 162°52′W
Pilsen *see* Plzeň
111 K18 **Pilsko** ▲ N Slovakia 49°31′N 19°21′E
Pilten *see* Piltene
118 D8 **Piltene** *Ger.* Pilten. Ventspils, W Latvia 57°14′N 21°41′E
111 M16 **Pilzno** Podkarpackie, SE Poland 49°58′N 21°18′E
Pilzno *see* Plzeň
37 N14 **Pima** Arizona, SW USA 32°49′N 109°50′W
58 H13 **Pimenta** Pará, N Brazil 04°32′S 56°17′W
59 F16 **Pimenta Bueno** Rondônia, W Brazil 11°40′S 61°14′W
56 B11 **Pimentel** Lambayeque, W Peru 06°51′S 79°53′W
105 S6 **Pina** Aragón, NE Spain 41°28′N 00°31′W
119 I20 **Pina** ↝ SW Belarus
40 E2 **Pinacate, Sierra del** ▲ NW Mexico 31°49′N 113°30′W
63 H22 **Pináculo, Cerro** ▲ S Argentina 50°46′S 72°07′W
191 X11 **Pinaki** *atoll* Îles Tuamotu, E French Polynesia
37 N15 **Pinaleno Mountains** ▲▲ Arizona, SW USA
171 P4 **Pinamalayan** Mindoro, N Philippines 13°00′N 121°30′E
169 Q10 **Pinang** Borneo, C Indonesia 0°36′N 109°11′W
168 J7 **Pinang** *var.* Penang. ◆ *state* Peninsular Malaysia
Pinang *see* Pinang, Pulau, Peninsular Malaysia
Pinang *see* George Town
168 J7 **Pinang, Pulau** *var.* Penang, Pinang; *prev.* Prince of Wales Island. *island* Peninsular Malaysia
44 B5 **Pinar del Río** Pinar del Río, W Cuba 22°24′N 83°42′W
114 N11 **Pinarhisar** Kırklareli, NW Turkey 41°37′N 27°32′E
171 O3 **Pinatubo, Mount** ▲ Luzon, N Philippines 15°08′N 120°21′E
11 Y16 **Pinawa** Manitoba, S Canada 50°09′N 95°52′W
11 Q17 **Pincher Creek** Alberta, SW Canada 49°31′N 113°53′W
30 L16 **Pinckneyville** Illinois, N USA 38°04′N 89°22′W
Pincota *see* Pâncota
111 L15 **Pińczów** Świętokrzyskie, C Poland 50°30′N 20°30′E
149 U7 **Pind Dādan Khān** Punjab, E Pakistan 32°36′N 73°07′E
Píndhos/Píndhos Óros *see* Píndos
149 V8 **Pindi Bhattiān** Punjab, E Pakistan 31°54′N 73°20′E
149 U6 **Pindi Gheb** Punjab, E Pakistan 33°16′N 72°21′E
115 D15 **Píndos** *var.* Píndhos Óros, *Eng.* Pindus Mountains; *prev.* Píndhos. ▲▲ C Greece
Pindus Mountains *see* Píndos

◆ Country ● Country Capital ◇ Dependent Territory ○ Dependent Territory Capital ◆ Administrative Regions ✈ International Airport ▲ Mountain ▲▲ Mountain Range ⛰ Volcano ↝ River ◎ Lake ⊠ Reservoir
305

Pine Barrens – Pokharā

18 J16 **Pine Barrens** *physical region* New Jersey, NE USA
27 V12 **Pine Bluff** Arkansas, C USA 34°15′N 92°00′W
23 X11 **Pine Castle** Florida, SE USA 28°28′N 81°22′W
29 V7 **Pine City** Minnesota, N USA 45°49′N 92°55′W
181 P2 **Pine Creek** Northern Territory, N Australia 13°51′S 131°51′E
35 V4 **Pine Creek** ≈ Nevada, W USA
18 F13 **Pine Creek** ≈ Pennsylvania, NE USA
27 Q13 **Pine Creek Lake** ⊠ Oklahoma, C USA
33 T15 **Pinedale** Wyoming, C USA 42°52′N 109°51′W
11 X15 **Pine Dock** Manitoba, S Canada 51°34′N 96°47′W
11 Y16 **Pine Falls** Manitoba, S Canada 50°29′N 96°12′W
35 R10 **Pine Flat Lake** ⊠ California, W USA
125 N8 **Pinega** Arkhangel'skaya Oblast', NW Russian Federation 64°40′N 43°24′E
125 N8 **Pinega** ≈ NW Russian Federation
15 N12 **Pine Hill** Québec, SE Canada 45°44′N 74°30′W
11 T12 **Pinehouse Lake** ◎ Saskatchewan, C Canada
21 T10 **Pinehurst** North Carolina, SE USA 35°12′N 79°28′W
115 D19 **Pineiós** ≈ S Greece
115 E16 **Pineiós** *var.* Piniós; *anc.* Peneius. ≈ C Greece
29 W10 **Pine Island** Minnesota, N USA 44°12′N 92°39′W
23 V15 **Pine Island** *island* Florida, SE USA
194 K10 **Pine Island Glacier** *glacier* Antarctica
25 X9 **Pineland** Texas, SW USA 31°15′N 93°58′W
23 V13 **Pinellas Park** Florida, SE USA 27°50′N 82°42′W
10 M13 **Pine Pass** *pass* British Columbia, W Canada
8 J10 **Pine Point** Northwest Territories, W Canada 60°52′N 114°30′W
28 K12 **Pine Ridge** South Dakota, N USA 43°01′N 102°33′W
29 U6 **Pine River** Minnesota, N USA 46°43′N 94°24′W
31 Q8 **Pine River** ≈ Michigan, N USA
30 M4 **Pine River** ≈ Wisconsin, N USA
106 A8 **Pinerolo** Piemonte, NE Italy 44°56′N 07°21′E
115 I15 **Pínes, Akrotírio** *var.* Akrotírio Pínnes. *headland* N Greece 40°06′N 24°19′E
25 W6 **Pines, Lake O' the** ⊠ Texas, SW USA
Pines, The Isle of the *see* Juventud, Isla de la
Pine Tree State *see* Maine
21 N7 **Pineville** Kentucky, S USA 36°47′N 83°43′W
22 H7 **Pineville** Louisiana, S USA 31°19′N 92°25′W
27 R8 **Pineville** Missouri, C USA 36°36′N 94°23′W
21 R10 **Pineville** North Carolina, SE USA 35°04′N 80°53′W
21 Q6 **Pineville** West Virginia, NE USA 37°35′N 81°34′W
33 V8 **Piney Buttes** *physical region* Montana, NW USA
163 W9 **Ping'an** Jilin, NE China 44°36′N 127°13′E
160 H14 **Pingbian** *var.* Pingbian Miaozu Zizhixian, Yuping. Yunnan, SW China 22°51′N 103°28′E
Pingbian Miaozu Zizhixian *see* Pingbian
157 S9 **Pingdingshan** Henan, C China 33°52′N 113°20′E
161 R4 **Pingdu** Shandong, E China 36°50′N 119°55′E
189 W16 **Pingelap Atoll** *atoll* Caroline Islands, E Micronesia
160 K14 **Pingguo** *var.* Matou. Guangxi Zhuangzu Zizhiqu, S China 23°24′N 107°30′E
161 Q13 **Pinghe** *var.* Xiaoxi. Fujian, SE China 24°30′N 117°19′E
P'ing-hsiang *see* Pingxiang
161 N10 **Pingjiang** Hunan, S China 28°44′N 113°33′E
Pingkiang *see* Harbin
160 L8 **Pingli** Shaanxi, C China 32°27′N 109°21′E
159 W10 **Pingliang** *var.* Kongtong, P'ing-liang. Gansu, C China 35°27′N 106°38′E
P'ing-liang *see* Pingliang
159 W8 **Pingluo** Ningxia, N China 38°55′N 106°31′E
Pingma *see* Tiandong
167 O7 **Ping, Mae Nam** ≈ W Thailand
161 Q1 **Pingquan** Hebei, E China 41°02′N 118°35′E
29 P5 **Pingree** North Dakota, N USA 47°07′N 98°54′W
Pingsiang *see* Pingxiang
161 S14 **P'ingtung** *Jap.* Heitō. S Taiwan 22°40′N 120°30′E
160 I8 **Pingwu** *var.* Long'an. Sichuan, C China 32°33′N 104°32′E
160 J15 **Pingxiang** Guangxi Zhuangzu Zizhiqu, S China 22°03′N 106°44′E
161 O11 **Pingxiang** *var.* P'ing-hsiang; *prev.* Pingsiang. Jiangxi, S China 27°42′N 113°50′E
Pingxiang *see* Tongwei
161 S11 **Pingyang** *var.* Kunyang. Zhejiang, SE China 27°46′N 120°37′E
161 P5 **Pingyi** Shandong, E China 35°30′N 117°38′E
161 P5 **Pingyin** Shandong, E China 36°18′N 116°24′E
60 H13 **Pinhalzinho** Santa Catarina, S Brazil 26°53′S 52°57′W
60 I12 **Pinhão** Paraná, S Brazil 25°46′S 51°32′W
61 H17 **Pinheiro Machado** Rio Grande do Sul, S Brazil 31°34′S 53°22′W
104 I7 **Pinhel** Guarda, N Portugal 40°47′N 07°03′W
Piniós *see* Pineiós
168 I11 **Pini, Pulau** *island* Kepulauan Batu, W Indonesia
109 Y7 **Pinka** ≈ SE Austria
109 X7 **Pinkafeld** Burgenland, SE Austria 47°23′N 16°08′E
Pinkiang *see* Harbin
10 M12 **Pink Mountain** British Columbia, W Canada 57°10′N 122°36′W
166 M3 **Pinlebu** Sagaing, N Myanmar (Burma) 24°02′N 95°21′E
38 J12 **Pinnacle Island** *island* Alaska, USA
180 I12 **Pinnacles, The** *tourist site* Western Australia
182 K10 **Pinnaroo** South Australia 35°17′S 140°54′E
Pinne *see* Pniewy
100 I9 **Pinneberg** Schleswig-Holstein, N Germany 53°40′N 09°49′E
Pínnes, Akrotírio *see* Pínes, Akrotírio
Pinos, Isla de *see* Juventud, Isla de la
35 R14 **Pinos, Mount** ▲ California, W USA 34°48′N 119°09′W
105 R12 **Pinoso** País Valenciano, E Spain 38°25′N 01°02′W
105 N14 **Pinos-Puente** Andalucía, S Spain 37°16′N 03°46′W
41 Q17 **Pinotepa Nacional** *var.* Santiago Pinotepa Nacional. Oaxaca, SE Mexico 16°20′N 98°02′W
114 F13 **Pínovo** ▲ N Greece 41°06′N 22°19′E
187 R17 **Pins, Île des** *var.* Kunyé. *island* E New Caledonia
119 I20 **Pinsk** *Pol.* Pińsk. Brestskaya Voblasts', SW Belarus 52°07′N 26°07′E
14 D18 **Pins, Pointe aux** *headland* Ontario, S Canada 42°14′N 81°53′W
57 B16 **Pinta, Isla** *var.* Abingdon. *island* Galapagos Islands, Ecuador, E Pacific Ocean
125 Q12 **Pinyug** Kirovskaya Oblast', NW Russian Federation 60°12′N 47°45′E
57 B17 **Pinzón, Isla** *var.* Duncan Island. *island* Galapagos Islands, Ecuador, E Pacific Ocean
35 Y8 **Pioche** Nevada, W USA 37°57′N 114°30′W
106 F13 **Piombino** Toscana, C Italy 42°54′N 10°30′E
0 C9 **Pioneer Fracture Zone** *tectonic feature* NE Pacific Ocean
122 L5 **Pioner, Ostrov** *island* Severnaya Zemlya, N Russian Federation
118 A13 **Pionerskiy** *Ger.* Neukuhren. Kaliningradskaya Oblast', W Russian Federation 54°57′N 20°16′E
110 N13 **Pionki** Mazowieckie, C Poland 51°30′N 21°27′E
184 L9 **Piopio** Waikato, North Island, New Zealand 38°27′S 175°00′E
110 K13 **Piotrków Trybunalski** *Ger.* Petrikau, *Rus.* Petrokov. Łodzkie, C Poland 51°25′N 19°42′E
152 F12 **Pīpār Road** Rājasthān, N India 26°25′N 73°29′E
115 I16 **Pipéri** *island* Vóreies Sporádes, Greece, Aegean Sea
29 S10 **Pipestone** Minnesota, N USA 44°00′N 96°19′W
12 C9 **Pipestone** ≈ Ontario, C Canada
61 E21 **Pipinas** Buenos Aires, E Argentina 35°32′S 57°20′W
149 T7 **Piplān** *prev.* Liaqatabad. Punjab, E Pakistan 32°17′N 71°24′E
15 R5 **Pipmuacan, Réservoir** ⊠ Québec, SE Canada
Piqan *see* Shanshan
31 R13 **Piqua** Ohio, N USA 40°08′N 84°14′W
105 P5 **Piqueras, Puerto de** *pass* N Spain
60 H11 **Piquiri, Rio** ≈ S Brazil
60 L9 **Piracicaba** São Paulo, S Brazil 22°45′S 47°40′W
Piraeus/Piraiévs *see* Peiraías
60 K10 **Piraju** São Paulo, S Brazil 23°12′S 49°24′W
60 K9 **Pirajuí** São Paulo, S Brazil 21°58′S 49°27′W
63 G21 **Pirámide, Cerro** ▲ S Chile 49°06′S 73°32′W
Piramiva *see* Pyramíva
109 R13 **Piran** *It.* Pirano. SW Slovenia 45°35′N 13°35′E
62 N6 **Pirané** Formosa, N Argentina 25°42′S 59°06′W
59 J18 **Piranhas** Goiás, S Brazil 16°24′S 51°51′W
Pirano *see* Piran
142 I4 **Pīrānshahr** Āžarbāyjān-e Gharbī, NW Iran 36°41′N 45°08′E
59 M19 **Pirapora** Minas Gerais, NE Brazil 17°20′S 44°54′W
60 I9 **Pirapózinho** São Paulo, S Brazil 22°17′S 51°31′W
61 G19 **Piraraja** Lavalleja, S Uruguay 33°44′S 54°45′W
60 L9 **Pirassununga** São Paulo, S Brazil 21°58′S 47°23′W
45 V6 **Pirata, Monte** ▲ E Puerto Rico 18°06′N 65°33′W
60 I13 **Piratuba** Santa Catarina, S Brazil 27°26′S 51°47′W
114 I9 **Pirdop** *prev.* Strednogorie. Sofiya, W Bulgaria 42°44′N 24°09′E
191 P7 **Pirea** Tahiti, W French Polynesia
59 K18 **Pirenópolis** Goiás, S Brazil 15°48′S 49°00′W
153 S13 **Pirganj** Rajshahi, NW Bangladesh 25°51′N 88°25′E
Pirgi *see* Pyrgí
Pírgos *see* Pýrgos
61 F20 **Piriápolis** Maldonado, S Uruguay 34°51′S 55°15′W
114 G11 **Pirin** ▲▲ SW Bulgaria
Pirineos *see* Pyrenees
58 N13 **Piripiri** Piauí, E Brazil 04°15′S 41°46′W
118 H4 **Pirita** *var.* Pirita Jõgi. ≈ NW Estonia
Pirita Jõgi *see* Pirita
54 J6 **Píritu** Portuguesa, N Venezuela 09°21′N 69°16′W
93 L18 **Pirkkala** Länsi-Suomi, W Finland 61°27′N 23°47′E
101 F20 **Pirmasens** Rheinland-Pfalz, SW Germany 49°12′N 07°37′E
101 P16 **Pirna** Sachsen, E Germany 50°57′N 13°56′E
Piroe *see* Piru
113 Q15 **Pirot** Serbia, SE Serbia 43°12′N 22°34′E
152 H6 **Pīr Panjāl Range** ▲▲ NE India
43 W16 **Pirre, Cerro** ▲ SE Panama 07°54′N 77°42′W
137 Y11 **Pirsaat** *Rus.* Pirsagat. ≈ E Azerbaijan
Pirsagat *see* Pirsaat
143 V11 **Pīr Shūrān, Selseleh-ye** ▲ SE Iran
92 M12 **Pirttikoski** Lappi, N Finland 66°20′N 27°08′E
Pirttikylä *see* Pörtom
171 R13 **Piru** *prev.* Piroe. Pulau Seram, E Indonesia 03°01′S 128°10′E
Piryatin *see* Pyryatyn
Pis *see* Piis Moen
106 F11 **Pisa** *var.* Pisae. Toscana, C Italy 43°43′N 10°23′E
Pisae *see* Pisa
189 V12 **Pisar** *atoll* Chuuk Islands, C Micronesia
Pisaurum *see* Pesaro
14 M10 **Piscatosine, Lac** ◎ Québec, SE Canada
109 W7 **Pischeldorf** Steiermark, SE Austria 47°11′N 15°48′E
Pischk *see* Simeria
107 L19 **Pisciotta** Campania, S Italy 40°07′N 15°13′E
57 E16 **Pisco** Ica, SW Peru 13°46′S 76°12′W
116 G9 **Pişcolt** *Hung.* Piskolt. Satu Mare, NW Romania 47°35′N 22°18′E
57 E16 **Pisco, Río** ≈ E Peru
111 C18 **Písek** Budějovický Kraj, S Czech Republic 49°19′N 14°07′E
31 R14 **Pisgah** Ohio, N USA 39°19′N 84°22′W
Pisha *see* Ningnan
158 F9 **Pishan** *var.* Guma. Xinjiang Uygur Zizhiqu, NW China 37°36′N 78°45′E
117 N8 **Pishchanka** Vinnyts'ka Oblast', C Ukraine 48°12′N 28°52′E
113 K21 **Pishë** Fier, SW Albania 40°40′N 19°22′E
143 X14 **Pīshīn** Sīstān va Balūchestān, SE Iran 26°05′N 61°46′E
149 O9 **Pishin** North-West Frontier Province, NW Pakistan 30°33′N 67°01′E
149 N11 **Pishin Lora** *var.* Psein Lora, *Pash.* Pseyn Bowr. ≈ SW Pakistan
Pishma *see* Pizhma
Pishpek *see* Bishkek
171 O14 **Pising** Pulau Kabaena, C Indonesia 05°07′S 121°50′E
Pisino *see* Pazin
Piski *see* Simeria
Piskolt *see* Pişcolt
147 Q9 **Piskom** *Rus.* Pskem. ≈ E Uzbekistan
Piskom Tizmasi *see* Pskemskiy Khrebet
35 P13 **Pismo Beach** California, W USA 35°08′N 120°38′W
77 P12 **Pissila** C Burkina 13°07′N 00°51′W
62 H8 **Pissis, Monte** ▲ N Argentina 27°45′S 68°43′W
41 X12 **Piste** Yucatán, E Mexico 20°40′N 88°34′W
107 O18 **Pisticci** Basilicata, S Italy 40°23′N 16°33′E
106 F11 **Pistoia** *anc.* Pistoria, Pistoriæ. Toscana, C Italy 43°57′N 10°53′E
32 E15 **Pistol River** Oregon, NW USA 42°13′N 124°23′W
Pistoria/Pistoriæ *see* Pistoia
15 U5 **Pistuacanis** ≈ Québec, SE Canada
Pistyan *see* Piešt'any
104 M5 **Pisuerga** ≈ N Spain
110 N8 **Pisz** *Ger.* Johannisburg. Warmińsko-Mazurskie, NE Poland 53°37′N 21°49′E
76 I13 **Pita** NW Guinea 11°05′N 12°15′W
54 D12 **Pitalito** Huila, S Colombia 01°51′N 76°01′W
60 I11 **Pitanga** Paraná, S Brazil 24°45′S 51°43′W
182 M9 **Pitarpunga Lake** *salt lake* New South Wales, SE Australia
193 P10 **Pitcairn Island** *island* S Pitcairn Islands
193 P10 **Pitcairn Islands** ◇ *UK dependent territory* C Pacific Ocean
93 J14 **Piteå** Norrbotten, N Sweden 65°19′N 21°30′E
92 I13 **Piteälven** ≈ N Sweden
116 I13 **Piteşti** Argeş, S Romania 44°53′N 24°49′E
Pithagorio *see* Pythagóreio
180 I12 **Pithara** Western Australia 30°31′S 116°38′E
103 N6 **Pithiviers** Loiret, C France 48°10′N 02°15′E
152 L9 **Pithorāgarh** Uttarakhand, N India 29°35′N 80°12′E
188 B16 **Piti** W Guam 13°28′N 144°42′E
106 G13 **Pitigliano** Toscana, C Italy 42°38′N 11°40′E
40 F3 **Pitiquito** Sonora, NW Mexico 30°39′N 112°00′W
Pitkäranta *see* Pitkyaranta
38 M11 **Pitkas Point** Alaska, USA 62°01′N 163°17′W
124 H11 **Pitkyaranta** *Fin.* Pitkäranta. Respublika Kareliya, NW Russian Federation 61°34′N 31°27′E
96 J10 **Pitlochry** C Scotland, United Kingdom 56°47′N 03°48′W
18 I16 **Pitman** New Jersey, NE USA 39°43′N 75°06′W
146 I9 **Pitnak** *var.* Drujba, *Rus.* Druzhba. Xorazm Viloyati, W Uzbekistan 41°14′N 61°13′E
112 G8 **Pitomača** Virovitica-Podravina, NE Croatia 45°57′N 17°14′E
35 O2 **Pit River** ≈ California, W USA
63 G15 **Pitrufquén** Araucanía, S Chile 38°59′S 72°40′W
Pitsanulok *see* Phitsanulok
Pitschen *see* Byczyna
Pitsunda *see* Bichvint'a
109 X6 **Pitten** ≈ E Austria
10 J14 **Pitt Island** *island* British Columbia, W Canada
Pitt Island *see* Makin
22 M3 **Pittsboro** Mississippi, S USA 33°55′N 89°20′W
21 T9 **Pittsboro** North Carolina, SE USA 35°46′N 79°12′W
27 R7 **Pittsburg** Kansas, C USA 37°24′N 94°42′W
25 W6 **Pittsburg** Texas, SW USA 33°00′N 94°58′W
18 B14 **Pittsburgh** Pennsylvania, NE USA 40°26′N 80°W
30 J14 **Pittsfield** Illinois, N USA 39°36′N 90°48′W
19 R6 **Pittsfield** Maine, NE USA 44°46′N 69°22′W
18 L11 **Pittsfield** Massachusetts, NE USA 42°27′N 73°15′W
183 U3 **Pittsworth** Queensland, E Australia 27°43′S 151°36′E
62 I8 **Pituil** La Rioja, NW Argentina 28°33′S 67°24′W
56 A10 **Piura** Piura, NW Peru 05°11′S 80°41′W
56 A9 **Piura** *off.* Departamento de Piura. ◈ *department* NW Peru
Piura, Departamento de *see* Piura
35 S13 **Piute Peak** ▲ California, W USA 35°27′N 118°24′W
113 J15 **Piva** ≈ NW Montenegro
117 V5 **Pivdenne** Kharkivs'ka Oblast', E Ukraine 49°52′N 36°04′E
117 P8 **Pivdennyy Buh** *Rus.* Yuzhnyy Bug. ≈ S Ukraine
54 F5 **Pivijay** Magdalena, N Colombia 10°31′N 74°36′W
109 T13 **Pivka** *prev.* Šent Peter, *Ger.* Sankt Peter, *It.* San Pietro del Carso. SW Slovenia 45°41′N 14°12′E
117 U13 **Pivnichno-Kryms'kyy Kanal** *canal* S Ukraine
113 J15 **Pivsko Jezero** ◎ NW Montenegro
111 M18 **Piwniczna** Małopolskie, S Poland 49°26′N 20°43′E
35 R12 **Pixley** California, W USA 35°58′N 119°18′W
125 Q15 **Pizhma** *var.* Pishma. ≈ NW Russian Federation
13 U13 **Placentia** Newfoundland, Newfoundland and Labrador, SE Canada 47°12′N 53°58′W
Placentia *see* Piacenza
13 U13 **Placentia Bay** *inlet* Newfoundland, Newfoundland and Labrador, SE Canada
171 P5 **Placer** Masbate, N Philippines 11°54′N 123°54′E
35 P7 **Placerville** California, W USA 38°42′N 120°48′W
44 F5 **Placetas** Villa Clara, C Cuba 22°18′N 79°40′W
113 Q18 **Plačkovica** ▲▲ E Macedonia
36 L2 **Plain City** Utah, W USA 41°18′N 112°05′W
22 G4 **Plain Dealing** Louisiana, S USA 32°54′N 93°42′W
31 O14 **Plainfield** Indiana, N USA 39°42′N 86°18′W
18 K14 **Plainfield** New Jersey, NE USA 40°37′N 74°25′W
33 O8 **Plains** Montana, NW USA 47°27′N 114°52′W
24 L6 **Plains** Texas, SW USA 33°12′N 102°50′W
29 X10 **Plainview** Minnesota, N USA 44°10′N 92°10′W
29 Q13 **Plainview** Nebraska, C USA 42°21′N 97°47′W
25 N4 **Plainview** Texas, SW USA 34°12′N 101°43′W
26 K4 **Plainville** Kansas, C USA 39°13′N 99°18′W
115 I22 **Pláka** *var.* Mílos. Mílos, Kykládes, Greece, Aegean Sea 36°44′N 24°25′E
115 J15 **Pláka, Akrotírio** *headland* Límnos, E Greece 40°02′N 25°25′E
113 N19 **Plakenska Planina** ▲▲ SW Macedonia
44 K5 **Plana Cays** *islets* SE Bahamas
105 S12 **Plana, Isla** *var.* Nueva Tabarca. *island* E Spain
59 L18 **Planaltina** Goiás, S Brazil 15°35′S 47°28′W
83 O14 **Planalto Moçambicano** *plateau* N Mozambique
112 N10 **Plandište** Vojvodina, NE Serbia 45°13′N 21°07′E
100 N13 **Plane** ≈ NE Germany
54 E6 **Planeta Rica** Córdoba, NW Colombia 08°24′N 75°39′W
29 P11 **Plankinton** South Dakota, N USA 43°43′N 98°28′W
30 M11 **Plano** Illinois, N USA 41°39′N 88°32′W
25 U6 **Plano** Texas, SW USA 33°01′N 96°42′W
23 W12 **Plant City** Florida, SE USA 28°01′N 82°06′W
22 J9 **Plaquemine** Louisiana, S USA 30°17′N 91°13′W
104 K9 **Plasencia** Extremadura, W Spain 40°02′N 06°05′W
110 P7 **Plaska** Podlaskie, NE Poland 53°55′N 23°18′E
112 C10 **Plaški** Karlovac, C Croatia 45°04′N 15°21′E
113 N19 **Plasnica** SW FYR Macedonia 41°28′N 21°07′E
13 N14 **Plaster Rock** New Brunswick, SE Canada 46°55′N 67°24′W
107 J24 **Platani** *anc.* Halycus. ≈ Sicilia, Italy, C Mediterranean Sea
115 G17 **Plataniá** Thessalía, C Greece 39°09′N 23°15′E
115 G24 **Plátanos** Kríti, Greece, E Mediterranean Sea 35°27′N 23°34′E
65 H18 **Plata, Río de la** *var.* River Plate. *estuary* Argentina/Uruguay
77 V15 **Plateau** ◈ *state* C Nigeria
79 G19 **Plateaux** *var.* Région des Plateaux. ◈ *province* C Congo
Plateaux, Région des *see* Plateaux
Plate, Île *see* Flat Island
92 P1 **Platen, Kapp** *headland* NE Svalbard 80°30′N 22°46′E
Plate, River *see* Plata, Río de la
99 G22 **Plate Taille, Lac de la** *var.* L'Eau d'Heure. ◎ SE Belgium
Plathe *see* Płoty
39 N13 **Platinum** Alaska, USA 59°01′N 161°49′W
54 F5 **Plato** Magdalena, N Colombia 09°47′N 74°47′W
29 O11 **Platte** South Dakota, N USA 43°20′N 98°51′W
27 R3 **Platte City** Missouri, C USA 39°22′N 94°47′W
Plattensee *see* Balaton
27 R2 **Platte River** ≈ Iowa/Missouri, USA
29 Q15 **Platte River** ≈ Nebraska, C USA
37 T3 **Platteville** Colorado, C USA 40°13′N 104°49′W
30 K9 **Platteville** Wisconsin, N USA 42°44′N 90°27′W
101 N21 **Plattling** Bayern, SE Germany 48°45′N 12°52′E
27 R3 **Plattsburg** Missouri, C USA 39°33′N 94°27′W
18 L6 **Plattsburgh** New York, NE USA 44°42′N 73°29′W
29 S15 **Plattsmouth** Nebraska, C USA 41°00′N 95°52′W
101 M17 **Plauen** *var.* Plauen im Vogtland. Sachsen, E Germany 50°31′N 12°08′E
Plauen im Vogtland *see* Plauen
100 M10 **Plauer See** ◎ NE Germany
113 L16 **Plav** E Montenegro 42°36′N 19°57′E
118 I10 **Pļaviņas** *Ger.* Stockmannshof. Aizkraukle, S Latvia 56°37′N 25°40′E
126 K5 **Plavsk** Tul'skaya Oblast', W Russian Federation 53°42′N 37°21′E
41 Z12 **Playa del Carmen** Quintana Roo, E Mexico 20°37′N 87°04′W
40 J12 **Playa Los Corchos** Nayarit, SW Mexico 21°91′N 105°28′W
37 P16 **Playas Lake** ◎ New Mexico, SW USA
41 S15 **Playa Vicenté** Veracruz-Llave, SE Mexico 17°42′N 95°01′W
167 U11 **Plây Cu** *var.* Pleiku. Gia Lai, C Vietnam 13°57′N 108°01′E
28 L3 **Plaza** North Dakota, N USA 48°00′N 102°00′W
63 I15 **Plaza Huincul** Neuquén, C Argentina 38°55′S 69°14′W
36 L3 **Pleasant Grove** Utah, W USA 40°21′N 111°44′W
29 V14 **Pleasant Hill** Iowa, C USA 41°34′N 93°31′W
27 R4 **Pleasant Hill** Missouri, C USA 38°47′N 94°16′W
Pleasant Island *see* Nauru
36 K13 **Pleasant, Lake** ⊠ Arizona, SW USA
19 P8 **Pleasant Mountain** ▲ Maine, NE USA 44°01′N 70°47′W
27 R5 **Pleasanton** Kansas, C USA 38°09′N 94°43′W
25 R12 **Pleasanton** Texas, SW USA 28°58′N 98°28′W
185 G20 **Pleasant Point** Canterbury, South Island, New Zealand 44°16′S 171°09′E
19 R5 **Pleasant River** ≈ Maine, NE USA
18 J17 **Pleasantville** New Jersey, NE USA 39°22′N 74°31′W
103 N12 **Pléaux** Cantal, C France 45°08′N 02°10′E
111 B19 **Plechý** *var.* Plöckenstein. ▲ Austria/Czech Republic 48°45′N 13°50′E
Pleebo *see* Plibo
Pleihari *see* Pelaihari
Pleiku *see* Plây Cu
101 M16 **Pleisse** ≈ E Germany
Plencia *see* Plentzia
184 O7 **Plenty, Bay of** *bay* North Island, New Zealand
33 Y6 **Plentywood** Montana, NW USA 48°46′N 104°33′W
105 O2 **Plentzia** *var.* Plencia. País Vasco, N Spain 43°25′N 02°56′W
102 H5 **Plérin** Côtes d'Armor, NW France 48°33′N 02°46′W
124 M10 **Plesetsk** Arkhangel'skaya Oblast', NW Russian Federation 62°41′N 40°14′E
Pleshchenitsy *see* Plyeshchanitsy
Pleskau *see* Pskov
Pleskauer See *see* Pskov, Lake
Pleskava *see* Pskov
112 E8 **Pleso International** ✈ (Zagreb) Zagreb, NW Croatia 45°45′N 16°00′E
Pless *see* Pszczyna
15 Q11 **Plessisville** Québec, SE Canada 46°14′N 71°46′W
110 H12 **Pleszew** Wielkopolskie, C Poland 51°54′N 17°47′E
12 L10 **Plétipi, Lac** ◎ Québec, SE Canada
101 F15 **Plettenberg** Nordrhein-Westfalen, W Germany 51°13′N 07°52′E
114 I8 **Pleven** *prev.* Plevna. Pleven, N Bulgaria 43°25′N 24°36′E
114 I8 **Pleven** ◈ *province* N Bulgaria
Plevlja/Plevlje *see* Pljevlja
Plevna *see* Pleven
Plezzo *see* Bovec
Pliberk *see* Bleiburg
76 L17 **Plibo** *var.* Pleebo. SE Liberia 04°38′N 07°41′W
121 R11 **Pliny Trench** *undersea feature* C Mediterranean Sea
118 K13 **Plisa** *Rus.* Plissa. Vitsyebskaya Voblasts', N Belarus 55°13′N 27°57′E
Plissa *see* Plisa
112 D11 **Plitvica Selo** Lika-Senj, W Croatia 44°53′N 15°36′E
112 D11 **Plješevica** ▲ C Croatia
113 K14 **Pljevlja** *prev.* Plevlja, Plevlje. N Montenegro 43°21′N 19°21′E
Ploça *see* Ploçë
Plocce *see* Ploče
113 K22 **Ploçë** *var.* Ploça. Vlorë, SW Albania 40°24′N 19°41′E
113 G15 **Ploče** *It.* Plocce; *prev.* Kardeljevo. Dubrovnik-Neretva, SE Croatia 43°02′N 17°25′E
110 K11 **Płock** *Ger.* Plozk. Mazowieckie, C Poland 52°32′N 19°40′E
109 Q10 **Plöcken Pass** *Ger.* Plöckenpass, *It.* Passo di Monte Croce Carnico. *pass* SW Austria
Plöckenpass *see* Plöcken Pass
Plöckenstein *see* Plechý
99 B19 **Ploegsteert** Hainaut, W Belgium 50°45′N 02°52′E
102 H6 **Ploërmel** Morbihan, NW France 47°57′N 02°24′W
Ploeşti *see* Ploieşti
116 K13 **Ploieşti** *prev.* Ploeşti. Prahova, SE Romania 44°56′N 26°03′E
115 L17 **Plomári** *prev.* Plomárion. Lésvos, E Greece 38°58′N 26°24′E
Plomárion *see* Plomári
103 O12 **Plomb du Cantal** ▲ C France 45°03′N 02°48′E
183 V6 **Plomer, Point** *headland* New South Wales, SE Australia 31°19′S 153°00′E
100 J8 **Plön** Schleswig-Holstein, N Germany 54°10′N 10°25′E
110 L11 **Płońsk** Mazowieckie, C Poland 52°38′N 20°23′E
119 J20 **Plotnitsa** Brestskaya Voblasts', SW Belarus 52°03′N 26°39′E
110 E8 **Płoty** *Ger.* Plathe. Zachodnio-pomorskie, NW Poland 53°48′N 15°16′E
102 G7 **Plouay** Morbihan, NW France 47°54′N 03°14′W
111 D15 **Ploučnice** *Ger.* Polzen. ≈ NE Czech Republic
114 I10 **Plovdiv** *prev.* Eumolpias; *anc.* Evmolpia, Philippopolis, *Lat.* Trimontium. Plovdiv, C Bulgaria 42°09′N 24°47′E
114 I11 **Plovdiv** ◈ *province* C Bulgaria
30 L6 **Plover** Wisconsin, N USA 44°30′N 89°33′W
Plozk *see* Płock
27 U11 **Plumerville** Arkansas, C USA 35°09′N 92°38′W
19 P10 **Plum Island** *island* Massachusetts, NE USA
32 M9 **Plummer** Idaho, NW USA 47°19′N 116°54′W
83 J18 **Plumtree** Matabeleland South, SW Zimbabwe 20°30′S 27°50′E
118 D11 **Plungė** Telšiai, W Lithuania 55°55′N 21°53′E
113 J15 **Plužine** NW Montenegro 43°08′N 18°49′E
119 K14 **Plyeshchanitsy** *Rus.* Pleshchenitsy. Minskaya Voblasts', N Belarus 54°25′N 27°50′E
45 V10 **Plymouth** ○ (Montserrat) SW Montserrat 16°44′N 62°14′W
97 I24 **Plymouth** SW England, United Kingdom 50°23′N 04°10′W
31 O11 **Plymouth** Indiana, N USA 41°20′N 86°19′W
19 P12 **Plymouth** Massachusetts, NE USA 41°57′N 70°40′W
19 N8 **Plymouth** New Hampshire, NE USA 43°43′N 71°39′W
21 X9 **Plymouth** North Carolina, SE USA 35°53′N 76°46′W
30 M8 **Plymouth** Wisconsin, N USA 43°48′N 87°58′W
97 J20 **Plynlimon** ▲ C Wales, United Kingdom 52°27′N 03°48′W
124 G14 **Plyussa** Pskovskaya Oblast', W Russian Federation 58°27′N 29°21′E
111 B17 **Plzeň** *Ger.* Pilsen, *Pol.* Pilzno. Plzeňský Kraj, W Czech Republic 49°45′N 13°23′E
111 B17 **Plzeňský Kraj** ◈ *region* W Czech Republic
110 F11 **Pniewy** *Ger.* Pinne. Wielkolpolskie, W Poland 52°31′N 16°14′E
77 P13 **Pô** S Burkina 11°11′N 01°10′W
106 D8 **Po** ≈ N Italy
42 M13 **Poás, Volcán** ⛰ NW Costa Rica 10°12′N 84°12′W
77 S16 **Pobè** S Benin 07°00′N 02°41′E
123 S8 **Pobeda, Gora** ▲ NE Russian Federation 65°28′N 145°44′E
Pobeda Peak *see* Pobedy, Pik/Tomur Feng
147 Z7 **Pobedy, Pik** *Chin.* Tomür Feng. ▲ China/Kyrgyzstan 42°02′N 80°02′E *see also* Tomür Feng
Pobedy, Pik *see* Tomür Feng
110 H11 **Pobiedziska** *Ger.* Pudewitz. Wielkolpolskie, C Poland 52°30′N 17°19′E
Po, Bocche del *see* Po, Foci del
27 W9 **Pocahontas** Arkansas, C USA 36°15′N 91°00′W
29 U12 **Pocahontas** Iowa, C USA 42°44′N 94°40′W
33 Q15 **Pocatello** Idaho, NW USA 42°52′N 112°27′W
167 S13 **Pochentong** ✈ (Phnum Penh) Phnum Penh, S Cambodia 11°24′N 104°52′E
126 I6 **Pochep** Bryanskaya Oblast', W Russian Federation 52°56′N 33°20′E
126 H4 **Pochinok** Smolenskaya Oblast', W Russian Federation 54°21′N 32°29′E
41 R17 **Pochutla** *var.* San Pedro Pochutla. Oaxaca, SE Mexico 15°45′N 96°30′W
62 I6 **Pocitos, Salar** *var.* Salar Quiróm. *salt lake* NW Argentina
101 O22 **Pocking** Bayern, SE Germany 48°22′N 13°17′E
186 I10 **Pocklington Reef** *reef* SE Papua New Guinea
59 P15 **Poço da Cruz, Açude** ⊠ E Brazil
27 R11 **Pocola** Oklahoma, C USA 35°13′N 94°28′W
21 Y5 **Pocomoke City** Maryland, NE USA 38°04′N 75°34′W
59 L21 **Poços de Caldas** Minas Gerais, NE Brazil 21°48′S 46°33′W
124 H14 **Podberez'ye** Novgorodskaya Oblast', NW Russian Federation 58°42′N 31°22′E
Podbrodzie *see* Pabradė
125 U8 **Podcher'ye** Respublika Komi, NW Russian Federation 63°55′N 57°34′E
111 E16 **Poděbrady** *Ger.* Podiebrad. Středočeský Kraj, C Czech Republic 50°10′N 15°06′E
126 L9 **Podgorenskiy** Voronezhskaya Oblast', W Russian Federation 50°22′N 39°43′E
113 J17 **Podgorica** *prev.* Titograd. ● S Montenegro 42°25′N 19°16′E
113 K17 **Podgorica** ✈ S Montenegro 42°22′N 19°16′E
109 T13 **Podgrad** SW Slovenia 45°31′N 14°09′E
Podiebrad *see* Poděbrady
116 M5 **Podil's'ka Vysochina** *plateau* W Ukraine
Podium Anicensis *see* le Puy
122 L11 **Podkamennaya Tunguska** *Eng.* Stony Tunguska. ≈ C Russian Federation
111 N17 **Podkarpackie** ◈ *province* SW Poland
Pod Klošter *see* Arnoldstein
110 P9 **Podlaskie** ◈ *province* Mazowieckie, C Poland
127 Q8 **Podlesnoye** Saratovskaya Oblast', W Russian Federation 51°51′N 47°03′E
126 K4 **Podol'sk** Moskovskaya Oblast', W Russian Federation 55°24′N 37°30′E
76 H10 **Podor** N Senegal 16°40′N 14°57′W
125 P12 **Podosinovets** Kirovskaya Oblast', NW Russian Federation 60°15′N 47°06′E
124 I12 **Podporozh'ye** Leningradskaya Oblast', NW Russian Federation 60°52′N 34°00′E
Podravska Slatina *see* Slatina
112 J13 **Podromanlja** Republika Srpska, SE Bosnia and Herzegovina 43°55′N 18°46′E
Podsvil'ye *see* Padsvillye
116 L9 **Podu Iloaiei** *prev.* Podul Iloaiei. Iaşi, NE Romania 47°13′N 27°16′E
113 N15 **Podujevë** *Serb.* Podujevo. N Kosovo 42°56′N 21°13′E
Podujevo *see* Podujevë
Podul Iloaiei *see* Podu Iloaiei
Podunajská Rovina *see* Little Alföld
124 M12 **Podyuga** Arkhangel'skaya Oblast', NW Russian Federation 61°04′N 40°46′E
56 A9 **Poechos, Embalse** ◎ NW Peru
55 W10 **Poeketi** Sipaliwini, E Suriname
100 L8 **Poel** *island* N Germany
83 M20 **Poelela, Lagoa** ◎ S Mozambique
Poerwodadi *see* Purwodadi
Poerwokerto *see* Purwokerto
Poerworedjo *see* Purworejo
Poetovio *see* Ptuj
83 E23 **Pofadder** Northern Cape, W South Africa 29°09′S 19°25′E
106 I9 **Po, Foci del** *var.* Bocche del Po. ≈ NE Italy
116 E12 **Pogăniş** ≈ W Romania
Pogegen *see* Pagėgiai
106 G12 **Poggibonsi** Toscana, C Italy 43°28′N 11°09′E
107 I14 **Poggio Mirteto** Lazio, C Italy 42°17′N 12°42′E
109 V4 **Pöggstall** Niederösterreich, N Austria 48°19′N 15°10′E
116 L13 **Pogoanele** Buzău, SE Romania 44°55′N 27°00′E
Pogónion *see* Delvinákí
113 M21 **Pogradec** *var.* Pogradeci. Korçë, SE Albania 40°54′N 20°40′E
Pogradeci *see* Pogradec
123 S15 **Pogranichnyy** Primorskiy Kray, SE Russian Federation 44°18′N 131°33′E
38 M16 **Pogromni Volcano** ▲ Unimak Island, Alaska, USA 54°34′N 164°41′W
163 Z15 **P'ohang** *Jap.* Hokō. E South Korea 36°02′N 129°20′E
15 T9 **Pohénégamook, Lac** ◎ Québec, SE Canada
93 L20 **Pohja** *Swe.* Pojo. Etelä-Suomi, SW Finland 60°07′N 23°30′E
Pohjanlahti *see* Bothnia, Gulf of
189 U16 **Pohnpei** ◈ *state* E Micronesia
189 O12 **Pohnpei** ✈ Pohnpei, E Micronesia
189 O12 **Pohnpei** *prev.* Ponape Ascension Island. *island* E Micronesia
111 F19 **Pohořelice** *Ger.* Pohrlitz. Jihomoravský Kraj, SE Czech Republic 48°58′N 16°30′E
109 V10 **Pohorje** *Ger.* Bacher. ▲▲ N Slovenia
117 N6 **Pohrebyshche** Vinnyts'ka Oblast', C Ukraine 49°31′N 29°16′E
Pohrlitz *see* Pohořelice
161 P9 **Po Hu** ◎ E China
116 G15 **Poiana Mare** Dolj, S Romania 43°55′N 23°02′E
Poictiers *see* Poitiers
127 N6 **Poim** Penzenskaya Oblast', W Russian Federation 53°03′N 43°11′E
159 N15 **Poindo** Xigzang Zizhiqu, W China 29°58′N 91°20′E
195 Y13 **Poinsett, Cape** *headland* Antarctica 65°35′S 113°00′E
29 R9 **Poinsett, Lake** ◎ South Dakota, N USA
22 I10 **Point Au Fer Island** *island* Louisiana, S USA
39 X14 **Point Baker** Prince of Wales Island, Alaska, USA 56°19′N 133°31′W
25 U13 **Point Comfort** Texas, SW USA 28°40′N 96°33′W
Point de Galle *see* Galle
44 K10 **Pointe à Gravois** *headland* SW Haiti 18°00′N 73°53′W
22 L10 **Pointe a la Hache** Louisiana, S USA 29°34′N 89°48′W
45 Y6 **Pointe-à-Pitre** Grande Terre, C Guadeloupe 16°14′N 61°32′W
15 U7 **Pointe-au-Père** Québec, SE Canada 48°31′N 68°27′W
15 V5 **Pointe-aux-Anglais** Québec, SE Canada 49°40′N 67°09′W
45 T10 **Pointe Du Cap** *headland* N Saint Lucia 14°06′N 60°56′W
79 E21 **Pointe-Noire** Kouilou, S Congo 04°46′S 11°53′E
45 X6 **Pointe Noire** Basse Terre, W Guadeloupe 16°14′N 61°47′W
79 E21 **Pointe-Noire** ✈ Kouilou, S Congo 04°45′S 11°55′E
45 U15 **Point Fortin** Trinidad, Trinidad and Tobago 10°12′N 61°41′W
38 M6 **Point Hope** Alaska, USA 68°21′N 166°48′W
39 N5 **Point Lay** Alaska, USA 69°42′N 162°57′W
18 B16 **Point Marion** Pennsylvania, NE USA 39°44′N 79°53′W
18 K16 **Point Pleasant** New Jersey, NE USA 40°04′N 74°00′W
21 P4 **Point Pleasant** West Virginia, NE USA 38°53′N 82°07′W
45 R14 **Point Salines** ✈ (St. George's) SW Grenada 12°00′N 61°47′W
102 L9 **Poitiers** *prev.* Poictiers; *anc.* Limonum. Vienne, W France 46°35′N 00°19′E
102 K9 **Poitou** *cultural region* W France
102 K10 **Poitou-Charentes** ◈ *region* W France
103 N3 **Poix-de-Picardie** Somme, N France 49°47′N 01°58′E
Pojo *see* Pohja
37 S10 **Pojoaque** New Mexico, SW USA 35°52′N 106°01′W
152 E11 **Pokaran** Rājasthān, NW India 26°55′N 71°55′E
183 R4 **Pokataroo** New South Wales, SE Australia 29°37′S 148°43′E
119 P18 **Pokats'** *Rus.* Pokot'. ≈ SE Belarus
29 V5 **Pokegama Lake** ◎ Minnesota, N USA
184 L6 **Pokeno** Waikato, North Island, New Zealand 37°15′S 175°01′E
153 O11 **Pokharā** Western, C Nepal 28°14′N 84°E

◆ Country ● Country Capital ◇ Dependent Territory ○ Dependent Territory Capital ◈ Administrative Regions ✈ International Airport ▲ Mountain ▲▲ Mountain Range ⛰ Volcano ≈ River ◎ Lake ⊠ Reservoir

POKHVISTNEVO – PORT ROIS

127 T6 **Pokhvistnevo** Samarskaya Oblast', W Russian Federation *53°38′N 52°07′E*
55 W10 **Pokigron** Sipaliwini, C Suriname *04°31′N 55°23′W*
92 L10 **Pokka** *Lapp.* Bohkká. Lappi, N Finland *68°11′N 25°45′E*
79 N16 **Poko** Orientale, NE Dem. Rep. Congo *03°08′N 26°52′E*
Pokot' *see* Pokats'
Po-ko-to Shan *see* Bogda Shan
147 S7 **Pokrovka** Talasskaya Oblast', NW Kyrgyzstan *42°45′N 71°33′E*
Pokrovka *see* Kyzyl-Suu
117 V8 **Pokrovs'ke** *Rus.* Pokrovskoye. Dnipropetrovs'ka Oblast', E Ukraine *47°58′N 36°15′E*
Pokrovskoye *see* Pokrovs'ke
Pola *see* Pula
37 N10 **Polacca** Arizona, SW USA *35°49′N 110°21′W*
104 L2 **Pola de Laviana** Asturias, N Spain *43°15′N 05°33′W*
104 K2 **Pola de Lena** Asturias, N Spain *43°10′N 05°49′W*
104 L2 **Pola de Siero** Asturias, N Spain *43°24′N 05°39′W*
191 Y3 **Poland** Kiritimati, E Kiribati *01°52′N 157°33′W*
110 H12 **Poland** *off.* Republic of Poland, *var.* Polish Republic, *Pol.* Polska, Rzeczpospolita Polska; *prev. Pol.* Polska Rzeczpospolita Ludowa, The Polish People's Republic. ◆ *republic* C Europe
Poland, Republic of *see* Poland
Polangen *see* Palanga
110 G7 **Polanów** *Ger.* Pollnow. Zachodnio-pomorskie, NW Poland *54°07′N 16°38′E*
136 H13 **Polatlı** Ankara, C Turkey *39°34′N 32°08′E*
118 L12 **Polatsk** *Rus.* Polotsk. Vitsyebskaya Voblasts', N Belarus *55°29′N 28°47′E*
125 U14 **Polazna** Permskaya Oblast', NW Russian Federation *58°18′N 56°22′E*
110 F8 **Połczyn-Zdrój** *Ger.* Bad Polzin. Zachodnio-pomorskie, NW Poland *53°44′N 16°02′E*
149 R5 **Pol-e-'Alam** Lowgar, E Afghanistan *33°59′N 69°02′E*
Polekhatum *see* Pulhatyn
149 Q3 **Pol-e Khomrī** *var.* Pul-i-Khumri. Baghlān, NE Afghanistan *35°55′N 68°45′E*
197 S10 **Pole Plain** *undersea feature* Arctic Ocean
Pol-e-Safid *see* Pol-e Sefīd
143 P5 **Pol-e Sefīd** *var.* Pol-e-Safid, Pul-i-Sefid. Māzandarān, N Iran *36°05′N 53°01′E*
118 B13 **Polessk** *Ger.* Labiau. Kaliningradskaya Oblast', W Russian Federation *54°52′N 21°06′E*
Polesskoye *see* Polis'ke
171 N13 **Polewali** Sulawesi, C Indonesia *03°26′S 119°23′E*
114 G11 **Polezhan** ▲ SW Bulgaria *41°42′N 23°28′E*
78 F13 **Poli** Nord, N Cameroon *09°31′N 13°10′E*
Poli *see* Pólis
107 M19 **Policastro, Golfo di** *gulf* S Italy
110 D8 **Police** *Ger.* Politz. Zachodnio-pomorskie, NW Poland *53°34′N 14°34′E*
172 I17 **Police, Pointe** *headland* Mahé, NE Seychelles *04°48′S 55°31′E*
115 L17 **Polichnítos** *var.* Polihnitos, Políkhnitos. Lésvos, E Greece *39°04′N 26°10′E*
Poligiros *see* Polýgyros
107 P17 **Polignano a Mare** Puglia, SE Italy *40°59′N 17°13′E*
103 S9 **Poligny** Jura, E France *46°51′N 05°42′E*
Polihnitos *see* Polichnítos
Polikastro/Políkastron *see* Polýkastro
Políkhnitos *see* Polichnítos
171 O3 **Polillo Islands** *island group* N Philippines
109 Q9 **Polinik** ▲ SW Austria *46°54′N 13°10′E*
115 J15 **Políochni** *var.* Polýochni. *site of ancient city* Límnos, E Greece
121 O2 **Pólis** *var.* Poli. W Cyprus *35°02′N 32°27′E*
Polish People's Republic, The *see* Poland
Polish Republic *see* Poland
117 O3 **Polis'ke** *Rus.* Polesskoye. Kyyivs'ka Oblast', N Ukraine *51°16′N 29°27′E*
107 N22 **Polistena** Calabria, SW Italy *38°25′N 16°05′E*
Politz *see* Police
Políyiros *see* Polýgyros
29 V14 **Polk City** Iowa, C USA *41°46′N 93°42′W*
110 F13 **Polkowice** *Ger.* Heerwegen. Dolnośląskie, W Poland *51°32′N 16°06′E*
155 G22 **Pollāchi** Tamil Nādu, SE India *10°38′N 77°00′E*
109 W7 **Pöllau** Steiermark, SE Austria *47°18′N 15°46′E*
189 T13 **Polle** *atoll* Chuuk Islands, C Micronesia
105 X9 **Pollença** Mallorca, Spain, W Mediterranean Sea *39°52′N 03°01′E*
Pollnow *see* Polanów
29 N7 **Pollock** South Dakota, N USA *45°53′N 100°15′W*
92 L8 **Polmak** Finnmark, N Norway *70°01′N 28°04′E*
30 L10 **Polo** Illinois, N USA *41°59′N 89°34′W*
193 V15 **Poloa** *island* Tongatapu Group, N Tonga
42 E5 **Polochic, Río** ~ C Guatemala
Pologi *see* Polohy
117 V9 **Polohy** *Rus.* Pologi. Zaporiz'ka Oblast', SE Ukraine *47°30′N 36°18′E*
83 K20 **Polokwane** *prev.* Pietersburg. Limpopo, NE South Africa *23°54′S 29°23′E*
14 M10 **Polonais, Lac des** ◎ Québec, SE Canada
61 G20 **Polonio, Cabo** *headland* E Uruguay *34°22′S 53°46′W*
155 K24 **Polonnaruwa** North Central Province, C Sri Lanka *07°56′N 81°02′E*
116 L5 **Polonne** *Rus.* Polonnoye. Khmel'nyts'ka Oblast', NW Ukraine *50°10′N 27°30′E*
Polonnoye *see* Polonne
Polotsk *see* Polatsk
Polovinka *see* Ugleural'skiy
109 T7 **Pöls** *var.* Pölsbach. ~ E Austria
Pölsbach *see* Pöls
Polska/Polska, Rzeczpospolita/Polska Rzeczpospolita Ludowa *see* Poland
114 L10 **Polski Gradets** Stara Zagora, C Bulgaria *42°12′N 26°06′E*
114 K8 **Polski Trŭmbesh** Ruse, N Bulgaria *43°22′N 25°38′E*
33 P8 **Polson** Montana, NW USA *47°41′N 114°09′W*
117 T6 **Poltava** Poltavs'ka Oblast', NE Ukraine *49°33′N 34°32′E*
Poltava *see* Poltavs'ka Oblast'
117 R5 **Poltavs'ka Oblast'** *var.* Poltava, *Rus.* Poltavskaya Oblast'. ◐ *province* NE Ukraine
Poltavskaya Oblast' *see* Poltavs'ka Oblast'
Poltoratsk *see* Aşgabat
118 I5 **Põltsamaa** *Ger.* Oberpahlen. Jõgevamaa, E Estonia *58°40′N 26°00′E*
118 I4 **Põltsamaa** *var.* Põltsamaa Jõgi. ~ C Estonia
Põltsamaa Jõgi *see* Põltsamaa
122 I8 **Poluy** ~ N Russian Federation
118 J6 **Põlva** *Ger.* Pölwe. Põlvamaa, SE Estonia *58°04′N 27°06′E*
93 N16 **Polvijärvi** Itä-Suomi, SE Finland *62°53′N 29°20′E*
Pölwe *see* Põlva
115 I22 **Polýaigos** *island* Kykládes, Greece, Aegean Sea
115 I22 **Polyaígou Folégandrou, Stenó** *strait* Kykládes, Greece, Aegean Sea
124 J3 **Polyarnyy** Murmanskaya Oblast', NW Russian Federation *69°10′N 33°21′E*
124 I5 **Polyarnyye Zori** Murmanskaya Oblast', NW Russian Federation *67°22′N 32°31′E*
125 W5 **Polyarnyy Ural** ▲▲ NW Russian Federation
115 G14 **Polýgyros** *var.* Poligiros, Políyiros. Kentrikí Makedonía, N Greece *40°21′N 23°27′E*
114 F13 **Polýkastro** *var.* Polikastro; *prev.* Políkastron. Kentrikí Makedonía, N Greece *41°01′N 22°33′E*
193 O9 **Polynesia** *island group* C Pacific Ocean
Polýochni *see* Políochni
41 Y13 **Polyuc** Quintana Roo, E Mexico
109 V10 **Polzela** C Slovenia *46°18′N 15°04′E*
Polzen *see* Ploučnice
56 D12 **Pomabamba** Ancash, C Peru *08°48′S 77°30′W*
185 D23 **Pomahaka** ~ South Island, New Zealand
106 F12 **Pomarance** Toscana, C Italy *43°19′N 10°53′E*
104 G9 **Pombal** Leiria, C Portugal *39°55′N 08°38′W*
76 D9 **Pombas** Santo Antão, NW Cape Verde *17°09′N 25°02′W*
83 N19 **Pomene** Inhambane, SE Mozambique *22°57′S 35°34′E*
110 G8 **Pomerania** *cultural region* Germany/Poland
110 D7 **Pomeranian Bay** *Ger.* Pommersche Bucht, *Pol.* Zatoka Pomorska. *bay* Germany/Poland
31 T15 **Pomeroy** Ohio, N USA *39°01′N 82°01′W*
32 L10 **Pomeroy** Washington, NW USA *46°28′N 117°36′W*
117 Q8 **Pomichna** Kirovohrads'ka Oblast', C Ukraine *48°07′N 31°25′E*
186 H7 **Pomio** New Britain, E Papua New Guinea *05°31′S 151°30′E*
Pomir, Dar"yoi *see* Pamir/Pāmīr, Daryā-ye
27 T6 **Pomme de Terre Lake** ⊠ Missouri, C USA
29 S8 **Pomme de Terre River** ~ Minnesota, N USA
Pommersche Bucht *see* Pomeranian Bay
35 T15 **Pomona** California, W USA *34°03′N 117°45′W*
114 N9 **Pomorie** Burgas, E Bulgaria *42°32′N 27°39′E*
Pomorska, Zatoka *see* Pomeranian Bay
110 H8 **Pomorskie** ◐ *province* N Poland
125 Q4 **Pomorskiy Proliv** *strait* NW Russian Federation
125 T10 **Pomozdino** Respublika Komi, NW Russian Federation *62°11′N 54°13′E*
Pompaelo *see* Pamplona
23 Z15 **Pompano Beach** Florida, SE USA *26°14′N 80°06′W*
107 K18 **Pompei** Campania, S Italy *40°45′N 14°27′E*
33 V10 **Pompeys Pillar** Montana, NW USA *45°58′N 107°55′W*
Ponape Ascension Island *see* Pohnpei
29 R13 **Ponca** Nebraska, C USA *42°35′N 96°42′W*
27 O8 **Ponca City** Oklahoma, C USA *36°41′N 97°04′W*
45 T6 **Ponce** C Puerto Rico *18°01′N 66°36′W*
23 X10 **Ponce de Leon Inlet** *inlet* Florida, SE USA
22 K8 **Ponchatoula** Louisiana, S USA *30°26′N 90°26′W*
26 M8 **Pond Creek** Oklahoma, C USA *36°40′N 97°48′W*
155 J20 **Pondicherry** *var.* Puduchcheri, *Fr.* Pondichéry. Pondicherry, SE India *11°59′N 79°50′E*
151 I20 **Pondicherry** *var.* Puduchcheri, *Fr.* Pondichéry. ◐ *union territory* India
Pondichéry *see* Pondicherry
197 N11 **Pond Inlet** Baffin Island, Nunavut, NE Canada *72°37′N 77°56′W*
187 P16 **Ponérihouen** Province Nord, C New Caledonia *21°04′S 165°24′E*
104 J4 **Ponferrada** Castilla-León, NW Spain *42°33′N 06°35′W*
184 N13 **Pongaroa** Manawatu-Wanganui, North Island, New Zealand *40°36′S 176°08′E*
167 Q12 **Pong Nam Ron** Chantaburi, S Thailand *12°55′N 102°15′E*
81 C14 **Pongo** ~ S Sudan
152 I7 **Pong Reservoir** ⊠ N India
111 N14 **Poniatowa** Lubelskie, E Poland *51°11′N 22°05′E*
167 R12 **Pônley** Kâmpóng Chhnăng, C Cambodia *12°26′N 104°25′E*
155 I20 **Ponnaiyār** ~ SE India
11 Q15 **Ponoka** Alberta, SW Canada *52°42′N 113°33′W*
127 U6 **Ponomarevka** Orenburgskaya Oblast', W Russian Federation *53°16′N 54°10′E*
169 Q17 **Ponorogo** Jawa, C Indonesia *07°51′S 111°30′E*
124 M5 **Ponoy** Murmanskaya Oblast', NW Russian Federation *67°00′N 41°06′E*
122 F6 **Ponoy** ~ NW Russian Federation
102 K11 **Pons** Charente-Maritime, W France *45°31′N 00°31′W*
Pons *see* Ponts
Pons Aelii *see* Newcastle upon Tyne
Pons Vetus *see* Pontevedra
99 G20 **Pont-à-Celles** Hainaut, S Belgium *50°31′N 04°21′E*
102 K16 **Pontacq** Pyrénées-Atlantiques, SW France *43°11′N 00°06′W*
64 P3 **Ponta Delgada** São Miguel, Azores, Portugal, NE Atlantic Ocean *37°29′N 25°40′W*
64 P3 **Ponta Delgado** ✈ São Miguel, Azores, Portugal, NE Atlantic Ocean *37°28′N 25°40′W*
64 N2 **Ponta do Pico** ▲ Pico, Azores, Portugal, NE Atlantic Ocean *38°28′N 28°25′W*
60 J11 **Ponta Grossa** Paraná, S Brazil *25°07′S 50°09′W*
103 S5 **Pont-à-Mousson** Meurthe-et-Moselle, NE France *48°55′N 06°03′E*
103 T9 **Pontarlier** Doubs, E France *46°54′N 06°20′E*
106 G11 **Pontassieve** Toscana, C Italy *43°46′N 11°28′E*
102 L4 **Pont-Audemer** Eure, N France *49°22′N 00°31′E*
22 K9 **Pontchartrain, Lake** ◎ Louisiana, S USA
102 I8 **Pontchâteau** Loire-Atlantique, NW France *47°26′N 02°04′W*
103 R10 **Pont-de-Vaux** Ain, E France *46°25′N 04°57′E*
104 G4 **Ponteareas** Galicia, NW Spain *42°11′N 08°29′W*
106 J6 **Pontebba** Friuli-Venezia Giulia, NE Italy *46°32′N 13°18′E*
104 G4 **Ponte Caldelas** Galicia, NW Spain *42°23′N 08°30′W*
107 J16 **Pontecorvo** Lazio, C Italy *41°27′N 13°40′E*
104 G5 **Ponte da Barca** Viana do Castelo, N Portugal *41°48′N 08°25′W*
104 G5 **Ponte de Lima** Viana do Castelo, N Portugal *41°46′N 08°35′W*
106 F11 **Pontedera** Toscana, C Italy *43°40′N 10°38′E*
104 H10 **Ponte de Sor** Portalegre, C Portugal *39°15′N 08°01′W*
104 H2 **Pontedeume** Galicia, NW Spain *43°22′N 08°09′W*
106 F6 **Ponte di Legno** Lombardia, N Italy *46°16′N 10°31′E*
11 T17 **Ponteix** Saskatchewan, S Canada *49°43′N 107°22′W*
171 Q16 **Ponte Macassar** *var.* Pante Macassar, Pante Makasar, Pante Makassar. W East Timor *09°11′S 124°27′E*
59 N20 **Ponte Nova** Minas Gerais, NE Brazil *20°25′S 42°54′W*
59 G18 **Pontes e Lacerda** Mato Grosso, W Brazil *15°14′S 59°21′W*
104 G4 **Pontevedra** *anc.* Pons Vetus. Galicia, NW Spain *42°25′N 08°39′W*
104 G3 **Pontevedra** ◐ *province* Galicia, NW Spain
104 G4 **Pontevedra, Ría de** *estuary* NW Spain
30 M12 **Pontiac** Illinois, N USA *40°54′N 88°36′W*
31 R9 **Pontiac** Michigan, N USA *42°38′N 83°17′W*
169 P11 **Pontianak** Borneo, C Indonesia *0°05′S 109°16′E*
107 I16 **Pontino, Agro** *plain* C Italy
Pontisarae *see* Pontoise
102 H6 **Pontivy** Morbihan, NW France *48°04′N 02°58′W*
102 F6 **Pont-l'Abbé** Finistère, NW France *47°52′N 04°14′W*
103 N4 **Pontoise** *anc.* Briva Isarae, Cergy-Pontoise, Pontisarae. Val-d'Oise, N France *49°03′N 02°05′E*
11 W13 **Ponton** Manitoba, C Canada *54°36′N 99°02′W*
102 J5 **Pontorson** Manche, N France *48°33′N 01°31′W*
22 M2 **Pontotoc** Mississippi, S USA *34°15′N 89°00′W*
25 R9 **Pontotoc** Texas, SW USA *30°52′N 98°57′W*
106 E10 **Pontremoli** Toscana, C Italy *44°24′N 09°55′E*
108 J10 **Pontresina** Graubünden, S Switzerland *46°29′N 09°52′E*
105 U5 **Ponts** *var.* Pons. Cataluña, NE Spain *41°55′N 01°12′E*
103 R14 **Pont-St-Esprit** Gard, S France *44°15′N 04°37′E*
97 K21 **Pontypool** *Wel.* Pontypŵl. SE Wales, United Kingdom *51°43′N 03°02′W*
97 J22 **Pontypridd** S Wales, United Kingdom *51°37′N 03°22′W*
Pontypŵl *see* Pontypool
43 R17 **Ponuga** Veraguas, SE Panama *07°50′N 80°58′W*
184 L6 **Ponui Island** *island* N New Zealand
119 K14 **Ponya** ~ N Belarus
107 I17 **Ponza, Isola di** *Island* Isole Ponziane, S Italy
107 I17 **Ponziane, Isole** *island* C Italy
182 F7 **Poochera** South Australia *32°45′S 134°51′E*
97 L24 **Poole** S England, United Kingdom *50°43′N 01°59′W*
25 S6 **Poolville** Texas, SW USA *33°00′N 97°55′W*
Poona *see* Pune
182 M8 **Pooncarie** New South Wales, SE Australia *33°26′S 142°37′E*
183 N6 **Poopelloe Lake** *seasonal lake* New South Wales, SE Australia
57 K19 **Poopó** Oruro, C Bolivia *18°23′S 66°58′W*
57 K19 **Poopó, Lago** *var.* Lago Pampa Aullagas. ◎ W Bolivia
184 L3 **Poor Knights Islands** *island* N New Zealand
39 P10 **Poorman** Alaska, USA *64°05′N 155°34′W*
182 E3 **Pootnoura** South Australia *28°31′S 134°09′E*
147 R10 **Pop** *Rus.* Pap. Namangan Viloyati, E Uzbekistan *40°49′N 71°06′E*
117 X7 **Popasna** *Rus.* Popasnaya. Luhans'ka Oblast', E Ukraine *48°38′N 38°24′E*
Popasnaya *see* Popasna
54 D12 **Popayán** Cauca, SW Colombia *02°27′N 76°32′W*
99 B18 **Poperinge** West-Vlaanderen, W Belgium *50°52′N 02°44′E*
123 N7 **Popigay** Taymyrskiy (Dolgano-Nenetskiy) Avtonomnyy Okrug, N Russian Federation *71°54′N 110°45′E*
123 N7 **Popigay** ~ N Russian Federation
117 O5 **Popil'nya** Zhytomyrs'ka Oblast', N Ukraine *49°57′N 29°24′E*
182 K8 **Popiltah Lake** *seasonal lake* New South Wales, SE Australia
33 X7 **Poplar** Montana, NW USA *48°06′N 105°12′W*
11 Y14 **Poplar** ~ Manitoba, C Canada
27 X8 **Poplar Bluff** Missouri, C USA *36°45′N 90°23′W*
33 X6 **Poplar River** ~ Montana, NW USA
41 P14 **Popocatépetl** ⛰ S Mexico *18°59′N 98°37′W*
79 H21 **Popokabaka** Bandundu, SW Dem. Rep. Congo *05°42′S 16°35′E*
107 J15 **Popoli** Abruzzo, C Italy *42°09′N 13°51′E*
186 F9 **Popondetta** Northern, S Papua New Guinea *08°45′S 148°15′E*
112 F9 **Popovača** Sisak-Moslavina, NE Croatia *45°35′N 16°37′E*
114 L8 **Popovo** Tŭrgovishte, N Bulgaria *43°20′N 26°14′E*
Popovo *see* Iskra
Popper *see* Poprad
30 M5 **Popple River** ~ Wisconsin, N USA
111 L19 **Poprad** *Ger.* Deutschendorf, *Hung.* Poprád. Prešovský Kraj, E Slovakia *49°04′N 20°16′E*
111 L18 **Poprad** *Ger.* Popper, *Hung.* Poprád. ~ Poland/Slovakia
111 L19 **Poprad-Tatry** ✈ (Poprad) Prešovský Kraj, E Slovakia *49°04′N 20°21′E*
21 X7 **Poquoson** Virginia, NE USA *37°08′N 76°21′W*
149 O15 **Porāli** ~ SW Pakistan
184 N12 **Porangahau** Hawke's Bay, North Island, New Zealand *40°19′S 176°36′E*
59 K17 **Porangatu** Goiás, C Brazil *13°28′S 49°14′W*
119 G18 **Porazava** *Pol.* Porozow, *Rus.* Porozovo. Hrodzyenskaya Voblasts', W Belarus *52°56′N 24°22′E*
154 A11 **Porbandar** Gujarāt, W India *21°40′N 69°40′E*
10 I13 **Porcher Island** *island* British Columbia, SW Canada
104 M13 **Porcuna** Andalucía, S Spain *37°52′N 04°12′W*
14 F7 **Porcupine** Ontario, S Canada *48°31′N 81°07′W*
64 M6 **Porcupine Bank** *undersea feature* N Atlantic Ocean
11 V15 **Porcupine Hills** ▲▲ Manitoba/Saskatchewan, S Canada
30 L3 **Porcupine Mountains** *hill range* Michigan, N USA
64 M7 **Porcupine Plain** *undersea feature* E Atlantic Ocean *16°00′W 49°00′N*
8 G7 **Porcupine River** ~ Canada/USA
106 I7 **Pordenone** *anc.* Portenau. Friuli-Venezia Giulia, NE Italy *45°58′N 12°39′E*
54 H9 **Pore** Casanare, E Colombia *05°42′N 71°59′W*
112 A9 **Poreč** *It.* Parenzo. Istra, NW Croatia *45°16′N 13°36′E*
60 I9 **Porecatu** Paraná, S Brazil *22°46′S 51°22′W*
Porech'ye *see* Parechcha
127 P4 **Poretskoye** Chuvashskaya Respublika, W Russian Federation *55°12′N 46°20′E*
77 Q13 **Porga** N Benin *11°04′N 00°58′E*
186 B7 **Porgera** Enga, W Papua New Guinea *05°32′S 143°08′E*
93 K18 **Pori** *Swe.* Björneborg. Länsi-Suomi, SW Finland *61°28′N 21°50′E*
185 L14 **Porirua** Wellington, North Island, New Zealand *41°08′S 174°51′E*
92 I12 **Porjus** *Lapp.* Bårjås. Norrbotten, N Sweden *66°55′N 19°55′E*
124 G14 **Porkhov** Pskovskaya Oblast', W Russian Federation *57°46′N 29°27′E*
55 O4 **Porlamar** Nueva Esparta, NE Venezuela *10°57′N 63°51′W*
102 I8 **Pornic** Loire-Atlantique, NW France *47°07′N 02°07′W*
186 B7 **Poroma** Southern Highlands, W Papua New Guinea *06°15′S 143°34′E*
123 T13 **Poronaysk** Ostrov Sakhalin, Sakhalinskaya Oblast', SE Russian Federation *49°15′N 143°00′E*
115 G20 **Póros** Póros, S Greece *37°30′N 23°27′E*
115 C19 **Póros** Kefallinía, Iónia Nisiá, Greece, C Mediterranean Sea *38°09′N 20°46′E*
115 G20 **Póros** *island* S Greece
81 G24 **Poroto Mountains** ▲▲ SW Tanzania
112 B10 **Porozina** Primorje-Gorski Kotar, NW Croatia *45°07′N 14°17′E*
Porozovo/Porozow *see* Porazava
195 X15 **Porpoise Bay** *bay* Antarctica
65 G15 **Porpoise Point** *headland* NE Ascension Island *07°54′S 14°22′W*
108 C6 **Porrentruy** Jura, NW Switzerland *47°25′N 07°06′E*
106 F10 **Porretta Terme** Emilia-Romagna, C Italy *44°10′N 11°01′E*
Porriño *see* O Porriño
Pors *see* Porsangenfijorden
92 L7 **Porsangenfijorden** *Lapp.* Pors. *fjord* N Norway
92 K8 **Porsangerhalvøya** *peninsula* N Norway
95 G16 **Porsgrunn** Telemark, S Norway *59°08′N 09°38′E*
136 E13 **Porsuk Çayı** ~ C Turkey
Porsy *see* Boldumsaz
57 N18 **Portachuelo** Santa Cruz, C Bolivia *17°21′S 63°24′W*
182 I9 **Port Adelaide** South Australia *34°49′S 138°31′E*
97 F15 **Portadown** *Ir.* Port An Dúnáin. S Northern Ireland, United Kingdom *54°26′N 06°27′W*
31 P10 **Portage** Michigan, N USA *42°12′N 85°34′W*
18 D15 **Portage** Pennsylvania, NE USA *40°23′N 78°40′W*
30 K8 **Portage** Wisconsin, N USA *43°33′N 89°29′W*
30 M3 **Portage Lake** ◎ Michigan, N USA
11 X16 **Portage la Prairie** Manitoba, S Canada *49°58′N 98°20′W*
31 R11 **Portage River** ~ Ohio, N USA
27 Y8 **Portageville** Missouri, C USA *36°25′N 89°42′W*
28 L2 **Portal** North Dakota, N USA *48°57′N 102°33′W*
10 L17 **Port Alberni** Vancouver Island, British Columbia, SW Canada *49°11′N 124°49′W*
14 E15 **Port Albert** Ontario, S Canada *43°51′N 81°42′W*
104 I10 **Portalegre** *anc.* Ammaia, Amoea. Portalegre, E Portugal *39°17′N 07°25′W*
104 H10 **Portalegre** ◐ *district* C Portugal
37 V12 **Portales** New Mexico, SW USA *34°11′N 103°19′W*
39 X14 **Port Alexander** Baranof Island, Alaska, USA *56°15′N 134°39′W*
83 I25 **Port Alfred** Eastern Cape, S South Africa *33°31′S 26°55′E*
10 J16 **Port Alice** Vancouver Island, British Columbia, SW Canada *50°23′N 127°24′W*
22 J8 **Port Allen** Louisiana, S USA *30°27′N 91°12′W*
Port Amelia *see* Pemba
Port An Dúnáin *see* Portadown
32 G7 **Port Angeles** Washington, NW USA *48°06′N 123°26′W*
44 L12 **Port Antonio** NE Jamaica *18°10′N 76°27′W*
115 D16 **Pórta Panagiá** *religious building* Thessalía, C Greece
25 T14 **Port Aransas** Texas, SW USA *27°49′N 97°03′W*
97 E18 **Portarlington** *Ir.* Cúil an tSúdaire. Laois/Offaly, C Ireland *53°10′N 07°11′W*
183 P17 **Port Arthur** Tasmania, SE Australia *43°09′S 147°51′E*
25 Y11 **Port Arthur** Texas, SW USA *29°55′N 93°56′W*
96 G12 **Port Askaig** W Scotland, United Kingdom *55°51′N 06°06′W*
182 I7 **Port Augusta** South Australia *32°29′S 137°44′E*
44 M9 **Port-au-Prince** ● (Haiti) C Haiti *18°33′N 72°20′W*
44 M9 **Port-au-Prince** ✈ E Haiti *18°38′N 72°13′W*
22 I8 **Port Barre** Louisiana, S USA *30°33′N 91°57′W*
Port-Bergé *see* Boriziny
151 Q19 **Port Blair** Andaman and Nicobar Islands, SE India *11°40′N 92°44′E*
25 X12 **Port Bolivar** Texas, SW USA *29°21′N 94°45′W*
105 X4 **Portbou** Cataluña, NE Spain *42°26′N 03°10′E*
77 N17 **Port Bouet** ✈ (Abidjan) SE Ivory Coast *05°17′N 03°55′W*
182 I8 **Port Broughton** South Australia *33°39′S 137°55′E*
14 F17 **Port Burwell** Ontario, S Canada *42°39′N 80°47′W*
12 G17 **Port Burwell** Québec, NE Canada *60°25′N 64°49′W*
182 M13 **Port Campbell** Victoria, SE Australia *38°37′S 143°00′E*
15 V4 **Port-Cartier** Québec, SE Canada *50°00′N 66°55′W*
185 F23 **Port Chalmers** Otago, South Island, New Zealand *45°46′S 170°37′E*
23 W14 **Port Charlotte** Florida, SE USA *27°00′N 82°07′W*
38 L9 **Port Clarence** Alaska, USA *65°15′N 166°51′W*
10 I13 **Port Clements** Graham Island, British Columbia, SW Canada *53°37′N 132°12′W*
31 S11 **Port Clinton** Ohio, N USA *41°30′N 82°56′W*
14 H17 **Port Colborne** Ontario, S Canada *42°51′N 79°16′W*
15 Y7 **Port-Daniel** Québec, SE Canada *48°10′N 64°58′W*
Port Darwin *see* Darwin
183 O17 **Port Davey** *headland* Tasmania, SE Australia *43°19′S 145°54′E*
44 K8 **Port-de-Paix** NW Haiti *19°56′N 72°52′W*
181 W4 **Port Douglas** Queensland, NE Australia *16°33′S 145°27′E*
10 J13 **Port Edward** British Columbia, SW Canada *54°11′N 130°16′W*
83 K24 **Port Edward** KwaZulu/Natal, SE South Africa *31°03′S 30°14′E*
58 J12 **Portel** Pará, NE Brazil *01°58′S 50°45′W*
104 H12 **Portel** Évora, S Portugal *38°18′N 07°42′W*
14 E14 **Port Elgin** Ontario, S Canada *44°26′N 81°22′W*
45 Y14 **Port Elizabeth** Bequia, Saint Vincent and the Grenadines *13°01′N 61°15′W*
83 I26 **Port Elizabeth** Eastern Cape, S South Africa *33°58′S 25°36′E*
96 G13 **Port Ellen** W Scotland, United Kingdom *55°37′N 06°12′W*
Portenau *see* Pordenone
97 H16 **Port Erin** SW Isle of Man *54°05′N 04°47′W*
45 Q13 **Porter Point** *headland* Saint Vincent, Saint Vincent and the Grenadines *13°22′N 61°10′W*
185 G18 **Porters Pass** *pass* South Island, New Zealand
83 E25 **Porterville** Western Cape, SW South Africa *33°03′S 19°00′E*
35 R12 **Porterville** California, W USA *36°03′N 119°03′W*
Port-Étienne *see* Nouâdhibou
182 L13 **Port Fairy** Victoria, SE Australia *38°24′S 142°13′E*
184 M4 **Port Fitzroy** Great Barrier Island, Auckland, NE New Zealand *36°10′S 175°21′E*
Port Florence *see* Kisumu
Port-Francqui *see* Ilebo
79 C18 **Port-Gentil** Ogooué-Maritime, W Gabon *0°40′S 08°50′E*
182 I7 **Port Germein** South Australia *33°02′S 138°01′E*
22 J6 **Port Gibson** Mississippi, S USA *31°57′N 90°58′W*
39 Q13 **Port Graham** Alaska, USA *59°21′N 151°49′W*
77 U17 **Port Harcourt** Rivers, S Nigeria *04°43′N 07°02′E*
10 J16 **Port Hardy** Vancouver Island, British Columbia, SW Canada *50°41′N 127°30′W*
Port Harrison *see* Inukjuak
13 R14 **Port Hawkesbury** Cape Breton Island, Nova Scotia, SE Canada *45°36′N 61°22′W*
180 I6 **Port Hedland** Western Australia *20°23′S 118°40′E*
39 O15 **Port Heiden** Alaska, USA *56°54′N 158°40′W*
97 I19 **Porthmadog** *var.* Portmadoc. NW Wales, United Kingdom *52°55′N 04°08′W*
14 I15 **Port Hope** Ontario, SE Canada *43°58′N 78°18′W*
13 S9 **Port Hope Simpson** Newfoundland and Labrador, E Canada *52°30′N 56°18′W*
65 C24 **Port Howard Settlement** West Falkland, Falkland Islands
31 T9 **Port Huron** Michigan, N USA *42°58′N 82°25′W*
107 K17 **Portici** Campania, S Italy *40°48′N 14°20′E*
137 Y13 **Port-İliç** *Rus.* Port Il'ich. SE Azerbaijan *38°54′N 48°49′E*
Port Il'ich *see* Port-İliç
104 G14 **Portimão** *var.* Vila Nova de Portimão. Faro, S Portugal *37°08′N 08°32′W*
25 T17 **Port Isabel** Texas, SW USA *26°04′N 97°13′W*
18 J13 **Port Jervis** New York, NE USA *41°22′N 74°39′W*
55 S7 **Port Kaituma** NW Guyana *07°42′N 59°52′W*
126 K12 **Port Katon** Rostovskaya Oblast', SW Russian Federation *46°52′N 38°46′E*
183 S9 **Port Kembla** New South Wales, SE Australia *34°30′S 150°54′E*
182 F8 **Port Kenny** South Australia *33°09′S 134°38′E*
Port Klang *see* Pelabuhan Klang
Port Láirge *see* Waterford
183 S8 **Portland** New South Wales, SE Australia *33°24′S 150°00′E*
182 L13 **Portland** Victoria, SE Australia *38°21′S 141°38′E*
184 K4 **Portland** Northland, North Island, New Zealand *35°48′S 174°19′E*
31 Q13 **Portland** Indiana, N USA *40°25′N 84°58′W*
19 P8 **Portland** Maine, NE USA *43°41′N 70°16′W*
31 Q9 **Portland** Michigan, N USA *42°51′N 84°52′W*
29 Q4 **Portland** North Dakota, N USA *47°28′N 97°22′W*
32 G11 **Portland** Oregon, NW USA *45°31′N 122°41′W*
20 J8 **Portland** Tennessee, S USA *36°34′N 86°31′W*
25 T14 **Portland** Texas, SW USA *27°52′N 97°19′W*
32 G11 **Portland** ✈ Oregon, NW USA *45°36′N 122°34′W*
182 L13 **Portland Bay** *bay* Victoria, SE Australia
44 K13 **Portland Bight** *bay* S Jamaica
97 L24 **Portland Bill** *var.* Bill of Portland. *headland* S England, United Kingdom *50°31′N 02°28′W*
Portland, Bill of *see* Portland Bill
183 P15 **Portland, Cape** *headland* Tasmania, SE Australia *40°46′S 147°58′E*
10 J12 **Portland Inlet** *inlet* British Columbia, W Canada
184 P11 **Portland Island** *island* E New Zealand
65 F15 **Portland Point** *headland* SW Ascension Island
44 J13 **Portland Point** *headland* C Jamaica *17°42′N 77°10′W*
103 P16 **Port-la-Nouvelle** Aude, S France *43°01′N 03°04′E*
Portlaoighise *see* Port Laoise
97 E18 **Port Laoise** *var.* Portlaoise, *Ir.* Portlaoighise; *prev.* Maryborough. C Ireland *53°02′N 07°17′W*
Portlaoise *see* Port Laoise
25 U13 **Port Lavaca** Texas, SW USA *28°36′N 96°39′W*
182 G9 **Port Lincoln** South Australia *34°43′S 135°49′E*
39 Q14 **Port Lions** Kodiak Island, Alaska, USA *57°55′N 152°48′W*
76 I15 **Port Loko** W Sierra Leone *08°50′N 12°50′W*
65 E24 **Port Louis** East Falkland, Falkland Islands *51°31′S 58°07′W*
45 Y5 **Port-Louis** Grande Terre, N Guadeloupe *16°25′N 61°32′W*
173 X16 **Port Louis** ● (Mauritius) NW Mauritius *20°10′S 57°30′E*
Port Louis *see* Scarborough
Port-Lyautey *see* Kénitra
182 K12 **Port MacDonnell** South Australia *38°04′S 140°40′E*
183 U7 **Port Macquarie** New South Wales, SE Australia *31°26′S 152°55′E*
Portmadoc *see* Porthmadog
Port Mahon *see* Mahón
44 K12 **Port Maria** C Jamaica *18°22′N 76°54′W*
10 K16 **Port McNeill** Vancouver Island, British Columbia, SW Canada *50°34′N 127°06′W*
13 P11 **Port-Menier** Île d'Anticosti, Québec, E Canada *49°49′N 64°19′W*
39 N15 **Port Moller** Alaska, USA *56°00′N 160°31′W*
44 L13 **Port Morant** E Jamaica *17°53′N 76°20′W*
44 K13 **Portmore** C Jamaica *17°58′N 76°52′W*
186 D9 **Port Moresby** ● (Papua New Guinea) Central/National Capital District, SW Papua New Guinea *09°28′S 147°12′E*
Port Natal *see* Durban
25 Y11 **Port Neches** Texas, SW USA *29°59′N 93°57′W*
182 G9 **Port Neill** South Australia *34°06′S 136°19′E*
15 S6 **Portneuf** ~ Québec, SE Canada
15 R6 **Portneuf, Lac** ◎ Québec, SE Canada
83 D23 **Port Nolloth** Northern Cape, W South Africa *29°17′S 16°51′E*
18 J17 **Port Norris** New Jersey, NE USA *39°13′N 75°00′W*
Port-Nouveau-Québec *see* Kangiqsualujjuaq
104 G6 **Porto** *Eng.* Oporto; *anc.* Portus Cale. Porto, NW Portugal *41°09′N 08°37′W*
104 G6 **Porto** *var.* Pôrto. ◐ *district* N Portugal
104 G6 **Porto** ✈ Porto, W Portugal *41°09′N 08°37′W*
Pôrto *see* Porto
61 I16 **Porto Alegre** *var.* Pôrto Alegre. *state capital* Rio Grande do Sul, S Brazil *30°03′S 51°10′W*
Porto Alexandre *see* Tombua
82 B12 **Porto Amboim** Cuanza Sul, NW Angola *10°47′S 13°43′E*
Porto Amélia *see* Pemba
Porto Bello *see* Portobelo
43 T14 **Portobelo** *var.* Porto Bello, Puerto Bello. Colón, N Panama *09°33′N 79°37′W*
60 G10 **Pôrto Camargo** Paraná, S Brazil *23°23′S 53°47′W*
25 U13 **Port O'Connor** Texas, SW USA *28°26′N 96°26′W*
Pôrto de Mós *see* Porto de Moz
58 J12 **Porto de Moz** *var.* Pôrto de Mós. Pará, NE Brazil *01°45′S 52°15′W*
64 O5 **Porto do Moniz** Madeira, Portugal, NE Atlantic Ocean
59 H16 **Porto dos Gaúchos** Mato Grosso, W Brazil *11°32′S 57°16′W*
Porto Edda *see* Sarandë
107 J24 **Porto Empedocle** Sicilia, Italy, C Mediterranean Sea *37°13′N 13°32′E*
59 H20 **Porto Esperança** Mato Grosso do Sul, SW Brazil *19°36′S 57°24′W*
106 E13 **Portoferraio** Toscana, C Italy *42°49′N 10°18′E*
96 G6 **Port of Ness** NW Scotland, United Kingdom *58°29′N 06°15′W*
45 U14 **Port-of-Spain** ● (Trinidad and Tobago) Trinidad, Trinidad and Tobago *10°39′N 61°30′W*
Port of Spain *see* Piarco
103 X15 **Porto, Golfe de** *gulf* Corse, France, C Mediterranean Sea
Porto Grande *see* Mindelo
106 I7 **Portogruaro** Veneto, NE Italy *45°46′N 12°50′E*
35 P5 **Portola** California, W USA *39°48′N 120°28′W*
187 Q13 **Port-Olry** Espiritu Santo, C Vanuatu *15°03′S 167°04′E*
93 J17 **Pörtom** *Fin.* Pirttikylä. Länsi-Suomi, W Finland *62°42′N 21°40′E*
Port Omna *see* Portumna
59 G21 **Porto Murtinho** Mato Grosso do Sul, SW Brazil *21°42′S 57°52′W*
59 K16 **Porto Nacional** Tocantins, C Brazil *10°41′S 48°19′W*
77 S16 **Porto-Novo** ● (Benin) S Benin *06°29′N 02°37′E*
23 X10 **Port Orange** Florida, SE USA *29°06′N 80°59′W*
32 G8 **Port Orchard** Washington, NW USA *47°32′N 122°38′W*
Porto Re *see* Kraljevica
32 E15 **Port Orford** Oregon, NW USA *42°45′N 124°30′W*
Porto Rico *see* Puerto Rico
106 J13 **Porto San Giorgio** Marche, C Italy *43°10′N 13°47′E*
107 F14 **Porto San Stefano** Toscana, C Italy *42°26′N 11°09′E*
64 P5 **Porto Santo** *var.* Vila Baleira. Porto Santo, Madeira, Portugal, NE Atlantic Ocean *33°04′N 16°20′W*
64 Q5 **Porto Santo** ✈ Porto Santo, Madeira, Portugal, NE Atlantic Ocean *33°04′N 16°20′W*
64 P5 **Porto Santo** *var.* Ilha do Porto Santo. *island* Madeira, Portugal, NE Atlantic Ocean
Porto Santo, Ilha do *see* Porto Santo
60 H9 **Porto São José** Paraná, S Brazil *22°43′S 53°10′W*
59 O19 **Porto Seguro** Bahia, E Brazil *16°25′S 39°07′W*
107 B17 **Porto Torres** Sardegna, Italy, C Mediterranean Sea *40°50′N 08°23′E*
59 J23 **Porto União** Santa Catarina, S Brazil *26°15′S 51°04′W*
103 Y16 **Porto-Vecchio** Corse, France, C Mediterranean Sea *41°35′N 09°17′E*
59 E15 **Porto Velho** *var.* Velho. *state capital* Rondônia, W Brazil *08°45′S 63°54′W*
56 A6 **Portoviejo** *var.* Puertoviejo. Manabí, W Ecuador *01°03′S 80°31′W*
185 B26 **Port Pegasus** *bay* Stewart Island, New Zealand
14 H15 **Port Perry** Ontario, SE Canada *44°08′N 78°57′W*
183 N12 **Port Phillip Bay** *harbor* Victoria, SE Australia
182 I8 **Port Pirie** South Australia *33°11′S 138°01′E*
96 G9 **Portree** N Scotland, United Kingdom *57°26′N 06°12′W*
Port Rex *see* East London
Port Rois *see* Portrush

◆ Country
● Country Capital
◇ Dependent Territory
○ Dependent Territory Capital
◐ Administrative Regions
✈ International Airport
▲ Mountain
▲▲ Mountain Range
⛰ Volcano
~ River
◎ Lake
⊠ Reservoir

PORT ROYAL – PRYDZ BAY

44 K13 Port Royal E Jamaica 17°55′N 76°52′W
21 R15 Port Royal South Carolina, SE USA 32°22′N 80°41′W
21 R15 Port Royal Sound inlet South Carolina, SE USA
97 F14 Portrush Ir. Port Rois. N Northern Ireland, United Kingdom 55°12′N 06°40′W
Port Said see Būr Sa'īd
23 R9 Port Saint Joe Florida, SE USA 29°49′N 85°18′W
23 Y11 Port Saint John Florida, SE USA 28°28′N 80°46′W
103 R16 Port-St-Louis-du-Rhône Bouches-du-Rhône, SE France 43°22′N 04°48′E
44 K10 Port Salut SW Haiti 18°04′N 73°55′W
65 E24 Port Salvador inlet East Falkland, Falkland Islands
65 D24 Port San Carlos East Falkland, Falkland Islands 51°30′S 58°59′W
13 S10 Port Saunders Newfoundland, Newfoundland and Labrador, SE Canada 50°40′N 57°17′W
83 K24 Port Shepstone KwaZulu/Natal, E South Africa 30°44′S 30°28′E
45 O11 Portsmouth var. Grand-Anse. NW Dominica 15°34′N 61°27′W
97 N24 Portsmouth S England, United Kingdom 50°48′N 01°05′W
19 P10 Portsmouth New Hampshire, NE USA 43°04′N 70°47′W
31 S15 Portsmouth Ohio, N USA 38°43′N 83°00′W
21 X7 Portsmouth Virginia, NE USA 36°50′N 76°18′W
14 E17 Port Stanley Ontario, S Canada 42°39′N 81°12′W
Port Stanley see Stanley
65 B25 Port Stephens inlet West Falkland, Falkland Islands
65 B25 Port Stephens Settlement West Falkland, Falkland Islands
97 F14 Portstewart Ir. Port Stíobhaird. N Northern Ireland, United Kingdom 55°11′N 06°43′W
Port Stíobhaird see Portstewart
83 K24 Port St. Johns Eastern Cape, SE South Africa 31°37′S 29°32′E
80 I7 Port Sudan Red Sea, NE Sudan 19°37′N 37°14′E
22 L10 Port Sulphur Louisiana, S USA 29°28′N 89°41′W
Port Swettenham see Klang/Pelabuhan Klang
97 J22 Port Talbot S Wales, United Kingdom 51°36′N 03°47′W
92 L11 Porttipahdan Tekojärvi ◎ N Finland
32 G7 Port Townsend Washington, NW USA 48°07′N 122°45′W
104 H9 Portugal off. Portuguese Republic. ◆ republic SW Europe
105 O2 Portugalete País Vasco, N Spain 43°19′N 03°01′W
54 J6 Portuguesa off. Estado Portuguesa. ◈ state N Venezuela
Portuguesa, Estado see Portuguesa
Portuguese East Africa see Mozambique
Portuguese Guinea see Guinea-Bissau
Portuguese Republic see Portugal
Portuguese Timor see East Timor
Portuguese West Africa see Angola
97 D18 Portumna Ir. Port Omna. Galway, W Ireland 53°06′N 08°13′W
Portus Cale see Porto
Portus Magnus see Almería
Portus Magonis see Mahón
103 P17 Port-Vendres var. Port Vendres. Pyrénées-Orientales, S France 42°31′N 03°06′E
182 H9 Port Victoria South Australia 34°34′S 137°31′E
187 Q14 Port-Vila var. Vila. ● (Vanuatu) Éfaté, C Vanuatu 17°45′S 168°21′E
Port Vila see Bauer Field
182 I9 Port Wakefield South Australia 34°13′S 138°10′E
31 N8 Port Washington Wisconsin, N USA 43°23′N 87°54′W
57 J14 Porvenir Pando, NW Bolivia 11°15′S 68°43′W
63 I24 Porvenir Magallanes, S Chile 53°18′S 70°22′W
61 D18 Porvenir Paysandú, W Uruguay 32°23′S 57°59′W
93 M19 Porvoo Swe. Borgå. Etelä-Suomi, S Finland 60°25′N 25°40′E
Porzecze see Parechcha
104 M10 Porzuna Castilla-La Mancha, C Spain 39°10′N 04°10′W
61 E14 Posadas Misiones, NE Argentina 27°27′S 55°52′W
104 L13 Posadas Andalucía, S Spain 37°48′N 05°06′W
Poschega see Požega
108 J11 Poschiavino ≈ Italy/Switzerland
108 J10 Poschiavo Ger. Puschlav. Graubünden, S Switzerland 46°19′N 10°02′E
112 D12 Posedarje Zadar, SW Croatia 44°12′N 15°27′E
Posen see Poznań
124 L14 Poshekhon'ye Yaroslavskaya Oblast', W Russian Federation 58°31′N 39°07′E
92 M13 Posio Lappi, NE Finland 66°06′N 28°16′E
Poskam see Zepu
Posnania see Poznań
1713 O12 Poso Sulawesi, C Indonesia 01°23′S 120°45′E
171 O12 Poso, Danau ◎ Sulawesi, C Indonesia
137 R10 Posof Ardahan, NE Turkey 41°30′N 42°33′E
25 R6 Possum Kingdom Lake ⊠ Texas, SW USA
25 N6 Post Texas, SW USA 33°14′N 101°24′W
Postavy/Postawy see Pastavy
12 I7 Poste-de-la-Baleine Québec, NE Canada 55°13′N 77°54′W
99 M17 Posterholt Limburg, SE Netherlands 51°07′N 06°02′E
83 G22 Postmasburg Northern Cape, N South Africa 28°20′S 23°05′E
Pôsto Diuarum see Campo de Diauarum
59 I16 Pôsto Jacaré Mato Grosso, W Brazil 12°S 53°27′W
109 T12 Postojna Ger. Adelsberg, It. Postumia. SW Slovenia 45°48′N 14°12′E
Postumia see Postojna
29 X12 Postville Iowa, C USA 43°04′N 91°34′W
Pöstyén see Piešt'any
113 G14 Posušje Federacija Bosna I Hercegovina, SW Bosnia and Herzegovina 43°28′N 17°20′E
171 O16 Pota Flores, C Indonesia 08°21′S 120°50′E
115 G23 Potamós Antikýthira, S Greece 35°53′N 23°17′E
55 S9 Potaru River ≈ C Guyana
83 I21 Potchefstroom North-West, N South Africa 26°42′S 27°06′E
27 R11 Poteau Oklahoma, C USA 35°03′N 94°36′W
25 R12 Poteet Texas, SW USA 29°02′N 98°34′W
115 G14 Poteidaia site of ancient city Kentrikí Makedonía, N Greece
Potentia see Potenza
107 M18 Potenza anc. Potentia. Basilicata, S Italy 40°40′N 15°50′E
185 A24 Poteriteri, Lake ◎ South Island, New Zealand
104 M2 Potes Cantabria, N Spain 43°10′N 04°41′W
Potgietersrus see Mokopane
25 S12 Poth Texas, SW USA 29°04′N 98°04′W
32 J9 Potholes Reservoir ⊠ Washington, NW USA
137 Q9 P'ot'i W Georgia 42°10′N 41°42′E
77 X13 Potiskum Yobe, NE Nigeria 11°38′N 11°07′E
Potkozarje see Ivanjska
32 M9 Potlatch Idaho, NW USA 46°55′N 116°51′W
33 N9 Pot Mountain ▲ Idaho, NW USA 46°44′N 115°24′W
113 H14 Potoci Federacija Bosna I Hercegovina, S Bosnia and Herzegovina 43°24′N 17°52′E
21 V3 Potomac River ≈ NE USA
57 L20 Potosí Potosí, S Bolivia 19°35′S 65°51′W
42 H9 Potosí Chinandega, NW Nicaragua 12°58′N 87°30′W
27 W6 Potosi Missouri, C USA 37°57′N 90°49′W
57 K21 Potosí ◈ department SW Bolivia
62 H7 Potrerillos Atacama, N Chile 26°30′S 69°25′W
42 H5 Potrerillos Cortés, NW Honduras 15°10′N 87°58′W
62 H8 Potro, Cerro del ▲ N Chile 28°22′S 69°34′W
100 N12 Potsdam Brandenburg, NE Germany 52°24′N 13°04′E
18 J7 Potsdam New York, NE USA 44°40′N 74°58′W
109 X5 Pottendorf Niederösterreich, E Austria 47°55′N 16°23′E
109 X5 Pottenstein Niederösterreich, E Austria 47°58′N 16°07′E
18 I15 Pottstown Pennsylvania, NE USA 40°15′N 75°39′W
18 H14 Pottsville Pennsylvania, NE USA 40°40′N 76°10′W
155 L25 Pottuvil Eastern Province, SE Sri Lanka 06°53′N 81°49′E
149 U6 Potwar Plateau plateau NE Pakistan
102 J7 Pouancé Maine-et-Loire, W France 47°46′N 01°11′W
15 R6 Poulin de Courval, Lac ◎ Québec, SE Canada
18 L9 Poultney Vermont, NE USA 43°31′N 73°12′W
187 O16 Poum Province Nord, W New Caledonia 20°15′S 164°03′E
59 L21 Pouso Alegre Minas Gerais, NE Brazil 22°13′S 45°56′W
192 I16 Poutasi Upolu, SE Samoa 14°00′S 171°43′W
167 R12 Poŭthĭsăt prev. Pursat. Poŭthĭsăt, W Cambodia 12°32′N 103°55′E
167 R12 Poŭthĭsăt, Stœng prev. Pursat. ≈ W Cambodia
102 J9 Pouzauges Vendée, NW France 46°47′N 00°54′W
Po, Valle del see Po Valley
106 F8 Po Valley It. Valle del Po. valley N Italy
111 I19 Považská Bystrica Ger. Waagbistritz, Hung. Vágbeszterce. Trenčiansky Kraj, W Slovakia 49°07′N 18°26′E
124 J10 Povenets Respublika Kareliya, NW Russian Federation 62°50′N 34°47′E
184 Q9 Poverty Bay inlet North Island, New Zealand
112 K12 Povlen ▲ W Serbia
104 G6 Póvoa de Varzim Porto, NW Portugal 41°22′N 08°46′W
127 N8 Povorino Voronezhskaya Oblast', W Russian Federation 51°10′N 42°16′E
Povungnituk see Puvirnituq
12 J3 Povungnituk, Rivière de ≈ Québec, NE Canada
14 H11 Powassan Ontario, S Canada 46°05′N 79°21′W
35 U17 Poway California, W USA 32°57′N 117°02′W
33 W14 Powder River Wyoming, C USA 43°01′N 106°57′W
33 Y10 Powder River ≈ Montana/Wyoming, NW USA
32 L12 Powder River ≈ Oregon, NW USA
33 W13 Powder River Pass pass Wyoming, C USA
33 U12 Powell Wyoming, C USA 44°45′N 108°45′W
65 I22 Powell Basin undersea feature NW Weddell Sea
36 M8 Powell, Lake ◎ Utah, W USA
37 R4 Powell, Mount ▲ Colorado, C USA 39°25′N 106°20′W
10 L17 Powell River British Columbia, SW Canada 49°54′N 124°34′W
31 N5 Powers Michigan, N USA 45°40′N 87°29′W
28 K2 Powers Lake North Dakota, N USA 48°33′N 102°37′W
21 V6 Powhatan Virginia, NE USA 37°33′N 77°56′W
31 V13 Powhatan Point Ohio, N USA 39°49′N 80°49′W
97 J20 Powys cultural region E Wales, United Kingdom
187 P17 Poya Province Nord, C New Caledonia 21°19′S 165°07′E
161 P10 Poyang Hu ◎ S China
30 L7 Poygan, Lake ◎ Wisconsin, N USA
109 Y2 Poysdorf Niederösterreich, NE Austria 48°40′N 16°38′E
112 N11 Požarevac Ger. Passarowitz. Serbia, NE Serbia 44°37′N 21°11′E
41 Q13 Poza Rica var. Poza Rica de Hidalgo. Veracruz-Llave, E Mexico 20°34′N 97°26′W
Poza Rica de Hidalgo see Poza Rica
112 L13 Požega prev. Slavonska Požega, Ger. Poschega, Hung. Pozsega. Požega-Slavonija, NE Croatia 45°19′N 17°42′E
112 H9 Požega-Slavonija off. Požeško-Slavonska Županija. ◈ province NE Croatia
Požeško-Slavonska Županija see Požega-Slavonija
125 U13 Pozhva Komi-Permyatskiy Avtonomnyy Okrug, NW Russian Federation 59°07′N 56°04′E
110 G11 Poznań Ger. Posen, Posnania. Wielkolpolskie, C Poland 52°24′N 16°56′E
105 O13 Pozo Alcón Andalucía, S Spain 37°43′N 02°55′W
62 H3 Pozo Almonte Tarapacá, N Chile 20°16′S 69°50′W
104 L12 Pozoblanco Andalucía, S Spain 38°23′N 04°48′W
105 Q11 Pozo Cañada Castilla-La Mancha, C Spain 38°49′N 01°45′W
62 N5 Pozo Colorado Presidente Hayes, C Paraguay 23°26′S 58°51′W
63 J20 Pozos, Punta headland S Argentina 47°55′S 65°46′W
Pozsega see Požega
Pozsony see Bratislava
55 N5 Pozuelos Anzoátegui, NE Venezuela 10°11′N 64°39′W
107 L26 Pozzallo Sicilia, Italy, C Mediterranean Sea 36°44′N 14°51′E
107 K17 Pozzuoli anc. Puteoli. Campania, S Italy 40°49′N 14°07′E
77 P17 Pra ≈ S Ghana
111 C19 Prachatice Ger. Prachatitz. Jihočeský Kraj, S Czech Republic 49°01′N 14°02′E
Prachatitz see Prachatice
167 P11 Prachin Buri var. Prachinburi. Prachin Buri, C Thailand 14°05′N 101°23′E
Prachinburi see Prachin Buri
Prachuab Girikhand see Prachuap Khiri Khan
167 O12 Prachuap Khiri Khan var. Prachuab Girikhand. Prachuap Khiri Khan, SW Thailand 11°50′N 99°49′E
111 H16 Praděd Ger. Altvater. ▲ NE Czech Republic 50°06′N 17°14′E
54 D11 Pradera Valle del Cauca, SW Colombia 03°23′N 76°11′W
103 O17 Prades Pyrénées-Orientales, S France 42°36′N 02°22′E
59 O19 Prado Bahia, SE Brazil 17°13′S 39°15′W
54 E11 Prado Tolima, C Colombia 03°45′N 74°55′W
Prado del Ganso see Goose Green
Prae see Phrae
95 I24 Præstø Storstrøm, SE Denmark 55°08′N 12°03′E
Prag/Praga/Prague see Praha
27 O10 Prague Oklahoma, C USA 35°29′N 96°40′W
111 D16 Praha Eng. Prague, Ger. Prag, Pol. Praga. ● (Czech Republic) Středočeský Kraj, NW Czech Republic 50°06′N 14°26′E
116 J13 Prahova ◈ county SE Romania
116 J13 Prahova ≈ S Romania
76 E10 Praia ● (Cape Verde) Santiago, S Cape Verde 14°55′N 23°31′W
83 M21 Praia do Bilene Gaza, S Mozambique 25°18′S 33°10′E
83 M20 Praia do Xai-Xai Gaza, S Mozambique 25°04′S 33°43′E
116 J10 Praid Hung. Parajd. Harghita, C Romania 46°33′N 25°06′E
26 J3 Prairie Dog Creek ≈ Kansas/Nebraska, C USA
30 J9 Prairie du Chien Wisconsin, N USA 43°02′N 91°08′W
27 J9 Prairie Grove Arkansas, C USA 35°58′N 94°19′W
31 P10 Prairie River ≈ Michigan, N USA
Prairie State see Illinois
25 V11 Prairie View Texas, SW USA 30°05′N 95°59′W
167 Q10 Prakhon Chai Buri Ram, E Thailand 14°36′N 103°04′E
109 R4 Pram ≈ N Austria
109 S4 Prambachkirchen Oberösterreich, N Austria 48°18′N 13°50′E
118 H2 Prangli island N Estonia
154 J13 Prānhita ≈ C India
127 O14 Praskoveya Stavropol'skiy Kray, SW Russian Federation 44°45′N 44°11′E
172 I15 Praslin island Inner Islands, NE Seychelles
115 O23 Prasonísi, Akrotírio cape Ródos, Dodekánisa, Greece, Aegean Sea
111 I14 Praszka Opolskie, S Poland 51°05′N 18°29′E
152 M13 Pratāpgarh Uttar Pradesh, N India 25°53′N 81°56′E
Pratas Island see Tungsha Tao
119 M18 Pratasy Rus. Protasy. Homyel'skaya Voblasts', SE Belarus 52°47′N 29°05′E
167 Q10 Prathai Nakhon Ratchasima, E Thailand 15°31′N 102°42′E
Prathet Thai see Thailand
Prathum Thani see Pathum Thani
63 F21 Prat, Isla island S Chile
106 G11 Prato Toscana, C Italy 43°53′N 11°05′E
103 O17 Prats-de-Mollo-la-Preste Pyrénées-Orientales, S France 42°25′N 02°28′E
26 L6 Pratt Kansas, C USA 37°40′N 98°45′W
108 E6 Pratteln Basel-Land, NW Switzerland 47°32′N 07°42′E
193 O2 Pratt Seamount undersea feature N Pacific Ocean 56°09′N 142°30′W
23 P5 Prattville Alabama, S USA 32°27′N 86°27′W
Praust see Pruszcz Gdański
119 B14 Pravdinsk Ger. Friedland. Kaliningradskaya Oblast', W Russian Federation 54°26′N 21°01′E
104 K2 Pravia Asturias, N Spain 43°30′N 06°06′W
118 L12 Prazaroki Rus. Prozoroki. Vitsyebskaya Voblasts', N Belarus 55°18′N 28°13′E
Prázsmár see Prejmer
167 S11 Preăh Vihéar Preăh Vihéar, N Cambodia 13°57′N 104°48′E
116 J12 Predeal Hung. Predeál. Braşov, C Romania 45°30′N 25°31′E
109 S8 Predlitz Steiermark, SE Austria 47°04′N 13°54′E
11 V15 Preeceville Saskatchewan, S Canada 51°58′N 102°40′W
Preenkuln see Priekule
102 K6 Pré-en-Pail Mayenne, NW France 48°27′N 00°15′W
109 T4 Pregarten Oberösterreich, N Austria 48°21′N 14°31′E
54 H7 Pregonero Táchira, NW Venezuela 08°02′N 71°35′W
118 J10 Preiļi Ger. Preli. Preiļi, SE Latvia 56°17′N 26°52′E
116 J12 Prejmer Ger. Tartlau, Hung. Prázsmár. Braşov, S Romania 45°42′N 25°49′E
113 J16 Prekornica ▲ C Montenegro
Preli see Preiļi
Prëmet see Përmet
100 M12 Premnitz Brandenburg, NE Germany 52°33′N 12°22′E
25 S15 Premont Texas, SW USA 27°21′N 98°07′W
113 H14 Prenj ▲ S Bosnia and Herzegovina
Prenjas/Prenjasi see Përrenjas
22 L7 Prentiss Mississippi, S USA 31°36′N 89°52′W
Preny see Prienai
100 O10 Prenzlau Brandenburg, NE Germany 53°19′N 13°52′E
123 N11 Preobrazhenka Irkutskaya Oblast', C Russian Federation 60°01′N 108°00′E
166 J9 Preparis Island island SW Myanmar (Burma)
Prerau see Přerov
111 H18 Přerov Ger. Prerau. Olomoucký Kraj, E Czech Republic 49°27′N 17°27′E
Preschau see Prešov
14 M14 Prescott Ontario, SE Canada 44°43′N 75°33′W
36 K12 Prescott Arizona, SW USA 34°33′N 112°26′W
27 T13 Prescott Arkansas, C USA 33°49′N 93°25′W
32 L10 Prescott Washington, NW USA 46°17′N 118°21′W
30 H6 Prescott Wisconsin, N USA 44°46′N 92°45′W
185 A24 Preservation Inlet inlet South Island, New Zealand
112 O7 Preševo Serbia, SE Serbia 42°20′N 21°38′E
29 N10 Presho South Dakota, N USA 43°54′N 100°03′W
58 M13 Presidente Dutra Maranhão, E Brazil 05°17′S 44°30′W
60 I8 Presidente Epitácio São Paulo, S Brazil 21°45′S 52°07′W
62 N5 Presidente Hayes off. Departamento de Presidente Hayes. ◈ department C Paraguay
Presidente Hayes, Departamento de see Presidente Hayes
60 I9 Presidente Prudente São Paulo, S Brazil 22°09′S 51°24′W
Presidente Stroessner see Ciudad del Este
Presidente Vargas see Itabira
60 I8 Presidente Venceslau São Paulo, S Brazil 21°52′S 51°51′W
193 O10 President Thiers Seamount undersea feature C Pacific Ocean 24°39′S 145°50′W
24 J11 Presidio Texas, SW USA 29°33′N 104°22′W
Preslav see Veliki Preslav
111 M19 Prešov var. Preschau, Ger. Eperies, Hung. Eperjes. Prešovský Kraj, E Slovakia 49°N 21°14′E
111 M19 Prešovský Kraj ◈ region E Slovakia
113 N20 Prespa, Lake Alb. Liqen i Prespës, Gk. Límni Megáli Préspa, Límni Prespa, Mac. Prespansko Ezero, Serb. Prespansko Jezero. ◎ SE Europe
Prespa, Limni/Prespansko Ezero/Prespansko Jezero/Prespës, Liqen i see Prespa, Lake
19 S2 Presque Isle Maine, NE USA 46°40′N 68°01′W
18 B11 Presque Isle headland Pennsylvania, NE USA 42°09′N 80°06′W
Pressburg see Bratislava
77 P17 Prestea SW Ghana 05°22′N 02°07′W
111 B17 Přeštice Ger. Pschestitz. Plzeňský Kraj, W Czech Republic 49°36′N 13°19′E
97 K17 Preston NW England, United Kingdom 53°46′N 02°42′W
23 S6 Preston Georgia, SE USA 32°03′N 84°32′W
33 R16 Preston Idaho, NW USA 42°06′N 111°52′W
29 Z13 Preston Iowa, C USA 42°03′N 90°24′W
29 X11 Preston Minnesota, N USA 43°41′N 92°06′W
21 O6 Prestonsburg Kentucky, S USA 37°40′N 82°46′W
96 I13 Prestwick W Scotland, United Kingdom 55°31′N 04°39′W
83 I45 Pretoria var. Epitoli, Tshwane. ● Gauteng, NE South Africa 25°41′S 28°12′E see also Tshwane
Pretoria-Witwatersrand-Vereeniging see Gauteng
Pretusha see Pretushë
113 M21 Pretushë var. Pretusha. Korçë, SE Albania 40°50′N 20°45′E
Preussisch Eylau see Bagrationovsk
Preußisch Holland see Pasłęk
Preussisch-Stargard see Starogard Gdański
115 C17 Préveza Ípeiros, W Greece 38°59′N 20°44′E
37 V3 Prewitt Reservoir ⊠ Colorado, C USA
167 S13 Prey Vêng Prey Vêng, S Cambodia 11°30′N 105°20′E
144 M12 Priaral'skiy Karakumy, Peski desert SW Kazakhstan
123 P14 Priargunsk Chitinskaya Oblast', S Russian Federation 50°25′N 119°12′E
38 K14 Pribilof Islands island group Alaska, USA
113 K14 Priboj Serbia, W Serbia 43°34′N 19°33′E
111 C17 Příbram Ger. Pibrans. Středočeský Kraj, W Czech Republic 49°41′N 14°02′E
36 M4 Price Utah, W USA 39°35′N 110°49′W
37 N5 Price River ≈ Utah, W USA
23 N8 Prichard Alabama, S USA 30°44′N 88°04′W
25 R8 Priddy Texas, SW USA 31°39′N 98°30′W
105 P8 Priego Castilla-La Mancha, C Spain 40°26′N 02°19′W
104 M14 Priego de Córdoba Andalucía, S Spain 37°27′N 04°12′W
118 C10 Priekule Ger. Preenkuln. Liepāja, SW Latvia 56°26′N 21°36′E
118 C12 Priekulė Ger. Prökuls. Klaipėda, W Lithuania 55°36′N 21°16′E
119 F14 Prienai Pol. Preny. Kaunas, S Lithuania 54°37′N 23°56′E
83 G23 Prieska Northern Cape, C South Africa 29°40′S 22°45′E
32 M7 Priest Lake ⊠ Idaho, NW USA
32 M7 Priest River Idaho, NW USA 48°10′N 117°02′W
104 M3 Prieta, Peña ▲ N Spain 43°01′N 04°42′W
40 J10 Prieto, Cerro ▲ C Mexico 24°10′N 105°21′W
111 J19 Prievidza var. Priewitz, Ger. Priwitz, Hung. Privigye. Trenčiansky Kraj, W Slovakia 48°47′N 18°35′E
Priewitz see Prievidza
112 F10 Prijedor ◈ Republika Srpska, NW Bosnia and Herzegovina
113 K14 Prijepolje Serbia, W Serbia 43°24′N 19°39′E
Prikaspiyskaya Nizmennost' see Caspian Depression
113 O19 Prilep Turk. Perlepe. S FYR Macedonia 41°21′N 21°34′E
108 B9 Prilly Vaud, SW Switzerland 46°32′N 06°38′E
Priluki see Pryluky
62 L10 Primero, Río ≈ C Argentina
29 S12 Primghar Iowa, C USA 43°05′N 95°37′W
112 B9 Primorje-Gorski Kotar off. Primorsko-Goranska Županija. ◈ province NW Croatia
118 A13 Primorsk Ger. Fischhausen. Kaliningradskaya Oblast', W Russian Federation 54°45′N 20°00′E
124 G12 Primorsk Fin. Koivisto. Leningradskaya Oblast', NW Russian Federation 60°20′N 28°39′E
123 S14 Primorskiy Kray prev. Eng. Maritime Territory. ◈ territory SE Russian Federation
114 N10 Primorsko prev. Keupriya. Burgas, E Bulgaria 42°15′N 27°45′E
126 K13 Primorsko-Akhtarsk Krasnodarskiy Kray, SW Russian Federation 46°03′N 38°44′E
Primorsko-Goranska Županija see Primorje-Gorski Kotar
Primorsk/Primorskoye see Prymors'k
117 U13 Primors'kyy Respublika Krym, S Ukraine 45°09′N 35°33′E
113 D14 Primošten Šibenik-Knin, S Croatia 43°34′N 15°57′E
11 R13 Primrose Lake ◎ Saskatchewan, C Canada
11 T14 Prince Albert Saskatchewan, S Canada 53°09′N 105°43′W
83 G25 Prince Albert Western Cape, SW South Africa 33°13′S 22°03′E
8 J5 Prince Albert Peninsula peninsula Victoria Island, Northwest Territories, NW Canada
8 J6 Prince Albert Sound inlet Northwest Territories, N Canada
J5 8 Prince Alfred, Cape headland Northwest Territories, NW Canada
9 P6 Prince Charles Island island Nunavut, NE Canada
195 W6 Prince Charles Mountains ▲ Antarctica
Prince-Édouard, Île-du see Prince Edward Island
172 M13 Prince Edward Fracture Zone tectonic feature SW Indian Ocean
13 P14 Prince Edward Island Fr. Île-du Prince-Édouard. ◈ province SE Canada
13 Q14 Prince Edward Island Fr. Île-du Prince-Édouard. island SE Canada
173 M12 Prince Edward Islands island group S South Africa
21 X4 Prince Frederick Maryland, NE USA 38°32′N 76°35′W
10 M14 Prince George British Columbia, SW Canada 53°55′N 122°49′W
21 W6 Prince George Virginia, NE USA 37°13′N 77°13′W
197 O8 Prince Gustaf Adolf Sea sea Nunavut, N Canada
197 Q3 Prince of Wales, Cape headland Alaska, USA 65°39′N 168°12′W
181 V1 Prince of Wales Island island Queensland, E Australia
8 L5 Prince of Wales Island island Queen Elizabeth Islands, Nunavut, NW Canada
39 Y14 Prince of Wales Island island Alexander Archipelago, Alaska, USA
Prince of Wales Island see Pinang, Pulau
8 J5 Prince of Wales Strait strait Northwest Territories, N Canada
197 O8 Prince Patrick Island island Parry Islands, Northwest Territories, NW Canada
9 N5 Prince Regent Inlet channel Nunavut, N Canada
10 J13 Prince Rupert British Columbia, SW Canada 54°18′N 130°17′W
Prince's Island see Príncipe
21 Y5 Princess Anne Maryland, NE USA 38°12′N 75°42′W
181 W2 Princess Charlotte Bay bay Queensland, NE Australia
195 W7 Princess Elizabeth Land physical region Antarctica
10 J14 Princess Royal Island island British Columbia, SW Canada
45 U15 Princes Town Trinidad, Trinidad and Tobago 10°16′N 61°23′W
11 N17 Princeton British Columbia, SW Canada 49°25′N 120°35′W
30 L11 Princeton Illinois, N USA 41°22′N 89°27′W
31 N16 Princeton Indiana, N USA 38°21′N 87°33′W
29 Z14 Princeton Iowa, C USA 41°40′N 90°21′W
20 H7 Princeton Kentucky, S USA 37°06′N 87°52′W
29 V8 Princeton Minnesota, N USA 45°34′N 93°34′W
27 S1 Princeton Missouri, C USA 40°22′N 93°37′W
18 J15 Princeton New Jersey, NE USA 40°21′N 74°39′W
21 R6 Princeton West Virginia, NE USA 37°23′N 81°06′W
39 S12 Prince William Sound inlet Alaska, USA
67 P9 Príncipe var. Príncipe Island, Eng. Prince's Island. island N Sao Tome and Principe
Príncipe Island see Príncipe
32 I13 Prineville Oregon, NW USA 44°19′N 120°50′W
28 J11 Pringle South Dakota, N USA 43°34′N 103°34′W
25 N1 Pringle Texas, SW USA 35°55′N 101°28′W
99 H14 Prinsenbeek Noord-Brabant, S Netherlands 51°36′N 04°42′E
98 L6 Prinses Margriet Kanaal canal N Netherlands
195 R1 Prinsesse Astrid Kyst physical region Antarctica
195 T2 Prinsesse Ragnhild Kyst physical region Antarctica
195 U2 Prins Harald Kyst physical region Antarctica
92 N2 Prins Karls Forland island W Svalbard
43 N8 Prinzapolka Región Autónoma Atlántico Norte, NE Nicaragua 13°19′N 83°35′W
42 L8 Prinzapolka, Río ≈ NE Nicaragua
122 H9 Priob'ye Khanty-Mansiyskiy Avtonomnyy Okrug-Yugra, N Russian Federation 62°25′N 65°36′E
104 H1 Prior, Cabo headland NW Spain 43°33′N 08°21′W
29 V9 Prior Lake Minnesota, N USA 44°42′N 93°25′W
124 H11 Priozersk Fin. Käkisalmi. Leningradskaya Oblast', NW Russian Federation 61°02′N 30°07′E
119 J20 Pripet Bel. Prypyats', Ukr. Pryp"yat'. ≈ Belarus/Ukraine
119 J20 Pripet Marshes wetland Belarus/Ukraine
113 N16 Prishtinë Eng. Pristina, Serb. Priština. C Kosovo 42°40′N 21°10′E
126 J8 Pristen' Kurskaya Oblast', W Russian Federation 51°15′N 36°47′E
Priština see Prishtinë
Pristina see Prishtinë
100 M10 Pritzwalk Brandenburg, NE Germany 53°10′N 12°11′E
103 R13 Privas Ardèche, E France 44°45′N 04°35′E
107 I16 Priverno Lazio, C Italy 41°28′N 13°11′E
Privigye see Prievidza
112 C12 Privlaka Zadar, SW Croatia 44°15′N 15°07′E
124 M15 Privolzhsk Ivanovskaya Oblast', NW Russian Federation 57°24′N 41°16′E
127 P7 Privolzhskaya Vozvyshennost' var. Volga Uplands. ▲ W Russian Federation
127 P8 Privolzhskiy Saratovskaya Oblast', W Russian Federation 51°24′N 46°02′E
127 P8 Privolzhskoye Saratovskaya Oblast', W Russian Federation 51°08′N 45°57′E
Priwitz see Prievidza
127 N13 Priyutnoye Respublika Kalmykiya, SW Russian Federation 46°08′N 43°33′E
127 U5 Priyutovo Respublika Bashkortostan, W Russian Federation 53°54′N 53°56′E
113 M17 Prizren S Kosovo 42°14′N 20°46′E
107 I24 Prizzi Sicilia, Italy, C Mediterranean Sea 37°44′N 13°26′E
113 P18 Probištip NE FYR Macedonia 42°00′N 22°06′E
169 S16 Probolinggo Jawa, C Indonesia 07°45′S 113°12′E
Probstberg see Wyszków
111 F14 Prochowice Ger. Parchwitz. Dolnośląskie, SW Poland 51°15′N 16°22′E
29 W5 Proctor Minnesota, N USA 46°46′N 92°13′W
25 R8 Proctor Texas, SW USA 31°57′N 98°25′W
25 R8 Proctor Lake ⊠ Texas, SW USA
155 I18 Proddatūr Andhra Pradesh, E India 14°45′N 78°34′E
104 H9 Proença-a-Nova var. Proença a Nova. Castelo Branco, C Portugal 39°45′N 07°56′W
Proença a Nova see Proença-a-Nova
99 I21 Profondeville Namur, SE Belgium 50°22′N 04°52′E
41 W11 Progreso Yucatán, SE Mexico 21°14′N 89°41′W
123 R14 Progress Amurskaya Oblast', SE Russian Federation 49°40′N 129°30′E
127 O15 Prokhladnyy Kabardino-Balkarskaya Respublika, SW Russian Federation 43°48′N 44°02′E
Prokletije see North Albanian Alps
Prökuls see Priekulė
113 O15 Prokuplje Serbia, SE Serbia 43°15′N 21°35′E
124 H14 Proletariy Novgorodskaya Oblast', W Russian Federation 58°24′N 31°40′E
126 M12 Proletarsk Rostovskaya Oblast', SW Russian Federation 46°42′N 41°48′E
127 N13 Proletarskoye Vodokhranilishche salt lake SW Russian Federation
Prome see Pyay
60 J8 Promissão São Paulo, S Brazil 21°33′S 49°51′W
60 J8 Promissão, Represa de ⊠ S Brazil
125 V4 Promyshlennyy Respublika Komi, NW Russian Federation 67°36′N 64°E
119 O16 Pronya ≈ E Belarus
10 M11 Prophet River British Columbia, W Canada 58°07′N 122°39′W
30 K11 Prophetstown Illinois, N USA 41°40′N 89°56′W
Propinsi Kepulauan Riau see Kepulauan Riau
59 P16 Propriá Sergipe, E Brazil 10°15′S 36°51′W
103 X16 Propriano Corse, France, C Mediterranean Sea 41°41′N 08°54′E
Prościejów see Prostějov
Proskurov see Khmel'nyts'kyy
114 H12 Prosotsáni Anatolikí Makedonía kai Thráki, NE Greece 41°11′N 23°59′E
171 Q7 Prosperidad Mindanao, S Philippines 08°36′N 125°54′E
32 J10 Prosser Washington, NW USA 46°12′N 119°46′W
Prossnitz see Prostějov
111 G18 Prostějov Ger. Prossnitz, Pol. Prościejów. Olomoucký Kraj, E Czech Republic 49°29′N 17°08′E
117 V8 Prosyana Dnipropetrovs'ka Oblast', E Ukraine 48°07′N 36°22′E
111 L16 Proszowice Małopolskie, S Poland 50°12′N 20°15′E
Protasy see Pratasy
172 J11 Protea Seamount undersea feature SW Indian Ocean 36°50′S 18°05′E
115 D21 Próti island S Greece
114 N8 Provadiya Varna, E Bulgaria 43°10′N 27°29′E
103 T14 Provence cultural region SE France
103 S15 Provence prev. Marseille-Marignane. ✕ (Marseille) Bouches-du-Rhône, SE France 43°25′N 05°15′E
103 T14 Provence-Alpes-Côte d'Azur ◈ region SE France
20 H6 Providence Kentucky, S USA 37°23′N 87°47′W
19 N12 Providence state capital Rhode Island, NE USA 41°50′N 71°26′W
36 L1 Providence Utah, W USA 41°42′N 111°49′W
Providence see Fort Providence
Providence see Providence Atoll
67 X10 Providence Atoll var. Providence. atoll S Seychelles
14 D12 Providence Bay Manitoulin Island, Ontario, S Canada 45°39′N 82°16′W
23 R6 Providence Canyon valley Alabama/Georgia, S USA
22 I5 Providence, Lake ◎ Louisiana, S USA
35 X13 Providence Mountains ▲ California, W USA
43 Q7 Providencia, Isla de island NW Colombia, Caribbean Sea
44 L6 Providenciales island W Turks and Caicos Islands
19 Q12 Provincetown Massachusetts, NE USA 42°01′N 70°10′W
103 P5 Provins Seine-et-Marne, N France 48°34′N 03°18′E
36 L3 Provo Utah, W USA 40°14′N 111°39′W
11 R15 Provost Alberta, SW Canada 52°24′N 110°16′W
112 G13 Prozor Federacija Bosna I Hercegovina, SW Bosnia and Herzegovina 43°46′N 17°38′E
Prozoroki see Prazaroki
60 I11 Prudentópolis Paraná, S Brazil 25°12′S 50°58′W
39 R5 Prudhoe Bay Alaska, USA 70°16′N 148°18′W
39 R4 Prudhoe Bay bay Alaska, USA
111 H16 Prudnik Ger. Neustadt, Neustadt in Oberschlesien. Opole, SW Poland 50°20′N 17°34′E
119 J16 Prudy Minskaya Voblasts', C Belarus 53°47′N 26°32′E
101 D18 Prüm Rheinland-Pfalz, W Germany 50°15′N 06°27′E
101 D18 Prüm ≈ W Germany
Prusa see Bursa
110 J7 Pruszcz Gdański Ger. Praust. Pomorskie, N Poland 54°16′N 18°36′E
110 M12 Pruszków Ger. Kaltdorf. Mazowieckie, C Poland 52°09′N 20°49′E
116 K8 Prut Ger. Pruth. ≈ E Europe
Pruth see Prut
108 L8 Prutz Tirol, W Austria 47°07′N 10°42′E
Pružana see Pruzhany
119 G19 Pruzhany Pol. Prużana. Brestskaya Voblasts', SW Belarus 52°33′N 24°28′E
124 I11 Pryazha Respublika Kareliya, NW Russian Federation 61°42′N 33°39′E
117 U10 Pryazovs'ke Zaporiz'ka Oblast', SE Ukraine 46°43′N 35°39′E
Prychornomor'ska Nyzovyna see Black Sea Lowland
Prydniprovs'ka Nyzovyna/Prydnyaprowskaya Nizina see Dnieper Lowland
195 Y7 Prydz Bay bay Antarctica

◆ Country ● Country Capital ◇ Dependent Territory ○ Dependent Territory Capital ◈ Administrative Regions ✕ International Airport ▲ Mountain ▲ Mountain Range ⛰ Volcano ≈ River ◎ Lake ⊠ Reservoir

PRYLUKY – QAPQAL XIBE ZIZHIXIAN

117 R4 **Pryluky** *Rus.* Priluki. Chernihivs'ka Oblast', NE Ukraine 50°35′N 32°23′E
117 V10 **Prymors'k** *Rus.* Primorsk; *prev.* Primorskoye. Zaporiz'ka Oblast', SE Ukraine 46°44′N 36°19′E
27 Q9 **Pryor** Oklahoma, C USA 36°19′N 95°19′W
33 U11 **Pryor Creek** ≈ Montana, NW USA
Pryp"yat'/Prypyats' *see* Pripet
110 M10 **Przasnysz** Mazowieckie, C Poland 53°01′N 20°51′E
111 K14 **Przedbórz** Lodzkie, S Poland 51°04′N 19°51′E
111 P17 **Przemyśl** *Rus.* Peremyshl. Podkarpackie, C Poland 49°47′N 22°47′E
111 O16 **Przeworsk** Podkarpackie, SE Poland 50°04′N 22°30′E
Przheval'sk *see* Karakol
110 L13 **Przysucha** Mazowieckie, SE Poland 51°22′N 20°36′E
115 H18 **Psachná** *var.* Psahna, Psakhná. Évvoia, C Greece 38°35′N 23°39′E
Psahna/Psakhná *see* Psachná
115 K18 **Psará** *island* E Greece
115 I16 **Psathoúra** *island* Vóreies Sporádes, Greece, Aegean Sea
Pschestitz *see* Přeštice
Psein Lora *see* Pishin Lora
117 S5 **Psel** *Rus.* Psël. ≈ Russian Federation/Ukraine
Psël *see* Psel
115 M21 **Psérimos** *island* Dodekánisa, Greece, Aegean Sea
Pseyn Bowr *see* Pishin Lora
Pskem *see* Piskom
147 R8 **Pskemskiy Khrebet** *Uzb.* Piskom Tizmasi. ▲ Kyrgyzstan/Uzbekistan
124 F14 **Pskov** *Ger.* Pleskau, *Latv.* Pleskava. Pskovskaya Oblast', W Russian Federation 58°32′N 31°15′E
118 K6 **Pskov, Lake** *Est.* Pihkva Järv, *Ger.* Pleskauer See, *Rus.* Pskovskoye Ozero. ◎ Estonia/Russian Federation
124 F15 **Pskovskaya Oblast'** ❖ *province* W Russian Federation
Pskovskoye Ozero *see* Pskov, Lake
112 G9 **Psunj** ▲ NE Croatia
111 J17 **Pszczyna** *Ger.* Pless. Śląskie, S Poland 49°59′N 18°54′E
Ptačnik/Ptacsnik *see* Vtáčnik
115 D17 **Ptéri** ▲ C Greece 39°08′N 21°32′E
Ptich' *see* Ptsich
115 E14 **Ptolemaïda** *prev.* Ptolemaïs. Dytikí Makedonía, N Greece 40°34′N 21°42′E
Ptolemaïs *see* Ptolemaïda, Greece
Ptolemaïs *see* 'Akko, Israel
119 M19 **Ptsich** *Rus.* Ptich'. Homyel'skaya Voblasts', SE Belarus 52°11′N 28°49′E
119 M18 **Ptsich** *Rus.* Ptich'. ≈ SE Belarus
109 X10 **Ptuj** *Ger.* Pettau; *anc.* Poetovio. NE Slovenia 46°26′N 15°54′E
61 A23 **Puán** Buenos Aires, E Argentina 37°35′S 62°45′W
192 H15 **Pu'apu'a** Savai'i, C Samoa 13°32′S 172°09′W
192 G15 **Puava, Cape** *headland* Savai'i, NW Samoa
Pubao *see* Baingoin
56 F12 **Pucallpa** Ucayali, C Peru 08°21′S 74°33′W
57 J17 **Pucarani** La Paz, NW Bolivia 16°25′S 68°29′W
Pučarevo *see* Novi Travnik
157 U12 **Pucheng** Shaanxi, SE China 35°00′N 109°34′E
160 L6 **Pucheng** *var.* Nanpu. Fujian, C China 27°59′N 118°31′E
125 N16 **Puchezh** Ivanovskaya Oblast', W Russian Federation 56°58′N 43°08′E
111 I19 **Púchov** *Hung.* Puhó. Trenčiansky Kraj, W Slovakia 49°08′N 18°15′E
116 J13 **Pucioasa** Dâmbovița, S Romania 45°04′N 25°23′E
110 I6 **Puck** Pomorskie, N Poland 54°43′N 18°24′E
30 L8 **Puckaway Lake** ◎ Wisconsin, N USA
63 G15 **Pucón** Araucanía, S Chile 39°18′S 71°52′W
93 M14 **Pudasjärvi** Oulu, C Finland 65°20′N 27°02′E
148 L8 **Pūdeh Tal, Shelleh-ye** ≈ SW Afghanistan
127 S1 **Pudem** Udmurtskaya Respublika, NW Russian Federation 58°18′N 52°08′E
Pudewitz *see* Pobiedziska
124 K11 **Pudozh** Respublika Kareliya, NW Russian Federation 61°48′N 36°30′E
97 M17 **Pudsey** N England, United Kingdom 53°48′N 01°40′W
Puduchcheri *see* Pondicherry
151 H21 **Pudukkottai** Tamil Nādu, SE India 10°23′N 78°47′E
171 Z13 **Pue** Papua, E Indonesia 02°42′S 140°36′E
41 P14 **Puebla** *var.* Puebla de Zaragoza. Puebla, S Mexico 19°02′N 98°13′W
41 P15 **Puebla** ❖ *state* S Mexico
104 L11 **Puebla de Alcocer** Extremadura, W Spain 38°59′N 05°14′W
Puebla de Don Fabrique *see* Puebla de Don Fadrique
105 P13 **Puebla de Don Fadrique** *var.* Puebla de Don Fabrique. Andalucía, S Spain 37°58′N 02°25′W
104 J11 **Puebla de la Calzada** Extremadura, W Spain 38°54′N 06°38′W
104 J5 **Puebla de Sanabria** Castilla-León, N Spain 42°04′N 06°38′W
Puebla de Trives *see* A Pobla de Trives
Puebla de Zaragoza *see* Puebla
37 T6 **Pueblo** Colorado, C USA 38°15′N 104°37′W
37 N10 **Pueblo Colorado Wash** *valley* Arizona, SW USA
61 C16 **Pueblo Libertador** Corrientes, NE Argentina 30°13′S 59°23′W
40 J10 **Pueblo Nuevo** Durango, C Mexico 23°24′N 105°21′W
42 J8 **Pueblo Nuevo** Estelí, NW Nicaragua 13°21′N 86°30′W
54 J3 **Pueblo Nuevo** Falcón, N Venezuela 11°59′N 69°57′W
42 B6 **Pueblo Nuevo Tiquisate** *var.* Tiquisate. Escuintla, SW Guatemala 14°16′N 91°21′W
41 Q11 **Pueblo Viejo, Laguna de** *lagoon* E Mexico
63 J14 **Puelches** La Pampa, C Argentina 38°08′S 65°56′W
104 L14 **Puente-Genil** Andalucía, S Spain 37°23′N 04°45′W
105 Q3 **Puente la Reina** *Bas.* Gares. Navarra, N Spain 42°40′N 01°49′W
104 L12 **Puente Nuevo, Embalse de** ⊠ S Spain
57 D14 **Puente Piedra** Lima, W Peru 11°49′S 77°01′W
160 F14 **Pu'er** *var.* Ning'er. Yunnan, SW China 23°09′N 100°58′E
45 V6 **Puerca, Punta** *headland* E Puerto Rico 18°13′N 65°36′W
37 R12 **Puerco, Rio** ≈ New Mexico, SW USA
57 J17 **Puerto Acosta** La Paz, W Bolivia 15°33′S 69°15′W
63 G19 **Puerto Aisén** Aisén, S Chile 45°24′S 72°42′W
41 R17 **Puerto Ángel** Oaxaca, SE Mexico 15°39′N 96°29′W
Puerto Argentino *see* Stanley
41 T17 **Puerto Arista** Chiapas, SE Mexico 15°55′N 93°47′W
43 O16 **Puerto Armuelles** Chiriquí, SW Panama 08°19′N 82°51′W
Puerto Arrecife *see* Arrecife
54 D14 **Puerto Asís** Putumayo, SW Colombia 0°31′N 76°31′W
54 L9 **Puerto Ayacucho** Amazonas, SW Venezuela 05°45′N 67°37′W
57 C18 **Puerto Ayora** Galapagos Islands, Ecuador, E Pacific Ocean 0°45′S 90°19′W
57 C18 **Puerto Baquerizo Moreno** *var.* Baquerizo Moreno. Galapagos Islands, Ecuador, E Pacific Ocean 0°54′S 89°37′W
42 G4 **Puerto Barrios** Izabal, E Guatemala 15°42′N 88°34′W
Puerto Bello *see* Portobelo
54 F8 **Puerto Berrío** Antioquia, C Colombia 06°28′N 74°28′W
54 F9 **Puerto Boyaca** Boyacá, C Colombia 05°58′N 74°36′W
54 K4 **Puerto Cabello** Carabobo, N Venezuela 10°29′N 68°02′W
43 N7 **Puerto Cabezas** *var.* Bilwi. Región Autónoma Atlántico Norte, NE Nicaragua 14°05′N 83°22′W
54 L9 **Puerto Carreño** Vichada, E Colombia 06°08′N 67°30′W
54 E4 **Puerto Colombia** Atlántico, N Colombia 10°59′N 74°57′W
42 H4 **Puerto Cortés** Cortés, NW Honduras 15°50′N 87°55′W
54 J4 **Puerto Cumarebo** Falcón, N Venezuela 11°29′N 69°21′W
Puerto de Cabras *see* Puerto del Rosario
55 Q5 **Puerto de Hierro** Sucre, NE Venezuela 10°40′N 62°03′W
64 O11 **Puerto de la Cruz** Tenerife, Islas Canarias, Spain, NE Atlantic Ocean 28°24′N 16°33′W
64 Q11 **Puerto del Rosario** *var.* Puerto de Cabras. Fuerteventura, Islas Canarias, Spain, NE Atlantic Ocean 28°29′N 13°52′W
63 J20 **Puerto Deseado** Santa Cruz, SE Argentina 47°45′S 65°53′W
40 F8 **Puerto Escondido** Baja California Sur, NW Mexico 25°48′N 111°20′W
41 R17 **Puerto Escondido** Oaxaca, SE Mexico 15°48′N 96°57′W
60 G12 **Puerto Esperanza** Misiones, NE Argentina 26°01′S 54°39′W
54 H10 **Puerto Gaitán** Meta, C Colombia 04°20′N 72°10′W
Puerto Gallegos *see* Río Gallegos
60 G12 **Puerto Iguazú** Misiones, NE Argentina 25°39′S 54°35′W
56 F12 **Puerto Inca** Huánuco, N Peru 09°22′S 74°54′W
54 L11 **Puerto Inírida** *var.* Obando. Guainía, E Colombia 03°48′N 67°54′W
42 K13 **Puerto Jesús** Guanacaste, NW Costa Rica 10°08′N 85°26′W
41 Z11 **Puerto Juárez** Quintana Roo, SE Mexico 21°06′N 86°46′W
55 N5 **Puerto La Cruz** Anzoátegui, NE Venezuela 10°14′N 64°40′W
54 E14 **Puerto Leguízamo** Putumayo, S Colombia 0°14′S 74°45′W
43 N5 **Puerto Lempira** Gracias a Dios, E Honduras 15°14′N 83°48′W
Puerto Libertad *see* La Libertad
54 I11 **Puerto Limón** Meta, E Colombia 04°00′N 71°09′W
54 D13 **Puerto Limón** Putumayo, SW Colombia 01°02′N 76°30′W
Puerto Limón *see* Limón
105 N11 **Puertollano** Castilla-La Mancha, C Spain 38°41′N 04°07′W
63 K17 **Puerto Lobos** Chubut, SE Argentina 42°00′S 64°58′W
54 I3 **Puerto López** La Guajira, N Colombia 11°54′N 71°21′W
105 Q14 **Puerto Lumbreras** Murcia, SE Spain 37°35′N 01°49′W
41 V17 **Puerto Madero** Chiapas, SE Mexico 14°44′N 92°25′W
63 K17 **Puerto Madryn** Chubut, S Argentina 42°45′S 65°02′W
Puerto Magdalena *see* Bahía Magdalena
57 J15 **Puerto Maldonado** Madre de Dios, E Peru 12°37′S 69°11′W
Puerto Masachapa *see* Masachapa
Puerto México *see* Coatzacoalcos
63 G17 **Puerto Montt** Los Lagos, C Chile 41°28′S 72°57′W
41 Z12 **Puerto Morelos** Quintana Roo, SE Mexico 20°47′N 86°54′W
54 L10 **Puerto Nariño** Vichada, E Colombia 04°57′N 67°51′W
63 H23 **Puerto Natales** Magallanes, S Chile 51°42′S 72°28′W
43 X15 **Puerto Obaldía** Kuna Yala, NE Panama 08°38′N 77°26′W
44 H6 **Puerto Padre** Las Tunas, E Cuba 21°13′N 76°35′W
54 L9 **Puerto Páez** Apure, C Venezuela 06°10′N 67°30′W
40 E3 **Puerto Peñasco** Sonora, NW Mexico 31°20′N 113°35′W
55 N5 **Puerto Píritu** Anzoátegui, NE Venezuela 10°04′N 65°00′W
45 N8 **Puerto Plata** *var.* San Felipe de Puerto Plata. N Dominican Republic 19°46′N 70°42′W
45 N8 **Puerto Plata** ✈ N Dominican Republic 19°43′N 70°43′W
Puerto Presidente Stroessner *see* Ciudad del Este
171 N6 **Puerto Princesa** *off.* Puerto Princesa City. Palawan, W Philippines 09°48′N 118°43′E
Puerto Princesa City *see* Puerto Princesa
Puerto Príncipe *see* Camagüey
Puerto Quellón *see* Quellón
60 F13 **Puerto Rico** Misiones, NE Argentina 26°48′S 54°59′W
57 K14 **Puerto Rico** Pando, N Bolivia 11°07′S 67°32′W
54 E12 **Puerto Rico** Caquetá, S Colombia 01°54′N 75°13′W
45 U5 **Puerto Rico** *off.* Commonwealth of Puerto Rico; *prev.* Porto Rico. ◇ *US commonwealth territory* C West Indies
64 F11 **Puerto Rico** *island* C West Indies
Puerto Rico, Commonwealth of *see* Puerto Rico
64 G11 **Puerto Rico Trench** *undersea feature* NE Caribbean Sea
54 I8 **Puerto Rondón** Arauca, E Colombia 06°16′N 71°05′W
Puerto San José *see* San José
63 J21 **Puerto San Julián** *var.* San Julián. Santa Cruz, SE Argentina 49°14′S 67°41′W
63 I22 **Puerto Santa Cruz** *var.* Santa Cruz. Santa Cruz, SE Argentina 50°05′S 68°31′W
Puerto Sauce *see* Juan L. Lacaze
57 Q20 **Puerto Suárez** Santa Cruz, E Bolivia 18°59′S 57°47′W
54 D13 **Puerto Umbría** Putumayo, SW Colombia 0°52′N 76°36′W
40 J13 **Puerto Vallarta** Jalisco, SW Mexico 20°36′N 105°15′W
63 G16 **Puerto Varas** Los Lagos, C Chile 41°20′S 73°00′W
42 M13 **Puerto Viejo** Heredia, NE Costa Rica 10°27′N 84°00′W
Puertoviejo *see* Portoviejo
57 B18 **Puerto Villamil** *var.* Villamil. Galapagos Islands, Ecuador, E Pacific Ocean 0°57′S 91°00′W
54 F8 **Puerto Wilches** Santander, N Colombia 07°22′N 73°53′W
63 H20 **Pueyrredón, Lago** *var.* Lago Cochrane. ◎ S Argentina
127 R7 **Pugachëv** Saratovskaya Oblast', W Russian Federation 52°06′N 48°50′E
127 T3 **Pugachëvo** Udmurtskaya Respublika, NW Russian Federation 56°38′N 53°03′E
32 H8 **Puget Sound** *sound* Washington, NW USA
107 O17 **Puglia** *var.* Le Puglie, *Eng.* Apulia. ❖ *region* SE Italy
107 N17 **Puglia, Canosa di** *anc.* Canusium. Puglia, SE Italy 41°13′N 16°04′E
118 I6 **Puhja** *Ger.* Kawelecht. Tartumaa, SE Estonia 58°20′N 26°19′E
Puhó *see* Púchov
105 V4 **Puigcerdà** Cataluña, NE Spain 42°25′N 01°53′E
Puigmal *see* Puigmal d'Err
103 N17 **Puigmal d'Err** *var.* Puigmal. ▲ S France 42°24′N 02°07′E
76 I16 **Pujehun** S Sierra Leone 07°23′N 11°44′W
Puka *see* Pukë
185 E20 **Pukaki, Lake** ◎ South Island, New Zealand
38 F10 **Pukalani** Maui, Hawaii, USA, C Pacific Ocean 20°50′N 156°20′W
190 J13 **Pukapuka** *atoll* N Cook Islands
191 X9 **Pukapuka** *atoll* Îles Tuamotu, E French Polynesia
Pukari Neem *see* Purekkari Neem
191 X11 **Pukarua** *var.* Pukaruha. *atoll* Îles Tuamotu, E French Polynesia
Pukaruha *see* Pukarua
14 A7 **Pukaskwa** ≈ Ontario, S Canada
11 V12 **Pukatawagan** Manitoba, C Canada 55°46′N 101°14′W
191 X16 **Pukatikei, Maunga** Ѫ Easter Island, Chile, E Pacific Ocean
182 C1 **Pukatja** *var.* Ernabella. South Australia 26°18′S 132°13′E
163 Y12 **Pukch'ŏng** E North Korea 40°13′N 128°20′E
113 L18 **Pukë** *var.* Puka. Shkodër, N Albania 42°03′N 19°53′E
184 L6 **Pukekohe** Auckland, North Island, New Zealand 37°12′S 174°54′E
184 L7 **Pukemiro** Waikato, North Island, New Zealand 37°37′S 175°02′E
190 D12 **Puke, Mont** ▲ Île Futuna, W Wallis and Futuna
Puket *see* Phuket
185 C20 **Puketeraki Range** ▲ South Island, New Zealand
184 N13 **Puketoi Range** ▲ North Island, New Zealand
185 F21 **Pukeuri Junction** Otago, South Island, New Zealand 45°01′S 171°01′E
119 L16 **Pukhavichy** *Rus.* Pukhovichi. Minskaya Voblasts', C Belarus 53°32′N 28°15′E
Pukhovichi *see* Pukhavichy
124 M10 **Puksoozero** Arkhangel'skaya Oblast', NW Russian Federation 62°37′N 40°29′E
112 A10 **Pula** *It.* Pola; *prev.* Pulj. Istra, NW Croatia 44°53′N 13°51′E
Pula *see* Nyingchi
163 U14 **Pulandian** *var.* Xinjin. Liaoning, NE China 39°25′N 121°58′E
163 T14 **Pulandian Wan** *bay* NE China
189 O15 **Pulap Atoll** *atoll* Caroline Islands, C Micronesia
18 H9 **Pulaski** New York, NE USA 43°34′N 76°06′W
20 I10 **Pulaski** Tennessee, S USA 35°11′N 87°00′W
21 R7 **Pulaski** Virginia, NE USA 37°03′N 80°47′W
171 Y14 **Pulau, Sungai** ≈ Papua, E Indonesia
110 N13 **Puławy** *Ger.* Neu Amerika. Lubelskie, E Poland 51°25′N 21°57′E
146 I16 **Pulhatyn** *Rus.* Polekhatum; *prev.* Pul'-I-Khatum. Ahal Welaýaty, S Turkmenistan 36°01′N 61°08′E
101 E16 **Pulheim** Nordrhein-Westfalen, W Germany 51°00′N 06°48′E
155 J19 **Pulicat Lake** *lagoon* SE India
Pul'-I-Khatum *see* Pulhatyn
Pul-i-Khumri *see* Pol-e Khomrī
Pul-i-Sefid *see* Pol-e Sefid
Pulj *see* Pula
109 W2 **Pulkau** ≈ NE Austria
93 L15 **Pulkkila** Oulu, C Finland 64°15′N 25°53′E
122 C7 **Pulkovo** ✈ (Sankt-Peterburg) Leningradskaya Oblast', NW Russian Federation 60°06′N 30°23′E
32 M9 **Pullman** Washington, NW USA 46°43′N 117°10′W
108 B10 **Pully** Vaud, SW Switzerland 46°31′N 06°40′E
40 F7 **Púlpita, Punta** *headland* NW Mexico 25°30′N 111°28′W
110 M10 **Pułtusk** Mazowieckie, C Poland 52°41′N 21°04′E
158 H10 **Pulu** Xinjiang Uygur Zizhiqu, W China 36°10′N 81°29′E
137 P13 **Pülümür** Tunceli, E Turkey 39°30′N 39°54′E
189 N16 **Pulusuk** *island* Caroline Islands, C Micronesia
189 N16 **Puluwat Atoll** *atoll* Caroline Islands, C Micronesia
25 N11 **Pumpville** Texas, SW USA 29°55′N 101°43′W
191 P7 **Punaauia** *var.* Hakapehi. Tahiti, W French Polynesia 17°38′S 149°37′W
56 B8 **Puná, Isla** *island* SW Ecuador
185 G16 **Punakaiki** West Coast, South Island, New Zealand 42°07′S 171°21′E
153 T11 **Punakha** C Bhutan 27°38′N 89°50′E
57 L18 **Punata** Cochabamba, C Bolivia 17°32′S 65°50′W
155 E14 **Pune** *prev.* Poona. Mahārāshtra, W India 18°32′N 73°52′E
83 M17 **Pungoè, Rio** *var.* Púnguè, Pungwe. ≈ C Mozambique
21 X10 **Pungo River** ≈ North Carolina, SE USA
Púnguè/Pungwe *see* Pungoè, Rio
79 N19 **Punia** Maniema, E Dem. Rep. Congo 01°28′S 26°25′E
62 H8 **Punilla, Sierra de la** ▲ W Argentina
161 P14 **Puning** Guangdong, S China 23°24′N 116°14′E
62 G10 **Punitaqui** Coquimbo, C Chile 30°50′S 71°29′W
149 T9 **Punjab** *prev.* West Punjab, Western Punjab. ❖ *province* E Pakistan
152 H8 **Punjab** *state* NW India
129 Q9 **Punjab Plains** *plain* N India
93 O17 **Punkaharju** *var.* Punkasalmi. Itä-Suomi, E Finland 61°45′N 29°21′E
Punkasalmi *see* Punkaharju
57 I17 **Puno** Puno, SE Peru 15°53′S 70°03′W
57 H17 **Puno** *off.* Departamento de Puno. ❖ *department* S Peru
Puno, Departamento de *see* Puno
61 B24 **Punta Alta** Buenos Aires, E Argentina 38°54′S 62°01′W
63 H24 **Punta Arenas** *prev.* Magallanes. Magallanes, S Chile 53°10′S 70°56′W
45 T6 **Punta, Cerro de** ▲ C Puerto Rico 18°10′N 66°36′W
43 T15 **Punta Chame** Panamá, C Panama 08°39′N 79°42′W
57 G17 **Punta Colorada** Arequipa, SW Peru 16°17′S 72°31′W
40 F9 **Punta Coyote** Baja California Sur, NW Mexico
62 G8 **Punta de Díaz** Atacama, N Chile 28°03′S 70°36′W
61 G20 **Punta del Este** Maldonado, S Uruguay 34°59′S 54°58′W
63 K17 **Punta Delgada** Chubut, SE Argentina 42°46′S 63°40′W
55 O4 **Punta de Mata** Monagas, NE Venezuela 09°48′N 63°38′W
55 O4 **Punta de Piedras** Nueva Esparta, NE Venezuela 10°57′N 64°06′W
42 F4 **Punta Gorda** Toledo, SE Belize 16°07′N 88°47′W
43 N11 **Punta Gorda** Región Autónoma Atlántico Sur, SE Nicaragua 11°31′N 83°46′W
23 W14 **Punta Gorda** Florida, SE USA 26°55′N 82°03′W
42 M11 **Punta Gorda, Río** ≈ SE Nicaragua
62 H6 **Punta Negra, Salar de** *salt lake* N Chile
40 D5 **Punta Prieta** Baja California Norte, NW Mexico 28°56′N 114°11′W
42 L13 **Puntarenas** Puntarenas, W Costa Rica 09°58′N 84°50′W
42 L13 **Puntarenas** *off.* Provincia de Puntarenas. ❖ *province* W Costa Rica
Puntarenas, Provincia de *see* Puntarenas
80 P13 **Puntland** *cultural region* NE Somalia
54 J4 **Punto Fijo** Falcón, N Venezuela 11°42′N 70°13′W
105 S4 **Puntón de Guara** ▲ N Spain 42°18′N 00°13′W
18 D14 **Punxsutawney** Pennsylvania, NE USA 40°55′N 78°57′W
93 M14 **Puolanka** Oulu, C Finland 64°51′N 27°42′E
57 J17 **Pupuya, Nevado** ▲ W Bolivia 15°04′S 69°01′W
Puqi *see* Chibi
57 F16 **Puquio** Ayacucho, S Peru 14°44′S 74°07′W
122 J9 **Pur** ≈ N Russian Federation
186 D7 **Purari** ≈ S Papua New Guinea
27 N11 **Purcell** Oklahoma, C USA 35°00′N 97°21′W
11 O16 **Purcell Mountains** ▲ British Columbia, SW Canada
105 P14 **Purchena** Andalucía, S Spain 37°21′N 02°21′W
27 S8 **Purdy** Missouri, C USA 36°49′N 93°55′W
118 I2 **Purekkari Neem** *prev.* Pukari Neem. *headland* N Estonia 59°33′N 24°49′E
37 U7 **Purgatoire River** ≈ Colorado, C USA
Purgstall *see* Purgstall an der Erlauf
109 V5 **Purgstall an der Erlauf** *var.* Purgstall. Niederösterreich, NE Austria 48°01′N 15°08′E
154 O13 **Puri** *var.* Jagannath. Orissa, E India 19°52′N 85°49′E
Puriramya *see* Buriram
109 X4 **Purkersdorf** Niederösterreich, NE Austria 48°13′N 16°12′E
98 I9 **Purmerend** Noord-Holland, C Netherlands 52°30′N 04°56′E
151 G16 **Pūrna** ≈ C India
Purnea *see* Pūrnia
153 R13 **Pūrnia** *prev.* Purnea. Bihār, NE India 25°47′N 87°28′E
Pursat *see* Poŭthĭsăt, Stœng, W Cambodia
Pursat *see* Poŭthĭsăt, Poŭthĭsăt, W Cambodia
Purulia *see* Puruliya
150 L13 **Puruliya** *prev.* Purulia. West Bengal, NE India 23°20′N 86°24′E
47 G7 **Purus, Rio** *var.* Río Purús. ≈ Brazil/Peru
186 C9 **Purutu Island** *island* SW Papua New Guinea
93 N17 **Puruvesi** ◎ SE Finland
22 L7 **Purvis** Mississippi, S USA 31°08′N 89°24′W
114 J11 **Pŭrvomay** *prev.* Borisovgrad. Plovdiv, C Bulgaria 42°06′N 25°13′E
169 R16 **Purwodadi** *prev.* Poerwodadi. Jawa, C Indonesia 07°05′S 110°53′E
169 P16 **Purwokerto** *prev.* Poerwokerto. Jawa, C Indonesia 07°25′S 109°14′E
169 P16 **Purworejo** *prev.* Poerworedjo. Jawa, C Indonesia 07°45′S 110°04′E
20 H8 **Puryear** Tennessee, S USA 36°25′N 88°21′W
154 H13 **Pusad** Mahārāshtra, C India 19°56′N 77°40′E
163 Z16 **Pusan** *off.* Pusan-gwangyŏksi, *var.* Busan, *Jap.* Fusan. SE South Korea 35°11′N 129°04′E
Pusan *see* Kim Hae
Pusan-gwangyŏksi *see* Pusan
168 H7 **Pusatgajo, Pegunungan** ▲ Sumatera, NW Indonesia
Puschlav *see* Poschiavo
124 G13 **Pushkin** *prev.* Tsarskoye Selo. Leningradskaya Oblast', NW Russian Federation 59°42′N 30°24′E
126 L3 **Pushkino** Moskovskaya Oblast', W Russian Federation 55°57′N 37°45′E
127 Q8 **Pushkino** Saratovskaya Oblast', W Russian Federation 51°09′N 47°00′E
Pushkino *see* Biläsuvar
111 M22 **Püspökladány** Hajdú-Bihar, E Hungary 47°20′N 21°05′E
118 J3 **Püssi** *Ger.* Isenhof. Ida-Virumaa, NE Estonia 59°22′N 27°04′E
116 I5 **Pustomyty** L'vivs'ka Oblast', W Ukraine 49°43′N 23°55′E
124 F16 **Pustoshka** Pskovskaya Oblast', W Russian Federation 56°21′N 29°16′E
Pusztakalán *see* Călan
167 N1 **Putao** *prev.* Fort Hertz. Kachin State, N Myanmar (Burma) 27°22′N 97°24′E
184 M8 **Putaruru** Waikato, North Island, New Zealand 38°03′S 175°48′E
Puteoli *see* Pozzuoli
161 R12 **Putian** Fujian, SE China 25°32′N 119°02′E
107 O17 **Putignano** Puglia, SE Italy 40°51′N 17°08′E
Puting *see* De'an
Putivl' *see* Putyvl'
41 Q16 **Putla** *var.* Putla de Guerrero. Oaxaca, SE Mexico 17°01′N 97°56′W
Putla de Guerrero *see* Putla
19 N12 **Putnam** Connecticut, NE USA 41°56′N 71°52′W
25 Q7 **Putnam** Texas, SW USA 32°22′N 99°11′W
18 M10 **Putney** Vermont, NE USA 42°59′N 72°30′W
111 L20 **Putnok** Borsod-Abaúj-Zemplén, NE Hungary 48°18′N 20°25′E
Putorana, Gory/Putorana Mountains *see* Putorana, Plato
122 L8 **Putorana, Plato** *var.* Gory Putorana, *Eng.* Putorana Mountains. ▲ N Russian Federation
168 K9 **Putrajaya** ● (Malaysia) Kuala Lumpur, Peninsular Malaysia 02°57′N 101°42′E
62 H2 **Putre** Tarapacá, N Chile 18°11′S 69°30′W
155 J24 **Puttalam** North Western Province, W Sri Lanka 08°02′N 79°55′E
155 J24 **Puttalam Lagoon** *lagoon* W Sri Lanka
99 H17 **Putte** Antwerpen, C Belgium 51°04′N 04°39′E
94 E10 **Puttegga** ▲ S Norway 62°13′N 07°40′E
98 K11 **Putten** Gelderland, C Netherlands 52°15′N 05°36′E
100 K7 **Puttgarden** Schleswig-Holstein, N Germany 54°30′N 11°13′E
Puttiala *see* Patiāla
101 D20 **Püttlingen** Saarland, SW Germany 49°16′N 06°52′E
54 D14 **Putumayo** *off.* Intendencia del Putumayo. ❖ *province* S Colombia
Putumayo, Intendencia del *see* Putumayo
48 E7 **Putumayo, Río** *var.* Içá, Rio. ≈ NW South America *see also* Içá, Rio
Putumayo, Río *see* Içá, Rio
169 P11 **Putus, Tanjung** *headland* Borneo, N Indonesia 0°27′S 109°04′E
116 J8 **Putyla** Chernivets'ka Oblast', W Ukraine 47°59′N 25°04′E
117 S3 **Putyvl'** *Rus.* Putivl'. Sums'ka Oblast', NE Ukraine 51°21′N 33°53′E
93 M18 **Puula** ◎ SE Finland
93 N18 **Puumala** Itä-Suomi, E Finland 61°31′N 28°12′E
118 I5 **Puurmani** *Ger.* Talkhof. Jõgevamaa, E Estonia 58°36′N 26°17′E
99 G17 **Puurs** Antwerpen, N Belgium 51°05′N 04°17′E
38 F10 **Pu'u 'Ula'ula** *var.* Red Hill. ▲ Maui, Hawai'i, USA 20°42′N 156°16′W
38 A8 **Pu'uwai** *var.* Puuwai. Ni'ihau, Hawaii, USA, C Pacific Ocean 21°54′N 160°11′W
12 J4 **Puvirnituq** *prev.* Povungnituk. Québec, NE Canada 60°10′N 77°20′W
32 H8 **Puyallup** Washington, NW USA 47°11′N 122°17′W
161 O5 **Puyang** Henan, C China 35°40′N 115°00′E
161 R9 **Puyang Jiang** *var.* Tsien Tang. ≈ SE China
103 O11 **Puy-de-Dôme** ❖ *department* C France
103 N15 **Puylaurens** Tarn, S France 43°33′N 02°01′E
102 M13 **Puy-l'Evêque** Lot, S France 44°31′N 01°10′E
103 N17 **Puymorens, Col de** *pass* S France
56 C7 **Puyo** Pastaza, C Ecuador 01°30′S 77°58′W
185 A24 **Puysegur Point** *headland* South Island, New Zealand 46°09′S 166°38′E
148 J8 **Pūzak, Hāmūn-e** *Pash.* Hāmūn-i-Puzak. ◎ SW Afghanistan
Puzak, Hāmūn-i- *see* Pūzak, Hāmūn-e
81 J23 **Pwani** *Eng.* Coast. ❖ *region* E Tanzania
79 O23 **Pweto** Katanga, SE Dem. Rep. Congo 08°28′S 28°52′E
97 I19 **Pwllheli** NW Wales, United Kingdom 52°54′N 04°23′W
189 O14 **Pwok** Pohnpei, E Micronesia
122 I9 **Pyakupur** ≈ N Russian Federation
124 M6 **Pyalitsa** Murmanskaya Oblast', NW Russian Federation 66°17′N 39°56′E
124 K10 **Pyal'ma** Respublika Kareliya, NW Russian Federation 62°24′N 35°56′E
Pyandzh *see* Panj
124 I6 **Pyaozero, Ozero** ◎ NW Russian Federation
166 L9 **Pyapon** Ayeyarwady, SW Myanmar (Burma) 16°15′N 95°40′E
119 J15 **Pyarshai** *Rus.* Pershay. Minskaya Voblasts', C Belarus 54°02′N 26°41′E
122 K8 **Pyasina** ≈ N Russian Federation
114 I10 **Pyasŭchnik, Yazovir** ⊠ C Bulgaria
Pyatikhatki *see* P"yatykhatky
117 S7 **P"yatykhatky** *Rus.* Pyatikhatki. Dnipropetrovs'ka Oblast', E Ukraine 48°23′N 33°43′E
166 M6 **Pyawbwe** Mandalay, C Myanmar (Burma) 20°39′N 96°04′E
166 L7 **Pyay** *var.* Prome, Pye. Bago, C Myanmar (Burma) 18°50′N 95°14′E
127 T3 **Pychas** Udmurtskaya Respublika, NW Russian Federation 56°30′N 52°33′E
Pye *see* Pyay
166 K6 **Pyechin** Chin State, W Myanmar (Burma) 20°01′N 93°36′E
119 G17 **Pyeski** *Rus.* Peski. Hrodzyenskaya Voblasts', W Belarus 53°21′N 24°38′E
119 L19 **Pyetrykaw** *Rus.* Petrikov. Homyel'skaya Voblasts', SE Belarus 52°08′N 28°30′E
93 O17 **Pyhäjärvi** ◎ SE Finland
93 M16 **Pyhäjärvi** ◎ C Finland
93 L15 **Pyhäjoki** Oulu, W Finland 64°28′N 24°15′E
93 L15 **Pyhäjoki** ≈ W Finland
93 M15 **Pyhäntä** Oulu, C Finland 64°07′N 26°19′E
93 M16 **Pyhäsalmi** Oulu, C Finland 63°38′N 26°E
93 O17 **Pyhäselkä** ◎ SE Finland
93 M19 **Pyhtää** *Swe.* Pyttis. Etelä-Suomi, S Finland 60°29′N 26°40′E
166 M5 **Pyin-Oo-Lwin** *var.* Maymyo. Mandalay, C Myanmar (Burma) 22°03′N 96°30′E
115 N24 **Pylés** *var.* Piles. Kárpathos, SE Greece 35°31′N 27°08′E
115 D21 **Pýlos** *var.* Pilos. Pelopónnisos, S Greece 36°55′N 21°42′E
18 B12 **Pymatuning Reservoir** ⊠ Ohio/Pennsylvania, NE USA
163 X15 **P'yŏngt'aek** NW South Korea 37°00′N 127°04′E
163 V14 **P'yŏngyang** *var.* P'yŏngyang-si, *Eng.* Pyongyang. ● (North Korea) SW North Korea 39°04′N 125°46′E
P'yŏngyang-si *see* P'yŏngyang
35 Q4 **Pyramid Lake** ◎ Nevada, W USA
37 P15 **Pyramid Mountains** ▲ New Mexico, SW USA
37 R5 **Pyramid Peak** ▲ Colorado, C USA 39°04′N 106°57′W
115 D17 **Pyramíva** *var.* Piramiva. ▲ C Greece 39°08′N 21°18′E
Pyrenaei Montes *see* Pyrenees
86 B12 **Pyrenees** *Fr.* Pyrénées, *Sp.* Pirineos; *anc.* Pyrenaei Montes. ▲ SW Europe
102 J16 **Pyrénées-Atlantiques** ❖ *department* SW France
103 N17 **Pyrénées-Orientales** ❖ *department* S France
115 L19 **Pyrgí** *var.* Pirgi. Chíos, E Greece 38°13′N 26°01′E
115 D20 **Pýrgos** *var.* Pírgos. Dytikí Elláda, S Greece 37°40′N 21°27′E
Pyritz *see* Pyrzyce
115 E19 **Pyrros** ≈ S Greece
117 R4 **Pyryatyn** *Rus.* Piryatin. Poltavs'ka Oblast', NE Ukraine 50°14′N 32°31′E
110 D9 **Pyrzyce** *Ger.* Pyritz. Zachodnio-pomorskie, NW Poland 53°09′N 14°53′E
124 F15 **Pytalovo** *Latv.* Abrene; *prev.* Jaunlatgale. Pskovskaya Oblast', W Russian Federation 57°06′N 27°55′E
115 M20 **Pythagóreio** *var.* Pithagorio. Sámos, Dodekánisa, Greece, Aegean Sea 37°42′N 25°57′E
14 L11 **Pythonga, Lac** ◎ Québec, SE Canada
Pyttis *see* Pyhtää
Pyu *see* Phyu
166 M8 **Pyuntaza** Bago, SW Myanmar (Burma) 17°51′N 96°44′E
153 N11 **Pyuthān** Mid Western, W Nepal 28°09′N 82°50′E
110 H12 **Pyzdry** *Ger.* Peisern. Wielkopolskie, C Poland 52°10′N 17°42′E

Q

138 H13 **Qā' al Jafr** ◎ S Jordan
197 O11 **Qaanaaq** *var.* Qânâq, *Dan.* Thule. ❖ Avannaarsua, N Greenland
Qabanbay *see* Kabanbay
138 G7 **Qabb Eliâs** E Lebanon 33°46′N 35°49′E
Qabil *see* Al Qābil
Qabırrı *see* Iori
Qābis *see* Gabès
Qābis, Khalīj *see* Gabès, Golfe de
Qabqa *see* Gonghe
141 S14 **Qabr Hūd** C Yemen 16°02′N 49°36′E
Qacentina *see* Constantine
148 L4 **Qādes** Bādghīs, NW Afghanistan 34°48′N 63°26′E
139 T11 **Qādisīyah** Al Qādisīyah, S Iraq 31°43′N 44°28′E
139 Q6 **Qādisīyah, Buḩayrat al** ⊠ NW Iraq
143 O4 **Qā'emshahr** *prev.* 'Alīābad, Shāhī. Māzandarān, N Iran 36°31′N 52°49′E
143 U7 **Qā'en** *var.* Qain, Qāyen. Khorāsān-Razavī, E Iran 33°43′N 59°07′E
141 U13 **Qafa** *spring/well* SW Oman 17°46′N 52°55′E
Qafşah *see* Gafsa
163 Q12 **Qagan Nur** *var.* Xulun Hobot Qagan, Zhengxiangbai Qi. Nei Mongol Zizhiqu, N China 42°10′N 114°57′E
163 V9 **Qagan Nur** ◎ NE China
163 Q11 **Qagan Nur** ◎ N China
Qagan Us *see* Dulan
158 H13 **Qagcaka** Xizang Zizhiqu, W China 32°32′N 81°52′E
Qagchêng *see* Xiangcheng
Qahremānshahr *see* Kermānshāh
159 Q10 **Qaidam He** ≈ C China
156 L8 **Qaidam Pendi** *basin* C China
Qain *see* Qā'en
Qala Āhangarān *see* Chaghcharān
139 U3 **Qaļā Diza** *var.* Qal'at Dīzah. As Sulaymānīyah, NE Iraq 36°11′N 45°07′E
Qal'ah Sālih *see* Qal'at Şāliḩ
147 R13 **Qal'aikhum** *Rus.* Kalaikhum. S Tajikistan 38°28′N 70°49′E
Qala Nau *see* Qal'eh-ye Now
141 V17 **Qalansīyah** Suquṭrā, W Yemen 12°40′N 53°30′E
Qala Panja *see* Qal'eh-ye Panjeh
Qala Shāhar *see* Qal'eh Shahr
149 O8 **Qalāt** *Per.* Kalāt. Zābol, S Afghanistan 32°10′N 66°54′E
139 W9 **Qal'at Aḩmad** Maysān, E Iraq 32°24′N 46°46′E
141 N11 **Qal'at Bīshah** 'Asīr, SW Saudi Arabia 19°59′N 42°38′E
138 H4 **Qal'at Burzay** Ḩamāh, W Syria 35°37′N 36°16′E
Qal 'at Dīzah *see* Qaļā Diza
139 W9 **Qal'at Ḩusayn** Maysān, E Iraq 32°19′N 46°46′E
139 V10 **Qal'at Majnūnah** Al Qādisīyah, S Iraq 31°39′N 45°44′E
139 X11 **Qal'at Şāliḩ** *var.* Qal'ah Sālih. Maysān, E Iraq 31°30′N 47°24′E
139 V10 **Qal'at Sukkar** Dhī Qār, SE Iraq 31°52′N 46°05′E
Qalba Zhotasy *see* Kalbinskiy Khrebet
143 Q12 **Qal'eh Bīābān** Fārs, S Iran
149 N4 **Qal'eh Shahr** *Pash.* Qala Shāhar. Sar-e Pol, N Afghanistan 35°34′N 65°38′E
148 L4 **Qal'eh-ye Now** *var.* Qala Nau. Bādghīs, NW Afghanistan 35°N 63°08′E
149 T2 **Qal'eh-ye Panjeh** *var.* Qala Panja. Badakhshān, NE Afghanistan 36°56′N 72°15′E
Qalqaman *see* Kalkaman
Qalzhat *see* Kol'zhat
Qamar Bay *see* Qamar, Ghubbat al
141 U14 **Qamar, Ghubbat al** *Eng.* Qamar Bay. *bay* Oman/Yemen
141 V13 **Qamar, Jabal al** ▲ SW Oman
147 N12 **Qamashi** Qashqadaryo Viloyati, S Uzbekistan 38°52′N 66°30′E
Qambar *see* Kambar
159 R14 **Qamdo** Xizang Zizhiqu, W China 31°09′N 97°09′E
75 R7 **Qamīnis** NE Libya 31°48′N 20°04′E
Qamishly *see* Al Qāmishlī
Qânâq *see* Qaanaaq
Qandahār *see* Kandahār
80 Q11 **Qandala** Bari, NE Somalia 11°30′N 50°00′E
Qandyaghash *see* Kandyagash
138 L2 **Qanṭarī** Ar Raqqah, N Syria 36°24′N 39°16′E
Qapiciğ Daği *see* Qazangödağ
158 H5 **Qapqal** *var.* Qapqal Xibe Zizhixian. Xinjiang Uygur Zizhiqu, NW China 43°46′N 81°09′E
Qapqal Xibe Zizhixian *see* Qapqal

◆ Country ● Country Capital ◇ Dependent Territory ○ Dependent Territory Capital ❖ Administrative Regions ✈ International Airport ▲ Mountain ▲ Mountain Range Ѫ Volcano ≈ River ◎ Lake ⊠ Reservoir

Column 1

Qapshagay Böyeni see Kapchagayskoye Vodokhranilishche
Qapshaghay see Kapchagay
Qapugtang see Zadoi
196 M15 Qaqortoq Dan. Julianehåb. ◆ S Kitaa, S Greenland
139 T4 Qara Anjir At Ta'mīn, N Iraq 35°30'N 44°37'E
Qarabāgh see Qarah Bāgh
Qarabaū see Karabau
Qaraboget see Karaboget
Qarabulaq see Karabulak
Qarabutaq see Karabutak
139 U4 Qara Gol As Sulaymānīyah, NE Iraq 35°21'N 45°38'S
75 U8 Qārah var. Qārah. NW Egypt 29°34'N 26°28'E
Qarah see Qārah
148 J4 Qara Bāgh var. Qarabāgh. Herāt, NW Afghanistan 35°06'N 63°13'E
138 G7 Qaraoun, Lac de var. Buhayrat al Qir'awn. ☒ S Lebanon
Qaraoy see Karaoy
Qaraqoyyn see Karakoyyn, Ozero
Qara Qum see Garagum
Qarasū see Karasu
Qaratal see Karatal
Qarataū see Karatau, Khrebet, Kazakhstan
Qarataū see Karatau, Zhambyl, Kazakhstan
Qaraton see Karaton
Qarazhal see Karazhal
80 P13 Qardho var. Kardh, It. Gardo. Bari, N Somalia 09°34'N 49°30'E
142 M6 Qareh Chāy ☒ N Iran
142 K2 Qareh Sū ☒ NW Iran
Qariateine see Al Qaryatayn
Qarkilik see Ruoqiang
147 O13 Qarluq Rus. Karluk. Surkhondaryo Viloyati, S Uzbekistan 38°11'N 67°39'E
147 U12 Qarokül Rus. Karakul'. E Tajikistan 39°07'N 73°33'E
147 T12 Qarokül Rus. Ozero Karakul'. ☒ E Tajikistan
Qarqan see Qiemo
158 K9 Qarqan He ☒ NW China
Qarqannah, Juzur see Kerkenah, Îles de
Qarqaraly see Karkaralinsk
149 O1 Qarqin Jowzjān, N Afghanistan 37°25'N 66°03'E
Qars see Kars
Qarsaqbay see Karsakpay
146 M12 Qarshi Rus. Karshi; prev. Bek-Budi. Qashqadaryo Viloyati, S Uzbekistan 38°54'N 65°48'E
146 L12 Qarshi Cho'li Rus. Karshinskaya Step. grassland S Uzbekistan
146 M13 Qarshi Kanali Rus. Karshinsky Kanal. canal Turkmenistan/Uzbekistan
Qaryatayn see Al Qaryatayn
Qāsh, Nahr al see Gash
146 M12 Qashqadaryo Viloyati Rus. Kashkadar'inskaya Oblast'. ◆ province S Uzbekistan
Qasigianguit see Qasigiannguit
197 N13 Qasigiannguit var. Qasigianguit, Dan. Christianshåb. ◆ Kitaa, C Greenland
Qasim, Mintaqat see Al Qasim
75 V10 Qasr al Farāfirah var. Qasr Farāfra. W Egypt 27°00'N 27°59'E
139 P8 Qasr 'Amīj Al Anbār. C Iraq 33°30'N 41°52'E
139 R9 Qasr Darwīshāh Karbalā', C Iraq 32°36'N 43°27'E
142 J6 Qasr-e Shīrīn Kermānshāhān, W Iran 34°32'N 45°36'E
Qasr Farāfra see Qasr al Farāfirah
141 O16 Qa'tabah SW Yemen 13°51'N 44°42'E
138 H7 Qatanā var. Katana. Dimashq, S Syria 33°27'N 36°04'E
143 N15 Qatar off. State of Qatar, Ar. Dawlat Qatar. ◆ monarchy SW Asia
Qatar, State of see Qatar
Qatrana see Al Qatrānah
143 Q12 Qatrüyeh Fārs, S Iran 29°08'N 54°42'E
Qattara Depression/Qattārah, Munkhafad al see Qattārah, Munkhafad el
75 U8 Qattārah, Munkhafad el var. Munkhafad al Qattārah, Eng. Qattara Depression. desert NW Egypt
Qattâra, Monkhafad el see Qattārah, Munkhafad el
Qattinah, Buhayrat see Hims, Buhayrat
Qausuittuq see Resolute
Qaydar see Qeydar
Qāyen see Qā'en
147 Q11 Qayroqqum Rus. Kayrakkum. NW Tajikistan 40°16'N 69°46'E
147 Q10 Qayroqqum, Obanbori Rus. Kayrakkumskoye Vodokhranilishche. ☒ NW Tajikistan
159 O17 Qayü Xizang Zizhiqu, W China 28°35'N 92°46'E
137 V13 Qazangöldağ Rus. Gora Kapydzhik, Turk. Qapiciğ Daği. ▲ SW Azerbaijan 39°18'N 46°00'E
139 U7 Qazānīyah var. Dhū Shaykh. Diyālā, E Iraq 33°39'N 45°33'E
Qazaqstan/Qazaqstan Respublikasy see Kazakhstan
137 T9 Qazax Rus. Kazbegi. NE Georgia 42°39'N 44°36'E
149 P15 Qāzi Ahmad var. Kazi Ahmad. Sind, SE Pakistan 26°15'N 68°30'E
137 Y12 Qazimämmäd Rus. Kazi Magomed. SE Azerbaijan 40°03'N 48°56'E
142 M4 Qazvīn var. Kazvin. Qazvīn, N Iran
142 M5 Qazvīn ◆ province N Iran
187 Z13 Qelelevu Lagoon lagoon NE Fiji
Qena see Qinā

Column 2

113 L23 Qeparo Vlorë, S Albania 40°04'N 19°49'E
Qeqertarssuaq see Qeqertarsuaq
197 N13 Qeqertarsuaq var. Qeqertarssuaq, Dan. Godhavn. ◆ Kitaa, W Greenland
196 M13 Qeqertarsuaq island W Greenland
197 N13 Qeqertarsuup Tunua Dan. Disko Bugt. inlet W Greenland
Qerveh see Qorveh
143 S14 Qeshm Hormozgān, S Iran 26°58'N 56°17'E
143 R14 Qeshm var. Jazīreh-ye Qeshm, Qeshm Island. island S Iran
Qeshm Island/Qeshm, Jazīreh-ye see Qeshm
Qey see Kīsh, Jazīreh-ye
142 L4 Qezel Owzan var. Qïzïl Üzen. NW Iran 36°50'N 47°40'E
142 K5 Qezel Owzan, Rūd-e var. Ki Zil Uzen, Qï Zil Uzun. ☒ NW Iran
161 Q2 Qian Jilin, Hebei, E China 40°01'N 118°43'E
Qiandao Hu see Chun'an Shuiku
Qian Gorlo/Qian Gorlos/Qian Gorlos Mongolzu Zizhixian/Quianguozhen see Qianguo
163 V9 Qianguo var. Qian Gorlo, Qian Gorlos, Qian Gorlos Mongolzu Zizhixian, Quianguozhen. Jilin, NE China 45°05'N 124°52'E
161 N9 Qianjiang Hubei, C China 30°23'N 112°58'E
160 K10 Qianjiang Sichuan, C China 29°30'N 108°45'E
160 L14 Qian Jiang ☒ S China
160 G9 Qianning var. Gartar. Sichuan, C China 30°27'N 101°24'E
163 U13 Qian Shan ▲ NE China
160 H10 Qianwei var. Yujin. Sichuan, C China 29°15'N 103°52'E
160 J11 Qianxi Guizhou, S China 27°09'N 106°01'E
Qiaotou see Datong
Qiaowa see Muli
159 Q7 Qiaowan Gansu, N China 40°37'N 96°40'E
Qibili see Kebili
159 Q7 Qiemo var. Qarqan. Xinjiang Uygur Zizhiqu, NW China 38°09'N 85°30'E
160 J10 Qijiang var. Gunan. Chongqing Shi, C China 29°01'N 106°40'E
159 N5 Qijiaojing Xinjiang Uygur Zizhiqu, NW China 43°25'N 91°35'E
9 R5 Qikiqtarjuaq prev. Broughton Island. Nunavut, NE Canada 67°35'N 63°55'W
149 P9 Qila Saifullāh Baluchistān, SW Pakistan 30°45'N 68°08'E
159 S9 Qilian var. Babao. Qinghai, C China 38°09'N 100°08'E
159 N8 Qilian Shan var. Kilien Mountains. ▲ N China
197 O11 Qimusseriarsuaq Dan. Melville Bugt, Eng. Melville Bay. bay NW Greenland
75 X10 Qinā var. Qena; anc. Caene, Caenepolis. E Egypt 26°12'N 32°49'E
159 W11 Qin'an Gansu, C China 34°49'N 105°50'E
159 X10 Qingcheng Gansu, N China 36°01'N 107°53'E
Qincheng see Nanfeng
163 W7 Qing'an Heilongjiang, NE China 46°53'N 127°29'E
161 R5 Qingdao var. Ching-Tao, Ch'ing-tao, Tsingtao, Tsintao, Ger. Tsingtau. Shandong, E China 36°31'N 120°55'E
163 V8 Qinggang Heilongjiang, NE China 46°41'N 126°05'E
Qinggil see Qinghe
159 P11 Qinghai var. Chinghai, Koko Nor, Qing, Qinghai. Qinghai, C China ◆ province C China
159 S10 Qinghai Hu var. Ch'ing Hai, Tsing Hai, Mong. Koko Nor. ☒ C China
Qinghai Sheng see Qinghai
158 M3 Qinghe var. Qinggil. Xinjiang Uygur Zizhiqu, NW China 46°42'N 90°19'E
160 L4 Qinghe var. Kuanzhou; prev. Xiuyan. Shaanxi, C China 37°01'N 110°09'E
160 L9 Qing Jiang ☒ C China
161 Q3 Qingjiang see Huai'an
Qingkou see Ganyu
160 I12 Qinglong var. Liancheng. Guizhou, S China 25°49'N 105°10'E
161 Q2 Qinglong Hebei, E China 40°24'N 118°57'E
Qingshan see Wudalianchi
159 R12 Qingshuihe Qinghai, C China 33°47'N 97°10'E
159 X10 Qingyang var. Xifeng. Gansu, C China 35°46'N 107°35'E
161 N14 Qingyuan Guangdong, S China 23°42'N 113°02'E
163 V13 Qingyuan var. Shandan
Qingyuan Manzu Zizhixian see Qingyuan
163 V13 Qingyuan Gaoyuan var. Xizang Gaoyuan, Eng. Plateau of Tibet. plateau W China
161 Q4 Qingzhou prev. Yidu. Shandong, E China 36°41'N 118°29'E
157 N9 Qin He ☒ C China
161 Q2 Qinhuangdao Hebei, E China 39°57'N 119°31'E
161 N5 Qin Ling ☒ C China
161 N7 Qinxian var. Dingchang. Shanxi, C China 36°46'N 112°42'E
161 O8 Qin Xian see Qinxian
161 N6 Qinyang Henan, C China 35°07'N 112°58'E
160 K15 Qinzhou Guangxi Zhuangzu Zizhiqu, S China 22°09'N 108°36'E

Column 3

160 L17 Qionghai prev. Jiaji. Hainan, S China 19°12'N 110°26'E
160 H9 Qionglai Sichuan, C China 30°24'N 103°28'E
160 H8 Qionglai Shan ▲ C China
160 L17 Qiongshan var. Hongyuan
160 L17 Qiongzhou Haixia var. Hainan Strait. strait S China
163 V7 Qiqihar var. Ch'i-ch'i-ha-erh, Tsitsihar; prev. Lungkiang. Heilongjiang, NE China 47°23'N 123°57'E
163 H10 Qira Xinjiang Uygur Zizhiqu, NW China 37°05'N 80°45'E
Qir'awn, Buhayrat al see Qaraoun, Lac de
143 T3 Qiryat Gat see Kiryat Gat
Qiryat Shemona see Kiryat Shmona
Qishlaq see Garmsār
141 O16 Qishn SE Yemen 15°29'N 51°44'E
Qishon, Nahal see Kishon, Nahal
Qita Ghazzah see Gaza Strip
156 K5 Qitai Xinjiang Uygur Zizhiqu, NW China 44°00'N 89°34'E
163 Y8 Qitaihe Heilongjiang, NE China 45°45'N 130°53'E
141 W12 Qitbit, Wādī dry watercourse S Oman
161 O5 Qixian var. Qi Xian, Zhaoge. Henan, C China 35°35'N 114°12'E
Qi Xian see Qixian
Qizil Orda see Kyzylorda
147 V14 Qizilrabot Rus. Kyzylrabot. SE Tajikistan 37°29'N 74°44'E
146 J10 Qizilravote Rus. Kyzylrabat. Buxoro Viloyati, C Uzbekistan 40°35'N 62°09'E
Qi Zil Uzun see Qezel Owzan, Rūd-e
139 S4 Qizil Yār At Ta'mīn, N Iraq 35°26'N 44°12'E
Qoghaly see Kugaly
Qogir Feng see K2
143 R5 Qom var. Kum, Qum. Qom, N Iran 34°43'N 50°54'E
143 N6 Qom ◆ province N Iran
Qomisheh see Shahreza
Qomolangma Feng see Everest, Mount
142 M7 Qom, Rūd-e ☒ C Iran
65 B24 Qomsheh see Shahrezā
Qomul see Hami
Qondūz see Kondoz
159 N16 Qonggyai Xizang Zizhiqu, W China 29°01'N 91°39'E
146 J7 Qo'ng'irot Rus. Kungrad. Qoraqalpog'iston Respublikasi, NW Uzbekistan 43°01'N 58°49'E
Qongyrat see Konyrat
Qoqek see Tacheng
147 R10 Qo'qon var. Khokand, Rus. Kokand. Farg'ona Viloyati, E Uzbekistan 40°34'N 70°55'E
Qorabowur Kirlari see Karabaur', Uval
Qoradaryo see Karadar'ya
Qoradzhar Rus. Karadzhar. Qoraqalpog'iston
146 G6 Qorajar Rus. Karadzhar. Qoraqalpog'iston Respublikasi, NW Uzbekistan 43°34'N 58°35'E
146 K12 Qorao'l Rus. Karakul'. Buxoro Viloyati, C Uzbekistan 39°30'N 63°55'E
146 H7 Qorao'zak Rus. Karauzyak. Qoraqalpog'iston Respublikasi, NW Uzbekistan 43°07'N 60°03'E
Qoradaryo see Karadar'ya
146 E5 Qoraqalpog'iston Rus. Karakalpakya. Qoraqalpog'iston Respublikasi, NW Uzbekistan 44°45'N 56°06'E
146 G7 Qoraqalpog'iston Respublikasi Rus. Respublika Karakalpakstan. ◆ autonomous republic W Uzbekistan
Qorghalzhyn see Korgalzhyn
138 N6 Qornet es Saouda ▲ NE Lebanon 36°06'N 34°06'E
146 L12 Qorowulbozor Rus. Karaulbazar. Buxoro Viloyati, C Uzbekistan 39°28'N 64°49'E
142 K5 Qorveh var. Qerveh, Qurveh. Kordestān, W Iran 35°09'N 47°48'E
147 N13 Qo'shrabot Rus. Kushrabat. Samarqand Viloyati, C Uzbekistan 40°15'N 66°40'E
Qoskol see Koskol'
Qosshaghyl see Koschagyl
Qostanay/Qostanay Oblysy see Kostanay
143 P12 Qotbābād Fārs, S Iran 28°52'N 53°40'E
143 R13 Qotbābād Hormozgān, S Iran 27°09'N 56°31'E
138 N6 Qoubaiyāt var. Al Qubayyāt. N Lebanon 37°00'N 34°30'E
Qoussantina see Constantine
Qowowuyag see Cho Oyu
147 O11 Qo'ytosh Rus. Koytash. Jizzax Viloyati, C Uzbekistan 40°13'N 67°19'E
146 G7 Qozonketkan Qoraqalpog'iston Respublikasi, W Uzbekistan 42°59'N 59°21'E
146 H6 Qozoqdaryo Rus. Kazakdar'ya. Qoraqalpog'iston Respublikasi, NW Uzbekistan 43°23'N 58°35'E
19 S11 Quabbin Reservoir ☒ Massachusetts, NE USA
100 F12 Quakenbrück Niedersachsen, NW Germany 52°41'N 07°57'E
18 I15 Quakertown Pennsylvania, NE USA 40°26'N 75°17'W
182 M10 Quambatook Victoria, SE Australia 35°53'N 143°28'E
25 Q4 Quanah Texas, SW USA 34°17'N 99°46'W
167 V13 Quang Ngai var. Quangngai, Quang Nghia. Quang Ngai, C Vietnam 15°09'N 108°50'E
Quangngai see Quang Ngai
Quang Nghia see Quang Ngai
167 T9 Quang Tri var. Tri Hai. Quang Tri, C Vietnam 16°46'N 107°11'E
Quanjiang see Suichuan
Quan Long see Ca Mau
152 L4 Quanshuigou China/India
161 R13 Quanzhou var. Ch'uan-chou, Tsinkiang; prev. chiang. Fujian, SE China 24°56'N 118°36'E

Column 4

160 M12 Quanzhou Guangxi Zhuangzu Zizhiqu, S China 25°59'N 111°02'E
11 V16 Qu'Appelle ☒ Saskatchewan, S Canada
12 M3 Quaqtaq prev. Koartac. Québec, NE Canada
61 E16 Quaraí Rio Grande do Sul, S Brazil 30°48'S 56°27'W
59 H24 Quaraí, Rio Sp. Río Cuareim. ☒ Brazil/Uruguay see also Cuareim, Río
Quaraí, Río see Cuareim, Río
171 N13 Quarles, Pegunungan ▲ Sulawesi, C Indonesia
107 C20 Quartu Sant' Elena Sardegna, Italy, C Mediterranean Sea 39°15'N 09°12'E
29 X13 Quasqueton Iowa, C USA 42°23'N 91°45'W
73 X16 Quatre Bornes W Mauritius 20°15'S 57°28'E
172 I17 Quatre Bornes Mahé, NE Seychelles
137 X10 Quba Rus. Kuba. N Azerbaijan 41°22'N 48°30'E
Quba see Ba'qūbah
83 D9 Quibala Cuanza Sul, NW Angola 10°44'S 14°58'E
82 B11 Quibaxe var. Quibaxi. Cuanza Norte, NW Angola 08°30'S 14°36'E
Quibaxi see Quibaxe
54 D9 Quibdó Chocó, W Colombia 05°40'N 76°38'W
102 G7 Quiberon Morbihan, NW France 47°30'N 03°07'W
102 G7 Quiberon, Baie de bay NW France
54 J5 Quíbor Lara, N Venezuela 09°55'N 69°35'W
42 C4 Quiché ◆ department W Guatemala
Quiché, Departamento del see Quiché
99 E21 Quiévrain Hainaut, S Belgium 50°25'N 03°41'E
83 B14 Quilengues Huíla, SW Angola 14°09'S 14°04'E
57 G15 Quillabamba Cusco, C Peru 12°49'S 72°41'W
57 L18 Quillacollo Cochabamba, C Bolivia 17°26'S 66°16'W
105 S8 Quillan Aude, S France 42°52'N 02°11'E
62 G11 Quillota Valparaíso, C Chile 32°54'S 71°16'W
155 G23 Quilon var. Kollam. Kerala, SW India 08°57'N 76°37'E see also Kollam
181 V9 Quilpie Queensland, C Australia 26°39'S 144°15'E
149 O4 Quil-Qala Bāmīān, N Afghanistan 34°45'N 67°54'E
62 L7 Quimilí Santiago del Estero, C Argentina 27°35'S 62°25'W
57 O19 Quimome Santa Cruz, E Bolivia 17°45'S 61°15'W
102 F6 Quimper anc. Quimper Corentin. Finistère, NW France 48°00'N 04°05'W
Quimper Corentin see Quimper
102 G7 Quimperlé Finistère, NW France 47°52'N 03°33'W
32 F8 Quinault Washington, NW USA 47°27'N 123°53'W
32 F8 Quinault River ☒ Washington, NW USA
35 P5 Quincy California, W USA 39°56'N 120°56'W
23 S8 Quincy Florida, SE USA 30°35'N 84°34'W
30 J10 Quincy Illinois, N USA 39°56'N 91°24'W
19 O11 Quincy Massachusetts, NE USA 42°15'N 71°00'W
32 J9 Quincy Washington, NW USA 47°13'N 119°51'W
54 E10 Quindío off. Departamento del Quindío. ◆ province C Colombia
Quindío, Departamento del see Quindío
54 E10 Quindío, Nevado del ▲ C Colombia 04°42'N 75°25'W
62 J10 Quines San Luis, C Argentina 32°15'S 65°46'W
39 N13 Quinhagak Alaska, USA 59°45'N 161°55'W
76 G13 Quinhámel W Guinea-Bissau 11°52'N 15°52'W
82 D11 Quela Malanje, NW Angola 09°18'S 17°07'E
83 O16 Quelimane var. Kilimane, Kilmain, Quilimane. Zambézia, NE Mozambique 17°53'S 36°51'E
63 G18 Quellón var. Puerto Quellón. Los Lagos, S Chile 43°05'S 73°38'W
37 P12 Quemado New Mexico, SW USA 34°18'N 108°29'W
25 O12 Quemado Texas, SW USA 28°58'N 100°36'W
Quemoy see Chinmen Tao
62 K13 Quemú Quemú La Pampa, E Argentina 36°03'S 63°35'W
155 E17 Quepem Goa, W India 15°13'N 74°03'E
42 M14 Quepos Puntarenas, S Costa Rica 09°28'N 84°10'W
Que Que see Kwekwe
62 G13 Queilén Bío Bío, C Chile 36°15'S 72°35'W
55 D23 Quequén Buenos Aires, E Argentina 38°34'S 58°44'W
61 C23 Quequén Grande, Río ☒ E Argentina
41 N13 Querétaro Querétaro de Arteaga, C Mexico 20°36'N 100°24'W
41 N13 Querétaro de Arteaga ◆ state C Mexico
Querétaro see Que Que
100 N13 Querfurt Sachsen-Anhalt, C Germany 51°23'N 11°36'E
41 N13 Querobabi Sonora, NW Mexico 30°02'N 111°02'W
41 N13 Quiroga Michoacán de Ocampo, SW Mexico 19°40'N 101°31'W

Column 5

Quetzalcoalco see Coatzacoalcos
Quetzaltenango see Quezaltenango
56 B6 Quevedo Los Ríos, C Ecuador 01°02'S 79°27'W
42 B6 Quezaltenango var. Quezaltenango. Quezaltenango, W Guatemala 14°50'N 91°30'W
42 A2 Quezaltenango off. Departamento de Quezaltenango, var. Quezaltenango. ◆ department SW Guatemala
42 E6 Quezaltepeque Chiquimula, SE Guatemala 14°38'N 89°25'W
170 M6 Quezon Palawan, W Philippines 09°13'N 118°01'E
161 P5 Qufu Shandong, E China 35°37'N 117°05'E
83 B12 Quibala Cuanza Sul, NW Angola 10°44'S 14°58'E
82 B11 Quibaxe Cuanza Norte, NW Angola 08°30'S 14°36'E
54 D9 Quibdó Chocó, W Colombia 05°40'N 76°38'W
102 G7 Quiberon Morbihan, NW France 47°30'N 03°07'W
102 G7 Quiberon, Baie de bay NW France
54 J5 Quíbor Lara, N Venezuela 09°55'N 69°35'W
83 B14 Quilengues Huíla, SW Angola 14°09'S 14°04'E
57 G15 Quillabamba Cusco, C Peru 12°49'S 72°41'W
57 L18 Quillacollo Cochabamba, C Bolivia 17°26'S 66°16'W
103 N17 Quillan Aude, S France 42°52'N 02°11'E
11 U15 Quill Lakes ☒ Saskatchewan, S Canada
62 G11 Quillota Valparaíso, C Chile 32°54'S 71°16'W
155 G23 Quilon var. Kollam. Kerala, SW India 08°57'N 76°37'E see also Kollam
181 V9 Quilpie Queensland, C Australia 26°39'S 144°15'E
149 O4 Quil-Qala Bāmīān, N Afghanistan 34°45'N 67°54'E
62 L7 Quimilí Santiago del Estero, C Argentina 27°35'S 62°25'W
57 O19 Quimome Santa Cruz, E Bolivia 17°45'S 61°15'W
102 F6 Quimper anc. Quimper Corentin. Finistère, NW France 48°00'N 04°05'W
102 G7 Quimperlé Finistère, NW France 47°52'N 03°33'W
195 Y10 Queen Mary Coast physical region Antarctica
65 N24 Queen Mary's Peak ▲ C Tristan da Cunha
196 M8 Queen Maud Gulf gulf Arctic Ocean
195 P11 Queen Maud Mountains ▲ Antarctica
181 O7 Queen's County see Laois
181 U9 Queensland ◆ state N Australia
192 I9 Queensland Plateau undersea feature N Coral Sea
183 O16 Queenstown Tasmania, SE Australia 42°06'S 145°33'E
185 C22 Queenstown Otago, South Island, New Zealand 45°01'S 168°44'E
83 I24 Queenstown Eastern Cape, S South Africa 31°52'S 26°50'E
Queenstown see Cobh
32 F8 Queets Washington, NW USA 47°32'N 124°19'W
61 D18 Queguay Grande, Río ☒ W Uruguay
59 O16 Queimadas Bahia, E Brazil 10°59'S 39°38'W
82 D11 Quela Malanje, NW Angola 09°18'S 17°07'E
83 O16 Quelimane var. Kilimane, Kilmain, Quilimane. Zambézia, NE Mozambique 17°53'S 36°51'E
63 G18 Quellón var. Puerto Quellón. Los Lagos, S Chile 43°05'S 73°38'W
37 P12 Quemado New Mexico, SW USA 34°18'N 108°29'W
25 O12 Quemado Texas, SW USA 28°58'N 100°36'W
41 N13 Querétaro de Arteaga ◆ state C Mexico
155 E17 Quepem Goa, W India 15°13'N 74°03'E
42 M14 Quepos Puntarenas, S Costa Rica 09°28'N 84°10'W
62 K13 Quemú Quemú La Pampa, E Argentina 36°03'S 63°35'W
155 E17 Quepem Goa, W India 15°13'N 74°03'E
54 M14 Quepos Puntarenas, S Costa Rica 09°28'N 84°10'W
83 B15 Quipungo Huíla, C Angola 14°49'S 14°29'E
62 G13 Quirihue Bío Bío, C Chile 36°15'S 72°35'W
182 D11 Quirindi New South Wales, SE Australia 31°29'S 150°40'E
55 P5 Quíriquire Monagas, NE Venezuela 09°59'N 63°14'W
41 A10 Quiriquire ...
62 G13 Quirihue Bío Bío, C Chile 36°15'S 72°35'W
55 D23 Quequén Buenos Aires, E Argentina 38°34'S 58°44'W
59 O4 Quitaque Texas, SW USA 34°22'N 101°03'W
59 S9 Questa New Mexico, SW USA 36°41'N 105°37'W
41 K13 Quesnel British Columbia, SW Canada 52°59'N 122°30'W
41 N13 Querétaro Querétaro de Arteaga, C Mexico 20°36'N 100°24'W
23 T6 Quitman Georgia, SE USA 30°46'N 83°33'W

Column 6

22 M6 Quitman Mississippi, S USA 32°02'N 88°43'W
25 V6 Quitman Texas, SW USA
56 C6 Quito ● (Ecuador) Pichincha, N Ecuador 0°14'S 78°30'W
Quito see Mariscal Sucre
58 P13 Quixadá Ceará, E Brazil 04°57'S 39°04'W
83 Q15 Quixaxe Nampula, NE Mozambique 15°15'S 40°07'E
161 N13 Qujiang var. Maba. Guangdong, S China 24°44'N 113°34'E
160 J9 Qu Jiang ☒ C China
160 K10 Qu Jiang ☒ SE China
160 H12 Qujing Yunnan, SW China 25°39'N 103°52'E
Qulan see Kulan
163 T8 Qulin Gol prev. Chaor He. ☒ NE China
146 L10 QuljuqtovTog'lari Rus. Gory Kul'dzhuktau. ▲ C Uzbekistan
Qulsary see Kul'sary
Qulyndy Zhazyghy see Kulunda Steppe
Qum see Qom
Qumālisch see Lubartów
159 P11 Qumar He ☒ C China
159 Q12 Qumarlēb var. Yuegai; prev. Yuegaitan. Qinghai, C China 34°06'N 95°54'E
159 Q15 Qumdo Xizang Zizhiqu, W China 30°03'N 95°33'E
Qumisheh see Shahrezā
147 O14 Qumqo'rg'on Rus. Kumkurgan. Surkhondaryo Viloyati, S Uzbekistan
Qunaytirah/Qunaytirah, Muhāfazat al see Al Qunaytirah
189 V12 Quoi island Chuuk, C Micronesia
9 N8 Quoich ☒ Nunavut, NE Canada
83 E26 Quoin Point headland SW South Africa 34°48'S 19°39'E
182 I7 Quorn South Australia 32°22'S 138°03'E
19 Q12 Quabbin ...
147 P14 Qürghonteppa Rus. Kurgan-Tyube. SW Tajikistan
Qurlurtuuq see Kugluktuk
Qurveh see Qorveh
167 S14 Qurveh ...
167 S14 Quryq see Kuryk
76 J8 Qusair see Al Qusayr
Qusar see Al Qusayr
110 L10 Qusay see Al Qusayr
142 I2 Qüshchī Āzārbāijān-e Gharbī, N Iran 37°59'N 45°05'E
31 N9 Qusmuryn see Kushmurun, Kostanay, Kazakhstan
14 D7 Qusmuryn see Kushmurun, Kostanay, Kazakhstan
159 O16 Qusum Xizang Zizhiqu, W China 29°02'N 92°09'E
141 O15 Qutayfah/Qutayfe/Quteife see Al Qutayfah
Quthing see Moyeni
147 S10 Quvasoy Rus. Kuvasay. Farg'ona Viloyati, E Uzbekistan 40°17'N 71°53'E
Quwair see Guwēr
Quxar see Lhazê
Qu Xian see Quzhou
159 N16 Quxü Xoi. Xizang Zizhiqu, W China 29°25'N 90°43'E
167 V13 Quy Chanh Ninh Thuan, S Vietnam 11°28'N 108°53'E
167 V11 Quy Nhon var. Quinhon, Qui Nhon. Binh Đinh, C Vietnam 13°47'N 109°11'E
161 Q3 Quzhou var. Qu Xian. Zhejiang, SE China 28°55'N 118°54'E
95 H16 Qyteti Stalin see Kuçovë
Qyzylaghash see Kyzylagash
Qyzylorda see Kyzylorda
Qyzyltū see Kishkenekol'
Qyzylzhar see Kyzylzhar

R

173 R4 Raa Atoll var. North Maalhosmadulu Atoll. atoll N Maldives
109 R4 Raab Oberösterreich, N Austria 48°19'N 13°40'E
109 X8 Raab Hung. Rába. ☒ Austria/Hungary see also Rába
Raab see Győr
Raab see Rába
109 V2 Raabs an der Thaya Niederösterreich, E Austria 48°51'N 15°28'E
93 L14 Raahe Swe. Brahestad. Oulu, W Finland 64°24'N 24°31'E
98 M10 Raalte Overijssel, E Netherlands 52°23'N 06°16'E
99 I14 Raamsdonksveer Noord-Brabant, S Netherlands 51°42'N 04°54'E
92 L12 Raanujärvi Lappi, NW Finland 66°39'N 24°40'E
96 G9 Raasay island NW Scotland, United Kingdom
118 H3 Raasiku Ger. Rasik. N Estonia 59°22'N 25°11'E
112 B11 Rab It. Arbe. Primorje-Gorski Kotar, NW Croatia 44°46'N 14°46'E
112 B11 Rab It. Arbe. island NW Croatia
171 N16 Raba Sumbawa, S Indonesia 08°27'S 118°45'E
111 G22 Rába Ger. Raab. ☒ Austria/Hungary see also Raab
Rába see Raab
104 I2 Rábade Galicia, NW Spain 43°07'N 07°37'W
79 B21 Rabak White Nile, C Sudan 13°12'N 32°44'E
186 G9 Rabaraba Milne Bay, SE Papua New Guinea 09°58'S 149°50'E
76 K16 Rabastens-de-Bigorre Hautes-Pyrénées, S France 43°23'N 00°10'E
121 O16 Rabat ▲ W Malta 35°51'N 14°25'E
74 F6 Rabat var. al Dar al Baida. ● (Morocco) NW Morocco 34°02'N 06°51'W
Rabat see Victoria
186 H6 Rabaul New Britain, E Papua New Guinea 04°13'S 152°11'E
119 G15 Rabboah ... Hrodzyenskaya Voblasts', W Belarus 54°03'N 25°09'E

Column 7

28 K8 Rabbit Creek ☒ South Dakota, N USA
14 H10 Rabbit Lake ☒ Ontario, S Canada
187 Y14 Rabi prev. Rambi. island N Fiji
140 K9 Rābigh Makkah, W Saudi Arabia 22°51'N 39°00'E
42 D5 Rabinal Baja Verapaz, C Guatemala 15°05'N 90°26'W
168 G9 Rabi, Pulau island W Indonesia, East Indies
111 L17 Rabka Małopolskie, S Poland 49°38'N 20°E
155 F16 Rabkavi Karnātaka, W India 16°40'N 75°03'E
Rabnica see Ribnita
109 Y6 Rabnitz ☒ E Austria
124 J7 Rabocheostrovsk Respublika Kareliya, NW Russian Federation 64°58'N 34°46'E
23 U1 Rabun Bald ▲ Georgia, SE USA 34°58'N 83°18'W
75 S11 Rabyānah SE Libya 24°07'N 21°58'E
75 S11 Rabyānah, Ramlat var. Rebiana Sand Sea, Şaḥrā' Rabyānah. desert SE Libya
Rabyānah, Şaḥrā' see Rabyānah
116 L11 Răcăciuni Bacău, E Romania 46°20'N 27°02'E
Racaka see Riwoqê
107 J24 Racalmuto Sicilia, Italy, C Mediterranean Sea 37°25'N 13°44'E
116 J14 Răcari Dâmbovița, SE Romania 44°37'N 25°43'E
Răcari see Durankulak
116 F13 Răcăşdia Hung. Rakasd. Caraș-Severin, SW Romania 44°58'N 21°36'E
106 B9 Racconigi Piemonte, NE Italy 44°45'N 07°41'E
31 T15 Raccoon Creek ☒ Ohio, N USA
13 V13 Race, Cape headland Newfoundland, Newfoundland and Labrador, E Canada 46°40'N 53°05'W
22 K10 Raceland Louisiana, S USA 29°43'N 90°36'W
19 Q12 Race Point headland Massachusetts, NE USA
167 S14 Rach Gia Kiên Giang, S Vietnam 10°01'N 105°05'E
167 S14 Rach Gia, Vinh bay S Vietnam
76 J8 Rachid Tagant, C Mauritania 18°48'N 11°41'W
110 L10 Raciąż Mazowieckie, C Poland 52°46'N 20°04'E
111 I16 Racibórz Ger. Ratibor. Śląskie, S Poland 50°05'N 18°10'E
31 N9 Racine Wisconsin, N USA 42°42'N 87°50'W
14 D7 Racine Lake ☒ Ontario, S Canada
111 J23 Ráckeve Pest, C Hungary 47°10'N 18°58'E
Rácz-Becse see Bečej
141 O15 Radā' var. Rida'. W Yemen 14°24'N 44°49'E
113 O15 Radan ▲ SE Serbia 42°59'N 21°31'E
63 J19 Rada Tilly Chubut, S Argentina 45°10'S 67°33'W
116 K8 Rădăuti Ger. Radautz, Hung. Radóc. Suceava, N Romania 47°50'N 25°58'E
116 L8 Rădăuti-Prut Botoșani, NE Romania 48°14'N 26°47'E
Radautz see Rădăuti
112 A10 Radbuza see Radbusa
20 K6 Radbuza Ger. Radbusa. ☒ W Czech Republic
139 O2 Radcliff Kentucky, S USA 37°50'N 85°57'W
21 R7 Radford Virginia, NE USA 37°08'N 80°34'W
154 C9 Rādhanpur Gujarāt, W India 23°50'N 71°38'E
127 Q6 Radishchevo Ul'yanovskaya Oblast', W Russian Federation
12 I9 Radisson Québec, C Canada 53°47'N 77°35'W
11 P16 Radium Hot Springs British Columbia, SW Canada 50°39'N 116°09'W
116 F11 Radna Hung. Máriaradna. Arad, W Romania
114 K10 Radnevo Stara Zagora, C Bulgaria 42°17'N 25°58'E
97 J20 Radnor cultural region E Wales, United Kingdom
Radnót see Iernut
101 H24 Radolfzell am Bodensee Baden-Württemberg, S Germany 47°43'N 08°58'E
116 M13 Radom Mazowieckie, C Poland 51°23'N 21°09'E
79 I16 Radom ... SE Sudan
111 K14 Radomsko Rus. Novoradomsk. Łódzkie, C Poland 51°04'N 19°25'E
116 H13 Radomireşti Olt, S Romania 44°06'N 24°50'E
117 N4 Radomyshl' Zhytomyrs'ka Oblast', N Ukraine 50°30'N 29°14'E
113 P19 Radoviš prev. Radovište. E Macedonia
94 B13 Radøy island S Norway
109 R7 Radstadt Salzburg, NW Austria 47°24'N 13°31'E
182 E8 Radstock, Cape headland South Australia 33°11'S 134°18'E
31 U10 Radufa ▲ N Slovenia
119 G15 Radun' Hrodzyenskaya Voblasts', W Belarus 54°03'N 25°09'E

◆ Country | ◇ Dependent Territory | ◆ Administrative Regions | ▲ Mountain | ☒ Volcano | ○ Lake
● Country Capital | ○ Dependent Territory Capital | ✕ International Airport | ▲ Mountain Range | ☒ River | ▣ Reservoir

RADUZHNYY – RED RIVER

126 M3 **Raduzhnyy** Vladimirskaya Oblast', W Russian Federation *55°59'N 40°15'E*
118 F11 **Radviliškis** Šiaulai, N Lithuania *55°48'N 23°32'E*
11 U17 **Radville** Saskatchewan, S Canada *49°28'N 104°19'W*
140 K7 **Radwá, Jabal** ▲ W Saudi Arabia *24°31'N 38°21'E*
111 P16 **Radymno** Podkarpackie, SE Poland *49°57'N 22°49'E*
116 J5 **Radyvyliv** Rivnens'ka Oblast', NW Ukraine *50°07'N 25°12'E*
Radziechów *see* Radekhiv
110 I11 **Radziejów** Kujawsko-pomorskie, C Poland *52°36'N 18°33'E*
110 O12 **Radzyń Podlaski** Lubelskie, E Poland *51°48'N 22°37'E*
8 J7 **Rae** ≈ Nunavut, NW Canada
152 M13 **Rāe Bareli** Uttar Pradesh, N India *26°14'N 81°14'E*
Rae-Edzo *see* Edzo
21 T11 **Raeford** North Carolina, SE USA *34°59'N 79°15'W*
99 M19 **Raeren** Liège, E Belgium *50°42'N 06°06'E*
9 N7 **Rae Strait** *strait* Nunavut, N Canada
184 L11 **Raetihi** Manawatu-Wanganui, North Island, New Zealand *39°29'S 175°16'E*
Raevavae *see* Raivavae
Rafa *see* Rafah
62 M10 **Rafaela** Santa Fe, E Argentina *31°16'S 61°25'W*
138 E11 **Rafah** *var.* Rafa, Rafaḥ, *Heb.* Rafiah, Raphiah. SW Gaza Strip *31°18'N 34°15'E*
79 L15 **Rafaï** Mbomou, SE Central African Republic *05°01'N 23°51'E*
141 O4 **Rafḩah** Al Ḩudūd ash Shamālīyah, N Saudi Arabia *29°41'N 43°29'E*
Rafiah *see* Rafah
143 R10 **Rafsanjān** Kermān, C Iran *30°25'N 56°E*
80 B13 **Raga** Western Bahr el Ghazal, SW Sudan *08°28'N 25°41'E*
19 S8 **Ragged Island** *island* Maine, NE USA
44 J5 **Ragged Island Range** *island group* S Bahamas
184 L7 **Raglan** Waikato, North Island, New Zealand *37°48'S 174°54'E*
22 G8 **Ragley** Louisiana, S USA *30°31'N 93°13'W*
Ragnit *see* Neman
107 K25 **Ragusa** Sicilia, Italy, C Mediterranean Sea *36°56'N 14°42'E*
Ragusa *see* Dubrovnik
Ragusavecchia *see* Cavtat
171 P14 **Raha** Pulau Muna, C Indonesia *04°50'S 122°43'E*
119 N17 **Rahachow** *Rus.* Rogachëv. Homyel'skaya Voblasts', SE Belarus *53°03'N 30°03'E*
67 U6 **Rahad** *var.* Nahr ar Rahad. ≈ W Sudan
Rahad, Nahr ar *see* Rahad
Rahaeng *see* Tak
138 F11 **Rahat** Southern, C Israel *31°20'N 34°43'E*
140 L8 **Rahaṭ, Ḩarrat** *lava flow* W Saudi Arabia
149 S12 **Rahīmyār Khān** Punjab, SE Pakistan *28°27'N 70°21'E*
95 I14 **Råholt** Akershus, S Norway *60°16'N 11°10'E*
113 M17 **Rahovec** *Serb.* Orahovac. W Kosovo *42°24'N 20°40'E*
191 S10 **Raiatea** *island* Îles Sous le Vent, W French Polynesia
155 H16 **Rāichūr** Karnātaka, C India *16°15'N 77°20'E*
Raidestos *see* Tekirdağ
153 S13 **Rāiganj** West Bengal, NE India *25°38'N 88°11'E*
154 M11 **Raigarh** Chhattīsgarh, C India *21°53'N 83°28'E*
183 O16 **Railton** Tasmania, SE Australia *41°24'S 146°28'E*
36 L8 **Rainbow Bridge** *natural arch* Utah, W USA
23 Q3 **Rainbow City** Alabama, S USA *33°57'N 86°02'W*
11 N11 **Rainbow Lake** Alberta, W Canada *58°30'N 119°24'W*
21 R5 **Rainelle** West Virginia, NE USA *37°57'N 80°46'W*
32 G10 **Rainier** Oregon, NW USA *46°05'N 122°55'W*
32 H9 **Rainier, Mount** ※ Washington, NW USA *46°51'N 121°45'W*
23 Q2 **Rainsville** Alabama, S USA *34°29'N 85°51'W*
12 B11 **Rainy Lake** ◎ Canada/USA
12 A11 **Rainy River** Ontario, C Canada *48°44'N 94°33'W*
Raippaluoto *see* Replot
154 K12 **Raipur** Chhattīsgarh, C India *21°16'N 81°42'E*
154 H10 **Raisen** Madhya Pradesh, C India *23°21'N 77°49'E*
15 N13 **Raisin** ≈ Ontario, SE Canada
31 R11 **Raisin, River** ≈ Michigan, N USA
191 U13 **Raivavae** *var.* Raevavae. Îles Australes, SW French Polynesia
149 W9 **Rāiwind** Punjab, E Pakistan *31°14'N 74°10'E*
171 T12 **Raja Ampat, Kepulauan** *island group* E Indonesia
155 L16 **Rājahmundry** Andhra Pradesh, E India *17°05'N 81°42'E*
155 I18 **Rājampet** Andhra Pradesh, E India *14°09'N 79°10'E*
Rajang *see* Rajang, Batang
169 S9 **Rajang, Batang** *var.* Rajang. ≈ East Malaysia
149 S11 **Rājanpur** Punjab, E Pakistan *29°05'N 70°25'E*
155 H23 **Rājapālaiyam** Tamil Nādu, SE India *09°26'N 77°36'E*
152 E12 **Rājasthān** ◐ *state* NW India
153 T15 **Rajbari** Dhaka, C Bangladesh *23°47'N 89°39'E*
153 R12 **Rajbiraj** Eastern, E Nepal *26°34'N 86°52'E*
154 G9 **Rājgarh** Madhya Pradesh, C India *24°01'N 76°42'E*
152 H10 **Rājgarh** Rājasthān, NW India *28°38'N 75°21'E*
153 P14 **Rājgīr** Bihār, N India *25°01'N 85°26'E*
110 O8 **Rajgród** Podlaskie, NE Poland *53°43'N 22°40'E*
154 L12 **Rājim** Chhattīsgarh, C India *20°57'N 81°58'E*
112 C11 **Rajinac, Mali** ▲ W Croatia *44°47'N 15°04'E*
154 B10 **Rājkot** Gujarāt, W India *22°18'N 70°47'E*
153 R14 **Rājmahal** Jhārkhand, NE India *25°03'N 87°49'E*
153 Q14 **Rājmahāl Hills** *hill range* N India
154 K12 **Rāj Nāndgaon** Chhattīsgarh, C India *21°06'N 81°02'E*
154 E12 **Rājpīpla** Gujarāt, W India *21°49'N 73°36'E*
152 I8 **Rājpura** Punjab, NW India *30°29'N 76°40'E*
152 E14 **Rājsamand** Rājasthān, N India *23°04'N 73.53°00'E*
153 S14 **Rajshahi** *prev.* Rampur Boalia. Rajshahi, W Bangladesh *24°24'N 88°40'E*
153 S13 **Rajshahi** ◐ *division* NW Bangladesh
158 J16 **Raka** Xizang Zizhiqu, W China *29°27'N 85°48'E*
190 K13 **Rakahanga** *atoll* N Cook Islands
185 H19 **Rakaia** Canterbury, South Island, New Zealand *43°45'S 172°02'E*
185 G19 **Rakaia** ≈ South Island, New Zealand
152 H3 **Rakaposhi** ▲ N India *36°06'N 74°31'E*
Rakasd *see* Răcăşdia
169 N15 **Rakata, Pulau** *var.* Pulau Krakatau. *island* S Indonesia
141 U10 **Rakbah, Qalamat ar** *well* SE Saudi Arabia
Rakhine State *see* Arakan State
116 I8 **Rakhiv** Zakarpats'ka Oblast', W Ukraine *48°05'N 24°15'E*
141 V13 **Rakhyūt** SW Oman *16°41'N 53°09'E*
192 K9 **Rakiraki** Viti Levu, W Fiji *17°22'S 178°10'E*
126 J8 **Rakitnoye** Belgorodskaya Oblast', W Russian Federation *50°50'N 35°51'E*
Rakka *see* Ar Raqqah
118 I4 **Rakke** Lääne-Virumaa, NE Estonia *58°58'N 26°14'E*
95 I16 **Rakkestad** Østfold, S Norway *59°25'N 11°17'E*
110 F12 **Rakoniewice** *Ger.* Rakwitz. Wielkopolskie, C Poland *52°09'N 16°10'E*
Rakonitz *see* Rakovník
83 H18 **Rakops** Central, C Botswana *21°01'S 24°20'E*
111 C16 **Rakovník** *Ger.* Rakonitz. Středočeský Kraj, W Czech Republic *50°07'N 13°44'E*
114 J10 **Rakovski** Plovdiv, C Bulgaria *42°16'N 24°58'E*
Rakutō-kō *see* Naktong-gang
118 I3 **Rakvere** *Ger.* Wesenberg. Lääne-Virumaa, N Estonia *59°21'N 26°20'E*
Rakwitz *see* Rakoniewice
22 L6 **Raleigh** Mississippi, S USA *32°01'N 89°30'W*
21 U9 **Raleigh** *state capital* North Carolina, SE USA *35°46'N 78°38'W*
21 Y11 **Raleigh Bay** *bay* North Carolina, SE USA
21 U9 **Raleigh-Durham** ✈ North Carolina, SE USA *35°54'N 78°45'W*
189 S6 **Ralik Chain** *island group* Ralik Chain, W Marshall Islands
25 N5 **Ralls** Texas, SW USA *33°40'N 101°23'W*
18 G13 **Ralston** Pennsylvania, NE USA *41°29'N 76°57'W*
141 O16 **Ramādah** W Yemen *13°35'N 43°50'E*
Ramadi *see* Ar Ramādī
105 N2 **Ramales de la Victoria** Cantabria, N Spain *43°15'N 03°28'W*
138 F10 **Ramallah** C West Bank *31°55'N 35°12'E*
61 C19 **Ramallo** Buenos Aires, E Argentina *33°30'S 60°01'W*
155 H20 **Rāmanagaram** Karnātaka, E India *12°45'N 77°16'E*
155 I23 **Rāmanāthapuram** Tamil Nādu, SE India *09°23'N 78°53'E*
154 N12 **Rāmapur** Orissa, E India *21°48'N 84°00'E*
155 I14 **Rāmāreddi** *var.* Kāmāreddi, Kamareddy. Andhra Pradesh, C India *18°19'N 78°23'E*
138 F10 **Ramat Gan** Tel Aviv, W Israel *32°04'N 34°48'E*
103 T6 **Rambervillers** Vosges, NE France *48°15'N 06°50'E*
Rambi *see* Rabi
103 N5 **Rambouillet** Yvelines, N France *48°39'N 01°50'E*
186 E5 **Rambutyo Island** *island* N Papua New Guinea
153 Q12 **Ramechhāp** Central, C Nepal *27°20'N 86°05'E*
183 R12 **Rame Head** *headland* Victoria, SE Australia *37°48'S 149°30'E*
126 L4 **Ramenskoye** Moskovskaya Oblast', W Russian Federation *55°31'N 38°24'E*
124 J15 **Rameshki** Tverskaya Oblast', W Russian Federation *57°21'N 36°05'E*
153 P14 **Rāmgarh** Jhārkhand, N India *23°37'N 85°32'E*
152 D11 **Rāmgarh** Rājasthān, NW India *27°29'N 70°38'E*
142 M9 **Rāmhormoz** *var.* Ram Hormuz, Ramuz. Khūzestān, SW Iran *31°15'N 49°38'E*
Ram Hormuz *see* Rāmhormoz
Ram, Jebel *see* Ramm, Jabal
138 F10 **Ramla** *var.* Ramle, Ramleh, *Ar.* Er Ramle. Central, C Israel *31°56'N 34°52'E*
Ramle/Ramleh *see* Ramla
138 F14 **Ramm, Jabal** *var.* Jebel Ram. ▲ SW Jordan *29°34'N 35°24'E*
152 K10 **Rāmnagar** Uttarākhand, N India *29°23'N 79°07'E*
95 N15 **Ramnäs** Västmanland, C Sweden *59°46'N 16°16'E*
Râmnicul-Sărat *see* Râmnicu Sărat
116 L12 **Râmnicu Sărat** *prev.* Râmnicul-Sărat, Rîmnicu-Sărat. Buzău, E Romania *45°24'N 27°06'E*
116 I13 **Râmnicu Vâlcea** *prev.* Rîmnicu Vîlcea. Vâlcea, C Romania *45°04'N 24°32'E*
Ramokgwebana *see* Ramokgwebane
83 J18 **Ramokgwebane** *var.* Ramokgwebana. Central, NE Botswana *20°38'S 27°40'E*
126 L7 **Ramon'** Voronezhskaya Oblast', W Russian Federation *51°51'N 39°18'E*
35 V17 **Ramona** California, W USA *33°02'N 116°52'W*
56 A10 **Ramón, Laguna** ◎ NW Peru
14 G7 **Ramore** Ontario, S Canada *48°26'N 80°19'W*
40 M11 **Ramos** San Luis Potosí, C Mexico *22°48'N 101°55'W*
41 N8 **Ramos Arizpe** Coahuila, NE Mexico *25°35'N 100°59'W*
40 J9 **Ramos, Río de** ≈ C Mexico
83 J21 **Ramotswa** South East, S Botswana *24°56'S 25°50'E*
39 R8 **Rampart** Alaska, USA *65°30'N 150°10'W*
8 H8 **Ramparts** ≈ Northwest Territories, NW Canada
152 K10 **Rāmpur** Uttar Pradesh, N India *28°48'N 79°03'E*
154 F9 **Rāmpura** Madhya Pradesh, C India *24°30'N 75°32'E*
Rampura *see* Rudrapur
Rampur Boalia *see* Rajshahi
166 K6 **Ramree Island** *island* W Myanmar (Burma)
141 W6 **Rams** *var.* Ar Rams. Ra's al Khaymah, NE United Arab Emirates *25°52'N 56°01'E*
143 N4 **Rāmsar** *prev.* Sakhtsar. Māzandarān, N Iran *36°55'N 50°39'E*
93 H16 **Ramsele** Västernorrland, N Sweden *63°33'N 16°35'E*
21 T9 **Ramseur** North Carolina, SE USA *35°43'N 79°39'W*
97 I16 **Ramsey** NE Isle of Man *54°19'N 04°24'W*
97 I16 **Ramsey Bay** *bay* NE Isle of Man
14 E9 **Ramsey Lake** ◎ Ontario, S Canada
97 Q22 **Ramsgate** SE England, United Kingdom *51°20'N 01°25'E*
94 M10 **Ramsjö** Gävleborg, C Sweden *62°10'N 15°40'E*
154 I12 **Rāmtek** Mahārāshtra, C India *21°28'N 79°28'E*
Ramtha *see* Ar Ramthā
Ramuz *see* Rāmhormoz
118 G12 **Ramygala** Panevėžys, C Lithuania *55°30'N 24°18'E*
152 H14 **Rāna Pratāp Sāgar** ◎ N India
169 V7 **Ranau** Sabah, East Malaysia *05°56'N 116°43'E*
168 L14 **Ranau, Danau** ◎ Sumatera, W Indonesia
62 H12 **Rancagua** Libertador, C Chile *34°10'S 70°45'W*
99 G22 **Rance** Hainaut, S Belgium *50°09'N 04°16'E*
102 H6 **Rance** ≈ NW France
60 J9 **Rancharia** São Paulo, S Brazil *22°13'S 50°53'W*
153 P15 **Rānchi** Jhārkhand, N India *23°22'N 85°20'E*
61 D21 **Ranchos** Buenos Aires, E Argentina *35°32'S 58°22'W*
37 S9 **Ranchos De Taos** New Mexico, SW USA *36°21'N 105°36'W*
63 G16 **Ranco, Lago** ◎ C Chile
95 C16 **Randaberg** Rogaland, S Norway *59°00'N 05°38'E*
29 U7 **Randall** Minnesota, N USA *46°05'N 94°30'W*
107 L23 **Randazzo** Sicilia, Italy, C Mediterranean Sea *37°52'N 14°57'E*
95 G21 **Randers** Århus, C Denmark *56°28'N 10°03'E*
92 I12 **Randijaure** ◎ N Sweden
21 T9 **Randleman** North Carolina, SE USA *35°49'N 79°48'W*
19 O11 **Randolph** Massachusetts, NE USA *42°09'N 71°02'W*
29 Q13 **Randolph** Nebraska, C USA *42°25'N 97°05'W*
36 M1 **Randolph** Utah, W USA *41°40'N 111°10'W*
100 P9 **Randow** ≈ NE Germany
95 H14 **Randsfjorden** ◎ S Norway
92 K13 **Råneå** Norrbotten, N Sweden *65°52'N 22°17'E*
92 G12 **Ranelva** ≈ C Norway
93 F15 **Ranemsletta** Nord-Trøndelag, C Norway *64°36'N 11°55'E*
76 H10 **Ranérou** C Senegal *15°17'N 14°00'W*
Rånes *see* Ringvassøya
185 E22 **Ranfurly** Otago, South Island, New Zealand *45°07'S 170°06'E*
167 P17 **Rangae** Narathiwat, SW Thailand *06°15'N 101°45'E*
153 V16 **Rangamati** Chittagong, SE Bangladesh *22°40'N 92°10'E*
184 I2 **Rangaunu Bay** *bay* North Island, New Zealand
19 P6 **Rangeley** Maine, NE USA *44°58'N 70°37'W*
37 O4 **Rangely** Colorado, C USA *40°05'N 108°48'W*
25 R7 **Ranger** Texas, SW USA *32°28'N 98°40'W*
14 C9 **Ranger Lake** Ontario, S Canada *46°51'N 83°34'W*
14 C9 **Ranger Lake** ◎ Ontario, S Canada
153 V12 **Rangia** Assam, NE India *26°26'N 91°38'E*
185 I18 **Rangiora** Canterbury, South Island, New Zealand *43°19'S 172°34'E*
191 T9 **Rangiroa** *atoll* Îles Tuamotu, W French Polynesia
184 N9 **Rangitaiki** ≈ North Island, New Zealand
185 F19 **Rangitata** ≈ South Island, New Zealand
184 M12 **Rangitikei** ≈ North Island, New Zealand
184 L6 **Rangitoto Island** *island* N New Zealand
Rangkasbitoeng *see* Rangkasbitung
169 N16 **Rangkasbitung** *prev.* Rangkasbitoeng. Jawa, SW Indonesia *06°21'S 106°12'E*
167 P9 **Rang, Khao** ▲ C Thailand *16°13'N 99°03'E*
147 V13 **Rangkŭl** *Rus.* Rangkul'. SE Tajikistan *38°30'N 74°24'E*
Rangkul' *see* Rangkŭl
Rangoon *see* Yangon
153 T13 **Rangpur** Rajshahi, N Bangladesh *25°46'N 89°20'E*
155 F18 **Rānībennur** Karnātaka, W India *14°36'N 75°39'E*
153 R15 **Rānīganj** West Bengal, NE India *23°34'N 87°13'E*
149 Q13 **Rānīpur** Sind, SE Pakistan *27°17'N 68°34'E*
Rāniyah *see* Rānya
25 N9 **Rankin** Texas, SW USA *31°14'N 101°56'W*
9 O9 **Rankin Inlet** Nunavut, C Canada *62°52'N 92°14'W*
183 P8 **Rankins Springs** New South Wales, SE Australia *33°51'S 146°16'E*
Rankovićevo *see* Kraljevo
108 I7 **Rankweil** Vorarlberg, W Austria *47°17'N 09°40'E*
Rann *see* Brežice
127 T8 **Ranneye** Orenburgskaya Oblast', W Russian Federation *51°28'N 52°29'E*
96 I10 **Rannoch, Loch** ◎ C Scotland, United Kingdom
191 U17 **Rano Kau** *var.* Rano Kao. *crater* Easter Island, Chile, E Pacific Ocean
167 N14 **Ranong** Ranong, SW Thailand *09°59'N 98°40'E*
186 J8 **Ranongga** *var.* Ghanongga. *island* NW Solomon Islands
191 W16 **Rano Raraku** *ancient monument* Easter Island, Chile, E Pacific Ocean
171 V12 **Ransiki** Papua, E Indonesia *01°27'S 134°12'E*
92 K12 **Rantajärvi** Norrbotten, N Sweden *66°45'N 23°39'E*
93 N17 **Rantasalmi** Itä-Suomi, SE Finland *62°02'N 28°22'E*
169 U13 **Rantau** Borneo, C Indonesia *02°56'S 115°09'E*
158 L10 **Rantau, Pulau** *var.* Pulau Tebingtinggi. *island* W Indonesia
171 N13 **Rantepao** Sulawesi, C Indonesia *02°58'S 119°58'E*
30 M13 **Rantoul** Illinois, N USA *40°19'N 88°08'W*
93 L15 **Rantsila** Oulu, C Finland *64°31'N 25°40'E*
92 L13 **Ranua** Lappi, NW Finland *65°55'N 26°34'E*
139 T3 **Rānya** *var.* Rāniyah. As Sulaymānīyah, NE Iraq *36°15'N 44°53'E*
157 X3 **Raohe** Heilongjiang, NE China *46°49'N 134°00'E*
74 H9 **Raoui, Erg er** *desert* W Algeria
193 O10 **Rapa** *island* Îles Australes, S French Polynesia
191 V14 **Rapa Iti** *island* Îles Australes, SW French Polynesia
106 D10 **Rapallo** Liguria, NW Italy *44°21'N 09°13'E*
Rapa Nui *see* Pascua, Isla de
Raphiah *see* Rafah
21 V5 **Rapidan River** ≈ Virginia, NE USA
28 J10 **Rapid City** South Dakota, N USA *44°05'N 103°14'W*
15 P8 **Rapide-Blanc** Québec, SE Canada *47°48'N 72°57'W*
14 I8 **Rapide-Deux** Québec, SE Canada *47°56'N 78°33'W*
118 K6 **Räpina** *Ger.* Rappin. Põlvamaa, SE Estonia *58°06'N 27°27'E*
118 G4 **Rapla** *Ger.* Rappel. Raplamaa, NW Estonia *59°00'N 24°46'E*
118 G4 **Raplamaa** *var.* Rapla Maakond. ◐ *province* NW Estonia
Rapla Maakond *see* Raplamaa
21 X6 **Rappahannock River** ≈ Virginia, NE USA
Rappel *see* Rapla
108 G7 **Rapperswil** Sankt Gallen, NE Switzerland *47°14'N 08°50'E*
Rappin *see* Räpina
153 N12 **Rāpti** ≈ N India
57 K16 **Rapulo, Río** ≈ E Bolivia
Raqqah/Raqqah, Muḩāfaẓat al *see* Ar Raqqah
18 J8 **Raquette Lake** ◎ New York, NE USA
18 J6 **Raquette River** ≈ New York, NE USA
191 V10 **Raraka** *atoll* Îles Tuamotu, C French Polynesia
191 V10 **Raroia** *atoll* Îles Tuamotu, C French Polynesia
190 H15 **Rarotonga** ✈ Rarotonga, S Cook Islands, C Pacific Ocean *21°15'S 159°45'W*
190 H16 **Rarotonga** *island* S Cook Islands, C Pacific Ocean
147 P12 **Rarz** W Tajikistan *39°23'N 68°43'E*
Ras al 'Ain *see* Ra's al 'Ayn
139 N2 **Ra's al 'Ayn** *var.* Ras al'Ain. Al Ḩasakah, N Syria *36°52'N 40°05'E*
138 H3 **Ra's al Basīṭ** Al Lādhiqīyah, W Syria *35°57'N 35°55'E*
Ra's al-Hafǧī *see* Ra's al Khafjī
141 R5 **Ra's al Khafjī** *var.* Ra's al-Hafǧī. Ash Sharqīyah, NE Saudi Arabia *28°22'N 48°30'E*
Ras al-Khaimah/Ras al Khaimah *see* Ra's al Khaymah
143 R15 **Ra's al Khaymah** *var.* Ras al Khaimah. Ra's al Khaymah, NE United Arab Emirates *25°44'N 55°55'E*
143 R15 **Ra's al Khaymah** ✈ Ras al-Khaimah. Ra's al Khaymah, NE United Arab Emirates *25°37'N 55°51'E*
138 G13 **Ra's an Naqb** Ma'ān, S Jordan *30°00'N 35°29'E*
61 B26 **Rasa, Punta** *headland* E Argentina *40°50'S 62°15'W*
171 V12 **Rasawi** Papua, E Indonesia *02°04'S 134°02'E*
Râşcani *see* Rîşcani
80 J10 **Ras Dashen Terara** ▲ N Ethiopia *13°12'N 38°09'E*
Rasdhoo Atoll *see* Rasdu Atoll
151 K19 **Rasdu Atoll** *var.* Rasdhoo Atoll. *atoll* C Maldives
118 E12 **Raseiniai** Kaunas, C Lithuania *55°23'N 23°06'E*
75 X8 **Ra's Ghārib** *var.* Râs Ghârib. E Egypt *28°16'N 33°01'E*
Râs Ghârib *see* Ra's Ghārib
162 J6 **Rashaant** Hövsgöl, N Mongolia *49°08'N 101°27'E*
Rashaant *see* Delüün, Bayan-Ölgiy, Mongolia
Rashaant *see* Öldziyt, Dundgovĭ, Mongolia
80 F12 **Rashad** Southern Kordofan, C Sudan *11°55'N 31°05'E*
75 V7 **Rashīd** *Eng.* Rosetta. N Egypt *31°25'N 30°25'E*
139 Y11 **Rashīd** Al Başrah, E Iraq *31°15'N 47°31'E*
142 M3 **Rasht** *var.* Resht. Gīlān, NW Iran *37°18'N 49°33'E*
139 S2 **Rashwan** Arbil, N Iraq *36°28'N 43°54'E*
Rasik *see* Raasiku
143 W14 **Rāsk** Sīstān va Balūchestān, SE Iran *26°13'N 61°25'E*
113 M15 **Raška** Serbia, C Serbia *43°18'N 20°37'E*
119 P15 **Rasna** *Rus.* Ryasna. Mahilyowskaya Voblasts', E Belarus *54°01'N 31°12'E*
116 J12 **Râşnov** *prev.* Rîşno, Rozsnyó, *Hung.* Barcarozsnyó. Braşov, C Romania *45°35'N 25°27'E*
118 L11 **Rasony** *Rus.* Rossony. Vitsyebskaya Voblasts', N Belarus *55°53'N 28°50'E*
Ra's Shamrah *see* Ugarit
127 N7 **Rasskazovo** Tambovskaya Oblast', W Russian Federation *52°42'N 41°45'E*
119 O16 **Rasta** ≈ E Belarus
Rastadt *see* Rastatt
Rastâne *see* Ar Rastān
141 S6 **Ra's Tannūrah** *Eng.* Ras Tanura. Ash Sharqīyah, NE Saudi Arabia *26°44'N 50°04'E*
Ras Tanura *see* Ra's Tannūrah
101 G21 **Rastatt** *var.* Rastadt. Baden-Württemberg, SW Germany *48°51'N 08°13'E*
Rastenburg *see* Kętrzyn
149 V7 **Rasūlnagar** Punjab, E Pakistan *32°20'N 73°51'E*
189 U6 **Ratak Chain** *island group* Ratak Chain, E Marshall Islands
119 K15 **Ratamka** *Rus.* Ratomka. Minskaya Voblasts', C Belarus *53°56'N 27°21'E*
93 G17 **Ratan** Jämtland, C Sweden *62°28'N 14°35'E*
152 G11 **Ratangarh** Rājasthān, NW India *28°02'N 74°39'E*
Rat Buri *see* Ratchaburi
167 O11 **Ratchaburi** *var.* Rat Buri. Ratchaburi, W Thailand *13°30'N 99°50'E*
29 W15 **Rathbun Lake** ▣ Iowa, C USA
Ráth Caola *see* Rathkeale
166 K5 **Rathedaung** Rakhine State, W Myanmar (Burma) *20°30'N 92°48'E*
100 M12 **Rathenow** Brandenburg, NE Germany *52°37'N 12°21'E*
97 C19 **Rathkeale** *Ir.* Ráth Caola. Limerick, SW Ireland *52°32'N 08°56'W*
96 F13 **Rathlin Island** *Ir.* Reachlainn. *island* N Northern Ireland, United Kingdom
97 C20 **Ráth Luirc** *Ir.* An Ráth. Cork, SW Ireland *52°22'N 08°44'W*
Ratibor *see* Racibórz
Ratisbon/Ratisbona/Ratisbonne *see* Regensburg
Rätische Alpen *see* Rhaetian Alps
38 E17 **Rat Island** *island* Aleutian Islands, Alaska, USA
38 E17 **Rat Islands** *island group* Aleutian Islands, Alaska, USA
154 F10 **Ratlām** *prev.* Rutlam. Madhya Pradesh, C India *23°23'N 75°04'E*
155 D15 **Ratnāgiri** Mahārāshtra, W India *17°00'N 73°20'E*
155 K26 **Ratnapura** Sabaragamuwa Province, S Sri Lanka *06°41'N 80°25'E*
Ratne *see* Ratno
116 J2 **Ratno** *var.* Ratne. Volyns'ka Oblast', NW Ukraine *51°40'N 24°33'E*
Ratomka *see* Ratamka
37 U8 **Raton** New Mexico, SW USA *36°54'N 104°27'W*
139 O7 **Ratqah, Wādī ar** *dry watercourse* W Iraq
Ratschach *see* Radeče
167 O16 **Rattaphum** Songkhla, SW Thailand *07°07'N 100°16'E*
26 L6 **Rattlesnake Creek** ≈ Kansas, C USA
94 L13 **Rättvik** Dalarna, C Sweden *60°53'N 15°12'E*
100 K9 **Ratzeburg** Mecklenburg-Vorpommern, N Germany *53°41'N 10°48'E*
100 K9 **Ratzeburger See** ◎ N Germany
10 J10 **Ratz, Mount** ▲ British Columbia, SW Canada *57°22'N 132°17'W*
61 D22 **Rauch** Buenos Aires, E Argentina *36°45'S 59°05'W*
41 U16 **Raudales** Chiapas, SE Mexico
Raudhatain *see* Ar Rawdatayn
Raudnitz an der Elbe *see* Roudnice nad Labem
92 K1 **Raufarhöfn** Nordhurland Eystra, NE Iceland *66°27'N 15°58'W*
94 H13 **Raufoss** Oppland, S Norway *60°44'N 10°39'E*
Raukawa *see* Cook Strait
184 Q8 **Raukumara** ▲ North Island, New Zealand *37°46'S 178°07'E*
192 K11 **Raukumara Plain** *undersea feature* N Coral Sea
184 P8 **Raukumara Range** ▲▲ North Island, New Zealand
154 N11 **Räulakela** *var.* Raurkela; *prev.* Rourkela. Orissa, E India *22°13'N 84°53'E*
95 F15 **Rauland** Telemark, S Norway *59°41'N 07°57'E*
93 J19 **Rauma** *Swe.* Raumo. Länsi-Suomi, SW Finland *61°09'N 21°30'E*
94 F10 **Rauma** ≈ S Norway
Raumo *see* Rauma
118 H8 **Rauna** Cēsis, C Latvia *57°19'N 25°34'E*
169 T17 **Raung, Gunung** ▲ Jawa, S Indonesia *08°00'S 114°07'E*
Raurkela *see* Rāulakela
95 J22 **Raus** Skåne, S Sweden *56°01'N 12°48'E*
165 W3 **Rausu** Hokkaidō, NE Japan *44°00'N 145°06'E*
165 W3 **Rausu-dake** ▲ Hokkaidō, NE Japan *44°06'N 145°04'E*
116 M9 **Răut** *var.* Răuţel. ≈ C Moldova
93 M17 **Rautalampi** Itä-Suomi, C Finland *62°37'N 26°48'E*
93 N16 **Rautavaara** Itä-Suomi, C Finland *63°30'N 28°19'E*
Răuţel *see* Răut
93 O18 **Rautjärvi** Etelä-Suomi, SE Finland *61°21'N 29°20'E*
Rautu *see* Sosnovo
191 V11 **Ravahere** *atoll* Îles Tuamotu, C French Polynesia
107 J25 **Ravanusa** Sicilia, Italy, C Mediterranean Sea *37°16'N 13°59'E*
143 S9 **Rāvar** Kermān, C Iran *31°15'N 56°51'E*
147 Q11 **Ravat** Batkenskaya Oblast', SW Kyrgyzstan *39°54'N 70°06'E*
18 K11 **Ravena** New York, NE USA *42°28'N 73°49'W*
106 H10 **Ravenna** Emilia-Romagna, N Italy *44°28'N 12°15'E*
29 O15 **Ravenna** Nebraska, C USA *41°01'N 98°54'W*
31 U11 **Ravenna** Ohio, N USA *41°09'N 81°14'W*
101 I24 **Ravensburg** Baden-Württemberg, S Germany *47°47'N 09°37'E*
181 W4 **Ravenshoe** Queensland, NE Australia *17°29'S 145°28'E*
180 K13 **Ravensthorpe** Western Australia *33°37'S 120°03'E*
21 Q4 **Ravenswood** West Virginia, NE USA *38°57'N 81°45'W*
149 U9 **Rāvi** ≈ India/Pakistan
112 C9 **Ravna Gora** Primorje-Gorski Kotar, NW Croatia *45°20'N 14°54'E*
109 U10 **Ravne na Koroškem** *Ger.* Gutenstein. N Slovenia *46°33'N 14°57'E*
139 P6 **Rāwah** Al Anbār, W Iraq *34°32'N 41°54'E*
191 T4 **Rawaki** *prev.* Phoenix Island. *atoll* Phoenix Islands, C Kiribati
149 U6 **Rāwalpindi** Punjab, NE Pakistan *33°38'N 73°06'E*
110 L13 **Rawa Mazowiecka** Łódzkie, C Poland *51°47'N 20°16'E*
139 T2 **Rawāndiz** *var.* Rawandoz, Rawāndūz. Arbil, N Iraq *36°38'N 44°32'E*
Rawandoz/Rawāndūz *see* Rawāndiz
171 U12 **Rawas** Papua, E Indonesia *01°07'S 132°12'E*
139 O4 **Rawḑah** ◎ E Syria
110 G13 **Rawicz** *Ger.* Rawitsch. Wielkopolskie, C Poland *51°37'N 16°51'E*
Rawitsch *see* Rawicz
180 M11 **Rawlinna** Western Australia *31°01'S 125°36'E*
33 W16 **Rawlins** Wyoming, C USA *41°47'N 107°14'W*
63 K17 **Rawson** Chubut, SE Argentina *43°22'S 65°01'W*
159 R16 **Rawu** Xizang Zizhiqu, W China *29°30'N 96°42'E*
153 P12 **Raxaul** Bihār, N India *26°58'N 84°51'E*
28 K3 **Ray** North Dakota, N USA *48°19'N 103°11'W*
169 S11 **Raya, Bukit** ▲ Borneo, C Indonesia *0°40'S 112°40'E*
155 I18 **Rāyachoti** Andhra Pradesh, E India *14°03'N 78°43'E*
Rāyadrug *see* Rāyagada
155 M14 **Rāyagada** *prev.* Rāyadrug. Orissa, E India *19°10'N 83°28'E*
138 H7 **Rayak** *var.* Rayaq, Riyāq. E Lebanon *33°51'N 36°03'E*
Rayaq *see* Rayak
139 T2 **Rāyat** Arbil, E Iraq *36°39'N 44°56'E*
169 N12 **Raya, Tanjung** *cape* Pulau Bangka, W Indonesia
13 R13 **Ray, Cape** *headland* Newfoundland, Newfoundland and Labrador, E Canada *47°38'N 59°15'W*
123 Q13 **Raychikhinsk** Amurskaya Oblast', SE Russian Federation *49°47'N 129°19'E*
127 U5 **Rayevskiy** Respublika Bashkortostan, W Russian Federation *54°04'N 54°58'E*
11 Q17 **Raymond** Alberta, SW Canada *49°30'N 112°41'W*
22 K6 **Raymond** Mississippi, S USA *32°15'N 90°25'W*
32 F9 **Raymond** Washington, NW USA *46°41'N 123°43'W*
183 T8 **Raymond Terrace** New South Wales, SE Australia *32°47'S 151°45'E*
25 T17 **Raymondville** Texas, SW USA *26°30'N 97°48'W*
11 U16 **Raymore** Saskatchewan, S Canada *51°24'N 104°34'W*
39 Q8 **Ray Mountains** ▲▲ Alaska, USA
22 H9 **Rayne** Louisiana, S USA *30°13'N 92°15'W*
41 O12 **Rayón** San Luis Potosí, C Mexico *21°54'N 99°33'W*
40 G4 **Rayón** Sonora, NW Mexico *29°45'N 110°33'W*
167 P12 **Rayong** Rayong, S Thailand *12°42'N 101°17'E*
25 T5 **Ray Roberts, Lake** ◎ Texas, SW USA
18 E15 **Raystown Lake** ▣ Pennsylvania, NE USA
141 V13 **Raysūt** SW Oman *16°58'N 54°02'E*
27 R4 **Raytown** Missouri, C USA *39°00'N 94°27'W*
22 I5 **Rayville** Louisiana, S USA *32°29'N 91°45'W*
142 L5 **Razan** Hamadān, W Iran *35°22'N 48°58'E*
139 S9 **Razāzah, Buḩayrat ar** *var.* Baḩr al Milḩ. ◎ C Iraq
114 L9 **Razboyna** ▲ E Bulgaria *42°54'N 26°31'E*
Razdan *see* Hrazdan
Razdolnoye *see* Rozdol'ne
Razelm, Lacul *see* Razim, Lacul
139 U2 **Razga** As Sulaymānīyah, E Iraq *36°25'N 45°06'E*
114 L8 **Razgrad** Razgrad, N Bulgaria *43°33'N 26°31'E*
114 L8 **Razgrad** ◐ *province* NE Bulgaria
117 N13 **Razim, Lacul** *prev.* Lacul Razelm. *lagoon* NW Black Sea
114 G11 **Razlog** Blagoevgrad, SW Bulgaria *41°53'N 23°28'E*
118 K10 **Rāznas Ezers** ◎ SE Latvia
102 E6 **Raz, Pointe du** *headland* NW France *48°06'N 04°52'W*
Reachlainn *see* Rathlin Island
Reachrainn *see* Lambay Island
97 N22 **Reading** S England, United Kingdom *51°28'N 00°59'W*
18 H15 **Reading** Pennsylvania, NE USA *40°20'N 75°55'W*
48 C7 **Real, Cordillera** ▲▲ C Ecuador
62 K12 **Realicó** La Pampa, C Argentina *35°02'S 64°14'W*
25 R15 **Realitos** Texas, SW USA *27°26'N 98°31'W*
108 G9 **Realp** Uri, C Switzerland *46°36'N 08°32'E*
167 Q12 **Reăng Kesei** Bătdâmbâng, W Cambodia *12°57'N 103°15'E*
191 Y11 **Reao** *atoll* Îles Tuamotu, E French Polynesia
Reate *see* Rieti
Greater Antarctica *see* East Antarctica
180 L11 **Rebecca, Lake** ◎ Western Australia
Rebiana Sand Sea *see* Rabyānah, Ramlat
124 H8 **Reboly** *Fin.* Repola. Respublika Kareliya, NW Russian Federation *63°51'N 30°49'E*
165 S1 **Rebun** Rebun-tō, NE Japan *45°19'N 141°02'E*
165 S1 **Rebun-tō** *island* NE Japan
106 J12 **Recanati** Marche, C Italy *43°23'N 13°34'E*
Rechitsa *see* Rechytsa
109 Y7 **Rechnitz** Burgenland, SE Austria *47°19'N 16°26'E*
119 J20 **Rechytsa** *Rus.* Rechitsa. Brestskaya Voblasts', SW Belarus *51°51'N 26°48'E*
119 O19 **Rechytsa** *Rus.* Rechitsa. Homyel'skaya Voblasts', SE Belarus *52°22'N 30°23'E*
59 Q15 **Recife** *prev.* Pernambuco. *state capital* Pernambuco, E Brazil *08°06'S 34°53'W*
83 I26 **Recife, Cape** *Afr.* Kaap Recife. *headland* S South Africa *34°03'S 25°37'E*
Recife, Kaap *see* Recife, Cape
172 I16 **Récifs, Îles aux** *island* Inner Islands, NE Seychelles
101 E14 **Recklinghausen** Nordrhein-Westfalen, W Germany *51°37'N 07°12'E*
100 M8 **Recknitz** ≈ NE Germany
99 K23 **Recogne** Luxembourg, SE Belgium *49°56'N 05°20'E*
61 C15 **Reconquista** Santa Fe, C Argentina *29°08'S 59°38'W*
195 O6 **Recovery Glacier** *glacier* Antarctica
59 G15 **Recreio** Mato Grosso, W Brazil *08°13'S 58°15'W*
27 X9 **Rector** Arkansas, C USA *36°15'N 90°17'W*
110 E9 **Recz** *Ger.* Reetz Neumark. Zachodnio-pomorskie, NW Poland *53°16'N 15°32'E*
99 L24 **Redange** *var.* Redange-sur-Attert. Diekirch, W Luxembourg *49°46'N 05°53'E*
Redange-sur-Attert *see* Redange
18 C13 **Redbank Creek** ≈ Pennsylvania, NE USA
13 S9 **Red Bay** Québec, E Canada *51°40'N 56°37'W*
23 N2 **Red Bay** Alabama, S USA *34°26'N 88°08'W*
35 N4 **Red Bluff** California, W USA *40°09'N 122°14'W*
24 J8 **Red Bluff Reservoir** ▣ New Mexico/Texas, SW USA
30 K16 **Red Bud** Illinois, N USA *38°12'N 89°59'W*
30 J5 **Red Cedar River** ≈ Wisconsin, N USA
11 R17 **Redcliff** Alberta, SW Canada *50°06'N 110°48'W*
83 K17 **Redcliff** Midlands, C Zimbabwe *19°00'S 29°49'E*
182 L9 **Red Cliffs** Victoria, SE Australia *34°21'S 142°12'E*
29 P17 **Red Cloud** Nebraska, C USA *40°05'N 98°31'W*
22 L8 **Red Creek** ≈ Mississippi, S USA
11 P15 **Red Deer** Alberta, SW Canada *52°15'N 113°48'W*
11 Q16 **Red Deer** ≈ Alberta, SW Canada
39 O11 **Red Devil** Alaska, USA *61°45'N 157°18'W*
35 N3 **Redding** California, W USA *40°33'N 122°26'W*
97 L20 **Redditch** W England, United Kingdom *52°19'N 01°56'W*
29 P9 **Redfield** South Dakota, N USA *44°51'N 98°31'W*
24 J12 **Redford** Texas, SW USA *29°31'N 104°19'W*
45 V13 **Redhead** Trinidad, Trinidad and Tobago *10°44'N 60°58'W*
182 I8 **Red Hill** South Australia *33°34'S 138°13'E*
Red Hill *see* Pu'u 'Ula'ula
26 K7 **Red Hills** *hill range* Kansas, C USA
13 T12 **Red Indian Lake** ◎ Newfoundland, Newfoundland and Labrador, E Canada
124 J16 **Redkino** Tverskaya Oblast', W Russian Federation *56°41'N 36°07'E*
12 A10 **Red Lake** Ontario, C Canada *51°00'N 93°55'W*
36 I10 **Red Lake** *salt flat* Arizona, SW USA
29 S4 **Red Lake Falls** Minnesota, N USA *47°52'N 96°16'W*
29 R4 **Red Lake River** ≈ Minnesota, N USA
35 U15 **Redlands** California, W USA *34°03'N 117°10'W*
18 G16 **Red Lion** Pennsylvania, NE USA *39°53'N 76°36'W*
33 U11 **Red Lodge** Montana, NW USA *45°11'N 109°15'W*
32 H13 **Redmond** Oregon, NW USA *44°16'N 121°10'W*
36 L5 **Redmond** Utah, W USA *39°00'N 111°51'W*
32 H8 **Redmond** Washington, NW USA *47°40'N 122°07'W*
Rednitz *see* Regnitz
29 T15 **Red Oak** Iowa, C USA *41°00'N 95°10'W*
18 K12 **Red Oaks Mill** New York, NE USA *41°39'N 73°52'W*
102 I7 **Redon** Ille-et-Vilaine, NW France *47°39'N 02°05'W*
45 W10 **Redonda** *island* SW Antigua and Barbuda
104 G4 **Redondela** Galicia, NW Spain *42°17'N 08°36'W*
104 H11 **Redondo** Évora, S Portugal *38°38'N 07°32'W*
39 Q12 **Redoubt Volcano** ▲ Alaska, USA *60°29'N 152°44'W*
11 Y16 **Red River** ≈ Canada/USA
129 U12 **Red River** *var.* Yuan, *Chin.* Yuan Jiang, *Vtn.* Sông Hông Hà. ≈ China/Vietnam
25 W4 **Red River** ≈ S USA
22 H7 **Red River** ≈ Louisiana, S USA
30 M6 **Red River** ≈ Wisconsin, N USA

◆ Country ● Country Capital ◇ Dependent Territory ○ Dependent Territory Capital ◐ Administrative Regions ✈ International Airport ▲ Mountain ▲▲ Mountain Range ※ Volcano ≈ River ◎ Lake ▣ Reservoir

331

RED ROCK, LAKE – RIO DELL

Red Rock, Lake see Red Rock Reservoir
29 W14 Red Rock Reservoir var. Lake Red Rock. Iowa, C USA
80 H7 Red Sea state NE Sudan
75 Y9 Red Sea var. Sinus Arabicus. sea Africa/Asia
21 T11 Red Springs North Carolina, SE USA 34°49′N 79°10′W
8 I9 Redstone Northwest Territories, NW Canada
11 V17 Redvers Saskatchewan, S Canada 49°31′N 101°33′W
77 P13 Red Volta var. Nazinon, Fr. Volta Rouge. Burkina/Ghana
11 Q14 Redwater Alberta, SW Canada 53°57′N 113°06′W
28 M16 Red Willow Creek Nebraska, C USA
29 W9 Red Wing Minnesota, N USA 44°33′N 92°31′W
35 N9 Redwood City California, W USA 37°29′N 122°13′W
29 T9 Redwood Falls Minnesota, N USA 44°33′N 95°07′W
31 P7 Reed City Michigan, N USA 43°52′N 85°30′W
28 K6 Reeder North Dakota, N USA 46°03′N 102°55′W
35 R11 Reedley California, W USA 36°35′N 119°27′W
33 T11 Reedpoint Montana, NW USA 45°41′N 109°33′W
30 K8 Reedsburg Wisconsin, N USA 43°33′N 90°03′W
32 E13 Reedsport Oregon, NW USA 43°42′N 124°06′W
187 Q9 Reef Islands island group Santa Cruz Islands, E Solomon Islands
185 H16 Reefton West Coast, South Island, New Zealand 42°07′S 171°53′E
20 F8 Reelfoot Lake Tennessee, S USA
97 D17 Ree, Lough Ir. Loch Rí. C Ireland
Reengus see Rīngas
35 U4 Reese River Nevada, W USA
98 M8 Reest E Netherlands
Reetz Neumark see Recz
Reevhtse see Røsvatnet
137 N13 Refahiye Erzincan, C Turkey 39°54′N 38°45′E
23 N4 Reform Alabama, S USA 33°22′N 88°01′W
95 K20 Reftele Jönköping, S Sweden 57°10′N 13°34′E
25 T14 Refugio Texas, SW USA 28°19′N 97°18′W
110 E8 Rega NW Poland
Regar see Tursunzoda
101 O21 Regen Bayern, SE Germany 48°57′N 13°10′E
101 M20 Regen SE Germany
101 M21 Regensburg Eng. Ratisbon, Fr. Ratisbonne, hist. Ratisbona; anc. Castra Regina, Reginum. Bayern, SE Germany 49°01′N 12°06′E
101 M21 Regenstauf Bayern, SE Germany 49°06′N 12°07′E
74 I10 Reggane C Algeria 26°46′N 00°09′E
98 N9 Regge E Netherlands
Reggio see Reggio nell'Emilia
Reggio Calabria see Reggio di Calabria
107 M23 Reggio di Calabria var. Reggio Calabria, Gk. Rhegion; anc. Regium, Rhegium. Calabria, SW Italy 38°06′N 15°39′E
Reggio Emilia see Reggio nell'Emilia
106 F9 Reggio nell'Emilia var. Reggio Emilia, abbrev. Reggio; anc. Regium Lepidum. Emilia-Romagna, N Italy 44°42′N 10°37′E
116 I10 Reghin Ger. Sächsisch-Reen, Hung. Szászrégen; prev. Reghinul Săsesc, Ger. Sächsisch-Regen. Mureș, C Romania 46°46′N 24°41′E
Reghinul Săsesc see Reghin
11 U16 Regina province capital Saskatchewan, S Canada 50°25′N 104°39′W
55 Z10 Régina E French Guiana 04°20′N 52°07′W
11 U16 Regina ✈ Saskatchewan, S Canada 50°21′N 104°43′W
11 U16 Regina Beach Saskatchewan, S Canada 50°44′N 105°03′W
Reginum see Regensburg
Région du Haut-Congo see Haut-Congo
Registan see Rīgestān
60 L11 Registro São Paulo, S Brazil 24°30′S 47°50′W
Regium see Reggio di Calabria
Regium Lepidum see Reggio nell'Emilia
101 K19 Regnitz var. Rednitz. SE Germany
40 K10 Regocijo Durango, W Mexico 23°35′N 105°11′W
104 H12 Reguengos de Monsaraz Évora, S Portugal 38°25′N 07°32′W
101 M18 Rehau Bayern, E Germany 50°15′N 12°03′E
83 D19 Rehoboth Hardap, C Namibia 23°18′S 17°03′E
21 Z4 Rehoboth Beach Delaware, NE USA 38°42′N 75°03′W
138 F10 Rehovot; prev. Rehovot. Central, C Israel 31°54′N 34°49′E
Rehovot see Rehovot
81 J20 Rei spring/well S Kenya 03°24′S 39°18′E
Reichenau see Rychnov nad Kněžnou
Reichenau see Bogatynia, Poland
101 M17 Reichenbach var. Reichenbach im Vogtland. Sachsen, E Germany 50°36′N 12°18′E
Reichenbach see Dzierżoniów
Reichenbach im Vogtland see Reichenbach
Reichenberg see Liberec
181 O11 Reid Western Australia 30°49′S 128°24′E
23 V6 Reidsville Georgia, SE USA 32°05′N 82°07′W
21 T8 Reidsville North Carolina, SE USA 36°21′N 79°39′W
Reifnitz see Ribnica
97 O22 Reigate SE England, United Kingdom 51°14′N 00°13′W
Reikjavik see Reykjavík
102 I10 Ré, Île de island W France
37 N15 Reiley Peak ▲ Arizona, SW USA 32°24′N 110°09′W
103 Q4 Reims Eng. Rheims; anc. Durocortorum, Remi. Marne, N France 49°16′N 04°01′E
63 G23 Reina Adelaida, Archipiélago island group S Chile
45 O16 Reina Beatrix ✈ (Oranjestad) C Aruba 12°30′N 69°57′W
108 F7 Reinach Aargau, W Switzerland 47°16′N 08°12′E
108 E6 Reinach Basel-Land, NW Switzerland 47°30′N 07°36′E
64 O11 Reina Sofía ✈ (Tenerife) Tenerife, Islas Canarias, Spain, NE Atlantic Ocean
29 W13 Reinbeck Iowa, C USA 42°19′N 92°36′W
100 J10 Reinbek Schleswig-Holstein, N Germany 53°31′N 10°15′E
11 U12 Reindeer Saskatchewan, C Canada
11 U11 Reindeer Lake Manitoba/Saskatchewan, C Canada
Reine-Charlotte, Îles de la see Queen Charlotte Islands
Reine-Élisabeth, Îles de la see Queen Elizabeth Islands
94 F13 Reineskarvet ▲ S Norway 60°38′N 07°48′E
184 H1 Reinga, Cape headland North Island, New Zealand 34°24′S 172°40′E
105 N3 Reinosa Cantabria, N Spain 43°01′N 04°09′W
109 R8 Reisseck ▲ S Austria 46°57′N 13°21′E
21 W3 Reisterstown Maryland, NE USA 39°27′N 76°46′W
Reisui see Yŏsu
98 N5 Reitdiep NE Netherlands
191 V10 Reitoru atoll Îles Tuamotu, C French Polynesia
95 M17 Rejmyre Östergötland, S Sweden 58°49′N 15°55′E
Reka see Rijeka
Reka Ili see Ile/Ili He
95 N16 Rekarne Västmanland, C Sweden 59°25′N 16°04′E
Rekhovot see Rehovot
8 K9 Reliance Northwest Territories, C Canada 62°45′N 109°08′W
33 U16 Reliance Wyoming, C USA 41°42′N 109°13′W
74 I5 Relizane var. Ghelîzâne, Ghilizane. NW Algeria 35°45′N 00°33′E
182 I7 Remarkable, Mount ▲ South Australia 32°46′S 138°08′E
54 E8 Remedios Antioquia, N Colombia 07°02′N 74°42′W
43 Q16 Remedios Veraguas, W Panama 08°13′N 81°48′W
42 D8 Remedios, Punta headland SW El Salvador 13°31′N 89°48′W
Remi see Reims
99 N25 Remich Grevenmacher, SE Luxembourg 49°33′N 06°23′E
99 J19 Remicourt Liège, E Belgium 50°40′N 05°19′E
14 H8 Rémigny, Lac Québec, SE Canada
55 Z10 Rémire NE French Guiana 04°52′N 52°16′W
127 N13 Remontnoye Rostovskaya Oblast', SW Russian Federation 46°35′N 43°38′E
171 U14 Remoon Pulau Kur, E Indonesia 05°18′S 131°59′E
99 L20 Remouchamps Liège, E Belgium 50°29′N 05°43′E
103 R15 Remoulins Gard, S France 43°56′N 04°34′E
173 X16 Rempart, Mont du hill W Mauritius
101 E15 Remscheid Nordrhein-Westfalen, W Germany 51°10′N 07°11′E
29 S12 Remsen Iowa, C USA 42°48′N 95°58′W
94 I12 Rena Hedmark, S Norway 61°08′N 11°21′E
94 I11 Renåa S Norway
Renaix see Ronse
118 H7 Renceni Valmiera, N Latvia 57°43′N 25°25′E
118 D9 Renda Kuldīga, W Latvia 57°04′N 22°18′E
107 N20 Rende Calabria, SW Italy 39°19′N 16°10′E
99 K21 Rendeux Luxembourg, SE Belgium 50°15′N 05°28′E
Rendina see Rentína
30 L16 Rend Lake Illinois, N USA
186 K9 Rendova island New Georgia Islands, NW Solomon Islands
100 I8 Rendsburg Schleswig-Holstein, N Germany 54°18′N 09°40′E
108 B9 Renens Vaud, SW Switzerland 46°32′N 06°36′E
14 K12 Renfrew Ontario, SE Canada 45°28′N 76°44′W
96 I12 Renfrew cultural region SW Scotland, United Kingdom
168 L11 Rengat Sumatera, W Indonesia 0°26′S 102°38′E
153 W12 Rengma Hills ▲▲ NE India
62 H12 Rengo Libertador, C Chile 34°24′S 70°50′W
116 M12 Reni Odes'ka Oblast', SW Ukraine 45°30′N 28°18′E
80 F11 Renk Upper Nile, E Sudan 11°48′N 32°49′E
93 L19 Renko Etelä-Suomi, S Finland 60°52′N 24°16′E
98 L12 Renkum Gelderland, SE Netherlands 51°58′N 05°43′E
182 K9 Renmark South Australia 34°12′S 140°43′E
186 L10 Rennell var. Mu Nggava. island S Solomon Islands
181 Q4 Renner Springs Roadhouse Northern Territory, N Australia 18°12′S 133°48′E
102 I6 Rennes Bret. Roazon; anc. Condate. Ille-et-Vilaine, NW France 48°08′N 01°40′W
195 S16 Rennick Glacier glacier Antarctica
11 Y16 Rennie Manitoba, S Canada 49°51′N 95°28′W
35 Q5 Reno Nevada, W USA 39°32′N 119°49′W
106 H10 Reno N Italy
35 Q5 Reno-Cannon ✈ Nevada, W USA 39°26′N 119°42′W
83 F24 Renoster SW South Africa
15 T5 Renouard, Lac Québec, SE Canada
18 F13 Renovo Pennsylvania, NE USA 41°19′N 77°42′W
161 O3 Renqiu Hebei, E China 38°49′N 116°02′E
160 I9 Renshou Sichuan, C China 30°02′N 104°09′E
31 N12 Rensselaer Indiana, N USA 40°57′N 87°09′W
18 L11 Rensselaer New York, NE USA 42°38′N 73°44′W
Rentería see Errenteria
115 E17 Rentína var. Rendina. Thessalía, C Greece 39°04′N 21°58′E
29 T9 Renville Minnesota, N USA 44°48′N 95°13′W
77 O13 Réo W Burkina 12°20′N 02°28′W
15 O12 Repentigny Québec, SE Canada 45°42′N 73°28′W
146 K13 Repetek Lebap Welaýaty, E Turkmenistan 38°40′N 63°12′E
93 J16 Replot Fin. Raippaluoto. island W Finland
Repola see Reboly
Reppen see Rzepin
Reps see Rupea
27 T7 Republic Missouri, C USA 37°07′N 93°28′W
32 K7 Republic Washington, NW USA 48°39′N 118°44′W
27 N3 Republican River Kansas/Nebraska, C USA
9 O7 Repulse Bay Northwest Territories, N Canada 66°35′N 86°20′W
56 F9 Requena Loreto, NE Peru 05°05′S 73°52′W
105 R10 Requena País Valenciano, E Spain 39°29′N 01°08′W
103 O14 Réquista Aveyron, S France 44°00′N 02°31′E
136 M12 Reşadiye Tokat, N Turkey 40°24′N 37°19′E
Reschenpass see Resia, Passo di
Reschitza see Reşiţa
113 N20 Resen Turk. Resne. SW FYR Macedonia 41°07′N 21°00′E
60 J11 Reserva Paraná, S Brazil 24°40′S 50°52′W
11 V15 Reserve Saskatchewan, S Canada 52°24′N 102°37′W
37 P13 Reserve New Mexico, SW USA 33°42′N 108°45′W
Reshetilovka see Reshetylivka
117 S6 Reshetylivka Rus. Reshetilovka. Poltavs'ka Oblast', NE Ukraine 49°34′N 34°05′E
Resht see Rasht
106 F5 Resia, Passo di Ger. Reschenpass. pass Austria/Italy
Resicabánya see Reşiţa
62 N7 Resistencia Chaco, NE Argentina 27°27′S 58°56′W
116 F12 Reşiţa Ger. Reschitza, Hung. Resicabánya. Caraş-Severin, W Romania 45°14′N 21°58′E
Resne see Resen
197 N9 Resolute Inuit Qausuittuq. Cornwallis Island, Nunavut, N Canada 74°41′N 94°54′W
Resolution see Fort Resolution
9 T7 Resolution Island island Nunavut, NE Canada
185 A23 Resolution Island island SW New Zealand
15 W7 Restigouche Québec, SE Canada 48°02′N 66°42′W
11 W17 Reston Manitoba, S Canada 49°33′N 101°03′W
14 H11 Restoule Lake Ontario, S Canada
54 F10 Restrepo Meta, C Colombia 04°20′N 73°29′W
42 B6 Retalhuleu Retalhuleu, SW Guatemala 14°31′N 91°40′W
42 A1 Retalhuleu off. Departamento de Retalhuleu. department SW Guatemala
Retalhuleu, Departamento de see Retalhuleu
97 N18 Retford C England, United Kingdom 53°18′N 00°52′W
103 Q3 Rethel Ardennes, N France 49°31′N 04°22′E
Rethimno/Réthimnon see Réthymno
115 I25 Réthymno prev. Réthimno, Réthimnon. Kríti, Greece, E Mediterranean Sea 35°21′N 24°29′E
Retiche, Alpi see Rhaetian Alps
99 J16 Retie Antwerpen, N Belgium 51°18′N 05°05′E
111 J21 Rétság Nógrád, N Hungary 47°57′N 19°08′E
109 W2 Retz Niederösterreich, NE Austria 48°46′N 15°58′E
173 N15 Réunion off. La Réunion. French overseas department W Indian Ocean
128 L17 Réunion island W Indian Ocean
105 U6 Reus Cataluña, E Spain 41°10′N 01°06′E
108 F7 Reuss NW Switzerland
99 J15 Reusel Noord-Brabant, S Netherlands 51°21′N 05°10′E
Reutel see Ciuhuru
101 H22 Reutlingen Baden-Württemberg, S Germany 48°30′N 09°13′E
108 L7 Reutte Tirol, W Austria 47°30′N 10°44′E
99 M16 Reuver Limburg, SE Netherlands 51°17′N 06°05′E
28 K7 Reva South Dakota, N USA 45°30′N 103°03′W
Reval/Revel see Tallinn
124 J4 Revda Murmanskaya Oblast', NW Russian Federation 67°57′N 34°29′E
122 F6 Revda Sverdlovskaya Oblast', C Russian Federation 56°48′N 59°42′E
103 N16 Revel Haute-Garonne, S France 43°27′N 01°59′E
11 O16 Revelstoke British Columbia, SW Canada 51°02′N 118°12′W
43 N13 Reventazón, Río E Costa Rica
106 G9 Revere Lombardia, N Italy 45°03′N 11°07′E
39 Y14 Revillagigedo Island island Alexander Archipelago, Alaska, USA
193 R7 Revillagigedo Islands Mexico
103 R3 Revin Ardennes, N France 49°57′N 04°39′E
92 O3 Revnosa headland C Svalbard 78°03′N 18°52′E
Revolyutsii, Pik see Revolyutsiya, Qullai
147 T13 Revolyutsiya, Qullai Rus. Pik Revolyutsii. ▲ SE Tajikistan 38°40′N 72°26′E
111 L19 Revúca Ger. Grossrauschenbach, Hung. Nagyrőce. Banskobystrický Kraj, C Slovakia 48°40′N 20°10′E
154 K9 Rewa Madhya Pradesh, C India 24°32′N 81°18′E
152 I11 Rewāri Haryāna, N India 28°14′N 76°38′E
33 R14 Rexburg Idaho, NW USA 43°49′N 111°47′W
78 G13 Rey Bouba Nord, NE Cameroon 08°40′N 14°11′E
92 L3 Reydharfjördhur Austurland, E Iceland 65°02′N 14°12′W
57 K16 Reyes Beni, NW Bolivia 14°17′S 67°18′W
34 L8 Reyes, Point headland California, W USA 37°59′N 123°01′W
54 B12 Reyes, Punta headland SW Colombia 02°44′N 78°08′W
136 L17 Reyhanlı Hatay, S Turkey 36°16′N 36°35′E
43 U16 Rey, Isla del island Archipiélago de las Perlas, SE Panama
92 H2 Reykhólar Vestfirdhir, W Iceland 65°28′N 22°12′W
92 K2 Reykjahlídh Nordhurland Eystra, NE Iceland 65°37′N 16°54′W
92 I4 Reykjanes region SW Iceland
197 O16 Reykjanes Basin var. Irminger Basin. undersea feature N Atlantic Ocean 62°30′N 33°30′W
197 N17 Reykjanes Ridge undersea feature N Atlantic Ocean 62°00′N 27°00′W
92 H4 Reykjavík var. Reikjavik. ● (Iceland) Höfudhborgarsvaedhi, W Iceland 64°08′N 21°54′W
18 D13 Reynoldsville Pennsylvania, NE USA 41°04′N 78°51′W
41 P8 Reynosa Tamaulipas, C Mexico 26°03′N 98°19′W
Reẕā'īyeh see Orūmīyeh
Reẕā'īyeh, Daryācheh-ye see Orūmīyeh, Daryācheh-ye
102 I8 Rezé Loire-Atlantique, NW France 47°10′N 01°36′W
118 K10 Rēzekne Ger. Rositten; prev. Rus. Rezhitsa. Rēzekne, SE Latvia 56°31′N 27°22′E
Rezhitsa see Rēzekne
117 N9 Rezina NE Moldova 47°44′N 28°58′E
114 N11 Rezovo Turk. Rezve. Burgas, E Bulgaria 42°00′N 28°00′E
114 N11 Rezovska Reka Turk. Rezve Deresi. Bulgaria/Turkey see also Rezve Deresi
Rezovska Reka see Rezve Deresi
Rezve see Rezovo
114 N11 Rezve Deresi Bul. Rezovska Reka. Bulgaria/Turkey see also Rezovska Reka
Rezve Deresi see Rezovska Reka
Rhadames see Ghadāmis
Rhaedestus see Tekirdağ
108 J10 Rhaetian Alps Fr. Alpes Rhétiques, Ger. Rätische Alpen, It. Alpi Retiche. ▲▲ C Europe
108 I8 Rhätikon ▲▲ C Europe
101 G14 Rheda-Wiedenbrück Nordrhein-Westfalen, W Germany 51°51′N 08°17′E
98 M12 Rheden Gelderland, E Netherlands 52°01′N 06°03′E
Rhegion/Rhegium see Reggio di Calabria
Rheims see Reims
Rhein see Rhine
101 E17 Rheinbach Nordrhein-Westfalen, W Germany 50°37′N 06°57′E
100 F13 Rheine var. Rheine in Westfalen. Nordrhein-Westfalen, NW Germany 52°17′N 07°27′E
Rheine in Westfalen see Rheine
Rheinfeld see Rheinfelden
101 F24 Rheinfelden Baden-Württemberg, S Germany 47°34′N 07°46′E
108 E6 Rheinfelden var. Rheinfeld. Aargau, N Switzerland 47°33′N 07°47′E
101 E17 Rheinisches Schiefergebirge var. Rhine State Uplands, Eng. Rhenish Slate Mountains. ▲▲ W Germany
101 D18 Rheinland-Pfalz Eng. Rhineland-Palatinate, Fr. Rhénanie-Palatinat. state W Germany
101 G18 Rhein Main ✈ (Frankfurt am Main) Hessen, W Germany 50°03′N 08°33′E
Rhénanie du Nord-Westphalie see Nordrhein-Westfalen
Rhénanie-Palatinat see Rheinland-Pfalz
98 K12 Rhenen Utrecht, C Netherlands 52°01′N 06°02′E
Rhenish Slate Mountains see Rheinisches Schiefergebirge
Rhétiques, Alpes see Rhaetian Alps
100 N10 Rhin NE Germany
Rhin see Rhine
84 F10 Rhine Dut. Rijn, Fr. Rhin, Ger. Rhein. W Europe
30 L5 Rhinelander Wisconsin, N USA 45°39′N 89°23′W
Rhineland-Palatinate see Rheinland-Pfalz
Rhine State Uplands see Rheinisches Schiefergebirge
100 N11 Rhinkanal canal NE Germany
81 F17 Rhino Camp NW Uganda 02°58′N 31°24′E
74 D7 Rhir, Cap headland W Morocco 30°40′N 09°54′W
106 D7 Rho Lombardia, N Italy 45°32′N 09°02′E
19 N12 Rhode Island off. State of Rhode Island and Providence Plantations, also known as Little Rhody, Ocean State. state NE USA
19 O13 Rhode Island island Rhode Island, NE USA
19 O13 Rhode Island Sound sound Maine/Rhode Island, NE USA
Rhodes see Ródos
Rhode-Saint-Genèse see Sint-Genesius-Rode
84 L14 Rhodes Basin undersea feature E Mediterranean Sea 35°55′N 28°30′E
Rhodesia see Zimbabwe
114 I12 Rhodope Mountains var. Rodhópi Óri, Bul. Rhodope Planina, Rodopi, Gk. Orosirá Rodhópis, Turk. Dospad Dagh. ▲▲ Bulgaria/Greece
Rhodope Planina see Rhodope Mountains
101 I18 Rhön ▲▲ C Germany
103 Q10 Rhône department E France
86 C12 Rhône France/Switzerland
103 R12 Rhône-Alpes region E France
98 G13 Rhoon Zuid-Holland, SW Netherlands 51°52′N 04°25′E
96 G9 Rhum var. Rum. island W Scotland, United Kingdom
Rhuthun see Ruthin
97 J18 Rhyl NE Wales, United Kingdom 53°19′N 03°28′W
59 K18 Rialma Goiás, S Brazil 15°22′S 49°35′W
104 L3 Riaño Castilla-León, N Spain 42°59′N 05°00′W
105 O9 Riansáres C Spain
152 H6 Riāsi Jammu and Kashmir, NW India 33°03′N 74°51′E
168 K10 Riau off. Propinsi Riau. province W Indonesia
Riau Archipelago see Riau, Kepulauan
168 M11 Riau, Kepulauan var. Riau Archipelago, Dut. Riouw-Archipel. island group W Indonesia
Riau, Propinsi see Riau
105 O6 Riaza Castilla-León, N Spain 41°17′N 03°29′W
105 N6 Riaza N Spain
81 K17 Riba spring/well NE Kenya 01°56′N 40°38′E
104 H4 Ribadavia Galicia, NW Spain 42°17′N 08°08′W
104 J2 Ribadeo Galicia, NW Spain 43°32′N 07°04′W
104 L2 Ribadesella Asturias, N Spain 43°27′N 05°04′W
104 G10 Ribatejo former province C Portugal
83 P15 Ribáuè Nampula, N Mozambique 14°56′S 38°19′E
97 K17 Ribble NW England, United Kingdom
95 F23 Ribe Ribe, W Denmark 55°20′N 08°47′E
95 F23 Ribe off. Ribe Amt, var. Ripen. county W Denmark
Ribe Amt see Ribe
104 G3 Ribeira Galicia, NW Spain 42°33′N 09°01′W
64 O5 Ribeira Brava Madeira, Portugal, NE Atlantic Ocean 32°39′N 17°04′W
64 P3 Ribeira Grande São Miguel, Azores, Portugal, NE Atlantic Ocean 37°34′N 25°32′W
60 L8 Ribeirão Preto São Paulo, S Brazil 21°09′S 47°48′W
60 L11 Ribeira, Rio S Brazil
107 I24 Ribera Sicilia, Italy, C Mediterranean Sea 37°31′N 13°16′E
57 L14 Riberalta Beni, N Bolivia 11°01′S 66°04′W
105 W4 Ribes de Freser Cataluña, NE Spain 42°18′N 02°11′E
30 L6 Rib Mountain ▲ Wisconsin, N USA 44°55′N 89°41′W
109 U12 Ribnica Ger. Reifnitz. S Slovenia 45°46′N 14°40′E
117 N9 Ribniţa var. Râbniţa, Rus. Rybnitsa. NE Moldova 47°46′N 29°01′E
100 M8 Ribnitz-Damgarten Mecklenburg-Vorpommern, NE Germany 54°14′N 12°25′E
111 D16 Říčany Ger. Ritschan. Středočeský Kraj, W Czech Republic 49°59′N 14°40′E
29 U7 Rice Minnesota, N USA 45°42′N 94°10′W
30 J5 Rice Lake Wisconsin, N USA 45°33′N 91°43′W
14 I15 Rice Lake Ontario, SE Canada
14 E8 Rice Lake Ontario, S Canada
23 V3 Richard B. Russell Lake Georgia, SE USA
25 U6 Richardson Texas, SW USA 32°55′N 96°44′W
11 R11 Richardson Alberta, C Canada
10 I3 Richardson Mountains ▲▲ Yukon Territory, NW Canada
185 C21 Richardson Mountains ▲▲ South Island, New Zealand
42 F2 Richardson Peak ▲ SE Belize 16°34′N 88°46′W
76 G10 Richard Toll N Senegal 16°28′N 15°44′W
28 L5 Richardton North Dakota, N USA 46°52′N 102°19′W
14 F13 Rich, Cape headland Ontario, S Canada 44°42′N 80°37′W
102 L8 Richelieu Indre-et-Loire, C France 47°01′N 00°18′E
33 P15 Richfield Idaho, NW USA 43°03′N 114°11′W
36 K5 Richfield Utah, W USA 38°45′N 112°05′W
18 J10 Richfield Springs New York, NE USA 42°52′N 74°57′W
18 M6 Richford Vermont, NE USA 44°59′N 72°37′W
27 R6 Rich Hill Missouri, C USA 38°06′N 94°22′W
13 P14 Richibucto New Brunswick, SE Canada 46°42′N 64°54′W
108 G8 Richisau Glarus, NE Switzerland 47°00′N 08°54′E
23 S6 Richland Georgia, SE USA 32°05′N 84°40′W
27 U6 Richland Missouri, C USA 37°51′N 92°24′W
25 U8 Richland Texas, SW USA 31°55′N 96°25′W
32 K10 Richland Washington, NW USA 46°17′N 119°16′W
30 K8 Richland Center Wisconsin, N USA 43°22′N 90°24′W
21 W11 Richlands North Carolina, SE USA 34°52′N 77°33′W
21 Q7 Richlands Virginia, NE USA 37°05′N 81°47′W
25 R9 Richland Springs Texas, SW USA 31°16′N 98°56′W
183 S8 Richmond New South Wales, SE Australia 33°36′S 150°44′E
10 L17 Richmond British Columbia, SW Canada 49°07′N 123°09′W
14 L13 Richmond Ontario, SE Canada 45°12′N 75°49′W
15 Q12 Richmond Québec, SE Canada 45°39′N 72°07′W
185 I14 Richmond Tasman, South Island, New Zealand 41°25′S 173°04′E
35 N8 Richmond California, W USA 37°57′N 122°22′W
31 Q14 Richmond Indiana, N USA 39°50′N 84°51′W
20 M6 Richmond Kentucky, S USA 37°45′N 84°19′W
27 S4 Richmond Missouri, C USA 39°15′N 93°59′W
25 V11 Richmond Texas, SW USA 29°36′N 95°48′W
36 L1 Richmond Utah, W USA 41°55′N 111°51′W
21 W6 Richmond state capital Virginia, NE USA 37°33′N 77°28′W
14 H15 Richmond Hill Ontario, S Canada 43°51′N 79°24′W
185 J15 Richmond Range ▲▲ South Island, New Zealand
27 S12 Rich Mountain ▲ Arkansas, C USA 34°37′N 94°17′W
31 S13 Richwood Ohio, N USA 40°25′N 83°18′W
21 R5 Richwood West Virginia, NE USA 38°13′N 80°31′W
104 K5 Ricobayo, Embalse de NW Spain
Ricomagus see Riom
Ridā' see Radā'
145 X9 Ridder Kaz. Leningor. Vostochnyy Kazakhstan, E Kazakhstan 50°20′N 83°34′E
98 H13 Ridderkerk Zuid-Holland, SW Netherlands 51°52′N 04°35′E
33 N16 Riddle Idaho, NW USA 42°07′N 116°09′W
32 F14 Riddle Oregon, NW USA 42°57′N 123°21′W
14 L13 Rideau Ontario, SE Canada
35 T12 Ridgecrest California, W USA 35°37′N 117°40′W
18 L13 Ridgefield Connecticut, NE USA 41°16′N 73°30′W
22 K5 Ridgeland Mississippi, S USA 32°25′N 90°07′W
21 R15 Ridgeland South Carolina, SE USA 32°30′N 80°59′W
20 F8 Ridgely Tennessee, S USA 36°15′N 89°29′W
14 D17 Ridgetown Ontario, S Canada 42°27′N 81°52′W
21 R12 Ridgeway South Carolina, SE USA 34°17′N 80°56′W
Ridgeway see Ridgway
18 D13 Ridgway var. Ridgeway. Pennsylvania, NE USA 41°24′N 78°40′W
11 W16 Riding Mountain ▲▲ Manitoba, S Canada
Ried see Ried im Innkreis
109 R4 Ried im Innkreis var. Ried. Oberösterreich, NW Austria 48°13′N 13°29′E
109 X8 Riegersburg Steiermark, SE Austria 47°03′N 15°52′E
108 E6 Riehen Basel-Stadt, NW Switzerland 47°35′N 07°39′E
92 J9 Riehppegáisá var. Rieppe. ▲ N Norway 69°38′N 21°31′E
99 K18 Riemst Limburg, NE Belgium 50°49′N 05°36′E
Rieppe see Riehppegáisá
101 O15 Riesa Sachsen, E Germany 51°18′N 13°18′E
63 H24 Riesco, Isla island S Chile
107 K25 Riesi Sicilia, Italy, C Mediterranean Sea 37°17′N 14°05′E
83 F25 Riet SW South Africa
83 I23 Riet SW South Africa
118 D11 Rietavas Telšiai, W Lithuania 55°43′N 21°56′E
83 F19 Rietfontein Omaheke, E Namibia 21°58′S 20°58′E
107 I14 Rieti anc. Reate. Lazio, C Italy 42°24′N 12°51′E
84 D14 Rif var. Riff, Er Rif, Er Riff. ▲▲ N Morocco
Riff see Rif
37 Q4 Rifle Colorado, C USA 39°30′N 107°46′W
31 R7 Rifle River Michigan, N USA
81 H18 Rift Valley province Kenya
Rift Valley see Great Rift Valley
118 F9 Rīga Eng. Riga. ● (Latvia) Rīga, C Latvia 56°57′N 24°08′E
Rigaer Bucht see Riga, Gulf of
118 F6 Riga, Gulf of Est. Liivi Laht, Ger. Rigaer Bucht, Latv. Rīgas Jūras Līcis, Rus. Rizhskiy Zaliv; prev. Est. Riia Laht. gulf Estonia/Latvia
Rīgas Jūras Līcis see Riga, Gulf of
15 N12 Rigaud Ontario/Québec, SE Canada
33 R14 Rigby Idaho, NW USA 43°40′N 111°54′W
148 M10 Rīgestān var. Registan. desert region S Afghanistan
32 M11 Riggins Idaho, NW USA 45°24′N 116°18′W
13 R8 Rigolet Newfoundland and Labrador, NE Canada 54°10′N 58°25′W
78 G9 Rig-Rig Kanem, W Chad 14°16′N 14°21′E
118 F4 Riguldi Läänemaa, W Estonia 59°07′N 23°34′E
Riia Laht see Riga, Gulf of
93 L19 Riihimäki Etelä-Suomi, S Finland 60°45′N 24°45′E
195 O2 Riiser-Larsenisen ice shelf Antarctica
195 U2 Riiser-Larsen Peninsula peninsula Antarctica
65 P22 Riiser-Larsen Sea sea Antarctica
40 D2 Riíto Sonora, NW Mexico 32°06′N 114°57′W
112 B9 Rijeka Ger. Sankt Veit am Flaum, It. Fiume, Slvn. Reka; anc. Tarsatica. Primorje-Gorski Kotar, NW Croatia 45°20′N 14°26′E
99 I14 Rijen Noord-Brabant, S Netherlands 51°35′N 04°55′E
99 H15 Rijkevorsel Antwerpen, N Belgium 51°23′N 04°43′E
Rijn see Rhine
98 G11 Rijnsburg Zuid-Holland, W Netherlands 52°12′N 04°27′E
Rijssel see Lille
98 N10 Rijssen Overijssel, E Netherlands 52°19′N 06°30′E
98 G12 Rijswijk Eng. Ryswick. Zuid-Holland, W Netherlands 52°03′N 04°20′E
92 I10 Riksgränsen Norrbotten, N Sweden 68°24′N 18°15′E
165 U4 Rikubetsu Hokkaidō, NE Japan 43°30′N 143°43′E
165 R9 Rikuzen-Takata Iwate, Honshū, C Japan 39°03′N 141°38′E
27 O4 Riley Kansas, C USA 39°18′N 96°49′W
99 I17 Rillaar Vlaams Brabant, C Belgium 50°58′N 04°58′E
Rí, Loch see Ree, Lough
114 G11 Rilska Reka W Bulgaria
77 T12 Rima N Nigeria
141 N7 Rimah, Wādī ar var. Wādī ar Rummah. dry watercourse C Saudi Arabia
Rimaszombat see Rimavská Sobota
191 R12 Rimatara island Îles Australes, SW French Polynesia
111 L20 Rimavská Sobota Ger. Gross-Steffelsdorf, Hung. Rimaszombat. Bankobystrický Kraj, C Slovakia 48°24′N 20°01′E
11 Q15 Rimbey Alberta, SW Canada 52°39′N 114°10′W
95 P15 Rimbo Stockholm, C Sweden 59°44′N 18°21′E
95 M18 Rimforsa Östergötland, S Sweden 58°06′N 15°40′E
106 I11 Rimini anc. Ariminum. Emilia-Romagna, N Italy 44°03′N 12°33′E
Rîmnicu-Sărat see Râmnicu Sărat
Rîmnicu Vîlcea see Râmnicu Vâlcea
149 Y3 Rimo Muztāgh ▲▲ India/Pakistan
15 U7 Rimouski Québec, SE Canada 48°26′N 68°32′W
158 M16 Rinbung Xizang Zizhiqu, W China 29°15′N 89°40′E
Rinchinlhumbe see Dzöölön
62 I5 Rincón, Cerro ▲ N Chile 24°01′S 67°19′W
104 M15 Rincón de la Victoria Andalucía, S Spain 36°43′N 04°18′W
Rincón del Bonete, Lago Artificial de see Río Negro, Embalse del
105 Q4 Rincón de Soto La Rioja, N Spain 42°15′N 01°50′W
94 G8 Rindal Møre og Romsdal, S Norway 63°02′N 09°09′E
115 J20 Ríneia island Kykládes, Greece, Aegean Sea
152 H11 Rīngas prev. Reengus, Ringus. Rājasthān, N India 27°18′N 75°27′E
95 H24 Ringe Fyn, C Denmark 55°14′N 10°30′E
94 H11 Ringebu Oppland, S Norway 61°31′N 10°09′E
Ringen see Rõngu
186 K8 Ringgi Kolombangara, NW Solomon Islands 08°03′S 157°08′E
23 R1 Ringgold Georgia, SE USA 34°55′N 85°06′W
22 G5 Ringgold Louisiana, S USA 32°19′N 93°16′W
25 S5 Ringgold Texas, SW USA 33°47′N 97°56′W
95 E22 Ringkøbing Ringkøbing, W Denmark 56°04′N 08°22′E
95 E21 Ringkøbing var. Ringkøbing Amt. county W Denmark
Ringkøbing Amt see Ringkøbing
95 E22 Ringkøbing Fjord fjord W Denmark
33 S10 Ringling Montana, NW USA 46°15′N 110°48′W
27 N13 Ringling Oklahoma, C USA 34°12′N 97°35′W
94 H13 Ringsaker Hedmark, S Norway 60°54′N 10°45′E
95 I23 Ringsted Vestsjælland, E Denmark 55°28′N 11°48′E
Ringus see Rīngas
92 I9 Ringvassøya Lapp. Ráneš. island N Norway
18 K13 Ringwood New Jersey, NE USA 41°06′N 74°15′W
Rinn Duáin see Hook Head
100 H13 Rinteln Niedersachsen, NW Germany 52°10′N 09°04′E
115 E18 Río Dytikí Ellás, S Greece 38°18′N 21°48′E
Rio see Rio de Janeiro
56 C7 Riobamba Chimborazo, C Ecuador 01°44′S 78°40′W
60 P9 Rio Bonito Rio de Janeiro, SE Brazil 22°42′S 42°38′W
59 C16 Rio Branco state capital Acre, W Brazil 09°59′S 67°49′W
61 H18 Río Branco Cerro Largo, NE Uruguay 32°32′S 53°28′W
Rio Branco, Território de see Roraima
41 P8 Río Bravo Tamaulipas, C Mexico 25°57′N 98°03′W
63 G16 Río Bueno Los Lagos, C Chile 40°20′S 72°55′W
55 P5 Río Caribe Sucre, NE Venezuela 10°43′N 63°06′W
54 M5 Río Chico Miranda, N Venezuela 10°18′N 66°00′W
63 H18 Río Cisnes Aisén, S Chile 44°29′S 71°15′W
60 L9 Rio Claro São Paulo, S Brazil 22°19′S 47°35′W
45 V14 Rio Claro Trinidad, Trinidad and Tobago 10°18′N 61°11′W
54 J5 Río Claro Lara, N Venezuela 09°54′N 69°23′W
63 J15 Río Colorado Río Negro, E Argentina 39°01′S 64°05′W
62 K11 Río Cuarto Córdoba, C Argentina 33°06′S 64°20′W
60 P10 Rio de Janeiro var. Rio. state capital Rio de Janeiro, SE Brazil 22°53′S 43°17′W
60 P9 Rio de Janeiro off. Estado do Rio de Janeiro. state SE Brazil
Rio de Janeiro, Estado do see Rio de Janeiro
43 R17 Río de Jesús Veraguas, S Panama 07°58′N 81°01′W
34 K3 Rio Dell California, W USA 40°30′N 124°07′W

◆ Country
● Country Capital
◇ Dependent Territory
○ Dependent Territory Capital
Administrative Regions
✈ International Airport
▲ Mountain
▲▲ Mountain Range
Volcano
River
Lake
Reservoir

RIO DO SUL – ROSALIE

60 K13 **Rio do Sul** Santa Catarina, S Brazil 27°15´S 49°37´W
63 I23 **Río Gallegos** *var.* Gallegos, Puerto Gallegos. Santa Cruz, S Argentina 51°40´S 69°21´W
63 J24 **Río Grande** Tierra del Fuego, S Argentina 53°45´S 67°46´W
61 I18 **Rio Grande** *var.* São Pedro do Rio Grande do Sul. Rio Grande do Sul, S Brazil 32°03´S 52°08´W
40 L10 **Río Grande** Zacatecas, C Mexico 23°50´N 103°20´W
42 J9 **Río Grande** León, NW Nicaragua 12°59´N 86°34´W
45 V5 **Río Grande** E Puerto Rico 18°23´N 65°51´W
24 I9 **Rio Grande** ⇝ Texas, SW USA
25 R17 **Rio Grande City** Texas, SW USA 26°24´N 98°50´W
59 P14 **Rio Grande do Norte** *off.* Estado do Rio Grande do Norte. ◈ *state* E Brazil
Rio Grande do Norte, Estado do *see* Rio Grande do Norte
61 G15 **Rio Grande do Sul** *off.* Estado do Rio Grande do Sul. ◈ *state* S Brazil
Rio Grande do Sul, Estado do *see* Rio Grande do Sul
65 M17 **Rio Grande Fracture Zone** *tectonic feature* C Atlantic Ocean
65 J18 **Rio Grande Gap** *undersea feature* S Atlantic Ocean
Rio Grande Plateau *see* Rio Grande Rise
65 J18 **Rio Grande Rise** *var.* Rio Grande Plateau. *undersea feature* SW Atlantic Ocean 31°00´S 35°00´W
54 G4 **Ríohacha** La Guajira, N Colombia 11°23´N 72°47´W
43 S16 **Río Hato** Coclé, C Panama 08°21´N 80°10´W
25 T17 **Rio Hondo** Texas, SW USA 26°14´N 97°34´W
56 D10 **Rioja** San Martín, N Peru 06°02´S 77°10´W
41 Y11 **Río Lagartos** Yucatán, SE Mexico 21°35´N 88°08´W
103 P11 **Riom** *anc.* Ricomagus. Puy-de-Dôme, C France 45°54´N 03°06´E
104 F10 **Rio Maior** Santarém, C Portugal 39°20´N 08°55´W
103 O12 **Riom-ès-Montagnes** Cantal, C France 45°15´N 02°39´E
60 J12 **Rio Negro** Paraná, S Brazil 26°06´S 49°46´W
63 I15 **Río Negro** *off.* Provincia de Río Negro. ◈ *province* C Argentina
61 D18 **Río Negro** ◈ *department* W Uruguay
47 V12 **Río Negro, Embalse del** *var.* Lago Artificial de Rincón del Bonete. ⊠ C Uruguay
Río Negro, Provincia de *see* Río Negro
107 M17 **Rionero in Vulture** Basilicata, S Italy 40°55´N 15°40´E
137 S9 **Rioni** ⇝ W Georgia
105 P12 **Riópar** Castilla-La Mancha, C Spain 38°31´N 02°27´W
61 H16 **Rio Pardo** Rio Grande do Sul, S Brazil 29°41´S 52°25´W
37 R11 **Rio Rancho Estates** New Mexico, SW USA 35°14´N 106°40´W
42 L11 **Río San Juan** ◈ *department* S Nicaragua
54 E9 **Ríosucio** Caldas, W Colombia 35°26´N 75°44´W
54 C7 **Ríosucio** Chocó, NW Colombia 07°25´N 77°05´W
62 K10 **Río Tercero** Córdoba, C Argentina 32°15´S 64°08´W
42 K5 **Río Tinto, Sierra** ▲▲ NE Honduras
54 J5 **Río Tocuyo** Lara, N Venezuela 10°18´N 70°00´W
Riouw-Archipel *see* Riau, Kepulauan
59 J19 **Rio Verde** Goiás, C Brazil 17°50´S 50°55´W
41 O12 **Río Verde** *var.* Rioverde. San Luis Potosí, C Mexico 21°58´N 100°W
Rioverde *see* Río Verde
35 O8 **Rio Vista** California, W USA 38°09´N 121°42´W
112 M11 **Ripanj** Serbia, N Serbia 44°37´N 20°30´E
106 J13 **Ripatransone** Marche, C Italy 43°00´N 13°45´E
Ripen *see* Ribe
22 M2 **Ripley** Mississippi, S USA 34°43´N 88°57´W
31 R15 **Ripley** Ohio, N USA 38°45´N 83°51´W
20 F9 **Ripley** Tennessee, S USA 35°43´N 89°30´W
21 Q4 **Ripley** West Virginia, NE USA 38°49´N 81°44´W
105 W4 **Ripoll** Cataluña, NE Spain 42°12´N 02°12´E
97 M16 **Ripon** N England, United Kingdom 54°07´N 01°31´W
30 M7 **Ripon** Wisconsin, N USA 43°52´N 88°48´W
107 L24 **Riposto** Sicilia, Italy, C Mediterranean Sea 37°44´N 15°13´E
99 L14 **Rips** Noord-Brabant, SE Netherlands 51°31´N 05°49´E
54 D9 **Risaralda** *off.* Departamento de Risaralda. ◈ *province* C Colombia
Risaralda, Departamento de *see* Risaralda
116 L8 **Rîşcani** *var.* Râşcani, *Rus.* Ryshkany. NW Moldova 47°55´N 27°31´E
152 J9 **Rishikesh** Uttarakhand, N India 30°06´N 78°16´E
165 S1 **Rishiri-tō** *var.* Risiri Tô. *island* NE Japan
165 S1 **Rishiri-yama** ⊼ Rishiri-tō, NE Japan 45°11´N 141°11´E
25 R7 **Rising Star** Texas, SW USA 32°06´N 98°57´W
31 Q15 **Rising Sun** Indiana, N USA 38°58´N 84°53´W
Risiri Tô *see* Rishiri-tō
102 L4 **Risle** ⇝ N France
Rîşno *see* Râşnov
27 V13 **Rison** Arkansas, C USA 33°58´N 92°11´W
95 G17 **Risør** Aust-Agder, S Norway 58°44´N 09°15´E
92 H10 **Risøyhamn** Nordland, C Norway 69°06´N 15°37´E
101 I23 **Riss** ⇝ S Germany
118 G4 **Risti** *Ger.* Kreuz. Läänemaa, W Estonia 59°01´N 24°01´E
15 V8 **Ristigouche** ⇝ Québec, SE Canada
93 N18 **Ristiina** Itä-Suomi, E Finland 61°32´N 27°15´E
93 N14 **Ristijärvi** Oulu, C Finland 64°30´N 28°15´E
188 C14 **Ritidian Point** *headland* N Guam 13°39´N 144°51´E
Ritschan *see* Říčany
35 R9 **Ritter, Mount** ▲ California, W USA 37°40´N 119°10´W
31 T12 **Rittman** Ohio, N USA 40°58´N 81°46´W
32 L9 **Ritzville** Washington, NW USA 47°07´N 118°22´W
Riva *see* Riva del Garda
61 A21 **Rivadavia** Buenos Aires, E Argentina 35°29´S 62°59´W
106 F7 **Riva del Garda** *var.* Riva. Trentino-Alto Adige, N Italy 45°54´N 10°50´E
106 B8 **Rivarolo Canavese** Piemonte, W Italy 45°21´N 07°42´E
42 K11 **Rivas** Rivas, SW Nicaragua 11°26´N 85°50´W
42 J11 **Rivas** ◈ *department* SW Nicaragua
103 R11 **Rive-de-Gier** Loire, E France 45°31´N 04°36´E
61 A22 **Rivera** Buenos Aires, E Argentina 37°13´S 63°14´W
61 F16 **Rivera** Rivera, NE Uruguay 30°54´S 55°31´W
61 F17 **Rivera** ◈ *department* NE Uruguay
35 P9 **Riverbank** California, W USA 37°43´N 120°59´W
76 K17 **River Cess** SW Liberia 05°28´N 09°32´W
28 M4 **Riverdale** North Dakota, N USA 47°29´N 101°22´W
30 I6 **River Falls** Wisconsin, N USA 44°52´N 92°38´W
11 T16 **Riverhurst** Saskatchewan, S Canada 50°52´N 106°49´W
183 O10 **Riverina** *physical region* New South Wales, SE Australia
80 G8 **River Nile** ◈ *state* NE Sudan
63 F19 **Rivero, Isla** *island* Archipiélago de los Chonos, S Chile
11 W16 **Rivers** Manitoba, S Canada 50°02´N 100°14´W
77 U17 **Rivers** ◈ *state* S Nigeria
185 D23 **Riversdale** Southland, South Island, New Zealand 45°54´S 168°44´E
83 F26 **Riversdale** Western Cape, SW South Africa 34°05´S 21°15´E
35 U15 **Riverside** California, W USA 33°58´N 117°25´W
25 W9 **Riverside** Texas, SW USA 30°51´N 95°24´W
37 U3 **Riverside Reservoir** ⊠ Colorado, C USA
10 K15 **Rivers Inlet** British Columbia, SW Canada 51°43´N 127°19´W
10 K15 **Rivers Inlet** *inlet* British Columbia, SW Canada
11 X15 **Riverton** Manitoba, S Canada 51°00´N 97°00´W
185 C24 **Riverton** Southland, South Island, New Zealand 46°20´S 168°02´E
30 L13 **Riverton** Illinois, N USA 39°50´N 89°31´W
36 L3 **Riverton** Utah, W USA 40°32´N 111°57´W
33 V15 **Riverton** Wyoming, C USA 43°01´N 108°22´W
14 G10 **River Valley** Ontario, S Canada 46°36´N 80°09´W
13 P14 **Riverview** New Brunswick, SE Canada 46°03´N 64°47´W
103 O17 **Rivesaltes** Pyrénées-Orientales, S France 42°46´N 02°48´E
36 H11 **Riviera** Arizona, SW USA 35°06´N 114°36´W
25 S15 **Riviera** Texas, SW USA 27°15´N 97°48´W
23 Z14 **Riviera Beach** Florida, SE USA 26°46´N 80°03´W
15 Q10 **Rivière-à-Pierre** Québec, SE Canada 46°59´N 72°12´W
15 T9 **Rivière-Bleue** Québec, SE Canada 47°26´N 69°02´W
15 T8 **Rivière-du-Loup** Québec, SE Canada 47°49´N 69°32´W
173 Y15 **Rivière du Rempart** NE Mauritius 20°06´S 57°41´E
45 R12 **Rivière-Pilote** S Martinique 14°29´N 60°54´W
173 O17 **Rivière St-Etienne, Point de la** *headland* SW Réunion
13 S10 **Rivière-St-Paul** Québec, E Canada 51°26´N 57°52´W
Rivière Sèche *see* Bel Air
116 K4 **Rivne** *Pol.* Równe, *Rus.* Rovno. Rivnens'ka Oblast', NW Ukraine 50°37´N 26°16´E
Rivne *see* Rivnens'ka Oblast'
116 K3 **Rivnens'ka Oblast'** *var.* Rivne, *Rus.* Rovenskaya Oblast'. ◈ *province* NW Ukraine
106 B8 **Rivoli** Piemonte, NW Italy 45°04´N 07°31´E
159 Q14 **Riwoqê** *var.* Racaka. Xizang Zizhiqu, W China 31°10´N 96°25´E
99 H19 **Rixensart** Walloon Brabant, C Belgium 50°43´N 04°32´E
Riyadh/Riyāḍ, Minṭaqat ar *see* Ar Riyāḍ
Riyāq *see* Rayak
Rizaiyeh *see* Orūmīyeh
137 P11 **Rize** Rize, NE Turkey 41°03´N 40°33´E
137 P11 **Rize** *prev.* Çoruh. ◈ *province* NE Turkey
161 R5 **Rizhao** Shandong, E China 35°23´N 119°31´E
Rizhskiy Zaliv *see* Riga, Gulf of
Rizokarpaso/Rizokárpason *see* Dipkarpaz
107 O21 **Rizzuto, Capo** *headland* S Italy 38°54´N 17°05´E
95 F15 **Rjukan** Telemark, S Norway 59°54´N 08°33´E
95 D16 **Rjuven** ▲▲ S Norway
76 H9 **Rkiz** Trarza, W Mauritania 16°50´N 15°20´W
115 Q23 **Ro** *prev.* Ágios Geórgios. *island* SE Greece
95 H14 **Roa** Oppland, S Norway 60°16´N 10°38´E
105 N5 **Roa** Castilla-León, N Spain 41°42´N 03°55´W
45 T9 **Road Town** ○ (British Virgin Islands) Tortola, C British Virgin Islands 18°28´N 64°39´W
96 F6 **Roag, Loch** *inlet* NW Scotland, United Kingdom
37 O5 **Roan Cliffs** *cliff* Colorado/Utah, W USA
21 P9 **Roan High Knob** *var.* Roan Mountain. ▲ North Carolina/Tennessee, SE USA 36°09´N 82°07´W
Roan Mountain *see* Roan High Knob
103 Q10 **Roanne** *anc.* Rodunma. Loire, E France 46°03´N 04°04´E
23 R4 **Roanoke** Alabama, S USA 33°09´N 85°22´W
21 S7 **Roanoke** Virginia, NE USA 37°16´N 79°57´W
21 Z9 **Roanoke Island** *island* North Carolina, SE USA
21 W8 **Roanoke Rapids** North Carolina, SE USA 36°27´N 77°39´W
21 X9 **Roanoke River** ⇝ North Carolina/Virginia, SE USA
37 O4 **Roan Plateau** *plain* Utah, W USA
37 R5 **Roaring Fork River** ⇝ Colorado, C USA
25 O5 **Roaring Springs** Texas, SW USA 33°54´N 100°51´W
42 J4 **Roatán** *var.* Coxen Hole, Coxin Hole. Islas de la Bahía, N Honduras 16°19´N 86°33´W
42 I4 **Roatán, Isla de** *island* Islas de la Bahía, N Honduras
Roat Kampuchea *see* Cambodia
Roazon *see* Rennes
143 T7 **Robāṭ-e Chāh Gonbad** Yazd, E Iran 33°24´N 57°43´E
143 R7 **Robāṭ-e Khān** Yazd, C Iran 33°24´N 56°04´E
143 T7 **Robāṭ-e Khvosh Āb** Yazd, E Iran
143 R8 **Robāṭ-e Bādām** Yazd, NE Iran 33°01´N 55°34´E
143 Q8 **Robāṭ-e Rīzāb** Yazd, C Iran
175 S8 **Robbie Ridge** *undersea feature* W Pacific Ocean
21 T10 **Robbins** North Carolina, SE USA 35°25´N 79°35´W
183 N15 **Robbins Island** *island* Tasmania, SE Australia
21 N10 **Robbinsville** North Carolina, SE USA 35°18´N 83°49´W
182 J12 **Robe** South Australia 37°11´S 139°48´E
21 W9 **Robersonville** North Carolina, SE USA 35°49´N 77°15´W
25 P8 **Robert Lee** Texas, SW USA 31°50´N 100°30´W
35 V5 **Roberts Creek Mountain** ▲ Nevada, W USA 39°52´N 116°16´W
93 J15 **Robertsfors** Västerbotten, N Sweden 64°12´N 20°50´E
153 N14 **Robertsganj** Uttar Pradesh, N India 24°41´N 83°04´E
27 R11 **Robert S. Kerr Reservoir** ⊠ Oklahoma, C USA
38 L12 **Roberts Mountain** ▲ Nunivak Island, Alaska, USA 60°01´N 166°15´W
83 F26 **Robertson** Western Cape, SW South Africa 33°48´S 19°53´E
194 H4 **Robertson Island** *island* Antarctica
76 J16 **Robertsport** W Liberia 06°45´N 11°15´W
182 J8 **Robertstown** South Australia 34°00´S 139°04´E
Robert Williams *see* Caála
15 P7 **Roberval** Québec, SE Canada 48°31´N 72°16´W
31 N15 **Robinson** Illinois, N USA 39°00´N 87°44´W
193 U11 **Róbinson Crusoe, Isla** *island* Islas Juan Fernández, Chile, E Pacific Ocean
180 J9 **Robinson Range** ▲▲ Western Australia
182 M9 **Robinvale** Victoria, SE Australia 34°37´S 142°45´E
105 P11 **Robledo** Castilla-La Mancha, C Spain 38°45´N 02°27´W
54 G5 **Robles** *var.* La Paz, Robles La Paz. Cesar, N Colombia 10°24´N 73°11´W
Robles La Paz *see* Robles
11 V15 **Roblin** Manitoba, S Canada 51°15´N 101°20´W
11 S17 **Robsart** Saskatchewan, S Canada 49°22´N 109°15´W
11 N15 **Robson, Mount** ▲ British Columbia, SW Canada 53°09´N 119°16´W
25 T14 **Robstown** Texas, SW USA 27°47´N 97°40´W
25 P6 **Roby** Texas, SW USA 32°42´N 100°23´W
104 E11 **Roca, Cabo da** *cape* C Portugal
Rocadas *see* Xangongo
41 S14 **Roca Partida, Punta** *headland* C Mexico 18°43´N 95°11´W
47 X6 **Rocas, Atol das** *island* E Brazil
107 L18 **Roccadaspide** *var.* Rocca d'Aspide. Campania, S Italy 40°25´N 15°12´E
Rocca d'Aspide *see* Roccadaspide
107 K15 **Roccaraso** Abruzzo, C Italy 41°49´N 14°01´E
106 H10 **Rocca San Casciano** Emilia-Romagna, C Italy 44°06´N 11°51´E
106 G13 **Roccastrada** Toscana, C Italy 43°00´N 11°09´E
61 G20 **Rocha** Rocha, E Uruguay 34°30´S 54°22´W
61 G19 **Rocha** ◈ *department* E Uruguay
97 L17 **Rochdale** NW England, United Kingdom 53°38´N 02°09´W
102 L11 **Rochechouart** Haute-Vienne, C France 45°49´N 00°49´E
99 J22 **Rochefort** Namur, SE Belgium 50°10´N 05°13´E
102 J11 **Rochefort** *var.* Rochefort sur Mer. Charente-Maritime, W France 45°57´N 00°58´W
Rochefort sur Mer *see* Rochefort
125 N10 **Rochegda** Arkhangel'skaya Oblast', NW Russian Federation 62°37´N 43°21´E
30 L10 **Rochelle** Illinois, N USA 41°54´N 89°03´W
25 Q9 **Rochelle** Texas, SW USA 31°13´N 99°10´W
15 V3 **Rochers Ouest, Rivière aux** ⇝ Québec, SE Canada
97 O22 **Rochester** *anc.* Durobrivae. SE England, United Kingdom 51°24´N 00°30´E
31 O12 **Rochester** Indiana, N USA 41°03´N 86°13´W
29 W10 **Rochester** Minnesota, N USA 44°01´N 92°28´W
19 O9 **Rochester** New Hampshire, NE USA 43°18´N 70°58´W
18 F9 **Rochester** New York, NE USA 43°09´N 77°37´W
25 P5 **Rochester** Texas, SW USA 33°19´N 99°51´W
31 S9 **Rochester Hills** Michigan, N USA 42°39´N 83°04´W
Rocheuses, Montagnes/Rockies *see* Rocky Mountains
64 M6 **Rockall** *island* N Atlantic Ocean, United Kingdom
64 L6 **Rockall Bank** *undersea feature* N Atlantic Ocean
84 B8 **Rockall Rise** *undersea feature* N Atlantic Ocean 59°00´N 14°00´W
84 C9 **Rockall Trough** *undersea feature* N Atlantic Ocean 57°00´N 12°00´W
35 U2 **Rock Creek** ⇝ Nevada, W USA
25 T10 **Rockdale** Texas, SW USA 30°39´N 96°58´W
195 N12 **Rockefeller Plateau** *plateau* Antarctica
30 K11 **Rock Falls** Illinois, N USA 41°46´N 89°41´W
23 Q5 **Rockford** Alabama, S USA 32°53´N 86°11´W
30 L10 **Rockford** Illinois, N USA 42°16´N 89°06´W
15 Q12 **Rock Forest** Québec, SE Canada 45°21´N 71°58´W
11 T17 **Rockglen** Saskatchewan, S Canada 49°11´N 105°57´W
181 Y8 **Rockhampton** Queensland, E Australia 23°31´S 150°31´E
21 R11 **Rock Hill** South Carolina, SE USA 34°55´N 81°01´W
180 I13 **Rockingham** Western Australia 32°16´S 115°21´E
21 T11 **Rockingham** North Carolina, SE USA 34°56´N 79°47´W
30 J11 **Rock Island** Illinois, N USA 41°30´N 90°34´W
25 U12 **Rock Island** Texas, SW USA 29°31´N 96°33´W
14 C10 **Rock Lake** Ontario, S Canada 46°25´N 83°49´W
29 O2 **Rock Lake** North Dakota, N USA 48°45´N 99°12´W
14 I12 **Rock Lake** ◎ Ontario, SE Canada
14 M12 **Rockland** Ontario, SE Canada 45°33´N 75°16´W
19 R7 **Rockland** Maine, NE USA 44°08´N 69°06´W
182 L11 **Rocklands Reservoir** ⊠ Victoria, SE Australia
35 O7 **Rocklin** California, W USA 38°48´N 121°13´W
23 R3 **Rockmart** Georgia, SE USA 34°00´N 85°02´W
31 N16 **Rockport** Indiana, N USA 37°53´N 87°04´W
27 Q1 **Rock Port** Missouri, C USA 40°26´N 95°30´W
25 T14 **Rockport** Texas, SW USA 28°02´N 99°04´W
32 I7 **Rockport** Washington, NW USA 48°28´N 121°36´W
29 S11 **Rock Rapids** Iowa, C USA 43°25´N 96°10´W
30 K11 **Rock River** ⇝ Illinois/Wisconsin, N USA
44 I3 **Rock Sound** Eleuthera Island, C Bahamas 24°52´N 76°10´W
25 P11 **Rocksprings** Texas, SW USA 30°02´N 100°14´W
33 U17 **Rock Springs** Wyoming, C USA 41°35´N 109°12´W
55 T9 **Rockstone** C Guyana 05°58´N 58°33´W
29 S12 **Rock Valley** Iowa, C USA 43°12´N 96°17´W
31 N14 **Rockville** Indiana, N USA 39°45´N 87°15´W
21 W3 **Rockville** Maryland, NE USA 39°05´N 77°10´W
25 U6 **Rockwall** Texas, SW USA 32°56´N 96°27´W
29 U13 **Rockwell City** Iowa, C USA 42°24´N 94°37´W
31 S10 **Rockwood** Michigan, N USA 42°04´N 83°15´W
20 M9 **Rockwood** Tennessee, S USA 35°52´N 84°41´W
25 Q8 **Rockwood** Texas, SW USA 31°29´N 99°23´W
37 U6 **Rocky Ford** Colorado, C USA 38°03´N 103°45´W
14 D9 **Rocky Island Lake** ◎ Ontario, S Canada
21 V9 **Rocky Mount** North Carolina, SE USA 35°56´N 77°48´W
21 S7 **Rocky Mount** Virginia, NE USA 37°00´N 79°53´W
33 Q8 **Rocky Mountain** ▲ Montana, NW USA 47°45´N 112°46´W
11 P15 **Rocky Mountain House** Alberta, SW Canada 52°24´N 114°52´W
37 T3 **Rocky Mountain National Park** *national park* Colorado, C USA
2 E12 **Rocky Mountains** *var.* Rockies, *Fr.* Montagnes Rocheuses. ▲▲ Canada/USA
42 H1 **Rocky Point** *headland* NE Belize 18°21´N 88°04´W
83 A17 **Rocky Point** *headland* NW Namibia 19°01´S 12°27´E
95 F14 **Rødberg** Buskerud, S Norway 60°16´N 09°00´E
95 I25 **Rødby** Storstrøm, SE Denmark 54°42´N 11°24´E
95 I25 **Rødbyhavn** Storstrøm, SE Denmark 54°39´N 11°24´E
13 T10 **Roddickton** Newfoundland, Newfoundland and Labrador, SE Canada 50°51´N 56°03´W
95 F23 **Rødding** Sønderjylland, SW Denmark 55°22´N 09°04´E
95 M22 **Rödeby** Blekinge, S Sweden 56°16´N 15°35´E
98 N6 **Roden** Drenthe, NE Netherlands 53°08´N 06°26´E
62 H9 **Rodeo** San Juan, W Argentina 30°12´S 69°06´W
103 O14 **Rodez** *anc.* Segodunum. Aveyron, S France 44°21´N 02°34´E
Rodholívos *see* Rodolívos
Rodhópi Óri *see* Rhodope Mountains
Ródhos/Rodi *see* Ródos
107 N15 **Rodi Garganico** Puglia, SE Italy 41°54´N 15°51´E
101 N20 **Roding** Bayern, SE Germany 49°12´N 12°30´E
113 J19 **Rodinit, Kepi i** *headland* W Albania 41°35´N 19°27´E
116 I9 **Rodnei, Munţii** ▲▲ N Romania
184 L4 **Rodney, Cape** *headland* North Island, New Zealand 36°16´S 174°48´E
38 L9 **Rodney, Cape** *headland* Alaska, USA 64°39´N 166°24´W
124 M16 **Rodniki** Ivanovskaya Oblast', W Russian Federation 57°04´N 41°45´E
119 Q16 **Rodnya** Mahilyowskaya Voblasts', E Belarus 53°31´N 32°07´E
Rodó *see* José Enrique Rodó
114 H13 **Rodolívos** *var.* Rodholívos. Kentrikí Makedonía, NE Greece 40°55´N 24°00´E
Rodopi *see* Rhodope Mountains
115 O22 **Ródos** *var.* Ródhos, *Eng.* Rhodes, *It.* Rodi. Ródos, Dodekánisa, Greece, Aegean Sea 36°26´N 28°14´E
115 O22 **Ródos** *var.* Ródhos, *Eng.* Rhodes, *It.* Rodi; *anc.* Rhodos. *island* Dodekánisa, Greece, Aegean Sea
Rodosto *see* Tekirdağ
59 A14 **Rodrigues** Amazonas, W Brazil 06°50´S 73°45´W
173 P8 **Rodrigues** *var.* Rodriquez. *island* E Mauritius
Rodriquez *see* Rodrigues
Rodunma *see* Roanne
180 I7 **Roebourne** Western Australia 20°49´S 117°04´E
83 J20 **Roedtan** Limpopo, NE South Africa 24°37´S 29°05´E
98 H11 **Roelofarendsveen** Zuid-Holland, W Netherlands 52°12´N 04°37´E
Roepat *see* Rupat, Pulau
Roer *see* Rur
99 M16 **Roermond** Limburg, SE Netherlands 51°12´N 06°E
99 C18 **Roeselare** *Fr.* Roulers; *prev.* Rousselaere. West-Vlaanderen, W Belgium 50°57´N 03°08´E
9 P8 **Roes Welcome Sound** *strait* Nunavut, N Canada
Roeteng *see* Ruteng
Rofreit *see* Rovereto
Rogachëv *see* Rahachow
57 L15 **Rogagua, Laguna** ◎ NW Bolivia
95 C16 **Rogaland** ◈ *county* S Norway
25 Y9 **Roganville** Texas, SW USA 30°49´N 93°54´W
109 W11 **Rogaška Slatina** *Ger.* Rohitsch-Sauerbrunn; *prev.* Rogatec-Slatina. E Slovenia 46°13´N 15°38´E
Rogatec-Slatina *see* Rogaška Slatina
112 J13 **Rogatica** Republika Srpska, SE Bosnia and Herzegovina 43°50´N 18°55´E
Rogatin *see* Rohatyn
93 F17 **Rogen** ◎ C Sweden
27 S9 **Rogers** Arkansas, C USA 36°19´N 94°07´W
29 P5 **Rogers** North Dakota, N USA 47°03´N 98°12´W
25 T9 **Rogers** Texas, SW USA 30°53´N 97°10´W
31 R5 **Rogers City** Michigan, N USA 45°25´N 83°49´W
Roger Simpson Island *see* Abemama
35 T14 **Rogers Lake** *salt flat* California, W USA
21 Q8 **Rogers, Mount** ▲ Virginia, NE USA 36°39´N 81°32´W
33 O16 **Rogerson** Idaho, NW USA 42°11´N 114°36´W
11 O16 **Rogers Pass** *pass* British Columbia, SW Canada
21 O8 **Rogersville** Tennessee, S USA 36°26´N 83°01´W
99 L16 **Roggel** Limburg, SE Netherlands 51°16´N 05°55´E
Roggeveen *see* Roggewein, Cabo
193 R10 **Roggeveen Basin** *undersea feature* E Pacific Ocean 31°30´S 95°30´W
191 X16 **Roggewein, Cabo** *var.* Roggeveen. *headland* Easter Island, Chile, E Pacific Ocean 27°07´S 109°15´W
103 Y13 **Rogliano** Corse, France, C Mediterranean Sea 42°58´N 09°25´E
107 N21 **Rogliano** Calabria, SW Italy 39°09´N 16°18´E
92 G12 **Rognan** Nordland, C Norway 67°04´N 15°21´E
100 K10 **Rögnitz** ⇝ N Germany
Rogozhina/Rogozhinë *see* Rrogozhinë
110 G10 **Rogoźno** Wielkopolskie, C Poland 52°46´N 16°58´E
32 E15 **Rogue River** ⇝ Oregon, NW USA
116 I6 **Rohatyn** *Rus.* Rogatin. Ivano-Frankivs'ka Oblast', W Ukraine 49°25´N 24°35´E
189 O14 **Rohi** Pohnpei, E Micronesia
Rohitsch-Sauerbrunn *see* Rogaška Slatina
149 Q13 **Rohri** Sind, SE Pakistan 27°39´N 68°57´E
152 I10 **Rohtak** Haryāna, N India 28°57´N 76°38´E
Roi Ed *see* Roi Et
167 R9 **Roi Et** *var.* Muang Roi Et, Roi Ed. Roi Et, E Thailand 16°05´N 103°38´E
191 U9 **Roi Georges, Îles du** *island group* Îles Tuamotu, C French Polynesia
153 Y10 **Roing** Arunāchal Pradesh, NE India 28°06´N 95°46´E
118 E7 **Roja** Talsi, NW Latvia 57°31´N 22°44´E
61 B20 **Rojas** Buenos Aires, E Argentina 34°10´S 60°45´W
149 R12 **Rojhān** Punjab, E Pakistan 28°39´N 70°00´E
41 Q12 **Rojo, Cabo** *headland* C Mexico 21°33´N 97°19´W
45 Q10 **Rojo, Cabo** *headland* W Puerto Rico 17°57´N 67°10´W
168 K10 **Rokan Kiri, Sungai** ⇝ Sumatera, W Indonesia
118 I11 **Rokiškis** Panevėžys, NE Lithuania 55°58´N 25°35´E
165 R7 **Rokkasho** Aomori, Honshū, C Japan 40°59´N 141°22´E
111 B17 **Rokycany** *Ger.* Rokytzan. Plzeňský Kraj, W Czech Republic 49°45´N 13°36´E
117 P6 **Rokytne** Kyyivs'ka Oblast', N Ukraine 49°40´N 30°29´E
116 L3 **Rokytne** Rivnens'ka Oblast', NW Ukraine 51°19´N 27°09´E
Rokytzan *see* Rokycany
158 L11 **Rola Co** ◎ W China
29 V13 **Roland** Iowa, C USA 42°10´N 93°30´W
95 D15 **Røldal** Hordaland, S Norway 59°52´N 06°49´E
98 O7 **Rolde** Drenthe, NE Netherlands 52°58´N 06°39´E
29 O2 **Rolette** North Dakota, N USA 48°39´N 99°50´W
27 V6 **Rolla** Missouri, C USA 37°56´N 91°47´W
29 O2 **Rolla** North Dakota, N USA 48°51´N 99°37´W
108 A10 **Rolle** Vaud, W Switzerland 46°27´N 06°19´E
181 X8 **Rolleston** Queensland, E Australia 24°30´S 148°36´E
185 H19 **Rolleston** Canterbury, South Island, New Zealand 43°34´S 172°24´E
185 G18 **Rolleston Range** ▲▲ South Island, New Zealand
14 H8 **Rollet** Québec, SE Canada 47°56´N 79°14´W
22 J4 **Rolling Fork** Mississippi, S USA 32°54´N 90°52´W
20 L6 **Rolling Fork** ⇝ Kentucky, S USA
14 J11 **Rolphton** Ontario, SE Canada 46°09´N 77°43´W
Röm *see* Rømø
181 X10 **Roma** Queensland, E Australia 26°37´S 148°54´E
107 I15 **Roma** *Eng.* Rome. ● (Italy) Lazio, C Italy 41°53´N 12°30´E
95 P19 **Roma** Gotland, SE Sweden 57°31´N 18°28´E
21 T14 **Romain, Cape** *headland* South Carolina, SE USA 33°00´N 79°21´W
13 P11 **Romaine** ⇝ Newfoundland and Labrador/Québec, E Canada
25 R17 **Roma Los Saenz** Texas, SW USA 26°24´N 99°01´W
114 H8 **Roman** Vratsa, NW Bulgaria 43°09´N 23°56´E
116 L10 **Roman** *Hung.* Románvásár. Neamţ, NE Romania 46°46´N 26°56´E
64 M13 **Romanche Fracture Zone** *tectonic feature* E Atlantic Ocean
61 C15 **Romang** Santa Fe, C Argentina 29°30´S 59°46´W
171 R15 **Romang, Pulau** *var.* Pulau Roma. *island* Kepulauan Damar, E Indonesia
171 R15 **Romang, Selat** *strait* Nusa Tenggara, S Indonesia
116 J11 **Romania** *Bul.* Rumŭniya, *Ger.* Rumänien, *Hung.* Románia, *Rom.* România, *SCr.* Rumunjska, *Ukr.* Rumuniya, *prev.* Republica Socialistă România, Roumania, Rumania, Socialist Republic of Romania, *prev.Rom.* Romînia. ◆ *republic* SE Europe
România, Republica Socialistă *see* Romania
Romania, Socialist Republic of *see* Romania
117 T7 **Romaniv** *Rus.* Dneprodzerzhinsk, *prev.* Dniprodzerzhyns'k, *prev.* Kamenskoye. Dnipropetrovs'ka Oblast', E Ukraine 48°30´N 34°35´E
23 W16 **Romano, Cape** *headland* Florida, SE USA 25°51´N 81°40´W
44 G5 **Romano, Cayo** *island* C Cuba
123 O13 **Romanovka** Respublika Buryatiya, S Russian Federation 53°10´N 112°34´E
127 N8 **Romanovka** Saratovskaya Oblast', W Russian Federation 51°45´N 42°45´E
108 I6 **Romanshorn** Thurgau, NE Switzerland 47°34´N 09°23´E
103 R12 **Romans-sur-Isère** Drôme, E France 45°03´N 05°03´E
189 U12 **Romanum** *island* Chuuk, C Micronesia
Románvásár *see* Roman
39 S5 **Romanzof Mountains** ▲▲ Alaska, USA
Roma, Pulau *see* Romang, Pulau
103 S4 **Rombas** Moselle, NE France 49°15´N 06°04´E
23 R2 **Rome** Georgia, SE USA 34°01´N 85°02´W
18 I9 **Rome** New York, NE USA 43°13´N 75°28´W
Rome *see* Roma
31 S9 **Romeo** Michigan, N USA 42°48´N 83°00´W
Römerstadt *see* Rýmařov
Rometan *see* Romiton
103 P5 **Romilly-sur-Seine** Aube, N France 48°31´N 03°44´E
Rominia *see* Romania
146 L11 **Romiton** *Rus.* Rometan. Buxoro Viloyati, C Uzbekistan 39°56´N 64°21´E
21 U3 **Romney** West Virginia, NE USA 39°21´N 78°44´W
117 S4 **Romny** Sums'ka Oblast', NE Ukraine 50°45´N 33°30´E
95 E24 **Rømø** *Ger.* Röm. *island* SW Denmark
117 S5 **Romodan** Poltavs'ka Oblast', NE Ukraine 50°00´N 33°20´E
127 P5 **Romodanovo** Respublika Mordoviya, W Russian Federation 54°25´N 45°24´E
Romorantin *see* Romorantin-Lanthenay
103 N8 **Romorantin-Lanthenay** *var.* Romorantin. Loir-et-Cher, C France 47°22´N 01°44´E
94 F9 **Romsdal** *physical region* S Norway
94 F10 **Romsdalen** *valley* S Norway
94 E9 **Romsdalsfjorden** *fjord* S Norway
33 P8 **Ronan** Montana, NW USA 47°31´N 114°06´W
59 M14 **Roncador** Maranhão, E Brazil 05°48´S 45°08´W
186 M7 **Roncador Reef** *reef* N Solomon Islands
59 J17 **Roncador, Serra do** ▲▲ C Brazil
21 S6 **Ronceverte** West Virginia, NE USA 37°45´N 80°27´W
107 H14 **Ronciglione** Lazio, C Italy 42°16´N 12°15´E
104 L15 **Ronda** Andalucía, S Spain 36°45´N 05°10´W
94 G11 **Rondane** ▲▲ S Norway
104 L15 **Ronda, Serranía de** ▲▲ S Spain
95 H22 **Rønde** Århus, C Denmark 56°18´N 10°28´E
Ronde, Île *see* Round Island
Röndik *see* Rongrik Atoll
59 E16 **Rondônia** *off.* Estado de Rondônia; *prev.* Território de Rondônia. ◈ *state* W Brazil
Rondônia, Estado de *see* Rondônia
Rondônia, Território de *see* Rondônia
59 I18 **Rondonópolis** Mato Grosso, W Brazil 16°29´S 54°37´W
94 G11 **Rondslottet** ▲ S Norway 61°54´N 09°48´E
95 P20 **Ronehamn** Gotland, SE Sweden 57°10´N 18°30´E
160 L13 **Rong'an** *var.* Chang'an, Rongan. Guangxi Zhuangzu Zizhiqu, S China 25°14´N 109°20´E
Rongan *see* Rong'an
Rongcheng *see* Rongxian, Guangxi, China
Rongcheng *see* Jianli, Hubei, China
189 R4 **Rongelap Atoll** *var.* Rōnļap. *atoll* Ralik Chain, NW Marshall Islands
Rongerik *see* Rongrik Atoll
160 K12 **Rongjiang** *var.* Guzhou. Guizhou, S China 25°59´N 108°27´E
160 L13 **Rong Jiang** ⇝ S China
Rongjiang *see* Nankang
Rong, Kas *see* Rŭng, Kaôh
167 P8 **Rong Kwang** Phrae, NW Thailand 18°19´N 100°18´E
189 T4 **Rongrik Atoll** *var.* Rōndik, Rongerik. *atoll* Ralik Chain, N Marshall Islands
189 X2 **Rongrong** *island* SE Marshall Islands
160 L13 **Rongshui** *var.* Rongshui Miaozu Zizhixian. Guangxi Zhuangzu Zizhiqu, S China 25°05´N 109°09´E
Rongshui Miaozu Zizhixian *see* Rongshui
118 I6 **Rõngu** *Ger.* Ringen. Tartumaa, SE Estonia 58°10´N 26°17´E
Rongwo *see* Tongren
160 L15 **Rongxian** *var.* Rongzhou; *prev.* Rongcheng. Guangxi Zhuangzu Zizhiqu, S China 22°52´N 110°33´E
Rongzhag *see* Danba
Rongzhou *see* Rongxian
Roniu *see* Ronui, Mont
189 N13 **Ronkiti** Pohnpei, E Micronesia 06°48´N 158°10´E
Rōnļap *see* Rongelap Atoll
95 L24 **Rønne** Bornholm, E Denmark 55°07´N 14°43´E
95 M22 **Ronneby** Blekinge, S Sweden 56°12´N 15°18´E
194 J7 **Ronne Entrance** *inlet* Antarctica
194 L6 **Ronne Ice Shelf** *ice shelf* Antarctica
99 E19 **Ronse** *Fr.* Renaix. Oost-Vlaanderen, SW Belgium 50°45´N 03°36´E
191 R8 **Ronui, Mont** *var.* Roniu. ⊼ Tahiti, W French Polynesia 17°49´S 149°12´W
30 K14 **Roodhouse** Illinois, N USA 39°28´N 90°22´W
83 C19 **Rooibank** Erongo, W Namibia 23°04´S 14°34´E
Rooke Island *see* Umboi Island
65 N24 **Rookery Point** *headland* NE Tristan da Cunha 37°03´S 12°15´W
171 V13 **Roon, Pulau** *island* E Indonesia
173 V7 **Roo Rise** *undersea feature* E Indian Ocean
152 J9 **Roorkee** Uttarakhand, N India 29°51´N 77°54´E
99 H15 **Roosendaal** Noord-Brabant, S Netherlands 51°32´N 04°29´E
25 P10 **Roosevelt** Texas, SW USA 30°28´N 100°06´W
37 N3 **Roosevelt** Utah, W USA 40°18´N 109°59´W
47 T8 **Roosevelt** ⇝ W Brazil
195 O13 **Roosevelt Island** *island* Antarctica
10 L10 **Roosevelt, Mount** ▲ British Columbia, W Canada 58°28´N 125°22´W
11 P17 **Roosville** British Columbia, SW Canada 48°59´N 115°03´W
29 X10 **Root River** ⇝ Minnesota, N USA
Ropar *see* Rūpnagar
111 N16 **Ropczyce** Podkarpackie, SE Poland 50°04´N 21°31´E
181 Q3 **Roper Bar** Northern Territory, N Australia 14°45´S 134°30´E
24 M5 **Ropesville** Texas, SW USA 33°24´N 102°09´W
102 K14 **Roquefort** Landes, SW France 44°01´N 00°18´W
61 C21 **Roque Pérez** Buenos Aires, E Argentina 35°25´S 59°24´W
58 E10 **Roraima** *off.* Estado de Roraima; *prev.* Território de Rio Branco, Território de Roraima. ◈ *state* N Brazil
Roraima, Estado de *see* Roraima
58 F9 **Roraima, Mount** ▲ N South America 05°10´N 60°36´W
Roraima, Território de *see* Roraima
94 I9 **Røros** Sør-Trøndelag, S Norway 62°37´N 11°25´E
108 I7 **Rorschach** Sankt Gallen, NE Switzerland 47°28´N 09°30´E
93 E14 **Rørvik** Nord-Trøndelag, C Norway 64°54´N 11°15´E
119 G17 **Ros'** *Rus.* Ross'. Hrodzyenskaya Voblasts', W Belarus 53°25´N 24°24´E
185 F17 **Ross** West Coast, South Island, New Zealand 42°54´S 170°52´E
119 G17 **Ros'** *Rus.* Ross'. ⇝ W Belarus
10 J7 **Ross** ⇝ Yukon Territory, W Canada
117 O6 **Ros'** ⇝ N Ukraine
44 K7 **Rosa, Lake** ◎ Great Inagua, S Bahamas
32 M9 **Rosalia** Washington, NW USA 47°14´N 117°22´W
191 W15 **Rosalia, Punta** *headland* Easter Island, Chile, E Pacific Ocean 27°04´S 109°19´W
45 P12 **Rosalie** E Dominica 15°22´N 61°15´W

◆ Country ● Country Capital ◇ Dependent Territory ○ Dependent Territory Capital ◈ Administrative Regions ✈ International Airport ▲ Mountain ▲▲ Mountain Range ⊼ Volcano ⇝ River ◎ Lake ⊠ Reservoir

313

ROSAMOND – RYBNITSA

35 T14 Rosamond California, W USA 34°51′N 118°09′W
35 S14 Rosamond Lake salt flat California, W USA
96 H8 Ross and Cromarty cultural region N Scotland, United Kingdom
61 B18 Rosario Santa Fe, C Argentina 32°56′S 60°39′W
40 J11 Rosario Sinaloa, C Mexico 23°00′N 105°51′W
40 G6 Rosario Sonora, NW Mexico 27°53′N 109°18′W
62 O6 Rosario San Pedro, C Paraguay 24°26′S 57°06′W
61 E20 Rosario Colonia, SW Uruguay 34°20′S 57°26′W
54 H5 Rosario Zulia, NW Venezuela 10°18′N 72°19′W
Rosario see Nishino-shima
Rosario see Rosarito
40 B4 Rosario, Bahía del bay NW Mexico
62 K6 Rosario de la Frontera Salta, N Argentina 25°50′S 65°00′W
61 C18 Rosario del Tala Entre Ríos, E Argentina 32°20′S 59°10′W
61 F16 Rosário do Sul Rio Grande do Sul, S Brazil 30°15′S 54°55′W
59 H18 Rosário Oeste Mato Grosso, W Brazil 14°50′S 56°25′W
40 B1 Rosarito var. Rosario. Baja California Norte, NW Mexico 32°25′N 117°04′W
40 D5 Rosarito Baja California Norte, NW Mexico 28°27′N 113°58′W
40 F7 Rosarito Baja California Sur, NW Mexico 26°28′N 111°41′W
104 L9 Rosarito, Embalse del ⊠ W Spain
107 N22 Rosarno Calabria, SW Italy 38°29′N 15°59′E
56 B5 Rosa Zárate var. Quinindé. Esmeraldas, SW Ecuador 0°14′N 79°28′W
Roscianum see Rossano
29 O8 Roscoe South Dakota, N USA 45°24′N 99°19′W
25 P7 Roscoe Texas, SW USA 32°27′N 100°32′W
102 F5 Roscoff Finistère, NW France 48°43′N 04°00′W
Ros Comáin see Roscommon
97 C17 Roscommon Ir. Ros Comáin. C Ireland 53°38′N 08°11′W
31 Q7 Roscommon Michigan, N USA 44°30′N 84°35′W
97 C17 Roscommon Ir. Ros Comáin. cultural region C Ireland
Ros. Cré see Roscrea
97 D19 Roscrea Ir. Ros. Cré. C Ireland 52°57′N 07°47′W
14 H13 Rosseau Ontario, S Canada 45°15′N 79°38′W
45 X12 Roseau prev. Charlotte Town. ● (Dominica) SW Dominica 15°17′N 61°23′W
29 S2 Roseau Minnesota, N USA 48°51′N 95°45′W
173 Y16 Rose Belle SE Mauritius 20°24′S 57°36′E
183 O16 Rosebery Tasmania, SE Australia 41°51′S 145°33′E
21 U11 Roseboro North Carolina, SE USA 34°58′N 78°31′W
25 T9 Rosebud Texas, SW USA 31°04′N 96°58′W
33 W10 Rosebud Creek ≈ Montana, NW USA
32 F14 Roseburg Oregon, NW USA 43°13′N 123°21′W
22 J3 Rosedale Mississippi, S USA 33°51′N 91°01′W
99 H21 Rosée Namur, S Belgium 50°15′N 04°43′E
55 U8 Rose Hall E Guyana 06°14′N 57°30′W
173 X16 Rose Hill W Mauritius 20°14′S 57°29′E
80 H12 Roseires, Reservoir var. Lake Rusayris. ⊠ E Sudan
Rosenau see Rožnov pod Radhoštěm
Rosenau see Rožňava
25 V11 Rosenberg Texas, SW USA 29°33′N 95°48′W
Rosenberg see Olesno, Poland
Rosenberg see Ružomberok, Slovakia
100 I10 Rosengarten Niedersachsen, N Germany 53°24′N 09°54′E
101 M24 Rosenheim Bayern, S Germany 47°51′N 12°08′E
Rosenhof see Zilupe
105 X4 Roses Cataluña, NE Spain 42°15′N 03°11′E
105 X4 Roses, Golf de gulf NE Spain
107 K14 Roseto degli Abruzzi Abruzzo, C Italy 42°39′N 14°01′E
11 S16 Rosetown Saskatchewan, S Canada 51°34′N 107°59′W
Rosetta see Rashīd
35 O7 Roseville California, W USA 38°44′N 121°16′W
30 J12 Roseville Illinois, N USA 40°42′N 90°40′W
29 V8 Roseville Minnesota, N USA 45°00′N 93°09′W
29 R7 Rosholt South Dakota, N USA 45°51′N 96°42′W
106 F12 Rosignano Marittimo Toscana, C Italy 43°24′N 10°28′E
116 I14 Roșiori de Vede Teleorman, S Romania 44°06′N 25°00′E
114 K8 Rositsa ≈ N Bulgaria
Rositten see Rēzekne
95 J23 Roskilde Roskilde, E Denmark 55°39′N 12°07′E
95 I23 Roskilde off. Roskilde Amt. ◐ county E Denmark
Roskilde Amt see Roskilde
Ros Láir see Rosslare
126 H5 Roslavl' Smolenskaya Oblast', W Russian Federation 54°N 32°57′E
124 J3 Roslyakovo Murmanskaya Oblast', NW Russian Federation 69°03′N 33°12′E
32 I8 Roslyn Washington, NW USA 47°13′N 120°52′W
99 K14 Rosmalen Noord-Brabant, S Netherlands 51°43′N 05°21′E
Ros Mhic Thriúin see New Ross
113 P19 Rosoman C FYR Macedonia 41°31′N 21°55′E
102 F6 Rosporden Finistère, NW France 47°58′N 03°54′W
Ross' see Ros'
107 O20 Rossano anc. Roscianum. Calabria, SW Italy 39°35′N 16°38′E
22 L5 Ross Barnett Reservoir ⊠ Mississippi, S USA
11 W16 Rossburn Manitoba, S Canada 50°42′N 100°49′W
14 H13 Rosseau, Lake ◎ Ontario, S Canada
186 I10 Rossel Island prev. Yela Island. island SE Papua New Guinea
195 P12 Ross Ice Shelf ice shelf Antarctica
13 P16 Rossignol, Lake ◎ Nova Scotia, SE Canada
83 C19 Rössing Erongo, W Namibia 22°31′S 14°52′E
195 Q14 Ross Island island Antarctica
Rossitten see Rybachiy
Rossiyskaya Federatsiya see Russian Federation
11 N17 Rossland British Columbia, SW Canada 49°03′N 117°49′W
97 F20 Rosslare Ir. Ros Láir. Wexford, SE Ireland 52°16′N 06°23′W
97 F20 Rosslare Harbour Wexford, SE Ireland 52°15′N 06°20′W
101 M14 Rosslau Sachsen-Anhalt, E Germany 51°52′N 12°15′E
76 G10 Rosso Trarza, SW Mauritania 16°36′N 15°50′W
103 X14 Rosso, Cap headland Corse, France, C Mediterranean Sea 42°25′N 08°22′E
93 H16 Rossön Jämtland, C Sweden 63°54′N 16°21′E
97 K21 Ross-on-Wye W England, United Kingdom 51°55′N 02°34′W
Rossony see Rasony
126 L9 Rossosh' Voronezhskaya Oblast', W Russian Federation 50°10′N 39°34′E
181 Q7 Ross River Northern Territory, N Australia 23°36′S 134°30′E
10 J7 Ross River Yukon Territory, W Canada 61°57′N 132°26′W
195 O15 Ross Sea sea Antarctica
92 G13 Røssvatnet Lapp. Reevhtse. ◎ C Norway
23 R1 Rossville Georgia, SE USA 34°59′N 85°22′W
Rostak see Ar Rustāq
143 P14 Rostāq Hormozgān, S Iran 26°48′N 53°50′E
117 N5 Rostavytsya ≈ N Ukraine
11 T15 Rosthern Saskatchewan, S Canada 52°40′N 106°20′W
100 M8 Rostock Mecklenburg-Vorpommern, NE Germany 54°05′N 12°08′E
124 L16 Rostov Yaroslavskaya Oblast', W Russian Federation 57°11′N 39°19′E
Rostov see Rostov-na-Donu
126 L12 Rostov-na-Donu var. Rostov, Eng. Rostov-on-Don. Rostovskaya Oblast', SW Russian Federation 47°16′N 39°45′E
Rostov-on-Don see Rostov-na-Donu
126 L10 Rostovskaya Oblast' ◐ province SW Russian Federation
93 J14 Rosvik Norrbotten, N Sweden 65°26′N 21°48′E
23 S3 Roswell Georgia, SE USA 34°01′N 84°21′W
37 U14 Roswell New Mexico, SW USA 33°23′N 104°31′W
94 K12 Rot Dalarna, C Sweden 61°16′N 14°04′E
101 I23 Rot ≈ S Germany
104 J15 Rota Andalucía, S Spain 36°39′N 06°20′W
188 K9 Rota island S Northern Mariana Islands
25 P6 Rotan Texas, SW USA 32°51′N 100°28′W
Rotcher Island see Tamana
100 I11 Rotenburg Niedersachsen, NW Germany 53°06′N 09°25′E
Rotenburg see Rotenburg an der Fulda
101 I16 Rotenburg an der Fulda var. Rotenburg. Thüringen, C Germany 51°00′N 09°43′E
101 L18 Roter Main ≈ E Germany
101 K20 Roth Bayern, SE Germany 49°15′N 11°06′E
101 G16 Rothaargebirge ▲▲ W Germany
Rothenburg see Rothenburg ob der Tauber
101 J20 Rothenburg ob der Tauber var. Rothenburg. Bayern, S Germany 49°23′N 10°10′E
194 H6 Rothera UK research station Antarctica 67°28′S 68°31′W
185 I17 Rotherham Canterbury, South Island, New Zealand 42°42′S 172°56′E
97 M17 Rotherham N England, United Kingdom 53°26′N 01°20′W
96 H12 Rothesay W Scotland, United Kingdom 55°49′N 05°03′W
108 E7 Rothrist Aargau, N Switzerland 47°18′N 07°54′E
194 H6 Rothschild Island island Antarctica
171 P17 Roti, Pulau island S Indonesia
183 O8 Roto New South Wales, SE Australia 33°04′S 145°27′E
184 N8 Rotoiti, Lake ◎ North Island, New Zealand
Rotomagus see Rouen
107 N19 Rotondella Basilicata, S Italy 40°12′N 16°30′E
103 X15 Rotondo, Monte ▲ Corse, France, C Mediterranean Sea 42°15′N 09°03′E
185 I15 Rotoroa, Lake ◎ South Island, New Zealand
184 N8 Rotorua Bay of Plenty, North Island, New Zealand 38°10′S 176°14′E
184 N8 Rotorua, Lake ◎ North Island, New Zealand
101 N22 Rott ≈ SE Germany
108 F10 Rotten ≈ S Switzerland
109 T6 Rottenmann Steiermark, E Austria 47°31′N 14°18′E
98 H12 Rotterdam Zuid-Holland, SW Netherlands 51°55′N 04°30′E
18 K10 Rotterdam New York, NE USA 42°46′N 73°57′W
95 M21 Rottnen ◎ S Sweden
98 N4 Rottumeroog island Waddeneilanden, NE Netherlands
98 N4 Rottumerplaat island Waddeneilanden, NE Netherlands
101 G23 Rottweil Baden-Württemberg, S Germany 48°10′N 08°38′E
191 O7 Rotui, Mont ⩘ Moorea, W French Polynesia 17°30′S 149°50′W
103 P1 Roubaix Nord, N France 50°42′N 03°10′E
111 C15 Roudnice nad Labem Ger. Raudnitz an der Elbe. Ústecký Kraj, NW Czech Republic 50°25′N 14°14′E
102 M4 Rouen anc. Rotomagus. Seine-Maritime, N France 49°26′N 01°05′E
171 X13 Rouffaer Reserves reserve Papua, E Indonesia
15 N10 Rouge, Rivière ≈ Québec, SE Canada
20 J6 Rough River ≈ Kentucky, S USA
20 J6 Rough River Lake ⊠ Kentucky, S USA
Rouhaïbé see Ar Ruḩaybah
102 K11 Rouillac Charente, W France 45°46′N 00°04′W
Roulers see Roeselare
Roumania see Romania
173 Y15 Round Island var. Île Ronde. island NE Mauritius
14 J12 Round Lake ◎ Ontario, SE Canada
35 U7 Round Mountain Nevada, W USA 38°42′N 117°04′W
25 R10 Round Mountain Texas, SW USA 30°25′N 98°20′W
183 U5 Round Mountain ▲ New South Wales, SE Australia 30°22′S 152°13′E
25 S10 Round Rock Texas, SW USA 30°30′N 97°40′W
33 U10 Roundup Montana, NW USA 46°27′N 108°32′W
55 Y10 Roura NE French Guiana 04°44′N 52°16′W
Rourkela see Răulakela
96 J4 Rousay island N Scotland, United Kingdom
Rousselaere see Roeselare
103 O17 Roussillon cultural region S France
15 V7 Routhierville Québec, SE Canada 48°09′N 67°07′W
99 K25 Rouvroy Luxembourg, SE Belgium 49°33′N 05°28′E
14 I7 Rouyn-Noranda Québec, SE Canada 48°16′N 79°03′W
Rouyuan see Huachi
Rouyuanchengzi see Huachi
92 L12 Rovaniemi Lappi, N Finland 66°29′N 25°40′E
106 E7 Rovato Lombardia, N Italy 45°34′N 10°03′E
125 N11 Rovdino Arkhangel'skaya Oblast', NW Russian Federation 61°36′N 42°28′E
Roven'ki see Roven'ky
117 Y8 Roven'ky var. Roven'ki. Luhans'ka Oblast', E Ukraine 48°05′N 39°20′E
Rovenskaya Oblast' see Rivnens'ka Oblast'
Rovenskaya Sloboda see Rovyenskaya Slabada
106 G7 Rovereto Ger. Rofreit. Trentino-Alto Adige, N Italy 45°53′N 11°03′E
167 S12 Rôviĕng Tbong Preăh Vihéar, N Cambodia 13°18′N 105°06′E
Rovigno see Rovinj
106 H8 Rovigo Veneto, NE Italy 45°04′N 11°48′E
112 A10 Rovinj It. Rovigno. Istra, NW Croatia 45°06′N 13°39′E
54 E10 Rovira Tolima, C Colombia 04°15′N 75°15′W
Rovno see Rivne
127 P9 Rovnoye Saratovskaya Oblast', W Russian Federation 50°43′N 46°03′E
82 Q12 Rovuma, Rio var. Ruvuma. ≈ Mozambique/Tanzania see also Ruvuma
Rovuma, Rio see Ruvuma
119 O19 Rovyenskaya Slabada Rus. Rovenskaya Sloboda. Homyel'skaya Voblasts', SE Belarus 52°13′N 30°19′E
183 R5 Rowena New South Wales, SE Australia 29°51′S 148°55′E
21 T11 Rowland North Carolina, SE USA 34°32′N 79°17′W
9 P5 Rowley ≈ Baffin Island, Nunavut, NE Canada
9 P6 Rowley Island island Nunavut, NE Canada
173 W8 Rowley Shoals reef NW Australia
Równe see Rivne
171 O4 Roxas Mindoro, N Philippines 12°36′N 121°29′E
171 P5 Roxas City Panay Island, C Philippines 11°33′N 122°43′E
21 U8 Roxboro North Carolina, SE USA 36°24′N 79°00′W
185 D23 Roxburgh Otago, South Island, New Zealand 45°32′S 169°18′E
96 K13 Roxburgh cultural region SE Scotland, United Kingdom
182 H5 Roxby Downs South Australia 30°29′S 136°56′E
95 M17 Roxen ◎ S Sweden
25 V5 Roxton Texas, SW USA 33°33′N 95°43′W
15 P12 Roxton-Sud Québec, SE Canada 45°30′N 72°35′W
33 U8 Roy Montana, NW USA 47°19′N 108°55′W
37 U10 Roy New Mexico, SW USA 35°56′N 104°12′W
97 E17 Royal Canal Ir. An Chanáil Ríoga. canal C Ireland
30 L1 Royale, Isle island Michigan, N USA
37 S6 Royal Gorge valley Colorado, C USA
97 M20 Royal Leamington Spa var. Leamington, Leamington Spa. C England, United Kingdom 52°18′N 01°31′W
97 O23 Royal Tunbridge Wells var. Tunbridge Wells. SE England, United Kingdom 51°08′N 00°16′E
24 L9 Royalty Texas, SW USA 31°21′N 102°51′W
102 J11 Royan Charente-Maritime, W France 45°37′N 01°01′W
65 B24 Roy Cove Settlement West Falkland, Falkland Islands 51°32′S 60°23′W
103 O3 Roye Somme, N France 49°42′N 02°46′E
95 H15 Røyken Buskerud, S Norway 59°47′N 10°21′E
93 F14 Røyrvik Nord-Trøndelag, C Norway 64°53′N 13°30′E
25 U6 Royse City Texas, SW USA 32°58′N 96°19′W
97 O21 Royston E England, United Kingdom 52°05′N 00°01′W
23 U2 Royston Georgia, SE USA 34°17′N 83°06′W
114 L10 Roza prev. Gyulovo. Yambol, E Bulgaria 42°29′N 26°30′E
113 L16 Rožaje E Montenegro 42°51′N 20°11′E
110 M10 Różan Mazowieckie, C Poland 52°36′N 21°27′E
117 O10 Rozdil'na Odes'ka Oblast', SW Ukraine 46°51′N 30°03′E
117 S12 Rozdol'ne Rus. Razdolnoye. Respublika Krym, S Ukraine 45°45′N 33°27′E
145 Q9 Rozhdestvenka Akmola, C Kazakhstan 50°51′N 71°25′E
116 I6 Rozhnyativ Ivano-Frankivs'ka Oblast', W Ukraine 48°58′N 24°07′E
116 J3 Rozhyshche Volyns'ka Oblast', NW Ukraine 50°54′N 25°16′E
Roznau am Radhost see Rožnov pod Radhoštěm
111 L19 Rožňava Ger. Rosenau, Hung. Rozsnyó. Košický Kraj, E Slovakia 48°41′N 20°32′E
116 K10 Roznov Neamț, NE Romania 46°47′N 26°33′E
111 I18 Rožnov pod Radhoštěm Ger. Rosenau, Roznau am Radhost. Zlínský Kraj, E Czech Republic 49°28′N 18°09′E
Rózsahegy see Ružomberok
Rozsnyó see Râșnov, Romania
Rozsnyó see Rožňava, Slovakia
113 K18 Rranxë Shkodër, NW Albania 41°58′N 19°27′E
113 L18 Rrëshen var. Rresheni, Rrshen. Lezhë, C Albania 41°46′N 19°54′E
Rresheni see Rrëshen
Rrogozhina see Rrogozhinë
113 K20 Rrogozhinë var. Rogozhina, Rogozhinë, Rrogozhina. Tiranë, W Albania 41°04′N 19°40′E
Rrshen see Rrëshen
112 O13 Rtanj ▲ E Serbia 43°45′N 21°54′E
127 O7 Rtishchevo Saratovskaya Oblast', W Russian Federation 52°16′N 43°46′E
184 N12 Ruahine Range var. Ruarine. ▲▲ North Island, New Zealand
185 L14 Ruamahanga ≈ North Island, New Zealand
Ruanda see Rwanda
184 M10 Ruapehu, Mount ⩘ North Island, New Zealand 39°15′S 175°33′E
185 C25 Ruapuke Island island SW New Zealand
Ruarine see Ruahine Range
184 O9 Ruatahuna Bay of Plenty, North Island, New Zealand 38°38′S 176°56′E
184 Q8 Ruatoria Gisborne, North Island, New Zealand 37°54′S 178°18′E
184 K4 Ruawai Northland, North Island, New Zealand 36°08′S 174°04′E
15 N8 Ruban ≈ Québec, SE Canada
81 I22 Rubeho Mountains ▲▲ C Tanzania
165 U3 Rubeshibe Hokkaidō, NE Japan 43°49′N 143°37′E
Rubezhnoye see Rubizhne
113 L18 Rubik Lezhë, C Albania 41°46′N 19°48′E
54 H7 Rubio Táchira, W Venezuela 07°42′N 72°23′W
117 X6 Rubizhne Rus. Rubezhnoye. Luhans'ka Oblast', E Ukraine 49°01′N 38°22′E
81 F20 Rubondo Island island N Tanzania
122 I13 Rubtsovsk Altayskiy Kray, S Russian Federation 51°34′N 81°11′E
39 P9 Ruby Alaska, USA 64°44′N 155°29′W
35 W3 Ruby Dome ▲ Nevada, W USA 40°35′N 115°25′W
35 W4 Ruby Lake ◎ Nevada, W USA
35 W4 Ruby Mountains ▲▲ Nevada, W USA
33 Q12 Ruby Range ▲▲ Montana, NW USA
118 C10 Rucava Liepāja, SW Latvia 56°09′N 21°10′E
143 S13 Rūdān var. Dehbārez. Hormozgān, S Iran 27°30′N 57°10′E
Rudelstadt see Ciechanowiec
Rudensk see Rudzyensk
119 G14 Rūdiškės Vilnius, S Lithuania 54°31′N 24°49′E
95 H24 Rudkøbing Fyn, C Denmark 54°57′N 10°43′E
125 S13 Rudnichnyy Kirovskaya Oblast', NW Russian Federation 59°37′N 52°28′E
Rūdnichnyy see Koksu
Rudny see Rudnyy
126 H4 Rudnya Smolenskaya Oblast', W Russian Federation 54°55′N 31°10′E
127 O8 Rudnya Volgogradskaya Oblast', SW Russian Federation 50°54′N 44°27′E
144 M7 Rudnyy var. Rudny. Kostanay, N Kazakhstan 53°N 63°05′E
122 K3 Rudol'fa, Ostrov island Zemlya Frantsa-Iosifa, NW Russian Federation
Rudolf, Lake see Turkana, Lake
Rudolfswert see Novo mesto
101 L17 Rudolstadt Thüringen, C Germany 50°44′N 11°20′E
152 K9 Rudraprayāg Uttarakhand, N India 28°51′N 79°01′E
152 K10 Rudrapur var. Rampura. Uttarakhand, N India 28°58′N 79°23′E
31 Q4 Rudyard Michigan, N USA 46°15′N 84°36′W
33 S7 Rudyard Montana, NW USA 48°33′N 110°37′W
119 K16 Rudzyensk Rus. Rudensk. Minskaya Voblasts', C Belarus 53°36′N 27°52′E
104 L6 Rueda Castilla-León, N Spain 41°24′N 04°58′W
114 F10 Ruen ▲ Bulgaria/FYR Macedonia 42°10′N 22°31′E
80 G10 Rufa'a Gezira, C Sudan 14°49′N 33°21′E
102 L10 Ruffec Charente, W France 46°01′N 00°10′E
21 R14 Ruffin South Carolina, SE USA 33°00′N 80°48′W
81 J23 Rufiji ≈ E Tanzania
61 A20 Rufino Santa Fe, C Argentina 34°16′S 62°45′W
76 F11 Rufisque W Senegal 14°44′N 17°18′W
83 K14 Rufunsa Lusaka, C Zambia 15°02′S 29°35′E
118 J9 Rugāji Balvi, E Latvia 57°01′N 27°07′E
161 R7 Rugao Jiangsu, E China 32°27′N 120°35′E
97 M20 Rugby C England, United Kingdom 52°22′N 01°18′W
29 N3 Rugby North Dakota, N USA 48°24′N 100°00′W
100 N7 Rügen headland NE Germany 54°25′N 13°21′E
Ruhaybeh see Ar Ruḩaybah
81 E19 Ruhengeri NW Rwanda 01°39′S 29°16′E
Ruhja see Rūjiena
100 M10 Ruhner Berg hill N Germany
118 F7 Ruhnu var. Ruhnu Saar, Swe. Runö. island SW Estonia
Ruhnu Saar see Ruhnu
101 G15 Ruhr ≈ W Germany
91 W6 Ruhr Valley industrial region W Germany
161 S11 Rui'an var. Rui an. Zhejiang, SE China 27°51′N 120°39′E
Rui an see Rui'an
161 P10 Ruichang Jiangxi, S China 29°46′N 115°37′E
24 J11 Ruidosa Texas, SW USA 30°00′N 104°40′W
37 S14 Ruidoso New Mexico, SW USA 33°19′N 105°40′W
161 P12 Ruijin Jiangxi, S China 25°52′N 116°01′E
160 D13 Ruili Yunnan, SW China 24°04′N 97°49′E
98 N8 Ruinen Drenthe, NE Netherlands 52°46′N 06°19′E
99 D17 Ruiselede West-Vlaanderen, W Belgium 51°03′N 03°21′E
64 P5 Ruivo de Santana, Pico ▲ Madeira, Portugal, NE Atlantic Ocean 32°46′N 16°57′W
40 J12 Ruiz Nayarit, SW Mexico 22°00′N 105°09′W
54 E10 Ruiz, Nevado del ⩘ W Colombia 04°53′N 75°22′W
138 J9 Rujaylah, Ḩarrat ar salt lake N Jordan
Rujen see Rūjiena
118 H7 Rūjiena Est. Ruhja, Ger. Rujen. Valmiera, N Latvia 57°54′N 25°22′E
79 I18 Ruki ≈ W Dem. Rep. Congo
81 E22 Rukwa ◐ region SW Tanzania
81 F23 Rukwa, Lake ◎ SE Tanzania
25 P6 Rule Texas, SW USA 33°10′N 99°53′W
22 K3 Ruleville Mississippi, S USA 33°43′N 90°33′W
Rum see Rhum
112 K10 Ruma Vojvodina, N Serbia 45°02′N 19°51′E
Rumadiya see Ar Ramādī
141 Q7 Rumāḩ Ar Riyāḑ, C Saudi Arabia 25°35′N 47°09′E
Rumaitha see Ar Rumaythah
Rumania/Rumänien see Romania
Rumänisch-Sankt-Georgen see Sângeorz-Băi
139 Y13 Rumaylah Al Başrah, SE Iraq 30°16′N 47°22′E
139 P2 Rumaylah, Wādī dry watercourse NE Syria
171 U13 Rumbati Papua, E Indonesia 02°44′S 132°04′E
81 E14 Rumbek El Buhayrat, S Sudan 06°50′N 29°42′E
Rumburg see Rumburk
111 D14 Rumburk Ger. Rumburg. Ústecký Kraj, NW Czech Republic 50°58′N 14°35′E
44 J4 Rum Cay island C Bahamas
99 M26 Rumelange Luxembourg, S Luxembourg 49°28′N 06°02′E
99 D20 Rumes Hainaut, SW Belgium 50°33′N 03°19′E
19 P7 Rumford Maine, NE USA 44°31′N 70°31′W
110 I6 Rumia Pomorskie, N Poland 54°36′N 18°21′E
113 J17 Rumija ▲▲ S Montenegro
103 T11 Rumilly Haute-Savoie, E France 45°52′N 05°57′E
139 O6 Rūmīyah Al Anbār, W Iraq 34°28′N 41°17′E
Rummah, Wādī ar see Rimah, Wādī ar
Rummelsburg in Pommern see Miastko
165 S3 Rumoi Hokkaidō, NE Japan 43°57′N 141°40′E
82 M12 Rumphi var. Rumpi. Northern, N Malawi 11°00′S 33°51′E
Rumpi see Rumphi
29 V7 Rum River ≈ Minnesota, N USA
188 F16 Rumung island Caroline Islands, W Micronesia
Rumuniya/Rumŭniya/Rumunjska see Romania
185 G16 Runanga West Coast, South Island, New Zealand 42°25′S 171°15′E
184 P7 Runaway, Cape headland North Island, New Zealand 37°33′S 177°59′E
97 K18 Runcorn C England, United Kingdom 53°20′N 02°44′W
118 K10 Rundāni var. Rundāni. Ludza, E Latvia 56°19′N 27°51′E
Rundāni see Rundāni
83 L18 Runde var. Lundi. ≈ SE Zimbabwe
83 E16 Rundu var. Runtu. Okavango, NE Namibia 17°55′S 19°45′E
93 I16 Rundvik Västerbotten, N Sweden 63°31′N 19°22′E
81 G20 Runere Mwanza, N Tanzania 03°06′S 33°18′E
25 S13 Runge Texas, SW USA 28°52′N 97°42′W
167 Q13 Rŭng, Kaôh prev. Kas Rong. island SW Cambodia
79 O16 Rungu Orientale, NE Dem. Rep. Congo 03°11′N 27°52′E
81 F23 Rungwa Rukwa, W Tanzania 07°18′S 31°40′E
81 G22 Rungwa Singida, C Tanzania 06°54′S 33°33′E
94 M14 Runn ◎ C Sweden
24 M4 Running Water Draw valley New Mexico/Texas, SW USA
Runö see Ruhnu
Runtu see Rundu
189 V12 Ruo island Caroline Islands, C Micronesia
158 L9 Ruoqiang var. Jo-ch'iang, Uigh. Charkhlik, Charkhliq, Qarkilik. Xinjiang Uygur Zizhiqu, NW China 38°59′N 88°08′E
159 S7 Ruo Shui ≈ N China
92 L8 Ruostekfielbmá var. Rustefjelbma Finnmark. Finnmark, N Norway 70°25′N 28°10′E
93 L18 Ruovesi Länsi-Suomi, W Finland 61°59′N 24°05′E
112 B9 Rupa Primorje-Gorski Kotar, NW Croatia 45°29′N 14°15′E
182 M11 Rupanyup Victoria, SE Australia 36°38′S 142°37′E
168 K9 Rupat, Pulau prev. Roepat. island W Indonesia
168 K10 Rupat, Selat strait Sumatera, W Indonesia
116 J11 Rupea Ger. Reps, Hung. Kőhalom; prev. Cohalm. Brașov, C Romania 46°02′N 25°13′E
99 G17 Rupel ≈ N Belgium
Rupella see la Rochelle
33 P15 Rupert Idaho, NW USA 42°37′N 113°40′W
21 R5 Rupert West Virginia, NE USA 37°57′N 80°40′W
Rupert House see Waskaganish
12 J10 Rupert, Rivière de ≈ Québec, C Canada
152 I8 Rūpnagar var. Ropar. Punjab, India
194 M13 Ruppert Coast physical region Antarctica
100 N11 Ruppiner Kanal canal NE Germany
55 S11 Rupununi River ≈ S Guyana
101 D16 Rur Dut. Roer. ≈ Germany/Netherlands
58 H13 Rurópolis Presidente Medici Pará, N Brazil 04°05′S 55°26′W
191 S12 Rurutu island Îles Australes, SW French Polynesia
Rusaddir see Melilla
83 L17 Rusape Manicaland, E Zimbabwe 18°32′S 32°07′E
Rusayris, Lake see Roseires, Reservoir
Ruschuk/Rusçuk see Ruse
114 K7 Ruse var. Ruschuk, Rustchuk, Turk. Rusçuk. Ruse, N Bulgaria 43°50′N 25°59′E
109 W10 Ruše NE Slovenia 46°31′N 15°30′E
114 L7 Ruse ◐ province N Bulgaria
114 K7 Rusenski Lom ≈ N Bulgaria
97 G17 Rush Ir. An Ros. Dublin, E Ireland 53°32′N 06°06′W
161 S4 Rushan var. Xiacun. Shandong, E China 36°55′N 121°26′E
Rushan see Rŭshon
Rushanskiy Khrebet see Rushon, Qatorkŭhi
29 V7 Rush City Minnesota, N USA 45°41′N 92°56′W
37 V5 Rush Creek ≈ Colorado, C USA
29 X10 Rushford Minnesota, N USA 43°48′N 91°45′W
154 N13 Rushikulya ≈ E India
14 D8 Rush Lake ◎ Ontario, S Canada
30 M7 Rush Lake ◎ Wisconsin, N USA
28 J10 Rushmore, Mount ▲ South Dakota, N USA 43°52′N 103°27′W
147 S13 Rŭshon Rus. Rushan. S Tajikistan 37°58′N 71°31′E
147 S14 Rushon, Qatorkŭhi Rus. Rushanskiy Khrebet. ▲▲ SE Tajikistan
26 M12 Rush Springs Oklahoma, C USA 34°46′N 97°57′W
45 V15 Rushville Trinidad, Trinidad and Tobago 10°07′N 61°03′W
30 J13 Rushville Illinois, N USA 40°07′N 90°33′W
28 K12 Rushville Nebraska, C USA 42°41′N 102°28′W
183 O11 Rushworth Victoria, SE Australia 36°36′S 145°03′E
25 W8 Rusk Texas, SW USA 31°49′N 95°11′W
93 I14 Ruskele Västerbotten, N Sweden 64°49′N 18°55′E
118 C12 Rusnė Klaipėda, W Lithuania 55°18′N 21°19′E
114 M10 Rusokastrenska Reka ≈ E Bulgaria
Russadir see Melilla
109 X3 Russbach ≈ NE Austria
11 V16 Russell Manitoba, S Canada 50°47′N 101°17′W
184 K2 Russell Northland, North Island, New Zealand 35°17′S 174°07′E
26 L4 Russell Kansas, C USA 38°54′N 98°51′W
21 O4 Russell Kentucky, S USA 38°30′N 82°43′W
20 L7 Russell Springs Kentucky, S USA 37°02′N 85°03′W
23 O2 Russellville Alabama, S USA 34°30′N 87°43′W
27 T11 Russellville Arkansas, C USA 35°17′N 93°06′W
20 J7 Russellville Kentucky, S USA 36°50′N 86°54′W
101 G18 Rüsselsheim Hessen, W Germany 50°00′N 08°25′E
Russia see Russian Federation
Russian America see Alaska
122 J11 Russian Federation off. Russian Federation, var. Russia, Latv. Krievija, Rus. Rossiyskaya Federatsiya. ◆ republic Asia/Europe
Russian Federation see Russian Federation
39 N11 Russian Mission Alaska, USA 61°48′N 161°23′W
34 M7 Russian River ≈ California, W USA
122 J5 Russkaya Gavan' Novaya Zemlya, Arkhangel'skaya Oblast', N Russian Federation 76°13′N 62°48′E
122 J5 Russkiy, Ostrov island N Russian Federation
109 Y5 Rust Burgenland, E Austria 47°48′N 16°42′E
Rustaq see Ar Rustāq
137 U10 Rust'avi SE Georgia 41°36′N 45°00′E
21 T7 Rustburg Virginia, NE USA 37°17′N 79°07′W
Rustchuk see Ruse
Rustefjelbma Finnmark see Ruostekfielbmá
83 I21 Rustenburg North-West, N South Africa 25°40′S 27°15′E
22 H5 Ruston Louisiana, S USA 32°31′N 92°38′W
81 E21 Rutana SE Burundi 04°01′S 30°01′E
62 I4 Rutana, Volcán ⩘ N Chile 22°43′S 67°52′W
Rutanzige, Lake see Edward, Lake
Rutba see Ar Ruţbah
104 M14 Rute Andalucía, S Spain 37°20′N 04°23′W
171 N16 Ruteng prev. Roeteng. Flores, C Indonesia 08°35′S 120°28′E
194 L8 Rutford Ice Stream ice feature Antarctica
35 X6 Ruth Nevada, W USA 39°15′N 115°00′W
101 G15 Rüthen Nordrhein-Westfalen, W Germany 51°30′N 08°28′E
14 D17 Rutherford Ontario, S Canada 42°39′N 82°06′W
21 Q10 Rutherfordton North Carolina, SE USA 35°23′N 81°57′W
97 J18 Ruthin Wel. Rhuthun. NE Wales, United Kingdom 53°05′N 03°18′W
108 G7 Rüti Zürich, N Switzerland 47°16′N 08°51′E
Rutlam see Ratlām
18 M9 Rutland Vermont, NE USA 43°37′N 72°59′W
97 N19 Rutland cultural region C England, United Kingdom
21 N8 Rutledge Tennessee, S USA 36°16′N 83°31′W
158 G12 Rutog var. Rutög, Rutok. Xizang Zizhiqu, W China 33°27′N 79°43′E
Rutok see Rutog
79 P19 Rutshuru Nord-Kivu, E Dem. Rep. Congo 01°11′S 29°28′E
98 L8 Rutten Flevoland, N Netherlands 52°49′N 05°44′E
127 Q17 Rutul Respublika Dagestan, SW Russian Federation 41°35′N 47°30′E
93 L14 Ruukki Oulu, C Finland 64°40′N 25°35′E
98 N11 Ruurlo Gelderland, E Netherlands 52°04′N 06°27′E
143 S15 Ru'ūs al Jibāl cape Oman/United Arab Emirates
138 I7 Ru'ūs aţ Ţiwāl, Jabal ▲▲ W Syria
81 H23 Ruvuma ◐ region SE Tanzania
81 I25 Ruvuma var. Rio Rovuma. ≈ Mozambique/Tanzania see also Rovuma, Rio
Ruvuma see Rovuma, Rio
Ruwais see Ar Ruways
138 L9 Ruwayshid, Wadi ar dry watercourse NE Jordan
141 Z10 Ruways, Ra's ar headland E Oman 20°58′N 59°00′E
79 P18 Ruwenzori ▲▲ Dem. Rep. Congo/Uganda
141 Y8 Ruwi NE Oman 23°33′N 58°31′E
114 F9 Ruy ▲ Bulgaria/Serbia 42°52′N 22°35′E
Ruya see Luia, Rio
81 E20 Ruyigi E Burundi 03°28′S 30°19′E
127 P5 Ruzayevka Respublika Mordoviya, W Russian Federation 54°04′N 44°56′E
119 G18 Ruzhany Brestskaya Voblasts', SW Belarus 52°52′N 24°53′E
114 I10 Růžhevo Konare Plovdiv, C Bulgaria 42°16′N 24°58′E
Ruzhin see Ruzhyn
114 G7 Ruzhintsi Vidin, NW Bulgaria 43°38′N 22°50′E
161 N6 Ruzhou Henan, C China 34°10′N 112°51′E
117 N5 Ruzhyn Rus. Ruzhin. Zhytomyrs'ka Oblast', N Ukraine 49°42′N 29°01′E
111 K19 Ružomberok Ger. Rosenberg, Hung. Rózsahegy. Žilinský Kraj, N Slovakia 49°04′N 19°19′E
111 C16 Ruzyně ✖ (Praha) Praha, C Czech Republic
81 D19 Rwanda off. Rwandese Republic; prev. Ruanda. ◆ republic C Africa
Rwandese Republic see Rwanda
95 G22 Ry Århus, C Denmark 56°06′N 09°46′E
Ryasna see Rasna
126 L5 Ryazan' Ryazanskaya Oblast', W Russian Federation 54°37′N 39°37′E
126 L5 Ryazanskaya Oblast' ◐ province W Russian Federation
126 M6 Ryazhsk Ryazanskaya Oblast', W Russian Federation 53°42′N 40°09′E
118 B13 Rybachiy Ger. Rossitten. Kaliningradskaya Oblast', W Russian Federation 55°09′N 20°49′E
124 J2 Rybachiy, Poluostrov peninsula NW Russian Federation
Rybach'ye see Balykchy
124 L15 Rybinsk prev. Andropov. Yaroslavskaya Oblast', W Russian Federation 58°03′N 38°53′E
124 K14 Rybinskoye Vodokhranilishche Eng. Rybinsk Reservoir, Rybinsk Sea. ⊠ W Russian Federation
Rybinsk Reservoir/Rybinsk Sea see Rybinskoye Vodokhranilishche
111 I16 Rybnik Śląskie, S Poland 50°05′N 18°31′E
Rybnitsa see Rîbniţa

◆ Country
● Country Capital
◇ Dependent Territory
○ Dependent Territory Capital
◐ Administrative Regions
✖ International Airport
▲ Mountain
▲▲ Mountain Range
⩘ Volcano
≈ River
◎ Lake
⊠ Reservoir

RYCHNOV NAD KNĚŽNOU – ST. JOSEPH, LAKE

111 F16 **Rychnov nad Kněžnou** *Ger.* Reichenau. Královéhradecký Kraj, N Czech Republic *50°10′N 16°17′E*
110 I12 **Rychwał** Wielkopolskie, C Poland *52°04′N 18°10′E*
11 O13 **Rycroft** Alberta, W Canada *55°45′N 118°42′W*
95 L21 **Ryd** Kronoberg, S Sweden *56°27′N 14°44′E*
95 L20 **Rydaholm** Jönköping, S Sweden *56°57′N 14°19′E*
194 I8 **Rydberg Peninsula** *peninsula* Antarctica
97 P23 **Rye** SE England, United Kingdom *50°57′N 00°42′E*
33 T10 **Ryegate** Montana, NW USA *46°21′N 109°12′W*
35 S3 **Rye Patch Reservoir** ⊠ Nevada, W USA
95 D15 **Ryfylke** *physical region* S Norway
95 H16 **Rygge** Østfold, S Norway *59°22′N 10°45′E*
110 N13 **Ryki** Lubelskie, E Poland *51°38′N 21°57′E*
Rykovo *see* Yenakiyeve
126 I7 **Ryl'sk** Kurskaya Oblast', W Russian Federation *51°34′N 34°41′E*
183 S8 **Rylstone** New South Wales, SE Australia *32°48′S 149°58′E*
111 H17 **Rýmařov** *Ger.* Römerstadt. Moravskoslezský Kraj, E Czech Republic *49°56′N 17°15′E*
144 E11 **Ryn-Peski** *desert* W Kazakhstan
165 N10 **Ryōtsu** *var.* Ryôtu. Niigata, Sado, C Japan *38°06′N 138°28′E*
Ryôtu *see* Ryōtsu
110 K10 **Rypin** Kujawsko-pomorskie, C Poland *53°03′N 19°25′E*
Ryshkany *see* Rîşcani
Ryssel *see* Lille
Ryswick *see* Rijswijk
95 M24 **Rytterknægten** *hill* E Denmark
Ryukyu Islands *see* Nansei-shotō
192 G5 **Ryukyu Trench** *var.* Nansei Syotō Trench. *undersea feature* S East China Sea *24°45′N 128°00′E*
110 D11 **Rzepin** *Ger.* Reppen. Lubuskie, W Poland *52°20′N 14°48′E*
111 N16 **Rzeszów** Podkarpackie, SE Poland *50°03′N 22°01′E*
124 I16 **Rzhev** Tverskaya Oblast', W Russian Federation *56°17′N 34°22′E*
Rzhishchev *see* Rzhyshchiv
117 P5 **Rzhyshchiv** *Rus.* Rzhishchev. Kyyivs'ka Oblast', N Ukraine *49°58′N 31°02′E*

S

138 E11 **Sa'ad** Southern, W Israel *31°27′N 34°31′E*
109 P7 **Saalach** 〰 W Austria
101 L14 **Saale** 〰 C Germany
101 L17 **Saalfeld** *var.* Saalfeld an der Saale. Thüringen, C Germany *50°39′N 11°22′E*
Saalfeld *see* Zalewo
Saalfeld an der Saale *see* Saalfeld
108 C8 **Saane** 〰 W Switzerland
101 D19 **Saar** *Fr.* Sarre. 〰 France/Germany
101 E20 **Saarbrücken** *Fr.* Sarrebruck. Saarland, SW Germany *49°13′N 07°01′E*
Saarburg *see* Sarrebourg
118 D6 **Sääre** *var.* Sjar. Saaremaa, W Estonia *57°57′N 21°53′E*
Saare *see* Saaremaa
118 D5 **Saaremaa** *off.* Saare Maakond. ◈ *province* W Estonia
118 E6 **Saaremaa** *Ger.* Oesel, Ösel; *prev.* Saare. *island* W Estonia
Saare Maakond *see* Saaremaa
92 L12 **Saarenkylä** Lappi, N Finland *66°31′N 25°51′E*
Saargemund *see* Sarreguemines
93 L17 **Saarijärvi** Länsi-Suomi, C Finland *62°42′N 25°16′E*
Saar in Mähren *see* Žd'ár nad Sázavou
92 M10 **Saariselkä** *Lapp.* Suoločielgi. Lappi, N Finland *68°27′N 27°29′E*
92 L10 **Saariselkä** *hill range* NE Finland
101 D20 **Saarland** *Fr.* Sarre. ◈ *state* SW Germany
Saarlautern *see* Saarlouis
101 D20 **Saarlouis** *prev.* Saarlautern. Saarland, SW Germany *49°19′N 06°45′E*
108 E11 **Saaser Vispa** 〰 S Switzerland
137 X12 **Saatlı** *Rus.* Saatly. C Azerbaijan *39°57′N 48°24′E*
Saatly *see* Saatlı
Saaz *see* Žatec
45 V9 **Saba** *island* N Netherlands Antilles
138 J7 **Sab' Ābār** *var.* Sab'a Biyar, Sa'b Bi'ār. Ḥimş, C Syria *33°46′N 37°41′E*
Sab'a Biyar *see* Sab' Ābār
112 K11 **Šabac** Serbia, W Serbia *44°45′N 19°42′E*
105 W5 **Sabadell** Cataluña, E Spain *41°33′N 02°07′E*
164 K12 **Sabae** Fukui, Honshū, SW Japan *36°00′N 136°12′E*
169 V7 **Sabah** *prev.* British North Borneo, North Borneo. ◈ *state* East Malaysia
168 J8 **Sabak** *var.* Sabak Bernam. Selangor, Peninsular Malaysia *03°45′N 100°59′E*
Sabak Bernam *see* Sabak
38 D16 **Sabak, Cape** *headland* Agattu Island, Alaska, USA *52°21′N 173°43′E*
81 J20 **Sabaki** 〰 S Kenya
142 L2 **Sabalān, Kuhhā-ye** ▲ NW Iran *38°21′N 47°47′E*
154 H7 **Sabalgarh** Madhya Pradesh, C India *26°13′N 77°28′E*
44 E4 **Sabana, Archipiélago de** *island group* C Cuba
42 H7 **Sabanagrande** *var.* Sabana Grande. Francisco Morazán, S Honduras *13°48′N 87°15′W*
Sabana Grande *see* Sabanagrande
54 E5 **Sabanalarga** Atlántico, N Colombia *10°38′N 74°55′W*
41 W14 **Sabancuy** Campeche, SE Mexico *18°58′N 91°11′W*
45 N8 **Sabaneta** NW Dominican Republic *19°30′N 71°21′W*
54 J4 **Sabaneta** Falcón, N Venezuela *11°17′N 70°00′W*
188 H4 **Sabaneta, Puntan** *prev.* Ushi Point. *headland* Saipan, S Northern Mariana Islands *15°17′N 145°49′E*
171 X14 **Sabang** Papua, E Indonesia *04°33′S 138°42′E*
116 L10 **Săbăoani** Neamţ, NE Romania *47°01′N 26°51′E*
155 J26 **Sabaragamuwa** ◈ *province* C Sri Lanka
Sabaria *see* Szombathely
154 D10 **Sābarmati** 〰 NW India
171 S10 **Sabatai** Pulau Morotai, E Indonesia *02°04′N 128°23′E*
141 Q15 **Sab'atayn, Ramlat as** *desert* C Yemen
107 I16 **Sabaudia** Lazio, C Italy *41°17′N 13°02′E*
57 J19 **Sabaya** Oruro, S Bolivia *19°09′S 68°21′W*
Sa'b Bi'ār *see* Sab' Ābār
Sabbioncello *see* Orebić
148 I8 **Şāberī, Hāmūn-e** *var.* Daryācheh-ye Hāmun, Daryācheh-ye Sīstān. ◎ Afghanistan/Iran *see also* Sīstān, Daryācheh-ye
Şāberī, Hāmūn-e *see* Sīstān, Daryācheh-ye
27 P2 **Sabetha** Kansas, C USA *39°54′N 95°48′W*
75 P10 **Sabhā** C Libya *27°02′N 14°26′E*
67 V13 **Sabi** *var.* Save. 〰 Mozambique/Zimbabwe *see also* Save
Sabi *see* Save
118 E8 **Sabile** *Ger.* Zabeln. Talsi, NW Latvia *57°03′N 22°33′E*
31 R14 **Sabina** Ohio, N USA *39°29′N 83°38′W*
40 I3 **Sabinal** Chihuahua, N Mexico *30°59′N 107°29′W*
25 Q12 **Sabinal** Texas, SW USA *29°19′N 99°28′W*
25 Q11 **Sabinal River** 〰 Texas, SW USA
105 S4 **Sabiñánigo** Aragón, NE Spain *42°31′N 00°22′W*
41 N6 **Sabinas** Coahuila, NE Mexico *27°52′N 101°04′W*
41 O8 **Sabinas Hidalgo** Nuevo León, NE Mexico *26°29′N 100°09′W*
41 N6 **Sabinas, Río** 〰 NE Mexico
22 F9 **Sabine Lake** ◎ Louisiana/Texas, S USA
92 O3 **Sabine Land** *physical region* C Svalbard
25 W7 **Sabine River** 〰 Louisiana/Texas, SW USA
137 X12 **Sabirabad** C Azerbaijan *40°00′N 48°27′E*
Sabkha *see* As Sabkhah
171 O4 **Sablayan** Mindoro, N Philippines *12°48′N 120°48′E*
13 P16 **Sable, Cape** *headland* Newfoundland and Labrador, SE Canada *43°21′N 65°40′W*
23 X17 **Sable, Cape** *headland* Florida, SE USA *25°12′N 81°06′W*
13 R16 **Sable Island** *island* Nova Scotia, SE Canada
14 L11 **Sables, Lac des** ◎ Québec, SE Canada
14 E10 **Sables, Rivière aux** 〰 Ontario, S Canada
102 K7 **Sable-sur-Sarthe** Sarthe, NW France *47°49′N 00°19′W*
125 U7 **Sablya, Gora** ▲ NW Russian Federation *64°46′N 58°52′E*
77 U14 **Sabon Birnin Gwari** Kaduna, C Nigeria *10°43′N 06°39′E*
77 V11 **Sabon Kafi** Zinder, C Niger *14°37′N 08°46′E*
104 I6 **Sabor, Rio** 〰 N Portugal
14 J8 **Sabourin, Lac** ◎ Québec, SE Canada
102 J14 **Sabres** Landes, SW France *44°07′N 00°46′W*
195 X13 **Sabrina Coast** *physical region* Antarctica
140 M11 **Sabt al Ulayā** 'Asīr, SW Saudi Arabia *19°33′N 41°58′E*
104 I8 **Sabugal** Guarda, N Portugal *40°20′N 07°05′W*
29 Z13 **Sabula** Iowa, C USA *42°04′N 90°10′W*
141 N13 **Şabyā** Jīzān, SW Saudi Arabia *17°50′N 42°50′E*
Sabzawar *see* Sabzevār
Sabzawaran *see* Jīroft
143 S4 **Sabzevār** *var.* Sabzawar. Khorāsān-Razavī, NE Iran *36°13′N 57°38′E*
Sabzvārān *see* Jīroft
Sacajawea Peak *see* Matterhorn
82 C9 **Sacandica** Uíge, NW Angola *06°01′S 15°57′E*
42 A2 **Sacatepéquez** *off.* Departamento de Sacatepéquez. ◈ *department* S Guatemala
Sacatepéquez, Departamento de *see* Sacatepéquez
104 F11 **Sacavém** Lisboa, W Portugal *38°47′N 09°06′W*
29 T13 **Sac City** Iowa, C USA *42°25′N 94°59′W*
105 P8 **Sacedón** Castilla-La Mancha, C Spain *40°29′N 02°44′W*
116 J12 **Săcele** *Ger.* Vierdörfer, *Hung.* Négyfalu; *prev. Ger.* Sieben Dörfer, *Hung.* Hétfalu. Braşov, C Romania *45°36′N 25°40′E*
12 C8 **Sachigo** Ontario, C Canada *53°52′N 92°16′W*
12 C7 **Sachigo** 〰 Ontario, C Canada
12 C8 **Sachigo Lake** ◎ Ontario, C Canada
163 Y16 **Sach'ŏn** *Jap.* Sansenhō; *prev.* Samch'ŏnpŏ. S South Korea *34°55′N 128°07′E*
101 O15 **Sachsen** *Eng.* Saxony, *Fr.* Saxe. ◈ *state* E Germany
101 K14 **Sachsen-Anhalt** *Eng.* Saxony-Anhalt. ◈ *state* C Germany
109 R9 **Sachsenburg** Salzburg, S Austria *46°49′N 13°23′E*
Sachsenfeld *see* Žalec
8 I5 **Sachs Harbour** *var.* Ikaahuk. Banks Island, Northwest Territories, N Canada *72°N 125°14′W*
Sächsisch-Reen/Sächsisch-Regen *see* Reghin
18 H8 **Sackets Harbor** New York, NE USA *43°57′N 76°06′W*
13 P14 **Sackville** New Brunswick, SE Canada *45°54′N 64°23′W*
19 P9 **Saco** Maine, NE USA *43°32′N 70°25′W*
19 P8 **Saco River** 〰 Maine/New Hampshire, NE USA
35 O7 **Sacramento** *state capital* California, W USA *38°35′N 121°30′W*
37 T14 **Sacramento Mountains** ▲▲ New Mexico, SW USA
35 N6 **Sacramento River** 〰 California, W USA
35 N5 **Sacramento Valley** *valley* California, W USA
36 I10 **Sacramento Wash** *valley* Arizona, SW USA
105 N15 **Sacratif, Cabo** *headland* S Spain *36°41′N 03°30′W*
116 F9 **Săcueni** *prev.* Săcuieni, *Hung.* Székelyhid. Bihor, W Romania *47°20′N 22°05′E*
Săcuieni *see* Săcueni
105 R4 **Sádaba** Aragón, NE Spain *42°15′N 01°16′W*
Sá da Bandeira *see* Lubango
138 I6 **Şadad** Ḥimş, W Syria *34°19′N 36°52′E*
141 O13 **Şa'dah** NW Yemen *16°59′N 43°45′E*
167 O16 **Sadao** Songkhla, SW Thailand *06°39′N 100°30′E*
142 L8 **Sadd-e Dez, Daryācheh-ye** ◎ W Iran
19 S3 **Saddleback Mountain** *hill* Maine, NE USA
19 P6 **Saddleback Mountain** ▲ Maine, NE USA *44°57′N 70°27′W*
141 W13 **Sadḥ** S Oman *17°11′N 55°08′E*
76 J11 **Sadiola** Kayes, W Mali *13°48′N 11°47′W*
149 R12 **Sādiqābād** Punjab, E Pakistan *28°16′N 70°10′E*
153 Y10 **Sadiya** Assam, NE India *27°49′N 95°38′E*
139 W9 **Sa'dīyah, Hawr as** ◎ E Iraq
165 N9 **Sado** *var.* Sadoga-shima. *island* C Japan
Sadoga-shima *see* Sado
104 F12 **Sado, Rio** 〰 S Portugal
114 I8 **Sadovets** Pleven, N Bulgaria *43°19′N 24°21′E*
114 J11 **Sadovo** Plovdiv, C Bulgaria *42°07′N 24°56′E*
127 O11 **Sadovoye** Respublika Kalmykiya, SW Russian Federation *47°51′N 44°34′E*
105 W9 **Sa Dragonera** *var.* Isla Dragonera. *island* Islas Baleares, Spain, W Mediterranean Sea
105 P9 **Saelices** Castilla-La Mancha, C Spain *39°55′N 02°49′W*
Saena Julia *see* Siena
Saetabicula *see* Alzira
114 O12 **Safaalan** Tekirdağ, NW Turkey *41°26′N 28°07′E*
Safad *see* Tsefat
Şafāqis *see* Sfax
143 P10 **Şafāshahr** *var.* Deh Bīd. Fārs, C Iran *30°50′N 53°50′E*
192 I16 **Safata Bay** *bay* Upolo, Samoa, C Pacific Ocean
Safed *see* Tsefat
139 X11 **Şaffāf, Ḥawr aş** *marshy lake* S Iraq
95 J16 **Säffle** Värmland, C Sweden *59°08′N 12°55′E*
37 N15 **Safford** Arizona, SW USA *32°46′N 109°41′W*
74 E7 **Safi** W Morocco *32°19′N 09°14′W*
126 I4 **Safonovo** Smolenskaya Oblast', W Russian Federation *55°05′N 33°12′E*
136 H11 **Safranbolu** Karabük, NW Turkey *41°16′N 32°41′E*
139 Y13 **Safwān** Al Başrah, SE Iraq *30°06′N 47°44′E*
158 J16 **Saga** *var.* Gya'gya. Xizang Zizhiqu, W China *29°22′N 85°19′E*
164 C14 **Saga** Saga, Kyūshū, SW Japan *33°14′N 130°16′E*
164 C13 **Saga** *off.* Saga-ken. ◈ *prefecture* Kyūshū, SW Japan
165 P10 **Sagae** Yamagata, Honshū, C Japan *38°22′N 140°12′E*
166 L3 **Sagaing** Sagaing, C Myanmar (Burma) *21°55′N 95°56′E*
166 L5 **Sagaing** ◈ *division* N Myanmar (Burma)
Saga-ken *see* Saga
165 N13 **Sagamihara** Kanagawa, Honshū, S Japan *35°34′N 139°22′E*
165 N14 **Sagami-nada** *inlet* SW Japan
Sagan *see* Żagań
29 Y3 **Saganaga Lake** ◎ Minnesota, N USA
155 F18 **Sāgar** Karnātaka, W India *14°09′N 75°02′E*
154 I9 **Sāgar** *prev.* Saugor. Madhya Pradesh, C India *23°53′N 78°46′E*
15 S8 **Sagard** Québec, SE Canada *48°01′N 70°03′W*
Sagarmāthā *see* Everest, Mount
Sagebrush State *see* Nevada
143 V11 **Sāghand** Yazd, C Iran *32°33′N 55°12′E*
19 N14 **Sag Harbor** Long Island, New York, NE USA *40°59′N 72°15′W*
Saghez *see* Saqqez
Saghyz *see* Sagiz
31 R8 **Saginaw** Michigan, N USA *43°25′N 83°57′W*
31 R8 **Saginaw Bay** *lake bay* Michigan, N USA
144 H11 **Sagiz** *Kaz.* Saghyz. Atyrau, W Kazakhstan *48°12′N 54°56′E*
64 H6 **Saglek Bank** *undersea feature* W Labrador Sea
13 P5 **Saglek Bay** *bay* SW Labrador Sea
Saglouc/Sagluk *see* Salluit
103 X15 **Sagonne, Golfe de** *gulf* Corse, France, C Mediterranean Sea
105 P13 **Sagra** ▲ S Spain *37°59′N 02°33′W*
104 F14 **Sagres** Faro, S Portugal *37°01′N 08°56′W*
37 S7 **Saguache** Colorado, C USA *38°05′N 106°05′W*
44 J7 **Sagua de Tánamo** Holguín, E Cuba *20°38′N 75°14′W*
44 E5 **Sagua la Grande** Villa Clara, C Cuba *22°48′N 80°06′W*
15 R7 **Saguenay** 〰 Québec, SE Canada
74 C9 **Saguia al Hamra** *var.* As Saqia al Hamra. 〰 N Western Sahara
105 S9 **Sagunto** *Cat.* Sagunt, *Ar.* Murviedro; *anc.* Saguntum. País Valenciano, E Spain *39°40′N 00°17′W*
Sagunt/Saguntum *see* Sagunto
158 L16 **Sa'gya** Xizang Zizhiqu, W China *28°51′N 88°00′E*
138 H10 **Saḥāb** 'Ammān, NW Jordan *31°52′N 36°00′E*
54 E6 **Sahagún** Córdoba, NW Colombia *08°58′N 75°30′W*
104 L4 **Sahagún** Castilla-León, N Spain *42°23′N 05°02′W*
141 X8 **Saḥam** N Oman *24°06′N 56°52′E*
68 F9 **Sahara** *desert* Libya/Algeria
Sahara el Gharbîya *see* Şaḥrā' al Gharbīyah
75 X9 **Sahara el Sharqîya** *var.* Aş Şaḥrā' ash Sharqīyah, *Eng.* Arabian Desert, Eastern Desert. *desert* E Egypt
Saharan Atlas *see* Atlas Saharien
152 J9 **Sahāranpur** Uttar Pradesh, N India *29°58′N 77°33′E*
64 L10 **Saharan Seamounts** *var.* Saharian Seamounts. *undersea feature* E Atlantic Ocean *25°00′N 20°00′W*
Saharian Seamounts *see* Saharan Seamounts
153 Q13 **Saharsa** Bihār, NE India *25°54′N 86°36′E*
67 O7 **Sahel** *physical region* C Africa
153 R14 **Sāhibganj** Jhārkhand, NE India *25°15′N 87°40′E*
80 N12 **Sahil** *off.* Gobolka Sahil. ◈ *region* N Somalia
139 Q7 **Sahīlīyah** Al Anbār, C Iraq *33°43′N 42°42′E*
138 H4 **Sāḥilīyah, Jibāl as** ▲▲ NW Syria
114 M13 **Şahin** Tekirdağ, NW Turkey *41°01′N 26°51′E*
149 U8 **Sāhīwāl** Punjab, E Pakistan *31°57′N 72°22′E*
149 U9 **Sāhīwāl** *prev.* Montgomery. Punjab, E Pakistan *30°40′N 73°05′E*
141 W11 **Saḥmah, Ramlat as** *desert* C Oman
75 U9 **Şaḥrā' al Gharbīyah** *var.* Sahara el Gharbîya, *Eng.* Western Desert. *desert* C Egypt
139 T13 **Şaḥrā' al Ḥijārah** *desert* S Iraq
40 H5 **Sahuaripa** Sonora, NW Mexico *29°02′N 109°14′W*
36 M16 **Sahuarita** Arizona, SW USA *31°24′N 110°55′W*
40 L13 **Sahuayo** *var.* Sahuayo de José Mariá Morelos; *prev.* Sahuayo de Díaz, Sahuayo de Porfirio Díaz. Michoacán, SW Mexico *20°05′N 102°42′W*
Sahuayo de Díaz/Sahuayo de José Mariá Morelos/Sahuayo de Porfirio Díaz *see* Sahuayo
173 W8 **Sahul Shelf** *undersea feature* N Timor Sea
167 P17 **Sai Buri** Pattani, SW Thailand *06°42′N 101°37′E*
74 I6 **Saïda** NW Algeria *34°50′N 00°10′E*
138 G7 **Saïda** *var.* Şaydā, Sayida; *anc.* Sidon. W Lebanon *33°20′N 35°24′E*
Sa'īdābād *see* Sīrjān
80 B13 **Sa'id Bundas** Western Bahr el Ghazal, SW Sudan *08°24′N 24°53′E*
186 E7 **Saidor** Madang, N Papua New Guinea *05°38′S 146°28′E*
153 S13 **Saidpur** *var.* Syedpur. Rajshahi, NW Bangladesh *25°48′N 89°E*
149 U5 **Saidu Sharif** *var.* Mingora, Mongora. North-West Frontier Province, N Pakistan *34°45′N 72°21′E*
108 C7 **Saignelégier** Jura, NW Switzerland *47°18′N 07°03′E*
164 H11 **Saigō** Shimane, Dōgo, SW Japan *36°12′N 133°18′E*
Saigon *see* Hô Chi Minh
163 P11 **SaihanTal** *var.* Sonid Youqi. Nei Mongol Zizhiqu, N China *42°45′N 112°36′E*
162 I12 **Saihan Toroi** Nei Mongol Zizhiqu, N China *41°44′N 100°29′E*
Sai Hun *see* Syr Darya
92 M11 **Saija** Lappi, NE Finland *67°07′N 28°46′E*
164 G14 **Saijō** Ehime, Shikoku, SW Japan *33°55′N 133°10′E*
164 E15 **Saiki** Ōita, Kyūshū, SW Japan *32°57′N 131°52′E*
93 N18 **Saimaa** ◎ SE Finland
93 N18 **Saimaa Canal** *Fin.* Saimaan Kanava, *Rus.* Saymenskiy Kanal. *canal* Finland/Russian Federation
Saimaan Kanava *see* Saimaa Canal
40 L10 **Saín Alto** Zacatecas, C Mexico *23°36′N 103°14′W*
96 L12 **St Abb's Head** *headland* SE Scotland, United Kingdom *55°54′N 02°07′W*
11 Y16 **St. Adolphe** Manitoba, S Canada *49°39′N 96°55′W*
103 O15 **St-Affrique** Aveyron, S France *43°57′N 02°52′E*
15 Q10 **St-Agapit** Québec, SE Canada *46°22′N 71°37′W*
97 O21 **St Albans** *anc.* Verulamium. E England, United Kingdom *51°46′N 00°21′W*
18 L6 **Saint Albans** Vermont, NE USA *44°49′N 73°07′W*
21 Q5 **Saint Albans** West Virginia, NE USA *38°21′N 81°47′W*
St. Alban's Head *see* St Aldhelm's Head
11 Q14 **St. Albert** Alberta, SW Canada *53°38′N 113°38′W*
97 M24 **St Aldhelm's Head** *var.* St. Alban's Head. *headland* S England, United Kingdom *50°34′N 02°04′W*
15 O11 **St-Alexis-des-Monts** Québec, SE Canada *46°30′N 73°08′W*
103 P2 **St-Amand-les-Eaux** Nord, N France *50°27′N 03°25′E*
103 O9 **St-Amand-Montrond** *var.* St-Amand-Mont-Rond. Cher, C France *46°43′N 02°29′E*
173 P16 **St-André** NE Réunion
14 M12 **St-André-Avellin** Québec, SE Canada *45°45′N 75°04′W*
Saint-André, Cap *see* Vilanandro, Tanjona
102 K12 **St-André-de-Cubzac** Gironde, SW France *45°01′N 00°26′W*
96 K11 **St Andrews** E Scotland, United Kingdom *56°20′N 02°49′W*
23 Q9 **Saint Andrews Bay** *bay* Florida, SE USA
23 W7 **Saint Andrew Sound** *sound* Georgia, SE USA
Saint Anna Trough *see* Svyataya Anna Trough
44 J11 **St. Ann's Bay** C Jamaica *18°26′N 77°12′W*
13 T10 **St. Anthony** Newfoundland and Labrador, SE Canada *51°22′N 55°34′W*
33 R13 **Saint Anthony** Idaho, NW USA *43°56′N 111°38′W*
182 M11 **Saint Arnaud** Victoria, SE Australia *36°39′S 143°15′E*
185 I15 **St.Arnaud Range** ▲▲ South Island, New Zealand
13 R10 **St-Augustin** Québec, E Canada *51°13′N 58°39′W*
23 X9 **Saint Augustine** Florida, SE USA *29°54′N 81°19′W*
97 H24 **St Austell** SW England, United Kingdom *50°21′N 04°47′W*
103 T4 **St-Avold** Moselle, NE France *49°06′N 06°43′E*
103 N17 **St-Barthélemy** ▲▲ S France
102 L17 **St-Béat** Haute-Garonne, S France *42°55′N 00°39′E*
97 I15 **St Bees Head** *headland* NW England, United Kingdom *54°30′N 03°39′W*
173 P16 **St-Benoit** E Réunion
103 T13 **St-Bonnet** Hautes-Alpes, SE France *44°41′N 06°04′E*
St.Botolph's Town *see* Boston
97 G21 **St Brides Bay** *inlet* SW Wales, United Kingdom
102 H5 **St-Brieuc** Côtes d'Armor, NW France *48°31′N 02°45′W*
102 H5 **St-Brieuc, Baie de** *bay* NW France
102 L7 **St-Calais** Sarthe, NW France *47°55′N 00°48′E*
15 Q10 **St-Casimir** Québec, SE Canada *46°40′N 72°05′W*
14 H16 **St. Catharines** Ontario, S Canada *43°10′N 79°15′W*
45 S14 **St. Catherine, Mount** ▲ N Grenada *12°10′N 61°41′W*
64 C11 **St Catherine Point** *headland* E Bermuda
23 X6 **Saint Catherines Island** *island* Georgia, SE USA
97 M24 **St Catherine's Point** *headland* S England, United Kingdom *50°34′N 01°17′W*
103 N13 **St-Céré** Lot, S France *44°52′N 01°53′E*
108 A10 **St. Cergue** Vaud, W Switzerland *46°25′N 06°10′E*
103 R11 **St-Chamond** Loire, E France *45°29′N 04°32′E*
33 S16 **Saint Charles** Idaho, NW USA *42°05′N 111°23′W*
27 X4 **Saint Charles** Missouri, C USA *38°48′N 90°29′W*
103 P13 **St-Chély-d'Apcher** Lozère, S France *44°51′N 03°16′E*
Saint Christopher and Nevis, Federation of *see* Saint Kitts and Nevis
Saint Christopher-Nevis *see* Saint Kitts and Nevis
31 S9 **Saint Clair** Michigan, N USA *42°49′N 82°29′W*
183 O17 **St. Clair, Lake** ◎ Tasmania, SE Australia
14 C17 **St. Clair, Lake** *var.* Lac à L'Eau Claire. ◎ Canada/USA
31 S10 **Saint Clair Shores** Michigan, N USA *42°30′N 82°53′W*
103 S10 **St-Claude** *anc.* Condate. Jura, E France *46°23′N 05°52′E*
45 X6 **St-Claude** Basse Terre, SW Guadeloupe *16°02′N 61°42′W*
23 X12 **Saint Cloud** Florida, SE USA *28°15′N 81°15′W*
29 U8 **Saint Cloud** Minnesota, N USA *45°34′N 94°10′W*
45 T9 **Saint Croix** *island* S Virgin Islands (US)
30 J4 **Saint Croix Flowage** ⊠ Wisconsin, N USA
19 T5 **Saint Croix River** 〰 Canada/USA
29 W7 **Saint Croix River** 〰 Minnesota/Wisconsin, N USA
45 S14 **St.David's** SE Grenada *12°01′N 61°40′W*
97 H21 **St David's** SW Wales, United Kingdom *51°53′N 05°16′W*
97 G21 **St David's Head** *headland* SW Wales, United Kingdom *51°54′N 05°19′W*
64 C12 **St David's Island** *island* E Bermuda
173 O16 **St-Denis** ○ (Réunion) NW Réunion *20°55′S 14°34′E*
103 U6 **St-Dié** Vosges, NE France *48°17′N 06°57′E*
103 R5 **St-Dizier** *anc.* Desiderii Fanum. Haute-Marne, N France *48°39′N 05°00′E*
15 N11 **St-Donat** Québec, SE Canada *46°19′N 74°15′W*
15 N11 **Ste-Adèle** Québec, SE Canada *45°58′N 74°10′W*
15 N11 **Ste-Agathe-des-Monts** Québec, SE Canada *46°03′N 74°19′W*
11 Y16 **Ste. Anne** Manitoba, S Canada *49°40′N 96°40′W*
45 R12 **Ste-Anne** Grande Terre, E Guadeloupe *16°13′N 61°23′W*
45 Y6 **Ste-Anne** SE Martinique *14°26′N 60°53′W*
15 Q10 **Ste-Anne** 〰 Québec, SE Canada
172 I16 **Sainte Anne** *island* Inner Islands, NE Seychelles
15 W6 **Ste-Anne-des-Monts** Québec, SE Canada *49°07′N 66°29′W*
14 M10 **Ste-Anne-du-Lac** Québec, SE Canada *46°51′N 75°20′W*
15 S10 **Ste-Apolline** Québec, SE Canada *46°47′N 70°15′W*
15 R10 **Ste-Claire** Québec, SE Canada *46°30′N 70°40′W*
15 Q10 **Ste-Croix** Québec, SE Canada *46°36′N 71°42′W*
108 B8 **Ste. Croix** Vaud, SW Switzerland *46°50′N 06°31′E*
103 P14 **Ste-Énimie** Lozère, S France *44°21′N 03°26′E*
27 Y6 **Sainte Genevieve** Missouri, C USA *37°57′N 90°01′W*
103 S12 **St-Egrève** Isère, E France *45°15′N 05°41′E*
39 T12 **Saint Elias, Cape** *headland* Kayak Island, Alaska, USA *59°48′N 144°36′W*
39 U11 **St Elias, Mount** ▲ Alaska, USA *60°18′N 140°57′W*
10 G8 **Saint Elias Mountains** ▲▲ Canada/USA
55 Y10 **St-Élie** N French Guiana *04°50′N 53°21′W*
103 O10 **St-Eloy-les-Mines** Puy-de-Dôme, C France *46°07′N 02°50′E*
15 R10 **Ste-Marie** Québec, SE Canada *46°28′N 71°00′W*
45 Q11 **Ste-Marie** NE Martinique *14°47′N 61°00′W*
173 P16 **Ste-Marie** NE Réunion
103 U6 **Ste-Marie-aux-Mines** Haut-Rhin, NE France *48°16′N 07°12′E*
Sainte Marie, Cap *see* Vohimena, Tanjona
102 L8 **Ste-Maure-de-Touraine** Indre-et-Loire, C France *47°06′N 00°38′E*
103 R4 **Ste-Menehould** Marne, NE France *49°06′N 04°54′E*
Ste-Perpétue *see* Ste-Perpétue-de-l'Islet
15 S9 **Ste-Perpétue-de-l'Islet** *var.* Ste-Perpétue. Québec, SE Canada *47°02′N 69°58′W*
45 X11 **Ste-Rose** Basse Terre, N Guadeloupe *16°20′N 61°42′W*
173 P16 **Ste-Rose** E Réunion
11 W15 **Ste. Rose du Lac** Manitoba, S Canada *51°04′N 99°31′W*
102 J11 **Saintes** *anc.* Mediolanum. Charente-Maritime, W France *45°45′N 00°37′W*
45 X7 **Saintes, Canal des** *channel* SW Guadeloupe
Saintes, Îles des *see* les Saintes
173 P16 **Ste-Suzanne** N Réunion
15 P10 **Ste-Thècle** Québec, SE Canada *46°48′N 72°31′W*
103 Q12 **St-Étienne** Loire, E France *45°26′N 04°23′E*
102 M4 **St-Étienne-du-Rouvray** Seine-Maritime, N France *49°22′N 01°07′E*
Saint Eustatius *see* Sint Eustatius
15 R7 **Ste-Marguerite** 〰 Québec, SE Canada
14 M11 **Ste-Véronique** Québec, SE Canada *46°30′N 74°58′W*
15 P7 **St-Félicien** Québec, SE Canada *48°38′N 72°29′W*
15 O11 **St-Félix-de-Valois** Québec, SE Canada *46°10′N 73°26′W*
103 Y14 **St-Florent** Corse, France, C Mediterranean Sea *42°41′N 09°19′E*
103 Y14 **St-Florent, Golfe de** *gulf* Corse, France, C Mediterranean Sea
103 P6 **St-Florentin** Yonne, C France *48°00′N 03°46′E*
103 N9 **St-Florent-sur-Cher** Cher, C France *47°00′N 02°13′E*
103 P12 **St-Flour** Cantal, C France *45°02′N 03°05′E*
26 H2 **Saint Francis** Kansas, C USA *39°45′N 101°31′W*
83 H26 **St. Francis, Cape** *headland* S South Africa *34°11′S 24°45′E*
27 X10 **Saint Francis River** 〰 Arkansas/Missouri, C USA
22 J8 **Saint Francisville** Louisiana, S USA *30°46′N 91°22′W*
45 Y6 **St-François** Grande Terre, E Guadeloupe *16°15′N 61°17′W*
15 Q12 **St-François** 〰 Québec, SE Canada
27 X7 **Saint Francois Mountains** ▲▲ Missouri, C USA
St-Gall *see* St-Gall/Saint Gall/St.Gallen
St-Gall/Saint Gall/St. Gallen *see* Sankt Gallen
102 L16 **St-Gaudens** Haute-Garonne, S France *43°07′N 00°43′E*
15 R12 **St-Gédéon** Québec, SE Canada *45°51′N 70°36′W*
181 X10 **Saint George** Queensland, E Australia *28°05′S 148°40′E*
64 B12 **St George** N Bermuda *32°24′N 64°42′W*
38 K15 **Saint George** Saint George Island, Alaska, USA *56°34′N 169°30′W*
21 S14 **Saint George** South Carolina, SE USA *33°12′N 80°34′W*
36 J8 **Saint George** Utah, W USA *37°06′N 113°35′W*
13 R12 **St. George, Cape** *headland* Newfoundland and Labrador, E Canada *48°26′N 59°17′W*
186 I6 **St. George, Cape** *headland* New Ireland, NE Papua New Guinea *04°49′S 152°52′E*
38 J15 **Saint George Island** *island* Pribilof Islands, Alaska, USA
23 S10 **Saint George Island** *island* Florida, SE USA
99 J19 **Saint-Georges** Liège, E Belgium *50°36′N 05°20′E*
15 R11 **St-Georges** Québec, SE Canada *46°08′N 70°40′W*
55 Z11 **St-Georges** E French Guiana *03°55′N 51°49′W*
45 R14 **St. George's** ● (Grenada) SW Grenada *12°04′N 61°45′W*
13 R12 **St. George's Bay** *inlet* Newfoundland and Labrador, E Canada
97 G21 **Saint George's Channel** *channel* Ireland/Wales, United Kingdom
186 H6 **St. George's Channel** *channel* NE Papua New Guinea
64 B11 **St George's Island** *island* E Bermuda
99 I21 **Saint-Gérard** Namur, S Belgium *50°20′N 04°47′E*
St-Germain *see* St-Germain-en-Laye
15 P12 **St-Germain-de-Grantham** Québec, SE Canada *45°49′N 72°32′W*
103 N5 **St-Germain-en-Laye** *var.* St-Germain. Yvelines, N France *48°53′N 02°04′E*
102 H8 **St-Gildas, Pointe du** *headland* NW France *47°09′N 02°25′W*
103 R15 **St-Gilles** Gard, S France *43°41′N 04°24′E*
102 I9 **St-Gilles-Croix-de-Vie** Vendée, NW France *46°41′N 01°55′W*
173 O16 **St-Gilles-les-Bains** W Réunion *21°02′S 55°14′E*
102 M16 **St-Girons** Ariège, S France *42°58′N 01°07′E*
Saint Gotthard *see* Szentgotthárd
108 G9 **St. Gotthard Tunnel** *tunnel* Ticino, S Switzerland
97 H22 **St Govan's Head** *headland* SW Wales, United Kingdom *51°35′N 04°55′W*
34 M7 **Saint Helena** California, W USA *38°29′N 122°30′W*
65 F24 **Saint Helena** ◇ *UK dependent territory* C Atlantic Ocean
67 O12 **Saint Helena** *island* C Atlantic Ocean
65 M16 **Saint Helena Fracture Zone** *tectonic feature* C Atlantic Ocean
34 M7 **Saint Helena, Mount** ▲ California, W USA *38°40′N 122°39′W*
21 S15 **Saint Helena Sound** *inlet* South Carolina, SE USA
31 Q7 **Saint Helen, Lake** ◎ Michigan, N USA
183 Q16 **Saint Helens** Tasmania, SE Australia *41°21′S 148°15′E*
97 K18 **St Helens** NW England, United Kingdom *53°28′N 02°44′W*
32 G10 **Saint Helens** Oregon, NW USA *45°54′N 122°50′W*
32 H10 **Saint Helens, Mount** 🌋 Washington, NW USA *46°24′N 121°49′W*
97 L26 **St Helier** ○ (Jersey) S Jersey, Channel Islands *49°12′N 02°07′W*
15 S9 **St-Hilarion** Québec, SE Canada *47°34′N 70°24′W*
99 K22 **Saint-Hubert** Luxembourg, SE Belgium *50°02′N 05°23′E*
15 P12 **St-Hyacinthe** Québec, SE Canada *45°38′N 72°57′W*
St.Iago de la Vega *see* Spanish Town
31 Q4 **Saint Ignace** Michigan, N USA *45°53′N 84°44′W*
15 O10 **St-Ignace-du-Lac** Québec, SE Canada *46°43′N 73°49′W*
12 D12 **St. Ignace Island** *island* Ontario, S Canada
108 C7 **St. Imier** Bern, W Switzerland *47°09′N 06°55′E*
97 G25 **St Ives** SW England, United Kingdom *50°12′N 05°29′W*
29 U10 **Saint James** Minnesota, N USA *44°00′N 94°36′W*
10 I15 **St. James, Cape** *headland* Graham Island, British Columbia, SW Canada *51°57′N 131°04′W*
15 O13 **St-Jean** *var.* St-Jean-sur-Richelieu. Québec, SE Canada *45°15′N 73°16′W*
55 X9 **St-Jean** NW French Guiana *05°25′N 54°05′W*
Saint-Jean-d'Acre *see* Akko
102 K11 **St-Jean-d'Angély** Charente-Maritime, W France *45°57′N 00°31′W*
103 N7 **St-Jean-de-Braye** Loiret, C France *47°54′N 01°58′E*
102 I16 **St-Jean-de-Luz** Pyrénées-Atlantiques, SW France *43°24′N 01°40′W*
103 T12 **St-Jean-de-Maurienne** Savoie, E France *45°17′N 06°21′E*
102 I9 **St-Jean-de-Monts** Vendée, NW France *46°45′N 02°00′W*
103 Q14 **St-Jean-du-Gard** Gard, S France *44°06′N 03°49′E*
15 Q7 **St-Jean, Lac** ◎ Québec, SE Canada
102 I16 **St-Jean-Pied-de-Port** Pyrénées-Atlantiques, SW France *43°10′N 01°14′W*
15 S9 **St-Jean-Port-Joli** Québec, SE Canada *47°13′N 70°16′W*
St-Jean-sur-Richelieu *see* St-Jean
15 N12 **St-Jérôme** Québec, SE Canada *45°47′N 74°01′W*
25 T5 **Saint Jo** Texas, SW USA *33°42′N 97°33′W*
13 O15 **St. John** New Brunswick, SE Canada *45°16′N 66°03′W*
26 L6 **Saint John** Kansas, C USA *37°59′N 98°44′W*
19 Q2 **Saint John** *Fr.* Saint-John. 〰 Canada/USA
76 K16 **Saint John** 〰 C Liberia
45 T9 **Saint John** *island* C Virgin Islands (US)
Saint-John *see* Saint John
22 I6 **Saint John, Lake** ◎ Louisiana, S USA
45 W10 **St John's** ● (Antigua and Barbuda) Antigua, Antigua and Barbuda *17°06′N 61°50′W*
13 V12 **St. John's** *province capital* Newfoundland and Labrador, E Canada *47°34′N 52°41′W*
37 O12 **Saint Johns** Arizona, SW USA *34°28′N 109°22′W*
31 Q9 **Saint Johns** Michigan, N USA *43°01′N 84°31′W*
13 V12 **St. John's** ✈ Newfoundland and Labrador, E Canada *47°22′N 52°45′W*
23 X11 **Saint Johns River** 〰 Florida, SE USA
103 Q11 **St-Jost-St-Rambert** Loire, E France *45°30′N 04°13′E*
45 N12 **St. Joseph** W Dominica *15°24′N 61°26′W*
173 P17 **St-Joseph** S Réunion
22 J6 **Saint Joseph** Louisiana, S USA *31°56′N 91°14′W*
31 O10 **Saint Joseph** Michigan, N USA *42°05′N 86°30′W*
27 R3 **Saint Joseph** Missouri, C USA *39°46′N 94°49′W*
20 I10 **Saint Joseph** Tennessee, S USA *35°02′N 87°29′W*
22 R9 **Saint Joseph Bay** *bay* Florida, SE USA
15 R11 **St-Joseph-de-Beauce** Québec, SE Canada *46°20′N 70°52′W*
12 C10 **St. Joseph, Lake** ◎ Ontario, C Canada

◆ Country
● Country Capital
◇ Dependent Territory
○ Dependent Territory Capital
◈ Administrative Regions
✈ International Airport
▲ Mountain
▲▲ Mountain Range
🌋 Volcano
〰 River
◎ Lake
⊠ Reservoir

31 Q11 **Saint Joseph River** ≈ N USA

14 C11 **Saint Joseph's Island** island Ontario, S Canada

15 N11 **St-Jovite** Québec, SE Canada 46°07′N 74°35′W

121 P16 **St Julian's** N Malta 35°55′N 14°29′E

St-Julien see St-Julien-en-Genevois

103 T10 **St-Julien-en-Genevois** var. St-Julien. Haute-Savoie, E France 46°07′N 06°06′E

102 M11 **St-Junien** Haute-Vienne, C France 45°52′N 00°54′E

96 D8 **St Kilda** island NW Scotland, United Kingdom

45 V10 **Saint Kitts** island Saint Kitts and Nevis

45 U10 **Saint Kitts and Nevis** off. Federation of Saint Christopher and Nevis, var. Saint Christopher-Nevis. ◆ commonwealth republic E West Indies

11 X16 **St. Laurent** Manitoba, S Canada 50°20′N 97°55′W

St-Laurent see St-Laurent-du-Maroni

55 X9 **St-Laurent-du-Maroni** var. St-Laurent. NW French Guiana 05°29′N 54°03′W

St-Laurent, Fleuve see St. Lawrence

102 J12 **St-Laurent-Médoc** Gironde, SW France 45°11′N 00°50′W

13 N12 **St. Lawrence** Fr. Fleuve St-Laurent. ≈ Canada/USA

13 Q12 **St. Lawrence, Gulf of** gulf NW Atlantic Ocean

38 K10 **Saint Lawrence Island** island Alaska, USA

14 M14 **Saint Lawrence River** ≈ Canada/USA

99 L25 **Saint-Léger** Luxembourg, SE Belgium 49°36′N 05°39′E

13 N14 **St. Léonard** New Brunswick, SE Canada 47°10′N 67°55′W

15 P11 **St-Léonard** Québec, SE Canada 46°06′N 72°18′W

173 O17 **St-Leu** W Réunion 21°09′S 55°17′E

102 J4 **St-Lô** anc. Briovera, Laudus. Manche, N France 49°07′N 01°08′W

11 T15 **St. Louis** Saskatchewan, S Canada 52°50′N 105°43′W

103 V7 **St-Louis** Haut-Rhin, NE France 47°35′N 07°34′E

173 O17 **St-Louis** S Réunion

76 G10 **Saint Louis** NW Senegal 15°59′N 16°30′W

27 X4 **Saint Louis** Missouri, C USA 38°38′N 90°15′W

29 W5 **Saint Louis River** ≈ Minnesota, N USA

103 T7 **St-Loup-sur-Semouse** Haute-Saône, E France 47°53′N 06°15′E

15 O12 **St-Luc** Québec, SE Canada 45°19′N 73°18′W

45 X13 **Saint Lucia** ◆ commonwealth republic SE West Indies

47 S3 **Saint Lucia** island SE West Indies

83 L22 **St. Lucia, Cape** headland E South Africa 28°29′S 32°26′E

45 Y13 **Saint Lucia Channel** channel Martinique/Saint Lucia

23 Y14 **Saint Lucie Canal** canal Florida, SE USA

23 Z13 **Saint Lucie Inlet** inlet Florida, SE USA

96 L2 **St Magnus Bay** bay N Scotland, United Kingdom

102 K10 **St-Maixent-l'École** Deux-Sèvres, W France 46°24′N 00°13′W

11 Y16 **St. Malo** Manitoba, S Canada 49°16′N 96°58′W

102 I5 **St-Malo** Ille-et-Vilaine, NW France 48°39′N 02°W

102 H4 **St-Malo, Golfe de** gulf NW France

44 L9 **St-Marc** C Haiti 19°08′N 72°41′W

44 L9 **St-Marc, Canal de** channel W Haiti

103 S12 **St-Marcellin-le-Mollard** Isère, E France 45°12′N 05°18′E

55 Y12 **Saint-Marcel, Mont** ▲ S French Guiana 2°32′N 53°00′E

96 K5 **St Margaret's Hope** NE Scotland, United Kingdom 58°50′N 02°57′W

32 M9 **Saint Maries** Idaho, NW USA 47°19′N 116°37′W

23 T9 **Saint Marks** Florida, SE USA 30°09′N 84°12′W

108 D11 **St. Martin** Valais, SW Switzerland 46°09′N 07°27′E

Saint Martin see Sint Maarten

31 O5 **Saint Martin Island** island Michigan, N USA

22 I9 **Saint Martinville** Louisiana, S USA 30°09′N 91°51′W

185 E20 **St. Mary, Mount** ▲ South Island, New Zealand 44°16′S 169°42′E

186 E8 **St. Mary, Mount** ▲ S Papua New Guinea 08°06′S 147°00′E

182 I6 **Saint Mary Peak** ▲ South Australia 31°25′S 138°39′E

183 Q16 **Saint Marys** Tasmania, SE Australia 41°34′S 148°13′E

14 E16 **St. Marys** Ontario, S Canada 43°15′N 81°08′W

38 M11 **Saint Marys** Alaska, USA 62°03′N 163°10′W

23 W8 **Saint Marys** Georgia, SE USA 30°44′N 81°30′W

27 P4 **Saint Marys** Kansas, C USA 39°09′N 96°00′W

31 Q4 **Saint Marys** Ohio, N USA 40°31′N 84°22′W

21 R3 **Saint Marys** West Virginia, NE USA 39°24′N 81°13′W

23 W8 **Saint Marys River** ≈ Florida/Georgia, SE USA

31 Q4 **Saint Marys River** ≈ Michigan, N USA

102 D6 **St-Mathieu, Pointe** headland NW France 48°17′N 04°56′W

38 J12 **Saint Matthew Island** island Alaska, USA

21 R13 **Saint Matthews** South Carolina, SE USA 33°40′N 80°44′W

St.Matthew's Island see Zadetkyi Kyun

186 G4 **St.Matthias Group** island group NE Papua New Guinea

108 C11 **St. Maurice** Valais, SW Switzerland 46°09′N 07°28′E

15 P9 **St-Maurice** ≈ Québec, SE Canada

102 J13 **St-Médard-en-Jalles** Gironde, SW France 44°54′N 00°43′W

39 N10 **Saint Michael** Alaska, USA 63°28′N 162°02′W

15 N10 **St-Michel-des-Saints** Québec, SE Canada 46°39′N 73°54′W

103 S5 **St-Mihiel** Meuse, NE France 48°57′N 05°33′E

108 J10 **St. Moritz** Ger. Sankt Moritz, Rmsch. San Murezzan. Graubünden, SE Switzerland 46°30′N 09°51′E

102 H8 **St-Nazaire** Loire-Atlantique, NW France 47°17′N 02°12′W

Saint Nicholas see São Nicolau

Saint-Nicolas see Sint-Niklaas

103 N1 **St-Omer** Pas-de-Calais, N France 50°45′N 02°15′E

102 J11 **Saintonge** cultural region W France

15 S9 **St-Pacôme** Québec, SE Canada 47°22′N 69°56′W

15 S10 **St-Pamphile** Québec, SE Canada 46°57′N 69°46′W

15 S9 **St-Pascal** Québec, SE Canada 47°32B 69°48′W

14 J11 **St-Patrice, Lac** ◎ Québec, SE Canada

11 R14 **St. Paul** Alberta, SW Canada 54°00′N 111°18′W

173 O16 **St-Paul** NW Réunion

38 K14 **Saint Paul** Saint Paul Island, Alaska, USA 57°08′N 170°13′W

29 V8 **Saint Paul** state capital Minnesota, N USA 45°N 93°10′W

29 P15 **Saint Paul** Nebraska, C USA 41°13′N 98°26′W

21 P7 **Saint Paul** Virginia, NE USA 36°53′N 82°18′W

77 Q17 **Saint Paul, Cape** headland S Ghana 05°44′N 00°55′E

103 O17 **St-Paul-de-Fenouillet** Pyrénées-Orientales, S France 42°49′N 02°29′E

65 K14 **Saint Paul Fracture Zone** tectonic feature E Atlantic Ocean

38 J14 **Saint Paul Island** island Pribilof Islands, Alaska, USA

102 J15 **St-Paul-les-Dax** Landes, SW France 43°45′N 01°01′W

21 U11 **Saint Pauls** North Carolina, SE USA 34°45′N 78°56′W

Saint Paul's Bay see San Pawl il-Baħar

191 R16 **St Paul's Point** headland Pitcairn Island, Pitcairn Islands

29 U10 **Saint Peter** Minnesota, N USA 44°21′N 93°58′W

97 L26 **St Peter Port** ○ (Guernsey) C Guernsey, Channel Islands 49°28′N 02°33′W

23 V13 **Saint Petersburg** Florida, SE USA 27°47′N 82°37′W

Saint Petersburg see Sankt-Peterburg

23 V13 **Saint Petersburg Beach** Florida, SE USA 27°43′N 82°43′W

173 P17 **St-Philippe** SE Réunion 21°21′S 55°46′E

45 Q11 **St-Pierre** NW Martinique 14°44′N 61°11′W

173 O17 **St-Pierre** SW Réunion

13 S13 **St-Pierre and Miquelon** Fr. Îles St-Pierre et Miquelon. ◇ French territorial collectivity NE North America

15 P11 **St-Pierre, Lac** ◎ Québec, SE Canada

102 F5 **St-Pol-de-Léon** Finistère, NW France 48°42′N 04°00′W

103 O2 **St-Pol-sur-Ternoise** Pas-de-Calais, N France 50°22′N 02°21′E

St. Pons see St-Pons-de-Thomières

103 O16 **St-Pons-de-Thomières** var. St. Pons. Hérault, S France 43°28′N 02°48′E

103 P10 **St-Pourçain-sur-Sioule** Allier, C France 46°19′N 03°16′E

15 S11 **St-Prosper** Québec, SE Canada 46°14′N 70°28′W

103 P3 **St-Quentin** Aisne, N France 49°51′N 03°17′E

15 R10 **St-Raphaël** Québec, SE Canada 46°47′N 70°46′W

103 U15 **St-Raphaël** Var, SE France 43°26′N 06°46′E

15 Q10 **St-Raymond** Québec, SE Canada 46°53′N 71°49′W

33 O9 **Saint Regis** Montana, NW USA 47°18′N 115°06′W

18 J7 **Saint Regis River** ≈ New York, NE USA

103 R15 **St-Rémy-de-Provence** Bouches-du-Rhône, SE France 43°48′N 04°49′E

102 M9 **St-Savin** Vienne, W France 46°34′N 00°53′E

Saint-Sébastien,Cap see Anorontany, Tanjona

23 X7 **Saint Simons Island** island Georgia, SE USA

191 Y2 **Saint Stanislas Bay** bay Kiritimati, E Kiribati

13 O15 **St. Stephen** New Brunswick, SE Canada 45°12′N 67°18′W

39 X12 **Saint Terese** Alaska, USA 58°28′N 134°46′W

14 E17 **St. Thomas** Ontario, S Canada 42°46′N 81°12′W

29 Q2 **Saint Thomas** North Dakota, N USA 48°37′N 97°28′W

45 T9 **Saint Thomas** island W Virgin Islands (US)

Saint Thomas see São Tomé, Sao Tome and Principe

Saint Thomas see Charlotte Amalie, Virgin Islands (US)

15 P10 **St-Tite** Québec, SE Canada 46°42′N 72°32′W

Saint-Trond see Sint-Truiden

103 U16 **St-Tropez** Var, SE France 43°16′N 06°39′E

Saint Ubes see Setúbal

102 L3 **St-Valéry-en-Caux** Seine-Maritime, N France 49°53′N 00°42′E

103 Q9 **St-Vallier** Saône-et-Loire, C France 46°39′N 04°19′E

106 B7 **St-Vincent** Valle d'Aosta, NW Italy 45°47′N 07°42′E

45 Q14 **Saint Vincent** island N Saint Vincent and the Grenadines

Saint Vincent see São Vicente

45 W14 **Saint Vincent and the Grenadines** ◆ commonwealth republic SE West Indies

Saint-Vincent, Cap see Ankaboa, Tanjona

Saint Vincent, Cape see São Vicente, Cabo de

102 I15 **St-Vincent-de-Tyrosse** Landes, SW France 43°39′N 01°16′W

182 I9 **Saint Vincent, Gulf** gulf South Australia

23 R10 **Saint Vincent Island** island Florida, SE USA

45 T12 **Saint Vincent Passage** passage Saint Lucia/Saint Vincent and the Grenadines

183 N18 **Saint Vincent, Point** headland Tasmania, SE Australia 43°19′S 145°50′E

Saint-Vith see Sankt-Vith

11 S14 **St. Walburg** Saskatchewan, S Canada 53°38′N 109°12′W

St Wolfgangsee see Wolfgangsee

102 M11 **St-Yrieix-la-Perche** Haute-Vienne, C France 45°31′N 01°12′E

Saint Yves see Setúbal

188 H5 **Saipan** island ● (Northern Mariana Islands) S Northern Mariana Islands

188 H6 **Saipan Channel** channel S Northern Mariana Islands

188 H6 **Saipan International** ✈ Saipan, S Northern Mariana Islands

74 G6 **Sais** ✈ (Fès) C Morocco 33°58′N 04°48′W

Saishū see Cheju-do

Saishū see Cheju

102 J16 **Saison** ≈ SW France

169 R10 **Sai, Sungai** ≈ Borneo, N Indonesia

165 N13 **Saitama** off. Saitama-ken. ◈ prefecture Honshū, S Japan

Saitama see Urawa

Saitama-ken see Saitama

Saiyid Abid see Sayyid 'Abīd

57 J19 **Sajama, Nevado** ▲ W Bolivia 17°57′S 68°51′W

141 V13 **Sājir, Ras** headland S Oman 16°42′N 53°40′E

111 M20 **Sajószentpéter** Borsod-Abaúj-Zemplén, NE Hungary 48°13′N 20°43′E

83 F24 **Sak** ≈ SW South Africa

81 J18 **Saka** Coast, E Kenya 0°11′S 39°27′E

167 P11 **Sa Kaeo** Prachin Buri, C Thailand 13°47′N 102°03′E

164 J14 **Sakai** Ōsaka, Honshū, SW Japan 34°35′N 135°28′E

164 H14 **Sakaide** Kagawa, Shikoku, SW Japan 34°19′N 133°50′E

164 H12 **Sakaiminato** Tottori, Honshū, SW Japan 35°34′N 133°12′E

140 M3 **Sakākah** Al Jawf, NW Saudi Arabia 29°56′N 40°10′E

28 L4 **Sakakawea, Lake** ▣ North Dakota, N USA

12 J9 **Sakami, Lac** ◎ Québec, C Canada

79 O26 **Sakania** Katanga, SE Dem. Rep. Congo 12°44′S 28°34′E

146 K12 **Sakar** Lebap Welaýaty, E Turkmenistan 38°57′N 63°46′E

172 H7 **Sakaraha** Toliara, SW Madagascar 22°54′S 44°31′E

146 I14 **Sakarçäge** var. Sakarchäge, Rus. Sakar-Chaga. Mary Welaýaty, C Turkmenistan 37°40′N 61°33′E

Sakar-Chaga/Sakarchäge see Sakarçäge

Sak'art'velo see Georgia

136 F11 **Sakarya** ◈ province NW Turkey

136 F12 **Sakarya Nehri** ≈ NW Turkey

165 P9 **Sakata** Yamagata, Honshū, C Japan 38°54′N 139°51′E

145 S11 **Saken Seyfullin** Kaz. Säken Seyfüllīn; prev. Zharyk. Karaganda, C Kazakhstan 48°52′N 72°51′E

Säken Seyfüllīn see Saken Seyfullin

123 P9 **Sakha (Yakutiya), Respublika** var. Respublika Yakutiya, Eng. Yakutia. ◈ autonomous republic NE Russian Federation

Sakhalin see Sakhalin, Ostrov

192 I3 **Sakhalin, Ostrov** var. Sakhalin. island SE Russian Federation

123 U12 **Sakhalinskaya Oblast'** ◈ province SE Russian Federation

123 T12 **Sakhalinskiy Zaliv** gulf E Russian Federation

Sakhnovshchina see Sakhnovshchyna

117 U6 **Sakhnovshchyna** Rus. Sakhnovshchina. Kharkivs'ka Oblast', E Ukraine 49°08′N 35°52′E

Sakhon Nakhon see Sakon Nakhon

Sakhtsar see Rāmsar

137 W10 **Şäki** Rus. Sheki; prev. Nukha. NW Azerbaijan 41°09′N 47°10′E

Saki see Saky

118 E13 **Šakiai** Ger. Schaken. Marijampolė, S Lithuania 54°57′N 23°04′E

165 O16 **Sakishima-shotō** var. Sakisima Syotô. island group SW Japan

Sakisima Syotô see Sakishima-shotō

Sakiz see Saqqez

Sakiz-Adasi see Chíos

155 F19 **Sakleshpur** Karnātaka, E India 12°58′N 75°45′E

167 S9 **Sakon Nakhon** var. Muang Sakon Nakhon, Sakhon Nakhon. Sakon Nakhon, E Thailand 17°10′N 104°08′E

149 P15 **Sakrand** Sind, SE Pakistan 26°06′N 68°20′E

83 F24 **Sak River** Afr. Sakrivier. Northern Cape, W South Africa 30°49′S 20°24′E

Sakrivier see Sak River

Saksaul'skiy see Saksaul'skoye

144 K13 **Saksaul'skoye** var. Saksaul'skiy, Kaz. Sekseūil. Kzylorda, S Kazakhstan 47°07′N 61°06′E

95 I25 **Sakskøbing** Storstrøm, SE Denmark 54°48′N 11°39′E

165 N12 **Saku** Nagano, Honshū, S Japan 36°17′N 138°29′E

117 S13 **Saky** Rus. Saki. Respublika Krym, S Ukraine 45°09′N 33°36′E

76 E9 **Sal** island Ilhas de Barlavento, NE Cape Verde

127 N12 **Sal** ≈ SW Russian Federation

111 I21 **Sal'a** Hung. Sellye, Vágsellye. Nitriansky Kraj, SW Slovakia 48°09′N 17°51′E

95 N15 **Sala** Västmanland, C Sweden 59°55′N 16°38′E

15 N13 **Salaberry-de-Valleyfield** var. Valleyfield. Québec, SE Canada 45°15′N 74°07′W

118 G7 **Salacgrīva** Est. Salatsi. Limbaži, N Latvia 57°45′N 24°21′E

107 M18 **Sala Consilina** Campania, S Italy 40°23′N 15°35′E

40 C2 **Salada, Laguna** ◎ NW Mexico

61 D14 **Saladas** Corrientes, NE Argentina 28°15′S 58°40′W

61 C21 **Saladillo** Buenos Aires, E Argentina 35°40′S 59°50′W

61 B16 **Saladillo, Río** ≈ C Argentina

25 T9 **Salado** Texas, SW USA 30°57′N 97°32′W

63 J16 **Salado, Arroyo** ≈ SE Argentina

61 D21 **Salado, Río** ≈ E Argentina

62 J12 **Salado, Río** ≈ C Argentina

41 N7 **Salado, Río** ≈ NE Mexico

37 Q12 **Salado, Rio** ≈ New Mexico, SW USA

143 N6 **Salafchegān** var. Sarafjagān. Quom, N Iran 34°28′N 50°28′E

77 Q15 **Salaga** C Ghana 08°31′N 00°37′W

139 S6 **Şalāḩ ad Dīn** ◈ governorate C Iraq

192 G5 **Sala'ilua** Savai'i, W Samoa 13°39′S 172°33′W

116 G9 **Sălaj** ◈ county NW Romania

83 H20 **Salajwe** Kweneng, SE Botswana 23°40′S 24°46′E

78 H9 **Salal** Kanem, W Chad 14°48′N 17°12′E

80 I6 **Salala** Red Sea, NE Sudan 21°17′N 36°16′E

141 V13 **Şalālah** SW Oman 17°01′N 54°04′E

42 D5 **Salamá** Baja Verapaz, C Guatemala 15°06′N 90°18′W

42 J6 **Salamá** Olancho, C Honduras 14°48′N 86°34′W

62 G10 **Salamanca** Coquimbo, C Chile 31°47′S 70°58′W

41 N13 **Salamanca** Guanajuato, C Mexico 20°34′N 101°12′W

104 K7 **Salamanca** anc. Helmantica, Salmantica. Castilla-León, NW Spain 40°58′N 05°40′W

18 D11 **Salamanca** New York, NE USA 42°09′N 78°43′W

104 J7 **Salamanca** ◈ province Castilla-León, W Spain

63 J19 **Salamanca, Pampa de** plain S Argentina

78 J12 **Salamat** off. Préfecture du Salamat. ◈ prefecture SE Chad

78 I12 **Salamat, Bahr** ≈ S Chad

Salamat, Préfecture du see Salamat

54 F5 **Salamina** Magdalena, N Colombia 10°30′N 74°48′W

115 G19 **Salamína** var. Salamís. Salamína, C Greece 37°58′N 23°29′E

115 G19 **Salamína** island C Greece

Salamís see Salamína

138 I5 **Salamīyah** var. As Salamīyah. Ḩamāh, W Syria 35°01′N 37°02′E

31 P12 **Salamonie Lake** ▣ Indiana, N USA

31 P12 **Salamonie River** ≈ Indiana, N USA

Salang see Phuket

192 I16 **Salani** Upolu, SE Samoa 14°00′S 171°35′W

118 C11 **Salantai** Klaipėda, NW Lithuania 56°05′N 21°36′E

104 K2 **Salas** Asturias, N Spain 43°25′N 06°15′W

105 O5 **Salas de los Infantes** Castilla-León, N Spain 42°02′N 03°17′W

102 M16 **Salat** ≈ S France

189 V13 **Salat** island Chuuk, C Micronesia

169 Q16 **Salatiga** Jawa, C Indonesia 07°15′S 110°34′E

189 V13 **Salat Pass** passage W Pacific Ocean

Salatsi see Salacgrīva

167 T10 **Salavan** var. Saravan, Saravane. Salavan, S Laos 15°43′N 106°26′E

127 V6 **Salavat** Respublika Bashkortostan, W Russian Federation 53°20′N 55°54′E

56 C12 **Salaverry** La Libertad, N Peru 08°14′S 78°55′W

171 T12 **Salawati, Pulau** island E Indonesia

193 R10 **Sala y Gomez** island Chile, E Pacific Ocean

Sala y Gomez Fracture Zone see Sala y Gomez Ridge

193 S10 **Sala y Gomez Ridge** var. Sala y Gomez Fracture Zone. tectonic feature SE Pacific Ocean

61 A22 **Salazar** Buenos Aires, E Argentina 36°20′S 62°11′W

54 G7 **Salazar** Norte de Santander, N Colombia 07°46′N 72°46′W

Salazar see N'Dalatando

173 P16 **Salazie** C Réunion 21°02′S 55°33′E

103 N8 **Salbris** Loir-et-Cher, C France 47°25′N 02°02′E

57 G15 **Salcantay, Nevado** ▲ C Peru 13°21′S 72°31′W

45 O8 **Salcedo** N Dominican Republic 19°26′N 70°25′W

39 S9 **Salcha River** ≈ Alaska, USA

119 H15 **Šalčininkai** Vilnius, SE Lithuania 54°20′N 25°26′E

Saldae see Béjaïa

54 E11 **Saldaña** Tolima, C Colombia 03°57′N 75°01′W

104 M4 **Saldaña** Castilla-León, N Spain 42°31′N 04°44′W

83 E25 **Saldanha** Western Cape, SW South Africa 33°00′S 17°56′E

Salduba see Zaragoza

61 B23 **Saldungaray** Buenos Aires, E Argentina 38°15′S 61°45′W

118 D9 **Saldus** Ger. Frauenburg. Saldus, W Latvia 56°40′N 22°29′E

183 P13 **Sale** Victoria, SE Australia 38°06′S 147°06′E

74 F6 **Salé** NW Morocco 34°07′N 06°40′W

74 F6 **Salé** ✈ (Rabat) W Morocco 34°09′N 06°30′W

Salehābād see Andīmeshk

170 M16 **Saleh, Teluk** bay Nusa Tenggara, S Indonesia

122 H8 **Salekhard** prev. Obdorsk. Yamalo-Nenetskiy Avtonomnyy Okrug, N Russian Federation 66°33′N 66°35′E

192 H16 **Sālelologa** Savai'i, C Samoa 13°42′S 172°10′W

155 H21 **Salem** Tamil Nādu, SE India 11°38′N 78°08′E

27 V9 **Salem** Arkansas, C USA 36°21′N 91°49′W

30 L15 **Salem** Illinois, N USA 38°37′N 88°57′W

31 P15 **Salem** Indiana, N USA 38°38′N 86°06′W

19 P11 **Salem** Massachusetts, NE USA 42°30′N 70°51′W

27 V6 **Salem** Missouri, C USA 37°39′N 91°32′W

18 I16 **Salem** New Jersey, NE USA 39°33′N 75°26′W

31 U12 **Salem** Ohio, N USA 40°52′N 80°51′W

32 G12 **Salem** state capital Oregon, NW USA 44°57′N 123°01′W

29 Q11 **Salem** South Dakota, N USA 43°43′N 97°23′W

36 L4 **Salem** Utah, W USA 40°03′N 111°40′W

21 S7 **Salem** Virginia, NE USA 37°16′N 80°00′W

21 R3 **Salem** West Virginia, NE USA 39°15′N 80°32′W

107 H23 **Salemi** Sicilia, Italy, C Mediterranean Sea 37°48′N 12°48′E

Salemy see As Sālimī

94 K12 **Sälen** Dalarna, C Sweden 61°11′N 13°14′E

107 Q18 **Salentina, Campi** Puglia, SE Italy 40°23′N 18°01′E

107 Q18 **Salentina, Penisola** peninsula SE Italy

107 L18 **Salerno** anc. Salernum. Campania, S Italy 40°40′N 14°44′E

107 L18 **Salerno, Golfo di** Eng. Gulf of Salerno. gulf S Italy

Salerno, Gulf of see Salerno, Golfo di

Salernum see Salerno

97 K17 **Salford** NW England, United Kingdom 53°30′N 02°16′W

Salgir see Salhyr

111 K21 **Salgótarján** Nógrád, N Hungary 48°07′N 19°47′E

59 O15 **Salgueiro** Pernambuco, E Brazil 08°04′S 39°05′W

94 C13 **Salhus** Hordaland, S Norway 60°30′N 05°15′E

117 T12 **Salhyr** Rus. Salgir. ≈ S Ukraine

171 Q9 **Salibabu, Pulau** island N Indonesia

37 S6 **Salida** Colorado, C USA 38°29′N 105°57′W

102 J15 **Salies-de-Béarn** Pyrénées-Atlantiques, SW France 43°28′N 00°55′W

136 C14 **Salihli** Manisa, W Turkey 38°29′N 28°08′E

119 K18 **Salihorsk** Rus. Soligorsk. Minskaya Voblasts', S Belarus 52°48′N 27°32′E

119 K18 **Salihorskaye Vodaskhovishcha** ▣ C Belarus

83 N14 **Salima** Central, C Malawi 13°44′S 34°21′E

166 L5 **Salin** Magway, W Myanmar (Burma) 20°30′N 94°40′E

27 N4 **Salina** Kansas, C USA 38°53′N 97°36′W

36 L5 **Salina** Utah, W USA 38°57′N 111°54′W

41 S17 **Salina Cruz** Oaxaca, SE Mexico 16°11′N 95°12′W

107 L22 **Salina, Isola** island Isole Eolie, S Italy

44 J5 **Salina Point** headland Acklins Island, SE Bahamas 22°10′N 74°16′W

56 A7 **Salinas** Guayas, W Ecuador 02°15′S 80°58′W

40 M11 **Salinas** var. Salinas de Hidalgo. San Luis Potosí, C Mexico 22°36′N 101°41′W

45 T6 **Salinas** C Puerto Rico 17°57′N 66°18′W

35 O10 **Salinas** California, W USA 36°41′N 121°40′W

Salinas, Cabo de see Salines, Cap de ses

Salinas de Hidalgo see Salinas

82 A13 **Salinas, Ponta das** headland W Angola 12°50′S 12°57′E

45 O10 **Salinas, Punta** headland S Dominican Republic 18°11′N 70°32′W

Salinas, Río see Chixoy, Río

35 O11 **Salinas River** ≈ California, W USA

22 H6 **Saline Lake** ◎ Louisiana, S USA

25 R17 **Salineno** Texas, SW USA 26°29′N 99°06′W

27 V14 **Saline River** ≈ Arkansas, C USA

30 M17 **Saline River** ≈ Illinois, N USA

105 X10 **Salines, Cap de ses** var. Cabo de Salinas. headland Mallorca, Spain, W Mediterranean Sea 39°15′N 03°03′E

Salisburg see Mazsalaca

45 O12 **Salisbury** var. Baroui. W Dominica 15°26′N 61°27′W

97 M23 **Salisbury** var. New Sarum. S England, United Kingdom 51°05′N 01°48′W

21 Y4 **Salisbury** Maryland, NE USA 38°22′N 75°37′W

27 T3 **Salisbury** Missouri, C USA 39°25′N 92°48′W

21 S9 **Salisbury** North Carolina, SE USA 35°40′N 80°28′W

Salisbury see Harare

9 Q7 **Salisbury Island** island Nunavut, NE Canada

Salisbury, Lake see Bisina, Lake

97 L23 **Salisbury Plain** plain S England, United Kingdom

21 R14 **Salkehatchie River** ≈ South Carolina, SE USA

138 I9 **Şalkhad** As Suwaydā', SW Syria 32°29′N 36°42′E

92 M12 **Salla** Lappi, NE Finland 66°50′N 28°40′E

Sállan see Sørøya

103 U11 **Sallanches** Haute-Savoie, E France 45°55′N 06°37′E

105 V5 **Sallent** Cataluña, NE Spain 41°48′N 01°52′E

61 A22 **Salliqueló** Buenos Aires, E Argentina 36°45′S 62°55′W

27 R10 **Sallisaw** Oklahoma, C USA 35°27′N 94°49′W

80 I7 **Sallom** Red Sea, NE Sudan 19°17′N 37°02′E

12 J2 **Salluit** prev. Saglouc, Sagluk. Québec, NE Canada 62°10′N 75°40′W

Sallyana see Şalyān

13 S11 **Sally's Cove** Newfoundland and Labrador, E Canada 49°43′N 58°00′W

139 W9 **Salmān Bin 'Arāzah** Maysān, E Iraq 32°33′N 46°36′E

Salmantica see Salamanca

142 I2 **Salmās** prev. Dilman, Shāpūr. Āžarbāyjān-e Gharbī, NW Iran 38°13′N 44°50′E

124 I11 **Salmi** Respublika Kareliya, NW Russian Federation 61°21′N 31°55′E

33 P12 **Salmon** Idaho, NW USA 45°10′N 113°54′W

11 N16 **Salmon Arm** British Columbia, SW Canada 50°41′N 119°18′W

192 L5 **Salmon Bank** undersea feature N Pacific Ocean 26°55′N 176°28′W

Salmon Leap see Leixlip

34 L2 **Salmon Mountains** ▲▲ California, W USA

14 J15 **Salmon Point** headland Ontario, SE Canada 43°51′N 77°15′W

33 N11 **Salmon River** ≈ Idaho, NW USA

18 K6 **Salmon River** ≈ New York, NE USA

33 N12 **Salmon River Mountains** ▲▲ Idaho, NW USA

18 I9 **Salmon River Reservoir** ▣ New York, NE USA

93 K19 **Salo** Länsi-Suomi, SW Finland 60°23′N 23°10′E

106 F7 **Salò** Lombardia, N Italy 45°37′N 10°30′E

Salona/Salonae see Solin

103 S15 **Salon-de-Provence** Bouches-du-Rhône, SE France 43°39′N 05°05′E

Salonica/Salonika see Thessaloníki

115 I14 **Salonikiós, Akrotírio** var. Akrotírio Salonikós. headland Thásos, E Greece 40°34′N 24°39′E

Salonikós, Akrotírio see Salonikiós, Akrotírio

116 F10 **Salonta** Hung. Nagyszalonta. Bihor, W Romania 46°49′N 21°40′E

104 I9 **Salor** ≈ W Spain

105 U6 **Salou** Cataluña, NE Spain 41°05′N 01°08′E

76 H11 **Saloum** ≈ C Senegal

42 H4 **Sal, Punta** headland NW Honduras 15°55′N 87°36′W

92 N3 **Salpynten** headland W Svalbard 78°12′N 12°11′E

138 I3 **Salqīn** Idlib, W Syria 36°09′N 36°27′E

93 F14 **Salsbruket** Nord-Trøndelag, C Norway 64°49′N 11°48′E

126 M13 **Sal'sk** Rostovskaya Oblast', SW Russian Federation 46°30′N 41°31′E

107 K25 **Salso** ≈ Sicilia, Italy, C Mediterranean Sea

107 J25 **Salso** ≈ Sicilia, Italy, C Mediterranean Sea

106 E9 **Salsomaggiore Terme** Emilia-Romagna, N Italy 44°49′N 09°58′E

Salt see As Salţ

62 J6 **Salta** Salta, NW Argentina 24°47′S 65°23′W

62 K6 **Salta** off. Provincia de Salta. ◈ province N Argentina

Salta, Provincia de see Salta

97 I24 **Saltash** SW England, United Kingdom 50°26′N 04°14′W

24 I8 **Salt Basin** basin Texas, SW USA

11 V16 **Saltcoats** Saskatchewan, S Canada 51°06′N 102°12′W

30 L13 **Salt Creek** ≈ Illinois, N USA

24 J9 **Salt Draw** ≈ Texas, SW USA

97 F21 **Saltee Islands** island group SE Ireland

92 G12 **Saltfjorden** inlet C Norway

24 I8 **Salt Flat** Texas, SW USA 31°43′N 105°05′W

27 N8 **Salt Fork Arkansas River** ≈ Oklahoma, C USA

31 T13 **Salt Fork Lake** ▣ Ohio, N USA

26 J11 **Salt Fork Red River** ≈ Oklahoma/Texas, C USA

95 J23 **Saltholm** island E Denmark

41 N8 **Saltillo** Coahuila, NE Mexico 25°30′N 101°W

182 L5 **Salt Lake** salt lake New South Wales, SE Australia

37 V15 **Salt Lake** ◎ New Mexico, SW USA

36 K2 **Salt Lake City** state capital Utah, W USA 40°45′N 111°54′W

61 C20 **Salto** Buenos Aires, E Argentina 34°18′S 60°17′W

61 D17 **Salto** Salto, N Uruguay 31°23′S 57°58′W

61 E17 **Salto** ◈ department N Uruguay

107 I14 **Salto** ≈ C Italy

62 Q6 **Salto del Guairá** Canindeyú, E Paraguay 24°06′S 54°22′W

61 D17 **Salto Grande, Embalse de** var. Lago de Salto Grande. ▣ Argentina/Uruguay

Salto Grande, Lago de see Salto Grande, Embalse de

35 W16 **Salton Sea** ◎ California, W USA

60 I12 **Salto Santiago, Represa de** ▣ S Brazil

149 U7 **Salt Range** ▲▲ E Pakistan

36 M13 **Salt River** ≈ Arizona, SW USA

20 L5 **Salt River** ≈ Kentucky, S USA

27 V3 **Salt River** ≈ Missouri, C USA

95 F17 **Saltrød** Aust-Agder, S Norway 58°28′N 08°49′E

95 P16 **Saltsjöbaden** Stockholm, C Sweden 59°15′N 18°20′E

92 G12 **Saltstraumen** Nordland, C Norway 67°16′N 14°42′E

21 Q7 **Saltville** Virginia, NE USA 36°52′N 81°48′W

Saluces/Saluciae see Saluzzo

21 Q12 **Saluda** South Carolina, SE USA 34°00′N 81°47′W

21 X6 **Saluda** Virginia, NE USA 37°36′N 76°36′W

21 Q12 **Saluda River** ≈ South Carolina, SE USA

Salûm see As Sallūm

152 F14 **Sālūmbar** Rājasthān, N India 24°16′N 74°04′E

Salûm, Gulf of see Khalīj as Sallūm

171 O11 **Salumpaga** Sulawesi, N Indonesia 01°18′N 120°58′E

155 M14 **Sālūr** Andhra Pradesh, E India 18°31′N 83°16′E

55 Y9 **Salut, Îles du** island group N French Guiana

106 A9 **Saluzzo** Fr. Saluces; anc. Saluciae. Piemonte, NW Italy 44°39′N 07°29′E

63 F23 **Salvación, Bahía** bay S Chile

59 P17 **Salvador** prev. São Salvador. state capital Bahia, E Brazil 12°58′S 38°29′W

65 E24 **Salvador** East Falkland, Falkland Islands 51°28′S 58°22′W

22 K10 **Salvador, Lake** ◎ Louisiana, S USA

Salvaleón de Higüey see Higüey

104 F10 **Salvaterra de Magos** Santarém, C Portugal 39°01′N 08°47′W

41 N13 **Salvatierra** Guanajuato, C Mexico 20°14′N 100°52′W

105 P3 **Salvatierra** Basq. Agurain. País Vasco, N Spain 42°52′N 02°23′W

Salwa/Salwah see As Salwā

166 M7 **Salween** Bur. Thanlwin, Chin. Nu Chiang, Nu Jiang. ≈ SE Asia

137 Y12 **Salyan** Rus. Sal'yany. SE Azerbaijan 39°36′N 48°57′E

153 N11 **Şalyān** var. Sallyana. Mid Western, W Nepal 28°22′N 82°10′E

Sal'yany see Salyan

21 O6 **Salyersville** Kentucky, S USA 37°43′N 83°06′W

109 V6 **Salza** ≈ E Austria

109 Q7 **Salzach** ≈ Austria/Germany

109 Q6 **Salzburg** anc. Juvavum. Salzburg, N Austria 47°48′N 13°03′E

109 O8 **Salzburg** off. Land Salzburg. ◈ state C Austria

Salzburg see Ocna Sibiului

Salzburg Alps see Salzburger Kalkalpen

109 Q7 **Salzburger Kalkalpen** Eng. Salzburg Alps. ▲▲ C Austria

Salzburg, Land see Salzburg

100 J13 **Salzgitter** prev. Watenstedt-Salzgitter. Niedersachsen, C Germany 52°07′N 10°24′E

101 G14 **Salzkotten** Nordrhein-Westfalen, W Germany 51°40′N 08°36′E

100 K11 **Salzwedel** Sachsen-Anhalt, N Germany 52°51′N 11°10′E

152 D11 **Sām** Rājasthān, NW India 26°50′N 70°30′E

Šamac see Bosanski Šamac

54 G9 **Samacá** Boyacá, C Colombia 05°28′N 73°33′W

40 I7 **Samachique** Chihuahua, N Mexico 27°17′N 107°28′W

141 Y8 **Şamad** NE Oman 22°47′N 58°12′E

Sama de Langreo see Sama, Spain

Samaden see Samedan

57 M19 **Samaipata** Santa Cruz, C Bolivia 18°08′S 63°53′W

167 T10 **Samakhixai** var. Attapu, Attopeu. Attapu, S Laos 14°48′N 106°51′E

Samakov see Samokov

42 B6 **Samalá, Río** ≈ SW Guatemala

40 J3 **Samalayuca** Chihuahua, N Mexico 31°25′N 106°30′W

155 L16 **Sāmalkot** Andhra Pradesh, E India 17°03′N 82°15′E

45 P8 **Samaná** var. Santa Bárbara de Samaná. E Dominican Republic 19°14′N 69°20′W

45 P8 **Samaná, Bahía de** bay E Dominican Republic

44 K4 **Samana Cay** island SE Bahamas

136 K17 **Samandağı** Hatay, S Turkey 36°07′N 35°55′E

149 P3 **Samangān** ◈ province N Afghanistan

Samangān see Āybak

165 T5 **Samani** Hokkaidō, NE Japan 42°07′N 142°57′E

54 C13 **Samaniego** Nariño, SW Colombia 01°22′N 77°35′W

171 Q5 **Samar** island C Philippines

127 S6 **Samara** prev. Kuybyshev. Samarskaya Oblast', W Russian Federation 53°15′N 50°15′E

127 T7 **Samara** ≈ W Russian Federation

127 S6 **Samara** ✈ Samarskaya Oblast', W Russian Federation 53°11′N 50°27′E

117 V7 **Samara** ≈ E Ukraine

186 G10 **Samarai** Milne Bay, SE Papua New Guinea 10°36′S 150°39′E

Samarang see Semarang

123 T14 **Samarga** Khabarovskiy Kray, SE Russian Federation 47°43′N 139°08′E

138 G9 **Samarian Hills** hill range N Israel

54 L9 **Samariapo** Amazonas, C Venezuela 05°16′N 67°43′W

169 V11 **Samarinda** Borneo, C Indonesia 0°30′S 117°09′E

Samarkand see Samarqand

Samarkandskaya Oblast' see Samarqand Viloyati

Samarkandski/Samarkandskoye see Temirtau

◆ Country
● Country Capital
◇ Dependent Territory
○ Dependent Territory Capital
◈ Administrative Regions
✈ International Airport
▲ Mountain
▲▲ Mountain Range
Volcano
≈ River
◎ Lake
▣ Reservoir

SAMAROBRIVA – SAN JUAN BAUTISTA TUXTEPEC

Samarobriva see Amiens
147 N11 **Samarqand** Rus. Samarkand. Samarqand Viloyati, C Uzbekistan 39°40′N 66°56′E
146 M11 **Samarqand Viloyati** Rus. Samarkandskaya Oblast'. ◈ province C Uzbekistan
139 S6 **Sāmarrā'** Ṣalāḥ ad Dīn, C Iraq 34°13′N 43°52′E
127 R7 **Samarskaya Oblast'** prev. Kuybyshevskaya Oblast'. ◈ province W Russian Federation
153 Q13 **Samastīpur** Bihār, N India 25°52′N 85°47′E
76 L14 **Samatiguila** NW Ivory Coast 09°51′N 07°36′W
Samawa see As Samāwah
137 Y11 **Şamaxı** Rus. Shemakha. E Azerbaijan 40°38′N 48°34′E
79 K18 **Samba** Equateur, NW Dem. Rep. Congo 0°13′N 21°17′E
79 N21 **Samba** Maniema, E Dem. Rep. Congo 04°41′S 26°23′E
152 H6 **Samba** Jammu and Kashmir, NW India 32°32′N 75°08′E
169 W10 **Sambaliung, Pegunungan** ▲▲ Borneo, N Indonesia
154 M11 **Sambalpur** Orissa, E India 21°28′N 84°04′E
67 X12 **Sambao** ∽ W Madagascar
169 Q10 **Sambas, Sungai** ∽ Borneo, N Indonesia
172 K2 **Sambava** Antsiranana, NE Madagascar 14°16′S 50°10′E
152 J10 **Sambhal** Uttar Pradesh, N India 28°35′N 78°34′E
152 H12 **Sāmbhar Salt Lake** ◎ N India
107 N21 **Sambiase** Calabria, SW Italy 38°58′N 16°16′E
116 H5 **Sambir** Rus. Sambor. L'vivs'ka Oblast', NW Ukraine 49°31′N 23°10′E
82 C13 **Sambo** Huambo, C Angola 13°07′S 16°06′E
Sambor see Sambir
61 E21 **Samborombón, Bahía** bay NE Argentina
99 H20 **Sambre** ∽ Belgium/France
43 V16 **Sambú, Río** ∽ SE Panama
163 Z14 **Samch'ŏk** Jap. Sanchoku. NE South Korea 37°21′N 129°12′E
Samch'ŏnpŏ see Sach'ŏn
81 I21 **Same** Kilimanjaro, NE Tanzania 04°04′S 37°41′E
108 J10 **Samedan** Ger. Samaden. Graubünden, S Switzerland 46°31′N 09°51′E
82 K12 **Samfya** Luapula, N Zambia 11°22′S 29°34′E
141 W13 **Samḥān, Jabal** ▲▲ SW Oman
115 C18 **Sámi** Kefallonía, Iónia Nisiá, Greece, C Mediterranean Sea 38°15′N 20°39′E
56 F10 **Samiria, Río** ∽ N Peru
Samirum see Semīrom
137 V11 **Şämkir** Rus. Shamkhor. NW Azerbaijan 40°51′N 46°03′E
167 S7 **Sam, Nam** Vtn. Sông Chu. ∽ Laos/Vietnam
Samnān see Semnān
Sam Neua see Xam Nua
75 P10 **Samnū** C Libya 27°19′N 15°01′E
192 H15 **Samoa** off. Independent State of Western Samoa, var. Sāmoa; prev. Western Samoa. ◆ monarchy W Polynesia
192 L9 **Samoa** island group American Samoa
Sāmoa see Samoa
175 T9 **Samoa Basin** undersea feature W Pacific Ocean
112 D8 **Samobor** Zagreb, N Croatia 45°48′N 15°38′E
114 H10 **Samokov** var. Samakov. Sofiya, W Bulgaria 42°19′N 23°34′E
111 H21 **Šamorín** Ger. Sommerein, Hung. Somorja. Trnavský Kraj, W Slovakia 48°01′N 17°18′E
115 M19 **Sámos** prev. Limín Vathéos. Sámos, Dodekánisa, Greece, Aegean Sea 37°45′N 26°58′E
115 M20 **Sámos** island Dodekánisa, Greece, Aegean Sea
Samosch see Szamos
168 I9 **Samosir, Pulau** island W Indonesia
Samothrace see Samothráki
115 K14 **Samothráki** Samothráki, NE Greece 40°28′N 25°31′E
115 J14 **Samothráki** anc. Samothrace. island NE Greece
115 A15 **Samothráki** island Iónia Nisiá, Greece, C Mediterranean Sea
Samotschin see Szamocin
Sampê see Xiangcheng
169 S13 **Sampit** Borneo, C Indonesia 02°30′S 112°30′E
169 S12 **Sampit, Sungai** ∽ Borneo, N Indonesia
Sampoku see Sanpoku
186 H7 **Sampun** New Britain, E Papua New Guinea 05°19′S 152°06′E
79 N24 **Sampwe** Katanga, SE Dem. Rep. Congo 09°17′S 27°22′E
25 X8 **Sam Rayburn Reservoir** ⊠ Texas, SW USA
158 H15 **Samsang** Xizang Zizhiqu, W China 30°23′N 82°49′E
167 Q6 **Sam Sao, Phou** ▲▲ Laos/Thailand
95 H22 **Samsø** island E Denmark
95 H23 **Samsø Bælt** channel E Denmark
167 T7 **Sâm Sơn** Thanh Hoa, N Vietnam 19°44′N 105°53′E
136 L11 **Samsun** anc. Amisus. Samsun, N Turkey 41°17′N 36°22′E
136 K11 **Samsun** ◈ province N Turkey
137 R9 **Samtredia** W Georgia 42°09′N 42°20′E
59 E15 **Samuel, Represa de** ⊠ W Brazil
167 O14 **Samui, Ko** island SW Thailand
Samundari see Samundri
149 U9 **Samundri** var. Samundari. Punjab, E Pakistan 31°04′N 72°58′E
137 X10 **Samur** ∽ Azerbaijan/Russian Federation
137 Y11 **Samur-Abşeron Kanalı** Rus. Samur-Apsheronskiy Kanal. canal E Azerbaijan
Samur-Apsheronskiy Kanal see Samur-Abşeron Kanalı
167 O11 **Samut Prakan** var. Muang Samut Prakan, Paknam. Samut Prakan, C Thailand 13°36′N 100°36′E
167 O11 **Samut Sakhon** var. Maha Chai, Samut Sakorn, Tha Chin. Samut Sakhon, C Thailand 13°31′N 100°15′E
Samut Sakorn see Samut Sakhon
167 O11 **Samut Songhram** prev. Meklong. Samut Songkhram, SW Thailand 13°25′N 100°01′E
77 N12 **San** Ségou, C Mali 13°21′N 04°57′W
111 O15 **San** ∽ SE Poland
141 O15 **Şan'ā'** Eng. Sana. ● (Yemen) W Yemen 15°24′N 44°14′E
112 F11 **Sana** ∽ NW Bosnia and Herzegovina
80 O12 **Sanaag** off. Gobolka Sanaag. ◈ region N Somalia
Sanaag, Gobolka see Sanaag
114 J8 **Sanadinovo** Pleven, N Bulgaria 43°33′N 25°00′E
195 P1 **Sanae** South African research station Antarctica 70°19′S 01°31′W
139 Y10 **Sanāf, Hawr as** ◎ S Iraq
79 E15 **Sanaga** ∽ C Cameroon
54 D12 **San Agustín** Huila, SW Colombia 01°53′N 76°14′W
171 R8 **San Agustin, Cape** headland Mindanao, S Philippines 06°17′N 126°12′E
37 Q13 **San Agustin, Plains of** plain New Mexico, SW USA
38 M16 **Sanak Islands** island Aleutian Islands, Alaska, USA
San Alessandro see Kita-Iō-jima
193 U10 **San Ambrosio, Isla** Eng. San Ambrosio Island. island W Chile
San Ambrosio Island see San Ambrosio, Isla
171 Q12 **Sanana** Pulau Sanana, E Indonesia 02°04′S 125°58′E
171 Q12 **Sanana, Pulau** island Maluku, E Indonesia
142 K5 **Sanandaj** prev. Sinneh. Kordestān, W Iran 35°18′N 47°01′E
35 P8 **San Andreas** California, W USA 38°10′N 120°40′W
2 C13 **San Andreas Fault** fault W USA
54 G8 **San Andrés** Santander, C Colombia 06°52′N 72°53′W
61 C20 **San Andrés de Giles** Buenos Aires, E Argentina 34°27′S 59°27′W
43 Q7 **San Andrés, Isla de** island NW Colombia, Caribbean Sea
43 Q7 **San Andrés y Providencia** ◈ province Colombia, Caribbean Sea
37 R14 **San Andres Mountains** ▲▲ New Mexico, SW USA
41 S15 **San Andrés Tuxtla** var. Tuxtla. Veracruz-Llave, E Mexico 18°28′N 95°15′W
25 P8 **San Angelo** Texas, SW USA 31°28′N 100°26′W
107 A20 **San Antioco, Isola di** island W Italy
42 F4 **San Antonio** Toledo, S Belize 16°13′N 89°02′W
62 G11 **San Antonio** Valparaíso, C Chile 33°35′S 71°38′W
188 H6 **San Antonio** Saipan, S Northern Mariana Islands
37 R13 **San Antonio** New Mexico, SW USA 33°53′N 106°52′W
25 R12 **San Antonio** Texas, SW USA 29°25′N 98°30′W
54 M11 **San Antonio** Amazonas, S Venezuela 03°31′N 66°47′W
54 I7 **San Antonio** Barinas, C Venezuela 07°24′N 71°28′W
55 O5 **San Antonio** Monagas, NE Venezuela 10°03′N 63°45′W
25 S12 **San Antonio** ✈ Texas, SW USA 29°31′N 98°11′W
San Antonio see San Antonio del Táchira
San Antonio Abad see Sant Antoni de Portmany
25 U13 **San Antonio Bay** inlet Texas, SW USA
61 E22 **San Antonio, Cabo** headland E Argentina 36°45′S 56°40′W
44 A5 **San Antonio, Cabo de** headland W Cuba 21°51′N 84°58′W
105 T11 **San Antonio, Cabo de** headland E Spain 38°50′N 00°09′E
54 H7 **San Antonio de Caparo** Táchira, W Venezuela 07°34′N 71°28′W
62 J5 **San Antonio de los Cobres** Salta, NE Argentina 24°10′S 66°17′W
54 H7 **San Antonio del Táchira** var. San Antonio. Táchira, W Venezuela 07°48′N 72°28′W
35 T15 **San Antonio, Mount** ▲ California, W USA 34°18′N 117°37′W
63 K16 **San Antonio Oeste** Río Negro, E Argentina 40°45′S 64°58′W
25 T13 **San Antonio River** ∽ Texas, SW USA
54 J5 **Sanare** Lara, N Venezuela 09°45′N 69°39′W
103 T16 **Sanary-sur-Mer** Var, SE France 43°07′N 05°48′E
25 X8 **San Augustine** Texas, SW USA 31°32′N 94°09′W
San Augustine see Minami-Iō-jima
141 T13 **Sanāw** var. Sanaw. NE Yemen 18°N 51°E
41 O11 **San Bartolo** San Luis Potosí, C Mexico 22°20′N 100°05′W
107 L16 **San Bartolomeo in Galdo** Campania, S Italy 41°24′N 15°01′E
106 K13 **San Benedetto del Tronto** Marche, C Italy 42°57′N 13°53′E
42 E3 **San Benito** Petén, N Guatemala 16°56′N 89°53′W
25 T17 **San Benito** Texas, SW USA 26°07′N 97°37′W
54 E6 **San Benito Abad** Sucre, N Colombia 08°56′N 75°02′W
35 P11 **San Benito Mountain** ▲ California, W USA 36°21′N 120°37′W
35 O10 **San Benito River** ∽ California, W USA
108 H10 **San Bernardino** Graubünden, S Switzerland 46°21′N 09°13′E
35 U15 **San Bernardino** California, W USA 34°06′N 117°15′W
35 U15 **San Bernardino Mountains** ▲▲ California, W USA
62 H11 **San Bernardo** Santiago, C Chile 33°37′S 70°45′W
40 J8 **San Bernardo** Durango, C Mexico 25°58′N 105°27′W
164 G12 **Sanbe-san** ▲ Kyūshū, SW Japan 35°09′N 132°36′E
San Bizenti-Barakaldo see San Vicente de Barakaldo
40 J12 **San Blas** Nayarit, C Mexico 21°35′N 105°20′W
40 H8 **San Blas** Sinaloa, C Mexico 26°05′N 108°44′W
San Blas see Kuna Yala
43 U14 **San Blas, Archipiélago de** island group NE Panama
23 Q10 **San Blas, Cape** headland Florida, SE USA 29°39′N 85°21′W
43 V14 **San Blas, Cordillera de** ▲▲ NE Panama
62 J8 **San Blas de los Sauces** Catamarca, NW Argentina 28°18′S 67°12′W
106 G8 **San Bonifacio** Veneto, NE Italy 45°22′N 11°14′E
29 S12 **Sanborn** Iowa, C USA 43°10′N 95°39′W
40 M7 **San Buenaventura** Coahuila, NE Mexico 27°04′N 101°32′W
105 S5 **San Caprasio** ▲ N Spain 41°45′N 00°26′W
62 G13 **San Carlos** Bío Bío, C Chile 36°25′S 71°58′W
40 E9 **San Carlos** Baja California Sur, NW Mexico 24°52′N 112°15′W
41 N5 **San Carlos** Coahuila, NE Mexico 29°00′N 100°51′W
41 P9 **San Carlos** Tamaulipas, C Mexico 24°36′N 98°42′W
42 L12 **San Carlos** Río San Juan, S Nicaragua 11°06′N 84°46′W
43 T16 **San Carlos** Panamá, C Panama 08°29′N 79°58′W
171 N3 **San Carlos** off. San Carlos City. Luzon, N Philippines 15°57′N 120°18′E
61 G20 **San Carlos** Maldonado, S Uruguay 34°46′S 54°58′W
36 M14 **San Carlos** Arizona, SW USA 33°21′N 110°27′W
54 K5 **San Carlos** Cojedes, N Venezuela 09°39′N 68°35′W
San Carlos see Quesada, Costa Rica
San Carlos see Luba, Equatorial Guinea
61 B17 **San Carlos Centro** Santa Fe, C Argentina 31°45′S 61°05′W
171 P6 **San Carlos City** Negros, C Philippines 10°34′N 123°24′E
San Carlos City see San Carlos
San Carlos de Ancud see Ancud
63 H16 **San Carlos de Bariloche** Río Negro, SW Argentina 41°08′S 71°15′W
61 B21 **San Carlos de Bolívar** Buenos Aires, E Argentina 36°15′S 61°06′W
54 H6 **San Carlos del Zulia** Zulia, W Venezuela 09°01′N 71°58′W
54 L12 **San Carlos de Río Negro** Amazonas, S Venezuela 01°54′N 67°54′W
San Carlos, Estrecho de see Falkland Sound
36 M14 **San Carlos Reservoir** ⊠ Arizona, SW USA
42 M12 **San Carlos, Río** ∽ N Costa Rica
65 D24 **San Carlos Settlement** East Falkland, Falkland Islands
61 C23 **San Cayetano** Buenos Aires, E Argentina 38°20′S 59°37′W
103 O8 **Sancerre** Cher, C France 47°19′N 02°53′E
158 G7 **Sanchakou** Xinjiang Uygur Zizhiqu, NW China 39°56′N 78°28′E
Sanchoku see Samch'ŏk
41 O12 **San Ciro** San Luis Potosí, C Mexico 21°40′N 99°50′W
105 P10 **San Clemente** Castilla-La Mancha, C Spain 39°24′N 02°25′W
35 T16 **San Clemente** California, W USA 33°25′N 117°36′W
61 E21 **San Clemente del Tuyú** Buenos Aires, E Argentina 36°22′S 56°43′W
35 S17 **San Clemente Island** island Channel Islands, California, W USA
103 O9 **Sancoins** Cher, C France 46°49′N 03°00′E
61 B16 **San Cristóbal** Santa Fe, C Argentina 30°20′S 61°14′W
44 B4 **San Cristóbal** Pinar del Río, W Cuba 22°43′N 83°03′W
45 O9 **San Cristóbal** var. Benemérita de San Cristóbal. S Dominican Republic 18°27′N 70°07′W
54 H7 **San Cristóbal** Táchira, W Venezuela 07°46′N 72°15′W
187 N10 **San Cristobal** var. Makira. island SE Solomon Islands
San Cristóbal see San Cristóbal de Las Casas
41 U16 **San Cristóbal de Las Casas** var. San Cristóbal. Chiapas, SE Mexico 16°44′N 92°40′W
187 N10 **San Cristóbal, Isla** var. Chatham Island. island Galapagos Islands, Ecuador, E Pacific Ocean
42 D5 **San Cristóbal Verapaz** Alta Verapaz, C Guatemala 15°21′N 90°22′W
44 F6 **Sancti Spíritus** Sancti Spíritus, C Cuba 21°54′N 79°27′W
103 O11 **Sancy, Puy de** ▲ C France 45°33′N 02°48′E
95 D15 **Sand** Rogaland, S Norway 59°28′N 06°16′E
169 W7 **Sandakan** Sabah, East Malaysia 05°52′N 118°04′E
182 K9 **Sandalwood** South Australia 34°51′S 140°13′E
Sandalwood Island see Sumba, Pulau
94 D11 **Sandane** Sogn Og Fjordane, S Norway 61°47′N 06°14′E
114 G12 **Sandanski** prev. Sveti Vrach. Blagoevgrad, SW Bulgaria 41°36′N 23°19′E
Sandaohezi see Shawan
75 J11 **Sandaré** Kayes, W Mali 14°36′N 10°22′W
95 J19 **Sandared** Västra Götaland, S Sweden 57°43′N 12°47′E
94 N12 **Sandarne** Gävleborg, C Sweden 61°15′N 17°10′E
186 B5 **Sandaun** prev. West Sepik. ◈ province NW Papua New Guinea
96 K4 **Sanday** island NE Scotland, United Kingdom
31 P15 **Sand Creek** ∽ Indiana, N USA
95 H15 **Sande** Vestfold, S Norway 59°34′N 10°13′E
95 H16 **Sandefjord** Vestfold, S Norway 59°10′N 10°15′E
77 O15 **Sandégué** E Ivory Coast 07°59′N 03°33′W
77 P14 **Sandema** N Ghana 10°42′N 01°17′W
37 O11 **Sanders** Arizona, SW USA 35°13′N 109°21′W
24 M11 **Sanderson** Texas, SW USA 30°08′N 102°25′W
23 U4 **Sandersville** Georgia, SE USA 32°58′N 82°48′W
92 H4 **Sandgerdhi** Sudhurland, SW Iceland 64°01′N 22°42′W
28 K14 **Sand Hills** ▲▲ Nebraska, C USA
25 S14 **Sandia** Texas, SW USA 27°59′N 97°52′W
35 T17 **San Diego** California, W USA 32°43′N 117°09′W
25 S14 **San Diego** Texas, SW USA 27°47′N 98°15′W
136 F14 **Sandıklı** Afyon, W Turkey 38°28′N 30°17′E
152 L12 **Sandila** Uttar Pradesh, N India 27°05′N 80°37′E
San Dimitri Point see San Dimitri, Ras
121 N15 **San Dimitri, Ras** var. San Dimitri Point. headland Gozo, NW Malta 36°04′N 14°12′E
168 J13 **Sanding, Selat** strait W Indonesia
30 J3 **Sand Island** island Apostle Islands, Wisconsin, N USA
95 C16 **Sandnes** Rogaland, S Norway 58°51′N 05°45′E
92 F13 **Sandnessjøen** Nordland, C Norway 66°00′N 12°37′E
Sandø see Sandoy
79 L24 **Sandoa** Katanga, S Dem. Rep. Congo 09°41′S 22°56′E
111 N15 **Sandomierz** Rus. Sandomir. Świętokrzyskie, C Poland 50°42′N 21°45′E
Sandomir see Sandomierz
54 C13 **Sandoná** Nariño, SW Colombia 01°13′N 77°28′W
106 I7 **San Donà di Piave** Veneto, NE Italy 45°38′N 12°34′E
124 K14 **Sandovo** Tverskaya Oblast', W Russian Federation 58°26′N 36°30′E
Sandoway see Thandwe
97 M24 **Sandown** S England, United Kingdom 50°40′N 01°11′W
95 B19 **Sandoy** Dan. Sandø. island C Faeroe Islands
39 N16 **Sand Point** Popof Island, Alaska, USA 55°20′N 160°30′W
32 M7 **Sandpoint** Idaho, NW USA 48°16′N 116°33′W
65 N24 **Sand Point** headland E Tristan da Cunha
31 R7 **Sand Point** headland Michigan, N USA 43°54′N 83°24′W
93 H14 **Sandsele** Västerbotten, N Sweden 65°16′N 17°40′E
10 I14 **Sandspit** Moresby Island, British Columbia, SW Canada 53°14′N 131°50′W
27 P9 **Sand Springs** Oklahoma, C USA 36°08′N 96°06′W
29 W7 **Sandstone** Minnesota, N USA 46°07′N 92°51′W
36 K15 **Sand Tank Mountains** ▲▲ Arizona, SW USA
31 S8 **Sandusky** Michigan, N USA 43°26′N 82°50′W
31 S11 **Sandusky** Ohio, N USA 41°27′N 82°42′W
31 S12 **Sandusky River** ∽ Ohio, N USA
83 D22 **Sandverhaar** Karas, S Namibia 26°50′S 17°25′E
95 L24 **Sandvig** Bornholm, E Denmark 55°15′N 14°45′E
95 H15 **Sandvika** Akershus, S Norway 59°54′N 10°29′E
94 N13 **Sandviken** Gävleborg, C Sweden 60°38′N 16°50′E
30 M11 **Sandwich** Illinois, N USA 41°39′N 88°37′W
Sandwich Island see Efate
Sandwich Islands see Hawaiian Islands
153 V16 **Sandwip** island S Bangladesh
11 U12 **Sandy Bay** Saskatchewan, C Canada 55°31′N 102°14′W
183 N16 **Sandy Cape** headland Tasmania, SE Australia 41°27′S 144°43′E
36 L3 **Sandy City** Utah, W USA 40°36′N 111°53′W
31 U12 **Sandy Creek** ∽ Ohio, N USA
21 O5 **Sandy Hook** Kentucky, S USA 38°05′N 83°09′W
18 K15 **Sandy Hook** headland New Jersey, NE USA 40°27′N 73°59′W
Sandykachi/Sandykgachy see Sandykgaçy
146 J15 **Sandykgaçy** var. Sandykgachy. Maryyskiy Velayat, S Turkmenistan 36°34′N 62°28′E
Sandykgachy see Sandykgaçy
146 J15 **Sandykgaçy** var. Sandykgachy, Rus. Sandykachi. Mary Welaýaty, S Turkmenistan 36°34′N 62°28′E
146 L13 **Sandykly Gumy** Rus. Peski Sandykly. desert E Turkmenistan
Sandykly, Peski see Sandykly Gumy
11 Q13 **Sandy Lake** Alberta, W Canada 55°50′N 113°30′W
12 B8 **Sandy Lake** Ontario, C Canada 53°00′N 93°25′W
12 B8 **Sandy Lake** ◎ Ontario, C Canada
65 N25 **Sandy Point** headland E Tristan da Cunha
23 S3 **Sandy Springs** Georgia, SE USA 33°57′N 84°23′W
24 H8 **San Elizario** Texas, SW USA 31°35′N 106°16′W
99 L25 **Sanem** Luxembourg, SW Luxembourg 49°33′N 05°56′E
42 K5 **San Esteban** Olancho, C Honduras 15°19′N 85°52′W
105 O6 **San Esteban de Gormaz** Castilla-León, N Spain 41°34′N 03°13′W
40 E5 **San Esteban, Isla** island NW Mexico
San Eugenio/San Eugenio del Cuareim see Artigas
62 H11 **San Felipe** var. San Felipe de Aconcagua. Valparaíso, C Chile 32°45′S 70°42′W
40 D3 **San Felipe** Baja California Norte, NW Mexico 31°03′N 114°52′W
40 N12 **San Felipe** Guanajuato, C Mexico 21°30′N 101°15′W
54 K5 **San Felipe** Yaracuy, NW Venezuela 10°25′N 68°40′W
44 B5 **San Felipe, Cayos de** island group W Cuba
San Felipe de Aconcagua see San Felipe
San Felipe de Puerto Plata see Puerto Plata
37 R11 **San Felipe Pueblo** New Mexico, SW USA 35°25′N 106°27′W
San Feliú de Guixols see Sant Feliu de Guixols
193 T10 **San Félix, Isla** Eng. San Felix Island. island W Chile
San Felix Island see San Félix, Isla
54 L11 **San Fernando de Atabapo** Amazonas, S Venezuela 04°00′N 67°42′W
40 C4 **San Fernando** var. Misión San Fernando. Baja California Norte, NW Mexico 29°58′N 115°14′W
41 P9 **San Fernando** Tamaulipas, C Mexico 24°50′N 98°10′W
171 N2 **San Fernando** Luzon, N Philippines 16°45′N 120°21′E
171 O3 **San Fernando** Luzon, N Philippines 15°01′N 120°41′E
104 J16 **San Fernando** prev. Isla de León. Andalucía, S Spain 36°28′N 06°12′W
45 U14 **San Fernando** Trinidad, Trinidad and Tobago 10°17′N 61°27′W
35 S15 **San Fernando** California, W USA 34°16′N 118°26′W
54 L7 **San Fernando** var. San Fernando de Apure. Apure, C Venezuela 07°54′N 67°28′W
San Fernando de Apure see San Fernando
62 L8 **San Fernando del Valle de Catamarca** var. Catamarca. Catamarca, NW Argentina 28°28′S 65°46′W
San Fernando de Monte Cristi see Monte Cristi
41 P9 **San Fernando, Río** ∽ C Mexico
23 X11 **Sanford** Florida, SE USA 28°48′N 81°16′W
19 P9 **Sanford** Maine, NE USA 43°26′N 70°46′W
21 T10 **Sanford** North Carolina, SE USA 35°29′N 79°10′W
25 N2 **Sanford** Texas, SW USA 35°42′N 101°31′W
39 T10 **Sanford, Mount** ▲ Alaska, USA 62°21′N 144°12′W
42 G8 **San Francisco** var. Gotera, San Francisco Gotera. Morazán, E El Salvador 13°41′N 88°06′W
43 R16 **San Francisco** Veraguas, C Panama 08°19′N 80°59′W
171 N2 **San Francisco** var. Aurora. Luzon, N Philippines 13°22′N 122°31′E
35 L8 **San Francisco** California, W USA 37°47′N 122°25′W
54 H5 **San Francisco** Zulia, NW Venezuela 10°36′N 71°39′W
34 M8 **San Francisco** ✈ California, W USA 37°37′N 122°23′W
35 N9 **San Francisco Bay** bay California, W USA
61 C24 **San Francisco de Bellocq** Buenos Aires, E Argentina 38°42′S 60°01′W
40 I6 **San Francisco de Borja** Chihuahua, N Mexico 27°57′N 106°42′W
42 J6 **San Francisco de la Paz** Olancho, C Honduras 14°55′N 86°14′W
40 J7 **San Francisco del Oro** Chihuahua, N Mexico 26°52′N 105°50′W
40 M12 **San Francisco del Rincón** Jalisco, SW Mexico 21°00′N 101°51′W
45 O8 **San Francisco de Macorís** C Dominican Republic 19°19′N 70°15′W
San Francisco de Satipo see Satipo
San Francisco Gotera see San Francisco
San Francisco Telixtlahuaca see Telixtlahuaca
107 K23 **San Fratello** Sicilia, Italy, C Mediterranean Sea 38°00′N 14°35′E
San Fructuoso see Tacuarembó
82 C12 **Sanga** Cuanza Sul, NW Angola 11°10′S 15°27′E
56 C5 **San Gabriel** Carchi, N Ecuador 0°35′N 77°48′W
159 S15 **Sa'ngain** Xizang Zizhiqu, W China 30°47′N 98°45′E
154 E13 **Sangamner** Mahārāshtra, W India 19°37′N 74°18′E
152 H12 **Sāngāner** Rājasthān, N India 26°48′N 75°48′E
Sangan, Koh-i- see Sangān, Kūh-e
149 N6 **Sangān, Kūh-e** Pash. Koh-i-Sangan. ▲ C Afghanistan
123 P10 **Sangar** Respublika Sakha (Yakutiya), NE Russian Federation 63°48′N 127°37′E
155 H18 **Sangāreddi** Andhra Pradesh, India 17°37′N 78°04′E
169 V11 **Sangasanga** Borneo, C Indonesia 0°36′S 117°12′E
103 N1 **Sangatte** Pas-de-Calais, N France 50°56′N 01°41′E
107 B19 **San Gavino Monreale** Sardegna, Italy, C Mediterranean Sea 39°33′N 08°47′E
57 D16 **Sangayan, Isla** island W Peru
30 L14 **Sangchris Lake** ⊠ Illinois, N USA
171 N16 **Sangeang, Pulau** island S Indonesia
116 I10 **Sângeorgiu de Pădure** prev. Erdăt-Sângeorz, Sîngeorgiu de Pădure, Hung. Erdőszentgyörgy. Mureș, C Romania 46°27′N 24°50′E
116 I9 **Sângeorz-Băi** var. Singeroz Băi, Ger. Rumänisch-Sankt-Georgen, Hung. Oláhszentgyőrgy; prev. Sîngeorz-Băi. Bistrița-Năsăud, N Romania 47°24′N 24°40′E
35 R10 **Sanger** California, W USA 36°42′N 119°33′W
25 T5 **Sanger** Texas, SW USA 33°21′N 97°10′W
Sângerei see Sîngerei
101 L15 **Sangerhausen** Sachsen-Anhalt, C Germany 51°29′N 11°18′E
45 S6 **San Germán** W Puerto Rico 18°05′N 67°02′W
San Germano see Cassino
161 N2 **Sanggan He** ∽ E China
169 Q11 **Sanggau** Borneo, C Indonesia 0°08′N 110°35′E
79 G17 **Sangha** ◈ province N Congo
79 H16 **Sangha** ∽ Central African Republic/Congo
79 G16 **Sangha-Mbaéré** ◈ prefecture SW Central African Republic
149 Q15 **Sānghar** Sind, SE Pakistan 26°10′N 68°59′E
115 F22 **Sangiás** ▲ S Greece 36°39′N 22°24′E
Sangihe, Kepulauan see Sangir, Kepulauan
171 Q9 **Sangihe, Pulau** var. Sangir. island N Indonesia
54 G8 **San Gil** Santander, C Colombia 06°35′N 73°08′W
106 F12 **San Gimignano** Toscana, C Italy 43°30′N 11°00′E
148 M8 **Sangin** var. Sangin. Helmand, S Afghanistan 32°03′N 64°50′E
Sangin see Sangin
107 O21 **San Giovanni in Fiore** Calabria, SW Italy 39°15′N 16°42′E
107 M16 **San Giovanni Rotondo** Puglia, SE Italy 41°43′N 15°44′E
106 G12 **San Giovanni Valdarno** Toscana, C Italy 43°34′N 11°31′E
Sangir see Sangihe, Pulau
171 Q10 **Sangir, Kepulauan** var. Kepulauan Sangihe. island group N Indonesia
Sangiyn Dalay see Erdenedalay, Dundgovĭ, Mongolia
Sangiyn Dalay see Erdene, Govĭ-Altay, Mongolia
Sangiyn Dalay see Nomgon, Ömnögovĭ, Mongolia
Sangiyn Dalay see Öldziyt, Övörhangay, Mongolia
163 Y15 **Sangju** Jap. Shōshū. C South Korea 36°26′N 128°09′E
167 R11 **Sangkha** Surin, E Thailand 14°36′N 103°43′E
169 W10 **Sangkulirang** Borneo, N Indonesia 01°00′N 117°56′E
169 W10 **Sangkulirang, Teluk** bay Borneo, N Indonesia
155 E16 **Sāngli** Mahārāshtra, W India 16°55′N 74°37′E
79 E16 **Sangmélima** Sud, S Cameroon 02°57′N 11°56′E
35 V15 **San Gorgonio Mountain** ▲ California, W USA 34°06′N 116°50′W
37 T8 **Sangre de Cristo Mountains** ▲▲ Colorado/New Mexico, C USA
61 A20 **San Gregorio** Santa Fe, C Argentina 34°18′S 62°02′W
61 F18 **San Gregorio de Polanco** Tacuarembó, C Uruguay 32°37′S 55°50′W
45 V14 **Sangre Grande** Trinidad, Trinidad and Tobago 10°35′N 61°08′W
159 N16 **Sangri** Xizang Zizhiqu, W China 29°17′N 92°01′E
152 H9 **Sangrūr** Punjab, NW India 30°16′N 75°52′E
158 K16 **Sangsang** Xizang Zizhiqu, W China 29°45′N 86°42′E
44 I11 **Sangster** off. Sir Donald Sangster International Airport, var. Montego Bay. ✈ (Montego Bay) W Jamaica 18°30′N 77°54′W
59 G17 **Sangue, Rio do** ∽ W Brazil
105 R4 **Sangüesa** Navarra, N Spain 42°34′N 01°17′W
61 C16 **San Gustavo** Entre Ríos, E Argentina 30°41′S 59°23′W
Sangyuan see Wuqiao
40 C6 **San Hipólito, Punta** headland NW Mexico 26°57′N 114°00′W
23 W15 **Sanibel** Sanibel Island, Florida, SE USA 26°27′N 82°01′W
23 V15 **Sanibel Island** island Florida, SE USA
60 F13 **San Ignacio** Misiones, NE Argentina 27°15′S 55°32′W
42 F2 **San Ignacio** prev. Cayo, El Cayo. Cayo, W Belize 17°09′N 89°02′W
57 L16 **San Ignacio** Beni, N Bolivia 14°54′S 65°35′W
57 O18 **San Ignacio** Santa Cruz, E Bolivia 16°23′S 60°59′W
42 M14 **San Ignacio** var. San Ignacio de Acosta. San José, W Costa Rica 09°46′N 84°10′W
40 E6 **San Ignacio** Baja California Sur, NW Mexico 27°18′N 112°51′W
40 J10 **San Ignacio** Sinaloa, W Mexico 23°55′N 106°25′W
56 B9 **San Ignacio** Cajamarca, N Peru 05°09′S 79°00′W
San Ignacio de Acosta see San Ignacio
40 D7 **San Ignacio, Laguna** lagoon W Mexico
12 I6 **Sanikiluaq** Belcher Islands, Nunavut, C Canada 55°20′N 77°50′W
171 O3 **San Ildefonso Peninsula** peninsula Luzon, N Philippines
Saniquillie see Sanniquellie
61 D20 **San Isidro** Buenos Aires, E Argentina 34°28′S 58°31′W
43 N14 **San Isidro** var. San Isidro de El General. San José, SE Costa Rica 09°28′N 83°42′W
San Isidro de El General see San Isidro
54 E5 **San Jacinto** Bolívar, N Colombia 09°53′N 75°06′W
35 U16 **San Jacinto** California, W USA 33°47′N 116°58′W
35 V15 **San Jacinto Peak** ▲ California, W USA 33°48′N 116°40′W
61 F14 **San Javier** Misiones, NE Argentina 27°50′S 55°06′W
61 C16 **San Javier** Santa Fe, C Argentina 30°35′S 59°59′W
105 S13 **San Javier** Murcia, SE Spain 37°49′N 00°50′W
61 D18 **San Javier** Río Negro, W Uruguay 32°41′S 58°08′W
61 C16 **San Javier, Río** ∽ C Argentina
160 L12 **Sanjiang** var. Guyi, Sanjiang Dongzu Zizhixian. Guangxi Zhuangzu Zizhiqu, S China 25°46′N 109°26′E
Sanjiang see Jinping, Guizhou
Sanjiang Dongzu Zizhixian see Sanjiang
Sanjiaocheng see Haiyan
165 N11 **Sanjō** var. Sanzyô. Niigata, Honshū, C Japan 37°39′N 139°00′E
57 M15 **San Joaquín** Beni, N Bolivia 13°06′S 64°46′W
55 O6 **San Joaquín** Anzoátegui, NE Venezuela 09°21′N 64°30′W
35 O9 **San Joaquin River** ∽ California, W USA
35 P10 **San Joaquin Valley** valley California, W USA
61 A18 **San Jorge** Santa Fe, C Argentina 31°50′S 61°50′W
40 D3 **San Jorge, Bahía de** bay NW Mexico
63 J19 **San Jorge, Golfo** var. Gulf of San Jorge. gulf S Argentina
San Jorge, Gulf of see San Jorge, Golfo
San Jorge, Isla de see Weddell Island
61 F14 **San José** Misiones, NE Argentina 27°46′S 55°47′W
57 P19 **San José** var. San José de Chiquitos. Santa Cruz, E Bolivia 14°13′S 68°05′W
42 M14 **San José** ● (Costa Rica) San José, C Costa Rica 09°55′N 84°05′W
42 C7 **San José** var. Puerto San José. Escuintla, S Guatemala 14°00′N 90°50′W
40 G6 **San José** Sonora, NW Mexico 27°32′N 110°09′W
188 K8 **San Jose** Tinian, S Northern Mariana Islands 15°00′S 145°38′E
105 U11 **San José** Eivissa, Spain, W Mediterranean Sea 38°55′N 01°18′E
35 N9 **San Jose** California, W USA 37°18′N 121°53′W
54 H5 **San José** Zulia, NW Venezuela 10°02′N 72°24′W
42 M14 **San José** off. Provincia de San José. ◈ province W Costa Rica
61 E19 **San José** ◈ department S Uruguay
42 M13 **San José** ✈ Alajuela, C Costa Rica 10°03′N 84°12′W
San José see San José del Guaviare, Colombia
San Jose see Oleai
San Jose see Sant Josep de sa Talaia, Ibiza, Spain
San José see San José de Mayo, Uruguay
171 O3 **San Jose City** Luzon, N Philippines 15°49′N 120°57′E
San José de Chiquitos see San José
San José de Cúcuta see Cúcuta
61 D16 **San José de Feliciano** Entre Ríos, E Argentina 30°26′S 58°46′W
55 O6 **San José de Guanipa** var. El Tigrito. Anzoátegui, NE Venezuela 08°54′N 64°10′W
62 I9 **San José de Jáchal** San Juan, W Argentina 30°15′S 68°46′W
40 G10 **San José del Cabo** Baja California Sur, NW Mexico 23°01′N 109°40′W
54 G12 **San José del Guaviare** var. San José. Guaviare, S Colombia 02°34′N 72°38′W
61 E20 **San José de Mayo** var. San José. San José, S Uruguay 34°20′S 56°42′W
54 I10 **San José de Ocuné** Vichada, E Colombia 04°10′N 70°21′W
41 O9 **San José de Raíces** Nuevo León, NE Mexico 24°32′N 100°15′W
63 K17 **San José, Golfo** gulf E Argentina
40 F9 **San José, Isla** island NW Mexico
43 U16 **San José, Isla** island SE Panama
25 U14 **San Jose Island** island Texas, SW USA
San José, Provincia de see San José
62 I10 **San Juan** San Juan, W Argentina 31°37′S 68°27′W
45 N9 **San Juan** var. San Juan de la Maguana. C Dominican Republic 18°49′N 71°12′W
57 E17 **San Juan** Ica, S Peru 15°22′S 75°07′W
45 U5 **San Juan** ○ (Puerto Rico) NE Puerto Rico 18°28′N 66°06′W
62 H10 **San Juan** off. Provincia de San Juan. ◈ province W Argentina
45 U5 **San Juan** var. Luis Muñoz Marín. ✈ NE Puerto Rico 18°27′N 66°05′W
San Juan see San Juan de los Morros
62 O7 **San Juan Bautista** Misiones, S Paraguay 26°40′S 57°08′W
35 O10 **San Juan Bautista** California, W USA 36°50′N 121°34′W
San Juan Bautista see Villahermosa
San Juan Bautista Cuicatlán see Cuicatlán
San Juan Bautista Tuxtepec see Tuxtepec

◆ Country ● Country Capital ◇ Dependent Territory ○ Dependent Territory Capital ◈ Administrative Regions ✈ International Airport ▲ Mountain ▲▲ Mountain Range Volcano ∽ River ◎ Lake ⊠ Reservoir

San Juan, Cabo – Santa Rosa

79 C17 **San Juan, Cabo** *headland* S Equatorial Guinea 01°09′N 09°25′E
105 S12 **San Juan de Alicante** País Valenciano, E Spain 38°26′N 00°27′W
54 H7 **San Juan de Colón** Táchira, NW Venezuela 08°02′N 72°17′W
40 L9 **San Juan de Guadalupe** Durango, C Mexico 25°12′N 100°50′W
San Juan de la Maguana *see* San Juan
54 G4 **San Juan del Cesar** La Guajira, N Colombia 10°45′N 73°00′W
40 L15 **San Juan de Lima, Punta** *headland* SW Mexico 18°34′N 103°40′W
42 I8 **San Juan de Limay** Estelí, NW Nicaragua 13°10′N 86°36′W
43 N12 **San Juan del Norte** *var.* Greytown. Río San Juan, SE Nicaragua 10°58′N 83°40′W
54 K4 **San Juan de los Cayos** Falcón, N Venezuela 11°11′N 68°27′W
40 M12 **San Juan de los Lagos** Jalisco, C Mexico 21°15′N 102°15′W
54 L5 **San Juan de los Morros** *var.* San Juan. Guárico, N Venezuela 09°53′N 67°23′W
40 K9 **San Juan del Río** Durango, C Mexico 25°12′N 100°50′W
41 O13 **San Juan del Río** Querétaro de Arteaga, C Mexico 20°24′N 100°00′W
42 J11 **San Juan del Sur** Rivas, SW Nicaragua 11°16′N 85°51′W
54 M9 **San Juan de Manapiare** Amazonas, S Venezuela 05°15′N 66°05′W
40 E7 **San Juanico** Baja California Sur, NW Mexico
40 D7 **San Juanico, Punta** *headland* NW Mexico 26°01′N 112°17′W
32 G6 **San Juan Islands** *island group* Washington, NW USA
40 I6 **San Juanito** Chihuahua, N Mexico
40 I12 **San Juanito, Isla** *island* C Mexico
37 R8 **San Juan Mountains** ▲ Colorado, C USA
54 E5 **San Juan Nepomuceno** Bolívar, NW Colombia 09°57′N 75°06′W
44 E5 **San Juan, Pico** ▲ C Cuba 21°58′N 80°10′W
San Juan, Provincia de *see* San Juan
191 W15 **San Juan, Punta** *headland* Easter Island, Chile, E Pacific Ocean 27°03′S 109°22′W
42 M12 **San Juan, Río** Costa Rica/Nicaragua
41 S15 **San Juan, Río** SE Mexico
37 O8 **San Juan River** Colorado/Utah, W USA
San Julián *see* Puerto San Julián
61 B17 **San Justo** Santa Fe, C Argentina 30°47′S 60°32′W
109 W5 **Sankt Aegyd am Neuwalde** Niederösterreich, E Austria 47°51′N 15°34′E
109 U9 **Sankt Andrä** *Slvn.* Šent Andraž. Kärnten, S Austria 46°46′N 14°49′E
Sankt Andrä *see* Szentendre
Sankt Anna *see* Sântana
108 K8 **Sankt Anton-am-Arlberg** Vorarlberg, W Austria 47°08′N 10°11′E
101 E16 **Sankt Augustin** Nordrhein-Westfalen, W Germany 50°46′N 07°10′E
Sankt-Bartholomäi *see* Palamuse
101 F24 **Sankt Blasien** Baden-Württemberg, SW Germany 47°43′N 08°09′E
109 R3 **Sankt Florian am Inn** Oberösterreich, N Austria 48°24′N 13°27′E
108 I7 **Sankt Gallen** *var.* St. Gallen, *Eng.* Saint Gall, *Fr.* St-Gall. Sankt Gallen, NE Switzerland 47°25′N 09°23′E
108 H8 **Sankt Gallen** *var.* St.Gallen, *Eng.* Saint Gall, *Fr.* St-Gall. *canton* NE Switzerland
108 J8 **Sankt Gallenkirch** Vorarlberg, W Austria 47°00′N 10°59′E
109 Q5 **Sankt Georgen** Salzburg, N Austria 47°59′N 12°57′E
Sankt Georgen *see* Đurđevac
Sankt-Georgen *see* Sfântu Gheorghe
109 R6 **Sankt Gilgen** Salzburg, NW Austria 47°46′N 13°21′E
Sankt Gotthard *see* Szentgotthárd
101 E20 **Sankt Ingbert** Saarland, SW Germany 49°17′N 07°07′E
Sankt-Jakobi *see* Viru-Jaagupi, Lääne-Virumaa, Estonia
Sankt-Jakobi *see* Pärnu-Jaagupi, Pärnumaa, Estonia
Sankt Johann *see* Sankt Johann in Tirol
109 T7 **Sankt Johann am Tauern** Steiermark, E Austria 47°20′N 14°27′E
109 Q7 **Sankt Johann im Pongau** Salzburg, NW Austria 47°22′N 13°13′E
109 P6 **Sankt Johann in Tirol** *var.* Sankt Johann. Tirol, W Austria 47°32′N 12°26′E
Sankt-Johannis *see* Järva-Jaani
108 L8 **Sankt Leonhard** Tirol, W Austria 47°05′N 10°53′E
Sankt Margarethen *see* Sankt Margarethen im Burgenland
109 Y5 **Sankt Margarethen im Burgenland** *var.* Sankt Margarethen. Burgenland, E Austria 47°49′N 16°38′E
Sankt Martin *see* Martin
109 X8 **Sankt Martin an der Raab** Burgenland, SE Austria 46°59′N 16°12′E
109 U7 **Sankt Michael in Obersteiermark** Steiermark, SE Austria 47°21′N 14°59′E
Sankt Michel *see* Mikkeli
Sankt Moritz *see* St. Moritz
108 E11 **Sankt Niklaus** Valais, S Switzerland 46°09′N 07°48′E
109 S7 **Sankt Nikolai** *var.* Sankt Nikolai im Sölktal. Steiermark, SE Austria 47°18′N 14°04′E
Sankt Nikolai im Sölktal *see* Sankt Nikolai
109 U9 **Sankt Paul** *var.* Sankt Paul im Lavanttal. Kärnten, S Austria 46°42′N 14°53′E
Sankt Paul im Lavanttal *see* Sankt Paul
Sankt Peter *see* Pivka
109 W9 **Sankt Peter am Ottersbach** Steiermark, SE Austria 46°49′N 15°48′E
124 J13 **Sankt-Peterburg** *prev.* Leningrad, Petrograd, *Eng.* Saint Petersburg, *Fin.* Pietari. Leningradskaya Oblast′, NW Russian Federation 59°55′N 30°25′E
100 H8 **Sankt Peter-Ording** Schleswig-Holstein, N Germany 54°18′N 08°37′E
109 V4 **Sankt Pölten** Niederösterreich, N Austria 48°14′N 15°38′E
109 W7 **Sankt Ruprecht** *var.* Sankt Ruprecht an der Raab. Steiermark, SE Austria 47°10′N 15°41′E
Sankt Ruprecht an der Raab *see* Sankt Ruprecht
Sankt-Ulrich *see* Ortisei
109 T4 **Sankt Valentin** Niederösterreich, C Austria 48°11′N 14°33′E
Sankt Veit am Flaum *see* Rijeka
109 T9 **Sankt Veit an der Glan** *Slvn.* Št. Vid. Kärnten, S Austria 46°47′N 14°22′E
99 M21 **Sankt-Vith** *var.* Saint-Vith. Liège, E Belgium 50°17′N 06°07′E
101 E20 **Sankt Wendel** Saarland, SW Germany 49°28′N 07°10′E
109 R6 **Sankt Wolfgang** Salzburg, NW Austria 47°43′N 13°30′E
79 K21 **Sankuru** C Dem. Rep. Congo
40 D8 **San Lázaro, Cabo** *headland* NW Mexico 24°46′N 112°15′W
137 O16 **Şanlıurfa** *prev.* Sanli Urfa, Urfa; *anc.* Edessa. şanlıurfa, S Turkey 37°08′N 38°45′E
137 O16 **Şanlıurfa** *prev.* Urfa. *province* SE Turkey
Sanli Urfa *see* Şanlıurfa
137 O16 **Şanlıurfa Yaylası** *plateau* SE Turkey
61 B18 **San Lorenzo** Santa Fe, C Argentina 32°45′S 60°45′W
57 M21 **San Lorenzo** Tarija, S Bolivia 21°25′S 64°45′W
56 C5 **San Lorenzo** Esmeraldas, N Ecuador 01°15′N 78°51′W
42 H8 **San Lorenzo** Valle, S Honduras 13°24′N 87°27′W
56 A6 **San Lorenzo, Cabo** *headland* W Ecuador 0°57′S 80°49′W
105 N8 **San Lorenzo de El Escorial** *var.* El Escorial. Madrid, C Spain 40°36′N 04°07′W
40 E5 **San Lorenzo, Isla** *island* NW Mexico
57 C14 **San Lorenzo, Isla** *island* W Peru
63 G20 **San Lorenzo, Monte** ▲ S Argentina 47°40′S 72°12′W
40 I9 **San Lorenzo, Río** C Mexico
104 J15 **Sanlúcar de Barrameda** Andalucía, S Spain 36°46′N 06°21′W
104 J14 **Sanlúcar la Mayor** Andalucía, S Spain 37°24′N 06°13′W
40 F11 **San Lucas** Baja California Sur, NW Mexico 22°50′N 109°52′W
40 E6 **San Lucas** *var.* Cabo San Lucas. Baja California Sur, NW Mexico 27°14′N 112°15′W
40 G11 **San Lucas, Cabo** *var.* San Lucas Cape. *headland* NW Mexico 22°52′N 109°53′W
San Lucas Cape *see* San Lucas, Cabo
62 J11 **San Luis** San Luis, C Argentina 33°18′S 66°18′W
42 E4 **San Luis** Petén, NE Guatemala 16°16′N 89°27′W
40 D2 **San Luis** *var.* San Luis Río Colorado. Sonora, NW Mexico 32°26′N 114°48′W
42 M7 **San Luis** Región Autónoma Atlántico Norte, NE Nicaragua 13°59′N 84°10′W
36 H15 **San Luis** Arizona, SW USA 32°27′N 114°45′W
37 T8 **San Luis** Colorado, C USA 37°09′N 105°24′W
54 J4 **San Luis** Falcón, N Venezuela 11°09′N 69°39′W
62 J11 **San Luis** *off.* Provincia de San Luis. *province* C Argentina
41 N12 **San Luis de la Paz** Guanajuato, C Mexico 21°15′N 100°33′W
40 K8 **San Luis del Cordero** Durango, C Mexico 25°25′N 104°09′W
40 D4 **San Luis, Isla** *island* NW Mexico
42 E6 **San Luis Jilotepeque** Jalapa, SE Guatemala 14°40′N 89°42′W
57 M16 **San Luis, Laguna de** NW Bolivia
35 P13 **San Luis Obispo** California, W USA 35°17′N 120°40′W
37 R7 **San Luis Peak** ▲ Colorado, C USA 37°59′N 106°55′W
41 N11 **San Luis Potosí** San Luis Potosí, C Mexico 22°10′N 100°57′W
41 N11 **San Luis Potosí** *state* C Mexico
San Luis, Provincia de *see* San Luis
35 O10 **San Luis Reservoir** California, W USA
San Luis Río Colorado *see* San Luis
37 S8 **San Luis Valley** *basin* Colorado, C USA
107 C19 **Sanluri** Sardegna, Italy, C Mediterranean Sea 39°34′N 08°54′E
61 D23 **San Manuel** Buenos Aires, E Argentina 37°47′S 58°50′W
36 M15 **San Manuel** Arizona, SW USA 32°36′N 110°37′W
106 F11 **San Marcello Pistoiese** Toscana, C Italy 44°03′N 10°46′E
107 N20 **San Marco Argentano** Calabria, SW Italy 39°31′N 16°07′E
54 E6 **San Marcos** Sucre, N Colombia 08°38′N 75°10′W
42 M14 **San Marcos** San José, C Costa Rica 09°39′N 84°00′W
42 B5 **San Marcos** San Marcos, W Guatemala 14°58′N 91°48′W
42 F6 **San Marcos** Ocotepeque, SW Honduras 14°23′N 88°57′W
41 O16 **San Marcos** Guerrero, S Mexico 16°45′N 99°22′W
25 S11 **San Marcos** Texas, SW USA 29°54′N 97°57′W
42 A5 **San Marcos** *off.* Departamento de San Marcos. *department* W Guatemala
San Marcos de Arica *see* Arica
San Marcos, Departamento de *see* San Marcos
40 E6 **San Marcos, Isla** *island* NW Mexico
106 H11 **San Marino** ● (San Marino) C San Marino 43°54′N 12°27′E
106 I11 **San Marino** *off.* Republic of San Marino. ◆ *republic* S Europe
San Marino, Republic of *see* San Marino
62 I11 **San Martín** Mendoza, C Argentina 33°05′S 68°28′W
54 F11 **San Martín** Meta, C Colombia 03°43′N 73°42′W
56 D11 **San Martín** *off.* Departamento de San Martín. *department* C Peru
194 I5 **San Martín** *Argentinian research station* Antarctica 68°18′S 67°03′W
63 H16 **San Martín de los Andes** Neuquén, W Argentina 40°11′S 71°22′W
San Martín, Departamento de *see* San Martín
104 M8 **San Martín de Valdeiglesias** Madrid, C Spain 40°21′N 04°24′W
63 G21 **San Martín, Lago** *var.* Lago O'Higgins. S Argentina
106 H6 **San Martino di Castrozza** Trentino-Alto Adige, N Italy 46°16′N 11°50′E
57 N16 **San Martín, Río** N Bolivia
San Martín Texmelucan *see* Texmelucan
35 N9 **San Mateo** California, W USA 37°33′N 122°19′W
55 O6 **San Mateo** Anzoátegui, NE Venezuela 09°48′N 64°36′W
42 B4 **San Mateo Ixtatán** Huehuetenango, W Guatemala 15°50′N 91°30′W
57 Q18 **San Matías** Santa Cruz, E Bolivia 16°20′S 58°24′W
63 K16 **San Matías, Golfo** *var.* Gulf of San Matías. *gulf* E Argentina
San Matías, Gulf of *see* San Matías, Golfo
15 O8 **Sanmaur** Québec, SE Canada 47°52′N 73°47′W
161 T10 **Sanmen Wan** *bay* E China
160 M6 **Sanmenxia** *var.* Shan Xian. Henan, C China 34°46′N 111°17′E
Sânmiclăuş Mare *see* Sânnicolau Mare
61 D14 **San Miguel** Corrientes, NE Argentina 28°02′S 57°41′W
57 L16 **San Miguel** Beni, N Bolivia 16°43′S 61°06′W
42 G8 **San Miguel** San Miguel, SE El Salvador 13°27′N 88°11′W
40 L6 **San Miguel** Coahuila, N Mexico 29°10′N 101°28′W
40 J9 **San Miguel** *var.* San Miguel de Cruces. Durango, C Mexico 24°25′N 105°55′W
43 U16 **San Miguel** Panamá, SE Panama 08°27′N 78°51′W
35 P12 **San Miguel** California, W USA 35°45′N 120°42′W
42 B9 **San Miguel** *department* E El Salvador
41 N13 **San Miguel de Allende** Guanajuato, C Mexico 20°56′N 100°48′W
San Miguel de Cruces *see* San Miguel
San Miguel de Ibarra *see* Ibarra
61 D21 **San Miguel del Monte** Buenos Aires, E Argentina 35°26′S 58°50′W
62 J7 **San Miguel de Tucumán** *var.* Tucumán. Tucumán, N Argentina 26°47′S 65°15′W
43 V16 **San Miguel, Golfo de** *gulf* S Panama
35 P15 **San Miguel Island** *island* California, W USA
42 L11 **San Miguelito** Río San Juan, S Nicaragua 11°22′N 84°54′W
43 T15 **San Miguelito** Panamá, C Panama 08°58′N 79°31′W
57 N18 **San Miguel, Río** E Bolivia
56 D6 **San Miguel, Río** Colombia/Ecuador
40 I7 **San Miguel, Río** N Mexico
42 G8 **San Miguel, Volcán de** SE El Salvador 13°27′N 88°18′W
161 Q12 **Sanming** Fujian, SE China 26°11′N 117°37′E
106 F11 **San Miniato** Toscana, C Italy 43°40′N 10°53′E
San Murezzan *see* St. Moritz
Sannār *see* Sennar
107 M15 **Sannicandro Garganico** Puglia, SE Italy 41°50′N 15°32′E
40 H6 **San Nicolás** Sonora, NW Mexico 28°31′N 109°24′W
61 C19 **San Nicolás de los Arroyos** Buenos Aires, E Argentina 33°20′S 60°13′W
35 R16 **San Nicolas Island** *island* Channel Islands, California, W USA
Sânnicolaul-Mare *see* Sânnicolau Mare
116 E11 **Sânnicolau Mare** *var.* Sânnicolaul-Mare, *Hung.* Nagyszentmiklós; *prev.* Sânmiclăuş Mare, Sînnicolau Mare. Timiş, W Romania 46°05′N 20°38′E
123 Q6 **Sannikova, Proliv** *strait* NE Russian Federation
76 K16 **Sanniquellie** *var.* Saniquillie. NE Liberia 07°24′N 08°45′W
165 R7 **Sannohe** Aomori, Honshū, C Japan 40°23′N 141°16′E
Sanntaler Alpen *see* Kamniško-Savinjske Alpe
111 O17 **Sanok** Podkarpackie, SE Poland 49°31′N 22°14′E
54 E5 **San Onofre** Sucre, NW Colombia 09°45′N 75°33′W
57 K21 **San Pablo** Potosí, S Bolivia 21°43′S 66°38′W
171 O4 **San Pablo** *off.* San Pablo City. Luzon, N Philippines 14°04′N 121°16′E
San Pablo Balleza *see* Balleza
35 N8 **San Pablo Bay** *bay* California, W USA
San Pablo City *see* San Pablo
40 C6 **San Pablo, Punta** *headland* NW Mexico 27°12′N 114°30′W
43 R16 **San Pablo, Río** C Panama
171 P4 **San Pascual** Burias Island, C Philippines 13°06′N 122°59′E
121 Q16 **San Pawl il-Baħar** *Eng.* Saint Paul's Bay. E Malta 35°57′N 14°24′E
61 C19 **San Pedro** Buenos Aires, E Argentina 33°43′S 59°45′W
62 K5 **San Pedro** Jujuy, N Argentina 24°12′S 64°55′W
60 G13 **San Pedro** Misiones, NE Argentina 26°38′S 54°12′W
42 H1 **San Pedro** Corozal, NE Belize 17°58′N 87°55′W
76 M17 **San-Pédro** S Ivory Coast 04°45′N 06°37′W
40 L8 **San Pedro** *var.* San Pedro de las Colonias. Coahuila, NE Mexico 25°47′N 102°57′W
62 O5 **San Pedro** San Pedro, SE Paraguay 24°08′S 57°08′W
62 O6 **San Pedro** *off.* Departamento de San Pedro. *department* C Paraguay
44 G6 **San Pedro** C Cuba
77 N16 **San Pedro** (Yamoussoukro) C Ivory Coast 06°49′N 05°14′W
San Pedro *see* San Pedro del Pinatar
42 D5 **San Pedro Carchá** Alta Verapaz, C Guatemala 15°30′N 90°12′W
35 S16 **San Pedro Channel** *channel* California, W USA
62 I5 **San Pedro de Atacama** Antofagasta, N Chile 22°52′S 68°10′W
San Pedro de Durazno *see* Durazno
40 G5 **San Pedro de la Cueva** Sonora, NW Mexico 29°17′N 109°47′W
San Pedro de las Colonias *see* San Pedro
56 B11 **San Pedro de Lloc** La Libertad, NW Peru 07°26′S 79°31′W
105 S13 **San Pedro del Pinatar** *var.* San Pedro. Murcia, SE Spain 37°50′N 00°47′W
45 P9 **San Pedro de Macorís** SE Dominican Republic 18°30′N 69°18′W
San Pedro, Departamento de *see* San Pedro
40 C3 **San Pedro Mártir, Sierra** ▲ NW Mexico
San Pedro Pochutla *see* Pochutla
42 D2 **San Pedro, Río** Guatemala/Mexico
40 K10 **San Pedro, Río** C Mexico
104 J10 **San Pedro, Sierra de** ▲ W Spain
42 G5 **San Pedro Sula** Cortés, NW Honduras 15°26′N 88°01′W
San Pedro Tapanatepec *see* Tapanatepec
62 I4 **San Pedro, Volcán** N Chile 21°46′S 68°13′W
106 E7 **San Pellegrino Terme** Lombardia, N Italy 45°53′N 09°42′E
25 T16 **San Perlita** Texas, SW USA 26°30′N 97°38′W
San Pietro *see* Supetar
San Pietro del Carso *see* Pivka
107 A20 **San Pietro, Isola di** *island* W Italy
32 K7 **Sanpoil River** Washington, NW USA
165 O9 **Sanpoku** *var.* Sampoku. Niigata, Honshū, C Japan 38°32′N 139°33′E
40 C3 **San Quintín** Baja California Norte, NW Mexico 30°28′N 115°58′W
40 B3 **San Quintín, Bahía de** *bay* NW Mexico
40 B3 **San Quintín, Cabo** *headland* NW Mexico 30°22′N 116°01′W
62 I12 **San Rafael** Mendoza, W Argentina 34°44′S 68°15′W
41 N9 **San Rafael** Nuevo León, NE Mexico 25°01′N 100°33′W
34 M8 **San Rafael** California, W USA 37°58′N 122°31′W
37 Q11 **San Rafael** New Mexico, SW USA 35°03′N 107°52′W
54 H4 **San Rafael** *var.* El Moján. Zulia, NW Venezuela 10°58′N 71°45′W
42 J8 **San Rafael del Norte** Jinotega, NW Nicaragua 13°12′N 86°06′W
42 J10 **San Rafael del Sur** Managua, SW Nicaragua 11°51′N 86°24′W
36 M5 **San Rafael Knob** ▲ Utah, W USA 38°46′N 110°45′W
35 Q14 **San Rafael Mountains** ▲ California, W USA
42 M13 **San Ramón** Alajuela, C Costa Rica 10°04′N 84°31′W
57 E14 **San Ramón** Junín, C Peru 11°08′S 75°18′W
61 F19 **San Ramón** Canelones, S Uruguay 34°18′S 55°55′W
62 K5 **San Ramón de la Nueva Orán** Salta, N Argentina 23°08′S 64°20′W
57 O16 **San Ramón, Río** E Bolivia
106 B11 **San Remo** Liguria, NW Italy 43°48′N 07°47′E
54 J3 **San Román, Cabo** *headland* NW Venezuela 12°10′N 70°01′W
61 C15 **San Roque** Corrientes, NE Argentina 28°35′S 58°45′W
188 I4 **San Roque** Saipan, S Northern Mariana Islands 15°15′S 145°47′E
104 K16 **San Roque** Andalucía, S Spain 36°13′N 05°23′W
25 R9 **San Saba** Texas, SW USA 31°13′N 98°44′W
25 Q9 **San Saba River** Texas, SW USA
61 D17 **San Salvador** Entre Ríos, E Argentina 31°38′S 58°30′W
42 F7 **San Salvador** ● (El Salvador) San Salvador, SW El Salvador 13°42′N 89°12′W
42 A10 **San Salvador** *department* C El Salvador
44 K4 **San Salvador** *prev.* Watlings Island. *island* E Bahamas
42 F8 **San Salvador** ✕ La Paz, S El Salvador 13°27′N 89°04′W
62 J5 **San Salvador de Jujuy** *var.* Jujuy. Jujuy, N Argentina 24°10′S 65°20′W
57 B18 **San Salvador, Isla** *island* Ecuador
42 F7 **San Salvador, Volcán de** C El Salvador 13°58′N 89°14′W
77 Q14 **Sansanné-Mango** *var.* Mango. N Togo 10°21′N 00°28′E
45 S5 **San Sebastián** W Puerto Rico 18°21′N 67°00′W
63 J24 **San Sebastián, Bahía** *bay* S Argentina
Sansenhō *see* Sach'ŏn
106 H12 **Sansepolcro** Toscana, C Italy 43°35′N 12°12′E
107 M16 **San Severo** Puglia, SE Italy 41°41′N 15°23′E
112 F11 **Sanski Most** Federacija Bosna I Hercegovina, NW Bosnia and Herzegovina
171 W12 **Sansundi** Papua, E Indonesia 0°42′S 135°48′E
162 K9 **Sant** *var.* Mayhan. Övörhangay, C Mongolia 46°02′N 104°00′E
104 K11 **Santa Amalia** Extremadura, W Spain 39°00′N 06°01′W
60 F13 **Santa Ana** Misiones, NE Argentina 27°22′S 55°34′W
57 L16 **Santa Ana** Beni, N Bolivia 13°43′S 65°37′W
42 E7 **Santa Ana** Santa Ana, NW El Salvador 13°59′N 89°34′W
40 F4 **Santa Ana** Sonora, NW Mexico 30°31′N 111°08′W
35 T16 **Santa Ana** California, W USA 33°45′N 117°52′W
55 N6 **Santa Ana** Nueva Esparta, NE Venezuela 09°15′N 64°39′W
42 A9 **Santa Ana** *department* NW El Salvador
Santa Ana de Coro *see* Coro
35 U16 **Santa Ana Mountains** ▲ California, W USA
42 E7 **Santa Ana, Volcán de** *var.* La Matepec. W El Salvador 13°49′N 89°36′W
42 G6 **Santa Bárbara** Santa Bárbara, W Honduras 14°56′N 88°11′W
40 J7 **Santa Barbara** Chihuahua, N Mexico 26°46′N 105°46′W
35 Q14 **Santa Barbara** California, W USA 34°24′N 119°40′W
54 L11 **Santa Bárbara** Amazonas, S Venezuela 03°55′N 67°06′W
54 I7 **Santa Bárbara** Barinas, W Venezuela 07°48′N 71°10′W
42 F5 **Santa Bárbara** *department* NW Honduras
Santa Bárbara *see* Iscuandé
35 Q15 **Santa Barbara Channel** *channel* California, W USA
Santa Bárbara de Samaná *see* Samaná
35 R16 **Santa Barbara Island** *island* Channel Islands, California, W USA
54 E5 **Santa Catalina** Bolívar, N Colombia 10°36′N 75°17′W
43 R15 **Santa Catalina** Ngöbe Bugle, W Panama 08°46′N 81°18′W
35 T17 **Santa Catalina, Gulf of** *gulf* California, W USA
43 Q7 **Santa Catalina, Isla** *island* NW Colombia, Caribbean Sea
40 F8 **Santa Catalina, Isla** *island* NW Mexico
35 S16 **Santa Catalina Island** *island* Channel Islands, California, W USA
41 N8 **Santa Catarina** Nuevo León, NE Mexico 25°39′N 100°30′W
60 H13 **Santa Catarina** *off.* Estado de Santa Catarina. *state* S Brazil
Santa Catarina de Tepehuanes *see* Tepehuanes
Santa Catarina, Estado de *see* Santa Catarina
60 L13 **Santa Catarina, Ilha de** *island* S Brazil
45 Q16 **Santa Catherina** Curaçao, C Netherlands Antilles 12°07′N 68°46′W
44 E5 **Santa Clara** Villa Clara, C Cuba 22°25′N 78°01′W
35 N9 **Santa Clara** California, W USA 37°20′N 121°57′W
36 J8 **Santa Clara** Utah, W USA 37°07′N 113°39′W
Santa Clara *see* Santa Clara de Olimar
61 F18 **Santa Clara de Olimar** *var.* Santa Clara. Cerro Largo, NE Uruguay 32°50′S 54°54′W
61 A17 **Santa Clara de Saguier** Santa Fe, C Argentina 31°21′S 61°50′W
Santa Coloma *see* Santa Coloma de Gramanet
105 X5 **Santa Coloma de Farners** *var.* Santa Coloma de Farnés. Cataluña, NE Spain 41°52′N 02°39′E
Santa Coloma de Farnés *see* Santa Coloma de Farners
105 W6 **Santa Coloma de Gramanet** *var.* Santa Coloma. Cataluña, NE Spain 41°28′N 02°14′E
104 G2 **Santa Comba** Galicia, NW Spain 43°02′N 08°49′W
Santa Comba *see* Uaco Cungo
104 H8 **Santa Comba Dão** Viseu, N Portugal 40°23′N 08°07′W
82 C10 **Santa Cruz** Uíge, NW Angola 06°56′S 16°25′E
57 N19 **Santa Cruz** *var.* Santa Cruz de la Sierra. Santa Cruz, C Bolivia 17°49′S 63°11′W
62 G12 **Santa Cruz** Libertador, C Chile 34°38′S 71°27′W
42 K13 **Santa Cruz** Guanacaste, W Costa Rica 10°15′N 85°35′W
44 I12 **Santa Cruz** W Jamaica 18°03′N 77°43′W
64 P6 **Santa Cruz** Madeira, Portugal, NE Atlantic Ocean 32°43′N 16°47′W
35 N10 **Santa Cruz** California, W USA 36°58′N 122°01′W
63 H20 **Santa Cruz** *off.* Provincia de Santa Cruz. *province* S Argentina
57 O18 **Santa Cruz** *department* E Bolivia
Santa Cruz *see* Puerto Santa Cruz
Santa Cruz *see* Viru-Viru
Santa Cruz Barillas *see* Barillas
59 O18 **Santa Cruz Cabrália** Bahia, E Brazil 16°17′S 39°03′W
Santa Cruz de El Seibo *see* El Seibo
64 N11 **Santa Cruz de la Palma** La Palma, Islas Canarias, Spain, NE Atlantic Ocean 28°41′N 17°46′W
Santa Cruz de la Sierra *see* Santa Cruz
105 O9 **Santa Cruz de la Zarza** Castilla-La Mancha, C Spain 39°59′N 03°10′W
42 C5 **Santa Cruz del Quiché** Quiché, W Guatemala 15°02′N 91°06′W
105 N8 **Santa Cruz del Retamar** Castilla-La Mancha, C Spain 40°08′N 04°14′W
Santa Cruz del Seibo *see* El Seibo
44 G7 **Santa Cruz del Sur** Camagüey, C Cuba 20°44′N 78°00′W
105 O11 **Santa Cruz de Mudela** Castilla-La Mancha, C Spain 38°37′N 03°27′W
64 Q11 **Santa Cruz de Tenerife** Tenerife, Islas Canarias, Spain, NE Atlantic Ocean 28°28′N 16°15′W
64 P11 **Santa Cruz de Tenerife** *province* Islas Canarias, Spain, NE Atlantic Ocean
60 K9 **Santa Cruz do Rio Pardo** São Paulo, S Brazil 22°52′S 49°37′W
61 H15 **Santa Cruz do Sul** Rio Grande do Sul, S Brazil 29°42′S 52°25′W
57 C17 **Santa Cruz, Isla** *var.* Indefatigable Island, Isla Chávez. *island* Galapagos Islands, Ecuador, E Pacific Ocean
40 F8 **Santa Cruz, Isla** *island* NW Mexico
35 Q15 **Santa Cruz Island** *island* California, W USA
187 Q10 **Santa Cruz Islands** *island group* E Solomon Islands
Santa Cruz, Provincia de *see* Santa Cruz
63 I22 **Santa Cruz, Río** S Argentina
36 L15 **Santa Cruz River** Arizona, SW USA
61 C17 **Santa Elena** Entre Ríos, E Argentina 30°58′S 59°47′W
42 F2 **Santa Elena** Cayo, W Belize 17°08′N 89°04′W
25 R16 **Santa Elena** Texas, SW USA 26°43′N 98°30′W
56 A7 **Santa Elena, Bahía de** *bay* W Ecuador
55 R10 **Santa Elena de Uairén** Bolívar, E Venezuela 04°40′N 61°03′W
42 K12 **Santa Elena, Península** *peninsula* NW Costa Rica
56 A7 **Santa Elena, Punta** *headland* W Ecuador 02°11′S 81°00′W
104 L11 **Santa Eufemia** Andalucía, S Spain 38°36′N 04°54′W
107 N21 **Santa Eufemia, Golfo di** *gulf* S Italy
105 S4 **Santa Eulalia de Gállego** Aragón, NE Spain 42°16′N 00°46′W
105 V11 **Santa Eulalia del Río** Ibiza, Spain, W Mediterranean Sea 39°00′N 01°33′E
61 B17 **Santa Fe** Santa Fe, C Argentina 31°36′S 60°47′W
44 C6 **Santa Fé** *var.* La Fe. Isla de la Juventud, W Cuba 21°45′N 82°45′W
43 R16 **Santa Fé** Veraguas, C Panama 08°29′N 80°50′W
105 N14 **Santa Fe** Andalucía, S Spain 37°11′N 03°43′W
37 S10 **Santa Fe** *state capital* New Mexico, SW USA 35°41′N 105°56′W
61 B15 **Santa Fe** *off.* Provincia de Santa Fe. *province* C Argentina
Santa Fe *see* Bogotá
Santa Fe de Bogotá *see* Bogotá
60 J7 **Santa Fé do Sul** São Paulo, S Brazil 20°13′S 50°56′W
57 B18 **Santa Fe, Isla** *var.* Barrington Island. *island* Galapagos Islands, Ecuador, E Pacific Ocean
Santa Fe, Provincia de *see* Santa Fe
23 V9 **Santa Fe River** Florida, SE USA
59 M15 **Santa Filomena** Piauí, E Brazil 09°06′S 45°52′W
40 G10 **Santa Genoveva** ▲ NW Mexico 23°07′N 109°56′W
153 S14 **Santahar** Rajshahi, NW Bangladesh 24°45′N 89°03′E
60 G11 **Santa Helena** Paraná, S Brazil 24°53′S 54°19′W
54 J5 **Santa Inés** Lara, N Venezuela 10°37′N 69°18′W
63 G24 **Santa Inés, Isla** *island* S Chile
62 J13 **Santa Isabel** La Pampa, C Argentina 36°11′S 66°59′W
43 U14 **Santa Isabel** Colón, N Panama 09°31′N 79°12′W
186 L8 **Santa Isabel** *var.* Bughotu. *island* N Solomon Islands
Santa Isabel *see* Malabo
58 D11 **Santa Isabel do Rio Negro** Amazonas, NW Brazil 0°40′S 64°56′W
61 C15 **Santa Lucia** Corrientes, NE Argentina 28°58′S 59°05′W
57 I17 **Santa Lucía** Puno, S Peru 15°45′S 70°34′W
61 F20 **Santa Lucía** *var.* Santa Lucia. Canelones, S Uruguay 34°26′S 56°25′W
42 B6 **Santa Lucía Cotzumalguapa** Escuintla, SW Guatemala 14°20′N 91°00′W
107 L23 **Santa Lucia del Mela** Sicilia, Italy, C Mediterranean Sea 38°08′N 15°17′E
35 O11 **Santa Lucia Range** ▲ California, W USA
40 D9 **Santa Margarita, Isla** *island* NW Mexico
62 J7 **Santa María** Catamarca, N Argentina 26°51′S 66°02′W
61 G15 **Santa Maria** Rio Grande do Sul, S Brazil 29°41′S 53°48′W
35 P13 **Santa Maria** California, W USA 34°56′N 120°25′W
64 Q4 **Santa Maria** ✕ Santa Maria, Azores, Portugal, NE Atlantic Ocean
64 P3 **Santa Maria** *island* Azores, Portugal, NE Atlantic Ocean
Santa Maria *see* Gaua
Santa María Asunción Tlaxiaco *see* Tlaxiaco
40 G9 **Santa María, Bahía** *bay* W Mexico
83 L21 **Santa Maria, Cabo de** *headland* S Mozambique 26°05′S 32°58′E
104 G15 **Santa Maria, Cabo de** *headland* S Portugal 36°57′N 07°55′W
44 J4 **Santa Maria, Cape** *headland* Long Island, C Bahamas 23°40′N 75°20′W
107 J17 **Santa Maria Capua Vetere** Campania, S Italy 41°05′N 14°15′E
104 G7 **Santa Maria da Feira** Aveiro, N Portugal 40°55′N 08°32′W
59 M17 **Santa Maria da Vitória** Bahia, E Brazil 13°26′S 44°09′W
55 N9 **Santa Maria de Erebato** Bolívar, SE Venezuela 05°09′N 64°50′W
55 N6 **Santa María de Ipire** Guárico, C Venezuela 08°51′N 65°21′W
Santa Maria del Buen Aire *see* Buenos Aires
40 J8 **Santa María del Oro** Durango, C Mexico 25°57′N 105°22′W
41 N12 **Santa María del Río** San Luis Potosí, C Mexico 21°48′N 100°42′W
Santa Maria di Castellabate *see* Castellabate
107 Q20 **Santa Maria di Leuca, Capo** *headland* SE Italy 39°48′N 18°21′E
108 K10 **Santa Maria-im-Munstertal** Graubünden, SE Switzerland 46°36′N 10°25′E
57 B18 **Santa María, Isla** *var.* Isla Floreana, Charles Island. *island* Galapagos Islands, Ecuador, E Pacific Ocean
40 J3 **Santa María, Laguna de** N Mexico
61 G16 **Santa Maria, Rio** S Brazil
43 R16 **Santa María, Río** C Panama
36 J12 **Santa Maria River** Arizona, SW USA
107 G15 **Santa Marinella** Lazio, C Italy 42°01′N 11°51′E
54 F4 **Santa Marta** Magdalena, N Colombia 11°14′N 74°13′W
104 J11 **Santa Marta** Extremadura, W Spain 38°37′N 06°39′W
54 F4 **Santa Marta, Sierra Nevada de** ▲ NE Colombia
Santa Maura *see* Lefkáda
35 S15 **Santa Monica** California, W USA 34°01′N 118°29′W
116 F10 **Sântana** *Ger.* Sankt Anna, *Hung.* Újszentanna; *prev.* Sîntana. Arad, W Romania 46°20′N 21°30′E
61 F16 **Santana, Coxilha de** *hill range* S Brazil
61 H16 **Santana da Boa Vista** Rio Grande do Sul, S Brazil 30°52′S 53°03′W
61 F16 **Santana do Livramento** *prev.* Livramento. Rio Grande do Sul, S Brazil 30°52′S 55°30′W
105 N2 **Santander** Cantabria, N Spain 43°28′N 03°48′W
54 F8 **Santander** *off.* Departamento de Santander. *province* C Colombia
Santander, Departamento de *see* Santander
Santander Jiménez *see* Jiménez
Sant'Andrea *see* Svetac
107 B20 **Sant'Antioco** Sardegna, Italy, C Mediterranean Sea 39°03′N 08°28′E
105 V11 **Sant Antoni de Portmany** *Cas.* San Antonio Abad. Ibiza, Spain, W Mediterranean Sea 38°58′N 01°18′E
105 Y10 **Santanyí** Mallorca, Spain, W Mediterranean Sea 39°22′N 03°07′E
104 J13 **Santa Olalla del Cala** Andalucía, S Spain 37°54′N 06°13′W
35 R15 **Santa Paula** California, W USA 34°21′N 119°03′W
36 L4 **Santaquin** Utah, W USA 39°58′N 111°46′W
58 I12 **Santarém** Pará, N Brazil 02°26′S 54°41′W
104 G10 **Santarém** *anc.* Scalabis. Santarém, W Portugal 39°14′N 08°40′W
104 G10 **Santarém** *district* C Portugal
44 F4 **Santaren Channel** *channel* W Bahamas
54 K10 **Santa Rita** Vichada, E Colombia 04°51′N 68°27′W
188 B16 **Santa Rita** SW Guam
42 H5 **Santa Rita** Cortés, NW Honduras 15°10′N 87°54′W
40 E9 **Santa Rita** Baja California Sur, NW Mexico 27°29′N 100°33′W
54 H5 **Santa Rita** Zulia, NW Venezuela 10°35′N 71°30′W
59 I19 **Santa Rita de Araguaia** Goiás, S Brazil 17°17′S 53°13′W
Santa Rita de Cassia *see* Cássia
61 D14 **Santa Rosa** Corrientes, NE Argentina 28°18′S 58°04′W

◆ Country
● Country Capital
◇ Dependent Territory
○ Dependent Territory Capital
Administrative Regions
✕ International Airport
▲ Mountain
Mountain Range
Volcano
River
Lake
Reservoir

SANTA ROSA – SATKHIRA

62 K13 Santa Rosa La Pampa, C Argentina 36°38′S 64°15′W
61 G14 Santa Rosa Rio Grande do Sul, S Brazil 27°50′S 54°29′W
58 E10 Santa Rosa Roraima, N Brazil 03°41′N 62°29′W
56 B8 Santa Rosa El Oro, SW Ecuador 03°29′S 79°57′W
57 I16 Santa Rosa Puno, S Peru 14°38′S 70°45′W
34 M7 Santa Rosa California, W USA 38°27′N 122°42′W
37 U11 Santa Rosa New Mexico, SW USA 34°54′N 104°43′W
55 O6 Santa Rosa Anzoátegui, NE Venezuela 09°37′N 64°20′W
42 A3 Santa Rosa off. Departamento de Santa Rosa. ◆ department SE Guatemala
Santa Rosa see Santa Rosa de Copán
63 J15 Santa Rosa, Bajo de basin E Argentina
42 F6 Santa Rosa de Copán var. Santa Rosa. Copán, W Honduras 14°48′N 88°43′W
54 E8 Santa Rosa de Osos Antioquia, C Colombia 06°40′N 75°27′W
Santa Rosa, Departamento de see Santa Rosa
35 Q15 Santa Rosa Island island California, W USA
23 O9 Santa Rosa Island island Florida, SE USA
40 E6 Santa Rosalía Baja California Sur, NW Mexico 27°20′N 112°20′W
54 K6 Santa Rosalía Portuguesa, NW Venezuela 09°02′N 69°01′W
188 C15 Santa Rosa, Mount ▲ NE Guam
35 V16 Santa Rosa Mountains ▲▲ California, W USA
35 T2 Santa Rosa Range ▲▲ Nevada, W USA
62 M8 Santa Sylvina Chaco, N Argentina 27°49′S 61°09′W
Santa Tecla see Nueva San Salvador
61 B19 Santa Teresa Santa Fe, C Argentina 33°30′S 60°45′W
59 O20 Santa Teresa Espírito Santo, SE Brazil 19°51′S 40°49′W
61 E21 Santa Teresita Buenos Aires, E Argentina 36°32′S 56°41′W
61 H19 Santa Vitória do Palmar Rio Grande do Sul, S Brazil 33°32′S 53°25′W
35 Q14 Santa Ynez River ∽ California, W USA
Sant Carles de la Rápida see Sant Carles de la Ràpita
105 U7 Sant Carles de la Ràpita var. Sant Carles de la Rápida. Cataluña, NE Spain 40°37′N 00°36′E
105 W5 Sant Celoni Cataluña, NE Spain 41°39′N 02°25′E
35 U17 Santee California, W USA 32°50′N 116°58′W
21 T13 Santee River ∽ South Carolina, SE USA
40 K15 San Telmo, Punta headland SW Mexico 18°19′N 103°30′W
107 O17 Santeramo in Colle Puglia, SE Italy 40°47′N 16°45′E
107 M23 San Teresa di Riva Sicilia, Italy, C Mediterranean Sea 38°00′N 15°25′E
105 X5 Sant Feliu de Guíxols var. San Felíu de Guixols. Cataluña, NE Spain 41°47′N 03°02′E
105 W6 Sant Feliu de Llobregat Cataluña, NE Spain 41°22′N 02°00′E
106 C7 Santhià Piemonte, NE Italy 45°21′N 08°11′E
61 F15 Santiago Rio Grande do Sul, S Brazil 29°11′S 54°52′W
62 H11 Santiago var. Gran Santiago. ● (Chile) Santiago, C Chile 33°30′S 70°40′W
45 N8 Santiago var. Santiago de los Caballeros. N Dominican Republic 19°27′N 70°42′W
40 G10 Santiago Baja California Sur, NW Mexico 23°32′N 109°47′W
41 O8 Santiago Nuevo León, NE Mexico 25°22′N 100°09′W
43 R16 Santiago Veraguas, S Panama 08°06′N 80°59′W
57 E16 Santiago Ica, SW Peru 14°14′S 75°44′W
104 G3 Santiago var. Santiago de Compostela, Eng. Compostella; anc. Campus Stellae. Galicia, NW Spain 42°52′N 08°33′W
62 H11 Santiago off. Región Metropolitana de Santiago, var. Metropolitan. ◆ region C Chile
76 D10 Santiago var. São Tiago. island Ilhas de Sotavento, S Cape Verde
62 H11 Santiago ✈ Santiago, C Chile 33°27′S 70°40′W
104 G3 Santiago ✈ Galicia, NW Spain
Santiago see Santiago de Cuba, Cuba
Santiago see Grande de Santiago, Río, Mexico
42 B6 Santiago Atitlán Sololá, SW Guatemala 14°39′N 91°12′W
43 Q16 Santiago, Cerro ▲ W Panama 08°27′N 81°42′W
Santiago de Compostela see Santiago
44 I8 Santiago de Cuba var. Santiago. Santiago de Cuba, E Cuba 20°01′N 75°51′W
Santiago de Guayaquil see Guayaquil
62 K8 Santiago del Estero Santiago del Estero, C Argentina 27°51′S 64°16′W
61 A15 Santiago del Estero off. Provincia de Santiago del Estero. ◆ province N Argentina
Santiago del Estero, Provincia de see Santiago del Estero
40 I8 Santiago de los Caballeros Sinaloa, W Mexico 25°33′N 107°22′W
Santiago de los Caballeros see Santiago, Dominican Republic
Santiago de los Caballeros see Ciudad de Guatemala, Guatemala
42 F8 Santiago de María Usulután, SE El Salvador 13°28′N 88°28′W
104 F12 Santiago do Cacém Setúbal, S Portugal 38°01′N 08°42′W
40 J12 Santiago Ixcuintla Nayarit, C Mexico 21°50′N 105°11′W
Santiago Jamiltepec see Jamiltepec
24 L11 Santiago Mountains ▲▲ Texas, SW USA
40 J9 Santiago Papasquiaro Durango, C Mexico 25°00′N 105°27′W
Santiago Pinotepa Nacional see Pinotepa Nacional
Santiago, Región Metropolitana de see Santiago
56 C8 Santiago, Río ∽ N Peru
40 M10 San Tiburcio Zacatecas, C Mexico 24°08′N 101°29′W
105 N2 Santillana Cantabria, N Spain 43°24′N 04°06′W
54 I5 San Timoteo Zulia, NW Venezuela 09°50′N 71°05′W
Santi Quaranta see Sarandë
Santissima Trinidad see Chilung
105 O12 Santisteban del Puerto Andalucía, S Spain 38°15′N 03°11′W
105 U7 Sant Jordi, Golf de gulf NE Spain
105 U11 Sant Josep de sa Talaia var. San Jose. Ibiza, Spain, W Mediterranean Sea 38°55′N 1°18′E
162 G6 Santmargats var. Holboo. Dzavhan, W Mongolia 48°35′N 95°25′E
105 T8 Sant Mateu País Valenciano, E Spain 40°28′N 00°10′E
25 S7 Santo Texas, SW USA 32°35′N 98°06′W
Santo see Espiritu Santo
60 M10 Santo Amaro, Ilha de island SE Brazil
61 G14 Santo Ângelo Rio Grande do Sul, S Brazil 28°17′S 54°15′W
76 C9 Santo Antão island Ilhas de Barlavento, N Cape Verde
60 J10 Santo Antônio da Platina Paraná, S Brazil 23°20′S 50°05′W
58 C13 Santo Antônio do Içá Amazonas, N Brazil 03°05′S 67°56′W
57 Q18 Santo Corazón, Río ∽ E Bolivia
44 E5 Santo Domingo Villa Clara, C Cuba 22°35′N 80°15′W
45 O9 Santo Domingo prev. Ciudad Trujillo. ● (Dominican Republic) SE Dominican Republic 18°30′N 69°57′W
40 E8 Santo Domingo Baja California Sur, NW Mexico 25°34′N 112°00′W
40 M10 Santo Domingo San Luis Potosí, C Mexico 23°18′N 101°42′W
42 L10 Santo Domingo Chontales, S Nicaragua 12°15′N 84°59′W
105 P4 Santo Domingo de la Calzada La Rioja, N Spain 42°26′N 02°57′W
56 B6 Santo Domingo de los Colorados Pichincha, NW Ecuador 0°13′S 79°09′W
Santo Domingo Tehuantepec see Tehuantepec
55 O6 San Tomé Anzoátegui, NE Venezuela 08°58′N 64°08′W
San Tomé de Guayana see Ciudad Guayana
105 R13 Santomera Murcia, SE Spain 38°03′N 01°05′W
105 O2 Santoña Cantabria, N Spain 43°27′N 03°28′W
Santorin see Santoríni
115 K22 Santoríni var. Santorin, prev. Thíra; anc. Thera. island Kykládes, Greece, Aegean Sea
60 M10 Santos São Paulo, S Brazil 23°56′S 46°22′W
65 J17 Santos Plateau undersea feature SW Atlantic Ocean 25°00′S 43°00′W
104 G6 Santo Tirso Porto, N Portugal 41°20′N 08°25′W
40 B2 Santo Tomás Baja California Norte, NW Mexico 31°32′N 116°26′W
42 L10 Santo Tomás Chontales, S Nicaragua 12°04′N 85°02′W
42 G5 Santo Tomás de Castilla Izabal, E Guatemala 15°40′N 88°36′W
40 B2 Santo Tomás, Punta headland NW Mexico 31°30′N 116°40′W
57 H16 Santo Tomás, Río ∽ C Peru
57 B18 Santo Tomás, Volcán ⛰ Galapagos Islands, Ecuador, E Pacific Ocean 0°46′S 91°01′W
61 F14 Santo Tomé Corrientes, NE Argentina 28°31′S 56°03′W
Santo Tomé de Guayana see Ciudad Guayana
98 H10 Santpoort Noord-Holland, W Netherlands 52°26′N 04°38′E
Santurce see Santurtzi
105 O2 Santurtzi var. Santurce, Santurzi. País Vasco, N Spain 43°20′N 03°03′W
Santurzi see Santurtzi
63 G20 San Valentín, Cerro ▲ S Chile 46°36′S 73°17′W
42 F8 San Vicente San Vicente, C El Salvador 13°38′N 88°42′W
40 C2 San Vicente Baja California Norte, NW Mexico 31°20′N 116°15′W
188 H6 San Vicente Saipan, S Northern Mariana Islands
42 B9 San Vicente ◆ department E El Salvador
104 I10 San Vicente de Alcántara Extremadura, W Spain 39°21′N 07°07′W
105 N2 San Vicente de Barakaldo var. Baracaldo, Basq. San Bizenti-Barakaldo. País Vasco, N Spain 43°17′N 02°59′W
57 E15 San Vicente de Cañete var. Cañete. Lima, W Peru 13°06′S 76°23′W
104 M2 San Vicente de la Barquera Cantabria, N Spain 43°23′N 04°24′W
54 E12 San Vicente del Caguán Caquetá, S Colombia 02°07′N 74°47′W
42 F8 San Vicente, Volcán de ▲ C El Salvador 13°34′N 88°50′W
43 O15 San Vito Puntarenas, SE Costa Rica 08°49′N 82°58′W
106 I7 San Vito al Tagliamento Friuli-Venezia Giulia, NE Italy 45°54′N 12°55′E
107 H23 San Vito, Capo headland Sicilia, Italy, C Mediterranean Sea 38°11′N 12°41′E
107 P18 San Vito dei Normanni Puglia, SE Italy 40°40′N 17°42′E
160 L17 Sanya var. Ya Xian. Hainan, S China 18°25′N 109°27′E
83 J16 Sanyati ∽ N Zimbabwe
25 Q16 San Ygnacio Texas, SW USA 27°04′N 99°26′W
160 L6 Sanyuan Shaanxi, C China 34°40′N 108°56′E
123 P11 Sanyyakhtakh Respublika Sakha (Yakutiya), NE Russian Federation 60°34′N 124°09′E
146 J15 S. A.Nyýazow Adyndaky Rus. Imeni S. A. Niyazova. Maryyskiy Velayat, S Turkmenistan 36°44′N 62°23′E
82 C10 Sanza Pombo Uíge, NW Angola 07°20′S 16°00′E
Sanzyô see Sanjō
104 G14 São Bartolomeu de Messines Faro, S Portugal 37°12′N 08°16′W
60 M10 São Bernardo do Campo São Paulo, S Brazil 23°45′S 46°34′W
61 F15 São Borja Rio Grande do Sul, S Brazil 28°35′S 56°01′W
104 H14 São Brás de Alportel Faro, S Portugal 37°09′N 07°55′W
60 M10 São Caetano do Sul São Paulo, S Brazil 23°37′S 46°34′W
60 L9 São Carlos São Paulo, S Brazil 22°02′S 47°53′W
59 P16 São Cristóvão Sergipe, E Brazil 10°59′S 37°10′W
61 F15 São Francisco de Assis Rio Grande do Sul, S Brazil 29°32′S 55°07′W
58 K13 São Félix Pará, NE Brazil 06°43′S 51°56′W
São Félix see São Félix do Araguaia
59 J16 São Félix do Araguaia var. São Félix. Mato Grosso, W Brazil 11°36′S 50°40′W
59 J14 São Félix do Xingu Pará, NE Brazil 06°38′S 51°59′W
60 Q9 São Fidélis Rio de Janeiro, SE Brazil 21°37′S 41°40′W
76 D10 São Filipe Fogo, S Cape Verde 14°52′N 24°29′W
60 K12 São Francisco do Sul Santa Catarina, S Brazil 26°17′S 48°39′W
60 K12 São Francisco, Ilha de island S Brazil
59 P16 São Francisco, Rio ∽ E Brazil
61 G16 São Gabriel Rio Grande do Sul, S Brazil 30°17′S 54°17′W
60 P10 São Gonçalo Rio de Janeiro, SE Brazil 22°48′S 43°03′W
81 H23 Sao Hill Iringa, S Tanzania 08°19′S 35°11′E
60 R9 São João da Barra Rio de Janeiro, SE Brazil 21°39′S 41°04′W
104 G7 São João da Madeira Aveiro, N Portugal 40°52′N 08°28′W
58 M12 São João de Cortes Maranhão, E Brazil 02°30′S 44°27′W
59 M21 São João del Rei Minas Gerais, NE Brazil 21°08′S 44°15′W
59 N15 São João do Piauí Piauí, E Brazil 08°21′S 42°14′W
59 N14 São João dos Patos Maranhão, E Brazil 06°29′S 43°44′W
58 C11 São Joaquim Amazonas, NW Brazil 0°08′S 67°10′W
61 J14 São Joaquim Santa Catarina, S Brazil 28°20′S 49°55′W
60 L7 São Joaquim da Barra São Paulo, S Brazil 20°36′S 47°50′W
64 N2 São Jorge island Azores, Portugal, NE Atlantic Ocean
61 K14 São José Santa Catarina, S Brazil 27°34′S 48°39′W
60 M8 São José do Rio Pardo São Paulo, S Brazil 21°37′S 46°52′W
60 K8 São José do Rio Preto São Paulo, S Brazil 20°50′S 49°20′W
60 N10 São José dos Campos São Paulo, S Brazil 23°07′S 45°52′W
61 I17 São Lourenço do Sul Rio Grande do Sul, S Brazil 31°25′S 52°00′W
58 M12 São Luís state capital Maranhão, NE Brazil 02°34′S 44°16′W
58 F11 São Luís Roraima, N Brazil 01°11′N 60°15′W
58 M12 São Luís, Ilha de island NE Brazil
61 F14 São Luiz Gonzaga Rio Grande do Sul, S Brazil 28°24′S 54°58′W
São Mandol see São Manuel, Rio
47 U8 São Manuel ∽ C Brazil
59 H15 São Manuel, Rio var. São Mandol, Teles Pirés. ∽ C Brazil
58 C11 São Marcelino Amazonas, NW Brazil 0°53′N 67°16′W
58 N12 São Marcos, Baía de bay N Brazil
59 O20 São Mateus Espírito Santo, SE Brazil 18°44′S 39°53′W
60 J12 São Mateus do Sul Paraná, S Brazil 25°58′S 50°29′W
64 P3 São Miguel island Azores, Portugal, NE Atlantic Ocean
60 G13 São Miguel d'Oeste Santa Catarina, S Brazil 26°45′S 53°34′W
45 P9 Saona, Isla island SE Dominican Republic
172 H12 Saondzou ▲ Grande Comore, NW Comoros
103 R10 Saône ∽ E France
103 Q9 Saône-et-Loire ◆ department C France
76 D9 São Nicolau Eng. Saint Nicholas. island Ilhas de Barlavento, N Cape Verde
60 M10 São Paulo state capital São Paulo, S Brazil 23°33′S 46°39′W
60 K9 São Paulo off. Estado de São Paulo. ◆ state S Brazil
São Paulo de Loanda see Luanda
São Paulo, Estado de see São Paulo
São Pedro do Rio Grande do Sul see Rio Grande
104 H7 São Pedro do Sul Viseu, N Portugal 40°46′N 07°58′W
64 K13 São Pedro e São Paulo undersea feature C Atlantic Ocean 01°25′N 28°54′W
59 M14 São Raimundo das Mangabeiras Maranhão, E Brazil 07°00′S 45°30′W
59 Q14 São Roque, Cabo de headland E Brazil 05°29′S 35°16′W
São Salvador see Salvador, Brazil
São Salvador/São Salvador do Congo see M'Banza Congo, Angola
60 N10 São Sebastião, Ilha de island S Brazil
83 N19 São Sebastião, Ponta headland C Mozambique 22°09′S 35°33′E
104 F13 São Teotónio Beja, S Portugal 37°30′N 08°41′W
São Tiago see Santiago
79 B18 São Tomé ● (Sao Tome and Principe) São Tomé, S Sao Tome and Principe 0°22′N 06°41′E
79 B18 São Tomé ✈ São Tomé, S Sao Tome and Principe 0°24′N 06°39′E
79 B18 São Tomé Eng. Saint Thomas. island S Sao Tome and Principe
79 B17 Sao Tome and Principe off. Democratic Republic of Sao Tome and Principe. ◆ republic E Atlantic Ocean
Sao Tome and Principe, Democratic Republic of see Sao Tome and Principe
74 H9 Saoura, Oued ∽ NW Algeria
60 M10 São Vicente Eng. Saint Vincent. São Paulo, S Brazil 23°55′S 46°25′W
64 O5 São Vicente Madeira, Portugal, NE Atlantic Ocean 32°48′N 17°03′W
76 C9 São Vicente Eng. Saint Vincent. island Ilhas de Barlavento, N Cape Verde
104 F14 São Vicente, Cabo de Eng. Cape Saint Vincent, Port. Cabode São Vicente. cape S Portugal
São Vicente, Cabo de see São Vicente, Cabo de
Sápai see Sápes
Sapaleri, Cerro see Zapaleri, Cerro
Saparoea see Saparua
171 S13 Saparua prev. Saparoea. Pulau Saparau, C Indonesia 03°35′S 128°37′E
168 L11 Sapat Sumatera, W Indonesia 0°18′S 103°18′E
77 U17 Sapele Delta, S Nigeria 05°54′N 05°43′E
23 X7 Sapelo Island island Georgia, SE USA
23 X7 Sapelo Sound sound Georgia, SE USA
114 K13 Sápes var. Sápai. Anatolikí Makedonía kai Thráki, NE Greece 41°02′N 25°44′E
Sapiénza see Sapiénza
115 D22 Sapiénza var. Sapiénza. island S Greece
138 F12 Sapir prev. Sappir. Southern, S Israel 30°43′N 35°11′E
61 I15 Sapiranga Rio Grande do Sul, S Brazil 29°39′S 50°58′W
114 K13 Sápka ▲▲ NE Greece
105 X9 Sa Pobla Mallorca, Spain, W Mediterranean Sea 39°46′N 03°03′E
56 D11 Saposoa San Martín, N Peru 06°53′S 76°45′W
119 F16 Sapotskin Pol. Sopockinie, Rus. Sapotskino, Sopotskin. Hrodzyenskaya Voblasts', W Belarus 53°50′N 23°39′E
77 P13 Sapoui var. Sapouy. S Burkina 11°34′N 01°44′W
Sapouy see Sapoui
Sappir see Sapir
165 S4 Sapporo Hokkaidō, NE Japan 43°05′N 141°21′E
107 M19 Sapri Campania, S Italy 40°05′N 15°36′E
169 T16 Sapudi, Pulau island S Indonesia
27 P9 Sapulpa Oklahoma, C USA 36°00′N 96°06′W
142 J4 Saqqez var. Saghez, Sakiz, Saqqiz. Kordestān, NW Iran 36°31′N 46°16′E
Saqqiz see Saqqez
139 U8 Sarābādī Wāsiţ, E Iraq 33°00′N 44°52′E
167 P10 Sara Buri var. Saraburi. Saraburi, C Thailand 14°32′N 100°53′E
Saraburi see Sara Buri
Sarafjagān see Salafchegān
24 K9 Saragosa Texas, SW USA 31°03′N 103°39′W
Saragossa see Zaragoza
Saragt see Sarahs
56 B8 Saraguro Loja, S Ecuador 03°42′S 79°18′W
146 I15 Sarahs var. Saragt, Rus. Serakhs. Ahal Welaýaty, S Turkmenistan 36°33′N 61°10′E
126 M6 Sarai Ryazanskaya Oblast', W Russian Federation 53°43′N 39°59′E
Sarai see Saráy
154 M12 Saraipāli Chhattīsgarh, C India 21°21′N 83°01′E
149 T9 Sarāi Sidhu Punjab, E Pakistan 30°35′N 72°02′E
93 M15 Säräisniemi Oulu, C Finland 64°25′N 26°50′E
113 I14 Sarajevo ● (Bosnia and Herzegovina) Federacija Bosna I Hercegovina, SE Bosnia and Herzegovina 43°53′N 18°24′E
112 I13 Sarajevo ✈ Federacija Bosna I Hercegovina, C Bosnia and Herzegovina 43°49′N 18°21′E
143 V4 Sarakhs Khorāsān-Razavī, NE Iran 36°50′N 61°00′E
115 H17 Sarakíniko, Akrotírio headland Évvoia, C Greece 38°46′N 23°43′E
115 I18 Sarakinó island Vóreies Sporádes, Greece, Aegean Sea
127 V7 Saraktash Orenburgskaya Oblast', W Russian Federation 51°46′N 56°23′E
30 L15 Sara, Lake ⊠ Illinois, N USA
23 N8 Saraland Alabama, S USA 30°49′N 88°04′W
55 V9 Saramacca ◆ district N Suriname
55 V10 Saramacca Rivier ∽ C Suriname
166 M2 Saramati ▲ N Myanmar (Burma) 25°46′N 95°01′E
145 R10 Saran' Kaz. Saran. Karaganda, C Kazakhstan 49°47′N 73°02′E
18 K7 Saranac Lake New York, NE USA 44°18′N 74°06′W
18 K7 Saranac River ∽ New York, NE USA
Saranda see Sarandë
113 L23 Sarandë var. Saranda, It. Porto Edda; prev. Santi Quaranta. Vlorë, S Albania 39°53′N 20°E
61 H14 Sarandi Rio Grande do Sul, S Brazil 27°57′S 52°58′W
61 F19 Sarandí del Yí Durazno, C Uruguay 33°18′S 55°38′W
61 F19 Sarandí Grande Florida, S Uruguay 33°43′S 56°19′W
171 Q8 Sarangani Islands island group S Philippines
127 P5 Saransk Respublika Mordoviya, W Russian Federation 54°11′N 45°10′E
115 C14 Sarantáporos ∽ N Greece
114 H9 Sarantsi Sofiya, W Bulgaria 42°43′N 23°46′E
127 T3 Sarapul Udmurtskaya Respublika, NW Russian Federation 56°26′N 53°52′E
Sarāqeb see Sarāqib
138 I3 Sarāqib Fr. Saraqeb. Idlib, N Syria 35°52′N 36°48′E
54 J5 Sarare Lara, N Venezuela 09°47′N 69°10′W
55 O10 Sarariña Amazonas, S Venezuela 04°10′N 64°31′W
143 S10 Sar Ashk Kermān, C Iran
23 V13 Sarasota Florida, SE USA 27°20′N 82°31′W
117 O11 Sarata Odes'ka Oblast', SW Ukraine 46°01′N 29°40′E
116 I10 Sărăţel Hung. Szeretfalva. Bistriţa-Năsăud, N Romania 47°02′N 24°24′E
25 X10 Saratoga Texas, SW USA 30°15′N 94°31′W
18 K10 Saratoga Springs New York, NE USA 43°04′N 73°47′W
127 P8 Saratov Saratovskaya Oblast', W Russian Federation 51°33′N 45°58′E
127 P8 Saratovskaya Oblast' ◆ province W Russian Federation
127 Q7 Saratovskoye Vodokhranilishche ⊠ W Russian Federation
143 X13 Sarāvān Sīstān va Balūchestān, SE Iran 27°11′N 62°35′E
Saravan/Saravane see Salavan
169 S9 Sarawak ◆ state East Malaysia
Sarawak see Kuching
139 U6 Saráy var. Sarāi. Diyālá, E Iraq 34°06′N 45°06′E
136 D10 Saray Tekirdağ, NW Turkey 41°27′N 27°56′E
76 J12 Saraya SE Senegal 12°50′N 11°45′W
143 W14 Sarbāz Sīstān va Balūchestān, SE Iran 26°38′N 61°13′E
143 U8 Sarbīsheh Khorāsān-e Janūbī, E Iran 32°35′N 59°50′E
111 J24 Sárbogárd Fejér, C Hungary 46°54′N 18°36′E
Sărcad see Sarkad
27 S7 Sarcoxie Missouri, C USA 37°04′N 94°07′W
152 L11 Sārda Nep. Kali. ∽ India/Nepal
152 G10 Sardārshahr Rājasthān, NW India 28°30′N 74°30′E
107 C18 Sardegna Eng. Sardinia. ◆ region Italy, C Mediterranean Sea
107 A18 Sardegna Eng. Sardinia. island Italy, C Mediterranean Sea
42 K13 Sardinal Guanacaste, NW Costa Rica 10°30′N 85°38′W
54 G7 Sardinata Norte de Santander, N Colombia 08°07′N 72°47′W
Sardinia see Sardegna
120 K8 Sardinia-Corsica Trough undersea feature Tyrrhenian Sea, C Mediterranean Sea
22 L2 Sardis Mississippi, S USA 34°25′N 89°55′W
22 L2 Sardis Lake ⊠ Mississippi, S USA
27 P12 Sardis Lake ⊠ Oklahoma, C USA
92 H12 Sarek ▲▲ N Sweden
92 H11 Sarektjåhkkå ▲ N Sweden 67°28′N 17°56′E
149 N3 Sar-e Pol var. Sar-i-Pul. Sar-e Pol, N Afghanistan 36°16′N 65°55′E
149 O3 Sar-e Pol ◆ province N Afghanistan
Sar-e Pol see Sar-e Pol-e Žahāb
142 J6 Sar-e Pol-e Žahāb var. Sar-e Pol, Sar-i Pul. Kermānshāhān, W Iran 34°28′N 45°52′E
Sarera, Teluk see Cenderawasih, Teluk
147 T13 Sarez, Kŭli Rus. Sarezskoye Ozero. ⊚ SE Tajikistan
Sarezskoye Ozero see Sarez, Kŭli
64 G10 Sargasso Sea sea W Atlantic Ocean
149 U8 Sargodha Punjab, NE Pakistan 32°06′N 72°48′E
78 I13 Sarh prev. Fort-Archambault. Moyen-Chari, S Chad 09°08′N 18°22′E
143 P4 Sārī var. Sari, Sāri. Māzandarān, N Iran 36°37′N 53°05′E
115 N23 Saría island SE Greece
Sariasiya see Sariosiyo
40 F3 Saric Sonora, NW Mexico 31°08′N 111°22′W
188 K6 Sarigan island C Northern Mariana Islands
136 D14 Sarıgöl Manisa, SW Turkey 38°16′N 28°41′E
139 T6 Sārihah At Ta'mīm, E Iraq 34°34′N 44°38′E
137 R12 Sarıkamış Kars, NE Turkey 40°18′N 42°36′E
169 R9 Sarikei Sarawak, East Malaysia 02°07′N 111°30′E
147 U12 Sarikol Range Rus. Sarykol'skiy Khrebet. ▲▲ China/Tajikistan
181 Y7 Sarina Queensland, NE Australia 21°34′S 149°12′E
Sarine see La Sarine
105 S5 Sariñena Aragón, NE Spain 41°47′N 00°10′W
147 O13 Sariosiyo Rus. Sariasiya. Surkhondaryo Viloyati, S Uzbekistan 38°25′N 67°51′E
Sar-i-Pul see Sar-e Pol, Afghanistan
Sar-i Pul see Sar-e Pol-e Žahāb, Iran
Sariqamish Kŭli see Sarygamyş Köli
149 V1 Sarī Qūl Rus. Ozero Zurkul', Taj. Zŭrkŭl. ⊚ Afghanistan/Tajikistan see also Zŭrkŭl
Sarī Qūl see Zŭrkŭl
75 Q12 Sarīr Tibistī var. Serir Tibesti. desert S Libya
25 S15 Sarita Texas, SW USA 27°14′N 97°48′W
163 W14 Sariwŏn SW North Korea 38°30′N 125°52′E
114 P12 Sarıyer İstanbul, NW Turkey 41°11′N 29°03′E
97 L26 Sark Fr. Sercq. island Channel Islands
111 N24 Sarkad Rom. Sărcad. Békés, SE Hungary 46°44′N 21°25′E
145 W14 Sarkand Kaz. Sarqan. Almaty, SW Kazakhstan 45°24′N 79°55′E
Sarkani see Krasnogorskoye
152 D11 Sarkāri Tala Rājasthān, NW India 27°39′N 70°52′E
136 G15 Şarkîkaraağaç var. Şarki Karaağaç. Isparta, SW Turkey 38°04′N 31°22′E
Şarki Karaağaç see Şarkîkaraağaç
136 L13 Şarkışla Sivas, C Turkey 39°21′N 36°27′E
136 C11 Şarköy Tekirdağ, NW Turkey 40°37′N 27°07′E
Sárköz see Livada
Sarlat see Sarlat-la-Canéda
102 M13 Sarlat-la-Canéda var. Sarlat. Dordogne, SW France 44°54′N 01°12′E
109 S3 Sarleinsbach Oberösterreich, N Austria 48°33′N 13°55′E
Šarma see Ash Sharmah
171 Y12 Sarmi Papua, E Indonesia 01°51′S 138°45′E
63 I19 Sarmiento Chubut, S Argentina 45°38′S 69°07′W
63 H25 Sarmiento, Monte ▲ S Chile 54°28′S 70°49′W
94 J11 Särna Dalarna, C Sweden 61°40′N 13°10′E
108 F8 Sarnen Obwalden, C Switzerland 46°54′N 08°15′E
108 F9 Sarner See ⊚ C Switzerland
14 D16 Sarnia Ontario, S Canada 42°58′N 82°23′W
116 L3 Sarny Rivnens'ka Oblast', NW Ukraine 51°20′N 26°35′E
171 O13 Saroako Sulawesi, C Indonesia 02°31′S 121°18′E
118 L13 Sarochyna Rus. Sorochino. Vitsyebskaya Voblasts', N Belarus 55°12′N 28°45′E
168 L12 Sarolangun Sumatera, W Indonesia 02°17′S 102°39′E
165 U3 Saroma Hokkaidō, NE Japan 44°01′N 143°43′E
165 V3 Saroma-ko ⊚ Hokkaidō, NE Japan
Saronic Gulf see Saronikós Kólpos
115 H20 Saronikós Kólpos Eng. Saronic Gulf. gulf S Greece
106 D7 Saronno Lombardia, N Italy 45°38′N 09°02′E
136 B11 Saros Körfezi gulf NW Turkey
111 N20 Sárospatak Borsod-Abaúj-Zemplén, NE Hungary 48°18′N 21°30′E
127 O4 Sarov prev. Sarova. Respublika Mordoviya, SW Russian Federation 54°39′N 43°09′E
Sarova see Sarov
127 P12 Sarpa Respublika Kalmykiya, SW Russian Federation 47°00′N 45°42′E
127 P12 Sarpa, Ozero ⊚ SW Russian Federation
113 M18 Šar Planina ▲▲ FYR Macedonia/Serbia
95 I16 Sarpsborg Østfold, S Norway 59°16′N 11°07′E
139 U5 Sarqalā At Ta'mīm, N Iraq
Sarqan see Sarkand
103 U4 Sarralbe Moselle, NE France 49°02′N 07°01′E
Sarre see Saar, France/Germany
Sarre see Saarland, Germany
103 U5 Sarrebourg Ger. Saarburg. Moselle, NE France 48°43′N 07°03′E
Sarrebruck see Saarbrücken
103 U4 Sarreguemines prev. Saargemund. Moselle, NE France 49°06′N 07°04′E
104 I3 Sarria Galicia, NW Spain 42°47′N 07°25′W
105 S8 Sarrión Aragón, NE Spain 40°09′N 00°49′W
42 F4 Sarstoon Sp. Río Sarstún. ∽ Belize/Guatemala
Sarstún, Río see Sarstoon
123 Q9 Sartang ∽ NE Russian Federation
103 X16 Sartène Corse, France, C Mediterranean Sea 41°38′N 08°58′E
102 K7 Sarthe ◆ department NW France
102 K7 Sarthe ∽ N France
115 H15 Sárti Kentrikí Makedonía, N Greece 40°05′N 24°E
Sartu see Daqing
165 T1 Sarufutsu Hokkaidō, NE Japan 45°20′N 142°03′E
Saruhan see Manisa
152 G9 Sarūpsar Rājasthān, NW India 29°25′N 73°50′E
137 U13 Şärur prev. Il'ichevsk. SW Azerbaijan 39°30′N 44°59′E
Sarvani see Marneuli
111 G23 Sárvár Vas, W Hungary 47°15′N 16°59′E
143 P11 Sarvestān Fārs, S Iran 29°16′N 53°13′E
171 W12 Sarwon Papua, E Indonesia 0°58′S 136°08′E
145 P17 Saryagash Kaz. Saryaghash. Yuzhnyy Kazakhstan, S Kazakhstan 41°29′N 69°10′E
Saryaghash see Saryagash
Saryarqa see Kazakhskiy Melkosopochnik
147 W8 Sary-Bulak Narynskaya Oblast', C Kyrgyzstan 41°56′N 75°44′E
147 U10 Sary-Bulak Oshskaya Oblast', SW Kyrgyzstan 40°49′N 73°44′E
117 S14 Sarych, Mys headland S Ukraine 44°23′N 33°44′E
147 Z7 Sary-Dzhaz var. Aksu He. ∽ China/Kyrgyzstan see also Aksu He
Sary-Dzhaz see Aksu He
146 F8 Sarygamyş Köli Rus. Sarykamyshkoye Ozero, Uzb. Sariqamish Kŭli. salt lake Kazakhstan/Uzbekistan
144 G13 Sarykamys Kaz. Saryqamys. Mangistau, SW Kazakhstan 45°58′N 53°30′E
Sarykamyshkoye Ozero see Sarygamyş Köli
145 N7 Sarykol' prev. Uritskiy. Kustanay, N Kazakhstan 53°19′N 65°34′E
Sarykol'skiy Khrebet see Sarikol Range
144 M10 Sarykopa, Ozero ⊚ C Kazakhstan
145 V15 Saryozek Kaz. Saryözek. Almaty, SE Kazakhstan 44°22′N 77°57′E
Saryqamys see Sarykamys
145 S13 Saryshagan Kaz. Saryshaghan. Karaganda, SE Kazakhstan 46°05′N 73°38′E
Saryshaghan see Saryshagan
145 O13 Sarysu ∽ S Kazakhstan
147 T11 Sary-Tash Oshskaya Oblast', SW Kyrgyzstan 39°44′N 73°14′E
145 T12 Saryterek Karaganda, C Kazakhstan 47°46′N 74°06′E
Saryyazynskoye Vodokhranilishche see Saryýazy Suw Howdany
146 J15 Saryýazy Suw Howdany Rus. Saryyazynskoye Vodokhranilishche. ⊠ S Turkmenistan
145 T14 Saryyesik-Atyrau, Peski desert E Kazakhstan
106 E10 Sarzana Liguria, NW Italy 44°07′N 09°59′E
188 B17 Sasalaguan, Mount ▲ S Guam
153 O14 Sasarām Bihār, N India 24°58′N 84°01′E
186 M8 Sasari, Mount ▲ Santa Isabel, N Solomon Islands 08°09′S 159°32′E
164 C13 Sasebo Nagasaki, Kyūshū, SW Japan 33°10′N 129°42′E
14 I9 Saseginaga, Lac ⊚ Québec, SE Canada
Saseno see Sazan
11 R13 Saskatchewan ◆ province SW Canada
11 U14 Saskatchewan ∽ Manitoba/Saskatchewan, C Canada
11 T15 Saskatoon Saskatchewan, S Canada 52°10′N 106°40′W
11 T15 Saskatoon ✈ Saskatchewan, S Canada 52°15′N 107°05′W
123 N7 Saskylakh Respublika Sakha (Yakutiya), NE Russian Federation 71°56′N 114°07′E
42 L7 Saslaya, Cerro ▲ N Nicaragua 13°52′N 85°06′W
38 G17 Sasmik, Cape headland Tanaga Island, Alaska, USA 51°36′N 177°55′W
119 N19 Sasnovy Bor Rus. Sosnovyy Bor. Homyel'skaya Voblasts', SE Belarus 52°32′N 29°35′E
127 N5 Sasovo Ryazanskaya Oblast', W Russian Federation 54°19′N 41°54′E
25 S12 Saspamco Texas, SW USA 29°13′N 98°18′W
109 W9 Sass var. Sassbach. ∽ SE Austria
76 M17 Sassandra S Ivory Coast 04°58′N 06°08′W
76 M17 Sassandra var. Ibo, Sassandra Fleuve. ∽ S Ivory Coast
Sassandra Fleuve see Sassandra
107 B17 Sassari Sardegna, Italy, C Mediterranean Sea 40°44′N 08°33′E
Sassbach see Sass
98 H11 Sassenheim Zuid-Holland, W Netherlands 52°14′N 04°31′E
Sassmacken see Valdemārpils
100 O7 Sassnitz Mecklenburg-Vorpommern, NE Germany 54°32′N 13°39′E
99 E16 Sas van Gent Zeeland, SW Netherlands 51°13′N 03°48′E
145 W12 Sasykkol', Ozero ⊚ E Kazakhstan
117 O12 Sasyk, Ozero Rus. Ozero Kunduk. ⊚ SW Ukraine
76 J12 Satadougou Kayes, SW Mali 12°40′N 11°25′W
164 C17 Sata-misaki Kyūshū, SW Japan
26 I7 Satanta Kansas, C USA 37°23′N 102°00′W
155 E15 Sātāra Mahārāshtra, W India 17°41′N 73°59′E
192 G15 Sātaua Savai'i, NW Samoa 13°26′S 172°40′W
188 M16 Satawal island Caroline Islands, C Micronesia
189 R17 Satawan Atoll atoll Mortlock Islands, C Micronesia
Sátbaev see Satpayev
23 Y12 Satellite Beach Florida, SE USA 28°10′N 80°35′W
95 M14 Säter Dalarna, C Sweden 60°21′N 15°45′E
Sathmar see Satu Mare
23 V7 Satilla River ∽ Georgia, SE USA
57 F14 Satipo var. San Francisco de Satipo. Junín, C Peru 11°19′S 74°37′W
122 F11 Satka Chelyabinskaya Oblast', C Russian Federation 55°08′N 58°54′E
153 T16 Satkhira Khulna, SW Bangladesh 22°43′N 89°06′E

◆ Country
● Country Capital
◇ Dependent Territory
○ Dependent Territory Capital
◆ Administrative Regions
✈ International Airport
▲ Mountain
▲▲ Mountain Range
⛰ Volcano
∽ River
⊚ Lake
⊠ Reservoir

ŞATLYK – SEHWĀN

146 J13 **Şatlyk** *Rus.* Shatlyk. Mary Welaýaty, C Turkmenistan 37°55′N 61°00′E
154 K9 **Satna** *prev.* Sutna. Madhya Pradesh, C India 24°33′N 80°50′E
103 R11 **Satolas** ✈ (Lyon) Rhône, E France 45°44′N 05°01′E
111 N20 **Sátoraljaújhely** Borsod-Abaúj-Zemplén, NE Hungary 48°24′N 21°39′E
145 O12 **Satpayev** *Kaz.* Sätbaev; *prev.* Nikol'skiy. Karaganda, C Kazakhstan 47°59′N 67°27′E
154 G11 **Sātpura Range** ▲▲ C India
Satsuma-Sendai *see* Sendai
167 P12 **Sattahip** *var.* Ban Sattahip, Ban Sattahipp. Chon Buri, S Thailand 12°36′N 100°56′E
92 L11 **Sattanen** Lappi, NE Finland 67°31′N 26°35′E
Satul *see* Satun
116 H9 **Satulung** *Hung.* Kővárhosszúfalu. Maramureş, N Romania 47°34′N 23°26′E
Satul-Vechi *see* Staro Selo
116 G8 **Satu Mare** *Ger.* Sathmar, *Hung.* Szatmárrnémeti. Satu Mare, NW Romania 47°46′N 22°55′E
116 G8 **Satu Mare** ◐ *county* NW Romania
167 N16 **Satun** *var.* Satul, Setul. Satun, SW Thailand 06°40′N 100°01′E
192 G16 **Satupa'iteau** Savai'i, W Samoa 13°46′S 172°26′W
Sau *see* Sava
14 F14 **Sauble** ≈ Ontario, S Canada
14 F13 **Sauble Beach** Ontario, S Canada 44°36′N 81°15′W
61 C16 **Sauce** Corrientes, NE Argentina 30°05′S 58°46′W
Sauce *see* Juan L. Lacaze
36 K15 **Sauceda Mountains** ▲▲ Arizona, SW USA
61 C17 **Sauce de Luna** Entre Ríos, E Argentina 31°15′S 59°09′W
63 L15 **Sauce Grande, Río** ≈ E Argentina
40 K6 **Saucillo** Chihuahua, N Mexico 28°01′N 105°17′W
95 D15 **Sauda** Rogaland, S Norway 59°38′N 06°23′E
145 Q16 **Saudakent** *Kaz.* Saūdakent; *prev.* Baykadam, *Kaz.* Bayqadam. Zhambyl, S Kazakhstan 43°49′N 69°56′E
92 J2 **Saudhárkrókur** Nordhurland Vestra, N Iceland 65°45′N 19°39′W
141 P9 **Saudi Arabia** *off.* Kingdom of Saudi Arabia, Al 'Arabīyah as Su'ūdīyah, *Ar.* Al Mamlakah al 'Arabīyah as Su'ūdīyah. ◆ *monarchy* SW Asia
Saudi Arabia, Kingdom of *see* Saudi Arabia
101 D19 **Sauer** *var.* Sûre. ≈ NW Europe *see also* Sûre
Sauer *see* Sûre
101 F15 **Sauerland** *forest* W Germany
14 F14 **Saugeen** ≈ Ontario, S Canada
18 K12 **Saugerties** New York, NE USA 42°04′N 73°55′W
Saugor *see* Sāgar
10 K15 **Saugstad, Mount** ▲ British Columbia, SW Canada 52°12′N 126°35′W
Sāūjbulāgh *see* Mahābād
102 J11 **Saujon** Charente-Maritime, W France 45°40′N 00°54′W
29 T7 **Sauk Centre** Minnesota, N USA 45°44′N 94°57′W
30 L8 **Sauk City** Wisconsin, N USA 43°16′N 89°43′W
29 U7 **Sauk Rapids** Minnesota, N USA 45°35′N 94°09′W
55 Y11 **Saül** C French Guiana 03°37′N 53°12′W
103 O7 **Sauldre** ≈ C France
101 I23 **Saulgau** Baden-Württemberg, SW Germany 48°03′N 09°28′E
103 Q8 **Saulieu** Côte d'Or, C France 47°15′N 04°15′E
118 G8 **Saulkrasti** Rīga, C Latvia 57°14′N 24°25′E
15 S6 **Sault-aux-Cochons, Rivière du** ≈ Québec, SE Canada
31 Q4 **Sault Sainte Marie** Michigan, N USA 46°29′N 84°22′W
12 F14 **Sault Ste. Marie** Ontario, S Canada 46°30′N 84°17′W
145 P7 **Saumalkol'** *prev.* Volodarskoye. Severnyy Kazakhstan, N Kazakhstan 53°19′N 68°05′E
190 E13 **Sauma, Pointe** *headland* Île Alofi, W Wallis and Futuna 14°21′S 177°58′W
171 T16 **Saumlaki** *var.* Saumlakki. Pulau Yamdena, E Indonesia 07°53′S 131°18′E
Saumlakki *see* Saumlaki
15 R12 **Saumon, Rivière au** ≈ Québec, SE Canada
102 K8 **Saumur** Maine-et-Loire, NW France 47°16′N 00°04′W
185 F23 **Saunders, Cape** *headland* South Island, New Zealand 45°53′S 170°40′E
195 N13 **Saunders Coast** *physical region* Antarctica
65 C24 **Saunders Island Settlement** Saunders Island, NW Falkland Islands 51°22′S 60°05′W
82 F11 **Saurimo** *Port.* Henrique de Carvalho, Vila Henrique de Carvalho. Lunda Sul, NE Angola 09°39′S 20°24′E
55 S11 **Sauriwaunawa** S Guyana 03°10′N 59°51′W
82 D12 **Sautar** Malanje, NW Angola 11°10′S 18°26′E
45 S13 **Sauteurs** N Grenada 12°14′N 61°38′W
102 K13 **Sauveterre-de-Guyenne** Gironde, SW France 44°43′N 00°02′W
119 O14 **Sava** Mahilyowskaya Voblasts', E Belarus 54°22′N 30°49′E
42 J5 **Savá** Colón, N Honduras 15°30′N 86°16′W
84 H11 **Sava** *Eng.* Save, *Ger.* Sau, *Hung.* Száva. ≈ SE Europe
33 Y8 **Savage** Montana, NW USA 47°28′N 104°17′W
183 N16 **Savage River** Tasmania, SE Australia 41°34′S 145°15′E
77 R15 **Savalou** S Benin 07°59′N 01°58′E
30 K10 **Savanna** Illinois, N USA 42°05′N 90°09′W
23 X6 **Savannah** Georgia, SE USA 32°02′N 81°01′W
27 R2 **Savannah** Missouri, C USA 39°57′N 94°49′W
20 H10 **Savannah** Tennessee, S USA 35°12′N 88°15′W
21 O12 **Savannah River** ≈ Georgia/South Carolina, SE USA
Savannakhét *see* Khanthabouli
44 H12 **Savanna-La-Mar** W Jamaica 18°13′N 78°08′W
12 B10 **Savant Lake** ◎ Ontario, S Canada
155 F17 **Savanūr** Karnātaka, W India 14°58′N 75°19′E
93 J16 **Sävar** Västerbotten, N Sweden 63°52′N 20°33′E
Savaria *see* Szombathely
154 C11 **Sāvarkundla** *var.* Kundla. Gujarāt, W India 21°21′N 71°20′E
116 F11 **Săvârşin** *Hung.* Soborsin; *prev.* Săvirşin. Arad, W Romania 46°00′N 22°15′E
136 C13 **Savaştepe** Balıkesir, W Turkey 39°20′N 27°38′E
147 P11 **Savat** *Rus.* Savat. Sirdaryo Viloyati, E Uzbekistan 40°03′N 68°35′E
Savat *see* Savat
Sávdijári *see* Skaulo
77 R15 **Savè** SE Benin 08°04′N 02°29′E
83 N18 **Save** Inhambane, E Mozambique 21°07′S 34°35′E
102 L16 **Save** ≈ S France
83 L17 **Save** *var.* Sabi. ≈ Mozambique/Zimbabwe *see also* Sabi
Save *see* Sava
Save *see* Sabi
142 M6 **Sāveh** Markazī, W Iran 35°00′N 50°22′E
116 L8 **Săveni** Botoşani, NE Romania 47°57′N 26°52′E
103 N16 **Saverdun** Ariège, S France 43°15′N 01°34′E
103 U5 **Saverne** *var.* Zabern; *anc.* Tres Tabernae. Bas-Rhin, NE France 48°45′N 07°22′E
106 B9 **Savigliano** Piemonte, NW Italy 44°39′N 07°39′E
Savigsivik *see* Savissivik
Savinichi *see* Savinichy
119 Q16 **Savinichy** *Rus.* Savinichi. Mahilyowskaya Voblasts', E Belarus 53°28′N 31°46′E
109 U10 **Savinja** ≈ N Slovenia
106 H11 **Savio** ≈ C Italy
Săvirşin *see* Săvârşin
197 O11 **Savissivik** *var.* Savigsivik. ◐ Avannaarsua, N Greenland
93 N18 **Savitaipale** Etelä-Suomi, SE Finland 61°12′N 27°43′E
113 J15 **Šavnik** C Montenegro 42°57′N 19°04′E
108 I9 **Savognin** Graubünden, S Switzerland 46°34′N 09°35′E
103 T12 **Savoie** ◐ *department* E France
106 C10 **Savona** Liguria, NW Italy 44°18′N 08°29′E
93 N17 **Savonlinna** *Swe.* Nyslott. Itä-Suomi, E Finland 61°51′N 28°56′E
93 N17 **Savonranta** Itä-Suomi, E Finland 62°10′N 29°10′E
38 K10 **Savoonga** Saint Lawrence Island, Alaska, USA 63°40′N 170°29′W
30 M13 **Savoy** Illinois, N USA 40°03′N 88°15′W
117 O8 **Savran'** Odes'ka Oblast', SW Ukraine 48°07′N 30°00′E
137 R11 **Şavşat** Artvin, NE Turkey 41°15′N 42°30′E
95 L19 **Sävsjö** Jönköping, S Sweden 57°25′N 14°40′E
Savu, Kepulauan *see* Sawu, Kepulauan
92 M11 **Savukoski** Lappi, NE Finland 67°17′N 28°14′E
Savu, Pulau *see* Sawu, Pulau
187 Y14 **Savusavu** Vanua Levu, N Fiji 16°48′S 179°20′E
171 O17 **Savu Sea** *Ind.* Laut Sawu. *sea* S Indonesia
83 H17 **Savute** North-West, N Botswana 18°33′S 24°06′E
139 N7 **Şawāb Uqlat'** *well* W Iraq
138 M7 **Sawāb, Wādī as** *dry watercourse* W Iraq
152 H13 **Sawāi Mādhopur** Rājasthān, N India 26°00′N 76°22′E
Sawakin *see* Suakin
167 R8 **Sawang Daen Din** Sakon Nakhon, E Thailand 17°28′N 103°27′E
167 O8 **Sawankhalok** *var.* Swankalok. Sukhothai, NW Thailand 17°19′N 99°50′E
165 P13 **Sawara** Chiba, Honshū, S Japan 35°52′N 140°31′E
37 R5 **Sawatch Range** ▲▲ Colorado, C USA
141 N12 **Sawdā', Jabal** ▲ SW Saudi Arabia 18°15′N 42°26′E
75 P9 **Sawdā', Jabal as** ▲▲ C Libya
Sawdirī *see* Sodiri
97 F14 **Sawel Mountain** ▲ C Northern Ireland, United Kingdom 54°49′N 07°04′W
75 X10 **Sawhāj** *var.* Sawhāj *var.* Sohâg, Suliag. C Egypt 26°28′N 31°44′E
Sawhāj *see* Sawhāj
77 O15 **Sawla** N Ghana 09°14′N 02°26′W
141 X12 **Şawqirah** *var.* Suqrah. S Oman 18°16′N 56°34′E
141 X12 **Şawqirah, Dawḩat** *var.* Ghubbat Sawqirah, Sukra Bay, Suqrah Bay. *bay* S Oman
Sawqirah, Ghubbat *see* Şawqirah, Dawḩat
183 V5 **Sawtell** New South Wales, SE Australia 30°22′S 153°04′E
138 K7 **Şawt, Wādī aş** *dry watercourse* S Syria
171 O17 **Sawu, Kepulauan** *var.* Kepulauan Savu. *island group* S Indonesia
Sawu, Laut *see* Savu Sea
171 O17 **Sawu, Pulau** *var.* Pulau Sawu. *island* Kepulauan Sawu, S Indonesia
105 S12 **Sax** País Valenciano, E Spain 38°33′N 00°49′W
Saxe *see* Sachsen
108 C11 **Saxon** Valais, SW Switzerland 46°07′N 07°09′E
Saxony *see* Sachsen
Saxony-Anhalt *see* Sachsen-Anhalt
77 R12 **Say** Niamey, SW Niger 13°08′N 02°20′E
15 V7 **Sayabec** Québec, SE Canada 48°33′N 67°42′W
Sayaboury *see* Xaignabouli
145 U12 **Sayak** *Kaz.* Sayaq. Karaganda, E Kazakhstan 46°54′N 77°17′E
57 D14 **Sayán** Lima, W Peru 11°10′S 77°08′W
129 T6 **Sayanskiy Khrebet** ▲▲ S Russian Federation
Sayaq *see* Sayak
146 K13 **Saýat** *Rus.* Sayat. Lebap Welaýaty, E Turkmenistan 38°44′N 63°51′E
42 D3 **Sayaxché** Petén, N Guatemala 16°34′N 90°14′W
Şaydā/Sayida *see* Saïda
162 J7 **Sayhan** *var.* Hüremt. Bulgan, C Mongolia 48°40′N 102°33′E
163 N10 **Sayhandulaan** *var.* Öldziyt. Dornogovĭ, SE Mongolia 44°42′N 109°10′E
162 K9 **Sayhan-Ovoo** *var.* Ongi. Dundgovĭ, C Mongolia 45°27′N 103°58′E
141 T15 **Sayḩūt** E Yemen 15°18′N 51°16′E
29 U14 **Saylorville Lake** ⊠ Iowa, C USA
Saymenskiy Kanal *see* Saimaa Canal
163 N10 **Saynshand** Dornogovĭ, SE Mongolia 44°51′N 110°07′E
Saynshand *see* Sevrey
Sayn-Ust *see* Hohmorĭt
Say-Ötesh *see* Say-Utës
138 J7 **Şayqal, Baḩr** ◎ S Syria
Sayrab *see* Sayrob
158 H4 **Sayram Hu** ◎ NW China
26 K11 **Sayre** Oklahoma, C USA 35°18′N 99°38′W
18 H12 **Sayre** Pennsylvania, NE USA 41°57′N 76°30′W
18 K15 **Sayreville** New Jersey, NE USA 40°27′N 74°19′W
147 N13 **Sayrob** *Rus.* Sayrab. Surkhondaryo Viloyati, S Uzbekistan 38°03′N 66°54′E
40 L13 **Sayula** Jalisco, SW Mexico 19°52′N 103°36′W
141 R14 **Say'ūn** *var.* Saywūn. C Yemen 15°53′N 48°32′E
144 G14 **Say-Utës** *Kaz.* Say-Ötesh. Mangistau, SW Kazakhstan 44°20′N 53°32′E
10 K16 **Sayward** Vancouver Island, British Columbia, SW Canada 50°20′N 126°01′W
Saywūn *see* Say'ūn
Sayyāl *see* As Sayyāl
139 U8 **Sayyid 'Abid** *var.* Saiyid Abid. Wāsiţ, E Iraq 32°51′N 45°07′E
113 J22 **Sazan** *var.* Ishulli i Sazanit, *It.* Saseno. *island* SW Albania
Sazanit, Ishulli i *see* Sazan
Sazau/Sazawa *see* Sázava
111 E17 **Sázava** *var.* Sazau, *Ger.* Sazawa. ≈ C Czech Republic
124 J14 **Sazonovo** Vologodskaya Oblast', NW Russian Federation 59°04′N 35°10′E
102 G6 **Scaër** Finistère, NW France 48°00′N 03°40′W
97 J15 **Scafell Pike** ▲ NW England, United Kingdom 54°26′N 03°10′W
Scalabis *see* Santarém
96 M2 **Scalloway** N Scotland, United Kingdom 60°10′N 01°17′W
38 M11 **Scammon Bay** Alaska, USA 61°50′N 165°34′W
Scammon Lagoon/ Scammon, Laguna *see* Ojo de Liebre, Laguna
84 F7 **Scandinavia** *geophysical region* NW Europe
Scania *see* Skåne
96 K5 **Scapa Flow** *sea basin* N Scotland, United Kingdom
107 K26 **Scaramia, Capo** *headland* Sicilia, Italy, C Mediterranean Sea 36°46′N 14°29′E
14 H15 **Scarborough** Ontario, SE Canada 43°46′N 79°14′W
45 Z16 **Scarborough** *prev.* Port Louis. Tobago, Trinidad and Tobago 11°11′N 60°45′W
97 N16 **Scarborough** N England, United Kingdom 54°17′N 00°24′W
185 I17 **Scargill** Canterbury, South Island, New Zealand 42°57′S 172°57′E
96 E7 **Scarp** *island* NW Scotland, United Kingdom
Scarpanto *see* Kárpathos
Scarpanto Strait *see* Karpathou, Stenó
107 G25 **Scauri** Sicilia, Italy, C Mediterranean Sea 36°45′N 12°06′E
Scealg, Bá na *see* Ballinskelligs Bay
Scebeli *see* Shebeli
100 K10 **Schaale** ≈ N Germany
100 K9 **Schaalsee** ◎ N Germany
99 G18 **Schaerbeek** Brussels, C Belgium 50°52′N 04°21′E
108 G6 **Schaffhausen** *Fr.* Schaffhouse. Schaffhausen, N Switzerland 47°42′N 08°38′E
108 G6 **Schaffhausen** *Fr.* Schaffhouse. ◐ *canton* N Switzerland
Schaffhouse *see* Schaffhausen
98 I8 **Schagen** Noord-Holland, NW Netherlands 52°47′N 04°47′E
Schaken *see* Šakiai
98 M10 **Schalkhaar** Overijssel, E Netherlands 52°16′N 06°10′E
109 R3 **Schärding** Oberösterreich, N Austria 48°27′N 13°26′E
100 G9 **Scharhörn** *island* NW Germany
Schässburg *see* Sighişoara
Schaulen *see* Šiauliai
30 M10 **Schaumburg** Illinois, N USA 42°01′N 88°04′W
Schebschi Mountains *see* Shebshi Mountains
98 P6 **Scheemda** Groningen, NE Netherlands 53°10′N 06°58′E
100 I10 **Scheessel** Niedersachsen, NW Germany 53°11′N 09°33′E
13 N8 **Schefferville** Québec, E Canada 54°50′N 67°W
Schelde *see* Scheldt
99 D18 **Scheldt** *Dut.* Schelde, *Fr.* Escaut. ≈ W Europe
35 X5 **Schell Creek Range** ▲▲ Nevada, W USA
18 K10 **Schenectady** New York, NE USA 42°48′N 73°57′W
99 I17 **Scherpenheuvel** *Fr.* Montaigu. Vlaams Brabant, C Belgium 51°00′N 04°57′E
98 K11 **Scherpenzeel** Gelderland, C Netherlands 52°07′N 05°30′E
25 S12 **Schertz** Texas, SW USA 29°33′N 98°16′W
98 G11 **Scheveningen** Zuid-Holland, W Netherlands 52°07′N 04°18′E
98 G12 **Schiedam** Zuid-Holland, SW Netherlands 51°55′N 04°25′E
99 M24 **Schieren** Diekirch, NE Luxembourg 49°50′N 06°06′E
98 M4 **Schiermonnikoog** *Fris.* Skiermûntseach. Friesland, N Netherlands 53°28′N 06°09′E
98 M4 **Schiermonnikoog** *Fris.* Skiermûntseach. *island* Waddeneilanden, N Netherlands
99 K14 **Schijndel** Noord-Brabant, S Netherlands 51°37′N 05°27′E
Schil *see* Jiu
99 H16 **Schilde** Antwerpen, N Belgium 51°14′N 04°35′E
Schillen *see* Zhilino
103 V5 **Schiltigheim** Bas-Rhin, NE France 48°38′N 07°47′E
106 G7 **Schio** Veneto, NE Italy 45°42′N 11°21′E
98 H10 **Schiphol** ✈ (Amsterdam) Noord-Holland, C Netherlands 52°18′N 04°48′E
Schippenbeil *see* Sępopol
Schiria *see* Şiria
Schivelbein *see* Świdwin
115 D22 **Schíza** *island* S Greece
175 U3 **Schjetman Reef** *reef* Antarctica
Schlackenwerth *see* Ostrov
109 R7 **Schladming** Steiermark, SE Austria 47°24′N 13°42′E
Schlan *see* Slaný
Schlanders *see* Silandro
100 I7 **Schlei** *inlet* N Germany
101 D17 **Schleiden** Nordrhein-Westfalen, W Germany 50°31′N 06°30′E
Schlelau *see* Szydłowiec
100 I7 **Schleswig** Schleswig-Holstein, N Germany 54°31′N 09°34′E
29 T13 **Schleswig** Iowa, C USA 42°10′N 95°27′W
100 H8 **Schleswig-Holstein** ◐ *state* N Germany
Schlettstadt *see* Sélestat
108 F7 **Schlieren** Zürich, N Switzerland 47°23′N 08°27′E
Schlochau *see* Człuchów
Schloppe *see* Człopa
101 I18 **Schlüchtern** Hessen, C Germany 50°19′N 09°27′E
101 J17 **Schmalkalden** Thüringen, C Germany 50°42′N 10°26′E
109 W2 **Schmida** ≈ NE Austria
65 P19 **Schmidt-Ott Seamount** *var.* Schmitt-Ott Seamount, Schmitt-Ott Tablemount. *undersea feature* SW Indian Ocean 39°37′S 13°00′E
Schmiegel *see* Śmigiel
Schmitt-Ott Seamount/ Schmitt-Ott Tablemount *see* Schmidt-Ott Seamount
15 V3 **Schmon** ≈ Québec, SE Canada
101 M18 **Schneeberg** ▲ W Germany 50°03′N 11°51′E
Schneeberg *see* Veliki Snežnik
Schnee-Eifel *see* Schneifel
Schneekoppe *see* Sněžka
Schneidemühl *see* Piła
101 D18 **Schneifel** *var.* Schnee-Eifel. *plateau* W Germany
Schnelle Körös/Schnelle Kreisch *see* Crişul Repede
100 I11 **Schneverdingen** *var.* Schneverdingen (Wümme). Niedersachsen, NW Germany 53°07′N 09°48′E
Schneverdingen (Wümme) *see* Schneverdingen
Schoden *see* Skuodas
45 Q12 **Schœlcher** W Martinique 14°37′N 61°08′W
18 K10 **Schoharie** New York, NE USA 42°40′N 74°20′W
18 K11 **Schoharie Creek** ≈ New York, NE USA
115 J21 **Schoinoússa** *island* Kykládes, Greece, Aegean Sea
100 L13 **Schönebeck** Sachsen-Anhalt, C Germany 52°01′N 11°45′E
Schöneck *see* Skarszewy
100 O12 **Schönefeld** ✈ (Berlin) Berlin, NE Germany 52°23′N 13°29′E
101 K24 **Schongau** Bayern, S Germany 47°49′N 10°54′E
100 K13 **Schöningen** Niedersachsen, C Germany 52°07′N 10°58′E
Schönlanke *see* Trzcianka
Schönsee *see* Kowalewo Pomorskie
31 P10 **Schoolcraft** Michigan, N USA 42°05′N 85°39′W
98 O8 **Schoonebeek** Drenthe, NE Netherlands 52°39′N 06°57′E
98 I12 **Schoonhoven** Zuid-Holland, C Netherlands 51°57′N 04°°51′E
98 H8 **Schoorl** Noord-Holland, NW Netherlands 52°42′N 04°40′E
Schooten *see* Schoten
101 F24 **Schopfheim** Baden-Württemberg, SW Germany 47°39′N 07°49′E
101 I21 **Schorndorf** Baden-Württemberg, S Germany 48°48′N 09°31′E
100 F10 **Schortens** Niedersachsen, NW Germany 53°31′N 07°57′E
99 H16 **Schoten** *var.* Schooten. Antwerpen, N Belgium 51°15′N 04°30′E
183 Q17 **Schouten Island** *island* Tasmania, SE Australia
186 C5 **Schouten Islands** *island group* NW Papua New Guinea
98 E13 **Schouwen** *island* SW Netherlands
Schreiberhau *see* Szklarska Poręba
109 U2 **Schrems** Niederösterreich, E Austria 48°48′N 15°05′E
101 L22 **Schrobenhausen** Bayern, SE Germany 48°33′N 11°14′E
18 L8 **Schroon Lake** ◎ New York, NE USA
108 J8 **Schruns** Vorarlberg, W Austria 47°04′N 09°54′E
Schubin *see* Szubin
25 U11 **Schulenburg** Texas, SW USA 29°40′N 96°54′W
Schuls *see* Scuol
108 E8 **Schüpfheim** Luzern, C Switzerland 47°02′N 07°23′E
35 S6 **Schurz** Nevada, W USA 38°55′N 118°48′W
101 I24 **Schussen** ≈ S Germany
Schüttenhofen *see* Sušice
29 R15 **Schuyler** Nebraska, C USA 41°25′N 97°04′W
18 L10 **Schuylerville** New York, NE USA 43°05′N 73°34′W
101 K20 **Schwabach** Bayern, SE Germany 49°20′N 11°02′E
Schwabenalb *see* Schwäbische Alb
101 I23 **Schwäbische Alb** *var.* Schwabenalb, *Eng.* Swabian Jura. ▲▲ S Germany
101 I22 **Schwäbisch Gmünd** *var.* Gmünd. Baden-Württemberg, SW Germany 48°49′N 09°48′E
101 I21 **Schwäbisch Hall** *var.* Hall. Baden-Württemberg, SW Germany 49°07′N 09°45′E
101 H16 **Schwalm** ≈ C Germany
109 V9 **Schwanberg** Steiermark, SE Austria 46°46′N 15°12′E
108 H8 **Schwanden** Glarus, E Switzerland 47°02′N 09°04′E
101 M20 **Schwandorf** Bayern, SE Germany 49°20′N 12°07′E
109 S5 **Schwanenstadt** Oberösterreich, NW Austria 48°03′N 13°47′E
169 S11 **Schwaner, Pegunungan** ▲▲ Borneo, N Indonesia
109 W5 **Schwarza** ≈ E Austria
109 P9 **Schwarzach** ≈ S Austria
101 M20 **Schwarzach** *Cz.* Černice. ≈ Czech Republic/Germany
Schwarzach *see* Schwarzach im Pongau
109 Q7 **Schwarzach im Pongau** *var.* Schwarzach. Salzburg, NW Austria 47°19′N 13°09′E
Schwarzawa *see* Svratka
101 N14 **Schwarze Elster** ≈ E Germany
Schwarze Körös *see* Crişul Negru
108 D9 **Schwarzenburg** Bern, W Switzerland 46°51′N 07°28′E
83 D21 **Schwarzrand** ▲▲ S Namibia
101 G23 **Schwarzwald** *Eng.* Black Forest. ▲▲ SW Germany
Schwarzwasser *see* Wda
39 P7 **Schwatka Mountains** ▲▲ Alaska, USA
109 N7 **Schwaz** Tirol, W Austria 47°21′N 11°44′E
109 Y4 **Schwechat** Niederösterreich, NE Austria 48°09′N 16°29′E
109 Y4 **Schwechat** ✈ (Wien) Wien, E Austria 48°04′N 16°31′E
100 P11 **Schwedt** Brandenburg, NE Germany 53°04′N 14°16′E
101 D19 **Schweich** Rheinland-Pfalz, SW Germany 49°49′N 06°44′E
Schweidnitz *see* Świdnica
101 J18 **Schweinfurt** Bayern, SE Germany 50°03′N 10°13′E
Schweiz *see* Switzerland
100 L9 **Schwerin** Mecklenburg-Vorpommern, N Germany 53°38′N 11°25′E
Schwerin *see* Skwierzyna
100 L9 **Schweriner See** ◎ N Germany
Schwertberg *see* Świecie
101 F15 **Schwerte** Nordrhein-Westfalen, W Germany 51°27′N 07°34′E
Schwiebus *see* Świebodzin
100 P13 **Schwielochsee** ◎ NE Germany
Schwihau *see* Švihov
Schwiz *see* Schwyz
108 G8 **Schwyz** *var.* Schwiz. Schwyz, C Switzerland 47°02′N 08°39′E
108 G8 **Schwyz** *var.* Schwiz. ◐ *canton* C Switzerland
14 J11 **Schyan** ≈ Québec, SE Canada
Schyl *see* Jiu
107 I24 **Sciacca** Sicilia, Italy, C Mediterranean Sea 37°31′N 13°05′E
Sciasciamana *see* Shashemenē
107 L26 **Scicli** Sicilia, Italy, C Mediterranean Sea 36°48′N 14°43′E
97 F25 **Scilly, Isles of** *island group* SW England, United Kingdom
111 H17 **Ščinawa** *Ger.* Steinau an der Elbe. Dolnośląskie, SW Poland 51°22′N 16°27′E
Scio *see* Chíos
31 S14 **Scioto River** ≈ Ohio, N USA
36 L5 **Scipio** Utah, W USA 39°15′N 112°06′W
33 X6 **Scobey** Montana, NW USA 48°47′N 105°25′W
183 T7 **Scone** New South Wales, SE Australia 32°02′S 150°51′E
Scoresby Sound/ Scoresbysund *see* Ittoqqortoormiit
Scoresby Sund *see* Kangertittivaq
Scorno, Punta dello *see* Caprara, Punta
34 K3 **Scotia** California, W USA 40°34′N 124°07′W
47 Y14 **Scotia Plate** *tectonic feature*
47 V15 **Scotia Ridge** *undersea feature* S Atlantic Ocean
194 H2 **Scotia Sea** *sea* SW Atlantic Ocean
29 Q12 **Scotland** South Dakota, N USA 43°09′N 97°43′W
25 R5 **Scotland** Texas, SW USA 33°37′N 98°27′W
96 H11 **Scotland** ◐ *national region* Scotland, U K
21 W8 **Scotland Neck** North Carolina, SE USA 36°07′N 77°25′W
195 R13 **Scott Base** *NZ research station* Antarctica 77°52′S 167°18′E
10 J16 **Scott, Cape** *headland* Vancouver Island, British Columbia, SW Canada 50°43′N 128°24′W
26 I5 **Scott City** Kansas, C USA 38°28′N 100°55′W
27 Y7 **Scott City** Missouri, C USA 37°13′N 89°31′W
195 R14 **Scott Coast** *physical region* Antarctica
18 C15 **Scottdale** Pennsylvania, NE USA 40°05′N 79°35′W
195 Y11 **Scott Glacier** *glacier* Antarctica
195 Q17 **Scott Island** *island* Antarctica
26 L11 **Scott, Mount** ▲ Oklahoma, USA 34°52′N 98°34′W
32 G15 **Scott, Mount** ▲ Oregon, NW USA 42°53′N 122°06′W
34 M1 **Scott River** ≈ California, W USA
28 I13 **Scottsbluff** Nebraska, C USA 41°52′N 103°40′W
23 Q2 **Scottsboro** Alabama, S USA 34°40′N 86°01′W
31 P15 **Scottsburg** Indiana, N USA 38°42′N 85°47′W
183 P16 **Scottsdale** Tasmania, SE Australia 41°13′S 147°30′E
36 L13 **Scottsdale** Arizona, SW USA 33°31′N 111°54′W
45 O12 **Scotts Head Village** *var.* Cachacrou. S Dominica 15°12′N 61°22′W
192 L14 **Scott Shoal** *undersea feature* S Pacific Ocean
20 K7 **Scottsville** Kentucky, S USA 36°45′N 86°11′W
29 U14 **Scranton** Iowa, C USA 42°01′N 94°33′W
18 I13 **Scranton** Pennsylvania, NE USA 41°25′N 75°40′W
186 B6 **Screw** ≈ NW Papua New Guinea
29 R14 **Scribner** Nebraska, C USA 41°40′N 96°40′W
Scrobesbyrig' *see* Shrewsbury
14 I14 **Scugog** ≈ Ontario, SE Canada
14 I14 **Scugog, Lake** ◎ Ontario, SE Canada
97 N17 **Scunthorpe** E England, United Kingdom 53°35′N 00°39′W
108 K9 **Scuol** *Ger.* Schuls. Graubünden, E Switzerland 46°51′N 10°21′E
Scupi *see* Skopje
Scutari *see* Shkodër
113 K17 **Scutari, Lake** *Alb.* Liqeni i Shkodrës, *SCr.* Skadarsko Jezero. ◎ Albania/ Montenegro
Scyros *see* Skýros
Scythopolis *see* Beit She'an
138 E11 **Sderot** *prev.* Sederot. Southern, S Israel 31°31′N 34°35′E
25 U13 **Seadrift** Texas, SW USA 28°25′N 96°42′W
21 Y4 **Seaford** *var.* Seaford City. Delaware, NE USA 38°39′N 75°35′W
Seaford City *see* Seaford
14 E15 **Seaforth** Ontario, S Canada 43°33′N 81°25′W
24 M6 **Seagraves** Texas, SW USA 32°56′N 102°33′W
11 X9 **Seal** ≈ Manitoba, C Canada
182 M10 **Sea Lake** Victoria, SE Australia 35°34′S 142°51′E
83 G26 **Seal, Cape** *headland* S South Africa 34°06′S 23°18′E
65 D26 **Sea Lion Islands** *island group* SE Falkland Islands
19 S8 **Seal Island** *island* Maine, NE USA
25 V11 **Sealy** Texas, SW USA 29°46′N 96°09′W
35 X12 **Searchlight** Nevada, W USA 35°27′N 114°54′W
27 V11 **Searcy** Arkansas, C USA 35°14′N 91°43′W
19 R7 **Searsport** Maine, NE USA 44°28′N 68°54′W
35 N10 **Seaside** California, W USA 36°36′N 121°51′W
32 F10 **Seaside** Oregon, NW USA 45°57′N 123°55′W
18 K16 **Seaside Heights** New Jersey, NE USA 39°56′N 74°03′W
32 H8 **Seattle** Washington, NW USA 47°35′N 122°20′W
32 H9 **Seattle-Tacoma** ✈ Washington, NW USA 47°04′N 122°27′W
185 J16 **Seaward Kaikoura Range** ▲▲ South Island, New Zealand
42 J9 **Sébaco** Matagalpa, W Nicaragua 12°51′N 86°08′W
19 P8 **Sebago Lake** ◎ Maine, NE USA
169 S13 **Sebangan, Teluk** *bay* Borneo, C Indonesia
169 S13 **Sebanganu, Teluk** *bay* Borneo, C Indonesia
Sebaste/Sebastia *see* Sivas
23 Y12 **Sebastian** Florida, SE USA 27°55′N 80°31′W
40 C5 **Sebastían Vizcaíno, Bahía** *bay* NW Mexico
19 R6 **Sebasticook Lake** ◎ Maine, NE USA
34 M7 **Sebastopol** California, W USA 38°22′N 122°50′W
Sebastopol *see* Sevastopol'
169 W8 **Sebatik, Pulau** *island* N Indonesia
19 R5 **Sebec Lake** ◎ Maine, NE USA
76 K12 **Sébékoro** Kayes, W Mali 13°00′N 09°03′W
Sebenico *see* Šibenik
40 G6 **Seberi, Cerro** ▲ NW Mexico 27°49′N 110°18′W
116 H11 **Sebeş** *Ger.* Mühlbach, *Hung.* Szászsebes; *prev.* Sebeşu Săsesc. Alba, W Romania 45°58′N 23°34′E
Sebes-Körös *see* Crişul Repede
Sebeşu Săsesc *see* Sebeş
31 R8 **Sebewaing** Michigan, N USA 43°43′N 83°27′W
124 F16 **Sebezh** Pskovskaya Oblast', W Russian Federation 56°19′N 28°31′E
137 N12 **Şebinkarahisar** Giresun, N Turkey 40°19′N 38°25′E
116 F11 **Sebiş** *Hung.* Borossebes. Arad, W Romania 46°21′N 22°09′E
Sebkra Azz el Matti *see* Azzel Matti, Sebkha
19 Q4 **Seboomook Lake** ◎ Maine, NE USA
74 G6 **Sebou** *var.* Sebu. ≈ N Morocco
20 I6 **Sebree** Kentucky, S USA 37°34′N 87°30′W
23 X13 **Sebring** Florida, SE USA 27°30′N 81°26′W
Sebta *see* Ceuta
Sebu *see* Sebou
169 U13 **Sebuku, Pulau** *island* N Indonesia
169 W8 **Sebuku, Teluk** *bay* Borneo, N Indonesia
106 F10 **Secchia** ≈ N Italy
10 L17 **Sechelt** British Columbia, SW Canada 49°25′N 123°37′W
56 C12 **Sechin, Río** ≈ W Peru
56 A10 **Sechura, Bahía de** *bay* NW Peru
185 A22 **Secretary Island** *island* SW New Zealand
155 I15 **Secunderābād** *var.* Sikandarabad. Andhra Pradesh, C India 17°30′N 78°33′E
57 L17 **Sécure, Río** ≈ C Bolivia
118 D10 **Seda** Telšiai, NW Lithuania 56°10′N 22°04′E
27 T5 **Sedalia** Missouri, C USA 38°42′N 93°15′W
103 R3 **Sedan** Ardennes, N France 49°42′N 04°56′E
27 P7 **Sedan** Kansas, C USA 37°07′N 96°11′W
105 N3 **Sedano** Castilla-León, N Spain 42°43′N 03°43′W
104 H10 **Seda, Ribeira de** *stream* C Portugal
185 K15 **Seddon** Marlborough, South Island, New Zealand 41°42′S 174°05′E
185 H15 **Seddonville** West Coast, South Island, New Zealand 41°35′S 171°59′E
143 U7 **Sedeh** Khorāsān-e Janūbī, E Iran 33°18′N 59°12′E
Sederot *see* Sderot
65 B23 **Sedge Island** *island* NW Falkland Islands
76 G12 **Sédhiou** SW Senegal 12°39′N 15°33′W
11 U16 **Sedley** Saskatchewan, S Canada 50°06′N 103°51′W
Sedlez *see* Siedlce
117 Q2 **Sedniv** Chernihivs'ka Oblast', N Ukraine 51°39′N 31°34′E
36 L11 **Sedona** Arizona, SW USA 34°52′N 111°45′W
Sedunum *see* Sion
118 F12 **Šeduva** Šiaulai, N Lithuania 55°45′N 23°46′E
141 Y8 **Seeb** *var.* Muscat Sīb Airport. ✈ (Masqaţ) NE Oman 23°36′N 58°27′E
Seeb *see* As Sīb
108 M7 **Seefeld-in-Tirol** Tirol, W Austria 47°19′N 11°16′E
83 E22 **Seeheim Noord** Karas, S Namibia 26°50′S 17°45′E
Seeland *see* Sjælland
195 N9 **Seelig, Mount** ▲ Antarctica 81°45′S 102°15′W
Seenu Atoll *see* Addu Atoll
Seeonee *see* Seoni
Seer *see* Dörgön
102 L5 **Sées** Orne, N France 48°36′N 00°11′E
101 J14 **Seesen** Niedersachsen, C Germany 51°54′N 10°11′E
Seesker Höhe *see* Szeska Góra
100 J10 **Seevetal** Niedersachsen, N Germany 53°24′N 10°01′E
109 V6 **Seewiesen** Steiermark, E Austria 47°37′N 15°16′E
136 J13 **Şefaatli** *var.* Kızılkoca. Yozgat, C Turkey 39°32′N 34°45′E
143 V9 **Sefīdābeh** Khorāsān-e Janūbī, E Iran 31°05′N 60°30′E
149 N3 **Sefīd, Darya-ye** *Pash.* Āb-i-safed. ≈ N Afghanistan
148 K5 **Sefīd Kūh, Selseleh-ye** *Eng.* Paropamisus Range. ▲ W Afghanistan 34°00′N 61°40′E
148 K5 **Sefīd Kūh, Selseleh-ye** *Eng.* Paropamisus Range. ▲▲ W Afghanistan
142 M4 **Sefīd, Rūd-e** ≈ NW Iran
74 G6 **Sefrou** N Morocco 33°51′N 04°49′W
185 E19 **Sefton, Mount** ▲ South Island, New Zealand 43°43′S 169°58′E
171 S13 **Segaf, Kepulauan** *island group* E Indonesia
169 W7 **Segama, Sungai** ≈ East Malaysia
168 L9 **Segamat** Johor, Peninsular Malaysia 02°30′N 102°48′E
77 S13 **Ségbana** NE Benin 10°56′N 03°42′E
Segestica *see* Sisak
Segesvár *see* Sighişoara
171 T12 **Seget** Papua, E Indonesia 01°21′S 131°04′E
Segewold *see* Sigulda
124 J9 **Segezha** Respublika Kareliya, NW Russian Federation 63°39′N 34°24′E
Seghedin *see* Szeged
Segna *see* Senj
107 I16 **Segni** Lazio, C Italy 41°41′N 13°02′E
Segodunum *see* Rodez
105 S9 **Segorbe** País Valenciano, E Spain 39°51′N 00°30′W
76 M12 **Ségou** *var.* Segu. Ségou, C Mali 13°26′N 06°12′W
76 M12 **Ségou** ◐ *region* SW Mali
54 E8 **Segovia** Antioquia, N Colombia 07°08′N 74°39′W
105 N7 **Segovia** Castilla-León, C Spain 40°57′N 04°07′W
104 M6 **Segovia** ◐ *province* Castilla-León, N Spain
Segoviao Wangkí *see* Coco, Río
124 J9 **Segozerskoye Vodokhranilishche** ◎ NW Russian Federation
102 J7 **Segré** Maine-et-Loire, NW France 47°41′N 00°51′W
105 U5 **Segre** ≈ NE Spain
Segu *see* Ségou
38 I17 **Seguam Island** *island* Aleutian Islands, Alaska, USA
38 I17 **Seguam Pass** *strait* Aleutian Islands, Alaska, USA
77 Y7 **Séguédine** Agadez, NE Niger 20°12′N 13°03′E
76 M15 **Séguéla** W Ivory Coast 07°58′N 06°44′W
25 S11 **Seguin** Texas, SW USA 29°34′N 97°58′W
38 E17 **Segula Island** *island* Aleutian Islands, Alaska, USA
62 K10 **Segundo, Río** ≈ C Argentina
105 Q12 **Segura** ≈ S Spain
105 P13 **Segura , Sierra de** ▲▲ S Spain
83 G18 **Sehithwa** North-West, N Botswana 20°28′S 22°43′E
154 H10 **Sehore** Madhya Pradesh, C India 23°12′N 77°08′E
186 G9 **Sehulea** Normanby Island, S Papua New Guinea 09°55′S 151°10′E
149 P15 **Sehwān** Sind, SE Pakistan 26°26′N 67°52′N

◆ Country
● Country Capital
◇ Dependent Territory
○ Dependent Territory Capital
◐ Administrative Regions
✈ International Airport
▲ Mountain
▲▲ Mountain Range
Volcano
≈ River
◎ Lake
⊠ Reservoir

SEIERSBERG – SHAHREZĀ

109 V8 **Seiersberg** Steiermark, SE Austria *47°01′N 15°22′E*
26 L9 **Seiling** Oklahoma, C USA *36°09′N 98°55′W*
103 S9 **Seille** ≈ E France
99 J20 **Seilles** Namur, SE Belgium *50°31′N 05°12′E*
93 K17 **Seinäjoki** *Swe.* Östermyra. Länsi-Suomi, W Finland *62°45′N 22°55′E*
12 B12 **Seine** ≈ Ontario, S Canada
102 M4 **Seine** ≈ N France
102 K4 **Seine, Baie de la** *bay* N France
Seine, Banc de la *see* Seine Seamount
103 O5 **Seine-et-Marne** ◈ *department* N France
102 L3 **Seine-Maritime** ◈ *department* N France
84 B14 **Seine Plain** *undersea feature* E Atlantic Ocean *34°00′N 12°15′W*
84 B15 **Seine Seamount** *var.* Banc de la Seine. *undersea feature* E Atlantic Ocean *33°45′N 14°25′W*
102 E6 **Sein, Île de** *island* NW France
171 Y14 **Seinma** Papua, E Indonesia *04°10′S 138°54′E*
Seisbierrum *see* Sexbierum
109 U5 **Seitenstetten Markt** Niederösterreich, C Austria *48°03′N 14°41′E*
Seiyo *see* Uwa
Seiyu *see* Chŏnju
95 H22 **Sejerø** *island* E Denmark
110 P7 **Sejny** Podlaskie, NE Poland *54°09′N 23°21′E*
81 G20 **Seke** Shinyanga, N Tanzania *03°16′S 33°31′E*
164 L13 **Seki** Gifu, Honshū, SW Japan *35°30′N 136°54′E*
161 U12 **Sekibi-sho** *island* China/Japan/Taiwan
165 U3 **Sekihoku-tōge** *pass* Hokkaidō, NE Japan
Sekondi *see* Sekondi-Takoradi
77 P17 **Sekondi-Takoradi** *var.* Sekondi. S Ghana *04°55′N 01°45′W*
80 J11 **Sek'ot'a** Āmara, N Ethiopia *12°41′N 39°05′E*
Sekseüil *see* Saksaul'skoye
32 I9 **Selah** Washington, NW USA *46°39′N 120°31′W*
168 J8 **Selangor** *var.* Negeri Selangor Darul Ehsan. ◈ *state* Peninsular Malaysia
Selânik *see* Thessaloníki
168 K10 **Selapanjang** Pulau Rantau, W Indonesia *01°00′N 102°44′E*
167 R10 **Selaphum** Roi Et, E Thailand *16°00′N 103°54′E*
171 T16 **Selaru, Pulau** *island* Kepulauan Tanimbar, E Indonesia
171 U13 **Selassi** Papua, E Indonesia *03°16′S 132°50′E*
168 J7 **Selatan, Selat** *strait* Peninsular Malaysia
39 N8 **Selawik** Alaska, USA *66°36′N 160°00′W*
39 N8 **Selawik Lake** ◎ Alaska, USA
171 N14 **Selayar, Selat** *strait* Sulawesi, C Indonesia
95 C14 **Selbjørnsfjorden** *fjord* S Norway
94 H8 **Selbusjøen** ◎ S Norway
97 M17 **Selby** N England, United Kingdom *53°49′N 01°06′W*
29 N8 **Selby** South Dakota, N USA *45°30′N 100°01′W*
21 Z4 **Selbyville** Delaware, NE USA *38°28′N 75°12′W*
136 B15 **Selçuk** *var.* Akıncılar. İzmir, SW Turkey *37°56′N 27°25′E*
39 Q13 **Seldovia** Alaska, USA *59°26′N 151°42′W*
107 M18 **Sele** *anc.* Silarius. ≈ S Italy
83 J19 **Selebi-Phikwe** Central, E Botswana *21°58′S 27°48′E*
42 B5 **Selegua, Río** ≈ W Guatemala
129 X7 **Selemdzha** ≈ SE Russian Federation
129 U7 **Selenga** *Mong.* Selenge Mörön. ≈ Mongolia/Russian Federation
79 I19 **Selenge** Bandundu, W Dem. Rep. Congo *01°58′S 18°11′E*
162 K6 **Selenge** *var.* Ingettolgoy. Bulgan, N Mongolia *49°27′N 103°59′E*
162 L6 **Selenge** ◈ *province* N Mongolia
Selenge *see* Hyalganat, Bulgan, Mongolia
Selenge *see* Ih-Uul, Hövsgöl, Mongolia
Selenge Mörön *see* Selenga
123 N14 **Selenginsk** Respublika Buryatiya, S Russian Federation *52°00′N 106°40′E*
Selenica *see* Selenicë
113 K22 **Selenicë** *var.* Selenica. Vlorë, SW Albania *40°32′N 19°38′E*
123 Q8 **Selennyakh** ≈ NE Russian Federation
100 J8 **Selenter See** ◎ N Germany
Sele Sound *see* Soela Väin
103 U6 **Sélestat** *Ger.* Schlettstadt. Bas-Rhin, NE France *48°16′N 07°28′E*
Selety *see* Sileti
Seleucia *see* Silifke
92 I4 **Selfoss** Sudhurland, SW Iceland *63°56′N 20°59′W*
28 M7 **Selfridge** North Dakota, N USA *46°01′N 100°52′W*
76 I15 **Seli** ≈ N Sierra Leone
76 I11 **Sélibabi** *var.* Sélibaby. Guidimaka, S Mauritania *15°14′N 12°11′W*
Sélibaby *see* Sélibabi
Selidovka/Selidovo *see* Selydove
124 I15 **Seliger, Ozero** ◎ W Russian Federation
36 J11 **Seligman** Arizona, SW USA *35°20′N 112°56′W*
27 S8 **Seligman** Missouri, C USA *36°31′N 93°56′W*
80 E6 **Selima Oasis** *oasis* N Sudan
76 L13 **Sélingué, Lac de** ⊠ S Mali
Selinoús *see* Kréstena
18 G14 **Selinsgrove** Pennsylvania, NE USA *40°47′N 76°51′W*
Selishche *see* Syelishcha
124 I16 **Selizharovo** Tverskaya Oblast', W Russian Federation *56°50′N 33°24′E*
94 C10 **Selje** Sogn Og Fjordane, S Norway *62°02′N 05°22′E*
11 X16 **Selkirk** Manitoba, S Canada *50°10′N 96°52′W*
96 K13 **Selkirk** SE Scotland, United Kingdom *55°36′N 02°48′W*
96 K13 **Selkirk** *cultural region* SE Scotland, United Kingdom
11 O16 **Selkirk Mountains** ▲▲ British Columbia, SW Canada
193 T11 **Selkirk Rise** *undersea feature* SE Pacific Ocean
115 F21 **Sellasía** Pelopónnisos, S Greece *37°14′N 22°24′E*
44 M9 **Selle, Pic de la** *var.* La Selle. ▲ SE Haiti *18°18′N 71°55′W*
102 M8 **Selles-sur-Cher** Loir-et-Cher, C France *47°16′N 01°31′E*
36 K16 **Sells** Arizona, SW USA *31°54′N 111°52′W*
Sellye *see* Sal'a
23 P5 **Selma** Alabama, S USA *32°24′N 87°01′W*
35 Q11 **Selma** California, W USA *36°33′N 119°37′W*
20 G10 **Selmer** Tennessee, S USA *35°10′N 88°34′W*
173 N17 **Sel, Pointe au** *headland* W Réunion
Selselehye Kuhe Vākhān *see* Nicholas Range
127 S2 **Selty** Udmurtskaya Respublika, NW Russian Federation *57°19′N 52°09′E*
Selukwe *see* Shurugwi
62 L9 **Selva** Santiago del Estero, N Argentina *29°46′S 62°02′W*
11 T9 **Selwyn Lake** ◎ Northwest Territories/Saskatchewan, C Canada
10 K6 **Selwyn Mountains** ▲▲ Yukon Territory, NW Canada
181 T6 **Selwyn Range** ▲▲ Queensland, C Australia
117 W8 **Selydove** *var.* Selidovka, *Rus.* Selidovo. Donets'ka Oblast', SE Ukraine *48°06′N 37°16′E*
Selzaete *see* Zelzate
Seman *see* Semanit, Lumi i
168 M15 **Semangka, Teluk** *bay* Sumatera, SW Indonesia
113 D22 **Semanit, Lumi i** *var.* Seman. ≈ W Albania
169 Q16 **Semarang** *var.* Samarang. Jawa, C Indonesia *06°58′S 110°29′E*
169 Q10 **Sematan** Sarawak, East Malaysia *01°50′N 109°44′E*
171 P17 **Semau, Pulau** *island* S Indonesia
169 V8 **Sembakung, Sungai** ≈ Borneo, N Indonesia
79 G17 **Sembé** Sangha, NW Congo *01°38′N 14°35′E*
169 S13 **Sembulu, Danau** ◎ Borneo, N Indonesia
Semendria *see* Smederevo
117 R1 **Semenivka** Chernihivs'ka Oblast', N Ukraine *52°10′N 32°37′E*
117 S6 **Semenivka** *Rus.* Semenovka. Poltavs'ka Oblast', NE Ukraine *49°36′N 33°10′E*
127 O3 **Semenov** Nizhegorodskaya Oblast', W Russian Federation *56°47′N 44°27′E*
Semenovka *see* Semenivka
169 S17 **Semeru, Gunung** *var.* Mahameru. ▲ Jawa, S Indonesia *08°01′S 112°53′E*
Semey *see* Semipalatinsk
Semezhevo *see* Syemyezhava
126 L7 **Semiluki** Voronezhskaya Oblast', W Russian Federation *51°46′N 39°00′E*
33 W16 **Seminoe Reservoir** ⊠ Wyoming, C USA
27 O11 **Seminole** Oklahoma, C USA *35°13′N 96°40′W*
24 M6 **Seminole** Texas, SW USA *32°43′N 102°39′W*
23 S8 **Seminole, Lake** ⊠ Florida/Georgia, SE USA
Semiozernoye *see* Auliyekol'
145 V9 **Semipalatinsk** *Kaz.* Semey. Vostochnyy Kazakhstan, E Kazakhstan *50°26′N 80°16′E*
143 O9 **Semīrom** *var.* Samirum. Eşfahān, C Iran *31°20′N 51°50′E*
38 F17 **Semisopochnoi Island** *island* Aleutian Islands, Alaska, USA
169 R11 **Semitau** Borneo, C Indonesia *0°30′N 111°59′E*
81 E18 **Semliki** ≈ Uganda/Dem. Rep. Congo
143 P5 **Semnān** *var.* Samnān. Semnān, N Iran *35°37′N 53°21′E*
143 Q5 **Semnān** *off.* Ostān-e Semnān. ◈ *province* N Iran
Semnān, Ostān-e *see* Semnān
99 K24 **Semois** ≈ SE Belgium
108 E8 **Sempacher See** ◎ C Switzerland
Sena *see* Vila de Sena
30 L12 **Senachwine Lake** ◎ Illinois, N USA
59 O14 **Senador Pompeu** Ceará, E Brazil *05°30′S 39°25′W*
Sena Gallica *see* Senigallia
59 C15 **Sena Madureira** Acre, W Brazil *09°05′S 68°41′W*
155 L25 **Senanayake Samudra** ◎ E Sri Lanka
83 G15 **Senanga** Western, SW Zambia *16°09′S 23°16′E*
27 Y9 **Senath** Missouri, C USA *36°07′N 90°09′W*
22 L2 **Senatobia** Mississippi, S USA *34°37′N 89°58′W*
164 C16 **Sendai** *var.* Satsuma-Sendai. Kagoshima, Kyūshū, SW Japan *31°49′N 130°17′E*
165 Q10 **Sendai** Miyagi, Honshū, C Japan *38°16′N 140°52′E*
165 Q11 **Sendai-wan** *bay* E Japan
101 J23 **Senden** Bayern, S Germany *48°18′N 10°04′E*
154 F11 **Sendhwa** Madhya Pradesh, C India *21°38′N 75°04′E*
111 H21 **Senec** *Ger.* Wartberg, *Hung.* Szenc; *prev.* Szempcz. Bratislavský Kraj, W Slovakia *48°14′N 17°24′E*
27 P3 **Seneca** Kansas, C USA *39°50′N 96°04′W*
27 R8 **Seneca** Missouri, C USA *36°50′N 94°36′W*
32 K13 **Seneca** Oregon, NW USA *44°06′N 118°57′W*
21 O11 **Seneca** South Carolina, SE USA *34°41′N 82°57′W*
18 G11 **Seneca Lake** ◎ New York, NE USA
31 U13 **Senecaville Lake** ⊠ Ohio, N USA
76 G11 **Senegal** *off.* Republic of Senegal, *Fr.* Sénégal. ◆ *republic* W Africa
76 H9 **Senegal** *Fr.* Sénégal. ≈ W Africa
Senegal, Republic of *see* Senegal
31 O4 **Seney Marsh** *wetland* Michigan, N USA
101 P14 **Senftenberg** Brandenburg, E Germany *51°31′N 14°01′E*
82 L11 **Senga Hill** Northern, NE Zambia *09°26′S 31°12′E*
158 G13 **Sênggê Zangbo** ≈ W China
171 Z13 **Senggi** Papua, E Indonesia *03°26′S 140°46′E*
127 R5 **Sengiley** Ul'yanovskaya Oblast', W Russian Federation *53°54′N 48°51′E*
63 I19 **Senguerr, Río** ≈ S Argentina
83 J16 **Sengwa** ≈ C Zimbabwe
Senia *see* Senj
111 H19 **Senica** *Ger.* Senitz, *Hung.* Szenice. Trnavský Kraj, W Slovakia *48°40′N 17°22′E*
Seniça *see* Sjenica
106 J11 **Senigallia** *anc.* Sena Gallica. Marche, C Italy *43°43′N 13°13′E*
136 F15 **Senirkent** Isparta, SW Turkey *38°07′N 30°34′E*
Senitz *see* Senica
112 C10 **Senj** *Ger.* Zengg, *It.* Segna; *anc.* Senia. Lika-Senj, NW Croatia *44°58′N 14°55′E*
Senj *see* Örgön
92 H9 **Senja** *prev.* Senjen. *island* N Norway
Senjen *see* Senja
161 U12 **Senkaku-shotō** *island group* SW Japan
137 R12 **Şenkaya** Erzurum, NE Turkey *40°33′N 42°17′E*
83 I16 **Senkobo** Southern, S Zambia *17°38′S 25°58′E*
103 O4 **Senlis** Oise, N France *49°13′N 02°33′E*
167 T12 **Senmonorom** Môndól Kiri, E Cambodia *12°27′N 107°12′E*
80 G10 **Sennar** *var.* Sannār. Sinnar, C Sudan *13°31′N 33°38′E*
Senno *see* Syanno
Senones *see* Sens
109 W11 **Senovo** E Slovenia *46°01′N 15°24′E*
103 P6 **Sens** *anc.* Agendicum, Senones. Yonne, C France *48°12′N 03°17′E*
Sensburg *see* Mrągowo
167 S11 **Sên, Stœ̆ng** ≈ C Cambodia
42 F7 **Sensuntepeque** Cabañas, NE El Salvador *13°52′N 88°38′W*
112 L8 **Senta** *Hung.* Zenta. Vojvodina, N Serbia *45°57′N 20°04′E*
Šent Andraž *see* Sankt Andrä
171 Y13 **Sentani, Danau** ◎ Papua, E Indonesia
28 J5 **Sentinel Butte** ▲ North Dakota, N USA *46°52′N 103°50′W*
10 M13 **Sentinel Peak** ▲ British Columbia, W Canada *54°51′N 122°02′W*
59 N16 **Sento Sé** Bahia, E Brazil *09°51′S 41°56′W*
Šent Peter *see* Pivka
Št. Vid *see* Sankt Veit an der Glan
Seo de Urgel *see* La See d'Urgel
154 I7 **Seondha** Madhya Pradesh, C India *26°09′N 78°47′E*
154 J11 **Seoni** *prev.* Seeonee. Madhya Pradesh, C India *22°06′N 79°36′E*
Seoul *see* Sŏul
83 I17 **Sepako** Central, NE Botswana *19°50′S 26°29′E*
184 I13 **Separation Point** *headland* South Island, New Zealand *40°46′S 172°58′E*
169 V10 **Sepasu** Borneo, N Indonesia *0°44′N 117°38′E*
186 B6 **Sepik** ≈ Indonesia/Papua New Guinea
Sepone *see* Muang Xépôn
110 M7 **Sępopol** *Ger.* Schippenbeil. Warmińsko-Mazurskie, N Poland *54°16′N 21°09′E*
116 F10 **Şepreuş** *Hung.* Seprős. Arad, W Romania *46°34′N 21°44′E*
Seprős *see* Şepreuş
Şepşi-Sângeorz/Sepsiszentgyörgy *see* Sfântu Gheorghe
15 W4 **Sept-Îles** Québec, SE Canada *50°11′N 66°19′W*
105 N6 **Sepúlveda** Castilla-León, N Spain *41°18′N 03°45′W*
104 K8 **Sequeros** Castilla-León, N Spain *40°31′N 06°04′W*
104 L5 **Sequillo** ≈ NW Spain
32 G7 **Sequim** Washington, NW USA *48°04′N 123°06′W*
35 S11 **Sequoia National Park** *national park* California, W USA
137 Q14 **Şerafettin Dağları** ▲▲ E Turkey
127 N10 **Serafimovich** Volgogradskaya Oblast', SW Russian Federation *49°34′N 42°43′E*
127 U5 **Serafimovskiy** Respublika Bashkortostan, W Russian Federation *54°26′N 53°49′E*
171 Q10 **Serai** Sulawesi, N Indonesia *01°45′N 124°58′E*
99 K19 **Seraing** Liège, E Belgium *50°37′N 05°31′E*
Sêraitang *see* Baima
Serakhs *see* Sarahs
171 W13 **Serami** Papua, E Indonesia *02°11′S 136°46′E*
Seram, Laut *see* Ceram Sea
Serampore/Serampur *see* Shrīrāmpur
171 S13 **Seram, Pulau** *var.* Serang, *Eng.* Ceram. *island* Maluku, E Indonesia
169 N15 **Serang** Jawa, C Indonesia *06°07′S 106°09′E*
Serang *see* Seram, Pulau
169 P9 **Serasan, Pulau** *island* Kepulauan Natuna, W Indonesia
169 P9 **Serasan, Selat** *strait* Indonesia/Malaysia
112 M13 **Serbia** *off.* Federal Republic of Serbia; *prev.* Yugoslavia, *SCr.* Jugoslavija. ◆ *federal republic* SE Europe
112 M12 **Serbia** *Ger.* Serbien, *Serb.* Srbija. ◈ *republic* Serbia
Serbia, Federal Republic of *see* Serbia
Serbien *see* Serbia
Sercq *see* Sark
146 D12 **Serdar** *prev. Rus.* Gyzyrlabat, Kizyl-Arvat. Balkan Welaýaty, W Turkmenistan *39°02′N 56°15′E*
Serdica *see* Sofiya
Serdobol' *see* Sortavala
127 O7 **Serdobsk** Penzenskaya Oblast', W Russian Federation *52°30′N 44°16′E*
145 X9 **Serebryansk** Vostochnyy Kazakhstan, E Kazakhstan *49°44′N 83°16′E*
123 Q12 **Serebryanyy Bor** Respublika Sakha (Yakutiya), NE Russian Federation *56°40′N 124°46′E*
111 H20 **Sered'** *Hung.* Szered. Trnavský Kraj, W Slovakia *48°19′N 17°45′E*
117 S1 **Seredyna-Buda** Sums'ka Oblast', NE Ukraine *52°09′N 34°00′E*
118 E13 **Seredžius** Tauragė, C Lithuania *55°04′N 23°24′E*
136 I14 **Şereflikoçhisar** Ankara, C Turkey *38°56′N 33°31′E*
106 D7 **Seregno** Lombardia, N Italy *45°39′N 09°12′E*
103 P7 **Serein** ≈ C France
168 K9 **Seremban** Negeri Sembilan, Peninsular Malaysia *02°42′N 101°54′E*
81 H20 **Serengeti Plain** *plain* N Tanzania
82 K13 **Serenje** Central, E Zambia *13°12′S 30°15′E*
Seres *see* Sérres
116 J5 **Seret** ≈ W Ukraine
Seret/Sereth *see* Siret
115 I21 **Serfopoúla** *island* Kykládes, Greece, Aegean Sea
127 P4 **Sergach** Nizhegorodskaya Oblast', W Russian Federation *55°31′N 45°29′E*
29 S13 **Sergeant Bluff** Iowa, C USA *42°24′N 96°19′W*
163 P7 **Sergelen** Dornod, NE Mongolia *48°31′N 114°01′E*
Sergelen *see* Tuvshinshiree
168 H8 **Sergeulangit, Pegunungan** ▲▲ Sumatera, NW Indonesia
122 L5 **Sergeya Kirova, Ostrova** *island* N Russian Federation
Sergeyevichi *see* Syarhyeyevichy
145 O7 **Sergeyevka** Severnyy Kazakhstan, N Kazakhstan *53°53′N 67°25′E*
Sergiopol *see* Ayagoz
59 P16 **Sergipe** *off.* Estado de Sergipe. ◈ *state* E Brazil
Sergipe, Estado de *see* Sergipe
126 L3 **Sergiyev Posad** Moskovskaya Oblast', W Russian Federation *56°21′N 38°10′E*
124 K5 **Sergozero, Ozero** ◎ NW Russian Federation
146 J17 **Serhetabat** *prev. Rus.* Gushgy, Kushka. Mary Welaýaty, S Turkmenistan *35°19′N 62°17′E*
169 Q10 **Serian** Sarawak, East Malaysia *01°10′N 110°35′E*
115 I21 **Sérifos** *anc.* Seriphos. *island* Kykládes, Greece, Aegean Sea
115 I21 **Sérifou, Stenó** *strait* SE Greece
136 F16 **Serik** Antalya, SW Turkey *36°55′N 31°06′E*
106 E7 **Serio** ≈ N Italy
Seriphos *see* Sérifos
Serir Tibesti *see* Sarīr Tībistī
Sêrkog *see* Sêrtar
127 S5 **Sernovodsk** Samarskaya Oblast', W Russian Federation *53°56′N 51°16′E*
127 R2 **Sernur** Respublika Mariy El, W Russian Federation *56°55′N 49°09′E*
110 M11 **Serock** Mazowieckie, C Poland *52°30′N 21°03′E*
61 B18 **Serodino** Santa Fe, C Argentina *32°33′S 60°52′W*
Seroei *see* Serui
105 P14 **Serón** Andalucía, S Spain *37°20′N 02°28′W*
99 E14 **Serooskerke** Zeeland, SW Netherlands *51°42′N 03°52′E*
105 T6 **Seròs** Cataluña, NE Spain *41°27′N 00°24′E*
122 G10 **Serov** Sverdlovskaya Oblast', C Russian Federation *59°42′N 60°32′E*
83 I19 **Serowe** Central, SE Botswana *22°26′S 26°44′E*
104 H13 **Serpa** Beja, S Portugal *37°56′N 07°36′W*
Serpa Pinto *see* Menongue
182 A4 **Serpentine Lakes** *salt lake* South Australia
45 T15 **Serpent's Mouth, The** *Sp.* Boca de la Serpiente. *strait* Trinidad and Tobago/Venezuela
Serpiente, Boca de la *see* Serpent's Mouth, The
126 K4 **Serpukhov** Moskovskaya Oblast', W Russian Federation *54°54′N 37°26′E*
104 I10 **Serra de São Mamede** ▲ C Portugal *39°18′N 07°19′W*
60 K13 **Serra do Mar** ▲▲
Sérrai *see* Sérres
107 N22 **Serra San Bruno** Calabria, SW Italy *38°32′N 16°18′E*
103 S14 **Serres** Hautes-Alpes, SE France *44°26′N 05°42′E*
114 H13 **Sérres** *var.* Seres; *prev.* Sérrai. Kentrikí Makedonía, NE Greece *41°03′N 23°33′E*
62 J9 **Serrezuela** Córdoba, C Argentina *30°38′S 65°26′W*
59 O16 **Serrinha** Bahia, E Brazil *11°38′S 38°56′W*
59 M19 **Serro** *var.* Sêrro. Minas Gerais, NE Brazil *18°38′S 43°22′W*
Sêrro *see* Serro
Sert *see* Siirt
104 H9 **Sertã** *var.* Sertá. Castelo Branco, C Portugal *39°48′N 08°05′W*
Sertá *see* Sertã
60 L8 **Sertãozinho** São Paulo, S Brazil *21°04′S 47°55′W*
160 F7 **Sêrtar** *var.* Sêrkog. Sichuan, C China *32°18′N 100°18′E*
124 G12 **Sertolovo** Leningradskaya Oblast', NW Russian Federation *60°08′N 30°06′E*
171 W13 **Serui** *prev.* Seroei. Papua, E Indonesia *01°53′S 136°15′E*
83 J19 **Serule** Central, E Botswana *21°58′S 27°20′E*
169 S12 **Seruyan, Sungai** *var.* Sungai Pembuang. ≈ Borneo, N Indonesia
115 E14 **Sérvia** Dytikí Makedonía, N Greece *40°12′N 22°01′E*
160 E7 **Sêrxü** *var.* Jugar. Sichuan, C China *32°54′N 98°06′E*
123 R13 **Seryshevo** Amurskaya Oblast', SE Russian Federation *51°03′N 128°16′E*
Sesana *see* Sežana
169 V8 **Sesayap, Sungai** ≈ Borneo, N Indonesia
Sesdlets *see* Siedlce
79 N17 **Sese** Orientale, N Dem. Rep. Congo *02°13′N 25°52′E*
81 F18 **Sese Islands** *island group* S Uganda
83 H16 **Sesheke** *var.* Sesheko. Western, SE Zambia *17°28′S 24°20′E*
Sesheko *see* Sesheke
106 C8 **Sesia** *anc.* Sessites. ≈ NW Italy
104 F11 **Sesimbra** Setúbal, S Portugal *38°26′N 09°06′W*
115 N22 **Seskló** *island* Dodekánisa, Greece, Aegean Sea
30 L16 **Sesser** Illinois, N USA *38°05′N 89°03′W*
Sessites *see* Sesia
106 G11 **Sesto Fiorentino** Toscana, C Italy *43°50′N 11°12′E*
106 E7 **Sesto San Giovanni** Lombardia, N Italy *45°32′N 09°14′E*
106 A8 **Sestriere** Piemonte, NE Italy *45°00′N 06°54′E*
106 D10 **Sestri Levante** Liguria, NW Italy *44°16′N 09°22′E*
124 G12 **Sestroretsk** Leningradskaya Oblast', NW Russian Federation *60°05′N 29°57′E*
107 C20 **Sestu** Sardegna, Italy, C Mediterranean Sea *39°15′N 09°06′E*
112 E8 **Sesvete** Zagreb, N Croatia *45°50′N 16°03′E*
118 G12 **Šėta** Kaunas, C Lithuania *55°17′N 24°16′E*
Setabis *see* Xàtiva
165 Q4 **Setana** Hokkaidō, NE Japan *42°27′N 139°52′E*
103 Q16 **Sète** *prev.* Cette. Hérault, S France *43°24′N 03°42′E*
58 J11 **Sete Ilhas** Amapá, NE Brazil *01°06′N 52°06′W*
59 L20 **Sete Lagoas** Minas Gerais, NE Brazil *19°29′S 44°15′W*
60 G10 **Sete Quedas, Ilha das** *island* S Brazil
92 I10 **Setermoen** Troms, N Norway *68°51′N 18°20′E*
95 E17 **Setesdal** *valley* S Norway
43 W16 **Setetule, Cerro** ▲ SE Panama *07°51′N 77°37′W*
21 Q5 **Seth** West Virginia, NE USA *38°06′N 81°40′W*
Setia *see* Sezze
74 K5 **Sétif** *var.* Stif. N Algeria *36°11′N 05°24′E*
164 L5 **Seto** Aichi, Honshū, SW Japan *35°14′N 137°06′E*
164 G13 **Seto-naikai** *Eng.* Inland Sea. *sea* S Japan
165 V16 **Setouchi** *var.* Setoushi. Kagoshima, Amami-Ō-shima, SW Japan *44°19′N 142°58′E*
Setoushi *see* Setouchi
74 F6 **Settat** W Morocco *33°03′N 07°37′W*
79 D20 **Setté Cama** Ogooué-Maritime, SW Gabon *02°32′S 09°46′E*
11 W13 **Setting Lake** ◎ Manitoba, C Canada
97 L16 **Settle** N England, United Kingdom *54°04′N 02°17′W*
189 Y12 **Settlement** E Wake Island *19°17′N 166°38′E*
104 F11 **Setúbal** *Eng.* Saint Ubes, Saint Yves. Setúbal, W Portugal *38°31′N 08°54′W*
104 F11 **Setúbal** ◈ *district* S Portugal
104 F12 **Setúbal, Baía de** *bay* W Portugal
Setul *see* Satun
12 B10 **Seul, Lac** ◎ Ontario, S Canada
103 R8 **Seurre** Côte d'Or, C France *47°00′N 05°09′E*
137 U11 **Sevan** C Armenia *40°32′N 44°56′E*
137 V12 **Sevana Lich** *Eng.* Lake Sevan, *Rus.* Ozero Sevan. ◎ E Armenia
Sevan, Lake/Sevan, Ozero *see* Sevana Lich
77 N11 **Sévaré** Mopti, C Mali *14°32′N 04°06′W*
117 S14 **Sevastopol'** *Eng.* Sebastopol. Respublika Krym, S Ukraine *44°36′N 33°33′E*
25 R14 **Seven Sisters** Texas, SW USA *27°57′N 98°34′W*
10 K13 **Seven Sisters Peaks** ▲ British Columbia, SW Canada *54°57′N 128°10′W*
99 M15 **Sevenum** Limburg, SE Netherlands *51°25′N 06°01′E*
103 P14 **Séverac-le-Château** Aveyron, S France *44°18′N 03°03′E*
14 H13 **Severn** ≈ Ontario, S Canada
97 L21 **Severn** *Wel.* Hafren. ≈ England/Wales, United Kingdom
125 O11 **Severnaya Dvina** *var.* Northern Dvina. ≈ NW Russian Federation
127 N16 **Severnaya Osetiya-Alaniya, Respublika** *Eng.* North Ossetia; *prev.* Respublika Severnaya Osetiya, Severo-Osetinskaya SSR. ◈ *autonomous republic* SW Russian Federation
Severnaya Osetiya, Respublika *see* Severnaya Osetiya-Alaniya, Respublika
122 M5 **Severnaya Zemlya** *var.* Nicholas II Land. *island group* N Russian Federation
127 T5 **Severnoye** Orenburgskaya Oblast', W Russian Federation *54°03′N 52°31′E*
35 S3 **Severn Troughs Range** ▲▲ Nevada, W USA
125 W3 **Severnyy** Respublika Komi, NW Russian Federation *67°38′N 64°13′E*
144 I13 **Severnyy Chink Ustyurta** ▲▲ W Kazakhstan
125 Q13 **Severnyye Uvaly** *var.* Northern Ural Hills. *hill range* NW Russian Federation
145 O6 **Severnyy Kazakhstan** *off.* Severo-Kazakhstanskaya Oblast', *var.* North Kazakhstan, *Kaz.* Soltüstik Qazaqstan Oblysy. ◈ *province* N Kazakhstan
125 V9 **Severnyy Ural** ▲▲ NW Russian Federation
Severo-Alichurskiy Khrebet *see* Alichuri Shimolí, Qatorkŭhi
123 N12 **Severobaykal'sk** Respublika Buryatiya, S Russian Federation *55°39′N 109°17′E*
Severodonetsk *see* Syeverodonets'k
124 M8 **Severodvinsk** *prev.* Molotov, Sudostroy. Arkhangel'skaya Oblast', NW Russian Federation *64°32′N 39°50′E*
Severo-Kazakhstanskaya Oblast' *see* Severnyy Kazakhstan
123 U11 **Severo-Kuril'sk** Sakhalinskaya Oblast', SE Russian Federation *50°38′N 155°57′E*
124 J3 **Severomorsk** Murmanskaya Oblast', NW Russian Federation *69°00′N 33°16′E*
Severo-Osetinskaya SSR *see* Severnaya Osetiya-Alaniya, Respublika
122 M7 **Severo-Sibirskaya Nizmennost'** *var.* North Siberian Plain, *Eng.* North Siberian Lowland. *lowlands* N Russian Federation
122 G10 **Severoural'sk** Sverdlovskaya Oblast', C Russian Federation *60°09′N 59°58′E*
122 L11 **Severo-Yeniseyskiy** Krasnoyarskiy Kray, C Russian Federation *60°29′N 93°13′E*
122 J12 **Seversk** Tomskaya Oblast', C Russian Federation *53°37′N 84°47′E*
126 M11 **Severskiy Donets** *Ukr.* Sivers'kyy Donets'. ≈ Russian Federation/Ukraine *see also* Sivers'kyy Donets'
Severskiy Donets *see* Sivers'kyy Donets'
92 M9 **Sevettijärvi** Lappi, N Finland *69°31′N 28°40′E*
36 M5 **Sevier Bridge Reservoir** ⊠ Utah, W USA
36 J4 **Sevier Desert** *plain* Utah, W USA
36 J5 **Sevier Lake** ◎ Utah, W USA
21 N9 **Sevierville** Tennessee, S USA *35°53′N 83°34′W*
104 J14 **Sevilla** *Eng.* Seville; *anc.* Hispalis. Andalucía, SW Spain *37°24′N 05°59′W*
104 J13 **Sevilla** ◈ *province* Andalucía, SW Spain
Sevilla de Niefang *see* Niefang
43 O16 **Sevilla, Isla** *island* SW Panama
Seville *see* Sevilla
114 J9 **Sevlievo** Gabrovo, N Bulgaria *43°01′N 25°06′E*
Sevluš/Sevlyush *see* Vynohradiv
109 V11 **Sevnica** *Ger.* Lichtenwald. E Slovenia *46°00′N 15°20′E*
162 J11 **Sevrey** *var.* Saynshand. Ömnögovĭ, S Mongolia *43°30′N 102°08′E*
126 I7 **Sevsk** Bryanskaya Oblast', W Russian Federation *52°03′N 34°31′E*
76 J15 **Sewa** ≈ E Sierra Leone
39 R12 **Seward** Alaska, USA *60°06′N 149°26′W*
29 R15 **Seward** Nebraska, C USA *40°52′N 97°06′W*
10 G8 **Seward Glacier** *glacier* Yukon Territory, W Canada
197 Q3 **Seward Peninsula** *peninsula* Alaska, USA
Seward's Folly *see* Alaska
62 H12 **Sewell** Libertador, C Chile *34°05′S 70°25′W*
98 K5 **Sexbierum** *Fris.* Seisbierrum. Friesland, N Netherlands *53°13′N 05°28′E*
11 O13 **Sexsmith** Alberta, W Canada *55°18′N 118°45′W*
41 W13 **Seybaplaya** Campeche, SE Mexico *19°39′N 90°36′W*
173 N6 **Seychelles** *off.* Republic of Seychelles. ◆ *republic* W Indian Ocean
67 Z9 **Seychelles** *island group* NE Seychelles
173 N6 **Seychelles Bank** *var.* Le Banc des Seychelles. *undersea feature* W Indian Ocean *04°45′S 55°30′E*
Seychelles, Le Banc des *see* Seychelles Bank
Seychelles, Republic of *see* Seychelles
172 H17 **Seychellois, Morne** ▲ Mahé, NE Seychelles
92 L2 **Seydhisfjördhur** Austurland, E Iceland *65°15′N 14°00′W*
146 J12 **Seýdi** *Rus.* Seydi; *prev.* Neftezavodsk. Lebap Welaýaty, E Turkmenistan *39°31′N 62°53′E*
136 G16 **Seydişehir** Konya, SW Turkey *37°25′N 31°51′E*
136 J13 **Seyfe Gölü** ◎ C Turkey
Seyhan *see* Adana
136 K16 **Seyhan Barajı** ⊠ S Turkey
136 K17 **Seyhan Nehri** ≈ S Turkey
136 F13 **Seyitgazi** Eskişehir, W Turkey *39°27′N 30°42′E*
126 J7 **Seym** ≈ W Russian Federation
117 S3 **Seym** ≈ N Ukraine
123 T9 **Seymchan** Magadanskaya Oblast', E Russian Federation *62°54′N 152°27′E*
114 N12 **Seymen** Tekirdağ, NW Turkey *41°06′N 27°56′E*
183 O11 **Seymour** Victoria, SE Australia *37°01′S 145°10′E*
83 I25 **Seymour** Eastern Cape, S South Africa *32°33′S 26°46′E*
29 W16 **Seymour** Iowa, C USA *40°40′N 93°07′W*
27 U7 **Seymour** Missouri, C USA *37°09′N 92°46′W*
25 Q5 **Seymour** Texas, SW USA *33°36′N 99°16′W*
114 M12 **Şeytan Deresi** ≈ NW Turkey
109 S12 **Sežana** *It.* Sesana. SW Slovenia *45°42′N 13°52′E*
103 P5 **Sézanne** Marne, N France *48°43′N 03°41′E*
107 I16 **Sezze** *anc.* Setia. Lazio, C Italy *41°29′N 13°04′E*
Sfákia *see* Chóra Sfakíon
115 D21 **Sfaktiría** *island* S Greece
116 J11 **Sfântu Gheorghe** *Ger.* Sankt-Georgen, *Hung.* Sepsiszentgyörgy; *prev.* Şepşi-Sângeorz, Sfîntu Gheorghe. Covasna, C Romania *45°52′N 25°49′E*
117 N13 **Sfântu Gheorghe, Braţul** *var.* Gheorghe Braţul. ≈ E Romania
75 N6 **Sfax** *Ar.* Şafāqis. E Tunisia *34°45′N 10°45′E*
75 N6 **Sfax** ✈ E Tunisia *34°43′N 10°37′E*
Sfîntu Gheorghe *see* Sfântu Gheorghe
98 H13 **'s-Gravendeel** Zuid-Holland, SW Netherlands *51°48′N 04°36′E*
98 F11 **'s-Gravenhage** *var.* Den Haag, *Eng.* The Hague, *Fr.* La Haye. ● (Netherlands-seat of government) Zuid-Holland, W Netherlands *52°07′N 04°17′E*
98 G12 **'s-Gravenzande** Zuid-Holland, W Netherlands *52°00′N 04°10′E*
Shaan/Shaanxi Sheng *see* Shaanxi
159 X11 **Shaanxi** *var.* Shaan, Shaanxi Sheng, Shan-hsi, Shenshi, Shensi. ◈ *province* C China
Shaartuz *see* Shahrtuz
Shaba *see* Katanga
Shabani *see* Zvishavane
81 N17 **Shabeellaha Dhexe** *off.* Gobolka Shabeellaha Dhexe. ◈ *region* E Somalia
Shabeellaha Dhexe, Gobolka *see* Shabeellaha Dhexe
81 L17 **Shabeellaha Hoose** *off.* Gobolka Shabeellaha Hoose. ◈ *region* S Somalia
Shabeellaha Hoose, Gobolka *see* Shabeellaha Hoose
Shabeelle, Webi *see* Shebeli
114 O7 **Shabla** Dobrich, NE Bulgaria *43°33′N 28°31′E*
114 O7 **Shabla, Nos** *headland* NE Bulgaria *43°30′N 28°36′E*
13 N9 **Shabogama Lake** ◎ Newfoundland and Labrador, E Canada
79 N20 **Shabunda** Sud-Kivu, E Dem. Rep. Congo *02°42′S 27°20′E*
141 Q15 **Shabwah** C Yemen *15°09′N 46°46′E*
158 F8 **Shache** *var.* Yarkant. Xinjiang Uygur Zizhiqu, NW China *38°27′N 77°16′E*
Shacheng *see* Huailai
195 R12 **Shackleton Coast** *physical region* Antarctica
195 Z10 **Shackleton Ice Shelf** *ice shelf* Antarctica
Shaddādī *see* Ash Shadādah
28 K7 **Shadehill Reservoir** ⊠ South Dakota, N USA
122 G11 **Shadrinsk** Kurganskaya Oblast', C Russian Federation *56°08′N 63°18′E*
31 O12 **Shafer, Lake** ⊠ Indiana, N USA
35 R13 **Shafter** California, W USA *35°27′N 119°15′W*
24 J11 **Shafter** Texas, SW USA *29°49′N 104°18′W*
97 L23 **Shaftesbury** S England, United Kingdom *51°01′N 02°12′W*
185 F22 **Shag** ≈ South Island, New Zealand
145 V9 **Shagan** ≈ E Kazakhstan
39 O11 **Shageluk** Alaska, USA *62°40′N 159°33′W*
122 K14 **Shagonar** Respublika Tyva, S Russian Federation *51°31′N 93°06′E*
185 F22 **Shag Point** *headland* South Island, New Zealand *45°28′S 170°50′E*
144 J12 **Shagyray, Plato** *plain* SW Kazakhstan
Shāhābād *see* Eslāmābād
168 K9 **Shah Alam** Selangor, Peninsular Malaysia *03°02′N 101°31′E*
117 O12 **Shahany, Ozero** ◎ SW Ukraine
138 H9 **Shahbā'** *anc.* Philippopolis. As Suwaydā', S Syria *32°50′N 36°38′E*
Shahbān *see* Ad Dayr
149 P17 **Shāh Bandar** Sind, SE Pakistan *23°59′N 67°54′E*
149 P13 **Shahdād Kot** Sind, SW Pakistan *27°49′N 67°49′E*
143 T10 **Shahdād, Namakzār-e** *salt pan* E Iran
149 Q15 **Shāhdādpur** Sind, SE Pakistan *25°56′N 68°40′E*
154 K10 **Shahdol** Madhya Pradesh, C India *23°19′N 81°26′E*
161 N7 **Sha He** ≈ C China
Shahe *see* Linze
Shahepu *see* Linze
153 N13 **Shāhganj** Uttar Pradesh, N India *26°03′N 82°41′E*
152 C11 **Shāhgarh** Rājasthān, NW India *27°08′N 69°56′E*
Sha Hi *see* Orūmīyeh, Daryācheh-ye
Shāhī *see* Qā'emshahr
Shahjahanabad *see* Delhi
152 L11 **Shāhjahānpur** Uttar Pradesh, N India *27°53′N 79°55′E*
149 U7 **Shāhpur** Punjab, E Pakistan *32°15′N 72°32′E*
Shāhpur *see* Shāhpur Chākar
152 G13 **Shāhpura** Rājasthān, N India *25°38′N 75°01′E*
149 Q15 **Shāhpur Chākar** *var.* Shāhpur. Sind, SE Pakistan *26°11′N 68°44′E*
148 M5 **Shahrak** Ghowr, C Afghanistan *34°09′N 64°16′E*
143 Q11 **Shahr-e Bābak** Kermān, C Iran *30°08′N 55°04′E*
143 N8 **Shahr-e Kord** *var.* Shahr Kord. Chahār Maḩall va Bakhtīārī, C Iran *32°20′N 50°52′E*
143 O9 **Shahrezā** *var.* Qomisheh, Qumisheh, Shahriza; *prev.* Qomsheh. Eşfahān, C Iran *32°01′N 51°51′E*

◆ Country
● Country Capital
◇ Dependent Territory
○ Dependent Territory Capital
◈ Administrative Regions
✈ International Airport
▲ Mountain
▲▲ Mountain Range
⛰ Volcano
≈ River
◎ Lake
⊠ Reservoir

SHAHRIKHON – SHŌDO-SHIMA

147 S10 **Shahrikhon** *Rus.* Shakhrikhan. Andijon Viloyati, E Uzbekistan 40°42′N 72°03′E
147 P11 **Shahriston** *Rus.* Shakhristan. NW Tajikistan 39°45′N 68°47′E
Shahriza *see* Shahreẕā
Shahr-i-Zabul *see* Zābol
Shahr Kord *see* Shahr-e Kord
147 P14 **Shahrtuz** *Rus.* Shaartuz. SW Tajikistan 37°13′N 68°05′E
143 Q4 **Shāhrūd** *prev.* Emāmrūd, Emāmshahr. Semnān, N Iran 36°30′N 55°E
Shahsavār/Shahsawar *see* Tonekābon
Shaidara *see* Step' Nardara
Shaikh Ābid *see* Shaykh 'Ābid
Shaikh Fāris *see* Shaykh Fāris
Shaikh Najm *see* Shaykh Najm
138 K5 **Shā'ir, Jabal** ▲ C Syria 34°51′N 37°49′E
154 G10 **Shājāpur** Madhya Pradesh, C India 23°27′N 76°21′E
80 J8 **Shakal, Ras** *headland* NE Sudan 18°04′N 38°34′E
83 G17 **Shakawe** North West, NW Botswana 18°25′S 21°53′E
Shakhdarinskiy Khrebet *see* Shokhdara, Qatorkŭhi
Shakhrikhan *see* Shahrikhon
Shakhrisabz *see* Sharixon
Shakhristan *see* Shahriston
Shakhtërsk *see* Shakmars'k
145 R10 **Shakhtinsk** Karaganda, C Kazakhstan 49°40′N 72°37′E
126 L11 **Shakhty** Rostovskaya Oblast', SW Russian Federation 47°45′N 40°14′E
127 P2 **Shakhun'ya** Nizhegorodskaya Oblast', W Russian Federation 57°42′N 46°36′E
77 S15 **Shaki** Oyo, W Nigeria 08°37′N 03°25′E
81 J15 **Shakīso** Oromīya, C Ethiopia 05°33′N 38°48′E
117 X8 **Shakmars'k** *Rus.* Shakhtërsk. Donets'ka Oblast', SE Ukraine 48°02′N 38°18′E
29 V9 **Shakopee** Minnesota, N USA 44°48′N 93°31′W
165 R3 **Shakotan-misaki** *headland* Hokkaidō, NE Japan 43°22′N 140°28′E
39 N9 **Shaktoolik** Alaska, USA 64°19′N 161°05′W
81 J14 **Shala Hāyk'** ◎ C Ethiopia
124 M10 **Shalakusha** Arkhangel'skaya Oblast', NW Russian Federation 62°16′N 40°16′E
145 U8 **Shalday** Pavlodar, NE Kazakhstan 51°57′N 78°51′E
127 P16 **Shali** Chechenskaya Respublika, SW Russian Federation 43°03′N 45°55′E
141 W12 **Shalīm** *var.* Shelim. S Oman 18°07′N 55°39′E
Shaliuhe *see* Gangca
144 K12 **Shalkar** *var.* Chelkar. Aktyubinsk, W Kazakhstan 47°50′N 59°29′E
144 F9 **Shalkar, Ozero** *prev.* Chelkar Ozero. ◎ W Kazakhstan
21 V12 **Shallotte** North Carolina, SE USA 33°58′N 78°21′W
25 N5 **Shallowater** Texas, SW USA 33°41′N 102°00′W
124 K11 **Shal'skiy** Respublika Kareliya, NW Russian Federation 61°45′N 36°02′E
160 F9 **Shaluli Shan** ▲▲ C China
81 F22 **Shama** ≈ C Tanzania
11 Z11 **Shamattawa** Manitoba, C Canada 55°52′N 92°05′W
12 F8 **Shamattawa** ≈ Ontario, C Canada
Shām, Bādiyat ash *see* Syrian Desert
Shamiya *see* Ash Shāmīyah
141 X8 **Shām, Jabal ash** *var.* Jebel Sham. ▲ NW Oman 23°21′N 57°08′E
Sham, Jebel *see* Shām, Jabal ash
Shamkhor *see* Şämkir
18 G14 **Shamokin** Pennsylvania, NE USA 40°47′N 76°33′W
25 P2 **Shamrock** Texas, SW USA 35°12′N 100°15′W
Shana *see* Kuril'sk
Sha'nabī, Jabal ash *see* Chambi, Jebel
139 Y12 **Shanāwah** Al Başrah, E Iraq 30°57′N 47°25′E
Shancheng *see* Taining
159 T8 **Shandan** *var.* Qingyuan. Gansu, N China 38°50′N 101°08′E
Shandī *see* Shendi
161 Q5 **Shandong** *var.* Lu, Shandong Sheng, Shantung. ◆ *province* E China
161 R4 **Shandong Bandao** *var.* Shantung Peninsula. *peninsula* E China
Shandong Sheng *see* Shandong
139 U8 **Shandrūkh** Diyālá, E Iraq 33°20′N 45°19′E
83 J17 **Shangani** ≈ W Zimbabwe
161 O15 **Shangchuan Dao** *island* S China
Shangchuankou *see* Minhe
163 P12 **Shangdu** Nei Mongol Zizhiqu, N China 41°32′N 113°33′E
161 O11 **Shanggao** *var.* Aoyang. Jiangxi, S China 28°16′N 114°55′E
Shangguan *see* Daixian
161 S8 **Shanghai** *var.* Shang-hai. Shanghai Shi, E China 31°14′N 121°28′E
161 S8 **Shanghai Shi** *var.* Hu, Shanghai. ◆ *municipality* E China
161 P13 **Shanghang** *var.* Linjiang. Fujian, SE China 25°03′N 116°25′E
160 K14 **Shanglin** *var.* Dafeng. Guangxi Zhuangzu Zizhiqu, S China 23°26′N 108°32′E
160 L7 **Shangluo** *prev.* Shangxian, Shangzhou. Shaanxi, C China 33°51′N 109°55′E
83 G15 **Shangombo** Western, W Zambia 16/28′S 22°10′E
Shangpai/Shangpaihe *see* Feixi
161 O6 **Shangqiu** *var.* Zhuji. Henan, C China 34°24′N 115°37′E
161 Q10 **Shangrao** Jiangxi, S China 28°27′N 117°57′E
Shangxian *see* Shangluo
161 S9 **Shangyu** *var.* Baiguan. Zhejiang, SE China 30°03′N 120°52′E
163 X9 **Shangzhi** Heilongjiang, NE China 45°13′N 127°59′E
Shangzhou *see* Shangluo
Shanhe *see* Zhengning
163 W9 **Shanhetun** Heilongjiang, NE China 44°42′N 127°12′E
Shan-hsi *see* Shaanxi, China
Shan-hsi *see* Shanxi, China
159 O6 **Shankou** Xinjiang Uygur Zizhiqu, W China 42°02′N 94°08′E
184 M13 **Shannon** Manawatu-Wanganui, North Island, New Zealand 40°32′S 175°24′E
97 C17 **Shannon** *Ir.* An tSionainn. ≈ W Ireland
97 B19 **Shannon** ✈ W Ireland 52°42′N 08°57′W
167 N6 **Shan Plateau** *plateau* E Myanmar (Burma)
158 M6 **Shanshan** *var.* Piqan. Xinjiang Uygur Zizhiqu, NW China 42°53′N 90°18′E
Shansi *see* Shanxi
167 N5 **Shan State** ◆ *state* E Myanmar (Burma)
Shantar Islands *see* Shantarskiye Ostrova
123 S12 **Shantarskiye Ostrova** *Eng.* Shantar Islands. *island group* E Russian Federation
161 Q14 **Shantou** *var.* Shan-t'ou, Swatow. Guangdong, S China 23°23′N 116°39′E
Shan-t'ou *see* Shantou
Shantung *see* Shandong
Shantung Peninsula *see* Shandong Bandao
161 O15 **Shanwei** Guangdong, China 22°28′N 115°13′E
163 O14 **Shanxi** *var.* Jin, Shan-hsi, Shansi, Shanxi Sheng. ◆ *province* C China
161 P6 **Shanxian** *var.* Shan Xian. Shandong, E China 34°51′N 116°09′E
Shan Xian *see* Sanmenxia
Shan Xian *see* Shanxian
Shanxi Sheng *see* Shanxi
160 L7 **Shanyang** Shaanxi, C China 33°35′N 109°48′E
161 N13 **Shanyin** *var.* Daiyue. Shanxi, C China E Asia 39°30′N 112°56′E
161 O13 **Shaoguan** *var.* Shao-kuan, *Cant.* Kukong; *prev.* Ch'u-chiang. Guangdong, S China 24°57′N 113°38′E
Shao-kuan *see* Shaoguan
161 Q11 **Shaowu** Fujian, SE China 27°24′N 117°26′E
161 S9 **Shaoxing** Zhejiang, SE China 30°02′N 120°35′E
160 M11 **Shaoyang** *var.* Baoqing, Shao-yang; *prev.* Pao-king. Hunan, S China 27°13′N 111°31′E
160 M12 **Shaoyang** *var.* Tangdukou. Hunan, S China 26°54′N 111°14′E
Shao-yang *see* Shaoyang
96 K5 **Shapinsay** *island* NE Scotland, United Kingdom
125 S4 **Shapkina** ≈ NW Russian Federation
Shāpūr *see* Salmās
158 M4 **Shaqiuhe** Xinjiang Uygur Zizhiqu, W China 45°00′N 88°52′E
139 T2 **Shaqlāwa** *var.* Shaqlāwah. Arbīl, E Iraq 36°24′N 44°21′E
Shaqlāwah *see* Shaqlāwa
138 I8 **Shaqqā** As Suwaydā', S Syria 32°53′N 36°42′E
141 P7 **Shaqrā'** Ar Riyāḑ, C Saudi Arabia 25°11′N 45°08′E
Shaqrā *see* Shuqrah
145 W10 **Shar** *var.* Charsk. Vostochnyy Kazakhstan, E Kazakhstan 49°33′N 81°03′E
149 O6 **Sharan** Dāykondī, SE Afghanistan 33°28′N 66°19′E
149 Q7 **Sharan** *var.* Zareh Sharan. Paktīkā, E Afghanistan 33°08′N 68°47′E
Sharaqpur *see* Sharqpur
Sharbaqty *see* Shcherbakty
141 X12 **Sharbatāt** S Oman 17°57′N 56°14′E
Sharbatāt, Ra's *see* Sharbithāt, Ras
141 X12 **Sharbithāt, Ras** *var.* Ra's Sharbatāt. *headland* S Oman 17°55′N 56°30′E
14 K14 **Sharbot Lake** Ontario, SE Canada 44°45′N 76°46′W
145 P17 **Shardara** *var.* Chardara. Yuzhnyy Kazakhstan, S Kazakhstan 41°15′N 68°01′E
Shardara Dalasy *see* Step' Nardara
162 F8 **Sharga** Govĭ-Altay, W Mongolia 46°16′N 95°32′E
Sharga *see* Tsagaan-Uul
116 M7 **Sharhorod** Vinnyts'ka Oblast', C Ukraine 48°46′N 28°05′E
Sharhulsan *see* Mandal-Ovoo
165 V3 **Shari** Hokkaidō, NE Japan 43°54′N 144°42′E
Shari *see* Chari
139 T6 **Shārī, Buḩayrat** ◎ C Iraq
147 N12 **Sharixon** *Rus.* Shakhrisabz. Qashqadaryo Viloyati, S Uzbekistan 39°01′N 66°45′E
Sharjah *see* Ash Shāriqah
118 K12 **Sharkawshchyna** *var.* Sharkowshchyna, *Pol.* Szarkowszczyzna, *Rus.* Sharkovshchina. Vitsyebskaya Voblasts', NW Belarus 55°27′N 27°28′E
180 G9 **Shark Bay** *bay* Western Australia
141 Y9 **Sharkh** E Oman 21°20′N 59°04′E
Sharkovshchina/Sharkowshchyna *see* Sharkawshchyna
127 U6 **Sharlyk** Orenburgskaya Oblast', W Russian Federation 52°52′N 54°45′E
75 Y9 **Sharm ash Shaykh** *var.* Ofiral, Sharm el Sheikh. E Egypt 27°51′N 34°16′E
Sharm el Sheikh *see* Sharm ash Shaykh
18 B13 **Sharon** Pennsylvania, NE USA 41°12′N 80°28′W
26 H4 **Sharon Springs** Kansas, C USA 38°54′N 101°46′W
31 Q14 **Sharonville** Ohio, N USA 39°16′N 84°24′W
Sharourah *see* Sharūrah
29 O10 **Sharpe, Lake** ⊠ South Dakota, N USA
Sharqī, Al Jabal ash/Sharqi, Jebel esh *see* Anti-Lebanon
Sharqīyah, Al Minţaqah ash *see* Ash Sharqīyah
138 I6 **Sharqīyat an Nabk, Jabal** ▲▲ W Syria
149 W8 **Sharqpur** *var.* Sharaqpur. Punjab, E Pakistan 31°29′N 74°08′E
141 Q13 **Sharūrah** *var.* Sharourah. Najrān, S Saudi Arabia 17°29′N 47°05′E
125 O14 **Shar'ya** Kostromskaya Oblast', NW Russian Federation 58°22′N 45°30′E
145 V15 **Sharyn** *var.* Charyn. ≈ SE Kazakhstan
Sharyn *see* Charyn
122 K13 **Sharypovo** Krasnoyarskiy Kray, C Russian Federation 55°33′N 89°12′E
83 J18 **Shashe** Central, NE Botswana 21°25′S 27°28′E
83 J18 **Shashe** *var.* Shashi. ≈ Botswana/Zimbabwe
81 J14 **Shashemenē** *var.* Shashemenne, Shashhamana, *It.* Sciasciamana. Oromīya, C Ethiopia 07°16′N 38°38′E
Shashemenne/Shashhamana *see* Shashemenē
Shashi *see* Shashe
Shashi/Sha-shih/Shasi *see* Jingzhou, Hubei
35 N3 **Shasta Lake** ⊠ California, W USA
35 N2 **Shasta, Mount** ▲ California, W USA 41°24′N 122°11′W
127 O4 **Shatki** Nizhegorodskaya Oblast', W Russian Federation 55°09′N 44°04′E
Shatlyk *see* Şatlyk
Shatra *see* Ash Shaţrah
119 K17 **Shatsk** Minskaya Voblasts', C Belarus 53°25′N 27°41′E
127 N5 **Shatsk** Ryazanskaya Oblast', W Russian Federation 54°02′N 41°38′E
26 J9 **Shattuck** Oklahoma, C USA 36°16′N 99°52′W
145 P16 **Shaul'der** Yuzhnyy Kazakhstan, S Kazakhstan 42°45′N 68°21′E
11 S17 **Shaunavon** Saskatchewan, S Canada 49°49′N 108°25′W
Shavat *see* Shovot
Shaviyani Atoll *see* North Miladhunmadulu Atoll
158 K4 **Shawan** *var.* Sandaohezi. Xinjiang Uygur Zizhiqu, NW China 44°21′N 85°37′E
14 G12 **Shawanaga** Ontario, S Canada 45°29′N 80°16′W
30 M6 **Shawano** Wisconsin, N USA 44°46′N 88°38′W
30 M6 **Shawano Lake** ◎ Wisconsin, N USA
15 P10 **Shawinigan** *prev.* Shawinigan Falls. Québec, SE Canada 46°33′N 72°45′W
Shawinigan Falls *see* Shawinigan
15 P10 **Shawinigan-Sud** Québec, SE Canada 46°30′N 72°43′W
138 J5 **Shawmarīyah, Jabal ash** ▲▲ C Syria
27 O11 **Shawnee** Oklahoma, C USA 35°20′N 96°55′W
14 K12 **Shawville** Québec, SE Canada 45°37′N 76°31′W
145 Q16 **Shayan** *var.* Chayan. Yuzhnyy Kazakhstan, S Kazakhstan 42°59′N 69°22′E
Shaykh *see* Ash Shakk
139 W9 **Shaykh 'Ābid** *var.* Shaikh Ābid. Wāsiţ, E Iraq 32°40′N 46°09′E
139 Y10 **Shaykh Fāris** *var.* Shaikh Fāris. Maysān, E Iraq 32°06′N 47°39′E
139 T7 **Shaykh Ḩātim** Baghdād, E Iraq 33°29′N 44°15′E
Shaykh, Jabal ash *see* Hermon, Mount
139 X10 **Shaykh Najm** *var.* Shaikh Najm. Maysān, E Iraq 32°04′N 46°54′E
139 W9 **Shaykh Sa'd** Maysān, E Iraq 32°35′N 46°16′E
147 T14 **Shazud** SE Tajikistan 37°45′N 72°22′E
119 N18 **Shchadryn** *Rus.* Shchedrin. Homyel'skaya Voblasts', SE Belarus 52°53′N 29°33′E
119 H18 **Shchara** ≈ SW Belarus
Shchedrin *see* Shchadryn
Shcheglovsk *see* Kemerovo
126 K5 **Shchëkino** Tul'skaya Oblast', W Russian Federation 53°57′N 37°33′E
125 S7 **Shchel'yayur** Respublika Komi, NW Russian Federation 65°19′N 53°27′E
145 U8 **Shcherbakty** *Kaz.* Sharbaqty. Pavlodar, E Kazakhstan 52°28′N 78°00′E
126 K7 **Shchigry** Kurskaya Oblast', W Russian Federation 51°53′N 36°49′E
Shchitkovichi *see* Shchytkavichy
117 Q2 **Shchors** Chernihivs'ka Oblast', N Ukraine 51°49′N 31°58′E
117 T8 **Shchors'k** Dnipropetrovs'ka Oblast', E Ukraine 48°20′N 34°07′E
Shchuchin *see* Shchuchyn
145 Q7 **Shchuchinsk** *prev.* Shchuchye. Akmola, N Kazakhstan 52°57′N 70°10′E
Shchuchye *see* Shchuchinsk
119 G16 **Shchuchyn** *Pol.* Szczuczyn Nowogródzki, *Rus.* Shchuchin. Hrodzyenskaya Voblasts', W Belarus 53°36′N 24°45′E
119 K17 **Shchytkavichy** *Rus.* Shchitkovichi. Minskaya Voblasts', C Belarus 53°13′N 27°59′E
122 J13 **Shebalino** Respublika Altay, S Russian Federation 51°16′N 85°41′E
126 J9 **Shebekino** Belgorodskaya Oblast', W Russian Federation 50°25′N 36°55′E
Shebelē Wenz, Wabē *see* Shebeli
81 L14 **Shebeli** *Amh.* Wabē Shebelē Wenz, *It.* Scebeli, *Som.* Webi Shabeelle. ≈ Ethiopia/Somalia
113 M20 **Shebenikut, Maja e** ▲ E Albania 41°13′N 20°27′E
149 N2 **Sheberghān** *var.* Shibarghān, Shiberghan, Shiberghān. Jowzjān, N Afghanistan 36°41′N 65°45′E
144 F14 **Shebir** Mangistau, SW Kazakhstan 44°52′N 52°01′E
31 N8 **Sheboygan** Wisconsin, N USA 43°46′N 87°44′W
77 X15 **Shebshi Mountains** *var.* Schebschi Mountains. ▲▲ E Nigeria
Shechem *see* Nablus
Shedadi *see* Ash Shadādah
13 P14 **Shediac** New Brunswick, SE Canada 46°13′N 64°35′W
126 L15 **Shedok** Krasnodarskiy Kray, SW Russian Federation 44°12′N 40°49′E
80 N12 **Sheekh** Toghdeer, N Somalia 10°01′N 45°21′E
38 M11 **Sheenjek River** ≈ Alaska, USA
96 D13 **Sheep Haven** *Ir.* Cuan na gCaorach. *inlet* N Ireland
35 X10 **Sheep Range** ▲▲ Nevada, W USA
98 M13 **'s-Heerenberg** Gelderland, E Netherlands 51°52′N 06°15′E
97 P22 **Sheerness** SE England, United Kingdom 51°27′N 00°45′E
13 Q15 **Sheet Harbour** Nova Scotia, SE Canada 44°56′N 62°31′W
185 H18 **Sheffield** Canterbury, South Island, New Zealand 43°22′S 172°01′E
97 M18 **Sheffield** N England, United Kingdom 53°23′N 01°30′W
23 O2 **Sheffield** Alabama, S USA 34°46′N 87°42′W
29 V12 **Sheffield** Iowa, C USA 42°53′N 93°13′W
25 N10 **Sheffield** Texas, SW USA 30°42′N 101°49′W
63 H22 **Shehuen, Río** ≈ S Argentina
Shekhem *see* Nablus
149 V8 **Shekhūpura** Punjab, NE Pakistan 31°42′N 74°08′E
Sheki *see* Şäki
124 L14 **Sheksna** Vologodskaya Oblast', NW Russian Federation 59°11′N 38°32′E
123 T5 **Shelagskiy, Mys** *headland* NE Russian Federation 70°04′N 170°39′E
27 V3 **Shelbina** Missouri, C USA 39°41′N 92°02′W
13 P16 **Shelburne** Nova Scotia, SE Canada 43°47′N 65°20′W
14 G14 **Shelburne** Ontario, S Canada 44°04′N 80°12′W
33 R7 **Shelby** Montana, NW USA 48°30′N 111°52′W
21 Q10 **Shelby** North Carolina, SE USA 35°15′N 81°34′W
31 S12 **Shelby** Ohio, N USA 40°52′N 82°39′W
30 L14 **Shelbyville** Illinois, N USA 39°24′N 88°47′W
31 P14 **Shelbyville** Indiana, N USA 39°31′N 85°46′W
20 L5 **Shelbyville** Kentucky, S USA 38°13′N 85°12′W
27 V2 **Shelbyville** Missouri, C USA 39°48′N 92°01′W
20 J10 **Shelbyville** Tennessee, S USA 35°29′N 86°30′W
25 X8 **Shelbyville** Texas, SW USA 31°42′N 94°03′W
30 L14 **Shelbyville, Lake** ⊠ Illinois, N USA
29 S12 **Sheldon** Iowa, C USA 43°10′N 95°51′W
38 M11 **Sheldons Point** Alaska, USA 62°31′N 165°03′W
Shelek *see* Chilik
Shelekhov Gulf *see* Shelikhova, Zaliv
123 U9 **Shelikhova, Zaliv** *Eng.* Shelekhov Gulf. *gulf* E Russian Federation
39 P14 **Shelikof Strait** *strait* Alaska, USA
Shelim *see* Shalīm
11 T14 **Shellbrook** Saskatchewan, S Canada 53°14′N 106°24′W
28 L3 **Shell Creek** ≈ North Dakota, N USA
Shellif *see* Chelif, Oued
22 I10 **Shell Keys** *island group* Louisiana, S USA
30 I4 **Shell Lake** Wisconsin, N USA 45°44′N 91°56′W
29 W12 **Shell Rock** Iowa, C USA 42°42′N 92°34′W
185 C26 **Shelter Point** *headland* Stewart Island, New Zealand 47°04′S 168°13′E
18 L13 **Shelton** Connecticut, NE USA 41°19′N 73°06′W
32 G8 **Shelton** Washington, NW USA 47°13′N 123°06′W
Shemakha *see* Şamaxı
145 W9 **Shemonaikha** Vostochnyy Kazakhstan, E Kazakhstan 50°38′N 81°55′E
127 Q4 **Shemursha** Chuvashskaya Respublika, W Russian Federation 54°57′N 47°27′E
38 D16 **Shemya Island** *island* Aleutian Islands, Alaska, USA
29 T16 **Shenandoah** Iowa, C USA 40°46′N 95°23′W
21 U4 **Shenandoah** Virginia, NE USA 38°26′N 78°34′W
21 U4 **Shenandoah Mountains** *ridge* West Virginia, NE USA
21 V3 **Shenandoah River** ≈ West Virginia, NE USA
77 W15 **Shendam** Plateau, C Nigeria 08°52′N 09°30′E
80 G8 **Shendi** *var.* Shandī. River Nile, NE Sudan 16°41′N 33°22′E
76 I15 **Shenge** SW Sierra Leone 07°54′N 12°54′W
146 L10 **Shengeldi** *Rus.* Chingildi. Navoiy Viloyati, N Uzbekistan 40°59′N 64°13′E
145 U15 **Shengel'dy** Almaty, SE Kazakhstan 44°04′N 77°31′E
113 K18 **Shëngjin** *var.* Shëngjini. Lezhë, NW Albania 41°49′N 19°34′E
Shëngjini *see* Shëngjin
Shengking *see* Liaoning
Sheng Xian/Shengxian *see* Shengzhou
161 S9 **Shengzhou** *var.* Shengxian, Sheng Xian. Zhejiang, SE China 29°36′N 120°42′E
Shenking *see* Liaoning
125 N11 **Shenkursk** Arkhangel'skaya Oblast', NW Russian Federation 62°10′N 42°58′E
160 L3 **Shenmu** Shaanxi, C China 38°49′N 110°27′E
113 L19 **Shën Noj i Madh** ▲ C Albania 41°23′N 20°07′E
160 L8 **Shennong Ding** ▲ C China 31°24′N 110°16′E
Shenshi/Shensi *see* Shaanxi
163 V12 **Shenyang** *Chin.* Shen-yang, *Eng.* Moukden, Mukden; *prev.* Fengtien. *province capital* Liaoning, NE China 41°50′N 123°26′E
Shen-yang *see* Shenyang
161 O15 **Shenzhen** Guangdong, S China 22°39′N 114°02′E
154 G8 **Sheopur** Madhya Pradesh, C India 25°41′N 76°42′E
116 L5 **Shepetivka** *Rus.* Shepetovka. Khmel'nyts'ka Oblast', NW Ukraine 50°12′N 27°01′E
Shepetovka *see* Shepetivka
25 W10 **Shepherd** Texas, SW USA 30°30′N 95°00′W
187 R14 **Shepherd Islands** *island group* C Vanuatu
20 K5 **Shepherdsville** Kentucky, S USA 38°00′N 85°42′W
183 O11 **Shepparton** Victoria, SE Australia 36°25′S 145°26′E
97 P22 **Sheppey, Isle of** *island* SE England, United Kingdom
Sherabad *see* Sherobod
9 O4 **Sherard, Cape** *headland* Nunavut, N Canada 74°36′N 80°10′W
97 L23 **Sherborne** S England, United Kingdom 50°58′N 02°30′W
76 H16 **Sherbro Island** *island* SW Sierra Leone
15 Q12 **Sherbrooke** Québec, SE Canada 45°23′N 71°55′W
29 T11 **Sherburn** Minnesota, N USA 43°39′N 94°43′W
78 H6 **Sherda** Borkou-Ennedi-Tibesti, N Chad 20°04′N 16°48′E
80 G7 **Shereik** River Nile, N Sudan 18°44′N 33°37′E
126 K3 **Sheremet'yevo** ✈ (Moskva) Moskovskaya Oblast', W Russian Federation 56°05′N 37°10′E
153 P14 **Sherghāti** Bihār, N India 24°35′N 84°51′E
27 U12 **Sheridan** Arkansas, C USA 34°18′N 92°22′W
33 W12 **Sheridan** Wyoming, C USA 44°47′N 106°59′W
182 G8 **Sheringa** South Australia 33°51′S 135°13′E
25 U5 **Sherman** Texas, SW USA 33°39′N 96°35′W
194 J10 **Sherman Island** *island* Antarctica
19 S4 **Sherman Mills** Maine, NE USA 45°51′N 68°23′W
29 O15 **Sherman Reservoir** ⊠ Nebraska, C USA
147 N14 **Sherobod** *Rus.* Sherabad. Surkhondaryo Viloyati, S Uzbekistan 37°43′N 66°59′E
147 O13 **Sherobod** *Rus.* Sherabad. ≈ S Uzbekistan
153 T14 **Sherpur** Dhaka, N Bangladesh 25°00′N 90°01′E
37 T4 **Sherrelwood** Colorado, C USA 39°49′N 105°00′W
99 J14 **'s-Hertogenbosch** *Fr.* Bois-le-Duc, *Ger.* Herzogenbusch. Noord-Brabant, S Netherlands 51°41′N 05°19′E
28 M2 **Sherwood** North Dakota, N USA 48°55′N 101°36′W
11 Q14 **Sherwood Park** Alberta, SW Canada 53°34′N 113°04′W
56 F13 **Sheshea, Río** ≈ E Peru
143 T5 **Sheshtamad** Khorāsān-Razavī, NE Iran 36°03′N 57°45′E
29 S10 **Shetek, Lake** ◎ Minnesota, N USA
96 M2 **Shetland Islands** *island group* NE Scotland, United Kingdom
144 F14 **Shetpe** Mangistau, SW Kazakhstan 44°06′N 52°03′E
154 C11 **Shetrunji** ≈ W India
Shevchenko *see* Aktau
117 W5 **Shevchenkove** Kharkivs'ka Oblast', E Ukraine 49°40′N 37°13′E
81 H14 **Shewa Gīmīra** Southern Nationalities, S Ethiopia 07°12′N 35°49′E
161 Q9 **Shexian** *var.* Huicheng, She Xian. Anhui, E China 29°53′N 118°27′E
She Xian *see* Shexian
161 R6 **Sheyang** *prev.* Hede. Jiangsu, E China 33°49′N 120°13′E
29 O4 **Sheyenne** North Dakota, N USA 47°49′N 99°08′W
29 P4 **Sheyenne River** ≈ North Dakota, N USA
96 G7 **Shiant Islands** *island group* NW Scotland, United Kingdom
123 U12 **Shiashkotan, Ostrov** *island* Kuril'skiye Ostrova, SE Russian Federation
31 R9 **Shiawassee River** ≈ Michigan, N USA
141 R14 **Shibām** C Yemen 15°49′N 48°24′E
Shibarghān *see* Sheberghān
165 O10 **Shibata** *var.* Sibata. Niigata, Honshū, C Japan 37°57′N 139°20′E
Shiberghan/Shiberghān *see* Sheberghān
Shibh Jazīrat Sīnā' *see* Sinai
75 W8 **Shibīn al Kawm** *var.* Shibîn el Kôm. N Egypt 30°33′N 31°00′E
Shibîn el Kôm *see* Shibīn al Kawm
143 O13 **Shīb, Kūh-e** ▲▲ S Iran
12 D8 **Shibogama Lake** ◎ Ontario, C Canada
Shibotsu-jima *see* Zelënyy, Ostrov
164 B16 **Shibushi** Kagoshima, Kyūshū, SW Japan 31°27′N 131°05′E
189 U13 **Shichiyo Islands** *island group* Chuuk, C Micronesia
Shickshock Mountains *see* Chic-Chocs, Monts
145 S8 **Shiderti** *var.* Shiderty. Pavlodar, NE Kazakhstan 51°40′N 74°50′E
145 S9 **Shiderti** ≈ N Kazakhstan
Shiderty *see* Shiderti
Shīeli *see* Chiili
96 G10 **Shiel, Loch** ◎ N Scotland, United Kingdom
164 J13 **Shiga** *off.* Shiga-ken, *var.* Siga. ◆ *prefecture* Honshū, SW Japan
Shiga-ken *see* Shiga
Shigatse *see* Xigazê
141 U13 **Shiḩan** *oasis* NE Yemen
Shih-chia-chuang/Shihmen *see* Shijiazhuang
158 K4 **Shihezi** Xinjiang Uygur Zizhiqu, NW China 44°21′N 85°59′E
Shiichi *see* Shyichy
113 K19 **Shijak** *var.* Shijaku. Durrës, W Albania 41°21′N 19°34′E
Shijaku *see* Shijak
161 O4 **Shijiazhuang** *var.* Shih-chia-chuang; *prev.* Shihmen. *province capital* Hebei, E China 38°04′N 114°28′E
165 R5 **Shikabe** Hokkaidō, NE Japan 42°03′N 140°45′E
149 Q13 **Shikārpur** Sind, S Pakistan 27°59′N 68°39′E
127 Q7 **Shikhany** Saratovskaya Oblast', W Russian Federation 52°07′N 47°13′E
189 V12 **Shiki Islands** *island group* Chuuk, C Micronesia
164 G14 **Shikoku** *var.* Sikoku. *island* SW Japan
192 H5 **Shikoku Basin** *var.* Sikoku Basin. *undersea feature* N Philippine Sea 28°00′N 137°00′E
164 G14 **Shikoku-sanchi** ▲▲ Shikoku, SW Japan
165 X4 **Shikotan, Ostrov** *Jap.* Shikotan-tō. *island* NE Russian Federation
Shikotan-tō *see* Shikotan, Ostrov
165 R4 **Shikotsu-ko** *var.* Sikotu Ko. ◎ Hokkaidō, NE Japan
81 N15 **Shilabo** Sumalē, E Ethiopia 06°05′N 44°48′E
127 X7 **Shil'da** Orenburgskaya Oblast', W Russian Federation 51°46′N 59°48′E
139 V3 **Shilēr, Āw-e** ≈ E Iraq
153 S12 **Shiliguri** *prev.* Siliguri. West Bengal, NE India 26°46′N 88°24′E
Shiliu *see* Changjiang
129 V7 **Shilka** ≈ S Russian Federation
18 H15 **Shillington** Pennsylvania, NE USA 40°18′N 75°57′W
153 V13 **Shillong** *state capital* Meghālaya, NE India 25°37′N 91°54′E
126 M5 **Shilovo** Ryazanskaya Oblast', W Russian Federation 54°18′N 40°53′E
164 C14 **Shimabara** *var.* Simabara. Nagasaki, Kyūshū, SW Japan 32°48′N 130°20′E
164 C14 **Shimabara-wan** *bay* SW Japan
164 F12 **Shimane** *off.* Shimane-ken, *var.* Simane. ◆ *prefecture* Honshū, SW Japan
164 G11 **Shimane-hantō** *peninsula* Honshū, SW Japan
Shimane-ken *see* Shimane
123 Q13 **Shimanovsk** Amurskaya Oblast', SE Russian Federation 52°00′N 127°36′E
Shimanto *see* Nakamura
Shimbir Berris *see* Shimbiris
80 O12 **Shimbiris** *var.* Shimbir Berris. ▲ N Somalia 10°43′N 47°10′E
165 T4 **Shimizu** Hokkaidō, NE Japan 42°58′N 142°54′E
164 M14 **Shimizu** *var.* Simizu. Shizuoka, Honshū, S Japan 35°01′N 138°29′E
152 I8 **Shimla** *prev.* Simla. *state capital* Himāchal Pradesh, N India 31°07′N 77°09′E
165 N14 **Shimoda** *var.* Simoda. Shizuoka, Honshū, S Japan 34°40′N 138°55′E
165 O13 **Shimodate** *var.* Simodate. Ibaraki, Honshū, S Japan 36°20′N 140°00′E
155 F18 **Shimoga** Karnātaka, W India 13°56′N 75°31′E
164 C15 **Shimo-jima** *island* SW Japan
164 B15 **Shimo-Koshiki-jima** *island* SW Japan
81 J21 **Shimoni** Coast, S Kenya 04°40′S 39°22′E
164 D13 **Shimonoseki** *var.* Simonoseki, *hist.* Akamagaseki, Bakan. Yamaguchi, Honshū, SW Japan 33°57′N 130°54′E
124 G14 **Shimsk** Novgorodskaya Oblast', NW Russian Federation 58°12′N 30°43′E
141 W7 **Shināş** N Oman 24°45′N 56°24′E
148 J6 **Shīndand** Herāt, W Afghanistan 33°19′N 62°09′E
Shinei *see* Hsinying
162 H10 **Shinejinst** *var.* Dzalaa. Bayanhongor, C Mongolia 44°29′N 99°19′E
25 T12 **Shiner** Texas, SW USA 29°25′N 97°10′W
167 N1 **Shingbwiyang** Kachin State, N Myanmar (Burma) 26°40′N 96°14′E
145 W11 **Shingozha** Vostochnyy Kazakhstan, E Kazakhstan 47°46′N 80°38′E
164 J15 **Shingū** *var.* Singû. Wakayama, Honshū, SW Japan 33°41′N 135°57′E
14 F8 **Shining Tree** Ontario, S Canada 47°36′N 81°12′W
165 P9 **Shinjō** *var.* Sinzyô. Yamagata, Honshū, C Japan 38°47′N 140°17′E
96 I7 **Shin, Loch** ◎ N Scotland, United Kingdom
21 S3 **Shinnston** West Virginia, NE USA 39°22′N 80°19′W
138 I6 **Shinshār** *Fr.* Chinnchâr. Ḩimş, W Syria 34°36′N 36°45′E
Shinshū *see* Chinju
165 T4 **Shintoku** Hokkaidō, NE Japan 43°03′N 142°50′E
81 G20 **Shinyanga** Shinyanga, NW Tanzania 03°40′S 33°25′E
81 G20 **Shinyanga** ◆ *region* N Tanzania
165 Q10 **Shiogama** *var.* Siogama. Miyagi, Honshū, C Japan 38°19′N 141°00′E
164 M12 **Shiojiri** *var.* Sioziri. Nagano, Honshū, S Japan 36°08′N 137°58′E
164 I15 **Shiono-misaki** *headland* Honshū, SW Japan 33°25′N 135°45′E
165 Q12 **Shioya-zaki** *headland* Honshū, C Japan 37°00′N 140°57′E
114 J9 **Shipchenski Prokhod** *pass* C Bulgaria
160 G14 **Shiping** Yunnan, SW China 23°45′N 102°23′E
13 P13 **Shippagan** *var.* Shippegan. New Brunswick, SE Canada 47°45′N 64°44′W
Shippegan *see* Shippagan
18 F15 **Shippensburg** Pennsylvania, NE USA 40°03′N 77°31′W
37 P9 **Shiprock** New Mexico, SW USA 36°47′N 108°41′W
37 O9 **Ship Rock** ▲ New Mexico, SW USA 36°41′N 108°50′W
15 R6 **Shipshaw** ≈ Québec, SE Canada
123 V10 **Shipunskiy, Mys** *headland* E Russian Federation 53°04′N 159°57′E
160 K7 **Shiquan** Shaanxi, C China 33°05′N 108°15′E
122 K13 **Shira** Respublika Khakasiya, S Russian Federation 54°35′N 89°58′E
Shirajganj Ghat *see* Sirajganj
165 P12 **Shirakawa** *var.* Sirakawa. Fukushima, Honshū, C Japan 37°07′N 140°11′E
164 M13 **Shirane-san** ▲ Honshū, S Japan 35°39′N 138°13′E
165 U14 **Shiranuka** Hokkaidō, NE Japan 42°57′N 144°01′E
195 N12 **Shirase Coast** *physical region* Antarctica
165 U3 **Shirataki** Hokkaidō, NE Japan 43°55′N 143°14′E
143 O11 **Shīrāz** *var.* Shīrāz. Fārs, S Iran 29°38′N 52°34′E
83 N15 **Shire** *var.* Chire. ≈ Malawi/Mozambique
Shiree *see* Tsagaanhayrhan
Shireet *see* Bayandelger
165 W3 **Shiretoko-hantō** *headland* Hokkaidō, NE Japan 44°06′N 145°07′E
165 W3 **Shiretoko-misaki** *headland* Hokkaidō, NE Japan 44°20′N 145°19′E
127 N5 **Shiringushi** Respublika Mordoviya, W Russian Federation 53°50′N 42°49′E
148 M3 **Shīrīn Tagāb** Fāryāb, N Afghanistan 36°49′N 65°01′E
149 N2 **Shīrīn Tagāb** ≈ N Afghanistan
165 R6 **Shiriya-zaki** *headland* Honshū, C Japan 41°24′N 141°27′E
144 I12 **Shirkala, Gryada** *plain* W Kazakhstan
165 P10 **Shiroishi** *var.* Siroisi. Miyagi, Honshū, C Japan 38°00′N 140°38′E
Shirokoye *see* Shyroke
165 O10 **Shirone** *var.* Sirone. Niigata, Honshū, C Japan 37°46′N 139°00′E
164 L12 **Shirotori** Gifu, Honshū, SW Japan 35°53′N 136°52′E
197 T1 **Shirshov Ridge** *undersea feature* W Bering Sea
Shirshütür/Shirshyutyur, Peski *see* Şirşütür Gumy
143 T3 **Shīrvān** *var.* Shirwān. Khorāsān, NE Iran 37°25′N 57°55′E
Shirwa, Lake *see* Chilwa, Lake
Shirwān *see* Shīrvān
159 N5 **Shisanjianfang** Xinjiang Uygur Zizhiqu, W China 43°10′N 91°15′E
38 M16 **Shishaldin Volcano** ▲ Unimak Island, Alaska, USA 54°45′N 163°58′W
Shishchitsy *see* Shyshchytsy
83 G16 **Shishikola** North West, N Botswana 18°09′S 23°08′E
38 M8 **Shishmaref** Alaska, USA 66°15′N 166°04′W
Shisur *see* Ash Shişar
164 L13 **Shitara** Aichi, Honshū, SW Japan 35°06′N 137°33′E
152 D12 **Shiv** Rājasthān, NW India 26°11′N 71°14′E
Shivāji Sāgar *see* Konya Reservoir
154 H8 **Shivpuri** Madhya Pradesh, C India 25°28′N 77°41′E
36 J9 **Shivwits Plateau** *plain* Arizona, SW USA
Shiwalik Range *see* Siwalik Range
160 M8 **Shiyan** Hubei, C China 32°31′N 110°45′E
Shizilu *see* Junan
160 H13 **Shizong** *var.* Danfeng. Yunnan, SW China 24°53′N 104°E
165 R10 **Shizugawa** Miyagi, Honshū, NE Japan 38°40′N 141°26′E
159 W8 **Shizuishan** *var.* Dawukou. Ningxia, N China 39°04′N 106°22′E
165 T5 **Shizunai** Hokkaidō, NE Japan 42°20′N 142°24′E
165 M14 **Shizuoka** *var.* Sizuoka. Shizuoka, Honshū, S Japan 34°59′N 138°20′E
164 M13 **Shizuoka** *off.* Shizuoka-ken, *var.* Sizuoka. ◆ *prefecture* Honshū, S Japan
Shizuoka-ken *see* Shizuoka
Shklov *see* Shklow
119 N15 **Shklow** *Rus.* Shklov. Mahilyowskaya Voblasts', E Belarus 54°13′N 30°18′E
113 K18 **Shkodër** *var.* Shkodra, *It.* Scutari, *SCr.* Skadar. Shkodër, NW Albania 42°03′N 19°31′E
113 K17 **Shkodër** ◆ *district* NW Albania
Shkodra *see* Shkodër
Shkodrës, Liqeni i *see* Scutari, Lake
113 L20 **Shkumbinit, Lumi i** *var.* Shkumbî, Shkumbin. ≈ C Albania
Shkumbî/Shkumbin *see* Shkumbinit, Lumi i
Shligigh, Cuan *see* Sligo Bay
122 L4 **Shmidta, Ostrov** *island* Severnaya Zemlya, N Russian Federation
183 S10 **Shoalhaven River** ≈ New South Wales, SE Australia
11 W16 **Shoal Lake** Manitoba, S Canada 50°28′N 100°36′W
31 O15 **Shoals** Indiana, N USA 38°40′N 86°47′W
164 I13 **Shōdo-shima** *island* SW Japan

◆ Country
● Country Capital
◇ Dependent Territory
○ Dependent Territory Capital
◆ Administrative Regions
✈ International Airport
▲ Mountain
▲▲ Mountain Range
Volcano
≈ River
◎ Lake
⊠ Reservoir

SHŌKA – SINT EUSTATIUS

Shōka *see* Changhua
122 M5 **Shokal'skogo, Proliv** *strait* N Russian Federation
147 T14 **Shokhdara, Qatorkŭhi** *Rus.* Shakhdarinskiy Khrebet. ▲▲ SE Tajikistan
145 P15 **Sholakkorgan** *var.* Chulakkurgan. Yuzhnyy Kazakhstan, S Kazakhstan 43°45′N 69°10′E
145 N9 **Sholaksay** Kostanay, N Kazakhstan 51°45′N 64°45′E
Sholāpur *see* Solāpur
Sholdaneshty *see* Şoldăneşti
Shonzhy *see* Chundzha
Shoqpar *see* Chokpar
155 G21 **Shoranūr** Kerala, SW India 10°53′N 76°06′E
155 G16 **Shorāpur** Karnātaka, C India 16°34′N 76°48′E
147 O14 **Sho'rchi** *Rus.* Shurchi. Surkhondaryo Viloyati, S Uzbekistan 37°58′N 67°40′E
30 M11 **Shorewood** Illinois, N USA 41°31′N 88°12′W
Shorkazakhly, Solonchak *see* Kazakhlyshor, Solonchak
145 Q9 **Shortandy** Akmola, C Kazakhstan 51°45′N 71°01′E
Shortepa/Shor Tepe *see* Shūr Tappeh
186 J7 **Shortland Island** *var.* Alu. *island* Shortland Islands, NW Solomon Islands
Shosambetsu *see* Shosanbetsu
165 S2 **Shosanbetsu** *var.* Shosambetsu. Hokkaidō, NE Japan 44°31′N 141°47′E
33 O15 **Shoshone** Idaho, NW USA 42°56′N 114°24′W
35 T6 **Shoshone Mountains** ▲▲ Nevada, W USA
33 U12 **Shoshone River** ≈ Wyoming, C USA
83 I19 **Shoshong** Central, SE Botswana 23°02′S 26°31′E
33 V14 **Shoshoni** Wyoming, C USA 43°13′N 108°06′W
Shōshū *see* Sangju
117 S2 **Shostka** Sums'ka Oblast', NE Ukraine 51°52′N 33°30′E
185 C21 **Shotover** ≈ South Island, New Zealand
146 H9 **Shovot** *Rus.* Shavat. Xorazm Viloyati, W Uzbekistan 41°41′N 60°13′E
37 N12 **Show Low** Arizona, SW USA 34°15′N 110°01′W
Show Me State *see* Missouri
125 O4 **Shoyna** Nenetskiy Avtonomnyy Okrug, NW Russian Federation 67°50′N 44°09′E
124 M11 **Shozhma** Arkhangel'skaya Oblast', NW Russian Federation 61°57′N 40°10′E
117 Q7 **Shpola** Cherkas'ka Oblast', N Ukraine 49°00′N 31°27′E
Shqipëria/Shqipërisë, Republika e *see* Albania
22 G5 **Shreveport** Louisiana, S USA 32°32′N 93°45′W
97 K19 **Shrewsbury** *hist.* Scrobesbyrig'. W England, United Kingdom 52°43′N 02°45′W
152 D11 **Shri Mohangarh** *prev.* Sri Mohangorh. Rājasthān, NW India 27°17′N 71°18′E
153 S16 **Shrīrāmpur** *prev.* Serampore, Serampur. West Bengal, NE India 22°44′N 88°20′E
97 K19 **Shropshire** *cultural region* W England, United Kingdom
113 N17 **Shtime** *Serb.* Štimlje. C Kosovo 42°27′N 21°03′E
145 S16 **Shu** *Kaz.* Shū. Zhambyl, SE Kazakhstan 43°34′N 73°41′E
160 G13 **Shuangbai** *var.* Tuodian. Yunnan, SW China 24°45′N 101°38′E
163 W9 **Shuangcheng** Heilongjiang, NE China 45°20′N 126°21′E
Shuangcheng *see* Zherong
160 E14 **Shuangjiang** *var.* Weiyuan. Yunnan, SW China 23°28′N 99°43′E
Shuangjiang *see* Jiangkou
Shuangjiang *see* Tongdao
163 U10 **Shuangliao** *var.* Zhengjiatun. Jilin, NE China 43°31′N 123°32′E
Shuang-liao *see* Liaoyuan
Shuangshipu *see* Fengxian
163 Y7 **Shuangyashan** *var.* Shuang-ya-shan. Heilongjiang, NE China 46°37′N 131°10′E
Shuang-ya-shan *see* Shuangyashan
Shu'aymiah *see* Shu'aymīyah
141 W12 **Shu'aymīyah** *var.* Shu'aymiah. S Oman 17°55′N 55°39′E
144 I10 **Shubarkuduk** *Kaz.* Shubarqudyq. Aktyubinsk, W Kazakhstan 49°09′N 56°31′E
Shubarqudyq *see* Shubarkuduk
145 N12 **Shubar-Tengiz, Ozero** ◎ C Kazakhstan
39 S5 **Shublik Mountains** ▲▲ Alaska, USA
Shubrā al Khaymah *see* Shubrâ el Kheima
121 U13 **Shubrâ el Kheima** *var.* Shubrā al Khaymah. N Egypt 30°06′N 31°15′E
158 E8 **Shufu** *var.* Tuokezhake. Xinjiang Uygur Zizhiqu, NW China 39°18′N 75°43′E
147 S14 **Shughnon, Qatorkŭhi** *Rus.* Shugnanskiy Khrebet. ▲▲ SE Tajikistan
Shugnanskiy Khrebet *see* Shughnon, Qatorkŭhi
161 Q6 **Shu He** ≈ E China
Shuicheng *see* Lupanshui
Shuiding *see* Huocheng
Shuidong *see* Dianbai
Shuiji *see* Laixi
Shū-Ile Taūlary *see* Chu-Iliyskiye Gory
Shuilocheng *see* Zhuanglang
Shuiluo *see* Zhuanglang
149 T10 **Shujāābād** Punjab, E Pakistan 29°53′N 71°23′E
Shū, Kazakhstan *see* Shu
Shū, Kazakhstan/Kyrgyzstan *see* Chu
163 W9 **Shulan** Jilin, NE China 44°28′N 126°57′E
158 E8 **Shule** Xinjiang Uygur Zizhiqu, NW China 39°19′N 76°06′E
Shuleh *see* Shule He
159 Q8 **Shule He** *var.* Shuleh, Sulo. ≈ C China
30 K9 **Shullsburg** Wisconsin, N USA 42°37′N 90°12′W
Shulu *see* Xinji
39 N16 **Shumagin Islands** *island group* Alaska, USA
146 G7 **Shumanay** Qoraqalpog'iston Respublikasi, W Uzbekistan 42°42′N 58°56′E
114 M8 **Shumen** Shumen, NE Bulgaria 43°17′N 26°57′E
114 M8 **Shumen** ◈ *province* NE Bulgaria
127 P4 **Shumerlya** Chuvashskaya Respublika, W Russian Federation 55°31′N 46°24′E
122 G11 **Shumikha** Kurganskaya Oblast', C Russian Federation 55°12′N 63°09′E
118 M12 **Shumilina** *Rus.* Shumilino. Vitsyebskaya Voblasts', NE Belarus 55°18′N 29°37′E
Shumilino *see* Shumilina
123 V11 **Shumshu, Ostrov** *island* SE Russian Federation
116 K5 **Shums'k** Ternopil's'ka Oblast', W Ukraine 50°06′N 26°04′E
Shūnan *see* Tokuyama
39 O7 **Shungnak** Alaska, USA 66°53′N 157°08′W
Shunsen *see* Ch'unch'ŏn
Shuoxian *see* Shuozhou
161 N3 **Shuozhou** *var.* Shuoxian. Shanxi, C China 39°20′N 112°25′E
141 P16 **Shuqrah** *var.* Shaqrā. SW Yemen 13°26′N 45°44′E
Shurab *see* Shŭrob
Shurchi *see* Sho'rchi
147 R11 **Shŭrob** *Rus.* Shurab. NW Tajikistan 40°02′N 70°31′E
143 T10 **Shūr, Rūd-e** ≈ E Iran
149 O2 **Shūr Tappeh** *var.* Shortepa, Shor Tepe. Balkh, N Afghanistan 37°22′N 66°49′E
83 K17 **Shurugwi** *prev.* Selukwe. Midlands, C Zimbabwe 19°40′S 30°00′E
142 L8 **Shūsh** *anc.* Susa, *Bibl.* Shushan. Khūzestān, SW Iran 32°12′N 48°20′E
Shushan *see* Shūsh
142 L9 **Shūshtar** *var.* Shustar, Shushter. Khūzestān, SW Iran 32°03′N 48°51′E
Shushter/Shustar *see* Shūshtar
141 T9 **Shuṭfah, Qalamat** *well* E Saudi Arabia
139 V9 **Shuwayjah, Hawr ash** *var.* Hawr as Suwayqiyah. ◎ E Iraq
124 M16 **Shuya** Ivanovskaya Oblast', W Russian Federation 56°51′N 41°24′E
39 Q14 **Shuyak Island** *island* Alaska, USA
166 M4 **Shwebo** Sagaing, C Myanmar (Burma) 22°35′N 95°42′E
166 L7 **Shwedaung** Bago, W Myanmar (Burma) 18°44′N 95°12′E
166 M7 **Shwegyin** Bago, SW Myanmar (Burma) 17°56′N 96°59′E
167 N4 **Shweli** *Chin.* Longchuan Jiang. ≈ Myanmar (Burma)/China
166 M6 **Shwemyo** Mandalay, C Myanmar (Burma) 20°04′N 96°13′E
Shyghanaq *see* Chiganak
Shyghys Qazagastan Oblysy *see* Vostochnyy Kazakhstan
Shyghys Qongyrat *see* Vostochno-Kounradskiy
Shyghys Qongyrat *see* Shygys Konyrat
145 T12 **Shygys Konyrat** , *Kaz.* Shyghys Qongyrat. Karaganda, C Kazakhstan 47°01′N 75°05′E
119 M19 **Shyichy** *Rus.* Shiichi. Homyel'skaya Voblasts', SE Belarus 52°15′N 29°14′E
145 Q17 **Shymkent** *prev.* Chimkent. Yuzhnyy Kazakhstan, S Kazakhstan 42°19′N 69°36′E
Shyngghyrlaū *see* Chingirlau
152 J5 **Shyok** Jammu and Kashmir, NW India 34°13′N 78°12′E
117 S9 **Shyroke** *Rus.* Shirokoye. Dnipropetrovs'ka Oblast', E Ukraine 47°41′N 33°16′E
117 O9 **Shyryayeve** Odes'ka Oblast', SW Ukraine 47°21′N 30°11′E
117 S5 **Shyshaky** Poltavs'ka Oblast', C Ukraine 49°54′N 34°00′E
119 K17 **Shyshchytsy** *Rus.* Shishchitsy. Minskaya Voblasts', C Belarus 53°13′N 27°33′E
149 Y3 **Siachen Muztāgh** ▲▲ NE Pakistan
Siadehan *see* Tākestān
148 M13 **Siāhān Range** ▲▲ W Pakistan
142 I1 **Sīāh Chashmeh** *var.* Chālderān. Āẕarbāyjān-e Gharbī, N Iran 39°02′N 44°22′E
149 W7 **Siālkot** Punjab, NE Pakistan 32°29′N 74°35′E
186 E7 **Sialum** Morobe, C Papua New Guinea 06°02′S 147°37′E
Siam *see* Thailand
Siam, Gulf of *see* Thailand, Gulf of
Sian *see* Xi'an
Siang *see* Brahmaputra
Siangtan *see* Xiangtan
169 N8 **Siantan, Pulau** *island* Kepulauan Anambas, W Indonesia
54 H11 **Siare, Río** ≈ C Colombia
171 R6 **Siargao Island** *island* S Philippines
186 F72 **Siassi** Umboi Island, C Papua New Guinea 05°34′S 147°50′E
115 D14 **Siátista** Dytikí Makedonía, N Greece 40°16′N 21°34′E
166 K4 **Siatlai** Chin State, W Myanmar (Burma) 22°05′N 93°36′E
171 P6 **Siaton** Negros, C Philippines 09°03′N 123°03′E
171 P6 **Siaton Point** *headland* Negros, C Philippines 09°03′N 123°00′E
118 F11 **Šiauliai** *Ger.* Schaulen. Šiauliai, N Lithuania 55°55′N 23°21′E
118 E11 **Šiauliai** ◈ *province* N Lithuania
171 Q10 **Siau, Pulau** *island* N Indonesia
83 J15 **Siavonga** Southern, SE Zambia 16°33′S 28°42′E
Siazan' *see* Siyäzän
Sibah *see* As Sībah
107 N20 **Sibari** Calabria, S Italy 39°45′N 16°26′E
Sibata *see* Shibata
127 X6 **Sibay** Respublika Bashkortostan, W Russian Federation 52°40′N 58°39′E
93 M19 **Sibbo** *Fin.* Sipoo. Etelä-Suomi, S Finland 60°22′N 25°20′E
112 D13 **Šibenik** *It.* Sebenico. Šibenik-Knin, S Croatia 43°43′N 15°54′E
Sibenik *see* Šibenik-Knin
112 E13 **Šibenik-Knin** *off.* Šibenska Županija, *var.* Sibenik. ◈ *province* S Croatia
Šibenik-Knin *see* Drniš
Šibenska Županija *see* Šibenik-Knin
Siberia *see* Sibir'
Siberoet *see* Siberut, Pulau
168 H12 **Siberut, Pulau** *prev.* Siberoet. *island* Kepulauan Mentawai, W Indonesia
168 I12 **Siberut, Selat** *strait* W Indonesia
149 P11 **Sibi** Baluchistān, SW Pakistan 29°31′N 67°54′E
186 B9 **Sibidiri** Western, SW Papua New Guinea 08°58′S 142°14′E
123 N10 **Sibir'** *var.* Siberia. *physical region* NE Russian Federation
79 F20 **Sibiti** Lékoumou, S Congo 03°41′S 13°20′E
81 G21 **Sibiti** ≈ C Tanzania
116 I12 **Sibiu** *Ger.* Hermannstadt, *Hung.* Nagyszeben. Sibiu, C Romania 45°48′N 24°09′E
116 I11 **Sibiu** ◈ *county* C Romania
29 S11 **Sibley** Iowa, C USA 43°24′N 95°45′W
153 X11 **Sibsāgar** Assam, NE India 26°59′N 94°38′E
169 R9 **Sibu** Sarawak, East Malaysia 02°18′N 111°49′E
42 G2 **Sibun** ≈ E Belize
79 I15 **Sibut** *prev.* Fort-Sibut. Kémo, S Central African Republic 05°44′N 19°07′E
171 P4 **Sibuyan Island** *island* C Philippines
189 U1 **Sibylla Island** *island* N Marshall Islands
11 N16 **Sicamous** British Columbia, SW Canada 50°49′N 118°52′W
Sichelburger Gerbirge *see* Gorjanci
167 N14 **Sichon** *var.* Ban Sichon, Si Chon. Nakhon Si Thammarat, SW Thailand 09°03′N 99°51′E
Si Chon *see* Sichon
160 H9 **Sichuan** *var.* Chuan, Sichuan Sheng, Ssu-ch'uan, Szechuan, Szechwan. ◈ *province* C China
160 I9 **Sichuan Pendi** *basin* C China
Sichuan Sheng *see* Sichuan
103 S16 **Sicie, Cap** *headland* SE France 43°03′N 05°50′E
107 J24 **Sicilia** *Eng.* Sicily; *anc.* Trinacria. ◈ *region* Italy, C Mediterranean Sea
107 M24 **Sicilia** *Eng.* Sicily; *anc.* Trinacria. *island* Italy, C Mediterranean Sea
Sicilian Channel *see* Sicily, Strait of
107 H24 **Sicily, Strait of** *var.* Sicilian Channel. *strait* C Mediterranean Sea
42 K5 **Sico Tinto, Río** *var.* Río Negro. ≈ NE Honduras
57 H16 **Sicuani** Cusco, S Peru 14°21′S 71°13′W
112 J10 **Šid** Vojvodina, NW Serbia 45°07′N 19°13′E
115 A15 **Sidári** Kérkyra, Iónia Nisiá, Greece, C Mediterranean Sea 39°47′N 19°43′E
169 Q11 **Sidas** Borneo, C Indonesia 0°24′N 109°46′E
98 O5 **Siddeburen** Groningen, NE Netherlands 53°15′N 06°52′E
154 D9 **Siddhapur** *prev.* Siddhpur, Sidhpur. Gujarāt, W India 23°57′N 72°28′E
Siddhpur *see* Siddhapur
155 I15 **Siddipet** Andhra Pradesh, C India 18°10′N 78°54′E
77 N14 **Sidéradougou** SW Burkina 10°39′N 04°16′W
107 N23 **Siderno** Calabria, SW Italy 38°18′N 16°19′E
Siders *see* Sierre
154 L9 **Sidhi** Madhya Pradesh, C India 24°24′N 81°54′E
Sidhirókastron *see* Sidirókastro
Sidhpur *see* Siddhapur
75 U7 **Sîdi Barrâni** NW Egypt 31°38′N 25°58′E
74 I6 **Sidi Bel Abbès** *var.* Sidi bel Abbès, Sidi-Bel-Abbès. NW Algeria 35°12′N 00°43′W
74 E7 **Sidi-Bennour** W Morocco 32°39′N 08°28′W
74 M6 **Sidi Bouzid** *var.* Gammouda, Sīdī Bu Zayd. C Tunisia 35°05′N 09°20′E
Sīdī Bu Zayd *see* Sidi Bouzid
74 D8 **Sidi-Ifni** SW Morocco 29°33′N 10°04′W
74 G6 **Sidi-Kacem** *prev.* Petitjean. N Morocco 34°21′N 05°46′W
114 G12 **Sidirókastro** *prev.* Sidhirókastron. Kentrikí Makedonía, NE Greece 41°14′N 23°23′E
194 L12 **Sidley, Mount** ▲ Antarctica 76°39′S 124°48′W
29 S16 **Sidney** Iowa, C USA 40°45′N 95°39′W
33 Y7 **Sidney** Montana, NW USA 47°42′N 104°10′W
28 J15 **Sidney** Nebraska, C USA 41°09′N 102°57′W
18 I11 **Sidney** New York, NE USA 42°18′N 75°21′W
31 R13 **Sidney** Ohio, N USA 40°16′N 84°09′W
23 T2 **Sidney Lanier, Lake** ⊠ Georgia, SE USA
Sidon *see* Saïda
122 J9 **Sidorovsk** Yamalo-Nenetskiy Avtonomnyy Okrug, N Russian Federation 66°34′N 82°12′E
Sidra *see* Surt
Sidra/Sidra, Gulf of *see* Surt, Khalīj, N Libya
Siebenbürgen *see* Transylvania
Sieben Dörfer *see* Săcele
110 O12 **Siedlce** *Ger.* Sedlez, *Rus.* Sesdlets. Mazowieckie, C Poland 52°10′N 22°18′E
101 E16 **Sieg** ≈ W Germany
101 F16 **Siegen** Nordrhein-Westfalen, W Germany 50°53′N 08°02′E
109 X4 **Sieghartskirchen** Niederösterreich, E Austria 48°13′N 16°01′E
110 O11 **Siemiatycze** Podlaskie, NE Poland 52°27′N 22°52′E
167 T11 **Siĕmpang** Stœng Trêng, NE Cambodia 14°07′N 106°24′E
167 R11 **Siĕmréab** *prev.* Siemreap. Siĕmréab, NW Cambodia 13°21′N 103°50′E
Siemreap *see* Siĕmréab
106 G12 **Siena** *Fr.* Sienne; *anc.* Saena Julia. Toscana, C Italy 43°20′N 11°20′E
Sienne *see* Siena
92 K12 **Sieppijärvi** Lappi, NW Finland 67°09′N 23°58′E
110 J13 **Sieradz** Sieradz, C Poland 51°36′N 18°42′E
110 K10 **Sierpc** Mazowieckie, C Poland 52°51′N 19°44′E
24 I9 **Sierra Blanca** Texas, SW USA 31°10′N 105°22′W
37 S14 **Sierra Blanca Peak** ▲ New Mexico, SW USA 33°22′N 105°48′W
35 P5 **Sierra City** California, W USA 39°34′N 120°35′W
63 I16 **Sierra Colorada** Río Negro, S Argentina 40°37′S 67°48′W
63 J16 **Sierra Grande** Río Negro, E Argentina 41°34′S 65°21′W
76 G15 **Sierra Leone** *off.* Republic of Sierra Leone. ◆ *republic* W Africa
64 M13 **Sierra Leone Basin** *undersea feature* E Atlantic Ocean 05°00′N 17°00′W
66 K8 **Sierra Leone Fracture Zone** *tectonic feature* E Atlantic Ocean
Sierra Leone, Republic of *see* Sierra Leone
Sierra Leone Ridge *see* Sierra Leone Rise
64 L13 **Sierra Leone Rise** *var.* Sierra Leone Ridge, Sierra Leone Schwelle. *undersea feature* E Atlantic Ocean 05°30′N 21°00′W
Sierra Leone Schwelle *see* Sierra Leone Rise
40 L7 **Sierra Mojada** Coahuila, NE Mexico 27°13′N 103°42′W
37 N16 **Sierra Vista** Arizona, SW USA 31°33′N 110°18′W
108 D10 **Sierre** *Ger.* Siders. Valais, SW Switzerland 46°18′N 07°33′E
36 L16 **Sierrita Mountains** ▲▲ Arizona, SW USA
Siete Moai *see* Ahu Akivi
76 M15 **Sifié** W Ivory Coast 07°59′N 06°55′W
115 I21 **Sífnos** *anc.* Siphnos. *island* Kykládes, Greece, Aegean Sea
115 I21 **Sífnou, Stenó** *strait* SE Greece
Siga *see* Shiga
103 P16 **Sigean** Aude, S France 43°02′N 02°58′E
Sighet *see* Sighetu Marmaţiei
Sighetul Marmaţiei *see* Sighetu Marmaţiei
116 I8 **Sighetu Marmaţiei** *var.* Sighet, Sighetul Marmaţiei, *Hung.* Máramarossziget. Maramureş, N Romania 47°56′N 23°53′E
116 I11 **Sighişoara** *Ger.* Schässburg, *Hung.* Segesvár. Mureş, C Romania 46°12′N 24°48′E
168 G7 **Sigli** Sumatera, W Indonesia 05°21′N 95°56′E
92 J1 **Siglufjördhur** Nordhurland Vestra, N Iceland 66°09′N 18°56′W
101 H23 **Sigmaringen** Baden-Württemberg, S Germany 48°04′N 09°12′E
101 N20 **Signalberg** ▲ SE Germany 49°30′N 12°34′E
36 I13 **Signal Peak** ▲ Arizona, SW USA 33°20′N 114°03′W
Signan *see* Xi'an
194 H1 **Signy** *UK research station* South Orkney Islands, Antarctica 60°27′S 45°35′W
29 X15 **Sigourney** Iowa, C USA 41°19′N 92°12′W
115 K17 **Sígri, Akrotírio** *headland* Lésvos, E Greece 39°12′N 25°49′E
Sigsbee Deep *see* Mexico Basin
47 N2 **Sigsbee Escarpment** *undersea feature* N Gulf of Mexico 26°00′N 92°30′W
56 C8 **Sigsig** Azuay, S Ecuador 03°04′S 78°50′W
95 O15 **Sigtuna** Stockholm, C Sweden 59°36′N 17°44′E
42 H6 **Siguatepeque** Comayagua, W Honduras 14°39′N 87°48′W
105 P7 **Sigüenza** Castilla-La Mancha, C Spain 41°04′N 02°38′W
105 R4 **Sigües** Aragón, NE Spain 42°39′N 01°00′W
76 K13 **Siguiri** NE Guinea 11°26′N 09°08′W
118 G8 **Sigulda** *Ger.* Segewold. Rīga, C Latvia 57°08′N 24°51′E
Sihanoukville *see* Kâmpóng Saôm
108 G8 **Sihlsee** ◎ NW Switzerland
93 K18 **Siikainen** Länsi-Suomi, SW Finland 61°52′N 21°49′E
93 M16 **Siilinjärvi** Itä-Suomi, C Finland 63°05′N 27°40′E
137 R15 **Siirt** *var.* Sert; *anc.* Tigranocerta. Siirt, SE Turkey 37°56′N 41°56′E
137 R15 **Siirt** *var.* Sert. ◈ *province* SE Turkey
187 N8 **Sikaiana** *var.* Stewart Islands. *island group* W Solomon Islands
Sikandarabad *see* Secunderābād
152 J11 **Sikandra Rao** Uttar Pradesh, N India 27°42′N 78°21′E
10 M11 **Sikanni Chief** British Columbia, W Canada 57°16′N 122°44′W
10 M11 **Sikanni Chief** ≈ British Columbia, W Canada
152 H11 **Sīkar** Rājasthān, N India 27°33′N 75°12′E
76 M13 **Sikasso** Sikasso, S Mali 11°21′N 05°43′W
76 L13 **Sikasso** ◈ *region* SW Mali
167 N3 **Sikaw** Kachin State, C Myanmar (Burma) 23°50′N 97°04′E
83 H14 **Sikelenge** Western, W Zambia 14°51′S 24°13′E
27 Y7 **Sikeston** Missouri, C USA 36°52′N 89°35′W
93 J14 **Sikfors** Norrbotten, N Sweden 65°29′N 21°17′E
123 T14 **Sikhote-Alin', Khrebet** ▲▲ SE Russian Federation
Siking *see* Xi'an
115 J22 **Síkinos** *island* Kykládes, Greece, Aegean Sea
153 S11 **Sikkim** *Tib.* Denjong. ◈ *state* N India
111 I26 **Siklós** Baranya, SW Hungary 45°51′N 18°18′E
Sikoku *see* Shikoku
Sikoku Basin *see* Shikoku Basin
83 G14 **Sikongo** Western, W Zambia 15°03′S 22°07′E
Sikotu Ko *see* Shikotsu-ko
Sikouri/Sikoúrion *see* Sykoúrio
123 P8 **Siktyakh** Respublika Sakha (Yakutiya), NE Russian Federation 69°45′N 124°42′E
118 D12 **Šilalė** Taurage, W Lithuania 55°29′N 22°10′E
106 G5 **Silandro** *Ger.* Schlanders. Trentino-Alto Adige, N Italy 46°39′N 10°55′E
41 N12 **Silao** Guanajuato, C Mexico 20°56′N 101°28′W
Silarius *see* Sele
153 W14 **Silchar** Assam, NE India 24°49′N 92°48′E
108 G9 **Silenen** Uri, C Switzerland 46°49′N 08°39′E
21 T9 **Siler City** North Carolina, SE USA 35°43′N 79°27′W
33 U11 **Silesia** Montana, NW USA 45°32′N 108°52′W
110 F13 **Silesia** *physical region* SW Poland
74 K12 **Silet** S Algeria 22°45′N 04°51′E
145 R8 **Sileti** *var.* Selety. ≈ N Kazakhstan
Siletitengiz *see* Siletiteniz, Ozero
145 R7 **Siletiteniz, Ozero** *Kaz.* Siletitengiz. ◎ N Kazakhstan
172 H16 **Silhouette** *island* Inner Islands, SE Seychelles
136 I17 **Silifke** *anc.* Seleucia. İçel, S Turkey 36°22′N 33°57′E
Siliguri *see* Shiliguri
156 J10 **Siling Co** ◎ W China
Silinhot *see* Xilinhot
192 G14 **Silisili, Mauga** ▲ Savai'i, C Samoa 13°37′S 172°26′W
114 M6 **Silistra** *var.* Silistria; *anc.* Durostorum. Silistra, NE Bulgaria 44°06′N 27°17′E
114 M7 **Silistra** ◈ *province* NE Bulgaria
Silistria *see* Silistra
136 D10 **Silivri** İstanbul, NW Turkey 41°05′N 28°15′E
94 L13 **Siljan** ◎ C Sweden
95 G22 **Silkeborg** Århus, C Denmark 56°10′N 09°34′E
108 M8 **Sill** ≈ W Austria
105 S10 **Silla** País Valenciano, E Spain 39°22′N 00°25′W
62 H3 **Sillajguay, Cordillera** ▲ N Chile 19°45′S 68°39′W
118 K3 **Sillamäe** *Ger.* Sillamäggi. Ida-Virumaa, NE Estonia 59°23′N 27°45′E
Sillamäggi *see* Sillamäe
Sillein *see* Žilina
109 P9 **Sillian** Tirol, W Austria 46°45′N 12°25′E
112 B10 **Šilo** Primorje-Gorski Kotar, NW Croatia 45°09′N 14°39′E
27 R9 **Siloam Springs** Arkansas, C USA 36°11′N 94°32′W
25 X10 **Silsbee** Texas, SW USA 30°21′N 94°10′W
143 W15 **Sīlūp, Rūd-e** ≈ SE Iran
118 C12 **Šilutė** *Ger.* Heydekrug. Klaipėda, W Lithuania 55°20′N 21°30′E
137 Q15 **Silvan** Dıyarbakır, SE Turkey 38°08′N 41°E
108 J10 **Silvaplana** Graubünden, S Switzerland 46°27′N 09°45′E
Silva Porto *see* Kuito
58 M12 **Silva, Recife do** *reef* E Brazil
154 D12 **Silvassa** Dādra and Nagar Haveli, W India 20°13′N 73°03′E
29 X4 **Silver Bay** Minnesota, N USA 47°17′N 91°15′W
37 P15 **Silver City** New Mexico, SW USA 32°47′N 108°16′W
18 D10 **Silver Creek** New York, NE USA 42°32′N 79°10′W
37 N12 **Silver Creek** ≈ Arizona, SW USA
27 P4 **Silver Lake** Kansas, C USA 39°06′N 95°51′W
32 I14 **Silver Lake** Oregon, NW USA 43°07′N 121°04′W
35 T9 **Silver Peak Range** ▲▲ Nevada, W USA
21 W3 **Silver Spring** Maryland, NE USA 39°00′N 77°01′W
Silver State *see* Colorado
Silver State *see* Nevada
37 Q7 **Silverton** Colorado, C USA 37°48′N 107°39′W
18 K16 **Silverton** New Jersey, NE USA 40°00′N 74°09′W
32 G11 **Silverton** Oregon, NW USA 45°00′N 122°46′W
25 N4 **Silverton** Texas, SW USA 34°28′N 101°18′W
104 G14 **Silves** Faro, S Portugal 37°11′N 08°26′W
54 D12 **Silvia** Cauca, SW Colombia 02°37′N 76°24′W
108 J9 **Silvrettagruppe** ▲▲ Austria/Switzerland
Sily-Vajdej *see* Vulcan
108 L7 **Silz** Tirol, W Austria 47°17′N 11°00′E
172 I13 **Sima** Anjouan, SE Comoros 12°11′S 44°18′E
Simabara *see* Shimabara
83 H15 **Simakando** Western, W Zambia 16°43′S 24°46′E
Simane *see* Shimane
119 L20 **Simanichy** *Rus.* Simonichi. Homyel'skaya Voblasts', SE Belarus 51°53′N 28°05′E
160 F14 **Simao** Yunnan, SW China 22°30′N 101°06′E
153 P12 **Simarā** Central, C Nepal 27°14′N 85°00′E
14 I8 **Simard, Lac** ◎ Québec, SE Canada
136 D13 **Simav** Kütahya, W Turkey 39°05′N 28°59′E
136 D13 **Simav Çayı** ≈ NW Turkey
79 L18 **Simba** Orientale, N Dem. Rep. Congo 0°46′N 22°54′E
186 C7 **Simbai** Madang, N Papua New Guinea 05°12′S 144°33′E
Simbirsk *see* Ul'yanovsk
14 F17 **Simcoe** Ontario, S Canada 42°50′N 80°19′W
14 H14 **Simcoe, Lake** ◎ Ontario, S Canada
80 J11 **Sīmēn** ▲▲ N Ethiopia
114 K11 **Simeonovgrad** *prev.* Maritsa. Khaskovo, S Bulgaria 42°03′N 25°36′E
116 G11 **Simeria** *Ger.* Pischk, *Hung.* Piski. Hunedoara, W Romania 45°51′N 23°00′E
107 L24 **Simeto** ≈ Sicilia, Italy, C Mediterranean Sea
168 G9 **Simeulue, Pulau** *island* NW Indonesia
117 T13 **Simferopol'** Respublika Krym, S Ukraine 44°55′N 33°06′E
117 T13 **Simferopol'** ✈ Respublika Krym, S Ukraine 44°55′N 34°04′E
Simi *see* Sými
152 M9 **Simikot** Far Western, NW Nepal 30°02′N 81°49′E
54 F7 **Simití** Bolívar, N Colombia 07°57′N 73°57′W
114 G11 **Simitla** Blagoevgrad, SW Bulgaria 41°57′N 23°06′E
35 S15 **Simi Valley** California, W USA 34°16′N 118°47′W
Simizu *see* Shimizu
Simla *see* Shimla
Şimlăul Silvaniei/Şimleul Silvaniei *see* Şimleu Silvaniei
116 G9 **Şimleu Silvaniei** *Hung.* Szilágysomlyó; *prev.* Şimlăul Silvaniei, Şimleul Silvaniei. Sălaj, NW Romania 47°12′N 22°49′E
Simmer *see* Simmerbach
101 E19 **Simmerbach** *var.* Simmer. ≈ W Germany
101 F18 **Simmern** Rheinland-Pfalz, W Germany 50°00′N 07°30′E
22 I7 **Simmesport** Louisiana, S USA 30°58′N 91°48′W
119 F14 **Simnas** Alytus, S Lithuania 54°23′N 23°40′E
92 L13 **Simo** Lappi, NW Finland 65°40′N 25°04′E
Simoda *see* Shimoda
Simodate *see* Shimodate
92 M13 **Simojärvi** ◎ N Finland
92 L13 **Simojoki** ≈ NW Finland
41 U15 **Simojovel** *var.* Simojovel de Allende. Chiapas, SE Mexico 17°14′N 92°40′W
Simojovel de Allende *see* Simojovel
56 B7 **Simon Bolivar** *var.* Guayaquil. ✈ (Quayaquil) Guayas, W Ecuador 02°16′S 79°54′W
54 L5 **Simon Bolívar** ✈ (Caracas) Vargas, N Venezuela 10°33′N 66°54′W
Simonichi *see* Simanichy
14 M12 **Simon, Lac** ◎ Québec, SE Canada
Simonoseki *see* Shimonoseki
Šimonovany *see* Partizánske
Simonstad *see* Simon's Town
83 E26 **Simon's Town** *var.* Simonstad. Western Cape, SW South Africa 34°12′S 18°26′E
Simony *see* Partizánske
Simpeln *see* Simplon
99 M18 **Simpelveld** Limburg, SE Netherlands 50°50′N 05°59′E
108 E11 **Simplon** *var.* Simpeln. Valais, SW Switzerland 46°13′N 08°01′E
108 E11 **Simplon Pass** *pass* S Switzerland
106 C6 **Simplon Tunnel** *tunnel* Italy/Switzerland
Simpson *see* Fort Simpson
182 G1 **Simpson Desert** *desert* Northern Territory/South Australia
10 J9 **Simpson Peak** ▲ British Columbia, W Canada 59°43′N 131°29′W
9 N7 **Simpson Peninsula** *peninsula* Nunavut, NE Canada
21 P11 **Simpsonville** South Carolina, SE USA 34°44′N 82°15′W
95 L23 **Simrishamn** Skåne, S Sweden 55°34′N 14°20′E
123 U13 **Simushir, Ostrov** *island* Kuril'skiye Ostrova, SE Russian Federation
168 G9 **Sinabang** Sumatera, W Indonesia 02°27′N 96°24′E
81 N15 **Sina Dhaqa** Galguduud, C Somalia 05°21′N 46°21′E
75 X8 **Sinai** *var.* Sinai Peninsula, *Ar.* Shibh Jazirat Sīnā', Sīnā. *physical region* NE Egypt
116 J12 **Sinaia** Prahova, SE Romania 45°20′N 25°33′E
188 B16 **Sinajana** C Guam 13°28′N 144°45′E
40 H8 **Sinaloa** ◈ *state* C Mexico
54 H4 **Sinamaica** Zulia, NW Venezuela 11°06′N 71°52′W
163 X14 **Sinan-ni** SE North Korea 38°37′N 127°43′E
Sīnā/Sinai Peninsula *see* Sinai
Sīnāwan *see* Sīnāwin
75 N8 **Sīnāwin** *var.* Sīnāwan. NW Libya 31°00′N 10°37′E
83 J16 **Sinazongwe** Southern, S Zambia 17°14′S 27°27′E
166 L6 **Sinbaungwe** Magway, W Myanmar (Burma) 19°44′N 95°10′E
166 L5 **Sinbyugyun** Magway, W Myanmar (Burma) 20°38′N 94°40′E
54 E6 **Since** Sucre, NW Colombia 09°14′N 75°08′W
54 E6 **Sincelejo** Sucre, NW Colombia 09°17′N 75°23′W
166 J5 **Sinchaingbyin** *var.* Zullapara. Rakhine State, W Myanmar (Burma) 20°51′N 92°23′E
23 U4 **Sinclair, Lake** ⊠ Georgia, SE USA
10 M14 **Sinclair Mills** British Columbia, SW Canada 54°03′N 121°37′W
149 Q14 **Sind** *var.* Sindh. ◈ *province* SE Pakistan
154 I8 **Sind** ≈ N India
95 H19 **Sindal** Nordjylland, N Denmark 57°29′N 10°13′E
171 P7 **Sindañgan** Mindanao, S Philippines 08°09′N 122°59′E
79 D19 **Sindara** Ngounié, W Gabon 01°07′S 10°41′E
152 E13 **Sindari** *prev.* Sindri. Rājasthān, N India 25°32′N 71°58′E
114 N8 **Sindel** Varna, E Bulgaria 43°07′N 27°35′E
101 H22 **Sindelfingen** Baden-Württemberg, SW Germany 48°43′N 09°E
155 G16 **Sindgi** Karnātaka, C India 17°01′N 76°22′E
Sindh *see* Sind
118 G5 **Sindi** *Ger.* Zintenhof. Pärnumaa, SW Estonia 58°28′N 24°41′E
136 C13 **Sındırgı** Balıkesir, W Turkey 39°13′N 28°10′E
77 N14 **Sindou** SW Burkina 10°35′N 05°04′W
Sindri *see* Sindari
149 T9 **Sind Sāgar Doāb** *desert* E Pakistan
126 M11 **Sinegorskiy** Rostovskaya Oblast', SW Russian Federation 48°01′N 40°52′E
123 S9 **Sinegor'ye** Magadanskaya Oblast', E Russian Federation 62°04′N 150°33′E
114 O12 **Sinekli** İstanbul, NW Turkey 41°13′N 28°13′E
104 F12 **Sines** Setúbal, S Portugal 37°58′N 08°52′W
104 F12 **Sines, Cabo de** *headland* S Portugal 37°57′N 08°55′W
92 L12 **Sinettä** Lappi, NW Finland 66°39′N 25°25′E
186 H6 **Sinewit, Mount** ▲ New Britain, C Papua New Guinea 04°42′S 151°58′E
80 G11 **Singa** *var.* Sinja, Sinjah. Sinnar, E Sudan 13°11′N 33°55′E
78 J12 **Singako** Moyen-Chari, S Chad 09°52′N 19°31′E
Singan *see* Xi'an
168 K10 **Singapore** ● (Singapore) S Singapore 01°17′N 103°48′E
168 L10 **Singapore** *off.* Republic of Singapore. ◆ *republic* SE Asia
Singapore, Republic of *see* Singapore
169 U17 **Singaraja** Bali, C Indonesia 08°06′S 115°04′E
167 O10 **Sing Buri** *var.* Singhaburi. Sing Buri, C Thailand 14°56′N 100°21′E
101 H24 **Singen** Baden-Württemberg, S Germany 47°46′N 08°50′E
Sîngeorgiu de Pădure *see* Sângeorgiu de Pădure
Sîngeorz-Băi/Singeroz Băi *see* Sângeorz-Băi
116 M9 **Sîngerei** *var.* Sângerei; *prev.* Lazovsk. N Moldova 47°38′N 28°08′E
Singhaburi *see* Sing Buri
81 H21 **Singida** Singida, C Tanzania 04°45′S 34°48′E
81 G22 **Singida** ◈ *region* C Tanzania
Singidunum *see* Beograd
166 M2 **Singkaling Hkamti** Sagaing, N Myanmar (Burma) 26°00′N 95°43′E
171 N14 **Singkang** Sulawesi, C Indonesia 04°09′S 119°58′E
168 J11 **Singkarak, Danau** ◎ Sumatera, W Indonesia
169 N10 **Singkawang** Borneo, C Indonesia 0°57′N 108°57′E
168 M11 **Singkep, Pulau** *island* Kepulauan Lingga, W Indonesia
168 H9 **Singkilbaru** Sumatera, W Indonesia 02°18′N 97°47′E
183 T7 **Singleton** New South Wales, SE Australia 32°38′S 151°00′E
Singora *see* Songkhla
Singû *see* Shingū
Sining *see* Xining
107 D17 **Siniscola** Sardegna, Italy, C Mediterranean Sea 40°34′N 09°42′E
113 F14 **Sinj** Split-Dalmacija, SE Croatia 43°41′N 16°37′E
Sinjajevina *see* Sinjavina
139 P3 **Sinjār** Nīnawýa, NW Iraq 36°20′N 41°51′E
139 P2 **Sinjār, Jabal** ▲▲ N Iraq
Sinja/Sinjah *see* Singa
113 K15 **Sinjavina** *var.* Sinjajevina. ▲▲ C Montenegro
80 I7 **Sinkat** Red Sea, NE Sudan 18°52′N 36°51′E
Sinkiang/Sinkiang Uighur Autonomous Region *see* Xinjiang Uygur Zizhiqu
Sînmartin *see* Târnăveni
163 V13 **Sinmi-do** *island* NW North Korea
101 I18 **Sinn** ≈ C Germany
Sinnamarie *see* Sinnamary
55 Y9 **Sinnamary** *var.* Sinnamarie. N French Guiana 05°23′N 53°00′W
80 G11 **Sinnar** ◈ *state* E Sudan
Sinneh *see* Sanandaj
18 E13 **Sinnemahoning Creek** ≈ Pennsylvania, NE USA
Sînnicolau Mare *see* Sânnicolau Mare
Sinoe, Lacul *see* Sinoie, Lacul
Sinoia *see* Chinhoyi
117 N14 **Sinoie, Lacul** *prev.* Lacul Sinoe. *lagoon* SE Romania
59 H16 **Sinop** Mato Grosso, W Brazil 11°38′S 55°27′W
136 K10 **Sinop** *anc.* Sinope. Sinop, N Turkey 42°02′N 35°09′E
136 J10 **Sinop** ◈ *province* N Turkey
136 K10 **Sinop Burnu** *headland* N Turkey 42°02′N 35°12′E
Sinope *see* Sinop
Sino/Sinoe *see* Greenville
163 Y12 **Sinp'o** E North Korea 40°01′N 128°10′E
101 H20 **Sinsheim** Baden-Württemberg, SW Germany 49°15′N 08°53′E
Sîntana *see* Sântana
169 R11 **Sintang** Borneo, C Indonesia 0°03′N 111°31′E
99 F14 **Sint Annaland** Zeeland, SW Netherlands 51°36′N 04°07′E
98 L5 **Sint Annaparochie** Friesland, N Netherlands 53°20′N 05°45′E
45 V9 **Sint Eustatius** *Eng.* Saint Eustatius. *island* N Netherlands Antilles

◆ Country
● Country Capital
◇ Dependent Territory
○ Dependent Territory Capital
◈ Administrative Regions
✈ International Airport
▲ Mountain
▲▲ Mountain Range
⛰ Volcano
≈ River
◎ Lake
⊠ Reservoir

SINT-GENESIUS-RODE – SNÆKOLLUR

99 G19 **Sint-Genesius-Rode** *Fr.* Rhode-Saint-Genèse. Vlaams Brabant, C Belgium *50°45´N 04°21´E*
99 F16 **Sint-Gillis-Waas** Oost-Vlaanderen, N Belgium *51°14´N 04°08´E*
99 H17 **Sint-Katelijne-Waver** Antwerpen, C Belgium *51°05´N 04°31´E*
99 E18 **Sint-Lievens-Houtem** Oost-Vlaanderen, NW Belgium *50°55´N 03°52´E*
45 V9 **Sint Maarten** *Eng.* Saint Martin. *island* N Netherlands Antilles
99 F14 **Sint Maartensdijk** Zeeland, SW Netherlands *51°33´N 04°05´E*
99 L19 **Sint-Martens-Voeren** *Fr.* Fouron-Saint-Martin. Limburg, NE Belgium *50°46´N 05°49´E*
99 J14 **Sint-Michielsgestel** Noord-Brabant, S Netherlands *51°38´N 05°21´E*
Sîn-Miclăuş *see* Gheorgheni
45 O16 **Sint Nicholaas** S Aruba *12°25´N 69°52´W*
99 F16 **Sint-Niklaas** *Fr.* Saint-Nicolas. Oost-Vlaanderen, N Belgium *51°10´N 04°09´E*
99 K14 **Sint-Oedenrode** Noord-Brabant, S Netherlands *51°34´N 05°28´E*
25 T14 **Sinton** Texas, SW USA *28°02´N 97°33´W*
99 G14 **Sint Philipsland** Zeeland, SW Netherlands *51°37´N 04°11´E*
99 G19 **Sint-Pieters-Leeuw** Vlaams Brabant, C Belgium *50°47´N 04°16´E*
104 E11 **Sintra** *prev.* Cintra. Lisboa, W Portugal *38°48´N 09°22´W*
99 J18 **Sint-Truiden** *Fr.* Saint-Trond. Limburg, NE Belgium *50°48´N 05°13´E*
99 H14 **Sint Willebrord** Noord-Brabant, S Netherlands *51°33´N 04°35´E*
163 V13 **Sinŭiju** W North Korea *40°08´N 124°33´E*
80 P13 **Sinujiif** Nugaal, NE Somalia *08°33´N 49°05´E*
Sinus Aelaniticus *see* Aqaba, Gulf of
Sinus Gallicus *see* Lion, Golfe du
Sinyang *see* Xinyang
Sinyavka *see* Sinyawka
119 I18 **Sinyawka** *Rus.* Sinyavka. Minskaya Voblasts', SW Belarus *52°57´N 26°29´E*
Sinying *see* Hsinying
Sinyukha *see* Synyukha
Sinzyô *see* Shinjō
111 I24 **Sió** ≈ W Hungary
171 O7 **Siocon** Mindanao, S Philippines *07°37´N 122°09´E*
111 I24 **Siófok** Somogy, Hungary *46°54´N 18°03´E*
Siogama *see* Shiogama
83 G15 **Sioma** Western, SW Zambia *16°39´S 23°36´E*
108 D11 **Sion** *Ger.* Sitten; *anc.* Sedunum. Valais, SW Switzerland *46°15´N 07°23´E*
103 O11 **Sioule** ≈ C France
29 S12 **Sioux Center** Iowa, C USA *43°04´N 96°10´W*
29 R13 **Sioux City** Iowa, C USA *42°30´N 96°24´W*
29 R11 **Sioux Falls** South Dakota, N USA *43°33´N 96°45´W*
12 B11 **Sioux Lookout** Ontario, S Canada *49°27´N 94°06´W*
29 T12 **Sioux Rapids** Iowa, C USA *42°53´N 95°09´W*
Sioux State *see* North Dakota
Sioziri *see* Shiojiri
171 P6 **Sipalay** Negros, C Philippines *09°46´N 122°25´E*
55 V11 **Sipaliwini** ◈ *district* S Suriname
45 U15 **Siparia** Trinidad, Trinidad and Tobago *10°08´N 61°31´W*
Siphnos *see* Sífnos
163 V11 **Siping** *var.* Ssu-p'ing, Szeping; *prev.* Ssu-p'ing-chieh. Jilin, NE China *43°09´N 124°22´E*
11 X12 **Sipiwesk** Manitoba, C Canada *55°28´N 97°16´W*
11 W13 **Sipiwesk Lake** ◎ Manitoba, C Canada
195 O11 **Siple Coast** *physical region* Antarctica
194 K12 **Siple Island** *island* Antarctica
194 K13 **Siple, Mount** ▲ Siple Island, Antarctica *73°25´S 126°24´W*
Sipoo *see* Sibbo
112 G12 **Šipovo** Republika Srpska, W Bosnia and Herzegovina *44°16´N 17°05´E*
23 O4 **Sipsey River** ≈ Alabama, S USA
168 I13 **Sipura, Pulau** *island* W Indonesia
0 G16 **Siqueiros Fracture Zone** *tectonic feature* E Pacific Ocean
42 L10 **Siquia, Río** ≈ SE Nicaragua
43 N13 **Siquirres** Limón, E Costa Rica *10°05´N 83°30´W*
54 J5 **Siquisique** Lara, N Venezuela *10°36´N 69°45´W*
155 G19 **Sīra** Karnātaka, W India *13°46´N 76°54´E*
95 D16 **Sira** ≈ S Norway
167 P12 **Siracha** *var.* Ban Si Racha, Si Racha. Chon Buri, S Thailand *13°10´N 100°57´E*
Si Racha *see* Siracha
107 L25 **Siracusa** *Eng.* Syracuse. Sicilia, Italy, C Mediterranean Sea *37°04´N 15°17´E*
153 T14 **Sirajganj** *var.* Shirajganj Ghat. Rajshahi, C Bangladesh *24°27´N 89°42´E*
Sirakawa *see* Shirakawa
11 N14 **Sir Alexander, Mount** ▲ British Columbia, W Canada *54°00´N 120°33´W*
137 O12 **Şiran** Gümüşhane, NE Turkey *40°12´N 39°07´E*
77 Q12 **Sirba** ≈ E Burkina
143 O17 **Şīr Banī Yās** *island* W United Arab Emirates
95 D17 **Sirdalsvatnet** ◎ S Norway
Sir Darya/Sirdaryo *see* Syr Darya
147 P10 **Sirdaryo** Sirdaryo Viloyati, E Uzbekistan *40°46´N 68°34´E*
147 O11 **Sirdaryo Viloyati** *Rus.* Syrdar'inskaya Oblast'. ◈ *province* E Uzbekistan
Sir Donald Sangster International Airport *see* Sangster
181 S3 **Sir Edward Pellew Group** *island group* Northern Territory, NE Australia
116 K8 **Siret** *Ger.* Sereth, *Hung.* Szeret. Suceava, N Romania *47°55´N 26°05´E*
116 K8 **Siret** *var.* Siretul, *Ger.* Sereth, *Rus.* Seret. ≈ Romania/Ukraine
Siretul *see* Siret
140 K3 **Sirḩān, Wādī as** *dry watercourse* Jordan/Saudi Arabia
152 I8 **Sirhind** Punjab, N India *30°39´N 76°28´E*
116 F11 **Şiria** *Ger.* Schiria. Arad, W Romania *46°16´N 21°38´E*
Siria *see* Syria
143 S14 **Sīrīk** Hormozgān, SE Iran *26°32´N 57°07´E*
167 P8 **Sirikit Reservoir** ◎ N Thailand
58 K12 **Sirituba, Ilha** *island* NE Brazil
143 R11 **Sīrjān** *prev.* Sa'īdābād. Kermān, S Iran *29°29´N 55°39´E*
182 H9 **Sir Joseph Banks Group** *island group* South Australia
92 K11 **Sirkka** Lappi, N Finland *67°49´N 24°48´E*
Sirna *see* Sýrna
137 R16 **Şırnak** Şırnak, SE Turkey *37°33´N 42°27´E*
137 S16 **Şırnak** ◈ *province* SE Turkey
152 E14 **Sirohi** Rājasthān, N India *25°53´N 72°58´E*
Siroisi *see* Shiroishi
155 J14 **Sironcha** Mahārāshtra, C India *18°51´N 80°03´E*
Sirone *see* Shirone
Síros *see* Sýros
Sirotino *see* Sirotsina
118 M12 **Sirotsina** *Rus.* Sirotino. Vitsyebskaya Voblasts', N Belarus *55°23´N 29°37´E*
152 H9 **Sirsa** Haryāna, NW India *29°32´N 75°04´E*
173 Y17 **Sir Seewoosagur Ramgoolam** ✈ (port Louis) SE Mauritius
155 E18 **Sirsi** Karnātaka, W India *14°46´N 74°49´E*
146 K12 **Şirşütür Gumy** *var.* Shirshütür, *Rus.* Peski Shirshyutyur. *desert* E Turkmenistan
Sirte *see* Surt
182 A2 **Sir Thomas, Mount** ▲ South Australia *27°09´S 129°49´E*
Sirti, Gulf of *see* Surt, Khalīj
142 J5 **Sīrvān, Rūdkhāneh-ye** *var.* Nahr Diyālá, Sirwan. ≈ Iran/Iraq *see also* Diyālá, Nahr
Sīrvān, Rudkhaneh-ye *see* Diyālá, Sirwan Nahr
118 H13 **Širvintos** Vilnius, SE Lithuania *55°01´N 24°58´E*
Sīrwān *see* Diyālá, Nahr/Sīrvān, Rudkhaneh-ye
11 N15 **Sir Wilfrid Laurier, Mount** ▲ British Columbia, SW Canada *52°45´N 119°51´W*
14 M10 **Sir-Wilfrid, Mont** ▲ Québec, SE Canada *46°57´N 75°33´W*
Sisačko-Moslavačka Županija *see* Sisak-Moslavina
112 E9 **Sisak** *var.* Siscia, *Ger.* Sissek, *Hung.* Sziszek; *anc.* Segestica. Sisak-Moslavina, C Croatia *45°28´N 16°21´E*
167 R10 **Si Sa Ket** *var.* Sisaket, Sri Saket. Si Sa Ket, E Thailand *15°08´N 104°18´E*
Sisaket *see* Si Sa Ket
112 E9 **Sisak-Moslavina** *off.* Sisačko-Moslavačka Županija. ◈ *province* C Croatia
167 O8 **Si Satchanala** Sukhothai, NW Thailand
Siscia *see* Sisak
83 G22 **Sishen** Northern Cape, NW South Africa *27°47´S 22°59´E*
137 V13 **Sisian** SE Armenia *39°31´N 46°03´E*
197 N13 **Sisimiut** *var.* Holsteinborg, Holsteinsborg, Holstenborg, Holstensborg. Kitaa, S Greenland *67°07´N 53°42´W*
30 M1 **Siskiwit Bay** *lake bay* Michigan, N USA
34 L1 **Siskiyou Mountains** ▲▲ California/Oregon, W USA
167 Q11 **Sisŏphŏn** Bătdâmbâng, NW Cambodia *13°37´N 102°58´E*
108 E7 **Sissach** Basel-Land, NW Switzerland *47°28´N 07°48´E*
186 B5 **Sissano** Sandaun, NW Papua New Guinea *03°02´S 142°01´E*
Sissek *see* Sisak
29 R7 **Sisseton** South Dakota, N USA *45°39´N 97°03´W*
143 W9 **Sīstān, Daryācheh-ye** *var.* Daryācheh-ye Hāmūn, Hāmūn-e Şāberī. ◎ Afghanistan/Iran *see also* Şāberī, Hāmūn-e
Sīstān, Daryācheh-ye *see* Şāberī, Hāmūn-e
143 V12 **Sīstān va Balūchestān** *off.* Ostān-e Sīstān va Balūchestān, *var.* Balūchestān va Sīstān. ◈ *province* SE Iran
Sīstān va Balūchestān, Ostān-e *see* Sīstān va Balūchestān
103 T14 **Sisteron** Alpes-de-Haute-Provence, SE France *44°12´N 05°55´E*
32 H13 **Sisters** Oregon, NW USA *44°17´N 121°33´W*
65 G15 **Sisters Peak** ▲ N Ascension Island *07°56´S 14°23´W*
21 R3 **Sistersville** West Virginia, NE USA *39°33´N 81°00´W*
Sistova *see* Svishtov
Sitakund *see* Sitakunda
153 V16 **Sitakunda** *var.* Sitakund. Chittagong, SE Bangladesh *22°35´N 91°40´E*
153 P12 **Sītāmarhi** Bihār, N India *26°36´N 85°30´E*
152 L11 **Sītāpur** Uttar Pradesh, N India *27°33´N 80°40´E*
Sitaş Cristuru *see* Cristuru Secuiesc
115 L25 **Siteía** *var.* Sitía. Kríti, Greece, E Mediterranean Sea *35°13´N 26°06´E*
105 V6 **Sitges** Cataluña, NE Spain *41°14´N 01°49´E*
115 H15 **Sithoniá** *peninsula* NE Greece
Sitía *see* Siteía
54 F4 **Sitionuevo** Magdalena, N Colombia *10°46´N 74°43´W*
39 X13 **Sitka** Baranof Island, Alaska, USA *57°03´N 135°19´W*
39 Q15 **Sitkinak Island** *island* Trinity Islands, Alaska, USA
Sittang *see* Sittoung
99 L17 **Sittard** Limburg, SE Netherlands *51°N 05°52´E*
Sitten *see* Sion
108 H7 **Sitter** ≈ NW Switzerland
109 U10 **Sittersdorf** Kärnten, S Austria *46°31´N 14°34´E*
166 M7 **Sittoung** *var.* Sittang. ≈ S Myanmar (Burma)
166 K6 **Sittwe** *var.* Akyab. Rakhine State, W Myanmar (Burma) *22°09´N 92°51´E*
42 L8 **Siuna** Región Autónoma Atlántico Norte, NE Nicaragua *13°44´N 84°46´W*
153 R15 **Siuri** West Bengal, NE India *23°54´N 87°32´E*
Siut *see* Asyūţ
155 I23 **Sivaganga** Tamil Nādu, SE India *09°59´N 78°30´E*
123 Q13 **Sivaki** Amurskaya Oblast', SE Russian Federation *52°39´N 126°43´E*
136 M13 **Sivas** *anc.* Sebastia, Sebaste. Sivas, C Turkey *39°44´N 37°01´E*
136 M13 **Sivas** ◈ *province* C Turkey
137 O15 **Siverek** Şanlıurfa, S Turkey *37°46´N 39°19´E*
117 X6 **Sivers'k** Donets'ka Oblast', E Ukraine *48°52´N 38°07´E*
124 G13 **Siverskiy** Leningradskaya Oblast', NW Russian Federation *59°21´N 30°01´E*
117 X6 **Sivers'kyy Donets'** *Rus.* Severskiy Donets. ≈ Russian Federation/Ukraine *see also* Severskiy Donets
Sivers'kyy Donets' *see* Severskiy Donets
125 W5 **Sivomaskinskiy** Respublika Komi, NW Russian Federation *66°42´N 62°33´E*
136 G13 **Sivrihisar** Eskişehir, W Turkey *39°29´N 31°32´E*
99 F22 **Sivry** Hainaut, S Belgium *50°10´N 04°11´E*
123 V9 **Sivuchiy, Mys** *headland* E Russian Federation *56°45´N 163°13´E*
Siwa *see* Sīwah
75 U9 **Sīwah** *var.* Siwa. NW Egypt *29°11´N 25°32´E*
152 J9 **Siwalik Range** *var.* Shiwalik Range. ▲▲ India/Nepal
153 O13 **Siwān** Bihār, N India *26°14´N 84°21´E*
43 O14 **Sixaola, Río** ≈ Costa Rica/Panama
Six Counties, The *see* Northern Ireland
103 T16 **Six-Fours-les-Plages** Var, SE France *43°05´N 05°50´E*
161 Q7 **Sixian** *var.* Si Xian. Anhui, E China *33°29´N 117°53´E*
Si Xian *see* Sixian
22 J9 **Six Mile Lake** ◎ Louisiana, S USA
139 V3 **Siyāh Gūz** As Sulaymānīyah, E Iraq *35°49´N 45°45´E*
155 L25 **Siyambalanduwa** Uva Province, SE Sri Lanka *06°54´N 81°32´E*
137 Y10 **Siyäzän** *Rus.* Siazan'. NE Azerbaijan *41°05´N 49°05´E*
Sizebolu *see* Sozopol
Sizuoka *see* Shizuoka
95 I24 **Sjælland** *Eng.* Zealand, *Ger.* Seeland. *island* E Denmark
Sjar *see* Sääre
113 L15 **Sjenica** *Turk.* Seniça. Serbia, SW Serbia *43°16´N 20°01´E*
94 G11 **Sjoa** ≈ S Norway
95 K23 **Sjöbo** Skåne, S Sweden *55°37´N 13°45´E*
94 E9 **Sjøholt** Møre og Romsdal, S Norway *62°29´N 06°50´E*
92 O1 **Sjuøyane** *island group* N Svalbard
Skadar *see* Shkodër
Skadarsko Jezero *see* Scutari, Lake
117 R11 **Skadovs'k** Khersons'ka Oblast', S Ukraine *46°07´N 32°53´E*
95 I24 **Skælskør** Vestsjælland, E Denmark *55°16´N 11°18´E*
92 I2 **Skagaströnd** *prev.* Höfdhakaupstadhur. Nordhurland Vestra, N Iceland *65°49´N 20°18´W*
95 H19 **Skagen** Nordjylland, N Denmark *57°44´N 10°37´E*
Skagerak *see* Skagerrak
95 L16 **Skagern** ◎ C Sweden
197 T17 **Skagerrak** *var.* Skagerak. *channel* N Europe
94 G12 **Skaget** ▲ S Norway *61°19´N 09°07´E*
32 H7 **Skagit River** ≈ Washington, NW USA
39 W12 **Skagway** Alaska, USA *59°27´N 135°18´W*
92 K8 **Skaidi** Finnmark, N Norway *70°26´N 24°31´E*
115 F21 **Skála** Pelopónnisos, S Greece *36°51´N 22°39´E*
116 K6 **Skalat** *Pol.* Skałat. Ternopil's'ka Oblast', W Ukraine *49°27´N 25°59´E*
95 J22 **Skälderviken** *inlet* Denmark/Sweden
92 I12 **Skalka** ◎ N Sweden
114 I12 **Skalotí** Anatolikí Makedonía kai Thráki, NE Greece *41°24´N 24°16´E*
95 G22 **Skanderborg** Århus, C Denmark *56°02´N 09°57´E*
95 K22 **Skåne** *prev. Eng.* Scania. ◈ *county* S Sweden
75 N6 **Skanès** ✈ (Sousse) E Tunisia *35°36´N 10°56´E*
95 C15 **Skånevik** Hordaland, S Norway *59°43´N 06°35´E*
95 M18 **Skänninge** Östergötland, S Sweden *58°24´N 15°05´E*
95 J23 **Skanör med Falsterbo** Skåne, S Sweden *55°24´N 12°48´E*
115 H17 **Skantzoúra** *island* Vóreies Sporádes, Greece, Aegean Sea
95 K18 **Skara** Västra Götaland, S Sweden *58°23´N 13°25´E*
95 M17 **Skärblacka** Östergötland, S Sweden *58°34´N 15°54´E*
152 I5 **Skārdu** Jammu and Kashmīr, India *35°18´N 75°44´E*
95 I18 **Skärhamn** Västra Götaland, S Sweden *57°59´N 11°33´E*
95 I14 **Skarnes** Hedmark, S Norway *60°14´N 11°41´E*
119 M21 **Skarodnaye** *Rus.* Skorodnoye. Homyel'skaya Voblasts', SE Belarus *51°38´N 28°50´E*
110 I8 **Skarszewy** *Ger.* Schöneck. Pomorskie, NW Poland *54°04´N 18°25´E*
111 M14 **Skarżysko-Kamienna** Świętokrzyskie, C Poland *51°07´N 20°52´E*
95 K16 **Skattkärr** Värmland, C Sweden *59°25´N 13°42´E*
118 D12 **Skaudvilė** Tauragė, SW Lithuania *55°25´N 22°33´E*
92 J12 **Skaulo** *Lapp.* Sávdijári. Norrbotten, N Sweden *67°21´N 21°03´E*
111 K17 **Skawina** Małopolskie, S Poland *49°59´N 19°49´E*
10 K12 **Skeena** ≈ British Columbia, SW Canada
10 J11 **Skeena Mountains** ▲▲ British Columbia, W Canada
97 O18 **Skegness** E England, United Kingdom *53°10´N 00°21´E*
92 J4 **Skeidharársandur** *coast* S Iceland
93 J15 **Skellefteå** Västerbotten, N Sweden *64°45´N 20°58´E*
93 I14 **Skellefteälven** ≈ N Sweden
93 J15 **Skelleftehamn** Västerbotten, N Sweden *64°41´N 21°13´E*
25 O2 **Skellytown** Texas, SW USA *35°34´N 101°10´W*
95 J19 **Skene** Västra Götaland, S Sweden *57°30´N 12°34´E*
97 G17 **Skerries** *Ir.* Na Sceirí. Dublin, E Ireland *53°35´N 06°07´W*
95 H15 **Ski** Akershus, S Norway *59°43´N 10°50´E*
115 G17 **Skíathos** Skíathos, Vóreies Sporádes, Greece, Aegean Sea *39°10´N 23°30´E*
115 G17 **Skíathos** *island* Vóreies Sporádes, Greece, Aegean Sea
27 P9 **Skiatook** Oklahoma, C USA *36°22´N 96°00´W*
27 P9 **Skiatook Lake** ⊠ Oklahoma, C USA
97 B22 **Skibbereen** *Ir.* An Sciobairín. Cork, SW Ireland *51°33´N 09°15´W*
92 I9 **Skibotn** Troms, N Norway *69°22´N 20°18´E*
119 F16 **Skidal'** *Rus.* Skidel'. Hrodzyenskaya Voblasts', W Belarus *53°35´N 24°15´E*
97 K15 **Skiddaw** ▲ NW England, United Kingdom *54°37´N 03°07´W*
Skidel' *see* Skidal'
25 T14 **Skidmore** Texas, SW USA *28°13´N 97°40´W*
95 G16 **Skien** Telemark, S Norway *59°14´N 09°37´E*
Skiermûntseach *see* Schiermonnikoog
110 L12 **Skierniewice** Łódzkie, C Poland *51°58´N 20°10´E*
74 L5 **Skikda** *prev.* Philippeville. NE Algeria *36°51´N 07°E*
30 M16 **Skillet Fork** ≈ Illinois, N USA
95 L19 **Skillingaryd** Jönköping, S Sweden *57°27´N 14°05´E*
115 B19 **Skinári, Akrotírio** *headland* Iónia Nisiá, Greece *37°55´N 20°57´E*
95 M15 **Skinnskatteberg** Västmanland, C Sweden *59°50´N 15°41´E*
182 M12 **Skipton** Victoria, SE Australia *37°44´S 143°21´E*
97 L16 **Skipton** N England, United Kingdom *53°57´N 02°W*
Skiropoula *see* Skyropoúla
Skíros *see* Skýros
95 F21 **Skive** Viborg, NW Denmark *56°34´N 09°02´E*
94 F11 **Skjåk** Oppland, S Norway *51°52´N 08°21´E*
92 K2 **Skjálfandafljót** ≈ C Iceland
95 F22 **Skjern** Ringkøbing, W Denmark *55°57´N 08°30´E*
95 F22 **Skjern Å** *var.* Skjern Aa. ≈ W Denmark
Skjern Aa *see* Skjern Å
92 G12 **Skjerstad** Nordland, C Norway *67°14´N 15°00´E*
92 J8 **Skjervøy** Troms, N Norway *70°03´N 20°56´E*
92 I10 **Skjold** Troms, N Norway *69°03´N 19°18´E*
111 I17 **Skoczów** Śląskie, S Poland *49°49´N 18°45´E*
109 T11 **Škofja Loka** *Ger.* Bischoflack. NW Slovenia *46°12´N 14°16´E*
94 N12 **Skog** Gävleborg, C Sweden *61°10´N 16°49´E*
95 K16 **Skoghall** Värmland, C Sweden *59°20´N 13°30´E*
31 N10 **Skokie** Illinois, N USA *42°01´N 87°43´W*
116 H6 **Skole** L'vivs'ka Oblast', W Ukraine *49°04´N 23°29´E*
115 D19 **Skóllis** ▲ S Greece *37°58´N 21°33´E*
167 S13 **Skon** Kâmpóng Cham, C Cambodia *12°56´N 104°36´E*
115 H17 **Skópelos** Skópelos, Vóreies Sporádes, Greece, Aegean Sea *39°07´N 23°43´E*
115 H17 **Skópelos** *island* Vóreies Sporádes, Greece, Aegean Sea
126 L5 **Skopin** Ryazanskaya Oblast', W Russian Federation *53°46´N 39°37´E*
113 N18 **Skopje** *var.* Üsküb, *Turk.* Üsküp, *prev.* Skoplje; *anc.* Scupi. ● (FYR Macedonia) N FYR Macedonia *42°N 21°28´E*
113 O18 **Skopje** ✈ N FYR Macedonia *41°58´N 21°35´E*
Skoplje *see* Skopje
110 I8 **Skórcz** *Ger.* Skurz. Pomorskie, N Poland *53°46´N 18°43´E*
Skorodnoye *see* Skarodnaye
93 H16 **Skorped** Västernorrland, C Sweden *63°23´N 17°55´E*
95 G21 **Skørping** Nordjylland, N Denmark *56°50´N 09°55´E*
95 K18 **Skövde** Västra Götaland, S Sweden *58°24´N 13°52´E*
123 Q13 **Skovorodino** Amurskaya Oblast', SE Russian Federation *54°03´N 123°47´E*
19 Q6 **Skowhegan** Maine, NE USA *44°46´N 69°41´W*
11 W15 **Skownan** Manitoba, S Canada *51°55´N 99°34´W*
94 H13 **Skreia** Oppland, S Norway *60°37´N 11°00´E*
Skripón *see* Orchómenos
118 H9 **Skrīveri** Aizkraukle, S Latvia *56°39´N 25°08´E*
118 J11 **Skrudaliena** Daugvapils, SE Latvia *55°50´N 26°42´E*
118 D9 **Skrunda** Kuldīga, W Latvia *56°39´N 22°01´E*
95 C16 **Skudeneshavn** Rogaland, S Norway *59°10´N 05°16´E*
83 L20 **Skukuza** Mpumalanga, NE South Africa *25°01´S 31°35´E*
97 B22 **Skull** *Ir.* An Scoil. SW Ireland *51°32´N 09°34´W*
22 L3 **Skuna River** ≈ Mississippi, S USA
29 X15 **Skunk River** ≈ Iowa, C USA
Skuø *see* Skúvoy
118 C10 **Skuodas** *Ger.* Schoden, *Pol.* Szkudy. Klaipėda, NW Lithuania *56°16´N 21°30´E*
95 K23 **Skurup** Skåne, S Sweden *55°28´N 13°30´E*
Skurz *see* Skórcz
114 H8 **Skŭt** ≈ NW Bulgaria
94 O13 **Skutskär** Uppsala, C Sweden *60°39´N 17°25´E*
95 B19 **Skúvoy** *Dan.* Skuø. *island* C Faeroe Islands
Skvira *see* Skvyra
117 O5 **Skvyra** *Rus.* Skvira. Kyyivs'ka Oblast', N Ukraine *49°44´N 29°42´E*
39 Q11 **Skwentna** Alaska, USA *61°56´N 151°03´W*
110 E11 **Skwierzyna** *Ger.* Schwerin. Lubuskie, W Poland *52°37´N 15°27´E*
194 J7 **SkyBlu** *UK research station* Antarctica*74°51´N 71°77´W*
96 G9 **Skye, Isle of** *island* NW Scotland, United Kingdom
36 K13 **Sky Harbor** ✈ (Phoenix) Arizona, SW USA *32°26´N 112°00´W*
32 I8 **Skykomish** Washington, NW USA *47°40´N 121°20´W*
Skylge *see* Terschelling
63 F19 **Skyring, Peninsula** *peninsula* S Chile
63 H24 **Skyring, Seno** *inlet* S Chile
115 H17 **Skyropoúla** *var.* Skiropoula. *island* Vóreies Sporádes, Greece, Aegean Sea
115 I17 **Skýros** *var.* Skíros. Skńyros, Vóreies Sporádes, Greece, Aegean Sea *38°55´N 24°34´E*
115 I17 **Skýros** *var.* Skíros; *anc.* Scyros. *island* Vóreies Sporádes, Greece, Aegean Sea
118 J12 **Slabodka** *Rus.* Slobodka. Vitsyebskaya Voblasts', NW Belarus *55°41´N 27°11´E*
95 I23 **Slagelse** Vestsjælland, E Denmark *55°25´N 11°22´E*
93 I14 **Slagnäs** Norrbotten, N Sweden *65°36´N 18°10´E*
39 T10 **Slana** Alaska, USA *62°46´N 144°00´W*
97 F20 **Slaney** *Ir.* An tSláine. ≈ SE Ireland
116 J13 **Slănic** Prahova, SE Romania *45°14´N 25°58´E*
116 K11 **Slănic Moldova** Bacău, E Romania *46°12´N 26°23´E*
113 H16 **Slano** Dubrovnik-Neretva, SE Croatia *42°47´N 17°54´E*
124 F13 **Slantsy** Leningradskaya Oblast', NW Russian Federation *59°06´N 28°00´E*
111 C16 **Slaný** *Ger.* Schlan. Střední Čechy, NW Czech Republic *50°14´N 14°05´E*
111 K16 **Śląskie** ◈ *province* S Poland
12 C10 **Slate Falls** Ontario, S Canada *51°11´N 91°32´W*
27 T4 **Slater** Missouri, C USA *39°13´N 93°04´W*
112 H9 **Slatina** *Hung.* Szlatina; *prev.* Podravska Slatina. Virovitica-Podravina, NE Croatia *45°40´N 17°46´E*
116 I14 **Slatina** Olt, S Romania *45°27´N 24°21´E*
25 N5 **Slaton** Texas, SW USA *33°26´N 101°38´W*
95 H14 **Slattum** Akershus, S Norway *60°00´N 10°55´E*
11 R10 **Slave** ≈ Alberta/Northwest Territories, C Canada
68 E12 **Slave Coast** *coastal region* W Africa
11 P13 **Slave Lake** Alberta, SW Canada *55°17´N 114°46´W*
122 I13 **Slavgorod** Altayskiy Kray, S Russian Federation *52°55´N 78°46´E*
Slavgorod *see* Slawharad
Slavonia *see* Slavonija
112 G9 **Slavonija** *Eng.* Slavonia, *Ger.* Slawonien, *Hung.* Szlavonia, Szlavonország. *cultural region* NE Croatia
112 H10 **Slavonski Brod** *Ger.* Brod, *Hung.* Bród; *prev.* Brod, Brod na Savi. Brod-Posavina, NE Croatia *45°09´N 18°00´E*
Slavonski Brod-Posavina *see* Brod-Posavina
116 L4 **Slavuta** Khmel'nyts'ka Oblast', NW Ukraine *50°18´N 26°52´E*
117 P2 **Slavutych** Chernihivs'ka Oblast', N Ukraine *51°31´N 30°47´E*
123 R15 **Slavyanka** Primorskiy Kray, SE Russian Federation *42°46´N 131°19´E*
114 J8 **Slavyanovo** Pleven, N Bulgaria *43°28´N 24°52´E*
Slavyansk *see* Slov"yans'k
126 K14 **Slavyansk-na-Kubani** Krasnodarskiy Kray, SW Russian Federation *45°16´N 38°09´E*
119 N20 **Slavyechna** *Rus.* Slovechna. ≈ Belarus/Ukraine
119 O16 **Slawharad** *Rus.* Slavgorod. Mahilyowskaya Voblasts', E Belarus *53°27´N 31°00´E*
110 G7 **Sławno** Zachodnio-pomorskie, NW Poland *54°23´N 16°43´E*
Slawonien *see* Slavonija
29 S10 **Slayton** Minnesota, N USA *43°59´N 95°45´W*
97 N18 **Sleaford** E England, United Kingdom *52°59´N 00°28´W*
97 A20 **Slea Head** *Ir.* Ceann Sléibhe. *headland* SW Ireland *52°05´N 10°25´W*
96 G9 **Sleat, Sound of** *strait* NW Scotland, United Kingdom
Sledyuki *see* Slyedzyuki
12 I5 **Sleeper Islands** *island group* Nunavut, C Canada
31 O6 **Sleeping Bear Point** *headland* Michigan, N USA *44°54´N 86°02´W*
29 T10 **Sleepy Eye** Minnesota, N USA *44°18´N 94°43´W*
39 O11 **Sleetmute** Alaska, USA *61°42´N 157°10´W*
Sléibhe, Ceann *see* Slea Head
Slēmānī *see* As Sulaymānīyah
195 O5 **Slessor Glacier** *glacier* Antarctica
22 L9 **Slidell** Louisiana, S USA *30°16´N 89°46´W*
18 K12 **Slide Mountain** ▲ New York, NE USA *42°00´N 74°23´W*
98 I13 **Sliedrecht** Zuid-Holland, C Netherlands *51°50´N 04°46´E*
121 P16 **Sliema** N Malta *35°54´N 14°31´E*
97 G16 **Slieve Donard** ▲ SE Northern Ireland, United Kingdom *54°10´N 05°57´W*
Sligeach *see* Sligo
97 D16 **Sligo** *Ir.* Sligeach. Sligo, NW Ireland *54°17´N 08°28´W*
97 C16 **Sligo** *Ir.* Sligeach. *cultural region* NW Ireland
97 C15 **Sligo Bay** *Ir.* Cuan Shligigh. *inlet* NW Ireland
18 B13 **Slippery Rock** Pennsylvania, NE USA *41°02´N 80°02´W*
95 P19 **Slite** Gotland, SE Sweden *57°37´N 18°46´E*
114 L9 **Sliven** *var.* Slivno. Sliven, C Bulgaria *42°42´N 26°21´E*
114 L10 **Sliven** ◈ *province* C Bulgaria
114 G9 **Slivnitsa** Sofiya, W Bulgaria *42°51´N 23°01´E*
Slivno *see* Sliven
114 L7 **Slivo Pole** Ruse, N Bulgaria *43°57´N 26°15´E*
29 S13 **Sloan** Iowa, C USA *42°13´N 96°13´W*
35 X12 **Sloan** Nevada, W USA *35°56´N 115°13´W*
Slobodka *see* Slabodka
125 R14 **Slobodskoy** Kirovskaya Oblast', NW Russian Federation *58°43´N 50°12´E*
Slobodzeya *see* Slobozia
117 O10 **Slobozia** *Rus.* Slobodzeya. E Moldova *46°45´N 29°42´E*
116 L14 **Slobozia** Ialomiţa, SE Romania *44°34´N 27°23´E*
98 O5 **Slochteren** Groningen, NE Netherlands *53°13´N 06°48´E*
119 H17 **Slonim** *Pol.* Słonim. Hrodzyenskaya Voblasts', W Belarus *53°06´N 25°19´E*
Słonim *see* Slonim
98 K7 **Sloter Meer** ◎ N Netherlands
Slot, The *see* New Georgia Sound
97 N22 **Slough** S England, United Kingdom *51°31´N 00°36´W*
111 J20 **Slovakia** *off.* Slovenská Republika, *Ger.* Slowakei, *Hung.* Szlovákia, *Slvk.* Slovensko. ◆ *republic* C Europe
Slovak Ore Mountains *see* Slovenské rudohorie
Slovechna *see* Slavyechna
109 S12 **Slovenia** *off.* Republic of Slovenia, *Ger.* Slowenien, *Slvn.* Slovenija. ◆ *republic* SE Europe
Slovenia, Republic of *see* Slovenia
Slovenija *see* Slovenia
109 V10 **Slovenj Gradec** *Ger.* Windischgraz. N Slovenia *46°29´N 15°05´E*
109 W10 **Slovenska Bistrica** *Ger.* Windischfeistritz. NE Slovenia *46°21´N 15°27´E*
Slovenská Republika *see* Slovakia
109 W10 **Slovenske Konjice** E Slovenia *46°21´N 15°28´E*
111 K20 **Slovenské rudohorie** *Eng.* Slovak Ore Mountains, *Ger.* Slowakisches Erzgebirge, Ungarisches Erzgebirge. ▲▲ C Slovakia
Slovensko *see* Slovakia
117 Y7 **Slov"yanoserbs'k** Luhans'ka Oblast', E Ukraine *48°41´N 39°00´E*
117 W6 **Slov"yans'k** *Rus.* Slavyansk. Donets'ka Oblast', E Ukraine *48°51´N 37°38´E*
Slowakei *see* Slovakia
Slowakisches Erzgebirge *see* Slovenské rudohorie
Slowenien *see* Slovenia
110 D11 **Słubice** *Ger.* Frankfurt. Lubuskie, W Poland *52°20´N 14°35´E*
119 K19 **Sluch** *Rus.* Sluch'. ≈ C Belarus
116 L4 **Sluch** ≈ NW Ukraine
99 D16 **Sluis** Zeeland, SW Netherlands *51°18´N 03°22´E*
112 D10 **Slunj** *Hung.* Szluin. Karlovac, C Croatia *45°06´N 15°35´E*
110 I11 **Słupca** Wielkopolskie, C Poland *52°17´N 17°52´E*
110 G6 **Słupia** *Ger.* Stolpe. ≈ NW Poland
110 G6 **Słupsk** *Ger.* Stolp. Pomorskie, N Poland *54°28´N 17°01´E*
119 K18 **Slutsk** Minskaya Voblasts', S Belarus *53°02´N 27°32´E*
119 O16 **Slyedzyuki** *Rus.* Sledyuki. Mahilyowskaya Voblasts', E Belarus *53°35´N 30°22´E*
97 A17 **Slyne Head** *Ir.* Ceann Léime. *headland* W Ireland *53°25´N 10°11´W*
27 U14 **Smackover** Arkansas, C USA *33°21´N 92°43´W*
95 L20 **Småland** *cultural region* S Sweden
95 K20 **Smålandsstenar** Jönköping, S Sweden *57°10´N 13°24´E*
Small Malaita *see* Maramasike
13 O8 **Smallwood Reservoir** ◎ Newfoundland and Labrador, S Canada
119 N14 **Smalyany** *Rus.* Smolyany. Vitsyebskaya Voblasts', NE Belarus *54°36´N 30°04´E*
119 L15 **Smalyavichy** *Rus.* Smolevichi. Minskaya Voblasts', C Belarus *54°02´N 28°05´E*
74 C9 **Smara** *var.* Es Semara. N Western Sahara *26°45´N 11°44´W*
119 I14 **Smarhon'** *Pol.* Smorgonie, *Rus.* Smorgon'. Hrodzyenskaya Voblasts', W Belarus *54°29´N 26°24´E*
112 M11 **Smederevo** *Ger.* Semendria. Serbia, N Serbia *44°41´N 20°56´E*
112 M12 **Smederevska Palanka** Serbia, C Serbia *44°24´N 20°56´E*
95 M14 **Smedjebacken** Dalarna, C Sweden *60°08´N 15°25´E*
116 L13 **Smeeni** Buzău, SE Romania *45°00´N 26°52´E*
Smela *see* Smila
107 D16 **Smeralda, Costa** *cultural region* Sardegna, Italy, C Mediterranean Sea
111 J22 **Śmigiel** *Ger.* Schmiegel. Wielkopolskie, C Poland *52°02´N 16°33´E*
117 Q6 **Smila** *Rus.* Smela. Cherkas'ka Oblast', C Ukraine *49°15´N 31°54´E*
98 N7 **Smilde** Drenthe, NE Netherlands *52°57´N 06°28´E*
11 S16 **Smiley** Saskatchewan, S Canada *51°40´N 109°24´W*
25 T12 **Smiley** Texas, SW USA *29°16´N 97°38´W*
Smilten *see* Smiltene
118 I8 **Smiltene** *Ger.* Smilten. Valka, N Latvia *57°25´N 25°53´E*
123 T13 **Smirnykh** Ostrov Sakhalin, Sakhalinskaya Oblast', SE Russian Federation *49°43´N 142°48´E*
11 Q13 **Smith** Alberta, W Canada *55°06´N 113°57´W*
39 P4 **Smith Bay** *bay* Alaska, NW USA
12 I3 **Smith, Cape** *headland* Québec, NE Canada *60°50´N 78°06´W*
26 L3 **Smith Center** Kansas, C USA *39°46´N 98°46´W*
10 K13 **Smithers** British Columbia, SW Canada *54°45´N 127°10´W*
21 V10 **Smithfield** North Carolina, SE USA *35°30´N 78°21´W*
36 L1 **Smithfield** Utah, W USA *41°50´N 111°49´W*
21 X7 **Smithfield** Virginia, NE USA *36°41´N 76°38´W*
12 I3 **Smith Island** *island* Nunavut, C Canada
Smith Island *see* Sumisu-jima
20 H7 **Smithland** Kentucky, S USA *37°06´N 88°24´W*
21 T7 **Smith Mountain Lake** *var.* Leesville Lake. ⊠ Virginia, NE USA
34 L1 **Smith River** California, W USA *41°54´N 124°09´W*
33 R9 **Smith River** ≈ Montana, NW USA
14 L13 **Smiths Falls** Ontario, SE Canada *44°54´N 76°01´W*
33 N13 **Smiths Ferry** Idaho, NW USA *44°19´N 116°04´W*
20 K7 **Smiths Grove** Kentucky, S USA *37°01´N 86°14´W*
183 N15 **Smithton** Tasmania, SE Australia *40°54´S 145°06´E*
18 L14 **Smithtown** Long Island, New York, NE USA *40°52´N 73°13´W*
20 K9 **Smithville** Tennessee, S USA *35°59´N 85°49´W*
25 T11 **Smithville** Texas, SW USA *30°04´N 97°32´W*
Šmohor *see* Hermagor
35 Q4 **Smoke Creek Desert** *desert* Nevada, W USA
11 O14 **Smoky** ≈ Alberta, W Canada
182 E7 **Smoky Bay** South Australia *32°22´S 133°57´E*
183 V6 **Smoky Cape** *headland* New South Wales, SE Australia *30°54´S 153°06´E*
26 L4 **Smoky Hill River** ≈ Kansas, C USA
26 L4 **Smoky Hills** *hill range* Kansas, C USA
11 Q14 **Smoky Lake** Alberta, SW Canada *54°08´N 112°26´W*
94 E8 **Smøla** *island* W Norway
126 H4 **Smolensk** Smolenskaya Oblast', W Russian Federation *54°48´N 32°08´E*
126 H4 **Smolenskaya Oblast'** ◈ *province* W Russian Federation
Smolensk-Moscow Upland *see* Smolensko-Moskovskaya Vozvyshennost'
126 J3 **Smolensko-Moskovskaya Vozvyshennost'** *var.* Smolensk-Moscow Upland. ▲▲ W Russian Federation
Smolevichi *see* Smalyavichy
115 C15 **Smólikas** *var.* Smolikás. ▲ W Greece *40°06´N 20°54´E*
114 I12 **Smolyan** *prev.* Pashmakli. Smolyan, S Bulgaria *41°34´N 24°42´E*
114 I12 **Smolyan** ◈ *province* S Bulgaria
Smolyany *see* Smalyany
33 S15 **Smoot** Wyoming, C USA *42°37´N 110°55´W*
12 G12 **Smooth Rock Falls** Ontario, S Canada *49°17´N 81°37´W*
Smorgon'/Smorgonie *see* Smarhon'
114 M9 **Smyadovo** Shumen, NE Bulgaria *43°04´N 27°01´E*
95 K23 **Smygehamn** Skåne, S Sweden *55°19´N 13°25´E*
194 I7 **Smyley Island** *island* Antarctica
21 Y3 **Smyrna** Delaware, NE USA *39°18´N 75°36´W*
23 S3 **Smyrna** Georgia, SE USA *33°52´N 84°30´W*
20 J9 **Smyrna** Tennessee, S USA *36°00´N 86°30´W*
Smyrna *see* İzmir
97 I16 **Snaefell** ▲ C Isle of Man *54°15´N 04°29´W*
92 H3 **Snaefellsjökull** ▲ W Iceland *64°51´N 23°51´W*
92 J3 **Snækollur** ▲ C Iceland *64°38´N 19°18´W*

◆ Country
● Country Capital
◇ Dependent Territory
○ Dependent Territory Capital
◈ Administrative Regions
✈ International Airport
▲ Mountain
▲▲ Mountain Range
Volcano
≈ River
◎ Lake
⊠ Reservoir

SNAKE – SOURIS

10 *J4* **Snake** ≈ Yukon Territory, NW Canada
29 *O8* **Snake Creek** ≈ South Dakota, N USA
183 *P13* **Snake Island** *island* Victoria, SE Australia
35 *Y6* **Snake Range** ▲▲ Nevada, W USA
32 *K10* **Snake River** ≈ NW USA
29 *V6* **Snake River** ≈ Minnesota, N USA
28 *L12* **Snake River** ≈ Nebraska, C USA
33 *Q14* **Snake River Plain** *plain* Idaho, NW USA
93 *F15* **Snåsa** Nord-Trøndelag, C Norway *64°16′N 12°25′E*
21 *O8* **Sneedville** Tennessee, S USA *36°31′N 83°13′W*
98 *K6* **Sneek** Friesland, N Netherlands *53°02′N 05°40′E*
Sneeuw-gebergte *see* Maoke, Pegunungan
95 *F22* **Snejbjerg** Ringkøbing, C Denmark *56°08′N 08°55′E*
124 *J3* **Snezhnogorsk** Murmanskaya Oblast', NW Russian Federation *69°12′N 33°20′E*
122 *K9* **Snezhnogorsk** Taymyrskiy (Dolgano-Nenetskiy) Avtonomnyy Okrug, N Russian Federation *68°06′N 87°37′E*
Snezhnoye *see* Snizhne
111 *G15* **Sněžka** *Ger.* Schneekoppe, *Pol.* Śnieżka. ▲ N Czech Republic/Poland *50°42′N 15°55′E*
110 *N8* **Śniardwy, Jezioro** *Ger.* Spirdingsee. ◎ NE Poland
Sniečkus *see* Visaginas
Śnieżka *see* Sněžka
117 *R10* **Snihurivka** Mykolayivs'ka Oblast', S Ukraine *47°05′N 32°48′E*
116 *I5* **Snilov** ✈ (L'viv) L'vivs'ka Oblast', W Ukraine *49°45′N 23°59′E*
111 *O19* **Snina** *Hung.* Szinna. Prešovský Kraj, E Slovakia *49°N 22°10′E*
117 *Y8* **Snizhne** *Rus.* Snezhnoye. Donets'ka Oblast', SE Ukraine *48°01′N 38°46′E*
94 *G10* **Snøhetta** *var.* Snohetta. ▲ S Norway *62°22′N 09°08′E*
92 *G12* **Snøtinden** ▲ C Norway *66°39′N 13°50′E*
97 *I18* **Snowdon** ▲ NW Wales, United Kingdom *53°04′N 04°04′W*
97 *I18* **Snowdonia** ▲▲ NW Wales, United Kingdom
8 *K10* **Snowdrift** ≈ Northwest Territories, NW Canada
Snowdrift *see* Łutselk'e
37 *N12* **Snowflake** Arizona, SW USA *34°30′N 110°04′W*
21 *Y5* **Snow Hill** Maryland, NE USA *38°11′N 75°23′W*
21 *W10* **Snow Hill** North Carolina, SE USA *35°26′N 77°39′W*
194 *H3* **Snowhill Island** *island* Antarctica
11 *V13* **Snow Lake** Manitoba, C Canada *54°56′N 100°02′W*
37 *R5* **Snowmass Mountain** ▲ Colorado, C USA *39°07′N 107°04′W*
18 *M10* **Snow, Mount** ▲ Vermont, NE USA *42°56′N 72°52′W*
34 *M5* **Snow Mountain** ▲ California, W USA *39°44′N 123°01′W*
Snow Mountains *see* Maoke, Pegunungan
33 *N7* **Snowshoe Peak** ▲ Montana, NW USA *48°15′N 115°44′W*
182 *I8* **Snowtown** South Australia *33°49′S 138°13′E*
36 *K1* **Snowville** Utah, W USA *41°59′N 112°42′W*
35 *X3* **Snow Water Lake** ◎ Nevada, W USA
183 *Q11* **Snowy Mountains** ▲▲ New South Wales/Victoria, SE Australia
183 *Q12* **Snowy River** ≈ New South Wales/Victoria, SE Australia
44 *K5* **Snug Corner** Acklins Island, SE Bahamas *22°31′N 73°51′W*
167 *T13* **Snuŏl** Krâchéh, E Cambodia *12°04′N 106°26′E*
116 *J7* **Snyatyn** Ivano-Frankivs'ka Oblast', W Ukraine *48°30′N 25°50′E*
26 *L12* **Snyder** Oklahoma, C USA *34°37′N 98°56′W*
25 *O6* **Snyder** Texas, SW USA *32°43′N 100°54′W*
172 *H3* **Soalala** Mahajanga, W Madagascar *16°05′S 45°21′E*
172 *J4* **Soanierana-Ivongo** Toamasina, E Madagascar *16°53′S 49°35′E*
171 *R11* **Soasiu** *var.* Tidore. Pulau Tidore, E Indonesia *0°40′N 127°25′E*
54 *G8* **Soatá** Boyacá, C Colombia *06°23′N 72°40′W*
172 *I5* **Soavinandriana** Antananarivo, C Madagascar *19°09′S 46°43′E*
77 *V13* **Soba** Kaduna, C Nigeria *10°58′N 08°06′E*
163 *Y16* **Sobaek-sanmaek** ▲▲ S South Korea
80 *F13* **Sobat** ≈ E Sudan
171 *Z14* **Sobger, Sungai** ≈ Papua, E Indonesia
171 *V13* **Sobiei** Papua, E Indonesia *02°31′S 134°30′E*
126 *M3* **Sobinka** Vladimirskaya Oblast', W Russian Federation *56°00′N 39°55′E*
127 *S7* **Sobolevo** Orenburgskaya Oblast', W Russian Federation *51°57′N 51°42′E*
Soborsin *see* Săvârşin
164 *D15* **Sobo-san** ▲ Kyūshū, SW Japan *32°50′N 131°16′E*
111 *G14* **Sobótka** Dolnośląskie, SW Poland *50°53′N 16°48′E*
59 *O15* **Sobradinho** Bahia, E Brazil *09°33′S 40°56′W*
Sobradinho, Barragem de *see* Sobradinho, Represa de
59 *O16* **Sobradinho, Represa de** *var.* Barragem de Sobradinho. ⊠ E Brazil
58 *O13* **Sobral** Ceará, E Brazil *03°45′S 40°20′W*
105 *T4* **Sobrarbe** *physical region* NE Spain
109 *R10* **Soča** *It.* Isonzo. ≈ Italy/Slovenia
110 *L11* **Sochaczew** Mazowieckie, C Poland *52°15′N 20°15′E*
126 *L15* **Sochi** Krasnodarskiy Kray, SW Russian Federation *43°35′N 39°46′E*
114 *G13* **Sochós** *var.* Sohos, Sokhós. Kentrikí Makedonía, N Greece *40°49′N 23°23′E*
191 *R11* **Société, Archipel de la** *var.* Archipel de Tahiti, Îles de la Société, *Eng.* Society Islands. *island group* W French Polynesia
Société, Îles de la/Society Islands *see* Société, Archipel de la
21 *T11* **Society Hill** South Carolina, SE USA *34°28′N 79°54′W*
175 *W9* **Society Ridge** *undersea feature* C Pacific Ocean
62 *I5* **Socompa, Volcán** 🌋 N Chile *24°18′S 68°03′W*
Soconusco, Sierra de *see* Madre, Sierra
54 *G8* **Socorro** Santander, C Colombia *06°30′N 73°16′W*
37 *R13* **Socorro** New Mexico, SW USA *33°58′N 106°55′W*
Socotra *see* Suquṭrā
167 *S14* **Soc Trăng** *var.* Khanh Hung. Soc Trăng, S Vietnam *09°36′N 105°58′E*
105 *P10* **Socuéllamos** Castilla-La Mancha, C Spain *39°18′N 02°48′W*
35 *W13* **Soda Lake** *salt flat* California, W USA
92 *L11* **Sodankylä** Lappi, N Finland *67°26′N 26°35′E*
Sodari *see* Sodiri
33 *R15* **Soda Springs** Idaho, NW USA *42°39′N 111°36′W*
Soddo/Soddu *see* Sodo
20 *L10* **Soddy Daisy** Tennessee, S USA *35°14′N 85°11′W*
95 *N14* **Söderfors** Uppsala, C Sweden *60°23′N 17°14′E*
94 *N12* **Söderhamn** Gävleborg, C Sweden *61°19′N 17°10′E*
95 *N17* **Söderköping** Östergötland, S Sweden *58°28′N 16°20′E*
95 *N17* **Södermanland** ◈ *county* C Sweden
95 *O16* **Södertälje** Stockholm, C Sweden *59°11′N 17°39′E*
80 *D10* **Sodiri** *var.* Sawdirī, Sodari. Northern Kordofan, C Sudan *14°23′N 29°06′E*
81 *I14* **Sodo** *var.* Soddo, Soddu. Southern Nationalities, S Ethiopia *06°49′N 37°43′E*
94 *N11* **Södra Dellen** ◎ C Sweden
95 *M19* **Södra Vi** Kalmar, S Sweden *57°45′N 15°45′E*
18 *G9* **Sodus Point** *headland* New York, NE USA *43°16′N 76°59′W*
171 *Q17* **Soe** *prev.* Soë. Timor, C Indonesia *09°51′S 124°29′E*
Soebang *see* Subang
Soekaboemi *see* Sukabumi
169 *N15* **Soekarno-Hatta** ✈ (Jakarta) Jawa, S Indonesia
Soëla-Sund *see* Soela Väin
118 *E5* **Soela Väin** *prev. Eng.* Sele Sound, *Ger.* Dagden-Sund, Soëla-Sund. *strait* W Estonia
Soemba *see* Sumba, Pulau
Soembawa *see* Sumbawa
Soemenep *see* Sumenep
Soengaipenoeh *see* Sungaipenuh
Soerabaja *see* Surabaya
Soerakarta *see* Surakarta
101 *G14* **Soest** Nordrhein-Westfalen, W Germany *51°34′N 08°06′E*
98 *J11* **Soest** Utrecht, C Netherlands *52°10′N 05°20′E*
100 *F11* **Soeste** ≈ NW Germany
98 *J11* **Soesterberg** Utrecht, C Netherlands *52°07′N 05°17′E*
115 *E16* **Sofádes** *var.* Sofádhes. Thessalía, C Greece *39°20′N 22°06′E*
Sofádhes *see* Sofádes
83 *N18* **Sofala** Sofala, C Mozambique *20°04′S 34°43′E*
83 *N17* **Sofala** ◈ *province* C Mozambique
83 *N18* **Sofala, Baia de** *bay* C Mozambique
172 *J3* **Sofia** *seasonal river* NW Madagascar
Sofia *see* Sofiya
115 *G19* **Sofikó** Pelopónnisos, S Greece *37°46′N 23°04′E*
Sofi-Kurgan *see* Sopu-Korgon
114 *G10* **Sofiya** *var.* Sophia, *Eng.* Sofia, *Lat.* Serdica. ● (Bulgaria) Sofiya-Grad, W Bulgaria *42°42′N 23°20′E*
114 *H9* **Sofiya** ◈ *province* W Bulgaria
114 *G9* **Sofiya** ✈ Sofiya-Grad, W Bulgaria *42°42′N 23°26′E*
114 *G9* **Sofiya, Grad** ◈ *municipality* W Bulgaria
Sofiyevka *see* Sofiyivka
117 *S8* **Sofiyivka** *Rus.* Sofiyevka. Dnipropetrovs'ka Oblast', E Ukraine *48°04′N 33°55′E*
123 *R12* **Sofiysk** Khabarovskiy Kray, SE Russian Federation *51°32′N 139°46′E*
123 *R13* **Sofiysk** Khabarovskiy Kray, SE Russian Federation *52°20′N 133°37′E*
124 *I6* **Sofporog** Respublika Kareliya, NW Russian Federation *65°48′N 31°30′E*
115 *L23* **Sofraná** *prev.* Záfora. *island* Kykládes, Greece, Aegean Sea
165 *Y14* **Sōfu-gan** *island* Izu-shotō, SE Japan
156 *K10* **Sog** Xizang Zizhiqu, W China *31°52′N 93°40′E*
54 *G9* **Sogamoso** Boyacá, C Colombia *05°43′N 72°56′W*
136 *I11* **Soğanlı Çayı** ≈ N Turkey
94 *E12* **Sogn** *physical region* S Norway
Sogndal *see* Sogndalsfjøra
94 *E12* **Sogndalsfjøra** *var.* Sogndal. Sogn Og Fjordane, S Norway *61°13′N 07°05′E*
95 *E18* **Søgne** Vest-Agder, S Norway *58°05′N 07°49′E*
94 *D12* **Sognefjorden** *fjord* NE North Sea
94 *C12* **Sogn Og Fjordane** ◈ *county* S Norway
162 *I11* **Sogo Nur** ◎ N China
159 *T12* **Sogruma** Qinghai, W China *32°32′N 100°52′E*
163 *X17* **Sŏgwip'o** S South Korea *33°14′N 126°33′E*
Sohâg *see* Sawhāj
Sohar *see* Şuḩār
64 *H9* **Sohm Plain** *undersea feature* NW Atlantic Ocean
100 *H7* **Soholmer Au** ≈ N Germany
Sohos *see* Sochós
Sohrau *see* Żory
99 *F20* **Soignies** Hainaut, SW Belgium *50°35′N 04°04′E*
159 *R15* **Soila** Xizang Zizhiqu, W China *30°40′N 97°07′E*
103 *P4* **Soissons** *anc.* Augusta Suessionum, Noviodunum. Aisne, N France *49°23′N 03°20′E*
164 *H13* **Sōja** Okayama, Honshū, SW Japan *34°40′N 133°42′E*
152 *F13* **Sojat** Rājasthān, N India *25°53′N 73°45′E*
163 *W13* **Sŏjosŏn-man** *inlet* W North Korea
116 *I4* **Sokal'** *Rus.* Sokal. L'vivs'ka Oblast', NW Ukraine *50°29′N 24°17′E*
163 *Y14* **Sokch'o** N South Korea *38°07′N 128°34′E*
136 *B15* **Söke** Aydın, SW Turkey *37°46′N 27°24′E*
189 *N12* **Sokehs Island** *island* E Micronesia
79 *M24* **Sokele** Katanga, SE Dem. Rep. Congo *09°54′S 24°38′E*
147 *R11* **Sokh** *Uzb.* Sūkh. ≈ Kyrgyzstan/Uzbekistan
Sokh *see* So'x
Sokhós *see* Sochós
137 *Q8* **Sokhumi** *Rus.* Sukhumi. NW Georgia *43°02′N 41°01′E*
113 *O14* **Sokobanja** Serbia, E Serbia *43°39′N 21°51′E*
77 *R15* **Sokodé** C Togo *08°58′N 01°10′E*
123 *T10* **Sokol** Magadanskaya Oblast', E Russian Federation *59°51′N 150°56′E*
124 *M13* **Sokol** Vologodskaya Oblast', NW Russian Federation *59°26′N 40°09′E*
110 *P9* **Sokółka** Podlaskie, NE Poland *53°24′N 23°31′E*
76 *M11* **Sokolo** Ségou, W Mali *14°43′N 06°02′W*
111 *A16* **Sokolov** *Ger.* Falkenau an der Eger; *prev.* Falknov nad Ohří. Karlovarský Kraj, W Czech Republic *50°10′N 12°38′E*
111 *O16* **Sokołów Małopolski** Podkarpackie, SE Poland *50°12′N 22°07′E*
110 *O11* **Sokołów Podlaski** Mazowieckie, C Poland *52°26′N 22°14′E*
76 *G11* **Sokone** W Senegal *13°53′N 16°22′W*
77 *T12* **Sokoto** Sokoto, NW Nigeria *13°05′N 05°16′E*
77 *T12* **Sokoto** ◈ *state* NW Nigeria
77 *S12* **Sokoto** ≈ NW Nigeria
Sokotra *see* Suquṭrā
147 *U7* **Sokuluk** Chuyskaya Oblast', N Kyrgyzstan *42°53′N 74°19′E*
116 *L7* **Sokyryany** Chernivets'ka Oblast', W Ukraine *48°28′N 27°25′E*
95 *C16* **Sola** Rogaland, S Norway *58°53′N 05°36′E*
187 *R12* **Sola** Vanua Lava, N Vanuatu *13°51′S 167°34′E*
95 *C17* **Sola** ✈ (Stavanger) Rogaland, S Norway *58°54′N 05°36′E*
81 *H18* **Solai** Rift Valley, W Kenya *0°02′N 36°03′E*
152 *I8* **Solan** Himāchal Pradesh, N India *30°54′N 77°06′E*
185 *A25* **Solander Island** *island* SW New Zealand
Solano *see* Bahía Solano
155 *F15* **Solāpur** *var.* Sholāpur. Mahārāshtra, W India *17°43′N 75°54′E*
93 *H16* **Solberg** Västernorrland, C Sweden *63°48′N 17°40′E*
116 *K9* **Solca** *Ger.* Solka. Suceava, N Romania *47°40′N 25°50′E*
105 *O16* **Sol, Costa del** *coastal region* S Spain
106 *F5* **Solda** *Ger.* Sulden. Trentino-Alto Adige, N Italy *46°33′N 10°35′E*
117 *N9* **Şoldăneşti** *Rus.* Sholdaneshty. N Moldova *47°49′N 28°45′E*
Soldau *see* Wkra
108 *L8* **Sölden** Tirol, W Austria *46°58′N 11°01′E*
27 *P3* **Soldier Creek** ≈ Kansas, C USA
39 *R12* **Soldotna** Alaska, USA *60°29′N 151°03′W*
110 *I10* **Solec Kujawski** Kujawsko-pomorskie, C Poland *53°04′N 18°09′E*
61 *B16* **Soledad** Santa Fe, C Argentina *30°38′S 60°52′W*
55 *E4* **Soledad** Atlántico, N Colombia *10°54′N 74°48′W*
35 *O11* **Soledad** California, W USA *36°25′N 121°19′W*
55 *O7* **Soledad** Anzoátegui, NE Venezuela *08°10′N 63°36′W*
61 *H15* **Soledade** Rio Grande do Sul, S Brazil *28°50′S 52°30′W*
Isla Soledad *see* East Falkland
103 *Y15* **Solenzara** Corse, France, C Mediterranean Sea *41°55′N 09°24′E*
Soleure *see* Solothurn
94 *C12* **Solheim** Hordaland, S Norway *60°54′N 05°30′E*
125 *N14* **Soligalich** Kostromskaya Oblast', NW Russian Federation *59°05′N 42°15′E*
Soligorsk *see* Salihorsk
97 *L20* **Solihull** C England, United Kingdom *52°25′N 01°45′W*
125 *U13* **Solikamsk** Permskaya Oblast', NW Russian Federation *59°37′N 56°46′E*
127 *V8* **Sol'-Iletsk** Orenburgskaya Oblast', W Russian Federation *51°09′N 55°05′E*
57 *G17* **Solimana, Nevado** ▲ S Peru *15°24′S 72°49′W*
58 *E13* **Solimões, Rio** ≈ C Brazil
113 *E14* **Solin** *It.* Salona; *anc.* Salonae. Split-Dalmacija, S Croatia *43°33′N 16°29′E*
101 *E15* **Solingen** Nordrhein-Westfalen, W Germany *51°10′N 07°05′E*
Solka *see* Solca
93 *H16* **Sollefteå** Västernorrland, C Sweden *63°09′N 17°15′E*
95 *O15* **Sollentuna** Stockholm, C Sweden *59°26′N 17°56′E*
105 *X9* **Sóller** Mallorca, Spain, W Mediterranean Sea *39°46′N 02°42′E*
94 *L13* **Sollerön** Dalarna, C Sweden *60°55′N 14°34′E*
101 *I14* **Solling** *hill range* C Germany
95 *O16* **Solna** Stockholm, C Sweden *59°22′N 17°58′E*
126 *K3* **Solnechnogorsk** Moskovskaya Oblast', W Russian Federation *56°07′N 37°04′E*
123 *R10* **Solnechnyy** Khabarovskiy Kray, SE Russian Federation *50°41′N 136°42′E*
123 *S13* **Solnechnyy** Respublika Sakha (Yakutiya), NE Russian Federation *60°13′N 137°42′E*
Solo *see* Surakarta
107 *L17* **Solofra** Campania, S Italy *40°49′N 14°48′E*
168 *J11* **Solok** Sumatera, W Indonesia *0°45′S 100°42′E*
42 *C6* **Sololá** Sololá, W Guatemala *14°46′N 91°09′W*
42 *A2* **Sololá** *off.* Departamento de Sololá. ◈ *department* SW Guatemala
Sololá, Departamento de *see* Sololá
81 *J16* **Sololo** Eastern, N Kenya *03°31′N 38°39′E*
42 *C4* **Soloma** Huehuetenango, W Guatemala *15°38′N 91°25′W*
38 *M9* **Solomon** Alaska, USA *64°33′N 164°26′W*
27 *N4* **Solomon** Kansas, C USA *38°55′N 97°22′W*
187 *N9* **Solomon Islands** *prev.* British Solomon Islands Protectorate. ◆ *commonwealth republic* W Solomon Islands N Melanesia W Pacific Ocean
186 *L7* **Solomon Islands** *island group* Papua New Guinea/Solomon Islands
26 *M3* **Solomon River** ≈ Kansas, C USA
186 *H8* **Solomon Sea** *sea* W Pacific Ocean
31 *U11* **Solon** Ohio, N USA *41°23′N 81°26′W*
117 *T8* **Solone** Dnipropetrovs'ka Oblast', E Ukraine *48°12′N 34°49′E*
171 *P16* **Solor, Kepulauan** *island group* S Indonesia
126 *M4* **Solotcha** Ryazanskaya Oblast', W Russian Federation *54°43′N 39°50′E*
108 *D7* **Solothurn** *Fr.* Soleure. Solothurn, NW Switzerland *47°13′N 07°32′E*
108 *D7* **Solothurn** *Fr.* Soleure. ◈ *canton* NW Switzerland
124 *J7* **Solovetskiye Ostrova** *island group* NW Russian Federation
105 *V5* **Solsona** Cataluña, NE Spain *42°00′N 01°31′E*
113 *E14* **Šolta** *It.* Solta. *island* S Croatia
Solṭānābād *see* Kāshmar
142 *L4* **Solṭānīyeh** Zanjān, NW Iran *36°24′N 48°50′E*
100 *I11* **Soltau** Niedersachsen, NW Germany *52°59′N 09°50′E*
124 *G14* **Sol'tsy** Novgorodskaya Oblast', W Russian Federation *58°09′N 30°23′E*
Soltūstik Qazaqstan Oblysy *see* Severnyy Kazakhstan
Solun *see* Thessaloníki
113 *O19* **Solunska Glava** ▲ C FYR Macedonia *41°43′N 21°24′E*
95 *L22* **Sölvesborg** Blekinge, S Sweden *56°04′N 14°35′E*
97 *J15* **Solway Firth** *inlet* England/Scotland, United Kingdom
82 *I13* **Solwezi** North Western, NW Zambia *12°11′S 26°23′E*
165 *Q11* **Sōma** Fukushima, Honshū, C Japan *37°49′N 140°52′E*
136 *C13* **Soma** Manisa, W Turkey *39°10′N 27°36′E*
81 *O15* **Somalia** *off.* Somali Democratic Republic, *Som.* Jamuuriyada Demuqraadiga Soomaaliyeed, Soomaaliya; *prev.* Italian Somaliland, Somaliland Protectorate. ◆ *republic* E Africa
173 *N6* **Somali Basin** *undersea feature* W Indian Ocean *0°00′N 52°00′E*
Somali Democratic Republic *see* Somalia
80 *N12* **Somaliland** ◈ *disputed territory* N Somalia
Somaliland Protectorate *see* Somalia
67 *Y8* **Somali Plain** *undersea feature* W Indian Ocean *01°00′N 51°30′E*
112 *J8* **Sombor** *Hung.* Zombor. Vojvodina, NW Serbia *45°46′N 19°07′E*
99 *H20* **Sombreffe** Namur, S Belgium *50°32′N 04°39′E*
40 *L10* **Sombrerete** Zacatecas, C Mexico *23°38′N 103°40′W*
45 *V8* **Sombrero** *island* N Anguilla
151 *Q21* **Sombrero Channel** *channel* Nicobar Islands, India
116 *H9* **Şomcuta Mare** *Hung.* Nagysomkút; *prev.* Somcuţa Mare. Maramureş, N Romania *47°29′N 23°30′E*
Somcuţa Mare *see* Şomcuta Mare
167 *R9* **Somdet** Kalasin, E Thailand *16°41′N 103°44′E*
99 *L15* **Someren** Noord-Brabant, SE Netherlands *51°23′N 05°42′E*
93 *L19* **Somero** Länsi-Suomi, SW Finland *60°37′N 23°30′E*
33 *P7* **Somers** Montana, NW USA *48°04′N 114°16′W*
64 *A12* **Somerset** *var.* Somerset Village. W Bermuda *32°18′N 64°53′W*
37 *Q5* **Somerset** Colorado, C USA *38°55′N 107°27′W*
20 *M7* **Somerset** Kentucky, S USA *37°05′N 84°36′W*
19 *O12* **Somerset** Massachusetts, NE USA *41°46′N 71°07′W*
97 *K23* **Somerset** *cultural region* SW England, United Kingdom
Somerset East *see* Somerset-Oos
64 *A12* **Somerset Island** *island* W Bermuda
197 *N9* **Somerset Island** *island* Queen Elizabeth Islands, Nunavut, NW Canada
Somerset Nile *see* Victoria Nile
83 *I25* **Somerset-Oos** *var.* Somerset East. Eastern Cape, S South Africa *32°44′S 25°35′E*
Somerset Village *see* Somerset
83 *E26* **Somerset-Wes** *var.* Somerset West. Western Cape, SW South Africa *34°05′S 18°51′E*
Somerset West *see* Somerset-Wes
Somers Islands *see* Bermuda
18 *J17* **Somers Point** New Jersey, NE USA *39°18′N 74°34′W*
19 *P9* **Somersworth** New Hampshire, NE USA *43°15′N 70°52′W*
36 *H15* **Somerton** Arizona, SW USA *32°36′N 114°42′W*
18 *J14* **Somerville** New Jersey, NE USA *40°34′N 74°36′W*
20 *F10* **Somerville** Tennessee, S USA *35°14′N 89°24′W*
25 *U10* **Somerville** Texas, SW USA *30°21′N 96°31′W*
25 *T10* **Somerville Lake** ⊠ Texas, SW USA
Someş/Somesch/Someşul *see* Szamos
103 *N2* **Somme** ◈ *department* N France
103 *N2* **Somme** ≈ N France
95 *L18* **Sommen** Jönköping, S Sweden *58°07′N 14°58′E*
95 *M18* **Sommen** ◎ S Sweden
101 *K16* **Sömmerda** Thüringen, C Germany *51°10′N 11°07′E*
Sommerein *see* Šamorín
Sommerfeld *see* Lubsko
55 *Y11* **Sommet Tabulaire** *var.* Mont Itoupé. ▲▲ S French Guiana
111 *H25* **Somogy** *off.* Somogy Megye. ◈ *county* SW Hungary
Somogy Megye *see* Somogy
Somorja *see* Šamorín
105 *N7* **Somosierra, Puerto de** *pass* N Spain
187 *Y14* **Somosomo** Taveuni, N Fiji *16°46′S 179°57′W*
42 *I9* **Somotillo** Chinandega, NW Nicaragua *13°01′N 86°53′W*
42 *I8* **Somoto** Madriz, NW Nicaragua *13°29′N 86°36′W*
110 *I11* **Sompolno** Wielkopolskie, C Poland *52°24′N 18°30′E*
102 *J17* **Somport, Col du** *var.* Puerto de Somport, *Sp.* Somport; *anc.* Summus Portus. *pass* France/Spain *see also* Somport
99 *K15* **Son** Noord-Brabant, S Netherlands *51°32′N 05°34′E*
95 *H15* **Son** Akershus, S Norway *59°32′N 10°42′E*
154 *L9* **Son** *var.* Sone. ≈ C India
43 *R16* **Soná** Veraguas, W Panama *08°00′N 81°20′W*
Sonag *see* Zêkog
154 *M12* **Sonapur** *prev.* Sonepur. Orissa, E India *20°50′N 83°58′E*
95 *G24* **Sønderborg** *Ger.* Sonderburg. Sønderjylland, SW Denmark *54°55′N 09°48′E*
Sonderburg *see* Sønderborg
95 *F24* **Sønderjylland** *var.* Sønderjyllands Amt. ◈ *county* SW Denmark
Sønderjyllands Amt *see* Sønderjylland
101 *K15* **Sondershausen** Thüringen, C Germany *51°22′N 10°52′E*
Sondre Strømfjord *see* Kangerlussuaq
106 *E6* **Sondrio** Lombardia, N Italy *46°11′N 09°52′E*
Sone *see* Son
Sonepur *see* Sonapur
57 *K22* **Sonequera** ▲ S Bolivia *22°06′S 67°10′W*
167 *V12* **Sông Câu** Phu Yên, C Vietnam *13°26′N 109°12′E*
167 *R15* **Sông Đôc** Minh Hai, S Vietnam *09°03′N 104°51′E*
81 *H25* **Songea** Ruvuma, S Tanzania *10°42′S 35°39′E*
163 *X10* **Songhua Hu** ◎ NE China
163 *Y7* **Songhua Jiang** *var.* Sungari. ≈ NE China
161 *S8* **Songjiang** Shanghai Shi, E China *31°01′N 121°14′E*
Sŏngjin *see* Kimch'aek
167 *O16* **Songkhla** *var.* Songkla, *Mal.* Singora. Songkhla, SW Thailand *07°12′N 100°35′E*
Songkla *see* Songkhla
163 *T13* **Song Ling** ▲▲ NE China
129 *U12* **Sŏng Ma** *Laos* Ma, Nam. ≈ Laos/Vietnam
163 *W14* **Songnim** SW North Korea *38°43′N 125°40′E*
82 *B10* **Songo** Uíge, NW Angola *07°30′S 14°56′E*
83 *M15* **Songo** Tete, NW Mozambique *15°36′S 32°45′E*
79 *F21* **Songololo** Bas-Congo, SW Dem. Rep. Congo *05°40′S 14°05′E*
160 *H7* **Songpan** *var.* Jin'an, *Tib.* Sungpu. Sichuan, C China *32°49′N 103°39′E*
163 *Y17* **Sŏngsan** S South Korea
161 *R11* **Songxi** Fujian, SE China *27°33′N 118°46′E*
160 *M6* **Songxian** *var.* Song Xian. Henan, C China *34°11′N 112°04′E*
Song Xian *see* Songxian
161 *R10* **Songyang** *var.* Xiping; *prev.* Songyin. Zhejiang, SE China *28°29′N 119°27′E*
Songyin *see* Songyang
163 *V9* **Songyuan** *var.* Fu-yü, Petuna; *prev.* Fuyu. Jilin, NE China *45°10′N 124°52′E*
Sonid Youqi *see* SaihanTal
Sonid Zuoqi *see* Mandalt
152 *I10* **Sonīpat** Haryāna, N India *29°00′N 77°01′E*
93 *M15* **Sonkajärvi** Itä-Suomi, C Finland *63°40′N 27°30′E*
167 *R6* **Sơn La** Sơn La, N Vietnam *21°20′N 103°55′E*
149 *O16* **Sonmiāni** Baluchistān, S Pakistan *25°24′N 66°37′E*
149 *O16* **Sonmiāni Bay** *bay* S Pakistan
101 *K18* **Sonneberg** Thüringen, C Germany *50°22′N 11°10′E*
101 *N24* **Sonntagshorn** ▲ Austria/Germany *47°40′N 12°42′E*
Sonoita *see* Sonoyta
40 *E3* **Sonoita, Rio** *var.* Río Sonoyta. ≈ Mexico/USA
35 *N7* **Sonoma** California, W USA *38°16′N 122°28′W*
35 *T3* **Sonoma Peak** ▲ Nevada, W USA *40°50′N 117°34′W*
35 *P8* **Sonora** California, W USA *37°58′N 120°22′W*
25 *O10* **Sonora** Texas, SW USA *30°34′N 100°35′W*
40 *F5* **Sonora** ◈ *state* NW Mexico
35 *X17* **Sonoran Desert** *var.* Desierto de Altar. *desert* Mexico/USA *see also* Altar, Desierto de
40 *G5* **Sonora, Río** ≈ NW Mexico
40 *E2* **Sonoyta** *var.* Sonoita. Sonora, NW Mexico *31°49′N 112°50′W*
Sonoyta, Río *see* Sonoita, Rio
142 *K6* **Sonqor** *var.* Sunqur. Kermānshāhān, W Iran *34°45′N 47°39′E*
105 *N9* **Sonseca** *var.* Sonseca con Casalgordo. Castilla-La Mancha, C Spain *39°40′N 03°59′W*
Sonseca con Casalgordo *see* Sonseca
54 *E9* **Sonsón** Antioquia, W Colombia *05°45′N 75°18′W*
42 *E7* **Sonsonate** Sonsonate, W El Salvador *13°44′N 89°43′W*
42 *A9* **Sonsonate** ◈ *department* SW El Salvador
188 *A10* **Sonsorol Islands** *island group* S Palau
112 *J9* **Sonta** *Hung.* Szond; *prev.* Szonta. Vojvodina, NW Serbia *45°34′N 19°06′E*
167 *S6* **Sơn Tây** *var.* Sontay. Ha Tây, N Vietnam *21°06′N 105°32′E*
Sontay *see* Sơn Tây
101 *J25* **Sonthofen** Bayern, S Germany *47°31′N 10°16′E*
Soochow *see* Suzhou
80 *O13* **Sool** *off.* Gobolka Sool. ◈ *region* N Somalia
Soomaaliya/Soomaaliyeed, Jamuuriyada Demuqraadiga *see* Somalia
Soome Laht *see* Finland, Gulf of
23 *V5* **Soperton** Georgia, SE USA *32°22′N 82°35′W*
167 *S6* **Sop Hao** Houaphan, N Laos *20°33′N 104°25′E*
Sophia *see* Sofiya
171 *S10* **Sopi** Pulau Morotai, E Indonesia *02°36′N 128°32′E*
Sopianae *see* Pécs
171 *U13* **Sopinusa** Papua, E Indonesia *03°31′S 132°55′E*
81 *B14* **Sopo** ≈ W Sudan
Sopockinie/Sopotskin/Sopotskino *see* Sapotskin
114 *I9* **Sopot** Plovdiv, C Bulgaria *42°39′N 24°43′E*
110 *I7* **Sopot** *Ger.* Zoppot. Pomorskie, N Poland *54°26′N 18°33′E*
167 *O8* **Sop Prap** *var.* Ban Sop Prap. Lampang, NW Thailand *17°55′N 99°20′E*
111 *G22* **Sopron** *Ger.* Ödenburg. Győr-Moson-Sopron, NW Hungary *47°40′N 16°35′E*
147 *U11* **Sopu-Korgon** *var.* Sofi-Kurgan. Oshskaya Oblast', SW Kyrgyzstan *40°03′N 73°30′E*
152 *H5* **Sopur** Jammu and Kashmir, NW India *34°19′N 74°30′E*
107 *J15* **Sora** Lazio, C Italy *41°43′N 13°37′E*
154 *N13* **Sorada** Orissa, E India *19°46′N 84°29′E*
93 *H17* **Söråker** Västernorrland, C Sweden *62°32′N 17°32′E*
57 *J17* **Sorata** La Paz, W Bolivia *15°47′S 68°38′W*
Sorau/Sorau in der Niederlausitz *see* Żary
105 *Q14* **Sorbas** Andalucía, S Spain *37°06′N 02°06′W*
Sord/Sórd Choluim Chille *see* Swords
15 *O11* **Sorel** Québec, SE Canada *46°03′N 73°06′W*
183 *P17* **Sorell** Tasmania, SE Australia *42°49′S 147°34′E*
183 *O17* **Sorell, Lake** ◎ Tasmania, SE Australia
106 *E8* **Soresina** Lombardia, N Italy *45°17′N 09°51′E*
95 *D14* **Sørfjorden** *fjord* S Norway
94 *N11* **Sörforsa** Gävleborg, C Sweden *61°45′N 17°00′E*
103 *R14* **Sorgues** Vaucluse, SE France *44°N 04°52′E*
136 *K13* **Sorgun** Yozgat, C Turkey *39°49′N 35°10′E*
105 *P5* **Soria** Castilla-León, N Spain *41°47′N 02°26′W*
105 *P6* **Soria** ◈ *province* Castilla-León, N Spain
61 *D19* **Soriano** Soriano, SW Uruguay *33°25′S 58°21′W*
61 *D19* **Soriano** ◈ *department* SW Uruguay
92 *O4* **Sørkapp** *headland* SW Svalbard *76°34′N 16°33′E*
143 *T5* **Sorkh, Kūh-e** ▲▲ NE Iran
95 *I23* **Sorø** Vestsjælland, E Denmark *55°25′N 11°34′E*
Soro *see* Ghazal, Bahr el
116 *M8* **Soroca** *Rus.* Soroki. N Moldova *48°10′N 28°18′E*
60 *L10* **Sorocaba** São Paulo, S Brazil *23°29′S 47°27′W*
Sorochino *see* Sarochyna
127 *T7* **Sorochinsk** Orenburgskaya Oblast', W Russian Federation *52°26′N 53°10′E*
Soroki *see* Soroca
188 *H15* **Sorol** *atoll* Caroline Islands, W Micronesia
171 *T12* **Sorong** Papua, E Indonesia *0°49′S 131°16′E*
81 *G17* **Soroti** C Uganda *01°42′N 33°37′E*
Sørøy *see* Sørøya
92 *J8* **Sørøya** *var.* Sørøy, *Lapp.* Sállan. *island* N Norway
104 *G11* **Sorraia, Rio** ≈ C Portugal
92 *I10* **Sørreisa** Troms, N Norway *69°08′N 18°09′E*
107 *K18* **Sorrento** *anc.* Surrentum. Campania, S Italy *40°37′N 14°23′E*
104 *H10* **Sor, Ribeira de** *stream* C Portugal
195 *T3* **Sør Rondane** ▲▲ Antarctica
93 *H14* **Sorsele** Västerbotten, N Sweden *65°31′N 17°34′E*
107 *B17* **Sorso** Sardegna, Italy, C Mediterranean Sea *40°46′N 08°33′E*
171 *P4* **Sorsogon** Luzon, N Philippines *12°57′N 124°04′E*
105 *U4* **Sort** Cataluña, NE Spain *42°25′N 01°07′E*
124 *H11* **Sortavala** *prev.* Serdobol'. Respublika Kareliya, NW Russian Federation *61°45′N 30°37′E*
107 *L25* **Sortino** Sicilia, Italy, C Mediterranean Sea *37°10′N 15°02′E*
92 *G10* **Sortland** Nordland, C Norway *68°44′N 15°25′E*
94 *G9* **Sør-Trøndelag** ◈ *county* S Norway
95 *I15* **Sørumsand** Akershus, S Norway *59°58′N 11°13′E*
118 *D6* **Sõrve Säär** *headland* SW Estonia *57°54′N 22°02′E*
95 *K22* **Sösdala** Skåne, S Sweden *56°00′N 13°36′E*
105 *R4* **Sos del Rey Católico** Aragón, NE Spain *42°30′N 01°13′W*
93 *F15* **Sösjöfjällen** ▲ C Sweden *63°51′N 13°15′E*
126 *K7* **Sosna** ≈ W Russian Federation
62 *H12* **Sosneado, Cerro** ▲ W Argentina *34°44′S 69°52′W*
125 *S9* **Sosnogorsk** Respublika Komi, NW Russian Federation *63°33′N 53°55′E*
124 *J8* **Sosnovets** Respublika Kareliya, NW Russian Federation *64°25′N 34°23′E*
Sosnovets *see* Sosnowiec
127 *Q3* **Sosnovka** Chuvashskaya Respublika, W Russian Federation *56°18′N 47°14′E*
125 *S16* **Sosnovka** Kirovskaya Oblast', NW Russian Federation *56°15′N 51°20′E*
124 *M6* **Sosnovka** Murmanskaya Oblast', NW Russian Federation *66°28′N 40°31′E*
126 *M6* **Sosnovka** Tambovskaya Oblast', W Russian Federation *53°14′N 41°19′E*
124 *H12* **Sosnovo** *Fin.* Rautu. Leningradskaya Oblast', NW Russian Federation *60°30′N 30°13′E*
124 *G13* **Sosnovyy Bor** Leningradskaya Oblast', NW Russian Federation *59°53′N 29°07′E*
127 *V3* **Sosnovyy Bor** Respublika Bashkortostan, W Russian Federation *55°51′N 57°09′E*
Sosnovyy Bor *see* Sasnovy Bor
111 *J16* **Sosnowiec** *Ger.* Sosnowitz, *Rus.* Sosnovets. Śląskie, S Poland *50°16′N 19°07′E*
Sosnowitz *see* Sosnowiec
117 *R2* **Sosnytsya** Chernihivs'ka Oblast', N Ukraine *51°31′N 32°30′E*
109 *V10* **Šoštanj** N Slovenia *46°23′N 15°03′E*
122 *G10* **Sos'va** Sverdlovskaya Oblast', C Russian Federation *59°13′N 61°58′E*
54 *D12* **Sotará, Volcán** 🌋 S Colombia *02°04′N 76°40′W*
76 *D10* **Sotavento, Ilhas de** *var.* Leeward Islands. *island group* S Cape Verde
93 *N15* **Sotkamo** Oulu, C Finland *64°06′N 28°30′E*
109 *W11* **Sotla** ≈ E Slovenia
41 *P10* **Soto la Marina** Tamaulipas, C Mexico *23°44′N 98°10′W*
41 *P10* **Soto la Marina, Río** ≈ C Mexico
95 *B14* **Sotra** *island* S Norway
41 *X12* **Sotuta** Yucatán, SE Mexico *20°34′N 89°00′W*
79 *F17* **Souanké** Sangha, NW Congo *02°03′N 14°02′E*
76 *M17* **Soubré** S Ivory Coast *05°50′N 06°35′W*
115 *H24* **Soúda** *var.* Soúdha, *Eng.* Suda. Kríti, Greece, E Mediterranean Sea *35°29′N 24°04′E*
Soúdha *see* Soúda
Soueida *see* As Suwaydā'
114 *L12* **Souflí** *prev.* Souflíon. Anatolikí Makedonía kai Thráki, NE Greece *41°12′N 26°18′E*
Souflíon *see* Souflí
45 *S11* **Soufrière** W Saint Lucia *13°51′N 61°03′W*
45 *X6* **Soufrière** 🌋 Basse Terre, S Guadeloupe *16°03′N 61°39′W*
102 *M13* **Souillac** Lot, S France *44°53′N 01°29′E*
173 *Y17* **Souillac** S Mauritius *20°31′S 57°31′E*
74 *M5* **Souk Ahras** NE Algeria *36°14′N 08°00′E*
Souk el Arba du Rharb/Souk-el-Arba-du-Rharb/Souk-el-Arba-el-Rhab *see* Souk-el-Arba-Rharb
74 *E6* **Souk-el-Arba-Rharb** *var.* Souk el Arba du Rharb, Souk-el-Arba-du-Rharb, Souk-el-Arba-el-Rhab. NW Morocco *34°38′N 06°00′W*
Soukhné *see* As Sukhnah
163 *X14* **Sŏul** *off.* Sŏul-t'ŭkpyŏlsi, *Eng.* Seoul, *Jap.* Keijō; *prev.* Kyŏngsŏng. ● (South Korea) NW South Korea *37°30′N 126°58′E*
102 *J11* **Soulac-sur-Mer** Gironde, SW France *45°31′N 01°06′W*
Sŏul-t'ŭkpyŏlsi *see* Sŏul
99 *L19* **Soumagne** Liège, E Belgium *50°36′N 05°48′E*
18 *M14* **Sound Beach** Long Island, New York, NE USA *40°56′N 72°58′W*
95 *J22* **Sound, The** *Dan.* Øresund, *Swe.* Öresund. *strait* Denmark/Sweden
115 *H20* **Soúnio, Akrotírio** *headland* C Greece *37°39′N 24°01′E*
138 *F8* **Soûr** *var.* Şūr; *anc.* Tyre. SW Lebanon *33°18′N 35°30′E*
Sources, Mont-aux- *see* Phofung
104 *G8* **Soure** Coimbra, N Portugal *40°04′N 08°38′W*
11 *W17* **Souris** Manitoba, S Canada *49°38′N 100°17′W*
13 *Q14* **Souris** Prince Edward Island, SE Canada *46°22′N 62°16′W*

◆ Country
● Country Capital
◇ Dependent Territory
○ Dependent Territory Capital
◈ Administrative Regions
✈ International Airport
▲ Mountain
▲▲ Mountain Range
🌋 Volcano
≈ River
◎ Lake
⊠ Reservoir

SOURIS RIVER – STAMFORD

28 L2 **Souris River** *var.* Mouse River. ≈ Canada/USA
25 X10 **Sour Lake** Texas, SW USA 30°08′N 94°24′W
115 F17 **Soúrpi** Thessalía, C Greece 39°07′N 22°55′E
104 H11 **Sousel** Portalegre, C Portugal 38°57′N 07°40′W
75 N6 **Sousse** *var.* Sūsah. NE Tunisia 35°46′N 10°38′E
14 H11 **South** ≈ Ontario, S Canada
South *see* Sud
83 G23 **South Africa** *off.* Republic of South Africa, *Afr.* Suid-Afrika. ◆ *republic* S Africa
South Africa, Republic of *see* South Africa
46-47 **South America** *continent*
2 J17 **South American Plate** *tectonic feature*
97 M23 **Southampton** *hist.* Hamwih, *Lat.* Clausentum. S England, United Kingdom 50°54′N 01°23′W
19 N14 **Southampton** Long Island, New York, NE USA 40°52′N 72°22′W
9 P8 **Southampton Island** *island* Nunavut, NE Canada
151 P20 **South Andaman** *island* Andaman Islands, India, NE Indian Ocean
13 Q6 **South Aulatsivik Island** *island* Newfoundland and Labrador, E Canada
182 E4 **South Australia** ⬖ *state* S Australia
South Australian Abyssal Plain *see* South Australian Plain
192 G11 **South Australian Basin** *undersea feature* SW Indian Ocean 38°00′S 126°00′E
173 X12 **South Australian Plain** *var.* South Australian Abyssal Plain. *undersea feature* SE Indian Ocean
37 R13 **South Baldy** ▲ New Mexico, SW USA 33°59′N 107°11′W
23 Y14 **South Bay** Florida, SE USA 26°39′N 80°43′W
14 E12 **South Baymouth** Manitoulin Island, Ontario, S Canada 45°33′N 82°01′W
30 L10 **South Beloit** Illinois, N USA 42°29′N 89°02′W
31 O11 **South Bend** Indiana, N USA 41°40′N 86°15′W
25 R6 **South Bend** Texas, SW USA 32°58′N 98°39′W
32 F9 **South Bend** Washington, NW USA 46°38′N 123°48′W
South Beveland *see* Zuid-Beveland
South Borneo *see* Kalimantan Selatan
21 U7 **South Boston** Virginia, NE USA 36°42′N 78°58′W
182 F2 **South Branch Neales** *seasonal river* South Australia
21 U3 **South Branch Potomac River** ≈ West Virginia, NE USA
185 H19 **Southbridge** Canterbury, South Island, New Zealand 43°49′S 172°17′E
19 N12 **Southbridge** Massachusetts, NE USA 42°03′N 72°00′W
183 P17 **South Bruny Island** *island* Tasmania, SE Australia
18 L7 **South Burlington** Vermont, NE USA 44°27′N 73°08′W
44 M6 **South Caicos** *island* S Turks and Caicos Islands
South Cape *see* Ka Lae
23 V3 **South Carolina** *off.* State of South Carolina, *also known as* The Palmetto State. ⬖ *state* SE USA
South Carpathians *see* Carpaţii Meridionalii
South Celebes *see* Sulawesi Selatan
21 Q5 **South Charleston** West Virginia, NE USA 38°22′N 81°42′W
192 D7 **South China Basin** *undersea feature* SE South China Sea 15°00′N 115°00′E
169 R8 **South China Sea** *Chin.* Nan Hai, *Ind.* Laut Cina Selatan, *Vtn.* Biên Đông. *sea* SE Asia
33 Z10 **South Dakota** *off.* State of South Dakota, *also known as* The Coyote State, Sunshine State. ⬖ *state* N USA
23 X10 **South Daytona** Florida, SE USA 29°09′N 81°01′W
37 R10 **South Domingo Pueblo** New Mexico, SW USA 35°28′N 106°24′W
97 N23 **South Downs** *hill range* SE England, United Kingdom
83 I21 **South East** ⬖ *district* SE Botswana
65 H15 **South East Bay** *bay* Ascension Island, C Atlantic Ocean
183 O17 **South East Cape** *headland* Tasmania, SE Australia 43°36′S 146°52′E
38 K10 **Southeast Cape** *headland* Saint Lawrence Island, Alaska, USA 62°56′N 169°39′W
South-East Celebes *see* Sulawesi Tenggara
192 G12 **Southeast Indian Ridge** *undersea feature* Indian Ocean/Pacific Ocean 50°00′S 110°00′E
Southeast Island *see* Tagula Island
193 P13 **Southeast Pacific Basin** *var.* Belling Hausen Mulde. *undersea feature* SE Pacific Ocean 60°00′S 115°00′W
65 H15 **South East Point** *headland* SE Ascension Island
183 O14 **South East Point** *headland* Victoria, S Australia 39°10′S 146°21′E
44 L5 **Southeast Point** *headland* Mayaguana, SE Bahamas 22°15′N 72°44′W
191 Z3 **South East Point** *headland* Kiritimati, NE Kiribati 01°42′N 157°10′W
South-East Sulawesi *see* Sulawesi Tenggara
11 U12 **Southend** Saskatchewan, C Canada 56°20′N 103°14′W
97 P22 **Southend-on-Sea** E England, United Kingdom 51°33′N 00°43′E
83 H20 **Southern** *var.* Bangwaketse, Ngwaketze. ⬖ *district* SE Botswana
138 E13 **Southern** ⬖ *district* S Israel
83 N15 **Southern** ⬖ *region* S Malawi
155 J26 **Southern** ⬖ *province* S Sri Lanka
83 I15 **Southern** ⬖ *province* S Zambia
185 E19 **Southern Alps** ▲▲ South Island, New Zealand
190 K15 **Southern Cook Islands** *island group* S Cook Islands
180 K12 **Southern Cross** Western Australia 31°17′S 119°15′E
80 A12 **Southern Darfur** ⬖ *state* W Sudan
186 B7 **Southern Highlands** ⬖ *province* W Papua New Guinea
11 V11 **Southern Indian Lake** ◎ Manitoba, C Canada
80 E11 **Southern Kordofan** ⬖ *state* C Sudan
187 Z15 **Southern Lau Group** *island group* Lau Group, SE Fiji
81 I15 **Southern Nationalities** ⬖ *region* S Ethiopia
173 S13 **Southern Ocean** *ocean*
21 T10 **Southern Pines** North Carolina, SE USA 35°10′N 79°23′W
96 I13 **Southern Uplands** ▲▲ S Scotland, United Kingdom
Southern Urals *see* Yuzhnyy Ural
183 P16 **South Esk River** ≈ Tasmania, SE Australia
11 U16 **Southey** Saskatchewan, S Canada 50°53′N 104°27′W
27 V2 **South Fabius River** ≈ Missouri, C USA
31 S10 **Southfield** Michigan, N USA 42°28′N 83°12′W
192 K10 **South Fiji Basin** *undersea feature* S Pacific Ocean 26°00′S 175°00′E
97 Q22 **South Foreland** *headland* SE England, United Kingdom 51°08′N 01°22′E
35 P7 **South Fork American River** ≈ California, W USA
28 K7 **South Fork Grand River** ≈ South Dakota, N USA
35 T12 **South Fork Kern River** ≈ California, W USA
39 Q7 **South Fork Koyukuk River** ≈ Alaska, USA
39 Q11 **South Fork Kuskokwim River** ≈ Alaska, USA
26 H2 **South Fork Republican River** ≈ C USA
26 L3 **South Fork Solomon River** ≈ Kansas, C USA
31 P5 **South Fox Island** *island* Michigan, N USA
20 G8 **South Fulton** Tennessee, S USA 36°28′N 88°53′W
195 U10 **South Geomagnetic Pole** *pole* Antarctica
65 J20 **South Georgia** *island* South Georgia and the South Sandwich Islands, SW Atlantic Ocean
65 K21 **South Georgia and the South Sandwich Islands** ⬖ *UK Dependent Territory* SW Atlantic Ocean
47 Y14 **South Georgia Ridge** *var.* North Scotia Ridge. *undersea feature* SW Atlantic Ocean 54°00′S 40°00′W
181 Q1 **South Goulburn Island** *island* Northern Territory, N Australia
153 U16 **South Hatia Island** *island* SE Bangladesh
31 O10 **South Haven** Michigan, N USA 42°24′N 86°16′W
21 V7 **South Hill** Virginia, NE USA 36°43′N 78°07′W
South Holland *see* Zuid-Holland
21 P8 **South Holston Lake** ⊞ Tennessee/Virginia, S USA
175 N1 **South Honshu Ridge** *undersea feature* W Pacific Ocean
26 M6 **South Hutchinson** Kansas, C USA 38°01′N 97°56′W
151 K21 **South Huvadhu Atoll** *atoll* S Maldives
173 U14 **South Indian Basin** *undersea feature* Indian Ocean/Pacific Ocean 60°00′S 120°00′E
11 W11 **South Indian Lake** Manitoba, C Canada 56°48′N 98°56′W
81 I17 **South Island** *island* NW Kenya
185 C20 **South Island** *island* S New Zealand
South Kalimantan *see* Kalimantan Selatan
South Kazakhstan *see* Yuzhnyy Kazakhstan
163 X15 **South Korea** *off.* Republic of Korea, *Kor.* Taehan Min'guk. ◆ *republic* E Asia
35 Q6 **South Lake Tahoe** California, W USA 38°56′N 119°57′W
25 N6 **Southland** Texas, SW USA 33°16′N 101°31′W
185 B23 **Southland** *off.* Southland Region. ⬖ *region* South Island, New Zealand
Southland Region *see* Southland
29 N15 **South Loup River** ≈ Nebraska, C USA
151 K19 **South Maalhosmadulu Atoll** *atoll* N Maldives
14 E15 **South Maitland** ≈ Ontario, S Canada
192 E8 **South Makassar Basin** *undersea feature* E Java Sea
31 O6 **South Manitou Island** *island* Michigan, N USA
151 K18 **South Miladhunmadulu Atoll** *var.* Noonu. *atoll* N Maldives
21 X8 **South Mills** North Carolina, SE USA 36°28′N 76°18′W
8 H9 **South Nahanni** ≈ Northwest Territories, NW Canada
39 P13 **South Naknek** Alaska, USA 58°39′N 157°01′W
14 M13 **South Nation** ≈ Ontario, SE Canada
44 F9 **South Negril Point** *headland* W Jamaica 18°14′N 78°21′W
151 K20 **South Nilandhe Atoll** *var.* Dhaalu Atoll. *atoll* C Maldives
36 L2 **South Ogden** Utah, W USA 41°09′N 111°58′W
18 M14 **Southold** Long Island, New York, NE USA 41°03′N 72°24′W
194 H1 **South Orkney Islands** *island group* Antarctica
137 S9 **South Ossetia** *former autonomous region* SW Georgia
South Pacific Basin *see* Southwest Pacific Basin
19 P7 **South Paris** Maine, NE USA 44°14′N 70°33′W
189 U13 **South Pass** *passage* Chuuk Islands, C Micronesia
33 U15 **South Pass** *pass* Wyoming, C USA
20 K10 **South Pittsburg** Tennessee, S USA 35°00′N 85°42′W
28 K15 **South Platte River** ≈ Colorado/Nebraska, C USA
31 T16 **South Point** Ohio, N USA 38°25′N 82°35′W
65 G15 **South Point** *headland* S Ascension Island
31 R6 **South Point** *headland* Michigan, N USA 44°51′N 83°17′W
South Point *see* Ka Lae
195 Q9 **South Pole** *pole* Antarctica
183 P17 **Southport** Tasmania, SE Australia 43°26′S 146°57′E
97 K17 **Southport** NW England, United Kingdom 53°39′N 03°01′W
21 V12 **Southport** North Carolina, SE USA 33°55′N 78°00′W
19 P8 **South Portland** Maine, NE USA 43°38′N 70°14′W
14 H12 **South River** Ontario, S Canada 45°50′N 79°23′W
21 U11 **South River** ≈ North Carolina, SE USA
96 K5 **South Ronaldsay** *island* NE Scotland, United Kingdom
36 L2 **South Salt Lake** Utah, W USA 40°42′N 111°52′W
65 L21 **South Sandwich Islands** *island group* SW Atlantic Ocean
65 K21 **South Sandwich Trench** *undersea feature* SW Atlantic Ocean 56°30′S 25°00′W
11 S16 **South Saskatchewan** ≈ Alberta/Saskatchewan, S Canada
65 I21 **South Scotia Ridge** *undersea feature* S Scotia Sea
11 V10 **South Seal** ≈ Manitoba, C Canada
194 G4 **South Shetland Islands** *island group* Antarctica
65 H22 **South Shetland Trough** *undersea feature* Atlantic Ocean/Pacific Ocean 61°00′S 59°30′W
97 M14 **South Shields** NE England, United Kingdom 55°N 01°25′W
29 R13 **South Sioux City** Nebraska, C USA 42°28′N 96°24′W
192 J9 **South Solomon Trench** *undersea feature* W Pacific Ocean
183 V3 **South Stradbroke Island** *island* Queensland, E Australia
South Sulawesi *see* Sulawesi Selatan
South Sumatra *see* Sumatera Selatan
184 K11 **South Taranaki Bight** *bight* SE Tasman Sea
South Tasmania Plateau *see* Tasman Plateau
36 M15 **South Tucson** Arizona, SW USA 32°11′N 110°56′W
12 H9 **South Twin Island** *island* Nunavut, C Canada
96 E9 **South Uist** *island* NW Scotland, United Kingdom
149 R8 **South Wazīristān** ⬖ *federally administered tribal area* NW Pakistan
South-West *see* Sud-Ouest
South-West Africa/South West Africa *see* Namibia
65 F15 **South West Bay** *bay* Ascension Island, C Atlantic Ocean
183 N18 **South West Cape** *headland* Tasmania, SE Australia 43°34′S 146°01′E
185 B26 **South West Cape** *headland* Stewart Island, New Zealand 47°15′S 167°28′E
38 J10 **Southwest Cape** *headland* Saint Lawrence Island, Alaska, USA 63°19′N 171°27′W
Southwest Indian Ocean Ridge *see* Southwest Indian Ridge
173 N11 **Southwest Indian Ridge** *var.* Southwest Indian Ocean Ridge. *undersea feature* SW Indian Ocean 43°00′S 40°00′E
192 L10 **Southwest Pacific Basin** *var.* South Pacific Basin. *undersea feature* SE Pacific Ocean 40°00′S 150°00′W
44 H2 **Southwest Point** *headland* Great Abaco, N Bahamas 25°50′N 77°12′W
191 X3 **South West Point** *headland* Kiritimati, NE Kiribati 01°53′N 157°34′E
65 G25 **South West Point** *headland* SW Saint Helena 16°00′S 05°48′W
25 P5 **South Wichita River** ≈ Texas, SW USA
97 Q20 **Southwold** E England, United Kingdom 52°15′N 01°36′E
19 Q12 **South Yarmouth** Massachusetts, NE USA 41°38′N 70°09′W
116 J10 **Sovata** *Hung.* Szováta. Mureş, C Romania 46°36′N 25°04′E
107 N22 **Soverato** Calabria, SW Italy 38°40′N 16°31′E
121 O4 **Sovereign Base Area** *uk military installation* S Cyprus
Sovetabad *see* Ghafurov
126 C2 **Sovetsk** *Ger.* Tilsit. Kaliningradskaya Oblast', W Russian Federation 53°04′N 21°52′E
125 Q15 **Sovetsk** Kirovskaya Oblast', NW Russian Federation 57°37′N 49°02′E
127 N10 **Sovetskaya** Rostovskaya Oblast', SW Russian Federation 49°00′N 42°09′E
127 P3 **Sovetskiy** Respublika Mariy El, W Russian Federation 56°45′N 48°30′E
Sovetskoye *see* Ketchenery
146 I15 **Sovet"yab** *prev.* Sovet"yap. Ahal Welaýaty, S Turkmenistan 36°29′N 61°13′E
Sovet"yap *see* Sovet"yab
117 U12 **Sovyets'kyy** Respublika Krym, S Ukraine 45°20′N 34°54′E
83 I18 **Sowa** *var.* Sua. Central, NE Botswana 20°33′S 26°18′E
83 I18 **Sowa Pan** *var.* Sua Pan. *salt lake* NE Botswana
83 J21 **Soweto** Gauteng, NE South Africa 26°08′S 27°54′E
147 R11 **So'x** *Rus.* Sokh. Farg'ona Viloyati, E Uzbekistan 39°56′N 71°10′E
Sōya-kaikyō *see* La Perouse Strait
165 T1 **Sōya-misaki** *headland* Hokkaidō, NE Japan 45°31′N 141°55′E
125 N7 **Soyana** ≈ NW Russian Federation
146 A8 **Soye, Mys** *var.* Mys Suz. *headland* NW Turkmenistan 41°47′N 52°27′E
82 A10 **Soyo** Dem. Rep. Congo, NW Angola 06°07′S 12°18′E
80 J10 **Soyra** ▲ C Eritrea 14°46′N 39°29′E
Sozaq *see* Suzak
119 P16 **Sozh** ≈ NE Europe
114 N10 **Sozopol** *prev.* Sizebolu; *anc.* Apollonia. Burgas, E Bulgaria 42°25′N 27°42′E
99 L20 **Spa** Liège, E Belgium 50°29′N 05°52′E
194 I7 **Spaatz Island** *island* Antarctica
144 M14 **Space Launching Centre** *space station* Kzylorda, S Kazakhstan
105 O7 **Spain** *off.* Kingdom of Spain, *Sp.* España; *anc.* Hispania, Iberia, *Lat.* Hispana. ◆ *monarchy* SW Europe
Spain, Kingdom of *see* Spain
Spalato *see* Split
97 O19 **Spalding** E England, United Kingdom 52°49′N 00°06′W
14 D11 **Spanish** Ontario, S Canada 46°12′N 82°21′W
36 L3 **Spanish Fork** Utah, W USA 40°09′N 111°40′W
64 B12 **Spanish Point** *headland* C Bermuda 32°18′N 64°49′W
14 E9 **Spanish River** ≈ Ontario, S Canada
44 K13 **Spanish Town** *hist.* St.Iago de la Vega. C Jamaica 18°N 76°57′W
Spánta, Akrotírio *see* Spátha, Akrotírio
35 Q5 **Sparks** Nevada, W USA 39°32′N 119°45′W
Sparnacum *see* Épernay
95 N16 **Sparreholm** Södermanland, C Sweden 59°04′N 16°51′E
23 U4 **Sparta** Georgia, SE USA 33°16′N 82°58′W
30 K16 **Sparta** Illinois, N USA 38°07′N 89°42′W
31 P9 **Sparta** Michigan, N USA 43°09′N 85°42′W
21 R8 **Sparta** North Carolina, SE USA 36°30′N 81°07′W
20 L9 **Sparta** Tennessee, S USA 35°55′N 85°30′W
30 I7 **Sparta** Wisconsin, N USA 43°57′N 90°50′W
Sparta *see* Spárti
21 Q11 **Spartanburg** South Carolina, SE USA 34°56′N 81°57′W
115 F21 **Spárti** *Eng.* Sparta. Pelopónnisos, S Greece 37°05′N 22°25′E
107 B21 **Spartivento, Capo** *headland* Sardegna, Italy, C Mediterranean Sea 38°52′N 08°50′E
11 P17 **Sparwood** British Columbia, SW Canada 49°45′N 114°45′W
126 I4 **Spas-Demensk** Kaluzhskaya Oblast', W Russian Federation 54°22′N 34°16′E
126 M4 **Spas-Klepiki** Ryazanskaya Oblast', W Russian Federation 55°08′N 40°15′E
Spasovo *see* Kulen Vakuf
123 R15 **Spassk-Dal'niy** Primorskiy Kray, SE Russian Federation 44°34′N 132°52′E
126 M5 **Spassk-Ryazanskiy** Ryazanskaya Oblast', W Russian Federation 54°25′N 40°21′E
115 H19 **Spáta** Attikí, C Greece 37°58′N 23°55′E
121 Q11 **Spátha, Akrotírio** *var.* Akrotírio Spánta. *headland* Kríti, Greece, E Mediterranean Sea 35°42′N 23°44′E
Špatrjan *see* Paternion
28 I9 **Spearfish** South Dakota, N USA 44°29′N 103°51′W
25 O1 **Spearman** Texas, SW USA 36°12′N 101°13′W
65 C25 **Speedwell Island** *island* S Falkland Islands
65 G25 **Speery Island** *island* S Saint Helena
45 N14 **Speightstown** NW Barbados 13°15′N 59°39′W
106 I13 **Spello** Umbria, C Italy 43°00′N 12°41′E
39 R12 **Spenard** Alaska, USA 61°09′N 150°03′W
Spence Bay *see* Taloyoak
31 O14 **Spencer** Indiana, N USA 39°18′N 86°46′W
29 T12 **Spencer** Iowa, C USA 43°09′N 95°07′W
29 P12 **Spencer** Nebraska, C USA 42°52′N 98°42′W
21 S9 **Spencer** North Carolina, SE USA 35°41′N 80°26′W
20 L9 **Spencer** Tennessee, S USA 35°46′N 85°27′W
21 Q4 **Spencer** West Virginia, NE USA 38°48′N 81°22′W
30 K6 **Spencer** Wisconsin, N USA 44°46′N 90°17′W
182 G10 **Spencer, Cape** *headland* South Australia 35°17′S 136°52′E
39 V13 **Spencer, Cape** *headland* Alaska, USA 58°12′N 136°39′W
182 H9 **Spencer Gulf** *gulf* South Australia
18 F9 **Spencerport** New York, NE USA 43°11′N 77°48′W
31 Q12 **Spencerville** Ohio, N USA 40°42′N 84°21′W
115 E17 **Spercheiáda** *var.* Sperhiada, Sperkhiás. Stereá Ellás, C Greece 38°54′N 22°07′E
115 E17 **Spercheiós** ≈ C Greece
Sperhiada *see* Spercheiáda
95 G14 **Sperillen** ◎ S Norway
Sperkhiás *see* Spercheiáda
101 I18 **Spessart** *hill range* C Germany
Spétsai *see* Spétses
115 G21 **Spétses** *prev.* Spétsai. Spétses, S Greece 37°16′N 23°09′E
115 G21 **Spétses** *island* S Greece
96 J8 **Spey** ≈ NE Scotland, United Kingdom
101 G20 **Speyer** *Eng.* Spires; *anc.* Civitas Nemetum, Spira. Rheinland-Pfalz, SW Germany 49°18′N 08°26′E
101 G20 **Speyerbach** ≈ W Germany
107 N20 **Spezzano Albanese** Calabria, SW Italy 39°40′N 16°17′E
Spice Islands *see* Maluku
100 F9 **Spiekeroog** *island* NW Germany
109 W9 **Spielfeld** Steiermark, SE Austria 46°43′N 15°36′E
65 N21 **Spiess Seamount** *undersea feature* S Atlantic Ocean 53°00′S 02°00′W
108 E9 **Spiez** Bern, W Switzerland 46°42′N 07°41′E
98 G13 **Spijkenisse** Zuid-Holland, SW Netherlands 51°52′N 04°19′E
39 T6 **Spike Mountain** ▲ Alaska, USA 67°42′N 141°39′W
115 I25 **Spíli** Kríti, Greece, E Mediterranean Sea 35°12′N 24°33′E
108 D10 **Spillgerten** ▲ W Switzerland 46°34′N 07°25′E
118 F9 **Spilva** ✈ (Rīga) Rīga, C Latvia 56°55′N 24°03′E
107 N17 **Spinazzola** Puglia, SE Italy 40°58′N 16°06′E
149 O9 **Spīn Būldak** Kandahār, S Afghanistan 31°01′N 66°23′E
Spira *see* Speyer
Spirdingsee *see* Śniardwy, Jezioro
Spires *see* Speyer
29 T11 **Spirit Lake** Iowa, C USA 43°25′N 95°06′W
29 T11 **Spirit Lake** ◎ Iowa, C USA
11 N13 **Spirit River** Alberta, W Canada 55°46′N 118°51′W
11 S14 **Spiritwood** Saskatchewan, S Canada 53°18′N 107°33′W
27 R11 **Spiro** Oklahoma, C USA 35°14′N 94°37′W
111 L19 **Spišská Nová Ves** *Ger.* Neudorf, Zipser Neudorf, *Hung.* Igló. Košický Kraj, E Slovakia 48°58′N 20°35′E
137 T11 **Spitak** NW Armenia 40°51′N 44°17′E
92 O2 **Spitsbergen** *island* NW Svalbard
Spittal *see* Spittal an der Drau
109 R9 **Spittal an der Drau** *var.* Spittal. Kärnten, S Austria 46°48′N 13°30′E
109 V3 **Spitz** Niederösterreich, NE Austria 48°24′N 15°22′E
94 D9 **Spjelkavik** Møre og Romsdal, S Norway 62°28′N 06°22′E
25 W10 **Splendora** Texas, SW USA 30°13′N 95°09′W
113 E14 **Split** *It.* Spalato. Split-Dalmacija, S Croatia 43°31′N 16°27′E
113 E14 **Split** ✈ Split-Dalmacija, S Croatia 43°33′N 16°19′E
113 E14 **Split-Dalmacija** *off.* Splitsko-Dalmatinska Županija. ⬖ *province* S Croatia
11 X12 **Split Lake** ◎ Manitoba, C Canada
Splitsko-Dalmatinska Županija *see* Split-Dalmacija
108 H10 **Splügen** Graubünden, S Switzerland 46°33′N 09°18′E
Spodnji Dravograd *see* Dravograd
25 P12 **Spofford** Texas, SW USA 29°10′N 100°24′W
118 J11 **Špoģi** Daugvapils, SE Latvia 56°03′N 26°47′E
32 L8 **Spokane** Washington, NW USA 47°40′N 117°26′W
32 L8 **Spokane River** ≈ Washington, NW USA
106 I13 **Spoleto** Umbria, C Italy 42°44′N 12°44′E
30 I4 **Spooner** Wisconsin, N USA 45°51′N 91°49′W
30 K12 **Spoon River** ≈ Illinois, N USA
21 W5 **Spotsylvania** Virginia, NE USA 38°12′N 77°35′W
32 L8 **Sprague** Washington, NW USA 47°19′N 117°55′W
170 J5 **Spratly Island** *island* SW Spratly Islands
192 E6 **Spratly Islands** *Chin.* Nansha Qundao. ◇ *disputed territory* SE Asia
32 J12 **Spray** Oregon, NW USA 44°30′N 119°38′W
112 I11 **Spreča** ≈ N Bosnia and Herzegovina
100 P13 **Spree** ≈ E Germany
100 P13 **Spreewald** *wetland* NE Germany
101 P14 **Spremberg** Brandenburg, E Germany 51°34′N 14°22′E
25 W11 **Spring** Texas, SW USA 30°03′N 95°24′W
31 Q10 **Spring Arbor** Michigan, N USA 42°12′N 84°33′W
83 E23 **Springbok** Northern Cape, W South Africa 29°44′S 17°56′E
18 I15 **Spring City** Pennsylvania, NE USA 40°10′N 75°33′W
20 L9 **Spring City** Tennessee, S USA 35°41′N 84°51′W
36 L4 **Spring City** Utah, W USA 39°28′N 111°30′W
35 W3 **Spring Creek** Nevada, W USA 40°45′N 115°40′W
27 S9 **Springdale** Arkansas, C USA 36°11′N 94°07′W
31 Q14 **Springdale** Ohio, N USA 39°17′N 84°29′W
100 I13 **Springe** Niedersachsen, N Germany 52°13′N 09°33′E
37 U9 **Springer** New Mexico, SW USA 36°21′N 104°35′W
37 W7 **Springfield** Colorado, C USA 37°24′N 102°36′W
23 W5 **Springfield** Georgia, SE USA 32°21′N 81°20′W
30 K14 **Springfield** *state capital* Illinois, N USA 39°48′N 89°39′W
20 L6 **Springfield** Kentucky, S USA 37°42′N 85°18′W
18 M12 **Springfield** Massachusetts, NE USA 42°06′N 72°32′W
29 T10 **Springfield** Minnesota, N USA 44°15′N 94°58′W
27 T7 **Springfield** Missouri, C USA 37°13′N 93°18′W
31 R13 **Springfield** Ohio, N USA 39°55′N 83°49′W
32 G13 **Springfield** Oregon, NW USA 44°03′N 123°01′W
29 Q12 **Springfield** South Dakota, N USA 42°51′N 97°54′W
20 J8 **Springfield** Tennessee, S USA 36°30′N 86°54′W
18 M9 **Springfield** Vermont, NE USA 43°18′N 72°27′W
30 K14 **Springfield, Lake** ⊞ Illinois, N USA
55 T8 **Spring Garden** NE Guyana 06°58′N 58°34′W
30 K8 **Spring Green** Wisconsin, N USA 43°10′N 90°02′W
29 X11 **Spring Grove** Minnesota, N USA 43°33′N 91°38′W
13 P15 **Springhill** Nova Scotia, SE Canada 45°40′N 64°04′W
23 V12 **Spring Hill** Florida, SE USA 28°28′N 82°36′W
27 R4 **Spring Hill** Kansas, C USA 38°44′N 94°49′W
22 G4 **Springhill** Louisiana, S USA 33°01′N 93°27′W
20 I9 **Spring Hill** Tennessee, S USA 35°46′N 86°55′W
21 U10 **Spring Lake** North Carolina, SE USA 35°10′N 78°58′W
24 M4 **Springlake** Texas, SW USA 34°13′N 102°18′W
35 W11 **Spring Mountains** ▲▲ Nevada, W USA
27 W9 **Spring River** ≈ Arkansas/Missouri, C USA
27 S7 **Spring River** ≈ Missouri/Oklahoma, C USA
83 J21 **Springs** Gauteng, NE South Africa 26°16′S 28°26′E
185 H16 **Springs Junction** West Coast, South Island, New Zealand 42°21′S 172°11′E
181 X8 **Springsure** Queensland, E Australia 24°09′S 148°06′E
29 W11 **Spring Valley** Minnesota, N USA 43°41′N 92°23′W
18 K13 **Spring Valley** New York, NE USA 41°10′N 73°58′W
29 N12 **Springview** Nebraska, C USA 42°49′N 99°45′W
18 D11 **Springville** New York, NE USA 42°27′N 78°52′W
36 L3 **Springville** Utah, W USA 40°10′N 111°36′W
Sprottau *see* Szprotawa
15 V4 **Sproule, Pointe** *headland* Québec, SE Canada 49°47′N 67°02′W
11 Q14 **Spruce Grove** Alberta, SW Canada 53°36′N 113°55′W
21 T4 **Spruce Knob** ▲ West Virginia, NE USA 38°40′N 79°37′W
35 X3 **Spruce Mountain** ▲ Nevada, W USA 40°33′N 114°46′W
21 P9 **Spruce Pine** North Carolina, SE USA 35°55′N 82°03′W
98 G13 **Spui** ≈ SW Netherlands
107 O19 **Spulico, Capo** *headland* S Italy 39°57′N 16°38′E
25 O5 **Spur** Texas, SW USA 33°28′N 100°51′W
97 O17 **Spurn Head** *headland* E England, United Kingdom 53°34′N 00°06′E
99 H20 **Spy** Namur, S Belgium 50°29′N 04°43′E
95 I15 **Spydeberg** Østfold, S Norway 59°36′N 11°04′E
185 J17 **Spy Glass Point** *headland* South Island, New Zealand 42°33′S 173°31′E
10 L17 **Squamish** British Columbia, SW Canada 49°41′N 123°11′W
19 O8 **Squam Lake** ◎ New Hampshire, NE USA
19 S2 **Squa Pan Mountain** ▲ Maine, NE USA 46°36′N 68°09′W
39 N16 **Squaw Harbor** Unga Island, Alaska, USA 55°12′N 160°41′W
14 E11 **Squaw Island** *island* Ontario, S Canada
107 O22 **Squillace, Golfo di** *gulf* S Italy
107 Q18 **Squinzano** Puglia, SE Italy 40°26′N 18°03′E
Sráid na Cathrach *see* Milltown Malbay
167 S11 **Srâlau** Stœng Trêng, N Cambodia 14°03′N 105°46′E
Srath an Urláir *see* Stranorlar
112 G10 **Srbac** ⬖ Republika Srpska, N Bosnia and Herzegovina
Srbija *see* Serbia
Srbinje *see* Foča
112 K9 **Srbobran** *var.* Bácsszenttamás, *Hung.* Szenttamás. Vojvodina, N Serbia 45°33′N 19°46′E
Srbobran *see* Donji Vakuf
167 R13 **Srê Âmbĕl** Kaôh Kông, SW Cambodia 11°07′N 103°46′E
112 K13 **Srebrenica** Republika Srpska, E Bosnia and Herzegovina 44°04′N 19°18′E
112 I11 **Srebrenik** Federacija Bosna I Hercegovina, NE Bosnia and Herzegovina 44°42′N 18°30′E
114 K10 **Sredets** *prev.* Syulemeshlii. Stara Zagora, C Bulgaria 42°16′N 25°40′E
114 M10 **Sredets** *prev.* Grudovo. ⬖ Burgas, E Bulgaria
114 M10 **Sredetska Reka** ≈ SE Bulgaria
123 U9 **Sredinnyy Khrebet** ▲▲ E Russian Federation
114 N7 **Sredishte** *Rom.* Beibunar; *prev.* Knyazhevo. Dobrich, NE Bulgaria 43°51′N 27°30′E
114 I10 **Sredna Gora** ▲▲ C Bulgaria
123 R7 **Srednekolymsk** Respublika Sakha (Yakutiya), NE Russian Federation 67°28′N 153°52′E
126 K7 **Srednerusskaya Vozvyshennost'** *Eng.* Central Russian Upland. ▲▲ W Russian Federation
122 L9 **Srednesibirskoye Ploskogor'ye** *var.* Central Siberian Uplands, *Eng.* Central Siberian Plateau. ▲▲ N Russian Federation
125 V13 **Sredniy Ural** ▲▲ NW Russian Federation
167 T12 **Srê Khtŭm** Môndól Kiri, E Cambodia 12°10′N 106°52′E
110 G12 **Śrem** Wielkopolskie, C Poland 52°07′N 17°00′E
112 K10 **Sremska Mitrovica** *prev.* Mitrovica, *Ger.* Mitrowitz. Vojvodina, NW Serbia 44°58′N 19°37′E
167 R11 **Srêng, Stœng** ≈ NW Cambodia
167 R11 **Srê Noy** Siĕmréab, NW Cambodia 13°47′N 104°03′E
Srepok, Sông *see* Srêpôk, Tônle
167 T12 **Srêpôk, Tônle** *var.* Sông Srepok. ≈ Cambodia/Vietnam
123 P13 **Sretensk** Chitinskaya Oblast', S Russian Federation 52°14′N 117°33′E
169 R10 **Sri Aman** Sarawak, East Malaysia 01°13′N 111°25′E
117 R4 **Sribne** Chernihivs'ka Oblast', N Ukraine 50°40′N 32°55′E
Sri Jayawardanapura *see* Sri Jayewardanapura Kotte
155 I25 **Sri Jayewardanapura Kotte** *var.* Sri Jayawardanapura. Western Province, W Sri Lanka 06°54′N 79°58′E
155 M14 **Srīkākulam** Andhra Pradesh, E India 18°18′N 83°54′E
155 I25 **Sri Lanka** *off.* Democratic Socialist Republic of Sri Lanka; *prev.* Ceylon. ◆ *republic* S Asia
130 F14 **Sri Lanka** *island* S Asia
Sri Lanka, Democratic Socialist Republic of *see* Sri Lanka
153 V14 **Srimangal** Sylhet, E Bangladesh 24°19′N 91°40′E
Sri Mohangorh *see* Shri Mohangarh
152 H5 **Srīnagar** *state capital* Jammu and Kashmir, N India 34°07′N 74°50′E
167 N10 **Srinagarind Reservoir** ◎ W Thailand
155 F19 **Sringeri** Karnātaka, W India 13°26′N 75°13′E
155 K25 **Sri Pada** *Eng.* Adam's Peak. ▲ S Sri Lanka 06°49′N 80°25′E
Sri Saket *see* Si Sa Ket
111 G14 **Środa Śląska** *Ger.* Neumarkt. Dolnośląskie, SW Poland 51°10′N 16°30′E
110 H12 **Środa Wielkopolska** Wielkopolskie, C Poland 52°13′N 17°17′E
Srpska Kostajnica *see* Bosanska Kostajnica
113 G14 **Srpska, Republika** ⬖ *republic* Bosnia and Herzegovina
Srpski Brod *see* Bosanski Brod
Ssu-ch'uan *see* Sichuan
Ssu-p'ing/Ssu-p'ing-chieh *see* Siping
Stablo *see* Stavelot
99 G15 **Stabroek** Antwerpen, N Belgium 51°21′N 04°22′E
Stackeln *see* Strenči
96 I5 **Stack Skerry** *island* N Scotland, United Kingdom
100 I9 **Stade** Niedersachsen, NW Germany 53°36′N 09°29′E
94 C10 **Stadlandet** *peninsula* S Norway
109 R5 **Stadl-Paura** Oberösterreich, NW Austria 48°05′N 13°52′E
119 L20 **Stadolichy** *Rus.* Stodolichi. Homyel'skaya Voblasts', SE Belarus 51°44′N 28°30′E
98 P7 **Stadskanaal** Groningen, NE Netherlands 53°N 06°55′E
101 H16 **Stadtallendorf** Hessen, C Germany 50°49′N 09°01′E
101 K23 **Stadtbergen** Bayern, S Germany 48°21′N 10°50′E
108 G7 **Stäfa** Zürich, NE Switzerland 47°14′N 08°45′E
95 K23 **Staffanstorp** Skåne, S Sweden 55°38′N 13°13′E
101 K18 **Staffelstein** Bayern, C Germany 50°05′N 11°00′E
97 L19 **Stafford** C England, United Kingdom 52°48′N 02°07′W
26 L6 **Stafford** Kansas, C USA 37°57′N 98°36′W
21 W4 **Stafford** Virginia, NE USA 38°26′N 77°27′W
97 L19 **Staffordshire** *cultural region* C England, United Kingdom
19 N12 **Stafford Springs** Connecticut, NE USA 41°57′N 72°18′W
115 H14 **Stágira** Kentrikí Makedonía, N Greece 40°31′N 23°46′E
118 G7 **Staicele** Limbaži, N Latvia 57°52′N 24°48′E
Ştaierdorf-Anina *see* Anina
109 V8 **Stainz** Steiermark, SE Austria 46°55′N 15°18′E
Stájerlakanina *see* Anina
117 Y7 **Stakhanov** Luhans'ka Oblast', E Ukraine 48°30′N 38°42′E
108 E11 **Stalden** Valais, SW Switzerland 46°12′N 07°55′E
15 S8 **St-Alexandre** Québec, SE Canada 47°39′N 69°36′W
Stalin *see* Varna
Stalinabad *see* Dushanbe
Stalingrad *see* Volgograd
Staliniri *see* Ts'khinvali
Stalino *see* Donets'k
Stalinobod *see* Dushanbe
Stalinov Štít *see* Gerlachovský štít
Stalinsk *see* Novokuznetsk
Stalins'kaya Oblast' *see* Donets'ka Oblast'
Stalinski Zaliv *see* Varnenski Zaliv
Stalin, Yazovir *see* Iskŭr, Yazovir
111 N15 **Stalowa Wola** Podkarpackie, SE Poland 50°35′N 22°02′E
114 I11 **Stamboliyski** Plovdiv, C Bulgaria 42°09′N 24°32′E
114 J8 **Stamboliyski, Yazovir** ⊞ N Bulgaria
15 Q7 **St-Ambroise** Québec, SE Canada 48°35′N 71°19′W
97 N19 **Stamford** E England, United Kingdom 52°39′N 00°32′W

◆ Country
● Country Capital
◇ Dependent Territory
○ Dependent Territory Capital
⬖ Administrative Regions
✈ International Airport
▲ Mountain
▲▲ Mountain Range
Volcano
≈ River
◎ Lake
⊞ Reservoir

STAMFORD – STROUDSBURG

18 L14 **Stamford** Connecticut, NE USA 41°03′N 73°32′W
25 P6 **Stamford** Texas, SW USA 32°55′N 99°49′W
25 Q6 **Stamford, Lake** ⊠ Texas, SW USA
108 I10 **Stampa** Graubünden, SE Switzerland 46°21′N 09°35′E
Stampalia *see* Astypálaia
27 T14 **Stamps** Arkansas, C USA 33°22′N 93°30′W
92 G11 **Stamsund** Nordland, C Norway 68°07′N 13°50′E
27 R2 **Stanberry** Missouri, C USA 40°12′N 94°33′W
195 O3 **Stancomb-Wills Glacier** *glacier* Antarctica
83 K21 **Standerton** Mpumalanga, E South Africa 26°57′S 29°14′E
31 R7 **Standish** Michigan, N USA 43°59′N 83°58′W
20 M6 **Stanford** Kentucky, S USA 37°30′N 84°40′W
33 S9 **Stanford** Montana, NW USA 47°08′N 110°15′W
95 P19 **Stånga** Gotland, SE Sweden 57°16′N 18°30′E
94 I13 **Stange** Hedmark, S Norway 60°40′N 11°05′E
83 L23 **Stanger** KwaZulu/Natal, E South Africa 29°20′S 31°18′E
Stanimaka *see* Asenovgrad
Stanislau *see* Ivano-Frankivs'k
35 P8 **Stanislaus River** ≈ California, W USA
Stanislav *see* Ivano-Frankivs'k
Stanislavskaya Oblast' *see* Ivano-Frankivs'ka Oblast'
Stanisławów *see* Ivano-Frankivs'k
Stanke Dimitrov *see* Dupnitsa
183 O15 **Stanley** Tasmania, SE Australia 40°48′S 145°18′E
65 E24 **Stanley** *var.* Port Stanley, Puerto Argentino. ○ (Falkland Islands) East Falkland, Falkland Islands 51°45′S 57°56′W
33 O13 **Stanley** Idaho, NW USA 44°12′N 114°58′W
28 L3 **Stanley** North Dakota, N USA 48°19′N 102°23′W
21 U4 **Stanley** Virginia, NE USA 38°34′N 78°30′W
30 J6 **Stanley** Wisconsin, N USA 44°58′N 90°54′W
79 G21 **Stanley Pool** *var.* Pool Malebo. ◎ Congo/Dem. Rep. Congo
155 H20 **Stanley Reservoir** ⊠ S India
Stanleyville *see* Kisangani
42 G3 **Stann Creek** ◈ *district* SE Belize
Stann Creek *see* Dangriga
123 Q12 **Stanovoy Khrebet** ⛰ SE Russian Federation
108 F8 **Stans** Unterwalden, C Switzerland 46°57′N 08°23′E
97 O21 **Stansted** ✈ (London) Essex, E England, United Kingdom 51°53′N 00°15′E
183 U4 **Stanthorpe** Queensland, E Australia 28°35′S 151°52′E
21 N6 **Stanton** Kentucky, S USA 37°51′N 83°51′W
31 Q8 **Stanton** Michigan, N USA 43°19′N 85°04′W
29 Q14 **Stanton** Nebraska, C USA 41°57′N 97°13′W
28 L5 **Stanton** North Dakota, N USA 47°19′N 101°22′W
25 N7 **Stanton** Texas, SW USA 32°07′N 101°47′W
32 H7 **Stanwood** Washington, NW USA 48°14′N 122°22′W
117 Y7 **Stanychno-Luhans'ke** Luhans'ka Oblast', E Ukraine 48°39′N 39°30′E
108 K7 **Stanzach** Tirol, W Austria 47°24′N 10°36′E
98 M9 **Staphorst** Overijssel, E Netherlands 52°38′N 06°12′E
14 D18 **Staples** Ontario, S Canada 42°09′N 82°34′W
29 T6 **Staples** Minnesota, N USA 46°21′N 94°47′W
28 M14 **Stapleton** Nebraska, C USA 41°29′N 100°40′W
25 S8 **Star** Texas, SW USA 31°27′N 98°16′W
111 M14 **Starachowice** Świętokrzyskie, C Poland 51°04′N 21°02′E
Stara Kanjiža *see* Kanjiža
111 M18 **Stará L'ubovňa** *Ger.* Altlublau, *Hung.* Ólubló. Prešovský Kraj, E Slovakia 49°19′N 20°40′E
112 L10 **Stara Pazova** *Ger.* Altpasua, *Hung.* Ópazova. Vojvodina, N Serbia 44°59′N 20°10′E
Stara Planina *see* Balkan Mountains
114 L9 **Stara Reka** ≈ C Bulgaria
116 M5 **Stara Synyava** Khmel'nyts'ka Oblast', W Ukraine 49°39′N 27°35′E
116 I2 **Stara Vyzhivka** Volyns'ka Oblast', NW Ukraine 51°27′N 24°25′E
Staraya Belitsa *see* Staraya Byelitsa
119 M14 **Staraya Byelitsa** *Rus.* Staraya Belitsa. Vitsyebskaya Voblasts', NE Belarus 54°42′N 29°38′E
127 R5 **Staraya Mayna** Ul'yanovskaya Oblast', W Russian Federation 54°36′N 48°57′E
119 O18 **Staraya Rudnya** Homyel'skaya Voblasts', SE Belarus 52°50′N 30°17′E
124 H14 **Staraya Russa** Novgorodskaya Oblast', W Russian Federation 57°59′N 31°18′E
114 K10 **Stara Zagora** *Lat.* Augusta Trajana. Stara Zagora, C Bulgaria 42°26′N 25°39′E
114 K10 **Stara Zagora** ◈ *province* C Bulgaria
29 S8 **Starbuck** Minnesota, N USA 45°36′N 95°31′W
191 W4 **Starbuck Island** *prev.* Volunteer Island. *island* E Kiribati
27 V13 **Star City** Arkansas, C USA 33°56′N 91°52′W
112 F13 **Staretina** ⛰ W Bosnia and Herzegovina
Stargard in Pommern *see* Stargard Szczeciński
110 E9 **Stargard Szczeciński** *Ger.* Stargard in Pommern. Zachodnio-pomorskie, NW Poland 53°20′N 15°02′E
187 N10 **Star Harbour** *harbor* San Cristobal, SE Solomon Islands
Stari Bečej *see* Bečej
113 F15 **Stari Grad** *It.* Cittavecchia. Split-Dalmacija, S Croatia 43°11′N 16°36′E
124 J16 **Staritsa** Tverskaya Oblast', W Russian Federation 56°28′N 34°51′E
23 V9 **Starke** Florida, SE USA 29°56′N 82°07′W
22 M4 **Starkville** Mississippi, S USA 33°27′N 88°49′W
186 B7 **Star Mountains** *Ind.* Pegunungan Sterren. ⛰ Indonesia/Papua New Guinea
101 L23 **Starnberg** Bayern, SE Germany 48°00′N 11°19′E
101 L24 **Starnberger See** ◎ SE Germany
Starobel'sk *see* Starobil's'k
117 X8 **Starobesheve** Donets'ka Oblast', E Ukraine 47°45′N 38°01′E
117 Y6 **Starobil's'k** *Rus.* Starobel'sk. Luhans'ka Oblast', E Ukraine 49°16′N 38°56′E
119 K18 **Starobin** *var.* Starobyn. Minskaya Voblasts', S Belarus 52°44′N 27°28′E
Starobyn *see* Starobin
126 H6 **Starodub** Bryanskaya Oblast', W Russian Federation 52°30′N 32°56′E
110 I8 **Starogard Gdański** *Ger.* Preussisch-Stargard. Pomorskie, N Poland 53°57′N 18°29′E
145 P16 **Staroikan** Yuzhnyy Kazakhstan, S Kazakhstan 43°09′N 68°34′E
Starokonstantinov *see* Starokostyantyniv
116 L5 **Starokostyantyniv** *Rus.* Starokonstantinov. Khmel'nyts'ka Oblast', NW Ukraine 49°43′N 27°13′E
126 K12 **Starominskaya** Krasnodarskiy Kray, SW Russian Federation 46°31′N 39°03′E
114 L7 **Staro Selo** *Rom.* Satul-Vechi; *prev.* Star-Smil. Silistra, NE Bulgaria 43°58′N 26°32′E
126 K12 **Staroshcherbinovskaya** Krasnodarskiy Kray, SW Russian Federation 46°36′N 38°42′E
127 V6 **Starosubkhangulovo** Respublika Bashkortostan, W Russian Federation 53°05′N 57°22′E
35 S4 **Star Peak** ▲ Nevada, W USA 40°31′N 118°09′W
15 T8 **St-Arsène** Québec, SE Canada 47°55′N 69°21′W
Star-Smil *see* Staro Selo
97 J25 **Start Point** *headland* SW England, United Kingdom 50°13′N 03°38′W
Startsy *see* Kirawsk
Starum *see* Stavoren
119 L18 **Staryya Darohi** *Rus.* Staryye Dorogi. Minskaya Voblasts', S Belarus 53°02′N 28°16′E
Staryye Dorogi *see* Staryya Darohi
127 T2 **Staryye Zyattsy** Udmurtskaya Respublika, NW Russian Federation 57°22′N 52°42′E
117 U13 **Staryy Krym** Respublika Krym, S Ukraine 45°03′N 35°06′E
126 K8 **Staryy Oskol** Belgorodskaya Oblast', W Russian Federation 51°21′N 37°52′E
116 H6 **Staryy Sambir** L'vivs'ka Oblast', W Ukraine 49°27′N 23°00′E
101 L14 **Stassfurt** *var.* Staßfurt. Sachsen-Anhalt, C Germany 51°51′N 11°35′E
Staßfurt *see* Stassfurt
111 M15 **Staszów** Świętokrzyskie, C Poland 50°33′N 21°07′E
29 W13 **State Center** Iowa, C USA 42°01′N 93°09′W
18 E14 **State College** Pennsylvania, NE USA 40°48′N 77°52′W
18 K15 **Staten Island** *island* New York, NE USA
Staten Island *see* Estados, Isla de los
23 U8 **Statenville** Georgia, SE USA 30°42′N 83°00′W
23 W5 **Statesboro** Georgia, SE USA 32°28′N 81°47′W
States, The *see* United States of America
21 R9 **Statesville** North Carolina, SE USA 35°46′N 80°54′W
95 G16 **Stathelle** Telemark, S Norway 59°01′N 09°40′E
30 K15 **Staunton** Illinois, N USA 39°00′N 89°47′W
21 T5 **Staunton** Virginia, NE USA 38°10′N 79°05′W
95 C16 **Stavanger** Rogaland, S Norway 58°58′N 05°43′E
99 L21 **Stavelot** *Dut.* Stablo. Liège, E Belgium 50°24′N 05°56′E
95 G16 **Stavern** Vestfold, S Norway 58°58′N 10°01′E
Stavers Island *see* Vostok Island
98 J7 **Stavoren** *Fris.* Starum. Friesland, N Netherlands 52°52′N 05°22′E
115 K21 **Stavrí, Akrotírio** *var.* Akrotírio Stavrós. *headland* Náxos, Kykládes, Greece, Aegean Sea 37°12′N 25°32′E
126 M14 **Stavropol'** *prev.* Voroshilovsk. Stavropol'skiy Kray, SW Russian Federation 45°02′N 41°58′E
Stavropol' *see* Tol'yatti
126 M14 **Stavropol'skaya Vozvyshennost'** ⛰ SW Russian Federation
126 M14 **Stavropol'skiy Kray** ◈ *territory* SW Russian Federation
115 H14 **Stavrós** Kentrikí Makedonía, N Greece 40°39′N 23°43′E
115 J24 **Stavrós, Akrotírio** *headland* Kríti, Greece, E Mediterranean Sea 35°25′N 24°57′E
Stavrós, Akrotírio *see* Stavrí, Akrotírio
114 I12 **Stavroúpoli** *prev.* Stavroúpolis. Anatolikí Makedonía kai Thráki, NE Greece 41°12′N 24°45′E
Stavroúpolis *see* Stavroúpoli
117 O6 **Stavyshche** Kyyivs'ka Oblast', N Ukraine 49°23′N 30°10′E
182 M11 **Stawell** Victoria, SE Australia 37°06′S 142°52′E
110 N9 **Stawiski** Podlaskie, NE Poland 53°22′N 22°08′E
14 G14 **Stayner** Ontario, S Canada 44°25′N 80°05′W
14 D17 **St. Clair** ≈ Canada/USA
37 R3 **Steamboat Springs** Colorado, C USA 40°28′N 106°51′W
15 U4 **Ste-Anne, Lac** ◎ Québec, SE Canada
20 M8 **Stearns** Kentucky, S USA 36°39′N 84°27′W
39 N10 **Stebbins** Alaska, USA 63°30′N 162°15′W
15 U7 **Ste-Blandine** Québec, SE Canada 48°22′N 68°27′W
108 K7 **Steeg** Tirol, W Austria 47°15′N 10°18′E
27 Y9 **Steele** Missouri, C USA 36°04′N 89°49′W
29 N5 **Steele** North Dakota, N USA 46°51′N 99°55′W
194 J5 **Steele Island** *island* Antarctica
30 K16 **Steeleville** Illinois, N USA 38°00′N 89°39′W
27 W6 **Steelville** Missouri, C USA 37°57′N 91°21′W
99 G14 **Steenbergen** Noord-Brabant, S Netherlands 51°35′N 04°19′E
Steenkool *see* Bintuni
11 O10 **Steen River** Alberta, W Canada 59°37′N 117°17′W
98 M8 **Steenwijk** Overijssel, N Netherlands 52°47′N 06°07′E
174 J8 **Steep Point** *headland* Western Australia 26°09′S 113°11′E
116 L9 **Ştefăneşti** Botoşani, NE Romania 47°44′N 27°15′E
Stefanie, Lake *see* Ch'ew Bahir
8 L5 **Stefansson Island** *island* Nunavut, N Canada
117 O10 **Ştefan Vodă** *Rus.* Suvorovo. SE Moldova 46°33′N 29°39′E
63 H18 **Steffen, Cerro** ▲ S Chile 44°27′S 71°42′W
108 D9 **Steffisburg** Bern, C Switzerland 46°47′N 07°38′E
95 J24 **Stege** Storstrøm, SE Denmark 54°59′N 12°18′E
116 G10 **Ştei** *Hung.* Vaskohsziklás. Bihor, W Romania 46°34′N 22°28′E
Steier *see* Steyr
Steierdorf/Steierdorf-Anina *see* Anina
109 T7 **Steiermark** *off.* Land Steiermark, *Eng.* Styria. ◈ *state* C Austria
Steiermark, Land *see* Steiermark
101 J19 **Steigerwald** *hill range* C Germany
99 L17 **Stein** Limburg, SE Netherlands 50°58′N 05°45′E
Stein *see* Stein an der Donau
Stein *see* Kamnik, Slovenia
108 M8 **Steinach** Tirol, W Austria 47°07′N 11°30′E
Steinamanger *see* Szombathely
109 W3 **Stein an der Donau** *var.* Stein. Niederösterreich, NE Austria 48°25′N 15°35′E
Steinau an der Elbe *see* Ścinawa
11 Y16 **Steinbach** Manitoba, S Canada 49°32′N 96°40′W
Steiner Alpen *see* Kamniško-Savinjske Alpe
99 L24 **Steinfort** Luxembourg, W Luxembourg 49°39′N 05°55′E
100 H12 **Steinhuder Meer** ◎ NW Germany
93 E15 **Steinkjer** Nord-Trøndelag, C Norway 64°01′N 11°29′E
Stejarul *see* Karapelit
99 F16 **Stekene** Oost-Vlaanderen, NW Belgium 51°13′N 04°04′E
83 E26 **Stellenbosch** Western Cape, SW South Africa 33°56′S 18°51′E
98 F13 **Stellendam** Zuid-Holland, SW Netherlands 51°48′N 04°01′E
39 T12 **Steller, Mount** ▲ Alaska, USA 60°36′N 142°49′W
103 Y14 **Stello, Monte** ▲ Corse, France, C Mediterranean Sea 42°49′N 09°24′E
106 F5 **Stelvio, Passo dello** *pass* Italy/Switzerland
15 S7 **Ste-Marguerite Nord-Est** ≈ Québec, SE Canada
15 V4 **Ste-Marguerite, Pointe** *headland* Québec, SE Canada 50°01′N 66°43′W
12 J14 **Ste-Marie, Lac** ◎ Québec, S Canada
103 R3 **Stenay** Meuse, NE France 49°29′N 05°12′E
100 L12 **Stendal** Sachsen-Anhalt, C Germany 52°36′N 11°52′E
118 E8 **Stende** Talsi, NW Latvia 57°09′N 22°33′E
182 H10 **Stenhouse Bay** South Australia 35°15′S 136°58′E
95 J23 **Stenløse** Frederiksborg, E Denmark 55°47′N 12°13′E
95 L19 **Stensjön** Jönköping, S Sweden 57°36′N 14°42′E
95 K18 **Stenstorp** Västra Götaland, S Sweden 58°15′N 13°45′E
95 I18 **Stenungsund** Västra Götaland, S Sweden 58°05′N 11°49′E
Stepanakert *see* Xankändi
137 T11 **Step'anavan** N Armenia 41°00′N 44°27′E
100 K9 **Stepenitz** ≈ N Germany
29 O10 **Stephan** South Dakota, N USA 44°12′N 99°25′W
29 R3 **Stephen** Minnesota, N USA 48°27′N 96°54′W
27 T14 **Stephens** Arkansas, C USA 33°25′N 93°04′W
184 J13 **Stephens, Cape** *headland* D'Urville Island, Marlborough, SW New Zealand 40°42′S 173°56′E
21 V3 **Stephens City** Virginia, NE USA 39°03′N 78°10′W
182 L6 **Stephens Creek** New South Wales, SE Australia 31°51′S 141°30′E
184 K13 **Stephens Island** *island* C New Zealand
31 N5 **Stephenson** Michigan, N USA 45°27′N 87°36′W
13 S12 **Stephenville** Newfoundland, Newfoundland and Labrador, SE Canada 48°33′N 58°34′W
25 S7 **Stephenville** Texas, SW USA 32°12′N 98°13′W
145 P17 **Step' Nardara** *Kaz.* Shardara Dalasy; *prev.* Shaidara. *grassland* S Kazakhstan
145 R8 **Stepnogorsk** Akmola, C Kazakhstan 52°04′N 72°18′E
127 O15 **Stepnoye** Stavropol'skiy Kray, SW Russian Federation 44°18′N 44°34′E
145 Q8 **Stepnyak** Akmola, N Kazakhstan 52°52′N 70°49′E
192 J17 **Steps Point** *headland* Tutuila, W American Samoa 14°23′S 170°46′W
115 F17 **Stereá Elláda** *Eng.* Greece Central. ◈ *region* C Greece
83 J24 **Sterkspruit** Eastern Cape, SE South Africa 30°31′S 27°22′E
127 U6 **Sterlibashevo** Respublika Bashkortostan, W Russian Federation 53°19′N 55°12′E
39 R12 **Sterling** Alaska, USA 60°32′N 150°51′W
37 V3 **Sterling** Colorado, C USA 40°37′N 103°12′W
30 K11 **Sterling** Illinois, N USA 41°47′N 89°42′W
26 M5 **Sterling** Kansas, C USA 38°12′N 98°12′W
25 O8 **Sterling City** Texas, SW USA 31°50′N 101°00′W
31 S9 **Sterling Heights** Michigan, N USA 42°34′N 83°01′W
21 W3 **Sterling Park** Virginia, NE USA 39°00′N 77°24′W
37 V2 **Sterling Reservoir** ⊠ Colorado, C USA
22 I5 **Sterlington** Louisiana, S USA 32°42′N 92°05′W
127 U6 **Sterlitamak** Respublika Bashkortostan, W Russian Federation 53°39′N 56°00′E
Sternberg *see* Šternberk
111 H17 **Šternberk** *Ger.* Sternberg. Olomoucký Kraj, E Czech Republic 49°45′N 17°20′E
141 V17 **Stēroh** Suquṭrā, S Yemen 12°21′N 53°50′E
Sterren, Pegunungan *see* Star Mountains
110 G11 **Stęszew** Wielkopolskie, C Poland 52°16′N 16°41′E
Stettin *see* Szczecin
Stettiner Haff *see* Szczeciński, Zalew
11 Q15 **Stettler** Alberta, SW Canada 52°21′N 112°40′W
31 V13 **Steubenville** Ohio, N USA 40°21′N 80°37′W
97 O21 **Stevenage** E England, United Kingdom 51°55′N 00°14′W
23 Q1 **Stevenson** Alabama, S USA 34°52′N 85°50′W
32 H11 **Stevenson** Washington, NW USA 45°43′N 121°54′W
182 E1 **Stevenson Creek** *seasonal river* South Australia
39 Q13 **Stevenson Entrance** *strait* Alaska, USA
30 L6 **Stevens Point** Wisconsin, N USA 44°32′N 89°33′W
39 R8 **Stevens Village** Alaska, USA 66°01′N 149°02′W
33 P10 **Stevensville** Montana, NW USA 46°30′N 114°05′W
93 E25 **Stevns Klint** *headland* E Denmark 55°15′N 12°25′E
10 J12 **Stewart** British Columbia, W Canada 55°58′N 129°52′W
10 J6 **Stewart** ≈ Yukon Territory, NW Canada
10 I6 **Stewart Crossing** Yukon Territory, NW Canada 63°22′N 136°37′W
63 H25 **Stewart, Isla** *island* S Chile
185 B25 **Stewart Island** *island* S New Zealand
Stewart Islands *see* Sikaiana
181 W6 **Stewart, Mount** ▲ Queensland, E Australia 20°11′S 145°29′E
10 H6 **Stewart River** Yukon Territory, NW Canada 63°17′N 139°24′W
27 R3 **Stewartsville** Missouri, C USA 39°45′N 94°30′W
11 S16 **Stewart Valley** Saskatchewan, S Canada 50°34′N 107°47′W
29 W10 **Stewartville** Minnesota, N USA 43°51′N 92°29′W
Steyerlak-Anina *see* Anina
109 T5 **Steyr** *var.* Steier. Oberösterreich, N Austria 48°02′N 14°26′E
109 T5 **Steyr** ≈ NW Austria
15 T7 **St-Fabien** Québec, SE Canada 48°19′N 68°51′W
15 R11 **St-François, Lac** ◎ Québec, SE Canada
83 E25 **St. Helena Bay** *bay* SW South Africa
15 T8 **St-Hubert** Québec, SE Canada 47°46′N 69°15′W
29 P11 **Stickney** South Dakota, N USA 43°24′N 98°23′W
98 L5 **Stiens** Friesland, N Netherlands 53°15′N 05°45′E
Stif *see* Sétif
27 Q11 **Stigler** Oklahoma, C USA 35°16′N 95°08′W
107 N18 **Stigliano** Basilicata, S Italy 40°24′N 16°13′E
95 N17 **Stigtomta** Södermanland, C Sweden 58°48′N 16°47′E
10 I11 **Stikine** ≈ British Columbia, W Canada
Stilida/Stilís *see* Stylída
95 G22 **Stilling** Århus, C Denmark 56°04′N 10°00′E
29 W8 **Stillwater** Minnesota, N USA 45°03′N 92°48′W
27 O9 **Stillwater** Oklahoma, C USA 36°07′N 97°03′W
35 S5 **Stillwater Range** ⛰ Nevada, W USA
18 I8 **Stillwater Reservoir** ⊠ New York, NE USA
107 O22 **Stilo, Punta** *headland* S Italy 38°27′N 16°36′E
27 R10 **Stilwell** Oklahoma, C USA 35°48′N 94°37′W
Štimlje *see* Shtime
25 N1 **Stinnett** Texas, SW USA 35°49′N 101°27′W
113 P18 **Štip** E FYR Macedonia 41°45′N 22°10′E
Stira *see* Stýra
96 J12 **Stirling** C Scotland, United Kingdom 56°07′N 03°57′W
96 I12 **Stirling** *cultural region* C Scotland, United Kingdom
180 J14 **Stirling Range** ⛰ Western Australia
15 R8 **St-Jean** ≈ Québec, SE Canada
93 E16 **Stjørdalshalsen** Nord-Trøndelag, C Norway 63°27′N 10°57′E
83 L22 **St. Lucia** KwaZulu/Natal, E South Africa 28°22′S 32°25′E
Stochód *see* Stokhid
101 H24 **Stockach** Baden-Württemberg, S Germany 47°51′N 09°01′E
25 S12 **Stockdale** Texas, SW USA 29°14′N 97°57′W
109 X3 **Stockerau** Niederösterreich NE Austria 48°24′N 16°13′E
93 H20 **Stockholm** ● (Sweden) Stockholm, C Sweden 59°17′N 18°03′E
95 O15 **Stockholm** ◈ *county* C Sweden
Stockmannshof *see* Pļaviņas
97 L18 **Stockport** NW England, United Kingdom 53°25′N 02°10′W
65 K15 **Stocks Seamount** *undersea feature* C Atlantic Ocean 11°42′S 33°48′W
35 O8 **Stockton** California, W USA 37°56′N 121°19′W
26 L3 **Stockton** Kansas, C USA 39°27′N 99°17′W
27 S6 **Stockton** Missouri, C USA 37°43′N 93°49′W
30 K3 **Stockton Island** *island* Apostle Islands, Wisconsin, N USA
27 S7 **Stockton Lake** ⊠ Missouri, C USA
97 M15 **Stockton-on-Tees** *var.* Stockton on Tees. N England, United Kingdom 54°34′N 01°19′W
Stockton on Tees *see* Stockton-on-Tees
24 M10 **Stockton Plateau** *plain* Texas, SW USA
28 M16 **Stockville** Nebraska, C USA 40°33′N 100°20′W
93 H17 **Stöde** Västernorrland, C Sweden 62°27′N 16°34′E
Stodolichi *see* Stadolichy
113 M19 **Stogovo Karaorman** ⛰ W FYR Macedonia
Stoke *see* Stoke-on-Trent
97 L19 **Stoke-on-Trent** *var.* Stoke. C England, United Kingdom 53°N 02°10′W
182 M15 **Stokes Point** *headland* Tasmania, SE Australia 40°09′S 143°55′E
116 J2 **Stokhid** *Pol.* Stochód, *Rus.* Stokhod. ≈ NW Ukraine
Stokhod *see* Stokhid
92 I4 **Stokkseyri** Sudhurland, SW Iceland 63°49′N 21°00′W
92 G10 **Stokmarknes** Nordland, C Norway 68°34′N 14°55′E
Stol *see* Veliki Krš
113 H15 **Stolac** Federacija Bosna I Hercegovina, S Bosnia and Herzegovina 43°04′N 17°58′E
Stolbce *see* Stowbtsy
101 D16 **Stolberg** *var.* Stolberg im Rheinland. Nordrhein-Westfalen, W Germany 50°45′N 06°15′E
Stolberg im Rheinland *see* Stolberg
123 P6 **Stolbovoy, Ostrov** *island* NE Russian Federation
Stolbtsy *see* Stowbtsy
119 J20 **Stolin** Brestskaya Voblasts', SW Belarus 51°53′N 26°51′E
95 K14 **Stöllet** *var.* Norra Ny. Värmland, C Sweden 60°24′N 13°15′E
Stolp *see* Słupsk
Stolpe *see* Słupia
Stolpmünde *see* Ustka
115 F15 **Stómio** Thessalía, C Greece 39°51′N 22°45′E
14 J11 **Stonecliffe** Ontario, SE Canada 46°12′N 77°58′W
96 L10 **Stonehaven** NE Scotland, United Kingdom 56°59′N 02°14′W
97 M23 **Stonehenge** *ancient monument* Wiltshire, S England, United Kingdom
23 T3 **Stone Mountain** ▲ Georgia, SE USA 33°48′N 84°10′W
11 X16 **Stonewall** Manitoba, S Canada 50°08′N 97°20′W
21 S3 **Stonewood** West Virginia, NE USA 39°15′N 80°18′W
14 D17 **Stoney Point** Ontario, S Canada 42°18′N 82°32′W
92 H10 **Stonglandseidet** Troms, N Norway 69°03′N 17°06′E
65 N25 **Stonybeach Bay** *bay* Tristan da Cunha, SE Atlantic Ocean
35 N5 **Stony Creek** ≈ California, W USA
65 N25 **Stonyhill Point** *headland* S Tristan da Cunha
14 I14 **Stony Lake** ◎ Ontario, SE Canada
11 Q14 **Stony Plain** Alberta, SW Canada 53°31′N 114°04′W
21 R9 **Stony Point** North Carolina, SE USA 35°51′N 81°04′W
18 G8 **Stony Point** *headland* New York, NE USA 43°50′N 76°18′W
11 T10 **Stony Rapids** Saskatchewan, C Canada 59°14′N 105°48′W
39 P11 **Stony River** Alaska, USA 61°48′N 156°37′W
Stony Tunguska *see* Podkamennaya Tunguska
12 G10 **Stooping** ≈ Ontario, C Canada
100 I9 **Stör** ≈ N Germany
95 M15 **Storå** Örebro, S Sweden 59°44′N 15°10′E
95 J16 **Stora Gla** ◎ C Sweden
95 J16 **Stora Le** *Nor.* Store Le. ◎ Norway/Sweden
92 I12 **Stora Lulevatten** ◎ N Sweden
92 H13 **Storavan** ◎ N Sweden
93 I20 **Storby** Åland, SW Finland 60°12′N 19°33′E
94 E10 **Stordalen** Møre og Romsdal, S Norway 62°22′N 07°00′E
95 H23 **Storebælt** *var.* Store Bælt, *Eng.* Great Belt, Storebelt. *channel* Baltic Sea/Kattegat
Store Bælt *see* Storebælt
Storebelt *see* Storebælt
95 M19 **Storebro** Kalmar, S Sweden 57°36′N 15°30′E
95 J24 **Store Heddinge** Storstrøm, SE Denmark 55°19′N 12°24′E
Store Le *see* Stora Le
93 E16 **Støren** Sør-Trøndelag, S Norway 63°02′N 10°16′E
92 O4 **Storfjorden** *fjord* S Norway
95 L15 **Storfors** Värmland, C Sweden 59°33′N 14°16′E
92 G13 **Storforshei** Nordland, C Norway 66°25′N 14°25′E
Storhammer *see* Hamar
100 L10 **Störkanal** *canal* N Germany
93 F16 **Storlien** Jämtland, C Sweden 63°18′N 12°10′E
183 P17 **Storm Bay** *inlet* Tasmania, SE Australia
29 T12 **Storm Lake** Iowa, C USA 42°38′N 95°12′W
29 S13 **Storm Lake** ◎ Iowa, C USA
96 G7 **Stornoway** NW Scotland, United Kingdom 58°13′N 06°23′W
Storojineț *see* Storozhynets'
92 P1 **Storøya** *island* NE Svalbard
125 S10 **Storozhevsk** Respublika Komi, NW Russian Federation 61°56′N 52°18′E
Storozhinets *see* Storozhynets'
116 K8 **Storozhynets'** *Ger.* Storozynetz, *Rom.* Storojineț, *Rus.* Storozhinets. Chernivets'ka Oblast', W Ukraine 48°11′N 25°42′E
Storozynetz *see* Storozhynets'
92 H11 **Storriten** ▲ C Norway 68°09′N 17°12′E
19 N12 **Storrs** Connecticut, NE USA 41°48′N 72°15′W
94 I11 **Storsjøen** ◎ S Norway
94 N13 **Storsjön** ◎ C Sweden
93 F16 **Storsjön** ◎ C Sweden
92 J9 **Storslett** Troms, N Norway 69°45′N 21°03′E
94 H11 **Storsølnkletten** ▲ S Norway 61°52′N 11°32′E
92 I9 **Storsteinnes** Troms, N Norway 69°13′N 19°14′E
95 I24 **Storstrøm** *var.* Storstrøms Amt. ◈ *county* SE Denmark
Storstrøms Amt *see* Storstrøm
93 J14 **Storsund** Norrbotten, N Sweden 65°36′N 20°40′E
94 J9 **Storsylen** *Swe.* Sylarna. ▲ Norway/Sweden 63°00′N 12°14′E
92 H11 **Stortoppen** ▲ N Sweden 67°33′N 17°27′E
93 H14 **Storuman** Västerbotten, N Sweden 65°05′N 17°10′E
93 H14 **Storuman** ◎ N Sweden
94 N13 **Storvik** Gävleborg, C Sweden 60°37′N 16°30′E
95 O14 **Storvreta** Uppsala, C Sweden 59°58′N 17°42′E
29 V13 **Story City** Iowa, C USA 42°10′N 93°36′W
11 V17 **Stoughton** Saskatchewan, S Canada 49°40′N 103°01′W
19 O11 **Stoughton** Massachusetts, NE USA 42°07′N 71°06′W
30 L9 **Stoughton** Wisconsin, N USA 42°56′N 89°12′W
97 L23 **Stour** ≈ E England, United Kingdom
97 P21 **Stour** ≈ S England, United Kingdom
27 T5 **Stover** Missouri, C USA 38°26′N 92°59′W
95 G21 **Støvring** Nordjylland, N Denmark 56°53′N 09°52′E
119 J17 **Stowbtsy** *Pol.* Stołbce, *Rus.* Stolbtsy. Minskaya Voblasts', C Belarus 53°29′N 26°44′E
25 X11 **Stowell** Texas, SW USA 29°47′N 94°22′W
97 P20 **Stowmarket** E England, United Kingdom 52°05′N 00°54′E
114 N8 **Stozher** Dobrich, NE Bulgaria 43°27′N 27°49′E
97 E14 **Strabane** *Ir.* An Srath Bán. W Northern Ireland, United Kingdom 54°49′N 07°27′W
121 S11 **Strabo Trench** *undersea feature* C Mediterranean Sea
27 T7 **Strafford** Missouri, C USA 37°16′N 93°07′W
183 N17 **Strahan** Tasmania, SE Australia 42°10′S 145°18′E
111 C18 **Strakonice** *Ger.* Strakonitz. Jihočeský Kraj, S Czech Republic 49°14′N 13°55′E
Strakonitz *see* Strakonice
100 N8 **Stralsund** Mecklenburg-Vorpommern, NE Germany 54°18′N 13°06′E
99 L16 **Stramproy** Limburg, SE Netherlands 51°12′N 05°43′E
83 E26 **Strand** Western Cape, SW South Africa 34°06′S 18°50′E
94 E10 **Stranda** Møre og Romsdal, S Norway 62°18′N 06°56′E
97 G15 **Strangford Lough** *Ir.* Loch Cuan. *inlet* E Northern Ireland, United Kingdom
95 N16 **Strängnäs** Södermanland, C Sweden 59°22′N 17°02′E
97 E14 **Stranorlar** *Ir.* Srath an Urláir. NW Ireland 54°48′N 07°46′W
97 H14 **Stranraer** S Scotland, United Kingdom 54°54′N 05°02′W
11 U16 **Strasbourg** Saskatchewan, S Canada 51°05′N 104°58′W
103 V5 **Strasbourg** *Ger.* Strassburg; *anc.* Argentoratum. Bas-Rhin, NE France 48°35′N 07°45′E
109 T8 **Strassburg** Kärnten, S Austria 46°54′N 14°21′E
37 U4 **Strasburg** Colorado, C USA 39°42′N 104°13′W
29 N7 **Strasburg** North Dakota, N USA 46°07′N 100°10′W
31 U12 **Strasburg** Ohio, N USA 40°35′N 81°31′W
21 U3 **Strasburg** Virginia, NE USA 38°59′N 78°21′W
117 N10 **Strășeni** *var.* Strasheny. C Moldova 47°07′N 28°37′E
Strasheny *see* Strășeni
Strassburg *see* Strasbourg, France
Strassburg *see* Aiud, Romania
99 M25 **Strassen** Luxembourg, S Luxembourg 49°37′N 06°05′E
109 R5 **Strasswalchen** Salzburg, C Austria 47°59′N 13°19′E
14 F16 **Stratford** Ontario, S Canada 43°22′N 81°00′W
184 K10 **Stratford** Taranaki, North Island, New Zealand 39°20′S 174°16′E
35 Q11 **Stratford** California, W USA 36°10′N 119°47′W
29 V13 **Stratford** Iowa, C USA 42°16′N 93°55′W
27 O12 **Stratford** Oklahoma, C USA 34°48′N 96°57′W
25 N1 **Stratford** Texas, SW USA 36°21′N 102°05′W
30 K6 **Stratford** Wisconsin, N USA 44°53′N 90°13′W
Stratford *see* Stratford-upon-Avon
97 M20 **Stratford-upon-Avon** *var.* Stratford. C England, United Kingdom 52°12′N 01°41′W
183 O17 **Strathgordon** Tasmania, SE Australia 42°49′S 146°04′E
11 Q16 **Strathmore** Alberta, SW Canada 51°05′N 113°20′W
35 R11 **Strathmore** California, W USA 36°07′N 119°04′W
14 E16 **Strathroy** Ontario, S Canada 42°57′N 81°40′W
96 I6 **Strathy Point** *headland* N Scotland, United Kingdom 58°36′N 04°04′W
37 W4 **Stratton** Colorado, C USA 39°16′N 102°34′W
19 P6 **Stratton** Maine, NE USA 45°06′N 70°25′W
18 M10 **Stratton Mountain** ▲ Vermont, NE USA 43°05′N 72°55′W
101 N21 **Straubing** Bayern, SE Germany 48°53′N 12°35′E
100 O12 **Strausberg** Brandenburg, E Germany 52°34′N 13°52′E
32 K13 **Strawberry Mountain** ▲ Oregon, NW USA 44°18′N 118°43′W
29 X12 **Strawberry Point** Iowa, C USA 42°40′N 91°31′W
36 M3 **Strawberry Reservoir** ⊠ Utah, W USA
36 M4 **Strawberry River** ≈ Utah, W USA
25 R7 **Strawn** Texas, SW USA 32°33′N 98°30′W
113 P17 **Straža** ▲ Bulgaria/FYR Macedonia 42°16′N 22°13′E
111 I19 **Strážov** *Hung.* Sztrazsó. ▲ NW Slovakia 48°59′N 18°29′E
182 F7 **Streaky Bay** South Australia 32°49′S 134°13′E
182 E7 **Streaky Bay** *bay* South Australia
30 L12 **Streator** Illinois, N USA 41°07′N 88°50′W
Streckenbach *see* Świdnik
Strednogorie *see* Pirdop
111 C17 **Středočeský Kraj** ◈ *region* C Czech Republic
29 O6 **Streeter** North Dakota, N USA 46°37′N 99°23′W
25 U8 **Streetman** Texas, SW USA 31°52′N 96°19′W
116 G13 **Strehaia** Mehedinți, SW Romania 44°37′N 23°10′E
Strehlen *see* Strzelin
114 I10 **Strelcha** Pazardzhik, C Bulgaria 42°28′N 24°21′E
122 L12 **Strelka** Krasnoyarskiy Kray, C Russian Federation 58°05′N 92°54′E
124 L6 **Strel'na** ≈ NW Russian Federation
118 H7 **Strenči** *Ger.* Stackeln. Valka, N Latvia 57°38′N 25°42′E
15 V6 **St-René-de-Matane** Québec, SE Canada 48°42′N 67°22′W
108 K8 **Strengen** Tirol, W Austria 47°07′N 10°25′E
106 C6 **Stresa** Piemonte, NE Italy 45°52′N 08°32′E
Streshin *see* Streshyn
119 N18 **Streshyn** *Rus.* Streshin. Homyel'skaya Voblasts', SE Belarus 52°43′N 30°07′E
95 B18 **Streymoy** *Dan.* Strømø. *island* N Faeroe Islands
95 G23 **Strib** Fyn, C Denmark 55°33′N 09°47′E
111 A17 **Stříbro** *Ger.* Mies. Plzeňský Kraj, W Czech Republic 49°44′N 12°55′E
186 B7 **Strickland** ≈ SW Papua New Guinea
Striegau *see* Strzegom
Strigonium *see* Esztergom
98 H13 **Strijen** Zuid-Holland, SW Netherlands 51°45′N 04°34′E
63 H21 **Strobel, Lago** ◎ S Argentina
61 B25 **Stroeder** Buenos Aires, E Argentina 40°11′S 62°35′W
115 C20 **Strofádes** *island* Iónia Nisiá, Greece, C Mediterranean Sea
Strofilia *see* Strofyliá
115 G17 **Strofyliá** *var.* Strofilia. Évvoia, C Greece 38°49′N 23°25′E
100 O10 **Strom** ≈ NE Germany
107 L22 **Stromboli** 🌋 Isola Stromboli, SW Italy 38°48′N 15°13′E
107 L22 **Stromboli, Isola** *island* Isole Eolie, S Italy
96 H9 **Stromeferry** N Scotland, United Kingdom 57°20′N 05°35′W
96 J5 **Stromness** N Scotland, United Kingdom 58°57′N 03°18′W
Strømø *see* Streymoy
94 N11 **Strömsbruk** Gävleborg, C Sweden 61°52′N 17°19′E
29 Q15 **Stromsburg** Nebraska, C USA 41°06′N 97°36′W
95 K21 **Strömsnäsbruk** Kronoberg, S Sweden 56°35′N 13°45′E
95 I17 **Strömstad** Västra Götaland, S Sweden 58°56′N 11°11′E
93 G16 **Strömsund** Jämtland, C Sweden 63°51′N 15°35′E
93 G15 **Ströms Vattudal** *valley* N Sweden
27 V14 **Strong** Arkansas, C USA 33°06′N 92°19′W
Strongilí *see* Strongylí
107 O21 **Strongoli** Calabria, SW Italy 39°17′N 17°03′E
31 T11 **Strongsville** Ohio, N USA 41°18′N 81°50′W
115 Q23 **Strongylí** *var.* Strongilí. *island* SE Greece
96 K5 **Stronsay** *island* NE Scotland, United Kingdom
97 L21 **Stroud** C England, United Kingdom 51°46′N 02°15′W
27 O10 **Stroud** Oklahoma, C USA 35°45′N 96°39′W
18 I14 **Stroudsburg** Pennsylvania, NE USA 40°59′N 75°12′W

◆ Country ● Country Capital ◇ Dependent Territory ○ Dependent Territory Capital ◈ Administrative Regions ✈ International Airport ▲ Mountain ⛰ Mountain Range 🌋 Volcano ≈ River ◎ Lake ⊠ Reservoir

STRUER – SUROVIKINO

95 *F21* **Struer** Ringkøbing, W Denmark *56°29′N 08°37′E*
113 *M20* **Struga** SW FYR Macedonia *41°11′N 20°40′E*
Strugi-Kranyse *see* Strugi-Krasnyye
124 *G14* **Strugi-Krasnyye** *var.* Strugi-Kranyse. Pskovskaya Oblast', W Russian Federation *58°19′N 29°09′E*
114 *G11* **Struma** *Gk.* Strymónas. ≈ Bulgaria/Greece *see also* Strymónas
Struma *see* Strymónas
97 *G21* **Strumble Head** *headland* SW Wales, United Kingdom *52°01′N 05°05′W*
Strumeshnitsa *see* Strumica
113 *Q19* **Strumica** E FYR Macedonia *41°27′N 22°39′E*
113 *Q19* **Strumica** *Bulg.* Strumeshnitsa. ≈ Bulgaria/FYR Macedonia
114 *G11* **Strumyani** Blagoevgrad, SW Bulgaria *41°41′N 23°13′E*
31 *V12* **Struthers** Ohio, N USA *41°03′N 80°36′W*
114 *I10* **Stryama** ≈ C Bulgaria
114 *G13* **Strymónas** *Bul.* Struma. ≈ Bulgaria/Greece *see also* Struma
Strymónas *see* Struma
115 *H14* **Strymonikós Kólpos** *gulf* N Greece
116 *I6* **Stryy** L'vivs'ka Oblast', NW Ukraine *49°16′N 23°51′E*
116 *H6* **Stryy** ≈ W Ukraine
111 *F14* **Strzegom** *Ger.* Striegau. Wałbrzych, SW Poland *50°59′N 16°20′E*
110 *E10* **Strzelce Krajeńskie** *Ger.* Friedeberg Neumark. Lubuskie, W Poland *52°52′N 15°30′E*
111 *I15* **Strzelce Opolskie** *Ger.* Gross Strehlitz. Opolskie, SW Poland *50°31′N 18°19′E*
182 *K3* **Strzelecki Creek** *seasonal river* South Australia
182 *J3* **Strzelecki Desert** *desert* South Australia
111 *G15* **Strzelin** *Ger.* Strehlen. Dolnośląskie, SW Poland *50°48′N 17°03′E*
110 *I11* **Strzelno** Kujawsko-pomorski, C Poland *52°38′N 18°11′E*
111 *N17* **Strzyżów** Podkarpackie, SE Poland *49°52′N 21°46′E*
15 *S8* **St-Siméon** Québec, SE Canada *47°50′N 69°55′W*
Stua Laighean *see* Leinster, Mount
23 *Y13* **Stuart** Florida, SE USA *27°12′N 80°15′W*
29 *U14* **Stuart** Iowa, C USA *41°30′N 94°19′W*
29 *O13* **Stuart** Nebraska, C USA *42°36′N 99°08′W*
21 *S8* **Stuart** Virginia, NE USA *36°38′N 80°19′W*
10 *L13* **Stuart** ≈ British Columbia, SW Canada
39 *N10* **Stuart Island** *island* Alaska, USA
10 *L13* **Stuart Lake** ◎ British Columbia, SW Canada
185 *B22* **Stuart Mountains** ▲▲ South Island, New Zealand
182 *F3* **Stuart Range** *hill range* South Australia
Stubaital *see* Neustift im Stubaital
95 *I24* **Stubbekøbing** Storstrøm, SE Denmark *54°53′N 12°04′E*
45 *P14* **Stubbs** Saint Vincent, Saint Vincent and the Grenadines *13°08′N 61°09′W*
109 *V6* **Stübming** ≈ E Austria
114 *J11* **Studen Kladenets, Yazovir** ⊠ S Bulgaria
185 *G21* **Studholme** Canterbury, South Island, New Zealand *44°44′S 171°08′E*
Stuhlweissenberg *see* Székesfehérvár
Stuhm *see* Sztum
12 *C7* **Stull Lake** ◎ Ontario, C Canada
126 *L4* **Stupino** Moskovskaya Oblast', W Russian Federation *54°54′N 38°06′E*
27 *U4* **Sturgeon** Missouri, C USA *39°13′N 92°16′W*
14 *G10* **Sturgeon** ≈ Ontario, S Canada
31 *N6* **Sturgeon Bay** Wisconsin, N USA *44°51′N 87°21′W*
14 *G11* **Sturgeon Falls** Ontario, S Canada *46°22′N 79°57′W*
12 *C11* **Sturgeon Lake** ◎ Ontario, S Canada
30 *M3* **Sturgeon River** ≈ Michigan, N USA
20 *H6* **Sturgis** Kentucky, S USA *37°33′N 87°58′W*
31 *P11* **Sturgis** Michigan, N USA *41°48′N 85°25′W*
28 *J9* **Sturgis** South Dakota, N USA *44°24′N 103°30′W*
112 *D10* **Šturlić** ◈ Federacija Bosna I Hercegovina, NW Bosnia and Herzegovina
111 *J22* **Štúrovo** *Hung.* Párkány; *prev.* Parkan. Nitriansky Kraj, SW Slovakia *47°49′N 18°40′E*
182 *L4* **Sturt, Mount** *hill* New South Wales, SE Australia
181 *P4* **Sturt Plain** *plain* Northern Territory, N Australia
181 *T9* **Sturt Stony Desert** *desert* South Australia
83 *J25* **Stutterheim** Eastern Cape, S South Africa *32°35′S 27°26′E*
101 *H21* **Stuttgart** Baden-Württemberg, SW Germany *48°47′N 09°12′E*
27 *W12* **Stuttgart** Arkansas, C USA *34°30′N 91°32′W*
92 *H2* **Stykkishólmur** Vesturland, W Iceland *65°04′N 22°43′W*
115 *F17* **Stylída** *var.* Stilida, Stilís. Stereá Ellás, C Greece *38°55′N 22°37′E*
116 *K2* **Styr** *Rus.* Styr'. ≈ Belarus/Ukraine
115 *I19* **Stýra** *var.* Stira. Évvoia, C Greece *38°10′N 24°13′E*
Styria *see* Steiermark
15 *Y5* **St-Yvon** Québec, SE Canada *49°09′N 64°51′W*
Su *see* Jiangsu
Sua *see* Sowa
171 *Q17* **Suai** W East Timor *09°19′S 125°16′E*
54 *G9* **Suaita** Santander, C Colombia *06°07′N 73°30′W*
80 *I7* **Suakin** *var.* Sawakin. Red Sea, NE Sudan *19°06′N 37°17′E*
161 *T13* **Suao** *Jap.* Suō. N Taiwan *24°33′N 121°48′E*
Suao *see* Suau
Sua Pan *see* Sowa Pan
40 *G6* **Suaqui Grande** Sonora, NW Mexico *28°22′N 109°52′W*
61 *A16* **Suardi** Santa Fe, C Argentina *30°32′S 61°58′W*
54 *D11* **Suárez** Cauca, SW Colombia *02°55′N 76°41′W*
186 *G10* **Suau** *var.* Suao. Suaul Island, SE Papua New Guinea *10°39′S 150°03′E*
118 *G12* **Subačius** Panevėžys, NE Lithuania *55°46′N 24°45′E*
168 *K9* **Subang** *prev.* Soebang. Jawa, C Indonesia *06°32′S 107°45′E*
169 *O16* **Subang** ✈ (Kuala Lumpur) Pahang, Peninsular Malaysia
129 *S10* **Subansiri** ≈ NE India
118 *I11* **Subate** Daugvapils, SE Latvia *56°00′N 25°54′E*
139 *N5* **Subaykhān** Dayr az Zawr, E Syria *34°52′N 40°35′E*
Subei/Subei Mongolzu Zizhixian *see* Dangchengwan
169 *P9* **Subi Besar, Pulau** *island* Kepulauan Natuna, W Indonesia
Subiyah *see* Aş Şubayḩīyah
26 *I7* **Sublette** Kansas, C USA *37°28′N 100°52′W*
112 *K8* **Subotica** *Ger.* Maria-Theresiopel, *Hung.* Szabadka. Vojvodina, N Serbia *46°06′N 19°41′E*
116 *K9* **Suceava** *Ger.* Suczawa, *Hung.* Szucsava. Suceava, NE Romania *47°41′N 26°16′E*
116 *J9* **Suceava** ◈ *county* NE Romania
116 *K9* **Suceava** *Ger.* Suczawa. ≈ N Romania
112 *E12* **Sučevići** Zadar, SW Croatia *44°13′N 16°04′E*
111 *K17* **Sucha Beskidzka** Małopolskie, S Poland *49°44′N 19°36′E*
111 *M14* **Suchedniów** Świętokrzyskie, C Poland *51°01′N 20°49′E*
42 *A2* **Suchitepéquez** *off.* Departamento de Suchitepéquez. ◈ *department* SW Guatemala
Suchitepéquez, Departamento de *see* Suchitepéquez
Su-chou *see* Suzhou
Suchow *see* Xuzhou, Jiangsu, China
Suchow *see* Suzhou, Jiangsu, China
97 *D17* **Suck** ≈ C Ireland
Sucker State *see* Illinois
186 *F9* **Suckling, Mount** ▲ S Papua New Guinea *09°36′S 149°00′E*
57 *L19* **Sucre** *hist.* Chuquisaca, La Plata. ● (Bolivia-legal capital) Chuquisaca, S Bolivia *18°53′S 65°25′W*
54 *E6* **Sucre** Santander, N Colombia *08°50′N 74°22′W*
56 *A7* **Sucre** Manabí, W Ecuador *01°21′S 80°27′W*
54 *E6* **Sucre** *off.* Departamento de Sucre. ◈ *province* N Colombia
55 *O5* **Sucre** *off.* Estado Sucre. ◈ *state* NE Venezuela
Sucre, Departamento de *see* Sucre
Sucre, Estado *see* Sucre
56 *D6* **Sucumbíos** ◈ *province* NE Ecuador
113 *G15* **Sućuraj** Split-Dalmacija, S Croatia *43°07′N 17°10′E*
58 *K10* **Sucuriju** Amapá, NE Brazil *01°31′N 50°W*
Suczawa *see* Suceava
79 *E16* **Sud** *Eng.* South. ◈ *province* S Cameroon
124 *K13* **Suda** ≈ NW Russian Federation
Suda *see* Soúda
117 *U13* **Sudak** Respublika Krym, S Ukraine *44°52′N 34°57′E*
24 *M4* **Sudan** Texas, SW USA *34°04′N 102°32′W*
80 *C10* **Sudan** *off.* Republic of Sudan, *Ar.* Jumhuriyat as-Sudan; *prev.* Anglo-Egyptian Sudan. ◆ *republic* N Africa
Sudanese Republic *see* Mali
Sudan, Jumhuriyat as- *see* Sudan
Sudan, Republic of *see* Sudan
14 *F10* **Sudbury** Ontario, S Canada *46°29′N 81°W*
97 *P20* **Sudbury** E England, United Kingdom *52°04′N 00°43′E*
Sud, Canal de *see* Gonâve, Canal de la
80 *E13* **Sudd** *swamp region* S Sudan
100 *K10* **Sude** ≈ N Germany
Suderø *see* Sudhuroy
Sudest Island *see* Tagula Island
111 *E15* **Sudeten** *var.* Sudetes, Sudetic Mountains, *Cz./Pol.* Sudety. ▲▲ Czech Republic/Poland
Sudetes/Sudetic Mountains/Sudety *see* Sudeten
92 *G1* **Sudhureyri** Vestfirdhir, NW Iceland *66°08′N 23°31′W*
92 *J4* **Sudhurland** ◈ *region* S Iceland
95 *B19* **Sudhuroy** *Dan.* Suderø. *island* S Faeroe Islands
124 *M15* **Sudislavl'** Kostromskaya Oblast', NW Russian Federation *57°55′N 41°45′E*
Südkarpaten *see* Carpaţii Meridionalii
79 *N20* **Sud-Kivu** *off.* Région Sud Kivu. ◈ *region* E Dem. Rep. Congo
Sud Kivu, Région *see* Sud-Kivu
Südliche Morava *see* Južna Morava
100 *E12* **Süd-Nord-Kanal** *canal* NW Germany
126 *M3* **Sudogda** Vladimirskaya Oblast', W Russian Federation *55°58′N 40°57′E*
Sudostroy *see* Severodvinsk
79 *C15* **Sud-Ouest** *Eng.* South-West. ◈ *province* W Cameroon
173 *X17* **Sud Ouest, Pointe** *headland* SW Mauritius *20°27′S 57°18′E*
187 *P17* **Sud, Province** ◈ *province* S New Caledonia
126 *J8* **Sudzha** Kurskaya Oblast', W Russian Federation *51°12′N 35°19′E*
81 *D15* **Sue** ≈ S Sudan
105 *S10* **Sueca** País Valenciano, E Spain *39°13′N 00°19′W*
114 *I10* **Sŭedinenie** Plovdiv, C Bulgaria *42°14′N 24°36′E*
Suero *see* Alzira
75 *X8* **Suez** *Ar.* As Suways, El Suweis. NE Egypt *29°59′N 32°33′E*
75 *W7* **Suez Canal** *Ar.* Qanāt as Suways. *canal* NE Egypt
Suez, Gulf of *see* Khalīj as Suways
11 *R17* **Suffield** Alberta, SW Canada *50°15′N 111°05′W*
21 *X7* **Suffolk** Virginia, NE USA *36°44′N 76°37′W*
97 *P20* **Suffolk** *cultural region* E England, United Kingdom
142 *J2* **Şūfīān** Āžarbāyjān-e Sharqī, N Iran *38°15′N 45°59′E*
31 *N12* **Sugar Creek** ≈ Illinois, N USA
30 *L13* **Sugar Creek** ≈ Illinois, N USA
31 *R3* **Sugar Island** *island* Michigan, N USA
25 *V11* **Sugar Land** Texas, SW USA *29°37′N 95°37′W*
19 *P6* **Sugarloaf Mountain** ▲ Maine, NE USA *45°01′N 70°18′W*
65 *G24* **Sugar Loaf Point** *headland* N Saint Helena *15°54′S 05°43′W*
136 *G16* **Suğla Gölü** ◎ SW Turkey
123 *T8* **Sugoy** ≈ E Russian Federation
158 *F7* **Sugun** Xinjiang Uygur Zizhiqu, W China *39°46′N 76°45′E*
147 *U11* **Sugut, Gora** ▲ SW Kyrgyzstan *39°52′N 73°36′E*
169 *V6* **Sugut, Sungai** ≈ East Malaysia
159 *O9* **Suhai Hu** ◎ C China
162 *K14* **Suhait** Nei Mongol Zizhiqu, N China *39°29′N 105°11′E*
141 *X7* **Şuḩār** *var.* Sohar. N Oman *24°20′N 56°43′E*
113 *M17* **Suharekë** *Serb.* Suva Reka. S Kosovo *42°23′N 20°50′E*
162 *L6* **Sühbaatar** Selenge, N Mongolia *50°12′N 106°14′E*
163 *P8* **Sühbaatar** *var.* Haylaastay. Sühbaatar, E Mongolia *46°44′N 113°51′E*
163 *P9* **Sühbaatar** ◈ *province* E Mongolia
101 *K17* **Suhl** Thüringen, C Germany *50°37′N 10°43′E*
108 *F7* **Suhr** Aargau, N Switzerland *47°23′N 08°05′E*
Sui'an *see* Zhangpu
Suicheng *see* Suixi
161 *O12* **Suichuan** *var.* Quanjiang. Jiangxi, S China *26°26′N 114°34′E*
Suid-Afrika *see* South Africa
160 *L4* **Suide** *var.* Mingzhou. Shaanxi, C China *37°30′N 110°10′E*
Suidwes-Afrika *see* Namibia
163 *Y9* **Suifenhe** Heilongjiang, NE China *44°22′N 131°12′E*
Suigen *see* Suwŏn
163 *W8* **Suihua** Heilongjiang, NE China *46°40′N 127°00′E*
Súilí, Loch *see* Swilly, Lough
161 *Q6* **Suining** Jiangsu, E China *33°54′N 117°58′E*
160 *I9* **Suining** Sichuan, C China *30°31′N 105°33′E*
103 *Q4* **Suippes** Marne, N France *49°08′N 04°31′E*
97 *E20* **Suir** *Ir.* An tSiúir. ≈ S Ireland
165 *J13* **Suita** Ōsaka, Honshū, SW Japan *34°39′N 135°27′E*
160 *L16* **Suixi** *var.* Suicheng. Guangdong, S China *21°23′N 110°14′E*
Sui Xian *see* Suizhou
163 *T13* **Suizhong** Liaoning, NE China *40°19′N 120°22′E*
161 *N8* **Suizhou** *prev.* Sui Xian. Hubei, C China *31°46′N 113°20′E*
149 *P17* **Sujāwal** Sind, SE Pakistan *24°36′N 68°06′E*
169 *O16* **Sukabumi** *prev.* Soekaboemi. Jawa, C Indonesia *06°55′S 106°56′E*
169 *Q12* **Sukadana, Teluk** *bay* Borneo, W Indonesia
165 *P11* **Sukagawa** Fukushima, Honshū, C Japan *37°16′N 140°20′E*
Sukarnapura *see* Jayapura
Sukarno, Puntjak *see* Jaya, Puncak
Sŭkh *see* Sokh
114 *N8* **Sukha Reka** ≈ NE Bulgaria
114 *J8* **Sukhindol** Veliko Turnovo, N Bulgaria *43°11′N 24°10′E*
126 *J5* **Sukhinichi** Kaluzhskaya Oblast', W Russian Federation *54°06′N 35°22′E*
Sukhne *see* As Sukhnah
127 *S5* **Sukhodol** Samarskaya Oblast', W Russian Federation *53°53′N 51°13′E*
129 *Q4* **Sukhona** *var.* Tot'ma. ≈ NW Russian Federation
167 *O8* **Sukhothai** *var.* Sukotai. Sukhothai, W Thailand *17°00′N 99°51′E*
Sukhumi *see* Sokhumi
Sukkertoppen *see* Maniitsoq
149 *Q13* **Sukkur** Sind, SE Pakistan *27°45′N 68°46′E*
Sukotai *see* Sukhothai
Sukra Bay *see* Şawqirah, Dawḩat
125 *V15* **Suksun** Permskaya Oblast', NW Russian Federation *57°10′N 57°27′E*
165 *F15* **Sukumo** Kōchi, Shikoku, SW Japan *32°55′N 132°42′E*
94 *B12* **Sula** *island* S Norway
125 *Q5* **Sula** ≈ NW Russian Federation
117 *R5* **Sula** ≈ N Ukraine
42 *H6* **Sulaco, Río** ≈ NW Honduras
Sulaimaniya *see* As Sulaymānīyah
149 *S10* **Sulaimān Range** ▲▲ C Pakistan
127 *Q16* **Sulak** Respublika Dagestan, SW Russian Federation *43°19′N 47°28′E*
127 *Q16* **Sulak** ≈ SW Russian Federation
171 *Q13* **Sula, Kepulauan** *island group* C Indonesia
136 *I12* **Sulakyurt** *var.* Konur. Kırıkkale, N Turkey *40°10′N 33°42′E*
171 *P17* **Sulamu** Timor, S Indonesia *09°57′S 123°33′E*
96 *F5* **Sula Sgeir** *island* NW Scotland, United Kingdom
171 *N13* **Sulawesi** *Eng.* Celebes. *island* C Indonesia
Sulawesi, Laut *see* Celebes Sea
171 *N14* **Sulawesi Selatan** *off.* Propinsi Sulawesi Selatan, *Eng.* South Celebes, South Sulawesi. ◈ *province* C Indonesia
Sulawesi Selatan, Propinsi *see* Sulawesi Selatan
171 *P12* **Sulawesi Tengah** *off.* Propinsi Sulawesi Tengah, *Eng.* Central Celebes, Central Sulawesi. ◈ *province* N Indonesia
Sulawesi Tengah, Propinsi *see* Sulawesi Tengah
171 *O14* **Sulawesi Tenggara** *off.* Propinsi Sulawesi Tenggara, *Eng.* South-East Celebes, South-East Sulawesi. ◈ *province* C Indonesia
Sulawesi Tenggara, Propinsi *see* Sulawesi Tenggara
171 *P11* **Sulawesi Utara** *off.* Propinsi Sulawesi Utara, *Eng.* North Celebes, North Sulawesi. ◈ *province* N Indonesia
Sulawesi Utara, Propinsi *see* Sulawesi Utara
139 *T5* **Sulaymān Beg** At Ta'mīn, N Iraq
Sulaymānīyah, Muḩāfaẓat as *see* As Sulaymānīyah
95 *D15* **Suldalsvatnet** ◎ S Norway
Sulden *see* Solda
110 *E12* **Sulechów** *Ger.* Züllichau. Lubuskie, W Poland *52°05′N 15°37′E*
110 *E11* **Sulęcin** Lubuskie, W Poland *52°29′N 15°06′E*
77 *U14* **Suleja** Niger, C Nigeria *09°15′N 07°10′E*
111 *K14* **Sulejów** Łodzkie, S Poland *51°21′N 19°57′E*
96 *I5* **Sule Skerry** *island* N Scotland, United Kingdom
Suliag *see* Sawhāj
76 *J16* **Sulima** S Sierra Leone *06°59′N 11°34′W*
117 *O13* **Sulina** Tulcea, SE Romania *45°07′N 29°40′E*
117 *N13* **Sulina, Braţul** ≈ SE Romania
100 *H12* **Sulingen** Niedersachsen, NW Germany *52°40′N 08°48′E*
Sulisjielmmá *see* Sulitjelma
92 *H12* **Suliskongen** ▲ C Norway *67°10′N 16°16′E*
92 *H12* **Sulitjelma** *Lapp.* Sulisjielmmá. Nordland, C Norway *67°10′N 16°05′E*
56 *A9* **Sullana** Piura, NW Peru *04°54′S 80°42′W*
23 *N3* **Sulligent** Alabama, S USA *33°54′N 88°07′W*
30 *M14* **Sullivan** Illinois, N USA *39°36′N 88°36′W*
31 *N15* **Sullivan** Indiana, N USA *39°05′N 87°24′W*
27 *W5* **Sullivan** Missouri, C USA *38°12′N 91°09′W*
Sullivan Island *see* Lanbi Kyun
96 *M1* **Sullom Voe** NE Scotland, United Kingdom *60°24′N 01°09′W*
103 *O7* **Sully-sur-Loire** Loiret, C France *47°46′N 02°21′E*
Sulmo *see* Sulmona
107 *K15* **Sulmona** *anc.* Sulmo. Abruzzo, C Italy *42°03′N 13°56′E*
Sulo *see* Shule He
114 *M11* **Süloğlu** Edirne, NW Turkey *41°46′N 26°55′E*
22 *G9* **Sulphur** Louisiana, S USA *30°14′N 93°22′W*
27 *O12* **Sulphur** Oklahoma, C USA *34°31′N 96°58′W*
28 *K9* **Sulphur Creek** ≈ South Dakota, N USA
24 *M5* **Sulphur Draw** ≈ Texas, SW USA
25 *W5* **Sulphur River** ≈ Arkansas/Texas, SW USA
25 *V6* **Sulphur Springs** Texas, SW USA *33°09′N 95°36′W*
24 *M6* **Sulphur Springs Draw** ≈ Texas, SW USA
14 *D8* **Sultan** Ontario, S Canada *47°34′N 82°45′W*
Sultānābād *see* Arāk
Sultan Alonto, Lake *see* Lanao, Lake
136 *G15* **Sultan Dağları** ▲▲ C Turkey
114 *N13* **Sultanköy** Tekirdağ, NW Turkey *41°01′N 27°58′E*
171 *Q7* **Sultan Kudarat** *var.* Nuling. Mindanao, S Philippines *07°20′N 124°16′E*
152 *M13* **Sultānpur** Uttar Pradesh, N India *26°15′N 82°04′E*
171 *O9* **Sulu Archipelago** *island group* SW Philippines
192 *F7* **Sulu Basin** *undersea feature* SE South China Sea *08°00′N 121°30′E*
Sülüktü *see* Sulyukta
Sulu, Laut *see* Sulu Sea
169 *X6* **Sulu Sea** *var.* Laut Sulu. *sea* SW Philippines
145 *O15* **Sulutobe** *Kaz.* Sulūtöbe. Kzylorda, S Kazakhstan *44°31′N 66°17′E*
Sulūtöbe *see* Sulutobe
147 *Q11* **Sulyukta** *Kir.* Sülüktü. Batkenskaya Oblast', SW Kyrgyzstan *39°57′N 69°31′E*
Sulz *see* Sulz am Neckar
101 *G22* **Sulz am Neckar** *var.* Sulz. Baden-Württemberg, SW Germany *48°22′N 08°37′E*
101 *L20* **Sulzbach-Rosenberg** Bayern, SE Germany *49°30′N 11°43′E*
195 *N13* **Sulzberger Bay** *bay* Antarctica
Sumail *see* Summēl
81 *M14* **Sumalē** ◈ *federal region* E Ethiopia
113 *F15* **Sumartin** Split-Dalmacija, S Croatia *43°17′N 16°52′E*
32 *H6* **Sumas** Washington, NW USA *49°00′N 122°15′W*
168 *J10* **Sumatera** *Eng.* Sumatra. *island* W Indonesia
168 *J12* **Sumatera Barat** *off.* Propinsi Sumatera Barat, *Eng.* West Sumatra. ◈ *province* W Indonesia
Sumatera Barat, Propinsi *see* Sumatera Barat
168 *L13* **Sumatera Selatan** *off.* Propinsi Sumatera Selatan, *Eng.* South Sumatra. ◈ *province* W Indonesia
Sumatera Selatan, Propinsi *see* Sumatera Selatan
168 *H10* **Sumatera Utara** *off.* Propinsi Sumatera Utara, *Eng.* North Sumatra. ◈ *province* W Indonesia
Sumatera Utara, Propinsi *see* Sumatera Utara
Sumatra *see* Sumatera
Šumava *see* Bohemian Forest
Sumayl *see* Summēl
139 *U7* **Sumayr al Muḩammad** Diyālá, E Iraq *33°34′N 45°06′E*
171 *N17* **Sumba, Pulau** *Eng.* Sandalwood Island; *prev.* Soemba. *island* Nusa Tenggara, C Indonesia
146 *D12* **Sumbar** ≈ W Turkmenistan
192 *E9* **Sumbawa** *prev.* Soembawa. *island* Nusa Tenggara, C Indonesia
170 *L16* **Sumbawabesar** Sumbawa, S Indonesia *08°30′S 117°25′E*
81 *F23* **Sumbawanga** Rukwa, W Tanzania *07°57′S 31°37′E*
82 *B12* **Sumbe** *var.* N'Gunza, *Port.* Novo Redondo. Cuanza Sul, W Angola *11°13′S 13°53′E*
96 *M3* **Sumburgh Head** *headland* NE Scotland, United Kingdom *59°51′N 01°16′W*
111 *H23* **Sümeg** Veszprém, W Hungary *47°01′N 17°13′E*
80 *C12* **Sumeih** Southern Darfur, S Sudan *09°50′N 27°39′E*
169 *T16* **Sumenep** *prev.* Soemenep. Pulau Madura, C Indonesia *07°01′S 113°51′E*
Sumgait *see* Sumqayıtçay, Azerbaijan
Sumgait *see* Sumqayıt, Azerbaijan
165 *Y14* **Sumisu-jima** *Eng.* Smith Island. *island* SE Japan
139 *Q2* **Summēl** *var.* Sumail, Sumayl. Dahūk, N Iraq *36°52′N 42°51′E*
31 *O5* **Summer Island** *island* Michigan, N USA
32 *H15* **Summer Lake** ◎ Oregon, NW USA
11 *N17* **Summerland** British Columbia, SW Canada *49°35′N 119°45′W*
13 *P14* **Summerside** Prince Edward Island, SE Canada *46°24′N 63°46′W*
21 *R5* **Summersville** West Virginia, NE USA *38°17′N 80°52′W*
21 *R5* **Summersville Lake** ⊠ West Virginia, NE USA
21 *S13* **Summerton** South Carolina, SE USA *33°36′N 80°21′W*
23 *R2* **Summerville** Georgia, SE USA *34°28′N 85°21′W*
21 *S14* **Summerville** South Carolina, SE USA *33°01′N 80°10′W*
39 *R10* **Summit** Alaska, USA *63°21′N 148°50′W*
35 *V6* **Summit Mountain** ▲ Nevada, W USA *39°23′N 116°25′W*
37 *R8* **Summit Peak** ▲ Colorado, C USA *37°21′N 106°42′W*
Summus Portus *see* Somport, Col du
29 *X12* **Sumner** Iowa, C USA *42°51′N 92°05′W*
22 *K3* **Sumner** Mississippi, S USA *33°58′N 90°22′W*
185 *H17* **Sumner, Lake** ◎ South Island, New Zealand
37 *U12* **Sumner, Lake** ⊠ New Mexico, SW USA
111 *G17* **Šumperk** *Ger.* Mährisch-Schönberg. Olomoucký Kraj, E Czech Republic *49°58′N 17°00′E*
42 *F7* **Sumpul, Río** ≈ El Salvador/Honduras
137 *Z11* **Sumqayıt** *Rus.* Sumgait. E Azerbaijan *40°33′N 49°41′E*
137 *Y11* **Sumqayıtçay** *Rus.* Sumgait. ≈ E Azerbaijan
147 *R9* **Sumsar** Dzhalal-Abadskaya Oblast', W Kyrgyzstan *41°12′N 71°16′E*
117 *S3* **Sums'ka Oblast'** *var.* Sumy, *Rus.* Sumskaya Oblast'. ◈ *province* NE Ukraine
Sumskaya Oblast' *see* Sums'ka Oblast'
124 *J8* **Sumskiy Posad** Respublika Kareliya, NW Russian Federation *64°12′N 35°22′E*
21 *S12* **Sumter** South Carolina, SE USA *33°54′N 80°22′W*
117 *T3* **Sumy** Sums'ka Oblast', NE Ukraine *50°54′N 34°49′E*
Sumy *see* Sums'ka Oblast'
159 *Q15* **Sumzom** Xizang Zizhiqu, W China *29°45′N 96°14′E*
125 *R15* **Suna** Kirovskaya Oblast', NW Russian Federation *57°53′N 50°04′E*
124 *I10* **Suna** ≈ NW Russian Federation
165 *S3* **Sunagawa** Hokkaidō, NE Japan *43°30′N 141°55′E*
153 *V13* **Sunamganj** Sylhet, NE Bangladesh *25°04′N 91°24′E*
163 *W14* **Sunan** ✈ (P'yŏngyang) SW North Korea *39°12′N 125°40′E*
Sunan/Sunan Yugurzu Zizhixian *see* Hongwansi
19 *N9* **Sunapee Lake** ◎ New Hampshire, NE USA
139 *P4* **Sunaysilah** *salt marsh* N Iraq
20 *M8* **Sunbright** Tennessee, S USA *36°12′N 84°39′W*
33 *R6* **Sunburst** Montana, NW USA *48°51′N 111°54′W*
183 *N12* **Sunbury** Victoria, SE Australia *37°36′S 114°45′E*
21 *X8* **Sunbury** North Carolina, SE USA *36°27′N 76°34′W*
18 *G14* **Sunbury** Pennsylvania, NE USA *40°51′N 76°47′W*
61 *A17* **Sunchales** Santa Fe, C Argentina *30°58′S 61°35′W*
163 *W13* **Sunch'ŏn** SW North Korea *39°28′N 125°58′E*
163 *Y16* **Sunch'ŏn** *Jap.* Junten. S South Korea *34°56′N 127°29′E*
36 *K13* **Sun City** Arizona, SW USA *33°36′N 112°16′W*
19 *O9* **Suncook** New Hampshire, NE USA *43°07′N 71°25′W*
161 *P5* **Suncun** *prev.* Xinwen. Shandong, E China *35°49′N 117°36′E*
Sunda Islands *see* Greater Sunda Islands
33 *Z12* **Sundance** Wyoming, C USA *44°24′N 104°22′W*
153 *T17* **Sundarbans** *wetland* Bangladesh/India
154 *M11* **Sundargarh** Orissa, E India *22°07′N 84°02′E*
129 *U15* **Sunda Shelf** *undersea feature* S South China Sea *05°00′N 107°00′E*
Sunda Trench *see* Java Trench
129 *U17* **Sunda Trough** *undersea feature* E Indian Ocean *08°50′S 109°30′E*
95 *O16* **Sundbyberg** Stockholm, C Sweden *59°22′N 17°58′E*
97 *M14* **Sunderland** *var.* Wearmouth. NE England, United Kingdom *54°55′N 01°23′W*
101 *F15* **Sundern** Nordrhein-Westfalen, W Germany *51°19′N 08°00′E*
136 *F12* **Sündiken Dağları** ▲▲ C Turkey
24 *M5* **Sundown** Texas, SW USA *33°27′N 102°29′W*
11 *P16* **Sundre** Alberta, SW Canada *51°49′N 114°46′W*
14 *H12* **Sundridge** Ontario, S Canada *45°45′N 79°25′W*
93 *H17* **Sundsvall** Västernorrland, C Sweden *62°22′N 17°20′E*
26 *H4* **Sunflower, Mount** ▲ Kansas, C USA *39°01′N 102°02′W*
Sunflower State *see* Kansas
169 *N14* **Sungaibuntu** Sumatera, SW Indonesia *04°04′S 105°37′E*
168 *K12* **Sungaidareh** Sumatera, W Indonesia *0°58′S 101°30′E*
167 *P17* **Sungai Kolok** *var.* Sungai Ko-Lok. Narathiwat, SW Thailand *06°02′N 101°58′E*
Sungai Ko-Lok *see* Sungai Kolok
168 *K12* **Sungaipenuh** *prev.* Soengaipenoeh. Sumatera, W Indonesia *02°S 101°28′E*
169 *P11* **Sungaipinyuh** Borneo, C Indonesia *0°16′N 109°06′E*
Sungari *see* Songhua Jiang
Sungaria *see* Dzungaria
Sungei Pahang *see* Pahang, Sungai
167 *O8* **Sung Men** Phrae, NW Thailand *17°59′N 100°07′E*
83 *M15* **Sungo** Tete, NW Mozambique *16°31′S 33°58′E*
Sungpu *see* Songpan
168 *M13* **Sungsang** Sumatera, W Indonesia *02°22′S 104°50′E*
114 *M9* **Sungurlare** Burgas, E Bulgaria *42°47′N 26°46′E*
136 *J12* **Sungurlu** Çorum, N Turkey *40°10′N 34°23′E*
112 *F9* **Sunja** Sisak-Moslavina, C Croatia *45°21′N 16°33′E*
153 *Q12* **Sun Koshī** ≈ E Nepal
94 *F9* **Sunndalen** *valley* S Norway
94 *F9* **Sunndalsøra** Møre og Romsdal, S Norway *62°39′N 08°37′E*
95 *K15* **Sunne** Värmland, C Sweden *59°52′N 13°05′E*
95 *O15* **Sunnersta** Uppsala, C Sweden *59°46′N 17°40′E*
94 *C11* **Sunnfjord** *physical region* S Norway
95 *C15* **Sunnhordland** *physical region* S Norway
94 *D10* **Sunnmøre** *physical region* S Norway
37 *N4* **Sunnyside** Utah, W USA *39°33′N 110°23′W*
32 *J10* **Sunnyside** Washington, NW USA *46°01′N 119°58′W*
35 *N9* **Sunnyvale** California, W USA *37°22′N 122°02′W*
30 *L8* **Sun Prairie** Wisconsin, N USA *43°12′N 89°12′W*
Sunqur *see* Sonqor
25 *N1* **Sunray** Texas, SW USA *36°01′N 101°49′W*
22 *I8* **Sunset** Louisiana, S USA *30°24′N 92°04′W*
25 *S5* **Sunset** Texas, SW USA *33°24′N 97°45′W*
Sunset State *see* Oregon
181 *Z10* **Sunshine Coast** *cultural region* Queensland, E Australia
Sunshine State *see* Florida
Sunshine State *see* New Mexico
Sunshine State *see* South Dakota
123 *O10* **Suntar** Respublika Sakha (Yakutiya), NE Russian Federation *62°10′N 117°34′E*
39 *R10* **Suntrana** Alaska, USA *63°51′N 148°51′W*
148 *J15* **Suntsar** Baluchistān, SW Pakistan *25°30′N 62°03′E*
163 *W15* **Sunwi-do** *island* SW North Korea
163 *W6* **Sunwu** Heilongjiang, NE China *49°29′N 127°15′E*
77 *O16* **Sunyani** W Ghana *07°22′N 02°18′W*
Suō *see* Suao
93 *M17* **Suolahti** Länsi-Suomi, C Finland *62°32′N 25°51′E*
Suoločielgi *see* Saariselkä
Suomenlahti *see* Finland, Gulf of
Suomen Tasavalta/Suomi *see* Finland
93 *N14* **Suomussalmi** Oulu, E Finland *64°54′N 29°05′E*
165 *E13* **Suō-nada** *sea* SW Japan
93 *M17* **Suonenjoki** Itä-Suomi, C Finland *62°36′N 27°07′E*
167 *S13* **Suŏng** Kâmpóng Cham, C Cambodia *11°53′N 105°41′E*
124 *I10* **Suoyarvi** Respublika Kareliya, NW Russian Federation *62°02′N 32°24′E*
Supanburi *see* Suphan Buri
57 *D14* **Supe** Lima, W Peru *10°49′S 77°40′W*
15 *V7* **Supérieur, Lac** ◎ Québec, SE Canada
Supérieur, Lac *see* Superior, Lake
36 *M14* **Superior** Arizona, SW USA *33°17′N 111°06′W*
33 *O9* **Superior** Montana, NW USA *47°11′N 114°53′W*
29 *P17* **Superior** Nebraska, C USA *40°01′N 98°04′W*
30 *I3* **Superior** Wisconsin, N USA *46°42′N 92°04′W*
41 *S17* **Superior, Laguna** *lagoon* S Mexico
31 *N2* **Superior, Lake** *Fr.* Lac Supérieur. ◎ Canada/USA
36 *L13* **Superstition Mountains** ▲▲ Arizona, SW USA
113 *F14* **Supetar** *It.* San Pietro. Split-Dalmacija, S Croatia *43°22′N 16°34′E*
167 *O10* **Suphan Buri** *var.* Supanburi. Suphan Buri, W Thailand *14°29′N 100°10′E*
171 *V12* **Supiori, Pulau** *island* E Indonesia
188 *K2* **Supply Reef** *reef* N Northern Mariana Islands
195 *O7* **Support Force Glacier** *glacier* Antarctica
137 *R10* **Sup'sa** *var.* Supsa. ≈ W Georgia
Supsa *see* Sup'sa
Sūq 'Abs *see* 'Abs
139 *W12* **Sūq ash Shuyūkh** Dhī Qār, SE Iraq *30°53′N 46°28′E*
138 *H4* **Şuqaylibīyah** Ḩamāh, W Syria *35°21′N 36°24′E*
161 *Q6* **Suqian** Jiangsu, E China *33°57′N 118°18′E*
Suqrah *see* Şawqirah
Suqrah Bay *see* Şawqirah, Dawḩat
141 *V16* **Suquţrā** *var.* Sokotra, *Eng.* Socotra. *island* SE Yemen
141 *Z8* **Şūr** NE Oman *22°32′N 59°33′E*
Şūr *see* Soûr
127 *P5* **Sura** Penzenskaya Oblast', W Russian Federation *53°23′N 45°03′E*
127 *P4* **Sura** ≈ W Russian Federation
149 *N12* **Sūrāb** Baluchistān, SW Pakistan *28°28′N 66°15′E*
Surabaja *see* Surabaya
192 *E8* **Surabaya** *prev.* Surabaja, Soerabaja. Jawa, C Indonesia *07°14′S 112°45′E*
95 *N15* **Surahammar** Västmanland, C Sweden *59°43′N 16°13′E*
169 *Q16* **Surakarta** *Eng.* Solo; *prev.* Soerakarta. Jawa, S Indonesia *07°32′S 110°50′E*
Surakhany *see* Suraxanı
137 *S10* **Surami** C Georgia *41°59′N 43°36′E*
143 *X13* **Sūrān** Sīstān va Balūchestān, SE Iran *27°18′N 61°58′E*
111 *I21* **Šurany** *Hung.* Nagysurány. Nitriansky Kraj, SW Slovakia *48°05′N 18°10′E*
154 *D12* **Sūrat** Gujarāt, W India *21°10′N 72°54′E*
Suratdhani *see* Surat Thani
152 *G9* **Sūratgarh** Rājasthān, NW India *29°20′N 73°59′E*
167 *N14* **Surat Thani** *var.* Suratdhani. Surat Thani, SW Thailand *09°09′N 99°20′E*
119 *Q16* **Suraw** *Rus.* Surov. ≈ E Belarus
137 *Z11* **Suraxanı** *Rus.* Surakhany. E Azerbaijan *40°25′N 49°59′E*
141 *Y11* **Surayr** E Oman *19°56′N 57°47′E*
138 *K2* **Suraysāt** Ḩalab, N Syria *36°42′N 38°01′E*
118 *O12* **Surazh** Vitsyebskaya Voblasts', NE Belarus *55°25′N 30°44′E*
126 *H6* **Surazh** Bryanskaya Oblast', W Russian Federation *53°04′N 32°29′E*
191 *V17* **Sur, Cabo** *headland* Easter Island, Chile, E Pacific Ocean *27°11′S 109°26′W*
112 *L11* **Surčin** Serbia, N Serbia *44°48′N 20°19′E*
116 *H9* **Surduc** *Hung.* Szurduk. Sălaj, NW Romania *47°13′N 23°20′E*
113 *P16* **Surdulica** Serbia, SE Serbia *42°43′N 22°10′E*
99 *L24* **Sûre** *var.* Sauer. ≈ W Europe *see also* Sauer
Sûre *see* Sauer
154 *C10* **Surendranagar** Gujarāt, W India *22°44′N 71°43′E*
18 *K16* **Surf City** New Jersey, NE USA *39°21′N 74°24′W*
183 *V3* **Surfers Paradise** Queensland, E Australia *27°54′S 153°18′E*
21 *U13* **Surfside Beach** South Carolina, SE USA *33°36′N 78°58′W*
102 *J10* **Surgères** Charente-Maritime, W France *46°07′N 00°44′W*
122 *H10* **Surgut** Khanty-Mansiyskiy Avtonomnyy Okrug-Yugra, C Russian Federation *61°13′N 73°28′E*
122 *K10* **Surgutikha** Krasnoyarskiy Kray, N Russian Federation *64°44′N 87°13′E*
98 *M6* **Surhuisterveen** Friesland, N Netherlands *53°11′N 06°10′E*
105 *V5* **Súria** Cataluña, NE Spain *41°50′N 01°45′E*
143 *P10* **Sūrīān** Fārs, S Iran
155 *J15* **Suriāpet** Andhra Pradesh, C India *17°10′N 79°42′E*
171 *Q6* **Surigao** Mindanao, S Philippines *09°43′N 125°31′E*
167 *R10* **Surin** Surin, E Thailand *14°53′N 103°29′E*
Surinam *see* Suriname
55 *U11* **Suriname** *off.* Republic of Suriname, *var.* Surinam; *prev.* Dutch Guiana, Netherlands Guiana. ◆ *republic* N South America
Suriname, Republic of *see* Surinam
Sūrīya/Sūrīyah, Al-Jumhūrīyah al-'Arabīyah as- *see* Syria
Surkhab, Darya-i- *see* Kahmard, Daryā-ye
Surkhandar'inskaya Oblast' *see* Surxondaryo Viloyati
Surkhandar'ya *see* Surxondaryo
Surkhet *see* Birendranagar
147 *R12* **Surkhob** ≈ C Tajikistan
137 *P11* **Sürmene** Trabzon, NE Turkey *40°56′N 40°03′E*
Surov *see* Suraw
127 *N11* **Surovikino** Volgogradskaya Oblast', SW Russian Federation *48°39′N 42°46′E*

◆ Country ● Country Capital ◇ Dependent Territory ○ Dependent Territory Capital ◈ Administrative Regions ✈ International Airport ▲ Mountain ▲▲ Mountain Range Volcano ≈ River ◎ Lake ⊠ Reservoir

Sur, Point – Tagant

35 N11 Sur, Point headland California, W USA 36°18′N 121°54′W
187 N15 Surprise, Île island N New Caledonia
61 E22 Sur, Punta headland E Argentina 50°59′S 69°10′W
Surrentum see Sorrento
28 M3 Surrey North Dakota, N USA 48°13′N 101°05′W
97 O22 Surrey cultural region SE England, United Kingdom
21 X7 Surry Virginia, NE USA 37°08′N 81°34′W
108 F8 Sursee Luzern, W Switzerland 47°11′N 08°07′E
127 P6 Sursk Penzenskaya Oblast', W Russian Federation 53°06′N 45°46′E
127 P5 Surskoye Ul'yanovskaya Oblast', W Russian Federation 54°28′N 46°47′E
75 P8 Surt var. Sidra, Sirte. N Libya 31°13′N 16°35′E
95 I19 Surte Västra Götaland, S Sweden 57°49′N 12°01′E
75 Q8 Surt, Khalīj Eng. Gulf of Sidra, Gulf of Sirti, Sidra. gulf N Libya
92 I5 Surtsey island S Iceland
137 N17 Suruç Şanlıurfa, S Turkey 36°58′N 38°24′E
168 L13 Surulangun Sumatera, W Indonesia 02°35′S 102°47′E
147 P13 Surxondaryo Rus. Surkhandar'ya. Tajikistan/Uzbekistan
147 N13 Surxondaryo Viloyati Rus. Surkhandar'inskaya Oblast'. ◆ province S Uzbekistan
Süs see Susch
106 A8 Susa Piemonte, NE Italy 45°10′N 07°01′E
165 E12 Susa Yamaguchi, Honshū, SW Japan 34°35′N 131°34′E
Susa see Sūsah
113 E16 Sušac It. Cazza. island SW Croatia
Sūsah see Sousse
164 G14 Susaki Kōchi, Shikoku, SW Japan 33°22′N 133°13′E
165 I15 Susami Wakayama, Honshū, SW Japan 33°32′N 135°32′E
142 K9 Sūsangerd var. Susangird. Khūzestān, SW Iran 31°40′N 48°06′E
Susangird see Sūsangerd
35 P4 Susanville California, W USA 40°25′N 120°39′W
108 J9 Susch var. Süs. Graubünden, SE Switzerland 46°45′N 10°04′E
137 N12 Suşehri Sivas, N Turkey 40°11′N 38°06′E
Susiana see Khūzestān
111 B18 Sušice Ger. Schüttenhofen. Plzeňský Kraj, W Czech Republic 49°14′N 13°32′E
39 R11 Susitna Alaska, USA 61°32′N 150°30′W
39 R11 Susitna River Alaska, USA
127 Q3 Suslonger Respublika Mariy El, W Russian Federation 56°18′N 48°16′E
105 N14 Suspiro del Moro, Puerto del pass S Spain
18 H16 Susquehanna River New York/Pennsylvania, NE USA
13 O15 Sussex New Brunswick, SE Canada 45°43′N 65°32′W
18 J13 Sussex New Jersey, NE USA 41°12′N 74°34′W
21 W7 Sussex Virginia, NE USA 36°54′N 77°16′W
97 O23 Sussex cultural region S England, United Kingdom
183 S10 Sussex Inlet New South Wales, SE Australia 35°10′S 150°35′E
99 L17 Susteren Limburg, SE Netherlands 51°04′N 05°50′E
10 K12 Sustut Peak ▲ British Columbia, W Canada 56°25′N 126°34′W
123 S9 Susuman Magadanskaya Oblast', E Russian Federation 62°46′N 148°08′E
188 H6 Susupe ● (Northern Mariana Islands-judicial capital) Saipan, S Northern Mariana Islands
136 D12 Susurluk Balıkesir, NW Turkey 39°55′N 28°10′E
114 M13 Susuzmüsellim Tekirdağ, NW Turkey 41°04′N 27°03′E
136 F15 Sütçüler Isparta, SW Turkey 37°31′N 31°00′E
116 L13 Şuţeşti Brăila, SE Romania 45°13′N 27°27′E
83 F25 Sutherland Western Cape, SW South Africa 32°24′S 20°40′E
28 L15 Sutherland Nebraska, C USA 41°09′N 101°07′W
96 I7 Sutherland cultural region N Scotland, United Kingdom
185 B21 Sutherland Falls waterfall South Island, New Zealand
32 F14 Sutherlin Oregon, NW USA 43°23′N 123°18′W
149 V10 Sutlej India/Pakistan
Sutna see Satna
35 P7 Sutter Creek California, W USA 38°22′N 120°49′W
39 R11 Sutton Alaska, USA 61°42′N 148°53′W
29 Q16 Sutton Nebraska, C USA 40°36′N 97°52′W
21 R4 Sutton West Virginia, NE USA 38°41′N 80°43′W
12 F8 Sutton Ontario, C Canada
97 M19 Sutton Coldfield C England, United Kingdom 52°34′N 01°48′W
21 R4 Sutton Lake West Virginia, NE USA
15 P13 Sutton, Monts hill range Québec, SE Canada
12 F8 Sutton Ridges ▲▲ Ontario, C Canada
165 Q4 Suttsu Hokkaidō, NE Japan 42°46′N 140°12′E
39 P15 Sutwik Island island Alaska, USA
Süüj see Dashinchilen
118 H5 Suure-Jaani Ger. Gross-Sankt-Johannis. Viljandimaa, S Estonia 58°34′N 25°28′E
118 J7 Suur Munamägi var. Munamägi, Ger. Eier-Berg. ▲ SE Estonia 57°42′N 27°03′E
118 F5 Suur Väin Ger. Grosser Sund. strait W Estonia
147 U8 Suusamyr Chuyskaya Oblast', C Kyrgyzstan 42°07′N 73°55′E
187 X14 Suva ● (Fiji) Viti Levu, W Fiji 18°08′S 178°27′E
187 X15 Suva ✈ Viti Levu, C Fiji 18°01′S 178°30′E
113 N18 Suva Gora ▲ W FYR Macedonia
118 H11 Suvainiškis Panevėžys, NE Lithuania 56°09′N 25°15′E
Suvalkai/Suvalki see Suwałki
113 P15 Suva Planina ▲▲ SE Serbia
Suva Reka see Suharekë
126 K5 Suvorov Tul'skaya Oblast', W Russian Federation 54°08′N 36°33′E
117 N12 Suvorove Odes'ka Oblast', SW Ukraine 45°35′N 28°58′E
114 M8 Suvorovo Varna, E Bulgaria 43°19′N 27°26′E
Suvorovo see Ştefan Vodă
Suwaik see As Suwayq
Suwaira see Aş Şuwayrah
110 O7 Suwałki Lith. Suvalkai, Rus. Suvalki. Podlaskie, NE Poland 54°06′N 22°56′E
167 R10 Suwannaphum Roi Et, E Thailand 15°36′N 103°46′E
23 V8 Suwannee River Florida/Georgia, SE USA
Şuwār see Aş Şuwār
190 K14 Suwarrow atoll N Cook Islands
143 R16 Suwaydān var. Sweihan. Abū Ẓaby, E United Arab Emirates 24°30′N 55°19′E
Suwaydá/Suwaydā' see As Suwaydā'
Suwayqiyah, Hawr as see Shuwayjah, Hawr ash
Suways, Qanāt as see Suez Canal
Suweida see As Suwaydā'
Suweon see Suwŏn
163 X15 Suwŏn var. Suweon, Jap. Suigen. NW South Korea 37°17′N 127°03′E
Su Xian see Suzhou
143 R14 Sūzā Hormozgān, S Iran 26°50′N 56°05′E
145 P15 Suzak Kaz. Sozaq. Yuzhnyy Kazakhstan, S Kazakhstan 44°09′N 68°28′E
165 N12 Suzaka var. Suzaka. Nagano, Honshū, S Japan 36°38′N 138°20′E
Suzaka see Suzaka
126 M3 Suzdal' Vladimirskaya Oblast', W Russian Federation 56°27′N 40°29′E
161 P7 Suzhou var. Su Xian. Anhui, E China 33°38′N 117°02′E
161 R8 Suzhou var. Soochow, Su-chou, Suchow; prev. Wuhsien. Jiangsu, E China 31°23′N 120°34′E
Suzhou see Jiuquan
163 V12 Suzi He NE China
Suz, Mys see Soye, Mys
165 M10 Suzu Ishikawa, Honshū, SW Japan 37°24′N 137°12′E
165 K14 Suzuka Mie, Honshū, SW Japan 34°52′N 136°37′E
165 M10 Suzu-misaki headland Honshū, SW Japan 37°31′N 137°19′E
Svågälv see Svågan
94 M10 Svågan var. Svågälv. C Sweden
Svalava/Svaljava see Svalyava
92 O2 Svalbard ◇ Norwegian dependency Arctic Ocean
92 J2 Svalbardhseyri Nordhurland Eystra, N Iceland 65°43′N 18°03′W
95 K22 Svalöv Skåne, S Sweden 55°55′N 13°06′E
116 H7 Svalyava Cz. Svalava, Svaljava, Hung. Szolyva. Zakarpats'ka Oblast', W Ukraine 48°33′N 23°00′E
92 O2 Svanbergfjellet ▲ C Svalbard 78°40′N 18°10′E
95 M24 Svaneke Bornholm, E Denmark 55°07′N 15°08′E
95 L22 Svängsta Blekinge, S Sweden 56°16′N 14°46′E
95 J16 Svanskog Värmland, C Sweden 59°10′N 12°34′E
95 L16 Svartå Örebro, C Sweden 59°13′N 14°07′E
95 L15 Svartälven C Sweden
92 G12 Svartisen glacier C Norway
117 X6 Svatove Rus. Svatovo. Luhans'ka Oblast', E Ukraine 49°24′N 38°11′E
Svatovo see Svatove
Sväty Kríž nad Hronom see Žiar nad Hronom
167 Q11 Svay Chék, Stœng Cambodia/Thailand
167 S13 Svay Riěng Svay Riěng, S Cambodia 11°05′N 105°48′E
92 O3 Sveagruva Spitsbergen, W Svalbard 77°53′N 16°42′E
95 K23 Svedala Skåne, S Sweden 55°30′N 13°15′E
118 H12 Svėdesai Utena, NE Lithuania 55°42′N 25°22′E
93 G18 Sveg Jämtland, C Sweden 62°02′N 14°20′E
118 C12 Švėkšna Klaipėda, W Lithuania 55°31′N 21°37′E
94 C11 Svelgen Sogn Og Fjordane, S Norway 61°47′N 05°18′E
95 H15 Svelvik Vestfold, S Norway 59°37′N 10°24′E
118 I13 Švenčionėliai Pol. Nowo-Święciany. Vilnius, SE Lithuania 55°10′N 26°00′E
118 I13 Švenčionys Pol. Święciany. Vilnius, SE Lithuania 55°08′N 26°08′E
95 H24 Svendborg Fyn, C Denmark 55°04′N 10°38′E
95 K19 Svenljunga Västra Götaland, S Sweden 57°30′N 13°05′E
92 P2 Svenskøya island E Svalbard
93 G17 Svenstavik Jämtland, C Sweden 62°40′N 14°24′E
95 G20 Svenstrup Nordjylland, N Denmark 56°58′N 09°52′E
118 H12 Šventoji C Lithuania
117 Z8 Sverdlovs'k Rus. Sverdlovsk; prev. Imeni Sverdlova Rudnik. Luhans'ka Oblast', E Ukraine 48°05′N 39°37′E
Sverdlovsk see Yekaterinburg
127 W2 Sverdlovskaya Oblast' ◆ province C Russian Federation
122 K6 Sverdrupa, Ostrov island N Russian Federation
Sverige see Sweden
113 D15 Svetac prev. Sveti Andrea, It. Sant'Andrea. island SW Croatia
Sveti Andrea see Svetac
Sveti Nikola see Sveti Nikole
113 O18 Sveti Nikole prev. Sveti Nikola. C FYR Macedonia 41°54′N 21°55′E
Sveti Vrach see Sandanski
123 T14 Svetlaya Primorskiy Kray, SE Russian Federation 46°33′N 138°20′E
126 B2 Svetlogorsk Kaliningradskaya Oblast', W Russian Federation 54°56′N 20°09′E
122 K9 Svetlogorsk Krasnoyarskiy Kray, N Russian Federation 66°51′N 88°29′E
Svetlogorsk see Svyetlahorsk
127 N14 Svetlograd Stavropol'skiy Kray, SW Russian Federation 45°20′N 42°53′E
Svetlovodsk see Svitlovods'k
119 A14 Svetlyy Ger. Zimmerbude. Kaliningradskaya Oblast', W Russian Federation 54°42′N 20°07′E
127 Y8 Svetlyy Orenburgskaya Oblast', W Russian Federation 50°34′N 60°42′E
127 P7 Svetlyy Saratovskaya Oblast', W Russian Federation 51°42′N 45°40′E
124 G11 Svetogorsk Fin. Enso. Leningradskaya Oblast', NW Russian Federation 61°06′N 28°52′E
Svetozarevo see Jagodina
111 B18 Švihov Ger. Schwihau. Plzeňský Kraj, W Czech Republic 49°31′N 13°18′E
112 E13 Svilaja ▲▲ SE Croatia
112 N12 Svilajnac Serbia, C Serbia 44°15′N 21°12′E
114 L11 Svilengrad prev. Mustafa-Pasha. Khaskovo, S Bulgaria 41°45′N 26°14′E
Svinecea Mare, Munte see Svinecea Mare, Vârful
116 F13 Svinecea Mare, Vârful var. Munte Svinecea Mare. ▲ SW Romania 44°47′N 22°10′E
Svino see Svínoy
95 B18 Svínoy Dan. Svinø. island NE Faeroe Islands
147 N14 Svintsovyy Rudnik Turkm. Swintsowyy Rudnik. Lebap Welaýaty, E Turkmenistan 37°54′N 66°25′E
118 I13 Svir Rus. Svir'. Minskaya Voblasts', NW Belarus 54°51′N 26°24′E
124 I12 Svir' canal NW Russian Federation
Svir', Ozero see Svir, Vozyera
119 I14 Svir, Vozyera Rus. Ozero Svir'. C Belarus
114 J7 Svishtov prev. Sistova. Veliko Tŭrnovo, N Bulgaria 43°37′N 25°20′E
119 F18 Svislach Pol. Świsłocz, Rus. Svisloch'. Hrodzyenskaya Voblasts', W Belarus 53°02′N 24°06′E
119 M17 Svislach Rus. Svisloch'. Mahilyowskaya Voblasts', E Belarus 53°26′N 28°59′E
119 L17 Svislach Rus. Svisloch'. E Belarus
Svisloch' see Svislach
111 F17 Svitavy Ger. Zwittau. Pardubický Kraj, C Czech Republic 49°45′N 16°27′E
117 S6 Svitlovods'k Rus. Svetlovodsk. Kirovohrads'ka Oblast', C Ukraine 49°05′N 33°15′E
Svizzera see Switzerland
123 Q13 Svobodnyy Amurskaya Oblast', SE Russian Federation 51°24′N 128°05′E
114 G9 Svoge Sofiya, W Bulgaria 42°58′N 23°20′E
92 G11 Svolvær Nordland, C Norway 68°15′N 14°40′E
111 F18 Svratka Ger. Schwarzawa. SE Czech Republic
113 P14 Svrljig Serbia, E Serbia 43°26′N 22°07′E
197 U10 Svyataya Anna Trough var. Saint Anna Trough. undersea feature N Kara Sea
124 M4 Svyatoy Nos, Mys headland NW Russian Federation 68°07′N 39°49′E
119 N18 Svyetlahorsk Rus. Svetlogorsk. Homyel'skaya Voblasts', SE Belarus 52°38′N 29°46′E
149 U5 Swābi North-West Frontier Province, N Pakistan 34°07′N 72°28′E
Swabian Jura see Schwäbische Alb
97 P19 Swaffham E England, United Kingdom 52°39′N 00°40′E
23 V5 Swainsboro Georgia, SE USA 32°36′N 82°19′W
83 C19 Swakop W Namibia
83 C19 Swakopmund Erongo, W Namibia 22°40′S 14°34′E
97 M15 Swale N England, United Kingdom
Swallow Island see Nendö
99 M16 Swalmen Limburg, SE Netherlands 51°13′N 06°02′E
12 G8 Swan Ontario, C Canada
97 L24 Swanage S England, United Kingdom 50°37′N 01°59′W
182 M10 Swan Hill Victoria, SE Australia 35°23′S 143°37′E
11 P13 Swan Hills Alberta, W Canada 54°41′N 116°20′W
65 D24 Swan Island island C Falkland Islands
Swankalok see Sawankhalok
29 U10 Swan Lake Minnesota, N USA
21 Y10 Swanquarter North Carolina, SE USA 35°24′N 76°20′W
182 J9 Swan Reach South Australia 34°39′S 139°35′E
11 V15 Swan River Manitoba, S Canada 52°06′N 101°17′W
183 P17 Swansea Tasmania, SE Australia 42°09′S 148°03′E
97 J22 Swansea Wel. Abertawe. S Wales, United Kingdom 51°38′N 03°57′W
21 R13 Swansea South Carolina, SE USA 33°47′N 81°06′W
19 S7 Swans Island island Maine, NE USA
28 L17 Swanson Lake Nebraska, C USA
31 R11 Swanton Ohio, N USA 41°35′N 83°53′W
110 G11 Swarzędz Poznań, W Poland 52°24′N 17°05′E
Swatow see Shantou
83 L22 Swaziland off. Kingdom of Swaziland. ◆ monarchy S Africa
Swaziland, Kingdom of see Swaziland
93 G18 Sweden off. Kingdom of Sweden, Swe. Sverige. ◆ monarchy N Europe
Sweden, Kingdom of see Sweden
Swedru see Agona Swedru
25 V12 Sweeny Texas, SW USA 29°02′N 95°42′W
33 R6 Sweetgrass Montana, NW USA 48°58′N 111°58′W
32 G12 Sweet Home Oregon, NW USA 44°24′N 122°44′W
25 T12 Sweet Home Texas, SW USA 29°21′N 97°04′W
27 T4 Sweet Springs Missouri, C USA 38°57′N 93°24′W
20 M10 Sweetwater Tennessee, S USA 35°36′N 84°27′W
25 P7 Sweetwater Texas, SW USA 32°27′N 100°25′W
33 V15 Sweetwater River Wyoming, C USA
Sweiham see Suwaydān
83 F26 Swellendam Western Cape, SW South Africa 34°01′S 20°26′E
111 G15 Świdnica Ger. Schweidnitz. Wałbrzych, SW Poland 50°51′N 16°29′E
111 O14 Świdnik Ger. Streckenbach. Lubelskie, E Poland 51°14′N 22°41′E
110 F8 Świdwin Ger. Schivelbein. Zachodnio-pomorskie, NW Poland 53°47′N 15°44′E
111 F15 Świebodzice Ger. Freiburg in Schlesien, Swiebodzice. Wałbrzych, SW Poland 50°54′N 16°23′E
110 E11 Świebodzin Ger. Schwiebus. Lubuskie, W Poland 52°15′N 15°31′E
Święciany see Švenčionys
110 I9 Świecie Ger. Schwertberg. Kujawsko-pomorskie, C Poland 53°24′N 18°24′E
111 L15 Świętokrzyskie ◆ province S Poland
11 T16 Swift Current Saskatchewan, S Canada 50°17′N 107°49′W
98 K9 Swifterbant Flevoland, C Netherlands 52°36′N 05°33′E
183 Q12 Swifts Creek Victoria, SE Australia 37°17′S 147°41′E
96 E13 Swilly, Lough Ir. Loch Súilí. inlet N Ireland
97 M22 Swindon S England, United Kingdom 51°34′N 01°47′W
Swinemünde see Świnoujście
110 D8 Świnoujście Ger. Swinemünde. Zachodnio-pomorskie, NW Poland 53°54′N 14°13′E
Swintsowyy Rudnik see Svintsovyy Rudnik
Świsłocz see Svislach
Swiss Confederation see Switzerland
108 E9 Switzerland off. Swiss Confederation, Fr. La Suisse, Ger. Schweiz, It. Svizzera; anc. Helvetia. ◆ federal republic C Europe
97 F17 Swords Ir. Sord, Sórd Choluim Chille. Dublin, E Ireland 53°28′N 06°13′W
18 H13 Swoyersville Pennsylvania, NE USA 41°18′N 75°48′W
124 I10 Syamozera, Ozero NW Russian Federation
124 M13 Syamzha Vologodskaya Oblast', NW Russian Federation 60°02′N 41°09′E
118 N13 Syanno Rus. Senno. Vitsyebskaya Voblasts', NE Belarus 54°49′N 29°43′E
119 K16 Syarhyeyevichy Rus. Sergeyevichi. Minskaya Voblasts', C Belarus 53°30′N 27°45′E
124 I12 Syas'stroy Leningradskaya Oblast', NW Russian Federation 60°05′N 32°37′E
Sycaminum see Hefa
30 M10 Sycamore Illinois, N USA 41°59′N 88°41′W
126 J3 Sychëvka Smolenskaya Oblast', W Russian Federation 55°52′N 34°19′E
111 H14 Syców Ger. Gross Wartenberg. Dolnośląskie, SW Poland 51°18′N 17°42′E
14 E17 Sydenham Ontario, S Canada
Sydenham Island see Nonouti
183 T9 Sydney state capital New South Wales, SE Australia 33°55′S 151°10′E
13 R14 Sydney Cape Breton Island, Nova Scotia, SE Canada 46°10′N 60°10′W
Sydney Island see Manra
13 R14 Sydney Mines Cape Breton Island, Nova Scotia, SE Canada 46°14′N 60°19′W
Syedpur see Saidpur
119 K18 Syelishcha Rus. Selishche. Minskaya Voblasts', C Belarus 53°01′N 27°25′E
119 J18 Syemyezhava Rus. Semezhevo. Minskaya Voblasts', C Belarus 52°58′N 27°00′E
Syene see Aswân
117 X6 Syeverodonets'k Rus. Severodonetsk. Luhans'ka Oblast', E Ukraine 48°59′N 38°28′E
161 T6 Syiao Shan island SE China
100 H11 Syke Niedersachsen, NW Germany 52°55′N 08°49′E
94 D10 Sykkylven Møre og Romsdal, S Norway 62°23′N 06°35′E
Sykoúri see Sykoúrio
115 F15 Sykoúrio var. Sikouri, Sykoúri; prev. Sikoúrion. Thessalía, C Greece 39°46′N 22°35′E
125 R11 Syktyvkar prev. Ust'-Sysol'sk. Respublika Komi, NW Russian Federation 61°42′N 50°45′E
23 Q4 Sylacauga Alabama, S USA 33°10′N 86°15′W
Sylarna see Storsylen
153 V14 Sylhet Sylhet, NE Bangladesh 24°53′N 91°51′E
153 V13 Sylhet ◆ division NE Bangladesh
100 G6 Sylt island NW Germany
21 O10 Sylva North Carolina, SE USA 35°23′N 83°13′W
125 V15 Sylva NW Russian Federation
23 W5 Sylvania Georgia, SE USA 32°45′N 81°38′W
31 R11 Sylvania Ohio, N USA 41°43′N 83°42′W
11 Q15 Sylvan Lake Alberta, SW Canada 52°18′N 114°02′W
33 T13 Sylvan Pass pass Wyoming, C USA
23 T7 Sylvester Georgia, SE USA 31°31′N 83°50′W
25 P6 Sylvester Texas, SW USA 32°42′N 100°15′W
10 L11 Sylvia, Mount ▲ British Columbia, W Canada 58°03′N 124°26′W
122 K11 Sym C Russian Federation
115 N22 Sými var. Simi. island Dodekánisa, Greece, Aegean Sea
117 U8 Synel'nykove Dnipropetrovs'ka Oblast', E Ukraine 48°19′N 35°32′E
125 U6 Synya Respublika Komi, NW Russian Federation 65°21′N 58°01′E
117 P7 Synyukha Rus. Sinyukha. S Ukraine
195 V2 Syowa Japanese research station Antarctica 68°58′S 40°07′E
26 H6 Syracuse Kansas, C USA 38°00′N 101°43′W
29 S16 Syracuse Nebraska, C USA 40°39′N 96°11′W
18 H10 Syracuse New York, NE USA 43°03′N 76°09′W
Syracuse see Siracusa
Syrdar'inskaya Oblast' see Sirdaryo Viloyati
Syrdariya see Syr Darya
144 L14 Syr Darya var. Sai Hun, Sir Darya, Syrdarya, Kaz. Syrdariya, Rus. Syrdar'ya, Uzb. Sirdaryo; anc. Jaxartes. C Asia
Syrdarya see Syr Darya
138 J6 Syria off. Syrian Arab Republic, var. Siria, Syrie, Ar. Al-Jumhūrīyah al-'Arabīyah as-Sūrīyah, Sūrīya. ◆ republic SW Asia
Syrian Arab Republic see Syria
138 L9 Syrian Desert Ar. Al Hamad, Bādiyat ash Shām. desert SW Asia
Syrie see Syria
115 L22 Sýrna var. Sirna. island Kykládes, Greece, Aegean Sea
115 I20 Sýros var. Síros. island Kykládes, Greece, Aegean Sea
93 M18 Sysmä Etelä-Suomi, S Finland 61°28′N 25°37′E
125 R12 Sysola NW Russian Federation
Syulemeshlii see Sredets
127 S2 Syumsi Udmurtskaya Respublika, NW Russian Federation 57°07′N 51°35′E
114 K10 Syuyutliyka C Bulgaria
Syvash, Zaliv see Syvash, Zatoka
117 U12 Syvash, Zatoka Rus. Zaliv Syvash. inlet S Ukraine
127 Q6 Syzran' Samarskaya Oblast', W Russian Federation 53°10′N 48°23′E
Szabadka see Subotica
111 N21 Szabolcs-Szatmár-Bereg off. Szabolcs-Szatmár-Bereg Megye. ◆ county E Hungary
Szabolcs-Szatmár-Bereg Megye see Szabolcs-Szatmár-Bereg
110 G10 Szamocin Ger. Samotschin. Wielkopolskie, C Poland 53°02′N 17°04′E
116 H8 Szamos var. Someş, Someşul, Ger. Samosch, Somesch. Hungary/Romania
Szamosújvár see Gherla
110 G11 Szamotuły Poznań, W Poland 52°35′N 16°36′E
Szarkowszczyzna see Sharkawshchyna
111 M24 Szarvas Békés, SE Hungary 46°51′N 20°35′E
Szászmagyarós see Măieruş
Szászrégen see Reghin
Szászsebes see Sebeş
Szászváros see Orăştie
Szatmárrnémeti see Satu Mare
Száva see Sava
111 P15 Szczebrzeszyn Lubelskie, E Poland 50°43′N 23°00′E
110 D9 Szczecin Eng./Ger. Stettin. Zachodnio-pomorskie, NW Poland 53°25′N 14°32′E
110 G8 Szczecinek Ger. Neustettin. Zachodnio-pomorskie, NW Poland 53°43′N 16°40′E
110 D8 Szczeciński, Zalew var. Stettiner Haff, Ger. Oderhaff. bay Germany/Poland
111 K15 Szczekociny Śląskie, S Poland 50°38′N 19°46′E
110 N8 Szczuczyn Podlaskie, NE Poland 53°34′N 22°17′E
Szczuczyn Nowogródzki see Shchuchyn
110 M8 Szczytno Ger. Ortelsburg. Warmińsko-Mazurskie, NE Poland 53°34′N 21°E
Szechuan/Szechwan see Sichuan
111 K21 Szécsény Nógrád, N Hungary 48°07′N 19°30′E
111 L25 Szeged Ger. Szegedin, Rom. Seghedin. Csongrád, SE Hungary 46°17′N 20°06′E
Szegedin see Szeged
111 N23 Szeghalom Békés, SE Hungary 47°01′N 21°09′E
Székelyhid see Săcueni
Székelykeresztúr see Cristuru Secuiesc
111 I23 Székesfehérvár Ger. Stuhlweissenberg; anc. Alba Regia. Fejér, W Hungary 47°13′N 18°24′E
Szeklerburg see Miercurea-Ciuc
Szekler Neumarkt see Târgu Secuiesc
111 J25 Szekszárd Tolna, S Hungary 46°21′N 18°41′E
Szempcz/Szenc see Senec
Szenice see Senica
Szentágota see Agnita
111 J22 Szentendre Ger. Sankt Andrä. Pest, N Hungary 47°40′N 19°02′E
111 L24 Szentes Csongrád, SE Hungary 46°40′N 20°17′E
111 F23 Szentgotthárd Eng. Saint Gotthard, Ger. Sankt Gotthard. Vas, W Hungary 46°57′N 16°18′E
Szentgyörgy see Đurđevac
Szenttamás see Srbobran
Széphely see Jebel
Szeping see Siping
Szered see Sereď
111 N21 Szerencs Borsod-Abaúj-Zemplén, NE Hungary 48°10′N 21°11′E
Szeret see Siret
Szeretfalva see Sărăţel
110 N7 Szeska Góra var. Szeskie Wygórza, Ger. Seesker Höhe. hill NE Poland
Szeskie Wygórza see Szeska Góra
111 H25 Szigetvár Baranya, SW Hungary 46°01′N 17°50′E
Szilágysomlyó see Şimleu Silvaniei
Szinna see Snina
Sziszek see Sisak
Szitás-Keresztúr see Cristuru Secuiesc
111 E15 Szklarska Poręba Ger. Schreiberhau. Dolnośląskie, SW Poland 50°50′N 15°30′E
Szkudy see Skuodas
Szlatina see Slatina
Szlavonia/Szlavonország see Slavonija
Szlovákia see Slovakia
Szluin see Slunj
111 L23 Szolnok Jász-Nagykun-Szolnok, C Hungary 47°11′N 20°12′E
Szolyva see Svalyava
111 G23 Szombathely Ger. Steinamanger; anc. Sabaria, Savaria. Vas, W Hungary 47°14′N 16°38′E
Szond/Szonta see Sonta
Szováta see Sovata
110 F13 Szprotawa Ger. Sprottau. Lubuskie, W Poland 51°33′N 15°32′E
Sztálinváros see Dunaújváros
Sztrazsó see Strážov
110 J8 Sztum Ger. Stuhm. Pomorskie, N Poland 53°54′N 19°01′E
110 H10 Szubin Ger. Schubin. Kujawsko-pomorskie, C Poland 53°04′N 17°49′E
Szucsava see Suceava
Szurduk see Surduc
111 M14 Szydłowiec Ger. Schlelau. Mazowieckie, C Poland 51°14′N 20°50′E

T

190 I17 Taakoka island S Cook Islands
Taalintehdas see Dalsbruk
171 O4 Taal, Lake Luzon, NW Philippines
95 J23 Taastrup var. Tåstrup. København, E Denmark 55°39′N 12°19′E
111 I24 Tab Somogy, W Hungary 46°45′N 18°01′E
171 P4 Tabaco Luzon, N Philippines 13°22′N 123°42′E
186 G4 Tabalo Mussau Island, NE Papua New Guinea 01°22′S 149°37′E
104 K5 Tábara Castilla-León, N Spain 41°49′N 05°57′W
186 H5 Tabar Islands island group NE Papua New Guinea
Tabariya, Bahrat see Tiberias, Lake
143 S7 Ţabas var. Golshan. Yazd, C Iran 33°37′N 56°54′E
43 P15 Tabasará, Serranía de ▲▲ W Panama
41 U15 Tabasco ◆ state SE Mexico
Tabasco see Grijalva, Río
127 Q2 Tabashino Respublika Mariy El, W Russian Federation 57°00′N 47°47′E
58 B13 Tabatinga Amazonas, N Brazil 04°14′S 69°44′W
74 G9 Tabelbala W Algeria 29°22′N 03°01′W
11 Q17 Taber Alberta, SW Canada 49°48′N 112°09′W
171 V15 Taberfane Pulau Trangan, E Indonesia 06°14′S 134°08′E
95 L19 Taberg Jönköping, S Sweden 57°42′N 14°05′E
191 O3 Tabiteuea prev. Drummond Island. atoll Tungaru, W Kiribati
171 O5 Tablas Island island C Philippines
184 Q10 Table Cape headland North Island, New Zealand 39°07′S 178°00′E
13 S13 Table Mountain ▲ Newfoundland, Newfoundland and Labrador, E Canada 47°39′N 59°15′W
173 P17 Table, Pointe de la headland SE Réunion 21°19′S 55°49′E
27 S8 Table Rock Lake Arkansas/Missouri, C USA
36 K14 Table Top ▲ Arizona, SW USA 32°45′N 112°07′W
186 D8 Tabletop, Mount ▲ C Papua New Guinea 06°51′S 146°00′E
111 D18 Tábor Jihočeský Kraj, S Czech Republic 49°25′N 14°41′E
123 R7 Tabor Respublika Sakha (Yakutiya), NE Russian Federation 71°14′N 150°23′E
29 S15 Tabor Iowa, C USA 40°54′N 95°40′W
81 F21 Tabora Tabora, W Tanzania 05°04′S 32°49′E
81 F21 Tabora ◆ region C Tanzania
21 U12 Tabor City North Carolina, SE USA 34°09′N 78°52′W
147 Q10 Taboshar NW Tajikistan 40°37′N 69°33′E
76 L18 Tabou var. Tabu. S Ivory Coast 04°28′N 07°20′W
142 J2 Tabrīz var. Tebriz; anc. Tauris. Āžarbāyjān-e Sharqī, NW Iran 38°05′N 46°18′E
Tabu see Tabou
191 W1 Tabuaeran prev. Fanning Island. atoll Line Islands, E Kiribati
171 O2 Tabuk Luzon, N Philippines 17°26′N 121°25′E
140 J4 Tabūk Tabūk, NW Saudi Arabia 28°25′N 36°34′E
140 J5 Tabūk off. Minţaqat Tabūk. ◆ province NW Saudi Arabia
Tabūk, Minţaqat see Tabūk
187 Q13 Tabwemasana, Mount ▲ Espiritu Santo, W Vanuatu 15°22′S 166°44′E
95 O15 Täby Stockholm, C Sweden 59°29′N 18°04′E
41 N14 Tacámbaro Michoacán, SW Mexico 19°12′N 101°27′W
42 A5 Tacaná, Volcán Guatemala/Mexico 15°07′N 92°06′W
43 X16 Tacarcuna, Cerro ▲ SE Panama 08°08′N 77°15′W
Tachau see Tachov
158 J3 Tacheng var. Qoqek. Xinjiang Uygur Zizhiqu, NW China 46°45′N 82°55′E
54 H7 Táchira off. Estado Táchira. ◆ state W Venezuela
Táchira, Estado see Táchira
161 T13 Tachoshui N Taiwan 24°26′N 121°43′E
111 A17 Tachov Ger. Tachau. Plveňský Kraj, W Czech Republic 49°48′N 12°38′E
171 Q5 Tacloban off. Tacloban City. Leyte, C Philippines 11°15′N 125°E
Tacloban City see Tacloban
57 I19 Tacna Tacna, SE Peru 18°S 70°15′W
57 H18 Tacna off. Departamento de Tacna. ◆ department S Peru
Tacna, Departamento de see Tacna
32 H8 Tacoma Washington, NW USA 47°15′N 122°27′W
18 L11 Taconic Range ▲▲ NE USA
62 L6 Taco Pozo Formosa, N Argentina 25°35′S 63°15′W
57 M20 Tacsara, Cordillera de ▲▲ S Bolivia
61 F17 Tacuarembó prev. San Fructuoso. Tacuarembó, C Uruguay 31°42′S 56°W
61 E18 Tacuarembó ◆ department C Uruguay
61 F17 Tacuarembó, Río C Uruguay
83 I14 Taculi North Western, NW Zambia 14°17′S 26°51′E
171 Q8 Tacurong Mindanao, S Philippines 06°42′N 124°40′E
77 V8 Tadek NW Niger
74 J9 Tademaït, Plateau du plateau C Algeria
187 R17 Tadine Province des Îles Loyauté, E New Caledonia 21°33′S 167°54′E
80 M11 Tadjoura, Golfe de Eng. Gulf of Tajura. inlet E Djibouti
80 L11 Tadjourah E Djibouti 11°47′N 42°51′E
Tadmor/Tadmur see Tudmur
11 W10 Tadoule Lake Manitoba, C Canada
15 S8 Tadoussac Québec, SE Canada 48°09′N 69°43′W
155 H18 Tādpatri Andhra Pradesh, E India 14°55′N 77°59′E
Tadzhikabad see Tojikobod
Tadzhikistan see Tajikistan
163 Y14 T'aebaek-sanmaek ▲▲ E South Korea
163 V15 Taechŏng-do island NW South Korea
163 X13 Taedong-gang C North Korea
163 Y16 Taegu off. Taegu-gwangyŏksi, var. Daegu, Jap. Taikyū. SE South Korea 35°55′N 128°33′E
Taegu-gwangyŏksi see Taegu
Taehan-haehyŏp see Korea Strait
Taehan Min'guk see South Korea
163 Y15 Taejŏn off. Taejŏn-gwangyŏksi, Jap. Taiden. C South Korea 36°20′N 127°28′E
Taejŏn-gwangyŏksi see Taejŏn
193 Z13 Tafahi island N Tonga
105 Q4 Tafalla Navarra, N Spain 42°32′N 01°41′W
77 W7 Tafassâsset, Ténéré du desert N Niger
75 M12 Tafassâsset, Oued SE Algeria
55 U11 Tafelberg ▲ S Suriname 03°55′N 56°09′W
97 J21 Taff SE Wales, United Kingdom
Tafila/Ţafilah, Muḩāfaẓat aţ see Aţ Ţafilah
77 N15 Tafiré N Ivory Coast 09°04′N 05°10′W
142 M6 Tafresh Markazī, W Iran 34°40′N 50°00′E
143 Q9 Taft Yazd, C Iran 31°45′N 54°14′E
35 R13 Taft California, W USA 35°08′N 119°27′W
25 T14 Taft Texas, SW USA 27°58′N 97°24′W
143 W12 Taftān, Kūh-e ▲ SE Iran 28°38′N 61°06′E
35 R13 Taft Heights California, W USA 35°06′N 119°29′W
189 Y14 Tafunsak Kosrae, E Micronesia 05°21′N 162°58′E
192 G16 Tāga Savai'i, SW Samoa 13°46′S 172°31′W
149 O6 Tagāb Dāikondī, E Afghanistan 33°53′N 66°23′E
39 O8 Tagagawik River Alaska, USA
165 Q10 Tagajō var. Tagazyō. Miyagi, Honshū, C Japan 38°18′N 140°58′E
126 K12 Taganrog Rostovskaya Oblast', SW Russian Federation 47°10′N 38°55′E
126 K12 Taganrog, Gulf of Rus. Taganrogskiy Zaliv, Ukr. Tahanroz'ka Zatoka. gulf Russian Federation/Ukraine
Taganrogskiy Zaliv see Taganrog, Gulf of
76 J8 Tagant ◆ region C Mauritania

◆ Country ● Country Capital ◇ Dependent Territory ○ Dependent Territory Capital ◆ Administrative Regions ✈ International Airport ▲ Mountain ▲▲ Mountain Range Volcano River Lake Reservoir

TAGAS – TAPIRAPECÓ, SERRA

148 M14 Tagas Baluchistān, SW Pakistan 27°09′N 64°36′E
171 O4 Tagaytay Luzon, N Philippines 14°04′N 120°55′E
Tagazyō see Tagajō
171 P6 Tagbilaran var. Tagbilaran City. Bohol, C Philippines 09°41′N 123°54′E
Tagbilaran City see Tagbilaran
106 B10 Taggia Liguria, NW Italy 43°51′N 07°48′E
77 V9 Taghouaji, Massif de ▲ C Niger 17°13′N 08°37′E
107 J15 Tagliacozzo Lazio, C Italy 42°03′N 13°15′E
106 J7 Tagliamento ≈ NE Italy
149 N3 Tagow Bāy var. Bai. Sar-e Pol, N Afghanistan 35°41′N 66°01′E
146 H9 Tagta var. Tahta, Rus. Takhta. Daşoguz Welaýaty, N Turkmenistan 41°40′N 59°51′E
146 J16 Tagtabazar var. Takhtabazar. Mary Welaýaty, S Turkmenistan 35°57′N 62°49′E
59 L17 Taguatinga Tocantins, C Brazil 12°16′S 46°25′W
186 I10 Tagula Tagula Island, SE Papua New Guinea 11°21′S 153°11′E
186 I11 Tagula Island prev. Southeast Island, Sudest Island. island SE Papua New Guinea
171 Q7 Tagum Mindanao, S Philippines 07°22′N 125°51′E
54 C7 Tagún, Cerro elevation Colombia/Panama
105 P7 Tagus Port. Rio Tejo, Sp. Río Tajo. ≈ Portugal/Spain
64 M9 Tagus Plain undersea feature E Atlantic Ocean 37°30′N 12°00′W
191 S10 Tahaa island Îles Sous le Vent, W French Polynesia
191 U10 Tahanea atoll Îles Tuamotu, C French Polynesia
Tahanroz'ka Zatoka see Taganrog, Gulf of
74 K12 Tahat ▲ SE Algeria 23°15′N 05°34′E
163 U4 Tahe Heilongjiang, NE China 52°21′N 124°42′E
Tahilt see Tsogt
191 T10 Tahiti island Îles du Vent, W French Polynesia
Tahiti, Archipel de see Société, Archipel de la
118 E4 Tahkuna Nina headland W Estonia 59°06′N 22°35′E
148 K12 Tāhlāb ≈ W Pakistan
148 K12 Tāhlāb, Dasht-i desert SW Pakistan
27 R10 Tahlequah Oklahoma, C USA 35°57′N 94°58′W
35 Q6 Tahoe City California, W USA 39°09′N 120°09′W
35 P6 Tahoe, Lake ◎ California/Nevada, W USA
25 N6 Tahoka Texas, SW USA 33°10′N 101°47′W
32 F8 Taholah Washington, NW USA 47°19′N 124°17′W
77 T11 Tahoua Tahoua, W Niger 14°53′N 05°18′E
77 T11 Tahoua ◈ department W Niger
31 P3 Tahquamenon Falls waterfall Michigan, N USA
31 P4 Tahquamenon River ≈ Michigan, N USA
139 V10 Taḩrīr Al Qādisīyah, S Iraq 31°58′N 45°34′E
10 K17 Tahsis Vancouver Island, British Columbia, SW Canada 49°42′N 126°31′W
75 W9 Ṭahṭā var. Ṭahta. C Egypt 26°47′N 31°31′E
Tahta see Tagta
136 L15 Tahtalı Dağları ⛰ C Turkey
57 I14 Tahuamanu, Río ≈ Bolivia/Peru
56 F13 Tahuanía, Río ≈ E Peru
191 X7 Tahuata island Îles Marquises, NE French Polynesia
76 L17 Taï SW Ivory Coast 05°52′N 07°28′W
161 P5 Tai'an Shandong, E China 36°13′N 117°12′E
191 R8 Taiarapu, Presqu'île de peninsula Tahiti, W French Polynesia
Taibad see Tāybād
160 K7 Taibai Shan ▲ C China 33°57′N 107°31′E
105 Q12 Taibilla, Sierra de ⛰ S Spain
Taibus Qi see Baochang
Taichū see T'aichung
161 S13 T'aichung Jap. Taichū; prev. Taiwan. C Taiwan 24°09′N 120°40′E
Taiden see Taejŏn
185 E23 Taieri ≈ South Island, New Zealand
115 E21 Taïgetos ⛰ S Greece
161 N4 Taihang Shan ⛰ C China
184 M11 Taihape Manawatu-Wanganui, North Island, New Zealand 39°41′S 175°47′E
161 O7 Taihe Anhui, E China 33°14′N 115°35′E
161 O12 Taihe var. Chengjiang. Jiangxi, S China 26°47′N 114°52′E
Taihoku see T'aipei
161 P9 Taihu Anhui, E China 30°22′N 116°20′E
161 R8 Tai Hu ◎ E China
159 O9 Taikang var. Dorbod, Dorbod Mongolzu Zizhixian. Heilongjiang, NE China 46°50′N 124°25′E
161 O6 Taikang Henan, C China 34°01′N 114°59′E
165 T5 Taiki Hokkaidō, NE Japan 42°29′N 143°15′E
166 L8 Taikkyi Yangon, SW Myanmar (Burma) 17°16′N 95°55′E
Taikyū see Taegu
163 U8 Tailai Heilongjiang, NE China 46°25′N 123°25′E
168 I12 Taileleo Pulau Siberut, W Indonesia 01°45′S 99°06′E
182 J10 Tailem Bend South Australia 35°20′S 139°34′E
96 I8 Tain N Scotland, United Kingdom 57°49′N 04°04′W
161 S14 T'ainan Jap. Tainan; prev. Dainan. S Taiwan 23°01′N 120°05′E
115 E22 Taínaro, Akrotírio cape S Greece
161 Q11 Taining var. Shancheng. Fujian, SE China 26°55′N 117°13′E
191 W7 Taiohae prev. Madisonville. Nuku Hiva, NE French Polynesia 08°55′S 140°04′W
161 T13 T'aipei Jap. Taihoku; prev. Daihoku. ● (Taiwan) N Taiwan 25°02′N 121°28′E
168 J7 Taiping Perak, Peninsular Malaysia 04°54′N 100°42′E
Taiping see Chongzuo
163 S8 Taiping Ling ▲ NE China 47°27′N 120°27′E
165 Q4 Taisei Hokkaidō, NE Japan 42°13′N 139°52′E
165 G12 Taisha Shimane, Honshū, SW Japan 35°23′N 132°40′E
109 R4 Taiskirchen Oberösterreich, NW Austria 48°15′N 13°33′E
63 F20 Taitao, Peninsula de peninsula S Chile
Taitō see T'aitung
161 T14 T'aitung Jap. Taitō. S Taiwan 22°43′N 121°10′E
92 M13 Taivalkoski Oulu, E Finland 65°35′N 28°20′E
93 K19 Taivassalo Länsi-Suomi, SW Finland 60°35′N 21°36′E
161 T14 Taiwan off. Republic of China, var. Formosa, Formo'sa. ◆ republic E Asia
192 F5 Taiwan var. Formosa. island E Asia
Taiwan see T'aichung
T'aiwan Haihsia/Taiwan Haixia see Taiwan Strait
Taiwan Shan see Chungyang Shanmo
161 R13 Taiwan Strait var. Formosa Strait, Chin. T'aiwan Haihsia, Taiwan Haixia. strait China/Taiwan
161 N4 Taiyuan var. T'ai-yuan, T'ai-yüan; prev. Yangku. province capital Shanxi, C China 37°48′N 112°33′E
T'ai-yuan/T'ai-yüan see Taiyuan
161 R7 Taizhou Jiangsu, E China 32°36′N 119°52′E
161 S10 Taizhou var. Jiaojiang; prev. Haimen. Zhejiang, SE China 28°36′N 121°19′E
Taizhou see Linhai
141 O16 Ta'izz SW Yemen 13°36′N 44°04′E
141 O16 Ta'izz ✈ SW Yemen 13°40′N 44°10′E
75 P12 Tajarhī SW Libya 24°21′N 14°28′E
147 P13 Tajikistan off. Republic of Tajikistan, Rus. Tadzhikistan, Taj. Jumhurii Tojikiston; prev. Tajik S.S.R. ◆ republic C Asia
Tajikistan, Republic of see Tajikistan
Tajik S.S.R see Tajikistan
165 O11 Tajima Fukushima, Honshū, C Japan 37°10′N 139°46′E
Tajoe see Tayu
Tajo, Río see Tagus
42 B5 Tajumulco, Volcán ▲ W Guatemala 15°04′N 91°50′W
105 P7 Tajuña ≈ C Spain
Tajura, Gulf of see Tadjoura, Golfe de
167 O9 Tak var. Rahaeng. Tak, W Thailand 16°51′N 99°08′E
189 U4 Taka Atoll var. Tōke. atoll Ratak Chain, N Marshall Islands
165 P12 Takahagi Ibaraki, Honshū, S Japan 36°42′N 140°42′E
165 H13 Takahashi var. Takahasi. Okayama, Honshū, SW Japan 34°48′N 133°38′E
Takahasi see Takahashi
189 P12 Takaieu Island island E Micronesia
184 I13 Takaka Tasman, South Island, New Zealand 40°52′S 172°49′E
170 M14 Takalar Sulawesi, C Indonesia 05°28′S 119°24′E
165 H13 Takamatsu var. Takamatu. Kagawa, Shikoku, SW Japan 34°19′N 133°59′E
Takamatu see Takamatsu
165 D14 Takamori Kumamoto, Kyūshū, SW Japan 32°50′N 131°08′E
165 D16 Takanabe Miyazaki, Kyūshū, SW Japan 32°13′N 131°31′E
170 M16 Takan, Gunung ▲ Pulau Sumba, S Indonesia 08°52′S 117°32′E
165 Q7 Takanosu var. Kita-Akita. Akita, Honshū, C Japan 40°13′N 140°23′E
Takao see Kaohsiung
165 L11 Takaoka Toyama, Honshū, SW Japan 36°44′N 137°02′E
184 N12 Takapau Hawke's Bay, North Island, New Zealand 40°01′S 176°21′E
191 U9 Takapoto atoll Îles Tuamotu, C French Polynesia
184 L5 Takapuna Auckland, North Island, New Zealand 36°48′S 174°46′E
165 J13 Takarazuka Hyōgo, Honshū, SW Japan 34°49′N 135°21′E
191 U9 Takaroa atoll Îles Tuamotu, C French Polynesia
165 N12 Takasaki Gunma, Honshū, S Japan 36°20′N 139°00′E
164 L12 Takayama Gifu, Honshū, SW Japan 36°09′N 137°16′E
164 K12 Takefu var. Echizen, Takehu. Fukui, Honshū, SW Japan 35°55′N 136°11′E
Takehu see Takefu
164 C14 Takeo Saga, Kyūshū, SW Japan 33°13′N 130°00′E
Takeo see Takêv
164 C17 Take-shima island Nansei-shotō, SW Japan
142 M5 Tākestān var. Takistan; prev. Siadehan. Qazvīn, N Iran 36°02′N 49°40′E
164 D14 Taketa Ōita, Kyūshū, SW Japan 33°00′N 131°23′E
167 R13 Takêv prev. Takeo. Takêv, S Cambodia 10°59′N 104°47′E
167 O10 Tak Fah Nakhon Sawan, C Thailand
139 T13 Takhādīd well S Iraq
149 R3 Takhār ◈ province NE Afghanistan
Takhiatash see Taxiatosh
167 S13 Ta Khmau Kândal, S Cambodia 11°30′N 104°59′E
Takhta see Tagta
Takhtabazar see Tagtabazar
145 O8 Takhtabrod Severnyy Kazakhstan, N Kazakhstan 52°35′N 67°37′E
Takhtakupyr see Taxtako'pir
142 M8 Takht-e Shāh, Kūh-e ▲ C Iran
77 V12 Takiéta Zinder, S Niger 13°43′N 08°33′E
8 J8 Takijuq Lake ◎ Nunavut, NW Canada
165 S3 Takikawa Hokkaidō, NE Japan 43°35′N 141°54′E
165 U3 Takinoue Hokkaidō, NE Japan 44°10′N 143°09′E
Takistan see Tākestān
185 B23 Takitimu Mountains ⛰ South Island, New Zealand
Takkaze see Tekezē
165 R7 Takko Aomori, Honshū, C Japan 40°19′N 141°11′E
10 L13 Takla Lake ◎ British Columbia, SW Canada
Takla Makan Desert see Taklimakan Shamo
158 H9 Taklimakan Shamo Eng. Takla Makan Desert. desert NW China
167 T12 Takôk Môndól Kiri, E Cambodia 12°37′N 106°30′E
39 P10 Takotna Alaska, USA 62°59′N 156°03′W
Takow see Kaohsiung
123 O12 Taksimo Respublika Buryatiya, S Russian Federation 56°18′N 114°53′E
164 C13 Taku Saga, Kyūshū, SW Japan 33°19′N 130°06′E
10 I10 Taku ≈ British Columbia, W Canada
166 M15 Takua Pa var. Ban Takua Pa. Phangnga, SW Thailand 08°55′N 98°20′E
77 W16 Takum Taraba, E Nigeria 07°16′N 10°00′E
191 V10 Takume atoll Îles Tuamotu, C French Polynesia
190 L16 Takutea island S Cook Islands
186 K6 Takuu Islands prev. Mortlock Group. island group NE Papua New Guinea
119 L18 Tal' Minskaya Voblasts', S Belarus 52°52′N 27°58′E
40 L13 Tala Jalisco, C Mexico 20°39′N 103°45′W
61 F19 Tala Canelones, S Uruguay 34°24′S 55°45′W
Talabriga see Aveiro, Portugal
Talabriga see Talavera de la Reina, Spain
119 N14 Talachyn Rus. Tolochin. Vitsyebskaya Voblasts', NE Belarus 54°25′N 29°42′E
149 U7 Talagang Punjab, E Pakistan 32°55′N 72°29′E
105 V11 Talaiassa ▲ Ibiza, Spain, W Mediterranean Sea 38°55′N 1°17′E
155 J23 Talaimannar Northern Province, NW Sri Lanka 09°05′N 79°43′E
117 R3 Talalayivka Chernihivs'ka Oblast', N Ukraine 50°51′N 33°09′E
43 O15 Talamanca, Cordillera de ⛰ S Costa Rica
56 A9 Talara Piura, NW Peru 04°31′S 81°17′W
104 L11 Talarrubias Extremadura, W Spain 39°03′N 05°14′W
147 S8 Talas Talasskaya Oblast', NW Kyrgyzstan 42°29′N 72°21′E
147 S8 Talas ≈ NW Kyrgyzstan
186 G7 Talasea New Britain, E Papua New Guinea 05°20′S 150°01′E
Talas Oblasty see Talasskaya Oblast'
147 S8 Talasskaya Oblast' Kir. Talas Oblasty. ◈ province NW Kyrgyzstan
147 S8 Talasskiy Alatau, Khrebet ⛰ Kazakhstan/Kyrgyzstan
77 U12 Tal'ata Mafara Zamfara, NW Nigeria 12°33′N 06°01′E
171 R9 Talaud, Kepulauan island group E Indonesia
104 M9 Talavera de la Reina anc. Caesarobriga, Talabriga. Castilla-La Mancha, C Spain 39°58′N 04°50′W
104 J11 Talavera la Real Extremadura, W Spain 38°53′N 06°46′W
186 F7 Talawe, Mount ▲ New Britain, C Papua New Guinea 05°30′S 148°24′E
23 S5 Talbotton Georgia, SE USA 32°40′N 84°32′W
183 R7 Talbragar River ≈ New South Wales, SE Australia
62 G13 Talca Maule, C Chile 35°28′S 71°42′W
62 F13 Talcahuano Bío Bío, C Chile 36°43′S 73°07′W
154 O12 Tālcher Orissa, E India 20°57′N 85°13′E
25 W5 Talco Texas, SW USA 33°21′N 95°06′W
145 V14 Taldykorgan Kaz. Taldyqorghan; prev. Taldy-Kurgan. Taldykorgan, SE Kazakhstan 45°N 78°23′E
Taldy-Kurgan/Taldyqorghan see Taldykorgan
147 Y7 Taldy-Suu Issyk-Kul'skaya Oblast', E Kyrgyzstan 42°49′N 78°33′E
147 U10 Taldy-Suu Oshskaya Oblast', SW Kyrgyzstan 40°33′N 73°52′E
Tal-e Khosravī see Yāsūj
193 Y15 Taleki Tonga island Otu Tolu Group, C Tonga
193 Y15 Taleki Vavu'u island Otu Tolu Group, C Tonga
102 J13 Talence Gironde, SW France 44°49′N 00°35′W
145 U16 Talgar Kaz. Talghar. Almaty, SE Kazakhstan 43°17′N 77°15′E
Talghar see Talgar
171 Q12 Taliabu, Pulau island Kepulauan Sula, C Indonesia
115 L22 Taliarós, Akrotírio headland Astypálaia, Kykládes, Greece, Aegean Sea 36°31′N 26°18′E
Ta-lien see Dalian
27 Q12 Talihina Oklahoma, C USA 34°45′N 95°03′W
Talimardzhan see Tollimarjon
137 T12 T'alin Rus. Talin; prev. Verin T'alin. W Armenia 40°23′N 43°51′E
Talin see T'alin
81 E15 Tali Post Bahr el Gabel, S Sudan 05°55′N 30°44′E
Taliq-an see Tāloqān
Talış Dağları see Talish Mountains
142 L2 Talish Mountains Az. Talış Dağları, Per. Kūhhā-ye Ṭavālesh, Rus. Talyshskiye Gory. ⛰ Azerbaijan/Iran
170 M16 Taliwang Sumbawa, C Indonesia 08°45′S 116°55′E
119 L17 Tal'ka Minskaya Voblasts', C Belarus 53°22′N 28°21′E
39 R11 Talkeetna Alaska, USA 62°19′N 150°06′W
39 R11 Talkeetna Mountains ⛰ Alaska, USA
Talkhof see Puurmani
92 H2 Tálknafjörður Vestfirdhir, W Iceland 65°38′N 23°51′W
139 Q3 Tall 'Abṭah Nīnawá, N Iraq 35°52′N 42°40′E
138 M2 Tall Abyaḍ var. Tell Abiad. Ar Raqqah, N Syria 36°42′N 38°56′E
23 Q4 Talladega Alabama, S USA 33°26′N 86°06′W
139 Q2 Tall 'Afar Nīnawá, N Iraq 36°22′N 42°27′E
23 S8 Tallahassee prev. Muskogean. state capital Florida, SE USA 30°26′N 84°17′W
22 L2 Tallahatchie River ≈ Mississippi, S USA
Tall al Abyaḍ see At Tall al Abyaḍ
139 W12 Tall al Laḥm Dhī Qār, S Iraq 30°46′N 46°22′E
183 P11 Tallangatta Victoria, SE Australia 36°15′S 147°13′E
23 R4 Tallapoosa River ≈ Alabama/Georgia, S USA
103 T13 Tallard Hautes-Alpes, SE France 44°30′N 06°04′E
139 Q3 Tall ash Sha'īr Nīnawá, N Iraq 36°11′N 42°26′E
23 Q5 Tallassee Alabama, S USA 32°32′N 85°53′W
139 R4 Tall 'Azbah Nīnawá, NW Iraq 35°47′N 43°13′E
138 I5 Tall Bīsah Ḩimş, W Syria 34°50′N 36°44′E
139 R3 Tall Ḩassūnah Al Anbār, N Iraq 36°05′N 43°10′E
139 Q2 Tall Ḩuqnah var. Tell Huqnah. Nīnawá, N Iraq 36°33′N 42°34′E
Tallin see Tallinn
118 G3 Tallinn Ger. Reval, Rus. Tallin; prev. Revel. ● (Estonia) Harjumaa, NW Estonia 59°26′N 24°42′E
118 H3 Tallinn ✈ Harjumaa, NW Estonia 59°23′N 24°52′E
138 H5 Tall Kalakh var. Tell Kalakh. Ḩimş, C Syria 34°40′N 36°18′E
139 R2 Tall Kayf Nīnawá, NW Iraq 36°30′N 43°08′E
Tall Kūchak see Tall Kūshik
139 P2 Tall Kūshik var. Tall Kūchak. Al Ḩasakah, E Syria 36°48′N 42°01′E
31 U12 Tallmadge Ohio, N USA 41°06′N 81°26′W
22 J5 Tallulah Louisiana, S USA 32°22′N 91°12′W
139 Q2 Tall 'Uwaynāt Nīnawá, NW Iraq 36°43′N 42°18′E
139 Q2 Tall Zāhir Nīnawá, N Iraq 36°51′N 42°29′E
122 J13 Tal'menka Altayskiy Kray, S Russian Federation 53°55′N 83°26′E
122 K8 Talnakh Taymyrskiy (Dolgano-Nenetskiy) Avtonomnyy Okrug, N Russian Federation 69°26′N 88°27′E
117 P7 Tal'ne Rus. Tal'noye. Cherkas'ka Oblast', C Ukraine 48°55′N 30°40′E
Tal'noye see Tal'ne
80 E12 Talodi Southern Kordofan, C Sudan 10°40′N 30°25′E
188 B16 Talofofo SE Guam 13°21′N 144°45′E
188 B16 Talofofo Bay bay SE Guam
26 L9 Taloga Oklahoma, C USA 36°02′N 98°58′W
123 T10 Talon Magadanskaya Oblast', E Russian Federation 59°47′N 148°46′E
14 H11 Talon, Lake ◎ Ontario, S Canada
149 R2 Tāloqān var. Taliq-an. Takhār, NE Afghanistan 36°44′N 69°33′E
126 M8 Talovaya Voronezhskaya Oblast', W Russian Federation 51°07′N 40°46′E
9 N6 Taloyoak prev. Spence Bay. Nunavut, N Canada 69°30′N 93°25′W
25 Q8 Talpa Texas, SW USA 31°46′N 99°42′W
40 K13 Talpa de Allende Jalisco, C Mexico 20°22′N 104°51′W
23 S9 Talquin, Lake ⊠ Florida, SE USA
Talsen see Talsi
Talshand see Chandmanī
118 E8 Talsi Ger. Talsen. Talsi, NW Latvia 57°14′N 22°35′E
143 V11 Tal Sīāh Sīstān va Balūchestān, SE Iran 28°19′N 57°43′E
62 G6 Taltal Antofagasta, N Chile 25°22′S 70°27′W
8 K10 Taltson ≈ Northwest Territories, NW Canada
168 K11 Taluk Sumatera, W Indonesia 0°32′S 101°35′E
92 J8 Talvik Finnmark, N Norway 70°02′N 22°59′E
182 M7 Talyawalka Creek ≈ New South Wales, SE Australia
Talyshskiye Gory see Talish Mountains
29 W14 Tama Iowa, C USA 41°58′N 92°34′W
Tama Abu, Banjaran see Penambo, Banjaran
169 U9 Tamabo, Banjaran ⛰ East Malaysia
190 B16 Tamakautoga SW Niue 19°05′S 169°55′W
127 N7 Tamala Penzenskaya Oblast', W Russian Federation 52°32′N 43°18′E
77 P15 Tamale C Ghana 09°21′N 00°54′W
191 P3 Tamana prev. Rotcher Island. atoll Tungaru, W Kiribati
74 K12 Tamanrasset var. Tamenghest. S Algeria 22°49′N 05°32′E
74 J13 Tamanrasset wadi Algeria/Mali
166 M2 Tamanthi Sagaing, N Myanmar (Burma) 25°17′N 95°18′E
97 I24 Tamar ≈ SW England, United Kingdom
Tamar see Tudmur
54 H9 Támara Casanare, C Colombia 05°51′N 72°09′W
54 F7 Tamar, Alto de ▲ C Colombia 07°25′N 74°28′W
173 X16 Tamarin E Mauritius 20°20′S 57°22′E
105 T5 Tamarite de Litera var. Tararite de Llitera. Aragón, NE Spain 41°52′N 00°25′E
111 I24 Tamási Tolna, S Hungary 46°39′N 18°17′E
Tamatave see Toamasina
41 O9 Tamaulipas ◈ state C Mexico
41 P10 Tamaulipas, Sierra de ⛰ C Mexico
56 F12 Tamaya, Río ≈ E Peru
40 I9 Tamazula Durango, C Mexico 24°43′N 106°33′W
40 L14 Tamazula Jalisco, C Mexico 19°41′N 103°18′W
Tamazulápam see Tamazulapán
41 Q15 Tamazulapán var. Tamazulápam. Oaxaca, SE Mexico 17°41′N 97°33′W
41 P12 Tamazunchale San Luis Potosí, C Mexico 21°17′N 98°46′W
76 H11 Tambacounda SE Senegal 13°44′N 13°43′W
83 M16 Tambara Manica, C Mozambique 16°42′S 34°14′E
77 T13 Tambawel Sokoto, NW Nigeria 12°24′N 04°42′E
186 M9 Tambea Guadalcanal, C Solomon Islands 09°19′S 159°42′E
169 N10 Tambelan, Kepulauan island group W Indonesia
57 E15 Tambo de Mora Ica, W Peru 13°30′S 76°08′W
170 L16 Tambora, Gunung Ж Sumbawa, S Indonesia 08°16′S 117°59′E
61 E17 Tambores Paysandú, W Uruguay 31°50′S 56°17′W
56 F7 Tamboryacu, Río ≈ N Peru
126 M7 Tambov Tambovskaya Oblast', W Russian Federation 52°43′N 41°28′E
126 L6 Tambovskaya Oblast' ◈ province W Russian Federation
104 H3 Tambre ≈ NW Spain
169 V7 Tambunan Sabah, East Malaysia 05°40′N 116°22′E
81 C15 Tambura Western Equatoria, SW Sudan 05°38′N 27°30′E
Tamchaket see Tâmchekkeṭ
76 J9 Tâmchekkeṭ var. Tamchaket. Hodh el Gharbi, S Mauritania 17°23′N 10°37′W
167 T7 Tam Điệp Ninh Binh, N Vietnam 20°09′N 105°54′E
Tamdybulak see Tomdibuloq
54 H8 Tame Arauca, C Colombia 06°27′N 71°42′W
104 H6 Tâmega, Rio Sp. Río Támega. ≈ Portugal/Spain
Támega, Río see Tâmega, Rio
115 H20 Tamélos, Akrotírio headland Tziá, Kykládes, Greece, Aegean Sea 37°31′N 24°16′E
Tamenghest see Tamanrasset
77 V8 Tamgak, Adrar ▲ C Niger 19°10′N 08°39′E
76 I13 Tamgue ▲ NW Guinea 12°14′N 12°18′W
41 Q12 Tamiahua Veracruz-Llave, E Mexico 21°15′N 97°27′W
41 Q12 Tamiahua, Laguna de lagoon E Mexico
23 Y16 Tamiami Canal canal Florida, SE USA
188 F17 Tamil Harbor harbor Yap, W Micronesia
155 H21 Tamil Nādu prev. Madras. ◈ state SE India
Ta'mīm, Muḥāfaẓat at see At Ta'mīm
99 H20 Tamines Namur, S Belgium 50°27′N 04°37′E
116 E12 Tamiš Ger. Temesch, Hung. Temes. ≈ Romania/Serbia
167 U10 Tam Ky Quang Nam-Đa Nang, C Vietnam 15°32′N 108°30′E
Tammerfors see Tampere
Tammisaari see Ekenäs
95 N14 Tämnaren ◎ C Sweden
191 Q7 Tamotoe, Passe passage Tahiti, W French Polynesia
23 V12 Tampa Florida, SE USA 27°57′N 82°27′W
23 V12 Tampa ✈ Florida, SE USA 27°57′N 82°29′W
23 V13 Tampa Bay bay Florida, SE USA
93 L18 Tampere Swe. Tammerfors. Länsi-Suomi, W Finland 61°30′N 23°45′E
41 Q11 Tampico Tamaulipas, C Mexico 22°18′N 97°52′W
171 P14 Tampo Pulau Muna, C Indonesia 04°38′S 122°40′E
167 V11 Tam Quan Binh Đinh, C Vietnam 14°34′N 109°00′E
162 J13 Tamsag Muchang Nei Mongol Zizhiqu, N China 40°28′N 102°34′E
Tamsal see Tamsalu
118 I4 Tamsalu Ger. Tamsal. Lääne-Virumaa, NE Estonia 59°10′N 26°07′E
109 S8 Tamsweg Salzburg, SW Austria 47°08′N 13°49′E
41 P12 Tamuín San Luis Potosí, C Mexico 22°00′N 98°44′W
188 C15 Tamuning NW Guam 13°29′N 144°47′E
183 T6 Tamworth New South Wales, SE Australia 31°07′S 150°54′E
97 M19 Tamworth C England, United Kingdom 52°39′N 01°40′W
81 K19 Tana ≈ SE Kenya
Tana see Deatnu/Tana
164 I15 Tanabe Wakayama, Honshū, SW Japan 33°43′N 135°22′E
92 L8 Tana Bru Finnmark, N Norway 70°11′N 28°06′E
39 T10 Tanacross Alaska, USA 63°30′N 143°21′W
92 L7 Tanafjorden Lapp. Deanuvuotna. fjord N Norway
38 G17 Tanaga Island island Aleutian Islands, Alaska, USA
38 G17 Tanaga Volcano Ж Tanaga Island, Alaska, USA 51°53′N 178°08′W
107 M18 Tanagro ≈ S Italy
80 H11 T'ana Hāyk' var. Lake Tana. ◎ NW Ethiopia
168 H11 Tanahbela, Pulau island Kepulauan Batu, W Indonesia
171 H15 Tanahjampea, Pulau island W Indonesia
168 H11 Tanahmasa, Pulau island Kepulauan Batu, W Indonesia
Tanais see Don
152 L10 Tanakpur Uttarakhand, N India 29°04′N 80°06′E
Tana, Lake see T'ana Hāyk'
181 P5 Tanami Desert desert Northern Territory, N Australia
167 T14 Tân An Long An, S Vietnam 10°32′N 106°24′E
39 Q9 Tanana Alaska, USA 65°12′N 152°00′W
Tananarive see Antananarivo
39 Q9 Tanana River ≈ Alaska, USA
95 C16 Tananger Rogaland, S Norway 58°55′N 05°34′E
188 H5 Tanapag Saipan, S Northern Mariana Islands 15°14′S 145°45′E
188 H5 Tanapag, Puetton bay Saipan, S Northern Mariana Islands
106 C9 Tanaro ≈ N Italy
163 Y12 Tanch'ŏn E North Korea 40°22′N 128°49′E
40 M14 Tancítaro, Cerro Ж C Mexico 19°16′N 102°25′W
153 N12 Tānda Uttar Pradesh, N India 26°33′N 82°39′E
77 O15 Tanda E Ivory Coast 07°48′N 03°10′W
116 L14 Ţăndărei Ialomiţa, SE Romania 44°39′N 27°40′E
63 N14 Tandil Buenos Aires, E Argentina 37°18′S 59°10′W
78 H12 Tandjilé off. Préfecture du Tandjilé. ◈ prefecture SW Chad
Tandjilé, Préfecture du see Tandjilé
Tandjoeng see Tanjung
Tandjoengkarang see Bandar Lampung
Tandjoengpandan see Tanjungpandan
Tandjoengpinang see Tanjungpinang
Tandjoengredeb see Tanjungredeb
149 Q16 Tando Allāhyār Sind, SE Pakistan 25°28′N 68°44′E
149 Q17 Tando Bāgo Sind, SE Pakistan 24°48′N 68°59′E
149 Q16 Tando Muhammad Khān Sind, SE Pakistan 25°07′N 68°35′E
182 L7 Tandou Lake seasonal lake New South Wales, SE Australia
94 L11 Tandsjöborg Gävleborg, C Sweden 61°40′N 14°40′E
155 H15 Tāndūr Andhra Pradesh, C India 17°16′N 77°37′E
164 C17 Tanega-shima island Nansei-shotō, SW Japan
165 R7 Taneichi Iwate, Honshū, C Japan 40°23′N 141°42′E
Tanen Taunggyi see Tane Range
167 N8 Tane Range Bur. Tanen Taunggyi. ⛰ W Thailand
111 P15 Tanew ≈ SE Poland
21 W2 Taneytown Maryland, NE USA 39°39′N 77°10′W
74 H12 Tanezrouft desert Algeria/Mali
138 L7 Ţanf, Jabal at ▲ SE Syria 33°32′N 38°43′E
81 J21 Tanga Tanga, E Tanzania 05°07′S 39°05′E
81 I22 Tanga ◈ region E Tanzania
153 T14 Tangail Dhaka, C Bangladesh 24°15′N 89°55′E
186 I5 Tanga Islands island group NE Papua New Guinea
155 K26 Tangalla Southern Province, S Sri Lanka 06°02′N 80°47′E
Tanganyika and Zanzibar see Tanzania
68 J13 Tanganyika, Lake ◎ E Africa
56 E7 Tangarana, Río ≈ N Peru
191 V16 Tangaroa, Maunga Ж Easter Island, Chile, E Pacific Ocean
Tangdukou see Shaoyang
74 G5 Tanger var. Tangiers, Tangier, Fr./Ger. Tangerk, Sp. Tánger; anc. Tingis. NW Morocco 35°49′N 05°49′W
169 N15 Tangerang Jawa, C Indonesia 06°14′S 106°36′E
Tangerk see Tanger
100 M12 Tangermünde Sachsen-Anhalt, C Germany 52°35′N 11°57′E
159 O12 Tanggulashan var. Togton Heyan, Tuotuoheyan. Qinghai, C China 34°13′N 92°25′E
156 K10 Tanggula Shan var. Dangla, Tangla Range. ⛰ W China
159 N13 Tanggula Shan ▲ W China 33°18′N 91°10′E
156 K10 Tanggula Shankou Tib. Dang La. pass W China
161 N7 Tanghe Henan, C China 32°40′N 112°53′E
149 T5 Tāngi North-West Frontier Province, NW Pakistan 34°18′N 71°42′E
Tangier see Tanger
21 Y5 Tangier Island island Virginia, NE USA
Tangiers see Tanger
22 K8 Tangipahoa River ≈ Louisiana, S USA
Tangla Range see Tanggula Shan
164 J12 Tango-hantō peninsula Honshū, SW Japan
156 I10 Tangra Yumco var. Tangro Tso. ◎ W China
Tangro Tso see Tangra Yumco
157 T7 Tangshan var. T'ang-shan. Hebei, E China 39°39′N 118°15′E
T'ang-shan see Tangshan
77 R14 Tanguiéta NW Benin 10°35′N 01°19′E
163 X7 Tangwang He ≈ NE China
163 X7 Tangyuan Heilongjiang, NE China 46°45′N 129°52′E
92 M11 Tanhua Lappi, N Finland 67°31′N 27°30′E
159 R15 Taniantaweng Shan ⛰ W China
171 U16 Tanimbar, Kepulauan island group Maluku, E Indonesia
Tanintharyi see Tenasserim
139 U4 Tānjarō ≈ E Iraq
129 T15 Tanjong Piai headland Peninsular Malaysia
Tanjore see Thanjāvūr
169 U12 Tanjung prev. Tandjoeng. Borneo, C Indonesia 02°08′S 115°23′E
169 W9 Tanjungbatu Borneo, N Indonesia 02°19′N 118°03′E
Tanjungkarang/Tanjungkarang-Telukbetung see Bandar Lampung
169 N13 Tanjungpandan prev. Tandjoengpandan. Pulau Belitung, W Indonesia 02°44′S 107°36′E
168 M10 Tanjungpinang prev. Tandjoengpinang. Pulau Bintan, W Indonesia 0°55′N 104°28′E
169 V9 Tanjungredeb var. Tanjungredep; prev. Tandjoengredeb. Borneo, C Indonesia 02°09′N 117°29′E
Tanjungredep see Tanjungredeb
149 S8 Tānk North-West Frontier Province, NW Pakistan 32°14′N 70°29′E
187 S15 Tanna island S Vanuatu
93 F17 Tännäs Jämtland, C Sweden 62°27′N 12°40′E
Tannenhof see Krynica
108 K7 Tannheim Tirol, W Austria 47°30′N 10°32′E
Tannu-Tuva see Tyva, Respublika
171 Q12 Tano Pulau Taliabu, E Indonesia 01°51′S 124°55′E
77 O17 Tano ≈ S Ghana
152 D10 Tanot Rājasthān, NW India 27°44′N 70°17′E
77 V11 Tanout Zinder, C Niger 14°58′N 08°54′E
Tân Phu see Đinh Quan
41 P12 Tanquián San Luis Potosí, C Mexico 21°38′N 98°39′W
77 R13 Tansarga E Burkina 11°51′N 01°51′E
167 T13 Tan Son Nhat ✈ (Hô Chi Minh) Tây Ninh, S Vietnam 10°52′N 106°38′E
75 V8 Ṭanṭā var. Tanta, Ṭanṭā. N Egypt 30°42′N 31°00′E
74 D9 Tan-Tan SW Morocco 28°30′N 11°11′W
41 P12 Tantoyuca Veracruz-Llave, E Mexico 21°21′N 98°12′W
152 J12 Tāntpur Uttar Pradesh, N India 26°51′N 77°29′E
Tan-tung see Dandong
38 M12 Tanunak Alaska, USA 60°35′N 165°15′W
166 L5 Ta-nyaung Magway, W Myanmar (Burma) 20°49′N 94°40′E
167 S5 Tân Yên Tuyên Quang, N Vietnam 22°08′N 104°58′E
81 F22 Tanzania off. United Republic of Tanzania, Swa. Jamhuri ya Muungano wa Tanzania; prev. German East Africa, Tanganyika and Zanzibar. ◆ republic E Africa
Tanzania, Jamhuri ya Muungano wa see Tanzania
Tanzania, United Republic of see Tanzania
Tao'an see Taonan
163 T8 Tao'er He ≈ NE China
159 U11 Tao He ≈ C China
163 U9 Taonan var. Tao'an. Jilin, NE China 45°20′N 122°46′E
T'ao-nan see Baicheng
Taongi see Bokaak Atoll
107 M23 Taormina anc. Tauromenium. Sicilia, Italy, C Mediterranean Sea 37°54′N 15°18′E
37 S9 Taos New Mexico, SW USA 36°24′N 105°35′W
Taoudenit see Taoudenni
77 O6 Taoudenni var. Taoudenit. Tombouctou, N Mali 22°46′N 03°54′W
74 G6 Taounate N Morocco 34°33′N 04°39′N
Taoyang see Lintao
161 S13 T'aoyüan Jap. Tōen. N Taiwan 25°00′N 121°15′E
118 I3 Tapa Ger. Taps. Lääne-Virumaa, NE Estonia 59°15′N 26°E
41 V17 Tapachula Chiapas, SE Mexico 14°53′N 92°18′W
Tapaiu see Gvardeysk
59 H14 Tapajós, Rio var. Tapajóz. ≈ NW Brazil
Tapajóz see Tapajós, Rio
61 C21 Tapalqué var. Tapalquén. Buenos Aires, E Argentina 36°21′S 60°01′W
Tapalquén see Tapalqué
Tapanahoni see Tapanahony Rivier
55 W11 Tapanahony Rivier var. Tapanahoni. ≈ E Suriname
41 T16 Tapanatepec var. San Pedro Tapanatepec. Oaxaca, SE Mexico 16°23′N 94°09′W
185 D23 Tapanui Otago, South Island, New Zealand 45°55′S 169°16′E
59 E14 Tapauá Amazonas, N Brazil 05°42′S 64°15′W
47 R7 Tapauá, Rio ≈ W Brazil
185 I14 Tapawera Tasman, South Island, New Zealand 41°24′S 172°50′E
61 I16 Tapes Rio Grande do Sul, S Brazil 30°40′S 51°25′W
76 K16 Tapeta C Liberia 06°36′N 08°52′W
154 H11 Tāpi prev. Tāpti. ≈ W India
104 J2 Tapia de Casariego Asturias, N Spain 43°34′N 06°56′W
56 F10 Tapiche, Río ≈ N Peru
167 N15 Tapi, Mae Nam var. Luang. ≈ SW Thailand
186 E8 Tapini Central, S Papua New Guinea 08°16′S 146°09′E
Tapirapecó, Serra see Tapirapecó, Sierra

◆ Country ● Country Capital ◇ Dependent Territory ○ Dependent Territory Capital ◈ Administrative Regions ✈ International Airport ▲ Mountain ⛰ Mountain Range Ж Volcano ≈ River ◎ Lake ⊠ Reservoir

TAPIRAPECÓ, SIERRA – TEHRI

55 N13 **Tapirapecó, Sierra** *Port.* Serra Tapirapecó. ▲ Brazil/ Venezuela
77 R13 **Tapoa** ≈ Benin/Niger
188 H5 **Tapochau, Mount** ▲ Saipan, S Northern Mariana Islands
111 H24 **Tapolca** Veszprém, W Hungary *46°54′N 17°29′E*
21 X5 **Tappahannock** Virginia, NE USA *37°55′N 76°54′W*
31 U13 **Tappan Lake** ⊠ Ohio, N USA
165 Q6 **Tappi-zaki** *headland* Honshū, C Japan *41°15′N 140°19′E*
Taps *see* Tapa
Tāpti *see* Tāpi
Tapuaemanu *see* Maiao
185 J16 **Tapuaenuku** ▲ South Island, New Zealand *42°00′S 173°39′E*
171 N8 **Tapul Group** *island group* Sulu Archipelago, SW Philippines
58 E11 **Tapurmcuará** *var.* Tapuruquara. Amazonas, NW Brazil *0°17′S 65°00′W*
Tapuruquara *see* Tapurmcuará
192 J17 **Taputapu, Cape** *headland* Tutuila, W American Samoa *14°20′S 170°51′W*
141 W13 **Ṭāqah** S Oman *17°02′N 54°23′E*
139 T3 **Taqtaq** Arbīl, N Iraq *35°54′N 44°36′E*
61 J15 **Taquara** Rio Grande do Sul, S Brazil *29°36′S 50°46′W*
59 H19 **Taquari, Rio** ≈ C Brazil
60 L8 **Taquaritinga** São Paulo, S Brazil *21°22′S 48°29′W*
122 I11 **Tara** Omskaya Oblast', C Russian Federation *56°54′N 74°17′E*
83 I16 **Tara** Southern, S Zambia *16°56′S 26°53′E*
113 J15 **Tara** ≈ Montenegro
112 K13 **Tara** ▲▲ W Serbia
77 W15 **Taraba** ◈ *state* E Nigeria
77 X15 **Taraba** ≈ E Nigeria
75 O7 **Ṭarābulus** *var.* Ṭarābulus al Gharb, *Eng.* Tripoli. ● (Libya) NW Libya *32°54′N 13°11′E*
75 O7 **Ṭarābulus** ✈ NW Libya *32°37′N 13°07′E*
Ṭarābulus al Gharb *see* Ṭarābulus
Tarābulus/Ṭarābulus ash Shām *see* Tripoli
105 O7 **Taracena** Castilla-La Mancha, C Spain *40°39′N 03°08′W*
117 N12 **Taraclia** *Rus.* Tarakilya. S Moldova *45°55′N 28°40′E*
139 V10 **Tarād al Kahf** Dhī Qār, SE Iraq *31°58′N 45°58′E*
183 R10 **Tarago** New South Wales, SE Australia *35°04′S 149°40′E*
162 J8 **Taragt** *var.* Hüremt. Övörhangay, C Mongolia *46°18′N 102°27′E*
169 V8 **Tarakan** Borneo, C Indonesia *03°20′N 117°38′E*
169 V9 **Tarakan, Pulau** *island* N Indonesia
Tarakilya *see* Taraclia
165 P16 **Tarama-jima** *island* Sakishima-shotō, SW Japan
184 K10 **Taranaki** *off.* Taranaki Region. ◈ *region* North Island, New Zealand
184 K10 **Taranaki, Mount** *var.* Egmont. ⊼ North Island, New Zealand *39°16′S 174°04′E*
Taranaki Region *see* Taranaki
105 O9 **Tarancón** Castilla-La Mancha, C Spain *40°01′N 03°01′W*
188 M15 **Tarang Reef** *reef* C Micronesia
96 E7 **Taransay** *island* NW Scotland, United Kingdom
107 P18 **Taranto** *var.* Tarentum. Puglia, SE Italy *40°30′N 17°11′E*
107 O19 **Taranto, Golfo di** *Eng.* Gulf of Taranto. *gulf* S Italy
Taranto, Gulf of *see* Taranto, Golfo di
62 G3 **Tarapacá** *off.* Región de Tarapacá. ◈ *region* N Chile
Tarapacá, Región de *see* Tarapacá
187 N9 **Tarapaina** Maramasike Island, N Solomon Islands *09°28′S 161°24′E*
56 D10 **Tarapoto** San Martín, N Peru *06°31′S 76°23′W*
138 M6 **Ṭaraq an Na'jah** *hill range* E Syria
138 M6 **Ṭaraq Sidāwī** *hill range* E Syria
103 Q11 **Tarare** Rhône, E France *45°54′N 04°25′E*
Tararite de Llitera *see* Tamarite de Litera
184 M13 **Tararua Range** ▲▲ North Island, New Zealand
151 Q22 **Tarāsa Dwīp** *island* Nicobar Islands, India, NE Indian Ocean
103 Q15 **Tarascon** Bouches-du-Rhône, SE France *43°48′N 04°39′E*
102 M17 **Tarascon-sur-Ariège** Ariège, S France *42°51′N 01°35′E*
117 P6 **Tarashcha** Kyyivs'ka Oblast', N Ukraine *49°34′N 30°31′E*
57 L18 **Tarata** Cochabamba, C Bolivia *17°35′S 66°04′W*
57 I18 **Tarata** Tacna, SW Peru *17°30′S 70°06′W*
190 H2 **Tarawa** *atoll* Tungaru, W Kiribati
59 B15 **Tarauacá** Acre, W Brazil *08°06′S 70°45′W*
59 B15 **Tarauacá, Rio** ≈ NW Brazil
191 Q8 **Taravao** Tahiti, W French Polynesia *17°44′S 149°19′W*
191 R8 **Taravao, Baie de** *bay* Tahiti, W French Polynesia
191 Q8 **Taravao, Isthme de** *isthmus* Tahiti, W French Polynesia
103 X16 **Taravo** ≈ Corse, France, C Mediterranean Sea
190 I3 **Tarawa** ✈ Tarawa, W Kiribati *01°53′S 169°32′E*
190 H2 **Tarawa** *atoll* Tungaru, W Kiribati
184 N10 **Tarawera** Hawke's Bay, North Island, New Zealand *39°03′S 176°34′E*
184 N8 **Tarawera, Lake** ◎ North Island, New Zealand
184 N8 **Tarawera, Mount** ▲ North Island, New Zealand *38°13′S 176°29′E*
105 S8 **Tarayuela** ▲ N Spain *40°28′N 00°22′W*
145 R16 **Taraz** *prev.* Aulie Ata, Auliye-Ata, Dzhambul, Zhambyl. Zhambyl, S Kazakhstan *42°55′N 71°27′E*
105 Q5 **Tarazona** Aragón, NE Spain *41°54′N 01°44′W*
105 Q10 **Tarazona de la Mancha** Castilla-La Mancha, C Spain *39°16′N 01°55′W*
145 X12 **Tarbagatay, Khrebet** ▲▲ China/Kazakhstan
96 J8 **Tarbat Ness** *headland* N Scotland, United Kingdom *57°51′N 03°48′W*
149 U5 **Tarbela Reservoir** ⊠ N Pakistan
96 H12 **Tarbert** W Scotland, United Kingdom *55°52′N 05°26′W*
96 F7 **Tarbert** NW Scotland, United Kingdom *57°54′N 06°48′W*
102 K16 **Tarbes** *anc.* Bigorra. Hautes-Pyrénées, S France *43°14′N 00°04′E*
21 W9 **Tarboro** North Carolina, SE USA *35°54′N 77°34′W*
Tarca *see* Torysa
106 J6 **Tarcento** Friuli-Venezia Giulia, NE Italy *46°13′N 13°13′E*
182 F5 **Tarcoola** South Australia *30°44′S 134°34′E*
105 S5 **Tardienta** Aragón, NE Spain *41°58′N 00°31′W*
102 L11 **Tardoire** ≈ W France
183 U7 **Taree** New South Wales, SE Australia *31°56′S 152°29′E*
92 K12 **Tärendö** *Lapp.* Deargget. Norrbotten, N Sweden *67°10′N 22°40′E*
Tarentum *see* Taranto
74 C9 **Tarfaya** SW Morocco *27°56′N 12°55′W*
116 J13 **Târgoviște** *prev.* Tîrgoviște. Dâmbovița, S Romania *44°54′N 25°29′E*
Târgoviște *see* Tŭrgovishte
116 M12 **Târgu Bujor** *prev.* Tîrgu Bujor. Galați, E Romania *45°52′N 27°55′E*
116 H13 **Târgu Cărbunești** *prev.* Tîrgu. Gorj, SW Romania *44°57′N 23°32′E*
116 L9 **Târgu Frumos** *prev.* Tîrgu Frumos. Iași, NE Romania *47°12′N 27°00′E*
116 H13 **Targu Jiu** *prev.* Tîrgu Jiu. Gorj, W Romania *45°03′N 23°20′E*
116 H9 **Târgu Lăpuș** *prev.* Tîrgu Lăpuș. Maramureș, N Romania *47°28′N 23°54′E*
Târgul-Neamț *see* Târgu-Neamț
Târgul-Săcuiesc *see* Târgu Secuiesc
116 I10 **Târgu Mureș** *prev.* Oșorhei, Tîrgu Mures, *Ger.* Neumarkt, *Hung.* Marosvásárhely. Mureș, C Romania *46°33′N 24°36′E*
116 K9 **Târgu-Neamț** *var.* Târgul-Neamț; *prev.* Tîrgu-Neamț. Neamț, NE Romania *47°12′N 26°25′E*
116 K11 **Târgu Ocna** *Hung.* Aknavásár; *prev.* Tîrgu Ocna. Bacău, E Romania *46°17′N 26°37′E*
116 K11 **Târgu Secuiesc** *Ger.* Neumarkt, Szekler Neumarkt, *Hung.* Kezdivásárhely; *prev.* Chezdi-Oșorheiu, Târgul-Săcuiesc, Tîrgu Secuiesc. Covasna, E Romania *46°00′N 26°08′E*
145 X10 **Targyn** Vostochnyy Kazakhstan, E Kazakhstan *49°32′N 82°47′E*
Tar Heel State *see* North Carolina
186 C7 **Tari** Southern Highlands, W Papua New Guinea *05°52′S 142°58′E*
162 J6 **Tarialan** *var.* Badrah. Hövsgöl, N Mongolia *49°33′N 101°58′E*
162 I7 **Tariat** *var.* Horgo. Arhangay, C Mongolia *48°06′N 99°52′E*
143 P17 **Ṭarīf** Abū Ẓaby, C United Arab Emirates *24°02′N 53°47′E*
104 K16 **Tarifa** Andalucía, S Spain *36°01′N 05°36′W*
84 C14 **Tarifa, Punta de** *headland* SW Spain *36°01′N 05°39′W*
57 M21 **Tarija** Tarija, S Bolivia *21°33′S 64°42′W*
57 M21 **Tarija** ◈ *department* S Bolivia
141 R14 **Tarīm** C Yemen *16°N 48°50′E*
Tarim Basin *see* Tarim Pendi
81 G19 **Tarime** Mara, N Tanzania *01°20′S 34°24′E*
129 S8 **Tarim He** ≈ NW China
159 H8 **Tarim Pendi** *Eng.* Tarim Basin. *basin* NW China
149 N7 **Tarīn Kowt** *var.* Terinkot. Orūzgān, C Afghanistan *32°38′N 65°52′E*
171 O12 **Taripa** Sulawesi, C Indonesia *01°51′S 120°46′E*
117 Q12 **Tarkhankut, Mys** *headland* S Ukraine *45°20′N 32°32′E*
27 Q1 **Tarkio** Missouri, C USA *40°25′N 95°24′W*
122 J9 **Tarko-Sale** Yamalo-Nenetskiy Avtonomnyy Okrug, N Russian Federation *64°55′N 77°34′E*
77 P17 **Tarkwa** S Ghana *05°16′N 01°59′W*
171 O3 **Tarlac** Luzon, N Philippines *15°29′N 120°34′E*
95 F22 **Tarm** Ringkøbing, W Denmark *55°55′N 08°32′E*
57 E14 **Tarma** Junín, C Peru *11°28′S 75°41′W*
103 N15 **Tarn** ◈ *department* S France
103 M15 **Tarn** ≈ S France
111 L22 **Tarna** ≈ C Hungary
93 G13 **Tärnaby** Västerbotten, N Sweden *65°44′N 15°20′E*
149 P8 **Tarnak Rūd** ≈ SE Afghanistan
116 J11 **Târnava Mare** *Ger.* Grosse Kokel, *Hung.* Nagy-Küküllő; *prev.* Tîrnava Mare. ≈ S Romania
116 I11 **Târnava Mică** *Ger.* Kleine Kokel, *Hung.* Kis-Küküllo; *prev.* Tîrnava Mică. ≈ C Romania
116 I11 **Târnăveni** *Ger.* Marteskirch, Martinskirch, *Hung.* Dicsőszentmárton; *prev.* Sînmartin, Tîrnăveni. Mureș, C Romania *46°20′N 24°17′E*
102 L14 **Tarn-et-Garonne** ◈ *department* S France
105 P8 **Tarnica** ▲ SE Poland *49°05′N 22°43′E*
111 N15 **Tarnobrzeg** Podkarpackie, SE Poland *50°35′N 21°40′E*
125 N12 **Tarnogskiy Gorodok** Vologodskaya Oblast', NW Russian Federation *60°28′N 43°45′E*
Tarnopol *see* Ternopil'
111 M16 **Tarnów** Małopolskie, S Poland *50°01′N 20°59′E*
Tarnowice/Tarnowitz *see* Tarnowskie Góry
111 J16 **Tarnowskie Góry** *var.* Tarnowice, Tarnowskie Gory, *Ger.* Tarnowitz. Śląskie, S Poland *50°27′N 18°52′E*
95 N14 **Tärnsjö** Västmanland, C Sweden *60°10′N 16°57′E*
106 E9 **Taro** ≈ NW Italy
186 I6 **Taron** New Ireland, NE Papua New Guinea *04°22′S 153°04′E*
74 E8 **Taroudannt** *var.* Taroudant. SW Morocco *30°31′N 08°50′W*
Taroudant *see* Taroudannt
23 V12 **Tarpon, Lake** ◎ Florida, SE USA
23 V12 **Tarpon Springs** Florida, SE USA *28°09′N 82°45′W*
107 G14 **Tarquinia** *anc.* Tarquinii, *hist.* Corneto. Lazio, C Italy *42°23′N 11°45′E*
Tarquinii *see* Tarquinia
Tarraco *see* Tarragona
76 D10 **Tarrafal** Santiago, S Cape Verde *15°16′N 23°45′W*
105 V6 **Tarragona** *anc.* Tarraco. Cataluña, E Spain *41°07′N 01°15′E*
105 T7 **Tarragona** ◈ *province* Cataluña, NE Spain
183 O17 **Tarraleah** Tasmania, SE Australia *42°11′S 146°29′E*
23 P3 **Tarrant City** Alabama, S USA *33°34′N 86°45′W*
185 D21 **Tarras** Otago, South Island, New Zealand *44°48′S 169°25′E*
Tarrasa *see* Terrassa
105 U5 **Tàrrega** *var.* Tarrega. Cataluña, NE Spain *41°39′N 01°09′E*
21 W9 **Tar River** ≈ North Carolina, SE USA
Tarrong *see* Nyêmo
Tarsatica *see* Rijeka
136 J17 **Tarsus** İçel, S Turkey *36°52′N 34°52′E*
62 K4 **Tartagal** Salta, N Argentina *22°32′S 63°50′W*
137 V12 **Tärtär** *Rus.* Terter. ≈ SW Azerbaijan
102 J15 **Tartas** Landes, SW France *43°52′N 00°45′W*
Tartlau *see* Prejmer
Tartous/Tartouss *see* Ṭarṭūs
118 J5 **Tartu** *Ger.* Dorpat; *prev. Rus.* Yurev, Yury'ev. Tartumaa, SE Estonia *58°20′N 26°44′E*
118 I5 **Tartumaa** *off.* Tartu Maakond. ◈ *province* E Estonia
Tartu Maakond *see* Tartumaa
138 H5 **Ṭarṭūs** *Fr.* Tartouss; *anc.* Tortosa. Ṭarṭūs, W Syria *34°55′N 35°52′E*
138 H5 **Ṭarṭūs** *off.* Muḥāfaẓat Ṭarṭūs, *var.* Tartous, Tartus. ◈ *governorate* W Syria
Ṭarṭūs, Muḥāfaẓat *see* Ṭarṭūs
164 C16 **Tarumizu** Kagoshima, Kyūshū, SW Japan *31°30′N 130°40′E*
126 K4 **Tarusa** Kaluzhskaya Oblast', W Russian Federation *54°45′N 37°10′E*
117 N11 **Tarutyne** Odes'ka Oblast', SW Ukraine *46°11′N 29°09′E*
162 I7 **Tarvagatyn Nuruu** ▲▲ N Mongolia
106 J6 **Tarvisio** Friuli-Venezia Giulia, NE Italy *46°31′N 13°33′E*
Tarvisium *see* Treviso
57 O16 **Tarvo, Río** ≈ E Bolivia
14 G8 **Tarzwell** Ontario, S Canada *48°00′N 79°58′W*
40 K5 **Tasajera, Sierra de la** ▲▲ N Mexico
145 S13 **Tasaral** Karaganda, C Kazakhstan *46°17′N 73°54′E*
Tasböget *see* Tasbuget
145 N15 **Tasbuget** *Kaz.* Tasböget. Kzylorda, S Kazakhstan *44°46′N 65°38′E*
108 E11 **Tasch** Valais, SW Switzerland *46°04′N 07°43′E*
Tasek Kenyir *see* Kenyir, Tasik
122 J14 **Tashanta** Respublika Altay, S Russian Federation *49°42′N 89°15′E*
Tashauz *see* Daşoguz
Tashi Chho Dzong *see* Thimphu
153 U11 **Tashigang** E Bhutan *27°19′N 91°33′E*
137 T11 **Tashir** *prev.* Kalinino. N Armenia *41°07′N 44°16′E*
143 Q11 **Ṭashk, Daryācheh-ye** ◎ C Iran
Tashkent *see* Toshkent
Tashkentskaya Oblast' *see* Toshkent Viloyati
Tashkepri *see* Daşköpri
Tash-Kömür *see* Tash-Kumyr
147 S9 **Tash-Kumyr** *Kir.* Tash-Kömür. Dzhalal-Abadskaya Oblast', W Kyrgyzstan *41°22′N 72°09′E*
127 T7 **Tashla** Orenburgskaya Oblast', W Russian Federation *51°42′N 52°33′E*
Tashqurghan *see* Kholm
122 J13 **Tashtagol** Kemerovskaya Oblast', S Russian Federation *52°49′N 88°00′E*
95 H24 **Tåsinge** *island* C Denmark
12 M5 **Tasiujaq** Québec, E Canada *58°43′N 69°58′W*
77 W11 **Tasker** Zinder, C Niger *15°06′N 10°42′E*
145 W12 **Taskesken** Vostochnyy Kazakhstan, E Kazakhstan *47°15′N 80°45′E*
136 J10 **Taşköprü** Kastamonu, N Turkey *41°30′N 34°12′E*
Taskuduk, Peski *see* Tosquduq Qumlari
186 G5 **Taskul** New Ireland, NE Papua New Guinea *02°34′S 150°25′E*
137 S13 **Taşlıçay** Ağrı, E Turkey *39°37′N 43°23′E*
185 H14 **Tasman** *off.* Tasman District. ◈ *unitary authority* South Island, New Zealand
192 J12 **Tasman Basin** *var.* East Australian Basin. *undersea feature* S Tasman Sea
185 I14 **Tasman Bay** *inlet* South Island, New Zealand
Tasman District *see* Tasman
192 I13 **Tasman Fracture Zone** *tectonic feature* S Indian Ocean
185 E19 **Tasman Glacier** *glacier* South Island, New Zealand
Tasman Group *see* Nukumanu Islands
183 N15 **Tasmania** *prev.* Van Diemen's Land. ◈ *state* SE Australia
183 Q16 **Tasmania** *island* SE Australia
185 H14 **Tasman Mountains** ▲▲ South Island, New Zealand
183 P17 **Tasman Peninsula** *peninsula* Tasmania, SE Australia
192 I11 **Tasman Plain** *undersea feature* W Tasman Sea
192 I12 **Tasman Plateau** *var.* South Tasmania Plateau. *undersea feature* SW Tasman Sea
192 I11 **Tasman Sea** *sea* SW Pacific Ocean
116 G9 **Tășnad** *Ger.* Trestenberg, Trestendorf, *Hung.* Tasnád. Satu Mare, NW Romania *47°30′N 22°33′E*
136 L11 **Taşova** Amasya, N Turkey *40°45′N 36°20′E*
77 T10 **Tassara** Tahoua, W Niger *16°40′N 05°34′E*
12 K4 **Tassialouc, Lac** ◎ Québec, C Canada
Tassili du Hoggar *see* Tassili ta-n-Ahaggar
74 L11 **Tassili-n-Ajjer** *plateau* E Algeria
74 K14 **Tassili ta-n-Ahaggar** *var.* Tassili du Hoggar. *plateau* S Algeria
59 M15 **Tasso Fragoso** Maranhão, E Brazil *08°22′S 45°53′W*
Tåstrup *see* Taastrup
145 O9 **Tasty-Taldy** Akmola, C Kazakhstan *50°47′N 66°31′E*
143 W10 **Tāsūkī** Sīstān va Balūchestān, SE Iran
111 I22 **Tata** *Ger.* Totis. Komárom-Esztergom, NW Hungary *47°39′N 18°19′E*
74 E8 **Tata** SW Morocco *29°38′N 08°04′W*
Tataaihoa, Pointe *see* Vénus, Pointe
111 I22 **Tatabánya** Komárom-Esztergom, NW Hungary *47°33′N 18°23′E*
191 X10 **Tatakoto** *atoll* Îles Tuamotu, E French Polynesia
75 N7 **Tataouine** *var.* Taṭāwīn. SE Tunisia *32°48′N 10°27′E*
55 O5 **Tataracual, Cerro** ▲ NE Venezuela *10°13′N 64°20′W*
117 O12 **Tatarbunary** Odes'ka Oblast', SW Ukraine *45°50′N 29°37′E*
119 M17 **Tatarka** Mahilyowskaya Voblasts', E Belarus *53°15′N 28°50′E*
Tatar Pazardzhik *see* Pazardzhik
122 I12 **Tatarsk** Novosibirskaya Oblast', C Russian Federation *55°08′N 75°58′E*
Tatarskaya ASSR *see* Tatarstan, Respublika
123 T13 **Tatarskiy Proliv** *Eng.* Tatar Strait. *strait* SE Russian Federation
127 R4 **Tatarstan, Respublika** *prev.* Tatarskaya ASSR. ◈ *autonomous republic* W Russian Federation
Tatar Strait *see* Tatarskiy Proliv
Taṭāwīn *see* Tataouine
171 N12 **Tate** Sulawesi, N Indonesia *0°12′S 119°44′E*
141 N11 **Tathlīth** 'Asīr, S Saudi Arabia *19°38′N 43°32′E*
141 O11 **Tathlīth, Wādī** *dry watercourse* S Saudi Arabia
183 R11 **Tathra** New South Wales, SE Australia *36°45′S 149°58′E*
127 P8 **Tatishchevo** Saratovskaya Oblast', W Russian Federation *51°43′N 45°35′E*
39 S12 **Tatitlek** Alaska, USA *60°49′N 146°29′W*
10 L15 **Tatla Lake** British Columbia, SW Canada *51°56′N 124°39′W*
121 Q2 **Tatlısu** *Gk.* Akanthoú. N Cyprus *35°21′N 33°45′E*
11 Z10 **Tatnam, Cape** *headland* Manitoba, C Canada *57°16′N 91°03′W*
111 K18 **Tatra Mountains** *Ger.* Tatra, *Hung.* Tátra, *Pol./Slvk.* Tatry. ▲▲ Poland/Slovakia
Tatra/Tátra *see* Tatra Mountains
Tatry *see* Tatra Mountains
164 I13 **Tatsuno** *var.* Tatuno. Hyōgo, Honshū, SW Japan *34°54′N 134°30′E*
145 S16 **Tatti** *var.* Tatty. Zhambyl, S Kazakhstan *43°11′N 73°22′E*
Tatty *see* Tatti
60 L10 **Tatuí** São Paulo, S Brazil *23°21′S 47°49′W*
37 V14 **Tatum** New Mexico, SW USA *33°15′N 103°19′W*
25 X7 **Tatum** Texas, SW USA *32°19′N 94°31′W*
Ta-t'ung/Tatung *see* Datong
Tatuno *see* Tatsuno
137 R14 **Tatvan** Bitlis, SE Turkey *38°31′N 42°15′E*
95 C16 **Tau** Rogaland, S Norway *59°04′N 05°55′E*
192 L17 **Ta'ū** *var.* Tau. *island* Manua Islands, E American Samoa
193 W15 **Tau** *island* Tongatapu Group, N Tonga
59 O14 **Tauá** Ceará, E Brazil *06°04′S 40°26′W*
60 N10 **Taubaté** São Paulo, S Brazil *23°S 45°36′W*
101 I19 **Tauber** ≈ SW Germany
101 I19 **Tauberbischofsheim** Baden-Württemberg, C Germany *49°37′N 09°39′E*
144 E14 **Tauchik** *Kaz.* Taūshyq. Mangistau, SW Kazakhstan *44°17′N 51°22′E*
191 W10 **Tauere** *atoll* Îles Tuamotu, C French Polynesia
101 H17 **Taufstein** ▲ C Germany *50°31′N 09°18′E*
190 I17 **Taukoka** *island* SE Cook Islands
145 T15 **Taukum, Peski** *desert* SE Kazakhstan
184 L10 **Taumarunui** Manawatu-Wanganui, North Island, New Zealand *38°52′S 175°14′E*
59 A15 **Taumaturgo** Acre, W Brazil *08°54′S 72°48′W*
27 X6 **Taum Sauk Mountain** ▲ Missouri, C USA *37°34′N 90°43′W*
83 H22 **Taung** North-West, N South Africa *27°32′S 24°48′E*
166 L6 **Taungdwingyi** Magway, C Myanmar (Burma) *20°01′N 95°20′E*
166 M6 **Taunggyi** Shan State, C Myanmar (Burma) *20°47′N 97°00′E*
166 M7 **Taungoo** Bago, C Myanmar (Burma) *18°57′N 96°26′E*
166 L5 **Taungtha** Mandalay, C Myanmar (Burma) *21°16′N 95°25′E*
166 K7 **Taungup** Rakhine State, W Myanmar (Burma) *18°50′N 94°14′E*
149 S9 **Taunsa** Punjab, E Pakistan *30°43′N 70°41′E*
97 K23 **Taunton** SW England, United Kingdom *51°01′N 03°06′W*
19 O12 **Taunton** Massachusetts, NE USA *41°54′N 71°03′W*
101 F18 **Taunus** ▲▲ W Germany
101 G18 **Taunusstein** Hessen, W Germany *50°09′N 08°09′E*
184 N9 **Taupo** Waikato, North Island, New Zealand *38°42′S 176°05′E*
184 M9 **Taupo, Lake** ◎ North Island, New Zealand
109 R8 **Taurach** *var.* Taurachbach. ≈ E Austria
Taurachbach *see* Taurach
118 D12 **Tauragė** *Ger.* Tauroggen. Tauragė, SW Lithuania *55°16′N 22°17′E*
118 D13 **Tauragė** ◈ *province* Lithuania
54 G10 **Tauramena** Casanare, C Colombia *05°02′N 72°43′W*
184 N7 **Tauranga** Bay of Plenty, North Island, New Zealand *37°42′S 176°09′E*
15 O10 **Taureau, Réservoir** ⊠ Québec, SE Canada
107 N22 **Taurianova** Calabria, SW Italy *38°22′N 16°01′E*
Tauris *see* Tabrīz
184 I2 **Tauroa Point** *headland* North Island, New Zealand *35°09′S 173°02′E*
Tauroggen *see* Tauragė
Tauromenium *see* Taormina
Taurus Mountains *see* Toros Dağları
Taus *see* Domažlice
Taūshyq *see* Tauchik
105 R5 **Tauste** Aragón, NE Spain *41°55′N 01°15′W*
191 V16 **Tautara, Motu** *island* Easter Island, Chile, E Pacific Ocean
191 R8 **Tautira** Tahiti, W French Polynesia *17°45′S 149°10′W*
Tauz *see* Tovuz
Ṭavālesh, Kūhhā-ye *see* Talish Mountains
136 D15 **Tavas** Denizli, SW Turkey *37°33′N 29°04′E*
Tavastehus *see* Hämeenlinna
Tavau *see* Davos
122 G10 **Tavda** Sverdlovskaya Oblast', C Russian Federation *58°01′N 65°07′E*
122 G10 **Tavda** ≈ C Russian Federation
105 T11 **Tavernes de la Valldigna** País Valenciano, E Spain *39°03′N 00°13′W*
81 I20 **Taveta** Coast, S Kenya *03°23′S 37°40′E*
187 Y14 **Taveuni** *island* N Fiji
147 R13 **Tavildara** *Rus.* Tavil'dara, Tovil'-Dora. C Tajikistan *38°42′N 70°27′E*
Tavin *see* Adaatsag
104 H14 **Tavira** Faro, S Portugal *37°07′N 07°39′W*
97 I24 **Tavistock** SW England, United Kingdom *50°33′N 04°08′W*
Tavoy *see* Dawei
Tavoy Island *see* Mali Kyun
115 E16 **Tavropoú, Techníti Límni** ⊠ C Greece
136 E13 **Tavşanlı** Kütahya, NW Turkey *39°34′N 29°28′E*
187 X14 **Tavua** Viti Levu, W Fiji *17°27′S 177°51′E*
97 J23 **Taw** ≈ SW England, United Kingdom
185 L14 **Tawa** Wellington, North Island, New Zealand *41°10′S 174°50′E*
25 V6 **Tawakoni, Lake** ⊠ Texas, SW USA
153 V11 **Tawang** Arunāchal Pradesh, NE India *27°34′N 91°54′E*
169 R17 **Tawang, Teluk** *bay* Jawa, S Indonesia
31 R7 **Tawas Bay** ◎ Michigan, N USA
31 R7 **Tawas City** Michigan, N USA *44°16′N 83°33′W*
169 V8 **Tawau** Sabah, East Malaysia *04°16′N 117°54′E*
141 U10 **Ṭawīl, Qalamat aṭ** *well* SE Saudi Arabia
171 N9 **Tawitawi** *island* Tawitawi Group, SW Philippines
Ṭawkar *see* Tokar
Tawūq *see* Dāqūq
Tawzar *see* Tozeur
41 O15 **Taxco** *var.* Taxco de Alarcón. Guerrero, S Mexico *18°32′N 99°37′W*
Taxco de Alarcón *see* Taxco
146 H8 **Taxiatosh** *Rus.* Takhiatash. Qoraqalpog'iston Respublikasi, W Uzbekistan *42°27′N 59°27′E*
158 D9 **Taxkorgan** *var.* Taxkorgan Tajik Zizhixian. Xinjiang Uygur Zizhiqu, NW China *37°43′N 75°13′E*
Taxkorgan Tajik Zizhixian *see* Taxkorgan
146 H7 **Taxtako'pir** *Rus.* Takhtakupyr. Qoraqalpog'iston Respublikasi, NW Uzbekistan *43°04′N 60°23′E*
96 J10 **Tay** ≈ C Scotland, United Kingdom
143 V6 **Tāybād** *var.* Taibad, Tāyybād, Tayyebāt. Khorāsān-Razavī, NE Iran *34°48′N 60°46′E*
Taybert at Turkz *see* Ṭayyibat at Turkī
124 J3 **Taybola** Murmanskaya Oblast', NW Russian Federation *68°30′N 33°18′E*
81 M16 **Tayeeglow** Bakool, C Somalia *04°01′N 44°25′E*
96 K11 **Tay, Firth of** *inlet* E Scotland, United Kingdom
122 J12 **Tayga** Kemerovskaya Oblast', S Russian Federation *56°02′N 85°26′E*
Taygan *see* Delger
123 T9 **Taygonos, Mys** *headland* E Russian Federation *60°36′N 160°09′E*
96 I11 **Tay, Loch** ◎ C Scotland, United Kingdom
11 N12 **Taylor** British Columbia, W Canada *56°09′N 120°43′W*
29 O14 **Taylor** Nebraska, C USA *41°47′N 99°23′W*
18 I13 **Taylor** Pennsylvania, NE USA *41°22′N 75°41′W*
25 T10 **Taylor** Texas, SW USA *30°34′N 97°24′W*
37 Q11 **Taylor, Mount** ▲ New Mexico, SW USA *35°14′N 107°36′W*
37 R5 **Taylor Park Reservoir** ⊠ Colorado, C USA
37 R6 **Taylor River** ≈ Colorado, C USA
21 P11 **Taylors** South Carolina, SE USA *34°55′N 82°18′W*
20 L5 **Taylorsville** Kentucky, S USA *38°01′N 85°21′W*
21 R6 **Taylorsville** North Carolina, SE USA *35°56′N 81°10′W*
30 L14 **Taylorville** Illinois, N USA *39°33′N 89°17′W*
140 K5 **Taymā'** Tabūk, NW Saudi Arabia *27°39′N 38°32′E*
122 M10 **Taymura** ≈ C Russian Federation
123 O7 **Taymylyr** Respublika Sakha (Yakutiya), NE Russian Federation *72°32′N 121°54′E*
122 L7 **Taymyr, Ozero** ◎ N Russian Federation
122 M6 **Taymyr, Poluostrov** *peninsula* N Russian Federation
122 L8 **Taymyrskiy (Dolgano-Nenetskiy) Avtonomnyy Okrug** ◈ *autonomous district* Krasnoyarskiy Kray, N Russian Federation
167 S13 **Tây Ninh** Tây Ninh, S Vietnam *11°21′N 106°07′E*
122 L12 **Tayshet** Irkutskaya Oblast', S Russian Federation *55°51′N 98°04′E*
162 G8 **Tayshir** *var.* Tsagaan-Olom. Govĭ-Altay, C Mongolia *46°42′N 96°30′E*
171 N5 **Taytay** Palawan, W Philippines *10°49′N 119°30′E*
169 Q16 **Tayu** *prev.* Tajoe. Jawa, C Indonesia *06°32′S 111°02′E*
Tāyybād/Tayyebāt *see* Tāybād
138 L5 **Ṭayyibah** *var.* At Taybé. Ḥimṣ, C Syria *35°13′N 38°51′E*
138 I4 **Ṭayyibat at Turkī** *var.* Taybert at Turkz. Ḥamāh, W Syria *35°16′N 36°55′E*
145 P7 **Tayynsha** *prev.* Krasnoarmeysk. Severnyy Kazakhstan, N Kazakhstan *53°52′N 69°51′E*
122 J10 **Taz** ≈ N Russian Federation
74 G6 **Taza** NE Morocco *34°13′N 04°06′W*
139 T4 **Tāza Khurmātū** At Ta'mīn, E Iraq *35°18′N 44°22′E*
165 Q8 **Tazawa-ko** ◎ Honshū, C Japan
21 N8 **Tazewell** Tennessee, S USA *36°27′N 83°34′W*
21 Q7 **Tazewell** Virginia, NE USA *37°08′N 81°34′W*
75 S11 **Tāzirbū** SE Libya *25°43′N 21°16′E*
39 S11 **Tazlina Lake** ◎ Alaska, USA
122 J8 **Tazovskiy** Yamalo-Nenetskiy Avtonomnyy Okrug, N Russian Federation *67°33′N 78°21′E*
137 U10 **T'bilisi** *Eng.* Tiflis. ● (Georgia) SE Georgia *41°41′N 44°55′E*
137 T10 **T'bilisi** ✈ S Georgia *41°43′N 44°49′E*
79 E14 **Tchabal Mbabo** ▲ NW Cameroon *07°12′N 12°16′E*
Tchad *see* Chad
Tchad, Lac *see* Chad, Lake
77 S15 **Tchaourou** E Benin *08°58′N 02°40′E*
79 E20 **Tchibanga** Nyanga, S Gabon *02°49′S 11°00′E*
Tchien *see* Zwedru
77 Z6 **Tchigaï, Plateau du** ▲ NE Niger
77 V9 **Tchighozérine** Agadez, C Niger *17°15′N 07°48′E*
77 T10 **Tchin-Tabaradene** Tahoua, W Niger *15°57′N 05°49′E*
78 G13 **Tcholliré** Nord, NE Cameroon *08°48′N 14°00′E*
Tchongking *see* Chongqing
22 K4 **Tchula** Mississippi, S USA *33°10′N 90°13′W*
110 I7 **Tczew** *Ger.* Dirschau. Pomorskie, N Poland *54°05′N 18°46′E*
116 I10 **Teaca** *Ger.* Tekendorf, *Hung.* Teke; *prev. Ger.* Teckendorf. Bistrița-Năsăud, N Romania *46°55′N 24°30′E*
40 J11 **Teacapán** Sinaloa, C Mexico *22°33′N 105°44′W*
190 A10 **Teafuafou** *island* Funafuti Atoll, C Tuvalu
25 U8 **Teague** Texas, SW USA *31°37′N 96°16′W*
191 R9 **Teahupoo** Tahiti, W French Polynesia *17°51′S 149°15′W*
190 H15 **Te Aiti Point** *headland* Rarotonga, S Cook Islands *21°11′S 159°47′W*
185 B22 **Te Anau** Southland, South Island, New Zealand *45°25′S 167°45′E*
185 B22 **Te Anau, Lake** ◎ South Island, New Zealand
41 U15 **Teapa** Tabasco, SE Mexico *17°36′N 92°57′W*
184 Q7 **Te Araroa** Gisborne, North Island, New Zealand *37°37′S 178°21′E*
184 M7 **Te Aroha** Waikato, North Island, New Zealand *37°32′S 175°58′E*
Teate *see* Chieti
190 A9 **Te Ava Fuagea** *channel* Funafuti Atoll, SE Tuvalu
190 B8 **Te Ava I Te Lape** *channel* Funafuti Atoll, SE Tuvalu
190 B9 **Te Ava Pua Pua** *channel* Funafuti Atoll, SE Tuvalu
184 M8 **Te Awamutu** Waikato, North Island, New Zealand *38°00′S 177°18′E*
171 X12 **Teba** Papua, E Indonesia *01°27′S 137°54′E*
104 L15 **Teba** Andalucía, S Spain *36°59′N 04°54′W*
126 M15 **Teberda** Karachayevo-Cherkesskaya Respublika, SW Russian Federation *43°28′N 41°45′E*
74 M6 **Tébessa** NE Algeria *35°21′N 08°06′E*
62 O7 **Tebicuary, Río** ≈ S Paraguay
168 I8 **Tebingtinggi** Sumatera, N Indonesia *03°20′N 99°08′E*
168 L13 **Tebingtinggi** Sumatera, W Indonesia *03°33′S 103°00′E*
Tebingtinggi, Pulau *see* Rantau, Pulau
Tebriz *see* Tabrīz
137 U9 **Tebulosmta** *Rus.* Gora Tebulosmta. ▲ Georgia/Russian Federation *42°33′N 45°21′E*
Tebulosmta, Gora *see* Tebulosmta
41 Q14 **Tecamachalco** Puebla, S Mexico *18°52′N 97°44′W*
40 B1 **Tecate** Baja California Norte, NW Mexico *32°33′N 116°38′W*
136 M13 **Tecer Dağları** ▲▲ C Turkey
103 O17 **Tech** ≈ S France
77 P16 **Techiman** W Ghana *07°35′N 01°56′W*
117 N15 **Techirghiol** Constanța, SE Romania *44°03′N 28°37′E*
74 A12 **Techla** *var.* Techlé. SW Western Sahara *21°39′N 14°57′W*
Techlé *see* Techla
63 H18 **Tecka, Sierra de** ▲▲ SW Argentina
Teckendorf *see* Teaca
40 K13 **Tecolotlán** Jalisco, SW Mexico *20°10′N 104°07′W*
40 K14 **Tecomán** Colima, SW Mexico *18°53′N 103°54′W*
35 V12 **Tecopa** California, W USA *35°51′N 116°14′W*
40 G5 **Tecoripa** Sonora, NW Mexico *28°38′N 109°58′W*
41 N16 **Tecpan** *var.* Tecpan de Galeana. Guerrero, S Mexico *17°12′N 100°39′W*
Tecpan de Galeana *see* Tecpan
40 J11 **Tecuala** Nayarit, C Mexico *22°24′N 105°30′W*
116 L12 **Tecuci** Galați, E Romania *45°50′N 27°27′E*
31 R10 **Tecumseh** Michigan, N USA *42°00′N 83°57′W*
29 S16 **Tecumseh** Nebraska, C USA *40°22′N 96°12′W*
27 O11 **Tecumseh** Oklahoma, C USA *35°15′N 96°56′W*
Tedzhen *see* Harīrūd/Tejen
Tedzhen *see* Tejen
146 H15 **Tedzhenstroy** *Turkm.* Tejenstroy. Ahal Welaýaty, S Turkmenistan *36°57′N 60°49′E*
Teel *see* Öndör-Ulaan
97 L15 **Tees** ≈ N England, United Kingdom
14 E15 **Teeswater** Ontario, S Canada *44°00′N 81°17′W*
190 A10 **Tefala** *island* Funafuti Atoll, C Tuvalu
58 D13 **Tefé** Amazonas, N Brazil *03°24′S 64°45′W*
74 K11 **Tefedest** ▲▲ S Algeria
136 E16 **Tefenni** Burdur, SW Turkey *37°19′N 29°45′E*
58 D13 **Tefé, Rio** ≈ NW Brazil
169 P16 **Tegal** Jawa, C Indonesia *06°52′S 109°07′E*
100 O12 **Tegel** ✈ (Berlin) Berlin, NE Germany *52°33′N 13°16′E*
99 M15 **Tegelen** Limburg, SE Netherlands *51°20′N 06°09′E*
101 L24 **Tegernsee** ◎ SE Germany
107 M18 **Teggiano** Campania, S Italy *40°25′N 15°28′E*
77 U14 **Tegina** Niger, C Nigeria *10°06′N 06°10′E*
42 I7 **Tegucigalpa** ● (Honduras) Francisco Morazán, SW Honduras *14°04′N 87°11′W*
42 H7 **Tegucigalpa** ✈ Central District, C Honduras *14°03′N 87°20′W*
Tegucigalpa *see* Central District
Tegucigalpa *see* Francisco Morazán
77 U9 **Teguidda-n-Tessoumt** Agadez, C Niger *17°27′N 06°40′E*
64 Q11 **Teguise** Lanzarote, Islas Canarias, Spain, NE Atlantic Ocean *29°04′N 13°38′W*
122 K12 **Tegul'det** Tomskaya Oblast', C Russian Federation *57°16′N 87°58′E*
35 S13 **Tehachapi** California, W USA *35°07′N 118°27′W*
35 S13 **Tehachapi Mountains** ▲▲ California, W USA
Tehama *see* Tihāmah
Teheran *see* Tehrān
77 O14 **Tehini** NE Ivory Coast *09°36′N 03°40′W*
143 N5 **Tehrān** *var.* Teheran. ● (Iran) Tehrān, N Iran *35°44′N 51°27′E*
143 N6 **Tehrān** *off.* Ostān-e Tehrān, *var.* Tehran. ◈ *province* N Iran
Tehrān, Ostān-e *see* Tehrān
152 K9 **Tehri** *var.* New Tehri. Uttarakhand, N India *30°12′N 78°29′E*

◆ Country ● Country Capital ◇ Dependent Territory ○ Dependent Territory Capital ◈ Administrative Regions ✈ International Airport ▲ Mountain ▲▲ Mountain Range ⊼ Volcano ≈ River ◎ Lake ⊠ Reservoir

TEHRI – THAU, BASSIN DE

Tehri see Tīkamgarh
41 Q15 **Tehuacán** Puebla, S Mexico 18°29′N 97°24′W
41 S17 **Tehuantepec** var. Santo Domingo Tehuantepec. Oaxaca, SE Mexico 16°18′N 95°14′W
41 S17 **Tehuantepec, Golfo de** var. Gulf of Tehuantepec. gulf S Mexico
Tehuantepec, Gulf of see Tehuantepec, Golfo de
Tehuantepec, Isthmus of see Tehuantepec, Istmo de
41 T16 **Tehuantepec, Istmo de** var. Isthmus of Tehuantepec. isthmus SE Mexico
0 I16 **Tehuantepec Ridge** undersea feature E Pacific Ocean 13°30′N 98°00′W
41 S16 **Tehuantepec, Río** SE Mexico
191 W10 **Tehuata** atoll Îles Tuamotu, C French Polynesia
64 O11 **Teide, Pico del** ▲ Gran Canaria, Islas Canarias, Spain, NE Atlantic Ocean 28°16′N 16°39′W
97 I21 **Teifi** SW Wales, United Kingdom
80 B9 **Teiga Plateau** plateau W Sudan
97 J24 **Teignmouth** SW England, United Kingdom 50°34′N 03°29′W
Teisen see Chech'ŏn
116 H11 **Teiuş** Ger. Dreikirchen, Hung. Tövis. Alba, C Romania 46°12′N 23°40′E
169 U17 **Tejakula** Bali, C Indonesia 08°09′S 115°19′E
146 H14 **Tejen** Rus. Tedzhen. Ahal Welaýaty, S Turkmenistan 37°24′N 60°29′E
146 I15 **Tejen** Per. Harīrūd, Rus. Tedzhen. Afghanistan/Iran see also Harīrūd
Tejen see Harīrūd
Tejenstroy see Tedzhenstroy
35 S14 **Tejon Pass** pass California, W USA
Tejo, Rio see Tagus
41 O14 **Tejupilco** var. Tejupilco de Hidalgo. México, S Mexico 18°55′N 100°10′W
Tejupilco de Hidalgo see Tejupilco
184 P7 **Te Kaha** Bay of Plenty, North Island, New Zealand 37°45′S 177°42′E
29 S14 **Tekamah** Nebraska, C USA 41°46′N 96°13′W
184 I1 **Te Kao** Northland, North Island, New Zealand 34°40′S 172°57′E
185 F20 **Tekapo** South Island, New Zealand
185 F19 **Tekapo, Lake** ◎ South Island, New Zealand
184 P9 **Te Karaka** Gisborne, North Island, New Zealand 38°30′S 177°52′E
184 L7 **Te Kauwhata** Waikato, North Island, New Zealand 37°22′S 175°07′E
41 X12 **Tekax** var. Tekax de Álvaro Obregón. Yucatán, SE Mexico 20°07′N 89°10′W
Tekax de Álvaro Obregón see Tekax
136 A14 **Teke Burnu** headland W Turkey 38°06′N 26°35′E
114 M12 **Teke Deresi** NW Turkey
146 D10 **Tekedzhik, Gory** hill range NW Turkmenistan
145 V14 **Tekeli** Almaty, SE Kazakhstan 44°50′N 78°47′E
145 R7 **Teke, Ozero** ◎ N Kazakhstan
158 I5 **Tekes** Xinjiang Uygur Zizhiqu, NW China 43°15′N 81°43′E
145 W16 **Tekes** Almaty, SE Kazakhstan 42°40′N 80°01′E
Tekes see Tekes He
158 H5 **Tekes He** Rus. Tekes. China/Kazakhstan
Teke/Tekendorf see Teaca
80 I10 **Tekezē** var. Takkaze. Eritrea/Ethiopia
Tekhtin see Tsyakhtsin
136 C10 **Tekirdağ** It. Rodosto; anc. Bisanthe, Raidestos, Rhaedestus. Tekirdağ, NW Turkey 40°59′N 27°31′E
136 C10 **Tekirdağ** ◆ province NW Turkey
155 N14 **Tekkali** Andhra Pradesh, E India 18°37′N 84°15′E
115 K15 **Tekke Burnu** Turk. İlyasbaba Burnu. headland NW Turkey 40°03′N 26°12′E
137 Q13 **Tekman** Erzurum, NE Turkey 39°39′N 41°31′E
32 M9 **Tekoa** Washington, NW USA 47°13′N 117°05′W
190 H16 **Te Kou** ▲ Rarotonga, S Cook Islands 21°14′S 159°46′W
Tekrit see Tikrīt
171 P12 **Teku** Sulawesi, N Indonesia 0°46′S 123°25′E
184 L9 **Te Kuiti** Waikato, North Island, New Zealand 38°21′S 175°10′E
42 H4 **Tela** Atlántida, NW Honduras 15°46′N 87°25′W
138 F12 **Telalim** Southern, S Israel 30°58′N 34°47′E
Telanaipura see Jambi
137 U10 **T'elavi** E Georgia 41°55′N 45°29′E
138 F10 **Tel Aviv** ◆ district W Israel
Tel Aviv-Jaffa see Tel Aviv-Yafo
138 F10 **Tel Aviv-Yafo** var. Tel Aviv-Jaffa. Tel Aviv, C Israel 32°05′N 34°46′E
111 E18 **Telč** Ger. Teltsch. Vysočina, C Czech Republic 49°10′N 15°28′E
186 B6 **Telefomin** Sandaun, NW Papua New Guinea 05°08′S 141°31′E
10 J10 **Telegraph Creek** British Columbia, W Canada 57°56′N 131°10′W
190 B10 **Telele** island Funafuti Atoll, C Tuvalu
60 J11 **Telêmaco Borba** Paraná, S Brazil 24°20′S 50°44′W
95 E15 **Telemark** ◆ county S Norway
62 J13 **Telén** La Pampa, C Argentina 36°20′S 65°31′W
Telenesty see Teleneşti
116 M9 **Teleneşti** Rus. Teleneshty. C Moldova 47°35′N 28°20′E
104 J4 **Teleno, El** ▲ NW Spain 42°19′N 06°21′W
116 I15 **Teleorman** ◆ county S Romania
116 I14 **Teleorman** S Romania
25 V5 **Telephone** Texas, SW USA 33°48′N 96°00′W
35 U11 **Telescope Peak** ▲ California, W USA 36°09′N 117°03′W
Teles Pirés see São Manuel, Rio
97 L19 **Telford** W England, United Kingdom 52°42′N 02°28′W
108 L7 **Telfs** Tirol, W Austria 47°19′N 11°05′E
42 I9 **Telica** León, NW Nicaragua 12°30′N 86°52′W
42 J6 **Telica, Río** C Honduras
76 I13 **Télimélé** W Guinea 10°45′N 13°02′W
43 O14 **Telire, Río** Costa Rica/Panama
114 I8 **Telish** prev. Azizie. Pleven, N Bulgaria 43°20′N 24°15′E
41 R16 **Telixtlahuaca** var. San Francisco Telixtlahuaca. Oaxaca, SE Mexico 17°18′N 96°54′W
10 K13 **Telkwa** British Columbia, SW Canada 54°39′N 126°51′W
25 P4 **Tell** Texas, SW USA 34°18′N 100°20′W
Tell Abiad see Tall Abyaḍ
Tell Abiad/Tell Abyad see At Tall al Abyaḍ
31 O16 **Tell City** Indiana, N USA 37°56′N 86°47′W
38 M9 **Teller** Alaska, USA 65°15′N 166°21′W
Tell Huqnah see Tall Ḥuqnah
155 F20 **Tellicherry** var. Thalashsheri, Thalassery. Kerala, SW India 11°44′N 75°29′E see also Thalassery
20 M10 **Tellico Plains** Tennessee, S USA 35°19′N 84°18′W
Tell Kalakh see Tall Kalakh
Tell Mardikh see Ebla
54 E11 **Tello** Huila, C Colombia 03°06′N 75°08′W
Tell Shedadi see Ash Shadādah
37 Q7 **Telluride** Colorado, C USA 37°56′N 107°48′W
117 X9 **Tel'manove** Donets'ka Oblast', E Ukraine 47°24′N 38°03′E
Tel'man/Tel'mansk see Gubadag
162 H6 **Telmen** var. Övögdiy. Dzavhan, C Mongolia 48°38′N 97°39′E
162 H6 **Telmen Nuur** ◎ NW Mongolia
Teloekbetoeng see Bandar Lampung
41 O15 **Teloloapán** Guerrero, S Mexico 18°21′N 99°52′W
Telo Martius see Toulon
125 V8 **Telposiz, Gora** ▲ NW Russian Federation 63°52′N 59°15′E
Telschen see Telšiai
63 J17 **Telsen** Chubut, S Argentina 42°27′S 66°59′W
118 D11 **Telšiai** Ger. Telschen. Telšiai, NW Lithuania 55°59′N 22°21′E
118 D11 **Telšiai** ◆ province NW Lithuania
Teltsch see Telč
Telukbetung see Bandar Lampung
168 H10 **Telukdalam** Pulau Nias, W Indonesia 0°34′N 97°47′E
14 H9 **Temagami** Ontario, S Canada 47°03′N 79°47′W
14 G9 **Temagami, Lake** ◎ Ontario, S Canada
190 H16 **Te Manga** ▲ Rarotonga, S Cook Islands 21°13′S 159°45′W
191 W12 **Tematangi** atoll Îles Tuamotu, S French Polynesia
41 X11 **Temax** Yucatán, SE Mexico 21°10′N 88°53′W
171 E14 **Tembagapura** Papua, E Indonesia 04°10′S 137°19′E
129 U5 **Tembenchi** N Russian Federation
55 P6 **Temblador** Monagas, NE Venezuela 08°59′N 62°44′W
105 N9 **Tembleque** Castilla-La Mancha, C Spain 39°41′N 03°30′W
Temboni see Mitemele, Río
35 U16 **Temecula** California, W USA 33°29′N 117°09′W
168 K7 **Temengor, Tasik** ⊠ Peninsular Malaysia
112 L9 **Temerin** Vojvodina, N Serbia 45°25′N 19°54′E
Temeschburg/Temeschwar see Timişoara
Temes-Kubin see Kovin
Temes/Temesch see Tamiš
Temesvár/Temeswar see Timişoara
Teminaboean see Teminabuan
171 U12 **Teminabuan** prev. Teminaboean. Papua, E Indonesia 01°30′S 131°59′E
145 P17 **Temirlanovka** Yuzhnyy Kazakhstan, S Kazakhstan 42°36′N 69°17′E
145 R10 **Temirtau** prev. Samarkandski, Samarkandskoye. Karaganda, C Kazakhstan 50°05′N 72°55′E
14 H10 **Témiscaming** Québec, SE Canada 46°40′N 79°04′W
Témiscamingue, Lac see Timiskaming, Lake
15 T8 **Témiscouata, Lac** ◎ Québec, SE Canada
127 N5 **Temnikov** Respublika Mordoviya, W Russian Federation 54°39′N 43°09′E
191 Y13 **Temoe** island Îles Gambier, E French Polynesia
183 Q9 **Temora** New South Wales, SE Australia 34°28′S 147°33′E
40 H7 **Témoris** Chihuahua, W Mexico 27°16′N 108°15′W
40 I5 **Temósachic** Chihuahua, N Mexico 28°55′N 107°42′W
187 Q10 **Temotu** var. Temotu Province. ◆ province E Solomon Islands
Temotu Province see Temotu
36 L14 **Tempe** Arizona, SW USA 33°24′N 111°54′W
Tempelburg see Czaplinek
107 C17 **Tempio Pausania** Sardegna, Italy, C Mediterranean Sea 40°55′N 09°07′E
42 K12 **Tempisque, Río** NW Costa Rica
25 T9 **Temple** Texas, SW USA 31°06′N 97°22′W
100 O12 **Tempelhof** ✕ (Berlin) Berlin, NE Germany 52°28′N 13°24′E
97 D19 **Templemore** Ir. An Teampall Mór. Tipperary, C Ireland 52°48′N 07°50′W
100 O11 **Templin** Brandenburg, NE Germany 53°07′N 13°31′E
41 P12 **Tempoal** var. Tempoal de Sánchez. Veracruz-Llave, E Mexico 21°32′N 98°23′W
Tempoal de Sánchez see Tempoal
41 P13 **Tempoal, Río** C Mexico
83 E14 **Tempué** Moxico, C Angola 13°36′S 18°56′E
126 J14 **Temryuk** Krasnodarskiy Kray, SW Russian Federation 45°15′N 37°26′E
99 G17 **Temse** Oost-Vlaanderen, N Belgium 51°08′N 04°13′E
63 F15 **Temuco** Araucanía, C Chile 38°45′S 72°37′W
185 G20 **Temuka** Canterbury, South Island, New Zealand 44°14′S 171°17′E
189 P13 **Temwen Island** island E Micronesia
56 C6 **Tena** Napo, C Ecuador 01°00′S 77°48′W
41 W13 **Tenabo** Campeche, E Mexico 20°02′N 90°12′W
Tenaghau see Aola
25 X7 **Tenaha** Texas, SW USA 31°56′N 94°14′W
39 X13 **Tenake** Chichagof Island, Alaska, USA 57°46′N 135°13′W
155 K16 **Tenāli** Andhra Pradesh, E India 16°13′N 80°36′E
Tenan see Ch'ŏnan
41 O14 **Tenancingo** var. Tenencingo de Degollado. México, S Mexico 18°57′N 99°39′W
191 X12 **Tenararo** island Groupe Actéon, SE French Polynesia
167 N12 **Tenasserim** Tanintharyi, S Myanmar (Burma) 12°05′N 99°00′E
167 N11 **Tenasserim** var. Tanintharyi. ◆ division S Myanmar (Burma)
98 O5 **Ten Boer** Groningen, NE Netherlands 53°16′N 06°42′E
97 I21 **Tenby** SW Wales, United Kingdom 51°41′N 04°43′W
80 K11 **Tendaho** Āfar, NE Ethiopia 11°39′N 40°59′E
103 V14 **Tende** Alpes Maritimes, SE France 44°04′N 07°34′E
151 Q20 **Ten Degree Channel** strait Andaman and Nicobar Islands, India, E Indian Ocean
80 F11 **Tendelti** White Nile, E Sudan 13°01′N 31°55′E
76 G8 **Te-n-Dghâmcha, Sebkhet** var. Sebkha de Ndrhamcha, Sebkra de Ndaghamcha. salt lake W Mauritania
165 P10 **Tendō** Yamagata, Honshū, C Japan 38°22′N 140°22′E
74 H7 **Tendrara** NE Morocco 33°06′N 01°58′W
117 Q11 **Tendrivs'ka Kosa** spit S Ukraine
117 Q11 **Tendrivs'ka Zatoka** gulf S Ukraine
Tenencingo de Degollado see Tenancingo
77 N11 **Ténenkou** Mopti, C Mali 14°28′N 04°55′W
77 W9 **Ténéré** physical region C Niger
77 W9 **Ténére, Erg du** desert C Niger
64 O11 **Tenerife** island Islas Canarias, Spain, NE Atlantic Ocean
74 J5 **Ténès** NW Algeria 36°35′N 01°18′E
170 M15 **Tengah, Kepulauan** island group C Indonesia
Tengcheng see Tengxian
169 V11 **Tenggarong** Borneo, C Indonesia 0°23′S 117°00′E
162 J15 **Tengger Shamo** desert N China
168 L8 **Tenggul, Pulau** island Peninsular Malaysia
Tengiz Köl see Tengiz, Ozero
145 P9 **Tengiz, Ozero** Kaz. Tengiz Köl. salt lake C Kazakhstan
76 M14 **Tengréla** var. Tingréla. N Ivory Coast 10°26′N 06°20′W
160 M14 **Tengxian** var. Tengcheng, Tengxian, Teng Xian. Guangxi Zhuangzu Zizhiqu, S China 23°24′N 110°49′E
Teng Xian see Tengxian
Tengxian see Tengxian
155 H23 **Teni** var. Theni. Tamil Nādu, SE India 10°00′N 77°29′E
194 H2 **Teniente Rodolfo Marsh** Chilean research station South Shetland Islands, Antarctica 61°57′S 58°23′W
32 G9 **Tenino** Washington, NW USA 46°51′N 122°51′W
112 I9 **Tenja** Osijek-Baranja, E Croatia 45°30′N 18°45′E
188 B16 **Tenjo, Mount** ▲ W Guam
155 H23 **Tenkāsi** Tamil Nādu, SE India 08°58′N 77°22′E
79 N24 **Tenke** Katanga, SE Dem. Rep. Congo 10°34′S 26°12′E
Tenke see Tinca
123 Q7 **Tenkeli** Respublika Sakha (Yakutiya), NE Russian Federation 70°09′N 140°39′E
27 R10 **Tenkiller Ferry Lake** ⊠ Oklahoma, C USA
77 Q13 **Tenkodogo** S Burkina 11°54′N 00°19′W
181 Q5 **Tennant Creek** Northern Territory, C Australia 19°40′S 134°16′E
20 G9 **Tennessee** off. State of Tennessee, also known as The Volunteer State. ◆ state SE USA
37 R5 **Tennessee Pass** pass Colorado, C USA
20 H10 **Tennessee River** S USA
23 N2 **Tennessee Tombigbee Waterway** canal Alabama/Mississippi, S USA
99 K22 **Tenneville** Luxembourg, SE Belgium 50°05′N 05°31′E
92 M11 **Tenniöjoki** NE Finland
92 L9 **Tenojoki** Lapp. Deatnu, Nor. Tana. Finland/Norway see also Deatnu
169 U7 **Tenom** Sabah, East Malaysia 05°07′N 115°57′E
Tenos see Tínos
41 V15 **Tenosique** var. Tenosique de Pino Suárez. Tabasco, SE Mexico 17°30′N 91°24′W
Tenosique de Pino Suárez see Tenosique
22 I6 **Tensas River** Louisiana, S USA
23 O8 **Tensaw River** Alabama, S USA
74 E7 **Tensift** seasonal river W Morocco
171 O12 **Tentena** var. Tenteno. Sulawesi, C Indonesia 01°46′S 120°40′E
Tenteno see Tentena
183 U4 **Tenterfield** New South Wales, SE Australia 29°04′S 152°02′E
23 X16 **Ten Thousand Islands** island group Florida, SE USA
60 H9 **Teodoro Sampaio** São Paulo, S Brazil 22°30′S 52°13′W
59 N19 **Teófilo Otoni** var. Theophilo Ottoni. Minas Gerais, NE Brazil 17°52′S 41°31′W
116 K5 **Teofipol'** Khmel'nyts'ka Oblast', W Ukraine 50°00′N 26°22′E
191 Q8 **Teohatu** Tahiti, W French Polynesia
41 P14 **Teotihuacán** ruins México, S Mexico
Teotilán see Teotitlán del Camino
41 Q15 **Teotitlán del Camino** var. Teotilán. Oaxaca, S Mexico 18°10′N 97°08′W
190 G12 **Tepa** Île Uvea, E Wallis and Futuna 13°19′S 176°09′W
191 P8 **Tepaee, Récif** reef Tahiti, W French Polynesia
40 L14 **Tepalcatepec** Michoacán, SW Mexico 19°11′N 102°50′W
190 A16 **Tepa Point** headland SW Niue 19°07′S 169°56′E
40 L13 **Tepatitlán** var. Tepatitlán de Morelos. Jalisco, SW Mexico 20°50′N 102°46′W
Tepatitlán de Morelos see Tepatitlán
40 J9 **Tepehuanes** var. Santa Catarina de Tepehuanes. Durango, C Mexico 25°22′N 105°42′W
Tepelena see Tepelenë
113 L22 **Tepelenë** var. Tepelena, It. Tepeleni. Gjirokastër, S Albania 40°18′N 20°00′E
Tepeleni see Tepelenë
40 K12 **Tepic** Nayarit, C Mexico 21°30′N 104°55′W
111 C15 **Teplice** Ger. Teplitz; prev. Teplice-Šanov, Teplitz-Schönau. Ústecký Kraj, NW Czech Republic 50°38′N 13°49′E
Teplice-Šanov/Teplitz/Teplitz-Schönau see Teplice
117 O7 **Teplyk** Vinnyts'ka Oblast', C Ukraine 48°40′N 29°46′E
123 R10 **Teplyy Klyuch** Respublika Sakha (Yakutiya), NE Russian Federation 62°46′N 137°01′E
40 E5 **Tepoca, Cabo** headland NW Mexico 29°19′N 112°24′W
191 W9 **Tepoto** island Îles du Désappointement, C French Polynesia
92 L11 **Tepsa** Lappi, N Finland 67°34′N 25°36′E
190 B8 **Tepuka** atoll Funafuti Atoll, C Tuvalu
184 N7 **Te Puke** Bay of Plenty, North Island, New Zealand 37°48′S 176°19′E
40 L13 **Tequila** Jalisco, SW Mexico 20°52′N 103°48′W
41 O13 **Tequisquiapan** Querétaro de Arteaga, C Mexico 20°34′N 99°52′W
77 Q12 **Téra** Tillabéri, W Niger 14°01′N 00°45′E
104 J5 **Tera** NW Spain
191 V1 **Teraina** prev. Washington Island. atoll Line Islands, E Kiribati
81 F15 **Terakeka** Bahr el Gabel, S Sudan 05°26′N 31°45′E
107 J14 **Teramo** anc. Interamna. Abruzzi, C Italy 42°40′N 13°43′E
98 P7 **Ter Apel** Groningen, NE Netherlands 52°52′N 07°05′E
104 H11 **Tera, Ribeira de** S Portugal
185 K14 **Terawhiti, Cape** headland North Island, New Zealand 41°17′S 174°36′E
98 N12 **Terborg** Gelderland, E Netherlands 51°55′N 06°22′E
137 P13 **Tercan** Erzincan, NE Turkey 39°47′N 40°23′E
64 O2 **Terceira** ✕ Terceira, Azores, Portugal, NE Atlantic Ocean 38°43′N 27°13′W
64 O2 **Terceira** var. Ilha Terceira. island Azores, Portugal, NE Atlantic Ocean
Terceira, Ilha see Terceira
116 K6 **Terebovlya** Ternopil's'ka Oblast', W Ukraine 49°18′N 25°44′E
127 O15 **Terek** SW Russian Federation
Terekhovka see Tsyerakhowka
147 R9 **Terek-Say** Dzhalal-Abadskaya Oblast', W Kyrgyzstan 41°28′N 71°06′E
145 Z10 **Terekty** prev. Alekseevka, Alekseyevka. Vostochnyy Kazakhstan, E Kazakhstan 48°25′N 85°38′E
168 L7 **Terengganu** var. Trengganu. ◆ state Peninsular Malaysia
127 X7 **Terensay** Orenburgskaya Oblast', W Russian Federation 51°35′N 59°28′E
58 N13 **Teresina** var. Therezina. state capital Piauí, NE Brazil 05°09′S 42°46′W
60 P9 **Teresópolis** Rio de Janeiro, SE Brazil 22°25′S 42°59′W
110 P12 **Terespol** Lubelskie, E Poland 52°05′N 23°37′E
191 V16 **Terevaka, Maunga** Easter Island, Chile, E Pacific Ocean 27°05′S 109°23′W
103 P3 **Tergnier** Aisne, N France 49°39′N 03°18′E
43 O14 **Teribe, Río** NW Panama
124 K3 **Teriberka** Murmanskaya Oblast', NW Russian Federation 69°10′N 35°18′E
Terinkot see Tarīn Kowt
Terisaqqan see Tersakkan
24 K12 **Terlingua** Texas, SW USA 29°18′N 103°36′W
24 K11 **Terlingua Creek** Texas, SW USA
62 K7 **Termas de Río Hondo** Santiago del Estero, N Argentina 27°29′S 64°52′W
136 M11 **Terme** Samsun, N Turkey 41°12′N 37°00′E
Termez see Termiz
Termia see Kýthnos
107 J23 **Termini Imerese** anc. Thermae Himerenses. Sicilia, Italy, C Mediterranean Sea 37°59′N 13°42′E
41 V14 **Términos, Laguna de** lagoon SE Mexico
77 X10 **Termit-Kaoboul** Zinder, C Niger 15°34′N 11°31′E
147 O14 **Termiz** Rus. Termez. Surkhondaryo Viloyati, S Uzbekistan 37°17′N 67°12′E
107 L15 **Termoli** Molise, C Italy 42°00′N 14°58′E
Termonde see Dendermonde
98 O5 **Termunten** Groningen, NE Netherlands 53°18′N 07°02′E
171 R11 **Ternate** Pulau Ternate, E Indonesia 0°48′N 127°23′E
109 T5 **Ternberg** Oberösterreich, N Austria 47°57′N 14°22′E
99 E15 **Terneuzen** var. Neuzen. Zeeland, SW Netherlands 51°20′N 03°50′E
123 T14 **Terney** Primorskiy Kray, SE Russian Federation 45°03′N 136°43′E
107 I14 **Terni** anc. Interamna Nahars. Umbria, C Italy 42°34′N 12°38′E
109 X6 **Ternitz** Niederösterreich, E Austria 47°43′N 16°02′E
117 V7 **Ternivka** Dnipropetrovs'ka Oblast', E Ukraine 48°30′N 36°05′E
116 K6 **Ternopil'** Pol. Tarnopol, Rus. Ternopol'. Ternopil's'ka Oblast', W Ukraine 49°32′N 25°38′E
Ternopil' see Ternopil's'ka Oblast'
116 I6 **Ternopil's'ka Oblast'** var. Ternopil', Rus. Ternopol'skaya Oblast'. ◆ province NW Ukraine
Ternopol' see Ternopil'
Ternopol'skaya Oblast' see Ternopil's'ka Oblast'
123 U13 **Terpeniya, Mys** headland Ostrov Sakhalin, SE Russian Federation 48°37′N 144°40′E
Térraba, Río see Grande de Térraba, Río
10 J13 **Terrace** British Columbia, W Canada 54°31′N 128°32′W
12 D12 **Terrace Bay** Ontario, S Canada 48°47′N 87°06′W
107 I16 **Terracina** Lazio, C Italy 41°18′N 13°13′E
93 F14 **Terråk** Troms, N Norway 65°03′N 12°22′E
26 M13 **Terral** Oklahoma, C USA 33°55′N 97°54′W
107 B19 **Terralba** Sardegna, Italy, C Mediterranean Sea 39°47′N 08°35′E
Terranova di Sicilia see Gela
Terranova Pausania see Olbia
105 W5 **Terrassa** Cast. Tarrasa. Cataluña, E Spain 41°34′N 02°01′E
15 O12 **Terrebonne** Québec, SE Canada 45°42′N 73°37′W
22 J11 **Terrebonne Bay** bay Louisiana, SE USA
31 N14 **Terre Haute** Indiana, N USA 39°27′N 87°24′W
25 U6 **Terrell** Texas, SW USA 32°44′N 96°16′W
Terre Neuve see Newfoundland and Labrador
33 Q14 **Terreton** Idaho, NW USA 43°49′N 112°25′W
103 T7 **Territoire-de-Belfort** ◆ department E France
33 X9 **Terry** Montana, NW USA 46°46′N 105°16′W
28 I9 **Terry Peak** ▲ South Dakota, N USA 44°19′N 103°49′W
136 H14 **Tersakan Gölü** ◎ C Turkey
145 O10 **Tersakkan** Kaz. Terisaqqan. C Kazakhstan
98 J4 **Terschelling** Fris. Skylge. island Waddeneilanden, N Netherlands
78 H10 **Tersef** Chari-Baguirmi, C Chad 12°55′N 16°49′E
147 X8 **Terskey Ala-Too, Khrebet** ▲▲ Kazakhstan/Kyrgyzstan
Terter see Tärtär
105 R8 **Teruel** anc. Turba. Aragón, E Spain 40°21′N 01°06′W
105 R7 **Teruel** ◆ province Aragón, E Spain
114 M7 **Tervel** prev. Kurtbunar, Rom. Curtbunar. Dobrich, NE Bulgaria 43°45′N 27°25′E
93 M16 **Tervo** Itä-Suomi, C Finland 62°57′N 26°48′E
92 L13 **Tervola** Lappi, NW Finland 66°04′N 24°49′E
Tervueren see Tervuren
99 H18 **Tervuren** var. Tervueren. Vlaams Brabant, C Belgium 50°48′N 04°28′E
162 G5 **Tes** var. Dzür. Dzavhan, W Mongolia 49°37′N 95°46′E
112 H11 **Tešanj** Federacija Bosna I Hercegovina, N Bosnia and Herzegovina 44°37′N 18°00′E
Teschen see Cieszyn
83 M19 **Tesenane** Inhambane, S Mozambique 22°48′S 34°02′E
80 I9 **Teseney** var. Tessenei. W Eritrea 15°05′N 36°42′E
39 P5 **Teshekpuk Lake** ◎ Alaska, USA
162 K6 **Teshig** Bulgan, N Mongolia 49°51′N 102°45′E
165 T2 **Teshio** Hokkaidō, NE Japan 44°49′N 141°46′E
165 T2 **Teshio-sanchi** ▲▲ Hokkaidō, NE Japan
14 L7 **Tessier, Lac** ◎ Québec, SE Canada
Těšín see Cieszyn
Tesiyn Gol see Tes-Khem
129 T7 **Tes-Khem** var. Tesiyn Gol. Mongolia/Russian Federation
112 H11 **Teslić** Republika Srpska, N Bosnia and Herzegovina 44°35′N 17°50′E
10 I9 **Teslin** Yukon Territory, W Canada 60°12′N 132°44′W
10 I8 **Teslin** British Columbia/Yukon Territory, W Canada
77 Q8 **Tessalit** Kidal, NE Mali 20°12′N 00°58′E
77 V12 **Tessaoua** Maradi, S Niger 13°46′N 07°55′E
99 J17 **Tessenderlo** Limburg, NE Belgium 51°05′N 05°04′E
Tessenei see Teseney
Tessin see Ticino
97 M23 **Test** S England, United Kingdom
Testama see Tõstamaa
55 P4 **Testigos, Islas los** island group N Venezuela
37 S10 **Tesuque** New Mexico, SW USA 35°45′N 105°55′W
103 O17 **Têt** var. Tet. S France
Tet see Têt
54 G5 **Tetas, Cerro de las** ▲ NW Venezuela 09°58′N 73°00′W
83 M15 **Tete** Tete, NW Mozambique 16°14′S 33°34′E
83 M15 **Tete** off. Província de Tete. ◆ province NW Mozambique
11 N15 **Tête Jaune Cache** British Columbia, SW Canada 52°52′N 119°22′W
184 O8 **Te Teko** Bay of Plenty, North Island, New Zealand 38°03′S 176°48′E
186 K9 **Tetepare** island New Georgia Islands, NW Solomon Islands
Tete, Província de see Tete
Teterev see Teteriv
116 M5 **Teteriv** Rus. Teterev. N Ukraine
100 M9 **Teterow** Mecklenburg-Vorpommern, NE Germany 53°47′N 12°34′E
114 I9 **Teteven** Lovech, N Bulgaria 42°54′N 24°18′E
191 T10 **Tetiaroa** atoll Îles du Vent, W French Polynesia
105 P14 **Tetica de Bacares** ▲ S Spain 37°15′N 02°24′W
Tetiyev see Tetiyiv
117 O6 **Tetiyiv** Rus. Tetiyev. Kyyivs'ka Oblast', N Ukraine 49°21′N 29°40′E
39 T10 **Tetlin** Alaska, USA 63°08′N 142°31′W
33 R8 **Teton River** Montana, NW USA
74 G5 **Tétouan** var. Tetouan, Tetuán. N Morocco 35°33′N 05°22′W
Tetova/Tetovë see Tetovo
114 L7 **Tetovo** Razgrad, N Bulgaria 43°49′N 26°21′E
113 N18 **Tetovo** Alb. Tetova, Tetovë, Turk. Kalkandelen. NW FYR Macedonia 42°01′N 20°58′E
115 E20 **Tetrázio** ▲▲ S Greece
Tetschen see Děčín
Tetuán see Tétouan
191 Q8 **Tetufera, Mont** ▲ Tahiti, W French Polynesia 17°40′S 149°26′W
127 R4 **Tetyushi** Respublika Tatarstan, W Russian Federation 54°55′N 48°46′E
108 I7 **Teufen** Sankt Gallen, NE Switzerland 47°24′N 09°24′E
40 L12 **Teul** var. Teul de Gonzáles Ortega. Zacatecas, C Mexico 21°30′N 103°28′W
107 B21 **Teulada** Sardegna, Italy, C Mediterranean Sea 38°58′N 08°46′E
Teul de Gonzáles Ortega see Teul
11 X16 **Teulon** Manitoba, S Canada 50°20′N 97°14′W
42 I7 **Teupasenti** El Paraíso, S Honduras 14°13′N 86°42′W
165 S2 **Teuri-tō** island NE Japan
100 G13 **Teutoburger Wald** Eng. Teutoburg Forest. hill range NW Germany
Teutoburg Forest see Teutoburger Wald
93 K17 **Teuva** Swe. Östermark. Länsi-Suomi, W Finland 62°29′N 21°45′E
107 H15 **Tevere** Eng. Tiber. C Italy
Teverya see Tverya
96 K13 **Teviot** SE Scotland, United Kingdom
Tevli see Tewli
122 H11 **Tevriz** Omskaya Oblast', C Russian Federation 57°30′N 72°13′E
185 B24 **Te Waewae Bay** bay South Island, New Zealand
97 L21 **Tewkesbury** C England, United Kingdom 51°59′N 02°09′W
119 F19 **Tewli** Rus. Tevli. Brestskaya Voblasts', SW Belarus 52°20′N 24°15′E
159 U12 **Têwo** var. Dêngka; prev. Dêngkagoin. Gansu, C China 34°05′N 103°15′E
Tewulike see Hoxud
25 U12 **Texana, Lake** ◎ Texas, SW USA
27 S14 **Texarkana** Arkansas, C USA 33°26′N 94°02′W
25 X5 **Texarkana** Texas, SW USA 33°26′N 94°03′W
25 N9 **Texas** off. State of Texas, also known as Lone Star State. ◆ state S USA
25 W12 **Texas City** Texas, SW USA 29°23′N 94°55′W
41 P14 **Texcoco** México, C Mexico 19°32′N 98°52′W
98 I6 **Texel** island Waddeneilanden, NW Netherlands
26 H8 **Texhoma** Oklahoma, C USA 36°30′N 101°46′W
25 N1 **Texhoma** Texas, SW USA 36°30′N 101°46′W
37 W12 **Texico** New Mexico, SW USA 34°23′N 103°03′W
24 L1 **Texline** Texas, SW USA 36°22′N 103°01′W
41 P14 **Texmelucan** var. San Martín Texmelucan. Puebla, S Mexico 19°46′N 98°53′W
27 O13 **Texoma, Lake** ⊠ Oklahoma/Texas, C USA
25 N9 **Texon** Texas, SW USA 31°13′N 101°42′W
83 J23 **Teyateyaneng** NW Lesotho 29°04′S 27°51′E
124 M16 **Teykovo** Ivanovskaya Oblast', W Russian Federation 56°49′N 40°31′E
124 M16 **Teza** W Russian Federation
41 Q13 **Teziutlán** Puebla, S Mexico 19°49′N 97°22′W
153 W12 **Tezpur** Assam, NE India 26°39′N 92°47′E
153 Y11 **Tezu** Arunāchal Pradesh, NE India 27°55′N 96°09′E
Thaa Atoll see Kolhumadulu
9 N10 **Tha-Anne** Nunavut, NE Canada
83 K23 **Thabana Ntlenyana** var. Thabantshonyana, Mount Ntlenyana. ▲ E Lesotho 29°26′S 29°16′E
Thabantshonyana see Thabana Ntlenyana
83 J23 **Thaba Putsoa** ▲ C Lesotho 29°48′S 27°46′E
167 Q8 **Tha Bo** Nong Khai, E Thailand 17°52′N 102°34′E
103 T12 **Thabor, Pic du** ▲ E France 45°07′N 06°34′E
Tha Chin see Samut Sakhon
166 M7 **Thagaya** Bago, C Myanmar (Burma) 19°19′N 96°16′E
Thai, Ao see Thailand, Gulf of
167 T6 **Thai Binh** Thai Binh, N Vietnam 20°27′N 106°20′E
167 S7 **Thai Hoa** var. Nghia Dan. Nghê An, N Vietnam 19°21′N 105°26′E
167 P9 **Thailand** off. Kingdom of Thailand, Th. Prathet Thai; prev. Siam. ◆ monarchy SE Asia
167 P13 **Thailand, Gulf of** var. Gulf of Siam, Th. Ao Thai, Vtn. Vinh Thai Lan. gulf SE Asia
Thailand, Kingdom of see Thailand
Thai Lan, Vinh see Thailand, Gulf of
167 T6 **Thai Nguyên** Bắc Thai, N Vietnam 21°36′N 105°50′E
167 S8 **Thakhèk** var. Muang Khammouan. Khammouan, C Laos 17°25′N 104°51′E
153 S13 **Thakurgaon** Rajshahi, NW Bangladesh 26°05′N 88°34′E
149 S6 **Thal** North-West Frontier Province, NW Pakistan 33°24′N 70°32′E
166 M15 **Thalang** Phuket, SW Thailand 08°00′N 98°21′E
Thalashsheri see Tellicherry/Thalassery
155 F20 **Thalassery** var. Tellicherry, Thalashsheri. Kerala, SW India 11°44′N 75°29′E see also Tellicherry
167 Q10 **Thalat Khae** Nakhon Ratchasima, C Thailand 15°15′N 102°24′E
109 Q5 **Thalgau** Salzburg, NW Austria 47°49′N 13°19′E
108 G7 **Thalwil** Zürich, NW Switzerland 47°17′N 08°35′E
83 I20 **Thamaga** Kweneng, SE Botswana 24°41′S 25°31′E
Thamarid see Thamarīt
141 V13 **Thamarīt** var. Thamarid, Thumrayt. SW Oman 17°39′N 54°02′E
141 P16 **Thamar, Jabal** ▲ SW Yemen 13°46′N 45°32′E
184 M6 **Thames** Waikato, North Island, New Zealand 37°10′S 175°33′E
14 D17 **Thames** Ontario, S Canada
97 O22 **Thames** S England, United Kingdom
184 M6 **Thames, Firth of** gulf North Island, New Zealand
14 D17 **Thamesville** Ontario, S Canada 42°33′N 81°58′W
141 S13 **Thamūd** N Yemen 17°18′N 49°57′E
167 N9 **Thanbyuzayat** Mon State, S Myanmar (Burma) 15°58′N 97°44′E
166 K7 **Thandwe** var. Sandoway. Rakhine State, W Myanmar (Burma) 18°28′N 94°20′E
152 I9 **Thānesar** Haryāna, NW India 29°58′N 76°48′E
167 T7 **Thanh Hoa** Thanh Hoa, N Vietnam 19°49′N 105°48′E
Thanintari Taungdan see Bilauktaung Range
155 I21 **Thanjāvūr** prev. Tanjore. Tamil Nādu, SE India 10°46′N 79°09′E
Thanlwin see Salween
103 U7 **Thann** Haut-Rhin, NE France 47°51′N 07°04′E
167 O16 **Tha Nong Phrom** Phatthalung, SW Thailand 07°24′N 100°04′E
167 N13 **Thap Sakae** var. Thap Sakau. Prachuap Khiri Khan, SW Thailand 11°30′N 99°35′E
Thap Sakau see Thap Sakae
98 L10 **'t Harde** Gelderland, E Netherlands 52°25′N 05°53′E
152 D11 **Thar Desert** var. Great Indian Desert, Indian Desert. desert India/Pakistan
181 V10 **Thargomindah** Queensland, C Australia 28°00′S 143°47′E
150 D11 **Thar Pārkar** desert SE Pakistan
139 S7 **Tharthār al Furāt, Qanāt ath** canal C Iraq
139 R7 **Tharthār, Buḥayrat ath** ◎ C Iraq
139 R5 **Tharthār, Wādī ath** dry watercourse N Iraq
167 N13 **Tha Sae** Chumphon, SW Thailand
167 N15 **Tha Sala** Nakhon Si Thammarat, SW Thailand 08°43′N 99°54′E
114 I13 **Thásos** Thásos, E Greece 40°47′N 24°43′E
115 I14 **Thásos** island E Greece
37 N14 **Thatcher** Arizona, SW USA 32°47′N 109°46′W
167 T5 **That Khê** var. Tràng Dinh. Lang Sơn, N Vietnam 22°15′N 106°26′E
166 M8 **Thaton** Mon State, S Myanmar (Burma) 16°56′N 97°20′E
167 S9 **That Phanom** Nakhon Phanom, E Thailand 16°52′N 104°41′E
167 R10 **Tha Tum** Surin, E Thailand 15°18′N 103°39′E
103 P16 **Thau, Bassin de** var. Étang de Thau. ◎ S France

◆ Country ● Country Capital ◇ Dependent Territory ○ Dependent Territory Capital ◆ Administrative Regions ✕ International Airport ▲ Mountain ▲▲ Mountain Range Volcano River ◎ Lake ⊠ Reservoir

THAU, ÉTANG DE – TISA

Thau, Étang de *see* Thau, Bassin de
166 *L3* **Thaungdut** Sagaing, N Myanmar (Burma) *24°26′N 94°45′E*
167 *O8* **Thaungyin** *Th.* Mae Nam Moei. ≈ Myanmar (Burma)/Thailand
167 *R8* **Tha Uthen** Nakhon Phanom, E Thailand *17°32′N 104°34′E*
109 *W2* **Thaya** *var.* Dyje. ≈ Austria/Czech Republic *see also* Dyje
Thaya *see* Dyje
27 *V8* **Thayer** Missouri, C USA *36°31′N 91°34′W*
166 *L6* **Thayetmyo** Magway, C Myanmar (Burma) *19°20′N 95°10′E*
33 *S15* **Thayne** Wyoming, C USA *42°54′N 111°01′W*
166 *M5* **Thazi** Mandalay, C Myanmar (Burma) *20°50′N 96°04′E*
Thebes *see* Thíva
44 *L5* **The Carlton** *var.* Abraham Bay. Mayaguana, SE Bahamas *22°21′N 72°56′W*
45 *O14* **The Crane** *var.* Crane. S Barbados *13°06′N 59°27′W*
32 *I11* **The Dalles** Oregon, NW USA *45°36′N 121°10′W*
28 *M14* **Thedford** Nebraska, C USA *41°59′N 100°32′W*
The Flatts Village *see* Flatts Village
The Hague *see* 's-Gravenhage
Theiss *see* Tisa/Tisza
8 *M9* **Thelon** ≈ Northwest Territories, N Canada
Theni *see* Teni
11 *V15* **Theodore** Saskatchewan, S Canada *51°25′N 103°01′W*
23 *N8* **Theodore** Alabama, S USA *30°33′N 88°10′W*
36 *L13* **Theodore Roosevelt Lake** ⊠ Arizona, SW USA
Theodosia *see* Feodosiya
Theophilo Ottoni *see* Teófilo Otoni
11 *V13* **The Pas** Manitoba, C Canada *53°49′N 101°09′W*
31 *T14* **The Plains** Ohio, N USA *39°22′N 82°07′W*
Thera *see* Santoríni
172 *H17* **Thérèse, Île** *island* Inner Islands, NE Seychelles
Therezina *see* Teresina
115 *L20* **Thérma** Ikaría, Dodekánisa, Greece, Aegean Sea *37°37′N 26°18′E*
Thermae Himerenses *see* Termini Imerese
Thermae Pannonicae *see* Baden
Thermaic Gulf/Thermaicus Sinus *see* Thermaïkós Kólpos
121 *Q8* **Thermaïkós Kólpos** *Eng.* Thermaic Gulf; *anc.* Thermaicus Sinus. *gulf* N Greece
Thermiá *see* Kýthnos
115 *L17* **Thermís** Lésvos, E Greece *39°08′N 26°32′E*
115 *E18* **Thérmo** Dytikí Ellás, C Greece *38°32′N 21°42′E*
33 *V14* **Thermopolis** Wyoming, C USA *43°39′N 108°12′W*
183 *P10* **The Rock** New South Wales, SE Australia *35°18′S 147°07′E*
195 *O5* **Theron Mountains** ▲▲ Antarctica
The Sooner State *see* Oklahoma
115 *G18* **Thespiés** Stereá Ellás, C Greece *38°18′N 23°08′E*
115 *E16* **Thessalía** *Eng.* Thessaly. ◈ *region* C Greece
14 *C10* **Thessalon** Ontario, S Canada *46°15′N 83°34′W*
115 *G14* **Thessaloníki** *Eng.* Salonica, Salonika, *SCr.* Solun, *Turk.* Selânik. Kentrikí Makedonía, N Greece *40°38′N 22°58′E*
115 *G14* **Thessaloníki** ✈ Kentrikí Makedonía, N Greece *40°30′N 22°58′E*
Thessaly *see* Thessalía
84 *B12* **Theta Gap** *undersea feature* E Atlantic Ocean *12°40′W 43°30′N*
97 *P20* **Thetford** E England, United Kingdom *52°25′N 00°45′E*
15 *R11* **Thetford-Mines** Québec, SE Canada *46°07′N 71°16′W*
113 *K17* **Theth** *var.* Thethi. Shkodër, N Albania *42°25′N 19°45′E*
Thethi *see* Theth
99 *L20* **Theux** Liège, E Belgium *50°33′N 05°48′E*
45 *V9* **The Valley** ○ (Anguilla) E Anguilla *18°13′N 63°00′W*
27 *N10* **The Village** Oklahoma, C USA *35°33′N 97°33′W*
The Volunteer State *see* Tennessee
25 *W10* **The Woodlands** Texas, SW USA *30°09′N 95°27′E*
Thiamis *see* Kalamás
Thian Shan *see* Tien Shan
Thibet *see* Xizang Zizhiqu
22 *J9* **Thibodaux** Louisiana, S USA *29°48′N 90°49′W*
29 *S3* **Thief Lake** ◎ Minnesota, N USA
29 *S3* **Thief River** ≈ Minnesota, C USA
29 *S3* **Thief River Falls** Minnesota, N USA *48°07′N 96°10′W*
Thièle *see* La Thielle
32 *G14* **Thielsen, Mount** ▲ Oregon, NW USA *43°09′N 122°04′W*
Thielt *see* Tielt
106 *G7* **Thiene** Veneto, NE Italy *45°43′N 11°29′E*
Thienen *see* Tienen
103 *P11* **Thiers** Puy-de-Dôme, C France *45°51′N 03°33′E*
76 *F11* **Thiès** W Senegal *14°49′N 16°52′W*
81 *I19* **Thika** Central, S Kenya *01°03′S 37°05′E*
Thikombia *see* Cikobia
151 *K18* **Thiladhunmathi Atoll** *var.* Tiladummati Atoll. *atoll* N Maldives
Thimbu *see* Thimphu
153 *T11* **Thimphu** *var.* Thimbu; *prev.* Tashi Chho Dzong. ● (Bhutan) W Bhutan *27°28′N 89°37′E*
92 *H2* **Thingeyri** Vestfirdhir, NW Iceland *65°52′N 23°28′W*
92 *I3* **Thingvellir** Sudhurland, SW Iceland *64°15′N 21°06′W*
187 *Q17* **Thio** Province Sud, C New Caledonia *21°37′S 166°13′E*
103 *T4* **Thionville** *Ger.* Diedenhofen. Moselle, NE France *49°22′N 06°11′E*
77 *O12* **Thiou** NW Burkina *13°42′N 02°34′W*
115 *K22* **Thíra** Santorini, Kykládes, Greece, Aegean Sea *36°25′N 25°26′E*
Thíra *see* Santoríni
115 *J22* **Thirasía** *island* Kykládes, Greece, Aegean Sea
97 *M16* **Thirsk** N England, United Kingdom *54°07′N 01°17′W*
14 *F12* **Thirty Thousand Islands** *island group* Ontario, S Canada
155 *G24* **Thiruvanathapuram** *var.* Tiruvantapuram, Trivandrum. *state capital* Kerala, SW India *08°30′N 76°57′E*
155 *H22* **Thiruvārūr** *var.* Tiruvarur. Tamil Nādu, SE India *10°46′N 79°39′E*
95 *F20* **Thisted** Viborg, NW Denmark *56°58′N 08°42′E*
Thistil Fjord *see* Thistilfjördhur
92 *L1* **Thistilfjördhur** *var.* Thistil Fjord. *fjord* NE Iceland
182 *G9* **Thistle Island** *island* South Australia
Thithia *see* Cicia
Thiukhaoluang Phrahang *see* Luang Prabang Range
115 *G18* **Thíva** *Eng.* Thebes; *prev.* Thívai. Stereá Ellás, C Greece *38°19′N 23°19′E*
Thívai *see* Thíva
102 *M12* **Thiviers** Dordogne, SW France *45°24′N 00°54′E*
92 *J4* **Thjórsá** ≈ C Iceland
9 *N10* **Thlewiaza** ≈ Nunavut, NE Canada
8 *L10* **Thoa** ≈ Northwest Territories, NW Canada
99 *G14* **Tholen** Zeeland, SW Netherlands *51°31′N 04°13′E*
99 *F14* **Tholen** *island* SW Netherlands
26 *L10* **Thomas** Oklahoma, C USA *35°44′N 98°45′W*
21 *T3* **Thomas** West Virginia, NE USA *39°09′N 79°28′W*
27 *U3* **Thomas Hill Reservoir** ⊠ Missouri, C USA
23 *S5* **Thomaston** Georgia, SE USA *32°53′N 84°19′W*
19 *R7* **Thomaston** Maine, NE USA *44°06′N 69°10′W*
25 *T12* **Thomaston** Texas, SW USA *28°56′N 97°07′W*
23 *O6* **Thomasville** Alabama, S USA *31°54′N 87°42′W*
23 *T8* **Thomasville** Georgia, SE USA *30°49′N 83°57′W*
21 *S9* **Thomasville** North Carolina, SE USA *35°52′N 80°04′W*
35 *N5* **Thomes Creek** ≈ California, W USA
11 *W12* **Thompson** Manitoba, C Canada *55°45′N 97°54′W*
29 *R4* **Thompson** North Dakota, N USA *47°45′N 97°07′W*
0 *F8* **Thompson** ≈ Alberta/British Columbia, SW Canada
33 *O8* **Thompson Falls** Montana, NW USA *47°36′N 115°20′W*
29 *Q10* **Thompson, Lake** ◎ South Dakota, N USA
34 *M3* **Thompson Peak** ▲ California, W USA *41°00′N 123°01′W*
27 *S2* **Thompson River** ≈ Missouri, C USA
185 *A22* **Thompson Sound** *sound* South Island, New Zealand
8 *J5* **Thomsen** ≈ Banks Island, Northwest Territories, NW Canada
23 *V4* **Thomson** Georgia, SE USA *33°28′N 82°30′W*
103 *T10* **Thonon-les-Bains** Haute-Savoie, E France *46°22′N 06°30′E*
103 *O15* **Thoré** *var.* Thore. ≈ S France
Thore *see* Thoré
37 *P11* **Thoreau** New Mexico, SW USA *35°24′N 108°13′W*
Thorenburg *see* Turda
92 *J3* **Thórisvatn** ◎ C Iceland
92 *P4* **Thor, Kapp** *headland* S Svalbard *76°25′N 25°01′E*
92 *I4* **Thorlákshöfn** Sudhurland, SW Iceland *63°52′N 21°24′W*
Thorn *see* Toruń
25 *T10* **Thorndale** Texas, SW USA *30°36′N 97°12′W*
14 *H10* **Thorne** Ontario, S Canada *46°38′N 79°04′W*
97 *J14* **Thornhill** S Scotland, United Kingdom *55°13′N 03°46′W*
25 *U8* **Thornton** Texas, SW USA *31°24′N 96°34′W*
Thornton Island *see* Millennium Island
14 *H16* **Thorold** Ontario, S Canada *43°07′N 79°15′W*
32 *I9* **Thorp** Washington, NW USA *47°03′N 120°40′W*
Thorshavn *see* Tórshavn
195 *S3* **Thorshavnheiane** *physical region* Antarctica
92 *L1* **Thórshöfn** Nordhurland Eystra, NE Iceland *66°09′N 15°18′W*
Thospitis *see* Van Gölü
167 *S14* **Thôt Nôt** Cần Thơ, S Vietnam *10°17′N 105°31′E*
102 *K8* **Thouars** Deux-Sèvres, W France *46°59′N 00°13′W*
153 *X14* **Thoubal** Manipur, NE India *24°40′N 94°00′E*
102 *K9* **Thouet** ≈ W France
Thoune *see* Thun
18 *H7* **Thousand Islands** *island* Canada/USA
35 *S15* **Thousand Oaks** California, W USA *34°10′N 118°50′W*
114 *L12* **Thrace** *cultural region* SE Europe
114 *J13* **Thracian Sea** *Gk.* Thrakikó Pélagos; *anc.* Thracium Mare. *sea* Greece/Turkey
Thracium Mare/Thrakikó Pélagos *see* Thracian Sea
Thrá Lí, Bá *see* Tralee Bay
33 *R11* **Three Forks** Montana, NW USA *45°53′N 111°34′W*
162 *M8* **Three Gorges Dam** *dam* Hubei, C China
160 *L9* **Three Gorges Reservoir** ⊠ C China
11 *Q16* **Three Hills** Alberta, SW Canada *51°43′N 113°15′W*
183 *N15* **Three Hummock Island** *island* Tasmania, SE Australia
184 *H1* **Three Kings Islands** *island group* N New Zealand
175 *P10* **Three Kings Rise** *undersea feature* W Pacific Ocean
77 *O18* **Three Points, Cape** *headland* S Ghana *04°43′N 02°03′W*
31 *P10* **Three Rivers** Michigan, N USA *41°56′N 85°37′W*
25 *S13* **Three Rivers** Texas, SW USA *28°27′N 98°10′W*
83 *G24* **Three Sisters** Northern Cape, SW South Africa *31°51′S 23°04′E*
32 *H13* **Three Sisters** ▲ Oregon, NW USA *44°08′N 121°46′W*
187 *N10* **Three Sisters Islands** *island group* SE Solomon Islands
155 *G22* **Thrissur** *var.* Trichūr. Kerala, SW India *10°32′N 76°14′E* *see also* Trichūr
25 *Q6* **Throckmorton** Texas, SW USA *33°11′N 99°12′W*
180 *M10* **Throssell, Lake** *salt lake* Western Australia
115 *K25* **Thryptís** *var.* Thrýptis. ▲ Kríti, Greece, E Mediterranean Sea *35°06′N 25°51′E*
167 *T13* **Thu Dâu Môt** *var.* Phu Cŭơng. Sông Be, S Vietnam *10°58′N 106°40′E*
167 *S6* **Thu Do** ✈ (Ha Nôi) Ha Nôi, N Vietnam *21°13′N 105°46′E*
99 *G21* **Thuin** Hainaut, S Belgium *50°21′N 04°18′E*
149 *Q12* **Thul** Sind, SE Pakistan *28°14′N 68°50′E*
Thule *see* Qaanaaq
83 *J18* **Thuli** *var.* Tuli. ≈ S Zimbabwe
Thumrayt *see* Thamarīt
108 *D9* **Thun** *Fr.* Thoune. Bern, W Switzerland *46°46′N 07°38′E*
12 *C12* **Thunder Bay** Ontario, S Canada *48°27′N 89°12′W*
30 *M1* **Thunder Bay** *lake bay* S Canada
31 *R6* **Thunder Bay** *lake bay* Michigan, N USA
31 *R6* **Thunder Bay River** ≈ Michigan, N USA
27 *N11* **Thunderbird, Lake** ⊠ Oklahoma, C USA
28 *L8* **Thunder Butte Creek** ≈ South Dakota, N USA
108 *E9* **Thuner See** ◎ C Switzerland
167 *N15* **Thung Song** *var.* Cha Mai. Nakhon Si Thammarat, SW Thailand *08°10′N 99°41′E*
108 *H7* **Thur** ≈ N Switzerland
108 *G6* **Thurgau** *Fr.* Thurgovie. ◈ *canton* NE Switzerland
Thurgovie *see* Thurgau
Thuringe *see* Thüringen
108 *J7* **Thüringen** Vorarlberg, W Austria *47°12′N 09°48′E*
101 *J17* **Thüringen** *Eng.* Thuringia, *Fr.* Thuringe. ◈ *state* C Germany
101 *J17* **Thüringer Wald** *Eng.* Thuringian Forest. ▲▲ C Germany
Thuringia *see* Thüringen
Thuringian Forest *see* Thüringer Wald
97 *D19* **Thurles** *Ir.* Durlas. S Ireland *52°41′N 07°49′W*
21 *W2* **Thurmont** Maryland, NE USA *39°36′N 77°22′W*
Thurø *see* Thurø By
95 *H24* **Thurø By** *var.* Thurø. Fyn, C Denmark *55°03′N 10°43′E*
14 *M12* **Thurso** Québec, SE Canada *45°36′N 75°13′W*
96 *J6* **Thurso** N Scotland, United Kingdom *58°35′N 03°32′W*
194 *I10* **Thurston Island** *island* Antarctica
108 *I9* **Thusis** Graubünden, S Switzerland *46°40′N 09°27′E*
Thýamis *see* Kalamás
95 *E21* **Thyborøn** *var.* Tyborøn. Ringkøbing, W Denmark *56°40′N 08°12′E*
195 *U3* **Thyer Glacier** *glacier* Antarctica
115 *L20* **Thýmaina** *island* Dodekánisa, Greece, Aegean Sea
83 *N15* **Thyolo** *var.* Cholo. Southern, S Malawi *16°03′S 35°11′E*
183 *U6* **Tia** New South Wales, SE Australia *31°14′S 151°51′E*
54 *H5* **Tía Juana** Zulia, NW Venezuela *10°18′N 71°24′W*
Tiancheng *see* Chongyang
160 *J14* **Tiandong** *var.* Pingma. Guangxi Zhuangzu Zizhiqu, S China *23°37′N 107°06′E*
161 *O3* **Tianjin** *var.* Tientsin. Tianjin Shi, E China *39°13′N 117°06′E*
Tianjin *see* Tianjin Shi
161 *P3* **Tianjin Shi** *var.* Jin, Tianjin, T'ien-ching, Tientsin. ◈ *municipality* E China
159 *S10* **Tianjun** *var.* Xinyuan. Qinghai, C China *37°16′N 99°03′E*
160 *J13* **Tianlin** *var.* Leli. Guangxi Zhuangzu Zizhiqu, S China *24°27′N 106°03′E*
Tian Shan *see* Tien Shan
159 *W11* **Tianshui** Gansu, C China *34°33′N 105°51′E*
150 *I7* **Tianshuihai** Xinjiang Uygur Zizhiqu, W China *35°17′N 79°30′E*
161 *S10* **Tiantai** Zhejiang, SE China *29°11′N 121°01′E*
160 *J14* **Tianyang** *var.* Tianzhou. Guangxi Zhuangzu Zizhiqu, S China *23°50′N 106°52′E*
Tianzhou *see* Tianyang
159 *U9* **Tianzhu** *var.* Huazangsi, Tianzhu Zangzu Zizhixian. Gansu, C China *37°01′N 103°04′E*
Tianzhu Zangzu Zizhixian *see* Tianzhu
191 *Q7* **Tiarei** Tahiti, W French Polynesia *17°32′S 149°20′W*
74 *J6* **Tiaret** *var.* Tihert. NW Algeria *35°20′N 01°20′E*
77 *N17* **Tiassalé** S Ivory Coast *05°54′N 04°50′W*
192 *I16* **Ti'avea** Upolu, SE Samoa *13°58′S 171°30′W*
Tiba *see* Chiba
60 *J11* **Tibagi** *var.* Tibaji. Paraná, S Brazil *24°29′S 50°29′W*
60 *J10* **Tibagi, Rio** *var.* Rio Tibají. ≈ S Brazil
Tibaji *see* Tibagi
Tibají, Rio *see* Tibagi, Rio
139 *Q9* **Tibal, Wādī** *dry watercourse* S Iraq
54 *G9* **Tibaná** Boyacá, C Colombia *05°19′N 73°25′W*
79 *F14* **Tibati** Adamaoua, N Cameroon *06°25′N 12°33′E*
76 *K15* **Tibé, Pic de** ▲ SE Guinea *08°39′N 08°58′W*
Tiber *see* Tevere, Italy
Tiber *see* Tivoli, Italy
Tiberias *see* Tverya
138 *G8* **Tiberias, Lake** *var.* Chinnereth, Sea of Bahr Tabariya, Sea of Galilee, *Ar.* Bahrat Tabariya, *Heb.* Yam Kinneret. ◎ N Israel
67 *Q5* **Tibesti** *var.* Tibesti Massif, *Ar.* Tibistī. ▲▲ N Africa
Tibesti Massif *see* Tibesti
Tibet *see* Xizang Zizhiqu
Tibetan Autonomous Region *see* Xizang Zizhiqu
Tibet, Plateau of *see* Qingzang Gaoyuan
Tībistī *see* Tibesti
14 *K7* **Tiblemont, Lac** ◎ Québec, SE Canada
139 *X9* **Ţīb, Nahr aţ** ≈ S Iraq
Tibnī *see* At Tibnī
182 *L4* **Tibooburra** New South Wales, SE Australia *29°24′S 142°01′E*
95 *L18* **Tibro** Västra Götaland, S Sweden *58°25′N 14°11′E*
40 *E5* **Tiburón, Isla** *var.* Isla del Tiburón. *island* NW Mexico
Tiburón, Isla del *see* Tiburón, Isla
23 *W14* **Tice** Florida, SE USA *26°40′N 81°49′W*
Tichau *see* Tychy
114 *L8* **Ticha, Yazovir** ◎ NE Bulgaria
76 *K9* **Tîchît** *var.* Tichitt. Tagant, C Mauritania *18°26′N 09°31′W*
Tichitt *see* Tîchît
108 *G11* **Ticino** *Fr./Ger.* Tessin. ◈ *canton* S Switzerland
106 *D8* **Ticino** ≈ Italy/Switzerland
108 *H11* **Ticino** *Ger.* Tessin. ≈ SW Switzerland
Ticinum *see* Pavia
41 *X12* **Ticul** Yucatán, SE Mexico *20°22′N 89°30′W*
95 *K18* **Tidaholm** Västra Götaland, S Sweden *58°12′N 13°55′E*
Tidjikdja *see* Tidjikja
76 *J8* **Tidjikja** *var.* Tidjikdja; *prev.* Fort-Cappolani. Tagant, C Mauritania *18°31′N 11°24′W*
Tidore *see* Soasiu
171 *R11* **Tidore, Pulau** *island* E Indonesia
Tîdra, Ile *see* Et Tîdra
77 *N16* **Tiébissou** *var.* Tiebissou. C Ivory Coast *07°10′N 05°10′W*
Tiebissou *see* Tiébissou
Tiefa *see* Diaobingshan
108 *I9* **Tiefencastel** Graubünden, S Switzerland *46°40′N 09°33′E*
Tiegenhof *see* Nowy Dwór Gdański
T'ieh-ling *see* Tieling
98 *K13* **Tiel** Gelderland, C Netherlands *51°53′N 05°26′E*
163 *W7* **Tieli** Heilongjiang, NE China *46°57′N 128°01′E*
163 *V11* **Tieling** *var.* T'ieh-ling. Liaoning, NE China *42°19′N 123°52′E*
152 *L4* **Tielongtan** China/India *35°10′N 79°32′E*
99 *D17* **Tielt** *var.* Thielt. West-Vlaanderen, W Belgium *51°00′N 03°20′E*
T'ien-ching *see* Tianjin Shi
99 *I18* **Tienen** *var.* Thienen, *Fr.* Tirlemont. Vlaams Brabant, C Belgium *50°48′N 04°56′E*
Tiên Giang, Sông *see* Mekong
147 *X9* **Tien Shan** *Chin.* Thian Shan, Tian Shan, T'ien Shan, *Rus.* Tyan'-Shan'. ▲▲ C Asia
Tientsin *see* Tianjin
167 *U6* **Tiên Yên** Quang Ninh, N Vietnam *21°19′N 107°24′E*
95 *O14* **Tierp** Uppsala, C Sweden *60°20′N 17°30′E*
62 *H7* **Tierra Amarilla** Atacama, N Chile *27°28′S 70°17′W*
37 *R9* **Tierra Amarilla** New Mexico, SW USA *36°42′N 106°31′W*
41 *R15* **Tierra Blanca** Veracruz-Llave, E Mexico *18°28′N 96°21′W*
41 *O16* **Tierra Colorada** Guerrero, S Mexico *17°10′N 99°30′W*
63 *J17* **Tierra Colorada, Bajo de la** *basin* SE Argentina
63 *I25* **Tierra del Fuego** *off.* Provincia de la Tierra del Fuego. ◈ *province* S Argentina
63 *J24* **Tierra del Fuego** *island* Argentina/Chile
Tierra del Fuego, Provincia de la *see* Tierra del Fuego
54 *D7* **Tierralta** Córdoba, NW Colombia *08°10′N 76°04′W*
104 *K9* **Tiétar** ≈ W Spain
60 *L10* **Tietê** São Paulo, S Brazil *23°04′S 47°41′W*
60 *J8* **Tietê, Rio** ≈ S Brazil
32 *I9* **Tieton** Washington, NW USA *46°41′N 120°43′W*
32 *J6* **Tiffany Mountain** ▲ Washington, NW USA *48°40′N 119°55′W*
31 *S12* **Tiffin** Ohio, N USA *41°06′N 83°10′W*
31 *Q11* **Tiffin River** ≈ Ohio, N USA
Tiflis *see* T'bilisi
23 *U7* **Tifton** Georgia, SE USA *31°27′N 83°31′W*
171 *R13* **Tifu** Pulau Buru, E Indonesia *03°46′S 126°35′E*
38 *L17* **Tigalda Island** *island* Aleutian Islands, Alaska, USA
115 *I15* **Tigáni, Akrotírio** *headland* Límnos, E Greece *39°50′N 25°03′E*
169 *V6* **Tiga Tarok** Sabah, East Malaysia *06°57′N 117°07′E*
117 *O10* **Tighina** *Rus.* Bendery; *prev.* Bender. E Moldova *46°51′N 29°28′E*
145 *X9* **Tigiretskiy Khrebet** ▲▲ E Kazakhstan
79 *F14* **Tignère** Adamaoua, N Cameroon *07°24′N 12°35′E*
13 *P14* **Tignish** Prince Edward Island, SE Canada *46°58′N 64°03′W*
Tigranocerta *see* Siirt
80 *I11* **Tigray** ◈ *federal region* N Ethiopia
41 *O11* **Tigre, Cerro del** ▲ C Mexico *23°06′N 99°13′W*
56 *F8* **Tigre, Río** ≈ N Peru
139 *X10* **Tigris** *Ar.* Dijlah, *Turk.* Dicle. ≈ Iraq/Turkey
76 *G9* **Tiguent** Trarza, SW Mauritania *17°15′N 16°00′W*
74 *M10* **Tiguentourine** E Algeria *27°59′N 09°16′E*
77 *V10* **Tiguidit, Falaise de** *ridge* C Niger
141 *N13* **Tihāmah** *var.* Tehama. *plain* Saudi Arabia/Yemen
Tihert *see* Tiaret
Ti-hua/Tihwa *see* Ürümqi
41 *Q13* **Tihuatlán** Veracruz-Llave, E Mexico *20°44′N 97°30′W*
40 *B1* **Tijuana** Baja California Norte, NW Mexico *32°32′N 117°01′W*
42 *E2* **Tikal** Petén, N Guatemala *17°11′N 89°36′W*
154 *I9* **Tīkamgarh** *prev.* Tehri. Madhya Pradesh, C India *24°44′N 78°50′E*
158 *L7* **Tikanlik** Xinjiang Uygur Zizhiqu, NW China *40°34′N 87°37′E*
77 *P12* **Tikaré** N Burkina *13°16′N 01°39′W*
39 *O12* **Tikchik Lakes** *lakes* Alaska, USA
191 *T9* **Tikehau** *atoll* Îles Tuamotu, C French Polynesia
191 *V9* **Tikei** *island* Îles Tuamotu, C French Polynesia
126 *L13* **Tikhoretsk** Krasnodarskiy Kray, SW Russian Federation *45°51′N 40°07′E*
124 *I13* **Tikhvin** Leningradskaya Oblast', NW Russian Federation *59°37′N 33°30′E*
193 *P9* **Tiki Basin** *undersea feature* S Pacific Ocean
76 *K13* **Tikinsso** ≈ NE Guinea
184 *Q8* **Tikitiki** Gisborne, North Island, New Zealand *37°49′S 178°23′E*
79 *D16* **Tiko** Sud-Ouest, SW Cameroon *04°02′N 09°19′E*
139 *S6* **Tikrīt** *var.* Tekrit. Şalāḩ ad Dīn, N Iraq *34°36′N 43°42′E*
124 *I8* **Tiksha** Respublika Kareliya, NW Russian Federation *64°07′N 32°31′E*
124 *I6* **Tikshozero, Ozero** ◎ NW Russian Federation
123 *P7* **Tiksi** Respublika Sakha (Yakutiya), NE Russian Federation *71°40′N 128°47′E*
Tiladummati Atoll *see* Thiladhunmathi Atoll
42 *A6* **Tilapa** San Marcos, SW Guatemala *14°31′N 92°11′W*
42 *L13* **Tilarán** Guanacaste, NW Costa Rica *10°28′N 84°57′W*
99 *J14* **Tilburg** Noord-Brabant, S Netherlands *51°34′N 05°05′E*
14 *D17* **Tilbury** Ontario, S Canada *42°15′N 82°26′W*
182 *K4* **Tilcha** South Australia *29°37′S 140°52′E*
Tilcha Creek *see* Callabonna Creek
29 *Q14* **Tilden** Nebraska, C USA *42°03′N 97°49′W*
25 *R13* **Tilden** Texas, SW USA *28°27′N 98°43′W*
14 *H10* **Tilden Lake** Ontario, S Canada *46°35′N 79°36′W*
116 *G9* **Tileagd** *Hung.* Mezőtelegd. Bihor, W Romania *47°03′N 22°11′E*
77 *Q8* **Tîlemsi, Vallée de** ≈ C Mali
123 *V8* **Tilichiki** Koryakskiy Avtonomnyy Okrug, E Russian Federation *60°25′N 165°55′E*
Tiligul *see* Tilihul
Tiligul'skiy Liman *see* Tilihul's'kyy Lyman
117 *P9* **Tilihul** *Rus.* Tiligul. ≈ SW Ukraine
117 *P10* **Tilihul's'kyy Lyman** *Rus.* Tiligul'skiy Liman. ◎ S Ukraine
Tilimsen *see* Tlemcen
Tilio Martius *see* Toulon
77 *R11* **Tillabéri** *var.* Tillabéry. Tillabéri, W Niger *14°13′N 01°27′E*
77 *R11* **Tillabéri** ◈ *department* SW Niger
Tillabéry *see* Tillabéri
32 *F11* **Tillamook** Oregon, NW USA *45°28′N 123°50′W*
32 *E11* **Tillamook Bay** *inlet* Oregon, NW USA
151 *Q22* **Tillanchāng Dwīp** *island* Nicobar Islands, India, NE Indian Ocean
95 *N15* **Tillberga** Västmanland, C Sweden *59°41′N 16°37′E*
Tillenberg *see* Dyleń
21 *S10* **Tillery, Lake** ⊠ North Carolina, SE USA
77 *T10* **Tillia** Tahoua, W Niger *16°13′N 04°51′E*
23 *N8* **Tillmans Corner** Alabama, S USA *30°35′N 88°10′W*
14 *F17* **Tillsonburg** Ontario, S Canada *42°53′N 80°44′W*
115 *N22* **Tílos** *island* Dodekánisa, Greece, Aegean Sea
183 *N5* **Tilpa** New South Wales, SE Australia *30°56′S 144°24′E*
Tilsit *see* Sovetsk
31 *N13* **Tilton** Illinois, N USA *40°06′N 87°39′W*
126 *K7* **Tim** Kurskaya Oblast', W Russian Federation *51°39′N 37°11′E*
54 *D12* **Timaná** Huila, S Colombia *01°58′N 75°55′W*
Timan Ridge *see* Timanskiy Kryazh
125 *Q6* **Timanskiy Kryazh** *Eng.* Timan Ridge. *ridge* NW Russian Federation
185 *G20* **Timaru** Canterbury, South Island, New Zealand *44°23′S 171°15′E*
127 *S6* **Timashevo** Samarskaya Oblast', W Russian Federation *53°22′N 51°13′E*
126 *K13* **Timashevsk** Krasnodarskiy Kray, SW Russian Federation *45°37′N 38°57′E*
Timbaki/Timbákion *see* Tympáki
22 *K10* **Timbalier Bay** *bay* Louisiana, S USA
22 *K11* **Timbalier Island** *island* Louisiana, S USA
76 *L10* **Timbedgha** *var.* Timbédra. Hodh ech Chargui, SE Mauritania *16°17′N 08°14′W*
Timbédra *see* Timbedgha
32 *G10* **Timber** Oregon, NW USA *45°42′N 123°19′W*
181 *O3* **Timber Creek** Northern Territory, N Australia *15°35′S 130°21′E*
28 *M8* **Timber Lake** South Dakota, N USA *45°25′N 101°01′W*
54 *D12* **Timbío** Cauca, SW Colombia *02°20′N 76°40′W*
54 *C12* **Timbiquí** Cauca, SW Colombia *02°43′N 77°45′W*
83 *O17* **Timbue, Ponta** *headland* C Mozambique *18°49′S 36°22′E*
Timbuktu *see* Tombouctou
169 *W8* **Timbun Mata, Pulau** *island* E Malaysia
77 *P8* **Timétrine** *var.* Ti-n-Kâr. *oasis* C Mali
Timfi *see* Týmfi
Timfristos *see* Tymfristós
77 *V9* **Tîmia** Agadez, C Niger *18°07′N 08°49′E*
171 *X14* **Timika** Papua, E Indonesia *04°39′S 137°15′E*
74 *I9* **Timimoun** C Algeria *29°18′N 00°21′E*
Timiris, Cap *see* Timirist, Râs
76 *F8* **Timirist, Râs** *var.* Cap Timiris. *headland* NW Mauritania *19°18′N 16°28′W*
145 *O7* **Timiryazevo** Severnyy Kazakhstan, N Kazakhstan *53°45′N 66°33′E*
116 *E11* **Timiş** ◈ *county* SW Romania
14 *H9* **Timiskaming, Lake** *Fr.* Lac Témiscamingue. ◎ Ontario/Québec, SE Canada
116 *E11* **Timişoara** *Ger.* Temeschwar, Temeswar, *Hung.* Temesvár; *prev.* Temeschburg. Timiş, W Romania *45°46′N 21°17′E*
116 *E11* **Timisoara** ✈ Timiş, SW Romania *45°50′N 21°21′E*
Timkovichi *see* Tsimkavichy
77 *U8* **Ti-m-Meghsoï** ≈ NW Niger
100 *K8* **Timmerdorfer Strand** Schleswig-Holstein, N Germany *53°59′N 10°50′E*
14 *F7* **Timmins** Ontario, S Canada *48°09′N 80°01′W*
21 *S12* **Timmonsville** South Carolina, SE USA *34°07′N 79°56′W*
30 *K5* **Timms Hill** ▲ Wisconsin, N USA *45°27′N 90°12′W*
112 *P12* **Timok** ≈ E Serbia
58 *N13* **Timon** Maranhão, E Brazil *05°08′S 42°52′W*
171 *Q17* **Timor Sea** *sea* E Indian Ocean
Timor Timur *see* East Timor
Timor Trench *see* Timor Trough
192 *G8* **Timor Trough** *var.* Timor Trench. *undersea feature* NE Timor Sea
61 *A21* **Timote** Buenos Aires, E Argentina *35°22′S 62°13′W*
54 *I6* **Timotes** Mérida, NW Venezuela *08°57′N 70°46′W*
25 *X8* **Timpson** Texas, SW USA *31°54′N 94°24′W*
123 *Q11* **Timpton** ≈ NE Russian Federation
93 *H17* **Timrå** Västernorrland, C Sweden *62°29′N 17°20′E*
20 *J10* **Tims Ford Lake** ⊠ Tennessee, S USA
168 *L7* **Timur, Banjaran** ▲▲ Peninsular Malaysia
149 *T4* **Timurgara** North-West Frontier Province, N Pakistan *34°50′N 71°55′E*
171 *Q8* **Tinaca Point** *headland* Mindanao, S Philippines *05°35′N 125°18′E*
54 *K5* **Tinaco** Cojedes, N Venezuela *09°44′N 68°28′W*
64 *Q11* **Tinajo** Lanzarote, Islas Canarias, Spain, NE Atlantic Ocean *29°03′N 13°41′W*
187 *P10* **Tinakula** *island* Santa Cruz Islands, E Solomon Islands
54 *K5* **Tinaquillo** Cojedes, N Venezuela *09°57′N 68°20′W*
116 *F10* **Tinca** *Hung.* Tenke. Bihor, W Romania *46°46′N 21°58′E*
155 *J20* **Tindivanam** Tamil Nādu, SE India *12°15′N 79°41′E*
74 *E9* **Tindouf** W Algeria *27°43′N 08°09′W*
74 *E9* **Tindouf, Sebkha de** *salt lake* W Algeria
104 *J2* **Tineo** Asturias, N Spain *43°20′N 06°25′W*
77 *R9* **Ti-n-Essako** Kidal, E Mali *18°30′N 02°27′E*
183 *T5* **Tingha** New South Wales, SE Australia *29°56′S 151°13′E*
Tingis *see* Tanger
Tinglett *see* Tinglev
95 *F24* **Tinglev** *Ger.* Tinglett. Sønderjylland, SW Denmark *54°57′N 09°15′E*
56 *E12* **Tingo María** Huánuco, C Peru *09°10′S 76°00′W*
Tingréla *see* Tengréla
158 *K16* **Tingri** *var.* Xêgar. Xizang Zizhiqu, W China *28°40′N 87°04′E*
95 *M21* **Tingsryd** Kronoberg, S Sweden *56°30′N 15°E*
95 *P19* **Tingstäde** Gotland, SE Sweden *57°45′N 18°36′E*
62 *H12* **Tinguiririca, Volcán** ⛰ C Chile *34°52′S 70°24′W*
94 *F9* **Tingvoll** Møre og Romsdal, S Norway *62°55′N 08°13′E*
188 *K8* **Tinian** *island* S Northern Mariana Islands
Ti-n-Kâr *see* Timétrine
Tinnevelly *see* Tirunelveli
95 *G15* **Tinnoset** Telemark, S Norway *59°43′N 09°03′E*
95 *F15* **Tinnsjø** ◎ S Norway
Tino *see* Chino
115 *J20* **Tínos** Tínos, Kykládes, Greece, Aegean Sea *37°33′N 25°08′E*
115 *J20* **Tínos** *anc.* Tenos. *island* Kykládes, Greece, Aegean Sea
153 *R14* **Tinpahar** Jhārkhand, NE India *25°00′N 87°43′E*
153 *X11* **Tinsukia** Assam, NE India *27°28′N 95°20′E*
76 *K10* **Tîntâne** Hodh el Gharbi, S Mauritania *16°25′N 10°08′W*
62 *L7* **Tintina** Santiago del Estero, N Argentina *27°00′S 62°45′W*
182 *K10* **Tintinara** South Australia *35°54′S 140°04′E*
104 *I14* **Tinto** ≈ SW Spain
77 *S8* **Ti-n-Zaouâtene** Kidal, NE Mali *19°56′N 02°45′E*
Tiobraid Árann *see* Tipperary
28 *K3* **Tioga** North Dakota, N USA *48°24′N 102°56′W*
18 *G12* **Tioga** Pennsylvania, NE USA *41°54′N 77°07′W*
25 *T5* **Tioga** Texas, SW USA *33°28′N 96°55′W*
35 *Q8* **Tioga Pass** *pass* California, W USA
18 *G12* **Tioga River** ≈ New York/Pennsylvania, NE USA
Tioman Island *see* Tioman, Pulau
168 *M9* **Tioman, Pulau** *var.* Tioman Island. *island* Peninsular Malaysia
18 *C12* **Tionesta** Pennsylvania, NE USA *41°31′N 79°30′W*
18 *D12* **Tionesta Creek** ≈ Pennsylvania, NE USA
168 *J13* **Tiop** Pulau Pagai Selatan, W Indonesia *03°12′S 100°21′E*
18 *H11* **Tioughnioga River** ≈ New York, NE USA
74 *J5* **Tipasa** *var.* Tipaza. N Algeria *36°35′N 02°27′E*
Tipaza *see* Tipasa
42 *J10* **Tipitapa** Managua, W Nicaragua *12°08′N 86°04′W*
31 *R13* **Tipp City** Ohio, N USA *39°57′N 84°10′W*
31 *O12* **Tippecanoe River** ≈ Indiana, N USA
97 *D20* **Tipperary** *Ir.* Tiobraid Árann. S Ireland *52°29′N 08°10′W*
97 *D19* **Tipperary** *Ir.* Tiobraid Árann. *cultural region* S Ireland
35 *R12* **Tipton** California, W USA *36°02′N 119°19′W*
31 *P13* **Tipton** Indiana, N USA *40°19′N 86°00′W*
29 *Y14* **Tipton** Iowa, C USA *41°46′N 91°07′W*
27 *U5* **Tipton** Missouri, C USA *38°39′N 92°46′W*
36 *I10* **Tipton, Mount** ▲ Arizona, SW USA *35°32′N 114°11′W*
20 *F8* **Tiptonville** Tennessee, S USA *36°21′N 89°30′W*
12 *E12* **Tip Top Mountain** ▲ Ontario, S Canada *48°18′N 86°06′W*
155 *G19* **Tiptūr** Karnātaka, W India *13°17′N 76°31′E*
Tiquisate *see* Pueblo Nuevo Tiquisate
58 *L13* **Tiracambu, Serra do** ▲▲ E Brazil
Tirana *see* Tiranë
113 *K19* **Tirana Rinas** ✈ Durrës, W Albania *41°25′N 19°41′E*
113 *L20* **Tiranë** *var.* Tirana. ● (Albania) Tiranë, C Albania *41°20′N 19°50′E*
113 *K20* **Tiranë** ◈ *district* W Albania
140 *I5* **Tirān, Jazīrat** *island* Egypt/Saudi Arabia
106 *F6* **Tirano** Lombardia, N Italy *46°13′N 10°10′E*
182 *I2* **Tirari Desert** *desert* South Australia
117 *O10* **Tiraspol** *Rus.* Tiraspol'. E Moldova *46°50′N 29°35′E*
Tiraspol' *see* Tiraspol
184 *M8* **Tirau** Waikato, North Island, New Zealand *37°59′S 175°44′E*
136 *C14* **Tire** İzmir, SW Turkey *38°04′N 27°45′E*
137 *O11* **Tirebolu** Giresun, N Turkey *41°01′N 38°49′E*
96 *F11* **Tiree** *island* W Scotland, United Kingdom
Tîrgovişte *see* Târgovişte
Tîrgu *see* Târgu Cărbuneşti
Tîrgu Bujor *see* Târgu Bujor
Tîrgu Frumos *see* Târgu Frumos
Tîrgu Jiu *see* Targu Jiu
Tîrgu Lăpuş *see* Târgu Lăpuş
Tîrgu Mures *see* Târgu Mureş
Tîrgu-Neamţ *see* Târgu-Neamţ
Tîrgu Ocna *see* Târgu Ocna
Tîrgu Secuiesc *see* Târgu Secuiesc
149 *T3* **Tirich Mīr** ▲ NW Pakistan *36°12′N 71°51′E*
76 *J5* **Tiris Zemmour** ◈ *region* N Mauritania
Tirlemont *see* Tienen
127 *W5* **Tirlyanskiy** Respublika Bashkortostan, W Russian Federation *54°09′N 58°32′E*
Tîrnava Mare *see* Târnava Mare
Tîrnava Mică *see* Târnava Mică
Tîrnăveni *see* Târnăveni
Tírnavos *see* Týrnavos
Tirnovo *see* Veliko Tŭrnovo
154 *J11* **Tirodi** Madhya Pradesh, C India *21°40′N 79°44′E*
108 *K8* **Tirol** *off.* Land Tirol, *var.* Tyrol, *It.* Tirolo. ◈ *state* W Austria
Tirol, Land *see* Tirol
Tirolo *see* Tirol
Tirreno, Mare *see* Tyrrhenian Sea
107 *B19* **Tirso** ≈ Sardegna, Italy, C Mediterranean Sea
95 *H22* **Tirstrup** ✈ (Århus) Århus, C Denmark *56°17′N 10°36′E*
155 *I21* **Tiruchchirāppalli** *prev.* Trichinopoly. Tamil Nādu, SE India *10°50′N 78°43′E*
155 *H23* **Tirunelveli** *var.* Tinnevelly. Tamil Nādu, SE India *08°45′N 77°43′E*
155 *J19* **Tirupati** Andhra Pradesh, E India *13°39′N 79°25′E*
155 *I20* **Tiruppattūr** Tamil Nādu, SE India *12°28′N 78°31′E*
155 *H21* **Tiruppur** Tamil Nādu, SW India *11°05′N 77°20′E*
155 *J20* **Tiruvallūr** *var.* Tirvellore. Tamil Nādu, SE India *13°08′N 79°54′E*
Tiruvantapuram *see* Thiruvanathapuram/Trivandrum
Tiruvarur *see* Thiruvārūr
155 *I20* **Tiruyannāmalai** Tamil Nādu, SE India *12°13′N 79°07′E*
Tirvellore *see* Tiruvallūr
112 *L10* **Tisa** *Ger.* Theiss, *Hung.* Tisza, *Rus.* Tissa, *Ukr.* Tysa. ≈ SE Europe *see also* Tisza

◆ Country
● Country Capital
◇ Dependent Territory
○ Dependent Territory Capital
◈ Administrative Regions
✈ International Airport
▲ Mountain
▲▲ Mountain Range
⛰ Volcano
≈ River
◎ Lake
⊠ Reservoir

TISA – TORRINGTON

Tisa *see* Tisza
Tischnowitz *see* Tišnov
11 U14 **Tisdale** Saskatchewan, S Canada 52°51′N 104°01′W
27 O13 **Tishomingo** Oklahoma, C USA 34°15′N 96°41′W
95 M17 **Tisnaren** ◎ S Sweden
111 F18 **Tišnov** *Ger.* Tischnowitz. Jihomoravský Kraj, SE Czech Republic 49°22′N 16°24′E
Tissa *see* Tisa/Tisza
74 J6 **Tissemsilt** N Algeria 35°37′N 01°48′E
153 S12 **Tista** ≈ NE India
112 L8 **Tisza** *Ger.* Theiss, *Rom./Slvn./SCr.* Tisa, *Rus.* Tissa, *Ukr.* Tysa. ≈ SE Europe *see also* Tisa
Tisza *see* Tisa
111 L23 **Tiszaföldvár** Jász-Nagykun-Szolnok, E Hungary 47°00′N 20°16′E
111 M22 **Tiszafüred** Jász-Nagykun-Szolnok, E Hungary 47°38′N 20°45′E
111 L23 **Tiszakécske** Bács-Kiskun, C Hungary 46°56′N 20°04′E
111 M21 **Tiszaújváros** *prev.* Leninváros. Borsod-Abaúj-Zemplén, NE Hungary 47°56′N 21°03′E
111 N21 **Tiszavasvári** Szabolcs-Szatmár-Bereg, NE Hungary 47°56′N 21°21′E
57 I17 **Titicaca, Lake** ◎ Bolivia/Peru
190 H17 **Titikaveka** Rarotonga, S Cook Islands 21°16′S 159°45′W
154 M13 **Titilāgarh** *var.* Titlagarh. Orissa, E India 20°18′N 83°09′E
168 K8 **Titiwangsa, Banjaran** ▲▲ Peninsular Malaysia
Titlagarh *see* Titilāgarh
Titograd *see* Podgorica
Titose *see* Chitose
Titova Mitrovica *see* Mitrovicë
Titovo Užice *see* Užice
113 M18 **Titov Vrv** ▲ NW FYR Macedonia 41°58′N 20°49′E
94 F7 **Titran** Sør-Trøndelag, S Norway 63°40′N 08°20′E
31 Q8 **Tittabawassee River** ≈ Michigan, N USA
116 J13 **Titu** Dâmboviţa, S Romania 44°40′N 25°32′E
79 M16 **Titule** Orientale, N Dem. Rep. Congo 03°20′N 25°23′E
23 X11 **Titusville** Florida, SE USA 28°37′N 80°50′W
18 C12 **Titusville** Pennsylvania, NE USA 41°36′N 79°39′W
76 G11 **Tivaouane** W Senegal 14°59′N 16°50′W
113 I17 **Tivat** SW Montenegro 42°25′N 18°43′E
14 E14 **Tiverton** Ontario, S Canada 44°15′N 81°31′W
97 J23 **Tiverton** SW England, United Kingdom 50°54′N 03°30′W
19 O12 **Tiverton** Rhode Island, NE USA 41°38′N 71°10′W
107 I15 **Tivoli** *anc.* Tiber. Lazio, C Italy 41°58′N 12°45′E
25 U13 **Tivoli** Texas, SW USA 28°26′N 96°54′W
141 Z8 **Ţīwī** NE Oman 22°43′N 59°20′E
41 Y11 **Tizimín** Yucatán, SE Mexico 21°10′N 88°09′W
74 K5 **Tizi Ouzou** *var.* Tizi-Ouzou. N Algeria 36°44′N 04°05′E
Tizi-Ouzou *see* Tizi Ouzou
74 D8 **Tiznit** SW Morocco 29°43′N 09°39′W
95 F23 **Tjæreborg** Ribe, W Denmark 55°28′N 08°35′E
113 I14 **Tjentište** Republika Srpska, SE Bosnia and Herzegovina 43°23′N 18°42′E
98 L7 **Tjeukemeer** ◎ N Netherlands
Tjiamis *see* Ciamis
Tjiandjoer *see* Cianjur
Tjilatjap *see* Cilacap
Tjirebon *see* Cirebon
95 I18 **Tjörn** *island* S Sweden
92 O3 **Tjuvfjorden** *fjord* S Svalbard
Tkvarcheli *see* Tqvarch'eli
40 L8 **Tlahualillo** Durango, N Mexico 26°06′N 103°25′W
41 P14 **Tlalnepantla** México, C Mexico 19°34′N 99°12′W
41 Q13 **Tlapacoyán** Veracruz-Llave, E Mexico 19°58′N 97°13′W
41 P16 **Tlapa de Comonfort** Guerrero, S Mexico 17°33′N 98°33′W
40 L13 **Tlaquepaque** Jalisco, C Mexico 20°36′N 103°19′W
Tlascala *see* Tlaxcala
41 P14 **Tlaxcala** *var.* Tlascala, Tlaxcala de Xicohténcatl. Tlaxcala, C Mexico 19°17′N 98°16′W
41 P14 **Tlaxcala** ◐ *state* S Mexico
Tlaxcala de Xicohténcatl *see* Tlaxcala
41 P14 **Tlaxco** *var.* Tlaxco de Morelos. Tlaxcala, S Mexico 19°38′N 98°06′W
Tlaxco de Morelos *see* Tlaxco
41 Q16 **Tlaxiaco** *var.* Santa María Asunción Tlaxiaco. Oaxaca, S Mexico 17°18′N 97°42′W
74 I6 **Tlemcen** *var.* Tilimsen, Tlemsen. NW Algeria 34°53′N 01°21′W
Tlemsen *see* Tlemcen
138 L4 **Tlété Ouâte Rharbi, Jebel** ▲ N Syria
116 J7 **Tlumach** Ivano-Frankivs'ka Oblast', W Ukraine 48°53′N 25°00′E
127 P17 **Tlyarata** Respublika Dagestan, SW Russian Federation 42°10′N 46°30′E
116 K10 **Toaca, Vârful** *prev.* Vîrful Toaca. ▲ NE Romania 46°58′N 25°55′E
Toaca, Vîrful *see* Toaca, Vârful
187 R13 **Toak** Ambrym, C Vanuatu 16°21′S 168°16′E
172 J4 **Toamasina** *var.* Tamatave. Toamasina, E Madagascar 18°10′S 49°23′E
172 J4 **Toamasina** ◐ *province* E Madagascar
172 J4 **Toamasina** ✈ Toamasina, E Madagascar 18°10′S 49°23′E
21 X6 **Toano** Virginia, NE USA 37°22′N 76°46′W
191 U10 **Toau** *atoll* Îles Tuamotu, C French Polynesia
45 T6 **Toa Vaca, Embalse** ▨ C Puerto Rico
62 K13 **Toay** La Pampa, C Argentina 36°43′S 64°22′W
159 R14 **Toba** Xizang Zizhiqu, W China 31°17′N 97°37′E
164 K14 **Toba** Mie, Honshū, SW Japan 34°29′N 136°51′E
168 I9 **Toba, Danau** ◎ Sumatera, W Indonesia
45 Y16 **Tobago** *island* NE Trinidad and Tobago
149 Q9 **Toba Kākar Range** ▲▲ NW Pakistan
105 Q12 **Tobarra** Castilla-La Mancha, C Spain 38°36′N 01°41′W
149 U9 **Toba Tek Singh** Punjab, E Pakistan 30°54′N 72°30′E
171 R11 **Tobelo** Pulau Halmahera, E Indonesia 01°45′N 127°59′E
14 E12 **Tobermory** Ontario, S Canada 45°15′N 81°39′W
96 G10 **Tobermory** W Scotland, United Kingdom 56°37′N 06°12′W
165 S4 **Tōbetsu** Hokkaidō, NE Japan 43°12′N 141°28′E
180 M6 **Tobin Lake** ◎ Western Australia
11 U14 **Tobin Lake** ◎ Saskatchewan, C Canada
35 T4 **Tobin, Mount** ▲ Nevada, W USA 40°25′N 117°28′W
165 O9 **Tobi-shima** *island* C Japan
169 N13 **Toboali** Pulau Bangka, W Indonesia 03°00′S 106°30′E
144 M8 **Tobol** *Kaz.* Tobyl. Kustanay, N Kazakhstan 52°42′N 62°36′E
144 L8 **Tobol** *Kaz.* Tobyl. ≈ Kazakhstan/Russian Federation
122 H11 **Tobol'sk** Tyumenskaya Oblast', C Russian Federation 58°15′N 68°12′E
Tobruch/Tobruk *see* Ţubruq
125 R3 **Tobseda** Nenetskiy Avtonomnyy Okrug, NW Russian Federation 68°37′N 52°24′E
Tobyl *see* Tobol
125 Q6 **Tobysh** ≈ NW Russian Federation
54 F10 **Tocaima** Cundinamarca, C Colombia 04°30′N 74°38′W
59 K16 **Tocantins** *off.* Estado do Tocantins. ◐ *state* C Brazil
Tocantins, Estado do *see* Tocantins
59 K15 **Tocantins, Rio** ≈ N Brazil
23 T2 **Toccoa** Georgia, SE USA 34°34′N 83°19′W
165 O12 **Tochigi** *off.* Tochigi-ken, *var.* Totigi. ◐ *prefecture* Honshū, S Japan
Tochigi-ken *see* Tochigi
165 O11 **Tochio** *var.* Totio. Niigata, Honshū, C Japan 37°27′N 139°00′E
95 I15 **Töcksfors** Värmland, C Sweden 59°30′N 11°49′E
42 J5 **Tocoa** Colón, N Honduras 15°40′N 86°01′W
62 H4 **Tocopilla** Antofagasta, N Chile 22°06′S 70°08′W
62 I4 **Tocorpuri, Cerro de** ▲ Bolivia/Chile 22°26′S 67°53′W
183 O10 **Tocumwal** New South Wales, SE Australia 35°53′S 145°35′E
54 K4 **Tocuyo de La Costa** Falcón, NW Venezuela 11°04′N 68°23′W
152 H13 **Toda Rāisingh** Rājasthān, N India 26°02′N 75°35′E
106 H13 **Todi** Umbria, C Italy 42°47′N 12°25′E
108 G9 **Tödi** ▲ NE Switzerland 46°52′N 08°53′E
171 T12 **Todlo** Papua, E Indonesia 0°46′S 130°50′E
165 S9 **Todoga-saki** *headland* Honshū, C Japan 39°33′N 142°02′E
59 P17 **Todos os Santos, Baía de** *bay* E Brazil
40 F10 **Todos Santos** Baja California Sur, NW Mexico 23°28′N 110°14′W
40 B2 **Todos Santos, Bahía de** *bay* NW Mexico
Toeban *see* Tuban
Toekang Besi Eilanden *see* Tukangbesi, Kepulauan
Toeloengagoeng *see* Tulungagung
Tōen *see* T'aoyüan
185 D25 **Toetoes Bay** *bay* South Island, New Zealand
11 Q14 **Tofield** Alberta, SW Canada 53°22′N 112°39′W
10 K17 **Tofino** Vancouver Island, British Columbia, SW Canada 49°05′N 125°51′W
189 X17 **Tofol** Kosrae, E Micronesia
95 J20 **Tofta** Halland, S Sweden 57°10′N 12°19′E
95 H15 **Tofte** Buskerud, S Norway 59°31′N 10°33′E
95 F24 **Toftlund** Sønderjylland, SW Denmark 55°12′N 09°04′E
193 X15 **Tofua** *island* Ha'apai Group, C Tonga
187 Q12 **Toga** *island* Torres Islands, N Vanuatu
80 N13 **Togdheer** *off.* Gobolka Togdheer. ◐ *region* NW Somalia
Togdheer, Gobolka *see* Togdheer
Toghyzaq *see* Toguzak
164 L11 **Togi** Ishikawa, Honshū, SW Japan 37°06′N 136°44′E
39 N13 **Togiak** Alaska, USA 59°03′N 160°31′W
171 O11 **Togian, Kepulauan** *island group* C Indonesia
77 Q15 **Togo** *off.* Togolese Republic; *prev.* French Togoland. ◆ *republic* W Africa
Togolese Republic *see* Togo
162 F8 **Tögrög** Govĭ-Altay, SW Mongolia 45°51′N 95°04′E
162 F8 **Tögrög** *var.* Hoolt. Övörhangay, C Mongolia 45°31′N 103°06′E
Tögrög *see* Manhan
159 N12 **Togton He** *var.* Tuotuo He. ≈ C China
Togton Heyan *see* Tanggulashan
144 L7 **Toguzak** *Kaz.* Toghyzaq. ≈ Kazakhstan/Russian Federation
37 P10 **Tohatchi** New Mexico, SW USA 35°51′N 108°45′W
191 O7 **Tohiea, Mont** ⛰ Moorea, W French Polynesia 17°33′S 149°48′W
137 N14 **Tohma Çayı** ≈ C Turkey
93 O17 **Tohmajärvi** Itä-Suomi, SE Finland 62°12′N 30°19′E
93 L16 **Toholampi** Länsi-Suomi, W Finland 63°46′N 24°15′E
Töhöm *see* Mandah
23 X12 **Tohopekaliga, Lake** ◎ Florida, SE USA
164 M14 **Toi** Shizuoka, Honshū, S Japan 34°55′N 138°45′E
190 B15 **Toi** N Niue 18°57′S 169°51′W
93 L19 **Toijala** Länsi-Suomi, SW Finland 61°09′N 23°51′E
171 P12 **Toima** Sulawesi, N Indonesia 0°48′S 122°21′E
164 D17 **Toi-misaki** Kyūshū, SW Japan
171 Q17 **Toineke** Timor, S Indonesia 10°06′S 124°22′E
Toirc, Inis *see* Inishturk
35 U6 **Toiyabe Range** ▲▲ Nevada, W USA
Tojikiston, Jumhurii *see* Tajikistan
147 R12 **Tojikobod** *Rus.* Tadzhikabad. C Tajikistan 39°08′N 70°54′E
164 G12 **Tōjō** Hiroshima, Honshū, SW Japan 34°54′N 133°15′E
39 T10 **Tok** Alaska, USA 63°20′N 142°59′W
164 K13 **Tōkai** Aichi, Honshū, SW Japan 35°01′N 136°51′E
111 N21 **Tokaj** Borsod-Abaúj-Zemplén, NE Hungary 48°08′N 21°25′E
165 N11 **Tōkamachi** Niigata, Honshū, C Japan 37°08′N 138°44′E
185 D25 **Tokanui** Southland, South Island, New Zealand 46°33′S 169°02′E
80 I7 **Tokar** *var.* Ţawkar. Red Sea, NE Sudan 18°27′N 37°41′E
136 L12 **Tokat** Tokat, N Turkey 40°20′N 36°35′E
136 L12 **Tokat** ◐ *province* N Turkey
163 X15 **Tŏkchŏk-kundo** *island group* NW South Korea
Tōke *see* Taka Atoll
190 J9 **Tokelau** ◇ *NZ overseas territory* W Polynesia
Tőketerebes *see* Trebišov
Tokhtamyshbek *see* Tŭkhtamish
24 M6 **Tokio** Texas, SW USA 33°09′N 102°31′W
Tokio *see* Tōkyō
189 W11 **Toki Point** *point* NW Wake Island
Tokkuztara *see* Gongliu
147 V7 **Tokmak** *Kir.* Tokmok. Chuyskaya Oblast', N Kyrgyzstan 42°50′N 75°18′E
117 V9 **Tokmak** *var.* Velykyy Tokmak. Zaporiz'ka Oblast', SE Ukraine 47°13′N 35°43′E
Tokmok *see* Tokmak
184 Q8 **Tokomaru Bay** Gisborne, North Island, New Zealand 38°10′S 178°18′E
184 M8 **Tokoroa** Waikato, North Island, New Zealand 38°14′S 175°52′E
76 K14 **Tokounou** C Guinea 09°43′N 09°46′W
38 M12 **Toksook Bay** Alaska, USA 60°33′N 165°01′W
Toksu *see* Xinhe
Toksum *see* Toksun
158 L6 **Toksun** *var.* Toksum. Xinjiang Uygur Zizhiqu, NW China 42°47′N 88°38′E
147 T8 **Toktogul** Talasskaya Oblast', NW Kyrgyzstan 41°51′N 72°56′E
147 T9 **Toktogul'skoye Vodokhranilishche** ▨ W Kyrgyzstan
Toktomush *see* Tŭkhtamish
193 Y14 **Toku** *island* Vava'u Group, N Tonga
165 U16 **Tokunoshima** Kagoshima, Tokuno-shima, SW Japan
165 U16 **Tokuno-shima** *island* Nansei-shotō, SW Japan
164 I14 **Tokushima** *var.* Tokusima. Tokushima, Shikoku, SW Japan 34°04′N 134°28′E
164 H14 **Tokushima** *off.* Tokushima-ken, *var.* Tokusima. ◐ *prefecture* Shikoku, SW Japan
Tokushima-ken *see* Tokushima
Tokusima *see* Tokushima
164 E13 **Tokuyama** *var.* Shūnan. Yamaguchi, Honshū, SW Japan 34°04′N 131°48′E
165 N13 **Tōkyō** *var.* Tokio. ● (Japan) Tōkyō, Honshū, S Japan 35°40′N 139°45′E
165 O13 **Tōkyō** *off.* Tōkyō-to. ◐ *capital district* Honshū, S Japan
Tōkyō-to *see* Tōkyō
145 T12 **Tokyrau** ≈ C Kazakhstan
149 O3 **Tokzār** *Pash.* Tukzār. Sar-e Pol, N Afghanistan 35°47′N 66°28′E
145 W13 **Tokzhaylau** *prev.* Dzerzhinskoye. Almaty, SE Kazakhstan 45°49′N 81°04′E
145 W13 **Tokzhaylau** *var.* Dzerzhinskoye. Taldykorgan, SE Kazakhstan 45°49′N 81°04′E
189 U12 **Tol** *atoll* Chuuk Islands, C Micronesia
184 Q9 **Tolaga Bay** Gisborne, North Island, New Zealand 38°22′S 178°17′E
172 I7 **Tôlañaro** *prev.* Faradofay, Fort-Dauphin. Toliara, SE Madagascar
162 D6 **Tolbo** Bayan-Ölgiy, W Mongolia 48°22′N 90°22′E
Tolbukhin *see* Dobrich
60 G11 **Toledo** Paraná, S Brazil 24°45′S 53°41′W
54 G8 **Toledo** Norte de Santander, N Colombia 07°16′N 72°28′W
105 N9 **Toledo** *anc.* Toletum. Castilla-La Mancha, C Spain 39°52′N 04°02′W
30 M14 **Toledo** Illinois, N USA 39°16′N 88°15′W
29 W13 **Toledo** Iowa, C USA 42°00′N 92°34′W
31 R11 **Toledo** Ohio, N USA 41°40′N 83°33′W
32 F12 **Toledo** Oregon, NW USA 44°37′N 123°56′W
32 G9 **Toledo** Washington, NW USA 46°27′N 122°49′W
42 F3 **Toledo** ◐ *district* S Belize
104 M9 **Toledo** ◐ *province* Castilla-La Mancha, C Spain
25 Y7 **Toledo Bend Reservoir** ▨ Louisiana/Texas, SW USA
104 M10 **Toledo, Montes de** ▲▲ C Spain
106 J12 **Tolentino** Marche, C Italy 43°08′N 13°17′E
Toletum *see* Toledo
94 H10 **Tolga** Hedmark, S Norway 62°25′N 11°00′E
158 J3 **Toli** Xinjiang Uygur Zizhiqu, NW China 45°55′N 83°33′E
172 H7 **Toliara** *var.* Toliary; *prev.* Tuléar. Toliara, SW Madagascar 23°20′S 43°41′E
172 H7 **Toliara** ◐ *province* SW Madagascar
Toliary *see* Toliara
54 D11 **Tolima** *off.* Departamento del Tolima. ◐ *province* C Colombia
Tolima, Departamento del *see* Tolima
171 N11 **Tolitoli** Sulawesi, C Indonesia 01°05′N 120°50′E
95 K22 **Tollarp** Skåne, S Sweden 55°55′N 14°00′E
100 N9 **Tollense** ≈ NE Germany
100 N10 **Tollensesee** ◎ NE Germany
36 K13 **Tolleson** Arizona, SW USA 33°25′N 112°15′W
146 M13 **Tollimarjon** *Rus.* Talimardzhan. Qashqadaryo Viloyati, S Uzbekistan 38°22′N 65°31′E
Tolmein *see* Tolmin
106 J6 **Tolmezzo** Friuli-Venezia Giulia, NE Italy 46°27′N 13°01′E
109 S11 **Tolmin** *Ger.* Tolmein, *It.* Tolmino. W Slovenia 46°12′N 13°39′E
Tolmino *see* Tolmin
111 J25 **Tolna** *Ger.* Tolnau. Tolna, S Hungary 46°26′N 18°47′E
111 I24 **Tolna** *off.* Tolna Megye. ◐ *county* SW Hungary
Tolna Megye *see* Tolna
Tolnau *see* Tolna
79 I20 **Tolo** Bandundu, W Dem. Rep. Congo 02°57′S 18°35′E
Tolochin *see* Talachyn
190 D12 **Toloke** Île Futuna, W Wallis and Futuna
30 M13 **Tolono** Illinois, N USA 39°59′N 88°16′W
105 Q3 **Tolosa** País Vasco, N Spain 43°09′N 02°04′W
Tolosa *see* Toulouse
171 O13 **Tolo, Teluk** *bay* Sulawesi, C Indonesia
39 R9 **Tolovana River** ≈ Alaska, USA
123 U10 **Tolstoy, Mys** *headland* E Russian Federation 59°12′N 155°04′E
63 G15 **Toltén** Araucanía, C Chile 39°13′S 73°15′W
63 G15 **Toltén, Río** ≈ S Chile
54 E6 **Tolú** Sucre, NW Colombia 09°32′N 75°34′W
41 O14 **Toluca** *var.* Toluca de Lerdo. México, S Mexico 19°20′N 99°40′W
Toluca de Lerdo *see* Toluca
41 O14 **Toluca, Nevado de** ⛰ C Mexico 19°05′N 99°45′W
127 R6 **Tol'yatti** *prev.* Stavropol'. Samarskaya Oblast', W Russian Federation 53°32′N 49°27′E
77 O12 **Toma** NW Burkina 12°46′N 02°51′W
30 K7 **Tomah** Wisconsin, N USA 43°59′N 90°31′W
30 L5 **Tomahawk** Wisconsin, N USA 45°27′N 89°40′W
117 T8 **Tomakivka** Dnipropetrovs'ka Oblast', E Ukraine 47°47′N 34°45′E
165 S4 **Tomakomai** Hokkaidō, NE Japan 42°38′N 141°32′E
165 S2 **Tomamae** Hokkaidō, NE Japan 44°18′N 141°38′E
104 G9 **Tomar** Santarém, W Portugal 39°36′N 08°25′W
123 T13 **Tomari** Ostrov Sakhalin, Sakhalinskaya Oblast', SE Russian Federation 47°47′N 142°09′E
115 C16 **Tómaros** ▲ W Greece 39°31′N 20°45′E
Tomaschow *see* Tomaszów Mazowiecki
Tomaschow *see* Tomaszów Lubelski
61 E16 **Tomás Gomensoro** Artigas, N Uruguay 30°28′S 57°28′W
117 N7 **Tomashpil'** Vinnyts'ka Oblast', C Ukraine 48°32′N 28°31′E
Tomaszów *see* Tomaszów Mazowiecki
111 P15 **Tomaszów Lubelski** *Ger.* Tomaschow. Lubelskie, E Poland 50°29′N 23°23′E
Tomaszów Mazowiecka *see* Tomaszów Mazowiecki
110 L13 **Tomaszów Mazowiecki** *var.* Tomaszów Mazowiecka; *prev.* Tomaszów, *Ger.* Tomaschow. Łódzkie, C Poland 51°33′N 20°E
40 J13 **Tomatlán** Jalisco, C Mexico 19°53′N 105°18′W
81 F15 **Tombe** Jonglei, S Sudan 05°52′N 31°40′E
23 N4 **Tombigbee River** ≈ Alabama/Mississippi, S USA
82 A10 **Tomboco** Dem. Rep. Congo, NW Angola 06°50′S 13°20′E
77 O10 **Tombouctou** *Eng.* Timbuktu. Tombouctou, N Mali 16°47′N 03°03′W
77 N9 **Tombouctou** ◐ *region* W Mali
37 N16 **Tombstone** Arizona, SW USA 31°42′N 110°04′W
83 A15 **Tombua** *Port.* Porto Alexandre. Namibe, SW Angola 15°49′S 11°53′E
83 J19 **Tom Burke** Limpopo, NE South Africa 23°07′S 28°01′E
146 L9 **Tomdibuloq** *Rus.* Tamdybulak. Navoiy Viloyati, N Uzbekistan 41°48′N 64°33′E
146 L9 **Tomditov-Tog'lari** ▲▲ N Uzbekistan
62 G13 **Tomé** Bío Bío, C Chile 36°38′S 72°57′W
58 L12 **Tomé-Açu** Pará, NE Brazil 02°25′S 48°09′W
95 L23 **Tomelilla** Skåne, S Sweden 55°33′N 14°00′E
105 O10 **Tomelloso** Castilla-La Mancha, C Spain 39°09′N 03°01′W
14 H10 **Tomiko Lake** ◎ Ontario, S Canada
77 N12 **Tominian** Ségou, C Mali 13°18′N 04°39′W
171 N12 **Tomini, Gulf of** *var.* Teluk Tomini; *prev.* Teluk Gorontalo. *bay* Sulawesi, C Indonesia
Tomini, Teluk *see* Tomini, Gulf of
165 Q11 **Tomioka** Fukushima, Honshū, C Japan 37°19′N 140°57′E
113 G14 **Tomislavgrad** Federacija Bosna I Hercegovina, SW Bosnia and Herzegovina 43°43′N 17°15′E
181 O9 **Tomkinson Ranges** ▲▲ South Australia/Western Australia
123 Q11 **Tommot** Respublika Sakha (Yakutiya), NE Russian Federation 58°57′N 126°24′E
171 Q11 **Tomohon** Sulawesi, N Indonesia 01°19′N 124°49′E
54 K9 **Tomo, Río** ≈ E Colombia
113 L21 **Tomorrit, Mali i** ▲ S Albania 40°43′N 20°12′E
11 S17 **Tompkins** Saskatchewan, S Canada 50°03′N 108°49′W
20 K8 **Tompkinsville** Kentucky, S USA 36°43′N 85°41′W
171 N11 **Tompo** Sulawesi, N Indonesia 0°56′N 120°16′E
180 I8 **Tom Price** Western Australia 22°48′S 117°49′E
122 J12 **Tomsk** Tomskaya Oblast', C Russian Federation 56°30′N 85°05′E
122 I11 **Tomskaya Oblast'** ◐ *province* C Russian Federation
18 K16 **Toms River** New Jersey, NE USA 39°56′N 74°09′W
Tom Steed Lake *see* Tom Steed Reservoir
26 L12 **Tom Steed Reservoir** *var.* Tom Steed Lake. ▨ Oklahoma, C USA
171 U13 **Tomu** Papua, E Indonesia 02°07′S 133°01′E
158 H6 **Tomür Feng** *var.* Pobeda Peak, *Rus.* Pik Pobedy. ▲ China/Kyrgyzstan 42°02′N 80°07′E *see also* Pobedy, Pik
Tomür Feng *see* Pobedy, Pik
189 N13 **Tomworoahlang** Pohnpei, E Micronesia
41 U17 **Tonalá** Chiapas, SE Mexico 16°08′N 93°41′W
106 F6 **Tonale, Passo del** *pass* N Italy
164 I11 **Tonami** Toyama, Honshū, SW Japan 36°40′N 136°55′E
58 C12 **Tonantins** Amazonas, W Brazil 02°58′S 67°30′W
32 K6 **Tonasket** Washington, NW USA 48°41′N 119°27′W
55 Y9 **Tonate** *var.* Macouria. N French Guiana 05°00′N 52°28′W
18 D10 **Tonawanda** New York, NE USA 43°00′N 78°51′W
171 Q11 **Tondano** Sulawesi, C Indonesia 01°19′N 124°56′E
104 H7 **Tondela** Viseu, N Portugal 40°31′N 08°05′W
95 F24 **Tønder** *Ger.* Tondern. Sønderjylland, SW Denmark 54°57′N 08°53′E
Tondern *see* Tønder
143 N4 **Tonekābon** *var.* Shahsawar, Tonkābon; *prev.* Shahsavār. Māzandarān, N Iran 36°40′N 51°25′E
Tonezh *see* Tonyezh
193 Y14 **Tonga** *off.* Kingdom of Tonga, *var.* Friendly Islands. ◆ *monarchy* SW Pacific Ocean
175 R9 **Tonga** *island group* SW Pacific Ocean
83 K23 **Tongaat** KwaZulu/Natal, E South Africa 29°35′S 31°07′E
Tonga, Kingdom of *see* Tonga
161 Q13 **Tong'an** *var.* Datong, Tong an. Fujian, SE China 24°43′N 118°07′E
Tong an *see* Tong'an
27 Q4 **Tonganoxie** Kansas, C USA 39°06′N 95°05′W
39 Y13 **Tongass National Forest** *reserve* Alaska, USA
193 Y16 **Tongatapu** ✈ Tongatapu, S Tonga 21°10′S 175°10′W
193 Y16 **Tongatapu** *island* Tongatapu Group, S Tonga
193 Y16 **Tongatapu Group** *island group* S Tonga
175 S9 **Tonga Trench** *undersea feature* S Pacific Ocean
161 N8 **Tongbai Shan** ▲▲ C China
161 P8 **Tongcheng** Anhui, E China 31°16′N 117°00′E
160 L6 **Tongchuan** Shaanxi, C China 35°10′N 109°03′E
160 L12 **Tongdao** *var.* Tongdao Dongzu Zizhixian; *prev.* Shuangjiang. Hunan, S China 26°06′N 109°46′E
Tongdao Dongzu Zizhixian *see* Tongdao
159 T11 **Tongde** *var.* Gabasumdo. Qinghai, C China 35°13′N 100°39′E
99 K19 **Tongeren** *Fr.* Tongres. Limburg, NE Belgium 50°47′N 05°28′E
163 Y14 **Tonghae** NE South Korea 37°26′N 129°09′E
160 G13 **Tonghai** *var.* Xiushan. Yunnan, SW China 24°06′N 102°45′E
163 X8 **Tonghe** Heilongjiang, NE China 46°00′N 128°45′E
163 W11 **Tonghua** Jilin, NE China 41°45′N 125°50′E
163 Z6 **Tongjiang** Heilongjiang, NE China 47°39′N 132°29′E
163 Y13 **Tongjosŏn-man** *prev.* Broughton Bay. *bay* E North Korea
163 V7 **Tongken He** ≈ NE China
167 T7 **Tongking, Gulf of** *Chin.* Beibu Wan, *Vtn.* Vinh Băc Bô. *gulf* China/Vietnam
163 U10 **Tongliao** Nei Mongol Zizhiqu, N China 43°37′N 122°15′E
161 Q9 **Tongling** Anhui, E China 30°55′N 117°50′E
161 R9 **Tonglu** Zhejiang, SE China 29°50′N 119°38′E
187 R14 **Tongoa** *island* Shepherd Islands, S Vanuatu
62 G9 **Tongoy** Coquimbo, C Chile 30°16′S 71°31′W
160 L11 **Tongren** *var.* Rongwo. Guizhou, S China 27°44′N 109°10′E
159 T11 **Tongren** *var.* Rongwo. Qinghai, C China 35°31′N 101°58′E
Tongres *see* Tongeren
153 U11 **Tongsa** *var.* Tongsa Dzong. C Bhutan 27°33′N 90°30′E
Tongsa Dzong *see* Tongsa
Tongshan *see* Fuding, Fujian, China
Tongshan *see* Xuzhou, Jiangsu, China
Tongshi *see* Wuzhishan
159 P12 **Tongtian He** ≈ C China
96 I6 **Tongue** N Scotland, United Kingdom 58°30′N 04°25′W
44 H3 **Tongue of the Ocean** *strait* C Bahamas
33 X10 **Tongue River** ≈ Montana, NW USA
33 W11 **Tongue River Resevoir** ▨ Montana, NW USA
159 V11 **Tongwei** *var.* Pingxiang. Gansu, C China 35°09′N 105°15′E
159 W9 **Tongxin** Ningxia, N China 37°00′N 105°41′E
163 U9 **Tongyu** *var.* Kaitong. Jilin, NE China 44°49′N 123°08′E
160 J11 **Tongzi** *var.* Loushanguan. Guizhou, S China 28°08′N 106°49′E
162 F8 **Tonhil** *var.* Dzüyl. Govĭ-Altay, SW Mongolia 46°09′N 93°55′E
40 G5 **Tónichi** Sonora, NW Mexico 28°37′N 109°34′W
81 D14 **Tonj** Warab, SW Sudan 07°18′N 28°41′E
152 H13 **Tonk** Rājasthān, N India 26°10′N 75°50′E
Tonkābon *see* Tonekābon
27 N8 **Tonkawa** Oklahoma, C USA 36°40′N 97°18′W
167 Q12 **Tônlé Sap** *Eng.* Great Lake. ◎ W Cambodia
102 L14 **Tonneins** Lot-et-Garonne, SW France 44°21′N 00°21′E
103 Q7 **Tonnerre** Yonne, C France 47°50′N 04°00′E
Tonoas *see* Dublon
35 U8 **Tonopah** Nevada, W USA 38°04′N 117°13′W
164 H13 **Tonoshō** Okayama, Shōdo-shima, SW Japan 34°29′N 134°10′E
43 S17 **Tonosí** Los Santos, S Panama 07°23′N 80°26′W
95 H16 **Tønsberg** Vestfold, S Norway 59°16′N 10°25′E
39 T11 **Tonsina** Alaska, USA 61°39′N 145°10′W
95 D17 **Tonstad** Vest-Agder, S Norway 58°40′N 06°42′E
193 X15 **Tonumea** *island* Nomuka Group, W Tonga
137 O11 **Tonya** Trabzon, NE Turkey 40°52′N 39°17′E
119 K20 **Tonyezh** *Rus.* Tonezh. Homyel'skaya Voblasts', SE Belarus 51°50′N 27°48′E
36 L3 **Tooele** Utah, W USA 40°32′N 112°18′W
122 L13 **Toora-Khem** Respublika Tyva, S Russian Federation 52°25′N 96°01′E
183 O5 **Toorale East** New South Wales, SE Australia 30°29′S 145°25′E
83 H25 **Toorberg** ▲ S South Africa 32°02′S 24°02′E
118 G5 **Tootsi** Pärnumaa, SW Estonia 58°34′N 24°43′E
183 U3 **Toowoomba** Queensland, E Australia 27°35′S 151°54′E
27 Q4 **Topeka** *state capital* Kansas, C USA 39°03′N 95°41′W
122 J12 **Topki** Kemerovskaya Oblast', S Russian Federation 55°12′N 85°40′E
111 M18 **Topľa** *Hung.* Toplya. ≈ NE Slovakia
Toplicza *see* Toplița
116 J10 **Toplița** *Ger.* Töplitz, *Hung.* Marosheviz; *prev.* Toplița Română, *Hung.* Oláh-Toplicza, Toplicza. Harghita, C Romania 45°56′N 25°20′E
Toplița Română/Töplitz *see* Toplița
Toplya *see* Topľa
111 I20 **Topoľčany** *Hung.* Nagytapolcsány. Nitriansky Kraj, W Slovakia 48°33′N 18°10′E
40 G8 **Topolobampo** Sinaloa, C Mexico 25°36′N 109°04′W
116 I13 **Topoloveni** Argeș, S Romania 44°49′N 25°02′E
114 L11 **Topolovgrad** *prev.* Kavakli. Khaskovo, S Bulgaria 42°06′N 26°20′E
Topolya *see* Bačka Topola
124 I6 **Topozero, Ozero** ◎ NW Russian Federation
32 J10 **Toppenish** Washington, NW USA 46°22′N 120°18′W
181 P4 **Top Springs Roadhouse** Northern Territory, N Australia 16°37′S 131°49′E
189 U11 **Tora** *island* Chuuk, C Micronesia
Toraigh *see* Tory Island
189 U11 **Tora Island Pass** *passage* Chuuk Islands, C Micronesia
143 U5 **Torbat-e Ḩeydarīyeh** *var.* Turbat-i-Haidari. Khorāsān-Razavī, NE Iran 35°18′N 59°12′E
143 V5 **Torbat-e Jām** *var.* Turbat-i-Jam. Khorāsān-Razavī, NE Iran 35°16′N 60°36′E
39 Q11 **Torbert, Mount** ▲ Alaska, USA 61°30′N 152°15′W
31 P6 **Torch Lake** ◎ Michigan, N USA
Törcsvár *see* Bran
Torda *see* Turda
104 L6 **Tordesillas** Castilla-León, N Spain 41°30′N 05°00′W
92 K13 **Töre** Norrbotten, N Sweden 65°55′N 22°40′E
95 L17 **Töreboda** Västra Götaland, S Sweden 58°41′N 14°07′E
95 J21 **Torekov** Skåne, S Sweden 56°25′N 12°39′E
92 O3 **Torell Land** *physical region* SW Svalbard
117 Y8 **Torez** Donets'ka Oblast', SE Ukraine 48°00′N 38°38′E
101 N14 **Torgau** Sachsen, E Germany 51°34′N 13°01′E
Torgay *see* Turgay
Torgay Üstirti *see* Turgayskaya Stolovaya Strana
Torghay *see* Turgay
95 N22 **Torhamn** Blekinge, S Sweden 56°04′N 15°49′E
99 C17 **Torhout** West-Vlaanderen, W Belgium 51°04′N 03°06′E
106 B8 **Torino** *Eng.* Turin. Piemonte, NW Italy 45°03′N 07°39′E
165 U15 **Tori-shima** *island* Izu-shotō, SE Japan
81 F16 **Torit** Eastern Equatoria, S Sudan 04°27′N 32°31′E
186 H6 **Toriu** New Britain, E Papua New Guinea 04°39′S 151°42′E
148 M4 **Torkestān, Selseleh-ye Band-e** *var.* Bandi-i Turkistan. ▲▲ NW Afghanistan
104 L7 **Tormes** ≈ W Spain
Tornacum *see* Tournai
Torneå *see* Tornio
92 K12 **Torneälven** *var.* Torniojoki, *Fin.* Tornionjoki. ≈ Finland/Sweden
92 I11 **Torneträsk** ◎ N Sweden
13 O4 **Torngat Mountains** ▲▲ Newfoundland and Labrador, NE Canada
24 H8 **Tornillo** Texas, SW USA 31°26′N 106°06′W
92 K13 **Tornio** *Swe.* Torneå. Lappi, NW Finland 65°50′N 24°18′E
Torniojoki/Tornionjoki *see* Torneälven
61 B23 **Tornquist** Buenos Aires, E Argentina 38°08′S 62°15′W
104 L6 **Toro** Castilla-León, N Spain 41°31′N 05°24′W
62 H9 **Toro, Cerro del** ▲ N Chile 29°10′S 69°43′W
77 R12 **Torodi** Tillabéri, SW Niger 13°05′N 01°46′E
Törökbecse *see* Novi Bečej
186 J7 **Torokina** Bougainville Island, NE Papua New Guinea 06°12′S 155°04′E
111 L23 **Törökszentmiklós** Jász-Nagykun-Szolnok, E Hungary 47°11′N 20°26′E
42 G7 **Torola, Río** ≈ El Salvador/Honduras
Toronaíos, Kólpos *see* Kassándras, Kólpos
14 H15 **Toronto** *province capital* Ontario, S Canada 43°42′N 79°25′W
31 V12 **Toronto** Ohio, N USA 40°27′N 80°36′W
Toronto *see* Lester B. Pearson
27 P6 **Toronto Lake** ▨ Kansas, C USA
35 V16 **Toro Peak** ▲ California, W USA 33°31′N 116°25′W
124 H16 **Toropets** Tverskaya Oblast', W Russian Federation 56°29′N 31°37′E
81 G18 **Tororo** E Uganda 0°42′N 34°12′E
136 H16 **Toros Dağları** *Eng.* Taurus Mountains. ▲▲ S Turkey
183 N13 **Torquay** Victoria, SE Australia 38°21′S 144°18′E
97 J24 **Torquay** SW England, United Kingdom 50°28′N 03°30′W
104 M5 **Torquemada** Castilla-León, N Spain 42°02′N 04°17′W
35 S16 **Torrance** California, W USA 33°50′N 118°20′W
104 G12 **Torrão** Setúbal, S Portugal 38°18′N 08°13′W
104 H8 **Torre, Alto da** ▲ C Portugal 40°21′N 07°31′W
107 K18 **Torre Annunziata** Campania, S Italy 40°45′N 14°27′E
105 T8 **Torreblanca** País Valenciano, E Spain 40°14′N 00°12′E
104 L15 **Torrecilla** ▲ S Spain 36°38′N 04°54′W
105 P4 **Torrecilla en Cameros** La Rioja, N Spain 42°18′N 02°33′W
105 N13 **Torredelcampo** Andalucía, S Spain 37°45′N 03°52′W
107 K17 **Torre del Greco** Campania, S Italy 40°46′N 14°22′E
104 I6 **Torre de Moncorvo** *var.* Moncorvo, Tôrre de Moncorvo. Bragança, N Portugal 41°10′N 07°03′W
104 J9 **Torrejoncillo** Extremadura, W Spain 39°54′N 06°28′W
105 O8 **Torrejón de Ardoz** Madrid, C Spain 40°27′N 03°29′W
105 N7 **Torrelaguna** Madrid, C Spain 40°50′N 03°33′W
105 N2 **Torrelavega** Cantabria, N Spain 43°21′N 04°03′W
107 M16 **Torremaggiore** Puglia, SE Italy 41°42′N 15°17′E
104 M15 **Torremolinos** Andalucía, S Spain 36°38′N 04°30′W
182 I6 **Torrens, Lake** *salt lake* South Australia
105 S10 **Torrent** *Cas.* Torrente, *var.* Torrent de l'Horta. País Valenciano, E Spain 39°27′N 00°28′W
Torrent de l'Horta/Torrente *see* Torrent
40 L8 **Torreón** Coahuila, NE Mexico 25°47′N 103°21′W
105 R13 **Torre Pacheco** Murcia, SE Spain 37°43′N 00°57′W
106 A8 **Torre Pellice** Piemonte, NE Italy 44°49′N 07°12′E
105 O13 **Torreperogil** Andalucía, S Spain 38°02′N 03°17′W
61 J15 **Torres** Rio Grande do Sul, S Brazil 29°20′S 49°43′W
Torrès, Îles *see* Torres Islands
187 Q11 **Torres Islands** *Fr.* Îles Torrès. *island group* N Vanuatu
104 G9 **Torres Novas** Santarém, C Portugal 39°28′N 08°32′W
181 V1 **Torres Strait** *strait* Australia/Papua New Guinea
104 F10 **Torres Vedras** Lisboa, C Portugal 39°05′N 09°15′W
105 S13 **Torrevieja** País Valenciano, E Spain 37°59′N 00°40′W
186 B6 **Torricelli Mountains** ▲▲ NW Papua New Guinea
96 G8 **Torridon, Loch** *inlet* NW Scotland, United Kingdom
106 D9 **Torriglia** Liguria, NW Italy 44°31′N 09°08′E
104 M9 **Torrijos** Castilla-La Mancha, C Spain 39°59′N 04°18′W
18 L12 **Torrington** Connecticut, NE USA 41°48′N 73°07′W

◆ Country
● Country Capital
◇ Dependent Territory
○ Dependent Territory Capital
◐ Administrative Regions
✈ International Airport
▲ Mountain
▲▲ Mountain Range
⛰ Volcano
≈ River
◎ Lake
▨ Reservoir

TORRINGTON – TRUCHAS PEAK

33 Z15 **Torrington** Wyoming, C USA 42°04′N 104°10′W
Torröjen *see* Torrön
94 F16 **Torrön** *prev.* Torröjen. ◎ C Sweden
105 N15 **Torrox** Andalucía, S Spain 36°45′N 03°58′W
94 N13 **Torsåker** Gävleborg, C Sweden 60°31′N 16°30′E
95 N21 **Torsås** Kalmar, S Sweden 56°24′N 16°00′E
95 J14 **Torsby** Värmland, C Sweden 60°07′N 13°E
95 N16 **Torshälla** Södermanland, C Sweden 59°25′N 16°28′E
95 B19 **Tórshavn** *Dan.* Thorshavn. ○ Faeroe Islands 62°02′N 06°47′W
Torshiz *see* Kāshmar
146 I9 **To'rtko'l** *var.* Türtkül, *Rus.* Turtkul'; *prev.* Petroaleksandrovsk. Qoraqalpog'iston Respublikasi, W Uzbekistan 41°35′N 61°E
Tortoise Islands *see* Colón, Archipiélago de
45 T9 **Tortola** *island* C British Virgin Islands
106 D9 **Tortona** *anc.* Dertona. Piemonte, NW Italy 44°54′N 08°52′E
107 L23 **Tortorici** Sicilia, Italy, C Mediterranean Sea 38°02′N 14°49′E
105 U7 **Tortosa** *anc.* Dertosa. Cataluña, E Spain 40°49′N 00°31′E
Tortosa *see* Ṭarṭūs
105 U7 **Tortosa, Cap** *cape* E Spain
44 L8 **Tortue, Île de la** *var.* Tortuga Island. *island* N Haiti
55 Y10 **Tortue, Montagne** ▲▲ C French Guiana
Tortuga, Isla *see* La Tortuga, Isla
Tortuga Island *see* Tortue, Île de la
54 C11 **Tortugas, Golfo** *gulf* W Colombia
45 T5 **Tortuguero, Laguna** *lagoon* N Puerto Rico
137 Q12 **Tortum** Erzurum, NE Turkey 40°20′N 41°36′E
Torugart, Pereval *see* Turugart Shankou
137 O12 **Torul** Gümüşhane, NE Turkey 40°35′N 39°18′E
110 J10 **Toruń** *Ger.* Thorn. Toruń, Kujawsko-pomorskie, C Poland 53°02′N 18°36′E
95 K20 **Torup** Halland, S Sweden 56°57′N 13°04′E
118 I6 **Tõrva** *Ger.* Törwa. Valgamaa, S Estonia 58°00′N 25°54′E
Törwa *see* Tõrva
96 D13 **Tory Island** *Ir.* Toraigh. *island* NW Ireland
111 N19 **Torysa** *Hung.* Tarca. ≈ NE Slovakia
Törzburg *see* Bran
124 J16 **Torzhok** Tverskaya Oblast', W Russian Federation 57°04′N 34°55′E
164 F15 **Tosa-Shimizu** *var.* Tosasimizu. Kōchi, Shikoku, SW Japan 32°47′N 132°58′E
Tosasimizu *see* Tosa-Shimizu
164 G15 **Tosa-wan** *bay* SW Japan
83 H21 **Tosca** North-West, N South Africa 25°51′S 23°56′E
106 F12 **Toscana** *Eng.* Tuscany. ◆ *region* C Italy
107 E14 **Toscano, Archipelago** *Eng.* Tuscan Archipelago. *island group* C Italy
106 G10 **Tosco-Emiliano, Appennino** *Eng.* Tuscan-Emilian Mountains. ▲▲ C Italy
Tōsei *see* Tungshih
165 N15 **To-shima** *island* Izu-shotō, SE Japan
147 Q9 **Toshkent** *Eng./Rus.* Tashkent. ● Toshkent Viloyati, E Uzbekistan 41°19′N 69°17′E
147 Q9 **Toshkent** ✈ Toshkent Viloyati, E Uzbekistan 41°13′N 69°15′E
147 P9 **Toshkent Viloyati** *Rus.* Tashkentskaya Oblast'. ◆ *province* E Uzbekistan
124 H13 **Tosno** Leningradskaya Oblast', NW Russian Federation 59°34′N 30°48′E
159 Q10 **Toson Hu** ◎ C China
162 H6 **Tosontsengel** Dzavhan, NW Mongolia 48°42′N 98°14′E
162 J6 **Tosontsengel** *var.* Tsengel. Hövsgöl, N Mongolia 49°29′N 101°09′E
146 I8 **Tosquduq Qumlari** *var.* Goshquduq Qum, Taskuduk, Peski. *desert* W Uzbekistan
105 U4 **Tossal de l'Orri** *var.* Llorri. ▲ NE Spain 42°24′N 01°15′E
61 A15 **Tostado** Santa Fe, C Argentina 29°15′S 61°45′W
118 F6 **Tõstamaa** *Ger.* Testama. Pärnumaa, SW Estonia 58°20′N 23°59′E
100 I10 **Tostedt** Niedersachsen, NW Germany 53°16′N 09°42′E
136 J11 **Tosya** Kastamonu, N Turkey 41°02′N 34°02′E
95 F15 **Totak** ◎ S Norway
105 R13 **Totana** Murcia, SE Spain 37°45′N 01°30′W
94 H13 **Toten** *physical region* S Norway
83 G18 **Toteng** North-West, C Botswana 20°25′S 23°00′E
102 M3 **Tôtes** Seine-Maritime, N France 49°40′N 01°02′E
Totigi *see* Tochigi
Totio *see* Tochio
Totis *see* Tata
189 U13 **Totiw** *island* Chuuk, C Micronesia
125 N13 **Tot'ma** *var.* Totma. Vologodskaya Oblast', NW Russian Federation 59°58′N 42°42′E
Tot'ma *see* Sukhona
55 V9 **Totness** Coronie, N Suriname 05°53′N 56°19′W
42 C5 **Totonicapán** Totonicapán, W Guatemala 14°58′N 91°12′W
42 A2 **Totonicapán** *off.* Departamento de Totonicapán. ◆ *department* W Guatemala
Totonicapán, Departamento de *see* Totonicapán
61 B18 **Totoras** Santa Fe, C Argentina 32°35′S 61°11′W
187 Y15 **Totoya** *island* S Fiji
183 Q7 **Tottenham** New South Wales, SE Australia 32°16′S 147°23′E
164 I12 **Tottori** Tottori, Honshū, SW Japan 35°29′N 134°14′E
164 H12 **Tottori** *off.* Tottori-ken. ◆ *prefecture* Honshū, SW Japan
Tottori-ken *see* Tottori
76 I6 **Touâjîl** Tiris Zemmour, N Mauritania 22°03′N 12°40′W
76 L15 **Touba** W Ivory Coast 08°17′N 07°41′W
76 G11 **Touba** W Senegal 14°55′N 15°53′W
74 E7 **Toubkal, Jbel** ▲ W Morocco 31°00′N 07°50′W
32 K10 **Touchet** Washington, NW USA 46°03′N 118°40′W
103 P7 **Toucy** Yonne, C France 47°45′N 03°18′E
77 O12 **Tougan** W Burkina 13°06′N 03°03′W
74 L7 **Touggourt** NE Algeria 33°08′N 06°04′E
77 Q12 **Tougouri** N Burkina 13°22′N 00°25′W
76 J13 **Tougué** NW Guinea 11°29′N 11°48′W
76 K12 **Toukoto** Kayes, W Mali 13°27′N 09°52′W
103 S5 **Toul** Meurthe-et-Moselle, NE France 48°41′N 05°54′E
76 L16 **Toulépleu** *var.* Toulobli. W Ivory Coast 06°37′N 08°27′W
161 S14 **Touliu** C Taiwan 23°44′N 120°27′E
15 U3 **Toulnustouc** ≈ Québec, SE Canada
Toulobli *see* Toulépleu
103 T16 **Toulon** *anc.* Telo Martius, Tilio Martius. Var, SE France 43°07′N 05°56′E
30 K12 **Toulon** Illinois, N USA 41°05′N 89°54′W
102 M15 **Toulouse** *anc.* Tolosa. Haute-Garonne, S France 43°37′N 01°25′E
102 M15 **Toulouse** ✈ Haute-Garonne, S France 43°38′N 01°19′E
77 N16 **Toumodi** C Ivory Coast 06°34′N 05°01′W
74 G9 **Tounassine, Hamada** *hill range* W Algeria
Toungoo *see* Taungoo
102 L8 **Touraine** *cultural region* C France
Tourane *see* Đà Nẵng
103 P1 **Tourcoing** Nord, N France 50°44′N 03°10′E
104 F2 **Touriñán, Cabo** *headland* NW Spain 43°02′N 09°20′W
76 J6 **Tourine** Tiris Zemmour, N Mauritania 22°23′N 11°50′W
102 J3 **Tourlaville** Manche, N France 49°38′N 01°34′W
99 D19 **Tournai** *var.* Tournay, *Dut.* Doornik; *anc.* Tornacum. Hainaut, SW Belgium 50°36′N 03°24′E
102 L16 **Tournay** Hautes-Pyrénées, S France 43°10′N 00°16′E
Tournay *see* Tournai
103 R12 **Tournon** Ardèche, E France 45°05′N 04°49′E
103 R9 **Tournus** Saône-et-Loire, C France 46°33′N 04°53′E
59 Q14 **Touros** Rio Grande do Norte, E Brazil 05°10′S 35°29′W
102 L8 **Tours** *anc.* Caesarodunum, Turoni. Indre-et-Loire, C France 47°22′N 00°40′E
183 Q17 **Tourville, Cape** *headland* Tasmania, SE Australia 42°09′S 148°20′E
162 I8 **Töv** ◆ *province* C Mongolia
54 H7 **Tovar** Mérida, NW Venezuela 08°22′N 71°50′W
126 L5 **Tovarkovskiy** Tul'skaya Oblast', W Russian Federation 53°41′N 38°18′E
Tovil'-Dora *see* Tavildara
Tövis *see* Teiuș
137 V11 **Tovuz** *Rus.* Tauz. W Azerbaijan 40°58′N 45°41′E
165 R7 **Towada** Aomori, Honshū, C Japan 40°35′N 141°13′E
184 K3 **Towai** Northland, North Island, New Zealand 35°29′S 174°06′E
18 H12 **Towanda** Pennsylvania, NE USA 41°45′N 76°25′W
29 W4 **Tower** Minnesota, N USA 47°48′N 92°16′W
171 N12 **Towera** Sulawesi, N Indonesia 0°29′S 120°01′E
Tower Island *see* Genovesa, Isla
180 M13 **Tower Peak** ▲ Western Australia 33°23′S 123°27′E
35 U11 **Towne Pass** *pass* California, W USA
29 N3 **Towner** North Dakota, N USA 48°20′N 100°27′W
33 R10 **Townsend** Montana, NW USA 46°19′N 111°31′W
181 X6 **Townsville** Queensland, NE Australia 19°24′S 146°53′E
Towoeti Meer *see* Towuti, Danau
148 K4 **Towraghoudī** Herāt, NW Afghanistan 35°13′N 62°19′E
21 X3 **Towson** Maryland, NE USA 39°25′N 76°36′W
171 O13 **Towuti, Danau** *Dut.* Towoeti Meer. ◎ Sulawesi, C Indonesia
Toxkan He *see* Ak-say
24 K9 **Toyah** Texas, SW USA 31°18′N 103°47′W
165 R4 **Tōya-ko** ◎ Hokkaidō, NE Japan
164 L11 **Toyama** Toyama, Honshū, SW Japan 36°41′N 137°13′E
164 L11 **Toyama** *off.* Toyama-ken. ◆ *prefecture* Honshū, SW Japan
Toyama-ken *see* Toyama
164 L11 **Toyama-wan** *bay* W Japan
164 H15 **Tōyo** Kōchi, Shikoku, SW Japan 33°22′N 134°18′E
Toyohara *see* Yuzhno-Sakhalinsk
164 L14 **Toyohashi** *var.* Toyohasi. Aichi, Honshū, SW Japan 34°46′N 137°22′E
Toyohasi *see* Toyohashi
164 L14 **Toyokawa** Aichi, Honshū, SW Japan 34°47′N 137°24′E
164 I14 **Toyooka** Hyōgo, Honshū, SW Japan 35°35′N 134°48′E
164 L13 **Toyota** Aichi, Honshū, SW Japan 35°04′N 137°09′E
165 T1 **Toyotomi** Hokkaidō, NE Japan 45°07′N 141°45′E
147 Q10 **To'ytepa** *Rus.* Toytepa. Toshkent Viloyati, E Uzbekistan 41°04′N 69°22′E
Toytepa *see* To'ytepa
74 M6 **Tozeur** *var.* Tawzar. W Tunisia 34°00′N 08°09′E
39 Q8 **Tozi, Mount** ▲ Alaska, USA 65°45′N 151°01′W
137 Q9 **Tqvarch'eli** *Rus.* Tkvarcheli. NW Georgia 42°51′N 41°42′E
Trâblous *see* Tripoli
137 O11 **Trabzon** *Eng.* Trebizond; *anc.* Trapezus. Trabzon, NE Turkey 41°N 39°43′E
137 O11 **Trabzon** *Eng.* Trebizond. ◆ *province* NE Turkey
13 P13 **Tracadie** New Brunswick, SE Canada 47°32′N 64°57′W
Trachenberg *see* Żmigród
15 O11 **Tracy** Québec, SE Canada 45°59′N 73°07′W
35 O8 **Tracy** California, W USA 37°43′N 121°27′W
29 S10 **Tracy** Minnesota, N USA 44°14′N 95°37′W
20 K10 **Tracy City** Tennessee, S USA 35°15′N 85°44′W
106 D7 **Tradate** Lombardia, N Italy 45°43′N 08°57′E
84 F6 **Traena Bank** *undersea feature* E Norwegian Sea 66°15′N 09°45′E
29 W13 **Traer** Iowa, C USA 42°11′N 92°28′W
104 J16 **Trafalgar, Cabo de** *headland* SW Spain 36°10′N 06°03′W
Traiectum ad Mosam/ Traiectum Tungorum *see* Maastricht
Tráigh Mhór *see* Tramore
11 O17 **Trail** British Columbia, SW Canada 49°04′N 117°39′W
58 B11 **Traíra, Serra do** ▲▲ NW Brazil
109 V5 **Traisen** Niederösterreich, NE Austria 48°03′N 15°37′E
109 W4 **Traisen** ≈ NE Austria
109 X4 **Traiskirchen** Niederösterreich, NE Austria 48°01′N 16°18′E
Trajani Portus *see* Civitavecchia
Trajectum ad Rhenum *see* Utrecht
119 H14 **Trakai** *Ger.* Traken, *Pol.* Troki. Vilnius, SE Lithuania 54°39′N 24°58′E
Traken *see* Trakai
97 B20 **Tralee** *Ir.* Trá Lí. SW Ireland 52°16′N 09°42′W
97 A20 **Tralee Bay** *Ir.* Bá Thrá Lí. *bay* SW Ireland
Trá Lí *see* Tralee
Trälleborg *see* Trelleborg
Tralles Aydin *see* Aydın
61 J16 **Tramandaí** Rio Grande do Sul, S Brazil 30°01′S 50°11′W
108 C7 **Tramelan** Bern, W Switzerland 47°13′N 07°07′E
Trá Mhór *see* Tramore
97 E20 **Tramore** *Ir.* Tráigh Mhór, Trá Mhór. Waterford, S Ireland 52°10′N 07°10′W
95 L18 **Tranås** Jönköping, S Sweden 58°03′N 15°00′E
62 J7 **Trancas** Tucumán, N Argentina 26°11′S 65°20′W
104 I7 **Trancoso** Guarda, N Portugal 40°46′N 07°21′W
95 H22 **Tranebjerg** Århus, C Denmark 55°51′N 10°36′E
95 K19 **Tranemo** Västra Götaland, S Sweden 57°30′N 13°20′E
167 N16 **Trang** Trang, S Thailand 07°33′N 99°36′E
171 V15 **Trangan, Pulau** *island* Kepulauan Aru, E Indonesia
Trắng Dinh *see* Thất Khê
183 Q7 **Trangie** New South Wales, SE Australia 32°01′S 147°58′E
94 K12 **Trängslet** Dalarna, C Sweden 61°22′N 13°43′E
107 N16 **Trani** Puglia, SE Italy 41°17′N 16°25′E
61 F17 **Tranqueras** Rivera, NE Uruguay 31°13′S 55°45′W
63 G17 **Tranqui, Isla** *island* S Chile
39 V6 **Trans-Alaska pipeline** *oil pipeline* Alaska, USA
195 Q10 **Transantarctic Mountains** ▲▲ Antarctica
Transcarpathian Oblast *see* Zakarpats'ka Oblast'
122 E9 **Trans-Siberian Railway** *railway* Russian Federation
Transilvania *see* Transylvania
Transilvaniei, Alpi *see* Carpații Meridionali
Transjordan *see* Jordan
172 L11 **Transkei Basin** *undersea feature* SW Indian Ocean 35°30′S 29°00′E
117 O10 **Transnistria** *cultural region* E Moldavia
Transsylvanische Alpen/ Transylvanian Alps *see* Carpații Meridionali
94 K12 **Transtrand** Dalarna, C Sweden 61°06′N 13°19′E
116 G10 **Transylvania** *Eng.* Ardeal, Transilvania, *Ger.* Siebenbürgen, *Hung.* Erdély. *cultural region* NW Romania
167 S14 **Tra On** Vinh Long, S Vietnam 09°58′N 105°58′E
107 H23 **Trapani** *anc.* Drepanum. Sicilia, Italy, C Mediterranean Sea 38°02′N 12°32′E
167 S12 **Trâpeăng Vêng** Kâmpóng Thum, C Cambodia 12°37′N 104°58′E
Trapezus *see* Trabzon
114 L9 **Trapoklovo** Sliven, C Bulgaria 42°40′N 26°36′E
183 P13 **Traralgon** Victoria, SE Australia 38°15′S 146°36′E
76 H9 **Trarza** ◆ *region* SW Mauritania
Trasimenischersee *see* Trasimeno, Lago
106 H12 **Trasimeno, Lago** *Eng.* Lake of Perugia, *Ger.* Trasimenischersee. ◎ C Italy
95 J20 **Träslövsläge** Halland, S Sweden 57°02′N 12°18′E
Trás-os-Montes *see* Cucumbi
104 I6 **Trás-os-Montes e Alto Douro** *former province* N Portugal
167 Q12 **Trat** *var.* Bang Phra. Trat, S Thailand 12°16′N 102°30′E
Trá Tholl, Inis *see* Inishtrahull
Traù *see* Trogir
109 T4 **Traun** Oberösterreich, N Austria 48°14′N 14°15′E
109 S5 **Traun** ≈ N Austria
Traun, Lake *see* Traunsee
101 N23 **Traunreut** Bayern, SE Germany 47°58′N 12°36′E
109 S5 **Traunsee** *var.* Gmundner See, *Eng.* Lake Traun. ◎ N Austria
Trautenau *see* Trutnov
21 P11 **Travelers Rest** South Carolina, SE USA 34°58′N 82°26′W
182 L8 **Travellers Lake** *seasonal lake* New South Wales, SE Australia
31 P6 **Traverse City** Michigan, N USA 44°45′N 85°37′W
29 R7 **Traverse, Lake** ◎ Minnesota/South Dakota, N USA
185 I16 **Travers, Mount** ▲ South Island, New Zealand 42°01′S 172°46′E
11 P17 **Travers Reservoir** ⊠ Alberta, SW Canada
167 T14 **Tra Vinh** *var.* Phu Vinh. Tra Vinh, S Vietnam 09°57′N 106°20′E
25 S10 **Travis, Lake** ⊠ Texas, SW USA
112 H12 **Travnik** Federacija Bosna I Hercegovina, C Bosnia and Herzegovina 44°14′N 17°40′E
109 V11 **Trbovlje** *Ger.* Trifail. C Slovenia 46°10′N 15°03′E
23 V13 **Treasure Island** Florida, SE USA 27°46′N 82°46′W
Treasure State *see* Montana
186 I8 **Treasury Islands** *island group* NW Solomon Islands
106 D9 **Trebbia** *anc.* Trebia. ≈ NW Italy
100 N8 **Trebel** ≈ NE Germany
103 O16 **Trèbes** Aude, S France 43°12′N 02°26′E
Trebia *see* Trebbia
111 F18 **Třebíč** *Ger.* Trebitsch. Vysočina, C Czech Republic 49°13′N 15°52′E
113 I16 **Trebinje** Republika Srpska, S Bosnia and Herzegovina 42°42′N 18°19′E
Trebišnica *see* Trebišnjica
113 H16 **Trebišnjica** *var.* Trebišnica. ≈ S Bosnia and Herzegovina
111 N20 **Trebišov** *Hung.* Tőketerebes. Košický Kraj, E Slovakia 48°37′N 21°44′E
Trebitsch *see* Třebíč
Trebizond *see* Trabzon
Trebnitz *see* Trzebnica
109 V12 **Trebnje** SE Slovenia 45°54′N 15°01′E
111 D19 **Třeboň** *Ger.* Wittingau. Jihočeský Kraj, S Czech Republic 49°00′N 14°46′E
104 J15 **Trebujena** Andalucía, S Spain 36°52′N 06°11′W
100 I7 **Treene** ≈ N Germany
Tree Planters State *see* Nebraska
109 S9 **Treffen** Kärnten, S Austria 46°40′N 13°51′E
Trefynwy *see* Monmouth
102 G5 **Tréguier** Côtes d'Armor, NW France 48°50′N 03°12′W
61 G18 **Treinta y Tres** Treinta y Tres, E Uruguay 33°16′S 54°17′W
61 F18 **Treinta y Tres** ◆ *department* E Uruguay
122 F11 **Trëkhgornyy** Chelyabinskaya Oblast', C Russian Federation 54°42′N 58°25′E
114 F9 **Treklyanska Reka** ≈ W Bulgaria
102 K8 **Trélazé** Maine-et-Loire, NW France 47°27′N 00°28′W
63 K17 **Trelew** Chubut, SE Argentina 43°13′S 65°15′W
95 K23 **Trelleborg** *var.* Trälleborg. Skåne, S Sweden 55°22′N 13°10′E
113 P15 **Trem** ▲ SE Serbia 43°10′N 22°12′E
15 N11 **Tremblant, Mont** ▲ Québec, SE Canada 46°13′N 74°34′W
99 H17 **Tremelo** Vlaams Brabant, C Belgium 51°N 04°34′E
107 M15 **Tremiti, Isole** *island group* SE Italy
30 K12 **Tremont** Illinois, N USA 40°30′N 89°31′W
36 L1 **Tremonton** Utah, W USA 41°42′N 112°09′W
105 U4 **Tremp** Cataluña, NE Spain 42°09′N 00°53′E
30 J7 **Trempealeau** Wisconsin, N USA 44°00′N 91°25′W
15 P8 **Trenche** ≈ Québec, SE Canada
15 O7 **Trenche, Lac** ◎ Québec, SE Canada
111 I20 **Trenčiansky Kraj** ◆ *region* W Slovakia
111 I19 **Trenčín** *Ger.* Trentschin, *Hung.* Trencsén. Trenčiansky Kraj, W Slovakia 48°54′N 18°03′E
Trencsén *see* Trenčín
Trengganu *see* Terengganu
Trengganu, Kuala *see* Kuala Terengganu
61 A21 **Trenque Lauquen** Buenos Aires, E Argentina 36°01′S 62°47′W
14 J14 **Trent** ≈ Ontario, SE Canada
97 N18 **Trent** ≈ C England, United Kingdom
Trent *see* Trento
106 F5 **Trentino-Alto Adige** *prev.* Venezia Tridentina. ◆ *region* N Italy
106 G6 **Trento** *Eng.* Trent, *Ger.* Trient; *anc.* Tridentum. Trentino-Alto Adige, N Italy 46°05′N 11°08′E
14 J15 **Trenton** Ontario, SE Canada 44°07′N 77°34′W
23 V10 **Trenton** Florida, SE USA 29°36′N 82°49′W
23 R1 **Trenton** Georgia, SE USA 34°52′N 85°27′W
31 S10 **Trenton** Michigan, N USA 42°08′N 83°10′W
27 S2 **Trenton** Missouri, C USA 40°04′N 93°37′W
28 M17 **Trenton** Nebraska, C USA 40°10′N 101°00′W
18 J15 **Trenton** *state capital* New Jersey, NE USA 40°13′N 74°45′W
21 W10 **Trenton** North Carolina, SE USA 35°03′N 77°20′W
20 G9 **Trenton** Tennessee, S USA 35°59′N 88°59′W
36 L1 **Trenton** Utah, W USA 41°53′N 111°57′W
Trentschin *see* Trenčín
Treptow an der Rega *see* Trzebiatów
61 C23 **Tres Arroyos** Buenos Aires, E Argentina 38°22′S 60°17′W
61 J15 **Três Cachoeiras** Rio Grande do Sul, S Brazil 29°21′S 49°48′W
106 E7 **Trescore Balneario** Lombardia, N Italy 45°43′N 09°52′E
41 V17 **Tres Cruces, Cerro** ▲ SE Mexico 15°28′N 92°27′W
57 K18 **Tres Cruces, Cordillera** ▲▲ W Bolivia
113 N18 **Treska** ≈ NW FYR Macedonia
113 I14 **Treskavica** ▲▲ SE Bosnia and Herzegovina
59 J20 **Três Lagoas** Mato Grosso do Sul, SW Brazil 20°46′S 51°43′W
40 H12 **Tres Marías, Islas** *island group* C Mexico
59 M19 **Três Marias, Represa** ⊠ SE Brazil
63 F20 **Tres Montes, Península** *headland* S Chile 46°49′S 75°29′W
105 O3 **Trespaderne** Castilla-León, N Spain 42°47′N 03°24′W
60 G13 **Três Passos** Rio Grande do Sul, S Brazil 27°33′S 53°55′W
61 A23 **Tres Picos, Cerro** ▲ E Argentina 38°10′S 61°54′W
63 G17 **Tres Picos, Cerro** ▲ SW Argentina 42°22′S 71°51′W
60 I12 **Três Pinheiros** Paraná, S Brazil 25°25′S 51°57′W
59 M21 **Três Pontas** Minas Gerais, SE Brazil 21°33′S 45°18′W
Tres Puntas, Cabo *see* Manabique, Punta
60 P9 **Três Rios** Rio de Janeiro, SE Brazil 22°06′S 43°15′W
Tres Tabernae *see* Saverne
Trestenberg/Trestendorf *see* Tășnad
41 R15 **Tres Valles** Veracruz-Llave, SE Mexico 18°14′N 96°03′W
94 H12 **Tretten** Oppland, S Norway 61°19′N 10°19′E
Treuburg *see* Olecko
101 K21 **Treuchtlingen** Bayern, S Germany 48°57′N 10°55′E
100 N13 **Treuenbrietzen** Brandenburg, E Germany 52°06′N 12°52′E
95 F16 **Treungen** Telemark, S Norway 59°00′N 08°34′E
63 H17 **Trevelín** Chubut, SW Argentina 43°02′S 71°27′W
Treves/Trèves *see* Trier
106 I13 **Trevi** Umbria, C Italy 42°52′N 12°46′E
106 E7 **Treviglio** Lombardia, N Italy 45°32′N 09°35′E
104 J4 **Trevinca, Peña** ▲ NW Spain 42°10′N 06°49′W
105 P3 **Treviño** Castilla-León, N Spain 42°45′N 02°41′W
106 I7 **Treviso** *anc.* Tarvisium. Veneto, NE Italy 45°40′N 12°15′E
97 G24 **Trevose Head** *headland* SW England, United Kingdom 50°33′N 05°03′W
Trg *see* Feldkirchen in Kärnten
183 P17 **Triabunna** Tasmania, SE Australia 42°33′S 147°55′E
21 W4 **Triangle** Virginia, NE USA 38°30′N 77°17′W
83 L18 **Triangle** Masvingo, SE Zimbabwe 20°58′S 31°28′E
115 L23 **Tría Nisía** *island* Kykládes, Greece, Aegean Sea
Triberg *see* Triberg im Schwarzwald
101 G23 **Triberg im Schwarzwald** *var.* Triberg. Baden-Württemberg, SW Germany 48°07′N 08°13′E
153 P11 **Tribhuvan** ✈ (Kathmandu) Central, C Nepal
54 C9 **Tribugá, Golfo de** *gulf* W Colombia
181 W4 **Tribulation, Cape** *headland* Queensland, NE Australia 16°14′S 145°48′E
108 M8 **Tribulaun** ▲ SW Austria 46°59′N 11°18′E
11 U17 **Tribune** Saskatchewan, S Canada 49°16′N 103°50′W
26 H5 **Tribune** Kansas, C USA 38°27′N 101°46′W
107 N18 **Tricarico** Basilicata, S Italy 40°37′N 16°09′E
107 Q19 **Tricase** Puglia, SE Italy 39°56′N 18°21′E
Trichinopoly *see* Tiruchchirāppalli
115 D18 **Trichonída, Límni** ◎ C Greece
155 G22 **Trichūr** *var.* Thrissur. Kerala, SW India 10°32′N 76°14′E *see also* Thrissur
Tricorno *see* Triglav
183 O8 **Trida** New South Wales, SE Australia 33°02′S 145°03′E
35 S1 **Trident Peak** ▲ Nevada, W USA 41°52′N 118°22′W
Tridentum/Trient *see* Trento
109 T6 **Trieben** Steiermark, SE Austria 47°29′N 14°30′E
101 D19 **Trier** *Eng.* Treves, *Fr.* Trèves; *anc.* Augusta Treverorum. Rheinland-Pfalz, SW Germany 49°45′N 06°39′E
106 K7 **Trieste** *Slvn.* Trst. Friuli-Venezia Giulia, NE Italy 45°39′N 13°45′E
Trieste, Golfo di/Triest, Golf von *see* Trieste, Gulf of
106 J8 **Trieste, Gulf of** *Cro.* Tršćanski Zaljev, *Ger.* Golf von Triest, *It.* Golfo di Trieste, *Slvn.* Tržaški Zaliv. *gulf* S Europe
109 W4 **Triesting** ≈ W Austria
Triều Hai *see* Quang Tri
Trifail *see* Trbovlje
116 L9 **Trifești** Iași, NE Romania 47°30′N 27°31′E
109 S10 **Triglav** *It.* Tricorno. ▲ NW Slovenia 46°22′N 13°40′E
104 I14 **Trigueros** Andalucía, S Spain 37°24′N 06°50′W
115 E16 **Tríkala** *prev.* Trikkala. Thessalía, C Greece 39°33′N 21°46′E
115 E17 **Trikeriótis** ≈ C Greece
Trikkala *see* Tríkala
Trikomo/Trikomon *see* İskele
97 F17 **Trim** *Ir.* Baile Átha Troim. Meath, E Ireland 53°34′N 06°47′W
108 E7 **Trimbach** Solothurn, NW Switzerland 47°22′N 07°53′E
109 Q5 **Trimmelkam** Oberösterreich, N Austria 48°02′N 12°55′E
29 U11 **Trimont** Minnesota, N USA 43°45′N 94°42′W
Trimontium *see* Plovdiv
Trinacria *see* Sicilia
155 K24 **Trincomalee** *var.* Trinkomali. Eastern Province, NE Sri Lanka 08°34′N 81°13′E
65 K16 **Trindade, Ilha da** *island* Brazil, W Atlantic Ocean
47 Y9 **Trindade Spur** *undersea feature* SW Atlantic Ocean 21°00′S 35°00′W
111 J17 **Třinec** *Ger.* Trzynietz. Moravskoslezský Kraj, E Czech Republic 49°41′N 18°39′E
57 M16 **Trinidad** Beni, N Bolivia 14°52′S 64°54′W
54 H9 **Trinidad** Casanare, E Colombia 05°25′N 71°39′W
44 E6 **Trinidad** Sancti Spíritus, C Cuba 21°48′N 80°00′W
61 E19 **Trinidad** Flores, S Uruguay 33°35′S 56°54′W
37 U8 **Trinidad** Colorado, C USA 37°11′N 104°31′W
45 Y17 **Trinidad** *island* C Trinidad and Tobago
Trinidad *see* Jose Abad Santos
45 Y16 **Trinidad and Tobago** *off.* Republic of Trinidad and Tobago. ◆ *republic* SE West Indies
Trinidad and Tobago, Republic of *see* Trinidad and Tobago
63 F22 **Trinidad, Golfo** *gulf* S Chile
61 B24 **Trinidad, Isla** *island* E Argentina
107 N16 **Trinitapoli** Puglia, SE Italy 41°22′N 16°06′E
55 X10 **Trinité, Montagnes de la** ▲▲ C French Guiana
25 W9 **Trinity** Texas, SW USA 30°57′N 95°22′W
13 U12 **Trinity Bay** *inlet* Newfoundland, Newfoundland and Labrador, E Canada
39 P15 **Trinity Islands** *island group* Alaska, USA
35 N2 **Trinity Mountains** ▲▲ California, W USA
35 S4 **Trinity Peak** ▲ Nevada, W USA 40°13′N 118°43′W
35 S5 **Trinity Range** ▲▲ Nevada, W USA
35 N2 **Trinity River** ≈ California, W USA
25 V8 **Trinity River** ≈ Texas, SW USA
Trinkomali *see* Trincomalee
173 Y15 **Triolet** NW Mauritius 20°05′S 57°32′E
107 O20 **Trionto, Capo** *headland* S Italy 39°37′N 16°46′E
Tripití, Ákra *see* Trypití, Akrotírio
115 F20 **Trípoli** *prev.* Trípolis. Pelopónnisos, S Greece 37°31′N 22°22′E
138 G6 **Tripoli** *var.* Țarābulus, Țarābulus ash Shām, Trâblous; *anc.* Tripolis. N Lebanon 34°30′N 35°42′E
29 X12 **Tripoli** Iowa, C USA 42°48′N 92°15′W
Tripoli *see* Țarābulus
Trípolis *see* Trípoli, Greece
Tripolis *see* Tripoli, Lebanon
75 O8 **Tripolitania** ◆ *cultural region* NW Libya
29 Q12 **Tripp** South Dakota, N USA 43°12′N 97°57′W
153 V15 **Tripura** *var.* Hill Tippera. ◆ *state* NE India
108 K8 **Trisanna** ≈ W Austria
100 H8 **Trischen** *island* NW Germany
65 M24 **Tristan da Cunha** ◇ *dependency of Saint Helena* SE Atlantic Ocean
67 P15 **Tristan da Cunha** *island* SE Atlantic Ocean
65 L18 **Tristan da Cunha Fracture Zone** *tectonic feature* S Atlantic Ocean
167 S14 **Tri Tôn** An Giang, S Vietnam 10°26′N 105°01′E
167 W10 **Triton Island** *island* S Paracel Islands
155 G24 **Trivandrum** *var.* Thiruvanathapuram, Tiruvantapuram. *state capital* Kerala, SW India 08°30′N 76°57′E
111 H20 **Trnava** *Ger.* Tyrnau, *Hung.* Nagyszombat. Trnavský Kraj, W Slovakia 48°22′N 17°36′E
111 H20 **Trnavský Kraj** ◆ *region* W Slovakia
Trnovo *see* Veliko Tŭrnovo
Trobriand Island *see* Kiriwina Island
Trobriand Islands *see* Kiriwina Islands
11 Q16 **Trochu** Alberta, SW Canada 51°48′N 113°12′W
109 U7 **Trofaiach** Steiermark, SE Austria 47°25′N 15°01′E
93 F14 **Trofors** Troms, N Norway 65°31′N 13°19′E
113 E14 **Trogir** *It.* Traù. Split-Dalmacija, S Croatia 43°32′N 16°13′E
112 F13 **Troglav** ▲ Bosnia and Herzegovina/Croatia 44°00′N 16°36′E
107 M16 **Troia** Puglia, SE Italy 41°21′N 15°19′E
107 K24 **Troina** Sicilia, Italy, C Mediterranean Sea 37°47′N 14°37′E
173 O16 **Trois-Bassins** W Réunion 21°05′S 55°18′E
101 E17 **Troisdorf** Nordrhein-Westfalen, W Germany 50°49′N 07°09′E
74 H5 **Trois Fourches, Cap des** *headland* NE Morocco 35°27′N 02°58′W
15 T8 **Trois-Pistoles** Québec, SE Canada 48°08′N 69°10′W
99 L21 **Trois-Ponts** Liège, E Belgium 50°22′N 05°52′E
15 P11 **Trois-Rivières** Québec, SE Canada 46°21′N 72°34′W
55 Y12 **Trois Sauts** S French Guiana 02°15′N 52°52′W
99 M22 **Troisvierges** Diekirch, N Luxembourg 50°07′N 06°00′E
122 F11 **Troitsk** Chelyabinskaya Oblast', S Russian Federation 54°04′N 61°31′E
125 T9 **Troitsko-Pechorsk** Respublika Komi, NW Russian Federation 62°39′N 56°06′E
127 V7 **Troitskoye** Orenburgskaya Oblast', W Russian Federation 52°23′N 56°24′E
Troki *see* Trakai
94 F9 **Trolla** ▲ S Norway 62°41′N 09°47′E
95 J18 **Trollhättan** Västra Götaland, S Sweden 58°17′N 12°20′E
94 G9 **Trollheimen** ▲▲ S Norway
94 E9 **Trolltindane** ▲ S Norway 62°30′N 07°43′E
58 H11 **Trombetas, Rio** ≈ NE Brazil
128 L16 **Tromelin, Île** *island* N Réunion
92 I9 **Troms** ◆ *county* N Norway
92 I9 **Tromsø** *Fin.* Tromssa. Troms, N Norway 69°39′N 19°01′E
84 F5 **Tromsøflaket** *undersea feature* W Barents Sea 18°30′E 71°30′N
Tromssa *see* Tromsø
94 H10 **Tron** ▲ S Norway 62°12′N 10°46′E
35 U12 **Trona** California, W USA 35°46′N 117°21′W
63 G16 **Tronador, Cerro** ▲ S Chile 41°12′S 71°51′W
94 H8 **Trondheim** *Ger.* Drontheim; *prev.* Nidaros, Trondhjem. Sør-Trøndelag, S Norway 63°25′N 10°24′E
94 H7 **Trondheimsfjorden** *fjord* S Norway
Trondhjem *see* Trondheim
107 J14 **Tronto** ≈ C Italy
121 P3 **Troódos** *var.* Troodos Mountains. ▲▲ C Cyprus
Troodos *see* Ólympos
Troodos Mountains *see* Troódos
96 I13 **Troon** W Scotland, United Kingdom 55°32′N 04°41′W
107 M22 **Tropea** Calabria, SW Italy 38°40′N 15°52′E
36 L7 **Tropic** Utah, W USA 37°37′N 112°04′W
64 L10 **Tropic Seamount** *var.* Banc du Tropique. *undersea feature* E Atlantic Ocean 23°50′N 20°40′W
Tropique, Banc du *see* Tropic Seamount
Tropoja *see* Tropojë
113 L17 **Tropojë** *var.* Tropoja. Kukës, N Albania 42°25′N 20°09′E
Troppau *see* Opava
95 O16 **Trosa** Södermanland, C Sweden 58°54′N 17°35′E
118 H12 **Troškūnai** Utena, E Lithuania 55°36′N 24°55′E
101 G23 **Trossingen** Baden-Württemberg, SW Germany 48°04′N 08°37′E
117 T4 **Trostyanets'** *Rus.* Trostyanets. Sums'ka Oblast', NE Ukraine 50°30′N 34°59′E
117 N7 **Trostyanets'** *Rus.* Trostyanets. Vinnyts'ka Oblast', C Ukraine 48°35′N 29°10′E
Trostyanets *see* Trostyanets'
116 L11 **Trotuș** ≈ E Romania
44 M8 **Trou-du-Nord** N Haiti 19°34′N 71°57′W
25 W7 **Troup** Texas, SW USA 32°08′N 95°07′W
8 I10 **Trout** ≈ Northwest Territories, NW Canada
33 N8 **Trout Creek** Montana, NW USA 47°51′N 115°40′W
32 H10 **Trout Lake** Washington, NW USA 45°59′N 121°33′W
12 B9 **Trout Lake** ◎ Ontario, S Canada
33 T12 **Trout Peak** ▲ Wyoming, C USA 44°36′N 109°33′W
102 L4 **Trouville** Calvados, N France 49°21′N 00°07′E
97 L22 **Trowbridge** S England, United Kingdom 51°20′N 02°13′W
23 Q6 **Troy** Alabama, S USA 31°48′N 85°58′W
27 Q3 **Troy** Kansas, C USA 39°45′N 95°06′W
27 W4 **Troy** Missouri, C USA 38°59′N 90°59′W
18 L10 **Troy** New York, NE USA 42°43′N 73°37′W
21 S10 **Troy** North Carolina, SE USA 35°23′N 79°54′W
31 R13 **Troy** Ohio, N USA 40°02′N 84°12′W
25 T9 **Troy** Texas, SW USA 31°12′N 97°18′W
114 I9 **Troyan** Lovech, N Bulgaria 42°52′N 24°42′E
114 I9 **Troyanski Prokhod** *pass* N Bulgaria
145 N6 **Troyebratskiy** Severnyy Kazakhstan, N Kazakhstan 54°25′N 66°03′E
103 Q6 **Troyes** *anc.* Augustobona Tricassium. Aube, N France 48°18′N 04°04′E
117 X5 **Troyits'ke** Luhans'ka Oblast', E Ukraine 49°55′N 38°18′E
35 W7 **Troy Peak** ▲ Nevada, W USA 38°18′N 115°27′W
113 G15 **Trpanj** Dubrovnik-Neretva, S Croatia 43°00′N 17°18′E
Tršćanski Zaljev *see* Trieste, Gulf of
Trst *see* Trieste
113 N14 **Trstenik** Serbia, C Serbia 43°38′N 21°01′E
126 I6 **Trubchevsk** Bryanskaya Oblast', W Russian Federation 52°33′N 33°45′E
Trubchular *see* Orlyak
37 S10 **Truchas Peak** ▲ New Mexico, SW USA 35°57′N 105°38′W

◆ Country ● Country Capital ◇ Dependent Territory ○ Dependent Territory Capital ◆ Administrative Regions ✈ International Airport ▲ Mountain ▲▲ Mountain Range Volcano ≈ River ◎ Lake ⊠ Reservoir

TRUCIAL COAST – TURPAN DEPRESSION

143 P16 **Trucial Coast** *physical region* C United Arab Emirates
Trucial States *see* United Arab Emirates
35 Q6 **Truckee** California, W USA 39°18′N 120°10′W
35 R5 **Truckee River** 🌊 Nevada, W USA
127 Q13 **Trudfront** Astrakhanskaya Oblast', SW Russian Federation 45°56′N 47°42′E
14 I9 **Truite, Lac à la** ◎ Québec, SE Canada
42 K4 **Trujillo** Colón, NE Honduras 15°59′N 85°54′W
56 C12 **Trujillo** La Libertad, NW Peru 08°04′S 79°02′W
104 K10 **Trujillo** Extremadura, W Spain 39°28′N 05°53′W
54 I6 **Trujillo** Trujillo, NW Venezuela 09°20′N 70°38′W
54 I6 **Trujillo** *off.* Estado Trujillo. ◆ *state* W Venezuela
Trujillo, Estado *see* Trujillo
Truk *see* Chuuk
Truk Islands *see* Chuuk Islands
29 U10 **Truman** Minnesota, N USA 43°49′N 94°26′W
27 X10 **Trumann** Arkansas, C USA 35°40′N 90°30′W
36 J9 **Trumbull, Mount** ▲ Arizona, SW USA 36°22′N 113°09′W
114 F9 **Trŭn** Pernik, W Bulgaria 42°51′N 22°37′E
183 Q8 **Trundle** New South Wales, SE Australia 32°55′S 147°43′E
129 U13 **Trung Phân** *physical region* S Vietnam
Trupcilar *see* Orlyak
13 Q15 **Truro** Nova Scotia, SE Canada 45°24′N 63°18′W
97 H25 **Truro** SW England, United Kingdom 50°16′N 05°03′W
25 P5 **Truscott** Texas, SW USA 33°43′N 99°48′W
116 K9 **Truşeşti** Botoşani, NE Romania 47°45′N 27°01′E
116 H6 **Truskavets'** L'vivs'ka Oblast', W Ukraine 49°15′N 23°30′E
95 H22 **Trustrup** Århus, C Denmark 56°20′N 10°46′E
10 M11 **Trutch** British Columbia, W Canada 57°42′N 123°00′W
37 Q14 **Truth Or Consequences** New Mexico, SW USA 33°07′N 107°15′W
111 F15 **Trutnov** *Ger.* Trautenau. Královéhradecký Kraj, N Czech Republic 50°34′N 15°55′E
103 P13 **Truyère** 🌊 C France
114 K9 **Tryavna** Lovech, N Bulgaria 42°52′N 25°30′E
28 M14 **Tryon** Nebraska, C USA 41°33′N 100°57′W
115 J16 **Trypití, Akrotírio** *var.* Ákra Tripití. *headland* Ágios Efstrátios, E Greece 39°28′N 24°58′E
94 J12 **Trysil** Hedmark, S Norway 61°18′N 12°16′E
94 I11 **Trysilelva** 🌊 S Norway
112 D10 **Tržac** Federacija Bosna I Hercegovina, NW Bosnia and Herzegovina 44°58′N 15°48′E
Tržaški Zaliv *see* Trieste, Gulf of
110 G10 **Trzcianka** *Ger.* Schönlanke. Pila, Wielkopolskie, C Poland 53°02′N 16°24′E
110 E7 **Trzebiatów** *Ger.* Treptow an der Rega. Zachodnio-pomorskie, NW Poland 54°04′N 15°14′E
111 G14 **Trzebnica** *Ger.* Trebnitz. Dolnośląskie, SW Poland 51°19′N 17°03′E
109 T10 **Tržič** *Ger.* Neumarktl. NW Slovenia 46°22′N 14°17′E
Trzynietz *see* Třinec
83 G21 **Tsabong** *var.* Tshabong. Kgalagadi, SW Botswana 26°03′S 22°27′E
162 G7 **Tsagaanchuluut** Dzavhan, C Mongolia 47°06′N 96°40′E
162 M8 **Tsagaandelger** *var.* Haraat. Dundgovĭ, C Mongolia 46°30′N 107°39′E
Tsagaanders *see* Bayantümen
162 G7 **Tsagaanhayrhan** *var.* Shiree. Dzavhan, W Mongolia 47°30′N 96°48′E
Tsagaannuur *see* Halhgol
Tsagaan-Olom *see* Tayshir
Tsagaan-Ovoo *see* Nariynteel
Tsagaantüngi *see* Altantsögts
162 H6 **Tsagaan-Uul** *var.* Sharga. Hövsgöl, N Mongolia 49°33′N 98°36′E
162 J5 **Tsagaan-Üür** *var.* Bulgan. Hövsgöl, N Mongolia 50°30′N 101°28′E
127 P12 **Tsagan Aman** Respublika Kalmykiya, SW Russian Federation 47°37′N 46°43′E
23 V11 **Tsala Apopka Lake** ◎ Florida, SE USA
Tsamkong *see* Zhanjiang
Tsangpo *see* Brahmaputra
Tsant *see* Deren
Tsao *see* Tsau
172 I4 **Tsaratanana** Mahajanga, C Madagascar 16°46′S 47°40′E
114 N10 **Tsarevo** *prev.* Michurin. Burgas, E Bulgaria 42°10′N 27°51′E
Tsarigrad *see* İstanbul
Tsaritsyn *see* Volgograd
114 K7 **Tsar Kaloyan** Ruse, N Bulgaria 43°36′N 26°14′E
Tsarskoye Selo *see* Pushkin
117 T7 **Tsarychanka** Dnipropetrovs'ka Oblast', E Ukraine 48°56′N 34°29′E
83 H21 **Tsatsu** Southern, S Botswana 25°21′S 24°45′E
83 G17 **Tsau** *var.* Tsao. North-West, NW Botswana 20°08′S 22°29′E
81 J20 **Tsavo** Coast, S Kenya 02°59′S 38°28′E
83 E21 **Tsawisis** Karas, S Namibia 26°18′S 18°09′E
Tschakathurn *see* Čakovec
Tschaslau *see* Čáslav
Tschenstochau *see* Częstochowa
Tschernembl *see* Črnomelj
28 K6 **Tschida, Lake** ▣ North Dakota, N USA
Tschorna *see* Mustvee
162 G8 **Tseel** Govĭ-Altay, SW Mongolia 45°45′N 95°54′E
138 G8 **Tsefat** *var.* Safed, *Ar.* Safad; *prev.* Zefat. Northern, N Israel 32°57′N 35°27′E
126 M13 **Tselina** Rostovskaya Oblast', SW Russian Federation 46°31′N 41°01′E
Tselinograd *see* Astana
Tselinogradskaya Oblast *see* Akmola
Tsengel *see* Tosontsengel
162 J8 **Tsenher** *var.* Altan-Ovoo. Arhangay, C Mongolia 47°24′N 101°51′E
Tsenher *see* Mönhhayrhan
163 N8 **Tsenhermandal** *var.* Modot. Hentiy, C Mongolia 47°45′N 109°03′E
Tsentral'nyye Nyenyye Garagumy *see* Merkezi Garagumy
83 E21 **Tses** Karas, S Namibia 25°58′S 18°08′E
Tseshevlya *see* Tsyeshavlya
162 E7 **Tsetseg** *var.* Tsetsegnuur. Hovd, W Mongolia 46°30′N 93°16′E
Tsetsegnuur *see* Tsetseg
Tsetsen Khan *see* Öndörhaan
162 J8 **Tsetserleg** Arhangay, C Mongolia 47°29′N 101°19′E
162 H6 **Tsetserleg** *var.* Halban. Hövsgöl, N Mongolia 49°30′N 97°33′E
162 J8 **Tsetserleg** *var.* Hujirt. Övörhangay, C Mongolia 46°50′N 102°38′E
77 R16 **Tsévié** S Togo 06°25′N 01°13′E
Tshabong *see* Tsabong
83 G20 **Tshane** Kgalagadi, SW Botswana 24°05′S 21°54′E
Tshangalele, Lac *see* Lufira, Lac de Retenue de la
83 H17 **Tshauxaba** Central, C Botswana 19°56′S 25°09′E
79 F21 **Tshela** Bas-Congo, W Dem. Rep. Congo 04°56′S 13°02′E
79 K22 **Tshibala** Kasai-Occidental, S Dem. Rep. Congo 06°53′S 22°01′E
79 J22 **Tshikapa** Kasai-Occidental, SW Dem. Rep. Congo 06°23′S 20°47′E
79 L22 **Tshilenge** Kasai Oriental S Dem. Rep. Congo 06°17′S 23°48′E
79 L24 **Tshimbalanga** Katanga, S Dem. Rep. Congo 09°42′S 23°04′E
79 L22 **Tshimbulu** Kasai-Occidental, S Dem. Rep. Congo 06°27′S 22°54′E
Tshiumbe *see* Chiumbe
79 M21 **Tshofa** Kasai-Oriental, C Dem. Rep. Congo 05°13′S 25°13′E
79 K18 **Tshuapa** 🌊 C Dem. Rep. Congo
83 J21 **Tshwane** *var.* Epitoli; *prev.* Pretoria. ● Gauteng, NE South Africa 25°41′S 28°12′E ● *see also* Pretoria
114 G7 **Tsibritsa** 🌊 NW Bulgaria
Tsien Tang *see* Puyang Jiang
114 I12 **Tsigansko Gradishte** ▲ Bulgaria/Greece 41°24′N 24°41′E
Tsihombe *see* Tsiombe
8 H7 **Tsiigehtchic** *prev.* Arctic Red River. Northwest Territories, NW Canada 67°24′N 133°40′W
125 Q7 **Tsil'ma** 🌊 NW Russian Federation
119 J17 **Tsimkavichy** *Rus.* Timkovichi. Minskaya Voblasts', C Belarus 53°04′N 26°59′E
126 M11 **Tsimlyansk** Rostovskaya Oblast', SW Russian Federation 47°39′N 42°05′E
127 N11 **Tsimlyanskoye Vodokhranilishche** *var.* Tsimlyanskoye Vodokhranilishche, *Eng.* Tsimlyansk Reservoir. ▣ SW Russian Federation
Tsimlyansk Reservoir *see* Tsimlyanskoye Vodokhranilishche
Tsimlyansk Vodoskhovshche *see* Tsimlyanskoye Vodokhranilishche
Tsinan *see* Jinan
Tsing Hai *see* Qinghai Hu, China
Tsinghai *see* Qinghai, China
Tsingtao/Tsingtau *see* Qingdao
Tsingyuan *see* Baoding
Tsinkiang *see* Quanzhou
Tsintao *see* Qingdao
83 D17 **Tsintsabis** Otjikoto, N Namibia 18°45′S 17°51′E
172 H8 **Tsiombe** *var.* Tsihombe. Toliara, S Madagascar
123 O13 **Tsipa** 🌊 S Russian Federation
172 H5 **Tsiribihina** 🌊 W Madagascar
172 I5 **Tsiroanomandidy** Antananarivo, C Madagascar 18°44′S 46°02′E
189 U13 **Tsis** *island* Chuuk, C Micronesia
Tsitsihar *see* Qiqihar
127 Q3 **Tsivil'sk** Chuvashskaya Respublika, W Russian Federation 55°51′N 47°30′E
137 T9 **Ts'khinvali** *prev.* Staliniri. C Georgia 42°12′N 43°58′E
119 J19 **Tsna** 🌊 SW Belarus
124 I15 **Tsna** *var.* Zna. 🌊 W Russian Federation
162 G9 **Tsogt** *var.* Tahilt. Govĭ-Altay, W Mongolia 45°20′N 96°42′E
162 K10 **Tsogt-Ovoo** *var.* Doloon. Ömnögovĭ, S Mongolia 44°28′N 105°22′E
162 L10 **Tsogttsetsiy** *var.* Baruunsuu. Ömnögovĭ, S Mongolia 43°46′N 105°28′E
Tsoohor *see* Hürmen
164 K14 **Tsu** *var.* Tu. Mie, Honshū, SW Japan 34°41′N 136°30′E
165 O10 **Tsubame** *var.* Tubame. Niigata, Honshū, C Japan 37°40′N 138°56′E
165 V3 **Tsubetsu** Hokkaidō, NE Japan 43°43′N 144°01′E
165 O13 **Tsuchiura** *var.* Tutiura. Ibaraki, Honshū, S Japan 36°05′N 140°11′E
165 Q6 **Tsugaru-kaikyō** *strait* N Japan
164 E14 **Tsukumi** *var.* Tukumi. Ōita, Kyūshū, SW Japan 33°00′N 131°51′E
Tsul-Ulaan *see* Bayannuur
Tsul-Ulaan *see* Bayanuur
83 D17 **Tsumeb** Otjikoto, N Namibia 19°13′S 17°42′E
83 F17 **Tsumkwe** Otjozondjupa, NE Namibia 19°37′S 20°30′E
164 D15 **Tsuno** Miyazaki, Kyūshū, SW Japan 32°43′N 131°32′E
164 D12 **Tsuno-shima** *island* SW Japan
164 K12 **Tsuruga** *var.* Turuga. Fukui, Honshū, SW Japan 35°38′N 136°01′E
164 H12 **Tsurugi-san** ▲ Shikoku, SW Japan 33°50′N 134°04′E
165 P9 **Tsuruoka** *var.* Turuoka. Yamagata, Honshū, C Japan 38°44′N 139°48′E
164 C12 **Tsushima** *var.* Tsushima-tō, Tusima. *island group* SW Japan
Tsushima-tō *see* Tsushima
164 H12 **Tsuyama** *var.* Tuyama. Okayama, Honshū, SW Japan 35°04′N 134°01′E
83 G19 **Tswaane** Ghanzi, W Botswana 22°21′S 21°52′E
119 N16 **Tsyakhtsin** *Rus.* Tekhtin. Mahilyowskaya Voblasts', E Belarus 53°51′N 29°44′E
119 P19 **Tsyerakhowka** *Rus.* Terekhovka. Homyel'skaya Voblasts', SE Belarus 52°13′N 31°24′E
119 I17 **Tsyeshawlya** *Rus.* Cheshevlya, Tseshevlya. Brestskaya Voblasts', SW Belarus 53°14′N 25°49′E
Tsyurupinsk *see* Tsyurupyns'k
117 R10 **Tsyurupyns'k** *Rus.* Tsyurupinsk. Khersons'ka Oblast', S Ukraine 46°35′N 32°43′E
Tu *see* Tsu
186 C7 **Tua** 🌊 C Papua New Guinea
Tuaim *see* Tuam
184 L6 **Tuakau** Waikato, North Island, New Zealand 37°16′S 174°56′E
97 C17 **Tuam** *Ir.* Tuaim. Galway, W Ireland 53°31′N 08°50′W
185 K14 **Tuamarina** Marlborough, South Island, New Zealand 41°27′S 174°00′E
Tuamotu, Archipel des *see* Tuamotu, Îles
193 Q9 **Tuamotu Fracture Zone** *tectonic feature* E Pacific Ocean
191 W9 **Tuamotu, Îles** *var.* Archipel des Tuamotu, Dangerous Archipelago, Tuamotu Islands. *island group* N French Polynesia
Tuamotu Islands *see* Tuamotu, Îles
175 X10 **Tuamotu Ridge** *undersea feature* C Pacific Ocean
167 R5 **Tuân Giao** Lai Châu, N Vietnam 21°34′N 103°24′E
171 O2 **Tuao** Luzon, N Philippines 17°42′N 121°25′E
190 B15 **Tuapa** NW Niue 18°57′S 169°59′W
43 N7 **Tuapí** Región Autónoma Atlántico Norte, NE Nicaragua 14°10′N 83°20′W
126 K15 **Tuapse** Krasnodarskiy Kray, SW Russian Federation 44°08′N 39°07′E
169 U6 **Tuaran** Sabah, East Malaysia 06°12′N 116°12′E
104 I6 **Tua, Rio** 🌊 N Portugal
192 H15 **Tuasivi** Savai'i, C Samoa 13°38′S 172°08′W
185 B24 **Tuatapere** Southland, South Island, New Zealand 46°09′S 167°43′E
36 M9 **Tuba City** Arizona, SW USA 36°08′N 111°14′W
138 H11 **Ṭūbah, Qaṣr aṭ** *castle* 'Ammān, C Jordan
Tubame *see* Tsubame
169 R16 **Tuban** *prev.* Toeban. Jawa, C Indonesia 06°55′S 112°01′E
141 O16 **Tuban, Wādī** *dry watercourse* SW Yemen
61 K14 **Tubarão** Santa Catarina, S Brazil 28°29′S 49°00′W
98 O10 **Tubbergen** Overijssel, E Netherlands 52°25′N 06°46′E
Tubeke *see* Tubize
101 H22 **Tübingen** *var.* Tuebingen. Baden-Württemberg, SW Germany 48°32′N 09°04′E
127 W6 **Tubinskiy** Respublika Bashkortostan, W Russian Federation 52°48′N 58°18′E
99 G19 **Tubize** *Dut.* Tubeke. Walloon Brabant, C Belgium 50°43′N 04°14′E
76 J16 **Tubmanburg** NW Liberia 06°50′N 10°53′W
75 T7 **Ṭubruq** *Eng.* Tobruk, *It.* Tobruch. NE Libya 32°05′N 23°59′E
191 T13 **Tubuai** *island* Îles Australes, SW French Polynesia
Tubuai, Îles/Tubuai Islands *see* Australes, Îles
Tubuai-Manu *see* Maiao
40 F3 **Tubutama** Sonora, NW Mexico 30°51′N 111°31′W
54 K4 **Tucacas** Falcón, N Venezuela 10°50′N 68°22′W
59 P16 **Tucano** Bahia, E Brazil 10°52′S 38°48′W
57 P19 **Tucavaca, Río** 🌊 E Bolivia
110 H8 **Tuchola** Kujawsko-pomorskie, C Poland 53°36′N 17°50′E
111 M17 **Tuchów** Małopolskie, S Poland 49°53′N 21°04′E
23 S3 **Tucker** Georgia, SE USA 33°53′N 84°10′W
27 W10 **Tuckerman** Arkansas, C USA 35°43′N 91°12′W
64 B12 **Tucker's Town** E Bermuda 32°20′N 64°42′W
Tuckum *see* Tukums
36 M15 **Tucson** Arizona, SW USA 32°14′N 111°01′W
62 J7 **Tucumán** *off.* Provincia de Tucumán. ◆ *province* N Argentina
Tucumán *see* San Miguel de Tucumán
Tucumán, Provincia de *see* Tucumán
37 V11 **Tucumcari** New Mexico, SW USA 35°10′N 103°43′W
58 H13 **Tucuraré** Pará, N Brazil 05°15′S 55°49′W
55 Q6 **Tucupita** Delta Amacuro, NE Venezuela 09°02′N 62°04′W
58 K13 **Tucuruí, Represa de** ▣ NE Brazil
110 F9 **Tuczno** Zachodnio-pomorskie, NW Poland 53°12′N 16°08′E
Tuddo *see* Tudu
105 Q5 **Tudela** *Basq.* Tutera; *anc.* Tutela. Navarra, N Spain 42°04′N 01°37′W
104 M6 **Tudela de Duero** Castilla-León, N Spain 41°35′N 04°34′W
162 G6 **Tüdevtey** *var.* Oygon. Dzavhan, N Mongolia 48°57′N 96°33′E
138 K6 **Tudmur** *var.* Tadmur, Tamar, *Gk.* Palmyra, *Bibl.* Tadmor. Ḥimṣ, C Syria 34°36′N 38°15′E
118 J4 **Tudu** *Ger.* Tuddo. Lääne-Virumaa, NE Estonia 59°12′N 26°52′E
Tuebingen *see* Tübingen
122 J14 **Tuekta** Respublika Altay, S Russian Federation 50°51′N 85°52′E
104 I5 **Tuela, Rio** 🌊 N Portugal
153 X12 **Tuensang** Nāgāland, NE India 26°16′N 94°45′E
136 L15 **Tufanbeyli** Adana, C Turkey 38°15′N 36°13′E
Tüffer *see* Laško
186 F9 **Tufi** Northern, S Papua New Guinea 09°08′S 149°20′S
193 O3 **Tufts Plain** *undersea feature* N Pacific Ocean
Tugalan *see* Kolkhozobod
67 V14 **Tugela** 🌊 SE South Africa
21 P6 **Tug Fork** 🌊 S USA
39 P15 **Tugidak Island** *island* Trinity Islands, Alaska, USA
171 O2 **Tuguegarao** Luzon, N Philippines 17°37′N 121°48′E
123 S12 **Tugur** Khabarovskiy Kray, SE Russian Federation 53°43′N 137°00′E
161 P4 **Tuhai He** 🌊 E China
104 G4 **Tui** Galicia, NW Spain 42°02′N 08°37′W
77 O13 **Tui** *var.* Grand Balé. 🌊 W Burkina
57 J16 **Tuichi, Río** 🌊 W Bolivia
64 Q11 **Tuineje** Fuerteventura, Islas Canarias, Spain, NE Atlantic Ocean 28°18′N 14°03′W
43 X16 **Tuira, Río** 🌊 SE Panama
Tuisarkan *see* Tüysarkān
Tujiabu *see* Yongxiu
127 W5 **Tukan** Respublika Bashkortostan, W Russian Federation 53°58′N 57°29′E
171 P14 **Tukangbesi, Kepulauan** *Dut.* Toekang Besi Eilanden. *island group* C Indonesia
147 V13 **Tŭkhtamish** *Rus.* Toktomush; *prev.* Tokhtamyshbek. SE Tajikistan 37°51′N 74°41′E
184 O12 **Tukituki** 🌊 North Island, New Zealand
Tu-k'ou *see* Panzhihua
121 P12 **Tūkrah** NE Libya 32°32′N 20°35′E
8 H6 **Tuktoyaktuk** Northwest Territories, NW Canada 69°27′N 133°W
168 I9 **Tuktuk** Pulau Samosir, W Indonesia 02°32′N 98°43′E
Tukum *see* Tukums
118 E9 **Tukums** *Ger.* Tuckum. Tukums, W Latvia 56°58′N 23°12′E
81 G24 **Tukuyu** *prev.* Neu-Langenburg. Mbeya, S Tanzania 09°14′S 33°39′E
Tukzār *see* Tokzār
41 O13 **Tula** *var.* Tula de Allende. Hidalgo, C Mexico 20°01′N 99°21′W
41 O11 **Tula** Tamaulipas, C Mexico 22°59′N 99°43′W
126 K5 **Tula** Tul'skaya Oblast', W Russian Federation 54°11′N 37°39′E
Tulach Mhór *see* Tullamore
Tula de Allende *see* Tula
186 M9 **Tulaghi** *var.* Tulagi. Florida Islands, C Solomon Islands 09°04′S 160°09′E
Tulagi *see* Tulaghi
159 N10 **Tulagt Ar Gol** 🌊 W China
41 P13 **Tulancingo** Hidalgo, C Mexico 20°34′N 98°25′W
35 R11 **Tulare** California, W USA 36°12′N 119°21′W
29 P9 **Tulare** South Dakota, N USA 44°43′N 98°29′W
35 Q12 **Tulare Lake Bed** *salt flat* California, W USA
37 S14 **Tularosa** New Mexico, SW USA 33°04′N 106°01′W
37 P13 **Tularosa Mountains** ▲▲ New Mexico, SW USA
37 S15 **Tularosa Valley** *basin* New Mexico, SW USA
83 E25 **Tulbagh** Western Cape, SW South Africa 33°17′S 19°09′E
56 C5 **Tulcán** Carchi, N Ecuador 0°44′N 77°43′W
117 N13 **Tulcea** Tulcea, E Romania 45°11′N 28°49′E
117 N13 **Tulcea** ◆ *county* SE Romania
Tul'chin *see* Tul'chyn
117 N7 **Tul'chyn** *Rus.* Tul'chin. Vinnyts'ka Oblast', C Ukraine 48°40′N 28°49′E
Tuléar *see* Toliara
35 O1 **Tulelake** California, W USA 41°57′N 121°30′W
116 J10 **Tulgheş** *Hung.* Gyergyótölgyes. Harghita, C Romania 46°57′N 25°46′E
Tuli *see* Thuli
25 N4 **Tulia** Texas, SW USA 34°32′N 101°46′W
8 I9 **Tulita** *prev.* Fort Norman, Norman. Northwest Territories, NW Canada 64°55′N 125°29′W
20 J10 **Tullahoma** Tennessee, S USA 35°21′N 86°12′W
183 N12 **Tullamarine** ✈ (Melbourne) Victoria, SE Australia 37°40′S 144°46′E
183 Q7 **Tullamore** New South Wales, SE Australia 32°39′S 147°35′E
97 E18 **Tullamore** *Ir.* Tulach Mhór. Offaly, C Ireland 53°16′N 07°30′W
103 N12 **Tulle** *anc.* Tutela. Corrèze, C France 45°16′N 01°46′E
109 X3 **Tulln** *var.* Oberhollabrunn. Niederösterreich, NE Austria 48°20′N 16°02′E
109 W4 **Tulln** 🌊 NE Austria
22 H6 **Tullos** Louisiana, S USA 31°48′N 92°19′W
97 F19 **Tullow** *Ir.* An Tullach. Carlow, SE Ireland 52°48′N 06°44′W
181 W5 **Tully** Queensland, NE Australia 18°03′S 145°56′E
124 J3 **Tuloma** 🌊 NW Russian Federation
27 P9 **Tulsa** Oklahoma, C USA 36°09′N 96°W
153 N11 **Tulsipur** Mid Western, W Nepal 28°01′N 82°22′E
126 K6 **Tul'skaya Oblast'** ◆ *province* W Russian Federation
126 L14 **Tul'skiy** Respublika Adygeya, SW Russian Federation 44°26′N 40°12′E
186 E5 **Tulu** Manus Island, N Papua New Guinea 01°58′S 146°50′E
54 D10 **Tuluá** Valle del Cauca, W Colombia 04°01′N 76°16′W
116 M12 **Tulucești** Galați, E Romania 45°35′N 28°01′E
39 N12 **Tuluksak** Alaska, USA 61°06′N 160°57′W
41 Z12 **Tulum, Ruinas de** *ruins* Quintana Roo, SE Mexico
169 R17 **Tulungagung** *prev.* Toeloengagoeng. Jawa, C Indonesia 08°03′S 111°54′E
186 J6 **Tulun Islands** *var.* Kilinailau Islands; *prev.* Carteret Islands. *island group* NE Papua New Guinea
126 M4 **Tuma** Ryazanskaya Oblast', W Russian Federation 55°09′N 40°27′E
54 B12 **Tumaco** Nariño, SW Colombia 01°51′N 78°46′W
54 B12 **Tumaco, Bahía de** *bay* SW Colombia
Tuman-gang *see* Tumen
42 L8 **Tuma, Río** 🌊 N Nicaragua
95 O16 **Tumba** Stockholm, C Sweden 59°12′N 17°49′E
Tumba, Lac *see* Ntomba, Lac
169 S12 **Tumbangsenamang** Borneo, C Indonesia 01°17′S 112°21′E
183 Q10 **Tumbarumba** New South Wales, SE Australia 35°47′S 148°03′E
56 A8 **Tumbes** Tumbes, NW Peru 03°33′S 80°27′W
56 A9 **Tumbes** *off.* Departamento de Tumbes. ◆ *department* NW Peru
Tumbes, Departamento de *see* Tumbes
19 P5 **Tumbledown Mountain** ▲ Maine, NE USA 45°27′N 70°28′W
11 N13 **Tumbler Ridge** British Columbia, W Canada 55°06′N 120°51′W
167 Q12 **Tumbŏt, Phnum** ▲ W Cambodia 12°23′N 102°57′E
182 G9 **Tumby Bay** South Australia 34°22′S 136°05′E
163 Y10 **Tumen** Jilin, NE China 42°56′N 129°47′E
163 Y11 **Tumen** *Chin.* Tumen Jiang, *Kor.* Tuman-gang, *Rus.* Tumyn'tszyan. 🌊 E Asia
Tumen Jiang *see* Tumen
55 Q8 **Tumeremo** Bolívar, E Venezuela 07°17′N 61°30′W
155 G19 **Tumkūr** Karnātaka, W India 13°20′N 77°06′E
96 I10 **Tummel** 🌊 C Scotland, United Kingdom
188 B15 **Tumon Bay** *bay* W Guam
77 P14 **Tumu** NW Ghana 10°55′N 01°59′W
58 I10 **Tumuc-Humac Mountains** *var.* Serra Tumucumaque. ▲▲ N South America
Tumucumaque, Serra *see* Tumuc-Humac Mountains
183 Q10 **Tumut** New South Wales, SE Australia 35°20′S 148°14′E
158 F7 **Tumxuk** *var.* Urad Qianqi. Xinjiang Uygur Zizhiqu, NW China 78°40′N 39°54′E
Tumyn'tszyan *see* Tumen
Tün *see* Ferdows
45 U14 **Tunapuna** Trinidad, Trinidad and Tobago 10°38′N 61°23′W
60 K11 **Tunas** Paraná, S Brazil 24°57′S 49°05′W
Tunbridge Wells *see* Royal Tunbridge Wells
114 L11 **Tunca Nehri** *Bul.* Tundzha. 🌊 Bulgaria/Turkey *see also* Tundzha
Tunca Nehri *see* Tundzha
137 O14 **Tunceli** *var.* Kalan. Tunceli, E Turkey 39°07′N 39°34′E
137 O14 **Tunceli** ◆ *province* C Turkey
152 J12 **Tündla** Uttar Pradesh, N India 27°13′N 78°14′E
81 I25 **Tunduru** Ruvuma, S Tanzania 11°08′S 37°21′E
114 L10 **Tundzha** *Turk.* Tunca Nehri. 🌊 Bulgaria/Turkey *see also* Tunca Nehri
Tundzha *see* Tunca Nehri
162 I6 **Tünel** *var.* Bulag. Hövsgöl, N Mongolia 49°51′N 100°41′E
155 H17 **Tungabhadra** 🌊 S India
155 F17 **Tungabhadra Reservoir** ◎ S India
191 P2 **Tungaru** *prev.* Gilbert Islands. *island group* W Kiribati
171 P7 **Tungawan** Mindanao, S Philippines 07°33′N 122°22′E
Tungdor *see* Mainling
T'ung-shan *see* Xuzhou
161 Q16 **Tungsha Tao** *Chin.* Dongsha Qundao, *Eng.* Pratas Island. *island* S Taiwan
161 S13 **Tungshih** *Jap.* Tōsei. N Taiwan 24°13′N 120°54′E
8 H9 **Tungsten** Northwest Territories, W Canada 62°N 128°09′W
Tung-t'ing Hu *see* Dongting Hu
56 A13 **Tungurahua** ◆ *province* C Ecuador
95 F14 **Tunhovdfjorden** ◎ S Norway
22 K2 **Tunica** Mississippi, S USA 34°40′N 90°22′W
75 N5 **Tunis** *var.* Tūnis. ● (Tunisia) NE Tunisia 36°53′N 10°10′E
75 N5 **Tunis, Golfe de** *Ar.* Khalīj Tūnis. *gulf* NE Tunisia
75 N6 **Tunisia** *off.* Tunisian Republic, *Ar.* Al Jumhūrīyah at Tūnisīyah, *Fr.* République Tunisienne. ◆ *republic* N Africa
Tunisian Republic *see* Tunisia
Tunisienne, République *see* Tunisia
Tūnisīyah, Al Jumhūrīyah at *see* Tunisia
Tūnis, Khalīj *see* Tunis, Golfe de
54 G9 **Tunja** Boyacá, C Colombia 05°33′N 73°23′W
93 F14 **Tunnsjøen** *Lapp.* Dåtnejaevrie. ◎ C Norway
39 N12 **Tuntutuliak** Alaska, USA 60°21′N 162°40′W
197 P14 **Tunu** ◆ *province* E Greenland
147 U8 **Tunuk** Chuyskaya Oblast', C Kyrgyzstan 42°11′N 73°55′E
13 Q6 **Tunungayualok Island** *island* Newfoundland and Labrador, E Canada
62 H11 **Tunuyán** Mendoza, W Argentina 33°35′S 69°00′W
62 I11 **Tunuyán, Río** 🌊 W Argentina
Tunxi *see* Huangshan
Tuodian *see* Shuangbai
Tuoji *see* Zhongba
Tuokezhake *see* Shufu
35 P9 **Tuolumne River** 🌊 California, W USA
Tuong Buong *see* Tương Đương
167 R7 **Tương Đương** *var.* Tuong Buong. Nghệ An, N Vietnam 19°15′N 104°30′E
160 I13 **Tuoniang Jiang** 🌊 S China
Tuotiereke *see* Jeminay
Tuotuo He *see* Togton He
Tuotuoheyan *see* Tanggulashan
Tüp *see* Tyup
60 J9 **Tupã** São Paulo, S Brazil 21°57′S 50°28′W
191 S10 **Tupai** *var.* Motu Iti. *atoll* Îles Sous le Vent, W French Polynesia
61 G15 **Tupanciretã** Rio Grande do Sul, S Brazil 29°06′S 53°48′W
22 M2 **Tupelo** Mississippi, S USA 34°15′N 88°42′W
59 K18 **Tupiraçaba** Goiás, S Brazil 14°33′S 48°40′W
57 L21 **Tupiza** Potosí, S Bolivia 21°27′S 65°45′W
11 N13 **Tupper** British Columbia, W Canada 55°30′N 119°59′W
18 J8 **Tupper Lake** ◎ New York, NE USA
146 J10 **Tuproqqal'a** Khorazm Viloyati, W Uzbekistan 40°52′N 62°00′E
146 J10 **Tuproqqal'a** *Rus.* Turpakkla. Xorazm Viloyati, W Uzbekistan 40°52′N 62°00′E
62 H11 **Tupungato, Volcán** ⛰ W Argentina 33°27′S 69°42′W
163 T9 **Tuquan** Nei Mongol Zizhiqu, N China 45°21′N 121°36′E
54 C13 **Túquerres** Nariño, SW Colombia 01°06′N 77°37′W
153 U13 **Tura** Meghālaya, NE India 25°33′N 90°14′E
122 M10 **Tura** Evenkiyskiy Avtonomnyy Okrug, N Russian Federation 64°20′N 100°17′E
122 G10 **Tura** 🌊 C Russian Federation
140 M10 **Turabah** Makkah, W Saudi Arabia 22°00′N 42°00′E
55 O8 **Turagua, Cerro** ▲ C Venezuela 06°59′N 64°34′W
184 L12 **Turakina** Manawatu-Wanganui, North Island, New Zealand 40°03′S 175°13′E
185 K15 **Turakirae Head** *headland* North Island, New Zealand 41°26′S 174°54′E
186 B8 **Turama** 🌊 S Papua New Guinea
122 K13 **Turan** Respublika Tyva, S Russian Federation 52°11′N 93°40′E
184 M10 **Turangi** Waikato, North Island, New Zealand 39°01′S 175°47′E
146 F11 **Turan Lowland** *var.* Turan Plain, *Kaz.* Turan Oypaty, *Rus.* Turanskaya Nizmennost', *Turk.* Turan Pesligi, *Uzb.* Turan Pasttekisligi. *plain* C Asia
Turan Oypaty/Turan Pesligi/Turan Plain/Turanskaya Nizmennost' *see* Turan Lowland
Turan Pasttekisligi *see* Turan Lowland
138 K7 **Ṭurāq al 'Ilab** *hill range* S Syria
119 K20 **Turaw** *Rus.* Turov. Homyel'skaya Voblasts', SE Belarus 52°04′N 27°44′E
140 L2 **Ṭurayf** Al Ḥudūd ash Shamālīyah, NW Saudi Arabia 31°43′N 38°40′E
Turba *see* Teruel
54 E5 **Turbaco** Bolívar, N Colombia 10°20′N 75°25′W
148 K15 **Turbat** Baluchistān, SW Pakistan 26°02′N 62°56′E
Turbat-i-Haidari *see* Torbat-e Ḥeydarīyeh
Turbat-i-Jam *see* Torbat-e Jām
54 D7 **Turbo** Antioquia, NW Colombia 08°06′N 76°44′W
Turčianský Svätý Martin *see* Martin
116 H10 **Turda** *Ger.* Thorenburg, *Hung.* Torda. Cluj, NW Romania 46°35′N 23°50′E
142 M7 **Ṭūreh** Markazī, W Iran
191 X12 **Tureia** *atoll* Îles Tuamotu, SE French Polynesia
110 I12 **Turek** Wielkopolskie, C Poland 52°01′N 18°30′E
93 L19 **Turenki** Etelä-Suomi, SW Finland 60°55′N 24°38′E
Turfan *see* Turpan
145 R8 **Turgay** *Kaz.* Torghay. Akmola, W Kazakhstan 51°46′N 72°45′E
145 N10 **Turgay** *Kaz.* Torgay. 🌊 C Kazakhstan
144 M8 **Turgayskaya Stolovaya Strana** *Kaz.* Torgay Üstirti. *plateau* Kazakhstan/Russian Federation
Turgel *see* Türi
114 L8 **Türgovishte** *prev.* Eski Dzhumaya, Tărgovište. Türgovishte, N Bulgaria 43°15′N 26°34′E
114 L8 **Türgovishte** ◆ *province* N Bulgaria
136 C14 **Turgutlu** Manisa, W Turkey 38°30′N 27°43′E
136 L12 **Turhal** Tokat, N Turkey 40°23′N 36°05′E
118 H4 **Türi** *Ger.* Turgel. Järvamaa, N Estonia 58°48′N 25°28′E
105 S9 **Turia** 🌊 E Spain
58 M12 **Turiaçu** Maranhão, E Brazil 01°40′S 45°22′W
Turin *see* Torino
116 I3 **Turiys'k** Volyns'ka Oblast', NW Ukraine 51°05′N 24°31′E
Turja *see* Tur"ya
116 H6 **Turka** L'vivs'ka Oblast', W Ukraine 49°07′N 23°01′E
81 H16 **Turkana, Lake** *var.* Lake Rudolf. ◎ N Kenya
145 P16 **Turkestan** *Kaz.* Türkistan. Yuzhnyy Kazakhstan, S Kazakhstan 43°18′N 68°18′E
147 Q12 **Turkestan Range** *Rus.* Turkestanskiy Khrebet. ▲▲ C Asia
Turkestanskiy Khrebet *see* Turkestan Range
111 M23 **Túrkeve** Jász-Nagykun-Szolnok, E Hungary 47°06′N 20°42′E
25 O4 **Turkey** Texas, SW USA 34°23′N 100°54′W
136 H14 **Turkey** *off.* Republic of Turkey, *Turk.* Türkiye Cumhuriyeti. ◆ *republic* SW Asia
181 N4 **Turkey Creek** Western Australia 16°54′S 128°12′E
26 M9 **Turkey Creek** 🌊 Oklahoma, C USA
37 T9 **Turkey Mountains** ▲▲ New Mexico, SW USA
Turkey, Republic of *see* Turkey
29 X11 **Turkey River** 🌊 Iowa, C USA
127 N7 **Turki** Saratovskaya Oblast', W Russian Federation 52°00′N 43°16′E
121 O1 **Turkish Republic of Northern Cyprus** ◇ *disputed territory* Cyprus
Türkistan *see* Turkestan
Turkistan, Bandi-i *see* Torkestān, Selseleh-ye Band-e
Türkiye Cumhuriyeti *see* Turkey
146 K12 **Türkmenabat** *prev.* *Rus.* Chardzhev, Chardzhou, Chardzhui, Lenin-Turkmenski, *Turkm.* Chärjew. Lebap Welaýaty, E Turkmenistan 39°07′N 63°30′E
146 A11 **Türkmen Aylagy** *Rus.* Turkmenskiy Zaliv. *lake gulf* W Turkmenistan
Turkmenbashi *see* Türkmenbaşy
146 A10 **Türkmenbaşy** *Rus.* Turkmenbashi; *prev.* Krasnovodsk. Balkan Welaýaty, W Turkmenistan 40°N 53°04′E
146 A10 **Türkmenbaşy Aylagy** *prev. Rus.* Krasnovodskiy Zaliv, *Turkm.* Krasnowodsk Aylagy. *lake Gulf* W Turkmenistan
146 J14 **Türkmengala** *Rus.* Turkmen-kala; *prev.* Turkmen-Kala. Mary Welaýaty, S Turkmenistan 37°25′N 62°19′E
146 G13 **Turkmenistan**; *prev.* Turkmenskaya Soviet Socialist Republic. ◆ *republic* C Asia
Turkmen-kala/Turkmen-Kala *see* Türkmengala
Turkmenskaya Soviet Socialist Republic *see* Turkmenistan
Turkmenskiy Zaliv *see* Türkmen Aylagy
136 L16 **Türkoğlu** Kahramanmaraş, S Turkey 37°24′N 36°49′E
44 L6 **Turks and Caicos Islands** ◇ *UK dependent territory* N West Indies
64 G10 **Turks and Caicos Islands** *UK dependant territory* N West Indies
45 N6 **Turks Islands** *island group* SE Turks and Caicos Islands
93 K19 **Turku** *Swe.* Åbo. Länsi-Suomi, SW Finland 60°27′N 22°17′E
81 H17 **Turkwel** *seasonal river* NW Kenya
27 P9 **Turley** Oklahoma, C USA 36°14′N 95°58′W
35 P9 **Turlock** California, W USA 37°29′N 120°52′W
118 I12 **Turmantas** Utena, NE Lithuania 55°41′N 26°27′E
Turmberg *see* Wieżyca
54 L5 **Turmero** Aragua, N Venezuela South America 10°14′N 66°40′W
184 N13 **Turnagain, Cape** *headland* North Island, New Zealand 40°30′S 176°36′E
Turnau *see* Turnov
42 H2 **Turneffe Islands** *island group* E Belize
18 M11 **Turners Falls** Massachusetts, NE USA 42°36′N 72°31′W
11 P16 **Turner Valley** Alberta, SW Canada 50°43′N 114°19′W
99 I16 **Turnhout** Antwerpen, N Belgium 51°19′N 04°57′E
109 V5 **Türnitz** Niederösterreich, E Austria 47°56′N 15°26′E
11 S12 **Turnor Lake** ◎ Saskatchewan, C Canada
111 E15 **Turnov** *Ger.* Turnau. Liberecký Kraj, N Czech Republic 50°36′N 15°10′E
Tŭrnovo *see* Veliko Tŭrnovo
116 I15 **Turnu Măgurele** *var.* Turnu-Măgurele. Teleorman, S Romania 43°44′N 24°53′E
Turnu Severin *see* Drobeta-Turnu Severin
Turócszentmárton *see* Martin
Turoni *see* Tours
Turov *see* Turaw
Turpakkla *see* Tuproqqal'a
158 M6 **Turpan** *var.* Turfan. Xinjiang Uygur Zizhiqu, NW China 42°55′N 89°06′E
Turpan Depression *see* Turpan Pendi

◆ Country ◇ Dependent Territory ◆ Administrative Regions ▲ Mountain ⛰ Volcano ◎ Lake
● Country Capital ○ Dependent Territory Capital ✈ International Airport ▲▲ Mountain Range 🌊 River ▣ Reservoir

TURPAN PENDI – UMMAS SAMĪN

158 M6 **Turpan Pendi** *Eng.* Turpan Depression. *depression* NW China
158 M5 **Turpan Zhan** Xinjiang Uygur Zizhiqu, W China 43°10′N 89°06′E
Turpentine State *see* North Carolina
44 H8 **Turquino, Pico** ▲ E Cuba 19°54′N 76°55′W
27 Y10 **Turrell** Arkansas, C USA 35°22′N 90°13′W
43 N14 **Turrialba** Cartago, E Costa Rica 09°56′N 83°40′W
96 K8 **Turriff** NE Scotland, United Kingdom 57°32′N 02°28′W
139 V7 **Tursāq** Diyālá, E Iraq 33°27′N 45°47′E
Turshiz *see* Kāshmar
Tursunzade *see* Tursunzoda
147 P13 **Tursunzoda** *Rus.* Tursunzade; *prev.* Regar. W Tajikistan 38°30′N 68°10′E
Turt *see* Hanh
Tŭrtkŭl/Turtkul' *see* To'rtko'l
29 O9 **Turtle Creek** ≈ South Dakota, N USA
30 K4 **Turtle Flambeau Flowage** ⊠ Wisconsin, N USA
11 S14 **Turtleford** Saskatchewan, S Canada 53°21′N 108°48′W
28 M4 **Turtle Lake** North Dakota, N USA 47°31′N 100°53′W
92 K12 **Turtola** Lappi, NW Finland 66°39′N 23°55′E
122 M10 **Turu** ≈ N Russian Federation
Turuga *see* Tsuruga
147 V10 **Turugart Pass** *pass* China/Kyrgyzstan
158 E7 **Turugart Shankou** *var.* Pereval Torugart. *pass* China/Kyrgyzstan
122 K9 **Turukhan** ≈ N Russian Federation
122 K9 **Turukhansk** Krasnoyarskiy Kray, N Russian Federation 65°50′N 87°48′E
139 N3 **Ţurumbah** *well* NE Syria
Turuoka *see* Tsuruoka
144 H14 **Turush** Mangistau, SW Kazakhstan 45°24′N 56°02′E
60 K7 **Turvo, Rio** ≈ S Brazil
116 J2 **Tur"ya** *Pol.* Turja, *Rus.* Tur'ya. ≈ NW Ukraine
23 O4 **Tuscaloosa** Alabama, S USA 33°13′N 87°34′W
23 O4 **Tuscaloosa, Lake** ◎ Alabama, S USA
Tuscan Archipelago *see* Toscano, Archipelago
Tuscan-Emilian Mountains *see* Tosco-Emiliano, Appennino
Tuscany *see* Toscana
35 V2 **Tuscarora** Nevada, W USA 41°16′N 116°13′W
18 F15 **Tuscarora Mountain** *ridge* Pennsylvania, NE USA
30 M14 **Tuscola** Illinois, N USA 39°46′N 88°19′W
25 P7 **Tuscola** Texas, SW USA 32°12′N 99°48′W
23 O2 **Tuscumbia** Alabama, S USA 34°43′N 87°42′W
92 O4 **Tusenøyane** *island group* S Svalbard
144 K13 **Tushchybas, Zaliv** *prev.* Zaliv Paskevicha. *lake gulf* SW Kazakhstan
Tusima *see* Tsushima
171 Y15 **Tusirah** Papua, E Indonesia 06°46′S 140°19′E
23 Q5 **Tuskegee** Alabama, S USA 32°25′N 85°41′W
94 E8 **Tustna** *island* S Norway
39 R12 **Tustumena Lake** ◎ Alaska, USA
110 K13 **Tuszyn** Łódzkie, C Poland 51°36′N 19°31′E
137 S13 **Tutak** Ağrı, E Turkey 39°34′N 42°48′E
185 C20 **Tutamoe Range** ▲▲ North Island, New Zealand
Tutasev *see* Tutayev
124 L15 **Tutayev** *var.* Tutasev. Yaroslavskaya Oblast', W Russian Federation 57°51′N 39°29′E
Tutela *see* Tulle, France
Tutela *see* Tudela, Spain
Tutera *see* Tudela
155 H23 **Tuticorin** Tamil Nādu, SE India 08°48′N 78°10′E
113 L15 **Tutin** Serbia, S Serbia 43°00′N 20°20′E
184 O10 **Tutira** Hawke's Bay, North Island, New Zealand 39°14′S 176°53′E
Tutiura *see* Tsuchiura
122 K10 **Tutonchny** Evenkiyskiy Avtonomnyy Okrug, N Russian Federation 64°12′N 93°52′E
114 L6 **Tutrakan** Silistra, NE Bulgaria 44°03′N 26°38′E
29 N5 **Tuttle** North Dakota, N USA 47°07′N 99°58′W
26 M11 **Tuttle** Oklahoma, C USA 35°17′N 97°48′W
27 O3 **Tuttle Creek Lake** ⊠ Kansas, C USA
101 H23 **Tuttlingen** Baden-Württemberg, S Germany 47°59′N 08°49′E
171 R16 **Tutuala** East Timor 08°23′S 127°12′E
192 K17 **Tutuila** *island* W American Samoa
83 I18 **Tutume** Central, E Botswana 20°26′S 27°02′E
39 N7 **Tututalak Mountain** ▲ Alaska, USA 67°51′N 161°27′W
22 K3 **Tutwiler** Mississippi, S USA 34°00′N 90°25′W
162 L8 **Tuul Gol** ≈ N Mongolia
93 O16 **Tuupovaara** Itä-Suomi, E Finland 62°30′N 30°40′E
Tuva *see* Tyva, Respublika
190 E7 **Tuvalu** *prev.* Ellice Islands. ◆ *commonwealth republic* SW Pacific Ocean
Tuvinskaya ASSR *see* Tyva, Respublika
163 O9 **Tuvshinshiree** *var.* Sergelen. Sühbaatar, E Mongolia 46°12′N 111°48′E
141 P9 **Ţuwayq, Jabal** ▲▲ C Saudi Arabia
138 H13 **Ţuwayyil ash Shihāq** *desert* S Jordan
11 U16 **Tuxford** Saskatchewan, S Canada 50°33′N 105°32′W
167 U12 **Tu Xoay** Đăc Lăc, S Vietnam 12°18′N 107°33′E
40 L14 **Tuxpan** Jalisco, C Mexico 19°33′N 103°21′W
40 J12 **Tuxpan** Nayarit, C Mexico 21°57′N 105°12′W
41 Q12 **Tuxpán** *var.* Tuxpán de Rodríguez Cano. Veracruz-Llave, E Mexico 20°58′N 97°23′W
Tuxpán de Rodríguez Cano *see* Tuxpán
41 R15 **Tuxtepec** *var.* San Juan Bautista Tuxtepec. Oaxaca, S Mexico 18°02′N 96°05′W
41 U16 **Tuxtla** *var.* Tuxtla Gutiérrez. Chiapas, SE Mexico 16°44′N 93°03′W
Tuxtla *see* San Andrés Tuxtla
Tuxtla Gutiérrez *see* Tuxtla
Tuyama *see* Tsuyama
167 T5 **Tuyên Quang** Tuyên Quang, N Vietnam 21°48′N 105°18′E
167 U13 **Tuy Hoa** Binh Thuân, S Vietnam 11°03′N 108°12′E
167 V12 **Tuy Hoa** Phu Yên, S Vietnam 13°02′N 109°15′E
127 U5 **Tuymazy** Respublika Bashkortostan, W Russian Federation 54°36′N 53°40′E
Tuy Phong *see* Liên Hương
142 L6 **Tūysarkān** *var.* Tuisarkan, Tuyserkān. Hamadān, W Iran 34°31′N 48°30′E
Tuyserkān *see* Tūysarkān
145 W16 **Tuyuk** *Kaz.* Tuyyq. Taldykorgan, SE Kazakhstan 43°07′N 79°24′E
Tuyyq *see* Tuyuk
136 I14 **Tuz Gölü** ◎ C Turkey
125 Q15 **Tuzha** Kirovskaya Oblast', NW Russian Federation 57°37′N 48°02′E
113 K17 **Tuzi** S Montenegro 42°22′N 19°21′E
139 T5 **Tūz Khurmātū** At Ta'mīn, N Iraq 34°56′N 44°38′E
112 I11 **Tuzla** Federacija Bosna I Hercegovina, NE Bosnia and Herzegovina 44°33′N 18°40′E
117 N15 **Tuzla** Constanţa, SE Romania 43°58′N 28°38′E
137 T12 **Tuzluca** İgdır, E Turkey 40°02′N 43°39′E
95 J20 **Tvååker** Halland, S Sweden 57°04′N 12°25′E
95 F17 **Tvedestrand** Aust-Agder, S Norway 58°36′N 08°55′E
124 J16 **Tver'** *prev.* Kalinin. Tverskaya Oblast', W Russian Federation 56°53′N 35°52′E
126 I15 **Tverskaya Oblast'** ◈ *province* W Russian Federation
124 I15 **Tvertsa** ≈ W Russian Federation
138 G9 **Tverya** *var.* Tiberias; *prev.* Teverya. Northern, N Israel 32°48′N 35°32′E
110 H13 **Twardogóra** *Ger.* Festenberg. Dolnośląskie, SW Poland 51°21′N 17°27′E
14 J14 **Tweed** Ontario, SE Canada 44°29′N 77°19′W
96 K13 **Tweed** ≈ England/Scotland, United Kingdom
98 O7 **Tweede-Exloërmond** Drenthe, NE Netherlands 52°55′N 06°55′E
183 V3 **Tweed Heads** New South Wales, SE Australia 28°10′S 153°32′E
98 M11 **Twello** Gelderland, E Netherlands 52°14′N 06°07′E
35 W15 **Twentynine Palms** California, W USA 34°08′N 116°03′W
25 P9 **Twin Buttes Reservoir** ⊠ Texas, SW USA
33 O15 **Twin Falls** Idaho, NW USA 42°34′N 114°28′W
39 N13 **Twin Hills** Alaska, USA 59°06′N 160°21′W
11 O11 **Twin Lakes** Alberta, W Canada 57°47′N 117°30′W
33 O12 **Twin Peaks** ▲ Idaho, NW USA 44°37′N 114°24′W
185 I14 **Twins, The** ▲ South Island, New Zealand 41°14′S 172°38′E
29 S5 **Twin Valley** Minnesota, N USA 47°15′N 96°15′W
100 G11 **Twistringen** Niedersachsen, NW Germany 52°48′N 08°39′E
185 E20 **Twizel** Canterbury, South Island, New Zealand 44°04′S 171°12′E
29 X5 **Two Harbors** Minnesota, N USA 47°01′N 91°40′W
11 R14 **Two Hills** Alberta, SW Canada 53°40′N 111°43′W
31 N7 **Two Rivers** Wisconsin, N USA 44°10′N 87°33′W
116 H8 **Tyachiv** Zakarpats'ka Oblast', W Ukraine 48°02′N 23°35′E
Tyan'-Shan' *see* Tien Shan
166 L3 **Tyao** ≈ Myanmar (Burma)/India
117 R6 **Tyasmyn** ≈ N Ukraine
23 X6 **Tybee Island** Georgia, SE USA 32°00′N 80°51′W
Tyborøn *see* Thyborøn
111 J16 **Tychy** *Ger.* Tichau. Śląskie, S Poland 50°12′N 19°01′E
111 O16 **Tyczyn** Podkarpackie, SE Poland 49°58′N 22°03′E
94 I8 **Tydal** Sør-Trøndelag, S Norway 63°01′N 11°36′E
115 H24 **Tyflós** ≈ Kríti, Greece, E Mediterranean Sea
21 S3 **Tygart Lake** ⊠ West Virginia, NE USA
123 Q13 **Tygda** Amurskaya Oblast', SE Russian Federation 53°07′N 126°12′E
21 Q11 **Tyger River** ≈ South Carolina, SE USA
32 I11 **Tygh Valley** Oregon, NW USA 45°15′N 121°12′W
94 F12 **Tyin** ◎ S Norway
29 S10 **Tyler** Minnesota, N USA 44°16′N 96°07′W
25 W7 **Tyler** Texas, SW USA 32°21′N 95°18′W
25 W7 **Tyler, Lake** ⊠ Texas, SW USA
22 K7 **Tylertown** Mississippi, S USA 31°07′N 90°08′W
117 P10 **Tylihuls'kyy Lyman** ◎ SW Ukraine
Tylos *see* Bahrain
115 C15 **Týmfi** *var.* Timfi. ▲ W Greece 39°58′N 20°51′E
115 E17 **Tymfristós** *var.* Timfristos. ▲ C Greece 38°57′N 21°49′E
115 J25 **Tympáki** *var.* Timbaki; *prev.* Timbákion. Kríti, Greece, E Mediterranean Sea 35°04′N 24°47′E
123 Q12 **Tynda** Amurskaya Oblast', SE Russian Federation 55°09′N 124°44′E
29 Q12 **Tyndall** South Dakota, N USA 42°57′N 97°52′W
97 L14 **Tyne** ≈ N England, United Kingdom
97 M14 **Tynemouth** NE England, United Kingdom 55°01′N 01°24′W
97 L14 **Tyneside** *cultural region* NE England, United Kingdom
94 H10 **Tynset** Hedmark, S Norway 61°45′N 10°49′E
39 Q12 **Tyonek** Alaska, USA 61°04′N 151°08′W
Tyôsi *see* Chōshi
Tyras *see* Dniester
Tyras *see* Bilhorod-Dnistrovs'kyy
Tyre *see* Soûr
95 G14 **Tyrifjorden** ◎ S Norway
95 K22 **Tyringe** Skåne, S Sweden 56°09′N 13°35′E
123 R13 **Tyrma** Khabarovskiy Kray, SE Russian Federation 50°00′N 132°04′E
Tyrnau *see* Trnava
115 F15 **Týrnavos** *var.* Tírnavos. Thessalía, C Greece 39°45′N 22°18′E
127 N16 **Tyrnyauz** Kabardino-Balkarskaya Respublika, SW Russian Federation 43°19′N 42°55′E
Tyrol *see* Tirol
18 E14 **Tyrone** Pennsylvania, NE USA 40°41′N 78°12′W
97 E15 **Tyrone** *cultural region* W Northern Ireland, United Kingdom
Tyros *see* Bahrain
182 M10 **Tyrrell, Lake** *salt lake* Victoria, SE Australia
84 H14 **Tyrrhenian Basin** *undersea feature* Tyrrhenian Sea, C Mediterranean Sea 39°30′N 13°00′E
120 L8 **Tyrrhenian Sea** *It.* Mare Tirreno. *sea* N Mediterranean Sea
94 J12 **Tyrsil** ≈ Hedmark, S Norway
Tysa *see* Tisa/Tisza
116 J7 **Tysmenytsya** Ivano-Frankivs'ka Oblast', W Ukraine 48°54′N 24°50′E
95 C14 **Tysnesøya** *island* S Norway
95 C14 **Tysse** Hordaland, S Norway 60°23′N 05°46′E
95 D14 **Tyssedal** Hordaland, S Norway 60°07′N 06°36′E
95 O17 **Tystberga** Södermanland, C Sweden 58°51′N 17°15′E
118 E12 **Tytuvėnai** Šiaulai, C Lithuania 55°36′N 23°14′E
144 D14 **Tyub-Karagan, Mys** *headland* SW Kazakhstan 44°40′N 50°19′E
147 V8 **Tyugel'-Say** Narynskaya Oblast', C Kyrgyzstan 41°57′N 74°40′E
122 H11 **Tyukalinsk** Omskaya Oblast', C Russian Federation 55°56′N 72°02′E
127 V7 **Tyul'gan** Orenburgskaya Oblast', W Russian Federation 52°27′N 56°08′E
122 G11 **Tyumen'** Tyumenskaya Oblast', C Russian Federation 57°11′N 65°29′E
122 H11 **Tyumenskaya Oblast'** ◈ *province* C Russian Federation
147 Y7 **Tyup** *Kir.* Tüp. Issyk-Kul'skaya Oblast', NE Kyrgyzstan 42°44′N 78°18′E
122 L14 **Tyva, Respublika** *prev.* Tannu-Tuva, Tuva, Tuvinskaya ASSR. ◈ *autonomous republic* C Russian Federation
117 N7 **Tyvriv** Vinnyts'ka Oblast', C Ukraine 49°01′N 28°28′E
97 J21 **Tywi** ≈ S Wales, United Kingdom
97 I19 **Tywyn** W Wales, United Kingdom 52°35′N 04°06′W
83 K20 **Tzaneen** Limpopo, NE South Africa 23°50′S 30°09′E
Tzekung *see* Zigong
115 I20 **Tziá** *prev.* Kéa, Kéos; *anc.* Ceos. *island* Kykládes, Greece, Aegean Sea
41 X12 **Tzucacab** Yucatán, SE Mexico 20°04′N 89°03′W

U

82 B12 **Uaco Cungo** *var.* Waku Kungo, *Port.* Santa Comba. Cuanza Sul, C Angola 11°21′S 15°04′E
UAE *see* United Arab Emirates
191 X7 **Ua Huka** *island* Îles Marquises, NE French Polynesia
58 E10 **Uaiacás** Roraima, N Brazil 03°28′N 63°13′W
Uamba *see* Wamba
Uanle Uen *see* Wanlaweyn
191 W7 **Ua Pu** *island* Îles Marquises, NE French Polynesia
81 L17 **Uar Garas** *spring/well* SW Somalia 01°19′N 41°22′E
58 G12 **Uatumã, Rio** ≈ C Brazil
Ua Uíbh Fhailí *see* Offaly
58 C11 **Uaupés, Rio** *var.* Río Vaupés. ≈ Brazil/Colombia *see also* Vaupés, Río
Uaupés, Rio *see* Vaupés, Río
145 X9 **Uba** ≈ E Kazakhstan
145 N6 **Ubagan** *Kaz.* Obagan. ≈ Kazakhstan/Russian Federation
186 G7 **Ubai** New Britain, E Papua New Guinea 05°38′S 150°45′E
79 J15 **Ubangi** *Fr.* Oubangui. ≈ C Africa
Ubangi-Shari *see* Central African Republic
116 M3 **Ubarts'** *Ukr.* Ubort'. ≈ Belarus/Ukraine *see also* Ubort'
Ubarts' *see* Ubort'
54 F9 **Ubaté** Cundinamarca, C Colombia 05°20′N 73°50′W
60 N10 **Ubatuba** São Paulo, S Brazil 23°26′S 45°04′W
149 R12 **Ubauro** Sind, SE Pakistan 28°08′N 69°43′E
171 Q6 **Ubay** Bohol, C Philippines 10°02′N 124°29′E
103 U14 **Ubaye** ≈ SE France
Ubayid, Wadi al *see* Ubayyiḍ, Wādī al
139 N8 **Ubaylah** Al Anbār, W Iraq 33°06′N 40°13′E
139 O10 **Ubayyiḍ, Wādī al** *var.* Wadi al Ubayid. *dry watercourse* SW Iraq
98 L13 **Ubbergen** Gelderland, E Netherlands 51°49′N 05°54′E
164 E13 **Ube** Yamaguchi, Honshū, SW Japan 33°57′N 131°15′E
105 O13 **Ubeda** Andalucía, S Spain 38°01′N 03°22′W
109 V7 **Übelbach** *var.* Markt-Übelbach. Steiermark, SE Austria 47°13′N 15°15′E
59 L20 **Uberaba** Minas Gerais, SE Brazil 19°47′S 47°57′W
57 Q19 **Uberaba, Laguna** ◎ E Bolivia
59 K19 **Uberlândia** Minas Gerais, SE Brazil 18°17′S 48°17′W
101 H24 **Überlingen** Baden-Württemberg, S Germany 47°46′N 09°10′E
77 U16 **Ubiaja** Edo, S Nigeria 06°39′N 06°23′E
104 K3 **Ubiña, Peña** ▲ NW Spain 43°01′N 05°58′W
57 H17 **Ubinas, Volcán** ⛰ S Peru 16°16′S 70°49′W
Ubol Rajadhani/Ubol Ratchathani *see* Ubon Ratchathani
167 P9 **Ubolratna Reservoir** ⊠ C Thailand
167 S10 **Ubon Ratchathani** *var.* Muang Ubon, Ubol Rajadhani, Ubol Ratchathani, Udon Ratchathani. Ubon Ratchathani, E Thailand 15°15′N 104°50′E
119 L20 **Ubort'** *Bel.* Ubarts'. ≈ Belarus/Ukraine *see also* Ubarts'
Ubort' *see* Ubarts'
104 K15 **Ubrique** Andalucía, S Spain 36°42′N 05°27′W
Ubsu-Nur, Ozero *see* Uvs Nuur
79 M18 **Ubundu** Orientale, C Dem. Rep. Congo 0°24′S 25°30′E
146 J13 **Üçajy** *var.* Üchajy, *Rus.* Uch-Adzhi. Mary Welaýaty, C Turkmenistan 38°06′N 62°44′E
137 X11 **Ucar** *Rus.* Udzhary. C Azerbaijan 40°31′N 47°40′E
56 G13 **Ucayali** *off.* Departamento de Ucayali. ◈ *department* E Peru
Ucayali, Departamento de *see* Ucayali
56 F10 **Ucayali, Río** ≈ C Peru
Uccle *see* Ukkel
Uch-Adzhi/Üchajy *see* Üçajy
127 X4 **Uchaly** Respublika Bashkortostan, W Russian Federation 54°19′N 59°33′E
145 W13 **Ucharal** *Kaz.* Üsharal. Almaty, E Kazakhstan 46°08′N 80°55′E
164 C17 **Uchinoura** Kagoshima, Kyūshū, SW Japan 31°16′N 131°04′E
165 R5 **Uchiura-wan** *bay* NW Pacific Ocean
Uchkuduk *see* Uchquduq
147 S9 **Uchqo'rg'on** *Rus.* Uchkurghan. Namangan Viloyati, E Uzbekistan 41°06′N 72°04′E
146 K8 **Uchquduq** *Rus.* Uchkuduk. Navoiy Viloyati, N Uzbekistan 42°12′N 63°27′E
Uchsay *see* Uchsoy
146 G6 **Uchsoy** *Rus.* Uchsay. Qoraqalpog'iston Respublikasi, NW Uzbekistan 43°51′N 58°51′E
Uchtagan Gumy/Uchtagan, Peski *see* Uçtagan Gumy
123 R11 **Uchur** ≈ E Russian Federation
100 O10 **Uckermark** *cultural region* E Germany
10 K17 **Ucluelet** Vancouver Island, British Columbia, SW Canada 48°55′N 123°34′W
146 D10 **Uçtagan Gumy** *var.* Uchtagan Gumy, *Rus.* Peski Uchtagan. *desert* NW Turkmenistan
122 M13 **Uda** ≈ S Russian Federation
123 R12 **Uda** ≈ E Russian Federation
123 N6 **Udachnyy** Respublika Sakha (Yakutiya), NE Russian Federation 66°27′N 112°18′E
155 G21 **Udagamandalam** *var.* Ooty, Udhagamandalam; *prev.* Ootacamund. Tamil Nādu, SW India 11°28′N 76°42′E
152 F14 **Udaipur** *prev.* Oodeypore. Rājasthān, N India 24°35′N 73°41′E
Udayadhani *see* Uthai Thani
143 N16 **'Udayd, Khawr al** *var.* Khor al Udeid. *inlet* Qatar/Saudi Arabia
112 D11 **Udbina** Lika-Senj, W Croatia 44°33′N 15°46′E
95 I18 **Uddevalla** Västra Götaland, S Sweden 58°20′N 11°56′E
Uddjaur *see* Uddjaure
92 H13 **Uddjaure** *var.* Uddjaur. ◎ N Sweden
Udeid, Khor al *see* 'Udayd, Khawr al
99 K14 **Uden** Noord-Brabant, SE Netherlands 51°40′N 05°37′E
Uden *see* Udenhout
99 J14 **Udenhout** *var.* Uden. Noord-Brabant, S Netherlands 51°37′N 05°09′E
155 H14 **Udgīr** Mahārāshtra, C India 18°23′N 77°06′E
Udhagamandalam *see* Udagamandalam
152 H6 **Udhampur** Jammu and Kashmir, NW India 32°55′N 75°07′E
139 X14 **'Udhaybah, 'Uqlat al** *well* S Iraq
106 J7 **Udine** *anc.* Utina. Friuli-Venezia Giulia, NE Italy 46°05′N 13°10′E
175 T14 **Udintsev Fracture Zone** *tectonic feature* S Pacific Ocean
Udipi *see* Udupi
Udmurtia *see* Udmurtskaya Respublika
127 S2 **Udmurtskaya Respublika** *Eng.* Udmurtia. ◈ *autonomous republic* NW Russian Federation
124 J15 **Udomlya** Tverskaya Oblast', W Russian Federation 57°53′N 34°59′E
Udon Ratchathani *see* Ubon Ratchathani
167 Q8 **Udon Thani** *var.* Ban Mak Khaeng, Udorndhani. Udon Thani, N Thailand 17°25′N 102°45′E
Udorndhani *see* Udon Thani
189 U12 **Udot** *atoll* Chuuk Islands, C Micronesia
123 S12 **Udskaya Guba** *bay* E Russian Federation
123 R12 **Udskoye** Khabarovskiy Kray, SE Russian Federation 54°32′N 134°26′E
155 E19 **Udupi** *var.* Udipi. Karnātaka, SW India 13°18′N 74°46′E
Udzhary *see* Ucar
100 O9 **Uecker** ≈ NE Germany
100 P9 **Ueckermünde** Mecklenburg-Vorpommern, NE Germany 53°43′N 14°03′E
164 M12 **Ueda** *var.* Uyeda. Nagano, Honshū, S Japan 36°27′N 138°13′E
79 L16 **Uele** *var.* Welle. ≈ NE Dem. Rep. Congo
123 W5 **Uelen** Chukotskiy Avtonomnyy Okrug, NE Russian Federation 66°01′N 169°52′W
Uele (upper course) *see* Kibali, Dem. Rep. Congo
Uele (upper course) *see* Uolo, Río, Equatorial Guinea/Gabon
100 J11 **Uelzen** Niedersachsen, N Germany 52°58′N 10°34′E
164 J14 **Ueno** Mie, Honshū, SW Japan 34°45′N 136°08′E
127 V4 **Ufa** Respublika Bashkortostan, W Russian Federation 54°46′N 56°02′E
127 V4 **Ufa** ≈ W Russian Federation
Ufra *see* Kenar
83 C18 **Ugab** ≈ C Namibia
118 D8 **Ugāle** Ventspils, NW Latvia 57°16′N 21°58′E
81 F17 **Uganda** *off.* Republic of Uganda. ◆ *republic* E Africa
Uganda, Republic of *see* Uganda
138 G4 **Ugarit** *Ar.* Ra's Shamrah. *site of ancient city* Al Lādhiqīyah, NW Syria
39 O14 **Ugashik** Alaska, USA 57°30′N 157°24′W
107 Q19 **Ugento** Puglia, SE Italy 39°53′N 18°09′E
105 O15 **Ugíjar** Andalucía, S Spain 36°58′N 03°03′W
103 T11 **Ugine** Savoie, E France 45°45′N 06°25′E
123 R13 **Uglegorsk** Amurskaya Oblast', S Russian Federation 51°40′N 128°05′E
Ugleural'sk *see* Ugleural'skiy
125 V13 **Ugleural'skiy** *var.* Ugleural'sk, *earlier* Polovinka. Permskaya Oblast', NW Russian Federation 58°57′N 57°37′E
124 L15 **Uglich** Yaroslavskaya Oblast', W Russian Federation 57°33′N 38°23′E
126 I4 **Ugra** ≈ W Russian Federation
147 V9 **Ugyut** Narynskaya Oblast', C Kyrgyzstan 41°22′N 74°49′E
111 H19 **Uherské Hradiště** *Ger.* Ungarisch-Hradisch. Zlínský Kraj, E Czech Republic 49°05′N 17°26′E
111 H19 **Uherský Brod** *Ger.* Ungarisch-Brod. Zlínský Kraj, E Czech Republic 49°01′N 17°40′E
111 B17 **Úhlava** *Ger.* Angel. ≈ W Czech Republic
Uhorshchyna *see* Hungary
31 T13 **Uhrichsville** Ohio, N USA 40°23′N 81°21′W
Uhuru Peak *see* Kilimanjaro
96 G8 **Uig** N Scotland, United Kingdom 57°35′N 06°22′W
82 B10 **Uíge** *Port.* Carmona, Vila Marechal Carmona. Uíge, NW Angola 07°37′S 15°02′E
82 B10 **Uíge** ◈ *province* N Angola
193 Y15 **Uiha** *island* Ha'apai Group, C Tonga
189 U13 **Uijec** *island* Chuuk, C Micronesia
163 X14 **Ŭijŏngbu** *Jap.* Giseifu. NW South Korea 37°42′N 127°02′E
144 H10 **Uil** *Kaz.* Oyyl. Aktyubinsk, W Kazakhstan 49°06′N 54°41′E
144 H10 **Uil** *Kaz.* Oyyl. ≈ W Kazakhstan
36 M3 **Uinta Mountains** ▲▲ Utah, W USA
83 C18 **Uis** Erongo, NW Namibia 21°08′S 14°49′E
83 I25 **Uitenhage** Eastern Cape, S South Africa 33°44′S 25°27′E
98 H9 **Uitgeest** Noord-Holland, W Netherlands 52°32′N 04°43′E
98 I11 **Uithoorn** Noord-Holland, C Netherlands 52°14′N 04°50′E
98 O4 **Uithuizen** Groningen, NE Netherlands 53°24′N 06°40′E
98 O4 **Uithuizermeeden** Groningen, NE Netherlands 53°25′N 06°43′E
189 R6 **Ujae Atoll** *var.* Wūjae. *atoll* Ralik Chain, W Marshall Islands
Ujain *see* Ujjain
111 I16 **Ujazd** Opolskie, S Poland 50°22′N 18°20′E
Új-Becse *see* Novi Bečej
Ujda *see* Oujda
189 N5 **Ujelang Atoll** *var.* Wujlān. *atoll* Ralik Chain, W Marshall Islands
111 N21 **Újfehértó** Szabolcs-Szatmár-Bereg, E Hungary 47°48′N 21°40′E
Újgradiska *see* Nova Gradiška
164 J13 **Uji** *var.* Uzi. Kyōto, Honshū, SW Japan 34°54′N 135°48′E
81 E21 **Ujiji** Kigoma, W Tanzania 04°55′S 29°39′E
154 G10 **Ujjain** *prev.* Ujain. Madhya Pradesh, C India 23°11′N 75°50′E
Újlak *see* Ilok
'Ujmān *see* 'Ajmān
Újmoldova *see* Moldova Nouă
Újszentanna *see* Sântana
Ujungpandang *see* Makassar
Ujung Salang *see* Phuket
Újvidék *see* Novi Sad
UK *see* United Kingdom
154 E11 **Ukāi Reservoir** ⊠ W India
81 G19 **Ukara Island** *island* N Tanzania
'Ukash, Wādī *see* 'Akāsh, Wādī
81 F19 **Ukerewe Island** *island* N Tanzania
139 S9 **Ukhayḍir** Al Anbār, C Iraq 32°28′N 43°36′E
153 X13 **Ukhrul** Manipur, NE India 25°08′N 94°24′E
125 S9 **Ukhta** Respublika Komi, NW Russian Federation 63°31′N 53°48′E
34 L6 **Ukiah** California, W USA 39°07′N 123°14′W
32 K12 **Ukiah** Oregon, NW USA 45°06′N 118°57′W
99 G18 **Ukkel** *Fr.* Uccle. Brussels, C Belgium 50°47′N 04°19′E
118 G13 **Ukmergė** *Pol.* Wiłkomierz. Vilnius, C Lithuania 55°16′N 24°46′E
Ukraina *see* Ukraine
116 L6 **Ukraine** *off.* Ukraine, *Rus.* Ukraina, *Ukr.* Ukrayina; *prev.* Ukrainian Soviet Socialist Republic, Ukrainskay S.S.R. ◆ *republic* SE Europe
Ukraine *see* Ukraine
Ukrainian Soviet Socialist Republic *see* Ukraine
Ukrainskay S.S.R/Ukrayina *see* Ukraine
82 B13 **Uku** Cuanza Sul, NW Angola 11°25′S 14°18′E
164 B13 **Uku-jima** *island* Gotō-rettō, SW Japan
83 F20 **Ukwi** Kgalagadi, SW Botswana 23°41′S 20°26′E
118 M13 **Ula** *Rus.* Ulla. Vitsyebskaya Voblasts', N Belarus 55°14′N 29°15′E
136 C16 **Ula** Muğla, SW Turkey 37°08′N 28°25′E
118 M13 **Ula** *Rus.* Ulla. ≈ N Belarus
162 L7 **Ulaanbaatar** *Eng.* Ulan Bator; *prev.* Urga. ● (Mongolia) Töv, C Mongolia 47°55′N 106°57′E
Ulaan-Ereg *see* Bayanmönh
162 E5 **Ulaangom** Uvs, NW Mongolia 49°56′N 92°06′E
162 D5 **Ulaanhus** *var.* Bilüü. Bayan-Ölgiy, W Mongolia 48°54′N 89°40′E
Ulaantolgoy *see* Möst
Ulaan-Uul *see* Öldziyt, Bayanhongor, Mongolia
Ulaan-Uul *see* Erdene, Dornogovĭ, Mongolia
162 M14 **Ulan** *var.* Otog Qi. Nei Mongol Zizhiqu, N China 39°05′N 107°58′E
159 R10 **Ulan** *var.* Xireg; *prev.* Xiligou. Qinghai, C China 36°59′N 98°21′E
Ulan Bator *see* Ulaanbaatar
162 L13 **Ulan Buh Shamo** *desert* N China
Ulanhad *see* Chifeng
163 T8 **Ulanhot** Nei Mongol Zizhiqu, N China 46°02′N 122°E
127 Q14 **Ulan Khol** Respublika Kalmykiya, SW Russian Federation 45°27′N 46°48′E
163 P13 **Ulan Qab** *var.* Jining. Nei Mongol Zizhiqu, N China 40°59′N 113°08′E
162 M13 **Ulansuhai Nur** ◎ N China
123 N14 **Ulan-Ude** *prev.* Verkhneudinsk. Respublika Buryatiya, S Russian Federation 51°55′N 107°40′E
159 N12 **Ulan Ul Hu** ◎ C China
187 N9 **Ulawa Island** *island* SE Solomon Islands
138 J7 **'Ulayyānīyah, Bi'r al** *var.* Al Hilbeh. *well* S Syria
123 S12 **Ul'banskiy Zaliv** *strait* E Russian Federation
Ulbo *see* Olib
113 J18 **Ulcinj** S Montenegro 41°56′N 19°14′E
Uldz *see* Norovlin
Uleåborg *see* Oulu
Uleälv *see* Oulujoki
95 G16 **Ulefoss** Telemark, S Norway 59°17′N 09°15′E
Uleträsk *see* Oulujärvi
113 L19 **Ulëz** *var.* Ulëza. Dibër, C Albania 41°42′N 19°52′E
Ulëza *see* Ulëz
95 F22 **Ulfborg** Ringkøbing, W Denmark 56°16′N 08°21′E
98 N13 **Ulft** Gelderland, E Netherlands 51°53′N 06°23′E
162 G7 **Uliastay** *prev.* Jibhalanta. Dzavhan, W Mongolia 47°47′N 96°53′E
188 F8 **Ulimang** Babeldaob, N Palau
67 T10 **Ulindi** ≈ W Dem. Rep. Congo
188 H14 **Ulithi Atoll** *atoll* Caroline Islands, W Micronesia
112 N10 **Uljma** Vojvodina, NE Serbia 45°04′N 21°08′E
144 L11 **Ul'kayak** *Kaz.* Ölkeyek. ≈ C Kazakhstan
145 Q7 **Ul'ken-Karoy, Ozero** ◎ N Kazakhstan
Ülkenözen *see* Bol'shoy Uzen'
Ülkenqobda *see* Bol'shaya Khobda
104 G3 **Ulla** ≈ NW Spain
Ulla *see* Ula
183 S10 **Ulladulla** New South Wales, SE Australia 35°21′S 150°25′E
153 T14 **Ullapara** Rajshahi, W Bangladesh 24°20′N 89°34′E
96 H7 **Ullapool** N Scotland, United Kingdom 57°54′N 05°10′W
95 J20 **Ullared** Halland, S Sweden 57°07′N 12°45′E
105 T7 **Ulldecona** Cataluña, NE Spain 40°36′N 00°27′E
92 I9 **Ullsfjorden** *fjord* N Norway
97 K15 **Ullswater** ◎ NW England, United Kingdom
101 I22 **Ulm** Baden-Württemberg, S Germany 48°24′N 09°59′E
33 R8 **Ulm** Montana, NW USA 47°27′N 111°32′W
183 V5 **Ulmarra** New South Wales, SE Australia 29°37′S 153°06′E
116 K13 **Ulmeni** Buzău, C Romania 45°08′N 26°43′E
116 K14 **Ulmeni** Călăraşi, S Romania 44°08′N 26°43′E
42 L7 **Ulmukhuás** Región Autónoma Atlántico Norte, NE Nicaragua 14°20′N 84°30′W
188 C8 **Ulong** *var.* Aulong. *island* Palau Islands, N Palau
83 N14 **Ulonguè** *var.* Ulongwé. Tete, NW Mozambique 14°34′S 34°21′E
Ulongwé *see* Ulonguè
95 K19 **Ulricehamn** Västra Götaland, S Sweden 57°47′N 13°25′E
98 N5 **Ulrum** Groningen, NE Netherlands 53°24′N 06°20′E
163 Z16 **Ulsan** *Jap.* Urusan. SE South Korea 35°33′N 129°19′E
94 D10 **Ulsteinvik** Møre og Romsdal, S Norway 62°21′N 05°53′E
97 D15 **Ulster** ◈ *province* Northern Ireland, United Kingdom/Ireland
171 Q10 **Ulu** Pulau Siau, N Indonesia 02°46′N 125°22′E
123 Q11 **Ulu** Respublika Sakha (Yakutiya), NE Russian Federation 60°18′N 127°27′E
42 H5 **Ulúa, Río** ≈ NW Honduras
136 D12 **Ulubat Gölü** ◎ NW Turkey
136 E12 **Uludağ** ▲ NW Turkey 40°08′N 29°13′E
158 D7 **Ulugqat** Xinjiang Uygur Zizhiqu, W China 39°45′N 74°10′E
136 J16 **Ulukışla** Niğde, S Turkey 37°33′N 34°29′E
189 O15 **Ulul** *island* Caroline Islands, C Micronesia
83 L22 **Ulundi** KwaZulu/Natal, E South Africa 28°18′S 31°26′E
158 M3 **Ulungur He** ≈ NW China
158 K2 **Ulungur Hu** ◎ NW China
181 P8 **Uluru** *var.* Ayers Rock. *monolith* Northern Territory, C Australia
97 K16 **Ulverston** NW England, United Kingdom 54°13′N 03°08′W
183 O16 **Ulverstone** Tasmania, SE Australia 41°09′S 146°10′E
94 D13 **Ulvik** Hordaland, S Norway 60°34′N 06°53′E
93 J18 **Ulvila** Länsi-Suomi, W Finland 61°26′N 21°55′E
117 O8 **Ulyanivka** *Rus.* Ul'yanovka. Kirovohrads'ka Oblast', C Ukraine 48°18′N 30°15′E
Ul'yanovka *see* Ulyanivka
127 Q5 **Ul'yanovsk** *prev.* Simbirsk. Ul'yanovskaya Oblast', W Russian Federation 54°17′N 48°21′E
127 Q5 **Ul'yanovskaya Oblast'** ◈ *province* W Russian Federation
145 S10 **Ul'yanovskiy** Karaganda, C Kazakhstan 50°05′N 73°45′E
Ul'yanovskiy Kanal *see* Ul'yanow Kanali
146 M13 **Ul'yanow Kanali** *Rus.* Ul'yanovskiy Kanal. *canal* Turkmenistan/Uzbekistan
Ulyshylanshyq *see* Uly-Zhylanshyk
26 H6 **Ulysses** Kansas, C USA 37°36′N 101°23′W
145 O12 **Ulytau, Gory** ▲▲ C Kazakhstan
145 N11 **Uly-Zhylanshyk** *Kaz.* Ulyshylanshyq. ≈ C Kazakhstan
112 A9 **Umag** *It.* Umago. Istra, NW Croatia 45°25′N 13°32′E
Umago *see* Umag
41 W12 **Umán** Yucatán, SE Mexico 20°51′N 89°43′W
117 O7 **Uman'** *Rus.* Uman. Cherkas'ka Oblast', C Ukraine 48°45′N 30°10′E
189 V13 **Uman** *atoll* Chuuk Islands, C Micronesia
Uman *see* Uman'
Umanak/Umanaq *see* Uummannaq
'Umān, Khalīj *see* Oman, Gulf of
'Umān, Salṭanat *see* Oman
154 K10 **Umaria** Madhya Pradesh, C India 23°34′N 80°49′E
149 R16 **Umarkot** Sind, SE Pakistan 25°22′N 69°48′E
188 B17 **Umatac** SW Guam 13°17′N 144°40′E
188 A17 **Umatac Bay** *bay* SW Guam
139 S6 **Umayqah** Şalāḩ ad Dīn, C Iraq 34°32′N 43°45′E
124 J5 **Umba** Murmanskaya Oblast', NW Russian Federation 66°39′N 34°24′E
138 I8 **Umbāshī, Khirbat al** *ruins* As Suwaydā', S Syria
80 A12 **Umbelasha** ≈ W Sudan
106 H12 **Umbertide** Umbria, C Italy 43°16′N 12°21′E
61 B17 **Umberto** *var.* Humberto. Santa Fe, C Argentina 30°52′S 61°19′W
186 E7 **Umboi Island** *var.* Rooke Island. *island* C Papua New Guinea
124 J4 **Umbozero, Ozero** ◎ NW Russian Federation
106 H13 **Umbria** ◈ *region* C Italy
Umbrian-Machigian Mountains *see* Umbro-Marchigiano, Appennino
106 I12 **Umbro-Marchigiano, Appennino** *Eng.* Umbrian-Machigian Mountains. ▲▲ C Italy
93 J16 **Umeå** Västerbotten, N Sweden 63°50′N 20°15′E
93 H14 **Umeälven** ≈ N Sweden
39 Q5 **Umiat** Alaska, USA 69°22′N 152°09′W
83 K23 **Umlazi** KwaZulu/Natal, E South Africa 29°58′S 30°50′E
139 X10 **Umm al Baqar, Hawr** *var.* Birkat ad Dawaymah. *spring* S Iraq
139 Q5 **Umm al Faṭūr** *var.* Umm al Tūz. Şalāḩ ad Dīn, C Iraq 34°53′N 42°42′E
141 U12 **Umm al Ḩayt, Wādī** *var.* Wādī Amilḩayt. *seasonal river* SW Oman
Umm al Qaiwain *see* Umm al Qaywayn
143 R15 **Umm al Qaywayn** *var.* Umm al Qaiwain. Umm al Qaywayn, NE United Arab Emirates 25°43′N 55°55′E
Umm al Tūz *see* Umm al Faṭūr
138 J3 **Umm 'Āmūd** Ḩalab, N Syria 35°57′N 37°39′E
141 Y10 **Umm ar Ruşāş** *var.* Umm Ruşayş. W Oman 20°26′N 58°48′E
141 X9 **Ummas Samīn** *salt flat* C Oman

◆ Country
● Country Capital
◇ Dependent Territory
○ Dependent Territory Capital
◈ Administrative Regions
✈ International Airport
▲ Mountain
▲▲ Mountain Range
⛰ Volcano
≈ River
◎ Lake
⊠ Reservoir

Umm az Zumūl – Vågø

141 V9 **Umm az Zumūl** *oasis* E Saudi Arabia
80 A9 **Umm Buru** Western Darfur, W Sudan 15°01′N 23°35′E
80 A12 **Umm Dafag** Southern Darfur, W Sudan 10°28′N 23°20′E
Umm Durmān *see* Omdurman
138 F9 **Umm el Fahm** Haifa, N Israel 32°30′N 35°06′E
80 F9 **Umm Inderab** Northern Kordofan, C Sudan 15°12′N 31°54′E
80 C10 **Umm Keddada** Northern Darfur, W Sudan 13°36′N 26°42′E
140 J7 **Umm Lajj** Tabūk, W Saudi Arabia 25°02′N 37°19′E
138 L10 **Umm Maḥfur** ≈ N Jordan
139 Y13 **Umm Qaṣr** Al Baṣrah, SE Iraq 30°02′N 47°55′E
Umm Ruṣayṣ *see* Umm ar Ruṣāṣ
80 F11 **Umm Ruwaba** *var.* Umm Ruwābah, Um Ruwāba. Northern Kordofan, C Sudan 12°54′N 31°13′E
Umm Ruwābah *see* Umm Ruwaba
143 N16 **Umm Sa'īd** *var.* Musay'īd. S Qatar 24°57′N 51°32′E
139 Y10 **Umm Sawān, Hawr** ◎ S Iraq
138 K10 **Umm Ṭuways, Wādī** *dry watercourse* N Jordan
38 J17 **Umnak Island** *island* Aleutian Islands, Alaska, USA
32 F13 **Umpqua River** ≈ Oregon, NW USA
82 D13 **Umpulo** Bié, C Angola 12°43′S 17°42′E
154 I12 **Umred** Mahārāshtra, C India 20°54′N 79°19′E
Um Ruwāba *see* Umm Ruwaba
Umtali *see* Mutare
83 J24 **Umtata** Eastern Cape, SE South Africa 31°33′S 28°47′E
77 V17 **Umuahia** Abia, SW Nigeria 05°30′N 07°33′E
60 H10 **Umuarama** Paraná, S Brazil 23°45′S 53°20′W
Umvuma *see* Mvuma
83 K18 **Umzingwani** ≈ S Zimbabwe
112 D11 **Una** ≈ Bosnia and Herzegovina/Croatia
Una *see* Unna
112 E12 **Unac** ≈ W Bosnia and Herzegovina
23 T6 **Unadilla** Georgia, SE USA 32°15′N 83°44′W
18 I10 **Unadilla River** ≈ New York, NE USA
59 L18 **Unaí** Minas Gerais, SE Brazil 16°24′S 46°49′W
39 N10 **Unalakleet** Alaska, USA 63°52′N 160°47′W
38 K17 **Unalaska Island** *island* Aleutian Islands, Alaska, USA
185 I16 **Una, Mount** ▲ South Island, New Zealand 42°12′S 172°34′E
82 N13 **Unango** Niassa, N Mozambique 12°45′S 35°28′E
Unao *see* Unnão
92 L12 **Unari** Lappi, N Finland 67°07′N 25°37′E
141 O6 **'Unayzah** *var.* Anaiza. Al Qaṣīm, C Saudi Arabia 26°03′N 44°00′E
138 L10 **'Unayzah, Jabal** ▲ Jordan/Saudi Arabia 32°09′N 39°11′E
Unci *see* Almería
57 K19 **Uncía** Potosí, C Bolivia 18°30′S 66°29′W
37 Q7 **Uncompahgre Peak** ▲ Colorado, C USA 38°04′N 107°27′W
37 P6 **Uncompahgre Plateau** *plain* Colorado, C USA
95 L17 **Unden** ◎ S Sweden
28 M4 **Underwood** North Dakota, N USA 47°25′N 101°09′W
171 T13 **Undur** Pulau Seram, E Indonesia 03°41′S 130°38′E
Undur Khan *see* Öndörhaan
126 H6 **Unecha** Bryanskaya Oblast', W Russian Federation 52°51′N 32°38′E
39 N16 **Unga** Unga Island, Alaska, USA 55°14′N 160°34′W
Ungaria *see* Hungary
183 P8 **Ungarie** New South Wales, SE Australia 33°39′S 146°54′E
Ungarisch-Brod *see* Uherský Brod
Ungarisches Erzgebirge *see* Slovenské rudohorie
Ungarisch-Hradisch *see* Uherské Hradiště
Ungarn *see* Hungary
12 M4 **Ungava Bay** *bay* Québec, E Canada
12 J2 **Ungava, Péninsule d'** *peninsula* Québec, SE Canada
Ungeny *see* Ungheni
116 M9 **Ungheni** *Rus.* Ungeny. W Moldova 47°13′N 27°48′E
Unguja *see* Zanzibar
146 G10 **Üngüz Angyrsyndaky Garagum** *Rus.* Zaunguzskiye Garagumy. *desert* N Turkmenistan
146 H11 **Unguz, Solonchakovyye Vpadiny** *salt marsh* C Turkmenistan
Ungvár *see* Uzhhorod
60 I12 **União da Vitória** Paraná, S Brazil 26°13′S 51°05′W
111 G17 **Uničov** *Ger.* Mährisch-Neustadt. Olomoucký Kraj, E Czech Republic 49°48′N 17°05′E
110 J12 **Uniejów** Łódzkie, C Poland 51°58′N 18°46′E
112 A11 **Unije** *island* W Croatia
38 L16 **Unimak Island** *island* Aleutian Islands, Alaska, USA
38 L16 **Unimak Pass** *strait* Aleutian Islands, Alaska, USA
62 J12 **Unión** San Luis, C Argentina 35°09′S 65°55′W
27 W5 **Union** Missouri, C USA 38°27′N 91°01′W
32 L12 **Union** Oregon, NW USA 45°12′N 117°51′W
21 Q11 **Union** South Carolina, SE USA 34°42′N 81°37′W
21 R6 **Union** West Virginia, NE USA 37°36′N 80°34′W
61 B25 **Unión, Bahía** *bay* E Argentina
31 Q13 **Union City** Indiana, N USA 40°12′N 84°50′W
31 Q10 **Union City** Michigan, N USA 42°03′N 85°06′W
18 C12 **Union City** Pennsylvania, NE USA 41°54′N 79°51′W
20 G8 **Union City** Tennessee, S USA 36°26′N 89°03′W
32 G14 **Union Creek** Oregon, NW USA 42°54′N 122°26′W
83 G25 **Uniondale** Western Cape, SW South Africa 33°40′S 23°07′E
40 K13 **Unión de Tula** Jalisco, SW Mexico 19°58′N 104°16′W
30 M9 **Union Grove** Wisconsin, N USA 42°39′N 88°03′W
45 Y15 **Union Island** *island* S Saint Vincent and the Grenadines
Union of Myanmar *see* Burma
46 K5 **Union Reefs** *reef* SW Mexico
0 D7 **Union Seamount** *undersea feature* NE Pacific Ocean 49°35′N 132°45′W
23 Q6 **Union Springs** Alabama, S USA 32°08′N 85°43′W
20 H6 **Uniontown** Kentucky, S USA 37°46′N 87°55′W
18 C16 **Uniontown** Pennsylvania, NE USA 39°54′N 79°44′W
27 T1 **Unionville** Missouri, C USA 40°28′N 93°00′W
141 V8 **United Arab Emirates** *Ar.* Al Imārāt al 'Arabīyah al Muttaḥidah, *abbrev.* UAE; *prev.* Trucial States. ◆ *federation* SW Asia
United Arab Republic *see* Egypt
97 H14 **United Kingdom** *off.* United Kingdom of Great Britain and Northern Ireland, *abbrev.* UK. ◆ *monarchy* NW Europe
United Kingdom of Great Britain and Northern Ireland *see* United Kingdom
United Mexican States *see* Mexico
United Provinces *see* Uttar Pradesh
16 L10 **United States of America** *off.* United States of America, *var.* America, The States, *abbrev.* U.S., USA. ◆ *federal republic* North America
United States of America *see* United States of America
124 J10 **Unitsa** Respublika Kareliya, NW Russian Federation 62°31′N 34°31′E
11 S15 **Unity** Saskatchewan, S Canada 52°27′N 109°10′W
Unity State *see* Wahda
105 Q8 **Universales, Montes** ▲▲ C Spain
27 X4 **University City** Missouri, C USA 38°40′N 90°19′W
187 Q13 **Unmet** Malekula, C Vanuatu 16°09′S 167°16′E
101 F15 **Unna** Nordrhein-Westfalen, W Germany 51°32′N 07°41′E
152 H8 **Unna** *var.* Una. Uttarakhand, N India 31°27′N 76°16′E
Unnan *see* Kisuki
152 L12 **Unnão** *prev.* Unao. Uttar Pradesh, N India 26°32′N 80°30′E
187 R15 **Unpongkor** Erromango, S Vanuatu 18°48′S 169°01′E
Unruhstadt *see* Kargowa
96 M1 **Unst** *island* NE Scotland, United Kingdom
101 K16 **Unstrut** ≈ C Germany
Unterdrauburg *see* Dravograd
Unterlimbach *see* Lendava
101 L23 **Unterschleissheim** Bayern, SE Germany 48°16′N 11°34′E
101 H24 **Untersee** ◎ Germany/Switzerland
100 O10 **Unterueckersee** ◎ NE Germany
108 F9 **Unterwalden** ◈ *canton* C Switzerland
55 N12 **Unturán, Sierra de** ▲▲ Brazil/Venezuela
159 N11 **Unuli Horog** Qinghai, W China 35°10′N 91°50′E
136 M11 **Ünye** Ordu, W Turkey 41°08′N 37°14′E
Unza *see* Unzha
125 O14 **Unzha** *var.* Unza. ≈ NW Russian Federation
79 E17 **Uolo, Río** *var.* Eyo (lower course), Mbini, Uele (upper course), Woleu; *prev.* Benito. ≈ Equatorial Guinea/Gabon
55 Q10 **Uonán** Bolívar, SE Venezuela 04°33′N 62°10′W
161 T12 **Uotsuri-shima** *island* China/Japan/Taiwan
165 M11 **Uozu** Toyama, Honshū, SW Japan 36°50′N 137°25′E
42 L12 **Upala** Alajuela, NW Costa Rica 10°52′N 85°W
55 P7 **Upata** Bolívar, E Venezuela 08°02′N 62°25′W
79 M23 **Upemba, Lac** ◎ SE Dem. Rep. Congo
197 O12 **Upernavik** *var.* Upernivik. Kitaa, C Greenland 73°06′N 55°42′W
Upernivik *see* Upernavik
83 F22 **Upington** Northern Cape, W South Africa 28°28′S 21°14′E
Uplands *see* Ottawa
192 I16 **'Upolu** *island* SE Samoa
38 G11 **'Upolu Point** *var.* Upolu Point. *headland* Hawai'i, USA, C Pacific Ocean 20°15′N 155°51′W
Upper Austria *see* Oberösterreich
Upper Bann *see* Bann
14 M13 **Upper Canada Village** *tourist site* Ontario, SE Canada
18 I16 **Upper Darby** Pennsylvania, NE USA 39°57′N 75°15′W
28 L2 **Upper Des Lacs Lake** ⊠ North Dakota, N USA
185 L14 **Upper Hutt** Wellington, North Island, New Zealand 41°06′S 175°06′E
29 X11 **Upper Iowa River** ≈ Iowa, C USA
32 H15 **Upper Klamath Lake** ◎ Oregon, NW USA
34 M6 **Upper Lake** California, W USA 39°07′N 122°53′W
35 Q1 **Upper Lake** ◎ California, W USA
10 K9 **Upper Liard** Yukon Territory, W Canada 60°01′N 128°59′W
97 E16 **Upper Lough Erne** ◎ SW Northern Ireland, United Kingdom
80 F12 **Upper Nile** ◈ *state* E Sudan
29 T3 **Upper Red Lake** ◎ Minnesota, N USA
31 S12 **Upper Sandusky** Ohio, N USA 40°49′N 83°16′W
Upper Volta *see* Burkina
95 O15 **Upplandsväsby** *var.* Upplands Väsby. Stockholm, C Sweden 59°29′N 18°04′E
Upplands Väsby *see* Upplandsväsby
95 O15 **Uppsala** Uppsala, C Sweden 59°52′N 17°38′E
95 O14 **Uppsala** ◈ *county* C Sweden
38 J12 **Upright Cape** *headland* Saint Matthew Island, Alaska, USA 60°19′N 172°15′W
20 K6 **Upton** Kentucky, S USA 37°25′N 85°53′W
33 Y13 **Upton** Wyoming, C USA 44°06′N 104°37′W
141 N7 **'Uqlat aş Şuqūr** Al Qaşīm, W Saudi Arabia 25°51′N 42°13′E
Uqsuqtuuq *see* Gjoa Haven
Uqturpan *see* Wushi
54 C7 **Urabá, Golfo de** *gulf* NW Colombia
Uracas *see* Farallon de Pajaros
uradqianqi *see* Wulashan, N China
Uradar'ya *see* O'radaryo
Urad Qianqi *see* Xishanzui, N China
165 U5 **Urahoro** Hokkaidō, NE Japan 42°47′N 143°41′E
165 T5 **Urakawa** Hokkaidō, NE Japan 42°11′N 142°42′E
127 X6 **Ural** *Kaz.* Zayyq. ≈ Kazakhstan/Russian Federation
183 T6 **Uralla** New South Wales, SE Australia 30°39′S 151°30′E
Ural Mountains *see* Ural'skiye Gory
144 F8 **Ural'sk** *Kaz.* Oral. Zapadnyy Kazakhstan, NW Kazakhstan 51°12′N 51°17′E
Ural'skaya Oblast' *see* Zapadnyy Kazakhstan
127 W5 **Ural'skiye Gory** *var.* Ural'skiy Khrebet, *Eng.* Ural Mountains. ▲▲ Kazakhstan/Russian Federation
Ural'skiy Khrebet *see* Ural'skiye Gory
138 I3 **Urām aş Şughrá** Ḩalab, N Syria 36°10′N 36°55′E
183 P10 **Urana** New South Wales, SE Australia 35°22′S 146°16′E
11 S10 **Uranium City** Saskatchewan, C Canada 59°30′N 108°46′W
58 F10 **Uraricoera** Roraima, N Brazil 03°26′N 60°54′W
47 S5 **Uraricoera, Rio** ≈ N Brazil
Ura-Tyube *see* Ŭroteppa
165 O13 **Urawa** *var.* Saitama. Saitama, Honshū, S Japan 35°52′N 139°40′E
122 H10 **Uray** Khanty-Mansiyskiy Avtonomnyy Okrug-Yugra, C Russian Federation 60°07′N 64°38′E
141 R7 **'Uray'irah** Ash Sharqīyah, E Saudi Arabia 25°59′N 48°52′E
30 M13 **Urbana** Illinois, N USA 40°06′N 88°12′W
31 R13 **Urbana** Ohio, N USA 40°04′N 83°46′W
29 V14 **Urbandale** Iowa, C USA 41°37′N 93°42′W
106 I11 **Urbania** Marche, C Italy 43°40′N 12°33′E
106 I11 **Urbino** Marche, C Italy 43°45′N 12°38′E
57 H16 **Urcos** Cusco, S Peru 13°40′S 71°38′W
144 D10 **Urda** Zapadnyy Kazakhstan, W Kazakhstan 48°52′N 47°31′E
105 N10 **Urda** Castilla-La Mancha, C Spain 39°25′N 03°43′W
Urdgol *see* Chandmanī
105 O3 **Urduña** *var.* Orduña. País Vasco, N Spain 43°00′N 03°00′W
Urdunn *see* Jordan
145 X12 **Urdzhar** *Kaz.* Ürzhar. Vostochnyy Kazakhstan, E Kazakhstan 47°06′N 81°33′E
97 L16 **Ure** ≈ N England, United Kingdom
119 K18 **Urechcha** *Rus.* Urech'ye. Minskaya Voblasts', S Belarus 52°57′N 27°54′E
Urech'ye *see* Urechcha
127 P2 **Uren'** Nizhegorodskaya Oblast', W Russian Federation 57°30′N 45°48′E
122 J9 **Urengoy** Yamalo-Nenetskiy Avtonomnyy Okrug, N Russian Federation 65°52′N 78°42′E
184 K10 **Urenui** Taranaki, North Island, New Zealand 38°59′S 174°25′E
187 Q12 **Ureparapara** *island* Banks Islands, N Vanuatu
40 G5 **Ures** Sonora, NW Mexico 29°26′N 110°24′W
Urfa *see* Şanlıurfa
Urga *see* Ulaanbaatar
162 F6 **Urgamal** *var.* Hungiy. Dzavhan, W Mongolia 48°31′N 94°15′E
146 H9 **Urganch** *Rus.* Urgench; *prev.* Novo-Urgench. Xorazm Viloyati, W Uzbekistan 41°40′N 60°32′E
Urgench *see* Urganch
136 J14 **Ürgüp** Nevşehir, C Turkey 38°39′N 34°55′E
147 O12 **Urgut** Samarqand Viloyati, C Uzbekistan 39°26′N 67°15′E
158 K3 **Urho** Xinjiang Uygur Zizhiqu, W China 46°05′N 84°51′E
152 G5 **Uri** Jammu and Kashmir, NW India 34°05′N 74°03′E
108 G9 **Uri** ◈ *canton* C Switzerland
54 F11 **Uribe** Meta, C Colombia 03°01′N 74°33′W
54 H4 **Uribia** La Guajira, N Colombia 11°45′N 72°19′W
116 G12 **Uricani** *Hung.* Hobicaurikány. Hunedoara, SW Romania 45°18′N 23°03′E
57 M21 **Uriondo** Tarija, S Bolivia 21°43′S 64°40′W
40 I7 **Urique** Chihuahua, N Mexico 27°16′N 107°51′W
40 I7 **Urique, Río** ≈ N Mexico
56 E9 **Uritiyacu, Río** ≈ N Peru
Uritskiy *see* Sarykol'
98 K8 **Urk** Flevoland, N Netherlands 52°40′N 05°35′E
136 B14 **Urla** İzmir, W Turkey 38°19′N 26°47′E
116 K13 **Urlaţi** Prahova, SE Romania 44°59′N 26°15′E
127 V4 **Urman** Respublika Bashkortostan, W Russian Federation 54°53′N 56°52′E
147 P12 **Urmetan** W Tajikistan 39°27′N 68°13′E
Urmia *see* Orūmīyeh
Urmia, Lake *see* Orūmīyeh, Daryācheh-ye
Urmiyeh *see* Orūmīyeh
Uroševac *see* Ferizaj
147 P11 **Ŭroteppa** *Rus.* Ura-Tyube. NW Tajikistan 39°55′N 68°57′E
54 D8 **Urrao** Antioquia, W Colombia 06°16′N 76°10′W
Ursat'yevskaya *see* Xovos
Urt *see* Gurvantes
127 X7 **Urtazym** Orenburgskaya Oblast', W Russian Federation 52°12′N 58°48′E
59 K18 **Uruaçu** Goiás, C Brazil 14°38′S 49°06′W
40 M14 **Uruapan** *var.* Uruapan del Progreso. Michoacán, SW Mexico 19°26′N 102°04′W
Uruapan del Progreso *see* Uruapan
57 G15 **Urubamba, Cordillera** ▲▲ C Peru
57 G14 **Urubamba, Río** ≈ C Peru
58 G12 **Urucará** Amazonas, N Brazil 02°30′S 57°45′W
61 E16 **Uruguaiana** Rio Grande do Sul, S Brazil 29°45′S 57°05′W
Uruguai, Rio *see* Uruguay
61 E18 **Uruguay** *off.* Oriental Republic of Uruguay; *prev.* La Banda Oriental. ◆ *republic* E South America
61 E15 **Uruguay** *var.* Rio Uruguai, Río Uruguay. ≈ E South America
Uruguay, Oriental Republic of *see* Uruguay
Uruguay, Río *see* Uruguay
Urukthapel *see* Ngeruktabel
Urumchi *see* Ürümqi
Urumi Yeh *see* Orūmīyeh, Daryācheh-ye
158 L5 **Ürümqi** *var.* Tihwa, Urumchi, Urumqi, Urumtsi, Wu-lu-k'o-mu-shi, Wu-lu-mu-ch'i; *prev.* Ti-hua. Xinjiang Uygur Zizhiqu, NW China 43°52′N 87°31′E
Urumtsi *see* Ürümqi
Urundi *see* Burundi
183 V6 **Urunga** New South Wales, SE Australia 30°33′S 152°58′E
188 C15 **Uruno Point** *headland* NW Guam 13°37′N 144°50′E
123 U13 **Urup, Ostrov** *island* Kuril'skiye Ostrova, SE Russian Federation
141 P11 **'Uruq al Mawārid** *desert* S Saudi Arabia
Urusan *see* Ulsan
127 O16 **Urus-Martan** Chechenskaya Respublika, SW Russian Federation 43°08′N 45°33′E
127 T5 **Urussu** Respublika Tatarstan, W Russian Federation 54°34′N 53°23′E
184 K10 **Uruti** Taranaki, North Island, New Zealand 38°57′S 174°32′E
57 K19 **Uru Uru, Lago** ◎ W Bolivia
55 P9 **Uruyén** Bolívar, SE Venezuela 05°40′N 62°26′W
Ūrūzgān *see* Orūzgān
165 T3 **Uryū-gawa** ≈ Hokkaidō, NE Japan
165 T2 **Uryū-ko** ◎ Hokkaidō, NE Japan
127 N8 **Uryupinsk** Volgogradskaya Oblast', SW Russian Federation 50°51′N 41°59′E
Ürzhar *see* Urdzhar
125 R16 **Urzhum** Kirovskaya Oblast', NW Russian Federation 57°09′N 49°56′E
116 K13 **Urziceni** Ialomiţa, SE Romania 44°43′N 26°39′E
164 E14 **Usa** Ōita, Kyūshū, SW Japan 33°31′N 131°22′E
119 L16 **Usa** ≈ C Belarus
125 T6 **Usa** ≈ NW Russian Federation
136 E14 **Uşak** *prev.* Ushak. Uşak, W Turkey 38°42′N 29°25′E
136 D14 **Uşak** *var.* Ushak. ◈ *province* W Turkey
83 C19 **Usakos** Erongo, W Namibia 22°01′S 15°32′E
81 J21 **Usambara Mountains** ▲▲ NE Tanzania
81 G23 **Usangu Flats** *wetland* SW Tanzania
65 D24 **Usborne, Mount** ▲ East Falkland, Falkland Islands 51°35′S 58°57′W
100 O8 **Usedom** *island* NE Germany
99 M24 **Useldange** Diekirch, C Luxembourg 49°47′N 05°59′E
Ushachi *see* Ushachy
118 L13 **Ushachy** *Rus.* Ushachi. Vitsyebskaya Voblasts', N Belarus 55°11′N 28°37′E
Ushak *see* Uşak
122 L4 **Ushakova, Ostrov** *island* Severnaya Zemlya, N Russian Federation
Ushant *see* Ouessant, Île d'
Üsharal *see* Ucharal
164 B15 **Ushibuka** *var.* Usibuka. Kumamoto, Shimo-jima, SW Japan 32°12′N 130°00′E
Ushi Point *see* Sabaneta, Puntan
145 V14 **Ushtobe** *Kaz.* Üshtöbe. Almaty, SE Kazakhstan 45°15′N 77°59′E
Üshtöbe *see* Ushtobe
63 I25 **Ushuaia** Tierra del Fuego, S Argentina 54°48′S 68°19′W
39 R10 **Usibelli** Alaska, USA 63°54′N 148°41′W
Usibuka *see* Ushibuka
186 D7 **Usino** Madang, N Papua New Guinea 05°40′S 145°31′E
125 U6 **Usinsk** Respublika Komi, NW Russian Federation 66°01′N 57°37′E
97 K22 **Usk** *Wel.* Wysg. ≈ SE Wales, United Kingdom
Uskočke Planine/Uskokengebirge *see* Gorjanci
Uskoplje *see* Gornji Vakuf
Üsküb/Üsküp *see* Skopje
114 M11 **Üsküpdere** Kırklareli, NW Turkey 41°41′N 27°21′E
126 L7 **Usman'** Lipetskaya Oblast', W Russian Federation 52°04′N 39°41′E
118 D8 **Usmas Ezers** ◎ NW Latvia
125 U13 **Usol'ye** Permskaya Oblast', NW Russian Federation 59°27′N 56°33′E
41 T16 **Uspanapa, Río** ≈ SE Mexico
145 R11 **Uspenskiy** Karaganda, C Kazakhstan 48°45′N 72°46′E
103 O11 **Ussel** Corrèze, C France 45°33′N 02°18′E
163 Z6 **Ussuri** *var.* Usuri, Wusuri, *Chin.* Wusuli Jiang. ≈ China/Russian Federation
123 S15 **Ussuriysk** *prev.* Nikol'sk, Nikol'sk-Ussuriyskiy, Voroshilov. Primorskiy Kray, SE Russian Federation 43°48′N 131°59′E
136 J10 **Usta Burnu** *headland* N Turkey 41°58′N 34°30′E
149 P13 **Usta Muhammad** Baluchistān, SW Pakistan 28°07′N 68°00′E
123 V11 **Ust'-Bol'sheretsk** Kamchatskaya Oblast', E Russian Federation 52°48′N 156°12′E
127 N9 **Ust'-Buzulukskaya** Volgogradskaya Oblast', SW Russian Federation 50°12′N 42°06′E
111 C16 **Ustecký Kraj** ◈ *region* NW Czech Republic
108 G7 **Uster** Zürich, NE Switzerland 47°21′N 08°49′E
107 I22 **Ustica, Isola d'** *island* S Italy
122 M11 **Ust'-Ilimsk** Irkutskaya Oblast', C Russian Federation 57°57′N 102°30′E
111 C15 **Ústí nad Labem** *Ger.* Aussig. Ústecký Kraj, NW Czech Republic 50°41′N 14°04′E
111 F17 **Ústí nad Orlicí** *Ger.* Wildenschwert. Pardubický Kraj, C Czech Republic 49°58′N 16°24′E
Ustinov *see* Izhevsk
113 J14 **Ustiprača** ◈ Republika Srpska, SE Bosnia and Herzegovina
122 H11 **Ust'-Ishim** Omskaya Oblast', C Russian Federation 57°42′N 70°58′E
110 G6 **Ustka** *Ger.* Stolpmünde. Pomorskie, N Poland 54°35′N 16°50′E
123 V9 **Ust'-Kamchatsk** Kamchatskaya Oblast', E Russian Federation 56°14′N 162°28′E
145 X9 **Ust'-Kamenogorsk** *Kaz.* Öskemen. Vostochnyy Kazakhstan, E Kazakhstan 49°58′N 82°36′E
123 T10 **Ust'-Khayryuzovo** Koryakskiy Avtonomnyy Okrug, E Russian Federation 57°07′N 156°37′E
122 I14 **Ust'-Koksa** Respublika Altay, S Russian Federation 50°15′N 85°45′E
125 S11 **Ust'-Kulom** Respublika Komi, NW Russian Federation 61°42′N 53°42′E
123 Q8 **Ust'-Kuyga** Respublika Sakha (Yakutiya), NE Russian Federation 69°59′N 135°27′E
126 L14 **Ust'-Labinsk** Krasnodarskiy Kray, SW Russian Federation 44°40′N 40°46′E
123 R10 **Ust'-Maya** Respublika Sakha (Yakutiya), NE Russian Federation 60°27′N 134°28′E
123 R9 **Ust'-Nera** Respublika Sakha (Yakutiya), NE Russian Federation 64°28′N 143°01′E
123 P12 **Ust'-Nyukzha** Amurskaya Oblast', S Russian Federation 56°30′N 121°32′E
123 O7 **Ust'-Olenëk** Respublika Sakha (Yakutiya), NE Russian Federation 73°03′N 119°34′E
123 T9 **Ust'-Omchug** Magadanskaya Oblast', E Russian Federation 61°07′N 149°17′E
122 M13 **Ust'-Ordynskiy** Ust'-Ordynskiy Buryatskiy Avtonomnyy Okrug, S Russian Federation 52°50′N 104°42′E
122 M13 **Ust'-Ordynskiy Buryatskiy Avtonomnyy Okrug** ◈ *autonomous district* S Russian Federation
125 N8 **Ust'-Pinega** Arkhangel'skaya Oblast', NW Russian Federation 64°09′N 41°55′E
122 K8 **Ust'-Port** Taymyrskiy (Dolgano-Nenetskiy) Avtonomnyy Okrug, N Russian Federation 69°42′N 84°25′E
114 L11 **Ustrem** *prev.* Vakav. Yambol, E Bulgaria 42°01′N 26°28′E
111 O18 **Ustrzyki Dolne** Podkarpackie, SE Poland 49°26′N 22°36′E
Ust'-Sysol'sk *see* Syktyvkar
125 R7 **Ust'-Tsil'ma** Respublika Komi, NW Russian Federation 65°25′N 52°09′E
Ust Urt *see* Ustyurt Plateau
125 O11 **Ust'ya** ≈ NW Russian Federation
124 K6 **Ust'ye Varzugi** Murmanskaya Oblast', NW Russian Federation 66°16′N 36°47′E
123 V10 **Ust'yevoye** *prev.* Kirovskiy. Kamchatskaya Oblast', E Russian Federation 54°06′N 155°48′E
117 R8 **Ustynivka** Kirovohrads'ka Oblast', C Ukraine 47°58′N 32°32′E
144 H15 **Ustyurt Plateau** *var.* Ust Urt, *Uzb.* Ustyurt Platosi. *plateau* Kazakhstan/Uzbekistan
Ustyurt Platosi *see* Ustyurt Plateau
124 K14 **Ustyuzhna** Vologodskaya Oblast', NW Russian Federation 58°50′N 36°25′E
158 J4 **Usu** Xinjiang Uygur Zizhiqu, NW China 44°27′N 84°37′E
171 O13 **Usu** Sulawesi, C Indonesia 02°34′S 120°58′E
164 E14 **Usuki** Ōita, Kyūshū, SW Japan 33°07′N 131°48′E
42 G8 **Usulután** Usulután, SE El Salvador 13°20′N 88°26′W
42 B9 **Usulután** ◈ *department* SE El Salvador
41 W16 **Usumacinta, Río** ≈ Guatemala/Mexico
Usumbura *see* Bujumbura
Usuri *see* Ussuri
U.S./USA *see* United States of America
171 W14 **Uta** Papua, E Indonesia 04°28′S 136°03′E
36 K5 **Utah** *off.* State of Utah, *also known as* Beehive State, Mormon State. ◈ *state* W USA
36 L3 **Utah Lake** ◎ Utah, W USA
Utaidhani *see* Uthai Thani
93 M14 **Utajärvi** Oulu, C Finland 64°45′N 26°25′E
Utamboni *see* Mitemele, Río
Utaradit *see* Uttaradit
165 T3 **Utashinai** *var.* Utasinai. Hokkaidō, NE Japan 43°32′N 142°03′E
Utasinai *see* Utashinai
193 Y14 **'Uta Vava'u** *island* Vava'u Group, N Tonga
37 V9 **Ute Creek** ≈ New Mexico, SW USA
118 H12 **Utena** Utena, E Lithuania 55°30′N 25°34′E
118 H12 **Utena** ◈ *province* Lithuania
37 V10 **Ute Reservoir** ⊠ New Mexico, SW USA
167 O10 **Uthai Thani** *var.* Muang Uthai Thani, Udayadhani, Utaidhani. Uthai Thani, W Thailand 15°22′N 100°03′E
149 O15 **Uthal** Baluchistān, SW Pakistan 25°53′N 66°37′E
18 I10 **Utica** New York, NE USA 43°06′N 75°15′W
105 R10 **Utiel** País Valenciano, E Spain 39°33′N 01°13′W
11 O13 **Utikuma Lake** ◎ Alberta, W Canada
42 I4 **Utila, Isla de** *island* Islas de la Bahía, N Honduras
Utina *see* Udine
59 O17 **Utinga** Bahia, E Brazil 12°05′S 41°07′W
Utirik *see* Utrik Atoll
95 M22 **Utlängan** *island* S Sweden
117 U11 **Utlyuts'kyy Lyman** *bay* S Ukraine
95 P16 **Utö** Stockholm, C Sweden 58°55′N 18°19′E
25 Q12 **Utopia** Texas, SW USA 29°30′N 99°31′W
98 J11 **Utrecht** *Lat.* Trajectum ad Rhenum. Utrecht, C Netherlands 52°06′N 05°07′E
83 K22 **Utrecht** KwaZulu/Natal, E South Africa 27°40′S 30°20′E
98 I11 **Utrecht** ◈ *province* C Netherlands
104 K14 **Utrera** Andalucía, S Spain 37°10′N 05°47′W
189 V4 **Utrik Atoll** *var.* Utirik, Utrōk, Utrōnk. *atoll* Ratak Chain, N Marshall Islands
Utrōk/Utrōnk *see* Utrik Atoll
95 B16 **Utsira** *island* SW Norway
92 L8 **Utsjoki** *var.* Ohcejohka. Lappi, N Finland 69°54′N 27°01′E
165 O12 **Utsunomiya** *var.* Utunomiya. Tochigi, Honshū, S Japan 36°36′N 139°53′E
127 P13 **Utta** Respublika Kalmykiya, SW Russian Federation 46°22′N 46°03′E
167 O8 **Uttaradit** *var.* Utaradit. Uttaradit, N Thailand 17°38′N 100°05′E
152 J9 **Uttarakhand** ◈ *state* N India
152 J8 **Uttarkāshi** Uttarakhand, N India 30°45′N 78°19′E
152 K11 **Uttar Pradesh** *prev.* United Provinces, United Provinces of Agra and Oudh. ◈ *state* N India
45 T5 **Utuado** C Puerto Rico 18°17′N 66°41′W
158 K3 **Utubulak** Xinjiang Uygur Zizhiqu, W China 46°50′N 86°15′E
39 N5 **Utukok River** ≈ Alaska, USA
Utunomiya *see* Utsunomiya
187 P10 **Utupua** *island* Santa Cruz Islands, E Solomon Islands
144 G9 **Utva** ≈ NW Kazakhstan
189 Y15 **Utwe** Kosrae, E Micronesia
189 X15 **Utwe Harbor** *harbor* Kosrae, E Micronesia
Uubulan *see* Hayrhan
163 O8 **Uulbayan** *var.* Dzüünbulag. Sühbaatar, E Mongolia 46°30′N 112°22′E
118 G6 **Uulu** Pärnumaa, SW Estonia 58°15′N 24°32′E
197 N13 **Uummannaq** *var.* Umanak, Umanaq. ◈ Kitaa, C Greenland
Uummannarsuaq *see* Nunap Isua
162 E4 **Üüreg Nuur** ◎ NW Mongolia
Uusikaarlepyy *see* Nykarleby
93 J19 **Uusikaupunki** *Swe.* Nystad. Länsi-Suomi, SW Finland 60°48′N 21°25′E
127 S2 **Uva** Udmurtskaya Respublika, NW Russian Federation 56°41′N 52°15′E
155 K25 **Uva** ◈ *province* SE Sri Lanka
113 L14 **Uvac** ≈ W Serbia
25 Q12 **Uvalde** Texas, SW USA 29°14′N 99°49′W
119 O18 **Uvaravichy** *Rus.* Uvarovichi. Homyel'skaya Voblasts', SE Belarus 52°36′N 30°44′E
54 J11 **Uvá, Río** ≈ E Colombia
Uvarovichi *see* Uvaravichy
127 N7 **Uvarovo** Tambovskaya Oblast', W Russian Federation 51°58′N 42°13′E
122 H10 **Uvat** Tyumenskaya Oblast', C Russian Federation 59°11′N 68°37′E
190 G12 **Uvea, Île** *island* N Wallis and Futuna
81 E21 **Uvinza** Kigoma, W Tanzania 05°08′S 30°23′E
79 O20 **Uvira** Sud-Kivu, E Dem. Rep. Congo 03°24′S 29°05′E
162 E5 **Uvs** ◈ *province* NW Mongolia
162 F5 **Uvs Nuur** *var.* Ozero Ubsu-Nur. ◎ Mongolia/Russian Federation
Uxin Qi *see* Galutu, N China
164 F14 **Uwa** *var.* Seiyo. Ehime, Shikoku, SW Japan 33°22′N 132°29′E
164 F14 **Uwajima** *var.* Uwazima. Ehime, Shikoku, SW Japan 33°13′N 132°32′E
80 B5 **'Uwaynāt, Jabal al** *var.* Jebel Uweinat. ▲ Libya/Sudan 21°51′N 25°01′E
Uwazima *see* Uwajima
Uweinat, Jebel *see* 'Uwaynāt, Jabal al
14 H14 **Uxbridge** Ontario, S Canada 44°07′N 79°07′W
Uxellodunum *see* Issoudun
Uxin Qi *see* Dabqig, N China
41 X12 **Uxmal, Ruinas** *ruins* Yucatán, SE Mexico
129 Q5 **Uy** ≈ Kazakhstan/Russian Federation
144 K15 **Uyaly** Kzylorda, S Kazakhstan 44°22′N 61°16′E
123 R8 **Uyandina** ≈ NE Russian Federation
162 J8 **Uyanga** *var.* Ongi. Övörhangay, C Mongolia 46°30′N 102°18′E
Üydzen *see* Manlay
Uyeda *see* Ueda
122 K5 **Uyedineniya, Ostrov** *island* N Russian Federation
77 V17 **Uyo** Akwa Ibom, S Nigeria 05°00′N 07°57′E
162 D8 **Üyönch** Hovd, W Mongolia 46°04′N 92°05′E
145 Q15 **Uyuk** Zhambyl, S Kazakhstan 43°46′N 70°55′E
141 V13 **'Uyūn** SW Oman 17°19′N 53°50′E
57 K20 **Uyuni** Potosí, W Bolivia 20°27′S 66°48′W
57 J20 **Uyuni, Salar de** *wetland* SW Bolivia
146 I9 **Uzbekistan** *off.* Republic of Uzbekistan. ◆ *republic* C Asia
Uzbekistan, Republic of *see* Uzbekistan
158 D8 **Uzbel Shankou** *Rus.* Pereval Kyzyl-Dzhiik. *pass* China/Tajikistan
146 B11 **Uzboý** *prev. Rus.* Imeni 26 Bakinskikh Komissarov, *Turkm.* 26 Baku Komissarlary Adyndaky. Balkan Welaýaty, W Turkmenistan 39°24′N 54°04′E
119 J17 **Uzda** Minskaya Voblasts', C Belarus 53°29′N 27°10′E
103 N12 **Uzerche** Corrèze, C France 45°24′N 01°35′E
103 R14 **Uzès** Gard, S France 44°00′N 04°25′E
147 T10 **Uzgen** *Kir.* Özgön. Oshskaya Oblast', SW Kyrgyzstan 40°42′N 73°17′E
117 O3 **Uzh** ≈ N Ukraine
Uzhgorod *see* Uzhhorod
116 G7 **Uzhhorod** *Rus.* Uzhgorod; *prev.* Ungvár. Zakarpats'ka Oblast', W Ukraine 48°36′N 22°19′E
Uzi *see* Uji
112 K13 **Užice** *prev.* Titovo Užice. Serbia, W Serbia 43°52′N 19°51′E
Uzin *see* Uzyn
126 L5 **Uzlovaya** Tul'skaya Oblast', W Russian Federation 54°01′N 38°15′E
108 H7 **Uznach** Sankt Gallen, NE Switzerland 47°12′N 09°00′E
145 U16 **Uzunagach** Almaty, SE Kazakhstan 43°08′N 76°20′E
136 B10 **Uzunköprü** Edirne, NW Turkey 41°18′N 26°40′E
118 D11 **Užventis** Šiauliai, C Lithuania 55°49′N 22°38′E
117 P5 **Uzyn** *Rus.* Uzin. Kyyivs'ka Oblast', N Ukraine 49°52′N 30°27′E
145 N7 **Uzynkol'** Kostanay, N Kazakhstan
145 N7 **Uzynkol'** *prev.* Lenīn, Leninskoye. Kustanay, N Kazakhstan 54°05′N 65°23′E

V

Vääksy *see* Asikkala
83 H23 **Vaal** ≈ C South Africa
93 M14 **Vaala** Oulu, C Finland 64°34′N 26°49′E
93 N19 **Vaalimaa** Etelä-Suomi, SE Finland 60°34′N 27°49′E
99 M19 **Vaals** Limburg, SE Netherlands 50°46′N 06°01′E
93 J16 **Vaasa** *Swe.* Vasa; *prev.* Nikolainkaupunki. Länsi-Suomi, W Finland 63°07′N 21°39′E
98 L10 **Vaassen** Gelderland, E Netherlands 52°18′N 05°59′E
118 G11 **Vabalninkas** Panevėžys, NE Lithuania 55°59′N 24°45′E
Vabkent *see* Vobkent
111 J22 **Vác** *Ger.* Waitzen. Pest, N Hungary 47°46′N 19°08′E
61 I14 **Vacaria** Rio Grande do Sul, S Brazil 28°31′S 50°52′W
35 N7 **Vacaville** California, W USA 38°21′N 121°59′W
103 R15 **Vaccarès, Étang de** ◎ SE France
44 L10 **Vache, Île à** *island* SW Haiti
173 Y16 **Vacoas** W Mauritius 20°18′S 57°29′E
155 F21 **Vadakara** *var.* Badagara. Kerala, SW India 11°36′N 75°34′E *see also* Badagara
32 G10 **Vader** Washington, NW USA 46°23′N 122°58′W
94 D12 **Vadheim** Sogn Og Fjordane, S Norway 61°12′N 05°48′E
154 D11 **Vadodara** *prev.* Baroda. Gujarāt, W India 22°19′N 73°14′E
92 M8 **Vadsø** *Fin.* Vesisaari. Finnmark, N Norway 70°07′N 29°47′E
95 L17 **Vadstena** Östergötland, S Sweden 58°26′N 14°55′E
108 I8 **Vaduz** ● (Liechtenstein) W Liechtenstein 47°08′N 09°32′E
Vág *see* Váh
125 N12 **Vaga** ≈ NW Russian Federation
94 G11 **Vågåmo** Oppland, S Norway 61°52′N 09°06′E
112 D12 **Vaganski Vrh** ▲ W Croatia 44°24′N 15°32′E
95 A19 **Vágar** *Dan.* Vågø. *island* W Faeroe Islands
Vágbeszterce *see* Považská Bystrica
95 L19 **Vaggeryd** Jönköping, S Sweden 57°30′N 14°10′E
137 T12 **Vagharshapat** *var.* Ejmiadzin, Ejmiatsin, Etchmiadzin, *Rus.* Echmiadzin. W Armenia 40°10′N 44°17′E
95 O16 **Vagnhärad** Södermanland, C Sweden 58°57′N 17°32′E
Vågø *see* Vágar

◆ Country ● Country Capital ◇ Dependent Territory ○ Dependent Territory Capital ◈ Administrative Regions ✈ International Airport ▲ Mountain ▲▲ Mountain Range Volcano ≈ River ◎ Lake ⊠ Reservoir

VAGOS – VELIKONDA RANGE

104 G7 Vagos Aveiro, N Portugal 40°33′N 08°42′W
Vágsellye see Šaľa
92 H10 Vågsfjorden fjord N Norway
94 C10 Vågsøy island S Norway
Vágújhely see Nové Mesto nad Váhom
111 I21 Váh Ger. Waag, Hung. Vág. ≈ W Slovakia
93 K16 Vähäkyrö Länsi-Suomi, W Finland 63°04′N 22°05′E
191 X11 Vahitahi atoll Îles Tuamotu, E French Polynesia
Vahtjer see Gällivare
Vaidei see Vulcan
22 L4 Vaiden Mississippi, S USA 33°19′N 89°42′W
155 I23 Vaigai ≈ SE India
191 V16 Vaihu Easter Island, Chile, E Pacific Ocean 27°10′S 109°22′W
118 I6 Väike Emajõgi ≈ S Estonia
118 I4 Väike-Maarja Ger. Klein-Marien. Lääne-Virumaa, NE Estonia 59°07′N 26°16′E
Väike-Salatsi see Mazsalaca
37 R4 Vail Colorado, C USA 39°36′N 106°20′W
193 V15 Vaina Tongatapu, S Tonga 21°12′S 175°10′W
118 E5 Väinameri prev. Muhu Väin, Ger. Moon-Sund. sea E Baltic Sea
93 N18 Vainikkala Etelä-Suomi, SE Finland 60°54′N 28°18′E
118 D10 Vaiņode Liepāja, SW Latvia 56°25′N 21°52′E
155 H23 Vaippār ≈ SE India
191 W11 Vairaatea atoll Îles Tuamotu, C French Polynesia
191 R8 Vairao Tahiti, W French Polynesia 17°48′S 149°17′W
103 R14 Vaison-la-Romaine Vaucluse, SE France 44°15′N 05°04′E
190 G11 Vaitupu Île Uvea, E Wallis and Futuna 13°14′S 176°09′W
190 F7 Vaitupu atoll C Tuvalu
Vajdahunyad see Hunedoara
Vajdej see Vulcan
78 K12 Vakaga ◐ prefecture NE Central African Republic
114 H10 Vakarel Sofiya, W Bulgaria 42°35′N 23°40′E
Vakav see Ustrem
137 O11 Vakfıkebir Trabzon, NE Turkey 41°03′N 39°19′E
122 J10 Vakh ≈ C Russian Federation
Vakhon, Qatorkŭhi see Nicholas Range
147 P14 Vakhsh SW Tajikistan 37°46′N 68°48′E
147 Q12 Vakhsh ≈ SW Tajikistan
127 P1 Vakhtan Nizhegorodskaya Oblast', W Russian Federation 58°00′N 46°43′E
94 C13 Vaksdal Hordaland, S Norway 60°29′N 05°45′E
125 O8 Vaksha ≈ NW Russian Federation
Valachia see Wallachia
108 D11 Valais Ger. Wallis. ◐ canton SW Switzerland
113 M21 Valamarës, Mali i ▲ SE Albania 40°48′N 20°31′E
127 S2 Valamaz Udmurtskaya Respublika, NW Russian Federation 57°36′N 52°07′E
113 Q19 Valandovo SE FYR Macedonia 41°20′N 22°33′E
111 I18 Valašské Meziříčí Ger. Wallachisch-Meseritsch, Pol. Wałeckie Międzyrzecze. Zlínský Kraj, E Czech Republic 49°29′N 17°57′E
115 I17 Valáxa island Vóreies Sporádes, Greece, Aegean Sea
95 K16 Vålberg Värmland, C Sweden 59°24′N 13°12′E
116 H12 Vâlcea prev. Vîlcea. ◐ county SW Romania
63 J16 Valcheta Río Negro, E Argentina 40°42′S 66°08′W
15 P12 Valcourt Québec, SE Canada 45°28′N 72°18′W
Valdai Hills see Valdayskaya Vozvyshennost'
104 M3 Valdavia ≈ N Spain
124 I15 Valday Novgorodskaya Oblast', W Russian Federation 57°57′N 33°20′E
124 I15 Valdayskaya Vozvyshennost' var. Valdai Hills. hill range W Russian Federation
104 L9 Valdecañas, Embalse de ⊠ W Spain
118 E8 Valdemārpils Ger. Sassmacken. Talsi, NW Latvia 57°23′N 22°36′E
95 N18 Valdemarsvik Östergötland, S Sweden 58°13′N 16°35′E
105 N8 Valdemoro Madrid, C Spain 40°12′N 03°40′W
105 O11 Valdepeñas Castilla-La Mancha, C Spain 38°46′N 03°24′W
104 L5 Valderaduey ≈ NE Spain
104 L5 Valderas Castilla-León, N Spain 42°05′N 05°27′W
105 T7 Valderrobres var. Vall-de-roures. Aragón, NE Spain 40°53′N 00°08′E
63 K17 Valdés, Península peninsula SE Argentina
56 C5 Valdéz var. Limones. Esmeraldas, NW Ecuador 01°13′N 79°00′W
39 S11 Valdez Alaska, USA 61°08′N 146°21′W
Valdia see Weldiya
103 U11 Val d'Isère Savoie, E France 45°27′N 07°03′E
63 G15 Valdivia Los Lagos, C Chile 39°50′S 73°13′W
Valdivia Bank see Valdivia Seamount
65 P17 Valdivia Seamount var. Valdivia Bank. undersea feature E Atlantic Ocean 26°15′S 06°25′E
103 N4 Val-d'Oise ◐ department N France
14 J8 Val-d'Or Québec, SE Canada 48°06′N 77°42′W
23 U8 Valdosta Georgia, SE USA 30°49′N 83°16′W
94 G13 Valdres physical region S Norway
32 L13 Vale Oregon, NW USA 43°59′N 117°15′W
116 F9 Valea lui Mihai Hung. Érmihályfalva. Bihor, NW Romania 47°31′N 22°08′E
11 N15 Valemount British Columbia, SW Canada 52°46′N 119°17′W
59 O17 Valença Bahia, E Brazil 13°22′S 39°06′W
104 F4 Valença do Minho Viana do Castelo, N Portugal 42°02′N 08°38′W
59 N14 Valença do Piauí Piauí, E Brazil 06°26′S 41°46′W
103 N8 Valençay Indre, C France 47°10′N 01°31′E
103 R13 Valence anc. Valentia, Valentia Julia, Ventia. Drôme, E France 44°56′N 04°54′E
105 S10 Valencia País Valenciano, E Spain 39°29′N 00°24′W
54 K5 Valencia Carabobo, N Venezuela 10°12′N 68°02′W
105 R10 Valencia Cat. València. ◐ province País Valenciano, E Spain
105 S10 Valencia ✈ Valencia, E Spain
104 I10 Valencia de Alcántara Extremadura, W Spain 39°25′N 07°14′W
104 L4 Valencia de Don Juan Castilla-León, N Spain 42°17′N 05°31′W
105 U9 Valencia, Golfo de var. Gulf of Valencia. gulf E Spain
Valencia, Gulf of see Valencia, Golfo de
97 A21 Valencia Island Ir. Dairbhre. island SW Ireland
Valencia/València see País Valenciano
103 P2 Valenciennes Nord, N France 50°21′N 03°32′E
116 K13 Vălenii de Munte Prahova, SE Romania 45°11′N 26°02′E
Valentia see Valence, France
Valentia see País Valenciano
Valentia Julia see Valence
103 T8 Valentigney Doubs, E France 47°27′N 06°49′E
28 M12 Valentine Nebraska, C USA 42°53′N 100°31′W
24 J10 Valentine Texas, SW USA 30°35′N 104°30′W
Valentine State see Oregon
106 C8 Valenza Piemonte, NW Italy 45°01′N 08°37′E
94 I13 Våler Hedmark, S Norway 60°39′N 11°52′E
54 I6 Valera Trujillo, NW Venezuela 09°21′N 70°38′W
192 M11 Valerie Guyot S Pacific Ocean 33°00′S 164°00′W
Valetta see Valletta
118 I7 Valga Ger. Walk, Latv. Valka. Valgamaa, S Estonia 57°48′N 26°04′E
118 I7 Valgamaa var. Valga Maakond. ◐ province S Estonia
Valga Maakond see Valgamaa
43 Q15 Valiente, Península peninsula NW Panama
103 X16 Valinco, Golfe de gulf Corse, France, C Mediterranean Sea
112 L12 Valjevo Serbia, W Serbia 44°17′N 19°54′E
Valjok see Válljohka
118 I7 Valka Ger. Walk. Valka, N Latvia 57°48′N 26°01′E
Valka see Valga
93 L18 Valkeakoski Länsi-Suomi, W Finland 61°17′N 24°05′E
93 M19 Valkeala Etelä-Suomi, S Finland 60°55′N 26°49′E
99 L18 Valkenburg Limburg, SE Netherlands 50°52′N 05°50′E
99 K15 Valkenswaard Noord-Brabant, S Netherlands 51°21′N 05°29′E
119 G15 Valkininkai Alytus, S Lithuania 54°22′N 24°51′E
117 U5 Valky Kharkivs'ka Oblast', E Ukraine 49°51′N 35°40′E
41 Y12 Valladolid Yucatán, SE Mexico 20°39′N 88°13′W
104 M5 Valladolid Castilla-León, NW Spain 41°39′N 04°45′W
104 L5 Valladolid ◐ province Castilla-León, N Spain
103 U15 Vallauris Alpes-Maritimes, SE France 43°34′N 07°03′E
Vall-de-roures see Valderrobres
Vall D'Uxó see La Vall d'Uixó
95 E16 Valle Aust-Agder, S Norway 59°13′N 07°33′E
105 N2 Valle Cantabria, N Spain 43°14′N 04°16′W
42 H8 Valle ◐ department S Honduras
105 N8 Vallecas Madrid, C Spain 40°23′N 03°37′W
37 Q8 Vallecito Reservoir ⊠ Colorado, C USA
106 A7 Valle d'Aosta ◐ region NW Italy
41 O14 Valle de Bravo México, S Mexico 19°19′N 100°08′W
55 N5 Valle de Guanape Anzoátegui, N Venezuela 09°54′N 65°41′W
54 M6 Valle de La Pascua Guárico, N Venezuela 09°15′N 66°00′W
54 B11 Valle del Cauca off. Departamento del Valle del Cauca. ◐ province W Colombia
Valle del Cauca, Departamento del see Valle del Cauca
41 N13 Valle de Santiago Guanajuato, C Mexico 20°25′N 101°15′W
40 J7 Valle de Zaragoza Chihuahua, N Mexico 27°25′N 105°50′W
54 G5 Valledupar Cesar, N Colombia 10°31′N 73°16′W
76 G10 Vallée de Ferlo ≈ NW Senegal
57 M19 Vallegrande Santa Cruz, C Bolivia 18°30′S 64°06′W
41 P8 Valle Hermoso Tamaulipas, C Mexico 25°39′N 97°49′W
35 N8 Vallejo California, W USA 38°08′N 122°16′W
62 G8 Vallenar Atacama, N Chile 28°35′S 70°44′W
95 O15 Vallentuna Stockholm, C Sweden 59°32′N 18°05′E
121 P16 Valletta prev. Valetta. ● (Malta) E Malta 35°54′N 14°31′E
27 N6 Valley Center Kansas, C USA 37°49′N 97°22′W
29 Q5 Valley City North Dakota, N USA 46°57′N 97°58′W
32 I15 Valley Falls Oregon, NW USA 42°28′N 120°16′W
Valleyfield see Salaberry-de-Valleyfield
21 S4 Valley Head West Virginia, NE USA 38°33′N 80°01′W
25 T8 Valley Mills Texas, SW USA 31°36′N 97°27′W
75 W10 Valley of the Kings ancient monument E Egypt
29 R11 Valley Springs South Dakota, N USA 43°34′N 96°28′W
20 K5 Valley Station Kentucky, S USA 38°06′N 85°52′W
11 O13 Valleyview Alberta, W Canada 55°02′N 117°17′W
25 T5 Valley View Texas, SW USA 33°27′N 97°08′W
61 C21 Vallimanca, Arroyo ≈ E Argentina
92 L9 Válljohka var. Valjok. Finnmark, N Norway 69°40′N 25°52′E
107 M19 Vallo della Lucania Campania, S Italy 40°13′N 15°15′E
108 B9 Vallorbe Vaud, W Switzerland 46°43′N 06°21′E
105 V6 Valls Cataluña, NE Spain 41°18′N 01°15′E
94 N11 Vallsta Gävleborg, C Sweden 61°30′N 16°25′E
94 N12 Vallvik Gävleborg, C Sweden 61°10′N 17°15′E
11 T17 Val Marie Saskatchewan, S Canada 49°15′N 107°44′W
118 H7 Valmiera Est. Volmari, Ger. Wolmar. Valmiera, N Latvia 57°34′N 25°26′E
105 N3 Valnera ▲ N Spain 43°08′N 03°39′W
102 J3 Valognes Manche, N France 49°31′N 01°28′W
Valona see Vlorë
Valona Bay see Vlorës, Gjiri i
104 G6 Valongo var. Valongo de Gaia. Porto, N Portugal 41°11′N 08°30′W
Valongo de Gaia see Valongo
104 M5 Valoria la Buena Castilla-León, N Spain 41°48′N 04°33′W
119 J15 Valozhyn Pol. Wołożyn, Rus. Volozhin. Minskaya Voblasts', C Belarus 54°05′N 26°32′E
104 I5 Valpaços Vila Real, N Portugal 41°36′N 07°17′W
62 G11 Valparaíso Valparaíso, C Chile 33°05′S 71°18′W
40 L11 Valparaíso Zacatecas, C Mexico 22°49′N 103°28′W
23 P8 Valparaiso Florida, SE USA 30°30′N 86°28′W
31 N11 Valparaiso Indiana, N USA 41°28′N 87°04′W
62 G11 Valparaíso off. Región de Valparaíso. ◐ region C Chile
Valparaíso, Región de see Valparaíso
Valpo see Valpovo
112 I9 Valpovo Hung. Valpó. Osijek-Baranja, E Croatia 45°40′N 18°25′E
103 R14 Valréas Vaucluse, SE France 44°22′N 05°00′E
Vals see Vals-Platz
154 D12 Valsād prev. Bulsar. Gujarāt, W India 20°40′N 72°55′E
Valsbaai see False Bay
171 T12 Valse Pisang, Kepulauan island group E Indonesia
108 H9 Vals-Platz var. Vals. Graubünden, S Switzerland 46°39′N 09°09′E
171 X16 Vals, Tanjung headland Papua, SE Indonesia 08°26′S 137°35′E
93 N15 Valtimo Itä-Suomi, E Finland 63°39′N 28°49′E
115 D17 Váltou ▲▲ C Greece
127 O12 Valuyevka Rostovskaya Oblast', SW Russian Federation 46°48′N 43°49′E
126 K9 Valuyki Belgorodskaya Oblast', W Russian Federation 50°11′N 38°07′E
36 L2 Val Verda Utah, W USA 40°51′N 111°53′W
64 N12 Valverde Hierro, Islas Canarias, Spain, NE Atlantic Ocean 27°48′N 17°55′W
104 I13 Valverde del Camino Andalucía, S Spain 37°35′N 06°45′W
95 G23 Vamdrup Vejle, C Denmark 55°26′N 09°18′E
94 L12 Våmhus Dalarna, C Sweden 61°07′N 14°30′E
93 K18 Vammala Länsi-Suomi, SW Finland 61°20′N 22°55′E
Vámosudvarhely see Odorheiu Secuiesc
137 S14 Van Van, E Turkey 38°30′N 43°23′E
25 V7 Van Texas, SW USA 32°31′N 95°38′W
137 T14 Van ◐ province E Turkey
137 T11 Vanadzor prev. Kirovakan. N Armenia 40°49′N 44°29′E
25 U5 Van Alstyne Texas, SW USA 33°25′N 96°34′W
33 W10 Vananda Montana, NW USA 46°22′N 106°58′W
116 I11 Vânători Hung. Héjjasfalva; prev. Vînători. Mureş, C Romania 46°14′N 24°56′E
191 W12 Vanavana atoll Îles Tuamotu, SE French Polynesia
Vana-Vändra see Vändra
122 M11 Vanavara Evenkiyskiy Avtonomnyy Okrug, C Russian Federation 60°19′N 102°19′E
15 Q8 Van Bruyssel Québec, SE Canada 47°56′N 72°08′W
27 R10 Van Buren Arkansas, C USA 35°28′N 94°25′W
19 S1 Van Buren Maine, NE USA 47°07′N 67°57′W
27 W7 Van Buren Missouri, C USA 37°00′N 91°00′W
19 T5 Vanceboro Maine, NE USA 45°31′N 67°25′W
21 W10 Vanceboro North Carolina, SE USA 35°16′N 77°06′W
21 O4 Vanceburg Kentucky, S USA 38°36′N 84°40′W
Vanch see Vanj
10 L17 Vancouver British Columbia, SW Canada 49°13′N 123°06′W
32 G11 Vancouver Washington, NW USA 45°38′N 122°39′W
10 L17 Vancouver ✈ British Columbia, SW Canada 49°03′N 123°00′W
10 K16 Vancouver Island island British Columbia, SW Canada
Vanda see Vantaa
171 X13 Van Daalen ≈ Papua, E Indonesia
30 L15 Vandalia Illinois, N USA 38°57′N 89°05′W
27 V3 Vandalia Missouri, C USA 39°18′N 91°29′W
31 R13 Vandalia Ohio, N USA 39°53′N 84°12′W
25 U13 Vanderbilt Texas, SW USA 28°45′N 96°37′W
31 Q10 Vandercook Lake Michigan, N USA 42°11′N 84°23′W
10 L14 Vanderhoof British Columbia, SW Canada 53°54′N 124°00′W
18 K8 Vanderwhacker Mountain ▲ New York, NE USA 43°54′N 74°06′W
181 P1 Van Diemen Gulf gulf Northern Territory, N Australia
Van Diemen's Land see Tasmania
118 H5 Vändra Ger. Fennern; prev. Vana-Vändra. Pärnumaa, SW Estonia 58°39′N 25°00′E
Vandsburg see Więcbork
34 L4 Van Duzen River ≈ California, W USA
118 F13 Vandžiogala Kaunas, C Lithuania 55°07′N 23°55′E
41 N10 Vanegas San Luis Potosí, C Mexico 23°53′N 100°55′W
Vaner, Lake see Vänern
95 K17 Vänern Eng. Lake Vaner; prev. Lake Vener. ◎ S Sweden
95 J18 Vänersborg Västra Götaland, S Sweden 58°16′N 12°22′E
94 F12 Vang Oppland, S Norway 61°07′N 08°34′E
172 I7 Vangaindrano Fianarantsoa, SE Madagascar 23°21′S 47°35′E
137 S14 Van Gölü Eng. Lake Van; anc. Thospitis. salt lake E Turkey
186 L9 Vangunu island New Georgia Islands, NW Solomon Islands
24 J9 Van Horn Texas, SW USA 31°03′N 104°51′W
187 Q11 Vanikolo var. Vanikoro. island Santa Cruz Islands, E Solomon Islands
Vanikoro see Vanikolo
186 A5 Vanimo Sandaun, NW Papua New Guinea 02°40′S 141°17′E
123 T13 Vanino Khabarovskiy Kray, SE Russian Federation 49°10′N 140°18′E
155 G19 Vānīvilāsa Sāgara ⊠ SW India
147 S13 Vanj Rus. Vanch. S Tajikistan 38°22′N 71°27′E
116 G14 Vânju Mare prev. Vînju Mare. Mehedinţi, SW Romania 44°25′N 22°52′E
15 N12 Vankleek Hill Ontario, SE Canada 45°32′N 74°39′W
Van, Lake see Van Gölü
93 I16 Vännäs Västerbotten, N Sweden 63°54′N 19°43′E
93 I15 Vännäsby Västerbotten, N Sweden 63°55′N 19°53′E
102 H7 Vannes anc. Dariorigum. Morbihan, NW France 47°40′N 02°45′W
92 I8 Vannøya island N Norway
103 T12 Vanoise, Massif de la ▲▲ E France
83 E24 Vanrhynsdorp Western Cape, SW South Africa 31°36′S 18°45′E
21 P7 Vansant Virginia, NE USA 37°13′N 82°03′W
94 L13 Vansbro Dalarna, C Sweden 60°32′N 14°15′E
95 D18 Vanse Vest-Agder, S Norway 58°04′N 06°40′E
9 P7 Vansittart Island island Nunavut, NE Canada
93 M20 Vantaa Swe. Vanda. Etelä-Suomi, S Finland 60°18′N 25°01′E
93 L19 Vantaa ✈ (Helsinki) Etelä-Suomi, S Finland 60°18′N 25°01′E
32 J9 Vantage Washington, NW USA 46°55′N 119°55′W
187 Z14 Vanua Balavu prev. Vanua Mbalavu. island Lau Group, E Fiji
187 R12 Vanua Lava island Banks Islands, N Vanuatu
187 Y13 Vanua Levu island N Fiji
Vanua Mbalavu see Vanua Balavu
187 R12 Vanuatu off. Republic of Vanuatu; prev. New Hebrides. ◆ republic SW Pacific Ocean
175 P8 Vanuatu island group SW Pacific Ocean
Vanuatu, Republic of see Vanuatu
31 Q12 Van Wert Ohio, N USA 40°52′N 84°34′W
187 Q17 Vao Province Sud, S New Caledonia 22°40′S 167°29′E
Vapincum see Gap
117 N7 Vapnyarka Vinnyts'ka Oblast', C Ukraine 48°31′N 28°44′E
103 T15 Var ◐ department SE France
103 U14 Var ≈ SE France
95 J18 Vara Västra Götaland, S Sweden 58°16′N 12°57′E
Varadinska Županija see Varaždin
118 J10 Varakļāni Madona, C Latvia 56°36′N 26°40′E
106 C7 Varallo Piemonte, NE Italy 45°51′N 08°16′E
143 O5 Varāmīn var. Veramin. Tehrān, N Iran 35°19′N 51°40′E
153 N14 Vārānasi prev. Banaras, Benares, hist. Kasi. Uttar Pradesh, N India 25°20′N 83°E
125 T3 Varandey Nenetskiy Avtonomnyy Okrug, NW Russian Federation 68°48′N 57°54′E
92 M8 Varangerbotn Finnmark, N Norway 70°09′N 28°28′E
92 M8 Varangerfjorden Lapp. Várjjatvuotna. fjord N Norway
92 M8 Varangerhalvøya Lapp. Várnjárga. peninsula N Norway
Varannó see Vranov nad Topl'ou
107 M15 Varano, Lago di ◎ SE Italy
118 J13 Varapayeva Rus. Voropayevo. Vitsyebskaya Voblasts', NW Belarus 55°09′N 27°13′E
Varasd see Varaždin
112 E7 Varaždin Ger. Warasdin, Hung. Varasd. Varaždin, N Croatia 46°18′N 16°21′E
112 E7 Varaždin off. Varadinska Županija. ◐ province N Croatia
106 C10 Varazze Liguria, NW Italy 44°21′N 08°35′E
95 J20 Varberg Halland, S Sweden 57°06′N 12°15′E
149 P5 Vardak var. Wardak, Pash. Wardag. ◐ province E Afghanistan
113 Q19 Vardar Gk. Axiós. ≈ FYR Macedonia/Greece see also Axiós
Vardar see Axiós
95 F23 Varde Ribe, W Denmark 55°38′N 08°31′E
137 V12 Vardenis E Armenia 40°11′N 45°43′E
92 N8 Vardø Fin. Vuoreija. Finnmark, N Norway 70°22′N 31°06′E
115 E18 Vardoúsia ▲▲ C Greece
Vareia see Logroño
100 G10 Varel Niedersachsen, NW Germany 53°24′N 08°07′E
119 G15 Varėna Pol. Orany. Alytus, S Lithuania 54°13′N 24°35′E
15 O12 Varennes Québec, SE Canada 45°42′N 73°25′W
103 P10 Varennes-sur-Allier Allier, C France 46°17′N 03°24′E
112 I12 Vareš Federacija Bosna I Hercegovina, E Bosnia and Herzegovina 44°12′N 18°19′E
106 D7 Varese Lombardia, N Italy 45°49′N 08°50′E
116 J12 Vârful Moldoveanu var. Moldoveanul; prev. Vîrful Moldoveanu. ▲ C Romania 45°35′N 24°48′E
Varganzi see Warganza
95 J18 Vårgårda Västra Götaland, S Sweden 58°00′N 12°49′E
54 L4 Vargas off. Estado Vargas. ◐ state N Venezuela
95 J18 Vargön Västra Götaland, S Sweden 58°21′N 12°22′E
95 C17 Varhaug Rogaland, S Norway 58°37′N 05°39′E
Várjjatvuotna see Varangerfjorden
93 N17 Varkaus Itä-Suomi, C Finland 62°20′N 27°50′E
92 J2 Varmahlíð Nordhurland Vestra, N Iceland 65°32′N 19°33′W
95 J15 Värmland ◐ county C Sweden
95 K16 Värmlandsnäs peninsula S Sweden
114 N8 Varna prev. Stalin; anc. Odessus. Varna, E Bulgaria 43°14′N 27°56′E
114 N8 Varna ◐ province E Bulgaria
114 N8 Varna ✈ Varna, E Bulgaria 43°16′N 27°52′E
95 L20 Värnamo Jönköping, S Sweden 57°11′N 14°03′E
114 N8 Varnenski Zaliv prev. Stalinski Zaliv. bay E Bulgaria
114 N8 Varnensko Ezero estuary E Bulgaria
118 D11 Varniai Telšiai, W Lithuania 55°45′N 22°22′E
Várnjárga see Varangerhalvøya
Varnoús see Baba
111 D14 Varnsdorf Ger. Warnsdorf. Ústecký Kraj, NW Czech Republic 50°57′N 14°35′E
111 I23 Várpalota Veszprém, W Hungary 47°12′N 18°08′E
Varshava see Warszawa
118 K6 Värska Põlvamaa, SE Estonia 57°58′N 27°37′E
98 N12 Varsseveld Gelderland, E Netherlands 51°55′N 06°28′E
115 D19 Vartholomió prev. Vartholomión. Dytikí Ellás, S Greece 37°52′N 21°12′E
Vartholomión see Vartholomió
137 Q14 Varto Muş, E Turkey 39°10′N 41°28′E
95 K18 Vartofta Västra Götaland, S Sweden 58°06′N 13°40′E
93 O17 Värtsilä Itä-Suomi, E Finland 62°10′N 30°35′E
Värtsilä see Vyartsilya
117 R4 Varva Chernihivs'ka Oblast', NE Ukraine 50°31′N 32°43′E
59 H18 Várzea Grande Mato Grosso, SW Brazil 15°39′S 56°08′W
106 D9 Varzi Lombardia, N Italy 44°51′N 09°13′E
Varzimanor Ayni see Ayní
124 K5 Varzuga ≈ NW Russian Federation
103 P8 Varzy Nièvre, C France 47°22′N 03°22′E
111 G23 Vas off. Vas Megye. ◐ county W Hungary
Vasa see Vaasa
190 A9 Vasafua island Funafuti Atoll, C Tuvalu
111 O21 Vásárosnamény Szabolcs-Szatmár-Bereg, E Hungary 48°10′N 22°18′E
104 H13 Vascão, Ribeira de ≈ S Portugal
116 G10 Vaşcău Hung. Vaskoh. Bihor, NE Romania 46°28′N 22°30′E
Vascongadas, Provincias see País Vasco
Vashess Bay see Vaskess Bay
Vāsht see Khāsh
Vasilevichi see Vasilyevichy
115 G14 Vasilikí Kentrikí Makedonía, NE Greece 40°28′N 23°08′E
115 C18 Vasilikí Lefkáda, Iónia Nisiá, Greece, C Mediterranean Sea 38°36′N 20°37′E
115 K25 Vasilikí Kríti, Greece, E Mediterranean Sea 35°04′N 25°49′E
119 G16 Vasilishki Pol. Wasiliszki. Hrodzyenskaya Voblasts', W Belarus 53°47′N 24°51′E
Vasil Kolarov see Pamporovo
Vasil'kov see Vasyl'kiv
119 N19 Vasilyevichy Rus. Vasilevichi. Homyel'skaya Voblasts', SE Belarus 52°15′N 29°50′E
191 Y3 Vaskess Bay var. Vashess Bay. bay Kiritimati, E Kiribati
Vaskoh see Vaşcău
Vaskohsziklás see Ştei
116 M10 Vaslui Vaslui, C Romania 46°38′N 27°44′E
116 L11 Vaslui ◐ county NE Romania
Vas Megye see Vas
31 R8 Vassar Michigan, N USA 43°22′N 83°34′W
95 E15 Vassdalsegga ▲ S Norway 59°47′N 07°07′E
60 P9 Vassouras Rio de Janeiro, SE Brazil 22°24′S 43°38′W
95 N15 Västerås Västmanland, C Sweden 59°37′N 16°33′E
93 G15 Västerbotten ◐ county N Sweden
94 K12 Västerdalälven ≈ C Sweden
95 O16 Västerhaninge Stockholm, C Sweden 59°07′N 18°06′E
94 M10 Västernorrland ◐ county C Sweden
95 N19 Västervik Kalmar, S Sweden 57°44′N 16°40′E
95 M15 Västmanland ◐ county C Sweden
107 L15 Vasto anc. Histonium. Abruzzo, C Italy 42°07′N 14°43′E
95 J19 Västra Götaland ◐ county S Sweden
95 J16 Västra Silen ◎ S Sweden
111 G23 Vasvár Ger. Eisenburg. Vas, W Hungary 47°03′N 16°48′E
117 U9 Vasylivka Zaporiz'ka Oblast', SE Ukraine 47°26′N 35°18′E
117 O5 Vasyl'kiv var. Vasil'kov. Kyyivs'ka Oblast', N Ukraine 50°12′N 30°18′E
122 I11 Vasyugan ≈ C Russian Federation
103 N8 Vatan Indre, C France 47°06′N 01°49′E
Vaté see Efate
115 C18 Vathy prev. Itháki. Itháki, Iónia Nisiá, Greece, C Mediterranean Sea 38°22′N 20°43′E
107 G15 Vatican City off. Vatican City. ◆ papal state S Europe
Vatican City see Vatican City
107 M22 Vaticano, Capo headland S Italy 38°37′N 15°49′E
92 K3 Vatnajökull glacier SE Iceland
95 P15 Vätö Stockholm, C Sweden 59°48′N 18°55′E
187 Z16 Vatoa island Lau Group, SE Fiji
172 J5 Vatomandry Toamasina, E Madagascar 19°20′S 48°58′E
116 J9 Vatra Dornei Ger. Dorna Watra. Suceava, NE Romania 47°20′N 25°21′E
116 J9 Vatra Moldoviţei Suceava, NE Romania 47°37′N 25°36′E
Vatter, Lake see Vättern
95 L18 Vättern Eng. Lake Vatter; prev. Lake Vetter. ◎ S Sweden
187 X15 Vatulele island SW Fiji
117 P7 Vatutine Cherkas'ka Oblast', C Ukraine 49°01′N 31°04′E
187 W15 Vatu Vara island Lau Group, E Fiji
103 R14 Vaucluse ◐ department SE France
103 S5 Vaucouleurs Meuse, NE France 48°37′N 05°38′E
108 B9 Vaud Ger. Waadt. ◐ canton SW Switzerland
15 N12 Vaudreuil Québec, SE Canada 45°24′N 74°01′W
37 T12 Vaughn New Mexico, SW USA 34°36′N 105°12′W
54 I14 Vaupés off. Comisaría del Vaupés. ◐ province SE Colombia
Vaupés, Comisaría del see Vaupés
54 J13 Vaupés, Río var. Rio Uaupés. ≈ Brazil/Colombia see also Uaupés, Rio
Vaupés, Río see Uaupés, Rio
103 Q15 Vauvert Gard, S France 43°42′N 04°16′E
11 R17 Vauxhall Alberta, SW Canada 50°05′N 112°09′W
99 K23 Vaux-sur-Sûre Luxembourg, SE Belgium 49°55′N 05°34′E
172 J4 Vavatenina Toamasina, E Madagascar 17°25′S 49°11′E
193 Y14 Vava'u Group island group N Tonga
76 M16 Vavoua W Ivory Coast 07°23′N 06°29′W
127 S2 Vavozh Udmurtskaya Respublika, NW Russian Federation 56°48′N 51°53′E
155 K23 Vavuniya Northern Province, N Sri Lanka 08°45′N 80°30′E
119 G17 Vawkavysk Pol. Wołkowysk, Rus. Volkovysk. Hrodzyenskaya Voblasts', W Belarus 53°10′N 24°28′E
119 F17 Vawkavyskaye Wzvyshsha Rus. Volkovyskiye Vysoty. hill range W Belarus
95 P15 Vaxholm Stockholm, C Sweden 59°25′N 18°21′E
95 L21 Växjö var. Vexiö. Kronoberg, S Sweden 56°52′N 14°50′E
125 T1 Vaygach, Ostrov island NW Russian Federation
137 V13 Vayk' prev. Azizbekov. SE Armenia 39°41′N 45°28′E
Vazáš see Vittangi
125 P8 Vazhgort prev. Chasovo. Respublika Komi, NW Russian Federation 64°06′N 46°44′E
45 V10 V. C. Bird ✈ (St. John's) Antigua, Antigua and Barbuda 17°07′N 61°49′W
95 C16 Veavågen Rogaland, S Norway 59°18′N 05°13′E
29 Q7 Veblen South Dakota, N USA 45°50′N 97°17′W
98 N9 Vecht Ger. Vechte. ≈ Germany/Netherlands see also Vechte
Vecht see Vechte
100 G12 Vechta Niedersachsen, NW Germany 52°44′N 08°16′E
100 E12 Vechte Dut. Vecht. ≈ Germany/Netherlands see also Vecht
Vechte see Vecht
118 I8 Vecpiebalga Cēsis, C Latvia 57°03′N 25°47′E
118 G9 Vecumnieki Bauska, C Latvia 56°36′N 24°30′E
Vedāvati see Hagari
95 J20 Veddige Halland, S Sweden 57°16′N 12°19′E
116 J15 Vedea ≈ S Romania
127 P16 Vedeno Chechenskaya Respublika, SW Russian Federation 42°57′N 46°02′E
95 C16 Vedvågen Rogaland, S Norway 59°18′N 05°13′E
98 O6 Veendam Groningen, NE Netherlands 53°05′N 06°53′E
98 K12 Veenendaal Utrecht, C Netherlands 52°03′N 05°33′E
99 E14 Veere Zeeland, SW Netherlands 51°33′N 03°40′E
24 M2 Vega Texas, SW USA 35°14′N 102°26′W
92 E13 Vega island C Norway
45 T5 Vega Baja C Puerto Rico 18°27′N 66°23′W
38 D17 Vega Point headland Kiska Island, Alaska, USA 51°49′N 177°19′E
95 F17 Vegår ◎ S Norway
99 K14 Veghel Noord-Brabant, S Netherlands 51°37′N 05°33′E
Veglia see Krk
114 E13 Vegorítida, Límni var. Límni Vegorítis. ◎ N Greece
Vegorítis, Límni see Vegorítida, Límni
11 Q14 Vegreville Alberta, SW Canada 53°30′N 112°02′W
95 K21 Veinge Halland, S Sweden 56°33′N 13°04′E
61 B21 Veinticinco de Mayo var. 25 de Mayo. Buenos Aires, E Argentina 35°27′S 60°11′W
63 I14 Veinticinco de Mayo La Pampa, C Argentina 37°45′S 67°40′W
119 F15 Veisiejai Alytus, S Lithuania 54°06′N 23°42′E
95 F23 Vejen Ribe, W Denmark 55°29′N 09°13′E
104 K16 Vejer de la Frontera Andalucía, S Spain 36°15′N 05°58′W
95 G23 Vejle Vejle, C Denmark 55°43′N 09°33′E
95 F23 Vejle off. Vejle Amt. ◐ county C Denmark
Vejle Amt see Vejle
114 M7 Vekilski Shumen, NE Bulgaria 43°33′N 27°19′E
54 G3 Vela, Cabo de la headland NE Colombia 12°14′N 72°13′W
Vela Goa see Goa
113 F15 Vela Luka Dubrovnik-Neretva, S Croatia 42°57′N 16°43′E
61 G19 Velázquez Rocha, E Uruguay 34°05′S 54°16′W
101 E15 Velbert Nordrhein-Westfalen, W Germany 51°22′N 07°03′E
109 S9 Velden Kärnten, S Austria 46°37′N 13°59′E
Veldes see Bled
99 K15 Veldhoven Noord-Brabant, S Netherlands 51°24′N 05°24′E
112 C11 Velebit ▲▲ C Croatia
114 N11 Veleka ≈ SE Bulgaria
109 V10 Velenje Ger. Wöllan. N Slovenia 46°22′N 15°07′E
190 E12 Vele, Pointe headland Île Futuna, S Wallis and Futuna
113 O18 Veles Turk. Köprülü. C FYR Macedonia 41°43′N 21°49′E
113 M20 Veleshta SW FYR Macedonia 41°16′N 20°37′E
115 F16 Velestíno prev. Velestínon. Thessalía, C Greece 39°23′N 22°45′E
Velestínon see Velestíno
Velevshchina see Vyelyewshchyna
54 F9 Vélez Santander, C Colombia 06°02′N 73°43′W
105 Q13 Vélez Blanco Andalucía, S Spain 37°43′N 02°07′W
104 M17 Vélez de la Gomera, Peñon de island group S Spain
105 N15 Vélez-Málaga Andalucía, S Spain 36°47′N 04°06′W
105 Q13 Vélez Rubio Andalucía, S Spain 37°39′N 02°04′W
Velha Goa see Goa
Velho see Porto Velho
112 E8 Velika Gorica Zagreb, N Croatia 45°43′N 16°03′E
112 C9 Velika Kapela ▲▲ NW Croatia
Velika Kikinda see Kikinda
112 D10 Velika Kladuša Federacija Bosna I Hercegovina, NW Bosnia and Herzegovina 45°10′N 15°48′E
112 N11 Velika Morava var. Glavn'a Morava, Morava, Ger. Grosse Morava. ≈ C Serbia
112 N12 Velika Plana Serbia, C Serbia 44°20′N 21°01′E
109 U10 Velika Raduha ▲ N Slovenia 46°24′N 14°46′E
123 V7 Velikaya ≈ NE Russian Federation
124 F15 Velikaya ≈ W Russian Federation
Velikaya Berestovitsa see Vyalikaya Byerastavitsa
Velikaya Lepetikha see Velyka Lepetykha
Veliki Bečkerek see Zrenjanin
112 P12 Veliki Krš var. Stol. ▲ E Serbia 44°10′N 22°09′E
114 L8 Veliki Preslav prev. Preslav. Shumen, NE Bulgaria 43°09′N 26°50′E
112 B9 Veliki Risnjak ▲ NW Croatia 45°30′N 14°31′E
109 T13 Veliki Snežnik Ger. Schneeberg, It. Monte Nevoso. ▲ SW Slovenia 45°36′N 14°25′E
112 J13 Veliki Stolac ▲ E Bosnia and Herzegovina 43°55′N 19°15′E
Velikiy Bor see Vyaliki Bor
124 G16 Velikiye Luki Pskovskaya Oblast', W Russian Federation 56°20′N 30°27′E
124 H14 Velikiy Novgorod prev. Novgorod. Novgorodskaya Oblast', W Russian Federation 58°32′N 31°15′E
125 P12 Velikiy Ustyug Vologodskaya Oblast', NW Russian Federation 60°46′N 46°18′E
112 N11 Veliko Gradište Serbia, NE Serbia 44°46′N 21°28′E
155 I18 Velikonda Range ▲ SE India

◆ Country ● Country Capital ◇ Dependent Territory ○ Dependent Territory Capital ◐ Administrative Regions ✈ International Airport ▲ Mountain ▲▲ Mountain Range Volcano ≈ River ◎ Lake ⊠ Reservoir
339

VELIKO TŬRNOVO – VILA MARECHAL CARMONA

114 K9 **Veliko Tŭrnovo** *prev.* Tirnovo, Trnovo, Tŭrnovo. Veliko Tŭrnovo, N Bulgaria *43°05′N 25°40′E*
114 K8 **Veliko Tŭrnovo** ⬖ *province* N Bulgaria
Velikovec *see* Völkermarkt
125 R5 **Velikovisochnoye** Nenetskiy Avtonomnyy Okrug, NW Russian Federation *67°13′N 52°00′E*
76 H12 **Vélingara** C Senegal *15°00′N 14°39′W*
76 H11 **Vélingara** S Senegal *13°12′N 14°05′W*
114 H11 **Velingrad** Pazardzhik, C Bulgaria *42°01′N 24°00′E*
126 H3 **Velizh** Smolenskaya Oblast', W Russian Federation *55°30′N 31°06′E*
111 F16 **Velká Deštná** *var.* Deštná, Grosskoppe, *Ger.* Deschnaer Koppe. ▲ NE Czech Republic *50°18′N 16°25′E*
111 F18 **Velké Meziříčí** *Ger.* Grossmeseritsch. Vysočina, C Czech Republic *49°22′N 16°02′E*
92 N1 **Velkomstpynten** *headland* NW Svalbard *79°51′N 11°37′E*
111 K21 **Vel'ký Krtíš** Banskobystrický Kraj, C Slovakia *48°13′N 19°21′E*
186 J8 **Vella Lavella** *var.* Mbilua. *island* New Georgia Islands, NW Solomon Islands
107 I15 **Velletri** Lazio, C Italy *41°41′N 12°47′E*
95 K23 **Vellinge** Skåne, S Sweden *55°29′N 13°00′E*
155 I19 **Vellore** Tamil Nādu, SE India *12°56′N 79°09′E*
Velobriga *see* Viana do Castelo
115 G21 **Velopoúla** *island* S Greece
98 M12 **Velp** Gelderland, SE Netherlands *52°00′N 05°59′E*
Velsen *see* Velsen-Noord
98 H9 **Velsen-Noord** *var.* Velsen. Noord-Holland, W Netherlands *52°27′N 04°40′E*
125 N12 **Vel'sk** *var.* Velsk. Arkhangel'skaya Oblast', NW Russian Federation *61°03′N 42°01′E*
Velsuna *see* Orvieto
98 K10 **Veluwemeer** *lake channel* C Netherlands
28 M3 **Velva** North Dakota, N USA *48°03′N 100°55′W*
Velvendos/Velvendós *see* Velventós
115 E14 **Velventós** *var.* Velvendos, Velvendós. Dytikí Makedonía, N Greece *40°15′N 22°04′E*
117 S5 **Velyka Bahachka** Poltavs'ka Oblast', C Ukraine *49°46′N 33°44′E*
117 S9 **Velyka Lepetykha** *Rus.* Velikaya Lepetikha. Khersons'ka Oblast', S Ukraine *47°09′N 33°59′E*
117 O10 **Velyka Mykhaylivka** Odes'ka Oblast', SW Ukraine *47°07′N 29°49′E*
117 W8 **Velyka Novosilka** Donets'ka Oblast', E Ukraine *47°49′N 36°49′E*
117 S9 **Velyka Oleksandrivka** Khersons'ka Oblast', S Ukraine *47°17′N 33°16′E*
117 T4 **Velyka Pysarivka** Sums'ka Oblast', NE Ukraine *50°25′N 35°28′E*
116 G6 **Velykyy Bereznyy** Zakarpats'ka Oblast', W Ukraine *48°54′N 22°27′E*
117 W4 **Velykyy Burluk** Kharkivs'ka Oblast', E Ukraine *50°04′N 37°25′E*
Velykyy Tokmak *see* Tokmak
173 P7 **Vema Fracture Zone** *tectonic feature* W Indian Ocean
65 P18 **Vema Seamount** *undersea feature* SW Indian Ocean *31°38′S 08°19′E*
93 F17 **Vemdalen** Jämtland, C Sweden *62°26′N 13°50′E*
95 N19 **Vena** Kalmar, S Sweden *57°31′N 16°00′E*
41 N11 **Venado** San Luis Potosí, C Mexico *22°56′N 101°05′W*
62 L11 **Venado Tuerto** Entre Ríos, E Argentina *33°45′S 61°56′W*
61 A19 **Venado Tuerto** Santa Fe, C Argentina *33°46′S 61°57′W*
107 K16 **Venafro** Molise, C Italy *41°28′N 14°03′E*
55 Q9 **Venamo, Cerro** ▲ E Venezuela *05°56′N 61°25′W*
106 B8 **Venaria** Piemonte, NW Italy *45°09′N 07°40′E*
103 U15 **Vence** Alpes-Maritimes, SE France *43°45′N 07°07′E*
104 H5 **Venda Nova** Vila Real, N Portugal *41°40′N 07°58′W*
104 G11 **Vendas Novas** Évora, S Portugal *38°41′N 08°27′W*
102 J9 **Vendée** ⬖ *department* NW France
103 Q6 **Vendeuvre-sur-Barse** Aube, NE France *48°08′N 04°17′E*
102 M7 **Vendôme** Loir-et-Cher, C France *47°48′N 01°04′E*
Venedig *see* Venezia
Vener, Lake *see* Vänern
106 I8 **Veneta, Laguna** *lagoon* NE Italy
Venetia *see* Venezia
39 S7 **Venetie** Alaska, USA *67°00′N 146°25′W*
106 H8 **Veneto** *var.* Venezia Euganea. ⬖ *region* NE Italy
114 M7 **Venets** Shumen, NE Bulgaria *43°33′N 26°56′E*
126 L5 **Venev** Tul'skaya Oblast', W Russian Federation *54°18′N 38°16′E*
106 I8 **Venezia** *Eng.* Venice, *Fr.* Venise, *Ger.* Venedig; *anc.* Venetia. Veneto, NE Italy *45°26′N 12°20′E*
Venezia Euganea *see* Veneto
Venezia, Golfo di *see* Venice, Gulf of
Venezia Tridentina *see* Trentino-Alto Adige
54 K8 **Venezuela** *off.* Republic of Venezuela; *prev.* Estados Unidos de Venezuela, United States of Venezuela. ◆ *republic* N South America
Venezuela, Cordillera de *see* Costa, Cordillera de la
Venezuela, Estados Unidos de *see* Venezuela
54 I4 **Venezuela, Golfo de** *Eng.* Gulf of Maracaibo, Gulf of Venezuela. *gulf* NW Venezuela
Venezuela, Gulf of *see* Venezuela, Golfo de
64 F11 **Venezuelan Basin** *undersea feature* E Caribbean Sea
Venezuela, Republic of *see* Venezuela
Venezuela, United States of *see* Venezuela
155 D16 **Vengurla** Mahārāshtra, W India *15°55′N 73°39′E*
39 O15 **Veniaminof, Mount** ▲ Alaska, USA *56°12′N 159°24′W*
23 V14 **Venice** Florida, SE USA *27°06′N 82°27′W*
22 L10 **Venice** Louisiana, S USA *29°15′N 89°20′W*
Venice *see* Venezia
106 J8 **Venice, Gulf of** *It.* Golfo di Venezia, *Slvn.* Beneški Zaliv. *gulf* N Adriatic Sea
Venise *see* Venezia
94 K13 **Venjan** Dalarna, C Sweden *60°58′N 13°55′E*
94 K13 **Venjansjön** ◎ C Sweden
155 J18 **Venkatagiri** Andhra Pradesh, E India *14°00′N 79°39′E*
99 M15 **Venlo** *prev.* Venloo. Limburg, SE Netherlands *51°22′N 06°11′E*
Venloo *see* Venlo
95 E18 **Vennesla** Vest-Agder, S Norway *58°15′N 08°00′E*
107 M17 **Venosa** *anc.* Venusia. Basilicata, S Italy *40°57′N 15°49′E*
Venoste, Alpi *see* Ötztaler Alpen
Venraij *see* Venray
99 M14 **Venray** *var.* Venraij. Limburg, SE Netherlands *51°32′N 05°59′E*
118 C8 **Venta** *Ger.* Windau. 〰 Latvia/Lithuania
Venta Belgarum *see* Winchester
40 G9 **Ventana, Punta Arena de la** *var.* Punta de la Ventana. *headland* NW Mexico *24°03′N 109°49′W*
Ventana, Punta de la *see* Ventana, Punta Arena de la
61 B23 **Ventana, Sierra de la** *hill range* E Argentina
Ventia *see* Valence
191 S11 **Vent, Îles du** *var.* Windward Islands. *island group* Archipel de la Société, W French Polynesia
191 R10 **Vent, Îles Sous le** *var.* Leeward Islands. *island group* Archipel de la Société, W French Polynesia
106 B11 **Ventimiglia** Liguria, NW Italy *43°47′N 07°37′E*
97 M24 **Ventnor** S England, United Kingdom *50°36′N 01°11′W*
18 J17 **Ventnor City** New Jersey, NE USA *39°19′N 74°27′W*
103 S14 **Ventoux, Mont** ▲ SE France *44°12′N 05°21′E*
118 C8 **Ventspils** *Ger.* Windau. Ventspils, NW Latvia *57°22′N 21°34′E*
54 M10 **Ventuari, Río** 〰 S Venezuela
35 R15 **Ventura** California, W USA *34°15′N 119°18′W*
182 F8 **Venus Bay** South Australia *33°15′S 134°42′E*
Venusia *see* Venosa
191 P7 **Vénus, Pointe** *var.* Pointe Tataaihoa. *headland* Tahiti, W French Polynesia *17°28′S 149°29′W*
41 V16 **Venustiano Carranza** Chiapas, SE Mexico *16°21′N 92°33′W*
41 N7 **Venustiano Carranza, Presa** ▣ NE Mexico
61 B15 **Vera** Santa Fe, C Argentina *29°28′S 60°10′W*
105 Q14 **Vera** Andalucía, S Spain *37°15′N 01°51′W*
63 K18 **Vera, Bahía** *bay* E Argentina
41 R14 **Veracruz** *var.* Veracruz Llave. Veracruz-Llave, E Mexico *19°10′N 96°09′W*
Veracruz *see* Veracruz-Llave
41 Q13 **Veracruz-Llave** *var.* Veracruz. ⬖ *state* E Mexico
Veracruz Llave *see* Veracruz
43 Q16 **Veraguas** *off.* Provincia de Veraguas. ⬖ *province* W Panama
Veraguas, Provincia de *see* Veraguas
Veramin *see* Varāmīn
154 B12 **Verāval** Gujarāt, W India *20°54′N 70°22′E*
106 C6 **Verbania** Piemonte, NW Italy *45°56′N 08°34′E*
107 N20 **Verbicaro** Calabria, SW Italy *39°44′N 15°51′E*
108 D11 **Verbier** Valais, SW Switzerland *46°06′N 07°14′E*
Vercellae *see* Vercelli
106 C8 **Vercelli** *anc.* Vercellae. Piemonte, NW Italy *45°19′N 08°25′E*
103 S13 **Vercors** *physical region* E France
Verdal *see* Verdalsøra
93 E16 **Verdalsøra** *var.* Verdal. Nord-Trøndelag, C Norway *63°47′N 11°27′E*
Verde, Cabo *see* Cape Verde
44 J5 **Verde, Cape** *headland* Long Island, C Bahamas *22°51′N 75°50′W*
104 M2 **Verde, Costa** *coastal region* N Spain
Verde Grande, Río/Verde Grande y de Belem, Río *see* Verde, Río
100 H11 **Verden** Niedersachsen, NW Germany *52°55′N 09°14′E*
57 P16 **Verde, Río** 〰 Bolivia/Brazil
59 J19 **Verde, Rio** 〰 SE Brazil
40 M12 **Verde, Río** *var.* Río Verde Grande, Río Verde Grande y de Belem. 〰 C Mexico
41 Q16 **Verde, Río** 〰 SE Mexico
36 L13 **Verde River** 〰 Arizona, SW USA
Verdhikoúsa/Verdhikoússa *see* Verdikoússa
27 Q8 **Verdigris River** 〰 Kansas/Oklahoma, C USA
115 E15 **Verdikoússa** *var.* Verdhikoúsa, Verdhikoússa. Thessalía, C Greece *39°47′N 21°59′E*
103 S15 **Verdon** 〰 SE France
15 O12 **Verdun** Québec, SE Canada *45°27′N 73°36′W*
103 S4 **Verdun** *var.* Verdun-sur-Meuse; *anc.* Verodunum. Meuse, NE France *49°09′N 05°25′E*
Verdun-sur-Meuse *see* Verdun
83 J21 **Vereeniging** Gauteng, NE South Africa *26°41′S 27°56′E*
Veremeyki *see* Vyeramyeyki
125 T14 **Vereshchagino** Permskaya Oblast', NW Russian Federation *58°06′N 54°38′E*
76 G14 **Verga, Cap** *headland* W Guinea *10°12′N 14°27′W*
61 G18 **Vergara** Treinta y Tres, E Uruguay *32°58′S 53°54′W*
108 G11 **Vergeletto** Ticino, S Switzerland *46°13′N 08°34′E*
18 L8 **Vergennes** Vermont, NE USA *44°09′N 73°13′W*
Veria *see* Véroia
104 I5 **Verín** Galicia, NW Spain *41°55′N 07°26′W*
Verin T'alin *see* T'alin
118 K6 **Veriora** Põlvamaa, SE Estonia *57°57′N 27°23′E*
117 T7 **Verkhivtseve** Dnipropetrovs'ka Oblast', E Ukraine *48°27′N 34°15′E*
Verkhnedvinsk *see* Vyerkhnyadzvinsk
122 K10 **Verkhneimbatsk** Krasnoyarskiy Kray, N Russian Federation *63°06′N 88°03′E*
124 I3 **Verkhnetulomskiy** Murmanskaya Oblast', NW Russian Federation *68°37′N 31°46′E*
124 I3 **Verkhnetulomskoye Vodokhranilishche** ▣ NW Russian Federation
Verkhneudinsk *see* Ulan-Ude
123 P10 **Verkhnevilyuysk** Respublika Sakha (Yakutiya), NE Russian Federation *63°44′N 119°59′E*
127 W5 **Verkhniy Avzyan** Respublika Bashkortostan, W Russian Federation *53°31′N 57°26′E*
127 Q11 **Verkhniy Baskunchak** Astrakhanskaya Oblast', SW Russian Federation *48°14′N 46°43′E*
127 W3 **Verkhniye Kigi** Respublika Bashkortostan, W Russian Federation *55°25′N 58°40′E*
117 T9 **Verkhniy Rohachyk** Khersons'ka Oblast', S Ukraine *47°16′N 34°16′E*
123 Q11 **Verkhnyaya Amga** Respublika Sakha (Yakutiya), NE Russian Federation *59°34′N 127°07′E*
125 V6 **Verkhnyaya Inta** Respublika Komi, NW Russian Federation *65°55′N 60°07′E*
125 O10 **Verkhnyaya Toyma** Arkhangel'skaya Oblast', NW Russian Federation *62°12′N 44°57′E*
126 K6 **Verkhov'ye** Orlovskaya Oblast', W Russian Federation *52°49′N 37°20′E*
116 I8 **Verkhovyna** Ivano-Frankivs'ka Oblast', W Ukraine *48°09′N 24°48′E*
123 P8 **Verkhoyanskiy Khrebet** ▲▲ NE Russian Federation
117 T7 **Verkn'odniprovs'k** Dnipropetrovs'ka Oblast', E Ukraine *48°40′N 34°17′E*
101 G14 **Verl** Nordrhein-Westfalen, NW Germany *51°52′N 08°30′E*
92 N1 **Verlegenhuken** *headland* N Svalbard *80°03′N 16°15′E*
82 A9 **Vermelha, Ponta** *headland* NW Angola *05°40′S 12°09′E*
103 P7 **Vermenton** Yonne, C France *47°40′N 03°43′E*
11 R14 **Vermilion** Alberta, SW Canada *53°21′N 110°52′W*
31 T11 **Vermilion** Ohio, N USA *41°25′N 82°21′W*
22 I10 **Vermilion Bay** *bay* Louisiana, S USA
29 V4 **Vermilion Lake** ◎ Minnesota, N USA
14 F9 **Vermilion River** 〰 Ontario, S Canada
30 L12 **Vermilion River** 〰 Illinois, N USA
29 R12 **Vermillion** South Dakota, N USA *42°46′N 96°55′W*
29 R12 **Vermillion River** 〰 South Dakota, N USA
15 O9 **Vermillon, Rivière** 〰 Québec, SE Canada
115 E14 **Vérmio** ▲▲ N Greece
18 L8 **Vermont** *off.* State of Vermont, *also known as* Green Mountain State. ⬖ *state* NE USA
113 K16 **Vermosh** *var.* Vermoshi. Shkodër, N Albania *42°37′N 19°42′E*
Vermoshi *see* Vermosh
37 O3 **Vernal** Utah, W USA *40°27′N 109°31′W*
14 G11 **Verner** Ontario, S Canada *46°24′N 80°04′W*
102 M5 **Verneuil-sur-Avre** Eure, N France *48°44′N 00°55′E*
114 D13 **Vérno** ▲▲ N Greece
11 N17 **Vernon** British Columbia, SW Canada *50°17′N 119°19′W*
102 M4 **Vernon** Eure, N France *49°04′N 01°28′E*
23 N3 **Vernon** Alabama, S USA *33°45′N 88°06′W*
31 P15 **Vernon** Indiana, N USA *38°59′N 85°39′W*
25 Q4 **Vernon** Texas, SW USA *34°11′N 99°17′W*
32 G10 **Vernonia** Oregon, NW USA *45°51′N 123°11′W*
14 G12 **Vernon, Lake** ◎ Ontario, S Canada
22 G7 **Vernon Lake** ▣ Louisiana, S USA
23 Y13 **Vero Beach** Florida, SE USA *27°38′N 80°24′W*
Verőcze *see* Virovitica
Verodunum *see* Verdun
115 E14 **Véroia** *var.* Veria, Vérroia, *Turk.* Karaferiye. Kentrikí Makedonía, N Greece *40°32′N 22°11′E*
106 E8 **Verolanuova** Lombardia, N Italy *45°20′N 10°06′E*
14 K14 **Verona** Ontario, SE Canada *44°30′N 76°42′W*
106 G8 **Verona** Veneto, NE Italy *45°27′N 11°E*
29 P6 **Verona** North Dakota, N USA *46°19′N 98°03′W*
30 L9 **Verona** Wisconsin, N USA *42°59′N 89°33′W*
61 E20 **Verónica** Buenos Aires, E Argentina *35°25′S 57°16′W*
22 J9 **Verret, Lake** ◎ Louisiana, S USA
Vérroia *see* Véroia
103 N5 **Versailles** Yvelines, N France *48°48′N 02°08′E*
31 P15 **Versailles** Indiana, N USA *39°04′N 85°16′W*
20 M5 **Versailles** Kentucky, S USA *38°02′N 84°45′W*
27 U5 **Versailles** Missouri, C USA *38°25′N 92°51′W*
31 Q13 **Versailles** Ohio, N USA *40°13′N 84°28′W*
Versecz *see* Vršac
108 A10 **Versoix** Genève, SW Switzerland *46°17′N 06°10′E*
15 Z6 **Verte, Pointe** *headland* Québec, SE Canada *48°36′N 64°10′W*
111 I22 **Vértes** ▲▲ NW Hungary
44 G6 **Vertientes** Camagüey, C Cuba *21°18′N 78°11′W*
114 G13 **Vertískos** ▲▲ N Greece
102 I8 **Vertou** Loire-Atlantique, NW France *47°10′N 01°28′W*
Verulamium *see* St Albans
99 L19 **Verviers** Liège, E Belgium *50°36′N 05°52′E*
103 Y14 **Vescovato** Corse, France, C Mediterranean Sea *42°30′N 09°27′E*
99 L20 **Vesdre** 〰 E Belgium
117 U10 **Vesele** *Rus.* Veseloye. Zaporiz'ka Oblast', S Ukraine *47°00′N 34°52′E*
111 D18 **Veselí nad Lužnicí** *var.* Weseli an der Lainsitz, *Ger.* Frohenbruck. Jihočeský Kraj, S Czech Republic *49°11′N 14°40′E*
114 M9 **Veselinovo** Shumen, NE Bulgaria *43°01′N 27°02′E*
126 L12 **Veselovskoye Vodokhranilishche** ▣ SW Russian Federation
Veseloye *see* Vesele
117 Q9 **Veselynove** Mykolayivs'ka Oblast', S Ukraine *47°21′N 31°15′E*
Veseya *see* Vyasyeya
126 M10 **Veshenskaya** Rostovskaya Oblast', SW Russian Federation *49°37′N 41°43′E*
127 Q5 **Veshkayma** Ul'yanovskaya Oblast', W Russian Federation *54°04′N 47°06′E*
Vesisaari *see* Vadsø
Vesontio *see* Besançon
103 T7 **Vesoul** *anc.* Vesulium, Vesulum. Haute-Saône, E France *47°37′N 06°09′E*
95 J20 **Vessigebro** Halland, S Sweden *56°58′N 12°40′E*
95 D17 **Vest-Agder** ⬖ *county* S Norway
23 P4 **Vestavia Hills** Alabama, S USA *33°27′N 86°47′W*
84 F6 **Vesterålen** *island* NW Norway
92 G10 **Vesterålen** *island group* N Norway
87 V3 **Vestervig** Viborg, NW Denmark *56°46′N 08°20′E*
92 H2 **Vestfirdhir** ⬖ *region* NW Iceland
92 G11 **Vestfjorden** *fjord* C Norway
95 G16 **Vestfold** ⬖ *county* S Norway
Vestmanhavn *see* Vestmanna
95 B18 **Vestmanna** *Dan.* Vestmanhavn. Streymoy, N Faeroe Islands *62°09′N 07°11′W*
92 I4 **Vestmannaeyjar** Sudhurland, S Iceland *63°26′N 20°14′W*
94 E9 **Vestnes** Møre og Romsdal, S Norway *62°39′N 07°00′E*
95 I23 **Vestsjælland** *off.* Vestsjællands Amt. ⬖ *county* E Denmark
Vestsjællands Amt *see* Vestsjælland
92 H3 **Vesturland** ⬖ *region* W Iceland
92 G11 **Vestvågøya** *island* C Norway
Vesulium/Vesulum *see* Vesoul
Vesuna *see* Périgueux
107 K17 **Vesuvio** *Eng.* Vesuvius. ⛰ S Italy *40°48′N 14°29′E*
Vesuvius *see* Vesuvio
124 K14 **Ves'yegonsk** Tverskaya Oblast', W Russian Federation *58°40′N 37°13′E*
111 I23 **Veszprém** *Ger.* Veszprim. Veszprém, W Hungary *47°06′N 17°54′E*
111 H23 **Veszprém** *off.* Veszprém Megye. ⬖ *county* W Hungary
Veszprém Megye *see* Veszprém
Veszprim *see* Veszprém
Vetka *see* Vyetka
95 M19 **Vetlanda** Jönköping, S Sweden *57°26′N 15°05′E*
127 P1 **Vetluga** Nizhegorodskaya Oblast', W Russian Federation *57°51′N 45°45′E*
125 P14 **Vetluga** 〰 NW Russian Federation
125 O14 **Vetluzhskiy** Kostromskaya Oblast', NW Russian Federation *58°21′N 45°25′E*
127 P2 **Vetluzhskiy** Nizhegorodskaya Oblast', W Russian Federation *57°10′N 45°07′E*
114 K7 **Vetovo** Ruse, N Bulgaria *43°42′N 26°16′E*
107 H14 **Vetralla** Lazio, C Italy *42°18′N 12°03′E*
Vetrino *see* Vyetryna
122 L7 **Vetrovaya, Gora** ▲ N Russian Federation *73°54′N 95°00′E*
Vetter, Lake *see* Vättern
106 J13 **Vettore, Monte** ▲ C Italy *42°49′N 13°15′E*
99 A17 **Veurne** *var.* Furnes. West-Vlaanderen, W Belgium *51°04′N 02°40′E*
31 Q15 **Vevay** Indiana, N USA *38°45′N 85°08′W*
108 C10 **Vevey** *Ger.* Vivis; *anc.* Vibiscum. Vaud, SW Switzerland *46°28′N 06°51′E*
Vexiö *see* Växjö
103 S13 **Veynes** Hautes-Alpes, SE France *44°33′N 05°51′E*
103 N11 **Vézère** 〰 W France
114 I9 **Vezhen** ▲ C Bulgaria *42°45′N 24°22′E*
136 K11 **Vezirköprü** Samsun, N Turkey *41°09′N 35°27′E*
57 J18 **Viacha** La Paz, W Bolivia *16°40′S 68°17′W*
27 R10 **Vian** Oklahoma, C USA *35°30′N 94°56′W*
Viana de Castelo *see* Viana do Castelo
104 H12 **Viana do Alentejo** Évora, S Portugal *38°20′N 08°00′W*
104 I4 **Viana do Bolo** Galicia, NW Spain *42°10′N 07°06′W*
104 G5 **Viana do Castelo** *var.* Viana de Castelo; *anc.* Velobriga. Viana do Castelo, NW Portugal *41°41′N 08°50′W*
104 G5 **Viana do Castelo** *var.* Viana de Castelo. ⬖ *district* N Portugal
98 J12 **Vianen** Utrecht, C Netherlands *52°N 05°06′E*
167 Q8 **Viangchan** *Eng./Fr.* Vientiane. ● (Laos) C Laos *17°58′N 102°38′E*
167 P6 **Viangphoukha** *var.* Vieng Pou Kha. Louang Namtha, N Laos *20°41′N 101°03′E*
104 K13 **Viar** 〰 SW Spain
106 E11 **Viareggio** Toscana, C Italy *43°52′N 10°15′E*
103 O14 **Viaur** 〰 S France
Vibiscum *see* Vevey
95 G21 **Viborg** Viborg, NW Denmark *56°28′N 09°25′E*
29 R12 **Viborg** South Dakota, N USA *43°10′N 97°04′W*
95 F21 **Viborg** *off.* Viborg Amt. ⬖ *county* NW Denmark
Viborg Amt *see* Viborg
107 N22 **Vibo Valentia** *prev.* Monteleone di Calabria; *anc.* Hipponium. Calabria, SW Italy *38°40′N 16°06′E*
105 W5 **Vic** *var.* Vich; *anc.* Ausa, Vicus Ausonensis. Cataluña, NE Spain *41°56′N 02°16′E*
102 K16 **Vic-en-Bigorre** Hautes-Pyrénées, S France *43°23′N 00°04′E*
40 K10 **Vicente Guerrero** Durango, C Mexico *23°30′N 104°24′W*
41 P10 **Vicente Guerrero, Presa** *var.* Presa de las Adjuntas. ▣ NE Mexico
Vicentia *see* Vicenza
106 G8 **Vicenza** *anc.* Vicentia. Veneto, NE Italy *45°32′N 11°31′E*
Vich *see* Vic
54 J10 **Vichada** *off.* Comisaría del Vichada. ⬖ *province* E Colombia
Vichada, Comisaría del *see* Vichada
54 K10 **Vichada, Río** 〰 E Colombia
61 G17 **Vichadero** Rivera, NE Uruguay *31°45′S 54°41′W*
Vichegda *see* Vychegda
124 M16 **Vichuga** Ivanovskaya Oblast', W Russian Federation *57°13′N 41°51′E*
103 P10 **Vichy** Allier, C France *46°08′N 03°26′E*
26 K9 **Vici** Oklahoma, C USA *36°09′N 99°18′W*
31 P10 **Vicksburg** Michigan, N USA *42°07′N 85°31′W*
22 J5 **Vicksburg** Mississippi, S USA *32°21′N 90°52′W*
103 O12 **Vic-sur-Cère** Cantal, C France *45°00′N 02°36′E*
59 I21 **Víctor** Mato Grosso do Sul, SW Brazil *21°39′S 53°21′W*
29 X14 **Victor** Iowa, C USA *41°45′N 92°18′W*
182 I10 **Victor Harbor** South Australia *35°33′S 138°37′E*
61 C18 **Victoria** Entre Ríos, E Argentina *32°40′S 60°10′W*
10 L17 **Victoria** *province capital* Vancouver Island, British Columbia, SW Canada *48°25′N 123°22′W*
45 R14 **Victoria** NW Grenada *12°12′N 61°42′W*
42 H6 **Victoria** Yoro, NW Honduras *15°01′N 87°28′W*
121 O15 **Victoria** *var.* Rabat. Gozo, NW Malta *36°02′N 14°14′E*
116 I12 **Victoria** *Ger.* Viktoriastadt. Brașov, C Romania *45°44′N 24°41′E*
172 H17 **Victoria** ● (Seychelles) Mahé, SW Seychelles *04°38′S 28°28′E*
25 U13 **Victoria** Texas, SW USA *28°47′N 96°59′W*
183 N12 **Victoria** ⬖ *state* SE Australia
174 K7 **Victoria** 〰 Western Australia
Victoria *see* Labuan, East Malaysia
Victoria *see* Masvingo, Zimbabwe
Victoria Bank *see* Vitória Seamount
11 Y15 **Victoria Beach** Manitoba, S Canada *50°40′N 96°30′W*
Victoria de Durango *see* Durango
Victoria de las Tunas *see* Las Tunas
83 I16 **Victoria Falls** Matabeleland North, W Zimbabwe *17°55′S 25°51′E*
83 I16 **Victoria Falls** *waterfall* Zambia/Zimbabwe
83 I16 **Victoria Falls** ✈ Matabeleland North, W Zimbabwe *18°03′S 25°48′E*
Victoria Falls *see* Iguaçu, Salto do
63 F19 **Victoria, Isla** *island* Archipiélago de los Chonos, S Chile
8 K6 **Victoria Island** *island* Northwest Territories/Nunavut, NW Canada
182 L8 **Victoria, Lake** ◎ New South Wales, SE Australia
68 I12 **Victoria, Lake** *var.* Victoria Nyanza. ◎ E Africa
195 S13 **Victoria Land** *physical region* Antarctica
187 X14 **Victoria, Mount** ▲ Viti Levu, W Fiji *17°37′S 178°00′E*
166 L5 **Victoria, Mount** ▲ W Myanmar (Burma) *21°13′N 93°53′E*
186 E9 **Victoria, Mount** ▲ S Papua New Guinea *08°51′S 147°36′E*
81 F17 **Victoria Nile** *var.* Somerset Nile. 〰 C Uganda
Victoria Nyanza *see* Victoria, Lake
42 G3 **Victoria Peak** ▲ SE Belize *16°50′N 88°38′W*
185 H16 **Victoria Range** ▲▲ South Island, New Zealand
181 O3 **Victoria River** 〰 Northern Territory, N Australia
181 P3 **Victoria River Roadhouse** Northern Territory, N Australia *15°37′S 131°07′E*
15 Q11 **Victoriaville** Québec, SE Canada *46°04′N 71°57′W*
Victoria-Wes *see* Victoria West
83 G24 **Victoria West** *Afr.* Victoria-Wes. Northern Cape, W South Africa *31°25′S 23°08′E*
62 J13 **Victorica** La Pampa, C Argentina *36°15′S 65°25′W*
Victor, Mount *see* Belgicafjella
35 U14 **Victorville** California, W USA *34°32′N 117°17′W*
62 G9 **Vicuña** Coquimbo, N Chile *30°00′S 70°44′W*
62 K11 **Vicuña Mackenna** Córdoba, C Argentina *33°53′S 64°25′W*
Vicus Ausonensis *see* Vic
Vicus Elbii *see* Viterbo
33 X7 **Vida** Montana, NW USA *47°52′N 105°30′W*
23 V6 **Vidalia** Georgia, SE USA *32°13′N 82°24′W*
22 J7 **Vidalia** Louisiana, S USA *31°34′N 91°25′W*
95 F22 **Videbæk** Ringkøbing, C Denmark *56°08′N 08°38′E*
60 I13 **Videira** Santa Catarina, S Brazil *27°00′S 51°08′W*
116 J14 **Videle** Teleorman, S Romania *44°15′N 25°27′E*
Videm-Krško *see* Krško
Vídeň *see* Wien
104 H12 **Vidigueira** Beja, S Portugal *38°12′N 07°48′W*
114 J9 **Vidima** 〰 N Bulgaria
114 G7 **Vidin** *anc.* Bononia. Vidin, NW Bulgaria *44°00′N 22°52′E*
114 F8 **Vidin** ⬖ *province* NW Bulgaria
154 H10 **Vidisha** Madhya Pradesh, C India *23°30′N 77°50′E*
25 Y10 **Vidor** Texas, SW USA *30°07′N 94°01′W*
95 L20 **Vidöstern** ◎ S Sweden
92 J13 **Vidsel** Norrbotten, N Sweden *65°49′N 20°31′E*
118 H9 **Vidzemes Augstiene** ▲▲ C Latvia
118 J12 **Vidzy** Vitsyebskaya Voblasts', NW Belarus *55°24′N 26°38′E*
63 L16 **Viedma** Río Negro, E Argentina *40°50′S 62°58′W*
63 H22 **Viedma, Lago** ◎ S Argentina
45 O11 **Vieille Case** *var.* Itassi. N Dominica *15°36′N 61°24′W*
104 M2 **Vieja, Peña** ▲ N Spain *43°09′N 04°47′W*
24 J10 **Vieja, Sierra** ▲▲ Texas, SW USA
40 E4 **Viejo, Cerro** ▲ NW Mexico *30°16′N 112°18′W*
56 B9 **Viejo, Cerro** ▲ N Peru *04°54′S 79°24′W*
118 E10 **Viekšniai** Telšiai, NW Lithuania *56°14′N 22°33′E*
105 U3 **Vielha** *var.* Viella. Cataluña, NE Spain *42°41′N 00°47′E*
Viella *see* Vielha
99 L21 **Vielsalm** Luxembourg, E Belgium *50°17′N 05°55′E*
Vieng Pou Kha *see* Viangphoukha
23 T6 **Vienna** Georgia, SE USA *32°05′N 83°48′W*
30 L17 **Vienna** Illinois, N USA *37°24′N 88°55′W*
27 V5 **Vienna** Missouri, C USA *38°12′N 91°59′W*
21 Q3 **Vienna** West Virginia, NE USA *39°19′N 81°33′W*
Vienna *see* Wien, Austria
Vienna *see* Vienne, France
103 R11 **Vienne** *anc.* Vienna. Isère, E France *45°32′N 04°53′E*
102 L10 **Vienne** ⬖ *department* W France
102 L9 **Vienne** 〰 W France
Vientiane *see* Viangchan
Vientos, Paso de los *see* Windward Passage
45 V6 **Vieques** *var.* Isabel Segunda. E Puerto Rico *18°08′N 65°25′W*
45 V6 **Vieques, Isla de** *island* E Puerto Rico
45 V6 **Vieques, Pasaje de** *passage* E Puerto Rico
45 V5 **Vieques, Sonda de** *sound* E Puerto Rico
Vierdörfer *see* Săcele
93 M15 **Vieremä** Itä-Suomi, C Finland *63°42′N 27°02′E*
99 M14 **Vierlingsbeek** Noord-Brabant, SE Netherlands *51°36′N 06°01′E*
101 G20 **Viernheim** Hessen, W Germany *49°32′N 08°35′E*
101 D15 **Viersen** Nordrhein-Westfalen, W Germany *51°16′N 06°24′E*
108 G8 **Vierwaldstätter See** *Eng.* Lake of Lucerne. ◎ C Switzerland
103 N8 **Vierzon** Cher, C France *47°13′N 02°04′E*
40 L8 **Viesca** Coahuila, NE Mexico *25°25′N 102°45′W*
118 H10 **Viesīte** *Ger.* Eckengraf. Jēkabpils, S Latvia *56°21′N 25°30′E*
107 N15 **Vieste** Puglia, SE Italy *41°52′N 16°11′E*
167 T8 **Vietnam** *off.* Socialist Republic of Vietnam, *Vtn.* Công Hoa Xa Hôi Chu Nghia Viêt Nam. ◆ *republic* SE Asia
Vietnam, Socialist Republic of *see* Vietnam
167 S5 **Viêt Quang** Ha Giang, N Vietnam *22°24′N 104°48′E*
Vietri *see* Viêt Tri
167 S6 **Viêt Tri** *var.* Vietri. Vinh Phu, N Vietnam *21°20′N 105°26′E*
30 L4 **Vieux Desert, Lac** ◎ Michigan/Wisconsin, N USA
45 Y13 **Vieux Fort** S Saint Lucia *13°43′N 60°57′W*
45 X6 **Vieux-Habitants** Basse Terre, SW Guadeloupe *16°04′N 61°45′W*
119 G14 **Vievis** Vilnius, S Lithuania *54°46′N 24°51′E*
171 N2 **Vigan** Luzon, N Philippines *17°34′N 102°21′E*
106 D8 **Vigevano** Lombardia, N Italy *45°19′N 08°51′E*
107 N18 **Viggiano** Basilicata, S Italy *40°21′N 15°54′E*
58 L12 **Vigia** Pará, NE Brazil *0°50′S 48°07′W*
41 Y12 **Vigía Chico** Quintana Roo, SE Mexico *19°49′N 87°31′W*
45 T11 **Vigie** *prev.* George F L Charles. ✈ (Castries) NE Saint Lucia *14°01′N 60°59′W*
102 K17 **Vignemale** *var.* Pic de Vignemale. ▲ France/Spain *42°48′N 00°06′W*
Vignemale, Pic de *see* Vignemale
106 G10 **Vignola** Emilia-Romagna, C Italy *44°28′N 11°00′E*
104 G4 **Vigo** Galicia, NW Spain *42°15′N 08°44′W*
104 G4 **Vigo, Ría de** *estuary* NW Spain
94 D9 **Vigra** *island* S Norway
95 C17 **Vigrestad** Rogaland, S Norway *58°34′N 05°42′E*
93 L15 **Vihanti** Oulu, C Finland *64°29′N 25°E*
149 U10 **Vihāri** Punjab, E Pakistan *30°03′N 72°32′E*
102 K8 **Vihiers** Maine-et-Loire, NW France *47°09′N 00°37′W*
111 O19 **Vihorlat** ▲ E Slovakia *48°54′N 22°09′E*
93 L19 **Vihti** Etelä-Suomi, S Finland *60°25′N 24°16′E*
Viipuri *see* Vyborg
93 M16 **Viitasaari** Länsi-Suomi, C Finland *63°05′N 25°52′E*
118 K3 **Viivikonna** Ida-Virumaa, NE Estonia *59°19′N 27°41′E*
155 K16 **Vijayawāda** *prev.* Bezwada. Andhra Pradesh, SE India *16°34′N 80°40′E*
Vijosa/Vijosë *see* Aóos, Albania/Greece
Vijosa/Vijosë *see* Vjosës, Lumi i, Albania/Greece
92 J4 **Vík** Sudhurland, S Iceland *63°25′N 18°58′W*
Vik *see* Vikøyri
94 L13 **Vika** Dalarna, C Sweden *60°55′N 14°30′E*
92 L12 **Vikajärvi** Lappi, N Finland *66°37′N 26°10′E*
94 L13 **Vikarbyn** Dalarna, C Sweden *60°57′N 15°00′E*
95 J22 **Viken** Skåne, S Sweden *56°09′N 12°36′E*
95 L17 **Viken** ◎ C Sweden
95 G15 **Vikersund** Buskerud, S Norway *59°58′N 09°59′E*
114 G11 **Vikhren** ▲ SW Bulgaria *41°45′N 23°24′E*
11 R15 **Viking** Alberta, SW Canada *53°07′N 111°50′W*
84 E7 **Viking Bank** *undersea feature* N North Sea *60°35′N 02°35′E*
95 M14 **Vikmanshyttan** Dalarna, C Sweden *60°19′N 15°55′E*
94 D12 **Vikøyri** *var.* Vik. Sogn Og Fjordane, S Norway *61°04′N 06°34′E*
93 H17 **Viksjö** Västernorrland, C Sweden *62°45′N 17°30′E*
Viktoriastadt *see* Victoria
Vila *see* Port-Vila
Vila Arriaga *see* Bibala
Vila Artur de Paiva *see* Cubango
Vila Baleira *see* Porto Santo
Vila Bela da Santissima Trindade *see* Mato Grosso
58 B12 **Vila Bittencourt** Amazonas, NW Brazil *01°25′S 69°24′W*
Vila da Ponte *see* Cubango
64 O2 **Vila da Praia da Vitória** Terceira, Azores, Portugal, NE Atlantic Ocean *38°44′N 27°04′W*
Vila de Aljustrel *see* Cangamba
Vila de Almoster *see* Chiange
Vila de João Belo *see* Xai-Xai
Vila de Macia *see* Macia
Vila de Manhiça *see* Manhiça
Vila de Manica *see* Manica
Vila de Mocímboa da Praia *see* Mocímboa da Praia
83 N16 **Vila de Sena** *var.* Sena. Sofala, C Mozambique *17°25′S 34°59′E*
104 F14 **Vila do Bispo** Faro, S Portugal *37°05′N 08°53′W*
104 G6 **Vila do Conde** Porto, NW Portugal *41°21′N 08°45′W*
Vila do Maio *see* Maio
64 P3 **Vila do Porto** Santa Maria, Azores, Portugal, NE Atlantic Ocean *36°57′N 25°10′W*
83 K15 **Vila do Zumbo** *prev.* Vila do Zumbu, Zumbo. Tete, NW Mozambique *15°36′S 30°30′E*
Vila do Zumbu *see* Vila do Zumbo
104 I6 **Vila Flor** *var.* Vila Flôr. Bragança, N Portugal *41°18′N 07°09′W*
105 V6 **Vilafranca del Penedès** *var.* Villafranca del Panadés. Cataluña, NE Spain *41°21′N 01°42′E*
104 F10 **Vila Franca de Xira** *var.* Vilafranca de Xira. Lisboa, C Portugal *38°57′N 08°59′W*
Vila Gago Coutinho *see* Lumbala N'Guimbo
104 G3 **Vilagarcía de Arousa** *var.* Villagarcía de Arosa. Galicia, NW Spain *42°35′N 08°45′W*
Vila General Machado *see* Camacupa
Vila Henrique de Carvalho *see* Saurimo
102 I7 **Vilaine** 〰 NW France
Vila João de Almeida *see* Chibia
118 K8 **Viļaka** *Ger.* Marienhausen. Balvi, NE Latvia *57°12′N 27°43′E*
104 I2 **Vilalba** Galicia, NW Spain *43°17′N 07°41′W*
Vila Marechal Carmona *see* Uíge

◆ Country
● Country Capital
◇ Dependent Territory
○ Dependent Territory Capital
⬖ Administrative Regions
✈ International Airport
▲ Mountain
▲▲ Mountain Range
⛰ Volcano
〰 River
◎ Lake
▣ Reservoir

Vila Mariano Machado – Volta Rouge

Vila Mariano Machado see Ganda
172 G3 Vilanandro, Tanjona Fr. Cap Saint-André. headland W Madagascar 16°10′S 44°27′E
Vilanculos see Vilankulo
118 J10 Viļāni Rēzekne, E Latvia 56°33′N 26°55′E
83 N19 Vilankulo var. Vilanculos. Inhambane, E Mozambique 22°01′S 35°19′E
Vila Norton de Matos see Balombo
104 G6 Vila Nova de Famalicão var. Vila Nova de Famalicao. Braga, N Portugal 41°24′N 08°31′W
104 I6 Vila Nova de Foz Côa var. Vila Nova de Fozcôa. Guarda, N Portugal 41°05′N 07°09′W
Vila Nova de Fozcôa see Vila Nova de Foz Côa
104 F6 Vila Nova de Gaia Porto, NW Portugal 41°08′N 08°37′W
Vila Nova de Portimão see Portimão
105 V6 Vilanova i La Geltrú Cataluña, NE Spain 41°15′N 01°42′E
Vila Pereira de Eça see N'Giva
104 H6 Vila Pouca de Aguiar Vila Real, N Portugal 41°30′N 07°38′W
104 H6 Vila Real var. Vila Rial. Vila Real, N Portugal 41°17′N 07°45′W
104 H6 Vila Real ◆ district N Portugal
Vila-real de los Infantes see Villarreal
104 H14 Vila Real de Santo António Faro, S Portugal 37°12′N 07°25′W
104 J7 Vilar Formoso Guarda, N Portugal 40°37′N 06°50′W
Vila Rial see Vila Real
59 J15 Vila Rica Mato Grosso, W Brazil 09°52′S 50°44′W
Vila Robert Williams see Caála
Vila Salazar see N'Dalatando
Vila Serpa Pinto see Menongue
Vila Teixeira da Silva see Bailundo
Vila Teixeira de Sousa see Luau
104 H9 Vila Velha de Ródão Castelo Branco, C Portugal 39°39′N 07°40′W
104 G5 Vila Verde Braga, N Portugal 41°39′N 08°27′W
104 H11 Vila Viçosa Évora, S Portugal 38°46′N 07°25′W
57 G15 Vilcabamba, Cordillera de ▲ C Peru
Vîlcea see Vâlcea
122 J4 Vil'cheka, Zemlya Eng. Wilczek Land. island Zemlya Frantsa-Iosifa, NW Russian Federation
95 F22 Vildbjerg Ringkøbing, C Denmark 56°12′N 08°47′E
Vileyka see Vilyeyka
93 H15 Vilhelmina Västerbotten, N Sweden 64°38′N 16°40′E
59 F17 Vilhena Rondônia, W Brazil 12°40′S 60°08′W
115 G19 Vília Attikí, C Greece 38°09′N 23°21′E
119 I14 Viliya Lith. Neris. W Belarus
Viliya see Neris
118 H5 Viljandi Ger. Fellin. Viljandimaa, S Estonia 58°22′N 25°30′E
118 H5 Viljandimaa var. Viljandi Maakond. ◆ province SW Estonia
Viljandi Maakond see Viljandimaa
119 E14 Vilkaviškis Pol. Wyłkowyszki. Marijampolė, SW Lithuania 54°39′N 23°03′E
118 F13 Vilkija Kaunas, C Lithuania 55°02′N 23°36′E
197 V9 Vil'kitskogo, Proliv strait N Russian Federation
Vilkovo see Vylkove
57 L21 Villa Abecia Chuquisaca, S Bolivia 21°00′S 65°18′W
41 N5 Villa Acuña var. Ciudad Acuña. Coahuila, NE Mexico 29°18′N 100°58′W
40 J4 Villa Ahumada Chihuahua, N Mexico 30°38′N 106°30′W
45 O9 Villa Altagracia C Dominican Republic 18°43′N 70°13′W
56 L13 Villa Bella Beni, N Bolivia 10°21′S 65°25′W
104 J3 Villablino Castilla-León, N Spain 42°55′N 06°21′W
54 K6 Villa Bruzual Portuguesa, N Venezuela 09°20′N 69°06′W
105 O9 Villacañas Castilla-La Mancha, C Spain 39°38′N 03°20′W
105 O12 Villacarrillo Andalucía, S Spain 38°07′N 03°05′W
104 M7 Villacastín Castilla-León, N Spain 40°46′N 04°25′W
Villa Cecilia see Ciudad Madero
109 S9 Villach Slvn. Beljak. Kärnten, S Austria 46°36′N 13°49′E
107 B20 Villacidro Sardegna, Italy, C Mediterranean Sea 39°28′N 08°43′E
Villa Concepción see Concepción
104 L4 Villada Castilla-León, N Spain 42°15′N 04°59′W
40 M10 Villa de Cos Zacatecas, C Mexico 23°20′N 102°20′W
54 L5 Villa de Cura var. Cura. Aragua, N Venezuela 10°00′N 67°30′W
Villa del Nevoso see Ilirska Bistrica
Villa del Pilar see Pilar
104 M13 Villa del Río Andalucía, S Spain 37°59′N 04°17′W
Villa de Méndez see Méndez
42 H6 Villa de San Antonio Comayagua, W Honduras 14°24′N 87°37′W
105 N4 Villadiego Castilla-León, N Spain 42°31′N 04°01′W
105 T8 Villafamés País Valenciano, E Spain 40°07′N 00°03′W
41 U16 Villa Flores Chiapas, SE Mexico 16°12′N 93°16′W
104 J3 Villafranca del Bierzo Castilla-León, N Spain 42°36′N 06°49′W
105 S8 Villafranca del Cid País Valenciano, E Spain 40°25′N 00°15′W
104 J11 Villafranca de los Barros Extremadura, W Spain 38°34′N 06°20′W
105 N10 Villafranca de los Caballeros Castilla-La Mancha, C Spain 39°26′N 03°21′W
Villafranca del Panadés see Vilafranca del Penedès
106 F8 Villafranca di Verona Veneto, NE Italy 45°22′N 10°51′E
107 J23 Villafrati Sicilia, Italy, C Mediterranean Sea 37°53′N 13°30′E
Villagarcía de Arosa see Vilagarcía de Arousa
41 O9 Villagrán Tamaulipas, C Mexico 24°29′N 99°30′W
61 C17 Villaguay Entre Ríos, E Argentina 31°55′S 59°01′W
62 O6 Villa Hayes Presidente Hayes, S Paraguay 25°05′S 57°25′W
41 U15 Villahermosa prev. San Juan Bautista. Tabasco, SE Mexico 17°56′N 92°50′W
105 O11 Villahermosa Castilla-La Mancha, C Spain 38°46′N 02°52′W
64 O11 Villahermoso Gomera, Islas Canarias, Spain, NE Atlantic Ocean 28°06′N 17°20′W
Villa Hidalgo see Hidalgo
105 T12 Villajoyosa Cat. La Vila Joíosa. País Valenciano, E Spain 38°31′N 00°14′W
Villa Juárez see Juárez
Villalba see Collado Villalba
41 N8 Villaldama Nuevo León, NE Mexico 26°29′N 100°27′W
104 L5 Villalón de Campos Castilla-León, N Spain 42°05′N 05°03′W
61 A25 Villalonga Buenos Aires, E Argentina 39°55′S 62°35′W
104 L5 Villalpando Castilla-León, N Spain 41°51′N 05°25′W
40 K9 Villa Madero var. Francisco I. Madero. Durango, C Mexico 24°28′N 104°20′W
41 O9 Villa Mainero Tamaulipas, C Mexico 24°32′N 99°39′W
Villamaña see Villamañán
104 L4 Villamañán var. Villamaña. Castilla-León, N Spain 42°19′N 05°35′W
62 L10 Villa María Córdoba, C Argentina 32°23′S 63°15′W
61 C17 Villa María Grande Entre Ríos, E Argentina 31°39′S 59°54′W
57 K21 Villa Martín Potosí, SW Bolivia 20°46′S 67°45′W
104 K15 Villamartín Andalucía, S Spain 36°52′N 05°38′W
62 J8 Villa Mazán La Rioja, NW Argentina 28°43′S 66°25′W
62 J11 Villa Mercedes var. Mercedes. San Luis, C Argentina 33°40′S 65°25′W
Villamil see Puerto Villamil
Villa Nador see Nador
54 G5 Villanueva La Guajira, N Colombia 10°37′N 72°58′W
42 H5 Villanueva Cortés, NW Honduras 15°14′N 88°00′W
40 L11 Villanueva Zacatecas, C Mexico 22°24′N 102°53′W
42 I9 Villa Nueva Chinandega, NW Nicaragua 12°58′N 86°46′W
37 T11 Villanueva New Mexico, SW USA 35°18′N 105°20′W
104 M12 Villanueva de Córdoba Andalucía, S Spain 38°20′N 04°38′W
105 O12 Villanueva del Arzobispo Andalucía, S Spain 38°10′N 03°00′W
104 K11 Villanueva de la Serena Extremadura, W Spain 38°58′N 05°48′W
104 L5 Villanueva del Campo Castilla-León, N Spain 41°59′N 05°25′W
105 O11 Villanueva de los Infantes Castilla-La Mancha, C Spain 38°45′N 03°01′W
61 C14 Villa Ocampo Santa Fe, C Argentina 28°28′S 59°22′W
40 J8 Villa Ocampo Durango, C Mexico 26°29′N 105°30′W
40 J7 Villa Orestes Pereyra Durango, C Mexico 26°30′N 105°38′W
105 N3 Villarcayo Castilla-León, N Spain 42°56′N 03°34′W
104 L5 Villardefrades Castilla-León, N Spain 41°43′N 05°15′W
105 S9 Villar del Arzobispo País Valenciano, E Spain 39°44′N 00°50′W
105 Q6 Villaroya de la Sierra Aragón, NE Spain 41°28′N 01°46′W
105 T9 Villarreal var. Vila-real de los Infantes. País Valenciano, E Spain 39°56′N 00°08′W
62 P6 Villarrica Guairá, SE Paraguay 25°45′S 56°28′W
63 G15 Villarrica, Volcán S Chile 39°28′S 71°57′W
105 P10 Villarrobledo Castilla-La Mancha, C Spain 39°16′N 02°36′W
105 N10 Villarrubia de los Ojos Castilla-La Mancha, C Spain 39°14′N 03°36′W
18 J17 Villas New Jersey, NE USA 39°01′N 74°54′W
105 O3 Villasana de Mena Castilla-León, N Spain 43°05′N 03°16′W
107 M23 Villa San Giovanni Calabria, S Italy 38°12′N 15°39′E
61 D18 Villa San José Entre Ríos, E Argentina 32°01′S 58°20′W
Villa Sanjurjo see Al-Hoceïma
105 P6 Villasayas Castilla-León, N Spain 41°19′N 02°36′W
107 C20 Villasimius Sardegna, Italy, C Mediterranean Sea 39°10′N 09°30′E
41 N6 Villa Unión Coahuila, NE Mexico 28°18′N 100°43′W
40 K10 Villa Unión Durango, C Mexico 23°59′N 104°01′W
40 J10 Villa Unión Sinaloa, C Mexico 23°10′N 106°12′W
62 K12 Villa Valeria Córdoba, C Argentina 34°21′S 64°56′W
105 N8 Villaverde Madrid, C Spain 40°21′N 03°43′W
54 F10 Villavicencio Meta, C Colombia 04°09′N 73°38′W
104 L2 Villaviciosa Asturias, N Spain 43°29′N 05°26′W
104 L12 Villaviciosa de Córdoba Andalucía, S Spain 38°04′N 05°00′W
57 L22 Villazón Potosí, S Bolivia 22°05′S 65°35′W
14 J8 Villebon, Lac ◎ Québec, SE Canada
Ville de Kinshasa see Kinshasa
102 J5 Villedieu-les-Poêles Manche, N France 48°51′N 01°12′W
Villefranche see Villefranche-sur-Saône
103 N16 Villefranche-de-Lauragais Haute-Garonne, S France 43°24′N 01°42′E
103 N14 Villefranche-de-Rouergue Aveyron, S France 44°21′N 02°02′E
103 R10 Villefranche-sur-Saône var. Villefranche. Rhône, E France 46°00′N 04°40′E
14 H9 Ville-Marie Québec, SE Canada 47°21′N 79°26′W
102 M15 Villemur-sur-Tarn Haute-Garonne, S France 43°50′N 01°32′E
105 S11 Villena País Valenciano, E Spain 38°39′N 00°52′W
Villeneuve-d'Agen see Villeneuve-sur-Lot
102 L13 Villeneuve-sur-Lot var. Villeneuve-d'Agen, hist. Gajac. Lot-et-Garonne, SW France 44°24′N 00°43′E
103 P6 Villeneuve-sur-Yonne Yonne, C France 48°04′N 03°21′E
22 H8 Ville Platte Louisiana, S USA 30°41′N 92°16′W
103 R11 Villeurbanne Rhône, E France 45°46′N 04°54′E
101 G23 Villingen-Schwenningen Baden-Württemberg, S Germany 48°04′N 08°27′E
29 T15 Villisca Iowa, C USA 40°55′N 94°58′W
Villmanstrand see Lappeenranta
Vilna see Vilnius
119 H15 Vilnius ◆ province Lithuania
119 H14 Vilnius Pol. Wilno, Ger. Wilna; prev. Rus. Vilna. ● (Lithuania) Vilnius, SE Lithuania 54°41′N 25°20′E
119 H14 Vilnius ✈ Vilnius, SE Lithuania 54°33′N 25°17′E
117 S7 Vil'nohirs'k Dnipropetrovs'ka Oblast', E Ukraine 48°31′N 34°01′E
117 U8 Vil'nyans'k Zaporiz'ka Oblast', SE Ukraine 47°56′N 35°22′E
93 L17 Vilppula Länsi-Suomi, W Finland 62°02′N 24°30′E
101 M20 Vils SE Germany
118 C5 Vilsandi island W Estonia
117 P8 Vil'shanka Rus. Olshanka. Kirovohrads'ka Oblast', C Ukraine 48°12′N 30°54′E
101 O22 Vilshofen Bayern, SE Germany 48°36′N 13°10′E
155 J20 Viluppuram Tamil Nādu, SE India 12°54′N 79°40′E
113 I16 Vilusi W Montenegro 42°44′N 18°34′E
99 G18 Vilvoorde Fr. Vilvorde. Vlaams Brabant, C Belgium 50°56′N 04°25′E
Vilvorde see Vilvoorde
119 J14 Vilyeyka Pol. Wilejka, Rus. Vileyka. Minskaya Voblasts', NW Belarus 54°30′N 26°55′E
122 V11 Vilyuchinsk Kamchatskaya Oblast', E Russian Federation 52°55′N 158°28′E
123 P10 Vilyuy NE Russian Federation
123 P10 Vilyuysk Respublika Sakha (Yakutiya), NE Russian Federation 63°42′N 121°20′E
123 N10 Vilyuyskoye Vodokhranilishche ⊞ NE Russian Federation
104 G2 Vimianzo Galicia, NW Spain 43°06′N 09°03′W
95 M19 Vimmerby Kalmar, S Sweden 57°40′N 15°50′E
102 L5 Vimoutiers Orne, N France 48°56′N 00°10′E
93 L16 Vimpeli Länsi-Suomi, W Finland 63°10′N 23°50′E
79 G14 Vina Cameroon/Chad
62 G11 Viña del Mar Valparaíso, C Chile 33°02′S 71°35′W
19 R8 Vinalhaven Island island Maine, NE USA
105 T8 Vinaròs País Valenciano, E Spain 40°29′N 00°28′E
Vînători see Vânători
31 N15 Vincennes Indiana, N USA 38°42′N 87°30′W
195 Y12 Vincennes Bay bay Antarctica
25 O7 Vincent Texas, SW USA 32°30′N 101°10′W
95 H24 Vindeby Fyn, C Denmark 54°55′N 11°09′E
93 I15 Vindeln Västerbotten, N Sweden 64°11′N 19°45′E
95 F21 Vinderup Ringkøbing, C Denmark 56°29′N 08°48′E
Vindhya Mountains see Vindhya Range
153 N14 Vindhya Range var. Vindhya Mountains. ▲ N India
Vindobona see Wien
20 K6 Vine Grove Kentucky, S USA 37°48′N 85°58′W
18 J17 Vineland New Jersey, NE USA 39°29′N 75°02′W
116 E11 Vinga Arad, W Romania 46°00′N 21°14′E
95 M16 Vingåker Södermanland, C Sweden 59°02′N 15°52′E
167 S8 Vinh Nghê An, N Vietnam 18°42′N 105°41′E
104 I5 Vinhais Bragança, N Portugal 41°50′N 07°00′W
167 T9 Vinh Linh Quang Tri, C Vietnam 17°02′N 107°03′E
Vinh Loi see Bac Liêu
167 S14 Vinh Long var. Vinhlong. Vinh Long, S Vietnam 10°15′N 105°59′E
Vinhlong see Vinh Long
113 Q18 Vinica NE FYR Macedonia 41°53′N 22°30′E
109 V13 Vinica SE Slovenia 45°28′N 15°12′E
114 G8 Vinishte Montana, NW Bulgaria 43°30′N 23°04′E
27 Q8 Vinita Oklahoma, C USA 36°38′N 95°09′W
Vînju Mare see Vânju Mare
98 I11 Vinkeveen Utrecht, C Netherlands 52°13′N 04°55′E
116 L6 Vin'kivtsi Khmel'nyts'ka Oblast', W Ukraine 49°02′N 27°13′E
112 I10 Vinkovci Ger. Winkowitz, Hung. Vinkovcze. Vukovar-Srijem, E Croatia 45°18′N 18°45′E
Vinkovcze see Vinkovci
Vinnitsa see Vinnytsya
Vinnitskaya Oblast' see Vinnyts'ka Oblast'
116 M7 Vinnyts'ka Oblast' var. Vinnytsya, Rus. Vinnitskaya Oblast'. ◆ province C Ukraine
117 N6 Vinnytsya Rus. Vinnitsa. Vinnyts'ka Oblast', C Ukraine 49°14′N 28°30′E
117 N6 Vinnytsya ✈ Vinnyts'ka Oblast', N Ukraine 49°13′N 28°40′E
Vinogradov see Vynohradiv
194 L8 Vinson Massif ▲ Antarctica 78°45′S 85°19′W
94 G11 Vinstra Oppland, S Norway 61°36′N 09°45′E
116 K12 Vintilă Vodă Buzău, SE Romania 45°28′N 26°43′E
29 X13 Vinton Iowa, C USA 42°10′N 92°01′W
22 F9 Vinton Louisiana, S USA 30°10′N 93°37′W
155 J17 Vinukonda Andhra Pradesh, E India 16°03′N 79°41′E
Vioara see Ocnele Mari
83 E23 Vioolsdrif Northern Cape, SW South Africa 28°50′S 17°38′E
109 S12 Vipava Italy/Slovenia
82 M13 Viphya Mountains ▲ C Malawi
171 Q4 Virac Catanduanes Island, N Philippines 13°39′N 124°17′E
124 K8 Virandozero Respublika Kareliya, NW Russian Federation 63°59′N 36°00′E
137 P16 Viranşehir Şanlıurfa, SE Turkey 37°13′N 39°32′E
154 D13 Virār Mahārāshtra, W India 19°30′N 72°48′E
11 W16 Virden Manitoba, S Canada 49°50′N 100°57′W
30 K14 Virden Illinois, N USA 39°30′N 89°46′W
Virdois see Virrat
102 J5 Vire Calvados, N France 48°50′N 00°53′W
102 J4 Vire N France
83 A15 Virei Namibe, SW Angola 15°43′S 12°54′E
Vîrful Moldoveanu see Vârful Moldoveanu
35 R5 Virginia Peak ▲ Nevada, W USA 39°46′N 119°26′W
45 U9 Virgin Gorda island C British Virgin Islands
83 I22 Virginia Free State, C South Africa 28°06′S 26°53′E
30 K13 Virginia Illinois, N USA 39°57′N 90°12′W
29 W4 Virginia Minnesota, N USA 47°31′N 92°32′W
21 T6 Virginia off. Commonwealth of Virginia, also known as Mother of Presidents, Mother of States, Old Dominion. ◆ state NE USA
21 Y7 Virginia Beach Virginia, NE USA 36°51′N 75°59′W
33 R11 Virginia City Montana, NW USA 45°17′N 111°54′W
35 Q6 Virginia City Nevada, W USA 39°19′N 119°39′W
14 H8 Virginiatown Ontario, S Canada 48°09′N 79°35′W
Virgin Islands see British Virgin Islands
45 T9 Virgin Islands (US) var. Virgin Islands of the United States; prev. Danish West Indies. ◇ US unincorporated territory E West Indies
Virgin Islands of the United States see Virgin Islands (US)
45 T9 Virgin Passage passage Puerto Rico/Virgin Islands (US)
35 Y10 Virgin River Nevada/Utah, W USA
Virihaur see Virihaure
92 H12 Virihaure var. Virihaur. ◎ N Sweden
167 T11 Virôchey Rôtânôkiri, NE Cambodia 13°59′N 106°49′E
93 N19 Virolahti Etelä-Suomi, S Finland 60°33′N 27°37′E
30 J8 Viroqua Wisconsin, N USA 43°33′N 90°54′W
112 G8 Virovitica Ger. Virovititz, Hung. Verőcze; prev. Ger. Werowitz. Virovitica-Podravina, NE Croatia 45°49′N 17°25′E
112 G8 Virovitica-Podravina off. Virovitičko-Podravska Županija. ◆ province NE Croatia
Virovitičko-Podravska Županija see Virovitica-Podravina
Virovititz see Virovitica
113 J17 Virpazar S Montenegro 42°15′N 19°06′E
93 L17 Virrat Swe. Virdois. Länsi-Suomi, W Finland 62°14′N 23°50′E
95 M20 Virserum Kalmar, S Sweden 57°17′N 15°18′E
99 K25 Virton Luxembourg, SE Belgium 49°34′N 05°32′E
118 F5 Virtsu Ger. Werder. Läänemaa, W Estonia 58°35′N 23°33′E
56 C12 Virú La Libertad, C Peru 08°24′S 78°40′W
Virudhunagar see Virudunagar
155 H23 Virudunagar var. Virudhunagar; prev. Virudupatti. Tamil Nādu, SE India 09°35′N 77°57′E
Virudupatti see Virudunagar
118 I3 Viru-Jaagupi Ger. Sankt-Jakobi. Lääne-Virumaa, NE Estonia 59°14′N 26°29′E
57 N19 Viru-Viru var. Santa Cruz. ✈ (Santa Cruz) Santa Cruz, C Bolivia 17°49′S 63°12′W
113 E15 Vis It. Lissa; anc. Issa. island S Croatia
Vis see Fish
118 I12 Visaginas prev. Sniečkus. Utena, E Lithuania 55°36′N 26°22′E
155 M15 Visākhapatnam var. Vishakhapatnam. Andhra Pradesh, SE India 17°45′N 83°19′E
35 R11 Visalia California, W USA 36°19′N 119°19′W
Vişău see Vişeu
95 P19 Visby Ger. Wisby. Gotland, SE Sweden 57°37′N 18°20′E
197 N9 Viscount Melville Sound prev. Melville Sound. sound Northwest Territories, N Canada
99 L19 Visé Liège, E Belgium 50°44′N 05°42′E
112 K13 Višegrad Republika Srpska, SE Bosnia and Herzegovina 43°46′N 19°18′E
58 L12 Viseu Pará, NE Brazil 01°10′S 46°09′W
104 H7 Viseu prev. Vizeu. Viseu, N Portugal 40°40′N 07°55′W
104 H7 Viseu var. Vizeu. ◆ district N Portugal
116 I8 Vişeu Hung. Visó; prev. Vişău. NW Romania
116 I8 Vişeu de Sus var. Vişeul de Sus, Ger. Oberwischau, Hung. Felsővisó. Maramureş, N Romania 47°43′N 23°24′E
Vişeul de Sus see Vişeu de Sus
Vishakhapatnam see Visākhapatnam
125 R10 Vishera NW Russian Federation
95 J19 Viskafors Västra Götaland, S Sweden 57°37′N 12°50′E
95 J20 Viskan S Sweden
95 L21 Vislanda Kronoberg, S Sweden 56°46′N 14°30′E
Vislinskiy Zaliv see Vistula Lagoon
Visó see Vişeu
112 H13 Visoko ◆ Federacija Bosna I Hercegovina, C Bosnia and Herzegovina
106 A9 Viso, Monte ▲ NW Italy 44°42′N 07°04′E
108 E10 Visp Valais, SW Switzerland 46°18′N 07°53′E
108 E10 Vispa S Switzerland
95 M21 Vissefjärda Kalmar, S Sweden 56°31′N 15°34′E
100 I11 Visselhövede Niedersachsen, NW Germany 52°58′N 09°36′E
95 G23 Vissenbjerg Fyn, C Denmark 55°23′N 10°08′E
35 U17 Vista California, W USA 33°12′N 117°14′W
58 C11 Vista Alegre Amazonas, NW Brazil 01°23′N 68°13′W
114 J13 Vistonída, Límni ◎ NE Greece
92 K12 Visttasjohka N Sweden
Vistula see Wisła
119 A14 Vistula Lagoon Ger. Frisches Haff, Pol. Zalew Wiślany, Rus. Vislinskiy Zaliv. lagoon Poland/Russian Federation
114 I8 Vit NW Bulgaria
Vitebsk see Vitsyebsk
Vitebskaya Oblast' see Vitsyebskaya Voblasts'
107 H14 Viterbo anc. Vicus Elbii. Lazio, C Italy 42°25′N 12°08′E
112 H12 Vitez Federacija Bosna I Hercegovina, C Bosnia and Herzegovina 44°08′N 17°47′E
167 S14 Vi Thanh Cần Thơ, S Vietnam 09°45′N 105°28′E
Viti see Fiji
186 E7 Vitiaz Strait strait NE Papua New Guinea
104 J7 Vitigudino Castilla-León, N Spain 41°00′N 06°26′W
187 W15 Viti Levu island W Fiji
123 O11 Vitim C Russian Federation
123 O12 Vitimskiy Irkutskaya Oblast', C Russian Federation 58°12′N 113°10′E
109 V2 Vitis Niederösterreich, N Austria 48°45′N 15°09′E
59 O20 Vitória state capital Espírito Santo, SE Brazil 20°19′S 40°21′W
Vitoria see Vitoria-Gasteiz
Vitoria Bank see Vitória Seamount
59 N18 Vitória da Conquista Bahia, E Brazil 14°53′S 40°52′W
105 P3 Vitoria-Gasteiz var. Vitoria, Eng. Vittoria. País Vasco, N Spain 42°51′N 02°40′W
65 J16 Vitória Seamount var. Victoria Bank, Vitoria Bank. undersea feature C Atlantic Ocean 18°48′S 37°24′W
112 F13 Vitorog ▲ SW Bosnia and Herzegovina 44°06′N 17°03′E
102 J6 Vitré Ille-et-Vilaine, NW France 48°07′N 01°12′W
103 R5 Vitry-le-François Marne, N France 48°43′N 04°36′E
114 D13 Vítsi var. Vítsoi. ▲ N Greece 40°39′N 21°23′E
Vítsoi see Vítsi
118 N13 Vitsyebsk Rus. Vitebsk. Vitsyebskaya Voblasts', NE Belarus 55°11′N 30°10′E
118 K13 Vitsyebskaya Voblasts' prev. Rus. Vitebskaya Oblast'. ◆ province N Belarus
92 J11 Vittangi Lapp. Vazáš. Norrbotten, N Sweden 67°40′N 21°39′E
103 R8 Vitteaux Côte d'Or, C France 47°24′N 04°31′E
103 S6 Vittel Vosges, NE France 48°13′N 05°57′E
95 N15 Vittinge Västmanland, C Sweden 59°52′N 17°04′E
107 K25 Vittoria Sicilia, Italy, C Mediterranean Sea 36°56′N 14°30′E
Vittoria see Vitoria-Gasteiz
106 I7 Vittorio Veneto Veneto, NE Italy 45°59′N 12°18′E
175 Q9 Vitu Levu island W Fiji
175 Q7 Vityaz Trench undersea feature W Pacific Ocean
108 G8 Vitznau Luzern, W Switzerland 47°01′N 08°28′E
104 I1 Viveiro Galicia, NW Spain 43°39′N 07°35′W
105 S9 Viver País Valenciano, E Spain 39°55′N 00°36′W
103 Q13 Viverais, Monts du ▲ C France
122 L9 Vivi N Russian Federation
22 F4 Vivian Louisiana, S USA 32°52′N 93°59′W
29 N10 Vivian South Dakota, N USA 43°53′N 100°16′W
103 R13 Viviers Ardèche, E France 44°31′N 04°40′E
Vivis see Vevey
83 K19 Vivo Limpopo, NE South Africa 22°58′S 29°13′E
102 L10 Vivonne Vienne, W France 46°25′N 00°15′E
Vizakna see Ocna Sibiului
105 O2 Vizcaya Basq. Bizkaia. ◇ province País Vasco, N Spain
Vizcaya, Golfo de see Biscay, Bay of
136 C10 Vize Kırklareli, NW Turkey 41°34′N 27°45′E
122 K4 Vize, Ostrov island Severnaya Zemlya, N Russian Federation
Vizeu see Viseu
155 M15 Vizianagaram var. Vizianagram. Andhra Pradesh, E India 18°07′N 83°25′E
Vizianagram see Vizianagaram
103 S12 Vizille Isère, E France 45°05′N 05°46′E
125 R11 Vizinga Respublika Komi, NW Russian Federation 61°06′N 50°09′E
116 M13 Viziru Brăila, SE Romania 45°00′N 27°43′E
113 K21 Vjosës, Lumi i var. Vijosa, Vijosë, Gk. Aóos. Albania/Greece see also Aóos
Vjosës, Lumi i see Aóos
99 H18 Vlaams Brabant ◆ province C Belgium
Vlaanderen see Flanders
98 G12 Vlaardingen Zuid-Holland, SW Netherlands 51°55′N 04°21′E
116 F10 Vlădeasa, Vârful prev. Vîrful Vlădeasa. ▲ NW Romania 46°45′N 22°46′E
Vlădeasa, Vîrful see Vlădeasa, Vârful
113 P16 Vladičin Han Serbia, SE Serbia 42°44′N 22°04′E
127 O16 Vladikavkaz prev. Dzaudzhikau, Ordzhonikidze. Respublika Severnaya Osetiya, SW Russian Federation 42°58′N 44°41′E
126 M3 Vladimir Vladimirskaya Oblast', W Russian Federation 56°09′N 40°21′E
144 M7 Vladimirovka Kostanay, N Kazakhstan 53°30′N 64°02′E
Vladimirovka see Yuzhno-Sakhalinsk
126 L3 Vladimirskaya Oblast' ◆ province W Russian Federation
126 I3 Vladimirskiy Tupik Smolenskaya Oblast', W Russian Federation 55°45′N 33°25′E
Vladimir-Volynskiy see Volodymyr-Volyns'kyy
123 Q7 Vladivostok Primorskiy Kray, SE Russian Federation 43°09′N 131°53′E
117 U13 Vladyslavivka Respublika Krym, S Ukraine 45°09′N 35°25′E
98 P6 Vlagtwedde Groningen, NE Netherlands 53°02′N 07°07′E
Vlajna see Kukavica
112 J12 Vlasenica ◆ Republika Srpska, E Bosnia and Herzegovina
112 G12 Vlašić ▲ C Bosnia and Herzegovina 44°18′N 17°40′E
111 D17 Vlašim Ger. Wlaschim. Středočeský Kraj, C Czech Republic 49°42′N 14°54′E
113 P15 Vlasotince Serbia, SE Serbia 42°58′N 22°07′E
123 Q7 Vlasovo Respublika Sakha (Yakutiya), NE Russian Federation 70°41′N 134°49′E
98 I11 Vleuten Utrecht, C Netherlands 52°07′N 05°01′E
98 I5 Vlieland Fris. Flylân. island Waddeneilanden, N Netherlands
98 I5 Vliestroom strait NW Netherlands
99 J14 Vlijmen Noord-Brabant, S Netherlands 51°42′N 05°14′E
99 E15 Vlissingen Eng. Flushing, Fr. Flessingue. Zeeland, SW Netherlands 51°26′N 03°34′E
Vlodava see Włodawa
Vlonë/Vlora see Vlorë
113 K22 Vlorë prev. Vlonë, It. Valona, Vlora. Vlorë, SW Albania 40°28′N 19°31′E
113 K22 Vlorë ◆ district SW Albania
113 K22 Vlorës, Gjiri i var. Valona Bay. bay SW Albania
Vlotslavsk see Włocławek
111 C16 Vltava Ger. Moldau. W Czech Republic
126 K3 Vnukovo ✈ (Moskva) Gorod Moskva, W Russian Federation 55°30′N 36°52′E
146 L11 Vobkent Rus. Vabkent. Buxoro Viloyati, C Uzbekistan 40°01′N 64°25′E
25 Q9 Voca Texas, SW USA 30°58′N 99°09′W
109 R5 Vöcklabruck Oberösterreich, NW Austria 48°01′N 13°38′E
112 D13 Vodice Šibenik-Knin, S Croatia 43°46′N 15°46′E
124 K10 Vodlozero, Ozero ◎ NW Russian Federation
112 A10 Vodnjan It. Dignano d'Istria. Istra, NW Croatia 44°57′N 13°51′E
125 S9 Vodnyy Respublika Komi, NW Russian Federation 63°31′N 53°21′E
95 G20 Vodskov Nordjylland, N Denmark 57°07′N 10°02′E
92 H4 Vogar Suðurland, SW Iceland 63°58′N 22°20′W
Vogelkop see Doberai, Jazirah
77 X15 Vogel Peak prev. Dimlang. ▲ E Nigeria 08°16′N 11°44′E
101 H17 Vogelsberg ▲ C Germany
106 D8 Voghera Lombardia, N Italy 44°59′N 09°01′E
112 I13 Vogošća Federacija Bosna I Hercegovina, SE Bosnia and Herzegovina 43°55′N 18°20′E
101 M17 Vogtland historical region E Germany
125 V12 Vogul'skiy Kamen', Gora ▲ NW Russian Federation 60°10′N 58°41′E
187 P16 Voh Province Nord, C New Caledonia 20°57′S 164°41′E
Vohémar see Iharaña
172 H8 Vohimena, Tanjona Fr. Cap Sainte Marie. headland S Madagascar 25°20′S 45°06′E
172 J6 Vohipeno Fianarantsoa, SE Madagascar 22°21′S 47°51′E
118 H5 Võhma Ger. Wõchma. Viljandimaa, S Estonia 58°37′N 25°34′E
81 J20 Voi Coast, S Kenya 03°23′S 38°35′E
76 K15 Voinjama N Liberia 08°25′N 09°42′W
103 S12 Voiron Isère, E France 45°22′N 05°35′E
109 V8 Voitsberg Steiermark, SE Austria 47°04′N 15°09′E
95 F24 Vojens Ger. Woyens. Sønderjylland, SW Denmark 55°15′N 09°19′E
112 K9 Vojvodina Ger. Wojwodina. Vojvodina, N Serbia
15 S6 Volant Québec, SE Canada
Volaterrae see Volterra
43 P15 Volcán var. Hato del Volcán. Chiriquí, W Panama 08°45′N 82°38′W
Volcano Islands see Kazan-rettō
Volchansk see Vovchans'k
Volchya see Vovcha
94 D10 Volda Møre og Romsdal, S Norway 62°07′N 06°04′E
98 J9 Volendam Noord-Holland, C Netherlands 52°30′N 05°04′E
124 L15 Volga Yaroslavskaya Oblast', W Russian Federation 57°56′N 38°23′E
29 R10 Volga South Dakota, N USA 44°19′N 96°55′W
122 C11 Volga NW Russian Federation
Volga-Baltic Waterway see Volgo-Baltiyskiy Kanal
Volga Uplands see Privolzhskaya Vozvyshennost'
124 L13 Volgo-Baltiyskiy Kanal var. Volga-Baltic Waterway. canal NW Russian Federation
126 M12 Volgodonsk Rostovskaya Oblast', SW Russian Federation 47°35′N 42°03′E
127 O10 Volgograd prev. Stalingrad, Tsaritsyn. Volgogradskaya Oblast', SW Russian Federation 48°42′N 44°29′E
127 N9 Volgogradskaya Oblast' ◆ province SW Russian Federation
127 P10 Volgogradskoye Vodokhranilishche ⊞ SW Russian Federation
101 J19 Volkach Bayern, C Germany 49°51′N 10°15′E
109 U9 Völkermarkt Slvn. Velikovec. Kärnten, S Austria 46°40′N 14°38′E
124 I12 Volkhov Leningradskaya Oblast', NW Russian Federation 59°56′N 32°19′E
101 D20 Völklingen Saarland, SW Germany 49°15′N 06°51′E
Volkovysk see Vawkavysk
Volkovyskiye Vysoty see Vawkavyskaye Wzvyshsha
83 K22 Volksrust Mpumalanga, E South Africa 27°22′S 29°54′E
98 L8 Vollenhove Overijssel, N Netherlands 52°40′N 05°58′E
119 L16 Volma C Belarus
Volmari see Valmiera
117 W9 Volnovakha Donets'ka Oblast', SE Ukraine 47°36′N 37°32′E
116 K6 Volochys'k Khmel'nyts'ka Oblast', W Ukraine 49°32′N 26°14′E
117 O6 Volodarka Kyyivs'ka Oblast', N Ukraine 49°31′N 29°55′E
117 W9 Volodars'ke Donets'ka Oblast', E Ukraine 47°11′N 37°19′E
127 R13 Volodarskiy Astrakhanskaya Oblast', SW Russian Federation 46°23′N 48°39′E
Volodarskoye see Saumalkol'
117 N8 Volodars'k-Volyns'kyy Zhytomyrs'ka Oblast', N Ukraine 50°37′N 28°28′E
116 K3 Volodymerets' Rivnens'ka Oblast', NW Ukraine 51°24′N 25°52′E
116 I3 Volodymyr-Volyns'kyy Pol. Włodzimierz, Rus. Vladimir-Volynskiy. Volyns'ka Oblast', NW Ukraine 50°51′N 24°19′E
124 L14 Vologda Vologodskaya Oblast', W Russian Federation 59°10′N 39°55′E
124 L12 Vologodskaya Oblast' ◆ province NW Russian Federation
126 K3 Volokolamsk Moskovskaya Oblast', W Russian Federation 56°03′N 35°57′E
126 K9 Volokonovka Belgorodskaya Oblast', W Russian Federation 50°30′N 37°54′E
115 G16 Vólos Thessalía, C Greece 39°21′N 22°58′E
124 M11 Voloshka Arkhangel'skaya Oblast', NW Russian Federation 61°19′N 40°06′E
Vološinovo see Novi Bečej
116 H7 Volovets' Zakarpats'ka Oblast', W Ukraine 48°42′N 23°12′E
Volozhin see Valozhyn
127 Q7 Vol'sk Saratovskaya Oblast', W Russian Federation 52°04′N 47°20′E
77 Q17 Volta SE Ghana
Volta Blanche see White Volta
77 P16 Volta, Lake ⊞ SE Ghana
Volta Noire see Black Volta
60 O9 Volta Redonda Rio de Janeiro, SE Brazil 22°31′S 44°05′W
Volta Rouge see Red Volta

◆ Country
● Country Capital
◇ Dependent Territory
○ Dependent Territory Capital
◆ Administrative Regions
✈ International Airport
▲ Mountain
▲ Mountain Range
Volcano
River
◎ Lake
⊞ Reservoir

VOLTERRA – WALK

106 F12 **Volterra** *anc.* Volaterrae. Toscana, C Italy 43°23′N 10°52′E
107 K17 **Volturno** 〰 S Italy
113 I15 **Volujak** ▲▲ NW Montenegro
Volunteer Island *see* Starbuck Island
114 H13 **Vólvi, Límni** ◎ N Greece
Volyn *see* Volyns'ka Oblast'
116 I3 **Volyns'ka Oblast'** *var.* Volyn, *Rus.* Volynskaya Oblast'. ◈ *province* NW Ukraine
Volynskaya Oblast' *see* Volyns'ka Oblast'
127 Q3 **Volzhsk** Respublika Mariy El, W Russian Federation 55°53′N 48°21′E
127 O10 **Volzhskiy** Volgogradskaya Oblast', SW Russian Federation 48°49′N 44°40′E
172 I7 **Vondrozo** Fianarantsoa, SE Madagascar 22°50′S 47°20′E
39 P10 **Von Frank Mountain** ▲ Alaska, USA 63°36′N 154°29′W
115 C17 **Vónitsa** Dytikí Ellás, W Greece 38°55′N 20°53′E
118 J6 **Võnnu** *Ger.* Wendau. Tartumaa, SE Estonia 58°17′N 27°06′E
98 G12 **Voorburg** Zuid-Holland, W Netherlands 52°04′N 04°22′E
98 H11 **Voorschoten** Zuid-Holland, W Netherlands 52°08′N 04°26′E
98 M11 **Voorst** Gelderland, E Netherlands 52°10′N 06°10′E
98 K11 **Voorthuizen** Gelderland, C Netherlands 52°12′N 05°36′E
92 L2 **Vopnafjördhur** Austurland, E Iceland 65°45′N 14°51′W
92 L2 **Vopnafjördhur** *bay* E Iceland
Vora *see* Vorë
119 H15 **Voranava** *Pol.* Werenów, *Rus.* Voronovo. Hrodzyenskaya Voblasts', W Belarus 54°09′N 25°19′E
108 I8 **Vorarlberg** *off.* Land Vorarlberg. ◈ *state* W Austria
Vorarlberg, Land *see* Vorarlberg
109 X7 **Vorau** Steiermark, E Austria 47°22′N 15°55′E
98 N11 **Vorden** Gelderland, E Netherlands 52°07′N 06°18′E
108 H9 **Vorderrhein** 〰 SE Switzerland
92 J2 **Vordhufell** ▲ N Iceland 65°42′N 18°45′W
95 I24 **Vordingborg** Storstrøm, SE Denmark 55°01′N 11°55′E
113 K19 **Vorë** *var.* Vora. Tiranë, W Albania 41°23′N 19°37′E
115 H17 **Vóreies Sporádes** *var.* Vóreioi Sporádes, Vórioi Sporádhes, *Eng.* Northern Sporades. *island group* E Greece
Vóreioi Sporádes *see* Vóreies Sporádes
115 J17 **Vóreion Aigaíon** *Eng.* Aegean North. ◈ *region* SE Greece
115 G18 **Vóreios Evvoïkós Kólpos** *var.* Voreiós Evvoïkós Kólpos. *gulf* E Greece
197 S16 **Voring Plateau** *undersea feature* N Norwegian Sea 67°00′N 04°00′E
Vórioi Sporádhes *see* Vóreies Sporádes
125 W4 **Vorkuta** Respublika Komi, NW Russian Federation 67°27′N 64°E
95 I14 **Vorma** 〰 S Norway
118 E4 **Vormsi** *var.* Vormsi Saar, *Ger.* Worms, *Swed.* Ormsö. *island* W Estonia
Vormsi Saar *see* Vormsi
127 N7 **Vorona** 〰 W Russian Federation
126 L7 **Voronezh** Voronezhskaya Oblast', W Russian Federation 51°40′N 39°13′E
126 L7 **Voronezh** 〰 W Russian Federation
126 K8 **Voronezhskaya Oblast'** ◈ *province* W Russian Federation
Voronovitsya *see* Voronovytsya
Voronovo *see* Voranava
117 N6 **Voronovytsya** *Rus.* Voronovitsya. Vinnyts'ka Oblast', C Ukraine 49°06′N 28°49′E
122 K7 **Vorontsovo** Taymyrskiy (Dolgano-Nenetskiy) Avtonomnyy Okrug, N Russian Federation 71°45′N 83°31′E
124 K3 **Voron'ya** 〰 NW Russian Federation
Voropayevo *see* Varapayeva
Voroshilov *see* Ussuriysk
Voroshilovgrad *see* Luhans'ka Oblast', Ukraine
Voroshilovgrad *see* Luhans'k, Ukraine
Voroshilovgradskaya Oblast' *see* Luhans'ka Oblast'
Voroshilovsk *see* Stavropol', Russian Federation
Voroshilovsk *see* Alchevs'k
137 V13 **Vorotan** *Az.* Bärguşad. 〰 Armenia/Azerbaijan
127 P3 **Vorotynets** Nizhegorodskaya Oblast', W Russian Federation 56°06′N 46°06′E
117 S3 **Vorozhba** Sums'ka Oblast', NE Ukraine 51°10′N 34°15′E
117 T5 **Vorskla** 〰 Russian Federation/Ukraine
99 I17 **Vorst** Antwerpen, N Belgium 51°06′N 05°01′E
83 G21 **Vorstershoop** North-West, N South Africa 25°46′S 22°57′E
118 H6 **Võrtsjärv** *Ger.* Wirz-See. ◎ SE Estonia
118 J7 **Võru** *Ger.* Werro. Võrumaa, SE Estonia 57°51′N 27°01′E
147 R11 **Vorukh** N Tajikistan 39°51′N 70°34′E
118 I7 **Võrumaa** *off.* Võru Maakond. ◈ *province* SE Estonia
Võru Maakond *see* Võrumaa
83 G24 **Vosburg** Northern Cape, W South Africa 30°35′S 22°52′E
147 Q14 **Vose'** *Rus.* Vose; *prev.* Aral. SW Tajikistan 37°51′N 69°31′E
103 S6 **Vosges** ◈ *department* NE France
103 U6 **Vosges** ▲▲ NE France
124 K13 **Voskresenkoye** Vologodskaya Oblast', NW Russian Federation 59°25′N 37°56′E
126 L4 **Voskresensk** Moskovskaya Oblast', W Russian Federation 55°19′N 38°42′E
127 P2 **Voskresenskoye** Nizhegorodskaya Oblast', W Russian Federation 57°00′N 45°33′E
127 V6 **Voskresenskoye** Respublika Bashkortostan, W Russian Federation 53°07′N 56°07′E
94 D13 **Voss** Hordaland, S Norway 60°38′N 06°25′E
94 D13 **Voss** *physical region* S Norway
99 I16 **Vosselaar** Antwerpen, N Belgium 51°19′N 04°55′E
94 D13 **Vosso** 〰 S Norway
Vostochno-Kazakhstanskaya Oblast' *see* Vostochnyy Kazakhstan
145 T12 **Vostochno-Kounradskiy** *Kaz.* Shyghys Qongyrat. Zhezkazgan, C Kazakhstan
123 S5 **Vostochno-Sibirskoye More** *Eng.* East Siberian Sea. *sea* Arctic Ocean
145 X10 **Vostochnyy Kazakhstan** *off.* Vostochno-Kazakhstanskaya Oblast', *var.* East Kazakhstan, *Kaz.* Shyghys Qazagastan Oblysy. ◈ *province* E Kazakhstan
Vostochnyy Sayan *see* Eastern Sayans
Vostock Island *see* Vostok Island
195 U10 **Vostok** *Russian research station* Antarctica 77°18′S 105°32′E
191 X5 **Vostok Island** *var.* Vostock Island; *prev.* Stavers Island. *island* Line Islands, SE Kiribati
127 T2 **Votkinsk** Udmurtskaya Respublika, NW Russian Federation 57°04′N 54°00′E
125 U15 **Votkinskoye Vodokhranilishche** *var.* Votkinsk Reservoir. ⊠ NW Russian Federation
Votkinsk Reservoir *see* Votkinskoye Vodokhranilishche
60 J7 **Votuporanga** São Paulo, S Brazil 20°26′S 49°53′W
104 H7 **Vouga, Rio** 〰 N Portugal
115 E14 **Voúrinos** ▲▲ N Greece
115 G24 **Voúxa, Akrotírio** *headland* Kríti, Greece, E Mediterranean Sea 35°37′N 23°34′E
103 R4 **Vouziers** Ardennes, N France 49°24′N 04°42′E
117 V7 **Vovcha** *Rus.* Volchya. 〰 E Ukraine
117 V4 **Vovchans'k** *Rus.* Volchansk. Kharkivs'ka Oblast', E Ukraine 50°19′N 36°55′E
103 N6 **Voves** Eure-et-Loir, C France 48°18′N 01°39′E
79 M14 **Vovodo** 〰 S Central African Republic
94 M12 **Voxna** Gävleborg, C Sweden 61°21′N 15°35′E
94 L11 **Voxnan** 〰 C Sweden
114 F7 **Voynishka Reka** 〰 NW Bulgaria
125 T9 **Voyvozh** Respublika Komi, NW Russian Federation 62°54′N 54°52′E
124 M12 **Vozhega** Vologodskaya Oblast', NW Russian Federation 60°27′N 40°11′E
124 L12 **Vozhe, Ozero** ◎ NW Russian Federation
117 Q9 **Voznesens'k** *Rus.* Voznesensk. Mykolayivs'ka Oblast', S Ukraine 47°34′N 31°21′E
124 J12 **Voznesen'ye** Leningradskaya Oblast', NW Russian Federation 61°00′N 35°24′E
144 J14 **Vozrozhdeniya, Ostrov** *Uzb.* Wozrojdeniye Oroli. *island* Kazakhstan/Uzbekistan
95 G20 **Vrå** *var.* Vraa. Nordjylland, N Denmark 57°21′N 09°57′E
Vraa *see* Vrå
114 H9 **Vrachesh** Sofiya, W Bulgaria 42°52′N 23°45′E
115 C19 **Vrachíonas** ▲ Zákynthos, Iónia Nisiá, Greece, C Mediterranean Sea 37°49′N 20°43′E
117 P8 **Vradiyivka** Mykolayivs'ka Oblast', S Ukraine 47°51′N 30°37′E
113 G14 **Vran** ▲ SW Bosnia and Herzegovina 43°35′N 17°30′E
116 K12 **Vrancea** ◈ *county* E Romania
147 T14 **Vrang** SE Tajikistan 37°03′N 72°26′E
123 T4 **Vrangelya, Ostrov** *Eng.* Wrangel Island. *island* NE Russian Federation
112 H13 **Vranica** ▲ C Bosnia and Herzegovina 43°57′N 17°43′E
113 O16 **Vranje** Serbia, SE Serbia 42°33′N 21°55′E
Vranov *see* Vranov nad Topl'ou
111 N19 **Vranov nad Topl'ou** *var.* Vranov, *Hung.* Varannó. Prešovský Kraj, E Slovakia 48°54′N 21°41′E
114 H8 **Vratsa** Vratsa, NW Bulgaria 43°13′N 23°34′E
114 H8 **Vratsa** ◈ *province* NW Bulgaria
114 F10 **Vrattsa** *prev.* Mirovo. Kyustendil, W Bulgaria 42°15′N 22°33′E
112 G11 **Vrbanja** 〰 NW Bosnia and Herzegovina
112 K9 **Vrbas** Vojvodina, NW Serbia 45°34′N 19°39′E
112 G13 **Vrbas** 〰 N Bosnia and Herzegovina
112 E8 **Vrbovec** Zagreb, N Croatia 45°53′N 16°24′E
112 C9 **Vrbovsko** Primorje-Gorski Kotar, NW Croatia 45°22′N 15°06′E
111 E15 **Vrchlabí** *Ger.* Hohenelbe. Královéhradecký Kraj, N Czech Republic 50°38′N 15°35′E
83 J22 **Vrede** Free State, E South Africa 27°25′S 29°10′E
100 E13 **Vreden** Nordrhein-Westfalen, NW Germany 52°01′N 06°50′E
83 E25 **Vredenburg** Western Cape, SW South Africa 32°55′S 18°00′E
99 I23 **Vresse-sur-Semois** Namur, SE Belgium 49°52′N 04°56′E
95 L16 **Vretstorp** Örebro, C Sweden 59°03′N 14°51′E
113 G15 **Vrgorac** *prev.* Vrhgorac. Split-Dalmacija, SE Croatia 43°10′N 17°24′E
Vrhgorac *see* Vrgorac
109 T12 **Vrhnika** *Ger.* Oberlaibach. W Slovenia 45°57′N 14°18′E
155 I21 **Vriddhāchalam** Tamil Nādu, SE India 11°33′N 79°18′E
98 N6 **Vries** Drenthe, NE Netherlands 53°04′N 06°34′E
98 O10 **Vriezenveen** Overijssel, E Netherlands 52°25′N 06°37′E
95 L20 **Vrigstad** Jönköping, S Sweden 57°19′N 14°30′E
108 H9 **Vrin** Graubünden, S Switzerland 46°40′N 09°06′E
112 E13 **Vrlika** Split-Dalmacija, S Croatia 43°54′N 16°24′E
113 M14 **Vrnjačka Banja** Serbia, C Serbia 43°36′N 20°55′E
Vrondádhes/Vrondados *see* Vrontádos
115 L18 **Vrontádos** *var.* Vrondados; *prev.* Vrondádhes. Chíos, E Greece 38°25′N 26°08′E
98 N9 **Vroomshoop** Overijssel, E Netherlands 52°28′N 06°35′E
112 N10 **Vršac** *Ger.* Werschetz, *Hung.* Versecz. Vojvodina, NE Serbia 45°08′N 21°18′E
112 M10 **Vršački Kanal** *canal* N Serbia
83 H21 **Vryburg** North-West, N South Africa 26°57′S 24°44′E
83 K22 **Vryheid** KwaZulu/Natal, E South Africa 27°45′S 30°48′E
111 I18 **Vsetín** *Ger.* Wsetin. Zlínský Kraj, E Czech Republic 49°21′N 17°57′E
111 J20 **Vtáčnik** *Hung.* Madaras, Ptacsnik; *prev.* Ptačnik. ▲ W Slovakia 48°38′N 18°38′E
Vuadil' *see* Wodil
114 I11 **Vŭcha** 〰 SW Bulgaria
Vučitrn *see* Vushtrri
99 J14 **Vught** Noord-Brabant, S Netherlands 51°37′N 05°19′E
117 W8 **Vuhledar** Donets'ka Oblast', E Ukraine 47°48′N 37°11′E
112 I9 **Vuka** 〰 E Croatia
113 K17 **Vukël** *var.* Vukli. Shkodër, N Albania 42°29′N 19°39′E
Vukli *see* Vukël
112 J9 **Vukovar** *Hung.* Vukovár. Vukovar-Srijem, E Croatia 45°18′N 18°45′E
Vukovarsko-Srijemska Županija *see* Vukovar-Srijem
112 I10 **Vukovar-Srijem** *off.* Vukovarsko-Srijemska Županija. ◈ *province* E Croatia
125 U8 **Vuktyl** Respublika Komi, NW Russian Federation 63°49′N 57°07′E
11 Q17 **Vulcan** Alberta, SW Canada 50°27′N 113°12′W
116 G12 **Vulcan** *Ger.* Wulkan, *Hung.* Zsilyvajdevulkán; *prev.* Crivadia Vulcanului, Vaidei, *Hung.* Sily-Vajdej, Vajdej. Hunedoara, W Romania 45°22′N 23°16′E
116 M12 **Vulcănești** *Rus.* Vulkaneshty. S Moldova 45°41′N 28°25′E
107 L22 **Vulcano, Isola** *island* Isole Eolie, S Italy
114 G7 **Vŭlchedrŭm** Montana, NW Bulgaria 43°42′N 23°25′E
114 N8 **Vŭlchidol** *prev.* Kurt-Dere. Varna, E Bulgaria 43°25′N 27°33′E
Vulkaneshty *see* Vulcănești
123 V11 **Vulkannyy** Kamchatskaya Oblast', R Russian Federation 53°01′N 158°26′E
36 J13 **Vulture Mountains** ▲▲ Arizona, SW USA
167 T14 **Vung Tau** *prev. Fr.* Cape Saint Jacques, Cap Saint-Jacques. Ba Ria-Vung Tau, S Vietnam 10°21′N 107°04′E
187 X15 **Vunisea** Kadavu, SE Fiji 19°04′S 178°10′E
Vuohčču *see* Vuotso
93 N15 **Vuokatti** Oulu, C Finland 64°08′N 28°16′E
93 M15 **Vuolijoki** Oulu, C Finland 64°09′N 27°00′E
Vuolleriebme *see* Vuollerim
92 J13 **Vuollerim** *Lapp.* Vuolleriebme. Norrbotten, N Sweden 66°24′N 20°36′E
Vuoreija *see* Vardø
92 L10 **Vuotso** *Lapp.* Vuohčču. Lappi, N Finland 68°04′N 27°05′E
114 J11 **Vŭrbitsa** *prev.* Filevo. Khaskovo, S Bulgaria 42°02′N 25°25′E
114 J12 **Vŭrbitsa** 〰 S Bulgaria
127 Q4 **Vurnary** Chuvashskaya Respublika, W Russian Federation 55°30′N 46°59′E
114 G8 **Vŭrshets** Montana, NW Bulgaria 43°14′N 23°20′E
113 N16 **Vushtrri** *Serb.* Vučitrn. N Kosovo 42°49′N 21°00′E
119 F17 **Vyalikaya Byerastavitsa** *Pol.* Brzostowica Wielka, *Rus.* Bol'shaya Berëstovitsa; *prev.* Velikaya Berestovitsa. Hrodzyenskaya Voblasts', SW Belarus 53°12′N 24°03′E
119 N20 **Vyaliki Bor** *Rus.* Velikiy Bor. Homyel'skaya Voblasts', SE Belarus 52°02′N 29°56′E
119 J18 **Vyaliki Rozhan** *Rus.* Bol'shoy Rozhan. Minskaya Voblasts', S Belarus 52°46′N 27°07′E
124 H10 **Vyartsilya** *Fin.* Värtsilä. Respublika Kareliya, NW Russian Federation 62°07′N 30°43′E
119 K17 **Vyasyeya** *Rus.* Veseya. Minskaya Voblasts', C Belarus 53°04′N 27°41′E
125 R15 **Vyatka** 〰 NW Russian Federation
Vyatka *see* Kirov
125 S16 **Vyatskiye Polyany** Kirovskaya Oblast', NW Russian Federation 56°15′N 51°06′E
123 S14 **Vyazemskiy** Khabarovskiy Kray, SE Russian Federation 47°28′N 134°39′E
126 I4 **Vyaz'ma** Smolenskaya Oblast', W Russian Federation 55°09′N 34°20′E
127 N3 **Vyazniki** Vladimirskaya Oblast', W Russian Federation 56°15′N 42°06′E
127 O8 **Vyazovka** Volgogradskaya Oblast', SW Russian Federation 50°57′N 43°57′E
119 J14 **Vyazyn'** Minskaya Voblasts', NW Belarus 54°25′N 27°10′E
124 G11 **Vyborg** *Fin.* Viipuri. Leningradskaya Oblast', NW Russian Federation 60°44′N 28°47′E
125 P11 **Vychegda** *var.* Vichegda. 〰 NW Russian Federation
125 P11 **Vychegodskiy** Arkhangel'skaya Oblast', NW Russian Federation 61°14′N 46°53′E
119 L14 **Vyelyewshchyna** *Rus.* Velevshchina. Vitsyebskaya Voblasts', N Belarus 54°44′N 28°35′E
119 P16 **Vyeramyeyki** *Rus.* Veremeyki. Mahilyowskaya Voblasts', E Belarus 53°46′N 31°17′E
118 K11 **Vyerkhnyadzvinsk** *Rus.* Verkhnedvinsk. Vitsyebskaya Voblasts', N Belarus 55°47′N 27°56′E
119 P18 **Vyetka** *Rus.* Vetka. Homyel'skaya Voblasts', SE Belarus 52°33′N 31°10′E
118 L12 **Vyetryna** *Rus.* Vetrino. Vitsyebskaya Voblasts', N Belarus 55°25′N 28°28′E
Vygonovskoye, Ozero *see* Vyhanawskaye, Vozyera
124 J9 **Vygozero, Ozero** ◎ NW Russian Federation
Vyhanashchanskaye Vozyera *see* Vyhanawskaye, Vozyera
119 I18 **Vyhanawskaye, Vozyera** *var.* Vyhanashchanskaye Vozyera, *Rus.* Ozero Vygonovskoye. ◎ SW Belarus
127 N4 **Vyksa** Nizhegorodskaya Oblast', W Russian Federation 55°21′N 42°10′E
117 O12 **Vylkove** *Rus.* Vilkovo. Odes'ka Oblast', SW Ukraine 45°24′N 29°37′E
125 R9 **Vym'** 〰 NW Russian Federation
116 H8 **Vynohradiv** *Cz.* Sevluš, *Hung.* Nagyszöllös, *Rus.* Vinogradov; *prev.* Sevlyush. Zakarpats'ka Oblast', W Ukraine 48°09′N 23°01′E
124 G13 **Vyritsa** Leningradskaya Oblast', NW Russian Federation 59°25′N 30°20′E
97 J19 **Vyrnwy** *Wel.* Afon Efyrnwy. 〰 E Wales, United Kingdom
145 X9 **Vyshe Ivanovskiy Belak, Gora** ▲ E Kazakhstan 50°16′N 83°46′E
117 P4 **Vyshhorod** Kyyivs'ka Oblast', N Ukraine 50°36′N 30°28′E
124 I15 **Vyshniy Volochek** Tverskaya Oblast', W Russian Federation 57°37′N 34°33′E
111 G18 **Vyškov** *Ger.* Wischau. Jihomoravský Kraj, SE Czech Republic 49°17′N 17°01′E
111 E18 **Vysočina** *prev.* Jihlavský Kraj. ◈ *region* N Czech Republic
119 E19 **Vysokaye** *Rus.* Vysokoye. Brestskaya Voblasts', SW Belarus 52°20′N 23°18′E
111 F17 **Vysoké Mýto** *Ger.* Hohenmauth. Pardubický Kraj, C Czech Republic 49°57′N 16°10′E
117 S9 **Vysokopillya** Khersons'ka Oblast', S Ukraine 47°28′N 33°30′E
126 K3 **Vysokovsk** Moskovskaya Oblast', W Russian Federation 56°12′N 36°42′E
Vysokoye *see* Vysokaye
124 K12 **Vytegra** Vologodskaya Oblast', NW Russian Federation 60°59′N 36°27′E
116 J8 **Vyzhnytsya** Chernivets'ka Oblast', W Ukraine 48°14′N 25°10′E

W

77 O14 **Wa** NW Ghana 10°07′N 02°28′W
Waadt *see* Vaud
Waag *see* Váh
Waagbistritz *see* Považská Bystrica
Waagneustadtl *see* Nové Mesto nad Váhom
81 M16 **Waajid** Gedo, SW Somalia 03°37′N 43°19′E
98 L13 **Waal** 〰 S Netherlands
187 O16 **Waala** Province Nord, W New Caledonia 19°46′S 163°41′E
99 I14 **Waalwijk** Noord-Brabant, S Netherlands 51°42′N 05°04′E
99 E16 **Waarschoot** Oost-Vlaanderen, NW Belgium 51°09′N 03°35′E
186 C7 **Wabag** Enga, W Papua New Guinea 05°28′S 143°40′E
15 N7 **Wabano** 〰 Québec, SE Canada
11 P11 **Wabasca** 〰 Alberta, SW Canada
31 P12 **Wabash** Indiana, N USA 40°47′N 85°48′W
29 X9 **Wabasha** Minnesota, N USA 44°22′N 92°01′W
31 N13 **Wabash River** 〰 N USA
14 C7 **Wabatongushi Lake** ◎ Ontario, S Canada
81 L15 **Wabē Gestro Wenz** 〰 SE Ethiopia
14 B9 **Wabos** Ontario, S Canada 46°48′N 84°06′W
11 W13 **Wabowden** Manitoba, C Canada 54°57′N 98°38′W
110 J9 **Wąbrzeźno** Kujawsko-pomorskie, C Poland 53°18′N 18°55′E
21 U12 **Waccamaw River** 〰 South Carolina, SE USA
23 U11 **Waccasassa Bay** *bay* Florida, SE USA
99 F16 **Wachtebeke** Oost-Vlaanderen, NW Belgium 51°10′N 03°52′E
25 T8 **Waco** Texas, SW USA 31°33′N 97°10′W
26 M3 **Waconda Lake** *var.* Great Elder Reservoir. ⊠ Kansas, C USA
Wadai *see* Ouaddaï
Wad Al-Hajarah *see* Guadalajara
164 I12 **Wadayama** Hyōgo, Honshū, SW Japan 35°19′N 134°51′E
80 D10 **Wad Banda** Western Kordofan, C Sudan 13°08′N 27°56′E
75 P9 **Waddān** NW Libya 29°10′N 16°08′E
98 J4 **Waddeneilanden** *Eng.* West Frisian Islands. *island group* N Netherlands
98 J6 **Waddenzee** *var.* Wadden Zee. *sea* SE North Sea
Wadden Zee *see* Waddenzee
10 L16 **Waddington, Mount** ▲ British Columbia, SW Canada 51°17′N 125°16′W
98 H12 **Waddinxveen** Zuid-Holland, C Netherlands 52°03′N 04°38′E
11 U15 **Wadena** Saskatchewan, S Canada 51°57′N 103°48′W
29 T6 **Wadena** Minnesota, N USA 46°27′N 95°07′W
108 G7 **Wädenswil** Zürich, N Switzerland 47°14′N 08°41′E
21 S11 **Wadesboro** North Carolina, SE USA 34°59′N 80°03′W
155 G16 **Wādi** Karnātaka, C India 17°00′N 76°58′E
138 G10 **Wādī as Sīr** *var.* Wadi es Sir. ʻAmmān, NW Jordan 31°57′N 35°49′E
Wadi es Sir *see* Wādī as Sīr
80 F5 **Wadi Halfa** *var.* Wādī Ḩalfā'. Northern, N Sudan 21°46′N 31°17′E
138 G13 **Wādī Mūsā** *var.* Petra. Ma'ān, S Jordan 30°19′N 35°29′E
23 V4 **Wadley** Georgia, SE USA 32°52′N 82°24′W
Wad Madanī *see* Wad Medani
80 G10 **Wad Medani** *var.* Wad Madanī. Gezira, C Sudan 14°24′N 33°30′E
80 F10 **Wad Nimr** White Nile, C Sudan 14°32′N 32°10′E
165 U16 **Wadomari** Kagoshima, Okinoerabu-jima, SW Japan 27°25′N 128°40′E
111 K17 **Wadowice** Małopolskie, S Poland 49°54′N 19°29′E
35 R5 **Wadsworth** Nevada, W USA 39°39′N 119°16′W
31 T12 **Wadsworth** Ohio, N USA 41°01′N 81°43′W
25 T11 **Waelder** Texas, SW USA 29°42′N 97°16′W
Waereghem *see* Waregem
163 U13 **Wafangdian** *var.* Fuxian, Fu Xian. Liaoning, NE China 39°36′N 122°00′E
171 R13 **Waflia** Pulau Buru, E Indonesia 03°10′S 126°05′E
Wagadugu *see* Ouagadougou
98 K12 **Wageningen** Gelderland, SE Netherlands 51°58′N 05°40′E
55 V9 **Wageningen** Nickerie, NW Suriname 05°44′N 56°45′W
9 O8 **Wager Bay** *inlet* Nunavut, N Canada
183 P10 **Wagga Wagga** New South Wales, SE Australia 35°11′S 147°22′E
180 J13 **Wagin** Western Australia 33°16′S 117°26′E
108 H8 **Wägitaler See** ◎ SW Switzerland
29 P12 **Wagner** South Dakota, N USA 43°04′N 98°17′W
27 Q9 **Wagoner** Oklahoma, C USA 35°58′N 92°23′W
37 U10 **Wagon Mound** New Mexico, SW USA 36°00′N 104°42′W
32 J14 **Wagontire** Oregon, NW USA 43°15′N 119°51′W
110 H10 **Wągrowiec** Wielkopolskie, C Poland 52°49′N 17°11′E
149 U6 **Wāh** Punjab, NE Pakistan 33°50′N 72°44′E
171 S13 **Wahai** Pulau Seram, E Indonesia 02°48′S 129°29′E
169 V10 **Wahau, Sungai** 〰 Borneo, C Indonesia
Wahaybah, Ramlat Al *see* Wahībah, Ramlat Āl
80 D13 **Wahda** *var.* Unity State. ◈ *state* S Sudan
38 D9 **Wahiawā** *var.* Wahiawa. O'ahu, Hawaii, USA, C Pacific Ocean 21°30′N 158°01′W
Wahībah, Ramlat Ahl *see* Wahībah, Ramlat Āl
141 Y9 **Wahībah, Ramlat Āl** *var.* Ramlat Ahl Wahībah, Ramlat Al Wahaybah, *Eng.* Wahībah Sands. *desert* N Oman
Wahībah Sands *see* Wahībah, Ramlat Āl
101 E16 **Wahn** ✈ (Köln) Nordrhein-Westfalen, W Germany 50°51′N 07°09′E
29 R15 **Wahoo** Nebraska, C USA 41°12′N 96°37′W
29 R6 **Wahpeton** North Dakota, N USA 46°16′N 96°36′W
Wahran *see* Oran
36 J6 **Wah Wah Mountains** ▲▲ Utah, W USA
38 D9 **Waialua** O'ahu, Hawaii, USA, C Pacific Ocean 21°34′N 158°07′W
38 D9 **Wai'anae** *var.* Waianae. O'ahu, Hawaii, USA, C Pacific Ocean 21°26′N 158°11′W
184 Q8 **Waiapu** 〰 North Island, New Zealand
185 I17 **Waiau** Canterbury, South Island, New Zealand 42°39′S 173°03′E
185 I17 **Waiau** 〰 South Island, New Zealand
185 B23 **Waiau** 〰 South Island, New Zealand
101 H21 **Waiblingen** Baden-Württemberg, S Germany 48°49′N 09°19′E
Waidhofen *see* Waidhofen an der Thaya, Niederösterreich, Austria
Waidhofen *see* Waidhofen an der Ybbs, Niederösterreich, Austria
109 V2 **Waidhofen an der Thaya** *var.* Waidhofen. Niederösterreich, NE Austria 48°49′N 15°17′E
109 U5 **Waidhofen an der Ybbs** *var.* Waidhofen. Niederösterreich, E Austria 47°58′N 14°47′E
171 T11 **Waigeo, Pulau** *island* Maluku, E Indonesia
184 L5 **Waiheke Island** *island* N New Zealand
184 M7 **Waihi** Waikato, North Island, New Zealand 37°22′S 175°51′E
185 C20 **Waihou** 〰 North Island, New Zealand
Waikaboebak *see* Waikabubak
171 N17 **Waikabubak** *prev.* Waikaboebak. Pulau Sumba, C Indonesia 09°40′S 119°25′E
185 D23 **Waikaia** 〰 South Island, New Zealand
185 D23 **Waikaka** Southland, South Island, New Zealand 45°55′S 168°59′E
184 L13 **Waikanae** Wellington, North Island, New Zealand 40°52′S 175°03′E
184 M7 **Waikare, Lake** ◎ North Island, New Zealand
184 O9 **Waikaremoana, Lake** ◎ North Island, New Zealand
185 I17 **Waikari** Canterbury, South Island, New Zealand 42°50′S 172°41′E
184 L8 **Waikato** *off.* Waikato Region. ◈ *region* North Island, New Zealand
184 M8 **Waikato** 〰 North Island, New Zealand
Waikato Region *see* Waikato
182 J9 **Waikerie** South Australia 34°12′S 139°57′E
185 F23 **Waikouaiti** Otago, South Island, New Zealand 45°36′S 170°39′E
38 H11 **Wailea** Hawaii, USA, C Pacific Ocean 19°53′N 155°07′W
38 F10 **Wailuku** Maui, Hawaii, USA, C Pacific Ocean 20°53′N 156°30′W
185 H18 **Waimakariri** 〰 South Island, New Zealand
38 D9 **Waimānalo Beach** *var.* Waimanalo Beach. O'ahu, Hawaii, USA, C Pacific Ocean 21°20′N 157°42′W
185 G15 **Waimangaroa** West Coast, South Island, New Zealand 41°41′S 171°49′E
185 G21 **Waimate** Canterbury, South Island, New Zealand 44°44′S 171°03′E
38 G11 **Waimea** *var.* Kamuela. Hawaii, USA, C Pacific Ocean 20°02′N 155°20′W
38 D9 **Waimea** *var.* Maunawai. O'ahu, Hawaii, USA, C Pacific Ocean 21°39′N 158°04′W
38 B8 **Waimea** Kaua'i, Hawaii, USA, C Pacific Ocean 21°57′N 159°40′W
99 M20 **Waimes** Liège, E Belgium 50°25′N 06°10′E
154 J11 **Wainganga** *var.* Wain River. 〰 C India
Waingapoe *see* Waingapu
171 N17 **Waingapu** *prev.* Waingapoe. Pulau Sumba, C Indonesia 09°40′S 120°16′E
55 S7 **Waini** 〰 N Guyana
55 S7 **Waini Point** *headland* NW Guyana 08°24′N 59°48′W
Wain River *see* Wainganga
11 R15 **Wainwright** Alberta, SW Canada 52°50′N 110°51′W
39 O5 **Wainwright** Alaska, USA 70°38′N 160°02′W
184 K4 **Waiotira** Northland, North Island, New Zealand 35°56′S 174°11′E
184 M11 **Waiouru** Manawatu-Wanganui, North Island, New Zealand 39°28′S 175°41′E
171 W14 **Waipa** Papua, E Indonesia 03°47′S 136°16′E
184 L8 **Waipa** 〰 North Island, New Zealand
184 P9 **Waipaoa** 〰 North Island, New Zealand
185 D25 **Waipapa Point** *headland* South Island, New Zealand 46°39′S 168°51′E
185 I18 **Waipara** Canterbury, South Island, New Zealand 43°04′S 172°45′E
184 N12 **Waipawa** Hawke's Bay, North Island, New Zealand 39°57′S 176°36′E
184 K4 **Waipu** Northland, North Island, New Zealand 35°58′S 174°25′E
184 N12 **Waipukurau** Hawke's Bay, North Island, New Zealand 40°01′S 176°34′E
171 U14 **Wair** Pulau Kai Besar, E Indonesia 05°16′S 133°09′E
Wairakai *see* Wairakei
184 N9 **Wairakei** *var.* Wairakai. Waikato, North Island, New Zealand 38°37′S 176°05′E
185 M14 **Wairarapa, Lake** ◎ North Island, New Zealand
185 J15 **Wairau** 〰 South Island, New Zealand
184 P10 **Wairoa** Hawke's Bay, North Island, New Zealand 39°03′S 177°26′E
184 P10 **Wairoa** 〰 North Island, New Zealand
184 J4 **Wairoa** 〰 North Island, New Zealand
184 N9 **Waitahanui** Waikato, North Island, New Zealand 38°48′S 176°04′E
184 M6 **Waitakaruru** Waikato, North Island, New Zealand 37°14′S 175°22′E
185 F21 **Waitaki** 〰 South Island, New Zealand
184 K10 **Waitara** Taranaki, North Island, New Zealand 39°01′S 174°14′E
184 M7 **Waitoa** Waikato, North Island, New Zealand 37°36′S 175°37′E
184 L8 **Waitomo Caves** Waikato, North Island, New Zealand 38°17′S 175°06′E
184 L11 **Waitotara** Taranaki, North Island, New Zealand 39°49′S 174°43′E
184 L11 **Waitotara** 〰 North Island, New Zealand
32 L10 **Waitsburg** Washington, NW USA 46°16′N 118°09′W
Waitzen *see* Vác
184 L6 **Waiuku** Auckland, North Island, New Zealand 37°15′S 174°45′E
164 L10 **Wajima** *var.* Wazima. Ishikawa, Honshū, SW Japan 37°23′N 136°53′E
81 K17 **Wajir** North Eastern, NE Kenya 01°46′N 40°05′E
79 J17 **Waka** Equateur, NW Dem. Rep. Congo 01°04′N 20°11′E
81 I14 **Waka** Southern Nationalities, S Ethiopia 07°12′N 37°19′E
14 D9 **Wakami Lake** ◎ Ontario, S Canada
164 I12 **Wakasa** Tottori, Honshū, SW Japan 35°18′N 134°25′E
164 J12 **Wakasa-wan** *bay* C Japan
185 C22 **Wakatipu, Lake** ◎ South Island, New Zealand
11 T15 **Wakaw** Saskatchewan, S Canada 52°40′N 105°45′W
164 I14 **Wakayama** Wakayama, Honshū, SW Japan 34°12′N 135°09′E
164 I15 **Wakayama** *off.* Wakayama-ken. ◈ *prefecture* Honshū, SW Japan
Wakayama-ken *see* Wakayama
26 K4 **Wa Keeney** Kansas, C USA 39°02′N 99°53′W
185 I14 **Wakefield** Tasman, South Island, New Zealand 41°24′S 173°03′E
97 M17 **Wakefield** N England, United Kingdom 53°42′N 01°29′W
27 O4 **Wakefield** Kansas, C USA 39°12′N 97°00′W
30 L4 **Wakefield** Michigan, N USA 46°27′N 89°55′W
21 U9 **Wake Forest** North Carolina, SE USA 35°58′N 78°30′W
Wakeham Bay *see* Kangiqsujuaq
189 Y11 **Wake Island** ◇ *US unincorporated territory* NW Pacific Ocean
189 Y12 **Wake Island** ✈ NW Pacific Ocean
189 Y12 **Wake Island** *atoll* NW Pacific Ocean
189 X12 **Wake Lagoon** *lagoon* Wake Island, NW Pacific Ocean
166 L8 **Wakema** Ayeyarwady, SW Myanmar (Burma) 16°36′N 95°11′E
Wakhan *see* Khandūd
164 H14 **Waki** Tokushima, Shikoku, SW Japan 34°04′N 134°10′E
165 T1 **Wakkanai** Hokkaidō, NE Japan 45°25′N 141°39′E
83 K22 **Wakkerstroom** Mpumalanga, E South Africa 27°21′S 30°10′E
14 C10 **Wakomata Lake** ◎ Ontario, S Canada
183 N10 **Wakool** New South Wales, SE Australia 35°30′S 144°22′E
Wakra *see* Al Wakrah
Waku Kungo *see* Uaco Cungo
186 J7 **Wakunai** Bougainville Island, NE Papua New Guinea 05°52′S 155°10′E
Walachei/Walachia *see* Wallachia
155 K26 **Walawe Ganga** 〰 S Sri Lanka
111 F15 **Wałbrzych** *Ger.* Waldenburg, Waldenburg in Schlesien. Dolnośląskie, SW Poland 50°45′N 16°20′E
183 T6 **Walcha** New South Wales, SE Australia 31°01′S 151°38′E
101 K24 **Walchensee** ◎ SE Germany
99 D14 **Walcheren** *island* SW Netherlands
29 Z14 **Walcott** Iowa, C USA 41°34′N 90°46′W
33 W16 **Walcott** Wyoming, C USA 41°46′N 106°46′W
99 G21 **Walcourt** Namur, S Belgium 50°16′N 04°26′E
110 G9 **Wałcz** *Ger.* Deutsch Krone. Zachodnio-pomorskie, NW Poland 53°17′N 16°29′E
108 H7 **Wald** Zürich, N Switzerland 47°17′N 08°56′E
109 U3 **Waldaist** 〰 N Austria
180 I9 **Waldburg Range** ▲▲ Western Australia
37 R3 **Walden** Colorado, C USA 40°43′N 106°16′W
18 K13 **Walden** New York, NE USA 41°35′N 74°09′W
Waldenburg/Waldenburg in Schlesien *see* Wałbrzych
11 T15 **Waldheim** Saskatchewan, S Canada 52°38′N 106°35′W
Waldia *see* Weldiya
101 M23 **Waldkraiburg** Bayern, SE Germany 48°10′N 12°23′E
27 T14 **Waldo** Arkansas, C USA 33°21′N 93°18′W
23 V9 **Waldo** Florida, SE USA 29°47′N 82°07′W
19 R7 **Waldoboro** Maine, NE USA 44°06′N 69°22′W
21 W4 **Waldorf** Maryland, NE USA 38°36′N 76°54′W
32 F12 **Waldport** Oregon, NW USA 44°25′N 124°04′W
27 S11 **Waldron** Arkansas, C USA 34°54′N 94°09′W
195 Y13 **Waldron, Cape** *headland* Antarctica 66°08′S 116°00′E
101 F24 **Waldshut-Tiengen** Baden-Württemberg, S Germany 47°37′N 08°13′E
171 P12 **Walea, Selat** *strait* Sulawesi, C Indonesia
Wałeckie Międzyrzecze *see* Valašské Meziříčí
108 H8 **Walensee** ◎ NW Switzerland
38 L8 **Wales** Alaska, USA 65°36′N 168°03′W
97 J20 **Wales** *Wel.* Cymru. ◈ *national region* Wales, United Kingdom
9 O7 **Wales Island** *island* Nunavut, NE Canada
77 P14 **Walewale** N Ghana 10°21′N 00°48′W
99 M24 **Walferdange** Luxembourg, C Luxembourg 49°39′N 06°08′E
183 Q5 **Walgett** New South Wales, SE Australia 30°02′S 148°14′E
194 K10 **Walgreen Coast** *physical region* Antarctica
29 Q2 **Walhalla** North Dakota, N USA 48°55′N 97°55′W
21 O11 **Walhalla** South Carolina, SE USA 34°46′N 83°05′W
79 O19 **Walikale** Nord-Kivu, E Dem. Rep. Congo 01°29′S 28°05′E
Walk *see* Valga, Estonia

◆ Country
● Country Capital
◇ Dependent Territory
○ Dependent Territory Capital
◈ Administrative Regions
✈ International Airport
▲ Mountain
▲▲ Mountain Range
⩘ Volcano
〰 River
◎ Lake
⊠ Reservoir

WALK – WELLINGBOROUGH

Walk see Valka, Latvia
29 U5 Walker Minnesota, N USA 47°06'N 94°35'W
15 V4 Walker, Lac ◎ Québec, SE Canada
35 S7 Walker Lake ◎ Nevada, W USA
35 R6 Walker River ⇝ Nevada, W USA
28 K10 Wall South Dakota, N USA 43°58'N 102°12'W
173 U9 Wallaby Plateau undersea feature E Indian Ocean
33 N8 Wallace Idaho, NW USA 47°28'N 115°55'W
21 V11 Wallace North Carolina, SE USA 34°42'N 77°59'W
14 D17 Wallaceburg Ontario, S Canada 42°34'N 82°22'W
22 F5 Wallace Lake ▣ Louisiana, S USA
11 P13 Wallace Mountain ▲ Alberta, W Canada 54°50'N 115°57'W
116 J14 Wallachia var. Walachia, Ger. Walachei, Rom. Valachia. cultural region S Romania
Wallachisch-Meseritsch see Valašské Meziříčí
183 U4 Wallangarra New South Wales, SE Australia 28°56'S 151°57'E
182 I8 Wallaroo South Australia 33°56'S 137°38'E
32 L10 Walla Walla Washington, NW USA 46°03'N 118°20'W
45 V9 Wall Blake ✈ (The Valley) C Anguilla 18°12'N 63°02'W
101 H19 Walldürn Baden-Württemberg, SW Germany 49°34'N 09°22'E
100 F12 Wallenhorst Niedersachsen, NW Germany 52°21'N 08°01'E
Wallenthal see Haţeg
109 S4 Wallern Oberösterreich, N Austria 48°13'N 13°58'E
Wallern see Wallern im Burgenland
109 Z5 Wallern im Burgenland var. Wallern. Burgenland, E Austria 47°44'N 16°57'E
18 M9 Wallingford Vermont, NE USA 43°27'N 72°56'W
25 V11 Wallis Texas, SW USA 29°38'N 96°05'W
Wallis see Valais
192 K9 Wallis and Futuna Fr. Territoire de Wallis et Futuna. ◇ French overseas territory C Pacific Ocean
108 G7 Wallisellen Zürich, N Switzerland 47°25'N 08°36'E
Wallis et Futuna, Territoire de see Wallis and Futuna
190 H11 Wallis, Îles island group N Wallis and Futuna
31 Q5 Walloon Lake ◎ Michigan, N USA
32 K10 Wallula Washington, NW USA 46°03'N 118°54'W
32 K10 Wallula, Lake ◎ Washington, NW USA
21 S8 Walnut Cove North Carolina, SE USA 36°18'N 80°08'W
35 N8 Walnut Creek California, W USA 37°52'N 122°04'W
26 K5 Walnut Creek ⇝ Kansas, C USA
27 W9 Walnut Ridge Arkansas, C USA 36°06'N 90°56'W
25 S7 Walnut Springs Texas, SW USA 32°05'N 97°42'W
182 L10 Walpeup Victoria, SE Australia 35°09'S 142°01'E
187 R17 Walpole, Île island SE New Caledonia
39 N13 Walrus Islands island group Alaska, USA
97 L19 Walsall C England, United Kingdom 52°35'N 01°58'W
37 T7 Walsenburg Colorado, C USA 37°37'N 104°46'W
11 S17 Walsh Alberta, SW Canada 49°58'N 110°03'W
37 W7 Walsh Colorado, C USA 37°20'N 102°17'W
100 I11 Walsrode Niedersachsen, NW Germany 52°52'N 09°36'E
Waltenberg see Zalău
21 R14 Walterboro South Carolina, SE USA 32°54'N 80°21'W
Walter F.George Lake see Walter F.George Reservoir
23 R6 Walter F. George Reservoir var. Walter F.George Lake. ▣ Alabama/Georgia, SE USA
26 M12 Walters Oklahoma, C USA 34°22'N 98°18'W
101 J16 Waltershausen Thüringen, C Germany 50°53'N 10°33'E
173 N10 Walters Shoal var. Walters Shoals. reef S Madagascar
Walters Shoals see Walters Shoal
22 M3 Walthall Mississippi, S USA 33°36'N 89°16'W
20 M4 Walton Kentucky, S USA 38°52'N 84°36'W
18 J11 Walton New York, NE USA 42°10'N 75°07'W
159 R16 Walung Xizang Zizhiqu, W China 28°07'N 97°00'E
79 O20 Walungu Sud-Kivu, E Dem. Rep. Congo 02°40'S 28°37'E
Walvisbaai see Walvis Bay
83 C19 Walvis Bay Afr. Walvisbaai. Erongo, NW Namibia 22°59'S 14°31'E
83 B19 Walvis Bay bay NW Namibia
Walvish Ridge see Walvis Ridge
65 O17 Walvis Ridge var. Walvish Ridge. undersea feature E Atlantic Ocean 28°00'S 03°00'E
171 X16 Wamal Papua, E Indonesia 08°00'S 139°06'E
171 U15 Wamar, Pulau island Kepulauan Aru, E Indonesia
79 O17 Wamba Orientale, NE Dem. Rep. Congo 02°10'N 27°59'E
77 V15 Wamba Nassarawa, C Nigeria 08°57'N 08°35'E
79 H22 Wamba var. Uamba. ⇝ Angola/Dem. Rep. Congo
27 P4 Wamego Kansas, C USA 39°12'N 96°18'W
18 I10 Wampsville New York, NE USA 43°03'N 75°40'W
42 K6 Wampú, Río ⇝ E Honduras
171 X16 Wan Papua, E Indonesia 08°15'S 138°00'E
Wan see Anhui
183 N4 Wanaaring New South Wales, SE Australia 29°42'S 144°07'E
185 D21 Wanaka Otago, South Island, New Zealand 44°42'S 169°09'E
185 D20 Wanaka, Lake ◎ South Island, New Zealand
171 W14 Wanapiri Papua, E Indonesia 04°21'S 135°52'E
14 F9 Wanapitei ⇝ Ontario, S Canada
14 F10 Wanapitei Lake ◎ Ontario, S Canada
18 K14 Wanaque New Jersey, NE USA 41°02'N 74°17'W
171 U12 Wanau Papua, E Indonesia 01°20'S 132°40'E
185 F22 Wanbrow, Cape headland South Island, New Zealand 45°07'S 170°59'E
Wancheng see Wanning
Wanchuan see Zhangjiakou
171 W13 Wandai var. Komeyo. Papua, E Indonesia 03°35'S 136°15'E
163 Z8 Wanda Shan ▲▲ NE China
197 R11 Wandel Sea sea Arctic Ocean
160 D13 Wanding var. Wandingzhen. Yunnan, SW China 24°01'N 98°00'E
Wandingzhen see Wanding
99 H20 Wanfercée-Baulet Hainaut, S Belgium 50°27'N 04°37'E
184 L12 Wanganui Manawatu-Wanganui, North Island, New Zealand 39°56'S 175°02'E
184 L11 Wanganui ⇝ North Island, New Zealand
183 P11 Wangaratta Victoria, SE Australia 36°22'S 146°17'E
160 J8 Wangcang var. Donghe; prev. Fengjiaba, Hongjiang. Sichuan, C China 32°15'N 106°16'E
Wangda see Zogang
101 I24 Wangen im Allgäu Baden-Württemberg, S Germany 47°40'N 09°49'E
Wangerin see Węgorzyno
100 F9 Wangerooge island NW Germany
171 W13 Wanggar Papua, E Indonesia 03°22'S 135°15'E
160 J13 Wangmo var. Fuxing. Guizhou, S China 25°08'N 106°08'E
Wangolodougou see Ouangolodougou
161 S9 Wangpan Yang sea E China
163 Y10 Wangqing Jilin, NE China 43°19'N 129°42'E
167 P8 Wang Saphung Loei, C Thailand 17°18'N 101°45'E
167 O6 Wan Hsa-la Shan State, E Myanmar (Burma) 20°27'N 98°39'E
55 W9 Wanica ◆ district N Suriname
79 M18 Wanie-Rukula Orientale, C Dem. Rep. Congo 0°13'N 25°34'E
Wankie see Hwange
Wanki, Río see Coco, Río
81 N17 Wanlaweyn var. Wanle Weyn, It. Uanle Uen. Shabeellaha Hoose, SW Somalia 02°36'N 44°47'E
Wanle Weyn see Wanlaweyn
180 I12 Wanneroo Western Australia 31°40'S 115°35'E
160 L17 Wanning var. Wancheng. Hainan, S China 18°55'N 110°27'E
167 Q8 Wanon Niwat Sakon Nakhon, E Thailand 17°39'N 103°45'E
155 H16 Wanparti Andhra Pradesh, C India 16°19'N 78°06'E
Wansen see Wiązów
160 L11 Wanshan Guizhou, S China 27°45'N 109°12'E
99 M14 Wanssum Limburg, SE Netherlands 51°31'N 06°04'E
184 N12 Wanstead Hawke's Bay, North Island, New Zealand 40°09'S 176°31'E
Wanxian see Wanzhou
188 F16 Wanyaan Yap, Micronesia
160 K8 Wanyuan Sichuan, C China 32°05'N 108°08'E
161 O11 Wanzai var. Kangle. Jiangxi, S China 28°06'N 114°27'E
99 J20 Wanze Liège, E Belgium 50°32'N 05°16'E
160 K9 Wanzhou var. Wanxian. Chongqing Shi, C China 30°48'N 108°21'E
31 R12 Wapakoneta Ohio, N USA 40°34'N 84°11'W
12 D7 Wapaseese ⇝ Ontario, C Canada
32 I10 Wapato Washington, NW USA 46°27'N 120°25'W
29 Y15 Wapello Iowa, C USA 41°10'N 91°13'W
11 N13 Wapiti ⇝ Alberta/British Columbia, SW Canada
27 X7 Wappapello Lake ▣ Missouri, C USA
18 K13 Wappingers Falls New York, NE USA 41°36'N 73°54'W
29 X13 Wapsipinicon River ⇝ Iowa, C USA
14 L9 Wapus ⇝ Québec, SE Canada
160 H7 Waqên Sichuan, C China 33°05'N 102°34'E
21 Q7 War West Virginia, NE USA 37°18'N 81°39'W
80 D13 Warab Warab, SW Sudan 08°08'N 28°37'E
81 D14 Warab ◆ state SW Sudan
155 J15 Warangal Andhra Pradesh, C India 18°N 79°35'E
Warasdin see Varaždin
183 O16 Waratah Tasmania, SE Australia 41°28'S 145°34'E
183 O14 Waratah Bay bay Victoria, SE Australia
101 H15 Warburg Nordrhein-Westfalen, W Germany 51°30'N 09°11'E
182 I1 Warburton Creek seasonal river South Australia
180 M9 Warburton Western Australia 26°17'S 126°18'E
99 M20 Warche ⇝ E Belgium
Wardag/Wardak see Vardak
32 K9 Warden Washington, NW USA 46°58'N 119°02'W
154 I12 Wardha Mahārāshtra, W India 20°41'N 78°40'E
Wardija Point see Wardija, Ras il-
121 N15 Wardija, Ras il- var. Wardija Point. headland Gozo, NW Malta 36°03'N 14°11'E
139 P3 Wardiyah Nīnawá, N Iraq 36°18'N 41°45'E
185 E19 Ward, Mount ▲ South Island, New Zealand 43°49'S 169°54'E
10 L11 Ware British Columbia, W Canada 57°26'N 125°41'W
99 D18 Waregem var. Waereghem. West-Vlaanderen, W Belgium 50°53'N 03°26'E
99 J19 Waremme Liège, E Belgium 50°41'N 05°15'E
100 N10 Waren Mecklenburg-Vorpommern, NE Germany 53°32'N 12°42'E
171 W13 Waren Papua, E Indonesia 02°13'S 136°21'E
101 F14 Warendorf Nordrhein-Westfalen, W Germany 51°57'N 08°00'E
21 P12 Ware Shoals South Carolina, SE USA 34°24'N 82°15'W
98 N4 Warffum Groningen, NE Netherlands 53°22'N 06°34'E
81 O15 Wargalo Mudug, E Somalia 06°06'N 47°40'E
146 M12 Warganza Rus. Varganzi. Qashqadaryo Viloyati, S Uzbekistan 39°18'N 66°00'E
Wargla see Ouargla
183 T4 Warialda New South Wales, SE Australia 29°34'S 150°35'E
154 F13 Wāri Godri Mahārāshtra, C India 19°28'N 75°43'E
167 R10 Warin Chamrap Ubon Ratchathani, E Thailand 15°11'N 104°51'E
25 R11 Waring Texas, SW USA 29°56'N 98°48'W
39 O8 Waring Mountains ▲▲ Alaska, USA
110 M12 Warka Mazowieckie, E Poland 51°45'N 21°12'E
184 L5 Warkworth Auckland, North Island, New Zealand 36°23'S 174°42'E
171 U12 Warmandi Papua, E Indonesia 0°21'S 132°38'E
83 E22 Warmbad Karas, S Namibia 28°29'S 18°41'E
98 H8 Warmenhuizen Noord-Holland, NW Netherlands 52°43'N 04°45'E
110 M8 Warmińsko-Mazurskie ◆ province C Poland
97 L22 Warminster S England, United Kingdom 51°13'N 02°12'W
18 I15 Warminster Pennsylvania, NE USA 40°11'N 75°04'W
35 V8 Warm Springs Nevada, W USA 38°10'N 116°21'W
32 H12 Warm Springs Oregon, NW USA 44°51'N 121°24'W
21 S5 Warm Springs Virginia, NE USA 38°03'N 79°48'W
100 M8 Warnemünde Mecklenburg-Vorpommern, NE Germany 54°10'N 12°03'E
27 Q10 Warner Oklahoma, C USA 35°29'N 95°18'W
35 Q2 Warner Mountains ▲▲ California, W USA
23 T5 Warner Robins Georgia, SE USA 32°38'N 83°38'W
57 N18 Warnes Santa Cruz, C Bolivia 17°30'S 63°11'W
100 M9 Warnow ⇝ NE Germany
Warnsdorf see Varnsdorf
98 M11 Warnsveld Gelderland, E Netherlands 52°08'N 06°14'E
154 I13 Warora Mahārāshtra, C India 20°12'N 79°01'E
182 L11 Warracknabeal Victoria, SE Australia 36°17'S 142°26'E
183 O13 Warragul Victoria, SE Australia 38°11'S 145°55'E
183 O4 Warrego River seasonal river New South Wales/ Queensland, E Australia
183 Q6 Warren New South Wales, SE Australia 31°41'S 147°51'E
11 X16 Warren Manitoba, S Canada 50°05'N 97°33'W
27 V14 Warren Arkansas, C USA 33°38'N 92°05'W
31 S10 Warren Michigan, N USA 42°29'N 83°02'W
29 R3 Warren Minnesota, N USA 48°12'N 96°46'W
31 U11 Warren Ohio, N USA 41°14'N 80°49'W
18 D12 Warren Pennsylvania, NE USA 41°52'N 79°09'W
25 X10 Warren Texas, SW USA 30°33'N 94°24'W
97 G16 Warrenpoint Ir. An Pointe. SE Northern Ireland, United Kingdom 54°07'N 06°16'W
27 S4 Warrensburg Missouri, C USA 38°46'N 93°44'W
83 H22 Warrenton Northern Cape, N South Africa 28°07'S 24°51'E
23 U4 Warrenton Georgia, SE USA 33°24'N 82°39'W
27 W4 Warrenton Missouri, C USA 38°48'N 91°08'W
21 V8 Warrenton North Carolina, SE USA 36°24'N 78°11'W
21 V4 Warrenton Virginia, NE USA 38°43'N 77°48'W
77 U17 Warri Delta, S Nigeria 05°26'N 05°34'E
97 L18 Warrington C England, United Kingdom 53°24'N 02°37'W
23 O9 Warrington Florida, SE USA 30°22'N 87°16'W
23 P3 Warrior Alabama, S USA 33°49'N 86°49'W
182 L13 Warrnambool Victoria, SE Australia 38°23'S 142°30'E
29 T2 Warroad Minnesota, N USA 48°55'N 95°18'W
183 S6 Warrumbungle Range ▲▲ New South Wales, SE Australia
154 J12 Wārsa Mahārāshtra, C India 20°42'N 79°58'E
31 P11 Warsaw Indiana, N USA 41°13'N 85°52'W
20 L4 Warsaw Kentucky, S USA 38°47'N 84°55'W
27 T5 Warsaw Missouri, C USA 38°14'N 93°23'W
18 E10 Warsaw New York, NE USA 42°44'N 78°06'W
21 V10 Warsaw North Carolina, SE USA 35°00'N 78°05'W
21 X5 Warsaw Virginia, NE USA 37°57'N 76°46'W
Warsaw/Warschau see Warszawa
81 N17 Warshiikh Shabeellaha Dhexe, C Somalia 02°22'N 45°52'E
101 G15 Warstein Nordrhein-Westfalen, W Germany 51°27'N 08°21'E
110 M11 Warszawa Eng. Warsaw, Ger. Warschau, Rus. Varshava. ● (Poland) Mazowieckie, C Poland 52°15'N 21°E
110 J13 Warta Sieradz, C Poland 51°43'N 18°37'E
110 D11 Warta Ger. Warthe. ⇝ W Poland
Wartberg see Senec
20 M9 Wartburg Tennessee, S USA 36°08'N 84°37'W
108 J7 Warth Vorarlberg, NW Austria 47°16'N 10°11'E
Warthe see Warta
169 U12 Waru Borneo, C Indonesia 01°24'S 116°37'E
171 T13 Waru Pulau Seram, E Indonesia 03°24'S 130°38'E
139 N6 Wa'r, Wādī al dry watercourse E Syria
183 U3 Warwick Queensland, E Australia 28°12'S 152°E
15 Q11 Warwick Québec, SE Canada 45°55'N 72°00'W
97 M20 Warwick C England, United Kingdom 52°17'N 01°34'W
18 K13 Warwick New York, NE USA 41°15'N 74°21'W
29 P4 Warwick North Dakota, N USA 47°49'N 98°42'W
19 O12 Warwick Rhode Island, NE USA 41°40'N 71°21'W
97 L20 Warwickshire cultural region C England, United Kingdom
14 G14 Wasaga Beach Ontario, S Canada 44°30'N 80°00'W
77 U13 Wasagu Kebbi, NW Nigeria 11°25'N 05°48'E
36 M2 Wasatch Range ▲▲ W USA
35 R12 Wasco California, W USA 35°34'N 119°20'W
29 V10 Waseca Minnesota, N USA 44°04'N 93°30'W
14 H13 Washago Ontario, S Canada 44°46'N 78°48'W
19 S2 Washburn Maine, NE USA 46°46'N 68°08'W
28 M5 Washburn North Dakota, N USA 47°15'N 101°02'W
30 K3 Washburn Wisconsin, N USA 46°41'N 90°53'W
31 S14 Washburn Hill hill Ohio, N USA
154 H13 Wāshīm Mahārāshtra, C India 20°06'N 77°08'E
97 M14 Washington NE England, United Kingdom 54°54'N 01°31'W
23 U3 Washington Georgia, SE USA 33°44'N 82°44'W
30 L12 Washington Illinois, N USA 40°42'N 89°24'W
31 N15 Washington Indiana, N USA 38°40'N 87°10'W
29 X15 Washington Iowa, C USA 41°18'N 91°41'W
27 O3 Washington Kansas, C USA 39°49'N 97°03'W
27 W5 Washington Missouri, C USA 38°31'N 91°01'W
21 X9 Washington North Carolina, SE USA 35°33'N 77°04'W
18 B15 Washington Pennsylvania, NE USA 40°11'N 80°16'W
25 V10 Washington Texas, SW USA 30°18'N 96°08'W
36 J8 Washington Utah, W USA 37°07'N 113°30'W
21 V4 Washington Virginia, NE USA 38°43'N 78°11'W
32 I9 Washington off. State of Washington, also known as Chinook State, Evergreen State. ◆ state NW USA
Washington see Washington Court House
31 S14 Washington Court House var. Washington. Ohio, NE USA 39°32'N 83°29'W
21 W4 Washington DC ● (USA) District of Columbia, NE USA 38°54'N 77°02'W
31 O5 Washington Island island Wisconsin, N USA
Washington Island see Teraina
19 O7 Washington, Mount ▲ New Hampshire, NE USA 44°16'N 71°18'W
26 M11 Washita River ⇝ Oklahoma/Texas, C USA
97 O18 Wash, The inlet E England, United Kingdom
32 L9 Washtucna Washington, NW USA 46°44'N 118°19'W
Wasiliszki see Vasilishki
110 P9 Wasilków Podlaskie, NE Poland 53°12'N 23°15'E
39 R11 Wasilla Alaska, USA 61°34'N 149°26'W
139 V9 Wāsiţ ◆ governorate E Iraq
55 U9 Wasjabo Sipaliwini, NW Suriname 05°09'N 57°09'W
12 I10 Waskaganish prev. Fort Rupert, Rupert House. Québec, SE Canada 51°30'N 79°45'W
11 X11 Waskaiowaka Lake ◎ Manitoba, C Canada
11 T14 Waskesiu Lake Saskatchewan, C Canada 53°56'N 106°05'W
25 X7 Waskom Texas, SW USA 32°28'N 94°03'W
110 G13 Wąsosz Dolnośląskie, SW Poland 51°36'N 16°30'E
42 M6 Waspam var. Waspán. Región Autónoma Atlántico Norte, NE Nicaragua 14°41'N 84°04'W
Waspán see Waspam
165 T3 Wassamu Hokkaidō, NE Japan 44°01'N 142°25'E
108 G9 Wassen Uri, C Switzerland 46°42'N 08°34'E
98 G11 Wassenaar Zuid-Holland, W Netherlands 52°09'N 04°23'E
99 N24 Wasserbillig Grevenmacher, E Luxembourg 49°43'N 06°30'E
Wasserburg see Wasserburg am Inn
101 M23 Wasserburg am Inn var. Wasserburg. Bayern, SE Germany 48°02'N 12°12'E
101 I17 Wasserkuppe ▲ C Germany 50°30'N 09°55'E
103 R5 Wassy Haute-Marne, N France 48°32'N 04°54'E
171 N14 Watampone var. Bone. Sulawesi, C Indonesia 04°33'S 120°20'E
171 R13 Watawa Pulau Buru, E Indonesia 03°36'S 127°13'E
Watenstedt-Salzgitter see Salzgitter
18 M13 Waterbury Connecticut, NE USA 41°33'N 73°01'W
21 R11 Wateree Lake ▣ South Carolina, SE USA
21 R12 Wateree River ⇝ South Carolina, SE USA
97 E20 Waterford Ir. Port Láirge. Waterford, S Ireland 52°15'N 07°08'W
31 S9 Waterford Michigan, N USA 42°42'N 83°24'W
97 E20 Waterford Ir. Port Láirge. cultural region S Ireland
97 E21 Waterford Harbour Ir. Cuan Phort Láirge. inlet S Ireland
98 G12 Wateringen Zuid-Holland, W Netherlands 52°02'N 04°16'E
99 G19 Waterloo Walloon Brabant, C Belgium 50°43'N 04°24'E
14 F16 Waterloo Ontario, S Canada 43°28'N 80°32'W
15 P12 Waterloo Québec, SE Canada 45°20'N 72°28'W
30 K16 Waterloo Illinois, N USA 38°20'N 90°09'W
29 X13 Waterloo Iowa, C USA 42°31'N 92°16'W
18 G10 Waterloo New York, NE USA 42°54'N 76°51'W
30 L4 Watersmeet Michigan, N USA 46°16'N 89°10'W
23 V9 Watertown Florida, SE USA 30°11'N 82°36'W
18 I8 Watertown New York, NE USA 43°37'N 75°56'W
29 R9 Watertown South Dakota, N USA 44°54'N 97°07'W
30 M8 Watertown Wisconsin, N USA 43°12'N 88°44'W
22 L3 Water Valley Mississippi, S USA 34°09'N 89°37'W
27 O3 Waterville Kansas, C USA 39°41'N 96°45'W
17 V6 Waterville Maine, NE USA 44°34'N 69°41'W
29 V10 Waterville Minnesota, N USA 44°13'N 93°34'W
18 I10 Waterville New York, NE USA 42°55'N 75°18'W
14 E16 Watford Ontario, S Canada 42°57'N 81°51'W
97 N21 Watford E England, United Kingdom 51°39'N 00°24'W
28 K4 Watford City North Dakota, N USA 47°48'N 103°16'W
141 X12 Wāţif S Oman 18°34'N 56°31'E
18 G11 Watkins Glen New York, NE USA 42°23'N 76°53'W
Watlings Island see San Salvador
171 U15 Watnil Pulau Kai Kecil, E Indonesia 05°45'S 132°39'E
26 M10 Watonga Oklahoma, C USA 35°52'N 98°26'W
11 T16 Watrous Saskatchewan, S Canada 51°40'N 105°29'W
37 T10 Watrous New Mexico, SW USA 35°48'N 104°58'W
79 P16 Watsa Orientale, NE Dem. Rep. Congo 03°00'N 29°31'E
31 N12 Watseka Illinois, N USA 40°46'N 87°44'W
79 J19 Watsikengo Equateur, C Dem. Rep. Congo 0°49'S 20°34'E
182 C5 Watson South Australia 30°32'S 131°29'E
11 U15 Watson Saskatchewan, S Canada 52°13'N 104°30'W
195 O10 Watson Escarpment ▲ Antarctica
10 K9 Watson Lake Yukon Territory, W Canada 60°05'N 128°47'W
35 N10 Watsonville California, W USA 36°53'N 121°43'W
167 Q8 Wattay ✈ (Viangchan) Viangchan, C Laos 18°03'N 102°36'E
109 N7 Wattens Tirol, W Austria 47°18'N 11°37'E
20 M9 Watts Bar Lake ▣ Tennessee, S USA
108 H7 Wattwil Sankt Gallen, NE Switzerland 47°18'N 09°06'E
171 T14 Watubela, Kepulauan island group E Indonesia
101 N24 Watzmann ▲ SE Germany 47°32'N 12°56'E
186 E8 Wau Morobe, C Papua New Guinea 07°22'S 146°40'E
81 D14 Wau var. Wāw. Western Bahr el Ghazal, S Sudan 07°43'N 28°01'E
29 Q8 Waubay South Dakota, N USA 45°19'N 97°18'W
29 Q8 Waubay Lake ◎ South Dakota, N USA
183 U7 Wauchope New South Wales, SE Australia 31°30'S 152°46'E
23 W13 Wauchula Florida, SE USA 27°33'N 81°48'W
30 M10 Wauconda Illinois, N USA 42°15'N 88°08'W
182 J7 Waukaringa South Australia 32°19'S 139°27'E
31 N10 Waukegan Illinois, N USA 42°21'N 87°50'W
30 M9 Waukesha Wisconsin, N USA 43°01'N 88°14'W
29 X11 Waukon Iowa, C USA 43°16'N 91°28'W
30 L8 Waunakee Wisconsin, N USA 43°13'N 89°28'W
30 L7 Waupaca Wisconsin, N USA 44°23'N 89°04'W
30 M8 Waupun Wisconsin, N USA 43°40'N 88°43'W
26 M13 Waurika Oklahoma, C USA 34°10'N 98°00'W
26 M12 Waurika Lake ▣ Oklahoma, C USA
30 L6 Wausau Wisconsin, N USA 44°58'N 89°40'W
31 R11 Wauseon Ohio, N USA 41°33'N 84°08'W
30 L7 Wautoma Wisconsin, N USA 44°05'N 89°17'W
30 M9 Wauwatosa Wisconsin, N USA 43°03'N 88°03'W
22 L9 Waveland Mississippi, S USA 30°17'N 89°22'W
97 Q20 Waveney ⇝ E England, United Kingdom
184 L11 Waverley Taranaki, North Island, New Zealand 39°45'S 174°35'E
29 W12 Waverly Iowa, C USA 42°43'N 92°28'W
27 T4 Waverly Missouri, C USA 39°12'N 93°31'W
29 R15 Waverly Nebraska, C USA 40°56'N 96°27'W
18 G12 Waverly New York, NE USA 42°00'N 76°33'W
20 H8 Waverly Tennessee, S USA 36°04'N 87°49'W
21 W7 Waverly Virginia, NE USA 37°02'N 77°06'W
99 H19 Wavre Walloon Brabant, C Belgium 50°43'N 04°37'E
166 M8 Waw Bago, SW Myanmar (Burma) 17°26'N 96°40'E
Wāw see Wau
14 B7 Wawa Ontario, S Canada 47°59'N 84°43'W
77 T14 Wawa Niger, W Nigeria 09°52'N 04°33'E
75 Q11 Wāw al Kabīr S Libya 25°21'N 16°41'E
43 N7 Wawa, Río var. Río Huahua. ⇝ NE Nicaragua
186 B8 Wawoi ⇝ SW Papua New Guinea
25 T7 Waxahachie Texas, SW USA 32°23'N 96°52'W
158 L9 Waxxari Xinjiang Uygur Zizhiqu, NW China 38°43'N 87°11'E
Wayaobu see Zichang
23 V7 Waycross Georgia, SE USA 31°13'N 82°21'W
180 K10 Way, Lake ◎ Western Australia
31 P9 Wayland Michigan, N USA 42°40'N 85°38'W
29 R13 Wayne Nebraska, C USA 42°13'N 97°01'W
18 K14 Wayne New Jersey, NE USA 40°57'N 74°16'W
21 P5 Wayne West Virginia, NE USA 38°14'N 82°27'W
23 V4 Waynesboro Georgia, SE USA 33°04'N 82°01'W
22 M7 Waynesboro Mississippi, S USA 31°40'N 88°39'W
20 H10 Waynesboro Tennessee, S USA 35°20'N 87°49'W
21 U5 Waynesboro Virginia, NE USA 38°04'N 78°54'W
18 B16 Waynesburg Pennsylvania, NE USA 39°51'N 80°10'W
27 U6 Waynesville Missouri, C USA 37°48'N 92°11'W
21 O10 Waynesville North Carolina, SE USA 35°29'N 82°59'W
26 L8 Waynoka Oklahoma, C USA 36°36'N 98°53'W
Wazan see Ouazzane
Wazima see Wajima
149 V7 Wazīrābād Punjab, NE Pakistan 32°28'N 74°04'E
Wazzan see Ouazzane
110 I8 Wda var. Czarna Woda, Ger. Schwarzwasser. ⇝ N Poland
187 Q16 Wé Province des Îles Loyauté, E New Caledonia 20°55'S 167°15'E
97 O23 Weald, The lowlands SE England, United Kingdom
186 A9 Weam Western, SW Papua New Guinea 08°33'S 141°10'E
97 L15 Wear ⇝ N England, United Kingdom
Wearmouth see Sunderland
26 L10 Weatherford Oklahoma, C USA 35°31'N 98°42'W
25 S6 Weatherford Texas, SW USA 32°47'N 97°48'W
34 M3 Weaverville California, W USA 40°42'N 122°57'W
27 R7 Webb City Missouri, C USA 37°07'N 94°28'W
192 G8 Weber Basin undersea feature S Ceram Sea
Webfoot State see Oregon
18 F9 Webster New York, NE USA 43°12'N 77°25'W
29 Q8 Webster South Dakota, N USA 45°19'N 97°31'W
29 V13 Webster City Iowa, C USA 42°28'N 93°49'W
27 X5 Webster Groves Missouri, C USA 38°32'N 90°20'W
21 S4 Webster Springs var. Addison. West Virginia, NE USA 38°29'N 80°52'W
171 S11 Weda, Teluk bay Pulau Halmahera, E Indonesia
65 B25 Weddell Island var. Isla de San Jorge. island W Falkland Islands
65 K22 Weddell Plain undersea feature SW Atlantic Ocean 65°00'S 40°00'W
65 K23 Weddell Sea sea SW Atlantic Ocean
182 M11 Wedderburn Victoria, SE Australia 36°26'S 143°37'E
100 I9 Wedel Schleswig-Holstein, N Germany 53°35'N 09°42'E
92 N3 Wedel Jarlsberg Land physical region SW Svalbard
100 I12 Wedemark Niedersachsen, NW Germany 52°33'N 09°43'E
10 M17 Wedge Mountain ▲ British Columbia, SW Canada 50°10'N 122°43'W
23 R4 Wedowee Alabama, S USA 33°16'N 85°28'W
171 U15 Weduar Pulau Kai Besar, E Indonesia 05°55'S 132°51'E
35 N2 Weed California, W USA 41°26'N 122°24'W
15 Q12 Weedon Centre Québec, SE Canada 45°40'N 71°28'W
18 E13 Weedville Pennsylvania, NE USA 41°15'N 78°28'W
100 F10 Weener Niedersachsen, NW Germany 53°09'N 07°19'E
29 S16 Weeping Water Nebraska, C USA 40°52'N 96°08'W
99 L16 Weert Limburg, SE Netherlands 51°15'N 05°43'E
98 I10 Weesp Noord-Holland, C Netherlands 52°18'N 05°03'E
183 S5 Wee Waa New South Wales, SE Australia 30°16'S 149°27'E
110 N7 Węgorzewo Ger. Angerburg. Warmińsko-Mazurskie, NE Poland 54°12'N 21°49'E
110 E9 Węgorzyno Ger. Wangerin. Zachodnio-pomorskie, NW Poland 53°34'N 15°35'E
110 N11 Węgrów Ger. Bingerau. Mazowieckie, C Poland 52°22'N 22°00'E
98 N5 Wehe-Den Hoorn Groningen, NE Netherlands 53°20'N 06°29'E
98 M12 Wehl Gelderland, E Netherlands 51°58'N 06°13'E
Wehlau see Znamensk
168 F7 Weh, Pulau island NW Indonesia
Wei see Weifang
161 P1 Weichang prev. Zhuizishan. Hebei, E China 41°55'N 117°45'E
Weichang see Weishan
Weichsel see Wisła
101 M16 Weida Thüringen, C Germany 50°46'N 12°05'E
Weiden see Weiden in der Oberpfalz
101 M19 Weiden in der Oberpfalz var. Weiden. Bayern, SE Germany 49°40'N 12°10'E
161 Q4 Weifang var. Wei, Wei-fang; prev. Weihsien. Shandong, E China 36°44'N 119°10'E
161 S4 Weihai Shandong, E China 37°30'N 122°04'E
160 K6 Wei He ⇝ C China
Weihsien see Weifang
101 G17 Weilburg Hessen, W Germany 50°31'N 08°18'E
101 K24 Weilheim in Oberbayern Bayern, SE Germany 47°50'N 11°09'E
183 P4 Weilmoringle New South Wales, SE Australia 29°13'S 146°51'E
101 L16 Weimar Thüringen, C Germany 50°59'N 11°20'E
25 U11 Weimar Texas, SW USA 29°42'N 96°46'W
160 L6 Weinan Shaanxi, C China 34°30'N 109°30'E
108 H6 Weinfelden Thurgau, NE Switzerland 47°33'N 09°09'E
101 I24 Weingarten Baden-Württemberg, S Germany 47°49'N 09°37'E
101 G20 Weinheim Baden-Württemberg, SW Germany 49°33'N 08°40'E
160 H11 Weining var. Caohai, Weining Yizu Huizu Miaozu Zizhixian. Guizhou, S China 26°51'N 104°16'E
Weining Yizu Huizu Miaozu Zizhixian see Weining
181 V2 Weipa Queensland, NE Australia 12°43'S 142°01'E
11 Y11 Weir River Manitoba, C Canada 56°44'N 94°06'W
21 R1 Weirton West Virginia, NE USA 40°24'N 80°37'W
32 M13 Weiser Idaho, NW USA 44°15'N 116°58'W
160 F12 Weishan var. Weichang. Yunnan, SW China 25°22'N 100°19'E
161 P6 Weishan Hu ◎ E China
101 M15 Weisse Elster Eng. White Elster. ⇝ Czech Republic/ Germany
Weisse Körös/Weisse Kreisch see Crişul Alb
108 L7 Weissenbach am Lech Tirol, W Austria 47°27'N 10°39'E
Weissenburg see Wissembourg, France
Weissenburg see Alba Iulia, Romania
101 K21 Weissenburg in Bayern Bayern, SE Germany 49°02'N 10°59'E
101 M15 Weissenfels var. Weißenfels. Sachsen-Anhalt, C Germany 51°12'N 11°58'E
109 R9 Weissensee ◎ S Austria
Weissenstein see Paide
108 E11 Weisshorn var. Flüela Wisshorn. ▲ SW Switzerland 46°06'N 07°43'E
Weisskirchen see Bela Crkva
23 R3 Weiss Lake ▣ Alabama, S USA
101 Q14 Weisswasser Lus. Běla Woda. Sachsen, E Germany 51°30'N 14°37'E
99 M22 Weiswampach Diekirch, N Luxembourg 50°08'N 06°05'E
109 U2 Weitra Niederösterreich, N Austria 48°41'N 14°54'E
161 O4 Weixian var. Wei Xian. Hebei, E China 36°59'N 115°15'E
Wei Xian see Weixian
159 V11 Weiyuan var. Qingyuan. Gansu, C China 35°07'N 104°12'E
Weiyuan see Shuangjiang
160 F14 Weiyuan Jiang ⇝ SW China
109 W7 Weiz Steiermark, SE Austria 47°13'N 15°38'E
Weizhou see Wenchuan
160 K16 Weizhou Dao island S China
110 I6 Wejherowo Pomorskie, NW Poland 54°36'N 18°12'E
27 Q8 Welch Oklahoma, C USA 36°52'N 95°06'W
24 M6 Welch Texas, SW USA 32°52'N 102°06'W
21 Q6 Welch West Virginia, NE USA 37°26'N 81°36'W
45 O14 Welchman Hall C Barbados 13°10'N 59°34'W
80 J11 Weldiya var. Waldia, It. Valdia. Āmara, N Ethiopia 11°45'N 39°39'E
21 W8 Weldon North Carolina, SE USA 36°25'N 77°35'W
25 V9 Weldon Texas, SW USA 31°00'N 95°33'W
99 M19 Welkenraedt Liège, E Belgium 50°40'N 05°58'E
193 O2 Welker Seamount undersea feature N Pacific Ocean 55°07'N 140°18'W
83 I22 Welkom Free State, C South Africa 27°59'S 26°44'E
14 H16 Welland Ontario, S Canada 42°59'N 79°14'W
14 G16 Welland ⇝ Ontario, S Canada
97 O19 Welland ⇝ C England, United Kingdom
14 H17 Welland Canal canal Ontario, S Canada
155 K25 Wellawaya Uva Province, SE Sri Lanka 06°44'N 81°07'E
Welle see Uele
181 T4 Wellesley Islands island group Queensland, N Australia
99 J22 Wellin Luxembourg, SE Belgium 50°06'N 05°05'E
97 N20 Wellingborough C England, United Kingdom 52°19'N 00°42'W

◆ Country ● Country Capital ◇ Dependent Territory ○ Dependent Territory Capital ◆ Administrative Regions ✈ International Airport ▲ Mountain ▲▲ Mountain Range Volcano ⇝ River ◎ Lake ▣ Reservoir

343

WELLINGTON – WILCZEK LAND

183 R7 **Wellington** New South Wales, SE Australia *32°33′S 148°59′E*
14 J15 **Wellington** Ontario, SE Canada *43°59′N 77°21′W*
185 L14 **Wellington** ● Wellington, North Island, New Zealand *41°17′S 174°47′E*
83 E26 **Wellington** Western Cape, SW South Africa *33°39′S 19°00′E*
37 T2 **Wellington** Colorado, C USA *40°42′N 105°00′W*
27 N7 **Wellington** Kansas, C USA *37°17′N 97°25′W*
35 R7 **Wellington** Nevada, W USA *38°45′N 119°22′W*
31 T11 **Wellington** Ohio, N USA *41°10′N 82°13′W*
25 P3 **Wellington** Texas, SW USA *34°52′N 100°13′W*
36 M4 **Wellington** Utah, W USA *39°31′N 110°45′W*
185 M14 **Wellington** *off.* Wellington Region. ◈ *region* (New Zealand) North Island, New Zealand
185 L14 **Wellington** ✈ Wellington, North Island, New Zealand *41°19′S 174°48′E*
Wellington *see* Wellington, Isla
63 F22 **Wellington, Isla** *var.* Wellington. *island* S Chile
183 P12 **Wellington, Lake** ⊚ Victoria, SE Australia
Wellington Region *see* Wellington
29 X14 **Wellman** Iowa, C USA *41°27′N 91°50′W*
24 M6 **Wellman** Texas, SW USA *33°03′N 102°25′W*
97 K22 **Wells** SW England, United Kingdom *51°13′N 02°39′W*
29 V11 **Wells** Minnesota, N USA *43°45′N 93°43′W*
35 X2 **Wells** Nevada, W USA *41°07′N 114°58′W*
25 W8 **Wells** Texas, SW USA *31°28′N 94°54′W*
18 F12 **Wellsboro** Pennsylvania, NE USA *41°43′N 77°39′W*
21 R1 **Wellsburg** West Virginia, NE USA *40°15′N 80°37′W*
184 K4 **Wellsford** Auckland, North Island, New Zealand *36°17′S 174°30′E*
180 L9 **Wells, Lake** ⊚ Western Australia
181 N4 **Wells, Mount** ▲ Western Australia *17°39′S 127°08′E*
97 P18 **Wells-next-the-Sea** E England, United Kingdom *52°58′N 00°48′E*
31 T15 **Wellston** Ohio, N USA *39°07′N 82°31′W*
27 O10 **Wellston** Oklahoma, C USA *35°41′N 97°03′W*
18 E11 **Wellsville** New York, NE USA *42°06′N 77°55′W*
31 V12 **Wellsville** Ohio, N USA *40°36′N 80°39′W*
36 L1 **Wellsville** Utah, W USA *41°38′N 111°55′W*
36 I14 **Wellton** Arizona, SW USA *32°40′N 114°09′W*
109 S4 **Wels** *anc.* Ovilava. Oberösterreich, N Austria *48°10′N 14°02′E*
99 K15 **Welschap** ✈ (Eindhoven) Noord-Brabant, S Netherlands *51°27′N 05°22′E*
100 P10 **Welse** ≈ NE Germany
22 H9 **Welsh** Louisiana, S USA *30°12′N 92°49′W*
97 K19 **Welshpool** *Wel.* Y Trallwng. E Wales, United Kingdom *52°38′N 03°06′W*
97 O21 **Welwyn Garden City** E England, United Kingdom *51°48′N 00°13′W*
79 K18 **Wema** Equateur, NW Dem. Rep. Congo *0°25′S 21°33′E*
81 G21 **Wembere** ≈ C Tanzania
11 N13 **Wembley** Alberta, W Canada *55°07′N 119°12′W*
12 I9 **Wemindji** *prev.* Nouveau-Comptoir, Paint Hills. Québec, C Canada *53°00′N 78°42′W*
99 G18 **Wemmel** Vlaams Brabant, C Belgium *50°54′N 04°18′E*
32 J8 **Wenatchee** Washington, NW USA *47°50′N 120°48′W*
160 M17 **Wenchang** Hainan, S China *19°34′N 110°46′E*
161 R11 **Wencheng** *var.* Daxue. Zhejiang, SE China *27°48′N 120°01′E*
77 P16 **Wenchi** W Ghana *07°45′N 02°02′W*
Wen-chou/Wenchow *see* Wenzhou
160 H8 **Wenchuan** *var.* Weizhou. Sichuan, C China *31°29′N 103°39′E*
Wendau *see* Võnnu
Wenden *see* Cēsis
161 S4 **Wendeng** Shandong, E China *37°10′N 122°00′E*
81 J14 **Wendo** Southern Nationalities, S Ethiopia *06°34′N 38°28′E*
36 J2 **Wendover** Utah, W USA *40°41′N 114°00′W*
14 D9 **Wenebegon** ≈ Ontario, S Canada
14 D8 **Wenebegon Lake** ⊚ Ontario, S Canada
108 E9 **Wengen** Bern, W Switzerland *46°38′N 07°57′E*
161 O13 **Wengyuan** *var.* Longxian. Guangdong, S China *24°22′N 114°06′E*
189 P15 **Weno** *prev.* Moen. Chuuk, C Micronesia
189 V12 **Weno** *prev.* Moen. *atoll* Chuuk Islands, C Micronesia
158 N13 **Wenquan** Qinghai, C China *33°16′N 91°44′E*
159 H4 **Wenquan** *var.* Arixang, Bogeda'er. Xinjiang Uygur Zizhiqu, NW China *45°00′N 81°02′E*
Wenquan *see* Yingshan
160 H14 **Wenshan** *var.* Kaihua. Yunnan, SW China *23°22′N 104°21′E*
158 H6 **Wensu** Xinjiang Uygur Zizhiqu, W China *41°15′N 80°11′E*
182 L8 **Wentworth** New South Wales, SE Australia *34°04′S 141°53′E*
27 W4 **Wentzville** Missouri, C USA *38°48′N 90°51′W*
159 V12 **Wenxian** *var.* Wen Xian. Gansu, C China *32°57′N 104°42′E*
Wen Xian *see* Wenxian
161 S10 **Wenzhou** *var.* Wen-chou, Wenchow. Zhejiang, SE China *28°02′N 120°36′E*
34 L4 **Weott** California, W USA *40°19′N 123°57′W*
99 I20 **Wépion** Namur, SE Belgium *50°24′N 04°53′E*
100 O11 **Werbellinsee** ⊚ NE Germany
99 L21 **Werbomont** Liège, E Belgium *50°22′N 05°43′E*
83 G20 **Werda** Kgalagadi, S Botswana *25°13′S 23°16′E*
81 N14 **Werder** Sumalē, E Ethiopia *06°59′N 45°20′E*
Werder *see* Virtsu
Werenów *see* Voranava
171 U13 **Weri** Papua, E Indonesia *03°10′S 132°39′E*
98 I13 **Werkendam** Noord-Brabant, S Netherlands *51°48′N 04°54′E*
101 M20 **Wernberg-Köblitz** Bayern, SE Germany *49°31′N 12°10′E*
101 J18 **Werneck** Bayern, C Germany *50°00′N 10°06′E*
101 K14 **Wernigerode** Sachsen-Anhalt, C Germany *51°51′N 10°48′E*
Werowitz *see* Virovitica
101 J16 **Werra** ≈ C Germany
183 N12 **Werribee** Victoria, SE Australia *37°55′S 144°39′E*
183 T6 **Werris Creek** New South Wales, SE Australia *31°22′S 150°40′E*
Werro *see* Võru
Werschetz *see* Vršac
101 K23 **Wertach** ≈ S Germany
101 I19 **Wertheim** Baden-Württemberg, SW Germany *49°45′N 09°31′E*
98 J8 **Wervershoof** Noord-Holland, NW Netherlands *52°43′N 05°09′E*
Wervicq *see* Wervik
99 C18 **Wervik** *var.* Wervicq, Werwick. West-Vlaanderen, W Belgium *50°47′N 03°03′E*
Werwick *see* Wervik
101 D14 **Wesel** Nordrhein-Westfalen, W Germany *51°39′N 06°37′E*
Weseli an der Lainsitz *see* Veselí nad Lužnicí
Wesenberg *see* Rakvere
100 H12 **Weser** ≈ NW Germany
Wes-Kaap *see* Western Cape
25 S17 **Weslaco** Texas, SW USA *26°09′N 97°59′W*
14 J13 **Weslemkoon Lake** ⊚ Ontario, SE Canada
181 R1 **Wessel Islands** *island group* Northern Territory, N Australia
29 P9 **Wessington** South Dakota, N USA *44°27′N 98°40′W*
29 P10 **Wessington Springs** South Dakota, N USA *44°02′N 98°33′W*
25 T8 **West** Texas, SW USA *31°48′N 97°05′W*
West *see* Ouest
30 M9 **West Allis** Wisconsin, N USA *43°01′N 88°00′W*
182 E8 **Westall Point** *headland* South Australia *32°54′S 134°04′E*
194 M10 **West Antarctica** *var.* Lesser Antarctica. *physical region* Antarctica
14 G11 **West Arm** Ontario, S Canada *46°16′N 80°25′W*
West Australian Basin *see* Wharton Basin
West Azerbaijan *see* Āzarbāyjān-e Gharbī
11 N17 **Westbank** British Columbia, SW Canada *49°50′N 119°37′W*
138 F10 **West Bank** *disputed region* SW Asia
14 E11 **West Bay** Manitoulin Island, Ontario, S Canada *45°48′N 82°09′W*
22 L11 **West Bay** *bay* Louisiana, S USA
30 M8 **West Bend** Wisconsin, N USA *43°26′N 88°13′W*
153 R16 **West Bengal** ◈ *state* NE India
West Borneo *see* Kalimantan Barat
29 Y14 **West Branch** Iowa, C USA *41°40′N 91°21′W*
31 R7 **West Branch** Michigan, N USA *44°16′N 84°14′W*
18 F13 **West Branch Susquehanna River** ≈ Pennsylvania, NE USA
97 L20 **West Bromwich** C England, United Kingdom *52°29′N 01°59′W*
19 P8 **Westbrook** Maine, NE USA *43°42′N 70°21′W*
29 T10 **Westbrook** Minnesota, N USA *44°02′N 95°26′W*
29 Y15 **West Burlington** Iowa, C USA *40°49′N 91°09′W*
96 L2 **West Burra** *island* NE Scotland, United Kingdom
30 J8 **Westby** Wisconsin, N USA *43°39′N 90°52′W*
44 L6 **West Caicos** *island* W Turks and Caicos Islands
185 A24 **West Cape** *headland* South Island, New Zealand *45°51′S 166°26′E*
174 L4 **West Caroline Basin** *undersea feature* SW Pacific Ocean *04°00′N 138°00′E*
18 I16 **West Chester** Pennsylvania, NE USA *39°56′N 75°35′W*
185 E18 **West Coast** *off.* West Coast Region. ◈ *region* South Island, New Zealand
West Coast Region *see* West Coast
25 V12 **West Columbia** Texas, SW USA *29°08′N 95°39′W*
29 W10 **West Concord** Minnesota, N USA *44°09′N 92°54′W*
29 V14 **West Des Moines** Iowa, C USA *41°35′N 93°42′W*
37 Q6 **West Elk Peak** ▲ Colorado, C USA *38°43′N 107°12′W*
44 F1 **West End** Grand Bahama Island, N Bahamas *26°36′N 78°55′W*
44 F1 **West End Point** *headland* Grand Bahama Island, N Bahamas *26°40′N 78°58′W*
98 O7 **Westerbork** Drenthe, NE Netherlands *52°49′N 06°36′E*
98 N3 **Westereems** *strait* Germany/Netherlands
98 O9 **Westerhaar-Vriezenveensewijk** Overijssel, E Netherlands *52°28′N 06°38′E*
100 G6 **Westerland** Schleswig-Holstein, N Germany *54°54′N 08°19′E*
99 I17 **Westerlo** Antwerpen, N Belgium *51°05′N 04°55′E*
19 N13 **Westerly** Rhode Island, NE USA *41°22′N 71°45′W*
81 G18 **Western** ◈ *province* W Kenya
153 N11 **Western** ◈ *zone* C Nepal
186 A8 **Western** ◈ *province* SW Papua New Guinea
186 J8 **Western** *off.* Western Province. ◈ *province* NW Solomon Islands
155 J26 **Western** ◈ *province* SW Sri Lanka
83 G15 **Western** ◈ *province* SW Zambia
180 K8 **Western Australia** ◈ *state* W Australia
80 A13 **Western Bahr el Ghazal** ◈ *state* SW Sudan
Western Bug *see* Bug
83 F25 **Western Cape** *off.* Western Cape Province, *Afr.* Wes-Kaap. ◈ *province* SW South Africa
Western Cape Province *see* Western Cape
80 A11 **Western Darfur** ◈ *state* W Sudan
Western Desert *see* Şaḩrā' al Gharbīyah
118 G9 **Western Dvina** *Bel.* Dzvina, *Ger.* Düna, *Latv.* Daugava, *Rus.* Zapadnaya Dvina. ≈ W Europe
81 D15 **Western Equatoria** ◈ *state* SW Sudan
155 E16 **Western Ghats** ▲▲ SW India
186 C7 **Western Highlands** ◈ *province* C Papua New Guinea
Western Isles *see* Outer Hebrides
80 C12 **Western Kordofan** ◈ *state* C Sudan
21 T3 **Westernport** Maryland, NE USA *39°29′N 79°03′W*
Western Province *see* Western
Western Punjab *see* Punjab
74 B10 **Western Sahara** ◇ *disputed territory* N Africa
Western Samoa *see* Samoa
Western Samoa, Independent State of *see* Samoa
Western Sayans *see* Zapadnyy Sayan
Western Scheldt *see* Westerschelde
Western Sierra Madre *see* Madre Occidental, Sierra
99 E15 **Westerschelde** *Eng.* Western Scheldt; *prev.* Honte. *inlet* S North Sea
31 S13 **Westerville** Ohio, N USA *40°07′N 82°55′W*
101 F17 **Westerwald** ▲▲ W Germany
65 C25 **West Falkland** *var.* Gran Malvina, Isla Gran Malvina. *island* W Falkland Islands
29 R5 **West Fargo** North Dakota, N USA *46°49′N 96°51′W*
188 M15 **West Fayu Atoll** *atoll* Caroline Islands, C Micronesia
18 C11 **Westfield** New York, NE USA *42°18′N 79°34′W*
30 L7 **Westfield** Wisconsin, N USA *43°56′N 89°31′W*
West Flanders *see* West-Vlaanderen
27 S10 **West Fork** Arkansas, C USA *35°55′N 94°11′W*
29 P16 **West Fork Big Blue River** ≈ Nebraska, C USA
29 U12 **West Fork Des Moines River** ≈ Iowa/Minnesota, C USA
25 S5 **West Fork Trinity River** ≈ Texas, SW USA
30 L16 **West Frankfort** Illinois, N USA *37°54′N 88°55′W*
98 I8 **West-Friesland** *physical region* NW Netherlands
West Frisian Islands *see* Waddeneilanden
19 T5 **West Grand Lake** ⊚ Maine, NE USA
18 M12 **West Hartford** Connecticut, NE USA *41°44′N 72°45′W*
18 M13 **West Haven** Connecticut, NE USA *41°16′N 72°57′W*
27 X12 **West Helena** Arkansas, C USA *34°33′N 90°38′W*
28 M2 **Westhope** North Dakota, N USA *48°54′N 101°01′W*
195 Y8 **West Ice Shelf** *ice shelf* Antarctica
47 R2 **West Indies** *island group* SE North America
West Irian *see* Papua
West Java *see* Jawa Barat
36 L3 **West Jordan** Utah, W USA *40°37′N 111°55′W*
West Kalimantan *see* Kalimantan Barat
99 D14 **Westkapelle** Zeeland, SW Netherlands *51°32′N 03°26′E*
West Kazakhstan *see* Zapadnyy Kazakhstan
31 O13 **West Lafayette** Indiana, N USA *40°24′N 86°54′W*
31 T13 **West Lafayette** Ohio, N USA *40°16′N 81°45′W*
West Lake *see* Kagera
29 Y14 **West Liberty** Iowa, C USA *41°34′N 91°15′W*
21 O5 **West Liberty** Kentucky, S USA *37°56′N 83°16′W*
Westliche Morava *see* Zapadna Morava
10 J13 **Westlock** Alberta, SW Canada *54°12′N 113°50′W*
14 E17 **West Lorne** Ontario, S Canada *42°36′N 81°35′W*
96 J12 **West Lothian** *cultural region* S Scotland, United Kingdom
99 H16 **Westmalle** Antwerpen, N Belgium *51°18′N 04°40′E*
192 G6 **West Mariana Basin** *var.* Perece Vela Basin. *undersea feature* W Pacific Ocean *15°00′N 137°00′E*
97 E17 **Westmeath** *Ir.* An Iarmhí, Na H-Iarmhidhe. *cultural region* C Ireland
27 Y11 **West Memphis** Arkansas, C USA *35°09′N 90°11′W*
21 W2 **Westminster** Maryland, NE USA *39°34′N 77°00′W*
21 O11 **Westminster** South Carolina, SE USA *34°39′N 83°06′W*
22 I5 **West Monroe** Louisiana, S USA *32°31′N 92°09′W*
18 D15 **Westmont** Pennsylvania, NE USA *40°16′N 78°55′W*
27 O3 **Westmoreland** Kansas, C USA *39°23′N 96°30′W*
35 W17 **Westmorland** California, W USA *33°02′N 115°37′W*
186 E6 **West New Britain** ◈ *province* E Papua New Guinea
West New Guinea *see* Papua
83 K18 **West Nicholson** Matabeleland South, S Zimbabwe *21°06′S 29°25′E*
29 T14 **West Nishnabotna River** ≈ Iowa, C USA
175 P11 **West Norfolk Ridge** *undersea feature* W Pacific Ocean
25 P12 **West Nueces River** ≈ Texas, SW USA
West Nusa Tenggara *see* Nusa Tenggara Barat
29 T11 **West Okoboji Lake** ⊚ Iowa, C USA
33 R16 **Weston** Idaho, NW USA *42°01′N 119°29′W*
21 R4 **Weston** West Virginia, NE USA *39°03′N 80°28′W*
97 J22 **Weston-super-Mare** SW England, United Kingdom *51°21′N 02°59′W*
23 Z14 **West Palm Beach** Florida, SE USA *26°43′N 80°03′W*
West Papua *see* Papua
188 E9 **West Passage** *passage* Babeldaob, N Palau
23 O9 **West Pensacola** Florida, SE USA *30°25′N 87°16′W*
27 V8 **West Plains** Missouri, C USA *36°44′N 91°51′W*
35 P7 **West Point** California, W USA *38°21′N 120°33′W*
23 R5 **West Point** Georgia, SE USA *32°52′N 85°10′W*
22 M3 **West Point** Mississippi, S USA *33°36′N 88°39′W*
29 R14 **West Point** Nebraska, C USA *41°50′N 96°42′W*
21 X6 **West Point** Virginia, NE USA *37°31′N 76°48′W*
182 G10 **West Point** *headland* South Australia *35°01′S 135°58′E*
23 R4 **West Point Lake** ⊠ Alabama/Georgia, SE USA
97 B16 **Westport** *Ir.* Cathair na Mart. Mayo, W Ireland *53°48′N 09°32′W*
185 G15 **Westport** West Coast, South Island, New Zealand *41°46′S 171°37′E*
32 F10 **Westport** Oregon, NW USA *46°07′N 123°22′W*
32 F9 **Westport** Washington, NW USA *46°53′N 124°06′W*
31 S15 **West Portsmouth** Ohio, N USA *38°45′N 83°01′W*
West Punjab *see* Punjab
11 V14 **Westray** Manitoba, C Canada *53°30′N 101°19′W*
96 J4 **Westray** *island* NE Scotland, United Kingdom
14 F9 **Westree** Ontario, S Canada *47°25′N 81°32′W*
97 L16 **West Riding** *cultural region* N England, United Kingdom
West River *see* Xi Jiang
30 J7 **West Salem** Wisconsin, N USA *43°54′N 91°04′W*
65 H21 **West Scotia Ridge** *undersea feature* W Scotia Sea
West Sepik *see* Sandaun
173 N4 **West Sheba Ridge** *undersea feature* W Indian Ocean *12°45′N 48°15′E*
West Siberian Plain *see* Zapadno-Sibirskaya Ravnina
31 S11 **West Sister Island** *island* Ohio, N USA
West-Skylge *see* West-Terschelling
West Sumatra *see* Sumatera Barat
98 J5 **West-Terschelling** *Fris.* West-Skylge. Friesland, N Netherlands *53°23′N 05°15′E*
64 J7 **West Thulean Rise** *undersea feature* N Atlantic Ocean
29 X12 **West Union** Iowa, C USA *42°57′N 91°48′W*
31 R15 **West Union** Ohio, N USA *38°47′N 83°33′W*
21 R3 **West Union** West Virginia, NE USA *39°18′N 80°47′W*
31 N13 **Westville** Illinois, N USA *40°02′N 87°38′W*
21 R3 **West Virginia** *off.* State of West Virginia, ***also known as*** Mountain State. ◈ *state* NE USA
99 A17 **West-Vlaanderen** *Eng.* West Flanders. ◈ *province* W Belgium
35 R7 **West Walker River** ≈ California/Nevada, W USA
35 P4 **Westwood** California, W USA *40°18′N 121°02′W*
183 P9 **West Wyalong** New South Wales, SE Australia *33°56′S 147°10′E*
171 Q16 **Wetar, Pulau** *island* Kepulauan Damar, E Indonesia
Wetar, Selat *see* Wetar Strait
171 R16 **Wetar Strait** *var.* SelatWetar. *strait* Nusa Tenggara, S Indonesia
11 Q15 **Wetaskiwin** Alberta, SW Canada *52°57′N 113°20′W*
81 K21 **Wete** Pemba, E Tanzania *05°03′S 39°41′E*
166 M4 **Wetlet** Sagaing, C Myanmar (Burma) *22°43′N 95°22′E*
37 T6 **Wet Mountains** ▲▲ Colorado, C USA
101 E15 **Wetter** Nordrhein-Westfalen, W Germany *51°22′N 07°24′E*
101 H17 **Wetter** ≈ W Germany
99 F17 **Wetteren** Oost-Vlaanderen, NW Belgium *51°06′N 03°59′E*
108 F7 **Wettingen** Aargau, N Switzerland *47°28′N 08°20′E*
27 P11 **Wetumka** Oklahoma, C USA *35°14′N 96°14′W*
23 Q5 **Wetumpka** Alabama, S USA *32°32′N 86°12′W*
108 G7 **Wetzikon** Zürich, N Switzerland *47°19′N 08°48′E*
101 G17 **Wetzlar** Hessen, W Germany *50°33′N 08°30′E*
99 C18 **Wevelgem** West-Vlaanderen, W Belgium *50°48′N 03°12′E*
38 M6 **Wevok** *var.* Wewuk. Alaska, USA *68°52′N 166°05′W*
23 R9 **Wewahitchka** Florida, SE USA *30°06′N 85°12′W*
186 C6 **Wewak** East Sepik, NW Papua New Guinea *03°35′S 143°35′E*
27 O11 **Wewoka** Oklahoma, C USA *35°09′N 96°30′W*
Wewuk *see* Wevok
97 F20 **Wexford** *Ir.* Loch Garman. SE Ireland *52°21′N 06°31′W*
97 F20 **Wexford** *Ir.* Loch Garman. *cultural region* SE Ireland
30 L7 **Weyauwega** Wisconsin, N USA *44°16′N 88°54′W*
11 U17 **Weyburn** Saskatchewan, S Canada *49°39′N 103°51′W*
Weyer *see* Weyer Markt
109 U5 **Weyer Markt** *var.* Weyer. Oberösterreich, N Austria *47°52′N 14°39′E*
100 H11 **Weyhe** Niedersachsen, NW Germany *53°00′N 08°52′E*
97 L24 **Weymouth** S England, United Kingdom *50°36′N 02°28′W*
19 P11 **Weymouth** Massachusetts, NE USA *42°13′N 70°56′W*
99 H18 **Wezembeek-Oppem** Vlaams Brabant, C Belgium *50°51′N 04°28′E*
98 M9 **Wezep** Gelderland, E Netherlands *52°28′N 06°E*
184 M9 **Whakamaru** Waikato, North Island, New Zealand *38°27′S 175°48′E*
184 O8 **Whakatane** Bay of Plenty, North Island, New Zealand *37°58′S 177°E*
184 O8 **Whakatane** ≈ North Island, New Zealand
9 O9 **Whale Cove** Nunavut, C Canada *62°14′N 92°10′W*
96 M2 **Whalsay** *island* NE Scotland, United Kingdom
184 L11 **Whangaehu** ≈ North Island, New Zealand
184 M6 **Whangamata** Waikato, North Island, New Zealand *37°13′S 175°54′E*
184 Q9 **Whangara** Gisborne, North Island, New Zealand *38°34′S 178°12′E*
184 K3 **Whangarei** Northland, North Island, New Zealand *35°44′S 174°18′E*
184 K3 **Whangaruru Harbour** *inlet* North Island, New Zealand
25 V12 **Wharton** Texas, SW USA *29°19′N 96°08′W*
173 U8 **Wharton Basin** *var.* West Australian Basin. *undersea feature* E Indian Ocean
185 E18 **Whataroa** West Coast, South Island, New Zealand *43°17′S 170°20′E*
8 J9 **Wha Ti** Northwest Territories, W Canada *63°10′N 117°12′W*
8 K10 **Wha Ti** *prev.* Lac la Martre. Northwest Territories, W Canada *63°10′N 117°12′W*
184 K6 **Whatipu** Auckland, North Island, New Zealand *37°17′S 174°44′E*
33 Y16 **Wheatland** Wyoming, C USA *42°03′N 104°57′W*
14 D18 **Wheatley** Ontario, S Canada *42°06′N 82°27′W*
30 M10 **Wheaton** Illinois, N USA *41°52′N 88°06′W*
29 R7 **Wheaton** Minnesota, N USA *45°48′N 96°30′W*
37 T4 **Wheat Ridge** Colorado, C USA *39°44′N 105°06′W*
25 P2 **Wheeler** Texas, SW USA *35°26′N 100°17′W*
23 O2 **Wheeler Lake** ⊠ Alabama, S USA
35 Y6 **Wheeler Peak** ▲ Nevada, W USA *39°00′N 114°17′W*
37 T9 **Wheeler Peak** ▲ New Mexico, SW USA *36°34′N 105°25′W*
31 S15 **Wheelersburg** Ohio, N USA *38°43′N 82°51′W*
21 R2 **Wheeling** West Virginia, NE USA *40°05′N 80°43′W*
97 L16 **Whernside** ▲ N England, United Kingdom *54°13′N 02°27′W*
182 F9 **Whidbey, Point** *headland* South Australia *34°36′S 135°08′E*
180 I7 **Whim Creek** Western Australia *20°51′S 117°54′E*
10 L17 **Whistler** British Columbia, SW Canada *50°07′N 122°57′W*
21 W8 **Whitakers** North Carolina, SE USA *36°06′N 77°43′W*
14 H15 **Whitby** Ontario, S Canada *43°52′N 78°56′W*
97 N15 **Whitby** N England, United Kingdom *54°29′N 00°37′W*
10 G6 **White** ≈ Yukon Territory, W Canada
13 T11 **White Bay** *bay* Newfoundland, Newfoundland and Labrador, E Canada
20 I8 **White Bluff** Tennessee, S USA *36°06′N 87°13′W*
28 J6 **White Butte** ▲ North Dakota, N USA *46°23′N 103°18′W*
19 R5 **White Cap Mountain** ▲ Maine, NE USA *45°33′N 69°15′W*
22 J9 **White Castle** Louisiana, S USA *30°10′N 91°09′W*
182 M5 **White Cliffs** New South Wales, SE Australia *30°52′S 143°04′E*
31 P8 **White Cloud** Michigan, N USA *43°34′N 85°47′W*
11 P14 **Whitecourt** Alberta, SW Canada *54°10′N 115°38′W*
25 O2 **White Deer** Texas, SW USA *35°26′N 101°10′W*
White Elster *see* Weisse Elster
24 M5 **Whiteface** Texas, SW USA *33°36′N 102°36′W*
18 K7 **Whiteface Mountain** ▲ New York, NE USA *44°22′N 73°54′W*
29 W5 **Whiteface Reservoir** ⊠ Minnesota, N USA
33 O7 **Whitefish** Montana, NW USA *48°24′N 114°20′W*
31 N9 **Whitefish Bay** Wisconsin, N USA *43°09′N 87°54′W*
31 Q3 **Whitefish Bay** *lake bay* Canada/USA
14 E11 **Whitefish Falls** Ontario, S Canada *46°06′N 81°42′W*
14 B7 **Whitefish Lake** ⊚ Ontario, S Canada
29 U6 **Whitefish Lake** ⊚ Minnesota, C USA
31 Q3 **Whitefish Point** *headland* Michigan, N USA *46°46′N 84°57′W*
31 O4 **Whitefish River** ≈ Michigan, N USA
25 O4 **Whiteflat** Texas, SW USA *34°06′N 100°55′W*
27 V12 **White Hall** Arkansas, C USA *34°18′N 92°05′W*
30 K14 **White Hall** Illinois, N USA *39°26′N 90°24′W*
31 O8 **Whitehall** Michigan, N USA *43°24′N 86°21′W*
18 L9 **Whitehall** New York, NE USA *43°33′N 73°24′W*
31 S13 **Whitehall** Ohio, N USA *39°58′N 82°53′W*
30 J7 **Whitehall** Wisconsin, N USA *44°22′N 91°20′W*
97 J15 **Whitehaven** NW England, United Kingdom *54°33′N 03°35′W*
10 I8 **Whitehorse** *territory capital* Yukon Territory, W Canada *60°41′N 135°08′W*
184 O7 **White Island** *island* NE New Zealand
14 K13 **White Lake** ⊚ Ontario, SE Canada
22 H10 **White Lake** ⊚ Louisiana, S USA
186 G7 **Whiteman Range** ▲▲ New Britain, E Papua New Guinea
183 Q15 **Whitemark** Tasmania, SE Australia *40°10′S 148°01′E*
35 S9 **White Mountains** ▲▲ California/Nevada, W USA
19 N7 **White Mountains** ▲▲ Maine/New Hampshire, NE USA
80 F11 **White Nile** ◈ *state* C Sudan
67 U7 **White Nile** *var.* Bahr el Jebel. ≈ S Sudan
81 E14 **White Nile** *Ar.* Al Baḩr al Abyaḑ, An Nīl al Abyaḑ, Bahr el Jebel. ≈ SE Sudan
25 W5 **White Oak Creek** ≈ Texas, SW USA
10 H9 **White Pass** *pass* Canada/USA
32 I9 **White Pass** *pass* Washington, NW USA
21 O9 **White Pine** Tennessee, S USA *36°06′N 83°17′W*
18 K14 **White Plains** New York, NE USA *41°01′N 73°45′W*
37 N13 **Whiteriver** Arizona, SW USA *33°50′N 109°57′W*
28 M11 **White River** South Dakota, N USA *43°34′N 100°45′W*
27 W12 **White River** ≈ Arkansas, SE USA
37 P3 **White River** ≈ Colorado/Utah, C USA
31 N15 **White River** ≈ Indiana, N USA
31 O8 **White River** ≈ Michigan, N USA
28 K11 **White River** ≈ South Dakota, N USA
25 O5 **White River** ≈ Texas, SW USA
18 M8 **White River** ≈ Vermont, NE USA
25 O5 **White River Lake** ⊠ Texas, SW USA
32 H11 **White Salmon** Washington, NW USA *45°43′N 121°29′W*
18 I10 **Whitesboro** New York, NE USA *43°07′N 75°17′W*
25 T5 **Whitesboro** Texas, SW USA *33°39′N 96°54′W*
21 O7 **Whitesburg** Kentucky, S USA *37°07′N 82°52′W*
White Sea *see* Beloye More
White Sea-Baltic Canal/White Sea Canal *see* Belomorsko-Baltiyskiy Kanal
63 I25 **Whiteside, Canal** *channel* S Chile
33 S10 **White Sulphur Springs** Montana, NW USA *46°33′N 110°54′W*
21 R6 **White Sulphur Springs** West Virginia, NE USA *37°48′N 80°18′W*
20 J6 **Whitesville** Kentucky, S USA *37°40′N 86°48′W*
32 I10 **White Swan** Washington, NW USA *46°22′N 120°46′W*
21 U12 **Whiteville** North Carolina, SE USA *34°20′N 78°42′W*
20 F10 **Whiteville** Tennessee, S USA *35°19′N 89°09′W*
77 Q13 **White Volta** *var.* Nakambé, *Fr.* Volta Blanche. ≈ Burkina/Ghana
30 M9 **Whitewater** Wisconsin, N USA *42°51′N 88°43′W*
37 P14 **Whitewater Baldy** ▲ New Mexico, SW USA *33°19′N 108°38′W*
23 X17 **Whitewater Bay** *bay* Florida, SE USA
31 Q14 **Whitewater River** ≈ Indiana/Ohio, N USA
11 V16 **Whitewood** Saskatchewan, S Canada *50°19′N 102°16′W*
28 J9 **Whitewood** South Dakota, N USA *44°27′N 103°38′W*
25 U5 **Whitewright** Texas, SW USA *33°30′N 96°23′W*
97 I15 **Whithorn** S Scotland, United Kingdom *54°44′N 04°26′W*
184 M6 **Whitianga** Waikato, North Island, New Zealand *36°50′S 175°42′E*
19 N11 **Whitinsville** Massachusetts, NE USA *42°06′N 71°40′W*
20 M8 **Whitley City** Kentucky, S USA *36°45′N 84°29′W*
21 Q11 **Whitmire** South Carolina, SE USA *34°30′N 81°36′W*
31 R10 **Whitmore Lake** Michigan, N USA *42°26′N 83°44′W*
195 N9 **Whitmore Mountains** ▲▲ Antarctica
14 I12 **Whitney** Ontario, SE Canada *45°29′N 78°11′W*
25 T8 **Whitney** Texas, SW USA *31°56′N 97°20′W*
25 S8 **Whitney, Lake** ⊠ Texas, SW USA
35 S11 **Whitney, Mount** ▲ California, W USA *37°45′N 119°55′W*
181 Y6 **Whitsunday Group** *island group* Queensland, E Australia
25 S6 **Whitt** Texas, SW USA *32°55′N 98°01′W*
29 U12 **Whittemore** Iowa, C USA *43°03′N 94°25′W*
39 R12 **Whittier** Alaska, USA *60°46′N 148°40′W*
35 T15 **Whittier** California, W USA *33°58′N 118°01′W*
83 I25 **Whittlesea** Eastern Cape, S South Africa *32°08′S 26°51′E*
20 K10 **Whitwell** Tennessee, S USA *35°12′N 85°31′W*
8 L10 **Wholdaia Lake** ⊚ Northwest Territories, NW Canada
182 H7 **Whyalla** South Australia *33°04′S 137°34′E*
Whydah *see* Ouidah
14 F13 **Wiarton** Ontario, S Canada *44°44′N 81°10′W*
171 O13 **Wiau** Sulawesi, C Indonesia *03°08′S 121°22′E*
111 H15 **Wiązów** *Ger.* Wansen. Dolnośląskie, SW Poland *50°49′N 17°13′E*
33 Y8 **Wibaux** Montana, NW USA *46°57′N 104°11′W*
27 N6 **Wichita** Kansas, C USA *37°42′N 97°20′W*
25 R5 **Wichita Falls** Texas, SW USA *33°55′N 98°30′W*
26 L11 **Wichita Mountains** ▲▲ Oklahoma, C USA
25 R5 **Wichita River** ≈ Texas, SW USA
96 K6 **Wick** N Scotland, United Kingdom *58°26′N 03°06′W*
36 K13 **Wickenburg** Arizona, SW USA *33°57′N 112°41′W*
24 L8 **Wickett** Texas, SW USA *31°34′N 103°00′W*
180 I7 **Wickham** Western Australia *20°40′S 117°11′E*
182 M14 **Wickham, Cape** *headland* Tasmania, SE Australia *39°36′S 143°55′E*
20 G7 **Wickliffe** Kentucky, S USA *36°58′N 89°04′W*
97 G19 **Wicklow** *Ir.* Cill Mhantáin. E Ireland *52°59′N 06°03′W*
97 F19 **Wicklow** *Ir.* Cill Mhantáin. *cultural region* E Ireland
97 G19 **Wicklow Head** *Ir.* Ceann Chill Mhantáin. *headland* E Ireland *52°57′N 06°00′W*
97 F18 **Wicklow Mountains** *Ir.* Sléibhte Chill Mhantáin. ▲▲ E Ireland
14 H10 **Wicksteed Lake** ⊚ Ontario, S Canada
Wida *see* Ouidah
65 G15 **Wideawake Airfield** ✈ (Georgetown) SW Ascension Island
97 K18 **Widnes** NW England, United Kingdom *53°22′N 02°44′W*
110 H9 **Więcbork** *Ger.* Vandsburg. Kujawsko-pomorskie, C Poland *53°21′N 17°31′E*
101 E17 **Wied** ≈ W Germany
101 F16 **Wiehl** Nordrhein-Westfalen, W Germany *50°57′N 07°33′E*
111 L17 **Wieliczka** Małopolskie, S Poland *50°N 20°02′E*
110 H12 **Wielkopolskie** ◈ *province* SW Poland
111 J14 **Wieluń** Sieradz, C Poland *51°14′N 18°33′E*
109 X4 **Wien** *Eng.* Vienna, *Hung.* Bécs, *Slvk.* Vídeň, *Slvn.* Dunaj; *anc.* Vindobona. ● (Austria) Wien, NE Austria *48°13′N 16°22′E*
109 X4 **Wien** *off.* Land Wien, *Eng.* Vienna. ◈ *state* NE Austria
109 X5 **Wiener Neustadt** Niederösterreich, E Austria *47°49′N 16°08′E*
Wien, Land *see* Wien
110 G7 **Wieprza** *Ger.* Wipper. ≈ NW Poland
98 O10 **Wierden** Overijssel, E Netherlands *52°22′N 06°35′E*
98 I7 **Wieringerwerf** Noord-Holland, NW Netherlands *52°51′N 05°01′E*
Wieruschow *see* Wieruszów
111 I14 **Wieruszów** *Ger.* Wieruschow. Łódzkie, C Poland *51°18′N 18°09′E*
109 V9 **Wies** Steiermark, SE Austria *46°40′N 15°16′E*
Wiesbachhorn *see* Grosses Weiesbachhorn
101 G18 **Wiesbaden** Hessen, W Germany *50°06′N 08°14′E*
Wieselburg and Ungarisch-Altenburg/Wieselburg-Ungarisch-Altenburg *see* Mosonmagyaróvár
Wiesenhof *see* Ostrołęka
101 G20 **Wiesloch** Baden-Württemberg, SW Germany *49°18′N 08°42′E*
100 F10 **Wiesmoor** Niedersachsen, NW Germany *53°22′N 07°46′E*
110 I7 **Wieżyca** *Ger.* Turmberg. *hill* Pomorskie, N Poland
97 L17 **Wigan** NW England, United Kingdom *53°33′N 02°38′W*
37 U3 **Wiggins** Colorado, C USA *40°11′N 104°03′W*
22 M8 **Wiggins** Mississippi, S USA *30°50′N 89°09′W*
Wigorna Ceaster *see* Worcester
97 I14 **Wigtown** S Scotland, United Kingdom *54°53′N 04°27′W*
97 H14 **Wigtown** *cultural region* SW Scotland, United Kingdom
97 I15 **Wigtown Bay** *bay* SW Scotland, United Kingdom
98 L13 **Wijchen** Gelderland, SE Netherlands *51°48′N 05°44′E*
92 N1 **Wijdefjorden** *fjord* NW Svalbard
98 M10 **Wijhe** Overijssel, E Netherlands *52°22′N 06°07′E*
98 J12 **Wijk bij Duurstede** Utrecht, C Netherlands *51°58′N 05°21′E*
98 J13 **Wijk en Aalburg** Noord-Brabant, S Netherlands *51°46′N 05°06′E*
99 H16 **Wijnegem** Antwerpen, N Belgium *51°13′N 04°32′E*
14 E11 **Wikwemikong** Manitoulin Island, Ontario, S Canada *45°46′N 81°43′W*
108 H7 **Wil** Sankt Gallen, NE Switzerland *47°28′N 09°03′E*
29 R16 **Wilber** Nebraska, C USA *40°28′N 96°57′W*
32 K8 **Wilbur** Washington, NW USA *47°45′N 118°42′W*
27 Q11 **Wilburton** Oklahoma, C USA *34°57′N 95°20′W*
182 M6 **Wilcannia** New South Wales, SE Australia *31°34′S 143°23′E*
18 D12 **Wilcox** Pennsylvania, NE USA *41°34′N 78°40′W*
Wilczek Land *see* Vil'cheka, Zemlya

◆ Country
● Country Capital
◇ Dependent Territory
○ Dependent Territory Capital
◈ Administrative Regions
✈ International Airport
▲ Mountain
▲▲ Mountain Range
⛰ Volcano
≈ River
⊚ Lake
⊠ Reservoir

WILDALPEN – WULKA

109 U6 **Wildalpen** Steiermark, E Austria 47°40′N 14°54′E
31 O13 **Wildcat Creek** ≈ Indiana, N USA
108 L9 **Wilde Kreuzspitze** *It.* Picco di Croce. ▲ Austria/Italy 46°53′N 10°51′E
Wildenschwert *see* Ústí nad Orlicí
98 O6 **Wildervank** Groningen, NE Netherlands 53°04′N 06°52′E
100 G11 **Wildeshausen** Niedersachsen, NW Germany 52°54′N 08°26′E
108 D10 **Wildhorn** ▲ SW Switzerland 46°21′N 07°22′E
11 R17 **Wild Horse** Alberta, SW Canada 49°00′N 110°19′W
27 N12 **Wildhorse Creek** ≈ Oklahoma, C USA
28 L14 **Wild Horse Hill** ▲ Nebraska, C USA 41°52′N 101°56′W
109 W8 **Wildon** Steiermark, SE Austria 46°53′N 15°29′E
24 M2 **Wildorado** Texas, SW USA 35°12′N 102°10′W
29 R6 **Wild Rice River** ≈ Minnesota/North Dakota, N USA
Wilejka *see* Vilyeyka
195 Y9 **Wilhelm II Coast** *physical region* Antarctica
195 X9 **Wilhelm II Land** *physical region* Antarctica
55 U11 **Wilhelmina Gebergte** ▲▲ C Suriname
18 B13 **Wilhelm, Lake** ⊠ Pennsylvania, NE USA
92 O2 **Wilhelmøya** *island* C Svalbard
Wilhelm-Pieck-Stadt *see* Guben
109 W4 **Wilhelmsburg** Niederösterreich, E Austria 48°07′N 15°37′E
100 G10 **Wilhelmshaven** Niedersachsen, NW Germany 53°31′N 08°07′E
Wilia/Wilja *see* Neris
18 H13 **Wilkes Barre** Pennsylvania, NE USA 41°15′N 75°50′W
21 R9 **Wilkesboro** North Carolina, SE USA 36°08′N 81°09′W
195 W15 **Wilkes Coast** *physical region* Antarctica
189 W12 **Wilkes Island** *island* N Wake Island
195 X12 **Wilkes Land** *physical region* Antarctica
11 S15 **Wilkie** Saskatchewan, S Canada 52°27′N 108°42′W
194 I6 **Wilkins Ice Shelf** *ice shelf* Antarctica
182 D4 **Wilkinsons Lakes** *salt lake* South Australia
Wiłkomierz *see* Ukmergė
182 K11 **Willalooka** South Australia 36°24′S 140°20′E
32 G11 **Willamette River** ≈ Oregon, NW USA
183 O8 **Willandra Billabong Creek** *seasonal river* New South Wales, SE Australia
32 F9 **Willapa Bay** *inlet* Washington, NW USA
27 T7 **Willard** Missouri, C USA 37°18′N 93°25′W
37 S12 **Willard** New Mexico, SW USA 34°36′N 106°01′W
31 S12 **Willard** Ohio, N USA 41°03′N 82°43′W
36 L1 **Willard** Utah, W USA 41°23′N 112°01′W
186 G6 **Willaumez Peninsula** *headland* New Britain, E Papua New Guinea 05°03′S 150°04′E
37 N15 **Willcox** Arizona, SW USA 32°13′N 109°49′W
37 N16 **Willcox Playa** *salt flat* Arizona, SW USA
99 G17 **Willebroek** Antwerpen, C Belgium 51°04′N 04°22′E
99 G14 **Willemstad** Noord-Brabant, S Netherlands 51°40′N 04°27′E
45 P16 **Willemstad** ○ (Netherlands Antilles) Curaçao, Netherlands Antilles 12°07′N 68°54′W
11 S11 **William** ≈ Saskatchewan, C Canada
23 O6 **William "Bill" Dannelly Reservoir** ⊠ Alabama, S USA
182 G3 **William Creek** South Australia 28°55′S 136°23′E
181 T15 **William, Mount** ▲ South Australia
36 K11 **Williams** Arizona, SW USA 35°15′N 112°11′W
29 X14 **Williamsburg** Iowa, C USA 41°39′N 92°00′W
20 M8 **Williamsburg** Kentucky, S USA 36°44′N 84°10′W
31 R15 **Williamsburg** Ohio, N USA 39°00′N 84°02′W
21 X6 **Williamsburg** Virginia, NE USA 37°17′N 76°43′W
10 M15 **Williams Lake** British Columbia, SW Canada 52°08′N 122°09′W
21 P6 **Williamson** West Virginia, NE USA 37°42′N 82°16′W
31 N13 **Williamsport** Indiana, N USA 40°18′N 87°18′W
18 G13 **Williamsport** Pennsylvania, NE USA 41°16′N 77°03′W
21 W9 **Williamston** North Carolina, SE USA 35°53′N 77°05′W
21 P11 **Williamston** South Carolina, SE USA 34°37′N 82°28′W
20 M4 **Williamstown** Kentucky, S USA 38°39′N 84°32′W
18 L10 **Williamstown** Massachusetts, NE USA 42°41′N 73°11′W
18 J16 **Willingboro** New Jersey, NE USA 40°01′N 74°52′W
11 Q14 **Willingdon** Alberta, SW Canada 53°49′N 112°08′W
25 W10 **Willis** Texas, SW USA 30°25′N 95°28′W
108 F8 **Willisau** Luzern, W Switzerland 47°07′N 08°00′E
83 F24 **Williston** Northern Cape, W South Africa 31°20′S 20°52′E
23 V10 **Williston** Florida, SE USA 29°23′N 82°27′W
28 J3 **Williston** North Dakota, N USA 48°07′N 103°37′W
21 Q13 **Williston** South Carolina, SE USA 33°24′N 81°25′W
10 L12 **Williston Lake** ⊠ British Columbia, W Canada
34 L5 **Willits** California, W USA 39°24′N 123°22′W
29 T8 **Willmar** Minnesota, N USA 45°07′N 95°02′W
10 K11 **Will, Mount** ▲ British Columbia, W Canada 57°31′N 128°48′W
31 T11 **Willoughby** Ohio, N USA 41°38′N 81°24′W
11 U17 **Willow Bunch** Saskatchewan, S Canada 49°30′N 105°41′W
32 J11 **Willow Creek** ≈ Oregon, NW USA
39 R11 **Willow Lake** Alaska, USA 61°44′N 150°02′W
8 I9 **Willowlake** ≈ Northwest Territories, NW Canada
83 H25 **Willowmore** Eastern Cape, S South Africa 33°18′S 23°30′E
30 L5 **Willow Reservoir** ⊠ Wisconsin, N USA
35 N5 **Willows** California, W USA 39°28′N 122°12′W
27 V7 **Willow Springs** Missouri, C USA 36°59′N 91°58′W
182 I7 **Wilmington** South Australia 32°42′S 138°08′E
21 Y2 **Wilmington** Delaware, NE USA 39°45′N 75°33′W
21 V12 **Wilmington** North Carolina, SE USA 34°14′N 77°55′W
31 R14 **Wilmington** Ohio, N USA 39°27′N 83°49′W
20 M6 **Wilmore** Kentucky, S USA 37°51′N 84°39′W
29 R8 **Wilmot** South Dakota, N USA 45°24′N 96°51′W
Wilna/Wilno *see* Vilnius
101 G16 **Wilnsdorf** Nordrhein-Westfalen, W Germany 50°49′N 08°06′E
99 G16 **Wilrijk** Antwerpen, N Belgium 51°11′N 04°25′E
100 I10 **Wilseder Berg** *hill* NW Germany
67 Z12 **Wilshaw Ridge** *undersea feature* W Indian Ocean 17°30′S 56°30′E
21 V9 **Wilson** North Carolina, SE USA 35°43′N 77°56′W
25 N5 **Wilson** Texas, SW USA 33°21′N 101°44′W
182 A7 **Wilson Bluff** *headland* South Australia/Western Australia 31°41′S 129°01′E
35 Y7 **Wilson Creek Range** ▲▲ Nevada, W USA
23 O1 **Wilson Lake** ⊠ Alabama, S USA
26 M4 **Wilson Lake** ⊠ Kansas, SE USA
37 P7 **Wilson, Mount** ▲ Colorado, C USA 37°50′N 107°59′W
183 P13 **Wilsons Promontory** *peninsula* Victoria, SE Australia
29 Y14 **Wilton** Iowa, C USA 41°35′N 91°01′W
19 P7 **Wilton** Maine, NE USA 44°35′N 70°15′W
28 M5 **Wilton** North Dakota, N USA 47°09′N 100°46′W
97 L22 **Wiltshire** *cultural region* S England, United Kingdom
99 M23 **Wiltz** Diekirch, NW Luxembourg 49°58′N 05°56′E
180 K9 **Wiluna** Western Australia 26°34′S 120°14′E
99 M23 **Wilwerwiltz** Diekirch, NE Luxembourg 49°59′N 06°00′E
29 P5 **Wimbledon** North Dakota, N USA 47°08′N 98°25′W
42 K7 **Wina** *var.* Güina. Jinotega, N Nicaragua 14°00′N 85°14′W
31 O12 **Winamac** Indiana, N USA 41°03′N 86°37′W
81 G19 **Winam Gulf** *var.* Kavirondo Gulf. *gulf* SW Kenya
83 I22 **Winburg** Free State, C South Africa 28°31′S 27°01′E
19 N10 **Winchendon** Massachusetts, NE USA 42°41′N 72°01′W
14 M13 **Winchester** Ontario, SE Canada 45°07′N 75°19′W
97 M23 **Winchester** *hist.* Wintanceaster, *Lat.* Venta Belgarum. S England, United Kingdom 51°04′N 01°19′W
32 M10 **Winchester** Idaho, NW USA 46°13′N 116°35′W
30 J14 **Winchester** Illinois, N USA 39°38′N 90°28′W
31 Q13 **Winchester** Indiana, N USA 40°11′N 84°57′W
20 M5 **Winchester** Kentucky, S USA 38°00′N 84°10′W
18 M10 **Winchester** New Hampshire, NE USA 42°46′N 72°21′W
20 K10 **Winchester** Tennessee, S USA 35°11′N 86°06′W
21 V3 **Winchester** Virginia, NE USA 39°11′N 78°12′W
99 L22 **Wincrange** Diekirch, NW Luxembourg 50°03′N 05°55′E
10 I5 **Wind** ≈ Yukon Territory, NW Canada
183 S8 **Windamere, Lake** ◎ New South Wales, SE Australia
Windau *see* Ventspils, Latvia
Windau *see* Venta, Latvia/Lithuania
18 D15 **Windber** Pennsylvania, NE USA 40°12′N 78°47′W
23 T3 **Winder** Georgia, SE USA 33°59′N 83°43′W
97 K15 **Windermere** NW England, United Kingdom 54°24′N 02°54′W
14 C7 **Windermere Lake** ◎ Ontario, S Canada
31 U11 **Windham** Ohio, N USA 41°14′N 81°03′W
83 D19 **Windhoek** *Ger.* Windhuk. ● (Namibia) Khomas, C Namibia 22°34′S 17°06′E
83 D20 **Windhoek** ✕ Khomas, C Namibia 22°31′S 17°04′E
Windhuk *see* Windhoek
15 O8 **Windigo** Québec, SE Canada 47°45′N 73°19′W
15 O8 **Windigo** ≈ Québec, SE Canada
Windischfeistritz *see* Slovenska Bistrica
109 T6 **Windischgarsten** Oberösterreich, W Austria 47°42′N 14°21′E
Windischgraz *see* Slovenj Gradec
37 T16 **Wind Mountain** ▲ New Mexico, SW USA 32°01′N 105°35′W
29 T10 **Windom** Minnesota, N USA 43°52′N 95°07′W
37 Q7 **Windom Peak** ▲ Colorado, C USA 37°37′N 107°35′W
181 U9 **Windorah** Queensland, C Australia 25°25′S 142°41′E
37 O10 **Window Rock** Arizona, SW USA 35°40′N 109°03′W
31 N9 **Wind Point** *headland* Wisconsin, N USA 42°46′N 87°46′W
33 U14 **Wind River** ≈ Wyoming, C USA
13 P15 **Windsor** Nova Scotia, SE Canada 45°00′N 64°09′W
14 C17 **Windsor** Ontario, S Canada 42°18′N 83°W
15 Q12 **Windsor** Québec, SE Canada 45°34′N 72°00′W
97 N22 **Windsor** S England, United Kingdom 51°29′N 00°39′W
37 T3 **Windsor** Colorado, C USA 40°28′N 104°54′W
18 M12 **Windsor** Connecticut, NE USA 41°51′N 72°38′W
27 T5 **Windsor** Missouri, C USA 38°31′N 93°31′W
21 X9 **Windsor** North Carolina, SE USA 36°00′N 76°57′W
18 M12 **Windsor Locks** Connecticut, NE USA 41°55′N 72°37′W
25 R5 **Windthorst** Texas, SW USA 33°34′N 98°26′W
45 Z14 **Windward Islands** *island group* E West Indies
Windward Islands *see* Barlavento, Ilhas de, Cape Verde
Windward Islands *see* Vent, Îles du, Archipel de la Société, French Polynesia
44 K8 **Windward Passage** *Sp.* Paso de los Vientos. *channel* Cuba/Haiti
55 T9 **Wineperu** C Guyana 06°10′N 58°34′W
23 O3 **Winfield** Alabama, S USA 33°55′N 87°49′W
29 Y15 **Winfield** Iowa, C USA 41°07′N 91°26′W
27 O7 **Winfield** Kansas, C USA 37°14′N 97°00′W
25 W6 **Winfield** Texas, SW USA 33°10′N 95°06′W
21 Q4 **Winfield** West Virginia, NE USA 38°30′N 81°54′W
29 N5 **Wing** North Dakota, N USA 47°06′N 100°16′W
183 U7 **Wingham** New South Wales, SE Australia 31°52′S 152°24′E
12 G16 **Wingham** Ontario, S Canada 43°54′N 81°19′W
33 T8 **Winifred** Montana, NW USA 47°33′N 109°26′W
12 E9 **Winisk Lake** ◎ Ontario, C Canada
24 L8 **Wink** Texas, SW USA 31°45′N 103°09′W
36 M14 **Winkelman** Arizona, SW USA 32°59′N 110°46′W
11 X17 **Winkler** Manitoba, S Canada 49°12′N 97°55′W
109 Q9 **Winklern** Tirol, W Austria 46°54′N 12°54′E
Winkowitz *see* Vinkovci
32 G9 **Winlock** Washington, NW USA 46°29′N 122°56′W
77 P17 **Winneba** SE Ghana 05°22′N 00°38′W
29 U11 **Winnebago** Minnesota, N USA 43°46′N 94°10′W
29 R13 **Winnebago** Nebraska, C USA 42°14′N 96°28′W
30 M7 **Winnebago, Lake** ◎ Wisconsin, N USA
30 M7 **Winneconne** Wisconsin, N USA 44°07′N 88°44′W
35 T3 **Winnemucca** Nevada, W USA 40°59′N 117°44′W
35 R4 **Winnemucca Lake** ◎ Nevada, W USA
101 H21 **Winnenden** Baden-Württemberg, SW Germany 48°52′N 09°22′E
29 N11 **Winner** South Dakota, N USA 43°22′N 99°51′W
33 U9 **Winnett** Montana, NW USA 47°00′N 108°18′W
14 I9 **Winneway** Québec, SE Canada 47°35′N 78°33′W
22 H6 **Winnfield** Louisiana, S USA 31°55′N 92°38′W
29 U4 **Winnibigoshish, Lake** ◎ Minnesota, N USA
25 X11 **Winnie** Texas, SW USA 29°49′N 94°22′W
11 Y16 **Winnipeg** *province capital* Manitoba, S Canada 49°53′N 97°10′W
11 X16 **Winnipeg** ✕ Manitoba, S Canada 49°56′N 97°16′W
0 J8 **Winnipeg** ≈ Manitoba, S Canada
11 X16 **Winnipeg Beach** Manitoba, S Canada 50°25′N 96°59′W
11 W14 **Winnipeg, Lake** ◎ Manitoba, C Canada
11 W15 **Winnipegosis** Manitoba, S Canada 51°36′N 99°59′W
11 W15 **Winnipegosis, Lake** ◎ Manitoba, C Canada
19 O8 **Winnipesaukee, Lake** ◎ New Hampshire, NE USA
22 I6 **Winnsboro** Louisiana, S USA 32°09′N 91°43′W
21 R12 **Winnsboro** South Carolina, SE USA 34°22′N 81°05′W
25 W6 **Winnsboro** Texas, SW USA 33°01′N 95°16′W
29 X10 **Winona** Minnesota, N USA 44°03′N 91°37′W
22 L4 **Winona** Mississippi, S USA 33°30′N 89°42′W
27 W7 **Winona** Missouri, C USA 37°00′N 91°19′W
25 W7 **Winona** Texas, SW USA 32°29′N 95°10′W
18 M7 **Winooski River** ≈ Vermont, NE USA
98 P6 **Winschoten** Groningen, NE Netherlands 53°09′N 07°03′E
100 J10 **Winsen** Niedersachsen, N Germany 53°22′N 10°13′E
36 M11 **Winslow** Arizona, SW USA 35°01′N 110°42′W
19 Q7 **Winslow** Maine, NE USA 44°33′N 69°35′W
18 M12 **Winsted** Connecticut, NE USA 41°55′N 73°03′W
32 F14 **Winston** Oregon, NW USA 43°07′N 123°24′W
21 S9 **Winston Salem** North Carolina, SE USA 36°06′N 80°15′W
98 N5 **Winsum** Groningen, NE Netherlands 53°20′N 06°31′E
Wintanceaster *see* Winchester
23 W11 **Winter Garden** Florida, SE USA 28°34′N 81°35′W
10 J16 **Winter Harbour** Vancouver Island, British Columbia, SW Canada 50°28′N 128°03′W
23 W12 **Winter Haven** Florida, SE USA 28°01′N 81°43′W
23 X11 **Winter Park** Florida, SE USA 28°36′N 81°20′W
25 P8 **Winters** Texas, SW USA 31°57′N 99°57′W
29 U15 **Winterset** Iowa, C USA 41°19′N 94°00′W
98 O12 **Winterswijk** Gelderland, E Netherlands 51°58′N 06°44′E
108 G6 **Winterthur** Zürich, NE Switzerland 47°30′N 08°43′E
29 U9 **Winthrop** Minnesota, N USA 44°32′N 94°22′W
32 J7 **Winthrop** Washington, NW USA 48°28′N 120°13′W
181 V7 **Winton** Queensland, E Australia 22°22′S 143°04′E
185 C24 **Winton** Southland, South Island, New Zealand 46°08′S 168°20′E
21 X8 **Winton** North Carolina, SE USA 36°24′N 76°57′W
101 K15 **Wipper** ≈ C Germany
101 K14 **Wipper** ≈ C Germany
Wipper *see* Wieprza
182 G6 **Wirraminna** South Australia 31°10′S 136°13′E
182 F4 **Wirrida** South Australia 29°34′S 134°33′E
182 F7 **Wirrulla** South Australia 32°27′S 134°33′E
Wirsitz *see* Wyrzysk
Wirz-See *see* Võrtsjärv
97 O19 **Wisbech** E England, United Kingdom 52°39′N 00°08′E
Wisby *see* Visby
19 Q8 **Wiscasset** Maine, NE USA 44°01′N 69°41′W
Wischau *see* Vyškov
30 J5 **Wisconsin** *off.* State of Wisconsin, *also known as* Badger State. ◆ *state* N USA
30 L8 **Wisconsin Dells** Wisconsin, N USA 43°37′N 89°43′W
30 L8 **Wisconsin, Lake** ⊠ Wisconsin, N USA
30 L7 **Wisconsin Rapids** Wisconsin, N USA 44°24′N 89°50′W
30 L7 **Wisconsin River** ≈ Wisconsin, N USA
33 P11 **Wisdom** Montana, NW USA 45°36′N 113°27′W
21 P7 **Wise** Virginia, NE USA 37°00′N 82°36′W
39 Q7 **Wiseman** Alaska, USA 67°24′N 150°06′W
96 J12 **Wishaw** W Scotland, United Kingdom 55°47′N 03°56′W
29 O6 **Wishek** North Dakota, N USA 46°12′N 99°33′W
32 I11 **Wishram** Washington, NW USA 45°40′N 120°53′W
111 J17 **Wisła** Śląskie, S Poland 49°39′N 18°50′E
110 K11 **Wisła** *Eng.* Vistula, *Ger.* Weichsel. ≈ C Poland
Wiślany, Zalew *see* Vistula Lagoon
111 M16 **Wisłoka** ≈ SE Poland
100 L9 **Wismar** Mecklenburg-Vorpommern, N Germany 53°54′N 11°28′E
29 R14 **Wisner** Nebraska, C USA 41°59′N 96°54′W
103 V4 **Wissembourg** *var.* Weissenburg. Bas-Rhin, NE France 49°03′N 07°57′E
30 J6 **Wissota, Lake** ⊠ Wisconsin, N USA
97 O18 **Witham** ≈ E England, United Kingdom
97 O17 **Withernsea** E England, United Kingdom 53°46′N 00°01′W
37 Q13 **Withington, Mount** ▲ New Mexico, SW USA 33°52′N 107°29′W
23 U8 **Withlacoochee River** ≈ Florida/Georgia, SE USA
110 H11 **Witkowo** Wielkopolskie, C Poland 52°27′N 17°49′E
97 M21 **Witney** S England, United Kingdom 51°47′N 01°30′W
101 E15 **Witten** Nordrhein-Westfalen, W Germany 51°25′N 07°19′E
101 N14 **Wittenberg** Sachsen-Anhalt, E Germany 51°53′N 12°39′E
30 L6 **Wittenberg** Wisconsin, N USA 44°53′N 89°20′W
100 L11 **Wittenberge** Brandenburg, N Germany 52°59′N 11°45′E
103 U7 **Wittenheim** Haut-Rhin, NE France 47°49′N 07°19′E
180 I7 **Wittenoom** Western Australia 22°17′S 118°22′E
Wittingau *see* Třeboň
100 K12 **Wittingen** Niedersachsen, C Germany 52°42′N 10°43′E
101 E18 **Wittlich** Rheinland-Pfalz, SW Germany 49°59′N 06°54′E
100 F9 **Wittmund** Niedersachsen, NW Germany 53°34′N 07°46′E
100 M10 **Wittstock** Brandenburg, NE Germany 53°10′N 12°29′E
186 F6 **Witu Islands** *island group* E Papua New Guinea
110 O7 **Wiżajny** Podlaskie, NE Poland 54°22′N 22°51′E
55 W10 **W. J. van Blommesteinmeer** ⊠ E Suriname
110 L11 **Wkra** *Ger.* Soldau. ≈ C Poland
110 I6 **Władysławowo** Pomorskie, N Poland 54°48′N 18°25′E
Wlaschim *see* Vlašim
111 E14 **Wleń** *Ger.* Lähn. Dolnośląskie, SW Poland 51°00′N 15°39′E
110 J11 **Włocławek** *Ger./Rus.* Vlotslavsk. Kujawsko-pomorskie, C Poland 52°39′N 19°03′E
110 P13 **Włodawa** *Rus.* Vlodava. Lubelskie, SE Poland 51°33′N 23°31′E
Włodzimierz *see* Volodymyr-Volyns'kyy
111 K15 **Włoszczowa** Świętokrzyskie, C Poland 50°51′N 19°58′E
83 C19 **Wlotzkasbaken** Erongo, W Namibia 22°26′S 14°30′E
15 R12 **Woburn** Québec, SE Canada 45°22′N 70°52′W
19 O11 **Woburn** Massachusetts, NE USA 42°28′N 71°09′W
Wocheiner Feistritz *see* Bohinjska Bistrica
Wöchma *see* Võhma
147 S11 **Wodil** *var.* Vuadil'. Farg'ona Viloyati, E Uzbekistan 40°10′N 71°43′E
181 V14 **Wodonga** Victoria, SE Australia 36°11′S 146°55′E
111 I17 **Wodzisław Śląski** *Ger.* Loslau. Śląskie, S Poland 49°59′N 18°27′E
98 I11 **Woerden** Zuid-Holland, C Netherlands 52°06′N 04°54′E
98 I8 **Wognum** Noord-Holland, NW Netherlands 52°40′N 05°01′E
Wohlau *see* Wołów
108 F7 **Wohlen** Aargau, NW Switzerland 47°21′N 08°17′E
195 R2 **Wohlthat Massivet** ▲▲ Antarctica
Wojerecy *see* Hoyerswerda
Wōjjā *see* Wotje Atoll
Wojwodina *see* Vojvodina
171 V15 **Wokam, Pulau** *island* Kepulauan Aru, E Indonesia
97 N22 **Woking** SE England, United Kingdom 51°20′N 00°34′W
Woldenberg Neumark *see* Dobiegniew
188 K15 **Woleai Atoll** *atoll* Caroline Islands, W Micronesia
Woleu *see* Uolo, Río
79 E17 **Woleu-Ntem** *off.* Province du Woleu-Ntem, *var.* Le Woleu-Ntem. ◆ *province* W Gabon
Woleu-Ntem, Province du *see* Woleu-Ntem
32 F15 **Wolf Creek** Oregon, NW USA 42°40′N 123°22′W
26 K9 **Wolf Creek** ≈ Oklahoma/Texas, SW USA
37 R7 **Wolf Creek Pass** *pass* Colorado, C USA
19 O9 **Wolfeboro** New Hampshire, NE USA 43°34′N 71°10′W
25 U5 **Wolfe City** Texas, SW USA 33°22′N 96°04′W
14 L15 **Wolfe Island** *island* Ontario, SE Canada
101 M14 **Wolfen** Sachsen-Anhalt, E Germany 51°40′N 12°16′E
100 J13 **Wolfenbüttel** Niedersachsen, C Germany 52°10′N 10°33′E
109 T4 **Wolfern** Oberösterreich, N Austria 48°06′N 14°16′E
109 Q6 **Wolfgangsee** *var.* Abersee, St Wolfgangsee. ◎ N Austria
39 P9 **Wolf Mountain** ▲ Alaska, USA 65°20′N 154°08′W
33 X7 **Wolf Point** Montana, NW USA 48°05′N 105°40′W
22 L8 **Wolf River** ≈ Mississippi, S USA
30 M7 **Wolf River** ≈ Wisconsin, N USA
109 U9 **Wolfsberg** Kärnten, SE Austria 46°50′N 14°50′E
100 K12 **Wolfsburg** Niedersachsen, N Germany 52°25′N 10°47′E
57 B17 **Wolf, Volcán** ⛰ Galapagos Islands, Ecuador, E Pacific Ocean 0°01′N 91°22′W
100 O8 **Wolgast** Mecklenburg-Vorpommern, NE Germany 54°04′N 13°47′E
108 F8 **Wolhusen** Luzern, W Switzerland 47°04′N 08°06′E
110 D8 **Wolin** *Ger.* Wollin. Zachodnio-pomorskie, NW Poland 53°52′N 14°35′E
109 Y3 **Wolkersdorf** Niederösterreich, NE Austria 48°24′N 16°31′E
Wołkowysk *see* Vawkavysk
Wöllan *see* Velenje
8 J6 **Wollaston, Cape** *headland* Victoria Island, Northwest Territories, NW Canada 71°00′N 118°21′W
63 J25 **Wollaston, Isla** *island* S Chile
11 U11 **Wollaston Lake** Saskatchewan, C Canada 58°05′N 103°38′W
11 T10 **Wollaston Lake** ◎ Saskatchewan, C Canada
8 J6 **Wollaston Peninsula** *peninsula* Victoria Island, Northwest Territories/Nunavut NW Canada
Wollin *see* Wolin
183 S9 **Wollongong** New South Wales, SE Australia 34°25′S 150°52′E
Wolmar *see* Valmiera
100 L13 **Wolmirstedt** Sachsen-Anhalt, C Germany 52°15′N 11°37′E
110 M11 **Wołomin** Mazowieckie, C Poland 52°20′N 21°11′E
110 G13 **Wołów** *Ger.* Wohlau. Dolnośląskie, SW Poland 51°21′N 16°40′E
Wołożyn *see* Valozhyn
14 G11 **Wolseley Bay** Ontario, S Canada 46°05′N 80°16′W
29 P10 **Wolsey** South Dakota, N USA 44°22′N 98°28′W
110 F12 **Wolsztyn** Wielkopolskie, C Poland 52°07′N 16°07′E
98 M7 **Wolvega** *Fris.* Wolvegea. Friesland, N Netherlands 52°53′N 06°E
Wolvegea *see* Wolvega
97 K19 **Wolverhampton** C England, United Kingdom 52°36′N 02°08′W
Wolverine State *see* Michigan
99 G18 **Wolvertem** Vlaams Brabant, C Belgium 50°55′N 04°19′E
99 H16 **Wommelgem** Antwerpen, N Belgium 51°12′N 04°32′E
186 D7 **Wonenara** *var.* Wonerara. Eastern Highlands, C Papua New Guinea 06°46′S 145°54′E
Wonerara *see* Wonenara
Wongalara Lake *see* Wongalarroo Lake
183 N6 **Wongalarroo Lake** *var.* Wongalara Lake. *seasonal lake* New South Wales, SE Australia
163 Y15 **Wŏnju** *Jap.* Genshū. N South Korea 37°21′N 127°57′E
10 M12 **Wonowon** British Columbia, W Canada 56°46′N 121°54′W
163 X13 **Wŏnsan** SE North Korea 39°11′N 127°21′E
183 O13 **Wonthaggi** Victoria, SE Australia 38°38′S 145°37′E
23 N2 **Woodall Mountain** ▲ Mississippi, S USA 34°47′N 88°14′W
23 W7 **Woodbine** Georgia, SE USA 30°58′N 81°43′W
29 S14 **Woodbine** Iowa, C USA 41°44′N 95°42′W
18 J17 **Woodbine** New Jersey, NE USA 39°12′N 74°47′W
21 W4 **Woodbridge** Virginia, NE USA 38°40′N 77°17′W
183 V4 **Woodburn** New South Wales, SE Australia 29°07′S 153°23′E
32 G11 **Woodburn** Oregon, NW USA 45°08′N 122°51′W
20 K9 **Woodbury** Tennessee, S USA 35°49′N 86°06′W
183 V5 **Wooded Bluff** *headland* New South Wales, SE Australia 29°24′S 153°22′E
183 V3 **Woodenbong** New South Wales, SE Australia 28°24′S 152°39′E
35 R11 **Woodlake** California, W USA 36°24′N 119°06′W
35 N7 **Woodland** California, W USA 38°41′N 121°46′W
19 T5 **Woodland** Maine, NE USA 45°10′N 67°25′W
32 G10 **Woodland** Washington, NW USA 45°54′N 122°44′W
37 T5 **Woodland Park** Colorado, C USA 38°59′N 105°03′W
186 I9 **Woodlark Island** *var.* Murua Island. *island* SE Papua New Guinea
Woodle Island *see* Kuria
11 T17 **Wood Mountain** ▲▲ Saskatchewan, S Canada
30 K15 **Wood River** Illinois, N USA 38°51′N 90°06′W
29 P16 **Wood River** Nebraska, C USA 40°48′N 98°33′W
39 R9 **Wood River** ≈ Alaska, USA
39 O13 **Wood River Lakes** *lakes* Alaska, USA
182 C1 **Woodroffe, Mount** ▲ South Australia 26°19′S 131°42′E
21 P11 **Woodruff** South Carolina, SE USA 34°44′N 82°02′W
30 K4 **Woodruff** Wisconsin, N USA 45°55′N 89°41′W
25 T14 **Woodsboro** Texas, SW USA 28°14′N 97°19′W
31 U13 **Woodsfield** Ohio, N USA 39°45′N 81°07′W
181 P4 **Woods, Lake** ◎ Northern Territory, N Australia
11 Z16 **Woods, Lake of the** *Fr.* Lac des Bois. ◎ Canada/USA
25 Q6 **Woodson** Texas, SW USA 33°00′N 99°01′W
13 N14 **Woodstock** New Brunswick, SE Canada 46°10′N 67°38′W
14 F16 **Woodstock** Ontario, S Canada 43°07′N 80°46′W
30 M10 **Woodstock** Illinois, N USA 42°18′N 88°27′W
18 M9 **Woodstock** Vermont, NE USA 43°37′N 72°33′W
21 U4 **Woodstock** Virginia, NE USA 38°55′N 78°31′W
19 N8 **Woodsville** New Hampshire, NE USA 44°08′N 72°02′W
184 M12 **Woodville** Manawatu-Wanganui, North Island, New Zealand 40°22′S 175°59′E
22 J7 **Woodville** Mississippi, S USA 31°06′N 91°18′W
25 X9 **Woodville** Texas, SW USA 30°47′N 94°26′W
26 K9 **Woodward** Oklahoma, C USA 36°26′N 99°25′W
29 O5 **Woodworth** North Dakota, N USA 47°06′N 99°19′W
171 W12 **Wool** Papua, E Indonesia 01°38′S 135°34′E
183 V5 **Woolgoolga** New South Wales, E Australia 30°04′S 153°09′E
182 H6 **Woomera** South Australia 31°12′S 136°52′E
19 O12 **Woonsocket** Rhode Island, NE USA 41°58′N 71°27′W
29 P10 **Woonsocket** South Dakota, N USA 44°03′N 98°16′W
31 T12 **Wooster** Ohio, N USA 40°48′N 81°56′W
80 L12 **Woqooyi Galbeed** *off.* Gobolka Woqooyi Galbeed. ◆ *region* NW Somalia
Woqooyi Galbeed, Gobolka *see* Woqooyi Galbeed
108 E8 **Worb** Bern, C Switzerland 46°54′N 07°36′E
83 F26 **Worcester** Western Cape, SW South Africa 33°41′S 19°22′E
97 L20 **Worcester** *hist.* Wigorna Ceaster. W England, United Kingdom 52°11′N 02°13′W
19 N11 **Worcester** Massachusetts, NE USA 42°17′N 71°48′W
97 L20 **Worcestershire** *cultural region* C England, United Kingdom
32 H16 **Worden** Oregon, NW USA 42°04′N 121°50′W
109 O6 **Wörgl** Tirol, W Austria 47°29′N 12°04′E
171 V15 **Workai, Pulau** *island* Kepulauan Aru, E Indonesia
97 J15 **Workington** NW England, United Kingdom 54°39′N 03°33′W
98 K7 **Workum** Friesland, N Netherlands 52°58′N 05°25′E
33 V13 **Worland** Wyoming, C USA 44°01′N 107°57′W
see São João de Cortes
Wormatia *see* Worms
99 N25 **Wormeldange** Grevenmacher, E Luxembourg 49°37′N 06°25′E
98 I9 **Wormer** Noord-Holland, C Netherlands 52°30′N 04°50′E
101 G19 **Worms** *anc.* Augusta Vangionum, Borbetomagus, Wormatia. Rheinland-Pfalz, SW Germany 49°38′N 08°22′E
Worms *see* Vormsi
101 K21 **Wörnitz** ≈ S Germany
25 U8 **Wortham** Texas, SW USA 31°47′N 96°27′W
101 G21 **Wörth am Rhein** Rheinland-Pfalz, SW Germany 49°04′N 08°16′E
109 S9 **Wörther See** ◎ S Austria
97 O23 **Worthing** SE England, United Kingdom 50°48′N 00°23′W
29 S11 **Worthington** Minnesota, N USA 43°37′N 95°37′W
31 S13 **Worthington** Ohio, N USA 40°05′N 83°01′W
35 W8 **Worthington Peak** ▲ Nevada, W USA 37°57′N 115°32′W
171 Y13 **Wosi** Papua, E Indonesia 03°55′S 138°54′E
171 V13 **Wosimi** Papua, E Indonesia 02°44′S 134°34′E
189 R5 **Wotho Atoll** *var.* Wōtto. *atoll* Ralik Chain, W Marshall Islands
189 V5 **Wotje Atoll** *var.* Wōjjā. *atoll* Ratak Chain, E Marshall Islands
Wotoe *see* Wotu
Wottawa *see* Otava
Wōtto *see* Wotho Atoll
171 O13 **Wotu** *prev.* Wotoe. Sulawesi, C Indonesia 02°34′S 120°46′E
98 K11 **Woudenberg** Utrecht, C Netherlands 52°05′N 05°25′E
98 I13 **Woudrichem** Noord-Brabant, S Netherlands 51°49′N 05°E
43 N8 **Wounta** *var.* Huaunta. Región Autónoma Atlántico Norte, NE Nicaragua 13°30′N 83°32′W
171 P14 **Wowoni, Pulau** *island* C Indonesia
81 J17 **Woyamdero Plain** *plain* E Kenya
Woyens *see* Vojens
Wozrojdeniye Oroli *see* Vozrozhdeniya, Ostrov
Wrangel Island *see* Vrangelya, Ostrov
39 Y13 **Wrangell** Wrangell Island, Alaska, USA 56°28′N 132°22′W
38 C15 **Wrangell, Cape** *headland* Attu Island, Alaska, USA 52°55′N 172°28′E
39 S11 **Wrangell, Mount** ▲ Alaska, USA 62°00′N 144°01′W
39 T11 **Wrangell Mountains** ▲▲ Alaska, USA
197 S7 **Wrangel Plain** *undersea feature* Arctic Ocean
96 H6 **Wrath, Cape** *headland* N Scotland, United Kingdom 58°37′N 05°01′W
37 W3 **Wray** Colorado, C USA 40°01′N 102°12′W
44 K13 **Wreck Point** *headland* C Jamaica 17°50′N 76°55′W
83 C23 **Wreck Point** *headland* W South Africa 28°52′S 16°17′E
23 V4 **Wrens** Georgia, SE USA 33°12′N 82°23′W
97 K18 **Wrexham** NE Wales, United Kingdom 53°03′N 03°W
27 R13 **Wright City** Oklahoma, C USA 34°03′N 95°00′W
194 J12 **Wright Island** *island* Antarctica
13 N9 **Wright, Mont** ▲ Québec, E Canada 52°36′N 67°40′W
25 X5 **Wright Patman Lake** ⊠ Texas, SW USA
36 M16 **Wrightson, Mount** ▲ Arizona, SW USA 31°42′N 110°51′W
23 U5 **Wrightsville** Georgia, SE USA 32°43′N 82°43′W
21 W12 **Wrightsville Beach** North Carolina, SE USA 34°12′N 77°48′W
35 T15 **Wrightwood** California, W USA 34°21′N 117°37′W
8 H9 **Wrigley** Northwest Territories, W Canada 63°16′N 123°39′W
111 G14 **Wrocław** *Eng./Ger.* Breslau. Dolnośląskie, SW Poland 51°07′N 17°01′E
110 F10 **Wronki** *Ger.* Fronicken. Wielkopolskie, C Poland 52°42′N 16°22′E
110 H11 **Września** Wielkopolskie, C Poland 52°19′N 17°34′E
110 F12 **Wschowa** Lubuskie, W Poland 51°49′N 16°15′E
Wsetin *see* Vsetín
161 O5 **Wu'an** Hebei, E China 36°45′N 114°12′E
180 I12 **Wubin** Western Australia 30°05′S 116°43′E
163 W9 **Wuchang** Heilongjiang, NE China 44°55′N 127°13′E
Wuchang *see* Wuhan
Wu-chou/Wuchow *see* Wuzhou
160 M16 **Wuchuan** *var.* Meilu. Guangdong, S China 21°28′N 110°49′E
160 K10 **Wuchuan** *var.* Duru, Gelaozu Miaozu Zhizhixian. Guizhou, S China 28°40′N 108°04′E
163 O13 **Wuchuan** Nei Mongol Zizhiqu, N China 41°04′N 111°28′E
163 V6 **Wudalianchi** *var.* Qingshan; *prev.* Dedu. Heilongjiang, NE China 48°40′N 126°06′E
159 O11 **Wudaoliang** Qinghai, C China 35°16′N 93°03′E
141 Q13 **Wuday'ah** *spring/well* S Saudi Arabia 17°03′N 47°06′E
77 V13 **Wudil** Kano, N Nigeria 11°46′N 08°49′E
160 G12 **Wuding** *var.* Jincheng. Yunnan, SW China 25°30′N 102°21′E
182 G8 **Wudinna** South Australia 33°06′S 135°30′E
Wudu *see* Longnan
160 L9 **Wufeng** Hubei, C China 30°09′N 110°31′E
161 O11 **Wugong Shan** ▲▲ S China
157 P7 **Wuhai** *var.* Haibowan. Nei Mongol Zizhiqu, N China 39°40′N 106°48′E
161 O9 **Wuhan** *var.* Han-kou, Han-k'ou, Hanyang, Wuchang, Wu-han; *prev.* Hankow. *province capital* Hubei, C China 30°35′N 114°19′E
Wu-han *see* Wuhan
161 Q7 **Wuhe** Anhui, E China 33°05′N 117°55′E
Wuhsien *see* Suzhou
Wuhsi/Wu-his *see* Wuxi
161 Q8 **Wuhu** *var.* Wu-na-mu. Anhui, E China 31°23′N 118°25′E
Wūjae *see* Ujae Atoll
160 K11 **Wu Jiang** ≈ C China
158 L5 **Wujiaqu** Xinjiang Uygur Zizhiqu, NW China 44°11′N 87°30′E
Wujlān *see* Ujelang Atoll
77 W15 **Wukari** Taraba, E Nigeria 07°51′N 09°49′E
Wulan *see* Jingyuan
152 H4 **Wular Lake** ◎ NE India
162 M13 **Wulashan** Nei Mongol Zizhiqu, N China 40°43′N 108°45′E
160 H11 **Wulian Feng** ▲▲ SW China
160 F13 **Wuliang Shan** ▲▲ SW China
160 K11 **Wuling Shan** ▲▲ S China
109 Y5 **Wulka** ≈ E Austria

◆ Country
● Country Capital
◇ Dependent Territory
○ Dependent Territory Capital
◆ Administrative Regions
✕ International Airport
▲ Mountain
▲▲ Mountain Range
⛰ Volcano
≈ River
◎ Lake
⊠ Reservoir

WULKAN – YARENSK

Wulkan see Vulcan
109 T3 Wullowitz Oberösterreich, N Austria 48°37′N 14°27′E
Wu-lu-k'o-mu-shi/Wu-lu-mu-ch'i see Ürümqi
79 D14 Wum Nord-Ouest, NE Cameroon 06°24′N 10°04′E
160 H12 Wumeng Shan ▲▲ SW China
160 K14 Wuming Guangxi Zhuangzu Zizhiqu, S China 23°12′N 108°11′E
100 I10 Wümme ≈ NW Germany
Wu-na-mu see Wuhu
171 X13 Wunen Papua, E Indonesia 03°40′S 138°31′E
12 D9 Wunnummin Lake ◎ Ontario, C Canada
80 D13 Wun Rog Warab, S Sudan 09°00′N 28°20′E
101 M18 Wunsiedel Bayern, E Germany 50°02′N 12°00′E
100 I12 Wunstorf Niedersachsen, NW Germany 52°25′N 09°25′E
166 M3 Wuntho Sagaing, N Myanmar (Burma) 23°52′N 95°43′E
101 F15 Wupper ≈ W Germany
101 E15 Wuppertal prev. Barmen-Elberfeld. Nordrhein-Westfalen, W Germany 51°16′N 07°12′E
160 K5 Wuqi Shaanxi, C China 36°57′N 108°15′E
158 E7 Wuqia Xinjiang Uygur Zizhiqu, NW China 39°50′N 75°19′E
161 P4 Wuqiao var. Sangyuan. Hebei, E China 37°40′N 116°21′E
101 L23 Würm ≈ SE Germany
77 T12 Wurno Sokoto, NW Nigeria 13°15′N 05°24′E
101 I19 Würzburg Bayern, SW Germany 49°48′N 09°56′E
101 N15 Wurzen Sachsen, E Germany 51°21′N 12°48′E
159 V11 Wushan Gansu, C China 34°42′N 104°53′E
160 L9 Wu Shan ▲▲ C China
158 G7 Wushi var. Uqturpan. Xinjiang Uygur Zizhiqu, NW China 41°07′N 79°09′E
Wusih see Wuxi
65 N18 Wüst Seamount undersea feature S Atlantic Ocean 32°00′S 00°06′E
Wusuli Jiang/Wusuri see Ussuri
161 N3 Wutai Shan var. Beitai Ding. ▲ C China 39°00′N 114°00′E
160 H10 Wutongqiao Sichuan, C China 29°21′N 103°48′E
159 P6 Wutongwozi Quan spring NW China
99 H15 Wuustwezel Antwerpen, N Belgium 51°24′N 04°34′E
186 B4 Wuvulu Island island NW Papua New Guinea
159 U9 Wuwei var. Liangzhou. Gansu, C China 37°58′N 102°40′E
161 R8 Wuxi var. Wuhsi, Wu-hsi, Wusih. Jiangsu, E China 31°35′N 120°19′E
Wuxing see Huzhou
160 L14 Wuxuan Guangxi Zhuangzu Zizhiqu, S China 23°40′N 109°41′E
Wuyang see Zhenyuan
160 K11 Wuyang He ≈ S China
163 X6 Wuyiling Heilongjiang, NE China 48°36′N 129°24′E
161 Q11 Wuyishan prev. Chong'an. Fujian, SE China 27°48′N 118°03′E
157 T12 Wuyi Shan ▲▲ SE China
162 M13 Wuyuan Nei Mongol Zizhiqu, N China 41°05′N 108°15′E
160 L17 Wuzhishan prev. Tongshi. Hainan, S China 18°37′N 109°34′E
160 L17 Wuzhi Shan ▲ S China 18°52′N 109°36′E
159 W8 Wuzhong Ningxia, N China 37°58′N 106°09′E
160 M14 Wuzhou var. Wu-chou, Wuchow. Guangxi Zhuangzu Zizhiqu, S China 23°30′N 111°21′E
18 H12 Wyalusing Pennsylvania, NE USA 41°40′N 76°13′W
182 M10 Wycheproof Victoria, SE Australia 36°06′S 143°13′E
97 K21 Wye Wel. Gwy. ≈ England/Wales, United Kingdom
Wyłkowyszki see Vilkaviškis
97 P19 Wymondham E England, United Kingdom 52°29′N 01°10′E
29 R17 Wymore Nebraska, C USA 40°07′N 96°39′W
182 E5 Wynbring South Australia 30°34′S 133°27′E
181 N3 Wyndham Western Australia 15°28′S 128°08′E
29 R6 Wyndmere North Dakota, N USA 46°16′N 97°07′W
27 X11 Wynne Arkansas, C USA 35°14′N 90°48′W
27 N12 Wynnewood Oklahoma, C USA 34°39′N 97°09′W
183 O15 Wynyard Tasmania, SE Australia 40°57′S 145°33′E
11 U15 Wynyard Saskatchewan, S Canada 51°46′N 104°10′W
33 V11 Wyola Montana, NW USA 45°07′N 107°23′W
182 A4 Wyola Lake salt lake South Australia
31 P9 Wyoming Michigan, N USA 42°54′N 85°42′W
33 V14 Wyoming off. State of Wyoming, also known as Equality State. ◆ state C USA
33 S15 Wyoming Range ▲▲ Wyoming, C USA
183 T8 Wyong New South Wales, SE Australia 33°18′S 151°27′E
110 G9 Wyrzysk Ger. Wirsitz. Wielkopolskie, C Poland 53°09′N 17°15′E
Wysg see Usk
110 O10 Wysokie Mazowieckie Łomża, E Poland 52°54′N 22°34′E
110 M11 Wyszków Ger. Probstberg. Mazowieckie, NE Poland 52°36′N 21°28′E
110 L11 Wyszogród Mazowieckie, C Poland 52°24′N 20°14′E
21 R7 Wytheville Virginia, NE USA 36°57′N 81°07′W
111 L15 Wyżyna Małopolska plateau

X

80 Q12 Xaafuun It. Hafun. Bari, NE Somalia 10°25′N 51°17′E
80 Q12 Xaafuun, Raas var. Ras Hafun. cape NE Somalia
Xàbia see Jávea
42 C4 Xaclbal, Río var. Xalbal. ≈ Guatemala/Mexico
137 Y10 Xaçmaz Rus. Khachmas. N Azerbaijan 41°26′N 48°47′E
80 O12 Xadeed var. Haded. physical region N Somalia
159 O14 Xagquka Xizang Zizhiqu, W China 31°47′N 92°46′E
167 Q6 Xai var. Muang Xay, Muong Sai. Oudômxai, N Laos 20°41′N 102°00′E
158 F10 Xaidulla Xinjiang Uygur Zizhiqu, W China 36°27′N 77°46′E
167 Q7 Xaignabouli prev. Muang Xaignabouri, Fr. Sayaboury. Xaignabouli, N Laos 19°16′N 101°43′E
167 R7 Xai Lai Leng, Phou ▲ Laos/Vietnam 19°13′N 104°09′E
158 L15 Xainza Xizang Zizhiqu, W China 30°54′N 88°36′E
158 L16 Xaitongmoin Xizang Zizhiqu, W China 29°27′N 88°13′E
83 F17 Xaixai var. Caecae. North-West, NW Botswana 19°52′S 21°04′E
83 M20 Xai-Xai prev. João Belo, Vila de João Belo. Gaza, S Mozambique 25°01′S 33°37′E
Xalbal see Xaclbal, Río
80 P13 Xalin Sool, N Somalia 09°16′N 49°00′E
146 H7 Xalqobod Rus. Khalkabad. Qoraqalpog'iston Respublikasi, W Uzbekistan 42°42′N 59°46′E
167 R6 Xam Nua var. Sam Neua. Houaphan, N Laos 20°24′N 104°03′E
82 D11 Xá-Muteba Port. Cinco de Outubro. Lunda Norte, NE Angola 09°34′S 17°50′E
Xangda see Nangqên
83 C16 Xangongo Port. Rocadas. Cunene, SW Angola 16°43′S 15°01′E
137 W12 Xankändi Rus. Khankendi; prev. Stepanakert. SW Azerbaijan 39°50′N 46°44′E
137 V11 Xanlar Rus. Khanlar. NW Azerbaijan 40°37′N 46°18′E
114 J13 Xánthi Anatolikí Makedonía kai Thráki, NE Greece 41°09′N 24°54′E
60 H13 Xanxerê Santa Catarina, S Brazil 26°52′S 52°25′W
81 O15 Xarardheere Mudug, E Somalia 04°45′N 47°54′E
137 Z11 Xärä Zirä Adası Rus. Ostrov Bulla. Island E Azerbaijan
162 K13 Xar Burd prev. Bayan Nuru. Nei Mongol Zizhiqu, N China 40°09′N 104°48′E
163 T11 Xar Moron ≈ NE China
163 T11 Xar Moron ≈ N China
Xarsingma see Chomo/Yadong
Xarra see Xarrë
113 L23 Xarrë var. Xarra. Vlorë, S Albania 39°45′N 20°01′E
82 D12 Xassengue Lunda Sul, NW Angola 10°28′S 18°32′E
105 S11 Xàtiva Cas. Xátiva; anc. Setabis, var. Jativa. País Valenciano, E Spain 39°00′N 00°32′W
Xauen see Chefchaouen
60 K10 Xavantes, Represa de var. Represa de Chavantes. ◎ Brazil
158 I7 Xayar Xinjiang Uygur Zizhiqu, W China 41°16′N 82°52′E
Xäzär Dänizi see Caspian Sea
167 S8 Xé Bangfai ≈ C Laos
167 T9 Xé Banghiang var. Bang Hieng. ≈ S Laos
Xégar see Tingri
31 R14 Xenia Ohio, N USA 39°40′N 83°55′W
Xeres see Jeréz de la Frontera
115 E15 Xeriás ≈ C Greece
115 G17 Xeró ▲ Évvoia, C Greece 38°52′N 23°18′E
Xhumo see Cum
161 N15 Xiachuan Dao island S China
Xiacun see Rushan
Xiaguan see Dali
159 U11 Xiahe var. Labrang. Gansu, C China 35°12′N 102°28′E
161 Q13 Xiamen var. Hsia-men; prev. Amoy. Fujian, SE China 24°28′N 118°05′E
160 L6 Xi'an var. Changan, Sian, Signan, Siking, Singan, Xian. province capital Shaanxi, C China 34°16′N 108°54′E
160 L10 Xianfeng var. Gaoleshan. Hubei, C China 29°45′N 109°10′E
Xiang see Hunan
161 N7 Xiangcheng Henan, C China 33°51′N 113°27′E
160 F10 Xiangcheng var. Sampê, Tib. Qagchêng. Sichuan, C China 28°52′N 99°45′E
160 M8 Xiangfan var. Xiangyang. Hubei, C China 32°07′N 112°00′E
Xianggang see Hong Kong
161 N10 Xiang Jiang ≈ S China
Xiangkhoang see Pèk
167 Q7 Xiangkhoang, Plateau de var. Plain of Jars. plateau N Laos
161 N11 Xiangtan var. Hsiang-t'an, Siangtan. Hunan, S China 27°53′N 112°55′E
161 N11 Xiangxiang Hunan, S China 27°50′N 112°31′E
Xiangyang see Xiangfan
161 S10 Xianju Zhejiang, SE China 28°53′N 120°41′E
161 O9 Xianning Hubei, C China 29°53′N 114°10′E
Xianshui see Dawu
160 F8 Xianshui He ≈ C China
161 N9 Xiantao var. Mianyang. Hubei, C China 30°20′N 113°31′E
161 R10 Xianxia Ling ▲▲ SE China
160 K6 Xianyang Shaanxi, C China 34°26′N 118°40′E
158 L5 Xiaocaohu Xinjiang Uygur Zizhiqu, W China 45°44′N 90°07′E
161 O9 Xiaogan Hubei, C China 30°55′N 113°54′E
Xiaogang see Dongxiang
163 W6 Xiao Hinggan Ling Eng. Lesser Khingan Range. ▲▲ NE China
160 M6 Xiao Shan ▲▲ C China
160 M12 Xiao Shui ≈ S China
Xiaoxi see Pinghe
161 P6 Xiaoxian var. Longcheng, Xiao Xian. Anhui, E China 34°11′N 116°56′E
Xiao Xian see Xiaoxian
160 G11 Xichang Sichuan, C China 27°52′N 102°16′E
41 P11 Xicoténcatl Tamaulipas, C Mexico 22°59′N 98°54′W
Xieng Khouang see Pèk
Xieng Ngeun see Muong Xiang Ngeun
160 J11 Xifeng var. Yongjing. Guizhou, S China 27°15′N 106°44′E
Xifeng see Qingyang
Xigang see Helan
158 L16 Xigazê var. Jih-k'a-tse, Shigatse, Xigaze. Xizang Zizhiqu, W China 29°18′N 88°50′E
159 W11 Xihe var. Hanyuan. Gansu, C China 34°00′N 105°24′E
160 I8 Xi He ≈ C China
Xihuachi see Heshui
159 W10 Xiji Ningxia, N China 36°02′N 105°33′E
160 M14 Xi Jiang var. Hsi Chiang, Eng. West River. ≈ S China
159 Q7 Xijian Quan spring NW China
160 K15 Xijin Shuiku ◎ S China
Xilagani see Xylaganí
Xiligou see Ulan
160 I13 Xilin var. Bada. Guangxi Zhuangzu Zizhiqu, S China 24°30′N 105°00′E
163 Q10 Xilinhot var. Silinhot. Nei Mongol Zizhiqu, N China 43°58′N 116°07′E
Xilinji see Mohe
Xilokastro see Xylókastro
Xin see Xinjiang Uygur Zizhiqu
Xin'an see Anlong
161 R10 Xin'anjiang Shuiku var. Qiandao Hu. ◎ SE China
Xin'anzhen see Xinyi
Xin Barag Youqi see Altan Emel
Xin Barag Zuoqi see Amgalang
163 W12 Xinbin var. Xinbin Manzu Zizhixian. Liaoning, NE China 41°44′N 125°02′E
Xinbin Manzu Zizhixian see Xinbin
161 O7 Xincai Henan, C China 32°47′N 114°58′E
Xincheng see Zhaojue
Xindu see Luhuo
161 O13 Xinfeng var. Jiading. Jiangxi, S China 25°23′N 114°48′E
161 O14 Xinfengjiang Shuiku ◎ S China
Xing'an see Ankang
Xingba see Lhünzê
163 T13 Xingcheng Liaoning, NE China 40°38′N 120°47′E
Xingcheng see Xingning
82 E11 Xinge Lunda Norte, NE Angola 09°44′S 19°10′E
161 P12 Xingguo var. Lianjiang. Jiangxi, S China 26°25′N 115°22′E
159 S11 Xinghai var. Ziketan. Qinghai, C China 35°12′N 102°28′E
161 R7 Xinghua Jiangsu, E China 32°54′N 119°48′E
Xingkai Hu see Khanka, Lake
161 P13 Xingning var. Xingcheng. Guangdong, S China 24°05′N 115°47′E
160 I13 Xingren Guizhou, S China 25°26′N 105°08′E
161 O4 Xingtai Hebei, E China 37°08′N 114°29′E
59 J14 Xingu, Rio ≈ C Brazil
159 P6 Xingxingxia Xinjiang Uygur Zizhiqu, NW China 41°48′N 95°01′E
160 I13 Xingyi Guizhou, S China 25°04′N 104°51′E
158 I6 Xinhe var. Toksu. Xinjiang Uygur Zizhiqu, NW China 41°32′N 82°39′E
163 Q10 Xin Hot Nei Mongol Zizhiqu, N China 43°58′N 114°59′E
Xinhua see Funing
163 T12 Xinhui var. Aohan Qi. Nei Mongol Zizhiqu, N China 42°12′N 119°57′E
159 T10 Xining var. Hsining, Hsi-ning, Sining. province capital Qinghai, C China 36°37′N 101°46′E
161 O4 Xinji prev. Shulu. Hebei, E China 37°55′N 115°14′E
161 P10 Xinjian Jiangxi, S China 28°37′N 115°46′E
Xinjiang see Xinjiang Uygur Zizhiqu
162 D8 Xinjiang Uygur Zizhiqu var. Sinkiang, Sinkiang Uighur Autonomous Region, Xin, Xinjiang. ◆ autonomous region NW China
160 H9 Xinjin var. Meixing, Tib. Zainlha. Sichuan, C China 30°27′N 103°46′E
Xinjin see Pulandian
Xinjing see Jingxi
163 U12 Xinmin Liaoning, NE China 41°58′N 122°51′E
160 M12 Xinning var. Jinshi. Hunan, S China 26°34′N 110°57′E
Xinning see Ningxian
Xinning see Fusui
Xinpu see Lianyungang
Xinshan see Anyuan
161 P5 Xintai Shandong, E China 35°54′N 117°44′E
Xinwen see Suncun
Xin Xian see Xinzhou
161 N6 Xinxiang Henan, C China 35°13′N 113°48′E
161 O8 Xinyang var. Hsin-yang, Sinyang. Henan, C China 32°09′N 114°04′E
161 Q6 Xinyi var. Xin'anzhen. Jiangsu, E China 34°17′N 118°14′E
161 Q6 Xinyi He ≈ E China
161 O11 Xinyu Jiangxi, S China 27°51′N 115°00′E
158 I5 Xinyuan var. Künes. Xinjiang Uygur Zizhiqu, NW China 43°25′N 83°12′E
Xinyuan see Tianjun
162 M13 Xinzhao Shan ▲ N China 39°37′N 107°51′E
161 N3 Xinzhou var. Xin Xian. Shanxi, C China 38°24′N 112°43′E
Xinzhou see Longlin
104 H4 Xinzo de Limia Galicia, NW Spain 42°05′N 07°45′W
Xions see Książ Wielkopolski
161 O7 Xiping Henan, C China 33°22′N 114°00′E
Xiping see Songyang
159 T11 Xiqing Shan ▲ C China
59 N16 Xique-Xique Bahia, E Brazil 10°47′S 42°44′W
Xireg see Ulan
115 E14 Xirovoúni ▲ N Greece 40°31′N 21°58′E
162 M13 Xishanzui prev. Urad Qianqi. Nei Mongol Zizhiqu, N China 40°43′N 108°41′E
160 J11 Xishui var. Donghuang. Guizhou, S China 28°24′N 106°09′E
Xi Ujimqin Qi see Bayan Ul
160 K11 Xiushan var. Zhonghe. Chongqing Shi, C China 28°23′N 108°52′E
Xiushan see Tonghai
161 O10 Xiu Shui ≈ S China
Xiuyan see Qingjian
146 H9 Xiva Rus. Khiva, Khiwa. Xorazm Viloyati, W Uzbekistan 41°22′N 60°22′E
158 J16 Xixabangma Feng ▲ W China 28°25′N 85°47′E
160 M7 Xixia Henan, C China 33°30′N 111°25′E
Xixón see Gijón
Xixona see Jijona
Xizang see Xizang Zizhiqu
Xizang Gaoyuan see Qingzang Gaoyuan
160 E9 Xizang Zizhiqu var. Thibet, Tibetan Autonomous Region, Xizang, Eng. Tibet. ◆ autonomous region W China
163 U14 Xizhong Dao island N China
Xoi see Qüxü
146 H8 Xo'jayli Rus. Khodzheyli. Qoraqalpog'iston Respublikasi, W Uzbekistan 42°23′N 59°27′E
Xolotlán see Managua, Lago de
147 I9 Xonqa var. Khonqa, Rus. Khanka. Xorazm Viloyati, W Uzbekistan 41°31′N 60°39′E
146 H9 Xorazm Viloyati Rus. Khorezmskaya Oblast'. ◆ province W Uzbekistan
159 N9 Xorkol Xinjiang Uygur Zizhiqu, NW China 38°45′N 91°07′E
147 P11 Xovos var. Ursat'yevskaya, Rus. Khavast. Sirdaryo Viloyati, E Uzbekistan 40°14′N 68°46′E
41 X14 Xpujil Quintana Roo, E Mexico 18°30′N 89°24′W
161 Q8 Xuancheng var. Xuanzhou. Anhui, E China 30°57′N 118°53′E
167 T9 Xuân Đuc Quang Binh, C Vietnam 17°19′N 106°38′E
160 L9 Xuan'en var. Zhushan. Hubei, C China 30°03′N 109°26′E
160 K8 Xuanhan Sichuan, C China 31°25′N 107°41′E
161 O2 Xuanhua Hebei, E China 40°36′N 115°01′E
161 P4 Xuanhui He ≈ E China
H12 Xuanwei Yunnan, China 26°08′N 104°04′E
Xuanzhou see Xuancheng
161 N7 Xuchang Henan, C China 34°03′N 113°48′E
Xucheng see Xuwen
137 X10 Xudat Rus. Khudat. NE Azerbaijan 41°37′N 48°39′E
81 M16 Xuddur var. Hudur, It. Oddur. Bakool, SW Somalia 04°07′N 43°47′E
80 O13 Xudun Sool, N Somalia 09°12′N 47°34′E
160 L11 Xuefeng Shan ▲▲ S China
147 O13 Xufar Surkhondaryo Viloyati, S Uzbekistan 38°31′N 67°45′E
Xulun Hobot Qagan see Qagan Nur
42 F2 Xunantunich ruins Cayo, W Belize
163 W6 Xun He ≈ NE China
160 L7 Xun He ≈ C China
160 L14 Xun Jiang ≈ S China
163 W5 Xunke var. Bianjing; prev. Qike. Heilongjiang, NE China 49°36′N 128°25′E
161 P13 Xunwu var. Changning. Jiangxi, S China 24°59′N 115°33′E
161 O3 Xushui Hebei, E China 39°01′N 115°38′E
160 L16 Xuwen var. Xucheng. Guangdong, S China 20°21′N 110°09′E
160 I11 Xuyong var. Yongning. Sichuan, C China 28°17′N 105°21′E
161 P6 Xuzhou var. Hsu-chou, Suchow, Tongshan; prev. T'ung-shan. Jiangsu, E China 34°17′N 117°09′E
114 K13 Xylaganí var. Xilagani. Anatolikí Makedonía kai Thráki, NE Greece 40°58′N 25°27′E
115 F19 Xylókastro var. Xilokastro. Pelopónnisos, S Greece 38°04′N 22°36′E

Y

160 H9 Ya'an var. Yaan. Sichuan, C China 30°N 102°57′E
182 L10 Yaapeet Victoria, SE Australia 35°48′S 142°03′E
79 D15 Yabassi Littoral, W Cameroon 04°30′N 09°59′E
81 J15 Yabēlo Oromīya, C Ethiopia 04°53′N 38°01′E
114 H9 Yablanitsa Lovech, N Bulgaria 43°01′N 24°06′E
43 N7 Yablis Región Autónoma Atlántico Norte, NE Nicaragua 14°08′N 83°44′W
123 O14 Yablonovyy Khrebet ▲▲ S Russian Federation
142 J4 Yabrai Shan ▲▲ NE China
45 U6 Yabucoa E Puerto Rico 18°02′N 65°53′W
160 J11 Yachi He ≈ S China
32 H10 Yacolt Washington, NW USA 45°49′N 122°22′W
54 M10 Yacuaray Amazonas, S Venezuela 04°12′N 66°30′W
57 M22 Yacuiba Tarija, S Bolivia 22°00′S 63°43′W
57 K16 Yacuma, Río ≈ C Bolivia
155 H16 Yādgīr Karnātaka, C India 16°46′N 77°09′E
21 R8 Yadkin River ≈ North Carolina, SE USA
21 R9 Yadkinville North Carolina, SE USA 36°07′N 80°40′W
158 L17 Yadong var. Xarsingma. Xizang Zizhiqu, W China 27°31′N 88°58′E see also Chomo
127 P3 Yadrin Chuvashskaya Respublika, W Russian Federation 55°55′N 46°10′E
Yaegama-shotō see Yaeyama-shotō
Yaeme-saki see Paimi-saki
165 O16 Yaeyama-shotō var. Yaegama-shotō. island group SW Japan
75 O8 Yafran NW Libya 32°04′N 12°31′E
165 S2 Yagashiri-tō island NE Japan
65 H21 Yaghan Basin undersea feature SE Pacific Ocean
123 S9 Yagodnoye Magadanskaya Oblast', E Russian Federation 62°37′N 149°18′E
Yagotin see Yahotyn
78 G12 Yagoua Extrême-Nord, NE Cameroon 10°23′N 15°13′E
159 Q11 Yagradagzê Shan ▲ C China 35°06′N 95°41′E
Yaguachi see Yaguachi Nuevo
56 B7 Yaguachi Nuevo var. Yaguachi. Guayas, W Ecuador 02°06′S 79°43′W
Yaguarón, Río see Jaguarão, Rio
117 Q11 Yahorlyts'kyy Lyman bay S Ukraine
117 Q5 Yahotyn Rus. Yagotin. Kyyivs'ka Oblast', N Ukraine 50°15′N 31°48′E
40 L12 Yahualica Jalisco, SW Mexico 21°11′N 102°29′W
79 L17 Yahuma Orientale, N Dem. Rep. Congo 01°12′N 23°00′E
136 K15 Yahyalı Kayseri, C Turkey 38°08′N 35°23′E
167 N15 Yai, Khao ▲ SW Thailand 08°45′N 99°32′E
164 M14 Yaizu Shizuoka, Honshū, S Japan 34°52′N 138°20′E
160 G9 Yajiang var. Hekou, Tib. Nyagquka. Sichuan, C China 30°05′N 100°57′E
119 O14 Yakawlyevichi Rus. Yakovlevichi. Vitsyebskaya Voblasts', NE Belarus 54°20′N 30°31′E
163 S6 Yakeshi Nei Mongol Zizhiqu, N China 49°16′N 120°42′E
32 I9 Yakima Washington, NW USA 46°36′N 120°30′W
32 J10 Yakima River ≈ Washington, NW USA
Yakkabag see Yakkabog'
147 N12 Yakkabog' Rus. Yakkabag. Qashqadaryo Viloyati, S Uzbekistan 38°57′N 66°35′E
148 L12 Yakmach Baluchistān, SW Pakistan 28°48′N 63°48′E
77 O12 Yako W Burkina 12°59′N 02°15′W
39 W13 Yakobi Island island Alexander Archipelago, Alaska, USA
79 K16 Yakoma Equateur, N Dem. Rep. Congo 04°04′N 22°23′E
114 H11 Yakoruda Blagoevgrad, SW Bulgaria 42°01′N 23°40′E
Yakovlevichi see Yakawlyevichi
127 T2 Yakshur-Bod'ya Udmurtskaya Respublika, NW Russian Federation 57°10′N 53°10′E
165 Q5 Yakumo Hokkaidō, NE Japan 42°18′N 140°15′E
164 B17 Yaku-shima island Nansei-shotō, SW Japan
39 V12 Yakutat Alaska, USA 59°33′N 139°44′W
39 U12 Yakutat Bay inlet Alaska, USA
Yakutia/Yakutiya, Respublika see Sakha (Yakutiya), Respublika
123 Q10 Yakutsk Respublika Sakha (Yakutiya), NE Russian Federation 62°10′N 129°50′E
167 O17 Yala Yala, SW Thailand 06°32′N 101°19′E
182 D6 Yalata South Australia 31°30′S 131°53′E
31 S9 Yale Michigan, N USA 43°07′N 82°45′W
180 I11 Yalgoo Western Australia 28°23′S 116°43′E
114 O12 Yalıköy İstanbul, NW Turkey 41°29′N 28°19′E
79 L14 Yalinga Haute-Kotto, C Central African Republic 06°47′N 23°09′E
119 M17 Yalizava Rus. Yelizovo. Mahilyowskaya Voblasts', E Belarus 53°24′N 29°01′E
44 L13 Yallahs Hill ▲ E Jamaica 17°53′N 76°31′W
22 L3 Yalobusha River ≈ Mississippi, S USA
79 H15 Yaloké Ombella-Mpoko, W Central African Republic 05°15′N 17°12′E
160 E7 Yalong Jiang ≈ C China
136 E11 Yalova Yalova, NW Turkey 40°40′N 29°17′E
136 E11 Yalova ◆ province NW Turkey
Yaloveny see Ialoveni
Yalpug see Ialpug
Yalpug, Ozero see Yalpuh, Ozero
117 N12 Yalpuh, Ozero Rus. Ozero Yalpug. ◎ SW Ukraine
117 T14 Yalta Respublika Krym, S Ukraine 44°30′N 34°09′E
163 W12 Yalu Chin. Yalu Jiang, Jap. Oryokko, Kor. Amnok-kang. ≈ China/North Korea
Yalu Jiang see Yalu
136 F14 Yalvaç Isparta, SW Turkey 38°16′N 31°09′E
165 R9 Yamada Iwate, Honshū, C Japan 39°27′N 141°56′E
165 D14 Yamaga Kumamoto, Kyūshū, SW Japan 33°02′N 130°41′E
165 P10 Yamagata Yamagata, Honshū, C Japan 38°15′N 140°19′E
165 P9 Yamagata off. Yamagata-ken. ◆ prefecture Honshū, C Japan
Yamagata-ken see Yamagata
164 C16 Yamagawa Kagoshima, Kyūshū, SW Japan 31°12′N 130°37′E
164 E13 Yamaguchi var. Yamaguti. Yamaguchi, Honshū, SW Japan 34°11′N 131°26′E
164 E13 Yamaguchi off. Yamaguchi-ken, var. Yamaguti. ◆ prefecture Honshū, SW Japan
Yamaguchi-ken see Yamaguchi
Yamaguti see Yamaguchi
125 X5 Yamalo-Nenetskiy Avtonomnyy Okrug ◆ autonomous district N Russian Federation
122 J7 Yamal, Poluostrov peninsula N Russian Federation
165 N13 Yamanashi off. Yamanashi-ken, var. Yamanasi. ◆ prefecture Honshū, S Japan
Yamanashi-ken see Yamanashi
Yamanasi see Yamanashi
Yamanīyah, Al Jumhūrīyah al see Yemen
127 W5 Yamantau ▲ W Russian Federation 53°11′N 57°30′E
Yamasaki see Yamazaki
15 P12 Yamaska ≈ Québec, SE Canada
192 G4 Yamato Ridge undersea feature S Sea of Japan 39°20′N 135°00′E
164 I13 Yamazaki var. Yamasaki. Hyōgo, Honshū, SW Japan 35°00′N 134°31′E
183 V5 Yamba New South Wales, SE Australia 29°28′S 153°22′E
81 D16 Yambio var. Yambiyo. Western Equatoria, S Sudan 04°34′N 28°21′E
Yambiyo see Yambio
114 L10 Yambol Turk. Yanboli. Yambol, E Bulgaria 42°29′N 26°30′E
114 M11 Yambol ◆ province E Bulgaria
79 M17 Yambuya Orientale, N Dem. Rep. Congo 01°22′N 24°21′E
171 T15 Yamdena, Pulau prev. Jamdena. island Kepulauan Tanimbar, E Indonesia
165 O14 Yame Fukuoka, Kyūshū, SW Japan 33°14′N 130°32′E
166 M6 Yamethin Mandalay, C Myanmar (Burma) 20°24′N 96°08′E
186 C6 Yaminbot East Sepik, NW Papua New Guinea 04°34′S 143°56′E
181 U9 Yamma Yamma, Lake ◎ Queensland, C Australia
76 M16 Yamoussoukro ● (Ivory Coast) C Ivory Coast 06°51′N 05°21′W
37 P3 Yampa River ≈ Colorado, C USA
117 S2 Yampil' Sums'ka Oblast', NE Ukraine 51°57′N 33°49′E
116 M8 Yampil' Vinnyts'ka Oblast', C Ukraine 48°15′N 28°18′E
123 T9 Yamsk Magadanskaya Oblast', E Russian Federation 59°33′N 154°04′E
152 J8 Yamuna prev. Jumna. ≈ N India
152 I9 Yamunānagar Haryāna, N India 30°07′N 77°17′E
Yamundá see Nhamundá, Rio
145 U8 Yamyshevo Pavlodar, NE Kazakhstan 51°49′N 77°28′E
159 N16 Yamzho Yumco ◎ W China
123 Q8 Yana ≈ NE Russian Federation
186 H9 Yanaba Island island SE Papua New Guinea
155 L16 Yanam var. Yanaon. Pondicherry, E India 16°45′N 82°16′E
160 L5 Yan'an var. Yanan. Shaanxi, C China 36°35′N 109°27′E
Yanaon see Yanam
127 U3 Yanaul Respublika Bashkortostan, W Russian Federation 56°15′N 54°57′E
118 O12 Yanavichy Rus. Yanovichi. Vitsyebskaya Voblasts', NE Belarus 55°17′N 30°42′E
Yanboli see Yambol
140 K8 Yanbu' al Baḥr Al Madīnah, W Saudi Arabia 24°07′N 38°03′E
21 T8 Yanceyville North Carolina, SE USA 36°25′N 79°22′W
161 R7 Yancheng Jiangsu, E China 33°28′N 120°10′E
159 W8 Yanchi Ningxia, N China 37°49′N 107°24′E
160 L5 Yanchuan Shaanxi, C China 36°54′N 110°04′E
183 O10 Yanco Creek seasonal river New South Wales, SE Australia
183 O6 Yanda Creek seasonal river New South Wales, SE Australia
182 K4 Yandama Creek seasonal river New South Wales/South Australia
161 S11 Yandang Shan ▲▲ SE China
159 O6 Yandun Xinjiang Uygur Zizhiqu, W China 42°24′N 94°08′E
76 L13 Yanfolila Sikasso, SW Mali 11°08′N 08°12′W
79 M18 Yangambi Orientale, N Dem. Rep. Congo 0°46′N 24°24′E
158 M15 Yangbajain Xizang Zizhiqu, W China 30°05′N 90°35′E
Yangcheng see Yangshan, Guangdong, S China
Yangchow see Yangzhou
160 M15 Yangchun var. Chuncheng. Guangdong, S China 22°16′N 111°49′E
161 N2 Yanggao var. Longquan. Shanxi, C China 40°24′N 113°51′E
Yanggeta see Yaqeta
Yangiabad see Yangiobod
Yangibazar see Dzhany-Bazar, Kyrgyzstan
Yangi-Bazar see Kofarnihon, Tajikistan
Yangiklshak see Yangiqishloq
146 M13 Yangi-Nishon Rus. Yang-Nishan. Qashqadaryo Viloyati, S Uzbekistan 38°37′N 65°39′E
147 Q9 Yangiobod Rus. Yangiabad. Toshkent Viloyati, E Uzbekistan 41°10′N 70°10′E
147 O10 Yangiqishloq Rus. Yangiklshak. Jizzax Viloyati, C Uzbekistan 40°27′N 67°06′E
147 P11 Yangiyer Sirdaryo Viloyati, E Uzbekistan 40°19′N 68°48′E
147 P9 Yangiyo'l Rus. Yangiyul'. Toshkent Viloyati, E Uzbekistan 41°12′N 69°05′E
Yangiyul' see Yangiyo'l
160 M15 Yangjiang Guangdong, S China 21°50′N 112°02′E
Yangku see Taiyuan
Yang-Nishan see Yangi-Nishon
166 L8 Yangon Eng. Rangoon. Yangon, S Myanmar (Burma) 16°50′N 96°11′E
166 M8 Yangon Eng. Rangoon. ◆ division SW Myanmar (Burma)
161 N4 Yangquan Shanxi, C China 37°52′N 113°29′E
161 N13 Yangshan var. Yangcheng. Guangdong, S China 24°32′N 112°36′E
167 U12 Yang Sin, Chu ▲ S Vietnam 12°23′N 108°25′E
Yangtze see Chang Jiang/Jinsha Jiang
Yangtze see Jinsha Jiang
Yangtze Kiang see Chang Jiang
161 R7 Yangzhou var. Yangchow. Jiangsu, E China 32°22′N 119°22′E
160 L5 Yan He ≈ C China
163 Y10 Yanji Jilin, NE China 42°54′N 129°31′E
Yanji see Longjing
Yanjing see Yanyuan
29 Q12 Yankton South Dakota, N USA 42°52′N 97°24′W
161 O12 Yanling prev. Lingxian, Ling Xian. Hunan, S China 26°32′N 113°48′E
Yannina see Ioánnina
123 Q7 Yano-Indigirskaya Nizmennost' plain NE Russian Federation
Yanovichi see Yanavichy
155 K24 Yan Oya ≈ N Sri Lanka
158 K6 Yanqi var. Yanqi Huizu Zizhixian. Xinjiang Uygur Zizhiqu, NW China 42°04′N 86°32′E
Yanqi Huizu Zizhixian see Yanqi
161 Q10 Yanshan var. Hekou. Jiangxi, S China 28°18′N 117°43′E
160 H14 Yanshan var. Jiangna. Yunnan, SW China 23°36′N 104°20′E
161 P2 Yan Shan ▲▲ E China
163 X8 Yanshou Heilongjiang, NE China 45°27′N 128°19′E
123 Q7 Yanskiy Zaliv bay N Russian Federation
183 O4 Yantabulla New South Wales, SE Australia 29°22′S 145°00′E
161 R4 Yantai var. Yan-t'ai; prev. Chefoo, Chih-fu. Shandong, E China 37°30′N 121°22′E
118 A13 Yantarnyy Ger. Palmnicken. Kaliningradskaya Oblast', W Russian Federation 54°53′N 19°59′E
114 J9 Yantra Gabrovo, N Bulgaria 42°58′N 25°19′E
114 K9 Yantra ≈ N Bulgaria
160 G11 Yanyuan var. Yanjing. Sichuan, C China 27°30′N 101°22′E
161 P5 Yanzhou Shandong, E China 35°35′N 116°53′E
79 E16 Yaoundé var. Yaunde. ● (Cameroon) Centre, S Cameroon 03°51′N 11°31′E
188 I14 Yap ◆ state W Micronesia
188 F16 Yap island Caroline Islands, W Micronesia
57 M18 Yapacani, Rio ≈ C Bolivia
171 W14 Yapa Kopra Papua, E Indonesia 04°18′S 135°05′E
Yapan see Yapen, Selat
Yapanskoye More see East Sea/Japan, Sea of
77 P15 Yapei N Ghana 09°10′N 01°08′W
12 M10 Yapeitso, Mont ▲ Québec, E Canada 52°18′N 70°24′W
171 W12 Yapen, Pulau prev. Japen. island E Indonesia
171 W12 Yapen, Selat var. Yapan. strait Papua, E Indonesia
61 E15 Yapeyú Corrientes, NE Argentina 29°28′S 56°50′W
136 I11 Yapraklı Çankırı, N Turkey 40°45′N 33°46′E
174 M3 Yap Trench var. Yap Trough. undersea feature SE Philippine Sea 08°30′N 138°00′E
Yap Trough see Yap Trench
Yapurá see Caquetá, Río, Brazil/Colombia
Yapurá see Japurá, Rio, Brazil/Colombia
197 I12 Yaqaga island N Fiji
197 H12 Yaqeta prev. Yanggeta. island Yasawa Group, NW Fiji
40 G6 Yaqui Sonora, NW Mexico 27°21′N 109°59′W
32 E12 Yaquina Bay bay Oregon, NW USA
40 G6 Yaqui, Río ≈ NW Mexico
54 K5 Yaracuy off. Estado Yaracuy. ◆ state NW Venezuela
Yaracuy, Estado see Yaracuy
146 E13 Yarajy Rus. Yaradzhi. Ahal Welaýaty, C Turkmenistan 38°12′N 57°40′E
Yaradzhi see Yarajy
125 Q15 Yaransk Kirovskaya Oblast', NW Russian Federation 57°18′N 47°52′E
136 F17 Yardımcı Burnu headland SW Turkey 36°10′N 30°25′E
97 Q19 Yare ≈ E England, United Kingdom
125 S9 Yarega Respublika Komi, NW Russian Federation 63°27′N 53°28′E
116 I7 Yaremcha Ivano-Frankivs'ka Oblast', W Ukraine 48°27′N 24°34′E
189 Q9 Yaren SW Nauru 0°33′S 166°54′E
125 Q10 Yarensk Arkhangel'skaya Oblast', NW Russian Federation 62°09′N 49°03′E

◆ Country ● Country Capital ◇ Dependent Territory ○ Dependent Territory Capital ◆ Administrative Regions ✈ International Airport ▲ Mountain ▲▲ Mountain Range ⛰ Volcano ≈ River ◎ Lake ◎ Reservoir

YARGATTI – YUNFU

155 F16 **Yargatti** Karnātaka, W India 16°07′N 75°11′E
164 M12 **Yariga-take** ▲ Honshū, S Japan 36°20′N 137°38′E
141 O15 **Yarīm** W Yemen 14°15′N 44°23′E
54 F14 **Yarí, Río** SW Colombia
54 K5 **Yaritagua** Yaracuy, N Venezuela 10°05′N 69°07′W
Yarkand *see* Yarkant He
Yarkant *see* Shache
158 E9 **Yarkant He** *var.* Yarkand. NW China
149 U3 **Yarkhūn** NW Pakistan
Yarlung Zangbo Jiang *see* Brahmaputra
116 L6 **Yarmolyntsi** Khmel'nyts'ka Oblast', W Ukraine 49°13′N 26°53′E
13 O16 **Yarmouth** Nova Scotia, SE Canada 43°53′N 66°09′W
Yarmouth *see* Great Yarmouth
Yaroslav *see* Jarosław
124 L15 **Yaroslavl'** Yaroslavskaya Oblast', W Russian Federation 57°38′N 39°53′E
124 K14 **Yaroslavskaya Oblast'** ◐ *province* W Russian Federation
123 N11 **Yaroslavskiy** Respublika Sakha (Yakutiya), NE Russian Federation 60°10′N 114°12′E
183 P13 **Yarram** Victoria, SE Australia 38°36′S 146°40′E
183 O11 **Yarrawonga** Victoria, SE Australia 36°04′S 145°58′E
182 L4 **Yarriarraburra Swamp** *wetland* New South Wales, SE Australia
122 I8 **Yar-Sale** Yamalo-Nenetskiy Avtonomnyy Okrug, N Russian Federation 66°52′N 70°42′E
122 K11 **Yartsevo** Krasnoyarskiy Kray, C Russian Federation 60°15′N 90°09′E
126 I4 **Yartsevo** Smolenskaya Oblast', W Russian Federation 55°03′N 32°46′E
54 E8 **Yarumal** Antioquia, NW Colombia 06°59′N 75°25′W
187 W14 **Yasawa Group** *island group* NW Fiji
77 V12 **Yashi** Katsina, N Nigeria 12°21′N 07°56′E
77 S14 **Yashikera** Kwara, W Nigeria 09°40′N 03°19′E
147 T14 **Yashilkŭl** *Rus.* Ozero Yashil'kul'. ◎ SE Tajikistan
Yashil'kul', Ozero *see* Yashilkŭl
165 P9 **Yashima** Akita, Honshū, C Japan 39°10′N 140°10′E
127 P13 **Yashkul'** Respublika Kalmykiya, SW Russian Federation 46°09′N 45°22′E
146 F13 **Yashlyk** Ahal Welaýaty, C Turkmenistan 37°46′N 58°51′E
Yasinovataya *see* Yasynuvata
114 N10 **Yasna Polyana** Burgas, E Bulgaria 42°18′N 27°35′E
167 R10 **Yasothon** Yasothon, E Thailand 15°46′N 104°12′E
183 R10 **Yass** New South Wales, SE Australia 34°52′S 148°55′E
Yassy *see* Iasi
164 H12 **Yasugi** Shimane, Honshū, SW Japan 35°25′N 133°12′E
143 N10 **Yāsūj** *var.* Yasuj; *prev.* Tal-e Khosravī. Kohkīlūyeh va Būyer Aḩmad, C Iran 30°40′N 51°34′E
136 M11 **Yasun Burnu** *headland* N Turkey 41°07′N 37°40′E
117 X8 **Yasynuvata** *Rus.* Yasinovataya. Donets'ka Oblast', SE Ukraine 48°05′N 37°57′E
136 C15 **Yatağan** Muğla, SW Turkey 37°22′N 28°08′E
165 Q7 **Yatate-tōge** *pass* Honshū, C Japan
187 Q17 **Yaté** Province Sud, S New Caledonia 22°10′S 166°56′E
27 P6 **Yates Center** Kansas, C USA 37°54′N 95°44′W
185 B21 **Yates Point** *headland* South Island, New Zealand 44°30′S 167°49′E
9 N9 **Yathkyed Lake** ◎ Nunavut, NE Canada
171 T16 **Yatoke** Pulau Babar, E Indonesia 07°51′S 129°49′E
79 M18 **Yatolema** Orientale, N Dem. Rep. Congo 0°25′N 24°35′E
164 C15 **Yatsushiro** *var.* Yatusiro. Kumamoto, Kyūshū, SW Japan 32°30′N 130°34′E
164 C15 **Yatsushiro-kai** *bay* SW Japan
138 F11 **Yatta** *var.* Yuta. S West Bank 31°29′N 35°10′E
81 J20 **Yatta Plateau** *plateau* SE Kenya
Yatusiro *see* Yatsushiro
57 F17 **Yauca, Río** SW Peru
45 S6 **Yauco** W Puerto Rico 18°02′N 66°51′W
Yaunde *see* Yaoundé
Yavan *see* Yovon
Yavari *see* Javari, Rio
56 G9 **Yavari Mirim, Río** NE Peru
40 G7 **Yavaros** Sonora, NW Mexico 26°40′N 109°32′W
154 I13 **Yavatmāl** Mahārāshtra, C India 20°22′N 78°11′E
54 M9 **Yaví, Cerro** ▲ C Venezuela 05°43′N 65°51′W
43 W16 **Yaviza** Darién, SE Panama 08°09′N 77°41′W
138 F10 **Yavne** Central, W Israel 31°52′N 34°45′E
116 H5 **Yavoriv** *Pol.* Jaworów, *Rus.* Yavorov. L'vivs'ka Oblast', NW Ukraine 49°57′N 23°22′E
Yavorov *see* Yavoriv
164 F14 **Yawatahama** Ehime, Shikoku, SW Japan 33°27′N 132°24′E
Ya Xian *see* Sanya
136 L17 **Yayladaği** Hatay, S Turkey 35°55′N 36°00′E
125 V13 **Yayva** Permskaya Oblast', NW Russian Federation 59°19′N 57°15′E
125 V12 **Yayva** NW Russian Federation
143 Q9 **Yazd** *var.* Yezd. Yazd, C Iran 31°55′N 54°22′E
143 Q8 **Yazd** *off.* Ostān-e Yazd, *var.* Yezd. ◐ *province* C Iran
Yazd, Ostān-e *see* Yazd
Yazgulemskiy Khrebet *see* Yazgulom, Qatorkŭhi
147 S13 **Yazgulom, Qatorkŭhi** *Rus.* Yazgulemskiy Khrebet. ▲▲ S Tajikistan
22 K5 **Yazoo City** Mississippi, S USA 32°51′N 90°24′W
22 K5 **Yazoo River** Mississippi, S USA
127 Q5 **Yazykovka** Ul'yanovskaya Oblast', W Russian Federation 54°19′N 47°22′E
109 U4 **Ybbs** Niederösterreich, NE Austria 48°10′N 15°03′E
109 U4 **Ybbs** C Austria
95 G22 **Yding Skovhøj** *hill* C Denmark
115 G20 **Ýdra** *var.* Ídhra, Idra. Ýdra, S Greece 37°20′N 23°28′E
115 G21 **Ýdra** *var.* Ídhra. *island* Ýdra, S Greece
115 G20 **Ýdras, Kólpos** *strait* S Greece
167 N10 **Ye** Mon State, S Myanmar (Burma) 15°15′N 97°50′E
183 O12 **Yea** Victoria, SE Australia 37°15′S 145°27′E
Yebaishou *see* Jianping
78 I5 **Yebbi-Bou** Borkou-Ennedi-Tibesti, N Chad 21°12′N 17°55′E
158 F9 **Yecheng** *var.* Kargilik. Xinjiang Uygur Zizhiqu, NW China 37°54′N 77°26′E
105 R11 **Yecla** Murcia, SE Spain 38°36′N 01°07′W
40 H6 **Yécora** Sonora, NW Mexico 28°23′N 108°56′W
Yedintsy *see* Edineţ
124 J13 **Yefimovskiy** Leningradskaya Oblast', NW Russian Federation 59°32′N 34°34′E
126 K6 **Yefremov** Tul'skaya Oblast', W Russian Federation 53°10′N 38°02′E
159 T11 **Yêgainnyin** *var.* Henan Mongolzu Zizhixian. Qinghai, C China 34°42′N 101°36′E
137 U12 **Yegbhegis** *Rus.* Yekhegis. C Armenia
137 U12 **Yeghegnadzor** C Armenia 39°45′N 45°20′E
145 T10 **Yegindybulak** *Kaz.* Egindibulaq. Karaganda, C Kazakhstan 49°45′N 75°45′E
126 L4 **Yegor'yevsk** Moskovskaya Oblast', W Russian Federation 55°29′N 39°03′E
Yehuda, Haré *see* Judaean Hills
81 E15 **Yei** S Sudan
161 P8 **Yeji** *var.* Yejiaji. Anhui, E China 31°52′N 115°58′E
Yejiaji *see* Yeji
122 G10 **Yekaterinburg** *prev.* Sverdlovsk. Sverdlovskaya Oblast', C Russian Federation 56°52′N 60°35′E
Yekaterinodar *see* Krasnodar
Yekaterinoslav *see* Dnipropetrovs'k
123 R13 **Yekaterinoslavka** Amurskaya Oblast', SE Russian Federation 50°23′N 129°03′E
127 O7 **Yekaterinovka** Saratovskaya Oblast', W Russian Federation 52°01′N 44°11′E
76 K16 **Yekepa** NE Liberia 07°35′N 08°32′W
Yekhegis *see* Yegbhegis
127 T3 **Yelabuga** Respublika Tatarstan, W Russian Federation 55°46′N 52°07′E
Yela Island *see* Rossel Island
127 O8 **Yelan'** Volgogradskaya Oblast', SW Russian Federation 51°00′N 43°40′E
117 Q9 **Yelanets'** *Rus.* Yelanets. Mykolayivs'ka Oblast', S Ukraine 47°40′N 31°51′E
126 L7 **Yelets** Lipetskaya Oblast', W Russian Federation 52°37′N 38°29′E
125 W4 **Yeletskiy** Respublika Komi, NW Russian Federation 67°03′N 64°05′E
76 J11 **Yélimané** Kayes, W Mali 15°06′N 10°43′W
Yelisavetpol *see* Gäncä
Yelizavetgrad *see* Kirovohrad
123 T12 **Yelizavety, Mys** *headland* SE Russian Federation 54°20′N 142°39′E
Yelizovo *see* Yalizava
127 S5 **Yelkhovka** Samarskaya Oblast', W Russian Federation 53°51′N 50°16′E
96 M1 **Yell** *island* NE Scotland, United Kingdom
155 E17 **Yellāpur** Karnātaka, W India 15°06′N 74°50′E
11 U17 **Yellow Grass** Saskatchewan, S Canada 49°51′N 104°09′W
Yellowhammer State *see* Alabama
11 O15 **Yellowhead Pass** *pass* Alberta/British Columbia, SW Canada
8 K10 **Yellowknife** *territory capital* Northwest Territories, W Canada 62°30′N 114°29′W
8 K9 **Yellowknife** Northwest Territories, NW Canada
23 P8 **Yellow River** Alabama/Florida, S USA
30 J6 **Yellow River** Wisconsin, N USA
30 K7 **Yellow River** Wisconsin, N USA
30 I4 **Yellow River** Wisconsin, N USA
Yellow River *see* Huang He
157 V8 **Yellow Sea** *Chin.* Huang Hai, *Kor.* Hwang-Hae. *sea* E Asia
33 S13 **Yellowstone Lake** ◎ Wyoming, C USA
33 T13 **Yellowstone National Park** *national park* Wyoming, NW USA
33 Y8 **Yellowstone River** Montana/Wyoming, NW USA
96 L1 **Yell Sound** *strait* N Scotland, United Kingdom
27 U9 **Yellville** Arkansas, C USA 36°12′N 92°41′W
126 I4 **Yel'nya** Smolenskaya Oblast', W Russian Federation 54°34′N 33°11′E
122 K10 **Yeloguy** C Russian Federation
Yëloten *see* Yolöten
119 M20 **Yel'sk** Homyel'skaya Voblasts', SE Belarus 51°48′N 29°09′E
77 T13 **Yelwa** Kebbi, W Nigeria 10°52′N 04°46′E
21 R15 **Yemassee** South Carolina, SE USA 32°41′N 80°51′W
141 O15 **Yemen** *off.* Republic of Yemen, *Ar.* Al Jumhuriyah al Yamaniyah, Al Yaman. ◆ *republic* SW Asia
Yemen, Republic of *see* Yemen
116 M4 **Yemil'chyne** Zhytomyrs'ka Oblast', N Ukraine 50°51′N 27°49′E
124 M10 **Yemtsa** Arkhangel'skaya Oblast', NW Russian Federation 63°04′N 40°18′E
124 M10 **Yemtsa** NW Russian Federation
125 R10 **Yemva** *prev.* Zheleznodorozhnyy. Respublika Komi, NW Russian Federation 62°38′N 50°59′E
77 U17 **Yenagoa** Bayelsa, S Nigeria 4°58′N 6°16′E
117 X7 **Yenakiyeve** *Rus.* Yenakiyevo; *prev.* Ordzhonikidze, Rykovo. Donets'ka Oblast', E Ukraine 48°13′N 38°13′E
Yenakiyevo *see* Yenakiyeve
166 L6 **Yenangyaung** Magway, W Myanmar (Burma) 20°28′N 94°54′E
167 S5 **Yên Bai** Yên Bai, N Vietnam 21°43′N 104°54′E
183 P9 **Yenda** New South Wales, SE Australia 34°16′S 146°15′E
77 Q14 **Yendi** NE Ghana 09°30′N 00°01′W
Yêndum *see* Zhag'yab
158 E8 **Yengisar** Xinjiang Uygur Zizhiqu, NW China 38°50′N 76°11′E
136 H11 **Yenice Çayı** *var.* Filyos Çayı. N Turkey
121 R1 **Yenierenköy** *var.* Yialousa, *Gk.* Agialoúsa. NE Cyprus 35°33′N 34°13′E
Yenipazar *see* Novi Pazar
136 E12 **Yenişehir** Bursa, NW Turkey 40°17′N 29°38′E
Yenisei Bay *see* Yeniseyskiy Zaliv
122 K12 **Yeniseysk** Krasnoyarskiy Kray, C Russian Federation 58°23′N 92°06′E
197 W10 **Yeniseyskiy Zaliv** *var.* Yenisei Bay. *bay* N Russian Federation
127 Q12 **Yenotayevka** Astrakhanskaya Oblast', SW Russian Federation 47°16′N 47°01′E
124 L4 **Yenozero, Ozero** ◎ NW Russian Federation
Yenping *see* Nanping
39 Q11 **Yentna River** Alaska, USA
180 M10 **Yeo, Lake** *salt lake* Western Australia
183 R7 **Yeoval** New South Wales, SE Australia 32°45′S 148°39′E
97 K23 **Yeovil** SW England, United Kingdom 50°57′N 02°39′W
40 H6 **Yepachic** Chihuahua, N Mexico 28°27′N 108°25′W
181 Y8 **Yeppoon** Queensland, E Australia 23°05′S 150°42′E
126 M5 **Yeraktur** Ryazanskaya Oblast', W Russian Federation 54°45′N 41°09′E
Yeraliyev *see* Kuryk
146 F12 **Yerbent** Ahal Welaýaty, C Turkmenistan 39°19′N 58°34′E
123 N11 **Yerbogachën** Irkutskaya Oblast', C Russian Federation 61°07′N 108°03′E
137 T12 **Yerevan** *Eng.* Erivan. ● (Armenia) C Armenia 40°12′N 44°31′E
137 U12 **Yerevan** ✈ C Armenia 40°07′N 44°34′E
145 R9 **Yereymentau** *var.* Jermentau, *Kaz.* Ereymentaū. Akmola, C Kazakhstan 51°38′N 73°10′E
127 O12 **Yergeni** *hill range* SW Russian Federation
Yeriho *see* Jericho
35 R6 **Yerington** Nevada, W USA 38°58′N 119°10′W
136 J13 **Yerköy** Yozgat, C Turkey 39°39′N 34°28′E
114 L13 **Yerlisu** Edirne, NW Turkey 40°45′N 26°38′E
Yermak *see* Aksu
145 R9 **Yermentau, Gory** ▲▲ C Kazakhstan
125 R5 **Yërmitsa** Respublika Komi, NW Russian Federation 66°57′N 52°15′E
35 V14 **Yermo** California, W USA 34°54′N 116°49′W
123 P13 **Yerofey Pavlovich** Amurskaya Oblast', SE Russian Federation 53°58′N 121°49′E
99 F15 **Yerseke** Zeeland, SW Netherlands 51°30′N 04°03′E
127 Q8 **Yershov** Saratovskaya Oblast', W Russian Federation 51°18′N 48°16′E
125 P9 **Yërtom** Respublika Komi, NW Russian Federation 63°27′N 47°52′E
56 D13 **Yerupaja, Nevado** ▲ C Peru 10°23′S 76°58′W
Yerushalayim *see* Jerusalem
105 R4 **Yesa, Embalse de** ▣ NE Spain
144 F9 **Yesensay** Zapadnyy Kazakhstan, NW Kazakhstan 49°59′N 51°19′E
144 F9 **Yesensay** Zapadnyy Kazakhstan, NW Kazakhstan 49°59′N 51°19′E
145 V15 **Yesik** *Kaz.* Esik; *prev.* Issyk. Almaty, SE Kazakhstan 42°23′N 77°25′E
145 O8 **Yesil'** *Kaz.* Esil. Akmola, C Kazakhstan 51°58′N 66°24′E
136 K15 **Yeşilhisar** Kayseri, C Turkey 38°22′N 35°08′E
136 L11 **Yeşilırmak** *var.* Iris. N Turkey
37 U12 **Yeso** New Mexico, SW USA 34°25′N 104°36′W
Yeso *see* Hokkaidō
127 N15 **Yessentuki** Stavropol'skiy Kray, SW Russian Federation 44°06′N 42°51′E
122 M9 **Yessey** Evenkiyskiy Avtonomnyy Okrug, N Russian Federation 68°18′N 101°49′E
105 P12 **Yeste** Castilla-La Mancha, C Spain 38°21′N 02°18′W
Yesuj *see* Yāsūj
183 T4 **Yetman** New South Wales, SE Australia 28°56′S 150°47′E
76 L4 **Yetti** *physical region* N Mauritania
166 M4 **Ye-u** Sagaing, C Myanmar (Burma) 22°49′N 95°26′E
102 H9 **Yeu, Île d'** *island* NW France
Yevlakh *see* Yevlax
137 W11 **Yevlax** *Rus.* Yevlakh. C Azerbaijan 40°36′N 47°10′E
117 S13 **Yevpatoriya** Respublika Krym, S Ukraine 45°12′N 33°23′E
Ye Xian *see* Laizhou
126 K12 **Yeya** SW Russian Federation
158 I10 **Yeyik** Xinjiang Uygur Zizhiqu, W China 36°44′N 83°14′E
126 K12 **Yeysk** Krasnodarskiy Kray, SW Russian Federation 46°41′N 38°15′E
Yezd *see* Yazd
Yezerishche *see* Yezyaryshcha
Yezhou *see* Jianshi
Yezo *see* Hokkaidō
118 N11 **Yezyaryshcha** *Rus.* Yezerishche. Vitsyebskaya Voblasts', NE Belarus 55°50′N 29°59′E
Yialí *see* Gyalí
Yialousa *see* Yenierenköy
163 V7 **Yi'an** Heilongjiang, NE China 47°52′N 125°13′E
Yiannitsá *see* Giannitsá
160 I10 **Yibin** Sichuan, C China 28°50′N 104°35′E
158 K13 **Yibug Caka** ◎ W China
160 M9 **Yichang** Hubei, C China 30°37′N 111°02′E
160 L5 **Yichuan** *var.* Danzhou. Shaanxi, C China 36°05′N 110°02′E
157 W3 **Yichun** Heilongjiang, NE China 47°41′N 129°10′E
161 O11 **Yichun** Jiangxi, S China 27°45′N 114°22′E
160 M9 **Yidu** *prev.* Zhicheng. Hubei, C China 30°21′N 111°27′E
Yidu *see* Qingzhou
188 C15 **Yigo** NE Guam 13°33′N 144°53′E
161 Q5 **Yi He** E China
163 X8 **Yilan** Heilongjiang, NE China 46°18′N 129°36′E
136 C9 **Yıldız Dağları** ▲▲ NW Turkey
136 L13 **Yıldızeli** Sivas, N Turkey 39°52′N 36°37′E
163 U4 **Yilehuli Shan** ▲▲ NE China
163 S7 **Yimin He** NE China
159 W8 **Yinchuan** *var.* Yinch'uan, Yin-ch'uan, Yinchwan. *province capital* Ningxia, N China 38°30′N 106°19′E
Yinchwan *see* Yinchuan
Yindu He *see* Indus
Yingcheng *see* Yingde
161 N14 **Yingde** *var.* Yingcheng. Guangdong, S China 24°08′N 113°21′E
161 O7 **Ying He** C China
163 U13 **Yingkou** *var.* Ying-k'ou, Yingkow; *prev.* Newchwang, Niuchwang. Liaoning, NE China 40°40′N 122°17′E
Yingkow *see* Yingkou
161 P9 **Yingshan** *var.* Wenquan. Hubei, C China 30°45′N 115°41′E
Yingshan *see* Guangshui
161 Q10 **Yingtan** Jiangxi, S China 28°17′N 117°03′E
Yin-hsien *see* Ningbo
158 H5 **Yining** *var.* I-ning, *Uigh.* Gulja, Kuldja. Xinjiang Uygur Zizhiqu, NW China 43°53′N 81°18′E
160 K11 **Yinjiang** *var.* Yinjiang Tujiazu Miaozu Zizhixian. Guizhou, S China 28°22′N 108°07′E
Yinjiang Tujiazu Miaozu Zizhixian *see* Yinjiang
166 L4 **Yinmabin** Sagaing, C Myanmar (Burma) 22°05′N 94°57′E
163 N13 **Yin Shan** ▲▲ N China
Yin-tu Ho *see* Indus
159 P15 **Yi'ong Zangbo** W China
Yioúra *see* Gyáros
81 J14 **Yirga 'Alem** *It.* Irgalem. Southern Nationalities, S Ethiopia 06°43′N 38°24′E
61 E19 **Yí, Río** C Uruguay
81 E14 **Yirol** El Buhayrat, S Sudan 06°34′N 30°33′E
163 S8 **Yirshi** *var.* Yirxie. Nei Mongol Zizhiqu, N China 47°16′N 119°51′E
Yirxie *see* Yirshi
Yishan *see* Guanyun
Yishi *see* Linyi
161 Q5 **Yishui** Shandong, E China 35°50′N 118°39′E
Yisrael/Yisra'el *see* Israel
Yíthion *see* Gýtheio
Yitiaoshan *see* Jingtai
163 W10 **Yitong** *var.* Yitong Manzu Zizhixian. Jilin, NE China 43°23′N 125°19′E
Yitong Manzu Zizhixian *see* Yitong
159 P5 **Yiwu** *var.* Aratürük. Xinjiang Uygur Zizhiqu, NW China 43°16′N 94°38′E
163 U12 **Yiwulü Shan** ▲ N China
163 T12 **Yixian** *var.* Yizhou. Liaoning, NE China 41°29′N 121°21′E
161 N10 **Yiyang** Hunan, S China 28°39′N 112°10′E
161 Q10 **Yiyang** Jiangxi, S China 28°21′N 117°23′E
161 N13 **Yizhang** Hunan, S China 25°24′N 112°51′E
Yizhou *see* Yixian
93 K19 **Yläne** Länsi-Suomi, SW Finland 60°51′N 22°26′E
93 L14 **Yli-Ii** Oulu, C Finland 65°21′N 25°55′E
93 L14 **Ylikiiminki** Oulu, C Finland 65°00′N 26°10′E
92 N13 **Yli-Kitka** ◎ NE Finland
93 K17 **Ylistaro** Länsi-Suomi, W Finland 62°58′N 22°30′E
92 K13 **Ylitornio** Lappi, NW Finland 66°19′N 23°40′E
93 L15 **Ylivieska** Oulu, W Finland 64°05′N 24°30′E
93 L18 **Ylöjärvi** Länsi-Suomi, W Finland 61°31′N 23°37′E
95 N17 **Yngaren** ◎ C Sweden
25 T12 **Yoakum** Texas, SW USA 29°18′N 97°09′W
77 X13 **Yobe** ◐ *state* NE Nigeria
165 R3 **Yobetsu-dake** Hokkaidō, NE Japan 43°15′N 140°27′E
80 L11 **Yoboki** C Djibouti 11°30′N 42°04′E
22 M4 **Yockanookany River** Mississippi, S USA
22 L2 **Yocona River** Mississippi, S USA
171 Y15 **Yodom** Papua, E Indonesia 07°12′S 139°24′E
169 Q16 **Yogyakarta** *prev.* Djokjakarta, Jogjakarta, Jokyakarta. Jawa, C Indonesia 07°48′S 110°24′E
169 P17 **Yogyakarta** *off.* Daerah Istimewa Yogyakarta, *var.* Djokjakarta, Jogjakarta, Jokyakarta. ◐ *autonomous district* S Indonesia
Yogyakarta, Daerah Istimewa *see* Yogyakarta
165 Q3 **Yoichi** Hokkaidō, NE Japan 43°11′N 140°45′E
42 G6 **Yojoa, Lago de** ◎ NW Honduras
79 G16 **Yokadouma** Est, SE Cameroon 03°26′N 15°06′E
164 K13 **Yokkaichi** *var.* Yokkaiti. Mie, Honshū, SW Japan 34°58′N 136°38′E
Yokkaiti *see* Yokkaichi
79 E15 **Yoko** Centre, C Cameroon 05°29′N 12°19′E
165 V15 **Yokoate-jima** *island* Nansei-shotō, SW Japan
165 R6 **Yokohama** Aomori, Honshū, C Japan 41°04′N 141°14′E
165 O14 **Yokosuka** Kanagawa, Honshū, S Japan 35°18′N 139°39′E
164 G12 **Yokota** Shimane, Honshū, SW Japan 35°10′N 133°03′E
165 Q9 **Yokote** Akita, Honshū, C Japan 39°20′N 140°33′E
77 Y14 **Yola** Adamawa, E Nigeria 09°08′N 12°24′E
79 L19 **Yolombo** Equateur, C Dem. Rep. Congo 01°36′S 23°13′E
146 J14 **Yolöten** *Rus.* Yëloten; *prev.* Iolotan'. Mary Welaýaty, S Turkmenistan 37°15′N 62°18′E
165 Y15 **Yome-jima** *island* Ogasawara-shotō, SE Japan
76 K16 **Yomou** SE Guinea 07°30′N 09°13′W
171 Y15 **Yomuka** Papua, E Indonesia 07°25′S 138°36′E
188 C16 **Yona** E Guam 13°24′N 144°46′E
164 H12 **Yonago** Tottori, Honshū, SW Japan 35°30′N 134°15′E
165 N16 **Yonaguni** Okinawa, SW Japan 24°29′N 123°00′E
165 N16 **Yonaguni-jima** *island* Nansei-shotō, SW Japan
165 T16 **Yonaha-dake** ▲ Okinawa, SW Japan 26°43′N 128°13′E
163 X14 **Yŏnan** SW North Korea 37°50′N 126°15′E
165 P10 **Yonezawa** Yamagata, Honshū, C Japan 37°56′N 140°06′E
161 Q12 **Yong'an** *var.* Yongan. Fujian, SE China 25°58′N 117°26′E
Yong'an *see* Fengjie
159 T9 **Yongchang** Gansu, N China 38°15′N 101°56′E
161 P7 **Yongcheng** Henan, C China 33°56′N 116°21′E
163 Z15 **Yŏngch'ŏn** *Jap.* Eisen. SE South Korea 35°56′N 128°55′E
160 J10 **Yongchuan** Chongqing Shi, C China 29°27′N 105°56′E
159 U10 **Yongdeng** Gansu, C China 35°58′N 103°27′E
Yongding *see* Yongren
129 W9 **Yongding He** E China
161 P11 **Yongfeng** *var.* Enjiang. Jiangxi, S China 27°19′N 115°23′E
158 L5 **Yongfengqu** Xinjiang Uygur Zizhiqu, W China 43°28′N 87°09′E
160 L13 **Yongfu** Guangxi Zhuangzu Zizhiqu, S China 24°57′N 109°59′E
163 X13 **Yŏnghŭng** E North Korea 39°31′N 127°14′E
159 U10 **Yongjing** *var.* Liujiaxia. Gansu, C China 36°00′N 103°30′E
Yongjing *see* Xifeng
163 Y15 **Yŏngju** *Jap.* Eishū. C South Korea 36°48′N 128°37′E
Yongning *see* Xuyong
160 E12 **Yongping** Yunnan, SW China 25°30′N 99°28′E
160 G12 **Yongren** *var.* Yongding. Yunnan, SW China 26°09′N 101°40′E
160 L10 **Yongshun** *var.* Lingxi. Hunan, S China 29°02′N 109°46′E
161 P10 **Yongxiu** *var.* Tujiabu. Jiangxi, S China 29°09′N 115°47′E
160 M12 **Yongzhou** *var.* Lengshuitan. Hunan, S China 26°13′N 111°36′E
Yongzhou *see* Zhishan
18 K14 **Yonkers** New York, NE USA 40°56′N 73°51′W
103 Q7 **Yonne** ◐ *department* C France
103 P6 **Yonne** C France
54 H9 **Yopal** *var.* El Yopal. Casanare, C Colombia 05°20′N 72°19′W
158 E8 **Yopurga** *var.* Yukuriawat. Xinjiang Uygur Zizhiqu, NW China 39°13′N 76°44′E
147 S11 **Yordon** *var.* Jordan, *Rus.* Jardan. Farg'ona Viloyati, E Uzbekistan 39°59′N 71°44′E
180 J12 **York** Western Australia 31°55′S 116°52′E
97 M16 **York** *anc.* Eboracum, Eburacum. N England, United Kingdom 53°58′N 01°05′W
23 N5 **York** Alabama, S USA 32°29′N 88°18′W
29 Q15 **York** Nebraska, C USA 40°52′N 97°35′W
18 G16 **York** Pennsylvania, NE USA 39°57′N 76°44′W
21 R11 **York** South Carolina, SE USA 34°59′N 81°14′W
14 J13 **York** Ontario, SE Canada
15 X6 **York** Québec, SE Canada
181 V1 **York, Cape** *headland* Queensland, NE Australia 10°40′S 142°36′E
182 I9 **Yorke Peninsula** *peninsula* South Australia
182 I9 **Yorketown** South Australia 35°01′S 137°38′E
19 P9 **York Harbor** Maine, NE USA 43°10′N 70°37′W
York, Kap *see* Innaanganeq
21 X6 **York River** Virginia, NE USA
97 M16 **Yorkshire** *cultural region* N England, United Kingdom
97 L16 **Yorkshire Dales** *physical region* N England, United Kingdom
11 V16 **Yorkton** Saskatchewan, S Canada 51°12′N 102°29′W
25 T12 **Yorktown** Texas, SW USA 28°58′N 97°30′W
21 X6 **Yorktown** Virginia, NE USA 37°14′N 76°32′W
30 M11 **Yorkville** Illinois, N USA 41°38′N 88°27′W
42 I5 **Yoro** Yoro, C Honduras 15°08′N 87°10′W
42 H5 **Yoro** ◐ *department* N Honduras
165 T16 **Yoron-jima** *island* Nansei-shotō, SW Japan
77 N13 **Yorosso** Sikasso, S Mali 12°21′N 04°47′W
35 R8 **Yosemite National Park** *national park* California, W USA
127 Q3 **Yoshkar-Ola** Respublika Mariy El, W Russian Federation 56°38′N 47°54′E
Yösönbulag *see* Altay
162 K8 **Yösöndzüyl** *var.* Mönhbulag. Övörhangay, C Mongolia 46°48′N 103°25′E
171 Y16 **Yos Sudarso, Pulau** *var.* Pulau Dolak, Pulau Kolepom; *prev.* Jos Sudarso. *island* E Indonesia
163 Y17 **Yŏsu** *Jap.* Reisui. S South Korea 34°45′N 127°41′E
165 R4 **Yotei-zan** ▲ Hokkaidō, NE Japan 42°50′N 140°46′E
97 D21 **Youghal** *Ir.* Eochaill. Cork, S Ireland 51°57′N 07°50′W
97 D21 **Youghal Bay** *Ir.* Cuan Eochaille. *inlet* S Ireland
18 C15 **Youghiogheny River** Pennsylvania, NE USA
160 K14 **You Jiang** S China
183 Q9 **Young** New South Wales, SE Australia 34°19′S 148°20′E
11 T15 **Young** Saskatchewan, S Canada 51°44′N 105°44′W
61 E18 **Young** Río Negro, W Uruguay 32°44′S 57°36′W
182 G5 **Younghusband, Lake** *salt lake* South Australia
182 J10 **Younghusband Peninsula** *peninsula* South Australia
184 Q10 **Young Nicks Head** *headland* North Island, New Zealand 39°38′S 177°03′E
185 D20 **Young Range** ▲▲ South Island, New Zealand
191 Q15 **Young's Rock** *island* Pitcairn Island, Pitcairn Islands
11 R16 **Youngstown** Alberta, SW Canada 51°32′N 111°12′W
31 V12 **Youngstown** Ohio, N USA 41°06′N 80°39′W
159 N9 **Youshashan** Qinghai, C China 38°12′N 90°58′E
Youth, Isle of *see* Juventud, Isla de la
77 N11 **Youvarou** Mopti, C Mali 15°19′N 04°15′W
160 K10 **Youyang** *var.* Zhongduo. Chongqing Shi, C China 28°48′N 108°48′E
163 Y7 **Youyi** Heilongjiang, NE China 46°51′N 131°54′E
147 P13 **Yovon** *Rus.* Yavan. SW Tajikistan 38°19′N 69°02′E
136 J13 **Yozgat** Yozgat, C Turkey 39°49′N 34°48′E
136 K13 **Yozgat** ◐ *province* C Turkey
62 O6 **Ypacaraí** *var.* Ypacaray. Central, S Paraguay 25°23′S 57°16′W
Ypacaray *see* Ypacaraí
62 P5 **Ypané, Río** C Paraguay
Ypres *see* Ieper
114 I13 **Ypsário** *var.* Ipsario. ▲ Thásos, E Greece 40°43′N 24°39′E
31 R10 **Ypsilanti** Michigan, N USA 42°12′N 83°36′W
34 M1 **Yreka** California, W USA 41°43′N 122°39′W
Yrendagüé *see* General Eugenio A. Garay
Yrghyz *see* Irgiz
186 G5 **Ysabel Channel** *channel* N Papua New Guinea
14 K8 **Yser, Lac** ◎ Québec, SE Canada
147 Y8 **Yshtyk** Issyk-Kul'skaya Oblast', E Kyrgyzstan 41°34′N 78°21′E
109 U4 **Ysper** N Austria
Yssel *see* IJssel
103 Q12 **Yssingeaux** Haute-Loire, C France 45°09′N 04°07′E
95 K23 **Ystad** Skåne, S Sweden 55°25′N 13°51′E
Ysyk-Köl *see* Issyk-Kul', Ozero
Ysyk-Köl *see* Balykchy
Ysyk-Köl Oblasty *see* Issyk-Kul'skaya Oblast'
96 L8 **Ythan** NE Scotland, United Kingdom
Y Trallwng *see* Welshpool
94 C13 **Ytre Arna** Hordaland, S Norway 60°28′N 05°25′E
94 B12 **Ytre Sula** *island* S Norway
93 G17 **Ytterhogdal** Jämtland, C Sweden 62°10′N 14°55′E
Yu *see* Henan
Yuan *see* Red River
Yuancheng *see* Heyuan, Guangdong, S China
Yuan Jiang *see* Red River
161 S13 **Yüanlin** *Jap.* Inrin. C Taiwan 23°57′N 120°33′E
161 N3 **Yuanping** Shanxi, C China 38°26′N 112°42′E
Yuanquan *see* Anxi
Yuanshan *see* Lianping
161 O11 **Yuan Shui** S China
35 O6 **Yuba City** California, W USA 39°07′N 121°40′W
35 O6 **Yuba River** California, W USA
80 H13 **Yubdo** Oromīya, C Ethiopia 09°05′N 35°28′E
41 X12 **Yucatán** ◐ *state* SE Mexico
47 O3 **Yucatan Basin** *var.* Yucatan Deep. *undersea feature* N Caribbean Sea 20°00′N 84°00′W
Yucatán, Canal de *see* Yucatan Channel
41 Y10 **Yucatan Channel** *Sp.* Canal de Yucatán. *channel* Cuba/Mexico
Yucatan Deep *see* Yucatan Basin
Yucatan Peninsula *see* Yucatán, Península de
41 X13 **Yucatán, Península de** *Eng.* Yucatan Peninsula. *peninsula* Guatemala/Mexico
36 I11 **Yucca** Arizona, SW USA 34°49′N 114°06′W
35 V15 **Yucca Valley** California, W USA 34°06′N 116°30′W
161 P4 **Yucheng** Shandong, E China 37°01′N 116°37′E
Yuci *see* Jinzhong
129 X5 **Yudoma** E Russian Federation
161 P12 **Yudu** *var.* Gongjiang. Jiangxi, C China 26°02′N 115°24′E
Yue *see* Guangdong
Yuecheng *see* Yuexi
160 M12 **Yuecheng Ling** ▲▲ S China
Yuegai *see* Qumarlêb
Yuegaitan *see* Qumarlêb
181 P7 **Yuendumu** Northern Territory, N Australia 22°19′S 131°51′E
Yue Shan, Tai *see* Lantau Island
160 H10 **Yuexi** *var.* Yuecheng. Sichuan, C China 28°50′N 102°36′E
161 N10 **Yueyang** Hunan, S China 29°24′N 113°08′E
125 U14 **Yug** Permskaya Oblast', NW Russian Federation 57°49′N 56°08′E
125 P13 **Yug** NW Russian Federation
123 R10 **Yugorënok** Respublika Sakha (Yakutiya), NE Russian Federation 59°46′N 137°36′E
122 H9 **Yugorsk** Khanty-Mansiyskiy Avtonomnyy Okrug-Yugra, C Russian Federation 61°17′N 63°25′E
122 H7 **Yugorskiy Poluostrov** *peninsula* NW Russian Federation
Yugoslavia *see* Serbia
146 K14 **Yugo-Vostochnyye Garagumy** *prev.* Yugo-Vostochnyye Karakumy. *desert* E Turkmenistan
Yugo-Vostochnyye Karakumy *see* Yugo-Vostochnyye Garagumy
Yuhu *see* Eryuan
161 S10 **Yuhuan Dao** *island* SE China
160 L14 **Yu Jiang** S China
Yujin *see* Qianwei
123 S7 **Yukagirskoye Ploskogor'ye** *plateau* NE Russian Federation
118 L11 **Yukhavichy** *Rus.* Yukhovichi. Vitsyebskaya Voblasts', N Belarus 56°02′N 28°39′E
126 J4 **Yukhnov** Kaluzhskaya Oblast', W Russian Federation 54°43′N 35°15′E
Yukhovichi *see* Yukhavichy
79 J20 **Yuki** *var.* Yuki Kengunda. Bandundu, W Dem. Rep. Congo 03°57′S 19°30′E
Yuki Kengunda *see* Yuki
26 M10 **Yukon** Oklahoma, C USA 35°30′N 97°45′W
0 F4 **Yukon** Canada/USA
Yukon *see* Yukon Territory
39 S7 **Yukon Flats** *salt flat* Alaska, USA
Yukon, Territoire du *see* Yukon Territory
10 I5 **Yukon Territory** *var.* Yukon, *Fr.* Territoire du Yukon. ◐ *territory* NW Canada
137 T16 **Yüksekova** Hakkâri, SE Turkey 37°35′N 44°17′E
123 N10 **Yukta** Evenkiyskiy Avtonomnyy Okrug, C Russian Federation 63°16′N 106°04′E
165 O13 **Yukuhashi** *var.* Yukuhasi. Fukuoka, Kyūshū, SW Japan 33°41′N 131°00′E
Yukuhasi *see* Yukuhashi
Yukuriawat *see* Yopurga
125 O9 **Yula** NW Russian Federation
181 P8 **Yulara** Northern Territory, N Australia 25°15′S 130°57′E
127 W6 **Yuldybayevo** Respublika Bashkortostan, W Russian Federation 52°22′N 57°55′E
23 W8 **Yulee** Florida, SE USA 30°37′N 81°36′W
158 K7 **Yuli** *var.* Lopnur. Xinjiang Uygur Zizhiqu, NW China 41°24′N 86°12′E
161 T14 **Yüli** C Taiwan 23°23′N 121°18′E
160 L15 **Yulin** Guangxi Zhuangzu Zizhiqu, S China 22°37′N 110°08′E
160 L4 **Yulin** Shaanxi, C China 38°14′N 109°48′E
161 T14 **Yüli Shan** ▲ E Taiwan 23°23′N 121°14′E
160 F11 **Yulong Xueshan** ▲ SW China 27°09′N 100°10′E
36 H14 **Yuma** Arizona, SW USA 32°40′N 114°38′W
37 W3 **Yuma** Colorado, C USA 40°07′N 102°43′W
54 K5 **Yumare** Yaracuy, N Venezuela 10°37′N 68°41′W
63 G14 **Yumbel** Bío Bío, C Chile 37°05′S 72°40′W
79 N19 **Yumbi** Maniema, E Dem. Rep. Congo 01°14′S 26°14′E
159 Q7 **Yumen** *prev.* Yumenzhen. Gansu, N China 40°19′N 97°12′E
Yumenzhen *see* Yumen
158 J3 **Yumin** *var.* Karabura. Xinjiang Uygur Zizhiqu, NW China 46°14′N 82°52′E
Yun *see* Yunnan
136 G14 **Yunak** Konya, W Turkey 38°50′N 31°42′E
45 O8 **Yuna, Río** E Dominican Republic
38 I17 **Yunaska Island** *island* Aleutian Islands, Alaska, USA
160 M6 **Yuncheng** Shanxi, C China 35°07′N 110°58′E
Yuncheng *see* Yunfu
161 N14 **Yunfu** *var.* Yuncheng. Guangdong, S China 22°55′N 112°02′E

◆ Country ● Country Capital ◇ Dependent Territory ○ Dependent Territory Capital ◐ Administrative Regions ✈ International Airport ▲ Mountain ▲▲ Mountain Range Volcano River ◎ Lake ▣ Reservoir

YUNGAS – ZHANADAR'YA

57 L18 **Yungas** *physical region* E Bolivia
Yungki *see* Jilin
Yung-ning *see* Nanning
160 I12 **Yungui Gaoyuan** *plateau* SW China
Yunjinghong *see* Jinghong
160 M15 **Yunkai Dashan** ▲ S China
Yunki *see* Jilin
160 E11 **Yun Ling** ▲ SW China
Yunling *see* Yunxiao
161 N9 **Yunmeng** Hubei, C China *31°04′N 113°45′E*
157 N14 **Yunnan** *var.* Yun, Yunnan Sheng, Yünnan, Yun-nan. ◆ *province* SW China
Yunnan *see* Kunming
Yunnan Sheng *see* Yunnan
Yünnan/Yun-nan *see* Yunnan
165 P15 **Yunomae** Kumamoto, Kyūshū, SW Japan *32°16′N 131°00′E*
161 N8 **Yun Shui** ⚘ C China
182 J7 **Yunta** South Australia *32°37′S 139°33′E*
161 Q14 **Yunxiao** *var.* Yunling. Fujian, SE China *23°56′N 117°16′E*
160 K9 **Yunyang** Sichuan, C China *31°03′N 109°43′E*
Yunzhong *see* Huairen
193 S9 **Yupanqui Basin** *undersea feature* E Pacific Ocean
Yuping *see* Libo, Guizhou, China
Yuping *see* Pingbian, Yunnan, China
Yuratishki *see* Yuratsishki
119 I15 **Yuratsishki** *Pol.* Juraciszki, *Rus.* Yuratishki. Hrodzyenskaya Voblasts', W Belarus *54°02′N 25°56′E*
Yurev *see* Tartu
122 J12 **Yurga** Kemerovskaya Oblast', S Russian Federation *55°42′N 84°59′E*
Yurihonjō *see* Honjō
56 E10 **Yurimaguas** Loreto, N Peru *05°54′S 76°07′W*
127 P3 **Yurino** Respublika Mariy El, W Russian Federation *56°19′N 46°15′E*
41 N13 **Yuriria** Guanajuato, C Mexico *20°12′N 101°09′W*
125 T13 **Yurla** Komi-Permyatskiy Avtonomnyy Okrug, NW Russian Federation *59°18′N 54°19′E*
Yuruá, Río *see* Juruá, Rio
114 M13 **Yürük** Tekirdağ, NW Turkey *40°58′N 27°09′E*
158 G10 **Yurungkax He** ⚘ W China
125 Q14 **Yur'ya** *var.* Jarja. Kirovskaya Oblast', NW Russian Federation *59°01′N 49°22′E*
Yury'ev *see* Tartu
125 N16 **Yur'yevets** Ivanovskaya Oblast', W Russian Federation *57°19′N 43°01′E*
126 M3 **Yur'yev-Pol'skiy** Vladimirskaya Oblast', W Russian Federation *56°28′N 39°39′E*
117 V7 **Yur"yivka** Dnipropetrovs'ka Oblast', E Ukraine *48°45′N 36°01′E*
42 I7 **Yuscarán** El Paraíso, S Honduras *13°55′N 86°51′W*
161 P12 **Yu Shan** ▲ S China
124 I7 **Yushkozero** Respublika Kareliya, NW Russian Federation *64°46′N 32°13′E*
124 I7 **Yushkozerskoye Vodokhranilishche** *var.* Ozero Kujto. ◎ NW Russian Federation
169 W9 **Yushu** Jilin, China E Asia *44°48′N 126°31′E*
159 R13 **Yushu** *var.* Gyêgu. Qinghai, C China *33°04′N 97°E*
127 P12 **Yusta** Respublika Kalmykiya, SW Russian Federation *47°06′N 46°16′E*
124 I10 **Yustozero** Respublika Kareliya, NW Russian Federation *62°44′N 33°31′E*
137 Q11 **Yusufeli** Artvin, NE Turkey *40°50′N 41°31′E*
164 F14 **Yusuhara** Kōchi, Shikoku, SW Japan *33°22′N 132°52′E*
125 T14 **Yus'va** Permskaya Oblast', NW Russian Federation *58°48′N 54°59′E*
Yuta *see* Yatta
161 P2 **Yutian** Hebei, E China *39°52′N 117°44′E*
158 H10 **Yutian** *var.* Keriya, Mugalla. Xinjiang Uygur Zizhiqu, NW China *36°49′N 81°31′E*
62 K5 **Yuto** Jujuy, NW Argentina *23°35′S 64°28′W*
62 P7 **Yuty** Caazapá, S Paraguay *26°31′S 56°20′W*
160 G13 **Yuxi** Yunnan, SW China *24°22′N 102°28′E*
161 O2 **Yuxian** *prev.* Yu Xian. Hebei, E China *39°50′N 114°33′E*
Yu Xian *see* Yuxian
165 Q9 **Yuzawa** Akita, Honshū, C Japan *39°11′N 140°29′E*
125 N16 **Yuzha** Ivanovskaya Oblast', W Russian Federation *56°34′N 42°00′E*
Yuzhno-Alichurskiy Khrebet *see* Alichuri Janubí, Qatorkŭhi
Yuzhno-Kazakhstanskaya Oblast' *see* Yuzhnyy Kazakhstan
123 T13 **Yuzhno-Sakhalinsk** *Jap.* Toyohara; *prev.* Vladimirovka. Ostrov Sakhalin, Sakhalinskaya Oblast', SE Russian Federation *46°58′N 142°45′E*
127 P14 **Yuzhno-Sukhokumsk** Respublika Dagestan, SW Russian Federation *44°43′N 45°32′E*
145 Z10 **Yuzhnyy Altay, Khrebet** ▲ E Kazakhstan
Yuzhnyy Bug *see* Pivdennyy Buh
145 O15 **Yuzhnyy Kazakhstan** *off.* Yuzhno-Kazakhstanskaya Oblast', *Eng.* South Kazakhstan, *Kaz.* Ongtüstik Qazaqstan Oblysy; *prev.* Chimkentskaya Oblast'. ◆ *province* S Kazakhstan
123 U10 **Yuzhnyy, Mys** *headland* E Russian Federation *57°44′N 156°49′E*
127 W6 **Yuzhnyy Ural** *var.* Southern Urals. ▲ W Russian Federation
159 V10 **Yuzhong** Gansu, C China *35°52′N 104°09′E*
Yuzhou *see* Chongqing
103 N5 **Yvelines** ◆ *department* N France
108 B9 **Yverdon** *var.* Yverdon-les-Bains, *Ger.* Iferten; *anc.* Eborodunum. Vaud, W Switzerland *46°47′N 06°38′E*
Yverdon-les-Bains *see* Yverdon
102 M3 **Yvetot** Seine-Maritime, N France *49°37′N 00°48′E*
Ýylanly *see* Gurbansoltan Eje

Z

147 T12 **Zaalayskiy Khrebet** *Taj.* Qatorkŭhi Pasi Oloy. ▲ Kyrgyzstan/Tajikistan
Zaamin *see* Zomin
Zaandam *see* Zaanstad
98 I10 **Zaanstad** *prev.* Zaandam. Noord-Holland, C Netherlands *52°27′N 04°49′E*
Zabadānī *see* Az Zabdānī
119 L18 **Zabalatstsye** *Rus.* Zabolot'ye. Homyel'skaya Voblasts', SE Belarus *52°40′N 28°34′E*
112 L9 **Žabalj** *Ger.* Josefsdorf, *Hung.* Zsablya; *prev.* Józseffalva. Vojvodina, N Serbia *45°22′N 20°01′E*
Zāb aş Şaghīr, Nahraz *see* Little Zab
123 P14 **Zabaykal'sk** Chitinskaya Oblast', S Russian Federation *49°37′N 117°20′E*
Zāb-e Kūchek, Rūdkhāneh-ye *see* Little Zab
Zabeln *see* Sabile
Zabéré *see* Zabré
Zabern *see* Saverne
141 N16 **Zabīd** W Yemen *14°N 43°E*
141 O16 **Zabīd, Wādī** *dry watercourse* SW Yemen
Žabinka *see* Zhabinka
Ząbkowice *see* Ząbkowice Śląskie
111 G15 **Ząbkowice Śląskie** *var.* Ząbkowice, *Ger.* Frankenstein, Frankenstein in Schlesien. Dolnośląskie, SW Poland *50°35′N 16°48′E*
110 P10 **Zabłudów** Podlaskie, NE Poland *53°00′N 23°21′E*
112 D8 **Zabok** Krapina-Zagorje, N Croatia *46°00′N 15°48′E*
143 W9 **Zābol** *var.* Shahr-i-Zabul, Zabul; *prev.* Nasratabad. Sīstān va Balūchestān, E Iran *31°N 61°32′E*
149 O7 **Zābol** *Pash.* Zābul. ◆ *province* SE Afghanistan
143 W13 **Zābolī** Sīstān va Balūchestān, SE Iran *27°09′N 61°32′E*
Zabolot'ye *see* Zabalatstsye
77 Q13 **Zabré** *var.* Zabéré. S Burkina *11°13′N 00°34′W*
111 G17 **Zábřeh** *Ger.* Hohenstadt. Olomoucký Kraj, E Czech Republic *49°52′N 16°53′E*
111 J16 **Zabrze** *Ger.* Hindenburg, Hindenburg in Oberschlesien. Śląskie, S Poland *50°18′N 18°47′E*
Zabul/Zābul *see* Zābol
42 E6 **Zacapa** Zacapa, E Guatemala *14°59′N 89°33′W*
42 A3 **Zacapa** *off.* Departamento de Zacapa. ◆ *department* E Guatemala
Zacapa, Departamento de *see* Zacapa
40 M14 **Zacapú** Michoacán, SW Mexico *19°49′N 101°48′W*
41 V14 **Zacatal** Campeche, SE Mexico *18°40′N 91°52′W*
40 M11 **Zacatecas** Zacatecas, C Mexico *22°46′N 102°33′W*
40 L10 **Zacatecas** ◆ *state* C Mexico
42 F8 **Zacatecoluca** La Paz, S El Salvador *13°29′N 88°51′W*
41 P15 **Zacatepec** Morelos, S Mexico *18°40′N 99°11′W*
41 Q13 **Zacatlán** Puebla, S Mexico *19°56′N 97°58′W*
144 F8 **Zachagansk** *Kaz.* Zashaghan. Zapadnyy Kazakhstan, NW Kazakhstan *51°04′N 51°13′E*
115 D20 **Zacháro** *var.* Zaharo, Zakháro. Dytikí Ellás, S Greece *37°29′N 21°40′E*
22 J8 **Zachary** Louisiana, S USA *30°39′N 91°09′W*
117 U6 **Zachepylivka** Kharkivs'ka Oblast', E Ukraine *49°13′N 35°15′E*
Zachist'ye *see* Zachystsye
110 E9 **Zachodnio-pomorskie** ◆ *province* NW Poland
119 L14 **Zachystsye** *Rus.* Zachist'ye. Minskaya Voblasts', NW Belarus *54°24′N 28°45′E*
40 L13 **Zacoalco** *var.* Zacoalco de Torres. Jalisco, SW Mexico *20°14′N 103°33′W*
Zacoalco de Torres *see* Zacoalco
41 P13 **Zacualtipán** Hidalgo, C Mexico *20°39′N 98°42′W*
112 C12 **Zadar** *It.* Zara; *anc.* Iader. Zadar, SW Croatia *44°07′N 15°15′E*
112 C12 **Zadar** *off.* Zadarsko-Kninska Županija, Zadar-Knin. ◆ *province* SW Croatia
Zadar-Knin *see* Zadar
Zadarsko-Kninska Županija *see* Zadar
166 M14 **Zadetkyi Kyun** *var.* St.Matthew's Island. *island* Mergui Archipelago, S Myanmar (Burma)
67 Q9 **Zadié** *var.* Djadié. ⚘ NE Gabon
159 Q13 **Zadoi** *var.* Qapugtang. Qinghai, C China *32°56′N 95°21′E*
126 L7 **Zadonsk** Lipetskaya Oblast', W Russian Federation *52°25′N 38°55′E*
Za'farâna *see* Za'farānah
75 X8 **Za'farānah** *var.* Za'farâna. E Egypt *29°06′N 32°34′E*
149 W7 **Zafarwāl** Punjab, E Pakistan *32°20′N 74°53′E*
121 Q1 **Zafer Burnu** *var.* Cape Andreas, Cape Apostolas Andreas, *Gk.* Akrotíri Apostólou Andréa. *cape* NE Cyprus
107 J23 **Zafferano, Capo** *headland* Sicilia, Italy, C Mediterranean Sea *38°06′N 13°31′E*
114 M7 **Zafirovo** Silistra, NE Bulgaria *44°00′N 26°51′E*
Záfora *see* Sofraná
104 J12 **Zafra** Extremadura, W Spain *38°25′N 06°27′W*
110 E13 **Żagań** *var.* Zagań, Żegań, *Ger.* Sagan. Lubuskie, W Poland *51°37′N 15°20′E*
118 F10 **Žagarė** *Pol.* Żagory. Šiaulai, N Lithuania *56°22′N 23°16′E*
Zagazig *see* Az Zaqāzīq
74 M5 **Zaghouan** *var.* Zaghwān. NE Tunisia *36°26′N 10°05′E*
Zaghwān *see* Zaghouan
115 G16 **Zagorá** Thessalía, C Greece *39°27′N 23°06′E*
Zagorod'ye *see* Zaharoddzye
Żagory *see* Žagarė
Zágráb *see* Zagreb
112 E8 **Zagreb** *Ger.* Agram, *Hung.* Zágráb. ● (Croatia) Zagreb, N Croatia *45°48′N 15°58′E*
112 E8 **Zagreb** *prev.* Grad Zagreb. ◆ *province* N Croatia
142 L7 **Zāgros, Kūhhā-ye** *Eng.* Zagros Mountains. ▲ W Iran
Zagros Mountains *see* Zāgros, Kūhhā-ye
112 O12 **Žagubica** Serbia, E Serbia *44°13′N 21°47′E*
Zagunao *see* Lixian
111 L22 **Zagyva** ⚘ N Hungary
Zaharo *see* Zacháro
119 G19 **Zaharoddzye** *Rus.* Zagorod'ye. *physical region* SW Belarus
143 W11 **Zāhedān** *var.* Zahidan; *prev.* Duzdab. Sīstān va Balūchestān, SE Iran *29°31′N 60°51′E*
Zahidan *see* Zāhedān
Zahlah *see* Zahlé
138 H7 **Zahlé** *var.* Zaḩlah. C Lebanon *33°51′N 35°54′E*
146 J14 **Zähmet** *Rus.* Zakhmet. Mary Welaýaty, C Turkmenistan *37°48′N 62°33′E*
111 O20 **Záhony** Szabolcs-Szatmár-Bereg, NE Hungary *48°26′N 22°11′E*
141 N13 **Ẓahrān** 'Asīr, S Saudi Arabia *17°48′N 43°28′E*
139 R12 **Ẓahrat al Baṭn** *hill range* S Iraq
120 H11 **Zahrez Chergui** *var.* Zahrez Chergúi. *marsh* N Algeria
Zainlha *see* Xinjin
127 S4 **Zainsk** Respublika Tatarstan, W Russian Federation *55°12′N 52°01′E*
82 A10 **Zaire** *prev.* Congo. ◆ *province* NW Angola
Zaire *see* Congo (river)
Zaire *see* Congo (Democratic Republic of)
112 P13 **Zaječar** Serbia, E Serbia *43°54′N 22°16′E*
83 L18 **Zaka** Masvingo, E Zimbabwe *20°20′S 31°29′E*
122 M14 **Zakamensk** Respublika Buryatiya, S Russian Federation *50°18′N 102°57′E*
116 G7 **Zakarpats'ka Oblast'** *Eng.* Transcarpathian Oblast, *Rus.* Zakarpatskaya Oblast'. ◆ *province* W Ukraine
Zakarpatskaya Oblast' *see* Zakarpats'ka Oblast'
Zakataly *see* Zaqatala
Zakháro *see* Zacháro
Zakhidnyy Buh/Zakhodni Buh *see* Bug
Zakhmet *see* Zähmet
139 Q1 **Zākhō** *var.* Zākhū. Dahūk, N Iraq *37°09′N 42°40′E*
Zākhū *see* Zākhō
Zákinthos *see* Zákynthos
111 L18 **Zakopane** Małopolskie, S Poland *49°17′N 19°57′E*
78 J12 **Zakouma** Salamat, S Chad *10°47′N 19°51′E*
115 L25 **Zákros** Kríti, Greece, E Mediterranean Sea *35°06′N 26°12′E*
115 C19 **Zákynthos** *var.* Zákinthos. Zákynthos, W Greece *37°47′N 20°54′E*
115 C20 **Zákynthos** *var.* Zákinthos, *It.* Zante. *island* Iónia Nísoi, Greece, C Mediterranean Sea
115 C19 **Zakýnthou, Porthmós** *strait* SW Greece
111 G24 **Zala** *off.* Zala Megye. ◆ *county* W Hungary
111 G24 **Zala** ⚘ W Hungary
138 M4 **Zalābiyah** Dayr az Zawr, C Syria *35°39′N 39°51′E*
111 G24 **Zalaegerszeg** Zala, W Hungary *46°51′N 16°49′E*
104 K11 **Zalamea de la Serena** Extremadura, W Spain *38°38′N 05°37′W*
104 J13 **Zalamea la Real** Andalucía, S Spain *37°41′N 06°40′W*
Zala Megye *see* Zala
163 U7 **Zalantun** *var.* Butha Qi. Nei Mongol Zizhiqu, N China *47°58′N 122°44′E*
111 G23 **Zalaszentgrót** Zala, SW Hungary *46°57′N 17°05′E*
Zalatna *see* Zlatna
116 G9 **Zalău** *Ger.* Waltenberg, *Hung.* Zilah; *prev. Ger.* Zillenmarkt. Sălaj, NW Romania *47°11′N 23°03′E*
109 V10 **Žalec** *Ger.* Sachsenfeld. C Slovenia *46°15′N 15°08′E*
110 K8 **Zalewo** *Ger.* Saalfeld. Warmińsko-Mazurskie, NE Poland *53°54′N 19°39′E*
141 N9 **Ẓalim** Makkah, W Saudi Arabia *22°46′N 42°12′E*
80 A11 **Zalingei** *var.* Zalinje. Western Darfur, W Sudan *12°51′N 23°29′E*
Zalinje *see* Zalingei
116 K7 **Zalishchyky** Ternopil's'ka Oblast', W Ukraine *48°40′N 25°43′E*
Zallah *see* Zillah
98 J13 **Zaltbommel** Gelderland, C Netherlands *51°49′N 05°15′E*
124 H15 **Zaluch'ye** Novgorodskaya Oblast', NW Russian Federation *57°40′N 31°45′E*
Zamak *see* Zamakh
141 Q14 **Zamakh** *var.* Zamak. N Yemen *16°26′N 47°35′E*
136 K15 **Zamantı Irmağı** ⚘ C Turkey
Zambesi/Zambeze *see* Zambezi
83 G14 **Zambezi** North Western, W Zambia *13°34′S 23°08′E*
83 K15 **Zambezi** *var.* Zambesi, *Port.* Zambeze. ⚘ S Africa
83 O15 **Zambézia** *off.* Província da Zambézia. ◆ *province* C Mozambique
Zambézia, Província da *see* Zambézia
83 I14 **Zambia** *off.* Republic of Zambia; *prev.* Northern Rhodesia. ◆ *republic* S Africa
Zambia, Republic of *see* Zambia
171 O8 **Zamboanga** *off.* Zamboanga City. Mindanao, S Philippines *06°56′N 122°03′E*
Zamboanga City *see* Zamboanga
54 E5 **Zambrano** Bolívar, N Colombia *09°45′N 74°50′W*
110 N10 **Zambrów** Łomża, E Poland *52°59′N 22°14′E*
83 L14 **Zâmbuè** Tete, NW Mozambique *15°03′S 30°49′E*
77 T13 **Zamfara** ⚘ NW Nigeria
Zamkog *see* Zamtang
56 C9 **Zamora** Zamora Chinchipe, S Ecuador *04°04′S 78°52′W*
104 K6 **Zamora** Castilla-León, NW Spain *41°30′N 05°45′W*
104 K5 **Zamora** ◆ *province* Castilla-León, NW Spain
Zamora *see* Barinas
56 A13 **Zamora Chinchipe** ◆ *province* S Ecuador
40 M13 **Zamora de Hidalgo** Michoacán, SW Mexico *20°N 102°18′W*
111 P15 **Zamość** *Rus.* Zamoste. Lubelskie, E Poland *50°44′N 23°16′E*
Zamoste *see* Zamość
160 G7 **Zamtang** *var.* Zamkog; *prev.* Gamba. Sichuan, C China *32°19′N 100°55′E*
75 O8 **Zamzam, Wādī** *dry watercourse* NW Libya
79 F20 **Zanaga** Lékoumou, S Congo *02°50′S 13°53′E*
41 T16 **Zanatepec** Oaxaca, SE Mexico *16°28′N 94°24′W*
105 P9 **Záncara** ⚘ C Spain
Zancle *see* Messina
158 G14 **Zanda** Xizang Zizhiqu, W China *31°29′N 79°50′E*
98 H10 **Zandvoort** Noord-Holland, W Netherlands *52°22′N 04°31′E*
39 P8 **Zane Hills** *hill range* Alaska, USA
31 T13 **Zanesville** Ohio, N USA *39°55′N 82°02′W*
Zanga *see* Hrazdan
Zangkaxa *see* Domar
142 L4 **Zanjān** *var.* Zenjan, Zinjan. Zanjān, NW Iran *36°40′N 48°30′E*
142 L4 **Zanjān** *off.* Ostān-e Zanjān, *var.* Zenjan, Zinjan. ◆ *province* NW Iran
Zanjān, Ostān-e *see* Zanjān
Zante *see* Zákynthos
81 J22 **Zanzibar** Zanzibar, E Tanzania *06°10′S 39°12′E*
81 J22 **Zanzibar** ◆ *region* E Tanzania
81 J22 **Zanzibar** *Swa.* Unguja. *island* E Tanzania
81 J22 **Zanzibar Channel** *channel* E Tanzania
81 J23 **Zanzibar North** ◆ *region* E Tanzania
81 J23 **Zanzibar South** ◆ *region* E Tanzania
81 J23 **Zanzibar West** ◆ *region* E Tanzania
161 N8 **Zaoyang** Hubei, C China *32°10′N 112°45′E*
165 P10 **Zaō-zan** ▲ Honshū, C Japan *38°06′N 140°27′E*
124 J2 **Zaozërsk** Murmanskaya Oblast', NW Russian Federation *69°25′N 32°25′E*
161 Q6 **Zaozhuang** Shandong, E China *34°53′N 117°38′E*
28 L4 **Zap** North Dakota, N USA *47°18′N 101°55′W*
112 L13 **Zapadna Morava** *Ger.* Westliche Morava. ⚘ C Serbia
124 H16 **Zapadnaya Dvina** Tverskaya Oblast', W Russian Federation *56°17′N 32°03′E*
Zapadnaya Dvina *see* Western Dvina
Zapadno-Kazakhstanskaya Oblast' *see* Zapadnyy Kazakhstan
122 I9 **Zapadno-Sibirskaya Ravnina** *Eng.* West Siberian Plain. *plain* C Russian Federation
Zapadnyy Bug *see* Bug
144 E9 **Zapadnyy Kazakhstan** *off.* Zapadno-Kazakhstanskaya Oblast', *Eng.* West Kazakhstan, *Kaz.* Batys Qazaqstan Oblysy; *prev.* Ural'skaya Oblast'. ◆ *province* NW Kazakhstan
122 K13 **Zapadnyy Sayan** *Eng.* Western Sayans. ▲ S Russian Federation
63 H15 **Zapala** Neuquén, W Argentina *38°54′S 70°06′W*
62 I4 **Zapaleri, Cerro** *var.* Cerro Sapaleri. ▲ N Chile *22°51′S 67°10′W*
25 Q16 **Zapata** Texas, SW USA *26°57′N 99°17′W*
44 D5 **Zapata, Península de** *peninsula* W Cuba
61 G19 **Zapicán** Lavalleja, S Uruguay *33°31′S 54°55′W*
65 J19 **Zapiola Ridge** *undersea feature* SW Atlantic Ocean
65 L19 **Zapiola Seamount** *undersea feature* S Atlantic Ocean *38°15′S 26°15′W*
124 I2 **Zapolyarnyy** Murmanskaya Oblast', NW Russian Federation *69°24′N 30°53′E*
117 U8 **Zaporizhzhya** *Rus.* Zaporozh'ye; *prev.* Aleksandrovsk. Zaporiz'ka Oblast', SE Ukraine *47°47′N 35°12′E*
Zaporizhzhya *see* Zaporiz'ka Oblast'
117 U9 **Zaporiz'ka Oblast'** *var.* Zaporizhzhya, *Rus.* Zaporozhskaya Oblast'. ◆ *province* SE Ukraine
Zaporozhskaya Oblast' *see* Zaporiz'ka Oblast'
Zaporozh'ye *see* Zaporizhzhya
40 L14 **Zapotiltic** Jalisco, SW Mexico *19°40′N 103°29′W*
158 G13 **Zapug** Xizang Zizhiqu, W China
137 V10 **Zaqatala** *Rus.* Zakataly. NW Azerbaijan *41°38′N 46°38′E*
159 P13 **Zaqên** Qinghai, W China *33°23′N 94°31′E*
159 Q13 **Za Qu** ⚘ C China
136 M13 **Zara** Sivas, C Turkey *39°55′N 37°44′E*
Zara *see* Zadar
Zarafshan *see* Zarafshon
147 P12 **Zarafshon** *Rus.* Zeravshan. W Tajikistan *39°12′N 68°36′E*
146 L9 **Zarafshon** *Rus.* Zarafshan. Navoiy Viloyati, N Uzbekistan *41°33′N 64°09′E*
Zarafshon *see* Zeravshan
147 O12 **Zarafshon, Qatorkŭhi** *Rus.* Zeravshanskiy Khrebet, *Uzb.* Zarafshon Tizmasi. ▲ Tajikistan/Uzbekistan
Zarafshon Tizmasi *see* Zarafshon, Qatorkŭhi
54 E7 **Zaragoza** Antioquia, N Colombia *07°30′N 74°52′W*
40 I5 **Zaragoza** Chihuahua, N Mexico *29°36′N 107°41′W*
41 N6 **Zaragoza** Coahuila, NE Mexico *28°31′N 100°54′W*
41 O10 **Zaragoza** Nuevo León, NE Mexico *23°59′N 99°49′W*
105 R5 **Zaragoza** *Eng.* Saragossa; *anc.* Caesaraugusta, Salduba. Aragón, NE Spain *41°39′N 00°54′W*
105 R6 **Zaragoza** ◆ *province* Aragón, NE Spain
105 R5 **Zaragoza** ✈ Aragón, NE Spain *41°38′N 00°53′W*
143 S10 **Zarand** Kermān, C Iran *30°50′N 56°35′E*
148 J9 **Zaranj** Nīmrūz, SW Afghanistan *30°59′N 61°54′E*
118 I11 **Zarasai** Utena, E Lithuania *55°44′N 26°17′E*
62 N12 **Zárate** *prev.* General José F.Uriburu. Buenos Aires, E Argentina *34°06′S 59°03′W*
105 Q2 **Zarautz** *var.* Zarauz. País Vasco, N Spain *43°17′N 02°10′W*
Zarauz *see* Zarautz
Zaravecchia *see* Biograd na Moru
Zarāyīn *see* Zarēn
126 L4 **Zaraysk** Moskovskaya Oblast', W Russian Federation *54°48′N 38°54′E*
55 N6 **Zaraza** Guárico, N Venezuela *09°23′N 65°20′W*
Zarbdar *see* Zarbdor
147 P11 **Zarbdor** *Rus.* Zarbdar. Jizzax Viloyati, C Uzbekistan *40°04′N 68°10′E*
142 M8 **Zard Kūh** ▲ SW Iran *32°19′N 50°03′E*
124 I5 **Zarechensk** Murmanskaya Oblast', NW Russian Federation *66°39′N 31°27′E*
127 P6 **Zarechnyy** Penzenskaya Oblast', W Russian Federation *53°12′N 45°12′E*
Zareh Sharan *see* Sharan
39 Y14 **Zarembo Island** *island* Alexander Archipelago, Alaska, USA
139 V4 **Zarēn** *var.* Zarāyīn. As Sulaymānīyah, E Iraq *35°16′N 45°43′E*
149 Q7 **Zarghūn Shahr** *var.* Katawaz. Paktīkā, SE Afghanistan *32°40′N 68°20′E*
77 V13 **Zaria** Kaduna, C Nigeria *11°06′N 07°42′E*
116 K2 **Zarichne** Rivnens'ka Oblast', NW Ukraine *51°49′N 26°09′E*
122 J13 **Zarinsk** Altayskiy Kray, S Russian Federation *53°34′N 85°22′E*
116 J12 **Zărneşti** *Hung.* Zernest. Braşov, C Romania *45°34′N 25°18′E*
115 J25 **Zarós** Kríti, Greece, E Mediterranean Sea *35°08′N 24°54′E*
100 O9 **Zarow** ⚘ NE Germany
Zarqa *see* Az Zarqā'
Zarqa/Muḩāfaẓat az Zarqā' *see* Az Zarqā'
111 G20 **Záruby** ▲ W Slovakia *48°30′N 17°24′E*
56 B8 **Zaruma** El Oro, SW Ecuador *03°46′S 79°38′W*
110 E13 **Żary** *Ger.* Sorau, Sorau in der Niederlausitz. Lubuskie, W Poland *51°44′N 15°09′E*
54 D10 **Zarzal** Valle del Cauca, W Colombia *04°24′N 76°01′W*
42 I7 **Zarzalar, Cerro** ▲ S Honduras *14°15′N 86°49′W*
Zashaghan *see* Zachagansk
152 I5 **Zāskār** ⚘ NE India
152 I5 **Zāskār Range** ▲ NE India
119 K15 **Zaslawye** Minskaya Voblasts', C Belarus *54°01′N 27°16′E*
116 K7 **Zastavna** Chernivets'ka Oblast', W Ukraine *48°30′N 25°51′E*
111 B16 **Žatec** *Ger.* Saaz. Ústecký Kraj, NW Czech Republic *50°20′N 13°35′E*
Zaumgarten *see* Chrzanów
Zaunguzskiye Garagumy *see* Üngüz Angyrsyndaky Garagum
25 X9 **Zavalla** Texas, SW USA *31°09′N 94°25′W*
99 H18 **Zaventem** Vlaams Brabant, C Belgium *50°53′N 04°28′E*
99 H18 **Zaventem** ✈ (Brussel/Bruxelles) Vlaams Brabant, C Belgium *50°55′N 04°28′E*
Zavertse *see* Zawiercie
114 L7 **Zavet** Razgrad, NE Bulgaria *43°46′N 26°40′E*
127 O12 **Zavetnoye** Rostovskaya Oblast', SW Russian Federation *47°10′N 43°54′E*
156 M3 **Zavhan Gol** ⚘ W Mongolia
112 H12 **Zavidovići** Federacija Bosna I Hercegovina, N Bosnia and Herzegovina *44°26′N 18°07′E*
123 R13 **Zavitinsk** Amurskaya Oblast', SE Russian Federation *50°23′N 128°57′E*
Zawia *see* Az Zāwiyah
111 K15 **Zawiercie** *Rus.* Zavertse. Śląskie, S Poland *50°29′N 19°24′E*
75 P11 **Zawīlah** *var.* Zuwaylah, *It.* Zueila. C Libya *26°10′N 15°07′E*
138 I4 **Zāwiyah, Jabal az** ▲ NW Syria
109 Y3 **Zaya** ⚘ NE Austria
166 M8 **Zayatkyi** Bago, C Myanmar (Burma) *17°48′N 96°27′E*
145 Y11 **Zaysan** Vostochnyy Kazakhstan, E Kazakhstan *47°30′N 84°55′E*
Zaysan Köl *see* Zaysan, Ozero
145 Y11 **Zaysan, Ozero** *Kaz.* Zaysan Köl. ◎ E Kazakhstan
159 R16 **Zayü** *var.* Gyigang. Xizang Zizhiqu, W China *28°36′N 97°25′E*
Zayyq *see* Ural
44 F6 **Zaza** ⚘ C Cuba
116 K5 **Zbarazh** Ternopil's'ka Oblast', W Ukraine *49°40′N 25°47′E*
116 J5 **Zboriv** Ternopil's'ka Oblast', W Ukraine *49°40′N 25°07′E*
111 F18 **Zbraslav** Jihomoravský Kraj, SE Czech Republic *49°13′N 16°19′E*
116 K6 **Zbruch** ⚘ W Ukraine
Žďár *see* Žďár nad Sázavou
111 F17 **Žďár nad Sázavou** *Ger.* Saar in Mähren; *prev.* Žďár. Vysočina, C Czech Republic *49°34′N 16°00′E*
116 K4 **Zdolbuniv** *Pol.* Zdołbunów, *Rus.* Zdolbunov. Rivnens'ka Oblast', NW Ukraine *50°33′N 26°15′E*
Zdolbunov *see* Zdolbuniv
Zdołbunów *see* Zdolbuniv
110 J13 **Zduńska Wola** Sieradz, C Poland *51°37′N 18°57′E*
117 O4 **Zdvizh** ⚘ N Ukraine
Zdzięciół *see* Dzyatlava
111 I16 **Zdzieszowice** *Ger.* Odertal. Opolskie, SW Poland *50°24′N 18°06′E*
Zealand *see* Sjælland
188 K6 **Zealandia Bank** *undersea feature* C Pacific Ocean
63 H20 **Zeballos, Monte** ▲ S Argentina *47°04′S 71°32′W*
83 K20 **Zebediela** Limpopo, NE South Africa *24°16′S 29°21′E*
113 L18 **Zebë, Mal** *var.* Mali i Zebës. ▲ NE Albania *41°57′N 20°16′E*
Zebës, Mali i *see* Zebë, Mal
21 V9 **Zebulon** North Carolina, SE USA *35°49′N 78°19′W*
112 K8 **Žednik** *Hung.* Bácsjózseffalva. Vojvodina, N Serbia *45°58′N 19°40′E*
99 C15 **Zeebrugge** West-Vlaanderen, NW Belgium *51°20′N 03°13′E*
183 N16 **Zeehan** Tasmania, SE Australia *41°54′S 145°19′E*
99 L14 **Zeeland** Noord-Brabant, SE Netherlands *51°42′N 05°40′E*
29 N7 **Zeeland** North Dakota, N USA *45°57′N 99°49′W*
99 E14 **Zeeland** ◆ *province* SW Netherlands
83 I21 **Zeerust** North-West, N South Africa *25°33′S 26°06′E*
98 K10 **Zeewolde** Flevoland, C Netherlands *52°20′N 05°32′E*
Zefat *see* Tsefat
Żegań *see* Żagań
Zehden *see* Cedynia
100 O11 **Zehdenick** Brandenburg, NE Germany *52°58′N 13°19′E*
Zē-i Bādīnān *see* Great Zab
Zeiden *see* Codlea
146 M14 **Zeidskoye Vodokhranilishche** ⊠ E Turkmenistan
Zē-i Kōya *see* Little Zab
181 P7 **Zeil, Mount** ▲ Northern Territory, C Australia *23°31′S 132°41′E*
98 J12 **Zeist** Utrecht, C Netherlands *52°05′N 05°15′E*
101 M16 **Zeitz** Sachsen-Anhalt, E Germany *51°03′N 12°08′E*
159 T11 **Zêkog** *var.* Zequ; *prev.* Sonag. Qinghai, C China *35°03′N 101°30′E*
Zelaya Norte *see* Atlántico Norte, Región Autónoma
Zelaya Sur *see* Atlántico Sur, Región Autónoma
99 F17 **Zele** Oost-Vlaanderen, NW Belgium *51°04′N 04°02′E*
110 N12 **Żelechów** Lubelskie, E Poland *51°49′N 21°57′E*
113 H14 **Zelena Glava** ▲ SE Bosnia and Herzegovina *43°32′N 17°55′E*
113 P20 **Zelen Breg** ▲ S Macedonia *41°10′N 22°14′E*
113 I14 **Zelengora** ▲ S Bosnia and Herzegovina
124 I5 **Zelenoborskiy** Murmanskaya Oblast', NW Russian Federation *66°52′N 32°25′E*
127 R3 **Zelenodol'sk** Respublika Tatarstan, W Russian Federation *55°52′N 48°49′E*
117 S9 **Zelenodol's'k** Dnipropetrovs'ka Oblast', E Ukraine *47°38′N 33°41′E*
122 J12 **Zelenogorsk** Krasnoyarskiy Kray, C Russian Federation *56°08′N 94°29′E*
126 K3 **Zelenograd** Moskovskaya Oblast', W Russian Federation *56°02′N 37°08′E*
118 B13 **Zelenogradsk** *Ger.* Cranz, Kranz. Kaliningradskaya Oblast', W Russian Federation *54°58′N 20°30′E*
127 O15 **Zelenokumsk** Stavropol'skiy Kray, SW Russian Federation *44°22′N 43°48′E*
165 X4 **Zelënyy, Ostrov** *var.* Shibotsu-jima. *island* NE Russian Federation
Železna Kapela *see* Eisenkappel
Železna Vrata *see* Demir Kapija
112 L11 **Železniki** Serbia, N Serbia *44°45′N 20°23′E*
98 N12 **Zelhem** Gelderland, E Netherlands *52°00′N 06°21′E*
113 N18 **Želino** NW FYR Macedonia *42°00′N 21°06′E*
113 M14 **Željin** ▲ C Serbia
101 K17 **Zella-Mehlis** Thüringen, C Germany *50°40′N 10°40′E*
109 P7 **Zell am See** *var.* Zell-am-See. Salzburg, S Austria *47°19′N 12°47′E*
Zell-am-See *see* Zell am See
109 N7 **Zell am Ziller** Tirol, W Austria *47°13′N 11°52′E*
Zelle *see* Celle
109 W2 **Zellerndorf** Niederösterreich, NE Austria *48°40′N 15°57′E*
109 U7 **Zeltweg** Steiermark, S Austria *47°12′N 14°46′E*
119 G17 **Zel'va** *Pol.* Zelwa. Hrodzyenskaya Voblasts', W Belarus *53°09′N 24°49′E*
118 H13 **Želva** Vilnius, C Lithuania *55°13′N 25°07′E*
Zelwa *see* Zel'va
99 E16 **Zelzate** *var.* Selzaete. Oost-Vlaanderen, NW Belgium *51°12′N 03°49′E*
118 E11 **Žemaičių Aukštumas** *physical region* W Lithuania
118 C12 **Žemaičių Naumiestis** Klaipėda, SW Lithuania *55°22′N 21°39′E*
119 L14 **Zembin** *var.* Zyembin. Minskaya Voblasts', C Belarus *54°22′N 28°13′E*
127 N6 **Zemetchino** Penzenskaya Oblast', W Russian Federation *53°31′N 42°35′E*
79 M15 **Zémio** Haut-Mbomou, E Central African Republic *05°04′N 25°07′E*
41 R16 **Zempoaltepec, Cerro** ▲ SE Mexico *17°04′N 95°54′W*
99 G17 **Zemst** Vlaams Brabant, C Belgium *50°59′N 04°28′E*
112 L11 **Zemun** Serbia, N Serbia *44°52′N 20°25′E*
Zendajan *see* Zendeh Jan
148 J5 **Zendeh Jan** *var.* Zendajan, Zindajān. Herāt, NW Afghanistan *34°55′N 61°53′E*
Zengg *see* Senj
112 H12 **Zenica** Federacija Bosna I Hercegovina, C Bosnia and Herzegovina *44°12′N 17°53′E*
Zenjan *see* Zanjān
Zen'kov *see* Zin'kiv
Zenshū *see* Chŏnju
Zenta *see* Senta
82 B11 **Zenza do Itombe** Cuanza Norte, NW Angola *09°22′S 14°10′E*
112 H12 **Žepče** Federacija Bosna I Hercegovina, N Bosnia and Herzegovina *44°26′N 18°00′E*
23 W12 **Zephyrhills** Florida, SE USA *28°13′N 82°10′W*
158 F9 **Zepu** *var.* Poskam. Xinjiang Uygur Zizhiqu, NW China *38°10′N 77°18′E*
Zequ *see* Zêkog
147 Q12 **Zeravshan** *Taj./Uzb.* Zarafshon. ⚘ Tajikistan/Uzbekistan
Zeravshan *see* Zarafshon
Zeravshanskiy Khrebet *see* Zarafshon, Qatorkŭhi
101 M14 **Zerbst** Sachsen-Anhalt, E Germany *51°57′N 12°05′E*
145 P8 **Zerenda** Akmola, N Kazakhstan *52°56′N 69°09′E*
110 H12 **Żerków** Wielkopolskie, C Poland *52°03′N 17°33′E*
108 E11 **Zermatt** Valais, SW Switzerland *46°00′N 07°45′E*
Zernest *see* Zărneşti
108 J9 **Zernez** Graubünden, SE Switzerland *46°42′N 10°06′E*
126 L12 **Zernograd** Rostovskaya Oblast', SW Russian Federation *46°52′N 40°13′E*
Zestafoni *see* Zestap'oni
137 S9 **Zestap'oni** *Rus.* Zestafoni. C Georgia *42°09′N 43°00′E*
98 H12 **Zestienhoven** ✈ (Rotterdam) Zuid-Holland, SW Netherlands *51°57′N 04°30′E*
113 J16 **Zeta** ⚘ C Montenegro
8 L6 **Zeta Lake** ◎ Victoria Island, Northwest Territories, N Canada
Zêtang *see* Nêdong
98 L12 **Zetten** Gelderland, SE Netherlands *51°55′N 05°43′E*
101 M17 **Zeulenroda** Thüringen, C Germany *50°40′N 11°58′E*
100 H10 **Zeven** Niedersachsen, NW Germany *53°17′N 09°16′E*
98 M12 **Zevenaar** Gelderland, SE Netherlands *51°55′N 06°05′E*
99 H14 **Zevenbergen** Noord-Brabant, S Netherlands *51°39′N 04°36′E*
129 X6 **Zeya** ⚘ SE Russian Federation
Zeya Reservoir *see* Zeyskoye Vodokhranilishche
143 T11 **Zeynalābād** Kermān, C Iran *29°56′N 57°29′E*
123 R12 **Zeyskoye Vodokhranilishche** *Eng.* Zeya Reservoir. ⊠ SE Russian Federation
104 H8 **Zêzere, Rio** ⚘ C Portugal
Zgerzh *see* Zgierz
138 H6 **Zgharta** N Lebanon *34°24′N 35°54′E*
110 K12 **Zgierz** *Ger.* Neuhof, *Rus.* Zgerzh. Łódź, C Poland *51°55′N 19°20′E*
111 E14 **Zgorzelec** *Ger.* Görlitz. Dolnośląskie, SW Poland *51°10′N 15°E*
119 F19 **Zhabinka** *Pol.* Žabinka. Brestskaya Voblasts', SW Belarus *52°12′N 24°01′E*
Zhaggo *see* Luhuo
159 R15 **Zhag'yab** *var.* Yêndum. Xizang Zizhiqu, W China *30°42′N 97°33′E*
144 L9 **Zhailma** *Kaz.* Zhayylma. Kostanay, N Kazakhstan *51°34′N 61°39′E*
Zhalagash *see* Dzhalagash
145 V16 **Zhalanash** Almaty, SE Kazakhstan *43°04′N 78°08′E*
145 S7 **Zhalauly, Ozero** ◎ NE Kazakhstan
144 E9 **Zhalpaktal** *Kaz.* Zhalpaqtal; *prev.* Furmanovo. Zapadnyy Kazakhstan, W Kazakhstan *49°43′N 49°28′E*
Zhalpaqtal *see* Zhalpaktal
119 G16 **Zhaludok** *Rus.* Zheludok. Hrodzyenskaya Voblasts', W Belarus *53°36′N 24°59′E*
Zhaman-Akkol', Ozero *see* Akkol', Ozero
145 Q14 **Zhambyl** *off.* Zhambylskaya Oblast', *Kaz.* Zhambyl Oblysy; *prev.* Dzhambulskaya Oblast'. ◆ *province* S Kazakhstan
Zhambyl *see* Taraz
Zhambyl Oblysy/Zhambylskaya Oblast' *see* Zhambyl
Zhamo *see* Bomi
145 S12 **Zhamshy** ⚘ C Kazakhstan
144 M15 **Zhanadar'ya** Kyzylorda, S Kazakhstan *44°41′N 64°39′E*

◆ Country ● Country Capital ◇ Dependent Territory ○ Dependent Territory Capital ◆ Administrative Regions ✈ International Airport ▲ Mountain ▲ Mountain Range ⛰ Volcano ⚘ River ◎ Lake ⊠ Reservoir

ZHANAKORGAN – ZYRYANOVSK

145 O15 **Zhanakorgan** *Kaz.* Zhangaqorghan. Kzylorda, S Kazakhstan 43°57′N 67°14′E
159 N16 **Zhanang** *var.* Chatang. Xizang Zizhiqu, W China 29°15′N 91°20′E
145 T12 **Zhanaortalyk** Karaganda, C Kazakhstan 47°31′N 75°42′E
144 F15 **Zhanaozen** *Kaz.* Zhangaözen; *prev.* Novyy Uzen'. Mangistau, W Kazakhstan 43°22′N 52°50′E
145 Q16 **Zhanatas** Zhambyl, S Kazakhstan 43°36′N 69°43′E
Zhangaözen *see* Zhanaozen
Zhangaqazaly *see* Ayteke Bi
Zhangaqorghan *see* Zhanakorgan
161 O2 **Zhangbei** Hebei, E China 41°13′N 114°43′E
Zhang-chia-k'ou *see* Zhangjiakou
Zhangdian *see* Zibo
Zhanggu *see* Danba
163 X9 **Zhangguangcai Ling** ▲▲ NE China
145 W10 **Zhangiztobe** Vostochnyy Kazakhstan, E Kazakhstan 49°15′N 81°16′E
159 W11 **Zhangjiachuan** Gansu, N China 34°55′N 106°26′E
160 L10 **Zhangjiajie** *var.* Dayong. Hunan, S China 29°10′N 110°22′E
161 O2 **Zhangjiakou** *var.* Changkiakow, Zhang-chia-k'ou, *Eng.* Kalgan; *prev.* Wanchuan. Hebei, E China 40°48′N 114°51′E
161 Q13 **Zhangping** Fujian, SE China 25°21′N 117°29′E
161 Q13 **Zhangpu** *var.* Sui'an. Fujian, SE China 24°08′N 117°36′E
163 U11 **Zhangwu** Liaoning, NE China 42°21′N 122°32′E
159 S8 **Zhangye** *var.* Ganzhou. Gansu, N China 38°58′N 100°30′E
161 Q13 **Zhangzhou** Fujian, SE China 24°31′N 117°40′E
163 W6 **Zhan He** ≋ NE China
Zhänibek *see* Dzhanibek
160 L16 **Zhanjiang** *var.* Chanchiang, Chan-chiang, *Cant.* Tsamkong, *Fr.* Fort-Bayard. Guangdong, S China 21°10′N 110°20′E
Zhansügirov *see* Dzhansugurov
163 V8 **Zhaodong** Heilongjiang, NE China 46°03′N 125°58′E
Zhaoge *see* Qixian
160 H11 **Zhaojue** *var.* Xincheng. Sichuan, C China 28°03′N 102°50′E
161 N14 **Zhaoqing** Guangdong, S China 23°08′N 112°26′E
Zhaoren *see* Changwu
158 H5 **Zhaosu** *var.* Mongolküre. Xinjiang Uygur Zizhiqu, NW China 43°09′N 81°07′E
160 H11 **Zhaotong** Yunnan, SW China 27°20′N 103°29′E
163 V9 **Zhaoyuan** Heilongjiang, NE China 45°30′N 125°05′E
163 V9 **Zhaozhou** Heilongjiang, NE China 45°42′N 125°11′E
145 X13 **Zharbulak** Vostochnyy Kazakhstan, E Kazakhstan 46°04′N 82°05′E
158 J15 **Zhari Namco** ◎ W China
144 I12 **Zharkamys** *Kaz.* Zharqamys. Aktyubinsk, W Kazakhstan 47°58′N 56°33′E
145 W15 **Zharkent** *prev.* Panfilov. Taldykorgan, SE Kazakhstan 44°10′N 80°01′E
124 H17 **Zharkovskiy** Tverskaya Oblast', W Russian Federation 55°51′N 32°19′E
145 W11 **Zharma** Vostochnyy Kazakhstan, E Kazakhstan 48°48′N 80°55′E
144 F14 **Zharmysh** Mangistau, SW Kazakhstan 44°12′N 52°27′E
Zharqamys *see* Zharkamys
118 L13 **Zhary** Vitsyebskaya Voblasts', N Belarus 55°05′N 28°40′E
Zharyk *see* Saken Seyfullin
Zhaslyk *see* Jasliq
158 J14 **Zhaxi Co** ◎ W China
Zhayylma *see* Zhailma
Zhdanov *see* Beyläqan
Zhdanov *see* Mariupol'
Zhe *see* Zhejiang
161 R10 **Zhejiang** *var.* Che-chiang, Chekiang, Zhe, Zhejiang Sheng. ◐ *province* SE China
Zhejiang Sheng *see* Zhejiang
145 S7 **Zhelezinka** Pavlodar, N Kazakhstan 53°35′N 75°16′E
119 C14 **Zheleznodorozhnyy** *Ger.* Gerdauen. Kaliningradskaya Oblast', W Russian Federation 54°21′N 21°17′E
Zheleznodorozhnyy *see* Yemva
122 K12 **Zheleznogorsk** Krasnoyarskiy, C Russian Federation 56°20′N 93°36′E
126 J7 **Zheleznogorsk** Kurskaya Oblast', W Russian Federation 52°22′N 35°21′E
127 N15 **Zheleznovodsk** Stavropol'skiy Kray, SW Russian Federation 44°12′N 43°01′E
Zhëltyye Vody *see* Zhovti Vody
Zheludok *see* Zhaludok
Zhem *see* Emba
160 K7 **Zhenba** Shaanxi, C China 32°42′N 107°55′E
160 I13 **Zhenfeng** *var.* Mingu. Guizhou, S China 25°27′N 105°38′E
Zhengjiatun *see* Shuangliao
159 X10 **Zhengning** *var.* Shanhe. Gansu, N China 35°29′N 108°21′E
Zhengxiangbai Qi *see* Qagan Nur
161 N6 **Zhengzhou** *var.* Ch'eng-chou, Chengchow; *prev.* Chenghsien. *province capital* Henan, C China 34°45′N 113°38′E
161 R8 **Zhenjiang** *var.* Chenkiang. Jiangsu, E China 32°08′N 119°30′E
163 U9 **Zhenlai** Jilin, NE China 45°52′N 123°11′E
160 I11 **Zhenxiong** Yunnan, SW China 27°31′N 104°52′E
160 K11 **Zhenyuan** *var.* Wuyang. Guizhou, S China 27°07′N 108°33′E
161 R11 **Zherong** *var.* Shuangcheng. Fujian, SE China 27°16′N 119°54′E
145 U15 **Zhetigen** *prev.* Nikolayevka. Almaty, SE Kazakhstan 43°39′N 77°10′E
Zhetiqara *see* Zhitikara
144 F15 **Zhetybay** Mangistau, SW Kazakhstan 43°35′N 52°05′E
145 P17 **Zhetysay** *var.* Dzhetysay. Yuzhnyy Kazakhstan 40°45′N 68°18′E
160 M11 **Zhexi Shuiku** ⊠ C China
145 O12 **Zhezdy** Karaganda, C Kazakhstan 48°06′N 67°01′E
145 O12 **Zhezkazgan** *Kaz.* Zhezqazghan; *prev.* Dzhezkazgan. Karaganda, C Kazakhstan 47°49′N 67°44′E
Zhezqazghan *see* Zhezkazgan
Zhicheng *see* Yidu
Zhidachov *see* Zhydachiv
159 Q12 **Zhidoi** *var.* Gyaijêpozhanggê. Qinghai, C China 33°55′N 95°39′E
122 M13 **Zhigalovo** Irkutskaya Oblast', S Russian Federation 54°47′N 105°00′E
127 R6 **Zhigulevsk** Samarskaya Oblast', W Russian Federation 53°24′N 49°30′E
118 D13 **Zhilino** *Ger.* Schillen. Kaliningradskaya Oblast', W Russian Federation 54°55′N 21°54′E
Zhiloy, Ostrov *see* Çiloy Adası
127 O8 **Zhirnovsk** Volgogradskaya Oblast', SW Russian Federation 51°01′N 44°49′E
160 M12 **Zhishan** *prev.* Yongzhou. Hunan, S China 26°12′N 111°36′E
144 L8 **Zhitikara** *Kaz.* Zhetiqara; *prev.* Džetygara. Kostanay, NW Kazakhstan 52°14′N 61°12′E
Zhitkovichi *see* Zhytkavichy
Zhitomir *see* Zhytomyr
Zhitomirskaya Oblast' *see* Zhytomyrs'ka Oblast'
126 J5 **Zhizdra** Kaluzhskaya Oblast', W Russian Federation 53°38′N 34°39′E
119 N18 **Zhlobin** Homyel'skaya Voblasts', SE Belarus 52°53′N 30°01′E
Zhmerinka *see* Zhmerynka
116 M7 **Zhmerynka** *Rus.* Zhmerinka. Vinnyts'ka Oblast', C Ukraine 49°00′N 28°02′E
149 R9 **Zhob** *var.* Fort Sandeman. Baluchistān, SW Pakistan 31°21′N 69°31′E
149 R8 **Zhob** ≋ C Pakistan
Zhodino *see* Zhodzina
119 L15 **Zhodzina** *Rus.* Zhodino. Minskaya Voblasts', C Belarus 54°06′N 28°21′E
123 Q5 **Zhokhova, Ostrov** *island* Novosibirskiye Ostrova, NE Russian Federation
Zholkev/Zholkva *see* Zhovkva
Zhondor *see* Jondor
158 I15 **Zhongba** *var.* Tuoji. Xizang Zizhiqu, W China 29°37′N 84°11′E
Zhongba *see* Jiangyou
160 F11 **Zhongdian** *var.* Larang. Yunnan, SW China 27°48′N 99°41′E
Zhongduo *see* Youyang
Zhonghe *see* Xiushan
Zhonghua Renmin Gongheguo *see* China
159 V9 **Zhongning** Ningxia, N China 37°26′N 105°40′E
Zhongping *see* Huize
161 N15 **Zhongshan** Guangdong, S China 22°30′N 113°20′E
195 X7 **Zhongshan** *Chinese research station* Antarctica 69°23′S 76°34′E
160 M6 **Zhongtiao Shan** ▲▲ C China
159 V9 **Zhongwei** Ningxia, N China 37°31′N 105°10′E
160 K9 **Zhongxian** *var.* Zhongzhou. Chongqing Shi, C China 30°16′N 108°03′E
161 N9 **Zhongxiang** Hubei, C China 31°12′N 112°35′E
Zhongzhou *see* Zhongxian
Zhosaly *see* Dzhusaly
161 O7 **Zhoukou** *var.* Zhoukouzhen. Henan, C China 33°32′N 114°40′E
Zhoukouzhen *see* Zhoukou
161 S9 **Zhoushan** Zhejiang, S China
Zhoushan Islands *see* Zhoushan Qundao
161 S9 **Zhoushan Qundao** *Eng.* Zhoushan Islands. *island group* SE China
116 I5 **Zhovkva** *Pol.* Zółkiew, *Rus.* Zholkev, Zholkva; *prev.* Nesterov. L'vivs'ka Oblast', NW Ukraine 50°04′N 24°E
117 S7 **Zhovti Vody** *Rus.* Zhëltyye Vody. Dnipropetrovs'ka Oblast', E Ukraine 48°24′N 33°30′E
117 Q10 **Zhovtneve** *Rus.* Zhovtnevoye. Mykolayivs'ka Oblast', S Ukraine 46°50′N 32°00′E
Zhovtnevoye *see* Zhovtneve
114 K9 **Zhrebchevo, Yazovir** ⊠ C Bulgaria
163 V13 **Zhuanghe** Liaoning, NE China 39°42′N 123°00′E
159 W11 **Zhuanglang** *var.* Shuiluo; *prev.* Shuilocheng. Gansu, C China 35°06′N 106°21′E
145 P15 **Zhuantobe** *Kaz.* Zhūantöbe. Yuzhnyy Kazakhstan, S Kazakhstan 44°45′N 68°50′E
161 Q5 **Zhucheng** Shandong, E China 35°58′N 119°24′E
159 V12 **Zhugqu** Gansu, C China 33°51′N 104°14′E
161 N15 **Zhuhai** Guangdong, S China 22°16′N 113°30′E
Zhuizishan *see* Weichang
Zhuji *see* Shangqiu
126 I5 **Zhukovka** Bryanskaya Oblast', W Russian Federation 53°33′N 33°48′E
161 N7 **Zhumadian** Henan, C China 32°58′N 114°03′E
Zhuo Xian *see* Zhuozhou
161 O3 **Zhuozhou** *prev.* Zhuo Xian. Hebei, E China 39°22′N 115°40′E
162 L14 **Zhuozi Shan** ▲ N China 39°28′N 106°58′E
113 M17 **Zhur** *Serb.* Žur. S Kosovo 42°10′N 20°37′E
Zhuravichi *see* Zhuravichy
119 O17 **Zhuravichy** *Rus.* Zhuravichi. Homyel'skaya Voblasts', SE Belarus 53°15′N 30°33′E
145 Q8 **Zhuravlevka** Akmola, N Kazakhstan 52°00′N 69°59′E
117 Q4 **Zhurivka** Kyyivs'ka Oblast', N Ukraine 50°28′N 31°48′E
144 J11 **Zhuryn** Aktyubinsk, W Kazakhstan 49°13′N 57°36′E
145 T15 **Zhusandala, Step'** *grassland* SE Kazakhstan
160 L8 **Zhushan** Hubei, C China 32°11′N 110°05′E
Zhushan *see* Xuan'en
Zhuyang *see* Dazhu
161 N11 **Zhuzhou** Hunan, S China 27°52′N 112°52′E
116 I6 **Zhydachiv** *Pol.* Żydaczów, *Rus.* Zhidachov. L'vivs'ka Oblast', NW Ukraine 49°20′N 24°08′E
144 G9 **Zhympity** *Kaz.* Zhympīty; *prev.* Dzhambeyty. Zapadnyy, W Kazakhstan 50°16′N 52°34′E
119 K19 **Zhytkavichy** *Rus.* Zhitkovichi. Homyel'skaya Voblasts', SE Belarus 52°14′N 27°52′E
117 N4 **Zhytomyr** *Rus.* Zhitomir. Zhytomyrs'ka Oblast', NW Ukraine 50°17′N 28°40′E
Zhytomyr *see* Zhytomyrs'ka Oblast'
116 M4 **Zhytomyrs'ka Oblast'** *var.* Zhytomyr, *Rus.* Zhitomirskaya Oblast'. ◐ *province* N Ukraine
153 U15 **Zia** ✈ (Dhaka) Dhaka, C Bangladesh
149 P10 **Ziārat** Baluchistān, SW Pakistan 30°23′N 67°43′E
111 J20 **Žiar nad Hronom** *var.* Sväty Kríž nad Hronom, *Ger.* Heiligenkreuz, *Hung.* Garamszentkereszt. Banskobystrický Kraj, C Slovakia 48°36′N 18°52′E
161 Q4 **Zibo** *var.* Zhangdian. Shandong, E China 36°51′N 118°01′E
160 L4 **Zichang** *prev.* Wayaobu. Shaanxi, C China 37°08′N 109°40′E
Zichenau *see* Ciechanów
111 G15 **Ziębice** *Ger.* Münsterberg in Schlesien. Dolnośląskie, SW Poland 50°37′N 17°01′E
Ziebingen *see* Cybinka
Ziegenhais *see* Głuchołazy
110 E12 **Zielona Góra** *Ger.* Grünberg, Grünberg in Schlesien, Grüneberg. Lubuskie, W Poland 51°56′N 15°31′E
99 F14 **Zierikzee** Zeeland, SW Netherlands 51°39′N 03°55′E
160 I10 **Zigong** *var.* Tzekung. Sichuan, C China 29°20′N 104°48′E
76 G12 **Ziguinchor** SW Senegal 12°34′N 16°20′W
41 N16 **Zihuatanejo** Guerrero, S Mexico 17°39′N 101°33′W
Ziketan *see* Xinghai
Zilah *see* Zalău
127 W7 **Zilair** Respublika Bashkortostan, W Russian Federation 52°12′N 57°15′E
136 L12 **Zile** Tokat, N Turkey 40°18′N 35°52′E
111 J18 **Žilina** *Ger.* Sillein, *Hung.* Zsolna. Zlínský Kraj, N Slovakia 49°13′N 18°44′E
111 J19 **Žilinský Kraj** ◐ *region* N Slovakia
75 Q9 **Zillah** *var.* Zallah. C Libya 28°30′N 17°33′E
Zillenmarkt *see* Zalău
109 N7 **Ziller** ≋ W Austria
Zillertal Alps *see* Zillertaler Alpen
109 N8 **Zillertaler Alpen** *Eng.* Zillertal Alps, *It.* Alpi Aurine. ▲▲ Austria/Italy
118 K10 **Zilupe** *Ger.* Rosenhof. Ludza, E Latvia 56°10′N 28°06′E
41 O13 **Zimapán** Hidalgo, C Mexico 20°45′N 99°21′W
83 I16 **Zimba** Southern, S Zambia 17°20′S 26°11′E
83 J17 **Zimbabwe** *off.* Republic of Zimbabwe; *prev.* Rhodesia. ◆ *republic* S Africa
Zimbabwe, Republic of *see* Zimbabwe
116 H10 **Zimbor** *Hung.* Magyarzsombor. Sălaj, NW Romania 47°00′N 23°16′E
Zimmerbude *see* Svetlyy
116 J15 **Zimnicea** Teleorman, S Romania 43°39′N 25°21′E
114 L9 **Zimnitsa** Yambol, E Bulgaria 42°34′N 26°37′E
127 N12 **Zimovniki** Rostovskaya Oblast', SW Russian Federation 47°07′N 42°29′E
Zindajān *see* Zendeh Jan
77 V12 **Zinder** Zinder, S Niger 13°47′N 09°02′E
77 W11 **Zinder** ◐ *department* S Niger
77 P12 **Ziniaré** C Burkina 12°35′N 01°18′W
Zinjan *see* Zanjān
141 P16 **Zinjibār** SW Yemen 13°08′N 45°23′E
117 T4 **Zin'kiv** *var.* Zen'kov. Poltavs'ka Oblast', NE Ukraine 50°11′N 34°22′E
Zinov'yevsk *see* Kirovohrad
Zintenhof *see* Sindi
31 N10 **Zion** Illinois, N USA 42°27′N 87°49′W
54 F10 **Zipaquirá** Cundinamarca, C Colombia 05°03′N 74°01′W
Zipser Neudorf *see* Spišská Nová Ves
111 H23 **Zirc** Veszprém, W Hungary 47°16′N 17°52′E
113 D14 **Žirje** *It.* Zuri. *island* S Croatia
Zirknitz *see* Cerknica
108 M7 **Zirl** Tirol, W Austria 47°17′N 11°16′E
101 K20 **Zirndorf** Bayern, SE Germany 49°27′N 10°57′E
153 Y11 **Ziro** Arunāchal Pradesh, NE India 27°35′N 93°50′E
160 M11 **Zi Shui** ≋ C China
109 Y3 **Zistersdorf** Niederösterreich, NE Austria 48°32′N 16°45′E
41 O14 **Zitácuaro** Michoacán, SW Mexico 19°28′N 100°21′W
Zito *see* Lhorong
101 Q16 **Zittau** Sachsen, E Germany 50°53′N 14°48′E
112 I12 **Živinice** Federacija Bosna I Hercegovina, E Bosnia and Herzegovina 44°26′N 18°39′E
Ziwa Magharibi *see* Kagera
81 J14 **Ziway Hāyk'** ◎ C Ethiopia
161 N12 **Zixing** Hunan, S China 26°01′N 113°25′E
127 W7 **Ziyanchurino** Orenburgskaya Oblast', W Russian Federation 51°36′N 56°58′E
160 K8 **Ziyang** Shaanxi, C China 32°33′N 108°27′E
111 I20 **Zlaté Moravce** *Hung.* Aranyosmarót. Nitriansky Kraj, SW Slovakia 48°24′N 18°20′E
112 K13 **Zlatibor** ▲▲ W Serbia
114 L9 **Zlati Voyvoda** Sliven, C Bulgaria 42°36′N 26°13′E
116 G11 **Zlatna** *Ger.* Kleinschlatten, *Hung.* Zalatna; *prev. Ger.* Goldmarkt. Alba, C Romania 46°08′N 23°11′E
114 I8 **Zlatna Panega** Lovech, N Bulgaria 43°07′N 24°09′E
114 N8 **Zlatni Pyasŭtsi** Dobrich, NE Bulgaria 43°19′N 28°03′E
122 F11 **Zlatoust** Chelyabinskaya Oblast', C Russian Federation 55°12′N 59°33′E
111 M19 **Zlatý Stôl** *Ger.* Goldener Tisch, *Hung.* Aranyosasztal. ▲ C Slovakia 48°45′N 20°39′E
113 P18 **Zletovo** NE FYR Macedonia 42°00′N 22°14′E
111 H18 **Zlín** *prev.* Gottwaldov. Zlínský Kraj, E Czech Republic 49°14′N 17°40′E
111 H19 **Zlínský Kraj** ◐ *region* E Czech Republic
75 O7 **Zlīṭan** W Libya 32°28′N 14°34′E
110 F9 **Złocieniec** *Ger.* Falkenburg in Pommern. Zachodnio-pomorskie, NW Poland 53°31′N 16°01′E
110 J13 **Złoczew** Sieradz, S Poland 51°24′N 18°36′E
Złoczów *see* Zolochev
111 F14 **Złotoryja** *Ger.* Goldberg. Dolnośląskie, W Poland 51°08′N 15°57′E
110 G9 **Złotów** Wielkopolskie, C Poland 53°22′N 17°02′E
110 G13 **Żmigród** *Ger.* Trachenberg. Dolnośląskie, SW Poland 51°31′N 16°55′E
126 J6 **Zmiyevka** Orlovskaya Oblast', W Russian Federation 52°39′N 36°20′E
117 V5 **Zmiyiv** Kharkivs'ka Oblast', E Ukraine 49°40′N 36°22′E
Zna *see* Tsna
Znaim *see* Znojmo
126 M7 **Znamenka** Tambovskaya Oblast', W Russian Federation 52°24′N 42°28′E
Znamenka *see* Znam"yanka
119 C14 **Znamens** Astrakhanskaya Oblast', W Russian Federation 54°37′N 21°13′E
127 P10 **Znamensk** *Ger.* Wehlau. Kaliningradskaya Oblast', W Russian Federation 48°33′N 46°18′E
117 R7 **Znam"yanka** *Rus.* Znamenka. Kirovohrads'ka Oblast', C Ukraine 48°41′N 32°40′E
110 H10 **Żnin** Kujawsko-pomorskie, C Poland 52°50′N 17°41′E
111 F19 **Znojmo** *Ger.* Znaim. Jihomoravský Kraj, SE Czech Republic 48°52′N 16°04′E
79 N16 **Zobia** Orientale, N Dem. Rep. Congo 02°57′N 25°55′E
83 N15 **Zóbuè** Tete, NW Mozambique 15°36′S 34°26′E
98 G12 **Zoetermeer** Zuid-Holland, W Netherlands 52°04′N 04°30′E
108 E7 **Zofingen** Aargau, N Switzerland 47°18′N 07°57′E
159 R15 **Zogang** *var.* Wangda. Xizang Zizhiqu, W China 29°41′N 97°54′E
106 E7 **Zogno** Lombardia, N Italy 45°49′N 09°42′E
142 M10 **Zohreh, Rūd-e** ≋ SW Iran
160 H7 **Zoigê** *var.* Dagcagoin. Sichuan, C China 33°44′N 102°57′E
Zółkiew *see* Zhovkva
108 D8 **Zollikofen** Bern, W Switzerland 47°00′N 07°24′E
116 J5 **Zolochev** *Pol.* Złoczów, *Rus.* Zolochiv. L'vivs'ka Oblast', W Ukraine 49°48′N 24°51′E
117 U4 **Zolochiv** *Rus.* Zolochev. Kharkivs'ka Oblast', E Ukraine 50°16′N 35°58′E
Zolochiv *see* Zolochev
117 X7 **Zolote** *Rus.* Zolotoye. Luhans'ka Oblast', E Ukraine 48°42′N 38°33′E
117 Q6 **Zolotonosha** Cherkas'ka Oblast', C Ukraine 49°39′N 32°05′E
Zolotoye *see* Zolote
Zólyom *see* Zvolen
83 N15 **Zomba** Southern, S Malawi 15°22′S 35°23′E
Zombor *see* Sombor
99 D17 **Zomergem** Oost-Vlaanderen, NW Belgium 51°07′N 03°31′E
147 P11 **Zomin** *Rus.* Zaamin. Jizzax Viloyati, C Uzbekistan 39°56′N 68°16′E
79 I15 **Zongo** Equateur, N Dem. Rep. Congo 04°18′N 18°42′E
136 G10 **Zonguldak** Zonguldak, NW Turkey 41°26′N 31°47′E
136 H10 **Zonguldak** ◐ *province* NW Turkey
99 K17 **Zonhoven** Limburg, NE Belgium 50°59′N 05°22′E
142 J2 **Zonūz** Āzarbāyjān-e Khāvarī, NW Iran 38°32′N 45°54′E
103 Y16 **Zonza** Corse, France, C Mediterranean Sea 41°49′N 09°13′E
Zoppot *see* Sopot
Zorgho *see* Zorgo
77 Q13 **Zorgo** *var.* Zorgho. C Burkina 12°15′N 00°37′W
104 K10 **Zorita** Extremadura, W Spain 39°18′N 05°42′W
147 U14 **Zorkŭl** *Rus.* Ozero Zorkul'. ◎ SE Tajikistan
Zorkul', Ozero *see* Zorkŭl
56 A8 **Zorritos** Tumbes, N Peru 03°43′S 80°42′W
111 J16 **Żory** *var.* Zory, *Ger.* Sohrau. Śląskie, S Poland 50°04′N 18°42′E
76 K15 **Zorzor** N Liberia 07°46′N 09°28′W
99 E18 **Zottegem** Oost-Vlaanderen, NW Belgium 50°52′N 03°49′E
77 R15 **Zou** ≋ S Benin
78 H6 **Zouar** Borkou-Ennedi-Tibesti, N Chad 20°25′N 16°28′E
76 J6 **Zouérat** *var.* Zouérate, Zouîrât. Tiris Zemmour, N Mauritania 22°44′N 12°29′W
Zouérate *see* Zouérat
Zoug *see* Zug
Zouîrât *see* Zouérat
76 M16 **Zoukougbeu** C Ivory Coast 09°47′N 06°50′W
98 M5 **Zoutkamp** Groningen, NE Netherlands 53°22′N 06°17′E
99 J18 **Zoutleeuw** *Fr.* Léau. Vlaams Brabant, C Belgium 50°49′N 05°06′E
112 L9 **Zrenjanin** *prev.* Petrovgrad, Veliki Bečkerek, *Ger.* Grossbetschkerek, *Hung.* Nagybecskerek. Vojvodina, N Serbia 45°23′N 20°24′E
112 E10 **Zrinska Gora** ▲▲ C Croatia
Zsablya *see* Žabalj
101 N16 **Zschopau** ≋ E Germany
Zsebely *see* Jebel
Zsibó *see* Jibou
Zsilyvajdevulkán *see* Vulcan
Zsil/Zsily *see* Jiu
Zsolna *see* Žilina
Zsombolya *see* Jimbolia
Zsupanya *see* Županja
55 N7 **Zuata** Anzoátegui, NE Venezuela 08°24′N 65°13′W
105 N14 **Zubia** Andalucía, S Spain 37°10′N 03°36′W
127 N5 **Zubova Polyana** Respublika Mordoviya, W Russian Federation 54°05′N 42°50′E
65 P16 **Zubov Seamount** *undersea feature* E Atlantic Ocean 20°45′S 08°45′E
124 I16 **Zubtsov** Tverskaya Oblast', W Russian Federation 56°10′N 34°34′E
108 M8 **Zuckerhütl** ▲ SW Austria 46°57′N 11°07′E
Zueila *see* Zawīlah
76 M16 **Zuénoula** C Ivory Coast 07°26′N 06°03′W
105 S5 **Zuera** Aragón, NE Spain 41°52′N 00°47′W
141 V13 **Ẓufār** *Eng.* Dhofar. *physical region* SW Oman
108 G8 **Zug** *Fr.* Zoug. Zug, C Switzerland 47°11′N 08°31′E
108 G8 **Zug** *Fr.* Zoug. ◐ *canton* C Switzerland
137 R9 **Zugdidi** W Georgia 42°30′N 41°52′E
108 G8 **Zuger See** ◎ NW Switzerland
101 K25 **Zugspitze** ▲ S Germany 47°25′N 10°58′E
99 E15 **Zuid-Beveland** *var.* South Beveland. *island* SW Netherlands
98 K10 **Zuidelijk-Flevoland** *polder* C Netherlands
Zuider Zee *see* IJsselmeer
98 G12 **Zuid-Holland** *Eng.* South Holland. ◐ *province* W Netherlands
98 N5 **Zuidhorn** Groningen, NE Netherlands 53°15′N 06°25′E
98 O6 **Zuidlaardermeer** ◎ NE Netherlands
98 O6 **Zuidlaren** Drenthe, NE Netherlands 53°06′N 06°41′E
99 K14 **Zuid-Willemsvaart Kanaal** *canal* S Netherlands
98 N8 **Zuidwolde** Drenthe, NE Netherlands 52°40′N 06°25′E
Zuitai/Zuitaizi *see* Kangxian
105 O14 **Zújar** Andalucía, S Spain 37°33′N 02°52′W
104 L11 **Zújar** ≋ W Spain
104 L11 **Zújar, Embalse del** ⊠ W Spain
80 J9 **Zula** E Eritrea 15°19′N 39°40′E
54 G6 **Zulia** *off.* Estado Zulia. ◐ *state* NW Venezuela
Zulia, Estado *see* Zulia
Zullapara *see* Sinchaingbyin
Züllichau *see* Sulechów
105 P3 **Zumárraga** País Vasco, N Spain 43°05′N 02°19′W
112 D8 **Žumberačko Gorje** *var.* Gorjanči, Uskocke Planine, Žumberak, *Ger.* Uskokengebirge; *prev.* Sichelburger Gerbirge. ▲ Croatia/Slovenia *see also* Gorjanci
Žumberak *see* Gorjanci/Žumberačko Gorje
194 K7 **Zumberge Coast** *coastal feature* Antarctica
Zumbo *see* Vila do Zumbo
29 W10 **Zumbro Falls** Minnesota, N USA 44°15′N 92°25′W
29 W10 **Zumbro River** ≋ Minnesota, N USA
29 W10 **Zumbrota** Minnesota, N USA 44°18′N 92°37′W
99 H15 **Zundert** Noord-Brabant, S Netherlands 51°28′N 04°40′E
Zungaria *see* Dzungaria
77 U14 **Zungeru** Niger, C Nigeria 09°49′N 06°10′E
161 P2 **Zunhua** Hebei, E China 40°10′N 117°58′E
37 O11 **Zuni** New Mexico, SW USA 35°03′N 108°52′W
37 P11 **Zuni Mountains** ▲▲ New Mexico, SW USA
160 J11 **Zunyi** Guizhou, S China 27°40′N 106°56′E
160 J15 **Zuo Jiang** ≋ China/Vietnam
108 J9 **Zuoz** Graubünden, SE Switzerland 46°37′N 09°58′E
112 I10 **Županja** *Hung.* Zsupanya. Vukovar-Srijem, E Croatia 45°03′N 18°42′E
Žur *see* Zhur
127 T2 **Zura** Udmurtskaya Respublika, NW Russian Federation 57°36′N 53°19′E
139 V8 **Zurbāṭīyah** Wāsiṭ, E Iraq 33°13′N 46°07′E
Zuri *see* Žirje
108 F7 **Zürich** *Eng./Fr.* Zurich, *It.* Zurigo. Zürich, N Switzerland 47°23′N 08°33′E
108 G6 **Zürich** *Eng./Fr.* Zurich. ◐ *canton* N Switzerland
Zurich, Lake *see* Zürichsee
108 G7 **Zürichsee** *Eng.* Lake Zurich. ◎ NE Switzerland
Zurigo *see* Zürich
149 V1 **Zŭrkŭl** *Pash.* Sarī Qūl, *Rus.* Ozero Zurkul'. ◎ Afghanistan/Tajikistan *see also* Sarī Qūl
Zŭrkŭl *see* Sarī Qūl
Zurkul', Ozero *see* Sarī Qūl/Zŭrkŭl
110 K10 **Żuromin** Mazowieckie, C Poland 53°00′N 19°54′E
108 J8 **Zürs** Vorarlberg, W Austria 47°11′N 10°11′E
77 T13 **Zuru** Kebbi, W Nigeria 11°28′N 05°13′E
108 F6 **Zurzach** Aargau, N Switzerland 47°33′N 08°21′E
101 J22 **Zusam** ≋ S Germany
98 M11 **Zutphen** Gelderland, E Netherlands 52°09′N 06°12′E
75 N7 **Zuwārah** NW Libya 32°56′N 12°06′E
Zuwaylah *see* Zawīlah
125 R14 **Zuyevka** Kirovskaya Oblast', NW Russian Federation 58°24′N 51°08′E
161 N10 **Zuzhou** Hunan, S China 27°52′N 113°00′E
Zvenigorodka *see* Zvenyhorodka
117 P6 **Zvenyhorodka** *Rus.* Zvenigorodka. Cherkas'ka Oblast', C Ukraine 49°05′N 30°58′E
123 N12 **Zvezdnyy** Irkutskaya Oblast', C Russian Federation 56°43′N 106°22′E
125 U14 **Zvëzdnyy** Permskaya Oblast', NW Russian Federation 57°45′N 56°20′E
83 K18 **Zvishavane** *prev.* Shabani. Matabeleland South, S Zimbabwe 20°20′S 30°02′E
111 J20 **Zvolen** *Ger.* Altsohl, *Hung.* Zólyom. Banskobystrický Kraj, C Slovakia 48°35′N 19°06′E
112 J12 **Zvornik** E Bosnia and Herzegovina 44°24′N 19°07′E
98 M5 **Zwaagwesteinde** *Fris.* De Westerein. Friesland, N Netherlands 53°16′N 06°08′E
98 H10 **Zwanenburg** Noord-Holland, C Netherlands 52°22′N 04°44′E
98 L8 **Zwarte Meer** ◎ N Netherlands
98 M9 **Zwarte Water** ≋ N Netherlands
98 M8 **Zwartsluis** Overijssel, E Netherlands 52°39′N 06°04′E
76 L17 **Zwedru** *var.* Tchien. E Liberia 06°04′N 08°07′W
98 O8 **Zweeloo** Drenthe, NE Netherlands 52°48′N 06°45′E
101 E20 **Zweibrücken** *Fr.* Deux-Ponts, *Lat.* Bipontium. Rheinland-Pfalz, SW Germany 49°15′N 07°22′E
108 D9 **Zweisimmen** Fribourg, W Switzerland 46°33′N 07°22′E
101 M15 **Zwenkau** Sachsen, E Germany 51°11′N 12°19′E
109 V3 **Zwettl** Wien, NE Austria 48°28′N 14°17′E
109 T3 **Zwettl an der Rodl** Oberösterreich, N Austria 48°28′N 14°17′E
99 D18 **Zwevegem** West-Vlaanderen, W Belgium 50°48′N 03°20′E
101 M17 **Zwickau** Sachsen, E Germany 50°43′N 12°31′E
101 N16 **Zwickauer Mulde** ≋ E Germany
101 O21 **Zwiesel** Bayern, SE Germany 49°02′N 13°14′E
98 H13 **Zwijndrecht** Zuid-Holland, SW Netherlands 51°49′N 04°39′E
Zwischenwässern *see* Medvode
Zwittau *see* Svitavy
110 N13 **Zwoleń** Mazowieckie, SE Poland 51°21′N 21°37′E
98 M9 **Zwolle** Overijssel, E Netherlands 52°31′N 06°06′E
22 G6 **Zwolle** Louisiana, S USA 31°37′N 93°38′W
110 K12 **Żychlin** Łódzkie, C Poland 52°15′N 19°38′E
Żydaczów *see* Zhydachiv
Zyembin *see* Zembin
Zyôetu *see* Jōetsu
110 L12 **Żyrardów** Mazowieckie, C Poland 52°02′N 20°28′E
123 S8 **Zyryanka** Respublika Sakha (Yakutiya), NE Russian Federation 65°45′N 150°43′E
145 Y9 **Zyryanovsk** Vostochnyy Kazakhstan, E Kazakhstan 49°45′N 84°16′E

◆ Country ● Country Capital ◇ Dependent Territory ○ Dependent Territory Capital ◐ Administrative Regions ✈ International Airport ▲ Mountain ▲▲ Mountain Range Volcano ≋ River ◎ Lake ⊠ Reservoir

DORLING KINDERSLEY *would like to express their thanks to the following individuals, companies, and institutions for their help in preparing this atlas.*

Earth Resource Mapping Ltd., Egham, Surrey
Brian Groombridge, World Conservation Monitoring Centre, Cambridge
The British Library, London
British Library of Political and Economic Science, London
The British Museum, London
The City Business Library, London
King's College, London
National Meteorological Library and Archive, Bracknell
The Printed Word, London
The Royal Geographical Society, London
University of London Library
Paul Beardmore
Philip Boyes
Hayley Crockford
Alistair Dougal
Reg Grant
Louise Keane
Zoe Livesley
Laura Porter
Jeff Eidenshink
Chris Hornby
Rachelle Smith
Ray Pinchard
Robert Meisner
Fiona Strawbridge

PICTURE CREDITS

Every effort has been made to trace the copyright holders and we apologize in advance for any unintentional omissions. We would be pleased to insert the appropriate acknowledgment in any subsequent edition of this publication.

Adams Picture Library: 86CLA; **G Andrews:** 186CR; **Ardea London Ltd:** K Ghana 150C; M Iljima 132TC; R Waller 148TR; Art Directors **Aspect Picture Library:** P Carmichael 160TR; 131CR(below); G Tompkinson 190TRB; **Axiom:** C Bradley 148CA, 158CA; J Holmes xivCRA, xxivBCR, xxviiCRB, 150TCR, 165C(below), 166TL, J Morris 75TL, 77CRB, J Spaull 134BL; **Bridgeman Art Library, London / New York:** Collection of the Earl of Pembroke, Wilton House xxBC; **The J. Allan Cash Photolibrary:** xlBR, xliiCLA, xlivCL, 10BC, 60CL, 69CLB, 70CL, 72CLB, 75BR, 76BC, 87BL, 109BR, 138BCL, 141TL, 154CR, 178BR, 181TR; **Bruce Coleman Ltd:** 86BC, 98CL, 100TC; S Alden 192BC(below); Atlantide xxviTCR, 138BR; E Bjurstrom 141BR; S Bond 96CRB; T Buchholz xvCL, 92TR, 123TCL; J Burton xxiiiC; J Cancalosi 181TRB; B J Coates xxvBL, 192CL; B Coleman 63TL; B & C Colhoun 2TR, 36CB; A Compost xxiiiCBR; Dr S Coyne 45TL; G Cubitt xviTCL, 169BR, 178TR, 184TR; P Davey xxviiCLB, 121TL(below); N Devore 189CBL; S J Doylee xxiiCRR; H Flygare xviiCRA; M P L Fogden 17C(above) ; Jeff Foott Productions xxiiiCRB, 11CRA; M Freeman 91BRA; P van Gaalen 86TR; G Gualco 140C; B Henderson 194CR; Dr C Henneghien 69C; HPH Photography, H Van den Berg 69CR; C Hughes 69BCL; C James xxxixTC; J Johnson 39CR, 197TR; J Jurka 91CA; S C Kaufman 28C; S J Krasemann 33TR; H Lange 10TRB, 68CA; C Lockwood 32BC; L C Marigo xxiiBC, xxviiCLA, 49CRA, 59BR; M McCoy 187TR; D Meredith 3CR; J Murray xvCR, 179BR; Orion Press 165CR(above); Orion Services & Trading Co. Inc. 164CR; C Ott 17BL; Dr E Pott 9TR, 40CL, 87C, 93TL, 194CLB; F Prenzel 186BC, 193BC; M Read 42BR, 43CRB; H Reinhard xxiiCR, xxviiTR, 194BR; L Lee Rue III 151BCL; J Shaw xixTL; K N Swenson 194BC; P Terry 115CR; N Tomalin 54BCL; P Ward 78TC; S Widstrand 57TR; K Wothe 91C, 173TCL; J T Wright 127BR; **Colorific:** Black Star / L Mulvehil 156CL; Black Star / R Rogers 57BR; Black Star / J Rupp 161BCR; Camera Tres / C. Meyer 59BRA; R Caputo / Matrix 78CL; J. Hill 117CLB; M Koene 55TR; G Satterley xliiCLAR; M Yamashita 156BL, 167CR(above); **Comstock:** 108CRB; Corbis UK Ltd: 170TR, 170BL; **D Cousens:** 147 CRA; **Corbis:** Bob Daemmrich 6BL; **Sue Cunningham Photographic:** 51CR; S Alden 192BC(below) **James Davis Travel Photography:** xxxviTCB, xxxviTR, xxxviCL, 13CA, 19BC, 49TLB, 56BCR, 57CLA, 61BCL, 93BC, 94TC, 102TR, 120CB, 158BC, 179CRA, 191BR; **Dorling Kindersley:** Paul Harris xxiiTR; Nigel Hicks xxiiBM; Jamie Marshall 181TR; Bharath Ramamrutham 155BR; Colin Sinclair 133BMR; George Dunnet: 124CA; **Environmental Picture Library:** Chris Westwood 126C; **Eye Ubiquitous:** xlCA; L. Fordyce 12CLA; L Johnstone 6CRA, 28BLA, 30CB; S. Miller xxiCA; M Southern 73BLA; **Chris Fairclough Colour Library:** xliBR; **Ffotograff:** N. Tapsell 158CL; **FLPA -Images of nature:** 123TR; **Geoscience Features:** xviBCR, xviBR, 102CL, 108BC, 122BR; Solar Film 64TC; **Getty Images:** Kim Steele 161BCL; **gettyone stone**: 131BC, 133BR, 164CR(above); G Johnson 130BL; R Passmore 120TR; D Austen 187CL; G Allison 186CL; L Ulrich 17TL; M Vines 17BL; R Wells 193BL; **Robert Harding Picture Library:** xviiTC, xxivCR, xxxC, xxxvTC, 2TLB, 3CA, 15CRB, 15CR, 37BC, 38CRA, 50BL, 95BR, 99CR, 114CR, 122BL, 131CLA, 142CB, 143TL, 147TR, 168TR, 168CA, 166BR; P G. Adam 13TCB; D Atchison-Jones 70BLA; J Bayne 72BCL; B Schuster 80CR; C Bowman 50BR, 53CA, 62CL, 70CRL; C Campbell xxiBC; G Corrigan 159CRB, 161CRB; P Craven xxxvBL; R Cundy 69BR; Delu 79BC; A Durand 111BR; Financial Times 142BR; R Frerck 51BL; T Gervis 3BCL, 7CR; I Griffiths xxxCL, 77TL; T Hall 166CRA; D Harney 142CA; S Harris xliiiBCL; G Hellier xvCRB, 135BL; F Jackson 137BCR; Jacobs xxxviiTL; P Koch 139TR; F Joseph Land 122TR; Y Marcoux 9BR; S Massif xvBC; A Mills 88CLB; L Murray 114TR; R Rainford xlivBL; G Renner 74CB, 194C; C Rennie 48CL, 116BR; R Richardson 118CL; P Van Riel 48BR; E Rooney 124TR; Sassoon xxivCL, 148CLB; Jochen Schlenker 193CL; P Scholey 176TR; M Short 137TL; E Simanor xxviiCR; V Southwell 139CR; J Strachan 42TR, 111BL, 132BCR; C Tokeley 131CLA; A C Waltham 161C; T Waltham xviiBL, xxiiCLLL, 138CRB; Westlight 37CR; N Wheeler 139BL; A Williams xxxviiiBR, xlTR; A Woolfitt 95BRA; Paul Harris: 168TC; **Hutchison Library:** 131CR (above) 6BL; P. Collomb 137CR; C. Dodwell 130TR; S Errington 70BCL; P. Hellyer 142BC; J. Horner xxxiTC; R. Ian Lloyd 134CRA; N. Durrell McKenna xxviBCR; J. Nowell 135CLB, 143TC; A Zvoznikov xxiiCL; **Image Bank:** 87BR; J Banagan 190BCA; A Becker xxivBCL; M Khansa 121CR, M Isy-Schwart 193CR(above), 191CL; Khansa K Forest 163TR; Lomeo xxivTCR; T Madison 170TL(below); C Molyneux xxiiCRRR; C Navajas xviiiTR; Ocean Images Inc. 192CLB; J van Os xviiTCR; S Proehl 6CL; T Rakke xixTC, 64CL; M Reitz 196CA; M Romanelli 166CL(below); G A Rossi 151BCR, 176BLA; B Roussel 109TL; S Satushek xviiBCR; Stock Photos / J M Spielman xxivTRL; **Images Colour Library:** xxiiCLL, xxxixTR, xliCR, xliiiBL, 3BR, 19BR, 37TL, 44TL, 62TC, 91BR, 102CLB, 103CR, 150CL, 180CA; 164BC, 165TL; **Impact Photos:** J & G Andrews 186BL; C. Bluntzer 156BR; Cosmos / G. Buthaud 65BC; S Franklin 126BL; A. le Garsmeur 131C; A Indge xxviiTC; C Jones xxxiCB, 70BL; V. Nemirousky 137BR; J Nicholl 76TCR; C. Penn 187C(below); G Sweeney xviiBR, 196CB, 196TR, J & G Andrews 186TR; **JVZ Picture Library:** T Nilson 135TC; **Frank Lane Picture Agency:** xxiTCR, xxiiiBL, 93TR; A Christiansen 58CRA; J Holmes xivBL; S. McCutcheon 3C; Silvestris 173TCR; D Smith xxiiBCL; W Wisniewsli 195BR; **Leeds Castle Foundation:** xxxviiBC; **Magnum:** Abbas 83CR, 136CA; S Franklin 134CRB; D Hurn 4BCL; P. Jones-Griffiths 191BL; H Kubota xviBCL, 156CLB; F Maver xviBL; S McCurry 73CL, 133BCR; G. Rodger 74TR; C Steele Perkins 72BL; **Mountain Camera / John Cleare:** 153TR; C Monteath 153CR; **Nature Photographers:** E.A. Janes 112CL; **Natural Science Photos:** M Andera 110C; **Network Photographers Ltd.:** C Sappa / Rapho 119BL; **N.H.P.A.:** N. J. Dennis xxiiiCL; D Heuchlin xxiiiCLA; S Krasemann 15BL, 25BR, 38TC; K Schafer 49CB; R Tidman 160CLB; D Tomlinson 145CR; M Wendler 48TR; **Nottingham Trent University:** T Waltham xivCL, xvBR; **Novosti:** 144BLA; **Oxford Scientific Films:** D Allan xxiiTR; H R Bardarson xviiiBC; D Bown xxiiiCBLL; M Brown 140BL; M Colbeck 147CAR; W Faidley 3TL; L Gould xxiiiTRB; D Guravich xxiiiTR; P Hammerschmidy / Okapia 87CLA; M Hill 57TL, 195TR; C Menteath ; J Netherton 2CRB; S Osolinski 82CA; R Packwood 72CA; M Pitts 179TC; N Rosing xxiiiCBL, 9TR, 197BR; D Simonson 57C; Survival Anglia / C Catton 137TR; R Toms xxiiiBR; K Wothe xxiBL, xviiCLA; **Panos Pictures:** B Aris 133C; P Barker xxivBR; T Bolstao 153BR; N Cooper 82CB, 153TC; J-L Dugast 166C(below), 167BR; J Hartley 73CA, 90CL; J Holmes 149BC; J Morris 76CLB; M Rose 146TR; D Sansoni 155CL; C Stowers 163TL; **Edward Parker:** 49TL, 49CLB; **Pictor International:** xivBR, xvBRA, xixTCL, xxCL, 3CLA, 17BR, 20TR, 20CRB, 23BCA, 23CL, 26CB, 27BC, 30CA, 33TRB, 34BC, 34BR, 34CR, 38CB, 38CL, 43CL, 63BR, 65TC, 82CL, 83CLB, 99BR, 107CLA, 166TR, 171CL(above), 180CLB, 185TL; **Pictures Colour Library:** xxiBCL, xxiiBR, xxviBCL, 6BR, 15TR, 8TR, 16CL(above), 19TL, 20BL, 24C, 24CLA, 27TR, 32TRB, 36BC, 41CA, 43CRA, 68BL, 90TCB, 94BL, 99BL, 106CA, 107CLB, 107CR, 107BR, 117BL, 164BC, 192BL, K Forest 165TL(below); **Planet Earth Pictures:** 193CR(below); D Barrett 148CB, 184CA; R Coomber 16BL; G Douwma 172BR; E Edmonds 173BR; J Lythgoe 196BL; A Mounter 172CR; M Potts 6CA; P Scoones xxTR; J Walencik 110TR; J Waters 53BCL; **Popperfoto:** Reuters / J Drake xxxiiCLA; **Rex Features:** 165CR; Antelope xxxiiCLB; M Friedel xxiCR; I McIlgorm xxxCBR; J Shelley xxxCR; Sipa Press xxxCR; Sipa Press / Alix xxxCBL; Sipa Press / Chamussy 176BL; **Robert Harding Picture Library:** C. Tokeley 131TL; J Strachan 132BL; Franz Joseph Land 122TR; Franz Joseph Land 364/7088 123BL, 169C(above), 170C(above), 168CL, Tony Waltham 186CR(below), Y Marcoux 9BR; **Russia & Republics Photolibrary:** M Wadlow 118CR, 119CL, 124BC, 124CL, 125TL, 125BR, 126TCR; **Science Photo Library:** Earth Satellite Corporation xixTRB, xxxiCR, 49BCL; F Gohier xiCR; J Heseltine xviTCB; K Kent xvBLA; P Menzell xvBL; N.A.S.A. xBC; D Parker xivBC; University of Cambridge Collection Air Pictures 87CLB; RJ Wainscoat / P Arnold, Inc. xiBC; D Weintraub xiBL; **South American Pictures:** 57BL, 62TR; R Francis 52BL; Guyana Space Centre 50TR; T Morrison 49CRB, 49BL, 50CR, 52TR, 54TR, 60BL, 61C; **Southampton Oceanography:** xviiiBL; **Sovofoto / Eastfoto:** xxxiiCBR; **Spectrum Colour Library:** 50BC, 160BC; J King 145BR; **Frank Spooner Pictures:** Gamma-Liason/Vogel 131CL(above); 26CRB; E. Baitel xxxiiBC; Bernstein xxxiCL; Contrast 112CR; Diard / Photo News 113CL; Liaison / C. Hires xxxiiTCB; Liaison / Nickelsberg xxxiiTR; Marleen 113TL; Novosti 116CA; P. Piel xxxCA; N Quidu 135CL; H Stucke 188CLB, 190CA; Torrengo / Figaro 78BR; A Zamur 113BL; **Still Pictures:** C Caldicott 77TC; A Crump 189CL; M & C Denis-Huot xxiiBL, 78CR, 81BL; M Edwards xxiCRL, 53BL, 64CR, 69BLA, 155BR; J Frebet 53CLB; H Giradet 53TC; E Parker 52CL; M Gunther 121BC; **Tony Stone Images:** xxviTR, 4CA, 7BL, 7CL, 13CRB, 39BR, 58C, 97BC, 101BR, 106TR, 109CL, 109CRB, 164CLB, 165C,180CB, 181BR, 188BC, 192TR; G Allison 18TR, 31CRB, 187CRB; D Armand 14TCB; D Austen 180TR, 186CL, 187CL; J Beatty 74CL; O Benn xxviBR; K Biggs xxiTL; R Bradbury 44BR; R A Butcher xxviTL; J Callahan xxviiCRA; P Chesley 185BCL, 188C; W Clay 30BL, 31CRA; J Cornish 96BL, 107TL; C Condina 41CB; T Craddock xxivTR; P Degginger 36CLB; Demetrio 5BR; N DeVore xxivBC; A Diesendruck 60BR; S Egan 87CRA, 96BR; R Elliot xxiiBCR; S Elmore 19C; J Garrett 73CR; S Grandadam 14BR; R Grosskopf 28BL; D Hanson 104BC; C Harvey 69TL; G Hellier 110BL, 165CR; S Huber 103CRB; D Hughs xxxiBR; A Husmo 91TR; G Irvine 31BC; J Jangoux 58CL; D Johnston xviiTR; A Kehr 113C; R Koskas xviTR; J Lamb 96CRA; J Lawrence 75CRA; L Lefkowitz 7CA; M Lewis 45CLA; S Mayman 55BR; Murray & Associates 45CR; G Norways 104CA; N Parfitt xxviiCL, 68TCR, 81TL; R Passmore 121TR; N Press xviBCA; E Pritchard 88CA, 90CLR; T Raymond 21BL, 29TR; L Resnick 74BR; M Rogers 80BR; A Sacks 28TCB; C Saule 90CR; S Schulhof xxivTC; P Seaward 34CL; M Segal 32BL; V Shenai 152CL; R Sherman 26CL; H Sitton 136CR; R Smith xxvBLA, 56C; S Studd 108CLA; H Strand 49BR, 63TR; P Tweedie 177CR; L Ulrich 17BL; M Vines 17TC; A B Wadham 60CR; J Warden 63CLB; R Wells 23CRA, 193BL; G Yeowell 34BL; **Telegraph Colour Library:** 61CRB, 61TCR, 157TL; R Antrobus xxxixBR; J Sims 26BR; **Topham Picturepoint:** xxxiCBL, 162BR, 168TR, 168BC; **Travel Ink:** A Cowin 88TR; **Trip:** 140BR, 144CA, 155CRA; B Ashe 159TR; D Cole 190BCL, 190CR; D Davis 89BL; I Deineko xxxiTR; J Dennis 22BL; Dinodia 154CL; Eye Ubiquitous / L Fordyce 2CLB; A Gasson 149CR; W Jacobs 43TL, 54BL, 177BC, 178CLA, 185BCR, 186BL; P Kingsbury 112C; K Knight 177BR; V Kolpakov 147BL; T Noorits 87TL, 119BR, 146CL; R Power 41TR; N Ray 166BL, 168TC; C Rennie 116CLB; V Sidoropolev 145TR; E Smith 183BC, 183TL; **Woodfin Camp & Associates:** 92BLR; **World Pictures:** xvCRA, xviiCRA, 9CRB, 22CL, 23BC, 24BL, 35BL, 40TR, 51TR, 71BR, 80TCR, 82TR, 83BL, 86BCR, 96TC, 98BL, 100CR, 101CR, 103BC, 105TC, 157BL, 161BCL, 162CLB, 172CLB, 172BC, 179BL, 182CB, 183C, 184CL, 185CR; 121BR, 121TT; **Zefa Picture Library:** xviBLR, xviiBCL, xviiiCL, 3CL, 8BC, 8CT, 9CR, 13BC, 14TC, 16TR, 21TL, 22CRB, 25BL, 32TCR, 36BCR, 59BCL, 65TCL, 69CLA, 79TL, 81BR, 87CRB, 92C, 98C, 99TL, 100BL, 107TR, 118CRB, 120BL; 122C(below), 124CLA, 164BR, 183TR; Anatol 113BR; Barone 114BL; Brandenburg 5C; A J Brown 44TR; H J Clauss 55CLB; Damm 71BC; Evert 92BL; W Felger 3BL; J Fields 189CRA; R Frerck 4BL; G Heil 56BR; K Heibig 115BR; Heilman 28BC; Hunter 8C; Kitchen 10TR, 8CL, 8BL, 9TR; Dr H Kramarz 7BLA, 123CR(below); Mehlio 155BL; J F Raga 24TR; Rossenbach 105BR; Streichan 89TL; T Stewart 13TR, 19CR; Sunak 54BR, 162TR; D H Teuffen 95TL; B Zaunders 40BC. **Additional Photography:** Geoff Dann; Rob Reichenfeld; H Taylor; Jerry Young.

MAP CREDITS

World Population Density map, page xxiv:

Source:LandScanTM Global Population Database. Oak Ridge, TN; Oak Ridge National Laboratory.
Available at http://www.ornl.gov/landscan/.

NORTH AMERICA

CANADA
Pages 8–15

UNITED STATES OF AMERICA
Pages 16–39

MEXICO
Pages 40–41

BELIZE
Pages 42–43

COSTA RICA
Pages 42–43

EL SALVADOR
Pages 42–43

GUATEMALA
Pages 42–43

HONDURAS
Pages 42–43

SOUTH AMERICA

GRENADA
Pages 44–45

HAITI
Pages 44–45

JAMAICA
Pages 44–45

ST KITTS & NEVIS
Pages 44–45

ST LUCIA
Pages 44–45

ST VINCENT & THE GRENADINES
Pages 44–45

TRINIDAD & TOBAGO
Pages 44–45

COLOMBIA
Pages 54–55

AFRICA

URUGUAY
Pages 60–61

CHILE
Pages 62–63

PARAGUAY
Pages 62–63

ALGERIA
Pages 74–75

EGYPT
Pages 74–75

LIBYA
Pages 74–75

MOROCCO
Pages 74–75

TUNISIA
Pages 74–75

LIBERIA
Pages 76–77

MALI
Pages 76–77

MAURITANIA
Pages 76–77

NIGER
Pages 76–77

NIGERIA
Pages 76–77

SENEGAL
Pages 76–77

SIERRA LEONE
Pages 76–77

TOGO
Pages 76–77

BURUNDI
Pages 80–81

DJIBOUTI
Pages 80–81

ERITREA
Pages 80–81

ETHIOPIA
Pages 80–81

KENYA
Pages 80–81

RWANDA
Pages 80–81

SOMALIA
Pages 80–81

SUDAN
Pages 80–81

EUROPE

SOUTH AFRICA
Pages 82–83

SWAZILAND
Pages 82–83

ZAMBIA
Pages 82–83

ZIMBABWE
Pages 82–83

DENMARK
Pages 92–93

FINLAND
Pages 92–93

ICELAND
Pages 92–93

NORWAY
Pages 92–95

MONACO
Pages 102–103

ANDORRA
Pages 104–105

PORTUGAL
Pages 104–105

SPAIN
Pages 104–105

ITALY
Pages 106–107

SAN MARINO
Pages 106–107

VATICAN CITY
Pages 106–107

AUSTRIA
Pages 108–109

LIECHTENSTEIN
Pages 108–109

CROATIA
Pages 112–113

KOSOVO (disputed)
Pages 112–113

MACEDONIA
Pages 112–113

MONTENEGRO
Pages 112–113

SERBIA
Pages 112–113

BULGARIA
Pages 114–115

GREECE
Pages 114–115

MOLDOVA
Pages 116–117

ASIA

ARMENIA
Pages 136–137

AZERBAIJAN
Pages 136–137

GEORGIA
Pages 136–137

TURKEY
Pages 136–137/114–115

IRAQ
Pages 138–139

ISRAEL
Pages 138–139

JORDAN
Pages 138–139

LEBANON
Pages 138–139

IRAN
Pages 142–143

KAZAKHSTAN
Pages 144–145

KYRGYZSTAN
Pages 146–147

TAJIKISTAN
Pages 146–147

TURKMENISTAN
Pages 146–147

UZBEKISTAN
Pages 146–147

AFGHANISTAN
Pages 148–149

PAKISTAN
Pages 148–151

TAIWAN
Pages 160–161

JAPAN
Pages 164–165

MYANMAR
Pages 166–167

CAMBODIA
Pages 166–167

LAOS
Pages 166–167

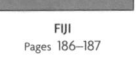
PHILIPPINES
Pages 166–167

THAILAND
Pages 166–167

VIETNAM
Pages 166–167

AUSTRALASIA & OCEANIA

MAURITIUS
Pages 172–173

SEYCHELLES
Pages 172–173

AUSTRALIA
Pages 180–183

NEW ZEALAND
Pages 184–185

PAPUA NEW GUINEA
Pages 186–187

FIJI
Pages 186–187

SOLOMON ISLANDS
Pages 186–187

VANUATU
Pages 186–187